Reading Zukofsky's *80 Flowers*

Reading Zukofsky's *80 Flowers*

Michele J. Leggott

THE JOHNS HOPKINS UNIVERSITY PRESS
BALTIMORE AND LONDON

This book has been brought to publication with the generous assistance of the Andrew W. Mellon Foundation.

The Johns Hopkins University Press, 701 West 40th Street,
Baltimore, Maryland 21211
The Johns Hopkins Press Ltd., London

The paper used in this publication meets the minimum requirements of American National Standard for Information Sciences—Permanence of Paper for Printed Library Materials, ANSI Z39.48-1984.

LIBRARY OF CONGRESS CATALOGING-IN-PUBLICATION DATA

Leggott, Michele J.
  Reading Zukofsky's 80 flowers.

  Bibliography: p.
  Includes index.
  1. Zukofsky, Louis, 1904–1978. 80 flowers. I. Title.
II. Title: Reading Zukofsky's eighty flowers.
PS3549.U47E3636   1988   811'.52   88-6769
ISBN 0-8018-3368-x (alk. paper)

Madeleine's

cadence
chance
the falling voice as befalls,
falls, as happened happens

L.Z., 19 September 1967.
From the black notebook, p. 9

Contents

Preface

Louis Zukofsky: poet, 1904–78, born and lived in New York City nearly all his life, of Russian-Jewish parentage and independent habits of mind. Friend and younger contemporary of William Carlos Williams, Ezra Pound, and Basil Bunting, driving his art over the years to the limits of an eye's appreciation of what a voice must do to bring the movement of words to an ear. Poet extraordinary of the delicate relations governing retina, larynx, tympanum, and cerebrum. Poet.

But also historian, lyricist, fiction writer, translator, essayist, anthologist, critic, scholar, and teacher. Zukofsky began the long poem "A" in 1928 when he was twenty-four, planning it then in twenty-four numbered movements and a life's time. It was finished, some eight hundred pages of ceaseless experiment, in 1974 when he was seventy. Robert Creeley: "Zukofsky says one writes one poem all one's life."[1] The one on one (on one) alignment of poet, poem, and life is fundamental to Zukofsky's work. In pragmatic terms it means that the end of one project is always a bridgehead to the next.

"A" was complete in the sense that the requirements of its structure had been met by September 1974; but its business, or Zukofsky's business at seventy years of age, was by no means finished ("Nothing is ever finished, / Complete," "A"-12, p. 181).[2] The project in the wings, planned since 1968 and prepared for in the last-written movements of "A," was 80 Flowers, a book of poems intended to comprehend by condensation all Zukofsky's previous writing. 80 Flowers was to be small but highly condensate—eighty-one short poems inwreathing time past with time present in the form of flowerings, wild and cultivated, of the plants with which Zukofsky had recently familiarized himself. The book was to be a present for his eightieth birthday, and its composition was scheduled over the intervening decade. However, as with many things in those retirement years, enthusiasm took hold and the Flowers were done by early 1978. The first edition of eighty privately printed copies was in press when Louis

Zukofsky died 12 May 1978. His widow, Celia, published *80 Flowers* a month later.

> *80 Flowers.* After he retired from Poly, he started that. And for that he spent, oh, hours, weeks, months just on research. And when [Louis] started on research there was no stopping him. Then he just went to the bitter end, every definition, every connotation, every annotation, it just went on and on. (Celia Zukofsky, 1978)

> They knew, to begin with, the name of simply everything, notably every sprig of vegetation, every flower . . . Beyond the name (and naturally the Linnean binomial) they also knew, especially Louis knew, every remote shading . . . recorded for 1,500 years' usage: likewise associated legends and private lore. And in "Eighty Flowers," which he'd meant for his 80th birthday (1984) but luckily finished before his death this year, you'll also have to remember that "flowers" can be a verb. That was one of his pleasures with English, anything could be any part of speech. (Hugh Kenner, 1978)

> When Guy Davenport wrote recently that Zuk. was engaged on a finite series of flower poems projected into an unending future (only flowers he knew firsthand of course) I didn't stop to think that this was the ploy of a man who smelled his end. Now it just seems possible. (Harold Schimmel, 1978)

> Pound left us, in Canto 120, with a vision of paradise and the despair of one who cannot enter paradise. Zukofsky left us with a black hole, *80 Flowers,* an impossible density that few will ever attempt to penetrate. (Eliot Weinberger, 1983)

> On the whole, you know when Louis would first write some of these things . . . I was talking with Hugh about *80 Flowers,* and he said, "It's difficult to get into." But all of Louis' stuff, when he first wrote it, seemed . . . ah, who will . . . (Celia Zukofsky, 1978)

> a breeze sweet rampant pulse
> scald scold honor the bard
>
> (Louis Zukofsky, 1978)[3]

These are the voices one finds, looking for news of *80 Flowers* in places where there is an audience for Zukofsky's poetry. The formidable underpinning of the *Flowers* was to be expected (as were its difficulties) with the later movements of *"A"* to go by. But potential readers then had little opportunity of letting elucidation leach its way out of the poems, because copies of the book were so scarce. My object here is to begin the elucidation Zukofsky might have wished for his last poems. My own efforts to understand how they work are research; ways to read *80 Flowers,* explorations of the material from which the poems were made, and attempts to account for the breath-taking aural delight that draws listeners long before the poems need to be understood intellectually. The job has been made at once easier and more complex because of the manuscripts to which I have had access. These blueprint the composition of *80 Flowers* from notes to final text and show that it is possible by an act of concentration to make excellent sense of the poetry. In so concentrating, we repeat in part a process that hones the edge of contemporary poetic expression.

Because the *Flowers'* passage through time present (the seasons of late 1974 to early 1978) is among the chief ordering principles of the book, any study of it is virtually compelled to proceed in the same direction. One starts, with Zukofsky, at the beginning and works, as he worked (picking up ever greater quantities of material), through to the end. I have tried, chapter by chapter, to preserve a sense of temporal development.

Part one deals with preliminaries (associated manuscripts, plans, and Zukofsky's immediate pre-*Flowers* poetry) and moves on to discuss the first five poems of the sequence as a means of getting a feel for technique, subject matter, scope, and so forth. Part two looks at some groupings to be found in *80 Flowers*—groups distinguished by common undertexts (Shakespeare, Henry James, Thomas Hardy) but standing together mostly as poems of a particular season written in a particular year. By the time discussion has followed the *Flowers* through one winter, three springs, a summer, and a fall, the sequence has arrived at its last ten poems. Part three is an exegesis of a finale that winds in paradise, time, the end of the alphabet—and the beginning of a book of "90 Trees" planned for the year 2000.

Acknowledgments

I should like to acknowledge the help and encouragement this work received from my doctoral research supervisor, Peter Quartermain, who gave freely of his time and resources throughout. To Jenny Penberthy I owe many pleasant and productive afternoons of Zukofsky conversation, which were the start of an enduring friendship. My thanks also to Peter Crisp for a voluminous and enlivening series of trans-Pacific letters on the subject of Zukofsky's meter, and for keen perceptions since. Thanks also to Robert Bringhurst for advice about Greek and botany. All of these people read the manuscript at various stages and offered suggestions and sound criticism; I am deeply grateful for their help.

My thanks to Cathy Henderson, research librarian at the Harry Ransom Humanities Research Center, University of Texas at Austin; and to Serge Brethé for generously comparing notes about the Zukofsky Collection there. Thanks also to Charles Watts, of Special Collections at Simon Fraser University, British Columbia.

I am most grateful to C. Freeman Keith, vice-president of the Stinehour Press, Lunenburg, Vermont, who sent the Zukofsky material in Stinehour's archive on loan. Also to Bard College, Annandale-on-Hudson, New York, for information relevant to Zukofsky's 1977 honorary doctorate. Also to Breck's Bulbs, Peoria, Illinois, to George W. Park Seed Co., Greenwood, South Carolina, and W. Atlee Burpee Co., Warminster, Pennsylvania, which kindly sent seed catalogs at my request. Thanks also to Burton Hatlen and Carroll F. Terrell of *Sagetrieb*, who printed an adapted version of the opening section of chapter 3 in their Spring 1985 issue; and to the Association of Universities and Colleges of Canada for the Commonwealth Scholarship that supported me and the research for this book from 1980 to 1985.

My special admiration goes to Mark, who survived calmly the invasive trauma of thesis and then book growing big in small spaces; and to my son, James, who was born *in medias res* and who slept just often enough to allow work to continue.

I would like to thank Eric Halpern and Jane Warth, editors at the Johns Hopkins University Press, for their enthusiasm and the painstaking care they gave this manuscript. Thanks also to Hugh Kenner, who initiated its progress from thesis to book form and supplied advice and information on a number of occasions. Martha Farlow designed this book. She and Village Typographers, Inc., have done an extraordinary job, and I am very grateful to them, as well as to Michael Kalen Smith, who produced the index.

All quotation of Louis Zukofsky manuscripts at Texas and elsewhere appears by permission of Paul Zukofsky, whom I also wish to thank for reading the manuscript. All Louis Zukofsky manuscripts are copyright Paul Zukofsky. All Celia Zukofsky and Paul Zukofsky materials are also copyright Paul Zukofsky. Zukofsky material may not be quoted from this book by third parties without the express permission of the copyright holder. Published Zukofsky material also appears with the permission of Paul Zukofsky.

Abbreviations

Libraries

SFU

> The Louis Zukofsky–Cid Corman Correspondence, 29 July 1960–21 December 1976, Contemporary Literature Collection, Simon Fraser University, Burnaby, British Columbia.

TxU

> The Harry Ransom Humanities Research Center, University of Texas at Austin, which houses the Louis Zukofsky Collection.

Manuscripts Held in the Zukofsky Collection at TxU
(see also pp. 4–31)

b.n.b.

> The black notebook. Loose-leaf notes for *"A,"* 1964–74.

"A" 22 *&* 23 Spiral

> Spiral notebook containing chronologies and notes for *"A"* 22 *&* 23, 1971–74.

"A"-22 Spiral

> Spiral notebook containing double draft of *"A"*-22 on facing pages, 1970; 1972–73.

"A"-23 Spiral

> Spiral notebook containing double draft of *"A"*-23 on facing pages, 1973–74.

(*80 Flowers*) Schema

> A two-page plan for *80 Flowers*, 1974, with additions 1975.

80 Fl. Notes

> Loose-leaf notes for *80 Flowers*, 1968–77.

80 Fl. Drafts
    Loose-leaf drafts of the *80 Flowers* poems, 1974–78.

First List (of 80 Flowers)
    The initial eighty candidates, October 1974.

1st Abb. List
    First Abbreviated List of 80 Flowers, sixty-five options, August 1975.

2nd Abb. List
    Second Abbreviated List of 80 Flowers, forty-six options, May 1976.

3rd Abb. List (or Third List)
    Third Abbreviated List of 80 Flowers, thirty options, October 1976.
    Extends, with more material, to April 1977.

In Process Notes
    Separate notes for most of the *Flowers* written in spring and summer
    1977.

Americana
    Separate distillation of notes from the extended Third List intended for
    use in composing the last 10 *Flowers.*

"Gamut" Notes, 1st seq.
    Loose-leaf notes for "Gamut: 90 Trees," 1969–75.

"Gamut" Notes, 2nd seq.
    Loose-leaf notes for "Gamut," 1976–78.

Other (see Select Bibliography for details)

Century
    The Century Dictionary

Enquiry
    Theophrastus, *Enquiry into Plants*

Gray
    Gray's Manual of Botany

L.Z.: Man and Poet
    Louis Zukofsky: Man and Poet, ed. C. F. Terrell

L.Z. Paideuma
    Paideuma 7, no. 3 (Winter 1978)

MJL thesis
  M. J. Leggott, "Reading Zukofsky's *80 Flowers*"

Neilson
  Complete Poems and Plays of William Shakespeare, ed. W. A. Neilson and C. J. Hill

Taylor
  Taylor's Encyclopedia of Gardening, Horticulture, and Landscape Design, ed. Norman Taylor

Part One

Time, Place, Voice, and the First Five *Flowers*

—The First, First Abbreviated, Second Abbreviated, and Third Abbreviated Lists of 80 Flowers, made at various stages 1974–77 during the composition of the *Flowers*. Also the Americana notes derived from the Third List.

- *80 Flowers* Drafts: another set of loose-leaf, December 1974–January 1978, containing in chronological order drafts of each *Flower*; 117 pages. Interleaved with these are In Process Notes from 1977, as well as sundry pages concerning the last poems of the sequence.
- *80 Flowers* Spiral: a spiral notebook containing fair copies of all eighty-one poems, signed and dated. Included here also is the front matter and a fair copy of the first poem of "Gamut: 90 Trees," the book that was to have followed the *Flowers*.
- The typed master copy of *80 Flowers,* made by Celia Zukofsky in 1978; 30 pages, three poems per page (carbon at the Stinehour Press).
- The Stinehour Galleys, 1978; 17 pages (master proofs at Stinehour).[4]

"Gamut: 90 Trees" Materials
- References in the *80 Flowers* Schema (1975) to the intended form of "Gamut."
- "Gamut" Notes: two sets of loose-leaf notes, the first sequence, 4 pages, covering 1969–75; the second sequence, 12 pages, covering 1976–78. Included in the later notes is the draft of an epigraph subsequently discarded.
- The fair copy of #1 Much Ado About Trees, February 1978, at the back of the *80 Flowers* Spiral.

The story of these materials is also an account of Zukofsky's days. One serves as a practical, if intricate, introduction to the other.

The *"A"* Materials

The Black Notebook (b.n.b.)

Zukofsky was in the habit of using narrow-ruled loose-leaf that clipped into a pocket-size ring binder. The set of loose-leaf headed "A-notes 8/19/64–9/17/74," 115 pages plus scraps and interleavings, is what Zukofsky refers to as "the black notebook," "black looseleaf," "black n.b.," or simply "b.n.b." The notes were originally accompanied by a host of brochures and clippings from newspapers and magazines, which tucked into the back pocket of the black ring binder; these are also at Texas though the black binder is not.

Into the black notebook went chronological entries concerning everything from Norbert Wiener's *Cybernetics* to the first moon landing to Guy

Davenport's cat. There is also more literary data—Theophrastus and Stendhal, Henry James and Geoffrey Chaucer, Dafydd ap Gwilym and Hazlitt, Rabelais and (once) a Bob Dylan song. It is a rich mix, stirred along by Zukofsky in his own character noting an anniversary, recording family talk, commenting on events of the day, and, constantly, planning the late movements of "A" which will give the poem its final shape. There are also places where he works the raw materials of perception (and reading) into lyric form, and there is the occasional observation that goes unaltered into the body of "A."

The dates of the notebook are deceptive, however. There is indeed material, though not very much of it, from 1964–66; and there are some notes for the last section of "A"-23, composed September 1974. But the main chronological drive begins in March 1967 and breaks off in August 1971. In those years, after retiring in 1965 from teaching at the Brooklyn Polytechnic Institute, Zukofsky completed "A"-18 and "A"-19 (1966) and concentrated his energies on finishing the "translation" of Catullus's *Carmina,* which had occupied him (and Celia) since 1958.[5] Early in February 1966, Catullus was done with and Zukofsky moved straight on to compose "A"-21 (1966–67), which pivots on an idiosyncratic Englishing of Plautus's comedy *Rudens.* Then he revised an earlier fragment of fiction and went on (1967–69) to expand it into the novel *Little: For Careenagers.*[6] Both "A"-21 and *Little* were written within the black notebook's main span, but, because they stand somewhat apart from the chief object of Zukofsky's thought, their relationship to the notebook is limited to one or two relevant entries apiece.

Zukofsky was preoccupied by the completion of "A," a job for which he scheduled himself five years of reading followed by three of composition:

5/23/70—Two sets of five keep it together—5 years
   of reading, little talking . . . and 5 words to the
   line[7]

(b.n.b., p. 90)

Earlier, writing to Cid Corman about the reading he planned to do, Zukofsky had said: "I want to go slow and let the life say it" (LZ to CC, 24 October 1967; SFU), a remark that reconfirms the symbiotic relationship between the materials of life and poem.[8] A few weeks later he was surmising to Corman: "and 5, 10, 15 years more? (not on paper till it's down) on 'A' 22–24—no hurry. Let life fill it & take long" (LZ to CC, 20 November 1967; SFU). It is interesting to learn that the last movements of "A" were projected so early in quintuple terms.

The reading and note-taking went much as scheduled, with the pleasing find in 1968 (Zukofsky's eye for serendipity) of *"A"*-24 ready-made in Celia's surprise gift to him of the "L.Z. Masque," a setting of some of her husband's works to music—his constant wish for them. There were visits to Wisconsin (May 1968) and Texas (October and November 1969), which receive mention in the black notebook. There was the Zukofskys' May 1969 trip to England, the record of which was copied into the notebook from field notes torn out of a small pad and then interleaved between pages 58–59. In 1970, the beginnings of *"A"*-22 manifested themselves with the composition of "AN ERA" and the hundred-line lyric that follows it—and the black notebook contains the genesis of both. Then, a month or so after a summer vacation at the Mansfield Center in July 1971, the record stops in midpage. That there was more loose-leaf to the black notebook than we now have seems likely, but the "missing" record is perhaps a matter of transferral rather than loss. By August 1971, with "5 years of reading, little talking" almost at an end, Zukofsky was warming up to begin *"A"*-22 proper.

The *"A"* 22 & 23 Spiral

The black notebook was the primary record; the spiral notebook Zukofsky began 19 August 1971 organizes that record and adds new material as the shape of the last movements fleshes out in the poet's mind. Without entering into a discussion of *"A"* 22 & 23 at this stage, it is necessary to know that Zukofsky intended to cover six thousand years of historical record in a highly unusual manner, which involved, in the finished poem, chronologies without dates or names. Not one chronology, but two; each movement has its century-by-century dateline, pre-3000 B.C. to the present, in the spiral notebook. To deal briefly with the two chronologies— both are still full of dates and names carried over from the black notebook, now meticulously arranged in a kind of transcultural chronicle. Many entries are simply dates indexed by page number to their originals in the black notebook. Many are checked, indicating that there is "no need to refer to orig. text" because the entry has been "abstracted in this spiral or black looseleaf" (*"A"* 22 & 23 Spiral, title-page note). The condensing process has begun; texts ingested into Zukofsky's system of notebooks have had their links with other kinds of historical reality severed; from this point they are materials for Zukofsky history, to be further condensed and marshaled as plans develop. New information entering the record also goes under Zukofsky's editing pencil, marked with green felt-tip for *"A"*-22 and blue for *"A"*-23. The notebook is full of underlinings, margin emphases, checks, and circled 22's and 23's. As composition progresses, a second check will appear beside the first, meaning that the entry has been used somewhere; eventually whole pages are crossed out diagonally to show that Zukofsky has finished with the information there.

The system, once grasped, is easy enough to follow, and the basic pattern of notes, condensation(s), designation, use, and then cancellation is duplicated in the *80 Flowers* material. But if the system itself was orderly, the complexities of each project made for anything but orderly manuscripts. In the *"A"* 22 & 23 Spiral, Zukofsky's relentless pursuit of condensation meant, for example, that everything had to fit into the double-page spread allocated each century—which was adequate space for the eighth century A.D. but proved hopelessly tight as the record swelled. The twentieth century is as fine a mass of Zukofsky's tiny many-colored script as anything in the Texas archive. There are, however, pages for the overflows and they are well-signposted.

The chronologies filled up concurrently 1971–74. The last entry is noted on the Spiral's title page as 17 September 1974, which is when Zukofsky began writing the final twenty-six lines of *"A"*-23. Coincidentally, this is also the terminus date of the black notebook. When we recall that the *"A"* 22 & 23 Spiral was begun August 1971 just before the black notebook cuts off, it begins to look as if the Spiral is phase two of the 1964–74 *"A"*-notes. It organizes and indexes the five-year read, 1967–71 (the black notebook), and then keeps adding to the record during the period of composition, 1972–74.

For the most part, as working plan rather than daybook, there was no place in the Spiral for observations of the sort that make the black notebook almost at times a diary. However, when the Zukofskys visited Bermuda in January 1972, the *"A"* 22 & 23 Spiral went with them; and near the back, some dozen pages beyond *"A"*-23's twentieth century, Zukofsky kept a miniaturized daily chronicle of sights, incidents, and commentary. A lot of this concerns the exotic flora of the island. After returning home, Zukofsky made infrequent entries, but when he and Celia traveled to Bellagio, Italy, in November 1972 the Spiral was again used for daily record. Although the composition of *"A"*-22 was in full swing, Zukofsky found time to make notes about what he found growing in the gardens of the Villa Serbelloni. The botanical and horticultural discoveries of 1972 were to have lasting effects not only on *"A"* 22 & 23 but also on *80 Flowers* and "Gamut."

The final pages of this Spiral are another rich resource; page 159 is headed "unused notes for 'A'-23," and a nearby parenthesis comments that the notes have been "(weeded)"—the gardening metaphor is appropriate because this overflow is headed straight for *80 Flowers*. All the entries

Zukofsky is still interested in and which did not receive the double check of admission to "A" 22 & 23 are listed here; bridgehead material.

The "A"-22 Spiral

The front matter of Zukofsky's notebooks tends to be a repository of useful information, and the spiral notebook containing the holograph manuscripts of "A"-22 is no exception. Its title page has a breakdown of the places and (some) dates of composition, which tell us that its first section of 103 lines was begun 14 February 1970 at 77 Seventh Avenue, New York City, that "notes only" were made in Bermuda (January 1972), and that the second section was started at "Belle Terre, Pt. Jefferson, L.I." (March 1972). Port Jefferson is a small town on Long Island Sound, where the Zukofskys stayed from time to time in an outlying district named Belle Terre. Composition of "A"-22 continued through 1972, at Seventh Avenue and Belle Terre and then (July onward) at 240 Central Park South, New York City.[9] In November came the trip to Bellagio, where they were the guests of the Rockefeller Foundation at the Villa Serbelloni on Lake Como, 9 November–14 December. Just over one hundred lines of "A"-22 were written in Bellagio ("A," pp. 524–27).[10] The balance of the poem was written at Central Park South, beginning 23 January 1973 (Zukofsky's birthday) and finishing 14 April that year.

The "A"-22 Spiral is a double manuscript. On each verso page are rough drafts and margin notes for about twenty-five lines of the poem; on each recto page is a fair copy of the same twenty-five lines. The facing pages are numbered alike, pages 1–39; the draft page contains start and finishing dates for passages ranging from two or three lines to several dozen long. It will often give the place of composition, the source of the margin notes (b.n.b. or the "A" 22 & 23 Spiral); and sometimes a piece of ad hoc chronology will appear as Zukofsky details an upcoming passage to himself. There are usually no more than two drafts of any passage and often a single attempt—heavily overwritten—gets the poem as Zukofsky wants it.[11]

At the foot of each fair-copy page is the number of its last line; there are minor revisions throughout the fair-copy text, but, when these and the clarifications of odd lines are taken together, the poem as it appears on the recto pages of the "A"-22 Spiral is virtually identical to the printed text. Because Zukofsky did not type, his fair copies are scrupulously legible; any alterations are precisely detailed and any doubtful orthography is cleared up. He rarely revised in typescript, so the fair copy of a given work, with its painstaking attentions to detail, is almost always an authoritative text.

The "*A*"-23 Spiral

The second manuscript spiral of the late "*A*" is set up like its predecessor, this time with forty double-numbered pages and more stapled interleavings; on the inside cover we find information about times and places again. Augmenting these with others to be found on the verso pages of the notebook, we can reconstruct the composing of "*A*"-23 thus: it was begun 13 April 1973 (a day before the finish of "*A*"-22) and the writing flowed smoothly at Central Park South through 15 May, when the first section (another hundred-line unit) was completed. Work began on the second section 9 July; in August the Zukofskys were at Belle Terre, and in September they returned to Central Park South. Composition stopped near the three-hundred-line mark in early October ("tying winter into summer," "*A*"-23, p. 544), and later that month (23 October) Louis and Celia shifted house to 306 East Broadway in Port Jefferson. The move was to be a permanent one.

Once installed there, they rarely left, even to go to the city; the onset of aches and pains had made travel increasingly uncomfortable for both over the years, and Zukofsky accepted fewer and fewer engagements, finally giving up public readings altogether after 1975.[12] The Port Jefferson Zukofsky is the "stabled horse" of "*A*"-22 (p. 535), "old in / a greenhouse," who "sings sometimes"—a masterly piece of understatement. The horse was singing constantly, that strength at least undiminished, absorbed by his present project, maturing the next one, and thinking about one beyond that:

> Only forever is previous
> And not a horse's forever.
> If someone stole off with its body
> Be sure that its spirits
> Canter forever.
>
>   ("*A*"-12, p. 181)

The arthritic Zukofsky hung out all the signs of mortal reclusiveness; the other Zukofsky was going to live the 120 years of his Jewish patrimony, and more.[13] The double time scale is important.

Meanwhile, after settling in at East Broadway, Zukofsky took up "*A*"-23 again in late December 1973 and wrote continuously through September 1974. The final twenty-six lines of the movement were begun 17 September, which Zukofsky noted as the first day of Rosh Hashana ("*A*"-23 Spiral, p. 39). Five days later he wrote beneath the last line of the movement, now also the last-composed line of "*A*":

"A"-23 completed 12.30 pm Sat Sept 21/74   Louis Zukofsky
                                          Pt Jefferson NY 11777
                         ("A"-23 Spiral, p. 40)

Forty-six years of "A" were at an end.

The *80 Flowers* Materials

The work of a lifetime was complete, but the life of course continued, and with it the poetry. Zukofsky promptly turned his attention to the growing body of notes for *80 Flowers*. There are some references in the black notebook to "*New Poems, this notebook*" which at first suggest an unrecovered cache of manuscript poems (perhaps this is why the black notebook is curiously truncated?). But "*New Poems,*" though it was clearly once part of the black notebook, may not have meant drafts of poems but notes for them. In context, the material referred to is in all likelihood notes for the embryonic *80 Flowers:*

> 12/23/68—See under 80 Poems first page of
> * * *~~12/25/68~~————(New Poems—this notebook
> (b.n.b., p. 51)

> 7/16/71—See *80 Flowers* (list) growing out of
>   ALL & *A* 1–21, same date (7/16/71) this
>   notebook, *New Poems.*
> (b.n.b., p. 114)

The second entry was made at the Mansfield Center; page 113 of the black notebook is devoted to notes taken from an edition of John Gerard's *Herball,* which Zukofsky consulted there.[14] In the *80 Flowers* Notes, which are written on the same sized loose-leaf as the black notebook, the entry for 16 July 1971 does indeed give a list of flora from *All,* Zukofsky's collected short poems, and from "*A*" 1–21.[15] More than that, the *80 Flowers* entry for 16 July 1971 duplicates the Gerard material from the black notebook entry of the same date (*80 Fl.* Notes, pp. 1–2). *New Poems* is *80 Flowers,* growing right there in the black notebook, probably beyond page 115. On 17 September 1974 (that date again) Zukofsky carried across from the "*A*" 22 & 23 Spiral the overflow list from "*A*"-23 (*80 Fl.* Notes, pp. 3–5), and it is presumably at or about this time that the black-notebook loose-leaf parted company from the *New Poems* loose-leaf. The former was probably filed; the latter became the *80 Flowers* Notes, perhaps inheriting the black pocket-size ring binder.

Whether Zukofsky bought another ring binder and transferred his *80*

Flowers material or whether he simply removed the "A" notes from the one he was already using, we have no way of knowing. Both sets turned up at Texas in marked envelopes; as did the "Gamut" Notes, which are written on the same size loose-leaf. The point is that until September 1974, notes for "A" 22 & 23 and *80 Flowers* were contingent, whatever their housing or respective titles.

The *80 Flowers* Notes, some sixty-six pages, are in several distinct parts. To take these in the order they are preserved in at Texas: a schema for the sequence and a fair copy of #9 Privet; three lists of the eighty flowers followed by twenty-eight pages of notes and condensations of notes, plus a fourth list of flowers, which fills out into a twenty-six-page catalog. To make the best sense of this material, however, is to treat it chronologically and therefore in tandem with the *80 Flowers* Drafts when they begin in December 1974.

The *80 Flowers* Schema

On 30 September 1974, Zukofsky took an unlined piece of paper without punch holes (did it reside afterward in the back pocket of the binder?) and headed it "*80 Flowers*." Then he wrote:

√

> *Plan.* Beginning at 70 to finish for my 80th
>   birthday a book of songs called *80 Flowers*.
>
> *Substance.* Only those flowers I have actually
>   seen and whatever botany I can learn
>   in 10 years. ("drive"—horses cf *Anew* poem
>   33 & "A"-7)
>
> *Form.* 8-line songs of 5-word lines : 40 words
>   to each poem, growing out of and *con-*
>   *densing* my previous books, "A", *All*,
>   *Arise, arise, Bottom: On Shakespeare,*
>   *Catullus, Little* etc.

We perceive another reason (*the* reason?) "A" was to be completed by 1974, the year Zukofsky turned seventy. A decade-long songbook was to follow it, characteristically a mixture of observation and erudition, to be "driven" (powered) by the spirit of a small poem from the 1946 collection, *Anew*:[16]

> Drive, fast kisses,
> no need to see
> hands or eyelashes
> a mouth at her ear

trees or leaves
night or the days.

(All, p. 105)

The Schema had said " 'drive'—horses," but there is nothing equine here—except perhaps "Drive" if one knows about Zukofsky's passion for horses. However, the tenderness of the lyric and the year it was written (1939) suggest something more. Louis and Celia were married 20 August 1939; given the already very personal dimensions of the *80 Flowers* plan, may not a small poem written in a significant year contribute its drive to a celebration of the poet's years?[17] As for *"A"*-7, the other source of the "drive"-horses mentioned by the Schema, it was composed 1928–30; in it seven sawhorses are transfigured as poetic drive-horses in the course of seven incrementally frenetic sonnets. The seventh movement is talismanic to Zukofsky: " 'A.' Quoting the dictionary. Remembering my sawhorses, my little a.'s," he wrote in 1932, beginning the prose piece "Thanks to the Dictionary."[18] And in 1950–51, with almost twelve movements of *"A"* completed:

—Look, Paul, where
The sawhorses of *"A"*-7
Have brought me.

("A"-12, p. 228)

It was typical of Zukofsky to cite early work in order to illuminate his intentions for a much later project, particularly one that (by condensing all the works—poetry, fiction, drama, criticism—into just eighty songs) is about to demonstrate his contention that a poet writes one poem all his life. Even in 1950–51, Zukofsky was saying of some discarded work: "not much in it interests me now / If it can't be turned into poetry" (*"A"*-12, p. 252); and in 1972, introducing his fiction to an audience, he twice remarked that he worked at prose the same way he worked at poetry, finding and making no distinction between genres.[19]

The Schema went on to elaborate the form of *80 Flowers* further:

As to "40 words" c.f. Old Testament;
tetraktys (*"A"*-19 p. 166 of *"A"* 13–21
Cape or Paris Rev. edtn.) Also adding
integers $4 + o = 4$. Eight lines $= 2 \times 4$
("two-by-fours" 'I's (pronounced
eyes' p. 218 *All,* Norton Lib. edtn).
Eight 8-line songs per year would $=$
$8^2 = 64$, and adding integers again

= 10 (years); 8 × 10 years = 80 and
again adding integers 8 + 0 = 8 (cf 'A'-8
pp. 53 and 98 re. the number 8.
"A" *1–12* Cape or Paris Rev edtn)

Louis Zukofsky

Port Jefferson, NY   Sept. 30/74
11777²⁰

Number-tumbling is usually near the heart of Zukofsky's poetry ("I've counted words, // selected all my / life," *"A"*-14, p. 353). Numbers are something to work against, a form to transform as number-generated writing takes on its own life, spawning more numbers, other ratios. And so, owing a little everywhere—the Old Testament, *I's (Pronounced Eyes)*, *"A"*-8—and not conspicuously bound by any of it, the template of *80 Flowers* is drawn up, a new context for the conjunction of older members of the canon.

And the sources Zukofsky mentions? In the Old Testament, forty was the number of years in a generation (Judg. 3:30; 5:31) and was so frequently used because of this connection that it came to be looked on as rather sacrosanct.²¹ The *tetraktys* had already figured in *"A"*:

> all
> contests decided
> before the outcome
> by the
> Pythagoreans' Four
> justice the
> first perfect
> square product
> of equals
> holy holy
> tetraktys root
> and source
> generate gods
> and men
> (bless us)
> divine number begins
>
> with one
> until it
> comes to
> Four then

numbers themselves could not accommodate. The first addendum to the
Schema reads:

> note 12/18/74   opening epigraph using *thyme*
> (pronounced *time*) and thread the play
> of sound on both thru the 80 flowers
> that follow—thus making with the epigraph
> 81 poems (Adding integers, 8 + 1 = 9, The Muses, etc)
> Let time determine the book sequence of
> the 80—and their "order"—that is the
> chronology of *their writing*.

Thyme = time; something of the sort was likely to happen, given the
scope of the *Flowers*. Numbers will also be time-numbers during the
projected decade of writing, the series from one to eighty integrating with
a count of months and seasons. This is the time-present coordinate of *80
Flowers;* the cycles of these years will in addition contain anniversaries of
events from the past. If Zukofsky had followed his intention to take ten
years over the book it should have been possible to make out a fourfold
groundswell—winter, spring, summer, fall—ten times over in *80 Flowers*.
Forty seasons (whose generation?), 4 + 0, or "Four for balance," as "A"-22
puts it (p. 514). The extra poem, which introduces a Musing and universal
9 (8 + 1) and is placed first and explicitly thematic in the sequence, is
clearly going to require special scrutiny.

But there is more yet to the Schema. On its verso we read:

> Anticipating in *80 Flowers,* and
> while planning it since 12/29/68,
> a book entitled ~~Gamut, Trees ninety~~
> *Gamut: Trees ninety 5's* ⁎
> —that is,(for the year 2000)
>   five-word
> 90 poems of 5-~~word~~   lines
> each.
>   ⁎final title
> showed to Hugh Kenner   decided
> Baltimore, Md.   Apr 20/75
> Sat. Dec 13/75   LZ

The planning of *80 Flowers* which Zukofsky refers to is easily cross-
checked by consulting the black notebook's entries for December 1968,
where we find:

> 12/25/68 Gk ἄρτος [artos]; bread
>   (b.n.b., p. 52)

This reappears as the first entry of the *80 Flowers* Notes, dated, however, 29 December 1968—the same date given by the Schema. There is no black notebook entry for 29 December 1968, so the change of date looks like an error of transmission. *80 Flowers,* then, is in process as of Christmas Day 1968; and Christmas 1968 was distinguished in the imagination of many Americans by the voices of the *Apollo 8* crew reading, in turn, the first ten verses of Genesis from lunar orbit on Christmas Eve.

Zukofsky had followed the space race from its beginnings, repelled by its militarist overtones, intrigued by the men riding the rockets and by the feats they accomplished. The astronaut Christmas of 1968 is recorded on pages 51–52 of the black notebook, one entry before the *artos* note; Zukofsky notes the astronauts' descriptions of the moon in some detail (this was the first manned lunar orbit) and also mentions the Genesis reading. Is there a connection between the momentous flight of *Apollo 8* (there's another 8) in 1968 and the inception (genesis) of *80 Flowers?* Timing would suggest one, and timing is the crux of the project, but the heart of the matter rests in the full significance of the *artos* note that initiated the sequence six years later in December 1974.

In December 1968 the book was little more than a provisional title, "80 Poems" (b.n.b., p. 51; 12/23/68), plus an entry ostensibly about Greek bread. Zukofsky declares in retrospect (the Schema of 1974) that *80 Flowers* was initiated at this point, and certainly its first title implies that the ten-year time scheme was already present; but whether flowers were involved is impossible to tell. The first floral indication shows up in May 1969 in the notes Zukofsky made in England. Both field and written-up versions include the observation:

> London May 23/69. If we live to write a book of flowers:
> "pond pox"—see Akenfield by Ronald Blythe
> of Selbourne[23]

(b.n.b., p. 57)

The Blythe reference does not surface in *80 Flowers,* but the intimation that the book was to be a joint project and that the Zukofskys were undertaking it somewhat in the spirit of a race against time is interesting. Celia's assistance to Louis had ranged over the years from typing manuscripts and correspondence to making lucid criticism of works in progress, with stops in between for preparation of the Latin pony from which the translations of Catullus were worked, 1958–66. This time her skills were to be called on as co-observer (the comments on London flora derive from mutual outings, as do later observations in Bermuda and Bellagio) and as gardener; Zukofsky was taking seriously his intention in the Schema of using only flowers, wild or cultivated, that he had actually seen. It was

Celia, by her own admission, who took on the houseplants and, in Port Jefferson, the practicalities of a garden.[24] Louis kept record in the *80 Flowers* Drafts of plantings and blossomings.

To move on to the matter of "Gamut" brought up in the Schema; no actual date of inception is given, but there is an implication that plans for the book of trees grew alongside the *Flowers*. It was to be set up on similar lines—years, numbers, and natural growth—and the title Zukofsky eventually settled on (at some date after 20 April 1975) was "Gamut: 90 Trees," which is closer to *"80 Flowers"* than his original choice, "Gamut: Trees Ninety 5's." Most interesting at this stage is the whole notion of envisaging a book for one's ninety-sixth year; once again we are in the presence of the poet whose drive knows no bounds: "He wants impossible liveforever," as Zukofsky expressed it in *"A"*-12 (p. 237). Liveforever, the sovereign flower of *"A,"* will turn up again in *80 Flowers*. I have suggested that the desire to go on living forever was associated with the 120 years a Jewish blessing confers on the newborn, but it could equally well derive from the Pythagorean lifespan of a century, neatly quartered:

> Pith or gore has 4
> seasons, 20 yet boy, 40
> young, 60 ripe, 80 aged[25]
>
>   (*"A"*-22, p. 517)

The alignment of human with seasonal cycles is commonplace, but the hundred-year grid on which Zukofsky laid them out looks as if it should be a matter of ratio rather than physiological probability. However, the numbers are there in Pythagoras, and, if Zukofsky cared to take them literally, then writing a book of trees for his ninety-fifth birthday in 1999, "for the year 2000" (Schema), was a logical outgrowth of the figure. The attempt on liveforever is seen to be undiminished; realizing its projects, though, was in some ways a question of beating the clock.

The First List of 80 Flowers (October 1974)

By the end of September 1974, Zukofsky had determined how *80 Flowers* was to be structured and written. His next action was to make an eighty-item alphabetical list, which became the reservoir he selected flowers from as occasion dictated ("Let time determine the book sequence of the 80—and their 'order' "). The list contained flowers (and some trees) that had accrued individual significance to him over the years and those that casual observation or the garden at Port Jefferson brought into present range. *Taylor's Encyclopedia of Gardening* (4th ed.) was crucial to the arrangement of the list and continued to be a textbook for the entire project. Another stand-by, *Gray's Manual of Botany* (8th ed.), was the source of more technical information, usually concerning family relationships among the eighty candidates.[26]

The list, Aloe to Zinnia, is six pages long, each entry double-spaced to allow room for notes. This is where things warm up, because the list effectively became Zukofsky's first working plan for the *Flowers*. Information from Taylor, from Gray, from other notebooks, from "*A*" and the rest of the published work, from plant identification guides he was using—some or all of this was written into the First List as page references or abbreviated notes. After composition began in December, Zukofsky would write "done" against a used entry and give the sequence number of the poem in which the information appeared; he also checked such entries and, when the list was entirely superseded, the familiar diagonal lines canceled each page. All of this serves to enhance the impression that the First List was to *80 Flowers* what the "*A*" 22 & 23 Spiral was to "*A*" 22 & 23; organization and index of material, the working plan that moved with the writing.

At about this time the matter of combination began altering the shape of the First List. Zukofsky had probably always intended to deal with more than one flower per poem; the "80" of the title might be a sum of his years but there are patently more flowers than years in anyone's history, impinging more than one at a time and often in striking combination—and this is the basis of the phrase "work with," which appeared with increasing frequency as the First List grew older. As some entries were subsumed into others, Zukofsky inserted "substitutes" in their places; the contents of the alphabetical reservoir were thus changed, and the overloaded pages became increasingly difficult to read.

Beyond the sixth page of the First List was an addendum headed "Weeds," and, from late November 1974 until the following July, Zukofsky made many entries on these most virulent of all flowers, setting up a category outside the original eighty candidates. One reason for this interest was his son Paul's presentation to him in August 1971 of *Common Weeds of the United States*—a gift recorded in the black notebook (p. 115).[27] This was a reprint of a USDA handbook; it provided Zukofsky with exhaustive identification guides, and its provenance assured it an important place in the source material of *80 Flowers*. Zukofsky enjoyed feeling that any project of his was open to family interest and participation.

The *80 Flowers* Notes and the *80 Flowers* Drafts (December 1974–August 1975)

Actual note-taking for the *Flowers* occupies a relatively small proportion of the loose-leaf material gathered under the heading of *80 Flowers* Notes.

It begins, as we know, in 1968; the first four pages cover (sparsely) the years to 1974 and include the 1971 material on Gerard's *Herball* and the floral lists from *"A"* and *All,* plus the September 1974 carry-over of unused *"A"*-23 notes. From page 5 onward, the notes run concurrently with the *80 Flowers* Drafts, which Zukofsky kept in a separate sequence, presumably lodged before or after the Notes in whichever ring binder he was using.[28]

The pattern of the Drafts is characteristically orderly. Each poem is headed up with a sequence number, title, and starting date; then follow notes from Taylor and/or Gray concerning horticultural and botanical details of the selected flower(s), and perhaps notes from other plant books. Sometimes all this information is compressed into a verso margin, in other places it spreads comfortably over a page or more; sometimes it is missing altogether. Additional material from the Notes, usually literary and with varying degrees of recognizable connection to the *Flower* in hand, goes into the already crowded margins or is (more legibly) appended to the page-wide botanical notes. There are *Flowers* lacking this material and others where it is written straight in, by-passing the filter of the Notes. By far the commonest source of this latter kind is Shakespeare, whom Zukofsky could quote on most occasions.

Next, eight lines will be numbered off and a pencil draft begun, to the right of any note-crammed margin or directly beneath full-page notes. The first draft is worked on, usually with many erasures, until it fairly well resembles in a rough and overwritten state the final version. Sometimes there will be two or even three drafts before the poem is copied out in (ball-point) ink immediately below, on lines again numbered from one to eight. As the sequence progresses, there is rarely more than one pencil draft before the ink version. The finishing date is then noted, and most poems also include the starting date of the ink draft. As with *"A"* 22 & 23, Zukofsky has left a very precise record of composition.

The Drafts begin 25 December 1974 (six years to the day since the *artos* note and the astronaut Christmas), and they continue steadily to #15 Zebrina Etc, completed 26 August 1975. There is a minor hiatus (twenty-nine days) in June, the month Zukofsky attended the Ezra Pound Symposium at the University of Orono, Maine.[29] The Notes over these months continue sporadically, the biggest blocks from Rachel Carson's *The Sea around Us* (*80 Fl.* Notes, pp. 6–9) and some quotation and translation from Virgil's *Georgics* (*80 Fl.* Notes, p. 10). It is now late August and fifteen of the eighty are finished; the plan to write eight songs a year has gone by the board in the face of Zukofsky's energy ("drive"), and the rapidly changing shape of the project requires an updated working plan.

The Revised (First) Abbreviated List of 80 Flowers (28 August 1975)

The list of 28 August 1975 is two pages and a few lines long; its entries are single-spaced, and into this reduced area Zukofsky transferred the essentials of his original list ever more minutely. He retained the original list numbers, omitting the fifteen entries that had been used; substitutes for specific entries noted in the original list were integrated alphabetically and then at the extreme left the list was renumbered, from one to sixty-five. "Weeds" now became part of the list proper, and the abundance of weed information from the old list was packed tightly into the last page of the new one. Also on that page is a query:

> [#71, 77, 78, 80 i.e. Thyme, Weeds, Wistaria, Zinnia
> in that order to close *80 Flowers?* we'll see—Sept 2/75]
> (80 Fl. Notes, p. 10A)

Obviously Zukofsky had not renumbered by 2 September (or Thyme would have been #62 and Zinnia #65), but what is interesting is the projected closing sequence, which is already leaning toward an alphabetical conclusion. Zinnia, or something similarly Z-full, was perhaps to be expected, but the presence of Thyme (time) there at the final curtain sends the significance count soaring; Weeds are already slated for detailed treatment if the volume of note-taking is anything to go by; Wistaria is the only unknown.

**The *80 Flowers* Notes and the *80 Flowers* Drafts
(September 1975–May 1976)**

Composition got under way again early in September 1975 with #16 Four o'clock, and by 12 December Zukofsky had finished #22 Bayberry. The next day, in Baltimore, at the Johns Hopkins University, he recorded in a private reading all twenty-three *Flowers* so far completed—the only record we have of the work in performance.[30] On the same tape Zukofsky spoke to Hugh Kenner at some length about #22 Bayberry, which was naturally still fresh in his mind. To listen to him talk is to hear the quiet interlocking of Notes with Drafts, and, although he stays with materials and sources, enough is said to let a listener deduce the processes by which these things become songs. The Johns Hopkins tape is an invaluable resource to any student of *80 Flowers*.

We may recall that 13 December 1975 was also the date Zukofsky showed the *80 Flowers* Schema to Kenner (see above). This was the second time Kenner had seen material from the *Flowers;* there is a copy of #9 Privet on a scrap of unlined paper that accompanies the Notes, and on the verso Zukofsky has written: "Shown to Hugh Kenner June 17/75 Orono,

Me." Checking the Drafts (pp. 14–15), we discover that #9 Privet was the last poem written before the Pound Symposium at Orono. In this instance, too, Zukofsky was concerned to show his very latest work.[31]

The note-taking over this period becomes complicated. On a page marked "10A–2," Zukofsky begins condensing the notes of the previous ten pages. Rather as the First List was trimmed down, so Carson, Virgil, and the rest are compressed into a radically smaller space (*80 Fl.* Notes, pp. 10A–2, 10B). The date for this appears to be 1 November 1975, and the condensing carries over to a page "to be filed as pg. 10C." Late in December, condensation is dropped in favor of full-scale note-taking again as Zukofsky reads Henri Fabre's *Social Life in the Insect World,* some Henry James (*The Princess Casamassima, The Ambassadors*) and then, in April 1976, *The Diary and Autobiography of John Adams,* followed by more James (*Watch and Ward, Roderick Hudson, William Wetmore Story and His Friends*), April through June. James material began appearing consistently in the *Flowers* at #30 Violet, composed near the end of April 1976. When he had finished #34 Lily-of-the-Valley late in May, Zukofsky made another list. The old one had reached the overwritten state of its predecessor.

The Second Abbreviated List of 80 Flowers (29 May 1976)

There remained forty-six poems to write; the Second Abbreviated List took what had not been used and the entries were renumbered from one to forty-six. Everything now fitted into two pages, again with some Weeds addenda numbered from one to thirteen. The closing sequence had developed a stage further: #44 is Thyme, #45 is Vines, and #46 is a conglomerate—Weeds, Yucca, and Zinnia. Wistaria has been replaced by a Y-flower; or to be more precise, it has been subsumed into #45 Vines.

The *80 Flowers* Notes and the *80 Flowers* Drafts (June 1976–October 1976)

From June to October 1976 Zukofsky wrote another sixteen poems, finishing #50 Chokecherry 22 October, Paul's thirty-third birthday. At the same time he continued to read and make notes from Henry James (*William Wetmore Story, The Portrait of a Lady*), and then he turned to Thomas Hardy (*Desperate Remedies, A Pair of Blue Eyes,* and *Far from the Madding Crowd*). Hardy begins to feature in *80 Flowers* at #44 Queen Anne's Lace, written late August–early September. The poems in this part of the sequence nearly all contain James or Hardy references, and three of them host both novelists (#38 Phlox, #47 Dahlia, #49 Slipperwort).

Another round of condensation was taking place in the Notes. In mid-June Zukofsky condensed pages 11–20 (those large tracts of Fabre and

Adams, plus the first James novels) into a page and a half of Condensed Notes, pp. 1–2. He continued to write up the remaining James material and the Hardy that followed in this severely impacted manner (*80 Fl.* Notes, pp. 3–4, Condensed Notes), finishing with both early in September.

The Third Abbreviated List of 80 Flowers (27 October 1976)

With thirty *Flowers* to go, the next list duly contained thirty unused options, their numbers carried over from the Second Abbreviated List. There was generally more space for the ever-present and multiplying minutiae; this list ran to four pages, the last of them almost entirely taken up with notes on the thirteen candidates for the Weeds poem.

But the Third Abbreviated List is the joker of the pack. The list of thirty was completed 27 October or soon afterward, in four pages—but each of the twenty-two pages beyond that is also scrupulously headed "3rd Abbreviated List of 80 Flowers." A better idea of their function is to be found in the heading:

> Notes for preceding final 30 especially
> numbers 45, 46***unless "better" substitutes
> come up prob. better to handle 45 in two poems and
> 46 Weeds . . . at least two; yucca zinnia one each[32]
> (3rd Abb. List, p. 5)

The outsize list is an extension of the Notes.

The *80 Flowers* Notes (November 1976–April 1977) and the Americana Notes

Zukofsky wrote no *Flower* poems over the five months that followed—the longest break in composition throughout the project. But silence did not signal inactivity; his attention was concentrated on other things.

One of these was probably the making of an index for the upcoming University of California Press edition of "*A.*" Celia's "Year By Year" section of the updated *Bibliography* gives only "1976" as the date of compilation for the index. He was thoroughly occupied by the *Flowers* until 22 October, and indexing "*A,*" even if it was to be done a few pages at a time over an extended period, was no light task. Zukofsky's indexes were customarily idiosyncratic; by means of unlikely entries and curious emphases they give directions about how to read the work being indexed (seventy-three cited instances of "the" in "*A,*" for example; eventually we have to wonder why the bulk of them occur in "*A*" 12–23 and why the page numbers dovetail so neatly with the seventy-one cited "a"s and the forty "an"s). Indexing was a special kind of composition to Zukofsky, alphabetical to boot. The impact of a full rereading of *"A"* on the composition of *80 Flowers* must be taken into account; the last thirty poems could well be expected to show traces of the reading Zukofsky did for his index.

Whatever else Zukofsky was doing in November 1976, he continued to make notes for *80 Flowers* in the Third Abbreviated List. First up was a condensation of the remaining unused material from the Condensed Notes of the previous June; Adams, Horace, Virgil (3rd Abb. List, p. 3). Then followed some entries on Hardy's *The Hand of Ethelberta, A Laodicean,* and (January 1977) *The Dynasts.* Karl von Frisch's *Animal Architecture* got expansive quarter-page treatment on page 6. Then on page 7, beginning 20 January 1977, Zukofsky made notes from *Taylor's Gardening Encyclopedia.* He started at "E" and for the next two and a half months made practically day-by-day entries on little else but Taylor's alphabet, ending at Zinnia, 4 April 1977 (3rd Abb. List, p. 24), and elaborating on Yaupon, Yucca, and Heather for two pages beyond that.

What are we to make of this huge new reservoir of plants, coming at a stage when Zukofsky's efforts seem otherwise strenuously directed at condensation? Did the indexing of *"A"* prompt it? Or did he simply feel that his botanical material needed shaking out? Certainly all twenty-six pages of the Third Abbreviated List were used in the ensuing composition, judging by the many checks and sequence numbers throughout. In fact, they were exhaustively used; near the top of each page is a double check and the word "done." We might guess that the (many) asterisked entries of the Third List represent yet another selection process, especially when the bulk of them turn up in *80 Flowers* either as title flowers or worked with title flowers. When we also discover that the set of interleavings headed "Americana" is a selection of the Third List's asterisked entries, and that some of the Third List was eventually added to the "Gamut" Notes, the heavily worked appearance of those twenty-six pages is explained. "Done" signifies not only material used in *80 Flowers* but also material transferred to other places, other lists. It is probably the last thing Zukofsky wrote on his notes for *80 Flowers,* sometime between January and May 1978.

The *80 Flowers* Drafts (April 1977–January 1978)

The date Zukofsky chose to begin composing again was 11 April 1977, the anniversary of his father's death in 1950. Once he had started there were no breaks above a few days, and sometimes notes for one poem were collected before composition of the previous one was complete.

The drafts of #51 Snowdrop through #80 Zinnia are distinguished from their predecessors in two ways. The first concerns the collection of notes; this had been an informal prelude to each poem almost from the outset, but after April 1977 Zukofsky began dating the collecting period, and sometimes it was longer than the combined drafts that followed. The amount of material which had not shaken down through the Notes also seemed on the increase. Obviously, no amount of condensation or list-making was going to get in the way of time present's right to order the *Flowers*.

Second, Zukofsky was also working from the surviving In Process Notes (his term) of the project. As the spring of 1977 brought up flowers in the garden at East Broadway, Zukofsky (still engaged on his Taylor list) noted the dates of blossoming on the backs of old checkbooks, which he ruled into columns headed "Blossoms" (the flowering date), "Name or Title" (usually as it was to appear in *80 Flowers*), and "Notes" (mostly Taylor and Gray, but also personal observations of the blossoming and cross-references to material already gathered in the Notes). By the time all this had been squeezed in, the In Process lists had turned into yet another instance of the condensing drive. There are six pages of the check-sized lists spanning March-September 1977 and their correct place in the Drafts is a matter of conjecture. Like the various lists of *80 Flowers*, they would have moved as the sequence progressed and so perhaps they are best grouped as an appendage to the Drafts, rather as Zukofsky grouped the first three lists of 80 Flowers together at the beginning of the Notes.

The order preserved on the In Process cards is almost exactly the order of *80 Flowers,* #51 Snowdrop through #72 Raspberry—a progress of spring into late summer; the whole 1977 growing season. The five-month hiatus of 1976–77, we realize in retrospect, was late fall and winter.

The last ten poems are organized differently. #71 Aster and #72 Raspberry derive from the In Process Notes, but for the others Zukofsky was using the Americana notes and unused literary material from the Third List; there was also the normal quota of newly introduced data. Why "Americana"? What time ordered the writing of the last ten *Flowers?* These are questions we shall consider later. One thing at least is sure; the closer Zukofsky came to the end, the more extensive were his preparations for each poem. For #76 Vines through #80 Zinnia, more check backs and scraps of paper are interleaved with the Drafts; each of the truly con-glomerate poems (#76 Vines, #77 Weeds, #78 "X") has a separate sum-mary of contents, and all five have separate collections of notes, which accounts for the scarcity of notes written into the Drafts themselves at this point. Most of the work for the end of *80 Flowers*, it would seem, was carried out on these miscellaneous scraps; there are even the beginnings of a draft of #80 Zinnia on one of them and some in-process scribblings for it on another. This is the one occasion in the project when lines written outside of the orderly sequence of the Drafts have survived; if Zukofsky was working from scraps during the composition period—and this was a characteristic of his earlier work—he took care to remove them from the material that later went to Texas.

On 21 January 1978, *80 Flowers* was completed. It had taken slightly over three years to write (although there is almost a decade-span counting from the *artos* note of 1968) and the date was Celia's birthday. For a work written around a count of the poet's own years there are a remarkable number of compositional dates in *80 Flowers* commemorating others' birthdays; not once is a poem started or finished on his own birthday, 23 January.

The *80 Flowers* Spiral, the Typescript, and Stinehour

The *80 Flowers* Spiral in which Zukofsky made fair copies of the *Flowers* from the ink drafts has been mentioned previously. Presumably the poems were copied as they were completed; each one is fully signed, then "Port Jefferson NY 11777" appears below the signature, and the dates of composition are entered below that. Everything suggests that these are the formal final manuscript versions of the work. Opposite or underneath the signature, Zukofsky sometimes added an observation, often a dedication and apparently connected to the dates of composition (see Appendix A). Knowing what we do about the personal dimension of *80 Flowers,* the dedications and anniversaries do not come altogether as a surprise. Nor does their suppression from the printed text, knowing what we do about Zukofsky's penchant for concealed figures.

There are very few variants between the ink drafts and the Spiral copies; most of them are matters of punctuation and spelling.[33] And there is only one variant between the Spiral and the master typed copy Celia made from it; ironically, that variant altered the sense of the line it was in and has to be counted as the only erratum in the first edition of *80 Flowers.* #61 Bearded Iris begins in the ink draft and in the Spiral:

Gay ore geek con candlelows

Four-fifths of this is the transliterated title of Virgil's *Georgics—Georgi-con,* a perfect phonetic match. However, the published text reads:

Gay ore gook con candlelows

Suddenly the tongue has a much harder time getting around the words and the Latin becomes indistinct. At the bottom of this change was a typing error; Celia had typed "gook" and then corrected by overtyping "geek" without erasing the first attempt. The top copy of the typescript (now at Texas) shows the word as "geok"; if Zukofsky did the proofing he must have seen "geek." But the printers at Stinehour, working from a carbon of this typescript, saw a much heavier imprint of "o"s ("gook") and set the word as "gook." Whoever read galley proof did not pick up the error; the master proofs were duly initialed by Zukofsky, and the altered line passed into the text.

Zukofsky had initiated proceedings with the Stinehour Press 21 December 1977 by writing to C. Freeman Keith, "at the suggestion of John Cage that you might be interested in printing my latest poems."[34] He requested an estimate of costs for publication in 1978, specified the font he wanted and that the edition be *"strictly* limited to eighty (80) copies." He then described the format of the poems and suggested a page approximately 6½″ × 5½″, ninety pages to the book, which was to have stitched-board binding so that it would open flat. The first three poems of *80 Flowers* were enclosed with the letter for Freeman Keith's inspection— perhaps a copy of page 1 of the typescript?

Stinehour's specifications, for a "nice little edition using good materials and workmanship but not fancy or ostentatious in any way" (Freeman Keith, letter of 4 January 1978), were as follows:

edition: 80
trim size: 6⅜ by 5½
length: 88 pages
paper: Curtis Rag Laid sub 75 (sample enclosed)
type: Monotype Bembo 13/18
ink: black throughout
binding: smythsewn, headbands, colored endleaves, cased in .070 boards with either one-piece paper or boards with cloth, printed or stamped spine only, inserted into .070 two-piece slipcase covered with unprinted colored text

The edition was to cost about $1,600 paperbound, $1,700 clothbound, and publication could be assured in mid-1978 if copy was received in January. The Zukofskys accepted Stinehour's specifications and opted for a hardcover edition.

Completion of *80 Flowers* was now only three poems distant, and Zukofsky worked the final pair in tandem from 14 January; #79 Yaupon was completed 17 January and #80 Zinnia, as we know, 21 January. The typescript must have been completed and dispatched a few days later because Freeman Keith's next communication (undated; a draft letter of either late January or early February) thanked Zukofsky for the receipt of the manuscript and promised galleys in late February and delivery of the book by late June.

The Zukofskys received their galleys presumably as scheduled and

read proof; apart from the #61 Bearded Iris mishap, which passed unnoticed, all was in order and there are no corrections on the master proof.
On the copy now at Texas, the only marks are penciled "i"s in the margin
every time "i" is preceded in the text by "f"; the proofreader here was
objecting to the apparently dotless "i" that an "fi" ligature produces in
Monotype Bembo (the ligature persists in the published version). The
galleys were returned, and production was well under way when Zukofsky died 12 May.

A publication announcement for June 1978 appeared in the *L.Z.
Paideuma* describing *80 Flowers* as, "with epigraph 81 new short poems
that have not been printed or read in public." The book was obtainable
only from Celia Zukofsky and the price, as already noted, was $150. In
place of Louis's signature, Celia inscribed each copy:

Atque in Perpetuum L.Z.
January 23, 1904 – May 12, 1978
C.

There were of course still six years before Zukofsky's eightieth birthday and the proper occasion of the book.

"Gamut: 90 Trees"

As *80 Flowers* was inextricable in its early stages from *"A"* 22 & 23, so
"Gamut: 90 Trees" is initially part of the *Flowers* corpus. The Schema
indicated as much and the sixteen pages of extant notes at Texas confirm
it. They also shed light on later note-taking for the *Flowers*.

The "Gamut" Notes are divided (by Zukofsky) into two parts. First
come four pages of the familiar loose-leaf, labeled at the bottom of the
fourth page as old notes dating from 1969 to 1975. Sure enough, the first
entry is an old friend from the black notebook's record of the London trip.
The following entries are scattered (two apiece for 1973 and 1974) until
1975, when trees that have appeared in the course of the *80 Flowers* Notes
reappear. The last note, 1 June 1975, is an identification of chokecherry,
the shrubby tree that became the title "flower" of #50 Chokecherry.

The second part of the "Gamut" Notes (same loose-leaf) is designated,
again on page 4 of the first sequence, as fourteen pages dating from 1969
to 1978. If this is a separate sequence, the first page of it is missing because
the loose-leaf numbering beyond page 4 (first sequence) starts in October
1976 at (another) page 3. Interestingly enough, the precise date is 28
October and the entry is Acer rubrum, red maple; it is followed by
Aconite, Anacardiaceae, Aralia racemosa, Araucaria, and so forth. It
seems this is the beginning of an alphabetical list of trees (and some

flowers), and the source of it is not long appearing: *Taylor's Encyclopedia of Gardening*.

Zukofsky made the four-page Third Abbreviated List on 27 October 1976; very few notes went into its continuation, November-December, but the pace quickened 20 January 1977, when he started the alphabetical list from Taylor, at "E." And what is happening in "Gamut," January 1977? On page 4 of the second sequence is the rough draft of an epigraph for "Gamut" entitled "The Overworld"; it is dated 16 January 1977 and incorporates material from *The Dynasts* by Thomas Hardy. Below it the alphabetical sequence from Taylor resumes with Elaeagnus, Elm, and Empetrum; the date is 20 January. From this point until 6 April and the end of the alphabet, note-taking for "Gamut" and *80 Flowers* is perfectly in step. In the winter and early spring of 1977, waiting for the flowers to come up so the *Flowers* could start again, Zukofsky was making a double list—flowers for the immediate future, trees for the long-term—so that the last list of one project blended into the first list for the next. And all through the pages of the outsize Third Abbreviated List of 80 Flowers as it was worked April 1977 to January 1978, there are references to "Gamut" and directions to leave unused material for the new book. No doubt if there were ever more notes for "Gamut," a condensation of unused *80 Flowers* material would have been among the immediate post–January 1978 pages.

How closely "Gamut" and *80 Flowers* are related in terms of actual text is evidenced in two places. The first concerns the "Gamut" epigraph of January 1977; Zukofsky was not satisfied with his attempt and made a note on the draft to rework it. The reworking, however, turns up in *80 Flowers* as part of #54 Windflower, the fourth poem to be composed after Zukofsky returned to the *Flowers* in April 1977 (see chap. 8). A second appropriation occurs when a "Gamut" entry of 17 January 1978 quoting Shakespeare's Sonnet 56 is carried bodily over into #80 Zinnia, which was being written at the time; there is a note on the draft of #80 Zinnia to check the "Gamut" entry—where the Shakespeare has been punctiliously annotated as having been used in *80 Flowers* ("Gamut" Notes, 2nd seq., p. 14).

Clearly, "Gamut" was set up to go as soon as the *Flowers* were out of the way. What is surprising, given Zukofsky's work habits, is that we have no notes after January 1978 and just one finished poem (and that only by accident of the *80 Flowers* Spiral). #1 Much Ado About Trees was written 5–11 February 1978; there are no drafts of it, and only a few scattered references in the "Gamut" Notes might help us elucidate it. The loose-leaf at Texas is obviously not all there was to "Gamut: 90 Trees," and because the work is so similar to the *Flowers*, for which we have ample evidence of

Zukofsky's late modes of composition, it is possible to construct a scenario January through May 1978.

First, the Taylor list in the "Gamut" Notes has been well worked over; there are checks, crosses, and diagonal page cancellations. Zukofsky's first action after finishing *"A"* 22 & 23 in 1974 was to make the first list of *80 Flowers* "from previous notes" (First List, p. vi); might not the Taylor alphabet in the "Gamut" Notes be raw material for a First List of 90 Trees? made sometime after 21 January 1978, and beginning the phase of active work on the trees project? Did Zukofsky then remove all the *80 Flowers* loose-leaf from the ring binder, leaving just the "Gamut" material? (shades of 1974). However, if he did that, why do we have the "Gamut" Notes but not the list of trees or any drafts that would have come after them?

The answer may lie with the nature of the Notes we do have. The configuration of the identificatory note on page 4 of the first sequence is ambiguous: the word "old" has been added *above* the description of the sequences (number of pages in each, duration of entries), and this may mean that *both* sequences are old notes; that is, they have been super-seded—and therefore removed from the ring binder to the marked enve-lope in which they survive at Texas. And this seems to be the case; both sequences are heavily checked and crossed with the sort of markings Zukofsky habitually made to indicate that entries have been used—or transferred for further use. This proposes the existence of another set of loose-leaf "Gamut" Notes (current, working notes) to go with the conjec-tural list of 90 Trees, the drafts of #1 Much Ado About Trees, plus those of any poems that followed it. By all accounts, Zukofsky was not incapaci-tated until a few days before his death, and it is hard to imagine that the "singing horse" would not be pushing ahead with his latest liveforever project as long as he was able to. Somewhere in Zukofsky's private papers there may be a pocket-size ring binder containing work in progress; three months' worth of "Gamut: 90 Trees."

What, in sum, does the material for *"A"* 22 & 23, *80 Flowers*, and "Gamut" tell us about the way Zukofsky worked his late poetry? Most obviously that it was comprehensively organized and that the organiza-tion was recorded in all its parts with keen attention to method, time, and place. The impulse to plan and record was partly instinctive (and the nature of the late work, particularly the *Flowers* and "Gamut," welcomed these attentions); it was also partly meant as elucidation of a difficult work.

Conventional wisdom would have it that notes and draft materials are unnecessary to the reading of a poem, and in most cases wisdom has its way—Zukofsky said often enough that paying sufficient attention elucidates a work. But what happens when that work is a radical departure not only from current modes but also from the very work that has preceded it? Zukofsky was ready to concede that the shape of "A" fell into three parts: "A" 1-21, "A" 22 & 23, and "A"-24.[35] The difficulty of the last-written movements was of an order to baffle and eventually alienate all but the most persistent of readers. The condescension of explanations was as distasteful as ever to Zukofsky, but just the same there was a real risk of losing his audience altogether. The solution, as Zukofskian as those quiet indexes that critique the poet's work without seeming to do anything more than give page numbers, was to legitimize use of the draft material by housing it in a public collection.

Zukofsky knew that all the manuscript he cared to preserve would find a home in the Texas archive. The black notebook was already there; there can be little doubt that the "A" 22 & 23 spirals and the *80 Flowers* materials were headed in the same direction—when the poet felt ready to release them. Texas was in effect written into the history of the work; Texas was an ultimate insurance against the black holes of neglect into which the very difficult too readily falls.

Zukofsky had put forty-six years into the writing of "A"; for a large part of that time his efforts were unrecognized and rarely published ("A" *1-12* did not appear until 1959, for example; thirty years after the composition of its first movements). He took most of this with the good grace of one secure in the knowledge that what he does is important, but the overly quiet years had a cumulative effect. The bitterness in parts of "A"-21 (composed 1966–67) has a parallel expression in the diary-like pages of the black notebook:

> Oct 23/67   Why do the young poets insist on sending
> their work, or showing me how they play, when
> near Shakespeare or Chaucer or Homer on the shelf
> the poets of one's youth ~~are~~ have become only sometimes an
> interest of how one's friends played, how ~~they~~ we
> lived ~~their~~ our lives. It took a long time to get to
> Z in an alphabetical order of a world such as
> it is.
>
> (b.n.b., p. 11)

"Getting to Z" was a figure Zukofsky took seriously (the passage above is marked for inclusion in either "A"-22 or "A"-23), and it serves to illustrate the point that although he wanted acclaim for his work, he was not going to make concessions to fashion or his audience to get it.

The world of poetry finally "got to Z" in the late 1960s, cued by the enthusiasm of a generation after Zukofsky's own: Robert Duncan, Robert

Creeley, and others, the slightly older brothers of the "young poets" mentioned above. By that time Zukofsky was retired and fully occupied with preparations for *"A"* 22 & 23 ("5 years of reading, little talking"). He enjoyed the slightly awed attentions of the fraternity but what might have pleased him even more was the prospect of a readership for the late *"A."* People wanted to read (and publish) the rest of the poem as it came to hand. This interest must have stimulated Zukofsky's poetic faculties enormously—and confirmed him in the belief that he had been on the right track all along.

But having been thirty years ahead of his time once, and having paid for it, Zukofsky was shrewd enough to know that a second radical jump would leave behind even the most perceptive and dedicated of his new-found readers. He made the jump anyway—but he blueprinted the process in minute detail, knowing he was constructing a time capsule: a contingency plan against mortality ("When I am dead in the empty ear / you might ask what he was like," *"A"*-18, p. 393). The notebooks now at Texas are part of Louis Zukofsky's intention to go on living forever; they preserve the details of a most remarkable poetic and it is time to use them, the better to read the poetry.

2

"The Happy New Years": Zukofsky's Late Poetic

"AN ERA" and "Initial": The "An"-Song Sings

The era of Zukofsky's late poetry gets under way 14 February 1970, when the valentine that later came to stand at the head of "A"-22 was composed. This was the ninth time a movement of "A" had led off with a lyric beginning "An," and this particular "An"-song (the term is Zukofsky's, from the notebooks) had the distinct appearance of an epigraph:

> AN ERA
> ANY TIME
> OF YEAR
>
> ("A"-22, p. 508)

Boldface capitals, two words per line, three justified lines; six words intricately linked by associations of sound and sense. Or "sight, sound, and intellection," as Zukofsky would have it, that test of pleasure's range in a poem.[1] Roughly, this poem could be saying—*start (from here) anytime* (an *era*, according to the *Century Dictionary* is, among other things, a date or event forming the beginning of a distinct period).[2] Or perhaps: "Tell us about it, my Light, / Start where you please" ("A"-12, p. 261). *Begin, anytime, from this point* (love's festival); no hearts, no snow, none of the red and white (warmth for the cold) to be found in some of Zukofsky's earlier valentines.[3] When "AN ERA" was printed later in 1970 by Unicorn Press of Santa Barbara as a poetry postcard, its blue uppercase type rode a ground of yellow—chromographic specifications concisely described by Zukofsky in the fourth line of "A"-22 proper: "blow blue up against yellow."[4] Blue and yellow persist in these first 103 lines of "A"-22, to be joined only at the last by the third primary, February's own red:

> cherries, knave of a valentine,
> were ever blue of yellow,
> birds, harp in three trees—

34

now summer happy new year
any time of year—

("A"-22, p. 511)

Three colors, three trees, three Zukofskys (the valentines were always
family-inclusive), and an odd mixing of seasons and greeting (cherries in
February? New Year's in summer?) for which "AN ERA" seems partly
responsible—"ANY TIME / OF YEAR." "AN ERA"'s extension across the
calendar is apparently to be taken literally; its occasion, Valentine's Day, is
simply a starting point that somehow manages to take in summer and
New Year's. What is going on?

The poem is deceptively simple. It is mellifluous, which surely has
something to do with the regular push and pull of vowels against consonants in a confined space. Three vowel sounds to each short line leave
precious little time for the two or three consonants to be anything but
springboards for a melody of A ("AN"), E ("ERA," "ANY," "ANY," "YEAR"), I
("TIME"), O ("OF"), and ə ("ERA").[5] Slow down the three lines to be
reminded, "as the Book Bahir says, 'the vowels abide in consonants like
souls in bodies'" (*Bottom: On Shakespeare*, p. 421).[6] Or, musically,
Zukofsky's notation in "4 Other Countries":

The vowels
    abide
in consonants
    like

Souls
    in
bodies—
    paradise is his

Hand,
    paradise
our
    speech.

(*All*, p. 181)

So these vowels hand over three nouns about chronology—ERA, TIME,
YEAR—in a column, the right half of the poem. And on the left are three
particles, two of them wide open to possibility—AN, ANY—and the other
one attaching and possessive—OF. The manner in which "AN ERA" is
arranged encourages the curious eye to notice this stacking of components, right and left, and then to search the justified margins for lexical
significance: AAO on the left, AER on the right; an abundance of vowels

without immediate significance. The only thing worth checking up on right away seems to be ERA.

The *Century* lets us know that the Latin root *aera* (item of account) was a singular noun formed from the plural of *aes* (ore, brass, money); all to do with counting. Some authorities refer the word *aera* to the Gothic *jēr*, our English YEAR—an item of potential Zukofskian interest in that connection. Semantically, ERA is a blend of fixity and seriation; the *Century* lists three senses ranging from "a series of years having some distinctive historical character" to "loosely, an epoch from which time is reckoned, or a point of time noted for some event or occurrence." Generally though, ERA is used in the third of the *Century*'s senses, as a *succession* of time containing certain *points* of time: "A tale or count of years from a fixed epoch; a period during which . . . years are numbered and dates are reckoned from a particular point of time in the past, generally determined by some historical event."

Notions of demarcation hang about ERA, perhaps the inevitable consequence of an etymology full of counters and counting. The drift of all this, Zukofsky-wise, seems to be that we are counting time, duration *and* events—ERA, TIME, YEAR. Phonetically, *aera* also points at a respectable (if antique) identity for that right-hand acrostic, AER; *aer* (air) signifies particularly the lower, hazier atmosphere as opposed to the pure upper air, or *aether* (ether), of the ancients.

Some of this begins to make sense when we start reading in the body of "*A*"-22 or, to be precise, in the hundred-line lyric originally entitled "Initial," which Zukofsky uses (with "AN ERA") to begin the twenty-second movement:

> Others letters a sum owed
> ages account years each year[7]

("A"-22, p. 508)

Some play going on here between ERA's old and newer meanings. The next stop is Zukofsky's black notebook (p. 74), a half-page entry for 14 February 1970. "An era / any time / of year" is already extant near the top of the page, and "A Happy New Year any time / of year" tucked in just below and bracketed with it; Zukofsky has the beginning and the end of his projected lyric. The entry itself is an exploration of ERA's Latin and (some) Greek antecedents; referring us to *aera* (second meaning) and *aes* in Zukofsky's standard source of Latin know-how, Lewis and Short's dictionary.[8]

The entry for *aera* gives basically what the *Century* did, but in greater philological detail. *Aes* is more gratifying; *aes alienum* is "the money of another, a sum owed, a debt"; *aes* can be "wages" ("a sum owed / ages") or "pay"; it can also be "reward." We try the opening lines of "Initial" again:

> Others letters a sum owed
> ages account years each year
> out of old fields, permute
> blow blue up against yellow
> —scapes welcome young birds—initial
>
> transmutes itself, swim near and
> read a weed's reward—grain
> an omen a good omen
> the chill mists greet woods
> ice, flowers—their soul's return
>
> ("*A*"-22, p. 508)

"Initial" rapidly begins to sound like commentary and expansion upon "AN ERA." It is still puzzling, but among the things permuting and transmuting are several dictionary-definition senses of *aera* and *aes*. The first meaning of *aera* in Lewis and Short is from the Greek *aira*, "a weed among grain; darnel, tare, cockle": "read a weed's reward—grain"—*aira* tangled up in *aera*. Checking *aer*, we find it has a poetic usage meaning "cloud, vapor, mist"; also poetical is the phrase *aer summus* (the highest point; an airy summit?) *arboris* (of the trees)—"the chill mists greet woods / ice"? Maybe that *summus* permutes in Zukofskian frames of reference to *summer's* (any time of year) trees? A long shot. Continuing with "Initial":

> let me live here ever,
> sweet now, silence foison to
> on top of the weather
> it has said it before
> why that was you that
>
> is how you weather division
>
> ("*A*"-22, p. 508)

Aer, another meaning, is also weather; "on top of the weather"—*aer summus?*

Now more familiar material is coming into the poem, voices from *The Tempest* at that exact point where an airy spectacle is being performed for the lovers. Prospero ("Sweet, now, silence!" *Tmp*. IV.i.124) masterminds it, Ariel (permute, Aerial) stage-manages it, and Ferdinand wonders aloud what Prospero wants to hear:

> Let me live here ever;
> So rare a wond'red father and a wise
> Makes this place Paradise.[9]

(Tmp. IV.i.122)

"Paradise"—the bottom line of Ferdinand's thought appears, capitalized the same, a few lines later: "Paradise / the swept brain blood warmer" ("A"-22, p. 509). And Ceres, lady of grain herself, has just sung a fulsome marriage blessing. No weedy *aira,* in this era:

> Earth's increase, foison plenty,
> Barns and garners never empty,
> Vines, with clust'ring bunches growing,
> Plants with goodly burden bowing.
> Spring come to you at the farthest
> In the very end of harvest!
> Scarcity and want shall shun you;
> Ceres' blessing so is on you.

(Tmp. IV.i.110)

From chill mists and ice, "Initial" has moved in the space of half a line, and with the assistance of *The Tempest,* to assurance of abundant, paradisal summer; an airy assurance, certainly, but we are never given reason to doubt the efficacy of Prospero's spirits. Even the marriage song conspires in Zukofsky's switchbacking of seasons with a wish for spring at the end of harvest. Does paradise tolerate winter? Is paradise summer and spring, "ANY TIME / OF YEAR"?

Shakespeare is not the only singing presence in "Initial." The other half of the 14 February 1970 note concerns Chaucer's *Parlement of Foules,* for two reasons bearing closely on "AN ERA" and "Initial." First, the *Parlement* is not only a dream vision (more "ayrie" *aer*) but also a Valentine's Day poem. By ancient tradition the birds convene 14 February each year to choose mates; the occasion affords Chaucer the opportunity to engineer a debate between the exponents of courtly love and those of procreative urgency. Chaucer's birds supply winged voices for Zukofsky's airy *aers,* also musical airs, a conceit in "A" since its seventh movement: "airs, birds / Of words" ("A"-7, p. 39). Second, the annual character of the parliament and its conventions is stressed throughout the poem by means of a small (permuting) phrase, "yeer to yere" and "yeer by yere." Zukofsky lit on this ("Others letters a sum owed / ages account years each year / out of old fields"), homing in on the very first occurrence of the phrase:

For out of old feldes, as men seith,
Cometh al this newe corn fro yeer to yere;
And out of olde bokes, in good feith,
Cometh al this newe science that men lere.[10]

(*Parlement,* 22–25)

More corn, more bounty. Zukofsky is also nodding across forty-four years
to his own "Poem Beginning 'The'" (1926); the epigraph of its first section
was: *"And out of olde bokes, in good feith"* (*All,* p. 12). " 'The'" was
Zukofsky's first attempt at cohering a lengthy poem, and it became
something of a gatehouse in his work; it stands first in *All,* and the
Chaucerian epigraph is therefore a gatehouse to the gatehouse. When
Zukofsky came to the *Parlement* in 1970 for its seasonal associations (14
February), he was about to plunge again into the difficulties of a departure
from what had gone before, *"A"* 1–21. It must have struck him as peculiarly
appropriate to pick up the other half of a figure calling new out of old
which he had used in his youth. The poet keeps writing the same (newly
different) poem all his life.

The first half of the aphorism that Chaucer put into the mouth of his
Dreamer is grainy enough for Zukofsky's purposes; but also of interest is
the kind of garden in which the Dreamer finds Nature and her assembled
birds. It is (of course) verdant despite the calendar; Nature's fairness is
"somer-sonne shene" (*Parlement,* 299), and when the birds' debate is
resolved they sing a roundel welcoming, rather than spring, the warm
season generally known at that time as "somer":[11]

Qui bien aime a tarde oublie

"Now welcom somer, with thy sonne softe,
That hast this wintres weders over-shake,
And driven awey the longe nightes blake!

Seynt Valentyn, that art ful hy on-lofte;—
Thus singen smale foules for thy sake—
 Now welcom somer, with thy sonne softe,
 That hast this wintres weders over-shake.

Wel han they cause for to gladen ofte,
Sith ech of hem recovered hath his make;
Ful blisful may they singen whan they wake;
 Now welcom somer, with thy sonne softe,
 That hast this wintres weders over-shake
 And driven awey the longe nightes blake."

(*Parlement,* 680–92)

From this Zukofsky distilled "welcome young birds" ("*A*"-22, p. 508) at one end of "Initial," and "birds, harp in three trees— / now summer" ("*A*"-22, p. 511) at the other. Driving out long black nights, "over-shaking" winter's weathers, is the roundel's refrain ("it has said it before") about getting "on top of the weather"; weathering it, so to speak. So even if the cold season is in retreat, there is a kind of winter in this prospect of spring and summer; there is the vague uneasiness of "an omen" before it is dispelled—driven out—by the assurance, "a good omen" (Zukofsky, reading the line, always emphasized the adjective).[12] There was also weed in the dictionary's corn; and Prospero warning Ferdinand and Miranda that an untimely consummation of their union would bestrew the marriage bed with "weeds so loathly / That you shall hate it both" (*Tmp.* IV.i.21). There is the unexplained matter of a debt owed (to whom? of what?), which is heaviness before the welcome presence of the birds (e)scapes it with a flourish of air and sun; blue and yellow. And the Dreamer hesitates before a double inscription on the gate to the dream garden, one half of it promising entrance where "grene and lusty May shal ever endure" (*Parlement*, 130), and then:

> "Thorgh me men goon," than spak that other syde,
> "Unto the mortal strokes of the spere,
>   Of which Disdayn and Daunger is the gyde,
>   Ther tree shal nevere fruyt ne leves bere.
>   This streem you ledeth to the sorweful were,
>   Ther as the fish in prison is al drye;
>   Th'eschewing is only the remedye."
>
> (*Parlement*, 134–40)

The Dreamer is torn: "No wit had I, for errour, for to chese" (*Parlement*, 146). And in "Initial" the dilemma is brought down to a breath-taking three-and-a-half lines:

> fish purl in the weir:
> we are caught by our
> own knowing, barb yellow hard
> ever yet—[13]
>
> ("*A*"-22, p. 510)

Paradise's catch. Zukofsky's wary sense of the paradisal seems to nose out a negative field, some poignancy of knowing more than appearances are telling. It is a dualism that appears from time to time in the plans for "*A*" 22 & 23, and one intriguing allusion to it is present in the note of 14 February 1970, crammed into the top right corner:

ie

vs. negativity

beg. of A-22

use positively

⎡An era / any time / of year / —re era ⎤   at
⎣A Happy New Year any time / of year —→ ⎥   end
see Lewis & Short aera, aes (all definitions)   ⎦ Aes

(b.n.b., p. 74)

Negativity at the beginning and positivity at the end of a projected poem to ravel out the nuances of "AN ERA" (AERA, *aira,* AER, AES)? From indebtedness to the weed's reward, airy music, a happy new year. Any time of year? How? To answer such questions we should perhaps note that the primary defintion of *aes,* according to Lewis and Short, is: "Any crude metal dug out of the earth, except gold and silver." (But the Latin *aurum* is connected to it, "with the common notion of brightness; c.f. *aurora,* etc.") Brightness, dug from the earth, tossed into the air, then? Certainly a figure to fit "Initial" as far as we have read. To go further, we must dig (as Zukofsky did) deeper into "AN ERA."

The little poem has the air of a *fait accompli* from which Zukofsky extrapolated, in "Initial," several different stories, in order to discover what it was he had written 14 February 1970. All of these stories have dictionary roots—even Shakespeare and Chaucer are etymological spin-offs—and they all turned out to be surprisingly inwreathed; Prospero may just have met his match in the liberal arts of design and management. And the story potential of "AN ERA" is by no means exhausted. After making the first set of etymological explorations after the compositional fact, Zukofsky set about finding out what else was going on in the poem from the configurations of its letters. The result is to be found as part of an undated diagrammatic note opposite the title page of the "A"-22 Spiral:

others by
Etymology (L \ Gk.) Prov. / permutation
9 vowels   9 consonants

	AN	(ERA)	(5)	A	E	A	N R	
18 letters	ANY TIME		(7)	A	I	E	N (Y)	T M
	OF YEAR		(6)	O	E	A	F Y R	

4 A's	1 F
3 E's	1 M
1 I	2 N's
1 O	2 R's
	2 Y's

We might have been alerted to some of the numerological felicities after hearing the vowel song of the poem, but it takes Zukofsky to step in and perform the operation of adding integers, thus compounding the three-squaredness of "AN ERA." We might note that 18 resolves into a 9 if its integers are added; 9 is significant as the sum of three (divine) threes—nine planets, nine Muses, and so forth. And so, *by counting*, more of "AN ERA" is disclosed; stretching it, the poem is "a sum owed" to "Others' letters" (my apostrophe), also "a sum ode" (an ode of sums) of "Others' letters," the "Others" being Romans, Greeks, and apparently Provençals from whom Zukofsky has extracted stories (histories, etymologies) for ERA.[14]

The "*A*"-22 Spiral (p. 1) indicates that the Unicorn Press poetry postcard of "AN ERA" was published 4 May 1970. Alan Brilliant of Unicorn had complied as closely as possible with Zukofsky's specifications (26 February 1970; TxU) that the text be: "*capitals*, printed or drawn, forming a square (or nearly so) of themselves, centered approximately in the glossy yellow background; spaces between the lines about equal, feeling of both hieroglyphics and 'Old English' illumination, legible *capitals* that are also of *today*."[15]

The type selected (by Unicorn) was twenty-four-point Perpetua, and the text occupies a space $2\frac{1}{4}'' \times 1\frac{1}{2}''$—not quite the square ($3 \times 3$?) Zukofsky had in mind. As for colors, he had equally firm ideas that indicate "Initial" was already taking shape. The letter of 26 February 1970 continues: "The yellow should rest, so to speak wash the eye, not glare; Chaucer's 'summer' that is late spring, early summer. The 'midnight blue' should be pure blue, in any light if that's possible. Or the feeling in my mind as I project it into a postcard is if it comes over to others as to me, that of the 'lute pear' song, pages 47, 48, 'A' 13–21."

So Zukofsky was indeed aware of the spread of a medieval "somer." Alan Brilliant chose chrome yellow (not glossy; was Zukofsky thinking of sun*shine*?) and process blue, and he no doubt read the section of "*A*"-13 to which the letter referred:

> Five strings of twisted silk ply of elements
> Five notes planets from the lute pear—
> Mercury, Jupiter, Saturn, Venus, Mars—
> *Yü*—North's black winter water
> *Chiao*—East's blue spring wood
> *Kung*—Compass' center yellow prevails
>   over all four seasons' earth
> *Shang*—West's white autumn metal
> *Chi*—South's red summer fire.
>
> ("*A*"-13, p. 300)

I do not know the source of the "lute pear" song, but its harmony of colors and seasons, especially the "blue spring wood" and the central position of a divine prevailing yellow, speaks eloquently to the concerns of "AN ERA" and "Initial." The Unicorn colors must have satisfied Zukofsky; in a subsequent effort to have the poem come across to others as to himself, *Poetry* magazine (which first published "*A*"-22 in its July 1973 and April 1974 numbers) was asked to print "AN ERA" in the blue and yellow of its postcard form, and a cutdown sample of the card was sent to editor Daryl Hine. *Poetry* could not oblige, and Hine returned the card with his letter of 14 March (TxU).[16]

Zukofsky wanted "AN ERA" published before Thanksgiving 1970; he had it by May. Imagine then, the poet sitting down with the blue-blown-up-against-yellow poem, now artifact, in front of him. Whether the diagrammatic note of its components has been made yet is not impor-tant—Zukofsky must know from hearing the sounds and their distribu-tion that the poem is an audio-semantic gold mine. He begins to permute the components of "AN ERA," entirely covering page 88 of the black notebook—which is dated 4−5 May 1970.

Almost all the vowel and consonant groupings are considered for potential contributions to the odd but already interrelated matrices of counting (time, money? ore? reward? letters), weed and grain (seasons, catches in paradise), and air (voices, breathings, mists, birds, singing). But the top candidates for permutation, the ones Zukofsky concentrates on as he extracts more Latin and Greek (and some Provençal) from the eighteen available letters, are AN and ANY.

Among the block-capital combinations that turn up on page 88 is ANNO, which Zukofsky must have come by much as we found AER in the poem's right margin. With a little ingenuity:

$$\boxed{\text{AN}} \quad \text{ERA}$$
$$\text{AN}\boxed{\text{Y}} \quad \text{TIME}$$
$$\boxed{\text{O}}\text{F} \quad \text{YEAR}$$

Lewis and Short indicate that *anno* can be dative or ablative of *annus* (year), so there is an immediate Latin-English mesh of interests and a swift return to eras, times, years. There is a sizeable group of these AN-derived words—ANNO, ANNONA, ANNUO, ANNUE, ANA, NEYO, ANANEYO, ANA-NÉOMAI, NA.

ANNO as a Latin verb can mean "to pass through a year"; ANNONA is "yearly produce, the annual income of natural products" (with emphasis on the grain crop as a standard unit of measure). But ANNO can also mean "to swim to, toward, or alongside": "swim near and / read a weed's reward—grain." More properly the verb is ADNO, and we feel how that prefix supplies a notion of motion toward.[17] Similarly, ANNUO (to nod to, point out by a sign, give assent or approval by nodding) is better ADNUO. The imperative form of the same verb is ANNUE, or ADNUE.

ANA is transliterated Greek; here we turn to Liddell and Scott's *Lexicon*, Zukofsky's Greek equivalent of Lewis and Short.[18] ANA is *ana*, related to *a*, whose force, according to the dictionary, "must be learnt from the constructions which contain it." Usually *ana* has the sense of upward movement or rising and it is commonly found as a prefix. With an English eye, the same word transliterated contains both forms of the indefinite article: AN, A.

ANANEYO (ANA + NEYO; all the letters are contained in "AN ERA") is more transliterated Greek, either for *ananeo*, "to come to the surface, float"; or for *ananeyo*, "to throw back the head in token of denial" (which we express by "shaking the head"), "to give signs of refusal." So ANANEYO and ANNUO are much the same word, passing a Greek nod into Latin, one negative, the other affirmative. Their common root is transliterated by Zukofsky as NEYO; generally, "to incline in any direction"; specifically, "to nod or beckon, as a sign, to nod or bow in token of assent." Both nods are more affirmative than negative at the root, then; "an omen a good omen."

ANANÉOMAI (all of it there in "AN ERA") means "to mount up" (like float [up], come to the surface; "swim near"?). Zukofsky wrote "rise" under ANANÉOMAI and arrowed the word to the phrase "moon rise" just above it. He was no doubt heading for this passage in "Initial":

an affair with the moon
it looked as if it
looked up someway above earth
a hectic of an instant

("A"-22, p. 509)

NA, which looks as if it should be an inversion of the dominant motif and perhaps a negative in one of those other languages, is the first of the Provençal permutations alluded to in the diagrammatic note. Zukofsky has marked it so and written beside it "nay," pronunciation rather than meaning. NA is "lady" (from *domina*); EN, "lord" (from *domine*, an inversion of the last syllable), is also an audible and lexical presence in "AN ERA" but Zukofsky did not choose to list it.[19] NA (lady) appears to be an outsider, a one-off permutation of the sort that also produced, on page 88 of the black notebook, the Greek word TIMAO (to honor, revere, cherish) and the Hebrew word EMET (truth; a translation that crops up in *Bottom*, p. 119). All of these are good valentine material but lack the capacity for multiple linkage which distinguishes the AN-group.

To look back a moment at that group; something interesting is going on between ANNO and ANNUE. Zukofsky seems to be trying to conflate them by means of the latter's Greek ancestor, NEYO (nod):

ANNO[Y]U
ANNOY[ ]Y   a happy
ANNO[Y]U
New Year any time of
Year

                                                    (b.n.b., p. 88)

Further down the same page he tries a different tack:

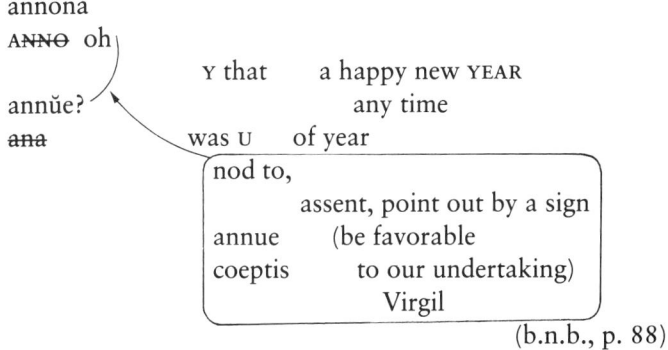

annōna
ANNO oh
                    Y that   a happy new YEAR
annŭe?   any time
ana   was U   of year
                    nod to,
                                assent, point out by a sign
                    annue   (be favorable
                    coeptis   to our undertaking)
                                Virgil
                                                    (b.n.b., p. 88)

The crux, if only we can read it correctly. Zukofsky has ANNO (year); and he has ANNUE (imperative assent by nodding), phonetically not an improbable match in English for "a new." If one can just be brought alongside the other ("swim near and / read"), he will have a happy Greco-Latin-English new year. *Adnue coeptis* ("be favorable to our undertaking") is part of Lewis and Short's example of usage for ANNUO, a phrase from *Georgics* I.40, where Virgil is invoking the powers that be to assist at the labor he is beginning. He asks, "audacibus adnue coeptis" (*bold* enterprises) for a sign (an omen?), a blessing (a *good* omen; the nod of approval). And in NEYO's benevolent nod, is an Englished Y that was a Greek U (upsilon): "why that was you that // is how you weather division." In A HAPPY NEW YEAR is A(HAPPY)NUE YEAR (division of languages?).

Any time of year? Following Zukofsky's lead, it could go something like this: ANNUE (happy) YEAR; and if Latin U becomes English Y, ANY YEAR. Any time? ANNUE TIME (is happy) (begins) . . . AN ERA / ANY TIME / OF YEAR. It is a delicate, precarious elaboration, this Happy Greco-Latin-English New Year. And now, quite silently, it acquires reinforcement from another quarter. The glossary of the Provençal anthology that gave us NA (lady) is found to contain both AN and ERA. The first means "year" (French, *l'an*) and the second, as a variant of AR rather than ESSER (to be), means "now." By straight juxtaposition, AN ERA spoken in Provençal might say YEAR NOW (any time of year) (now). That Zukofsky was juxtaposing languages on page 88 of the black notebook is to be seen in his rendering there of AER ARA as "air now," where the Latin word is joined to another variant of the Provençal AR.

These are fine discoveries but they are not all that Provence has to tell; in the same glossary is ANNOU and it means—New Year's (*le jour de l'an, le nouvel an*). ANNUE (happy nod), ANNOU (New Year's), a HAPPY NEW YEAR ANY TIME (now, ERA) OF YEAR (AN, ANNO).

"One air then a host / an air not my own" (*"A"*-22, p. 509)—"Initial" continues to comment on the process of permutation; "not my own" sounding on "Others letters" of line one, raw material of the elaboration. Letters as alphabet, not epistle or learning. There is a reference concerning them near the top left corner of page 88:

Erigena   the letters permute
Grammar begins
with the letter
        (Bottom
            117

                              (b.n.b., p. 88)

Sure enough, on page 117 of *Bottom* is John Scotus Erigena "(circa 810– 877)," saying in *The Division of Nature* (Zukofsky's ellipses): ". . . motion terminates at no other end save its own beginning . . . in order to cease and rest in it . . . In the intelligible world . . . Grammar begins with the letter, from which all writing is derived and into which it is all resolved."[20] Erigena misses by one "g" being a bona fide permutation of "AN ERA" himself, but an echo of his thought is nonetheless present in "Initial":

a peacocks grammar perching—[21]

                              (*"A"*-22, p. 508)

Because the word *grammar* derives from *gramma* (letter), we see that Erigena is as much the literalist in these matters as Zukofsky could wish. If grammar begins and ends with the letter, then all those labors over the components of "AN ERA" are etymologically justified; letters, not phonemes or morphemes, are the smallest items of account in writing (what is writing anyway but the transpositions of an alphabet?).

Erigena was a louder voice in the early composition of "Initial," as the very first draft of the fourth stanza shows:

~~Grammar begins with the letter~~
~~into which all letters resolve~~
birds fly into the letter

("A"-22 Spiral, p. 1)

The third line derives from the first two and becomes, in a second draft (on the same page): "a ~~dizzy~~ bird's grammar perching," and then: "a peacock's grammar perching" (the possessive apostrophe is struck out before the poem reaches final draft). There were peacocks in *The Tempest*'s airy masque (Juno's "peacocks fly amain," *Tmp*. IV.i.74), as well as in the dream parliament of birds ("The pecok, with his aungels fethres brighte," *Parlement*, 356)—but what is "a peacock's grammar"? peacock letters? birds' letters? (peacock-)blue letters perching on the yellow ground (air?) of a postcard? Zukofsky, in another aside on page 88, wrote:

his story not
in ~~history~~ ~~when~~ alone
but [illeg.] under ~~the~~
sun ~~under~~ of into peacock-blue
sky alone

(b.n.b., p. 88)

The combination of sky, sun, and history as "his story" is important further on in "A"-22. Meanwhile, though it is difficult to see how Erigena supplied that vivid flash of blue in the fourth stanza of "Initial," his thought of letter-grammar plainly connects in some way with Zukofsky's elusive birds:

a peacocks grammar perching—and
perhaps think that they see
or they fly thru a
window not knowing it there

("A"-22, p. 508)

Do the flyers see falsely? (they do not notice the pane). Or do they see rather better (for making no obstacle of it)? Are we talking about real birds, who fly through only *open* windows without paying the price of optical deception (thud); or are we talking about mind-birds over glass-matter? Questions of perception, to which there are no answers, only further complexity, perplexity:

the window could they sing
it broken need not bleed
one proof of its strength
a need birds cannot feign
persisting for flight as when

they began to exist—error
if error vertigo their sun
eyes delirium—both initial together
rove into the blue initial
surely it carves a breath

("A"-22, p. 508)

If they were real, corporeal birds they could, yes, fly through a broken window unhurt; but if they were corporeal birds they could not, really, "sing / it broken," bleeding or otherwise. What kind of a window is broken as a proof of its strength? And "broken need," to take out the implicit comma of singing it broken, does not sound like those confident, singing fliers. Error (in this era)? eyes' delirium? (Chaucer's Dreamer had no wit, "for errour" to choose his way when the same gate promised heaven and hell.) But the dizzying altitude of the birds suddenly has enough height, blue blown up against yellow, to be initialing the initial— the one literal letter in which everything is possible and into which, as now, it can be seen to make a return.

What is the letter, the initial? Nowhere in the poem does Zukofsky explicitly disclose its identity. Barry Ahearn thinks it might be the "O" of "Others letters."[22] I think it is an unseen "C" arrived at by means of the hardly less circumspect "I" (my/eye) of "Initial," the eye so vulnerable to error but also capable, if clear, of seeing all the way to paradise. I want to return to that particular thought but for now it is enough to know that the initial is also Erigena's letter, very likely acting in its capacities as source, multiple, and resolution.

It is time to look, or listen, more closely to the particle AN, which was at the base of the host of airs elaborated some time ago. Purely as an English part of speech, **an** holds several attractions for Zukofsky. To begin with, it is part of his diminutive trinity, *"an, a, the"* ("A"-18, p. 397), small words that sway the manner in which we perceive all objects. A *poem* is any poem, wide-open; anonymity, definition without specificity, easy singularity. **An** does the same for nouns with an initial vowel; a consonantal body for one vowel to run into and the next to take off from, avoiding hiatus (*an era*). **The,** by contrast (*the poem*), is particularized, finger-pointing identity, sometimes even emphatic about uniqueness (*the* poem).

In 1946 Zukofsky wrote that "a case can be made out for the poet giving some of his life to the use of the words *the* and *a:* both of which are weighted with as much epos and historical destiny as one man can perhaps resolve. Those who do not believe this are too sure that the little words mean nothing among so many other words."[23] His own "Poem Beginning 'The'" and *"A"* itself testified to an enduring preoccupation with little words. The 1976 index of *"A,"* with its seventy-one "a"s and seventy-three "the"s—favorite words of a poet then in his early seventies?—cues us to the importance they assumed in the life's poem. In 1968, Zukofsky was prepared to distinguish the indefinite article from the definite on unabashedly ideological grounds:

> a
>
> an historical = *an*historical?
>
> sick of history——Cases standing for
>
> 4/28/68 *An* v.s. *the* (vide HK⟩ & lack of ⎰ kinds
>
> cf A-18 (*"An"* faring no cause to an
>
> article in Latin) impersonal, infinite, infinitesimal
>
> A, an   The   ⎱ unowned end
>
> possibility v.s. predatory insistence ??? the hunt
>
> cf Little she *entertained* probability if she let it be possible
>
> for *probability in both empi*rical and mathematical
>
> thinking today [Reword all this *simply* without
>
> philosophical jargon e.g. Stalin—*the* Stalin . . .
>
> (b.n.b., p. 40)

"HK" is Hugh Kenner in a 1967 essay, discussing Zukofsky's concern for the little words. Kenner quotes the 1946 statement and comments (my emphasis): "It is a curious possibility the whole poem [*"A"*] may be an exegesis of the indefinite article, and so of *cases standing for kinds,* and so of a tension between the kind of reality kinds have and our stubborn pragmatic intuition that our need for a filing system has merely devised them. . . . And as to the little words being weighted with history, we may note Charles Williams's speculation . . . that the inability of a *Latin devoid of articles* to distinguish between 'the' and 'a' malign spirit may have hastened the conception of the devil."[24]

Zukofsky linked Kenner's words to *"A"*-18 (p. 393): " *'An':* faring no cause to an unowned end," and to a speculation about possibility and probability in *Little,* the novel he was completing 1967–69.[25] Most interesting though, is the jotting "a an historical = *an*historical?"; here a neologism is coined by mixing the usage of **an** before an initial, silent **h** ("an hotel") with the **an** that derives from the Greek a-privative in a similar position. By chance (probability?), the indefinite article **a** is made to assist Zukofsky's conviction ("sick of history") that an alternative view of things is possible. *Anhistorical,* suggesting *without* history ("faring no cause to an unowned end"), is somehow stronger than *unhistorical,* perhaps by analogy with words like *anarchy* (without a ruler), *anemia* (without blood), *anharmonic, anhydrous,* and so forth.

Concentrating on **an** became a preoccupation of Zukofsky's after "*A*"-14 declared that its opening lines were:

> *First of*
> *eleven songs*
> *beginning An*
>
> (*"A"*-14, p. 315)

Some of the reasons for this fascination we have already looked at, but there are others. Grammatically, **an** is vowel property, and Zukofsky takes particular delight in the vowel song of his lyrics. Like **a** and **the, an** is ubiquitous and often goes unfelt in constructions that the speaker of idiomatic English handles without a second thought. But unlike **the** and more extensively than **a, an** (those two letters) is a force in other languages; its appearance may signal the onset of semantic revelries of a rare order. And where did Zukofsky pick up the idea of pushing one (rich) word into so many translingual situations? There was always the dictionary, with its information about eras of the language, but, more than that, in the late fifties and early sixties Zukofsky was "translating" the *Carmina* of Catullus in such a way that degrees of semantic and phonetic identity between English and Latin were very much on his mind: "I'm trying to read the old passionate guy's lips like an ignorant American," he explained once.[26] In 1964, the English "*An*" that led off "*A*"-14 was in line for permutation as a Latin or Greek **an** somewhere in the ensuing eleven songs. We saw that taking place (and the lengths to which it could be taken) as Zukofsky raveled "Initial" out of "AN ERA."

Numbers. The *Century* notes that **an** and **one** were once the same word, Anglo-Saxon *an.* **One,** another of the big little words, is important to Zukofsky. It is the signature of origin, of deity; it is point or unit, the start of the number series and the principle of its construction. In Pythagorean terms, **one** is both even and odd and it is outside of all number. Its fascination lies in being simultaneously individuation and homogeneity, Many-as-One, One-as-Many. Zukofsky put it like this:

> One single number should determine our life: 1.
> Greater has no peace or rest,
>
> (*"A"*-12, p. 172)

We remember Erigena: "motion terminates at no other end save its own beginning . . . in order to cease and rest in it," from which proposition the letter-grammar analogy stemmed. The ninth-century Irishman was the last of a line of medieval thinkers whose Greek derived from Plato through the church fathers; after Erigena, Greek thought lost itself in a filter of Latin, but his comprehension of number and generation—stressing motion rather than reduction—is in the tradition of Heraclitus and those who followed him. It was also congenial to Zukofsky, who nevertheless saw that part of the trouble with philosophy was the all-too-common manner in which it "looks for solace in thinking of the great world of *all* things as if one were One and alone. *Consider* had meant *to observe the stars*— together. *Contemplate* had in past times a meaning of augurs who saw a *templum,* a space marked out in the sky that eyes could regard" (*Bottom,* p. 115).

Thus it was with the idea of multiplicity *unbowed* by homogeneity that *"A"*-22 and *"A"*-23 were projected at 1,000 lines apiece; adding integers again, 1. Or Anglo-Saxon *an*. Ending *"A"*-23 with "one" was among several options Zukofsky was considering in 1971 for the close of his part of *"A";* on Christmas Day that year, he recorded one of his more minimal poems to date:

12/25/71   one & all

(*"A"* 22 & 23 Spiral, p. 129)

Idiom is catching in more than it could know, including Zukofsky's collection of short poems, *All,* and the single poem of his life, *"A."* As it happened, "one" was scrapped in favor of another ending plan, so that *"A"*-23's last word is the less ambiguous "us" of family. However, "one" did get its moment of emphasis as the ultimate word of *"A"*-23's "An"-song; as Handel is about to be brought into the Bach music of *"A,"* and as languages are about to be brought together by more of Zukofsky's "lip-reading" translations, the activity is identified as:

> —the saving history
> not to deny the gifts
> of time where those who
> never met together may hear
> this other time sound *one.*

(*"A"*-23, p. 539)

"A"-22 and *"A"*-23 are both 1,000 lines long; each movement begins with a 100-line lyric (100 is, by addition of integers, 1) in 5-line stanzas, 5 words per line. Five is the "conjugal or wedding number" (*"A"*-22, p. 531) and also the 5 notes of the lute pear (*"A"*-13, p. 300). It is the number of

generation, marriage, and reproduction in Pythagorean number meta-physic and perhaps the number of seasonal harmony in oriental thought. These 100-line lyrics are the ninth and tenth "An"-songs of "*A*"; in the case of "*A*"-22, the song is 103 lines, the sum of "AN ERA" plus "Initial." Next in each movement comes an 800-line body of uninterrupted verse, followed by a final 100 lines. In "*A*"-22 these take the form of more 5-line stanzas, and the section is 97 lines long to balance the 103 lines taken up by "Initial." In "*A*"-23, the final 100 lines are the eleventh (as promised) "An"-song of "*A*"—no stanzas but the last 26 lines are an alphabetic crescendo drawing in the signal passions of the poem.

Threeness within the numerous One is also in the planning of these movements. As he prepares to write "*A*" 22 & 23, Zukofsky designates various portions of his extensive notes "M," "H," and "M2" (green felt-tip pen for "*A*"-22, blue for "*A*"-23), which correspond to the tripartite structure and signify "Music," "History," and "Music 2."

Materials and Mode: Contingencies and Condensation

"*A*" is a textbook of histories. Zukofsky constantly unearthed and brought into the intense light of his poetry all sorts of arcana. The source material alone in "*A*" 1–19 is keeping Zukofsky scholars occupied, never mind the poetry. "*A*"-20 (composed 1963) is homage to Paul Zukofsky on his twentieth birthday; "*A*"-21, the made-over *Rudens* (composed 1966–67), might be passed off as a *Catullus* in drama, the next exercise of the poet's ever-growing fascination with "sounding" Latin in English, except for the mysterious Voice Off sections (at least one of which Zukofsky calls "my own chorus in Plautus") presenting lyric interludes of pointed if imperme-able commentary.[27]

Then comes "*A*" 22 & 23 (1970; 1972–74) after an interval of almost five years (nonstop gathering and planning on Zukofsky's part), and the problem of impermeability seems to have compounded itself tenfold. Syntax is now totally idiosyncratic; readers grab at what they can—see our efforts at applying single lines (or partial lines) of "Initial" to the diction-ary sense they evidently stem from. To "make sense" of syntax this difficult is really a matter of holding as many cards as Zukofsky holds. Failing that (and who does not, notebooks at Texas regardless), all we can do is listen hard and puzzle connections with what is available.

And there are no names; hearing "*A*"-7 (p. 39): "but / They have no manes," always wanting to exchange those consonants (names for manes) but Zukofsky insisting on horse sense. There are no names in "*A*" 22 & 23, though there is history of some sort being recounted as soon as we get to the eight-hundred-line middle section of "A"-22. Shortly after it starts there is a passage of categorical information:

> History's best emptied of names'
> impertinence met on the ways:
> shows then the little earth
> at regard of the heavens
> unfolding tract and flying congregate
> birds their hiding valentine's day.
>
> ("A"-22, p. 511)

Those birds again, Zukofsky's and Chaucer's. If this sounds like twentieth-century images of earth from space as well as a fourteenth-century poem about a parliament of birds, so much the better for history. Chaucer has his Dreamer paraphrase Cicero's *Somnium Scipionis* (dream within the dream), and, with a magnificent but well-precedented leap of imagination, Chaucerian English soars into the cosmos:

> Than shewed he him the litel erthe, that heer is,
> At regard of the hevenes quantite.
>
> (*Parlement,* 57–58)

Scipio is being instructed by his ancestor Africanus in the finer points of the vantage that will be his at the end of a hard-working and virtuous life; the *Somnium Scipionis* is the last part of *De Re Publica,* a work Cicero modeled on Plato's *Republic*—which also closes with "an account of a mystical experience which carries the reader beyond the boundaries of the present life," as Cicero's Loeb editor puts it, citing parallels between the two works.[28] Plato is a ghostly presence extending the Zukofsky-Chaucer-Cicero figure back another three hundred years or so—rather as he is also a shadowy figure behind Erigena's thought as it surfaces in Zukofsky's reading.

Africanus continues Scipio's celestial education with numbers whose significance has endured the Plato-Zukofsky span and longer:

> And after shewed he him the nyne speres,
> And after that the melodye herde he
> That cometh of thilke speres thryes three,
> That welle is of musyke and melodye
> In this world heer, and cause of armonye.
>
> (*Parlement,* 59–63)

So that history, emptied of names and here transformed into a kind of revealed cosmogeny, leads straight back to musical intervals. But now

Zukofsky's Chaucer is being glossed in that "sterry place" by the language *his* story is coming from:

> the heavens
> unfolding tract and flying congregate
> birds their hiding valentine's day.

("A"-22, p. 511)

> *Explicit tractatus de congregacione Volucrum*
> *die sancti Valentini.*

(Parlement, colophon)

The Latin is medieval ("Here finishes—literally, *has unfolded*—the treatise concerning the parliament of birds [on] St. Valentine's Day"), but Chaucer's colophon is the one place in the fourteenth-century poem where Cicero, source, could literally hear Chaucer, reteller, speaking his language. Both Chaucer and Cicero listening to *"A"*-22 could perhaps at this point in Zukofsky's poem hear their common language—but only Zukofsky, designer, could tell them why they are both part of a valentine alignment in 1970 and why these birds fly so dizzyingly high in it.

Each author is, to most intents and purposes, hidden; does that "hiding" come out of *sancti,* the only word unaccounted for in Zukofsky's "translation" of the colophon? *sanctus* (saint), breathing on English *sanctuary?* The point is that they are present as voices rather than names. "If I'm to reveal any secrets," Zukofsky told an audience in 1973, "all of *"A"*-22 sounds whatever history I've found trying to read over the six thousand years of it, coming through—oh, various languages. That way I feel a kind of noise that persists through all time that's perhaps worth listening to."[29]

What did Zukofsky have against conventional history that he wanted it "emptied of names"? We remember the "sick of history" and "an historical = *an*historical?" jottings and "*his story* not alone but . . . under the sun . . . into peacock blue sky alone," the little aside on page 88 of the black notebook. In this context, two lines of *"A"*-22 begin to answer our question:

> Scribes conceive history as tho
> sky, sun, men never were.

("A"-22, p. 522)

What get recorded and endure, Zukofsky is saying, are names and dates, reigns and incursions; **the**'s not **a**'s, and certainly not the breathings of men, or any one man. History ("*his story*") (hear the breath) is "a story made and not known except for the order or disorder of story" (b.n.b., p.

100); the implication is that we can all follow a story. As for orders and disorders, when he read Wallace Stevens for three months on end in 1971, Zukofsky had this to say about Stevens's exactitude:

> His care for *particulars*, the wars, etc., spurred one of his clearest inductions in the opening lines of "Connoisseur of Chaos":
>
> > A. A violent order is disorder; and
> > B. A great disorder is an order. These
> > Two things are one. (Pages of illustrations.)
>
> (That is: A. The particulars elate or hurt / B. If you don't expect too much from the universe maybe it's an order. / Both A. and B. are only propositions *about* a singular activity whose particulars are countless.) (*Prepositions*, p. 33)

One and all, no less. If the particulars are countless and also the only proper subject (your **a**'s and **an**'s) for a breathing, noisy history, how do you get six thousand years of the record into just two thousand lines? From Zukofsky's point of view, the apparently monolithic blocks of verse that form the history sections of "A"-22 and "A"-23 were myriad assemblages of bright lyric citation, paraphrase, and quotation; a density of Babel comprehended. "Condensation," he wrote in *A Test of Poetry* (p. 81), "is more than half of composition. The rest is proper breathing space, ease, grace." This impulse to the little and lyrical is central to his art; the process usually went something like this: DISCOVER (find, be impinged upon, perceive), CONDENSE (concentrate, the essentials), and SCORE (essentials are designs; designs have rhythms; rhythms can be recorded). In the case of "AN ERA," the process was reversed—the score arrived, condensate, inviting discovery.

The material? No chronological plod went into the "reading over" of six thousand years, which is not to say the reading was not thorough. It was; and the spread of voices talking about "sky, sun, men" was later plotted along the two datelines, pre-3000 B.C. to the twentieth century, one for each movement, in the "A" 22 & 23 Spiral. But the real delight of the reading (and we might guess this from what has gone before) was the unearthing of contingencies, those places where one voice had been, or seemed to have been, listening to another. Zukofsky-Chaucer-Cicero-Plato on cosmic perspective, for example.

If the mode of Zukofsky's poetry is condensation, its material is the staggering incidence of such contingency. Contingency is a term that is forever cropping up in his notes, poetry, letters, essays, and conversation; "Contingencies' flowers," a phrase from the black notebook (p. 60), is synonymous with "the gifts / of time" ("A"-23, p. 539). Both expressions linger in the mind aware of Zukofsky's interest in growth and duration in "A" 22 & 23 and beyond.

Zukofsky started to read for "A" 22 & 23 with an idea about history as a persistent sound rather than names, and with a bias against the kind of events that "named" and "dated" history goes in for. Nowhere is this more apparent than in the division between the preparatory material for the last two movements and the finished product; the black notebook is, in part, a chronicle of the kind of history Zukofsky eschewed—the Arab-Israeli war, Vietnam, Kent State, the killings of Martin Luther King, Jr., and Robert F. Kennedy, the moon race, politics of the Johnson and Nixon eras— Zukofsky notes them all, time present interleaved with his reading of the past. But none of them gets into "A" 22 & 23 as names and dates in the way that contemporary events are part of the earlier "A" ("Rather a noted statesman hump TV- / free face between a pumpkin and a shark," "A"-18, p. 392), and this is not just because the greater part of "A" 22 & 23 is taken up with pre-twentieth-century material. In the summer of 1970, composing "Initial" and thinking about the character that the last movements would assume as amalgams of music and history, Zukofsky made a series of entries in the black notebook (pp. 100–102) which show that "nameless" history is conceived on the human scale of people talking to one another—contingencies. (How else does a man's news of himself—his sky, his sun—travel?)

There was the observation about history being "a story made and not known except for the order or disorder of story" (b.n.b., p. 100; 4 July 1970); more curiously, in the same entry it is also "a picture window never clean, if sometimes (often) washed." The chronology was to be continued, raw material with names, but:

> 7/28/70 . . . (*don't* use "sick of history"—just imply by omission
> of names—stress the sense of the good that is
> *now* (Aquinas)[30]
>
> (b.n.b., p. 101)

The Aquinas that Zukofsky had in mind is not specified, but the idea receives further medieval support at a later date in the "A" 22 & 23 Spiral:

> 10/9/71 For if history relates good things of good men
> the attentive hearer is excited to imitate that which is
> good . . . shunning that which is hurtful & perverse . .
> is the more earnestly excited to perform these things
> which he knows to be good—Bede, Preface
>
> ("A" 22 & 23 Spiral, p. 2)

An interlineation of 9 August 1970 on the 28 July 1970 note clarifies the position Zukofsky intends to adopt: "the good things said thru 6000 years—the present chronology not the names   their story" (b.n.b., p. 101). Pursuing this line of thought, by 13 August 1970 Zukofsky had formulated the relation of History sections to Music sections thus:

> . . . continue with history, without proper names, from
> earliest time to present—relieved by (mostly)
> seasonal (or "house") lyrical episodes—giving only the
> good things.
>
> (b.n.b., p. 101)

To this a margin note, undated, added: "the good things chronology working in with images seen out of the window, around me, etc i.e. if love be present why remember it?" Love so present as to be unforgettable ("If love exists, why remember it?" "A"-12, p. 170) seems to tie in with another crossover of history with personal concerns in the interlineation: "10/1/71—Do not insult the married with names" (b.n.b., p. 101). Marriage, we guess, is another kind of contingency.

Zukofsky's plans for "A" 22 & 23 had to be weighed against a product of his own marriage, "A"-24. The initial problem of how to end "A" had been solved in 1968 when Zukofsky recognized in Celia's "L.Z. Masque" an appropriately polyphonic conclusion to the poem. Celia Zukofsky, a musician and composer, had set simultaneous excerpts from her husband's poetry, fiction, drama, and critical prose to Handel's Harpsichord Pieces, structuring the work around elements of Zukofsky's 1936 play, *Arise, arise*.[31] The "L.Z. Masque" became "A"-24 and left Zukofsky with the job of discovering the details of its felicitousness and how they might best assist him in planning the intervening movements. "AN ERA" was not, therefore, the first time a primary act of recognition was followed up by elucidation.

By October 1970, Zukofsky had the whole shape of "A" in his head:

> 10/31/70—"A"-24 = answer to "A"-6's question,
> *can* / the design / of the fugue / Be transferred / To
> poetry?" Full cycle, then, after 40 years. A-22
> = emptying history "of all but the good, and "A"-23
> more of the street scenes of the city, the lyrical freshness,
> intimacies of the lonely walks, interests of the earlier life
> taken up (again) in C's *L.Z. Masque*. The whole poem
> dividing into 3rds ie A 1–21, A 22 & 23, A-24.[32]
>
> (b.n.b., p. 102)

The note confirms our sense that "A" 22 & 23 are a departure from the movements that preceded them; it also divides everything once more into threes, and it has us well on the way to identifying the paradise sensed in "Initial" (and drawn out of "AN ERA") as being concomitant with the tender history, "the good things," Zukofsky is about to undertake record of, and for which he has already *(adnue coeptis)* asked blessing. An earthly paradise ("let me live here ever") of one man's content? Why not?—if he keeps breathing it to others, and realizes that his is "a singular activity whose particulars are countless" ("For Wallace Stevens," *Prepositions*, p. 33).

What went into the tender history? If scribes recorded "as tho / sky, sun, men never were," we could guess that redressing the balance should involve men's accounts (stories, histories) of how these things came to be. "Initial" was full of sky and sun, and the History section of *"A"*-22 gets under way with the birth of a volcanic island, Surtsey, off the Icelandic coast:

> Late later and much later
> surge sea erupts boiling molten
> lava island from ice, land
> seen into color thru day
> and night: voiced, once unheard
> earth beginning idola of years
> that love well forget late.

(*"A"*-22, p. 511)

Voices? Instead of a half-expected "In the beginning—" we are listening to the boiling hyperbole of a CBS advertisement Zukofsky clipped from the *New York Times* of 10 April 1969, adding it to the cuttings and brochures that accompany the *"A"* 22 & 23 Spiral. "VOLCANO: BIRTH OF AN ISLAND," is the legend superimposed on the large photograph of a pillar of fire from earth to lightning-struck heaven, reflected in an eerily calm sea. The ad continues below: "An incredible return to our planet at its very beginning. Surtsey Island. Born 1963 in a cataclysmic boiling up of molten lava from storm-blown Icelandic waters. Now, primitive life is beginning to evolve. Much as it may have billions of years ago. Perhaps this is the way our world was formed. See it happen before your eyes as Charles Kuralt reports in a CBS News Special."

"Late later and much later," we watch a "once unheard / earth beginning" "voiced" by a TV special ("seen into color"). In another line or so we will make that fourteenth-across-twentieth-century zoom into the heavens, to be shown "the little earth" that even NASA's astronauts waxed lyrical over. Binding these perspectives is the hidden valentine legacy of

"Initial" and "AN ERA"; the bridge, "that love well forget late," with its idea of duration and attachment, is the Zukofsky-translated title of the French air to which Chaucer's roundel was sung by the birds— *"Que bien aime a tard oublie"* (see above). And so music persists in history.

Surtsey is one kind of creation, accompanied by technology's voices. For another account and a detailed look at how Zukofsky "lip-reads" his non-standard-English voices, we go to *"A"*-23, the *Beowulf* section, where the well-known and very lovely Hymn of Creation appears, transliteratively:

> Dragged thole
> load—sea-dark bided, day urged
> merriment harp-swag Almighty earthen worth,
> sea-water bŏwed, sun and moon,
> lumine lighted land beings' hum
> tree-limb, leaf, all-welcome shape quick
> so that men life don
> heartily.
>
> *("A"*-23, p. 556)

Behind seven-and-a-half lines of Zukofsky we "hear" fourteen lines of Anglo-Saxon (direct transliteration is indicated by an unbroken line, translation by a broken rule):

> Đā se ellengǣst   earfoðlīce
> þrāge geþolode,   sē þe in þȳstrum bād,
> þæt hē dōgora gehwām   drēam gehȳrde
> hlūdne in healle;   þǣr wæs hearpan swēg,
> swutol sang scopes.   Sægde sē þe cūþe
> frumsceaft fīra   feorran reccan,
> cwæð þæt se Ælmihtiga   eorðan worh(te),
> wlitebeorhtne wang,   swā wæter bebūgeð,
> gesette sigehrēþig   sunnan ond mōnan
> lēoman tō lēohte   landbūendum,
> ond gefrætwade   foldan scēatas
> leomum ond lēafum,   līf ēac gesceōp
> cynna gehwylcum   þāra ðe cwice hwyrfaþ.—
> Swā ðā drihtguman   drēamum lifdon,
> ēadiglīce.[33]
>
> *(Beowulf*, 86–100)

Or, in language scarcely less contorted by literality than Zukofsky's:

Then the powerful demon	with torture
a long time suffered,	he who in darkness waited
for he of days each one	joy heard
loud mirth in hall;	there was of harp the sound,
sweet song of the minstrel.	Spoke he who knew how
[of the] creation of men	from long ago to tell,
he told how the Almighty	the earth wrought,
a fair-shining field,	which water encompasses,
he set triumphant	the sun and moon
luminaries to light	the land-dwellers
and he adorned	of earth the regions
[with] branches and leaves,	life moreover he made
of race each kind	which move about in a living manner.—
So the warriors	in joy lived,
happily³⁴	

The spectacle of the Marsh-walker outside the firelight where men recount their beginnings is one of *Beowulf*'s most powerful images. Dark terror is about to close in on the builders of Heorot, which heightens the effect of the song. And dancing between two eras of the same language, Zukofsky makes (a kind of) sense to both. The relation is intricate; for example, the outlandish "Dragged thole / load" is faithful first to its phonic original and the sense therein: Grendel "dragged [th' / whole] load" of his exclusion from Heorot and the race of men. Second, the phrase incorporates the modern English *thole* (to suffer, endure), which is a direct descendant of "geþolode" in line eighty-seven. Third (and working again out of the *Century*), the noun *thole* happens to be the pin on a gunwale, against which the oar rests—a continuum for "sea-dark" in Zukofsky's retelling of a sea-voyaging people's epic. "Sea-dark" otherwise comes out of "sē" (simple transliteration, no semantic carry-over) and "þȳstrum" (simple translation, no phonetic carry-over). Zukofsky's perfect audience "met together" here would be a hall of Anglo-Saxon thanes with backgrounds in twentieth-century poetics and modern philology. Some contingency.

Both the *Beowulf* passage and the "unfolding tract and flying congregate" Latin aim at rendering sound as sense, or sense through sound. But Zukofsky's transliterations are not always semantically accommodating. Look, for instance, at what happens to the celebrated first line of *Beowulf*, "Hwaet, wē gār-dena in gēardagum" ("Yes, we of the Spear-Danes, in former days"); at Zukofsky's touch it becomes a horticultural opener for the Anglo-Saxon section of "A"-23 (p. 556): "What we garden / ah in year-day home." Which is non-sensical, purely phonetic transliteration, re-producing the phrase full-size (no condensation) but saying nothing to the sense of its original. "What we garden," and so forth, does however contribute to the prevailing horticultural feel of "A"-23 at this point. Though we can see or hear no etymological reason for those gardening Spear-Danes, we can certainly see that the base language (Anglo-Saxon) is fueling the apparent surface (Zukofskian English), which wants to talk about gardening.

There are at least two types of transliteration then. Sensical translitera-tion by and large continues the compression of material into Zukofskian lyric molds ("harp-swag" for "hearpan swēg"; "lumine lighted" for "lēo-man tō lēohte," etc.). Anti-sensical transliteration, by contrast, affords some fine opportunities for stretching the limits of etymological credulity (*did* the Spear-Danes garden?). Both kinds are at work in Zukofsky's late poetry, and a sudden switch to the anti-sensical mode is one of its most disconcerting features. Zukofsky is in the habit of sudden switching.

The Happy New Years

Eight hundred lines at a stretch is a lot of history, however musical it can be made. Zukofsky was careful to vary his voices and to lift them in and out of aural focus; try: "Cart a new / case: fritt'll lose? Stave lucre" ("A"-23, p. 552), against: "Wistaria plights flute song unbroken, / Mayfly larvae launched rice husk / on sea" ("A"-22, p. 526), which is transliterated Roman pragmatism sounding against an evocation of oriental lyricism.[35] It helped that the history he was after seemed increasingly amenable to expression as inflorescence and growing things generally; the natural end of that determination to give "sky, sun, men" historical being—but also a natural beginning for *80 Flowers*. Zukofsky, as we know, liked to "in-wreathe" his work, so one project gestated (as plans, lists, notes) in the body of another's composition. The *Flowers* are very much an outgrowth of "A" 22 & 23—particularly "A"-23, where they are mentioned by number and name in both Music sections.

This brings up another function of the four Music sections. We know already that they are intended to be leavening, drawing on the poet's perception of his surroundings and their impingement on his work—"seasonal (or 'house') lyrical episodes" as Zukofsky puts it (b.n.b., p. 101; 8/13/70), complements to the chronology of "good things" amassed in the History sections. The subject of one man's content is a longstanding theme of Zukofsky's; "A"-12 is the other great inwreathing of time present and particular (summers of the late forties and early fifties spent at Old Lyme, Connecticut; record of family talk) with wide-ranging meditations on history and perception (Aristotle, Spinoza, Wittgenstein). So it is not really surprising to find Zukofsky making the following note early in 1970:

> 2/13/70—Handle (arrangements (objects around the house (via A
>
> 8/25/67
> 13, A-14) in "A"-22   /A-23 as part of history (See Oct 15/67)
> also M2?   12/2/67
> also 5/17/68
> (b.n.b., p. 73)

The host of pre-1970 cross-references indicates that this handling of domestic icons went back a long way in the planning of "A" 22 & 23. To take the one most germane to our purposes:

> cushions
> Oct 15/67   Playing house: the ~~pillows~~ on the / legs-that-have
> cut off
> been
> rush bottom chair (back cushion animalcule
> (Shakti)(Parati)⤳
> design/ tho never intended ⎰ Hindu armed goddess, & the seat
> under the plant thread for the animal above);
> sweeping rather caressing the floor with a
> rag wrapped over the broom) etc.   these
> are the things of our (history (lives, these we live with[36]
> (b.n.b., p. 10)

This was the source in part of a passage in the first Music section of "A"-23:

> oak-ilex
> holm: the rushbottom chair legs
> shortened accord seat and back
>
> cushions—2 crewel threads flowers,
> 1 worsted thread animalcule or
> purposely minimal armed goddess caressing
> the floor—wholeness over broom—
> her logic's unanswerable refurnishing from
>
> nothing:[37]
> ("A"-23, p. 538)

Colon to colon, the passage is a poem within the poem. Reading the black notebook, we are made aware that the Music sections are built up from entries with personal rather than literary hearts—which is not to say that there was no interpenetration of the two; the broom wielder's "unanswerable" logic, for example, is made-over D. H. Lawrence from the notebook's next entry (b.n.b., p. 10)—a nice touch of poetic refurnishing.

Not all the colon-enclosed lyrics in each Music section emanate the tranquility of things known or quantities perceived; uneasiness was also part of the plan. In March 1970 Zukofsky makes an observation that shows his awareness of the special place that "AN ERA" is to hold in the scheme of "A" 22 & 23, and what it is up against:

3/19/70
> Looking from 12th story window an illusion of the corner lamp
> as a crescent on the asphalt—then one sees the lamppost.
> Use these short occasional poems . . . as connecting links
> involving the doubt (skepticism) of the eye not seeing
> with the perception of an era / any time / of year
> the "confusion"—history—vs. the sureness, the certainty
> (b.n.b., p. 78)

Here is the window again, specifically the view from what Zukofsky called his "high riser" (b.n.b., pp. 40, 41, 66; *80 Fl.* Notes, p. 3), the apartment at 77 Seventh Avenue, New York City; but also perhaps the window of history that was "sometimes (often) washed but never clean"—perhaps engendering illusions akin to those perceptual gaffes the eye finds itself making twelve floors up.

It is near-vertiginous altitude, however, that will release the birds of "Initial" from the perceptual dilemma of whether or not it is possible to fly through a window "not knowing it there" ("A"-22, p. 508). And "Initial" will spend a lot of time building altitude toward such clear vision—the Greek *an-* that denotes upward motion, the up-nods of assent in ANNUE, getting on top of the airy weather, sunrise, moonrise, and everywhere the birds of music-making and Valentine's Day which cannot feign their need for flight. Could they be in error? Is vertigo delirium?

The terms are Spinoza's as quoted in *Bottom* (pp. 343–44), part of the blessed Baruch's thought about appearances and realities. Condensing Zukofsky's condensation from the *Tractatus de Intellectus Emendatione* (1677), we read (double-dot ellipses are Zukofsky's edits, triple-dot ellipses are mine): " '. . when we say, let us suppose that this burning candle is not burning, or let us suppose that it burns in some imaginary space where there are no bodies . . nothing is feigned . . . the less men know of nature, the more easily they can feign things . . . But error . . is a waking man's dream, and if it become too prominent it is called delirium'" (*Bottom*, pp. 343, 344).[38] How this is to be applied to the flying birds I am not sure, though vocabulary insists that it must be done. It might have something to do with Baruch's neighbor, "Crying his hall's flown into the bird" ("*A*"-9, p. 108), and Spinoza saying later in "*A*":

> I grant no one is deceived
> In so far as he perceives.
> The imaginations of the mind
> > in themselves
> Involve no error.
>
> > > ("*A*"-12, p. 189)

Where does error creep in then? Is the confusion in the eye or in the mind? *No error*, says Spinoza, in what a man perceives (the bird flying into the hall), but the mind may attend to perceptions confusedly (fly the hall into the bird; get its objects at wrong ends of the action).

Seeing clear, the consuming problem of *Bottom*'s 470 pages, is somehow the prerogative of "AN ERA." What perception engendered the clear-eyed poem is not revealed; we may guess that it was one of those convergences—contingencies—of circumstance and expression which the poet chose to keep essentially private, in this case as a valentine. We can also note, however, that earlier valentines have treated of clarity and error, in particular the 1953 pair. First:

> I
>
> > With
> > a Valentine
> > (the 12 February)
>
> Hear, her
> Clear
> Mirror,
> Care
> His error.
> In her
> Care
> Is clear.
>
> > > (*All*, p. 151)

And on this Zukofsky plays ("With a Valentine / [the 14 February]," *All*, p. 152) punctuational and lineal variations five times over, until the terms ring in the reading brain, attaching and detaching from each other. The basic conceit is, of course, a figure of hearing and seeing—clearly—and it turns on the "C" (**see**) of Celia, enduring, we may suppose, all the way to 1970 and a poem 100 lines long; a quiet Latin C, or (adding Arabic integers) a seminal 1. "Have I said it before . . . There is her constant initial," Zukofsky writes in the black notebook (p. 100), and he tries out some titles in the margins of his draft for this C/see (almost "CZ") poem: *The Initial Love, The Lovely Initial* ("A"-22 Spiral, p. 1)—titles that were pared away not to the letter itself but to the word intimating that such a letter *starts* things: "Initial." Better still, "Initial"'s initial ("I") is an eye to that action, the I's eye or the eye's I. Try putting back the permuting "C" [see] [sea] wherever the word "initial" crops up in the poem: "[C] // transmutes itself, swim near and / read" (transmutes to **sea**, and finally there is a context for ANANEYO which might be *ananeo*, swimming toward or alongside); "eyes delirium—both [see] together / rove into the blue [C] [sea?] / surely it carves a breath"; "fear thawed reach three-fingered chord / sweet treble hold lovely—[C]" ("A"-22, pp. 508–11).

Whatever peregrinations "Initial" makes over its hundred lines, it does not move out of earshot of the initial, so to speak, melody. And why should that melody be so concealed? The black notebook again:

12/18/70—"A"-22 (3 section) (after H: M2)
anticipating A-23 = H *thru* M thruout
(song as H—from earliest song to
present (so includes "Rejoice" & Smart etc
as part of the "chronology"); the
main "hidden" melody; family as
developed thruout A-11 thru A-24 incl.
C's 5 voices M / T / D / S / P[39]

(b.n.b., p. 106)

Zukofsky is thinking specifically of "A"-22's second Music section, but the tenor of the note tells us more about why "Initial" and three subsequent Music sections are at once so beatific and elusive. They are in direct line of descent from those other places in "A" where Zukofsky surfaced the "hidden" melody of the poem, the very best of one poet's "good things" not easily expressed or necessarily comprehended as anything but ineffable light. What comes to mind is "A"-11, large parts of "A"-12, "A"-18's "An Unearthing," "A"-19's "An other / song." "AN ERA" and "Initial" are, together, the valentine that spread ("ANY TIME / OF YEAR") across 1970.

What of the other Music sections? "Between grape bay and hungry / bay" ("A"-22, p. 532) was composed April 1973 and brings together Prospero's *still-vext Bermoothes*—the compound adjective is important—and the winter flowers of Bellagio, Italy. The Zukofskys visited both places in 1972, and each supplied a winter/summer opposition of the kind inaugurated by "Initial." The section clearly conforms to Zukofsky's intention to relieve history with seasonal lyrical episodes of personal significance. April-May 1973 also saw the composition of "An unforeseen delight a round" ("A"-23, p. 536), which began the job of moving "A" one step closer to its twenty-fourth section with an assemblage of largely domestic fragments—those "house" lyrics Zukofsky had in mind in 1970, some of them the equivocal window images of perception and confusion. "An art of honor, laud—" ("A"-23, p. 560) was written September 1974, and it completed the transition to "A"-24 by inwreathing Paul, Celia, and Louis into "A"-23 at the exact point of contact with the "L.Z. Masque," to which all three had contributed.[40]

The chief contribution of the four Music sections, however, is concealed. Reading "A" 22 & 23 as passages of music and history (at times history *through* music, song *as* history), we become aware that the initial desire to empty names from the record is replaced, at the halfway point, by "a dream of named history" ("A"-22, p. 535) in the poet's mind. Quietly marking the change is a tiny "An"-song, the concluding line of "A"-22 (p. 535): "*there / she's hid:* an arm embraces." We must suspect that more than Alonso's ship is meant; that an arm of the sea is also "C"'s arm, everything resolving once more into a single, all-embracing letter. And is that "C" also responsible for the "dream of named history"? Twenty-six lines from the termination of "A"-23 is "A living calendar, names inwreath'd" (p. 562). There are no names in "A" 22 & 23—except in this calendar, which is full of them: named names—Bach, Handel, (Richard) Eden (since whom "gardens labor," a neat conceit on his *History of Travaile* [1577], also mentioned in *Bottom*, p. 101); inwreathed names— "Land or," "Most art," "donn'd one"; and the "voiced" names we have been listening to throughout. "*Kalenderes enlumined*" quotes the opening of the K-stanza of Chaucer's "An A.B.C."; "For / series distributes harmonies" is Charles Fourier, his epitaph; "doubts' / passionate Judgement, passion the task" is Henry James; "thrice-urged / *posato* (poised) 'support from the / source' . . . 'to / rethink the Caprices'" is Paul Zukofsky; "*sawhorses silver / all these fruit-tree tops*" is Louis Zukofsky (switch!) William Shakespeare; "consonances / and dissonances only of degree" is Schönberg; "impossible's / sort-of think-cramp work x" is Wittgenstein; "music, thought, drama, story, poem" is Celia's arrangement of Louis's work; "are but us" is Arbutus Path, where Paul's Port Jefferson residence was.[41] As for "21-2-3," these are dates lit by special symmetry; as Chaucer would have it:

Kalenderes enlumined ben they
That in this world ben lighted with thy name

("An A.B.C.")

The names attached to the dates? Celia's birthday is 21 January, Paul's is 22 October, and Louis's is 23 January—with a glance at the "names" of "A"'s last movements. This is Zukofsky's "dream of named history," music and history lying so close as to be practically indistinguishable, brought there by the agency of breathing contingencies, that agency inspired by the contingency of family, family represented condensately by the intricacies and simplicities of a three-line poem and one significant letter.

Small wonder then, that Zukofsky used "AN ERA" (the postcard) extensively as salutation and greeting in the seventies and was in the habit of invoking the associated "happy new year / any time of year" when writing letters December through January. "AN ERA" was a signature; concise, public but with a private genesis that could be elaborated an enigmatic hundred lines and keynote nineteen hundred lines beyond that; aurally, typographically, intellectually, and (as a postcard) chromatically stimulating. But it was not the only felicity to come Zukofsky's way, though it is certainly of a high order. Scattered through the notebooks are lines and phrases, sometimes with lineation markings, always easily distinguishable from the note-taking and planning that surround them. "One & all," from Christmas Day 1971 ("A" 22 & 23 Spiral, p. 129), is one such piece, a *daruma* of a poem, as Zukofsky would say, *"found object"* for a new context.[42] Some others:

12/31/67 Happiness / New Year [1968] / end / so on

(b.n.b., p. 18)

4/16/68 [in re Easter] Happy / spring / to / all

(b.n.b., p. 35)

1/1/72 *(end 23)* and live it over

("A" 22 & 23 Spiral, p. 129)

lovely All composed

(3/24/75; for Gerard Malanga)[43]

These are not fragments; they embody Zukofsky's genius for recognizing lyric condensation. They may be contrasted to the other kind of lyric he wrote, whose smallness was the result of much paring; for example, some of the perception poems in "A"-23's first Music section, whose raw materials and subsequent drafts cover up to two pages of the black notebook at a time. Or "A"-24's dedication (to Celia), which went through many drafts—some of which are preserved among the last pages of the black notebook—in order to achieve by ellipsis the singing enigma inherent in "AN ERA":

> the gift—
> she hears
> the work
> in its recurrence

("A"-24, p. 806)

What we should observe in the *darumas* set out above, as opposed to the "pared" lyrics, is a generic likeness in tone and content to the twin poles of "A"-22, "AN ERA / ANY TIME / OF YEAR" and its "happy new year / any time of year." All are wishes and salutations, the ringing of Zukofskian changes on standard greetings: at the year's end, for the new year, at Easter. All are bent on conferring continuance, recurrence, wanting to "live it over"— many happy returns, in fact. "Happy" and "all" are their common note, tied here to specific occasions. How this benign spirit spread across Zukofsky's calendar makes an intriguing counterpoint to the poetry of the years 1970–78.

It begins right on cue in 1970. Zukofsky was in the habit of initialing family copies of his books and reading programs, and on the flyleaf of a copy of the pirated *Louis Zukofsky at the American Embassy* is the following inscription:

> L's
>   C's
>   & P's
>
> to happy new
>   years
> any time of
>   year
>
> L
> 12/30/70[44]

The wish has multiplied, year to years (faint echo of Chaucer, "yeer to yere"), and it springs from a second thought about that North American contraction, *New Year's*, for New Year's Day or the celebration that welcomes a new year. Zukofsky has retained the possessive ending but elided its apostrophe, triggering the appearance (it *appears*) of a plural, which in turn starts to even out "Happy New Year's" (the greeting, stress falling on "New") as "happy new years" (lots of them, stress falling on both adjectives); the sense of the wish lingers, multiplied. Exactly the point, we guess, behind Zukofsky's greeting of 20 December 1971 (SFU) to Cid Corman: "Happy New Years to you & Shizumi." A year later, the greeting is repeated, complete with underscored *s* (LZ to CC, 16 December 1972; SFU). A few days later, in black or blue ball-point on the all-red surface of Aram Saroyan's "Red Postcard" (postmarked 19 December 1972 on the reverse; TxU), Zukofsky wrote to David Farmer:

Happy New Years

Celia & Louis[45]

The triple score, emphasis, is significant in terms of what follows. In 1976, writing to Corman just before Christmas, Zukofsky's note had almost the appearance of a poem:

Tues
12-21-1976

Dear Cid,
      'S here 's today. Comment 's best
      confined these years to the years
                  &

Happy 1977

            both
            of us
            to you
            both

            Louis
            (LZ to CC, 21 December 1976; SFU)

The eyecatching underscore is red-blue-yellow in both instances. Drafting a reply to Bruce Jaffe of Johns Hopkins, who had sent a videocassette of the May 1975 reading there, Zukofsky wrote:

                  on postcard
                  Dec 24/76

Dear Mr Jaffe
      Thanks for the video here today
            Happy New Years

      and to Dick Macksey & family
            Sincerely
                  LZ————[46]

The tricolor of the emphatic (this time blue-red-yellow) is instantly recognizable from the drafts of *80 Flowers*. Ever since 29 December 1974, when he finished the Epigraph, Zukofsky had been marking the completion of each *Flower* with a three-color rule:

It does not seem to matter in which order the colors appear (usually the first line contrasts with the prevailing color of the final ink draft, which is either blue or red ball-point), but there are always three and they are always red, blue, and yellow. The ball-point colors are set off by the brilliance (sunshine?) of the yellow felt-tip pen. Which brings us, full circle, to the colors drawn out of "AN ERA" 's three lines by "Initial":

> cherries, knave of a valentine,
> were ever blue of yellow,
> birds, harp in three trees—
> now summer happy new year
> any time of year—so
>
> ("A"-22, p. 511)

This stanza is followed by "Initial" 's conclusion:

> no piper lead with nonsense
> before its music don't, horse,
> brag of faith too much—
> fear thawed reach three-fingered chord
> sweet treble hold lovely—initial
>
> ("A"-22, p. 511)

How a piper gets into the lead is not clear, but the horse—the horse of constant plod who saw as far back as "A"-12 (p. 175) that he was repeating all known cultures and probably some unknown to him, kin to the horses Zukofsky wished "could but sing Bach" in 1926 ("Poem Beginning 'The,' " *All,* p. 19), and the same horse, now stabled, to be heard "old in / a greenhouse" singing sometimes ("A"-22, p. 535)—this horse is the poet, hoping to bring off the poem (the life), apprehensive of pitfalls and pratfalls, trusting the melody of family (that three-fingered chord), trusting ultimately the beauty of its top note—a high C.

One last occurrence of the red-blue-yellow motif is in the *80 Flowers* Spiral. At the back, two pages after #80 Zinnia, is the fair copy of the first poem of "Gamut," #1 Much Ado About Trees; it is also Zukofsky's final valentine (an era ended), but what concerns us here is the dedication of the new book:

Paul's
to ≋
years

Out of context, this is as enigmatic as any Zukofsky *daruma*. But with the eight-year matrix it is perfectly simple—an elision along the lines of the pared-away dedication of *"A"*-24. As *80 Flowers* was Celia's (a plain "to C" [to see?] on its dedication page), so "Gamut" is Paul's and the wish, the dedication, is: to [happy new] years [any time of year]. Year$_=$, that is.

80 Flowers was an outgrowth of *"A"* 22 & 23; its five-word lines continued the pattern set by those movements, emphasizing anew the symbolism of the number—generation, marriage, growth, all close to the heart of Zukofsky's lyric impulse (the five-word lines of "Gamut" would have connected that work more closely to the Music sections of *"A"* 22 & 23). The declared form (songs) of *80 Flowers* and its intention to sound time (as thyme) give a fair idea of the kind of lyric density to expect; the *Flowers* are going to continue the "hidden" melody of family as Zukofsky sounds the happy new years of the present and inwreathes those that went before. At seventy, a poet has accumulated many anniversaries; his year is full (any time) of dates—and (this is important) he apparently still "wants impossible liveforever" (*"A"*-12, p. 237).

Living forever by sounding time is Zukofsky's enduring theme. When the *Flowers* project is brought up in *"A"*-23's first Music section, it is in conjunction with *"A"*-24:

rendered his requiem

alive (white gold-autumn-leafed mat cut
down to 1-foot circle and
tasseled) would praise when 80
flowers the new lives' descant
thought's rarer air, act, story

words earth—the saving history
not to deny the gifts
of time where those who
never met together may hear
this other time sound *one*.

(*"A"*-23, pp. 538–39)

(How the works of the household's presiding goddess intermingle, refurnishing and resetting.) Zukofsky was thinking of Bach and Handel, those exact contemporaries who never met, but particularly he was thinking of Bach, who wrote an unfinished fugue upon the letters of his own name, whose motifs Zukofsky worked into "A"-12. The twentieth-century master of inwreathing, who recognized in "A"-24 the answer to his question about fugues in poetry, once remarked that he felt fortunate to be able to attend his own requiem in *this* life;[47] a comment made partly in homage and partly in the spirit of an aside in the Wallace Stevens lecture: "like Stravinsky accused of imitating Mozart, [I] answer (at least to myself) *no, I stole Mozart*" (*Prepositions*, p. 31).

The real point of aligning "A"-24 with the *Flowers* is to indicate that "A," though complete, is not ended; the ongoing music will be a descant of praise on everything that goes before it. There was an early plan (March 1970) to finish "A"-23 by naming all eighty flowers, "16 lines of 5 each" (b.n.b., p. 78), which was transmuted, I think, into an East-West-North-South description of the grounds at 306 East Broadway; ("A"-23, p. 554). The gardening that is so prominent in the later parts of "A" 22 & 23 is partially a reflection of the garden that grew alongside the plans for *80 Flowers*. The description occurs in "A"-23's History section; no doubt there was good reason to modify the notion of history a little further to include one man's garden at that point. Then, in the second Music section, the *Flowers* get their second mention:

> two centuries touching cold-ridge inventoried
> abreast of '10 years—80 flowers'.
>
> ("A"-23, p. 562)

Another historical contingency, and a named one: Coleridge's list of flowers (notebook of 1800), touches Zukofsky's intention to write "a book of songs called *80 Flowers*" (Schema), 1974–84.[48] To comprehend such a project, we start at the beginning, in time.

3

"See how the roses burn!": The Epigraph and #1 Starglow

The Epigraph

It is winter in Port Jefferson, December 1974. "A"-23 is three months old, the Schema and the First List of 80 Flowers are two months old, and notes for the project so far consist of a little more than four pages of material carried over from the black notebook and the "A" 22 & 23 Spiral. Zukofsky is seventy and it is time, according to the *80 Flowers* Schema, to start writing the book of songs for his eightieth birthday. This time there will be minimal preparatory reading and note-taking; by contrast to "A" 22 & 23, much of the prospective material for the *Flowers* is already present in Zukofsky's mind ("growing out of and *condensing* my previous books," Schema), and his botanical knowledge ("whatever . . . I can learn in 10 years," Schema) will be picked up along the way, generated by observation ("Only those flowers I have actually seen," Schema) rather than systematic study. Whatever notes for *80 Flowers* are in the offing, they will clearly be concurrent with the book's composition.

How does one make a start? By permuting the original plan with some subsequent thought about the shape of the project. The process had begun almost as soon as the First List of 80 Flowers was complete. On a piece of loose-leaf marked "I A-B," Zukofsky began to note "possible substitutes for the 80 listed on pp. I–VI"; that is, the First List.[1] These substitutes were for the most part plants growing in or around 306 East Broadway—celandine (little and great), lavender cotton, spearmint, spider plant, thyme, costmary, sweet-fern, wild geranium, sour gum, catnip, Japanese honeysuckle, Virginia pepperweed, and prostrate knotweed. The last two, plus a list of page references to *Common Weeds of the United States*, represent the beginnings of the Weeds addendum to the First List (pp. vii–viii), which was started 24 November 1974 with the Virginia pepperweed entry. All of the others are to be found either among the titles of the first twenty or so *Flowers* (see Appendix A) or embedded in the texts of the same poems, with the exception of sour gum, a tree, which was trans-

ferred to the "Gamut" Notes, and Japanese honeysuckle, which lost its
adjective to the generic Honeysuckle of subsequent lists.

Of the "possible substitutes" growing there in the garden, the thyme
bush (planted August-September of that year) suggested itself to Zukofsky
as a potentially appropriate start to *80 Flowers,* and 18 December saw the
first addition to the Schema. It is worth quoting once more in full:

> note 12/18/74   opening epigraph using *thyme*
> (pronounced *time*)   and thread the play
> of sound on both thru the 80 flowers
> that follow—thus making with the epigraph
> 81 poems (Adding integers, 8 + 1 = 9, The Muses, etc)
> Let time determine the book sequence of
> the 80—and their "order"—that is the
> chronology of *their writing.*

As noted earlier, this became the operative principle of selection for the
Flowers. Exactly one week later, 25 December and the sixth anniversary of
the *artos* note, Zukofsky began the Epigraph by assembling a medley of
thyme-related notes. He started to draft the poem 27 December; it was
finished in the same draft 29 December:

[EPIGRAPH]

Heart us invisibly thyme time
round rose bud fire downland
bird tread quagmire dry gill-over-the-ground
stem-square leaves-cordate earth race horsethyme
breath neighbors a mace nays
sorrow of harness pulses pent
thus fruit pod split four
one-fourth *ripens* unwithering gaping

There is a lot going on here, some of it accessible by associational
music, some of it by scrutiny of the Notes and Drafts, some of it
inaccessible. The poem sounds like an invocation, an exhortation in which
thyme (time) and roses (more fragrance) speed over (what?) ground
(why?). It sounds like a race, a horse race with a bursting (victorious?)
climax. Somehow it also sounds like a paced process of inflorescence,
maturation, and dehiscence. Predominant are the related motifs of fragrance, breath, and fire; good running mates for opening a book of songs
about thyme/time.

"Heart us invisibly"? Here at the beginning of the poems (as it is at the
beginning of the Notes) is the mysterious Greek *artos,* or (one of Zukof-

sky's transliterations) *hartos*. The word means "bread" according to Zukofsky, and according also to Liddell and Scott, who note that it is used frequently by Greek writers, and give several instances of its usage in the *Odyssey* and elsewhere. None of these seems to have any bearing on the present context, and there is nothing in the *80 Flowers* Notes or the original entry in the black notebook (p. 52) to suggest how Zukofsky came by the Greek or why it appealed to his sense of appropriate openings. *Artos.* Bread. Heart us. Flowers. Flours. *Flour* and *flower* are of course the same word; the *Century* gives, under the third sense of the noun *flower:* "The best or finest of a number of persons or things, or the choice part of a thing." Flower of wheat, originally fine meal produced by grinding the choice part of the plant, underwent a change of spelling and eventually meaning so that now *flowery* and *floury* signify quite different states. *Artos,* bread, flour, flower, *anthos,* anthology? Word-association games lead no further. We may guess that the "us" is a private community of two or three; two for the gardeners-cum-botanists of 306 East Broadway ("If we live to write a book of flowers," b.n.b., p. 58; 5/23/69) whose names (both) appear on the copyright page of *80 Flowers.* Three if we put the first line of the new book alongside the final lines of *"A"*-23:

> parks' sunburst—animals, grace notes—
> z-sited path are but us.
>
> *("A"-23, p. 563)*

> Heart us invisibly thyme time
>
> (Epigraph, *80 Flowers*)

The lifetime conversation of the poem is continuing. Here are the (three?) Z's of "us," decidedly sited in Port Jefferson in a context of *beatus ille,* z-cited as being "z-sited," also z-sighted—no ordinary gift. With Paul living on Arbutus Path, Port Jefferson, and his initials acrostically present in the last two lines of *"A"*-23, we might discern in "path" a literal lead into first *"A"*-24 and then *80 Flowers,* both so oriented, in their separate ways, to the family. This is guesswork; we have no line on "sited" except the obvious locative sense noted in the *Century* and the standard freedom to hear as many variants on it as sense permits.[2] If "sited" is *cited* and also *sighted,* that canny Zukofsky vision, what better post-*"A"* note to resume on than a wish to heart "z"s invisibly, out of sight; another concealment of the personal.

"Heart us"—give us strength, passion; an address, an invocation. Zukofsky did consider the transliteration "art us" (*80 Fl.* Notes, p. 1; also *80 Fl.* Drafts, p. 3), but he preferred to hear the Greek breathe an aspirate, and the implications of *heart,* semantic and lexical—it contains not only *art* but also *hear* and *ear,* all important to a lyric sequence—swung the balance in favor of sensibility. "Heart us invisibly" is fair warning of subtleties to come; "invisibly" itself is only half-visible, derived from an earlier phrase, "sounds invisibly," an ear/eye paradox of the order of *cited* (noise) and *sighted* (vision) present in "sited" (place). "Sounds invisibly" comes from the "Gamut" Notes (p. 1, 1st seq.) and is Zukofsky's condensed translation of a passage from a Vedic hymn to Vắta, god of the wind, more conventionally rendered as: "his sounds are heard, his form not seen." The wind and Zukofsky both.[3]

Visibility problems abound already. In the collected notes for the Epigraph is an item that reads:

√ —[the Nine] i.e. heart us invisibly

(*80 Fl.* Drafts, p. 3)

Everything after the brackets is in red ball-point, an addition, probably made after the composition of line one (further down the same page are "sounds invisibly" and "ἄρτος [Gk bread] heart us, ~~art us~~-"; consecutive entries but as yet not amalgamated). "The Nine" has been checked, in its brackets, so it is somehow incorporated, and from the Schema we know that it will be related to the nine Muses who are among the genii of this first poem. Perhaps it is these nine (invisible) (parenthetic) presences Zukofsky is addressing if the invocation is not simply reflexive? By means of another almost invisible entrant, he brings the relevant numbers into the Epigraph. Alongside the *artos* note on page 3 of the Drafts is a reference to *Antony and Cleopatra* III.xiii.178, which, checked, turns out to be Antony saying: "I will be treble-sinew'd, hearted, breath'd." Meaning, to Zukofsky, 3×3; for Muses or good Zukofsky hearts, winds, stamina. And though only a third of it is actually in the poem (heart), the other two-thirds is there as context; the invisible wind god ("gill-over-the-ground"), and then:

stem-square leaves-cordate earth race horsethyme
breath neighbors a mace nays
sorrow of harness pulses pent

A race with rather than against time is on; "Heart us invisibly thyme time" indicates not an enemy but a pace for the project, or a presiding presence rather like a Muse (or nine of them).

With the near-invisible nine safely threaded into this first poem of *80 Flowers,* which is numberless (first but also eighty-first) (or the 80's first), and with the family three reiterated in the process, Zukofsky allows other numbers to enter the play. The most obvious of these is four; the divine four of "A"-19 (see chap. 1), and particularly "Four for balance" and "Pith or gore has 4 / seasons" of "A"-22 (pp. 514, 517). The latter, with its inextricables of plant and animal nature, might have something to say to the flower/horse race figure of the Epigraph; and as for numbers, try "A"-22 against *80 Flowers:*

> Pith or gore has 4
> seasons, 20 yet boy, 40
> young, 60 ripe, 80 aged
>
> ("A"-22, p. 517)
>
> *thus* fruit pod split four
> .one-fourth *ripens* unwithering gaping
>
> (Epigraph, *80 Flowers*)

Setting aside for a moment the "pith" component in order to look at the implied "gore"; at sixty a man goes on ripening through his third quarter until at eighty he is "aged"—maturation rather than decrepitude. He is "unwithering"; Zukofsky talks about an "unwithering Cleopatra" in *Bottom* (p. 35), an allusion to the famous "Age cannot wither her, nor custom stale / Her infinite variety" (*Ant.* II.ii.240). And if "gaping" at last suggests toothless gums, why shouldn't they also be those of the newborn, gaped for food or attention (nurture)?

The insistent four of the Epigraph works against the quiet five of each line's official word count (hyphenations, we quickly gather, count as a unit) until by the eighth line there are four words, not five, and the rule of word count has been altered by immediate circumstances. However, if we were to count every word in the Epigraph, the thirty-nine of the hyphenated version would leap to an interesting forty-five. That is nine multiplied by five; nine lines of a standard five-word line; or perhaps a standard eight-line poem plus one extra line, as this is an "extra" (though fully integrated) poem. When integers are added, 45 brings back the 9, and the integers themselves point back to the four-word maverick line (if we hyphenate again) alongside the five-word lines. Nine is that unique number whose multiples from one to ten always add up to nine. The series looks like a palindrome:

9 18 27 36 45 54 63 72 81 90

We begin to see why *80 Flowers* is 81 poems long and why "Gamut: 90 Trees" started without an epigraph. Ten might have been the Pythagorean central fire, but for Zukofsky's purposes nine was more useful, a truly encompassing number. We remember:

seven words heaven, eight love, nine universe, longing
that innocence at nine

("A"-18, p. 406)

and find that nine is another of the mystical numbers. One strand of
Pythagorean thought asserts that man is a full chord of eight notes, and
deity is therefore nine, a "perfect plural" (three, a trinity, is a perfect unity;
six is a perfect dual).[4] There were nine spheres in the Ptolemaic universe,
and inventions such as Muses to the order of nine derived from this
scheme. Apollo was their later Primum Mobile when tastes ran to a
decimal universe.

"Heart us invisibly thyme time"—what about the botanical ("pith")
implications of the line? How do they relate to the rest of the Epigraph?
Common thyme, *Thymus vulgaris,* is a member of the mint family,
Labiatae, distinguished by two-lipped corollas and square stems ("two-
by-four's"? at any rate associated with the quaternary elements of the
poem). Thyme. Time. *Thymus.* Teem us, like "Heart us," or "team us"
(apposition—"our team"? or just, "cohere this," "[let us] live to write a
book of flowers"?). But not "thime" or "thy me" (us?) out of our English
thyme except in fun. To recover the value of that "th" which was aped
from Latin and which Latin took from the Greek, we must go to Liddell
and Scott and find that Greek thyme is *thýmon* or *thýmos,* deriving from
thyō, a word signifying either rushing, excitement, or burning, burning
sacrifice. Liddell and Scott suggest that *thýmos* belongs to the latter sense
because of its sweet smell or because it was first used to burn on an altar.
Burnt offering or sacrifice was signified by *thyos,* a word that later became
synonymous with incense. That sweet smell and the fire were more or less
inseparable.

Two things in the Epigraph immediately suggest that we are on the
right track; "fire" in the second line and *"thus"* in the seventh. *Thus* is
Latin for Greek incense; the italics help point out the otherwise inconspicuous word and open it up to non-English possibilities. So far so
good. Thyme is etymologically connected with fire and fragrance. However, there is another very similar word, *thymós,* deriving from that same
root *thyō* but in its sense of rushing, excitement, commotion; *thymós* (the
sound is different from *thýmos,* the appearance near-identical) means
"soul, spirit, thought, passion, animation"—and "heart":

Heart us invisibly thyme time

"Heart us" is transliteration of *artos* plus part-translation, part-transliteration of *thymós,* thyme's warm Greek heart. The connection is

invisible, lovely, apparently breadless, and a perfect touchstone for *80 Flowers* as it sets about resuming the "hidden melody" of "*A*."

If we want more links with "*A*"-23's "living calendar," consider that "z-sited" could be tongue-in-cheek Greek (xanthina, xylosteum, xiphium, xanthium) for a Latin *ex*-cited, x-cited. Excitement of exit? Heart still pounding?

> parks' sunburst—animals, grace notes—
> z-sited path are but us.

The Latin equivalent of *thymós* is *anima*, to which "animals" lose nothing when we turn to Jaime de Angulo's *Indian Tales*, a book Zukofsky made use of in his preparations for "*A*" 22 & 23. He condensed an account of a Pit River creation myth being told to Angulo by an Indian; according to this myth, Fox and Coyote sing the world into existence, and then (Zukofsky's ellipses, emphasis, and parentheses):

> [Fox throws the clump of sod
> thru the clouds & wishes Stretch! Stretch (They look down
> & it stretches to mts, valleys, trees, rocks & everything) . . not
>   people Indians
> much later . . after the world was spoiled by a crazy woman,
>   Loon . .
> ~~but~~ [Angulo points to inconsistency, but there were no people
> & the reply is] Ain't animals people, the word for animal =
> world-over, all-living . . [includes] earth, rocks . . white people
> think everything is dead "They are dead themselves, I don't call that
> people" . . smart . . but don't know anything[5]
> ("*A*" 22 & 23 Spiral, p. 144)

Suddenly "*A*"-23's last two lines, at first glance so Zukofsky-exclusive, indicate human family and then some—"the great hem of the extended / World" is lifted as it was with similar figures in "*A*"-11's movement toward cosmos; "sunburst" and "grace notes" fit its Celia- and Paul-related music, light, honor and grace, as do "animals" of either the Angulo mold or the strange musico-hunting lines:

> Art new, hurt old: revealing
> The slackened bow as the stinging
> Animal dies, thread gold stringing
> The fingerboard pressed in my honor.
> ("*A*"-11, p. 124)

Coming back to the Epigraph and its plant life, we look at the rose of line two: "round rose bud fire downland" (how many nouns acting as verbs? or verbs acting as nouns? the syntax reforms itself half a dozen times). Round rosebuds? There is an enigmatic entry on page 1 of the *80 Flowers* Notes (11 February 1970), "circles the rose," repeated on the page of notes collected for the Epigraph. The note of February 1970 occurs directly after an undated but perhaps relevant reference:

re-read—Cecco: see *Rossetti   Dante & his Circle*
(*80 Fl.* Notes, p. 1)

Cecco's sonnets figure much later in *80 Flowers* (#48 Impatiens) and do not seem to be of special importance to the Epigraph. But perhaps the title of Rossetti's book is meaningful here: a circle, around Dante of the beatific rose—and what is "Rossetti" to the literal mind if not "a little rose," also named Dante? The Epigraph's "round rose bud fire" (that syntax refusing to keep still) has its affinities with the Dante-inspired climax of "Little Gidding":

And all shall be well and
All manner of thing shall be well
When the tongues of flame are in-folded
Into the crowned knot of fire
And the fire and the rose are one.[6]

But Eliot's fire and rose are resolution and symbol, whereas Zukofsky's are twin elements in a poem initiating a sequence to be based on observed phenomena. And so it is that we find their immediate location in Zukofsky's own garden; another of the assembled notes for the Epigraph reads:

circles the rose
"—and grows by the rose tree(s) bud fire"
(*80 Fl.* Drafts, p. 3)

If we are reading correctly, thyme (time) is planted near the rosebush. The rosy fire thus appears to have gained a phenomenal basis; by 1974, directly after "circles the rose" in the Notes (February 1970), is the entry:

2/19/71—an instant's illusion the red blossom
of the shardy green opens, a tiny rose
(*80 Fl.* Notes, p. 1)

This reported February observation (an illusion, note) is characteristically backed up by literary reference—also the report of an illusion:

11/13/69—"The ~~first~~ frozen Norwegians on the first
   sight of roses, dared not touch what they conceived
   were trees budding with fire." Isaac D'Israeli
   Introd. Of Tea, Coffee, Chocolate.[7]

                        (*80 Fl.* Notes, p. 1)

Zukofsky had the D'Israeli quote well before perceptual experience added
its verifications of the fiery rose illusion. Knowing firsthand how roses
might be taken for fire, seeing it happen, then legitimized for him some
allusion in *80 Flowers* to the widely held association of roses with (sweet-
smelling) fire—"See how the roses burn!" is Emerson's translation of the
Persian poet Hafiz (1320–91), quoted by Zukofsky in *Bottom* (p. 141).

    The fire and the rose of the Epigraph occur near "downland," and to
find a lead on this we need to go further in the poem:

Heart us invisibly thyme time
round rose bud fire downland
bird tread quagmire dry gill-over-the-ground

The figure in the carpet here is John Gerard (1545–1611/12), the celebrated Elizabethan herbalist, but his relationship to the poem is complicated. The starting point is (I think) "gill-over-the-ground," which Taylor,
Gray, and the *Century* all give as an old name for ground ivy, *Nepeta
hederacea* alias *Nepeta glechoma,* another member of the mint family
(*glechoma* is from the Greek for pennyroyal, a species of mint; *hederacea*
means "ivylike"). Gerard calls the plant "Ground-Ivy, Ale-hoofe, Gill-go-
by-ground, Tune-hoof, and Cats-foot," and his list has a remarkable
number of affinities with the elements of the Epigraph.[8] Alehoof and
tunehoof sound as if they might contribute to the horse parts of the poem
and, with catsfoot, add something to "bird tread." As for the ground(ed)
ivy, surely it will be pertinent to "downland," "tread," "quagmire," and
"dry," all underfoot. The connection comes by way of Marcus Woodward's introduction to his edition of Gerard's *Herball* (the text Zukofsky
used at the Mansfield Center in July 1971; see chap. 1). Woodward quoted
W. H. Hudson on the subject of Gerard: "The old author is simple, not
concerning himself over much about the reason of things, or as he would
say he loveth not to dance in quagmires."[9]

    The source of Hudson's remarks is his book *Nature in Downland.*[10]
Zukofsky noted this and the passage quoted in the black notebook (p. 113)
and then again in the *80 Flowers* Notes (pp. 1–2), clearly struck by
Gerard's figure of the dance; "tread a measure" followed by "bird(s)
tread" in the list of collected notes for the Epigraph indicate how Gerard

and the dance of dry-ground sense meshed with Zukofsky's conception of his book of songs. "Bird tread" is probably bird's-foot trefoil (*Lotus corniculatus* of the Leguminosae or pea family), a ground-hugging weed named for its triply divided leaves. Glancing at the First List, we find the plant listed as Corniculatus and the information that Zukofsky had come across it, or reference to it, at Bellagio in 1972. Trefoil, in Gerard's book (and mentioned again in Woodward's introduction) is a charm against the biting of any venomous beast, and it does not look out of place in a poem of invocation. As for treading a measure with Gerard, Zukofsky inscribed the title page of the *80 Flowers* Drafts:

> Working drafts
> of 80 flowers
> (including the Epigraph)
> (making it 81
>   for good measure)
>
>   LZ Jan 21/75
>   for C.

The date is Celia's birthday. The inscription "to C" (to see?) appears on the dedication page of the published text; evidently the hidden melody of the lifetime poem is also a dance.

The *Nepeta* of ground ivy supplies the next important step in the Epigraph; Taylor believes the word derives from the name of an ancient Etrurian city, Nepete. But it develops more interesting possibilities for Zukofsky when he discovers that the other common plant of the genus is *Nepeta cataria,* the catmint or catnip (catnip, we recall, was on the list of possible substitutes). The *Century* discounts any etymological connection between the "nip" of *catnip* and the "nep" of *Nepeta,* but it is *Nepeta cataria* just the same which is being described (out of Taylor) in most of the fourth line of the Epigraph: "stem-square leaves-cordate earth race horse-thyme." Both *Nepeta*s are of a creeping "earth race" (*race* of course connected with root); and, if genus is abruptly transformed to track and field competition, everything is still in the family because horsethyme is either another name for *Thymus vulgaris* (common as—horses?), or for what the *Century* calls *Calamintha clinopodium.* Gray includes both halves of this as old names for the genus *Satureja* (the savorys, which are also mints) and offers a species named *Satureja calamintha* (*calamintha* means "beautiful mint"), the basil-thyme, with a variety *nepeta.* Cross-checking, we establish that the *Century* also lists basil-thyme—as *Calamintha nepeta.* At the bottom of this tail-chasing nomenclature is another "beautiful mint," closely related to catnip and ground ivy while retaining the thyme label and anticipating the horse motif of the poem.

Catnip is the third or perhaps fourth empirical base of the Epigraph. The first was the Zukofskys' thyme bush, listed in the substitutes on page 1 of the *80 Flowers* Drafts; the second is a rosebush, which sounds as if it is planted nearby. The third is ground ivy, the twenty-ninth entry of the First List of 80 Flowers, included probably by virtue of its previous appearance in *"A"*-23 (p. 554): "in / the ground ivy half a / house-wren's egg pink-white" (this is the section in which the Zukofsky garden is described; see chap. 2). Now catnip appears, also on the substitutes list, identified as ground ivy. Zukofsky presumably corrected himself after looking more closely at Taylor, Gray, and the *Century* (that maze of *glechoma, hederacea* and *nepeta*), for there are certainly two *Nepeta*s in the Epigraph—though there may well have been only one, *Nepeta hederacea,* growing at 306 East Broadway. It was *Nepeta cataria* (catnip), however, that recalled for Zukofsky a passage from Melville:

> unwithering   "The catnip and the
> unfading → amaranth!—man's earthly household
>   peace & the ever encroaching appetite for God."
>   Melville, *Pierre* Book xxv IV (p. 386 Signet ed)[11]
>   (*80 Fl.* Drafts, p. 1)

The context is a description of the "Mount of Titans," whose uplands are covered in a "small white amaranthine flower," which, as the epithet suggests, never dies. Amaranth is from the Greek *amarantos,* a compound of *a*-privative plus *marainein* (to wither, fade) (*Century*). The imaginary amaranth of the poets was supposed to be unfading even after being picked. Melville's encroaching weed is styled amaranthine for its hardy persistence in contrast to the homely catnip, which is found around ruined farmhouses of the region, dying off each autumn and conceding ground to the "celestial" but also "sterile" and "inodorous" flower. If living forever is to be equated with appetite for God, then Melville's sympathies are clearly with the mortal, aromatic catnip.

Committed to the fire and fragrance of "thyme time," does Zukofsky still want "impossible liveforever" on amaranthine terms? Amaranth is in the Epigraph ("unwithering"), with a nod to Cleopatra, but in this context at least the mortal herbs are pervasive—and it is the ripening of a *Nepeta* which is described in line seven: "fruit pod split four," from Taylor's "Fruit a 2-celled capsule, which when ripe splits into 4 parts." Nothing about "one-fourth *ripens,*" but the dehiscence (from Latin *dehiscere,* "to gape, open") is practically acted out by the pacing of the line:

thus fruit pod split four

This emphatic rupture is followed—1–2–3–4—by the four-way split:

one-fourth *ripens* unwithering gaping

(one quarter continues in its own good polysyllabic time). As for "gaping," Gerard described ground-ivy flowers "gaping like little hoods,"[12] and Zukofsky's note on page 3 of the Drafts corroborates the botanical reading: "—gaping (bot. of pod) flower." However, the word apparently has connections with *"ripens";* Zukofsky remarks in the margin of the Epigraph notes that Latin *ripa* is a riverbank, a shore, a seashore, and then directs attention to "Plautus re- breast feeding." Gaping *ripae?* The association is not at all clear. There are two Plautus citations in Lewis and Short under *ripa,* but neither pertains obviously to breast-feeding. We might guess that the reference is to be found somewhere in *"A"*-21, the translation-transliteration of Plautus's *Rudens.*

It is time to look at the horse of the Epigraph; the first mention occurs ("horsethyme") at the end of line four, but the rhythm of hooves is apparent to the ear almost as soon as the quiet tread of birds gets onto hard ground and into multiple word units:

bird tread quagmire dry gill-over-the-ground
stem-square leaves-cordate earth race horsethyme
breath neighbors a mace nays
sorrow of harness pulses pent
thus

Horsethyme, the herb, has been discussed already; but horse time, the interval? One of the relevant glosses is a statement Celia Zukofsky brought to light in 1978 after Louis's death: "Louis best summed up his life when he wrote: 'There exists in the labors of any valid artist the sadness of the horse plodding with blinkers and his direction filled with the difficulty of keeping a pace. My wife Celia and son Paul have been the only reason for the poet's persistence.'"[13]

The poet's time is horse time, race or plod ("To plod is not hobble," *"A"*-12, p. 180, from that most notable horse-poet section of *"A"*). He breathes his labors (think of the noisy, breathing history of *"A"* 22 & 23); he declares trebled breath (and heart, and sinew) for this project, invokes a Hindu wind deity who is also the breath of the gods, one who "wafts healing and prolongs life; for he has the treasure of immortality in his house. . . . His swiftness often supplies a comparison for the speed of the gods or of mythical steeds."[14] More perspectives on living (breathing?) forever?

The horse's breath neighs his labors—they are (ahem) neighbors. They also "nay" the sorrow of his harness, his pent pulses. The phrase "nays / sorrow" is almost straight translation of *nepenthes,* the entry preceding *nepeta* in the *Century; ne* (not), plus *penthos* (sorrow, grief); the name of an Egyptian drug fabled to drive away sorrows. Nepenthes (or nepenthe) is there in the Epigraph, translated *and* transliterated—take the "neigh" of "neighbors" and prefix it to "pent / *thus*"; neighing or naying sorrow. The "sorrow of harness" might be unavoidable and all too apparent to the horse, but his recompense and relief are at hand in almost the same breath.

The source of the harness figure is Albert Einstein, who in his old age made a remark very much in the mood of Zukofsky's own piece of autobiography quoted by Celia. Louis condensed from the review of a 1972 biography of Einstein by Banesh Hoffmann as follows:

> Nov 4/72 * Einstein (old age) uncertain "any single
> concept will stand firm" . . that he is "on the right track"
> described himself *"a horse for single harness, not*
> cut out *for tandem* or team work" . . *"his peculiar*
> popularity among those
> *who do n*ot *understand h*im[15]
>
> ("A" 22 & 23 Spiral, p. 130)

There was Einstein, the architect since 1905 of modern concepts of time and space, expressing the arduousness of a life's labor in horse terms. Zukofsky must have been delighted.

There are still some loose ends in the Epigraph: "pulses" as yet lacks a specific referent, though it fits comfortably enough into the race proceedings and is a word Zukofsky uses frequently in "A" and elsewhere, synonymous with the "drive" motif of the *80 Flowers* Schema.[16] The English is both noun and verb; the Latin root *pulsus* (phonetic twin of "pulses") is from *pellere,* "to strike, drive, push" (*Century*). Botanically, pulses are peas, beans, lentils; all the leguminous fruits of a pod (*"thus* fruit pod split"), and this word comes from the Greek *poltos,* where it already means "pottage of beans, peas, etc; porridge" (*Century*) and has nothing to do with any Latin striking or driving. Botanical pulses in the Epigraph might also reflect on bird's-foot trefoil, that other leguminous outsider in the prevailing pattern of mints and aromatics.

Zukofsky intended a meshing of physiological and botanical pulses, etymology notwithstanding (more "pith" and "gore"; or, earlier, thinking fit to bust: "—Measure woo't burst the bean / Mere pulse is heir to," "A"-13, p. 276). There is a passage in *Bottom* (p. 103) which seems to prefigure a good deal of the Epigraph's dynamic: "Pythagoras, in whom green pulse of pod and flame seeded nine spheres of number and tone, saw thru the hindsight of five Changes of himself his incarnation before Troy and heard his latest voice, that of Zarates the Chaldean."

Here we are, back with numbers and that fertile nine; also with Pythagoras, who wanted to measure all of creation in ratios and intervals. Who also, apocryphally, was reputed to have remembered five previous lives (a fair attempt at living forever), and to have journeyed to Zoroaster (Zarates), the Chaldean magus. His name is also linked with the Pythagorean or sacred bean of the Egyptians and Hindus, which the *Century* identifies as the fruit of the lotus, *Nelumbium specioscum* (botanically not a pulse at all). Perhaps the explanation of why this "bean" attached itself to the name of Pythagoras has something to do with the well-known Pythagorean abstinence from beans.[17]

There is another instance of physiological/botanical pulses in a poem of Zukofsky's which keeps measure mortal though still Greek. It is a neat analog of "pulses pent" and the circumscriptions of winter (or age), also their (measured) compensations:

XENOPHANES

Water, cold, and sweet, and pure
And yellow loaves are near at hand,
Wine that makes a rosy hand
Fire in winter, the little pulse.

Eating a little pulse, who are you?
How old? The hands of all are clean.
Why first pour wine into the cup?
Water first and the wine above.

Better than the strength of horses,
I come back to my other words;
The hound, "Stop beating him, I said,
I knew him when I heard his voice."

For now the floor and cups are clean,
The aired earth at the feet is seen,
The rainbow, violet, red, pale green,
Men making merry should first hymn—

(*All*, p. 130)

Celia set the first stanza of this to music 25 December 1949, and the piece was later included in *Autobiography* (p. 55). Again, dates and seasons are important; the music was a Christmas gift, from Celia to Louis, returning the gift of that year's valentine ("Xenophanes" was written 10 February 1949), from Louis to Celia and Paul. The poem itself is connected with Zukofsky's commentary on Xenophanes in the "Continents" section of *Bottom,* leading straight on from Pythagoras and his five incarnations (p. 103): "Xenophanes was simpler. He talked with the Medes among whom he wandered, the strays, had the rainbowed earth—for his feet. Clean cup and table, sang the season—winter. A good glance—*Stop beating that dog, he's a friend, I knew as I heard his voice;* the words reproachful." This, like the poem, is a condensate of several of the fragments, which are all that is extant of the writings of Xenophanes, the most poetic of the early Greek thinkers.[18] As for the 1949 poem containing both kinds of pulse, loaves, horses, and "a rosy hand" made "Fire in winter"—who could doubt that its warm invisible heart (no outward indication of the occasion) speaks across twenty-five years (a quarter of a century, "one-fourth"), "unwithering," to the Epigraph of *80 Flowers?*

All this is an attempt to locate "pulses"; the absence of a specific source has generated many possible contexts—and the feeling that the word is generic in Zukofsky's vocabulary, expressing perfectly the dynamic ("drive") of the *Flowers.* Now, though, there is the matter of what to make of "mace" in line five: "breath neighbors a mace nays." Suddenly adrift again syntactically and unable to make associational sense, we might take a hint from "breath" and suspect some non-English noise in the line. This is the case, though discovering its source, in this instance at least, is not immediately helpful. Among the Epigraph notes is one we have not touched on, a rendering of several lines by "Palládas" about grafting a wild pear-tree. Some search in the *"A" 22 & 23* Spiral (pp. 96, 97) reveals that Palladas was a fourth-century Alexandrian whose epigrams are collected in the *Greek Anthology.* Zukofsky's condensations of some of these, the usual blend of translation-cum-transliteration, are to be found in *"A"*-23 (p. 553) beginning "Naked at birth . . ." through ". . . Awe together deterrent." The pear-tree epigram is Palladas's first in volume 3 of the Loeb edition of the *Anthology,* and it translates as follows: "This pear-tree is the sweet result of the labour of my hand, with which in summer I fixed the graft in its moist bark. The slip, rooted on the tree by the incision, has changed its fruit, and though it is still a pyraster below, it is a fragrant-fruited pear-tree above."[19]

Fragrance and fruit fit the general shapes of the Epigraph, and the differentiation between wild and cultivated forms (a pyraster is a wild pear-tree) is something Zukofsky becomes preoccupied with in the course of *80 Flowers.* However, the Palladas component in the Epigraph does not stem from anything so obvious; the note in question reads:

ochnay⌐ hand, skill of an artist
  —Palládas ὄχνη, χειρὸς ἐμῆς
    sweet   working, handiwork
    γλυκερὸς πόνος [ponus]
    pear tree my handiwork
    (grafting the wild pear-tree (pyraster Αχρὰς)
               fruit
    in summer to ~~make~~ the upper stem
    fragrant ~~fruited~~)

                           (*80 Fl.* Drafts, p. 3)

"Breath neighbors a mace nays / sorrow"? Zukofsky has chosen to trans-
literate ἐμῆς (*emēs*) as "a mace"; ἐμῆς means "my" in connection with
"handiwork." Χειρὸς (*cheiros*) itself is nowhere to be heard in the line but
there are part-echoes of ὄχνη (*ochnēy*), "pear-tree," in "neighbors" and
"nays." If Zukofsky's transliteration "ochnay" is pushed in the direction of
the improbable, we might hear a "breath" (O, oh, och) of (Gaelic?)
"sorrow" (och nay, oh no). And the line might say: "breath neigh"
(*ochnēy*—pear-tree) "-bors a mace" (*emēs*—my) "nays / sorrow." Translinguistic mongrel for something like "my happy pear-tree"? Or—"pear-
tree my handiwork," the artist's *hand-work* elided in the felicity of the
result; an obvious enough parallel with the labors that produce these
poems from wild word-wood.

    If the pear-tree is there it is well-concealed, and so is the pronoun
claiming the artistry of its cultivation. The surface of the line presents
"mace," another aromatic component closely associated with nutmeg
(literally, "musked [scented] nut"; *Century*). Mace is the outer covering or
arillode of the nutmeg as it comes off the tree. Zukofsky's margin note on
page 3 of the Drafts: "mace   nutmeg," confirms his knowledge of the
connection but adds nothing else. Is it helpful to know that the fleshy fruit
of *Myristica fragrans,* the Indian nutmeg tree, splits in two or four sections
when ripe to disclose, gaping, the combination seed that will be processed
as mace and nutmeg? Is it helpful to know that mace is also an ale-
flavoring just as ground ivy, Gerard's alehoof, once was? *Mace-ale* and
alehoof both appear in the *Century*. The *hoof* of alehoof (and for that
matter of tunehoof, another of Gerard's names) is a corruption of *hove*
(i.e., ground ivy), and the *ale* is a simulation of the earlier *haihove*
(literally, "hedge-ivy"). The leaves were used in ale-making before the
introduction of hops, and the practice made *ale* out of the unrelated *hai*
(hedge). No horses in the ground ivy, then. Tunehoof also turns out to be
associated with ale-making rather than musical horses—a *tun* is a vat used

in brewing. Is ale a drink to take away sorrows? brewed in the year's ripening quarter? We recall: "ale's sorrow cheer poured" ("A"-23, p. 562).

Historical etymology may not allow for horses in the ground ivy, but history does not constrain Zukofsky once a word is admitted to his lexicon; hoof may indicate ivy and, just as happily, horse. We cannot even be sure he ever read Gerard's *Herball* on ground ivy; the only Gerard audible in the *Flowers* comes out of the notes made at the Mansfield Center in 1971. These are taken exclusively from the introductory material of Woodward's edition, and ground ivy is not included there. It may well be that Zukofsky did not pursue Woodward any further and was therefore technically unaware of Gerard's horsey aliases for the plant. The alehoof-tunehoof connections, rising out of an attempt to account for the "mace" of line five in terms of what we know to be already in the poem (ground ivy, horses)—these are the kinds of connections Zukofsky welcomed whether they were made before or after the act of composition.

There is one more mace-nutmeg consideration, this time from a source Zukofsky could hardly fail to recall, *The Winter's Tale*. The Clown busies himself with a shopping list for the sheep-shearing festivities: "I must have saffron, to colour the warden pies; mace, dates—none; that's out of my note;—nutmegs seven; a race or two of ginger but that I may beg" (*WT* IV.ii.46). Mace, a spice, and race, a root—as close here as they are in the Epigraph. The spices are for Perdita's baking; wardens are long-keeping pears, fruit of the summer-grafted tree for a winter feast, pies aromatic and oven-warm against the cold.

We have examined the Epigraph in almost exhaustive detail, confirming initial impressions by scrutiny of the source, history, and associations of nearly every word, bringing as much material to bear on the poem as possible, helped in the exercise by a remarkably comprehensive set of notes collected for its composition. We were baffled just the same whenever these clues failed to produce the next step in the sequence of word events. So much connects, read correctly, that a conviction arises of total, multimoded sense—if we could just listen hard enough and stay alert to the crossovers. It is like learning a new, difficult (but not alien) language. And the net gain of fluency? Hearing the intricate play of word sounds one against the other (none of the syntactic comfort that tends to be so much aural wadding), we pay attention, constantly and on many levels. And so, chasing semantics, we regain the histories that have disappeared beneath the surfaces of words (and events), and our attention is another way of keeping history—noisy, breathing, polyglot—alongside.

The Epigraph's many voices offer a commentary on *making:* delight and darkness, unavoidable and unstoppable concoction, activity of intime lives, the continuum; particularized by one poet's present intentions and continuing obsessions. Because one of these happens to be "liveforever," we also observe several attempts on the other kind of continuum: amaranth and Cleopatra "living forever"; the wind sounding (invisibly) the breath of gods (or horses) (poets); Pythagoras "living it over"—that phrase from the *"A" 22 & 23* Spiral which Zukofsky at one time thought of using as the final line of *"A"*-23 (see chap. 2). These attempts are rooted in the continuum (time/thyme), perhaps indicating that any way of "living forever" is going to be metaphor rather than literal escape from the measures. *80 Flowers,* its time seasonal, cyclical (endless recurrences), is set up precisely so as to address both halves of the matter. The poems that follow the Epigraph continue to play on thyme/time and at the same time keep a stream of liveforever motifs flowing into the book. Prominent among these is the rose, curiously meshed with thyme's fire (time's fire), as illusive and elusive as on its first appearance.

The Epigraph's considerable plays with concealment indicate how *80 Flowers* will work; as words (and events) lie visible on the surface, so some of the poem's components explain themselves and their connections or antecedents—with some knowledge of Zukofsky's reference sources. But just as a lot of history has vanished beneath the surface of words (and events), so the Epigraph is an iceberg of a poem, proportionally, and eightninths (suitable figure) of it is submerged. There is nothing wrong with staying on the surface and admiring the configurations, just as there is nothing wrong with being an appreciative, fluent speaker of one's own language. But the how-why-when-where of that speech is the underwater ice Zukofsky has always been fascinated by and which now becomes the base of a book also intended to comprehend earlier works and present projects.

#1 Starglow

The Epigraph, with its collection of notes, is a primer for *80 Flowers;* #1 Starglow, by contrast, plunges us into the difficulties of the work—one draft (begun 7 January 1975), one fair copy (finished 21 January), and no notes except the bits and pieces to be found in and around relevant entries of the First List of 80 Flowers. What are those entries? What is Starglow? To judge by a preliminary reading, the second poem of the book, across the page from the first, is inversely mirroring it. In the Epigraph, thyme circled a rose; now focus closes in on the rose but does not preclude thyme/time:

#1 STARGLOW

Starglow dwarf china rose shrubthorn
lantern fashion-fare airing car-tire crushed
young's churching old rambler's flown
to sky cane cut back
a crown transplanted patient of
drought sun's gold firerimmed branched
greeting thyme's autumn sprig head
happier winter sculpt white rose

In terms of the poem at least, a rose named Starglow now encircles "thyme's autumn sprig head"—that is, the plant that went into the Zukofskys' garden in August-September 1974. As for "firerimmed branched" (the eye almost sees, and the ear almost hears, "fiery-rimmed"), the D'Israeli quotation about rose trees budding deceptive fire may be taken for a first try at the sense. The poem appears to move from autumn into winter, so perhaps in more literal terms a low winter sun silhouettes the rosebush, rimming its branches fierily (another perceptual anchor for a fiery, roseate illusion). Is that "sculpt white rose" real in the depths of a Long Island winter? a memory? an ice-rose, the sculpture of frozen plants? One of the poems in *All* often read publicly by Zukofsky (because it is also part of *Autobiography*) is "Song 8" of *55 Poems,* which echoes now in the mind:[20]

Happier, happier, now
For whom in snowsleet barberries see;
   If not that, if not that, how
Are red berries for their windsleights free?
The glaze of mind, winter of eyes,
   Snow's berries, meet!
The Void of mind, the fall of thighs,
   Cold winds heat.

                                                          (*All,* p. 50)

The second strophe plays variations on this, and it is the notion of "Cold winds heat," already familiar to us from the valentines (fire and snow), which connects with #1 Starglow. The repetition of images also specifies the point of contact; the poem concludes:

The fall of thighs; love's discrete forehead
   Happier.

                                                          (*All,* p. 50)

The "discretion" of #1 Starglow corresponds to the concealments of the Epigraph: one poem is addressed, more or less, to time, thyme, heart, animating passion; the other is for Celia, perhaps Zukofsky's specific instance of fire and fragrance. Its finishing date, 21 January, is sufficient indication of the dedication even without "for C." inscribed on the ink drafts (*80 Fl.* Drafts, p. 4); the same inscription is crossed out in the *80 Flowers* Spiral version, and is of course omitted in the published text.

So #1 Starglow is a quiet birthday poem for Celia. It is no accident that the composition of *80 Flowers* began when it did; we have already noted that the Epigraph was started on the sixth anniversary of the book's inception, a date allowing time for a winter prelude, which took the Zukofskys from Christmas to New Year's through to their season of personal festivities—Celia's birthday, Louis's birthday two days later, and Valentine's Day soon after that. The Zukofsky calendar (the horse's own time) is determining the nature of *80 Flowers* at its outset.

Roses? *Rosa chinensis minima,* the fairy rose (faery rose? fiery rose?), is "a dwarf shrub . . . with small, single or double, rose-red flowers," according to Taylor, and "from this and other plants has come the Baby Rambler"—"dwarf china rose shrubthorn," with a remembrance of Rossetti, the Dantean "little rose," and with a mental note to remember the rambler when we get to line three, something about old ramblers and young churching. *Rosa chinensis,* the China or Bengal rose, is the stock from which continually blooming roses were developed (persisting into winter?). "Old Crimson Rambler," as Taylor styles it, is a familiar climbing rose, one of the Multifloras that "need the removal each year at their base of old canes immediately after flowering. The plant then renews itself with new canes." Zukofsky: "old rambler's flown / to sky cane cut back." The hard "k" monosyllables chop back the length of line four with appropriate care for future developments.[21]

There seems to be an implied red as well as a white rose in #1 Starglow, with "sun's gold firerimmed" as some sort of middle term in the coloration of the poem. But what is happening to the roses in line two?

> *Starglow* dwarf china rose shrubthorn
> lantern fashion-fare airing car-tire crushed

Proceeding linearly, we look at "lantern," once spelt *lanthorn* in supposed allusion to the transparent plates of horn which formed the sides of lanterns (*Century*). Besides providing a sort of submerged rhyme over the line break—shrubthorn/lanthorn—this suggests a link with one of Zukofsky's favorite Shakespearean stamping grounds, the play within a play of *A Midsummer Night's Dream,* where Starveling presents Moonshine "with lanthorn, dog, and bush of thorn" (*MND* V.i.136). Well before Zukofsky thought to play *thorn* against its component *horn*, Shakespeare had spotted their mutual connection with light:

> This lanthorn doth the horned moon present;
> Myself the man i' the moon do seem to be.
>
> (MND V.i.248)

Horn in a more natural ("horned") state nevertheless gives off light and gets closer to the puncturing thorns of a man in the moon's bush—and #1 Starglow's "shrubthorn," a rose/bush. Is "shrubthorn / lantern" a moon-shine (starglow) rosebush?

Lantern is from the Greek *lamptēr,* the stand or grate for pine or other wood used for lighting rooms (*Century*), and the underlying verb is *lampō,* "to give light, shine, beam, be bright, brilliant, radiant." All of this connects with the various lights of the poem—sun, fire, star, moon—and all of it is a possible cipher for Celia's benign influence.

What of "fashion-fare airing car-tire crushed"? fashion fair (event) or fare (fodder)? A look at the First List's sixty-fourth entry, Rose, begins to untangle the bush of thorns (it also points out Taylor's fairy rose and baby rambler, and the link with *A Midsummer Night's Dream*). Zukofsky wanted to make a distinction between wild or native roses and the cultivated hybrids, and his gloss reads: "native persisting—fashions changing" (First List, p. v). Old-fashioned roses (like Crimson Rambler) endure in the face of changing tastes; the hybrid varieties run to thousands in number, and many, "while popular for a year or two," says Taylor, "are probably destined to oblivion." They are "fashion-fare," having been fashion fair (adjective), obliterated as effectively as whatever was crushed (disconcerting note) under the "car-tire" of line two.[22]

What is "Starglow" then? Works about popular rose varieties list a highly rated miniature named Starglo, producing fragrant "double blooms with a 'glo' of cream and with pointed petal tips (the 'star')."[23] If this is Zukofsky's rose, it sounds like a hybrid, the result of some cross with *Rosa chinensis;* but the Rose note in the First List continues, somewhat elliptically:

<pre>
        minimal china bush
        Miniature rose (medieval)
wed thorn [illeg.]
                        tire (W.S. [illeg.])
sun <s>blossom</s>   "starglow"   car rode
over it)(not frail
</pre>

(First List, p. v)

Difficult, and not helped by the faintness of the interlineations. The sun seems to have more impact than we initially thought. Some first steps toward a resolution come from another interlinear instruction in the same note to refer to Chaucer's *Merchant's Tale,* lines 975–78; enter the medieval component. *The Merchant's Tale* is the story of Januarie and May, the *senex amans* duped by a lusty young wife who has her lover sit up in a pear-tree while she walks in the orchard with her old blind husband:

> Bright was the day, and blew the firmament,
> Phebus of gold his stremes doun hath sent,
> To gladen every flour with his warmnesse.
> He was that tyme *in Geminis,* as I gesse,
> But litel fro his declinacion
> Of Cancer, Iovis exaltacion.
>
> (*Merchant's Tale,* 975–80)

Here is "sun's gold" again, and the date, circumlocutionally, is, according to Skeat's notes, 8 June—a date of extreme personal significance to Zukofsky, nowhere specified but frequently alluded to and usually in connection with Celia. We must guess at an anniversary of some sort, private, to be marked "invisibly" by such embedded references as the present one. It looks like another case of a happy new year any time of year: June roses in a January poem, summer in winter, May and Januarie. Perhaps Starglow was a token somehow implicated in the still enigmatic "fashion-fare airing car-tire crushed" (a rose-and-glove interlude?). And perhaps the Zukofsky rose linked itself by happy accident to the *Century*'s observation that a *rose-festival* (of French origin) is celebrated 8 June, and customarily a girl (*La Rosière*) is "selected from the most distinguished for feminine virtues." She is adorned ("crowned"?) with roses held together by a silver clasp and led to the church, where she hears a sermon in a place of honor ("young's churched"? after being searched out?).

We have the yellow of the sun (or "sun fire" as the Rose note evolves it from an interlineation: "Sun yellow-red   [alive anew]"), and also a version of the blue firmament, spelt by Chaucer "blew," permuted by Zukofsky "flown": "young's churching old rambler's flown / to sky cane cut back." Young May certainly "churched" old Januarie, and it is she who will presently "fly" up into the pear-tree, there to be swyved by Damian.[24]

This implicit pear-tree reminds us of another one, equally invisible, in the Epigraph, with its intimations about the sweet fruit-bearing branch grafted onto the vigorous stock of a wild form. Mirror-imaging between the Epigraph and #1 Starglow apparently continues; and if we are to draw an inference from the former, then cultivated forms are to be looked on as augmentation, rather than dilution, of the wild stock. What this has to do with the Zukofsky component is anyone's guess, but the figure was clearly an enduring one—it reappears in the "Gamut" Notes (p. 3, 1st seq.) as an entry of 8 January 1975, the day after Zukofsky began drafting #1 Starglow. The entry cites part of line 973 of *The Merchant's Tale,* the narrator saying: "And thus I lete him *sitte up-on the pyrie*" (Zukofsky's excerpt italicized). A pyrie is a pear-tree and "him" is the lover, Damian. Then follows a cross-reference to the Palladas epigram, dated 25 December 1974 (Zukofsky began collecting notes for the Epigraph on that date) and repeating most of the "pear-tree my handiwork" translation. It seems that the pear-tree was slated for a third appearance, this time probably more visible, in "Gamut: 90 Trees."[25]

Meanwhile, back with #1 Starglow, we may speculate about Zukofsky's reasons for using these vanished pear-trees. A Chaucerian motif of cuckoldry hardly fits the poem's purposes, so we conclude that his interest here concerns the summer date supplied by the story and the Merchant's description of the balmy season—in which a pear-tree happens to feature. The crux of the affair seems to be the Palladian grafting; perhaps the pear-tree maps onto some private episode, perhaps it is merely the link between Palladas (the graft) and Chaucer (8 June). And what of the graft? The commonplace figure would align raw poetic vigor with beneficent cultivation for a fruitful union. Palladas's next epigram, following the one already discussed, makes figurative capital of the motif: "I was a pyraster; thy hand hath made me a fragrant pear-tree by inserting a graft, and I reward thee for thy kindness."[26]

However, any grafting in #1 Starglow seems to concern roses rather than pear-trees, by way of the odd note, still under Rose in the First List: "wed thorn sun fire." Earlier in the same note we read: "Jeff: 'Keep the thorn . . wed,'" and this is an echo from another 1931 poem, "Madison, Wis., remembering the bloom of Monticello (1931)," which intersperses quotation from Thomas Jefferson's *Garden Book* with the same sort of oblique intimacy to be found in the snow-barberries-happier piece. It begins:

No empty bed blues—
    between these walls
I can lie—
    your thigh, me—

(All, p. 45)

(Is it just sensitivity to the present context which sees "thigh, me" and thinks "thyme" or "thymy"? "I know a bank where the wild thyme blows," etc.) The last strophe is something of a recapitulation:

Empty Bed
  Blues—"keep the
thorn constantly
  wed."   (*All*, p. 46)

A search in the *Garden Book* turns up the phrase in Jefferson's letter of
13 May 1807 to one Edmund Bacon in which, directing "plantation
affairs," he urges: "Keep the thorns constantly clean wed."[27] Wed?
weeded? or married (grafted)? Is "thorns" synecdoche for rosebushes? or
simply a reference to Jefferson's extensive box-thorn hedges ("*May*, the
flower, as haw is the fruit, of the thorn," wrote Basil Bunting; and
suddenly May's sharp wits assume new overtones).[28] How much and
what kinds of grafting were undertaken at Monticello? In Zukofsky's
figure ("keep the thorn wed"), the verb is about binding and almost
implies hurt or injury, not necessarily to a plant. Jefferson's plurality of
thorns, by contrast, is not sharply pointed at one breast, could not be
mistaken for anything but the botanical.

The single most interesting word here is "wed," the way Zukofsky
chooses to resurrect it forty-four years after whatever circumstances gave
rise to the Monticello poem. These were not pertinent to Celia, whom he
did not meet until 1933,[29] but Zukofsky was fond of the sort of revisions
that history is able to work on its products. He was going to incorporate
"wed" into #1 Starglow as the tail of "white sculpted" ("sculptwed"), the
initial version of the "sculpt white" winter rose of line eight. This time it
may have been intended as a gloss on the marriage that took place in
August 1939, and this is a surmise that takes root in something more
visible in the draft material than the finished poem.

Looking again at "fashion-fare airing," and taking the time to roll it
thoughtfully over the tongue, we discover a couple of phonetic presences
inaudible at ordinary reading speed: "fairy" and "ring"—so contingent as
to be practically attached at the point of contact. Fairy rose, yes, but also
(and it is there in the first draft) "fayery": "lanthorne of fayerye" (*80 Fl.
Drafts*, p. 4), already crossed out in favor of the superscription: "fairing
fashion airing," one step closer to the final text. (Is a "lanthorne of
fayerye" a thorny fairy rose by the luminous name of Starglow?) (No rose
without a thorn, etc.)

Fayery; a medieval word for another medieval reference, *The Squire's
Tale*, with its story of Canacee's magic ring afterward "completed" by
Spenser in—*The Faerie Queene* IV.iii. Zukofsky also "completes" the
Canacee tale (in another poem), but here it acts primarily as a marker for
the later development, incidentally reiterating the "fairy" motif of the rose
and the ring, which is part of both stories. In Chaucer's account four

magic gifts arrive at the court of King Cambinskan, brought by a knight on a wonderful horse of brass that can fly or vanish as its rider wishes; the horse is the first of the gifts sent by the king of "Arabie and of Inde." The knight then presents a mirror that will show its owner only truth and find out deceit, and a ring with the virtue of letting its wearer understand the languages of the birds and be knowledgeable about the healing powers of herbs. Both mirror and ring are given to Canacee, Cambinskan's daughter. The fourth gift is a sword of immense strength, which will heal any wound it makes if its flat is applied to the hurt. The fairy ring becomes the immediate focus of the story as Canacee listens to the lament of a noble lady hawk and heals her wounds; the tale then breaks off.

In #1 Starglow there is a hidden ring, a submerged date, an enigmatic rose, a strong hint of augmentive grafting almost using the term *wed*. Thinking about the fairy ring with its powers of understanding and healing, and about the other gifts, we discover something like two of them in poems to either side of #1 Starglow. The Epigraph contains a vanishing horse which (as poet) is a kind of latter-day Pegasus (who kicked the Muses' hill and out spouted Hippocrene, the "horse-fountain" of poetic inspiration). In "unwithering" we may hear ("with her ring") the horse's side and that marvelous ring. The thyme (time) that circles the rose(bush) is another ring, and a corresponding "ring of roses" is found elsewhere in the sequence (see chaps. 7 and 8). The mirror begins appearing in #2 Mountain Laurel when Zukofsky brings the Spenser version of the story into play, and it comes into full view at the close of #3 Honesty, honestly mirroring "luck's horseshoe."

The fourth element of Chaucer's story, the wounding and healing sword, is nowhere obvious in these poems, and this is puzzling until we read Spenser and discover that he conflated sword powers with ring powers, so when Canacee gives the ring to her brother, Cambalo (or Cambello), as he goes out to fight her suitors, she is conferring on him invulnerability, or at least the faculty of self-healing. Neither magic mirror nor horse figures in Spenser, but a supernatural intervention in the form of a fairy sister of Priamond (Cambalo's last adversary) is suddenly borne into the fight in a lion-drawn chariot, intent on making peace with a brimming cup—of nepenthe:

Nepenthe is a drinck of souerayne grace,
  Deuized by the Gods, for to asswage
  Harts grief, and bitter gall away to chace,
  Which stirs vp anguish and contentious rage:
  In stead thereof sweet peace and quiet age
  It doth establish in the troubled mynd.

> Few men, but such as sober are and sage,
> Are by the Gods to drinck thereof assynd;
> But such as drinck, eternall happinesse do fynd.[30]
>
> (*Faerie Queene* IV.iii.xliii)

All is resolved in the story by dosing the antagonists with nepenthe and having them marry each other's sister (both of whom, incidentally, are expert herbalists—shades of Chaucer's Canacee). The proliferation of siblings in Spenser also obviates a slur on the classical Canacee which says (Ovid, *Heroides* XI) that she bore a child to her brother. As for a Zukofskian application, the verse about nepenthe is the kind of commentary we needed to make sense of the drug's place in the Epigraph. From "Harts grief" to "thereof assynd," Spenser could be describing the progress of Zukofsky's years; the final line then expresses that hoped-for connection with "impossible liveforever" in a manner that has none of the chilling overtones of Melville's amaranthine flower.

Chaucer and Spenser. Chaucer, we might reflect, was a voice in the beginning of "A" 22 & 23 (the song from *The Parlement of Foules* in "Initial") and then again at its conclusion (Zukofsky's "living calendar" patterned on "An A.B.C."). Now he reappears, just across the bridgehead, bringing in sky and sun, a pear-tree, a significant date, and the magic tokens of horse, ring, and mirror. For both Zukofsky and Pound, Geoffrey Chaucer is the English lyricist *par excellence;* in his *ABC of Reading* (1934), Pound dealt at some length with Chaucer, saying that the French (i.e., European) fourteenth-century lyric mode in Chaucer's hands produced: "English lyric, the technique for singing already complete, no augmentation of singability from Chaucer's days to our own. . . . Idiom has changed, but no greater *fitness to be sung* has been attained. Not even by Shakespeare with the aid of later Italian song-books" (*ABC*, p. 106).[31]

Zukofsky would have quarreled with that last point, but in all other respects his conclusions about "Master Geoffrey" dovetail with Pound's. *A Test of Poetry* (published 1948 but compiled 1935–40) uses for its examples of Chaucer's work exactly those lyrics pinpointed by Pound, grouping them mostly under the "Consideration" (i.e., selection rationale) of Song.[32] *A Test* comments on the contrast between "singable" Chaucerian lyric and a wooden nineteenth-century translation of François Villon's "Rondeau." Zukofsky's note: "Simplicity of utterance and song go together . . . The fitting of words to musical composition seems to have reached its maximum development in English poetry as early as the 14th century" (*A Test*, p. 65).

The chief difference between Pound and Zukofsky on this score was not evaluative but presentational. At the beginning of his "Exhibits" section, Pound regretted that presenting quotations without comment (the ideal mode) would be "too revolutionary. By long and wearing experience I have learned that in the present imperfect state of the world, one MUST tell the reader" (*ABC*, p. 95). The spirit of breezy opinionation therefore pervades his book. Zukofsky actually took the risk of minimal commentary by removing names and dates from two-thirds of *A Test* (the voice-only chronologies of *"A"* 22 & 23 are obviously long-term evolutions). The other third contains annotations to the poems selected.

To return to 1975 and the first poems of *80 Flowers;* it is clear that Chaucer still represents to Zukofsky the point at which song got into the English tradition. The Chaucerian elements of *"A"* 22 & 23 are in the Music sections of that poem for good reason, and who better to lead off a "book of songs" about a lifetime than Geoffrey Chaucer, who laced his lyric gift with insight into, and gusto for, the animating peculiarities of the world? When Pound says (*ABC*, p. 106): "Chaucer wrote when reading was no disgrace," and praises the compendiousness of his work (*ABC*, p. 92): "The Tales have lasted through centuries while the long-winded mediaeval narratives went into museums" (compendiums are people's trimmings and condensations and recordings of what has come down to them), we may be sure that Zukofsky is appreciative of the parallels with his own methods. Indeed, we are reminded of Zukofsky when Pound talks of Chaucer's citizenship in the European civilization of his age and his appropriation of its rich resources of language and material: "He is Le Grand Translateur. He had found a new language, he had it largely to himself, with the grand opportunity. Nothing spoiled, nothing worn out" (*ABC*, p. 101).

Nor for the poet of *Catullus, "A"*-21, the polyglot *"A"* 22 & 23 — and *80 Flowers;* nothing spoiled, nothing worn out, grand opportunity for a *grand translateur.* Even the earlier parts of *"A"* (the fifteenth movement in particular, but snatches of it throughout) demonstrate Zukofsky's interest in the carry-over of degrees of sound and sense; an interest sustained probably since childhood and the multilingual environment of the Lower East Side.[33] Translation is the first "Consideration" of *A Test,* which then has six sections on the variations of translating classical authors before it strikes the native English lyric, and after that (one section later) Geoffrey Chaucer.

Pound teams Chaucer and Shakespeare on one count, their "insuperable courage in tackling any, but absolutely any, thing that arouses their interest" (*ABC*, p. 102), but he prefers the fourteenth-century poet for his breadth and urbanity. Zukofsky saw the difference for himself (as Pound had directed; *ABC*, p. 99) in the thirteen years it took him to write *Bottom,* and the results will be heard again in *80 Flowers.* For the moment, though, Chaucer is the ideal voice for a starting point, with Pound in the background saying: "You would not be far out if you chose to consider Chaucer as the father of 'litterae humaniores' for Europe" (*ABC*, p. 103).

There is another voice in #1 Starglow, one that bridges the botanical/literary gap; Theophrastus, who wrote, among other things, the treatise *Peri Phyton Historias,* or *Enquiry into Plants.*[34] Theophrastus (370–ca. 285 B.C.) was a pupil first of Plato and then of Aristotle, his near-contemporary and close friend. He was responsible for the first philosophical meditations on the nature of plant structure and gathered a prodigious amount of plant lore, which he mixed with narrow-eyed personal observation, evolving a system of plant classification which had its roots in Platonic and Aristotelian methods. Theophrastus wrote his treatises as research rather than textbooks, and this led Arthur Hort, translator of the 1916 Loeb *Enquiry,* to remark of his style: "There is no literary charm; the sentences are mostly compressed and highly elliptical, to the point sometimes of obscurity. It follows that translation, as with Aristotle, must be to some extent paraphrase" (*Enquiry,* intro., p. xxi). The similarity to his own style was doubtless not lost upon Zukofsky, who carried that compression and ellipsis into *80 Flowers* and intensified it further. That the dense style of Theophrastus was deliberate rather than simply expedient was to be expected of an associate of Aristotle, who gave Theophrastus the name we know him by (it means, roughly, "divine stylist"). Benedict Einarson, translator of the 1976 Loeb edition of *De Causis Plantarum* (the work that succeeded the *Enquiry*), is closer to Aristotle than Hort in his evaluation of Theophrastus's style: "Theophrastus writes the *Kunstprosa* or euphonic prose of the day, such as we see it in the *Constitution of Athens.* Such prose endeavours to borrow the graces of poetry without ceasing to be prose. It remains prose by avoiding all poetical or non-current words and all oddities of syntax or idiom, and it seeks to please the ear by avoiding hiatus and having a certain rhythm and balanced structure of its own."[35] What was once considered charmless finds historical explanation and consequent appreciation. Zukofsky, reading Theophrastus and writing before Einarson, saw and heard the Greek's elliptic "poetry" first.[36]

Theophrastus held attractions for Zukofsky outside the botanical and stylistic. According to Diogenes Laertius, he lived to be eighty-five and preached by example a doctrine of hard work: "It is said that his disciples asked him if he had any last message for them, to which he replied: 'Nothing else but this, that many of the pleasures which life boasts are but in the seeming. For when we are just beginning to live, lo! we die. Nothing then is so unprofitable as the love of glory. Farewell, and may you be happy. Either drop my doctrine, which involves a world of labour, or stand forth its worthy champions, for you will win great glory. Life holds more disappointment than advantage . . . do you go on with the inquiry into right conduct.'"[37] This has affinities with Zukofsky's own "sorrow of harness," particularly when taken with another of Diogenes' reports which states that Theophrastus said: "An unbridled horse ought to be trusted sooner than a badly-arranged discourse."[38] This remark had been part of the Zukofsky canon at least since 1964, when it was voiced in "A"-14 (p. 319): " 'better // trust an / unbridled horse / than undigested // harangue.' " The "digestion" (or digest) of the remark was to be continued in 1977 with #59 Spirea of *80 Flowers*, the fifth line of which reads: "sun-steed water unbridled harangue maybe / argued." Another reputed remark of Theophrastus conveyed to us by Diogenes must have gained significance to Zukofsky as he pushed ahead with the writing of *80 Flowers*: "Nothing costs us so dear as the waste of time."[39]

Theophrastus also had distinctive theories about the nature of wild and cultivated plant forms and the associated matter of fruit-ripening. Zukofsky brings up these concerns in a prolonged burst of Theophrastian translation (some transliteration) in "A"-22. The section leads off:

> Annual in all parts annual—
> mere regard won't carp, own
> fruit sees history as
> *defined, once understood by another.*
> With plants as with men
> as to wild and cultivated:
> cautioning fast and hard *definitions*—
>
> ("A"-22, p. 520)

The four seasons of a man are implicit here and particularly that quarter ("one-fourth") which ripens fruit to a point where the plant can reproduce itself; *mechri gar ton karpon e physis* ("mere regard won't carp, own / fruit sees") is Theophrastus saying (the translation of Zukofsky's transliteration is italicized): "while it is plain that in annual plants *all* the parts are annual; for the end of their being is attained *when the fruit is produced*" (*Enquiry* I.ii.2).

The distinction between wild and cultivated plants and trees also centers on their relative degrees of ripening and stirs up questions about the nature and function of fruit. In his introduction to *De Causis Plantarum*, Einarson summarizes the matter of fruit and ripening, wild and cultivated, thus:

Nature, like art, is purposive, and the goal of the plant's nature is to ripen the fruit and reproduce. Here the distinction drawn between concoction—an old term derived from cooking and used of ripening and digestion—of the pericarpion and "concoction" (here not the accepted word) of the fruit or seed is of capital importance. The pericarpion is for human use, and "fruit" (seed) for the plant's own propagation. Plato had said that plants were created to serve man as food . . . and the language in current use coincides with this view. So wild trees are said to fail to "concoct" or "ripen" their fruit, because they do not make it edible . . . Theophrastus' distinction between the two concoctions gets rid of the notion that the goal of a plant is to feed man, although the notion passes uncontradicted when the "fruit" (a non-committal term which can mean the seed with the pericarpion or the one or the other alone) is made the goal of the plant.[40]

Theophrastus is curious about the distinctions between wild forms and cultivated ones because of his interest in man's "improvements" on nature and what this might signify about man himself: "Now in using the terms 'cultivated' and 'wild' we must make these on the one hand our standard, and on the other that which is in the truest sense 'cultivated.' Now Man, if he is not the only thing to which this name is strictly appropriate, is at least that to which it most applies" (*Enquiry* I.iii.6).

The matter of cultivation and fully matured fruit is clearly something Zukofsky also wants to work into *80 Flowers*, and the Theophrastus in #1 Starglow concerns the cultivation of roses and thyme. Of roses, Theophrastus's commentary is pertinent rather than integral to #1 Starglow: "If the bush is burnt or cut over, it bears better flowers; for, if left to itself, it grows luxuriantly and makes too much wood. Also it has to be often transplanted; for then, they say, the roses are improved" (*Enquiry* VI.vi.6). Roses are listed among the coronary plants: "cane cut back / a crown transplanted" paraphrases Theophrastus neatly and, with an incipient vision of rose crowns, touches again on the circled or circling rose of the Epigraph; one more variant on the ring shape. But "transplanted" is the prompt for thyme's entry into #1 Starglow: "The season for planting most of [the different sorts of thyme] is autumn, and then men hasten to plant them as early as possible . . . All of them love shade, water, and especially dung; however, thyme is patient of drought and, in general, needs moisture less than the others . . . it is said that they should often be transplanted, for that improves them" (*Enquiry* VI.vii.6). And Zukofsky, on the simultaneous cultivation of roses and thyme as practiced at 306 East Broadway (is this an instance of companion-planting?):

> cane cut back
> a crown transplanted patient of

> drought sun's gold firerimmed branched
> greeting thyme's autumn sprig head

A sprig of thyme, cut back for winter like the rose growing above it, both backlit (fiery-rimmed?) by the sun? And the "sculpt white rose" with which the poem ends is not Theophrastus, Taylor, Gray, Chaucer, Spenser; it cannot be anything but Zukofsky's private vision of the rose, Starglow—something flourishing, having survived setbacks ("car-tire crushed") and benefited from cutbacks, perhaps even from a transplanting. As the poem gains a familiar altitude ("flown / to sky," "sun's gold firerimmed"), so the rose itself rises, the first of many times it will use the conceit of its name to do so.

The Epigraph and the first *Flower* are a matched pair; the two poems that come after them, #2 Mountain Laurel and #3 Honesty, are similarly concatenated. As the winter of 1974–75 persists, Zukofsky continues to draw on the flowers of memory and anniversary. We follow him into that winter again.

4

The Ring and the Mirror: #2 Mountain Laurel and #3 Honesty

#2 Mountain Laurel

The first thing to notice in reading #2 Mountain Laurel is that many of its components are familiar: word repeats, more thyme, another trefoil, the same winter as in the earlier poems (but with a spring clearly in the wings). Most of all, there are hints that the undertexts of those poems (Chaucer and Spenser in particular) are surfacing:

#2 MOUNTAIN LAUREL

Known color grown mountain laurel
broadleaf of acid earth margin
entire green winter years hoarfrost
mooned pod *honesty* open unvoiced
May-grown acute 5-petal calicoflower cluster
10-slender rods spring seed sway
trefoil birds throat *Not thyme's*
spur-flower calico clusters laurelled well

Leaving for a while the stories, we concentrate first on the botanical and horticultural components. From Taylor, Gray, the *Century,* and cues in the draft material—this is a poem that went through three drafts and has its notes crammed into the margins of the same page (*80 Fl.* Drafts, p. 5)—we can quickly establish that mountain laurel is *Kalmia latifolia* of the Ericaceae or heath family, a native American shrub also known as calico bush, ivy bush, broadleaved ivy, spoonwood, and American laurel. From these names it is possible to gather that *Kalmia* is an evergreen of laurel- or ivy-like appearance ("ample shining leaves," as the *Century* puts it) with flowers the color of calico ("very showy flowers varying from nearly white to deep pink," *Century*), and with hard wood from which implements including tool handles and spoons can be turned. The shrub prefers acidic soils, and its leathery green leaves are untoothed—"margin / *entire*"; the italics plus a cross-reference in Taylor prompt us to look up the term, yielding: "Whole; as wholly without teeth, as are many leaf margins." *Kalmia* is "green" the *"entire" "winter,"* "hoarfrost" notwithstanding. As for "May-grown acute 5-petal calicoflower cluster," mountain laurel flowers from late May to mid-July, its blooms occur in terminal clusters, and each gamopetalous corolla is "acutely 5-lobed" (Gray). This last means that the limb of each corolla (that part above its "throat," to pick up a botanical reference in line seven of the poem) terminates in five sharply pointed sections. The fully expanded corolla is shallowly cuplike in shape.

The line "10-slender rods spring seed sway" (*not*, note, "away" as the sense demands and the eye virtually reads) continues the description of *Kalmia*'s inflorescence. Quoting again from the *Century:* "The anthers have the peculiarity (though free in the early bud) of becoming embedded in specialized pits or pockets of the corolla as it expands, the filaments bending over and acquiring tension, and finally straightening elastically, withdrawing the anthers suddenly and projecting pollen some distance over adjacent flowers." These "10 slender stamens" (Taylor) spring their pollen, which may loosely be called their seed; they spring it away and then sway with the recoil of the action. For the second time in *80 Flowers* a plant has shot seed as we listened, remembering: *"thus* fruit pod split four." But the Epigraph's action belongs to an emphatic syntax rather than botanical fact—*Nepeta cataria* does not actually fire its pod apart. Contrast that syntactic salvo with the long elasticity of *Kalmia*'s filaments springing their seeds (**way** into the air?).

Kalmia is a near-perfect Euro-American emblem, indigenous but identified by, and later named in honor of, Pehr Kalm (1716–79), a botanist who traveled extensively in North America 1748–51 for the Swedish Academy of Sciences. Kalm had been a pupil of Karl von Linné (1701–78), the great Linnaeus, whose binomial system of plant classification—one name for genus, one for species—is still the basis of botanical nomenclature. Linnaeus himself named the American mountain laurel *Kalmia latifolia* (broadleaved; Zukofsky—"broadleaf"), thus completing the transaction, phenomena for expertise, between the Old World and the New.

Kalm kept diaries of his American experiences, and it was a two-volume edition of *Peter Kalm's Travels in North America* that Paul Zukofsky presented to his father in 1971, along with the USDA handbook *Common Weeds*, and *The Travels of William Bartram.*[1] Zukofsky was interested in travelers who left lively records of their North American passage, and he made notes from both Kalm and Bartram in the "A" 22 *&* 23 Spiral.

The Swedes wanted to know what North American flora might thrive in their latitudes, with an eye to economic and agricultural improvements; and Kalm was their faithful, systematic scout. That he was also a Linnean botanist must have intimated to Zukofsky the prospect of a trained eye finding itself in earthly paradise—a whole new world to be systematically explored, recorded, and its flora brought under the classifications Linnaeus was developing at the time. *Species Plantarum* and *Genera Plantarum,* the two works that pioneered the binomial system, were published 1753 and 1754, respectively. And so it is that, having worked Theophrastus into #1 Starglow, Zukofsky now inserts another giant of botanical literature at the beginning of *80 Flowers*—by means of an American connection. Enlightenment science is seen to bridge Old World and New, its emblem a vigorous evergreen, which is, however, not the European laurel.

Of *Kalmia* itself, Kalm wrote a full report, observing that the Swedes of New Jersey called the shrub a spoon tree because Indians made spoons and other items from its wood; it was the English who called the tree a laurel. He noted that *Kalmia* grew best on north-facing hillsides; and here, apparently, is the basis of the later descriptive, "mountain" laurel. He also commented that the further up a hillside *Kalmia* shrubs grew, the shorter they were; in fact, they appear in his journal as "American dwarf laurel." His description tallies with what we have already found in Zukofsky's poem:

> They have the quality of preserving their fine green leaves throughout the winter, so that when all other trees have lost their ornaments, and stand quite naked, these adorn the woods with their green foliage. About the month of May they begin to flower in these parts, and then their beauty rivals that of most of the known trees in nature. The flowers are innumerable, and grow in great clusters. Before they open they have a fine red color, but as they expand, the sun bleaches them so that some are almost white; many keep the color of roses. Their shape is singular, for they resemble ancient cups. Their scent, however, is none of the most agreeable. In some places it is customary to decorate the churches on Christmas Day or New Year's Day with the fine branches of this tree.[2]

Beauty rivaling most of the known trees in nature; flowers keeping the color of roses; leaves so persistently evergreen they suggested ornament for winter festivals to the early Americans. Add to such credentials the fact that the Zukofskys had a mountain laurel in their own garden:

> yew, flame-azalea,
> box-like shrub holly, kalmia more

you, díscolor willow with the
lilac.

("A"-23, p. 554)

Certainly the foliage of such a plant, others standing "quite naked"
around it (the willow, the lilac), must have suggested to Zukofsky an
appropriate subject for this late-January poem. Mountain laurel was
already on the First List of 80 Flowers; its time had obviously arrived.

However, there are other flowers in the poem. For example, line four,
"mooned pod *honesty* open unvoiced," abruptly introduces the subject of
the fourth poem, #3 Honesty, then just as suddenly leaves it. And in lines
seven and eight we make out thyme and the shadowy bird's-foot trefoil
("bird tread") of the Epigraph:

> trefoil birds throat *Not thyme's*
> *spur-flower calico clusters laurelled well*

What "throat" does in such close proximity to the "trefoil birds" is not
altogether clear; botanically, it sits more comfortably with the cuplike
Kalmia flower. However, if we think about "birds throat" and hear
"throat" as a verb (one of its *Century*-listed senses), then perhaps what
follows is birdsong and the italics are what is throated. If this is so, the
lyric is a complicated one: *"Not thyme's / spur-flower"* it begins, and
already we are in trouble. Does this mean there is no thyme here? But the
only spurred flower in #2 Mountain Laurel (shades of horses—or birds—
or the acute tips of *Kalmia*'s corolla) is bird's-foot trefoil, whose botanical
name, *Lotus corniculatus,* recognizes in the species a clawlike petal:
corniculatus means "horned" (it is also the name under which bird's-foot
trefoil is entered in the First List of 80 Flowers). This gets us no further
with *"Not thyme's,"* which turns out to be an elliptic scrap of Theophrastus (reenter the Old World). The margin notes of the drafts lead us
eventually to the exact source: "Savory, and still more marjoram, has a
conspicuous fruitful seed, but in thyme it is not easy to find, being
somehow mixed up with the flower; for men sow the flower and plants
come up from it" (*Enquiry* VI.ii.3). This is why the spectacular pollination
mechanism of *Kalmia latifolia,* involving "seed" rather than pollen, was
evoked a line earlier; the showy mountain laurel shows how it is done, but
the seeds of thyme are not easily discoverable. The seeds of time are
hidden in a flower.

The almost-presence of thyme elusively scents this poem about a shrub
with flowers that may have the color of roses but not their incomparable
fragrance. One thymy whiff, then we are back with the visual splendor of
Kalmia (which the birds are singing about?): *"calico clusters laurelled*

well." Laurelled dwell? laurel dwell? Come May and its full glory, the calico bush will be *"laurelled well"*; now, in January, it is also a handsome sight.

Here we should take notice of an addition to the mountain laurel entry in the First List which specifies that the *Kalmia* poem is not to include "bay wreath etc."; that is, Zukofsky does not want to get onto the territory of *Laurocerasus*, the European Laurel, which has its own literary heritage. There are no allusions to Apollo and Daphne here, and no wreaths or crowns; this is an American laurel, a notable flowerer—and it is time to look at those blossoms:

May-grown acute 5-petal calicoflower cluster

Compounds wind into the line a bunchy tension made up of "k" and "l" sounds aimed at that final term, "cluster," a word that also manages to include the "t" of those acute petal tips. Then the flower springs its pollen in a shower of sibilants anchored by vibrant "n" sounds—"10," "slender," "spring"—which give way to the long, easy vowels of release—"seed," "sway." And the next time *Kalmia* flowers are brought into view, the terms of the repeat are separated words and the pace of the line is serene due to an infusion of "l"s:

spur-flower calico clusters laurelled well

"And all shall be well and / All manner of thing shall be well"; there is the faintest hint of a benison.[3] For Eliot, backed up by the liturgy, exchange the brightness of a Shakespearean comedy, *All's Well That Ends Well*. This poem literally ends "well."

With some working knowledge now of the greenery in #2 Mountain Laurel, we turn to its undertexts. Continuation first; there is a carry-over from #1 Starglow of the protagonists in Chaucer's pear-tree story. A quotation from *The Merchant's Tale* in the mountain laurel entry of the First List alerts us to the presence of old Januarie, who boasted to his friends about his virility:

> I fele me nowher hoor but on myn heed;
> Myn herte and alle my limes been as grene
> As laurer thurgh the yeer is for to sene.
>
> (*Merchant's Tale,* 219–21)

This condenses, losing nothing to either botany or Chaucer, as: *"entire green winter years hoarfrost."* What amounts to a laurel crown has appeared in Zukofsky's poem at the exact moment it dives from New World botany into Old World literature; that is, from the description of *Kalmia*'s visible characteristics into undertextual doublings of them. So the European laurel exemplifying winter greenness is drawn into #2 Mountain Laurel, but what Zukofsky extracts from Januarie's speech is not his simile so much as his white hairs—hoarfrost on the laurel, age on the lover. Chaucer double-edged his portrait of Januarie (is this why his *senex amans* is named for Janus's month?) so as to establish some sympathy for an old man about to be roundly hoodwinked. But there can be no doubt that Chaucer had fun at Januarie's expense, and especially over his sexual boasting; and it is in the spirit of the tale that Zukofsky follows suit.

"*Entire* green winter years hoarfrost"; the italics repeat Januarie's pointed allusion to "alle my limes." In the *Century, entire* derives from *integer,* meaning "whole" (e.g., numbers), or, literally, "untouched." The Latin root is *in*-privative + *tangere,* "to touch." Whole or untouched—the *Century*'s full string of synonyms is: "untouched, unhurt, unchanged, sound, fresh, whole, entire, pure, honest"; and suddenly emotional dignity is restored to the line. An *entire horse,* continues the *Century,* is a stallion as distinguished from a gelding, "uncut." This brings old Januarie's boast to mind (pathos, comedy), and the slender seed-springing rods of line six assume new overtones. However, between the hoarfrosted old laurel and the firing of seed is: "May-grown acute." Remove the hyphen and there is Januarie's young wife, playing "*honesty* open" to her husband's suspicions, and managing at the same time to put herself in the way of a more congenial seed-springer, Damian in his pear-tree.

All ends "well" in the tale thanks to the quick intervention of Lady Proserpina, who champions May (and the wits of women) against Pluto's distaste for the deception being played upon Januarie. May, having hinted that pregnancy drove her desire for the "smale peres grene" in the first place (diplomatic nod to Januarie's procreative powers), has with no little sophistry convinced the old man that he did not see what his magically restored eyes thought they saw: "Was no-thing bet to make yow to see / Than strugle with a man up-on a tree," she says (*Merchant's Tale,* 1129–30). If May was not pregnant before she climbed into the pear-tree, there is a chance she is now—and Januarie, taken in by this as well as the other ruse, delightedly pats her belly and considers himself still green.

Pluto and Proserpina, the supernatural components of the Merchant's cheerfully ribald tale, have been medievalized from classical legend as the king and queen of "Fayerye"; in medieval fashion, they dispute the honesty of women and Proserpina wins, as she will shortly win May's victory. Not many underworld trappings are obvious as the pair sit themselves down with a fairy entourage on the far side of Januarie's orchard, but reference is made to Proserpina's ravishing from Ethna, "Whil that she gadered floures in the mede" (*Merchant's Tale,* 987). This echoes another piece of Chaucer which goes into the making of Zukofsky's phrase "Known color grown," the lead of #2 Mountain Laurel. The Chaucer, pointed out by a margin note in the Drafts (p. 5), is from *The Franklin's Prologue*. Excusing himself for being of "rude speche" and ignorant of "Colours of rethoryk," the Franklin says:

> Colours ne knowe I none, with-outen drede,
> But swiche colours as growen in the mede.
>
> *(Franklin's Prologue*, 51–52)

As with Proserpina, an association of innocence with flowers is taking place. "Known color grown" also has a perceptual basis; generally because Zukofsky knows firsthand the flowers he is writing about ("Only those flowers I have actually seen," Schema), and specifically because he knows the color May will bring to the January mountain laurel. Cross that line of thought with *The Merchant's Tale* for further variations on the themes of fertility and staying green. The uppercase "K" of "Known," incidentally, is the only sign of the mountain laurel's Latin identity to show up in the poem, although a plenitude of "k" and "l" sounds in the lines about *Kalmia latifolia* let us hear that Zukofsky has the binomial in mind.

Between *The Franklin's Prologue* and *The Merchant's Tale* in Skeat's Chaucer is *The Squire's Tale,* that story about magical gifts and the king's daughter, Canacee. The bottom margin of the #2 Mountain Laurel drafts contains a series of quotations from *The Squire's Tale,* mainly concerned with the virtues of Canacee's ring (understanding of bird languages and herb lore), along with a note to use the material in #3 Honesty, the next *Flower*. This is the second time the *Squire's Tale* material has been shifted ahead; it was originally intended for inclusion in the mountain laurel poem, to judge by a reference immediately following the drafts of #1 Starglow. However, the forward shift does not mean that Canacee has vanished altogether from #2 Mountain Laurel. Traces of her survive in the singing birds of line seven and by means of Spenser's treatment of the story in book 4 of *The Faerie Queene* (another "fayerye" queen in the undertexts of #2 Mountain Laurel). The Spenser connection comes via a quotation Zukofsky writes into the left margin of the drafts; Triamond, last and most powerful of the brother-suitors, fights Cambalo with astonishing (and magical) power (Zukofsky's quotation in the drafts in italics):

> He stroke, he soust, he foynd, he hewd, he lasht,
> And did his yron brond so fast applie,
> That from the same the *fierie sparkles flasht,*
> *As fast as water-sprinkles gainst a rocke are dasht.*
>
> *(Faerie Queene* IV.iii.xxv)

The image of a spray or sprinkling is one we have already encountered in #2 Mountain Laurel. To the fertile shower of pollen (Danae's golden rain) is added the spectacle of flashing "fierie sparkles" and sparkling "water-sprinkles." An earlier candidate for the place "spring" now occupies in the line "10-slender rods spring seed sway" was "sparkle." The same word was also an early component of the line "mooned pod *honesty* open unvoiced," occurring somewhere between "mooned" and "pod." Water sparkles, fire sparks; pollen may shower as a simile of either, but can the moon be said to "sparkle"? A run-on line in the poem suggests that on a still, frosty night it can: "hoarfrost / mooned pod *honesty* open unvoiced." Hoarfrost, as Zukofsky notes (in part from the *Century*), is made up of silvery white ice needles and forms on still, clear nights, which can of course be moonlit.

The actual "sparkle" of seed shower or icy moonlight does not surface in the final text of #2 Mountain Laurel, but it does provide a starting point for considering the implications of that "mooned pod" which is the plant known botanically as *Lunaria annua* and popularly as honesty, moonwort, and a host of other names associated with the silvery sheen of its circular seedpods. Sometimes by confusion, *Lunaria* is also identified as moon trefoil, a plant the *Century* lists as *Medicago arborea* of the pea family; and so there is an alternative identity for the trefoil of line seven.[4] (What now of the neighboring "birds throat"?)

The "mooned pod" line has a complex set of antecedents. On the draft page of #2 Mountain Laurel, it (and the trefoil) stem from yet another margin note:

moon
  dust
  had
  danced
   there
    unvoiced
     throated
      picking
     up
      deep
   bottle
    green
  moon
(trefoil
(honesty)
moonwort

                     (*80 Fl.* Drafts, p. 5)

Notice the conflation of moon plants. Most of this note comes in turn from an early entry in the *80 Flowers* Notes:

(in pocket)

11/24/69—Moondust[got their throats .]. picking
(had danced there)   (moon
up (ginger-ale) bottle green on the moon]trefoil)

(*80 Fl.* Notes, p. 1)

The three-way conflation of honesty, moonwort, and moon trefoil occurs some time later (1974?) as Zukofsky is making notes for the final section of "*A*"-23, on the checkbook blanks that accompany the black notebook. From one of these, undated:

moondust in his pocket = honesty
had danced there   moonwort

moon
trefoil
(b.n.b., loose-leaf after p. 115)

This note is the immediate source of the "moonwort" in the tail end of "*A*"-23:

—impossible's
sort-of think-cramp work x: moonwort:
music, thought, drama, story, poem

("*A*"-23, p. 563)

But that used up only one of the moony aliases, so in the overflow of "*A*"-23 notes Zukofsky transferred to the *80 Flowers* Notes in September 1974, he wrote:

see 11/24/69
 moondust
in pocket
moon trefoil
 had danced
  there

(*80 Fl.* Notes, p. 3)

This meant, of course, that the note of 1969 was still live material. Where did the moon trefoil come from? Christopher Smart's *Jubilate Agno*, the poem Zukofsky "named" just prior to the beginning of the "living calendar" ("Jubilant agony," "*A*"-23, p. 562), contains a line about the plant: "Let Hashum rejoice with Moon-Trefoil." According to his editor, Smart drew heavily on *The Gardener's Dictionary*, by Philip Miller, for his botanical material; and Miller lists moon trefoil under *Lunarium*.[5]

Whether Zukofsky knew this makes little difference; a plant whose name incorporated not only a lunar motif but also tripleness (that lucky, familial, perfect three) was meant to join forces with honesty and moon-wort.

What of the moon dust and dancing references in the note of 24 November 1969? They were certainly used in *80 Flowers* as part of the composite moon-plant figure—"open unvoiced . . . trefoil . . . throat," in #2 Mountain Laurel, for example—but it is not easy to tell from this what Zukofsky had in mind. The key to the 1969 note is its date and the phrase "on the moon"; 24 November 1969 was the day *Apollo 12*'s astronauts splashed down after the second successful moon landing. The moon walkers had spent a lot of time complaining about lunar dust ("And the dust! Dust got into everything," Pete Conrad wrote later);[6] and although none of the transcripts mentions moon dust getting specifically into throats or pockets, it was enough of a problem to make Conrad and Alan Bean stay in their moon suits between the walks rather than scrambling messily in and out of them in the confines of the lunar module *Intrepid*. (Is "mooned pod" Zukofsky for "lunar module"? Is *"honesty"* the name of a private craft?) Zukofsky shared a then-common curiosity about the nature of the lunar surface. From 1964:

Ranger VII
photos landing
on the

moon
how deep
its dust?

crater whose
base is
shoal? Egypt

Sumer's works
whose foot
has disappeared?

("A"-14, pp. 315–16)

"Moondust got their throats" (they were "unvoiced"?) might simply be impressionistic note-taking on Zukofsky's part. Who does not remember the crackly voices from the moon? and the eerie green of color photography on the lunar surface, as if the lens were peering through a (bottle-green) filter? It was a phenomenon noticed by more spectators than Zukofsky; the *New York Times* of 19 November 1969 carried a story on *Apollo 12*'s TV transmission, part of which reads: "In Monday night's color transmission from lunar orbit, there was a greenish tinge over the whole screen, which was similar to the color that predominated in the color movie films taken during the Apollo descent in July by Col. Edwin E. Aldrin, Jr. . . . The difference between the spacemen's impressions and what the television viewer sees on his screen is due, according to a spokesman for the Columbia Broadcasting System, to the transmission, lighting conditions, the angle from which the picture is taken, and reflection from the sun."[7]

Color TV became a major issue in the course of *Apollo 12*'s moon landing when the astronauts' TV camera failed a few minutes into the first walk, which Zukofsky noted, 19 November 1969, in the black notebook (p. 68), along with a general opinion that the camera's color tube had been burnt out by inadvertent exposure to the direct heat of the sun on the atmosphereless surface of the moon. The TV watchers at home were left with nothing but the scratchy voice record as Conrad and Bean swung into exhaustive description of what they were seeing and picking up (rocks, moon dust) (moon trefoil?), partially to compensate for the lack of visual pickup.

Dancing? In gravity one-sixth of the earth's all the moon walks were slow-motion ballets. Of the *Apollo 11* descent, Zukofsky had written:

"~~one small step for man, one giant leap for mankind~~"
July 20/69—Moonlanding (with man's bug with 4 legs)
("*Eagle* has landed") "Tranquility Base, man on the moon"
The best "abstract" dance I've seen
July 24/69—Splashdown after an abstract of dance.
(b.n.b., p. 63)

Four months later, writing the "moondust" entry in the *80 Flowers* Notes, with the descriptions of *Apollo 12*'s moon walks fresh in mind, he inserted the dance motif again. But there is also a possibility that the insertion took place even later and as a result of a different set of moon references, which draw in that parenthesized and as yet unexplained "pocket" in the note of 24 November 1969. A near illegible margin note in the black notebook reads:

7/22/70—and it is over (∗) crater rocks but I did dance
    drop in my pocket   there
                                   (via
                                     rock,
                                   jumped
                                   jimmied[8]
                                   (b.n.b., p. 52)

Each half of this is arrowed to another entry in the main part of page 52; the dance to Zukofsky's description of the astronaut Christmas of 1968, *Apollo 8* disappearing around the dark side of the moon after the Genesis reading. The pocket is arrowed to a quotation from Laurence Sterne's *Sentimental Journey*, about an affair with the moon. We shall come back to the Sterne, which was written into "Initial" July-August 1970, along with NASA's moon dancers:

> an affair with the moon
> it looked as if it
> looked up someway above earth
> a hectic of an instant
>
> until computed in the metal—
> tidal waves also timing it
> moon's day and earth's month
> figured closer—blazed sun, white
> under weightless dancing
>
> ("A"-22, pp. 509–10)

The moon dance was in "Initial" by 1970, and moonwort was in the last lines of "A"-23 by 1974; the moon dust (in pocket, in throat), moon trefoil, and honesty were left for *80 Flowers*. It is difficult to see why the moon and its plants come into #2 Mountain Laurel one poem before their logical place in the sequence, #3 Honesty; difficult, that is, until we realize that the mirroring principle which operates between the Epigraph and #1 Starglow could also be working cross-page between #2 Mountain Laurel and #3 Honesty. Here there also seems to be an inverse effect built into the mirror, for if the moon in #2 Mountain Laurel is associated first with hoarfrost and wintry moonlight and then by extension with the intense cold of the lunar shade, #3 Honesty is full of blazing sun images. Extremes of heat and cold lie one against the other on the daytime lunar surface, 250° F in the sun, −250° F in the shade, truly a thermal mirror image.

The mirror principle seems to derive from Canacee's glass (a "mirror-ring" principle indeed), which will show only truth (honesty) and find out deceit. We should remember that #2 Mountain Laurel's most prominent undertext is a story about successful deceit—right across the page from a poem called "Honesty," a plant also paradoxically present in the poem that deals with Januarie and the smooth-tongued May. A mirror, though honest, is never simple.

Canacee survives in the poem; we discern the effects of her mirror and the presence of her ring (in "spring"), which makes sense of the birds' throatings. From Spenser's version, there are vestiges of her story in the shower of seed which Zukofsky thought of comparing to sparkles of water or sparks of fire. Although the process is in part speculative, Canacee's actual presence in #2 Mountain Laurel can be established; perhaps its strongest recommendation is that the speculation is ultimately dependent upon an analogy of sound. It is also rooted in the last "story" of the poem, which is the matter of its dedication.

Zukofsky began composing #2 Mountain Laurel 25 January 1975; he finished it 29–30 January and inscribed the final draft: "for Chana Z."—a dedication that was not repeated in the *80 Flowers* Spiral. Zukofsky's opinion of dedications is characteristic; he thought they should be built into the piece of work thus being offered as a kind of gift to the dedicatee. The receiver should be able to read there signs of contact or intimacy between himself and the giver, obviating the need for labels on something he regarded as essentially a private matter.[9] Printed dedications tend to focus attention on one aspect of a poem at the expense of others; Zukofsky is by and large unwilling to risk such a narrowing of scope, though he does occasionally dedicate a poem where acknowledgment is due (*Catullus* 95 to Pound) or to a close friend (*Catullus* 102 to Bunting).

"Chana Z." of the ink draft, whose association with the poem has been left until last in deference to the erasure of the dedication in every place but one, is Louis Zukofsky's mother, Chana Zukofsky, née Pruss.[10] She died 29 January 1927 as Louis turned twenty-three, and he felt the loss deeply; it is written obliquely into "A"-5 (composed 1930) and dramatized in *Arise, arise,* the play of 1936 in which a mother dies on her son's birthday. Zukofsky's birthday was 29 January; at least, it was the birthday he celebrated before finding he had misread the figure on the birth certificate unearthed in order to fix the date his parents had simply approximated.[11]

The dedication of #2 Mountain Laurel to Chana Zukofsky is made in the finishing date of its composition; and this, perhaps because it is a matter of time and therefore part of the book's proper subject matter (at least in draft) does get into the *80 Flowers* Spiral, a silent ("unvoiced") dedication to the poet's mother in the only poem of *80 Flowers* which could also be a birthday poem for himself. #2 Mountain Laurel conceals an intense, familial curve of birth and death. Mountain laurel per se does not appear in the 1936 play or in "A"-5, but the latter does contain some intriguing echoes of the second-numbered *Flower:*

> (New York, tonight, the rat-lofts
>   light
>   with the light of a trefoil);

> Purple clover,
> She wore her shoes three years—

> (The soles new as the sunned black
>   of her grave-turf);
>
> . . .
>
> New are, the trees,
> Purple in the violets' swath,
> Birds—birds—birds.
>
> ("A"-5, pp. 18, 19)

"Trefoil birds throat" (they sing in clover? the light of clover?). *"Not thyme's / spur-flower"* (they "throat" trefoil rather than thyme? why?). Or do "trefoil birds" sing the entire italicization? What is a trefoil bird? (body and two outspread wings, more of a fleur-de-lis) (bird of a trefoil window, flying through, not knowing it there, singing it broken like the birds of "Initial"—a trefoil window is certainly a window of history). The birds, their trefoil, their throats or throating are still elusive; they do, however, appear with the purple clover again in *"A"*-7's recapitulation of the six movements before it, especially in the reiteration ("Birds—birds—," *"A"*-7, p. 40), which brings them close to transformation as *words,* those singing airs.

This sounds like the link with Canacee's magic ring, which granted understanding of and fluency in the language of the birds (Zukofsky's words?) because *Chana Z.,* associated in death with the birds and flowers of a spring field, is a phonetic doublet of *Canacee.* Zukofsky seems to be gifting his mother with supralinguistic powers of understanding languages (e.g., his poetry) she knew nothing of in life; extension or restatement of lines in the 1926 "Poem Beginning 'The'":

> If horses could but sing Bach, mother,—
> Remember how I wished it once—
> Now I kiss you who could never sing Bach,
>   never read Shakespeare.
>
> (*All,* p. 19)

Zukofsky fashioned Bach-singing horses for himself; why not poetry-singing birds for his mother?

There is another linguistic dimension to the Canacee-Chana Z. overlay, again speculative and again intriguing. Liddell and Scott offer a number of related words that seem to contribute to the figure Zukofsky has set up. The Greek rendering of Canacee's name (she was a figure of classical literature) is *Kanachē.* Zukofsky would not have found the name in Liddell and Scott, but he might well have seen instead a number of similarly sounded words: *kanachē* is a sharp sound, especially the ring or clang of metal but also the sound of flutes or lyres; *kanachēs* is the plashing of water; *kanacheō* is a verb expressing various sounds—ringing, clashing, plashing, and so forth; *kanassō* means "to make a sharp gurgling sound with water." The root of *kanassō* (and of *kanachē*) is *kan*, which is the ultimate source of the Latin verb *cano*, "to sing." If Zukofsky was aware of these connections of sound—water plashing, metal ringing, flute and lyre reminiscent of both—then we are looking at another underpinning of the passage from Spenser's Canacee story where the sound of battle produces fiery sparkles like rock-dashed water droplets. From somewhere in the plashing/ringing Greek emerges music, eventually Latin song. And from somewhere in Zukofsky's sparkle-spring-moon continuum emerges birdsong in unspecified relation to honesty, a trefoil, thyme (time), and mountain laurel.

The other side of the mirror might tell us more about this.

#3 Honesty

Honesty, the third *Flower* and fourth poem of the book, is also the 1975 valentine, for "C + P" (Celia and Paul), as Zukofsky initials the ink draft. We could expect to find in it the dense blend of public and private material typical of the "family" *Flowers* to date, and of Zukofsky's past valentines (particularly "AN ERA").

On the face of it, though, not much is being given away. The silvery beauty of the seed pod is obviously in the poet's eye, but the moonshine is mixed up with other, sublunary material of an enigmatic nature:

#3   HONESTY

Honesty lunar year annual anew
birdsong your lifelode blazing sunned
moon Lionmane Sickle quiet waiting
strings inner pegbox no angry
dew more alive once believed
picklock unshodding horseshoes from lofting
hooves iron zeal each lentilled
seedpod somehow mirrors luck's horseshoe

Taylor establishes that honesty is *Lunaria annua,* "moonwort, satinpod, or satinflower. An annual"—and already we have uncovered a Latin transliteration that reflects the sense of its Latin sound: "lunar year annual"; "annual anew" further describes the plant's life span. *Anew* is in addition the title of Zukofsky's 1946 collection, and so the drawing-in of the canon goes on. For the same reason we should notice two previous references in

"*A*" to the herb honesty. It belongs to the Cruciferae or mustard family, and this is the point behind an association of moon, herb, and Shakespeare which occurs in "*A*"-14:

> *Lunaria annua honesty*
>
> this side the
> moon's. *Good Master*
> *Mustardseed I desire*
>
> *you more acquaintance.*
>
> ("*A*"-14, p. 356)

(This section of "*A*"-14 is written in three-line stanzas, three words per line; a formally suitable predecessor for #3 Honesty.) More acquaintance with Mustardseed's kin, the Crucifers, is offered by the close of "*A*"-15:

> *negritude* no nearer or further
> than the African violet
> not deferred to
> or if white, Job
> white pods of *honesty*
> *satinflower*
>
> ("*A*"-15, p. 375)

Zukofsky is driving at a black/white contrast here, and it is transformed in *80 Flowers* as a gold/silver opposition: "blazing sunned / moon Lionmane Sickle"—if these last terms can be imagined as the shapes of sun and crescent moon, respectively.

This much said, we must deal with the array of information presented by #3 Honesty. As in the earlier *Flowers,* some of it makes sense of the plant's physical appearance: "each lentilled / seedpod" and "strings inner pegbox," for example. The arrangement of *Lunaria*'s lentil-like seeds in the translucent pod bears resemblance to the head of a fiddle (its pegbox). The strings are "quiet waiting . . . [in a] pegbox" (an open string, unvoiced [quiet] because it is waiting?). Or perhaps "quiet waiting" (adjective + noun) (or noun + verb) is stringing an inner pegbox? heartstrings? Whatever else, there is an allusion to patience in the "*A*"-15 phrase "Job / white pods of *honesty.*"

The seed pod could certainly be said to "somehow mirror" (that satiny sheen) the almost circular shape of a horseshoe. There are two "horseshoes" in the poem, and there is another "mooned pod" reflecting from across the page in #2 Mountain Laurel. Moon and mirror, music and horses; the music is stringed, recalling the bowings of "*A*"-11 and the "An"-song of "*A*"-19, each of them related to Paul, violinist, and to Celia, his earliest tutor and a composer herself. Zukofsky *père* is once again bringing his music to that of his valentines.

The horses of #3 Honesty are neither simple figures nor easily separable from their surrounding syntax:

> no angry
> dew more alive once believed
> picklock unshodding horseshoes from lofting
> hooves iron zeal

There are two early notes for *80 Flowers* which might help sort out this odd assortment of motifs. The first is an entry made on New Year's Day 1969:

> 1/1/69—her greatest beauty of a flower
> an angry dew
>
> (*80 Fl*. Notes, p. 1)

On the same page is another note, written 8 June 1969, that anniversary of great personal significance in the Zukofsky calendar:

> 6/8/69—Lunaria annua (see Century Dict.)
> the pod than there's nothing more alive.[12]
>
> (*80 Fl*. Notes, p. 1)

So we consult the *Century* and happen (in a roundabout way) on an explanation of honesty's link with horses. *Lunaria annua* has a long history of magical association because of the moonlike appearance of its pods; it was one of two herbs once called "lunary." However, it is the other lunary, *Botrychium lunaria* or moonwort, whose also magical past provides horses for Zukofsky.[13] The *Century* notes that moonwort "was formerly supposed to have the power of opening locks and drawing the shoes from the feet of horses," and it then refers us to a quotation under *lunatic*. From Sir Thomas Browne, 1646: "That ferrum equinum [lunary] . . . hath a vertu attractive of iron to break lockes and draw off the shooes of a horse that passeth over it . . . Which strange and magicall conceit seemes unto me to have no deeper root in reason than the figure of its seed, for therein indeed it somewhat resembles an horseshoe, which notwithstanding Baptista Porta hath . . . raised the same unto a lunatic representation" (*Pseudo Epigraphia* ii.6).

This makes preliminary sense of "once believed / picklock unshodding horseshoes from lofting / hooves iron zeal," although it is hard to see how "zeal" fits into the condensation of Browne's information, and the *Century* has nothing to say about an "angry dew" (jew?), "more alive" or otherwise. Both Zukofsky's 1969 notebook entries resume their hermetic aspect; and the case should perhaps rest there—two private observations, conjecturally concerning Celia ("her greatest beauty," etc.), conflated and then embedded in a valentine.

However, the "angry dew" has a forerunner in the second Music section of "A"-22, the personal lyric that begins: "Between grape bay and hungry / bay." Here Zukofsky is recalling the Bermuda trip of 1972, a vacation that was interrupted by news of the death of his sister Fanny. Near the outset of the section we perceive an undercurrent of emotional trauma in the gorgeous Bermuda setting:

merely—ocean blued windows sweat
between soused bitten cliff and
that—we're freed by silence,
anger lights windflower, tears': or
a mad gist always glad?

("A"-22, p. 533)

Here are "anger" and "tears" but nothing to connect them to the "angry dew" of #3 Honesty until we reflect (and it was never far from Zukofsky's Shakespeare-ridden mind) that these are the "still-vex'd Bermoothes" where Prospero once dispatched Ariel to fetch dew (*Tmp.* I.ii.229) in days ("once") when dew was decidedly "more alive" to those who knew what to do with it. We are not mistaken, because Ariel's voice is heard in the last four lines of the section, also the closing moments of the poem:

contént with *still-vext Bermoothes . . where*
once thou call'dst me up

. . to fetch dew . . tears: *there*
she's hid an arm embraces.

("A"-22, p. 535)

So: "anger" and "tears," and now "*dew*" and "tears." The last section of "A"-22 encompasses two family deaths ("Min," whose identity is not specified further but who seems connected with Fanny, and died three weeks after her; Zukofsky notes ["A" 22 & 23 Spiral, p. 141] they were both about eighty-four or eighty-five).[14] The same section also hints at an "angry dew" close to the heart of the Zukofsky household; the notes made in Bermuda incorporate references to earlier material, one of which reads:

10/30/68: To say nothing seems too
much, the sorrows remain human

("A" 22 & 23 Spiral, p. 140)

This elucidates part of the stanza about Bermuda quoted earlier: "we're freed by silence . . . and sorrows dissolve—human" ("*A*"-22, p. 533). A second note from 1969 turns out to be familiar material, somewhat amplified:

(cf 1/1/69 p. 52 black notebook—the greatest beauty of a face in
        its anger the light shining thru the windflower of

                                              its

                                           tears.

                        ("*A*" 22 *&* 23 Spiral, p. 140)

This explains "*A*"-22's "anger lights windflower, tears' " —condensation of an already condensed note. We begin to see where #3 Honesty's "angry dew" comes from, but the phrase as a whole ("no angry / dew more alive") remains elusive. Digging even deeper into the strata of "*A*," we consult page 52 of the black notebook, as instructed—and find all on the same page what appear to be the original versions of three notes relevant to *80 Flowers* and the present discussion.

First there is the *artos* note of Christmas 1968; then an entry made five days later:

12/30/68   To say ~~anything~~ nothing seems too much & the
     sorrows remain human[15]

                               (b.n.b., p. 52)

(Does the "freed by silence" of "*A*"-22 reach as far as "open unvoiced" of #2 Mountain Laurel and "quiet waiting" of #3 Honesty?) The next black notebook entry, partly illegible and with a note that it is to be used also in *80 Flowers,* is the "angry dew" of New Year's 1969:

       greatest   transfer   ~~shining~~
  1/1/69—the / beauty of ~~the~~ face in its anger, ~~the~~(light shone
                                   thru)
                             (delicate)
  [illeg.   ] ~~transparency of its love~~   the wind
  flower of its tears.

                                (b.n.b., p. 52)

One of the things to notice about these three entries is their Christmas–New Year's locus; significance of date seems to have produced a corresponding enigma or complexity of referent. This feeling is reinforced when we find the original version of the "pod than there's nothing more alive" a few pages further on in the black notebook, of course dated 8 June 1969:

—This flower dead / tho nothing is more alive to

nod to the

me, integrity, lunaria annua, moon, sign to

the moon is

the moon / favorable to its undertaking, appointed to the moon

(b.n.b., p. 60)

A student of "A"-22 leaps several feet into the air (aer, ayre, etc.), because the second half of this entry connects with "AN ERA / ANY TIME / OF YEAR," composed eight months later, 14 February 1970. Here, then, is a definite indication that the 1970 valentine is linked to the 1975 valentine by an anniversary that also seems to involve the moon.[16] *Annue* was a Latin nod or sign of assent, and "audacibus adnue coeptis" (*Georgics* I.40) meant "be favorable to, smile on our bold undertakings." *Lunaria annua,* translated literally as "nod to the moon, sign to the moon," is Zukofsky's substitution of *annue* (nod) for *annua,* the yearly phenomenon. And so an etymological conceit is produced whereby the moon plant's old magical powers are made to include a benevolent influence over human (whose?) undertakings. *Botrychium lunaria,* the other lunary, belongs to the tribe Alyssinae *(Century),* the Greek root of which means "not madness"; no lunacy whichever moonwort we choose.

Look at, and sound again, the first line of #3 Honesty:

Honesty lunar year annual anew

And reflect that 1969, when Zukofsky made the original entry for *Lunaria annua* on page 60 of the black notebook, was truly a "lunar year": four Apollo missions were flown, and the first moon landing took place 20 July. But phonetically the line is rendering even more. Suddenly, by sleight of eye and ear moving independently over the words, we are hearing an "era," two "an"s, and two "new"s. Put together that aural/visual information and the line is saying:

Honesty lunary era anew all anew

There is honesty's old alias, lunary, preparing the way for *Botrychium*'s horses. The contemporary "lunary era," we might say, was boosted to new heights in the public imagination by the successful undertakings of Apollo. Alternatively, the line is sounding:

Honesty lunary era a new all anew

Both versions leave the lunary era (or lunar year) in first place, but at the same time they seem to bring in more personal considerations. A conviction that moon-related references are also Celia-related grows stronger as we realize what else is in the line. "All" is a favorite of Zukofsky's among words whose brevity belies their importance. Here in the transliterative versions of #3 Honesty's opening line, "all" is making an appearance between a doubling of "anew," which is another target for Zukofskian wordplay. The lunary era, that public but also private phenomenon, could be A NEW ALL, ANEW—or ANEW, ALL ANEW—or, to add another component, A NEW ALL, A NEW / BIRDSONG. However we hear it, there is a potent line-up of Zukofsky's titles, and their potential for multiple entendre creates a semantic maze with surprisingly few blind alleys. There is sense coming out of every combination and an intransigent "*Honesty*" anchoring each permutation—no accident, that.

Whatever sense we choose, there is also an "An"-song in the line, and it is tied up with some kind of lunar blessing ("moon / loon / bless / light," as Zukofsky puts it in that most moonlit of movements, "*A*"-14, pp. 314–15). The "An"-songs of the later "*A*" are being invoked, particularly those of "Initial," which proliferate, tiny but charged with the significance of amplifying "AN ERA" (perhaps of defining an era?):

an omen a good omen

an air not my own
an earth of three trees

with an assemblage of naught

definite as an aching nerve

an affair with the moon

a hectic of an instant

("A"-22, pp. 508–9)

"Initial" was full of sky and sun, but it also included a passage about the moon and moon timing, as the last two of these "An"-songs should remind us. Moon time is important in "Initial"; Zukofsky overlaid America's "affair with the moon" with the whimsy of Laurence Sterne: "—for there is no regular reasoning upon the ebbs and flows of our humours, they may depend upon the same causes, for ought I know, which influence the tides themselves;—'twould oft be no discredit to us, to suppose it was so: I'm sure at least for myself, that in many a case I should be more highly satisfied, to have it said by the world, 'I had an affair with the moon, in which there was neither sin nor shame,' than to have it pass altogether as my own act and deed, wherein there was so much of both."[17]

The old moon (of lovers, of lunacy) was preserved and at the same time the new moon (of space technology, of the rush to plant an American footprint in its dust) was acknowledged. Even before the events of July 1969 changed the moon forever, translunar flights had given us perspectives of both moon and earth as startling as the science that had made them possible. Apparently none of this was at odds with the out-of-time flights that Zukofsky's valentines have a habit of making; the moon passage of "Initial" is worth quoting again, this time in full:

> an affair with the moon
> it looked as if it
> looked up someway above earth
> a hectic of an instant
>
> until computed in the metal—
> tidal waves also timing it
> moon's day and earth's month
> figured closer—blazed sun, white
> under weightless dancing after the
>
> predictable vaguer with time's increase,
> seemed to say: the same
> earth gaze returns to them
> weightless, inkling of outlines, unearthing
> always only their past futures
>
> ("A"-22, pp. 509–10)

The allusion to "A"-18's ethereal "An Unearthing" is significant, especially in view of Sterne's second contribution to Zukofsky's lyric: "—it look'd forwards; but look'd, as if it look'd at something beyond this world."[18] Sterne is talking about the face of a beggar monk. Zukofsky has placed the remark in apposition to the moon and turned it into—a moonrise? moon rising, "looking" quite literally at "something beyond this world" (the sun whose light it reflects), also "unearthing" itself by rising, its face (a full moon) still ruddy in the east, "someway above earth." Sterne again: "The poor Franciscan made no reply: a hectic of a moment pass'd across his cheek, but could not tarry—."[19] And Zukofsky modifies again ("an instant" instead of "a moment") so as to have a seventh "An"-song in "Initial."

Suns also figure prominently in the "An"-songs, from: "An / orange / our / sun / fire / pulp" ("A"-14, p. 314), to the bōwing/bŏwing son of "A"-19, to the "blazed sun, white / under weightless dancing" in "Initial." Now in 1975 comes another valentine, complete with "An"-songs picking up sun and moon, sun *on* the moon: "blazing sunned / moon" has to remind us of *Apollo 12*'s unfortunate camera. But it might also remind us of the Sterne-Zukofsky moonrise, one face reflecting the light of another.

If #3 Honesty's moon is a mirror (and the shine of *Lunaria*'s seed pods suggest that it is), then we should look carefully at "birdsong" in line two. The line has an abundance of Chaucerian overtones reaching back at least as far as 1970, "AN ERA," and "Initial." Both poems have already said plenty about the 1975 valentine, so it is quite possible that the birds which keep flying and singing through "Initial" are also responsible for #3 Honesty's "birdsong." Springing immediately to mind now is the roundel Chaucer's birds sing at the end of their valentine dispute about the proper nature of love and marriage, which begins "Now welcom somer, with thy sonne softe" (see chap. 2). This is birdsong, it concerns the dominion of the sun over the warm season, and it is sung by birds whose speech we and the Dreamer understand.

Zukofsky's use of the Canacee story in 1975 extends these concerns: #1 Starglow set up the motifs of honest mirror and bird-language ring, those magic gifts. In #2 Mountain Laurel, Canacee herself was an under-textual presence along with honesty, a reflection from across the page, and with some birds to "throat" a song whose lyrics we understood more as word music than as coherent syntax; bird words. The material from *The Squire's Tale* which Zukofsky used in part but also moved ahead to #3 Honesty lets us appreciate the full significance of the latter's "birdsong." The relevant lines from Chaucer are as follows (Zukofsky's actual quotation in italics, *80 Fl. Drafts*, p. 5):

> Ther cam *a knight up-on a stede of bras,*
> *And in his hand a brood mirour of glas.*
> Upon his thombe he hadde of gold a ring
> . . .
> *The vertu of the ring,* if ye wol here,
> Is this; that, if hir lust it for to were
> Up-on her thombe, or in her purs it bere,
> Ther is *no foul that fleeth under the hevene*
> *That she* ne *shal wel understonde his stevene,*
> And knowe his mening openly and pleyn,
> *And answere him in his langage ageyn.*
> (*Squire's Tale*, 73–75; 138–44)

Canacee will understand "openly and pleyn"; and the mirror will show the king "openly" who is friend and who is foe, will show his daughter "openly" the worth of any lover. The mirror, reflecting rather than telling, is (Zukofsky) "*honesty* open unvoiced"; but the ring is a gift of comprehension by language (a gift also of fluency in that language), literally the language of the birds, birdsong. It seems that the bird/words of *"A"*-7, "Initial," #2 Mountain Laurel, and #3 Honesty all contribute to Zukofsky's enduring fascination with sounding languages, one over another. Birds of words fly up (to the condition of music), and in their sound (song) is comprehension of their language.

As for #3 Honesty, there is this birdsong and a blazing lunar surface as well as a "Sickle" moon to look favorably upon the annually renewed feast of lovers:

> *Honesty* lunar year annual anew
> birdsong your lifelode blazing sunned
> moon Lionmane Sickle

"Lifelode" is a medievalism (more support for a Chaucerian cast to the "birdsong"); it appears, among other places, in *Piers Plowman* and in Chaucer and it means livelihood, literally "life load" or "life labor." "Birdsong your lifelode" could be an allusion to Zukofskian artistic endeavors, which tended to be long and often arduous affairs. We might notice that "your" also conceals "our." But the original burdensomeness of the word is transformed in two ways; first by modern English, which sees "lode" and thinks of precious metals and magnetic north (those iron horseshoes drawn off by lunary) and then, figuratively, of constancy and other sterling qualities. Second, the word "lifelode" is affected by its surroundings in the poem, and *they* head straight into glorious orbit: "birdsong your lifelode blazing sunned / moon." Making a habitual Zukofskian substitution of "son" for "sun," and noting that Paul was once Celia's "lifelode" in the sense of a full-time occupation and responsibility, we find more evidence of "C + P"'s luminous presence in the valentine dedicated to them. Of course, "your lifelode" can be aimed in any one of three directions, all of them combinations of music and composition.

The ramifications of "lifelode" introduce another concern in #3 Honesty, which explains, at least partially, two more out-of-the-way words in the poem. "Lionmane" is a fanciful allusion to the shape of the (blazing) sun and somehow partner to the also-capitalized "Sickle"; "zeal" in line seven does not really fit with "lofting / hooves" before it or "each lentilled / seedpod" after it. The key to both is the number of words in the poem which begin with the letter "l"; notes for #3 Honesty (*80 Fl.* Drafts, p. 6) list a couple of dozen "l"-words, all from the *Century*. "Lifelode" is one of them (also "lodestar" and "lodestone," which show the direction Zukofsky's mind was taking with "lifelode"); "lens" is another (Latin *lens* is also a lentil; an optical lens is conventionally lentil-shaped); "landscape mirror" is another (sometimes known as "Claude Lorrain glass," a mirror that condenses an image and projects it perspectively onto a canvas). "Light," "lute," "labor," "luminary," "luminous," "loft," "leaven," "look," "luck"—some of these bear on the eventual vocabulary of #3 Honesty. "Lionmane," oddly enough, is not present; but the archaism "lele" (loyal, true) is, and it survives in early versions of line seven right through to the ink draft where a margin note ("leal   zeal?") accompanies its cancellation and the substitution in its place of "zeal." "Z" presumably for a loyal and true Zukofsky, as in true north or "true as truest horse," one of his favorite Shakespearean tags. "Hooves iron zeal," syntactically a difficult phrase, connects #3 Honesty's horses with the magnetic undercurrents of "lifelode." And "zeal"? "For Z is zeal," proclaimed Christopher Smart in *Jubilate Agno* (his "L," no surprise, was: "love, God in every language," alluding to the Hebrew for God, *el*).[20]

So many "l"s in #3 Honesty and now this zealous "z"; do we hear a buzz of Louis Zukofsky's initials in the poem? There are two actual "z"s, in "zeal" and "blazing"; there are another four "z"-sounds produced by the sibilant endings of "strings," "horseshoes," "hooves," "mirrors" (and almost another in the possessive "luck's"). That small catalog by itself outlines the content of #3 Honesty, especially if we hear the Latin *lux* (light) in "luck's."

"Lionmane," the unresolved "l"-word, and "Sickle" are the teasers of the poem. I offer a tentative explanation of "Lionmane," but if I am right the connection is a silent one; the notebooks have no comment and I see no other clues in the poetry. My contention is that "Lionmane" perhaps conceals a transliteration of *leman* or *lemman*, a medieval "l"-word for "dear one," "sweetheart," or "lover" (does the "l"-play in #3 Honesty revolve around Love's initial letter?). But a better phonetic match, and one that returns to the lunisolar drive of the line, is a possible translation of the Anglo-Saxon *lēoman* (luminary, light, gleam); think how many light-related words there were on Zukofsky's "l"-list. And we recall a phrase from *Beowulf*, part of the Hymn of Creation: "sunnan ond mōnan / lēoman tō lēohte" (two lit lions there), which became in *"A"*-23 (p. 556): "sun and moon, / lumine lighted" (see chap. 2). "Lionmane"/*lēoman;* it can only remain conjectural, but the context fits snugly enough. "Lionmane Sickle"—two luminaries lighting Zukofsky's life? But also *Leoman*, lion-man, lion-mane (corolla of light); Zukofsky had a translinguistic affinity for lions, as he explained in the Wallace Stevens address of 1971: "A strange case of this feeling of duration recently happened to me. I was again reading Luis De Leon's book called *The Perfect Wife*, which I read about 1944 not particularly impressed then. He lived about the time of Shakespeare. But now the parallels were uncanny; his first name Luis like my first name; the patrilineal De Leon like my Hebrew surname. I don't feel like a lion, but for some reason in Hebrew the word lion repetitiously precedes the sense of my given name" (*Prepositions,* p. 25).[21]

And "Sickle"? The single reference to it occurs in the draft notes for the poem, in the middle of, if not actually attached to a raft of sun- and moon-related information:

lunisolar
12 or 13 mos.
(13 = embolismic
yr). In every
cycle of 19 yrs
the 3rd, 6th, 8, 11, 14
17, 19 have 13 mos
—the rest 12
  scythe
  sickle
—lunar year
  Hebrew calendar

(80 Fl. Drafts, p. 6)

It looks as if "scythe" (too strong an association with mortality?) was an early synonym here for "Sickle." As for the rest of the note, it seems we may have been too hasty in turning #3 Honesty's "lunar year" into the Latin *Lunaria* and hearing that second transliteration, "lunary era." This is one occasion when Zukofsky's transliteration also contributes face-value sense to what is going on. The calculation of a "lunar year" seems pertinent to whatever numbers are running in #3 Honesty.

Before we examine the "lunisolar" material proper (it is a condensation of a compound entry, *Hebrew year,* in the *Century*), some alphanumerical tumbling is in order. "L," Love's initial and much on Zukofsky's mind as he composes #3 Honesty, is the 12th letter of the alphabet. Adding integers, 12 promptly turns up a 3. What three signifies personally to Zukofsky has been touched on several times; there is indeed a valentine on the subject, from 1951:

TO MY VALENTINES

From one to two
is one step up
and one and two
spell three
and we agree

three is the sum
      a run
of two and one.

(All, p. 140)

"Gaelic *run*, *rune* = *beloved* or *mystery*, Dala meditated"—and the meditation (*Little*, p. 50) uncovers a further dimension of the valentine. Third, then, is an excellent position in *80 Flowers* for a valentine to take up.

Back to the "lunar year," which like a solar (i.e., earth) year has 12 months, though they are shorter because the moon's year has only 354 days (3 + 5 + 4 = 12). A lunisolar calendar, therefore, periodically has thirteen months instead of twelve to make up the difference. A year with thirteen months is an embolismic or leap year, and in every lunar cycle of nineteen years, as Zukofsky noted from the *Century*, the third, sixth, eighth, eleventh, fourteenth, seventeenth, and nineteenth are embolismic. By Jewish reckoning, 17 September 1974 had seen the onset of the sixteenth year of such a cycle, something Zukofsky probably knew or could easily find out; he had, after all, noted the date as the first day of Rosh Hashana as he began "*A*"-23's "living calendar." This particular year was 5735; and February, the month in which Zukofsky composed #3 Honesty, falls within the lunar months Shevet (14 January 1975–12 February 1975) and Adar (13 February–12 March 1975).[22] Rather as February supplies an intercalation of one day every four years to round out the 365¼ days of a solar year, so it is at the end of Adar that the embolismic month Adar II is inserted. Neither 1975 nor 5735 was a leap year; but the whole matter of leap years is still implicit in #3 Honesty's phrase, "lofting / hooves"—and September 1975 marked the start of the next Jewish leap year. At first sight, and with Sir Thomas Browne's help, we discerned horseshoes being drawn off hooves galloping over lunary. However, "lofting" is related to the archaic noun *loft* (sky, air) (Saint Valentine in Chaucer's roundel is "on-lofte," *Parlement*, 683), and it is this sense of *loft* which Zukofsky recorded in his "l"-listing of the word. These "lofting / hooves," then, are leaping sky-high.

"Hooves" contributes to that altitude because as a verb it can mean "to lift, heave"; "lofting / hooves iron zeal" (noun + verb + adjective + noun)—is that more uplift for true grit? A second, obsolete meaning of "hooves" as a verb is "to be fit, meet for"; "lofting / hooves iron zeal"—all this lofting and lifting befits the unswerving Zukofskian labor? ("labor" was another item on the "l"-list).

Regretfully, these other meanings of "hooves" do not make sense outside the line fragment. In context, the word is quickly reappropriated by its horses:

> picklock unshodding horseshoes from lofting
> hooves iron zeal

Listen though, to how the gallop becomes a gentler pace just at the moment it reaches "lofting"; there is a smooth leap over the line break into long vowels, sibilants, and the slide into a terminal liquid. All of which may or may not signify the sweetness of justified zeal (not liking to give up on "hooves," the old verb), but the change of pace provides a sedate enough lead-in to the glassy sheens of the poem's final line and a half:

> each lentilled
> seedpod somehow mirrors luck's horseshoe

On the subject of sheen, we return to "Sickle," that important moon term for which no precise source is apparent. The "lunisolar" note pointed us in the direction of Jewish tradition, and, looking closer at the Jewish significance of sun and moon, we discover that special ceremonies were attached to them as God's luminaries and visible manifestation of his sovereignty. The Blessing of the Sun occurs at the beginning of each twenty-eight-year solar cycle. The Blessing of the Moon, however, takes place each month at the first sighting of the new moon. According to the *Encyclopedia Judaica*, the Jews based their calendar on the lunar year, "since they have a portion in this world and the world to come, like the moon which can be seen both by day and by night. An eclipse of the moon is therefore considered an evil omen for Israel."[23] Conversely, the periodical reappearance of the moon's crescent is hailed with a prayer of thanksgiving, which is the Blessing of the Moon. This seems to link up with #3 Honesty's "Sickle" and the lunary blessing we glimpsed behind the substitution of *annue* for *annua*. The impression is strengthened as the *Judaica* continues: "In the mishnaic period, the proclamation of the new month by the rabbinical court was celebrated with dancing and rejoicing. It is still customary to rise on the tips of the toes in the direction of the moon while reciting three times 'As I dance toward thee, but cannot touch thee, so shall none of my evil-inclined enemies be able to touch me.'"[24] Such unearthliness touches, somehow, other aspects of that longstanding "affair with the moon" which #3 Honesty is intent on exploring; we recall the American moon dancers and their abstract ballet on the lunar surface.

Should the stars be brought in too? The *Century*, unearthing a capitalized *Sickle*, informs us that in the constellation of Leo is a sickle-shaped configuration of stars forming the neck and mane of the lion, the sign of

Leo being ♌, a symbol "showing the lion's mane"—a true "Lionmane Sickle." Zukofsky's self-proclaimed linguistic identification with lions comes to mind (the capitalization of "Lionmane Sickle" almost suggests some kind of nomenclature). Contingencies in the drafts of the poem show how, when, and in what form the elusive pair became part of #3 Honesty. There are four versions of line three, earliest jotting to ink draft:

(1) Lion's mane sickle virtue Sun's
        spangles
(2) alight/ moon Lionmane Sickle lustrous
        waiting
(3) moon
        ~~spangling~~   ~~shining (wound~~
            moon Lion-mane Sickle ~~lustrous~~ waiting
                                        ~~lofted~~
(4)   quiet
        moon Lionmane S̲ickle ~~waiting~~ waiting
                                (*80 Fl.* Drafts, pp. 6–7)

The news that "Lionmane" was originally "Lion's mane" triggers a startling chain of association—why not Lion's *name* (Louis) (De Leon)? like that pressure the horses' *manes* in *"A"*-7 exerts on the eye and ear, which badly want to see and hear *names*. Both of Zukofsky's identifications with animals have manes, but only the lion also has his name. But "Lion's mane" in the draft may also be pointing indirectly at the "angry dew." There is a passage in *Troilus and Cressida* quoted in *Bottom* (p. 399) as follows:

> Sweet, rouse yourself; and the weak wanton Cupid
> Shall from your neck unloose his amorous fold,
> And, like a dew-drop from the lion's mane,
> Be shook to ayrie ayre   *T. & C.*, III. iii. 22[25]

Is it possible that Shakespeare's association of dew, lion's mane, and air was at the back of Zukofsky's composing mind? Dew was once believed ("once believed"—there is #3 Honesty's cue for magic) to originate in the moon. In *A Midsummer Night's Dream*, directly after Bottom, desiring more acquaintance, has spoken to Mustardseed, Titania breaks in:

> Come, wait upon him; lead him to my bower.
> The moon methinks looks with a wat'ry eye;
> And when she weeps, weeps every little flower,

Lamenting some enforced chastity.
Tie up my love's tongue, bring him silently.

(MND III.i.205)

Zukofsky, assisted by Ariel, perceived tears as dew near the close of "A"-22; Shakespeare, here, makes dew into tears. The moon is close at hand either way the analogy goes and so is a silent (or silenced?) lover. Here also is another fairy queen, whose special attribute is moonlight, for *80 Flowers* (Proserpina, thinking about it, is also Luna, goddess of the moon) (and the Faerie Queene herself, Elizabeth, was constantly compared to both sun and moon; she is also alluded to in the *Dream* [II.i.157], where moonbeams quenched the love dart Cupid loosed, thus preserving her chastity). Titania fancies that dewy flowers weep, lamenting enforced chastity; her moonlight is sensuous, perhaps sensual when all is peaceable in the fairy kingdom.

Returning to the drafts of line three, this time to examine "Sickle," we find that the discarded "lustrous" and "shining" and "spangles" and "spangling" confirm our early supposition that the word signifies *moon* rather than *blade*. The sparkle of moonlit hoarfrost in #2 Mountain Laurel is mirror-imaged at the dew-point as spangled moonlight in #3 Honesty. But perhaps there are elements of the sickle blade in the figure too—the nearby "wound" (also crossed out) could have brought us by an alternative route to the "angry dew" with, remember, a face *shining* through the windflower of its tears—wounded?

"Wound" itself is an interesting choice for Zukofsky to have considered. First, it has a connection with Spenser's story of the ring with great healing powers, a story that also supplies mortal wounds for the ring to overcome. Second, it connects directly with *Botrychium lunaria*. The alleged remover of horseshoes was also esteemed for curing wounds. This was one of the virtues of the plant listed by Gerard, and though he was as skeptical as Browne about the horseshoe stories ("in truth they are all but drowsie dreames and illusions"), Gerard did put some stock in the herb's vulnerary properties: "but it is singular for wounds as aforesaid."[26] So if there is a wound in #3 Honesty, the chances are that the means to heal it are also at hand. We may be reminded here of the Epigraph horse's "sorrow of harness" mitigated in the same breath by the means—also familial—to "nay sorrow."

Third (and this is *Century* work), *wound* has a covert connection with *bless,* that sacramental verb with the Anglo-Saxon root meaning literally "to make bloody." There is a more overt link when *bless* means "to hurt, wound," a medievalism that survives in the modern French *blesser.* Once more the intimation of a blessing hovers in #3 Honesty, this time close to the "angry dew" of tears and perhaps an emotional wounding. Is "Sickle" the vestigial member of a bless-wound configuration, retained in the poem because of its ability to point both ways (moon first, then blade), quietly preserving the enigma of that "angry dew"? Bless, *blesser,* blest, blessed. There is a subtext in #3 Honesty and it has an aura of Celia, that "quiet waiting" (but exquisitely musical) presence in Zukofsky's poetry:

> Blest
> Ardent   good,
> Celia,   speak simply, rarely   scarce, seldom—
> Happy,   immeasurable love
>
> >   ("A"-12, p. 127)

Could it be that the "blaze" of #3 Honesty's "blazing sunned / moon" (such radiance) is also a partial echo of the bless figure? In addition, *blaze* is (as the *Century* indicates) a horse word, but "only in the past participle *blazed,*" and this sense (of a white spot on the forehead) derives from a Germanic root *blass* (shining). If we want to bring in the "wound" component again, only consider that blazing (a tree, a trail) customarily involves cutting, marking, slashing.

The lurking question is, do these double figures of hurt and heal have to do with Zukofsky's valentines? The specifics are unguessable, but the paradox itself belongs to countless descriptions of love likened to light and heat that alternately illumines and scorches. Regulating the blaze is the great impossible preoccupation of a lifetime:

> But true love is a durable fire,
>   In the mind ever burning,
> Never sick, never dead, never cold,
>   From itself never turning.

Zukofsky worked this last stanza of "Walsinghame" (a poem he had cited in *A Test of Poetry,* p. 69, as a perfect example of folk art) into "A"-12 (p. 131). "Walsinghame" is ten stanzas' agony of love for this one crowning vindication, and though Zukofsky's personal estimate of love's balance is nobody's business but his own, the bittersweet quality of "A"-11, the first of the "family" movements, shows that the hurt/heal paradox has been present in his art a long time. In "A"-11 there are a surprising number of #3 Honesty's trace elements:

> Take care, song, that what stars' imprint you mirror
> Grazes their tears; draw speech from their nature or
> Love in you—faced to your outer stars—purer
> Gold than tongues make without feeling

> Art new, hurt old: revealing
> The slackened bow as the stinging
> Animal dies, thread gold stringing
> The fingerboard pressed in my honor.
>
> ("A"-11, p. 124)

Song, stars, mirror, grazes, tears; art, hurt, bow, stringed fingerboard. It continues:

> Honor, song, sang the blest is delight knowing
> We overcome ills by love. Hurt, song, nourish
> Eyes, think most of whom you hurt. For the flowing
> River 's poison
>
> ("A"-11, p. 124)

What hurt, hurts, or is hurting who (or what)? The deliberate ambivalence of "A"-11 is a forerunner of #3 Honesty's "angry dew."

What do we have, then, in the fourth poem of *80 Flowers?* A valentine song about the moon, the sun, light, delight, labor, music, tears, time, love, luck (that magic) and lions—all of this under the aegis of honesty, a herb that mirrored to Zukofsky luminous signs of the quality for which it is named. The song's antecedents run a complicated weave from at least 1968, possibly earlier, drawing in and on previous valentines and Valentine's Day literature. At the center of the poem, as at the center of its predecessors in the sequence, is a cluster of private images; what do we know, for all the to-ing and fro-ing between notebooks and texts, about the circumstances of that "angry dew," or the exact source of "Sickle"? We can get close to the intensity of the poet's private emotions, close enough to feel the extraordinary power and grace their expression calls from him, without risking an invasion of that privacy. What we comprehend, what Zukofsky intends that we should comprehend, is "birdsong."

Honesty and honesty; herb and virtue, virtues of the herb. Honesty the virtue has been implicit in many of the things (light, delight, labor, etc.) that honesty the herb brought into the poem. "Virtue," we might remind ourselves, was a term in the first draft of line three: "Lion's mane sickle virtue Sun's / spangles." Sir Thomas Browne and John Gerard both use the word in writing about the properties of moon plants; but Zukofsky's most immediate source is the Chaucer he noted on page 5 of the Drafts, the last of the quotations from *The Squire's Tale* and the one most clearly earmarked for inclusion in #3 Honesty. Canacee is listening to the story of a gentle lady hawk deserted by her false lover; the lady takes his first departure stoically (Zukofsky quotes in part):

> And reson wolde eek that he moste go
> For his honour, as ofte it happeth so,
> *That I made a vertu of necessitee,*
> *And took it wel, sin that it moste be*
>
> *(Squire's Tale, 583–86)*

By "vertu" of the magic ring, Canacee listens to a tale of virtue deceived; honor and honesty are the principles at stake. In Zukofsky's poem we feel strongly that honesty, the shining moon-mirror plant, is a visible metaphor of the virtue. No authority offers explanation of the herb honesty's name; there is, however, Gerard's spare comment: "We call this herbe in English, Penny floure, or Mony-floure, Silver Plate, Pricksong-wort; in Norfolke, Sattin, and white Sattin; and among our women it is called Honestie."[27] This suggests that women recognized a truth-reflecting symbol when they saw it. Gerard is talking about what he lists as Satinflower or Bolbonac (our *Lunaria annua*), as distinct from Moon-wort, the picklock (*Botrychium*), which he describes several entries later. No moons for the honest herb from Gerard, then; but everywhere else in #3 Honesty the moon governs and is the means by which the virtue is seen to be immanent in the herb.

The moon governs #3 Honesty. It is responsible, among other things, for the horses that gallop into the poem and for the music (word music, bird music) that animates it. If these motifs suggest Louis and Paul, then the moon belongs to Celia as she is perceived by Louis. The moon ("Why is it wonderful / That the moon is inevitable?" *"A"*-12, p. 165) is at the heart of #3 Honesty as much as Celia is at the heart of the family triad, explicitly a luminary:

> Tell us about it, my Light,
> Start where you please.
>
> *("A"*-12, p. 261)

> *It is not night when I do see your face.*[28]
>
> *("A"*-13, p. 296)

This is indeed "an affair with the moon"; Zukofsky, like Sterne's Senti-mental Traveller before him, supposed there was no discredit in owning oneself to be governed by lunar influence. Indeed, commonplaces of lunar changeableness have no place in his thinking. Against Juliet's frantic "O, swear not by the moon, the inconstant moon!" (*Rom.* II.ii.109), Zukofsky preserves Romeo's lovely initial image of a "blessed" body plus his own vision of the (moonlit?) "latticed orchards" of *"A"*-7: "*sawhorses sil-ver / all these fruit-tree tops*" (*"A"*-23, p. 563). This is the last Shake-spearean tag in the "living calendar" and therefore in *"A"*-23; it is also the poem's final glimpse of Zukofsky's transformative horses.

The moon in all its phases is in #3 Honesty. Celia in as many guises gets into "A." Knowing something of the larger work's intricate mesh of moon with woman sensitizes us to intimations of the same thing in #3 Honesty, so, when a full moon gleams in the seed pods of *Lunaria annua,* we may recall how one shining face conjures another for Zukofsky (reflection again):

> The full moon rose. Flowed in the water.
>   The harbor
> Had the sea's face: C's face as expected.
>
> ("A"-12, p. 190)

A half-moon for the poem is concealed in the second "lunary," *Botrychium lunaria;* according to Culpeper's *Herbal,* the compound leaves of what he lists as "Moonwort" are: "broad forwards, pointed and round, resembling therein a half moon, from whence it took the name."[29] *Botrychium* lets into the poem Louis's horses (their lucky shoes) and the suggestions of healing after hurt associated with Celia in "A" since its eleventh movement.

Then there is the crescent moon, the "Sickle" that is important to the calculation of lunar time, to Jewish ceremony (more blessings), and to a folk tradition that counts new moons and horseshoes as omens of good luck. Horseshoe luck is contingent upon new-moon luck; an iron crescent looks something like the lunar crescent—and the new moon has been a timeless symbol of good fortune.[30] And for Zukofsky? "We are as you have said / Lucky," he tells Celia in "A"-12 (p. 238). So the new moon is addressed as a sign of hope and renewal amid the strain of bitterness that runs in "A"-21; (a passage that has drawn attention before in connection with an 8 June entry in the black notebook; see n.16, this chapter):

> *The moon washes all the*
> *air:* crescent, dear, come out
> for all of us. Of
> the God in the table:
> that you cannot make it
> eat grass. 'Signed and *dayed.*'
> Dated? No not an erratum—
> a felicity.[31]
>
> ("A"-21, p. 474)

This is part of the Voice Off section in "A"-21 which Zukofsky specifically described as his own chorus in Plautus (see chap. 2, n.27). If this is the case, who but Celia is being identified with the moon's redemptive power? If there are tears and a hinted-at wound in #3 Honesty, who but Celia has the means also to redeem them?

Her initial is a crescent if not a new moon; and crescent shapes have reminded Zukofsky before of the moon and:

Honesty *for* us

grave the
black glyphs
new moon

adz
(sail?)—

("A"-14, p. 358)

There is honesty—probably the plant but also the virtue—close to the moon again, close to the "us," which is in all likelihood Louis and Celia. "This flower dead," Zukofsky wrote in the black notebook (p. 60) 8 June 1969, "tho nothing is more alive to me, integrity, lunaria annua, nod to the moon." The personal mixes with the literary in a note made earlier the same year:

1/16/68—Wyatt letter to his son on his marriage ca. 1536
Honesty . . (your grandfather . . had rather left to me
than all the lands he did leave me) . . as light follow-
eth fire, tho it were kindled for warmth.[32]

(b.n.b., p. 18)

Honesty, integrity (remember the *Century*'s synonyms for *integer*, root of #2 Mountain Laurel's *"entire"*: untouched, unhurt, unchanged, sound, fresh, whole, entire, pure, honest; a veritable checklist of Zukofsky's Celia terms). And now marriage, honesty, fire, light. This piece of Wyatt was incorporated into the second Music section of "A"-23; rubbing shoulders with the courtly Englishman are Rabelais—and Luis de Leon, also condensed to a conglomerate line or two apiece in Zukofsky's supremely economic anthology of sixteenth-century European letters. The gist of it, keeping in mind what Zukofsky chose to record from Wyatt's letters, is reasonably clear:

An art of honor, laud—
"pleasures do" wit's joys accord:
so on hand-vowed integrities, unaltered
syllables, the fended wrist, fires'
light rest.

("A"-23, p. 560)

Rabelais (the first two lines) supplies the honor coordinate; Fra Luis (the third line) supplies integrities (from *The Perfect Wife?*); and Wyatt (end of the third line to the fifth) gives us the "fires' / light" of honesty (information from the "A"-23 Spiral, p. 37). This is another "An"-song, with honor, integrity, and honesty in its first four and a half lines, signaling once again the onset of matters close to Zukofsky's heart.

Considering how often poets pair honor and honesty (check, for example, any Shakespeare concordance), it is a felicity to discover that of course they stem from the same Latin root, *honor* or *honos* (honor, repute). So honesty derives from honor (as Canacee's lady hawk could have told us), and honor is another of Zukofsky's bywords for Celia's graciousness; current since his extended play on the word in "A"-11 and its extension in turn from mother to son and husband. The poet's special feeling for a herb called honesty, an honor-named moon plant is at last clear.

A quick review of all the herb honesty's appearances in "A" confirms that Zukofsky's 1975 valentine has been many years in the making. Mustardseed's *Lunaria annua* occurs in "A"-14 (p. 356), to be followed a little later (p. 358) by the new moon/adz figure (a private Zukofskian glyph for honesty, the virtue?). "A"-15's *"satinflower"* (p. 375) is in some way associated with that movement's exploration of the Job story (a patience we surmised might have to do with the "quiet waiting" of #3 Honesty). Both "A"-14 and "A"-15 were composed in 1964. In "A"-18, written 1964–66, half a page after a recipe for an aphrodisiac containing powdered pear-tree wood (another pear-tree) mixed with "flower of the *moon* plant" (which one?) is the following:

> only in my love's
> room did her plants not burn: in world's
> hangar great room *honesty* a shade gray
> the unminded plant burned with all others where
> white is at least as false as true
> that fittest survives.

("A"-18, p. 399)

Celia and Louis have been watching a televised report of the self-immolation of Roger Allen La Porte.[33] Honesty, Celia's special quality, is being stood against the world's honesty, which is stuck with its ash-gray outer casings. Nothing in the world, Zukofsky seems to be saying, can be black or white (African violet versus satinflower at the end of "A"-15); but Celia, honesty's paradigm, is fire's light (star's glow), the inner surface of *Lunaria*'s seed pod, "thinne and cleere shining, like a shred of white Sattin newly cut from the piece," as Gerard puts it.[34]

For the last time the figure appears in "A," a passage we have already looked at, a moon plant we have already identified as part of a triad:

> *sawhorses silver*
> *all these fruit-tree tops:* consonances
> and dissonances only of degree, never-
> Unfinished hairlike water of notes
> vital free as Itself—impossible's
> sort-of think-cramp work x: moonwort:
> music, thought, drama, story, poem
> parks' sunburst—animals, grace notes—
> z-sited path are but us.
>
> ("A"-23, p. 563)

Moonwort ∷ Celia; her upcoming "L.Z. Masque" of five voices. A "sunburst" near the PZ acrostic, the animals and grace notes (or do these things grace certain notes?) from "A"-11 (written when Paul was seven years old, already a musician), moving to the evergreen arbutus (Paul's 1974 address). So sun/son and moon are there in the close of "A"-23; Paul and Celia. And Louis, who saw horses silver orchards in 1928–30 ("A"-7) and sees them still at it forty-six years later? What better description of his own poetic than the lines just quoted:

> consonances
> and dissonances only of degree, never-
> Unfinished hairlike water of notes
> vital free as Itself—impossible's
> sort-of think-cramp work x:
>
> ("A"-23, p. 563)

This is a matter to return to. Meanwhile, we should observe of the "living calendar" generally that its inwreathed names and what they have to say voice Zukofsky at his heart; the technique also of *80 Flowers*.

5

Sounding and Measuring Time: #4 Liveforever

On Valentine's Day 1975, Zukofsky began composing the fifth poem of *80 Flowers, #4* Liveforever. The pencil draft is squeezed into the last quarter of page 7 of the *80 Flowers* Drafts, along with a sprinkling of margin notes—Chaucer (out of the *Century*), Taylor, Shakespeare, Zukofsky's own references—before the clean draft emerges at the top of the next page, dated 19 February. So there is minimal on-page preparation for what we might expect to be a most important *Flower;* Zukofsky and liveforever go back a long way, and there will be occasion to look in some detail at the plant's appearances in *"A"* since 1928 as they bear on this poem of 1975.

Before examining time past, however, it is as well to look around time present and to ask what prompted Zukofsky to place the liveforever poem where and when he did. Liveforever (four syllables, one of them a phonetic "four") stands in the fourth-numbered position of *80 Flowers*. And given the presumed implications of its name, 14 February is an auspicious starting date. But the poem is not the 1975 valentine, it misses that distinction by one place; and after three poems celebrating wife, mother, and valentines, the fourth is apparently without occasion. However, as the Epigraph lacked a dedication but was clearly addressed to the *80 Flowers* project itself, we could expect that #4 Liveforever has some invisible object, and that its placement just shy of the valentine position and so close to the "family" *Flowers* will entail a similar density of reference. The move from a family three to a Pythagorean four is also a consideration. Four is:

> justice the
> first perfect
> square product
> of equals
> holy holy
> tetraktys root

and source
generate gods
and men

("A"-19, p. 419)

Gods live forever. And men? Four is the "tetraktys root," and the *tetraktys* is (appropriate *apo koinou*): "root / and source" of all generation.[1] The Pythagorean oath, which bound its swearers to secrecy, is solemnized: "By him who handed down to us the tetractys, source and root of everlasting nature."[2] And the Pythagoreans believed, of course, in the transmigration of souls ("eternal flowing creation," as Zukofsky put it in *"A"*-15, p. 368), based on the infinitely generative properties of number.

Putting aside the botanical referents of the third- and fourth-numbered poems of *80 Flowers,* we could weigh "honesty" against "liveforever" and speculate that the latter may be heading away from personal qualities into territory so far hinted at only in the Epigraph, another portentous but opaque poem centered on an equation of thyme/time, in which four signals the approach of a near-invisible liveforever (see chap. 3):

thus fruit pod split four
one-fourth *ripens* unwithering gaping

And yet (catnip and thyme both "stem-square"), the same four seems associated with earthly time. Pythagoras, "in whom green pulse of pod and flame seeded nine spheres of number and tone" (*Bottom,* p. 103), apparently reconciled the paradox; remember "pulses pent," the "pod," and the "fire" of the Epigraph and its curious, submerged connection with "the Nine." We should also keep in mind the continuation of the rosy fire motif in #1 Starglow and its association with thyme/time. Preliminaries under way, we turn to the latest *Flower* itself:

#4   LIVEFOREVER

Wild time *liveforever* horsethyme ice
by shard green red-purple thyrse
shadowed stone or a flurry
troth *orpine* kin *acre* yellow-red
mossy stonecrop love-entangle your kind's
roof houseleek old-man-and-woman who woo
thatch song quicksilver cold would
won't know All *sedum* no

Still thinking about time present and remembering that Louis and Celia planted a thyme bush at Port Jefferson, which has shown up already in *80 Flowers*, we might wonder if they also have a "liveforever" plant and whether some garden event, contemporary or remembered, has prompted a poem about liveforever in mid-February. The answer in each case is a qualified yes. To find out that the Zukofskys may have had such a plant in 1975, we check the First List of 80 Flowers (p. iv), where entry #43, Liveforever, is tagged as *Sedum telephium* (a succulent of the Crassulaceae or orpine family). The identification comes from Taylor, backed by Gray and by the *Century*. There is no mention in the First List or in Zukofsky's scant notes for #4 Liveforever itself of a planting or flowering, but if we go to #68 Telephus Sedum (composed 25 September–2 October 1977), Zukofsky's In Process Notes for the period show that a *Sedum* began flowering in the garden 4 July that year. No doubt the date pleased him, because #68 Telephus Sedum (an Anglicized *Sedum telephium*) was intended to be a continuation of #4 Liveforever, according to a note on the drafts of the 1977 poem (*80 Fl.* Drafts, p. 91). It seems possible that this 1977 plant, under its alias "liveforever," is the immediate referent of the 1975 poem—but it is also conceivable that the entry in the First List was at this early stage of the project simply a plant with which Zukofsky was familiar.

It was something actually *seen,* though not necessarily in his own garden, that provided the poet with a flower for the liveforever plant in the middle of February. A direction in the pencil draft—"See #43   Note 2/19/71"—has us reaching for the *80 Flowers* Notes, having been already to the First List (entry #43) to identify the plant:

2/11/70—circles the rose
2/19/71—an instant's illusion the red blossom
    of the shardy green opens, a tiny rose

(80 Fl. Notes, p. 1)

The 1970 note went into the Epigraph ("time / round rose bud") and probably into #1 Starglow ("a crown transplanted . . . greeting thyme's autumn sprig head"); a sensory perception, transformed. The 1971 note, which is canceled and has a checked "4" beside it (i.e., #4 Liveforever), is the basis of "shard green red-purple" in line two of #4 Liveforever. What Zukofsky saw four years previously on 19 February (finishing date of this poem; a coincidental anniversary?) may or may not have been an out-of-season *Sedum telephium* flower, but it *was* a flash of red in the thick of winter-green foliage sufficiently vivid to make real Isaac D'Israeli's report, quoted two entries earlier on the same page of the Notes, about rose trees budding fire (see chap. 3).

Seen by "frozen Norwegians," roses were fire. Seen by a wintering Zukofsky, the flash of an unseasonable red blossom is a tiny rose. He has realized for himself the illusion of fire and rose, heightened against a background of winter: "ice / by shard green red-purple thyrse." The flower of *Sedum telephium* is carried on a "thyrsiform" stalk (Gray). By the time the illusion of 1971 enters the poem of 1975, it is not overtly a "tiny rose" at all; "shardy green" (1971) is making a contribution to the iciness of the locale rather than just describing the thick, platelike (glass-like? sharded?) leaves of an orpine; and the "red blossom" (1971) has been chromatically refined as "red-purple," which is the color of *Sedum tele-phium*'s flower according to Taylor ("reddish-purple") and Gray ("purple-red to deep roseate").[3]

The elusiveness and illusiveness of the liveforever flower and its appearance in #4 Liveforever (as in the Epigraph) in conjunction with time and thyme, the ordering principles of the sequence, is important:

Wild time *liveforever* horsethyme ice

Horsethyme is familiar to us from the Epigraph, common thyme or the poet's own measure of time—which is a "Wild time" not so much in the vernacular as in the sense an etymological byway affords. Written into the margin of the ink draft of #4 Liveforever is Zukofsky's pointer:

wild (root prob. *will*—as used in
Langland, Chaucer etc = *wish*
desire. L. *volo*.

(*80 Fl.* Drafts, p. 8)

Willed time, wished-for time, wanted time; volition and desire—all of these describe the horse's attempts at "living forever" through his own (good) (persistent) time. His constancy ("As true as truest horse") is a version of endurance different but still attached to the magical-sounding liveforever. "Wild time *liveforever* horsethyme ice" is botanically a list—the cadence falls that way—with plays on time and *thymus* at either end. As the description of a poetic, the line is a conjunction of elements whose exact relation to one another can be guessed at but not ascertained. Juxtaposition is proximity, but it leaves further definition up in the air; the poem itself immediately turns to the red-green particulars of a flower mysteriously observed in winter and then ("shadowed stone") to the sculptural effect of the orpine's basal rosette of leaves under bright light.

Can we find out what liveforever means to Zukofsky and why a couple of light touches resonate so profoundly that the rest of the poem spends its time apparently walking away from the matter, for the most part recounting a catalog of names? Here begins #4 Liveforever's engagement with time past. Even on its first appearance, the plant (flower? not specified) is presented as a measure of perfection. After Zukofsky's exhilaration at hearing an Easter 1928 performance of the *St. Matthew Passion,* the doldrums:

> The next day the reverses
> As if the music were only a taunt:
> As if it had not kept, flower-cell, liveforever,
>   before the eyes, perfecting.
>
> ("A"-1, p. 4)

The association with music is pursued in "A"-2, beginning in a buoyant, vitreous element:

> Till the moon, one afternoon,
> Launches with sea-whorl,
> Opening leaf within leaf floats, green,
> On waves: liveforever.
> Hyaline cushions it, sun,
> In one's own head.
>
> ("A"-2, p. 7)

A vision? Moon reflection fallen on sunlit water that, tremulous, breaks the image into a widening, multifoliate whorl? To get a syntactically clearer idea of what Zukofsky was seeing in 1928, we go to the original version of "A"-2, published 1932 in *Poetry:*

> Till of an afternoon
> Launches the moon upon sea-whorl; green, flowering, open-
>   ing leaf within leaf
> Floats upon wave-edge; liveforever,
>   pearl-clean, giant-size,
> Green leathery leaf within leathery vision—
> Hyaline cushions it, sunned, as of sand-gold—
> (All imagined)[4]

Zukofsky revised "A" 1–6 in 1942 according to Celia's *Bibliography* (p. 49), and the later versions, though more concise and perhaps more poetically effective, are not the original stuff of 1928. The 1942 liveforever is more vision than transformed perception, and the moon/sea/flower connection is markedly more ambiguous. In trying to determine what liveforever meant to Zukofsky by its first appearances in "A," it is a good idea to use both texts.[5]

In both versions, but more particularly in 1942, the eye-catching motif of the passage quoted above is "hyaline." The *OED* cites as a major poetic usage of the noun *hyaline* its meaning as "the smooth sea, the clear sky, or any transparent substance." The dictionary derives this meaning by way of the King James Version of Revelation's *thalassa hyalinē* as: "A sea of glass like unto crystal" (4:6); *hyalinos* means "of glass or crystal," root of the Latin adjective *hyalinus,* from which the English word stems. The point is that, for classicists at least, the sea and crystal were early associated—Milton, for example, practically retranslates the epithet:

> Witness this new-made world, another heav'n
> From heaven gate not far, founded in view
> On the clear hyaline, the glassy sea.[6]

The *OED* quotes this in part. John saw the throne of God (floating?) on a sea of glass (a glassy sea? or sealike glass?) before having a new heaven and a new earth revealed to him. Milton's Paradise apparently floats on the same substance; as does Zukofsky's liveforever. Did he also know that to anatomists hyaline cartilage—glassy, transparent, purest form of all cartilages—is most typical of the fetal skeleton? So that this vision of liveforever/paradise is so new (so revelatory?) that it is still proceeding (with fetal inexorability) toward full birth? It is an intriguing thought, and quite within the bounds of Zukofsky's nose for etymology. His extended use of the hyaline figure (it will return to "A"-2 in a moment) and his apparent consideration of the implications of its usage suggest that he was taking it beyond Pound's more casual application in *Canto* 2, where sea becomes glassy solid:

> Lithe turning of water,
>   sinews of Poseidon,
> Black azure and hyaline,
>   glass wave over Tyro.[7]

Zukofsky was not picking up the motif from Pound; he remarked to Cid Corman in a letter of 15 January 1959 (TxU): "And some day when the historians get their dates straight they'll find out that the draft of XXX Cantos wasn't out yet when I was working on 'A' in 1928—." Earlier in the 1950s he had elaborated the chronology to Lorine Niedecker (undated frag.; TxU):

> Earliest A i.e. 1–4 done by 1928. I had *not* seen any of Cantos at that time, tho the first 16 had been pubd. in expensive folio edtn in Paris in 1925, & 17–27 same way, same place in 1927. It was these copies I saw in 1930 (found in rare book room of N.Y. Pubic [*sic*] Lib. when I [was] interested in E.P.), certainly not before 1929, when I wrote the Criterion essay on E.P. . . . First letter E.P. sent me wuz in Aug 1927 about *The* & no mention of *Cantos* ever for years . . . It was in 1930 that I first became aware of the *early* draft of Cantos in *Lustra* (1917)—the Browningese had kept me away from that part of the book—[8]

"Hyaline," a high-profile word that looks to the casual reader of "A"-2 as if it has undergone a sophisticated philological spin with Zukofsky after an incidental appearance in Pound, is a case in point for the definition of "influence" and its corollary of arbiter-and-followers as expounded by Zukofsky in the same letter to Niedecker: "So that there's no direct influence except wut wuz in air of a time that affects young & elder alike to make the same shapes. But that's what influence is? Yes. And who gets affected first gets patent rights."

Does hyaline persist in the poem of 1975? In a manner of speaking, yes, although in deference to the season (perhaps also to the advance of years) it has been transformed from fluid to solid state, from crystalline sea to icy shard, and from support medium to part of the plant itself. This option is actually present in "A"-2, where the ambiguity of "Hyaline cushions it" leaves room for perceiving support as external (the sea) or internal (mucus). Does Zukofsky now think of hyaline as the mucilagenous tissue ("flower-cell, liveforever") visible when the leaf of a succulent is snapped? Hyaline cushions it internally, botanically—a nice analogy with Zukofsky's own increased botanical knowledge.[9]

Ambiguity has been the essence of liveforever from the start; even in 1928 the flower is not quite of this world, an image engendered between moon, sea, and sun. The vision is splendid: "sun, / In one's own head" ("A"-2, p. 7), or "(All imagined)" as the 1928 version puts it. This sounds rather like the liveforever of 1975 as first glimpsed in the Epigraph, an amaranthine flower, barely visible in the text. Are we getting closer to discovering why the title flower of #4 Liveforever is vestigial in that poem, its presence covered over by a raft of other names?

Back to "A"-2, where Fibonacci relations between botanical sequences (the imbricated spiral of a basal rosette) and musical intervals are being identified. The wording of 1928 differs only minimally from that of 1942 given here:

> As in Johann Sebastian,
> Listen, Kay . . .
> The music is in the flower,
> Leaf around leaf ranged around the center;
> Profuse but clear outer leaf breaking on space.
>
> ("A"-2, p. 7)

Centrifugal is (simultaneously?) centripetal, supportive and supporting:

> There is space to step to the central heart:
> The music is in the flower,
> It is not the sea but hyaline cushions the flower—

Liveforever, everlasting.
The leaves never topple from each other,
Each leaf a buttress flung for the other.

("A"-2, p. 7)

It is as well to realize that this liveforever, vision now being fleshed with some botanical structure, is not the *Sedum telephium* of 1975 but a plant from a related genus, *Sempervivum*—probably *Sempervivum tectorum,* the common houseleek (which also appears, *"roof houseleek,"* in #4 Liveforever). This plant is an uncommonly tenacious succulent; its generic name means "always-living," or (Zukofsky): "Liveforever, everlasting." It can grow in almost any crevice and survive on no food but its own fallen leaves. Houseleek is often planted on roofs in Europe, particularly thatched or tiled roofs, where it builds up great clusters of near-spherical rosettes; *tectorum* means "of the roofs," and the plant traditionally protects the house from lightning.[10] *Sempervivum*'s rosettes look flowerlike, especially when the tip of each imbricated leaf is tinged with red (the actual flowers blossom, like those of *Sedum telephium,* atop a thyrsiform stalk sent out by the rosette). When Zukofsky says "flower" in "A"-2 he means not the inflorescence but the flowerlike basal rosette, which is not flat so much as fat (an orb):

Ankle, like fetlock, at the center leaf—
Looked into the mild orbs of the flower,
Eyes drowned in the mild orbs.

("A"-2, p. 7)

The orb of the moon, disc-shaped but actually spherical, is just such a figure. Zukofsky's 1928 "A"-2 had described the pearliness of the liveforever image ("pearl-clean, giant-size"), which, nacreous on the glass wave, might have looked rather like the gray-green foliage of a *Sempervivum.* Stepping to the heart of this hyaline-supported vision is the poet, also (already) horse. Simpler in 1928, the same lines read:

I have stepped with haired ankle,
As with fetlock, to the center leaf,
I have looked into the mild orbs of the flower,
My eyes have drowned in the mild orbs.

With typically less first-person explanatory linkage, 1942 continues:

Hair falling over ankle, hair falling over forehead,
What is at my lips,
The flower bears rust lightly.

("A"-2, p. 7)

"It is green yet graciously ferruginous," (those red tips) chimes in a line from 1928; and then: "The flower is the steel piston at my chest." Something erotic is going on here, but also rather sacred. From 1942:

No air stirs, but the music steeps in the center—
It is not the sea, but what floats over it.[11]

("A"-2, p. 7)

What floats over it is the (hyaline) liveforever, which inspires an un-sacrilegious poetry in the young Zukofsky walking out on Easter Sunday:

This is my face
This is my form.
Faces and forms, I would write
                    you down
In a style of leaves growing.

("A"-2, p. 8)

Not forgetting that other (wriggling) passion, rosette turned full-blown rose:

A sign behind trees read (blood red as intertwined
        Rose of the Passion)
                        Wrigleys.
Boy and girl with crosses of straw for their nosegays
Impinged upon field as on ocean;
Breath fast as in love's lying close,
Crouched, high—O my God, into the flower!

("A"-2, p. 8)

"Boy and girl" in the flower or in their flower in 1928; in 1975 maybe *old-man-and-woman*—another name for *Sempervivum tectorum*, "A"-2's liveforever.

How about conjecturing now that the "instant's illusion" of a tiny red rose in the "shardy green" of 1971 occurred as Zukofsky caught sight of the red-tipped rosette of a *Sempervivum?* Many species become red-tinged in fall, and some produce entirely red rosettes amid their red-and-green whorls. It would not be the first time the liveforever rosette had led on to rosy vision, after all. When liveforever appears in "A"-7, its identification with the rose is reaffirmed. Before this, only traces of the motif are visible in "A"-5 and "A"-6; however, the original versions of these movements, composed 1930 and first published by Pound in his *Active Anthology* (1933), reveal a higher visibility, especially in "A"-5:

Liveforever! flower in flower heart;
                   Design
And past the leaf's edge
(Not in the central heart)
Two voices:[12]

This was reduced by the 1942 revision to the last three lines, with the substitution of "Our" for "Two" (*"A"*-5, p. 17). Similarly, a second live-forever in *"A"*-5 was cut back to an elliptic reference:

And then, Sleep, yet the face open,
    the Flower, sea of Waves Shut, calm, looking
        Outward
The edges of no one like it looking; everlasting;
Of an afternoon.

                             (*Active Anthology*, p. 126)

And besides it, asleep, the face open,
Edges of no one like it: Everlasting.

                                (*"A"*-5, p. 18)

This cut was to have repercussions in *"A"*-7, where the flower actually starts out as a (kind of) rose. The preliminary signals are metamorphic; first a sawhorse (seen horse?) turning equine:

Speaks: My face at where its forehead might be,
The plank's end 's a forehead, waving a rose—

                                (*"A"*-7, p. 40)

Another remarkable closeness of poet to horse. The rose had been a red lamp before the passionate advance of metamorphosis caught up with it:

Says you! Then I, Singing, It is not the sea
But what floats over: hang from necks or where could
Be necks, blood red, red lamps (Night), Launder me,
Mary! Sea of horses that once were wood,
Green and, and leaf on leaf, and dancing bucks,
Who take liveforever! Taken a pump
And shaped a flower. "Street Closed" on their stomachs.
But the street has moved; at each block a stump
That blossoms red

                                (*"A"*-7, p. 41)

As did the winter plant of 1971, "blossoming"—no less a miracle, no less an illusion. The red and the green, that vision of liveforever's perfect abutments, also incorporates its hyaline support; at the last, foreshadowed by the passage above, *"A"*-7's rose is beatific:

> each face as
> Of a Sea looking Outward (Rose the Glass
> Broken), Each a reflection of the other.
>
> > (*"A"*-7, p. 42)

The transfiguration is all the more enigmatic because the 1930 lines from *"A"*-5 ("the Flower, sea of Waves Shut, calm, looking / Outward," etc.) do not survive to provide the link. As for "Rose the Glass / Broken" (mirror? crystal? or swirl of moon-reflection?), are we being shown a very early prototype of "Initial" 's birds rising up to clear perception by singing broken the window they fly through? A perceptual concern Zukofsky carried over in *80 Flowers* with birdsong, light, mirrors—and (timely) roses.

Zukofsky wrote to Carl Rakosi in 1930 that he was glad the latter had liked "Poem Beginning 'The'" and *"A"* (the seven movements then complete in their original versions): "I like the last [i.e., *"A"*] more," he went on, "—covers more—less the 'sea' and more what 'floats over'" (LZ to CR, 3 December 1930; TxU). *What floats over* might be hyaline, that special state of the sea, but more logically it is the vision of liveforever. One supports the other, and in some lights (as vitreous tissue) they can be seen to be one and the same thing. What matters is the idea of a lucid, lucent poetic ("I would write / you down / In a style of leaves growing") bent on paradise:

> On that morning when everything
> > will be clear,
> Greeting myself, despite glasses,
> The world's earth a rose,
> > rose every particle
> The palm open,
> > earth's lily,
> One will see
> > gravel in gravel
> Stray bits
> > of burnt matches
> Glass,
> > disused rubber,
> Scrape heels of shoes,
> > and not trip,

> Not that one will get, see
> more than particulars.

("A"-6, p. 27)

These lines, virtually unchanged from 1930 to 1942, go part of the way toward clarifying "A"-7's beatific moment. They also show that when Zukofsky thinks about it, even paradise is going to be gritty, the glass (-rose?) broken. The lovely vision of liveforever, his purest apprehension of the paradisal, is cautious with ambiguity and ethereality (is it, finally, flower or reflection?) as if it may not bear out against the grim stack of contemporary particulars which looms in the early movements of "A." Zukofsky had remarked to Niedecker apropos of the differences between the opening of "A" and the *Cantos*: "I start from a sitooation—the performance at Carnegie & lead to a world back—forward. Ez. starts with trans. of Homer in hell—my hell is what's wrong today" (LZ to LN, undated frag.; TxU). The vision of liveforever was heaven, and Zukofsky's constant goal to be thoroughly of his time was going to involve achieving paradise without leaving purgatory ("Not that one will get, see / more than particulars").[13] We know that over forty years or so Zukofsky came to recognize the special case of his family's love as paradise and that the "hidden melody" of "A" recorded stages of this realization ("A"-11, parts of "A"-12, the "An"-songs "A"-14 through "A"-23). So what became of the inspiring liveforever motif, which preceded the family paradise historically but was also its clearest intimation?

In 1942, as we have already seen, particulars of the initial perception were condensed, and the result was a liveforever that lived up to the possibilities of its improbable name to the point where a reader of "A"-2 could be forgiven for assuming that what Zukofsky saw was a *Sempervivum* afloat at the waves' edge. (Does the houseleek float?) The changes in "A"-5 show the poet concentrating on the leaf/music analogy at the expense of the "flower" itself, especially its name. Similarly, in "A"-6 one low-key reference endures unaltered from 1930; the principles of nature-creator and nature-created are juxtaposed, and then:

> He who creates
> Is a mode of these inertial systems—
> The flower—leaf around leaf wrapped
> around the center leaf,
>
> Environs—the sea

("A"-6, p. 23)

Whereas another allusion, more visibly attached to the name of the plant, is deleted altogether from the 1942 text:

His environs? (it's a joke, Ricky,) but in eternity
                he marries the flower,
Or following a real fiction his attitude towards the flower
           exercises influence.
                             (*Active Anthology*, p. 131)

"*A*"-7, where leaf and flower attributes of the motif are brought together in metamorphosis, was not altered in 1942, a circumstance that could be put down to the greater formal exigencies of the movement. "*A*"-7's sonnet stanzas were two years in the making (1928–30), and their carefully worked rhythms would tolerate little substantive change.

The liveforever's next named appearance in "*A*" is one we have already looked at in support of the idea that "living forever" by sounding time (thyme) is a strong theme in *80 Flowers:* "He wants impossible liveforever" ("*A*"-12, p. 237; see chap. 1). That is, the artist, in his time and sounding it (plumbline, voice), is not so much chasing immortality as pursuing a vision of what might be achieved (gritty earthly paradise) if he could only realize his artistic goals. In 1928, the name Zukofsky found for the vision was liveforever, a buoyant, vital, tantalizing image. In 1942, rearranging the early voices of "*A*," he modified the liveforever vision; its role in the scheme of things had obviously changed in the fourteen intervening years. By 1950 the very name is being treated with caution; earlier in "*A*"-12 the component parts had appeared, once in a conceit upon Genesis:

> In Hebrew "In the beginning"
> Means literally *from the head?*
> A source creating
> The heaven and the earth
> And every plant in the field
> Before it was in the earth.
> Sweet shapes from a head
> Whose thought must live forever—
> Be the immortelle—
> Before it is thought
>
>   ("*A*"-12, p. 142)

Immortelle is the name of several kinds of "everlastings," those flowers in which the dry calyx and bracts do not wither, much used in dried-flower arrangements. Among them is the globe-amaranth (*Gomphrena globosa*); a different, amaranthine "mild orb" ("*A*"-2, p. 7) in which to observe creation's ratios? The other "creator," in time, makes his appearance:

So year to year—
Nor do the arts
Ever end.
How can man say
"I am certain"
For certain and uncertain
Do not make certain.
Only forever is previous
And not a horse's forever.
If someone stole off with its body
Be sure that its spirits
Canter forever.
Blacksmith, creator, shapes his shoe
Into substance.

("*A*"-12, pp. 180–81)

Horse time again, cantering (singing), indefinitely projective. The horse-shoe reminds us twenty-five years later of #3 Honesty and the shining pods that are also an immortelle. But certainty for a man (for an artist?) is not part of the figure. We should look again at the "impossible liveforever" line, this time in context:

Making friends from self-probing, quite lonely
Until we know love is loyal to one person,
Happiness is not present at the start
Like a piece of property and is only
Accidentally concerned with the good
Of the artist—failing he must blame himself—
He wants impossible liveforever
While justice is to persons as well as to things.
Nothing is better for being eternal
Or more white than white that dies of a day.
To be is better than not to be. To
Live—

C elia.

    Over coffee.

("*A*"-12, p. 237)

Fortunate in personal happiness (easier syntax than the chopped-about juxtapositions of "*A*" 1–7 but still worth paraphrasing), the artist may still hanker after an earlier vision; he wants (the) impossible liveforever (flower), unwilling or unable to realize that he has artistic as well as personal bliss (one consequent upon the other), if he would only see the equation. (Here is the difference between 1928–30 and 1950–51, with 1942—three years married—a kind of intermediary step, not exactly rewriting the earlier vision but recasting its emphasis.) To continue blind is to chase a chimera; he wants (the) impossible (i.e., to) live forever. Implied solipsis.

There is no flower in the 1950 passage except memory of the early liveforever and the hope it stood for then; an evocation, transformed by time. The very shape of *Sempervivum tectorum* allowed for addition: "Profuse but clear outer leaf breaking on space" (*"A"*-2, p. 7). Or, like the house Zukofsky was talking about in *"A"*-12 just before liveforever cropped up: "It does not leave off making space, / Its building is an agreeable habit" (*"A"*-12, p. 237).

The next liveforever in *"A"* is difficult to sort out without close knowledge of the Hebrew Book of Job, which Zukofsky transliterates all around the suddenly lucid fragment in which the motif occurs. From 1964:

> He neigh ha lie low h'who y'he gall mood
> So roar cruel hire
> Lo to achieve an eye leer rot off
> Mass th'lo low o loam echo
> How deal me many coeval yammer
> Naked on face of white rock—sea.
> *Then* I said: Liveforever my nest
> is arable   hymn
> Shore she   root to water
> Dew anew to branch.

$$(\textit{"A"}\text{-15, p. 359})$$

Using only the King James Version and surmising that the wild noise around and about contributes also to a synopsis of Job, we find (29:18): "Then I said, I shall die in my nest, and I shall multiply my days as the sand." Job, in the time of his prosperity, thought he could never be moved from his place and that his days were without number. Zukofsky's version—"*Then* I said: Liveforever my nest / is arable"—runs the two figures into one; why bring in (barren) sand when "living forever" is a counting of everything nearest and dearest to that nest? Job 29:19 continues: "My root was spread out by the waters, and the dew lay all night upon my branch." What is a nest but the place of nurture? And Job 29:20: "My glory was fresh in me and my bow was renewed in my hand"—the Hebrew, according to a margin reference in the King James Version, allows the alternative translation "new" for "fresh." Zukofsky took "fresh," "new," and "renewed," and combined them under the personally significant "anew."

Job was a man sorely afflicted, recalling the innocent pride of his prosperity—which was that it should go on forever. Now he wants only to die: "I would not live alway" (Job 7:16).[14] Zukofsky, quoting Job, was at sixty a man who had had more than his share of affliction by neglect; who had been at twenty-four confident in his abilities and inspired (fresh glory and a new bow) with a vision of liveforever. Who had been at forty-six aware that "living forever" was a vanity because "justice is to persons as well as to things," and had accordingly perceived that the stuff of live-forever was in all likelihood his emotional prosperity. Is 1964 the darkest-yet hour of the motif? Implying that even the "arable nest," its happiness, is a pride that hindsight will regret? "Where a / nest is tears may flow / no key to the tangle"; *"A"*-22 (p. 518) seems to gloss 1964. We should be wary of identifying Zukofsky wholesale with the Job he is transliterating, but this new appearance of liveforever signals some degree of attachment to the early vision and its subsequent modifications.

However, the thing about liveforever, motif and plant, is its endurance and consequent adaptability. By 1972, Zukofsky had reorganized the name of his early vision to match its changed nature. Near the beginning of "Initial" and with a flourish of Shakespeare (see chap. 2), winter and summer coalesce:

> the chill mists greet woods
> ice, flowers—their soul's return
>
> let me live here ever,
> sweet now, silence foison to
> on top of the weather
> it has said it before

> ("*A*"-22, p. 508)

No longer liveforever but (let me) live (here) ever; an exclamation in the face of another vision, also a request—continuing wonderment and a certain humility. Early in 1971, Zukofsky was going to segue "*A*"-23 into "*A*"-24 with the old phrase "liveforever everlasting," thinking of flowers past and upcoming and of Celia's gift to him of the "L.Z. Masque" (b.n.b., p. 109). A year later the plan was to finish with "and live it over" (see chap. 2), an obvious rhyme on "Initial" 's "live here ever," taken a step further in the direction of one poet's content.

When the motif returns for the last time in "*A*" it is highly noticeable (eight occurrences in 138 lines) and at the same time defused because the recurring word is not "liveforever" but its erstwhile synonym "everlasting." In "A"-23 (pp. 540–43) Zukofsky retells the Gilgamesh epic as part of that movement's pre-3000–2000 B.C. section; the text he reworks is Nancy K. Sandars's prose version, which is based on combined translations out of the Akkadian, Hittite, and Sumerian originals.[15] Zukofsky's exercise here is selective editing rather than transliteration. Of the translations Sandars combines, it is the earliest recension, Sumerian cuneiform, that fixes the date of the epic for Zukofsky; Sandars states (intro., p. 19) that the cycle of poems centered on the exploits of the god-king Gilgamesh of Uruk in Mesopotamia was probably the creation of a proto-literate Sumerian people at the beginning of the third millennium and was only written down centuries later, perhaps as late as 2000 B.C. The world described in *Gilgamesh* is, according to Sandars, discernibly located in the early and middle third millennium.

Gilgamesh is mortal despite his two-thirds divinity, and alternating acceptance and rejection of his lot underlies most of the episodes of the cycle, particularly after the death of his bosom friend, Enkidu (Zukofsky: "One Kid," "A"-23, p. 540). Gilgamesh then searches for everlasting life, going the road the sun takes between its setting and rising, reaching the gem garden of the gods: "hedges / flower carnelian, bud sapphires— quests: / 'Everlasting Garden yet death smell / mine'" ("A"-23, p. 542). He also crosses the waters of death in the company of a ferryman. At each stage of the journey he is warned of the futility of his quest, finally reaching his spiritual father Utnapishtim (Zukofsky: "Everlasting," "A"-23, p. 543), a Noah figure who survived the Sumerian deluge and with his wife was placed by the gods "in the distance, at the mouth of the rivers" (Sandars, p. 110). When Gilgamesh questions Utnapishtim concerning the living and the dead, he is told that mortality is inescapable and irrevocable:

> Eternal's forever,
> everlasting came after, and no
> part-fulness contracts forever.
>
> ("A"-23, p. 543)

That is, only the gods are eternal; they granted one man everlasting life under extraordinary circumstances, and being two-thirds divine will not save Gilgamesh. The echoes this passage sounds on "liveforever" and the message it spells out are important to the continuing history of the motif in "A"; it sounds like an ultimate pronouncement.

Yet the sheer volume of the "everlasting" refrain in "A"-23 makes us wonder if the word is more than a jeer at Gilgamesh's blunt attempts on immortality. In the first instance, "everlasting" comes out of Sandars, who uses the word seven times in her account (it would be interesting to discover the word being translated in each case; this is the sort of thing Zukofsky would be likely to work transliteratively into his editing of Sandars, but the indications are that he did not check the Sumerian).[16] However, Zukofsky's eight "everlasting"s do point in a more optimistic direction than those of their immediate source. Utnapishtim, after relating the story of the Flood, promises Gilgamesh everlasting life if the hero can stay awake seven days and seven nights (he tries and fails). Then the Distant One prepares him for return to Uruk, and to ease the hardship of the journey offers him a magic plant, saying: "Gilgamesh, I shall reveal a secret thing, it is a mystery of the gods that I am telling you. There is a plant that grows under the water, it has a prickle like a thorn, like a rose; it will wound your hands, but if you succeed in taking it, then your hands will hold that which restores his lost youth to a man" (Sandars, p. 113). Not immortality, note, but rejuvenation. The distinction is important.

Gilgamesh dives in the deepest channel of the sea for the roselike plant, gets it, resolves to take it back to Uruk and give it to the old men to eat, saying: "Its name shall be 'The Old Men Are Young Again'; and at last I shall eat it myself and have back all my lost youth" (Sandars, p. 113). But the plant is lost en route for Uruk—The Everlasting had after all said only that Gilgamesh would hold the plant in his hands; no promises about restored youth, no revocation of the lecture. Gilgamesh returns to Uruk empty-handed and in a later part of the cycle dies. Zukofsky, though, terminates the story at Utnapishtim's double-edged gift:

> Take home my gift, my
> secret, the plant you shall
> name, this journey as under
> water, 'Alive-Old-Stay-Young.'
>
> ("A"-23, p. 543)

Notice that Utnapishtim here seems to say that the secret of his own immortality is the magic plant, whereas in Sandars the plant was simply one of the divine mysteries and the gods themselves had conferred his everlasting life. Zukofsky's Utnapishtim is holding out not just rejuvenation but, perhaps, immortality. Subsequent loss and imminent death may still be the implication (Zukofsky is not stopping anyone from reading *Gilgamesh* to its conclusion) but, in terms of immediate surroundings, this "everlasting" is feeding into "A" 22 & 23's conception of paradise garden, a place in which (to wish) to live ever; in which to "praise when 80 / flowers the new lives' descant" ("A"-23, pp. 538–39); in which, importantly, the *old-man-and-woman* will stay vigorous, "at 90 and 81" ("A"-18, p. 391), tending their ongoing projects.

Zukofsky has renewed the liveforever motif on his own terms in retelling *Gilgamesh,* an epic that in other sections not touched on by *"A"*-23 dwells at length on the horrors of the land of the dead and man's helpless destiny. Even given Zukofsky's treatment and truncation of the story (in line presumably with that self-imposed injunction to relate the good things of history—here the brilliance and the beauty of a Sumerian glimpse of paradise), we cannot read "liveforever everlasting" now without experiencing anew the resounding irony of the phrase. Does Utnapishtim's gift hold good? Is knowing how to stay young the only kind of "everlasting life" possible for mortals? Or are we to perceive the gift as already lost? One more time liveforever compounds itself.

1975. Does it please Zukofsky's sense of compression that the essentials of liveforever's history in *"A"* can be packed not just into a small lyric but into one line of it? "Wild time *liveforever* horsethyme ice"; by enclosing liveforever between two thymes, also times (wished for, and actual plod), Zukofsky emblematically presents the enduring dynamics of his poetic. If #4 Liveforever has any dedicatee, it must be that poetic; the title commands it, the first line confirms it, the second line contains a buried rose that is cognate and update of the first of liveforever's transformations. The rest of the poem has other, contemporary business.

There is one last question to be asked before stepping with Zukofsky into time present: Why, after taking so many pains to modify the vision as the poetic developed—even to the point of altering its name—did Zukofsky call the fourth-numbered poem of *80 Flowers* "Liveforever"? To begin with he was not going to; the original title was #4 Everlasting and the opening line was to have begun: "Wild time *everlasting* . . ." (*80 Fl.* Drafts, p. 7)—which would have taken us back through *"A"*-23 to the early, bright vision of *"A"*-2 quite as effectively as the eventual opening, but without perhaps stirring as many memories of the motif.

The change of mind and thus of title came about, I think, for two reasons. First, the qualities and subtleties (and risks) of the poetic are more readily conjured by "liveforever" than by the less evocative (because less presumptuous?) "everlasting." Second, Zukofsky had discovered that the flower of 1928 had truly eluded him in a pragmatic sense; according to the authorities he was consulting in 1975 (Taylor on horticulture, Gray on botany), "liveforever" was not at all the *Sempervivum* he had taken it to be but a *Sedum,* perhaps *telephium.* The old confusion of plants and names and a desire to set the record straight without rewriting *"A"* prompted a poem proliferating with new information; this was #4 Liveforever—and the exercise was duplicated, with variations and extensions, two years later:

#68   TELEPHUS SEDUM

Tell of us sedum comic
course a zone *everlasting* fuses
hue green questions cosmos nods
tell of him sempiternal octobers
seat white-purpling house-roof *hen-'n'-chicks* or
no anthers a kor homer
grass-widow's *goldenmoss* weigh little lovely
rosette-climbing-3's two-lip dropper bred true

It is necessary to distinguish the "flurry" of names in the two poems. We start with the family itself, Crassulaceae (from *crassulus,* "thick," in reference to the fleshy leaves); the family's English name is orpine and it includes the genus *Sedum* (the stonecrops or—confusingly—orpines) and the genus *Sempervivum* (the houseleeks). *Sempervivum tectorum,* the common houseleek, is also popularly called old-man-and-woman or hen-and-chicks; its flower is pinkish red to rose-purple, and the tips of its basal rosette of leaves sometimes turn red in fall. This was probably the plant Zukofsky called "liveforever" in 1928, and it may have been the basis of his 1971 "illusion" of a tiny red rose.

Next come the *Sedums* (from *sedere,* "to sit," because of their easy attachment to walls, rocks, crevices, etc.). They do not have basal rosettes. Zukofsky nods to the genus itself (*"sedum,"* "seat") as well as detailing several species. Two of these stand out in the poems—*telephium* and *acre. Sedum telephium,* the botanical liveforever, is also called livelong, orpine, and garden orpine, and its flowers range from greenish yellow and creamy (Gray) to reddish purple (Taylor) in the variety sometimes distinguished separately as *Sedum purpureum* (see n. 3, this chapter). The epithet "red-purple" in line two of #4 Liveforever most likely refers to this plant; if it does, Zukofsky is layering over his 1971 illusion of the red rose (and its connection with his earlier illusion, the vision of the *Sempervivum* live-forever) with this new, accurate description of the "real" liveforever's inflorescence. The name *telephium* alludes to Telephus, son of Hercules, and the Greek story is wound into #68 Telephus Sedum, which in addition contains a number of Greek transliterations. No botanical authority accounts for the link between Telephus and the plant; Zukofsky appears to use the name for its associations with Apollodorus's version of the tale.[17]

Sedum acre (*acer,* "pungent-tasting") is known as mossy stonecrop, love-entangle, and golden moss. Zukofsky uses these names and elements of two others—wallpepper and peppergrass ("know **All**," "grass-widow's"; my emphasis). The flower is bright yellow: "*orpine* kin *acre* yellow-red."

Sempervivum tectorum, Sedum telephium, and *Sedum acre* are present in both poems in a varied blaze of red, purple, pink, cream, and yellow. The other *Sedums* Zukofsky brings in occur only in the 1977 poem; perhaps a measure of his increasing botanical interest (there are three full pages of notes for #68 Telephus Sedum [*80 Fl.* Drafts, pp. 91–94], in contrast to #4 Liveforever's scanty margin references). There is *Sedum pulchellum* (Gray: "beautiful and little"; Zukofsky: "little lovely"), which is called widow's-cross or flowering moss ("-widow's *goldenmoss*"), a plant the Zukofskys had in their garden, according to the notes for #68 Telephus Sedum. And there is *Sedum ternatum* (Gray: "in threes"; Zukofsky: "rosette-climbing-3's"—a distillation of Gray's "fertile branches arising from the sterile rosettes").

Then come the less visible plants. *Sedum aizoon* is present in "course a zone" (*aizoon* is the Greek name of the houseleek; i.e., a *Sedum* reminiscent of the *Sempervivums*). *Sedum anopetalum* (Gray: "with upturned petals") undergoes a process of filtration through Theophrastus, who uses the epithet *ananthē* (flowerless) to describe a stonecrop, *epipetron* (*Enquiry* VII.vii.4), which the glossary identifies as *Sedum anopetalum.* Zukofsky, his ear simultaneously attuned to Greek and Latin sound, his intellection mixing sound and sense in Greek, Latin, and English, came up with "no anthers." *Anopetalum. Ananthe.* No petals, no anthers, flowerless; a stonecrop indeed. Lastly, there is a possible transliterative reference to *Sedum acre* in "a kor."

Aizoon, descriptive of the houseleek in Taylor, is of course the houseleek itself in Theophrastus (*Enquiry* VII.xv.2). Its nature (*physis*) is always to remain moist (*hygron*) and green; or, Zukofsky: "a zone *everlasting* fuses / hue green." This is liveforever, the houseleek, in Greek dress for a poem incorporating a Greek story, #68 Telephus Sedum.

Kinds and kinship among the orpines are not the easiest of matters to keep track of: "would / won't know All *sedum* no"—with a wry glance perhaps at the "know-all" of 1928 who mixed up his *Sedums* and *Sempervivums.* There is more to #4 Liveforever's time present, however, than the catalog of names, extensive as it is. The first extranominal sign occurs before the names begin; "or a flurry" changes the pace of line three, coming off faster than "shadowed stone," which retains somehow (semantic weight?) a trace of its manuscript articulation as "shade owed stone" (*80 Fl.* Drafts, p. 7). Still looking at a clump of *Sempervivum* which might have inspired line two's vision of a tiny red rose, we see that the rosettes are in one sense static, sculptural. But in another sense the dynamics of their structure (those marvelous spirals) and their very proximity (clustered one upon the other) produce a vivid impression of whorls; they are indeed "a flurry." And perhaps beneath "or a flurry" we can hear—what? Latin? *aura* (air, breeze, breath of heaven), a flurry of paradisal airs? where wild thyme blows? or maybe *ora* (border, brim, margin; especially sea-coast), flurry of liveforever at the waves' edge? or *hora,* hour, flurry of an hour against timeless liveforever? And could that "flurry" conceal a flowery, fleury, flowing antecedent? Zukofsky has left no indication of his source. One thing is certain: the image of "thyrse / shadowed stone" (in which, when we read over the line break, the flowering stalk of our *Sempervivum,* not yet withered completely, casts its shadow across the winter-lit rosette?) is about to be joined by a flurry of *Sedums* that pile up as spectacularly as an old houseleek. A "troth *orpine*" could be either liveforever; *Sempervivum* ("*old-man-and-woman* who woo") or *Sedum telephium* (liveforever, livelong). Close "kin" is *Sedum acre* ("*love-en-tangle*").

The yellow-red color that *Sedum acre* introduces also derives from the word *orpine.* Zukofsky directs us to the *Century* here, interested in *orpine*'s descent from *orpiment* (Latin, *auripigmentum;* gold + pigment), which is arsenic trisulphide. The *Century*'s example of usage is from *The Canon's Yeoman's Tale,* and the alchemical context plugs in another component of #4 Liveforever. Chaucer's hapless apprentice:

> I wol yow telle, as was me taught also,
> The foure spirites and the bodies sevene,
> By ordre, as ofte I herde my lord hem nevene.
> The firste spirit quik-silver called is,
> The second orpiment, the thridde, y-wis,
> Sal armoniak, and the ferthe brimstoon.
> The bodies sevene eek, lo! hem heer anoon:
> Sol gold is, and Luna silver we threpe,
> Mars yren, Mercurie quik-silver we clepe,
> Saturnus leed, and Iupiter is tin,
> And Venus coper, by my fader kin!
>
> (*Canon's Yeoman's Tale,* 819)

From orpine to orpiment to quicksilver; golden *Sedum* to silvery mercury; botany to alchemy. If Mercury is Hermes (enter also Trismegistos?) and Hermes is the Egyptian Thoth, may we not hear the name faintly in "troth"? The *Century* informs us that a thyrse can be a small earthenware vessel and gives as example a passage from a handbook on Persian art: "From their resemblance to pine cones they have been called thyrses, and are supposed to have been used for holding mercury." Pine cones ("*pine* kin"?) because the Dionysian wand was tipped with one; Hermes/Mercury of course carried the caduceus, a different kind of thyrse (the Greek, *thyrsos,* means "stalk, stem") but his quick spirit still manages to find its way into the word.

The "quicksilver cold" of #4 Liveforever takes us back to the icy vision of lines one and two, and with other hints in the poem, plus a guiding line or two from Zukofsky's draft notes, we uncover Hiems's song from the conclusion of *Love's Labour's Lost:*

When icicles hang by the wall

(#4 Liveforever: "ice / by," "w All"):

And Dick the shepherd blows his nail
And Tom bears logs into the hall
    And milk comes frozen home in pail,
When blood is nipp'd and ways be foul,
Then nightly sings the staring owl,
            "Tu-whit, tu-who!"—

(#4 Liveforever: "who woo") (and perhaps "know All"?):

A merry note,
While greasy Joan doth keel the pot.
                                    (*LLL* V.ii.922)

That Zukofsky considers the songs of spring and winter as the high point and resolution of *Love's Labour's Lost* is clear from his condensed synopsis of the play's temper in *Bottom* (p. 282; the ellipses are Zukofsky's): "What is there left to a feast of language seeing the day of wrong thru the little hole of discretion—scraps and alms, basket of words—but to forget what conceit obscured and to see the seasons, Hiems and Ver, as they are: *And cuckoo-buds . . . When icicles hang by the wall:* the Mozartian song of it, generous, gentle, humble to listen to, that merry note makes as if to see into lovers' ears—some forecast of the seasonable in any time of year in the country of Watteau painting and Boucher textile print; more France than its history." ("Any time of year"—spring and winter spread across the calendar again.) Even in fragments, Hiems's song casts a warm glow over Zukofsky's February poem (he once wrote to Pound: "I'd rather be . . . one of Shakes' Songs than any long poem 'built on a plan'").[18] Zukofsky has not finished with the play, though; its last lines, spoken by Armado, also resonate in #4 Liveforever:

The words of Mercury are harsh after the songs of Apollo,
You that way: we this way.
                                    (*LLL* V.ii.940)

Zukofsky: "song quicksilver cold would / won't." Armado means not winter after spring (Ver's song is, after all, the harsher of the two), but plain speech after songs and the play, a descent. Mercury/Hermes/Thoth was the inventor of written characters; before literacy there was orality, song, Apollo's craft, a golden age. (There is a Latin adjective, *aurifluus,* flowing with gold, which might be at the back of "or a flurry," before the quicksilver gets in.) Silver after gold? Age after youth? Words after music? But Zukofsky's intent is words *as* music—"song quicksilver," and age as youth—*"old-man-and-woman* who woo." The beauty of silver is no greater than the beauty of gold, to judge by appearances here and in #3 Honesty ("Lionmane Sickle"). Whoever "would" put one before the other "won't know All," that collection of lyric poems, words as song. Music has reappeared in the liveforever figure and the sounding of time will continue. Mercury, we might also observe, is the god of speech; silver-tongued.

A postscript: the "All" in line eight, capitalized, refers us not only to Zukofsky's short poems but also to other places where he uses the small word weightily: "Happy / spring / to / all" (1968); "one & all" (1971); and the poem for Gerard Malanga: "lovely All composed" (1975) (see chap. 2, n.43). The Malanga poem was in fact composed 24 March, a little over a month after #4 Liveforever, and it would be interesting to be able to follow Zukofsky's thought from one to the other, to find out how the "All" of poetic and photographic composition connected with the "All" of liveforever, wanting it, or ("contént," *"A"*-22, p. 535) having it.

A more accessible sense of #4 Liveforever's "All" is the possible gloss it makes on a well-known line from Shakespeare. Sounding out and slowing down the poem's last two words, we may hear (*"sedum* no") "see—dumb—know," Zukofsky for Prospero's admonition: "No tongue! all eyes! Be silent" (*Tmp.* IV.i.59). Again the vision of a paradise to live in is evoked.

Part Two

Presences: Shakespeare, James, Hardy, Greeks and Romans

6

"The sweet o' the year": Spring 1975 and 1976

Spring 1975, and Shakespeare

80 Flowers' first spring, forecast in the winter poems of family, memory, and evergreen motifs, took its time to actually arrive in the sequence. #5 Lavender Cotton, for Bach's birthday, 21 March, draws on flowers planted by the Zukofskys the previous fall.[1] #6 Spider or Ribbon Plant, written in March but anticipating 11 April, the anniversary of Reb Pinchos's death, describes one of Zukofsky's houseplants and a related lily.[2] Both these poems contain flowers that may have been blossoming February-March (celandine in #5; lily-of-the-valley in #6), but the emphasis is not yet on the advancing season. Nor is it in #7 Sprengeri, a combination of the houseplant *Asparagus sprengeri* and the evergreen or English ivy.[3] However, #8 Pussy Willow is unmistakably a spring poem, as its title announces and its content quickly confirms; the gold of willow catkins flowers just ahead of tender green leaves, which Zukofsky (with assistance from Theophrastus) concentrates on rather than the familiar velvety gray buds. Nonetheless, male and female principles are hard at work in the poem (young female catkins, still at bud stage, are the pussy willows of popular terminology).

There is green and gold springiness; white and gray withiness. *Salix discolor* (the species name means "two-colored"), the pussy willow, derives its generic name from the Latin *salio,* "to leap, spring, bound, jump, leap"; it is a withy willow, and Zukofsky winds in the epithet across a word break: "with thyme."[4] And in time, 1 May 1975 now, we come to #9 Privet and hear spring break out in earnest:

#9 PRIVET

League gust strum ovally folium
looped leaf nodes winter icejewel
platinum stoneseed true ebony berries
gray-jointed persistent thru green hedge
ash-or-olive order white panicles heavy

with daffodil doxy red blood pale
reign paired leaves without tooth
on edge primmed private *privet*[5]

Four lines of wintering privet, one line anticipating its summer blossom, and then a blast of red and yellow Shakespearean song, from *The Winter's Tale* but about the advent of spring. #9 Privet, ninth-numbered *Flower* and tenth poem, seasonally encapsulates and recapitulates all ("the Nine") which have gone before it; symmetrically (3 × 3), it looks back to #3 Honesty (Celia and Paul), then to #6 Spider or Ribbon Plant (Reb Pinchos, literally Zukofsky's "root / and source," *"A"*-19, p. 419). It celebrates now the birthday of William Shakespeare, probably Zukofsky's most important lyric mentor; both ink draft and Spiral copy, as well as the copy written out and shown to Hugh Kenner in Maine that June, state that #9 Privet is "intended W.S. Apr 26/75."

As usual, the poem is a blend of personal and literary referents. Most of the personal associations center on the privet itself; we start in 1973 with what looks like the germ of Zukofsky's winter perception of the plant:

12/18/73 The ice still platinum (-[minus] *like*)
     on the privet and opal on the grass
                              (*"A"* 22 *&* 23 Spiral, p. 154)

This observation, recorded during the Zukofskys' first Port Jefferson winter, did not make its way into *"A"*-23, to judge by its reappearance near the end of the Spiral with other materials that subsequently turned up in *80 Flowers:* "the ice platinum on privet, opal on grass" (*"A"* 22 *&* 23 Spiral, p. 160). The simile-suffix *"-like"* has indeed gone (did that "-[minus]" mean also degrees below [centigrade] freezing point?). By the time it turns up in the *80 Flowers* Notes (p. 4; 17 September 1974), the opalescence has dropped out too and the way is clear to: "winter ice-jewel / platinum stoneseed."

The 1973 privet is the descendant-by-association of a hedge that appears earlier in Zukofsky's poetry, first in 1950:

AIR

How my city has grown!
Privet close at the window,
We have seen
New stone at the old thrown down,

Springs coiled; iron rib, spade
The excavation for the tunnel
Over which
The approaches meet at grade.

For all their metal we are not alone—
Hedge and human
As it were winds met on Sunday
High up and in a street of stone.

This Egypt, a downtown never to go
But, under bridge a river, to harbor
With a thought
Of ashlar to arbor.

My father praying at my mother's grave
Heard his father's song
Love and book
Not their dust where we don't pray.

We are so much alive, child, were
All his city's old graves to go
Out of sight, its harbor
Would still carry his old air.

(*All,* pp. 139–40)

Sun, air song; a son's song about his father's air, #6 Spider or Ribbon
Plant had picked up the patriarchal singing in its allusion to the Song of
Songs: "*familial-lily* not fathers' song -of-the-valley," a line that rises in
part from the verse: "I am the rose of Sharon, and the lily of the valleys,"
Song. of Sol. 2:1. The privet that seems to stand, "Hedge and human,"
with "Love and book," is party to the old song's flow "to harbor / With a
thought / Of ashlar to arbor." The poem was written 24 December 1950,
eight months after Reb Pinchos's death.[6] In 1957, again in winter but this
time with more of an eye to the physical appearance of the hedge,
Zukofsky composed the following, which became the third poem of
Barely and Widely (1958):[7]

The green leaf that will outlast the winter
        because sheltered in the open:
the wall, transverse, and diagonal ribs
        of the privet that pocket air
            around the air inside them

> and cover but with walls of wind:
> it happens wind colors like glass shelter,
>   as the light's aire from a vault
>   which has a knob of sun.
>
> (*All,* p. 169)

Or, 1973–75: "looped leaf nodes . . . gray-jointed persistent thru green hedge" (but see 1957's privet *literally* pocketing that air, the line getting further and further from its left margin). Sun, wind, air (and perhaps "light's aire"—a wind song) come in from the earlier poem. The composition date of "The green leaf" is 1 January 1957; the Zukofskys were still living at 30 Willow Street, as they had been since 1946, and, if this residence is to be identified with the brownstone in *Little,* then we are looking again at the privet as recalled by Zukofsky writing in 1969: "Verchadet and Little worked in the garden on the upper level of their city back yard. Dala wrote in the shadow of the privet, his eggshell (he called it) protected, under his Borsalino, from neuralgia the sun's direct rays always caused at a small table on the uneven pavement of the damp terrace below. She clipped a blossoming spray of the privet hanging over the neighbor's wire fence, but kept it arching for shade and for them" (*Little,* p. 143).

Summer and winter, privet was a familiar sight to Zukofsky. The opening line of #9 Privet indicates that the plant at Port Jefferson was identified as *Ligustrum ovalifolium,* California privet, which as its name suggests has ovally shaped leaves. They are borne opposite (i.e., in pairs) and have unserrated margins: "paired leaves without tooth." Privet belongs to the natural order Oleaceae ("ash-or-olive order"), which therefore "orders" the heavy white panicles of strongly scented flowers in June-July. These are succeeded by clusters of fruit, "black, lustrous, ovoid . . . 6–8 mm long" (Gray). Zukofsky seems to draw an interline parallel between the rolled-up "icejewel / platinum" leaves and the actual fruits of the privet, described in line three as "platinum stoneseed true ebony berries." The *Century* refers us to the Hebrew *hobnīn* (ebony), "so called in allusion to its hardness, from *eben,* a stone." Buried in the word *ebony* is a Hebrew stone; berried in true ebony black is the privet's stoneseed. Somewhere there is a stirring of privet and stone against the song of Hebrew fathers. Hearing also "League gust strum" (Zukofsky is at pains to enunciate separately the "-gue gu" and "-st st," English sense taking precedence over Latin undertext), we might discern another wind song—through privet leaves? or (winter) branches?—over a great distance.

The *Century* has another contribution to make; not only is "folium" a Latin leaf, it is a leaf-shaped geometric oval: "a loop being part of a curve

terminated at both ends by the same node." In the dictionary's illustration
of the Folium of Descartes, Zukofsky saw an analogy of his perception of
the rolled-up privet icejewels; 1957 poem and 1973 observation come
together as botany ("ovally folium / looped leaf nodes") once more aligns
itself with configurations of number (an "ovally folium"):

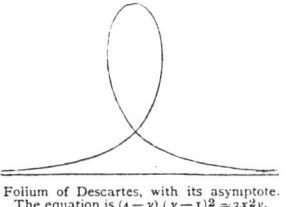

Folium of Descartes, with its asymptote.
The equation is $(4-y)(y-1)^2 = 3x^2y$.

Enter Shakespeare. The time of year is as important to Zukofsky's
choice of the song as it is in the play itself; we have seen with what care he
brings winter (icejeweled leaves and berries, sound of wind through them),
and the promise of spring and summer (ordering of the white panicles, the
same wind through summer leaves) into the first half of #9 Privet. Now,
from a play set in winter, he takes Autolycus's anticipation of spring
delights:

When daffodils begin to peer,
   With heigh! the doxy over the dale,
Why, then comes in the sweet o' the year;
   For the red blood reigns in the winter's pale.

The white sheet bleaching on the hedge,
   With heigh! the sweet birds, O, how they sing!
Doth set my pugging tooth on edge;
   For a quart of ale is a dish for a king.

The lark, that tirra-lyra chants,
   With heigh! with heigh! the thrush and the jay,
Are summer songs for me and my aunts,
   While we lie tumbling in the hay.

(*WT* IV.iii.1)

Like Zukofsky, Autolycus looks as far ahead as summer. His second verse,
its white on a green hedge, was probably what prompted Zukofsky to link
the two songs, so that again poetry is glossing botany: "paired leaves
without tooth / on edge." But it is the first verse, its glamorous yellow and
red, that gets most play in #9 Privet.

Autolycus is #9 Privet's answer to Hiems, each of them representing a
season's robustness. Zukofsky rewrites icicles hanging by the wall in his

vision of the winter privet, then swaps the winter fire for Autolycus's red and yellow spring. Both blazes are vital, convivial: " 'For the red blood reigns in the winter's pale. / . . . let's be red with mirth' "; *Bottom* (p. 340) makes a connection between two scenes of *The Winter's Tale* which picks up the ambiguity of the earlier line. Autolycus is welcoming the rise of red blood after months of less strenuous activity (denoted by winter's "pale" blood) or relative confinement (within winter's "pale"; i.e., enclosure, domain). At the same time he seems to say that red blood reigns *even* in the winter's pale—a construction that accords with the spirit of the *Tale*, and with Hiems's song. Zukofsky wants both nuances and gets them: "with daffodil doxy red blood pale." Line six condenses daffodils, girl, and inspiring blood; it is also perfectly descriptive of a narcissus flower, either the common daffodil (in which the trumpet can be a rich yellow-red orange) or the poet's narcissus with its orange-red corona and creamy petals. There are six words to line six; lilies typically have six petals, a point Zukofsky has already made (by the same means) in #6 Spider or Ribbon Plant:

familial-lily not fathers' song   -of-the-valley
so shone argued *narcissus king's rose*

At issue here is a textual crux in the Song of Songs centered on the verse mentioned earlier: "I am the rose of Sharon, and the lily of the valleys." Aramaic recensions render the flower of the first half of this as *narqīs* (narcissus), and commentators point out that the rose had not been introduced to Palestine at the time of the Song's composition (the flower in question is generally taken to be some kind of crocus). However, at least two famous twelfth-century Hebrew scholars, Joseph Kimḥi and Abraham ibn Ezra, supported Greek renderings of the Hebrew as *kalykōsis,* rosebud, or *rhodon,* rose. This, together with *šārôn* (plain), evolved into the traditional "rose of Sharon"; thus the narcissus was argued to be Solomon's (*"king's"*) rose—and *80 Flowers* gains another ambivalent rose.[8] A similar ambiguity surrounds the translation of *šôšannāh* as "lily of the valleys." Certainly the plant is a lily (as is, *"familial,"* the narcissus), and translators agree on the epithet "of the valleys," but scholarship points to a lotus. *Šôšannāh* ("so shone argued") is supposed to be related to the numeral *šēš* (six) in connection with the number of its petals.

Returning to #9 Privet and its narcissus; is Zukofsky making a roundabout comparison, via his own choice of texts, with the songs of his father? We have heard that voice's association with sun, wind, stone, and privet; and we have heard wind in the privet itself ("League gust strum"). Now we must hear it in Shakespeare's daffodils. Perdita:

O Proserpina,
For the flowers now, that frighted thou let'st fall
From Dis's waggon! daffodils,
That come before the swallow dares, and
Take the winds of March with beauty.

(WT IV.iv.116)

This is a more evocative picture than Wordsworth's, and one that times precisely the appearance of the daffodils. #6 Spider or Ribbon Plant was a March poem with a textual heart of narcissus; #9 Privet is a May poem intended for April, with a spread of motifs running from winter ice through narcissus gold to heavily scented summer privet blossom.

There is another Shakespeare-cum-philological component in the poem: "primmed private *privet*," its excellently repeating conclusion. Prim or prim-print is an old name for privet (*Century;* also Taylor), and privet hedges traditionally (primly?) surrounded gardens, making them private. Etymologically, no link is proposed between *privet* and *private,* and there does not seem to be a connection between *prim* (adjective) and *privet.* But all three flow into one another (prim private privet), and the illustration Zukofsky takes from *Twelfth Night,* that of Malvolio saying, in Olivia's garden, "Let me enjoy my private" (*TN* III.iv.99), reinforces the conviction—especially when we know that, as a verb, *prim* means "to deck with great nicety; form or dispose with affected preciseness; prink; make prim" *(Century);* thinking of those cross-gartered yellow stockings.

Prim privets enclose (even their winter leaves pocket air), they make private; we are reminded of the summer garden in *Little,* where privet shaded Dala at his writing. Then there is Zukofsky saying to Corman in a letter of 6 October 1958 (TxU): "I am orderly—primly orderly of habits—"; and Verchadet/Celia clipping a spray of blossoming privet hanging over the neighbor's fence but making sure the hedge is kept arching for shade (protection for the "eggshell"), and for the family. A private privet, apart from whatever public. The ninth-numbered *Flower* looks back at the third, the private valentine for Celia and Paul, as well as the sixth, a quiet celebration of Reb Pinchos's singing. It also initiates the poems about spring 1975, and its clear Shakespearean song announces a presence in the *Flowers* which will remain constant throughout the growing season of that year and which never really leaves the sequence thereafter.

In Shakespeare we have an excellent example of Zukofsky's assimilation habits. The Shakespeare in *80 Flowers* is not quotation so much as appropriation—*stealing Mozart,* as Zukofsky would want to say again with Stravinsky (*Prepositions,* p. 31); or, to Corman, wondering where he had cribbed a phrase in *Bottom:* "I'm inclined to forget these things, like

Shixes himself, when the theft has become part of me" (LZ to CC, 16 June 1960; TxU). Zukofsky emerged from the thirteen-year odyssey of *Bottom* with knowledge not only of Shakespeare's poetry but also of his sources (actual and probable) and with a list of things the Bard might have enjoyed reading, or thieving, post-1616 (Spinoza, Bach, Wittgenstein, and so on). This is the idea of contingency again, of one thinker reading another and finding chronology no barrier to conversation. To draw in all of Zukofsky's works, as *80 Flowers* proposed to do, meant comprehending Shakespeare as Shakespeare persisted in Zukofsky's vocabulary; and quoting Shakespeare was an almost undifferentiated step away from quoting his own work. As mentioned in chapter 1, Shakespeare references occur in the *80 Flowers* Drafts rather than the Notes; they are a permanent resource, drawn on as fit application occurs to Zukofsky during the assemblage of each *Flower.* References to his own poetry and prose are the only other literary source materials treated in this way.

A single word out of his own or Shakespeare's work could be sufficient recall of its precise literary (and personal) context. Shakespeare, we recall, was the merest subtextual note in the trebled hearts, sinews, and wind of the Epigraph; he was a light touch in #1 Starglow ("Midsummer's thorns and a lantern," as *"A"*-12 might put it, p. 226); he was considered but then discarded from the list of "l"-words for #3 Honesty. We first heard Shakespearean song distinctly in #4 Liveforever, a poem "about" Zukofsky's own poetic. But #9 Privet is the true debut of Shakespeare in the book, and he appears in a context thoroughly assimilated to the circumstances in hand: the song from *The Winter's Tale* speaks to Zukofsky's perceptions of the privet hedge; the occasion of the song (located between winter and spring, celebrating the vitality of both) appealed to his sense of *80 Flowers'* time-ordered advance. The song's content allowed him a reflection on the yellows and reds of #1 Starglow's sun-fire and #4 Liveforever's orpines (also the implied warmth of Hiems's song). The same yellow and red allowed reflection of the possible affinities of Zukofsky's song (its antecedents) with the singing of his father, perhaps fathers, as conjectured by the narcissus of #6 Spider or Ribbon Plant. The private nature of these associations was reaffirmed by another piece of Shakespeare (Malvolio), dovetailed with the privet motif. Finally, the whole poem, Zukofsky and Shakespeare inextricable, is one's gift to the other, 26 April 1975, the occasion of Shakespeare's 411th birthday. Time-specific, as we have come to expect of *80 Flowers.*

Shakespeare's voice in the poems of spring, summer, and fall 1975, and in the *Flowers* beyond, is sometimes obvious and more often not. Guided mostly by Zukofsky's cues in the Drafts, I have found Shakespearean material in fifty-one of the eighty-one poems, but not all of this material surfaces in the text.⁹ Sometimes it will underlie a poem (as in the Epigraph); on at least two occasions it slips away from the finished product entirely (#3 Honesty, #43 Lilies). Often Zukofsky does not cue a reference and its presence must be inferred from a reader's own knowledge of Shakespeare (fernseed in #7 Sprengeri, for example; though the *Century*'s example of usage here would have sounded an alert). Then again, but for a hint from Zukofsky, many of the one-word references would go ·unnoticed ("private" in #9 Privet). Thus there are poems where the Shakespeare component is simple to distinguish (e.g., #9 Privet), others in which it is a convoluted presence, and still others in which it is a mere nod. Examples of the Shakespearean nod occur in #12 Cinquefoil and #22 Bayberry; convolution and its implications will enliven a detailed discussion of #10 Charlock Per Winkle. But first we should think more specifically about how Zukofsky chooses his Shakespeare and what governs his choices; the best way to do this is to stay with the post–#9 Privet poems in which Shakespeare is simple to distinguish.

To date, following the rationale has been relatively easy: trebleness for the Epigraph, lanthorn for #1 Starglow, winter's song for #4 Liveforever, fernseed for an asparagus fern in #7 Sprengeri, and the daffodil song for spring's arrival. The poems after this in which Shakespearean material is present continue to put it to obvious use; #11 Heart's Ease utilizes the song "Heart's ease, Heart's ease!" from *Romeo and Juliet* and brings in love-in-idleness, the magic flower of *A Midsummer Night's Dream*. #13 Venus's Looking-Glass, which includes other members of the Campanulaceae or bell-flower family, uses both *Cymbeline*'s "azur'd harebell" and, less visibly, the ending of *Venus and Adonis*, where the goddess flies away (into the blue). #14 Spearmint, taking advantage of the title flower's connection with other members of the Labiatae, introduces Perdita's "Hot lavender, mints, savory, marjoram," together with a couple of less conspicuous mint references. #17 Cockle lends itself to quotations concerning cockleshell boats (*Pericles*), cockled snails (*Love's Labour's Lost*), and the cockle plant itself (*Love's Labour's Lost* again).

The connection in #18 Petunia is not as simple, though the Shakespeare is loud and clear; the poem begins: "What's in a name." In this case the naming has little to do with Juliet's rose (though here is another equivocal rose in the source material for *80 Flowers*) and much to do with a confusion between arrowhead and arrowroot, both linked to the title flower, petunia, by virtue of their indigenous American habit. In addition, arrowhead roots were native potatoes, and petunia belongs to the Solanaceae, the potato or nightshade family. The same combination of loud Shakespeare and quiet connection occurs in #19 Wild Geranium, which begins: "Not a friend hated time / must friend or end," a curious amalgam of speeches from Much Ado about Nothing and Troilus and Cressida which plays on the thyme/time motif of the sequence; pennyroyal and ground ivy, both mints, appear alongside the wild geranium, and thyme/time comes in again at the close with a reference to Cymbeline's "Fear no more the heat o' the sun."

The other Shakespeare poems of 1975 offer varying degrees of difficulty. Who, for example, would detect a Shakespearean undertone in the opening lines of #12 Cinquefoil:

> Potent tiller reck to copper
> silveryyellow sulphur notched hearts rose

The connection is "sulphur," and Zukofsky arrived at it via the Century's quote from Coriolanus in which sulphur is used in the sense of being the substance of lightning (fire and brimstone from the heavens). Volumnia:

> To tear with thunder the wide cheeks o'th' air
> And yet to charge thy sulphur with a bolt
> That should but rive an oak.
>
> (Cor. V.iii.149)

Within #12 Cinquefoil we can make out a possible association of this sulphur with the (Theophrastian) summer rainstorm that ends the poem: "minting white-thyme assures bees roses / summersun honeyyield together rained upon."[10] The Century provides the link between "copper" in line one and "sulphur" in line two by pointing out an etymological fancy that late Sanskrit çulvāri derives from çulva (copper), plus the suffix -ari (hostile); that is, "hostile to copper." Despite this, the two substances are often found in compounds.

Why did Zukofsky look up sulphur in the first place? His reasons are respectably, connectedly, botanical: "silveryyellow" in line two accurately describes Potentilla argentea, silvery cinquefoil (Gray). And "silveryyellow sulphur," besides providing a visual impression of sulphur itself, also refers to Potentilla sulphurea, which is included in Gray's description of Potentilla recta, shrubby cinquefoil: "Potent tiller reck to copper / silveryyellow sulphur notched hearts rose" (the cinquefoils are rosaceous; their petals are notched at the outer edge and therefore heart-shaped; sulphur is of course a "wreck" to copper).[11] Even a nod to Shakespeare involves the usual complex grounding.

#22 Bayberry's Shakespearean nods are much easier to comprehend. First, line seven: "standstill plummet unprotected laurel crown" ("And deeper than did ever plummet sound / I'll drown my book . . . There stand / For you are spell-stopp'd," Tmp. V.i.56, 60). The Prospero of "A"-22 reemerges to sound old themes, not the least of them a bay (bottoming a bay?) from the poem in *Anew* called *"che di lor suona su nella tua vita"* (*All*, p. 85). The plummet, preceded by a standstill, also anticipates the birds in line seven of #22 Bayberry which might hang and swoop over any bay. A second snippet of Shakespeare occurs in line eight as Zukofsky winds in Henry Compton (1632–1713), English bishop and patron of botany, for whom *Comptonia peregrina*, the sweet-fern, is named: "sand-iced willows *compt* gibbous moons" (the sweet-fern is related to bayberry; both belong to the Myricaceae or wax myrtle family). What is most interesting here, though, is the nature of the citations made in the Drafts concerning the Shakespearean *"compt"*—a list of line references (no actual quotation) which gives us occasion to think that even Zukofsky sometimes consulted a concordance. The list looks like this:

	Mac I. vi. 26
	Oth V. ii. 272
compt W.S.	AW V iii 57
	Tim II. i. 35

(80 Fl. Drafts, p. 28)

(The *Century*, possible source of such a list—but would it be so extensive?—offers no Shakespeare for *compt*.) If we take the order of these as *All's Well That Ends Well*, *Timon of Athens*, *Macbeth*, and then *Othello*, we have the order of the plays as they occur in the Globe edition and its descendants—which is also the order of Bartlett's *Concordance* (1896), the standard reference before Spevack's computerized work (1968–70).[12] We can ascertain that Zukofsky was using Bartlett (or something similar) rather than Spevack by noticing that the latter omits the *Timon* reference.

We cannot expect to follow into every reach of Zukofsky's intimacy with Shakespeare's words, but it is fascinating work to take on one of the poems with clear Shakespearean elements threaded through a text that appears to swallow them up. #10 Charlock Per Winkle is the ultimate Shakespearean convolution among the poems of 1975:

#10   CHARLOCK PER WINKLE

A skein bottoms them together
brassy core crux fiery yellow
fourpetal fivepetal salver blue solitary
winkle springgreen wellwintered leaves bright
trails creep white thyme times
fieldmustard with myrtle dogbane minor
quillet praises lacquer truemustard ox-beef
weeps *uncrossed charlock bluer winkle*

After the clarion of Autolycus this is more subtle, but it is not difficult to make out Bottom and his conversation with the fairies, in particular with Mustardseed. The Shakespeare link starts with Mustardseed once Zukofsky has decided to compose a poem about myrtle (an entry in the First List, p. iv) and field-mustard, a weedy flower identified in Port Jefferson, 29 April 1975 (First List, p. viii). The original title of #10 was "Field Mustard & Myrtle," which became "Charlock Per Winkle" after Zukofsky discovered that periwinkle, the "myrtle" he had in mind, was named *vinca-pervinca* by Pliny; the *Century* notes that it was "a peculiarly formed name, apparently from *vinca*, a twist, + *per*, through, + *vinca*, a twist." Common periwinkle, today known as *Vinca minor*, spreads by creeping stems; twist through twist. Zukofsky took charlock, another common name for the field-mustard, *Brassica kaber*, and twisted it through (*per*) his periwinkle, formerly called *perwinkle* (*Century*), to come up with an inwound title, which the first line immediately begins explaining: "A skein bottoms them together."

Shakespeare is prefigured here already in the verb *bottom*, "To wind round something, as in making a ball of thread" (*Century*; and gives a Shakespearean example of usage, *TGV* III.ii.51). The *OED* is even closer to Zukofsky's mark: "To wind (as a skein)," and a *skein* in the same dictionary consists of eighty (80!) turns of thread upon a wheel fifty-four inches in circumference. *Bottom*, the noun, can be "a clue or nucleus on which to wind thread; the thread so wound," and the *Century* goes on to quote Grumio mock-seriously imploring Petruchio: "beat me to death with a bottom of brown thread" (*Shr.* IV.iii.137). From all of this it is apparent that Shakespeare had his reasons for naming the weaver Bottom. Apart from being an occupational epithet (Quince, Flute, Snout, Starveling, and Snug are too), Bottom is the name of the character who skeins together fairies and mortals, fairies and fairies; is even (as chief mouth of the rude mechanicals' play, equally at home lecturing Peter Quince or his noble audience) the skeiner of mortals and mortals. Moreover, as another kind of *bottom* he is fundamental to all parts of the *Dream;* he makes the joke himself in deciding to call his adventure: " 'Bottom's Dream,' because it hath no bottom" (*MND* IV.i.220). In yet another sense his bottoming together of the play's elements reflects a strength latent in his name; *bottom*, noun, can be "Power of endurance; stamina, native strength: as, a horse of good bottom" (*Century*). One step away from Pyramus, "As true as truest horse that yet would never tire" (*MND* III.i.98). (Are we to hear an echo of this in line seven's "truemustard," fragmentary conversation of Bottom and Mustardseed?) Bottom's skeining will not break; Zukofsky could hardly have settled on a better connective for charlock and periwinkle.

For the moment, Bottom's presence sketched in, the poem moves away from Shakespeare to concentrate on the promised inwreathing: "brassy core crux fiery yellow" contains an almost perfect phonetic cognate of *brassica* and Cruciferae, or perhaps Crucifer. *Brassica kaber* (the generic name means "cabbage," the species name is of Persian origin; Gray) is a bright yellow-flowered member of the Cruciferae or mustards; "fourpetal fivepetal salver blue solitary / winkle" leads from that brassy yellow cross-flower ("fourpetal") borne in clusters, to the blue periwinkle, "salver-shaped, solitary" (Taylor), which is five-petaled, with "springgreen well-wintered leaves bright / trails creep." Glossy leaves, evergreen; flowers appearing early in spring. These last few lines describe "fieldmustard with myrtle dogbane minor" (common periwinkle belongs to the Apocynaceae or dogbanes); but something else—another creeper—has entered the picture, wound about with periwinkle and adding twists of its own:

> winkle springgreen wellwintered leaves bright
> trails creep white thyme times
> fieldmustard with myrtle dogbane minor
> quillet praises lacquer truemustard ox-beef

How does the thyme get in, "timing" the other two flowers? (shades of the Epigraph, and #4 Liveforever). Charlock and periwinkle might literally grow together, flower together; one is a weed, the other a successful garden escape. But thyme, particularly white thyme, is a cultivated plant though of wild origin (remember Theophrastus's summer-flowering white thyme in #12 Cinquefoil). Here is John Gerard again, in time and on thyme: "Of which kinde I found another sort, with floures as white as snow, and have planted it in my garden, where it becommeth an herbe of great beauty. This wilde Time that bringeth forth white floures differeth not from the other, but onely in the colour of the floures, whence it may be called *Serpillum vulgare flore albo*: White floured Wilde Time."[13] *Serpillum*, an old generic name that survives in the species-descriptive of *Thymus serpyllum*, mother-of-thyme or creeping thyme, furthers the winding (snakelike?) and twisting motifs in Zukofsky's poem.

Gerard is also present in "quillet praises lacquer," bottomed with his near-contemporary, Shakespeare, in a complex series of associations (Shakespeare, we should note, is known to have drawn on Gerard's *Herball* for some of his plant lore).[14] Starting at the far end of the phrase, "lacquer" is straight out of Zukofsky's paraphrase of W. H. Hudson in Woodward's introduction to the *Herball*. Hudson, praising Gerard's prose, writes: "The colour of his style is never overworn, and he is for ever fresh and full of variety and agreeable surprises, like Nature herself, who maketh her plants not for meat and medicine only, but some to be esteemed for beauty alone, and as garlands and crowns for pleasure. Indeed, there is not seldom a lustre in his words that serves to remind one of the red whortle he greatly admired, which is full of juice of so orient and beautiful a colour to limn withal that India lacca cannot be compared thereunto."[15] Hudson, in his turn, is paraphrasing Gerard's entry "Of Worts or Whortle berries"; "lacca" or "lacquer," its modern spelling, therefore comes to *80 Flowers* via four authors and almost four hundred years: Gerard in his *Herball* admires the red whortle; Hudson in *Nature in Downland* praises Gerard's descriptive powers, using in part the old herbalist's own words; Woodward admires Hudson's style, then includes the whortle quote in the section of his introduction called "Eulogy of Gerard"; Zukofsky cuts through these layers of preservation to the voice of Gerard himself: "the red whortle . . juice . . a color . . India lacca cannot compare thereunto" (*80 Fl.* Notes, p. 2). Eventually he condenses the whole business, voice and voices, as "praises lacquer." Gerard "praises lacquer" (verb + noun), but the phrase also describes the preservation of his words (praise's lacquer).

There is no rich red in #10 Charlock Per Winkle apart from Gerard's startling "lacquer" (one strong red among the blues and yellows), and there is nothing botanical that is praiseworthily shiny unless it is the bright leaves of the periwinkle. But "quillet praises lacquer" (difficult syntax) does draw on Shakespeare, specifically on Bottom walking up and down after his transformation, convinced his co-actors have run off to fright him, and singing to prove to them that he is not afraid. The song is about birds, and the line that wakes Titania is: "The wren with little quill—" (*MND* III.i.131). "Quill" to "quillet" is a step Zukofsky accomplishes with the aid of Skeat's *Etymological Dictionary,* first looking up *quill* and finding more to please him under *quillet,* "a sly trick in argument . . L. short for quidlibet anything you choose (that pleases you)" (*80 Fl.* Drafts, p. 16).[16] The element of caprice seems to justify the word's inclusion in #10 Charlock Per Winkle. But perhaps more important is the context of Bottom's tune, because it connects with the Gerard around it in the poem in an unsuspected manner. Making preliminary notes in the margin of the First List around the entry on Myrtle, Zukofsky wrote:

```
    use           Gray—purple or whitish flowers. Gk thyein to burn
    note 7/7/71    John Gerard Herbal re. white thyme
use sense only of I Borage Bring alwaies
courage
Lord Zouch
sent him seeds
from Italy Spain Crete
```

(First List, p. iv)

The note of 7 July 1977 is the Gerard material gathered at the Mansfield Center and passed on to *80 Flowers* via the black notebook (see chap. 3); Lord Zouch rates a mention in the *80 Flowers* Notes (p. 1), along with a "(sic)" from Zukofsky; and the entry of *white* thyme into the poem is apparently based on the fact that periwinkle flowers range from blue through pink to white. The enjambement of periwinkle against thyme in the poem now assumes more significance: "bright / trails creep white thyme times." Zukofsky's observation about thyme's fiery Greek root connects not only with the "fiery yellow" crucifer (hot as mustard?) but also with previous incidences of thyme and fire in *80 Flowers*. However, the most important part of the information quoted above, as far as Shakespeare is concerned, is the directive to use the *sense* of the adage quoted by Gerard and requoted by Woodward in his introduction, about borage, the bringer of courage, promoter of merriment and joy. For here is Bottom, walking up and down, trying to get rid of the blues (those minor chords) that dog him.

Why doesn't borage itself come into the poem? In one sense because its blue is already present in the brave show of periwinkle's flowers, *"bluer winkle"* in the green (one of *Vinca minor*'s old names was "joy of the ground").[17] *These* blues signify cheer. In addition, borage has already made a lyrical appearance in *"A"-23*'s first Music section:

> second
> paradise turnsole suns again, borage
> corolla clear blue, anthers sapphire
> after a night thinking sun
>
> *("A"-23, p. 538)*

"Life's a long / Second paradise," as *"A"-12* expressed it (p. 146). Blue and yellow again, sky and sun, here illuminating a night (sky) spent thinking, composing; Zukofsky's note in the *"A"-23* Spiral (p. 3 verso, stapled in) states that these lines were finished 13 May 1973 between 12:30 and 1:00 A.M. The second paradise of *"A"-11* and *"A"-12* is identified here with sun, sky, and flowers that image both. The blues and yellows of "Initial" (reified in the postcard "AN ERA") have persisted through *"A"-23* to emerge in the *Flowers*—as we might have expected, looking at the red-yellow-blue line that terminates each poem in the Drafts. #10 Charlock Per Winkle winds blue and yellow together (with the oriently beautiful red lacca); #11 Heart's Ease, mostly about gold, nevertheless mentions the "bluepurple white yellow" of *Viola tricolor;* #12 Cinquefoil is full of yellow flowers (but, rosaceous, also brings in a rose-colored cactus); #13 Venus' Looking-Glass, in some ways its mirror-opposite (copper for sulphur) is about azure-blue flowers; #15 Zebrina Etc's most vivid color is that of the sky-blue day-flower.

Did Zukofsky know that in many cultures lapis lazuli and gold were taken to be the substance of the land of the dead? They signified respectively the river of oblivion and paradise beyond, a figure sometimes interpreted as having cosmic origins.[18] Reading six thousand years of "sky, sun, men" ("A"-22, p. 522), Zukofsky could scarcely escape such a recurrent motif, and consequently "A" 22 & 23 is full of Stygian or Lethe blues and paradisal golds for historical as well as personal reasons. When Gilgamesh has a statue made of the dead Enkidu, for example, it is "fashioned with a great weight of lapis lazuli for the breast and of gold for the body. A table of hardwood was set out, and on it a bowl of carnelian filled with honey, and a bowl of lapis lazuli filled with butter. These [Gilgamesh] exposed and offered to the Sun; and weeping he went away" (Sandars, p. 93). This Zukofsky rendered:

A hardwood table, two bowls:
carnelian blushes honey, sapphire swims
butter in sunlight for Stronger,
sapphire breast in gold body
becoming his monument.

("A"-23, p. 542)

These jeweled colors are repeated in the gem garden of the gods a few lines on ("hedges / flower carnelian, bud sapphires—") as Gilgamesh goes the sun's road to find everlasting life. Note in each case a carnelian red among the golds and lapis lazuli (Zukofsky's "sapphire" maps onto Sandars's lapis lazuli via the *Century*'s etymology of the former: "[*sapheiros*], sapphire, or more probably lapis lazuli").

Meanwhile, back with Bottom and his courage-making song backed up by periwinkle blue and the presence of Gerard, contact with Titania's fairies is about to be made. This is a routine Zukofsky has rehearsed, verbatim, twice before; once in "A"-12 (pp. 132–34), where essentials of the dialogue are reproduced from the moment of Bottom's transformation until his greeting of Mustardseed. The second occurrence is in *Bottom* (pp. 370, 371), where conversations with Peaseblossom and Mustardseed are repeated. At stake in both instances (and therefore in #10 Charlock Per Winkle?) is Bottom's manifest ability to "gleek upon occasion"; to play the antic and at the same time draw out its sense. So that when we come across "quillet praises lacquer truemustard ox-beef / weeps" and have trouble seeing an association between its parts (knowledge of individual sources notwithstanding), I think we have to suspect some Bottomish idiolect at work—particularly given the clue (nucleus upon which to wind some threads?) that Bottom's wren's quill (pipe) has been transformed as a demagogic trick meaning literally: "anything you choose (that pleases you)." (Interesting that in reading #10 Charlock Per Winkle Zukofsky says "quill'd praises"—penned? sung? standard pronunciation does not grant *quillet* this option.) Are "quillet praises" (adjective + noun) the kind Bottom strews on the fairies, lacquering them (varnishing truth)? Or are they *small* praises (the wren with *little* quill), coming after the small periwinkle ("dogbane minor")? Another meaning of *quillet,* origin obscure, is: "1. A furrow . . . 2. A croft, or small separate piece of ground" (*Century*). Small, rural, or idiosyncratic praises from Bottom, least hempen of the homespuns? What about the other praiser in the scene, Titania, whose voice might imaginably be as tiny as that of Bottom's wren; one of her fairies, after all, is named for the type of minuteness, mustardseed, and becomes the butt of Bottom's pleasantries about fairy sizes and giant sizes:

> Good Master Mustardseed, I know your patience well. That same cowardly, giant-like ox-beef hath devoured many a gentleman of your house. I promise you your kindred hath made my eyes water ere now. I desire you more acquaintance, good Master Mustardseed. (*MND* III.i.196)

Perhaps: "quillet praises lacquer" (noun + verb + noun)? Why? No bottoming this configuration. Besides, Zukofsky's reading inserts a caesura after "praises" and another, smaller, after "lacquer"; the latter is intentionally isolated in midline, inscrutable in a context of Shakespeare, tractable only as it pertains to Gerard, who has his own courage-inspiring business with the *Dream.*

Beef and mustard; Bottom is ringing changes on who eats what. Has Zukofsky noticed that Grumio's protestation in *The Taming of the Shrew* comes just after an argument about whether Kate shall have "a piece of beef and mustard" (*Shr.* IV.iii.23)? Fiery mustard has made Bottom's eyes water ere now, and Zukofsky's substitution, "weeps," shifts matters along to Titania's closure of the interview, a passage already discussed in connection with dew, flowers, and love's silence (see chap. 4):

> The moon, methinks, looks with a wat'ry eye;
> And when she weeps, weeps every little flower,
> Lamenting some enforced chastity.
> Tie up my love's tongue, bring him silently.
>
> (*MND* III.i.203)

Zukofsky notes the last line of this among the materials for #10 Charlock Per Winkle (*80 Fl. Drafts,* p. 16) with the query "(via Ovid?)" and the observation that the Quarto text has "lovers" for "love's." Acting on this hint, we find that Diana, disturbed at her bath, is called Titania in the *Metamorphoses* (III.173) and turns Actaeon into a speechless stag with the words: "Now you are free to tell that you have seen me all unrobed—if you can tell."[19] Silence. We remember the command preceding a magic vision:

"No tongue! all eyes! Be silent!" (*Tmp*. IV.i.59), which Zukofsky worked (silently) into #4 Liveforever as "see—dumb—know." It would seem that privacy is essential to love's inner sanctum as praise-singing is appropriate to its outward-looking aspects. "Her face the book of—love delights in—praises" is Zukofsky's combination title (from *Pericles* and *Two Gentlemen*) for a poem dealing with the nature of praise, poetry, music, and love (*All*, p. 209). In this 1975 poem "about" courageous singing and love's praises, there is just one hint—"weeps"—of love's other face, the one we encountered so enigmatically in #3 Honesty. *80 Flowers* continues to insist on a certain amount of invisibility (silence, privacy) amid the singing.

The remainder of #10 Charlock Per Winkle's final line, "*uncrossed charlock bluer winkle*," seems to untangle at least the flowers. Charlock, the crucifer, is mysteriously *un*crossed—until we hear in "weeps *uncrossed*" a golden solar parallel to the earlier "brassy core" and "crux fiery yellow." Then—in the twinkling of an eye?—periwinkle becomes "*bluer*," the wink/twinkle association implicit since "blue solitary / winkle spring-green." Zukofsky had contemplated working in the garden song from *Cymbeline* which begins "Hark, hark! the lark at heaven's gate sings," continuing: "And winking Mary-buds begin / To ope their golden eyes" (*Cym*. II.ii.21). At first glance the song is a good candidate for inclusion in #10 Charlock Per Winkle; bird, sun, sun's horses, winking flowers. But on reflection the winking eyes (for the *Vinca*) that Zukofsky wants here are blue, not golden, and the introduction of winking marigolds into the careful skeining of yellow flower with blue would have confused the issue. Field-mustard and periwinkle are both spring flowers; marigolds, according to the gardening books and Perdita, are the flowers of middle summer. Once again, considerations of time (and exactitude) governed a decision in the composition of the *Flowers*.

The mary-buds were discarded, as was a thought to include Pyramus/Bottom's "O Fates, come come / Cut thread and thrum" (*MND* V.i.290). One skein in the poem was sufficient to put the weaving motif in place? Or was *cutting* threads (especially life's threads) antagonistic to the *Flower*'s drift? Also written into the Draft notes, and checked for inclusion in the poem, is the *Century*'s example of usage for *skein*:

> God winds us off the skein, that he may weave us up
> into the whole piece.
>
> Donne, Sermons, xi.

Skeining visible in the poem; weaving implicit.

Zukofsky's last Shakespearean twist in #10 Charlock Per Winkle is hard to follow; "*uncrossed*," the crucifer word, stems from Belarius's speech about the virtues of independence:

> O, this life
> Is nobler than attending for a check,
> Richer than doing nothing for a bribe,
> Prouder than rustling in unpaid-for silk.
> Such gains the cap of him that makes him fine,
> Yet keeps his book uncross'd. No life to ours.
>
> (*Cym.* III.iii.21)

An "uncross'd book" is an unpaid account. What link Zukofsky makes between this and his poem is a crux I see no way of uncrossing. Again the unobvious word has been selected; looking at its context, we might wonder if he also included the sense, somehow, of: "No life to ours."

This brings to a close discussion of the Shakespeare poems of 1975, a sample group that shows the variety of entrances that Zukofskian Shakespeare makes in *80 Flowers*. As noted already, the Bard never really fades out of the sequence (just as he never fades out of Zukofsky's vocabulary); but not until the summer of 1977, as the book nears completion, is there such a series of Shakespeare-infused *Flowers*—and by that time a multitude of presences are at work in the poems and thus Shakespeare is just one element among many.

Now, though, back with the *Flowers* of 1975, there are signs of the season's turning; the twenty-first *Flower* (composed 28 October–13 November 1975) is Chrysanthemum and the title flower itself is a late-blooming perennial. #22 Bayberry (16 November–12 December 1975) concerns a shrub with inconspicuous flowers but evergreen leaves and aromatic berries; sweet-fern is likewise admired for its scented foliage rather than its insignificant flowers. Then, December through January, the poems concern indoor plants—#23 White Begonia, #24 African Violet, #25 Coleus—all heavily dependent on Taylor and with few visible signs of other material (no Shakespeare, for example). It is as if, with the finish of the 1975 growing season, Zukofsky's own resources and inspiration wore correspondingly thin—in contrast to the winter poems of 1974–75, which brim with long-accumulated material, memories, and invocations. Certainly, a change of direction ("drive") becomes obvious.

The storehouses were being replenished, however. Zukofsky was reading Henri Fabre December 1975–January 1976. And there are signs that he began on Henry James as early as November 1975, although the bulk of this reading and note-taking took place in the spring of 1976. More importantly, a new strategy for the selection of upcoming *Flowers* was in the offing.

Another Unearthing: Spring 1976

Composed almost one year after the Epigraph, #22 Bayberry stands in
Zukofsky's mind as a marker. Among the notes that precede its writing is
the record of its source: "Sudden recall of *Anew* I & Note 1 esp.   2
'bay' (the feeling of Port Jefferson terrain, Dante   prophetic full cycle)
gibbous gibbose" (*80 Fl.* Drafts, p. 28). The first poem of *Anew*, "*che di lor
suona su nella tua vita*" (written 1937), is the aftermath of a dream's
action constructed upon many shades of the word *bay*—"but more
specifically two meanings that seemed to include all the others . . . an arm
of the sea and a recess of low land between hills," as the accompanying
Note puts it (*All*, p. 113).[20] A line from Dante, translated "which sounds of
them, up in that life of thine," best accounted for the mood of the dream
and provided the poem with a title. Thirty-eight years later and living in a
coastal town, Zukofsky felt anew the enduring figure of his dream and
composed another poem inwreathed with Dante (whose name means
"deerskin," and alternatively can be short for *durante*, "enduring"):

#22 BAYBERRY

Candleberry bayberry spice resinwax green
durant leaf moor in key
dour attested deer-wit winds survive
days *hippos* rampant *wooden* ancient
standstill plummet unprotected laurel crown
trust sweet-fern of your family
bring birds alula sound coast-floes
sand-iced willows *compt* gibbous moons[21]

Persistent bay and inwreathed poet; Prospero requiring a little more magic
before drowning his book, the *"compt"* (Shakespearean account) at hand
but perhaps not yet of the moment (a gibbous moon is not quite full). If
ever Zukofsky wrote a poem about the passage of time, this is it.
Undercurrents in the line "standstill plummet unprotected laurel crown"
spell mortality in the same breath that evokes consummate poetic power
(remembering hoarfrost on the crown in #2 Mountain Laurel).[22]

Still Zukofsky, poised on the edge of winter, is looking at spring; the
"sand-iced" willows (willows growing in sandy soil) recall for us the first
spring poem of 1975, #8 Pussy Willow. Talking about "birds alula,"
Zukofsky said on the Johns Hopkins tape: "The alula, you know, are the
wings that can't open and fly; they're rather the counterpart of the thumb
in a human being. They're right near the breast. You find that in any

dictionary, but I found a picture of it, I don't know—many years ago—in the *Century Dictionary* and I always wanted to use that. It's a nice sound there. And besides, we're talking about spring, and so there they are, whatever spring it is. We trust. That is kind of personal."[23]

#22 Bayberry was not the only *Flower* of fall and winter 1975–76 with a vernal aspect. The last line of #21 Chrysanthemum reads: "East spring winter hearts renew," four-fifths of which is made-over Campion, a line from the song "And would you see my Mistris face?":

> It is faire beauties freshest youth,
>   it is the fain'd Elizium's truth:
> The spring that winter'd harts renu'th;
>   and this is that my soule pursu'th.[24]

Once again Zukofsky is replaying (by song) red blood reigning in the winter's pale. But the last lines of #23 White Begonia go beyond spring: "zinnias arm perennial rays summers / white begonia suns 5-lobed indoor." In "suns" we are hearing another fragment of Campion, this time making a solar devotion:

> Is shee come? O, how neare is shee?
>   How farre yet from this friendly place?
> How many steps from me?
>   When shall I her imbrace?
> These armes Ile spred, which onely at her sight shall close,
> Attending as the starry flowre that the Suns noone-tide knowes.[25]

Campion's flower is heliotrope; Zukofsky's poem is written 19–23/24 December 1975, at the winter solstice ("How farre yet . . ." etc.).[26] #24 African Violet continues the pattern of forward-looking last lines: "temperate tempered sanctum tho no / land or violet spring brings." Spring may not bring an African violet, which after all is (line one of the poem) an "Open rosette flowering continually"—indoors—but it will bring other kinds of violets, and the intimation has been present in Zukofsky's notes for the Drafts since #22 Bayberry.

At the foot of the #22 Bayberry draft is, as has become usual since #6 Spider or Ribbon Plant, a projected sequence of the next few poems. This time the projection is more outline than enumeration:

> In spring—pachysandra, azalea, Japanese holly whatever blooms
>   first etc
>
> (*80 Fl.* Drafts, p. 28)

The idea is elaborated at the foot of the #23 White Begonia draft:

> winter
> plants
> African violet
>   Coleus
>   Spring: Iris orig. list 38; and/or time they blossom: pachysandra
>   azalea, Japanese holly, whatever comes up first.
>
> (*80 Fl.* Drafts, p. 29)

When the worst of winter was over, Zukofsky put his anticipated chronology into operation; but first he wrote #26 Tulip and #27 Crocus, noting on the draft of the former:

>   after the blizzard upturned the soil
> In warm winter sun / tulip
>   ⌠woodchuck searching
> and crocus bulbs appear like the ⌡groundhog chancing his shadow
> w. Valentines early Valentine   ⟋pachysandra, azalea
> etc in the order spring '76 brings NB. ⟋ thyme, lavender
> cotton, myrtle, Japanese holly (crenata, fortunei, convexa)
> thriving esp. persistent in rock garden as late as Jan 14
> begin 28 saying they did?
>
> (*80 Fl.* Drafts, p. 31)

(We remember "spring brings" from the close of #24 African Violet; Zukofsky had been thinking about this ordering for some time. Spring touches in the winter poems begin to look more than incidental.) And the *Flowers* after #27 Crocus are #28 Forsythia (which includes Japanese holly, thyme, and the "myrtle," periwinkle), #29 Pachysandra, #30 Violet, #31 Deutzia, #32 Lilac, and #33 Azalea—a sequence that moves *80 Flowers* through March-May 1976, a much earlier spring than the previous year.

It starts off, as the above note indicates, with a pair of facing poems, both about bulbs. One title signifies conventionally red flowers (#26 Tulip), the other typically yellow flowers (#27 Crocus), but each bursts with other early spring flowers, white, yellow, and green:

#26   TULIP

Blizzard sun upturn tulips chances
bare earth guess near in
honor breed true as the
lilies wakerobin naked bulb turban
wejack shadow *early* crocus iris

thinnest leafblade many seed air-thread
still livid tulip to leaf
green blue pointed heart valentines

#27   CROCUS

Hear it tease question will
the snowdrop come up nodding
green in white crome asea
navvies long a crook tip
strung alack riches look o
into scaleless bulbs a false
spring snowpits measure hours sative
crocus furnace sandy yellows cloth-of-gold

The first of these, begun on Groundhog Day (2 February) and finished 11 February for Valentine's Day 1976, revolves around the folklore of seasonal change. If the groundhog (or woodchuck; from a simulation of the American Indian *wejack*) emerges from hibernation 2 February and sees its shadow, it goes underground for another six weeks, implying that "warm, sunshiny weather very early in the spring, or in February, arousing the woodchuck from its torpidity, is likely to be followed by a cold or late season" (*Century*). This "Blizzard sun" (treachery?) brings up the bulbs; they take a chance on the bare earth but risk a cold snap just the same. Crocus (a member of the Iridaceae, irises) pushes up grasslike leaves along with the blue-green two-leafed ("to leaf") tulip. The latter, a lily with a pointed bulb and a flower that derives its name from the Arabic for *turban (dulband),* is a popular symbol of Valentine's Day—but see how Zukofsky chromatically transforms the red-heart flower ("green blue pointed heart valentines") while still playing with the tulips/two lips conceit. In line one, "tulips" is adjacent to "chances," suggesting one possible twinning of initial sounds ("tʃ"); then, in line seven, "tulip to leaf" releases the other (a dental "t")—and immediately "to" (hearing of course "two") attaches itself to "lip" ("tulip") as well as to "leaf."

Tulipa gesneriana ("guess near in / honor") is the Persian-Armenian ancestor of most garden tulips. According to Taylor, the majority of garden tulips do not breed true; that is, they must be propagated by their bulbs. "Species" tulips, however, do breed true. And Zukofsky's flower, "guess near in / honor breed true as the / lilies," implies that the tulip he has in mind is a garden variety, probably one of the early-flowering tulips (*"early,"* in line five; though apparently linked with the crocus) that "open their flowers on sunny days almost as soon as the leaves push through the ground" (Taylor). But breeding true, in connection with the transliterative "honor," gives notice of extrahorticultural considerations—particularly when we know the poem is working in valentine motifs with its garden information. "Honor" is the family keynote of "A"-11; #3 Honesty dwelt on true-bred valentine honor, and in "true as the / lilies" is the faintest echo of the true horse that canters through "A" and 80 Flowers. In "honor breed true as the / lilies," is the 1976 update of Zukofsky's private valentine figures. It may be significant that the very next word is "wakerobin," a popular name for the trillium—another lily that comes up early in spring, leaves and flowers arranged in threes as the Latin trillium would suggest. (Counting through the poem there are three flowers being described—tulip, trillium, and crocus.)

In #26 Tulip, spring bulbs "unearth" themselves like the groundhog from whose day the poem takes its start; a most American valentine. In "air-thread" (line six) we are hearing some genuine American sound unearthed; Zukofsky includes among his notes for #26 Tulip the quotation: "a man ain't born like a woodchuck to live in the ~~earth~~ airth" (80 Fl. Drafts, p. 31). No source is given, but checking Mitford M. Mathews's Dictionary of Americanisms, a work Zukofsky used later in his preparations for the Flowers, we find the same quotation under woodchuck and relevant etymological information under wejack.[27] The "thread" of airth/"air-thread" (a Southern drawl) most likely refers to the filaments of the crocus flower, from which saffron is derived.

Was early February 1976 so warm that the groundhogs turned tail on the sun—and on the bulbs its warmth had brought up? A spell of mild weather may well have had the tulips up, but any groundhog who surfaced 2 February 1976 would have had good reason, at least traditionally, to stay above ground; a "near-blizzard" storm made front-page news the next day in the New York Times. "Blizzard sun upturn tulips chances," a line written on Long Island the day of the storm, means exactly what it says; no early tulips this year. The price, one had to hope (nursing winter aches and pains), of spring not too far off.

Perhaps Zukofsky had his eye also on the ubiquitous potted tulips forced for Valentine's Day (aligning the twenty-sixth Flower with its indoor predecessors?). The point is that neither tulip nor crocus features explicitly in the chronology of flowers expected in the garden at Port Jefferson—though Zukofsky may have observed them elsewhere if the weather had indeed been as mild (before the storm) as both the poem ("Blizzard sun") and the "warm winter sun" note would indicate.

The "early crocus iris" is #26 Tulip's in-text link with #27 Crocus; it is the kind of name prefigurement Zukofsky had carried out in the Epigraph (for #1 Starglow), in #2 Mountain Laurel (for #3 Honesty), and in #6 Spider or Ribbon Plant (for the "family lilies" of #7 Sprengeri). The phrase provokes thought even before we follow its lead into #27 Crocus. The three words are a concise summary of the plant—always early flowering, a member of the Iridaceae, yellow as the saffron processed from its anthers but also (*Crocus vernus,* the common spring-blooming crocus) coming in a veritable rainbow of colors: "white, white with purple and violet stripes, lavenders, lilacs, gray-blues, rosy purples, and deep, warm purples darkening in the throat" (Taylor). All these, in addition, are iris colors. But also we must hear, run-on in "crocus iris"—what? "Osiris"? (how does that fit?). Or, a pretty blend of antecedents, the Greek *krokos,* which Zukofsky once transliterated/translated from a Homeric Hymn to Demeter as: "crocus-eye color violet" (*"A"*-23, p. 545); "eye color" is the property of an (optical) iris—1976's "crocus iris" catches all of these nuances.[28]

#27 Crocus seems to concern itself more with snowdrops than with its title flower, which has already been botanically covered in #26 Tulip by: "thinnest leafblade many seed air-thread," and perhaps: "still livid tulip to leaf"; two lines that mix tulip and crocus details. The "thinnest leafblade" belongs to a crocus; "many seed" is the tulip's fruit capsule, as described by Taylor; we have already surmised that "air-thread" is connected with the crocus—which then merges with the tulip, "still livid" (brightness after blizzard? calm and color?). We could suspect some transliteration or translation in this, but nothing shows the way to identifying it. This is also the case with "Hear it tease question," the opening of #27 Crocus. Who or what is "Hear-it-tease"? The "question," however, is put plainly enough: "will / the snowdrop come up nodding / green in white." To discover the answer, we must go to the notes for #51 Snowdrop (composed 11 April–1 May 1977), where Zukofsky records that a snowdrop planted early in 1975 failed to flower in 1976, blossoming finally 27 March 1977 (*80 Fl. Drafts,* p. 58) and thereby supplying the occasion of the fifty-first *Flower.*

In 1976, Zukofsky may have found reason for pairing crocus and snowdrop in that both are sometimes called "Candlemas Bells" (Taylor; *Century,* in its entry on *Galanthus nivalis,* the snowdrop). Candlemas is celebrated 2 February, the same date as Groundhog Day; and so the linking of #26 Tulip and #27 Crocus continues, now with bells and light to add to the snows of early February.[29] As for the snowdrop question, in February-March 1976 it was unanswerable (a tease?). Zukofsky may have seen bulbs in other gardens but his own had not unearthed any flowers, and this could be why #27 Crocus spends so much of its time with two literary snowdrops. The first of these is Theophrastus, writing about snowdrops and some related plants that he perceives as belonging to a wider class of bulbs. The translation reads: "These belong to this class only in having round roots; for in colour they are white, and the bulbs are not formed of scales" (*Enquiry* VII.xiii.9). From this Zukofsky evolves "scaleless bulbs," a phrase that also fits Taylor's description of *corms,* underground stems resembling bulbs but without scales; crocus is cited by Taylor as a typical example, though snowdrop is not specifically mentioned as reproducing by corms. However, there is more Theophrastus in #27 Crocus than translation and to get at it we must go to the Greek of the passage quoted above:

> *Bolbōdē de tauta hoti strongula tais rhizais*
> *epei tois ge chrōmasi leuka kai ou lepuriōdē.*

This, the sound of it, gives us "crome asea" (*chromasi,* "color") right after "green in white." (A crome is a crook or staff—"a crook tip"—specifically, a kind of rake with a long handle, used for pulling weeds out of water; *Century.*) *Leuka* (white) is rendered by Zukofsky: "look o"; and if we look at the Greek for snowdrop (mentioned by Theophrastus in the sentence preceding the one just quoted), and find *to leukoïon* (literally "white violet"), we may run over the line break and hear a Greek noun precede its article: "look o / into." In "riches" is *rhizais* (roots); and in "strung alack" is *strongula* (round). Round roots are the snowdrop's distinctive characteristic, according to Theophrastus.

From here Zukofsky moves sideways, via Liddell and Scott, to arrive at "navvies long a"—plainly a transliteration of Latin *navis longa* (warship). The route (and root) is convolute and largely unsignposted: under *strongula* in Liddell and Scott is the compound *strongulos naus,* a merchant ship, so called "from its round, roomy shape, as opposed to the long narrow ship-of-war (*makra naus*)." Why Zukofsky chose to bring the warship rather than the merchant ship into this poem is not clear, nor is its transformation from a Greek to a Latin vessel.[30] Perhaps "navvies" suited his purposes too well to be passed up, looking one way at *navies* that might ("asea") sail a green 'n' ("in") white ocean either militarily or as a merchant marine; looking the other way at *navvies* who might wield rakes, crooks, or cromes. (The Latin snowdrop, *Galanthus nivalis,* is literally a snowy milkflower; perhaps Zukofsky wanted some aural vestige of that snow (*nivalis*) in the poem as well as the Greek (*leukoïon*).

We leave Theophrastus's snowdrop (temporarily) on encountering the phrase "a false / spring." This points back at the "Blizzard sun" of #26 Tulip, enticing up the bulbs only to "upturn [their] chances / [in the] bare earth." The Zukofskys' snowdrops may have got above ground but they did not ("alack riches") make it into flower in 1976, and by the sound of it winter descended with a vengeance: "snowpits measure hours." The snowpits derive from note-taking Zukofsky had done the previous April

from a translation of Xenophon's *Persian Expedition*. On the great march
back to Greece, the remains of Cyrus's army cross the mountains of
Armenia, heading toward the Black Sea. Zukofsky:

> 4/21/75—Xenophon IV 5 (Marching thru the snow)
> (nightfires in camp) When the fires were made
> great pits formed reaching down to the ground as the
> snow melted . . giving one a chance of measuring
> the depth of the snow. [condense!][31]
>
> > (*80 Fl.* Notes, p. 6)

Condensed some pages later, the same entry reads: "campnightfires . .
~~melting~~ thawing snowpits . . measure—Z." (*80 Fl.* Notes, p. 10A-2); the
initial puts a proprietary seal on the editing. So, in terms of the poem,
spring bulbs may push up through snow (or it may treacherously descend
on them pushing up) but the more literal message delivered by the fire-
melted snow of Xenophon/Zukofsky is of a different kind of—"snowdrop."

Time measure is once again to the fore. Xenophon's is wreathed with
Shakespeare's Salarino, fearing for the safety of his ship at the outset of
The Merchant of Venice:

> I should not see the sandy hour-glass run
> But I should think of shallows and of flats,
> And see my wealthy Andrew dock'd in sand.
>
> > (*MV* I.i.25)

Zukofsky incorporated the sense of this in "measure hours" and the sound
of it in "sandy yellows" (sandy shallows):

> spring snowpits measure hours sative
> crocus furnace sandy yellows cloth-of-gold

Here is a merchant ship "wealthy" with cargo; in Xenophon warships
(*makra naus*) transport the Greeks once they reach the coast. Round and
roomy or sleek and fast, both kinds of vessel appear to be part of #27
Crocus. Further to the theme of mercantile anxiety, "alack riches" has a
Shakespearean ring to it; Salarino anxious of losing them? Shylock about
to lose his ("My daughter! O my ducats!" *MV* II.viii.15) in a play all about
the worth or otherwise of golden wealth? Here also is a crocus (*Crocus
susianus*) named "cloth-of-gold" and another, *Crocus sativus*, the saffron
crocus, sometimes known as Vegetable Gold (Taylor). A "sative / crocus
furnace" might offer the sight of garden-sown yellow crocuses blazing in
the snow, which their brilliance seems to melt away (in pits?). Fire in a
wintry season again.

Then there is the element of song, present in the poem by means of some more Shakespeare. First thoughts spring to Ariel, "Come unto these yellow sands" (*Tmp.* I.ii.376), who helped bring a king's ship to what looked like grief. But Zukofsky, intent on backing up his transliterations with a sense pertinent to the poem, found three other passages that pleased him. On top of the Greek that sounded "strung alack riches" is Shakespeare writing about music: first Biron, on Love that is "as sweet and musical / As bright Apollo's lute strung with his hair" (*LLL* IV.iii.242); then more myth from Proteus:

> For Orpheus' lute was strung with poets' sinews,
> Whose golden touch could soften steel and stones,
> Make tigers tame, and huge leviathans
> Forsake unsounded deeps to dance on sands.
>
> (*TGV* III.ii.78)

More gold, more "sandy yellows," and a distant (deep) sound of Prospero's vow; all in a context of music. Finally, there is Juno's song (actual music) dropping benison upon lovers for whom the "sandy hour-glass" means only increase:

> Honour, riches, marriage-blessing,
> Long continuance and increasing,
> Hourly joys be still upon you!
> Juno sings her blessings on you.
>
> (*Tmp.* IV.ii.106)

(And there, "riches," is Shakespearean quotation acting as transliterative cover for Theophrastus's *rhizais*.) Juno's benison affirms that the snow-pits' measured hours and the false spring are incidents in a life's musical time; #27 Crocus's proximity to the 1976 valentine shows clearly.

One final musical note (literally) is indicated by the phrase "a crook tip." We have already established the relationship between "crook" in line four and "crome" in line three, but the *Century* also lists a meaning for *crome* as "eighth note, quaver," from the Italian *croma* (crook). Looking at the eighth note ♪ (eyes for once ahead of ears), we see immediately its distinguishing "crook tip." The prevalence of music in what at first seems to be a poem concerned with other things is probably explained by the dedication "for J.S.B. 3/21/76," which is found only in the *80 Flowers* Spiral; #27 Crocus is the second birthday poem for Bach in the sequence.

Returning, though, to the matter of valentines; the crocus has come close at least once before to the private family heart. In a strophe of "A"-18, set against a multitude of dishearteners, occurs a potent if not patent hope:

                    Then in myself
her look in an areaway said 'the spring's
one white crocus Eden no friends to share'
. . .
be it but a line or a dot let it persist
at that solely with the unearthing crocus

                                        ("A"-18, p. 403)

This directs us straight away to the movement's opening "An"-song, a
different kind of unearthing:

An unearthing
my valentine
if I say it now will
it always be said.
I always know
it is I who have died
yet in that state

sorrow for you
by yourself.
Thinking of you
without me
without years
of hours
that time is.
Selfish of
me to wish you
to merely
live long

to fulfill
no time
where your
thought for
me has no sense
for with
that thought
it is I have died.
I mean don't cry
in that sense
I cannot now
get around
thinking I am dead

where with you
now I have no place
as I say
it now
and you sense
it always said.

("A"-18, pp. 389–90)

As it happened, "An Unearthing" was not composed in any February and
is a valentine rather in the spirit of: "if I say it now will / it always be said";
time's measure "unearthed" spreads over the calendar as "AN ERA / ANY
TIME / OF YEAR" did a few years later.[32] And yet "unearthed," brought out
of the ground (as opposed to wheeling away from its surface realities into
some "A"-11 cosmos) is also very time-specific, as Zukofsky acknowledges
by bringing the crocus into "A"-18 and by devoting the first two *Flowers* of
spring 1976 to the business of unearthing which underlies the season—
whether it is a question of snowdrops blossoming in the Zukofskys' yard
or Persephone picking roses, crocus, iris, hyacinth, and then a deceiving
narcissus in the meadows of Nysa; being seized there by Hades, to be
unearthed with her flowers each year.

The snowdrops did not show, but in #28 Forsythia there are signs at
last of Zukofsky's spring chronology. Recalling the note about "thyme,
lavender cotton, myrtle, Japanese holly (crenata fortunei convexa),"
thriving and persistent in the rock garden as late as mid-January, we may
see for ourselves that Zukofsky did compose the twenty-eighth *Flower*,
saying so:

#28   FORSYTHIA

Forced yellow spring before crenated
green unfolding fortune eye holly-
ember firethorn winter low stonecrop
thyme bluewinkle lilac forsythia suspense-arched
glance 4-petal goldenbell closer strapped
vine pith stem arch aged
branches root their height steep
smoke breathe olive branch dove

The chronology is puzzling because it seems to indicate not the spring of
1976, still struggling to begin, but a series of plants from the "spring
before": we recognize thyme, lavender cotton, and periwinkle from the
poems of 1975; stonecrop, too—although its presence might denote the
rock garden as well as the plant (which one?) itself. Most of these are

evergreens, all of them are at least persistent through winter, and this is what Zukofsky has in mind when he says they are "thriving . . . as late as Jan 14." To his 1975 plants he added another handsome evergreen, *Ilex crenata fortunei,* the Japanese holly, which bears not red but black fruit. This is the "box-like shrub holly" of *"A"*-23's Zukofsky-garden section (p. 554), a description that incidentally confirms Zukofsky was working out of Taylor ("box-like habit and foliage") before *80 Flowers* was begun.

The one plant of #28 Forsythia unmistakably in blossom is the title flower, another shrub; though again there is a chance the blossoming is a memory: "Forced yellow spring before crenated / green unfolding." Taylor observes that forsythia is useful for forcing, and that some varieties flower before the unfolding of the leaves ("crenated" more plausibly belongs with the Japanese holly, but a new leaf-cluster unfolding could be so described). Thus "Forced yellow spring" could mean any forsythia presaging spring "before . . . green unfolding"; that is, that "before" does not necessarily compound with "spring" to mean 1975.

Whatever year Zukofsky has in mind, yellow forsythia presides in this poem ("for" resounds in its first four lines—"Forced," "before," "fortune," "forsythia"). The species concerned is *Forsythia suspensa,* the weeping golden bell: "the tips of the long, arching hollow branches often pendulous and, in age, rooting at the tip" (Taylor). Speaking of forsythia blossom, Taylor also notes: "Corolla bell-shaped below, but split into 4 strap-shaped lobes which look casually like 4 separate petals"; and of the genus at large: "Most of them stand smoke better than such decorative shrubs usually do." The last half of Zukofsky's poem draws almost entirely on these passages and on the remark that *Forsythia suspensa,* if left unpruned, "may sometimes act like a vine over a wall." Stonecrop proverbially sits on walls and likes, of course, rock gardens. The "low wall / ranges" are perhaps the rock garden Zukofsky speaks of in the spring chronology note (*80 Fl.* Drafts, p. 31). Certainly the plants of 1973 correspond to some of those mentioned as thriving there (pachysandra, azalea, Japanese holly) in the winter of 1976.

As for the "olive branch dove" that ends the poem (has the bad weather lasted *that* long?), forsythia is a member of the Oleaceae—like privet (both are noted for their easy rooting); also like the lilac that appears in line four, at first sight an adjective of "bluewinkle" (periwinkle flowers are violet-blue). Finding two privet-related shrubs in #28 Forsythia leads to something that also accounts for "firethorn" in line three. Privet, in the First List of 80 Flowers, was to have been combined with Pyracantha, the firethorn, a member of the Rosaceae; as we know, Pyracantha was supplanted by the red and yellow of spring daffodils and Shakespearean song. In the First Abbreviated List (which Zukofsky was working from, #15 Zebrina Etc through #34 Lily-of-the-Valley), Pyracantha was teamed with Cotoneaster (also rosaceous), and the title of the projected poem was to have been "Firethorn," next incarnation of the fiery rose. But the same entry included a cross-reference to Forsythia, where we find:

forced spring   olive f.
    yellow   24. *Forsythia* planted Pt J 6/7/75; w. firethorn eg *Ember*
                                           Eves
                    (1st Abb. List, p. [1])

This time Forsythia came in ahead of Cotoneaster, and for the moment the Firethorn became part of the twenty-eighth *Flower*'s figure of sharp spines and fiery colors. The connection Zukofsky found to link Forsythia and Pyracantha was *Ilex crenata;* "holly- / ember" is aligned with "firethorn," and the spectacle of the firethorn with its showy red berries and evergreen foliage transforms by juxtaposition the Japanese holly's black berries into something nearer the traditional red; "holly-ember" mirror-images "firethorn."

Firethorn, via *Bottom,* brings Shakespeare into the poem; Gower intoning:

To sing a song that old was sung,
From ashes ancient Gower is come,
Assuming man's infirmities,
To glad your ear and please your eyes.
It hath been sung at festivals,
On ember-eves and holidays.

                                 (*Per.* I.i.1)

"Ember Eves," the fifth section of *Bottom*'s Alphabet of Subjects, is a meditation on flame, fire, and light as "An image in history," starting with the Zohar and progressing (always by lateral reference to Shakespeare) through quotations from Francis Bacon, Georges de la Tour (a painting), Descartes, Spinoza, Berkeley, Faraday, Henry Adams, and a voice from 1960 which is Zukofsky's commentary. The emphasis is on what the eye looks at when it sees flame (fire's light), but the section closes with a rehearsal, from the 1623 Folio text, of the Moonshine sequence in the rude mechanicals' performance of *Pyramus and Thisbe.* Starveling's presentation of moonshine—bush of thorns, dog, and lantern standing for moonlight—seems to fascinate Zukofsky and to provide contrast with or parallel to the philosophical (also lyrical) explanations of the physical phenomenon of light and fire which precede it in "Ember Eves." We saw the same combination of fire and light in #1 Starglow, where Starveling's "lanthorn" connected fiery rose and thorny light in celebration of Zukofsky's particular source of emotional and artistic light, Celia. The motifs of fire and light, with their corollaries of light and time (thyme), have been present in *80 Flowers* since its inception, along with a sometimes insistent association with thorns. In #28 Forsythia, with the introduction of the rosaceous firethorn, we are witnessing a marriage of motifs mirrored from the Greek *Pyracantha;* that the "fire" refers to the scarlet berries rather than the shrub's flower and that its "thorns" are spiny twigs make it a mate for the Japanese holly Zukofsky had observed thriving in his rock garden; and the holly was in turn teamed with the bright golden "fire" of the forsythia. In each case the nature of the fire/light entering *80 Flowers* is akin to the illusion of roses as fire which started things off—the light implicit in both kinds of Candlemas Bells is a continuation of the same concern. This is probably the appropriate place to mention that #28 Forsythia, written 31 March–3 April 1976, was dedicated (again, only in the *80 Flowers* Spiral) to Reb Pinchos: "for April 11/76." The singing Gower, the light-filled construct Zukofsky built upon Gower's "ember-eves," and its extension in the forsythia poem all accord well with what we know of Zukofsky's esteem for his father.

That the firethorn in #28 Forsythia was intended to be the debut of a powerful motif in the *Flowers* is borne out by the continued presence of the shrub in subsequent Lists. In the Second Abbreviated List it rejoins Cotoneaster and the title of the poem is still to be "Firethorn." In the Third Abbreviated List the same entry appears, but with a note that Pyracantha will be substituted for Cotoneaster and possibly combined with Larkspur. However, the firethorn poem never eventuates, though the matter does not drop from sight entirely. First Cotoneaster and later Pyracantha reappear in the lists for "Gamut," the latter marked with three asterisks suggesting imminent inclusion in the new book—and the continuation of one of *80 Flowers'* major concerns.

#29 Pachysandra concerns a ground cover also in the Zukofskys' garden. It is worth quoting again part of the 1973 description of the garden, noting that among the next few *Flowers* are #32 Lilac and #33 Azalea:

> —as
> the eyes turn North lilac
> blue-red, white too, right-angled facing
> stone porch whose low wall
> ranges (pachysandra mingling) yew, flame-azalea,
> box-like shrub holly, kalmia, more
> you, díscolor willow with the
> lilac.
>
> ("A"-23, p. 554)

Familiarity with the Zukofskys' northern aspect is one thing this part of the *Flowers* is building up in good measure. And what of pachysandra itself, a member of the Buxaceae, boxes? The sort known as Japanese spurge (another "Japanese" "box" to match #28 Forsythia's *Ilex crenata*) is *Pachysandra terminalis,* easily propagated by cuttings "planted in a mixture of ½ sand and ½ soil, in a cold frame which should be well-watered and shaded until cuttings are rooted" (Taylor):

#29   PACHYSANDRA

Naked spike chocolaty men white
lances girl sewing-awl down stem
flowers join over evergreen saw-edge
upsúrge pack in sandy rows
cover ground sun shade the
term it all is box-leaf
winterer white blossom East spurge
when *spring beauty* goes quicked

Pachysandra terminalis is evergreen, with partly serrated leaves and white flowers in naked terminal spikes from three to four inches long. *Pachysandra* is from the Greek *pachys* (thick), and *andros,* used here (according to Gray) for *stamen* (Zukofsky's "pack in sandy rows" acknowledges this phonetically). However, Taylor says that the second element of the name *pachysandra* derives from the Greek for "men," an etymology Zukofsky has also picked up in line one. Whichever authority is correct, pachysandra flowers are monoecious (stamens and pistils in separate flowers on the same plant); the staminate flowers have long, thick filaments, the pistillate flowers have thick awl-shaped styles, which are "stigmatic down their whole inner side" (Gray)—that is, the pollen-receiving mechanisms are arranged all ("awl") down the style ("stem"). To Zukofsky's eye, these stigmata in the female ("girl") inflorescence look like stitch marks; the male (staminate) flower has separate stamens (whence "men"?), which the poet sees as "white / lances." The sexual figure is plain, with a "Naked spike" (the brownish common axis of all the flowers) transferring its phallic shape to the "white / lances" that fertilize the stigmatic pistillate flowers. When we discover that *stamen* is Latin for "thread, string, fiber" (*Century*), the conjugation of male and female is completed somewhere in "white / lances girl sewing-awl down stem"—an ingenious meshing of botanical with human reproductive procedures. #29 Pachysandra is heavily dependent on Gray's minutely descriptive botany, but its interpretation is all Zukofsky.

What about "chocolaty men"? A note in the Drafts (p. 39) says simply: "chocolate soldiers." Is this a colloquial (or private) name for pachysandra? Or does it enter the poem unattached to the title flower except by force of circumstance; that is, timing? #29 Pachysandra was written 20–25 April 1976; does chocolate suggest Easter treats? Remembering the reported Pound in *"A"*-13 (pp. 264–65): *"Thanks / for passover delicacies / specially the black bambino / . . . Aint tasted / that kind of ADmired chocolate / for 40 years—."* Easter Sunday fell on 18 April in 1976.

Zukofsky was thinking forward as he composed #29 Pachysandra; exactly twenty poems after #9 Privet, it is another poem for Shakespeare's birthday, designated so on both the ink draft and in the *80 Flowers* Spiral (Valentine's Day, Bach, Reb Pinchos, Shakespeare 1976; the yearly cycle of anniversaries paces the season's flowers again). This time there is no Shakespearean quotation (chocolate is no part of Elizabethan England either), and even the title flower is one of the less memorable plants of the sequence. It is as if, having pulled out the Shakespearean stops in 1975, Zukofsky has reverted to his more customary practice of making silent dedications, poem not visibly associated with dedicatee except by private watchword. This also seems the case with #28 Forsythia (Reb Pinchos), #27 Crocus (Bach), and (to some extent) #26 Tulip (Valentine's Day). What #29 Pachysandra's Zukofsky/Shakespeare key might be is not deducible from the text or its preparatory material; we could guess that it occurs somehow in the last line, "when *spring beauty* goes quicked," simply on the grounds that this introduces the flower *Claytonia virginica*, by name and nature different to the prosaic Gray and Taylor–derived pachysandra.

The last line means what it says; we catch a mere glimpse of the spring beauty before it disappears—just as the meadowflower itself is "very fleeting, and wilting at once if picked" (Taylor). Zukofsky's rhyming condensation of this is: "goes quicked" (but the flower so alive with spring?). *Claytonia virginica* had been identified in Port Jefferson 18 June 1975, Zukofsky noting its alternative names: good-morning-spring, mayflower, and grassflower (First List, p. v). Seven days later he identified a closely related plant, *Claytonia caroliniana* (First List, p. i). It is these 1975 flowerings that are used in #29 Pachysandra; by the time #35 Grassflower is composed (2–8 June 1976), the Zukofskys' own plant has flowered (13 May). The introductory glimpse in the earlier poem reminds us of the firethorn situation—except that here the planned title poem does materialize.

Why team pachysandra and spring beauty? The connection is once more a product of combination-changes in the First List: the original fifty-ninth entry was Portulaca of the purslane family, or Portulaceae; and Portulaca was to have been teamed with Spring Beauty, also a purslane. When Zukofsky substituted Pachysandra in the fifty-ninth place, Spring Beauty stayed on—no doubt as that introductory note for the grassflower poem Zukofsky was hoping to write once his own *Claytonia* bloomed.

Enter Henry James

The next four *Flowers* are linked not only by the sequential order of their 1976 blossoming but also by a voice from Zukofsky's recent reading. He had made notes from Henry James for *80 Flowers* in November the year before, but the single quotation from *The Princess Casamassima* was an isolated instance (see n.22, this chapter). The same novel was picked up again near the end of January 1976 with another note; then, March through April, Zukofsky read and made notes from *The Ambassadors* (1903), *William Wetmore Story and His Friends* (1903), *Watch and Ward* (1878), *Roderick Hudson* (1875), and *The Portrait of a Lady* (1881). Were these first-time readings? It seems likely, despite Zukofsky's long-standing acquaintance with James's work and thought.[33] In letters to Cid Corman, Zukofsky had admitted his problem with novelistic prose: "I gotta have it at least like the first chapter of *Great Expectations* beyond which I never got in my reading it's so final as language. I ain't no novel reader" (LZ to CC, 26 November 1959; TxU). In fact, he was "reserving all novels for the dream paradise of old age" (LZ to CC, 24 January 1959; TxU). That reference to a "dream paradise" is crucial to the late work. As for novel-reading, he was as good as his word; a systematic perusal of James and Hardy was under way by the mid-seventies, to judge by entries in the *"A"* 22 & 23 Spiral and the *80 Flowers* Notes.

The nature of Zukofsky's selections from James's novels and the use to which they are put in the poems of *80 Flowers* make an interesting comparison with the treatment Shakespeare received. Both enter as spring voices in the sequence but whereas Shakespeare is Zukofsky's long-time familiar, James (in the present instance at least) is a product of contingency, 1975–76. The distinction is important.

We begin with the violet, a flower Zukofsky notes as blossoming in Port Jefferson (in his garden?) 13 April 1976 (*80 Fl.* Drafts, p. 39):

#30 VIOLET

Viol lace each stilled note
color two-petal pairs out of
five one heart cup yearly
white violet-streaks leave pointed-scoop

greener other more a round
purple gold centers down white
tree shadow if no rose
too near to be bruised

And this, in its concern with music, colors, and petal-counting, refers quite deliberately to #11 Heart's Ease, a poem occasioned by the planting of pansies in the Zukofskys' garden 8 April 1975 (First List, p. v) and perhaps by their blossoming later that season. In the First Abbreviated List, Zukofsky also teams the violet with African violet, though the link is harder to appreciate except as contrast between an everblooming indoor plant and the delicate spring perennial.

#30 Violet has smaller lines than either #11 Heart's Ease or #24 African Violet; the difference is surely intentional. #30 Violet begins with the family name, Violaceae, and goes on to encompass the larger *Viola tricolor hortensis* (the garden pansy or hearts-ease), whose corolla differs from other *Violas* in being "flattish and roundish," with overlapping petals (Taylor). Zukofsky: "greener other more a round / purple gold centers down white." But "other" violets are also present, among them the well-known sweet violet (*Viola odorata*) with its deep purple petals and gold center, the white violet (*Viola blanda*), and a white form of the sweet violet, *Viola odorata alba,* which has purple streaks.

The famous heart-shaped flower of the Violaceae is drawn in from #11 Heart's Ease—"four in pairs unbleeding heart aflower / the lower fifth twice-spurred nectar" is reworked as: "two-petal pairs out of / five one heart cup yearly / white violet-streaks leave pointed-scoop"; that is, the calyx (a Greek "cup") gathers all five petals into a multicolored heart from which projects (from the lower petal) the pointed scoop of a nectar-bearing spur. That "pointed" rings faintly on the "pointed heart valentines" of #26 Tulip; and so by means of a differently configured heart the motif is extended.

The appearance of a rose in #30 Violet, anticipated by the "rosette" in #24 African Violet and perhaps by some "pinked-white" coloring among the purples, blues, golds, and whites there, saves the violet poem from being merely a restatement of #11 Heart's Ease. For one thing, the association of violets with roses provides a lyrical base, whether we start with "Roses are red, violets are blue" or one of Zukofsky's favorite pieces of Herrick. From "Violets":

You're the maiden posies
    And so graced
    To be placed
'Fore damask roses

These lines are part of the section of *A Test of Poetry* (pp. 79–81), where Zukofsky notes that condensation is more than half of composition—the rest is proper breathing space, ease, grace; a dictum we have observed in action over and over again in his own late work.[34] But the teaming in #30 Violet is also the result of some judicious selection from Henry James's early novel *Watch and Ward*. First, from the scene of a tryst: "At the base of a tree, on its little bed of sparse raw verdure, he suddenly spied the first violet of the year. He stooped and picked it; its mild firm tint was the colour of friendship."[35] Then a few pages later: "He had become, in the brief space of a moment, the man she once had loved; but if he was no longer the rose, he stood too near it to be wantonly bruised" (*Watch and Ward*, p. 231). With the sight of his own first violet for 1976 in mind, and reading near the end of James's novel, Zukofsky condensed these passages 19 April:

> p. 218 the base of a tree . .
> the first violet of the year . . the colour of friendship . .
>   [f. violaceae viol lacy
> p. 231 if no longer the rose . . too near to be
> bruised
>
> (*80 Fl.* Notes, p. 19)

He composed #30 Violet 27–30 April, incorporating the James-derived "yearly," "violet," "tree shadow," and: "if no rose / too near to be bruised." Once more the rose is there and not there—a figure of speech in James; at least partly an allusion to or comparison with the proverbial "shrinking violet" as James is invoked by Zukofsky.

As if to make up for the neat dovetailing of novel with poem in #30 Violet, Zukofsky goes on to throw a puzzling Jamesian "lotus" into the first line of his next poem, which by title concerns a spring-blossoming member of the saxifrages, *Deutzia gracilis campanulata*. In 1976, the deutzia flowered in Port Jefferson 21 April according to the First Abbreviated List (p. [1]); the poem Zukofsky derived from that observation:

#31   DEUTZIA

Lotus of toy china bells
numerous pent amorous white blossoms
recurved gracile japanned gray yellow
stems dewed see your oblong
bluish leaves green cities sacks
if rage scent drugged roadsides
lotus fruit spins oaths a
night amulet hardby white deutzia

Did the graceful white deutzia blossom remind Zukofsky of ornamental (and oriental) flowering cherry trees? ("Lotus [lots] of toy china bells / . . . recurved gracile japanned"). Because there is, besides the mysterious lotus, another white and spectacular blossom in the poem, *Prunus spinosa* of the Rosaceae, the sloe or European blackthorn, which sounds as if it grows (also in Port Jefferson?) "hardby" the white deutzia.[36] Zukofsky had first identified the deutzia 22 May 1975 on a roadside in Port Jefferson (First List, p. ii; under Dandelion); proximity of locale as well as of flowering date has been sufficient cause before now in *80 Flowers* for two candidates to be worked together.

The *spinosa*/Spinoza overlap was too good to pass up, especially when Zukofsky connected it, "swift . . . sloe slow" (*80 Fl.* Drafts, p. 35), to a remark of the philosopher's he had once excerpted for possible inclusion in "A"-23:

12/21/68—transition to 23 & to 24 [illeg.] A-12 A 14
(in a twinkling) & Spinoza "moving or still, swift or slow
(A mode that occupies) actual & nothing else

(b.n.b., p. 51)

If this piece of Spinoza assists at the transition of "A"-23 into "A"-24, it is not obvious (though it is just one of a number of strategies Zukofsky contemplated to shift his poem toward its final movement; and it is an early option). What sounds like the same Spinoza proposition had already appeared at the close of *Bottom*'s second section (p. 94): " 'The object of the idea constituting the human mind is the body, or a certain mode of extension actually existing and nothing else' (*Ethics, Part II, Prop. XIII*)." The links this has with #31 Deutzia are subtextual but not tenuous. The "spin oaths a" Spinoza is a touchstone for any or all of Zukofsky's previous dealings with the philosopher—and the association of *spinosa*/ sloe/slow-swift with Spinoza is a typical Zukofskian salute to the thought of a mind with which he had long since established contingency.

Deutzia and rosaceous blackthorn; the third white flower in #31 Deutzia is a lotus. It is a compound figure, appearing in the poem primarily because of timing. To judge by his note-taking, Zukofsky was near the end of *Watch and Ward* by 19 April; he then started *Roderick Hudson* and had read about a hundred pages by 29 April, when he began making notes on it. But there is one undated *Roderick Hudson* quotation from early in the novel entered in the First Abbreviated List (p. [1]) under Deutzia, and it seems reasonable to assume it is there because Zukofsky ran across it the same day he noticed and recorded the blossoming of the deutzia (21 April). The note is brief: "H.J. Rod. Hud. 24. lotuses . . . on rococo china," and it is repeated verbatim in the minimal notes for #31 Deutzia (*80 Fl.* Drafts, p. 35) with the addition "4/21/76"—which confirms our deductions. The "china" lotus in question, however, turns out to be the product of wordplay Zukofsky works from the *Roderick Hudson* passage. Speaking of the good life to be lived in Rome, Rowland Mallett tells his cousin Cecilia: "It's always lotus-eating, only you sit down at table and the lotuses are served up on rococo china."[37] Not exactly *Nelumbium nelumbo* then, the lotus of the Hindus, Chinese, and Egyptians, a water plant with scented pink or rose-colored flowers that close up at night (but can we see—or sniff?—traces of it in "scent" and "night"?). Rowland is referring to the Homeric *lotophagi* (were they "scent drugged" as well as amnesiac, eating the "lotus fruit"?); Taylor says that *Zizyphus lotus,* a jujube tree, was probably the source of the lotus-eaters' wonderful fruit; Theophrastus, too, describes the tree as such (*Enquiry* IV.iii.1–2).

Zukofsky has in mind yet another sort of lotus (even Theophrastus admits that many plants called lotus have nothing in common but the name; *Enquiry* VII.xv.3). *Nymphaea lotus* is also a water lily, called by Taylor the Egyptian white lotus; its flowers open at night, closing nearly at noon next day. It is some variety of *Nymphaea* that Theophrastus calls "Egyptian bean" and describes as having a receptacle "like a round wasps' nest, and in each of the cells is a 'bean,' which slightly projects from it" (*Enquiry* IV.viii.7). The sacred Egyptian lotus and the Sacred or Pythagorean bean are one and the same thing; is there a sacred lotus sitting (invisibly) among the "pulses" of the Epigraph (see chap. 3, n.17)?

Lotus, the water lily *Nymphaea,* is on the First List and the First Abbreviated List of 80 Flowers with the annotation: "Old Lyme"; "ca. 1947–50" adds the entry on the Second Abbreviated List, its presence there proving that lotus was still an option for a title flower, #31 Deutzia notwithstanding. Like the projected Firethorn, Lotus did not materialize in the *Flowers* as a title poem; and like Pyracantha, Lotus (as *Nelumbo*) appeared in the "Gamut" Notes (p. 8), also an addition to the main sequence of trees. The Zukofskys spent their summers "ca. 1947–50" at Old Lyme, Connecticut, which served as a model for the hamlet of Sweetsider in *Little.* Cattails and the aquatic arrowroot were prominent in the marshes of Old Lyme/Sweetsider, and there is at least one poem written out of this locale ("Chloride of Lime and Charcoal," *All,* p. 131) which suggests that water lilies were also part of the Zukofsky summer world at that time. After a description of some garden zinnias, Zukofsky abruptly has a classical lotus appear in "Chloride" 's concluding lines:

So: these are your lancet leaves, tubular stems
Stopped in the lotus or artichoke of your sepals
Of Egypt.[38]

(*All,* p. 132)

The environs of Sweetsider include "the Egyptian lotus pond on the estate of Antonio Viertel Achtel" (*Little,* p. 32), a feature Dala and Verchadet resolve to duplicate in sort on the property they buy, Verchadet saying: "That arrowroot in the rivulet like Viertel Achtel's lotus, Lada, if landscaped could be white . . . It'll be white and float" (*Little,* p. 37).

One reference to the lotus in a day's reading of Henry James was sufficient impulse to bring many histories into the poem occasioned by the same-day record of the deutzia's flowering.

#32 Lilac and #33 Azalea were intended as another facing pair. Both belong to that northern aspect of the garden described in *"A"*-23; the Shakespeare slated for one spills into the other; a Jamesian quotation in one is a Jamesian flavor in the other; and the two poems were worked in close succession, #32 Lilac 8–14 May, #33 Azalea 16–23 May 1976. Even the manner of their entrances into the sequence are linked, though to discuss this it is necessary to know something of the other plants that are teamed with the title flowers. First however, *Syringa,* once known as Pipe:

#32   LILAC

Sere ring a pipe wood
lodging sweet by tempest lodged
nose knows two colors pale
and deep lilac blossom breezed
pruned some red fall-scattered bloom
hesperis purple mother-of-evening gone spring
angels in bustles deep lilac
pales lilac angels for white

It was another genus altogether, *Philadelphus* (mock orange), which was originally named *Syringa* from the Greek *syrinx* "pipe" (Gray), though the *Century* says that straight shoots of lilac were also easily hollowed out for pipe stems; the "Sere ring," for which Zukofsky immediately develops lilac fragrance by invoking a Shakespearean instruction: "And burn sweet wood to make the lodging sweet" (*TS,* induction, i.49). A variation on the sweet fire of thyme and roses; the knowing nose is kept busy in #32 Lilac.

Pipe, however, may also mean music. Syrinx was the name of a nymph pursued by Pan, and she prayed to be turned into a river reed—from which the god subsequently fashioned his pipes. When Basil Bunting begins a short poem: "A thrush in the syringa sings," the bird's voice is already complement to the tree it sits in. Bunting's "i"s take the ear from "syringa" to "sings," "wings," and "things"; ringing.[39]

#32 Lilac is an exquisite lyric with an emphasis on doubling as variation that may well get its start in the two different lilacs at East Broadway. In line two, "lodging" is placed against "lodged"—a juxtaposition of two separate Shakespearean fragments (the second is from 2H6 III.ii.176: "Like to the summer's corn by tempest lodg'd") which mimics the "sweet wood" and "lodging sweet" of the line from the *Shrew* induction. Other doubles work homonymic, syntactic, and chromatic variations: "pale / and deep lilac," "deep lilac / pales"; "angels in bustles deep lilac," "lilac angels for white." It is not stated anywhere in the poem, but the sheer incidence of doubling makes it likely that at least one of the Zukofskys' lilacs (the white? commonly a double form) was a double-flowered variety.

Fragrance and color characterize lilac, and both concerns are carried over into the second flower of the poem, *Hesperis matronalis,* a purple night-scented member of the mustard family, variously known as dame's rocket, dame's violet, garden rocket (Taylor); or as summer lilac (*Funk and Wagnalls*).[40] This last is possibly glossed (with a memory of the quick-going spring beauty) by "gone spring." Zukofsky intended to use a different rocket with the lilac, the weed *Barbarea vulgaris* or yellow rocket; but the scent, color, and name of the garden plant must have changed this plan (the yellow rocket was used in #34 Lily-of-the-Valley), though neither the Lists, Notes, nor Drafts have any record of *Hesperis matronalis'* entrance into the project.

The lilac, "tempest lodged" (one of the trees knocked over by a storm?) and "blossom breezed," "some red fall-scattered bloom" cast on the ground, gives way to a poem where winds and storms still rage, with some assistance from Shakespeare:

#33   AZALEA

Foul weather sighs old time
may is so unfurnished walls
drown tears azalea wills barrens
dry long heath be friend
south lion's-ear tale red north
chalices leaf winter greener wet
azalea longs no dry death
climbs crimson treading roman shades

The source of this tempest is the Greek root of azalea *azaleos* (dry), in allusion to the old (and false, adds Taylor) idea that the shrub requires a dry site. Zukofsky found in Liddell and Scott a metaphorical meaning of the verb from which the adjective derives: in the passive, according to a note in the margin of the azalea poem, *azo* can mean "to be parched up, pine away (through grief)" (*80 Fl.* Drafts, p. 37). This was Zukofsky's chance to introduce grief from the Shakespearean overflow of #32 Lilac— first the Duchess of Gloucester crying: "Alack, and what shall good old York there seè / But empty lodgings and unfurnish'd walls" (*R2* I.ii.67). Then Hermione, with "That honourable grief lodg'd here which burns / Worse than tears drown" (*WT* II.i.110). And then Richard himself saying:

> We'll make foul weather with despised tears.
> Our sighs and they shall lodge the summer corn,
> And make a dearth in this revolting land.
>
> (R2 III.iii.161)

To the melee of tears, sighs, lodgings, and storms, Zukofsky added a logical complement, Gonzalo's sardonic (but heartfelt) parting shots in the face of the Prospero-raised tempest:

> Now would I give a thousand furlongs of sea for an acre of barren ground, long heath, brown furze, anything. The wills above be done! but I would fain die a dry death. (*Tmp.* I.i.69)

It is hardly surprising, given the density and vocabulary overlaps of the Shakespeare in #33 Azalea, that the poem echoes with repeats, whether they are literal ("dry," "dry"; "long," "longs") or partial rhymes ("walls," "wills"; "heath," "death") or semantic pairs ("sighs," "tears"; "barrens," "heath"—thinking particularly of pine barrens, pining). The drown/dry figure is extended first one way ("dry long heath") then another ("longs no dry death").

What, very distinct, is left over from this flurry of quotation? "Old time / may is," which sounds "old Timaeus." What Plato is doing here with his treatise on the creation of the universe is not at all clear (unless we surmise that out of chaos will eventuate cosmos, as always in Shakespeare; as also with Zukofsky's words). Taking a different view, we could say that the time is May (a foul-weathered May? a very dry May? difficult to tell). The Zukofskys' flame-azalea (*Azalea calendulacea*) is a member of the Ericaceae or heath family (one more tie with Gonzalo's dry ground); but by 1975 at least one other species had been planted—*Azalea obtusa,* red-flowered and recorded as being in bloom 25 April 1976 (1st Abb. List, p. [1]). It would still be flowering in May.

From *Azalea obtusa,* "red" and "crimson . . . shades" come into the poem; did Zukofsky know of the color called Roman Lake (cited in the *OED*), its powerful scarlet deriving etymologically as well as chromatically from *lac,* Gerard's "lacca"? *Azalea calendulacea* supplies the yellow of flame; and *Leonotis leonurus,* the lion's-ear or lion's-tail, combines red and yellow in its "orange-red" (Taylor). *Leonotis* (another lion for Louis) is a mint—maybe that "time" in line one is also, fierily, "thyme"?—that Zukofsky had made notes on from Bailey's *Cyclopedia of Horticulture* in Bellagio.[41] Had he seen it flowering there in November, a "winter bloomer under glass" (*"A"* 22 & 23 Spiral, p. 142)? Certainly Taylor was consulted later to find out that as an outdoor plant *Leonotis* is hardy only in southern climates, "but it can be cultivated outdoors northward all summer and then brought into the cool greenhouse, where it will flower in November-December." Zukofsky: "south lion's-ear tale red north," noting also that flame-azalea is in the northern quarter of the garden.

Line seven, "climbs crimson treading roman shades," while according with the colors of the poem, is not wholly convincing as a description either of azalea or of *Leonotis,* for neither is a climber. On a first glance into the *80 Flowers* Notes, "climbs crimson treading roman shades" appears to be the product of some more James; on page 19 there is an entry from the biography *William Wetmore Story and His Friends,* which produces in #32 Lilac the phrase "angels in bustles."[42] Immediately afterward is an entry concerned with "roman shades (blinds)" and a perception of tall green trees—and we may be forgiven for supposing that this too is from the biography, perhaps something to do with William Wetmore Story's Roman sojourn. Subsequent entries, on page 20 of the Notes, do indeed come from this source. In the interests of symmetry, a final line incorporating *William Wetmore Story* in #33 Azalea would complement #32 Lilac's play with the charming "angels in tournures"; Italian crimsons (Roman lakes?) for New England lilacs.

This is not to be the case. On closer examination, the "roman shades" entry has no page reference and appears to be the record of Zukofsky's own observation, as usual worked over even as he formulates it. The note is made midway through the composition period of #33 Azalea and it runs across a page break:

May 21/76   roman shades (blinds)
   *   climbing thru (the) slats of (the) *Romans* tall green trees [over]

May 21/76 (cont) ~~the eye~~
                 ~~climbing slat~~   shades
                 the eye climbing slats of roman ~~blinds~~
                 up tall green trees
                                    (*80 Fl.* Notes, pp. 19–20)

Henry James appears in five more *Flowers* of summer and fall 1976, three times in tandem with Thomas Hardy, Zukofsky's other novelistic engagement of the period. On each occasion the connection with the poem in hand is traceable if not obvious. Nothing, though, is so transparent as violets and roses for #30 Violet, where the contingency of reading and blossoming seems to have been responsible for the transparency of the conjunction; time and timing.

The core of the matter is to determine why Zukofsky selected as he did from his reading of James. As with the majority of his literary sources, James's novels were quoted speculatively—though apparently with an eye to the directions of the project—and then fitted to the chronology of *80 Flowers*. By examining the specifics of each application, we might in time arrive at some general pattern in Zukofsky's attraction to certain features of Jamesian style and subject (floral motifs are only part of that story).

We do know from the instances discussed so far that James is a voice from the past made over as one of *80 Flowers*' time-present coordinates. James is here because Zukofsky was reading him in 1976; he appears first in #30 Violet, #31 Deutzia, and #32 Lilac because that reading is concurrent with the chronology of flowers at last in blossom at 306 East Broadway. Later in the same seasonal ordering, Zukofsky is writing from memory and from notes of the blossomings (e.g., #33 Azalea was not written until three weeks had passed since the flowering of the azalea bush)—and from the James notes he had made in the spring and early summer. To a large extent, the order of flowerings and James is preserved in their integration with each other in successive poems, though other things (time present's latest gifts) do tend to get in the further away composition is from the flowering date.

After writing #34 Lily-of-the-Valley (24–28 May), Zukofsky felt the need of a new list, and as the year turned toward summer the Second Abbreviated List became the operative reservoir of *80 Flowers*' composition—with, however, a new corollary.

7

The *Flowers* of Summer and Fall 1976

The In Process Notes of 1976

The Second Abbreviated List of 80 Flowers, made 29 May 1976, marshals forty-six remaining options and their projected running mates, plus the usual number of compressed notes concerning each. But among these notes are definite signs that the lists were no longer entirely responsible for prompting Zukofsky's sense of the *Flowers'* advance. Under Clover is the injunction: "see in process spring blossoming notes Pt J. 1976." Under Celandine is a similar reference with the addition: "May 20"; also under Iris, noting that the Dutch White had flowered 25 May; and for Marigold, flowering 9 June; also Phlox, flowering 24 May. This is alphabetical ordering; if we rearrange the entries by chronological sequence of flowering, we see: Celandine, Phlox, Iris, and Marigold, with Clover's place unspecified. In rough outline—#38 Phlox, #39 Dutch White Iris, #42 Marigold (celandine appears as an ancillary in #40 Snowflake)—another sequence in the 1976 *Flowers* apparently ordered by dates of blossoming of the title flowers. It is easy enough to search for other flowering dates in the Second List and among the Drafts and to come up with the following:

#36 Clover
Flowered 12 May 1976 (1st Abb. List); cross-reference to In Process Notes (2nd Abb. List). Poem composed 13–15 June.

#37 Roses
"New species" flowered 22–26 May, wild roses in flower 2–23 June (2nd Abb. List). Poem composed 23–25 June.

#38 Phlox
Flowered 24 May; cross-reference to In Process Notes (2nd Abb. List). Poem composed 26–27 June.

#39 Dutch White Iris
Flowered 25 May; cross-reference to In Process Notes (2nd Abb. List). Poem composed 30 June–3 July.[1]

#40 Snowflake	Flowered 28 May (*80 Fl.* Drafts, p. 42), teamed with celandine, which flowered 20 May, with a cross-reference to In Process Notes (2nd Abb. List). Poem composed 6–8 July.
#41 Honeysuckle	Flowered 7 June; cross-reference to In Process Notes (*80 Fl.* Drafts, p. 44). Poem composed 16–23 July.
#42 Marigold	Flowered 9 June; cross-reference to In Process Notes (2nd Abb. List). Poem composed 18–20 July.
#43 Lilies	Orange day lily flowered 12 June, plantain lily flowered 20 June; cross-reference to In Process Notes (*80 Fl.* Drafts, p. 48). Poem composed 23–25 July.

Zukofsky is adhering (again) to the letter of his time-ordered vision of *80 Flowers*. The 1976 In Process Notes are not at Texas (removed once they had served their purpose?) but from their 1977 counterparts (which are still with the Drafts) we can guess that they were organized according to date of blossoming, name of flower, and notes concerning it (see chap. 1). Zukofsky was careful to transfer some of this information to the alphabetical Second Abbreviated List—and now we might guess that "Abbreviated" means abbreviated from the In Process Notes as well as from the earlier alphabetical Lists.

This brings up an interesting point; exactly when did Zukofsky begin keeping In Process records? The pre–29 May alphabetical reservoir was also an "Abbreviated" List, the first one. Does this mean Zukofsky was working out of In Process Notes as early as August 1975? Unlikely. Even the garden sequence of spring 1976, where we first made out a systematic chronology-by-flowering, seems to have been arrived at mostly by ad hoc projections in the Drafts. The idea of a flowering chronology most certainly originated in early 1976, but the record keeping was probably not organized by In Process Notes until around May—when the season brought up more flowers in quick succession than Zukofsky could hope to keep compositional pace with. Hence the record.

I want to select two *Flowers* written in the early summer of 1976, one with minimal notes and some history in the sequence (#37 Roses) and one with extensive notes and no previous *Flower*-history (#38 Phlox). What binds these two is a continuation of the rose and fire motifs, which seem fundamental to the sequence.

#37 Roses and #38 Phlox

The roses poem, which we turn to with the kind of expectations that attended an earlier scrutiny of #4 Liveforever, proves to be as bland-faced as was (at first sight, anyway) the liveforever poem. Zukofsky has employed catalog strategy again:

37   ROSES

Roses hardy as clover return
the wild no quirk-thorobred notched
5-petal evening-shining knit to the
pasture valley-scent *old teas damask*
pink *sweetbriar eglantine* white today
miniatures floribunda grandiflora tho new
restore purple-rose *Angel Face Handel* white
figures redoubled *climber* pink-edging invests

A poem about wild roses and old roses in a world taken over by successful hybrids? Memories of #1 Starglow are very dim (Zukofsky clearly admiring, there, the hybrid rose). But, as ever, the sympathetic text is to be found one step to the side—in a rosaceous rather than a rose poem, #12 Cinquefoil, which we looked at before, in part, for the Shakespeare it contains (see chap. 6). Zukofsky takes the cinquefoil's "wild rose" characteristics ("notched hearts rose / with the wild roses field / roadside") and works them into his combined evocation of *Rosa nitida* and *Rosa carolina* (the pasture rose) in #37 Roses: *"the wild . . . notched /* 5-petal evening-shining knit to the / *pasture* valley-scent." *Nitida* means "shining" and, according to Gray, the rose flowers "in evening with fragrance of Convallaria"; that is, lily-of-the-valley. Rosaceous cinquefoil is a meadow-flower, and when Zukofsky comes to start his roses poem, he not only begins with wild roses—he likens their persistence to another common meadowflower, clover. This links #37 Roses with its facing neighbor, #36 Clover, but also looks at #12 Cinquefoil's "assures bees roses." Thyme and clover are renowned bee plants (that fragrance); roses are also.

Scent leads the first five lines of #37 Roses: *Rosa nitida* with its evening fragrance; *Rosa carolina*, located by its common name in the same fields and meadows ("knit to the / *pasture* valley-scent"); and so on to the sweetly scented old-fashioned tea rose (*Rosa odorata*); then the damask rose (*Rosa damascena*, European source of attar of roses); and the sweetbriar (*Rosa eglanteria*, eglantine). And all of these so far named are not only fragrant but also pink—mostly rose-pink (though *Rosa odorata* may also come in white and yellow, and *Rosa damascena* may be red).

They are rose-colored roses; and so the poem's title takes on a second meaning; palette. 37 roses? Flowers, or hues, 37 Junes have passed since 1939, the year of the Zukofskys' marriage. This rose poem, composed 23–25 June 1976, takes its place in the sequence by virtue of the date Zukofsky noted their "new species" in bloom (he could as easily have used the later date of the wild roses and we would have a poem called #41 Roses). It looks as if the time-ordering principle can to some extent be arranged to fit circumstances, particularly when circumstances are going to bring roses to June, and progress in *80 Flowers* is nearing the number of years in an anniversary.

Returning to the roses, wild and hybrid, of the poem; their respective provenances map significantly. There are two native Americans (*nitida* and *carolina*), as well as an import from China (*odorata*), one from Asia Minor (*damascena*), and one from Europe (*eglanteria*) now commonly naturalized in the United States. Brought to the same ground by historical circumstance and Zukofsky's mustering of them, the roses cross and proliferate; pink bred "white today," then *"miniatures floribunda grandiflora"* (tiny, many, giant-size; a bunch of options, bunchily sounded). We already have some acquaintance with miniatures (the Fairy Rose, *Rosa minima chinensis,* in #1 Starglow); floribundas are a class of Polyantha hybrids with a tendency to recurrent flowering from the Chinese part of their ancestry; grandifloras are floribunda types crossed with hybrid teas to produce large-flowered, long-stemmed roses in few-flowered clusters.

These are all new terms for newly derived plants in the long history of the cultivated rose. The new names give us (and the Zukofskys?) roses called Angel Face ("purple-rose" in the poem) and Handel ("white"). Angel Face is a well-known floribunda and was an All-America Rose Selection of 1969: "The deep lavender color is enlivened by rose tints and is beautifully complemented by bronze-tinged deep green foliage. Ruffled, very double, fragrant blooms. Spreading plant."[2] A rosy purple rose. Handel is a large-flowered climber (*"grandiflora"?*) introduced in 1965; its blooms are slightly fragrant, semidouble, and clustering; in color they are "creamy pink, edged in reddish pink."[3] Zukofsky had noted that Handel is a "recurrent climber" (*80 Fl.* Drafts, p. 41), and in the poem this leads to other kinds of currency: "figures redoubled *climber* pink-edging invests." Contemporaneity and horticultural commerce. Did the "new species" recorded flowering in the Zukofskys' garden 22–26 May cost them dearly? If they were buying by names it is easy to see why a rose named Handel was planted at 306 East Broadway.

Zukofsky's sympathies do eventually come down with the once-blooming native and old-fashioned roses: "no quirk-thorobred" is a phrase he initialed "Z." (another horse) in the margin notes for the poem.

It recalls the sense of "fashion-fare airing" in #1 Starglow. Roses were entered on the Second Abbreviated List 2 June 1976, a few days before the anniversary of 8 June, which was celebrated once before with roses and "wed" thorns. This year a June poem gathers together May-flowering species roses and June-flowering wild varieties. "Hardy as clover," the wild roses return each year, and the anniversary is marked each year—by luck, by light, and this year by fragrance prefiguring the sweetness of honey, a product of unremitting industry. (A bee pictured with a sprig of thyme was a medieval device for double activity; in ancient Greece the scent of thyme was thought to be an energy restorer.)[4] But there is no fire in any of this until we turn the page and find:

38   PHLOX

Flux ablaze flog a new
wine look now's fast lamp-lighting
corymb high poop of ships
fires ring rose blood ruby
branching raise round ladders leaves
clasp full flame in sight
valerian purple papule *wild sweet*
william jack-pudding trumpets *jacob's ladder charity*

Much Greek fire/light here, beginning with *phlox* (flame, blaze). "Flux ablaze"—light's fluency? the kind of fire/light we most readily associate with *80 Flowers?* Hearing clustered liquids, doubled ə sounds, and an "x" giving way to its Greekish "z" buzz. But "flog a new / wine"? Let the continuation of "fl" and ə sounds guide us to more Greek, a phrase under the same entry in Liddell and Scott: *phlox oinou,* "the fiery strength of wine." Intoxicating fire. No sign of flowers except for the discovery that phlox took its name straight from the Greek flame—for color, perhaps also for bouquet, that most volatile (fleeting, fluent) of properties? This seems to be what Zukofsky is getting at, with the weight of previous thyme and fire figures behind his phrase about fiery wine.

If flames and wine-drinking suggest convivial light, what better foil for them than gathering darkness: "look now's fast lamp-lighting / corymb"? A bright cluster of flowers, lamplike; their lamplight derived via Gray, who says that phlox was the ancient name for *Lychnis,* another flamelike flower. And *lychnis* has a bright scarlet flower once used for garlands; but it may also be a precious stone that emits light, "probably the ruby," add Liddell and Scott. We make out this doubling in #38 Phlox as it moves toward fire and light, but also (jumping over a line or so) the red (lights) of "fires . . . rose . . . ruby." However, *lychnis* has a close dictionary neighbor (a likeness?) in *lychnos* (a portable light, a lamp), and this light seems a better phonetic match for "look now's" than the flower/ruby (reminded here of the *thýmos/thymós* coalescence that underlay "Heart us invisibly thyme time"). Indeed, another quick scan of Liddell and Scott's entry for *lychnos* turns up the phrase *peri lychnōn haphas,* which means "about lamp-lighting time, i.e. towards nightfall"—when lights blaze, wine flows, and a cluster of scarlet flowers might glow against the dark. Fragments of the Greek sounds survive in Zukofsky's second line ("look no ... fast"), wound about with the nominative form ("look now's") and the sense of the phrase as a whole: "look now's fast lamp-lighting."

On to "corymb high poop of ships." Phlox flowers are corymbic, but the dissociation of sense here is familiar enough to send us back to Liddell and Scott for more Greek. This time it proves to be meaning rather than sound—*korymbos* (from *koros,* "helmet," says the *Century*) is the uppermost point, end, or head, once used by Homer for the high-pointed sterns of ships (*Iliad* IX.241). High-pointed; "high poop." Do the ships at Troy connect in any way with the family Polemoniaceae (the phloxes), whose name is surmised by some authorities to derive from the Greek *polemos* (war)? Certainly a Trojan atmosphere could be drawn out of: "fires ring rose blood ruby."

That line, however, has an independent history in *80 Flowers* stemming from the thyme-ringed rosebush of the Epigraph and #1 Starglow and its literary analog in D'Israeli's rosy fire. What is new here is the "blood ruby," introduced via light-emitting Greek and the phlox's own coloration beneath that. Blood rubies come specifically designated—pigeon's blood ruby; beef blood ruby (*Century*)—why not (and more attractively): "rose blood ruby"? Rubies, after all, are the type of red (Latin *rubus*), whether synonymous with blood:

Paled pearls and rubies red as blood.
          (Shakespeare, "A Lover's Complaint," l.198)

Or a sign of (precious) health:

      You can behold such sights,
And keep the natural ruby of your cheeks,
When mine is blanch'd with fear.
          (*Mac.* III.iv.115)

Or inspiring stimulants:

Butler, fetch the ruby wine
Which with sudden greatness fills us.
          (Emerson, From Hafiz)

All three quotations are taken entire from the *Century*'s examples of usage, but it is the last that connects most forcibly with #38 Phlox, more so when we recall Zukofsky's admiration for that other line of Emerson-translated Hafiz: "See how the roses burn!"—and find that it too contributes to Hafiz's typical scheme of music, delight, passion, and feasting:

> "See how the roses burn!
>   Bring wine to quench the fire!
> Alas! the flames come up with us,
>   We perish with desire."[5]

Zukofsky quoted only the first line of this stanza in *Bottom* (p. 141), perhaps because he had just given Emerson's rendition of Hafiz's "Revelation":

> ". . . because of a drop of wine
> Is creation's heart,
> Wash with wine those eyes of thine—
> Nothing is hid . . ."

> *(Bottom, p. 141)*

"The fiery strength of wine" ("flog a new / wine"), in its sacred rather than profane aspect. As for flowers, another Emerson-Hafiz couplet runs: "The rose in the hour of gloaming / Flamed like a lamp hard-by." And Emerson himself wrote: "The rose of beauty burns," and "Like fiery honey sucked from roses"; and also: "In the ring of thy rose-lips, / My heart forgets to pray."[6] All of this adds up to a fair, if coincidental, parallel of "fires ring rose blood ruby." Light and vitality.

The same line begins the description proper of the phlox flower, a red variety; then "branching raise round ladders leaves / clasp" moves into description of the plant's structure, first its corymb of branching flowers (that cluster of course the rounded-out head, or high point, of the plant), then the lance-shaped opposite leaves, which climb their stems in pairs, producing the ladderlike effect typical of phloxes. We have to hear "round" in two ways; as the roundness of that head of flowers, but also (to make some kind of syntax in the line) as a contraction of "around." The phlox is raising its clustered flower heads *around* the laddered leaves, more precisely the ladders made by these clasping leaves. This construction gets rid of the problem of how to envisage "round ladders," which arises if the adjective cannot also be a preposition as we read forward in the line. The word "branching" also indicates the variety Zukofsky has in mind: *Phlox divaricata* ("strongly divergent; from the branching of the inflorescence"; Gray), known as Wild Sweet William or Blue Phlox. From red flames to blue, then? Or even purple?—because a second plant called Wild Sweet William is *Phlox maculata* ("spotted"; Gray), with pink or purple flowers and purple-spotted stems ("purple papule *wild sweet / william*"; Zukofsky). And if red, blue, and purple, why not more familial phlox color? Jacob's Ladder, or Charity, is a plant with clasping leaves and blue flowers; the botanical name is *Polemonium caeruleum*. Another popular name, Greek Valerian, suggests a reason for the plant's inclusion in the poem; herbalists mistook it for the valerian of the ancient Greeks (which had powerful medicinal virtues) and named it *Valeriana Graeca* (*Century*). Thus the plant has a Greco-Latin matrix of force—as the warlike *Polemonium,* or the supposed Greek strength of *Valeriana* (from Latin *valere,* "to be strong").

Valerian, William, Jacob, Charity—all proper names connected with the "full flame" of the phlox family (and doesn't a Jacob's ladder suggest angelic "trumpets" [line eight] not too far off? prompted by the sight of those long corolla-tubes opening salverlike in the genus *Phlox*). But what about "jack-pudding"? Another flower name? Not according to the *Century,* where Zukofsky found it (noting the dictionary's usages from Milton and John Gay; *80 Fl.* Drafts, p. 40[a]).[7] A *jack-pudding,* like a *Hanswurst* or a *Jean-potage,* is "a buffoon, a merry-andrew, being combinations of a characteristic national nickname with a characteristic national article of food" (*Century*). Hardly connected with phlox or *Polemonium* yet; the intermediate step is an inference from Henry James.

The novel this time is *Roderick Hudson,* and its leading lady is Christina Light. When Zukofsky made notes on the book April-May 1976, he copied out six passages, three of which were worked into the light-filled #38 Phlox. One was the sculptor Gloriani saying: "I've been carrying about in my head for years an idea for a creature as fine as a flower-stem and yet as full as a flame, but it has always stayed there for want of a tolerable model" (*Roderick Hudson,* p. 132). Another was Mrs Light saying of her daughter: "She never raised a finger for herself, she breathed nothing but perfumes, she walked, she slept upon flowers. She never was out of my sight, and from that day to this I've never said a nasty word to her" (*Roderick Hudson,* p. 169). Treated by Zukofsy (perceiving the mesh of images surrounding Christina) in a poem about fire, light, and fragrance, this comes out in line six of #38 Phlox as: "clasp full flame in sight."

With the James fitted to a logical purpose, Zukofsky went one step further with a third passage from the novel where Roderick meets Christina for the first time, and conversation turns to her great white poodle, Stenterello. Archetypically, Stenterello is the commedia dell'arte buffoon—an Italian jack-pudding. Zukofsky noted this when he first made the *Roderick Hudson* reference (*80 Fl.* Notes, p. 19); "jack-pudding," like "alula" in #22 Bayberry, was a word he had found in the *Century* at some earlier date, and James's Stenterello gave him an opportunity to use it. The exact use seems to have been suggested by the swirl of proper names in the final lines of #38 Phlox, plus the fact that other *Roderick Hudson* material was already there. Stenterello was written into the phlox poem as "jack-pudding," buffoon among the flowers—but we can also make out a nuance of the Italian, preserved by the adjacent "trumpets." This buffoon, Stenterello, is a "little Stentor," and in the *Iliad* (V.785) Stentor was the Greek herald whose voice was as loud as fifty men combined. Stentorian; trumpeting. More Greek underlay.

#38 Phlox has another parallel with #22 Bayberry in the matter of prefigurement. We remember that James made his first appearance in *80 Flowers* in the bayberry poem, months before the debut proper in #30 Violet and the poems that followed it. Similarly, a presentiment of Thomas Hardy is included, though quite by accident, in #38 Phlox. The poem was composed 26–27 June 1976; Zukofsky started his reading of Hardy's novels near the end of July, and in August he came across Mrs Worm and Mrs Smith on the subject of the latter's garden in a *A Pair of Blue Eyes* (p. 258):[8]

> "What's that long-favoured flower under the hedge?"
> "They? O, they are the horrid Jacob's ladders! Instead of praising 'em, I am mad wi' 'em for being so ready to grow where they are not wanted. They are very well in their way, but I do not care for things that neglect won't kill. Do what I will, dig, drag, scrap, pull, I get too many of 'em. I chop the roots: up they'll come, treble strong . . . When John wanted to use [the manure mixen, where the Jacob's ladders had been planted] about the garden, he said, 'Nation seize them Jacob's ladders of yours, Maria! They've eat the goodness out of every morsel of my manure, so that 'tis no better than sand itself!' Sure enough the hungry mortals had. 'Tis my belief that in the secret souls of 'em, Jacob's ladders are weeds, and not flowers at all, if the truth was known."

In the margin of his notes on this, Zukofsky wrote: "anticipates L.Z. F. #38."

"Weeds dress earth": Thomas Hardy and the *Flowers* of Fall 1976

It may be pure coincidence (but it may also be the result of some thought about emergent patterning) that the poems which introduce Hardy in *80 Flowers* are, at least to begin with, all about weeds. We left the sequence near the end of June as it turned, with the aid of the 1976 In Process Notes, to the flowers of late spring and early summer. Through July, Zukofsky composed #39 Dutch White Iris, #40 Snowflake (midpoint of *80 Flowers,* with an unprecedentedly irregular word count in four of its eight lines, perhaps to mark the fact), #41 Honeysuckle, #42 Marigold, and #43 Lilies.[9] All the liliaceous *Flowers* of this group include at least one six-word line, but #41 Honeysuckle, though its title flower is five-petaled, has two six-word lines—further indication of the midsequence mark? Three of the poems contain Greek transliteration as well as the usual botanical Latin plays; the same three (#40, #41, #43) incorporate fragments of James; and all five contain Shakespearean references.

Zukofsky completed #43 Lilies 25 July; at the same time he was making notes on *The Portrait of a Lady* (he had used his notes on *William Wetmore Story,* vol. 2, in the composition of the lilies poem). Four days later, the first Hardy note, from *Desperate Remedies,* appears in the *80 Flowers* Notes (p. 2 Condensed Notes), and from late July through August no poems are written as Zukofsky reads and makes notes on *Desperate Remedies* (1871), *A Pair of Blue Eyes* (1873), and *Far from the Madding Crowd* (1874), Hardy's first, third, and fourth published novels. (He had read the second, *Under the Greenwood Tree* [1872], in October 1971 according to an entry in the *"A" 22 & 23* Spiral, p. 60.) More systematically than with James, Zukofsky was taking on another novelist in the "dream paradise of old age"—and finding plenty of material for poetry. Like James, Hardy was no stranger to Zukofsky (except as a novelist), and we should remember the considerable influence Hardy exerted as a poet. Mention of his death occurs in a conversational aside in *"A"-1* (p. 3), where it marks the end of one era and the beginning of another (Zukofsky's). Nevertheless (new out of old), Zukofsky could write to Niedecker of his formative years: "Music guided as always—'run over lines' because of a resolution or uptake of cadence etc—wanted to get away from rhyme & write quantitative verse like Horace, Catullus, etc but never scholarly mastery of Latin meters—just what I thought English cd. sound like with Latin & Greek sound as exemplars—And via Hardy crazy about rhyme all the same, so I never missed a chance at interior (hidden rhyming) within lines, long carry over of one line into other stanzas" (LZ to LN, undated frag.; TxU).

The break in composition which took place as Zukofsky read Hardy was something of a summer recess after the exhausting pace of the previous months—four poems in June, four in May, three in April. When the writing of *80 Flowers* resumed 31 August with #44 Queen Anne's Lace, the trajectory of the sequence had altered slightly, for here (with Thomas Hardy) are three weeds (*hardy?*) followed by two recently planted flowers, one recently substituted flower, and a shrubby tree that is noted as a transition to "Gamut." After #50 Chokecherry, Zukofsky stopped again, this time for the five-month winter hiatus already noted (see chap. 1).

What is happening? Conjecturally, the 1976 In Process Notes have been used up; #43 Lilies is the last *Flower* in which preparatory material refers to an entry on the In Process records. When the sequence comes back, it is concerned with summertime roadside flowers, then with June- and September-planted flowers, then with slipperwort and chokecherry. Obviously the In Process Notes, in 1976, were a phenomenon of spring and its overflow into early summer; another kind of time is ordering the *Flowers* now.

Thomas Hardy marks the onset of this late summer—early fall order (as Henry James marked the 1976 spring ordering, as Shakespeare marked the 1975 spring). In view of the changes we have noticed, #44 Queen Anne's Lace, #45 Chicory, and #46 Dandelion seem to have been deliberately selected for what they can add to Zukofsky's "anticipation" of Hardy in #38 Phlox's weedy Jacob's ladder (was ever a garden flower "hardier," by Maria Smith's testimony?). Zukofsky was of course intending to use Hardy in *80 Flowers,* but it is a fairly safe bet that the "anticipation" showed him the direction to be taken. For once, time in the background reading for *80 Flowers* seems to have dictated time present's selection of flowers. And from a decision to use weeds as title flowers, it was an easy step to look around and find them in flower. Everywhere; "weeds dress earth" was Zukofsky's pun in #19 Wild Geranium. And considering how many "wildflowers" are technically weeds or weedy, nevertheless dressing the earth for delighted eyes, we may hear in Zukofsky's phrase an (unintentional?) echo of Gerard in the dedication of his *Herball:* "for if delight may provoke mens labor, what greater delight is there than to behold the earth apparelled with plants, as with a robe of embroidered worke, set with Orient pearls and garnished with great diversitie of rare and costly jewels?"[10]

The living-gem garden again; preciousness of the spectacle. And we recall gold, silver, quicksilver, bronze, platinum, and brass already in the *Flowers;* also icejewel, ebony, azure (lapis lazuli), cloth-of-gold, and ruby. Now in the Queen Anne's Lace poem comes a weed whose flower was used by courtiers of Queen Anne as substitute lace for their costumes-of-a-day. More pragmatically, *Daucus carota* is the ancestor of the garden carrot and a member of the Umbelliferae or parsley, carrot, and celery family. Zukofsky's poem (composed 31 August–5 September) swings between court and garden, rather as the weed is both flower and pest—rank, vital, successful, a hoyden:

#44   QUEEN ANNE'S LACE

Top-turfy gimp fiery oes eyes
light white flat lacy heads
centrums purple many uneven small
flowers each whorl umbel if
awry ladies songflawed wit pretty 's
well queen unwanted princess throws
horse prize wild carrot autumn
hurdle stands jackdaw-course carried her

Wild carrot was a pre-eighteenth-century name. The carroty foliage, "rather bristly, much-divided or compound leaves, the ultimate segments fern-like" (Taylor), is indeed "Top-turfy gimp"—green lace. The *Century*'s explanation of *gimp* starts off with an etymology concerning its descent from the French *guimpe* ("a nun's wimple, or lower part of the hood, gathered in folds about the neck"), but there is room to think that the word is better associated with *guipure,* a kind of corded lace. *Gimp* itself is: "A coarse thread used in some kinds of pillow-lace to form the edges or outlines of the design," or "A flat trimming made of silk, worsted, or other cord, usually stiffened by wire and more or less open in design, used for borders for curtains or furniture, trimming for women's gowns etc." As a verb, *gimp* means (again lacily?) to jag or denticulate (lace, in French, is *la dentelle*).

Green lace of carrot leaves. But is Zukofsky also playing on "carrot-top," which means not green at all but (carroty) orange, red, auburn— "Top-turfy gimp fiery"? If this is the case, the redhead lasts no longer than the turfy green as the line passes its implication of laciness into a quarter we were expecting: "Top-turfy gimp fiery oes eyes / light white flat lacy heads." Each little flower is an "eye," an "o" (*un oeil? des yeux?* eye rhymes and ear rhymes) in the flat-topped "head" of Queen Anne's Lace. The flowers are light white; they also light (up) the clusters, illuminate them. If the fire/lace/light connection sits somewhat uneasily, we may want to think about some nonbotanical underpinning—may have found it in the "Ember Eves" quotation of Francis Bacon, courtly if not of Anne's era. From *Of Masques and Triumphs,* as quoted in *Bottom* (p. 343): "Let the scenes abound with light, specially colored and varied . . . the colors that show best by candlelight are white, carnation, and a kind of sea-water green; and oes and spangs as they are of no great cost, so they are of most glory."

Bacon's white, red, and green are not exactly synonymous with Zukofsky's turf, carrot, and lace, but the flame-light illuminating them and beglittering the "oes and spangs" is definitely in #44 Queen Anne's Lace. When the *OED* adds that gimp trimming is sometimes covered with beads and spangles, Bacon is drawn closer to Zukofsky's poem. When we notice that one of the *OED*'s examples of usage is out of *Far from the Madding Crowd* ("The rowel of the spur had . . . wound itself among the gimp cords [of a lady's dress]"; *OED* ellipses and brackets), we can make a connection with the note on page 50 of the *80 Flowers* Drafts: "Hardy Gimp & notes 8/11." The notes of 11 August enter into the poem a few lines further on, but they concern *A Pair of Blue Eyes* and have nothing to do with gimp of any kind. Zukofsky, researching lace for the forty-fourth *Flower*, seems to have come across the *OED*'s *gimp* citation while his reading of *Far from the Madding Crowd* was fresh in mind (he was at chap. 31 by 30 August and still reading as he began composition of #44 Queen Anne's Lace the next day). Hardy's "gimp," a true gift of time present, was duly wound into the poem. The lady whose gimp trim was so entangled is Bathsheba Everdene, whose fortunes are prominent in this part of *80 Flowers*.

Oes and spangs, fire and light, spangled gimp, spurs and tangles, a progress through Bacon, the dictionary, and Thomas Hardy. But "fiery oes eyes / light" has yet another source, nowhere alluded to in the notes for the poem but discernible if we are looking out for other "oes" in Zukofsky. From the "living calendar":

> smiles ray *immaterial Nimbus* . . *Oes*
> sun-pinned to red threads—
>
> ("A"-23, p. 563)

These (sun-spangled) oes, so decorative, so festive (in Bacon's light), derive from *A Midsummer Night's Dream*, according to a margin note in the "A"-23 Spiral (p. 40) which pinpoints just the single word "*Oes*." The context is Lysander telling Hermia of his love for:

> Fair Helena, who more engilds the night
> Than all yon fiery oes and eyes of light.
>
> (*MND* III.ii.187)

Oes being orbs or circles (Neilson's gloss), "fiery oes eyes / light" is a composite metaphor, in its Shakespearean context, for stars. Queen Anne's Lace resembling, look at it, a galaxy in small; just that random star-cluster effect—"each whorl umbel if / awry." An umbel is the kind of inflorescence where flower stalks spread from a common center, their summits forming a level, convex, concave, or globose surface. The family Latin ("umbel if / awry") is feeding precisely into Zukofsky's description of the (starry) flower head (though he has appropriated "whorl" from

Taylor's "whorl of leaf-like bracts," which is situated below the flat-topped umbel). Similarly, he has modified Gray's "flowers white or whit-ish . . . the central one usually dark purple," to produce: "centrums pur-ple"; and he has mixed it with a description noted from a work given only as *Field Flowers:* "flowers small, uneven size" ("many uneven small / flowers").[11] The skewed umbel is the focusing shape of the poem—and its dark central flower has been a source of comment by herbalists and botanists alike, from Gybson's "lytell reed pryche," and Gerard's "middle most parte . . . a deep purple," to Lewis J. Clark's "single brown, purple, or pink variant . . . thought to represent a bull's-eye on which insects may 'zero-in' for a landing."[12] Early observers were also zeroing in on nature's device for facilitating reproductive action. Punctuation, which is a flight path for pollinating insects, has sparked poetic imagination as well as botanical explanation, for Zukofsky would scarcely have forgotten Wil-liams's poem:

QUEEN ANNE'S LACE

Her body is not so white as
anemone petals nor so smooth—nor
so remote a thing. It is a field
of the wild carrot taking
the field by force; the grass
does not raise above it.
Here is no question of whiteness,
white as can be, with a purple mole
at the center of each flower.
Each flower is a hand's span
of her whiteness. Wherever
his hand has lain there is
a tiny purple blemish. Each part
is a blossom under his touch
to which the fibres of her being
stem one by one, each to its end,
until the whole field is a
white desire, empty, a single stem,
a cluster, flower by flower,
a pious wish to whiteness gone over—
or nothing.[13]

Williams, too, never forgets the flower's luxuriance is that of a weed; his feel for the fact manifests itself in "her" whiteness (ambivalently "white as can be") and availability ("—nor / so remote a thing"). His wild carrot takes "the field by force"; it is (terminology playing into the poet's hands here) passion's force field—and so erotic sensibility is attributed to the weed's vitality. Zukofsky, having set up the wild carrot as lacy but rank ("umbel if / awry" must also refer to the flower's gimpy symmetry), now brings in grace and femininity, though somewhat ambivalently:

> awry ladies songflawed wit pretty 's
> well queen unwanted princess throws

Ladies awry; their pretty wit (all very well, but) "songflawed." Beneath "ladies" is *A Pair of Blue Eyes* (p. 174), Mrs Swancourt telling Stephen Knight in the conservatory of the rectory at Wendelstow (the essentials of this are copied into the *80 Flowers* Notes, p. 3 Condensed Notes): "But oleanders, though they are such bulky shrubs, are so very easily wounded as to be unprunable—giants with the sensitiveness of young ladies. O, here is Elfride!" And a pair of blue, sensitive eyes enters the scene; Elfride Swancourt is demonstrably pretty and has wit enough, though it is not obviously "songflawed."

"Songflawed wit" is an autonomous phrase in Zukofsky's notebook, though it has distinct allegiances to the words on either side of it in the poem; "awry ladies" leads the eye to "songflawed," and "wit" walks on to "pretty 's / well." The pivot, "songflawed wit," is an amalgam of earlier observations concerning two lyrics of Thomas Campion: "she sings and therefore knows," and "a much flawed pathos the wit" (*80 Fl.* Notes, p. 11).[14] This Campion and Williams's potent field of wild carrot together put us in mind of the first Campion song Zukofsky used in *80 Flowers:* "And would you see my Mistris face? / it is a flowrie garden place . . ." but also "It is a Meadow yet unshorne, / whome thousand flowers do adorne."[15] Fieldflower women, we note, have been around as long as garden beauties—or hothouse sensitives.

Finding Hardy again in #44 Queen Anne's Lace is no real surprise, though the balance of "gimp" 's antecedents against those of "ladies" is nice; Bathsheba Everdene against Elfride Swancourt. However, Campion arrives in the poem by a circuitous route, which also manages to implicate Hardy by a completely different provenance. Once again, the key to the poem's components is to be found in their progress through the Lists of flowers.

The first stop is an uncomplicated entry in the First List (p. v), which makes Queen Anne's Lace the sixty-first entry, with a parenthetic note to use lowercase. Perhaps Zukofsky was planning to team the plant with something else rather than make it a full-scale title flower; certainly in the First Abbreviated List, the same entry (its uppercase still intact) is hemmed in by potential substitutes: Chinese quince and shadbush. In the Second

Abbreviated List, the one Zukofsky was working out of when he wrote the forty-fourth *Flower*, Queen Anne's Lace seems to have vanished from the alphabetical sequences (Shadbush has appeared a few places further on). But closer scrutiny reveals the wild carrot now linked with Moss Campion, which is bracketed with an adjacent (alphabetical) entry, Oleander. A margin note points out the Hardy reference concerning Mrs Swancourt and her oleanders, those unprunable giants of ladylike sensitivity.

Moss campion was a plant Zukofsky saw in Bellagio in November 1972; he had seen oleanders in Paget, Bermuda, the previous January; the Hardy (but not hardy) oleanders apparently prompted him to utilize the two entries in conjunction with the hardy weed, Queen Anne's Lace—which had been a title option once and could be so again if time present dictated.

We have already surmised that Zukofsky was planning a weed-flower debut for Hardy; here, then (with a little ingenuity), was a potential grouping for such a poem: Queen Anne's Lace would resume its title role; Oleander would bring in Hardy and a taste of the exotic (oleanders in Wessex; Zukofsky in Bermuda); and Oleander, by alphabetical affinity and another geographical contingency of 1972, would introduce Moss Campion, which Zukofsky was probably even then intending to use as a cipher for Thomas Campion in *80 Flowers*. A tender Hardy for a hardy weed; why not the musical Campion for a mossy campion? Add to this that Zukofsky had planned from an early stage to use Oleander in conjunction with John Gerard because the shrub is a dogbane, and dogbane is the family of *Vinca minor*, the periwinkle. #10 Charlock Per Winkle alluded to Gerard's "lacca"-colored red whortle in context of a quotation which centered on the idea that "weeds dress earth." In W. H. Hudson's paraphrase: "[Gerard] is forever fresh and full of variety and agreeable surprises, like Nature herself, who maketh her plants not for meat and medicine only, but some to be esteemed for beauty alone . . . there is not seldom a lustre in his words that serves to remind one of the red whortle he greatly admired, which is full of juice so orient and beautiful a colour to limn withal that Indian lacca cannot be compared thereunto."[16] Zukofsky, reading over Gerard/Hudson/Woodward again (and he had noted "meat and medicine" as well as the incomparable "Indian lacca"), was moved to remember a piece of antic Shakespeare, Holofernes in full voice:

> Of piercing a hogshead! a good lustre of conceit in a turf of earth; fire enough for a flint, pearl enough for a swine; 'tis pretty, it is well. (*LLL* IV.ii.88)[17]

Was a conceit's luster ("wit pretty 's / well") the root and direct source of "turfy" in line one of #44 Queen Anne's Lace? and flint to the spark that also brought in "fiery oes eyes / light"? All of these resting ultimately on the orient shine of another Elizabethan's language? Gerard's presence in #10 Charlock Per Winkle was convoluted; his role in #44 Queen Anne's Lace is complex to the point of tenuousness.

Or invisibility. The reappearance of Moss Campion and Oleander in the Third Abbreviated List, side by side and complete with notes on Hardy and Gerard ("for lacca cannot compare vs. uses as spice and medicine," 3rd Abb. List, p. 3), hints at the reason we never actually make out an oleander or a campion in #44 Queen Anne's Lace in the way, for example, that Jacob's ladder is plain in #38 Phlox or snowdrop is manifest in #27 Crocus. Zukofsky is reserving an opportunity to work oleander and moss campion in a poem *as flowers*. As literary motifs and punning allusions, they can make an appearance now (there is an occasion); as a pairing of 1972 geographical incidents and a pairing of 1975–76 alphabetical sequence, they can make that appearance together. But their rights to a title flower are evidently not complete because it is not time present that throws them (as flowers, not literature or language) into Zukofsky's path. He was projecting Oleander into "Gamut" soon after completing the Third Abbreviated List; it may have found a place there (it was in the preliminary lists for the new book; "Gamut" Notes, p. 8). It did not emerge as a title poem in *80 Flowers;* nor did Moss Campion.

So much for the components of #44 Queen Anne's Lace—their sum visible only in single words, and visible only if we have firm grasp of a considerable number of antecedents. Which among them is providing context for lines six to eight?

> well queen unwanted princess throws
> horse prize wild carrot autumn
> hurdle stands jackdaw-course carried her

Is Anne the "unwanted princess" who ascended a throne in the absence of male heirs? Or is it Helena, unwanted and then (unwonted) object of Lysander's desires: "O, let me kiss / This princess of pure white, this seal of bliss!"—having said a moment before: "That pure congealed white, high Taurus' snow, / Fann'd with the eastern wind, turns to crow" (*MND* III.ii.141–44). Crow? jackdaw? The same scene has Bottom's colleagues, in Puck's report, flying from him like "russet-pated choughs" (*MND* III.ii.21). And there is a "princess" with "ladies" (but perfectly level-headed) in *Love's Labour's Lost;* not, however, a "horse prize." Nothing covered so far accounts for the odd picture these lines present; Zukofsky's notes are silent; the lines apparently write themselves. Their most likely source is some part of Zukofsky's work which suggested a link with the concerns of #44 Queen Anne's Lace.

When Zukofsky came to start #45 Chicory, 9 September 1976 (completing it 16 September), the Hardy in the poem came from same-day notes on *Far from the Madding Crowd*—some tea for the coffeeweed, and the most audible Latin to date in *80 Flowers*. Because #45 Chicory and #46 Dandelion are undoubtedly a pair, we shall look at them together. They were worked in close succession, one's overflow was caught by the other, the same novel informs both, and they are both flowers of the daisy family, a memorable blue and a sunny yellow:

#45   CHICORY

Seacorps hint imbues blues *blue*
sailors blueweed blue dandelion monksbeard
low backward-bent leaves outdo lettuce
thinned bluetooth'd rays impassioned keek
core and mires steed *coffeeweed*
chicóryĕ succory 's bitter tea 's palaver
horse-seas bow kiss fill'em on
concur it ur hoar-eye memento

#46   DANDELION

No blanch witloof handbound dry
heart to racks a comb
lion's-teeth thistlehead *golden-hair earth nail*
flower-clock *up-by-pace* dandle lion won't
dwarf lamb closes night season
its long year *dumble-dor* bumbles
cure wine *blowball* black fall's-berry
madding sun mixen seeded rebus

Again directed by various names for each plant, Zukofsky is looking at appearances and use (dressing the earth; succoring humankind), as if anxious to move away from the pejorative tag "weed." #45 Chicory leads off with a two-line translingual rhapsody in blue: "Seacorps hint" (one of its best-known popular names is blue sailors) "imbues blues" (the blues? or simply the graduated shades of blue between young and old flowers?) *"blue / sailors blueweed blue dandelion"* (all blue names for chicory, the last of them tightening the bond Zukofsky is establishing between the blue daisy and the yellow) *"monksbeard"* (translation of *Barbe-de-capuchin,* "suggesting that the stems were as tough as the beard of a Capuchin monk," according to Minnie Watson Kamm, from whom Zukofsky is taking much of the plant's historical context).[18] And so *Cichorium intybus,* the chicory, is imbued by its English aliases with a characterizing chroma, and the "Seacorps hint" proceeds, in the poem, to color them in with that insistent blue. (Each touch another flower on the plant? as each name widens our perception of it? sea-blue; sailor-blue; blueweed; a dandelion look-alike.)

At *"monksbeard,"* focus shifts from flowers to tough stems and then to runcinate lower leaves: "low backward-bent leaves" is Zukofsky's version of Gray's gloss on *runcinate*—"Sharply incised, with the segments directed backwards." These leaves, surprisingly, "outdo lettuce"; for chicory was once a widely cultivated salad green. Kamm (pp. 224–25) reports that its monk-tough stem was never used: "but always cut away at the crown, and tender root leaves allowed to develop. These basal leaves, grown to large size, were bleached to avoid any trace of strong bitter flavor and to enhance the tenderness, and were popular as 'sallet-furniture' in the heyday of herbs."

Back to the inflorescence: "thinned bluetooth'd rays." Toothed by analogy to the dandelion? ray-flowers of each strap-shaped and thin? chicory more thinly radiated? (the class of Compositae to which chicory and dandelion belong has only ray-flowers; as does the lettuce, which is also a member). But "thinned" and "bluetooth'd," by their common suffix, announce business with the remainder of the line ("impassioned"), a rapid slide into transliteration of some sort:

> thinned bluetooth'd rays impassioned keek
> core and mires steed *coffeeweed*

Do the blue rays "keek" (a Scottish peek) "impassioned" from the central "core" of their flower? What about that bogged-down horse? But plunge in among Latin salad lovers and things become less opaque. First, Horace (prompted by Lewis and Short's citation for *cichorium*), *Carmina* I.31.16, which Zukofsky checked, finding: "me pascunt olivae, / me cichorea levesque malvae." The Loeb editor translates (Zukofsky noting it, *80 Fl. Drafts*, p. 52): "My fare is the olive, the endive, and the wholesome mallow."[19] This is part of the "Poet's Prayer" for homely contentment offered by simple foods; and in Zukofsky we hear "impassioned" ("me pascunt"; feeding it) "keek / core and" ("cichorea"). There are more fragments of the Horatian song scattered over these lines; from a preliminary transliteration Zukofsky made, something near-illegible to do with an impassioned kick and a horsey tooth (or is it hoof?), we gather that "bluetooth'd" has connections with "steed" and also with "horse-seas." Horsies? Horace's? Or whitecaps (white horses) for an impassioned and long-sighted poet? "The horse sees he is repeating / All known cultures" (*"A"*-12, p. 175); and shortly thereafter:

At last he finds
What he has never
Learned or seen:
Man a shape like
The satyrion root,
Chicory high
When the sun is in the sky
Its root a bird
After seven years.
If you know the answer
Keep still,
If you don't, try
Find out.

("*A*"-12, pp. 179–80)

The significance of the seven-year bird-root of chicory is not easily discoverable; that it counts in #45 Chicory we may infer from that extraordinary line of *seven* words (the only one in *80 Flowers*): "chicóryĕ succory 's bitter tea 's palaver." We do know that reference to chicory in combination with the satyrion root was intended early in the genesis of #45 Chicory, for in the First List (p. ii) Clover was to have been combined with Chicory plus: "(satyrion root compositae f.) atonement's coffee." An odd note because botanically satyrion is a species of orchis.

What stands out clearly is the horse's association with chicory. He sees, and now hears, not only Horace but also Horace's Greek underlay; Latin *cichorea,* heard as "keek / core and," from *kichorion* or *kichore.* And in the same moment the horse hears Virgil abutting at "and mires," which is part-translation, part-transliteration of a phrase from *Georgics* I.120: "et amaris intiba fibris" ("the bitter-fibred succory"). Kamm mentions the Virgil reference, and Lewis and Short pinpoint it under *intibus,* the Latin half of chicory's binomial; Zukofsky consulted his Virgil and found chicory or succory numbered among the besetting problems of husbandry.

Thus on the one hand we have Horace acclaiming *cichorium,* while on the other Virgil damns the weed *intibus,* and this is not simply a matter of Virgil being unaware that his plant could be made tender and edible. Kamm says (p. 225): "Chicory and the plant we call endive were confused in classic [*sic*] literature, both being used in salads." Looking to Taylor for clarification, we find that the other salad herb, closely related, is *Cichorium endivia.* When Horace writes "cichorea" we cannot say for certain whether his salad is chicory leaves or endive; Virgil's "intiba" sounds more like chicory (bitter fibers), but when Ovid has Baucis and Philemon set out olives and "cornel-cherries," then "intibaque et radix et lactis massa coacti / ovaque" for the visiting gods, translatory opinion gives us *endives* and radishes, cream cheese and eggs.[20] Again, a combination of Kamm plus Lewis and Short led Zukofsky to the *Metamorphoses.* The old man and woman who entertained the gods humbly ("bow kiss"), and proceeded to "fill'em on" honest fare, appear in place of their salad at line seven of the poem. They were also turned into trees at the same instant after a lifetime of conjugal contentment, by their own wish "dying" together into new life; "An Unearthing" is perhaps Zukofsky's version of that dread of parting they felt.

Chicory is both weed and salad herb; but also, updated, it is associated with the horse's beloved drink, the stimulant to which he works (impassioned or mired): "steed *coffeeweed*" (earlier, still with the salad, Kamm quoted Lucilius's praise of the endive, "stretching out with feet like horses" [p. 225]; those wide-spreading roots). The bitter principle of chicory root is a better coffee substitute (according to Kamm) than acorns, *horse*-chestnuts, turnips, or rye ("chicórye̬"?), all of which were tried when the tax on coffee first rose exorbitantly in England. Chicory does not of course contain the caffeine stimulant (it is a bitter tease), and this is the cue for Hardy's entrance in the poem, taken from Zukofsky's reading of *Far from the Madding Crowd.*

Bathsheba Everdene takes tea at a sheep fair, saying (Zukofsky quoting): "there's nothing so refreshing as a cup of tea."[21] To which Zukofsky adds: "B's palaver forever loves" (*80 Fl.* Notes, p. 3 Condensed Notes). And the line as it emerges in #45 Chicory, "chicórye̬ succory 's bitter tea 's palaver," winds up the context of Bathsheba's remark; she is a bitter tease to Boldwood, who has procured this cup of tea for her refreshment. Earlier in the novel her faculty for "palaver" has been evident, at times authorially remarked on as symptomatic of her moral equivocation: "There is a loquacity that tells nothing, which was Bathsheba's" (*Madding Crowd,* p. 167). (The *Century,* noting the word's provenance from the Portuguese *palavra,* meaning "talk, speech, word," surmises that it was picked up by English sailors on the West Coast of Africa. Blue sailor talk?) At the same time, this "bitter tea 's palaver" (possessive, but also contraction) is a palliative to Boldwood: it "succors" him to be near Bathsheba.

From *cichorium* came English *cikhorie,* afterward changed to *succory* by suggestion of medicinal properties: "Succory pounded and put under the left nipple eases the heart-ache" (*OED* quot. 1736). Succor, *au secours;* help for the sound of a (French) heart; and all through #45 Chicory there is an audible insistence on the "cor" sound out of the Latin *Cichorium:* "Seacorps" (more French influence); "core" ("Give me that man / That is not passion's slave, and I will wear him / In my heart's core, ay, in my heart of heart," *Ham* III.ii.76) (endive is the tied-up core of *Cichorium endivia*); then a double beat: "chicórye̊ succory 's" (long-"e" sounds also asserting themselves), "bitter tea 's palaver / horse-seas" (and we realize that we have been hearing as many "e"s as "cor"s all along, again because of the Latin *Cichorium*— "Sea," *"weed," "beard,"* "leaves," "keek," "steed," *"coffeeweed").*

There is one last, agreeable heart sound in *"concur,"* which brings us to the barely concealed Latin—Horace's, Hardy's, and now Zukofsky's—of line eight: *"concur it ur hoar-eye memento."* There is little difficulty in reconstructing "concurritur horae momento," a well-known Horatian quotation, its high profile in #45 Chicory a parallel for Hardy's use of it as the title of chapter 53 in *Far from the Madding Crowd.* The Loeb translation reads: "There is the battle clash, and in a moment of time [comes speedy death or joyous victory]"; and in chapter 53 Boldwood shoots Troy.[22] Zukofsky, working at the transliteration: "concurrence— hours memento"; or: "moment's horae time lapses quickly" (*80 Fl.* Notes, pp. 3–4 Condensed Notes). And a few days later: "lion time lapses quickly"; then: "concur? hurry memento" (*80 Fl.* Drafts, p. 52). The eventual form of the transliteration encompasses most of its prototypes, literally a running together of agreement (*"concur it"*), hours turned into old eyes (*"hoar-eye"*) (Baucis and Philemon? the old horse still watching?), a moment becoming a memory (*"memento"*). Is *"ur"* a primitive (the earliest, oldest)? a hoary moment of time? a (French) hour? When he was listing the contents of Theophrastus's entries on chicory (*80 Fl.* Drafts, p. 52), Zukofsky added a margin comment: "(like thyme)." Whether this is intended to apply to the whole listing or whether it is actually arrowed to: "grows again when the top of the stem is cut off i.e. the flower" is not quite clear. But if Zukofsky has in mind a similarity to thyme, then the Horace in #45 Chicory is less inscrutable. Thyme/time— "like thyme"—perhaps "lion time," with #46 Dandelion already in the wings? a (blue-)dandelion clock? Chicory does not blow hours like the dandelion seedhead, but certain of its mechanisms throughout the daylight hours make it a more reliable timepiece; the blue flowers are open from 7:00 A.M. to 12:00 M., after which they close up for the day. Bees apparently know this and visit the plant only between the hours of 5:00 A.M. and 12:00 M.[23]

Time and those efficient timekeepers, the bees, reappear in #46 Dandelion; but first in that poem stands an extension of endive, the salad heart that outdoes lettuce ("No blanch witloof handbound dry / heart"), followed by a string of dandelion names, which push thought toward history and usage ("lion's-teeth thistlehead *golden-hair earth nail* / flower-clock *up-by-pace* dandle lion"). Witloof chicory (Dutch for "white leaf") is the winter salad green also known as French endive; its large roots, according to the *Century*, are as good a coffee substitute as ordinary chicory. *Witloof* was a word Zukofsky found in Taylor, but it takes its place in the *Flowers* as part of recent plays he has made on "wit" in #40 Snowflake, #42 Marigold, and #44 Queen Anne's Lace. When the plant witloof appeared in the course of chicory-related research, it became an obvious candidate for inclusion in the chicory/dandelion nexus.

#46 Dandelion starts with a firm negative: "No blanch witloof hand-bound dry / heart." To obtain its crisp white leaf, endive must be kept away from light—in direct contrast to the sun-loving and sun-colored title flower. A dandelion is "No blanch witloof," though its leaves do "sometimes have to be boiled (blanched) to remove any residual bitterness." This is Taylor, who continues: "Many good growers [of endive] prefer to tie up each plant by hand . . . the real difficulty . . . is that if drops of water are left, or subsequently get into the heart of the plant, it will probably rot before it blanches." Witloof chicory is therefore an exceptionally good subject for the cellar garden; it can be forced, from roots brought in from the summer garden, and the plants come up creamy white, in the characteristic closed shape that lessens the danger of heart-rotting moisture getting in. Does the "handbound dry / heart" of endive then make its way "to racks" in produce stores? Hard to say, because at this point *Taraxacum officinale,* the common dandelion, is making an entrance; but *officinale* does mean, literally, "of the shops."

Taraxacum comes to botanical Latin by way of Persian antecedents, *tarasacon, tarkhashqūn, tarashqūq*—all names for wild succory or wild endive, the last of them also (possibly) for dandelion. So family ties insist on holding dandelion and chicory close. But "to racks a comb / lion's-teeth thistlehead *golden-hair earth nail*"? One may comb a head of hair whether golden or downy. And *dents-de-lion* is French fancy for the denticulated leaves (as "blue-tooth'd" was Zukofsky making a daisy-family analogy in #45 Chicory), whereas Golden Hair and Earth Nail, the poetic and the prosaic, are old Chinese names alluding to dandelion flower and root respectively (Kamm, p. 227). But when the *80 Flowers* Drafts (p. 53) give us: "lion's tooth [z: teeth]," we may suspect that Zukofsky is thinking not only of the dandelion but also of the problems he was experiencing with his own teeth.[24] The horse in #45 Chicory was "blue-tooth'd," and if Zukofsky was looking in the *OED* for chicory/succory information he would have come across this quotation of 1550: "The ioyce of succorye put into the eare or nostrel that is on the contrary syde to the grefe taketh away vtterly the tooth ache." In #46 Dandelion, the horse gives way to the Zukofsky lion, "racked" by the pain his dental work is causing. And *Taraxacum,* according to Taylor, derives from the Greek for disorder, disquiet; the plant's medicinal effectiveness against such things. The *Century* says *taraxis* means "trouble," from *tarassein* (to trouble, confound, or confuse). Condensately, "to racks"?

The dandelion's concerns with time are about to be made clear: "flower-clock *up-by-pace* dandle lion won't / dwarf lamb closes night season / its long year." Theophrastus's dandelion (*apapē*) is transformed— *"up-by-pace"*—by aural suggestion into the smart clip of a ticking clock ("Tick-Tack Uhr" does the same thing in *"A"*-12, pp. 228, 232). The dandelion flower is indeed a clock, opening between 5:00 and 6:00 A.M. and closing between 8:00 and 9:00 P.M., so punctual throughout its extended flowering season that Linnaeus included it in his celebrated floral clock (*Century*). Also in the *Century* is a dandling lion: "Sporting the lion ramp'd, and in his paw / Dandled the kid" (Milton, *Paradise Lost* iv.344). Eden was on Zukofsky's mind too, to judge by the note among the overflow from *"A"*-23 which is the source of the lion/lamb motif: "~~the plover~~ the crocodile's dentist, the wrasse, the goatfish (goldfish?) barber, the lion & the lamb may yet lie down together" (*80 Fl.* Notes, p. 3).[25] Does "dandle lion won't / dwarf lamb" imply a kind of paradisal equality which breeds affection, not just tolerance? The gentled lion puts us in mind of Zukofsky's characterization of himself and his family as gentle people; more specifically his assertions that certain insults over the years have been borne "with as much gentleness" as could be mustered (LZ to CC, 10 May 1968, 20 December 1971; SFU).

The same line has a botanical coloring though. When Dandelion appeared on the Second Abbreviated List after being teamed with Deutzia in the First List, then (in the First Abbreviated List) relegated to the various Compositae Zukofsky intended to work with Daisy, it was accompanied by a voice (Celia's?) saying (25 July 1976): "you can't dwarf a d—." Was this a weed puller's reaction to the news (from Gray, and the *Century*) that a related genus, *Krigia,* is known as dwarf dandelion? Gray was also the source of other dandelion names in the latter part of the poem, for instance *"dumble-dor,"* a Newfoundland term acknowledging the flower's status as a bee plant. *"Dumble dor* bumbles," as Zukofsky puts it, having looked up the *Century* and found that the same word, before it crossed the Atlantic, signified a bumblebee, from *dumble,* "stupid, very dull" (but also, imitatively, that buzzing mumble) (which might have been a dull dozing slumber?). Then there is *"blowball"* (Gray: blowballs), an obvious epithet contributing another kind of timekeeping to the "flower-clock." And "fall's-berry"—there is a false dandelion (*Pyrrhopappus;* "flame-colored pappus"); there is also a fall dandelion, *Leontodon autumnalis* ("lion's tooth of autumn"). When the wind or any other breath has airlifted dandelion pappus, each with its achene, off the seeded flower head, the enlarged ovary left behind looks like a "black autumn berry," according to Zukofsky's notes; "black fall's-berry" (false berry) in the poem. As for "cure wine," Kamm tells us (p. 227) that the dandelion is "widely favored to-day especially by Italians who visit the suburban areas in spring with trowel and basket for both foliage and flowers, the latter used principally in wine."

The final line of #46 Dandelion is a conflation of Zukofsky's excerpts from Hardy, with a flavoring of Chaucer:

madding sun mixen seeded rebus

The novel is easily spotted (*Far from the Madding Crowd*), but we shall try for some dandelion sense before taking on literary sources. A "madding sun" might be a memory of summer just past (this is a September poem), sun emblematic of the dandelion flowers "mixing" their gold with the blowball seedheads; "seeded rebus," those seeded things. Or, remembering that the madder family (Rubiaceae) is also the coffee family, "madding sun" (dandelion coffee again?) may be mixing it up with other seeded things, "rebus" linking with "berry" in the line above to produce a notion of (late summer's) blackberries, genus *Rubus* (not related to Rubiaceae).

Changing the angle once more, a "seeded rebus" may be a dandelion. A *rebus* is "a puzzle or riddle consisting of words or phrases represented by figures or pictures of objects whose names resemble in sound those words or phrases or the syllables of which they are composed" (*Century*). If words were represented "by things" (Latin, *rebus*) in #46 Dandelion, would you use a sartorial (dandy) lion? the contents (*les dents*) of its jaws? have the lion fondling (dandling) a kid, or a lamb? Obviously the form of *80 Flowers* precludes an entirely literal rebus, but just the same Zukofsky has been working rebuslike elements into his poem—"dandle lion" but also (hear the French), translatively, "lion's-teeth." The images evoked by these phrases substitute for the pictures of a conventional rebus.

Turning to line eight's literary antecedents, we discover Bathsheba Everdene's shearers in the madding sun of June, speculating on the probability of their mistress marrying Boldwood. A piece of rustic wisdom is elicited, " 'Well, better wed over the mixen than over the moor,' said Laban Tall, turning his sheep" (*Madding Crowd*, p. 171). Zukofsky, reading this 27 August, remembered from his notes of two weeks earlier the "mixen" on which Mrs Smith's invasive Jacob's ladders throve—and this time he looked up the archaic word in the *Century* and found that it was indeed related to his own preliminary rendering, "midden" (*80 Fl.*

Notes, p. 3 Condensed Notes). However, the dung hill gets into #46 Dandelion as "mixen" not "midden," perhaps because Zukofsky is interested in its passage through time. Hardy, in the novel, had been eulogizing the harmony of the shearers with their surroundings: "Five decades hardly modified the cut of a gaiter, the embroidery of a smock-frock, by the breadth of a hair. Ten generations failed to alter the turn of a single phrase" (*Madding Crowd*, p. 166). So Laban Tall's comment might easily have been already three hundred years old when reported to our ears; perhaps even older, because Zukofsky has chosen to include with the Wessex mixen elements of a Chaucerian usage he found in the *Century*. From *The Parson's Tale:* "Hooly writ nat have been defouled, na moore than the sonne that shyneth on the mixne." Chaucer, plus Hardy's acute ear for the authentic rusticity; Zukofsky's reading followed by a little research (did he notice "moore . . . mixne" echoing Tall's "mixen . . . moor"?), and there was "mixen" mixed into line eight of #46 Dandelion.[26] In 1975, *"compt"* had prevailed over the modern term, "account," in the composition of #22 Bayberry; in 1976, writing #32 Lilac, "bustles" wins over the older "tournures"—yet "mixen" is kept in place of the modern "midden" in the dandelion poem. "Madding sun *midden* seeded rebus" would have contributed another "d"-geminate to the line, but the trail followed through *Far from the Madding Crowd, A Pair of Blue Eyes,* and *The Parson's Tale,* plus the incremental "s"-drive of the line, decided in favor of the authentic word.

Mixens or moors, Bathsheba marries Troy not Boldwood, and it is he who tries to give her his natural father's watch, engraved in the back "Cedit amor rebus"; "Love yields to circumstance," as he translates for her—"Love ceded things [or better] ceded love's rebus," as Zukofsky puts it (*80 Fl.* Notes, p. 3 Condensed Notes). The "seeded rebus" that eventually appeared in the tail of #46 Dandelion touches both seeded things (dandelion clocks) and ceded things (Bathsheba, yielding?). As dandelion sense though, both homonyms have a direct (but silent) source in *"A"*-9. In the first half of the movement, remarking upon time's effect on labor and value:

> Unsorted, indrawn, but things that time ceded
> To life exceeded—not change, the mind pieces
> The expanse of labor in us when it ceases.
>
> (*"A"*-9, p. 107)

But it is the changes played by the second half of *"A"*-9 ("Virtue flames value, merriment love," p. 109) which really confirm the link between #46 Dandelion's "seeded rebus" and the watch's engraved motto:

> :impeded
> Not by things seeded from which strength increases;
> Remindful of its deaths as loves decreases;
> Happy with the dandelion unsorted,
> Well-sorted by imagination speeded
> To it, exceeded night lasts, the sun pieces
> Its necessary nature, error ceases
>
> ("A"-9, pp. 109–10)

Whatever implications the motto holds in the novel, in the poem it has been picked up for its rhymes with "A"-9's time-ceded things and love-seeded things. The watch itself, instigator of the parallel Zukofsky found between his own work and the Latin supplied by Hardy, is of course another timekeeper for #46 Dandelion. The position in the poem of the reference to its motto, and the very audible Latin of that motto and its concern with time (and, in some guise, love), puts us in mind of the final line of #44 Queen Anne's Lace: *"concur it ur hoar-eye memento"* (the rushing together of time's hours conspires to kill the would-be watch-giver). This parallel in turn brings to mind the "gimp" of #44 Queen Anne's Lace, the image of Bathsheba prophetically tangled up with Troy by her petticoats, Hardy (heavy-handed?) saying: "The rowel of the spur had so wound itself among the gimp cords in those few moments, that separation was likely to be a matter of time" (*Madding Crowd*, p. 185). Indeed. And the time of three *Flowers*.

Zukofsky went back to the garden for #47 Dahlia and #48 Impatiens; the dahlias, planted 1 June 1976, budded 12 August; and impatiens was planted 24 September. Both are beyond the scope of the 1976 In Process Notes. #47 Dahlia works more Hardy (*A Pair of Blue Eyes* and *Far from the Madding Crowd*) and some James (*The Portrait of a Lady*) into the same poem in a manner no different from the poems that include one or other of the novelists. #48 Impatiens inwreathes fragments of four sonnets by Cecco Angioliere in Rossetti's translation, *Dante and His Circle,* the work also associated with the thyme-circled rose of the Epigraph (see chap. 3).

In #49 Slipperwort, Hardy and James again appear together but our chief concern is the *Flower*'s provenance. Slipperwort, *Calceolaria crenatifolia* of the figworts, is not to be found in any of the Lists or Notes for *80 Flowers;* it appears in forty-ninth place on the strength (we have to assume) of some intervention by time present. Oddly enough, that intervention appears purely literary—a noted occurrence of calceolaria in *Desperate Remedies.* Zukofsky himself comments on the irregularity of considering the slipperwort for inclusion in *80 Flowers:*

7/29/76 Hardy *Desperate Remedies* p. 62 calceolaria
slipperwort . .
include in 80 Flowers w. after Chaucer Book of Duchesse
[l. 26 spirit of quickness
seen in a book, in Pt. J. tho slipperwort is not native
to Pt. J. nor seen here accdg to my plan to
include only those, but this wd be the one exception[27]
(*80 Fl*. Notes, p. 2 Condensed Notes)

For reasons perhaps clearer if we could make sense of the juxtapositions in this note, Zukofsky goes ahead and includes the slipperwort—as a title flower.

When he selects chokecherry, a late-flowering shrubby tree, as the subject of the fiftieth poem, his motives are clear enough. There is another tree in #49 Slipperwort, the paulownia, which had made an appearance once before on account of its name (*"A"*-13, p. 290). Both paulownia and what Zukofsky identified 1 June 1975 as chokecherry (First List, p. vii) are typically roadside escapes; *Prunus virginiana* blooms in Port Jefferson late September–October and Zukofsky began #50 Chokecherry 16 October, finishing it 22 October 1976. The Spiral copy of #49 Slipperwort (composed 7–14 October) had been annotated: "10/14 P: back from Motorola, Chicago," and the Spiral copy of #50 Chokecherry is dedicated: "for Paul's 33 birthday." Two "tree" poems composed with Paul in mind give added point to a note in the preparatory material for #50 Chokecherry that the poem is an anticipation of "Gamut," the book that is Paul's, dedicated to a count of years.

After the fiftieth *Flower* Zukofsky breaks off for almost six months; when he resumes with #51 Snowdrop, the date is 11 April 1977. The hiatus spans the distance between two of the most significant anniversaries in Zukofsky's calendar. In the *Flowers*, though, the poems for Paul and Reb Pinchos are placed quietly facing each other.

8

The Doublings
of Spring 1977

Wintering Over, 1976–1977

The desultory nature of the *Flower* selections of September-October 1976 suggests Zukofsky was ready to stop working on *80 Flowers* when the growing season ended. He made the cessation on his own terms, as the dates and dedication of #50 Chokecherry show, then he turned to the business of wintering over. The activities of this period have already been briefly outlined (see chap. 1): the making of the Third Abbreviated List of 80 Flowers (27 October), the start of serious note-taking for "Gamut" (28 October), and (conjecturally) the indexing of "A," which could have been fitted into the time left over from these ongoing but not all-absorbing tasks.

Looking a little closer at the four-page Third List and its twenty-two-page appendage in conjunction with events in the "Gamut" chronology, we recognize a familiar pattern of dovetailing. "Gamut"'s genesis has quite as much to do with *80 Flowers'* resolution as the beginnings of the *Flowers* themselves had to do with the end of "A." On page 5 of the Third List there is another condensation of unused notes on John Adams, Chaucer, Virgil, and Horace. On page 6 new material is entered—passages from Hardy's fifth and eighth novels, *The Hand of Ethelberta* (1876) and *A Laodicean* (1881), and notes from Karl von Frisch's *Animal Architecture* concerning apiculture. On page 7, probably as a result of recent rereadings of Virgil's comments on a bee flower identified as *Aster atticus,* there is an entry out of Taylor on *Chrysopsis* or golden aster. The date is 11 December 1976. The same date in "Gamut"'s alphabetical list from Taylor gives *Cladrastis lutea* (Kentucky yellow-wood); Zukofsky had started 28 October at *Acer rubrum* (the red maple) and had stopped 17 November at *Carludovica palmata* (Panama-hat plant), apparently to concentrate on the *Ethelberta* and *Laodicean* material for *80 Flowers.* On 7 December he took up the "Gamut" list again at *Cedrus* (cedar) and by 11 December was, as we have noted, at *Cladrastis.* For three days thereafter he made notes in tandem for "Gamut" and *80 Flowers'* Third List; *Crataegus* and *Cupressus* for the "Trees," *Cyclamen* for the *Flowers*. From 14 December to 15 January there is a complete break in both sets of notes. When they resume, both 16 January 1977, their mutual concern is "Gamut" 's proto-epigraph, written on that date, and entitled "The Overworld."

This poem, clearly a draft, is nine lines long (one stanza of six lines, one of three lines), and, though these vary in length from three words to six words, the overall word count comes out to forty. A most *Flower*-like beginning for a book of trees. How Zukofsky envisaged the poem as keynote to his new project is anyone's guess—but the starting point must be the first part of the book's title, "Gamut" (range). Discovering "The Overworld" 's associations with "90 Trees" looks considerably more difficult, as is reconciling its nine lines with the projected form of five lines of five words per line described in the *80 Flowers* Schema. Then there is the matter of tone. "The Overworld" sounds like the Zukofsky of an earlier period (say *"A"*-11 or *"A"*-12); it lacks the severely compressed syntax of later work and there is not a transliteration to be heard. The manner of its making is very reminiscent of *"A"*-12; the proto-epigraph is pure assemblage from Zukofsky's reading—this time Hardy's verse-drama *The Dynasts* (1904). From its "After Scene" (entitled "The Overworld"), where various spirits and choruses convene to comment on the action just passed, Zukofsky takes material from the opening speech of the Spirit of the Years (italic type indicates the editings that make up, in order, the assemblage):

> Thus doth the Great Foresightless mechanize
> In blank entrancement now as evermore
> Its *ceaseless artistries in Circumstance*
> *Of curious stuff and braid,* as just forthshown.
>   Yet but one flimsy riband of Its web
> Have we here watched in weaving—web Enorm,
> Whose *furthest hem and selvage* may extend
> To where the roars and plashings of the *flames*
> *Of earth-invisible suns* swell noisily,
> And onwards into ghastly gulfs of sky,
> Where hideous presences churn through the dark—
> Monsters of *magnitude without a shape,*
> Hanging amid deep wells of nothingness.[1]
> (The Dynasts III.521)

The incidence of Zukofsky's capitalizations in the proto-epigraph is explained; his poem duplicates Hardy's styling throughout. Its sixth line is drawn from the first semichorus of the Pities, as they address the implacable Spirit of the Years:

> To thee whose eye all Nature owns,
> *Who hurlest Dynasts from their thrones,*
> And liftest those of low estate
> We sing, with Her men consecrate!
>
> (The Dynasts III.522)

Hardy's footnote on line two of this is: "καθεῖλε ΔΥΝΆΣΤΑΣ 'απὸ θρόνων—Magnificat," acknowledging his own appropriation of the sense of the first clause of Luke 1:52, which the King James Version translates: "He hath put down the mighty from their seats, and exalted them of low degree." Zukofsky takes the Greek for line seven of his assemblage poem. The semichorus of the Years goes on to describe their presiding Spirit:

> *O Loveless, Hateless!*—past the sense
> Of kindly eyed benevolence,
> To what tune danceth this Immense?
>
> (The Dynasts III.524)

However, the play's final chorus (Years, Pities, and Spirits) offers vestigial relief from this rather pitiless cosmogeny:

> But—a stirring thrills the air
> Like to sounds of joyance there
> > That the rages
> > Of the ages
> Shall be cancelled, and deliverance offered from the
> > darts that were
> Consciousness the Will informing, *till It fashion all*
> > *things fair!*
>
> (The Dynasts III.525)

Zukofsky's same-day comments in the Third List (p. 7) on the *Dynasts* assemblage clarify his intentions for it: "use parts of my condensation in *80 Flowers?* also in Gamut: trees ninety 5's *perhaps* as *epigraph.*" The "poem" as it stands in the "Gamut" Notes is condensation, possibly to be used as epigraph, not ruling out some appearance in *80 Flowers* ("Gamut" has not yet received its final title). All of this bears on later additions to the piece—Zukofsky had also noted beside the composition date that it was potentially an epigraph, but this was later crossed out. An arrowed instruction of 21 March 1977 to condense the whole thing suggests that had it found a place in "Gamut" as an epigraph, alterations would have fitted it to comply with the 5 × 5 format. An additional instruction to try the Greek again suggests that further condensing would have included some transliteration—which is what happened when Zukofsky used the assemblage in #54 Windflower. The balance of "The Overworld"'s history belongs to a discussion of that *Flower* (see below).

Meanwhile, beginning 20 January 1977, the lists from Taylor were resumed in tandem and entries were made almost daily in both sets of notes through to April and "Z." Both start again at "E" (Edelweiss; Elaeagnus), omitting all of Taylor's "D" section; because there are no pages missing in this part of either set, we must assume that the move is deliberate. Perhaps the *Dynasts* poem, with its insistently uppercase ΔΥΝΆΣΤΑΣ, filled in for the missing "D" flora.

We turn to the Third List of 80 Flowers and the matter of its working. The original (four-page) Third List was simply a mustering of the thirty unused options from the Second List after the completion of #50 Chokecherry (even their Second List numeration was retained). Zukofsky must have felt limited by this selection, and he found a solution in the reading and note-taking being done for "Gamut"; he simply began adding flowers to the *Flowers* material while making up the "Trees" list. By April, a new *Flowers* reservoir had been added to the old one, and for the third year in a row the spring garden was ready to order the actual sequence of the *Flowers*.

For 1977, however, the Zukofskys had taken particular trouble over what would appear in their garden; they had planted, 4 October 1976, an extensive selection of spring bulbs ordered from the Breck's catalog of that year.[2] Zukofsky recorded the planting of "Breck's Dutch Bulbs" on page 4 of the Third List, together with the note: "1977 as they flower." Familiar shorthand. None of the bulbs was further identified, but when Zukofsky reached Tulip in the extended Third List he asterisked the entry heavily and added:

> Use Breck
> Hollands planted Fall 76? but cf Flwr #26
> & stress garden type (Darwin etc) vs "species" derived
> from wild breeding true NB Tulip
> dropper T 1234
>
> (3rd Abb. List, p. 22)

Whether the Zukofskys had had tulips in their garden in the spring of 1976 when #26 Tulip was composed is not determinable; but they were planning to have them for the following spring, and Zukofsky seems to have been contemplating a second tulip poem. It did not eventuate;

however, "two-lip dropper bred true" is the final phrase of #68 Telephus Sedum (see chap. 5), and the tulips are recorded as being in flower "after about June 10" (1977 In Process Notes, p. 1).

Tulips were planted, then, early in October 1976. The other Breck bulbs were revealed in flowering order by the 1977 In Process Notes, which began 27 March (Zukofsky was still occupied with his Taylor lists) with an unexpected candidate—the snowdrop, which had failed to flower the previous spring. Next up, 3 April, were Grecian windflower and grape-hyacinth, followed by hyacinth, 11 April. The sequence of the *Flowers* written after that date is: #51 Snowdrop, #52 Snow-Wreath, #53 Grecian Windflower, #54 Windflower, #55 Grape-Hyacinth, and #56 Hyacinth. The basis of the spring chronology is intact—but what are we to make of the "extras" (#52 Snow-Wreath, #54 Windflower), which turn that chronology into a neat pattern of doubles?

#51 Snowdrop and #52 Snow-Wreath

The configuration of *80 Flowers* after 11 April 1977 is shaped by at least three forces. The first is the fall 1976 bulb planting, which ensured an early garden start the following spring and provided Zukofsky with another set of potential candidates. The second is the Third Abbreviated List in its two parts, the thirty leftovers (among them Anemone and Hyacinth, the latter encompassing Grape-Hyacinth) plus the new Taylor listings (Snow-Wreath included here, plus Tulip). The third is the In Process Notes, which start as soon as spring begins bringing up the early bulbs. We could wonder if the sequence of blossomings recorded there—snowdrop, Grecian windflower, grape-hyacinth, hyacinth—suggested in its third and fourth elements a doubling Zukofsky thought to extend to the others. Grecian windflower, which he decided was not an anemone despite its name, was easily paired with the "real" Windflower already on the Third List (p. 1). Similarly, snowdrop (the sleeper of 1976) found a title-flower mate in the Third List (p. 18) among a group of snow-named plants entered there 25 March, just two days before the recalcitrant snowdrop flowered in Port Jefferson.

The innovation here is that Zukofsky chose to double his poems instead of working similar flowers together; for example, grape-hyacinth could have been included in a hyacinth poem (as originally intended). It seems to have been the spring's unearthing of one kind of hyacinth straight after the other (3 April, 11 April) which prompted Zukofsky to plan separate though closely connected poems. And because he could not have planned the hyacinth pair much before 11 April, it is likely that the date itself inspired the three doublings. This is (as yet) conjecture, but certainly the six poems form a distinct group in *80 Flowers,* largely but not entirely garden-determined, signaling the onset of spring 1977 rather as the entrances of Shakespeare and Henry James marked previous spring groups in the sequence. Beginning with #51 Snowdrop and #52 Snow-Wreath, I want to discuss two of these pairs in some detail for the different contributions they make to *80 Flowers* at the beginning of its final stretch of composition.

On reading #51 Snowdrop and #52 Snow-Wreath, we are increasingly convinced that their extraordinary form has to do with the new start. We recall that the midpoint of *80 Flowers,* also a poem with distinctive features to mark its place, was #40 Snowflake, another snow-named spring flower. It is remembered, twice, in the present pair:

#51   SNOWDROP

Snow names a wreath *snowdrop*
2-year-sleep look-on tie bulb Oh
say earthleaf lagnappe midwinter huddle
futural *snowflake* aft *snowdrift* sweet
alisoun not madness kneevalleys harp
snowtrillium woodland dwarf-white *snowpoppy* east
moss starry chickweed *snow-in-summer snow-on-the-mountain*
snowberry bears white-fruit *snow-wreath* nine

#52   SNOW-WREATH

From solitary flowerstalk some fingers
fragrance look down ridge-back enamel
leaves *snowdrop* impetal seagreen unseen
months *snowflake* unplanted *snowdrift* sweet
alyssum self-risen *snowtrillium* new valleys
east *snowpoppy snow-in-summer* starry grasswort
prairie *snow-on-the-mountain* wilding seacoast
snowberry-drupe snow-wreath earth-rounds bees' rose

Nine italicized "Snow names" in each; the same names in the same order. #51 Snowdrop starts out with snow-wreath, or at least a snow-named wreath; #52 Snow-Wreath begins with three lines of snowdrop description. Both end talking about the wreath. The other seven snow-flowers take what space they can for description by name, attributes, or garden history. At the exact center of each poem, running over the line break, is the same flower though in different spellings—"sweet / alisoun," "sweet / alyssum." The key to this patterning is to be found in the Notes column of the snowdrop entry in the In Process record:

Planted 1975 none '76
~~notes p. 18 3/25/77~~
Breck illust. ~~Theophrastus.~~
Double canzone 1)the Nine
      2)snowreath

(In Process Notes, p. 1)

The idea is elaborated near the end of the combined notes for #51 Snowdrop and #52 Snow-Wreath: "[w. double canzone after "A"-9 ending *snowreath* (rose f.)" (*80 Fl.* Drafts, p. 60). The abbreviation "w." means "work"; the imperative mood. So the nine snow-names of March-April 1977 reflect the Nine informing but invisible genii of the *Flowers'* Schema and Epigraph; and beyond that, formally, the intricacies of "A"-9. In each strophe of the second half of Zukofsky's virtuoso double canzone, the half that sets up its presiding value on Love, is a flower: sweet alyssum ("that not-madness"), the rose, the dandelion, jewelweed (*Impatiens*), the hyacinth, and, reiterated in the coda, sweet alyssum. All of these figure in *80 Flowers,* and, whether by coincidence or design, they pattern this part of the sequence—#46 Dandelion, #49 Impatiens, sweet alyssum in #51 Snowdrop and #52 Snow-Wreath, then #56 Hyacinth. Sweet alyssum is also the center of this grouping, and the rose of "A"-9, Second Half, is supplied by the rosaceous snow-wreath. The Second Half of "A"-9 marks a major turning point in "A"; it was written 1948–50, ten years after the First Half, and in the interim marriage and the birth of Paul had altered Zukofsky's outlook on many things. Most notably it had cemented the conjunction of poetry with personal happiness. Lyricism, which appears from time to time in "A"-1 through "A"-9, First Half, becomes a thoroughly dominant mode in the remainder of the lifework, and with it comes a change in Zukofsky's line, which begins a long road to the purely quantitative measure of "A" 22 & 23 and *80 Flowers.*[3]

In what sense, though, do two eight-line poems make a "double canzone"? It seems that, like everything else that goes into *80 Flowers,* a canzone may be condensed even when it is doubled. The salient feature of the form is repeat and variation—an intricate rhyme scheme intricately worked so that a listener hears sets of sounds returning as different semantic or syntactic units (ear hears repeat, brain registers variation). Zukofsky, with his catalog of snow-names conveniently at hand and a numerological motif to restate (the Nine) which also complements the source of his projected canzone, set out to compose a poem that lays the sound of "snow" nine times upon air and ear. As it does so, it lays down whiteness, lightness (brightness) at each touch of sound upon meaning—and each time there is a trailer flower that spells variation—nine entities, presented to the ear first as nine repetitions. This is the fascination underlying any list of compounds; at a very simple level, the mathematics of Zukofsky's latest "canzones" assert that $1 + 1 = 3$—an abundantly generative principle for poems designed to lead off a spring sequence.

But if birth, it is also the anniversary of death—and we are perhaps seeing part of the reason for Zukofsky's insistent use of the snow-wreath. Its wreathery is intended to weave in springtime anniversary of death as well as a nine-flower garland; both intentions are obliquely stated in the 11 April preparations for #51 Snowdrop:

Snow names a wreath *snowdrop snowflake*
snowdrift, snow-in-summer snowpoppy
snowtrillium snow-on-the-mountain snowberry
snowreath; snowdrop, after over two years
(defective sentence, defection, failure, wasting)
blossoms

(80 Fl. Drafts, p. 58)

Here, intact, is line one of the poem; in the tying of particular history to textual accident is the germ of lines two to three. Zukofsky, thinking of the Theophrastian snowdrop he had already made use of in #27 Crocus ("look o / into" sounding an inverted *to leukoïon, Enquiry* VII.xiii.9), reread or remembered the Greek and also an editorial comment about it in Theophrastus: the snowdrop reference does indeed occur in a defective sentence because the text is corrupt. As a nod to textual and horticultural dereliction, but also in recognition of the latter's eventual winning out, Zukofsky works in (from the defective sentence) *leukoïon* and immediately follows it with a partial rendering of *ta bolbōdē* from the preceding clause of the same sentence. The result looks like this:

2-year-sleep look-on tie bulb Oh
say

But why not "bulb Oh / day"? The change of suffix may have taken place because of a sudden switch from Greek into Latin for the sake of a semantic detail. *Ta bolbodes* means "bulb-like, bulb-shaped" (Liddell and Scott); the Loeb Theophrastus translates the first half of the sentence in question as: "There are also several kinds of plants of the same class as purse-tassels," because its index gives *ho bolbos* as "purse-tassel." Liddell and Scott, however, explain the word as "Latin *bulbus,* a certain bulbous root that grew wild in Greece and was much prized." Zukofsky, listening for description of the class rather than specific plant, took his cue from this, found *bulbosus, -a, -um* (bulbous) an entry or so away from *bulbus* in Lewis and Short; he found also *bulbosa, -us, -um* ("bearing bulbs") in Taylor. In a Greekish kind of Latin or a Latinate kind of Greek, "look-on tie bulb Oh / say" says what Theophrastus obviously meant, that snowdrop is a bulb-bearing plant.

As for transliterative sense, "2-year-sleep look-on tie bulb Oh / say earthleaf lagnappe midwinter huddle" has something to say about the long "nap" the Zukofskys' laggard snowdrop bulbs took. When the snowdrop did appear in 1977 it produced only "one nodding bell" and "2–3 basal leaves lagniappe for next warm Dec-Jan" (*80 Fl.* Drafts, p. 58). Leaves, not flowers, are the midwinter gift Zukofsky anticipates from the snowdrops; according to the *Century,* a *lagnappe* is a small complimentary item accompanying a purchase, Creole adaptation of the Spanish *la ñapa* (gift), to which we are then referred. But the *Century*'s cross-reference fails to appear between *nap* and *Napaean* (pertaining to nymphs of dells and glens, from a Greek adjective descriptive of wooded vales). What with napping and woodland vales, we might just discern the habit and habitat of the snowdrop; its disappearing trick is contagious, even in the pages of a dictionary.

To return to Zukofsky's preliminary snow-flower list from which the rest of #51 Snowdrop was evolved. Its first components, snowdrop and snowflake are obvious choices in obvious positions—current title flower and fortieth title flower, each with an appearance in the book already. Third is snowdrift, so (drop, flake, drift) snow forms fall musically upon the ear. Then snowtrillium and snowpoppy—(snow-)whiteness modifying a flower name in each case. Followed by snow-in-summer and snow-on-the-mountain, hyphenated metaphors for the scatter of snow and, incidentally, remnants of Zukofsky's original alphabetical listing. Then snowberry, brought into the present list from an entry two days later in the Third List under its Latin name, *Symphoricarpos albus.* Finally, joining the end of the garland with its beginning, is snow-wreath.

The wreathing of this snow garland after the poem's initial account of the title flower involves a familiar skeining of translation, transliteration, and garden history: "futural *snowflake*" (not up yet, April 1977; did not appear until May in 1976), "aft *snowdrift*"—*flake* coming after *drift* alphabetically, though not horticulturally (snowflake is the earlier of the two) (snowflakes also precede snowdrifts in the meteorological sense). Zukofsky is after euphony to lead further with his latest flower:

futural *snowflake* aft *snowdrift* sweet
alisoun not madness kneevalleys harp

The procession of "f," "t," and "ft" sounds wound about with long vowels and liquids lifts us effortlessly to the central, sane pivot of the song. Snowdrift is another name for sweet alyssum, and Zukofsky has chosen to extend the slow drift of his line by settling for an alternative spelling, "alisoun" ("alison" is the more usual variant), which gives more open vowels in slower measure than "alyssum" would. The medieval spelling draws out the name even further and cannot help but recall for us the late-thirteenth/early-fourteenth-century lyric "Alisoun," which Zukofsky printed in *A Test of Poetry* (pp. 61–62), its refrain a perfect exemplar of mellifluousness:

> From alle wymmen mi love is lent
> Ant lyht on Alysoun.

Lobularia maritima, sweet alyssum's Latin name, is similarly euphonious but, instead of transliterating that, Zukofsky settled again for translation of "Alyssum," which comes from the Greek *a*-privative and *lyssa* (rage, madness). Plants of the genus *Alyssum* were supposed to cure madness; *Alyssum* and *Lobularia* are both Crucifers, and *Lobularia maritima,* a bee plant looking like an *Alyssum* and once included in that very genus, added a honey scent to the sweetness of sanity. In *"A"*-9, sweet alyssum had suggested itself to Zukofsky as a metamorphosis of the drift of stars:

> Light is
> The night isolated by stars (poled mentors)
> Blossom eyelet enters pealing with such changes
> As sweet alyssum, that not-madness, (ranges
> In itself, there tho acting without right) is—
> Whose sight is rays, "I shall go; the frequenters
> That search our centers, love; Elysium exchanges
> No desires; its thought loves what hope estranges"[4]
>
> *("A"-9, pp. 108–9)*

Elysian calm out of star-drift, also snowdrift. The center of #51 Snowdrop is sweet and still by several provenances.

So to "kneevalleys harp / *snowtrillium* woodland dwarf-white"; where, leaving the coast (*maritima*), one may walk woodland valleys knee-deep in spring flowers. Except that snowtrillium is "dwarf-white," and "kneevalleys," suggestive of deep spring growth, conceals a further account of its color; the Latin is *Trillium nivale,* and the species name means "snowy." There is a distinct possibility that "kneevalleys," which sounds out *nivalis* as well as *nivale,* is harking back to (harping on?) the title flower. Snowdrop, as we know already from #27 Crocus, is *Galanthus nivalis,* a snowy milkflower. There are two trilliums present in #51 Snowdrop, *Trillium nivale* ("kneevalleys") and *Trillium cernuum* ("harp"). The latter, known as nodding trillium (*cernuum* is a Latin nod), ground lily, or Jew's-harp, grows up to eighteen inches in height (knee-high) and has white or pinkish flowers. Is this a walk among trilliums and snowdrops? The snowdrops are present only in a sounded suffix (*nivalis*)—as usual half-vanished, lagnappe of surrounding woods and vales.

Then: *"snowpoppy* east / moss starry chickweed *snow-in-summer snow-on-the-mountain."* *Eomecon chionantha* is a white, spring-blooming poppy; the genus name is Greek for "eastern poppy," in reference to its Chinese origin (Taylor), and the species name means "snow-flower." *Cerastium tomentosum* is a species of chickweed belonging to the Pink family and growing in large patches; in June it indeed resembles snow in summer, may be described as "starry chickweed"—if stars can be spilt milk, why not drifts of snow? Another species, *Cerastium arvense,* is called field chickweed or starry grasswort. Snow-on-the-mountain is a spurge, *Euphorbia marginata;* showy white bracts against the deep green of its lower leaves (the upper leaves are white-margined) suggest snow patches on a summer mountain, at once a parallel with *Cerastium tomentosum* in its flowering season and a contrast to it; solid mass against starry drift.

What of "moss"? Does it belong with *"snowpoppy* east" or "starry chickweed *snow-in-summer snow-on-the-mountain"*? There is a note, "(w. *moss muscus*)," between Zukofsky's entries on snow-on-the-mountain and snowpoppy (*80 Fl.* Drafts, p. 59), which does nothing further to explain what the word is doing at the beginning of line seven. Moss campion, musical accompaniment for "starry chickweed"? moss, music, muse; "the Nine"? The moss remains mysterious; "musically" it contributes another consonantal geminate that adds to the prevailing sibilance of both snow poems. "Moss starry" is as fine a snow/flower image as anything the popular names in the poem have supplied; once again the celestial territory of *"A"*-9's "not-madness" is approximated.

"Snowberry bears white-fruit"; it does, they are. The phrase is a rearrangement of *Symphoricarpos albus,* Greco-Latin for "white clustered-together fruit." Snowberry bears berries, but snow buries berries. The homonym "bury" could be the reason *Symphoricarpos albus* is positioned alongside *Neviusa alabamensis,* the snow-wreath; a light allusion to the funereal buried in the white inwreathing. Snowberry is a honeysuckle (*"bees visit it,"* Zukofsky comments; *80 Fl.* Drafts, p. 39),

and snow-wreath is a rose; more of that sweet "not-madness." The shrub with feathery white masses of petalless flowers (all stamens) completes the wreath and quietly voices its function: *"snow-wreath* nine"; that is, *snow-wreath* wreathes th' nine.

Zukofsky finished #51 Snowdrop 1 May 1977; its composition had taken him three weeks. By contrast, #52 Snow-Wreath was written in three days, 4–6 May, without any further notes. The doubling of the 1977 "canzone" apparently did not present the problems Zukofsky had faced in making the canzone on economics speak Love's value to an identical rhyme scheme. Once the strategy of essentializing canzone form as nine snow-names had been arrived at (each repeat with its variation) and the sequencing of those "rhymes" according to their associations had been carried out, doubling the form was a matter of varying the material between the rhymes. Variation included changes of syntactic attachment and the introduction of new information about each snow-named plant, but, because Zukofsky seems to have been intent on doubling as multiplication (rather than inverse or mirror image), #52 Snow-Wreath was relatively simple to assemble.

As for the implications of the doubling, it is reasonable to suppose that Zukofsky was deliberately providing by poetic means what had been beyond the powers of his single-blossomed snowdrop. There is a (slightly disconsolate?) note in the preparatory material for #51 Snowdrop which concerns the title flower itself: "single flowering not richly *doubled* Galanthus = milk + flower" (*80 Fl.* Drafts, p. 58). The Zukofskys had watched one plant produce its solitary blossom (of single form) after a two-year wait; snowdrops are typically, commonly profuse, often in a double-flowered form. Even the binomial doubles up its epithets—*Galanthus nivalis,* milky snowy white. In #51 Snowdrop, poetry had stepped in and supplied eight snowy analogs for the solitary flower; they in turn evoked midwinter flakes and drifts, springtime valleys of white flowers, summer stars and mountains, autumnal clusters of white berries—all wound in white profusion by the encircling snow-wreath. None of this exactly doubled the snowdrop, but its duplication in a second snow-flower poem did.

#52 Snow-Wreath starts out with three-and-one-fifth lines about *Galanthus nivalis* (so did #51 Snowdrop), appearance and scent rather than the wait for its unearthing:

From solitary flowerstalk some fingers
fragrance look down ridge-back enamel
leaves *snowdrop* impetal seagreen unseen
months

Is it the device of linked "f" sounds carried over from #51 Snowdrop ("futural *snowflake* aft *snowdrift*") which produces "fingers" at the end of line one? noun or verb? singular, plural, or (silent) possessive? looking back at the flowerstalk or running on to the fragrance its flower produces? "After 2 years dormant blossom awakes . . . unfingered," reads the opening note about the flower on page 59 of the Drafts. Perhaps, "unfingered" by anxious gardeners, the snowdrop put out its flowerstalk (finger-high), and a blossom with a fingerful of scent unfolded above the ridged shiny blue-green basal leaves. The flower itself "impetals" tiny spots of green and thus we "see green" on its inner segments. Then:

> *snowflake* unplanted *snowdrift* sweet
> alyssum self-risen *snowtrillium* new valleys

Was the Zukofskys' snowflake a self-planted flower (by contrast to the looked-for snowdrop), or is sweet alyssum a flower they have yet to plant (though it struck root long ago in Louis's work)? Like "fingers," "unplanted" extends its options in both directions. And if the snowdrift is "unplanted" (by gardeners) perhaps it could be described as "self-risen"? The beat of "alýssum" steps percussively on to shape (and claim) "selfrísen"—though botanically, "sélf-risen" is a more likely description of "*snówtrillium,*" the woodland flower. Do we allow ("not-madness") the snowdrift to inform line five simply on the basis of a name, alyssum, center stage and trailing "i" sounds, "l" sounds, and sibilants?

> alýssum self-rísen *snowtríllium* new válleys

This fits "new valleys" as the transliteration of *nivális,* but it quite removes emphasis from one of the nine snow rhymes of the poem (snowtríllium rather than snówtrillium). Voicing the line again, we could be guided instead by consonantal endings and the pauses (or run-ons) they imply: "*snówdrift* swéet / alýssum sélf-risen *snówtrillium* new valleys." This reinstates the rhyme (difficult to ignore the ninefold insistence of those italics) and gives back the trillium's self-rising at the cost of distancing "alyssum" slightly from "self-risen" and the "zn"/"sn"-"ym"/"ny" connectives that follow it. At the same time, aural memory of the strong "alýssum" is going to persist across the miniature caesura that follows it.

The poem continues: "east *snowpoppy*" (for #51 Snowdrop's "*snowpoppy* east") "*snow-in-summer* starry grasswort" (*Cerastium arvense* certainly present now) "prairie *snow-on-the-mountain* wilding seacoast" (*Euphorbia marginata* is a prairie plant now widely cultivated and spreading to waste places as far as the Atlantic seaboard; Gray). That "seacoast" may remind us of snow-in-summer, which will grow in pure sand, and of *Lobularia maritima,* the pervasive snowdrift. Finally:

snowberry-drupe snow-wreath earth-rounds bees' rose

The fruit of *Symphoricarpos albus* is indeed a drupe (pulpy flesh surrounding a hard "stone" in which the seed lies), though drupes are typically single-seeded (peach, plum, cherry, olive), whereas snowberry has two hard seed-stones. Gray calls them nutlets. The clustered white berries weigh down their slender leafless branches in late fall; *"snowberry-drupe"* may be describing that graceful arc as well as the weight that makes it. *"Snow-wreath* earth-rounds"—a partial inversing of sounds and a duplication of their spondaic beat—suggests the circular and cyclic aspects of garland and anniversary, which "bees' rose" lightens (as they fly up?) into the feathery whiteness of the flower itself. We must also remember, rising with the wild roses of #12 Cinquefoil, "minting white-thyme assures bees roses," and realize that #52 Snow-Wreath's title flower associates the double canzone with the whole matter of sweet rosy fire and thyme. How this sits with sweet alyssum's Elysian aspect is not clear, but, because the two are bee plants and important to Zukofsky's present scheme, we have to take account of the line in *"A"*-9's coda which runs (and Love is speaking): "Sweet alyssum sometimes is not of time"—though (Zukofsky might add in 1977) it will always be thymelike in its bee-attracting qualities. Thymelike, thymely, timely. When, as sweet "not-madness," it takes a cosmological leap into Elysium (the Greek derives from "I shall go," as Barry Ahearn observes),[5] or a step to the double center of canzones that (doubly) remember the death of Reb Pinchos and celebrate the onset of spring—then in all probability we are looking at another of Zukofsky's liveforever flowers, which are not so much time*less* as not *altogether* of time, for they always seem to have one or two terrestrial roots.

#53 Grecian Windflower and #54 Windflower

The snowdrop was probably not a Breck bulb (though Zukofsky referred to the firm's catalog for an illustration of the flower), but the Grecian windflower that came up 3 April 1977 certainly was. Much to the Zukofskys' chagrin, the bulb was not a garden success, and the poem about it spends a lot of time recording the disappointment:

#53   GRECIAN WINDFLOWER

Peer re foot own his
story as no grecian or
anemone *dutch bulb* starves promises
die anthers carry off fill

us sparse scent choose which
true name red-pink-purple rays yellowed
green discs keen ens seas
betrayed sold neglected ponent anemone

There was first of all the matter of determining what the flower was (Breck's catalog does not identify its garden varieties by the Latin of their original stock).[6] Zukofsky decided that what they had planted was neither Greek nor an anemone; does "Peer re foot own his / story" have the poet examining both bulb and dictionary for clues to its identity? After all, we—or he—had to "look down" the snowdrop's ridgeback leaves, and the snowdrop itself "looked on" for two seasons before it blossomed. Looking to identify a bulb, what does one do but peer at its roots ("re foot"), literal and etymological, to establish its "own his / story." Zukofsky concluded that his *"dutch bulb"* was a pink and therefore a member of the family that includes *Dianthus caryophyllus,* the sweet-scented carnation or clove pink, as well as the unfragrant *Dianthus barbatus* (called bunch pink or, more oddly, sweet william), and the faintly fragrant *Dianthus chinensis,* the China or Indian pink. The "sparse scent" of the Zukofskys' flower led them to identify it ("choose which / true name") as the last of these, which according to Taylor grows from twelve to eighteen inches high and produces red, white, or lilac flowers about an inch wide, "solitary or in sparse clusters." What appeared, on stems no more than six inches high ("stunted," Zukofsky commented, *80 Fl.* Drafts, p. 62, "prob. under-nourished before arrival") were flowers with pink, red, or purple rays and greenish-yellow central disks, which soon vanished—"sold short," Zukofsky noted, enjoying the pun; "starves promises," as the poem puts it, and "sold neglected." Alternatively: *"dutch bulb* starves" and "promises / die" (headlining the incident; a little tragedy). Anthers, sparse clusters, faint scent, all carried off within a few unsatisfactory days—"betrayed sold neglected." Caveat emptor.

There is some reason to believe, however, that the Zukofskys had not been sold as short as they imagined and that their expectations were in part the result of mistaken identification. For Breck's "Grecian wind-flower" is not a pink (pinks are not bulbous, and their flowers do not have the yellow central disk of Zukofsky's plant); it is in fact an anemone. *Anemone blanda,* according to Taylor, is: "Tuberous-rooted and usually less than 6″ high . . . resembling [*Anemone appenina* in having solitary flowers, about 1½″ wide] but with larger and darker blue flowers. Greece and Asia Minor." What Taylor does not give is its common name—Greek anemone, which Breck's apparently reorganized as "Grecian windflower."

Hybridizing accounts for the white-eyed pink, red, and purple flowers, illustrated in the catalog and blooming—fleetingly—at East Broadway.⁷

Ironically, the misidentification is in no way ruinous to the poem because although Zukofsky decided the flower was "no grecian or / anemone," he went ahead anyway and threaded both motifs through the *Dianthus* material to augment the garden "story." Or history. First, a blast of Greek transliteration so loud it barely makes "sense" as English: "Peer re foot own his / story as"; we remember the Latin of #45 Chicory, another prolonged burst closer to its original tongue than the one purportedly making sense of it. What Zukofsky is sounding out here is nothing less than the title of Theophrastus's treatise *Peri Phyton Historias: The Enquiry into Plants*. He copied out the Loeb edition's Greek title meticulously and began toying with transliteration cum translation of "Theophrastus": "(theo phrased thus) . . . (godly phrasing, godly intellect godly minded)" (*80 Fl.* Drafts, p. 62). Theophrastus has ended up in the poem characterized by his own history as a scrutinizer of things that lay in front of him (literally at his feet?); but a remnant of his godly name survives in the phrase "choose which," transliteration of "Zeus" as the god lingers in the name *Dianthus,* from *Dios* (Zeus; Jove; Jupiter; "choose which / true name") and *anthos:* "Jove's own flower," as Gray styles it. Zeus, in his "z"-spelt aspect, was linked with the pink that Theophrastus describes as having no scent (*Enquiry* VI.vi.2); thus Zukofsky: "sparse scent choose which." But Theophrastus's style, described by Aristotle as divinely sweet, is perhaps another reason for the inclusion in the poem of the very fragrant clove pink *Dianthus caryophyllus,* so the question of which *Dianthus* the Zukofskys thought they were seeing centers again on the issue of scent (*Anemone blanda*—the species name signifies whiteness rather than insipidity—is not particularly fragrant). When the flower is finally named as "keen ens seas" (*Dianthus chinensis*), a finely attuned nose twitches somewhere, picking up a faint essence of the flower over transoceanic distances. *Ens,* derived from the present participle of the Latin *esse* (to be), means: "That which in any sense is; an object; something that can be named and spoken of" (*Century*). This connects with the concreteness of Theophrastus's enquiries, shadowed by or shadowing Zukofsky's own "peering" at things botanical and etymological.

Greek, Grecians, and the clove pink figure in a poem about a barely fragrant bulb whose immediate origins are Dutch; what next to supply but its technically nonexistent (to Zukofsky) affiliation with the anemone? The preoccupation with fragrance in part anticipates the entrance of the windflower or "ponent anemone" in line eight, where it acts as a bridgehead to the fifty-fourth *Flower.* Zukofsky had had "ponent" in reserve at least since July 1976 (it appears as a note of 2 July 1976 among his condensations of Henry James, *80 Fl.* Notes, p. 2 Condensed Notes), intending to use it in an anemone poem (the note reappears in the Second and Third Abbreviated Lists under Anemone). *Ponent* came out of the *Century;* it is a rare word in English, meaning "western" from the Latin root *ponere,* "to set, put, lay down" (the west is the setting place of the sun), but it also has a poetic, intransitive sense: "to fall, abate" (of winds). The Italian *ponente* can signify the west wind; Milton's usage, which the *Century* cites (profiling the word also for Zukofsky), encompasses the sense of both languages:

> Forth rush the Levant and the Ponent winds
> Eurus and Zephyr.
>
> *(Paradise Lost* x.704)

This wind, though considerably decreased in force, is the zephyr that keeps *"A"*-16 airborne ("An inequality // wind flower," p. 376) and blows straight on (p. 377) into *"A"*-17's Coronal for Floss Williams: "Anemones . . . 'Anemones sprang where she pressed . . .' " Now the same breeze is blowing—fragrantly?—toward #54 Windflower (the Latin prefix *po-* signifies forward or downward motion).

The connection of "ponent" with "anemone" (Latinate wind, Greek flower) and the windflower's powerful association with the death of Williams suggests one other line of thought in #53 Grecian Windflower. It was Williams who in 1956 rendered the opening of Sappho's famous verses (mediated by Catullus in his Carmen 51) as:

> Peer of the gods is that man, who
> face to face, sits listening
> to your sweet speech and lovely
> > laughter.[8]

And it was Zukofsky who got into *his* version of Carmen 51a, Catullus's coda, the phrase "peers who died"—for the sound of "perdidit" (lost) in context of kings and cities, and the most graceful of nods to Williams (*Catullus,* p. [98]). "Peer re" is Theophrastus concerning himself *(peri)* with botanical phenomena, writing down its stories. The same phrase also has Zukofsky peering at bulbs under his feet and at history all around (his own and others'), one as full of "things" ("re") as the other. Why shouldn't the same "Peer" in its initial position and about to move on to divine flowers and godly phrasing also remind us of Williams's line from Sappho?

The effects of the 1976 reading for the index of the University of California Press edition of *"A"* make themselves felt in the poems that lead off the 1977 *Flowers;* "*A*"-9's canzones were acknowledged by number and doubled form in #51 Snowdrop and #52 Snow-Wreath, and now "*A*"-16 and "*A*"-17 partially inform the first (and, we could guess, the second) windflower poem. Zukofsky explicitly brings more "*A*" into the picture by including among a group of "literary notes" for use in the windflower poems the following lines from a lyric near the beginning of "*A*"-8 (italics indicate actual lines quoted, p. 62 of *80 Fl.* Drafts):

> For labor who will sing
> *When spring, the May,*
> *Is strength enough?*
>
> *The mirth of all this land*
> Browne, Morel and More
> (Who speed the plow in May!)
>
> *Rewarded with a sheaf or more*
> Of an
>   evening—
>
> The poor
>
> *Betrayed and sold.*
>
> ("*A*"-8, pp. 46–47)

Labor's May song is central to "*A*"-8 and is transformed by its passage through that movement into the final ballade, which foreshadows the complexities (and song) of "*A*"-9's economics canzone. But the use Zukofsky has in mind for the lyric in 1977 is mock-serious, more underlining for dead promises and starved bulbs (not starved proletariats) because spring's strength, "The mirth of all this land," has been insufficient to bring up Grecian windflowers of the caliber Zukofsky thought he had been promised; not even a sheaf of blooms.

Christ of the *St. Matthew Passion* was "*Betrayed and sold*"; the poor, whom he also championed, had suffered the same fate according to Marxist thinking. But the Zukofskys were sold short, a venial betrayal of resoundingly less significance. As "sold" twists in midline from adjectival participle ("betrayed sold neglected") to transitive verb ("sold neglected ponent anemones"), we watch mock-blasphemy (Christ, the poor—and *bulbs?*) divide into its proper parts; *betrayed,* the Zukofskys were *sold neglected* bulbs. Double complication: the (neglected) anemone bulbs they thought they were buying were (they thought) pinks—further treachery. But because the bulbs *were* anemones and did flower according to their lights, the only "real" betrayal was their failure to survive more than a few days in bloom.

From all the complication #53 Grecian Windflower draws about itself on account of the anemone/not anemone/but really anemone, we extricate a final lucid detail, a floral correlative for "neglected," which might have suggested itself even if Zukofsky had not written "(penance) 'neglected' Herrick" among the notes on page 62 of the Drafts. He was thinking of affinities the Latinate "ponent" offers with such words as "potent" and "penitent," realizing how much like Latin "ponent anemone" was going to sound. And this brought to mind another poem where a Latinate word falls as emphatic contrast to simple terms and dainty subject matter. Herrick's "Violets" again:

> Welcome, maids of honour,
>   You do bring
>   In the spring
> And wait upon her.
>
> She has virgins many,
>   Fresh and fair;
>   Yet you are
> More sweet than any.
>
> You're the maiden posies
>   And so graced
>   To be placed
> 'Fore damask roses.
>
> Yet, though thus respected
>   By-and-by
>   Ye do die,
> Poor girls, neglected.[9]

(quoted in *A Test,* p. 79)

The alignment of three Latinate words in the tail of #53 Grecian Wind-flower—"neglected ponent anemone"—is the felicity that points out the parallel, violets and anemones, of quickly fading flowers.

We have speculated that the plan for double poems was in the offing as early as 11 April 1977; if it was, the second windflower poem was being projected about the same time as an "answer" to the disappointment caused by the Grecian windflower's poor showing, 3 April. The fifty-third *Flower* was composed 20–24 May 1977 with the aid of a page and a half of notes that Zukofsky had begun assembling 10 May. From the same notes and from the proto-epigraph of "Gamut," he wrote #54 Windflower 27–31 May 1977:

#54 WINDFLOWER

Windflower overworld selvageflame sun coddle
lay dune ass toss opt
thrown own candle urge shade
unhated unloved unseen slight bud
windflower singled erst field-lily nods
unshaded whorled th'solitary flower suns
clouds summers asleep crowfoots spring-*rue*
anemone leaves flowers both earth

At the head of the pencil draft, Zukofsky wrote: "still to be found and
planted"—plainly convinced that Breck's Grecian windflower had nothing
to do with the real thing—and for the second time in this part of *80
Flowers,* he prepared to write a poem without immediate personal horticultural or botanical underpinning. In the case of #49 Slipperwort, some
circumstance had brought the title flower to the Zukofskys' attention;
with the windflower, years of casual acquaintance stepped in to take the
place of a firsthand observation in the spring of 1977. And yet Zukofsky
could not depart from his self-imposed criteria without leaving visible
signs that he was doing so; nor was it to be done without somehow
anchoring the writing of the poem in time present.

What appears is a *Flower* that avoids overt reference to *"A"*-16 or
"A"-17, and avoids (as they do) overt references to the Adonis myth
associated with anemones. Instead, Zukofsky presents the "ponent anemone," all wind and barely a flower, in a poem full of rushing sound derived
not from the flower at all but from the high windy verse ("magnitude
without a shape"?) of Hardy's Overworld. The assemblage of January, a
kind of poetic cultivation among Zukofsky's 1977 lists for "Gamut," was
in effect standing in for the garden subject that #54 Windflower lacked. He
had intended to make some use of it in *80 Flowers;* he ended up digging
almost all of it into the second windflower poem, pleased by the "ceaseless
artistries in / Circumstance" that suggested the amalgamation. This line
from Hardy, a fair assessment of Zukofsky's poetic, is one of the few
elements of "The Overworld" editings he chose *not* to transfer into #54
Windflower. It stands silently, descriptively, behind the transaction.

Hardy's Overworld and Zukofsky's windflower converge in the upper
air of "the extended / World that nothing can leave" (*"A"*-11, p. 125).
Hardy's cosmos is violent and gargantuan—its "furthest hem and selvage
may extend / To where the roars and plashings of the flames / Of earth-
invisible suns swell noisily" (*The Dynasts* III.521). By contrast, in Zukofsky's overworld of light, breath, and love that is not terminated by death,

one may "raise the great hem" of the Heraclitean scheme and perhaps begin to comprehend it. Hardy's conception owes more to Blake:

. . . These are the sons of Los! These the Visions of Eternity.
But we see only as it were the hem of their garments
When with our vegetable eyes we view these wond'rous Visions.[10]

Zukofsky's is a calm Dantean or Paracelsian paradiso where one may be instructed in mysteries, and then instruct them. The barely turbulent airs of "A"-16, another elegy, continue "A"-11's theme; so does the unearthing of "A"-18. But when Zukofsky went searching for new perspectives on the windflower, something to extend rather than restate his previous settings of it, Hardy's cosmos was there with its sound and fury, signifying—an absence. Not a death this time but absence of the actual flower.

> *Windflower* overworld selvageflame sun coddle
> lay dune ass toss opt
> thrown own candle urge shade
> unhated unloved unseen slight bud

The "selvageflame sun" is a particularly vivid image, brought just this side of the cosmological hem (was Zukofsky also remembering the hot yellow ache of Williams's "Love-Song," which ends: "you far off there under / the wine-red selvage of the west!"?).[11] But the subsequent burst of transliteration disrupts any coherence the first four words are establishing; now the words seem to "mean" nothing ("coddle / lay dune") except, sometimes, their bare chops of sound ("ass toss opt") and a violence drawing on to darkness ("thrown own candle urge shade"), then—finished with transliteration—indifference ("unhated, unloved, unseen"). Zukofsky has carried out his intention to make over the Greek that Hardy quoted (*katheile* DYNASTAS *apo thronōn*), merging "throne" and "thrown" to catch a modicum of its sense (dynasts hurled from their seats), trusting aural turbulence for the rest of the sound effects signifying heaven's shake-up.

As for the shaded candle (one poor sun against the wind and dark of cosmos?), its origins lie in another part of Hardy's works, the novel *A Laodicean*. The phrase is, as usual, a conjunction of condensed passages from the book; the first of these is a comparison of beauties, Paula Power and a casually eclipsed rival, "who lingered on in the background like a candle after sunrise."[12] The second is taken from a passage near the first where Dare and De Stancy meet and the former describes their defeat in terms of lineal extinction: " 'We are past and done for. Our line has had five hundred years of glory, and we ought to be content. *Enfin les renards se trouvent chez le pelletier.*' . . . Dare went his way, and after a while De Stancy went his. Both were soon lost in the shades" (*A Laodicean*, p. 367).

"Unhated unloved unseen" returns us to the *Dynasts* passage, with a stronger feeling than before of time's snuffing-out capacities. If the string of adjectives has a direct source in Hardy ("O Loveless, Hateless!—past the sense / Of kindly eyed benevolence") it also has Miltonic underpinning in Belial's grim picture of renewed conflict with heaven:

> while we perhaps
> Designing or exhorting glorious war,
> Caught in a fiery tempest shall be hurled
> Each on his rock transfixed, the sport and prey
> Of racking whirlwinds, or for ever sunk
> Under yon boiling ocean, wrapped in chains;
> There to converse with everlasting groans,
> Unrespited, unpitied, unreprieved . . .[13]

Lucifer and his crew are the first powers to be thrown down by the Almighty. (Did Zukofsky also see a pattern for his reiterated adjectives in the *Century*'s ten columns of words beginning with the prefix *un-* spread across almost two pages of the dictionary?)

At "unseen," the poem makes a move toward the floral—still dealing, however, in intangibles:

> unhated unloved unseen slight bud
> windflower singled erst field-lily nods
> unshaded whorled th'solitary flower suns
> clouds summers asleep crowfoots spring-*rue*
> *anemone* leaves flowers both earth

Zukofsky has not seen the windflower (he thinks), or (yet) *Anemone coronaria,* the poppy anemone, whose scarlet form is supposed to be ("erst field-lily") the biblical lily-of-the-field. It grows wild in Syria and Palestine and is also the flower associated with the cultic worship of Tammuz/Adonis (the Hebrew epithet of Adonis, *na᳋man,* "beautiful," is one explanation of the origins of the word *anemone*).[14] However, Zukofsky passes quickly over *Anemone coronaria* (perhaps because it will be the subject proper of #58 Poppy Anemone?) to get to two native American species, *Anemone quinquefolia,* the common wood anemone, and *Anemonella thalictroides,* the rue anemone. Both are delicate woodland plants with small white flowers; both need protection from undue sun and wind—unlike *Anemone coronaria* ("field-lily nods / unshaded"), which Pliny says is called windflower (from *anemos,* wind) because it never opens except when the wind is blowing.[15] The *Century* backs up Pliny's fanciful account of the name, if not his explanation of it; the herbalists who followed him preserved the story, so giving us an English "wind-flower" to translate the Greek-Latin "anemone." The survival of both names in English shows up in Breck's decision to market *Anemone blanda,* the Greek anemone, as Grecian windflower. The *Century* also points out that *anemos* (wind) is the root of the Latin *anima* (breath, spirit), therefore also of *animus* (mind, soul), an etymology we have looked at once before (see chap. 3). All of this suggests good reason for Zukofsky's adoption of the windflower in *"A"*-16 and strengthens that movement's associations with *"A"*-11. When he reconfigures the motif in *80 Flowers,* "ponent anemone" breathes the connection, the mighty animisms of Hardy's drama supply variation by tumult—and the delicate wildflowers of American home ground gentle it again. At "nods / un-shaded whorled," the tossing poppy anemone (whirled?) in its sunlit world blends into the shade-loving *Anemone quinquefolia;* a process beginning perhaps as early as "nods / unshaded," if we hear the run-on "nod sun" (*Anemone coronaria*) then "shaded whorled th'solitary flower suns / clouds summers asleep." *Anemone quinquefolia*'s midstalk leaves are arranged in a whorl below its solitary flower; as a bud, the flower head hangs down ("unseen slight bud / windflower singled . . . nods"?), but it opens upward in moderate amounts of sun, closing again in cloudy weather ("nods / unshaded whorled th'solitary flower suns / clouds"). At the height of summer the plant dies down and remains dormant until the following spring ("summers asleep . . . spring . . . leaves flowers both earth").

Anemonella thalictroides, the rue anemone, is a member of the butter-cup or crowfoot family and is closely related to the anemones; *Anemo-nella* is a diminutive. It flowers in clusters, a single central flower opening first ("singled erst"), and the ultimate segments of its compound basal leaves resemble those of the meadow rue, *Thalictrum. Woodland Flowers,* the source of Zukofsky's information here, obviously has something to say about the sequence of leaf and flower (the basal leaves develop after the flower and stem leaves in both *Anemone quinquefolia* and *Anemonella thalictroides*). Zukofsky makes a margin-cramped note: "of Goethe run like the meadow rue leaf to flower rise from the flower together" (*80 Fl.* Drafts, p. 62). The *Century* gives no help in unraveling this; perhaps it is coming from the elusive *Woodland Flowers?* (see chap. 7, n.11). Whatever it is, it also informs the last line of #54 Windflower: "*anemone* leaves flowers both earth."

On the one hand, botany has us imagining the anemone dying back after its spring flowering (*quinquefolia*). On the other, a different part of the cycle has us looking at the plant springing up from the earth, putting out flowers and then leaves (*quinquefolia, thalictroides*). This second view puts us almost inevitably in mind of the Adonis myth. There and not-there, like the windflower itself.

A Note on the Hyacinth Flowerings

In the hyacinth pair is solid ground for the conjecture that doubling of the spring 1977 poems was planned from 11 April. The Zukofskys' Breck hyacinth flowered on that date and was recorded in the In Process Notes after grape-hyacinth, also a Breck bulb, which blossomed 3 April.[16] When Zukofsky came to compose #56 Hyacinth (13–15 June), he noted that collecting material for it had taken him from 1–12 June; however, on the first draft of the poem is the revealing addition: "ideas for pencil draft beg. Apr 11/77 or earlier via 'A'-9" (80 Fl. Drafts, p. 66).

To reconstruct. On a deeply significant date, the Zukofskys' hyacinth blossoms, its associated myths concerning death and regeneration. Zukofsky has had tentative plans to write a hyacinth poem (garden permitting) since the previous fall plantings, and into that scheme has entered at some point the hyacinth of "A"-9, Second Half. When the flowering is recorded, Zukofsky also does a little preliminary transliteration: "ΎΑΚΙΝΘΟΣ who act'n'toss" (In Process Notes, p. 1). If we are right, he sees on the In Process list to date: a pair of hyacinths; next to them an "anemone" badly in need of poetic restoration to its position of dignity in "A"; and a lone snowdrop where multitudes should have appeared. If we can assume that the appearance of the hyacinth 11 April stirred thoughts of "A"-9, it becomes apparent that the idea for a double canzone built around the Nine was close at hand. From the crowded nature of the notes Zukofsky made alongside the snowdrop entry of 27 March in his In Process Notes—"Double canzone 1)the Nine 2)Snowreath Rose f."—it is reasonable to believe they were later additions—made 11 April? When this was done, Zukofsky acted upon his inspiration immediately, taking the date as a good omen, and began writing #51 Snowdrop.

The rest follows on as we have seen and then takes in #55 Grape-Hyacinth and #56 Hyacinth, another pair that sounds components back and forth to subtextual murmurs of Theophrastus, Breck's, Taylor and Gray, and the story of Hyacinthus and Apollo as played out in Ovid, also in "A"-9, Second Half. There, and in the present poems, grief inscribed on the hyacinth's petals (Ai ai) is transformed by Zukofsky (eye-eye; I-I) to clear, self-possessed vision.[17] The hyacinth poem is crowded with delphinium, gladiolus (a glad eye), and the poet's narcissus—the latter adds another mythological presence, Narcissus, to the Flowers of spring 1977 which already host Adonis and Hyacinthus. Amplifying the implicit theme of metamorphosis, Zukofsky winds in a reference to Cadmus's army of dragon-teeth warriors (the Sown Men), obviously intrigued by Ovid's description of the unearthing phalanx as a field of wheat. Zukofsky transfers that irruptive power to the hyacinth and its associated spring bulbs.

The Cadmean Sown Men cut themselves down and go back under the earth, which gave them birth (so do a number of the spring flowers we have looked at). The underearthing that precedes and then succeeds spring flowerings is crucial to the Greek stories, whereas Zukofsky is largely content to let symbolic interpretation alone. He invokes the stories, but the manner of their "telling" rests on botanical and horticultural detail that elucidates the *Flower* so the other is a light wind over and through it, blowing from personal anniversaries.[18]

Part Three

Making for Paradise:
The Last Ten *Flowers*

9

Aster, Raspberry, Daisy, Aloe, and Thyme

Overview: #57 Dogwood to #80 Zinnia

The "double" poems of spring 1977 occupied Zukofsky until mid-June, but they barely touched the flowering chronology built up in the In Process Notes over the same period. After 11 April, flowering date of the hyacinth and starting date of the 1977 *Flowers,* came a rapid succession of spring blooms in the garden—dogwood, poppy anemone, spirea, daffodils (narcissus), lily-of-the-valley fortunei, oxalis, alpine rosy bells—which took the spring to 18 May and the sequence from #57 Dogwood to #64 Alpine Rosy Bells, completed 24 August, a poem that included the summer history of the flower as its time-present coordinate. The Zukofskys' locust tree was in bloom 21 May, as was its neighboring mulberry; below both was oxalis, also flowering, which is why there are two trees in #63 Oxalis: "more ruse mulberry locust-flower shield" (*Morus* is a mulberry). From *"A"-23*'s garden section (p. 554) we can even locate this tableau: "East: / the old mulberry's escapes, wild / locust."

#65 Jade commemorated not a flowering but the planting, 25 May 1977, of a sprig of succulent from a local nursery. The chronology of flowerings then resumed with artemisia and greater celandine, both of which figure in #66 Artemisia. Then followed wild honeysuckle, *Sedum telephium,* and yarrow (#67 Wild Honeysuckle, #68 Telephus Sedum, #69 Yarrow), bringing the sequence to sixty-nine *Flowers.* The In Process Notes went on to record a raspberry in flower (18 July) followed by butter-and-eggs (1 September), a budding aster (5 September), and (undated) American holly, pipsissewa, and umbra. This upsets the book sequence somewhat (#70 Butter-and-Eggs, #71 Aster, #72 Raspberry) and introduces flowers that do not appear in *80 Flowers;* it also directs attention to a number of things about the use Zukofsky made of his In Process Notes.

First, the Notes themselves were selective rather than a record of every blossoming in the garden—such flowers as crocus, forsythia, pachysandra, deutzia, and lilac did not reappear in the 1977 Notes. What did was clearly

"In Process" of entrance into this part of the *Flowers;* that is, it had already passed its first selection test. Second, the six pages of 1977 In Process Notes show that Zukofsky was constantly clarifying the order of his selections; as one page became crowded and written-over, he would start another and write fuller notes on flowers that had previously been listed with only a date. The first two pages, therefore, are rather like an overview; "18 planned" says a note at the foot of page 1, and there are eighteen numbers spread over pages 1–2, but they include such things as wild strawberry, tigerlily, mimosa, American holly, and blackberry, which never became title flowers. Third, Zukofsky changed his mind over the title flowers but rarely did anything escape some sort of inclusion in *80 Flowers* once it had entered in the In Process lists. Thus a strawberry appears in #73 Daisy, tigerlily and American holly in #79 Yaupon, and blackberry in #72 Raspberry; mimosa was transferred to the "Gamut" lists (nothing is wasted), and when there was a reason for trees to be included (locust, mulberry) they were written into appropriate *Flowers*.

The fifth and sixth In Process pages pinpoint Zukofsky's compositional progress. One is headed: "beginning #67" and gives notes for three poems through to #69 Yarrow; the next begins at #70 and goes to #72 Raspberry—and here we learn that although the Zukofskys' raspberry had flowered 18 July (a circumstance that in the normal run of things would have placed it between #69 Yarrow and #70 Butter-and-Eggs), other events of the fall provided the final sequence date. A cultivated raspberry cane from their east neighbor was planted by the Zukofskys 21 September and reported thriving 26 September (In Process Notes, p. [6]). Zukofsky obviously took this as an auspicious sign and settled his raspberry poem on the new plant rather than the one whose fruit had been dry by the end of August.

So much for the garden. The nonhorticultural content of *80 Flowers* from #57 Dogwood to #70 Butter-and-Eggs includes routine entrances from Shakespeare in all but two of the fourteen poems. Greek and Latin material, which was increasingly evident in the early spring poems, continues to inform the *Flowers:* lots of Theophrastus, lots of backup from Liddell and Scott, more Greek input still from Diogenes Laertius (#59 Spirea), Apollodorus (#68 Telephus Sedum; see chap. 5 and n.17 of that chap.), and Hesiod (#70 Butter-and-Eggs). These are contingency appearances, primarily suggested by associations of the *Flower* in hand. With Latin components the case is different (except when Zukofsky is using Lewis and Short to augment his information about botanical names or to back up literary reference). The Latin is coming out of literary notes now condensed in the early pages of the Third Abbreviated List—passages from Virgil's *Georgics* (#61 Bearded Iris; #69 Yarrow) and the *Aeneid*

(#69 Yarrow), and from Horace's *Epistles* (#66 Artemisia), *Satires* (#67 Wild Honeysuckle; #69 Yarrow), and *Odes* (#69 Yarrow). The Virgil is mostly from long-standing entries in the *80 Flowers* Notes (the result of some reading of the *Georgics* and the *Aeneid?*), whereas the Horace derives mainly from quotations made by Johnson in *Lives of the Poets,* a work Zukofsky seems to have been reading February-April 1977.[1] It is this source that supplies #63 Oxalis with a Miltonic Latin pun on *Morus,* the mulberry. Other literary material in the poems of 1977 up to #70 includes snatches of Hebraic Old Testament (#62 Lily-of-the-Valley Fortunei), some Milton (#65 Jade), some Wordsworth (#69 Yarrow), and Hardy, Steele, and Sir Thomas Browne (#70 Butter-and-Eggs).

By the time he reached the seventy-first *Flower* (#70 Butter-and-Eggs was completed 18 October 1977), Zukofsky had used a good deal of the nonbotanical material in the Third List, and the In Process Notes had only two more candidates to offer as the growing season drew to a close. This year Zukofsky chose not to suspend composition until the following spring; instead he looked to his alternative resource, the extended Third List, and began organizing it into a manageable reservoir from which to select material for the last ten poems. Thus emerged the four surviving pages headed "Americana," which contain about thirty entries (mostly botanical) carried over alphabetically from the Third Abbreviated List, plus a couple of new candidates. It seems likely that two pages of the Americana are missing, for although the candidates we have run without serious alphabetical interruption from Delphinium to Yam, one folio is numbered page 1 and page 2 and the other page 5 and page 6. What happened to the intervening folio is not clear, nor is the make-up of its conjectural contents, but we should remember the gap and be cautious when talking about what got into the Americana from the Third List. "Follow pp in order for use of final 10 leave the rest for *Gamut*," reads a note across the top of the Americana, and then: "pp. 5–25 . . . notes for abbvt 3rd List 80 F condensed for #71–80." The Americana list was intended "for use of final 10"—not as a means of selecting title flowers. In this respect it is different from the In Process Notes, just as the Lists of 80 Flowers themselves (of which the Americana is the latest offshoot) have been reservoirs of potentially useful material rather than a means of ordering the *Flowers.*

Having provided himself with context for the projected winter composition, how did Zukofsky arrive at the sequence that concludes the book? And how did time present contribute to that ordering? From #71 Aster through #73 Daisy, the sequence is still garden-determined; #74 Aloe is occasioned by the memory of a special event earlier in 1977 and is also the "A" to place against the end-of-the-alphabet sequence that follows—#75 Thyme, #76 Vines, #77 Weeds, #78 "X," #79 Yaupon, and #80 Zinnia. As early as 1975 Zukofsky had been planning, tentatively, to finish in alphabetical fashion: "Thyme, Weeds, Wistaria, Zinnia in that order to close *80 Flowers?* we'll see Sept 2/75" (1st Abb. List, p. [3]). This plan of course had to be reconciled with the general rule of selection for the *Flowers* as it had evolved 1976–77, which decreed order by garden appearance, blossoming time, planting time, or some other immediate horticultural/botanical circumstance. As it happened, timing was (once more) on Zukofsky's side; he was ready to embark on the final decade just as fall began in earnest, was able to use what was left of the garden material and then turn to the long-projected alphabetical ordering. *80 Flowers'* first winter had produced poems based on the flowers of memory and anniversary; its final winter is worked on the alphabet, the abundance of material Zukofsky had amassed in three years—and a sense of finale that prompts the poet to end where he began, with *Flowers* about time and ("getting to Z") the family.

We move in to look at the last poems of *80 Flowers,* summarizing the three that are still garden-based and treating in detail those beyond them that make up the finale proper.[2]

From the Garden: #71 Aster to #73 Daisy

In the fall of 1976 the Zukofskys had planted a sprig of aster given to them by a neighbor. By 28 September 1977 the plant was in full flower, a Michaelmas daisy almost to the day, and Zukofsky had identified it as a New England aster. *Aster novae-angliae* is a North American native developed by European cultivators into the hybrid garden asters known as Michaelmas daisies. So the Zukofskys' aster is of American origin but garden-bred through Europe—and the poem constructed around it is decidedly of the Old World. Starry Greek and Latin asters appear from dictionary etymologies and from a meadowflower in Virgil's *Georgics* (IV.271). The Phoenician/Greek goddess of the moon, Ashtaroth/Astarte, is worked phonetically into the opening lines. As Venus (star and goddess), she then brings in terrestrial music-making as well as celestial mechanics. A women-starring play, *Love's Labour's Lost,* figures prominently—so too does Hardy's *A Laodicean,* in which the same Shakespearean comedy is staged by the novel's protagonists. The contingency of these things—Virgil's aster, Shakespeare's play, Hardy's novel—derives from their fortuitous appearance together early in the extended Third List. All of them are made to connect on many planes by means of the poem's running concern with beneficent stellar fire and cooling (annealing) heat. The movement between star and flower—which inaugurates patterns of fire, heat, and light, followed by coolings, healings, and tensile strengthen-ing—is one more instance of Zukofsky's working of love's hidden melody. Goddesses, a princess, and the presence of music confirm its place among the poems of quiet homage to Celia.

A transliterated Connecticut ("connect a cut") in #71 Aster returns the poem to North America (a New England state for a New England aster). But Zukofsky also has in mind a flower from the Park Seed catalog, Delphinium Connecticut Yankee—and suddenly New World blends with Old as Mark Twain's *A Connecticut Yankee at the Court of King Arthur* comes into view.[3] Perhaps the chief reason for the Connecticut reference, though, is to prepare for transition to the American bramble patch that is #72 Raspberry.

The seventy-second *Flower* is a romp; a tangle of compounds and hybrids loaded with fruit rather than flowers, full of fruit colors, tastes, textures (thorns among them—this is another rose poem), and at the last even a sound ("th'*raspberry*"). It is a veritable feast for the senses, drawing almost entirely on Taylor and Gray to back up garden experience and botanical identifications, mostly of native species. Thimbleberry, the Zu-kofskys' own raspberry, dewberry, blackberry, boysenberry, and logan-berry are all there. And somehow bound up with berry feasts and the cuplike receptacles of the fruit is an intriguing strain of wine and roses which makes its way from Jonson's "Drinke to me, onely, with thine eyes" ("I sent thee, late, a rosie wreath") to Zukofsky's address-in-reply, the poem beginning: "One lutenist played *look;* your thought was *drink*" (*All,* p. 85).[4] The title of the Jonson is, significantly, "Song. To Celia." The rose of *80 Flowers,* associated with fire and thyme (time), as well as with Hafiz's bucolic topery, extends now to Jonson's transformative cup and wreath by way of Zukofsky's previous reworkings of them.

Then the poem passes on to cranberry, red whortleberry, and huckle-berry (Samuel Langhorne Clemens makes a second entrance—"twain"—in *80 Flowers*); all of these belong to the heath family. The year had passed into cranberry season by the time Zukofsky came to write #72 Raspberry, and so he had two more oriently beautiful American reds to put alongside the native raspberry. The irreverent "raspberry" that ends the poem ("the sound a wound to the fragrance," *80 Fl.* Drafts, p. 102) seems an acknowledgment of the vernacular tradition represented by *Huckleberry Finn.*

A wild strawberry growing at East Broadway initially was to have been part of the raspberry poem. However, it failed to flower because of a spell of cold spring weather—a "blackberry winter" as Mathews's *Dictionary of Americanisms* expresses it. Zukofsky, finding the term there in his research for #72 Raspberry, noted it along with parallel phrases denoting cool weather in May. He reserved them, and the strawberry, for #73 Daisy as the most visible American components of a poem that ranges Old World and New with a freedom that is beginning to look typical of the last *Flowers,* Americana notes or no.

The last garden-derived *Flower* of 1977 is #73 Daisy; late in the season the Zukofskys had planted a variety of English daisy (*Bellis perennis*) locally known as a Montauk daisy (Montauk is the easternmost peninsula of Long Island). Zukofsky pursued English and then Irish elements associated with his daisy, plus a conceit on its Latin name which moved the "pretty perennial" to "perennial war" (his translations) and the battle of the sexes.

Eventually, dictionary work brought him up against the notion of seriation ("the formation of an orderly sequence or series," *Century*), more specifically of *thinking* as seriation. And so, connected as orderly sequence simply by thinking through their very light touches upon one another in Zukofsky's notebooks, are such diversities in #73 Daisy as Anglo-Saxon etymologies, Adam and Eve, a strawberry, the chamise lily *Erythronium grandiflorum* (also known as adder's tongue and dog's tooth violet), playwright William Congreve, philosopher G. H. Lewes, Hugh Kenner's gift of a piece of Irish verse for Saint Patrick's Day 1977, a Brehon lawyer stemming from it, and Ver's song from the end of *Love's Labour's Lost* beginning: "When daisies pied and violets blue . . ." The song seems Zukofsky's way, as it was Shakespeare's, of envisaging daisies in flower in a winter piece; looking forward of course to the spring that will bring the October-planted daisy into bloom.

#74 Aloe, #75 Thyme, and More Timing

The gift of verse that partly inspired #73 Daisy is paralleled by the gift of the plant that occasioned #74 Aloe. Aloe had been on all the Lists of 80 Flowers, always in first place; an "A" flower first observed by Zukofsky in Paget, Bermuda, 1972 (it appears—"sea-fig aloe"—in the Bermuda passage of "A"-22's second Music section, p. 534). When Helen Kelly gave the Zukofskys an aloe vera plant 4 June 1977, its place somewhere in the sequence was more or less assured. Putting together notes for the aloe poem, Zukofsky wrote:

> L.Z. note 12/10/77 Aloe seen in
> Bermoothes if not touched
> spiny tough etc but as gift
> touched soft
>
> (*80 Fl.* Drafts, p. 108)

Perhaps it is a happy accident that gifts from people with the initials "H.K." are commemorated by consecutive *Flowers,* or perhaps Zukofsky intended it. Certainly time condoned the juxtaposition; by including in #73 Daisy substantial amounts of Third List and Americana material plus a strong tie with 17 March 1977, Zukofsky was easing the sequence away from garden-grown subjects and at the same time preparing the way for a houseplant *Flower* with some Americana—but also the pleasing associations of 4 June 1977. This is the date Zukofsky received, in person, the honorary degree of Doctor of Letters from Bard College, Annandale-on-Hudson, New York. The award was the brainchild of Bard's Robert Kelly. It had been offered 26 October 1976; Zukofsky accepted 9 November and agreed to attend commencement ceremonies the following June.[5]

Both Louis and Celia went to Annandale and Zukofsky inscribed her copy of the commencement exercises booklet, adding a flourish of yellow:

C's

  6/4/77

   $\sim$

   Louis

The yellow felt-tip pen was still part of the tripartite rule that signaled completion of each *Flower* in the Drafts and was customarily drawn under the "s" of Zukofsky's wishes for Happy New Years (see chap. 2). The flourish above is special emphasis; yellow, traced through the years, is part of that wordless Zukofskian cipher for paradise.

So it is the date of the aloe gift that positions the poem beginning (with an A) the finale that will—Thyme, Vines, Weeds, Yaupon, Zinnia—bring *80 Flowers* to Z. Zukofsky has more to say about the Bard award in #75 Thyme and has already intimated its existence (ambiguously) in #63 Oxalis, a poem laced with Shakespeare, ending: "honor the bard." For the moment (11–16 December 1977), gift, award, and memories of the Bermudan plant combine to produce a *Flower* alight with manic and then magical Shakespeare:

#74 ALOE

Álow álow loo no words
Oliver-error Rowland to Tower came
eyebright monkeyshines monkey-wrench whitespotted eyetooth
Adder's-tongue juice 'll streak kill-courtesy
mule-bitter-aloes fanciers of boor succulence
Bermoothes thrust rapier's-point barb Ā-doze
stemless-lilies-internode more a lów E
mellows habit swept dust or

Neilson's *Complete Plays and Poems* (1942) formulates mad Edgar's howls on the heath as: "Alow, alow, loo, loo!" (*Lr.* III.iv.79). "No words," as Gloucester might put it (*Lr.* III.iv.186)—but Zukofsky heard differently, and there is the aloe (ă-low) in the middle of the hallowing hollowing and hallooing—"mere syllables to call attention . . . freely varied for sonorous effect" (*Century;* one of the variations cited there is *alow* and one of the examples of usage is Edgar's line). If Zukofsky wanted backup effects for his re-creation of the stormy heath, he had only to check the *Century's* *alow* to have Scottish fire there in a flash, the noise of it (a-lou) proposing a different rhyme for the opening line: "A-lou a-lou loo no words."

Howl gives way to fragmented babble ("Child Rowland to the dark tower came; / His word was still, 'Fie, foh, and fum, / I smell the blood of a British man,'" *Lr.* IV.iii.187), spliced by Zukofsky with the figure of speech "a Roland for an Oliver," which can find no distinction (blow for blow) between champions of balanced strength. So that it might have been Oliver coming to the dark tower though the legend specifies Rowland? Except that Oliver and Roland/Orlando belong to the tradition of Charlemagne, whereas Childe Rowland features in an old Scottish ballad that tells how he rescued his sister, Burd Ellen, from the fairies who had carried her off.[6] Zukofsky seems to have built a composite Franco-British hero, interested most of all in how the blending of stories gives him ("Oliver-error") the true aloe, *Aloe vera*. Happily surrounded by loyal heroes, Roland, Oliver, Childe Rowland, Edgar, Gloucester.

The fairies of the dark tower story have an immediate effect on the direction of the poem: "*eyebright* monkeyshines monkey-wrench whitespotted eyetooth / Adder's-tongue juice 'll streak kill courtesy." The gleam starts out impish and botanical; eyebright is *Mimulus ringens,* and *mimulus* is a diminutive of *mimus,* "buffoon" (Gray) or "mimic" (Taylor), from the grinning corolla of the flower (*ringens* means "gaping"). "Monkeyshines" is an inspired descriptive for the bright-eyed monkey-flower; "monkey-wrench" mimics the sound while refocusing attention on the jaw that first pointed the flower monkey-ward. At "whitespotted eyetooth / Adder's-tongue," we begin to move out of the Americana notes (where Mimulus follows on from Erythronium, the yellow adder's tongue or dog's tooth violet) into the midsummer night's magic of Oberon and Puck. *Mimulus ringens* is violet with dark markings resembling a monkey face; it is spotted but never "whitespotted"—except in the sense that occasionally a white variation is found (spotted?). The troublesome mark is coming from another direction: "You spotted snakes with double tongue, / . . . be not seen," begins the lullaby Titania's fairies sing (*MND* II.ii.9). Zukofsky already had adder's tongue and dog's tooth violet, those sharp-pointed names, from the #73 Daisy material; dog's tooth to canine to eyetooth was an easy transition that also preserved the gleam of a bright eye as the flash of a bared incisor, white below the eye (*Aloe vera*'s leaves are margined with tooth-shaped spines). As for the adder's tongue (eye-tooth-tongue), snake beauty is thoroughly wound about the midsummer wood. Titania's fairies might warn off snakes from her bower but Oberon has already remarked of it: "And there the snake throws her enamell'd skin, / Weed wide enough to wrap a fairy in" (*MND* II.i.255). He also has the flower Puck fetched:

And with the juice of this I'll streak her eyes,
And make her full of hateful fantasies.

(*MND* II.i.257)

Zukofsky's implication, "whitespotted eyetooth / Adder's-tongue juice 'll streak kill-courtesy," is that these sharp points are full of beautiful poisons that will ill-streak eyes when fairy magic gets to work. Puck, looking at Hermia and Lysander asleep (taking, incidentally, the wrong inference):

Pretty soul! she durst not lie
Near this lack-love, this kill-courtesy.
Churl, upon thy eyes I throw
All the power this charm doth owe.

(*MND* II.ii.76)

The poem also sours: "kill-courtesy / *mule-bitter-aloes* fanciers of boor succulence." Botanically, we are still talking about *Aloe vera,* which is sometimes known as Barbados aloe though it is a native of North Africa and is one source of bitter aloes, a well-known purgative. This is probably the substance alluded to in P. Vegetius's treatise *De Arte Veterinaria sive De Mulomedicina (The Art of Healing Domestic Animals,* or *Of Curing the Diseases of Mules)*—the first of Lewis and Short's references for *aloe.* Zukofsky copied it out (*80 Fl.* Drafts, p. 107), possibly drawn to the title because of its sick mules—a few steps distant from the sickness that makes Titania love an ass (or fancy a boor?). Oberon cared little at the outset of the prank whether his queen's affections fixed upon: "lion, bear, or wolf or bull, / On meddling monkey, or on busy ape" (*MND* II.i.180)—his own monkeyshines with the purple-stained Cupid's flower looking back at the purple *Mimulus.* The juice Oberon lays on eyes, from the plant called love-in-idleness (*Viola tricolor*), sickens the perceptions; "Dian's bud," which he uses to release Titania from her delusions, is some kind of purgative. The juice of *Aloe vera* purges sickness from beasts of burden, but we might reflect that it is not the translated Bottom who needs curing; rather, his native witticisms ("*mule-bitter-aloes*"?) make more sense in an eye-sick world than the pronouncements of anyone else in the play.

The proverbial bitterness of aloes is confused with its reputation in the Old Testament as the source of a perfume (Prov. 7:17; Song of Sol. 4:13–16); the *Century* explains that the Hebrew *akhālīm* or *akhālōth* signifies the fragrant resin or wood called *agallochum* or wood aloes, which Greek translators confused with the succulent.[7] Zukofsky, interested in the translinguistic misidentification, copied the King James Version of the verses pointed out by Lewis and Short, with a note considering possible Hebrew transliterations. If there is Hebrew in #74 Aloe, it is most likely in line five, centered on "boor," the only word for which no direct botanical or Shakespearean source is determinable. No direct noise, that is; there is a section of the preparatory notes (*80 Fl.* Drafts, p. 107) taken from the 1977 Park Seed catalog which describes the South African *Aloe variegata* and its showy red clustered flowers. Did this plant remind Zukofsky (more than the smaller, yellow-flowered *Aloe vera* described by Taylor) of the vivid, orange-trumpeted variety he had seen in Bermuda? hence "boor [Boer] succulence"? The unlikely choice of word still leaves room for a transliterative overlay. "Fanciers" might also be part of a transliteration, but it does have a direct antecedent in Taylor's comment that many species of aloe "are to be had from fanciers and specialists in succulents."

Time for more Shakespeare in the effort to point up *Aloe vera*'s most obvious physical attribute:

Bermoothes thrust rapier's-point barb Ā-doze

Sleepy magic at either end of the line, pricked by needle-sharp spines. The "rapier's-point," turning falsehood upon the heart where it was forged, is Fitzwater's threat to Aumerle (*R2* IV.i.40); some analog of the true aloe's virtues? Barbados may be *Aloe vera*'s Caribbean home, but for Zukofsky it was indelibly associated with Bermuda, where he and Celia had seen it in flower (*"A"* 22 & 23 Spiral, p. 140); and so, "Bermoothes," the scenario of January 1972 is re-created (see chap. 4). There is the hurt of the day that news of his sister's death reached them, and there is the curious balm made of it at the close of *"A"*-22 (Zukofsky's ellipses):

> . . in my mind
> a dream of named history
> content with *still-vext Bermoothes . . where*
> *once thou call'dst me up*
> . . *to fetch dew . . tears: there*
> *she's hid* an arm embraces

(*"A"*-22, p. 535)

Behind this personal "rapier's-point," though, is Ariel's description of the deep nook where he has hidden the king's ship and left its mariners asleep

("Ā-doze"?); that corner of the island where Prospero once called him at midnight to fetch (magical) dew from the stormy Bermudas. #74 Aloe brims with midnight enchantments and island magic, bringing together two of Zukofsky's favorite Shakespearean plays.

"Stemless-lilies-internode"—most aloes are stemless and all belong to the Liliaceae; an internode is the space between two knots or joints of a stem—not particularly relevant to the aloe. But the phrase drops another open vowel into proceedings that have been sibilant with "s" and "z" sounds: "Bermoothes thrust rapier's-point barb Ā-doze / stemless-lilies-"; hiss of—snake? rapier through air? swift-moving magic? Then the sibilance winds down: "-internode more a lōw E / mellows habit," though there is one last flick at the end of line eight: "swept dust or." The slow movement pitches itself ("a lōw E") at the deep end of any magic-curing music (lowest open string of a double bass); and "mellows habit" suggests a sweetening power in those low tones. All of this says something to the gist of the underlying Latin, a line from Juvenal (*Satires* VI.181) given in Lewis and Short's entry on *aloe* as an example of usage: "plus aloes quam mellis habet." As an aphorism, this translates: "He has in him more bitters than sweets," said of a writer with a sarcastic pen, according to Brewer's *Dictionary*. In context, however (and Zukofsky copied lines 178–81 of Juvenal's sixth *Satire* into the Drafts, pp. 107–8, along with some preliminary transliteration of them), the line is about the bitters and sweets of the marriage bed, and the metaphor of aloes and honey stands intact:

> quae tanti gravitas, quae forma, ut se tibi semper
> imputet? huius enim rari summique voluptas
> nulla boni, quotiens animo corrupta superbo
> plus aloes quam mellis habet.

Or: "For is any dignity in a wife, any beauty, worth the cost, if she is for ever reckoning up her merits against you? These high and transcendent qualities lose all their charm when spoilt by a pride that savours more of aloes than of honey."[8]

The sense of "plus aloes quam mellis habet" is continued in #74 Aloe, not in the transliteration of it (that low, sweetening note) but in *"mule-bitter-aloes."* We have found already that this phrase had literal business, via aloes, with the art of mule-doctoring; but the introduction of a Latin mule (*mulus*) so close in the dictionary to words denoting woman or wife alerted Zukofsky's translinguistic sense (*mulierosus,* "fond of women," is followed in Lewis and Short by *mulinus,* "of or belonging to a mule"). He had turned from *aloe* to *mulomedicina* to check that Vegetius's treatise concerned mule-medicine rather than wife-doctoring, but with Juvenal's phrase in mind he saw to it that *"mule-bitter-aloes"* held also the whiff of a mulish *mulier* (wife, woman): "La côte d'Adam contient plus d'aloès que de miel" is the French adaptation of Juvenal's witticism (Brewer). On top of it all, more bitters than sweets from the pen of a satirist, is the line's nod (as an aphorism) to Juvenal, perhaps also to the bittersweet logic of the ass Bottom.

The mule-*mulier* connection is an extension of similar dictionary work in a 1964 poem, "The Translation" (*All,* p. 235), written when Zukofsky was immersed (with Celia) in his transformation of Catullus. "The Trans-lation" tracks Lewis and Short's *mulier* through *mollier,* comparative of *mollis* (soft) and takes various sidesteps to check and then discard English homonyms (**mulley, mooley, moolea;** "harmless animal, cow") and Greek synonyms (*malakós,* "soft"; *amalós,* "weak"; *mōlus,* "soft, weak, feeble"; *blaychrós,* "weak, feeble, slight").[9] But somewhere between *mollis* ("mov-able / pliant / flexible / supple // soft / delicate / gentle / mild // pleasant— / not / bad / for // authority— / in / shorts") and *blaychrós* when applied to faint and gentle winds, and *malakòs leimown* ("a // soft / grassy / mead-ow / *amalós* // light / [slight / like / seductive]—"), Zukofsky constructs the etymology he wants for *mulier:*

> that
>   would
>
> be
>   *mulier*
> that
>   would
>
> be
>   *wife*
> that
>   would
>
> be
>   soft—
> a
>   sleeping
>
> breath
>   sof-
> t-
>   t

(All, p. 240)

Early in the poem, he had rejected ("*mule-* / *ier* / hardly / either-") the obvious transliteration, *mule ear.* In 1977 he brought mule and wife together by the agency of P. Vegetius and Juvenal (via Lewis and Short) with a context of Shakespeare—the mulish (to Oberon) Titania and the ass-headed but not ass-brained Bottom. In addition, there was the bittersweet to-do over right-sightedness, the effect of various plant juices upon love's bright eye, and the monkeying-about with that eye. There were the enchantments (dewy sleeps, brain-curing musics) of islands, at least one of them governed by a prescient magus. There were also the initial bitternesses of howling madness on the heath (*mule-Lear?*), though that was filially rather than conjugally inspired. Lear, to be taught love's value, had to lose his sight; the folk of *A Midsummer Night's Dream* act lighter scenarios of love and blindness. Prospero's revenge loses its thrust ("rapier's-point barb Ã-doze"), and he oversees with a benign eye the breaking of his enchantments with solemn music ("a lów E / mellows habit"), which is sweetness after embitterment, his own and others'.

"Swept dust or"? What sounds like transliteration is in fact the retreating voice of Robin Goodfellow ("I am sent with broom before, / To sweep the dust behind the door," *MND* V.i.396), who precedes the fairy train that pronounces final blessing on the bridal beds.

#74 Aloe was completed 16 December 1977; the next day Zukofsky began planning the seventy-fifth poem of the sequence, and the date determined not only the title flower but also to a large extent the content of #75 Thyme. Across the top of a fresh page of the Drafts (which from this point are unnumbered) he wrote:

> cf 12/18/74 pg A-1 *Plan* etc
>
> but trusts
> (75) this poem rounds out ⟨Thyme⟩ still greet
> the epigraph seven years
> sooner than expected, but C + me at
> 80_{10}
>
> (*80 Fl.* Drafts, p. [109])

Three years previously at this time, the addendum about thyme/time had been written into the Schema: "opening epigraph using *thyme* [pronounced *time*] and thread the play of sound on both thru the 80 flowers that follow . . . Let time determine the book sequence of the 80—and their 'order'—that is the chronology of *their writing*." Conjecturally, this note was the result of Zukofsky's discovery of the *thýmos/thymós* relation, which gave him thyme's warm Greek heart with which to lead off *80 Flowers* (see chap. 3). Since that eventful December discovery, thyme's fire and fragrance have acted as touchstones in the sequence, drawing to them roses, bees, and the horse who has made all of this his personal matrix.

The enlivening energy associated with thyme (remembering the medieval device of a bee circling a sprig of thyme, signifying double energy) has determined the pace of composition as well as the order of the *Flowers*. The horse, trusting, has followed time's directive and can contemplate alterations to his initial scheme with equanimity.

There are six *Flowers* to write, the alphabetical finale to be implemented, and the Americana notes to be used. Thyme had always led off that alphabetical closure, and time now conspired to anchor the thyme poem to the anniversary of its entrance in the *Flowers*. What was there to do but compose an anniversary poem?

#75   THYME

Takes time where wild the
thyme blows poor tom's a
cold relentless-vest muffler jacket coat
one bluegreen eye ate his
hope sevenyear fanned eyesack disrailing
birds'-tread hie *rose* tree-budding fire
moon's flight twice sun's spider-manor-borne
litter letter words-justice *thyme* righting

"*Thyme*," "*rose*," "*thyme*"; three maplike italicizations in the *Flower*. Here is the fiery rose again, budding flame in winter (Epigraph, #1 Starglow) in front of Isaac D'Israeli's credulous, frozen Norsemen (their eyes popping out?). Here is the "birds'-tread" dance ("bird tread," Epigraph), which assumes rose-sense as soon as we step from trefoil (a pulse, or a charm for every good purpose) to cinquefoil (a wild rose), compound leaves in each case looking like bird tracks. For the wild rose, bring in wild thyme and wild time, recalling: "Wild time *liveforever* horsethyme ice" (#4 Liveforever)—the line that also draws on Oberon's "I know a bank where the wild thyme blows" (*MND* II.ii.249). In #4 Liveforever there was an allusive fiery rose and the horse whose time is running (or being run by?) *80 Flowers*. There are no open indications of his presence in #75 Thyme but hints of it abound, from "time . . . wild . . . / *thyme*" of the opening to the comical wrapping up ("relentless-vest muffler jacket coat") of his mortal frame against the cold suddenly blowing out of the thymy bank. And then, "hope sevenyear," there is his projection of faith in time's design ("but trusts still greet C + me at 80"), which the last line of the poem elaborates.

The line from the *Dream* was perhaps to be expected as an opener; the ingenious turn that transforms blossoming thyme into wintry blizzard is a product of time present's influence. The storm is blowing out of #74

Aloe, the scene on the heath in *King Lear* where mad Edgar cavorted almost naked and babbled sense in nonsense. Now the same tempest has him howling "Poor Tom's a-cold" (*Lr.* III.iv.152) as the message of his bare flesh is borne upon Lear, who cries:

> Thou art the thing itself; unaccommodated man is no more but such a poor, bare, forked animal as thou art. Off, off, you lendings! come, unbutton here. (*Lr.* III.iv.110)

In #75 Thyme's storm, clothing goes on rather than comes off, most likely for good, seasonable reason. December storms had battered New York State earlier in the month #75 Thyme was composed, and the weather continued wintry as Zukofsky pressed on with the last *Flowers*.

No poor naked wretches here, then. The poem moves on: "one bluegreen eye ate his / hope sevenyear fanned." Once again literary reference is glossing the personal; the history Edgar makes up for himself as Poor Tom hints at some disaster that has reduced him to his present misery: "But mice and rats, and such small deer, / Have been Tom's food for seven long year" (*Lr.* III.iv.144). Zukofsky wanted the seven-year reference (though in his own case it lay before him, a hiatus to be filled before his eightieth birthday) but took care to turn aside any personal identification with the play's circumstances—"one bluegreen eye" is coming not from Shakespeare but from the first of several old notes worked into #75 Thyme. Its subject is a very different "Poor Tom," Guy Davenport's duplicitous and dinner-loving cat, Max. Zukofsky had had the story from Davenport in a letter that he copied into the black notebook, 30 November 1969; Davenport, edited by Zukofsky:

¶Speaking of Max, whom
we
I've had for two years—[B & I] discovered
the other evening that he is also the cat of some
people on Bell Court (a block away) who have been
wondering for two years who puts fresh flea
collars on him and doctors his chronic bad
[that]   bit
ear ([the result of] a squirrel [bite,] it turns out).
His name over there is Bunny. He is twelve
years old, pushing thirteen. ¶We were all
. . . amazed to uncover this very cat-like
duplicity in the old cooter, who had the grace I think
to be appalled to see his two families in the one
room. He even had two vets, and apparently sups
double daily, though he spends his nights [here] with us

Now I must check on the rumor which I paid no attention
to at the time that the widow down [Montgomery] street has a large
white cat with one blue eye and one green whose name
is Snowball. A triple identity would merit an article
in the Journal of the American Veterinarian Association,
surely, with photographs of the Master Confidence Cat as
                              Trinity
Max, Bunny, and Snowball. (Triplicity) more than
human & putting the humane by God in its deserved place.

(b.n.b., pp. 68–69)

The black notebook was sent to Texas in 1975, but not before Zukofsky
had abstracted this entry in the *"A"* 22 & 23 Spiral, first on page 131 and
then as part of the material that was eventually carried over into the
Flowers:

fresh flea collarer pitied wherever he's fed
                    "Snowball" one green eye one blue
           monologs ———
      cats don't live for dialogs ↘(word
                         (multiplied/multiple
      his cat sponged ~~multiplied~~ neighbors dinners

(*"A"* 22 & 23 Spiral, p. 161)

And, 17 September 1974, the story of feline sang-froid appeared for the
first time in the *80 Flowers* material:

Cat-one-green-eye-one-
blue ~~sponged~~ lived for
multiple dinners unknown & pitied
from neighbor to neighbor

(*80 Fl.* Notes, p. 4)

In the Second Abbreviated List (29 May 1976), the story had become
a margin note connected with another entry about the etymology of
cat (from Latin *feles,* "happy, fortunate") and the meaning of *catulus*
("whelp," diminutive of *canis*), a word one letter removed from Zukofsky's own preoccupying "Cat" of the mid-sixties (a positive monolog?).
Cats and dogs and multiplicity; the same material appears in the Third
Abbreviated List (October 1976), now connected to the thyme entry.
Davenport's story has been reconfigured thus:

Cat one-green-one-blue-eye | timing
pitied from neighbor to neighbor| ~~multiplying~~ dinners

(Third List, p. 4)

And so, multiple identities in a storm (raining cats and dogs?), Poor Tom victualing himself on mice and rats for seven long years, Shakespeare fits over the Davenport-Zukofsky material in #75 Thyme.[11]

But ("eye ate his / hope"), there is more to the passage; we are hearing: "hiatus / hope sevenyear fanned," that forward-looking glance at post–*80 Flowers* activities. On fire for the new project? Pausing a moment to check on *hiatus* in Lewis and Short, we find one sense of the word meaning "an eager desire, longing"—an apparently metaphoric extension of its literal sense of "an opening, aperture, cleft," which leads on to mean "gaping" (mouths).[12] Agape for the impending hiatus? Just as, in December 1974, the Epigraph had expressed an eager desire ("unwithering gaping") to be getting on with the *Flowers,* a thought of breast-feeding crossed with octogenarian gums; always new from the old. (Is it too much to connect the Latin *agape* [love] with the English *agape,* jaws wide open for it?) The Davenport story (1969) and its various condensations (1974, 1976) are glossed by *King Lear* and a 1977 storm in a poem about thyme which looks back to the start of the sequence (December 1974) while looking forward (over the hiatus) with a hope for 1984. Ever punctilious, Zukofsky makes sure that a grammatical hiatus is part of the figure, finding one latent in the term itself: "eye ate his."[13]

Still more from "eye ate his / hope"; are we hearing "hiatus hyssop"? or "eye ate hyssop"? or "I ate hyssop"? Certainly the plant is there, another interjection by time present, this time from the Americana notes. When Hyssop first appeared in the Third List (p. 9), Zukofsky had made a cross-reference to Kamm's explanations of the relationship between *Hyssopus officinalis* and the hyssop of the Bible (Kamm, pp. 141, 142–43). He had also written out the Hebrew for at least one instance of the biblical hyssop, probably from Psalm 51:7, David praying for forgiveness of his sins: "Purge me with hyssop, and I shall be clean: wash me, and I shall be whiter than snow." This hyssop (Hebrew: *ēzōph,* literally "aromatic plant") was part of the ceremonies of purification and was of considerable importance to Jewish tradition because God had directed Moses to tell the captive Israelites to brush their doorways with hyssop dipped in the blood of a sacrificed lamb to ensure their houses would be passed over as the last and most terrible plague was visited upon the Egyptians (Exod. 12). Kamm notes that eighteen herbs native to Palestine have been proposed as the biblical hyssop, including species of savory, marjoram, and thyme; she concludes that the most likely candidate is *Satureia thymus,* which is abundant in the area; neither Taylor nor Gray recognizes such a savory, but the *Century* mentions a Mediterranean species, *Satureia thymbra,* with a fragrance very like thyme. Whatever savory Kamm has in mind, it is a labiate and a highly aromatic bee plant; *Hyssopus officinalis* is also a labiate (the Greek *hyssōpos* translates as "aromatic plant"); it produces "long slender dark-green leaves with a mild mint odor and spikes of closely-set dark blue-purple flowers" (Kamm, p. 143). Quite thymelike.

Is it some aspect of the purification associations which leads Zukofsky to include hyssop (biblically) in #75 Thyme? (He has used the Psalms of David for their musical beauty before, in "Thanks to the Dictionary" [1932] and "Specifically, a writer of music . . ." [1934], *All*, p. 69.) Or is it simply the botanical affinity hyssop holds with thyme? Or, better still, both options—covered in the same breath by Shakespeare, in a speech of Iago's which had to arrive in *80 Flowers* at some point:

> Virtue! a fig! 'tis in ourselves that we are thus or thus. Our bodies are our gardens, to the which our wills are gardeners; so that if we will plant nettles or sow lettuce, set hyssop and weed up thyme, supply it with one gender of herbs or distract it with many, either to have it sterile with idleness or manured with industry, why, the power and corrigible authority of this lies in our wills. (*Oth.* I.iii.322)

"Wild time" (thyme) of #4 Liveforever was in at least one (Zukofsky-specified) sense *willed* time, horse time; and "horsethyme" is important not only in #4 Liveforever but also in the Epigraph, that direct ancestor of #75 Thyme. *80 Flowers* is of course the garden, "manured with industry," and brought forth by willed effort, in time.

Hyssop leads straight into thyme/time, and thyme/time leads on into the rosy fire of liveforever. The implication is there, along with D'Israeli's name and the report of his words:

> eyesack disrailing
> birds'-tread hie *rose* tree-budding fire
> moon's flight twice sun's

The oddity is "hie" (everything else traceable to the Epigraph or #1 Starglow)—and what is "hie *rose*" if not a high rose, even (*hierose?* a neologism, but credible) a sacred rose. Alternatively, choosing to go with the sense of "hie," we make out a verb for speed (timing?) among other vestiges of the Epigraph which ran with a bird tread over quagmires to dry ground—a dance that was also ("earth race horsethyme") a pace for *80 Flowers*. Should #3 Honesty, with its luminaries and lunarys, also be brought into the picture? "Moon's flight twice sun's" not only sounds like familiar territory—its Celia-related motifs conceivably link back to "hie" (how high the moon?) ("up someway above earth," *"A"*-22, p. 509). Hied up there, with birdsong.

The moon flight/sun flight comparison is another contribution of time past; Zukofsky is drawing on notes made 18 June 1975 from Rachel

Carson's *The Sea around Us.* The chapter concerned, "The Moving Tides," starts out with an epigraph from Bede: "In every country the moon keeps ever the rule of alliance with the sea which it once for all has agreed upon."[14] Carson is talking about the influence heavenly bodies exert on terrestrial waters ("Anyone who has lived near tidewater knows that the moon, far more than the sun, controls tides," p. 145). Zukofsky was living on Long Island Sound and was always conscious of moon time, literal or figurative; "Bede: moon's [allied] with sea (z)" was his condensation of Carson's epigraph; his own reworking—"(z)"—but also with an aura of Celia. Sounding the condensation: moon's [allied] with C (z). Eliding the elision: moon's with C, moon's with CZ. Time and tide, moon and sun (son?).

Carson continues (p. 145): "That the sun, with a mass 27 million times that of the moon, should have less influence over the tides than a small satellite of the earth is at first surprising. But in the mechanics of the universe, nearness counts for more than distant mass, and when all the mathematical calculations have been made we find that the moon's power over the tides is more than twice that of the sun." Zukofsky condensed this as: "moon's power twice the sun's" (*80 Fl.* Notes, p. 10A-2), one step from its manifestation in #75 Thyme, where "flight" is linked with the height of the moon (or of birds soaring and singing in "Initial" and #3 Honesty), as well as with the voyages to the moon which so captured Zukofsky's imagination in the later stages of "*A.*"

Mostly though, "moon's flight twice sun's" is present in the poem for its commentary on time; *tide* derives from the Anglo-Saxon *tid* (time, hour, season, opportunity) (*Century*)—and Carson launches into a discussion of how the terrestrial day has been lengthened over many millennia by the earth's slowing rotation. At the same time, tidal friction has pushed the (accelerating) moon out, and centrifugal force carries it further, lessening its influence over the tides. Eventually the length of the day will coincide with the (much increased) lunar month, the moon will be so far distant that it will cease to orbit the earth and there will be no lunar tides. The moon, such a powerful timepiece now, will in a sense destroy time as we know it.

Whether Zukofsky remembered the implications of Carson's pronouncements on time and tide is open to argument; he did not make notes on this section of the chapter, and his copy of *The Sea around Us* was sent to Texas in November 1975. By December 1977 and after several condensations, he was taking what Carson he had noted at its face value and therefore positioning moon and sun as arbiters of historical time, much as they appear in the "affair with the moon" passage of "Initial":

tidal waves also timing it
moon's day and earth's month

                                    ("*A*"-22, p. 510)

The whole of line seven, "moon's flight twice sun's spider-manor-
borne," concerns galactic trajectories. But spiders? manor-borne? (manner born?). The unlikely compound has come to #75 Thyme via a series of
notes leading back through Drafts, Third List, Notes, and "*A*" 22 & 23
Spiral. Throughout this progression, a spider pans (movie-camera use) to
the manner born, but it is only on page 161 of the Spiral that we find it with
some information about *Mariner* 9 approaching Mars. Checking the
Spiral again to find a dated entry, we come across the original note in the
twentieth-century section of the "*A*"-22 chronology:

                          pans
        8/18/73 . . spider manner born
    11/12/71 Mariner 9 approaching Mars
            in space [illeg.] without gravity stands to
                          reason uplifted . .
                needs no suit stronger than human
                            ("*A*" 22 & 23 Spiral, p. 64)

Recorded November 1971 as *Mariner* 9 journeyed toward Mars, condensed August 1973 for inclusion in "*A*"-23 (which never happened). What
we picture is a spiderlike *Mariner* ("manner") 9 spacecraft nearing the
object of its five-and-a-half-month, 248-million-mile voyage, cameras
sending back the first televised photos of the planet as the craft prepares to
become the first manmade object to orbit another planet.[15] The mission
was scheduled to last ninety days, during which *Mariner* 9 would continue
taking photos of Mars; the craft was expected to orbit the planet thereafter and transmit data for at least a further seventeen years—information
that may well have appealed to Zukofsky's well-developed sense for events
that characterize the history of an era. The observation about uplift in
zero gravity seems only tangentially concerned with the *Mariner* 9 flight
(which was unmanned), but it is the play on pressure suits and the suit of
humanity which produces in 1973 the phrase "manner born." *Mariner* 9's
TV cameras may have been panning the Martian surface flawlessly, but
included somehow in the condensate "spider pans to the manner born" is
the bare nakedness of the original human suit ("Thou art the thing itself;
unaccommodated man is no more but such a poor, bare, forked animal as
thou art"). Humility is something we apparently have to learn many times
over.

When Zukofsky came to use the 1971/1973 information, its passage
through the notebooks had supplied the elliptic casing through which he

(and no one else, without the notebooks) could still discern *Mariner* 9 and its historic flight. In 1977, the star-ship's name must have struck him as an appropriate extension of the Carson material. Line seven, with its densities of time and time-related motifs, could have been a hard act to follow except that there was still plenty of material to be worked into the poem. The last five words of #75 Thyme are freighted with individual and interrelated significance:

litter letter words-justice *thyme* righting

Zukofsky himself lays the first pointer to this: "line 8 hinting at Bard College doctor of letters degree," reads the last addition to the notes collected for the writing of the poem (*80 Fl.* Drafts, p. [109]). It is not the first hint (we recall #63 Oxalis' "honor the bard"), but it is the most intricate. It is stated in a context of amelioration—"words-justice *thyme* righting"; things are getting better (time is "doctoring" a certain wrong). Zukofsky's work has always been in a sense "time writing" (ahead of its time, concerned with its time, waiting for its time), never more so than in the years since 1974 and the start of *80 Flowers*. Now he has been made an honorary Doctor of Letters; the Latin citation that accompanied the degree admitted him "ad gradum doctoris in litteris"; and the poem comments: "litter letter words-justice." We remember Erigena's insistence, taken up by Zukofsky in the poem he carefully entitled "Initial" (one letter), that all grammar (words as sense) begins with the letter and finally resolves into it again. This poet is a superb doctor of letters; of letters, of the letter (corpus and smallest element): "A teacher, an instructor; a learned man; one skilled in a learned profession"—the *Century*'s first definition of *doctor* fits the circumstances perfectly. "Come, sit thou here, most learned justicer," Lear instructs Poor Tom, and: "Thou robed man of justice, take thy place" (*Lr.* III.vi.23, 38)—social inversion taking place as Lear hears sense in the madman's babble. Is Zukofsky taking another opportunity—"words-justice"—to gloss his own receipt of Bard's award with more words from the bard he has always honored? He is neither Poor Tom nor mad Lear, but the sense to be found in the non-sense of each talks to his poetic. Other conjunctions suggest that Zukofsky is bringing the mad scenes in *King Lear* as close as possible to #75 Thyme; though Tom's gamut of creepy-crawlies does not quite include spiders, he *has* been proud of heart and ridden a bay trotting horse, and been led through fire and flame over bog and quagmire (echoes of the Epigraph?). There is even a litter upon which Lear is to be laid and driven toward Dover.

Other kinds of litter are to be considered in Zukofsky's choice of the word. "Litter letter," Latin into English, first: perhaps the "litter" of words strewn over the storm scenes in *King Lear,* or (self-deprecation?) the

"litter" of fifty years' word work. But looking over the line break—
"borne / litter"—we make out not only Lear on his hurdle-bed but also
some kind of birth; not Shakespeare now but surely a backward glance at
the cats and dogs that were mixed with Zukofsky's abstract of the Max/
Bunny/Snowball story. They were Latin animals, unearthed as Zukofsky
checked the etymology of *cat* and found, in the *Century:* "the oldest
known forms being L., namely LL. *catus* . . . L. *catta* . . . ML. *cattus* . . . a
cat (a domestic cat, as opposed to *felis,* prop. a wildcat: see *Felis*), a word
found earlier in the dim. *catulus,* in common classical use in the extended
sense of 'the young of an animal, a kitten, cub, whelp, pup,' etc . . . and
esp. of a dog, being regarded in this sense as a dim. of *canis,* a dog: see
Canis)." This, as we have already remarked, supplied Zukofsky with a
feline grounding for the name of the poet whose work he translated over
seven years, lightly referring to it as his "Cats" (each poem one "Cat").
Lewis and Short agree with the *Century* on *catulus* and, under *catus,* give
as a primary meaning its adjectival sense of sharp to the hearing, clear-
sounding, shrill, which can be transferred to intellectual objects in a
positive sense (clear-sighted, intelligent, sagacious, wise; Catullian Cats?)
or in a negative one (sly, cunning, crafty, artful; the master confidence cat,
Max/Bunny/Snowball?). All, positive and negative, very catlike qualities.

Cross-checking *Felis,* in the *Century* we find more Zukofskian reason
for "borne / litter letter words-justice *thyme* righting." The root of the
word is *fe* (to produce or bear young), and the dictionary refers us to
felicity, fecund, and *fetus.* It was the first of these that caught Zukofsky's
eye and ("a felicity," *"A"*-21, p. 474) furthered his present intentions.
Felicity is from the Latin *felicita* (happiness), which derives from the
adjective *felix* ("happy, lucky, fortunate, in an earlier sense fruitful, fertile,
productive"). Hence the association with *fe.* Hence also ("borne / litter . . . *thyme* righting") the happiness produced by the Bard award and
the more generalized satisfaction with life in Port Jefferson and the project
being created out of it. In 1974 Zukofsky had told Corman in a letter of 21
February (SFU): "We expect more and more of quiet, including hushed
complaints such as over root-canal work and feet sensitive to weather days
ahead that sabotage the walks we once could take. But with so much sun,
clouds, stars, usw * (ice storms too) thru our windows, we should have left
the city ten years ago. It's a pleasure even to carry out the garbage."

Subsequent years had added to the Zukofskys' pleasure in their
surroundings and, perhaps sweetest of all, the world had finally "got to Z"
in a meaningful way. "It took a long time to get to Z in an alphabetical
order of a world such as it is," Zukofsky had written pointedly in the black
notebook (p. 11), 23 October 1967. In 1970, thinking of using the entry as
part of the transition to *"A"*-24, he recopied it on page 86 of the same

notebook, adding an indication of its original source: "4/8/70—C: (takes a long time). It took long to get to the letter Z." And near the end of *"A"*-23's History section (p. 558) the thought duly appears, minus the emphasis conceived for it, merely a parenthesis: "—a long time / to zee." The phrase takes its proper place in the quiet triumph of #75 Thyme, time now righting past wrongs as Zukofsky had been confident it would: "Takes time" begins the poem that celebrates the times of the *80 Flowers* project and begins its final progress to Z.

Thyme, roses, thyme. The emphases of the poem and what is associated with them—roses coupled with fire, coupled again with thyme and time, bees and horses circling near—prompt us to recall that Zukofsky has kept these motifs before us, in changing combination, throughout the sequence. For the most part, the cue seems rosaceous: where a rose is admitted, the other motifs are usually close at hand, but not since the Epigraph and #1 Starglow has the rose/thyme conjunction been so explicitly stated as in #75 Thyme. Over the last compositional phase of *80 Flowers,* from April 1977 on, it is possible to see (at least in retrospect) a certain building up of the concerns of the thyme poem—which had been the first item of the projected closing sequence early on in the planning of the *Flowers.* It is worth looking briefly at the poems that prepare its entrance.

To start with there is the snow-wreath (*Neviusa alabamensis*) of #51 Snowdrop and #52 Snow-Wreath, the latter ending "earth-rounds bees' rose." I have suggested in chapter 8 that this phrase displays in its first part the circular aspects of the garland each snow-flower poem makes and the cyclic aspects of the anniversary they commemorate together: "earth-rounds" are surely timekeepers, a feeling verified by the connection of "bees' rose" with #12 Cinquefoil's "minting white-thyme assures bees roses." In the same poem is the phrase: "rose / with the wild roses," that conceit Zukofsky capitalizes on to further the upward movement of the paradisal in his work ("birds'-tread hie *rose"*—it rose on high? as does "birdsong" in #3 Honesty, or bird-tread over quagmire in the Epigraph, or the singing and flight persistent in "Initial"). The roll of earth time, so closely associated with the cycles of sun and moon, is brought into #75 Thyme by the agency of a (fiery) rose just before *Mariner 9*'s epic journey through time and space spins us toward cosmos: "*rose* tree-budding fire / moon's flight twice sun's."

The next rose after the snow-wreath is #59 Spirea—appropriate because the title flower's name is derived from the Greek *speira,* a wreath or garland, and one of the varieties named in the poem is *Spirea prunifolia,* the (white) bridal wreath. It may have been this name that led Zukofsky to structure the nonbotanical content of the poem on the "unbridled horse" of Theophrastus's aphorism ("A"-14, p. 319; see also chap. 3) so that the *Flower* swarms with equine motifs on the one hand and (because the title flower is a rose?) bees on the other:

#59 SPIREA

Meadowsweet centuries friends allowably carol
lineal plinius names *spiry* thicket
old house-sites haul thick-ey'd horse
toméntose no-sting no honey mopus
sun-steed water unbridled harangue maybe
argued can nod dew day
hardhack steeplebush roseate or standing
smoke white thrive bridal wreath

The pertinent lines here run from "thick-ey'd horse" to "maybe / argued," the usual compound of botany, etymology, Greeks, and Shakespeare: "Why hast thou . . . given my treasures and my rights of thee / To thick-ey'd musing and curst melancholy?" Lady Percy asks Hotspur (1H4 II.iii.47). Is he, horse-obsessed, a "thick-ey'd horse," tormented? Is the poet, with his bad eyes, musing "thick-ey'd"? Or is the "horse / toméntose" simply Zukofskian transformation of *Spirea tomentosa*'s common names, hardhack and steeplebush—both fortuitously horsey?[16] Horse leads into honey by way of a second anecdote about Theophrastus, again told by Diogenes Laertius, again concerning bridles: "It is said that Aristotle applied to [Theophrastus] and Callisthenes what Plato had said of Xenocrates and himself . . . namely, that the one needed a bridle and the other a goad; for Theophrastus interpreted all his meaning with an excess of cleverness, whereas the other was naturally backward."[17]

It was not, however, the bridle (*chalinos*) that attracted Zukofsky's immediate attention but the goad (*myōpos*). Somehow he connected it with *mopus*, "a cant word from mopes a drone, a dreamer . . . & the male honeybee has no sting gathers no honey" (80 *Fl*. Drafts, p. 74). The definition came from Johnson's *Dictionary*, according to the same note, and the line that evolved from it was: "no-sting no honey mopus."[18] There is a curious twist of thought here by which a stingless drone is produced from a Greek goad; Johnson's *mopus* is coming out of a more usual form of the Greek *myōps*, a word that may signify "horsefly, gadfly" (most definitely with a sting) but also refers to the closing or contracting of the eyes by short-sighted (myopic) people in order to focus: the squint of a dull eye, hence by transferral, a dull or stupid person—Johnson's (metaphorical) drone. In one complicated derivation, we find goad, stingless and honeyless drone, horsefly, and myopic dreamer—another "thick-ey'd horse."

The ills of old age seldom overwhelmed the horse's drive, making him feel unstung and unproductive, but failing eyesight was among the chief irritations of those years and must have placed circumscriptions on what the spirit was perfectly willing to embrace. Perhaps this is why we also find in #59 Spirea hints of a Castalian infusion, to turn the musings sunny:

> Hark, hark! the lark at heaven's gate sings,
>   And Phoebus gins arise
> His steeds to water at those springs
>   On chalic'd flowers that lies.
>
> (Cym. II.ii.21)

"Sun-steed water unbridled harangue maybe / argued"—with that draught, spirits and output pick up; the horse now seems to need Theophrastian bridling, but it is likely his innate sense of decorum will prevail without it. Balance, after all, is the trademark of a "divine stylist" who can say: "better // trust an / unbridled horse / than / undigested // harangue" ("A"-14, p. 319). It was Aristotle who coined the name we know Theophrastus by; his suggestion of a bridle for that horse's enthusiasm sounds rueful rather than censorious (so much of a good thing?). Zukofsky's self-evaluation has the same ring to it.

Greek wreathery gives way to Latin; this time horses, bees, and thyme from Virgil, in a poem concerned to keep all of these things in the air (territory of the rainbow, Iris):

#61   BEARDED IRIS

> Gay ore geek con candlelows
> driveway west fanswordleaves equitant stride
> meteor aery creamwhite *falls bearded*
> pard-yellow spotted *standards* gules bees
> knuck to min hours crewroar
> thyme our booty us east
> bluepurple lapilli broad weigh Libra
> short month candelabrum amaryllis paper

An "equitant stride," horseback, arises out of the iris' fanned sword leaves, which enfold each other in two ranks. "Astride," Gray's glossary defines *equitant,* "as in *iris*" (the *Century*'s example of usage also specifies iris as the type of botanical equitance). But Zukofsky promptly lofts the figure ("meteor aery creamwhite") into the blue where (*ta meteōra,* literally "things in the air") it becomes a kind of Pegasus.[19] Given that the poem contains Virgilian bee lore taken from notes Zukofsky made July 1975, and that the other half of these is a list of line references to the horse sections of book 3 of the *Georgics,* it seems reasonable to think that the airborne horse is coming out of a passage such as: "Only upon those [horses] whom you mean to rear for the hope of the race, be sure to spend special pains, even from their early youth. From the first, the foal of a noble breed steps higher in the fields and brings his feet down lightly" (*Georgics* III.73). Or (and also listed by Zukofsky): "But when three summers are past and the fourth is come, let him soon begin to run round the circuit, to make his steps ring evenly, to bend his legs in alternating curves, and be as one hard labouring: then, then let him challenge the winds to a race, and, skimming over the open plains, as though free from reins, let him scarce plant his steps on the surface of the sand" (*Georgics* III.190). Virgil's bees are also young, also laboring, also in flight:

at fessae multa referunt se nocte minores,
crura thymo plenae; pascuntur et arbuta passim.
(*Georgics* IV.180)

("But the young betake them home in weariness, late at night, their thighs freighted with thyme; far and wide they feed on arbutus.") Bee thighs and horse legs (in both quotations) are signified by the same word: *crura.* Or, Zukofsky: "crewroar," the whole thymy swarm appearing in #61 Bearded Iris as: "gules bees / knuck to min hours crewroar / thyme our booty us." A beauteous sight. And some more flight description:

nec vero a stabulis pluvia impendente recedunt
longius, aut credunt caelo adventantibus Euris,
sed circum tutae sub moenibus urbis aquantur
excursusque brevis temptant, et saepe lapillos,
ut cumbae instabiles fluctu iactante saburram,
tollunt, his sese per inania nubila librant.
(*Georgics* IV.191)

"Nor yet, if rain impend, do they stray far from their stalls, or trust the sky when eastern gales are near, but round about, beneath the shelter of their city walls, draw water, and essay short flights; and often they raise tiny stones, as unsteady barques take up ballast in a tossing sea, and with these balance themselves amid the unsubstantial clouds." This Zukofsky works out to: "east / bluepurple lapilli broad weigh Libra"—balance become literally (celestial) scales in the face of (east?) winds. Just how close to home are these flights, some of them thyme (time) flights? The old worker ("us east . . . broad weigh") is to be found, never too far from his stall, at 306 East Broadway.

There was another horse passage, concerning the brilliant colt grown old, on Zukofsky's list of Virgil references: "Yet even such a steed, when, worn with disease or sluggish through years, he begins to fail, shut up indoors and pity not his inglorious age. Cold is his passion when old, vainly he strives at a thankless toil, and whenever he comes to the fray his ardour is futile, as in the stubble a great fire rages at times without strength. Therefore note above all their spirit and years" (*Georgics* III.95). Time's passage. It might almost be "thoughts' template" for the "sorrow of harness pulses pent" (Epigraph), asking no pity:

a nerve's aching respond to
energies not itself: old in
a greenhouse the stabled horse
sings sometimes, thoughts' template
somehow furthers a cento reading[20]

(*"A"*-22, p. 535)

Which parts of the horse are indomitable? When does his sense of balance call for a bridling of the ardor that pours out? When does the same shrewd self-evaluation recognize that age cannot sap the physical capacity for ardor without somehow affecting its spiritual coordinate? Is this the other face of the "dream paradise of old age" Zukofsky wrote of to Corman? There are no definite answers to such questions—only an unsettling ambivalence among the motifs of the last ten *Flowers*. The conundrum is restated, once more obliquely, in #63 Oxalis (even complaints were expected to be muted in the enveloping quiet of Port Jefferson), where elation and sharpnesses of one sort or another rub shoulders:

#63   OXALIS

Wood sorrel lady's-sorrel 3-hearts tow ox
a leese rapids whose soul
air-spring disperses thru water elator
ox lips mistaken for clover
more ruse mulberry locust-flower shield
welcome wanderer *óxalis* time primrose-yellow
a breeze sweet rampant pulse
scald scold honor the bard

Was it the combination of "sorrel" and finding out that the Greek *oxys* had more senses of sharpness than acidity, sourness, pungency (the leaves and stems of most oxalises are sour-juiced), that decided Zukofsky to bring in the horse again? Plus the resemblance of oxalis leaves (three leaflets, notched) to those of clover, the lucky leaf ("One's a lucky horse,"

"*A*"-12, p. 176)—more lucky to Zukofsky when its heart shapes number three rather than four? Each leaflet-heart comes to a sharp point at the mutual conjunction, or is "brought to a point" (*kyrbasias es oxy apēg-menas*); Zukofsky was looking at Liddell and Scott's entry for *oxys*. "Tow ox / a"? The vertex of a triangle is expressed in the phrase *to oxy*. The Greek point was also extended to the senses, and could signify sharp keen feeling, whether the blazing heat of the sun or stabs of pain or grief. Virgil's "rapidus sol" is cited by Liddell and Scott as an analog; Zukofsky checked Lewis and Short and found the reference under the literal sense (very rare, used only poetically) of *rapidus* as "tearing away, seizing." In the *Georgics,* the effects of burning-over are supposed to harden and therefore protect the soil from, among other things, "seizure" by the sun's heat:

> ne tenues pluviae rapidive potentia solis
> acrior aut Boreae penetrabile frigus adurat.
>
> > (*Georgics* I.92)

"So that the searching showers may not harm, or the blazing sun's fierce tyranny wither it, or the North-wind's piercing cold." Remembering "so much sun, clouds, stars usw∗(ice storms too) thru our windows, we should have left the city ten years ago"—Zukofsky is developing a landsman's sense of the elements, probably hearing with the poet's ear: "Fear no more the heat o' th' sun, / Nor the furious winter's rages" (*Cym.* IV.ii.258), or even: "The sun shall not smite thee by day, nor the moon by night" (Ps. 121:1). In #63 Oxalis, the sense of Virgil's "rapidus sol" and Liddell and Scott's citation of the trope is to be heard in: "rapids whose soul / air-spring disperses through water."

For *rapidus* in its more customary sense means "tearing or hurrying along, swift, quick, rapid"; and suddenly we see that the *oxys-rapidus* carryover has generated a multitude of meanings in #63 Oxalis, from the sharp points of (keen) hearts that may feel (or, unwittingly, inflict?) pain, grief, or other emotional blazes ("scald scold"), to the quick (and as sharply felt) elations sweeping those same rapid souls: "a breeze sweet rampant pulse." If this last, by means of the drive word "pulse," stirs powerful memories of the horse of the Epigraph, perhaps it is intended to, because the source of the line deals expressly with the issue of poetic inspiration. Johnson wrote of Milton's compositional technique: "Richardson, who . . . discovers always a wish to find Milton discriminated from other men, relates, that 'he would sometimes lie awake whole nights, but not a verse could he make; and on a sudden his poetical faculty would rush upon him with an *impetus* or *oestrum,* and his daughter was immediately called to secure what came.'"[21]

Oestrum, says the *Century,* is more properly *oestrus* and it means "vehement desire or emotion, passion, frenzy." *Oestrus,* from the Greek *oistros,* is "gadfly," or "breeze" and by extension "vehement urging, stimulus, desire"; in fact, "sting." *Oistros* is listed as a synonym for *myōps,* the goad/gadfly/squint of #59 Spirea. And so it is that a sweet breeze is another sharp point, this time rather like the Aristotelian goad, for the "rampant pulse" of the horse—whose imagination still seems to run with the wind whatever stable the old singer is compelled to inhabit, reaffirming: "If someone stole off with its body / Be sure that its spirits / Canter forever" (*"A"*-12, p. 181).

As for "honor the bard," the phrase with which #63 Oxalis closes, more than Shakespeare and a hint of the honorary doctorate is encompassed when we discover, as Zukofsky did when he checked the *Century* and found a fine illustration, that a *bard* can be medieval horse's armor. Bards are the defensive armor of a war-horse (an old war-horse, this poet looking at himself with a smile?), or they may be the decorative caparison used in tournaments, jousts, or processions, woven or embroidered with the rider's arms. We appear to have arrived at the ultimate inference of "honor the bard"—not exactly "honor the poet" (as, with a clear conscience, he could let the phrase do homage to Shakespeare), but (noun equivalence) "honor [is] the bard"; the caparison. Bard College had decorated the horse, honored him with an honorary Doctor of Letters— his very coat of arms ("relentless-vest muffler jacket coat," #75 Thyme).

There are stars and eyes in #66 Artemisia ("Art to me's hear stellary / honor . . . blur / old eyes-iris evergreen retainers sun"); there is "flora honey bees visit" and a "many days / paradise dim covert yellow heath / alight" in #67 Wild Honeysuckle. There are the stars, (Virgilian) bees, and eye restoratives in #71 Aster, a rosy cup and wine in #72 Raspberry, and a revolving set of Eden motifs in #73 Daisy. These things, put with the magic island and *Dream* enchantments of #74 Aloe and the renewed roses and fire of #75 Thyme (at a time of great personal fulfilment, not forgetting the thankless years), ensure that we move into the final five *Flowers* with all faculties alert for news of this often difficult passage through a paradise in constant process of definition.

10

The Composites: #76 Vines and #77 Weeds

#76 Vines

#75 Thyme was completed 20 December 1977; 21 December Zukofsky made his first approach to Freeman Keith of the Stinehour Press (see chap. 1), and 23 December he began collecting notes for #76 Vines. This meant first of all selecting from the Third List suitable candidates for the poem—a process that entailed at least two extra pages (both checkbook-sized, one of them actually the cardboard back of a checkbook), which were later interleaved with the *80 Flowers* Drafts. At the outset Zukofsky was considering more than a dozen vines for inclusion: "Select & collect max 13" reads a note at the top of one of these lists, and a similar instruction on one of the preliminary lists for #77 Weeds suggests there was more than random chance to the selection of the number. Zukofsky's affinity for 13 was well-established: "To answer on my lucky day—it being Friday the 13th," he wrote Corman in August 1965 (SFU), and in "*A*"-19 (with a vine to boot):

> The wistaria 's
> blessing: why
> you should
> have patience
> ranging random
> numbers (my
> luck is
> 13)

("*A*"-19, p. 420)

However, the thirteen candidates were weeded out to "6 vines only" as the list that then alphabetizes them on the verso of the checkbook back puts it. They were bittersweet, bougainvillea, clematis, grape, nasturtium, and wistaria. Why six? Taylor's entry on vines defines six classes of garden interest, and although the selection above covers only four of these—wall-top tumblers (bittersweet and clematis), woody vines (grape and wistaria), annuals (nasturtium), and greenhouse vines (bougainvillea)—it is not unreasonable to think that Zukofsky had the number in mind as he scaled down the original count.

The horticulturalist was on the job, then, but it was the Doctor of Letters who supervised preparations for the vines poem and placed it in the alphabetical countdown: "beg. *You vines* (see Allen & Greenough 1 6 & 5. pp. 1 & 3) history L. alphab. (takes care of U₂V)." This instruction (*80 Fl.* Drafts, p. [110]), correctly read, explains why the sequence apparently leaps from T (#75 Thyme) to V (#76 Vines) without an intervening U. *Allen and Greenough's New Latin Grammar* describes in its first section ("The Alphabet") the relation between consonantal "u" and vowel "u": the Latin alphabet did not distinguish between the two sounds, and the letter "v" was used to denote each. In modern texts, we use "u" for the vowel sound and "v" (pronounced with the sound of our consonant "w") for the consonant sound of the Latin "u." Thus *ius* (vowel "u"), *vir* (consonantal "u"), and *iuvenis* (vowel "u" succeeded by consonantal "u").[1] Zukofsky's distillation of this—and we remember the "y" that was "u" ("why that was you," *"A"*-22, p. 508) of the Greco-Latin alphabetizing in "Initial"—is "U₂V." Sounded, this is: "U to V," which is what happened to Latin consonantal "u"; which is what happens in English alphabetical sequence; which is about to happen, a quick skip, in the sequence of *80 Flowers.* Semantically, "U₂V" implies plurality (two "u"s, or "you" plural; i.e., "you two"), which is why #76 Vines was to begin "You vines." Or: "U Vines," as one of the preliminary list headings styles it. At this point we might recall that U is the sixth-to-last letter of the English alphabet. Six letters, six vines; wreathing:

#76   VINES

You vines wreathe sands printless
coil *bittersweet waxwork* most bound
free walls fall-arils scan dense
mushrooms gathered gentler than *grapevine*
columned pied *clematis* life's white
withywind *wistaria* nods *traveler's joy*
magenta-climb 3-bract *bougainvillea* seafroth floret
nasturtium-leaf what most it heart

"You vines wreathe"—"u," "v," "w"; and the English sequence reminds us that one Latin "v" (the consonantal "u") is voiced by us as "w"—more alphabetical wreathery. So that *vitis,* the Latin vine, is sounded "witus," which is why, eventually, the product of the vine is in English *wine.* And the force of that consonantal Latin "u" derives from the Greek *oinos* (wine), which according to Skeat (whom Zukofsky consulted) is allied to *oinē* (vine), with a common root WEI, to twine (to wind?). *Oinē*, vines, Vitaceae (U, V, W); Zukofsky's choice of subject for the seventy-sixth *Flower* could not have been better, given its position in the sequence and the wreathery of *80 Flowers*.

Who should be stage-managing that process but Prospero, bringing matters to a head with a last call on the rough magic that will draw the play's personnel to his cell, most of them to stand charmed within a circle they will step out of only by the curative power of music. The invocation:

> Ye elves of hills, brooks, standing lakes, and groves,
> And ye that on the sands with printless foot
> Do chase the ebbing Neptune, and do fly him
> When he comes back; you demi-puppets that
> By moonshine do the green sour ringlets make,
> Whereof the ewe not bites; and you whose pastime
> Is to make midnight mushrooms, that rejoice
> To hear the solemn curfew; by whose aid,
> Weak masters though ye be, I have bedimm'd
> The noontide sun, call'd forth the mutinous winds,
> And 'twixt the green sea and the azur'd vault
> Set roaring war; to the dread rattling thunder
> Have I given fire, and rifted Jove's stout oak
> With his own bolt; the strong-bas'd promontory
> Have I made shake; and by the spurs pluck'd up
> The pine and cedar; graves at my command
> Have wak'd their sleepers, op'd, and let 'em forth
> By my so potent art.
>
> (*Tmp.* V.i.33)

"You vines wreathe sands printless / coil"—the echoes ("keywords," Zukofsky calls them, *80 Fl.* Drafts, p. [110]) are unmistakable, the invocation overlaid with a mental image of vines near some shore where a wreathery of waves running up a beach imitates kinetically, constantly, the vegetative twists. Thoughts of Bermuda spring to mind, #74 Aloe's Prospero right there as the possible implications of "*bittersweet waxwork* most bound / free" work their way into the mind's eye long before we arrive ("*traveler's joy*"?) at "magenta-climb 3-bract *bougainvillea* seafroth floret" in line seven.

Bougainvillea is indeed one of the First List entrants, first seen in Paget, 1972; part of the island vividness Zukofsky associates with the intensity of emotions he experienced there. Bougainvillea was very likely a "seafroth floret" in the sense of being close to the Bermudan surf (it also flowers in great drifts of color). Then we learn from the notes made in Paget that a cottage the Zukofskys stayed in was called Sea Foam and next-door to it was one named Wind Song (*"A"* 22 & 23 Spiral, p. 140):

> Between grape bay and hungry
> bay wind song and sea
> foam, reef (stone beeves)—struck
> green kelp waves arms, dips
> tons my only eyes fear.

("A"-22, pp. 532–33)

The cottage was between the two bays, and the kelp (sea vines?) was clearly another memorable image of the ocean's motor power. Prospero's dominion over green sea and azured vault had included setting roaring war between them; we know the effect news of his sister's death had on Zukofsky's impressions of Bermuda, and it was wound into *"A"*-22's second Music section, to the rhythm of pounding surf: "ocean blued windows sweat / between soused bitten cliff and / *that* . . . sun burns thru the roars / dear eyes, *all eyes*" (*"A"*-22, p. 533).

The casting of an analogy between himself and the chief protagonist of *The Tempest* is a recurring feature of Zukofsky's old age, traceable in both correspondence and the poetry. It is inextricable from the implications of Prospero's name, as a 1964 letter to Charles Tomlinson, quoted by that poet, shows. Zukofsky had found Tomlinson's work valid, saying: "I can read it—which is to be moved—as Ez used to say. And for the rest Prospero had better shut up about Miranda's accomplishments—just go ahead and prosper."[2] This was echoed 1967, in the final Voice Off of *"A"*-21:

> And tho love starve
> carved mostly bones
> (not *those* young friends
> put to good use)
> if I'm not dead
> a dead mask smiles
> to all old friends
> still young where else
> it says *take care*
> *prosper*
> without my tongue
> only your own

("A"-21, p. 500)

The figure surfaces again in the last strophes of "Between grape bay and hungry / bay" as Paget's Prospero listens attentively to Bellagio's "peasant gardener" saying: " 'iberis prefers limestone—evonymus prospers' " ("A"-22, p. 535).[3] As he began "A"-23, the identification was sufficiently strong for Zukofsky to remark to Guy Davenport apropos of writing an endorsement for *Tatlin!:* "I'd be swamped under endless requests for blurbs. But Prospero's old mind would indeed be troubled both if he broke his vow not to write them and after all the time you've given me saw no way to get around a vow."[4]

The 1977 call on his Shakespearean alias was quite the conjuring of an old friend to step through a well-known role (we recall, too, other glimpses of Prospero in *80 Flowers* before this, notably in the time-measuring, plummet-sounding #22 Bayberry; see chap. 6). The book-drowning, art-abjuring aspects of the role are not so much stated as implied in #76 Vines, which concentrates on present powers. But then (line four) a link with the autobiographical movement of "Poem Beginning 'The' " is discovered, because "mushrooms gathered" is a condensate of:

Speaking about epics, mother,
How long ago is it since you gathered mushrooms,
Gathered mushrooms while you mayed.

(*All,* p. 18)

And "gathered" in #76 Vines must host the memory of 1926's appropriation, Robert Herrick's "Gather ye Rose-buds while ye may . . ."; a poem making much of time.[5] Wreathery. As usual, though, time present has something to add to the Prospero motif; Zukofsky's notes pick out for emphasis the magus' observation about plucking up pines and cedars by the spurs—"tree-roots," as he then clarifies it. And, perhaps drawn on by the appearance of trees so close to the start of "Gamut," or thinking of goads and breezes recently come the horse's way, he adds more Shakespeare, thickening the blend of arboreal and oblique personal reference:

I do note
That grief and patience, rooted in him both,
Mingle their spurs together.

(*Cym.* IV.ii.56)

To Guiderius's observation, Arviragus responds:

Grow, patience!
And let the stinking elder, grief, untwine
His perishing root with th'increasing vine!

(*Cym.* IV.ii.58)

The *Cymbeline* spur does not appear in #76 Vines but its under-earth presence contributes to *"bittersweet waxwork* most bound / free," a phrase that begins the winding together of *Celastrus scandens* ("scan dense"), which is the vine called bittersweet, waxwork, or fever-twig (Taylor), and the poetry of Phineas Fletcher (1580–1650).

A scrap of paper attached to one of the preliminary lists of vines is covered on both sides with lines from Fletcher excerpted from H. J. Massingham's *Treasury of Seventeenth-Century English Verse.*[6] One of Fletcher's several poems entitled "Love" is quoted at some length; it is a seventeenth-century corollary to Shakespeare's definition of love as traced by Zukofsky in *Bottom* (parts Zukofsky copied out are italicized);

LOVE

> *Love is the sire, dam, nurse, and seed*
> Of all that earth, air, waters breed:
> All these, earth, water, air, fire,
> Though contraries, in love conspire.
> Fond painters: Love is *not a lad*
> *With bow, and shafts,* and feathers clad,
> *As he is Fancied in the brain*
> *Of* some loose loving *idle swain.*
> *Much sooner* is he *felt than seen;*
> His *substance subtile,* slight, and thin.
> *Oft leaps* he *from the glancing eyes;*
> . . .
> Love with a thousand darts abounds,
> Surest and deepest virtue wounds;
> *Oft himself becomes a dart,*
> And love with love doth love impart.
> Thou *painful pleasure, pleasing pain,*
> Thou gainful loss, thou losing gain,
> *Thou bitter sweet, easing disease,*
> *How dost thou by displeasing please?*
> How dost thou thus *bewitch the heart,*
> *To love in hate, to joy in smart!*
> *To think itself most bound when free,*
> *And freest in its slavery?*
> *Every creature* is thy debtor;
> None but loves, some worse, some better:
> Only *in love* they *happy prove*
> *Who love what most deserves their love.*[7]

From Phineas Fletcher, whose name might signify viny arrows, and whose poem abounds in darts and spurs, #76 Vines takes material that works out to *"bittersweet . . . most bound / free"* and (final note) "what most it heart." Zukofsky has restated the old ambiguity we observed in "Initial" and #3 Honesty particularly, and which haunts the paradisal throughout his work.

The genus *Celastrus* is also known as staff-tree (Prospero: "I'll break my staff, / Bury it certain fathoms in the earth," *Tmp.* V.i.54), and *Celastrus scandens* (Latin, "climbing") is best planted on the tops of low walls, its chief beauty the brilliant crimson arils of the terminal clusters of its yellow fruit: "walls fall-arils scan dense." *Aril* derives ultimately from *aridus* (dry), via the intermediary *arilli* (dried grapes); and there, one line later, inwinding mushrooms, is the vine itself: "mushrooms gathered gentler than *grapevine*." That is, mushrooms are gathered (from the *Tempest* invocation) but perhaps rosebuds are too (from Herrick and "Poem Beginning 'The'"). And if rosebuds and Herrick, "gentler than *grapevine*," why not (more seventeenth century) a rosy wreath and Ben Jonson, "Drinke to me, onely, with thine eyes / . . . And ile not look for wine," asking for the soul's divine cup? That song, of course, "To Celia."

We might ask ourselves what has become of Zukofsky's stated intention to use more of the Americana. *Celastrus scandens* is North American and comes out of the Third List (under Staff-tree and Waxwork) but it is not part of the designated Americana. Mushroom is on both lists, with the reference to " 'The' "; was it Taylor's illustration of mushroom mycelia that encouraged Zukofsky to include the fungus in his vines poem?[8] Grape is a Third List candidate only, but Taylor's entry on it starts out by treating the twenty or thirty species of wild native grape at some length before moving on to discuss *Vitus vinifera*, the wine-making grape, which is European-derived. And clematis, wistaria, bougainvillea, nasturtium? None appears in the extant Americana, but the first two have North American varieties and the last two are natives of South America. Zukofsky has brought his vines poem to the New World by wrapping botany around a Shakespearean speech that personal circumstances and one of Ariel's midnight flights had already removed ("Initial") from its original setting to the Bermudas.

As usual, though, movement *between* Old World and New continues to inform the last poems of the sequence. At this point in #76 Vines are several sorts of clematis, the "slender vine" of the Greeks: "columned pied *clematis* life's white / withywind . . . *traveler's joy*." Zukofsky mentions "columnar clematis" on the scrap of paper where he also copied out the Fletcher verses; the phrase presumably comes from the description of clematis in one of the preliminary lists as (being trained over?) "pillars rose blue white, pink, lilac"—pied columns, no less. The pillar-twining also appears to link back over the line break to *"grapevine"* and to spur a thought of *climbing* roses gathered before that; an order that echoes: "unregretful minds / always sense roses, grape, clematis / twine" (*"A"*-23, p. 553).

The "pied *clematis*" could mean (covering those pillars) a splendid profusion of varieties; alternatively, it might be describing the "violet-purple" shade of *Clematis jackmani,* which is mentioned specifically (and close to the pillar reference) on the preliminary list of vines. However, "life's white / withywind" can signify only *Clematis vitalba,* an Old World species once called *Vitis alba* (the white vine), which name John Gerard objected to in favor of *Viorna, quasi vias ornans,* "of decking and adorning waies and hedges, where people trauell, and thereupon I have named it the Traueilers Ioie" (Gray's quotation of Gerard appropriately decked out in consonantal "u"s). Substituting *vita* (life) for *vitis* (vine) produced for Zukofsky a lively vine, its other common name (twining, flexible)—withywind. "Whiter galet then the white withie-wind"; the *Century* quotes Burton's *Anatomy of Melancholy,* observing that the word is identical to *withwind,* the bindweed *Convolvulus arvensis.* The information simply adds density to #76 Vines, because morning glory (*Ipomoea purpurea*) was among its original thirteen candidates, a close relative of the white-flowered field bindweed; "white / withywind" embraces both twiners, nodding (in the breeze?) at wistaria, the next woody vine. The joyous sight of Gerard's vine sits well with the exquisite lyricism of the spring-flowering pea's last appearance in *"A"*:

> Escaped conceptions clouds darken hang
> without violence, orioles dart and
> the rare flower opens, spring's
> green snow the moon above.
> Wistaria plights flute song unbroken,
> Mayfly larvae launched rice husk
> on sea. Three days rain
> and the cold thank god
> Who persists saying, *no,* nature.
> Nature says, this wet, vine.[9]
>
> (*"A"*-22, pp. 526–27)

An Asian vine in this context; joined in the next breath of #76 Vines by another *"traveler's joy,"* the bougainvillea, a tropical "seafroth floret," which in turn gives way to *"nasturtium*-leaf"—a salad green. But Zukofsky is not so much interested here in culinary as in etymological business. The true Latin is not *Nasturtium* (properly applied to the watercress, only by transferral to the also-delicious nasturtium) but *Tropaelum,* from the Greek for "trophy," "in allusion to the shield-shaped leaves" (Taylor). The word concerned is *tropaios;* according to the *Century* it means "of defeat, of change or turning," from *tropē* (defeat, rout), literally "a turning" (when it can mean a solstice; hence *tropic*). The winter solstice of 1977 has just passed; there is also a decidedly tropical air to #76 Vines because of its association with Bermuda—which lies north of the twenty-fourth parallel but supports a tropical climate.

How do we get from Greek turns to Latin shields? (other popular names for *Tropaelum* are trophy-cress and trophy-wort; *Century*). A trophy was originally a sign of victory, the monument of an enemy's defeat (Greek *tropaion;* Latin *tropaeum*): "It consisted of some of the arms and other spoils of the vanquished enemy hung upon the trunk of a tree or a pillar or upright by the victor" (*Century*). But Lewis and Short, under *tropaeum,* expand on this as "originally a trunk of a tree, on which were fixed the arms, shields, helmets, etc., taken from the enemy; afterwards made of stone and ornamented in the same manner." #76 Vines has found itself another pillar, coiled bittersweetly with tokens of victory to complement Fletcher's multiple images of love's martial strife, which resolves ("what most it heart") into happiness only when Love loves what most deserves its love. In addition, Zukofsky adds a reference—"Nasturtium-Pope Essay on Man Epistle IV. 303" (*80 Fl.* Drafts, p. [110])—that confirms the etymological nature of his investigations. The lines concerned deal with the false scale of happiness of "the rich, the honour'd, fam'd, and great":

> What greater bliss attends their close of life?
> Some greedy minion, or imperious wife,
> The trophy'd arches, story'd halls invade
> And haunt their slumbers in the pompous shade.[10]

" 'Virtue alone, is Happiness below' "; Pope's quotation seems to accord with what we know of Zukofsky's conditions for a paradisal community.

#77 Weeds

Marshaling components for the weeds poem proceeded along the same lines as the selection of vines, but the initial lists of weeds began earlier in the *80 Flowers* Notes. The idea for a composite weeds poem was in evidence soon after completion of the First List, born out of the identifications Zukofsky was making from the USDA handbook *Common Weeds,* late 1974 and 1975. This group was added to in the First Abbreviated List (August 1975) and then numbered from one to thirteen at the end of the

Second Abbreviated List (May 1976). The same group was recopied in the Third Abbreviated List (October 1976), and, when Zukofsky came to make some preliminary notes for #77 Weeds, he worked partly from the thirteen and partly from the extended Third List (some of which was also in the Americana notes), finishing with two more checkbook-sized pages about weeds (one of these bearing the instruction to select and collect a maximum of thirteen candidates from the Third List). Then there was a third page, a scrap headed "Order of Weeds" numbering the final eleven "weeds" (but some numbers included more than one plant). These eleven and their outriders are, in order, the flora of #77 Weeds. Most of them are italicized in the poem:

#77   WEEDS

Founderous wilding weeds endear paradise
smallhead *bluecurls* blue-wool'd *romero* defer-ah
bamboo-suh *downyrattlesnake* pact is pubescence
feed talk bananas great maulin'
favor'd *henbit chara* no wars
goldenrod solid-day go ponder otter
blue-boneset scut-redshank *ladysthumb* smilax *herb-patience*
ascending *tansy field-bindweed lady's-orchid-slipper* foison[11]

Choked with weeds? (consider the length and articulate the mouthfuls of those last two lines). The vines were sinuous in their embrace of each other; the weeds sprawl and pile up, name after name. Each poem "flourishes" according to the habit of its subject. But as we have come to expect of those *Flowers* that spend a lot of time apparently listing components, there is more to #77 Weeds than the pile of names; the beginning of its informing framework is almost as old as the first weed groupings of the Notes.

We recall that Zukofsky coined the phrase "Weeds dress earth," with its play on gorgeous clothing, in the Weeds addendum of the First List; with the weeds, it was transferred to the First Abbreviated List, to be joined there by two phrases that also look like Zukofsky originals: "wilding stemware (for a start)," and then, a later interlineation: "May 21/76 Weeds met in paradise." The three phrases set up an interesting figure; first and most important is the idea that weeds are more than the gardener's sworn enemy, which Taylor (of course) casts them as. When Zukofsky used "weeds dress earth" in line six of #19 Geranium, he was moving toward a vision of the paradisal via personal delight in such free-flowering profusion—delight backed up by Gerard's description of the earth appareled in an embroidered floral robe, which prompted thoughts of the paradisal gem garden of Gilgamesh's journey (see chap. 5). "Wild-ing stemware" (precious crystal?) is also (stemwear) an extension of the living dress the earth puts on without assistance from gardeners. As for "weeds met in paradise," the phrase is among other things confirming many shades of meaning to an "earthly paradise" (e.g., remember the darnel, *aira,* in the paradise of "Initial").

"Weeds dress earth" was used (in #19 Geranium) by 7 October 1975; by 20 September 1976 Zukofsky had written the weed poems that introduce Hardy to the sequence (#44 Queen Anne's Lace, #45 Chicory, #46 Dandelion), incidentally using some of the early weed candidates. #63 Oxalis, #69 Yarrow, and #72 Raspberry each took one of the group of thirteen, but still no poem had touched the paradise-met wilding stem-wear. Clearly those elements were destined for the composite weeds poem, and in the Third Abbreviated List Zukofsky finally amalgamates them: "LZ Wilding stemware weeds met in paradise [name 13]." Further down the same page, something new is introduced: "weeds so much is food." He had been making an entry on lamb's quarters (*Chenopodium album*), which is related to spinach; perhaps it was that spinachy relationship plus the butcher-shop popular name of the plant (meat and veg?) which prompted the observation about food. It also brought to mind more of Gerard's introductory remarks about the flora so painstakingly described in the *Herball:* "The delight is great, but the use greater, and joyned often with necessitie."[12] This was echoed in the Hudson-quoting-Gerard section of Woodward's introduction that Zukofsky had noted; nature making its plants "not for meat and medicine only," some to be esteemed for beauty alone—but meat and medicine nevertheless cropping up everywhere, as Zukofsky realized, making additions to his Third List.

So much is food. Does this account for the bamboo and the bananas in #77 Weeds, both "weedy" in their profuse growth? Meat and medicine— the latter accounting for the presence of goldenrod, blue-boneset, herb patience, and tansy? All of it a kind of harvest, summed up in the final word of the poem: "foison." A closer look at each component may answer some of our questions, but first (because of "Founderous," that opening word) we need to look in a different direction: the writing of John Adams as edited by Zukofsky reading the *Diary and Autobiography,* April 1976.[13]

Adams, writing in 1802, recalled a journey through rough country in the spring of 1765: "The Roads, where a wheel had never rolled from the Creation, were miry and founderous, incumbered with long Sloughs of Water."[14] Zukofsky, curious, consulted the *Century* and discovered that the rare word meant "Causing to founder, go lame, or be disabled"— "disabling" as he recast it from this definition (*80 Fl.* Notes, p. 18), probably admiring Adams's lexical exactitude as he did so—the next sentence of the *Autobiography* describes how dangerous the stump- and root-ridden road was for a horse's limbs as well as its rider's. Adams could reflect that by 1802 the same country was beautifully cultivated; and in the *Diary* of 1771 a similar progress toward cultivation is described in terms of highest approbation: "I have spent this Morning in Riding thro Paradise. My Eyes never beheld so fine a Country. From Bissills in Windsor to Hartford Ferry, 8 miles, is one continued Street—Houses all along, and a vast Prospect of level Country on each Hand, the Lands very rich and the Husbandry pretty good."[15]

Adams's "paradise" is civilization, not the barely touched American wilderness so "founderous" to early attempts at taming it; the Creation and paradise garden standing at opposite ends of an eighteenth-century outlook. Zukofsky noted the "founderous" entry and its 1802 codicil; he also noted the first sentence of the "paradise" entry—and its date: 8 June 1771. One paradise maps onto another. When the first line of #77 Weeds emerges in 1977 as: "Founderous wilding weeds endear paradise," we hear many things: those disabling (to the garden, to civilization) plants, springing up spontaneously and flourishing uncultivated, nonetheless endearing themselves to the gardeners of East Broadway, who looked upon them with more than a horticulturalist's eye and reflected that nobody planted out Eden or kept its weeds down. Turn the line another way and hear, characteristically, a shadow "in dear paradise," weeds choking something.

Mostly, however, we are to perceive the sunny paradisal glinting through Zukofsky's "wilding stemware weeds met in paradise" and his appreciation of Adams's two hundred-year-old heaven of 8 June. As if to reinforce the latter, one more piece of Adams is inserted in the poem—"no wars," and this has its origin in another *Diary* entry, 5 June 1771. Adams describes a conversation with one Doctor McKinstry (who is "superficial enough, and conceited enough, and enthusiastical enough to entertain"): "And when we were drinking Tea, I said, 500 Years hence there would be a great Number of Empires in America, independent of Europe and of each other.—Oh says he I have no Idea that the World will stand so long—not half 500 Years. The world is to conform to the Jewish Calculations, every seventh day was to be a day of Rest, every 7th year was to be a Jubilee, and the 7th. Thousand Years will be a Thousand Years of Rest and Jubilee—no Wars, no fightings, and there is but 230 wanting to compleat the 6000 Years. Till that Time, there will be more furious Warrs than ever."[16]

Was it the combination of prophecies which drew Zukofsky's attention to the passage (quoted in full, *80 Fl.* Notes, pp. 17–18)? Adams's foresight was correct (and in view of the coming revolution, poignant), but McKinstry's world order struck other chords in Zukofsky—who had wound almost six thousand years of recorded history into "A" 22 & 23, pointing it toward paradise, and was now finishing another time-ordered project and planning "Gamut" (another span) along similar lines for completion in the year 2000. Historically, it was only too evident that McKinstry's prognostication of ever more furious wars was correct and that some of those wars were taking place on the American continents, with the United States as a prime moving force. Zukofsky's abhorrence of the contemporary American scene is stated in the lines from "A"-22 (p. 522), which he pointed out to Asa Benveniste in 1977: "inflated state and abated / derelict pretend titular courage."[17] But still there was the numerologically generated hope held out by the arrival of the seventh (in Jewish terms) millennium; "no Wars, no fightings," Rest and Jubilee. It was a logical projection to make for a poet who had for many years believed that "Life's a long / Second paradise" ("A"-12, p. 146) and who talked constantly in his late works about the joys and difficulties of a *paradiso terrestre* ("Terrainal paradise's consolation," "A"-23, p. 560; is that apostrophe possessive or a contraction?).

It was not Adams but the "enthusiastical" McKinstry holding out another instance of the time scheme Zukofsky had worked so intensively into his late poetry; but the poet recognized in the statesman's personal writings an affinity he had long overlooked. Beginning to read the *Diary* after a dip into the *Autobiography,* Zukofsky wrote:

> Apr 15/76
> [-Vol I J. Adams Diary 1755–1770, c.f. "A"-12 not having read
> them then except for quotes here & there
> today it seems the contingency of my
>   mind I wasn't aware of was very close
> to him re- "natural philosophy" (axioms, science
> Sense, Ideas (chiefly via Aristotle, Plato, Spinoza
> Bacon), feeling for landscape "snowfall last night
> half leg deep" rather than arguments of theology
> church etc, (deism but undogmatic)—
> the true sceptic de[illeg.] innocent—E.P.'s
> stress on money only part of "my little
> school like the Great World made of Kings, Politicians
> Divines, L.D., Fops, Buffoons, Fidlers, etc . . [& these
> against "ardor and emulation" (ie. excellence)
>   (*80 Fl.* Notes, pp. 15–16)

Like Wallace Stevens, John Adams was admitted late to Zukofsky's troop of contingent minds; as with Stevens, once he began listening, there was more and more to interest him. He seems to have read three of the four volumes that contain the *Diary and Autobiography,* and excerpts from them spread over some four pages of the *80 Flowers* Notes. The reference to Pound's Adams *Cantos* (62–71), published 1940, uncovers one reason Zukofsky put off reading John Adams for so long. He never enjoyed the sense of competition with the *Cantos* which *"A"* seemed unfailingly to draw, and, if duplication was one charge that could be avoided by pursuing different source material, it stood to reason that John Adams was not likely to loom large in *"A."* By the time Zukofsky got to Adams, the world had got to Z, and Zukofsky's technique had become so idiosyncratic that comparisons with Pound are useful only on the broadest of bases. When Adams appears in *80 Flowers,* his words have been filtered through a dense set of considerations—literary, botanical, horticultural, and personal—which integrates them thoroughly with the present context: "Founderous," "paradise," "no wars." They are, nevertheless, an encapsulation by quotation of #77 Weeds' Adams subtext.

To return to the botanical surface of the poem; we pick it up at the second line: "smallhead *bluecurls* blue-wool'd *romero* defer-ah," which is describing the mint *Trichostema lanatum* (Greek for "hairy-stamens," plus Latin, "bearing wool, woolly"), a bee plant with half-inch blue or purple flowers that have arched protruding stamens, hence the popular name bluecurls. Hardly a weed but of course a "wilding." The species *Trichostema lanatum* is called ramero, a name Zukofsky mistranscribed in the Third List as "Romero," adding the enigmatic comment: "(Rapallo waster)" (Third List, p. 15). He continues to spell the name "Romero" and the clue to its significance (and the reason bluecurls was selected for inclusion in #77 Weeds? it was not one of the original thirteen) is perhaps to be found on a page of the Americana which is missing. We are directed to "see Americana," and bluecurls is not on the four surviving pages. Who or what is the "Rapallo waster"? a "smallhead"? What is the connection with Pound, and does it have anything to do with the 1976 allusion to the finance-riddled Adams *Cantos? "Romero* defer-ah" sounds like an Italian name. Who was at Rapallo in 1933, when Zukofsky summered there at Pound's invitation? When was Pound writing those ten *Cantos* and what was at work on him? What was happening at Rapallo when the Zukofskys visited Italy in 1957? The answer to the Romero/ramero question could lie in any of these places—or a dozen others.

"Defer-ah / *bamboo*-suh" (what is this, a throat-clearing Brit?). The transliteration beneath all the blowing is *bambusa,* Latinized bamboo, coming out of the Americana entry on Gramineae, the grass family. The bamboo is a one-word entrant in #77 Weeds; the poem sweeps on (with a

rattle of wind through canes?): *"downyrattlesnake* pact is pubescence,"
again straightforward partial transliteration. *Epipactis pubescens* is a
native orchid known as downy rattlesnake plantain or adder's violet; it is
entered in the Third List under *Goodyera,* and it is a wilding rather than a
weed, with a densely hairy spike *(pubescens;* downy). It was the "plantain" part of the name that drew Zukofsky's thoughts from weedy
plantains (genus *Plantago;* from *planta,* "footprint," in allusion to the leaf
shape) to the tropical plantain that gets its name from the plane-tree, is
edible, and is one related step away from the banana: "feed talk bananas."
Who's (talking) bananas? Not Zukofsky, who has discovered that both
plants belong to the family Musaceae. The *Century* explains that the
family name is probably derived from the Arabic *mūz* (banana), but
Zukofsky was not alone in recognizing its Castalian potential—the plantain, originally a native of India, is *Musa paradisiaca* ("endear paradise"),
from the fancy that it was the forbidden fruit of Eden. The banana itself is
Musa sapientum (a wise Muse?) from the same notion. Other genera of
the family are *Heliconia,* named for the seat of the Muses, and *Strelitzia,*
which includes the bird-of-paradise flower. The association of Muses and
paradise was readymade; Zukofsky, with customary ingenuity, added it to
the paradise mix of #77 Weeds using the double-signifying plantain (weed
but also fruit) ("weeds so much is food")—which does not even surface in
the poem though its presence is obvious once the connection between
bananas and *Epipactis pubescens* is understood.

Banana was not one of the eleven plants ultimately listed for appearance in #77 Weeds, nor was plantain; both are outriders of the third
candidate (the first two are bluecurls/ramero and bamboo), simply listed
as "downy rattlesnake." When we realize that mullein, though a weed, is
not mentioned in the Order of Weeds, we should suspect that it is also
somehow connected with the plantain/banana motif: "feed talk bananas
great maulin'." Writing notes for great mullein (*Verbascum thapsus;*
another downy, woolly plant) in the preliminary lists, Zukofsky transferred from the Third List a cross-reference to an early (1921) Williams
poem:

GREAT MULLEN

One leaves his leaves at home
being a mullen and sends up a lighthouse
to peer from: I will have my way,
yellow—A mast with a lantern, ten
fifty, a hundred, smaller and smaller
as they grow more—Liar, liar, liar!
You come from her! I can smell djer-kiss

on your clothes. Ha! you come to me,
you—I am a point of dew on a grass-stem.
Why are you sending heat down on me
from your lantern?—You are cowdung, a
dead stick with the bark off. She is
squirting on us both. She has had her
hand on you!—well?—She has defiled
ME.—Your leaves are dull, thick
and hairy.—Every hair on my body will
hold you off from me. You are a
dungcake, bird-lime on a fencerail.—
I love you, straight, yellow
finger of God pointing to—her!
Liar, broken weed, dungcake, you have—
I am a cricket waving his antennae
and you are high, grey and straight. Ha![18]

This is a pitched verbal battle, a "great maulin' "; even, on account and in partial simulation of its manic shrillness: "talk bananas great maulin'." And then: "favor'd *henbit chara* no wars" (does the bitchy spat favor that henpecked male presence? a great deal of noise covering no real *casus belli?*). Henbit, identified in Port Jefferson 22 May 1976 by means of *Common Weeds,* is another mint, *Lamium amplexicaule* (Greek for "throat," in allusion to the corolla; and the species name means "clasping"). Taylor and Gray call the plant dead nettle, and it is the first real weed of the Order of Weeds. Similarly, chara figures in *Common Weeds* as *Chara vulgaris,* an aquatic weed and type of the family Characeae. The *Century* maintains that the origin of the name (pronounced "kara") is Greek, from *chara,* "delight."[19] Hearing also *cara (mia?),* Zukofsky seems to have positioned the name next to *"henbit"* to amplify his gloss on Williams's poem ("I love you, straight, yellow / finger of God . . . / Liar, broken weed, dungcake"). He also checked Lewis and Short, found a *chara* there, referring to some root, probably a wild cabbage, mentioned in Caesar's *Bellum Civile.* Civil wars? ("no wars") (but no wars are civil, either). Zukofsky noted the reference and translated this *chara:* "dear (costly)." *Bellis perennis* of #73 Daisy had by conceit signified pretty, perennial war between the sexes; *chara,* by similar Latinate twistings and the context of Williams's poem, seems to indicate dear warfare: costing dearly, between dear ones.

Then comes goldenrod (*Solidago*), entangled with one of the bindweeds, *Ipomoea pandurata:* "*goldenrod* solid-day go ponder otter." Goldenrod has been headed for *80 Flowers* since 1971 when, in the list of flora derived from "A" and *All*, Zukofsky itemized it as: "(3-states flower)" (*80 Fl.* Notes, p. 2) and subsequently affixed it, with epithet, to all the lists of weeds. The three states concerned are Alabama, Kentucky, and Nebraska. A likely reference in *All* may be to the lines in "Poem Beginning 'The'" concerning the death of Whittaker Chambers's brother, Ricky:

> Lion-heart, frate mio, and so on in two languages
> the thing itself a shadow world.
> Goldenrod
> Of which he is a part,
> Sod
> He hurried over
> Underfoot,
> Make now
> His testament of sun and sky
> With clod
> To root what shoot
> It sends to run the sun,
> The sun-sky blood.
>
> (*All*, pp. 14–15)

A transformation after death, goldenrod part of a solid-state testament of sun and sky ("solid-day"?) echoing against Zukofsky's statement in the notes to " 'The' " that reference to the word sun in his poem signifies "Power of the Past, Present, and Future" (*All*, p. 11). It is a signification worth remembering. Goldenrod is not indexed in "A" and does not come immediately to mind in the way another instance of the plant in Zukofsky's work does. The first paragraph of "Thanks to the Dictionary," playing variations on words beginning *a, aa,* and *ab,* throws up the following chain of associations: "Perhaps next Ab, when the fast will not commemorate a Temple in ruins, Aaron's rod, the serpent to blossom, will grow, goldenrod which flowers on long stems in that vacation a part of July and of August" ("Thanks to the Dictionary," *It Was,* p. 99). Ab, the eleventh month of the Jewish calendar, in which falls the holy day commemorating (with fasting) the Destruction of the Temple, is "a part of July and of August." It is also when the goldenrod flowers, and goldenrod is one of several plants with tall stems and yellow blossoms called Aaron's rod. Another is great mullein, as Zukofsky found out years later from the *Century.* That he was indeed mindful in 1977 of the biblical association made in 1932 becomes evident looking into the etymology of the plant bound with goldenrod in #77 Weeds, *Ipomoea pandurata:*

> *goldenrod* solid-day go ponder otter

Ipomoea literally means "resembling a worm" ("Greek *ips,* a worm, and *homoios,* resembling; from the twining habit"; Gray). The first mention of Aaron's rod, before it budded and flowered, appointing Aaron and his brothers keepers of the tabernacle (Num. 17:8, 18:3), occurred when he cast it down before Pharaoh and it turned into a serpent which swallowed up the rods-also-turned-serpents of the Egyptian enchanters (Exod. 7:10–12)—"serpent to blossom," as Zukofsky encapsulated the two incidents in 1932. And he reversed the order in 1977, with an elided serpent (*Ipomoea*) twining around a golden rod (an Aaron's rod, in architectural ornament, can be a rod wound with one serpent; a caduceus has two; *Century*). A second snake, all but invisible, in the paradise of #77 Weeds. The downy rattlesnake of line two barely emerged as a serpentine presence, we were drawn on so quickly to the elliptic plantain it was pointing out. Here again we are not permitted to dwell on possible snaky implications because— "ponder otter"—we have to puzzle at the other half of the bindweed's name.

The transliteration comes from notes made in preparation for #76 Vines, where Zukofsky was going to use *Ipomoea,* the manroot, as "aye poor me-a ponder otter." Its passage into the weeds poem is legitimate enough; the plant is a weed as well as a vine, and Zukofsky wanted his goldenrod serpentinely tangled. But "ponder otter," the phrase itself, is a mystery in relation to the plant and to the epithet it transliterates. For *pandurata* means "fiddle-shaped," describing the leaf form (and this bindweed's foliage, though normally heart-shaped, is occasionally fiddle-shaped, according to Taylor; also Gray). Zukofsky consulted Lewis and Short, found that the *pandura* was a three-stringed musical instrument invented by the god Pan, noted this beside the sixth entry on the Order of Weeds, which reads: "6. goldenrod (ponder otter = pandura)"—and elucidated the otter/fiddle connection no further. Private association? etymological joke? The nearest we can get to it without privileged information is to hear a musical note in the otter's Latin name, *Lutra.* We could "go ponder otter" a long time without turning up more.

Pondering the otter, we are precipitated into the floral riot of the last two lines, which cover the seventh to eleventh entries on the Order of Weeds:

> *blue-boneset* scut-redshank *ladysthumb* smilax *herb-patience*
> ascending *tansy field-bindweed lady's-orchid-slipper* foison

Red and blue, and ascending yellow; bone, shank, thumb, slipper; a lady's smiling patience with herbs (her green thumb?); another orchid; truly a heaped-up benison. Blue boneset is the second medicinal plant of the poem (*Solidago,* goldenrod, derives its name from *solidus,* "whole," in reference to its supposed powers of drawing together, strengthening, making whole). The boneset is *Eupatorium coelestinum* (sky-blue), a member of the Compositae, and it was identified 14 June 1976 on Belle Terre Road, along with a close relative, *Eupatorium purpureum* (purple), the joe pye weed, among the weeds appended to the First Abbreviated List. One of the blue boneset's other names (Zukofsky has noted it alongside the plant in the Order of Weeds) is hardy ageratum—*ageratum* is from the Greek for "not growing old," so a hardy ageratum would seem to be double resistance to the depredations of time.[20] Liveforever motifs begin to show among the flowers of the earthly paradise. The next plant in the Order of Weeds is ladysthumb, one of the knotweeds or smartweeds, pink-flowered and many-jointed: *Polygonum persicaria* (small, with many joints). But what, intervening between the boneset and the lady's thumb, is "scut-redshank"?

In the pencil draft of #77 Weeds, crossing out *"joe-pye"* in order to substitute *"blue-boneset,"* Zukofsky canceled "scut" by accident (the underscoring of *"blue-boneset"* inadvertently went through the third word of the line). So that when he copied out the ink draft on the same page (*80 Fl.* Drafts, p. [111]), the "scut" originally hyphenated to "red-shank" disappeared, to be reinserted only in the Spiral copy of the poem as an interlineation. That Zukofsky had intended the phrase as a hyphenation all along is clear from its origin in the Notes; on the last page of the Third List in a discussion of heathers (wild and uncultivated plants, Zukofsky observes, if not weeds), there is a quotation from Robert Burton's *Anatomy of Melancholy,* specified by edition and page number. The passage in question, part of Burton's disquisition on Remedies of Love, in particular the "Cure of Love-Melancholy, by Labour, Diet, Physick, Fasting, Etc," reads: "By this means those Indian Brachmanes kept themselves continent, they lay upon the ground covered with skins, as the Redshanks [or Highlanders] do on Hadder [or Heather], and dieted themselves sparingly on one dish, which Guianerius would have all young men put in practice; and if that will not serve, Gordonius would have them soundly whipped, or, to cool their courage, kept in prison, and there be fed with bread and water, till they acknowledge their error, and become of another mind."[21] Zukofsky added, among the notes for #77 Weeds and apparently still on the trail of Americana: "scut-redshank, i.e. American Indian and Brahmins." The connection is apparently a stoicism running from India to Scotland to aboriginal North America. Redshanks to redskins? It is not as improbable as it sounds when we add Zukofsky's note concerning the banana (information from Taylor): "India redskin fruit cluster *ladyfinger* small very thin skin" (*80 Fl.* Drafts, p. [111]).

Redskins from India; thin-skinned lady-finger (thumb?) bananas behind the standard variety.

Zukofsky had come by the Burton via a *Century* example of usage for *heather;* he had looked up the full passage in the *Anatomy,* perhaps wondering if "Indian Brachmanni" (*Century* spelling) covered with skins were Native Americans. Writing #77 Weeds, he acknowledged the Scottish link ("scut"), having also looked up *redshanks* and found not only an explanation of its origin (derogatory, an allusion to bare highland legs) but also the Burton passage repeated in part. He compounded the joke on kilts by introducing a spelling that images bare-tailed Scots—and arranged the whole figure alongside *Polygonum persicaria,* the ladysthumb (in the nose?), because the *Century* had in addition disclosed another name for the jointed weed—redshanks.

Ladysthumb had been in the weeds grouping since the First Abbreviated List, probably an identification of summer 1975. Its relative, herb patience (*Rumex patientia*) is a type of sorrel (a patient horse?) and is used in soups and salads. The identification of *Rumex* also dates from the summer of 1975 (First List, p. viii), but the variety *Rumex patientia* appears to be an entrant selected specifically for #77 Weeds. We could guess that the common name has something to do with its position in the poem, hearing: "lady's . . . smile . . . her . . . patience ascending." Zukofsky has made sure that relatives will not easily be separated—the smilax that appears between them is another remnant of the vines poem; it is commonly called greenbrier, catbrier, or horsebrier, and one of its classical identities is bindweed, according to the *Century;* according also to Lewis and Short, who (also) call the plant withwind. Smilax is thus a liliaceous vine with one horsey common name and an etymology that continues the binding we have been conscious of since first encountering the flora of #76 Vines. Looking ahead to line eight of #77 Weeds, we find more evidence of the same principle at work: *"field-bindweed,"* the most tenacious convolvulus of them all, is set between tansy and another orchid:

ascending *tansy field-bindweed lady's-orchid-slipper* foison

Tansy, one more yellow-flowered plant to add to the yellows of goldenrod and great mullein (perhaps even bananas, those golden Muses), is used to make a bitter tansy tea and is the chief ingredient of a traditional dish called a tansy, "made with eggs, cream, sugar, rose-water, and the juice of tansy, to which that of spinach, sorrel, or other herbs was sometimes added" (*Century*); here is one possible reason for tansy's position in #77 Weeds immediately after the sorrel sometimes known as spinach-dock. However, Zukofsky's present interest in *Tanacetum vulgare* concerns its name, which can be traced to the herb's Crimean and Greek origins through the Old French *tanaisie* or *athanasie* to Middle Latin *athanasia,* and so to the Greek *athanasia,* literally "immortality," from *a*-privative and *thanatos* (death); "cf. liveforever and immortelle," adds the *Century.* The bitter tansy turns out to be Zukofsky's latest liveforever flower, "ascending" into the paradise that is earthly, perhaps difficult. No source explains why tansy should signify immortality (is it some kind of golden bough?), which could be why Zukofsky's appropriation appears in a poem that already figures the death-transforming goldenrod and is full of the yellows and blues that could be sun and sky, those paradise colors. It is also, from years before, the setting for the celestial body that represents "Power of the Past, Present, and Future."

Ascending, as does the sun, but not dominant. The tansy is rapidly wound about with a weed of the field (*Convolvulus arvensis*) which is a morning glory (some of the family close up their flowers at midday). The bindweed then wraps around *"lady's-orchid-slipper,"* compound for the lady's-slipper, *Cypripedium* (incorrectly Latinized Greek for "Venus's shoe"), a genus of hardy native orchids, also (more aptly?) known as moccasin flower. It seems this kind of orchid, supremely beautiful without the agency of man, and growing wild in the North American woodland the same kind of flower we have come to associate exclusively with greenhouses and sophisticated hybridization, represents for Zukofsky a high point of the term *wildflower*—a term recast for the purpose of this poem as "wilding weeds." And, as always, the most beautiful is at most risk; Taylor observes that native orchids are in danger of extinction in the wild unless commercial propagation from seed is developed to counter the heavy collecting by dealers which presently (1961) takes place. Wild-flowers could do without this kind of harvesting. But "foison," the last word of #77 Weeds, concerns more than native orchids; it is a summation of the whole paradise discussion to date because it condenses the begin-ning of Zukofsky's late treatment of the theme, "Initial." We remember (blowing blue up against yellow):

> let me live here ever,
> sweet now, silence foison to
> on top of the weather
> it has said it before

> ("A"-22, p. 508)

The paradise of the island, Prospero-created, Prospero-directed—for a common prosperity, plenty, foison. Ceres bestowed the original blessing, in terms of grain and harvest; Zukofsky added the complicating weed but left the prospect of paradise open ("read a weed's reward—grain / an omen a good omen," "A"-22, p. 508)—and brought the family Gramineae (the grasses and grains) into #77 Weeds, which he was filling with a host of medicinal and edible plants. Much in the way valentine red finally took its place with the paradisal yellows and blues of "Initial," completing the triple emphasis of the wish for happy new years, a botanical red appears among the blue and yellow flowers of #77 Weeds—"redshanks." Spinning off it is the possibility of redskinned bananas—Indian Muses? "And to paradise," as a 1928 poem put it, "which is a port"—Jefferson, Zukofsky might well have added mentally in 1977. He had thought of the old poem ("cf LZ   and to paradise," *80 Fl.* Notes, p. 18) as he copied out, in 1976, Adams's account of the blissful June-morning ride. The two moods, two hundred years apart, are analogous; from 1928:

> And to paradise which is a port
> And over water-trestle,
> And as over a sea so over: and by the way
>   of this train's movement
>
> Water-staves,
> Moorings, spread blue coats of water,
> Long,
> Along,
> Long.

(All, p. 29)

("Life's a long / Second paradise"—the echo comes years later; *"A"*-12, p. 146.) The 1928 train could well have been crossing to Long Island, a port, a paradise. The pencil draft of #77 Weeds was completed 1 January 1978, the ink draft next day, thus making the latest (and, as happened, the last) expression of Zukofsky's wish for happy new years at New Year.

II

XYZ: #78 "X," #79 Yaupon, and #80 Zinnia

The pencil draft of the seventy-eighth *Flower* precedes the notes that accompany it (*80 Fl.* Drafts, p. [112]). These notes are concise and line-specific—they cite sources and give references; they are in effect an index to the poem that has just been written out. The same thing had happened in #77 Weeds, where the notes acted as a summary of the various preliminary lists of flora, at the same time highlighting the nonbotanical inferences drawn from that information. When Zukofsky came to write #79 Yaupon, the line-referenced information was more terse, crammed into a few lines between pencil and ink drafts; and for # 80 Zinnia, each line was annotated, again between two near-identical drafts.

The strategy tells us a couple of things about the composition of *80 Flowers* December 1977 through January 1978. For a start, the pace had quickened to the point where although Zukofsky was dealing with *Flowers* that embraced more material than ever, he did not feel leisured enough to spend several days covering several pages of the Drafts with preliminary notes (which had been the case with most of the poems written since April 1977). Now preliminaries were taking the form of lists, a logical step in dealing with the big composite poems, and the lists were made on pieces of paper outside of the Drafts sequence. Perhaps Zukofsky was also constructing ur-drafts on similar scraps (traces of such a process survive in the material for #80 Zinnia) before penciling each *Flower* into the sequence of Drafts, summarizing his references line by line, and then within a few days completing the ink draft.

What was the hurry? We can be fairly certain that it was a self-imposed deadline, at least initially; *80 Flowers* was to be complete by Celia's birthday. Then the Stinehour contract added its impetus; soon after 4 January 1978, the Zukofskys received Freeman Keith's proposal for a June publication date if the manuscript was in Lunenburg by the end of January (see chap. 1). At the time, Louis would have been working on #78 "X" (composed 4–13 January 1978); the accelerated pace—three more poems to write before 21 January—showed itself in the cleaner-than-usual pencil drafts and the brisk summaries of content. When Zukofsky worked fast, he worked out of notes and lists that may or may not have been intended to survive, but the sense of documentation associated with the *80 Flowers* project would not let him omit from the Drafts some record of each set of preliminaries.

Thus there are lots of references for the last poems and usually some botanical lists, which are helpful in ascertaining the make-up of each piece but do not necessarily tell us why the contents should be what they are. That, of course, is where documentation stops and interpretation begins. As we turn to the "X" poem that initiates the last stage of the finale—XYZ is somehow analogous to and as much an ontological unit as ABC (is it the rhyme? or the 1-2-3? or both?)—the feeling arises that from here on interpretation will be particularly challenging. The expectation is partly due to being faced with a title that says "unknown quantity"—reinforced by the reminder (from the *Century*) that x is the first of the three algebraic variable or unknown quantities x y z. Then there is the added realization that the Z that *80 Flowers* has been so long getting to will play heavily on variables and enigma because it will no doubt be closest to the tripartite family heart. Zukofsky wrote in 1930:

> Asked Albert who introduced relativity—
> "And what is the formula for success?"
> "X = work, y = play, Z = keep your mouth shut."
> "What about Johann Sebastian? The same formula."
>
> ("A"-6, p. 23)

His interest in Bach, also Einstein's beloved Bach, had increased with the years; his interest in Einstein, the horse for single (but musical) harness, had also kept pace. Does Einstein's "formula for success" persist in Zukofsky's mind as he begins the end of *80 Flowers*? The "X" poem makes a start on the answer:

#78   "x"

Of thousands grown climb head-on-head
A "X" unknown stand indued
no glue kiss'd peon knee
freesia's iris grass-tropical true scourge
bees earthflight magnetic north 4-native
dial-canter excellence scent one-thousandth-in
one-night *lady's-eardrops-fuchsia* seaborne northeast unnailed
papyrus-bath-nut *trailing arbutus fringed-gentian hydrangea*

The scrap of paper headed "summary 'X'" (on its verso is the Order of Weeds) lists in order the five flowers italicized here—freesia, fuchsia, trailing arbutus, fringed gentian, and hydrangea. As usual we can see (and hear) other flora ranged about these principals—peony, iris, grass, and papyrus. And with the reference to bees and horses, we guess that more Zukofsky orientation is in the offing. That supposition gathers support as we look at line two and find an uppercase A italicized (a sixth "flower"?) next to an X in quotes; Zukofsky appears to be placing the life poem in apposition to the name of some other composition—not *"An* 'X,'" mind, but (difficult): *"A* 'X.'" And the "X" is "unknown," perhaps an "unknown stand" (position or location) "indued" (dowered? gifted? invested?) (with what?). Alternatively, the unknown "X" itself may "stand indued"—"Of thousands grown climb head-on-head"? Is "X" in one of its manifestations the choice Zukofsky made eighty times among his multiplying candidates for title flowers? Made many times more among the lists of flora that piled up over the years? An X laid on its side, the *Century* tells us, signifies 1,000; with a dash over the upright position (X̄) it means 10,000. Certainly the "X" poem had held for Zukofsky the notion of multiplicity for some time; the two pages of preliminary botanical listings simply take unused options from the Third Abbreviated List with the blanket instruction: "include." What is interesting is that the listings proper begin: Aloe, Andromeda, Arbutus, Bougainvillea, Clematis— which tells us they were made prior to the composition of #74 Aloe and #76 Vines. The "X" summary, made much closer to the writing of #78 "X," picks up the unused Arbutus but for the most part sticks with options from the latter half of the preliminary list (Freesia, Fuchsia, Gentian). (Hydrangea, the fifth entrant, enters directly from the Third Abbreviated List, p. 2.)

So "X" may mean choice or choosing, may 'stand for the process by which Zukofsky filled his floral options—a thousand variables intervening between start and finish. But the quotation marks, insistent on some titular value, and punctiliously marked in by the poet—there are two sets of them, top and bottom, on the "X" summary which gives the figure a distinct kinetic quality "X"—these quotes direct our attention to other possibilities. The most intriguing of them is suggested by a note on the *80 Flowers* Spiral copy of the poem which reads: "P's *work.*" We remember "X = work"; we recall the *"A"* alongside this current "X"; we hear Celia in interview saying: "Louis was very intense, and worked and worked and worked, always on his own work. And Louis didn't care if the rest of the world just suddenly vanished, and he were left working. But Paul is not Louis. He is a very intense worker too, but he wants to be in the world, this world."[1] And we think of Louis's observation in the black notebook (p.

111) about an "old chip off the block" as he made a note concerning Paul's recording of the Paganini Caprices. This note ended up in the "p" section of "A"-23's alphabetical crescendo—next to an example of Louis's own rethinking of a Shakespearean caprice:

>   —thrice-urged
> *posato* (poised) 'support from the
> source'—horn-note out of a
> string (Quest returns answer—'to
> rethink the Caprices') *sawhorses silver*
> *all these fruit-tree tops.*
>
>   ("A"-23, p. 563)[2]

Not quite three lines further on, the final winding-in of family accomplishments begins. We knew already the XYZ of this included figures of Celia and her work ("moonwort: / music, thought, drama, story, poem") and of Paul ("z-sited path are but us"; plus the acrostic "pz"), all of it wreathed with Louis's own work and vision. But now we must hear also the signature, "x," which allies all art as work, as quests (sometimes) returning answers. The "living calendar" continues:

>   consonances
> and dissonances only of degree, never-
> Unfinished hairlike water of notes
> vital free as Itself—impossible's
> sort-of think-cramp work x: moonwort:
> music, thought, drama, story, poem
> parks' sunburst—animals, grace notes—
> z-sited path are but us.
>
>   ("A"-23, p. 563)

This is Schönberg, Bach, Leonardo, Tolstoy, Wittgenstein, Celia, and the "LZ Masque" (see chap. 2 and n.41) and the three Z's sited, open-eyed, in Port Jefferson. What takes our attention now is: "impossible's / sort-of think-cramp work x," not only because it might describe the odds Zukofsky work takes on and the kinds of compression and intensity involved, but also because in "work x" we have such a clear restatement of the "A"-6 XYZ. Tracing the "A"-23 version of *work* and *x* leads through the "A"-23 Spiral (p. 40: "LW Foundations of Math") to the "A" 22 & 23 Spiral, in which a search in the twentieth-century sections produces an entry concerning Wittgenstein's *Remarks on the Foundations of Mathematics*. Zukofsky, working out of a German text, translated a sentence from this treatise; then the translation was pushed toward the transliteration we hear in "A"-23. The remark that prefaces this operation and that Zukofsky has been careful to link to the Wittgenstein (for comment? as context?) is most interesting:

$$\text{LZ : everything labors (Eccl)} \begin{cases} \text{only} \\ \text{except} \\ \text{but liveforever} \end{cases}$$

Foundations of Math's
L.W. Grundlagen der Mathematik (1937–44) I 132 : Man kann sich auch (even) in eine Art Denk-krampf versetzen, in welchem man tut : als versuchte man, das Unmögliche zu denken und es gelänge nicht

$$\text{Art} = \binom{\text{coll. } \textit{sort of}}{\text{species}}\text{[but transliterate] } \textit{tut} \text{ (math.} = \text{to permute}$$

colloquial *does* "als versuchte man es   e.g.(i.e.?)
one proposes to think the Impossible and it won't work can't be done (accomplished) [L.Z. An art thought cramped Impossible works out (accomplished now does)[3]

("A" 22 & 23 Spiral, p. 159)

One tries the impossible; "One can even get oneself into a thinking-cramp, in which one *does* someone trying to think the impossible and not succeeding," runs the English translation. But "impossible's / sort-of think-cramp work x" conveys more immediately that double-think situation of accomplishing a thought of the impossible not being accomplished. And we see that "work x" is as much Zukofsky (from "A"-6 and with thanks to Einstein) as it is transliterated Wittgenstein ("versetzen"), another brilliant thinker, whose name is transliterated "wit can shine" elsewhere in the "A" 22 & 23 Spiral (p. 154).

One *works it out* because "everything labors." "If you know the answer / Keep still, / If you don't, try / Find out" ("A"-12, p. 180) is the 1950 update on "A"-6's work/play/keep-your-mouth-shut; and in 1974 there is the same dictum, closing one labor ("impossible's / sort-of think-cramp") and beginning another ("sorrow of harness pulses pent"). Then in 1978, the same bridgehead and the continuation of work ("A 'X'")— visible also in the drive of the son to whom the next project is dedicated. The *80 Flowers* Spiral annotations frequently concern the whereabouts and activities of Paul—concerts, a symposium and its reviews, excursions to Iceland, the edition of a Steuermann violin solo—so the *Flowers* poems, though as a rule not "dedicated" to these events, do form a running index to "P's *work*," as the note to #78 "X" finally expressed it.

Then there is the other half of the Ecclesiastes-Zukofsky note to be considered; "everything labors . . . except liveforever." From "A"-6 (p. 27) we recall the vision of the beatific rose ("On that morning when everything / will be clear") which accompanies so many grubby particulars; from "*A*"-12 (p. 237) the difficulties facing the artist wanting "impossible liveforever"; from "*A*" 22 & 23 the history of men's good voices built as an analog to the hidden melody of one man's life; and from *80 Flowers* the ongoing business of working out an earthly paradise in time and with time. This might be called "liveforever" in the sense of its untiring optimism and because durability attends the labors of articulation.

It seems increasingly likely that "*A* 'X' unknown stand indued" is intended to embrace a common working habit and the tendency to take on impossibles and unthinkables, and work them out. (This is Zukofskian livelihood, in the sense given by #3 Honesty's "lifelode," literally life-labor, life-load; see chap. 4). At the same time, the line acknowledges differences between father and son, to go by its Shakespearean contexts, which bestow credit more lavishly than Zukofsky would have wished on himself. The unknown, standing indued, is an amalgam of two fragments (so the line references on p. [112] of the Drafts tell us); the first is from *Two Gentlemen of Verona*, Valentine saying:

These banish'd men that I have kept withal
Are men endu'd with worthy qualities.
                                        (*TGV* V.iv.152)

The second, from *Coriolanus*, concerns the consular election:

Menenius: You have stood your limitation, and the tribunes
Endue you with the people's voice.
. . . .
Sicinius: How now, my masters! have you chose this man?
1st Citizen: He has our voices, sir.
Brutus: We pray the gods he may deserve your loves.
2nd Citizen: Amen, sir. To my poor unworthy notice,
He mock'd us when he begg'd our voices.
. . . .
1st Citizen: No, 'tis his kind of speech; he did not mock us.
                                        (*Cor.* II.iii.146, 163, 169)

Endue, says the *Century*, is now usually spelt *indue;* it is a synonym of *endow*, but the two words have distinct applications. *Enduement* is used of spiritual and moral qualities, viewed as given rather than acquired ("men endu'd with worthy qualities"); *endowment* pertains to the body, to external things, or to mental gifts ("the Tribunes / Endue you with the people's voice"). The Zukofsky enterprise, that difficult idiosyncratic music, stands indued by trial of time, its latest exponent endowed with abilities (and with the "excellence" Louis characterized as "ardor and emulation" in his John Adams notes) that will take it in new directions: "My wife Celia and son Paul have been the only reason for the poet's persistence," we hear Zukofsky saying near the close of *Autobiography* (p. 59). "Paul is a violinist and composer. I trust, considering his gifts, that his art will be welcomed sooner than mine." There is, then, a relationship in Zukofsky's mind between gifts and the (hard) working of them; the first sentence of the *Autobiography* passage also reappears in the statement Celia quoted in 1978 as best summing up Louis's life: "There exists in the labors of any valid artist the sadness of the horse plodding with blinkers and his direction filled with the difficulty of keeping a pace. My wife Celia and son Paul have been the only reason for the poet's persistence."⁴ One reason the musical horse ("dial-canter") appears later in #78 "X"?

Turning now to look at the "X" flowers, we discover them to be a diverse collection brought together out of the Third Abbreviated List, having come through earlier lists unused. These are the five italicized flowers; around them are others whose histories in the material for *80 Flowers* date only from the extended Third List. The first of this latter group is a peony—"glue kiss'd peon knee"—which Zukofsky looked up in Theophrastus after finding out in Taylor that the name derives from Paian, a Greek god of healing. The *Enquiry* confirmed that the peony held some medicinal value to the ancients; moreover (as the *Century* points out), that its root was regarded by some as a charm. Not, however, by Theophrastus: "On the other hand the following ideas may be considered farfetched and irrelevant; for instance they say that the peony, which some call *glykyside,* should be dug up at night, for, if a man does it in the daytime and is observed by a woodpecker while he is gathering the fruit, he risks the loss of his eyesight; and, if he is cutting the root at the time, he gets *prolapsus ani*" (*Enquiry* IX.viii.6).

Zukofsky zeroed in on *glykysidē,* the synonym for peony (*paiōnia*), which, as the surrounding entries in Liddell and Scott would have informed him, alluded to the flower's sweetness—probably in the metaphorical sense of delight or dearness, because peonies are not fragrant. So the "X" poem starts horticulturally with a delightful healer—and, concealed a little further inside its Greek healing name, is Apollo, poetry, and a music of thanksgiving. The *Century* says that *Paion* is an epithet of Apollo, first applied (by Homer) to the physician of the gods; hymns of thanksgiving to Apollo, particularly after a successful battle, began in ancient times with the invocation *Io Paean!* Compositions honoring the god came to be known as *paeons;* later the term signified a song of thanksgiving to a deity; later still it meant any song of joy, praise, or thanksgiving—an evolution that suits Zukofsky's purposes.

So why "peon" in #78 "X" and not "paean"? Why the curious (sticky? sweet?) surface presented by "no glue kiss'd peon knee"? Why is the transliteration not one of the five named candidates of the "X" poem? The answers lie in the discovery that Peony is to be found, a margin addition, in the preliminary list for "Gamut." We cannot tell when it was transferred there, but because Zukofsky specifically notes the tree peony (*Paeonia suffruticosa*) in the extended Third List, we get the impression that he was considering the genus for full treatment in "Gamut" rather than the *Flowers*. The margin note on page 8 of the "Gamut" Notes cites Taylor's Paian reference, to which is added (in parentheses) Zukofsky's initials and the comment that Paian is a son of Aescapuleius; that is, a physician. He obviously intended to follow up the Greek healing lead.[5] In *80 Flowers*, then, the peony is making one of those momentary appearances characteristic of plants for which Zukofsky has further plans. Perhaps the "Gamut" peony poem would have shed retrospective light on the still mysterious reasons for this peony's inclusion in #78 "X."

We could conjecture sweetness as one of those reasons; and now visual beauty is succeeded by the delight of fragrance: "*freesia*'s iris grass-tropical." The freesia *is* an iris (the peony, as Zukofsky had observed, is "only a buttercup"—family Ranunculaceae—for all its showiness; *80 Fl.* Drafts, p. [112]). Freesias have the iris's grasslike leaves and are South African in origin: "(native *tropics* S. Africa)," as Zukofsky puts it in the "X" poem summary. This led him to the hot-and-cold conceit suggested by the name (*Freesia* honors a Swedish botanist, Elias Magnus Fries), and then to a personal association with climate the flower had held for him since the May 1969 trip to London. Freesia's appearances in the lists for *80 Flowers* nearly all carry a reference to 13 May 1969, London; this may be a tag for the whole sojourn (Zukofsky's field notes cover the whole stay, 13–27 May; b.n.b., interleavings between pp. 57 and 58), because the notes on London flora are actually dated 14 May:

> Grosvenor Sq, Berkley, Bedford, Parks
> the flowers, laburnum, linden thriving on the
> damp, the English sky, the clouds of London,
> one minute of blue and sun followed by ~~complete~~
> mountainous cumulus, and a downpour, the background heat
> of Adam's Georgian (& Queen Anne's?) houses cannot warm: grass
> greener, a chill of flowers thriving.
>
> (b.n.b., p. 56)

These memories of London spring, warmth and chill, were rendered in "A"-23's first Music section:

damp cannot warm the houses—
linden thrives, one minute of
blue and sun then downpour—
treecolumned greensward greener, man empty

spaces in cells sounds thick
gardens, digs up, plants may—

("*A*"-23, p. 537)

Linden and London were thriving; freezing but thriving—what better flower to signify the paradox than the spring-blooming freesia? There is no evidence that the Zukofskys actually saw freesias in London or gardened them thereafter; "X" is also the domain of the possible, and in this part of *80 Flowers* we are once more among flowers of memory and anniversary.

This is why a poem featuring the freesia was certainly going to include a fuchsia; the two had been linked since the Second Abbreviated List, when Zukofsky wrote a reference concerning the poet David Jones on the subject of fuchsias into the Freesia entry. Again, the link is London, May 1969; Louis and Celia visited Jones in his lodgings at Harrow on the Hill 25 May. Zukofsky recognized in the Welshman a "meeting of 3 roots of history—Hebraic, Roman, Celtic (Xian)" (b.n.b., p. 59). When he read Colin Wilcockson's "Notes on Some Letters of David Jones" in a 1976 issue of *Agenda*, the probing, polyglot erudition (rather like his own) was brought vividly to mind again and Jones's remark about the origins of the fuchsia was keyed into the *80 Flowers* material. Wilcockson, to whom the letters are addressed, had described the landscape of County Donegal, Ireland; and Jones replied, December 1956: "I was interested about the fuchsias growing wild—I remember that & also they did that on that Welsh island, Caldey, off Tenby—the hedges there were full of fuchsia. I wonder who planted them in these places, for clearly they can't be native." Then he added (in different-colored ink) what Wilcockson calls "the familiar marginal gloss": "I find they were introduced from America late in the 18th century to Kew Gardens—but it's a long way to Tipperary, Iona & Inys Pyr."[6]

Zukofsky would have been interested for a variety of reasons; first, because the holograph letter Wilcockson quotes from is reproduced in the *Agenda* article, and marginal glosses and different colored inks are a Zukofskian epistolary trait as well as a Jonesian one. Second, there was the link with Kew Gardens (locale of at least one of those "freesia" London days). Third, there was the eastward transatlantic direction of the flower's history. Fuchsias, like the Zukofskys, were once Americans in a London garden; they had naturalized on Irish and Welsh coasts—and

Louis and Celia had found common ground with a Welsh poet whose roots crossed Zukofsky's own. "Contingencies' flowers," that comment from later in the London diary (b.n.b., p. 60), aptly describes the meeting with Jones.

Freesia and fuchsia were old associates in the notes for *80 Flowers,* but in #78 "X" they occur several lines apart and a number of other concerns intervene. One of these is a puzzling addition to the freesia line:

freesia's iris grass-tropical true scourge

Whippy grass-leaves? another stinging goad for the horse? A source has been provided—"true scourge cf I Kings ch 12:11" (*80 Fl.* Drafts, p. [112])—but it does not shed much light. Rehoboam, son of Solomon, ignores the counsel of the old men and answers the request of the children of Israel for clemency in the new reign thus: "And now whereas my father did lade you with a heavy yoke, I will add to your yoke: my father hath chastised you with whips, but I will chastise you with scorpions" (1 Kings 12:11). We might guess that the reference is coming into the poem via some other context in Zukofsky's work; that if we could find it, this ominous note among the flowers would be less troubling. We cannot associate it particularly with the freesia; it suggests no obvious link with David Jones, his work or his fuchsia. Nor does it seem to be connected with what follows:

bees earthflight magnetic north 4-native
dial-canter excellence scent one-thousandth-in
one-night

This returns us to the bright lyrical world of flowers, fragrance, sweetness—and that sense of being at ease with one's place which is orientation. The bees met with to date in *80 Flowers* have come from Theophrastus and Virgil; these ones proceed from the writing of German naturalist Karl von Frisch in his 1974 work *Tiere als Bauermeister,* published in English as *Animal Architecture.* The excerpt Zukofsky copied into the extended Third List (p. 6) 26 November 1976 was later condensed and transferred to the Americana notes (p. 1), so the "X" poem's quota of Americana begins with Euro-American translation of European scientific observation:

orientation of bees—influenced by earth's magnetic field (on moving from old hive to a new, even when the natural magnetic field is artificially disturbed & deflected 40° between the first & second field with the aid of a magnet placed outside the 2nd hive: the directions of the new combs differed from the previous by the same angle of 40°. (Third List, p. 6)[7]

Zukofsky straightaway condensed this: "[Z: bees flight earth's magnet North]" (Third List, p. 6), which is how it looks in the Americana—to be only slightly rearranged in #78 "X." Bees, like tides, are influenced by forces that keep the cosmic dance in balance; "bees earthflight" sounds upon "moon's flight twice sun's" (#75 Thyme) and provokes memory of "earth-rounds bees' rose" (#52 Snow-Wreath) and "minting white-thyme assures bees roses / summersun honeyyield" (#12 Cinquefoil), also the "crewroar" of thyme-covered bees night-flying around their citadels (#61 Bearded Iris). Zukofsky is extending once more the thyme-roses-fire-horse-bees figure out of which he distills the conditions of paradise. As Spinoza observed (Zukofsky quoting in *Bottom*, p. 29): "The more an image is associated with many other things, the more often it flourishes. . . . The more causes there are by which it can be excited."

The von Frisch-derived line (a beeline from all points of the compass? homing in?) ends "4-native," and, counting, we discover that four of the five flowers of the Summary are native Americans. Fuchsias are from tropical America (and so Jones's fuchsia appropriates the freesia's epithet "tropical"; never a particularly apt designation, by itself, of South African heritage). Trailing arbutus and fringed gentian are North American, and *Hydrangea arborescens,* which Zukofsky pinpoints in the extended Third List (p. 17), is the wild hydrangea or sevenbark.

Now the poem turns again in earnest to its undertext, the subject of that "X": "dial-canter excellence." The dial might be a compass, it might be a clock (it might tell location, it might tell time; if it was a sundial it would do both). However, the compound, with its suggestion of time at a gallop, brings us down in favor of timing (as does the presence of those thymy bees?)—and Zukofsky's note on the phrase illuminates it further: "Line 6 dial (clock) canter—horse's leaping pace e.g. metronome timing" (*80 Fl.* Drafts, p. [112]). Canter, one of Zukofsky's oldest horse-music conceits, has been allied with the time-measure, and the horse paces—easily now?—into the last stretches of this project, nostrils wide: "excellence scent one-thousandth-in / one-night." One-in-a-thousand excellence, sniffed out? Once more the issue is fragrance, and this time the horse is extracting scent where none exists botanically; doing it, as usual, by etymological means. The line is an approach to *"lady's-eardrops-fuchsia";* fuchsia belongs to the Onagraceae or evening primrose family, and, though the tropical American is itself scentless, the family fragrance begins in its name, which the *Century* derives from *onagra,* apparently a dubious reading for *oinagra: oinos* (wine) + *agra* (a hunting). Hunting, scenting, seeking out wine? The name is linked to that of the evening primrose itself, *Oenothera,* which Taylor translates as "wine-scenting." Lewis and Short say that the juice of a plant of this name was drunk in wine, producing sleep; Liddell and Scott say that its root was used to flavor wine—or that it smells of wine. Wine-scenting or wine-scented, the combination of another "rose," its night-fragrance, and the bouquet of wine was enough to win *Oenothera* a place in *80 Flowers*. Zukofsky was also remembering the evening-scented wild roses of #37 Roses and the winey blaze of night-fragrant flowers in #38 Phlox. He had contrived to blend the motifs of fire, roses and night bouquet there (see chap. 7), and here was *Oenothera* offering the same mix, a primrose-yellow flower opening at nightfall and, according to Zukofsky's *Field Flowers,* falling at sunrise: "each flower lasts only one night, and new buds are [rings?], visited at dusk by moths draining the nectar down long tubes. Use as an example of thousands in one night." This note, on page 2 of the "X" poem preliminaries, suddenly provides text not only for "one-thousandth-in" (which in addition contains a part-sounding of *Oenothera*) and "one-night," but also for the opening of the poem: "Of thousands grown climb head-on-head." *Oenothera* is a larger presence in #78 "X" than we suspected; another "rose" appearing and then vanishing, its "excellence" the night scent that draws nectar-seekers. If Zukofsky was thinking of *celsus* (high, lofty, raised), the root of his X-sounding approbation, "excellence," then *Oenothera* rises with all the other wild roses of *80 Flowers.*

Before we get to the posy that ends the "X" poem, there is other business, some of it related to the remaining flowers, some not:

one-night *lady's-eardrops-fuchsia* seaborne northeast unnailed
papyrus-bath-nut *trailing arbutus fringed-gentian hydrangea*

Fuchsia was carried to England from America ("seaborne northeast"), and an "unnailed" hydrangea will not turn blue—perhaps the failure of the blue hydrangea planted by the Zukofskys in 1975 (First List, p. vii) was being attributed to a lack of iron nails dug under its roots? In 1977 they tried again with more success, and by June Zukofsky could report some rooted sprigs (Third List, p. 2); presumably this time the plants were "nailed," as recommended in the Hydrangea entries of all lists of 80 Flowers from the First Abbreviated on. Though a horticultural inference is to be drawn from "unnailed," the choice of word was apparently dictated by other concerns. Zukofsky had come across it in the *Century* and had copied out the example of usage—" 'Whiles Joseph of Arimathaea and Nicodemus unnail our Lord,' Evelyn, *Perfection of Painting"*—with the comment: *"unnailed* i.e. tactility of Christ." That "unnailed" should pick up connotations of the Passion leads us to reconsider the implications of "true scourge" a few lines earlier (should we voice "A 'X' " as "a cross"?). Also to remember the thorns and barbs of #72 Raspberry and the "thrust rapier's-point barb" of #74 Aloe. Tactility, though not necessarily of the godhead, has been at issue in each case—a matter we might link up with the goads and stings the horse encounters in earlier poems of the sequence, and perhaps even with thorns of the roses that run throughout. The important point is the realization we first made when looking at "Initial"—that hurt does not vanish even in the making of a paradise; that nothing earthly is a seamless beatific smile. In the hoariest of cliches: no rose without a thorn.

There is also no line of #78 "X" without a genuine *x* quantity; in line eight, the inclusion of "papyrus-bath-nut" just before the flowers that end the poem. The *what* of this is, with the assistance of Zukofsky's notes, easily determinable; the *why* is another matter entirely. We are working out of the Americana entry Graminea, which with the comment "nothing's typical" (from Taylor) lists a number of grasses and grasslike genera, among them the Cyperaceae or sedges. *Cyperus papyrus* is the Egyptian paper plant, an aquatic sedge that does not, however, grow in deep water—as Theophrastus noted (*Enquiry* IV.viii.3): *Phyetai de ho papyros ouk en bathei;* bath-depth. *Cyperus esculentus* ("excellence," in line six?) has an edible rootstock and is known as chufa, earthnut, and earth-almond. *Cyperus,* in its Greek manifestation *kyperos,* was an aromatic plant used in embalming, probably (according to the *Century* and to Liddell and Scott) the same thing as *kypeiros,* the name of a sweet-smelling marsh plant. Even the grasses of #78 "X" contribute (etymological) fragrance—but "papyrus-bath-nut" alludes more immediately to their utility, taking up again the theme of meat and medicine first noticed in #76 Vines and #77 Weeds.

There is a note attached to the last entry of the Third Abbreviated List (p. 4): "46. Weeds Yucca Zinnia (w. grasses)," which goes some way toward explaining Zukofsky's interest in Gramineae and grassiness in the last poems of *80 Flowers:* the bamboo in #77 Weeds, an English meadow in #73 Daisy, a "grass-tropical" iris in #78 "X"—and the full harvest implied by Ceres' "foison" at the close of #77 Weeds. The family in which no genus is typical—ranging from cereals, pasture and lawn grasses, and sugar-producers to ornamental grasses, drug-producing plants, and pernicious weeds—is, as Taylor comments, of supreme importance and world-wide distribution. We could suspect that its appearance in #78 "X" has to do with its also extreme variability. Was Zukofsky remembering in addition a small poem of Lorine Niedecker's which pays homage to the author of *Gray's Manual of Botany?*:

Asa Gray wrote Increase Lapham:
pay particular attention
to my pets, the grasses.[8]

And, all in a bunch, to *"trailing arbutus fringed-gentian hydrangea"*; two blues and a fragrant white flower, all three natives (if we add *Hydrangea arborescens* to the "cultivated blue" Zukofsky mentions in his "X" summary), and all three are the object of a sudden conservationist concern voiced in the summary. There Zukofsky notes that trailing arbutus has been "picked indiscriminately by predatory collectors etc"; that fringed gentian is not generally perennial in East Coast meadows and should not be dug from the wild unless it is a biennial that may grow hardy enough to be classified as a perennial; and that hydrangea (never content to stay long with pure botany) sounds "hide ranger"—which the neologist took to mean, with a mixture of British and American usage, one who ranges, wanders over, or is keeper of a royal forest (the original function of a ranger; as one original meaning of *hide* was a unit of land-ownership). Or, in modern North America, "a state forest ranger" as the summary evolves it; one who takes an interest in preserving native flora from overzealous collectors of wild flowers.

We are not done with the Euro-American swing, however, because in *"arbutus"* is a wealth of bee and honey-bearing significance. The arbutus of the Old World was as fragrant as its New World counterparts; we recall the bee passage from Virgil (*Georgics* IV.180) which describes the young workers returning to the hive late at night, "their thighs freighted with thyme; far and wide they feed on arbutus, on pale-green willows, on cassia and ruddy crocus, on the rich linden, and the dusky hyacinth." Part of this was incorporated into #61 Bearded Iris (see chap. 9). When Zukofsky made notes on Arbutus in the Abbreviated Third List (p. 1), both *Epigaea repens,* the trailing American wild flower, and *Arbutus,* the evergreen tree, were included—as was the information that *Arbutus menziesi,* the madrona, is an important source of honey to California bee-keepers (as its Virgilian equivalent was to European apiarists). Zukofsky wrote in the Virgil reference and he had already inserted references to two passages from Henri Fabre. The first of these concerns Fabre's introduction of his chief "assistant" in the field:

> This is my son, little Paul, aged seven . . . he knows better than any one of his age the secrets of the Cigale, the Cricket, and especially of the dung-beetle, his great delight. At a distance of twenty yards his clear sight distinguishes the refuse-tip of a beetle's burrow from a chance lump of earth; his fine ear will catch the chirping of a grasshopper inaudible to me. He lends me his sight and hearing, and I in return make him free of my thoughts, which he welcomes attentively, raising his wide blue eyes questioningly to mine.
>
> What an adorable thing is the first blossoming of the intellect! Best of all ages is that when the candid curiosity awakens and commences to acquire knowledge of every kind.
>
> . . .

> Little Paul and I will study as much as possible in the open country, among the rosemary bushes and arbutus. There we shall gain vigour of body and of mind; we shall find the true and beautiful better than in school-books.⁹

The rhyme of a little Paul, his keen sight and hearing, and the fragrance of arbutus, was readymade for Zukofsky's purposes, which spanned memory and continuing appreciation of his son (compare Fabre's description with those sections of "A"-12 which concern the American Paul's "first blossoming of the intellect"; also the charming, precocious Little). Here was another contingency, and its natural place was a poem that considered the son's work as an extension in kind of the father's.

The second Fabre excerpt is not as clearcut in its application to #78 "X," but Zukofsky's interest in it as part of the Arbutus material leads us to consider possible connections. This time Fabre is writing of the night he imprisoned a female emperor moth in his study and the house was besieged by courting males: "Candle in hand, we entered the room. What we saw is unforgettable. With a soft *flic-flac* the great night-moths were flying around the wire-gauze cover, alighting, taking flight, returning, mounting to the ceiling, re-descending. They rushed at the candle and extinguished it with a flap of the wing; they fluttered on our shoulders, clung to our clothing, grazed our faces. My study had become a cave of a necromancer, the darkness alive with creatures of the night! Little Paul, to reassure himself, held my hand much tighter than usual."¹⁰ The moths had negotiated screens of plane trees, lilacs, rose trees, pines, and cypresses to reach the house, and it is this implication of nighttime fragrance, added to Fabre's description of the moths as suitors of the "maiden princess" in his study, that lends the anecdote a fairytale air—and makes us think that "one-thousandth-in / one-night" has about it an air of *The Arabian Nights,* just as "Of thousands grown climb head-on-head" suggests those exotic, frantic moths. Fabre calls the episode "The Night of the Great Peacock," and when we recall Zukofsky's note about the nectar-drinking moths that drain the flowers of *Oenothera,* the night-scent of fairytale seems to connect full circle. Von Frisch's *Animal Architecture* (1974) is from "P's library," according to Zukofsky's note on p. [112] of the Drafts; perhaps Fabre's *Social Life in the Insect World* has a similar provenance.

By associations of scent both real and imaginary, #78 "X" has characterized itself as *ex*otic. It has also thrown up a surprising number of trees in the course of its eight lines—a tree peony, a tree hydrangea, even a tree primrose (one of the *Century*'s names for the evening primrose); all of them literally tree/flowers and probably suggested by the double incarnation of the arbutus. "Gamut" presses close.

First there is Y for Yaupon, and if X was "work," why shouldn't Y be Albert's "play"? or even child's play?

#79   YAUPON

Children nurs'd woods tilled rock
red totem dances blacks drink
under eyes threshold index thunder
Yaupon flower-scurried buds eyes glance
magnified throb aye lex foam't
horse a full bolus leaf-wave-edged
evergreen prove if berries hardy-bred
'junivals' gulp'm tiger-numb current-red

Children and strange dances; eyes and lenses; horse at the sea's edge; currents and currants, gulped. We seem to have retreated from the paradisal into an opaque, prickly place as cryptic as the entrance of Yaupon itself into the *Flowers*. Since the First List, the Y candidate had been Yucca; Yaupon appears as a late entry inserted into the extended Third List (p. 24) with a cross-reference to a half-page of notes (p. 25). On the same page, notes on *Carpentaria* and carpenter's square are to be "work[ed] with Yucca," so perhaps yaupon was to be part of the same poem. But one spiny native American ousted the other, and, somewhere between Third List and Drafts, the seventy-ninth title flower became *Ilex vomitoria,* the southern holly sometimes called cassena, more properly true yaupon; an evergreen shrub bearing small scarlet berries (branches are sent north as winter decoration, according to the *Century*), which in Texas grows into a tree—"and so is transition to *Gamut,"* as Zukofsky observes (Third List, p. 25). A native holly tree for the wintry American end of *80 Flowers,* which is spreading so much warmth and light across the bridgehead to "Gamut"? Zukofsky found more linkage still in the information (again from the *Century*) that yaupon leaves have an emetic and purgative property (hence *vomitoria*): "and a decoction of them was the famous black drink of the southern Indians. Its use was both ceremonial and medicinal, and to partake of it large numbers of them went down to the coast every spring." Zukofsky: "red totem dances blacks drink"—but the line was speaking also to a personal memory that seems to hinge on that *Century* derivation of *totem,* from the Algonquin *nt' otem,* "my family token." ("A child said to father / or totem: you're a horse"; these lines out of *"A"*-21, p. 474, contribute family weight.) The totems Zukofsky had in mind were three childhood paintings by Paul which had hung in the Central Park South apartment:

1972 (240 CPS) P's 3 pictures[to each side]over C's desk-A child's own graph ~~history~~ of culture: 1)woods 2)rock & hard tilling 3)the ethnic dances. civilized (alas) "~~primitives~~" primitives[11]

("A" 22 & 23 Spiral, p. 162)

Versions of this appear in the *80 Flowers* Notes (pp. 4, 10B); and in the drafts for #79 Yaupon Zukofsky's comment on his use of the material described the "totems" further:

line 2 blacks(= print

with P's *child's* graph of culture in mind; his three
paintings (crayons, ca 1948–9)

(*80 Fl.* Drafts, p. [113])

We cannot know exactly why the subjects of these drawings suggested to Zukofsky a "graph of culture" analogous to the one he plotted in *Bottom,* also in the late forties (except that the "X" poem has already alerted us to the number of son-father links concerning "work"). Zukofsky *père* had entitled Part Two of *Bottom* (p. 33): "*Music's master:* notes for Her music and a graph of culture," but the index reveals that the graphing extends well beyond the second section of the book: "Culture, a graph, 33–443." This takes in the rest of volume 1 and Zukofsky's part in the work, including that Alphabet of Subjects with the long C (for "Continents") section out of which Zukofsky delivered, among other things, an enigmatic "X" (p. 441), then speaking progeny in "Young" (p. 441), and an A-Z compass in "Z (signature)" (p. 442). Family. Well before this, directly after finishing the "Continents" section in late 1958, Zukofsky began "Definition," also lengthy, a dialog between one "Son" and "I" (play the possibilities), which he described to Corman as starting off lyrically "—a conversation between Paul and me" (LZ to CC, 1 January 1959; TxU). This is reminiscent of the walking talk between Louis and Paul which leads off the second part of "A"-14 (p. 274); Zukofsky had remarked to Corman (LZ to CC, 6 September 1959; TxU) that *Bottom* was the place "into which so much of [the] future 'A' has gone"—a place to store more of the hidden melody of family and the graph of culture (human family) which found its most comprehensive expression in the six-thousand-year spans of "A"-22 and "A"-23.

The "civilized primitives" of Paul's drawings and his father's observation, who are apparently dancers, map onto similar figures in "A" 22 & 23, whether they are races appearing out of the geological record in "A"-22 (p. 512), "unconsciously sounding / skills as of bees in / a hive," or the Arapaho singing and the primitive dancing following it ("for honey has she danced / ahead there, pipes and flute, / let her dance ahead," p. 539) at the beginning of "A"-23's History section. Or, to bring matters nearer the tea-drinking Indians of #79 Yaupon:

> West redskins' talk grammars older
> than East's. Tongues: lark's wings:
> '*hi!*' requires a serious answer
> agglutinative questions when no redskins
> lust white gospel in red-tongue.[12]
>
> ("A"-23, p. 561)

Whether language of dance or of tongues, the graph is concerned with registering cultural nuance. That it reaches into #79 Yaupon we may deduce from the "index thunder" (line three) produced by the appearance of Paul's "graph of culture" paintings. "Ay me," cries Gertrude in the face of Hamlet's accusations of gross misconduct, "what act, / That roars so loud and thunders in the index?" (*Ham.* III.iv.50). Meaning, in a now-obsolete sense of the word, what prelude or prolog (and the *Century* gives the line from *Hamlet* as its example of that usage). But Zukofsky has twice before used this particular "index" to gloss indexes of his own, once as epigraph to the index of *Bottom* (p. 445), then, talking about it in "A"-14:

> 'That thunders in
> the Index' Imagine,
> said Celia, selling
>
> the movie rights
> to *Bottom : on*
> *Shakespeare.* No
>
> index was whole
> so our index
> will sometimes lead
>
> us to us
>
> ("A"-14, p. 336–37)

"Culture, a graph, 33–443" led us to Louis's work, all of it, on *Bottom* and to the extension of the graph thereafter; it also led to Paul's "own graph"—or Louis was led back to that graph (a drawing; graphic), contemplating parallels of work and nurture. Indeed, one piece of Shakespeare produced another; not the " 'junivals' " of line eight, which sound as if they should bear some relation to Pyramus/Bottom, that "Most brisky juvenal" (*MND* III.i.97), but the opening phrase of #79 Yaupon:

Children nurs'd woods tilled rock

Closely abutted here to the first two titles of the "child's own graph" is some Shakespeare Zukofsky identifies as coming from Sonnet 77—which also supplies the "blacks" of line two which permute the ceremonial "black drink" of the Indians to: "blacks drink / under eyes threshold." "Blacks" is the Quarto spelling of what Theobald emended to "blanks," and what Zukofsky, quoting the sonnet in *Bottom*, preferred to let be:

77

(To himself)

'Thy glasse will shew thee how thy beauties were,
Thy dyall how thy pretious mynuits waste,
The vacant leaues thy mindes imprint will beare,
And of this booke, this learning maist thou taste.
The wrinckles which thy glasse will truly show,
Of mouthed graues will give thee memorie,
Thou by thy dyals shady stealth maist know,
Times theeiush progresse to eternitie.
Looke what thy memorie cannot containe,
Commit to these waste blacks, and thou shalt finde
Those children nurst, deliuerd from thy braine,
To take a new acquaintance of thy minde.
   These offices, so oft as thou wilt looke,
   Shall profit thee and much inrich thy booke.'
(quoted in Bottom, p. 437)

According to Zukofsky's criterion, 77 is one of the eight sonnets "in which a lifetime appears to be made of their *definition of love,* that is a life's eyes to look and then write—" (*Bottom*, p. 337). Of "Thy glasse will shew thee," he remarked: "I believe the poet speaks to himself, as his memory forgets and his mind rereads his work anew" (*Bottom*, p. 337). A life's eyes looking and then writing also describes Zukofsky's poetic, and *80 Flowers* reads all his work anew, taking delight in and new acquaintance of the record. The mirror's honesty is not without brightness and luck; the dial's canter is inexorable but also inherently musical; blanks will take the mind's imprint, blacks (print) will tell it over to the rereading eye—which will also see richness in the preservation. The brain's children have been "nursed" by time—"under eyes threshold"? Does that mean all-but-invisibly, waiting for the rereading? ("Heart us invisibly thyme time.")

Literally, "under eyes threshold" seems to have its source in some part of the three paintings. The note on page 10B of the *80 Flowers* Notes reads: "C's desk paintgs Graph of culture *woods;* rock; & *hard* tilling:

thought's threshold *dances,* ~~the~~ a *child's* ~~own~~ *graph."* Thought's threshold is Paul remembered at age six ("What an adorable thing is the first blossoming of the intellect! Best of all ages . . .", Fabre). Then the phrase reappears as "flowers under sight's threshold" on a scrap of paper whose reverse side is covered with notes for the yaupon poem. And what has happened to the sense of it? We might guess that Zukofsky's attention has been led from Paul's paintings to a thought of their location over Celia's desk—"C's desk," where one *sees* them, more or less at eye-level, while sitting there, working or thinking; a place that is also thought's threshold. But "under sight's threshold" means also *below* the eye's capacity, and when Zukofsky prefixes "flowers" to it, thought turns promptly to the tiny, inconspicuous flowers of the holly—and discerns some kind of gloss in the lines that follow:

> *Yaupon* flower-scurried buds eyes glance
> magnified throb aye lex foam't
> horse

The talk of magnifying (aid for chronic eye-strain; "throb aye"?) seems to follow on from "under eyes threshold" by means of a working draft of some lines to be found on the verso of the yaupon scrap. Along with a preliminary draft of the first line of #80 Zinnia appears the following notation:

                    no lens perceives
                                        hints
                        no man's glance sees
    ~~budding~~
    flower-scurried buds
                            lens
                no crystalline ~~stone~~
                    ~~may~~ glas (sees)
                            glance
            glance
                            hints
        no low sense
                except it magnify

No hint of a source is given in the line synopsis of the poem, which notes that material in lines four to seven is to be found in Taylor and Gray—and in Theophrastus, whose index gives a list of references to *kēlastros,* the holly *Ilex aquifolium* ("leaf-wave-edged") (and the family is Aquifoliaceae). None of these elucidates the rather beautiful working that seeks to take the poem from tiny yaupon buds to the implications of inadequate (failing?) eyesight brought up by their minuteness. Perhaps it is the term "crystalline" that spurs a thought of the hyaline vision of 1928 and the poet's keen, lensing eye: "Liquid crystal is only as it must be," Zukofsky wrote later, "an incalculable pleasure of optics" (*Bottom*, p. 75). Now that vision (spectacle and eyesight) (spectacles?) seems to have something to do with a magnifying glance or glass; are we to hear transliteration (*megalos*) in that tentative "may glas"?

To return to Zukofsky's line references—Theophrastus is indeed present in #79 Yaupon; *kēlastros,* according to Liddell and Scott, is the classical name of some evergreen tree, either holly or privet. The Loeb translator chooses holly (so does Zukofsky), and the "evergreen" of line seven refers to its distinctive trait. The Greek for evergreen is *aeiphyllos*, a term Theophrastus uses in opposition to *phyllobolus*, literally "shedding leaves"; that is, deciduous (*Enquiry* I.ix.3; III.iii.3). What we can hear in #79 Yaupon is not *aeiphyllos* but *phyllobolos*—or rather ("a full bolus"), Zukofsky's coining of a term (*a*-privative + *phyllobolos*) that, logically, means "not shedding leaves"; that is, "evergreen." (He was close; Liddell and Scott's word for the same idea is *aphyllorrous*.) It seems that the "bolus" sound held some attraction for the horse; perhaps a connection with the emetic properties of yaupon (a *bolus*, figuratively, is "anything disagreeable, as an unpalatable doctrine or argument, that has to be accepted or tolerated," *Century*). Some balance between throwing up and keeping down, echoed by "gulp'm" of line eight and suggested by the "yaup" of the plant name itself, whether as noise ("I sound my barbaric yawp over the roofs of the world"; Whitman) or hunger; yelp or gape.[13] And finding that *gape* is indeed the root of one sense of *yaup*, we are invited to think of the role that gaping has played in *80 Flowers*, from the Epigraph's "unwithering gaping" to #75 Thyme's hiatus ("eye ate his"), mouth wide; agape for love. #79 Yaupon begins "Children nurs'd," and more than Shakespearean nurture is being alluded to: Zukofsky singled out Theophrastus's *therapeia*, meaning "cultivation," in a passage concerning the holly's resistance to human attentions (*Enquiry* I.iii.6); the same word in a different context may signify "fostering, tending, nurturing, generally caring for." Here is one such context.

For similar reasons of lexical shift, we have not yet finished with *bolus*. As the word comes to us from the Greek *bōlos* (a clod or lump of earth), it becomes in Latin "clay, lump"—but also "a choice bit, nice morsel" (Lewis and Short); palatable rather than not. In this sense, "a full bolus" does not sound so much like a grim exercise in subduing a rising gorge. Then both Latin and Greek dictionaries put another *bolus* into the play, its root this time is *bolos*, meaning "throw, cast," as of a net, a haul of fish (hence gain, profit, or advantage), or a throw of dice. It can mean the cast itself or the thing caught ("a full bolus," drawing in the horse's catch) (but also the choice bits? the flower of his achievements?). It can also mean, in the sense of *phyllobolos,* "casting away, shedding." Did Zukofsky notice in the dictionary an Aristotelian usage signifying a casting of teeth? Did he let it settle, with a grimace, over other boluses the horse has had business with, thinking privately of the dental agonies of the Port Jefferson years and earlier? It all adds up; from *"A"*-21, which is all about the catch of a "fisheRman's sea net":

> A child said to father
> or totem: you're a horse.
> An old toothless walks: gap,
> drivel, gab—diagnosed muscular and
> skeletal aches, says: gadgets—I
> look but don't want 'em.
>
>   (*"A"*-21, p. 474)

There was a third Theophrastan holly reference Zukofsky took interest in, which at first sight seems as if it might be connected with the frailties of age; Theophrastus observes (*Enquiry* V.vii.7) that the wood of *kēlastros* (holly) is used for making walking sticks, *baktērias.* However, "light sticks and canes for old men" are fashioned not from holly wood but from the bay tree; Liddell and Scott define *baktēria* or *baktron* as a staff or cane, specifically as a badge of office. The dictionary's wording suddenly makes clear a connection we might otherwise have passed by; if the holly is a staff tree rather than a walking-stick tree, what should come to mind (from #76 Vines) but *Celastrus scandens,* the bittersweet, also known as staff tree. *Celastrus,* "from the Greek for some evergreen tree" (Taylor), is of course a Latinized form of *kēlastros,* the evergreen that Theophrastus's translators chose to give as holly. A walking stick (or staff) made from the wood of an evergreen clearly struck Zukofsky as a nice touch (even old men's canes came from the evergreen *Laurus nobilis*). And a staff does not necessarily prop up diminished strength; it can be an active man's support, a formidable weapon, or the sign of his authority—the *Century* distinguishes its synonyms carefully on this score: a *cane* or *stick* is ornamental or defensive, a *stay* or *prop* buttresses something stationary, but a *staff* is "a substantial support for one who is in motion." Quite.

We begin to think more carefully about sticks, staffs, and rods in *80 Flowers.* Most recently there was the goldenrod of #77 Weeds, which led straight to a biblical emblem of authority via its other popular name of Aaron's rod (serpent and blossom) and which in Zukofsky's early poetry seems some sort of golden bough. In #43 Lilies there is a *"jacob's rod sceptre,"* naming the tall, yellow-flowered *Asphodeline,* the asphodel of the ancients, according to Taylor. The flower of the dead was possibly most interesting to Zukofsky as yet another rod-flower; he transliterates (and translates) in #43 Lilies a passage from Theophrastus describing the asphodel as having the tallest of all stems. In addition, he follows up the Latin *narthex* (rod; according to Taylor), which is the root of *Narthecium,* the bog-asphodel, finding in Lewis and Short that *narthex* is a shrub also known as *ferula*—and *ferula* is: "the plant fennel-giant . . . in the pith of which Prometheus is feigned to have preserved the fire which he stole from heaven." A *ferula,* by transferral, is the thin slender branch of a tree, a whip or a rod, a staff or walking stick, or an attribute of the god Sylvanus; really every sense of a rod/staff Zukofsky could wish for.

More prosaically, in #31 Deutzia there was the blackthorn, *Prunus spinosa,* its wood famous for fine walking sticks. Earlier still in the sequence there was a thyrse in #4 Liveforever, implying Dionysian presence, and there was an actual presence of the god Mercury, bringing with it implications of his sleep-inducing and snake-wound caduceus. This in turn puts us in mind of Aesculapius, concealed deep in the (concealed) peony of #78 "X," who carried a snaky rod of healing. Snakes seem to have a traditional affinity for rods, their lively energy perhaps elaborating the vigor of a living shoot—which (shoot or slender stem), says the *Century,* is the primary meaning of *rod,* suiting the botanical surface of *80 Flowers.* As for staffs, one in particular has kept coming back, an emblem of power about to be relinquished: "and, when I have requir'd / Some heavenly music . . . / To work mine end upon their senses . . . / . . . I'll break my staff, / Bury it certain fathoms in the earth" (*Tmp.* V.i.51). Prospero; the old man as magus, forever about to cast off his power (but the staff is not broken nor the book drowned in our hearing). Did it seem peculiarly apt to Zukofsky that the poem in which the *80 Flowers* magus first introduced mention of Prospero's retirement—"standstill plummet unprotected laurel crown"—should be #22 Bayberry, with its allusion to the bay tree that furnishes not only laurels for crowns but also walking sticks (or staffs?) for old men (or magi)?

Perhaps the figure of the powerful staff goes even further back in the sequence, to the enigmatic Greek bread, *artos;* the staff of life? ("a substantial support for one who is in motion"). "Heart us invisibly . . ."; Zukofsky takes up another project, calling on invisible presences for inspiration, for poetic nourishment ("so much is food"), which is his very life support. Many of the staffs and rods of *80 Flowers* are "invisible" in the poems, nevertheless influential to their business; in #79 Yaupon there is no outward trace of the *baktēria,* merely the slightest whiff of its implications in "evergreen prove if berries hardy-bred"; bred to enduring greenness, hardy-bred life, hardy *bread* (proving, rising); that staff. But also, describing the upcoming line eight, Hardy-bred; " 'junivals' gulp'm tiger-numb current-red" is Zukofsky's final distillation from *A Pair of Blue Eyes*, Mrs Worm and Mrs Smith again: " 'What beautiful tiger-lilies!' said Mrs Worm. 'Yes, they are very well, but such a trouble to me on account of the children that come here. They will go eating the berries on the stem, and call 'em currants. Taste wi' juvinals is quite fancy, really' " (*A Pair of Blue Eyes*, p. 258).

Holly berries are poisonous, and the "berries" of *Lilium tigrinum* presumably do young stomachs no good either (gulped, produce a numbing sensation?). To find out why the tiger lily is here at all, we go back to the In Process Notes of spring 1977, where the plant is listed (p. 1) as the eleventh of "18 planned" *Flowers*. There is, however, no blossoming date and page 2 of the In Process Notes tells us why; the bulb had failed. Probably because of this, the tiger lily never became a title flower, but it was picked up as an ancillary thanks to the Hardy reference Zukofsky had copied into the Notes, July 1977 (p. 3 Condensed Notes), most likely before finding out that his own plant was not flourishing. Hardy's tiger lily reappeared among the unused literary material copied into the Third Abbreviated List (p. 4); Zukofsky must have noticed it there and gone back to the novel to read over the passage, because the reference to "juvinals" is not part of the original note. (Why does he enclose the word in quotation marks and spell it "junivals"? private coinage? a family joke? or a quotation from elsewhere in the canon?)

Incentive to include the tiger lily in #79 Yaupon may have come from its proximity to American holly in the In Process Notes. *Ilex opaca* is the fourteenth of the eighteen garden subjects planned for upcoming poems, planted 1 March 1975 as recorded also in the "Gamut" Notes (p. 3, 1st seq.), where it seems to be a gift from Philip Yannella.[14] The Zukofskys had more luck with their holly; it was in flower 26 May 1976, and "opaca" reappears as a candidate twice more in the lists. Exactly how the switch from *Ilex opaca* to *Ilex vomitoria* was made we cannot be sure, except that it had something to do with the nativeness of both and the initial letter of the latter's common name. That #79 Yaupon is full of holly could be construed as a gesture to the season (Christmas just past), although yaupon's distinctively southern habit works against traditional wintriness. The poem is playful; it is full of play between child and old man (each nurturing the other) but remains ultimately opaque (despite magnifying eyes glancing or glassing over its lexical subtleties), which is perhaps the contribution of the holly from Zukofsky's garden, *Ilex opaca*.

The poet is also gesturing at #80 Zinnia as he composes the yaupon poem, as evidenced by the horse at an ocean's edge ("foam't / horse a full bolus leaf-wave-edged"), casting teeth but with a rich haul to think about, or savor. When Zukofsky changed "currant-red," the last word of the seventy-ninth *Flower* as it stood in both pencil and ink drafts, to "current-red" (the alteration occurs silently between the ink draft and Spiral copy), he was stepping deliberately into the final poem of a book dedicated "to C." There is an air of *"A"*-2 about, where at the sea's edge the horse first encountered the perfect beauty of liveforever on hyaline: "There is space to step to the central heart: / The music is in the flower, / . . . Ankle, like fetlock, at the center leaf—" (*"A"*-2, p. 7). Or, 1928, an explicitness later lost to compression: "I have stepped with haired ankle, / As with fetlock, to the center leaf, / I have looked . . ." The final "C" poem of *80 Flowers* is reverent in its vocabulary and resonant with motifs the sequence has taught us to recognize:

#80   ZINNIA

With prayer-plant eyes annually winter-leggy
zinnia miracles itself perennial return
blest interim strength lengthening coreopsis'-summers
actual some time whereso near
zebra-fragrant sharpened wave currents tide
new moon to full sunrise
sunset enable ships seaworth slow-rounds
rosette lancers speared-yucca's white night

Prayer, miracles, perennial return, blest interim, lengthening strength, "z" fragrance; then tides, moons, sun, a rosette, music, and a dance. A "C"-worthy lyric indeed, assembled as a movement through time, beginning ("With prayer-") at the sight of those "eyes" on a wide-open leaf of *Maranta leuconeura kerchoveana,* the plant that rolls up its leaves as darkness approaches. The prayer plant's eyes are open (it is daylight), and they trigger association with another "day's eye" (that recurring conceit), the zinnia; family, Compositae. Zinnia, the "z" flower, is an annual with an exceptionally long flowering period, summer through fall, which puts it almost in the everblooming category. Remembering that "winter-leggy outdoor / zinnias arm perennial rays summers" (#23 White Begonia)—evolved from Zukofsky's observation that their own zinnias were still in bloom 22 November 1975 (1st Abb. List, p. [2])—we can easily make sense of this day's eye: "annually winter-leggy / *zinnia* miracles itself perennial return." And the "blest interim" (that time when little else flowers? winter of Zukofskian content?) when the zinnia grows, leggy, toward another growing season is "strength lengthening"; or else the "blest interim strength" lengthens the summer flowering into fall, almost into winter. Zinnia and Zukofsky strength or length (staying power?), but also that of coreopsis, another daisy flowering early to late fall, perennial in habit, brilliant yellow in color. The 1977 Park Seed catalog pictures three sunny golden coreopsis blooms on a blue ground (coreopsis varieties have names like Sunray, Baby Sun, Double New Gold). Suddenly we see that zinnia with its eye of gold and coreopsis with its ragged-edged yellow ray-flowers make up, compositely, a sun-flower. Pragmatically, horticulturally, both daisies thrive in the full sun their shapes and colors mimic; poetically, they bring in the gold and imply the blue foil of Zukofsky's paradise.

Literary sources support this notion. The line references for #80 Zinnia point out that "miracles itself" derives from *Cymbeline;* Belarius, musing aloud on a paradise of sons, and provoked by the conversations of Guiderius and Arviragus:

> Nature hath meal and bran, contempt and grace.
> I'm not their father; yet who this should be
> Doth miracle itself, lov'd before me.—
>
> (*Cym.* IV.ii.27)

Then ("blest interim") another piece of Shakespeare is pinpointed, and its context proves relevant to #80 Zinnia:

> Sweet loue, renew thy force, be it not said
> Thy edge should blunter be then apetite,
> Which but too daie by feeding is alaied,
> To morrow sharpned in his former might.
> So loue be thou; although too daie thou fill
> Thy hungrie eies, euen till they winck with fulnesse,
> Too morrow see againe, and doe not kill
> The spirit of Loue, with a perpetual dulnesse:
> Let this sad *Intrim* like the Ocean be
> Which parts the shore, where two contracted new,
> Come daily to the banckes, that when they see:
> Returne of loue, more blest may be the view.
>   As cal it Winter, which being ful of care,
>   Makes Somers welcome, thrice more wish'd, more rare.[15]
>
> (Son. 56)

Sonnet 56 is another of the eight sonnets perceived by Zukofsky as embodying the definition of love, "that is a life's eyes to look and then write" (*Bottom,* p. 337). It has much to say to the zinnia poem and to the concerns of *80 Flowers* generally, beginning with the renewal of love, which is likened to a hunger that must be perpetually fed (think of the recent interest Zukofsky has shown in food-flowers). It is characterized as a hunger of the eyes, and eyes will close with fullness of looking (or of eating; the conceit is neatly doubled), but they will open wide again, wanting more, as surely as day follows night. When the sun is up, eyes must be at their business, which is attentiveness and the record of attentiveness (looking and then writing):

> —It means, Paul,
> If a man sees a thing
>   when alone
> He goes right away
> To look for someone
> To show it
> So he may hear
> More and more of it.
> —You see, that's why
> I don't want any of us
>   to sleep late.
>
>   (Knavery)
>
> ("A"-12, p. 227)

No dullness; another description of Zukofsky's credo, personal and poetic—no dullness and a drive to record. "A"-12 ends (p. 260) with the poet at work ("—Still awake, still pothering? / —What, goddess?"), reminded by Celia that all things are due their season ("—So long as sleep comes in the night, Penelope said"). "A"-12 finally hands on the enterprise to Paul, who does not sleep late ("It's so simple, / Telemachos rose from his bed / And dressed," p. 261), and it honors Celia, who is a deity in their everyday lives ("Blest / Ardent / Celia / unhurt and / Happy," p. 261). "A"-23, a second watershed in the poem, finishes with three-way "z" work and "z" sight; moonwort and sunburst and the "impossible's / sort-of think-cramp work x" ("A"-23, p. 563). Now *80 Flowers,* through which sun and moon have threaded a commentary on time and season, is culminating in a poem that again pays homage to love's open eyes, reasonable, seasonable, timely, and looking out on an earthly paradise.

Shakespeare's "sad *Intrim*" (time when eyes are closed or lovers parted) has merged with the blest view of returned love (of eyes open, "feeding"), so "blest interim" accurately describes for Zukofsky not only the time of year (winter, full of care) but also the special significance of the season (Celia's birthday, his own, Valentine's Day coming up; summer's welcome—"thrice . . . wish'd"—in winter). Bleak January is lit by out-of-season wishes, just as Valentine's Day was cheered by a happy new year at the start of *"A"*-22 and heralded there with the roundel from Chaucer beginning:

> 'Now welcom somer, with thy sonne softe,
> That hast this wintres weders over-shake,
> And driven away the longe nightes blake!
> (*Parlement,* 680–82)

"Somer" meant spring as well but even so, at five weeks before the equinox, the birds are premature in their welcome. So are lyric poets, anticipating light and delight from the depths of a winter season; Thomas Campion's poems in the *Flowers* of late 1975 come to mind—a mistress's face is: "The spring that winter'd harts renu'th; / and this is that my soule pursu'th," and becomes, in #21 Chrysanthemum: "East spring winter hearts renew."[16] In 1977 Zukofsky was looking at the same vocabulary, this time in Shakespeare ("Sweet loue, renew thy force . . . As cal it Winter, which being ful of care, / Makes Somers welcome, thrice more wish'd, more rare"), and choosing to let it rest, a subtext marked economically in the zinnia poem by the phrase "blest interim." Was he thinking also (with more immediate reference to #80 Zinnia) of the other Campion piece he had used, in the other poem with zinnias in it, #23 White Begonia?

> Is shee come? O, how neare is shee?
>> How farre yet from this friendly place?
> How many steps from me?
>> When shall I her imbrace?
> These armes Ile spred, which onely at her sight shall close,
> Attending as the starry flowre that the Suns noone-tide knowes.[17]

In 1975, "suns" had stood for the gist of these lines; in 1977 Zukofsky invoked it with the sun-flowers of #80 Zinnia and with more lyricism to match Campion's context of yearning and anticipation. The two anonymous medieval lyrics Zukofsky edited and then conflated to produce "whereso near" in line four of #80 Zinnia are older than "Sweet loue, renew . . ." but have a similar force. The first is a refrain:

> *A, a, a, a,*
> *Yet I love wher-so I go*[18]

It is understandable that the refrain's first line attracted the poet's attention, and it was typical of him to select the unobvious word (*"wher-so"*) for inclusion in #80 Zinnia—enjoying the silent *"A"* of a cotext in the Z poem of *80 Flowers* as he did so. "Whereso" widens the poem, with love and a singing voice, while "near" renews its concern with intimacy. The conjunction "whereso near" compounds that intimacy across the word break ("so near")—and is Zukofsky's gist of the second medieval lyric, a fragment:

> Lie thou me neer, lemman,
> In thyne armes . . .[19]

The arms, "so near" at last, are about to close on love. And it is "actual some time whereso near / zebra-fragrant," signaling that the referent is personal; *Some Time* is the collection in which a pre–*80 Flowers* zinnia poem appears, in the second part of the 1949 sequence, "Chloride of Lime and Charcoal."[20] The section begins: "Zinnias you look so much like Gentiles" (*All*, p. 131), and goes on to consider the cultural implications of a gift of flowers made to the Zukofskys at their Old Lyme cottage, apparently by the couple from whom the property had been purchased. "Some time," however, is also the epigraph lyric of the 1956 collection, a tribute to wife, son, and the family music:

> Some time has gone
> Since these were written:
> The cause runs off—
> A child's mitten.
>
> But hear play the
> Fingers of his hand
> Celia perpends—
> To understand
>
> (All, p. 116)

Thus Zukofsky inserts, by allusion, his own "love" poem in the lyrical matrix of #80 Zinnia. As an added felicity, that allusion manages to bring in the signal motif of the *Flowers*, time—and to say once more: "Some time has gone" since the poems of *80 Flowers* were begun.

The stamp of the personal is even stronger if we append the unlikely-looking (smelling?) "zebra-fragrant" to the blest interim of perennial coreopsis summers, which are "actual some time whereso near." The fragrance Zukofsky speaks of is time (thyme) rather than zinnia or coreopsis, those scentless daisies. It is of course (perennial) Zukofsky time, a "z" fragrance of some strength, as we discover from the *Century's* definition of *zebra*, which the horse must have read with amusement:

> The general form is light and symmetrical, like that of most wild asses, and seems to indicate speed rather than bottom. The zebra is one of the most

beautiful of animals, as it is also one of the wildest and least tractable. It has often been kept in confinement, and occasionally tamed, but generally retains its indomitable temper. It inhabits in herds the hilly and mountainous countries of South Africa, seeking the most secluded places; so that from the nature of its haunts, as well as its watchfulness, swiftness, and the acuteness of its senses, it is difficult to capture. It is, however, much hunted, and seems destined to extermination.

Perfect! And a rich ground for variations, from the subgenus name *Hippotigris* (tiger horse) to the information about habit, temperament, and the family connection with both horse and ass. Graceful, asslike lines may indicate speed rather than bottom (strength) to the *Century* zoologists, but to Zukofsky the zebra is the ultimate "z" horse because its speed and grace *are* its strength.[21] Also because this bottom indicates that other poetic ass, Bottom, whose long ears do not disqualify him as one of the horse's alter egos—often with flowers:

> Millennium of sun—
> Beast of the field,—
> Kissing the beast upon both ears—
>
> O who will pluck geranium
> With smiles before this ass's face
> And tie it to his cranium
> To match the ass's grace!
>
> (*All*, p. 31)

Strength, or bottom, has been a key concern of *80 Flowers*. We recall an early bottoming strength in #10 Charlock Per Winkle, for example; more recently, the colt grown old (but not inglorious) of the *Georgics*. Strength—durability—is important to the horse in #80 Zinnia (Zukofsky could not have missed the popular name of *Zinnia elegans* in Taylor, an allusion to its extended blooming season: youth-and-old-age). Now, "strength lengthening" the blest interim so that summer's delight extends right across the calendar of Zukofsky's days, the horse seems to have lasted the distance with honors. But still he cannot resist privately undercutting triumph with hints of its price; "strength" in line three of #80 Zinnia is drawn from another Shakespearean sonnet, according to the line synopsis. The reference looks like "69" or "68" in Zukofsky's hand (*80 Fl.* Drafts, p. [114]), but neither includes the word "strength." Sonnet 66, however, does: "And strength by limping sway disabled" is part of a list of the world's evils. If this is indeed the line Zukofsky has in mind, then "strength" in the Zinnia poem is a severely compromised term—until we read further in Sonnet 66:

Tir'd with all these, from these I would be gone,
Save that, to die, I leave my love alone.

What looks like another admission of waning strength turns into a statement of tenacity. So that in #80 Zinnia, publicly at least, "strength" is to be taken at face value, and we are left in no doubt as to the acuteness of the "z" horse, evidently also a seahorse:

zebra-fragrant sharpened wave currents tide
new moon to full sunrise
sunset enable ships seaworth slow-rounds

Not unexpected; after all, the horse's first encounter with the live-forever flower is prefaced with just such a blending (horse and sea) as hooves break onto the hyaline element:

Half-human, half-equestrian, clatter of waves,
Fabulous sea-horses up blind alleys,
Never appeased, desire to break thru the walls
                            of alleyways:
Till the moon, one afternoon,
Launches with sea-whorl,
Opening leaf within leaf floats, green,
On waves: liveforever.

                                       ("*A*"-2, p. 7)

The horse then steps (no clattering), to the center leaf, witness to and part of the liveforever vision (a *see*-horse?) ("*A*"-7's sawhorses), his pivotal role established. The 1978 version of this connection with the sea, also with the "C" whom subsequent years brought on the scene, draws on material from *The Sea around Us* originally intended for inclusion in #75 Thyme. Our guess that "zebra-fragrance" signified another time/thyme figure is confirmed by the time/tide material from Rachel Carson.

    This begins at "sharpened wave," which is Zukofsky for Carson's observation (p. 112) that it is possible to distinguish several types of wave: "Young waves, only recently shaped by the wind, have a steep, peaked shape even well out at sea." This, from the chapter "Wind and Water," is copied out fully in the *80 Flowers* Notes (p. 7), and the material around it is the basis of the next few lines of #80 Zinnia. However, "sharpened," the word Zukofsky uses to describe Carson's young waves, acts as a bridge between *The Sea around Us* and other material of the poem. The "sharp-ened wave" is reminiscent of the "leaf-wave-edged" (*Aquifolium*) of #79 Yaupon's hollies; and we are surely to recall, from Sonnet 56, a different kind of sharpness, an appetite satisfied daily but "To morrow sharpned in his former might" (oceanic strength is a variation of the figure later in the poem). Finally, reading from the start of line five, the acumen of the "z" horse (youth-and-old-age) is alluded to in: "zebra-fragrant sharpened wave currents tide." Sharp points in *80 Flowers* are a sure indication that the horse, laboring or singing, is nearby.

Read as a list, "wave currents tide" itemizes Carson's discussion of wind-generated waves, the planetary currents, and the sun- and moon-influenced tides. But Zukofsky's syntax suggests that it is the blest interim, "actual some time" and so near a "zebra-fragrant sharpened wave," which is activated by forces appropriate to its "z" principals: "currents tide / new moon to full sunrise / sunset." Carson says that when currents cross the path of waves or move in direct opposition to them, they are responsible for some of the sea's most terrible displays of power; so "currents" cuts across "wave," swinging the poem onto a track that considers time as tide, and tide as (the power of) time. Among the notes summarized for #75 Thyme is the remark: "tidal's human life (tide)" (*80 Fl.* Drafts, p. [109]), a compression of Carson's discussion of the sea's effect on its shores: "Unlike the slow geologic changes that bring about the flooding of half a continent, the work of the waves is attuned to the brief span of human life, and so the sculpturing of the continent's edge is something each of us can see for ourselves" (*The Sea around Us*, p. 119). We can see also a briefer work, the two-week process that "tides" the moon from crescent to orb ("new moon to full"), those points of the lunar cycle which produce the big tides (known as "springs") because moon and sun are in direct line with the earth and their combined pull brings water high onto the beaches.[22]

Reading the lines again, though, "sharpened wave currents" (depths chopping up surfaces) tide a "new moon to full sunrise"—a night-span in which the tides have time to rise and fall once, and then complete their (lunar) daily cycle between "sunrise / sunset." The length of the lunar day is twenty-four hours and fifty minutes, and so the tides are roughly an hour later each (terrestrial) day. How compelling this lunar clock is among tidal creatures Carson illustrates (and Zukofsky notes) with the example of a sea-worm, which, even removed to a tideless aquarium, will rise up from its sand as the tide is ebbing and sink down again as the tide turns. This moon-attuned rhythm, living creation following the sea's own help-less attunement, appealed to Zukofsky. The cycles turn musically within each other:

new moon to full sunrise
sunset enable ships seaworth slow-rounds

The reference to lunisolar-enabled ships is more Carson, and the subject is again waves: "Furthermore, the water that composes a wave does not advance with it across the sea; each water particle describes a circular or elliptical orbit with the passage of the wave form, but returns very nearly to its original position. And it is fortunate that this is so, for if the huge masses of water that comprise a wave actually moved across the sea, navigation would be impossible" (*The Sea around Us,* p. 110). With even water particles describing orbits, the apparently random ocean wave is brought within the pattern of cycles and circles which starts, or finishes, with the grand wheelings of moon and sun; "slow-rounds." But specifically "seaworth slow-rounds," encompassing the slowly circling planetary currents and their deeper, even slower, counterparts. Carson on oceanic "slow-rounds":

> The flow of these deep waters is hardly a "flow" at all; its pace is ponderously slow, the measured creep of icy, heavy water. But the volumes involved are prodigious, and the areas covered world-wide . . .
>
> There is, then, no water that is wholly of the Pacific, or wholly of the Atlantic, or of the Indian or the Antarctic. The surf that we find exhilarating at Virginia Beach or at La Jolla today may have lapped at the base of antarctic icebergs or sparkled in the Mediterranean sun, years ago, before it moved through dark and unseen waterways to the place we find it now. It is by the deep, hidden currents that the oceans are made one. (*The Sea around Us,* pp. 142–43)[23]

Zukofsky's "slow-rounds" are also a pervasive music (of the spheres?): "the musical form intended here," as he annotates it (*80 Fl.* Drafts, p. [114]). Retrospectively, this casts new meaning on #52 Snow-Wreath's "earth-rounds," making music of the seasons' turning, and of the globe's (another circle within a circle; Zukofsky's phrase matches the concentric principle perceived everywhere).

In #80 Zinnia the wheels are "seaworth," but the term, by association with what has gone before, ascends toward the celestial and cosmic even without Zukofsky's explanation of the coinage: "L.Z. = seaworthy + . . . worth, evalued by 'God's' sea (whatever's providence, nature or creation)" (*80 Fl.* Drafts, p. [114]). The private analog, made so intricately in "Initial" and kept with light insistence before us since then (see-worthy, and all *Around Us*) is "C"-worth; seen, all around (gentle daily orbit, life's time), seaworth and seaworthy (durable; worthy of the sea). Is this the ultimate cipher of durability (Celia's) intended to match that set up for the horse of good bottom (Louis)?[24] The sea's moon is also "C" 's moon and, with a quick refocus, "C" is [the] moon. Hence the situation in #80 Zinnia, where the sea appears to direct the affairs of the moon ("currents tide / new moon to full"). However, if the sea is "C," and "C" is also the moon (looking on the sea) (seeing), then Zukofsky has deduced a figure in constant motion between heaven and earth to parallel the conjunctions and oppositions of earthly and heavenly bodies.

High as such implications take us, there is still one line of #80 Zinnia left—and, typically, it appears to strike out in a new direction:

rosette lancers speared-yucca's white night

We are back on the ground, with another plant to consider; one that was scheduled to have been the title flower of the seventy-ninth poem, reported first from Bermuda in 1972 ("A" 22 & 23 Spiral, p. 140), planted at East Broadway in the fall of 1974 (First List, p. vi), variety *Yucca filamentosa* ("bearing slender threads," Gray) according to the First Abbreviated List, which also gives the alternative popular names of Adam's-needle and bear grass, and notes that it blossoms at night. The yucca is a native American lily, and its flowers are white or cream, rising from the familiar basal rosette of "sword-shaped leathery leaves" (Taylor). Another popular name is Spanish bayonet, and the *Century* embellishes the spikiness of Taylor's name as "Adam's Needle and Thread" or "Eve's Thread." Zukofsky must have been pleased to receive another Eden reference into the *Flowers*, especially one that brought with it an allusion to thread when the poem already included some bottoming; he wrote "(unravelling)" next to the description of *Yucca filamentosa*'s leaves as thready-margined.

All of this somewhat accounts for line eight of #80 Zinnia but, dancing around or above the botanical components, is more of the poem's hidden melody. The clue is "rosette," just over the line break from "seaworth slow-rounds"; the yucca's rosette of leaves provokes a memory of *Sempervivum tectorum*'s rosy-pointed basal rosette, essence of the liveforever vision that has taken to itself images of the multifoliate rose on several occasions. Zinnias also may be rosettes, and multifoliate; there is even a green-flowered variety, many-petaled and orblike, illustrated in the 1977 Park Seed catalog, which may have put Zukofsky in mind of his original liveforever flower. In fact, it may have been Park's full-page heading— "Giant Cactus-Flowered Zinnia"—that brought yucca, a plant requiring the same culture as desert cacti, into the zinnia poem.[25]

Once the yucca was there, its sharpness and night fragrance fitted well: "speared-yucca" is a Zukofskian step away from the swords, bayonets, and daggers of other imaginations. And "lancers"? At one level we are talking about more sharp-pointed weaponry (is a "lancer" a "white [k]night"?) with overtones of botanical description; yucca leaves are "sword-shaped," zinnia leaves are "lance-shaped." Zukofsky as good as used Taylor's term years before in the zinnia poem of *Some Time*: "So; these are your lancet leaves" (*All*, p. 132). But while this memory is meant to adhere to "lancers," the exact configuration of the term derives from some *80 Flowers* note-taking, specifically an entry of October 1975. It starts in the *Century* with *pool,* meaning in one sense a set of players; and the example of usage Zukofsky noticed was from Jane Austen:

> She had also asked him to dine at Rosings, and had sent for him only the Saturday before, to make up her pool of quadrille in the evening. (*Pride and Prejudice*, p. xiv)

Curious, Zukofsky looked up *quadrille,* and found that it was the name of a card game (four players, forty cards) as well as the more familiar square dance or the music for it. All of this was noted down (*80 Fl.* Notes, p. 10A), though the source was not identified or the sequence of operations made clear. The quadrille reference then prompted the thought of *Lancers,* "A popular set of quadrilles, first used in England about 1820 . . . Music for such a set of dances" (*Century*)—"Therefore metaphorically together," Zukofsky observed, linking *pool, quadrille,* and *lancers.* The note stayed on page 10A, untransferred, uncondensed, and unused until musical form and lancet leaves coalesced near the close of #80 Zinnia and Zukofsky remembered the reference that would bring in dance as well. With "lancers" in the poem, *80 Flowers* has come full circle from treading a measure with John Gerard, the man who had better things to do than dance in quagmires. The dance, circles and cycles, is now something of a cosmic hoedown.

The *Pride and Prejudice* note is cited among the line references for #80 Zinnia even though Austen's quadrille is a card game rather than a dance; and this nineteenth-century provenance of "lancers" (and *quadrille*) is paralleled by the final literary reference of the poem, which is not Shakespeare, James, Hardy, or any of the other big figures of *80 Flowers'* undertexts; "white night," that most evocative expression of the yucca's nighttime scent, is almost the exact title of Dostoevsky's 1811 collection *"White Nights" and Other Stories.*[26] This title derives from its first piece, "White Nights: A Sentimental Story from the Diary of a Dreamer." Zukofsky makes the connection laconically: "white night—Fyodor 'Dusty,'" (*80 Fl.* Drafts, p. [114]); the first and also the last time Dostoevsky enters the *Flowers.* A chance association? a memory of the story? Or was Zukofsky reading the collection early in 1978? Whatever the link, the thing about a white night is that one spends it awake. Dostoevsky's story concerns a series of rendezvous between the diary-keeper and a young woman; the setting is Saint Petersburg by night, the season is high summer, and the narrator remains sleepless throughout, wound up to fever pitch by the meetings.

We recall again the close of "A"-12, poet "still pothering" deep into the night; and the late working of "A"-23's first "An"-song, that part of it finished 13 May 1973 between 12:30 and 1:00 A.M., ending:

                    second
paradise turnsole suns again, borage
corolla clear blue, anthers sapphire
after a night thinking sun

("A"-23, p. 538)

"A"-23 was finished, with a "sunburst" and more flowers (one of them moonwort), at 12:30 P.M. on 21 September 1974, which is more or less an equinox and was certainly close to the Jewish New Year. Now *80 Flowers* is ending with a night-blooming flower that keeps the senses wakeful and delighted after the perennial daisies and their day's eye have closed. We can be certain that the moon's eye looks on this white night of conjectural summer, or *somer;* a warm season always coming; a blest interim.

Coda

Time

"By some miracle of fourth-dimensional topology," Hugh Kenner wrote in 1978, "Zukofsky routinely folded universes into matchboxes."[1] Did Kenner know then that time (thyme) was the ordering principle of Zukofsky's last completed matchbox/universe, *80 Flowers,* the one that brought him closest to the millennial jubilee of the year 2000 (paradise) at which "Gamut" was projected? The six thousand years of recorded history—gamut of voices, breath, and music—is Zukofsky's lifelong subject; its summation in the year 2000 (almost the start of a promised thousand-year of Rest and Jubilee; nothing ends without beginning) is prepared for at the close of *"A"* where a "living calendar" starts (in 1974) at line 1,974 of *"A"* 22 & 23 and finishes 26 lines later, alphabetical gamut standing in for a count of years to come (this *is* a calendar), at line 2,000. The Jewish coordinate in this count of Gregorian years is to be found in the composition dates of the "living calendar": 17 September 1974 was Jewish New Year 5735; and 21 September, as mentioned already, is near the autumnal equinox—moon time—upon which the Hebrew calendar is calculated in part.

80 Flowers writes the first phase of this post-*"A"* future. Looking into the minutiae of the *Flowers,* we discovered everywhere the shapes of time past worked as the detail of time present. The fourth-dimensional miracle Kenner speaks of is Zukofsky's ability to make condensation ("which is more than half of composition," *A Test,* p. 81) the agent of an extraordinary lyricism ("proper breathing space, ease, grace"—a long-established blueprint). The beauty of it is in the listening and the looking, and in the power these activities have of exciting or inciting attention—to universes, their stars, their flowers. Sight, sound, and intellection.

Thyme

As I write it is summer and there are minute flowers appearing on the herbs outside the window. Looking at them, I am reminded of Lorine Niedecker saying in a letter of 25 July 1948 (TxU): "The little mint [family] is what intrigues me, tho. Some of it has flowers so tiny they remind me of the notes of LZ in his watchpocket."[2] This serves to bring us from considerations of time and scale to talk about thyme and another time scale.

We have explored in detail the association in *80 Flowers* of thyme with fire (light and heat), roses (thorns and fragrance), bees (energetic workers of sweetness), and horses (Pegasus colts to harnessed laborers). A word needs to be said about the relation this bears to the liveforever it is connected to but also (thyme, time) somewhat at odds with. At stake here is that notion of paradise Zukofsky developed over the years; its roots are set in the vision of liveforever, and the vision was a roselike configuration, the imbrication of petals (or leaves) supplying a visible metaphor of ratio and addition. As Zukofsky's sense of the paradisal became oriented to his family rather than an abstract goal of artistic perfection, "living forever" became a matter of exploring and recording the "long / Second paradise" (*"A"*-12, p. 146) of life. It was not a simple thing, either to live or to write about, especially (as the years passed) with a sense of physical frailty encroaching on the domain of the possible. When Zukofsky's fascination with growing things deepened (fortunately in proportion to Celia's willingness to garden), he found in the cycles of growth and decay the link needed to reconcile living forever with an earthly paradise created over the years.

Paradise is a delight and a garden, but to Zukofsky it is not somewhere to sit down without first checking the ground for whatever might have sprung up (or got in) overnight.[3] That is, paradises are subject to flux; things happen or there would be no story. The growing going on in paradise garden stands for this; if it is to be a delight worth the name, there must be variation and change, or else, earthly, we will find paradise a bore. The garden must be like a real garden, with cycles of growth; blossomings and witherings. Recurrence, living it over, is the "forever" of such a paradise; and of a poet like Zukofsky. By the time *"A"* finishes, liveforever has become the poet saying "let me live here ever" (*"A"*-22, p. 508) in a place from which everything can be lived over ("ever" is now "over") as the seasons turn, bringing anniversaries and new unearthings.

In *80 Flowers*, taking up the idea in earnest, thyme (time) co-opts the flower liveforever for its rosaceous shape and as a rosy extension of its own fragrance and burning energy. As Zukofsky's wreatheries proceed,

fiery rose and rosy fire dance a fine line between garden reality and icon—
precisely the ground prepared for them. In personal terms, the most
important development of the liveforever "rose" is its alignment in *80
Flowers* with the real roses of the 8 June anniversary (recurrence); it is
their scent that pervades the private undertext of the sequence, with the
sweet fiery smell of thyme close by. That central privacy, a silence where
words leave off (and flowers bloom?) is unassailable; we are properly
directed to love's outer, praise-singing face, and only hints of the other are
audible in the songs from time to time.

Technique

Formally, *80 Flowers* is the tour de force of Zukofsky's late style of
condensed lyricism in which words freed from conventional syntax invite
or demand that an audience make what aural or semantic connections it
can. Each word has a certain historical weight that contributes to the
poem; but it is also a unit in the syntax Zukofsky forges by balancing these
histories (the noise they make) and the actual noise of words against
tympanum. When the poet reads his *Flowers*, we hear him making definite
syntactical choices; indeed, he will start again when he feels he is losing the
sense of lines that to a casual reader may look like random aggregates. The
point is that by reading aloud, Zukofsky is mapping one semantic option
among the several that this poetry habitually offers. As an audience,
listening, we can perhaps make out the play of backward- and forward-
looking words (the ear remembers their sounds, registers their associations). When, as readers, we come to the texts of these poems, Zukofsky's
visual strategies come into play: almost purely visual devices like "th[e]
nine" written across the break of #51 Snowdrop's last two words, or the
italics that foreground *thyme, rose,* and *thyme* as the scope of #75 Thyme.
Then there are the strategies inhabiting a region between ear and eye,
speaking to one and then the other, one impossible to perform without the
other: for example, the "lunary era" to be heard (but also almost spelt) in
"lunar year annual," the first line of #3 Honesty. What starts out as a
largely aural transformation then turns into "lunary era a new all anew,"
and the double use of the initial "a" of "annual" ("era **a** new all") is the
result of the eye casting back even as the voice reads forward.

Compounding such intricacies in the endlessly kinetic lines of *80
Flowers* is the lack of punctuation. Conventions of punctuation are
present even as late as *"A" 22 & 23;* but in the *Flowers* they are missing
(except for a few apostrophes and the occasional inflection mark) because
Zukofsky apparently wants to push us, readers, back to the sound of these
words, wants us to sound them in the effort to establish the sense (or

multiplicity of sense) our ears, hearing melody (an order), insist is there. It is perhaps significant that the *80 Flowers* poems reached their audience first as a taped recording; there was no text until 1978, and Celia's advertisement for the book is quick to point out that none of it had been printed (or read in public)—unusual, because Zukofsky normally allowed magazine publication of work as it reached final form, and the *80 Flowers* Spiral was receiving each poem as authoritative text from December 1974 on.

As listeners and readers, then, we derive delight from the complicated verse of the *Flowers*. Think what Zukofsky, reading out loud or to himself, must have got from them as condensation touched off wealths of associative detail. The investigations made here touch only a fraction of that richness; everywhere, though, they open up possibilities for taking a poem one way or another—and that, the increment, is pure Zukofsky.

As for the role of quotation and transliteration in *80 Flowers*, much of it falls into the category of "breathed history"—verbatim record of men's voices, preserved freshly. This is nothing new to modern poetry, which has been making new out of old for the best part of seventy years; Zukofsky's peculiar contribution is the quotation he chooses to use. His brand of transliteration amounts to "quoting" classical authors in the sound of their original language using English words (and their superadded sense, which may or may not gloss the underlying language). In *80 Flowers* this fascination with languages laid over one another continues to develop; at the outset, most of the transliterations concern the Latin (and sometimes Greekish Latin) binomials of Linnean classification—though there are odd bits of Latin, Greek, Hebrew, and even transliterated English ("some mule purchase" in #11 Heart's Ease is Samuel Purchas, via a *Century* quotation). By midway in *80 Flowers,* as the result of constant recourse to Theophrastus and of saturation by the *Century*'s etymologies, but most of all because of a (re?)reading of Virgil and Horace, the incidence of Latin and Greek transliteration is much greater. It is not unusual to find Greek inwreathed with or directly abutting Latin as Zukofsky sounds a name through its history: "keek / core and" in #45 Chicory, for example, containing both Virgil's *cichorea* and the Greek *kichorē* or *kichorion*. And as he winds not just names or single terms but whole phrases into the poems (the craftsman of *Catullus* unable to resist new challenge?), transliteration begins to show ever more markedly in the "English" of the *Flowers*. From the straightforward (as English) "Heart us" (*artos*), *"thus"* (*thus*), or "a mace" (*emēs*) of the Epigraph, or the Italian and Greek plays Zukofsky describes in the #22 Bayberry exposition, we move to the complexities and sustained strangeness of "coddle / lay dune ass toss opt / thrown own" (*katheile Dynastas apo thronōn*) in #54 Windflower, or "bees / knuck to min hours crewroar / thyme our booty us" (*se nocte minores crura thymo . . . arbut[us]*) in #61 Bearded Iris.

The strategy reaches a peak with: "leg it / toles odd astral eaves rust / sticks urban miraculous ditty whinnied / to few gains . . . knows weathers flame," which is #69 Yarrow's potpourri of Horace ("leg[it] . . . tollis ad astra levis . . . rusticus urbem") and Virgil ("mirabile dictu . . . hinnatu fugiens . . . adgnosco veteris vestigia flammae"). The density of this extended transliteration in the poems from mid-sequence to #69 Yarrow is a result of what also filled earlier poems with quotation first from James and then from Hardy: Zukofsky is using notes on his reading of Virgil and Horace. When they are exhausted, the sequence turns back to the "normalities" of largely binomial transliteration.

There is another kind of quotation in *80 Flowers* which attracts attention because of its nonliterary, almost mundane, nature. Why, we might ask, is a poet lifting material verbatim from a gardening encyclopedia (Taylor) and a botany manual (Gray)? The answer lies in Zukofsky's respect for languages of specialization, and the precision and expertise they imply; his attachment to the *Century* is based on a similar respect. Getting authority's voices into the contemporary and American botanical/horticultural aspects of this book about keen observation is at least as important as getting in the voices of Virgil, Horace, Theophrastus, and others as keen observers of other eras. Actual quotation of Taylor and Gray is generally restricted to one- or two-word phrases; though as information sources (made over in Zukofsky's cadence), they inform a sizeable proportion of nearly every poem.

"Gamut: 90 Trees"

80 Flowers is a finale in the way "A"-23's "living calendar" was; it celebrates work to date and prefigures work to be written. The best possible way to "finish" a study of the *Flowers* would be to go on to the "Trees," as Zukofsky himself did.

The surviving poem of "Gamut," #1 Much Ado About Trees, sounds an intriguing pattern of repetition and variation which is delight for the ear and work for the attentive eye.[4] Remarkably, it contains not a single tree—only lichen, alga, and fungus, and a little information about their interdependence. Then follows a transliteration of *Diodia teres*, the plant commonly known as buttonweed and drawn in this instance from the USDA Agricultural Handbook *Common Weeds,* as is the last floral component of the poem, poor joe of the madder or coffee family. Snow, alongside poor joe in the last line, has an agricultural origin; it is Taylor's "poor man's manure," and so the names merge. But snow also reminds us of *80 Flowers'* double canzone of snow-named flowers and of their critical position in the sequence, starting off spring (in 1951 Niedecker wrote a poem beginning: "In February almost March a snow-blanket / is good manure," which was shown to Zukofsky for comment and criticism; did he remember it?).[5] In addition, snow reminds us of earlier valentines addressed to Celia and Paul; the warmth of red hearts is evoked here by the implied conviviality of Sunday coffee and the cold/warmth of a snow/ blanket, nurturing the earth.

There are no trees though (*Much Ado About—Nothing?*), only trees' lichen hugging bark (or rocks). Lichen contains alga and fungus, which live off each other, according to Taylor, whom Zukofsky summarized on page 6 of the "Gamut" Notes. "The process involves complicated chemical reactions," Taylor continues, "some of which result in the extremely slow disintegration of rocks into soil. Lichens are thus one of the first agencies in changing rock into soil. Sometimes used in terraria." Zukofsky's absorption of this information shows up in the fourth line of the poem as he transliterates *Diodia teres* by bringing in the rhymes of a dear *terra* (earth); a terraced terrarium standing in for a *belle terre*(?) or even for a *paradiso terrestre* and its slow, often difficult metamorphosis of quotidian detail.

There is another line of investigation which, in customary Zukofskian fashion, links the start of "Gamut" with the body of *80 Flowers,* its reference books and notes. It begins with some thought about the title, "Gamut," and the ear's memory of an unused piece of information located next to something that eventually went into the first poem of the *Flowers,* having started out in the "Gamut" Notes:

> Nov 8/74—zygote fertilized cell (= male + female)
>   gametes [sex cells joined] (sigh goat
>   (game meat) gam meet
>   gam
> 12/24/74 sounds invisibly (from 90 Trees p. 1)
>   (*80 Fl.* Notes, p. 5)

Looking at the *Century*'s etymology for *gamete,* an inkling of Zukofsky's interest in the word stands forth: "[< Gr. (*gametē*), a wife, (*gametēs*), a husband, < (*gamein*), marry, < (*gamos*), marriage]." A marriage of partners produces—a zygote; which, says the *Century*, is the same as a zygospore, from *zygon* (yoke) and *spora* (seed). Z-yoked gametes, in Zukofsky parlance? Did he see also the definition of a *zygospore:* "In botany, a spore formed in the process of reproduction in some algae and fungae by the union or conjugation of two similar gametes." "Gamut," encompassing the musical gamma-ut and the gamut of years which will take it into the twenty-first century and the seventh millennium, may conceivably make the first step of that trajectory by alluding to gametes that find each other (they "meet" for a "gam"—endless talk?) in order then to "marry" and make of themselves a "z" yoke, a zygote, a zygospore; the seed of things to come. Perhaps even a book of trees.

Appendix A

Contents of *80 Flowers,* Listed and Dated by Composition

Dates of composition are taken from the *80 Flowers* Drafts (D), which sometimes include time spent collecting notes for a poem, and from the *80 Flowers* Spiral (S), where Zukofsky dated each poem as he copied it in. Page numbers at far right indicate that the poem has been quoted whole in this work.

363

FLOWER	COMPOSITION	DEDICATION	PAGE QUOTED
Epigraph	27–29 Dec. 1974	—	—
#1 Starglow	7–21 Jan. 1975	"for C" (D)	91
#2 Mountain Laurel	25–29/30 Jan. 1975 (D) 29–30 Jan. 1975 (S)	"for Chana Z." (D)	104
#3 Honesty	31 Jan.–9 Feb. 1975 (D) 9 Feb. 1975 (S)	"for Fri Feb 14 C + P Valentine's Day Song 1975" (D) "Valentine 1975" (S)	118
#4 Liveforever	14–19 Feb. 1975		
#5 Lavender Cotton	22 Feb.–10 Mar. 1975	"for JSB's Birthday Mar 21" (S)	142
#6 Spider or Ribbon Plant	10–29 Mar. 1975	"anticipating Apr. 11" (D) (S)	
#7 Sprengeri	30 Mar.–15 Apr. 1975		
#8 Pussy Willow	11–29 Apr. 1975		
#9 Privet	1–29 May 1975	"intended W.S. April 26/75" (D) (S)	167
#10 Charlock Per Winkle	27 June–4 July 1975		177
#11 Heart's Ease	5–11 July 1975		
#12 Cinquefoil	13–19 July 1975	"pōpulus or populus" (S)	
#13 Venus's Looking-Glass	22 July–1 Aug. 1975		
#14 Spearmint	4–15 Aug. 1975		
#15 Zebrina Etc	20–26 Aug. 1975		
#16 Four-o'clock	4–10 Sept. 1975		
#17 Cockle	8–22 Sept. 1975		
#18 Petunia	23–25 Sept. 1975 (D) 23–26 Sept. 1975 (S)	"D.P. (née Z.) Dora Pruss d. 1913" (S)	
#19 Wild Geranium	28 Sept.–7 Oct. 1975		
#20 Rose-of-Sharon	19–27 Oct. 1975	"for Oct 22/75" (S)	

FLOWER	COMPOSITION	DEDICATION	PAGE QUOTED
#44 Queen Anne's Lace	31 Aug.–5 Sept. 1976		223
#45 Chicory	9–16 Sept. 1976		229
#46 Dandelion	16–20 Sept. 1976		229
#47 Dahlia	17–25 Sept. 1976	"Rosh Hashana 5737" (S)	
#48 Impatiens	26 Sept.–6 Oct. 1976	"10/14 P: back from Motorola, Chicago" (S)	
#49 Slipperwort	7–14 Oct. 1976	"for Paul's 33 birthday" (S)	
#50 Chokecherry	16–22 Oct. 1976		
#51 Snowdrop	11 Apr.–1 May 1977	"for P's Mountain State College, N.J. Symposium (Fri 6/Sat 7) CP2" (S)	245
#52 Snow-Wreath	4–6 May 1977		245
#53 Grecian Windflower	20–24 May 1977. Notes collected b. 10 May (D)	"CP2 Symposium reviews in Mountain & Paterson, N.J. rc'd." (S)	253
#54 Windflower	27–31 May 1977		
#55 Grape-Hyacinth	6–8 June 1977. Notes collected b. 1 June (D)	"Salute P's Oldsmobile by coincidence acquired June 8" (S)	259
#56 Hyacinth	13–15 June 1977. "ideas for pencil draft beg. Apr 11/77 or earlier via 'A'-9" (D)		
#57 Dogwood	18–21 June 1977. Notes collected 16–17 June (D)	"Paul: Iceland Lvs 9.30 arr Sun 6:19" (D)	
#58 Poppy Anemone	24–27 June 1977. Notes collected 21–22 June (D)	"for Paul 10 days Iceland beg June 18 -Fri)" (S)	

FLOWER	COMPOSITION	DEDICATION	PAGE QUOTED
#72 Raspberry	30 Nov.–4 Dec. 1977 (D). Notes collected 27–29 Nov. (D), 27 Nov.–4 Dec. (S)	"P. Iceland back 12/18 or earlier" (S)	
#73 Daisy	6–11 Dec. 1977. Notes collected 5–7 Dec. (D)		
#74 Aloe	13–16 Dec. 1977. Notes collected 11 Dec. (D)	"Personal: Aloe vera, Helen Kelly's gift June 4/77" (D) "Paul back Dec 14 with gifts from Iceland C. turtle neck L. matching gloves" (S)	273
#75 Thyme	17–20 Dec. 1977. Notes collected 17 Dec. (D)	[17 Dec.] "Paul here for pre-Xmas dinner" (D)	280
#76 Vines	23–28 Dec. 1977. Notes collected 23–28 Dec. (D)		297
#77 Weeds	30 Dec. 1977–2 Jan. 1978 (D).		—
—	Notes collected b. 30 Dec. (D), 23–28 Dec. 1977 (S)	"P. here for dinner New Years Day" (D) "Paul here during New Year's day" (S)	305
#78 "X"	4–13 Jan. 1978. Notes collected 4–13 Jan. (D)	"P's *work*" (S)	319
#79 Yaupon	14–17 Jan. 1978. Notes collected 26 Mar. 1977–17 Jan. 78 (D)		333
#80 Zinnia	4–21 Jan. 1978. Notes collected 9 Aug. 1977–21 Jan. 1978 (D)	"C's b." (S)	342

Appendix B
Zukofsky on #22 Bayberry

"80 Flowers—#22 Bayberry," Louis Zukofsky interviewed by Hugh Kenner, at the Johns Hopkins University, Baltimore, Maryland, 13 December 1975. First transcribed by Andy Campbell, University of Kentucky, Lexington, Summer 1982. N.B.: Square brackets indicate transcriber's information. I have silently corrected minor mistranscriptions after listening to the tape. This material is copyright Paul Zukofsky.

#22 BAYBERRY

Candleberry bayberry spice resinwax green
durant leaf moor in key
dour attested deer-wit winds survive
days *hippos* rampant *wooden* ancient
standstill plummet unprotected laurel crown
trust sweet-fern of your family
bring birds alula sound coast-floes
sand-iced willows *compt* gibbous moons

LZ: The source of this is really the first poem in *Anew,* if you remember. The one that has the footnote about the bay . . .

HK: Yea, uh-huh.

LZ: You remember that?

HK: I remember that.

LZ: Ah—And all the variations. As Guy [Davenport] said, he asked, "Which do you mean?" and I said, "All the connotations a reader can get out of it, that's up to him," you know, and I gave him various ideas of bay, you know, an inlet of the sea, a bay horse, a bay, you know, all kinds, a window bay; I don't know, there are probably at least a dozen. And we planted some bayberry, and of course it is used as a spice, and it has this resin wax on it, on the underleaf; there are little spots of wax, resin, you know. And there are the family of bayberry, Linnaeus-wise, there are only two genera of the family which is Myricaceae. So there's the *Myrica* bayberry, which is called candleberry, sometimes wax myrtle; those are the popular names for it. The second genus is *Comptonia* named after a guy called Compton I guess, or something, in America. And sweet-fern; and it's really not a fern. People get confused. It's really of the same family as the bayberry but the leaves are sort of pinnated, you know, divided, and it hugs the bark very closely. The flowers of both of these things are just inconspicuous; sometimes you don't see them at all. It's only when, you know, you look at it, with a microscope.

Now, so I've used that information. I start with candleberry because they're also used to make candles. In fact, Carruth sent me one I think, a few years ago. So it starts with "Candleberry bayberry spice." I get the nature of it because it's used as a spice. "Resinwax," that's obvious. "Green durant leaf." "Durant," and that's where Dante comes in. You remember, I start "che di lor suona su nella," which sounds up into "la tua vita," which sounds up into "the life of thine," as I translate it, which is—where does that come from? I don't know. I give the source in the footnote there in *Anew*. I guess it's the *Inferno* probably. The name Dante: do you know what that means?

HK: No.

LZ: It's still used today: it's deer-skin. And it's enduring. It presumably holds. So it's "durant leaf."

Where I get the "moor in key"? Not only does it grow on moor, you know swampland, and so on, the bayberry, and near the ocean, but that is the old Greek word, not for bayberry, which tended to be bulbous or drab or tawny, which is the same word, and it's also waxy and spotted. They think that was the Greek word for tamarisk [*myrikinos:* tamarisk bough, *Iliad* 6.39]. It's like all these things, I look up Theophrastus. All that goes into a word. Celia sees me lugging the *Century Dictionary* or this dictionary [and she says] "When you gonna stop?" And then she has better moods.

Alright: "durant leaf," so that's where I get Dante in; "moor in key," you have your Greek. "Dour." D—O—U—R is Scotch for hardened. Of course, the more vulgar meaning is sour, you know, sour-puss, or something like that, but really used all the time for hardened, tested by life, enduring life, and so on. "Deer wit . . . (and that of course) . . . winds survive." You know the winds do better than the hides of deer.

"Days *hippos*"—those are the only three words I underline, that I use italics, *hippos, wooden, compt.* I'll explain each one. *Hippos* is non-slang, if you don't know. It means deceptions, trickster, you know, anybody who cheats, and so on. The "rampant" I have in the early *Anew* poem, "Waters / At the ramp / Running away." I worked that in. My original source, that's my private knowledge.

"*Wooden*" is the other word I underlined. That comes right in out of the *Odyssey*, book 8, 493, where it's mentioned only once. It's one of those rarities. He talks about "the wooden." And it's the wooden horse he's referring to. The Greek of that is *dourateos*. So you see I already have the *dour* there: "dour attested," witnessed, you see, and if you say it a little faster, I've got Homer in there. But you don't and—it's the only time it's this "wooden"; he mentions it by an adjective. And that's the way A. J. [B.] Wace interprets it and all the Homeric scholars, a word that he used once. They have a term for that; I don't know [the term is *hapax legomenon*]. So, that is in there. But a few lines later on, line 516 [actually 512], he mentions *hippos*, that is the—very indignant, you know!—about the Trojan deception and he mentions *hippos*. So finally we get back to the line before and you know what *wooden* is because he has an adjective substitute for a noun. So that's *"wooden."*

"Ancient standstill plummet," that is out of *The Tempest*. A standstill is, well, it's a *stand*still, is a waiting, nothing happens. "Plummet," right out of *The Tempest* then, how, I don't know—I can't remember the exact—but it's in Prospero's speech when he throws his book away and so on . . .

HK: "Deeper than did plummet sound."

LZ: "Deeper than did ever plummet sound." Memory! Alright. Now *compt* is used a number of times and I wanted to get this man Compt—, the botanical name *Comptonia* in, and Shakespeare uses it a number of times, and especially as the Day of Compt, at the end of *Othello* there, the day of judgment. You see, he'll stand there, and it's the Day of Compt, really "account." And, shall I use this? This is a kind of "A"-11 situation I argued again; shall I revive this old word and the hell with what people make of it or shall I use "account"? It's just too corny for me today. So I had a hard time getting that in.

The willow business . . . do I mention willow?

Well, the "birds alula." The alula, you know, are the wings that can't open and fly; they're rather the counterpart of the thumb in a human being. They're right near the breast. You find that in any dictionary, but I found a picture of it, I don't know—many years ago—in the *Century Dictionary* and I always wanted to use that. It's a nice sound there. And besides, we're talking about spring, and so there they are, whatever spring it is. We trust. That is kind of personal.

alula (al′ū-lä̤), *n*.; pl. *alulæ* (-lē). [NL., dim. of *ala*, wing: see *aisle*.] 1 In *ornith*., the winglet, bastard wing, or ala spuria of a bird; the packet of small feathers which grows upon the so-called thumb of a bird's wing.

Alula (the shaded part in the figure).

The feathers are rather stiff, resembling primaries to some extent, but always smaller, and contribute to the smoothness and evenness of the border of the wing.
2. In *entom*.: (*a*) The small membranous appendage or scale situated at the base of each wing of many dipterous insects, above the halteres or poisers. (*b*) A similar appendage beneath each elytron of some water-beetles. Also called *alulet* and *cueilleron*.

In certain water beetles (Dytiscidæ) a pair of *alulæ*, or winglets, are developed at the inner angle of the elytra.
Encyc. Brit., VI. 127.

We found this bit of sweet-fern and a lady who is a rose specialist identified it and she said, "No, that's not a fern." One of the other specialists said, "That's a sweet-fern; everybody knows that." It grows by the roadside. Wonderful dark green leaf above, you know, pinnated-like, you know, jagged, because you call the whole thing a leaf no matter how many cuttings it has, and underneath it's this beautiful brown. And of course we loved it right away; we planted it. It never grew, but I think it's growing now next to the bayberry because I sniffed it the other day and, boy, it's pungent and really *alive*. So we hope the spring brings it up.

The willows are interesting. The willows are what you call dioecious in botany, that is, the sexes grow on different trees or different parts of the tree in some of them. If there's a male willow around, there is probably a female there too. So that's sort of interesting.

So there it is. Now, when you get back to it, you see how it sounds. [Rereads poem, inserting at the last line] Willows always growing in the sandy region.

And the "gibbous" is brought in at the end because, you know what gibbous is? The arms of the moon are convex—both of them—and it's this irregular shape which is approaching, well, it's between a half-moon and a full moon.

Now, the only other thing, the "unprotected laurel crown," there is the other bay; now that other bay, that's underwater "than ever plummet . . ."

So alright. This is how Zukofsky amuses himself. They say, they ask me, do I amuse myself? God, no! But when it's done, well then, it's—at least it's out of the way, damn it.

Appendix C
Shakespeare in *80 Flowers*

This appendix traces the passage of Shakespearean quotation from notes to text in those *Flowers* discussed and quoted fully in chapters 3–6. Each entry has three parts: (1) title of the *Flower* and those lines of it containing Shakespearean material; direct quotations appear in boldface, (2) Zukofsky's notes indicating Shakespearean reference, and (3) relevant passage(s) from Shakespeare. The text used is W. A. Neilson and C. J. Hill's New Cambridge edition (1942) of the *Complete Poems and Plays* (see chap. 2, n.9). When Zukofsky has come to a quotation via a *Century Dictionary* example of usage, or *Bottom: On Shakespeare,* this will be noted. N.B.: Two-dot ellipses (. .) in quotation are Zukofsky's; three-dot ellipses (. . .) are mine.

EPIGRAPH

LZ: "A & C III. xiii. 178"
                                                          (*80 Fl.* Drafts, p. 3)
WS: 1. *Antony:* I will be treble-sinew'd, hearted, breath'd
                                                          (*Ant.* III.xiii.178)

#1   STARGLOW

Starglow dwarf china rose shrub**thorn**
lantern fashion-fare airing car-tire crushed
                                                          (ll. 1–2)
LZ: "*Bottom:* bush of thorns & a lantern thorned? lanthorne"
                                                          (First List of 80 Fl., p. v)
WS: 1. *Quince:* Ay; or else one must come in with a bush of thorns and a
          lantern, and say he comes to disfigure, or to present the person of
          Moonshine. (*MND* III.i.60)

#3   HONESTY

LZ: "W.S CE iii. 2. 37 why labour . . wander in an unknown field *Macb* II.
          2. 38 care . . sore labour's bath . . . (MND latched [charmed] the
          Athenian's eyes" (*80 Fl.* Drafts, p. 6)

373

WS: 1. *Antipholus:* Against my soul's pure truth why labour you
          To make it wander in an unknown field?

([via Century] Err. III.ii.37)

    2. *Macbeth:* Sleep that knits up the ravell'd sleave of care,
          The death of each day's life, sore labour's bath.

([via Century] Mac. II.ii.38)

    3. *Oberon:* But hast thou yet latch'd the Athenian's eyes
          With the love-juice, as I did bid thee do?

([via Century] MND III.ii.36)

#4 LIVEFOREVER

Wild time *liveforever* horsethyme **ice**
by shard green red-purple thyrse

(ll. 1–2)

roof houseleek old-man-and-woman **who woo**
thatch **song** quicksilver cold would
won't know **All** *sedum* no

(ll. 6–8)

LZ: "LLL When icicles, also the words of Mercury are harsh after the
     songs of Apollo" (*80 Fl.* Drafts, p. 7)

WS: 1. *Winter:* When icicles hang by the wall . . .
          Then nightly sings the staring owl,

"Tu-whit, tu-who!"—

          A merry note
          While greasy Joan doth keel the pot.
          Armado: The words of Mercury are harsh after the songs
          of Apollo. You that way: we, this way.

(LLL V.ii.922)

#9 PRIVET

with **daffodil doxy red blood pale**
reign paired leaves without **tooth**
on edge primmed **private** *privet*

(ll. 6–8)

LZ: "Autolycus IV. iii. daffodils . . peer heigh the doxy over the dale why,
     then comes in the sweet o' the year For the red blood reigns in the
     winter's pale . . my *pugging* tooth *on edge* . . . T.N. Mal III. iv. 101 let
     me enjoy *my private* (privacy)" (*80 Fl.* Drafts, p. 14)

WS: 1.   *Autolycus' Song*
        "When daffodils begin to peer,
          With heigh! the doxy over the dale,
        Why, then comes in the sweet o' the year;
          For the red blood reigns in the winter's pale.

        "The white sheet bleaching on the hedge,
          With heigh! the sweet birds, O, how they sing!

375 co Shakespeare in 80 Flowers

Doth set my pugging tooth on edge;
    For a quart of ale is a dish for a king."

(WT IV.iii.1)

2. *Malvolio:* Go off; I discard you. Let me enjoy my private. Go off.
(*TN* III.iv.99)

#10   CHARLOCK PER WINKLE

A **skein bottoms** them together

(l. 1)

quillet praises lacquer true-**mustard ox-beef**
weeps *uncrossed charlock bluer winkle*

(ll. 7–8)

LZ: "And winking mary-buds (Cymbeline) . . . uncrossed (Cymb. III. iii.
26 . . . re *"Bottom, a Weaver"* (the word *bottom Century* = clue (or
clew) for winding thread or the the thread itself. *Onions* . . And beat
me to death with a bottom of brown thread *Tam Shrew* IV. iii. 137.
M.N.D. III. i. 21 ff . . translated . . Bottom: knavery . . to make an ass
of me . . to *fright* me, if they could. I will *not stir* from *this* place . . will
walk up & down here . . and sing . . not afraid the wren with little
quill (pipe? or feather v.i. Skeat) reason & love . . I can gleek upon
occasion Good Master Mustardseed . . I know your patience well your
kindred hath made my eyes water ere now . . . ox-beef hath devoured
gentlemen of your house *Titania* (via Ovid?) Tie up my love's tongue
(Folio, but Q *lovers*) tongue . . bring him silently . . . (Bottom) MND V.
1. 291 cut thread & thrum . . . used as a verb—Two Gent. Verona III. ii.
53 Thurio: as you unwind your love from him . . [provide to] bottom it
on me." (*80 Fl.* Drafts, pp. 15–16)

WS: 1. *Song* Hark, hark! the lark at heaven's gate sings,
    And Phoebus gins arise
    His steeds to water at those springs
    On chalic'd flowers that lies;
    And winking Mary-buds begin
    To ope their golden eyes.

(Cym. II.ii.21 [discarded])

2. *Belarius:* Such gain the cap of him that makes 'em fine,
    Yet keeps his book uncross'd; no life to ours.

(Cym. III.iii.25)

3. *Grumio:* Master, if ever I said loose-bodied gown, sew me in the
skirts of it, and beat me to death with a bottom of brown thread. I
said a gown. (*TS* IV.iii.137)

4. *Quince:* Bless thee, Bottom! bless thee! thou art translated.
Bottom: I see their knavery; this is to make an ass of me, to fright
me if they could. But I will not stir from this place, do what they
can. I will walk up and down here, and I will sing, that they shall
hear I am not afraid . . . [sings] " . . . The wren with little

quill," . . . and yet to say the truth, reason and love keep little
company together now-a-days . . . Nay, I can gleek upon
occasion . . . Good Master Mustardseed, I know your patience well.
That same cowardly, giant-like ox-beef hath devoured many a
gentleman of your house. I promise you, your kindred hath made
my eyes water ere now.
Titania: The moon, methinks, looks with a wat'ry eye;
And when she weeps, weeps every little flower,
Lamenting some enforced chastity.
Tie up my love's tongue, bring him silently.

(MND III.i.121ff.)

5. *Pyramus:* O Fates, come, come,
   Cut thread and thrum.

(MND V.i.290 [discarded])

6. *Thurio:* Therefore, as you unwind her love from him,
   Lest it should ravel and be good to none,
   You must provide to bottom it on me.

(TGV III.ii.51)

#22 BAYBERRY

standstill plummet unprotected laurel crown

(l. 5)

sand-iced willows ***compt*** gibbous moons

(l. 8)

LZ: "*compt* W.S. Mac I. vi. 26 Oth. V. ii. 272 AW V. iii. 57 Tim. II. i.
35 . . break my staff / Bury it certain fathoms in the earth / And deeper
than did ever *plummet sound* / I'll drown my book" (*80 Fl.* Drafts, p.
28)

WS: 1. *Lady Macbeth:*   Your servants ever
   Have theirs, themselves, and what is theirs, in compt,
   To make their audit

([via Concordance?] Mac. I.vi.26)

2. *Othello:*   When we shall meet at compt,
   This look of thine will hurl my soul from heaven,

([via Concordance?] Oth. V.ii.273)

3. *King:* That thou didst love her, strikes some scores away
   From the great compt;

([via Concordance?] AWW V.iii.56)

4. *Senator:* Take the bonds along with you,
   And have the dates in compt.

([via Concordance?] Tim. II.i.34)

5. *Prospero:*   I'll break my staff,
   Bury it certain fathoms in the earth,
   And deeper than did ever plummet sound
   I'll drown my book.

   . . .   There stand
For you are spell-stopp'd.

                           (*Tmp.* V.i.54, 60)

#27 CROCUS
strung alack **riches** look o

                           (l. 5)

spring snowpits measure **hours** sative
crocus furnace **sandy** yellows cloth-of-gold

                         (ll. 7–8)

LZ: "∗W.S. strung W.S. TGV III. ii. 78. LLL IV. iii. 343 hour-glass MV I. i. 25 I should not see the sandy hourglass run But I wd think of shallows & of flats T IV. i. 108 hourly joys be still upon you" (*80 Fl.* Drafts, p. 32)

WS: 1. *Proteus:* For Orpheus' lute was strung with poets' sinews,
        Whose golden touch could soften steel and stones,
        Make tigers tame, and huge leviathans
        Forsake unsounded deeps to dance on sands.

                         (*TGV* III.ii.78)

    2. *Biron:*   as sweet and musical
        As bright Apollo's lute strung with his hair

                     (*LLL* IV.iii.342)

    3. *Salarino:* I should not see the sandy hour-glass run
        But I should think of shallows and of flats,
        And see my wealthy Andrew dock'd in sand.

                   (*MV* I.i.25)

    4. *Juno:* Honour, riches, marriage-blessing,
        Long continuance, and increasing,
        Hourly joys be still upon you!
        Juno sings her blessings on you.

                  (*Tmp.* IV.ii.106)

    5. *Ariel:* Come unto these yellow sands
          And then take hands.
        Curtsied when you have kiss'd—
          The wild waves whist—
        Foot it featly here and there

                 (*Tmp.* I.ii.375)

#28 FORSYTHIA
ember firethorn winter low stonecrop

                         (l. 3)

LZ: "w. firethorn—fire flames cf. ember eves" (*80 Fl.* Drafts, p. 33)
WS: *Gower:* It hath been sung at festivals,
        On ember-eves and holidays

           ([via *Bottom*, p. 342] *Per.* I.i.5)

#32   LILAC

Sere ring a pipe **wood**
lodging sweet by tempest lodged

(ll. 1–2)

LZ: "T.S. *Induction* i. 49—And *burn sweet wood* to make the lodging
sweet; R.II, I. iv. 68—empty lodgings unfurnished walls W.S. WT II. i.
111 (Hermione) *honourable* grief *lodg'd* here which burns worse than
tears drown; R.II. iii. 161 foul weather . . sighs . . (trans) lodge the
summer corn; II HVI III. ii. 176 summer's corn, *by tempest
lodg'd* . . . Per III. ii. 12 Our lodgings standing bleak upon the sea; KL
II. ii. 179 (Kent) this shameful lodging" (*80 Fl.* Drafts, p. 36)

WS: 1. *Lord:* And burn sweet wood to make the lodging sweet

(*Shr.* induction. i.49)

  2. *Duchess of Gloucester:* Alack, and what shall good old York there
   see
   But empty lodgings and unfurnish'd walls.

(*R2* I.ii.67 [see #33 Azalea])

  3. *Hermione:*   but I have
   That honourable grief lodg'd here which burns
   Worse than tears drown.

(*WT* II.i.110 [see #33 Azalea])

  4. *Richard:* We'll make foul weather with despised tears.
   Our sighs and they shall lodge the summer corn,
   And make a dearth in this revolting land.

(*R2* III.iii.161 [see #33 Azalea])

  5. *Warwick:* His well-proportion'd beard made rough and rugged,
   Like to the summer's corn by tempest lodg'd.

(*2H6* III.ii.176)

  6. *1st Gentleman:* Our lodgings, standing bleak upon the sea,
   Shook as the earth did quake.

(*Per.* III.ii.14)

  7. *Kent:* Take vantage, heavy eyes, not to behold
   This shameful lodging.

(*Lr.* II.ii.178)

#33   AZALEA

Foul weather sighs old time
may is so **unfurnished walls**
drown tears azalea **wills barrens**
dry long heath be friend

(ll. 1–4)

azalea **longs** no **dry death**

(l. 7)

LZ: "T. I. i. 71. Gon (honest counsellor) Now would I give a thousand
furlongs of sea for an acre of barren ground, long heath, brown furze

anything. The wills above be done but I would fain die a dry
death . . . & Lear 'heath'" (*80 Fl.* Drafts, p. 37)

ws: 1. *Gonzalo:* Now would I give a thousand furlongs of sea for an acre
of barren ground, long heath, brown furze, anything. The wills
above be done! but I would fain die a dry death. (*Tmp.* I.i.69)

[See also, under #32 Lilac: *R2* I.ii.67; *WT* II.i.110; and *R2* III.iii.161.]

Notes

Preface

1. Robert Creeley, "A Note." Prefatory note to Zukofsky's "A" 1–12, Paris Review Editions (Garden City, N.Y.: Doubleday, 1967), p. vii. "A" was published in four parts before the complete edition appeared in 1978; see Select Bibliography for details.

2. Louis Zukofsky, "A" (Berkeley and Los Angeles: University of California Press). All references are to this, the complete edition of "A," and will be cited in the text. Movement number will accompany page number in each case.

3. Celia Zukofsky, in "Conversations with Celia," by Carroll F. Terrell, Paideuma 7, no. 3 (Winter 1978): 598 (this memorial issue of the journal will be cited hereafter as the L.Z. Paideuma); Hugh Kenner, "Louis Zukofsky: All the Words," L.Z. Paideuma, 388; Harold Schimmel, "Zuk. Yehoash David Rex," L.Z. Paideuma, 559; Eliot Weinberger, "At the Death of Kenneth Rexroth," Sagetrieb 2, no. 3 (Winter 1983): 51; Celia Zukofsky, in "Two Conversations with Celia Zukofsky," ed. Barry Ahearn, Sagetrieb 2, no. 1 (Spring 1983): 118; Louis Zukofsky, #63 Oxalis, 80 Flowers (see chap. 1, n.1). The poems are best referred to by number and title, without quotation marks around the latter; this is the styling Zukofsky used. (See Appendix A for a full list of title flowers.)

1. How, When, Where, What, and Why: The 80 Flowers Project

1. Louis Zukofsky, 80 Flowers (Lunenburg, Vt.: Stinehour Press for Louis and Celia Zukofsky, 1978). Draft material for the Flowers and for "A" 22 & 23 (New York: Grossman, 1975; London: Trigram, 1977) arrived at TxU in June 1979 after Zukofsky's death the previous year. It is still among the uncatalogued manuscripts of the Louis Zukofsky Collection in the Harry Ransom Humanities Research Center at the University of Texas (TxU). Permission to quote from this and from other Zukofsky manuscript material held at Texas and elsewhere is given by Paul Zukofsky; all such material is copyright Paul Zukofsky and may not be quoted from this book by third parties without the express permission of the copyright holder.

2. David Levi Strauss, "Approaching 80 Flowers," in Code of Signals: Recent Writings in Poetics, ed. Michael Palmer (Berkeley: North Atlantic Books, 1983), pp. 79–102.

3. The black notebook is the only item discussed here which is not part of the June 1979 bequest. It belongs to material that arrived at TxU in November 1975 and is also among the uncatalogued Zukofsky manuscripts.

4. My thanks to C. Freeman Keith of the Stinehour Press, who generously allowed me to examine the Zukofsky documents in the press archive. A full list of these appears in appendix C of my doctoral thesis, "Reading Zukofsky's *80 Flowers*" (University of British Columbia, 1985), hereafter referred to as MJL thesis.

5. Louis Zukofsky and Celia Zukofsky, trans., *Catullus (Gai Valeri Catulli Veronensis Liber)* (London: Cape Goliard, 1969). Once a work of Zukofsky's has been cited, further references to it will be given in the text.

6. Louis Zukofsky, *Little: For Careenagers* (New York: Grossman, 1970).

7. The five years of reading were presumably 1967–71. Zukofsky completed "A"-21 in 1967 and began the bulk of "A"-22 early in March 1972. The following three years were originally scheduled for one movement each. N.B.: A three-dot ellipsis (. . .) in quotation is my editing; a two-dot ellipsis (. .) is Zukofsky's distinctive editorial mark.

8. The Zukofsky-Corman correspondence (1960–76) is in the Contemporary Literature Collection at Simon Fraser University, Burnaby, British Columbia (SFU). Citations of letters held at TxU and SFU will be made in the text, in this format. See the List of Abbreviations for details of collections. This material is copyright Paul Zukofsky.

9. The Central Park South address was an apartment house, not a residential hotel as Robert Creeley describes it in "For L.Z.," L.Z. *Paideuma*, 384. (Information from Paul Zukofsky.)

10. In manuscript, "A"-22 and "A"-23 are numbered by lines but the published text is not. Where the location of a particular passage is important, page numbers will be followed by the first and last lines of the excerpt.

11. The major exception to this is the hundred-line first section of "A"-22 (pp. 508–11), entitled *Initial* when it was separately published in 1970 (see chap. 2, n.7). The drafts consist of the usual verso and recto versions, but Zukofsky continued to work on the recto (fair) version and eventually had to recopy the update onto sheets, which he then stapled over the recto pages of the notebook. This section will be hereafter cited in the text as "Initial."

12. The Johns Hopkins engagements of May and December 1975 and the Pound Symposium in June that year were Zukofsky's last major reading and speaking appearances.

13. "A"-12, p. 143: "Bless him, may he live / 120 years." The voice is that of Reb Pinchos, Zukofsky's father, talking about the grandson, Paul, who has been named for him.

14. John Gerard, *Gerard's Herball: The Essence Thereof Distilled . . . From the Edition of Th. Johnson, 1636,* ed. Marcus Woodward (London: Gerald Howe, 1927).

15. Louis Zukofsky, *All: The Collected Short Poems, 1923–1964* (New York: Norton, 1966). Reference to Zukofsky's short poems will be given from *All* unless the date or title of the original collection is necessary.

16. Louis Zukofsky, *Anew* (Prairie City, Ill.: James A. Decker, 1946).

17. Dates of composition are to be found in the "Year by Year" section of Celia Zukofsky's *A Bibliography of Louis Zukofsky* (Los Angeles: Black Sparrow, 1969), pp. 47–52. An update appears in her "Year by Year Bibliography of Louis Zukofsky," L.Z. *Paideuma*, 603–10. Dates of composition given in the text are taken from these sources unless stated otherwise.

18. Louis Zukofsky, "Thanks to the Dictionary," in *It Was* (Kyoto: Origin, 1961), pp. 99–132.

19. Louis Zukofsky, reading at Glassboro State College, N.J., 17 October 1972. He was beginning the second half of the program, "which I suppose everybody would

call prose, but my way of working at it has always been the poet's work, so I make no distinctions." And at Bard College, Annandale-on-Hudson, N.Y., 2 November 1972: "I've always worked at prose the way I work at poetry; I find no distinction except that one seems to be a little longer getting there." All citations of taped readings concern tapes now at TxU unless otherwise specified.

20. The complete (University of California Press) *"A"* had not yet appeared, hence the tracking back and forth between its published parts; page equivalents to this edition will be given as each reference is discussed here. *I's (Pronounced Eyes)* was published in 1963 by Trobar Press.

21. Information from Professor Alec Globe (University of British Columbia), who notes that because of the forty years the Israelites spent in the desert, the number became suggestive of punishment or fasting (Examination notes on MJL thesis, October 1985). *Brewer's Dictionary of Phrase and Fable* (ed. Ivor H. Evans, Centenary ed. [London: Cassell, 1970]) supports this with a host of biblical and secular references. Zukofsky's interest, however, seems to rest solely in the generational significance of the number.

22. *Brewer's Dictionary* cites as examples of such tetragrams JHVH, Zeus, Jove, Deus, Gott, Deva, Dios, Odin, and Lord.

23. Ronald Blythe, *Akenfield: Portrait of an English Village* (London: Allen Lane/ Penguin Press, 1969). The "pond pox" reference occurs on p. 14 in connection with village sanitation; its relevance to Zukofsky's intention of 23 May to write a book of flowers is not clear.

24. Ahearn, "Two Conversations with Celia Zukofsky," 126–27.

25. The source of this is Diogenes Laertius writing about Pythagoras in *Lives of Eminent Philosophers,* trans. R. D. Hicks, Loeb Classical Library (London: Heinemann; New York: Putnam, 1925), 2:329. The lines that follow in *"A"*-22 are excerpted from the same chapter; 2:320–67.

26. Norman Taylor, ed., *Taylor's Encyclopedia of Gardening, Horticulture, and Landscape Design,* 4th ed. (Boston: Houghton Mifflin, 1961). Merritt Lyndon Fernald, ed., *Gray's Manual of Botany,* 8th ed. (New York: American Book Co., 1950). Hereafter cited in the text respectively as Taylor and Gray.

27. U.S. Department of Agriculture, Agricultural Research Service, *Common Weeds of the United States* (1970; reprint, New York: Dover, 1971). The original edition of 1970 was USDA Agricultural Handbook No. 366, entitled *Selected Weeds of the United States.*

28. I am assuming, for the sake of convenience, that Zukofsky kept both the Notes and Drafts in the same ring binder. He could have been using two binders.

29. Zukofsky finished #9 Privet 29 May 1975; the Pound Symposium, at which he was a panelist, took place 15–17 June. #10 Charlock Per Winkle was begun 27 June.

30. Louis Zukofsky, reading and talking privately at Johns Hopkins University, Baltimore, Md., 13 December 1975. Side 1: *80 Flowers,* Epigraph through #22 Bayberry, followed by conversation with Hugh Kenner about #22 Bayberry. Side 2: *"A"*-11, from *"A"*-15, *"A"*-20, from *"A"*-21, "It's a good life," "A foin lass bodders." The tape was made by Hugh Kenner; see Appendix B for the transcription of the Bayberry talk. This material is copyright Paul Zukofsky.

31. Was the copy of #9 Privet kept with the Schema because those two documents were the only parts of the work in progress to be shown "outside"? or because they are the only non–loose-leaf material in the Notes and were probably stowed together in the back pocket of the ring binder?

32. The closing sequence of *80 Flowers* is #76 Vines, #77 Weeds, #78 "X," #79 Yaupon, #80 Zinnia. Zukofsky managed to fit all the vines and weeds into one poem apiece.

33. See MJL thesis, appendix B, for these as well as word count, line count, and irregular lines in the *Flowers*.

34. LZ to CFK, 21 December 1977. This letter is in the Stinehour archive, as are the other parts of the correspondence quoted here.

35. Zukofsky, b.n.b., p. 102: "The whole poem dividing into 3rds? i.e. A 1–21, A 22 & 23, A-24."

2. "The Happy New Years": Zukofsky's Late Poetic

1. Louis Zukofsky, preface to *A Test of Poetry* (1948; reprint, New York: C.Z. Publications, 1980), n.p.

2. *The Century Dictionary: An Encyclopedic Lexicon of the English Language*, 10 vols. (1889–91; reprint, New York: Century, 1895). This was Zukofsky's favorite dictionary, acquired about 1950 and much used by him for its etymological detail and examples of usage. The first edition was in 6 vols.; Zukofsky specifies his own as 1895 (LZ to CC, 31 January 1968; SFU). Paul Zukofsky confirms that the dictionary in the house was in 10 vols. (letter to author, 29 August 1984). This edition included in its final volumes *The Century Cyclopedia of Names* (1894) and a world atlas. Hereafter cited in the text as the *Century*.

3. In particular, "On Valentine's Day to Friends," composed 1952 (*All*, p. 141). Zukofsky wrote one or more Valentine's Day poems a year from about 1942. Many of them are in *All*, identifiable by their titles or content.

4. Louis Zukofsky, AN ERA / ANY TIME / OF YEAR, Poetry Postcard (Santa Barbara: Unicorn, 1970). In context of *"A,"* the poem will be styled "AN ERA."

5. I am itemizing a North American pronunciation; other voicings might alter the vowel song. For example, a British or British-affiliated articulation could add ə to the second half of "YEAR," rhyming it with the vowel in the second syllable of "ERA."

6. Louis Zukofsky, *Bottom: On Shakespeare*, vol. 1 (Austin: Ark Press/Humanities Research Center, University of Texas, 1963). Vol. 2 of the boxed set is Celia Zukofsky's *Music to Shakespeare's Pericles*. The Book Bahir is an ancient Cabbalistic text of the first century C.E.

7. Louis Zukofsky, *Initial*, Oblong Octavo Series, no. 12 (New York: Phoenix Bookshop, 1970). In context of *"A,"* the poem will be styled "Initial." It was composed 5 July–11 August 1970, according to dated drafts in the *"A"*-22 Spiral, pp. 1–5.

8. Charlton D. Lewis and Charles Short, eds., *A Latin Dictionary, Founded on Andrews' Edition of Freund's Latin Dictionary* (Oxford: Clarendon, 1879). This book will be hereafter cited as Lewis and Short.

9. Shakespearean quotation throughout is taken unless otherwise stated from the New Cambridge *Complete Poems and Plays of William Shakespeare*, ed. W. A. Neilson and C. J. Hill (Cambridge, Mass.: Houghton Mifflin/Riverside, 1942). This text fits the description of Zukofsky's *Shakespeare* given on p. 266 of *Bottom* and is the edition now in the collection of Zukofsky's personal books at TxU.

10. I follow Walter W. Skeat, ed., *The Complete Works of Geoffrey Chaucer*, 7 vols. (Oxford: Clarendon, 1894); this is the text Zukofsky used, to judge by the spelling in his quotation of Chaucer. That "olde feldes" is the direct source of Zukofsky's "old fields" is obvious as soon as the Chaucer is read over "Initial"; but this does not invalidate Barry Ahearn's speculation (*Zukofsky's "A": An Introduction* [Berkeley and

Los Angeles: University of California Press, 1983], p. 185) that the Long Island village of Old Field, near Stonybrook, was at the back of the phrase. The poet would hear with pleasure the part-echo of twentieth-century topography on fourteenth-century art.

11. Skeat's glossary gives *somer-sesoun* as "spring, early summer."

12. Zukofsky read from *"A"*-22 on a number of occasions between 1970 and 1975. "AN ERA" and "Initial" feature in the following taped readings at TxU: (1) the Wallace Stevens Memorial Series, University of Connecticut, Storrs, 29 April 1971; (2) YM-YWHA, New York City, 15 October 1973; (3) Franconia College, Franconia, N.H., 9 May 1974; and (4) the Turnbull Memorial Series, Johns Hopkins University, Baltimore, 8 May 1975.

13. University of California Press' "every yet" is an erratum; the final draft of "Initial" in the *"A"*-22 Spiral gives "ever yet" (p. 4), which is followed by the Phoenix Bookshop *Initial* (1970) and all subsequent publications of *"A"* 22 & 23.

14. The phrase *is* "Others' letters" in draft (*"A"*-22 Spiral, p. 1) but loses its possessive in the two succeeding drafts—a deliberate blurring of definition (and widening of semantic possibilities). The same thing happened to "a peacock's grammar perching" farther on in the poem.

15. There are typed carbons at TxU of three pieces of correspondence with Alan Brilliant, February-March 1970.

16. I wish to thank Peter Quartermain for pointing out this and the correspondence with Alan Brilliant.

17. Lewis and Short's entry for *adn-* advises: "For all words in *adn-* not found here, v. under *an-*." The assimilation of "d" before "n" was commonplace.

18. Henry George Liddell and Robert Scott, eds., *A Greek-English Lexicon,* 9th ed. (Oxford: Clarendon, 1968). This book will be hereafter cited as Liddell and Scott.

19. I am using the glossary of Raymond Hill and Thomas Bergin's *Anthology of the Provençal Troubadours,* Yale Romanic Studies, 17 (New Haven: Yale University Press, 1941). In 1930–31, Zukofsky was studying (among other things) *"Old Provençal"* during his stay in Madison, Wis.; see Barry Ahearn, ed., "Ezra Pound and Louis Zukofsky: Letters 1928–1930," *Montemora,* no. 8 (Summer 1982): 170.

20. Zukofsky is using a translation by George Bosworth Burch, according to the citation on p. 119 of *Bottom.* This is Burch's *Early Mediaeval Philosophers* (New York: King's Crown, 1951), and the passage quoted appears on pp. 9–10. Burch's account of Erigena's philosophy (pp. 1–30) depends heavily on paraphrase and translated quotation. Zukofsky has quoted a passage that is both—"motion terminates . . . rest in it" is given by Burch as quotation, and the remainder is paraphrase.

21. University of California Press' "grammer" is an erratum; the final draft of "Initial" in the *"A"*-22 Spiral gives the word as "grammar" (p. 1), which is followed by the Phoenix Bookshop *Initial* (1970) and all subsequent publications of *"A"* 22 & 23.

22. Ahearn, *Zukofsky's "A,"* p. 183.

23. Louis Zukofsky, "Poetry: For My Son When He Can Read," in *Prepositions: The Collected Critical Essays,* enl. ed. (Berkeley and Los Angeles: University of California Press, 1981), p. 10.

24. Hugh Kenner, "Of Notes and Horses," *Poetry* 140, no. 2 (November 1967): 112–21; reprint in *Louis Zukofsky: Man and Poet,* ed. Carroll F. Terrell (Orono: National Poetry Foundation/University of Maine, 1979), pp. 187–94. This book will hereafter be cited as *L.Z.: Man and Poet.*

25. See *Little: For Careenagers,* p. 110.

26. Reading at Bard College, 2 November 1972.

27. This remark accompanied the Wallace Stevens Lecture, 29 April 1971 (see n.

12). Zukofsky was preparing to read *"A"*-21, pp. 473–74: "A concept of culture joyed . . . a felicity."

28. Clinton Walker Keyes, trans., introduction to *De Re Publica,* in *Cicero: De Re Publica, De Legibus,* Loeb Classical Library (Cambridge, Mass.: Harvard University Press; London: Heinemann, 1928), p. 7.

29. Reading at YM-YWHA, 15 October 1973.

30. The phrase "sick of history" occurs first on p. 90 of the black notebook and seems to be a quotation.

31. Louis Zukofsky, *Arise, arise* (New York: Grossman, 1973).

32. *"A"*-6 was written 1930, and the passage referred to is on p. 38 near the conclusion of the movement that introduces a wealth of particulars to the poem and wonders, in its last line, what is to be done with them: "With all this material / To what distinction—."

33. I follow Franz Klaeber's *Beowulf and the Fight at Finnsburg,* 3rd ed. (Lexington, Mass.: D. C. Heath, 1950).

34. The translation is mine. Zukofsky made a similar one (*"A"* 22 & 23 Spiral, pp. 103–4), which is more working notes than reproducible text.

35. The Latin is Martial, *Epigrams* XIII.i.7–8 (boldface indicates Zukofsky's base for transliteration):

haec mihi **charta nuces,** haec est mihi charta **fritillus;**
alea nec damnum nec facit ista **lucrum.**

("this paper is my nuts, this paper is my dice-box; hazard that brings me no loss nor yet any gain.") Zukofsky is using the Loeb edition of the *Epigrams,* trans. Walter C. A. Ker, Loeb Classical Library, 2 vols. (London: Heinemann; New York: Putnam, 1919), according to a note in the *"A"*-22 Spiral. The wistaria passage is derived from translations in Herbert A. Giles, *A History of Chinese Literature* (New York: D. Appleton, 1901). See chap. 10, n.9.

36. The rush-bottomed chair, according to the note of 25 August 1967 mentioned in the cross-references (b.n.b., p. 7), is Paul Zukofsky's "two-finial rush bottom black painted baby chair." The same note describes other family possessions, including the refurbished cushions.

37. The holm-oak (*Quercus ilex*) choreographs this passage. It is a "home" oak, and perhaps the chair itself is oaken; certainly it is sturdy. Looking again, holm oak is **holly**-oak (*ilex*), "wholly" oak (sturdiness), or "wholeness." Over a broom? or broom? What is flowering in the world outside the window?

38. Zukofsky's Spinoza has been identified as *Ethics and "De Intellectus Emendatione,"* an Everyman's Library translation by Andrew Boyle, with an introduction by George Santayana (London: J. M. Dent, 1910). See Ahearn, *Zukofsky's "A,"* p. 105n.

39. Celia's "5 voices" are the components of *"A"*-24—Music (Handel), Thought (*Prepositions*), Drama (*Arise, arise*), Story (*It Was*), and Poem (*"A"*). Christopher Smart's *Jubilate Agno* (*Rejoice in the Lamb: A Song from Bedlam,* ed. William Force Stead [London: Jonathan Cape, 1939]) was to have been a key text in *"A"*-22's second Music section, but Zukofsky reserved the full force of its ecstatic "rejoice" theme for the finale of *"A"*-23.

40. Paul Zukofsky loaned his copy of the Handel for *"A"*-24 and made suggestions concerning the typography of the movement (*"A"*-24, p. 806).

41. The sources of the "living calendar" are for the most part noted alongside the draft of it in the *"A"*-23 Spiral, pp. 39–40. They are drawn from all parts of the material for *"A"* 22 & 23, and some of them will be discussed as they bear on *80 Flowers.*

42. "Daruma / *found object* / that is art // for good luck" (*All*, p. 223). Zukofsky tells Lorine Niedecker in an undated letter of 1962 (TxU) that *daruma* is equivalent to the Zen Buddhist concept of *dharma*. Robert Bringhurst explains in conversation that *daruma* is a transliteration of the character called *fa* (Chinese) or *ho* (Japanese), and is short for *Bodhidharma*, the name of the sage who brought Zen Buddhism from India to China. A statement upon which Zen Buddhists reflect at length is: "All *dharmas* are empty," when *dharma* (or *daruma*) means "any thing"; that is (for Zukofsky), a "*found object.*"

43. Gerard Malanga published the first (Music) section of "*A*"-23 in *Transatlantic Review*, no. 52 (Autumn 1975): 5–8. There is a six-item Zukofsky-Malanga correspondence at TxU, January-July 1975, in the course of which Malanga asks (and receives) permission to photograph the Zukofskys at home in Port Jefferson as part of a projected book of photographic portraits of poets and writers. Following the photo session of 24 March 1975, Zukofsky wrote to Malanga thanking him for some contact prints and enclosing the signed holograph original of "lovely All composed" as his contribution to events of that afternoon.

44. *Louis Zukofsky at the American Embassy, London, May 21, 1969* (Newcastle-upon-Tyne: Ultima Thule, 1969). The substance of this was later revised by Zukofsky and published as "About the Gas Age" in *Journal of Modern Literature* 4, no. 1 (September 1974). It appears in the expanded edition of *Prepositions* (pp. 169–72). Zukofsky habitually requested copies of anything published by or about him; he refers to these as "the usual three (family) copies" in a note on Gilbert Sorrentino's letter to him (15 April 1977, TxU).

45. Aram Saroyan, "Red Postcard," [1972?].

46. Bruce Jaffe's letter, on which Zukofsky drafted his reply, is still enclosed with the color videocassette now at TxU.

47. Zukofsky, reading at Bard College, 2 November 1972. He made a similar comment, also introducing "*A*"-24, at the Paley Library Cultural Series, Temple University, Philadelphia, 16 October 1972: "as I told Phil [Philip Yannella], I'd like to be present at my own requiem."

48. *The Notebooks of Samuel Taylor Coleridge, 1794–1804*, ed. Kathleen Coburn, Bollingen Series, 50 (New York: Pantheon, 1957), #863. This is a list of flowers, copied from the index of William Withering's *An Arrangement of British Plants* (1796). Coburn also refers to an entry of 24 October 1803 in which Coleridge writes: "O surely I might make a noble Poem of all my Youth nay *all my life*—one section on plants and flowers, my passion for them always deadened by their learned names." Zukofsky, of course, found a means of utilizing those names in *80 Flowers*. Where he came across Coleridge's list (and whether he knew about the 1803 comment that serves to bring it into close parallel with the *Flowers*), I do not know. The first mention of the list occurs in the "*A*" 22 & 23 Spiral, p. 125, 13 May 1974.

3. "See how the roses burn!": The Epigraph and #1 Starglow

1. The loose-leaf folio marked "1 A-B" (2 pp.) was an addition to the First List of 80 Flowers, dating from October-November 1974. It was probably kept with the First List until composition began in December; then it was reheaded "Notes & orig. drafts" (pp. 1, 2), and the next page (*80 Fl.* Drafts, p. 3) contains the material collected for the writing of the Epigraph; the *80 Flowers* Drafts are under way.

2. Zukofsky appears to draw "sited" at least initially from the *Century*. On p. 40 of the "*A*"-23 Spiral, there is a margin note acknowledging the examples of usage taken

from Jonson's *Sejanus* (IV.1) and Robert Burton's *Anatomy of Melancholy* (To the Reader). Neither quotation overrides the personal significance contributed by the "z" of "z-sited."

3. The "sounds invisibly" entry was transferred to the *80 Fl.* Notes (p. 4) 24 December 1974, the day before Zukofsky began assembling materials for the Epigraph. He is using Arthur A. Macdonell's *A Vedic Reader for Students, containing thirty hymns of the Rigveda in the original Saṃhitā and Pada texts, with transliteration, translation, explanatory notes, introduction, vocabulary* (Madras: Oxford University Press, 1917). This is the "gift of a Vedic Reader" referred to in the black notebook (p. 21; 2/1/68), which Zukofsky thanks Cid Corman for in a letter of 16 February 1968 (SFU). Zukofsky made some notes from it and later copied passages into the *"A" 22 & 23* Spiral. In 1973, some of the Spiral notes were transferred, with other material from the *Reader,* to the "Gamut" Notes, where Zukofsky worked on the Vāta passage to produce "sounds invisibly" as follows: Macdonell (pp. 218–19) transliterates and then translates: "ghósa id asya śrnvire, ná rūpám"; that is, "His sounds are heard (but) his form not (seen)." Which Zukofsky improves on first by an attempt of his own at transliterating the transliteration—"goes a shrubbery rue palm"—before opting for the condensate translation: "he sounds invisibly."

4. *Brewer's Dictionary,* s.v. "Nine." For comments on Zukofsky's fascination with Pythagorean number theory, see Ahearn, "Two Conversations with Celia Zukofsky," p. 120.

5. The condensation is from Jaime de Angulo, "Indian Religion," appendix in *Indian Tales* (New York: Hill and Wang, 1953), pp. 241–42. Notes from Angulo appear in the black notebook (pp. 101, 110) and the *"A" 22 & 23* Spiral (pp. 144–45).

6. T. S. Eliot, "Little Gidding," in *Collected Poems 1909–1962* (London: Faber and Faber, 1963), p. 223.

7. Isaac D'Israeli, "Introduction of Tea, Coffee, and Chocolate," in his *Curiosities of Literature,* ed. Benjamin D'Israeli, rev. ed. (London: Routledge, Warne, and Routledge, 1863), 2:317.

8. *Gerard's Herball,* p. 200.

9. Marcus Woodward, introduction to ibid., p. vii.

10. W. H. Hudson, *Nature in Downland* (London: Longmans, Green, 1900), p. 51. Hudson, an American on the London literary scene in the era of compatriots Henry James and Whistler, was a much-admired figure. Zukofsky enjoyed reading his work, according to a letter of 20 November 1967 to Corman (SFU).

11. Herman Melville, *Pierre: Or, The Ambiguities,* Signet Classics (New York: New American Library, 1964).

12. *Gerard's Herball,* p. 200.

13. Celia Zukofsky, "1927–1972," L.Z. *Paideuma,* 371. Part of Zukofsky's statement (the last sentence) is also to be found in *Autobiography* (New York: Grossman, 1970), p. 59.

14. Macdonell, *Vedic Reader,* p. 216.

15. Zukofsky is using Einstein quotes that appear in Martin J. Klein and Robert K. Merton, "A Passion to Understand the Order in the World," a review of Banesh Hoffmann's *Albert Einstein: Creator and Rebel* (New York: Viking, 1972), in *New York Times Book Review* (5 November 1972): 3. Zukofsky had translated (anonymously) Anton Reiser's *Albert Einstein: A Biographical Portrait* in 1930, and his eye would have been caught by Klein and Merton's mention of "distinguished early biographies by Anton Reiser, Carl Seelig," which in the opinion of the reviewers

nonetheless failed to explain "what Einstein himself sadly described as his 'peculiar popularity.'"

16. See instances of Zukofsky's use of the word in *"A"*-12, connecting horse, poet, and era (all so alive), on pp. 126, 137, 169, 215.

17. W.K.C. Guthrie, *The Earlier Presocratics and the Pythagoreans*, vol. 1 of *A History of Greek Philosophy* (London: Cambridge University Press, 1962), p. 164 (the magic forty again, this time with powers of transformation): "Heraclides explains the Pythagorean ban on beans by the curious superstition that if a bean is laid on a new tomb and covered with dung for forty days, it takes on the appearance of a man."

18. The 1949 poem was prompted by reading translations of Xenophanes' fragments in Milton C. Nahm, ed., *Selections from Early Greek Philosophy*, 3rd ed. (New York: Appleton-Century-Crofts, 1947), pp. 109–13. Zukofsky mentioned this and the book concerned in a letter to Lorine Niedecker of 11 February 1949 (TxU); information from Jenny Penberthy. "Xenophanes" is almost entirely quotation of the philosopher's words; the passage in *Bottom* was written in the late fifties.

19. W. R. Paton, trans., *The Greek Anthology*, Loeb Classical Library (London: Heinemann; New York: Putnam, 1915), 3:5. The material used in *"A"*-23 is from vols. 3 and 4 of the *Anthology;* in order, it is as follows: bk. 10:58; bk. 9:168; bk. 9:180–83; bk. 9:395; bk. 9:489.

20. Louis Zukofsky, *55 Poems* (Prairie City, Ill.: James A. Decker, 1941). When Zukofsky read short poems in public after 1970, he nearly always selected from *Autobiography*, prefacing the poems with some remarks about Celia's musical settings and commenting that *Autobiography* contained all that he wanted known about his personal life.

21. There is also a climbing rose named Paul's Scarlet, a continuous bloomer, which appears in the *"A"* 22 & 23 Spiral, p. 154; not forgetting the early association of Paul with rambling roses in *"A"*-12, p. 156–57.

22. "Car-tire crushed" assumes a somewhat grisly aspect as we scrutinize the draft of #1 Starglow, where there is a reference, much overwritten, to the "blood of [illeg.] farm hand," repeated as "blood of farm   rambler." What this means and how it fits into the poem I do not know, but the unsettling note sounded amid happiness and celebration is a Zukofskian trademark.

23. Philip Edinger, ed., *How to Grow Roses*, Sunset Books (Menlo Park, Calif.: Lane, 1982), p. 59. See also Charles Harden Fitch, *The Complete Book of Miniature Roses* (New York: Hawthorne, 1977), p. 72 and color photo.

24. The immediate source of this phrase, "young's churching," appears to be an entry in the *"A"* 22 & 23 Spiral, p. 64:

> #churching
> 11/21/71 young are   ~~searching~~

The obvious inference is a play on *chercher*, but where the comment comes from is not indicated, so we lack the context to make precise sense of its place in #1 Starglow.

25. Flowering fruit trees were to have figured in *80 Flowers*. Zukofsky, culling flora from *"A"* and *All* 16 July 1971, wrote in the *80 Fl.* Notes (p. 2): "—fruit tree blossoms cherry, apple, crab, peach, pear, quince, etc." He later canceled the entry, adding: "use in Gamut."

26. Palladas, *The Greek Anthology*, 3:5.

27. *Thomas Jefferson's Garden Book: 1766–1824. With Relevant Extracts from His Other Writings*, ed. Edwin Morris Betts, vol. 22 of the *Memoirs* (Philadelphia:

390 ɔɔ Notes to Pages 96–108

American Philosophical Society, 1944), p. 348. Zukofsky's acquaintance with the *Garden Book* goes back at least to 1930; writing to Pound 5 November that year, he observed: "What interests me is how J. uses the names of flowers in his garden book— and so we talk." Quoted in Ahearn, "Ezra Pound and Louis Zukofsky," 170.

28. Basil Bunting, note to "Briggflats" in his *Collected Poems,* 2nd ed. (Oxford: Oxford University Press, 1978), p. 148.

29. Terrell, "Conversations with Celia," in L.Z. *Paideuma,* 588.

30. I follow *Spenser's "Faerie Queene,"* ed. J. C. Smith, 2 vols. (Oxford: Clarendon, 1909); spelling and line references in the Drafts indicate that Zukofsky used this edition. References will be cited in the text.

31. Ezra Pound, *ABC of Reading* (1934; reprint, New York: New Directions, 1960). Hereafter cited in the text as *ABC.*

32. Zukofsky's Chaucer selections are: (1) "I have of sorwe so gret woon," (2) "Hyd, Absolon, thy gilte tresses clere," (3) *Balade, Lak of Stedfastnesse,* including *Lenvoy to King Richard,* and (4) "Madamé, ye ben of al beauté shryne." Zukofsky also uses "So hath your beautè fro your herte chaced" [no. 2 of *A Triple Roundel*]; Pound uses no. 1.

33. See Ahearn, *Zukofsky's "A,"* p. 5. Chapter 1 (pp. 1–37) is an excellent account of the formative effect of Zukofsky's early surroundings.

34. Theophrastus, *Enquiry into Plants,* trans. Arthur Hort, Loeb Classical Library, 2 vols. (London: Heinemann; Cambridge, Mass.: Harvard University Press, 1916). This is the edition Zukofsky used, and further references to it will be cited in the text.

35. Benedict Einarson, trans., introduction to Theophrastus's *De Causis Plantarum,* Loeb Classical Library (London: Heinemann; Cambridge, Mass.: Harvard University Press, 1976), 1:xxix.

36. Zukofsky's knowledge of Greek was apparently acquired when Paul was being instructed (by Celia) in Latin, Greek, Hebrew, and several modern Romance languages. Niedecker writes (13 November 1952): "—but you want Latin and greek *yrself!!* [What] a household"; and again (7 August 1953): "You and [Paul] learning Greek!" (See Jenny Penberthy, "Lorine Niedecker and Louis Zukofsky: Her Poems and Letters" [Ph.D. Diss., University of British Columbia, 1985], pp. 307, 317.) Zukofsky was reading and making notes from Theophrastus in the early seventies; there is material from vol. 1 of the *Enquiry* in the *"A"* 22 & 23 Spiral (pp. 20, 23), which became the basis of the passage in *"A"*-22 (pp. 520–21), "Annual in all parts annual— . . . close to the twig."

37. Diogenes Laertius, *Lives of Eminent Philosophers,* trans. R. D. Hicks, Loeb Classical Library (London: Heinemann; New York: Putnam, 1925), 1:487.

38. Ibid.

39. See Hort, introduction to *Enquiry* 1:xxii.

40. Einarson, introduction to *De Causis Plantarum* 1:xviii.

4. The Ring and the Mirror: #2 Mountain Laurel and #3 Honesty

1. *The America of 1750: Peter Kalm's Travels in North America. The English Version of 1770,* ed. Adolph B. Benson, 2 vols. (1937; reprint, New York: Dover, 1966); *The Travels of William Bartram,* ed. Mark Van Doren (New York: Dover, 1928), first published in 1791. Paul gave the books to his father 27 August 1971, according to the last entry in the black notebook (p. 115).

2. *Peter Kalm's Travels in North America,* 1:177.

3. T. S. Eliot, "Little Gidding," p. 223.

4. Taylor and Gray list no species *arborea* under *Medicago* (the *Century* is occasionally anachronistic in its botany). Zukofsky's chief concern, though, was not botanical exactitude but the play that flower names afforded; if the *Century* offered him a moon trefoil, the chances are he would make use of it.

5. Smart, *Rejoice in the Lamb*, p. 137; and see editorial notes on section 21. I follow Philip Miller, *The Gardener's Dictionary*, 2nd ed., 1733. Miller's explanation of the name "Moon Trefoil" derives from the plant's leguminous seedpod: "a plain orbiculated Fruit, shap'd somewhat like a Half Moon." This *Lunarium* of Miller's is not the modern *Lunaria annua*, and the description does not fit *Botrychium lunaria* (see n. 13, this chapter).

6. Charles ("Pete") Conrad, in *Apollo Expeditions to the Moon*, ed. Edgar M. Cortright (Washington, D.C.: NASA, Scientific and Technical Information Office, 1975), p. 226.

7. Fred Feretti, "At Undocking, Fiery Orange Replaces Moon Gray," *New York Times*, 19 November 1969.

8. The moondust/pocket/dancing motifs were part of a collection of notes from 1970 in the *"A"* 22 & 23 Spiral. The entry is still enigmatic, but it does prove that the material of 24 November 1969 is related to events in the American space program:

(3) moondust in my
         pocket re-*astronaut* but did

                         dance there
                         (*"A"* 22 & 23 Spiral, p. 159)

9. Zukofsky: "I can't remember a time when I dedicated a poem using a poet's name or even its initials—the actual dedication is I hope . . . recognized in the reading," draft letter to Deba P. Patnik, 8 October 1977 (TxU).

10. Carroll F. Terrell, "Louis Zukofsky: An Eccentric Profile," in *L.Z.: Man and Poet*, p. 35. Terrell's information is from "established record" and from tapes and correspondence with Celia Zukofsky (p. 35n).

11. See Ahearn, *Zukofsky's "A,"* pp. 9–10. Information from a conversation with Zukofsky, who regarded himself as (Ahearn is quoting) "a man with three birthdays"; that is, the approximate date his parents fixed on; 29 January (misreading of the birth certificate); and 23 January.

12. The notes of 1 January 1969 and 8 June 1969 are reproduced, slightly modified, on p. 6 of the *80 Flowers* Drafts as part of the material for #3 Honesty.

13. *Botrychium lunaria* is a grape fern of the Ophioglossaceae (adder's-tongue family). But the "moonwort" that appeared at the end of *"A"*-23 was equated with *Lunaria annua*, as was moon trefoil. Again, Zukofsky's interest is in the moon figure rather than botanical exactitude.

14. See Terrell, "Louis Zukofsky: An Eccentric Profile," p. 35, for details of Zukofsky's immediate family. Pertinent here is the observation that Louis's surviving elder sisters and brother were born 1888 [Fanny], 1890 [Dora, who died in 1913, according to a note on the *80 Fl.* Spiral copy of #18 Petunia; see Appendix A], and 1892 [Morris Ephraim, to whose memory *"A"*-21 (1967) is dedicated].

15. The same entry in the *"A"* 22 & 23 Spiral was dated, note, 10/30/68. The error of transmission is perhaps due to a line running through the date 12/30/68 on p. 52 of the black notebook, which makes the "12" look like "10." Zukofsky is apparently quoting a letter he wrote Cid Corman, 30 December 1968 (SFU), which begins: "To say anything seems too much—your father, Tom Merton dying alone—the sorrows remain human."

16. There is also a lunar aspect to part of Zukofsky's entry in the black notebook for 8 June 1968 (the *"A"*-21 passage is on p. 474):

A-14
A sign of hope - (A-21 - the moon come out for all of
   of the God in / that it   a table *to eat* on
us ~~but~~ the Table/ will not eat grass /) a felicity

17. Laurence Sterne, *A Sentimental Journey through France and Italy, By Mr Yorick,* ed. Gardner D. Stout, Jr. (Berkeley and Los Angeles: University of California Press, 1967), p. 70. Zukofsky does not mention which edition he was using.

18. Ibid., p. 71.

19. Ibid., p. 74.

20. Smart, *Rejoice in the Lamb,* p. 121.

21. The book Zukofsky was reading in 1944 was *The Perfect Wife: Translated from the Spanish of Friar Luis De Leon, 1583,* trans. Alice Philena Hubbard (Denton: College Press, Texas State College for Women, Department of Foreign Languages, 1943). The work is an exposition of Proverbs 31:10–31. Zukofsky had been sent a copy by an enthusiastic William Carlos Williams, who wrote (3 January 1943, TxU) that its author, Sister Felicia, a nun, was a distant cousin of his, and that he considered the translation a first-rate contribution to American literature in its direct but still scholarly language. My thanks to Peter Quartermain for this information.

22. See Frank Parise, ed., *The Book of Calendars* (New York: Facts on File, 1982), pp. 12–13, 40. Zukofsky was in the habit of noting the dates of Rosh Hashana, Yom Kippur, Kol Nidrě, and so forth throughout the notebooks, which testifies more to his highly developed sense of anniversaries and festivals than to vestigial religious convictions. Whether his acquaintance with Jewish reckoning went beyond high holidays is not something I have been able to find out.

23. *Encyclopedia Judaica,* s.v. "Moon" (Jerusalem: Keter; New York: Macmillan, 1972).

24. Ibid., s.v. "Moon, Blessing of the."

25. The *Troilus and Cressida* citation is incorrect and should read: "*T. & C.,* III. iii. 221."

26. *Gerard's Herball,* p. 103.

27. Ibid., p. 113.

28. The quotation is Shakespeare, *MND* II.i.221, Helena to Demetrius.

29. Nicholas Culpeper, *Culpeper's Complete Herbal and English Physician* (Manchester: J. Gleave, 1826; fac. reprint, Harvey Sales, 1981), p. 98. There is no evidence that Zukofsky ever read Culpeper (1652), but it is listed among several herbals on p. 113 of the black notebook.

30. See E. Radford and M. A. Radford, s.v. "Horseshoe," *Encyclopedia of Superstitions,* ed. Christina Hole, rev. ed. (London: Hutchinson, 1961).

31. The quotation is Shakespeare again, *MND* II.i.103, Titania speaking.

32. The letter in question is to be found in Kenneth Muir's *Life and Letters of Sir Thomas Wyatt* (Liverpool: Liverpool University Press, 1963), p. 38. The keyword *honesty* rings in its opening sentences.

33. See Ahearn, "Two Conversations with Celia Zukofsky," pp. 119–20, for explanation of the La Porte reference.

34. *Gerard's Herball,* p. 113.

5. Sounding and Measuring Time: #4 Liveforever

1. See Peter Quartermain, " 'Actual Word Stuff, Not Thoughts For Thoughts,' " *Credences*, n.s. 2, no. 1 (Summer 1982): 108 and note, for an explanation of *apo koinou* ("a grammatical/syntactic play known to students of classical Greek") as evidenced in the poems of Williams and Zukofsky. The device, "where the end-word of a line . . . ends one statement, but unpunctuated also starts the next, acting as the pivot on which the next line turns," is a trademark of *80 Flowers*, where it operates not merely over line breaks but also between components of the same line. The difficulties we experience trying to "make sense" of the *Flowers* are due in large part to this simultaneously backward- and forward-looking, which may change a word's function in the line several times over.

2. Quoted in Guthrie, *History of Greek Philosophy*, 1:225.

3. Gray's description occurs under *Sedum purpureum*, which he then notes is better considered as a variety of *Sedum telephium*.

4. Louis Zukofsky, " 'A'—Second Movement," *Poetry* 40, no. 1 (April 1932): 27. Further references will be given in the text.

5. The 1942 revision stood as the text to *"A"* 1–6 in the 1959 edition (*"A" 1–12* [Kyoto: Origin Press]) and in all subsequent editions, including the 1978 University of California Press *"A."* Earlier versions will be differentiated as such when quoted.

6. John Milton, *Paradise Lost* VII.617. I am using *Milton: Poetical Works* (London: Oxford University Press, 1966); the editor, Douglas Bush, glosses "hyaline" as "the waters above the firmament" (p. 354n), which reinforces the otherness of the substance.

7. Ezra Pound, *The Cantos* (London: Faber and Faber, 1975), p. 9.

8. See also Zukofsky's letter of 12 December 1930 to Pound (Ahearn, "Ezra Pound and Louis Zukofsky," pp. 177–78), which gives much the same account but also addresses the problem he faced, after reading *The Cantos*, of making *"A"* substantially different and his own.

9. Hyaline endured in Zukofsky's vocabulary of wonder, as evidenced by a passage in *Bottom* (p. 75) describing the "liquid crystal of [Shakespeare's] lines' self-argument—its musical and verbal liquefactions dissolving finely as it were anterior crystalline, visible properties . . . Liquid crystal is only as it must be, an incalculable pleasure of optics."

10. See Geoffrey Grigson, *The Englishman's Flora, Illustrated with Woodcuts from Sixteenth-Century Herbals* (London: Phoenix House, 1955), pp. 198–99. I am grateful to Harry Gilonis for pointing out Grigson's work as a useful source of literary/botanical reference.

11. The *Poetry* version of this passage (p. 28) reads:

Hair falling over ankle, hair falling over forehead.
What is at my lips, have I kissed the flower,
It is green yet graciously ferruginous,
The flower bears the iron-rust lightly,
The flower is the steel piston at my chest,
No air stirs, but, hear . . . the music steeps in the center—
It is not the sea, but what floats over it—

12. Zukofsky, "From 'A,' " in *Active Anthology*, ed. Ezra Pound (London: Faber and Faber, 1933), p. 125. Pound printed the fifth, sixth, and seventh movements. Further references to this will be given in the text.

13. LZ to CC (27 December 1959; TxU): "I follow out of Walt [Whitman] more than I realized, especially in the sense that I am more of my time, as he was of his, than are my immediate elders born ca. 1875–1894. I assume less attitude I think than any of them & come out more person—whatever that's worth—even in the regular meter & I'm of this time (covering the first half of the century) (and anticipating like Walt)—my elders rather end off something European."

14. The Revised Standard Version gives: "I would not live for ever." However, Zukofsky's exhaustive knowledge of the Old and New Testaments was based on the King James Version (see Terrell, "Conversations with Celia," p. 599). His copy of the King James–derived *Pocket Bible* (New York: Pocket Books, 1941) is at TxU, heavily annotated.

15. Nancy K. Sandars, *The Epic of Gilgamesh: An English Version,* Penguin Classics (Harmondsworth: Penguin, 1960). Zukofsky made notes from the text in the *"A" 22 & 23* Spiral, pp. 69–72, 75, and his copy of Sandars is now among the books from his personal library held at TxU. Further references will be made in the text.

16. Zukofsky did note Sandars's translation sources, but the *"A" 22 & 23* Spiral does not contain material from any of them, and almost all of the Gilgamesh section in *"A"-23* can be directly traced to the note-taking from Sandars. The only exceptions are, significantly, parenthetic: one is Vedic transliteration, the other a Zukofskian etymological play (see MJL thesis, appendix D).

17. Zukofsky's reference (*80 Fl.* Drafts, pp. 93–94) is to the Loeb edition of Apollodorus's *The Library,* trans. Sir J. G. Frazer, 2 vols. (London: Heinemann; New York: Putnam, 1921). Zukofsky transcribes Frazer's summary of the story (1:252–57 and notes), which involves Telephus's fulfilment of an oracle ("bred true") that he would kill his mother's brothers. The silence of Telephus was proverbial; Frazer cites a passage from the comic poet Alexis describing a glutton: "he dines like speechless Telephus, answering all questions put to him only with nods." This is the source of Zukofsky's "Tell of us . . . comic . . . questions . . . nods."

18. Ahearn, "Ezra Pound and Louis Zukofsky," p. 177.

6. "The sweet o' the year": Spring 1975 and 1976

1. According to the list of "possible substitutes" (*80 Fl.* Drafts, p. 1), the Zukofskys planted greater celandine and lavender cotton 18 October 1974. Both plants were worked into #5 Lavender Cotton, composed 22 February–10 March 1975, and annotated "for J.S.B.'s Birthday Mar 21" in the *80 Flowers* Spiral.

2. The Zukofskys had a spider (or ribbon) plant (see Ahearn, "Two Conversations with Celia Zukofsky," p. 126) and Zukofsky combined it in the poem with lily-of-the-valley. #6 Spider or Ribbon Plant was written 10–29 March 1975, annotated "anticipating April 11" (see *"A"-12,* p. 154) in both the *80 Flowers* Drafts (p. 10) and the Spiral.

3. Asparagus fern was presumably another houseplant; Zukofsky notes it 1 March 1975 (*80 Fl.* Notes, p. 5), and inserts it, with Ivy, into the First List under Vines. Ivy occurs several times in *"A"* (indexed), notably in a (Zukofsky?) family lyric in *"A"-12* (p. 194) and as the subject of nine-year-old Paul's composition quoted in *"A"-20.* #7 Sprengeri was written 30 March–15 April 1975; no dedication.

4. The pussy willow appears in the Zukofsky-garden section of *"A"-23* (p. 554): "—as / the eyes turn North lilac / blue-red, white too . . . discolor willow with the / lilac" (two differently-colored lilacs, two-colored willow; "with the" also conceals a play on "withy"). Theophrastian material in #8 Pussy Willow comes from the following passages of the *Enquiry:* III.xiii.7; IV.x.6; V.vii.7; and V.ix.4.

5. #9 Privet was composed 1–29 May 1975 (*80 Fl.* Drafts, p. 14).

6. So dated on the manuscript held at TxU. Dates of composition cited in the text which include day and month are taken from manuscripts at Texas. Year of composition only indicates Celia Zukofsky's "Year by Year" section in *A Bibliography of Louis Zukofsky* and its update in the L.Z. *Paideuma,* 603–10.

7. Louis Zukofsky, *Barely and Widely* (New York: C.Z. Publications, 1958).

8. Zukofsky indicates his knowledge of the crux in some notes for the poem under Lily-of-the-valley in the First List of 80 Flowers (p. iv). No source is given, and I have used Marvin H. Pope's close textual commentary in *"Song of Songs": A New Translation,* vol. 7C of *The Anchor Bible* (Garden City, N.Y.: Doubleday, 1977), pp. 367–68, to unravel these lines in #6 Spider or Ribbon Plant.

9. See Appendix C for details of Shakespearean quotation in the *Flowers* discussed in chapters 3–6. See MJL thesis, appendix E, for Shakespearean detail in all *Flowers* quoted in that work.

10. Theophrastus is not directly mentioned in the Draft material of #12 Cinquefoil; it is only by referring to the *80 Flowers* Notes (p. 5) that we find comprehensive notes on Theophrastus's remarks about thyme plus a margin note about their distribution in #1 Starglow, #2 Mountain Laurel, #5 Lavender Cotton, #8 Pussy Willow, and #12 Cinquefoil; the threading of thyme/time continues. In #12 Cinquefoil, the passage concerned is VI.ii.3: "There is a black and a white thyme, and it flowers very freely: it is in bloom about the summer solstice. It is from this flower that the bee gets the honey, and by it beekeepers say it is made known whether they have a good yield of honey or not; for, if the thyme flowers abundantly, they have a good yield, but the bloom is injured or even destroyed if it is rained upon."

11. Zukofsky identified *Potentilla recta* in Port Jefferson 4 June 1975, according to an entry in the Weeds section of the First List (p. viii). #12 Cinquefoil was composed 13–19 July 1975, the height of summer; also of thyme's blooming season.

12. John Bartlett, *A New and Complete Concordance . . . to Shakespeare* (New York: Macmillan, 1896); Marvin Spevack, *A Complete and Systematic Concordance to the Works of Shakespeare,* 9 vols. (Hildesheim: Georg Olms, 1968–70).

13. *Gerard's Herball,* p. 129. Zukofsky had copied (*80 Fl.* Notes, p. 1) a passage from Woodward's introduction concerning the rarities grown in Gerard's own garden, among them white thyme and double-flowered peach.

14. See Mats Rydén, *Shakespearian Plant Names: Identifications and Interpretations,* Stockholm Studies in English, 43 (Stockholm: Almqvist and Wiksell International, 1978), p. 18 and note. Rydén lists various critics who follow up the Shakespeare-Gerard links.

15. Woodward, Introduction to *Gerard's Herball,* p. vii. Woodward identifies the "red whortle" in his notes as cowberry (p. 299). Taylor lists cowberry as *Vaccinium vitis-idea,* closely related to cranberry and blueberry.

16. Walter W. Skeat, *An Etymological Dictionary of the English Language,* rev. ed. (Oxford: Clarendon, 1963). Zukofsky does not specify the edition used in the composition of the *Flowers;* preparation for #10 Charlock Per Winkle indicates that he looked at Skeat's entries on *quill, quillet,* and *bottom.*

17. Alice M. Coats, *Flowers and Their Histories* (New York: Pitman, 1956), p. 262, quoting a fourteenth-century medical manuscript.

18. See Giorgio de Santillana and Hertha von Dechend, *Hamlet's Mill: An Essay on Myth and the Frame of Time* (Boston: Gambit, 1969), pp. 194, 200–201, 292.

19. Frank Justus Miller, trans., *Ovid: "Metamorphoses,"* Loeb Classical Library (London: Heinemann; Cambridge, Mass.: Harvard University Press, 1916), 1:137.

20. The poem itself, composed 4 February 1937 (ms. at TxU), is on p. 85 of *All:*

    che di lor suona su nella tua vita

I walked out, before
"Break of Day"
And saw
Four cabins in the hay.

Blue sealed glasses
Of preserves—four—
In the window-sash
In the yard on the bay.

Further:
The waters
At the ramp
Running away.

21. Bayberry is *Myrica cerifera* (waxy) or *Myrica pensylvanica* of the Myricaceae or bayberry family. The plant is sometimes known as wax myrtle or candleberry. Sweet-fern is *Comptonia peregrina* ("foreign," to Linnaeus who named it), another myri-caceous shrub that the Zukofskys had in their garden. *Myrica,* according to Gray, is from the Greek name of the tamarisk, which Zukofsky looked up in Theophrastus (*myrikē; Enquiry* V.iv.8, concerning the hardness of Arabian tamarisk wood) and wound into his poem as: "moor in key" (an Arabian touch?). Liking, obviously, the association of fragrance and another kind of endurance. For Zukofsky's account of the motifs drawn into #22 Bayberry, see Appendix B.

22. Is it significant that "unprotected," that one admission of vulnerability, comes from a new quarter in Zukofsky's note-taking, Henry James? Zukofsky was reading the Harper Torchbook edition of *The Princess Casamassima* (1866; reprint, New York: Harper, 1959) November 1975–January 1976, and this first note (of two) is a quotation from p. 117, Hyacinth saying to Pinnie: "Oh, I'm unprotected in the nature of things." The note was made 27 November 1975 (*80 Fl.* Notes, p. 11); #22 Bayberry was written 16 November–12 December, so the James was an in-composition addition. The timing must have struck Zukofsky as somehow appropriate.

23. See the figure of alula in Appendix B.

24. *The Works of Thomas Campion: Complete Songs, Masques, and Treatises, with a Selection of Latin Verse,* ed. Walter R. Davis (Garden City, N.Y.: Doubleday, 1967), p. 451. This lyric is classed among the poems of doubtful authenticity—no object to Zukofsky, who took his authors as and where he heard their distinctive voices.

25. Ibid., p. 108.

26. The zinnias of #23 White Begonia look both ways; a long-range view of summer to come and a recollection of the season just gone. On 22 November 1975, when Zukofsky substituted Begonia for Baby's Breath (1st Abb. List, p. [1]), he also noted, under Impatience on the same List, that the zinnia in the garden was still blooming. Later he teamed begonia and zinnias on account of this date.

27. Mitford M. Mathews, ed., *A Dictionary of Americanisms on Historical Principles* (Chicago: University of Chicago Press, 1956): "*woodchuck* ... 1938 *New Orleans Picayune* 17 Feb. 2/4: A man wasn't born like a woodchuck to live in the airth."

28. See MJL thesis, p. 546, for details of the process by which the Loeb Hesiod's Hymn to Demeter entered "A"-23.

29. *Century,* s.v. "Candlemas": "The feast takes its name from the custom, as old as the seventh century, of carrying lighted candles in procession in memory of Simeon's words at the presentation of the infant [Christ] (Luke ii.32), 'a light to lighten the Gentiles, and the glory of thy people Israel.' "

30. The notes for #27 Crocus (*80 Fl.* Drafts, p. 32) record the basic steps of this Greek and Latin play. Snowdrop is there as *leukoïon* and *Galanthus nivalis; strongula rhizais* diverges into *strongula naus* and then *makra naus.* There is no indication of the break to Latin at this point.

31. Zukofsky is quoting Rex Warner's translation of Xenophon's *Anabasis* entitled *The Persian Expedition* (Harmondsworth: Penguin, 1949), p. 150. This book was among the items of Zukofsky's personal library sent to TxU in November 1975, so by the time he came to use the Xenophon material its source was no longer at hand. The autonomy of his editings is demonstrated once more.

32. "An Unearthing" was composed 26 December 1964 (ms. at TxU). It was published May 1965 in an edition of seventy-seven and printed by the Adams House and Lowell House Printers in Harvard Yard. In June 1965, twenty copies of another excerpt from *"A"*-18 were printed by "LHS" of Harvard Yard as *I Sent Thee Late.*

33. Henry James is an indexed presence in *"A"* and *Bottom* and an important Euro-American gauge to Zukofsky (see Ahearn, *Zukofsky's "A,"* pp. 1–4). He is also a voice in *"A"*-23's "living calendar," saying: "doubts' / passionate Judgement, passion the task" (p. 563), which is Zukofsky's condensation of a passage from the short story "The Middle Years" (Henry James, *Selected Stories,* ed. Gerard Hopkins [London: Oxford University Press, 1957], 2:139). James, speaking in the person of an elderly dying novelist: "We work in the dark—we do what we can—we give what we have. Our doubt is our passion and our passion is our task. The rest is the madness of art." This was copied into the black notebook (p. 51) 23 December 1968. Other James material (not from the novels) also made its way through this notebook, the *"A"* 22 & 23 Spiral, and the *80 Flowers* Notes, but it does not appear to have been used in the poems. These quotations, apparently selected for their aphoristic qualities, are markedly different from the passages Zukofsky noted in his reading of 1975–76.

34. There is an interesting juxtaposition of violets and roses in *"A"*-23 (p. 551), the result of Zukofsky's inwreathing of three flower passages from classical literature. See MJL thesis, p. 269 and notes.

35. Henry James, *Watch and Ward,* introduction by Leon Edel (1878; reprint, New York: Grove, 1960), p. 218. This is the edition Zukofsky was using according to a citation of p. 19 in the *80 Flowers* Notes. References to this and other James novels will be given in the text after an initial citation.

36. The only indication that "spin oaths a" denotes the sloe is given in the margin notes for #31 Deutzia (*80 Fl.* Drafts, p. 35); *Prunus spinosa* does not appear on any of the Lists and is not mentioned in the Notes. Its appearance seems spontaneous.

37. Henry James, *Roderick Hudson,* introduction by Leon Edel, Harper Torchbooks (1875; reprint, New York: Harper, 1960), p. 24. Zukofsky cites this edition as he begins note-taking from the novel, *80 Flowers* Notes, p. 19.

38. See also *"A"*-12 (p. 176) for an Egyptian lotus reference, and *"A"*-23 (p. 536) for metamorphosis of the hieratic motif.

39. Bunting, *Collected Poems,* p. 113. There is a strong association of bird, song, and syringa in the poetic mind. See, for example, Whitman's "When Lilacs Last in the Dooryard Bloom'd," in *"Leaves of Grass": Comprehensive Reader's Edition,* ed. Harold W. Blodgett and Sculley Bradley (New York: Norton, 1965), p. 328. Also Mina

Loy's "The Song of the Nightingale Is Like the Scent of Syringa," in *The Last Lunar Baedeker,* ed. Roger L. Conover (Highlands, N.C.: Jargon, 1982), p. 218.

40. *Funk and Wagnalls New Standard Dictionary of the English Language,* s.v. "Lilac" (New York: Funk and Wagnalls, 1965).

41. Liberty Hyde Bailey, *The Standard Cyclopedia of Horticulture,* 3 vols. (New York: Macmillan, 1935). Zukofsky consulted this at the Villa Serbelloni, November 1972, and made some notes from it in the *"A"* 22 & 23 Spiral, p. 142.

42. The original phrase "angels in tournures" occurs on p. 48 of James's *William Wetmore Story and His Friends, From Letters, Diaries, and Recollections,* 2 vols. (Boston: Houghton Mifflin, 1903). This is the edition Zukofsky used. The substitution of "bustles" for "tournures" in #32 Lilac is an example of Zukofsky's preference (in this case) for the contemporary and comprehensible over the obsolete and perhaps obscure. For the dilemma such niceties of balance plunged him into, see Appendix B, the discussion of #22 Bayberry's *"compt."*

7. The *Flowers* of Summer and Fall 1976

1. The preparatory notes for #39 Dutch White Iris (*80 Fl.* Drafts, p. 41) record the 1976 flowering date as 25 June. This would throw the poem out of sequence, and the entry on the Second Abbreviated List has the date as "5/25/76"; it is therefore reasonable to assume that in copying from List to Drafts, Zukofsky mistook the faintly formed 5 (May) for a 6 (June). We could also notice that blue-eyed grass, identified in June, is noted as flowering "June 13 along with D. Wh." (*80 Fl.* Drafts, p. 41), which suggests the May date for the iris's flowering.

2. Edinger, *How to Grow Roses,* p. 51.

3. Ibid., p. 56. Additional information from S. Millar Gault and Patrick M. Synge, eds., *A Dictionary of Roses in Colour* (London: Ebury and Michael Joseph, 1971), p. 132; illustration, p. 46.

4. See Claire Powell, *The Meaning of Flowers: A Garland of Plant Lore and Symbolism from Popular Custom and Literature* (London: Jupiter, 1977), p. 126.

5. Ralph Waldo Emerson, trans., quoting from an unnamed poem of Hafiz in his essay "Persian Poetry," in *Letters and Social Aims,* vol. 8 of *Emerson's Complete Works* (London: Routledge, 1883), p. 232. This is the essay Zukofsky was using for some of his references to Hafiz's poetry in *Bottom* ("Emerson's little bouquet of Persians," p. 120; and the Emerson translations pp. 141–42).

6. Emerson, "Persian Poetry," pp. 244, 247; and from "Waldeinsamheit" and "Initial Love" in *The Poems,* ed. Walter Lewin (London: Walter Scott, 1886), pp. 188, 107.

7. Zukofsky misnumbered two pages of the Drafts, repeating pp. 40 and 41. I have styled these repeats p. 40[a] and p. 41[a]; they cover part of the material for #38 Phlox and #39 Dutch White Iris. Following p. 41[a], the page numbering proceeds normally from p. 42.

8. Thomas Hardy, *A Pair of Blue Eyes* (1873; reprint, New York: Macmillan, 1927). Zukofsky copies from this passage generously (*80 Fl.* Notes, p. 3, Condensed Notes). This is not the edition he was reading; unlike James's novels, Hardy's are not cited in the Notes and are difficult to track down. I use standard editions when Zukofsky's are not to be found. References to this and other Hardy novels will be given in the text after the first citation.

9. The fortieth *Flower,* for all its "irregularity," contains exactly the regulation 40

words in lines respectively 5, 6, 4, 6, 4, 5, 5, and 5 words long. For a list of irregular lines in *80 Flowers,* see MJL thesis, appendix B.

10. *Gerard's Herball,* p. 1.

11. There are two books, *Field Flowers* and *Woodland Flowers,* which Zukofsky uses extensively for their illustrations and botanical information. They are probably handbooks or identification guides, but I have been unable to match page numbers with any such works and no further identification of them is given in the Notes or Drafts.

12. Lewis J. Clark, *Wild Flowers of the Pacific Northwest, from Alaska to Northern California,* ed. John G. Trelawny (Sidney, B.C.: Gray, 1976), p. 340. Clark quotes both Gybson (1539) and Gerard (1597).

13. William Carlos Williams, *Selected Poems,* 2nd ed. (New York: New Directions, 1968), p. 16.

14. According to his notes, Zukofsky was commenting on Campion's fifteenth song in the *Second Book of Ayres* and the twenty-sixth song in the *Third Book.* (Campion, *Works,* pp. 105, 162.)

15. Campion, *Works,* p. 451; and see chap. 6.

16. Woodward, introduction to *Gerard's Herball,* p. vii.

17. Zukofsky notes the passage in his preparations for the poem (*80 Fl.* Drafts, p. 50). Here he is not reading Neilson's text, which uses an emendation, "tuft," in place of the (Folio-derived) "turf." Most modern editors favor the latter.

18. Minnie Watson Kamm, *Old-time Herbs for Northern Gardens* (Boston: Little, Brown, 1938), p. 224. Zukofsky used Kamm for the range of historical quotations on herbs her work provides. Further references are in the text.

19. Horace, *The Odes and Epodes,* trans. C. E. Bennett, rev. ed. (Cambridge, Mass.: Harvard University Press; London: Heinemann, 1964), pp. 84, 85.

20. Ovid, *Metamorphoses* VIII.666 (Loeb trans.).

21. Thomas Hardy, *Far from the Madding Crowd* (1874; reprint, New York: Harper and Row, 19[?]), p. 399. Zukofsky read this edition or a reprint of it, to judge by the page numbers he notes.

22. Horace, *Satire* I.i.7, in *Satires, Epistles, and Ars Poetica,* trans. H. Rushton Fairclough, rev. ed., Loeb Classical Library (London: Heinemann; Cambridge, Mass.: Harvard University Press, 1929), p. 5.

23. Clark, *Wild Flowers,* p. 537n.

24. Dentistry is a subject that crops up often in Zukofsky's correspondence of the mid-seventies. In 1974, for example, he was having root-canal work done (LZ to CC, 21 February 1974; SFU), and later that year he speaks of "a cruel spring with M.D.'s and D.D.S." slowing up work on *"A"*-23 (LZ to CC, June 1974; SFU).

25. No source is given for this. In the *"A"* 22 & 23 Spiral it appears on p. 159 as part of a summary of unused notes from 1969; again, no source is given.

26. The Chaucer quotation appears directly after Zukofsky's transcription of Laban Tall's speech (*80 Fl.* Notes, p. 3, Condensed Notes).

27. Thomas Hardy, *Desperate Remedies* (1871; reprint, London: Macmillan, 1966), p. 71: "But the vivacity of spirit which had hitherto enlivened her was fast ebbing . . . and the warm scarlet of the geraniums, glowing most conspicuously, and mingling with the vivid cold red and green of the verbenas, the rich depth of the dahlia, and the ripe mellowness of the calceolaria . . . were to a great extent, lost upon her eyes." (Not the edition Zukofsky was using.) We might notice the proximity of dahlia and calceolaria in Hardy's summer show, as well as in Zukofsky's sequence.

8. The Doublings of Spring 1977

1. Thomas Hardy, *The Dynasts, An Epic-Drama* (London: Macmillan, 1904), 3:521–22. This is the text Zukofsky worked from; Celia was going to use it as part of "Marginalia," a compilation of Louis's annotations which was to have been published by C.Z. Publications. See MJL thesis, appendix C.

2. Breck's, a long-established Dutch-American firm, packages and ships mail-order bulbs from Holland. Each year the company puts out a full-color advance sale catalog. The Zukofskys would have ordered from the 1976 catalog; Breck's was unable to find a copy of this in 1984 but kindly sent me the 1977 one. As the bulb selections do not change radically (*Breck's 1984 Advance Sale* is offering much the same flowers as it was in 1977), we have a close approximation of what Zukofsky was ordering from and consulting, 1976–77.

3. The issue of quantity in Zukofsky's verse is a dissertation topic in itself, which will be ably treated when Peter Crisp (now of Napier, New Zealand) resumes his study of "A." To him I owe what understanding I have of Zukofsky's meter; information generously shared in a series of letters 1984–85. Concerning "A"-9:

> The "quantitative interest" that develops in "A" I have to my own satisfaction traced to the specific point where "A"-9 Second Half takes over from "A"-9 First Half. A comparison of the two halves shows a far more percussive, stress-accented first half compared to the sudden change heard in the more evenly paced and accented second half . . . Phrases [in "A"-9 Second Half] like "this sole lee is love," define the ear against the comparative "bounce" of "labor, lowlier" in the matching line of the first stretch. "The foci of production" generated an apt, but different sound from "The foci of things timelessly reflected" (again the echo of line against line). And of course the flowers come in and the song for ever leaves "A"-8 and naked labor for more involved intertwinings, reaching away from "the material clef" to a more abstract music of words now fully aware of how they connect as quantities of sound and sense. (Letter to author, 1 October 1984)

> Fumbling for the "unmistakable" point where "A" starts becoming quantitative in earnest, I hold by what I (finally) wrote about "A"-9 as the hinged diptych, as it were, *where it actually happens;* with an appropriateness one can only praise in the distinct switch of register from labor to love, and so from the concerns of "A"-8 to the central key of "A"-11, "A"-12. And thereafter, a concentrated intertwining, with different emphases from movement to movement but never again as "black and white" as the earlier "chunked" strategy would have it. The new measure so perfectly matches the new, more integral focus, yet also so plainly *continues* what precedes, as the echoes and cross-references insist, that one is tempted again to raise the single question of the metric of "A" as the true, disembodied "hero" of the poem's adventures. Certainly metric as a way of measuring and clarifying—quantifying—a life sounded in words is central to "A" in no fanciful way. (Letter to author, 7 November 1984)

4. See Ahearn's discussion of "A"-9 Second Half, *Zukofsky's "A,"* pp. 104–7.

5. Ahearn, *Zukofsky's "A,"* pp. 106–7.

6. The *Breck's Dutch Bulb Handbook* (Peoria, Ill.: Breck's Bulbs, 1983), which now accompanies a bulb order, does. This publication was not available to the Zukofskys, so they had to identify the specific varieties of their bulbs by other means.

7. Grecian windflowers are still offered by Breck's, and the *Dutch Bulb Handbook* confirms that they are cultivars of *Anemone blanda.*

8. William Carlos Williams, *Paterson* (New York: New Directions, 1963), p. 217. The translation starts off the second movement of "Paterson V."

9. Most texts give the final lines as "Ye do lie, / Poor girls, neglected." Pound's *ABC* (p. 142) gives "die"—one more point of contact between *A Test* and the *ABC*. Zukofsky's "die" brings the poem closer to the circumstances of #53 Grecian Windflower.

10. William Blake, *Milton*, ed. Kay Parkhurst Easson and Roger R. Easson (Boulder, Colo.: Shambala; New York: Random House, 1978), 1.26.10–12. I am indebted to Charles Bernstein's discussion of "Blake's Vision, Zukofsky's Sight," which foregrounds this quotation, in the essay "Words and Pictures," *Sagetrieb* 2, no. 1 (Spring 1983): 9–34.

11. Williams, *Selected Poems*, p. 14.

12. Thomas Hardy, *A Laodicean: Or, The Castle of the De Stancys. A Story of Today* (1881; reprint, New York: Peter Fenelon Collier, 1912), p. 358. This edition was not used by Zukofsky.

13. Milton, *Paradise Lost* II.178–85.

14. Pope, *Song of Songs*, p. 368.

15. Pliny, *Natural History*, trans. W.H.S. Jones (Cambridge, Mass.: Harvard University Press; London: Heinemann, 1938), 6:xxi, 164. Lewis and Short quote the sense of the passage under *anemone*.

16. The notes for #53 Grecian Windflower and #55 Grape-Hyacinth give each bulb's flowering date as "31 April"—an error of transmission from p. 1 of the In Process Notes, where a stroke next to the 3 of "April 3" makes the number into (an impossible) 31.

17. Levi Strauss chooses #56 Hyacinth as one of two *Flowers* that he takes apart, line by line, with a dictionary (the *OED*) in "Approaching *80 Flowers*," pp. 89–96. This approach yields a gist of the poem but it lacks the enrichment contributed by "*A*"-9 and the intricate Theophrastian underlay carried over from #55 Grape-Hyacinth.

18. See MJL thesis, pp. 350–62, for detailed discussion of #55 Grape-Hyacinth and #56 Hyacinth.

9. Aster, Raspberry, Daisy, Aloe, and Thyme

1. Samuel Johnson, *Lives of the English Poets*, introduction by Arthur Waugh, World's Classics, 2 vols. (London: Oxford University Press, 1952). This is referred to as "W.C. ed" a number of times in the Notes and Drafts, and once (Third List, p. 14) Zukofsky gives the page reference according to "my copy of Johnson's *Lives*."

2. See MJL thesis, pp. 369–94, for detailed treatment of #71 Aster, #72 Raspberry, and #73 Daisy.

3. *Park Seed 1977: Flowers and Vegetables*. Catalog. (Greenwood, S.C.: George W. Park Seed Co., 1977), p. 43. Zukofsky was using this and *Burpee Gardens 1977*. Catalog. (Warminster, Pa.: W. Atlee Burpee Co., 1977), for color photographs of the garden plants Taylor describes but does not usually illustrate. My thanks to Park Seed for supplying a 1977 catalog, and to Burpee Seed for searching, unsuccessfully, for a copy of theirs. The 1985 catalogs that both companies sent show that current selections are similar to those being offered eight years previously, so it is usually possible to find the Burpee references or close approximations of them.

4. Ben Jonson, in *Seventeenth-Century Poetry: The Schools of Donne and Jonson*, ed. Hugh Kenner (New York: Holt, Rinehart and Winston, 1964), p. 85. This is a text

Zukofsky is likely to have owned, given his respect for Kenner's scholarship and the friendship that developed over the years.

5. Material concerning the Bard award is at TxU among the uncatalogued Zukofsky papers. It consists of correspondence; the commencement program with Zukofsky's holograph notes about what he would read for the occasion if asked to do so (a passage from "A"-22); two inscribed copies of the commencement booklet; a photocopy of the citation; and a photocopy of the Latin diploma.

6. See Brewer, s.v. "Roland"; also W. J. Craig, ed., *King Lear,* 3rd ed., The Arden Shakespeare (London: Methuen, 1921), p. 146n, for the probable source of the ballad "Childe Rowland and Burd Ellen."

7. Agallochum is also called lign aloes, and sometimes Paradise Shoots, because, according to Brewer, it is "said to be the only plant descended to us from the Garden of Eden. When Adam left Paradise he took a shoot of this tree, and from it the lign aloes have been propagated." Zukofsky may not have been aware of this paradisal link but it fits comfortably into the last ten *Flowers.*

8. Juvenal, *Satires* VI.178–81, in *Juvenal and Persius,* trans. G. G. Ramsay, rev. ed., Loeb Classical Library (Cambridge, Mass.: Harvard University Press; London: Heinemann, 1940), pp. 96, 97.

9. I have reproduced Zukofsky's transliterations, Greek to English alphabet, in discussing this poem.

10. "Trusts still greet C + me at 80" echoes Zukofsky's comment about willows in the #22 Bayberry exposition: "And besides, we're talking about Spring, and so there they are, whatever spring it is. We trust. That is kind of personal" (see Appendix B).

11. Guy Davenport to Peter Quartermain, 22 June 1985:

> Fascinating indeed, the "Thyme" of *80 Flowers* containing Max. . . . For what it's worth:
>
> poor tom's a-cold: Max was enticed into the house on a day so bitter that he had ice between his toes, and clicked when he walked. We'd seen him in the snow, and thought he was homeless. BJ patiently held a saucer of meat and gravy until he got up the courage to come in.
>
> eye ate his (hiatus)
>
> moon's flight: Max saw Commander Armstrong step onto the moon on a rented TV set (only one ever in my house) and peed all over me while I held him to the screen.
>
> ate his hope—may refer to Max having to eat catfood placed in a turkey carcass. We cleaned all meat off the turkey for days after a Thanksgiving, which Max so enjoyed that he refused non-turkey meals, butting the refrigerator in which he thought the great bird lived.
>
> Is there an undertext?

12. The Latin verb *hio* from which *hiatus* derives covers all these possibilities. It means "to open, stand, or be open, to gape, in particular to open the mouth, to gape, to yawn." Figuratively it can mean (of speech) "to be badly connected, to leave a hiatus"; or "to gape (with longing, wonder, or curiosity), to be eager, to long (for anything), to be amazed" (Lewis and Short).

13. See Alex Preminger, ed., *Princeton Encyclopedia of Poetry and Poetics,* enl. ed. (Princeton: Princeton University Press, 1974); *hiatus* (b): "Grammar and prosody: a break between two vowels coming together without an intervening consonant in successive words or syllables to prevent vowel clash. . . . In English the indefinite article may be altered by addition of a nasal to prevent hiatus: *an action.*"

14. I could not find a copy of Zukofsky's New American Library edition (1963; a

reprint of the revised edition). Therefore I follow the Oxford University Press revised edition of *The Sea around Us* (New York, 1961); the present quotation is on p. 144. Further references will be given in the text. Zukofsky copied extensive passages from Carson (*80 Fl.* Notes, pp. 6, 7–9), which were subsequently condensed (*80 Fl.* Notes, pp. 10A-2, 10C).

15. The *New York Times* of 12 November 1971 reported that the first televised photos of Mars transmitted by *Mariner 9* showed the planet obscured by haze and dust; one day later the spacecraft was ready to enter Martian orbit. Schematic diagrams of *Mariner 9* show a windmill-shaped craft with a central core that somewhat resembles a spider—especially when the filaments of its orbital flight paths are diagrammatically described. Information from the *New York Times Index 1971: A Book of Record*.

16. "Hardhack" alludes to the hardness of spirea's wood (tough cutting) and "steeplebush" refers to the spire-shaped flower. By analogy with *hack* and *steeplechase*, the two names, close together in the poem, appear more equine than they are.

17. Diogenes Laertius, *Lives of Eminent Philosophers*, 1:485.

18. Samuel Johnson, *A Dictionary of the English Language* (1755): "MOPUS. [A cant word from MOPE.] Drone; dreamer." The balance of Zukofsky's note appears to be his own inference.

19. Zukofsky copies out the *Century*'s etymology of *meteor* (*80 Fl.* Drafts, p. 78). The dictionary was probably responsible for a much earlier note concerning the same word: "9/27/67—meteor (GK: a thing in the air)" (b.n.b., p. 9).

20. "Cento" is literally a patchwork, but we can be sure that it was the *Century*'s example of the word's figurative use that took Zukofsky's eye on account of its authorship and the relevance of the term to the techniques of the late "A." From Isaac D'Israeli's *Curiosities of Literature*, 1:392: "A cento primarily signifies a cloak made of patches. In poetry it denotes a work wholly composed of verses or passages promiscuously taken from other authors; only disposed in a new form or order, so as to compose a new work and a new meaning. . . . The pieces may be taken either from the same poet, or from several, and the verses may either be taken entire, or divided into two, one half to be connected with another half taken elsewhere, but two verses are never to be taken together."

21. Johnson, *Lives*, 1:97. Zukofsky copied this passage into the Third List (p. 10) and followed it with the comment: "[L.Z. breeze, gadfly, horsefly—any *poet*]."

10. The Composites: #76 Vines and #77 Weeds

1. J. B. Greenough et al., eds., *Allen and Greenough's New Latin Grammar for Schools and Colleges, Founded on Comparative Grammar*, rev. ed. (Boston: Ginn, 1916), pp. 1, 3. Zukofsky refers to this work in his letter of 5 November 1930 to Pound; see Ahearn, "Ezra Pound and Louis Zukofsky," p. 171. N.B.: Ahearn mistranscribes Zukofsky's handwriting (or Zukofsky himself cites the author incorrectly) in giving "Greenbaugh's" for "Greenough's."

2. Quoted in Charles Tomlinson, "Objectivists: Zukofsky and Oppen, a Memoir," L.Z. *Paideuma*, 435.

3. Zukofsky acknowledged his debt to the gardener of the Villa Serbelloni in a letter of 16 December 1972 to the Rockefeller Foundation, which had funded the sojourn there. From a carbon copy now at TxU: "By happy contingency the landscaping of the villa grounds offered a sequence of context I had in mind beginning this movement of 'A' three years ago. I am especially grateful for a conversation with Mario Ferrario, the gardener."

4. Guy Davenport, *Tatlin! Six Stories* (New York: Scribner's, 1974). Apparently the matter was taken no further.

5. Robert Herrick, "To the Virgins, To Make Much of Time," in *Poems,* ed. L. C. Martin (London: Oxford University Press, 1965), p. 84.

6. Harold John Massingham, ed., *A Treasury of Seventeenth-Century English Verse, from the Death of Shakespeare to the Restoration (1616–1660)* (London: Macmillan, 1919), pp. 107–10.

7. Ibid., pp. 109–10.

8. Mushrooms have been part of the *Flowers* material since 1971, when Zukofsky transferred various botanical references in *"A"* and *All* into the embryonic *80 Flowers* Notes (p. 2). The entry in question reads: "—mushrooms *mayed* (verb c.f. . . . Poem Beg. The." Zukofsky obviously appreciative of Herrick's doubling use of the verb *may*.

9. This passage is a condensation of the work (in translation) of two lyricists, Ssŭ-k'ung Tu (834–908) and Su Shih (1036–1101); Zukofsky was working from Giles, *History of Chinese Literature,* pp. 179–88, 222–26. His initial note-taking from Giles for the passage appears in the *"A"* 22 & 23 Spiral, pp. 40–44. (N.B.: The wistaria seems to be Zukofsky's own contribution to the pervasive lyricism.)

10. Alexander Pope, "An Essay on Man," in *Poetical Works,* ed. Herbert Davis (Oxford: Oxford University Press, 1966), p. 277.

11. The Order of Weeds as listed on the scrap of paper originally stapled into the Notes:

1. bluecurls romero
2. bamboo   3 string
3. downy-rattlesnake   / musical
4. henbit   / instrument
5. chara
6. goldenrod (ponder otter = pandura
7. blue boneset ("hardy ageratum"
   compositae, var. purpureum
   = joe-pye
8. ladysthumb (Penna.) persicaria
   (Rumex, sorrel) var. *herb patience*
9. (ascending) *tansy* ~~bitter buttons~~
10. field-bindweed
11. lady's-orchid-slipper

12. *Gerard's Herball,* p. 1.

13. *Diary and Autobiography of John Adams,* ed. L. H. Butterfield, Series 1 (Diaries) of *The Adams Papers,* 4 vols. (Cambridge, Mass.: Belknap/Harvard University Press, 1961).

14. *Diary and Autobiography of John Adams,* III:281. This passage is from the *Autobiography.*

15. Ibid., II:28.

16. Ibid., II:25. McKinstry's 230 years is a Gregorian estimate; by Jewish reckoning the seventh millennium will begin 2239 C.E.

17. Asa Benveniste of Trigram Press corresponded with Zukofsky in the course of producing the British edition of *"A"* 22 & 23 (1977). The Zukofsky/Benveniste exchange, half a dozen items, is among the uncatalogued Zukofsky material at TxU.

18. Williams, *Selected Poems,* p. 22. The poem is representative of the temper of the 1921 collection, *Sour Grapes,* in which it first appeared.

19. For a possible addition chara (as Greek delight) is making to the paradisal aspects of #77 Weeds, consider that the Hebrew for *Eden* meant literally "pleasure or delight" (*Century*). See Coda, n.3.

20. Ageratum is also an entry on one of the preliminary lists for #78 "X"—a list compiled at least before #74 Aloe was written because several of its candidates (Aloe, Bougainvillea, Clematis) were drafted into *Flowers* earlier than the "X" poem (see chap. 11).

21. Robert Burton, *The Anatomy of Melancholy*, ed. Floyd Dell and Paul Jordan Smith (New York: Tudor, 1927), p. 767.

11. XYZ: #78 "X," #79 Yaupon, and #80 Zinnia

1. Celia Zukofsky, quoted in Ahearn's "Two Conversations with Celia Zukofsky," p. 130.

2. The first mention of the Paganini occurs in the black notebook (p. 111), where Louis copies material from the jacket notes of Paul Zukofsky's *Niccolò Paganini: The 24 Caprices for Solo Violin (Complete)*, Vanguard Cardinal Series, VCS-10093/4, 1970.

3. Zukofsky was probably working from the bilingual edition entitled *Bemerkungen über die Grundlagen der Mathematik/Remarks on the Foundations of Mathematics*, ed. G. H. von Wright, R. Rees, and G.E.M. Anscombe; trans. G.E.M. Anscombe (Oxford: Basil Blackwell, 1956). The paragraph under discussion is on p. 41.

4. Zukofsky, quoted by Celia Zukofsky in "1927–1972," *L.Z. Paideuma*, 371.

5. Liddell and Scott give the phrase *Asklēpiadēs* ("son of Aesculapius") and note its origin in the *Iliad*. Lewis and Short describe Aesculapius (in Greek, Asklepios) as follows: "According to fable, the son of Apollo and the nymph Coronis, deified after his death on account of his great knowledge of medicine . . . Serpents, probably as symbols of prudence and renovation, were everywhere connected with his worship."

6. David Jones, quoted in Colin Wilcockson's "Notes on Some Letters of David Jones," *Agenda* 14, no. 2 (Summer 1976): 83.

7. See Karl von Frisch, *Animal Architecture*, trans. Lisbeth Gombrich, with Otto von Frisch (New York: Harcourt Brace Jovanovich, 1974), pp. 93–94.

8. Lorine Niedecker, *New Goose* (Prairie City, Ill.: James A. Decker, 1946), p. 42.

9. Henri Fabre, *Social Life in the Insect World*, trans. Bernard Miall (Harmondsworth: Penguin, 1937), p. 140. This is the edition Zukofsky cites (*80 Fl.* Notes, p. 11), observing that the first edition appeared in 1911. The "little Paul" passage was edited and copied into the Notes, p. 13.

10. Fabre, *Insect World*, p. 80. Zukofsky condensed the whole story of the emperor moth in the *80 Flowers* Notes, p. 13.

11. The three paintings hung in the apartment at Central Park South; from Barry Ahearn's observation of 1978 it seems as though they were also installed in Port Jefferson: "On the walls hung Paul's childhood paintings; the Patchens had encouraged his young artistic efforts" (Ahearn, "Two Conversations with Celia Zukofsky," p. 113).

12. Celia's analog for this passage is an excerpt from Cotton Mather's *Life of John Eliot* (*American Friends*, comp. Celia Zukofsky [New York: C.Z. Publications, 1979], p. 13; CZ's ellipses): ". . . if their *Alphabet* be *short* . . . the *Words* composed of it are long enough to tire the Patience of any Scholar. . . . they are Sesquipedalia Verba . . . growing ever since *Babel*, unto the Dimensions to which they are now extended . . . if my Reader will count how many *Letters* there are in this one Word *Nummatchekodtantamoonganunnonash*, when he has done . . . I'll tell him, it signifies no more than *our Lusts*, and . . . *our Loves* . . . nothing shorter than *Noowoman-*

tammoonkanunonnash." The "*A*"-22 Spiral corroborates the Eliot reference (p. 38) and cites as well *Peter Kalm's Travels in North America,* Hawthorne, and Thoreau; also Jefferson's *Notes on Virginia* (p. 37). This density of source material is typical of the final hundred lines of "*A*"-23.

13. Whitman, "Song of Myself," p. 89.

14. The "Gamut" reference is clearly connected with an entry of the same date in the *80 Flowers* Notes (p. 5) concerning an *Asparagus sprengeri* plant, with the parenthetic comment: "Taffy Yannella" (see also chap. 6, n.3). The Yannellas appear to have given the Zukofskys a holly bush and an asparagus fern 1 March 1975 ("Gamut" Notes, p. 3, 1st seq.). Zukofsky's 1972 reading at Temple University, Philadelphia, was organized by Yannella (see chap. 2, n.47).

15. Sonnet 56 was originally slated for use in "Gamut," as a partial quotation of it on p. 14 of the "Gamut" Notes shows. A margin comment indicating that the entry had been reread 17 January 1978 perhaps gives us the date of transferral to *80 Flowers.* The same lines are copied out on one of the preliminary sheets for #79 Yaupon and marked conspicuously for "Gamut." Maybe Zukofsky had not finished with the sonnet, and its appearance at the close of the *Flowers* was to be mirrored by one at the beginning of "Gamut."

16. Campion, *Works,* p. 451.

17. Ibid., p. 108.

18. Robert D. Stevick, ed., *One Hundred Middle English Lyrics* (Indianapolis: Bobbs-Merrill, 1964), p. 141. Zukofsky makes his selection of lines from two poems of the book at the end of the Third Abbreviated List (p. 24) along with his Zinnia and Zebra material. It is probably significant that the "*A, a, a, a,*" poem is no. 81 of Stevick's anthology; #80 Zinnia is (technically) the eighty-first *Flower.*

19. Stevick, *One Hundred Middle English Lyrics,* p. 175. Remember also the discussion of #3 Honesty's "Lionmane" as a possible homonym for "lemman"; see chap. 4.

20. Louis Zukofsky, *Some Time* (Stuttgart: Jonathan Williams, 1956).

21. Zukofsky seems to deliberately misread the *Century* here; the zebra information as it first appears in the Third Abbreviated List (p. 24): "speed = bottom (i.e. strength) Zebra (see Century Dict."

22. Carson discusses this (p. 145) and Zukofsky condenses the passage (*80 Fl.* Notes, p. 9).

23. Zukofsky copied only "in the deep hidden currents . . the oceans are made one" (*80 Fl.* Notes, p. 8); sufficient material for his drift in #80 Zinnia.

24. The mind casts back to #45 Chicory's "horse-seas," a phrase we were unable to associate with the remainder of the line: "bow kiss fill'em on." Why not "horse—C's," complementing the classical epitome of married contentment?

25. *Park Seed 1977,* p. 93. The green-flowered zinnia is pictured on p. 92.

26. Fyodor Dostoevsky, *"White Nights" and Other Stories,* trans. Constance Garnett (London: Heinemann, 1918).

Coda

1. Hugh Kenner, "Loove in Brooklyn," L.Z. *Paideuma,* 419.

2. Quoted in Penberthy, "Niedecker and Zukofsky," p. 266.

3. The etymology of *paradise* from the Persian for a park or garden, which later became the garden enclosed of Christian theology is well-known. Not so commonplace, and something Zukofsky undoubtedly knew, was the derivation of *Eden*

from the Hebrew *ēden*, literally "pleasure, delight." The *Century* records the steps of its passage into English.

4. Cid Corman printed a pirated text of #1 Much Ado About Trees in his article "Gamut," *Origin*, 5th ser., no. 4 (Fall 1984): 51–54.

5. Lorine Niedecker, *My Life by Water: Collected Poems 1936–1968* (London: Fulcrum, 1970), p. 70. For commentary, see Penberthy, "Niedecker and Zukofsky," p. 285.

Select Bibliography

Primary Sources

Books by Louis Zukofsky

Anon. trans. *Albert Einstein: A Biographical Portrait*. By Anton Reiser. New York: Boni, 1930.

55 Poems. Prairie City, Ill.: James A. Decker, 1941.

Anew. Prairie City, Ill.: James A. Decker, 1946.

A Test of Poetry. New York: Objectivist Press, 1948; London: Routledge and Kegan Paul, 1952; New York: Jargon/Corinth, 1964; New York: C.Z. Publications, 1980.

Some Time. Stuttgart: Jonathan Williams, 1956.

Barely and Widely. New York: C.Z. Publications, 1958.

"A" 1–12. With an essay on poetry by the author and a final note by William Carlos Williams. Kyoto: Origin, 1959; London: Jonathan Cape, 1966. Reprint, with "foreword" by Zukofsky and "A Note" by Robert Creeley. Paris Review Editions. Garden City, N.Y.: Doubleday, 1967.

It Was. Kyoto: Origin, 1961.

Bottom: On Shakespeare. Vol. 1. Austin: Ark Press/Humanities Research Center, University of Texas, 1963. Vol. 2 is Celia Zukofsky's *Music to Shakespeare's Pericles*.

I's (Pronounced Eyes). New York: Trobar, 1963.

An Unearthing. Cambridge, Mass.: Adams House and Lowell House Printers, 1965.

I Sent Thee Late. Cambridge, Mass.: LHS, 1965.

All: The Collected Short Poems, 1923–1964. New York: Norton, 1966.

Prepositions: The Collected Critical Essays. London: Rapp and Carroll, 1967; New York: Horizon, 1968. Expanded ed. Berkeley and Los Angeles: University of California Press, 1981.

Ferdinand, Including "It Was." London: Jonathan Cape, 1968; New York: Grossman, 1968.

"A" 13–21. London: Jonathan Cape, 1969; Paris Review Editions. Garden City, N.Y.: Doubleday, 1969.

With Celia Zukofsky, trans. *Catullus (Gai Valeri Catulli Veronensis Liber)*. London: Cape Goliard, 1969.

Louis Zukofsky at the American Embassy, London, May 21, 1969. Newcastle-upon-Tyne: Ultima Thule, 1969.
AN ERA / ANY TIME / OF YEAR. Poetry Postcard. Santa Barbara: Unicorn, 1970.
Autobiography. New York: Grossman, 1970.
Initial. Oblong Octavo Series, no. 12. New York: Phoenix Bookshop, 1970.
Little: For Careenagers. New York: Grossman, 1970.
"A"-24. New York: Grossman, 1972.
Arise, arise. New York: Grossman, 1973.
"A" 22 & 23. New York: Grossman, 1975; London: Trigram, 1977.
"A." Berkeley and Los Angeles: University of California Press, 1978.
80 Flowers. New York: Stinehour Press for Louis and Celia Zukofsky, 1978.

Prose and Poetry by Zukofsky Cited Separately in This Work

" 'A'-Second Movement." *Poetry* 40, no. 1 (April 1932): 26–29.
"From 'A.' " In *Active Anthology.* Ed. Ezra Pound. London: Faber and Faber, 1933.
"Poetry: For My Son When He Can Read." *Cronos* 2, no. 4 (March 1946); *Prepositions*, enl. ed., pp. 3–11.
"Thanks to the Dictionary." In *It Was*, pp. 99–132.
"A"-22, Part 1. *Poetry* 122, no. 4 (July 1973): 215–34.
"A"-22, Part 2. *Poetry* 124, no. 1 (April 1974): 35–44.
"About the Gas Age." *Journal of Modern Literature* 4, no. 1 (September 1974); *Prepositions*, enl. ed., pp. 169–72.
"From 'A'-23." *Transatlantic Review*, no. 52 (Autumn 1975): 5–8.
"For Wallace Stevens." In *Prepositions*, enl. ed., pp. 23–38.

Zukofsky Manuscripts at TxU and SFU

The Louis Zukofsky–Cid Corman Correspondence, 29 July 1960–21 December 1976. Contemporary Literature Collection, SFU.
The black notebook. Notes for *"A,"* 1964–74. Item 2 of #6836 Uncat. L.Z. Mss. at TxU.
"A" 22 & 23 Spiral. Notes for *"A" 22 & 23*, 1971–74. Item 1 of #8463 Uncat. L.Z. Mss. at TxU.
"A"-22 Spiral. Drafts of *"A"-22*, 1970; 1972–73. Item 2 of #8463 Uncat. L.Z. Mss. at TxU.
"A"-23 Spiral. Drafts of *"A"-23*, 1973–74. Item 3 of #8463 Uncat. L.Z. Mss. at TxU.
80 Flowers Notes and *80 Flowers* Drafts, 1968–78. Including: *80 Flowers* Schema, 1974–75; First, First Abbreviated, Second Abbreviated, and Third Abbreviated Lists of 80 Flowers, 1974–77; In Process Notes, 1977; Americana Lists, 1977. Item 10 of #8463 Uncat. L.Z. Mss. at TxU.
80 Flowers Spiral. Original handwritten ms. of *80 Flowers* plus front matter and first poem of "Gamut: 90 Trees." Item 12 of #8463 Uncat. L.Z. Mss. at TxU.
80 Flowers Typescript and Stinehour Press printer's galleys, 1978. Item 13 of #8463 Uncat. L.Z. Mss. at TxU.
"Gamut" Notes. Notes for "Gamut: 90 Trees," 1969–75; 1976–78. Item 15 of #8463 Uncat. L.Z. Mss. at TxU.

Readings 1971–1975

The Wallace Stevens Memorial Series, University of Connecticut, Storrs, 29 April 1971. Tape: Item 26 of #6836 Uncat. L.Z. Mss. at TxU.

The Paley Library Cultural Series, Temple University, Philadelphia, 16 October 1972. Tape: Item 22A of #6836 Uncat. L.Z. Mss. at TxU.

Glassboro State College, N.J., 17 October 1972. Tape: Item 22B of #6836 Uncat. L.Z. Mss. at TxU.

Bard College, Annandale-on-Hudson, N.Y., 2 November 1972. Tape: Item 22C of #6836 Uncat. L.Z. Mss. at TxU.

YM-YWHA, N.Y.C., 15 October 1973. Tape: Item 27 of #6836 Uncat. L.Z. Mss. at TxU.

Franconia College, Franconia, N.H., 9 May 1974. Videotape: Item 28 of #6839 Uncat. L.Z. Mss. at TxU.

The Turnbull Memorial Series, Johns Hopkins University, Baltimore, 8 May 1975. Tape: Item 29 of #6836. Color videocassette: Item 8 of #8463. Uncat. L.Z. Mss. at TxU.

Private reading of *80 Flowers,* Epigraph through #22 Bayberry; conversations with Hugh Kenner about #22 Bayberry; various excerpts from *"A."* Tape made by Hugh Kenner at Johns Hopkins University, 13 December 1975, now in the possession of Paul Zukofsky.

Secondary Sources

Note: an asterisked entry (*) indicates that the work is an edition identified by Zukofsky in the notebooks and so forth, or traceable by page or line references there. Entries marked (T) indicate that the book is part of Zukofsky's personal library now at TxU.

*Adams, John. *Diary and Autobiography.* Ed. L. H. Butterfield. Series 1 (Diaries) of *The Adams Papers.* 4 vols. Cambridge, Mass.: Belknap/Harvard University Press, 1961.

Ahearn, Barry, ed. "Ezra Pound and Louis Zukofsky: Letters 1928–1930." *Montemora,* no. 8 (Summer 1982): 149–83.

———. *Zukofsky's "A": An Introduction.* Berkeley and Los Angeles: University of California Press, 1983.

———. "Two Conversations with Celia Zukofsky." *Sagetrieb* 2, no. 1 (Spring 1983): 113–31.

*Angulo, Jaime de. *Indian Tales.* New York: Hill and Wang, 1953.

*Apollodorus. *The Library.* Trans. Sir J. G. Frazer. Loeb Classical Library. 2 vols. London: Heinemann; New York: Putnam, 1921.

*Bailey, Liberty Hyde. *The Standard Cyclopedia of Horticulture.* 3 vols. New York: Macmillan, 1935.

Bartlett, John. *A New and Complete Concordance . . . to Words, Phrases, and Passages in the Dramatic Works of Shakespeare; with a Supplementary Concordance to the Poems.* New York: Macmillan, 1896.

*Bartram, William. *The Travels of William Bartram.* Ed. Mark Van Doren. New York: Dover, 1928.

Bernstein, Charles. "Words and Pictures." *Sagetrieb* 2, no. 1 (Spring 1983): 9–34.

(T)Bible. *The Pocket Bible: The King James Version of the Old and New Testaments, the original wording unchanged; the text specially edited, abridged, for reading enjoyment.* New York: Pocket Books, 1941.

Blake, William. *Milton.* Ed. Kay Parkhurst Easson and Roger R. Easson. Boulder, Colo.: Shambala; New York: Random House, 1978.

*Blythe, Ronald. *Akenfield: Portrait of an English Village.* London: Allen Lane/ Penguin Press, 1969.

Breck's 1976 Advance Sale. Catalog. Peoria, Ill.: Breck's Bulbs, 1976.

Breck's 1977 Advance Sale. Catalog. Peoria, Ill.: Breck's Bulbs, 1977.

Breck's 1984 Advance Sale. Catalog. Peoria, Ill.: Breck's Bulbs, 1984.

Breck's Dutch Bulb Handbook. Peoria, Ill.: Breck's Bulbs, 1983.

Brewer, Ebenezer Cobham. *Brewer's Dictionary of Phrase and Fable.* Ed. Ivor H. Evans. Centenary ed. London: Cassell, 1970.

Bunting, Basil. *Collected Poems.* 2nd ed. Oxford: Oxford University Press, 1978.

*Burch, George Bosworth. *The Early Mediaeval Philosophers.* New York: King's Crown, 1951.

Burpee Gardens 1977. Catalog. Warminster, Pa.: W. Atlee Burpee Co., 1977.

*Burton, Robert. *The Anatomy of Melancholy.* Ed. Floyd Dell and Paul Jordan Smith. New York: Tudor, 1927.

*Campion, Thomas. *The Works of Thomas Campion: Complete Songs, Masques, and Treatises, with a Selection of Latin Verse.* Ed. Walter R. Davis. Garden City, N.Y.: Doubleday, 1967.

(T)Carson, Rachel. *The Sea around Us.* Rev. ed. New York: Oxford University Press, 1961. Zukofsky's text: rev. ed. Signet Science Library. New York: New American Library, 1963.

The Century Dictionary: An Encyclopedic Lexicon of the English Language. Ed. William Dwight Whitney. 10 vols. 1889–91; New York: Century, 1895.

*Chaucer, Geoffrey. *The Complete Works.* Ed. Walter W. Skeat. 7 vols. Oxford: Clarendon, 1894.

Clark, Lewis J. *Wild Flowers of the Pacific Northwest, from Alaska to Northern California.* Ed. John G. Trelawny. Sidney, B.C.: Gray, 1976.

Coats, Alice M. *Flowers and Their Histories.* New York: Pitman, 1956.

Coleridge, Samuel T. *The Notebooks of Samuel Taylor Coleridge, 1794–1804.* Ed. Kathleen Coburn. Bollingen Series, 50. New York: Pantheon, 1957.

Corman, Cid. "Gamut." *Origin*, 5th ser., no. 4 (Fall 1984): 51–54.

Cortright, Edgar M. *Apollo Expeditions to the Moon.* Washington, D.C.: National Aeronautics and Space Administration, Scientific and Technical Information Office, 1975.

Craig, W. J., ed. *King Lear.* 3rd ed. The Arden Shakespeare. London: Methuen, 1921.

Creeley, Robert. "A Note." Prefatory note to Zukofsky's *"A" 1–12.* Paris Review Editions. Garden City, N.Y.: Doubleday, 1967.

———. "For L. Z." L.Z. *Paideuma*, 383–85.

Crisp, Peter. Letters to author. 1 October 1984; 7 October 1984.

Culpeper, Nicholas. *Culpeper's Complete Herbal and English Physician.* 1652; Manchester: J. Gleave, 1826; facsimile reprint, Harvey Sales, 1981.

Davenport, Guy. *Tatlin! Six Stories.* New York: Scribner's, 1974.

———. Letter to Peter Quartermain. 22 June 1985.

Diogenes Laertius. *Lives of Eminent Philosophers.* Trans. R. D. Hicks. Loeb Classical Library. 2 vols. London: Heinemann; New York: Putnam, 1925.

D'Israeli, Isaac. "Introduction of Tea, Coffee, and Chocolate." In *Curiosities of Literature.* Ed. Benjamin D'Israeli. Vol. 2, 317–26. Rev. ed. London: Routledge, Warne, and Routledge, 1863.

Dostoevsky, Fyodor. *"White Knights" and Other Stories.* Trans. Constance Garnett. London: Heinemann, 1918.

Edinger, Philip, ed. *How to Grow Roses.* Sunset Books. Menlo Park, Calif.: Lane, 1982.

Eliot, T. S. *Collected Poems 1909–1962.* London: Faber and Faber, 1963.

*Emerson, Ralph Waldo. "Persian Poetry." In *Letters and Social Aims.* Vol. 8 of *Emerson's Complete Works,* 225–51. London: Routledge, 1883.

———. *The Poems.* Ed. Walter Lewin. London: Walter Scott, 1886.

Encyclopedia Judaica. 16 vols. Jerusalem: Keter; New York: Macmillan, 1972.

*Fabre, Henri. *Social Life in the Insect World.* Trans. Bernard Miall. 1911; Harmondsworth: Penguin, 1937.

Feretti, Fred. "At Undocking, Fiery Orange Replaces Moon Gray." *New York Times,* 19 November 1969.

Fitch, Charles Harden. *The Complete Book of Miniature Roses.* New York: Hawthorne, 1977.

*Frisch, Karl von. *Animal Architecture.* Trans. Lisbeth Gombrich, with Otto von Frisch. New York: Harcourt Brace Jovanovich, 1974.

Funk and Wagnalls New Standard Dictionary of the English Language. New York: Funk and Wagnalls, 1965.

Gault, S. Millar, and Patrick M. Synge, eds. *A Dictionary of Roses in Colour.* London: Ebury and Michael Joseph, 1971.

*Gerard, John. *Gerard's Herball: The Essence Thereof Distilled . . . From the Edition of Th. Johnson, 1636.* Ed. Marcus Woodward. London: Gerald Howe, 1927.

*Giles, Herbert A. *A History of Chinese Literature.* New York: D. Appleton, 1901, 1928.

Globe, Alexander V. Examination notes on MJL thesis. October 1985.

Gray's Manual of Botany. Ed. Merritt Lyndon Fernald. 8th ed. New York: American Book Co., 1950.

*Greenough, J. B., et al., eds. *Allen and Greenough's New Latin Grammar for Schools and Colleges, Founded on Comparative Grammar.* Rev. ed. Boston: Ginn, 1916.

Grigson, Geoffrey. *The Englishman's Flora, Illustrated with Woodcuts from Sixteenth-Century Herbals.* London: Phoenix House, 1955.

Guthrie, W.K.C. *The Earlier Presocratics and the Pythagoreans.* Vol. 1 of *A History of Greek Philosophy.* London: Cambridge University Press, 1962.

Hardy, Thomas. *Desperate Remedies.* 1871; London: Macmillan, 1966.

———. *A Pair of Blue Eyes.* 1873; New York: Macmillan, 1927.

*————. *Far from the Madding Crowd.* 1874; New York: Harper & Row, 19[?].

————. *A Laodicean; Or, The Castle of the De Stancys. A Story of Today.* 1881; New York: Peter Fenelon Collier, 1912.

*————. *The Dynasts, An Epic-Drama.* 3 vols. London: Macmillan, 1904.

Herrick, Robert. *Poems.* Ed. L. C. Martin. London: Oxford University Press, 1965.

Hill, Raymond, and Thomas Bergin, eds. *Anthology of the Provençal Troubadours.* Yale Romanic Studies, 17. New Haven: Yale University Press, 1941.

Hoffmann, Banesh. *Albert Einstein: Creator and Rebel.* With Helen Dukas. New York: Viking, 1972.

Horace (Quintus Horatius Flaccus). *The Odes and Epodes.* Trans. C. E. Bennett. Rev. ed. Loeb Classical Library. Cambridge, Mass.: Harvard University Press; London: Heinemann, 1964.

————. *Satires, Epistles, and Ars Poetica.* Trans. H. Rushton Fairclough. Rev. ed. Loeb Classical Library. London: Heinemann; Cambridge, Mass.: Harvard University Press, 1929.

Hudson, W. H. *Nature in Downland.* London: Longmans, Green, 1900.

*James, Henry. *Roderick Hudson.* Introduction by Leon Edel. Harper Torchbooks. New York: Harper, 1960. First published 1875.

*————. *Watch and Ward.* Introduction by Leon Edel. New York: Grove, 1960. First published 1878.

*————. *The Princess Casamassima.* Harper Torchbooks. New York: Harper, 1959. First published 1886.

*————. *William Wetmore Story and His Friends, From Letters, Diaries, and Recollections.* 2 vols. Boston: Houghton Mifflin, 1903.

————. "The Middle Years." Vol. 2, *Selected Stories.* Ed. Gerard Hopkins, 118–39. London: Oxford University Press, 1957.

Jefferson, Thomas. *Thomas Jefferson's Garden Book: 1766–1824: With Relevant Extracts from His Other Writings.* Ed. Edwin Morris Betts. Vol. 22, *Memoirs.* Philadelphia: American Philosophical Society, 1944.

Johnson, Samuel. *A Dictionary of the English Language.* 1755.

*————. *Lives of the English Poets.* Introduction by Arthur Waugh. World's Classics. 2 vols. London: Oxford University Press, 1952.

Juvenal (D. Junius Juvenalis). *Satires.* In *Juvenal and Persius.* Trans. G. G. Ramsay. Rev. ed. Loeb Classical Library. Cambridge, Mass.: Harvard University Press; London: Heinemann, 1940.

*Kalm, Peter. *The America of 1750: Peter Kalm's Travels in North America. The English Version of 1770.* Ed. Adolph B. Benson. 2 vols. 1937; New York: Dover, 1966.

*Kamm, Minnie Watson. *Old-Time Herbs for Northern Gardens.* Boston: Little, Brown, 1938.

Kenner, Hugh, ed. *Seventeenth-Century Poetry: The Schools of Donne and Jonson.* New York: Holt, Rinehart and Winston, 1964.

————. "Of Notes and Horses." *Poetry* 140, no. 2 (November 1967): 112–21; *L.Z.: Man and Poet,* ed. Terrell, pp. 187–94.

————. "Louis Zukofsky: All the Words." *New York Times Book Review* (18 June 1978): 11; L.Z. *Paideuma,* 386–89.

————. "Loove in Brooklyn." L.Z. *Paideuma,* 413–20.

Keyes, Clinton Walker, trans. Introduction to *De Re Publica*. In *Cicero: De Re Publica, De Legibus*, 2–11. Loeb Classical Library. Cambridge, Mass.: Harvard University Press; London: Heinemann, 1928.

Klaeber, Franz, ed. *Beowulf and the Fight at Finnsburg*. 3rd ed. Lexington, Mass.: D. C. Heath, 1950.

*Klein, Martin J., and Robert K. Merton. "A Passion to Understand the Order in the World." Review of *Albert Einstein: Creator and Rebel* by Banesh Hoffmann. *New York Times Book Review* (5 November 1972): 3.

Leggott, Michele. "Reading Zukofsky's *80 Flowers*." Ph.D. Diss., University of British Columbia, 1985.

———. " 'See how the roses burn!': The Epigraph of Zukofsky's *80 Flowers*." *Sagetrieb* 4, no. 1 (Spring 1985): 115–36.

Leon, Luis de. *The Perfect Wife: Translated from the Spanish of Friar Luis de Leon. 1583*. Trans. Alice Philena Hubbard. Denton: College Press, Texas State College for Women, Dept. of Foreign Languages, 1943.

Levi Strauss, David. "Approaching *80 Flowers*." In *Code of Signals: Recent Writings in Poetics*, ed. Michael Palmer, 79–102. Berkeley: North Atlantic Books, 1983.

*Lewis, Charlton D., and Charles Short, eds. *A Latin Dictionary, Founded on Andrews' Edition of Freund's Latin Dictionary*. Oxford: Clarendon, 1879.

*Liddell, Henry George, and Robert Scott, eds. *A Greek-English Lexicon*. 9th ed. Oxford: Clarendon, 1968.

Loy, Mina. *The Last Lunar Baedeker*. Ed. Roger L. Conover. Highlands, N.C.: Jargon, 1982.

*Macdonell, Arthur A. *A Vedic Reader for Students, containing thirty hymns of the Rigveda in the original Saṃhitā and Pada texts, with transliteration, explanatory notes, introduction, vocabulary*. Madras: Oxford University Press, 1917.

*Martial (M. Valerius Martialus). *Epigrams*. Trans. Walter C. A. Ker. Loeb Classical Library. 2 vols. London: Heinemann; New York: Putnam, 1919.

*Massingham, Harold John, ed. *A Treasury of Seventeenth-Century English Verse, from the Death of Shakespeare to the Restoration (1616–1660)*. London: Macmillan, 1919.

Mathews, Mitford M., ed. *A Dictionary of Americanisms on Historical Principles*. Chicago: University of Chicago Press, 1956.

*Melville, Herman. *Pierre: Or, The Ambiguities*. Signet Classics. New York: New American Library, 1964.

Miller, Philip. *The Gardener's Dictionary*. 2nd ed. 1733.

Milton, John. *Poetical Works*. Ed. Douglas Bush. London: Oxford University Press, 1966.

Muir, Kenneth. *The Life and Letters of Sir Thomas Wyatt*. Liverpool: Liverpool University Press, 1963.

*Nahm, Milton C., ed. *Selections from Early Greek Philosophy*. 3rd ed. New York: Appleton-Century-Crofts, 1947.

New York Times. Advertisement for CBS News Special, "Volcano: Birth of an Island." 10 April 1969.

New York Times Index 1971: A Book of Record 59. New York: New York Times, 1972.

*Niedecker, Lorine. *New Goose*. Prairie City, Ill.: James A. Decker, 1946.

———. *My Life by Water: Collected Poems 1936–1968*. London: Fulcrum, 1970.

Ovid (Publius Ovidius Naso). *Metamorphoses*. Trans. Frank Justus Miller. Loeb Classical Library. 2 vols. London: Heinemann; Cambridge, Mass.: Harvard University Press, 1916.

The Oxford English Dictionary, Being a Corrected Re-issue . . . of a New English Dictionary on Historical Principles . . . Ed. James A. H. Murray et al. 12 vols. Oxford: Clarendon, 1933. First published 1884–1928 in 10 vols.

Paideuma 7, no. 3 (Winter 1978): 371–625. Louis Zukofsky memorial issue.

Parise, Frank, ed. *The Book of Calendars*. New York: Facts on File, 1982.

Park Seed 1977: Flowers and Vegetables. Catalog. Greenwood, S.C.: George W. Park Seed Co., 1977.

*Paton, W. R., trans. *The Greek Anthology*. Loeb Classical Library. 5 vols. London: Heinemann; New York: Putnam, 1915.

Penberthy, Jenny. "Lorine Niedecker and Louis Zukofsky: Her Poems and Letters." Ph.D. Diss., University of British Columbia, 1985.

Pliny (Caius Plinius Secundus). *Natural History*. Trans. W.H.S. Jones. Loeb Classical Library. Vol. 6. London: Heinemann; Cambridge, Mass.: Harvard University Press, 1938.

Pope, Alexander. *Poetical Works*. Ed. Herbert Davis. Oxford: Oxford University Press, 1966.

Pope, Marvin H., ed. *"Song of Songs": A New Translation*. Vol. 7C of *The Anchor Bible*. Garden City, N.Y.: Doubleday, 1977.

Pound, Ezra. *ABC of Reading*. 1934; New York: New Directions, 1960.

———. *The Cantos*. London: Faber and Faber, 1975.

Powell, Claire. *The Meaning of Flowers: A Garland of Plant Lore and Symbolism from Popular Custom and Literature*. London: Jupiter, 1977.

Preminger, Alex, ed. *Princeton Encyclopedia of Poetry and Poetics*. Enl. ed. Princeton: Princeton University Press, 1974.

Quartermain, Peter. " 'Actual Word Stuff, Not Thoughts for Thoughts.' " *Credences*, n.s. 2, no. 1 (Summer 1982): 104–22.

Radford, E., and M. A. Radford. *Encyclopedia of Superstitions*. Ed. Christina Hole. Rev. ed. London: Hutchinson, 1961.

*Rossetti, Dante Gabriel, trans. *Dante and His Circle, with the Italian Poets Preceding Him (1100–1200–1300): A Collection of Lyrics*. Preface by W. M. Rossetti. Rev. ed. London: Ellis and Elvey, 1892.

Rydén, Mats. *Shakespearian Plant Names: Identifications and Interpretations*. Stockholm Studies in English, 43. Stockholm: Almqvist and Wiksell International, 1978.

(T)Sandars, Nancy K. *The Epic of Gilgamesh: An English Version*. Penguin Classics. Harmondsworth: Penguin, 1960.

Santillana, Giorgio de, and Hertha von Dechend. *Hamlet's Mill: An Essay on Myth and the Frame of Time*. Boston: Gambit, 1969.

Saroyan, Aram. "Red Postcard." [1972?]

Schimmel, Harold. "Zuk. Yehoash David Rex." L.Z. *Paideuma,* 559–69; *L.Z.: Man and Poet,* pp. 235–45.

(T)Shakespeare, William. *Complete Poems and Plays.* Ed. W. A. Neilson and C. J. Hill. New Cambridge Edition. Cambridge, Mass.: Houghton Mifflin/Riverside, 1942.

*Skeat, Walter W. *An Etymological Dictionary of the English Language.* Rev. ed. Oxford: Clarendon, 1963.

Smart, Christopher. *Rejoice in the Lamb: A Song from Bedlam.* Ed. William Force Stead. London: Jonathan Cape, 1939.

*Spenser, Edmund. *Spenser's "Faerie Queene."* Ed. J. C. Smith. 2 vols. Oxford: Clarendon, 1909.

Spevack, Marvin. *A Complete and Systematic Concordance to the Works of Shakespeare.* 9 vols. Hildesheim: Georg Olms, 1968–70.

*Spinoza, Baruch de. *Ethics and "De Intellectus Emendatione."* Trans. Andrew Boyle. Introduction by George Santayana. Everyman's Library. London: J. M. Dent, 1910.

Sterne, Laurence. *A Sentimental Journey through France and Italy, by Mr Yorick.* Ed. Gardner D. Stout, Jr. Berkeley and Los Angeles: University of California Press, 1967.

*Stevick, Robert D., ed. *One Hundred Middle English Lyrics.* Indianapolis: Bobbs-Merrill, 1964.

Taylor, Norman, ed. *Taylor's Encyclopedia of Gardening, Horticulture, and Landscape Design.* 4th ed. Boston: Houghton Mifflin, 1961.

Terrell, Carroll F. "Conversations with Celia." L.Z. *Paideuma,* 585–600.

———. "Louis Zukofsky: An Eccentric Profile." In *L.Z.: Man and Poet,* ed. Terrell, pp. 31–74.

———, ed. *Louis Zukofsky: Man and Poet.* Orono: National Poetry Foundation/University of Maine at Orono, 1979.

*Theophrastus. *Enquiry into Plants.* Trans. Arthur Hort. Loeb Classical Library. 2 vols. London: Heinemann; Cambridge, Mass.: Harvard University Press, 1916.

———. *De Causis Plantarum.* Trans. Benedict Einarson. Loeb Classical Library. Vol. 1. London: Heinemann; Cambridge, Mass.: Harvard University Press, 1976.

Tomlinson, Charles. "Objectivists: Zukofsky and Oppen, a Memoir." L.Z. *Paideuma,* 429–45; *L.Z.: Man and Poet,* ed. Terrell, pp. 79–95.

*U.S. Department of Agriculture, Agricultural Research Service. *Common Weeds of the United States.* New York: Dover, 1971. Reprint of *Selected Weeds of the United States.* Agricultural Handbook No. 366. USDA, 1970.

(T)Virgil (Publius Vergilius Maro). *The Works of Virgil: A Literal Translation.* Trans. A. Hamilton Bryce. Bohn's Classical Library. London: G. Bell, 1897.

*———. *Virgil.* Trans. H. Rushton Fairclough. Rev. ed. Loeb Classical Library. 2 vols. London: Heinemann; Cambridge, Mass.: Harvard University Press, 1935.

Weinberger, Eliot. "At the Death of Kenneth Rexroth." *Sagetrieb* 2, no. 3 (Winter 1983): 45–52.

Whitman, Walt. *"Leaves of Grass": Comprehensive Reader's Edition.* Ed. Harold
    W. Blodgett and Sculley Bradley. New York: Norton, 1965.
*Wilcockson, Colin. "Notes on Some Letters of David Jones." *Agenda* 14, no. 2
    (Summer 1976): 67–87.
Williams, William Carlos. *Paterson.* New York: New Directions, 1963.
————. *Selected Poems.* 2nd ed. New York: New Directions, 1968.
Wittgenstein, Ludwig. *Bemerkungen über die Grundlagen der Mathematik/Re-
    marks on the Foundations of Mathematics.* Ed. G. H. von Wright, R. Rees, and
    G.E.M. Anscombe. Trans. G.E.M. Anscombe. Oxford: Basil Blackwell, 1956.
(T)Xenophon. *The Persian Expedition.* Trans. Rex Warner. Penguin Classics.
    Harmondsworth: Penguin, 1949.
Zukofsky, Celia. *Music to Shakespeare's Pericles.* Vol. 2 of *Bottom: On Shake-
    speare* by Louis Zukofsky. Austin: Ark Press/Humanities Research Center,
    University of Texas, 1963.
————. *A Bibliography of Louis Zukofsky.* Los Angeles: Black Sparrow, 1969.
————. "1927–1972." L.Z. *Paideuma,* 371–72.
————. "Year by Year Bibliography of Louis Zukofsky." L.Z. *Paideuma,* 603–10.
————, comp. *American Friends.* New York: C.Z. Publications, 1979.
Zukofsky, Paul. Jacket Notes. *Niccolò Paganini: The 24 Caprices for Solo Violin
    (Complete).* Vanguard Cardinal Series, VCS-10093/4, 1970.

Untraced Secondary Sources

Field Flowers
Woodland Flowers

Index

All book or poem titles listed without an author's name are by Zukofsky. Entries for numbered flower poems are listed numerically under 80 Flowers.

University of Texas: Louis Zukofsky
Collection at, 3–5, 8, 12, 27, 32–33

Valentines: Zukofsky and, 64–65, 91, 118,
123, 125, 134, 135, 141, 194–96
Vegetius, P., 275, 279
Venus and Adonis (Shakespeare): and
allusions in #13 Venus's Looking-Glass,
175
Verbascum thapsus. See Great mullein; *80
Flowers*—#77 Weeds
Vinca minor. See Periwinkle; *80 Flowers*—
#10 Charlock Per Winkle
Violaceae. See Violets; *80 Flowers*—#30
Violet
Violets: botanical data, 203; and #11
Heart's Ease, 203
"Violets" (Herrick), 203–4, 258
Virgil, 240, 327, 359; *Aeneid,* 268–69;
Georgics, 21, 23, 25, 45, 268–69, 270,
292–94, 331; influence on #61 Bearded
Iris, 291–92

Watch and Ward (James), 202, 204
Weeds: list for *80 Flowers,* 20
"White Nights: A Sentimental Story from
the Diary of a Dreamer" (Dostoevsky),
352
Wilcockson, Colin: "Notes on Some
Letters of David Jones," 326
Williams, Floss, 256, 260
Williams, William Carlos: "Great Mullen,"
310–11; "Peer of the gods," 256;
"Queen Anne's Lace," 225–26
William Wetmore Story and His Friends
(James), 23, 202, 210, 221
Winter's Tale, The (Shakespeare), 89; and
allusions in #9 Privet, 171–74
Wistaria: proposed for poem and rejected,
22, 23
"With a Valentine," 64
Withwind: in #76 Vines, 303
Wittgenstein, Ludwig: *Remarks on the
Foundations of Mathematics,* 321–22
Woodward, Marcus, 81–82
Word play. *See as subheading*
Wordsworth, William, 269
Wyatt, Sir Thomas, 138–39

"Xenophanes": and Epigraph, 86–87
Xenophon: *Persian Expedition,* 193

Yannella, Philip, 341
Yaupon: botanical data, 333
Yucca: botanical data, 351; in #80 Zinnia,
333, 351; proposed for poem and
rejected, 23, 24
Yucca filamentosa. See Yucca

Zebra: in #80 Zinnia, 346–48
Zinnia: botanical data, 342–43
Zinnia elegans. See Zinnia; *80 Flowers*—
#80 Zinnia
Zukofsky, Celia, xiv, 3, 6–8, 10, 13, 18–19,
24, 27, 29, 65, 79, 85, 86–87, 94, 118,
119, 121, 168, 173, 235, 273, 276, 278,
324, 337, 344, 360; and *"A"*-12,
136–37; and *"A"*-13, 136; birthday,
66–67, 92, 318, 344; *80 Flowers*
dedicated to, 71, 82; and #3 Honesty,
124, 127, 134, 138; on Louis Zukofsky,
xiv, 84, 320, 324; "L.Z. Masque," 7, 57,
66, 140, 321; marriage to Louis
Zukofsky, 96; #1 Starglow as birthday
poem for, 92–93; on Paul Zukofsky,
320; #80 Zinnia dedicated to, 342, 350
Zukofsky, Chana: death of, 116; #2
Mountain Laurel dedicated to, 116–17
Zukofsky, Fanny: death of, 121
Zukofsky, Louis: on "A", 6; on "A",
151–52; on *Apollo 11* mission, 114;
background, xiii; birthday, 66–67, 116,
344; Celia Zukofsky on, xiv, 84, 320,
324; on Chaucer, 98–99; condensation
in his work, 23–24, 55, 63, 67, 73, 100,
129, 159, 172, 204, 242–43, 246, 256,
285, 328; Creeley on, xiii; death of, xiv,
3, 29, 31, 84; on De Leon, 128–29; and
his audience, 31–32; on his literary
sources, 221; and history, 355; on
history, 54–55; and horses, 13, 52, 70,
84–85, 101; indexes *"A"*, 24–25, 49,
240, 256; interest in grammatical
articles, 48–50; interest in space
program, 18, 113–15; Kenner
interviews, 22; Kenner on, 355; on
literary dedications, 116; on literary
influences, 146–47; marriage to Celia,
96; and New Year's greetings, 67–69,
122, 273, 317; on novels, 202; on #22
Bayberry, 22, 186–87; number play,
13–14; on Paul Zukofsky, 324; on
Pound, 146–47, 152; receives honorary

Designed by Martha Farlow

Composed by Village Typographers, Inc., in Sabon

Printed by Edwards Brothers, Inc., on 50-lb. Glatfelter B-16 and
bound in Joanna Arrestox A with Multicolor Antique endsheets

Funk & Wagnalls

Standard
(REG. U.S. PAT. OFF.)

Desk

Dictionary

Funk & Wagnalls

Standard _(REG. U.S. PAT. OFF.)

Desk

Dictionary

A Funk & Wagnalls Book
Published by Thomas Y. Crowell
New York

TABLE OF CONTENTS

PREFACE

This dictionary contains over 100,000 entries, offering comprehensive coverage of the general vocabulary and including many scientific and technical terms seldom found in dictionaries of comparable size. Based upon the considerably larger Standard College Dictionary, it represents an up-to-date survey of the English language, and includes, apart from the main body of vocabulary words, a wide selection of idioms and figurative expressions, as well as many common slang terms and meanings. It also includes a large number of usage notes, marked off in the dictionary proper by this symbol [◆], which give helpful information and counsel on a variety of traditionally troublesome words, such as *can* and *may*, *lay* and *lie*, *infer* and *imply*.

Following the main vocabulary section is *A Pronouncing Gazetteer*, including all places in the United States and Canada having a population of 5000 or over (based upon the latest census figures available), as well as all the countries of the world and the major foreign cities, and indicating political status, location, and, if appropriate, ZIP Code number. A separate section, *Biographies*, lists and pronounces the names of, and gives information about, people of the past and present who have distinguished themselves in the arts and sciences, in world affairs, or in other areas of endeavor. *Abbreviations*, which immediately follows the biographical section, is a comprehensive list of abbreviations and acronyms that one is most likely to encounter, whether in business practice or in everyday affairs.

Finally, the *Secretarial Handbook* includes sections on usage, punctuation, business correspondence, and forms of address that should be of considerable help not only to secretaries but to anyone who is sometimes puzzled by the complexities of English grammar and usage, or who is called upon to write an important business letter.

For a more complete account of these sections as well as other features of this book, and for valuable discussions of pronunciation, restrictive labels, etymologies, and synonyms and antonyms, the reader is urged to read the *Guide to This Dictionary* beginning on p. v.

The Editors

EDITORIAL STAFF

Funk & Wagnalls' Editorial Board for Dictionaries consists of Albert H. Marckwardt, Chairman, Professor of English and Linguistics, Princeton University; Frederic G. Cassidy, Professor of English, University of Wisconsin; S. I. Hayakawa, Professor of English, San Francisco State College; and James B. McMillan, Professor of English, University of Alabama. Each of these scholars has contributed an essay in his field of special competence to the *Guide to This Dictionary*. In addition, many other authorities in a variety of fields have given us the benefit of their specialized knowledge and advice in formulating the definitions that appear in this book.

Editor in Chief: Sidney I. Landau

General Editors: Sheila C. Brantley, Samuel Davis, Ruth Koenigsberg

Science Editor: Harold Ward

Geography Editor: Harold A. Rodgers, Jr.

Production Editor: Jack Doenias

Associate Editors: Veronica P. Collings, Alma E. Graham

Office Staff: Maxine Edelstein, Bruce Chalnick, Wendy Duveen, Seth Malin

Illustrations: Stephen J. Voorhies

GUIDE TO THIS DICTIONARY

The following explanatory material deals with the different kinds of information given in this dictionary and with their arrangement within each entry. A careful reading of the thirteen items discussed below, and of the essays on **Pronunciations, Level and Style Labels, Etymologies,** and **Synonyms** that begin on page vii, will help the reader use this dictionary effectively. Items 1–13 are listed in roughly the same order in which the information they describe appears in most individual entries:

1. The Main Entry	7. Collateral Adjectives
2. Pronunciations	8. Variant Forms
3. Parts of Speech	9. Cross-references
4. Inflected Forms	10. Etymologies
5. Definitions	11. Run-on Derivatives
6. Restrictive Labels	12. Usage Notes

13. Synonyms and Antonyms

1. The Main Entry

The main entry word or words have been printed in large, boldface type, set slightly into the left-hand margin so as to be easily found. Uncapitalized spellings precede capitalized forms, as **harlequin,** then **Harlequin.** Words spelled the same but different in meaning and origin are entered separately and differentiated by a superior figure, as **pink**[1] (color) and **pink**[2] (stab). Biographical entries, geographical entries, and abbreviations appear in separate alphabetical lists following the main vocabulary.

A center period is used to indicate division in main entry words, as **par·ti·cip·i·al.** In other boldface entries, such as run-on derivatives and variant forms, the center period is eliminated wherever the primary and secondary syllable stresses are marked, as **par'ti·cip'i·al·ly.** Phrasal entries, as **intelligence quotient,** are not divided when the elements are individually entered elsewhere.

2. Pronunciations

Pronunciations are shown in parentheses immediately following the boldface main entry, as **di·chot·o·my** (dī·kot′ə·mē). The pronunciation system used in this dictionary utilizes, with a few exceptions, the letters of the alphabet, combined with certain standard diacritical marks, such as the macron for the so-called "long vowels" (ā, ē, ī, ō, yōō). The "short vowels" have no diacritical marks. The breve is retained in the one symbol (oŏ), the vowel in *book,* to avoid confusion with the vowel in *pool,* for which the macron is used (ōō). The dieresis is used for one symbol (ä), and the circumflex for three (â, ô, û). The schwa (ə) is used for the unstressed neutral vowel, however spelled. This pronunciation key is based on phonemic principles to the extent that each symbol represents a single sound or closely associated cluster of sounds, and no sound is transcribed with more than one symbol.

The pronunciation key appears in full on p. xii and inside the front cover; an abbreviated key is given at the foot of every odd-numbered page in the main vocabulary section. For a fuller discussion of the treatment given pronunciation in this dictionary, see p. vii.

3. Parts of Speech

These are shown in italics following the pronunciation for main entries, and are abbreviated as follows: *n.* (noun), *v.* (verb), *pron.* (pronoun), *adj.* (adjective), *adv.* (adverb), *prep.* (preposition), *conj.* (conjunction), *interj.* (interjection). When more than one part of speech is entered under a main entry, the additional designations are run in and preceded by a boldface dash, as **cor·ner** (kôr′nər) *n.* . . . — *v.t.* . . . — *v.i.* . . . — *adj.* . . . .

Verbs used transitively are identified as *v.t.,* those intransitively as *v.i.;* those used both transitively and intransitively in all senses are designated *v.t. & v.i.*

4. Inflected Forms

These include the past tense, past participle, and present participle of verbs, the plural of nouns, and the comparative and superlative of adjectives and adverbs. Inflected forms are entered wherever there is some irregularity in spelling or form. They are shown in boldface type, with syllabication, immediately after the part-of-speech designation. Only the syllable affected is shown, unless ambiguity may occur, as **com·pute** (kəm·pyōot′) *v.t. & v.i.* **·put·ed, ·put·ing.** An inflected form that requires pronunciation or is alphabetically distant from the main entry will also be separately entered and pronounced in its proper vocabulary place.

Principal parts of verbs The order in which the principal parts are shown is past tense, past participle, and present participle, as **come** (kum) *v.i.* **came, come, com·ing.** Where the past tense and past participle are identical, only two forms are entered, as **bake** (bāk) *v.* **baked, bak·ing.** When alternative forms are given, the first form indicated is usually the one preferred, as **grov·el** (gruv′əl, grov′-) *v.i.* **grov·eled** or **·elled, grov·el·ing** or **·el·ling.** Principal parts entirely regular in formation — those that add *-ed* and *-ing* directly to the infinitive without spelling modification — are not shown.

Plurals of nouns Irregular forms are here preceded by the designation *pl.,* as **a·lum·nus** (ə·lum′nəs) *n. pl.* **·ni** (-nī); **co·dex** (kō′deks) *n. pl.* **co·di·ces** (kō′də·sēz, kod′ə-); **deer** (dir) *n. pl.* **deer.** When alternative plurals are given, the first shown is the preferred form, as **buf·fa·lo** (buf′ə·lō) *n. pl.* **·loes** or **·los; chrys·a·lis** (kris′ə·lis) *n. pl.* **chrys·a·lis·es** or **chry·sal·i·des** (kri·sal′ə·dēz).

Comparison of adjectives and adverbs The comparatives and superlatives of adjectives and adverbs are shown immediately after the part of speech when there is some spelling modification or a complete change of form, as **mer·ry** (mer′ē) *adj.* **·ri·er, ·ri·est; bad**[1] (bad) *adj.* **worse, worst; well**[2] (wel) *adv.* **bet·ter, best.**

5. Definitions

In entries for words having several senses, the definition appearing first is the one most frequently used. Successive definitions are listed, wherever possible, in order of declining frequency of use rather than according to semantic evolution. Each such definition is distinguished by a boldface numeral, the numbering starting anew after each part-of-speech designation when more than one sense follows. Closely related meanings, especially those within a specific field or area of study, are defined under the same number and set apart by boldface letters.

6. Restrictive Labels

No restrictive label is required for those general-purpose words and meanings, usable in any context, which make up the bulk of the English language as it is spoken and written throughout the world. Words or particular senses of words, however, which have any restriction of use are labeled. A number of different types of labels are used in this dictionary to indicate where, by whom, or in what context a particular word or expression is most commonly used. For a full discussion of **Level and Style Labels,** including the labels *Informal, Dial.* (for *dialectal*), *Slang,* and *Illit.* (for *illiterate*), see p. viii. The following are other types of labels found in this dictionary:

Currency Labels Both standard and nonstandard words may be in less than general currency. If these are included they are labeled *Rare, Archaic,* or *Obs.* (obsolete). (See the definitions of these words in the body of the dictionary.)

Locality Labels These identify the geographical region of the English-speaking world in which a word or meaning, either standard or nonstandard, is used exclusively or more characteristically than it is in other regions. (For example, *elevator* is labeled *U.S.*, while the synonymous *lift* is labeled *Brit.*)

Field Labels These identify the field of learning or of activity in which a word or sense belongs. (Some common examples are *Bot., Chem., Mil., Photog.* — see the list of abbreviations.) Because of the frequent overlapping between fields, however, these labels can be applied only broadly.

Foreign-language Labels These identify the source of words or phrases not fully naturalized into English. Because these retain the foreign spelling and pronunciation, though used in English context, they should be italicized when written. (Examples are *joie de vivre* labeled *French, Weltschmerz* labeled *German.*)

7. Collateral Adjectives

Because of extensive borrowing in English from Norman French and Medieval Latin, we find a good many English nouns which have adjectives closely connected with them in meaning, but not in form, such as *arm* and *brachial, horse* and *equine, dog* and *canine, day* and *diurnal,* etc. These functionally related adjectives are defined in this dictionary in their alphabetic place, but as an added convenience many of them are also shown with their associated nouns. Collateral adjectives follow the sense or senses of the noun to which they apply, and are introduced with a diamond symbol:

arm (ärm) *n.* **1.** *Anat.* **a** The upper limb of the human body. . . . ◆ Collateral adjective: *brachial.*

8. Variant Forms

Some words have more than one standard spelling or form, as *center, centre; algebraic, algebraical.* Sometimes, completely different forms have the same meaning, as *bachelor's-button* and *cornflower.* These variants are listed in two ways: (1) When the variant form is alphabetically close to the commoner form, it is entered with the main entry in boldface type, syllabicated, stressed, and, where necessary, pronounced; (2) When the variant is alphabetically distant, it is shown in italic print under the main entry, and is also listed in its proper alphabetic place with a cross-reference to the main entry.

bach·e·lor (bach′ə·lər, bach′lər) *n.* . . . **3.** A young knight serving under another's banner: also **bach′e·lor-at-arms′** . . . .
bas-re·lief (bä′ri·lēf′, bas′-) *n.* That type of sculpture in which the figures project . . . : also called *low relief.*

Forms that have some restricted usage are labeled accordingly, as **hon·or** . . . . Also *Brit.* **hon′our.**

9. Cross-references

Cross-references are directions to see another entry for additional information. The entry to be sought is generally indicated in small capital letters, as **car·a·cul** . . . See KARAKUL; **cor·po·ra** . . . Plural of CORPUS; **Vulgar Latin** See under LATIN.
Some entries are defined by citing another form:

cach·a·lot (kash′ə·lot, -lō) *n.* The sperm whale.
cou·gar (kōō′gər) *n.* The puma.
fog chamber *Physics* A cloud chamber.

Complete information will be found under the word or term used in the definition.
Cross-references are also used to indicate where more information may be found, or when an important semantic distinction might otherwise be missed, as **petit mal** . . . : distinguished from *grand mal*; **Brunhild.** . . . Compare BRUNNHILDE.
For information about cross-references used in the etymologies, see p. ix.

10. Etymologies

Etymologies are given in brackets at the end of each entry. For a full discussion of the treatment given etymology in this dictionary, see p. ix.

11. Run-on Derivatives

Words that are actually or apparently derived from other words by the addition or replacement of a suffix, and whose sense can be inferred from the meaning of the main word, are run on, in smaller boldface type, at the end of the appropriate main entries. The run-on entries are preceded by a heavy dash and followed by a part-of-speech designation. They are syllabicated and stressed, and, when necessary, a full or partial pronunciation is indicated:

in·sip·id (in·sip′id) *adj.* . . . — **in·si·pid·i·ty** (in′si·pid′ə·tē), in·sip′id·ness** *n.* — **in·sip′id·ly** *adv.*

12. Usage Notes

Special points of grammar and idiom, when essential to correct usage, are included, following a colon, after the particular sense of a word to which they apply, as **anx·ious** ... **3.** Intent; eagerly desirous: with *for* or the infinitive.... More extensive notes consisting of supplementary information on grammar, accepted usage, the relative status of variant forms, etc., are entered at the end of the relevant entries and prefaced with the symbol ◆. Examples may be found under the entries **Asiatic, gotten,** and **me.**

13. Synonyms and Antonyms

Extended discussions of the differentiation in shades of meaning within a group of related words are given at the end of relevant entries in paragraphed form. They are introduced by the abbreviation **Syn.** Since a word may have distinct synonyms for each of several senses, the discussions are numbered, where necessary, to accord with the numbering of relevant definitions in the preceding entry. In addition to the discussions, lists of synonyms and antonyms are entered in cases where the distinctions between the words in question are easily ascertained from the definitions. For a full discussion of the treatment given synonyms in this dictionary, see p. x.

Pronunciations by James B. McMillan

A pronunciation is correct when it is normally and unaffectedly used by cultivated people. Strictly, any pronunciation is correct when it serves the purposes of communication and does not call unfavorable attention to the speaker, but the user of a desk dictionary does not need or expect to find every pronunciation of every word that may be heard in the smallest, most isolated communities. He expects to find the pronunciations that he can use comfortably before educated audiences.

We do not have in the English-speaking world a standard of pronunciation like the standard specimens of meters, liters, feet, and gallons that national bureaus of standards keep to preserve and enforce uniformity. It would be technically simple to have a professional speaker record on magnetic tape his pronunciation of every word in a dictionary and to store the tapes in libraries where they could be heard, even in distant cities, by dialing the telephone number of a computer that would select and play back the pronunciation of any desired word. But choosing the model speaker would not be simple. Should he pronounce *forest* as it sounds in Boston? Or Chicago? Or Atlanta? Or Spokane? If he pronounced *dew* and *do* differently, would educated people who pronounce the two words alike change to conform? Or if he pronounced both (dōō), would educated people who distinguish the two words be willing to give up their distinction? Simple inanimate quart jars and foot rulers can easily be taken to a government bureau and compared with a standard measure, but pronunciations are articulations of sounds by individual human vocal organs, with all the diversity of human beings. One standard of correctness is impractical, unenforceable, impossible.

Correctness in pronunciation is so flexible and pronunciations are so varied that a desk dictionary cannot list nearly all the acceptable forms of even common words; for this reason the absence of a pronunciation, for example *said* as (sād), rhyming with *laid*, does not mean that the pronunciation is necessarily "incorrect," but simply that there is not space to record every minor-

ity practice. The editors do not include (bûr′ē) for *bury* (rhyming with *hurry*) because they have heard it very rarely, and not usually in cultivated speech. On the other hand, when a pronunciation is listed the dictionary user can be confident that the pronunciation is in actual use among educated people. Disagreements that arise because two people do not pronounce the key words alike cannot be settled; the fact that every user has to interpret the pronunciation symbols in terms of his own pronunciation of the key words makes each one, in a sense, his own standard.

Because words are listed in a dictionary as separate items, not as segments of a flow of speech, the pronunciations given are for words pronounced in isolation; for example the pronunciation (fāt) is what one would say in answering "How do you pronounce the word spelled *f-e-t-e*?" In the stream of speech, many words, particularly pronouns, articles, and auxiliaries, occur in shortened or changed form when they are weakly stressed. Thus the words (tel), (him), (hē), (haz), (tōō), (sē), (hûr) may appear in sentence form as (tel·im·ē·has·tə·sē·ər). The changed pronunciations that actual utterance produces are not normally listed.

Syllabication in pronunciation follows, in general, the breaks heard in speech, rather than the conventional division of the boldface entry, as **hid·ing** (hī′ding), **lat·er** (lā′tər), **of·fi·cial** (ə·fish′əl). Syllable boundaries are sometimes impossible to set with certainty and are sometimes variable. Thus words like **met·ric** (met′rik) and **cad·re** (kad′rē) are divided between the consonants, although many people pronounce both consonants in the second syllable (me′trik) and (ka′drē), as the contrast between *metric* and *met Rick* will show.

Three levels of stress are indicated in the pronunciations. Syllables with weakest stress are not marked; every word with two or more syllables has one primary stress marked, as *editor* (ed′it·ər); and words with three or more syllables frequently have a secondary stress marked by a light symbol, as *acceleration* (ak·sel′ə·rā′shən), or a secondary stress indicated simply by a vowel, as in the final syllable of *ameliorate* (ə·mēl′yə·rāt). These three levels correspond to the primary, tertiary (*not* secondary), and weak levels in the four-stress system commonly used by linguists. The secondary level of the four-stress system is not used here because it occurs only in phrases or other word groups, not in single words.

Because a dictionary records and reports the pronunciations of educated people, and all educated people do not pronounce identically, a dictionary must list variant forms of thousands of words. When two or more pronunciations are indicated for a word, the one that the editors believe must frequent in the northern and western sections of the United States is listed first, but other pronunciations are equally reputable. (The dictionary does not list socially substandard pronunciations, no matter how common they may be.)

Pronunciation differences are of seven principal kinds:
(1) Different consonants may be used in the same word; e.g. some people pronounce *exit* (ek′sit), others (eg′zit); some pronounce *blouse* (blous), others (blouz).
(2) Different vowels may be used in the same word; e.g. for some people the word *lever* rhymes with *clever* (klev′ər), for others it rhymes with *beaver* (bē′vər); the first syllable of *economics* may rhyme with *peck* (ek·ə·nom′iks) or with *peak* (ē·kə·nom′iks).
(3) A word may have different syllables stressed; e.g. *altimeter* (al·tim′ə·tər) or (al′tə·mē′tər), and *abdomen* (ab′də·mən) or (ab·dō′mən).
(4) The same consonant may be used in a word, but it may be articulated very differently; e.g. the /t/* in *metal*, or *writer*, or *winter*, or the /r/ in *very* (sometimes humorously written *veddy*).

*The symbols printed between virgules represent phonemes.

(5) The same vowel may be used in a word, but it may be articulated very differently; e.g. the /ô/ in *raw*, the /ou/ in *house*, the /ī/ in *ice*, and the /ä/ in *park*, which have wide regional variations.

(6) Although all dialects of American English seem to have the same twenty-four consonants, some have fewer vowels than others; e.g., the contrasts made in some regions between *morning* and *mourning*, *cot* and *caught*, *burred* and *bird*, and *Cary*, *Kerry*, and *Carrie* are not made in other regions.

(7) The same vowel or consonant may not occur in the same positions in all varieties; e.g., some speakers pronounce /y/ before /ōō/ in *cute* (kyōōt) but not in *new* (nōō) or *due* (dōō) or *tune* (tōōn), while others of equal education pronounce these words (nyōō), (dyōō), and (tyōōn). Some speakers have /zh/ normally between vowels, as in *pleasure* (plezh′ər) and *vision* (vizh′ən) but not at the ends of words, so that *garage* is both (gə·räzh′) and (gə·raj′).

Some differences in pronunciation can be correlated with geography, and others are purely personal. No dictionary can pick one pronunciation of *dog*, or *either*, or *room* and ignore other pronunciations of equal repute. The principal variants must be acknowledged. For rare words, such as terms in the arts and sciences that are not learned vernacularly, analogy and the pattern of source languages provide the pronunciations listed.

Two methods of providing variants are used, (1) multiple pronunciations, as *fog* (fog, fôg), and (2) variable symbols keyed to common words, such as /â/ as in *dare, fair*; it is assumed that when a dictionary user looks up *parterre* and finds (pär·târ′) he will pronounce the first syllable to rhyme with *bar* and the second syllable to rhyme with *dare, air*, since /ä/ is keyed to the word *father*, and /â/ is keyed to the words *dare, air*. The dictionary does not tell the user how to pronounce the key words, assuming that they represent stable basic patterns.

When a variant pronunciation differs only in part from the first pronunciation recorded, only the differing syllable or syllables are shown, provided there is no possibility of misinterpretation, as **eq·ua·ble** (ek′wə·bəl, ē′kwə-).

Phrasal entries of two or more words are not pronounced if the individual elements are separately entered in proper alphabetic place.

Sometimes a word will differ in its pronunciation depending on its use as a noun, verb, etc., or in some particular sense. The differing pronunciations are shown immediately after the entry word, with the applications clearly indicated, as follows:

ad·dress (ə·dres′; *for n. defs. 2, 3, also* ad′res)
re·ject (*v.* ri·jekt′; *n.* rē′jekt)

A few foreign words occur with sufficient frequency in English to require dictionary entry; as their use increases they usually become adapted to English pronunciation patterns. For the dictionary user who speaks the language from which a word is imported, no pronunciation is necessary; he recognizes the word or can pronounce it from his knowledge of the spelling of the foreign language. However, the dictionary user who does not speak the foreign language may wish to pronounce a word in a recognizable approximation of its native form. Such words are respelled with the English vowels and consonants that are closest to the foreign phonemes, plus a handful of symbols for French and German sounds that have no counterparts in English. Thus the French word *chef-d'oeuvre* is respelled (shedoe′vr′), which warns that a non-English vowel occurs in the second syllable and that the /r/ at the end is voiceless. It is assumed that the consonants /sh/, /d/, and /v/, and the vowel /e/ will be reasonably similar to the corresponding (but not identical) French sounds, and that the stress on the second syllable will be lighter than English primary stress.

Level and Style Labels by Frederic G. Cassidy

The language is often thought of as existing on two "levels of usage," the standard and the nonstandard. This distinction rests on the fact that, though there is nothing intrinsically higher or lower, better or worse in one word than in another *considered as words* (language signals), every speech community nevertheless responds more or less favorably toward individual words and senses on the basis of association, habit, imposed value judgments, and the like. The language of cultivation, being that normally used by the leading part of the community, and that most widely understood within the English-speaking world, has high prestige and is considered to be of the "upper" level. This is *Standard English*. In contrast, the language of limited, local, or uncultivated use is nonstandard and of "lower" level. The following scheme represents the relative positions of various types of discourse and the corresponding labels used in this dictionary.

Standard English	Throughout the English-speaking world (No label)
	Characteristic of a national division of English Labels: *U.S., Brit., Scot., Austral.*, etc.
	Characteristic of a broad region of a national division Labels: *Southern U.S., SW U.S.*, etc.
	Characteristic of general informal use Label: *Informal*
Nonstandard English	Used within a small geographical area, and often rural and traditional Label: *Dial.*
	Used to express a humorous, racy, and irreverent attitude, often within a particular group Label: *Slang*
	Used within a group in connection with a common activity, trade, or profession (No label or a field label)
	Used by the least educated, and considered incorrect by most users of Standard English Label: *Illit.*

The dictionary concentrates on standard words and meanings; only those nonstandard ones are included which have wide currency or which deserve notice for some other reason (e.g., their relationship to standard words). Lines of distinction cannot always be sharply drawn between the various types of nonstandard words or meanings. It is sometimes necessary also to combine the labels (e.g., *Brit. Dial., U.S. Slang*) for precise discriminations.

In addition, since the response to words depends in part upon the stylistic context in which they are used, the dictionary maker must take this response into consideration in applying labels. Two distinct styles are generally recognized: Formal and Informal.*

Formal style is that appropriate to all public and serious expression; to spoken use in legislative assemblies, in courts, in the pulpit; to "belles lettres" or artistic literature; to legal and scientific writing. Because its users belong to the cultivated and literate part of the public it tends to be more deliberate, precise, discriminating, and orderly than the casual usage normal to everyday discourse, even that carried on by this same cultivated group.

---

*The label *Colloq.* (colloquial — see its definition in the body of the dictionary) is now so widely misunderstood by the public as to be no longer serviceable and is therefore not used in this dictionary.

Informal style, that employed by most people a great part of the time in both speaking and writing, differs from the formal in being less consciously controlled, less precise, less complex and compact, less careful in diction — though quite acceptable within its sphere, and more appropriate to relaxed situations than formal style would be.

In pronunciation the formal style is more controlled, with conscious use of prosodic features (pitch, pause, stress) and with clear articulation and syllabication (though without restressing, spelling-pronunciation, or other distortions). In grammar it is conservative; in sentence form it has more variety and range than everyday discourse has. Its vocabulary is far broader and richer, demanding sharper distinctions and more sensitive choice. In overall structure it is orderly, consciously articulated, intellectually directed.

In pronunciation the informal style is easy, relaxed; it admits a degree of slurring and ellipsis, though not to the point of becoming unclear. It makes fuller use of voice qualifiers (indicating emotional attitudes) than does formal style; it is therefore far more personal. In grammar it is less conservative, reflecting contemporary tendencies in the development of the language. In sentence form it is less complex and varied, and in vocabulary less discriminating, than is formal style: it experiments with neologisms, slang, and the livelier words of current vogue. It is given to abbreviation and contraction. In overall structure it is likely to be casual, not closely knit, additive rather than integral.

New scientific and literary words are apt to enter the sphere of standard usage at once; new popular words, by contrast, tend to remain nonstandard for a time — perhaps always; but they may and sometimes do rapidly gain status and enter the standard sphere.

Since "formal" and "informal" properly describe *styles* of discourse, the application of one of these terms to an individual word or meaning indicates only that such an item is appropriate to the one style or the other. If a word of one style is employed in a context not its own, it will give some effect of its own style to that context. Further, since no meaning is irrevocably fixed, the connotation of a word repeatedly used in a stylistic context not its own may change.

A word or meaning labeled *Informal* is therefore one which, though as well known as any other standard one, is less acceptable (i.e., less accepted at any given time) for formal use than for informal. The actual usage of cultivated writers and speakers is the only valid test of such status. Words not labeled are appropriate to formal use.

The "levels" and "styles" do not coincide exactly. Their relationship may best be expressed by the following diagram, in which the sphere of Standard English is represented by a circle, the nonstandard lying outside it.

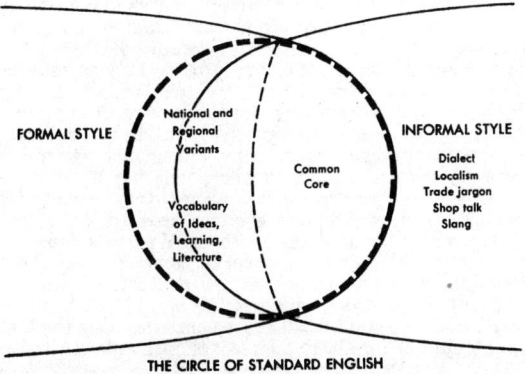

THE CIRCLE OF STANDARD ENGLISH

The circle is broken to indicate that nonstandard usages sometimes enter and become standard, and that formerly standard words also drop out into nonstandard usage or disappear altogether. Elliptical lines to left and right, drawn through the circle of Standard English, set off those parts that are appropriate respectively to formal and informal style. The Common Core comprises those words and senses which are used in all types of English.

Distinctions within the levels of language can be made nowadays with a considerable degree of objectivity. Distinctions of style, on the other hand, are partly esthetic and subjective. In every case an accurate application of labels must rest on the investigation of the situations in which any word or sense is actually used, the kind of people who do or do not use it, and the kind of response (apart from that of its denotative meaning) which it is likely to elicit in any linguistic community. Ultimately, however, it must also depend to some extent upon the judgment of the lexicographer.

Etymologies by Albert H. Marckwardt

Etymology is the systematic study of word origins, or in a particular sense the facts relating to the derivation or formation of a word. To illustrate, *etymology* is a borrowing of French *étymologie*, which developed from Latin *etymologia*, itself a borrowing from the Greek. The Greek form may be divided into two parts, *etymon* a form of the adjective "true" and *logos* "word, study, account." Thus we have the elements which entered into the formation of this word and the languages through which it passed into English.

The etymology of a word is given after the definition. It appears in square brackets, and precedes the boldface listing of derivative forms. The following three symbols are used: < "derived from"; + "and" or "combined with"; ? "possible." Abbreviations used in the etymologies are given inside the front cover.

Native words that were present in the earliest period of the language (450–1050) are shown in their Old English form.

> **bed·rid·den . . .** [Earlier *bedrid* < OE *bedrida* < *bed* bed + *rida* rider]

For borrowed words, the immediate source is given first, followed by those intermediate forms and languages which show significant changes.

> **pi·ra·nha . . .** [< Pg. (Brazilian) < Tupi, toothed fish]

If the specific language of origin cannot be determined but the general provenance is known, a linguistic family or a geographical area is indicated as the source.

> **ba·nan·a . . .** [< Sp. < native African name]

Words of unknown or uncertain origin are so marked. If there is a Middle English form for a word of obscure origin, it is cited. Even though the origin of a word cannot be determined, it is sometimes possible to give cognate forms from related languages. Be careful to note the difference between the mark < which means "derived from" and the abbreviation *cf.* which indicates a cognate relationship but not a derivation.

> **bud . . .** [ME *budde*; origin uncertain]
> **gloat . . .** [Cf. ON *glotta* to grin]

In order to avoid repetition and to present as much information as possible within a limited space, cross-references are occasionally used to direct attention to main entries where detailed information may be found.

> **de·cep·tion . . .** [See DECEIVE.]
> **de·ceive . . .** [< OF < L < *de-* away, down + *capere* to take]

The etymologies of words representing various types of combinations of free and bound forms (*wildcat, prejudge, goodness*) may be found under the main entries for *wild, cat; pre-, judge; good, -ness.*

Etymologies of a somewhat unusual character, especially those connecting words with particular people, places, or events are recorded with additional notes explaining the historic background of the word. For examples of this see *buncombe, gerrymander, knickerbocker.* Acronyms and blends are shown by placing the portions of the source words which have survived in the new formation in distinctive type. Back formations and instances of folk etymology are so labeled. See *donate, legislate, woodchuck.*

A knowledge of etymology can be useful in many ways. If, for example, those words which have come into English from any one language are considered as a group, they often reveal much about the nature of the cultural impact of that language and the people who speak it upon English. The fact that so many of our mineralogical terms come from German suggests the preeminence of that nation in the development of the science and our indebtedness to its scientists. The same might be said with respect to the Italian origin of our musical terminology. The common and intimate character of many of the Scandinavian borrowings in English tells us something of the nature of the relationship between the Norse and the English during the tenth and eleventh centuries.

It may also be true that in certain instances a knowledge of the etymology of a word may give the individual speaker or writer a surer sense of its meaning and use. A word like *supercilious* would seem, at least, to be more vivid to someone who can connect it with raised eyebrows than to the person for whom it is merely a polysyllable with a general implication of superiority of attitude. The word *equinox* will be employed with a greater feeling of certainty by one who connects the component parts of the word with the simple facts behind them.

A note of warning is called for, however. Etymology, informative and interesting though it may be, is not a valid criterion of present meaning or determiner of use. Meaning is determined by present usage; the meanings assigned to the words included in this dictionary were determined by a careful and systematic examination of their use in actual context.

The fact that *dilapidated* contains a form of *lapis* "stone" does not signify that this word can be applied only to stone structures. The word *etymology* itself is an excellent illustration of this point. Despite the fact that its first element is the neuter form of *etymos* "true," the etymology of a word is not the sole determiner of a single "true" or correct meaning, however much light it may shed upon aspects of its significance.

Synonyms *by S. I. Hayakawa*

The English language is unusually rich in synonyms and near-synonyms. This richness is due to the fact that the vocabulary of English, a language especially hospitable to loan-words, is drawn from many sources. The vocabulary of Anglo-Saxon, already containing loanwords from Celtic, Latin, and Scandinavian, was just about doubled after the Norman Conquest by borrowings from French, to form the Middle English vocabulary. From the sixteenth century on, with the revival of classical learning, there was vast borrowing from Latin and Greek. Wherever English-speaking people have subsequently gone, in war, travel, or colonization, they have added new words to the language, and they continue to do so today. Thus, one may give a *speech* or *talk*

(Anglo-Saxon words), a *lecture* or *address* or *harangue* (French words), an *oration* (Latin), or a *homily* (Greek). One may live on a wide and open *plain* (Old French), *steppe* (Russian), *prairie* (French), *tundra* (Lapp), *pampas* (South American Indian), or *savanna* (Spanish). A person may adhere to a *teaching* (Anglo-Saxon), a *doctrine* (French), a *tenet* (Latin), a *dogma* (Greek). Some words were borrowed more than once, at different times and in different forms, like *warden* and *warranty* (Norman French) as compared with *guardian* and *guarantee* (Central French); like *loyal* and *legal*, *royal* and *regal*, *fancy* and *fantasy*, *count* and *compute*, *gentle* and *genteel*, *priest* and *presbyter*. Some of these "doublets" are alike in meaning, some are quite different.

Often the borrowings were in a strict sense unnecessary; many that remain today are simply relics of the sixteenth-century fad of embellishing one's speech and writing with Latinisms. Certainly it is possible to talk about *kissing* without using the word *osculatory*, about *day* without *diurnal*. Nevertheless, the availability of foreign and learned vocabularies, even if they partly duplicate the native vocabulary, is a tremendous asset to any language. An advanced civilization needs, in addition to a language of everyday life (from which emerges the language of poetry), a language for law and social organization and the discussion of policy, and an even more abstract language for scientific and philosophical discourse. These many distinct needs are more easily met by a language that has had a long history of borrowing than by a language (like Gaelic) whose speakers insist on a fanatical "purity" of vocabulary, such as can only result in a poverty of things to talk about.

Are there any *exact* synonyms? The general semanticists, who assert that "no word ever has exactly the same meaning twice," would seem to assert that a word cannot even be synonymous with itself. What they mean is that the word *apple*, for example, cannot be applied twice to *exactly* the same referent, because every apple is different from every other apple, and because each apple is itself changing from moment to moment. However, in a dictionary we are concerned not so much with referents as with *verbal* equivalences: what word or phrase or circumlocution can serve as an equivalent for the word defined. Thus, *entire* means "having no part missing; whole; complete." Insofar as certain words can be substituted for others without affecting the meaning of a sentence, one can indeed speak of exact synonyms. "The *entire* (*whole, complete*) cast was invited to the party." The test for exact synonymy, then, is interchangeability. Despite Hilaire Belloc's haughty distinction, "what Anglo-Saxons call a *foreword*, but gentlemen a *preface*," these terms are also genuinely interchangeable in most contexts. But interchangeability in certain contexts does not mean interchangeability in all. "The cast is now *complete*" — not *whole*, or *entire*. A skirmish may be a *preface* to a battle, but not a *foreword*.

Hence interchangeability is by no means the whole story on synonyms. What are treated as synonyms in this dictionary are more often words that point to the same facts but convey different attitudes on the part of the speaker. An individual's regard for himself may be termed *egotism*, *conceit*, or *self-esteem*, depending on whether or not the speaker approves of it. Other synonyms point to similar actions or events, but in different contexts or applications: a *journey* is usually by land, a *voyage* by water; a short journey, whether by land or water, is a *trip*; an *excursion* is a short trip (usually for pleasure) from which one soon returns to a starting point; a military excursion is a *sortie*. We *accompany* our equals, *attend* those whom we serve, *conduct* those whom we guide, *escort* those whom we protect, except for merchant ships, which we *convoy*. It would be simpler if *go with* could be used in all these contexts. But the language would be infinitely poorer if these shades of meaning, expressive of innumerable nuances of human relationships, attitudes, and perceptions, were to be lost.

Occupational and regional differences also account for many synonyms. Is a *loch* a *lake*? Is an *arroyo* a *dry wash*? Is a *billabong* the same as an *oxbow*? What is the difference between the *headmaster* of a school and a *principal*, between a *dining room* and a *mess*, between being *cashiered, disbarred, unfrocked,* and *drummed out*? Words

not only point to things and events and ideas; they also advertise our social affiliations and reinforce our self-concepts. It is as important for a sailor to refer to a privy as a *head* as it is for him to wear his uniform; indeed, his nautical vocabulary is part of his uniform. The richness of English synonymy attests to the variety of adventures of both body and mind encountered by speakers of English in many climes over many centuries.

PRONUNCIATION KEY

The primary stress mark (ʹ) is placed after the syllable bearing the heavier stress or accent; the secondary stress mark (ˊ) follows a syllable having a somewhat lighter stress, as in com·men·da·tion (kom′en·daʹshen).

a	add, map	m	move, seem	u	up, done		
ā	ace, rate	n	nice, tin	û(r)	urn, term		
â(r)	care, air	ng	ring, song	yōō	use, few		
ä	palm, father						
b	bat, rub	o	odd, hot	v	vain, eve		
ch	check, catch	ō	open, so	w	win, away		
d	dog, rod	ô	order, jaw	y	yet, yearn		
		oi	oil, boy	z	zest, muse		
e	end, pet	ou	out, now	zh	vision, pleasure		
ē	even, tree	ōō	pool, food				
f	fit, half	o͝o	took, full	ə	the schwa, an un-stressed vowel representing the sound spelled		
g	go, log				*a* in *above*		
h	hope, hate	p	pit, stop		*e* in *sicken*		
i	it, give	r	run, poor		*i* in *clarity*		
ī	ice, write	s	see, pass		*o* in *melon*		
		sh	sure, rush		*u* in *focus*		
j	joy, ledge	t	talk, sit				
k	cool, take	th	thin, both				
l	look, rule	t͟h	this, bathe				

The schwa (ə) varies widely in quality from a sound close to the (u) in *up* to a sound close to the (i) in *it* as heard in pronunciations of such words as *ballot, custom, landed, horses*.

The (r) in final position as in *star* (stär) and before a consonant as in *heart* (härt) is regularly indicated in the respellings, but pronunciations without (r) are unquestionably reputable. Standard British is much like the speech of Eastern New England and the Lower South in this feature.

In a few words, such as *button* (butʹn) and *sudden* (sudʹn), no vowel appears in the unstressed syllable because the (n) constitutes the whole syllable.

FOREIGN SOUNDS

à   as in French *ami, patte*. This is a vowel midway in quality between (a) and (ä).

œ   as in French *peu*, German *schön*. Round the lips for (ō) and pronounce (ā).

ü   as in French *vue*, German *grün*. Round the lips for (ōō) and pronounce (ē).

ᴋʜ   as in German *ach*, Scottish *loch*. Pronounce a strongly aspirated (h) with the tongue in position for (k) as in *cool* or *keep*.

ṅ   This symbol indicates that the preceding vowel is nasal. The nasal vowels in French are œṅ (*brun*), aṅ (*main*), äṅ (*chambre*), ôṅ (*dont*).

ʹ   This symbol indicates that a preceding (l) or (r) is voiceless, as in French *fin-de-siècle* (fan·de·syeʹkl') or *fiacre* (fyàʹkr'); that a preceding (y) is pronounced consonantly in a separate syllable followed by a slight schwa sound, as in French *fille* (fēʹy'); or that a consonant preceding a (y) is palatalized, as in Russian *oblast* (ôʹblesty').

NOTE ON THE ACCENTUATION OF FOREIGN WORDS

Many languages do not employ stress in the manner of English; only an approximation can be given of the actual situation in such languages. As it is not possible to reproduce the tones of Chinese in a work of this kind, Chinese names have been here recorded with primary stress on each syllable and may be so pronounced. Japanese and Korean have been shown without stress and may be pronounced with a level accent throughout. French words are shown convention-ally with a primary stress on the last syllable; however, this stress tends to be evenly divided among the syllables (except for those that are completely unstressed), with slightly more force and higher pitch on the last syllable.

TABLE OF ENGLISH SPELLINGS

FOLLOWING is a list of words exemplifying the possible spellings for the sounds of English. The sounds represented by these spellings are shown in the pronunciation symbols used in this dictionary, followed by their equivalents in the International Phonetic Alphabet.

DICTIONARY KEY	IPA SYMBOL	EXAMPLES
a	æ	cat, plaid, calf, laugh
ā	eɪ,e	mate, bait, gaol, gauge, pay, steak, skein, weigh, prey
â(r)	ɛ,er	dare, fair, prayer, where, bear, their
á	a	bar, ask, cot (a vowel midway in quality between [æ] and [ɑ], used in some regional American speech)
ä	ɑ	dart, ah, sergeant, heart
b	b	boy, rubber
ch	tʃ	chip, batch, righteous, bastion, structure
d	d	day, ladder, called
e	ɛ	many, aesthete, said, says, bet, steady, heifer, leopard, friend, foetid
ē	i	Caesar, quay, scene, meat, see, seize, people, key, ravine, grief, phoebe, city
f	f	fake, coffin, cough, half, phase
g	g	gate, beggar, ghoul, guard, vague
h	h	hot, whom
hw	hwʍ,	whale
i	ɪ	pretty, been, tin, sieve, women, busy, guilt, lynch
ī	aɪ	aisle, aye, sleight, eye, dime, pie, sigh, guile, buy, try, lye
j	dʒ	edge, soldier, modulate, rage, exaggerate, joy
k	k	can, accost, saccharine, chord, tack, acquit, king, talk, liquor
l	l	let, gall
m	m	drachm, phlegm, palm, make, limb, grammar, condemn
n	n	gnome, know, mnemonic, note, banner, pneumatic
ng	ŋ	sink, ring, meringue
o	ɑ, ɒ	watch, pot
ō	ou,o	beau, yeoman, sew, over, soap, roe, oh, brooch, soul, though, grow
ô	ɔ	ball, balk, fault, dawn, cord, broad, ought
oi	ɔɪ	poison, toy
ou	aʊ	out, bough, cow
o͞o	u	rheum, drew, move, canoe, mood, group, through, fluke, sue, fruit
o͝o	ʊ	wolf, foot, could, pull
p	p	map, happen
r	r	rose, rhubarb, marry, diarrhea, wriggle
s	s	cite, dice, psyche, saw, scene, schism, mass
sh	ʃ	ocean, chivalry, vicious, pshaw, sure, schist, prescience, nauseous, shall, pension, tissue, fission, potion
t	t	walked, thought, phthisic, ptarmigan, tone, Thomas, butter
th	θ	thick
th	ð	this, bathe
u	ʌ	some, does, blood, young, sun
yo͞o	ju,ɪu	beauty, eulogy, queue, pew, ewe, adieu, view, fuse, cue, youth, yule
û(r)	ɝ r, ɚ	yearn, fern, err, girl, worm, journal, burn, guerdon, myrtle
v	v	of, Stephen, vise, flivver
w	w	choir, quilt, will
y	j	onion, hallelujah, yet
z	z	was, scissors, xylophone, zoo, muzzle
zh	ʒ	rouge, pleasure, incision, seizure, glazier
ə	ə	above, fountain, darken, clarity, parliament, cannon, porpoise, vicious, locus
ər	ər, ɚ	mortar, brother, elixir, donor, glamour, augur, nature, zephyr

Funk & Wagnalls

Standard
(REG. U.S. PAT. OFF.)

Desk

Dictionary

A

a, A (ā) *n. pl.* **a's** or **as, A's** or **As, aes** (āz) **1.** The first letter of the English alphabet. **2.** Any sound represented by the letter *a*. — *symbol* **1.** Primacy in class. **2.** A substitute for the numeral 1. **3.** *Music* **a** One of a series of tones, the sixth in the natural diatonic scale of C, or the first note in the related minor scale. **b** A written note representing this tone. **c** The scale built upon A. **4.** *Chem.* Argon (symbol A).

a¹ (ə, *stressed* ā) *indefinite article* or *adj.* In each; to each; for each: one dollar *a* bushel. [OE *on, an* in, on, at]

a² (ə, *stressed* ā) *indefinite article* or *adj.* One; any; some; each: expressing singleness, unity, etc., more or less indefinitely. It is used: **1.** Before a noun expressing an individual object or idea: *a* bird; *a* hope. **2.** Before an abstract noun used concretely: to show *a* kindness. **3.** Before a collective noun: *a* crowd. **4.** Before a proper noun denoting a type: He is *a* Hercules in strength. **5.** Before plural nouns with *few, great many,* or *good many: a* few books. **6.** After *on, at,* or *of,* denoting oneness, sameness: birds of *a* feather. ◆ Before vowel sounds the form becomes *an*. See note under AN¹. [Reduced form of AN¹ used before consonant sounds]

a-¹ *prefix* In; on; at: *aboard, asleep, agog, agoing.* [OE *on, an* in, on, at]

a-² *prefix* Up; on; away: *arise, abide.* [OE *ā-* up, on, away]

a-³ *prefix* Of; from: *athirst, akin, anew.* [OE *of* off, of]

a-⁴ *prefix* **1.** Without; not: *achromatic.* **2.** Apart from; unconcerned with: *amoral.* [Reduced form of AN-¹]

a-⁵ Reduced var. of AB-¹.

a-⁶ Reduced var. of AD-.

aard·vark (ärd′värk′) *n.* A burrowing, ant-eating African mammal. [< Afrikaans < Du. *aarde* earth + *vark* pig]

aard·wolf (ärd′woolf′) *n.* A hyenalike mammal of Africa. [< Afrikaans < Du. *aarde* earth + *wolf* wolf]

Aar·on (âr′ən, ar′ən) The first high priest of the Hebrews, older brother of Moses. *Ex.* xxviii 1–4.

ab-¹ *prefix* Off; from; away: *absolve, abduct, abrogate.* Also: *a-* before *m, p, v,* as in *avocation; abs-* before *c, t,* as in *abscess, abstract.* [< L < *ab* from]

ab-² Var. of AD-.

Ab (äb) *n.* The eleventh month of the Hebrew year. See (Hebrew) CALENDAR.

ab·a·ca (ab′ə·kä, ä′bə·kä′) *n.* **1.** A banana plant of the Philippines. **2.** The inner fiber of this plant, used for cordage. Also **ab′a·ka.** [< Tagalog]

a·back (ə·bak′) *adv. Naut.* Back against the mast: said of sails so blown by the wind. — **taken aback** Disconcerted, as by a sudden check. [OE *on bæc* on or to the back]

ab·a·cus (ab′ə·kəs) *n. pl.* **·cus·es** or **·ci** (-sī) **1.** A calculator with sliding counters. **2.** *Archit.* A slab forming the top of a capital. [< L < Gk. *abax* counting table]

a·baft (ə·baft′, ə·bäft′) *Naut. adv.* Toward the stern; aft. — *prep.* Further aft than; astern of. [OE < *on* on, at + *be* by + *æftan* aft, back]

ab·a·lo·ne (ab′ə·lō′nē) *n.* An edible shellfish having a shell lined with mother-of-pearl. [< Am. Sp.]

a·ban·don (ə·ban′dən) *v.t.* **1.** To give up wholly; desert; forsake. **2.** To surrender or give over: with *to.* **3.** To yield (oneself) without restraint, as to an emotion. — *n.* Utter surrender to one's feelings or natural impulses. [< OF *abandoner* < *a bandon* under one's control] — **a·ban′don·er** *n.* — **a·ban′don·ment** *n.*

a·ban·doned (ə·ban′dənd) *adj.* **1.** Deserted; forsaken. **2.** Unrestrained. **3.** Profligate; shameless.

a·base (ə·bās′) *v.t.* **a·based, a·bas·ing** To lower in position, rank, prestige, or estimation; cast down; humble. [< LL *abassare* to lower] — **a·bas·ed·ly** (ə·bā′sid·lē) *adv.* — **a·bas′ed·ness** *n.* — **a·base′ment** *n.* — **a·bas′er** *n.*

a·bash (ə·bash′) *v.t.* To deprive of self-possession; disconcert; make ashamed or confused. [< AF < OF *esbaïr* to astonish] — **a·bash·ed·ly** (ə·bash′id·lē) *adv.* — **a·bash′ment** *n.*

a·bate (ə·bāt′) *v.* **a·bat·ed, a·bat·ing** *v.t.* **1.** To make less; reduce in quantity, value, force, or intensity. **2.** To deduct. **3.** *Law* To do away with (a nuisance); annul (a writ). — *v.i.* **4.** To become less, as in strength or degree. **5.** *Law* To fail; become void. — **Syn.** See ANNUL, DECREASE. [< OF *abatre* to beat down] — **a·bat·a·ble** (ə·bā′tə·bəl) *adj.* — **a·bat′er** *n.* — **a·bate′ment** *n.*

ab·ba·cy (ab′ə·sē) *n. pl.* **·cies** The office, term of office, dignity, or jurisdiction of an abbot.

ab·bé (ab′ā, *Fr.* à·bā′) *n.* **1.** In France, a title given to a priest or other cleric. **2.** An abbot. [< F]

ab·bess (ab′is) *n.* The female superior of a community of nuns connected with an abbey. [ME < OF *abbesse*]

ab·bey (ab′ē) *n. pl.* **·beys 1.** A monastery or convent under the jurisdiction of an abbot or abbess. **2.** A church or building attached to an abbey. [ME < OF < LL < Gk. < Aramaic *abbā* father]

ab·bot (ab′ət) *n.* The superior of a community of monks. [OE < LL < Gk. < Aramaic *abbā* father] — **ab′bot·cy, ab′bot·ship** *n.*

ab·bre·vi·ate (ə·brē′vē·āt) *v.t.* **·at·ed, ·at·ing 1.** To condense or make briefer. **2.** To shorten, as a word or expression, esp. by omission or contraction. [< L < *ad-* to + *breviare* to shorten] — **ab·bre′vi·a′tor** *n.*

— **Syn.** shorten, curtail, abridge, contract.

ab·bre·vi·a·tion (ə·brē′vē·ā′shən) *n.* **1.** A shortened form of a word or phrase, used to represent the full form: Mr. is an *abbreviation* of Mister. **2.** The act of abbreviating, or the state of being abbreviated.

— **Syn. 1.** An *abbreviation* is a shortening by any method. A *contraction* is made by omitting certain medial elements (whether sounds or letters) and bringing together the first and last elements. *Rec't* for *receipt* is a written *contraction* as well as *abbreviation; Am.* for *American* is a written *abbreviation,* but not a *contraction.*

ABC (ā′bē′sē′) *pl.* **ABC's 1.** *Usually pl.* The alphabet. **2.** The rudiments, elements, or basic facts (of a subject).

Ab·di·as (ab·dī′əs) The Douai Bible name for OBADIAH.

ab·di·cate (ab′də·kāt) *v.* **·cat·ed, ·cat·ing** *v.t.* **1.** To give up formally; renounce, as a throne, power, or rights. — *v.i.* **2.** To relinquish power, sovereignty, or rights. [< L *abdicare* to renounce] — **ab·di·ca·ble** (ab′di·kə·bəl) *adj.* — **ab′di·ca′tion** *n.* — **ab′di·ca′tive** *adj.* — **ab′di·ca′tor** *n.*

ab·do·men (ab′də·mən, ab·dō′mən) *n.* **1.** In mammals, the body cavity between the diaphragm and the pelvic floor containing the viscera. **2.** In other vertebrates, the region or cavity that contains the viscera. **3.** In insects and other arthropods, the hindmost of the main body divisions. [< L] — **ab·dom·i·nal** (ab·dom′ə·nəl) — **ab·dom′i·nal·ly** *adv.*

ab·duct (ab·dukt′) *v.t.* **1.** To carry away wrongfully, as by force or fraud; kidnap. **2.** *Physiol.* To draw aside or away from the original position. [< L < *ab-* away + *ducere* to lead] — **ab·duc′tion** *n.* — **ab·duc′tor** *n.*

a·beam (ə·bēm′) *adv. Naut.* **1.** At right angles to the keel of a vessel. **2.** At or off the side of a vessel: with *of.*

a·bed (ə·bed′) *adv.* In bed; on a bed; to bed.

A·bel (ā′bəl) Second son of Adam. *Gen.* iv 2.

ab·er·rant (ab·er′ənt, ab′ər·ənt) *adj.* **1.** Straying from the right way or usual course; wandering. **2.** Varying from type; abnormal; exceptional. [< L < *ab-* from + *errare* to wander] — **ab·er′rance, ab·er′ran·cy** *n.*

ab·er·ra·tion (ab′ə·rā′shən) *n.* **1.** Deviation from a right, customary, prescribed, or natural course or condition. **2.** Partial mental derangement.

a·bet (ə·bet′) *v.t.* **a·bet·ted, a·bet·ting** To encourage and support; esp., to support wrongdoing or a wrongdoer. [< OF < *a-* to + *beter* to tease, bait] — **a·bet′ment, a·bet′tal** *n.*

a·bet·tor (ə·bet′ər) *n.* One who abets. Also **a·bet′ter.**

a·bey·ance (ə·bā′əns) *n.* **1.** Suspension or temporary inaction. **2.** *Law* An undetermined condition, as of an estate not legally assigned. Also **a·bey′an·cy.** [< AF < OF < *a-* to, at + *bair* to gape] — **a·bey′ant** *adj.*

ab·hor (ab·hôr′) *v.t.* **·horred, ·hor·ring** To regard with re-

---

CHINESE ABACUS
The counters in the lower compartment have five times the value of those above.

pugnance; detest; loathe. — **Syn.** See HATE. [< L *ab-* from + *horrere* to shudder] — **ab·hor′rer** *n.*

ab·hor·rence (ab-hôr′əns, -hor′-) *n.* **1.** A feeling of utter loathing. **2.** Something loathsome or repugnant.

ab·hor·rent (ab-hôr′ənt, -hor′-) *adj.* **1.** Repugnant or detestable. **2.** Opposed: with *to.* **3.** Feeling repulsion. — **ab·hor′rent·ly** *adv.*

a·bide (ə-bīd′) *v.* **a·bode** or **a·bid·ed, a·bid·ing** *v.i.* **1.** To continue in a place; remain. — *v.t.* **2.** To look for; wait for. **3.** To endure; put up with. — **to abide by 1.** To behave in accordance with; adhere to, as a promise or rule. **2.** To accept the consequences of; submit to. [OE *ābīdan*] — **a·bi′dance** *n.* — **a·bid′er** *n.* — **a·bid′ing·ly** *adv.*

a·bil·i·ty (ə-bil′ə-tē) *n.* *pl.* **·ties 1.** The state or quality of being able; capacity. **2.** *pl.* Talents. **3.** Competence or skill. [< OF < L < *habilis* suitable < *habere* to have, hold]

ab·ir·ri·tant (ab-ir′ə-tənt) *n.* A soothing agent; medicine that eases irritation. — *adj.* Relieving irritation; soothing.

ab·ir·ri·tate (ab-ir′ə-tāt) *v.t.* **·tat·ed, ·tat·ing** *Med.* To diminish sensibility or irritation in. — **ab·ir′ri·ta′tion** *n.*

ab·ject (ab′jekt, ab·jekt′) *adj.* **1.** Sunk to a low condition; groveling; mean; despicable. **2.** Hopelessly low; disheartening. [< L < *ab-* away + *jacere* to throw] — **ab·jec′tive** *adj.* — **ab′ject·ly** *adv.* — **ab′ject·ness, ab·jec′tion** *n.*

ab·jure (ab-jŏŏr′) *v.t.* **·jured, ·jur·ing 1.** To renounce under oath; forswear. **2.** To retract or recant, as an opinion. — **Syn.** See RENOUNCE. [< L < *ab-* away + *jurare* to swear] **ab·ju·ra′tion** *n.* — **ab·jur·a·to·ry** (ab-jŏŏr′ə-tôr′ē, -tō′rē) *adj.* — **ab·jur′er** *n.*

ab·la·tive (ab′lə-tiv) *adj. Gram.* In some inflected languages, as Latin and Sanskrit, pertaining to a case expressing separation, position, motion from, instrumentality, etc. — *n.* **1.** The ablative case. **2.** A word in this case. [< L, *ablatus*, pp. of *aufferre* < *ab-* away + *ferre* to carry]

a·blaze (ə-blāz′) *adv.* On fire. — *adj.* **1.** Flaming. **2.** Zealous; ardent.

a·ble (ā′bəl) *adj.* **a·bler** (ā′blər), **a·blest** (ā′blist) **1.** Having adequate power. **2.** Having or exhibiting superior abilities; skillful: an *able* writer. [< OF < L *habilis* suitable, fit < *habere* to have, hold] — **a′bly** *adv.*

-able *suffix* **1.** Given to; tending to; likely to: *changeable.* **2.** Fit to; able to; capable of; worthy of: *eatable, solvable.* Also spelled *-ble, -ible.* [< F < L *-abilis, -ibilis, -bilis*]

a·ble-bod·ied (ā′bəl-bod′ēd) *adj.* Having a sound, strong body; competent for physical service; robust.

able-bodied seaman An experienced and skilled seaman.

able seaman *pl.* **·men 1.** In the Royal Canadian Navy the fourth lowest grade. **2.** One who holds this grade.

a·bloom (ə-blōōm′) *adj. & adv.* Blooming; in blossom.

ab·lu·tion (ab-lōō′shən) *n.* **1.** A washing or cleansing of the body; a bath. **2.** *Eccl.* **a** A ceremonial washing of the priest's hands or of the chalice and paten during the Eucharist. **b** The liquid used for this. [< L < *ab-* away + *luere* to wash] — **ab·lu′tion·ar′y** *adj.*

-ably *suffix* Like; in the manner of: *peaceably:* used to form adverbs from adjectives ending in *-able.*

ab·ne·gate (ab′nə-gāt) *v.t.* **·gat·ed, ·gat·ing** To deny; renounce. [< L < *ab-* away + *negare* to deny] — **ab′ne·ga′tion** *n.* — **ab′ne·ga′tor** *n.*

ab·nor·mal (ab-nôr′məl) *adj.* Not according to rule; different from the average; unusual; irregular. [< F < Med.L < L < *ab-* from + *norma* rule] — **ab·nor′mal·ly** *adv.*

ab·nor·mal·i·ty (ab′nôr-mal′ə-tē) *n. pl.* **·ties 1.** The state of being abnormal. **2.** An abnormal thing.

a·board (ə-bôrd′, ə-bōrd′) *adv.* **1.** On board; into, in, or on a ship, train, etc. **2.** Alongside. — **all aboard!** Get on board! Get in!: a warning to passengers. — *prep.* **1.** On board of; upon or within. **2.** Alongside of.

a·bode (ə-bōd′) Past tense and past participle of ABIDE. — *n.* **1.** A place of abiding; dwelling; home. **2.** The state or act of abiding; sojourn; stay. [OE *ābād*]

a·bol·ish (ə-bol′ish) *v.t.* To do away with; put an end to; annul; destroy. [< F < *abolere* to destroy] — **a·bol′ish·a·ble** *adj.* — **a·bol′ish·er** *n.* — **a·bol′ish·ment** *n.*

ab·o·li·tion (ab′ə-lish′ən) *n.* **1.** The act of abolishing, or the state of being abolished. **2.** *Sometimes cap.* The abolishing of slavery in the United States. — **ab′o·li′tion·al, ab′o·li′tion·ar′y** *adj.* — **ab′o·li′tion·ism** *n.* — **ab′o·li′tion·ist** *n.*

ab·o·ma·sum (ab′ə-mā′səm) *n. pl.* **·sa** (-sə) The fourth or true digestive stomach of a ruminant: also called *reed.* Also **ab·o·ma·sus** (ab′ə-mā′səs). [< NL < L *ab-* away from + *omasum* bullock's tripe]

A-bomb (ā′bom′) *n.* An atomic bomb.

a·bom·i·na·ble (ə-bom′in·ə-bəl) *adj.* **1.** Very hateful; loathsome. **2.** Extremely disagreeable; bad. — **a·bom′i·na·ble·ness** *n.* — **a·bom′i·na·bly** *adv.*

a·bom·i·nate (ə-bom′ə-nāt) *v.t.* **·nat·ed, ·nat·ing 1.** To regard with loathing; abhor. **2.** To dislike strongly. — **Syn.** See HATE. [< L *abominari* to abhor as an ill omen] — **a·bom′i·na′tion** *n.* — **a·bom′i·na′tor** *n.*

ab·o·rig·i·nal (ab′ə-rij′ə-nəl) *adj.* **1.** Of or pertaining to aborigines. **2.** Native; indigenous. — *n. Austral.* An aborigine. — **ab′o·rig′i·nal·ly** *adv.*

ab·o·rig·i·ne (ab′ə-rij′ə-nē) *n.* **1.** One of the original native inhabitants of a country. **2.** *pl.* Flora and fauna indigenous to a geographical area. [< L *ab origine* from the beginning]

a·bort (ə-bôrt′) *v.i.* **1.** To bring forth young prematurely; miscarry. **2.** To fail of complete development. — *v.t.* **3.** To cause to have a miscarriage. **4.** To bring to a premature or unsuccessful conclusion. [< L *aboriri* to miscarry]

a·bor·tion (ə-bôr′shən) *n.* **1.** The expulsion of a fetus prematurely, when it is nonviable; miscarriage. **2.** A miscarriage produced artificially. **3.** The defective result of a premature birth. **4.** Partial or complete arrest of development in anything. — **a·bor′tion·al** *adj.*

a·bor·tion·ist (ə-bôr′shən·ist) *n.* One who causes abortion.

a·bor·tive (ə-bôr′tiv) *adj.* **1.** Coming to naught; failing. **2.** Brought forth or born prematurely. **3.** Imperfectly developed; rudimentary. **4.** *Med.* Causing abortion. — **Syn.** See FUTILE. — **a·bor′tive·ly** *adv.* — **a·bor′tive·ness** *n.*

a·bound (ə-bound′) *v.i.* **1.** To be in abundance; be plentiful. **2.** To have plenty; be rich. **3.** To be full; teem. [< OF < L < *ab-* from + *undare* to flow in waves]

a·bout (ə-bout′) *adv.* **1.** Approximately; nearly. **2.** *Informal* Almost; not quite. **3.** Nearby; in the vicinity. **4.** To a reversed position; around. **5.** In rotation; around and around. **6.** In every direction; to all sides. **7.** Here and there, as without direction. **8.** Astir; in motion; active. **9.** On every side; around. — *prep.* **1.** On every side of; encircling. **2.** Near; within; on some side of. **3.** Here and there in or upon. **4.** Near; close to. **5.** Engaged in. **6.** Concerning; in reference to. **7.** In one's possession. **8.** Attached to (a person) as an attribute. **9.** On the point of; ready to. [OE < *on, a* on + *būtan* outside]

a·bout-face (*n.* ə·bout′fās′; *v.* ə-bout′fās′) *n.* **1.** *Mil.* A pivoting turn to the rear executed when halted. **2.** Any turning around or reversal, as of opinion or point of view. — *v.i.* **-faced, -fac·ing** To perform an about-face.

a·bove (ə-buv′) *adv.* **1.** In or to a higher place; overhead; up. **2.** Superior in rank or position. **3.** In an earlier section of something written. **4.** In heaven. — *adj.* Given, said, named, etc., in what is above; preceding: The *above* men were acquitted. — *n.* That which is higher up or just before: preceded by *the.* — *prep.* **1.** Directly over; on top of. **2.** Higher than; rising beyond. **3.** Farther north than. **4.** More than, in number, quantity, degree, etc.; beyond. **5.** Superior to in authority or power. **6.** Beyond the influence or reach of. [ME *abofen* < OE *onbufan*]

a·bove·board (ə-buv′bôrd′, -bōrd′) *adj. & adv.* In open sight; without concealment, fraud, or trickery.

ab·ra·ca·dab·ra (ab′rə-kə-dab′rə) *n.* **1.** Any spell or incantation. **2.** Jargon or nonsensical words. [< L]

a·brade (ə-brād′) *v.t.* **a·brad·ed, a·brad·ing** To rub or wear off by friction; scrape away. [< L < *ab-* away + *radere* to scrape] — **a·bra′dant** *adj. & n.* — **a·brad′er** *n.*

A·bra·ham (ā′brə·ham) The progenitor of the Hebrews; first called A·bram (ā′brəm). *Gen.* xvii 5.

a·bran·chi·al (ā·brang′kē·əl) *adj. Zool.* Without gills. Also **a·bran·chi·ate** (ā·brang′kē·it, -āt). [< A-⁴ without + Gk. *branchia* gills]

a·bra·sion (ə-brā′zhən) *n.* **1.** A wearing or rubbing away, as of rocks by glaciers. **2.** An abraded area, as on the skin.

a·bra·sive (ə-brā′siv, -ziv) *adj.* Abrading or tending to abrade. — *n.* An abrading substance, as emery or sand.

a·breast (ə-brest′) *adv. & adj.* Side by side. — **abreast of** (or **with**) Side by side with.

a·bridge (ə-brij′) *v.t.* **a·bridged, a·bridg·ing 1.** To give the substance of in fewer words; condense. **2.** To shorten, as in time. **3.** To curtail or lessen, as rights. **4.** To deprive. [< OF < L *abbreviare* < *ad-* to + *brevis* short] — **a·bridg′a·ble** or **a·bridge′a·ble** *adj.* — **a·bridg′er** *n.*

a·bridg·ment (ə-brij′mənt) *n.* **1.** The act of abridging, or the state of being abridged. **2.** A condensation, as of a book; epitome; abstract. Also **a·bridge′ment.**

—**Syn. 2.** An *abridgment* gives the most important portions of a work substantially as they stand. An *abstract, digest,* or *précis* is an independent statement of what a book or an article contains, the *abstract* closely following the main heads, the *digest* or *précis* giving careful consideration of all the contents.

a·broad (ə-brôd′) *adv.* **1.** Out of one's home or abode; out-of-doors. **2.** In or to foreign lands. **3.** At large; in circulation. **4.** Broadly; widely. **5.** Wide of the mark. [ME]

ab·ro·gate (ab′rə-gāt) *v.t.* **·gat·ed, ·gat·ing** To annul by authority, as a law; abolish; repeal. — **Syn.** See ANNUL. [< L < *ab-* away + *rogare* to propose a law] — **ab′ro·ga·ble** (ab′rə-gə-bəl) *adj.* — **ab′ro·ga′tion** *n.* — **ab′ro·ga′tive** *adj.* — **ab′ro·ga′tor** *n.*

a·brupt (ə-brupt′) *adj.* **1.** Beginning, ending, or changing suddenly; unexpected. **2.** Unceremonious; rude, as in speech or departure. **3.** Unconnected, as literary style. **4.** Steep, as a cliff. — **Syn.** See BLUNT. [< L < *ab-* off + *rumpere* to break] — **a·brupt′ly** *adv.* — **a·brupt′ness** *n.*

abs- Var. of AB-[1].

Ab·sa·lom (ab'sə·ləm) The favorite and rebellious son of David. II *Sam.* xiii–xix.

ab·scess (ab'ses) *Pathol. n.* A collection of pus in any part of the body, often inflamed — *v.i.* To form an abscess. [< L < *ab*- away + *cedere* to go] — **ab'scessed** *adj.*

ab·scis·sa (ab·sis'ə) *n. pl.* **ab·scis·sas** or **ab·scis·sae** (-sis'ē) *Math.* The distance of any point from the vertical or Y-axis in a coordinate system, measured on a line parallel to the horizontal or X-axis. [< L (*linea*) *abscissa* (line) cut off < *ab*- off + *scindere* to cut]

ab·scis·sion (ab·sizh'ən, -sish'ən) *n.* **1.** The act of cutting off or removing. **2.** In rhetoric, an abrupt breaking off for effect, as in the middle of a sentence. [< L < *ab*- off + *scindere* to cut]

ABSCISSA
AB: *x* axis.
AC: *y* axis.
Ae abscissa
of point *f.*

ab·scond (ab·skond') *v.i.* To depart suddenly and secretly, esp. to escape the law. [< L < *ab*- away + *condere* to store away, conceal] — **ab·scond'er** *n.*

ab·sence (ab'səns) *n.* **1.** The state of being absent. **2.** The period of being away. **3.** Lack.

ab·sent (*adj.* ab'sənt; *v.* ab·sent') *adj.* **1.** Not present; away. **2.** Lacking; nonexistent. **3.** Inattentive; absent-minded. — *v.t.* To take or keep (oneself) away. [< L < *ab*- away + *esse* to be] — **ab·sent'er** *n.* — **ab'sent·ly** *adv.* — **ab'sent·ness** *n.*

ab·sen·tee (ab'sən·tē') *n.* One who is absent, as from a job. — *adj.* Temporarily absent. — **ab'sen·tee'ism** *n.*

ab·sent-mind·ed (ab'sənt·mīn'did) *adj.* Inattentive to one's immediate surroundings or business because of preoccupation of the mind; forgetful. — **ab'sent-mind'ed·ly** *adv.* — **ab'sent-mind'ed·ness** *n.*

absent without leave *Mil.* Absent without authorization but not intending to desert. *Abbr. a.w.o.l., A.W.O.L.*

ab·sinthe (ab'sinth) *n.* **1.** A green, bitter liqueur having the flavor of licorice and wormwood. **2.** Wormwood. Also **ab'sinth.** [< F < L *absinthium* wormwood]

ab·so·lute (ab'sə·lōōt) *adj.* **1.** Free from restriction; unlimited; unconditional. **2.** Complete; perfect. **3.** Unadulterated; pure. **4.** Not relative to anything else; independent. **5.** Positive; certain. **6.** *Gram.* **a** Free from the usual relations of syntax or construction with other words in the sentence, as *It being late* in *It being late, we started home.* **b** Of a transitive verb, having no object expressed, as *That professor inspires and stimulates.* **c** Of an adjective standing without a noun, as *the brave and the fair.* — *n.* That which is absolute or perfect. — **the Absolute** *Philos.* The ultimate basis of all thought, reasoning, or being. [< L < *ab*- from + *solvere* to loosen] — **ab·so·lute'ness** *n.*

ab·so·lute·ly (ab'sə·lōōt'lē, *emphatic* ab'sə·lōōt'lē) *adv.* **1.** Completely; unconditionally. **2.** Positively. **3.** *Gram.* So as not to take an object: to use a verb *absolutely.*

absolute pitch *Music* The ability to produce or name the pitch of any note sounded or asked for: also *perfect pitch.*

absolute zero That temperature at which a body contains no heat, and at which a perfect gas exerts no pressure, equivalent to about −273.16° C. or −459.7° F.

ab·so·lu·tion (ab'sə·lōō'shən) *n.* **1.** The act of absolving, as from guilt. **2.** *Eccl.* **a** A remission of sin and its penalties pronounced by a priest. **b** A formula declaring the forgiveness of sin. [< L < *ab*- from + *solvere* to loosen]

ab·so·lut·ism (ab'sə·lōō·tiz'əm) *n.* In government, the doctrine or practice of unlimited authority and control; despotism. — **ab'so·lut'ist** *n.* — **ab'so·lu·tis'tic** *adj.*

ab·solve (ab·solv', -zolv', əb-) *v.t.* **·solved, ·solv·ing** **1.** To free from the penalties or consequences of an action. **2.** To release, as from an obligation. **3.** *Eccl.* To grant a remission of sin. [< L < *ab*- from + *solvere* to loosen.] — **ab·solv'a·ble** *adj.* — **ab·sol'vent** *adj. & n.* — **ab·solv'er** *n.*

ab·sorb (ab·sôrb', -zôrb') *v.t.* **1.** To drink in or suck up, as through or into pores. **2.** To engross completely. **3.** To take up or in by chemical or molecular action, as gases, heat, liquid, light, etc.: distinguished from *adsorb.* **4.** To take in and incorporate. **5.** To receive the force or action of; intercept. [< L < *ab*- from + *sorbere* to suck in] — **ab·sorb·a·bil'i·ty** *n.* — **ab·sorb'a·ble** *adj.* — **ab·sorb'er** *n.* — **ab·sorb'ing** *adj.* — **ab·sorb'ing·ly** *adv.*

ab·sor·bent (ab·sôr'bənt, -zôr'-) *adj.* Absorbing or tending to absorb. — *n.* A substance, duct, etc., that absorbs. — **ab·sor'ben·cy** *n.*

absorbent cotton Cotton from which all fatty matter has been removed, used in surgical dressings, etc.

ab·sorp·tion (ab·sôrp'shən, -zôrp'-) *n.* **1.** The act of absorbing, or the condition of being absorbed. **2.** Assimilation, as by the digestive process. **3.** Preoccupation of the mind. — **ab·sorp'tive** *adj.* — **ab·sorp'tive·ness, ab'sorp·tiv'i·ty** *n.*

ab·stain (ab·stān') *v.i.* To keep oneself back; refrain voluntarily: with *from.* [< OF < L *abstinere* to hold back < *ab*- from + *tenere* to hold] — **ab·stain'er** *n.*

ab·ste·mi·ous (ab·stē'mē·əs) *adj.* Eating and drinking sparingly; abstinent; temperate. [< L < *ab*- from + root of *temetum* intoxicating drink] — **ab·ste'mi·ous·ly** *adv.* — **ab·ste'mi·ous·ness** *n.*

ab·sten·tion (ab·sten'shən) *n.* An abstaining. — **ab·sten'·tious** *adj.*

ab·sti·nence (ab'stə·nəns) *n.* **1.** The act or practice of abstaining, as from food, pleasure, etc. **2.** Abstention from alcoholic beverages. [< F < L *abstinere* < *ab*- from + *tenere* to hold] — **ab'sti·nent** *adj.* — **ab'sti·nent·ly** *adv.*

ab·stract (*adj.* ab·strakt', ab'strakt; *n.* ab'strakt; *v. defs. 1–4* ab·strakt'; *v. def. 5* ab'strakt) *adj.* **1.** Considered apart from matter or from specific examples; not concrete. **2.** Theoretical; ideal, as opposed to practical. **3.** Abstruse. **4.** Considered or expressed without reference to particular example, as numbers, attributes, or qualities. **5.** In art, generalized or universal, as opposed to concrete, specific, or representational. — *n.* **1.** A summary or epitome, as of a document. **2.** The essence of some larger object or whole. **3.** An abstract idea or term. *Abbr. abs.* — **Syn.** See ABRIDGMENT. — **in the abstract** Apart from concrete relation or embodiment; abstractly. — *v.t.* **1.** To take away; remove. **2.** To take away secretly; purloin. **3.** To withdraw or disengage (the attention, interest, etc.). **4.** To consider apart from particular or material instances. **5.** To make an abstract of; summarize. [< L < *ab*- away + *trahere* to draw] — **ab·stract'er** *n.* — **ab·stract'ly** *adv.* — **ab·stract'ness** *n.*

ab·stract·ed (ab·strak'tid) *adj.* **1.** Lost in thought; absent-minded. **2.** Separated from all else; apart. — **ab·stract'·ed·ly** *adv.* — **ab·stract'ed·ness** *n.*

ab·strac·tion (ab·strak'shən) *n.* **1.** The process of abstracting. **2.** A product of this process; a concept. **3.** A visionary or impractical theory. **4.** The act of withdrawing; separation. **5.** Absence of mind; preoccupation. **6.** An art form or work of art in which the qualities are abstract.

ab·strac·tive (ab·strak'tiv) *adj.* **1.** Of, pertaining to, or tending to abstraction. **2.** Having the power of abstraction; epitomizing. — **ab·strac'tive·ly** *adv.* — **ab·strac'tive·ness** *n.*

abstract noun *Gram.* A noun that names a quality, idea, etc., as *goodness, democracy, reputation.*

ab·struse (ab·strōōs') *adj.* Hard to understand. — **Syn.** See COMPLEX, MYSTERIOUS. [< L < *ab*- away + *trudere* to thrust] — **ab·struse'ly** *adv.* — **ab·struse'ness** *n.*

ab·surd (ab·sûrd', -zûrd') *adj.* Irrational; ridiculous. [< F < L < *ab*- completely + *surdus* deaf, dull] — **ab·surd'ly** *adv.* — **ab·surd'ness** *n.*

ab·surd·i·ty (ab·sûr'də·tē, -zûr'-) *n. pl.* **·ties 1.** The quality of being absurd. **2.** Something absurd.

a·bun·dance (ə·bun'dəns) *n.* **1.** A plentiful or overflowing supply. **2.** Wealth; affluence.

a·bun·dant (ə·bun'dənt) *adj.* **1.** Existing in plentiful supply; ample. **2.** Abounding. — **Syn.** See PLENTIFUL. [< OF < L *abundare.* See ABOUND.] — **a·bun'dant·ly** *adv.*

a·buse (*v.* ə·byōōz'; *n.* ə·byōōs') *v.t.* **a·bused, a·bus·ing** **1.** To use improperly or injuriously; misuse. **2.** To hurt by treating wrongly; injure. **3.** To speak in coarse or bad terms of or to; revile. — *n.* **1.** Improper or injurious use; misuse. **2.** Ill-treatment; injury. **3.** Vicious conduct, practice, or action. **4.** Abusive language; slander. [< F < L < *ab*- away + *uti* to use] — **a·bus'er** *n.*

a·bu·sive (ə·byōō'siv) *adj.* **1.** Mistreating. **2.** Insulting; vituperative. — **a·bu'sive·ly** *adv.* — **a·bu'sive·ness** *n.*

a·but (ə·but') *v.i.* **a·but·ted, a·but·ting** To touch, join, or adjoin at the end or side; border: with *on, upon,* or *against.* [< OF < *a*- to + *bout* end] — **a·but'ter** *n.*

a·but·ment (ə·but'mənt) *n.* **1.** The act of abutting. **2.** Something that abuts, the thing abutted upon, or the point of junction. **3.** A supporting or buttressing structure.

a·bys·mal (ə·biz'məl) *adj.* Unfathomable; immeasurable; extreme: an *abysmal* ignorance. — **a·bys'mal·ly** *adv.*

a·byss (ə·bis') *n.* **1.** A bottomless gulf; chasm. **2.** Any profound depth or void. **3.** The depths of the sea. [< L < Gk. < *a*- without + *byssos* bottom] — **a·bys'sal** *adj.*

Ab·ys·sin·i·an (ab'ə·sin'ē·ən) *adj. & n.* Ethiopian.

ac- Assimilated var. of AD-.

-ac *suffix* **1.** Having; affected by: *demoniac.* **2.** Pertaining to; of: *cardiac.* [< Gk. *-akos* or L *-acus* or F *-aque*]

a·ca·cia (ə·kā'shə) *n.* **1.** Any of various flowering, leguminous trees and shrubs of the tropics and warm temperate regions. **2.** The locust tree. **3.** Gum arabic. [< L < Gk. *akakia,* a thorny tree < *akē* point]

ac·a·dem·ic (ak'ə·dem'ik) *adj.* **1.** Pertaining to an academy, college, or university; scholarly. **2.** *U.S.* Offering or having to do with liberal rather than vocational or technical studies. **3.** Theoretical, as opposed to practical. **4.** Pedantic. Also **ac·a·dem/i·cal.** — *n.* A college or university student or faculty member. — **ac/a·dem/i·cal·ly** *adv.*

a·cad·e·mi·cian (ə-kad/ə-mish/ən, ak/ə-də-) *n.* A member of an academy of art, science, or literature.

ac·a·dem·i·cism (ak/ə-dem/ə-siz/əm) *n.* Pedantic formalism, as in art. Also **a·cad·e·mism** (ə-kad/ə-miz/əm).

a·cad·e·my (ə-kad/ə-mē) *n. pl.* **·mies 1.** A secondary school, usually a private one. **2.** A school giving instruction in some science or art. **3.** A learned society for the advancement of arts or sciences. [< F < L < Gk. *Akadēmeia* the grove where Plato taught]

A·ca·di·a (ə-kā/dē·ə) A former name for a region in eastern Canada, including Nova Scotia and New Brunswick.

A·ca·di·an (ə-kā/dē·ən) *adj.* Of or pertaining to Acadia or Nova Scotia. — *n.* One of the early French settlers of Acadia or their descendants. See CAJUN.

acantho- *combining form* Thorn or thorny; spine, point. Also, before vowels, **acanth-.** [< Gk. *akantha* thorn]

a·can·thus (ə-kan/thəs) *n. pl.* **·thus·es** or **·thi** (-thī) **1.** A plant having large spiny leaves, common in the Mediterranean region. **2.** *Archit.* A decorative representation of its leaf, characteristic of the Corinthian capital. [< L < Gk. *akē* thorn] — **a·can/thine** (-thin) *adj.*

a cap·pel·la (ä/ kə-pel/ə, *Ital.* ä/ käp-pel/lä) *Music* Sung without accompaniment. [< Ital., in chapel style]

ACANTHUS (*def.* 2)

ac·cede (ak-sēd/) *v.i.* **·ced·ed, ·ced·ing 1.** To give one's consent or adherence; agree; assent: with *to.* **2.** To come into or enter upon an office or dignity: with *to.* [< L < *ad-* to + *cedere* to yield]

ac·cel·er·an·do (ak-sel/ə-ran/dō, *Ital.* ät-chā/lä-rän/dō) *Music adj.* Gradually quickening in time. — *adv.* In gradually quickening tempo. [< Ital.]

ac·cel·er·ant (ak-sel/ər-ənt) *n.* That which accelerates.

ac·cel·er·ate (ak-sel/ə-rāt) *v.* **·at·ed, ·at·ing** *v.t.* **1.** To cause to act or move faster. **2.** To hasten the natural or usual course of. **3.** To cause to happen ahead of time. — *v.i.* **4.** To move or become faster. [< L < *ad-* to + *celerare* to hasten] — **ac·cel/er·a·ble** *adj.* — **ac·cel/er·a/tive** *adj.*

ac·cel·er·a·tion (ak-sel/ə-rā/shən) *n.* **1.** The act of accelerating or being accelerated. **2.** *Physics* The rate at which the velocity of a body increases per unit of time.

ac·cel·er·a·tor (ak-sel/ə-rā/tər) *n.* **1.** One who or that which accelerates. **2.** *Physics* Any of various devices for accelerating the velocity of atomic particles: also called *atom smasher.* **3.** *Mech.* The foot throttle of an automobile.

ac·cent (*n.* ak/sent; *v.* ak/sent, ak-sent/) *n.* **1.** The prominence given in speech to a particular sound, syllable, or word. **2.** A mark used to indicate the place of accent in a word. The **primary accent** notes the chief stress, and the **secondary accent** a somewhat weaker stress. **3.** A mark used in some languages to show the quality of a vowel. In French, the accents are acute (´), grave (`), and circumflex (ˆ). **4.** A modulation of the voice. **5.** Mode of utterance; pronunciation: a Southern *accent.* **6.** In prosody, the stress determining the rhythm of poetry. **7.** *Music* An emphasis given to one tone or chord. **8.** *pl.* Speech; words. — *v.t.* **1.** To speak, pronounce, play, or sing with an accent; stress. **2.** To write a mark indicating accent. **3.** To accentuate or emphasize. [< L < *ad-* to + *cantus* a singing]

ac·cen·tu·al (ak-sen/chōo-əl) *adj.* **1.** Of or pertaining to accent. **2.** In prosody, having a stress accent. — **ac·cen/tu·al·ly** *adv.*

ac·cen·tu·ate (ak-sen/chōo-āt) *v.t.* **·at·ed, ·at·ing 1.** To strengthen or heighten the effect of; emphasize. **2.** To mark or pronounce with an accent. — **ac·cen/tu·a/tion** *n.*

ac·cept (ak-sept/) *v.t.* **1.** To receive with favor, willingness, or consent. **2.** To give an affirmative answer to. **3.** To receive as satisfactory or sufficient. **4.** To take with good grace; submit to. **5.** In commerce, to agree to pay, as a draft. **6.** To believe in. [< L < *ad-* to + *capere* to take] — **ac·cept/er** *n.*

ac·cept·a·ble (ak-sep/tə-bəl) *adj.* Worthy of acceptance. — **ac·cept/a·ble·ness, ac·cept/a·bil/i·ty** *n.* — **ac·cept/a·bly** *adv.*

ac·cep·tance (ak-sep/təns) *n.* **1.** The act of accepting. **2.** The state of being accepted or acceptable. **3.** Favorable reception; approval. **4.** Assent; belief. **5.** In commerce, an agreement to pay a bill of exchange, etc.; also, the paper showing this. Also **ac·cep/tan·cy.** — **ac·cep/tant** *adj.*

ac·cep·ta·tion (ak/sep-tā/shən) *n.* The accepted meaning of a word or expression.

ac·cept·ed (ak-sep/tid) *adj.* Commonly recognized, believed, or approved; popular.

ac·cess (ak/ses) *n.* **1.** The act of coming to or near. **2.** A passage; path. **3.** The state or quality of being approachable; accessibility. **4.** A sudden attack of a disease. **5.** An outburst of emotion, etc. [< L *accedere* to yield]

ac·ces·si·ble (ak-ses/ə-bəl) *adj.* **1.** Easy of access; ap-

proachable. **2.** Attainable; obtainable. **3.** Open to the influence of. — **ac·ces/si·bil/i·ty** *n.* — **ac·ces/si·bly** *adv.*

ac·ces·sion (ak-sesh/ən) *n.* **1.** The act of attaining an office, dignity, or right. **2.** An increase by something added. **3.** Assent; agreement. — *v.t.* To record, as additions to a library or museum. — **ac·ces/sion·al** *adj.*

ac·ces·so·ry (ak-ses/ər-ē) *n. pl.* **·ries 1.** Something added for convenience, display, etc., as to an automobile or to one's attire. **2.** *Law* A person who, though absent during the perpetration of a felony, instigates, aids, or encourages another to commit the felony (**accessory before the fact**), or knowingly comforts, conceals, or assists the felon (**accessory after the fact**). — *adj.* **1.** Aiding the principal design, or assisting subordinately the chief agent, as in the commission of a crime. **2.** Contributory; supplemental; additional. Also **ac·ces/sa·ry.** [< LL < L *accedere* to yield] — **ac/ces·so/ri·al** *adj.* — **ac·ces/so·ri·ly** *adv.* — **ac·ces/so·ri·ness** *n.*

— **Syn.** (noun) **2.** In law, an *accessory* assists in planning or concealing a crime, though he is not present when it is committed. An *accomplice* is actively or constructively present during the act itself. *Confederate* is a general term for one who assists another.

ac·ci·dent (ak/sə-dənt) *n.* **1.** Anything occurring unexpectedly, or without known cause. **2.** Any unpleasant or unfortunate occurrence involving injury, loss, or death. **3.** Chance; fortune. **4.** Any nonessential attribute. [< L < *ad-* upon + *cadere* to fall]

ac·ci·den·tal (ak/sə-den/təl) *adj.* **1.** Happening or coming by chance. **2.** Nonessential; subordinate; incidental. **3.** *Music* Pertaining to or indicating a sharp, natural, flat, etc., elsewhere than in the signature. — **ac/ci·den/tal·ly** *adv.*

ac·claim (ə-klām/) *v.t.* **1.** To proclaim with applause; hail: They *acclaimed* him victor. **2.** To shout approval of. — *v.i.* **3.** To applaud; shout approval. — *n.* A shout of applause. — **Syn.** See PRAISE. [< L < *ad-* to + *clamare* to shout] — **ac·claim/a·ble** *adj.* — **ac·claim/er** *n.*

ac·cla·ma·tion (ak/lə-mā/shən) *n.* **1.** The act of acclaiming or of being acclaimed. **2.** A shout of applause or welcome. **3.** An oral vote, as in public assembly. **4.** *Canadian* Election without opposition. — **ac·clam·a·to·ry** (ə-klam/ə-tôr/ē, -tō/rē) *adj.*

ac·cli·mate (ə-klī/mit, ak/lə-māt) *v.t. & v.i.* **·mat·ed, ·mat·ing** *Chiefly U.S.* To adapt or become adapted to a new climate or environment. [< F < *à-* to + *climat* climate] — **ac·cli·ma·ta·ble** (ə-klī/mə-tə-bəl) *adj.* — **ac·cli·ma·tion** (ak/lə-mā/shən), **ac·cli·ma·ta·tion** (ə-klī/mə-tā/shən) *n.*

ac·cli·ma·tize (ə-klī/mə-tīz) *v.t. & v.i.* **·tized, ·tiz·ing** To acclimate. — **ac·cli/ma·ti·za/tion** *n.*

ac·cliv·i·ty (ə-kliv/ə-tē) *n. pl.* **·ties** An upward slope: opposed to *declivity.* [< L < *ad-* to + *clivus* hill] — **ac·cliv/i·tous, ac·cli·vous** (ə-klī/vəs) *adj.*

ac·co·lade (ak/ə-lād/, -läd/) *n.* **1.** The salutation (at first an embrace, now a light blow with a sword) in conferring knighthood. **2.** A conferring of praise; an honor. [< F < Ital. *accollare* to embrace about the neck]

ac·com·mo·date (ə-kom/ə-dāt) *v.* **·dat·ed, ·dat·ing** *v.t.* **1.** To do a favor for; oblige; help. **2.** To provide for; give lodging to. **3.** To be suitable for; contain comfortably. **4.** To adapt or modify, as to new conditions. **5.** To reconcile or settle, as conflicting opinions. — *v.i.* **6.** To be or become adjusted, as the eye to distance. [< L < *ad-* to + *commodare* to make fit, suit] — **ac·com/mo·da/tive** *adj.* — **ac·com/mo·da/tive·ness** *n.*

ac·com·mo·dat·ing (ə-kom/ə-dā/ting) *adj.* Disposed to make adjustment; obliging. — **ac·com/mo·dat/ing·ly** *adv.*

ac·com·mo·da·tion (ə-kom/ə-dā/shən) *n.* **1.** The act of accommodating, or the state of being accommodated; adjustment; adaptation. **2.** Reconciliation; compromise. **3.** Anything that supplies a need; convenience. **4.** *Usu. pl. U.S.* Lodging, board, etc. **5.** Willingness to please or help.

ac·com·pa·ni·ment (ə-kum/pə·ni·mənt, ə-kump/ni-) *n.* **1.** Anything that accompanies something. **2.** *Music* A subordinate part supporting a leading part.

ac·com·pa·nist (ə-kum/pə-nist, ə-kump/nist) *n.* One who plays or sings the accompaniment. Also **ac·com/pa·ny·ist.**

ac·com·pa·ny (ə-kum/pə-nē) *v.t.* **·nied, ·ny·ing 1.** To go with; attend; escort. **2.** To be or coexist with. **3.** To supplement. **4.** To play a musical accompaniment to or for. [< F < *à-* to + *compagne* companion]

ac·com·plice (ə-kom/plis) *n.* An associate in wrongdoing; partner in crime. — **Syn.** See ACCESSORY. [< *a,* indefinite article + F *complice* accomplice]

ac·com·plish (ə-kom/plish) *v.t.* To bring to pass or to completion. [< OF < LL < L *ad-* to + *complere* to fill up, complete] — **ac·com/plish·a·ble** *adj.*

ac·com·plished (ə-kom/plisht) *adj.* **1.** Completed; done. **2.** Proficient; skilled. **3.** Trained in the social graces.

ac·com·plish·ment (ə-kom/plish-mənt) *n.* **1.** The act of accomplishing. **2.** Something accomplished; achievement. **3.** An acquirement or attainment, esp. a social skill. — **Syn.** See ATTAINMENT.

ac·cord (ə-kôrd/) *v.t.* **1.** To render as due; grant. **2.** To make harmonize or agree. — *v.i.* **3.** To agree; harmonize. — *n.* **1.** Harmony, as of sentiment, colors, sounds, etc.; agreement. **2.** A settlement of any difference, as between governments. — **Syn.** See HARMONY. — **of one's own accord** By one's own choice. [< OF < LL < L < *ad-* to + *cor* heart] — **ac·cord·a·ble** *adj.* — **ac·cord′er** *n.*

ac·cord·ance (ə·kôr′dəns) *n.* Agreement; conformity. — **ac·cord′ant** *adj.* — **ac·cord′ant·ly** *adv.*

ac·cord·ing (ə·kôr′ding) *adj.* Being in accordance or agreement; harmonizing. — *adv.* Accordingly. — **according as** **1.** In proportion as; just as. **2.** Depending on whether. — **according to 1.** In accordance with. **2.** As stated by; on the authority of. **3.** In proportion to.

ac·cord·ing·ly (ə·kôr′ding·lē) *adv.* **1.** In accord; correspondingly. **2.** Consequently; so.

ac·cor·di·on (ə·kôr′dē·ən) *n.* A portable musical wind instrument with metallic reeds and a keyboard, the air for which is furnished by a bellows operated by the performer. [< Ital. *accordare* to harmonize] — **ac·cor′di·on·ist** *n.*

ac·cost (ə·kôst′, ə·kost′) *v.t.* To speak to first; address; greet. [< F < L < *ad-* to + *costa* rib]

ac·couche·ment (ə·kōōsh′mənt, *Fr.* à·kōōsh·mäṅ′) *n.* Confinement; childbirth. [< F *accoucher* to put to bed]

ac·count (ə·kount′) *v.t.* **1.** To hold to be; consider; estimate. — *v.i.* **2.** To provide a reckoning, as of funds paid or received: with *to* or *with* (someone), *for* (something). **3.** To give a rational explanation: with *for*. **4.** To be responsible; answer: with *for*. **5.** To cause death, capture, or incapacitation: with *for*. — *n.* **1.** A record of events; narrative; description. **2.** A statement of causes; explanation. **3.** A record of monetary transactions. **4.** Worth; importance. **5.** Judgment; estimation. **6.** Profit; advantage. — **on account of** Because of. — **on no account** Under no circumstances. [< OF < LL < L *ad-* to + *computare* to reckon together]

ac·count·a·ble (ə·koun′tə·bəl) *adj.* **1.** Liable to be called to account; responsible. **2.** Capable of being explained. — **ac·count·a·bil′i·ty** *n.* — **ac·count′a·bly** *adv.*

ac·count·ant (ə·koun′tənt) *n.* One whose business is to keep or examine books, as of a mercantile or banking house. — **ac·count′an·cy** *n.*

ac·count·ing (ə·koun′ting) *n.* The art or system of recording, classifying, and summarizing commercial transactions.

ac·cou·ter (ə·kōō′tər) *v.t.* To furnish with dress or trappings; equip, as for military service. Also *Brit.* **ac·cou′tre.** [< F *accoutrer*; ult. origin uncertain]

ac·cou·ter·ment (ə·kōō′tər·mənt) *n.* **1.** *pl.* Equipment; trappings; especially, the equipment of a soldier other than arms and dress. **2.** The act of accoutering.

ac·cred·it (ə·kred′it) *v.t.* **1.** To give credit to as the owner, author, or creator of; attribute to: with *with*. **2.** To accept as true; believe. **3.** To bring into credit; vouch for. **4.** To furnish or send with credentials. **5.** To certify as fulfilling official requirements. [< F < L < *ad-* to + *credere* to believe, trust]

ac·cred·i·ta·tion (ə·kred′ə·tā′shən) *n. U.S.* The granting of approved status to an academic institution.

ac·cre·tion (ə·krē′shən) *n.* **1.** Growth by external additions or by adhesion or inclusion. **2.** An external addition; something added. **3.** Increase by natural growth.

ac·crue (ə·krōō′) *v.i.* **·crued, ·cru·ing** **1.** To come as a natural result or increment, as by growth: with *to*. **2.** To accumulate, as the interest on money: with *from*. [< F < L < *ad-* to + *crescere* to grow] — **ac·cru′al, ac·crue′ment** *n.*

ac·cu·mu·late (ə·kyōōm′yə·lāt) *v.* **·lat·ed, ·lat·ing** *v.t.* **1.** To heap or pile up; amass; collect. — *v.i.* **2.** To become greater in quantity or number; increase. [< L < *ad-* to + *cumulare* to heap] — **ac·cu′mu·la·ble** (-lə·bəl) *adj.*

ac·cu·mu·la·tion (ə·kyōōm′yə·lā′shən) *n.* **1.** The act or process of accumulating. **2.** That which is accumulated. **3.** The addition of earnings or profits to capital.

ac·cu·mu·la·tive (ə·kyōōm′yə·lā′tiv, -lə·tiv) *adj.* **1.** Tending to accumulate. **2.** Arising from accumulation. — **ac·cu′mu·la′tive·ly** *adv.* — **ac·cu′mu·la′tive·ness** *n.*

ac·cu·mu·la·tor (ə·kyōōm′yə·lā′tər) *n.* **1.** A person or thing that accumulates. **2.** *Brit.* A storage battery.

ac·cu·ra·cy (ak′yər·ə·sē) *n.* The condition or quality of being accurate; exactness; precision; correctness.

ac·cu·rate (ak′yər·it) *adj.* Conforming exactly to truth or to a standard; without error; precise; exact. [< L < *ad-* to + *cura* care] — **ac′cu·rate·ly** *adv.* — **ac′cu·rate·ness** *n.*

ac·curs·ed (ə·kûr′sid, ə·kûrst′) *adj.* **1.** Lying under a curse; doomed. **2.** Deserving a curse; detestable. Also **ac·curst′.** — **ac·curs′ed·ly** *adv.* — **ac·curs′ed·ness** *n.*

ac·cu·sa·tion (ak′yōō·zā′shən) *n.* **1.** The act of accusing or the state of being accused. **2.** The crime or act charged. Also **ac·cu·sal** (ə·kyōō′zəl) *n.* — **ac·cu·sa·to·ry** (ə·kyōō′zə·tôr′ē, -tō′rē) *adj.*

ac·cu·sa·tive (ə·kyōō′zə·tiv) *Gram. adj.* Denoting, in inflected languages, the case or relation of the direct object of a verb or preposition, or the goal toward which an action is directed; objective. Also **ac·cu·sa·ti·val** (ə·kyōō′zə·tī′vəl). — *n.* **1.** The case of Latin and Greek nouns corresponding to the English objective. **2.** A word in this case. [< L *accusativus,* trans. of Gk. (*ptōsis*) *aitiatikē* (the case) of the effect < *aitiatos* effected] — **ac·cu′sa·tive·ly** *adv.*

ac·cuse (ə·kyōōz′) *v.* **·cused, ·cus·ing** *v.t.* **1.** To charge with fault or error; blame; censure. **2.** To bring charges against: with *of.* — *v.i.* **3.** To make accusation; utter charges. [< OF < L < *ad-* to + *causa* a cause, lawsuit] — **ac·cus′er** *n.* — **ac·cus′ing·ly** *adv.*
— **Syn. 2.** *Accuse* is a general word for declaring a person guilty of a fault; *charge* is more formal and stresses the serious or criminal nature of an act: to *accuse* a man of lying, to *charge* him with perjury. An *accused* man is *indicted* by a grand jury, and *arraigned* before a court to answer the indictment. *Incriminate* implies involvement in a serious crime.

ac·cused (ə·kyōōzd′) *n. Law* The defendant or defendants in a criminal case: preceded by *the.*

ac·cus·tom (ə·kus′təm) *v.t.* To familiarize by custom or use; habituate or inure: with *to*: to *accustom* oneself to noise.

ac·cus·tomed (ə·kus′təmd) *adj.* **1.** Habitual; usual. **2.** Wont; used: *accustomed* to hard work.

ace (ās) *n.* **1.** A playing card, die, etc., having a single spot. **2.** A very small amount, distance, or degree: within an *ace* of death. **3.** One who excels in a particular field, especially a combat flyer. **4.** In tennis and similar games, a point won by a single stroke, as upon the service. — **ace in the hole** *U.S. Slang* A hidden advantage. — *v.t.* **aced** (āst), **ac·ing** To score a point against in a single stroke, as in tennis. [< OF < L *as* unity, unit]

-acea *suffix Zool.* Used in forming names of classes and orders of animals. [< L, neut. pl. of *-aceus*]

-aceae *suffix Bot.* Used in forming names of families of plants. [< L, fem. pl. of *-aceus*]

a·ce·di·a (ə·sē′dē·ə) *n.* **1.** Extreme mental or spiritual torpor. **2.** Sloth regarded as one of the seven deadly sins. [< LL < Gk. < *a-* without + *kēdos* care]

a·cen·tric (ā·sen′trik) *adj.* Without a center; off center.

-aceous *suffix* Of the nature of; belonging or pertaining to; like: used to form adjectives corresponding to nouns in *-acea, -aceae.* [< L *-aceus* of the nature of]

ac·er·bate (as′ər·bāt) *v.t.* **·bat·ed, ·bat·ing** **1.** To make sour; embitter. **2.** To exasperate. [< L *acerbus* sharp]

a·cer·bi·ty (ə·sûr′bə·tē) *n. pl.* **·ties** **1.** Sourness, bitterness, as that of unripe fruit. **2.** Severity, as of temper, etc.; harshness. Also **a·cer·bi·tude** (ə·sûr′bə·tōōd, -tyōōd).

acet- Var. of ACETO-.

ac·e·tab·u·lum (as′ə·tab′yə·ləm) *n. pl.* **·la** (-lə) *Anat.* The socket in the hip in which the head of the femur rests and revolves. [< L, a vinegar cup < *acetum* vinegar]

ac·e·tal (as′ə·tal) *n. Med.* A volatile, colorless liquid, $C_6H_{14}O_2$, having hypnotic properties.

ac·et·an·i·lide (as′ə·tan′ə·lid, -lid) *n. Chem.* A derivative of aniline, C_8H_9ON, used as a sedative and antipyretic.

ac·e·tate (as′ə·tāt) *n. Chem.* A salt or ester of acetic acid.

a·ce·tic (ə·sē′tik, ə·set′ik) *adj.* Pertaining to or like vinegar; sour. [< L *acetum* vinegar + -IC]

acetic acid *Chem.* A colorless, pungent liquid, $C_2H_4O_2$, occurring in a dilute form in vinegar.

a·cet·i·fy (ə·set′ə·fī) *v.t. & v.i.* **·fied, ·fy·ing** To change into acid or vinegar. — **a·cet′i·fi·ca′tion** *n.* — **a·cet′i·fi′er** *n.*

aceto- *combining form* Of, pertaining to, or from acetic acid or acetyl. Also, before vowels, *acet-.* [< L *acetum* vinegar]

ac·e·tone (as′ə·tōn) *n. Chem.* A clear, flammable liquid, C_3H_6O, used as a solvent for fats, camphor, and resins. — **ac·e·ton·ic** (as′ə·ton′ik) *adj.*

a·cet·y·lene (ə·set′ə·lēn) *n. Chem.* A colorless hydrocarbon gas, C_2H_2, used as an illuminant and for cutting metals.

a·ce·tyl·sal·i·cyl·ic acid (as′ə·til·sal′ə·sil′ik, ə·sē′təl-) Aspirin.

ace·y·deuc·y (ā′sē·dōō′sē, -dyōō′sē) *n.* A variety of backgammon.

A·chae·an (ə·kē′ən) *adj.* Pertaining to Achaea, its people, or their culture. — *n.* **1.** A member of one of the four major tribes of ancient Greece. **2.** A Greek. Also **A·cha·ian** (ə·kā′ən, -kī-).

ache (āk) *v.i.* **ached** (ākt), **ach·ing** **1.** To suffer dull, continued pain; be in pain or distress. **2.** *Informal* To yearn; be eager; with *for* or the infinitive. — *n.* A local, dull, and protracted pain. [OE *acan*] — **ach′ing·ly** *adv.*

a·chene (ā·kēn′) *n. Bot.* A small, dry, one-seeded pericarp, as in the dandelion, buttercup, etc.: also spelled *akene.* [< NL < A-⁴ not + Gk. *chainein* to gape] — **a·che′ni·al** *adj.*

Ach·e·ron (ak′ə·ron) **1.** In Greek and Roman mythology,

the river of woe, one of the rivers surrounding Hades.
2. Hades. [< L < Gk. *Acherōn*]

a·chieve (ə·chēv′) *v.* **a·chieved, a·chiev·ing** *v.t.* **1.** To accomplish; do successfully. **2.** To win or attain, as by effort or skill. —*v.i.* **3.** To accomplish something. [< OF < LL *ad caput* (*venire*) (to come) to a head, finish] —**a·chiev′a·ble** *adj.* —**a·chiev′er** *n.*

a·chieve·ment (ə·chēv′mənt) *n.* **1.** Something accomplished. **2.** The act of achieving. —Syn. See ACT.

A·chil·les (ə·kil′ēz) In the *Iliad*, the foremost Greek hero of the Trojan War, who killed Hector and was killed by an arrow Paris shot into his right heel, his only vulnerable spot. —**Ach·il·le·an** (ak′ə·lē′ən) *adj.*

Achilles' heel A vulnerable point.

Achilles' tendon *Anat.* The tendon connecting the calf muscles to the heel bone.

ach·ro·mat·ic (ak′rə·mat′ik) *adj.* **1.** *Optics* Free from color or iridescence; transmitting light without separating it into its constituent colors, as a lens. **2.** *Music* Diatonic; without accidentals. [< Gk. *a-* without + *chrōma* color] —**ach′ro·mat′i·cal·ly** *adv.* —**a·chro·ma·tism** (ā·krō′mə·tiz′əm), **a·chro·ma·tic·i·ty** (ā·krō′mə·tis′ə·tē) *n.*

a·chro·ma·tin (ā·krō′mə·tin) *n. Biol.* The substance in the cell nucleus that does not readily take color from stains.

a·chro·ma·tize (ā·krō′mə·tīz) *v.t.* **·tized, ·tiz·ing** To make achromatic.

a·chro·mic (ā·krō′mik) *adj.* Colorless. Also **a·chro′mous.**

ac·id (as′id) *adj.* **1.** Sharp and biting to the taste, as vinegar; sour. **2.** *Chem.* Pertaining to or like an acid. **3.** *Geol.* Acidic. **4.** Sharp-tempered; biting. —*n.* **1.** Any sour substance. **2.** *Chem.* A compound containing hydrogen in which all or a part of the hydrogen may be exchanged for a metal or a basic radical, forming a salt. Aqueous solutions of acids are sour, and redden litmus. **3.** *Slang* LSD. —Syn. See SOUR. [< L *acidus*] —**ac′id·ly** *adv.* —**ac′id·ness** *n.*

ac·id-fast (as′id·fast′, -fäst′) *adj.* Not readily decolorized by acids when stained: said of bacteria, epithelial tissue, etc.

a·cid·ic (ə·sid′ik) *adj.* **1.** *Geol.* Containing a high percentage of silica: said of rocks. **2.** *Chem.* Acid.

a·cid·i·fy (ə·sid′ə·fī) *v.t. & v.i.* **·fied, ·fy·ing** To make or become acid; change into an acid. —**a·cid′i·fi′a·ble** *adj.* —**a·cid′i·fi·ca′tion** *n.* —**a·cid′i·fi′er** *n.*

a·cid·i·ty (ə·sid′ə·tē) *n.* **1.** The state or quality of being acid. **2.** Degree of acid strength. **3.** *Chem.* The combining power of a base with reference to an acid. **4.** Hyperacidity.

ac·i·do·sis (as′ə·dō′sis) *n. Pathol.* Acid intoxication due to faulty metabolism. —**ac·i·dot·ic** (as′ə·dot′ik) *adj.*

acid test A final, decisive test, as of worth or integrity.

a·cid·u·late (ə·sij′o̅o̅·lāt) *v.t.* **·lat·ed, ·lat·ing** To make somewhat acid or sour. —**a·cid′u·la′tion** *n.*

a·cid·u·lous (ə·sij′o̅o̅·ləs) *adj.* Slightly acid; sour. Also **a·cid′u·lent.** [< L *acidulus* slightly sour]

ac·i·nus (as′ə·nəs) *n., pl.* **·ni** (-nī) **1.** *Bot.* One of the small parts of a fruit, as of the raspberry. **2.** A berry, as a grape, growing in bunches; a bunch of such berries. [< L, grape]

-acious *suffix of adjectives* Abounding in; characterized by; given to: *pugnacious, vivacious.* [< L *-ax, -acis* + -OUS]

-acity *suffix* Quality or state of: used to form abstract nouns corresponding to adjectives in *-acious.* [< L *-acitas*]

ack-ack (ak′ak′) *n.* Antiaircraft fire. [British radio operator's code for *A.A.* (antiaircraft)]

ac·knowl·edge (ak·nol′ij) *v.t.* **·edged, ·edg·ing** **1.** To admit the truth or fact of; confess. **2.** To recognize as or avow to be. **3.** To admit the validity of, as a claim or right. **4.** To show appreciation of or admit obligation for; express thanks for. **5.** To report receipt or arrival of. —Syn. See CONFESS. [Earlier *aknowledge* < obs. *aknow* to admit, confess] —**ac·knowl′edge·a·ble** *adj.* —**ac·knowl′edg·er** *n.*

ac·knowl·edg·ment (ak·nol′ij·mənt) *n.* **1.** The act of admitting; confession. **2.** Recognition of the existence or truth of something. **3.** Something done or given in return. **4.** *Law* A formal certificate. Also **ac·knowl′edge·ment.**

ac·me (ak′mē) *n.* The highest point. [< Gk. *akmē* point]

ac·ne (ak′nē) *n. Pathol.* A skin disease marked by pimples, chiefly on the face. [? Alter. of Gk. *akmē* point]

ac·o·lyte (ak′ə·līt) *n.* **1.** An attendant or assistant. **2.** An altar boy. **3.** In the Roman Catholic Church, a member of the highest minor order. [< Med.L < Gk. *akolouthos* follower, attendant]

ac·o·nite (ak′ə·nīt) *n.* **1.** The monkshood, or any similar plant. **2.** An extract of this plant, used as a sedative. Also **ac·o·ni·tum** (ak′ə·nī′təm). [< F < L < Gk. *akoniton*]

a·corn (ā′kôrn, ā′kərn) *n.* The fruit of the oak, a one-seeded nut, fixed in a woody cup. [OE *æcern*]

a·cous·tic (ə·ko̅o̅s′tik) *adj.* **1.** Pertaining to the act or sense of hearing, heard sound, or the science of sound. **2.** Adapted for conveying sound or aiding hearing. Also **a·cous′ti·cal.** [< F < Gk. *akouein* to hear] —**a·cous′ti·cal·ly** *adv.*

a·cous·tics (ə·ko̅o̅s′tiks) *n.pl.* (construed as *sing.* in def. 1) **1.** The branch of physics that treats of sound. **2.** The sound-transmitting qualities of an auditorium, room, etc.

ac·quaint (ə·kwānt′) *v.t.* **1.** To make familiar or conversant. **2.** To cause to know; inform. [< OF < LL < L *ad-* to + *cognitus*, pp. of *cognoscere* to know]

ac·quain·tance (ə·kwān′təns) *n.* **1.** Knowledge of any person or thing. **2.** A person or persons with whom one is acquainted. —**ac·quain′tance·ship** *n.*

ac·quaint·ed (ə·kwān′tid) *adj.* Having acquaintance; having personal knowledge: with *with.*

ac·qui·esce (ak′wē·es′) *v.i.* **·esced** (-est′), **·esc·ing** To consent or concur tacitly; assent; comply. [< MF < L < *ad-* to + *quiescere* to rest] —**ac′qui·esc′ing·ly** *adv.*

ac·qui·es·cence (ak′wē·es′əns) *n.* Quiet submission; passive consent. —**ac′qui·es′cent** *adj.* —**ac′qui·es′cent·ly** *adv.*

ac·quire (ə·kwīr′) *v.t.* **·quired, ·quir·ing** **1.** To obtain by one's own endeavor or action. **2.** To come to possess; receive. —Syn. See GET, RECEIVE. [< L < *ad-* to + *quaerere* to seek] —**ac·quir′a·ble** *adj.* —**ac·quir′er** *n.*

acquired character *Biol.* A noninheritable change in an organism resulting from environmental influences.

ac·quire·ment (ə·kwīr′mənt) *n.* **1.** The act of acquiring. **2.** Something acquired, as a skill; an attainment.

ac·qui·si·tion (ak′wə·zish′ən) *n.* **1.** The act of acquiring. **2.** Anything gained or acquired.

ac·quis·i·tive (ə·kwiz′ə·tiv) *adj.* Able or inclined to acquire (money, property, etc.); grasping. —**ac·quis′i·tive·ly** *adv.* —**ac·quis′i·tive·ness** *n.*

ac·quit (ə·kwit′) *v.t.* **·quit·ted, ·quit·ting** **1.** To free or clear, as from an accusation. **2.** To relieve, as of an obligation. **3.** To repay or return. **4.** To conduct (oneself); behave. [< OF < L *ad-* to + *quietare* to settle, quiet] —**ac·quit′tal** *n.* —**ac·quit′ter** *n.*

ac·quit·tance (ə·kwit′ns) *n.* **1.** A release, as from a debt. **2.** Satisfaction of indebtedness or obligation. **3.** A receipt.

a·cre (ā′kər) *n.* **1.** A measure of land, equal to 43,560 square feet. **2.** *pl.* Lands; estate. [OE *æcer* field]

a·cre·age (ā′kər·ij, -krij) *n.* Area in acres; acres collectively.

a·cred (ā′kərd) *adj.* Comprising or owning acres of land.

ac·rid (ak′rid) *adj.* **1.** Cutting or burning to the taste or smell. **2.** Sharp and satirical, as speech. [< L *acer, acris*] —**a·crid·i·ty** (ə·krid′ə·tē), **ac′rid·ness** *n.* —**ac′rid·ly** *adv.*

ac·ri·mo·ny (ak′rə·mō′nē) *n., pl.* **·nies** Sharpness or bitterness of speech or temper; acridity. [< L < *acer* sharp] —**ac·ri·mo·ni·ous** (ak′rə·mō′nē·əs) *adj.* —**ac′ri·mo′ni·ous·ly** *adv.* —**ac′ri·mo′ni·ous·ness** *n.*

acro- *combining form* **1.** At the tip or end of. **2.** *Med.* Pertaining to the extremities. [< Gk. *akros* at the end]

ac·ro·bat (ak′rə·bat) *n.* One skilled in feats requiring muscular coordination, as in tightrope walking, tumbling, trapeze performing, etc.; a gymnast. [< F < Gk. *akrobatos* walking on tiptoe < *akros* at the tip + *bainein* to walk, go] —**ac·ro·bat′ic** or **·i·cal** *adj.* —**ac′ro·bat′i·cal·ly** *adv.*

ac·ro·bat·ics (ak′rə·bat′iks) *n.pl.* The skills or activities of an acrobat, as in gymnastics.

ac·ro·gen (ak′rə·jən) *n. Bot.* A plant growing at the tip only, as ferns, mosses, etc. —**ac·ro·gen·ic** (ak′rə·jen′ik), **a·crog·e·nous** (ə·kroj′ə·nəs) *adj.* —**a·crog′e·nous·ly** *adv.*

ac·ro·meg·a·ly (ak′rō·meg′ə·lē) *n. Pathol.* A disorder of the pituitary gland characterized by an enlargement of the extremities, thorax, and face, including both soft and bony parts. [< F < Gk. *akros* at the tip + *megas, megalou* big] —**ac·ro·me·gal·ic** (ak′rō·mi·gal′ik) *adj. & n.*

ac·ro·nym (ak′rə·nim) *n.* A word formed by combining initial letters (*Eniac, UNESCO*) or syllables and letters (*radar, sonar*) of a series of words or a compound term. [< ACRO- + *-nym* name, as in *homonym*]

a·crop·o·lis (ə·krop′ə·lis) *n.* The citadel of an ancient Greek city. —**the Acropolis** The citadel of Athens. [< Gk. < *akros* at the top + *polis* city]

a·cross (ə·krôs′, ə·kros′) *adv.* **1.** From one side to the other. **2.** On or at the other side. **3.** Crosswise; crossed, as arms. —*prep.* **1.** On or from the other side of; beyond; over. **2.** Through or over the surface of. **3.** From side to side of. [< A-¹ on, in + CROSS]

a·cros·tic (ə·krôs′tik, ə·kros′-) *n.* A poem or other composition in which initial or other letters, taken in order, form a word or phrase. —*adj.* Of or resembling an acrostic. [< L < Gk. < *akros* at the end + *stichos* line of verse] —**a·cros′ti·cal·ly** *adv.*

A·crux (ā′kruks) *n.* One of the 20 brightest stars, 1.05 magnitude; Alpha in the constellation Crux.

a·cryl·ic acid (ə·kril′ik) *Chem.* Any of a series of acids having a sharp, acrid odor, and used in plastics.

act (akt) *v.t.* **1.** To play the part of; impersonate, as in a drama. **2.** To perform on the stage, as a play. **3.** To perform as if on a stage; feign the character of. **4.** To behave as suitable to. —*v.i.* **5.** To behave or conduct oneself. **6.** To carry out a purpose or function; perform. **7.** To produce an effect: often with *on.* **8.** To serve temporarily or as a substitute, as in some office or capacity. **9.** To perform on the stage; be an actor. **10.** To pretend; play a part so as to appear. **11.** To serve for theatrical performance or use: This scene *acts* well. **— to act on** (or **upon**) To order one's conduct in accordance with; obey: to *act on* someone's advice. **— to act up** *Informal* To behave mischievously; appear troublesome. **—** *n.* **1.** The exertion of mental or physical power; the performance of a function or process; a doing: taken in the very *act*. **2.** Something done; a deed; action. **3.** An enactment or edict, as of a legislative body. **4.** *Often pl.* A formal written record or statement of a transaction, action taken, etc. **5.** One of the main divisions of a play or opera. **6.** A short theatrical performance. **7.** *Informal* Something feigned; a pose. [< L *actum* a thing done] **— Syn.** (noun) **2.** *Act* and *deed* are both used for something done, while *action* refers more to the doing of it. *Acts* and *deeds* may be good or bad, but a *deed* is commonly great or notable. A *feat* requires daring and skill, and usually involves physical *action. Achievement* is usually notable and distinguished.

act·a·ble (ak′tə-bəl) *adj.* That can be acted, as a role in a play. **— act′a·bil′i·ty** *n.*

ACTH A pituitary hormone that stimulates the secretion of cortisone by the adrenal cortex.

act·ing (ak′ting) *adj.* **1.** Operating or officiating, especially in place of another: *acting* secretary. **2.** Functioning; working. **—** *n.* **1.** The occupation of an actor. **2.** Pretense or simulation.

ac·tin·i·a (ak·tin′ē-ə) *n.* A sea anemone. Also **ac·tin′i·an.** [< NL < Gk. *aktis, aktinos* ray]

actinic rays Those wavelengths of violet and ultraviolet light capable of effecting chemical changes.

ac·ti·nide series (ak′ti-nīd) *Physics* A series of radioactive elements beginning with actinium, atomic number 89, and ending with lawrencium, atomic number 103.

ac·tin·ism (ak′tin-iz′əm) *n.* **1.** The property of radiant energy that effects chemical changes. **2.** The production of such change. **— ac·tin′ic** *adj.*

ac·tin·i·um (ak·tin′ē-əm) *n.* A radioactive element (symbol Ac), isolated from pitchblende, and having a half life of about 13 years. See ELEMENT.

ac·ti·noid (ak′ti-noid) *adj.* Having the form of rays; radiate, as a starfish.

ac·ti·non (ak′ti-non) *n.*, *Chem.* A radioactive isotope of radon, with a half life of nearly four seconds. [< NL]

ac·ti·no·zo·an (ak′ti-nə-zō′ən) *n.* *Zool.* An anthozoan. [< Gk. *aktis* ray + *zōion* animal] **— ac′ti·no·zo′al** *adj.*

ac·tion (ak′shən) *n.* **1.** The process of acting, doing, or working; operation. **2.** The result of putting forth power; a deed; act. **3.** *pl.* Habitual behavior; conduct. **4.** Activity; energy. **5.** The exertion of power; influence. **6.** *Physiol.* The performance by an organ of its proper function. **7.** *Mech.* **a** The mechanism by which a machine operates. **b** The movement of the parts of a machine. **8.** *Mil.* A battle; combat. **9.** *Law* A lawsuit. **10.** The posture and gestures of an actor or orator. **11.** In literature, the series of connected events that form the plot in a story or play. **12.** In sculpture or painting, gesture or attitude intended to express passion or sentiment. **13.** *Slang* Lively or exciting social activity; excitement: where the *action* is. **— Syn.** See ACT, BATTLE. [< F < L *agere* to do]

ac·tion·a·ble (ak′shən-ə-bəl) *adj.* Affording ground for prosecution, as a trespass or a libel. **— ac′tion·a·bly** *adv.*

ac·ti·vate (ak′tə-vāt) *v.t.* **·vat·ed, ·vat·ing 1.** To make active. **2.** To organize (a military unit) for its assigned function. **3.** *Physics* To make radioactive. **4.** *Chem.* To promote or hasten a reaction in, as by heat. **5.** To purify by aeration, as sewage. **— ac′ti·va′tion** *n.* **— ac′ti·va′tor** *n.*

ac·tive (ak′tiv) *adj.* **1.** Abounding in or exhibiting action; busy. **2.** Being in or pertaining to a state of action; not extinct or quiescent. **3.** Agile; quick; nimble. **4.** Characterized by much activity; brisk; lively. **5.** Causing or promoting action or change; not contemplative. **6.** Bearing interest: *active* investments. **7.** In business, busy; productive: *active* accounts. **8.** *Gram.* Designating a voice of the verb that indicates that the subject of the sentence is performing the action. **—** *n.* *Gram.* The active voice. Abbr. *a.* [< F < L *activus < agere* to do] **— ac′tive·ly** *adv.* **— ac′tive·ness** *n.*

ac·tiv·i·ty (ak·tiv′ə-tē) *n.*, *pl.* **·ties 1.** The state of being active; action. **2.** Brisk or vigorous movement or action; liveliness; energy. **3.** A particular action or sphere of action.

act of God *Law* An event caused by the operations of nature unmixed with human agency or human negligence.

ac·tor (ak′tər) *n.* **1.** A player on the stage, in motion pictures, etc. **2.** One who does something.

ac·tress (ak′tris) *n.* A woman who acts, as on the stage.

Acts of the Apostles The fifth book of the New Testament. Also **Acts.**

ac·tu·al (ak′chōō-əl) *adj.* **1.** Existing in fact; real. **2.** Being in existence or action now; existent; present. [< F < LL < L *actus* a doing] **— ac′tu·al·ness** *n.*

ac·tu·al·i·ty (ak′chōō-al′ə-tē) *n.*, *pl.* **·ties 1.** The state or quality of being actual; reality; realism. **2.** *pl.* Actual circumstances or conditions.

ac·tu·al·ize (ak′chōō-əl-īz′) *v.t.* **·ized, ·iz·ing 1.** To make real; realize in action, as a possibility. **2.** To make seem real; represent realistically. **— ac′tu·al·i·za′tion** *n.*

ac·tu·al·ly (ak′chōō-əl-ē) *adv.* As a matter of fact; really.

ac·tu·ar·y (ak′chōō-er′ē) *n.*, *pl.* **·ar·ies** A statistician who calculates and states risks, premiums, etc., for insurance purposes. [< L *actuarius* clerk] **— ac·tu·ar′i·al** (ak′chōō-âr′ē-əl) *adj.* **— ac·tu·ar′i·al·ly** *adv.*

ac·tu·ate (ak′chōō-āt) *v.t.* **·at·ed, ·at·ing 1.** To set into action or motion, as a mechanism. **2.** To incite or influence to action: *actuated* by motives of kindness. [< Med.L < L *actus* a doing] **— ac′tu·a′tion** *n.* **— ac′tu·a′tor** *n.* **— Syn. 2.** *Actuate* and *impel* both imply mental or moral reasons for acting, while *urge* more often involves persuasion by others or from without.

acu- *combining form* Needle; point. [< L *acus*]

a·cu·i·ty (ə-kyōō′ə-tē) *n.* Acuteness; sharpness. [< MF < Med.L < L *acus* needle]

ac·u·men (ə-kyōō′mən,ak′yōō-mən) *n.* Quickness of insight or discernment. [< L < *acuere* to sharpen] **— Syn. 1.** *Sharpness, acuteness,* and *insight,* however keen, and *perception,* however deep, fall short of the meaning of *acumen,* which belongs to an astute and discriminating mind.

a·cu·mi·nate (ə-kyōō′mə-nāt; for *adj.,* also ə-kyōō′mə-nit) *v.t.* **·nat·ed, ·nat·ing** To sharpen; make pointed. **—** *adj.* Ending in a long, tapering point: also a·cu′mi·nat′ed. [< L *acuminare* to point] **— a·cu′mi·na′tion** *n.*

a·cu·punc·ture (ak′yōō-pungk′chər) *n.* The practice, orig. Chinese, of puncturing the body at certain points with fine needles as a medical treatment. [< ACU- + PUNCTURE]

a·cute (ə-kyōōt′) *adj.* **1.** Coming to a crisis quickly; violent: said of a disease: opposed to *chronic.* **2.** Of the greatest importance; crucial. **3.** Affecting keenly; poignant; intense. **4.** Keenly discerning or sensitive. **5.** *Music* High in pitch; shrill. [< L *acutus,* pp. of *acuere* to sharpen] **— a·cute′ly** *adv.* **— a·cute′ness** *n.*

acute accent See ACCENT (def. 3).

acute angle *Geom.* An angle less than a right angle.

-acy *suffix of nouns* Forming nouns of quality, state, or condition from adjectives in *-acious,* and nouns and adjectives in *-ate: fallacy, celibacy, curacy.* [< F *-atie* < L *-acia, -atia* < Gk. *-ateia*; or directly < L or < Gk.]

ad (ad) *n.* **1.** *Informal* An advertisement. **2.** In tennis, advantage.

ad- *prefix* To; toward; near: *adhere:* also spelled a-, ab-, ac-, af-, ag-, al-, an-, ap-, ar- before various consonants. [< L *ad- < ad* to]

-ad *suffix of nouns* Of or pertaining to; used to form: **a** Collective numerals: *triad.* **b** Names of poems: *Iliad.* [< Gk. *-as, -ados*]

ad·age (ad′ij) *n.* A maxim; proverb. **— Syn.** See PROVERB. [< F < L < *ad-* to + root of *aio* I say]

a·da·gio (ə-dä′jō, -zhē-ō, -zhō) *Music adj.* Slow. **—** *adv.* Slowly. **—** *n.* A composition in adagio time. [< Ital.]

Ad·am (ad′əm) In the Bible, the first man, progenitor of the human race. *Gen.* ii 7. **—** *n.* Mankind collectively: **the old Adam** Unregenerate human nature.

ad·a·mant (ad′ə-mant, -mənt) *n.* A very hard legendary mineral, later identified with the diamond or lodestone. **—** *adj.* **1.** Immovable; unyielding. **2.** Very hard. [< OF < L < Gk. < *a-* not + *damaein* to conquer] **— ad·a·man·tine** (ad′ə-man′tin, -tēn, -tīn) *adj.*

Adam's apple The prominence made by the thyroid cartilage at the front of the human throat, conspicuous in males.

a·dapt (ə-dapt′) *v.t.* **1.** To fit for a new use; make suitable: with *for.* **2.** To adjust (oneself or itself) to a new situation or environment. **—** *v.i.* **3.** To become adjusted to a circumstance or environment. [< F < L *ad* to + *aptare* to fit]

a·dapt·a·ble (ə-dap′tə-bəl) *adj.* **1.** Capable of being adapted. **2.** Able to change easily to meet new circumstances. **— a·dapt′a·bil′i·ty, a·dapt′a·ble·ness** *n.*

ad·ap·ta·tion (ad′ap-tā′shən) *n.* **1.** The act of adapting or the state of being adapted. **2.** Anything produced by adapting. **— ad′ap·ta′tion·al** *adj.* **— ad′ap·ta′tion·al·ly** *adv.*

a·dapt·er (ə-dap′tər) *n.* **1.** A person or thing that adapts. **2.** *Mech.* **a** A device that connects parts not designed to fit together. **b** A device that extends or alters the function of an apparatus. Also **a·dap′tor.** Abbr. *ad.*

a·dap·tive (ə-dap′tiv) *adj.* Capable of, fit for, or manifesting adaptation. **— a·dap′tive·ly** *adv.* **— a·dap′tive·ness** *n.*

A·dar (ə-där′, ä′där) *n.* The sixth month of the Hebrew year. See (Hebrew) CALENDAR.

add (ad) *v.t.* **1.** To join or unite, so as to increase the importance, size, quantity, or scope: with *to.* **2.** To find the sum of, as a column of figures. **3.** To say or write further.

— *v.i.* **4.** To make or be an addition: with *to*. **5.** To perform the arithmetical process of addition. — **to add up 1.** To accumulate to a total. **2.** *Informal* To make sense. [< L *ad*- to + *dare* to give, put] — **add/a·ble** or **add/i·ble** *adj*.
— **Syn.** *Add* denotes the joining of one thing to another to increase it. To *append* is to add something supplemental; *annex* indicates that the addition is subordinate, and often remains distinct. Compare INCREASE.

ad·dend (ad/ənd, ə·dend/) *n. Math.* A quantity or number that is to be added to another.

ad·den·dum (ə·den/dəm) *n. pl.* **·da** (-də) **1.** A thing added, or to be added. **2.** A supplement, as to a book; appendix. [< L, neut. gerundive of *addere* to add]

ad·der (ad/ər) *n.* **1.** A viper, esp. the common European viper. **2.** Any of various other snakes, as the puff adder. [OE *nǣdre* (*a nadder* in ME becoming *an adder*)]

ad·der's-tongue (ad/ərz·tung/) *n.* **1.** A fern with a narrow spike. **2.** The dogtooth violet.

ad·dict (*v.* ə·dikt/; *n.* ad/ikt) *v.t.* To apply or devote (oneself) habitually: with *to*. — *n.* One who is given to some habit, esp. to the use of narcotic drugs. [< L *ad*- to + *dicere* to say] — **ad·dic/tion, ad·dict/ed·ness** *n.*

ad·dict·ed (ə·dik/tid) *adj.* Given over to a pursuit, practice, or habit: with *to*: *addicted* to drugs.
— **Syn.** *Addicted* suggests a pathological weakness; *given*, a tendency or usual practice. Both words may apply to good or bad things, but usually to bad: *addicted* to alcohol, *given* to lying.

ad·di·tion (ə·dish/ən) *n.* **1.** The act of adding. **2.** That which is added. **3.** The uniting of two or more quantities in one sum. — **ad·di/tion·al** *adj.* — **ad·di/tion·al·ly** *adv.*

ad·di·tive (ad/ə·tiv) *n.* Something added or to be added to a product or device. — *adj.* That is to be added; serving or tending to increase. — **ad/di·tive·ly** *adv.*

ad·dle (ad/l) *v.t. & v.i.* **·dled, ·dling 1.** To become or cause to become confused. **2.** To spoil, as eggs. — *adj.* **1.** Confused; mixed up: now generally in compounds: *addlepated*. **2.** Spoiled, as eggs; rotten. [OE *adela* liquid filth]

ad·dle-brained (ad/l·brānd/) *adj.* Confused; mixed up. Also **ad/dle·head/ed, ad/dle·pat/ed, ad/dle·wit/ted.**

ad·dress (ə·dres/; *for n. defs. 2, 3, also* ad/res) *v.t.* **dressed, ·dress·ing 1.** To speak to. **2.** To deliver a set discourse to. **3.** To direct, as spoken or written words, to the attention of: with *to*: to *address* prayers to God. **4.** To devote the energy or force of (oneself): with *to*: to *address* oneself to a task. **5.** To mark with a destination, as a letter. **6.** To consign, as a cargo to a merchant. **7.** To aim or direct. **8.** To pay court to, as a lover; woo. **9.** To assume a preparatory stance toward (a golf ball, etc.). — *n.* **1.** A set or formal discourse. **2.** The writing on an envelope, etc., indicating its destination. **3.** The name, place, residence, etc., of a person. **4.** The manner of a person; bearing. **5.** *Chiefly pl.* Any courteous or devoted attention; wooing. **6.** Adroitness; tact. [< OF < L *ad*- to + *directus* straight] — **ad·dress/er, ad·dress/or** *n.*

ad·dress·ee (ad/res·ē/, ə·dres/ē/) *n.* One to whom mail, etc., is addressed.

ad·duce (ə·dōōs/, ə·dyōōs/) *v.t.* **·duced, ·duc·ing** To present for proof or consideration, as an example; cite; allege. [< L *ad*- to + *ducere* to lead] — **ad·duce/a·ble** or **ad·duc/i·ble** *adj.*

ad·duct (ə·dukt/) *v.t. Physiol.* To draw toward the axis: said of muscles. — **ad·duc/tion** *n.* — **ad·duc/tive** *adj.*

ad·duc·tor (ə·duk/tər) *n.* An adducting muscle.

-ade¹ *suffix of nouns* **1.** Act or action: *cannonade*. **2.** A person or group concerned in an action or process: *cavalcade*. **3.** That which is produced by an action or process: *pomade*. **4.** A beverage made with or containing a fruit juice: *lemonade*. [< F < L *-ata*, fem. pp. ending]

-ade² *suffix of nouns* Relating to; pertaining to: *decade*. See -AD¹. [< F *-ade* < Gk. *-as, -ados*]

adeno- *combining form* Gland. Also, before vowels, **aden-**. [< Gk. *adēn* gland]

ad·e·noid (ad/ə·noid) *adj.* Of or like a gland; glandular. Also **ad/e·noi/dal.** — *n. Usually pl. Pathol.* An enlarged lymphoid growth behind the pharynx.

ad·e·no·ma (ad/ə·nō/mə) *n. Pathol.* A tumor of glandular origin or structure. — **ad·e·nom·a·tous** (ad/ə·nom/ə·təs) *adj.*

a·dept (ə·dept/; *for n., also* ad/ept) *adj.* Highly skilled; proficient: an *adept* worker. — *n.* One fully skilled in any art; an expert. [< L *ad*- to + *apisci* to get] — **a·dept/ly** *adv.* — **a·dept/ness** *n.*

ad·e·quate (ad/ə·kwit) *adj.* **1.** Equal to what is required; fully sufficient. **2.** Barely sufficient. [< L *ad*- to + *aequus* equal] — **ad/e·qua·cy** *n.* — **ad/e·quate·ness** *n.* — **ad/e·quate·ly** *adv.*
— **Syn. 1.** *Adequate* is applied to ability or power; *sufficient*, to quantity or number. A man is *adequate* to a situation; a supply is *sufficient* for a need. A thing is *satisfactory* if it measures up, more or less; it is *equal* if it is exactly commensurate. The connotation of these terms varies widely in contexts. An actor called *adequate* is usually regarded as mediocre. A *sufficient* reason may range from

ADENOIDS *(a)*

the flimsiest pretext to the surest demonstration. *Satisfactory* is a term in many grading systems, varying from passing to good.

ad·here (ad·hir/) *v.i.* **·hered, ·her·ing 1.** To stick fast or together. **2.** To be attached or devoted to a party or faith. **3.** To follow closely or without deviation. [< L *ad*- to + *haerere* to stick] — **ad·her/ence** *n.* — **ad·her/er** *n.*

ad·her·ent (ad·hir/ənt) *adj.* Clinging or sticking fast. — *n.* One who is devoted or attached, as to a cause or leader; a follower. — **ad·her/ent·ly** *adv.*
— **Syn.** (noun) *Adherent* is the weakest term. A *follower* is more fervid in his attachment. A *disciple* has a pupil-teacher relationship with the one he follows. A *supporter* is one who aids in any way, while a *partisan* is militant in his support.

ad·he·sion (ad·hē/zhən) *n.* **1.** The act of adhering, or the state of being joined. **2.** Firm attachment, as to a cause; fidelity. **3.** *Physics* The binding force exerted by molecules of unlike substances in contact: distinguished from *cohesion*. **4.** *Med.* Abnormal surface union of dissimilar tissues as a result of inflammation, etc. [See ADHERE.]

ad·he·sive (ad·hē/siv) *adj.* **1.** Tending to adhere; sticky. **2.** Prepared to adhere; gummed. — *n.* A substance that causes adhesion. — **ad·he/sive·ly** *adv.* — **ad·he/sive·ness** *n.*

adhesive tape A piece or strip of fabric coated with adhesive material, used for bandages, dressings, etc.

ad hoc (ad hok/) *Latin* For this purpose.

ad·i·a·bat·ic (ad/ē·ə·bat/ik, ā/dē·ə-) *adj. Physics* Pertaining to a thermodynamic system in which changes are effected without gain or loss of heat. [< Gk. < *a*- not + *dia-* through + *bainein* to go + -IC]

a·dieu (ə·dōō/, ə·dyōō/; *Fr.* à·dyœ/) *n. pl.* **a·dieus,** *Fr.* **a·dieux** (à·dyœ/) A farewell. — *interj.* Good-by; farewell: literally, to God (I commend you). [< F]

ad in·fi·ni·tum (ad in/fə·nī/təm) *Latin* Endlessly; forever.

ad in·ter·im (ad in/tər·im) *Latin* In the meantime.

a·di·os (ä/dē·ōs/, ad/ē·ōs/; *Sp.* ä·thyōs/) *interj.* Farewell; good-by: literally, to God (I commend you). [< Sp.]

ad·i·pose (ad/ə·pōs) *adj.* Of or pertaining to fat; fatty: also **ad·i·pous** (ad/ə·pəs). — *n.* Fat. [< NL < L *adeps, adipis* fat] — **ad/i·pose/ness, ad·i·pos·i·ty** (ad/ə·pos/ə·tē) *n.*

ad·ja·cen·cy (ə·jā/sən·sē) *n. pl.* **·cies 1.** The state of being adjacent; contiguity. **2.** That which is adjacent.

ad·ja·cent (ə·jā/sənt) *adj.* Lying near or close at hand; adjoining; contiguous. Abbr. *adj.* [< L *ad*- near + *jacere* to lie] — **ad·ja·cent·ly** *adv.*

adjacent angle *Geom.* An angle having a common side with another angle and the same vertex.

ad·jec·tive (aj/ik·tiv) *n. Gram.* Any of a class of words used to limit or qualify a noun: one of the eight traditional parts of speech. — *adj. Gram.* Functioning as an adjective; depending upon or standing in adjunct relation to a noun. Abbr. *a., adj.* [< L *adjicere* to add to < *ad*- to + *jacere* to throw] — **ad·jec·ti·val** (aj/ik·tī/vəl, aj/ik·ti·vəl) *adj.* — **ad/jec·ti/val·ly** *adv.*

adjective clause *Gram.* A dependent clause usually introduced by a relative pronoun and qualifying its antecedent, as *who painted my house in the man who painted my house*: also called *relative clause*. Also **adjectival clause.**

ad·join (ə·join/) *v.t.* **1.** To be next to; border upon. **2.** To join to; append; unite: with *to*. — *v.i.* **3.** To lie close together; be in contact. [< OF < L < *ad*- to + *jungere* to join]

ad·join·ing (ə·joi/ning) *adj.* Lying next; contiguous.

ad·journ (ə·jûrn/) *v.t.* **1.** To put off to another day or place, as a meeting or session; postpone. — *v.i.* **2.** To postpone or suspend proceedings for a specified time. **3.** *Informal* To move or go to another place. — **Syn.** See POSTPONE. [< OF < LL < L *ad*- to + *diurnus* daily < *dies* day] — **ad·journ/ment** *n.*

ad·judge (ə·juj/) *v.t.* **·judged, ·judg·ing 1.** To determine or decide judicially, as a case. **2.** To pronounce or order by law: His testimony was *adjudged* perjury. **3.** To condemn or sentence: with *to*. **4.** To award by law, as damages. [< OF < L < *ad*- to + *judicare* to judge]

ad·ju·di·cate (ə·jōō/də·kāt) *v.* **·cat·ed, ·cat·ing** *v.t.* **1.** To determine judicially, as a case; adjudge. — *v.i.* **2.** To act as a judge. — **ad·ju·di·ca/tion** *n.* — **ad·ju/di·ca/tor** *n.*

ad·junct (aj/ungkt) *n.* **1.** Something joined to something else, but in an auxiliary or subordinate position. **2.** A helper; assistant. **3.** *Gram.* A modifier. **4.** *Logic* Any nonessential quality of a thing. — *adj.* Joined subordinately; auxiliary. [See ADJOIN.] — **ad·junc·tive** (ə·jungk/tiv) *adj.* — **ad·junc/tive·ly** *adv.*

ad·jure (ə·jōōr/) *v.t.* **·jured, ·jur·ing 1.** To charge or entreat solemnly, as under oath or penalty. **2.** To appeal to earnestly. [< L *ad*- to + *jurare* to swear] — **ad·ju·ra·tion** (aj/ōō·rā/shən) *n.* — **ad·jur·a·to·ry** (ə·jōōr/ə·tôr/ē, -tō/rē) *adj.* — **ad·jur/er** or **ad·ju/ror** *n.*

ad·just (ə·just/) *v.t.* **1.** To arrange so as to fit or match. **2.** To harmonize or compose, as differences. **3.** To regulate or make accurate. **4.** To determine the amount to be paid in settlement of (an insurance claim). **5.** To arrange in order. — *v.i.* **6.** To adapt oneself; conform, as to a new environment. [< OF < L *ad-* to + *juxta* near; refashioned on F *juste* right < L *justus*] **— ad·just'a·ble** *adj.* **— ad·just'er** or **ad·jus'tor** *n.* **— ad·jus'tive** *adj.*

ad·just·ment (ə·just'mənt) *n.* **1.** The act of adjusting or the state of being adjusted. **2.** An instrument or means of adjusting. **3.** The amount to be paid in settling a claim.

ad·ju·tant (aj'ōō·tənt) *n.* **1.** *Mil.* A staff officer who assists a commanding officer in administrative duties. Abbr. *adj.* **2.** A carrion-eating East Indian stork: also called *marabou:* also **adjutant stork, adjutant crane.** [< L *adjutare* to assist] **— ad'ju·tan·cy, ad'ju·tant·ship** *n.*

adjutant general *pl.* **adjutants general** The adjutant of a military unit having a general staff. **— The Adjutant General** The major general in charge of the administrative branch of the United States Army.

ad-lib (ad'lib') *Informal v.t. & v.i.* **-libbed, -lib·bing** To improvise, as words or gestures not called for in the script. **—** *n.* An instance of this. [< AD LIBITUM]

ad lib·i·tum (ad lib'ə·təm) **1.** *Latin* As one pleases. **2.** *Music* Freely: a direction indicating that a section may be played as the performer wishes.

ad·meas·ure (ad·mezh'ər) *v.t.* **·ured, ·ur·ing** To apportion. [< OF < LL < *ad-* to + *mensurare* to measure] **— ad·meas'ur·er** *n.* **— ad·meas'ure·ment** *n.*

ad·min·is·ter (ad·min'is·tər) *v.t.* **1.** To have the charge or direction of; manage. **2.** To supply or provide with; apply, as medicine or treatment. **3.** To inflict; mete out; dispense. **4.** *Law* To act as executor or trustee of. **5.** To tender, as an oath. **—** *v.i.* **6.** To contribute help; minister: with *to.* **7.** To carry out the functions of an administrator. [< OF < L < *ad-* to + *ministrare* to serve] **— ad·min·is·te'ri·al** (ad·min'is·tir'ē·əl) *adj.* **— ad'min·is·tra·ble** *adj.*

ad·min·is·trate (ad·min'is·trāt) *v.t.* **·trat·ed, ·trat·ing** To administer.

ad·min·is·tra·tion (ad·min'is·trā'shən) *n.* **1.** The act of administering, or the state of being administered. **2.** The executive personnel of a government, institution, etc.: also, their policies. **3.** The term of office of such a government. **4.** *Law* The legal management of an estate.

ad·min·is·tra·tive (ad·min'is·trā'tiv) *adj.* Pertaining to administration; executive. **— ad·min'is·tra'tive·ly** *adv.*

ad·min·is·tra·tor (ad·min'is·trā'tər) *n.* **1.** One who administers something; an executive. **2.** *Law* One commissioned by a competent court to administer the personal property of a deceased or incompetent person. [< L] **— ad·min'is·tra'tor·ship** *n.*

ad·min·is·tra·trix (ad·min'is·trā'triks) *n.* *pl.* **·tra·trix·es** or **·tra·tri·ces** (-trā'trə·sēz, -trə·trī'sēz) A woman administrator. Also **ad·min'is·tra'tress.**

ad·mi·ra·ble (ad'mər·ə·bəl) *adj.* Worthy of admiration; excellent. **— ad'mi·ra·ble·ness, ad'mi·ra·bil'i·ty** *n.* **— ad'mi·ra·bly** *adv.*

ad·mi·ral (ad'mər·əl) *n.* **1.** The supreme commander of a navy or fleet. **2.** In the U.S. Navy and Royal Canadian Navy, an officer of the next to highest rank, equivalent to a general; also, loosely, a rear admiral or a vice admiral. [< OF < Arabic *amīr-al* commander of the]

Admiral of the Fleet The highest rank in the U.S. and Royal Canadian Navies, corresponding to General of the Army or Field Marshal. Also **Fleet Admiral.**

ad·mi·ral·ty (ad'mər·əl·tē) *n.* *pl.* **·ties 1.** The office or functions of an admiral. **2.** *Law* Maritime law or courts.

Ad·mi·ral·ty (ad'mər·əl·tē) *n.* **1.** A department of the British government having charge of naval affairs. **2.** The building in London housing this department.

ad·mi·ra·tion (ad'mə·rā'shən) *n.* **1.** A feeling of wonder and approbation, as at the sight of anything rare, excellent, or sublime. **2.** High esteem. **3.** That which is admired.

ad·mire (ad·mīr') *v.* **·mired, ·mir·ing** *v.t.* **1.** To regard with wonder, pleasure, and approbation. **2.** To have respect or esteem for. **—** *v.i.* **3.** To feel or express admiration. [< F < L < *ad-* at + *mirari* to wonder] **— ad·mir'er** *n.* **— ad·mir'ing** *adj.* **— ad·mir'ing·ly** *adv.*

ad·mis·si·ble (ad·mis'ə·bəl) *adj.* **1.** Worthy of being considered; allowable. **2.** Such as may be admitted. [< L] **— ad·mis'si·bil'i·ty, ad·mis'si·ble·ness** *n.* **— ad·mis'si·bly** *adv.*

ad·mis·sion (ad·mish'ən) *n.* **1.** The act of admitting, or the state of being admitted. **2.** Authority to enter. **3.** An entrance fee. **4.** A confession. **5.** Anything conceded.

ad·mis·sive (ad·mis'iv) *adj.* Characterized by, implying, or granting admission. Also **ad·mis·so·ry** (ad·mis'ər·ē).

ad·mit (ad·mit') *v.* **·mit·ted, ·mit·ting** *v.t.* **1.** To allow to enter. **2.** To be the means or channel of admission to; let in. **3.** To allow to join. **4.** To have room for; contain. **5.** To leave room for; permit: His impatience *admits* no delay. **6.** To concede or grant as valid. **7.** To acknowledge or avow. **—** *v.i.* **8.** To afford possibility or opportunity: This problem *admits* of several solutions. **9.** To afford entrance; open on:

with *to:* This gate *admits* to the garden. **— Syn.** See CONFESS. [< OF < L < *ad-* to + *mittere* to send]

ad·mit·tance (ad·mit'ns) *n.* **1.** The act of admitting, or the state or fact of being admitted; entrance. **2.** Right or permission to enter. **3.** Actual entrance; admission. **4.** *Electr.* The ability of a circuit to carry an alternating current, combining the effects of conductance and susceptance.

ad·mit·ted·ly (ad·mit'id·lē) *adv.* By admission; confessedly.

ad·mix (ad·miks') *v.t. & v.i.* **·mixed** or **·mixt, ·mix·ing** To mingle or mix with something else. [ME < L *ad-* to + *miscere* to mix]

ad·mix·ture (ad·miks'chər) *n.* **1.** The act of mixing, or the state of being mixed. **2.** Anything added in mixing.

ad·mon·ish (ad·mon'ish) *v.t.* **1.** To administer mild reproof to. **2.** To caution against danger or error; warn. **3.** To charge authoritatively; exhort; urge. [< OF < LL < L < *ad-* to + *monere* to warn] **— ad·mon'ish·er** *n.*

ad·mo·ni·tion (ad'mə·nish'ən) *n.* **1.** The act of admonishing. **2.** A gentle reproof. Also **ad·mon'ish·ment.**

ad·mon·i·tor (ad·mon'ə·tər) *n.* One who admonishes. [< L] **— ad·mon'i·to·ry** (ad·mon'ə·tôr'ē, -tō'rē) *adj.*

ad nau·se·am (ad nô'zē·əm, -sē-, -zhē-, -shē-; äd) *Latin* To the point of nausea or disgust.

a·do (ə·dōō') *n.* Activity; bustle; fuss. [ME *at do* to do]

a·do·be (ə·dō'bē) *n.* **1.** An unburnt, sun-dried brick. **2.** The mixed earth or sandy, calcareous clay of which such bricks are made. **3.** A structure made of such bricks. [< Sp.]

ad·o·les·cence (ad'ə·les'əns) *n.* **1.** The period of growth from puberty to adulthood. **2.** The quality or condition of being adolescent.

ad·o·les·cent (ad'ə·les'ənt) *adj.* **1.** Approaching adulthood. **2.** Characteristic of or pertaining to youth. **—** *n.* A person in the period of adolescence. **— Syn.** See YOUTHFUL. [< L < *ad-* to + *alescere* to grow]

A·don·is (ə·don'is, ə·dō'nis) In Greek mythology, a youth beloved by Aphrodite for his beauty and killed by a wild boar. **—** *n.* Any man of rare beauty.

a·dopt (ə·dopt') *v.t.* **1.** To take into some new relationship, as that of son, heir, etc. **2.** To take into one's family or as one's child by legal measures. **3.** To take and follow as one's own, as a course of action. **4.** To take up from someone else and use as one's own. **5.** To vote to accept, as a motion. [< MF < L < *ad-* to + *optare* to choose] **— a·dopt'a·ble** *adj.* **— a·dopt'er** *n.* **— a·dop'tion** *n.*

a·dop·tive (ə·dop'tiv) *adj.* **1.** Of or characterized by adoption. **2.** Related by adoption. **— a·dop'tive·ly** *adv.*

a·dor·a·ble (ə·dôr'ə·bəl, ə·dōr'-) *adj.* **1.** Worthy of adoration. **2.** *Informal* Delightful; lovable. **— a·dor'a·ble·ness, a·dor'a·bil'i·ty** *n.* **— a·dor'a·bly** *adv.*

ad·o·ra·tion (ad'ə·rā'shən) *n.* **1.** The act of adoring, as in worship. **2.** A feeling of profound admiration and devotion. **3.** An act of homage to a person or object.

a·dore (ə·dôr', ə·dōr') *v.* **a·dored, a·dor·ing** *v.t.* **1.** To render divine honors to; worship as divine. **2.** To love or honor with intense devotion. **3.** *Informal* To like especially. **—** *v.i.* **4.** To worship. **— Syn.** See VENERATE. [< OF < L < *ad-* to + *orare* to speak, pray] **— a·dor'er** *n.*

a·dorn (ə·dôrn') *v.t.* **1.** To increase the beauty of; enhance. **2.** To furnish or decorate with or as with ornaments. [< OF < L < *ad-* to + *ornare* to deck out] **— a·dorn'er** *n.* **— a·dorn'ment** *n.*

ad·re·nal (ə·drē'nəl) *Physiol. n.* An adrenal gland. **—** *adj.* **1.** Near or upon the kidneys. **2.** Of or from the adrenal glands. [< AD- + L *renes* kidneys + -AL³]

adrenal gland One of a pair of small ductless glands situated on the kidneys of most vertebrates, in man secreting epinephrine and cortin: also called *suprarenal gland.*

Ad·ren·a·lin (ə·dren'ə·lin) *n.* Proprietary name for a brand of epinephrine. Also **ad·ren·a·lin** (ə·dren'ə·lin).

ad·re·no·cor·ti·co·tro·pic hormone (ə·drē'nō·kôr'ti·kō·trō'pik) *Physiol.* ACTH.

A·dri·at·ic (ā'drē·at'ik) *adj.* Of or pertaining to the Adriatic Sea or to the inhabitants of its coastal regions.

a·drift (ə·drift') *adv. & adj.* Without moorings; drifting.

a·droit (ə·droit') *adj.* Skillful; expert. [< F < à to + *droit* right] **— a·droit'ly** *adv.* **— a·droit'ness** *n.*

ad·sorb (ad·sôrb', -zôrb') *v.t. Chem.* To condense and hold by adsorption: distinguished from *absorb.* [< AD- + L *sorbere* to suck in] **— ad·sor'bent** *n. & adj.*

ad·sorp·tion (ad·sôrp'shən, -zôrp'-) *n. Chem.* The action of a body, as charcoal, in condensing and holding a gas or soluble substance upon its surface. **— ad·sorp'tive** *adj.*

ad·u·late (aj'ōō·lāt) *v.t.* **·lat·ed, ·lat·ing** To flatter or praise extravagantly. [< L *adulari* to fawn] **— ad'u·la'tion** *n.* **— ad'u·la'tor** *n.* **— ad·u·la·to·ry** (aj'ōō·lə·tôr'ē, -tō'rē) *adj.*

a·dult (ə·dult', ad'ult) *n.* **1.** A person who has attained the age of maturity or legal majority. **2.** *Biol.* A fully developed animal or plant. **—** *adj.* **1.** Pertaining to mature life;

full-grown. **2.** Of or for mature people. [< L < *ad-* to + *alescere* to grow] **— a·dult'ness** *n.* **— a·dult'hood** *n.*

a·dul·ter·ant (ə·dul'tər·ənt) *n.* An adulterating substance. **—** *adj.* Adulterating.

a·dul·ter·ate (ə·dul'tə·rāt; *for adj., also* ə·dul'tər·it) *v.t.* **·at·ed, ·at·ing** To make impure or inferior by admixture of other ingredients; corrupt. **—** *adj.* Corrupted; debased. [< L < *ad-* to + *alter* other, different] **— a·dul'ter·a'tion** *n.* **— a·dul'ter·a'tor** *n.*

a·dul·ter·er (ə·dul'tər·ər) *n.* One who commits adultery. **— a·dul'ter·ess** (-tər·is, -tris) *n. fem.*

a·dul·ter·ous (ə·dul'tər·əs) *adj.* Of, pertaining to, or given to adultery; illicit. **— a·dul'ter·ous·ly** *adv.*

a·dul·ter·y (ə·dul'tər·ē) *n.* *pl.* **·ter·ies** The voluntary sexual intercourse of a married person with someone not the spouse; unfaithfulness. [< L *adulterium*]

ad·um·brate (ad·um'brāt, ə·dum'-) *v.t.* **·brat·ed, ·brat·ing** **1.** To represent the mere shadow of; outline sketchily. **2.** To overshadow; darken. [< L < *ad-* to + *umbrare* to shade] **— ad'um·bra'tion** *n.* **— ad·um'bra·tive** *adj.*

ad va·lo·rem (ad və·lôr'əm, -lō'rəm) *Latin* According or in proportion to the value. Abbr. *adv., ad val.*

ad·vance (ad·vans', -väns') *v.* **·vanced, ·vanc·ing** *v.t.* **1.** To move or cause to go forward or upward. **2.** To offer; propose. **3.** To further; promote. **4.** To put in a better or more advantageous rank, position, or situation. **5.** To make occur earlier; accelerate. **6.** To raise (a rate, price, etc.). **7.** To pay, as money or interest, before legally due. **8.** To lend, as money. **9.** *Law* To provide an advancement for. **—** *v.i.* **10.** To move or go forward. **11.** To make progress; rise or improve. **—** *adj.* **1.** Being before in time; early. **2.** Being or going before; in front. **—** *n.* **1.** The act of going forward; progress. **2.** Improvement; promotion. **3.** An increase or rise, as of prices. **4.** *pl.* Personal approaches; overtures. **5.** The supplying of goods, money, etc., on credit. **6.** The goods or money so supplied; a loan. **7.** The payment of money before it is legally due. **8.** *U.S.* The front or foremost part. Abbr. *adv.* **— in advance 1.** Before due; beforehand. [ME < OF *avancier* < L < *ab-* away + *ante* before] **— ad·vanc'er** *n.*

ad·vanced (ad·vanst', -vänst') *adj.* **1.** In advance of others, as in progress or thought. **2.** In front; moved forward. **3.** At a late or forward stage, as of life, time, etc.

ad·vance·ment (ad·vans'mənt, -väns'-) *n.* **1.** The act of advancing, or the state of being advanced. **2.** Progression; promotion; preferment. **3.** An advance of property or money.

ad·van·tage (ad·van'tij, -vän'-) *n.* **1.** Any circumstance, state, or condition favoring success. **2.** Benefit or gain; profit. **3.** A better state or position; superiority. **4.** In tennis, the first point scored after deuce. **— to advantage** To good effect; favorably. **— to take advantage of 1.** To avail oneself of. **2.** To impose upon; use selfishly. **—** *v.t.* **·taged, ·tag·ing** To give advantage or profit to. [< OF < *avant* before < L *ab ante* from before]

ad·van·ta·geous (ad'vən·tā'jəs) *adj.* Affording advantage; profitable; favorable; beneficial. **— ad'van·ta'geous·ly** *adv.* **— ad'van·ta'geous·ness** *n.*

ad·vec·tion (ad·vek'shən) *n.* *Meteorol.* Heat transfer by the horizontal motion of air. [< L < *ad-* to + *vehere* to carry] **— ad·vec'tive** *adj.*

ad·vent (ad'vent) *n.* A coming or arrival. [< L < *ad-* to + *venire* to come]

Ad·vent (ad'vent) *n.* **1.** The birth of Christ. **2.** The Second Advent. **3.** The season prior to Christmas.

Ad·vent·ist (ad'ven·tist, ad·ven'-) *n.* A member of a denomination that believes the Second Advent is imminent. The largest U.S. Adventist bodies are the **Advent Christian Church** and the **Seventh-Day Adventists.**

ad·ven·ti·tious (ad'ven·tish'əs) *adj.* Not inherent; accidentally acquired; extrinsic. **— ad'ven·ti'tious·ly** *adv.* **— ad'ven·ti'tious·ness** *n.*

ad·ven·tive (ad·ven'tiv) *adj.* Occurring away from the natural habitat; exotic.

ad·ven·ture (ad·ven'chər) *n.* **1.** A hazardous or perilous undertaking. **2.** A stirring or thrilling experience. **3.** Risky or exciting activity. **4.** A commercial venture; speculation. **—** *v.* **tured, ·tur·ing** *v.t.* **1.** To venture upon; take the chance of. **—** *v.i.* **2.** To venture upon daring or dangerous undertakings. [< OF < L *adventura* about to happen]

ad·ven·tur·er (ad·ven'chər·ər) *n.* **1.** One who seeks after or takes part in adventures. **2.** One who seeks his fortune in war; a soldier of fortune. **3.** A speculator in commerce. **4.** A person who seeks advancement by questionable means. **— ad·ven'tur·ess** *n. fem.*

ad·ven·tur·ous (ad·ven'chər·əs) *adj.* **1.** Disposed to seek adventures or take risks; venturesome. Also **ad·ven'ture·some** (-səm). **2.** Attended with risk; hazardous. **— ad·ven'tur·ous·ly** *adv.* **— ad·ven'tur·ous·ness** *n.*

ad·verb (ad'vûrb) *n.* *Gram.* Any of a class of words used to modify the meaning of a verb, adjective, or other adverb, in regard to time, place, manner, means, cause, degree, etc. [< L < *ad-* to + *verbum* verb] **— ad·ver'bi·al** *adj.* **— ad·ver'bi·al·ly** *adv.*

adverb clause *Gram.* A dependent clause that functions as an adverb in a sentence, as *when the guests arrive* in *We will eat when the guests arrive:* also **adverbial clause.**

ad·ver·sar·y (ad'vər·ser'ē) *n. pl.* **·sar·ies** One actively hostile to another; an opponent; enemy. **— Syn.** See ENEMY.

ad·ver·sa·tive (ad·vûr'sə·tiv) *adj.* Expressing opposition or antithesis. **—** *n.* An antithetic word or proposition. [< L *adversatus* opposite] **— ad·ver'sa·tive·ly** *adv.*

ad·verse (ad·vûrs', ad'vûrs) *adj.* **1.** Opposed; antagonistic. **2.** Unpropitious; detrimental. **3.** Opposite. [< L < *ad-* to + *vertere* to turn] **— ad·verse'ly** *adv.* **— ad·verse'ness** *n.*

ad·ver·si·ty (ad·vûr'sə·tē) *n. pl.* **·ties 1.** A condition of hardship or affliction. **2.** *Often pl.* A misfortune.

ad·vert (ad·vûrt') *v.i.* To call attention; refer: with *to.* [< L *advertere* < *ad-* to + *vertere* to turn]

ad·ver·tent (ad·vûr'tənt) *adj.* Giving attention; heedful. **— ad·ver'tence, ad·ver'ten·cy** *n.* **— ad·ver'tent·ly** *adv.*

ad·ver·tise (ad'vər·tīz, ad'vər·tīz') *v.* **·tised, ·tis·ing** *v.t.* **1.** To make known by public notice; proclaim the qualities of, as by publication or broadcasting, generally in order to sell. **—** *v.i.* **2.** To inquire by public notice, as in a newspaper: to *advertise* for a house. **3.** To distribute or publish advertisements. Also **ad've·tize.** [< MF < L *advertere* to direct one's attention to] **— ad'ver·tis'er** *n.*

ad·ver·tise·ment (ad'vər·tīz'mənt, ad·vûr'tis·mənt, -tiz-) *n.* A public notice, as in a newspaper or on a radio program. Also **ad'ver·tize'ment.** Abbr. *ad., adv., advt.*

ad·ver·tis·ing (ad'vər·tī'zing) *n.* **1.** Advertisements collectively. **2.** The business of writing and publicizing advertisements. Also **ad'ver·tiz'ing.**

ad·vice (ad·vīs') *n.* **1.** Counsel given to encourage or dissuade; suggestion. **2.** *Often pl.* Information; notification. [< OF < LL < L *ad-* to + *videre* to see]

ad·vis·a·ble (ad·vī'zə·bəl) *adj.* Proper to be advised or recommended; sensible. **— Syn.** See EXPEDIENT. **— ad·vis'a·bil'i·ty, ad·vis'a·ble·ness** *n.* **— ad·vis'a·bly** *adv.*

ad·vise (ad·vīz') *v.* **·vised, ·vis·ing** *v.t.* **1.** To give advice to; counsel. **2.** To recommend. **3.** To notify; inform, as of a transaction: with *of.* **—** *v.i.* **4.** To take counsel: with *with:* **5.** To give advice. Abbr. *adv.* [< OF < LL < L *ad-* to + *videre* to see]

ad·vised (ad·vīzd') *adj.* **1.** Planned; deliberate: chiefly in *ill-advised, well-advised.*

ad·vis·ed·ly (ad·vī'zid·lē) *adv.* With forethought or advice.

ad·vise·ment (ad·vīz'mənt) *n.* Consultation; deliberation.

ad·vis·er (ad·vī'zər) *n.* **1.** One who advises. **2.** A teacher in a school or college who counsels students about their studies, careers, etc. Also **ad·vi'sor.**

ad·vi·so·ry (ad·vī'zər·ē) *adj.* **1.** Having power to advise. **2.** Containing or given as advice; not mandatory.

ad·vo·ca·cy (ad'və·kə·sē) *n.* The act of advocating or pleading a cause; vindication; defense.

ad·vo·cate (*v.* ad'və·kāt; *n.* ad'və·kit, -kāt) *v.t.* **cat·ed, ·cat·ing** To speak or write in favor of; defend; recommend. **—** *n.* **1.** One who pleads the cause of another; an intercessor. **2.** One who espouses or defends a cause by argument: an *advocate* of slavery. [< OF < L < *ad-* to + *vocare* to call] **— ad'vo·ca'tor** *n.* **— ad·voc·a·to·ry** (ad·vok'ə·tôr'ē, -tō'rē) *adj.*

adz (adz) *n.* A hand cutting tool with its blade at right angles to its handle and usually curved inward, used for dressing timber, etc. Also **adze.** [OE *adesa*]

ae- For those words not entered below see under E-.

æ 1. A ligature of Latin origin, equivalent to Greek *ai:* usually printed *ae.* It is sometimes retained in the spelling of Greek and Latin proper names and in certain scientific terms, but, in modern use, is generally reduced to *e.* **2.** A character in Old English, representing the sound of *a* in modern *hat.*

ADZES
a Sculptor's.
b Cooper's.
c Carpenter's.

a·e·des (ā·ē'dēz) *n.* A mosquito that carries yellow fever: formerly called *stegomyia.* [< NL < Gk. < *a-* not + *hēdys* sweet]

Ae·ge·an (i·jē'ən) *adj.* Of or pertaining to the Aegean Islands or the Aegean Sea.

Æ·gir (ā'jər, ā'jər) The Norse god of the sea. Also **Æ'ger.**

ae·gis (ē'jis) *n.* **1.** In Greek mythology, the breastplate of Zeus and Athena. **2.** Any shield or armor. **3.** A protecting influence. Also spelled *egis.* [< Gk. *aigis* goatskin]

-aemia See -EMIA.

Ae·ne·as (i·nē'əs) In classical legend, a Trojan warrior and hero of the *Aeneid.* After the sack of Troy he wandered for seven years before reaching Latium.

Ae·ne·id (i·nē'id) A Latin epic poem by Vergil, narrating the adventures of Aeneas.

ae·o·li·an (ē·ō'lē·ən) *adj.* Pertaining to or caused by the winds; wind-borne: also spelled *eolian.*

Aeolian harp A stringed instrument so constructed as to produce musical sounds when exposed to a current of air.

Ae·o·lus (ē′ə·ləs) In Greek mythology, the god of the winds.

ae·on (ē′ən, ē′on), **ae·o·ni·an** (ē·ō′nē·ən) See EON, etc.

aer- Var. of AERO-.

aer·ate (âr′āt, ā′ə·rāt) v.t. **·at·ed, ·at·ing** 1. To supply or charge with air or gas. 2. To purify by exposure to air. — **aer·a′tion** n. — **aer′a·tor** n.

aeri- Var. of AERO-.

aer·i·al (âr′ē·əl, ā·ir′ē·əl) adj. 1. Of or in the air. 2. Living or moving in the air. 3. Extending into the air; lofty. 4. Light as air; airy. 5. Unsubstantial; intangible; imaginary. 6. Of, by, or pertaining to aircraft, or to flying. — n. An antenna, as in television. [< L aer air] — **aer′i·al·ly** adv.

aer·i·al·ist (âr′ē·əl·ist, ā·ir′ē·əl-) n. One who performs on a tightrope, trapeze, etc.

aer·ie (âr′ē, ir′ē) n. 1. The nest of a predatory bird, as the eagle, on a crag. 2. The brood or young of such a bird. 3. A house or stronghold situated on a height. Also spelled *aery, eyrie, eyry.* [< Med.L < OF < L *area* open space]

aer·i·fy (âr′ə·fī, ā′ə·fī) v.t. **·fied, ·fy·ing** 1. To aerate. 2. To change into a gaseous form. — **aer′i·fi·ca′tion** n.

aero- *combining form* 1. Air; of the air. 2. Of aircraft or flying. 3. Gas; of gases. Also *aer-, aeri-.* [< Gk. *aēr* air]

aer·obe (âr′ōb, ā′ər-ōb) n. A microorganism that can live only in air or free oxygen. [< AERO- + Gk. *bios* life] — **aer·o′bic** adj.

aer·o·drome (âr′ə·drōm, ā′ər-ə-) n. An airdrome.

aer·o·dy·nam·ics (âr′ō·dī·nam′iks, ā′ər-ō-) n.pl. (construed as sing.) The branch of physics that treats of the laws of motion of gases, under the influence of gravity and other forces. — **aer′o·dy·nam′ic** adj.

aer·o·gramme (âr′ə·gram, ā′ər-ə-) n. An international airmail letter consisting of a single folded sheet. [< Fr.]

aer·o·lite (âr′ə·līt, ā′ər-ə-) n. A meteorite containing more stone than iron. Also **aer′o·lith** (-lith). [< AERO- + Gk. *lithos* stone] — **aer′o·lit′ic** (-lit′ik) adj.

aer·ol·o·gy (âr·ol′ə·jē, ā′ə·rol′-) n. *pl.* **·gies** The scientific study of the atmosphere and its phenomena. — **aer·o·log′ic** (âr′ə·loj′ik, ā′ər-ə-) or **·i·cal** adj. — **aer·ol′o·gist** n.

aer·o·me·chan·ics (âr′ō·mə·kan′iks, ā′ər-ō-) n.pl. (construed as sing.) The science that treats of equilibrium and motion of air and gases. — **aer′o·me·chan′ic** adj. & n.

aer·o·naut (âr′ə·nôt, ā′ər-ə-) n. One who pilots a balloon or dirigible. [< F < Gk. *aēr* air + *nautēs* sailor]

aer·o·nau·tics (âr′ə·nô′tiks, ā′ər-ə-) n.pl. (construed as sing.) 1. The science or art of navigating aircraft. 2. That branch of engineering that deals with the design, construction, operation, and performance of aircraft. — **aer′o·nau′tic, aer′o·nau′ti·cal** adj.

aer·o·pause (âr′ə·pôz, ā′ər-ə-) n. *Meteorol.* The region of the atmosphere near outer space.

aer·o·phyte (âr′ə·fīt, ā′ər-ə-) n. An epiphyte.

aer·o·plane (âr′ə·plān, ā′ər-ə-) n. *Brit.* Airplane.

aer·o·sol (âr′ə·sōl, -sol, ā′ər-ə-) n. A suspension of solid or liquid particles in a gas.

aerosol bomb A small spraying can holding a liquid, as an insecticide, etc., under gas pressure.

aer·o·space (âr′ō·spās, ā′ər-ō-) n. 1. The earth's atmosphere and outer space, considered as a single region in the operation of spacecraft. 2. The study of this region.

aerospace medicine The branch of medicine that deals with conditions and disorders associated with space flight.

aer·o·sphere (âr′ə·sfir, ā′ər-ə-) n. The entire atmosphere considered as a single gaseous shell surrounding the earth.

aer·o·stat (âr′ə·stat, ā′ər-ə-) n. Any lighter-than-air craft, as a balloon or dirigible. [< F < Gk. *aēr* air + *statos* standing] — **aer′o·stat′ic** or **·i·cal** adj.

aer·o·stat·ics (âr′ə·stat′iks, ā′ər-ə-) n.pl. (construed as sing.) The branch of physics that treats of the mechanical properties of air and gases in equilibrium.

aer·y (âr′ē, ir′ē) See AERIE.

Aes·cu·la·pi·us (es′kyə·lā′pē·əs) In Roman mythology, the god of medicine: identified with the Greek *Asclepius.*

Æ·sir (ā′sir, ē′-) n. *pl.* of **As** (äs) The gods of the Norse pantheon collectively.

aes·thete (es′thēt), **aes·thet·ic** (es·thet′ik), etc. See ESTHETE, etc.

aes·ti·val (es′tə·vəl, es·tī′-), **aes·ti·vate** (es′tə·vāt), etc. See ESTIVAL, etc.

ae·ther (ē′thər) See ETHER (defs. 3 and 4).

ae·ti·ol·o·gy (ē′tē·ol′ə·jē) See ETIOLOGY.

af- Assimilated var. of AD-.

a·far (ə·fär′) adv. At, from, or to a distance; remotely.

af·fa·ble (af′ə·bəl) adj. Easy to approach and speak to; friendly; courteous. [< F < L < *ad-* to + *fari* to speak] — **af′fa·bil′i·ty, af′fa·ble·ness** n. — **af′fa·bly** adv.

af·fair (ə·fâr′) n. 1. Anything done or to be done; business; concern. 2. *pl.* Matters of business or concern. 3. A thing or occurrence. 4. A love affair. 5. A social event, as a wedding reception. [< OF < L *ad* to + *facere* to do]

af·fect¹ (v. ə·fekt′; n. af′ekt) v.t. 1. To act upon or have an effect upon; influence. 2. To touch or move emotionally. — n. *Psychol.* Emotion; feeling. [< L < *ad-* to + *facere* to do; noun < G *affekt*]

af·fect² (ə·fekt′) v.t. 1. To show a preference for by wearing, using, etc.; fancy: to *affect* large hats. 2. To imitate or assume: to *affect* a British accent. [< F < L *affectare* to aim at. See AFFECT¹.] — **af·fect′er** n.

af·fec·ta·tion (af′ek·tā′shən) n. 1. A studied pretense; display: with *of.* 2. Artificiality of manner or behavior.

af·fec·ted¹ (ə·fek′tid) adj. 1. Acted upon, as by a drug. 2. Moved emotionally. 3. Attacked, as by disease.

af·fect·ed² (ə·fek′tid) adj. 1. Artificial; feigned. 2. Showing affectation. [pp. of AFFECT²] — **af·fect′ed·ly** adv. — **af·fect′ed·ness** n.

af·fect·ing (ə·fek′ting) adj. Having power to move the feelings; touching; pathetic. — **af·fect′ing·ly** adv.

af·fec·tion (ə·fek′shən) n. 1. Fond attachment or kind feeling. 2. *Often pl.* A mental state brought about by any influence; an emotion or feeling. 3. An abnormal state of the body; disease. 4. The act of affecting or the state of being affected.

af·fec·tion·ate (ə·fek′shən·it) adj. Having or expressing affection; loving; fond. — **af·fec′tion·ate·ly** adv. — **af·fec′tion·ate·ness** n.

af·fer·ent (af′ər·ənt) adj. *Physiol.* Conducting inward, or toward the center, as nerves that transmit sensory stimuli to the central nervous system: opposed to *efferent.* [< L < *ad-* to + *ferre* to bear]

af·fi·ance (ə·fī′əns) v.t. **·anced, ·anc·ing** To promise in marriage; betroth. — n. A betrothal; pledge of faith. [< OF *afiance* trust, confidence] — **af·fi′an·cer** n.

af·fi·da·vit (af′ə·dā′vit) n. *Law* A sworn, written declaration, made before competent authority. — Syn. See TESTIMONY. [< Med.L, he has pledged on oath]

af·fil·i·ate (v. ə·fil′ē·āt; n. ə·fil′ē·it) v. **·at·ed, ·at·ing** v.t. 1. To associate or unite, as a member or branch to a larger or principal body: with *to* or *with.* 2. To join or associate (oneself): with *with.* 3. To determine the source or relations of. — v.i. 4. To associate or ally oneself: with *with.* — n. An affiliated person, company, etc. [< L *affiliare* to adopt < *ad-* to + *filius* son] — **af·fil′i·a′tion** n.

af·fin·i·ty (ə·fin′ə·tē) n. *pl.* **·ties** 1. A natural attraction or inclination. 2. Any close relation or agreement; kinship in general; similarity. 3. Relationship by marriage. 4. An attraction between certain persons, esp. of opposite sexes; also, the person exerting such attraction. 5. *Chem.* The property by which differing chemical elements or groups of elements unite to form a new compound. [< L *affinis* adjacent, related < *ad-* to + *finis* end]

af·firm (ə·fûrm′) v.t. 1. To declare or state positively. 2. To confirm or ratify. — v.i. 3. *Law* To make a formal judicial declaration, but not under oath. [< OF < L < *ad-* to + *firmare* to make firm] — **af·firm′a·ble** adj. — **af·firm′a·bly** adv. — **af·firm′ance** n. — **af·firm′ant** adj & n. — **af·firm′er** n.

af·fir·ma·tion (af′ər·mā′shən) n. 1. The act of affirming; assertion. 2. That which is affirmed or asserted. 3. A solemn declaration made before a competent officer, in place of a judicial oath. — Syn. See OATH.

af·firm·a·tive (ə·fûr′mə·tiv) adj. 1. Characterized by affirmation; asserting that the fact is so. 2. Positive. Also **af·firm·a·to·ry** (ə·fûr′mə·tôr′ē, -tō′rē). — adv. Yes; that is so: a military usage. — n. 1. A word or expression of affirmation or assent. 2. The side in a debate that affirms the proposition debated. — **af·firm′a·tive·ly** adv.

af·fix (v. ə·fiks′; n. af′iks) v.t. 1. To fix or attach; fasten; append. 2. To connect with or lay upon, as blame, responsibility, etc. — n. 1. That which is attached, appended, or added. 2. A prefix, suffix, or infix. [< L *affigere* < *ad-* to + *figere* to fasten]

af·fla·tus (ə·flā′təs) n. Any creative inspiration or impulse. [< L < *ad-* to + *flare* to blow]

af·flict (ə·flikt′) v.t. To distress with continued suffering; trouble greatly. [< L < *ad-* + *fligere* to dash, strike] — **af·flict′er** n. — **af·flic′tive** adj. — **af·flic′tive·ly** adv.

af·flic·tion (ə·flik′shən) n. 1. The state of being afflicted; sore distress of body or mind. 2. A misfortune; calamity.

af·flu·ence (af′lōō·əns) n. Riches; wealth.

af·flu·ent (af′lōō·ənt) adj. 1. Abounding; abundant. 2. Wealthy; opulent. — n. A stream that flows into another. [< L < *ad-* to + *fluere* to flow] — **af′flu·ent·ly** adv.

af·ford (ə·fôrd′, ə·fōrd′) v.t. 1. To have sufficient means for;

be able to meet the expense of.   **2.** To incur without detriment.   **3.** To spare.   **4.** To provide, yield, or furnish.   [OE *geforthian* to further, promote]   — **af·ford'a·ble** *adj.*

af·fray (ə·frā') *n.* A public brawl.   [< OF, *effrei, esfrei*]

af·fri·cate (af'ri·kit) *n. Phonet.* A sound consisting of a stop followed by the fricative release of breath at the point of contact, as *ch* in *match.*   [< L < *ad-* against + *fricare* to rub]   — **af·fric·a·tive** (ə·frik'ə·tiv) *n. & adj.*

af·front (ə·frunt') *v.t.* **1.** To insult openly; treat with insolence.   **2.** To confront in defiance; accost.   — *n.* An open insult or indignity.   — **Syn.** See OFFEND.   [< OF < LL *affrontare* to strike against]   — **af·fron'tive** *adj.*

af·ghan (af'gən, -gan) *n.* A soft wool coverlet, knitted or crocheted, often in many-colored geometrical patterns.

Af·ghan (af'gən, -gan) *n.* A native of Afghanistan.   — *adj.* Of or pertaining to Afghanistan, its inhabitants, etc.

a·fi·cio·na·do (ə·fish'ə·nä'dō, ə·fis'ē-, ə·fē'ē·ə-; *Sp.* ä·fē·thyō·nä'thō, -fē·syō-) *n. pl.* **·dos** (-dōz, *Sp.* -thōs) An avid follower or fan, as of a sport or activity; devotee.   [< Sp.]

a·field (ə·fēld') *adv.* **1.** In or to the field; abroad.   **2.** Off the track; astray.

a·fire (ə·fīr') *adv. & adj.* On fire.   [ME]

a·flame (ə·flām') *adv. & adj.* Flaming; glowing.

a·float (ə·flōt') *adv. & adj.* **1.** Floating.   **2.** Not aground or ashore; at sea.   **3.** In circulation: Rumors were *afloat.*   **4.** Overflowed; flooded, as the deck of a ship.   **5.** Adrift.

a·foot (ə·fŏŏt') *adv.* **1.** On foot.   **2.** In motion or progress; on the move; astir.   [ME *on fot*]

a·fore·men·tioned (ə·fôr'men'shənd, ə·fōr'-) *adj.* Mentioned previously.

a·fore·said (ə·fôr'sed', ə·fōr'-) *adj.* Mentioned before.

a·fore·thought (ə·fôr'thôt', ə·fōr'-) *adj.* Intended beforehand: now chiefly in the phrase *malice aforethought.*

a·fore·time (ə·fôr'tīm', ə·fōr'-) *adv.* At a previous time.

a·foul (ə·foul') *adv. & adj.* In entanglement or collision; entangled.   — **to run** (or **fall**) **afoul of** To become entangled with; get into difficulties with.

a·fraid (ə·frād') *adj.* Filled with fear or apprehension; apprehensive; fearful: often used to soften an unpleasant statement: I'm *afraid* you're wrong.   [Orig. pp. of AFFRAY]

A-frame (ā'frām') *n.* A structural framework, as of a house, in the form of a triangle or an A.

a·fresh (ə·fresh') *adv.* Once more; anew; again.

Af·ri·can (af'ri·kən) *adj.* Of or pertaining to Africa, or its inhabitants.   — *n.* **1.** A native inhabitant of Africa.   **2.** A member of one of the African peoples; a Negro or Negrito.

Af·ri·kaans (af'ri·käns', -känz') *n.* The Dutch dialect spoken in South Africa.

Af·ri·ka·ner (af'ri·kä'nər) *n.* An Afrikaans-speaking South African of Dutch ancestry. Also **Af'ri·kan'der** (-kan'dər).

Af·ro (af'rō) *n. pl.* **Af·ros** A hair style in which bushy hair is shaped into a full, rounded mass.

Afro- *combining form* Africa; African.

Af·ro-A·mer·i·can (af'rō·ə·mer'ə·kən) *adj.* Of or pertaining to Americans of black African descent.   — *n.* An Afro-American person.

aft (aft, äft) *Naut. adj.* Of or near the stern of a vessel.   — *adv.* At, toward, or near the stern.   [OE *æftan* behind]

af·ter (af'tər, äf'-) *prep.* **1.** In the rear of; farther back than; following: He came *after* me.   **2.** In search or pursuit of: Strive *after* wisdom.   **3.** In relation to; concerning: to inquire *after* one's health.   **4.** Subsequently to; at a later period than.   **5.** In succession to; following repeatedly: day *after* day.   **6.** As a result of; subsequently to and because of.   **7.** Notwithstanding; subsequently to and in spite of: *After* the best endeavors, one may fail.   **8.** Next below in order or importance: *after* the king in power.   **9.** According to the nature, wishes, or customs of; in conformity with: a man *after* my own heart.   **10.** In imitation of; in the manner of.   **11.** In honor, remembrance, or observance of.   **12.** *U.S.* Of time by the clock, past.   — *adv.* **1.** In the rear; behind.   **2.** At a later time.   — *adj.* **1.** Following in time or place; later.   **2.** *Naut.* Toward the stern; farther aft.   — *conj.* Following the time that: *After* I went home, I ate.   [OE *æfter*]

af·ter·birth (af'tər·bûrth', äf'-) *n.* The placenta and fetal membranes expelled from the uterus after childbirth.

af·ter·bod·y (af'tər·bod'ē, äf'-) *n. Aerospace* A section of a rocket or missile that continues to trail the nose cone or satellite from which it was separated in flight.

af·ter·brain (af'tər·brān', äf'-) *n. Anat.* Metencephalon.

af·ter·burn·er (af'tər·bûr'nər, äf'-) *n. Aeron.* A device for injecting extra fuel into the exhaust system of a jet engine as a means of increasing the thrust.   — **af'ter·burn'ing** *n.*

af·ter·deck (af'tər·dek', äf'-) *n. Naut.* That part of a deck aft of amidships.

af·ter·ef·fect (af'tər·ə·fekt', äf'-) *n.* An effect succeeding its cause after an interval.

af·ter·glow (af'tər·glō', äf'-) *n.* A glow after a light has disappeared, as in the western sky after sunset.

af·ter·im·age (af'tər·im'ij, äf'-) *n. Physiol.* The persistence of an image after the withdrawal of direct stimulation.

af·ter·math (af'tər·math, äf'-) *n.* Result; consequence.

af·ter·most (af'tər·mōst, äf'-) *adj.* **1.** *Naut.* Nearest the stern: also **aft'most.**   **2.** Last.

af·ter·noon (af'tər·nōōn', äf'-) *n.* **1.** The part of the day between noon and sunset.   **2.** The closing part: the *afternoon* of life.   — *adj.* Of, for, or occurring in the afternoon.

af·ter·taste (af'tər·tāst', äf'-) *n.* A taste persisting in the mouth, as after a meal.

af·ter·thought (af'tər·thôt', äf'-) *n.* **1.** An expedient, explanation, etc., that occurs to one after decision or action.   **2.** A subsequent or second thought.

af·ter·ward (af'tər·wərd, äf'-) *adv.* In time following; subsequently. Also **aft'er·wards.**   [OE *æfterweard*]

ag- Assimilated var. of AD-.

a·gain (ə·gen', *esp. Brit.* ə·gān') *adv.* **1.** Another time; once more; anew.   **2.** Once repeated.   **3.** To the same place or over the same course; back, as in a previous condition.   **4.** Further; moreover.   **5.** On the other hand.   [OE *ongegn*]

a·gainst (ə·genst', *esp. Brit.* ə·gānst') *prep.* **1.** In the opposite direction to; counter to.   **2.** In contact or collision with; upon.   **3.** In contact with and pressing upon.   **4.** In opposition to; contrary to.   **5.** In contrast or comparison with.   **6.** In preparation for.   **7.** In hostility to.   **8.** In resistance to.   **9.** To the debit of.   **10.** Directly opposite; facing: now usu. *over against.*   [OE *ongegn* + *-es,* adverbial suffix]

Ag·a·mem·non (ag'ə·mem'non, -nən) In Greek legend, king of Mycenae and chief of the Greek army in the Trojan War.

a·gape (ə·gāp', ə·gap') *adv. & adj.* In a gaping state; gaping.

a·gar-a·gar (ā'gär·ā'gär, ä'gär-, ä'gär·, ag'ər-) *n.* A gelatinous substance obtained from seaweeds, used as a laxative and in the cultivation of bacteria. Also **a'gar.**   [< Malay]

ag·a·ric (ag'ə·rik, ə·gar'ik) *n.* Any of several mushrooms, esp. the common edible variety.   [< L < Gk. *Agaria,* a town in Sarmatia]   — **a·gar·i·ca·ceous** (ə·gar'i·kā'shəs) *adj.*

ag·ate (ag'it) *n.* **1.** A variegated waxy quartz or chalcedony, in which the colors are usually in bands.   **2.** A child's playing marble.   **3.** *Printing* A size of type, 5½ points.   [< F < L < Gk. *Achatēs,* a river in Sicily]

a·ga·ve (ə·gä'vē) *n.* Any desert plant of the amaryllis family, as the century plant.   [< Gk. *Agauē,* a proper name]

a·gaze (ə·gāz') *adv.* Gazing.

age (āj) *n.* **1.** The period of existence of a person, thing, nation, etc., particularly as measured by the time past.   **2.** The entire span of life of any being or thing.   **3.** The time of life marked by maturity and discretion; adulthood; esp., that age when full civil rights or certain personal rights can be legally exercised, usually 18 or 21 years: also called *legal age.*   **4.** Any period of life which, by reason of natural development or custom, fits or unfits for anything.   **5.** Any distinct stage of life.   **6.** The closing period of life; the state of being old.   **7.** Any great period of time in the history of man, of the earth, etc., marked off by certain distinctive features or characters.   **8.** The people alive at a given time; a generation.   **9.** *Informal* A long time.   — **mental age** *Psychol.* The level of mental development as measured against the chronological age at which this level is reached by the average child. Abbr. *MA, M.A.*   — *v.* **aged, ag·ing** or **age·ing** *v.t.* **1.** To make or cause to grow mature or old.   — *v.i.* **2.** To assume or show some characteristics of age; ripen.   [< OF < L *aetas* age, a span of life]

-age *suffix of nouns* **1.** Collection or aggregate of: *leafage.*   **2.** Condition, office, service, or other relation or connection of: *haulage.*   [< OF < L *-aticum,* neut. adj. suffix]

a·ged (ā'jid for defs. 1 & 2; ājd for def. 3) *adj.* **1.** Advanced in years; old.   **2.** Of, like, or characteristic of old age.   **3.** Of or at the age of: a child, *aged* six.   — **Syn.** See OLD.   — **the aged** Those who are old.   — **a'ged·ly** *adv.*   — **a'ged·ness** *n.*

age·ing (ā'jing) See AGING.

age·less (āj'lis) *adj.* **1.** Not seeming to grow old.   **2.** Having no limits of duration; eternal.

age·long (āj'lông', -long') *adj.* Lasting for a long time.

a·gen·cy (ā'jən·sē) *n. pl.* **·cies** **1.** Active power or operation; activity.   **2.** Means; instrumentality.   **3.** A firm or establishment where business is done for others.   **4.** The office or function of an agent.   [< L < *agere* to do]

a·gen·da (ə·jen'də) *n. pl.* of **a·gen·dum** (ə·jen'dəm) (*usu.* construed as *sing.*) A list of things to be done; esp., a program of business at a meeting.   [< L *agere* to do]

♦ *Agenda,* originally the plural of the Latin *agendum,* now has a regular English plural *agendas.*

a·gent (ā'jənt) *n.* **1.** One who or that which acts or has power to act; an efficient cause of anything.   **2.** One who acts for or by the authority of a government, company, etc.   **3.** Any force, substance, or organism that causes a material change.   **4.** A means by which something is done; instrument.   **5.** *Informal* A traveling salesman.   [< L *agens, agentis,* ppr. of *agere* to do]   — **a·gen·tial** (ā·jen'shəl) *adj.*

a·gent pro·vo·ca·teur (à·zhän' prô·vô·kà·tœr') *pl.* **a·gents pro·vo·ca·teurs** (à·zhän' prô·vô·kà·tœr') *French* A secret agent planted in a trade union, political party, etc., to incite actions or declarations that will incur punishment.

Ag·ge·us (ə·gē′us) The Douai Bible name for HAGGAI.

ag·glom·er·ate (ə·glom′ə·rāt; *for adj. & n., also* -ər·it) *v.t. & v.i.* **·at·ed, ·at·ing** To gather, form, or grow into a ball or rounded mass. — *adj.* Gathered into a mass or heap; clustered densely. — *n.* A heap or mass of things thrown together indiscriminately. [< L < *ad-* to + *glomerare* to gather into a ball] **— ag·glom′er·a′tion** *n.* **— ag·glom′er·a′tive** *adj.*

ag·glu·ti·nant (ə·glōō′tə·nənt) *adj.* Tending to cause adhesion; uniting. — *n.* Any sticky substance.

ag·glu·ti·nate (ə·glōō′tə·nāt; *for adj., also* -nit) *v.t. & v.i.* **·nat·ed, ·nat·ing** 1. To unite, as with glue; join by adhesion. 2. *Ling.* To form (words) by agglutination. 3. *Physiol.* To mass together, as bacteria. — *adj.* Joined by adhesion. [< L < *ad-* to + *glutinare* to glue] **— ag·glu′ti·na′tive** *adj.*

ag·glu·ti·na·tion (ə·glōō′tə·nā′shən) *n.* 1. Adhesion of distinct parts; also, a mass formed by adhesion. 2. *Ling.* A combining of words into compounds in which the constituent elements retain their characteristic forms.

ag·glu·ti·nin (ə·glōō′tə·nin) *n. Biochem.* An antibody in blood serum that causes the red corpuscles or any bacteria it touches to coalesce into floccules.

ag·gran·dize (ə·gran′dīz, ag′rən·dīz) *v.t.* **·dized, ·diz·ing** 1. To make great or greater; enlarge or intensify. 2. To make appear greater; exalt. [< F < L *ad-* to + *grandire* to make great] **— ag·gran·dize·ment** (ə·gran′diz·mənt) *n.* **— ag′gran′diz·er** *n.*

ag·gra·vate (ag′rə·vāt) *v.t.* **·vat·ed, ·vat·ing** 1. To make worse; intensify, as an illness. 2. To make heavier or more burdensome, as a duty. 3. *Informal* To provoke or exasperate. [< L < *ad-* to + *gravare* to make heavy] **— ag′gra·vat′ing** *adj.* **— ag′gra·vat′ing·ly** *adv.* **— ag·gra·va′tion** (ag′rə·vā′shən) *n.* **— ag′gra·va′tive** *adj.*

ag·gre·gate (*v.* ag′rə·gāt; *adj. & n.* -git) *v.t.* **gat·ed, ·gat·ing** 1. To bring or gather together, as into a mass, sum, or body. 2. To amount to; form a total of. — *adj.* Collected into a sum or mass; gathered into a whole. — *n.* The entire number, mass, or quantity of anything; amount; total. — **in the aggregate** Collectively; as a whole. [< L < *ad-* to + *gregare* to collect] **— ag·gre·ga·tion** (ag′rə·gā′shən) *n.* **— ag′gre·ga′tive** *adj.* **— ag′gre·ga′tor** *n.*

ag·gress (ə·gres′) *v.i.* To undertake an attack; begin a quarrel. [< L < *ad-* + *gradi* to step, go]

ag·gres·sion (ə·gresh′ən) *n.* 1. An unprovoked attack or encroachment. 2. Habitual aggressive action or practices.

ag·gres·sive (ə·gres′iv) *adj.* 1. Of or characterized by aggression or attack. 2. Disposed to vigorous activity; assertive. **— ag·gres′sive·ly** *adv.* **— ag·gres′sive·ness** *n.*

ag·gres·sor (ə·gres′ər) *n.* One who commits an aggression.

ag·grieve (ə·grēv′) *v.t.* **·grieved, ·griev·ing** 1. To cause sorrow to; distress or afflict. 2. To give cause for just complaint, as by injustice. [< OF < L *aggravare*]

a·ghast (ə·gast′, ə·gäst′) *adj.* Struck dumb with horror. [ME < OE *ā* + *gæstan* to terrify; spelling infl. by *ghost*]

ag·ile (aj′əl, aj′īl) *adj.* Able to move or act quickly and easily; active. [< F < L *agere* to move] **— ag′ile·ly** *adv.*

a·gil·i·ty (ə·jil′ə·tē) *n.* Quickness in movement.

ag·ing (ā′jing) *n.* 1. The process or the effects of growing mature or old. 2. Any artificial process for producing the effects of age. Also, *Brit.*, **ageing.**

ag·i·tate (aj′ə·tāt) *v.* **·tat·ed, ·tat·ing** *v.t.* 1. To disturb or shake irregularly. 2. To set or keep moving. 3. To excite or stir up; perturb. 4. To keep before the public, as a controversial issue. — *v.i.* 5. To excite, or endeavor to excite, public interest and action. [< L *agitare* to set in motion]

ag·i·ta·tion (aj′ə·tā′shən) *n.* 1. Violent motion; commotion. 2. Strong emotional disturbance.

ag·i·ta·tor (aj′ə·tā′tər) *n.* One who or that which agitates; esp., one who persists in political or social agitation.

a·gleam (ə·glēm′) *adv. & adj.* Bright; gleaming.

a·glit·ter (ə·glit′ər) *adv. & adj.* Glittering.

a·glow (ə·glō′) *adv. & adj.* In a glow; glowing.

ag·no·men (ag·nō′mən) *n. pl.* **ag·nom·i·na** (ag·nom′ə·nə) A nickname. [< L < *ad-* to + (*g*)*nomen* name] **— ag·nom′i·nal** *adj.*

ag·nos·tic (ag·nos′tik) *adj.* Of or pertaining to agnostics or agnosticism. — *n.* One who holds the theory of agnosticism. **— Syn.** See SKEPTIC. [< Gk. < *a-* not + *gignōskein* to know]

ag·nos·ti·cism (ag·nos′tə·siz′əm) *n.* The doctrine and philosophical theory that man cannot know God, first truths, or anything beyond material phenomena.

Ag·nus De·i (ag′nəs dē′ī, dä′ē) 1. *Eccl.* A figure of a lamb, as an emblem of Christ, often bearing a cross and banner. 2. *Eccl.* **a** A Eucharistic prayer beginning with *Agnus Dei.* **b** Its music. [< LL, Lamb of God. See *John* i 29.]

a·go (ə·gō′) *adv.* In the past; since: long *ago.* — *adj.* Gone by; past: a year *ago.* [OE *āgān* past, gone away]

a·gog (ə·gog′) *adv. & adj.* In a state of eager curiosity; excited; expectant. [< MF *en gogues* in a merry mood]

-agogue *combining form* Leading, promoting, or inciting: *demagogue, pedagogue.* Also **-agog.** [< Gk. *agein* to lead]

ag·o·nize (ag′ə·nīz) *v.* **·nized, ·niz·ing** *v.i.* 1. To be in or suffer extreme pain or anguish. 2. To make convulsive efforts; strive. — *v.t.* 3. To subject to agony; torture. [< F < Med.L < Gk. *agōnizesthai* to contend, strive]

ag·o·ny (ag′ə·nē) *n. pl.* **·nies** 1. Intense suffering of body or mind; anguish. 2. Any intense or sudden emotion. 3. The suffering that precedes death. 4. Violent striving. [< L < Gk. *agōn* contest]

ag·o·ra (ag′ər·ə) *n. pl.* **ag·o·rae** (-ər·ē) *or* **ag·o·ras** 1. In ancient Greece, a popular assembly. 2. Any place of popular assembly, esp. a market place. [< Gk.]

a·gou·ti (ə·gōō′tē) *n. pl.* **·tis** *or* **·ties** A tropical American rodent of grayish color, with slender limbs and three hind toes. Also **a·gou′ty.** [< F < Sp. *aguti* < Tupi]

a·grar·i·an (ə·grâr′ē·ən) *adj.* 1. Pertaining to land or the distribution of lands. 2. Organizing or furthering agricultural interests. — *n.* One who advocates equal distribution of lands or equalizing farm income. [< L < *ager* field] **— a·grar′i·an·ism** *n.*

a·gree (ə·grē′) *v.* **a·greed, a·gree·ing** *v.i.* 1. To give consent; accede: with *to* or the infinitive. 2. To come into or be in harmony. 3. To be of one mind; concur: often with *with.* 4. To come to terms, as in the details of a transaction: with *about* or *on.* 5. To be acceptable; suit: with *with.* 6. *Gram.* To correspond in person, number, case, or gender. — *v.t.* 7. To grant as a concession: with a noun clause. [< OF < L *ad* to + *gratus* pleasing]

a·gree·a·ble (ə·grē′ə·bəl) *adj.* 1. Pleasant to the mind or senses. 2. Being in accordance or conformity. 3. Ready or willing to agree. **— a·gree′a·bil′i·ty, a·gree′a·ble·ness** *n.* **— a·gree′a·bly** *adv.*

a·greed (ə·grēd′) *adj.* 1. In agreement. 2. Settled by consent, bargain, or contract. 3. Granted: used as a rejoinder.

a·gree·ment (ə·grē′mənt) *n.* 1. The act of coming into accord. 2. The state of being in accord; conformity. 3. A contract. 4. *Gram.* Correspondence in person, number, case, or gender.

ag·ri·cul·ture (ag′rə·kul′chər) *n.* The science and art of the cultivation of the soil, the breeding and raising of livestock, etc.; tillage; farming. Abbr. *agr., agric.* **— Department of Agriculture** An executive department of the U.S. government headed by the Secretary of Agriculture, that administers loans and grants in aid to farmers and assists in production, irrigation, etc. [< F < L *ager* field + *cultura* cultivation] **— ag′ri·cul′tur·al** *adj.* **— ag′ri·cul′tur·al·ly** *adv.*

ag·ri·cul·tur·ist (ag′rə·kul′chər·ist) *n.* 1. An expert in agriculture. 2. A farmer: also **ag′ri·cul′tur·al·ist.**

agro- *combining form* Of or pertaining to fields or agriculture: *agronomy.* [< Gk. < *agros* field]

ag·ro·bi·ol·o·gy (ag′rō·bī·ol′ə·jē) *n.* The quantitative study of plant life, esp. in relation to the yields of cultivated plants. **— ag′ro·bi·o·log·ic** (ag′rō·bī′ə·loj′ik) *or* **·i·cal** *adj.* **— ag′ro·bi·o·log′i·cal·ly** *adv.* **— ag′ro·bi·ol′o·gist** *n.*

ag·ro·nom·ics (ag′rə·nom′iks) *n.pl.* (*construed as sing.*) Agronomy.

a·gron·o·my (ə·gron′ə·mē) *n.* The application of scientific principles to the cultivation of land. [< Gk. < *agros* field + *nemein* to distribute, manage] **— ag·ro·nom·ic** (ag′rə·nom′ik) *or* **·i·cal** *adj.* **— a·gron′o·mist** *n.*

a·ground (ə·ground′) *adv. & adj.* On the shore or bottom, as a vessel; stranded.

a·gue (ā′gyōō) *n.* 1. *Pathol.* A periodic malarial fever marked by intermittent chills. 2. A chill or paroxysm. [< OF < L (*febris*) *acuta* acute (fever)] **— a′gu·ish** *adj.*

ah (ä) *interj.* An exclamation expressive of various emotions, as surprise, triumph, satisfaction, contempt, etc. [ME]

a·ha (ä·hä′) *interj.* An exclamation expressing surprise, triumph, or mockery. [ME]

a·head (ə·hed′) *adv.* 1. At the head or front. 2. In advance. 3. Onward; forward. **— ahead of** In advance of, as in time, rank, achievement, etc. **— to be ahead** *U.S. Informal* To have as profit or advantage; be winning. **— to get ahead** To make one's way socially, financially, etc.

a·hem (ə·hem′) *interj.* An exclamation similar to the sound of clearing the throat, made to attract attention.

a·hoy (ə·hoi′) *interj.* Ho there!: a call used in hailing.

aid (ād) *v.t. & v.i.* To render assistance (to); help. — *n.* 1. Assistance; help. 2. A person or thing that affords assistance. 3. An aide. [< OF < L < *ad-* to + *juvare* to help] **— aid′er** *n.*

aide (ād) *n.* 1. An aide de camp. 2. An assistant. [< F]

aide-de-camp (ād′də·kamp′) *n. pl.* **aides-de-camp** A military or naval officer on the personal staff of a superior officer

---

in a high command as his confidential assistant and secretary: also *aide.* Also *U.S.* **aid′-de-camp′.** [< F *aide de camp,* lit., field assistant]

ai·grette (ā′gret, ā-gret′) *n.* **1.** The tail plume of the egret. **2.** A tuft of feathers or gems, worn on a helmet, headdress, etc. Also **ai′gret.** [< F, a heron]

ail (āl) *v.t.* **1.** To cause uneasiness or pain to; trouble; make ill. — *v.i.* **2.** To be somewhat ill; feel pain. [OE *eglan*]

ai·lan·thus (ā-lan′thəs) *n.* A large, deciduous tree of the quassia family, having malodorous, greenish flowers. [< NL, genus name] — **ai·lan′thic** *adj.*

ai·le·ron (ā′lə·ron) *n. Aeron.* Any of several movable surfaces of an airplane wing, used to bank the airplane. [< F]

ail·ing (ā′ling) *adj.* Sick; ill. — **Syn.** See SICK.

ail·ment (āl′mənt) *n.* A slight illness.

aim (ām) *v.t.* **1.** To direct, as a weapon, remark, or act, toward or against some object or person. — *v.i.* **2.** To have a purpose; try: with the infinitive. **3.** To direct a missile, weapon, etc. — *n.* **1.** The act of aiming. **2.** The line of direction of anything aimed. **3.** Design; purpose. [< OF < L *aestimare* to estimate]

aim·less (ām′lis) *adj.* Wanting in aim or purpose. — **aim′· less·ly** *adv.* — **aim′less·ness** *n.*

ain't (ānt) *Illit. & Dial.* Am not: also used for *are not, is not, has not,* and *have not.*

◆ **ain't, aren't I?** *Ain't* is now nonstandard, although users of standard English sometimes say or write it for amusing effect when they are sure it will not be taken as their normal usage. *Aren't I?* is an ungrammatical locution used to avoid *Ain't I?* when one means *Am I not?*

air (âr) *n.* **1.** The mixture of gases that forms the atmosphere of the earth, consisting chiefly of oxygen and nitrogen very nearly in the proportions one to four. **2.** The open space around and above the earth; sky. **3.** An atmospheric movement or current; wind; breeze. **4.** Utterance abroad; publicity: to give *air* to one's feelings. **5.** Peculiar or characteristic appearance; mien; manner: an honest *air.* **6.** *pl.* Assumed manner; affectation: to put on *airs.* **7.** *Music* A melody; tune. **8.** The medium through which radio signals are sent. — **in the air 1.** Prevalent; abroad; as gossip. **2.** In the making, as plans. — **on the air** Now broadcasting or transmitting, as by radio; being broadcast. — **up in the air** *Informal* Undecided. — *v.t.* **1.** To expose to the air; admit air into so as to purify or dry; ventilate. **2.** To make public; display; exhibit. [< OF < L < Gk. *aēr* air, mist]

air base A base for operations by aircraft.

air bladder 1. *Zool.* In fishes, a sac filled with air, aiding them to maintain an equilibrium in the water: also called *sound, swimming bladder.* **2.** Any vesicle filled with air.

air·borne (âr′bôrn′, -bōrn′) *adj.* **1.** Carried through the air, as bacteria, pollen, etc. **2.** Transported in aircraft: *airborne* infantry. **3.** In flight; flying.

air brake A brake operated by compressed air.

air·brush (âr′brush′) *n.* A kind of atomizer for spraying paint or other liquids by compressed air. Also **air brush.**

air·bus (âr′bus′) *n.* A large passenger airplane designed to accommodate hundreds of people. [< AIR(PLANE) + BUS]

air castle A visionary project; a daydream.

air chamber An enclosed space containing, or designed to contain, air, esp. in hydraulics.

air chief marshal In the Royal, Royal Canadian, and other Commonwealth air forces, an officer of the next to highest rank. See table at GRADE.

air coach *U.S.* The second-best and cheaper class of accommodations in commercial aircraft. Also **air-coach** (âr′cōch′).

air commodore In the Royal, Royal Canadian, and other Commonwealth air forces, an officer ranking next above group captain. See table at GRADE.

air-con·di·tion (âr′kən-dish′ən) *v.t.* To equip with or ventilate by air conditioning. — **air′-con·di′tioned** *adj.*

air conditioner Any of various air-conditioning devices.

air conditioning A system for treating air in buildings, etc., so as to maintain those conditions of temperature, humidity, and purity best adapted to personal comfort, etc.

air-cool (âr′kool′) *v.t.* To cool, as the cylinders of an engine, with a flow of air instead of liquid. — **air′-cooled** *adj.*

air·craft (âr′kraft′, -kräft′) *n. pl.* **·craft** Any form of craft designed for flight through or navigation in the air.

aircraft carrier *Naval* A large ship designed to carry aircraft, having a flight deck for landing and taking off.

air·craft·man (âr′kraft′mən, kräft′-) *n. pl.* **·men** *Brit.* Any of the four lower grades in the Royal or Royal Canadian Air Force. See table at GRADE.

air·drome (âr′drōm) *n. Chiefly Brit.* An airport.

air·drop (âr′drop′) *n.* Aerial delivery of supplies and equipment from an aircraft in flight. — *v.t. & v.i.* **·dropped**, **·drop·ping** To drop (supplies, etc.) from an aircraft.

Aire·dale (âr′dāl) *n.* A large terrier with a wiry tan coat. [after *Airedale,* the Aire river valley, England]

air·field (âr′fēld′) *n.* An airport.

air·foil (âr′foil′) *n. Aeron.* A surface, as a wing, aileron, etc., designed to provide the maximum aerodynamic advantage for an airplane in flight.

air force The air arm of a country's defense forces. — **United States Air Force** The air force of the United States.

air gun A gun impelling a charge by compressed air.

AIREDALE
(About 23 inches high at shoulder)

air hole 1. A hole containing, or made by or for, gas or air. **2.** A flaw in a casting. **3.** An opening in the ice over a body of water. **4.** *Aeron.* An air pocket.

air·i·ly (âr′ə·lē) *adv.* In a light or airy manner; jauntily.

air·ing (âr′ing) *n.* **1.** An exposure to air, as for drying. **2.** Public exposure or discussion. **3.** Exercise in the air.

air lane A route regularly used by airplanes.

air·less (âr′lis) *adj.* Destitute of air or of fresh air.

air letter 1. An airmail letter. **2.** A sheet of lightweight paper for airmail letters. **3.** *Brit.* An aérogramme.

air·lift (âr′lift′) *n.* The transporting of passengers and cargo by aircraft. — *v.t. & v.i.* To transport by airplane.

air·line (âr′līn′) *n.* A business organization that transports passengers and freight by air. — **air′lin′er** *n.*

air lock An airtight antechamber, as of a caisson, for maintaining the air pressure.

air mail 1. Mail carried by airplane. **2.** A system of carrying mail by airplane. — **air′-mail′, air′mail′** *adj.*

air·man (âr′mən) *n. pl.* **·men** (-mən) An aviator; flyer.

air marshal In the Royal, Royal Canadian, and other Commonwealth air forces, an officer ranking next below air chief marshal. See table at GRADE.

air mass *Meteorol.* A body of air having essentially uniform conditions of temperature, humidity, etc.

Air Medal A decoration awarded by the U.S. Air Force for meritorious achievement during flight. See DECORATION.

air·plane (âr′plān′) *n.* A heavier-than-air, powered flying craft having fixed wings. Also, *Brit.,* **aeroplane.**

air pocket *Aeron.* A sinking mass of cooled air.

air·port (âr′pôrt′, -pōrt′) *n.* A field laid out as a base for aircraft, including all structures and appurtenances necessary for operation, housing, storage, and maintenance.

air power The strength of a nation in terms of its command of the air in peace and war.

air·proof (âr′proof′) *adj.* Impenetrable by air. — *v.t.* To make airproof.

air raid An attack by military aircraft, esp. by bombers.

air-raid shelter A place set aside and equipped for the protection of people during an air raid.

air sac *Ornithol.* One of the membranous sacs filled with air in different parts of the body in birds and communicating with the lungs.

air shaft An open shaft intended to provide ventilation.

air·ship (âr′ship′) *n.* A lighter-than-air, powered flying craft.

air·sick·ness (âr′sik′nis) *n.* Motion sickness caused by air travel. — **air′sick′** *adj.*

air·space (âr′spās′) *n.* That portion of the atmosphere overlying a designated space, considered as subject to territorial jurisdiction or international law.

air speed The speed of an airplane with relation to the air.

air·strip (âr′strip′) *n.* A flat surface used as an airfield.

air·tight (âr′tīt′) *adj.* **1.** Not allowing air to escape or enter. **2.** Having no weak places; flawless: an *airtight* case.

air vice-marshal (vīs′mär′shəl) In the Royal, Royal Canadian, and other Commonwealth air forces, an officer ranking next below air marshal. See table at GRADE.

air·way (âr′wā′) *n.* **1.** Any passageway for air, as the ventilating passage of a mine. **2.** *Aeron.* An air lane.

air·wor·thy (âr′wûr′thē) *adj.* Being in fit condition to fly: said of aircraft. — **air′wor′thi·ness** *n.*

air·y (âr′ē) *adj.* **air·i·er, air·i·est 1.** Of or pertaining to the air. **2.** Like or resembling air; immaterial. **3.** Thin or light as air; delicate. **4.** Light or buoyant in manner; lively; gay. **5.** Unsubstantial as air; unreal; empty. **6.** Dealing with fancies; visionary; speculative. **7.** Open to the air; breezy. **8.** Performed in the air; aerial. **9.** *Informal* Giving oneself airs; affected. — **air′i·ness** *n.*

aisle (īl) *n.* **1.** A passageway between rows of seats. **2.** A division of a church, usu. divided from the nave by a range of columns or piers. [< MF < L *ala* wing]

a·jar¹ (ə-jär′) *adv. & adj.* Partly open, as a door. [ME *a-on + char,* OE *cier* turn]

a·jar² (ə-jär′) *adv. & adj.* Not in harmony.

a·kim·bo (ə-kim′bō) *adv. & adj.* With hands on hips and elbows outward. [ME *in kenebowe* in a sharp bow]

a·kin (ə-kin′) *adj. & adv.* **1.** Of the same kin; related by blood. **2.** Of similar nature or qualities. [< A⁻³ + KIN]

al-¹ *prefix* The Arabic definite article, seen in words of Arabic origin, as *Alkoran, algebra.*

al-² Assimilated var. of AD-.

-al¹ *suffix of adjectives and nouns* Of or pertaining to; characterized by: *personal, musical.* [< L *-alis*]

-al² *suffix of nouns* The act or process of, used in nouns formed from verbs: *betrayal, refusal.* [< OF < L *-alis*]

-al³ *suffix Chem.* Denoting a compound having the properties of or derived from an aldehyde: *chloral.* [< AL(DEHYDE)]

a·la (ā′lə) *n. pl.* **a·lae** (ā′lē) A wing or a winglike part. [< L, wing]

à la (ä′ lä, ä′ lə; *Fr.* à là) After the manner or in the style of. Also **a la.** [< F]

al·a·bam·ine (al′ə·bam′ēn, -in) *n.* A hypothetical element of atomic number 85; replaced by astatine. [*Alabama*]

al·a·bas·ter (al′ə·bas′tər, -bäs′-) *n.* **1.** A white or tinted fine-grained gypsum. **2.** A banded variety of calcite. —*adj.* Made of or like alabaster; smooth and white: also **al′a·bas′trine** (-trin). [< L < Gk. *alabast(r)os* alabaster box]

à la carte (ä′ lə kärt′) By the bill of fare; each item having a separate price. Compare TABLE D'HÔTE. [< F]

a·lac·ri·ty (ə·lak′rə·tē) *n.* Cheerful willingness and promptitude; liveliness. [< L *alacer* lively] — **a·lac′ri·tous** *adj.*

A·lad·din (ə·lad′n) In the *Arabian Nights*, a boy who can summon a jinni by rubbing a magic lamp or a magic ring.

à la king (ä′ lə king′) Cooked in a cream sauce, with pimiento or green pepper, mushrooms, etc.

Al·a·mo (al′ə·mō) A Franciscan mission building, San Antonio, Texas; besieged and taken by Mexicans, 1836.

à la mode (ä′ lə mōd′, al′ ə mōd′) **1.** In style; fashionable. **2.** In cookery: **a** Served with ice cream: said of pie. **b** Braised with vegetables and served in a rich gravy. [< F]

à la New·burg (ä′ lə nōō′bûrg, nyōō′bûrg) Cooked with a sauce made of egg yolks, cream, sherry, and butter.

a·lar (ā′lər) *adj.* Having or pertaining to an ala or wing; wing-shaped. [< L *ala* wing]

a·larm (ə·lärm′) *n.* **1.** Sudden fear or apprehension caused by awareness of danger. **2.** Any sound or signal intended to awaken or apprise of danger; a warning. **3.** Any device, as a bell, for giving such a signal. **4.** A call to arms, to meet danger or attack. —*v.t.* **1.** To strike with sudden fear. **2.** To arouse to a sense of danger; give warning to. [< OF < Ital. *all' arme* to arms] — **a·larm′a·ble** *adj.*

alarm clock A clock fitted with a device to sound a bell or buzzer when the hands reach a predetermined hour.

a·larm·ing (ə·lär′ming) *adj.* Exciting alarm; causing fear and apprehension; disturbing. — **a·larm′ing·ly** *adv.*

a·larm·ist (ə·lär′mist) *n.* **1.** One who needlessly excites or tries to excite alarm. **2.** One who is easily alarmed.

a·las (ə·las′, ə·läs′) *interj.* An exclamation of regret, sorrow, etc. [< OF *a* ah! + *las* wretched]

a·late (ā′lāt) *adj. Bot.* Winged, as a stem, petiole, or fruit. Also **a′lat·ed.** [< L *ala* wing]

alb (alb) *n. Eccl.* A white linen eucharistic vestment reaching to the ankles, close-sleeved and girded at the waist. [OE < L *alba* (*vestis*) white garment]

al·ba·core (al′bə·kôr, -kōr) *n.* Any of various tunas or large related fishes of the Atlantic. [< Pg. < Arabic *al* the + *bukr* young camel]

Al·ba·ni·an (al·bā′nē·ən, -bān′yən) *adj.* Of or pertaining to Albania, its people, or their language. —*n.* **1.** A native or inhabitant of Albania. **2.** The language of Albania.

al·ba·tross (al′bə·trôs, -tros) *n. pl.* **·tross·es** or **tross** A large, web-footed sea bird, with long, narrow wings and a hooked beak. [Orig. *alcatras* frigate bird < Sp., Pg. *alcatraz*]

al·be·it (ôl·bē′it) *conj.* Even though; although. [ME *al be it* although it be]

al·bes·cent (al·bes′ənt) *adj.* Growing white or moderately white; becoming whitish. [< L *albescens, -entis*, ppr. of *albescere* to become white] — **al·bes′cence** *n.*

Al·bi·gen·ses (al′bə·jen′sēz) *n.pl.* A sect of religious reformers during the 11th to 13th centuries in the south of France, suppressed as heretics. [< Med.L, after *Albi*, a town in southern France] — **Al′bi·gen′si·an** (-sē·ən, -shən) *adj. & n.*

al·bi·no (al·bī′no) *n. pl.* **·nos 1.** A person lacking pigment in the skin, hair, and eyes. **2.** Any plant or animal lacking normal pigmentation. [< Pg. < L *albus* white] — **al·bin·ic** (al·bin′ik) *adj.* — **al·bin·ism** (al′bə·niz′əm) *n.*

ALBATROSS
(About 40 inches long; wingspread 10 to 12 feet)

al·bum (al′bəm) *n.* **1.** A booklike container for stamps, pictures, phonograph records, etc. **2.** A set of phonograph records stored in such a container. [< L, blank tablet]

al·bu·men (al·byōō′mən) *n.* **1.** The white of an egg. **2.** *Bot.* The nutritive material in a seed between the embryo and the seed coats. **3.** Albumin. [< L < *albus* white]

al·bu·min (al·byōō′mən) *n. Biochem.* Any of a class of water-soluble protein substances found in many animal and vegetable tissues and fluids. They contain carbon, oxygen, nitrogen, hydrogen, and sulfur. [< F < L *albumen* white of an egg] — **al·bu′mi·nous** *adj.*

al·bu·min·ize (al·byōō′mən·īz) *v.t.* **·ized, ·iz·ing** *Biochem.* To convert into or coat with albumin.

al·ca·zar (al′kə·zär; *Sp.* äl·kä′thär) *n.* A Moorish castle in Spain. — **the Alcazar** A Moorish palace in Seville, later used by the Spanish kings. [< Sp. < Arabic *al-qasr* the castle]

al·che·mist (al′kə·mist) *n.* One skilled in or practicing alchemy. — **al′che·mis′tic** or **·ti·cal** *adj.*

al·che·mize (al′kə·mīz) *v.t.* **·mized, ·miz·ing** To transmute by or as by alchemy.

al·che·my (al′kə·mē) *n.* **1.** The chemistry of the Middle Ages, concerned primarily with the transmutation of base metals into gold. **2.** Any power or process of transmutation. Also **al′chy·my.** [< OF < Med.L *alchimia* < Gk. *cheein* to pour] — **al·chem·ic** (al·kem′ik) *adj.* — **al·chem′i·cal·ly** *adv.*

al·co·hol (al′kə·hôl, -hol) *n.* **1.** Either of two volatile, flammable, pungent liquids, ethanol, the intoxicating principle of wines and liquors, and methanol, or wood alcohol. **2.** Any drink containing alcohol. **3.** *Chem.* Any of a group of organic compounds derived from the alkanes by the substitution of one hydroxyl radical for one hydrogen atom. [< Med.L < Arabic *al-kohl* the fine powder (of antimony)]

al·co·hol·ic (al′kə·hôl′ik, -hol′-) *adj.* **1.** Containing or using alcohol. **2.** Caused by alcohol or alcoholism. **3.** Suffering from alcoholism. —*n.* One who suffers from alcoholism.

al·co·hol·ism (al′kə·hôl′iz·əm, -hol′-) *n. Pathol.* A diseased condition resulting from the excessive or persistent use of alcoholic beverages.

al·co·hol·ize (al′kə·hôl·īz′, -hol-) *v.t.* **·ized, ·iz·ing 1.** To change into alcohol. **2.** To mix or saturate with alcohol. — **al′co·hol′i·za′tion** *n.*

Al·co·ran (al′kō·rän′, -ran′) *n.* The Koran.

al·cove (al′kōv) *n.* **1.** A recess at the side of a larger room. **2.** Any secluded spot. [< F < Sp. < Arabic *al-qobbah* the vaulted chamber]

Al·deb·a·ran (al·deb′ə·rən) *n.* A red star, one of the 20 brightest, 1.06 magnitude, Alpha in the constellation Taurus.

al·de·hyde (al′də·hīd) *n.* **1.** *Chem.* Any of a group of compounds derived from the alcohols, and intermediate between the alcohols and the acids. **2.** Acetaldehyde.

al·der (ôl′dər) *n.* A shrub or small tree of the birch family, growing in wet ground and bearing small catkins. [OE *alor*]

al·der·man (ôl′dər·mən) *n. pl.* **·men 1.** *U.S.* In many municipalities, a member of the governing body. **2.** In England and Ireland a member of the higher branch of a municipal or borough council. [OE *eald* old, senior + *man*] — **al′der·man·ship′** *n.* — **al′der·man′ic** (-man′ik) *adj.*

Al·der·ney (ôl′dər·nē) *n.* One of a breed of cattle originally peculiar to the island of Alderney.

ale (āl) *n.* A fermented malt flavored with hops, resembling beer but generally having more body. [OE *ealu*]

a·le·a·to·ry (ā′lē·ə·tôr′ē, -tō′rē) *adj.* Dependent on gambling or luck. [< L *aleator* gambler]

a·lee (ə·lē′) *adv. Naut.* At, on, or to the lee side. [< ON]

ale·house (āl′hous′) *n.* A public place where ale is sold.

a·lem·bic (ə·lem′bik) *n.* **1.** An apparatus of glass or metal formerly used in distilling. **2.** Anything that tests, purifies, or transforms. [< Arabic < Gk. *ambix* a cup]

A·len·çon lace (ə·len′sən, *Fr.* à·län·sôn′) A fine needlepoint lace. [after *Alençon*, France]

a·lert (ə·lûrt′) *adj.* **1.** Keenly watchful; ready for sudden action; vigilant. **2.** Lively; nimble. **3.** Intelligent; bright. —*n.* **1.** A warning against attack; esp., a signal to prepare for an air raid. **2.** The time during which such a warning is in effect. — **on the alert** On the lookout; vigilant. —*v.t.* To warn, as of a threatened attack or raid. [< Ital. *all'erta* on the watch] — **a·lert′ly** *adv.* — **a·lert′ness** *n.*

-ales *suffix Bot.* A feminine plural used to form the scientific names of plant orders. [< pl. of *-alis*]

A·le·ut (al′ē·ōot) *n. pl.* **Al·e·uts** or **Al·e·ut 1.** A native of the Aleutian Islands. **2.** The language of the Aleuts. — **A·leu·tian** (ə·lōō′shən), **A·leu′tic** *adj.*

ale·wife (āl′wīf′) *n. pl.* **·wives** A small North American herring-like fish. [Origin unknown]

Al·ex·an·dri·an (al′ig·zan′drē·ən, -zän′-) *adj.* **1.** Of Alexandria in Egypt. **2.** Of Alexander the Great, his reign, or his conquests. **3.** In prosody, Alexandrine. —*n.* **1.** An inhabitant of Alexandria. **2.** An Alexandrine verse.

Al·ex·an·drine (al′ig·zan′drin, -drēn, -zän′-) *n.* In prosody, a line of verse having six iambic feet with the caesura generally after the third. —*adj.* Of, composed of, or characterized by Alexandrines. Also *Alexandrian.*

al·fal·fa (al·fal′fə) *n.* A cloverlike plant of the bean family, used as forage. Also, *Brit.*, *lucerne.* [< Sp. < Arabic *al-fasfasah*, the best kind of fodder]

al·fres·co (al-fres′kō) *adv.* In the open air. — *adj.* Occurring outdoors, as a meal. Also **al fresco.** [< Ital.]

al·ga (al′gə) *n.* *pl.* **·gae** (-jē) Any of various primitive, chlorophyll-bearing plants widely distributed in fresh and salt water and moist lands, including the seaweeds and kelps. [< L, seaweed] — **al·gal** (al′gəl) *adj.*

al·ge·bra (al′jə-brə) *n.* The branch of mathematics that treats of quantity and the relations of numbers in the abstract, and in which calculations are performed by means of letters and symbols. [< Ital. < Arabic *al-jebr* the reunion of broken parts, bonesetting] — **al·ge·bra·ic** (al′jə-brā′ik) or **·i·cal** *adj.* — **al·ge·bra′i·cal·ly** *adv.* — **al′ge·bra′ist** *n.*

Al·ge·ri·an (al-jir′i-ən) *adj.* Of or pertaining to Algeria or its people. — *n.* A citizen or inhabitant of Algeria.

-algia *suffix* Pain: *neuralgia.* [< Gk. *algos* pain]

al·gid (al′jid) *adj.* Cold. [< F < L *algere* to be cold]

al·gin (al′jin) *n.* The dried, gelatinous form of various seaweeds, used as an emulsifier, etc. [< ALGA]

Al·gon·qui·an (al-gong′kwē-ən) *n.* 1. A family of North American Indian languages, including Arapaho, Blackfoot, Cheyenne, Cree, Ojibwa, Micmac, Delaware, and Massachusett. 2. A member of an Algonquian-speaking peoples. — *adj.* Of these languages. Also **Al·gon′ki·an** (-kē-ən).

Al·gon·quin (al-gong′kwin) *n.* 1. A member of certain Algonquian peoples formerly living along the Ottawa River. 2. The Algonquian language. Also **Al·gon′kin** (-kin).

al·go·rithm (al′gə-rith′əm) *n.* A step-by-step problem-solving procedure, as with a computer. [after *al-Khwarizmi*, 9th c. Arabian mathematician] — **al′go·rith′mic** *adj.*

Al·ham·bra (al-ham′brə) The palace of the Moorish kings at Granada, Spain, built in the 13th and 14th centuries. [< Sp. < Arabic *al-hamrā′* the red (house)]

a·li·as (ā′lē-əs) *n.* *pl.* **a·li·as·es** An assumed name. — **Syn.** See PSEUDONYM. — *adv.* Called by an assumed name: Miller, *alias* Brown. [< L, at another time]

al·i·bi (al′ə-bī) *n.* *pl.* **·bis** 1. *Law* A form of defense by which an accused person attempts to show that he was elsewhere when the crime was committed. 2. *U.S. Informal* An excuse. — *v.i.* **·bied**, **·bi·ing** *U.S. Informal* To make excuses for oneself. [< L, elsewhere]

al·ien (āl′yən, ā′lē-ən) *adj.* 1. Owing allegiance to another country; unnaturalized; foreign. 2. Of or related to aliens. 3. Not one's own; strange. 4. Not consistent with; incongruous; opposed: with *to.* — *n.* 1. An unnaturalized foreign resident. 2. A member of a foreign nation, tribe, people, etc. 3. One estranged or excluded. [< L *alius* another]
— **Syn.** (adj.) 4. extrinsic, extraneous, irrelevant. — (noun) 1. An *alien* is not a citizen of the country in which he resides. A *foreigner* is not a native of the country where he lives, but he may become a naturalized citizen.

al·ien·a·ble (āl′yən-ə-bəl, ā′lē-ən-) *adj.* *Law* Capable of being transferred in ownership. — **al′ien·a·bil′i·ty** *n.*

al·ien·ate (āl′yən-āt, ā′lē-ən-) *v.t.* **·at·ed**, **·at·ing** 1. To make indifferent or unfriendly; estrange. 2. To cause to feel estranged or withdrawn from society. 3. To turn away: to *alienate* the affections. 4. *Law* To transfer, as property. [< L *alienare* to estrange] — **al′ien·a′tor** *n.*

al·ien·a·tion (āl′yən-ā′shən, ā′lē-ən-) *n.* 1. The act of alienating, or the state of being alienated; estrangement: the growing *alienation* of students. 2. Insanity.

al·ien·ee (āl′yən-ē′, ā′lē-ən-ē′) *n.* *Law* One to whom property is transferred.

al·ien·ist (āl′yən-ist, ā′lē-ən-) *n.* A doctor skilled in the treatment of mental disorders: used chiefly in medical jurisprudence. [< F < L *alienus* insane] — **al′ien·ism** *n.*

al·ien·or (āl′yən-ər, ā′lē-ən-ôr′) *n.* *Law* One who alienates property to another; a vendor. Also **al′ien·er.** [< AF]

al·i·form (al′ə-fôrm, ā′lə-fôrm) *adj.* Wing-shaped; alar. [< F *ala* wing + -FORM]

a·light¹ (ə-līt′) *v.i.* **a·light·ed** or **a·lit**, **a·light·ing** 1. To descend and come to rest; settle, as after flight. 2. To dismount. 3. To come by accident: with *on* or *upon.* [OE *ālīhtan* < ā- out, off + *līhtan* to alight]

a·light² (ə-līt′) *adj.* & *adv.* Lighted; burning.

a·lign (ə-līn′) *v.t.* 1. To bring into a straight line. 2. To put (oneself, one's party, etc.) on one side of an issue, controversy, etc. — *v.i.* 3. To fall into line. Also spelled *aline.* [< F *aligner* < *a-* to + *ligner* to place in line]

a·lign·ment (ə-līn′mənt) *n.* 1. Position, place, or arrangement in a straight line. 2. A line or lines so made. 3. The state of being on one side of an issue, controversy, etc.

a·like (ə-līk′) *adj.* Having resemblance; like one another: used predicatively: The family are all *alike.* — *adv.* In the same or like manner; equally. [Fusion of ON *ālīkr* and OE *gelīc*, *anlīc*] — **a·like′ness** *n.*

al·i·ment (al′ə-mənt) *n.* 1. Food for body or mind; nutriment. 2. That which sustains or supports. — *v.t.* To furnish with food; nourish. [< L *alere* to nourish] — **al·i·men·tal** (al′ə-men′təl) *adj.* — **al′i·men′tal·ly** *adv.*

al·i·men·ta·ry (al′ə-men′trē, -tə-rē) *adj.* 1. Supplying nourishment. 2. Connected with food or the function of nutrition. 3. Providing support; sustaining.

alimentary canal The food canal between the mouth and the anus, including esophagus, stomach, and intestines.

al·i·men·ta·tion (al′ə-men-tā′shən) *n.* 1. The act or process of supplying or receiving nourishment. 2. Maintenance; support. — **al·i·men·ta·tive** (al′ə-men′tə-tiv) *adj.*

al·i·mo·ny (al′ə-mō′nē) *n.* *Law* The allowance made to a woman from her husband's estate or income after a divorce or legal separation. [< L *alere* to nourish]

a·line (ə-līn′), **a·line·ment** (ə-līn′mənt) See ALIGN, etc.

al·i·quant (al′ə-kwənt) *adj.* *Math.* Not dividing evenly into another number: 4 is an *aliquant* part of 11. [< L *alius* other + *quantus* how large, how much]

al·i·quot (al′ə-kwət) *adj.* *Math.* Dividing evenly into another number: 4 is an *aliquot* part of 12. [< L *alius* other + *quot* how many]

a·lit (ə-lit′) Alternative past tense and past participle of ALIGHT¹.

a·live (ə-līv′) *adj.* 1. In a living or functioning state; having life. 2. In existence or operation: to keep hope *alive.* 3. In lively action; animated: *alive* with enthusiasm. 4. Aware; sensitive: with *to.* 5. Abounding. [OE *on līfe* in life]

a·liz·a·rin (ə-liz′ə-rin) *n.* *Chem.* An orange-red compound, $C_{14}H_8O_4$, formerly prepared from madder, used as a dye. Also **a·liz·a·rine** (ə-liz′ə-rin, -rēn). [< F < Arabic *al-asārah* juice]

al·ka·li (al′kə-lī) *n.* *pl.* **·lis** or **·lies** *Chem.* 1. A hydroxide of any of the alkali metals, soluble in water and capable of neutralizing acids and of turning red litmus paper blue. 2. Any compound that will neutralize an acid, as lime, magnesia, etc. [< MF < Arabic *al-galiy* the ashes of saltwort]

al·ka·li·fy (al′kə-lə-fī′, al-kal′ə-fī) *v.t.* & *v.i.* **·fied**, **·fy·ing** To change into or become alkaline or an alkali.

alkali metals *Chem.* A group of elements including lithium, sodium, potassium, rubidium, cesium, and francium.

al·ka·line (al′kə-lin, -līn) *adj.* Of, like, or containing an alkali. Also **al′ka·lin.** — **al′ka·lin′i·ty** *n.*

alkaline earths *Chem.* The oxides of calcium, strontium, barium, and sometimes magnesium.

al·ka·lize (al′kə-līz) *v.t.* & *v.i.* **·lized**, **·liz·ing** To convert into or become alkali or alkaline. — **al′ka·li·za′tion** *n.*

al·ka·loid (al′kə-loid) *n.* *Chem.* Any of a class of nitrogenous organic bases, especially one of vegetable origin, having a physiological effect on animals and man, as strychnine or morphine. — **al′ka·loi′dal** *adj.*

Al·ko·ran (al′kō-rän′, -ran′) *n.* The Koran. — **Al′ko·ran′ic** (-ran′ik) *adj.* [< Arabic *al-qurān* the reading]

al·kyl (al′kil) *n.* *Chem.* A univalent radical obtained by removing one hydrogen atom from an aliphatic compound. — **al·kyl·a·tion** (al′kə-lā′shən) *n.* *Chem.* The introduction of an alkyl group into an organic compound.

all (ôl) *adj.* 1. The entire substance or extent of: *all* Europe. 2. The entire number of: known to *all* men. 3. The greatest possible: in *all* haste. 4. Any and every: *all* doubt. 5. Every: used in phrases with *manner, sorts,* and *kinds*: *all* manner of men. 6. Nothing except: He was *all* skin and bones. — *n.* 1. Everything that one has: to give one's *all.* 2. Whole being; totality. — *pron.* 1. Everyone: *All* are condemned. 2. Everything: *All* is lost. 3. Every part, as of a whole: *All* of it is gone. — **above all** Primarily. — **after all** Everything else being considered; nevertheless. — **all in all** Taken as a whole. — **at all** 1. In any way: I can't come *at all.* 2. To any degree or extent: no luck *at all.* — **for all** To the degree that: *For all* I care, you can go alone. — **for all of** As for: You can leave now, *for all of* me. — **in all** Including everything; all told: ten books *in all.* — *adv.* 1. Wholly; entirely: fallen *all* to bits. 2. Exclusively; only: This desk is *all* for me. 3. For each; on each side: a score of three *all.* — **all but** Almost; on the verge of. — Every one except. — **all in** *Informal* Wearied. — **all out** Making every effort: *all out* for victory. — **all the** (better, more, etc.) So much the (better, more, etc.). [OE]

Al·lah (al′ə, ä′lə) In Islam, the one supreme being; God. [< Arabic]

all-A·mer·i·can (ôl′ə-mer′ə-kən) *adj.* 1. Composed of the best in the United States: an *all-American* football team. 2. Of or composed of Americans or American products exclusively. — *n.* A player selected for an all-American team.

all-a·round (ôl′ə-round′) *adj.* All-round.

al·lay (ə-lā′) *v.t.* **·layed**, **·lay·ing** 1. To lessen the violence or reduce the intensity of. 2. To lay to rest, as fears; pacify; calm. [OE < ā- away + *lecgan* to lay] — **al·lay′er** *n.*

all clear The signal indicating that an air raid is over.

al·le·ga·tion (al′ə-gā′shən) *n.* 1. The act of alleging. 2. That which is alleged. 3. Something alleged without proof. 4. *Law* The assertion that a party to a suit undertakes to prove. [< L < *ad-* to + *legare* to commission]

al·lege (ə-lej′) *v.t.* **·leged**, **·leg·ing** 1. To assert to be true without proving; affirm. 2. To plead as an excuse, in support of or in opposition to a claim or accusation. [< AF < OF < L *ex-* out + *litigare* to sue] — **al·lege'a·ble** *adj.* — **al·leged'** (ə·lejd', ə·lej'id) *adj.* — **al·leg'er** *n.*

al·leg·ed·ly (ə·lej'id·lē) *adv.* According to allegation.

al·le·giance (ə·lē'jəns) *n.* 1. Fidelity, or an obligation of fidelity, to a government or sovereign. 2. Fidelity in general, as to a principle. [ME < *a-* to + OF *liege* liege]

al·le·gor·ic (al'ə·gôr'ik, -gor'-) *adj.* Pertaining to, appearing in, or containing allegory; figurative. Also **al'le·gor'i·cal.** — **al'le·gor'i·cal·ly** *adv.*

al·le·go·rist (al'ə·gôr'ist, -gō'rist, al'ə·gər·ist) *n.* One who composes or uses allegories.

al·le·go·ris·tic (al'ə·gə·ris'tik) *adj.* Allegorizing.

al·le·go·rize (al'ə·gə·rīz') *v.* **·rized, ·riz·ing** *v.t.* 1. To turn into an allegory; relate in the manner of an allegory. 2. To explain or interpret as an allegory. — *v.i.* 3. To make or use allegory. — **al·le·go·ri·za·tion** (al'ə·gôr'ə·zā'shən, -gor'-) *n.* — **al'le·go·riz'er** *n.*

al·le·go·ry (al'ə·gôr'ē, -gō'rē) *n.* *pl.* **·ries** 1. A story or narrative, as a fable, in which a moral principle or truth is presented by means of fictional characters, events, etc. 2. The presentation of a truth or moral by such stories. 3. Loosely, any symbolic representation in literature or art. [< L < Gk. *allos* other + *agoreuein* to speak publicly]

al·le·gret·to (al'ə·gret'ō, *Ital.* äl'lā·gret'tō) *Music adj. & adv.* Rather fast. — *n.* *pl.* **·tos** A composition, movement, etc., in such tempo. [< Ital., dim. of *allegro* lively]

al·le·gro (ə·lā'grō, ə·leg'rō; *Ital.* äl·lā'grō) *Music adj. & adv.* Lively. — *n.* *pl.* **·gros** A composition, movement, etc., in such tempo. [< Ital.]

al·lele (ə·lēl') *n. Genetics* One of a series of hereditary characters alternative to each other. Also **al·le·lo·morph** (ə·lē'lə·môrf, ə·lel'ə-). [< Gk. *allēlōn* of one another + *morphē* form] — **al·le·lo·mor'phic** *adj.* — **al·le·lo·mor'phism** *n.*

al·le·lu·ia (al'ə·lōō'yə) *n. & interj.* Hallelujah: the Latin spelling and more common liturgic form. Also **al'le·lu'iah.**

al·ler·gen (al'ər·jən) *n.* Any substance capable of producing allergy. Also **al'ler·gin.** — **al·ler·gen·ic** (al'ər·jen'ik) *adj.*

al·ler·gic (ə·lûr'jik) *adj.* 1. Of, pertaining to, or having an allergy. 2. *Informal* Having an aversion: *allergic* to work.

al·ler·gist (al'ər·jist) *n.* A specialist in the diagnosis and treatment of allergies.

al·ler·gy (al'ər·jē) *n.* *pl.* **·gies** *Med.* A condition of heightened sensitivity to a substance, as food, pollen, dust, etc. [< NL < Gk. *allos* other + *ergon* work]

al·le·vi·ate (ə·lē'vē·āt) *v.t.* **·at·ed, ·at·ing** To make lighter or easier to bear. [< L < *ad-* to + *levis* light, not heavy]

al·le·vi·a·tive (ə·lē'vē·ā'tiv, ə·lē'vē·ə·tiv) *adj.* Tending to alleviate. Also **al·le·vi·a·to·ry** (ə·lē'vē·ə·tôr'ē, -tō'rē), — *n.* Anything that alleviates.

al·ley (al'ē) *n.* 1. A narrow passageway; esp., a narrow way between or behind city buildings. 2. A bowling alley. 3. A walk bordered with trees or shrubbery. [< OF *alee* a going, passage < *aler* to go]

al·ley·way (al'ē·wā') *n.* A passageway between buildings.

All Fools' Day The first of April, a day on which jokes and tricks are commonly practiced: also *April Fools' Day.*

all fours The four legs of a quadruped, or the arms and legs of a person. — **to go** (or **be**) **on all fours** To rest or crawl on all four limbs.

All·hal·low·mas (ôl'hal'ō·məs) *n.* All Saints' Day. Also **All·hal·lows** (ôl'hal'ōz).

al·li·ance (ə·lī'əns) *n.* 1. The state or condition of being allied. 2. The relationship or union brought about by marriage. 3. Any union, coalition, or agreement between parties, sovereigns, nations, etc., in their common interest. 4. Relationship in qualities or characteristics; affinity. [< OF < L < *ad-* to + *ligare* to bind]

al·lied (ə·līd', al'īd) *adj.* 1. United, confederated, or leagued. 2. Closely related: *allied* interests.

Al·lies (al'īz, ə·līz') *n.pl.* 1. The twenty-seven nations allied against the Central Powers in World War I; esp., Russia, France, Great Britain, Italy, and the United States. 2. The nations and governments-in-exile known as the United Nations in World War II. — **Al·lied** (ə·līd', al'īd) *adj.*

al·li·ga·tor (al'ə·gā'tər) *n.* 1. A large crocodilian reptile found only in the southern United States and in the Yangtze river, China, having a shorter, blunter snout than the crocodile. 2. Leather made from the skin of the alligator. [< Sp. *el lagarto* < L *lacertus* lizard]

ALLIGATOR
(To 16 feet long)

alligator pear The fruit of the avocado.

all-im·por·tant (ôl'im·pôr'tənt) *adj.* Very important.

all-in·clu·sive (ôl'in·klōō'siv) *adj.* Including everything.

al·lit·er·ate (ə·lit'ə·rāt) *v.* **·at·ed, ·at·ing** *v.i.* 1. To use alliteration. 2. To contain alliteration. — *v.t.* 3. To make alliterative. [< AL-² to + L *littera* a letter (of the alphabet)]

al·lit·er·a·tion (ə·lit'ə·rā'shən) *n.* The occurrence, in a phrase or line, of two or more words having the same initial sound or sound cluster, as in "A fair field full of folk."

al·lit·er·a·tive (ə·lit'ə·rā'tiv, -ər·ə·tiv) *adj.* Of or like alliteration. — **al·lit'er·a'tive·ly** *adv.* — **al·lit'er·a'tive·ness** *n.*

allo- *combining form* 1. Other; alien. 2. Extraneousness; difference from or opposition to the normal: *allopathy*. [< Gk. *allos* other]

al·lo·cate (al'ə·kāt) *v.t.* **·cat·ed, ·cat·ing** 1. To set apart for a special purpose, as funds. 2. To apportion; assign as a share or in shares. 3. To locate or localize, as a person or event. [< Med.L < L *ad-* to + *locare* to place] — **al·lo·ca·ble** (al'ə·kə·bəl) *adj.* — **al'lo·ca'tion** *n.*

al·lom·er·ism (ə·lom'ər·iz'əm) *n. Crystall.* Constancy of crystalline form with variation in chemical constitution. [< ALLO- + Gk. *meros* a part] — **al·lom'er·ous** *adj.*

al·lo·path (al'ə·path) *n.* One who practices or favors allopathy. Also **al·lo·path·ist** (ə·lop'ə·thist).

al·lop·a·thy (ə·lop'ə·thē) *n.* A system of treatment that seeks to cure a disease by producing a condition different from the effects of the disease. — **al·lo·path·ic** (al'ə·path'ik) *adj.* — **al'lo·path'i·cal·ly** *adv.*

al·lot (ə·lot') *v.t.* **·lot·ted, ·lot·ting** 1. To assign by lot; distribute. 2. To apportion or assign: with *to.* [< OF < *a-* to + *loter* to apportion]

al·lot·ment (ə·lot'mənt) *n.* 1. The act of allotting, or that which is allotted. 2. *U.S. Mil.* A portion of a serviceman's pay regularly assigned, as to a member of his family.

al·lo·trope (al'ə·trōp) *n. Chem.* One of the forms assumed by an allotropic substance.

al·lot·ro·py (ə·lot'rə·pē) *n. Chem.* The variation in properties shown by elements or their compounds without change of chemical composition. Also **al·lot·ro·pism** (ə·lot'rə·piz'əm). [< Gk. *allos* other + *tropos* turn, manner] — **al·lo·trop·ic** (al'ə·trop'ik) or **·i·cal** *adj.* — **al'lo·trop'i·cal·ly** *adv.*

al·lot·tee (ə·lot'ē) *n.* One to whom anything is allotted.

all-out (ôl'out') *adj.* Complete and entire; total.

all·o·ver (*adj.* ôl'ō'vər; *n.* ôl'ō'vər) *adj.* Extending over the whole or surface of anything: the *allover* effect. — *n.* A fabric or other substance having an allover pattern.

al·low (ə·lou') *v.t.* 1. To permit to occur or do. 2. To concede; admit. 3. To make allowance or provision for: to *allow* an hour for lunch. 4. To make concession of: to *allow* a month to pay. 5. To grant; allot. 6. *U.S. Dial* To say; declare. — *v.i.* 7. To permit or admit: with *of:* Your remark *allows* of several interpretations. 8. To make concession or due allowance: with *for.* [< OF *alouer* to place, use, assign < Med.L < L < *ad-* to + *laudare* to praise]

al·low·a·ble (ə·lou'ə·bəl) *adj.* Permissible; admissible. — **al·low'a·ble·ness** *n.* — **al·low'a·bly** *adv.*

al·low·ance (ə·lou'əns) *n.* 1. That which is allowed. 2. A definite sum of money given at regular intervals. 3. A discount, as for a purchase in volume, a trade-in, etc. 4. The act of allowing; toleration; sanction. 5. Admission; acceptance. — **to make allowance(s) for** To take into account or to excuse because of modifying circumstances. — *v.t.* **·anced, ·anc·ing** 1. To put on an allowance; limit to a regular amount. 2. To supply in limited quantities.

al·low·ed·ly (ə·lou'id·lē) *adv.* Admittedly.

al·loy (*n.* al'oi, ə·loi'; *v.* ə·loi') *n.* 1. *Metall.* **a** A mixture or combination formed by the fusion of two or more metals or of a metal and a nonmetal. **b** A baser metal mixed or combined with a finer one. 2. Anything that reduces purity. — *v.t.* 1. To reduce the purity of, as a metal, by mixing with an alloy. 2. To mix (metals) so as to form into an alloy. 3. To modify or debase, as by mixture with something inferior. [< F < OF < L < *ad-* to + *ligare* to bind]

all-pur·pose (ôl'pûr'pəs) *adj.* Generally useful.

all-right (ôl'rīt') *adj. Slang* 1. Dependable; honest; loyal. 2. Good; excellent.

all right 1. Satisfactory. 2. Correct, as a sum in addition. 3. Uninjured. 4. Certainly. 5. Yes. See ALRIGHT.

all-round (ôl'round') *adj.* 1. *U.S.* Of comprehensive range or scope; complete in action or effect. 2. Excelling in all or many aspects; many-sided; versatile. Also *all-around.*

All Saints' Day *Eccl.* November 1, a festival commemorative of all saints and martyrs. Also **All Saints.**

All Souls' Day *Eccl.* November 2, a day of commemoration on which intercession is made for the souls of all the faithful departed. Also **All Souls.**

all·spice (ôl'spīs') *n.* 1. The aromatic dried berry of the pimento. 2. The sharply flavored spice made from it.

al·lude (ə·lōōd') *v.i.* **lud·ed, ·lud·ing** To refer without express mention; make indirect or casual reference: with *to.* [< L < *ad-* to + *ludere* to play]

---

al·lure (ə·lŏŏr′) *v.t.* & *v.i.* **·lured, ·lur·ing** To draw with or as with a lure; attract; entice. — *n.* That which allures. [< OF < *a-* to + *leurre* lure] — **al·lure′ment** *n.* — **al·lur′er** *n.*

al·lur·ing (ə·lŏŏr′ĭng) *adj.* Attractive; fascinating. — **al·lur′ing·ly** *adv.* — **al·lur′ing·ness** *n.*

al·lu·sion (ə·lōō′zhən) *n.* The act of alluding; indirect reference; suggestion. [< L *alludere* to play with, joke]

al·lu·sive (ə·lōō′sĭv) *adj.* Making allusion; suggestive. — **al·lu′sive·ly** *adv.* — **al·lu′sive·ness** *n.*

al·lu·vi·al (ə·lōō′vē·əl) *adj.* Pertaining to or composed of earth deposited by water. — *n.* Alluvial soil.

al·lu·vi·um (ə·lōō′vē·əm) *n.* *pl.* **·vi·a** (-vē·ə) or **·vi·ums** A deposit, as of sand or mud, transported and laid down by flowing water in river beds, flood plains, lakes, etc. [< L]

al·ly (ə·lī′, al′ī) *v.* **·lied, ·ly·ing** *v.t.* **1.** To connect by some relationship or bond: with *to* or *with*. **2.** To enter into alliance; become allied. — *n.* *pl.* **·lies 1.** A person or country connected with another, as by treaty or common action. **2.** Any friendly associate or helper. **3.** An organism or substance associated with another by similarity. [< OF < *a-* to + *ligare* to bind]

al·ma ma·ter (al′mə mä′tər, al′mə mā′tər, äl′mə mä′tər) The institution of learning that one has attended. Also **Al′ma Ma′ter.** [< L, fostering mother]

al·ma·nac (ôl′mə·nak) *n.* A yearly calendar giving weather forecasts, astronomical information, times of high and low tides, etc. [< Med.L < Sp. < Arabic *al-manākh*]

al·might·y (ôl·mīt′ē) *adj.* **1.** Able to do all things; omnipotent. **2.** *U.S. Informal* Great; extreme: an *almighty* noise. — *adv.* *U.S. Informal* Exceedingly: *almighty* mad. — **the Almighty** God; the Supreme Being. [OE *eal* all + *mihtig* mighty] — **al·might′i·ly** *adv.* — **al·might′i·ness** *n.*

al·mond (ä′mənd, am′ənd) *n.* **1.** A small tree of the rose family, widely cultivated in the warmer temperate regions. **2.** The kernel of the fruit of the almond tree. **3.** Anything having the pointed, oval shape of an almond. [< OF < LL < L < Gk. *amygdalē*]

al·mon·er (al′mən·ər, ä′mən-) *n.* An official dispenser of alms. Also **alm·ner** (alm′nər, äm′nər). [< OF < LL < L < Gk. *eleēmosynē* alms < *eleos* pity]

al·most (ôl′mōst, ôl·mōst′) *adv.* Approximately; very nearly; all but: *almost* complete. [OE *ealmǣst*]

alms (ämz) *n. sing.* & *pl.* A gift or gifts for the poor. ◆ Collateral adjective: *eleemosynary.* Some self-explanatory compounds have *alms* as their first element: **almsgiver, almsgiving, almsmoney,** etc. [OE < LL < Gk. *eleēmosynē* alms < *eleos* pity]

alms·house (ämz′hous′) *n.* A poorhouse.

al·oe (al′ō) *n.* *pl.* **·oes 1.** An Old World plant of the lily family, some species of which furnish a drug, and others valuable fiber. **2.** *pl.* (construed as sing.) A cathartic made from the juice of certain aloes. [OE < L < Gk. *aloē*] — **al·o·et·ic** (al′ō·et′ik) or **·et·i·cal** *adj.*

a·loft (ə·lôft′, ə·loft′) *adv.* **1.** In or to a high or higher place; on high; high up. **2.** *Naut.* At or to the higher parts of a ship's rigging. [< ON *ā lopt* in (the) air]

a·lo·ha (ə·lō′ə, ä·lō′hä) *n.* & *interj.* *Hawaiian* Love: used as a salutation and a farewell.

Aloha State Nickname of HAWAII.

a·lone (ə·lōn′) *adv.* & *adj.* **1.** Without company; solitary. **2.** Excluding all others; only: He *alone* survived. **3.** Without equal; unique; unparalleled: As an artist, he stands *alone.* [ME *al one* solitary]

a·long (ə·lông′, ə·long′) *adv.* **1.** Following the length or course of; lengthwise: usually with *by.* **2.** Progressively onward in a course; forward: The years roll *along* quickly. **3.** In company or association; together: usually with *with.* **4.** *U.S.* As a companion: Bring a friend *along.* **5.** *U.S. Informal* Advanced in its natural course. **6.** *U.S. Informal* Approaching a time, age, number, etc.: usually with *about.* — **all along** From the outset; throughout. — **to be along** *U.S. Informal* To arrive at a place; come. — **right along** *U.S. Informal* Without interruption. — *prep.* Throughout or over the length or course of. [OE *andlang* continuous]

a·long·shore (ə·lông′shôr′, ə·long′-, -shōr′) *adv.* Along the shore, either on the water or on the land.

a·long·side (ə·lông′sīd′, ə·long′-) *adv.* Close to or along the side. — *prep.* Side by side with; at the side of.

a·loof (ə·lōōf′) *adj.* Distant, esp. in manner; unsympathetic. — *adv.* At a distance; apart: to stand *aloof.* [< A-[1] + *loof* < Du. *loef* windward] — **a·loof′ly** *adv.* — **a·loof′ness** *n.*

a·loud (ə·loud′) *adv.* Loudly or audibly.

alp (alp) *n.* **1.** A lofty mountain. **2.** Any peak of the Alps. [Back formation < L *Alpes* the Alps.]

al·pac·a (al·pak′ə) *n.* **1.** A domesticated ruminant of South America, related to the llama and vicuña. **2.** Its long silky wool. **3.** A thin cloth made of or containing this wool. **4.** A glossy black fabric of cotton and wool. [< Sp. < Arabic *al* the + Peruvian *paco,* name of the animal]

al·pen·stock (al′pən·stok′) *n.* A long, iron-pointed staff used by mountain climbers. [< G]

al·pha (al′fə) *n.* **1.** The first letter in the Greek alphabet (A, α), corresponding to English *a.* See table for ALPHABET. **2.** The first of anything. [< Gk. < Hebrew *āleph* ox]

al·pha·bet (al′fə·bet) *n.* **1.** The letters that form the elements of written language, in an order fixed by usage. **2.** Any system of characters or symbols representing the sounds of speech. **3.** The simplest elements of anything. [< L < Gk. < Hebrew *āleph* ox + *beth* house]

al·pha·bet·i·cal (al′fə·bet′i·kəl) *adj.* **1.** Arranged in the order of the alphabet. **2.** Pertaining to or expressed by an alphabet. Also **al′pha·bet′ic.** — **al·pha·bet′i·cal·ly** *adv.*

al·pha·bet·ize (al′fə·bə·tīz′) *v.t.* **·ized, ·iz·ing 1.** To put in alphabetical order. **2.** To express by or furnish with an alphabet or alphabetic symbols. — **al·pha·bet·i·za·tion** (al′fə·bet′ə·zā′shən) *n.* — **al′pha·bet·iz′er** *n.*

al·pha·nu·mer·ic (al′fə·nōō·mer′ik, -nyōō-) *adj.* Consisting of or using the letters of the alphabet and numerals, as in a computer code. Also **al′pha·nu·mer′i·cal.**

alpha particle *Physics* The positively charged nucleus of the helium atom.

alpha ray *Physics* A stream of alpha particles.

alpha rhythm *Physiol.* The recurring cycles of electrical change in the brain, each cycle known as an **alpha wave.**

al·pine (al′pīn, -pin) *adj.* **1.** Like an alp; lofty and towering. **2.** *Biol.* Inhabiting or growing in mountain regions.

Al·pine (al′pīn, -pin) *adj.* Pertaining to or characteristic of the Alps. [< L *Alpes* the Alps]

al·pi·nist (al′pə·nist) *n.* A climber of alps; a mountaineer. Also **Al′pi·nist.** — **al′pi·nism, al′pi·nism** *n.*

al·read·y (ôl·red′ē) *adv.* Before or by the time mentioned.

al·right (ôl·rīt′) *adv.* All right: a spelling not yet considered acceptable.

Al·sa·tian (al·sā′shən) *adj.* **1.** Of or pertaining to Alsace. **2.** Of or pertaining to Alsatia. — *n.* **1.** A native or inhabitant of Alsace. **2.** A German shepherd dog.

al·so (ôl′sō) *adv.* In addition; besides; likewise. [OE *alswā, ealswā* all (wholly) so]

al·so·ran (ôl′sō·ran′) *n.* *U.S. Informal* **1.** A horse that fails to win, place, or show in a race. **2.** Any unsuccessful competitor.

Al·ta·ic (al·tā′ik) *adj.* Of the Altai Mountains or the languages spoken there. Also **Al·tai·an** (al·tā′ən, -tī′-) *adj.*

al·tar (ôl′tər) *n.* **1.** Any raised place or structure on which sacrifices may be offered or incense burned as an act of worship. **2.** *Eccl.* The structure of wood or stone on which the elements are consecrated in the Eucharist. [OE < L *altus* high]

altar boy An attendant at the altar; acolyte.

al·tar·piece (ôl′tər·pēs′) *n.* A painting, mosaic, or bas-relief over and behind the altar; a reredos.

al·ter (ôl′tər) *v.t.* **1.** To cause to be different. **2.** *U.S.* To castrate or spay. — *v.i.* **3.** To change. [< MF < Med.L < L *alter* other]

al·ter·a·ble (ôl′tər·ə·bəl) *adj.* Capable of alteration. — **al′ter·a·bil′i·ty, al′ter·a·ble·ness** *n.* — **al′ter·a·bly** *adv.*

al·ter·a·tion (ôl′tər·ā′shən) *n.* **1.** The act or process of altering. **2.** Any change. [< MF < Med.L < L *alter* other]

al·ter·a·tive (ôl′tər·ā′tiv) *adj.* **1.** Tending to produce change. **2.** *Med.* Tending to change gradually the bodily condition to a normal state. — *n.* *Med.* An alterative medicine or treatment. Also **al·ter·ant** (ôl′tər·ənt).

al·ter·cate (ôl′tər·kāt, al′-) *v.i.* **·cat·ed, ·cat·ing** To dispute vehemently. [< L *alter* other]

al·ter·ca·tion (ôl′tər·kā′shən, al′-) *n.* A heated dispute.

al·ter e·go (ôl′tər ē′gō, al′tər eg′ō) **1.** Another self; a double. **2.** An intimate friend. [< L, lit., other I]

al·ter·nant (ôl·tûr′nənt, ôl′tər·nənt) *adj.* Alternating.

al·ter·nate (*v.* ôl′tər·nāt, al′-; *adj.* & *n.* ôl′tər·nit, al′-) *v.* **·nat·ed, ·nat·ing** *v.i.* **1.** To follow one another by turns. **2.** To change from one place, condition, etc., to another and back again repeatedly. **3.** *Electr.* To reverse direction of flow repeatedly: said of a current. — *v.t.* **4.** To do or perform by turns. **5.** To cause to follow one another by turns. — *adj.* **1.** Existing, occurring, or following by turns. **2.** Referring or pertaining to every other of a series. **3.** Alternative: *alternate* plans. — *n.* A substitute or second. [< L *alternus* every second one] — **al′ter·nate·ly** (-nit·lē) *adv.* — **al′ter·nate·ness** *n.*

alternate angle *Geom.* Either of two nonadjacent interior or exterior angles formed on opposite sides of a line that crosses two other lines.

al·ter·na·tion (ôl′tər·nā′shən, al′-) *n.* Occurrence or action of two things in turn; passage from one place or state to another and back again.

al·ter·na·tive (ôl·tûr′nə·tiv, al-) *n.* **1.** A choice between two things: often loosely applied to more than two. **2.** Either of the two or more things to be chosen. **3.** The remaining choice. — *adj.* Affording or implying a choice between two (or sometimes more) things. — **al·ter′na·tive·ly** *adv.* — **al·ter′na·tive·ness** *n.* [< Med.L *alternativus*]

al·ter·na·tor (ôl′tər·nā′tər, al′-) *n. Electr.* A generator giving an alternating current. Also **al′ter·nat′er.**

al·the·a (al·thē′ə) *n.* Any of several plants of the mallow family, including the rose of Sharon. Also **al·thae′a.** [< L < Gk. *althainein* to heal]

alt·horn (alt′hôrn′) *n.* An alto flügelhorn or saxhorn.

al·though (ôl·thō′) *conj.* Notwithstanding the fact that; supposing that; though. Also **al·tho′.**

alti- *combining form* High. Also **alto-.** [< L < *altus* high]

al·tim·e·ter (al·tim′ə·tər, al′tə·mē′tər) *n.* 1. An aneroid barometer for determining altitudes. 2. Any instrument for determining altitude. — **al·tim·e·try** (al·tim′ə·trē) *n.*

al·ti·tude (al′tə·tōod, -tyōod) *n.* 1. Elevation above any given point, esp. above mean sea level; height. 2. *Astron.* Angular elevation above the horizon. 3. *Geom.* The vertical distance from the base of a figure to its highest point. 4. A high place or rank. [< L *altus* high] — **al·ti·tu′di·nal** *adj.*

al·to (al′tō) *Music n. pl.* **·tos** 1. The lowest female voice; contralto. 2. The highest male voice; countertenor. 3. A singer who has an alto voice. 4. A musical part for this voice. — *adj.* Of or for the alto. [< Ital. < L *altus* high]

alto- Var. of ALTI-.

al·to·geth·er (ôl′tə·geth′ər, ôl′tə·geth′ər) *adv.* 1. Completely; wholly; entirely. 2. With everything included. — *n.* A whole. — **in the altogether** *Informal* Nude.

al·tru·ism (al′trōo·iz′əm) *n.* Selfless devotion to the welfare of others. [< F < L *alter* other] — **al·tru·ist** *n.* — **al·tru·is·tic** (al′trōo·is′tik) *adj.* — **al′tru·is′ti·cal·ly** *adv.*

al·um (al′əm) *n. Chem.* An astringent, crystalline, double sulfate of aluminum and potassium, $K_2SO_4Al_2(SO_4)_3 \cdot 24H_2O$, used in medicine and industry. [< OF < L *alumen* alum]

a·lu·mi·na (ə·lōo′mə·nə) *n. Chem.* Aluminum oxide, Al_2O_3, occurring in the silicate minerals and as corundum in the sapphire and ruby. Also **al·u·min** (al′yə·min), **al·u·mine** (al′yə·mēn, -min). [< NL < L *alumen* alum]

a·lu·mi·nize (ə·lōo′mə·nīz) *v.t.* **·nized, ·niz·ing** To cover or treat with aluminum. Also **a·lu·me·tize** (ə·lōo′mə·tīz).

a·lu·mi·num (ə·lōo′mə·nəm) *n.* A light, bluish white, malleable and ductile metallic element (symbol Al) found only in combination. It is widely used in alloys. Also *Brit.* **al·u·min·i·um** (al′yə·min′ē·əm). See ELEMENT. [< NL < L *alumen* alum]

a·lum·na (ə·lum′nə) *n. pl.* **·nae** (-nē) *U.S.* A female graduate or former student of a college or school. [< L]

a·lum·nus (ə·lum′nəs) *n. pl.* **·ni** (-nī) *Chiefly U.S.* A male graduate or former student of a college or school. [< L, foster son, pupil < *alere* to nourish]

al·ve·o·lar (al·vē′ə·lər) *adj.* 1. *Anat.* Denoting that part of the jaws in which the teeth are set. 2. *Phonet.* Formed with the tongue tip touching or near the alveolar ridge, as (t), (d), and (s) in English. — *n. Phonet.* A sound so produced.

al·ve·o·late (al·vē′ə·lit, al′vē·ə-) *adj.* Having alveoli arranged like the cells of a honeycomb; deeply pitted. Also **al·ve·o·lat·ed** (al·vē′ə·lā′tid). — **al·ve·o·la′tion** *n.*

al·ve·o·lus (al·vē′ə·ləs) *n. pl.* **·li** (-lī) 1. A small cavity or pit, as an air cell of the lung. 2. The socket in which a tooth is set. 3. *pl.* The bony ridge holding the upper front teeth. [< L, dim. of *alveus* a hollow]

TABLE OF FOREIGN ALPHABETS

(1) ARABIC			(2) HEBREW			(3) GREEK			(4) RUSSIAN			(5) GERMAN			
ا	alif	–[1]	א	aleph	–[6]	Α α	alpha	ä	А а	ä	ä	Ꮶ a	ä	A a	
ب	ba	b	ב, בּ	beth	b, v	Β β	beta	b	Б б	be	b	B b	bā	B b	
ت	ta	t	ג, גּ	gimel	g, gh[3]	Γ γ	gamma	g	В в	ve	v	C c	tsä	C c	
ث	sa	th	ד, דּ	daleth	d, th	Δ δ	delta	d	Г г	ge	g	D d	dā	D d	
ج	jim	j	ה	he	h	Ε ε	epsilon	e	Д д	de	d	E e	ā[22]	E e	
ح	ha	h	ו	vav	v	Ζ ζ	zeta	z	Е е	ye	ye, e[12]	F f	ef	F f	
خ	kha	kh	ז	zayin	z	Η η	eta	ā	Ё ё	yô	yô, ô[12, 13]	G g	gā	G g	
د	dal	d	ח	heth	kh	Θ θ	theta	th[9]	Ж ж	zhe	zh[14]	H h	hä	H h	
ذ	zal	th	ט	teth	t	Ι ι	iota	ē	З з	ze	z	I i	ē	I i	
ر	ra	r	י	yod	y	Κ κ	kappa	k	И и	ē krät′. kə·ya	ē[15]	J j	yôt	J j	
ز	za	z	ך, כ, כּ[8]	kaph	k[5], kh	Λ λ	lambda	l	Й й	ē	ē[16]	K k	kä	K k	
سب	sin	s	ל	lamed	l	Μ μ	mu	m	К к	kä	k	L l	el	L l	
ش	shin	sh	ם, מ[8]	mem	m	Ν ν	nu	n	Л л	el	l	M m	em	M m	
ص	sad	s	ן, נ[8]	nun	n	Ξ ξ	xi	ks	М м	em	m	N n	en	N n	
ض	dad	d	ס	samek	s	Ο ο	omicron	o	Н н	en	n	O o	ō[22]	O o	
ط	ta	t	ע	ayin	–[7]	Π π	pi	p	О о	ô	ô	Ö ö	œ[21]	Ö ö	
ظ	za	z	ף, פ, פּ[8]	pe	p, f	Ρ ρ	rho	r	П п	pe	p	P p	pā	P p	
ع	ain	–[2]	ץ, צ[8]	sade	s	Σ σ, ς[8]	sigma	s	Р р	er	r	Q q	kōō	Q q	
غ	ghain	gh[3]	ק	koph	k[4]	Τ τ	tau	t	С с	es	s	R r	er	R r	
ف	fa	f	ר	resh	r	Υ υ	upsilon	ü, ōō	Т т	te	t	S ſ, s[8]	es	S s	
ق	qaf	k[4]	שׁ, שׂ	sin, shin	s, sh	Φ φ	phi	f[10]	У у	ōō	ōō	ß[22]	es′tset	ß[22], ss	
ك	kaf	k[5]	ת, תּ	tav	t, th	Χ χ	chi	kh[11]	Ф ф	ef	f	T t	tā	T t	
ل	lam	l				Ψ ψ	psi	ps	Х х	khä	kh	U u	ōō	U u	
م	mim	m				Ω ω	omega	ō	Ц ц	tse	ts[14]	Ü ü	ü[21]	Ü ü	
ن	nun	n							Ч ч	che	ch[17]	V v	fou	V v	
ه	ha	h							Ш ш	shä	sh[14]	W w	vä	W w	
و	waw	w							Щ щ	shchä	shch[17]	X x	iks	X x	
ي	ya	y							Ъ ъ	tvyôr′dē znäk	–[18]	Y y	üp′si·lôn	Y y	
									Ы ы		i[19]	Z z	tset	Z z	
									Ь ь	myäkh′. kyē znäk	–[20]				
									Э э	e	e				
									Ю ю	yōō	yōō, ōō[12]				
									Я я	yä	yä, ä[12]				

In each column the characters of the alphabet are given first, followed by their names. In columns 4 (Russian) and 5 (German) the names are printed in the phonetic system used in this dictionary. The last rows of columns 1 through 4 show the approximate sound represented by each character. Columns 3 through 5 show the upper- and lower-case letters.

The Arabic characters are given in their final, unconnected forms. The German style letter, called *fraktur*, has been gradually replaced by the Latin letter. The last row of column 5 gives the Latin equivalents.

[1] Functions as the bearer of *hamza* (the glottal stop), or as a lengthener of short *a*. [2] A voiced pharyngeal fricative. [3] A voiced velar fricative. [4] A uvular velar stop. [5] A voiceless velar stop. [6] A glottal stop, now usually silent, or pronounced according to the accompanying vowel points. [7] A pharyngeal fricative, now usually silent, or pronounced according to the accompanying vowel points. [8] The alternate form is restricted to the ends of words. [9, 10, 11] In classical Greek these were pronounced as aspirated stops, similar to the sounds in foothill, haphazard, and blockhouse. [12] Preceded by a y glide when initial, following a vowel, or following a previously palatalized consonant. The glide is otherwise omitted and the preceding consonant palatalized. [13] The diacritical mark is most often omitted. [14] Never palatalized. [15] Palatalizes the consonant preceding it. [16] A short vowel, as y in *boy*, used only as the second element of diphthongs. [17] Always palatalized. [18] No phonetic value, used to separate parts of compounds and indicate that the consonant preceding it is not palatalized; a hard sign. [19] No English equivalent, similar to *i* as in *kick* with the tongue drawn back. [20] Indicates that the preceding consonant is to be palatalized. [21] See UMLAUT in vocabulary section. [22] In German this vowel is not a diphthong. [23] Restricted to the ends of words.

PRONUNCIATION KEY: add, āce, câre, pälm; end, ēven; it, īce; odd, ōpen, ôrder; tŏŏk, pōōl; up, bûrn; ǝ = a in *above*, e in *sicken*, i in *flexible*, o in *melon*, u in *focus*; yōō = u in *fuse*; oil; pout; check; go; ring; thin; this; zh, vision. For à, œ, ü, kh, n̄, see inside front cover.

al·ways (ôl′wāz, -wiz) *adv.* **1.** Perpetually; for all time; ceaselessly. **2.** At every time; on all occasions. [ME *alles weyes* < OE *aelne weg*]

a·lys·sum (ə·lis′əm) *n.* **1.** Any plant of the mustard family, bearing white or yellow flowers. **2.** The sweet alyssum. [< NL < Gk. < *a-* not + *lyssa* madness]

am (am, *unstressed* əm) Present indicative, first person singular, of BE. [OE *eom, am*]

a·mah (ä′mə, am′ə) *n.* In India and the Orient, a female attendant for children; esp., a wet nurse. Also **a′ma.** [< Anglo-Indian < Pg. *ama* nurse]

a·mal·gam (ə·mal′gəm) *n.* **1.** An alloy or union of mercury with another metal. **2.** A silver-white, brittle compound of mercury and silver. **3.** Any combination of two or more things. [< MF < Med.L < Gk. *malagma* an emollient < *malassein* to soften]

a·mal·ga·mate (ə·mal′gə·māt) *v.t. & v.i.* **·mat·ed, ·mat·ing** **1.** To form an amalgam. **2.** To unite or combine. — **a·mal·ga·ma·ble** (ə·mal′gə·mə·bəl) *adj.* — **a·mal·ga·ma·tive** (ə·mal′gə·mā′tiv) *adj.* — **a·mal′ga·ma·tor** or **a·mal′ga·mat′er** *n.* — **a·mal′ga·ma′tion** *n.*

a·man·u·en·sis (ə·man′yōō·en′sis) *n.* *pl.* **·ses** (-sēz) One who copies manuscript or takes dictation; a secretary. [< L < (*servus*) *a manu* hand (servant), secretary]

am·a·ranth (am′ə·ranth) *n.* **1.** Any of various allied plants, as the love-lies-bleeding. **2.** *Poetic* An imaginary nonfading flower. [< L < Gk. < *a-* not + *marainein* to wither] — **am′a·ran′thine** *adj.*

am·a·ryl·lis (am′ə·ril′is) *n.* A bulbous plant, producing large, lily-like flowers. [< L < Gk. *Amaryllis*, fem. personal name]

a·mass (ə·mas′) *v.t.* To heap up, esp. wealth or possessions for oneself. [< OF < *a-* to + *masser* to pile up] — **a·mass′a·ble** *adj.* — **a·mass′er** *n.* — **a·mass′ment** *n.*

am·a·teur (am′ə·chŏŏr, -tŏŏr, -tyŏŏr, am′ə·tûr′) *n.* **1.** One who practices an art or science for his own pleasure, rather than as a profession. **2.** An athlete who has not engaged in contests for money. **3.** One who does something without professional skill or ease. — *adj.* **1.** Of, pertaining to, or done by an amateur. **2.** Not expert. [< F < L *amare* to love] — **am′a·teur·ism** *n.*
— **Syn.** (noun) **1.** In present usage, *amateur* is often used to indicate lack of skill, while *connoisseur* implies the ability to make discriminating judgments. A *dilettante* loves the arts, and often possesses great esthetic sensitivity, but lacks technical mastery.

am·a·teur·ish (am′ə·chŏŏr′ish, -tŏŏr′-, -tyŏŏr′-, -tûr′-) *adj.* Lacking the skill or perfection of an expert or professional. — **am′a·teur′ish·ly** *adv.* — **am′a·teur′ish·ness** *n.*

am·a·to·ry (am′ə·tôr′ē, -tō′rē) *adj.* Pertaining to, expressing, or exciting love, especially sexual love. — **Syn.** See AMOROUS. [< L *amare* to love]

a·maze (ə·māz′) *v.t.* **a·mazed, a·maz·ing** To overwhelm, as by wonder or surprise; astonish greatly. [OE *āmasian*] — **a·maz·ed·ly** (ə·mā′zid·lē) *adv.* — **a·maz′ed·ness** *n.*

a·maze·ment (ə·māz′mənt) *n.* Extreme wonder or surprise; astonishment.

a·maz·ing (ə·mā′zing) *adj.* Causing amazement; astonishing; wonderful. — **a·maz′ing·ly** *adv.*

Am·a·zon (am′ə·zon, -zən) *n.* **1.** In Greek mythology, one of a race of female warriors. **2.** Any large, strong or athletic woman or girl: also **am′a·zon.** [< L < Gk. *Amazōn* < Gk. *a-* without + *mazōs* breast, because of the fable that they cut off the right breast to facilitate the use of the bow] — **Am′a·zo′ni·an** (-zō′nē·ən) *adj.*

am·bas·sa·dor (am·bas′ə·dər, -dôr) *n.* **1.** An accredited diplomatic agent of the highest rank, appointed as the representative of one government to another. **2.** Any personal representative or messenger. — **ambassador-at-large** An ambassador accredited to no specific government. [< F, ult. < LL *ambactus* servant, goer about, prob. < Celtic] — **am·bas·sa·do·ri·al** (am·bas′ə·dôr′ē·əl, -dō′rē-) *adj.* — **am·bas′a·dress** (-dris) *n.fem.* — **am·bas′sa·dor·ship** *n.*
— **Syn.** **1.** A diplomatic representative of highest rank is an *ambassador*; one of lower rank is a *minister*. A minister sent on a special mission is called an *envoy*. A *nuncio* is a papal *ambassador*; a papal *envoy* is a *legate*.

am·ber (am′bər) *n.* **1.** A yellow or brownish-yellow fossilized vegetable resin, hard, brittle, and translucent, used in jewelry, etc. **2.** The color of amber. — *adj.* Pertaining to or like amber. [< OF < Arabic *anbar* ambergris]

am·ber·gris (am′bər·grēs, -gris) *n.* An opaque, grayish secretion of the sperm whale, sometimes found floating in the ocean, used in perfumery. [< F *ambre gris* gray amber]

ambi- *combining form* Both: *ambidextrous.* [< L *ambo* both]

am·bi·dex·trous (am′bə·dek′strəs) *adj.* **1.** Able to use both hands equally well. **2.** Very dexterous or skillful. **3.** Dissembling; double-dealing. — **am′bi·dex′trous·ly** *adv.* — **am′bi·dex·ter′i·ty** (-dek·ster′ə·tē), **am′bi·dex′trous·ness** *n.*

am·bi·ent (am′bē·ənt) *adj.* **1.** Surrounding; encircling; encompassing. **2.** Circulating. [< L < *ambi-* around + *ire* to go] — **am′bi·ence** *n.*

am·bi·gu·i·ty (am′bə·gyōō′ə·tē) *n.* *pl.* **·ties 1.** The quality of being ambiguous; doubtfulness. **2.** An expression, statement, situation, etc., that can be variously interpreted.

am·big·u·ous (am·big′yōō·əs) *adj.* **1.** Capable of being understood in more senses than one; having a double meaning. **2.** Doubtful or uncertain. [< L < *ambi-* around + *agere* to go] — **am·big′u·ous·ly** *adv.* — **am·big′u·ous·ness** *n.*

am·bi·tion (am·bish′ən) *n.* **1.** Eager desire to succeed, to achieve power, wealth, fame, etc. **2.** The object of aspiration or desire. — *v.t.* To desire and seek eagerly. [< L *ambitio, -onis* a going about (to solicit votes) < *ambi-* around + *ire* to go] — **am·bi′tion·less** *adj.*

am·bi·tious (am·bish′əs) *adj.* **1.** Actuated or characterized by ambition. **2.** Greatly desiring; eager for: with *of* or the infinitive. **3.** Challenging; difficult: an *ambitious* project. — **am·bi′tious·ly** *adv.* — **am·bi′tious·ness** *n.*

am·biv·a·lent (am·biv′ə·lənt) *adj.* **1.** Uncertain or changeful, esp. because affected by contradictory emotions. **2.** *Psychol.* Experiencing contradictory emotions, as love and hate, toward the same object. [< AMBI- + L *valens, -entis*, ppr. of *valere* to be strong, be worth] — **am·biv′a·lence** *n.*

am·ble (am′bəl) *v.i.* **·bled** (-bəld), **·bling 1.** To move, as a horse, by lifting the two feet on one side together, alternately with the two feet on the other. **2.** To walk or proceed leisurely. — *n.* **1.** The gait of a horse when ambling. **2.** Any movement resembling this. [< OF < L *ambulare* to walk] — **am′bler** *n.* — **am′bling·ly** *adv.*

am·bro·sia (am·brō′zhə, -zhē·ə) *n.* **1.** In classical mythology, the food of the gods, giving immortality. **2.** Any very delicious food or drink. [< L < Gk. < *a-* not + *brotos* mortal]

am·bro·sial (am·brō′zhəl, -zhē·əl) *adj.* **1.** Of or like ambrosia; fragrant; delicious. **2.** Worthy of the gods; heavenly. Also **am·bro·sian** (am·brō′zhən, -zhē·ən) — **am·bro′sial·ly** *adv.*

am·bu·lance (am′byə·ləns) *n.* **1.** A special vehicle equipped for conveying the sick and wounded. **2.** A moving or field hospital. [< F < L *ambulare* to walk]

am·bu·lant (am′byə·lənt) *adj.* Walking or moving about.

am·bu·late (am′byə·lāt) *v.i.* **·lat·ed, ·lat·ing** To walk about; move from place to place. [< L *ambulare* to walk] — **am′bu·la′tion** *n.*

am·bu·la·to·ry (am′byə·lə·tôr′ē, -tō′rē) *adj.* **1.** Of or for walking. **2.** Able to walk, as an invalid. **3.** Shifting; not fixed or stationary. **4.** *Law* Alterable; changeable. — *n.pl.* **·ries** A sheltered place for walking, as a cloister.

am·bus·cade (am′bəs·kād′) *n.* An ambush. — *v.t.* **·cad·ed, ·cad·ing** To ambush. [See AMBUSH.] — **am′bus·cad′er** *n.*

am·bush (am′bŏŏsh) *n.* **1.** A lying in wait to attack unawares; also, the attackers. **2.** Any unseen peril or snare. **3.** A secret position for surprise attack. Also **am′bush·ment.** — *v.t.* To attack from a hidden place; waylay. [< OF < Ital. < L *in-* in + *boscus* a wood] — **am′bush·er** *n.*

a·me·ba (ə·mē′bə) *n.* *pl.* **·bas** or **·bae** (-bē) A unicellular protozoan found in stagnant water or as a parasite, of indefinite shape, and reproducing by simple division: also spelled *amoeba.* [< NL < Gk. *amoibē* change] — **a·me·bic** (ə·mē′bik) *adj.*

a·me·boid (ə·mē′boid) *adj.* Resembling an ameba, as in its change of form: also spelled *amoeboid.*

a·meer (ə·mir′) See AMIR.

a·mel·io·rate (ə·mēl′yə·rāt) *v.t. & v.i.* **·rat·ed, ·rat·ing** To make or become better; meliorate; improve. [< F < L *ad-* to + *meliorare* to better] — **a·mel′io·ra·ble** (ə·mēl′yər·ə·bəl) *adj.* — **a·mel′io·rant** (-rənt) *n.* — **a·mel′io·ra′tion** *n.* — **a·mel′io·ra·tive** (ə·mēl′yə·rā′tiv, -rə·tiv) *adj.* — **a·mel′io·ra′tor** *n.*

a·men (ā′men′, ä′-) *interj.* So it is; so be it: used at the end of a prayer or statement to express agreement. — *n.* The word *amen* or any use of it. — *adv.* Verily; truly. [< L < Gk. < Hebrew *āmēn* verily]

a·me·na·ble (ə·mē′nə·bəl, ə·men′ə-) *adj.* **1.** Capable of being persuaded; submissive. **2.** Liable to be called to account; responsible to authority. **3.** Capable of being tested or judged by rule or law. [< AF < *a-* to + *mener* to lead < L *minare* to drive (with threats)] — **a·me′na·bil′i·ty, a·me′na·ble·ness** *n.* — **a·me′na·bly** *adv.*

a·mend (ə·mend′) *v.t.* **1.** To change for the better; improve; correct. **2.** To change or alter by authority. — *v.i.* **3.** To become better in conduct. [< OF < L *emendare* to free from faults] — **a·mend′a·ble** *adj.* — **a·mend′a·ble·ness** *n.* — **a·mend′er** *n.*

a·mend·a·to·ry (ə·men′də·tôr′ē, -tō′rē) *adj.* Tending to amend; corrective.

a·mend·ment (ə·mend′mənt) *n.* **1.** Change for the better. **2.** A removal of faults; correction. **3.** The changing, as of a law, bill, or motion. **4.** The statement of such a change.

a·mends (ə·mendz′) *n.pl.* Reparation, as in satisfaction or compensation for loss, etc. [< OF < L *mendum* fault]

AMBROSIA
(def. 4)
Common ragweed
(3 to 6 feet high)

a·men·i·ty (ə-men′ə-tē) *n. pl.* **·ties** **1.** Agreeableness; pleasantness. **2.** *Usu. pl.* An act or expression of courtesy; civility. [< L *amoenitas, -tatis* < *amoenus* pleasant]

a·merce (ə-mûrs′) *v.t.* **a·merced, a·merc·ing** **1.** To punish by an assessment or arbitrary fine. **2.** To punish, as by deprivation. [< AF < *a merci* at the mercy of] — **a·merce′·a·ble** *adj.* — **a·merce′ment** *n.* — **a·merc′er** *n.*

A·mer·i·can (ə-mer′ə-kən) *adj.* **1.** Pertaining to the United States of America, its history, government, people, etc. **2.** Pertaining to the continent or people of North or South America, or of the Western Hemisphere. — *n.* **1.** A citizen of the United States. **2.** An inhabitant of America.

A·mer·i·ca·na (ə-mer′ə-kä′nə, -kan′ə, -kā′nə) *n.pl.* Any collection of American literary papers, sayings, etc., that relate to America.

American eagle The bald eagle. See under EAGLE.

American English The English language as used or spoken in the United States.

American Expeditionary Forces United States troops sent to Europe in World War I.

American Federation of Labor A federation of trade unions, founded in 1886, in 1955 merged with the Congress of Industrial Organizations. *Abbr. AFL, A.F.L., A.F. of L.*

A·mer·i·can·ism (ə-mer′ə-kən·iz′əm) *n.* **1.** A trait, custom, or tradition especially characteristic of the people of the United States or of some of them. **2.** A word, phrase, or usage especially characteristic of American English. **3.** Devotion to the United States, its institutions, etc.

A·mer·i·can·ize (ə-mer′ə-kən·īz′) *v.t. & v.i.* **·ized, ·iz·ing** To make or become American in spirit, methods, speech, etc. — **A·mer′i·can·i·za′tion** *n.*

American League See under MAJOR LEAGUE.

American Revolution See under REVOLUTION.

American Standard Version or **American Revised Version** See under KING JAMES BIBLE.

am·er·i·ci·um (am′ə·rish′ē·əm) *n.* An unstable radioactive element (symbol Am), resulting from the bombardment of uranium and plutonium by high-energy helium ions. See ELEMENT. [< NL, after *America*]

Am·er·in·di·an (am′ə·rin′dē·ən) *adj.* Of or pertaining to the American Indians or the Eskimos. Also **Am′er·in′dic.** — *n.* An American Indian or Eskimo. Also **Am·er·ind** (am′ə·rind).

am·e·thyst (am′ə·thist) *n.* **1.** Quartz with clear purple or violet color, a semiprecious stone. **2.** A purple variety of sapphire or corundum used as a. gem: also called *Oriental amethyst.* **3.** A purplish violet. [< OF < L < Gk. < *a-* not + *methystos* drunken < *methy* wine; from the ancient belief that a wearer of the stone would be unaffected by wine]

am·e·thys·tine (am′ə·this′tin, -tīn) *adj.* Violet; purple.

a·mi (à·mē′) *n.masc. pl.* **a·mis** (à·mē′) *French* A friend. — **a·mie** (à·mē′) *n.fem.*

a·mi·a·ble (ā′mē·ə·bəl) *adj.* **1.** Pleasing in disposition; kindly. **2.** Free from irritation; friendly: an *amiable* rivalry. [< OF < L *amicabilis* friendly < *amicus* friend] — **a′mi·a·bil′i·ty, a′mi·a·ble·ness** *n.* — **a′mi·a·bly** *adv.*

am·i·ca·ble (am′i·kə·bəl) *adj.* Friendly; peaceable. [< L *amicabilis* friendly] — **am·i·ca·bil·i·ty** (am′i·kə·bil′ə·tē), **am′i·ca·ble·ness** *n.* — **am′i·ca·bly** *adv.*

a·mi·cus cu·ri·ae (ə·mē′kəs kyŏor′ē·ī) *Law* One who advises or is asked to advise a court upon a pending cause to which he is not a party. [< L, friend of the court]

a·mid (ə·mid′) *prep.* In the midst of; among. Also *amidst, midst.* [ME < OE *on middan* in the middle]

am·ide (am′īd, -id) *n. Chem.* **1.** Any compound of the type formula RCONH₂. **2.** A derivative of ammonia in which a metal replaces a hydrogen atom. Also **am·id** (am′id). — **a·mid·ic** (ə·mid′ik) *adj.*

amido- *combining form Chem.* **1.** Pertaining to or containing both the NH₂ radical and an acid radical. **2.** Less frequently, amino-. [< AMIDE]

am·i·dol (am′ə·dol, -dōl) *n.* A white crystalline powder, $C_6H_8N_2O·2HCl$, used in photography as a developer.

a·mid·ships (ə·mid′ships′) *adv. Naut.* Halfway between bow and stern; toward the middle of a ship: also *midships.*

a·midst (ə·midst′) *prep.* Amid. [ME *amidde* + -s³ + *t*]

a·mi·go (ə·mē′gō) *n. pl.* **·gos** A friend; comrade. [< Sp.]

a·mine (ə·mēn′, am′in) *n. Chem.* One of a class of organic compounds derived from ammonia by replacement of one or more of its hydrogen atoms by an alkyl radical. Also **am′in.**

a·mi·no (ə·mē′nō, am′ə·nō) *adj. Chem.* Of or pertaining to the NH₂ group combined with a nonacid radical. [< AMINE]

amino acid *Biochem.* Any of a group of organic compounds containing the amino group combined with the carboxyl radical and forming an essential part of the protein molecule.

a·mir (ə·mir′) *n.* **1.** A sovereign of Afghanistan. **2.** A Moslem prince or governor. Also spelled *ameer.* [< Arabic *amīr*]

Am·ish (am′ish, ä′mish) *adj.* Relating to or designating the adherents of Jacob Ammann, a 17th-century Mennonite. — *n.pl.* A sect of Mennonites, founded by Jacob Ammann.

a·miss (ə·mis′) *adj.* Out of order or relation; wrong; improper: used predicatively: Something is *amiss.* — *adv.* In a wrong or defective way; erroneously. — **to take amiss** To take offense at. [ME < *a-* at + *mis* failure]

am·i·to·sis (am′ə·tō′sis) *n. Biol.* Cell division without the formation and splitting of chromosomes; direct division. [< NL < A-⁴ without + MITOSIS] — **am·i·tot·ic** (am′ə·tot′ik) *adj.* — **am′i·tot′i·cal·ly** *adv.*

am·i·ty (am′ə·tē) *n. pl.* **·ties** Peaceful relations, as between nations; friendship. [< MF < L *amicus* friend]

am·me·ter (am′mē′tər) *n. Electr.* An instrument for measuring amperage.

am·mo·nia (ə·mōn′yə, ə·mō′nē·ə) *n.* **1.** A colorless, pungent, suffocating gas, NH₃, obtained chiefly by the synthesis of nitrogen and hydrogen. **2.** Spirits of hartshorn. [< NL < SAL AMMONIAC] — **am·mo′ni·ac** *adj.*

am·mo·ni·ac (ə·mō′nē·ak) *n.* The resinous gum of a tree found in Persia and western India, used in medicine: also *gum ammoniac.* [< F < L < Gk. *ammōniakon,* a resinous gum]

am·mo·ni·ate (*v.* ə·mō′nē·āt; *n.* ə·mō′nē·it) *v.t.* **·at·ed, ·at·ing** To treat or combine with ammonia.

am·mon·ite (am′ən·īt) *n. Paleontol.* A curved or spiral fossil cephalopod shell, commonly found in Mesozoic rocks. [< NL *ammonites* < L (*cornu*) *Ammonis* (horn) of Ammon]

am·mo·ni·um (ə·mō′nē·əm) *n. Chem.* The univalent radical NH₄, that in compounds formed from ammonia acts as an alkali metal.

ammonium hydroxide *Chem.* A compound, NH₄OH, formed in ordinary aqueous or caustic ammonia.

am·mu·ni·tion (am′yə·nish′ən) *n.* **1.** Any one of various articles used in the discharge of firearms and ordnance, as cartridges, shells, rockets, etc. **2.** Any resources for attack or defense. [< F < L *munire* to fortify]

am·ne·sia (am·nē′zhə, -zhē·ə) *n. Psychiatry* Partial or total loss or impairment of memory. [< NL < Gk. < *a-* not + *mnasthai* to remember] — **am·ne·sic** (am·nē′sik, -zik), **am·nes·tic** (am·nes′tik) *adj.*

am·nes·ty (am′nəs·tē) *n. pl.* **·ties** **1.** A general pardon by which a government absolves offenders. **2.** Intentional overlooking, esp. of wrongdoing; forgetfulness. — *v.t.* **tied, ·ty·ing** To pardon; grant amnesty to. [< F < L < Gk. < *a-* not + *mnasthai* to remember]

am·ni·on (am′nē·ən) *n. pl.* **·ni·ons** or **·ni·a** (-nē·ə) *Biol.* A membranous sac enclosing the embryo and fetus in mammals, birds, and reptiles. [< Gk. *amnion* the fetal envelope] — **am·ni·ot·ic** (am′nē·ot′ik), **am·ni·on·ic** (am′nē·on′ik) *adj.*

a·moe·ba (ə·mē′bə), **a·moe·bic** (ə·mē′bik), **a·moe·boid** (ə·mē′boid), etc. See AMEBA, etc.

am·oe·bae·an, am·oe·be·an (am′ə·bē′ən) See AMEBEAN.

amok (ə·muk′, ə·mok′) See AMUCK.

a·mong (ə·mung′) *prep.* **1.** In the midst of. **2.** In the class or number of: He was *among* the dead. **3.** Within or by the group of: a practice *among* the French. **4.** By the joint or concerted action of: *Among* us, we can build the wall. **5.** In portions for each of: to distribute money *among* the poor. **6.** Reciprocally between: disputes *among* friends. Also **a·mongst′.** ◆ See note under BETWEEN. [OE *on gemonge* in the crowd]

a·mon·til·la·do (ə·mon′tə·lä′dō, *Sp.* ä·mōn′tē·lyä′thō) *n.* A pale dry sherry. [< Sp., after *Montilla,* a town in Spain]

a·mor·al (ā·môr′əl, ə·môr′əl) *adj.* **1.** Not subject to or concerned with moral or ethical distinctions. **2.** Lacking a sense of right and wrong. — **Syn.** See IMMORAL. — **a·mo·ral·i·ty** (ā′mə·ral′ə·tē) *n.* — **a·mor′al·ly** *adv.*

am·o·rous (am′ər·əs) *adj.* **1.** Tending to fall in love; affectionate; loving. **2.** Of or related to love. **3.** Showing or arising from love or sexual desire; ardent. **4.** In love; enamored: often with *of: amorous* of the truth. [< OF < LL < L *amor* love] — **am′o·rous·ly** *adv.* — **am′o·rous·ness** *n.*
— **Syn. 1, 2.** *Amorous* is applied to persons and emotions; *amatory* refers to literature and other things that deal with love.

a·mor·phous (ə·môr′fəs) *adj.* **1.** Without definite form or shape. **2.** Of no fixed character; anomalous; unorganized. **3.** *Chem.* Uncrystallized. [< Gk. < *a-* without + *morphē* form] — **a·mor′phism** *n.* — **a·mor′phous·ly** *adv.* — **a·mor′phous·ness** *n.*

am·or·tize (am′ər·tīz, ə·môr′tīz) *v.t.* **tized, ·tiz·ing** To extinguish gradually, as a debt or liability, by installment payments or by a sinking fund. Also *Brit.* **am′or·tise.** [< OF < *amortir* to extinguish < L *ad-* to + *mors, mortis* death] — **am·or·tiz·a·ble** (am′ər·tīz′ə·bəl, ə·môr′tīz·ə·bəl) *adj.* — **am′or·ti·za′tion, a·mor·tize·ment** (ə·môr′tiz·mənt) *n.*

A·mos (ā′məs) Eighth-century B.C. Hebrew minor prophet. — *n.* A book of the Old Testament containing his prophecies.

a·mount (ə·mount′) *n.* **1.** A sum total of two or more quantities. **2.** The value of the principal with the interest upon it, as in a loan. **3.** The entire significance, value, or effect. **4.** Quantity: a considerable *amount* of discussion. — *v.i.* **1.** To reach in number or quantity: with *to*: to *amount* to ten dollars. **2.** To be equivalent in effect or importance: with *to*: It *amounts* to treason. [< OF < L *ad* to + *mons, montis* mountain]

a·mour (ə·mŏŏr′) *n.* A love affair, esp. an illicit one. [< F]

a·mour-pro·pre (a·mŏŏr′prôpr′) *n. French* Self-respect.

am·per·age (am·pir′ij, am′pər·ij) *n. Electr.* The strength of a current in amperes.

am·pere (am′pir, am·pir′) *n. Electr.* The practical unit of current strength; such a current as would be given by one volt through a wire having a resistance of one ohm. [after A. M. *Ampère*, 1775-1836, French physicist]

am·per·sand (am′pər·sand, am′pər·sand′) *n.* The character & or *&* or *&* meaning *and*. [< *and per se and*, lit., & by itself = and]

am·phet·a·mine (am·fet′ə·mēn, -min) *n.* An acrid liquid compound, $C_9H_{13}N$, used as a nasal spray. [< *a(lpha)-m(ethyl)-ph(enyl)-et(hyl)-amine*]

amphi- *prefix* **1.** On both or all sides; at both ends. **2.** Around: *amphitheater.* **3.** Of both kinds; in two ways. [< Gk. < *amphi* around]

am·phib·i·an (am·fib′ē·ən) *adj.* **1.** *Zool.* Of or pertaining to a class of cold-blooded, chiefly egg-laying vertebrates adapted for life both on land and in water, as frogs, newts, salamanders, etc. **2.** Amphibious. — *n.* **1.** An amphibian animal or plant. **2.** An airplane constructed to rise from and alight on either land or water. **3.** A vehicle capable of self-propulsion upon land and upon water.

am·phib·i·ous (am·fib′ē·əs) *adj.* **1.** Living or adapted to life on land or in water. **2.** Capable of operating or landing on land or water. **3.** Of a mixed nature. [< Gk. < *amphi-* of two kinds + *bios* life] — **am·phib′i·ous·ly** *adv.* — **am·phib′i·ous·ness** *n.*

am·phi·bole (am′fə·bōl) *n. Mineral.* Any of a class of variously colored hydrous silicates, consisting chiefly of calcium, magnesium, iron, aluminum, and sodium, as asbestos. [< F < L < Gk. < *amphi-* around + *ballein* to throw]

am·phi·bol·ic (am′fə·bol′ik) *adj.* Ambiguous; equivocal.

am·phi·ox·us (am′fē·ok′səs) *n. Zool.* The most primitive of the chordates, a lancelet. [< AMPHI- + Gk. *oxys* sharp]

am·phi·the·a·ter (am′fə·thē′ə·tər) *n.* **1.** An oval structure having tiers of seats built around an open space or arena. **2.** A level area surrounded by slopes. **3.** A place of contest. Also *Brit.* **am′phi·the′a·tre.** [< L < Gk. < *amphi-* around + *theatron* theater]

am·pho·ra (am′fə·rə) *n. pl.* **·rae** (-rē) In ancient Greece and Rome, a tall, two-handled earthenware jar for wine or oil, narrow at the neck and the base. [< L < Gk. < *amphi-* on both sides + *phoreus* bearer] — **am′pho·ral** *adj.*

am·pho·ter·ic (am′fə·ter′ik) *adj. Chem.* Exhibiting the characteristics of both an acid and a base. [< Gk. *amphoteros* both]

am·ple (am′pəl) *adj.* **1.** Of great dimension, capacity, amount, degree, etc.; large. **2.** More than enough; abundant. **3.** Fully sufficient; adequate. — **Syn.** See PLENTIFUL. [< F < L *amplus* large, abundant] — **am′ple·ness** *n.* — **am·ply** (am′plē) *adv.*

AMPHORAE

am·pli·fi·ca·tion (am′plə·fi·kā′shən) *n.* **1.** The act of extending or enlarging; also, that which is added. **2.** An extended statement, phrase, etc.

am·pli·fi·er (am′plə·fī′ər) *n.* **1.** One who or that which amplifies or increases. **2.** *Electronics* Any of a class of devices for reinforcing a signal by means of power supplied to the output from a source other than the input.

am·pli·fy (am′plə·fī) *v.* **·fied, ·fy·ing** *v.t.* **1.** To enlarge or increase in scope, significance, or power. **2.** To add to so as to make more complete, as by illustrations. **3.** To exaggerate; magnify. **4.** *Electronics* To increase the strength or amplitude of, as electromagnetic impulses. — *v.i.* **5.** To make additional remarks. [< F < L *amplus* large + *facere* to make] — **am·pli·fi·ca·tive** (am′plə·fi·kā′tiv, am·plif′i·kə·tiv), **am·plif′i·ca·to·ry** (am·plif′i·kə·tôr′ē, -tō′rē) *adj.*

am·pli·tude (am′plə·tōōd, -tyōōd) *n.* **1.** Greatness of extent; largeness; breadth. **2.** Fullness; abundance. **3.** Scope or range, as of mind. **4.** *Physics* **a** The extent of the swing of a vibrating body on each side of the mean position. **b** The peak value attained by a wave or an alternating current during one complete cycle. [< L *amplus* large]

amplitude modulation *Telecom.* That form of radio transmission in which the carrier wave is modulated by varying the amplitude above and below a standard value in accordance with the signals to be transmitted. Compare FREQUENCY MODULATION. Abbr. *AM, A-m, a.m., A.M.*

am·pule (am′pyōōl) *n. Med.* A sealed glass vial used as a container for one dose of a hypodermic solution. Also **am·poule** (am′pōōl), **am·pul** (am′pul, am′pōōl). [< F < L *ampulla* ampula (def. 1)]

am·pul·la (am·pul′ə) *n. pl.* **·pul·lae** (-pul′ē) **1.** An ancient Roman bottle or vase with slender neck and flattened mouth, used for oil, wine, or perfume. **2.** *Eccl.* **a** A cruet for wine or water at the Eucharist. [< L, dim. of *amphora* jar]

am·pu·tate (am′pyōō·tāt) *v.t. & v.i.* **·tat·ed, ·tat·ing** To cut off (a limb, etc.) by surgical means. [< L < *ambi-* around + *putare* to trim] — **am′pu·ta′tion** *n.* — **am′pu·ta′tor** *n.*

am·pu·tee (am′pyōō·tē′) *n.* One who has had a limb or limbs removed by amputation.

a·muck (ə·muk′) *adv.* In a murderous or frenzied manner: only in the phrase **to run amuck.** Also **amok.** [< Malay *amoq* engaging furiously in battle]

am·u·let (am′yə·lit) *n.* Anything worn about the person as protection against accident, evil, etc.; a charm. [< L *amuletum* charm; ult. origin unknown]

a·muse (ə·myōōz′) *v.t.* **a·mused, a·mus·ing 1.** To occupy pleasingly. **2.** To cause to laugh or smile. [< MF < *à* at + OF *muser* to stare] — **a·mus′a·ble** *adj.* — **a·mus′er** *n.*

a·muse·ment (ə·myōōz′mənt) *n.* **1.** The state of being amused. **2.** That which diverts or entertains.

amusement park A park having various devices for entertainment, as roller coasters, shooting galleries, etc.

a·mus·ing (ə·myōō′zing) *adj.* **1.** Entertaining, or diverting. **2.** Arousing laughter or mirth. — **a·mus′ing·ly** *adv.*

a·myg·da·la (ə·mig′də·lə) *n. pl.* **·lae** (-lē) **1.** *Anat.* Any almond-shaped structure or part; esp., a tonsil. **2.** An almond. [< L < Gk. *amygdalē* almond] — **a·myg′de·late** (-lit, -lāt), **a·myg′da·line** (-lin, -līn) *adj.*

am·yl (am′il) *n. Chem.* The univalent alcohol radical, C_5H_{11}, derived from pentane. [< Gk. *amylon* starch + -YL] — **a·myl·ic** (ə·mil′ik) *adj.*

am·y·la·ceous (am′ə·lā′shəs) *adj.* Of or like starch.

am·y·lase (am′ə·lās) *n. Biochem.* An enzyme, found in plant and animal tissue, that promotes the conversion of starch and glycogen into maltose.

am·y·loid (am′ə·loid) *n.* **1.** A gummy or starchlike substance formed in certain diseased plant and animal tissues. — *adj.* Like or containing starch: also **am′y·loi′dal.**

am·y·lum (am′ə·ləm) *n.* Starch (def. 1) [< L < Gk.]

Am·y·tal (am′ə·tal, -tôl) *n.* Proprietary name for a colorless, crystalline compound, $C_{11}H_{18}N_2O_3$, used as a sedative.

an *(an, unstressed* ən) *indefinite article or adj.* Equivalent to the article *a*, but used before words beginning with a vowel, as *an* eagle and sometimes before words beginning with *h* in an unstressed syllable, as *an* hotel. [OE *ān* one]

an-[1] *prefix* Without; not: *anarchy.* Also, before consonants (except *h*) *a-.* [< Gk.]

an-[2] Var. of ANA-.

an-[3] Assimilated var. of AD-.

-an *suffix* Used to form adjectives and nouns denoting connection with a country, person, group, doctrine, etc., as follows: **1.** Pertaining to; belonging to: *human, sylvan.* **2.** Originating in; living in: *Italian.* **3.** Adhering to; following: *Lutheran.* **4.** *Zool.* Belonging to a class or order: *amphibian.* See -IAN. [< L -*anus*]

ana- *prefix* **1.** Up; upward: *anadromous.* **2.** Back; backward: *anapest.* **3.** Anew: sometimes capable of being rendered *re-*, as *anabaptism, rebaptism.* **4.** Thoroughly: *analysis.* Also, before vowels an, *an-.* [< Gk. < *ana* up, back]

-ana *suffix* Pertaining to: added to the names of notable persons, places, etc., to indicate a collection of materials, such as writings or anecdotes, about the subject: *Americana.* Also -*iana.* [< L, neut. pl. of -*anus.* See -AN.]

An·a·bap·tist (an′ə·bap′tist) *n.* One of a sect that arose in Switzerland about 1520, who rejected infant baptism and limited church membership to adults baptized after a confession of faith. [< NL < LL < Gk. < *ana-* new + *baptizein* to baptize] — **An′a·bap′tism** *n.*

an·a·bi·o·sis (an′ə·bī·ō′sis) *n.* A return to life; resuscitation. [< NL < ANA- + Gk. *bios* life] — **an·a·bi·ot·ic** (an′ə·bī·ot′ic) *adj.*

a·nab·o·lism (ə·nab′ə·liz′əm) *n. Biol.* The process by which food is built up into protoplasm: opposed to *catabolism.* [< Gk. *anabolē* a heaping up] — **an·a·bol·ic** (an′ə·bol′ik) *adj.*

a·nach·ro·nism (ə·nak′rə·niz′əm) *n.* **1.** The assigning of an event, person, etc., to a wrong, esp. an earlier, date. **2.** Something out of its proper time. [< F < L < Gk. < *ana-* against + *chronos* time] — **a·nach′ro·nis′tic, a·nach′ro·nis′ti·cal, a·nach′ro·nous** *adj.*

an·a·con·da (an′ə·kon′də) *n.* **1.** A very large, nonvenomous tropical serpent that crushes its prey in its coils. **2.** Any boa constrictor. [? < Singhalese]

a·nad·ro·mous (ə·nad′rə·məs) *adj. Zool.* Of fishes, as the salmon, going from the sea up rivers to spawn. [< Gk. < *ana-* up + *dromos* a running, course]

a·nae·mi·a (ə·nē′mē·ə), **a·nae·mic** (ə·nē′mik), etc. See ANEMIA, etc.

an·aer·obe (an·âr′ōb, an·ā′ə·rōb) *n.* An anaerobic organism. [See ANAEROBIC]

an·aer·o·bic (an′âr·ō′bik, -ob′ik) *adj.* Living or functioning in the absence of free oxygen. [< NL < AN-¹ without + AERO- + Gk. *bios* life] —an'aer·o'bi·cal·ly *adv.*

an·aes·the·sia (an'is·thē'zhə, -zhē·ə), **an·aes·thet·ic** (an'·is·thet'ik), etc. See ANESTHESIA, etc.

an·a·gram (an'ə·gram) *n.* 1. A word or phrase formed by transposing the letters of another word or phrase. 2. *pl.* (construed as *sing.*) A game in which the players make words by transposing or adding letters. [< MF < LGk < Gk. < *ana-* backwards + *gramma* letter] —**an·a·gram·mat·ic** (an'·ə·grə·mat'ik) or **·i·cal** *adj.* —**an'a·gram·mat'i·cal·ly** *adv.*

an·a·gram·ma·tize (an'ə·gram'ə·tīz) *v.t.* **·tized, ·tiz·ing** To arrange as an anagram.

a·nal (ā'nəl) *adj. Anat.* Of, pertaining to, or situated in the region of the anus. [< L *anus* + -AL¹]

an·a·lects (an'ə·lekts) *n.pl.* Selections or fragments from a literary work or group of works. Also **an·a·lec·ta** (an'ə·lek'tə) [< L < Gk. < *ana-* up + *legein* to gather]

an·al·ge·si·a (an'əl·jē'zē·ə, -sē·ə) *n. Pathol.* Inability to feel pain. Also **an·al·gi·a** (an·al'jē·ə). [< NL < Gk. < *an-* without + *algos* pain]

an·al·ge·sic (an'əl·jē'zik, -sik) *Med. n.* A drug for the alleviation of pain. —*adj.* Promoting analgesia.

analog computer A computer that solves problems by substituting analogous quantities, as voltage, etc., for the variables of the problems. Compare DIGITAL COMPUTER.

a·nal·o·gous (ə·nal'ə·gəs) *adj.* 1. Resembling or comparable in certain respects. 2. *Biol.* Having a similar function but differing in origin and structure, as the wings of birds and insects: distinguished from *homologous.* —**a·nal'o·gous·ly** *adv.* —**a·nal'o·gous·ness** *n.*

an·a·logue (an'ə·lôg, -log) *n.* Anything analogous to something else. Also **an'a·log.**

a·nal·o·gy (ə·nal'ə·jē) *n. pl.* **·gies** 1. Agreement or resemblance in certain aspects. 2. *Biol.* A similarity in function and appearance, but not in origin. 4. *Logic* Reasoning in which relations or resemblances are inferred from others that are known or observed. Abbr. *anal.* [< L < Gk. < *ana-* according to + *logos* proportion]
— **Syn.** 1, 2. In careful usage, an *analogy* is drawn only between things clearly unlike in kind, form, or appearance, and refers to their similar properties, relations, behavior, etc. A *resemblance* is almost always a likeness in appearance, while *similarity* is usually a likeness in some external or superficial aspect or characteristic.

a·nal·y·sis (ə·nal'ə·sis) *n. pl.* **·ses** (-sēz) 1. The separation of a whole into its parts or elements: opposed to *synthesis.* 2. A statement of the results of this; logical synopsis. 3. A method of determining or describing the nature of a thing by separating it into its parts. 4. *Chem.* The determination of the kind, quantity, and proportions of constituents forming a compound or substance. 5. Psychoanalysis. [< Med.L. < Gk. < *ana-* throughout + *lyein* to loosen]

an·a·lyst (an'ə·list) *n.* 1. One who analyzes or is skilled in analysis. 2. A psychoanalyst.

an·a·lyt·ic (an'ə·lit'ik) *adj.* 1. Pertaining to or proceeding by analysis. 2. Separating into constituent parts or first principles. Also **an'a·lyt'i·cal.** —**an'a·lyt'i·cal·ly** *adv.*

an·a·lyt·ics (an'ə·lit'iks) *n.pl.* (construed as *sing.*) 1. The science or use of analysis. 2. The part of logic concerned with analysis.

an·a·lyze (an'ə·līz) *v.t.* **·lyzed, ·lyz·ing** 1. To separate into constituent parts or elements, especially so as to determine the nature, form, etc., of the whole by examination of the parts. 2. To examine critically or minutely. 3. To psychoanalyze. Also, *Brit.*, *analyse.* See ANALYSIS. —**an'a·lyz'a·ble** *adj.* —**an'a·ly·za'tion** *n.* —**an'a·lyz'er** *n.*

an·a·pest (an'ə·pest) *n.* 1. In prosody, a metrical foot consisting of two short or unaccented syllables followed by one long or accented syllable (˘˘ˊ). 2. A line of verse made up of such feet: Then the rāin | ǎnd thě trēe | wēre ǎlōne. Also **an'a·paest.** [< L < Gk. < *ana-* back + *paiein* to strike, so called because it is a reversed dactyl] —**an'a·pes'tic** *adj.*

an·ar·chic (an·är'kik) *adj.* 1. Pertaining to or like anarchy. 2. Advocating anarchy. 3. Inducing anarchy; lawless. Also **an·ar'chi·cal.** —**an·ar'chi·cal·ly** *adv.*

an·ar·chism (an'ər·kiz'əm) *n.* 1. The theory that all forms of government are incompatible with individual and social liberty and should be abolished. 2. The methods of anarchists. —**an·ar·chis·tic** (an'ər·kis'tik) *adj.*

an·ar·chist (an'ər·kist) *n.* 1. One who believes in and advocates anarchism. 2. One who encourages or furthers anarchy. Also **an·arch** (an'ärk).

an·ar·chy (an'ər·kē) *n.* 1. Absence of government. 2. Lawless confusion and political disorder. 3. General disorder. [< Gk. < *an-* without + *archos* leader]

an·as·tig·mat·ic (an·as'tig·mat'ik) *adj. Optics* Not astigmatic; esp., corrected for astigmatism, as a lens.

a·nas·to·mose (ə·nas'tə·mōz) *v.i.* **·mosed, ·mos·ing** To connect by anastomosis.

a·nas·to·mo·sis (ə·nas'tə·mō'sis) *n. pl.* **·ses** (-sēz) 1. *Physiol.* A union, interlacing, or running together, as of veins, nerves, or canals of animal bodies. 2. Any intercommunication, as of two or more rivers. [< NL < Gk. *anastomōsis* opening] —**a·nas'to·mot'ic** (-mot'ik) *adj.*

a·nath·e·ma (ə·nath'ə·mə) *n. pl.* **·mas** or **·ma·ta** (-mə·tə) 1. A formal ecclesiastical ban or curse, excommunicating a person or damning something, as a book or doctrine. 2. Any curse or imprecation. 3. One who or that which is excommunicated or damned. 4. One who or that which is greatly disliked. [< L < Gk. *anathema* a thing devoted to evil]

a·nath·e·ma·tize (ə·nath'ə·mə·tīz') *v.* **·tized, ·tiz·ing** *v.t.* 1. To pronounce an anathema against. —*v.i.* 2. To utter or express anathemas. —**a·nath'e·ma·ti·za'tion** *n.*

an·a·tom·i·cal (an'ə·tom'i·kəl) *adj.* Of or pertaining to anatomy. Also **an'a·tom'ic.** —**an'a·tom'i·cal·ly** *adv.*

a·nat·o·mist (ə·nat'ə·mist) *n.* One skilled in anatomy.

a·nat·o·mize (ə·nat'ə·mīz) *v.t.* **·mized, ·miz·ing** 1. To dissect (an animal or plant) for the purpose of investigating the structure, position, and interrelationships of its parts. 2. To examine minutely; analyze. **a·nat'o·mi·za'tion** *n.*

a·nat·o·my (ə·nat'ə·mē) *n. pl.* **·mies** 1. The structure of a plant or animal, or of any of its parts. 2. The science of the structure of plants or animals. 3. The art or practice of anatomizing. [< F < L < Gk. < *ana-* up + *temnein* to cut]

-ance *suffix of nouns* Used to form nouns of action, quality, state, or condition from adjectives in *-ant*, and also directly from verbs, as in *abundance, forbearance.* Compare -ANCY. [< F *-ance* < L *-antia, -entia*, a suffix used to form nouns]

an·ces·tor (an'ses·tər) *n.* 1. One from whom a person is descended; progenitor; forbear. 2. *Biol.* An organism from which later organisms have been derived. [< OF < L *ante-* before + *cedere* to go] —**an·ces·tress** (an'ses·tris) *n.fem.*

an·ces·tral (an·ses'trəl) *adj.* Of, pertaining to, or descending from an ancestor. Also **an·ces·to·ri·al** (an'ses·tôr'ē·əl, -tō'rē-). —**an·ces'tral·ly** *adv.*

an·ces·try (an'ses·trē) *n. pl.* **·tries** 1. A line or body of ancestors; ancestors collectively. 2. Ancestral lineage.

an·chor (ang'kər) *n.* 1. A heavy implement, usu. of iron or steel, with hooks or flukes to grip the bottom, attached to a cable and dropped from a ship or boat to hold it in place. 2. Any object used for a similar purpose. 3. Anything that makes stable or secure. —*at anchor* Anchored, as a ship. —*to drop* (or *cast*) *anchor* To put down the anchor in order to hold fast a vessel. —*to ride at anchor* To be anchored, as a ship. —*to weigh anchor* To take up the anchor so as to sail away. —*v.t.* 1. To secure or make secure by an anchor. 2. To fix firmly. —*v.i.* 3. To lie at anchor, as a ship. [OE < L < Gk. *ankyra*]

an·chor·age (ang'kər·ij) *n.* 1. A place for anchoring. 2. A coming to or lying at anchor. 3. A source or place of stability or security. 4. A fee charged for anchoring.

an·cho·rite (ang'kə·rīt) *n.* One who has withdrawn from the world for religious reasons; hermit. Also **an'cho·ret** (-rit, -ret). [< L < Gk. < *ana-* back + *chōreein* to withdraw] —**an'cho·rit'ic** (-rit'ik) *adj.*

an·cho·vy (an'chō·vē, -chə·vē, an·chō'vē) *n. pl.* **·vies** or **·vy** 1. A very small, herringlike fish inhabiting warm seas, valued as a delicacy. 2. *U.S.* Smelt. [< Sp., Pg. *anchova*]

an·chy·lose (ang'kə·lōs), **an·chy·lo·sis** (ang'kə·lō'sis) See ANKYLOSE, etc.

an·cien ré·gime (än·syän'rā·zhēm') *French* A former political and social system; esp., the system in France before the revolution of 1789. Also **Ancient Regime.**

an·cient (ān'shənt) *adj.* 1. Existing or occurring in times long past, esp. before the fall of the Western Roman Empire, in A.D. 476. 2. Having existed from remote antiquity; of great age. 3. Very old: said of persons. Abbr. *anc.* —*n.* 1. One who lived in ancient times. 2. An aged or venerable person. —*the ancients* 1. The ancient Greeks, Romans, Hebrews, or other civilized nations of antiquity. 2. The ancient authors of Greece and Rome. [< OF < LL < L *ante* before] —**an'cient·ness** *n.* —**an'cient·ly** *adv.*

an·cil·lar·y (an'sə·ler'ē) *adj.* Subordinate; auxiliary. [< L *ancilla* maid]

an·con (ang'kon) *n. pl.* **an·co·nes** (ang·kō'nēz) 1. *Anat.* The point of the elbow. 2. *Archit.* An elbow-shaped projection, as for an ornament on a keystone. Also **an·cone** (ang'kōn). [< L < Gk. *ankōn* a bend, the elbow] —**an·co·nal** (ang'kə·nəl), **an·co·ne·al** (ang·kō'nē·əl) *adj.*

-ancy *suffix of nouns* A modern variant of -ANCE: used to form new words expressing quality, state, or condition (*infancy, vacancy*), or to refashion older nouns of quality in *-ance* (*constancy*). [< L *-antia*]

an·cy·los·to·mi·a·sis (an'sə·lōs'tə·mī'ə·sis) *n.* A progressive anemia caused by nematode worms that suck the blood from the small intestine. Also called *hookworm disease.* [< NL < Gk. *ankylos* crooked + *stoma* mouth + -IASIS]

and (and, *unstressed* ənd, ən, 'n) *conj.* **1.** Also; added to; as well as: a particle denoting addition, emphasis, or union, used as a connective between words, phrases, clauses, and sentences: shoes *and* ships *and* sealing wax. **2.** As a result or consequence: Make one move *and* you are dead! **3.** To: with *come, go, try,* etc.: Try and stop me. [OE *ond, and*]

an·dan·te (an·dän′tē, än·dän′tā) *Music adj. & adv.* Moderately slow; slower than allegretto but faster than larghetto. — *n.* An andante movement or passage. [< Ital., walking]

an·dan·ti·no (an′dan·tē′nō, än′dän-) *Music adj. & adv.* Slightly quicker than andante; originally, slower than andante. — *n.* An andantino movement or passage. [< Ital., dim. of *andante*]

An·de·an (an·dē′ən, an′dē·ən) *adj.* Of the Andes.

and·i·ron (and′ī′ərn) *n.* One of two metal supports for holding wood in an open fireplace: also called *firedog.* [< OF *andier*; infl. by *iron*]

and/or Either *and* or *or,* according to the meaning intended.

andro- *combining form* **1.** Man in general. **2.** The male sex. **3.** *Bot.* Stamen; anther. [< Gk. *anēr, andros* man]

an·droe·ci·um (an·drē′shē·əm, -sē·əm) *n. pl.* **·ci·a** (-shē·ə, -sē·ə) *Bot.* The stamens of a flower collectively. [< NL < ANDRO- + Gk. *oikos* house] — **an·droe′cial** (-shəl) *adj.*

an·dro·gen (an′drə·jən) *n. Biochem.* Any of various hormones that control the development of masculine characteristics. — **an·dro·gen·ic** (an′drə·jen′ik) *adj.*

an·drog·y·nous (an·droj′ə·nəs) *adj.* **1.** Uniting the characteristics of both sexes; hermaphroditic. **2.** *Bot.* Having the male and female flowers in the same cluster. Also **an·drog·y·nal** (an·droj′ə·nəl), **an·dro·gyn·ic** (an′drə·jin′ik). [< L < Gk. < *anēr,* man + *gynē* woman] — **an·drog′y·ny** *n.*

An·drom·a·che (an·drom′ə·kē) In Greek legend, the wife of Hector, taken captive to Greece after the fall of Troy.

An·drom·e·da (an·drom′ə·də) In Greek mythology, a princess rescued from a sea monster by Perseus, who then married her. — *n.* A constellation containing the bright star Alpheratz.

an·dros·ter·one (an·dros′tə·rōn) *n. Biochem.* A male sex hormone. $C_{19}H_{30}O_2$.

-androus *suffix* **1.** *Bot.* Having a (specified) number or kind of stamens. **2.** Having a (given) number of husbands. [< Gk. *anēr, andros* man]

-ane¹ *suffix* Used primarily to differentiate words that have a corresponding form in -AN, as *human, humane.* [< L -*anus*]

-ane² *suffix Chem.* Denoting a hydrocarbon compound of the methane series: *pentane.* [An arbitrary formation]

an·ec·do·tal (an′ik·dōt′l) *adj.* Pertaining to, characterized by, or consisting of anecdotes.

an·ec·dote (an′ik·dōt) *n.* A brief account of an interesting or entertaining nature. [< Med.L < Gk. < *an-* not + *ekdotos* published < *ekdidonai* to give out, publish]

an·ec·dot·ic (an′ik·dot′ik) *adj.* **1.** Anecdotal. **2.** Habitually telling or given to anecdotes. Also **an′ec·dot′i·cal.**

an·ec·dot·ist (an′ik·dō′tist) *n.* One who collects, publishes, or is given to telling anecdotes.

a·ne·mi·a (ə·nē′mē·ə) *n. Pathol.* A deficiency in hemoglobin or the number of red corpuscles in the blood, characterized by pallor, loss of energy, etc. [< NL < Gk. < *an-* without + *haima* blood] — **a·ne′mic** *adj.*

a·nem·o·graph (ə·nem′ə·graf, -gräf) *n. Meteorol.* An instrument that makes a record of the velocity and direction of the wind. — **a·nem′o·graph′ic** *adj.*

an·e·mom·e·ter (an′ə·mom′ə·tər) *n. Meteorol.* An instrument for measuring the velocity of the wind. — **an·e·mo·met·ric** (an′ə·mō·met′rik) *or* **·ri·cal** *adj.*

an·e·mom·e·try (an′ə·mom′ə·trē) *n. Meteorol.* The technique of determining the velocity of the wind.

a·nem·o·ne (ə·nem′ə·nē) *n.* **1.** A plant having flowers with no petals but showy, multicolored sepals: also called *windflower.* **2.** *Zool.* The sea anemone. [< Gk. *anemos* wind]

ANEMOMETER

an·er·oid (an′ə·roid) *adj.* Not using liquid. — *n.* An aneroid barometer. [< F < Gk. *a-* not + *nēros* wet + -OID]

aneroid barometer An instrument for measuring atmospheric pressure through its effect upon the flexible top of a partially evacuated chamber.

an·es·the·sia (an′is·thē′zhə, -zhē·ə) *n.* Partial or total loss of physical sensation, particularly of pain, due to disease or certain drugs. Also **an·es·the·sis** (an′is·thē′sis). [< NL < Gk. < *an-* without + *aisthēsis* sensation]

an·es·thet·ic (an′is·thet′ik) *n.* A drug, gas, etc., that causes anesthesia. — *adj.* **1.** Pertaining to or like anesthesia. **2.** Producing anesthesia. Also spelled *anaesthetic.*

an·es·the·tist (ə·nes′thə·tist) *n.* A person trained to administer anesthetics: also spelled *anaesthetist.*

an·es·the·tize (ə·nes′thə·tīz) *v.t.* **·tized, ·tiz·ing** To render insensible, esp. to pain, by means of an anesthetic: also spelled *anaesthetize.* — **an·es′the·ti·za·tion** *n.*

an·eu·rysm (an′yə·riz′əm) *n. Pathol.* A dilatation of the wall of an artery, forming a sac. Also **an′eu·rism.** [< Gk. < *ana-* up + *eurys* wide] — **an·eu·rys·mal** (an′yə·riz′məl) *or* **·ris′mal** *adj.*

a·new (ə·nōō′, ə·nyōō′) *adv.* **1.** Again. **2.** Over again in a different way. [OE *of nīwe*]

an·ga·ry (ang′gə·rē) *n.* In international law, the right of a belligerent, in case of need, to seize, use, or destroy neutral property, esp. ships, subject to claim for full compensation. [< F < LL < Gk. *angaros* courier]

an·gel (ān′jəl) *n.* **1.** *Theol.* **a** A spiritual being attendant upon the Deity; a heavenly messenger. **b** A fallen spiritual being, also immortal. **2.** A conventional representation of an angel, usually a youthful winged human figure in white robes and with a halo. **3.** A person of real or fancied angelic qualities, as of character or beauty. **4.** *Informal* The financial backer of a play, etc. **5.** A former English gold coin. [OE < L < Gk. *angelos* messenger]

an·gel·fish (ān′jəl·fish′) *n. pl.* **·fish** *or* **·fish·es** **1.** A raylike shark having very large, winglike pectoral fins. **2.** A fish of warm seas having brilliant coloration, as the porgy.

angel food cake A delicate, spongy cake made without shortening or egg yolks. Also **angel cake.**

an·gel·ic (an·jel′ik) *adj.* **1.** Pertaining to, of, or consisting of angels; celestial. **2.** Like an angel; pure; beautiful. Also **an·gel′i·cal.** — **an·gel′i·cal·ly** *adv.*

an·gel·i·ca (an·jel′i·kə) *n.* **1.** A fragrant plant of the parsley family. **2.** The stalks of one species of this plant, often candied and used as a flavoring and an aromatic. [< Med.L (*herba*) *angelica* the angelic (herb)]

an·ge·lus (an′jə·ləs) *n. Eccl.* **1.** A devotional prayer used to commemorate the Annunciation. **2.** A bell rung at morning, noon, and night as a call to recite this prayer: also called **angelus bell.** Also **An′ge·lus.** [< L]

an·ger (ang′gər) *n.* A feeling of sudden and strong displeasure and antagonism directed against the cause of an assumed wrong or injury; wrath; ire. — *v.t.* To make angry; enrage. [< ON *angr* grief]

An·ge·vin (an′jə·vin) *adj.* **1.** Of or from Anjou. **2.** Of or pertaining to the Plantagenet kings of England. — *n.* **1.** A native or inhabitant of Anjou. **2.** A member of the royal house of Anjou. Also **An′ge·vine** (-vin, -vīn). [< F]

an·gi·na (an·jī′nə, an′jə·nə) *n. Pathol.* **1.** Any disease characterized by spasmodic suffocation, as croup. **2.** Angina pectoris. [< L, quinsy < *angere* to choke]

angina pec·to·ris (pek′tə·ris) *Pathol.* A defect of coronary circulation, characterized by paroxysmal pain below the sternum. [< NL, angina of the chest]

angio- *combining form* **1.** *Bot.* Seed vessel. **2.** *Med.* Blood vessel; lymph vessel. Also, before vowels, **angi-.** [< Gk. *angeion* case, vessel, capsule]

an·gi·o·ma (an′jē·ō′mə) *n. pl.* **·mas** *or* **·ma·ta** (-mə·tə) *Pathol.* A tumor consisting of dilated blood or lymph vessels. — **an·gi·om·a·tous** (an′jē·om′ə·təs) *adj.*

an·gi·o·sperm (an′jē·ə·spûrm′) *n.* Any of a class of plants having the seeds in a closed seed vessel. — **an·gi·o·sper′mal,** **an′gi·o·sper′ma·tous** (-spûr′mə·təs), **an′gi·o·sper′mous** *adj.*

an·gle¹ (ang′gəl) *v.i.* **·gled, ·gling** **1.** To fish with a hook and line. **2.** To try to get something slyly or artfully: with *for.* [< OE *angel* fishhook]

an·gle² (ang′gəl) *n.* **1.** *Geom.* **a** The figure formed by the divergence of two straight lines from a common point or of two or more planes from a common straight line. **b** The space between these lines or surfaces. **c** The amount of divergence of these lines or surfaces, measured in degrees. **2.** A projecting corner, as of a building. **3.** The point of view or aspect from which something is regarded. **4.** *U.S. Slang* Special selfish motive or interest. — *v.* **an·gled, an·gling** *v.t.* **1.** To move or turn at an angle or by angles. **2.** *Informal* To impart a particular bias or interpretation to, as a story or report. — *v.i.* **3.** To proceed or turn itself at an angle or by angles. [< F < L *angulus* a corner, angle]

ANGLES

1. Acute: *aeb, bec;* Right: *aec, ced;* Obtuse: *bed.* 2. Dihedral.

An·gle (ang′gəl) *n.* A member of a Germanic tribe that migrated to Britain in the fifth century. [< L *Anglus,* sing. of *Angli* < Gmc.] — **An′gli·an** *adj. & n.*

angle iron A piece of iron in the form of an angle, for joining or strengthening beams, girders, etc.

angle of incidence *Physics* The angle relative to the perpendicular drawn from the point of impact at which an object, beam of light, etc., strikes a surface.

an·gler (ang′glər) *n.* **1.** One who fishes with rod, hook, and line. **2.** A fish having antennalike filaments on its head.

an·gle·worm (ang'gəl·wûrm') *n.* An earthworm, commonly used as bait on fishhooks.

An·gli·can (ang'glə·kən) *adj.* Pertaining to or characteristic of the Church of England, or of the churches that agree with it in faith and order. — *n.* **1.** A member of an Anglican Church. [< Med.L *Anglicanus* < L *Angli* the Angles]

Anglican Church 1. The Church of England. **2.** A body of churches, including the Protestant Episcopal Church, mostly derived from the Church of England and in communion with it. — **An·gli·can·ism** (ang'glə·kən·iz'əm) *n.*

An·gli·cism (ang'glə·siz'əm) *n.* **1.** An idiom or turn of phrase peculiar to the English language. **2.** A Briticism. **3.** The state or quality of being English.

An·gli·cize (ang'glə·sīz) *v.* **·cized, ·ciz·ing** *v.t.* **1.** To give an English form, style, or idiom to. — *v.i.* **2.** To acquire some English trait or peculiarity; become like the English. Also *Brit.* **An·gli·cise.** — **An·gli·ci·za·tion** *n.*

An·gli·fy (ang'glə·fī) *v.t. & v.i.* **·fied, ·fy·ing** To Anglicize.

an·gling (ang'gling) *n.* The act or art of fishing with a hook, line, and rod.

Anglo- *combining form* English; English and: *Anglophile, Anglo-Norman.*

An·glo·ma·ni·a (ang'glō·mā'nē·ə) *n.* Overfondness for or imitation of English manners, speech, institutions, etc.

An·glo-Norman (ang'glō·nôr'mən) *adj.* Pertaining to the Normans who settled in England after the Norman Conquest, their descendants, or their language. — *n.* **1.** One of the Norman settlers in England after the Norman Conquest. **2.** The dialect of Old French of these settlers.

An·glo·phile (ang'glə·fil, -fīl) *n.* A lover of England or its people, customs, institutions, or manners. — *adj.* Of or like Anglophiles. Also **An'glo·phil** (fil).

An·glo·pho·bi·a (ang'glə·fō'bē·ə) *n.* Hatred or dread of England, its customs, people, or institutions. — **An'glo·phobe** *n. & adj.* — **An'glo·pho'bic** (-fō'bik, -fob'ik) *adj.*

An·glo-Sax·on (ang'glō·sak'sən) *n.* **1.** A member of one of the Germanic tribes (Angles, Saxons, and Jutes) that dominated England until the Norman Conquest. **2.** Their West Germanic language; Old English. **3.** A person of English nationality or descent. — *adj.* Of or pertaining to the Anglo-Saxons, their language or descendants.

An·go·ra (ang·gôr'ə, -gō'rə) *n.* **1.** A goat, originally from Ankara, having long, silky hair. **2.** A shawl, cloth, etc., made of Angora wool or its imitations. **3.** An Angora cat.

Angora cat A variety of cat with long, silky hair.

an·gos·tu·ra bark (ang'gəs·tŏŏr'ə, -tyŏŏr'ə) A bark from a South American tree, used in the preparation of a tonic and flavoring. Also **an'gos·tu'ra.** [after *Angostura,* former name of Ciudad Bolívar, Venezuela]

an·gry (ang'grē) *adj.* **ang·ri·er, an·gri·est 1.** Feeling, showing, or excited by anger; indignant. **2.** Showing signs of anger; wrathful. **3.** Seeming to be in anger. **4.** Badly inflamed. — **an·gri·ly** (ang'grə·lē) *adv.* — **an'gri·ness** *n.*

ang·strom (ang'strəm) *n.* A linear unit equal to 10^{-8} centimeter or 3.937×10^{-9} inch, used for minute measurements, as of wavelengths of light. Also **angstrom unit.** [after A. J. *Ångström,* 1814–75, Swedish physicist]

an·guish (ang'gwish) *n.* Excruciating mental or bodily pain; agony; torture. — *v.t. & v.i.* To affect or suffer with anguish. [< OF *anguisse* < L *angustia* tightness, difficulty]

an·gu·lar (ang'gyə·lər) *adj.* **1.** Having, forming, or constituting an angle or angles; sharp-cornered. **2.** Measured by an angle. **3.** Pertaining to angles. **4.** Bony; gaunt. **5.** Awkward or ungraceful. [< L < *angulus* corner, angle] — **an'gu·lar·ly** *adv.*

an·gu·lar·i·ty (ang'gyə·lar'ə·tē) *n.* *pl.* **·ties 1.** The state of being angular: also **an'gu·lar·ness. 2.** *pl.* Angular outlines or parts.

an·hy·dride (an·hī'drīd, -drid) *n. Chem.* **1.** Any organic or inorganic compound that has been dehydrated. **2.** A compound formed from another compound, especially an acid or base, by the removal of one or more molecules of water, the process being generally reversible. [See ANHYDROUS]

an·hy·drous (an·hī'drəs) *adj. Chem.* Pertaining to or designating a compound that has no water of crystallization in its composition. [< Gk. < *an-* without + *hydōr* water]

an·il (an'il) *n.* **1.** A West Indian indigo plant. **2.** The indigo dye made from this plant. [< F < Pg. < Arabic *al-nīl* the blue < Skt.]

an·i·line (an'ə·lin, -līn) *n. Chem.* A colorless oily, poisonous compound, $C_6H_5NH_2$, the base of many coal-tar dyes, chiefly made from nitrobenzene. Also called *phenylamine.* — *adj.* Made of, derived from, or pertaining to aniline. Also **an·i·lin** (an'ə·lin). [< ANIL + -INE²]

an·i·ma (an'ə·mə) *n.* The vital principle; soul. [< L]

an·i·mad·ver·sion (an'ə·mad·vûr'zhən, -shən) *n.* A censorious comment or reflection: with *on* or *upon.*

an·i·mad·vert (an'ə·mad·vûrt') *v.i.* To comment critically, usu. in an adverse sense: with *on* or *upon.* [< L < *animus* mind + *advertere* to turn to]

an·i·mal (an'ə·məl) *n.* **1.** A sentient living organism typically capable of voluntary motion and sensation: distinguished from *plant.* **2.** Any such creature as distinguished from man. **3.** A bestial human being. — *adj.* **1.** Of, characteristic of, derived from, or resembling animals. **2.** Carnal; sensual: *animal* appetites. [< L, < *anima* breath, soul, life]

an·i·mal·cule (an'ə·mal'kyōōl) *n.* An animal of microscopic smallness, as an ameba. Also **an'i·mal'cu·lum** (-kyə·ləm). [< L *animalculum,* dim. of *animal* animal] — **an'i·mal'cu·lar** (-kyə·lər) *adj.*

animal husbandry The branch of agriculture specializing in the breeding, raising, and care of farm animals.

an·i·mal·ism (an'ə·məl·iz'əm) *n.* **1.** The state or condition of a mere animal. **2.** Animal activity. **3.** The doctrine that man is entirely animal, having no soul. — **an'i·mal·ist** *n.* — **an'i·mal·is'tic** *adj.*

an·i·mal·i·ty (an'ə·mal'ə·tē) *n.* **1.** The nature or qualities of an animal. **2.** Animal life; the animal kingdom.

an·i·mal·ize (an'ə·məl·īz') *v.t.* **·ized, ·iz·ing** To render brutal; sensualize. — **an·i·mal·i·za·tion** (an'ə·mel·ə·zā'shən, -ī·zā'-) *n.*

animal kingdom Animal organisms collectively, as distinguished from plants.

an·i·mal·ly (an'ə·məl·ē) *adv.* Physically, as distinguished from spiritually or mentally.

animal magnetism Mesmerism.

an·i·mate (*v.* an'ə·māt; *adj.* an'ə·mit) *v.t.* **·mat·ed, ·mat·ing 1.** To impart life to; make alive. **2.** To move to action; incite; inspire. **3.** To produce activity or energy in. — *adj.* **1.** Possessing animal life; living. **2.** Full of life; vivacious; lively: also **an'i·mat'ed** (-mā'tid). [< L *anima* breath, soul] — **an'i·mat'ed·ly** *adv.* See CARTOON. — **an'i·ma'tor, an'i·ma'ter** *n.*

animated cartoon See CARTOON.

an·i·ma·tion (an'ə·mā'shən) *n.* **1.** The act of imparting life, or the state of possessing life. **2.** The quality of being lively or quick; vivacity. **3.** The process and technique of preparing animated cartoons.

a·ni·ma·to (ä'nē·mä'tō) *adj. & adv. Music* With animation. [< Ital.]

an·i·mism (an'ə·miz'əm) *n.* **1.** The belief in the existence of spirit or soul, as distinct from matter. **2.** The doctrine that natural objects and phenomena possess a soul. [< L *anima* soul] — **an'i·mist** *n.* — **an'i·mis'tic** *adj.*

an·i·mos·i·ty (an'ə·mos'ə·tē) *n. pl.* **·ties** Active and vehement enmity; hatred. [< L *animositas, -tatis* high spirit]

an·i·mus (an'ə·məs) *n.* **1.** Hostile feeling; animosity. **2.** The animating thought or purpose; intention. [< L]

an·i·on (an'ī'ən) *n. Chem.* A negative ion: opposed to *cation.* [< Gk. *anienai* to go up] — **an'i·on'ic** (-on'ik) *adj.*

an·ise (an'is) *n.* **1.** A small South European and North African plant that furnishes aniseed. **2.** Aniseed. [< OF < L < Gk. *anison*]

an·i·seed (an'i·sēd') *n.* The fragrant seed of the anise plant.

an·i·sette (an'ə·zet', -set') *n.* A cordial made from or flavored with aniseed. [< F,

an·kle (ang'kəl) *n.* **1.** The joint connecting the foot and the leg. **2.** The part of the leg between the foot and the calf near the ankle joint. [ME *ankel* < OE *ancleow*]

an·kle·bone (ang'kəl·bōn') *n.* The talus. Also **ankle bone.**

an·klet (ang'klit) *n.* **1.** An ornament or fetter for the ankle. **2.** A short sock reaching just above the ankle.

ankylo- *combining form* Bent; crooked: in anatomy, referring to adhesion of bones. [< Gk. *ankylos* crooked]

an·ky·lose (ang'kə·lōs) *v.t. & v.i.* **·losed, ·los·ing** To unite or join by ankylosis: also spelled *anchylose.*

an·ky·lo·sis (ang'kə·lō'sis) *n.* **1.** *Anat.* The fusing of bones or parts of bones. **2.** *Pathol.* The abnormal adhesion of bones, especially those forming a joint; stiffening of a joint. Also spelled *anchylosis.* [< NL < Gk. *ankylōsis* < *ankyloein* to bend < *ankylos* crooked] — **an'ky·lot'ic** (-lo t'ik) *adj.*

an·nal·ist (an'əl·ist) *n.* A writer of annals; a historian. — **an'nal·is'tic** *adj.*

an·nals (an'əlz) *n.pl.* **1.** A record of events in their chronological order, year by year. **2.** History or records. **3.** A periodical publication of discoveries, transactions, etc. [< L *annus* year]

An·na·mese (an'ə·mēz', -mēs') *n. pl.* **An·na·mese 1.** A native or inhabitant of Annam. **2.** Formerly, the Vietnamese language. — *adj.* Of Annam or the Annamese.

Anne, Saint Traditionally, the mother of the Virgin Mary.

an·neal (ə·nēl') *v.t.* **1.** To reduce the brittleness of, as glass and various metals, by heating and then slowly cooling. **2.** To toughen, as the will. [OE *onǣlan* to burn]

an·ne·lid (an'ə·lid) *Zool. adj.* Belonging to a phylum of segmented worms, including the earthworm and leeches. — *n.* An annelid worm. [< NL < F < L *annellus* a ring]

---

an·nex (*v.* ə·neks′; *n.* an′eks) *v.t.* **1.** To add or append, as an additional or minor part, to existing possessions; affix. **2.** To attach, as an attribute, condition, or consequence. — **Syn.** See ADD. — *n.* **1.** An addition to a building. **2.** An addition to a document; addendum. [< F < L < *ad-* to + *nectere* to tie] — **an·nex′a·ble** *adj.*

an·nex·a·tion (an′ek·sā′shən) *n.* **1.** The act of annexing. **2.** That which is added or attached. Also **an·nex′ment.**

an·ni·hi·late (ə·nī′ə·lāt) *v.t.* **·lat·ed, ·lat·ing** To destroy utterly. [< L *ad-* to + *nihil* nothing] — **an·ni′hi·la·ble** *adj.* — **an·ni′hi·la′tive** *adj.* — **an·ni·hi·la·tion** (ə·nī′ə·lā′shən) *n.* — **an·ni′hi·la′tor** *n.*

an·ni·ver·sa·ry (an′ə·vûr′sər·ē) *n. pl.* **·ries 1.** A day in the year on the date of which an event occurred in some preceding year. **2.** A celebration on such occasion. — *adj.* **1.** Recurring annually or at the same date every year. **2.** Pertaining to or occurring on an anniversary. [< L < *annus* year + *versus,* pp. of *vertere* to turn]

an·no Dom·i·ni (an′ō dom′ə·nī) *Latin* In the year of our Lord or of the Christian era. Abbr. *A.D.*

an·no·tate (an′ō·tāt) *v.t. & v.i.* **·tat·ed, ·tat·ing** To provide (a text, etc.) with explanatory or critical notes. [< L < *ad-* to + *notare* to note, mark] — **an′no·ta′tion** *n.* — **an′no·ta′tive** *adj.* — **an′no·ta′tor** *n.*

an·nounce (ə·nouns′) *v.t.* **·nounced, ·nounc·ing 1.** To make known publicly or officially; proclaim. **2.** To give notice of the approach or appearance of: to *announce* guests. **3.** To make known to the senses. **4.** To serve as the announcer for, as a radio program. [< OF < L < *ad-* to + *nuntiare* to report] — **an·nounce′ment** *n.*

an·nounc·er (ə·noun′sər) *n.* **1.** One who announces. **2.** A person who identifies the station from which a radio or television program is broadcast, introduces the performers, etc.

an·noy (ə·noi′) *v.t.* **1.** To be troublesome to; bother; irritate. **2.** To do harm to or injure. [< OF *anuier, anoier,* ult. < L *in odio* in hatred] — **an·noy′er** *n.*

an·noy·ance (ə·noi′əns) *n.* **1.** One who or that which annoys. **2.** The act of annoying or being annoyed.

an·noy·ing (ə·noi′ing) *adj.* Vexatious; troublesome. — **an·noy′ing·ly** *adv.* — **an·noy′ing·ness** *n.*

an·nu·al (an′yōō·əl) *adj.* **1.** Returning, performed, or occurring every year. **2.** Reckoned by the year. — *n.* **1.** A book or pamphlet issued once a year. **2.** *Bot.* A plant living for a single year or season. Abbr. *ann.* [< L *annualis* yearly] — **an′nu·al·ly** *adv.*

an·nu·i·tant (ə·nōō′ə·tənt, ə·nyōō′-) *n.* One receiving, or entitled to receive, an annuity.

an·nu·i·ty (ə·nōō′ə·tē, ə·nyōō′-) *n. pl.* **·ties 1.** An income paid yearly. **2.** The right to receive such an allowance, or the duty of paying it. **3.** Interest from an investment in yearly payments. [< OF < Med.L *annuitas, -tatis*]

an·nul (ə·nul′) *v.t.* **·nulled, ·nul·ling** To put an end to; nullify, esp. a marriage. [< OF < L *ad-* to + *nullus* none] — **an·nul′ment** *n.* — **an·nul′la·ble** *adj.*

— **Syn. 1.** *Annul* and *nullify* are general terms; *nullify* may also be used in an extralegal sense. A marriage is *annulled*; a law may be *nullified* by a new law, or by the effects of popular defiance. *Cancel, abate, void, vacate, quash, abrogate, repeal, rescind,* and *revoke* differ chiefly in technical usage. Typically, we *cancel* a lease, *abate* or *void* a writ, *vacate* an injunction, *quash* an indictment, *abrogate* a treaty, *repeal* a law, *rescind* a ruling, and *revoke* a will.

an·nu·lar (an′yə·lər) *adj.* Formed like a ring; ring-shaped. [< L *annularis < annulus, anulus* ring] — **an′nu·lar·ly** *adv.*

annular eclipse *Astron.* A solar eclipse in which a narrow ring of the sun is visible beyond the dark mass of the moon.

an·nu·late (an′yə·lit, -lāt) *adj.* Furnished with rings; ringed. [< L *annulatus < annulus* a ring] — **an′nu·la′tion** *n.*

an·nu·lus (an′yə·ləs) *n. pl.* **·li** (-lī) or **·lus·es** A ringlike part, body, or space. [< L, a ring]

an·nun·ci·ate (ə·nun′shē·āt, -sē-) *v.t.* **·at·ed, ·at·ing** To announce. [< L *annuntiare* to report]

an·nun·ci·a·tion (ə·nun′sē·ā′shən, -shē-) *n.* The act of announcing, or that which is announced; proclamation.

An·nun·ci·a·tion (ə·nun′sē·ā′shən, -shē-) *n.* **1.** *Eccl.* **1.** The announcement of the Incarnation to the Virgin Mary by an angel. *Luke* i 28–38. **2.** The festival (March 25) commemorating this event.

an·nun·ci·a·tor (ə·nun′shē·ā′tər, -sē-) *n.* **1.** An announcer. **2.** An electrical indicator used in hotels, etc., that shows a number or name when a bell is rung.

an·ode (an′ōd) *n. Electr.* **1.** The positive electrode toward which anions migrate in an electrolytic cell. **2.** The plate of an electron tube toward which electrons are attracted. [< Gk. *anodos* a way up] — **an·od·ic** (an·od′ik) *adj.*

an·o·dyne (an′ə·dīn) *adj.* Having power to allay pain; soothing. — *n. Med.* Anything that relieves pain or soothes. [< L < Gk. < *an-* without + *odynē* pain]

a·noint (ə·noint′) *v.t.* **1.** To smear with oil or ointment. **2.** To put oil on in a religious ceremony. [< OF < L < *in-* on + *ungere* to smear] — **a·noint′er** *n.* — **a·noint′ment** *n.*

a·nom·a·lous (ə·nom′ə·ləs) *adj.* Deviating from the common

rule; exceptional; abnormal. [< L < Gk. < *an-* not + *homalos* even] — **a·nom′a·lous·ly** *adv.* — **a·nom′a·lous·ness** *n.*

a·nom·a·ly (ə·nom′ə·lē) *n. pl.* **·lies 1.** Deviation from rule, type, or form; irregularity. **2.** Anything anomalous. — **a·nom′a·lism** *n.* — **a·nom·a·lis·tic** (ə·nom′ə·lis′tik) or **·ti·cal** *adj.*

a·non (ə·non′) *adv.* **1.** In a little while; soon. **2.** At another time; again. [OE *on ān* in one]

a·non·ym (an′ə·nim) *n.* **1.** An anonymous person or writer. **2.** A pseudonym.

a·non·y·mous (ə·non′ə·məs) *adj.* **1.** Having or bearing no name. **2.** Of unknown authorship or agency. [< Gk. < *an-* without + *onoma* name] — **a·no·nym·i·ty** (an′ə·nim′ə·tē), **a·non′y·mous·ness** *n.* — **a·non′y·mous·ly** *adv.*

a·noph·e·les (ə·nof′ə·lēz) *n.* A mosquito carrying the malaria parasite. [< NL < Gk. *anóphelēs* harmful] — **a·noph·e·line** (ə·nof′ə·lin, -lin) *adj.*

an·o·rex·i·a (an′ə·rek′sē·ə) *n. Med.* Loss of appetite. Also **an′o·rex′y.** [< NL < Gk. < *an-* without + *orexis* appetite] — **an·o·rec·tic** (an′ə·rek′tik), **an′o·rec′tous** *adj.*

an·oth·er (ə·nuth′ər) *adj.* **1.** An additional; one more. **2.** Not the same; different: *another* man. — *pron.* **1.** An additional one; one more. **2.** A different one. **3.** A similar or identical one. [< *an other*]

an·ox·i·a (an·ok′sē·ə) *n. Pathol.* An insufficient oxygen supply to the body tissues.

An·schluss (än′shlŏŏs) *n. German* Political union.

an·swer (an′sər, än′-) *v.i.* **1.** To reply or respond, as by words or actions. **2.** To be responsible or accountable: with *for.* **3.** To serve the purpose. **4.** To correspond or match, as in appearance: with *to.* — *v.t.* **5.** To speak, write, or act in response or reply to. **6.** To be sufficient for; fulfill. **7.** To pay for: to *answer* damages. **8.** To conform or correspond to; match. **9.** *Law* To reply favorably to, as a petition or petitioner. — **to answer back** To talk back, as in contradiction. — *n.* **1.** A reply. **2.** Any action in return or in kind; retaliation. **3.** The result of a calculation or solution. **4.** *Law* The defense of a defendant. **5.** *Music* The restatement of a musical theme or phrase. [OE *andswarian*] — **an′swer·er** *n.*

an·swer·a·ble (an′sər·ə·bəl, än′-) *adj.* **1.** Accountable; responsible. **2.** That may be answered. — **an·swer·a·ble·ness** *n.* — **an′swer·a·bly** *adv.*

ant (ant) *n.* A small insect, usu. wingless, and living in colonies. [OE *ǣmete*]

ant- Var. of ANTI-.

-ant *suffix* **1.** Forming adjectives that mean in the act or process of doing (what is denoted by the stem): *militant, litigant,* etc. **2.** One who or that which does (what is indicated by the stem): *servant,* one who serves. [< F < L *-ans, -ens,* present participial suffixes]

ant·ac·id (ant·as′id) *adj.* Correcting acidity. — *n.* An alkaline remedy for stomach acidity.

an·tag·o·nism (an·tag′ə·niz′əm) *n.* **1.** Mutual opposition or resistance; hostility. **2.** An opposing principle or force.

an·tag·o·nist (an·tag′ə·nist) *n.* **1.** An adversary; opponent. **2.** *Anat.* A muscle that acts counter to another muscle. — **Syn.** See ENEMY.

an·tag·o·nis·tic (an·tag′ə·nis′tik) *adj.* Opposed; hostile. — **an·tag′o·nis′ti·cal·ly** *adv.*

an·tag·o·nize (an·tag′ə·nīz) *v.* **·nized, ·niz·ing** *v.t.* **1.** To make unfriendly; make an enemy of. **2.** To struggle against; oppose. — *v.i.* **3.** To act antagonistically. [< Gk. < *anti-* against + *agōnizesthai* to struggle, strive]

ant·al·ka·li (ant·al′kə·lī) *n. pl.* **·lis** or **·lies** Any substance able to neutralize alkalis.

Ant·arc·tic (ant·ärk′tik, -är′tik) *adj.* Of or relating to the South Pole, or the regions within the Antarctic Circle. [< L < Gk. < *anti-* opposite + *arktos* the Bear (a northern constellation), the north]

An·tar·es (an·târ′ēz) *n.* A giant red star, one of the 20 brightest; Alpha in the constellation Scorpio. [< Gk.]

ant bear A mammal of tropical America feeding on ants.

an·te (an′tē) *v.t. & v.i.* **·ted** or **·teed, ·te·ing 1.** In poker, to put up (one's stake). **2.** *Slang* To pay (one's share). — *n.* **1.** In poker, the stake put up before receiving the hand. **2.** *Slang* One's share. [< L, before]

ante- *prefix* **1.** Before in time or order: *antemeridiem.* **2.** Before in position; in front of: *antechamber.* [< L *ante* before]

ANT BEAR
(8 feet long;
2 feet high)

ant·eat·er (ant′ē′tər) *n.* **1.** The ant bear. **2.** One of several other mammals that feed partly on ants, as the aardvark.

an·te·bel·lum (an′tē·bel′əm) *adj.* Before the war; esp., before the Civil War in the United States. [< L]

an·te·cede (an′tē·sēd′) *v.t. & v.i.* **·ced·ed, ·ced·ing** To go or come before. [< L < *ante-* before + *cedere* to go]

an·te·ce·dence (an′tə·sēd′ns) *n.* **1.** A going before; precedence; priority. **2.** *Astron.* The apparent retrograde motion of a planet. Also **an'te·ce'den·cy.**

an·te·ce·dent (an'tə·sēd'nt) *adj.* **1.** Prior; preceding. — *n.* **1.** One who or that which precedes. **2.** *Gram.* The word, phrase, or clause to which a pronoun refers. **3.** *pl.* The past events, circumstances, etc., of a person's life; also, ancestry. **4.** *Math.* The first term of a ratio; in a proportion, the first and third terms. **5.** *Logic* The condition on which a hypothetical proposition depends. [< L < *ante-* before + *cedere* to go] — **an'te·ce'dent·ly** *adv.*

an·te·cham·ber (an'ti·chām'bər) *n.* A room serving as an entranceway to another room

an·te·date (an'ti·dāt') *v.t.* **·dat·ed, ·dat·ing** **1.** To precede in time. **2.** To assign to a date earlier than the actual one. **3.** To cause to happen at an earlier date.

an·te·di·lu·vi·an (an'ti·di·lōō'vē·ən) *adj.* **1.** Before the Flood. **2.** Antiquated; primitive. — *n.* **1.** A person, animal, or plant that lived before the Flood. **2.** An old or old-fashioned person. [< ANTE- + L *diluvium* deluge]

an·te·lope (an'tə·lōp) *n.* *pl.* **·lope** or **·lopes** **1.** Any of various swift, hollow-horned animals, as the gazelle, chamois, gnu, etc. **2.** Leather made from its hide. **3.** *U.S.* The pronghorn. [< OF < Med.L < LGk. *antholops*]

an·te me·rid·i·em (an'tē mə·rid'ē·em) *Latin* Before noon. Abbr. *a.m., A.M.* — **an'te·me·rid'i·an** *adj.*

an·ten·na (an·ten'ə) *n.* *pl.* **·ten·nae** (-ten'ē) *for def. 1* **·ten·nas** *for def. 2* **1.** *Entomol.* One of the paired, movable sense organs on the head of an insect or other arthropod. **2.** *Telecom.* A system of wires, etc., for transmitting or receiving electromagnetic waves. [< L, a yard for a sail]

an·te·pe·nult (an'ti·pē'nult, -pi·nult') *n.* The last syllable but two in a word, as *te* in *antepenult.* [< L]

an·te·pe·nul·ti·mate (an'ti·pi·nul'tə·mit) *adj.* Pertaining to the last but two of any series. — *n.* The antepenult.

an·te·ri·or (an·tir'ē·ər) *adj.* **1.** Antecedent in time; prior. **2.** Farther front or forward in space. [< L, compar. of *ante* before] — **an·te'ri·or·ly** *adv.*

antero- *combining form* Anterior; placed in front. [< L *anterus* (assumed form)]

an·te·room (an'ti·rōōm', -rŏŏm') *n.* A waiting room.

anth- Var. of ANTI-.

an·them (an'thəm) *n.* **1.** A hymn of gladness or praise: a national *anthem.* **2.** A musical composition, usually set to words from the Bible. — *v.t.* To celebrate with an anthem. [OE < LL < Gk., < *anti-* against + *phōnē* voice]

an·ther (an'thər) *n.* *Bot.* The pollen-bearing part of a stamen. For illustration see FLOWER. [< F < L < Gk. *anthos* flower]

an·ther·id·i·um (an'thə·rid'ē·əm) *n.* *pl.* **·ther·id·i·a** (-thə·rid'ē·ə) *Bot.* The male sexual organ in cryptogams. [< NL, dim. of Gk. *anthēros* flowery] — **an'ther·id'i·al** *adj.*

antho- *combining form* Flower. [< Gk. *anthos* a flower]

an·thol·o·gize (an·thol'ə·jīz) *v.* **·gized, ·giz·ing** *v.i.* **1.** To make an anthology or anthologies. — *v.t.* **2.** To put into an anthology or make an anthology of.

an·thol·o·gy (an·thol'ə·jē) *n.* *pl.* **·gies** A collection of choice or representative literary extracts. [< L < Gk. < *anthos* flower + *legein* to gather] — **an·tho·log·i·cal** (an'thə·loj'i·kəl) *adj.* — **an·thol'o·gist** *n.*

an·tho·zo·an (an'thə·zō'ən) *Zool.* *adj.* Of or belonging to a class of marine animals including the sea anemones and corals. — *n.* An anthozoan animal. [< NL < ANTHO- + Gk. *zōion* animal] — **an'tho·zo'ic** *adj.*

an·thra·cene (an'thrə·sēn) *n.* *Chem.* A crystalline compound, $C_{14}H_{11}$, obtained from coal tar and used in manufacturing dyes. [< Gk. *anthrax, -akos* coal + -ENE]

an·thra·cite (an'thrə·sīt) *n.* Coal that burns slowly and with great heat: also called *hard coal.* [< L < Gk. *anthrax* coal] — **an·thra·cit·ic** (an'thr·sit'ik) *adj.*

an·thrax (an'thraks) *n.* *pl.* **·thra·ces** (-thrə·sēz) *Pathol.* An infectious, malignant disease of man and some animals, often with carbuncles; also, the carbuncle. [< Gk., coal]

anthropo- *combining form* Man; human: *anthropology.* Also, before vowels, **anthrop-.** [< Gk. *anthrōpos* man]

an·thro·po·cen·tric (an'thrə·pō·sen'trik) *adj.* Regarding man as the central fact or final aim of the universe.

an·thro·pog·e·ny (an'thrə·poj'ə·nē) *n.* The branch of anthropology that treats of the origin and development of man. Also **an·thro·po·gen·e·sis** (an'thrə·pō·jen'ə·sis).

an·thro·poid (an'thrə·poid) *adj.* Like a human being in form or other characteristics, as the gorilla, chimpanzee, and orang-utan. Also **an'thro·poi'dal.** — *n.* An ape.

an·thro·pol·o·gy (an'thrə·pol'ə·jē) *n.* **1.** The science treating of the physical, social, material, and cultural development of man, including his origin, evolution, distribution, customs, beliefs, folkways, etc. — **an·thro·po·log·i·cal** (an'thrə·pə·loj'i·kəl) or **·log'ic** *adj.* — **an'thro·po·log'i·cal·ly** *adv.* — **an'thro·pol'o·gist** *n.*

an·thro·pom·e·try (an'thrə·pom'ə·trē) *n.* The science and technique of human anatomical measurements. — **an·thro·po·met·ric** (an'thrə·pō·met'rik) or **·ri·cal** *adj.*

an·thro·po·mor·phic (an'thrə·pō·môr'fik) *adj.* Of or characterized by anthropomorphism.

an·thro·po·mor·phism (an'thrə·pō·môr'fiz·əm) *n.* The ascription of human form or characteristics to a deity, or to any being or thing not human. — **an'thro·po·mor'phist** *n.*

an·thro·po·mor·phize (an'thrə·pō·môr'fīz) *v.t. & v.i.* **·phized, ·phiz·ing** To ascribe human characteristics (to).

an·thro·po·mor·phous (an'thrə·pō·môr'fəs) *adj.* Having or resembling human form. [< Gk. < *anthrōpos* man + *morphē* form, shape]

an·ti (an'tī, an'tē) *n.* *pl.* **·tis** *Informal* One opposed to some policy, group, etc.

anti- A prefix having the following meanings: **1.** Against; opposed to, as in: *antitobacco, anti-Fascist.* **2.** Opposite to; reverse, as in: *anticyclic, antilogic.* **3.** *Med.* Counteracting; curative, as in: *antianemic, antivirus. Anti-* usu. changes to *ant-* before words beginning with a vowel, as in *antacid.* [< Gk. *anti* against]

an·ti·air·craft (an'tē·âr'kraft/, -âr'kräft/, an'tī-) *adj.* Used for defense against enemy aircraft. Abbr. *AA, A.A.*

an·ti·bi·o·sis (an'ti·bī·ō'sis) *n.* *Biol.* The condition of associated organisms in which one is detrimental to the other.

an·ti·bi·ot·ic (an'ti·bī·ot'ik, an'ti-, an'ti·bē·ot'ik) *n.* *Biochem.* Any of a large class of substances, as penicillin, streptomycin, etc., having the power of destroying or arresting the growth of microorganisms. [< ANTI- + Gk. *bios* life]

an·ti·bod·y (an'ti·bod'ē) *n.* *pl.* **·bod·ies** *Biochem.* Any of a class of proteins serving to immunize the body against specific antigens.

an·tic (an'tik) *n.* **1.** *Usually pl.* A prank; caper. **2.** A clown; buffoon. — *adj.* Odd; fantastic; ludicrous. — *v.i.* **an·ticked, an·tick·ing** To play the clown; perform antics. [< Ital. *antico* old, grotesque] — **an'tic·ly** *adv.*

an·ti·christ (an'ti·krist') *n.* *Often cap.* A denier or opponent of Christ or Christianity. — **an'ti·chris'tian** *adj. & n.*

An·ti·christ (an'ti·krist') *n.* The blasphemous antagonist of Christ. 1 *John* ii 18.

an·tic·i·pant (an·tis'ə·pənt) *adj.* Coming or acting in advance; anticipating; expectant. — *n.* One who anticipates.

an·tic·i·pate (an·tis'ə·pāt) *v.t.* **·pat·ed, ·pat·ing** **1.** To experience or realize beforehand. **2.** To look forward to. **3.** To act or arrive sooner than, especially so as to forestall. **4.** To foresee and fulfill beforehand, as desires. **5.** To make use of beforehand. **6.** To discharge, as a debt, before it is due. **7.** To cause to happen earlier. [< L < *ante-* before + *capere* to take] — **an·tic'i·pa'tor** *n.*

an·tic·i·pa·tion (an·tis'ə·pā'shən) *n.* **1.** The act of anticipating; also, that which is anticipated. **2.** An expectation. **3.** An intuitive prevision.

an·tic·i·pa·tive (an·tis'ə·pā'tiv) *adj.* Anticipating, or characterized by anticipation. — **an·tic'i·pa'tive·ly** *adv.*

an·tic·i·pa·to·ry (an·tis'ə·pə·tôr'ē, -tō'rē) *adj.* Of, showing, or embodying anticipation. — **an·tic'i·pa·to'ri·ly** *adv.*

an·ti·cler·i·cal (an'ti·kler'i·kəl) *adj.* Opposed to clerical influence in political and civic affairs. — **an'ti cler'i·cal·ism** *n.*

an·ti·cli·max (an'ti·klī'maks) *n.* **1.** In rhetoric, a ludicrous decrease in the importance or impressiveness of what is said. **2.** Any sudden descent or fall contrasted with a previous rise. — **an'ti·cli·mac'tic** (-klī·mak'tik) *adj.*

an·ti·cline (an'ti·klīn) *n.* *Geol.* A system of roughly parallel folds in stratified rock in which the folds slope downward from the crest in opposite directions. Compare SYNCLINE. [< ANTI- + Gk. *klinein* to slope] — **an'ti·cli'nal** *adj.*

ANTICLINE

an·ti·cy·clone (an'ti·sī'klōn) *n.* *Meteorol.* An atmospheric condition in which winds spiral outward from a central point of high pressure. — **an'ti·cy·clon'ic** (-klon'ik) *adj.*

an·ti·dote (an'ti·dōt) *n.* Anything that will counteract or remove the effects of poison, disease, or any evil. [< L < Gk. < *anti-* against + *didonai* to give] — **an'ti·do'tal** *adj.* — **an'ti·do'tal·ly** *adv.*

An·ti·fed·er·al·ist (an'ti·fed'ər·əl·ist, -fed'rəl-) *n.* A member of the political party that opposed the ratification of the U.S. Constitution. — **An'ti·fed'er·al** *adj.*

an·ti·freeze (an'ti·frēz') *n.* A liquid of low freezing point, added to or substituted for the cooling agent in combustion-engine radiators, to prevent freezing.

an·ti·gen (an'tə·jən) *n.* *Biochem.* Any of several substances that cause the development of antibodies. Also **an′ti·gene** (-jēn). — **an·ti·gen·ic** (an′tə·jen′ik) *adj.*

An·tig·o·ne (an·tig′ə·nē) In Greek legend, a daughter of Oedipus and Jocasta, who was sentenced to death for illegally burying her brother.

an·ti·he·ro (an′ti·hir′ō, -hē′rō) *n. pl.* **·roes** A principal male character in a drama, fictional work, etc., who lacks the virtues of a traditional hero.

an·ti·his·ta·mine (an′ti·his′tə·mēn, -min) *n. Med.* Any of certain drugs that neutralize the action of histamine in the treatment of hay fever, asthma, etc.

an·ti·knock (an′ti·nok′) *n.* A fuel additive that prevents premature combustion in an internal-combustion engine.

an·ti·log·a·rithm (an′ti·lôg′ə·rith̸əm, -log′-) *n. Math.* The number corresponding to a given logarithm. Also, in shortened form, **an·ti·log** (an′ti·lôg, -log).

an·ti·ma·cas·sar (an′ti·mə·kas′ər) *n.* A covering for the backs and arms of chairs and sofas to prevent soiling; a tidy.

an·ti·mat·ter (an′ti·mat′ər) *n. Physics* A form of matter composed of antiparticles.

an·ti·mo·ni·al (an′tə·mō′nē·əl) *adj.* Of or containing antimony. — *n.* A medicine containing antimony.

an·ti·mo·ny (an′tə·mō′nē) *n.* A silver-white, crystalline, metallic element (symbol Sb) used in chemistry, medicine, in alloys, etc.: also called *stibium.* See ELEMENT. ◆ Collateral adjective: *stibial.* [< Med.L *antimonium*]

an·ti·par·ti·cle (an′ti·pär′ti·kəl) *n. Physics* Any of a group of atomic particles having masses equal to the electron, proton, neutron, etc., but with opposite charges and magnetic characteristics.

an·ti·pas·to (än′tē·päs′tō) *n.* A course of smoked or salted meat, fish, vegetables, etc., served as an appetizer. [< Ital.]

an·ti·pa·thet·ic (an·tip′ə·thet′ik, an′ti·pə-) *adj.* Having a natural aversion; constitutionally opposed: often with *to.* Also **an·tip′a·thet′i·cal.** — **an·tip′a·thet′i·cal·ly** *adv.*

an·tip·a·thy (an·tip′ə·thē) *n. pl.* **·thies 1.** An instinctive feeling of aversion or dislike. **2.** The object of such a feeling. [< Gk. < *anti-* against + *pathein* to feel, suffer]

an·ti·per·son·nel (an′ti·pûr′sə·nel′, an′tī-) *adj. Mil.* Designating weapons that are employed against troops rather than against defenses or mechanized equipment.

an·ti·per·spi·rant (an′ti·pûr′spə·rənt, an′tī-) *n.* A skin astringent that prevents or diminishes perspiration.

an·ti·phlo·gis·tic (an′ti·flō·jis′tik) *Med. adj.* Capable of reducing inflammation. — *n.* A remedy for inflammation. [< ANTI- + Gk. *phlogizein* to burn]

an·ti·phon (an′tə·fon) *n.* A verse of a psalm or hymn said or chanted in response to another. [< LL < Gk. < *anti-* against + *phōnē* voice]

an·tiph·o·nal (an·tif′ə·nəl) *adj.* Of or like an antiphon; sung responsively. Also **an·tiph·on·ic** (an′tə·fon′ik). — *n.* An antiphonary. — **an·tiph′o·nal·ly** *adv.*

an·tiph·o·nar·y (an·tif′ə·ner′ē) *n. pl.* **·nar·ies** A book of antiphons. — *adj.* Of or pertaining to a book of antiphons.

an·tip·o·dal (an·tip′ə·dəl) *adj.* **1.** Pertaining to or situated on the opposite side of the earth. **2.** Diametrically opposed.

an·ti·pode (an′ti·pōd) *n.* An exact opposite.

an·tip·o·des (an·tip′ə·dēz) *n.* (*construed as sing. or pl.*) A place or region on the opposite side of the earth, or its inhabitants. [< L < Gk. < *anti-* opposite + *pous* foot]

an·ti·py·ret·ic (an′ti·pī·ret′ik) *Med. adj.* Reducing fever. — *n.* A medicine to reduce fever. [< ANTI- + Gk. *pyretos* fever]

an·ti·quar·i·an (an′ti·kwâr′ē·ən) *adj.* Pertaining to antiques or antiquaries. — *n.* An antiquary. — **an′ti·quar′i·an·ism** *n.*

an·ti·quar·y (an′ti·kwer′ē) *n. pl.* **·quar·ies** One who collects, deals in, or studies antiques or antiquities.

an·ti·quate (an′ti·kwāt) *v.t.* **·quat·ed, ·quat·ing 1.** To make old or out-of-date. **2.** To cause to look antique. [< L *antiquare* to make old] — **an′ti·qua′tion** *n.*

an·ti·quat·ed (an′ti·kwā′tid) *adj.* **1.** Out-of-date; old-fashioned; obsolete. **2.** Ancient; very old.

an·tique (an·tēk′) *adj.* **1.** Of or pertaining to ancient times. **2.** Of an earlier period: an *antique* chair. **3.** Old-fashioned; out-of-date. — *n.* **1.** The style of ancient art, or a specimen of it. **2.** Any old object, usually prized for its rarity, style or craft, etc. **3.** *Printing* A style of type with all the lines of nearly equal thickness. — *v.t.* **an·tiqued, an·ti·quing** To give the appearance of antiquity to. [< F < L *antiquus* ancient] — **an·tique′ly** *adv.* — **an·tique′ness** *n.*

an·tiq·ui·ty (an·tik′wə·tē) *n. pl.* **·ties 1.** The quality of being ancient. **2.** Ancient times, esp. before the Middle Ages. **3.** The people of ancient times collectively; the ancients. **4.** *Usually pl.* Ancient relics.

an·ti·Sem·i·tism (an′ti·sem′ə·tiz′əm, an′tī-) *n.* Opposition to, discrimination against, or intolerance of Jews, Jewish culture, etc. — **an′ti-Sem′ite** (-sem′īt) *n.* — **an′ti-Se·mit′ic** (-sə·mit′ik) *adj.* — **an′ti-Se·mit′i·cal·ly** *adv.*

an·ti·sep·sis (an′tə·sep′sis) *n.* The condition of being free of pathogenic bacteria; also, the method of obtaining this.

an·ti·sep·tic (an′tə·sep′tik) *adj.* **1.** Of, pertaining to, or used in antisepsis. **2.** Preventing or counteracting infection. Also **an′ti·sep′ti·cal.** — *n.* Any antiseptic substance. [< ANTI- + Gk. *sēpsis* putrefaction] — **an′ti·sep′ti·cal·ly** *adv.*

an·ti·se·rum (an′ti·sir′əm) *n.* A serum that provides immunity from specific diseases.

an·ti·slav·er·y (an′ti·slā′vər·ē, -slāv′rē, an′tī-) *adj.* Opposed to human slavery.

an·ti·so·cial (an′ti·sō′shəl, an′tī-) *adj.* **1.** Unsociable. **2.** Opposed to or disruptive of society or the general good.

an·ti·spas·mod·ic (an′ti·spaz·mod′ik) *Med. adj.* Relieving or checking spasms. — *n.* An antispasmodic agent.

an·tis·tro·phe (an·tis′trə·fē) *n.* In ancient Greek drama, the verses sung by the chorus while returning from left to right, in answer to the previous strophe. [< L < Gk. < *anti-* against, opposite + *strephein* to turn] — **an·ti·stroph·ic** (an′ti·strof′ik) *adj.*

an·ti·tank (an′ti·tangk′) *adj. Mil.* Designed to combat tanks and other armored vehicles: *antitank* guns. Abbr. *AT*

an·tith·e·sis (an·tith′ə·sis) *n. pl.* **·ses** (-sēz) **1.** The balancing of two contrasted words, ideas, or phrases against each other. Example: *My prayers go up; my thoughts remain below.* **2.** Opposition; contrast: the *antithesis* of peace and war. **3.** The direct opposite. **4.** One of the three categories found in the dialectic systems of Hegel, Marx, etc. [< L < Gk. < *anti-* against + *tithenai* to place] — **an·ti·thet·i·cal** (an′tə·thet′i·kəl) *adj.* — **an′ti·thet′i·cal·ly** *adv.*

an·ti·tox·in (an′ti·tok′sin) *n. Biochem.* A substance formed in the living tissues of an animal, that neutralizes a specific bacterial poison; also, serum containing this. Also **an′ti·tox′ine** (-tok′sin, -sēn). — **an′ti·tox′ic** *adj.*

an·ti·trade (an′ti·trād′) *n.* One of the upper air currents in the tropics, moving contrary to the trade winds.

an·ti·trust (an′ti·trust′) *adj.* Pertaining to the regulation of or opposition to trusts, cartels, monopolies, etc.

ant·ler (ant′lər) *n. Usu. pl.* Either of the branched horns on the head of members of the deer family. [< OF < L *ante-* before + *oculus* eye] — **ant′lered** *adj.*

ant lion An insect resembling a dragonfly, whose larva preys on ants and other insects.

an·to·nym (an′tə·nim) *n.* A word that is the opposite of another in meaning: opposed to *synonym.* Abbr. *ant.* [< Gk. < *anti-* opposite + *onoma, onyma* name]

an·trum (an′trəm) *n. pl.* **·tra** (-trə) *Anat.* A cavity, usually in a bone; esp., the cavity in the upper jaw opening into the nose. [< L < Gk. *antron* cave]

a·nus (ā′nəs) *n. Anat.* The excretory opening at the lower extremity of the alimentary canal. [< L, orig., a ring]

an·vil (an′vil, -vəl) *n.* **1.** A heavy block of iron or steel on which metal may be forged. **2.** *Anat.* The incus. — *v.t. & v.i.* **an·viled** or **·villed, an·vil·ing** or **·vil·ling** To work at or shape on an anvil. [OE *anfilt*]

anx·i·e·ty (ang·zī′ə·tē) *n. pl.* **·ties 1.** Disturbance of mind regarding some uncertain event; misgiving; worry. **2.** Strained or solicitous desire; eagerness. **3.** *Psychiatry* A tense emotional state characterized by fear and apprehension without apparent cause.

DOUBLE-BEAK ANVIL
a Rounded beak. *b* Flat beak. *c* Hardy hole, cutter, or chisel hole.

anx·ious (angk′shəs, ang′-) *adj.* **1.** Troubled in mind respecting some uncertain matter. **2.** Causing anxiety; distressing: an *anxious* matter. **3.** Intent; eagerly desirous: with *for* or the infinitive. [< L *angere* to choke, distress] — **anx′ious·ly** *adv.* — **anx′ious·ness** *n.*

an·y (en′ē) *adj.* **1.** One, no matter which; a or an, or (plural) some: Have we *any* choice? **2.** Some, however much or little: Did he eat *any* supper? **3.** Every: *Any* fool knows that. — *pron.* One or more persons or things of a number: Have *any* of the guests arrived? — *adv.* At all; to any extent: Are they *any* nearer? [OE *ǣnig* < *ān* one]

an·y·bod·y (en′i·bod′ē, -bud′ē) *pron.* Any person whatever; anyone. — *n. pl.* **·bod·ies** A person of importance.

an·y·how (en′i·hou′) *adv.* **1.** In any way whatever; by any means. **2.** Notwithstanding; in any case. **3.** Carelessly.

an·y·one (en′i·wun′, -wən) *pron.* Any person. ◆ **any one, anyone** *Any one* is used to distinguish one person from others in the same group or class: *Any one* of these men may be guilty. *Anyone* (indefinite pronoun) means any person at all.

an·y·thing (en′i·thing′) *pron.* Any thing, event, or matter whatever. — *n.* A thing of any kind. — *adv.* To any degree; in any way: now only in the expression **anything like.**

anything but By no means; far from: *anything but* safe.

an·y·way (en′i·wā′) *adv.* **1.** In any manner. **2.** Nevertheless; anyhow. **3.** Carelessly; haphazardly.

an·y·where (en′i·hwâr′) *adv.* In, at, or to any place.

an·y·wise (en′i·wīz′) *adv.* In any manner.

An·zac (an′zak) *adj.* Pertaining to the Australian and New Zealand Army Corps during World War I. — *n.* Any soldier from Australia or New Zealand.

A-one (ā′wun′) *adj. Informal* Excellent. Also **A-1.**

a·or·ta (ā·ôr′tə) *n. pl.* **·tas** or **·tae** (-tē) *Anat.* The great artery springing from the left ventricle of the heart and forming the main arterial trunk that distributes blood to all of the body except the lungs. [< NL < Gk. < *aeirein* to raise, heave] — **a·or′tal, a·or′tic** *adj.*

ap-¹ Assimilated var. of AD-.

ap-² Var. of APO-.

a·pace (ə·pās′) *adv.* Rapidly; quickly. [< A-¹ on + PACE]

a·pache (ə·päsh′, ə·pash′; *Fr.* à·pàsh′) *n.* A ruffian or gangster of Paris. [< F < APACHE]

A·pach·e (ə·pach′ē) *n. pl.* **A·pach·es** or **A·pach·e** One of a group of Indians, inhabiting the southern and SW U.S.

a·part (ə·pärt′) *adv.* **1.** Separated; not together. **2.** One from another. **3.** Separately for some use or purpose. **4.** Independently in logic or thought: Let us view this matter *apart.* **5.** Aside; to one side. **6.** In pieces or to pieces: The ship broke *apart.* — *adj.* Separate; distinct. [< MF < L *ad* to + *pars, partis* part]

a·part·heid (ə·pärt′hīt) *n.* In the Republic of South Africa, the official policy of political, social, and economic discrimination and segregation enforced against nonwhites. [< Afrikaans, apartness, separation]

a·part·ment (ə·pärt′mənt) *n.* **1.** Any of several suites of rooms in a building, each equipped for housekeeping; a flat. **2.** A room. Abbr. **apt.** (pl. **apts.**). [< F < Ital., ult. < L *ad* to + *pars, partis* part]

apartment house *U.S.* A multiple-dwelling building divided into a number of apartments.

ap·a·thet·ic (ap′ə·thet′ik) *adj.* **1.** Lacking emotion. **2.** Indifferent; unconcerned. Also **ap′a·thet′i·cal.** [< APATHY, on analogy with *sympathetic*] — **ap′a·thet′i·cal·ly** *adv.*

ap·a·thy (ap′ə·thē) *n. pl.* **·thies** **1.** Lack of emotion. **2.** Indifference. [< L < Gk. < *a-* without + *pathos* feeling] — **Syn. 1, 2.** *Apathy* may refer to a habitual lack of feeling, or it may be used in the sense of *indifference* to describe a temporary lack of interest caused by depression, sorrow, ignorance, despair, etc. *Insensibility* is a lack of feeling for other persons.

ape (āp) *n.* **1.** A large, tailless, Old World primate, as a gorilla or chimpanzee. **2.** Loosely, any monkey. **3.** A mimic. — *v.t.* **aped, ap·ing** To imitate; mimic. [OE *apa*]

a·pe·ri·ent (ə·pir′ē·ənt) *Med. adj.* Laxative. — *n.* A gentle purgative. Also **a·per·i·tive** (ə·per′ə·tiv). [< L *aperire* to open]

a·pé·ri·tif (à·pā·rē·tēf′) *n. French* A drink of alcoholic liquor or wine taken as an appetizer.

ap·er·ture (ap′ər·chŏŏr, -chər) *n.* **1.** An opening; orifice. **2.** *Optics* An opening, often adjustable in diameter, through which light enters the lens of a camera, etc. [< L *aperire* to open] — **ap′er·tur·al** *adj.* — **ap′er·tured** *adj.*

a·pex (ā′peks) *n. pl.* **a·pex·es** or **ap·i·ces** (ap′ə·sēz, ā′pə-) **1.** The highest point; tip; top. **2.** *Geom.* The vertex of an angle. **3.** Climax. [< L]

aph- Var. of APO-.

a·pha·sia (ə·fā′zhə, -zhē·ə) *n. Pathol.* Any partial or total loss of the power of articulate speech, usu. due to a brain lesion. [< NL < Gk. < *a-* not + *phanai* to speak] — **a·pha·sic** (ə·fā′zik, -sik), **a·pha·si·ac** (ə·fā′zē·ak) *adj. & n.*

a·phe·li·on (ə·fē′lē·ən) *n. pl.* **·li·a** (-lē·ə) *Astron.* The point in an orbit, as of a planet, farthest from the sun: opposed to *perihelion.* [< APH- (APO-) away from + Gk. *hēlios* sun] — **a·phe′li·an** (-ən) *adj.*

APHELION
P Perihelion.
S Sun. A Aphelion.

a·phid (ā′fid, af′id) *n.* A small, juice-sucking insect, injurious to plants: also called *plant louse.* Also **a′phis.** [Origin uncertain] — **a·phid·i·an** (ə·fid′ē·ən) *adj.*

aph·o·rism (af′ə·riz′əm) *n.* **1.** A brief statement of a truth or principle. **2.** A proverb; maxim. [< MF < Med.L < Gk. < *apo-* from + *horizein* to divide] — **aph′o·rist** *n.* — **aph′o·ris·tic** (af′ə·ris′tik) or **·i·cal** *adj.* — **aph′o·ris′ti·cal·ly** *adv.*

aph·ro·dis·i·ac (af′rə·diz′ē·ak) *adj.* Arousing or increasing sexual desire or potency. — *n.* An aphrodisiac drug, food, etc. [< Gk. *aphrodisiakos* < *Aphrodītē*, goddess of love]

Aph·ro·di·te (af′rə·dī′tē) *n.* In Greek mythology, the goddess of love and beauty, the daughter of Zeus: identified with the Roman *Venus.* [< Gk. *Aphrodītē* the foam-born]

a·pi·ar·i·an (ā′pē·âr′ē·ən) *adj.* Of or relating to bees or the keeping of bees. — *n.* An apiarist.

a·pi·a·rist (ā′pē·ər·ist) *n.* A beekeeper.

a·pi·a·ry (ā′pē·er′ē) *n. pl.* **·ar·ies** A place where bees are kept; a set of hives, bees, etc. [< L *apiarium* < *apis* bee]

ap·i·cal (ap′i·kəl, ā′pi-) *adj.* Situated at or belonging to the apex or top. [< L *apex, apicis* tip]

ap·i·ces (ap′ə·sēz, ā′pə-) Alternative plural of APEX.

a·pi·cul·ture (ā′pi·kul′chər) *n.* The raising and care of bees. [< L *apis* bee + CULTURE] — **a′pi·cul′tur·ist** *n.*

a·piece (ə·pēs′) *adv.* For or to each one; each.

ap·ish (ā′pish) *adj.* Like an ape; servilely imitative; foolish and tricky. — **ap′ish·ly** *adv.* — **ap′ish·ness** *n.*

a·plomb (ə·plom′, *Fr.* à·plôn′) *n.* Assurance; self-confidence. [< F < *à* according to + *plomb* plumb bob]

apo- *prefix* Off; from; away: *apostasy.* Also **ap-** before vowels; **aph-** before an aspirate. [< Gk. < *apo* from, off]

a·poc·a·lypse (ə·pok′ə·lips) *n.* A prophecy or revelation. [< L < Gk. < *apo-* from + *kalyptein* to cover]

A·poc·a·lypse (ə·pok′ə·lips) The book of Revelaton, the last book of the New Testament. Abbr. *Apoc.*

a·poc·a·lyp·tic (ə·pok′ə·lip′tik) *adj.* **1.** Of or of the nature of a revelation. **2.** Pertaining to the Apocalypse. Also **a·poc′a·lyp′ti·cal.** — **a·poc′a·lyp′ti·cal·ly** *adv.*

a·poc·o·pe (ə·pok′ə·pē) *n.* A cutting off or elision of the last sound or syllable of a word. [< Gk. *apokopē* < *apokoptein* to cut off < *apo-* off + *koptein* to cut]

A·poc·ry·pha (ə·pok′rə·fə) *n.pl.* (*often construed as sing.*) Those books of the Septuagint included in the Vulgate but rejected by Protestants as uncanonical because not in the Hebrew Scriptures. [< LL < Gk. *apokryphos* hidden]

a·poc·ry·phal (ə·pok′rə·fəl) *adj.* Having little or no authenticity. — **a·poc′ry·phal·ly** *adv.* — **a·poc′ry·phal·ness** *n.*

ap·o·gee (ap′ə·jē) *n.* **1.** *Astron.* That point in the orbit of a celestial body which is farthest from the earth: opposed to *perigee.* **2.** The highest point; climax. [< MF < L < Gk. < *apo-* away from + *gē, gaia* earth] — **ap·o·ge·al** (ap′ə·jē′əl), **ap′o·ge′an** *adj.*

APOGEE
P Moon at perigee. E Earth.
A Moon at apogee.

A·pol·lo (ə·pol′ō) In Greek and Roman mythology, the god of music, poetry, prophecy, and medicine, and later of the sun. — *n.* Any handsome young man.

a·pol·o·get·ic (ə·pol′ə·jet′ik) *adj.* **1.** Of the nature of an apology; excusing. **2.** Defending or explaining. Also **a·pol′o·get′i·cal.** — *n.* An apology or defense. [< F < L < Gk. < *apologia* a speech in defense] — **a·pol′o·get′i·cal·ly** *adv.*

a·pol·o·get·ics (ə·pol′ə·jet′iks) *n.pl.* (*construed as sing.*) The branch of theology that defends Christianity.

a·pol·o·gist (ə·pol′ə·jist) *n.* One who argues for a cause.

a·pol·o·gize (ə·pol′ə·jīz) *v.i.* **·gized, ·giz·ing** **1.** To offer an excuse; acknowledge, with regret, any offense. **2.** To make a formal defense in speech or writing. — **a·pol′o·giz′er** *n.*

ap·o·logue (ap′ə·lôg, -log) *n.* A fable or tale having a moral. Also **ap′o·log.** [< L < Gk. < *apo-* from + *logos* speech]

a·pol·o·gy (ə·pol′ə·jē) *n. pl.* **·gies** **1.** A statement or explanation expressing regret for some error or offense. **2.** A poor substitute. [< L < Gk. *apologia* a speech in defense]

ap·o·lune (ap′ə·loōn) *n.* In the orbit of a lunar satellite, the point farthest from the moon. [< *apo-* away from + Fr. *lune* moon]

ap·o·plec·tic (ap′ə·plek′tik) *adj.* Pertaining to, affected with, or tending toward apoplexy. Also **ap′o·plec′ti·cal.** — *n.* A person subject to apoplexy.

ap·o·plex·y (ap′ə·plek′sē) *n. Pathol.* Sudden paralysis and loss of sensation caused by a bloodclot or hemorrhage in the brain. [< Gk. < *apo-* from, off + *plēssein* to strike]

a·port (ə·pôrt′, ə·pōrt′) *adv. Naut.* On or toward the port side.

a·pos·ta·sy (ə·pos′tə·sē) *n. pl.* **·sies** Desertion of one's faith, party, or principles. Also **a·pos′ta·cy.** [< L < Gk. < *apo-* away + *stasis* a standing] — **a·pos′tate** *adj. & n.*

a·pos·ta·tize (ə·pos′tə·tīz) *v.i.* **·tized, ·tiz·ing** To forsake one's faith or principles; become an apostate.

a pos·te·ri·o·ri (ā′ pos·tir′ē·ôr′ī, -ō′rī) **1.** *Logic* Reasoning from facts to principles or from effect to cause. **2.** Inductive; empirical. [< L, from the later]

a·pos·tle (ə·pos′əl) *n.* **1.** One of the twelve disciples originally commissioned by Christ to preach the gospel (*Matt.* x 2–4). **2.** One of a class of missionaries in the early church (*I Cor.* xii 28). **3.** A Christian missionary who first evangelizes a nation or place. **4.** The earliest or foremost advocate of a cause. [OE *apostol* < L < Gk. a messenger]

Apostles' Creed A traditional and still widely accepted Christian confession of faith.

a·pos·to·late (ə·pos′tə·lit, -lāt) *n.* The dignity or office of an apostle. Also **a·pos′tle·ship.**

ap·os·tol·ic (ap′ə·stol′ik) *adj.* **1.** Of or pertaining to an apostle, the apostles, or their times. **2.** According to the doctrine or practice of the apostles. **3.** *Often cap.* Papal. Also **ap′os·tol′i·cal.**

Apostolic See **1.** The Church of Rome, regarded as having been founded by St. Peter. **2.** The papacy.

apostolic succession The transmission of authority from the apostles to bishops, claimed by various Christian churches.

---

a·pos·tro·phe[1] (ə·pos′trə·fē) *n.* A symbol (′) written above the line to mark the omission of a letter or letters from a word, to indicate the possessive case, and to denote certain plurals, as 5's, cross your t's. [< F < L < Gk. < *apo-* away + *strephein* to turn] — **ap·os·troph·ic** (ap′ə·strof′ik) *adj.*

a·pos·tro·phe[2] (ə·pos′trə·fē) *n.* A digression from a discourse; esp., a turning aside to speak to an absent person. — **ap·os·troph·ic** (ap′ə·strof′ik) *adj.*

a·pos·tro·phize[1] (ə·pos′trə·fīz) *v.t. & v.i.* **·phized, ·phiz·ing** To shorten (a word) by the omission of a letter or letters.

a·pos·tro·phize[2] (ə·pos′trə·fīz) *v.t. & v.i.* **·phized, ·phiz·ing** To speak or write an apostrophe (to).

apothecaries′ measure A system of liquid measure used in pharmacy. See table inside back cover. *Abbr. ap.*

apothecaries′ weight A system of weights used in pharmacy. See table inside back cover. *Abbr. ap.*

a·poth·e·car·y (ə·poth′ə·ker′ē) *n. pl.* **·car·ies** A druggist. [< OF < L < Gk. < *apo-* away + *tithenai* to put]

ap·o·thegm (ap′ə·them) *n.* A terse, instructive, practical saying; maxim: also spelled *apophthegm.* [< Gk. < *apo-* from + *phthengesthai* to utter] — **ap·o·theg·mat·ic** (ap′ə·theg·mat′ik) or **·i·cal** *adj.*

a·poth·e·o·sis (ə·poth′ē·ō′sis, ap′ə·thē′ə·sis) *n. pl.* **·ses** (-sēz) **1.** Exaltation to divine rank; deification. **2.** Supreme exaltation of any person, principle, etc. [< L < Gk. < *apo-* from + *theos* a god]

a·poth·e·o·size (ə·poth′ē·ə·sīz′, ap′ə·thē′ə·sīz) *v.t.* **·sized, ·siz·ing 1.** To deify. **2.** To glorify; exalt.

ap·pal (ə·pôl′) *v.t.* **·palled, ·pal·ling** *Brit.* Appall.

ap·pall (ə·pôl′) *v.t.* To fill with dismay or horror; shock: also, *Brit., appal.* [< OF *apallir* to pale < L *pallidus*]

ap·pal·ling (ə·pô′ling) *adj.* Causing dismay or terror; frightful. — **ap·pal′ling·ly** *adv.*

ap·pa·ra·tus (ap′ə·rā′təs, -rat′əs) *n. pl.* **·tus** or (rarely) **·tus·es 1.** A device, machine, or assembly of tools, instruments, etc., for a particular purpose. **2.** *Physiol.* Those organs and parts of the body by means of which natural processes are carried on. [< L < *ad-* to + *parare* to prepare]

ap·par·el (ə·par′əl) *n.* **1.** Clothing; attire. **2.** Equipment or furnishings, especially for a ship. — *v.t.* **·eled** or **·elled, ·el·ing** or **·el·ling.** To clothe; dress. [< OF *apareiller* to prepare, ult. < L *ad-* to + *par* equal]

ap·par·ent (ə·par′ənt, ə·pâr′-) *adj.* **1.** Readily perceived by the mind; evident; obvious. **2.** Easily seen; visible. **3.** Seeming, in distinction from real or actual. [< OF < L *apparere*] — **ap·par′ent·ness** *n.*

ap·par·ent·ly (ə·par′ənt·lē, ə·pâr′-) *adv.* **1.** Obviously; plainly. **2.** Seemingly.

ap·pa·ri·tion (ap′ə·rish′ən) *n.* **1.** A visual appearance of a disembodied spirit; phantom; ghost. **2.** Anything that appears, esp. if remarkable or startling. [< MF < L *apparitio, -onis* < *apparere* to appear] — **ap′pa·ri′tion·al** *adj.*

ap·peal (ə·pēl′) *n.* **1.** An earnest entreaty for aid, sympathy, or the like; prayer; supplication. **2.** The quality of being attractive. **3.** A resort to some higher power or final means, for sanction, proof, or aid. **4.** *Law* **a** The carrying of a case from a lower to a higher tribunal for a rehearing. **b** A case so carried. — *v.t.* **1.** *Law* To refer or remove, as a case, to a higher court. — *v.i.* **2.** To make an earnest supplication or request, as for sympathy, corroboration, or aid. **3.** To awaken a favorable response; be interesting. **4.** *Law* To remove a case, or request that a case be moved, to a higher court. **5.** To resort or have recourse: with *to.* [< OF < L *appellare* to accost, call upon] — **ap·peal′a·ble** *adj.* — **ap·peal′er** *n.* — **ap·peal′ing·ly** *adv.*

ap·pear (ə·pir′) *v.i.* **1.** To come into view; become visible. **2.** To seem, or seem likely. **3.** To be clear to the mind; be obvious. **4.** To come before the public; also, to be published, as a book. **5.** *Law* To come formally into court. [< OF < L < *ad-* to + *parere* to come forth, appear]

ap·pear·ance (ə·pir′əns) *n.* **1.** The act of appearing or coming into view. **2.** External or physical aspect; presence: a commanding *appearance.* **3.** *pl.* Circumstances or indications: *Appearances* are against him. **4.** Outward show; pretense. **5.** An apparition; phenomenon.

ap·pease (ə·pēz′) *v.t.* **·peased, ·peas·ing 1.** To placate by making concessions or yielding to demands. **2.** To satisfy or allay. [< OF *apaisier* < L *pax*] — **ap·peas′a·ble** *adj.* — **ap·peas′a·bly** *adv.* — **ap·peas′er** *n.* — **ap·peas′ing·ly** *adv.*

ap·pease·ment (ə·pēz′mənt) *n.* **1.** The act of appeasing or being appeased. **2.** The policy of making concessions to potential aggressors in order to maintain peace.

ap·pel·lant (ə·pel′ənt) *adj. Law* Of or pertaining to an appeal; appellate. — *n.* One who appeals, in any sense.

ap·pel·late (ə·pel′it) *adj. Law* Pertaining to or having jurisdiction of appeals: an *appellate court.*

ap·pel·la·tion (ap′ə·lā′shən) *n.* **1.** A name or title. **2.** The act of calling or naming.

ap·pel·la·tive (ə·pel′ə·tiv) *adj.* **1.** Serving to designate or name. **2.** *Gram.* Denoting a class: said of common nouns. — *n.* **1.** A title; appellation. **2.** A common noun. — **ap·pel′la·tive·ly** *adv.* — **ap·pel′la·tive·ness** *n.*

ap·pend (ə·pend′) *v.t.* **1.** To add, as something subordinate or supplemental. **2.** To hang or attach: to *append* a seal. — **Syn.** See ADD. [< L < *ad-* to + *pendere* to hang]

ap·pend·age (ə·pen′dij) *n.* **1.** Anything appended. **2.** *Zool.* Any part joined to or diverging from the axial trunk, as a limb.

ap·pen·dant (ə·pen′dənt) *adj.* **1.** Attached; adjunct. **2.** Hanging attached. **3.** Attendant; consequent. — *n.* Something appended or attached. Also **ap·pen′dent.**

ap·pen·dec·to·my (ap′ən·dek′tə·mē) *n. pl.* **·mies** *Surg.* The removal of the vermiform appendix.

ap·pen·di·ces (ə·pen′də·sēz) Alternative plural of APPENDIX.

ap·pen·di·ci·tis (ə·pen′də·sī′tis) *n. Pathol.* Inflammation of the vermiform appendix.

ap·pen·dix (ə·pen′diks) *n. pl.* **·dix·es** or **·di·ces** (-də·sēz) **1.** An addition or appendage, as of supplementary matter at the end of a book. **2.** *Anat.* **a** The vermiform appendix. **b** An outgrowth of an organ. [< L, an appendage]

ap·per·cep·tion (ap′ər·sep′shən) *n. Psychol.* Conscious perception. [< F *apercevoir* to see, recognize] — **ap′per·cep′tive** *adj.*

ap·per·tain (ap′ər·tān′) *v.i.* To pertain or belong as by custom, function, nature, right, or fitness; relate: with *to.* [< OF < LL < L *ad-* to + *pertinere* to reach to]

ap·pe·tence (ap′ə·təns) *n.* **1.** Strong craving or propensity. **2.** Instinct or tendency. Also **ap′pe·ten·cy.** [< L < *appetere* to seek] — **ap′pe·tent** *adj.*

ap·pe·tite (ap′ə·tīt) *n.* **1.** A desire for food or drink. **2.** Any physical craving or natural desire. **3.** A strong liking. [< OF < L < *ad-* to + *petere* to seek] — **ap′pe·ti′tive** *adj.*

ap·pe·tiz·er (ap′ə·tī′zər) *n.* Anything that excites appetite or gives relish before a meal. Also *Brit.* **ap′pe·tis·er.**

ap·pe·tiz·ing (ap′ə·tī′zing) *adj.* Stimulating or tempting to the appetite. Also *Brit.* **ap′pe·tis·ing.** [Orig. ppr. of rare *appetize*] — **ap′pe·tiz′ing·ly** *adv.*

ap·plaud (ə·plôd′) *v.t. & v.i.* **1.** To express approval (of) by clapping the hands. **2.** To commend; praise. — **Syn.** See PRAISE. [< L < *ad-* to + *plaudere* to clap hands, strike] — **ap·plaud′er** *n.* — **ap·plaud′ing·ly** *adv.*

ap·plause (ə·plôz′) *n.* Approval or commendation, esp. as shown by clapping the hands, shouting, etc. — **ap·plau·sive** (ə·plô′siv) *adj.* — **ap·plau′sive·ly** *adv.*

ap·ple (ap′əl) *n.* **1.** The fleshy, edible fruit of a widely distributed tree of the rose family, usually of a roundish or conical shape. **2.** The similar fruit of several allied species, as the crab apple. **3.** One of several fruits or plants with little or no resemblance to the apple. [OE *æppel*]

apple cart A handcart used for peddling apples, etc. — **to upset the apple cart** To ruin someone's plans.

ap·ple·jack (ap′əl·jak′) *n.* Brandy made from cider.

ap·ple·sauce (ap′əl·sôs′) *n.* **1.** Apples stewed to a pulp. **2.** *U.S. Slang* Nonsense; bunk.

Ap·ple·ton layer (ap′əl·tən) A region of the ionosphere about 150 miles above sea level that acts as a reflector of certain frequencies of radio waves: also called *F layer.* [after Sir E. V. *Appleton,* born 1892, English physicist.]

ap·pli·ance (ə·plī′əns) *n.* A device or instrument; esp., an electrically powered device for household work.

ap·pli·ca·ble (ap′li·kə·bəl, ə·plik′ə-) *adj.* Capable of or suitable for application; relevant; fitting. [< L *applicare* to apply + -ABLE] — **ap′pli·ca·bil′i·ty, ap′pli·ca·ble·ness** *n.* — **ap′pli·ca·bly** *adv.*

ap·pli·cant (ap′li·kənt) *n.* One who applies, as for a job.

ap·pli·ca·tion (ap′li·kā′shən) *n.* **1.** The act of applying. **2.** That which is applied, especially as a remedial agent. **3.** Employment for a special purpose or use. **4.** Capacity of being used; relevance. **5.** Close attention. **6.** A formal, written request, esp. for employment.

ap·pli·ca·tive (ap′li·kā′tiv) *adj.* Applicatory.

ap·pli·ca·tor (ap′li·kā′tər) *n.* An instrument or utensil for applying medication, etc.

ap·pli·ca·to·ry (ap′li·kə·tôr′ē, -tō′rē) *adj.* Fit for application; practical; applicative.

ap·plied (ə·plīd′) *adj.* Put in practice; utilized: opposed to *abstract, theoretical,* or *pure: applied* science.

ap·pli·qué (ap′li·kā′) *adj.* Applied: said of ornaments, as in needlework, sewn to the surface of another. — *n.* Decoration or ornaments so applied. — *v.t.* **·quéd** (-kād′), **·qué·ing** (-kā′ing) To decorate by appliqué work. [< F]

ap·ply (ə·plī′) *v.* **·plied, ·ply·ing** *v.t.* **1.** To bring into contact with something; put on or to. **2.** To devote or put to a particular use: to *apply* steam to navigation. **3.** To connect, as an epithet, with a particular person or thing. **4.** To give (oneself) wholly to; devote. — *v.i.* **5.** To make a request or petition; ask: with *for.* **6.** To be relevant: This order *applies* to all. [< OF < L < *ad-* to + *plicare* to fold]

ap·point (ə·point′) *v.t.* **1.** To name or select, as a person, a time and place, etc. **2.** To ordain, as by decree; command; prescribe. **3.** To fit out; equip: used chiefly in combination in the past participle: a *well-appointed* yacht. [< OF < LL < L *ad-* to + *punctum* a point]

ap·point·ee (ə·poin′tē′) *n.* One appointed to an office.

ap·poin·tive (ə·poin′tiv) *adj.* Filled by appointment.

ap·point·ment (ə·point′mənt) *n.* **1.** The act of appointing or placing in office. **2.** A position held by someone appointed. **3.** An agreement to meet someone or to be somewhere at a specified time; engagement. **4.** *Usually pl.* Furniture.

Ap·po·mat·tox (ap′ə·mat′əks) A village in central Virginia. At **Appomattox Court House** Lee surrendered to Grant, April 9, 1865, virtually ending the Civil War.

ap·por·tion (ə·pôr′shən, ə·pōr′-) *v.t.* To divide and assign proportionally; allot. [< OF < *a-* to + *portionner* to divide] — **ap·por′tion·ment** *n.*

ap·pose (ə·pōz′) *v.t.* **·posed, ·pos·ing 1.** To apply or put, as one thing to another: with *to:* to *appose* a seal to a document. **2.** To arrange side by side. [< OF < *a-* to + *poser* to put]

ap·po·site (ap′ə·zit) *adj.* Fit for or appropriate. [< L *apponere* to put near to] — **ap′po·site·ly** *adv.* — **ap′po·site·ness** *n.*

ap·po·si·tion (ap′ə·zish′ən) *n.* **1.** *Gram.* **a** The placing of one word beside another so that the second adds to or explains the first, and both have the same grammatical form, as *John, president* of the class. **b** The syntactical relationship between such words. **2.** An apposing or being apposed. — **ap′po·si′tion·al** *adj.* — **ap′po·si′tion·al·ly** *adv.*

ap·pos·i·tive (ə·poz′ə·tiv) *adj.* Of or in apposition. — *n.* A word or phrase in apposition. — **ap·pos′i·tive·ly** *adv.*

ap·prais·al (ə·prā′zəl) *n.* **1.** An appraising. **2.** An official valuation, as for sale, taxation, etc. Also **ap·praise′ment.**

ap·praise (ə·prāz′) *v.t.* **·praised, ·prais·ing 1.** To make an official valuation of; set a price or value on. **2.** To estimate the amount, quality, or worth of; judge. — **ap·prais′a·ble** *adj.* — **ap·prais′er** *n.*
— **Syn. 1.** evaluate, value, assess, assay.

ap·pre·ci·a·ble (ə·prē′shē·ə·bəl, -shə·bəl) *adj.* Capable of being valued or estimated. — **ap·pre′ci·a·bly** *adv.*

ap·pre·ci·ate (ə·prē′shē·āt) *v.* **·at·ed, ·at·ing** *v.t.* **1.** To be fully aware of the value, importance, magnitude, etc., of. **2.** To esteem adequately or highly. **3.** To be keenly sensible of or sensitive to. **4.** To show gratitude for. **5.** To increase the price or value of. **6.** To estimate the worth of. — *v.i.* **7.** To rise in value. [< LL < *ad-* to + *pretium* price] — **ap·pre′ci·a′tor** *n.*

ap·pre·ci·a·tion (ə·prē′shē·ā′shən) *n.* **1.** The act of placing an estimate on persons or things; judgment. **2.** Perception or awareness, as of qualities, values, etc. **3.** Gratitude. **4.** Increase in value.

ap·pre·ci·a·tive (ə·prē′shē·ā′tiv, -shə·tiv) *adj.* Capable of showing appreciation; manifesting appreciation. — **ap·pre′ci·a·tive·ly** *adv.* — **ap·pre′ci·a·tive·ness** *n.*

ap·pre·ci·a·to·ry (ə·prē′shē·ə·tôr′ē, -tō′rē, -shə-) *adj.* Appreciative. — **ap·pre′ci·a·to′ri·ly** *adv.*

ap·pre·hend (ap′rə·hend) *v.t.* **1.** To lay hold of or grasp mentally; understand; perceive. **2.** To expect with anxious foreboding; dread. **3.** To arrest; take into custody. **4.** *Obs.* To take hold of. — *v.i.* **5.** To understand. [< L < *ad-* to + *prehendere* to seize] — **ap′pre·hend′er** *n.*
— **Syn. 1.** To *apprehend* is merely to perceive, while to *comprehend* something is to grasp its meaning in its entirety. *Understand* is close in meaning to *comprehend*, but can also mean to have insight into or sympathy with.

ap·pre·hen·si·ble (ap′rə·hen′sə·bəl) *adj.* Capable of being apprehended. — **ap′pre·hen′si·bil′i·ty** *n.*

ap·pre·hen·sion (ap′rə·hen′shən) *n.* **1.** Foreboding; misgiving. **2.** The power of apprehending; understanding. **3.** An estimate; opinion. **4.** Arrest; capture. — **Syn.** See KNOWLEDGE.

ap·pre·hen·sive (ap′rə·hen′siv) *adj.* **1.** Fearful; anxious. **2.** Quick to apprehend or perceive. — **ap′pre·hen′sive·ly** *adv.* — **ap′pre·hen′sive·ness** *n.*

ap·pren·tice (ə·pren′tis) *n.* **1.** One who is bound by a legal agreement to serve another for a fixed period of time in order to learn a trade or business. **2.** Any learner or beginner. — *v.t.* **·ticed, ·tic·ing** To bind or take on as an apprentice. [< OF < L *apprehendere* to comprehend] — **ap·pren′tice·ship** *n.*

ap·prise (ə·prīz′) *v.t.* **·prised, ·pris·ing** To notify, as of an event; inform. Also **ap·prize′.** [< F < L *apprehendere* to comprehend] — **ap·prise′ment** *n.* — **ap·pris′er** *n.*

ap·prize (ə·prīz′) *v.t.* **·prized, ·priz·ing 1.** To appraise. Also **ap·prise′.** [Prob. < OF < *a-* on, to + *prisier* to value]

ap·proach (ə·prōch′) *v.i.* **1.** To come near or nearer in time or space. — *v.t.* **2.** To come near or nearer to. **3.** To come close to; approximate. **4.** To make advances to; offer a proposal, or bribe to. **5.** To cause to move nearer. **6.** To start to deal with: to *approach* a problem. — *n.* **1.** The act of approaching; a coming near. **2.** An approxi-

mation; nearness. **3.** A way or means of approaching; access. **4.** A method of beginning or accomplishing something. **5.** *Often pl.* An overture of friendship, etc.; advance. **6.** In golf, a stroke made after the tee shot, intended to land the ball on the putting green. [< OF < LL < L *ad-* to + *prope* near] — **ap·proach′a·ble** *adj.* — **ap·proach′a·bil′i·ty, ap·proach′a·ble·ness** *n.*

ap·pro·ba·tion (ap′rə·bā′shən) *n.* **1.** The act of approving; approval. **2.** Sanction. — **ap·pro·ba′tive, ap·pro·ba·to·ry** (ə·prō′bə·tôr′ē, -tō′rē) *adj.*

ap·pro·pri·ate (*adj.* ə·prō′prē·it; *v.* ə·prō′prē·āt) *adj.* Suitable; fit; proper; relevant. — *v.t.* **·at·ed, ·at·ing 1.** To set apart for a particular use. **2.** To take for one's own use. [< L < *ad-* to + *proprius* one's own] — **ap·pro′pri·ate·ly** *adv.* — **ap·pro′pri·ate·ness** *n.* — **ap·pro′pri·a′tor** *n.*

ap·pro·pri·a·tion (ə·prō′prē·ā′shən) *n.* **1.** The act of appropriating or setting apart. **2.** Anything, esp. money, set apart for a special use. — **ap·pro′pri·a′tive** *adj.*

ap·prov·al (ə·prōō′vəl) *n.* **1.** The act of approving; approbation. **2.** Official consent; sanction. **3.** Favorable opinion; praise, commendation. — **on approval** For (a customer's) examination without obligation to purchase.

ap·prove (ə·prōōv′) *v.* **·proved, ·prov·ing 1.** To regard as worthy, proper, or right. **2.** To confirm formally or authoritatively; sanction; ratify. — *v.i.* **3.** To show or state approval: often with *of.* [< OF < L < *ad-* to + *probare* to approve, prove] — **ap·prov′a·ble** *adj.* — **ap·prov′er** *n.* — **ap·prov′ing·ly** *adv.*

ap·prox·i·mate (*adj.* ə·prok′sə·mit; *v.* ə·prok′sə·māt) *adj.* **1.** Nearly exact, accurate, or complete. **2.** Like; resembling. **3.** Near; close together. — *v.* **·mat·ed, ·mat·ing** *v.t.* **1.** To come close to, as in quality, degree, or quantity. **2.** To cause to come near. — *v.i.* **3.** To come near in quality, degree, etc. [< L < *ad-* to + *proximus*, superl. of *prope* near] — **ap·prox′i·mate·ly** *adv.*

ap·prox·i·ma·tion (ə·prok′sə·mā′shən) *n.* **1.** The act or result of approximating. **2.** *Math.* A result sufficiently exact for a specified purpose.

ap·pur·te·nance (ə·pûr′tə·nəns) *n.* **1.** Something attached to another, more important thing. **2.** *pl.* Apparatus. **3.** *Law* Something passing as an incident to a principal thing. [< AF, OF < LL < L *ad-* to + *pertinere* to reach to]

ap·pur·te·nant (ə·pûr′tə·nənt) *adj.* Appertaining or belonging, as by right; accessory. — *n.* An appurtenance.

a·pri·cot (ā′pri·kot, ap′ri·kot) *n.* **1.** A yellow fruit of a tree, similar to a small peach. **2.** The tree bearing this fruit. **3.** A pinkish yellow color. [Earlier *apricock* (prob. directly < Pg.) < F < Pg. or Sp. < L *praecoquus* early ripe]

A·pril (ā′prəl) *n.* The fourth month of the year, containing 30 days. [< L *Aprilis*]

April fool The victim of a practical joke on April 1, known as **April (or All) Fools' Day.**

a pri·o·ri (ā′ prī·ō′rī, ā′ prē·ôr′ē) **1.** *Logic* Proceeding from cause to effect, or from an assumption to its logical conclusion. **2.** Based on theory rather than on experience or examination. [< L, from what is before] — **a·pri·or·i·ty** (ā′prī·ôr′ə·tē, -or′-) *n.*

a·pron (ā′prən, ā′pərn) *n.* **1.** A garment of cloth, leather, etc., worn to protect or adorn the front of a person's clothes. **2.** *Mech.* Any of various overlapping pieces protecting parts of machines. **3.** *Engin.* **a** The platform or sill at the entrance to a dock. **b** The platform below a dam or in a sluiceway. **4.** *Aeron.* A hard-surfaced area in front of and around a hangar or aircraft shelter. **5.** The part of a theater stage in front of the curtain. — *v.t.* To cover or furnish with an apron. [< OF < L *mappa* cloth, napkin]

ap·ro·pos (ap′rə·pō′) *adj.* Suited to the occasion; opportune: an *apropos* remark. — *adv.* **1.** With reference or regard; in respect: with *of: apropos* of spring. **2.** To the purpose; pertinently. **3.** By the way; incidentally: used to introduce a remark. [< F < *à* to + *propos* purpose]

apse (aps) *n.* *Archit.* An extending portion of an edifice, usually semicircular with a half dome; especially, the eastern or altar end of a church. [< L *apsis* arch]

apt (apt) *adj.* **1.** Inclined; liable; likely. **2.** Quick to learn; intelligent. **3.** Pertinent; relevant. [< L *aptus* fitted, suited] — **apt′ly** *adv.* — **apt′ness** *n.*

ap·ter·ous (ap′tər·əs) *adj.* *Biol.* Without wings; wingless.

ap·ter·yx (ap′tər·iks) *n.* A New Zealand bird with undeveloped wings, now nearly extinct: also called *kiwi.* [< NL < Gk. *a-* without + *pteryx* wing]

ap·ti·tude (ap′tə·tōōd, -tyōōd) *n.* **1.** Natural or acquired ability or bent. **2.** Quickness of understanding; intelligence. **3.** The state or quality of being apt or fitting. [< F < LL < L *aptus* fitted, suited]

aq·ua (ak′wə, ä′kwə) *n.* *pl.* **aq·uae** (ak′wē, ä′kwē) or **aq·uas** Water: in Latin phrases applied to different kinds of water. — *adj. & n.* Bluish green. [< L]

aqua for·tis (fôr'tis) Commercial nitric acid.

Aq·ua-Lung (ak'wə·lung') n. A scuba: a trade name. Also **aq'ua·lung'.**

aq·ua·ma·rine (ak'wə·mə·rēn') n. 1. A sea-green variety of precious beryl. 2. A bluish green color. — adj. Bluish green. [< L aqua marina sea water]

aq·ua·naut (ak'wə·nôt) n. One who is trained to live and work underwater over a period of time. [< L aqua water + -naut (< Gk. nautēs sailor), after aeronaut, astronaut]

aq·ua·plane (ak'wə·plān) n. A board on which one stands while being towed by a motorboat. — v.i. **·planed, ·plan·ing** To ride an aquaplane. [< L aqua water + PLANE⁴]

aqua re·gi·a (rē'jē·ə) A mixture of nitric and hydrochloric acid, a solvent for gold and platinum. [< L, royal water]

a·quar·i·um (ə·kwâr'ē·əm) n. pl. **a·quar·i·ums** or **a·quar·i·a** (ə·kwâr'ē·ə) 1. A tank, pond, or the like for the exhibition or study of aquatic animals or plants. 2. A public building containing such an exhibition. [< L aqua water]

A·quar·i·us (ə·kwâr'ē·əs) n. A constellation, the Water Bearer; also, a sign of the zodiac. See ZODIAC. [< L]

a·quat·ic (ə·kwat'ik, ə·kwot'-) adj. 1. Living or growing in or near water. 2. Performed on or in water. — n. An aquatic animal or plant. [< L aqua water]

aq·ua·tint (ak'wə·tint') n. 1. A technique of engraving by treating the surface of a copper plate with an acid to give the effect of a water color. 2. Such an engraving. — v.t. To etch by aquatint. [< F < Ital. < L aqua tincta]

aqua vi·tae (vī'tē) 1. Alcohol. 2. Whisky; brandy. [< L]

aq·ue·duct (ak'wə·dukt) n. 1. A water conduit, esp. one for supplying water to a community from a distance. 2. A structure supporting a canal carried across a river or over low ground. [< L aqua water + ducere to lead]

a·que·ous (ā'kwē·əs, ak'wē-) adj. 1. Of or like water; watery. 2. Composed of matter deposited by water.

aqueous humor Physiol. A clear fluid filling the space in the eye between the cornea and the lens.

aqui- combining form Water. [< L aqua]

aq·ui·line (ak'wə·līn, -lin) adj. 1. Of or like an eagle. 2. Curving or hooked: an aquiline nose. [< L aquila eagle]

ar- Assimilated var. of AD-.

-ar¹ suffix 1. Pertaining to; like: regular, singular. 2. The person or thing pertaining to: scholar. [< OF -er, -ier < L -aris (in nouns -are), var. of -alis, suffix of adjectives; or directly < L]

-ar² suffix A form of -ARY, -ER², refashioned in imitation of -AR¹: vicar, in ME vicary, viker.

-ar³ suffix A form of -ER¹, refashioned in imitation of -AR²: pedlar.

Ar·ab (ar'əb) n. 1. A native or inhabitant of Arabia. 2. Any of a Semitic-speaking people inhabiting Arabia. 3. A horse of a graceful, intelligent breed originally native to Arabia. — adj. Arabian.

ar·a·besque (ar'ə·besk') n. 1. An ornament or design, as used in Moorish architecture, of intertwined scrollwork, leaves or flowers, etc. 2. In ballet, a position in which the dancer extends one leg straight backward, one arm forward, and the other arm backward. — adj. Relating to, executed in, or resembling arabesque; fanciful; ornamental. [< F < Ital. Arabo Arab]

A·ra·bi·an (ə·rā'bē·ən) adj. Of or pertaining to Arabia or the Arabs. — n. An Arab (defs. 1 and 3).

ARABESQUE (def. 1)

Arabian Nights A collection of stories from Arabia, India, Persia, etc., from the tenth century.

Ar·a·bic (ar'ə·bik) adj. Of or pertaining to Arabia, the Arabs, their language, culture, etc. — n. The Southwest Semitic language of the Arabs.

Arabic numerals The symbols 1, 2, 3, 4, 5, 6, 7, 8, 9, and 0, in general use in Europe since about the tenth century.

ar·a·ble (ar'ə·bəl) adj. Capable of being plowed. — n. Arable land. [< L arare to plow] — **ar'a·bil'i·ty** n.

Arab League A confederation, established 1945, of the states of Iraq, Jordan (then Trans-Jordan), Lebanon, Saudi Arabia, the United Arab Republic (Egypt), Syria, and Yemen, joined by 1959 by Libya, Morocco, Sudan, and Tunisia, and in 1961 by Kuwait.

a·rach·nid (ə·rak'nid) n. Any of a class of arthropods, including the spiders, scorpions, mites, etc. [< NL < Gk. arachnē spider] — **a·rach·ni·dan** (ə·rak'nə·dən) adj. & n.

Ar·a·gon (ar'ə·gon) n. A former kingdom in Spain. — **Ar·a·go·nese** (ar'ə·gə·nēz', -nēs') adj. & n.

A·ram (âr'əm) n. The Biblical name of ancient Syria. Also **Ar·a·me·a** (ar'ə·mē'ə).

Ar·a·ma·ic (ar'ə·mā'ik) n. Any of a group of Semitic languages, including Syriac and the language spoken by Christ. **Ar·a·me·an** (ar'ə·mē'ən) adj. Of or pertaining to ancient Aram or Aramea, or its peoples, languages, etc. — n. 1. An inhabitant of Aram. 2. Aramaic. Also **Ar'a·mae'an.**

A·rap·a·ho (ə·rap'ə·hō) n. pl. **·ho** or **·hoes** A member of a nomadic Algonquian tribe, now dwelling primarily in Oklahoma and Wyoming. Also **A·rap'a·hoe.**

ar·ba·lest (är'bə·list) n. A medieval crossbow requiring a mechanical appliance to bend it. Also **ar'ba·list.** [< OF < L arcus a bow + ballista to throw] — **ar'ba·lest'er** n.

ar·bi·ter (är'bə·tər) n. 1. A chosen or appointed judge or umpire, as between parties in a dispute. 2. One who has matters under his sole control; an absolute and final judge. — **Syn.** See JUDGE. [< L < ad- to + bitere, betere to go] — **ar'bi·tress** n.fem. — **ar'bi·tral** (-trəl) adj.

ar·bi·tra·ble (är'bə·trə·bəl) adj. Subject to, capable of, or suitable for arbitration.

ar·bi·tra·ment (är·bit'rə·mənt) n. 1. Arbitration. 2. The decision of an arbitrator; an award. 3. The power or right to make such decision. Also **ar·bit're·ment.**

ar·bi·trar·y (är'bə·trer'ē) adj. 1. Based on or subject to one's opinion, judgment, prejudice, etc. 2. Absolute; despotic. 3. Law Not determined by statute. [See ARBITER.] — **ar'bi·trar'i·ly** adv. — **ar'bi·trar'i·ness** n.

ar·bi·trate (är'bə·trāt) v. **·trat·ed, ·trat·ing** v.t. 1. To decide as arbitrator. 2. To submit to or settle by arbitration. — v.i. 3. To act as arbitrator. 4. To submit a dispute to arbitration. — **ar'bi·tra'tive** adj.

ar·bi·tra·tion (är'bə·trā'shən) n. The settlement of a dispute by the decision of a third party or court.

ar·bi·tra·tor (är'bə·trā'tər) n. A person chosen to decide a dispute. — **Syn.** See JUDGE. [< L]

ar·bor¹ (är'bər) n. A bower, as of latticework, supporting vines or trees. Also **ar'bour.** [Earlier erber, herber < AF < L < herba grass, herb]

ar·bor² (är'bər) n. pl. **ar·bo·res** (är'bər·ēz) for def. 1; **ar·bors** for def. 2. 1. A tree: used chiefly in botanical names. 2. Mech. a A shaft, mandrel, spindle, or axle. b A principal support of a machine. [< L, tree]

ar·bo·re·al (är·bôr'ē·əl, -bō'rē-) adj. 1. Of or like a tree. 2. Inhabiting trees, or adapted to life in trees.

ar·bo·res·cent (är'bə·res'ənt) adj. Treelike; branching.

ar·bo·re·tum (är'bə·rē'təm) n. pl. **·tums** or **·ta** (-tə) A botanical garden exhibiting trees for display or study.

arbori- combining form Tree. [< L arbor tree]

ar·bor·vi·tae (är'bər·vī'tē) n. An evergreen shrub or tree of the pine family. [< L arbor vitae tree of life]

ar·bu·tus (är·byōō'təs) n. 1. An evergreen tree or shrub of the heath family. 2. The trailing arbutus. [< L, strawberry tree]

arc (ärk) n. 1. Anything in the shape of an arch, a curve, or a part of a circle; a bow; arch. 2. Geom. A part of any curve. 3. Electr. The bow of flame formed by the passage of an electric current across the gap between two conductors. 4. Astron. A part of the apparent path of a heavenly body. — v.i. **arced** (ärkt) or **arcked, arc·ing** (är'king) or **arck·ing** Electr. To form an arc. [< L arcus bow, arch]

ar·cade (är·kād') n. 1. Archit. A series of arches with supporting columns or piers, standing against the face of a wall or free. 2. A roofed passageway or street, esp. one having shops, etc., opening from it. — v.t. **cad·ed, ·cad·ing** To furnish with or form into an arcade or arcades. [< F < Med.L < L arcus bow, arch]

Ar·ca·di·a (är·kā'dē·ə) Any region of ideal rustic simplicity and contentment. Also **Ar·ca·dy** (är'kə·dē).

Ar·ca·di·an (är·kā'dē·ən) adj. 1. Of or pertaining to Arcadia. 2. Rural or simple; pastoral. — n. 1. A native of or dweller in Arcadia. 2. One with simple, pastoral tastes.

ar·cane (är·kān') adj. Secret; hidden. [< L arcanus hidden]

ar·ca·num (är·kā'nəm) n. pl. **·na** (-nə) An inner secret.

arch¹ (ärch) n. 1. A curved structure spanning an opening, formed of wedge-shaped parts resting on supports at the two extremities. 2. Any similar structure or object. 3. A bowlike curve. 4. Anat. A curved or archlike part, as of the foot. — v.t. 1. To cause to form an arch or arches. 2. To furnish with an arch or arches. 3. To span; extend over, as an arch. — v.i. 4. To form an arch or arches. [< OF < Med.L < L arcus bow, arch]

arch² (ärch) adj. 1. Cunning; roguish; sly. 2. Most eminent; chief. [< ARCH-] — **arch'ly** adv. — **arch'ness** n.

arch- prefix 1. Chief; principal. 2. Very great; extreme. Also **archi-.** [OE < L < Gk. archos ruler]

archaeo- See ARCHEO-.

ar·chae·ol·o·gy (är'kē·ol'ə·jē), etc. See ARCHEOLOGY, etc.

ar·cha·ic (är·kā'ik) adj. 1. Old-fashioned; antiquated. 2. Characterizing a word, an inflectional form, or a phrase no longer in current use. Also **ar·cha'i·cal.** — **Syn.** See OBSOLETE. [< Gk. archaios ancient]

ar·cha·ism (är'kē·iz'əm, -kā-) n. An archaic word, idiom, or style. — **ar'cha·ist** n. — **ar'cha·is'tic** adj.

arch·an·gel (ärk'ān'jəl) n. 1. An angel of highest rank. 2. The angelica. — **the Archangel** In Christian legend, usually Michael. [< LL < Gk. < arch- chief + angelos angel] — **arch·an·gel·ic** (ärk'an·jel'ik) or **·i·cal** adj.

arch·bish·op (ärch'bish'əp) n. Eccl. The chief bishop of a province. — **arch'bish'op·ric** n.

arch·dea·con (ärch′dē′kən)   *n. Eccl.*   A chief deacon, ranking just below a bishop.

arch·dea·con·ry (ärch′dē′kən·rē) *n. pl.* **·ries** 1. The jurisdiction or office of an archdeacon. Also **arch′dea′con·ate** (-it), **arch′dea′con·ship.** 2. An archdeacon's residence.

arch·di·o·cese (ärch′dī′ə·sēs, -sis)   *n.*   The diocese or jurisdiction of an archbishop.

arch·du·cal (ärch′dōō′kəl, -dyōō′-)   *adj.* Of or pertaining to an archduke or an archduchy.

arch·duch·ess (ärch′duch′is)   *n.* 1. The wife or widow of an archduke. 2. A princess of the former royal family of Austria.

arch·duch·y (ärch′duch′ē) *n. pl.* **·duch·ies** The territory ruled by an archduke. Also **arch′duke′dom.**

arch·duke (ärch′dōōk′, -dyōōk′) *n.* A chief duke, especially a prince of the former royal family of Austria. Abbr. *Archd.*

arched (ärcht) *adj.* 1. Having the form of an arch. 2. Covered or furnished with arches.

ar·che·go·ni·um (är′kə·gō′nē·əm) *n. pl.* **·ni·a** (-nē·ə) *Bot.* The female sexual organ of the higher cryptogams. Also **ar·che·gone** (är′kə·gōn). [< NL < Gk. < *archos* chief, first + *gonos* race, offspring] — **ar′che·go′ni·al** *adj.* **ar′che·go′ni·ate** *adj.*

archeo- *combining form* Ancient: *Archeozoic.* Also **archaeo-.** [< Gk. *archaios* ancient]

ar·che·ol·o·gy (är′kē·ol′ə·jē) *n.* The science or study of history from the remains of early human cultures as discovered chiefly by systematic excavations: also, *esp. Brit.,* **archaeology.** — **ar·che·o·log·i·cal** (är′kē·ə·loj′i·kəl) or **·log′ic** *adj.* — **ar′che·ol′o·gist** *n.*

Ar·che·o·zo·ic (är′kē·ə·zō′ik) *adj. Geol.* Of or pertaining to the oldest of the eras making up the geological record. See chart for GEOLOGY. Also spelled *Archaeozoic.* [< ARCHEO- + Gk. *zōion* animal]

arch·er (är′chər) *n.* One who shoots with a bow and arrow. [< AF < L *arcus* bow]

Arch·er (är′chər) *n.* The constellation and sign of the zodiac Sagittarius.

arch·er·y (är′chər·ē) *n.* 1. The art or sport of shooting with bow and arrows. 2. The weapons and outfit of an archer.

ar·che·type (är′kə·tīp) *n.* An original or standard pattern or model; a prototype. [< L < Gk. < *arche-* first + *typos* stamp, pattern] — **ar′che·typ′al** (-tī′pəl), **ar′che·typ′ic** (-tip′ik) or **·i·cal** *adj.*

archi- *prefix* 1. Var. of ARCH-. 2. *Biol.* Original; primitive: *archicarp.* [See ARCH-.]

ar·chi·e·pis·co·pate (är′kē·i·pis′kə·pit, -pāt) *n.* The office or tenure of an archbishop. — **ar′chi·e·pis′co·pal** *adj.*

Ar·chi·me·de·an (är′kə·mē′dē·ən, mə·dē′ən) *adj.* Of, discovered by, or pertaining to Archimedes.

ar·chi·pel·a·go (är′kə·pel′ə·gō) *n. pl.* **·goes** or **·gos** 1. A sea with many islands. 2. The islands in such a sea. [< Ital. < Gk. *archi-* chief + *pelagos* sea] — **ar·chi·pe·lag·ic** (är′kə·pə·laj′ik) *adj.*

ar·chi·tect (är′kə·tekt) *n.* 1. One whose profession is to design and draw up the plans for buildings, etc., and supervise their construction. 2. One who devises or creates anything. [< F < L < Gk. < *archi-* chief + *tektōn* worker]

ar·chi·tec·ton·ic (är′kə·tek·ton′ik) *adj.* 1. Pertaining to an architect or architecture; constructive. 2. Having architectural qualities of design and structure.

ar·chi·tec·ton·ics (är′kə·tek·ton′iks) *n.pl. (construed as sing.)* 1. The science of architecture. 2. Structural design, as in works of music or art.

ar·chi·tec·ture (är′kə·tek′chər) *n.* 1. The science, art, or profession of designing and constructing buildings or other structures. 2. A style or system of building: Gothic *architecture.* 3. Construction or structure generally. 4. A building, or buildings collectively. Abbr. **arch., archit.** — **ar′chi·tec′tur·al** *adj.* — **ar′chi·tec′tur·al·ly** *adv.*

ar·chi·trave (är′kə·trāv) *n. Archit.* 1. The part of an entablature that rests upon the column heads and supports the frieze. For illus. see COLUMN. 2. A molded ornament skirting the head and sides of a door or window. [< F < Ital. < Gk. < *archi-* chief + Ital. *trave* beam]

ar·chives (är′kīvz) *n.pl.* 1. A place where public records and historical documents are kept. 2. Public records, documents, etc., as kept in such a depository. [< LL < Gk. *archeion* a public office] — **ar·chi·val** (är·kī′vəl) *adj.*

ar·chi·vist (är′kə·vist) *n.* A keeper of archives.

arch·priest (ärch′prēst′) *n.* 1. Formerly, the senior priest of a cathedral chapter, serving as assistant to a bishop: later called *dean.* 2. A chief priest. — **arch′priest′hood.**

arch·way (ärch′wā′) *n.* A passage under an arch.

-archy *combining form* Rule; government: *monarchy.* [< Gk. *-archia* < *archos* ruler]

arc light A lamp in which light of high intensity is produced between two adjacent electrodes. Also **arc lamp.**

arc·tic (ärk′tik, är′tik) *adj.* Characteristic of the Arctic; extremely cold; frigid. [Earlier *artik* < OF < L < Gk. < *arktos* a bear]

Arctic Circle The parallel at 66°33′ north latitude; the boundary of the North Frigid Zone.

Arc·tu·rus (ärk·tōōr′əs, -tyōōr′-)   *n.*   An orange-red star, one of the 20 brightest, 0.24 magnitude; Alpha in the constellation Boötes. [< L < Gk. *arktos* a bear + *ouros* a guard]

-ard *suffix of nouns* One who does something to excess or who is to be disparaged: *drunkard, coward;* sometimes changed to *-art: braggart.* [< OF *-ard, -art* < G *-hard, -hart* hardy]

ar·den·cy (är′dən·sē) *n.* Intensity of emotion; ardor.

ar·dent (är′dənt) *adj.* 1. Passionate; zealous; intense. 2. Glowing; flashing. 3. Hot; burning. [< L *ardere* to burn] — **ar′dent·ly** *adv.* — **ar′dent·ness** *n.*

ar·dor (är′dər) *n.* 1. Warmth or intensity of passion or affection; eagerness; vehemence; zeal. 2. Great heat, as of fire. Also *Brit.* **ar′dour.** [< L *ardere* to burn]

ar·du·ous (är′jōō·əs) *adj.* 1. Involving great labor or hardship; difficult. 2. Toiling strenuously; energetic. 3. Steep; hard to climb or surmount. [< L *arduus* steep] — **ar′du·ous·ly** *adv.* — **ar′du·ous·ness** *n.*

are[1] (är, *unstressed* ər, r, ə) *v.* First, second, and third person plural, present indicative, of BE: also used as second person singular. [OE (Northumbrian) *aron*]

are[2] (âr, är) *n.* In the metric system, a surface measure equal to one hundred square meters; also spelled **ar.** See table inside back cover. [< F < L *area* area]

ar·e·a (âr′ē·ə) *n. pl.* **ar·e·as** 1. A particular portion of the earth's surface; region. 2. The surface included within a bounding line. 3. The extent or scope of anything. 4. The yard of a building. 5. Any flat, open space. [< L, an open space] — **ar′e·al** *adj.*

ar·e·a·way (âr′ē·ə·wā′) *n.* 1. A small sunken court before a basement door. 2. A passageway.

a·re·na (ə·rē′nə) *n.* 1. The oval space in a Roman amphitheater, where contests and shows were held. 2. Any place of this nature: a football *arena.* 3. A scene or sphere of action or contest: the political *arena.* [< L, sand, sandy place]

arena theater A stage in the center of an auditorium, surrounded by seats: also called *theater-in-the-round.*

aren't (ärnt) Are not.

aren't I ◆ See note under AIN'T.

areo- *combining form* Mars. [< Gk. *Arēs*]

a·re·o·la (ə·rē′ə·lə) *n. pl.* **·lae** (-lē) or **·las** 1. *Bot.* An interstice in a network of leaf veins. 2. *Anat.* The colored circle about a nipple or about a vesicle. Also **ar·e·ole** (âr′ē·ōl). [< L, dim. of *area* open space] — **a·re·o·lar, a·re·o·late** (ə·rē′ə·lit, -lāt) *adj.* — **ar·e·o·la·tion** (âr′ē·ə·lā′shən) *n.*

Ar·e·op·a·gus (ar′ē·op′ə·gəs) 1. A hill NW of the Acropolis on which the highest court of ancient Athens held its sessions; also, the court itself. 2. Any high law court. [< L < Gk. *Areios* of Ares + *pagos* hill]

Ar·es (âr′ēz) In Greek mythology, the god of war: identified with the Roman *Mars.*

ar·ga·li (är′gə·lē) *n. pl.* **·lis** or **·li** 1. An Asian wild sheep with large horns curved spirally outward. 2. Any of several other wild sheep. Also **ar·gal** (är′gəl). [< Mongolian]

ar·gent (är′jənt) *n. Archaic & Poetic* Silver. — *adj.* Like or made of silver; white; silvery: also **ar·gen·tal** (är·jen′təl). [< F < L *argentum* silver]

ar·gen·tine (är′jən·tin, -tīn) *adj.* Silvery. [< F < L *argentum* silver]

Ar·gen·tine (är′jən·tēn, -tīn) *adj.* Of or pertaining to Argentina. — *n.* A native or citizen of Argentina: also **Ar·gen·tin·e·an** (är′jən·tin′ē·ən).

ar·gen·tum (är·jen′təm) *n. Chem.* Silver. [< L]

ar·gil (är′jil) *n.* Potters' clay; white clay. [< MF < L < Gk. < *argos* white]

ar·gi·nine (är′jə·nēn, -nin, -nīn) *n. Biochem.* One of the amino acids essential to nutrition, $C_6H_{14}O_2N_4$. [< NL *argin-* < -INE[2]]

Ar·give (är′jīv, -gīv) *adj. & n.* Greek.

Ar·go (är′gō) *n.* In Greek legend, the ship in which Jason and the Argonauts sailed for the Golden Fleece.

ar·gol (är′gəl) *n.* Crude potassium bitartrate, the base of tartaric acid. [ME < AF *argoil*]

ar·gon (är′gon) *n.* A colorless, gaseous element (symbol Ar) present in the atmosphere, used in electric display signs and as a filter for incandescent electric lamps. [< NL < Gk. neut. of *argos* idle, inert + -ON]

Ar·go·naut (är′gə·nôt) *n.* 1. In Greek legend, one who sailed with Jason in the ship Argo to find the Golden Fleece. 2. One who went to California in 1849 to hunt gold. [< L

ARGALI
(4 feet high at shoulder)

PRONUNCIATION KEY: add, āce, câre, pälm; end, ēven; it, īce; odd, ōpen, ôrder; tōōk, pōōl; up, bûrn; ə = a in *above,* e in *sicken,* i in *flexible,* o in *melon,* u in *focus;* yōō = u in *fuse;* oil; pout; check; go; ring; thin; this; zh, vision. For à, œ, ü, kh, ń, see inside front cover.

< Gk. < *Argō*, the ship + *nautēs* sailor] **—ar′go·nau′tic** *adj.*

ar·go·sy (är′gə·sē) *n. pl.* **·sies** **1.** A large merchant ship. **2.** A fleet of merchant vessels. [Earlier *ragusy*, after *Ragusa*, Italian name of Dubrovnik, Yugoslav port]

ar·got (är′gō, -gət) *n.* The specialized vocabulary or jargon of any class or group, as that of the underworld. [< F] **—ar·got·ic** (är·got′ik) *adj.*

ar·gue (är′gyōō) *v.* **·gued, ·gu·ing** *v.i.* **1.** To present reasons to support or contest a measure or opinion. **2.** To contend in argument; quarrel. **—v.t. 3.** To present reasons for or against; discuss, as a proposal. **4.** To contend or maintain, by reasoning. **5.** To prove or indicate, as from evidence. **6.** To influence or convince, as by argument. [< OF < L *arguere* to prove] **—ar′gu·a·ble** *adj.* **—ar′gu·er** *n.*

ar·gu·ment (är′gyə·mənt) *n.* **1.** An angry discussion or quarrel. **2.** A reason or reasons offered for or against something. **3.** Discourse intended to persuade or to convince. **4.** A short summary of a piece of subject matter.

ar·gu·men·ta·tion (är′gyə·men·tā′shən) *n.* **1.** The methodical setting forth of premises and the drawing of conclusions therefrom. **2.** Discussion; debate.

ar·gu·men·ta·tive (är′gyə·men′tə·tiv) *adj.* **1.** Controversial. **2.** Given to argumentation; disputatious. **—ar′gu·men·ta·tive·ly** *adv.* **—ar′gu·men·ta·tive·ness** *n.*

Ar·gus (är′gəs) **1.** In Greek mythology, a giant with a hundred eyes, killed by Hermes. **2.** Any vigilant watchman.

Ar·gus-eyed (är′gəs-īd′) *adj.* Sharp-sighted; vigilant.

a·ri·a (ä′rē·ə, âr′ē·ə) *n.* **1.** An air; melody. **2.** An elaborate melody for single voice, as in an opera or oratorio, often with instrumental accompaniment. [< Ital. < L *aer* air]

-aria *suffix* Used in forming new Latin names, esp. in zoological and botanical classifications. [< NL < L *-arius*]

Ar·i·ad·ne (ar′ē·ad′nē) In Greek mythology, the daughter of Minos, who gave Theseus the thread by which he found his way out of the Labyrinth.

-arian *suffix* Used in forming adjectives and adjectival nouns denoting occupation, age, sect, beliefs, etc.: *nonagenarian, predestinarian.* [< L *-arius -ary* + -AN]

Ar·i·an (âr′ē·ən, ar′-, är′yən) See ARYAN.

Ar·i·an·ism (âr′ē·ən·iz′əm) *n. Theol.* The doctrine denying that Christ is of one substance with God the Father. [after *Arius*, 250?–336, Greek theologian] **—Ar′i·an** *adj. & n.*

ar·id (ar′id) *adj.* **1.** Parched with heat; dry. **2.** Without interest or feeling; dull. [< L *arere* to be dry] **—a·rid·i·ty** (ə·rid′ə·tē), **ar′id·ness** *n.* **—ar′id·ly** *adv.*

Ar·ies (âr′ēz, âr′i·ēz) *n.* A constellation, the Ram; also, the first sign of the zodiac. See ZODIAC. [< L]

a·right (ə·rīt′) *adv.* In a right way; correctly; rightly.

a·ri·o·so (ä·ryō′sō) *adj. Music* Characteristic of an aria. **—adv.** In the manner of an aria. **—n.** A passage, composition, etc., resembling an aria. [< Ital.]

-arious *suffix of adjectives* Connected with; pertaining to: *gregarious.* [< L *-arius -ary* + -OUS]

a·rise (ə·rīz′) *v.i.* **a·rose** (ə·rōz′), **a·ris·en** (ə·riz′ən), **a·ris·ing** **1.** To get up, as from a prone position. **2.** To rise; ascend. **3.** To come into being; originate; issue. **4.** To result; proceed. [OE < ā- up + *rīsan* to rise]

aristo- *combining form* Best; finest. [< Gk. *aristos*]

ar·is·toc·ra·cy (ar′is·tok′rə·sē) *n. pl.* **·cies** **1.** A hereditary nobility or privileged class. **2.** A state ruled by a privileged upper class, or by the nobility. **3.** Government by an upper class or the nobility. **4.** Originally, government by its best citizens or a state governed by its best citizens. **5.** Any preeminent group: the *aristocracy* of talent. [< L < Gk. < *aristos* best + *krateein* to rule]

a·ris·to·crat (ə·ris′tə·krat, ar′is·tə·krat′) *n.* **1.** A member of an aristocracy. **2.** A proud and exclusive person. **3.** One who prefers an aristocratic form of government. **—a·ris′to·crat′ic** or **·i·cal** *adj.* **—a·ris·to·crat′i·cal·ly** *adv.*

Ar·is·to·te·li·an (ar′is·tə·tē′lē·ən, -tēl′yən, ə·ris′tə-) *adj.* Pertaining to or characteristic of Aristotle or his philosophy. **—n.** An adherent of Aristotle's teachings; one who tends to be empirical or scientific in his method, rather than speculative. Also **Ar′is·to·te′le·an.** **—Ar′is·to·te′li·an·ism** *n.*

Aristotelian logic The deductive method of logic of Aristotle, characterized by the syllogism.

a·rith·me·tic (*n.* ə·rith′mə·tik; *adj.* ar′ith·met′ik) *n.* The science of computing with numbers by the operations of addition, subtraction, multiplication, and division. **—adj.** Of or pertaining to arithmetic: also **ar′ith·met′i·cal.** [< L < Gr. *arithmos* number] **—ar′ith·met′i·cal·ly** *adv.*

a·rith·me·ti·cian (ə·rith′mə·tish′ən, ar′ith-) *n.* One who uses or is skilled in arithmetic.

arithmetic mean (ar′ith·met′ik) *Math.* The sum of a set of numbers, divided by the number of terms in the set.

arithmetic progression (ar′ith·met′ik) *Math.* A sequence of terms in which each, except the first, differs from the preceding one by a constant quantity, as 2, 4, 6, 8.

-arium *suffix of nouns* **1.** A place for: *herbarium.* **2.** Connected with: *honorarium.* [< L *-arius*. See -ARY[1].]

ark (ärk) *n.* **1.** In the Bible: **a** The ship of Noah. *Gen.* vi–viii. **b** The chest containing the stone tablets bearing the Ten Commandments: also called **ark of the covenant.** *Ex.* xxv 10. **2.** A large, flat-bottomed or awkward boat; scow. [OE *arc* < L *arca* chest]

arm[1] (ärm) *n.* **1.** *Anat.* An upper limb of the human body, from the shoulder to the hand or wrist. ◆ Collateral adjective: *brachial.* **2.** The forelimb of certain other vertebrates. **3.** An armlike part or appendage. **4.** Something intended to support or cover the human arm. **5.** Anything branching out like an arm from a main body, as the end of a spar. **—at arm's length** At a distance. **—with open arms** Cordially; warmly. [OE *earm, arm*]

arm[2] (ärm) *n.* **1.** A weapon. **2.** A distinct branch of the military service: the air *arm.* **—v.t. 1.** To supply with weapons. **2.** To make secure, as with a protective covering. **—v.i. 3.** To supply or equip oneself with weapons. [< OF < L *arma* weapons] **—arm′er** *n.*

ar·ma·da (är·mä′də, -mā′-) *n.* A fleet of war vessels. **—the Armada** The fleet sent against England by Spain in 1588, defeated by the English navy: also **Invincible Armada, Spanish Armada.** [< Sp. < L *armare* to arm]

ar·ma·dil·lo (är′mə·dil′ō) *n. pl.* **·los** An American burrowing nocturnal mammal having an armor-like covering of jointed plates. [< Sp. < L *armare* to arm]

Ar·ma·ged·don (är′mə·ged′n) *n.* **1.** In Biblical prophecy, the scene of a great battle between the forces of good and evil, to occur at the end of the world. *Rev.* xvi 16. **2.** Any great or decisive conflict.

ARMADILLO
(30 inches long; tail 12 inches)

ar·ma·ment (är′mə·mənt) *n.* **1.** *Often pl.* The guns and other military equipment of a fortification, military unit, warship, etc. **2.** The act of arming or equipping for war. [< L *armare* to arm]

ar·ma·ture (är mə·chŏŏr) *n.* **1.** A piece of soft iron joining the poles of a magnet to prevent the loss of magnetic power. **2.** *Electr.* **a** In a dynamo or motor, the cylindrical, laminated iron core carrying the coils of insulated wire to be revolved through the magnetic field. **b** The part of a relay, as a buzzer or bell, that vibrates when activated. **3.** *Biol.* Protective covering, as the shells of animals. **4.** In sculpture, a framework to support the clay or other substance in modeling. **5.** Arms; armor. [< MF < L *armare* to arm]

arm·chair (ärm′châr′) *n.* A chair with supports for the arms.

armed (ärmd) *adj.* **1.** Provided with weapons. **2.** Having upper limbs: used in combination: *strong-armed.*

armed forces The military and naval forces of a nation.

Ar·me·ni·an (är·mē′nē·ən, -mēn′yən) *adj.* Of or pertaining to the country, people, or language of Armenia. **—n. 1.** A native of Armenia. **2.** The language of the Armenians.

arm·ful (ärm′fŏŏl) *n. pl.* **·fuls** That which is held, or as much as can be held, in the arm or arms.

Ar·min·i·an·ism (är·min′ē·ən·iz′əm) *n. Theol.* The doctrines holding a less rigorous view of predestination than Calvinism. [after Jacobus *Arminius*, 1560–1609, Dutch Protestant theologian] **—Ar·min′i·an** *adj. & n.*

ar·mi·stice (är′mə·stis) *n.* A temporary cessation of hostilities by mutual agreement; a truce. [< F < L < *arma* arms + *sistere* to stop, stand still]

Armistice Day See VETERANS DAY.

arm·let (ärm′lit) *n.* **1.** A little arm, as of the sea. **2.** A band worn around the arm. **3.** A small, short sleeve.

ar·moire (är·mwär′) *n.* A large, movable, often ornate cabinet or cupboard. [< F < OF < L *armarium* a chest]

ar·mor (är′mər) *n.* **1.** A defensive covering, as of metallic plates for a war vessel, a tank, etc. **2.** The armored vehicles of an army. **3.** Any protective covering, as the shell of a turtle. **—v.t. & v.i.** To furnish with or put on armor. Also *Brit.* **ar′mour.** [< OF *armeür* < L *armare* to arm]

ar·mored (är′mərd) *adj.* **1.** Protected by armor. **2.** Equipped with armored vehicles, as a military unit.

ar·mor·er (är′mər·ər) *n.* **1.** A maker or repairer, of arms or armor. **2.** A manufacturer of arms. **3.** *Mil.* An enlisted man in charge of small arms. Also *Brit.* **ar′mour·er.**

ar·mo·ri·al (är·môr′ē·əl, -mō′rē-) *adj.* Pertaining to heraldry.

armor plate A covering of very hard steel plating, used on warships, tanks, etc. **—ar·mor-plat·ed** (är′mər·plā′tid) *adj.*

ar·mor·y (är′mər·ē) *n. pl.* **·mor·ies** **1.** A place where arms are kept; arsenal. **2.** *U.S.* A building for the use of a body of militia, including storage for arms and equipment, drill rooms, etc. **3.** *U.S.* A factory for making firearms. Also *Brit.* **ar′mour·y.** [Prob. < ARMOR]

arm·pit (ärm′pit′) *n.* The cavity under the arm at the shoulder; axilla.

arms (ärmz) *n.pl.* **1.** Weapons collectively. **2.** Warfare. **3.** The official insignia of a state, etc. **4.** Heraldic symbols. **—to arms!** Make ready for battle! **—to bear arms 1.** To carry weapons. **2.** To serve in the armed forces. **—under arms** Provided with weapons; ready for war. **—up in arms** Aroused and ready to fight. [< F < L *arma* weapons]

ar·my (är'mē) *n. pl.* **·mies 1.** A large organized body of men armed for military service on land. **2.** The total military land forces of a country. **3.** Any large body of people, animals, etc.; host; multitude. [< OF < L *armare* to arm]

ar·ni·ca (är'ni·kə) *n.* **1.** A widely distributed herbaceous perennial of the composite family. **2.** A tincture prepared from this herb, used for sprains and bruises. [< NL]

a·ro·ma (ə·rō'mə) *n.* **1.** Fragrance, as from appetizing food, spices, etc.; agreeable odor. **2.** Characteristic quality or style. — **Syn.** See SMELL. [< L < Gk. *arōma, -atos* spice] — **a·ro·ma·tous** (ə·rō'mə·təs) *adj.*

ar·o·mat·ic (ar'ə·mat'ik) *adj.* Having an aroma; fragrant; spicy. Also **ar'o·mat'i·cal.** — *n.* Any vegetable or drug of agreeable odor. — **ar'o·mat'i·cal·ly** *adv.*

a·ro·ma·tize (ə·rō'mə·tīz) *v.t.* **·tized, ·tiz·ing** To make fragrant or aromatic.

a·rose (ə·rōz') Past tense of ARISE.

a·round (ə·round') *adv.* **1.** On all sides; in various directions: It is raining all *around.* **2.** In the opposite direction: to turn *around.* **3.** *U.S.* From place to place; here and there: to walk *around.* **4.** *U.S. Informal* Nearby; in the vicinity: Wait *around* till I call. **5.** In or to a particular place: Come *around* to see us again. — **to get around** *U.S. Informal* **1.** To be experienced and up to date. **2.** To overcome or cope with (someone or something). — **to get around to** *U.S. Informal* To give attention to or accomplish. — **to have been around** *U.S. Informal* To be experienced in the ways of the world. — *prep.* **1.** About the circumference or circuit of. **2.** On all sides of; surrounding or enveloping. **3.** *U.S. Informal* Here and there in: He wandered *around* the city. **4.** *U.S. Informal* Somewhere near or within. **5.** *U.S. Informal* Somewhere near in time, amount, etc.; about.

a·rouse (ə·rouz') *v.* **a·roused, a·rous·ing** *v.t.* **1.** To awaken. **2.** To excite, as to a state of high emotion. — *v.i.* **3.** To arouse oneself. [< A-² + ROUSE] — **a·rous'al** (-zəl) *n.*

ar·peg·gi·o (är·pej'ē·ō, -pej'ō) *n. pl.* **·gi·os** *Music* **1.** The sounding or playing of the notes of a chord in rapid succession. **2.** A chord so played. [< Ital. *arpa* a harp]

ar·que·bus (är'kwə·bəs) *n.* A harquebus.

ar·raign (ə·rān') *v.t. Law* To call into court and cause to answer to an indictment. **2.** To call upon for an answer; accuse. — **Syn.** See ACCUSE. [< AF < LL *arrationare* to call to account] — **ar·raign'er** *n.* — **ar·raign'ment** *n.*

ar·range (ə·rānj') *v.* **·ranged, ·rang·ing** *v.t.* **1.** To put in definite or proper order. **2.** To plan the details of; prepare for. **3.** To adjust, as a conflict or dispute; settle. **4.** *Music* To change or adapt for other instruments or voices. — *v.i.* **5.** To come to an agreement or understanding. **6.** To see about the details; make plans. [< OF *arangier* < *a-* to + *rangier* to put in order] — **ar·rang'er** *n.*

ar·range·ment (ə·rānj'mənt) *n.* **1.** The act of arranging, or the state of being arranged; disposition. **2.** That which is arranged. **3.** The style in which something is arranged; order. **4.** A settlement, as of a dispute; adjustment. **5.** *Usually pl.* The plans or preparations made, or measures taken, for a particular purpose. **6.** *Music* The adaptation of a composition to other voices or instruments.

ar·rant (ar'ənt) *adj.* Notoriously bad; unmitigated. [Var. of ERRANT] — **ar'rant·ly** *adv.*

ar·ras (ar'əs) *n.* **1.** A tapestry. **2.** A wall hanging, esp. of tapestry. [after *Arras*, France]

ar·ray (ə·rā') *n.* **1.** Regular or proper order, esp. of troops. **2.** The persons or things arrayed. **3.** Clothing; fine dress. — *v.t.* **1.** To draw up in order of battle; set in order. **2.** To adorn; dress, as for display. [< AF < OF *arei* < *a-* to + *rei* order]

ar·ray·al (ə·rā'əl) *n.* **1.** The act or process of arraying. **2.** Anything arrayed; an array.

ar·rear·age (ə·rir'ij) *n.* **1.** The state of being in arrears. **2.** The amount in arrears. **3.** A thing kept in reserve.

ar·rears (ə·rirz') *n.pl.* That which is behindhand; a part, as of a debt, overdue and unpaid. — **in arrears** (or **arrear**) Behind in meeting payment, completing work, etc. [< OF < L *ad-* to + *retro* backward]

ar·rest (ə·rest') *v.t.* **1.** To stop suddenly; check. **2.** To take into legal custody. **3.** To attract and fix, as the attention. — *n.* **1.** The act of arresting, or the state of being arrested. **2.** Seizure by legal authority. Also **ar·rest'ment.** **3.** A device for arresting motion. — **under arrest** In custody; arrested. [< OF < L *ad-* to + *restare* to stop, remain] — **ar·rest'er, ar·rest'or** *n.*

ar·ri·val (ə·rī'vəl) *n.* **1.** The act of arriving. **2.** One who or that which arrives or has arrived.

ar·rive (ə·rīv') *v.i.* **·rived, ·riv·ing 1.** To reach a destination or place. **2.** To come to a desired object, state, etc.: often with *at.* **3.** To attain success or fame. **4.** To come at length: The hour has *arrived.* [< OF < LL < L *ad-* to + *ripa* shore]

ar·ro·gance (ar'ə·gəns) *n.* The quality or state of being arrogant or haughty. Also **ar'ro·gan·cy, ar'ro·gant·ness.**

ar·ro·gant (ar'ə·gənt) *adj.* **1.** Overbearing; haughty. **2.** Characterized by or due to arrogance. [< OF < L < *ad-* to + *rogare* to ask] — **ar'ro·gant·ly** *adv.*

ar·ro·gate (ar'ə·gāt) *v.t.* **·gat·ed, ·gat·ing 1.** To claim or take without right. **2.** To ascribe to another without reason. [< L < *ad-* to + *rogare* to ask] — **ar'ro·ga'tion** *n.* — **ar'ro·ga'tive** *adj.*

ar·row (ar'ō, -ə) *n.* **1.** A slender shaft, generally feathered at one end and with a pointed head at the other, to be shot from a bow. **2.** Anything resembling an arrow in shape, speed, etc. **3.** A sign or figure in the shape of an arrow, used to indicate directions. [OE *earh, arwe*] — **ar·row·y** (ar'ō·ē) *adj.*

ar·row·head (ar'ō·hed', -ə-) *n.* **1.** The sharp-pointed head of an arrow. **2.** Something resembling an arrowhead, as a mark used to point direction, etc. **3.** *Bot.* An aquatic plant with arrow-shaped leaves.

ar·row·root (ar'ō·rōōt', -ə-, -rōōt') *n.* **1.** A nutritious starch obtained from a tropical American plant. **2.** The plant itself. [Plant so called because used to treat arrow wounds]

ar·roy·o (ə·roi'ō) *n. pl.* **·os** (-ōz) *SW U.S.* **1.** A deep, dry gully. **2.** A brook. [< Sp., ult. < L *arrugia* pit, shaft]

ar·se·nal (är'sə·nəl) *n.* **1.** A government facility for manufacturing and storing arms and munitions. **2.** A store of arms. [< Ital. < Arabic *dār aṣ-ṣin'ah* workshop]

ar·se·nic (är'sə·nik) *n.* A grayish white, brittle metallic element (symbol As), forming many poisonous compounds and used in medicine, industry, and the arts. [< OF < L < Gk. *arsenikon* yellow orpiment]

ar·sen·i·cal (är·sen'i·kəl) *adj.* Of or containing arsenic. Also **ar·sen'ic.** — *n.* Any arsenical insecticide or drug.

ar·son (är'sən) *n. Law* The crime of setting fire to a building or other property. [< OF < L *ardere* to burn]

ars po·et·i·ca (ärz pō·et'i·kə) *Latin* The art of poetry.

art¹ (ärt) *n.* **1.** An esthetically pleasing and meaningful arrangement of elements, as words, sounds, colors, shapes, etc. **2.** Literature, music, and esp. painting, sculpture, drawing, etc. **3.** Any system of rules and principles that facilitates skilled human accomplishment. **4.** A pursuit or occupation that depends upon the skilled application of such a system of rules and principles. **5.** Practical skill; dexterity: the *art* of a craftsman. **6.** *pl.* The liberal arts. **7.** *Usu. pl.* Cunning. [< OF < L *ars, artis* skill]

art² (ärt) *Archaic* or *Poetic* Second person singular present tense of BE: used with *thou.* [OE *eart*]

-art *suffix* Var. of -ARD.

Ar·te·mis (är'tə·mis) In Greek mythology, the goddess identified with the Roman *Diana.*

ar·te·ri·al (är·tir'ē·əl) *adj.* **1.** Of or pertaining to the arteries or an artery. **2.** *Physiol.* Pertaining to the bright red blood that has undergone aeration in the lungs. **3.** Resembling an artery: an *arterial* highway.

ar·te·ri·al·ize (är·tir'ē·əl·īz') *v.t.* **·ized, ·iz·ing** *Physiol.* To convert (venous blood) into arterial blood by oxygenation. Also *Brit.* **ar·te'ri·al·ise'.** — **ar·te'ri·al·i·za'tion** *n.*

arterio- *combining form* Artery. Also, before vowels, **arter-.** [< Gk. *artēria*]

ar·te·ri·o·scle·ro·sis (är·tir'ē·ō·sklə·rō'sis) *n. Pathol.* The thickening and hardening of the walls of an artery. — **ar·te'ri·o·scle·rot'ic** (-rot'ik) *adj.*

ar·ter·y (är'tər·ē) *n. pl.* **·ter·ies 1.** *Anat.* Any of a large number of muscular vessels conveying blood away from the heart to every part of the body. **2.** Any main channel or route. [< L *arteria* artery, windpipe]

ar·te·sian well (är·tē'zhən) A well that penetrates to a water-bearing stratum from a surface lower than the source of the water supply, so that the water pressure forces a flow of water out at the surface. [< F, after *Artois,* town in France]

ARTESIAN WELL (d)
a Precipitation. *b* Seepage.
c Water table.

art·ful (ärt'fəl) *adj.* **1.** Crafty; cunning. **2.** Skillful; ingenious. **3.** Artificial. — **art'ful·ly** *adv.* — **art'ful·ness** *n.*

ar·thri·tis (är·thrī'tis) *n. Pathol.* Inflammation of a joint or joints. [< L < Gk. *arthron* joint] — **ar·thrit·ic** (är·thrit'ik) *adj. & n.*

arthro- *combining form* Joint. Also, before vowels, **arthr-**. [< Gk. *arthron*]

ar·thro·pod (är′thrə·pod) *Zool. n.* Any of a large phylum of invertebrate animals having jointed legs and segmented body parts, including insects, spiders, and crabs. [< AR-THRO- + Gk. *pous, podos* foot] — **ar·throp·o·dous** (är-throp′ə·dəs), **ar·throp′o·dal** *adj.*

Ar·thur (är′thər) Legendary sixth-century British king; hero of the Round Table. [? < Celtic, high, admirable] — **Ar·thu′ri·an** (-thōōr′ē·ən) *adj.*

ar·ti·choke (är′tə·chōk) *n.* 1. A thistlelike garden plant. 2. Its flower head, used as a vegetable. 3. The Jerusalem artichoke. [< Ital. ult. < Arabic *al-kharshūf*]

ar·ti·cle (är′ti·kəl) *n.* 1. A particular object or substance; a thing. 2. An individual item in a class: an *article* of food. 3. A literary composition forming an independent part of a newspaper, magazine, etc. 4. A separate section in a document, as in a treaty, contract, statute, etc. 5. *Gram.* One of a class of auxiliary words inserted before a noun to limit or modify it in some way, as English *a, an* (**indefinite article**) and *the* (**definite article**). — *v.* **·cled, ·cling** *v.t.* 1. To bind to service by a written contract. 2. To accuse by formal articles. — *v.i.* 3. To make accusations: with *against.* [< F < L *artus* a joint]

ar·tic·u·lar (är·tik′yə·lər) *adj.* Pertaining to a joint or the joints. [< L *articularis*]

ar·tic·u·late (*adj.* är·tik′yə·lit; *v.* är·tik′yə·lāt) *adj.* 1. Able to speak, esp. well or expressively. 2. Clearly enunciated. 3. Coherent; well presented: an *articulate* thesis. 4. Jointed; segmented, as limbs. Also **ar·tic′u·lat′ed.** — **ar·tic′u·lat·ing** *v.t.* 1. To utter distinctly; enunciate. 2. To give utterance to; express in words. 3. To joint together; unite by joints. — *v.i.* 4. To speak distinctly. 5. *Phonet.* To produce a speech sound. [< L *articulare* to divide into joints, utter distinctly] — **ar·tic′u·late·ly** *adv.* — **ar·tic′u·late·ness** *n.*

ar·tic·u·la·tion (är·tik·yə·lā′shən) *n.* 1. A jointing or being jointed together. 2. The manner or method of jointing. 3. *Anat.* The union forming a joint, as of bones. 4. The utterance of speech sounds; enunciation. 5. *Phonet.* **a** A speech sound. **b** The movements of the organs of speech in producing a speech sound. 6. *Bot.* A node or the space between two nodes. — **ar·tic·u·la·tive** (är·tik′yə·lā′tiv, -lə·tiv) *adj.* — **ar·tic·u·la·to·ry** (är·tik′yə·lə·tôr′ē, -tō′rē) *adj.*

ar·tic·u·la·tor (är·tik′yə·lā′tər) *n.* One who or that which articulates.

ar·ti·fact (är′tə·fakt) *n.* Anything made by human work or art. Also **ar′te·fact.** [< L *ars, artis* art, skill + *facere* to make]

ar·ti·fice (är′tə·fis) *n.* 1. An ingenious expedient; stratagem; maneuver. 2. Subtle or deceptive craft; trickery. 3. Skill; ingenuity. [< F < L *ars, artis* art + *facere* to make]

ar·tif·i·cer (är·tif′ə·sər) *n.* 1. One who constructs with skill. 2. *Mil.* A skilled mechanic. 3. An inventor.

ar·ti·fi·cial (är′tə·fish′əl) *adj.* 1. Produced by human art. 2. Made in imitation of something natural. 3. Feigned; fictitious. 4. Not genuine or natural; affected. [See ARTIFICE.] — **ar′ti·fi′cial·ly** *adv.* — **ar′ti·fi′cial·ness** *n.*

artificial horizon *Aeron.* An instrument that shows the deviations of an aircraft from level flight.

artificial insemination Impregnation of the female without direct sexual contact.

ar·ti·fi·ci·al·i·ty (är′tə·fish′ē·al′ə·tē) *n. pl.* **·ties** 1. The quality or state of being artificial. 2. Something artificial.

ar·til·ler·y (är·til′ə·rē) *n.* 1. Guns of larger caliber than machine guns. 2. Military units armed with such guns. 3. A branch of the U.S. Army. 4. The science of gunnery. 5. *U.S. Slang* A firearm. [< OF *artiller* to fortify]

ar·til·ler·y·man (är·til′ə·rē·mən) *n. pl.* **·men** (-mən) A soldier in the artillery. Also **ar·til′ler·ist.**

ar·ti·san (är′tə·zən) *n.* A trained or skilled workman. [< F < Ital. < L *ars, artis* art]

ar·tist (är′tist) *n.* 1. One skilled in any of the fine arts, esp. the graphic arts. 2. One whose work exhibits artistic qualities and skill; a craftsman. 3. An artiste. [< F < Ital. < L *ars, artis* art]

ar·tiste (är·tēst′) *n.* 1. An entertainer, as a dancer or singer. 2. An artist: often used ironically.

ar·tis·tic (är·tis′tik) *adj.* 1. Of or pertaining to art or artists. 2. Conforming or conformable to the principles of art; tastefully executed. 3. Fond of or sensitive to art. Also **ar·tis′ti·cal.** — **ar·tis′ti·cal·ly** *adv.*

art·ist·ry (är′tis·trē) *n.* 1. Artistic workmanship or ability. 2. The pursuits or occupation of an artist.

art·less (ärt′lis) *adj.* 1. Lacking craft or deceit; guileless; naive. 2. Natural; simple. 3. Devoid of art or skill; clumsy. 4. Uncultured; ignorant. — **Syn.** See INGENUOUS. — **art′less·ly** *adv.* — **art′less·ness** *n.*

art·y (är′tē) *adj.* Ostentatiously claiming artistic worth or interest. — **art′i·ness** *n.*

ar·um (âr′əm) *n.* Any of a genus of Old World herbs, including the philodendron. [< L < Gk. *aron*]

-ary¹ *suffix of adjectives and nouns* 1. Connected with or pertaining to what is expressed in the root word: *elementary.* 2. A person employed as or engaged in: *apothecary.* 3. A thing connected with or a place dedicated to: *dictionary.* [< L *-arius, -arium*]

-ary² *suffix of adjectives* Of or pertaining to; belonging to: *military, salutary.* See -AR¹. [< L *-aris*]

Ar·y·an (âr′ē·ən, ar′-, är′yən) *n.* 1. A member or descendant of a prehistoric people who spoke Indo-European. 2. In Nazi ideology, a Caucasian gentile, esp. one of Nordic stock. — *adj.* 1. Of or pertaining to the Aryans or their languages. 2. In Nazi ideology, of or pertaining to Caucasian gentiles. Also spelled *Arian.* [< Skt. *ārya* noble]

Ar·y·an·ize (âr′ē·ən·īz′, ar′-, är′yən-) *v.t.* **·ized, ·iz·ing** In Nazi ideology, to make characteristically Aryan or to free from (so-called) non-Aryan influences, control, etc.

as¹ (az, *unstressed* əz) *adv.* To the same degree; equally. — *conj.* 1. To the same degree or extent that: often used in correlative constructions with *as* or *so* to denote equality or identity: *as* fair *as* the sun. 2. In the way that; in the same manner that: Do *as* I do. 3. In proportion that; to the degree in which: He became gentler *as* he grew older. 4. At the same time that; while. 5. Because; since. ♦ This sense, though standard, often involves an ambiguity in meaning, and should be used with care. In the sentence *As it was raining, we stayed at home, as* may mean *while, when,* or *because.* 6. With the result or purpose that: Speak louder, so *as* to make yourself heard. 7. For instance: used to introduce examples or illustrations: Some animals are cunning, *as* the fox. 8. Though; however: Bad *as* it was, it might have been worse. — **as for** (or **as to**) In the matter of; concerning. — **as if** (or **as though**) The same, or in the same manner, that it would be if. — **as is** *Informal* Just as it is; in its present condition. — *pron.* 1. That; who; which: after *same* and *such*: He lived in the same city *as* I did. 2. A fact which: He is dead, *as* everyone knows. — *prep.* 1. In the role or character of: to act *as* umpire. 2. In the manner of; like: to use a board *as* a hammer. [ME *as, als, alse,* OE *eatswā* entirely so, just as]

as- Assimilated var. of AD-.

As (äs) Singular of ÆSIR.

as·a·fet·i·da (as′ə·fet′ə·də) *n.* A fetid substance prepared from certain plants of the parsley family, formerly used in medicine as an antispasmodic. Also **as′a·foet′i·da.** [< Med.L *asa* gum + L *foetida,* fem., ill-smelling]

as·bes·tos (as·bes′təs, az-) *n.* 1. A white or light gray silicate mineral, occurring in long slender needles or fibrous masses that may be woven or shaped into acid-resisting, nonconducting, and fireproof articles. 2. A fireproof curtain, as in a theater. — *adj.* Of or made of asbestos. Also **as·bes′tus.** [< L < Gk., < *a-* not + *sbennynai* to quench] — **as·bes·tine** (as·bes′tin, az-), **as·bes′tic** *adj.*

as·ca·rid (as′kə·rid) *n. Zool.* A nematode worm parasitic in the intestines. [< Gk. *askaris, -idos*]

as·cend (ə·send′) *v.i.* 1. To go or move upward; rise. 2. To lie along an ascending slope. — *v.t.* 3. To mount; climb. [< L < *ad-* to + *scandere* to climb] — **as·cend′a·ble** or **as·cend′i·ble** *adj.* — **as·cen′sive** *adj.* — **as·cen′der** *n.*

as·cen·dan·cy (ə·sen′dən·sē) *n.* The quality, fact, or state of being in the ascendant; domination; sway. Also **as·cen′dance, as·cen′dence, as·cen′den·cy.**

as·cen·dant (ə·sen′dənt) *adj.* 1. Ascending; rising. 2. Superior; dominant. 3. *Astron.* Coming to or above the horizon. — *n.* A position of preeminence; domination. Also **as·cen′dent.** — **to be in the ascendant** To approach or occupy a predominating position.

as·cen·sion (ə·sen′shən) *n.* The act of ascending. — **the Ascension** *Theol.* The bodily assent of Christ into heaven after the Resurrection, commemorated on **Ascension Day,** the fortieth day after Easter. — **as·cen′sion·al** *adj.*

as·cent (ə·sent′) *n.* 1. The act of ascending in space; a rising, soaring, or climbing. 2. A rise in state, rank, or station; advancement. 3. A way or means of ascending; upward slope. 4. The degree of acclivity: an *ascent* of 30°.

as·cer·tain (as′ər·tān′) *v.t.* To learn with certainty; find out by experiment or investigation. [< OF < *a-* to (< L *ad-*) + *certain*] — **as′cer·tain′a·ble** *adj.* — **as′cer·tain′a·ble·ness** *n.* — **as′cer·tain′a·bly** *adv.* — **as′cer·tain′ment** *n.*

as·cet·ic (ə·set′ik) *n.* One who leads a very austere and self-denying life, esp. for religious purposes. — *adj.* 1. Pertaining to ascetics or asceticism. 2. Rigidly abstinent; austere. Also **as·cet′i·cal** *adj.* [< Gk. *askētēs* one who practices (self-denial), a monk] — **as·cet′i·cal·ly** *adv.*

as·cet·i·cism (ə·set′ə·siz′əm) *n.* Ascetic belief or conduct.

as·cid·i·an (ə·sid′ē·ən) *Zool.* One of a class of marine animals having a leathery sac; a tunicate. — *adj.* Of or pertaining to this class of animals. [< NL < ASCIDIUM]

as·cid·i·um (ə·sid′ē·əm) *n. pl.* **·cid·i·a** (-sid′ē·ə) *Bot.* A flask-shaped plant appendage. [< NL < Gk. *askos* bag]

As·cle·pi·us (as·klē′pē·əs) In Greek mythology, the god of medicine: identified with the Roman *Aesculapius.*

as·co·my·ce·tous (as′kə·mī·sē′təs) *adj. Bot.* Belonging to a large class of fungi, including mildews and yeasts. [< NL *Ascomycetes*]

a·scor·bic (ə·skôr′bik) *adj.* Antiscorbutic.

ascorbic acid *Biochem.* The scurvy-preventing vitamin C, a white, odorless, crystalline compound, $C_6H_8O_6$, present in citrus and other fresh fruits, tomatoes, potatoes, and green leafy vegetables, and also made synthetically.

as·cot (as′kət, -kot) *n.* A kind of necktie knotted so that the broad ends are laid one across the other. [after *Ascot*, a village in England.]

as·cribe (ə·skrīb′) *v.t.* **·cribed, ·crib·ing** 1. To attribute or impute, as to a cause or source: I *ascribe* his conduct to insanity. 2. To consider or declare as belonging (to); assign as a quality or attribute. — **Syn.** See ATTRIBUTE. [< L < *ad-* to + *scribere* to write] — **as·crib′a·ble** *adj.*

as·crip·tion (ə·skrip′shən) *n.* 1. The act of ascribing. 2. That which ascribes; esp., a text or sentence of praise to God.

-ase *suffix Chem.* Used in naming enzymes: *amylase, casease.*

a·sea (ə·sē′) *adv.* To or toward the sea; at sea.

a·sep·sis (ə·sep′sis, ā-) *n. Med.* 1. Absence of pathogenic organisms. 2. The prevention of infection by the use of sterilized instruments, dressings, etc. [< A-⁴ + SEPSIS]

a·sep·tic (ə·sep′tik, ā-) *adj.* Free of pathogenic microorganisms. — **a·sep′ti·cal·ly** *adv.*

a·sex·u·al (ā·sek′shoo·əl) *adj. Biol.* 1. Having no distinct sexual organs; without sex. 2. Occurring or performed without union of male and female gametes. — **a·sex·u·al·i·ty** (ā·sek′shoo·al′ə·tē) *n.* — **a·sex′u·al·ly** *adv.*

As·gard (as′gärd, äs′-) In Norse mythology, the home of the gods and of heroes slain in battle. Also **As·garth** (äs′gärth). [< ON < *āss* god + *gardhr* yard, dwelling]

ash¹ (ash) *n.* The powdery, whitish gray residue of a substance that has been burned. [OE *æsce, asce*]

ash² (ash) *n.* 1. A tree of the olive family. 2. The light, tough, elastic wood of this tree. — *adj.* Made of ash wood. [OE *æsc*]

a·shamed (ə·shāmd′) *adj.* 1. Feeling shame. 2. Deterred by fear of shame. [OE *āscamod,* pp. of *āscamian*] — **a·sham·ed·ly** (ə·shā′mid·lē) *adv.* — **a·sham′ed·ness** *n.*

ash·en¹ (ash′ən) *adj.* 1. Of, pertaining to, or like ashes. 2. Pale in color; gray.

ash·en² (ash′ən) *adj.* Pertaining to or made of ash wood.

ash·es (ash′iz) *n.pl.* 1. The grayish white, powdery particles remaining after something has been burned. 2. The remains of the human body after cremation. 3. Mortal remains. 4. Volcanic lava. [pl. of ASH¹]

ash·lar (ash′lər) *n.* 1. In masonry, a roughhewn block of stone. 2. A thin, dressed, squared stone, used for facing a wall. 3. Masonry made of such stones. Also **ash′ler.** [< OF < L *axis* board, plank]

a·shore (ə·shôr′, ə·shōr′) *adv. & adj.* 1. To or on the shore. 2. On land; aground.

Ash Wednesday The first day of Lent: from the sprinkling of ashes on the heads of penitents.

ash·y (ash′ē) *adj.* **ash·i·er, ash·i·est** 1. Of, pertaining to, or like ashes; ash-covered. 2. Ash-colored; ashen.

A·sian (ā′zhən, ā′shən) *adj.* Of or characteristic of Asia or its peoples. — *n.* A native or inhabitant of Asia.

A·si·at·ic (ā′zhē·at′ik, ā′shē-) *adj. & n.* Asian. ◆ In most cases, esp. in the ethnic sense, *Asian* is now preferred.

a·side (ə·sīd′) *adv.* 1. On or to one side; apart. 2. Out of thought or use: to put grief *aside.* 3. Away from the general company; in seclusion: He drew me *aside.* 4. Away from one's person; down. 5. In reserve. — **aside from** *U.S.* 1. Apart from. 2. Excepting. — *n.* Lines spoken privately by an actor and supposed to be heard by the audience but not by the other actors.

as·i·nine (as′ə·nīn) *adj.* Pertaining to or like an ass, considered a stupid, obstinate animal. [< L *asinus* ass] — **as′·i·nin·i·ty** *adv.* — **as·i·nin·i·ty** (as′ə·nin′ə·tē) *n.*

ask (ask, äsk) *v.t.* 1. To put a question to: Don't *ask* me. 2. To put a question about: to *ask* the time. 3. To make a request of or for; solicit. 4. To need or require: This job *asks* too much time. 5. To state the price of; demand. 6. To invite. — *v.i.* 7. To make inquiries: with *for, after,* or *about.* 8. To make a request: often with *for:* He *asked* for aid. [OE *āscian*] — **ask′er** *n.*

— **Syn.** 1. *Ask* is the most direct and inclusive term of putting a question to a person. *Query* suggests the effort to settle a doubt. To *question* is to put a series of questions; to *interrogate* is to *question* formally or by right of authority. We *quiz* as a test of knowledge. *Inquire* suggests the effort to ascertain facts or the truth. 3. *Ask* and *request* mean to urge that something desired be granted or handed over. *Ask* suggests the expectation of compliance; *request* is more formal, and allows for refusal.

a·skance (ə·skans′) *adv.* 1. With a side glance; sidewise. 2. Disdainfully; distrustfully. Also **a·skant′.** [Origin unknown]

a·skew (ə·skyoo′) *adj.* Oblique. — *adv.* In an oblique position or manner; to one side; awry.

a·slant (ə·slant′, ə·slänt′) *adj.* Slanting; oblique. — *adv.* At a slant; obliquely. — *prep.* Slantingly across or over.

a·sleep (ə·slēp′) *adj.* 1. In a state of sleep; sleeping. 2. Dormant; inactive. 3. Benumbed, as an arm or leg. 4. Dead. — *adv.* Into a sleeping condition: to fall *asleep.*

a·slope (ə·slōp′) *adj.* Sloping. — *adv.* At a slope.

a·so·cial (ā·sō′shəl) *adj.* 1. Avoiding society; not gregarious. 2. Heedless of one's fellow beings; self-centered.

asp (asp) *n.* The common European viper. [< L < Gk.]

as·par·a·gus (ə·spar′ə·gəs) *n.* 1. The succulent, edible shoots of a cultivated variety of a perennial herb of the lily family. 2. Any related plant. [< L < Gk. *aspharagos*]

as·pect (as′pekt) *n.* 1. The look of a person; facial expression. 2. Appearance to the eye; look: the pleasant *aspect* of a lake. 3. Appearance presented to the mind by circumstances, etc.; interpretation: all *aspects* of a problem. 4. A looking or facing in a given direction: the southern *aspect* of a house. 5. The side or surface facing in a certain direction: ventral *aspect.* 6. In astrology: a Any configuration of the planets. b The supposed influence of this for good or evil. — **Syn.** See PHASE. [< L < *ad-* at + *specere* to look]

asp·en (as′pən) *n.* Any of several species of poplar of North America or Europe with leaves that tremble in the slightest breeze. — *adj.* 1. Of the aspen. 2. Shaking, like aspen leaves. [OE *æspe*]

as·per·i·ty (as·per′ə·tē) *n. pl.* **·ties** 1. Roughness or harshness, as of surface, sound, etc. 2. Sharpness of temper; acrimony. [< OF < L *asper* rough]

as·perse (ə·spûrs′) *v.t.* **as·persed** (ə·spûrst′), **as·pers·ing** To spread false charges against; slander. [< L < *ad-* to + *spargere* to sprinkle] — **as·pers′er** or **as·per′sor** *n.* — **as·per′sive** (-siv) *adj.*

as·per·sion (ə·spûr′zhən, -shən) *n.* 1. A slandering; defamation. 2. A slanderous or damaging report; calumny.

as·phalt (as′fôlt, -falt) *n.* 1. A solid, brownish black, combustible mixture of bituminous hydrocarbons, found native in various parts of the world and also obtained as a residue in the refining of petroleum. 2. A mixture of this with sand or gravel, used for paving, etc. Also **as·phal·tum** (as·fal′təm), **as·phal′tus.** — *v.t.* To pave with asphalt. [< LL < Gk. *asphalton*] — **as·phal·tic** (as·fôl′tik, -fal′-) *adj.*

as·pho·del (as′fə·del) *n.* A plant of the lily family, bearing white, pink, or yellow flowers. [< L < Gk. *asphodelos*]

as·phyx·i·a (as·fik′sē·ə) *n. Pathol.* Unconsciousness caused by too little oxygen and too much carbon dioxide in the blood. [< NL < Gk. < *a-* not + *sphyzein* to beat] — **as·phyx′i·al** *adj.* — **as·phyx′i·ant** *adj. & n.*

as·phyx·i·ate (as·fik′sē·āt) *v.* **·at·ed, ·at·ing** *v.t.* 1. To cause asphyxia in; suffocate. — *v.i.* 2. To undergo asphyxia. — **as·phyx′i·a′tion** *n.* — **as·phyx′i·a′tor** *n.*

as·pic (as′pik) *n.* A jelly of meat or vegetable juices, served as a relish or as a mold for meat, vegetables, etc. [< F]

as·pi·dis·tra (as′pə·dis′trə) *n.* A stemless, Asian herb of the lily family, with large, glossy, evergreen leaves. [< NL < Gk. *aspis, aspidos* shield + *astron* star]

as·pi·rant (ə·spīr′ənt, as′pər·ənt) *n.* One who aspires, as after honors or place; a candidate. — *adj.* Aspiring.

as·pi·rate (*v.* as′pə·rāt; *n. & adj.* as′pər·it) *v.t.* **·rat·ed, ·rat·ing** 1. To utter with a puff of breath or as if preceded by an *h* sound. 2. To follow with a puff of breath, as *p,* (t), and (k) when before a vowel. 3. *Med.* To draw out with an aspirator. — *n.* An aspirated sound. — *adj. Phonet.* Uttered with an aspirate: also **as′pi·rat·ed** (-rā′tid). [See ASPIRE.]

as·pi·ra·tion (as′pə·rā′shən) *n.* 1. Exalted desire; high ambition. 2. The act of breathing; breath. 3. *Med.* The use of an aspirator. 4. *Phonet.* An aspirate.

as·pi·ra·tor (as′pə·rā′tər) *n. Med.* A device for drawing off fluid matter or gases from the body by suction.

as·pi·ra·to·ry (ə·spīr′ə·tôr′ē, -tō′rē) *adj.* Of, pertaining to, or adapted for breathing or suction.

as·pire (ə·spīr′) *v.i.* **spired, spir·ing** To have an earnest desire or ambition. [< L < *ad-* to + *spirare* to breathe] — **as·pir′er** *n.* — **as·pir′ing** *adj.* — **as·pir′ing·ly** *adv.*

as·pi·rin (as′pər·in, -prin) *n.* A white crystalline compound, the acetyl derivative of salicylic acid, $C_9H_8O_4$, used for the relief of fever, pain, etc. [< A(CETYL) + SPIR(AEIC ACID), former name of salicylic acid, + -IN]

a·squint (ə·skwint′) *adj. & adv.* With sidelong glance.

ass (as, äs) *n. pl.* **ass·es** 1. A long-eared quadruped smaller than the ordinary horse, used as a beast of burden; the donkey. 2. A stupid person; fool. [OE *assa* ? < OIrish < L *asinus*]

as·sail (ə·sāl′) *v.t.* To attack violently, as by force, argument, etc. — **Syn.** See ATTACK. [< OF < LL < L *ad-* to + *salire* to leap] — **as·sail′a·ble** *adj.* — **as·sail′a·ble·ness** *n.*

as·sail·ant (ə·sā′lənt) *n.* One who assails. Also **as·sail′er.** — *adj.* Attacking; hostile.

as·sas·sin (ə·sas′in) *n.* One who kills; esp., one who murders a political figure from fanaticism or for a price.

as·sas·si·nate (ə·sas′ə·nāt) *v.t.* **·nat·ed, ·nat·ing** 1. To kill by secret or surprise assault. 2. To destroy or injure by treachery, as a reputation. — **Syn.** See KILL. — **as·sas′si·na′tion** *n.* — **as·sas′si·na′tor** *n.*

as·sault (ə·sôlt′) *n.* 1. Any violent attack, as an act, speech, or writing. 2. *Law* An unlawful attempt or offer to do bodily injury to another. 3. A rape. 4. *Mil.* **a** An attack upon a fortified place. **b** A closing with the enemy. — *v.t. & v.i.* To attack with violence. — **Syn.** See ATTACK. [< OF < L ad- to + salire to leap]

assault and battery *Law* The carrying out of an assault with force and violence; a beating.

as·say (n. ə·sā′, as′ā; v. ə·sā′) *n.* 1. The analysis or testing of an alloy or ore to ascertain the ingredients and their proportions. 2. The substance to be so examined. 3. The result of such a test. 4. Any examination or testing. — *v.t.* 1. To subject to chemical analysis; make an assay of. 2. To prove; test. — *v.i.* 3. *U.S.* To show by analysis a certain value or proportion, as of a precious metal. [< OF assai, var. of essai trial] — **as·say′er** *n.*

as·sem·blage (ə·sem′blij, for def. 4, also Fr. à·sän·bläzh′) *n.* 1. The act of assembling, or the state of being assembled. 2. Any gathering of persons or things; collection; assembly. 3. A fitting together, as of the parts of a machine. 4. A work of art created by assembling materials and objects; also, the technique of making such works: compare COLLAGE. — **Syn.** See COMPANY. [< F]

as·sem·ble (ə·sem′bəl) *v.t. & v.i.* **·bled, ·bling** 1. To come or bring together; collect or congregate. 2. To fit or join together, as the parts of a mechanism. [< OF < L ad- to + simul together] — **as·sem′bler** *n.*

as·sem·bly (ə·sem′blē) *n. pl.* **·blies** 1. The act of assembling, or the state of being assembled. 2. A number of persons met together for a common purpose. 3. The act or process of fitting together the parts of a machine, etc.; also, the parts themselves. 4. *Mil.* The signal calling troops to form ranks.

assembly line An arrangement of industrial equipment and workers in which the product passes from one specialized operation to another until completed.

as·sem·bly·man (ə·sem′blē·mən) *n. pl.* **·men** (-men′, -mən) *U.S. & Canadian* A member of a legislative assembly, esp. of a State or Provincial legislature.

as·sent (ə·sent′) *v.i.* To express agreement; acquiesce; concur: usually with to. — *n.* 1. Mental concurrence or agreement. 2. Consent; sanction. [< OF < L ad- to + sentire to feel] — **as·sen·ta′tion** *n.* — **as·sent′er** *n.*

as·sert (ə·sûrt′) *v.t.* 1. To state positively; affirm; declare. 2. To maintain as a right or claim, as by words or force. — **to assert oneself** To put forward and defend one's own rights or claims. [< L ad- to + serere to bind] — **as·sert′a·ble** or **as·sert′i·ble** adj. — **as·sert′er** or **as·ser′tor** *n.*

as·ser·tion (ə·sûr′shən) *n.* 1. The act of asserting. 2. A positive declaration without attempt at proof.

as·ser·tive (ə·sûr′tiv) *adj.* Confident; aggressive. — **as·ser′tive·ly** *adv.* — **as·ser′tive·ness** *n.*

as·sess (ə·ses′) *v.t.* 1. To charge with a tax, fine, or other payment, as a person or property. 2. To determine the amount of, as a tax or other fine on a person or property. 3. To evaluate, as property, for taxation. [< OF < LL < L assidere to sit by (as a judge in court)] — **as·sess′a·ble** adj.

as·sess·ment (ə·ses′mənt) *n.* 1. The act of assessing. 2. An amount assessed.

as·ses·sor (ə·ses′ər) *n.* One who makes assessments, as for taxation. — **as·ses·so·ri·al** (as′ə·sôr′ē·əl, -sō′rē-) adj.

as·set (as′et) *n.* 1. An item of property. 2. A useful or valuable thing or quality.

as·sets (as′ets) *n.pl.* 1. In accounting, a balance sheet showing all the property or resources of a person or business, and money owed: opposed to liabilities. 2. *Law* All the property, real and personal, of a person, corporation, or partnership, that is or may be chargeable with their debts or legacies. [< OF < LL ad- to + satis enough]

as·sev·er·ate (ə·sev′ə·rāt) *v.t.* **·at·ed, ·at·ing** To affirm or declare emphatically or solemnly. [< L ad- to + severus serious] — **as·sev′er·a′tion** *n.*

as·si·du·i·ty (as′ə·dōō′ə·tē, -dyōō′-) *n. pl.* **·ties** Close and continuous application or effort; diligence.

as·sid·u·ous (ə·sij′ōō·əs) *adj.* 1. Devoted; attentive. 2. Unremitting; persistent: assiduous study. [< L ad- to + sedere to sit] — **as·sid′u·ous·ly** adv. — **as·sid′u·ous·ness** *n.*

as·sign (ə·sīn′) *v.t.* 1. To set apart, as for a particular function; designate: to assign a day for trial. 2. To appoint, as to or for a post or duty. 3. To allot as a task: to assign a lesson. 4. To ascribe or attribute; refer: to assign a monument to Roman times. 5. *Law* To transfer, as personal property, rights, or interests. — *v.i.* 6. To transfer property, espe-

cially for the benefit of creditors. — **Syn.** See ATTRIBUTE. — *n.* Law Usually pl. Assignee. [< OF < L < ad- to + signare make a sign] — **as·sign′a·bil·i·ty** *n.* — **as·sign′a·ble** adj. — **as·sign′a·bly** adv. — **as·sign′er,** Law **as·sign·or** (ə·sī′nôr′, as′ə·nôr′) *n.*

as·sig·na·tion (as′ig·nā′shən) *n.* 1. An appointment for meeting, esp. a secret or illicit one as made by lovers. 2. An assignment. [See ASSIGN.]

as·sign·ee (ə·sī′nē′, as′ə·nē′) *n.* Law A person to whom property, rights, or powers are transferred.

as·sign·ment (ə·sīn′mənt) *n.* 1. The act of assigning. 2. Anything assigned, as a lesson or task. 3. *Law* **a** The transfer of a claim, right, or property, or the instrument or writing of transfer. **b** The claim, right, or property transferred.

as·sim·i·la·ble (ə·sim′ə·lə·bəl) *adj.* Capable of being assimilated. — **as·sim′i·la·bil′i·ty** *n.*

as·sim·i·late (ə·sim′ə·lāt) *v.* **·lat·ed, ·lat·ing** *v.t.* 1. *Biol.* To take up and incorporate into living organisms, as food. 2. To make into a homogeneous part, as of a substance or system. 3. To make alike or similar; cause to resemble. — *v.i.* 4. To become alike or similar. 5. To become absorbed or assimilated. [< L < ad- to + similare to make like] — **as·sim′i·la·tive, as·sim·i·la·to·ry** (ə·sim′ə·lə·tôr′ē, -tō′rē) adj.

as·sim·i·la·tion (ə·sim′ə·lā′shən) *n.* 1. The act or process of assimilating. 2. *Biol.* The transformation of nutriment into an integral part of a plant or animal. 3. *Phonet.* The process whereby a sound is influenced by a neighboring sound, as when horseshoe is pronounced (hôrsh′shōō′).

as·sist (ə·sist′) *v.t.* 1. To give or render help to; relieve; succor. 2. To act as subordinate or deputy to. — *v.i.* 3. To give help or support. 4. In baseball, to aid a teammate in a put-out. — **to assist at** To be present at (a ceremony, etc.). — *n.* 1. An act of helping. 2. In baseball, a play that helps to put out a runner. [< MF < L < ad- to + sistere to cause to stand] — **as·sist′er,** Law **as·sis′tor** *n.*

as·sis·tance (ə·sis′təns) *n.* The act of helping, or the help given; aid; support.

as·sis·tant (ə·sis′tənt) *n.* One who assists; a subordinate or helper. — *adj.* 1. Holding a subordinate or auxiliary place, office, or rank. 2. Affording aid; assisting.

as·size (ə·sīz′) *n.* 1. Originally, a session of a legislative or judicial body. 2. pl. In England, one of the regular court sessions held in each county for the trial of civil and criminal cases by jury; also, the time and place of such sessions. [< OF < L assidere to sit by (as a judge at court)]

as·so·ci·ate (n. & adj. ə·sō′shē·it, -āt, -sē-; v. ə·sō′shē·āt, -sē-) *n.* 1. A companion. 2. A partner, colleague, or fellow employee. 3. Anything that habitually accompanies something else; a concomitant. 4. One admitted to partial membership in an association, society, or institution. — adj. 1. Joined with another or others in a common pursuit or office. 2. Having subordinate or secondary status: an associate professor. 3. Existing or occurring together; concomitant. — *v.* **·at·ed, ·at·ing** *v.t.* 1. To ally; unite. 2. To combine. 3. To connect mentally. — *v.i.* 4. To unite for a common purpose. 5. To keep or be in company: with with. [< L < ad- to + sociare to join]

Associated Press An organization for collecting news and distributing to member newspapers.

as·so·ci·a·tion (ə·sō′sē·ā′shən, -shē-) *n.* 1. The act of associating. 2. The state of being associated; fellowship; companionship. 3. A body of persons associated for some common purpose; society; league. Abbr. assn., assn., assoc. 4. *Ecol.* A group of plants or animals sharing a common habitat and similar geographic conditions. 5. The connection or relation of ideas, feelings, etc. — **as·so′ci·a′tion·al** adj.

association football Soccer.

as·so·ci·a·tive (ə·sō′shē·ā′tiv, -shē·ə-) *adj.* 1. Of or characterized by association. 2. Causing association. — **as·so′ci·a′tive·ly** adv.

as·so·nance (as′ə·nəns) *n.* 1. Resemblance in sound; especially, in prosody, correspondence of accented vowels, but not of consonants, as in main, came. 2. Rough likeness; approximation. [< F, ult. < L < ad- to + sonare to sound] — **as′so·nant** adj. & *n.*

as·sort (ə·sôrt′) *v.t.* 1. To distribute into groups according to kinds; classify. 2. To furnish, as a warehouse, with a variety of goods, etc. — *v.i.* 3. To fall into groups or classes of the same kind. 4. To associate: with with. [< OF < a- to + sorte sort] — **as·sort′er** *n.*

as·sort·ed (ə·sôr′tid) *adj.* 1. Containing or arranged in various sorts or kinds; miscellaneous. 2. Classified. 3. Matched.

as·sort·ment (ə·sôrt′mənt) *n.* 1. The act of assorting; classification. 2. A varied collection; miscellany.

as·suage (ə·swāj′) *v.t.* **·suaged, ·suag·ing** 1. To make less harsh or severe; alleviate. 2. To satisfy, as thirst. 3. To calm; pacify. [< OF < L ad- to + suavis sweet] — **as·suage′ment** *n.*

as·sume (ə·sōōm′) *v.t.* **·sumed, ·sum·ing** 1. To take on or adopt, as a style of dress, aspect, or character. 2. To undertake, as an office or duty. **3.** To usurp, as powers of state. **4.** To take for granted. **5.** To affect; feign. [< L < *ad-* to + *sumere* to take] — **as·sum·a·ble** (ə-sōō′mə-bəl) *adj.*

as·sump·tion (ə-sump′shən) *n.* **1.** The act of assuming, or that which is assumed. **2.** That which is taken for granted; a supposition. **3.** Presumption; arrogance. **4.** *Logic* A minor premise. — **Syn.** See HYPOTHESIS. — **the Assumption** A church feast, observed on August 15, commemorating the bodily ascent of the Virgin Mary into heaven. — **as·sump′·tive** *adj.* — **as·sump′tive·ly** *adv.*

as·sur·ance (ə-shŏŏr′əns) *n.* **1.** The act of assuring, or the state of being assured. **2.** A positive statement, intended to give confidence, encouragement, etc. **3.** Self-confidence. **4.** Boldness; effrontery. **5.** *Chiefly Brit.* Insurance.

as·sure (ə-shŏŏr′) *v.t.* **·sured, ·sur·ing 1.** To make sure or secure; establish firmly. **2.** To make (something) certain; guarantee. **3.** To cause to feel certain; convince. **4.** To promise; make positive declaration to. **5.** To encourage; reassure. **6.** To insure, as against loss. [< OF < LL < L *ad-* to + *securus* safe] — **as·sur′a·ble** *adj.* — **as·sur′er** *n.*

as·sured (ə-shŏŏrd′) *adj.* **1.** Made certain; undoubted; sure: His defeat is *assured.* **2.** Self-possessed; confident. **3.** Insured. — *n.* An insured person. — **as·sur·ed·ly** (ə-shŏŏr′id·lē) *adv.* — **as·sur′ed·ness** *n.*

As·syr·i·a (ə-sir′ē-ə) An ancient empire of western Asia; capital, Nineveh. — **As·syr′i·an** *adj. & n.*

as·ta·tine (as′tə-tēn, -tin) *n.* An unstable chemical element (symbol At) of atomic number 85, related to the halogens and occupying the place formerly assigned to alabamine. [< Gk. *astatos* unstable + -INE²]

as·ter (as′tər) *n.* A plant of the composite family, having flowers with white, purple, or blue rays and yellow disc. [< L < Gk. *astēr* star]

-aster *suffix* Little; inferior: *poetaster.* [< L *-aster,* dim. suffix]

as·ter·isk (as′tər·isk) *n. Printing* A starlike figure (*) used to indicate omissions, footnotes, references, etc. — *v.t.* To mark with an asterisk. [< L < Gk. *astēr* star]

a·stern (ə-stûrn′) *adv. & adj. Naut.* **1.** In the rear; at any point behind a vessel. **2.** To the rear; backward.

astero- *combining form* Of or related to a star. Also *aster-* (before vowels): also **asteri-**. [< Gk. *astēr* a star]

as·ter·oid (as′tə-roid) *adj.* Star-shaped. — *n.* **1.** *Astron.* Any of several hundred small planets between Mars and Jupiter: also called *planetoid.* **2.** A starfish. [< Gk. *astēr* a star] — **as′ter·oi′dal** *adj.*

asth·ma (az′mə, as′-) *n. Pathol.* A chronic respiratory disorder characterized by recurrent paroxysmal coughing and constriction of the chest. [< Gk. *azein* to breathe hard]

asth·mat·ic (az-mat′ik, as-) *adj.* Of, pertaining to, or affected with asthma. Also **asth·mat′i·cal.** — *n.* A person suffering from asthma. — **asth·mat′i·cal·ly** *adv.*

as·tig·mat·ic (as′tig-mat′ik) *adj.* Of, having, or correcting astigmatism.

a·stig·ma·tism (ə-stig′mə-tiz′əm) *n.* A defect of the eye or of a lens such that the rays of light from an object do not converge to a focus, thus causing imperfect vision or images. [< A-⁴ without + Gk. *stigma, -atos* mark, spot + -ISM]

a·stir (ə-stûr′) *adv. & adj.* Stirring; moving about.

a·ston·ish (ə-ston′ish) *v.t.* To affect with wonder and surprise; amaze; confound. [OF *estoner* < L *ex-* out + *tonare* to thunder] — **a·ston′ish·er** *n.* — **a·ston′ish·ing** *adj.* — **a·ston′ish·ing·ly** *adv.*

a·ston·ish·ment (ə-ston′ish-mənt) *n.* **1.** The state of being astonished. **2.** A cause of such emotion.

a·stound (ə-stound′) *v.t.* To overwhelm with wonder; confound. [ME < OF *estoner* < L *ex-* out + *tonare* to thunder] — **a·stound′ing** *adj.* — **a·stound′ing·ly** *adv.*

as·trag·a·lus (as-trag′ə-ləs) *n. pl. -li* (-lī) *Anat.* The talus. [< L < Gk. *astragalos*] — **as·trag′a·lar** (-lər) *adj.*

as·tra·khan (as′trə-kan, -kən) *n.* **1.** The black or gray, loosely curled fur made from the pelt of lambs raised near Astrakhan. **2.** A fabric with a curled pile imitative of this. Also **as·tra·chan.**

as·tral (as′trəl) *adj.* **1.** Of, pertaining to, coming from, or like the stars; starry. **2.** Of or designating a supposedly supernatural substance. — *n.* An astral body. [< LL < L < Gk. *astron* star] — **as′tral·ly** *adv.*

a·stray (ə-strā′) *adv. & adj.* Away from the right path; wandering. [< OF < L *extra-* beyond + *vagare* to wander]

a·stride (ə-strīd′) *adv. & adj.* **1.** With one leg on each side. **2.** With the legs far apart. — *prep.* With one leg on each side of: *astride* a horse.

as·trin·gent (ə-strin′jənt) *adj.* **1.** *Med.* Tending to contract or draw together organic tissues; binding; styptic. **2.** Harsh; stern; austere. — *n.* An astringent substance. [< L < *ad-* to + *stringere* to bind fast] — **as·trin′gen·cy** *n.* — **as·trin′gent·ly** *adv.*

astro- *combining form* **1.** Star. **2.** Of, pertaining to, occurring in, or characteristic of outer space: *astronautics.* [< Gk. *astron* star]

as·tro·dy·nam·ics (as′trō-dī·nam′iks) *n.pl.* (construed as *sing.*) The branch of dynamics concerned with the motions of celestial bodies.

as·tro·labe (as′trə-lāb) *n.* An instrument formerly used for obtaining the altitudes of planets and stars. [< OF < Med.L < Gk. *astron* star + *lambanein* to take]

as·trol·o·gy (ə-strol′ə-jē) *n.* The study professing to foretell the future and interpret the influence of the heavenly bodies upon the destinies of men. [< L < Gk. < *astron* star + *logos* discourse] — **as·trol′o·ger** *n.* — **as·tro·log·ic** (as′trə-loj′ik) or **-i·cal, as·trol′o·gous** (-gəs) *adj.* — **as′tro·log′i·cal·ly** *adv.*

as·tro·naut (as′trə-nôt) *n.* One who travels in space. [< ASTRO- + *-naut* (< Gk. *nautēs* sailor), after *aeronaut*]

as·tro·nau·tics (as′trə-nô′tiks) *n.pl.* (construed as *sing.*) The science and art of space travel. — **as′tro·nau′tic** or **-ti·cal** *adj.* — **as′tro·nau′ti·cal·ly** *adv.*

as·tron·o·mer (ə-stron′ə-mər) *n.* One learned or expert in astronomy. Abbr. *astr., astron.*

as·tro·nom·i·cal (as′trə-nom′i·kəl) *adj.* **1.** Of or pertaining to astronomy. **2.** Enormously or inconceivably large. Also **as′tro·nom′ic.** — **as′tro·nom′i·cal·ly** *adv.*

astronomical unit A space unit for expressing the distances of the stars, equal to the mean distance of the earth from the sun.

astronomical year The period between two passages of the sun through the same equinox, equal to about 365 days, 5 hours, 48 minutes, and 46 seconds.

as·tron·o·my (ə-stron′ə-mē) *n.* The science that treats of the heavenly bodies, their motions, magnitudes, distances, and constitution. [< OF < L < Gk. *astron* star + *nomos* law]

as·tro·phys·ics (as′trō-fiz′iks) *n.pl.* (construed as *sing.*) The branch of astronomy that treats of the physical constitution and properties of the heavenly bodies. — **as′tro·phys′i·cal** *adj.* — **as′tro·phys′i·cist** (as′trō-fiz′ə-sist) *n.*

as·tute (ə·stōōt′, ə·styōōt′) *adj.* Keen in discernment; acute; shrewd; cunning. [< L *astus* cunning] — **as·tute′ly** *adv.* — **as·tute′ness** *n.*

a·sun·der (ə-sun′dər) *adv.* **1.** Apart; into pieces. **2.** In or into a different place or direction. — *adj.* Separated; apart. [OE *on sundran*]

a·sy·lum (ə-sī′ləm) *n. pl.* **·lums** or **·la** (-lə) **1.** An institution for the care of the mentally ill, the aged, the destitute, etc. **2.** A place of refuge. **3.** An inviolable shelter from arrest or punishment, as a temple or church in ancient times. [< L < Gk. < *a-* without + *sylon* right of seizure]

a·sym·met·ric (ā′si-met′rik, as′i-) *adj.* **1.** Not symmetrical. **2.** *Chem.* Designating an unbalanced spatial arrangement of atoms and radicals within a molecule. Also **a′sym·met′ri·cal.** — **a′sym·met′ri·cal·ly** *adv.*

a·sym·me·try (ā-sim′ə-trē) *n.* Lack of symmetry.

as·ymp·tote (as′im-tōt) *n. Math.* A straight line that an indefinitely extended curve continually approaches as a tangent. [< Gk. < *a-* not + *syn-* together + *piptein* to fall] — **as′ymp·tot′ic** or **-i·cal** *adj.* — **as′ymp·tot′i·cal·ly** *adv.*

at (at, *unstressed* ət) *prep.* **1.** In or on the position of: *at* the center of the circle. **2.** Of time, on or upon the point or stroke of: *at* noon. **3.** During the course or lapse of: *at* night. **4.** In contact with; on; upon: *at* sea. **5.** To or toward: Look *at* that sunset! **6.** Through; by way of: Smoke came out *at* the windows. **7.** Within the limits of; present in: *at* home. **8.** Engaged or occupied in: *at* work. **9.** Attending: *at* a party. **10.** In the state or condition of: *at* war. **11.** In the region or vicinity of: *at* the door. **12.** With an interval of: *at* sixty paces. **13.** Having reference to; in connection with: He winced *at* the thought. **14.** In the manner of: *at* a trot. **15.** In pursuit or quest of; in the direction of; against: to catch *at* straws. **16.** Dependent upon: *at* an enemy's mercy. **17.** According to: Proceed *at* your discretion. **18.** Amounting to: interest *at* two percent. **19.** From; out of: to draw water *at* a well. **20.** On the occasion of. [OE *æt*] — **Syn. 2.** *At, in,* and *on* may be used with reference to time. An event occurs *at* an hour of the day, *in* a month or year, *on* a day of the week, a date, or a precise division of time: to arrive *on* the hour. **7.** *At, in,* and *on* may be used of spatial location. Something is *at* a place regarded as a point: *at* a city, displayed *at* the museum. It is *in* a place regarded as embracing it: *in* a country, *in* a suburb. A building is said to be *on* a street.

At·a·brine (at′ə-brin, -brēn) *n.* Proprietary name for a brand of quinacrine. Also **at′a·brine.**

at·a·rac·tic (at′ə-rak′tik) *n. Med.* A drug having the power to tranquilize and to lessen nervous tension. Also **at′a·rax′ic** (-rak′sik). [< NL < Gk. *ataraktein* to be calm]

at·a·vism (at′ə-viz′əm) *n.* **1.** Reversion to an earlier or primitive type. **2.** *Biol.* Reversion. [< F < L < *at-* beyond + *avus* grandfather] — **at′a·vist** *n*. — **at′a·vis′tic** *adj*.

a·tax·i·a (ə·tak′sē·ə) *n. Pathol.* Loss or failure of muscular coordination. Also **a·tax·y** (ə·tak′sē). [< NL < Gk. < *a*- not + *tattein* to arrange] — **a·tax′ic** *adj. & n.*

ate (āt, *chiefly Brit.* et) Past tense of EAT.

-ate[1] *suffix* Forming: **1.** Participial adjectives equivalent to those in *-ated*. **2.** Adjectives from nouns with the meaning "possessing or characterized by": *caudate*. **3.** Verbs, originally from stems of Latin verbs of the first conjugation, and, by analogy, extended to other stems: *fascinate*. **4.** *Chem.* Verbs with the meaning "combine or treat with": *chlorinate*. [< L *-atus*, pp. ending of 1st conjugation verbs]

-ate[2] *suffix* Forming: **1.** Nouns denoting office, function, or agent: *magistrate*. **2.** Nouns denoting the object or result of an action: *mandate*. [< L *-atus*, suffix of nouns]

at·el·ier (at′əl·yā, Fr. à·tə·lyä′) *n.* A workshop, esp. of an artist; studio. [< F]

a·the·ism (ā′thē·iz′əm) *n.* The belief that there is no God. [< MF < Gk. < *a*- without + *theos* god]

a·the·ist (ā′thē·ist) *n.* One who denies or disbelieves in the existence of God. — **a′the·is′tic** or **-tic·al** *adj.* — **a′the·is′ti·cal·ly** *adv.*

A·the·na (ə·thē′nə) In Greek mythology, the goddess identified with the Roman *Minerva*. Also **Athena Parthenos**, **A·the·ne** (ə·thē′nē). [< Gk. *Athēnē*]

ath·e·ne·um (ath′ə·nē′əm) *n.* **1.** A literary club, academy, or other institution for the promotion of learning. **2.** A reading room, library, etc. Also **ath′e·nae′um**.

A·the·ni·an (ə·thē′nē·ən) *adj.* Of or pertaining to Athens, or to its art or culture. — *n.* A native or citizen of Athens.

ath·er·o·scle·ro·sis (ath′ər·ō·sklə·rō′sis) *n. Pathol.* Hardening of the arteries, accompanied by the deposit of fat in the inner arterial walls. [< NL < Gk. *athērē* gruel + *sklēros* hard]

a·thirst (ə·thûrst′) *adj.* Keenly desirous; longing; eager: with *for*. [OE < *of*-, intensive + *thyrstan* to thirst]

ath·lete (ath′lēt) *n.* One trained in acts or feats of physical strength and agility, as in sports. [< L < Gk. *athleein* to contend for a prize]

athlete's foot Ringworm of the foot, caused by a fungus.

ath·let·ic (ath·let′ik) *adj.* **1.** Of, pertaining to, or befitting an athlete or athletics. **2.** Strong; vigorous; muscular. — **ath·let′i·cal·ly** *adv.* — **ath·let′i·cism** (ath·let′ə·siz′əm) *n.*

ath·let·ics (ath·let′iks) *n.pl.* Athletic games and exercises, as rowing, wrestling, etc.

ath·o·dyd (ath′ō·did) *n.* A jet engine consisting of a pipe to which air is admitted, heated, and expelled from the rear at high velocity.

at-home (ət·hōm′) *n.* An informal party or reception given at one's home.

a·thwart (ə·thwôrt′) *adv.* **1.** From side to side; across. **2.** So as to thwart; perversely. — *prep.* **1.** From side to side of. **2.** Contrary to. **3.** *Naut.* Across the course of.

-atic *suffix* Of; of the kind of: *erratic*. [< F < L < Gk. *-atikos*]

a·tilt (ə·tilt′) *adv. & adj.* In a tilted manner; tilted up.

-ation *suffix of nouns* **1.** Action or process of: *creation*. **2.** Condition or quality of: *affectation*. **3.** Result of: *reformation*. Also *-ion*, *-tion*. [< F *-ation* or L *-atio*, *-ationis*]

-ative *suffix* Denoting relation, tendency, or characteristic: *remunerative*. [< F *-atif*, masc., *-ative*, fem. or < L *-ativus*]

At·lan·tic (at·lan′tik) *adj.* Of, near, in, or pertaining to the Atlantic Ocean. [< L < Gk. *Atlantikos* pertaining to Atlas]

Atlantic Charter A statement issued in August, 1941, by Churchill and Roosevelt, setting forth the basic aims of the Allied Nations for the peace after World War II.

At·lan·tis (at·lan′tis) A mythical island west of Gibraltar, said by Plato to have been engulfed by the sea.

at·las (at′ləs) *n.* **1.** A volume of maps usu. bound together. **2.** Any book of tables or charts on a given subject.

At·las (at′ləs) *n.* **1.** In Greek mythology, a Titan who supported the heavens on his shoulders. **2.** An intercontinental ballistic missile of the U.S. Air Force.

at·man (ät′mən) *n.* In Hinduism, the soul; the divine life principle in man. — **Atman** The supreme soul, the source and goal of all individual souls. [< Skt.]

atmo- *combining form* Vapor. [< Gk. *atmos*]

at·mos·phere (at′məs·fir) *n.* **1.** The body of gases surrounding the earth or a celestial body. **2.** The particular climatic condition of any place or region. **3.** Any surrounding or pervasive element or influence. **4.** *Informal* A quality regarded as especially characteristic or interesting: This café has *atmosphere*. **5.** *Physics* A unit of pressure, equal to 14.69 pounds per square inch. [< NL < Gk. *atmos* vapor + *sphaira* sphere]

at·mos·pher·ic (at′məs·fer′ik) *adj.* **1.** Of or in the atmosphere. **2.** Dependent on or resulting from the atmosphere. Also **at′mos·pher′i·cal.** — **at′mos·pher′i·cal·ly** *adv.*

at·mos·pher·ics (at′məs·fer′iks) *n.pl. (construed as sing.)* In radio transmission, static.

at·oll (at′ōl, -ol, ə·tol′) *n.* A ring-shaped coral island and its associated reef, nearly or completely enclosing a lagoon. [? < Malayalam *adal* closing, uniting]

ATOLL
a Islets. *b* Barrier reef. *c* Fringing reef. *d* Lagoon. *e* Passage.

a·tom (at′əm) *n.* **1.** *Chem.* The smallest part of an element capable of existing alone or in combination, and that cannot be changed or destroyed in any chemical reaction. **2.** *Physics* One of the particles of which all matter is formed, regarded as an aggregate of nucleons and electrons variously organized within and around a central nucleus, and exhibiting complex mass-energy characteristics. **3.** A hypothetical entity admitting of no division into smaller parts. **4.** The smallest quantity or particle; iota. [< L < Gk. < *a*- not + *temnein* to cut]

a·tom·ic (ə·tom′ik) *adj.* **1.** Of or pertaining to an atom or atoms. Also **a·tom′i·cal.** **2.** Very minute; infinitesimal. — **a·tom′i·cal·ly** *adv.*

atomic age The era characterized by the use and growing importance of atomic energy.

atomic bomb A bomb of formidable destructive power using the energy released by the fission of atomic nuclei, esp. those of radioactive elements, as uranium: also called *A-bomb*. Also **atom bomb.**

atomic clock A high-precision instrument for the measurement of time by the vibration rate of suitable molecules.

atomic energy The energy contained within the nucleus of the atom, esp. when made available for human use by controlled nuclear fission or thermonuclear reactions.

atomic number *Physics* A number that represents the unit positive charges (protons) in the atomic nucleus of each element and corresponds to the number of extranuclear electrons. Hydrogen is assigned an atomic number of 1.

atomic power Atomic energy as a source of power.

atomic reactor Reactor (def. 4).

a·tom·ics (ə·tom′iks) *n.pl. (construed as sing.)* Nuclear physics, esp. in its practical applications.

atomic structure *Physics* The conception of the atom as a system of particles consisting of a central positive nucleus and a cluster of negatively charged electrons, the number and arrangement of the particles determining the energy relations within and between atoms.

atomic theory **1.** *Chem.* The doctrine that elements unite with one another, atom by atom, and in definite simple proportions by weight. **2.** *Physics* The modern concept of atomic structure as a complex of mass-energy relationships.

atomic weight *Chem.* **a** Since 1961, the weight of an atom of an element relative to that of an atom of carbon, taken as 12. **b** Formerly, the weight of an atom of an element relative to that of an atom of oxygen, taken as 16.

at·om·ize (at′əm·īz) *v.t.* **·ized, ·iz·ing** **1.** To reduce to atoms. **2.** To spray or reduce to a spray, as by an atomizer. Also *Brit.* **at′om·ise.** — **at′om·i·za′tion** *n.*

at·om·iz·er (at′əm·ī′zər) *n.* An apparatus for reducing a liquid, esp. medicine or perfume, to a spray.

atom smasher *Physics* An accelerator.

a·to·nal (ā·tō′nəl) *adj. Music* Without tonality; lacking key or tonal center. — **a·to′nal·ly** *adv.*

a·to·nal·i·ty (ā′tō·nal′ə·tē) *n. Music* The use of a system of tones, especially the chromatic scale, so that each tone is equal in its relation to the others and no one tone holds a central or primary position; absence of key or tonal center.

a·tone (ə·tōn′) *v.i.* **a·toned, a·ton·ing** To make expiation, as for sin or wrongdoing. [< earlier adverbial phrase *at one* in accord, short for *to set at one*, i.e., reconcile] — **a·ton′a·ble** or **a·tone′a·ble** *adj.* — **a·ton′er** *n.*

a·tone·ment (ə·tōn′mənt) *n.* **1.** Satisfaction, reparation, or expiation made for wrong or injury. **2.** *Usually cap. Theol.* The reconciliation between God and man effected by Christ.

a·ton·ic (ə·ton′ik, ā-) *adj.* **1.** Not accented, as a word or syllable. **2.** Lacking tone or vigor. [< Med.L < Gk. < *a*- not + *teinein* to stretch]

a·top (ə·top′) *adv. & adj.* On or at the top. — *prep. Chiefly U.S.* On the top of.

-ator *suffix of nouns* An agent; doer; actor; one who or that which: *arbitrator*, *mediator*. [< L]

-atory *suffix of adjectives* Characterized by; producing or produced by: *conciliatory*. [< L *-atorius*, adj. suffix]

at·ra·bil·ious (at′rə·bil′yəs) *adj.* Disposed to hypochondria; melancholy; splenetic. Also **at′ra·bil′i·ar** (-bil′ē·ər). [< L *atra bilis* black bile] — **at′ra·bil′ious·ness** *n.*

a·tri·um (ā′trē·əm) *n. pl.* **a·tri·a** (ā′trē·ə) **1.** The entrance hall or central open court of an ancient Roman house. **2.** A court or hall. **3.** *Anat.* One of the upper chambers of the heart: also called *auricle*. [< L, a hall] — **a′tri·al** *adj.*

a·tro·cious (ə·trō′shəs) *adj.* **1.** Very wicked, cruel, etc. **2.** *Informal* Very bad, or in bad taste. [< L *atrox, atrocis* harsh, cruel] — **a·tro′cious·ly** *adv.* — **a·tro′cious·ness** *n.*

a·troc·i·ty (ə·tros′ə·tē) *n. pl.* **·ties** **1.** The state or quality of being atrocious. **2.** An atrocious deed or act. **3.** *Informal.* Something in very bad taste.

at·ro·phy (at'rə-fē) *n.* *pl.* **·phies** *Pathol.* A wasting or failure in development of the body or any of its parts. **—** *v.* **·phied, ·phy·ing** *v.t.* **1.** To cause to waste away or wither. **—** *v.i.* **2.** To waste away; wither. [< F < L < Gk. < *a*- not + *trephein* to nourish] **— a·troph·ic** (ə-trof'ik) *adj.* **— at'ro·phied** *adj.*

at·ro·pine (at'rə-pēn, -pin) *n.* A crystalline, poisonous alkaloid, $C_{17}H_{23}O_3N$, found in the deadly nightshade and in certain other plants, used as an antispasmodic and to enlarge the pupil of the eye. Also **at'ro·pin** (-pin). [See ATROPOS.]

At·ro·pos (at'rə·pos) One of the three Fates. [< Gk., inflexible < *a*- not + *trepein* to turn]

at·tach (ə-tach') *v.t.* **1.** To make fast to something; fasten on; affix. **2.** To join on as a part or adjunct. **3.** To add or append, as a signature. **4.** To connect by personal ties, as of affection. **5.** To ascribe: with *to*. **6.** To appoint officially; assign. **7.** *Law* To secure for legal jurisdiction; seize by legal process: to *attach* an employee's salary. **—** *v.i.* **8.** To be attached; connect. [< OF < *a*- to + *tache* nail] **— at·tach'a·ble** *adj.*

at·ta·ché (at'ə·shā', *esp. Brit.* ə·tash'ā) *n.* A person officially attached to a diplomatic mission or staff in a specified capacity: military *attaché*. [< F, pp. of *attacher* to attach]

attaché case A boxlike hinged briefcase.

at·tach·ment (ə-tach'mənt) *n.* **1.** The act of attaching, or the state of being attached. **2.** A bond; band; tie. **3.** Affection; devoted regard. **4.** An appendage or adjunct. **5.** *Law* Seizure of a person or property.

at·tack (ə-tak') *v.t.* **1.** To set upon violently; begin battle or conflict with. **2.** To assail with hostile words; criticize. **3.** To begin work on; set about, as an undertaking. **4.** To begin to affect injuriously. **—** *v.i.* **5.** To make an attack; begin battle. **—** *n.* **1.** The act of attacking; assault; onset. **2.** The first movement toward any undertaking. **3.** A seizure, as by disease. [< F, ult. < same source as ATTACH] **— Syn.** (verb) **1.** *Attack* is applied loosely to any offensive action, but strictly means to begin hostilities. *Assault* always suggests close physical contact and extreme violence. To *assail* is to belabor with repeated words or blows. — (noun) **1.** assault, onslaught, onset, invasion, incursion, raid.

at·tain (ə-tān') *v.t.* **1.** To gain by exertion of body or mind; achieve. **2.** To come to, as in time; arrive at: He *attained* old age. **— to attain to** To arrive at with effort; succeed in reaching. [< OF < L < *ad*- to + *tangere* to touch]

at·tain·a·ble (ə-tā'nə-bəl) *adj.* That can be attained. **— at·tain'a·bil'i·ty, at·tain'a·ble·ness** *n.*

at·tain·der (ə-tān'dər) *n.* The loss of all civil rights consequent to a sentence of death or of outlawry for a capital offense. **— bill of attainder** Formerly, a legislative act inflicting attainder upon a person guilty of a capital offense. [< OF *ataindre* to attain, strike]

at·tain·ment (ə-tān'mənt) *n.* **1.** The act of attaining. **2.** That which is attained; an acquisition, as of skill.

at·taint (ə-tānt') *v.t.* **1.** To inflict attainder upon; condemn. **2.** To touch or affect injuriously; disgrace; taint. **—** *n.* **1.** Imputation; stigma. **2.** Attainder. [See ATTAIN.]

at·tar (at'ər) *n.* The fragrant essential oil extracted from the petals of flowers, esp. roses. [< Arabic *itr* perfume]

at·tempt (ə-tempt') *v.t.* **1.** To make an effort to do or accomplish; try. **2.** To try to take by force; attack: to *attempt* the life of someone. **—** *n.* **1.** A putting forth of effort; a trial; endeavor. **2.** An attack; assault. [< OF < L < *ad*- toward + *tendere* to stretch] **— at·tempt'a·bil'i·ty** *n.* **— at·tempt'a·ble** *adj.* **— at·tempt'er** *n.*

at·tend (ə-tend') *v.t.* **1.** To be present at, as a meeting. **2.** To wait upon or go with as an attendant; escort. **3.** To visit or minister to (a sick person). **4.** To accompany as a result. **5.** To give heed to; listen to. **—** *v.i.* **6.** To be present. **7.** To give heed; listen. **— to attend to 1.** To apply oneself to. **2.** To take care of; tend to. [< OF < L < *ad*- toward + *tendere* to stretch]

at·ten·dance (ə-ten'dəns) *n.* **1.** The act of attending. **2.** Those who attend; an audience or retinue.

at·ten·dant (ə-ten'dənt) *n.* **1.** One who attends, esp. as a servant. **2.** One who is present. **3.** A concomitant; consequence. **—** *adj.* Following or accompanying.

at·ten·tion (ə-ten'shən) *n.* **1.** Close or earnest attending. **2.** The power or faculty of mental concentration. **3.** Practical consideration; care: *attention* to one's appearance. **4.** *Usu. pl.* Acts of courtesy, esp. on the part of a lover. **5.** *Mil.* The prescribed position of readiness: to stand at *attention*; also, the order to take this position.

at·ten·tive (ə-ten'tiv) *adj.* **1.** Observant. **2.** Courteous or gallant. **— at·ten'tive·ly** *adv.* **— at·ten'tive·ness** *n.*

at·ten·u·ate (*v.* ə-ten'yŏŏ-āt; *adj.* ə-ten'yŏŏ-it) *v.* **·at·ed, ·at·ing** *v.t.* **1.** To make thin, small, or fine; draw out, as a wire.

2. To weaken; lessen. **3.** To reduce in density; rarefy, as a liquid or gas. **4.** *Bacteriol.* To weaken the virulence of (a microorganism). **—** *v.i.* **5.** To become thin, weak, rarefied, etc. **—** *adj.* Attenuated. [< L < *ad*- (intensive) + *tenuare* to make thin] **— at·ten'u·a·ble** *adj.*

at·ten·u·a·tion (ə-ten'yŏŏ-ā'shən) *n.* The act or process of attenuating, or the state of being attenuated.

at·test (ə-test') *v.t.* **1.** To confirm as accurate, true, or genuine; vouch for. **2.** To certify, as by signature or oath. **3.** To be proof of. **4.** To put upon oath. **—** *v.i.* **5.** To bear witness; testify: with *to*. **—** *n.* Attestation. [< MF < L < *ad*- to + *testari* to bear witness]

at·tes·ta·tion (at'es-tā'shən) *n.* **1.** The act of attesting. **2.** Testimony.

at·tic (at'ik) *n.* **1.** A low story beneath the roof of a building; a garret. **2.** *Archit.* A low structure, above a cornice or entablature. [< F < L *Atticus*, architectural term]

At·tic (at'ik) *adj.* **1.** Of Attica. **2.** Of or characteristic of Athens or the Athenians. **3.** Simple and graceful; delicate; refined: also **at'tic**. **—** *n.* The dialect of Attica. [< L < Gk. *Attikē* Attica]

At·ti·ca (at'i·kə) In ancient times, the region of Greece surrounding Athens.

Attic salt Delicate, refined, graceful wit. Also **Attic wit**.

at·tire (ə-tīr') *v.t.* **·tired, ·tir·ing** To dress; array; adorn. **—** *n.* Dress or clothing. [< OF *atirer* to arrange, adorn]

at·ti·tude (at'ə-tōōd, -tyōōd) *n.* **1.** Position of the body, as suggesting some thought or feeling. **2.** State of mind, behavior, or conduct regarding some matter, as indicating opinion or purpose. [< F < Ital. < LL < L *aptus* fitted, suited] **— at·ti·tu·di·nal** (at'ə-tōō'də·nəl, -tyōō'-) *adj.*

at·ti·tu·di·nize (at'ə-tōō'də-nīz, -tyōō'-) *v.i.* **·nized, ·niz·ing** To take a pose for effect. Also *Brit.* **at'ti·tu'di·nise**.

atto- *combining form* One quintillionth (10^{-18}) of a specific quantity or dimension.

at·tor·ney (ə-tûr'nē) *n.* A person empowered by another to act in his stead; esp., a lawyer. **— by attorney** By proxy. [< OF *atorner* to turn to, appoint] **— at·tor'ney·ship** *n.*

attorney at law A lawyer.

attorney general *pl.* **attorneys general, attorney generals** The chief law officer of a government. *Abbr.* A.G., Atty. Gen.

at·tract (ə-trakt') *v.t.* **1.** To draw to or cause to come near by some physical force, as magnetism. **2.** To draw, as the admiration or attention of. **—** *v.i.* **3.** To exert attractive influence. [< L < *ad*- toward + *trahere* to draw, drag] **— at·tract'a·ble** *adj.* **— at·tract'a·ble·ness, at·tract'a·bil'i·ty** *n.* **— at·trac'tor** or **at·tract'er** *n.*

at·trac·tion (ə-trak'shən) *n.* **1.** The act or power of attracting. **2.** Attractive quality or characteristic; enticement; charm. **3.** Something that attracts. **4.** *Physics* A force that, exerted between or among bodies, tends to make them approach each other or prevents their separating.

at·trac·tive (ə-trak'tiv) *adj.* **1.** Pleasing; winning; charming. **2.** Having the power to attract. **— at·trac'tive·ly** *adv.* **— at·trac'tive·ness** *n.*

at·trib·ute (ə-trib'yŏŏt) *v.t.* **·ut·ed, ·ut·ing** To ascribe as belonging to or resulting from: to *attribute* wisdom to old age. **— at·tri·bute** (at'rə·byŏŏt) *n.* **1.** A quality or characteristic of a person or thing. **2.** *Gram.* An adjective or its equivalent. **3.** In art and mythology, a distinctive mark or symbol. [< L < *ad*- to + *tribuere* to allot, give over] **— at·trib'ut·a·ble** *adj.* **— at·trib'u·ter** or **at·trib'u·tor** *n.* **— Syn.** (verb) *Attribute, impute,* and *ascribe* are largely interchangeable, but usually we *attribute* good things, *impute* bad, and *ascribe* either. We usually *assign* or *refer* a thing to a category, as time, place, cause, etc., rather than to a person.

at·tri·bu·tion (at'rə-byōō'shən) *n.* **1.** The act of attributing. **2.** An ascribed characteristic or quality; attribute.

at·trib·u·tive (ə-trib'yə-tiv) *adj.* **1.** Pertaining to or of the nature of an attribute. **2.** Ascribed, as a work of art: an *attributive* Vermeer. **3.** *Gram.* Designating an adjective or its equivalent that stands before the noun it modifies. **—** *n.* *Gram.* An attributive word or phrase. **— at·trib'u·tive·ly** *adv.* **— at·trib'u·tive·ness** *n.*

at·tri·tion (ə-trish'ən) *n.* **1.** A rubbing out or grinding down, as by friction. **2.** A gradual wearing down or weakening. [< L < *ad*- to, against + *terere* to rub]

at·tune (ə-tōōn') *v.t.* **·tuned, ·tun·ing** **1.** To bring into accord; harmonize. **2.** To tune.

a·typ·i·cal (ā-tip'i-kəl) *adj.* Not typical; differing from the type; irregular. Also **a·typ'ic**. **— a·typ'i·cal·ly** *adv.*

au·burn (ô'bûrn) *adj. & n.* Reddish brown. [< OF < LL < L *albus* white; infl. in meaning by ME *brun* brown]

au cou·rant (ō kōō-rän') *French* Up to date; well informed.

auc·tion (ôk'shən) *n.* **1.** A public sale in which the price is increased by bids until the highest bidder becomes the purchaser. **2.** The bidding in bridge. **—** *v.t.* To sell by or at auction: usually with *off*. [< L *augere* to increase]

auction bridge A variety of the game of bridge in which tricks made by the declarer in excess of the contract count toward game. Compare CONTRACT BRIDGE.

auc·tion·eer (ôk′shən·ir′) *n.* One who conducts an auction, usu. as a business. — *v.t.* To sell at auction.

au·da·cious (ô·dā′shəs) *adj.* **1.** Showing no fear; daring; bold. **2.** Shameless; impudent. [< L *audere* to dare + -OUS] — **au·da′cious·ly** *adv.* — **au·da′cious·ness** *n.*

au·dac·i·ty (ô·das′ə·tē) *n.* **1.** Boldness; daring. **2.** Impudence; shamelessness. — *Syn.* See TEMERITY.

au·di·ble (ô′də·bəl) *adj.* Perceptible by the ear; loud enough to be heard. [< Med.L *audire* to hear] — **au·di·bil′i·ty, au′di·ble·ness** *n.* — **au′di·bly** *adv.*

au·di·ence (ô′dē·əns) *n.* **1.** An assembly of listeners or spectators, as at a concert. **2.** Those who are reached by a book, television program, etc. **3.** A formal hearing, interview, or conference. **4.** Opportunity to be heard. [<OF < L *audire* to hear]

au·di·o (ô′dē·ō) *adj.* **1.** Of or pertaining to characteristics associated with sound waves. **2.** *Electronics* Designating devices used in transmission or reception of sound waves: in television, distinguished from *video*. [< L *audire* to hear]

audio- *combining form* Pertaining to hearing: Also **audi-**. [< L *audire* to hear]

audio frequency *Physics* A frequency of electrical, sound, or other wave vibrations within the range of normal human hearing, or from about 20 to 20,000 cycles a second.

au·di·o·vis·u·al aids (ô′dē·ō·vizh′ōō·əl) Motion pictures, photographs, recordings, etc., used as teaching devices.

au·dit (ô′dit) *v.t.* **1.** To examine, adjust, and certify, as accounts. **2.** *U.S.* To attend (a college course) as a listener and without earning credit. — *v.i.* **2.** To make an audit. — *n.* **1.** An examination of an accounting document and of the evidence in support of its correctness. **2.** A final statement of such an account. **3.** An adjustment and settling of accounts. [< L *audire* to hear]

au·di·tion (ô·dish′ən) *n.* **1.** The act or sense of hearing. **2.** A test or hearing, as of an actor or singer. — *v.t. & v.i.* To give an audition. [< L *audire* to hear]

au·di·tor (ô′də·tər) *n.* **1.** One who audits accounts. **2.** A listener. **3.** *U.S.* One who audits classes. [< L]

au·di·to·ri·um (ô′də·tôr′ē·əm, -tō′rē·əm) *n. pl.* **·to·ri·ums** or **·to·ri·a** (-tôr′ē·ə, -tō′rē·ə) **1.** The room or part of a school, church, theater, etc., occupied by the audience. **2.** A building for concerts, public meetings, etc. [< L, lecture room]

au·di·to·ry (ô′də·tôr′ē, -tō′rē) *adj.* Of or pertaining to hearing or the organs or sense of hearing. — *n. pl.* **·ries 1.** An audience. **2.** The nave of a church. [< L *audire* to hear]

auditory canal *Anat.* The passage leading from the auricle to the tympanic membrane. For illustration see EAR.

auf Wie·der·seh·en (ouf vē′dər·zā′ən) *German* Till we meet again; good-by for now.

Au·ge·an stables (ô·jē′ən) In Greek mythology, the stables that were cleaned in a day by Hercules.

au·gend (ô′jend) *n. Math.* A number to which another is to be added. See ADDEND. [< L *augere* to increase]

au·ger (ô′gər) *n.* Any of various tools for boring wood. [OE *nafugār*, < *nafu* nave of a wheel + *gār* borer, spear]

aught[1] (ôt) *n.* Anything; any part or item. — *adv.* By any chance; at all. [OE *āwiht, ōwiht* < *ā* ever + *wiht* thing]

aught[2] (ôt) *n.* The figure 0; cipher; a naught; nothing. [*a naught* taken as *an aught*]

aug·ment (*v.* ôg·ment′; *n.* ôg′ment) *v.t.* **1.** To make greater, as in size, number, or amount; enlarge; intensify. — *v.i.* **2.** To become greater, as in size. — *Syn.* See INCREASE. — *n.* Increase; enlargement. [< F < L *augere* to increase] — **aug·ment′a·ble** *adj.*

aug·men·ta·tion (ôg′men·tā′shən) *n.* **1.** The act of augmenting, or the state of being augmented. **2.** An addition.

aug·men·ta·tive (ôg·men′tə·tiv) *adj.* **1.** Having the quality or power of augmenting. **2.** *Gram.* Denoting greater size or intensity, as a suffix. — *n. Gram.* An augmentative form. Also **aug·men′tive**. Abbr. *aug.*

aug·ment·er (ôg·men′tər) *n.* One who or that which augments. **2.** *Aeron.* Afterburner.

au gra·tin (ō grä′tn, grat′n; *Fr.* ō grà·taṅ′) Sprinkled with bread crumbs or grated cheese and baked until brown. [< F]

au·gur (ô′gər) *n.* A prophet; soothsayer. — *v.t. & v.i.* **1.** To prophesy. **2.** To betoken; be an omen of. [< L *augere* to increase] — **au′gu·ral** *adj.*

au·gu·ry (ô′gyə·rē) *n. pl.* **·ries 1.** The art or practice of divination. **2.** A portent or omen.

au·gust (ô·gust′) *adj.* Inspiring awe, admiration, or reverence; majestic; imposing. [< L *augere* to increase, exalt] — **au·gust′ly** *adv.* — **au·gust′ness** *n.*

Au·gust (ô′gəst) *n.* The eighth month of the year, containing 31 days. Abbr. *Ag., Aug, Aug.* [< L *Augustus Caesar*]

Au·gus·tan (ô·gus′tən) *adj.* **1.** Of or pertaining to Augustus Caesar or to his times. **2.** Pertaining to any similar era. — *n.* A writer or artist of an Augustan age.

Augustan age 1. The period of the reign of Augustus Cae-sar, the golden age of Roman literature. **2.** A similar period in English literature during the reign of Queen Anne.

auk (ôk) *n.* A short-winged, web-footed diving bird of northern seas; the **razor-billed auk** of the North Atlantic. [< ON *ālka*]

auld lang syne (ōld′ lang sīn′, zīn′) *Scot.* Literally, old long since; long ago.

au na·tu·rel (ō nȧ·tü·rel′) *French* **1.** Plainly cooked; ungarnished. **2.** In the natural condition; nude.

aunt (ant, änt) *n.* A sister of one's father or mother, or the wife of one's uncle. [< OF *aunte, ante*]

au pair (ō pâr) *Chiefly Brit.* **1.** An arrangement whereby one receives room and board in a foreign household in exchange for doing certain chores, as caring for children: often used attributively: *au pair girls*. **2.** *Informal* An au pair girl. [< F, lit., at par, even (with)]

RAZOR-BILLED
AUK
(About 16 inches high)

au·ra (ôr′ə) *n. pl.* **au·ras** or **au·rae** (ôr′ē) **1.** An invisible emanation or exhalation. **2.** A distinctive air or quality enveloping or characterizing a person or thing. **3.** *Pathol.* The sensory, motor, or psychic manifestations preceding an epileptic attack or other paroxysm. [< L, breeze < Gk. *aurē* breath] — **au′ral** *adj.*

au·ral (ôr′əl) *adj.* Pertaining to the ear or the sense of hearing; auricular. [< L *auris* ear + -AL]

au·re·ate (ôr′ē·it) *adj.* **1.** Of the color of gold; golden. **2.** Splendid. [< L *aureus* < *aurum* gold]

au·re·ole (ôr′ē·ōl) *n.* **1.** In art, a halo. **2.** Any radiance or halo around a body. Also **au·re·o·la** (ô·rē′ə·lə). [< L *aureola* (*corona*) golden (crown) < *aurum* gold]

Au·re·o·my·cin (ôr′ē·ō·mī′sin) *n.* Proprietary name for a type of antibiotic. Also **au′re·o·my′cin**. [< L *aureus* golden + Gk. *mykes* fungus]

au re·voir (ō rə·vwȧr′) *French* Good-by; till we meet again.

au·ri·cle (ôr′i·kəl) *n.* **1.** *Anat.* **a** An atrium of the heart. **b** The external ear; pinna. **2.** An ear-shaped part. [< L *auricula*, dim. of *auris* ear] — **au′ri·cled** *adj.*

au·ric·u·lar (ô·rik′yə·lər) *adj.* **1.** Of or pertaining to the ear or the sense of hearing. **2.** Intended for the ear. **3.** Earshaped. **4.** Of or pertaining to an auricle.

au·rif·er·ous (ô·rif′ər·əs) *adj.* Containing gold. [< L < *aurum* gold + *ferre* to bear]

au·ri·form (ôr′ə·fôrm) *adj.* Ear-shaped.

Au·ri·ga (ô·rī′gə) *n.* A constellation, the Charioteer or Wagoner, containing the bright star Capella. [< L]

au·ro·ra (ô·rôr′ə, ô·rō′rə) *n.* **1.** *Meteorol.* A display of arcs, bands, streamers, etc., of light occasionally seen in the skies of polar latitudes. **2.** The dawn. [< L, dawn]

Au·ro·ra (ô·rôr′ə, ô·rō′rə) In Roman mythology, the goddess of the dawn: identified with the Greek *Eos.*

aurora aus·tra·lis (ôs·trā′lis) *Meteorol.* The aurora seen in far southern latitudes: also called *southern lights*. [< NL, southern aurora < L *auster* south wind]

aurora bo·re·a·lis (bôr′ē·al′is, -ā′lis, bō′rē-) *Meteorol.* The aurora seen in high northern latitudes: also called *northern lights.* [< NL, northern aurora < Gk. *boreas* north wind]

au·ro·ral (ô·rôr′əl, ô·rō′rəl) *adj.* **1.** Pertaining to or like the dawn; roseate. **2.** *Meteorol.* Of, like, or caused by an aurora.

au·rum (ôr′əm) *n.* Gold. [< L]

aus·cul·tate (ôs′kəl·tāt) *v.t. & v.i.* **·tat·ed, ·tat·ing** *Med.* To examine by auscultation. [< L *auscultare* to listen, give ear to] — **aus′cul·ta′tor** *n.*

aus·cul·ta·tion (ôs′kəl·tā′shən) *n.* **1.** *Med.* The act of listening, as with a stethoscope. **2.** A listening.

aus·pice (ôs′pis) *n. pl.* **aus·pi·ces** (ôs′pə·sēz) **1.** *Usu. pl.* Patronage. **2.** An omen, or sign. [< F < L *auspex*]

aus·pi·cious (ôs·pish′əs) *adj.* **1.** Of good omen; propitious. **2.** Prosperous; fortunate. — *Syn.* See PROPITIOUS. — **aus·pi′cious·ly** *adv.* — **aus·pi′cious·ness** *n.*

aus·tere (ô·stir′) *adj.* **1.** Severe, grave, or stern, as in aspect or conduct. **2.** Morally strict; abstemious; ascetic. **3.** Sour and astringent. **4.** Severely simple; unadorned. [< OF < L < Gk. *austēros* harsh, bitter] — **aus·tere′ly** *adv.*

aus·ter·i·ty (ô·ster′ə·tē) *n. pl.* **·ties 1.** The quality of being austere; severity of demeanor, way of life, etc.: also **aus·tere′ness**. **2.** *Usually pl.* Severe or ascetic acts.

aus·tral (ôs′trəl) *adj.* Southern; torrid. [< L *southern* < *auster* south wind]

Aus·tral·a·sian (ôs′tral·ā′zhən, -ā′shən) *n.* A native or inhabitant of Australasia. — *adj.* Of Australasia.

Aus·tral·ian (ôs·strāl′yən) *n.* A native or naturalized inhabitant of Australia. — *adj.* Of or pertaining to Australia or to its people.

Australian English The English language as spoken and written in Australia.

Aus·tri·an (ôs′trē·ən) *n.* An inhabitant or citizen of Austria. — *adj.* Of Austria or its people.

Austro- *combining form* **1.** Austrian. **2.** Australian.

Aus·tro·ne·sian (ôs′trō-nē′zhən, -shən) *adj.* Of or pertaining to Austronesia, its inhabitants, or their languages. — *n.* A family of languages of the Pacific comprising the Indonesian, Oceanic (including Melanesian and Micronesian), and Polynesian subfamilies. Also *Malayo-Polynesian.*

aut- Var. of AUTO-[1].

au·tar·chy (ô′tär·kē) *n.* *pl.* **·chies** 1. Absolute rule or sovereignty, or a country under such rule. 2. Self-government. 3. Autarky. [< Gk. < *autos* self + *archein* to rule] — **au·tar·chic** (ô·tär′kik) or **·chi·cal** *adj.*

au·tar·ky (ô′tär·kē) *n.* National economic self-sufficiency. [< Gk. *autarkeia* self-sufficiency] — **au·tar·kik** (ô·tär′kik) or **·ki·kal** *adj.*

au·then·tic (ô·then′tik) *adj.* 1. Authoritative; reliable. 2. Of undisputed origin; genuine. 3. *Law* Duly executed before the proper officer. Also **au·then′ti·cal.** [< OF < L < Gk. < *authentēs* the doer of a deed] — **au·then′ti·cal·ly** *adv.* — **Syn.** 1. true, veritable. 2. real, legitimate, authorized, accredited. — **Ant.** spurious, counterfeit, fictitious, false.

au·then·ti·cate (ô·then′ti·kāt) *v.t.* **·cat·ed, ·cat·ing** 1. To make authentic or authoritative. 2. To give legal validity to. 3. To establish the authenticity of. — **au·then′ti·ca′·tion** *n.* — **au·then′ti·ca′tor** *n.*

au·then·tic·i·ty (ô′thən·tis′ə·tē) *n.* The state or quality of being authentic, authoritative, or genuine.

au·thor (ô′thər) *n.* 1. The writer of a book, treatise, etc.; also, one who makes literary composition his profession. 2. One who begins or originates; creator. 3. An author's writings collectively. — *v.t.* *Informal* To be the author of; write. [< AF < L *auctor* originator, producer] — **au′thor·ess** *n.fem.* — **au·tho·ri·al** (ô·thôr′ē·əl, ô·thō′rē-) *adj.*

au·thor·i·tar·i·an (ə·thôr′ə·târ′ē·ən, ə·thor′-) *adj.* Favoring subjection to authority as opposed to individual freedom. — *n.* One who favors the principle of authority. — **au·thor′i·tar′i·an·ism** *n.*

au·thor·i·ta·tive (ə·thôr′ə·tā′tiv, ə·thor′-) *adj.* 1. Possessing or proceeding from proper authority; duly sanctioned. 2. Exercising authority; commanding; dictatorial. — **au·thor′i·ta′tive·ly** *adv.* — **au·thor′i·ta′tive·ness** *n.*

au·thor·i·ty (ə·thôr′ə·tē, ə·thor′-) *n.* *pl.* **·ties** 1. The right to command and to enforce obedience; the right to act, decide, etc. 2. Delegated right or power; authorization. 3. *pl.* Those having the power to govern or command. 4. Title to respect, confidence, etc.; personal influence. 5. A person, volume, etc., appealed to in support of action or belief. 6. One who has special knowledge; an expert. 7. An official or group having administrative control in a specified area. 8. An authoritative opinion, decision, or precedent. Abbr. *auth.* [< OF < L < *augere* to increase]

au·thor·ize (ô′thə·rīz) *v.t.* **·ized, ·iz·ing** 1. To confer authority upon; empower; commission. 2. To warrant; justify. 3. To sanction. [< OF < Med.L < L *auctor* originator] — **au′thor·i·za′tion** *n.* — **au′thor·iz′er** *n.*

au·thor·ized (ô′thə·rīzd) *adj.* 1. Endowed with authority; accepted as authoritative. 2. Formally or legally sanctioned.

au·thor·ship (ô′thər·ship) *n.* 1. The profession or occupation of an author. 2. Origin or source.

au·to (ô′tō) *U.S. Informal n.* An automobile. — *v.i.* **au·toed, au·to·ing** To ride in or travel by an automobile.

auto-[1] *combining form* 1. Arising from some process or action within the object; not induced by any stimulus from without; as in:

autoagglutination   autodiffusion   autoinduction

2. Acting, acted, or directed upon the self; as in:

autoanalysis   autodiagnosis   autolavage

Also, before vowels, **aut-**. [< Gk. *autos* self]

auto-[2] *combining form* Self-propelled. [< Gk. *autos* self]

au·to·bi·og·ra·phy (ô′tə·bī·og′rə·fē, -bē·og′-) *n.* *pl.* **·phies** The story of a person's life written by that person. — **au′to·bi·og′ra·pher** *n.* — **au·to·bi·o·graph·ic** (ô′tə·bī′ō·graf′ik) or **·i·cal** *adj.* — **au′to·bi′o·graph′i·cal·ly** *adv.*

au·to·clave (ô′tə·klāv) *n.* 1. An enclosed chamber for the sterilization of drugs, vaccines, instruments, etc. 2. A pressure cooker. [< F < *auto-* self + L *clavis* a key]

au·toc·ra·cy (ô·tok′rə·sē) *n.* *pl.* **·cies** 1. Absolute government by an individual; rule or authority of an autocrat. 2. A state ruled by an autocrat.

au·to·crat (ô′tə·krat) *n.* 1. A supreme ruler of unrestricted power. 2. An arrogant, dictatorial person. [< F < Gk. *autos* self + *kratos* power] — **au·to·crat′ic** or **·i·cal** *adj.* — **au′to·crat′i·cal·ly** *adv.*

au·to·da·fé (ô′tō·də·fā′, ou′-) *n.* *pl.* **au·tos·da·fé** (ô′tōz-, ou′tōz-) The public announcement and execution of a sentence of the Inquisition; esp., the burning of heretics at the stake. [< Pg., lit., act of the faith]

au·tog·e·nous (ô·toj′ə·nəs) *adj.* Self-produced or self-generated. Also **au·to·gen·ic** (ô′tō·jen′ik). [< Gk. *autogenēs* self-produced]

au·to·gi·ro (ô′tō·jī′rō) *n.* *pl.* **·ros** An airplane that is supported in the air chiefly by freely-turning rotors but is drawn forward by a conventional propeller. Also **au′to·gy′ro.** [< AUTO-[1] + Gk. *gyros* a circle]

au·to·graph (ô′tə·graf, -gräf) *n.* 1. One's own signature or handwriting. 2. A manuscript in the author's handwriting. — *v.t.* 1. To write one's name in or affix one's signature to. 2. To write in one's own handwriting. — *adj.* Written by one's own hand, as a will. [< L < Gk. < *autos* self + *graphein* to write] — **au′to·graph′ic** or **·i·cal** *adj.* — **au′to·graph′i·cal·ly** *adv.*

au·to·in·tox·i·ca·tion (ô′tō·in·tok′sə·kā′shən) *n.* Poisoning from noxious secretions of one's own body.

au·to·mat (ô′tə·mat) *n.* *U.S.* A restaurant in which food is automatically made available from a receptacle when coins are deposited in a slot alongside.

au·to·mate (ô′tə·māt) **·mat·ed, ·mat·ing** *v.t.* To adapt, as a machine, factory, or process, for automation. [Back formation < AUTOMATION]

au·to·mat·ic (ô′tə·mat′ik) *adj.* 1. Acting from forces inherent in itself; self-moving. 2. Self-acting and self-regulating, as machinery; mechanical. 3. *Psychol.* Done from force of habit or without volition. 4. Of firearms, extracting and ejecting the empty case and chambering the next round, using the force of recoil or of part of the exploding gas, and firing continuously until the trigger is released. Also (*except for def. 4*) **au′to·mat′i·cal, au·tom·a·tous** (ô·tom′ə·təs) — *n.* An automatic device, pistol, etc. [< Gk. *automatos* acting of oneself] — **au′to·mat′i·cal·ly** *adv.*

automatic pilot *Aeron.* An automatic-control mechanism designed to keep an aircraft level and on an even course.

automatic pistol A pistol using the force of recoil to extract and eject used shells and chamber the next round.

automatic rifle A rifle capable of automatic fire.

au·to·ma·tion (ô′tə·mā′shən) *n.* The automatic transfer of one unit of a complex industrial assembly to a succession of machines, each of which completes another stage in manufacture. — **au·to·ma·tive** (ô′tə·mā′tiv) *adj.*

au·tom·a·tism (ô·tom′ə·tiz′əm) *n.* 1. The state or quality of being automatic or of having no voluntary action. 2. *Physiol.* The functioning or power of functioning of muscular or other processes in response to external stimuli but independent of conscious control. — **au·tom′a·tist** *n.*

au·tom·a·ton (ô·tom′ə·ton, -tən) *n.* *pl.* **·tons** or **·ta** (-tə) 1. An apparatus that appears to function of itself by the action of a concealed mechanism. 2. Any living being whose actions are or appear to be involuntary or mechanical. 3. Anything capable of spontaneous movement or action. [< Gk. *automaton*, neut. of *automatos* acting of oneself, independent]

au·to·mo·bile (*n.* ô′tə·mə·bēl′, ô′tə·mə·bēl′, ô′tə·mō·bēl′; *adj.* ô′tə·mō′bil) *n.* A four-wheeled passenger vehicle that carries its own source of power and travels on roads or streets; motorcar. — *v.i.* **·biled, ·bil·ing** To ride in or drive an automobile. — *adj.* Automotive. [< F < Gk. *auto-* + *mobile* moving] — **au·to·mo·bil·ist** (ô′tə·mə·bēl′ist, -mō′·bil·ist) *n.*

au·to·mo·tive (ô′tə·mō′tiv) *adj.* 1. Self-propelling. 2. Of or for automobiles.

au·to·nom·ic (ô′tə·nom′ik) *adj.* 1. Autonomous. 2. *Physiol.* Pertaining to the autonomic nervous system. Also **au′to·nom′i·cal.** — **au′to·nom′i·cal·ly** *adv.*

autonomic nervous system A plexus of nerve ganglia and fibers originating in the spinal column and acting to innervate and control the efferent functions of all body tissues and organs not subject to voluntary control, as the heart, blood vessels, smooth muscle, glands, stomach, and intestines.

au·ton·o·mous (ô·ton′ə·məs) *adj.* 1. Independent; self-governing. 2. *Biol.* Independent. [< Gk. < *autos* self + *nomos* law, rule] — **au·ton′o·mous·ly** *adv.*

au·ton·o·my (ô·ton′ə·mē) *n.* *pl.* **·mies** 1. The condition or quality of being autonomous; esp., the power or right of self-government. 2. A self-governing community or group. 3. Self-determination. — **au·ton′o·mist** *n.*

au·top·sy (ô′top·sē, ô′təp-) *n.* *pl.* **·sies** Post-mortem examination of a human body, esp. when ordered by a coroner. [< NL < Gk. < *autos* self + *opsis* a seeing]

au·to·sug·ges·tion (ô′tō·səg·jes′chən) *n. Psychol.* Suggestion emanating from one's self only. — **au′to·sug·gest′i·bil′·i·ty** *n.* — **au′to·sug·ges′tive** *adj.*

au·tumn (ô′təm) *n.* 1. The season of the year occurring between summer and winter. Often called *fall.* 2. A time of maturity and incipient decline. [< OF < L *autumnus*]

au·tum·nal (ô·tum′nəl) *adj.* 1. Of, pertaining to, or like autumn. 2. Ripening or harvested in autumn. 3. Past maturity; declining. — **au·tum′nal·ly** *adv.*

autumnal equinox See under EQUINOX.

aux·il·ia·ry (ôg·zil′yər·ē, -zil′ər-) *adj.* 1. Giving or furnishing aid. 2. Subsidiary; accessory. 3. Supplementary; reserve. — *n.* *pl.* ·ries 1. One who or that which aids or helps; assistant; associate. 2. *Gram.* A verb that helps to express tense, mood, etc., as *have* in *We have gone:* also **auxiliary verb.** 3. *pl.* Foreign troops associated with those of a nation at war. [< L < *auxilium* help]

a·vail (ə·vāl′) *v.t.* 1. To assist or aid; profit. — *v.i.* 2. To be of value or advantage; suffice. — **to avail oneself of** To take advantage of; utilize. — *n.* 1. Utility for a purpose; benefit; good: His efforts were of no *avail.* 2. *pl.* Proceeds. [< OF < L *ad-* to + *valere* to be strong]

a·vail·a·ble (ə·vā′lə·bəl) *adj.* 1. Capable of being used; at hand; usable. 2. *Law* Valid. — **a·vail/a·bil/i·ty, a·vail/a·ble·ness** *n.* — **a·vail/a·bly** *adv.*

av·a·lanche (av′ə·lanch, -länch) *n.* 1. A large mass of snow or ice falling down a slope. 2. Something like an avalanche, as in power, destructiveness, etc. — *v.* ·lanched, ·lanch·ing *v.i.* 1. To fall or slide like an avalanche. — *v.t.* 2. To fall or come down upon like an avalanche. [< F < dial. F (Swiss) *lavenche* < L *ad vallem*]

a·vant-garde (ə·vänt′gärd′, *Fr.* å·väṅ·gȧrd′) *n.* The vanguard; esp., in art, the group regarded as most advanced or daring in technique and ideas. — *adj.* Of or pertaining to this group. [< F, lit., advance guard]

av·a·rice (av′ə·ris) *n.* Passion for acquiring and hoarding riches; greed. [< OF < L < *avere* to desire, crave]

av·a·ri·cious (av′ə·rish′əs) *adj.* Greedy of gain; grasping; miserly. — **av/a·ri/cious·ly** *adv.* — **av/a·ri/cious·ness** *n.*

a·vast (ə·vast′, ə·väst′) *interj.* *Naut.* Stop! hold! cease! [< Du. *hou' vast, houd vast* hold fast]

av·a·tar (av′ə·tär′) *n.* 1. In Hindu mythology, the incarnation of a god. 2. Any incarnation. [< Skt. *avatāra* descent]

a·ve (ä′ve, ä′vā) *interj.* 1. Hail! 2. Farewell! — *n.* The salutation *ave.* [< L, hail, farewell]

A·ve Ma·ri·a (ä′vā mə·rē′ə, ä′vē) A Roman Catholic prayer to the Virgin Mary; also called *Hail Mary.* Also **A/ve, Mar·y** (ä′vē mâr′ē). [< L, Hail, Mary]

a·venge (ə·venj′) *v.* **a·venged, a·veng·ing** *v.t.* 1. To take vengeance or exact exemplary punishment for or in behalf of. — *v.i.* 2. To take vengeance. [< OF < L < *ad-* to + *vindicare* to avenge] — **a·veng/er** *n.* — **a·veng/ing·ly** *adv.*

av·e·nue (av′ə·nōō, -nyōō) *n.* 1. A broad street. 2. A way of approach, as to a building, often bordered with trees. 3. A mode of access or attainment. [< F *avenue* < L < *ad-* toward + *venire* to come]

a·ver (ə·vûr′) *v.t.* **a·verred, a·ver·ring** 1. To declare confidently as fact; affirm. 2. *Law* To assert formally; prove or justify (a plea). [< OF < L *ad-* to + *verus* true] — **a·ver/ment** *n.* — **a·ver/ra·ble** *adj.*

av·er·age (av′rij, av′ər·ij) *n.* 1. *Math.* An arithmetic mean. 2. A mean, ratio, etc., showing a specific standing or accomplishment: batting *average*; B *average.* 3. The ordinary rank, degree, or amount; general type. 4. In marine law: **a** The loss arising by damage to a ship or cargo. **b** The proportion of such loss falling to a single person in an equitable distribution among those interested. — *adj.* 1. Obtained by calculating the mean of several. 2. Medium; ordinary. — *v.* ·aged, ·ag·ing *v.t.* 1. To fix or calculate as the mean. 2. To amount to or obtain an average of: He *averages* three dollars an hour. 3. To apportion on the average. — *v.i.* 4. To be or amount to an average. 5. To buy or sell more goods, shares, etc., in order to get a better average price. [< F *avarie* damage to a ship] — **av/er·age·ly** *adv.*

A·ver·nus (ä·ver′nəs) In Roman mythology, hell; Hades. — **A·ver/nal** *adj.*

a·verse (ə·vûrs′) *adj.* Opposed; unfavorable; reluctant: with *to.* [< L *aversus,* pp. of *avertere* to turn aside] — **a·verse/ly** *adv.* — **a·verse/ness** *n.*

a·ver·sion (ə·vûr′zhən, -shən) *n.* 1. Extreme dislike; opposition; antipathy. 2. A cause of repugnance or dislike.

a·vert (ə·vûrt′) *v.t.* 1. To turn or direct away or aside, as one's regard. 2. To prevent or ward off, as a danger. — **Syn.** See PREVENT. [< OF *avertir* < L *avertere* to turn aside < *ab-* away + *vertere* to turn] — **a·vert/ed·ly** *adv.* — **a·vert/i·ble** or **a·vert/a·ble** *adj.*

A·ves·ta (ə·ves′tə) The sacred writings of Zoroastrianism, written in **A·ves·tan,** (ə·ves′tən), an ancient Iranian language. See ZEND-AVESTA. — **A·ves/tan** *adj.*

avi- *combining form* Bird; of or related to birds. [< L *avis* bird]

a·vi·ar·y (ā′vē·er′ē) *n.* *pl.* ·ar·ies An enclosure or large cage for live birds. [< L < *avis* bird] — **a·vi·ar·ist** (ā′vē·er′ist, -ə·rist) *n.*

a·vi·a·tion (ā′vē·ā′shən, av′ē-) *n.* The act, science, or art of flying heavier-than-air aircraft. [< F < L *avis* bird]

a·vi·a·tor (ā′vē·ā′tər, av′ē-) *n.* An airplane pilot. — **a/vi·a/tress** (-tris) or **a·vi·a/trix** (ā′vē·ā′triks, av′ē-) *n.fem.*

av·id (av′id) *adj.* Very desirous; eager; greedy. [< L < *avere* to crave] — **a·vid·i·ty** (ə·vid′ə·tē) *n.* — **av/id·ly** *adv.*

a·vi·on·ics (ā′vē·on′iks, av′ē-) *n.pl.* (construed as *sing.*) The applications of electronics to aviation, astronautics, etc.

av·o·ca·do (av′ə·kä′dō, ä′və-) *n.* *pl.* ·dos 1. The pear-shaped fruit of a West Indian tree: also called *alligator pear.* 2. The tree bearing this fruit. [< Sp. < Nahuatl *ahuacatl*]

av·o·ca·tion (av′ə·kā′shən) *n.* A casual or occasional occupation; diversion; hobby. — **Syn.** See OCCUPATION. [< L < *ab-* away + *vocare* to call]

av·o·cet (av′ə·set) *n.* A long-legged shore bird having webbed feet and an upcurved bill. Also **av/o·set.** [< F < Ital. *avocetta*]

a·void (ə·void′) *v.t.* 1. To keep away or at a distance from; shun; evade. 2. *Law* To make void. [< OF < L *ex-* out + *viduare* to empty, deprive] — **a·void/a·ble** *adj.* — **a·void/a·bly** *adv.* — **a·void/ance** *n.*

av·oir·du·pois (av′ər·də·poiz′) *n.* 1. The ordinary system of weights of the U.S. and Great Britain in which 16 ounces avoirdupois make a pound. Abbr. *av., avdp., avoir.* See table inside back cover. 2. *Informal* Weight; corpulence. [< OF *avoir de pois* goods of (i.e., sold by) weight]

a·vouch (ə·vouch′) *v.t.* 1. To vouch for; guarantee. 2. To affirm positively; proclaim. 3. To acknowledge; avow. [< OF < L < *ad-* to + *vocare* to call]

a·vow (ə·vou′) *v.t.* To declare openly, as facts; own; acknowledge. [< OF < L *advocare* to summon] — **a·vow/a·ble** *adj.* — **a·vow/a·bly** *adv.* — **a·vow/er** *n.*

a·vow·al (ə·vou′əl) *n.* Frank admission or acknowledgment.

a·vowed (ə·voud′) *adj.* Openly acknowledged; plainly declared. — **a·vow·ed·ly** (ə·vou′id·lē) *adv.* — **a·vow/ed·ness** *n.*

a·vun·cu·lar (ə·vung′kyə·lər) *adj.* Of or pertaining to an uncle. [< L *avunculus* maternal uncle]

a·wait (ə·wāt′) *v.t.* 1. To wait for; expect. 2. To be ready or in store for. [< OF *awaitier* to watch for < *a-* to (< L *ad-*) + *waitier* to watch < OHG *wahtēn* to watch]

a·wake (ə·wāk′) *adj.* Not asleep; alert; vigilant. [< v.] — *v.* **a·woke** (Rare **a·waked**), **a·waked** (Rare **a·woke**), **a·wak·ing** *v.t.* 1. To arouse from sleep. 2. To stir up; excite. — *v.i.* 3. To cease to sleep; become awake. 4. To become alert or aroused. [OE *onwæcnan* rise from sleep]

a·wak·en (ə·wā′kən) *v.t.* & *v.i.* To awake. — **a·wak/en·er** *n.*

a·wak·en·ing (ə·wā′kən·ing) *adj.* Stirring; exciting. — *n.* 1. The act of waking. 2. A reviving, as of interest.

a·ward (ə·wôrd′) *v.t.* 1. To adjudge as due, as by legal decision. 2. To bestow as the result of a contest or examination, as a prize. — *n.* 1. A decision, as by a judge or arbitrator. 2. The document containing it. 3. That which is awarded, as a medal. [< AF, OF < *es-* out (< L *ex-*) + *guarder* to watch] — **a·ward/a·ble** *adj.* — **a·ward/er** *n.*

a·ware (ə·wâr′) *adj.* Conscious; cognizant: often with *of.* [OE *gewær* watchful] — **a·ware/ness** *n.*

a·wash (ə·wosh′, ə·wôsh′) *adv.* & *adj.* 1. Level with or just above the surface of the water. 2. Tossed or washed about by waves. 3. Covered or overflowed by water.

a·way (ə·wā′) *adv.* 1. From a given place; off. 2. Far; at or to a distance. 3. In another direction; aside. 4. Out of existence; at or to an end: to waste *away.* 5. On and on; continuously: to peg *away* at a task. 6. From one's keeping, attention, or possession: to give food *away.* 7. At once, without hesitation: Fire *away!* — **to do away with** 1. To get rid of. 2. To kill. — *adj.* 1. Absent. 2. At a distance. — *interj.* Begone! [OE *on weg* on (one's) way]

awe (ô) *n.* Reverential fear; dread mingled with veneration. — *v.t.* **awed, aw·ing** or **awe·ing** To impress with reverential fear. [< ON *agi* fear]

a·weigh (ə·wā′) *adv.* *Naut.* Hanging with the flukes just clear of the bottom: said of an anchor.

awe·some (ô′səm) *adj.* 1. Inspiring awe. 2. Characterized by or expressing awe; reverential. — **awe/some·ly** *adv.* — **awe/some·ness** *n.*

aw·ful (ô′fəl) *adj.* 1. *Informal* Exceedingly bad or unpleasant; ugly. 2. Inspiring awe; majestically or solemnly impressive. 3. Causing fear or dread. 4. *Informal* Very great. — **aw/ful·ness** *n.*

aw·ful·ly (ô′fəl·ē for def. 1; ô′flē for def. 2) *adv.* 1. In an awful manner. 2. *Informal* Excessively; very: *awfully* rich.

a·while (ə·hwīl′) *adv.* For a brief time. [OE *āne hwīle* a while]

awk·ward (ôk′wərd) *adj.* 1. Ungraceful in bearing. 2. Unskillful in action; bungling. 3. Embarrassing or perplexing. 4. Difficult or dangerous to deal with. 5. Inconvenient for use; uncomfortable. [< ON *ōfugr* turned the wrong way + -WARD] — **awk/ward·ly** *adv.* — **awk/ward·ness** *n.*

awl (ôl) *n.* A pointed instrument for making small holes, as in wood or leather. [ME *awel* < OE *æl*]

awn (ôn) *n.* *Bot.* A bristlelike appendage of certain grasses; beard, as of wheat or rye. [ME < ON *ōgn* chaff] — **awned** (ônd) *adj.* — **awn/less** *adj.* — **awn/y** *adj.*

awn·ing (ô′ning) *n.* A rooflike cover, as of canvas, for protection from sun or rain. [Origin unknown]

a·woke (ə·wōk′) Past tense of AWAKE.

AWOL (as an acronym pronounced ā′wôl) *Mil.* Absent or absence without leave. Also **awol, A.W.O.L., a.w.o.l.**

a·wry (ə·rī′) *adj.* & *adv.* 1. Toward one side; askew. 2. Out of the right course; amiss; wrong.

ax (aks) *n.* *pl.* **ax·es** A tool with a bladed head mounted on a handle, used for chopping, hewing, etc. **— to have an ax to grind** *Informal* To have a private purpose or interest to pursue. **—** *v.t.* **1.** To cut or trim with an ax. **2.** To behead with an ax. Also *Brit.* **axe.** [OE *æx*] **— ax′like′** *adj.*

ax·es[1] (ak′sēz) Plural of AXIS[1].

ax·es[2] (ak′siz) Plural of AX.

ax·i·al (ak′sē·əl) *adj.* **1.** Of, pertaining to, or forming an axis. **2.** Situated on or along an axis. Also **ax·ile** (ak′sil, -sīl).

ax·il (ak′sil) *n.* *Bot.* The cavity or angle formed by the junction of the upper side of a leafstalk, branch, etc., with a stem or branch. [< L *axilla* armpit]

ax·il·la (ak·sil′ə) *n.* *pl.* **ax·il·lae** (-sil′ē) **1.** *Anat.* The armpit. **2.** An axil. [< L]

ax·il·lar (ak′sə·lər) *adj.* Axillary.

ax·il·lar·y (ak′sə·ler′ē) *adj.* **1.** *Bot.* Of, pertaining to, or situated in an axil. **2.** *Anat.* Pertaining to the axilla.

ax·i·om (ak′sē·əm) *n.* **1.** A self-evident or universally recognized truth. **2.** An established principle or rule. **3.** *Logic & Math.* A self-evident proposition accepted as true without proof. [< L < Gk. < *axioein* to think worthy]

ax·i·o·mat·ic (ak′sē·ə·mat′ik) *adj.* **1.** Of, pertaining to, or resembling an axiom; self-evident. **2.** Aphoristic. Also **ax′·i·o·mat′i·cal.** **— ax′i·o·mat′i·cal·ly** *adv.*

ax·is[1] (ak′sis) *n.* *pl.* **ax·es** (ak′sēz) **1.** A line around which a turning body rotates or may be supposed to rotate. **2.** *Geom.* **a** A straight line through the center of a plane or solid figure, esp. the line in relation to which the figure is symmetrical. **b** A fixed line, as in a graph, along which distances are measured or to which positions are referred. **3.** The central line about which the parts of a body or thing are regularly arranged. **4.** An affiliation of two or more nations to promote and ensure mutual interest, cooperation, and solidarity in their foreign relations. [< axis, axle]

ax·le (ak′səl) *n.* **1.** A crossbar on which a wheel or wheels turn. **2.** An axletree. [< AXLETREE] **— ax′led** *adj.*

ax·le·tree (ak′səl·trē′) *n.* A bar or beam on the ends of which the opposite wheels of a carriage or wagon revolve. [< ON < *öxull* axle + *trē* tree, beam]

ax·man (aks′mən) *n.* *pl.* **·men** (-mən) One who wields an ax; a woodsman. Also **axe′man.**

Ax·min·ster (aks′min·stər) *n.* **1.** A carpet with a long, soft pile. **2.** A carpet made in imitation of this. [after *Axminster*, England, where first made]

ax·o·lotl (ak′sə·lot′l) *n.* A North American tailed amphibian that retains its external gills and breeds in a larval state. [< Sp. < Nahuatl, lit., servant of water]

ax·on (ak′son) *n.* *Physiol.* The central process of a neuron, usu. carrying impulses away from the cells. Also **ax·one** (ak′sōn). [< NL < Gk. *axōn* axis]

a·yah (ä′yə) *n.* *Anglo-Indian* A native nurse or lady's maid. [< Hind. *āyā* < Pg. *aia* nurse]

aye (ī) *n.* An affirmative vote or voter. **—** *adv.* Yes; yea. Also **ay.** [Origin unknown]

a·zal·ea (ə·zāl′yə) *n.* A flowering shrub of the heath family, esp. the **flame azalea**, with showy scarlet or orange flowers. [< NL < Gk. < *azein* to parch, dry up]

az·i·muth (az′ə·məth) *n.* **1.** The angular distance in a horizontal plane measured clockwise from true north to a given course or celestial object. **2.** In celestial navigation, the angle measured at the zenith, clockwise, from true north to a vertical plane passing through a heavenly body; in astronomy, measured clockwise from the south point. [< OF < Arabic *as-sumūt* the ways, pl. of *samt* way] **— az·i·muth·al** (az′ə·muth′əl) *adj.* **— az′i·muth′al·ly** *adv.*

az·o (az′ō, ā′zō) *adj.* *Chem.* Containing nitrogen. [< *azote*, former name for nitrogen]

a·zo·ic (ə·zō′ik) *adj.* *Geol.* Of or pertaining to those periods on earth before life appeared; without organic remains. [< Gk. < *a-* without + *zōē* life]

Az·tec (az′tek) *n.* **1.** One of a tribe of Indians of Nahuatlan stock, founders of an empire that was at its height when Cortés invaded Mexico in 1519. **2.** Nahuatl. **—** *adj.* Of or pertaining to the Aztec Indians, their language, culture, or empire: also **Az·tec·an** (az′tek·ən).

az·ure (azh′ər, ā′zhər) *adj.* Sky blue. **—** *n.* **1.** A clear, sky-blue color or pigment. **2.** *Poetic* The sky. [< OF < Arabic < Persian *lāzhward* lapis lazuli]

az·u·rite (azh′ə·rīt) *n.* A vitreous, monoclinic, azure-blue, basic copper carbonate, often used as a gemstone.

az·y·gous (az′i·gəs) *adj.* *Biol.* Occurring singly; not paired. [< Gk. < *a-* without + *zygon* a yoke]

B

b, B (bē) *n.* *pl.* **b's** or **bs, B's** or **Bs, bees** (bēz) **1.** The second letter of the English alphabet. **2.** The sound represented by the letter *b.* **— symbol 1.** *Music* **a** One of a series of tones, the seventh in the natural diatonic scale of C. **b** A written note representing it. **c** A scale built upon B. **2.** *Chem.* Boron (symbol B). **3.** The second in sequence, etc.

baa (bä, ba) *v.i.* **baaed, baa·ing** To bleat, as a sheep. **—** *n.* A bleat, as of a sheep. [Imit.]

Ba·al (bā′əl, bäl) *n.* *pl.* **Ba·al·im** (bā′əl·im) **1.** Any of several ancient Semitic gods of fertility and flocks; esp., the sun god of the Phoenicians. **2.** An idol or false god. [< Hebrew *ba'al* lord] **— Ba′al·ish** *adj.* **— Ba′al·ist, Ba′al·ite** *n.* **— Ba′al·ism** *n.*

bab·bitt (bab′it) *v.t.* To line, fill, etc., with Babbitt metal.

Bab·bitt (bab′it) *n.* A type of conventional American businessman who is mediocre and smug; philistine. [after Sinclair Lewis's novel *Babbitt* (1922)] **— Bab′bitt·ry** *n.*

Babbitt metal 1. A soft, white, antifriction alloy of tin, copper, and antimony. **2.** Any of a group of similar alloys. [after Isaac *Babbitt*, 1799–1862, U.S. metallurgist]

bab·ble (bab′əl) *v.* **·bled, ·bling** *v.i.* **1.** To utter inarticulate or meaningless sounds. **2.** To make a murmuring or rippling sound, as a stream. **3.** To talk unwisely or foolishly. **—** *v.t.* **4.** To utter unintelligibly. **5.** To blurt out thoughtlessly. **—** *n.* **1.** Inarticulate or confused speech. **2.** Prattle, as of an infant. **3.** A murmuring or rippling sound. [ME *babelen;* ult. origin unknown] **— bab′bler** *n.*

babe (bāb) *n.* **1.** An infant; baby. **2.** *U.S. Informal* An artless or inexperienced person. **3.** *U.S. Slang* A girl. [ME]

ba·bel (bā′bəl, bab′əl) *n.* A confusion of many voices or languages; tumult. Also **Ba′bel.** [after (*Tower of*) *Babel*]

Ba·bel (bā′bəl, bab′əl) In the Bible, an ancient city in Shinar, now identified with Babylon. **— Tower of Babel 1.** A

tower begun in Babel by the descendants of Noah and intended to reach heaven, but abandoned. *Gen.* xi 9. **2.** Any impractical scheme or structure.

ba·bies'-breath (bā′bēz·breth′) See BABY'S-BREATH.

ba·boon (ba·bōōn′) *n.* **1.** A large, terrestrial monkey of Africa and Asia, having a doglike muzzle and usu. a short tail. **2.** *Slang* A coarse or stupid person. [< OF *babuin*]

ba·bush·ka (bə·bŏŏsh′kə) *n.* A woman's scarf, worn over the head. [< Russian, grandmother]

ba·by (bā′bē) *n.* *pl.* **·bies 1.** A very young child of either sex; an infant. **2.** The youngest or smallest member of a family or group. **3.** One who looks or acts like a child. **4.** Any young animal. **5.** *Slang* A girl. **—** *adj.* **1.** For a baby. **2.** Childish; infantile. **3.** Small; diminutive; miniature. **—** *v.t.* **·bied, ·by·ing** To treat as a baby; pamper. [ME *baby,* dim. of *babe*] **— ba′by·hood** *n.* **— ba′by·like′** *adj.*

ba·by-blue-eyes (bā′bē·blōō′īz′) *n.* An annual plant with showy, sky-blue flowers. Also **baby blue-eyes.**

ba·by·ish (bā′bē·ish) *adj.* Childish; infantile. **— ba′by·ish·ly** *adv.* **— ba′by·ish·ness** *n.*

Bab·y·lon (bab′ə·lon, -lon) *n.* **1.** An ancient city of Mesopotamia on the Euphrates, capital of Babylonia from about 2100 B.C.; celebrated as a seat of wealth, luxury, and vice. **2.** Any city or place of great wealth, luxury, or vice.

Bab·y·lo·ni·a (bab′ə·lō′nē·ə) An ancient empire of Mesopotamia; capital, Babylon; conquered by Persia, 538 B.C. **— Bab′y·lo′ni·an** *adj. & n.*

ba·by's-breath (bā′bēz·breth′) *n.* **1.** An Old World perennial with numerous clusters of small, white or pink, fragrant flowers. **2.** Any of certain other fragrant herbs, as the wild madder. Also spelled *babies'-breath.*

baby-sit (bā′bē·sit′) *v.i.* **-sat, -sit·ting** To act as a baby sitter.

---

baby sitter A person employed to take care of young children while the parents are absent: also called *sitter*.

bac·ca·lau·re·ate (bak′ə·lôr′ē·it) *n.* **1.** The degree of bachelor of arts, bachelor of science, etc. **2.** An address to a graduating class at commencement: also **baccalaureate sermon.** [< Med.L < *baccalaureus,* var. of *baccalaris,* a young farmer; infl. in form by L *bacca lauri* laurel berry]

bac·ca·rat (bak′ə·rä′, bak′ə·rä) *n.* A gambling game in which winnings are decided by comparing cards held by the banker with those held by the players. Also **bac·ca·ra** (bak′-ə·rä′, bak′ə·rä). [< F *baccara,* a game of cards]

bac·cha·nal (bak′ə·nəl) *n.* **1.** A votary of Bacchus. **2.** A drunken reveler. **3.** *pl.* Bacchanalia. — *adj.* Bacchanalian. [< L *bacchanalis* of Bacchus]

bac·cha·na·li·a (bak′ə·nā′lē·ə, -nāl′yə) *n.pl.* Drunken revelries; orgies. [< L, neut. pl. of *bacchanalis* of Bacchus] — **bac·cha·na′li·an** *adj.* — **bac·cha·na′li·an·ism** *n.*

bac·chant (bak′ənt) *n. pl.* **bac·chants** or **bac·chan·tes** (bə·kan′tēz) **1.** A votary of Bacchus. **2.** A carouser; reveler. — *adj.* Given to drunkenness. — **bac·chan·te** (bə·kan′tē, bə·kant′, bak′ənt) *n. fem.*

bac·chic (bak′ik) *adj.* Riotous; orgiastic; drunken.

Bac·chus (bak′əs) In classical mythology, the god of wine and revelry: identified with *Dionysus.* — **Bac·chic** *adj.*

bacci- *combining form* Berry or berries. [< L *bacca* berry]

bach·e·lor (bach′ə·lər, bach′lər) *n.* **1.** An unmarried man. **2.** One who has taken his first university or college degree. **3.** A young knight serving under another's banner: also **bach′e·lor-at-arms′.** [< OF < Med.L *baccalaris,* a young farmer] — **bach′e·lor·hood′, bach′e·lor·ship′** *n.*

Bachelor of Arts **1.** A degree usu. given by a college or university to a person who has completed a four-year course in the humanities. **2.** One who has received this degree.

Bachelor of Science **1.** A degree given by a college or university to a person who has completed a four-year course in the sciences. **2.** One who has received this degree.

bach·e·lor's-but·ton (bach′ə·lərz·but′n, bach′lərz-) *n.* **1.** Any of several plants with button-shaped flowers or flower heads. **2.** The cornflower.

bac·il·lar·y (bas′ə·ler′ē) *adj.* **1.** Rod-shaped. **2.** Pertaining to or caused by bacilli. Also **ba·cil·lar** (bə·sil′ər).

ba·cil·lus (bə·sil′əs) *n. pl.* **·cil·li** (-sil′ī) **1.** *Bacteriol.* Any of a large class of straight, rod-shaped bacteria including both beneficial and pathogenic species. **2.** A bacterium. — Syn. See MICROBE. [< NL < L *baculus* stick]

back[1] (bak) *n.* **1.** The part of the body nearest the spine; in man the hinder, in quadrupeds the upper part, extending from the neck to the base of the spine. ◆ Collateral adjective: *dorsal.* **2.** The backbone. **3.** The rear or posterior part of anything. **4.** The farther or other side; the reverse. **5.** The part behind or opposite to the part used: the *back* of a knife. **6.** Anything to cover or support the back. **7.** The part of a garment covering the back. **8.** Physical strength: Put your *back* into it. **9.** In football, a player in a position behind the line of scrimmage. **10.** *Phonet.* The part of the tongue directly behind the front and below the velum. — **at one's back** Following closely. — **behind one's back** **1.** Secretly. **2.** Treacherously. — **in back of** Behind; at or to the rear of. — **to be (flat) on one's back** To be helplessly ill. — **to turn one's back on** **1.** To show contempt or ill feeling toward by ignoring. **2.** To renounce. — *v.t.* **1.** To cause to move backward; reverse the action of. **2.** To furnish with a back. **3.** To support, as by financing or by endorsing: to *back* a candidate; to *back* a business. **4.** To bet on. **5.** To form a background for. **6.** To mount, as a horse. **7.** To write on the back of. — *v.i.* **8.** To move backward. **9.** To shift counterclockwise: said of the wind. — **to back down** To withdraw from a position, abandon a claim, etc. — **to back off** To retreat, as from contact. — **to back out (of)** To withdraw from or refuse to carry out a promise, contest, etc. — *adj.* **1.** In the rear; behind. **2.** Distant; remote: the *back* country. **3.** Of or for a date earlier than the present: a *back* issue. **4.** In arrears; overdue: *back* taxes. **5.** In a backward direction. [OE *bæc*]

back[2] (bak) *adv.* **1.** At, to, or toward the rear. **2.** In, to, or toward a former place or condition. **3.** Into time past. **4.** In return or retort. **5.** In reserve or concealment. **6.** In check or hindrance. **7.** In withdrawal or repudiation. — **back and forth** First in one direction and then in the opposite. — **back of** *U.S.* Behind. — **to go back on** *Informal* **1.** To fail to keep (an engagement, promise, etc.). **2.** To desert or betray. [< ABACK]

back·bite (bak′bīt′) *v.t. & v.i.* **·bit, ·bit·ten** (*Informal* ·bit) **·bit·ing** To revile behind one's back; slander. — **back′bit′er** *n.*

back·board (bak′bôrd′, -bōrd′) *n.* **1.** A board forming or supporting the back of something. **2.** In basketball, the vertical board behind the basket.

back·bone (bak′bōn′) *n.* **1.** The spine or vertebral column. **2.** Something likened to a backbone in function or appearance. **3.** Strength of character. — **back′boned′** *adj.*

back·break·ing (bak′brā′king) *adj.* Physically exhausting.

back·door (bak′dôr′, -dōr′) *adj.* Clandestine; underhand.

back·drop (bak′drop′) *n.* The curtain hung at the rear of a stage, often representing a scene. Also **back cloth.**

backed (bakt) *adj.* Having a (specified kind of) back or backing: used in combination: *low-backed; cardboard-backed.*

back·er (bak′ər) *n.* **1.** One who supports with money; a patron. **2.** One who bets on a contestant.

back·field (bak′fēld′) *n.* In football, the players behind the line of scrimmage: the backs.

back·fire (bak′fīr′) *n.* **1.** A fire built to check an advancing forest or prairie fire by creating a barren area in its path. **2.** Premature explosion in the cylinder of an internal-combustion engine. **3.** An explosion of unburned fuel in the muffler of an internal combustion engine. **4.** An explosion in the back part of a gun. — *v.i.* **·fired, ·fir·ing** **1.** To set or use a backfire. **2.** To explode in a backfire. **3.** To react in an unexpected and unwelcome manner: His scheme *backfired.*

back formation *Ling.* **1.** The creation by analogy of a new word from an existing word. **2.** A word so formed, as *enthuse* from *enthusiasm.*

back·gam·mon (bak′gam′ən, bak′gam′ən) *n.* **1.** A game played by two persons, on a special board, the moves of the pieces being determined by dice throws. **2.** A victory in this game. — *v.t.* To win a backgammon from. [ME *back gammen* back game]

back·ground (bak′ground′) *n.* **1.** That part in a picture against which the principal elements, motifs, or subjects are represented. **2.** Ground in the rear or distance. **3.** A subordinate position; obscurity; retirement. **4.** The aggregate of one's experiences, education, etc. **5.** The events leading up to or causing a situation, event, etc. **6.** Music or sound effects employed in a motion picture, radio program, etc.

back·hand (bak′hand′) *n.* **1.** Handwriting that slopes toward the left. **2.** The hand turned backward in making a stroke, as with a racket. **3.** A stroke made with the hand turned backward, as in tennis. — *adj.* Backhanded. — *adv.* With a backhand stroke.

back·hand·ed (bak′han′did) *adj.* **1.** Delivered or made with the back of the hand turned forward, as a stroke in tennis. **2.** Insincere; equivocal: a *backhanded* compliment. **3.** Sloping to the left, as handwriting.

back·ing (bak′ing) *n.* **1.** Support or assistance. **2.** Supporters or promoters collectively. **3.** Endorsement. **4.** Motion backward. **5.** The back of anything, as for support.

back·lash (bak′lash′) *n.* **1.** *Mech.* **a** A jarring recoil, as of the parts of a machine when poorly fitted. **b** The amount of loose play in such parts. **2.** In angling, a snarl or tangle of line on a reel, caused by a faulty cast.

back·log (bak′lôg′, -log′) *n. U.S.* **1.** A large log at the back of an open fireplace to maintain and concentrate the heat. **2.** Any reserve supply, as of funds, business orders, etc.

back·most (bak′mōst) *adj.* Farthest to the rear; hindmost.

back number **1.** An old issue of a magazine or newspaper. **2.** *U.S. Informal* An old-fashioned person or thing.

back·pack (bak′pak′) *n.* A bag worn on the back, often having a lightweight frame, for carrying food and gear. — *v.t. & v.i.* **·packed, ·packing** To travel with a backpack; hike.

back·rest (bak′rest′) *n.* A support for or at the back.

back seat **1.** A seat in the rear, as of a vehicle, hall, etc. **2.** An inconspicuous or subordinate position.

back-seat driver (bak′sēt′) A passenger in an automobile who persists in directing and advising the driver.

back·side (bak′sīd′) *n.* **1.** The hind part. **2.** The rump.

back·slide (bak′slīd′) *v.i.* **·slid, ·slid** or **·slid·den, ·slid·ing** To return to wrong or sinful ways. — **back′slid′er** *n.*

back·spin (bak′spin′) *n.* Reverse rotation of a round object that is moving forward, as a golf ball, baseball, etc.

back·stage (*n., adv.* bak′stāj′; *adj.* bak′stāj′) *adv.* **1.** In or toward the portion of a theater behind the stage, including the wings, dressing rooms, etc. **2.** To or toward the back portion of the stage. — *n.* The back portion of the stage. — *adj.* Situated or occurring backstage.

back·stairs (bak′stârz′) *adj.* Indirect; underhand.

back·stay (bak′stā′) *n. Naut.* A stay supporting a mast on the aft side.

back·stitch (bak′stich′) *n.* A stitch made by carrying the thread back half the length of the preceding stitch. — *v.t. & v.i.* To sew with backstitches.

back·stop (bak′stop′) *n. U.S.* A fence, wire screen, or net to stop the ball from going too far, as in baseball, tennis, etc.

back·stretch (bak′strech′) *n.* That part of a racecourse farthest from the spectators, usually a straightaway.

back·stroke (bak′strōk′) *n.* **1.** A backhanded stroke. **2.** In swimming, a stroke executed while on one's back. — *v.* **·stroked, ·strok·ing** *v.t.* **1.** To strike, as a ball, with a backstroke. — *v.i.* **2.** To swim with a backstroke.

back talk Impudent retort; insolent answering back.

back·track (bak′trak′) *v.i. U.S.* **1.** To retrace one's steps. **2.** To withdraw from a position, undertaking, etc.

back·ward (bak′wərd) *adv.* **1.** Toward the back; to the rear. 2. With the back foremost. 3. In reverse order. 4. From better to worse. 5. To or into time past. Also **back′-wards.** — *adj.* 1. Turned to the back or rear; reversed. 2. Done the reverse or wrong way. 3. Behind in growth or development; retarded; slow. 4. Hesitating; reluctant; bashful. — **back′ward·ly** *adv.* — **back′ward·ness** *n.*

back·wash (bak′wosh′, -wôsh′) *n.* 1. Water moved backward, as by a boat. 2. A backward current or flow.

back·wa·ter (bak′wô′tər, -wot′ər) *n.* 1. Water turned or held back, as by a dam, a current, etc. 2. Any place or condition regarded as stagnant, backward, etc.

back·woods (bak′wŏŏdz′) *U.S. n.pl.* Wild, heavily wooded, or sparsely settled districts. — *adj.* In, from, or like the backwoods: also **back′wood′.** — **back′woods′man** (-mən) *n.*

ba·con (bā′kən) *n.* The salted and dried or smoked back and sides of the hog. — **to bring home the bacon** *U.S. Informal* 1. To provide food, etc. 2. To succeed. [< OF < OHG *bacho, bahho* ham, side of bacon]

Ba·co·ni·an (bā·kō′nē·ən) *adj.* Of or pertaining to Francis Bacon, his philosophy, or his literary style. — *n.* A believer in the Baconian theory.

Baconian theory The theory that Francis Bacon wrote the plays attributed to Shakespeare.

bac·te·ri·a (bak·tir′ē·ə) Plural of BACTERIUM.

bac·te·ri·cide (bak·tir′ə·sīd) *n.* An agent destructive of bacteria. — **bac·te′ri·ci′dal** *adj.*

bacterio- *combining form* Of or pertaining to bacteria. Also, before vowels, **bacter-.** Also **bacteri-, bactero-.** [< Gk. *baktron* rod, staff]

bac·te·ri·ol·o·gy (bak·tir′ē·ol′ə·jē) *n.* The branch of biology and medicine that deals with bacteria. — **bac·te′ri·o·log′i·cal** (bak·tir′ē·ə·loj′i·kəl) *adj.* — **bac·te′ri·o·log′i·cal·ly** *adv.* — **bac·te′ri·ol′o·gist** *n.*

bac·te·ri·o·phage (bak·tir′ē·ə·fāj′) *n. Bacteriol.* An ultramicroscopic filter-passing agent that has the power of destroying bacteria in a living organism.

bac·te·ri·um (bak·tir′ē·əm) *n. pl.* **·te·ri·a** (-tir′ē·ə) Any of numerous widely distributed unicellular microorganisms exhibiting both plant and animal characteristics, and ranging from the harmless and beneficial to those that cause disease. — *Syn.* See MICROBE. [< NL < Gk. *baktron* staff, stick] — **bac·te′ri·al** *adj.* — **bac·te′ri·al·ly** *adv.*

bad (bad) *adj.* **worse, worst** 1. Not good in any manner or degree. 2. Evil; wicked; immoral. 3. Defective; worthless: *bad* wiring. 4. Faulty or incorrect: *bad* grammar. 5. Not valid or sound. 6. Not sufficient; inadequate. 7. Lacking skill or proficiency: a *bad* poet. 8. Distressing; unfavorable: *bad* news. 9. Offensive; disagreeable: a *bad* taste. 10. Harmful; noxious: *bad* for the eyes. 11. Rotted; spoiled. 12. Severe: a *bad* storm. 13. Sick; in ill health. 14. Sorry; regretful: He felt *bad* about it. — **in bad** *Informal* 1. In difficulty. 2. In disfavor. — **not bad** Rather good: also **not half bad, not so bad.** — *n.* 1. That which is bad. 2. Those who are bad: with *the.* 3. A bad state or condition; wickedness. — *adv. Informal* Badly. [ME *bad, baddle,* ? < OE *bæddel* effeminate man] — **bad′ness** *n.*

bade (bad) Past tense of BID.

badge (baj) *n.* 1. Any device worn to indicate rank, office, membership in an organization, an award or prize, etc. 2. Any distinguishing mark, token, or insignia. — *v.t.* **badged, badg·ing** To decorate or provide with a badge. [ME *bage*]

badg·er (baj′ər) *n.* 1. A small, burrowing, nocturnal, carnivorous mammal, with a broad body, short legs, and long-clawed toes. 2. The fur of a badger, or a brush made of its hair. — *v.t.* To harass; nag at. [Origin unknown]

Badger State Nickname of WISCONSIN.

AMERICAN BADGER
(About 30 inches long; tail 6 inches)

bad·i·nage (bad′ə·näzh′, bad′ə·nij) *n.* Playful raillery; banter. — *v.t.* **·naged, ·nag·ing** To subject to or tease with badinage. [< F *badin* silly, jesting]

bad·lands (bad′landz′) *n.pl.* A barren area characterized by numerous ridges, peaks, and mesas cut by erosion.

Bad Lands An arid, eroded plateau in South Dakota and Nebraska. Also **Bad′lands.**

bad·ly (bad′lē) *adv.* 1. In a bad manner; improperly, imperfectly, or grievously. 2. *Informal* Very much; greatly.

bad·min·ton (bad′min·tən) *n.* A game played by batting a shuttlecock back and forth over a high, narrow net with a light racket. [after *Badminton,* an estate in England]

bad-tem·pered (bad′tem′pərd) *adj.* Cross; irritable.

Bae·de·ker (bā′di·kər) *n.* 1. Any of a series of travelers' guidebooks. 2. Loosely, any guidebook. [after Karl *Baedeker,* 1801–59, German publisher who issued them]

baf·fle (baf′əl) *v.* **·fled, ·fling** *v.t.* 1. To confuse mentally; perplex: The problem *baffled* him. 2. To foil or frustrate;

hinder. — *v.i.* 3. To struggle to no avail. — *n.* 1. A partition or wall used to control and direct sound effects in radio or motion pictures. 2. A partition or grating used to alter the flow of gases or liquids: also **baf·fle·plate** (baf′əl·plāt′). [Origin uncertain] — **baf′fle·ment** *n.* — **baf′fler** *n.* — **baf′fling** *adj.* — **baf′fling·ly** *adv.*

bag (bag) *n.* 1. A sack or pouch, usu. of paper, cloth, or leather, used as a receptacle. 2. The amount a bag will hold. 3. A woman's purse. 4. A suitcase or satchel. 5. The quantity of game caught or killed in hunting. 6. A bulging or baggy part, as of a sail. 7. A sac or similar part in various animals, as the udder of a cow. 8. In baseball slang, a base. 9. *U.S. Slang* A slovenly woman. — **in the bag** *U.S. Slang* Assured; certain. — **to be left holding the bag** *U.S. Informal* To be left to assume full responsibility or blame. — *v.* **bagged, bag·ging** *v.t.* 1. To put into a bag. 2. To cause to fill out or bulge like a bag. 3. To capture or kill, as game. — *v.i.* 4. To bulge or swell like a bag. 5. To hang loosely. [? < ON *baggi* pack, bundle]

bag and baggage *Informal* 1. With all one's possessions: He cleared out *bag and baggage.* 2. Entirely; completely.

ba·gasse (bə·gas′) *n.* The dry refuse of sugar cane after the juice has been expressed, used in making paper and fiberboard. Also **ba·gass′.** [< F < Sp. *bagazo* refuse of grapes, olives, etc., after pressing]

bag·a·telle (bag′ə·tel′) *n.* 1. A trifle. 2. A game similar to billiards. [< F < Ital. *bagatella,* dim of *baga* sack]

ba·gel (bā′gəl) *n.* A doughnut-shaped roll of yeast dough simmered in water and baked. [< Yiddish < *beigen* to twist]

bag·gage (bag′ij) *n.* 1. *Chiefly U.S.* The trunks, packages, etc., of a traveler. 2. An army's movable equipment. 3. A lively or impudent woman. [< MF < Med.L *baga* sack]

bag·ging (bag′ing) *n.* A coarse cloth for making bags.

bag·gy (bag′ē) *adj.* **bag·gi·er, bag·gi·est** Like a bag; loose; bulging. — **bag′gi·ly** *adv.* — **bag′gi·ness** *n.*

bagn·io (ban′yō, bän′-) *n.* 1. A brothel. 2. In the Orient, a prison. [< Ital. < L < Gk. *balaneion* bath]

bag·pipe (bag′pīp′) *n. Often pl.* A reed musical instrument having several pipes, the air being forced through them from an inflated leather bag. — **bag′pip′er** *n.*

ba·guette (ba·get′) *n.* A gem or crystal cut in long, narrow, rectangular form. Also **ba·guet′.** [< F < Ital. < L *baculum* staff, stick]

bah (bä, ba) *interj.* An exclamation of contempt or dismissal.

bail¹ (bāl) *n.* A scoop or bucket for dipping out fluids, as from a boat. — *v.t. & v.i.* 1. To dip (water) from a boat with a bail. 2. To clear (a boat) of water by dipping out. — **to bail out** To jump with parachute from an aircraft. [< OF < LL *baca, bacca* tub] — **bail′er** *n.*

bail² (bāl) *n.* In cricket, one of the crosspieces of the wicket. [< OF *bailler* to enclose]

bail³ (bāl) *Law n.* 1. One who becomes surety for the debt or default of another, esp. of a person under arrest. 2. The security or guaranty given or agreed upon. 3. Release, or the privilege of release, on bail. — **to go bail for** *U.S. Slang* To provide bail for. — *v.t.* To obtain the release of (an arrested person) by giving bail: often with *out.* [< OF < L *bajulare* to carry] — **bail′a·ble** *adj.* — **bail′ment** *n.*

bail⁴ (bāl) *n.* 1. The semicircular handle of a pail, kettle, etc. 2. An arch-shaped support, as for a canopy. — *v.t.* To provide with a bail or handle. [< ON *beygla* hook, ring]

bai·liff (bā′lif) *n.* 1. A court officer having custody of prisoners under arraignment. 2. A sheriff's deputy for serving processes and warrants of arrest. 3. One who oversees an estate for the owner; a steward. 4. *Brit.* A subordinate magistrate with jurisdiction limited to a certain district or to certain functions. [< OF < L *bajalus* porter, manager]

bai·li·wick (bā′lə·wik) *n.* 1. The office, jurisdiction, or district of a bailiff. 2. *U.S.* A person's own area of authority or competence. [ME *bailie* bailiff + *wick* village]

bails·man (bālz′mən) *n. pl.* **·men** (-mən) One who provides bail for another.

bairn (bârn) *n. Scot.* A young child; a son or daughter.

bait (bāt) *n.* 1. Food or other enticement placed as a lure in a trap, on a hook, etc. 2. Any allurement or enticement. 3. A halt for food or refreshment during a journey. — *v.t.* 1. To put food or some other lure on or in: to *bait* a trap. 2. To set dogs on for sport: to *bait* a bear. 3. To harass; torment. 4. To lure; entice. [< ON *beita* food] — **bait′er** *n.*

baize (bāz) *n.* A plain woolen fabric, usu. dyed green and napped to imitate felt, used for pool table covers, etc. [< OF *baies,* fem. pl. of *bai* chestnut brown]

bake (bāk) *v.* **baked, bak·ing** *v.t.* 1. To cook (bread, pastry, etc.) by dry heat, as in an oven. 2. To harden or vitrify by heat, as bricks or pottery. — *v.i.* 3. To bake bread, pastry, etc. 4. To become baked or hardened by heat, as soil. — *n.* A baking, or the amount baked. [OE *bacan*]

bake·house (bāk′hous′) *n.* A bakery.

Ba·ke·lite (bā′kə·līt) *n.* Any of a group of thermosetting plastics having many uses: a trade name. Also **ba′ke·lite**. [after Leo Hendrik *Baekeland*, 1863–1944, U.S. chemist]

bak·er (bā′kər) *n.* 1. One who bakes and sells bread, cake, etc. 2. A portable oven.

baker's dozen Thirteen.

bak·er·y (bā′kər·ē, bāk′rē) *n. pl.* **·er·ies** 1. A place for baking bread, cake, etc. 2. A shop where bread, cake, etc., are sold: also **bake′shop′**.

bak·ing (bā′king) *n.* 1. The act of one who or that which bakes. 2. The quantity baked.

baking powder A finely powdered mixture of baking soda and an acid salt, giving off carbon dioxide when moist, used as a leavening agent in baking.

baking soda Sodium bicarbonate.

bak·sheesh (bak′shēsh) *n.* In India, Turkey, etc., a gratuity or a gift of alms. — *v.t. & v.i.* To give a tip or alms (to). Also **bak′shish**. [< Persian *bakhshīdan* to give]

Ba·laam (bā′ləm) In the Bible, a prophet hired to curse the Israelites but who blessed them by God's command after his donkey spoke to him. *Num.* xxii.

bal·a·lai·ka (bal′ə·lī′kə) *n.* A Russian stringed instrument of the guitar family. [< Russian]

bal·ance (bal′əns) *n.* 1. *Sometimes pl.* An instrument for weighing; esp., a bar that pivots on a central point as weights are placed in the pans suspended from each end. 2. Figuratively, the scale by which deeds and principles are weighed and destinies determined. 3. The power or authority to decide and determine. 4. A state of equilibrium or equal relationship; equipoise. 5. Bodily poise. 6. Mental or emotional stability. 7. Harmonious proportion, as in the design or arrangement of parts in a whole. 8. Something used to produce an equilibrium; counterpoise. 9. The act of balancing or weighing. 10. In bookkeeping: **a** Equality between the debit and credit totals of an account. **b** A difference between such totals; the excess on either side. 11. *U.S.* Whatever is left over; remainder. 12. A balance wheel. 13. A movement in dancing. — **to strike a balance** To find or take an intermediate position; compromise. — *v.* **·anced, ·anc·ing** *v.t.* 1. To bring into or keep in equilibrium; poise. 2. To weigh in a balance. 3. To compare or weigh in the mind, as alternative courses of action. 4. To offset or counteract. 5. To place or keep in proportion. 6. To be equal or in proportion to. 7. In bookkeeping: **a** To compute the difference between the debit and credit sides of (an account). **b** To reconcile, as by making certain entries, the debit and credit sides of (an account). **c** To adjust (an account) by paying what is owed. — *v.i.* 8. To be or come into equilibrium. 9. To be equal. 10. To hesitate; tilt. [< F < L *bis* two + *lanx, lancis* dish, plate] — **bal′ance·a·ble** *adj.* — **bal′an·cer** *n.*

Bal·ance (bal′əns) *n.* The constellation and sign of the zodiac Libra.

balance of power A distribution of forces among nations such that none may acquire a degree of power dangerous to the others.

balance of trade The difference in value between exports and imports of a country.

balance sheet A statement in tabular form to show assets and liabilities, profit and loss, etc., of a business.

balance wheel The oscillating wheel of a watch or chronometer, that determines its rate of motion.

bal·a·ta (bal′ə·tə) *n.* The juice of one of several tropical American trees, used as an elastic gum for making golf balls, insulating wires, etc. [< Sp. < Tupi]

bal·bo·a (bal·bō′ə) *n.* A silver monetary unit of Panama, in 1960 worth $1.00. [after Vasco de *Balboa*]

bal·brig·gan (bal·brig′ən) *n.* 1. A fine, unbleached, knitted cotton fabric. 2. *pl.* Underwear and hose made of this fabric. [after *Balbriggan*, a town in Ireland]

bal·co·ny (bal′kə·nē) *n. pl.* **·nies** 1. A balustraded platform projecting from a wall of a building. 2. A projecting gallery in a theater or public building. [< Ital. < OHG *balcho* beam] — **bal′co·nied** *adj.*

bald (bôld) *adj.* 1. Without hair on the head. 2. Without natural covering or growth. 3. Unadorned. 4. Without disguise; forthright. 5. *Zool.* Having white feathers or fur on the head. [? < Welsh *bāl* white] — **bald′ly** *adv.* — **bald′ness** *n.*

BALCONY
(With balusters and balustrade)

Bal·der (bôl′dər) In Norse mythology, god of sunlight, spring, and joy; son of Odin. Also **Bal′dr**.

bal·der·dash (bôl′dər·dash) *n.* A meaningless flow of words; nonsense. [Origin uncertain]

bald·head (bôld′hed′) *n.* One whose head is bald. — **bald′head′ed** *adj.*

bald·pate (bôld′pāt′) *n.* 1. A baldheaded person. 2. See under WIDGEON. — **bald′pat′ed** *adj.*

bal·dric (bôl′drik) *n.* A belt worn over one shoulder and across the breast, to support a sword, bugle, etc. Also **bal′drick**. [Cf. OF *baldrei*, ult. < L *balteus* belt]

bale (bāl) *n.* A large package of bulky goods corded or otherwise prepared for transportation. — *v.t.* **baled, bal·ing** To make into a bale or bales. [< OF *bale* round package] — **bal′er** *n.*

ba·leen (bə·lēn′) *n.* Whalebone. [< F < L < Gk. *phalaina* whale]

bale·ful (bāl′fəl) *adj.* 1. Hurtful; malignant. 2. Ominous: *baleful* predictions of his political future. [OE *bealu* evil + -FUL] — **bale′ful·ly** *adv.* — **bale′ful·ness** *n.*

Ba·li·nese (bä′lə·nēz′, -nēs′) *adj.* Of or pertaining to Bali, its people, or their language. — *n. pl.* **·nese** 1. A native or inhabitant of Bali. 2. The Indonesian language of Bali.

balk (bôk) *v.i.* 1. To stop short and refuse to proceed or take action. — *v.t.* 2. To render unsuccessful; thwart; frustrate. — *n.* 1. A hindrance or check; defeat; disappointment. 2. An error or slip; blunder. 3. In baseball, an illegal motion made by the pitcher when one or more runners are on base. 4. A ridge between furrows. 5. A squared beam. Also spelled *baulk*. [OE *balca* bank, ridge]

Bal·kan (bôl′kən) *adj.* 1. Of or pertaining to the Balkan Peninsula, its people, or their customs. 2. Of or pertaining to the Balkan Mountains.

balk·y (bô′kē) *adj.* **balk·i·er, balk·i·est** Given to balking.

ball¹ (bôl) *n.* 1. A spherical or nearly spherical body. 2. Such a body, of any size and made of various substances, used in a number of games. 3. A game played with a ball, esp. baseball. 4. In sports, a ball moving, thrown, or struck in a specified manner. 5. In baseball, a pitch in which the ball fails to pass over the home plate between the batter's armpits and knees and is not struck at by him. 6. A roundish protuberance or part of something. 7. *Usu. pl. Slang* A testicle. — **to be on the ball** *U.S. Slang* To be alert or competent. — **to have something on the ball** *U.S. Slang* To have ability. — **to play ball** 1. To begin or resume playing a ball game or some other activity. 2. *U.S. Informal* To cooperate. — *v.t. & v.i.* To form, gather, or wind into a ball. — **to ball up** *Slang* To confuse. [< ON *böllr*]

ball² (bôl) *n.* A formal social dance. [< F *bal*]

bal·lad (bal′əd) *n.* 1. A narrative poem or song of popular origin in short stanzas, often with a refrain. 2. A sentimental song of several stanzas, in which the melody is usually repeated for each stanza. [Var. of BALLADE]

bal·lade (bə·läd′, ba-) *n.* 1. A verse form having three stanzas of eight or ten lines each and an envoy of four or five lines. The last line of each stanza and of the envoy is the same. 2. A musical composition of romantic or dramatic nature, usually for piano or orchestra. [< OF *balade* dancing song]

bal·lad·ry (bal′əd·rē) *n.* 1. Ballad poetry. 2. The art of making or singing ballads.

ball-and-sock·et joint (bôl′ən·sok′it) 1. *Mech.* A joint composed of a sphere in a bearing, permitting a degree of free turning in any direction. 2. *Anat.* An enarthrosis.

bal·last (bal′əst) *n.* 1. Any heavy substance, as sand, stone, etc., laid in the hold of a vessel or in the car of a balloon to steady it. 2. Gravel or broken stone laid down as a stabilizer for a rail bed. 3. That which gives stability to character, morality, etc. — *v.t.* 1. To provide or fill with ballast. 2. To steady with ballast; stabilize. [< ODan. *bar* bare, mere + *last* load]

ball bearing *Mech.* 1. A bearing in which a shaft bears on small metal balls that turn freely as it revolves. 2. A metal ball in such a bearing.

bal·le·ri·na (bal′ə·rē′nə) *n.* A female ballet dancer. [< Ital., fem. of *ballerino* dancer]

bal·let (bal′ā, ba·lā′) *n.* 1. An elaborate dramatic group dance using conventionalized movements, often for narrative effects. 2. The performers or troupe of such dancing. [< F, dim. of *bal* dance]

bal·lis·tic (bə·lis′tik) *adj.* Of or pertaining to projectiles or to ballistics.

ballistic missile A missile controlled to the apex of its trajectory, falling free thereafter.

bal·lis·tics (bə·lis′tiks) *n.pl.* (construed as *sing.*) 1. The science that deals with the motion of projectiles, either while they are still in the bore (**interior ballistics**) or after they leave the muzzle (**exterior ballistics**). 2. The study of the flight of all missiles. — **bal·lis·ti·cian** (bal′ə·stish′ən) *n.*

bal·loon (bə·lōōn′) *n.* 1. A large, impermeable bag, inflated with gas lighter than air, and designed to rise and float in the atmosphere; esp., such a bag having a car or basket attached, for carrying passengers, instruments, etc. 2. A small, inflatable rubber bag, used as a toy. — *v.i.* 1. To increase quickly in scope or magnitude; expand: The rumor threatened to *balloon* into a full-fledged scandal. 2. To swell out like a balloon, as a sail. 3. To ascend or travel in a balloon. — *v.t.* 4. To inflate or distend with air. — *adj.* Like a balloon. [< Ital. *balla* ball, sphere < Gmc.] — **bal·loon′ist** *n.*

bal·lot (bal′ət) *n.* **1.** A written or printed slip or ticket used in casting a secret vote. **2.** The total number of votes cast in an election. **3.** The act or system of voting secretly by ballots or by voting machines. **4.** A list of candidates for office; ticket. — *v.* **·lot·ed, ·lot·ing** *v.i.* **1.** To cast a ballot in voting. — *v.t.* **2.** To vote for or decide on by ballot. [< Ital. *ballotta,* dim. of *balla* ball]

ball·play·er (bôl′plā′ər) *n. U.S.* A baseball player.

ball-point pen (bôl′point′) A fountain pen having for a point a ball bearing that rolls to ink itself from a cartridge.

ball·room (bôl′rōōm′, -rŏŏm′) *n.* A large room for dancing.

ballroom dancing Social dancing for two people.

ball valve *Mech.* A valve controlled by a ball that is free to rise when the upward pressure exceeds gravity.

bal·ly·hoo (bal′ē-hōō′) *n. U.S. Informal* **1.** Blatant or sensational advertising; noisy propaganda. **2.** Clamor; uproar. — *v.t. & v.i.* **·hooed, ·hoo·ing** To advocate or promote by ballyhoo. [Origin unknown]

balm (bäm) *n.* **1.** An aromatic, resinous exudation from various trees or shrubs, used as medicine; balsam. **2.** Any oily, fragrant, resinous substance. **3.** A tree or shrub yielding such a substance. **4.** Any of various aromatic plants resembling mint. **5.** A pleasing fragrance. **6.** Anything that soothes. [< OF < L < Gk. *balsamon* balsam tree]

balm of Gilead **1.** The resinous, fragrant juice obtained from a small evergreen tree growing on the shores of the Red Sea. **2.** The balsam fir.

balm·y (bä′mē) *adj.* **balm·i·er, balm·i·est** **1.** Mild and soothing; soft. **2.** Having the fragrance of balm; aromatic. **3.** *Brit. Slang* Crazy. — **balm′i·ly** *adv.* — **balm′i·ness** *n.*

ba·lo·ney (bə-lō′nē) *n.* **1.** *Slang* Nonsense. **2.** Bologna sausage. Also spelled *boloney.* [def. 1 < BOLOGNA SAUSAGE]

bal·sa (bôl′sə, bäl′-) *n.* **1.** A tree of tropical America and the West Indies. **2.** The very light wood of this tree. **3.** A raft made of light logs. [< Sp. *balza*]

bal·sam (bôl′səm) *n.* **1.** Any of a group of fragrant oleoresins obtained chiefly from the exudations of various trees. **2.** Any tree yielding such a resinous substance, as the balsam fir. **3.** Any fragrant ointment, esp. one used medicinally. — *v.t.* To anoint with balsam. [< L < Gk. *balsamon* balsam] — **bal·sam·ic** (bôl-sam′ik) *adj.*

balsam fir A tree of the pine family, growing in the U.S. and Canada and yielding Canada balsam: also *balm of Gilead.*

Bal·tic (bôl′tik) *adj.* Of or pertaining to the Baltic Sea or the Baltic States.

Baltimore oriole An American oriole of which the male has orange and black plumage. [after the colors of the coat of arms of Lord *Baltimore*]

bal·us·ter (bal′əs-tər) *n.* One of a set of small pillars supporting a handrail. For illus. see BALCONY. [< MF < Ital. *balaustra* pomegranate flower]

bal·us·trade (bal′ə-strād′, bal′ə-strād) *n.* A handrail supported by balusters. For illus. see BALCONY. See BALUSTER.

bam·bi·no (bam-bē′nō) *n. pl.* **·ni** (-nē) or **·nos** **1.** A little child; a baby. **2.** A figure of the child Jesus. [< Ital., dim. of *bambo* simple, childish]

bam·boo (bam-bōō′) *n.* **1.** A tall, treelike or shrubby grass of tropical and semitropical regions. **2.** Its tough, hollow, jointed stem, used for furniture, etc. [< Malay *bambu*]

bam·boo·zle (bam-bōō′zəl) *v.* **·zled, ·zling** *Informal v.t.* **1.** To mislead; cheat. **2.** To perplex. — *v.i.* **3.** To practice trickery or deception. [Origin unknown] — **bam·boo′zle·ment** *n.* — **bam·boo′zler** *n.*

ban (ban) *v.t.* **banned, ban·ning** **1.** To proscribe or prohibit; forbid. **2.** To place under a ban; anathematize; interdict. — *n.* **1.** An official proclamation, especially of prohibition. **2.** *Eccl.* An edict of excommunication or interdiction. **3.** A sentence of outlawry. [< OE *bannan* to proclaim and ON *banna* to curse, prohibit]

ba·nal (bā′nəl, bə-nal′, ban′əl) *adj.* Hackneyed; trite. [< F < OF *ban* feudal summons hence, ordinary, common] — **ba·nal·i·ty** (bə-nal′ə-tē) *n.* — **ba′nal·ly** *adv.*

ba·nan·a (bə-nan′ə) *n.* **1.** The elongated, edible, pulpy fruit of a herbaceous plant of tropical regions, having an easily removed rind and growing in drooping clusters. **2.** The plant bearing this fruit. [< Sp. < native African name]

band¹ (band) *n.* **1.** A flat flexible strip of any material, often used for binding or securing. **2.** A strip of fabric used to finish, strengthen, or trim an article of dress: often in combination: *hatband.* **3.** Any broad stripe of contrasting color, material, or surface. **4.** *pl.* Geneva bands (which see). **5.** A high collar worn in the 16th and 17th centuries. **6.** *Telecom.* A range of frequencies or wavelengths between two stated limits. — *v.t.* **1.** To unite or tie with a band; encircle. **2.** To mark by attaching a band to. [< F *bande*.]

band² (band) *n.* **1.** A company of persons associated for a common purpose; a group, troop, or gang. **2.** A company of persons organized to play musical instruments. **3.** *Cana-*

dian A group of reservation Indians having elective chiefs. — *v.t. & v.i.* To unite in a band. [< MF *bande*]

band·age (ban′dij) *n.* A strip of soft cloth or other material used in dressing wounds, etc. — *v.t.* **·aged, ag·ing** To bind or cover with a bandage. [< F < *bande* band]

Band-Aid (band′ād′) *n.* An adhesive strip with a gauze patch for covering minor wounds: a trade name. Also **band′-aid′.**

ban·dan·na (ban-dan′ə) *n.* A large, brightly colored handkerchief decorated with spots or figures. Also **ban·dan′a.** [< Hind. *bāndhnū,* a method of dyeing]

band·box (band′boks′) *n.* A light round or oval box, originally used to hold collars, and now used for carrying hats.

ban·deau (ban-dō′, ban′dō) *n. pl.* **·deaux** (-dōz′, -dōz) **1.** A narrow band, esp. one worn about the hair. **2.** A narrow brassiere. [< F < OF *bande* band]

ban·di·coot (ban′di-kōōt) *n.* **1.** A large rat of India and Ceylon. **2.** A small marsupial of Australia, Tasmania, etc. [Alter. of Telugu *pandikokku* pig-rat]

ban·dit (ban′dit) *n. pl.* **ban·dits** or **ban·dit·ti** (ban-dit′ē) **1.** A robber. **2.** An outlaw; brigand. [< Ital. *bandire* to proscribe, outlaw] — **ban′dit·ry** *n.*

band·mas·ter (band′mas′tər, -mäs′tər) *n.* The conductor of a musical band.

ban·do·leer (ban′də-lir′) *n.* A broad belt fitted with loops or cases for holding cartridges, and worn over the shoulder. Also **ban′do·lier′.** [< MF < Ital. *banda* band]

band saw *Mech.* A saw consisting of a toothed endless belt mounted on pulleys.

band shell A bandstand having a concave hemispherical rear wall.

band·stand (band′stand′) *n.* A platform for a band of musicians, often roofed when outdoors.

band·wag·on (band′wag′ən) *n.* A high, decorated wagon used to carry a band in a parade. — **to climb** (hop, get, etc.) **on the bandwagon** *U.S. Informal* To give one's support to a principle or candidate apparently assured of success.

ban·dy (ban′dē) *v.t.* **·died, ·dy·ing** **1.** To give and take; exchange, as blows or words. **2.** To pass along; circulate: to *bandy* stories. **3.** To pass, throw, or knock back and forth, as a ball. — *n.pl.* **·dies** A game resembling hockey; also, a crooked stick used in this game. [Origin uncertain]

ban·dy-leg·ged (ban′dē-leg′id, -legd′) *adj.* Bowlegged.

bane (bān) *n.* **1.** Anything destructive or ruinous. **2.** Poison: now only in combination: *henbane.* [OE *bana* killer]

bane·ful (bān′fəl) *adj.* Poisonous; destructive. — **Syn.** See PERNICIOUS. — **bane′ful·ly** *adv.* — **bane′ful·ness** *n.*

bang¹ (bang) *n.* **1.** A heavy, noisy blow or thump. **2.** A sudden, loud noise or explosion. **3.** *Informal* A sudden spurt of activity: To start with a *bang.* **4.** *U.S. Slang* Thrill; enjoyment. — *v.t.* **1.** To beat or strike heavily and noisily. — *v.i.* **2.** To make a loud sound. **3.** To strike noisily; crash. — *adv.* Abruptly and loudly. [< ON *banga* to hammer]

bang² (bang) *n. Usu. pl.* A fringe of hair cut straight across the forehead. — *v.t.* To cut short and straight across. [< BANG¹, *adv.*; from the hair being cut off abruptly]

bang³ (bang) See BHANG.

ban·gle (bang′gəl) *n.* A decorative bracelet or anklet. [< Hind. *bangrī* glass bracelet]

bang-up (bang′up′) *adj. Slang* Excellent.

ban·ish (ban′ish) *v.t.* **1.** To compel to leave a country by political decree; exile. **2.** To expel, as from any customary or desired place; drive away; dismiss. [< OF < LL *bannire* to banish] — **ban′ish·er** *n.* — **ban′ish·ment** *n.*

ban·is·ter (ban′is-tər) *n.* **1.** *Often pl.* A balustrade. **2.** Loosely, a baluster. Also *bannister.* [BALUSTER]

ban·jo (ban′jō) *n. pl.* **·jos** or **·joes** A long-necked, four- or five-stringed musical instrument having a hoop-shaped body covered on top with stretched skin and played by plucking the strings with the fingers or a plectrum. [< a West African language; cf. Mandingo *bania*] — **ban′jo·ist** *n.*

bank¹ (bangk) *n.* **1.** Any moundlike formation or mass; ridge. **2.** A steep slope; rising ground. **3.** *Often pl.* The slope of land at the edge of a watercourse or of any cut or channel. — **Syn.** See SHORE. **4.** A raised portion of the ocean floor, a river bed, etc.; a shoal; shallow: the Newfoundland *banks.* **5.** Aeron. The controlled sidewise tilt of an airplane in a turn, used to prevent skidding. — *v.t.* **1.** To enclose, cover, or protect by a bank, dike, or border; embank. **2.** To heap up into a bank or mound. **3.** To give an upward lateral slope to, as the curve of a road. **4.** To tilt (an airplane) laterally in flight. **5.** In billiards and pool: To cause (a ball) to rebound at an angle from a cushion. — *v.i.* **6.** To form or lie in banks. **7.** To tilt an airplane laterally in flight. [ME *banke*]

BANJO

bank[2] (bangk) *n.* **1.** An institution for lending, borrowing, exchanging, issuing, or safeguarding money. **2.** An office or building used for such purposes. **3.** The funds of a gambling house or the fund held by the dealer or banker in some gambling games. **4.** A store or reserve supply of anything needed for future use: a blood *bank.* — *v.t.* **1.** To deposit in a bank. — *v.i.* **2.** To do business as or with a bank or banker. **3.** In gambling, to keep the bank in a game. — **to bank on** *Informal* To rely on; be sure about. [< F < Ital. *banca* money-changer's table, ult. < Gmc.]

bank[3] (bangk) *n.* **1.** A set of like articles arranged in a row. **2.** *Naut.* A rowers' bench or tier of oars in a galley. **3.** A rank of keys in a piano or organ. **4.** In journalism, lines under a headline; deck. — *v.t.* To arrange in a bank. [< OF < LL *bancus* bench, ult. < Gmc.]

bank account Money deposited in a bank to the credit of, and subject to withdrawal by, the depositor.

bank bill 1. A bank note. **2.** A draft drawn on one bank by another: also **banker's bill.**

bank·book (bangk′bŏŏk′) *n.* A book kept by a depositor in which his accounts are entered: also called *passbook.*

bank·er[1] (bangk′ər) *n.* **1.** An employee or officer of a bank. **2.** One who keeps the bank in certain gambling games.

bank·er[2] (bangk′ər) *n. U.S. & Canadian* A vessel or person engaged in cod fishing on the Newfoundland banks.

bank·ing (bangk′ing) *n.* The business of a bank or banker.

bank note A promissory note issued by a bank, payable on demand and serving as currency. Abbr. *B.N.*

bank·rupt (bangk′rupt) *n.* **1.** *Law* One who is judicially declared insolvent, his property being administered for and distributed among his creditors, under a bankruptcy law. **2.** Any person unable to pay his debts, or without resources. **3.** One ruined and unproductive in some way: a spiritual *bankrupt.* — *adj.* **1.** Subject to the conditions of a bankruptcy law; insolvent. **2.** Destitute; lacking: with *in.* — *v.t.* To make bankrupt. [< F < Ital. *rumpere* to break]

bank·rupt·cy (bangk′rupt·sē, -rəp·sē) *n. pl.* **·cies** The state of being bankrupt.

ban·ner (ban′ər) *n.* **1.** A flag or standard bearing a motto or device. **2.** In journalism, a headline extending across a newspaper page. — *adj.* Leading; foremost; outstanding. [< OF < LL *bandum* banner]

ban·nis·ter (ban′is·tər) See BANISTER.

banns (banz) *n.pl. Eccl.* A public announcement in church of a proposed marriage, usu. made on three successive Sundays. Also **bans.** [< BAN]

ban·quet (bang′kwit) *n.* **1.** A sumptuous feast. **2.** A formal or ceremonial dinner, often followed by speeches. — *v.t. & v.i.* To entertain at a banquet; feast sumptuously or formally. [< MF, dim. of *banc* table] — **ban′quet·er** *n.*

ban·quette (bang·ket′) *n.* **1.** *Mil.* A platform or bank behind a parapet, on which soldiers may stand and fire. **2.** An upholstered bench, as along a wall. **3.** A sidewalk. [< F < Ital. *banchetta,* dim. of *banca* bench]

ban·shee (ban′shē, ban·shē′) *n.* In Gaelic folklore, a spirit whose wailing was supposed to foretell a death. Also **ban′shie.** [< Irish *bean* woman + *sídhe* fairy]

ban·tam (ban′təm) *n.* **1.** *Often cap.* Any of various breeds of very small domestic fowl, characterized by combativeness. **2.** A small, pugnacious person. — *adj.* Like a bantam; small and combative. [after *Bantam,* Java]

ban·tam·weight (ban′təm·wāt′) *n.* A boxer or wrestler who weighs between 113 and 118 pounds.

ban·ter (ban′tər) *n.* Good-humored ridicule; raillery. — *v.t.* **1.** To tease good-naturedly. — *v.i.* **2.** To exchange good-natured repartee. [Origin unknown] — **ban′ter·er** *n.* — **ban′ter·ing·ly** *adv.*

Ban·tu (ban′tōō) *n. pl.* **·tu** or **·tus** (-tōōz) **1.** A member of any of numerous Negro tribes of central and southern Africa, including the Kaffirs, Zulus, Bechuanas, and Damaras. **2.** A family of languages spoken by these tribes. — *adj.* Of or pertaining to the Bantu tribes or their languages.

ban·yan (ban′yən) *n.* An East Indian fig-bearing tree whose branches send down roots that develop into new trunks. [< *banian,* Hindu merchant, from the use of the ground under the tree as a market place]

ban·zai (bän·zī) *Japanese* (May you live) ten thousand years: used as a cheer, battle cry, etc.

ba·o·bab (bā′ō·bab, bä′ō-) *n.* An African tree with a thick trunk, bearing edible fruit. [< native African name]

bap·tism (bap′tiz·əm) *n.* **1.** The act of baptizing or of being baptized; esp., the Christian sacrament of initiation into the Church. **2.** Any initiatory or purifying experience. [< OF < LL < Gk. *baptismos* immersion] — **bap·tis·mal** (bap·tiz′məl) *adj.* — **bap·tis′mal·ly** *adv.*

Bap·tist (bap′tist) *n.* **1.** A member of any of various Protestant denominations holding that baptism (generally by immersion) should be given only to professed believers. **2.** One who baptizes. — **the Baptist** John the Baptist.

bap·tis·ter·y (bap′tis·tər·ē, -tis·trē) *n. pl.* **·ter·ies** A part of a church set apart for baptism. Also **bap′tis·try** (-trē).

bap·tize (bap·tīz′, bap′tīz) *v.* **·tized, ·tiz·ing** *v.t.* **1.** To immerse in water or sprinkle water on in Christian baptism. **2.** To christen. **3.** To cleanse or initiate. — *v.i.* **4.** To administer baptism. Also *Brit.* **bap·tise′.** [< OF < LL < Gk. *baptizein* to immerse, wash] — **bap·tiz′er** *n.*

bar (bär) *n.* **1.** A piece of wood, metal, etc., evenly shaped and long in proportion to its width and thickness, used as a fastening, lever, etc. **2.** An oblong block of solid material, as of soap or a precious metal. **3.** Any barrier or obstacle. **4.** A bank, as of sand, at the entrance to a harbor or river. **5.** The railing about the place in a court occupied by the judge and lawyers, or where prisoners are brought to trial. **6.** A court of law. **7.** Lawyers collectively; also, the legal profession. **8.** Any tribunal or place of judgment. **9.** *Music* **a** The vertical line that divides a staff into measures. **b** A measure. **10** A counter or establishment serving drinks and food, esp. alcoholic drinks. **11.** A stripe, as of color. **12.** The metal mouthpiece of a horse's bridle. — *v.t.* **barred, bar·ring 1.** To fasten or secure with a bar. **2.** To prevent or prohibit. **3.** To obstruct or hinder. **4.** To exclude. **5.** To mark with stripes. — *prep.* Excepting: *bar none.* [< OF < LL *barra* bar]

Ba·rab·bas (bə·rab′əs) A thief released in place of Jesus at the demand of the multitude. *Matt.* xxvii 16–21.

barb[1] (bärb) *n.* **1.** A point projecting backward on a sharp weapon, as on an arrow, fishhook, or spear, intended to prevent easy extraction. **2.** Any similar sharp point, as on barbed wire. **3.** Pointedness; sting, as of wit; also, a stinging remark. **4.** *Ornithol.* One of the lateral processes of a bird's feather. — *v.t.* To provide with a barb or barbs: to *barb* an arrow. [< F < L *barba* beard]

barb[2] (bärb) *n.* A horse of the breed introduced by the Moors from Barbary into Spain. [< F < Arabic *Barbar* native of North Africa]

bar·bar·i·an (bär·bâr′ē·ən) *n.* **1.** One who belongs to a people, group, or tribe characterized by a primitive civilization. **2.** A rude, coarse, or brutal person. **3.** Formerly, a foreigner; esp., in ancient Greece, one who was non-Hellenic. — *adj.* **1.** Of or resembling a barbarian; uncivilized. **2.** Foreign. — **bar·bar′i·an·ism** *n.*

bar·bar·ic (bär·bar′ik) *adj.* **1.** Of or befitting barbarians; uncivilized. **2.** Coarse; unrestrained.

bar·ba·rism (bär′bə·riz′əm) *n.* **1.** The use of words or forms not approved or standard in a language. **2.** Such a word or form. **3.** A primitive stage of civilization. **4.** A trait, condition, act, etc., characteristic of such a stage.

bar·bar·i·ty (bär·bar′ə·tē) *n. pl.* **·ties 1.** Barbaric conduct. **2.** A barbaric act. **3.** Crudity in style or taste.

bar·ba·rize (bär′bə·rīz) *v.t. & v.i.* **·rized, ·riz·ing** To make or become barbarous or corrupt, as a language.

bar·ba·rous (bär′bər·əs) *adj.* **1.** Uncivilized; primitive. **2.** Lacking in refinement; coarse. **3.** Cruel; brutal. **4.** Rude or harsh in sound: *barbarous music.* **5.** Of language, abounding in barbarisms; also, not classical. **6.** Formerly, foreign; esp. in ancient Greece, non-Hellenic. [< L < Gk. *barbaros* non-Hellenic, foreign, rude] — **bar′ba·rous·ly** *adv.* — **bar′ba·rous·ness** *n.*

Bar·ba·ry (bär′bər·ē) North Africa west of Egypt, including the former Barbary States.

Barbary ape An easily trained, tailless ape of North Africa and southern Spain.

bar·bate (bär′bāt) *adj.* **1.** Bearded. **2.** *Bot.* Tufted with long hairs. [< L *barba* beard]

bar·be·cue (bär′bə·kyōō) *n.* **1.** *U.S.* A social gathering, usu. outdoors, at which animals are roasted whole over an open fire. **2.** A whole animal carcass or other meat roasted over an open fire. **3.** A grill, framework, or pit for roasting meat in this fashion. — *v.t.* **·cued, ·cu·ing** To roast (usu. beef or pork) in large pieces or whole over an open fire or in a trench, often using a highly seasoned sauce. [< Sp. *barbacoa* < Taino *barbacoa* framework of sticks]

barbed (bärbd) *adj.* **1.** Having a barb or barbs. **2.** Pointed, piercing, or wounding: a *barbed* remark.

barbed wire Fence wire having barbs at short intervals.

bar·bel (bär′bəl) *n.* **1.** One of the soft threadlike appendages to the jaws, chin, or nostrils of certain fishes, functioning as an organ of touch. **2.** A carplike, Old World fish. [< OF < LL *barba* beard]

bar·ber (bär′bər) *n.* One who cuts hair, shaves beards, etc., as a business. ◆ Collateral adjective: *tonsorial.* — *v.t.* To cut or dress the hair of; shave or trim the beard of. [< AF, ult. < L *barba* beard]

bar·ber·ry (bär′ber′ē, -bər·ē) *n. pl.* **·ries 1.** A shrub bearing yellow flowers and bright red, oblong berries. **2.** Its acid berry. [< Med.L *berberis, barbaris*]

bar·ber·shop (bär′bər·shop′) *n.* **1.** The place of business of a barber. — *adj. Informal* Characterized by close harmony and sentimentality of theme: said of a singing group.

bar·bi·can (bär′bi·kən) *n.* An outer fortification; outwork. [< OF *barbaquenne;* ult. origin uncertain]

bar·bi·tal (bär′bə·tôl, -tal) *n. Chem.* A white, odorless, crystalline powder, $C_8H_{12}O_3N_2$, with a bitter taste, used as a sedative and hypnotic. Also *Brit.* **bar′bi·tone** (-tōn).

bar·bit·u·rate (bär-bich′ər-it, bär′bə-tŏŏr′it, -tyŏŏr′it) *n.* *Chem.* A salt or ester of barbituric acid, esp. one used as a sedative or sleeping pill.

bar·bi·tu·ric acid (bär′bə-tŏŏr′ik, -tyŏŏr′-) *Chem.* A crystalline powder, $C_4H_4O_3N_2$, from which several sedative and hypnotic drugs are derived. [< NL (*Usnea*) *barbata* bearded (lichen) + -URIC]

bar·bule (bär′byōōl) *n.* **1.** A small barb or beard. **2.** *Ornithol.* A process fringing the barb of a feather. [< L *barbula,* dim. of *barba* beard]

bar·ca·role (bär′kə-rōl) *n.* **1.** A Venetian gondolier's song. **2.** A melody in imitation of this. Also **bar′ca·rolle.** [< F < Ital. *barcaruola* boatman's song]

bard (bärd) *n.* **1.** A Celtic poet and minstrel. **2.** A poet. [< Celtic] —**bard′ic** *adj.*

bare¹ (bâr) *adj.* **1.** Without clothing or covering; naked. **2.** Open to view; exposed. **3.** Without the usual furnishings or equipment; empty. **4.** Unadorned; plain; bald. **5.** Just sufficient; mere. **6.** Threadbare. —*v.t.* **bared, bar·ing** To make or lay bare; reveal; expose. [OE *bær*]

bare² (bâr) Archaic past tense of BEAR¹.

bare·back (bâr′bak′) *adj.* Riding a horse without a saddle. —*adv.* Without a saddle. —**bare′backed′** *adj.*

bare·faced (bâr′fāst′) *adj.* **1.** Having the face bare. **2.** Unconcealed; open. **3.** Impudent; audacious. —**bare·fac·ed·ly** (bâr′fā′sid·lē, -fāst′lē) *adv.* —**bare′fac′ed·ness** *n.*

bare·foot (bâr′fŏŏt′) *adj.* & *adv.* With the feet bare.

bare·foot·ed (bâr′fŏŏt′id) *adj.* Having the feet bare.

bare·hand·ed (bâr′han′did) *adj.* & *adv.* **1.** With the hands uncovered. **2.** Without a weapon, tool, etc.

bare·head·ed (bâr′hed′id) *adj.* & *adv.* With the head bare. Also **bare′head′.**

bare·leg·ged (bâr′leg′id, -legd′) *adj.* & *adv.* With the legs bare.

bare·ly (bâr′lē) *adv.* **1.** Only just; scarcely. **2.** Openly; boldly; plainly. **3.** Nakedly.

bar·gain (bär′gən) *n.* **1.** A mutual agreement between persons, especially an agreement to buy or sell goods. **2.** That which is agreed upon or the terms of the agreement. **3.** The agreement as it affects one of the parties: He made a bad *bargain.* **4.** An article bought or offered at a low price. —**into the bargain** In addition to what was agreed; besides. —**to strike a bargain** To come to an agreement on terms. —*v.i.* **1.** To discuss terms for selling or buying. **2.** To make a bargain; reach an agreement. **3.** To negotiate. —*v.t.* **4.** To trade or arrange by bargaining. —**to bargain for** To expect; count on: more than I *bargained for.* [< OF *bargaine*] —**bar′gain·er,** *Law* **bar′gain·or** *n.*

barge (bärj) *n.* **1.** A flat-bottomed freight boat or lighter for harbors and inland waters. **2.** A large boat, for pleasure, pageants, or for state occasions. **3.** *Naval* A ship's boat for the use of a flag officer. —*v.* **barged, barg·ing** *v.t.* **1.** To transport by barge. —*v.i.* **2.** To move clumsily and slowly. **3.** *Informal* To collide: with *into.* **4.** *Informal* To enter or intrude rudely or awkwardly. [< OF < LL *barga*]

barge·man (bärj′mən) *n.* *pl.* **·men** (-mən) One in charge of or employed on a barge. Also *Brit.* **bar·gee** (bär·jē′).

bar·ite (bâr′īt) *n.* A heavy, vitreous, usu. white, orthorhombic barium sulfate, $BaSO_4$: also called *heavy spar.*

bar·i·tone (bar′ə-tōn) *n.* **1.** A male voice of a register higher than bass and lower than tenor. **2.** One having such a voice. **3.** A brass instrument having a similar range. —*adj.* **1.** Of or pertaining to a baritone. **2.** Having the range of a baritone. [< Ital. < Gk. < *barys* deep + *tonos* tone]

bar·i·um (bâr′ē-əm) *n.* A silver white to yellow, malleable, metallic element (symbol Ba) occurring in combination and forming salts, of which the soluble ones and the carbonate are poisonous. See ELEMENT. [< NL < Gk. *barys* heavy] —**bar·ic** (bar′ik) *adj.*

barium sulfate An insoluble compound, $BaSO_4$, used to facilitate X-ray pictures of the stomach and intestines.

bark¹ (bärk) *n.* **1.** The short, abrupt, explosive cry of a dog. **2.** Any sound like this. —*v.i.* **1.** To utter a bark, as a dog, or to make a sound like a bark. **2.** *Informal* To cough. **3.** To speak loudly and sharply. **4.** *U.S. Slang* To solicit customers at the entrance to a show by proclaiming its attractions. —*v.t.* **5.** To say roughly and curtly: He *barked* an order. —**to bark up the wrong tree** *U.S. Informal* To be mistaken as to one's object or as to the means of attaining it. [OE *beorcan*]

bark² (bärk) *n.* The rind or covering of the stems, branches, and roots of a tree or other plant. —*v.t* **1.** To remove the bark from; scrape; girdle. **2.** To rub off the skin of. **3.** To tan or treat with an infusion of bark. [< Scand.]

bark³ (bärk) *n.* A sailing vessel of three or more masts, square-rigged on all but the mizzenmast, which is fore-and-aft-rigged. [< MF < LL *barca* bark]

bar·keep·er (bär′kē·pər) *n.* **1.** One who owns or manages a bar where alcoholic liquors are served. **2.** A bartender. Also **bar′keep′.**

bar·ken·tine (bär′kən·tēn) *n.* A sailing vessel of three or more masts, square-rigged on the foremast and fore-and-aft-rigged on the other masts: also spelled *barquentine.* [< BARK³, on analogy with *brigantine*]

BARK

bark·er (bär′kər) *n.* *U.S. Informal* One who advertises a show, etc., at its entrance.

bar·ley (bär′lē) *n.* **1.** A hardy cereal grass of temperate regions. **2.** The grain borne by this grass. [OE *bærlic*]

bar·ley·corn (bär′lē·kôrn) *n.* Barley, or a grain of barley.

Bar·ley·corn (bär′lē·kôrn), **John** A humorous personification of malt liquor, or of intoxicating liquors in general.

barm (bärm) *n.* The froth or foam rising on fermented malt liquors. [OE *beorma*]

bar·maid (bär′mād) *n.* A female bartender.

bar·man (bär′mən) *n.* *pl.* **·men** (mən) A bartender.

bar mitz·vah (bär mits′və) In Judaism, a boy commencing his thirteenth year, the age of religious duty; also, the ceremony celebrating this. [< Hebrew, son of the commandment]

barm·y (bär′mē) *adj.* **barm·i·er, barm·i·est 1.** Full of barm; frothy. **2.** *Brit. Slang* Silly; flighty. Also *Scot.* **barm′ie.**

barn (bärn) *n.* **1.** A building for storing hay, stabling livestock, etc. **2.** *Brit.* A building for storing grain. [OE *bern*]

bar·na·cle (bär′nə·kəl) *n.* **1.** A marine shellfish that attaches itself to rocks, ship bottoms, etc. **2.** A European wild goose of northern seas: also **barnacle goose. 3.** One who or that which clings tenaciously. [< ME *bernacle;* origin uncertain] —**bar′na·cled** *adj.*

barn dance A social dance held in a barn and usu. consisting of square dances with appropriate music and calls.

barn owl An owl of nearly world-wide distribution, often found in barns, where it preys on mice.

barn·storm (bärn′stôrm′) *v.i.* *U.S Informal* To tour rural districts, giving shows, political speeches, exhibitions of stunt flying, etc. —**barn′storm′er** *n.* —**barn′storm′ing** *adj.* & *n.*

barn·yard (bärn′yärd′) *n.* A yard adjoining a barn. —*adj.* Of or fit for a barnyard; broad; smutty.

baro- *combining form* Weight; atmospheric pressure: *barometer.* [< Gk. *baros* weight]

bar·o·gram (bar′ə-gram) *n.* The record of a barograph.

bar·o·graph (bar′ə-graf, -gräf) *n.* An automatically recording barometer. —**bar′o·graph′ic** *adj.*

ba·rom·e·ter (bə-rom′ə-tər) *n.* **1.** An instrument for measuring atmospheric pressure, used in forecasting weather, measuring elevations, etc. **2.** Anything that indicates changes. —**bar·o·met·ric** (bar′ə-met′rik) or **·ri·cal** *adj.* —**bar′o·met′ri·cal·ly** *adv.* —**ba·rom′e·try** *n.*

bar·on (bar′ən) *n.* **1.** A member of the lowest order of hereditary nobility in several European countries. **2.** *U.S.* One who has great power in a commercial field. [< OF < LL *baro, -onis* man < Gmc.] —**ba·ro·ni·al** (bə-rō′nē-əl) *adj.*

bar·on·age (bar′ən-ij) *n.* **1.** Barons collectively. **2.** The dignity or rank of a baron.

bar·on·ess (bar′ən-is) *n.* **1.** The wife or widow of a baron. **2.** A woman holding a barony in her own right.

bar·on·et (bar′ən-it, -net) *n.* **1.** An inheritable English title, below that of baron and not part of the nobility. **2.** The bearer of the title. —**bar′on·et·age, bar′on·et·cy** *n.*

bar·o·ny (bar′ə-nē) *n.* *pl.* **·nies** The rank, dignity, or domain of a baron.

ba·roque (bə-rōk′) *adj.* **1.** Of or characteristic of a style of art and architecture developed in Europe in the late 16th and 17th centuries, characterized by extravagantly contorted classical forms and curvilinear ornament. **2.** Fantastic in style; elaborately ornamented. **3.** Loosely, rococo. **4.** Irregular in shape: said of pearls. —*n.* **1.** The baroque style in art. **2.** An object, ornament, design, or composition in this style. [< F < Pg. *barroco* rough or imperfect pearl]

ba·rouche (bə-rōōsh′) *n.* A four-wheeled carriage with folding top, four inside seats, and an outside seat for the driver. [< G < Ital. < L *bis* twice + *rota* wheel]

barque (bärk), **bar·quen·tine** (bär′kən·tēn) See BARK³, BARKENTINE.

bar·racks (bar′əks) *n.pl.* (construed as *sing.* or *pl.*) **1.** A building or group

BAROQUE
ARCHITECTURE
(Church of Santa
Maria della Salute,
Venice, 1631–56)

of buildings for the housing of soldiers. **2.** Any large, plain building used for temporary housing. Also **bar′rack.** [< F *baraque* < Ital. *baracca* soldier's tent; ult. origin uncertain]

barracks bag A soldier's cloth bag with a draw cord, for holding clothing and equipment. Also **barrack bag.**

bar·ra·cu·da (bar′ə·kōō′də) *n. pl.* **·da** or **·das** A voracious pikelike fish of tropical seas. [< Sp.]

bar·rage (bə·räzh′) *n.* **1.** *Mil.* A curtain of fire designed to protect troops by impeding enemy movements across defensive lines or areas. **2.** Any overwhelming attack, as of words or blows. — *v.t. & v.i.* **·raged, ·rag·ing** To lay down or subject to a barrage. [< F (*tir de*) *barrage* barrage (fire)]

bar·ran·ca (bə·rang′kə) *n. SW U.S.* A deep ravine. [< Sp.]

bar·ra·try (bar′ə·trē) *n. pl.* **·tries** *Law* **1.** Any willful and unlawful act by the master or crew of a ship, whereby the owners sustain injury. **2.** The offense of exciting lawsuits, stirring up quarrels, etc. Also **bar′re·try.** [< OF < *barat* fraud] — **bar′ra·tor** *n.* — **bar′ra·trous** *adj.*

barred (bärd) *adj.* **1.** Having or secured with bars. **2.** Prohibited. **3.** Marked with bars or stripes.

bar·rel (bar′əl) *n.* **1.** A large, approximately cylindrical vessel usu. of wood, flat at the base and top and bulging slightly in the middle. **2.** As much as a barrel will hold, as the standard U.S. barrel containing 3.28 bushels dry measure, or 31.5 liquid measure. **3.** Something resembling or having the form of a barrel, as the tube of a gun, the drum of a windlass, the cylindrical box containing the mainspring of a watch, etc. — *v.* **bar·reled** or **·relled, bar·rel·ing** or **·rel·ling** **1.** To put or pack in a barrel. — *v.i.* **2.** *U.S. Slang* To move fast. [< OF *baril*]

bar·rel·house (bar′əl·hous′) *n. U.S. Slang* **1.** A cheap drinking house. **2.** *Music* An early style of jazz.

barrel organ A hand organ.

barrel roll *Aeron.* A maneuver in which an airplane rolls on its own axis as it spirals about its original path.

bar·ren (bar′ən) *adj.* **1.** Not producing or incapable of producing offspring; sterile. **2.** Not productive; unfruitful. **3.** Unprofitable, as an enterprise. **4.** Lacking in interest or attractiveness; dull. **5.** Empty; devoid. — *n. Usu. pl.* A tract of level, scrubby land. [< OF *baraigne*] — **bar′ren·ly** *adv.* — **bar′ren·ness** *n.*

bar·rette (bə·ret′) *n.* A small bar with a clasp used for keeping a woman's hair in place. [< F, dim. of *barre* bar]

bar·ri·cade (bar′ə·kād′, bar′ə·kād) *n.* **1.** A barrier hastily built for obstruction or defense. **2.** Any barrier or obstruction blocking passage. — *v.t.* **·cad·ed, ·cad·ing** To enclose, obstruct, or defend with a barricade or barricades. [< F < Sp. *barricada* barrier < *barrica* barrel; the first barricades were barrels filled with earth, stones, etc.] — **bar′ri·cad′er** *n.*

bar·ri·er (bar′ē·ər) *n.* **1.** A fence, wall, gate, etc., erected to bar passage. **2.** Any obstacle or obstruction, natural or otherwise. **3.** Something that separates or keeps apart: a *barrier* of suspicion. [< OF < *barre* bar]

barrier reef A long, narrow ridge of rock or coral parallel to the coast and close to or above the surface of the sea.

bar·ring (bär′ing) *prep.* Excepting; apart from.

bar·ris·ter (bar′is·tər) *n.* In England, a member of the legal profession who argues cases in the courts.

bar·room (bär′rōōm′, -rŏŏm′) *n.* A room where alcoholic liquors are served across a counter or bar.

bar·row[1] (bar′ō) *n.* **1.** A frame or tray with handles at either end by which it is carried, used for transporting loads. **2.** A wheelbarrow. **3.** The load carried on a barrow. **4.** *Brit.* A pushcart. [OE *bearwe* < *beran* to bear]

bar·row[2] (bar′ō) *n.* **1.** *Anthropol.* A mound of earth or stones built over a grave. **2.** A hill. [OE *beorg*]

bar sinister Erroneously, a bend sinister.

bar·tend·er (bär′ten′dər) *n.* A man who mixes and serves alcoholic drinks over a bar.

bar·ter (bär′tər) *v.i.* **1.** To trade by exchange of goods or services without use of money. — *v.t.* **2.** To trade (goods or services) for something of equal value. — *n.* **1.** The act of bartering; exchange of goods. **2.** Anything bartered. [< OF *barater* to exchange] — **bar′ter·er** *n.*

Bart·lett (bärt′lit) *n.* A variety of pear introduced by Enoch Bartlett of Massachusetts. Also **Bartlett pear.**

Bar·uch (bâr′ək) A book in the Old Testament Apocrypha.

bar·y·tes (bə·rī′tēz) *n.* Barite.

ba·sal (bā′səl) *adj.* **1.** Of, at, or forming the base. **2.** Basic; fundamental. — **ba′sal·ly** *adv.*

basal metabolism *Physiol.* The minimum energy required by the body at rest in maintaining essential vital activities, measured by the rate (**basal metabolic rate**) of oxygen intake and heat discharge.

ba·salt (bə·sôlt′, bas′ôlt) *n.* A dense, dark volcanic rock, having a columnar structure. [< L *basaltes* dark marble] — **ba·sal′tic** *adj.*

bas·cule (bas′kyool) *n.* A mechanical apparatus of which each end counterbalances the other, used in a kind of drawbridge (**bascule bridge**) operated by a counterpoise. [< F, seesaw]

base[1] (bās) *n.* **1.** The lowest or supporting part of anything; bottom. **2.** An underlying principle or foundation. **3.** The essential or preponderant element; chief or fundamental ingredient. **4.** Any point, line, or quantity from which an inference, measurement, or reckoning is made. **5.** *Archit.* The lowest member of a structure, as the basement of a building.

BASCULE BRIDGE
(Tower Bridge, London)

6. *Geom.* The side of a polygon or solid figure on which it appears to rest. **7.** *Math.* A number on which a numerical system depends: the *base* of the decimal system is 10. **8.** *Mil.* A locality or installation from which operations are projected or supported. **9.** *Chem.* A compound that is capable of so uniting with an acid as to neutralize it and form a salt. **10.** *Biol.* The point of attachment of an organ. **11.** In baseball, any of the four points of the diamond, or the bag or plate marking one of these. **12.** A base line. **13.** *Ling.* A form to which prefixes, suffixes, or infixes are added; root or stem. — **off base 1.** In baseball, not in contact with the base occupied: said of base runners. **2.** *U.S. Slang* Thinking, speaking, etc., erroneously. — *v.t.* **based, bas·ing 1.** To place on a foundation or basis; ground; establish: with *on* or *upon*. **2.** To form a base for. — *adj.* **1.** Serving as a base: a *base* line. **2.** Situated at or near the base: a *base* angle. [< OF < L < Gk. < *bainein* to go]

base[2] (bās) *adj.* **1.** Morally low; mean; vile; contemptible. **2.** Like or befitting an inferior person or thing; menial; degrading: *base* flattery. **3.** Comparatively low in value: said of metals. **4.** Debased, as money; counterfeit: *base* coin. **5.** Not classical; corrupted: said of languages. [< OF < LL *bassus* low] — **base′ly** *adv.* — **base′ness** *n.*

base·ball (bās′bôl′) *n.* **1.** A game played with a wooden bat and a hard ball by two teams of nine players each, one team being at bat and the other in the field, alternately, the object of the game being to make as many runs as possible within nine innings of play. **2.** The ball used in this game.

base·board (bās′bôrd′, -bōrd′) *n.* **1.** A board skirting the interior wall of a room, next to the floor. **2.** Any board forming a base.

base·born (bās′bôrn′) *adj.* **1.** Of humble birth; plebeian. **2.** Born out of wedlock. **3.** Mean; vile.

base burn·er (bās′bûr′nər) *n.* A coal stove or furnace in which the fuel is fed from above into a central fuel chamber.

base hit In baseball, a batted ball that enables the batter to reach a base unaided by a defensive error, an attempt to put out a preceding base runner, or a force play: also called *hit.*

base·less (bās′lis) *adj.* Without foundation in fact; unfounded; groundless. — **base′less·ness** *n.*

base line 1. In baseball, a path of definite width connecting successive bases. **2.** A line, value, etc., taken as a base for measurement or comparison.

base·ment (bās′mənt) *n.* **1.** The lowest story of a building, usu. wholly or partly underground and just beneath the main floor. **2.** The basal portion of any building.

base runner In baseball, a member of the team at bat who has reached a base.

bas·es[1] (bā′siz) Plural of BASE[1].

ba·ses[2] (bā′sēz) Plural of BASIS.

bash (bash) *Informal v.t.* To strike heavily; smash in. — *n.* A smashing blow. [? Akin to Dan. *baske* thwack]

bash·ful (bash′fəl) *adj.* **1.** Shrinking from notice; shy; timid; diffident. **2.** Characterized by or indicating sensitiveness and timid modesty: a *bashful* glance. [< *bash*, var. of ABASH + -FUL] — **bash′ful·ly** *adv.* — **bash′ful·ness** *n.*

ba·sic (bā′sik) *adj.* **1.** Pertaining to, forming, or like a base or basis; essential; fundamental. **2.** *Chem.* Of, pertaining to, or producing a base. — **ba′si·cal·ly** *adv.*

Basic English A simplified form of English, devised for use as an international language and in the teaching of English. It contains 850 words of general vocabulary, supplemented by an additional 150 for scientific purposes. Also **Basic.**

bas·il (baz′əl) *n.* An aromatic plant of the mint family, sometimes used in cooking. [< OF < L < Gk. *basilikon* (*phyton*) royal (plant), basil]

bas·i·lar (bas′ə·lər) *adj.* Pertaining to or situated at the base, esp. of the skull; basal. Also **bas·i·lar·y** (bas′ə·ler′ē).

ba·sil·i·ca (bə·sil′i·kə) *n.* **1.** In ancient Rome, a rectangular building divided by columns into a nave and two side aisles, used as a place of assembly. **2.** A building of this type used as a Christian church. [< L *basilikē* (*stoa*) royal (hall), fem. of *basilikos*] — **ba·sil′i·can** *adj.*

bas·i·lisk (bas′ə·lisk) *n.* **1.** A fabled reptile whose breath and look were said to be fatal. **2.** A tropical American lizard having an erectile crest on the head. [< L < Gk. *basiliskos*, dim. of *basileus* king]

ba·sin (bā′sən) *n.* **1.** A round, wide, shallow vessel, often with sloping sides, used for holding liquids. **2.** A vessel resembling this, as the scale or pan of a balance. **3.** The amount that a basin will hold. **4.** A sink or washbowl. **5.** *Geog.* **a** Any large depression in the earth's surface, as the bed of a lake or ocean. **b** The region drained by a river. **6.** An enclosed place or hollow containing water, as a cistern, pond, etc. [< OF < LL < *bacca* bowl] — **ba′sined** *adj.*

ba·sis (bā′sis) *n. pl.* **ba·ses** (bā′sēz) **1.** That on which anything rests; support; foundation; base. **2.** Fundamental principle; groundwork. **3.** The chief component or ingredient of a thing. [< L < Gk., base, pedestal]

bask (bask, bäsk) *v.i.* **1.** To lie in and enjoy a pleasant warmth, as of the sun or a fire. **2.** To enjoy or benefit from a similar warmth, as of regard: to *bask* in royal favor. — *v.t.* **3.** To expose to warmth. [< ON *badhask* to bathe oneself]

bas·ket (bas′kit, bäs′-) *n.* **1.** A container made of interwoven splints, rushes, strips of wood, etc. **2.** Something like a basket in form or use. **3.** The amount a basket will hold. **4.** In basketball: **a** One of the goals, consisting of a metal ring with a cord net suspended from it. **b** The point or points made by throwing the ball through the basket. [ME]

bas·ket·ball (bas′kit·bôl′, bäs′-) *n.* **1.** A game played by two teams of five men each, in which the object is to throw the ball through an elevated goal (basket) at the opponent's end of an oblong court. **2.** The ball used in this game.

bas·ket·ry (bas′kit·rē, bäs′-) *n.* **1.** Baskets collectively; basketwork. **2.** The art or craft of making baskets.

basket weave A weave with two or more warp and filling threads woven side by side to resemble a plaited basket.

bas·ket·work (bas′kit·wûrk′, bäs′-) *n.* Work made of or resembling interlaced osiers, twigs, etc.; wickerwork.

ba·so·phile (bā′sə·fil, -fil) *n. Biol.* A tissue or cell having a special affinity for basic staining dyes. Also **ba′si·phile.** — **ba·so·phil·ic** (bā′sə·fil′ik), **ba·soph·i·lous** (bā·sof′ə·ləs) *adj.*

basque (bask) *n.* A woman's closely fitting bodice, separate from the dress skirt.

Basque (bask) *n.* **1.** One of a people of unknown origin living in the western Pyrenees in Spain and France. **2.** The language of the Basque people. — *adj.* Of the Basques.

bas-re·lief (bä′ri·lēf′, bas′-) *n.* That type of sculpture in which the figures project only slightly from the background: also called *low relief*. [< F < Ital. *basso* low + *rilievo* relief]

bass[1] (bas) *n. pl.* **bass** or **bass·es** Any of various spiny-finned, marine and fresh-water food fishes. [OE *bærs*]

bass[2] (bās) *n. Music* **1.** The lowest-pitched male singing voice. **2.** The notes in the lowest register of the piano, pipe organ, etc. **3.** The lowest part in vocal or instrumental music; also, these parts collectively. **4.** One who sings or an instrument that plays such a part, esp., a bass viol. — *adj.* **1.** Low in pitch; having a low musical range. **2.** Of or for a bass or basses. [< OF *bas* low]

bass[3] (bas) *n.* **1.** The basswood or linden. **2.** Bast. [Alter. of BAST]

bass drum (bās) The largest of the drums, beaten on both heads and having a deep sound.

bas·set (bas′it) *n.* A hound characterized by a long, low body, long head and nose, and short, heavy, crooked forelegs. Also **basset hound.** [< OF *basset*, dim. of *bas* low]

bas·si·net (bas′ə·net′) *n.* A basket used as a baby's cradle, usu. with a hood over one end. [< F]

bas·so (bas′ō, bäs′ō; *Ital.* bäs′sō) *n. pl.* **bas·sos** (bas′ōz, bäs′ōz), *Ital.* **bas·si** (bäs′sē) **1.** A bass singer. **2.** The bass part. [< Ital., low]

bas·soon (ba·sōōn′, bə-) *n. Music* A large, low-pitched, double-reed woodwind instrument. [< F < It. *basso* low]

bass viol (bās) *Music* The double bass.

bass·wood (bas′wood′) *n.* The American linden. See under LINDEN. Also called *bass.*

bast (bast) *n. Bot.* The fibrous inner bark of trees, originally of the linden, used in making cordage: also called *bass*. [OE *bæst*]

bas·tard (bas′tərd) *n.* **1.** An illegitimate child. **2.** Any irregular, inferior, or counterfeit thing. **3.** *U.S. Slang* A worthless or cruel man. **4.** *Brit. Informal* A fellow; chap: a somewhat disparaging term. — *adj.* **1.** Born out of wedlock. **2.** False; spurious. **3.** Resembling but not typical of the genuine thing. **4.** Abnormal or irregular in size, shape, or proportion. [< OF < *fils de bast* packsaddle child] — **bas′tard·ly** *adj.* — **bas′tard·y** *n.*

bas·tard·ize (bas′tər·dīz) *v.* **·ized, ·iz·ing** *v.t.* **1.** To prove to be or proclaim to be a bastard. **2.** To make degenerate; debase. — *v.i.* **3.** To become debased. — **bas′tard·i·za′tion** *n.*

baste[1] (bāst) *v.t.* **bast·ed, bast·ing** To sew loosely together, as with long, temporary stitches. [< OF < OHG *bestan* to sew with bast]

baste[2] (bāst) *v.t.* **bast·ed, bast·ing** To moisten (meat or fish) with drippings, butter, etc., while cooking. [? < OF *basser* to soak, moisten]

baste[3] (bāst) *v.t.* **bast·ed, bast·ing** *Informal* **1.** To beat; thrash. **2.** To attack verbally; abuse. [Prob. < Scand.]

bas·tille (bas·tēl′) *n.* A prison, esp. one operated tyrannically. Also **bas·tile′.** [< OF < LL < *bastire* to build]

Bas·tille (bas·tēl′, *Fr.* bás·tē′y′) A fortress in Paris, stormed and destroyed in the French Revolution on July 14, 1789.

bas·ti·na·do (bas′tə·nā′dō) *n. pl.* **·does** **1.** A beating with a stick, usu. on the soles of the feet. **2.** A stick or cudgel. Also **bas′ti·nade′** (-nād′). [< Sp. < *baston* cudgel]

bast·ing (bās′ting) *n.* **1.** The act of sewing loosely together. **2.** The thread used for this purpose. **3.** *pl.* Long, loose, temporary stitches.

bas·tion (bas′chən, -tē·ən) *n.* **1.** In fortifications, a projecting part of a rampart. **2.** Any fortified position. [< MF < Ital. < *bastire* to build] — **bas′tioned** *adj.*

bat[1] (bat) *n.* **1.** In baseball, cricket, and similar games: **a** A stick or club for striking the ball. **b** The act of batting. **c** A turn at bat. **2.** In cricket, the batsman. **3.** In tennis, badminton, etc., a racket. **4.** Any heavy cudgel or club. **5.** *Informal* A blow, as with a stick. **6.** *Slang* A drunken spree. — **to go to bat for** *Informal* To defend or advocate the cause of. — *v.* **bat·ted, bat·ting** *v.i.* **1.** In baseball, cricket, and other games, to use a bat or take a turn at bat. — *v.t.* **2.** To strike with or as with a bat. **3.** To have a batting average of: to *bat* .400. — **to bat around** *Slang* **1.** To travel about. **2.** To discuss. [OE *batt* cudgel]

bat[2] (bat) *n.* A nocturnal flying mammal having elongated forelimbs and digits that support a thin wing membrane. — **blind as a bat** Altogether blind. — **to have bats in the belfry** *U.S. Slang* To be crazy. [ME *bakke*, ? < Scand.]

bat[3] (bat) *v.t.* **bat·ted, bat·ting** *Informal* To wink. — **not bat an eye** or **eyelash** *Informal* Not show surprise.

batch (bach) *n.* **1.** A quantity or number taken together. **2.** The amount of bread produced at one time. **3.** The quantity of material required for one operation. **4.** Any set of things made, done, etc., at one time. [ME *bacche*]

bate (bāt) *v.t. & v.i.* **bat·ed, bat·ing** To restrain; decrease. — **with bated breath** In a state of fear, suspense, expectation, etc. [Var. of ABATE]

ba·teau (ba·tō′) *n. pl.* **·teaux** (-tōz′) **1.** *U.S. & Canadian* A light, flat-bottomed boat. **2.** A pontoon for a floating bridge. [< F < OF *batel*, ult. < Gmc.]

bat·fish (bat′fish′) *n.* **1.** A North American marine fish having a batlike appearance. **2.** A sting ray.

bath (bath, bäth) *n. pl.* **baths** (bathz, bäthz; baths, bäths) **1.** A washing or immersing of something, esp. the body, in water or other liquid. **2.** The liquid used for this. **3.** The container for such a liquid; a bathtub. **4.** A bathroom. **5.** *Often pl.* A set of rooms or a building equipped for bathing. **6.** *Often pl.* An establishment or resort where bathing is part of a medical treatment. — *v.t. Brit.* To place or wash in a bath; immerse. [OE *bæth*]

bathe (bāth) *v.* **bathed, bath·ing** *v.t.* **1.** To place in liquid; immerse. **2.** To wash; wet. **3.** To apply liquid to for comfort or healing. **4.** To cover or suffuse as with liquid. — *v.i.* **5.** To wash oneself; take a bath. **6.** To be covered or suffused as if with liquid: to *bathe* in sunshine. — *n. Brit.* A swim. [< OE *bathian*] — **bath′a·ble** *adj.* — **bath′er** *n.*

bath·house (bath′hous′, bäth′-) *n.* **1.** A building with facilities for bathing. **2.** A small structure at a bathing resort used as a dressing room.

bath·ing suit (bāth′ing) A garment, sometimes consisting of two pieces, worn for swimming.

batho- *combining form* Depth. [< Gk. *bathos* depth]

bath·o·lith (bath′ə·lith) *n. Geol.* A large, irregular mass of igneous rock, often forming the core of mountain ranges. Also **bath′o·lite** (-līt). [< BATHO- + -LITH] — **bath′o·lith·ic** or **bath·o·lit′ic** (-lit′ik) *adj.*

ba·thos (bā′thos) *n.* **1.** A descent from the lofty to the commonplace in discourse; anticlimax. **2.** Insincere pathos; sentimentality. [< Gk. < *bathys* deep]

bath·robe (bath′rōb′, bäth′-) *n.* A long, loose garment for wear before and after bathing.

bath·room (bath′rōōm′, -rōōm′, bäth′-) *n.* **1.** A room in which to bathe. **2.** A toilet.

Bath·she·ba (bath·shē′ba, bath′shi·bə) In the Bible, the wife of Uriah and later of David; mother of Solomon. II *Sam.*

bath·tub (bath′tub′, bäth′-) *n.* A vessel in which to bathe, esp. one installed as a permanent fixture in a bathroom.

bathy- *combining form* Deep; of the sea or ocean depths: *bathysphere.* [< Gk. *bathys* deep]

bath·y·scaph (bath′ə·skaf) *n.* A free bathysphere with ballast and a gasoline-filled float to control depth, capable of ocean depths over 35,000 feet. Also **bath′y·scaphe** (-skāf′). [< BATHY- + Gk. *skaphē* bowl]

bath·y·sphere (bath′ə·sfir) *n.* A spherical diving bell equipped with windows for deep-sea observations.

ba·tik (bə·tēk′, bat′ik) *n.* 1. A process for coloring fabrics, in which the parts not to be dyed are covered with wax. 2. The fabric so colored. Also spelled *battik*. [< Malay]

ba·tiste (bə·tēst′) *n.* A fine cotton fabric in plain weave. [< F; after Jean *Baptiste*, 13th c. French linen weaver]

ba·ton (ba·ton′, bat′n; *Fr.* bȧ·tôn′) *n.* 1. A short staff or truncheon borne as an emblem of authority or privilege. 2. *Music* A slender stick or rod used by a conductor. [< F OF *baston* < LL *bastum* stick]

ba·tra·chi·an (bə·trā′kē·ən) *adj.* Of or pertaining to a former class of amphibians, esp. to frogs and toads; amphibian. — *n.* A frog or toad. [< NL < Gk. *batrachos* frog]

bats (bats) *adj. Slang* Batty.

bats·man (bats′mən) *n. pl.* **·men** (-mən) In baseball or cricket, the batter.

bat·tal·ion (bə·tal′yən) *n.* 1. *Mil.* **a** A unit consisting of a headquarters and two or more companies, batteries, or comparable units. **b** A body of troops. 2. *Usu. pl.* A large group or number. [< MF < Ital. < *battaglia* battle]

bat·ten¹ (bat′n) *v.i.* 1. To grow fat; thrive. — *v.t.* 2. To make fat, as cattle. [< ON *batna* to grow better, improve]

bat·ten² (bat′n) *n.* 1. A light strip of wood, as for covering a joint between boards. 2. A strip of sawed timber, used for flooring, scantling, etc. 3. *Naut.* A thin strip of wood placed in a sail to keep it flat or for fastening a tarpaulin over a hatch. — *v.t.* To fasten with battens: with *up* or *down*.

bat·ter¹ (bat′ər) *v.t.* 1. To strike with repeated, violent blows. 2. To damage or injure with such blows or with hard usage. — *v.i.* 3. To pound or beat with blow after blow; hammer. [Partly < OF < L *battuere* to beat]

bat·ter² (bat′ər) *n.* In baseball and cricket, the player whose turn it is to bat.

bat·ter³ (bat′ər) *n.* A mixture, as of eggs, flour, and milk, beaten for use in cookery. [? < OF < *battre* to beat]

bat·ter·ing-ram (bat′ər·ing·ram′) *n.* A long, stout beam, used in ancient warfare for battering down walls.

bat·ter·y (bat′ər·ē, ba′trē) *n. pl.* **·ter·ies** 1. Any unit, apparatus, or grouping in which a series or set of parts or components is assembled to serve a common end. 2. *Electr.* One or more cells operating together as a single source of direct current. 3. *Mil.* **a** An artillery unit equivalent to an infantry company. **b** A group of guns, rockets, or related equipment forming an artillery unit. 4. *Naval* The guns of a warship, or a specific group of them. 5. *Law* The illegal beating or touching of another person. [< OF < *battre* to beat]

bat·tik (bə·tēk′, bat′ik) See BATIK.

bat·ting (bat′ing) *n.* Wadded cotton or wool prepared in sheets or rolls, used for interlining, stuffing mattresses, etc.

bat·tle (bat′l) *n.* 1. A combat between hostile armies or fleets. 2. Any fighting, conflict, or struggle. — *v.* **·tled**, **·tling** *v.i.* 1. To contend in or as in battle; struggle; strive. — *v.t.* 2. *U.S.* To fight. [< OF < LL < L *battuere* to beat] — **bat′tler** *n.*

— **Syn.** (noun) 1. A *battle* is a more or less continuous fight and may last for many days, while a *skirmish* is brief and involves small groups of combatants. An *action* is one of the events in a *battle*, as by a part of the forces engaged. *Engagement* refers to a period of active combat, but may also be a complete *battle* or war.

bat·tle-ax (bat′l·aks′) *n.* 1. A large ax formerly used in battle; a broadax. 2. *U.S. Slang* A formidable, disagreeable woman. Also **bat′tle-axe′.**

battle cruiser *Naval* A war vessel having cruiser speed, but less heavily armored than a battleship.

battle cry 1. A shout uttered by troops in battle. 2. A slogan or distinctive phrase used in any conflict or contest.

bat·tle·dore (bat′l·dôr, -dōr) *n.* 1. A flat paddle or bat used to strike a shuttlecock. 2. A game in which a shuttlecock is battered back and forth: also **battledore and shuttlecock.** — *v.t. & v.i.* **·dored**, **·dor·ing** To volley or hurl back and forth. [? < Provençal *batedor*, an implement for beating laundry]

battle fatigue *Psychiatry* Combat fatigue.

bat·tle·field (bat′l·fēld′) *n.* The terrain on which a battle is fought. Also **bat′tle·ground′.**

bat·tle·ment (bat′l·mənt) *n.* A parapet indented along its upper line. [< OF < *ba(s)tillier* to fortify]

battle royal 1. A fight involving numerous combatants. 2. A protracted, vehement altercation.

bat·tle·ship (bat′l·ship′) *n. Naval* A warship of great size, belonging to the class with heaviest armor and armament.

bat·ty (bat′ē) *adj.* **·ti·er**, **·ti·est** *Slang* Crazy; odd.

bau·ble (bô′bəl) *n.* A worthless, showy trinket; gewgaw; toy. [< OF *baubel* toy, ? < L *bellus* pretty]

baulk (bôk), **baulk·y** (bô′kē) See BALK, BALKY.

baux·ite (bôk′sīt, bō′zīt) *n.* A white to red claylike substance containing aluminum oxide or hydroxide, the principal ore of aluminum. [after Les *Baux*, France]

Ba·var·i·an (bə·vâr′ē·ən) *adj.* Of or pertaining to Bavaria, its people, or their dialect. — *n.* 1. A native or inhabitant of Bavaria. 2. The High German dialect spoken in Bavaria.

bawd (bôd) *n.* The keeper of a brothel. [ME *bawde*]

bawd·y (bô′dē) *adj.* **bawd·i·er**, **bawd·i·est** Obscene; indecent. — **bawd′i·ly** *adv.* — **bawd′i·ness** *n.*

bawd·y·house (bô′dē·hous′) *n.* A brothel.

bawl (bôl) *v.t.* 1. To call out noisily; bellow. 2. To cry for sale. — *v.i.* 3. To cry or sob noisily. — **to bawl out** *U.S. Slang* To berate; scold. — *n.* A loud outcry. [Cf. Med.L *baulare* to bark and ON *baula* to low, moo] — **bawl′er** *n.*

bay¹ (bā) *n.* A body of water partly enclosed by land; an inlet of the sea. [< OF < *baie* < LL *baia*]

bay² (bā) *n.* 1. *Archit.* **a** A bay window. **b** A principal part or division of a structure. **c** An extension or wing of a building. 2. Any opening or recess in a wall. 3. *Aeron.* A compartment in an aircraft. [< OF < L *badare* to gape]

bay³ (bā) *adj.* Reddish brown: said esp. of horses. — *n.* 1. A reddish brown color. 2. A horse (or other animal) of this color. [< F *bai* < L *badius*]

bay⁴ (bā) *n.* 1. A deep bark or cry, as of dogs in hunting. 2. The position of or as of a hunted animal forced to turn and fight. 3. The condition of being kept off by or as by one's quarry. — **at bay** 1. Unable to escape; cornered. 2. Kept off, as by one's quarry. — *v.i.* 1. To utter a deep-throated, prolonged bark, as a hound. — *v.t.* 2. To utter with or as with such a bark. 3. To pursue or beset with barking. 4. To bring to bay. [< OF < L *badare* to gape]

bay⁵ (bā) *n.* 1. A laurel wreath, bestowed as a garland of honor, esp. on a poet. 2. *pl.* Fame; renown. 3. The bayberry. 4. Any of several plants resembling the laurels. [< F *baie* < L *bacca* berry]

bay·ber·ry (bā′ber′ē, -bər·ē) *n. pl.* **·ries** 1. A tree or shrub having aromatic berries, as the wax myrtle or laurel; also, its fruit. 2. A tropical tree yielding an oil used in bay rum.

bay leaf The leaf of the laurel, used as a cooking herb.

bay·o·net (bā′ə·nit, -net, bā′ə·net′) *n.* A daggerlike weapon attachable to the muzzle of a firearm, used in close fighting. — *v.t.* **·net·ed**, **·net·ing** To stab or pierce with a bayonet. [< F after *Bayonne*, France, where first made]

bay·ou (bī′ōō) *n. U.S.* A marshy inlet or outlet of a lake, river, etc. [< dial. F < Choctaw *bayuk* small stream]

Bayou State Nickname of Mississippi.

bay rum An aromatic liquid used in medicines and cosmetics, originally distilled from the leaves of the bayberry, but now also made from alcohol, water, and essential oils.

Bay State Nickname of Massachusetts.

bay window 1. A window structure projecting from the wall of a building and forming a recess within. 2. *Slang* A protruding belly, as of a fat person.

ba·zaar (bə·zär′) *n.* 1. An Oriental market or street of shops. 2. A shop or store for the sale of miscellaneous wares. 3. A sale of miscellaneous articles, as for charity. Also **ba·zar′.** [Ult. < Persian *bāzār* market]

ba·zoo·ka (bə·zōō′kə) *n. Mil.* A tubular, portable weapon that fires an explosive rocket, used against tanks and fortifications. [from *bazooka*, a comical musical instrument]

be (bē, *unstressed* bi) *v.i.* **been**, **be·ing** Present indicative: I **am**, he, she, it **is**, we, you, they **are**; past indicative: I, he, she, it **was**, we, you, they **were**; present subjunctive: **be**; past subjunctive: **were**; archaic forms: thou **art** (present), thou **wast** or **wert** (past) 1. As the substantive verb, *be* is used to mean: **a** To have existence, truth, or actuality: God *is*; There *are* bears in the zoo. **b** To take place; happen: The party *is* today. **c** To stay or continue: She *was* here for one week. **d** To belong; befall: a subjunctive use, often with *to* or *unto*: Joy *be* unto you. 2. As a copulative verb *be* forms a link between the subject and predicate nominative or qualifying word or phrase in sentences, and also forms infinitive and participial phrases: George *is* my friend; He *is* sick; the pleasure of *being* here. 3. As an auxiliary verb *be* is used: **a** With the present participle of other verbs to express continuous or progressive action: I *am* working. **b** With the past participle of transitive verbs to form the passive voice: He *was* injured. **c** With the past participle of intransitive verbs to form the perfect tense: Christ *is* come; I *am* finished. **d** With the infinitive or present participle to express purpose, duty, possibility, futurity, etc.: We *are* to start on Monday.

be- *prefix* Used to form words from nouns, adjectives, and verbs with the following meanings: 1. (*from verbs*) Around; all over; throughout; as in: **bedrape**; **befinger**. 2. (*from verbs*) Completely; thoroughly; as in: **bedrench**; **bemuddle**. 3. (*from verbs*) Off; away from; as in: **behead**. 4. (*from intransitive verbs*) About; at; on; over; against; for; as in: **becrawl**; **bethunder**. 5. (*from adjectives and nouns*) To make; cause to be; as in: **becripple**; **bedirty**. 6. (*from nouns*) To provide with; affect by; cover with; as in: **becarpet**; **bejewel**. 7. (*from nouns*, in the form of participial adjectives) Furnished with; as in: **bechained**; **beflowered**. [OE *be-*, *bi-*, var. of *bī* near, by]

beach (bēch) *n.* The sloping shore of a body of water; strand; esp., a sandy shore used for swimming. — **Syn.** See SHORE¹. — *v.t. & v.i.* To drive or haul up (a boat or ship) on a beach; strand. [Origin unknown]

beach·comb·er (bēch'kō'mər) n. 1. A vagrant living on what he can find or beg around the wharves and beaches of ports. 2. A long wave rolling upon the beach.

beach·head (bēch'hed') n. Mil. An area on a hostile shore established by an advance force for the landing of troops and supplies and the launching of subsequent operations.

bea·con (bē'kən) n. 1. A signal; esp., a signal fire or light on a hill, building, etc., intended as a warning or guide. 2. A light, buoy, etc., set on a shore, shoal, or similar place to guide or warn mariners. 3. A lighthouse. 4. Anything that warns or signals. 5. Aeron. A mark, light, or radio transmitter used to plot flight courses. — v.t. 1. To furnish with or guide by a beacon. — v.i. 2. To shine as a beacon. [OE bēacn sign, signal. Akin to BECKON.]

bead (bēd) n. 1. A small, usually round, piece of glass, wood, stone, etc., pierced for stringing on thread or attaching to fabric as decoration. 2. pl. A string of beads; necklace. 3. pl. A rosary. 4. Any small body resembling a bead, as a bubble or a drop of liquid. 5. Froth; foam. 6. A small knob used as the front sight of a gun. 7. Archit. A molding composed of a row of half-oval ornaments resembling a string of beads. — to draw a bead on To take careful aim at. — to tell (count, or say) one's beads To recite prayers with a rosary. — v.t. 1. To decorate with beads or beading. — v.i. 2. To collect in beads or drops. [OE gebed prayer]

bead·ing (bē'ding) n. 1. Ornamentation with beads. 2. Material consisting of or ornamented with beads. 3. Archit. A bead, or beads collectively.

bea·dle (bēd'l) n. In the Church of England, a lay officer who ushers or keeps order. [< OF bedel messenger]

beads·man (bēdz'mən) n. pl. ·men (-mən) One who prays for another. — **beads'wom'an** n.fem.

bead·work (bēd'wûrk') n. 1. Decorative work made with or of beads. 2. Archit. A bead.

bead·y (bē'dē) adj. bead·i·er, bead·i·est 1. Small and glittering: beady eyes. 2. Covered with beads. 3. Foamy.

bea·gle (bē'gəl) n. A small, short-coated hound with short legs and drooping ears. [ME begle]

beak (bēk) n. 1. The horny, projecting mouth parts of birds. 2. A beaklike part or organ, as the horny jaws of turtles. 3. Something resembling a bird's beak, as the spout of a pitcher. 4. Slang A person's nose. [< F bec < LL beccus] — **beaked** adj. — **beak'less** adj. — **beak'like'** adj.

BEAGLE
(About 15 inches high at shoulder)

beak·er (bē'kər) n. 1. A large, wide-mouthed drinking cup or goblet. 2. A cylindrical, flat-bottomed vessel of glass, aluminum, etc., with a lip for pouring, used in chemical analysis, etc. 3. The contents or capacity of a beaker. [< ON bikarr; spelling infl. by beak]

beam (bēm) n. 1. A long, heavy piece of wood, metal, or stone, shaped for use. 2. A horizontal piece forming part of the frame of a building or other structure. 3. Naut. a One of the heavy pieces of timber or iron set across a vessel to support the decks and stay the sides. b The greatest width of a vessel. c The shank of an anchor. 4. The bar of a balance; also, the balance. 5. A ray of light, or a group of nearly parallel rays. 6. Aeron. A radio beam. 7. The area of maximum sound clarity in front of a microphone. 8. The horizontal piece in a plow to which the share and handles are attached. 9. The widest part of anything. 10. Slang The hips: broad in the beam. — **off the beam** 1. Aeron. Not following the radio beam. 2. Informal On the wrong track; wrong. — **on the beam** 1. Naut. In a direction at right angles with the keel; abeam. 2. Aeron. Following the radio beam. 3. Informal In the right direction; just right; correct. — v.t. 1. To send out in beams or rays. 2. Telecom. To aim or transmit (a signal) in a specific direction. 3. Aeron. To guide (an airplane) by radio beams. — v.i. 4. To emit light. 5. To smile or grin radiantly. [OE bēam tree] — **beam'less** adj. — **beam'like'** adj.

beam-ends (bēm'endz') n.pl. Naut. The ends of a ship's beams. — **on her beam-ends** Of a ship, tipped over so far as to be in danger of capsizing.

beam·ing (bē'ming) adj. Radiant; bright; smiling; cheerful. — **beam'ing·ly** adv.

beam·y (bē'mē) adj. beam·i·er, beam·i·est 1. Sending out beams of light; radiant. 2. Like a beam; massive.

bean (bēn) n. 1. The oval, edible seed of any of various leguminous plants. 2. A plant that bears beans. 3. Any of several beanlike seeds or plants. 4. Slang The head. 5. Brit. Slang Person; chap. — v.t. U.S. Slang To hit on the head. [OE bēan]

bean·ie (bē'nē) n. A small, brimless cap.

bean·pole (bēn'pōl') n. 1. A tall pole for a bean plant to climb on. 2. Slang A tall, thin person.

bear¹ (bâr) v. bore (Archaic bare), borne, bear·ing v.t. 1. To support; hold up. 2. To carry; convey. 3. To show visibly; carry. 4. To conduct or guide. 5. To spread; disseminate. 6. To hold in the mind; maintain or entertain. 7. To suffer or endure; undergo. 8. To accept or acknowledge; assume, as responsibility or expense. 9. To produce; give birth to. ◆ In this sense, the participial form in the passive is **born**, except when followed by by. 10. To conduct or comport (oneself). 11. To manage or carry (oneself or a part of oneself). 12. To move by pressing against; drive. 13. To render; give: to bear witness. 14. To be able to withstand; allow. 15. To have or stand in (comparison or relation): with to: What relation does his story bear to yours? 16. To possess as a right or power: to bear title. — v.i. 17. To rest heavily; lean; press. 18. To endure patiently; suffer. 19. To produce fruit or young. 20. To carry burdens. 21. To move or lie in a certain direction; be pointed or aimed. 22. To be relevant; have reference. — **to bear down** 1. To force down; overpower or overcome. 2. To exert oneself; make an effort. — **to bear down on** (or **upon**) 1. To put pressure on; press hard on. 2. To make a great effort. 3. To approach, especially another vessel from windward. — **to bear out** To support; confirm; justify. — **to bear up** To keep up strength and spirits. [OE beran to carry, wear]

bear² (bâr) n. 1. A large mammal having a massive, thickly furred body and a very short tail, as the grizzly bear, polar bear, etc. ◆ Collateral adjective: ursine. 2. Any of various other animals resembling or likened to the bear: ant bear. 3. A gruff, ill-mannered, or clumsy person. 4. A speculator, esp. one in the stock exchange, who seeks to depress prices or who sells in the belief that a decline in prices is likely: opposed to bull. — **the Bear** Russia. — adj. Of, pertaining to, or caused by stock-market bears, or a decline in prices. — v.t. To endeavor to depress the price of (stocks etc.) by selling or offering to sell. [OE bera]

bear·a·ble (bâr'ə-bəl) adj. Capable of being borne; endurable. — **bear'a·ble·ness** n. — **bear'a·bly** adv.

bear·cat (bâr'kat') n. The panda (def. 1).

beard (bird) n. 1. The hair on a man's face, esp. on the chin, usu. excluding the mustache. 2. Any similar growth or appendage, as the long hair on the chin of some animals. 3. Bot. An awn. For illus. see WHEAT. — v.t. 1. To take by the beard; pull the beard of. 2. To defy courageously. 3. To furnish with a beard. [OE] — **beard'ed** adj. — **beard'less** adj. — **beard'less·ness** n. — **beard'like'** adj.

bear·er (bâr'ər) n. 1. One who or that which bears, carries, or upholds. 2. A person who bears or presents for payment a check, money order, etc. 3. A tree or vine producing fruit. 4. A carrier or porter. 5. A pallbearer.

bear·ing (bâr'ing) n. 1. Manner of conducting or carrying oneself; deportment. 2. The act, capacity, or period of producing. 3. That which is produced; crops; yield. 4. Endurance. 5. Mech. A part on which something rests, or in which a pin, journal, etc., turns. 6. The position or direction of an object or point. 7. Often pl. The situation of an object relative to that of another, or of other points or places: to lose one's bearings. 8. Reference or relation.

bear·ish (bâr'ish) adj. 1. Like a bear; rough; surly. 2. Tending toward, counting on, or causing a depression in the price of stocks. — **bear'ish·ly** adv. — **bear'ish·ness** n.

bear·skin (bâr'skin') n. The skin of a bear, or a coat or robe made of it.

beast (bēst) n. 1. Any animal except man; esp., any large, quadruped. 2. Animal characteristics or animal nature. 3. A cruel, rude, or filthy person. [< OF < LL < L bestia beast] — **beast'like'** adj.

beast·ly (bēst'lē) adj. ·li·er, ·li·est 1. Resembling a beast; bestial. 2. Informal Disagreeable or unpleasant; nasty. — adv. Brit. Slang Very. — **beast'li·ness** n.

beat (bēt) v. beat, beat·en or beat, beat·ing v.t. 1. To strike repeatedly; pound. 2. To punish by repeated blows; thrash; whip. 3. To dash or strike against. 4. To shape or break by blows. 5. To make flat by tramping or treading. 6. To make, as one's way, by or as by blows. 7. To flap; flutter, as wings. 8. To stir or mix rapidly so as to make lighter or frothier: to beat eggs. 9. To mark or measure as with a baton: to beat time. 10. To sound (a signal), as on a drum. 11. To hunt over; search. 12. To subdue or defeat; master. 13. To surpass; be superior to. 14. Informal To baffle; perplex: it beats me. 15. U.S. Slang To defraud; swindle. — v.i. 16. To strike repeated blows. 17. To strike or smite as if with blows: The sound beat on my ears. 18. To throb; pulsate. 19. To give forth sound, as when tapped or struck. 20. To sound a signal, as on a drum. 21. Physics To alternate in intensity so as to pulsate. 22. To be adaptable to beating. 23. To hunt through underbrush, etc., as for game. 24. To win a victory or contest. — **to beat about** To search by one means and then another. — **to beat**

about the bush To approach a subject in a roundabout way. **— to beat a retreat 1.** To give a signal for retreat, as by the beat of drums. **2.** To turn back; flee. **— to beat down** To force or persuade (a seller) to accept a lower price. **— to beat it** *Slang* To depart hastily. **— to beat off** To repel; drive away. **— to beat up** *Informal* To thrash thoroughly. **— n. 1.** A stroke or blow. **2.** A regular stroke, or its sound; pulsation; throb. **3.** *Physics* A regularly recurring pulsation or throb heard when two tones not quite in unison are sounded together, and caused by the interference of sound waves. **4.** *Music* **a** A regular pulsation; the basic unit of musical time. **b** The gesture or symbol designating this. **5.** The measured sound of verse; rhythm. **6.** A round, line, or district regularly traversed, as by a sentry, policeman, or reporter. **7.** *U.S.* A subdivision of a county, esp. in the South. **8.** In newspaper slang, a scoop. **9.** *U.S. Slang* A deadbeat. **10.** A beatnik. **— on the beat** *Music* In tempo. **— adj. 1.** *U.S. Informal* Fatigued; worn out. **2.** *Informal* Of or pertaining to beatniks. [OE *bēatan*] **— beat′er** *n.*

beat·en (bēt′n) Past participle of BEAT. **— adj. 1.** Shaped or made thin by beating. **2.** Mixed by beating. **3.** Worn by use; customary. **4.** Defeated; baffled. **5.** Exhausted.

be·a·tif·ic (bē′ə·tif′ik) *adj.* Imparting or expressing bliss or blessedness. **— be′a·tif′i·cal·ly** *adv.*

be·at·i·fi·ca·tion (bē·at′ə·fi·kā′shən) *n.* **1.** The act of beatifying, or the state of being beatified. **2.** In the Roman Catholic Church, an act of the pope declaring a deceased person beatified, usually the last step toward canonization.

be·at·i·fy (bē·at′ə·fi) *v.t.* **·fied, ·fy·ing 1.** To make supremely happy. **2.** In the Roman Catholic Church, to declare as blessed and worthy of public honor, by an act of the pope. **3.** To exalt above others. [< F < LL < L *beatus* happy + *facere* to make]

beat·ing (bē′ting) *n.* **1.** The act of one who or that which beats. **2.** Punishment by blows; flogging. **3.** Pulsation; throbbing, as of the heart. **4.** A defeat.

be·at·i·tude (bē·at′ə·tood, -tyood) *n.* Supreme blessedness or felicity. **— the Beatitudes** Eight declarations made by Jesus in the Sermon on the Mount. *Matt.* v 3–11. [< MF < L *beatitudo* blessedness]

beat·nik (bēt′nik) *n. Informal* One who acts and dresses in a manner calculated to be unconventional.

beau (bō) *n., pl.* **beaus** or **beaux** (bōz) **1.** A sweetheart or lover of a girl or woman. **2.** A dandy. [< OF, var. of *bel* < L *bellus* fine, pretty] **— beau′ish** *adj.*

Beau Brum·mell (brum′əl) A dandy or fop. [after George "Beau" Brummell, 1778–1840, English dandy]

Beau·fort scale (bō′fərt) *Meteorol.* A scale of wind velocities, ranging from 0 (calm) to 12 (hurricane). [after Sir Francis Beaufort, 1774–1857, British admiral]

beau monde (bō mônd′) *French* The fashionable world.

beau·te·ous (byoo′tē·əs) *adj.* Beautiful. **— beau′te·ous·ly** *adv.* **— beau′te·ous·ness** *n.*

beau·ti·cian (byoo·tish′ən) *n.* One who works in or operates a beauty parlor.

beau·ti·ful (byoo′tə·fəl) *adj.* Possessing the qualities or presenting an appearance of beauty, as in form or grace. **— beau′ti·ful·ly** *adv.* **— beau′ti·ful·ness** *n.*

beau·ti·fy (byoo′tə·fi) *v.t. & v.i.* **·fied, ·fy·ing** To make or grow beautiful. **— beau′ti·fi·ca′tion** *n.* **— beau′ti·fied** *adj.* **— beau′ti·fi′er** *n.*

beau·ty (byoo′tē) *n., pl.* **·ties 1.** The quality of objects, sounds, ideas, etc., that pleases and gratifies, as by their harmony, pattern, excellence, or truth. **2.** One who or that which is beautiful, esp. a woman. **3.** A special grace or charm. [< OF *beaute*, ult. < L *bellus* handsome, fine]

beauty parlor An establishment where women may go for hairdressing, complexion care, or other cosmetic treatment. Also **beauty salon, beauty shop.**

beauty spot 1. A small patch or mark put on the face to set off the whiteness of the skin. **2.** A mole or other natural mark resembling this. Also **beauty mark.**

beaux (bōz) Plural of BEAU.

beaux-arts (bō·zär′) *n.pl. French* The fine arts.

bea·ver¹ (bē′vər) *n.* **1.** An amphibious rodent with a scaly, flat, oval tail and webbed hind feet, valued for its fur, and noted for its skill in damming shallow streams. **2.** The fur of the beaver. **3.** A high silk hat. [OE *beofor*]

bea·ver² (bē′vər) *n.* **1.** A movable piece of medieval armor covering the lower face. **2.** The visor of a helmet. **3.** *Slang* A beard. [< OF *bavé* saliva]

bea·ver·board (bē′vər·bôrd′, -bōrd′) *n.* A light, stiff building material made of compressed or laminated wood pulp, used chiefly for walls and partitions.

Beaver State Nickname of Oregon..

be·calm (bi·käm′) *v.t. Naut.* **1.** To make (a sailing vessel) motionless for lack of wind. **2.** To make calm; quiet.

be·came (bi·kām′) Past tense of BECOME.

be·cause (bi·kôz′) *conj.* For the reason that; on account of the fact that; since. **— because of** By reason of; on account of. [ME *bi cause* by cause]

be·chance (bi·chans′, -chäns′) *v.t. & v.i.* **·chanced, ·chanc·ing** To befall; happen by chance.

beck (bek) *n.* A nod or other gesture of summons. **— at one's beck and call** Subject to one's slightest wish. **— v.t. & v.i.** To beckon. [Short for BECKON]

beck·on (bek′ən) *v.t. & v.i.* **1.** To signal, direct, or summon by sign or gesture. **2.** To entice or lure. **— n.** A summoning gesture; beck. [OE *bīecnan, bēacnian* to make signs to]

be·cloud (bē·kloud′) *v.t.* **1.** To obscure with clouds; darken. **2.** To confuse, as an issue: to *becloud* his senses.

be·come (bi·kum′) *v.* **·came, ·come, ·com·ing** *v.i.* **1.** To come to be; grow to be. **— v.t. 2.** To be appropriate to; befit. **3.** To be suitable to; show to advantage. **— to become of** To be the condition or fate of: What *became of* him? [OE *becuman* to happen, come about]

be·com·ing (bi·kum′ing) *adj.* **1.** Appropriate; suitable. **2.** Pleasing; attractive. **— n.** A coming to be. **— be·com′ing·ly** *adv.* **— be·com′ing·ness** *n.*

bed (bed) *n.* **1.** An article of furniture to rest or sleep on, consisting of a bedstead, mattress, spring, and bedclothes. **2.** Any place or thing used for resting or sleeping. **3.** A lodging, esp. for the night. **4.** A heap or mass resembling a bed. **5.** A plot of ground prepared for planting; also the plants themselves. **6.** The ground at the bottom of a body of water. **7.** A part or surface that serves as a foundation or support. **8.** *Geol.* Any layer in a mass of stratified rock; a seam. **— to get up on the wrong side of the bed** To be irritable, grouchy, or cross. **— to put** (or go) **to bed** *U.S. Slang* To go to press; be printed. **— v. bed·ded, bed·ding** *v.t.* **1.** To furnish with a bed. **2.** To put to bed. **3.** To make a bed for; provide with litter: often with *down*: to *bed down* cattle. **4.** To set out or plant in a bed of earth. **5.** To lay flat or arrange in layers: to *bed* oysters. **6.** To place firmly; embed. **— v.i. 7.** To go to bed. **8.** To form a closely packed layer; stratify. [OE] **— bed′der** *n.*

bed and board Lodging and meals.

be·daub (bi·dôb′) *v.t.* **1.** To smear or daub; besmirch; soil. **2.** To ornament vulgarly or excessively.

be·daz·zle (bi·daz′əl) *v.t.* **·zled, ·zling** To confuse or blind by dazzling.

bed·bug (bed′bug) *n.* A bloodsucking insect of reddish brown color, infesting houses and esp. beds.

bed·cham·ber (bed′chām′bər) *n.* A bedroom.

bed·clothes (bed′klōz′, -klōthz′) *n.pl.* Covering for a bed, as sheets, blankets, quilts, etc.

bed·ding (bed′ing) *n.* **1.** Mattress and bedclothes. **2.** Straw or other litter for animals to sleep on. **3.** That which forms a bed or foundation. **4.** *Geol.* Stratification of rocks.

be·deck (bi·dek′) *v.t.* To adorn.

be·dev·il (bi·dev′əl) *v.t.* **·iled** or **·illed, ·il·ing** or **·il·ling 1.** To treat diabolically; harass or torment. **2.** To worry or confuse; bewilder. **3.** To possess with or as with a devil; bewitch. **4.** To spoil; corrupt. **— be·dev′il·ment** *n.*

be·dew (bi·doo′, -dyoo′) *v.t.* To moisten with dew.

bed·fel·low (bed′fel′ō) *n.* **1.** One who shares a bed with another. **2.** A companion; associate.

be·dim (bi·dim′) *v.t.* **·dimmed, ·dim·ming** To make dim.

bed·lam (bed′ləm) *n.* **1.** A place or scene of noisy confusion. **2.** An incoherent uproar. **3.** A lunatic asylum. [after *Bedlam,* an old London hospital for the insane]

bed linen Sheets, pillowcases, etc., for beds.

Bed·ou·in (bed′oo·in) *n.* **1.** One of the nomadic Arabs of Syria, Arabia, etc. **2.** Any nomad or vagabond. **— adj. 1.** Of or pertaining to the Bedouins. **2.** Roving; nomadic. Also spelled *Beduin.* [< F < Arabic *badâwîn* desert dweller]

bed·pan (bed′pan′) *n.* **1.** A shallow vessel to be used as a toilet by one confined to bed. **2.** A warming pan.

be·drag·gle (bi·drag′əl) *v.t.* **·gled, ·gling** To make wet, soiled, or untidy, as by dragging through mire.

bed·rid·den (bed′rid′n) *adj.* Confined to bed. Also **bed′rid′.** [Earlier *bedrid* < OE *bedrida* < *bed* bed + *rida* rider]

bed·rock (bed′rok′) *n.* **1.** *Geol.* The solid rock underlying the looser materials of the earth's surface. **2.** The lowest level; bottom. **3.** Fundamental principles; foundation.

bed·roll (bed′rōl′) *n.* Bedding rolled to facilitate carrying.

bed·room (bed′room′, -room′) *n.* A room for sleeping.

bed·side (bed′sid′) *n.* The space beside a bed, especially of a sick person; the side of a bed. **— adj.** Placed beside a bed.

bed·sore (bed′sôr′, -sōr′) *n.* A sore caused by prolonged pressure against a bed, occurring among bedridden persons.

bed·spread (bed′spred′) *n.* A cloth covering for a bed, usually for ornament.

bed·spring (bed′spring′) *n.* The framework of springs supporting the mattress of a bed; also, any of such springs.

bed·stead (bed′sted′) *n.* A framework for supporting the springs and mattress of a bed.

bed·time (bed′tim′) *n.* The time for retiring to bed.

Bed·u·in (bed′oo·in) See BEDOUIN.

bed·wet·ting (bed′wet′ing) *n.* Urination in bed.

bee (bē) *n.* **1.** A four-winged insect feeding largely upon nectar and pollen, esp. the honey bee. **2.** *U.S.A* social

gathering for work, competition, entertainment, etc.: a quilting *bee.* — **to have a bee in one's bonnet** To be excessively concerned about or obsessed with one idea. [OE *bēo*]
bee·bread (bē/bred/) *n.* A mixture of pollen and certain proteins stored by bees for food.
beech (bēch) *n.* **1.** A tree of temperate regions with smooth, ash-gray bark, and bearing an edible nut. **2.** The wood of the beech. **3.** A tree similar to the beech, as the hornbeam. [OE *bēce*] — **beech/en** *adj.*
beech mast Beechnuts.
beech·nut (bēch/nut/) *n.* The edible nut of the beech.
beef (bēf) *n.* *pl.* **beeves** (bēvz) or **beefs** *for def. 2;* **beefs** *for def. 4* **1.** The flesh of a slaughtered adult bovine animal. **2.** Any adult bovine animal, as an ox, cow, steer, bull, etc., fattened for the table. **3.** *Informal* Muscle; brawn. **4.** *U.S. Slang* A complaint. — *v.i. U.S. Slang* To complain. [< OF < L *bos, bovis* ox]
beef·eat·er (bēf/ē/tər) *n* **1.** A yeoman of the guard, or one of the similarly uniformed warders of the Tower of London. **2.** *Slang* An Englishman.
beef·steak (bēf/stāk/) *n.* A slice of beef suitable for broiling.
beef tea A beverage made by boiling lean beef or made from a beef extract.
beef·y (bē/fē) *adj.* **beef·i·er, beef·i·est** **1.** Muscular and heavy. **2.** Beeflike. **3.** Stolid. — **beef/i·ness** *n.*
bee·hive (bē/hīv/) *n.* **1.** A hive for a colony of honeybees. **2.** A place full of activity.
Beehive State Nickname of UTAH.
bee·keep·er (bē/kē/pər) *n.* One who keeps bees; an apiarist.
bee·line (bē/līn/) *n.* The shortest course from one place to another: chiefly in the phrase **to make a beeline for.**
Be·el·ze·bub (bē·el/zə·bub) **1.** The prince of the demons; the devil. **2.** Any devil. [< Hebrew *ba'alzebūb* lord of flies]
been (bin, *Brit.* bēn) Past participle of BE.
beep (bēp) *n.* **1.** A short, piercing sound used as a signal or warning. — *v.i.* **1.** To make such a sound. — *v.t.* **2.** To sound (a horn). **3.** To transmit (a message) by beeps. [Imit.]
beer (bir) *n.* **1.** An alcoholic fermented beverage made from malt and hops. **2.** A beverage made from the roots, etc., of various plants: ginger *beer* [OE *bēor*]
Beer·she·ba (bir·shē/bə, bir/shi·ba) An ancient city in southwest Palestine.
beer·y (bir/ē) *adj.* **beer·i·er, beer·i·est** **1.** Of or like beer. **2.** Influenced by beer; tipsy. — **beer/i·ness** *n.*
beest·ings (bēs/tingz) *n.pl. & sing.* The first milk from a cow after calving; the colostrum: also *biestings.* [OE *bēost*]
bees·wax (bēz/waks/) *n.* A yellow fatty solid secreted by honeybees for honeycombs, used in medicine and the arts.
beet (bēt) *n.* **1.** The fleshy succulent root of a biennial herb of the goosefoot family, esp. the common or red beet, and the sugar beet. **2.** The plant itself. [OE < L *beta*]
bee·tle[1] (bēt/l) *n.* **1.** An insect having biting mouth parts and hard, horny front wings that serve as a cover for the posterior wings when at rest. **2.** Loosely, any insect resembling a beetle. — *adj.* Jutting; overhanging: a *beetle* brow: also **beet/ling.** — *v.i.* **·tled, ·tling** To jut out; overhang. [OE *bītan* to bite]
bee·tle[2] (bē/tl) *n.* **1.** A heavy instrument, usu. with a wooden head, for ramming paving stones, driving wedges, etc. **2.** A pestle or mallet for pounding, etc. — *v.t.* **·tled, ·tling** To beat or stamp with a beetle. [OE *bīetel* mallet]
bee·tle-browed (bēt/l-broud/) *adj.* **1.** Having prominent, overhanging eyebrows. **2.** Scowling; frowning.
beet sugar Sucrose obtained from the sugar beet.
beeves (bēvz) Alternative plural of BEEF.
be·fall (bi·fôl/) *v.* **·fell, ·fall·en, ·fall·ing** *v.i.* **1.** To come about; happen; occur. — *v.t.* **2.** To happen to. [OE *be-f(e)allan* to fall]
be·fit (bi·fit/) *v.t.* **·fit·ted, ·fit·ting** To be suited to; be appropriate for. — **be·fit/ting** *adj.* — **be·fit/ting·ly** *adv.*
be·fit·ting (bi·fit/ing) *adj.* Becoming; proper; suitable. — **be·fit·ting·ly** *adv.*
be·fog (bi·fôg/, -fog/) *v.t.* **fogged, ·fog·ging** **1.** To envelop in fog. **2.** To confuse; obscure.
be·fore (bi·fôr/, -fōr/) *adv.* **1.** In front; ahead. **2.** Preceding in time; previously. **3.** Earlier; sooner. — *prep.* **1.** In front of; ahead of. **2.** Earlier or sooner than. **3.** In advance of in development, rank, etc. **4.** In preference to; rather than. **5.** In the presence of; face to face with. **6.** Under the consideration or cognizance of: the issue *before* you. **7.** Ahead of; awaiting. — *conj.* **1.** Previous to the time when. **2.** Rather than. [OE *beforan* in front]
be·fore·hand (bi·fôr/hand/, -fōr/-) *adv. & adj.* In anticipation or advance; ahead of time.
be·foul (bi·foul/) *v.t* To make foul or dirty; sully.
be·friend (bi·frend/) *v.t.* To act as a friend to; help.
be·fud·dle (bi·fud/l) *v.t.* **·dled, ·dling** To confuse, as with liquor or glib arguments.

beg (beg) *v.* **begged, beg·ging** *v.t.* **1.** To ask for in charity: to *beg* alms. **2.** To ask for or of earnestly; beseech: to *beg* forgiveness. — *v.i.* **3.** To ask alms or charity; be a beggar. **4.** To ask humbly or earnestly. — **to beg off** To ask to be excused or released (from an engagement, obligation, etc.). — **to beg the question 1.** To take for granted the very matter in dispute. **2.** Loosely, to avoid answering directly. — **to go begging** To fail of acceptance, adoption, or use. [? < AF < OF *begard* mendicant friar]
be·gan (bi·gan/) Past tense of BEGIN.
be·get (bi·get/) *v.t.* **·got** (*Archaic* **·gat**), **·got·ten** or **·got, ·get·ting** **1.** To procreate; be the father of. **2.** To cause to be; occasion. [OE *begitan*] — **be·get/ter** *n.*
beg·gar (beg/ər) *n.* **1.** One who asks alms, or lives by begging. **2.** A poor person; pauper. **3.** A rogue; rascal. — *v.t.* **1.** To reduce to want; impoverish. **2.** To exhaust the resources of: It *beggars* analysis. [< OF *begard* mendicant friar] — **beg/gar·dom, beg/gar·hood** *n.*
beg·gar·ly (beg/ər·lē) *adj.* Appropriate for a beggar; miserably poor; mean; sordid. — **beg/gar·li·ness** *n.*
be·gin (bi·gin/) *v.* **·gan, ·gun, ·gin·ning** *v.i.* **1.** To start to do something; take the first step; commence. **2.** To come into being; arise. — *v.t.* **3.** To do the first act or part of; start to do. **4.** To give origin to; start; originate. [OE *beginnan*]
be·gin·ner (bi·gin/ər) *n.* **1.** One beginning to learn a trade, study a subject, etc.; a novice; tyro. — Syn. See NOVICE. **2.** One who begins or originates; a founder.
be·gin·ning (bi·gin/ing) *n.* **1.** The act of starting; commencement. **2.** The point in time at which a thing begins. **3.** Source or first cause; origin. **4.** The first part. **5.** *Usually pl.* The first or rudimentary stage. — *adj.* **1.** First; opening: the *beginning* chapter. **2.** Elementary; introductory: a *beginning* course in physics.
be·gird (bi·gûrd/) *v.t.* **·girt** or **·gird·ed, ·gird·ing** To gird; encircle. [OE *begyrdan*]
be·gon·ia (bi·gōn/yə) *n.* A plant having brilliantly colored leaves and showy flowers. [after Michel *Bégon,* 1638–1710, French colonial administrator]
be·got (bi·got/) Past tense and past participle of BEGET.
be·got·ten (bi·got/n) Alternative past participle of BEGET.
be·grime (bi·grīm/) *v.t.* **·grimed, ·grim·ing** To soil.
be·grudge (bi·gruj/) *v.t.* **·grudged, ·grudg·ing** **1.** To envy one the possession or enjoyment of (something). **2.** To give or grant reluctantly. — **be·grudg/ing·ly** *adv.*
be·guile (bi·gīl/) *v.t.* **·guiled, ·guil·ing** **1.** To deceive; mislead by guile. **2.** To cheat; defraud: with *of* or *out of.* **3.** To while away pleasantly, as time. **4.** To charm; divert. — **be·guile/ment** *n.* — **be·guil/er** *n*
be·gum (bē/gəm) *n.* A Moslem princess, or woman of rank in India. [< Hind. < Turkish *bigim* princess]
be·gun (bi·gun/) Past participle of BEGIN.
be·half (bi·haf/, -häf/) *n.* The interest, part, or defense: usu. preceded by *in* or *on* and followed by *of.* — Syn. See SAKE. [OE *be healfe* by the side (of)]
be·have (bi·hāv/) *v.* **·haved, ·hav·ing** *v.i* **1.** To act; conduct oneself or itself. **2.** To comport oneself properly. **3.** To react to stimuli or environment. — *v.t.* **4.** To conduct (oneself), esp. in a proper or suitable manner. [ME *behaven* < *be-* thoroughly + *have* to hold oneself, act]
be·hav·ior (bi·hāv/yər) *n.* **1.** Manner of conducting oneself; demeanor; deportment. **2.** The way a person, substance, machine, etc., acts under given circumstances. Also *Brit.* **be·hav/iour.**
be·hav·ior·ism (bi·hāv/yər·iz/əm) *n.* *Psychol.* The theory that the behavior of animals and man is determined by measurable external and internal stimuli acting independently. — **be·hav/ior·ist** *n.* — **be·hav/ior·is/tic** *adj.*
be·head (bi·hed/) *v.t.* To decapitate. [OE *behēafdian*]
be·held (bi·held/) Past tense and past participle of BEHOLD.
be·he·moth (bi·hē/məth, bē/ə-) *n.* **1.** In the Bible, a huge beast. **2.** Anything large. [< Hebrew *bēhēmāh* beast]
be·hest (bi·hest/) *n.* An authoritative request; command. [OE *behǣs* promise, vow]
be·hind (bi·hīnd/) *adv.* **1.** In, at, or toward the rear. **2.** In a place, condition, or time previously passed or departed from. **3.** In arrears; late. **4.** Slow, as a watch. — *prep.* **1.** At the back or rear of. **2.** Toward the rear of; backward from. **3.** In a place, condition, or time left by (one): Leave your problems *behind* you. **4.** After (a set time). **5.** Not so well advanced as; inferior to. **6.** Hidden by: What is *behind* your actions? **7.** Backing up; supporting: to be *behind* a venture. — *adj.* **1.** Following: the man *behind* **2.** In arrears. — *n. Informal* The buttocks. [OE *behindan*]
be·hind·hand (bi·hīnd/hand/) *adv. & adj.* **1.** Behind time; late. **2.** In arrears. **3.** Behind in development; backward.
be·hold (bi·hōld/) *v.t.* **·held, ·hold·ing** To look at or upon; observe. — *interj.* Look! See! [OE *beh(e)aldan* to hold] — **be·hold/er** *n.*

be·hold·en (bi-hōl′dən) *adj.* Indebted; obligated.

be·hoof (bi-hōōf′) *n.* That which benefits; advantage; use. [OE *behōf* advantage]

be·hoove (bi-hōōv′) *v.* **·hooved, ·hoov·ing** *v.t.* To be incumbent upon; be needful or right for: It *behooves* me to leave. Also *Brit.* **be·hove** (bi-hōv′). [OE *behōfian*]

beige (bāzh, bāj) *n.* The color of natural, undyed, unbleached wool; grayish tan. — *adj.* Of the color beige. [< F]

be·ing (bē′ing) Present participle of BE. — *n.* **1.** Existence, as opposed to nonexistence. **2.** Essential nature; substance: His whole *being* is musical. **3.** A living thing. **4.** A human individual; person. **5.** *Philos.* **a** Perfect or unqualified subsistence; essence. **b** That which has reality in time, space, or idea; anything that exists actually or potentially. **Be·ing** (bē′ing) *n.* The Supreme Being; God.

bel (bel) *n.* *Physics* A unit expressing the logarithmic ratio of the values of two amounts of power; a measure of sound intensity. Compare DECIBEL. [after A. G. *Bell*]

be·la·bor (bi-lā′bər) *v.t.* **1.** To beat soundly; assail with blows; drub. **2.** To assail verbally. Also *Brit.* **be·la′bour.** — **be·lat′ed·ness** *n.*

be·lat·ed (bi-lā′tid) *adj.* Late or too late. — **be·lat′ed·ly** *adv.* — **be·lat′ed·ness** *n.*

be·lay (bi-lā′) *v.t. & v.i.* **·layed, ·lay·ing 1.** *Naut.* To make fast (a rope) by winding on a cleat or pin (**belaying pin**). **2.** *Informal* To stop or hold: *Belay* there! [OE *belecgan*]

belch (belch) *v.i.* **1.** To eject wind noisily from the stomach through the mouth; eructate. **2.** To issue spasmodically from within; gush. **3.** To expel its contents violently, as a volcano. — *v.t.* **4.** To eject or throw forth violently; give vent to. — *n.* A belching. [OE *bealcian*] — **belch′er** *n.*

be·lea·guer (bi-lē′gər) *v.t.* **1.** To surround or shut in with an armed force. **2.** To surround; beset. [< Du. < *be-* about + *leger* camp] — **be·lea′guered** *adj.*

bel·fry (bel′frē) *n. pl.* **·fries** **1.** A tower in which a bell is hung. **2.** The part of a tower or steeple containing the bell. [< OF *berfrei* tower, infl. by BELL¹] — **bel′fried** *adj.*

Bel·gian (bel′jən, -jē-ən) *adj.* Of or pertaining to Belgium. — *n.* A native or citizen of Belgium.

Be·li·al (bē′lē-əl, bēl′yəl) In the Bible, the devil.

be·lie (bi-lī′) *v.t.* **·lied, ·ly·ing 1.** To misrepresent; disguise: His clothes *belie* his station. **2.** To prove false; contradict: Her actions *belied* her words. **3.** To fail to fulfill: to *belie* hopes. **4.** To slander. [OE *belēogan*] — **be·li′er** *n.*

be·lief (bi-lēf′) *n.* **1.** Acceptance of the truth or actuality of anything without certain proof. **2.** Something held to be true or actual. **3.** Trust in another person; confidence. **4.** A doctrine; creed. [ME < *bi-* complete + *leafe* belief] — **Syn. 1.** *Belief* denotes acceptance with or without proof or strong emotional feelings. *Faith* is always the acceptance of something not susceptible of proof, while *conviction* is strong *belief* arising from a deep feeling of certainty.

be·lieve (bi-lēv′) *v.* **·lieved, ·liev·ing** *v.t.* **1.** To accept as true or real. **2.** To credit (a person) with veracity. **3.** To think; assume: with a clause as object. — *v.i.* **4.** To accept the truth, existence, worth, etc., of something: with *in*: to *believe* in freedom. **5.** To have confidence; place one's trust: with *in*. **6.** To have religious faith. **7.** To think: I cannot *believe* badly of you. [ME *beleven* < OE *gelēfan* to believe] — **be·liev′a·ble** *adj.* — **be·liev′er** *n.*

be·lit·tle (bi-lit′l) *v.t.* **·tled, ·tling** To cause to seem small or less; disparage; minimize.

bell¹ (bel) *n.* **1.** A hollow metallic instrument, usu. cup-shaped, which gives forth a ringing sound when struck. **2.** Anything in the shape of or suggesting a bell. **3.** The lower termination of a tubular musical instrument. **4.** A bell-shaped flower or corolla. **5.** *Naut.* A stroke on a bell every half hour to mark the periods of the watch; also, each of these periods. — *v.t.* **1.** To put a bell on. **2.** To shape like a bell. — *v.i.* **3.** To take the shape of a bell. [OE *belle*]

bell² (bel) *v.i.* To cry, as a hound, rutting stag, etc. — *n.* The cry of a deer, bittern, etc. [OE *bellan* to bellow]

bel·la·don·na (bel′ə-don′ə) *n.* **1.** A perennial herb with purple-red flowers and black berries: also called *deadly nightshade*. **2.** A poisonous alkaloid, as atropine, used in medicine. [< Ital. *bella donna*, lit., beautiful lady]

bell·boy (bel′boi′) *n. U.S.* A boy or man employed by a hotel to answer calls for service, carry suitcases, etc.

belle (bel) *n.* A beautiful and attractive woman or girl; a reigning social beauty. [< F, fem. of *beau* beautiful]

belles-let·tres (bel′let′rə) *n.pl.* Literature having esthetic appeal, rather than didactic or informational value; poetry, drama, fiction, etc. [< F, fine letters] — **bel·let·rist** (bel′let′rist) *n.* — **bel·le·tris·tic** (bel′lə-tris′tik) *adj.*

bell·flow·er (bel′flou′ər) *n.* The campanula.

bell·hop (bel′hop′) *n. U.S. Informal* A bellboy.

bel·li·cose (bel′ə-kōs) *adj.* Pugnacious. [< L *bellum* war] — **bel′li·cose′ly** *adv.* — **bel·li·cos′i·ty** (-kos′ə·tē) *n.*

bel·lig·er·ence (bə-lij′ər-əns) *n.* **1.** The state or quality of being warlike. **2.** Belligerency.

bel·lig·er·en·cy (bə-lij′ər-ən-sē) *n.* The status of a belligerent; condition of being at war.

bel·lig·er·ent (bə-lij′ər-ənt) *adj.* **1.** Warlike; bellicose. **2.** Engaged in or pertaining to warfare. — *n.* A person or nation engaged in warfare or fighting. [< F < L *belligerare* to wage war] — **bel·lig′er·ent·ly** *adv.*

bell·man (bel′mən) *n. pl.* **·men** (-mən) A town crier.

bel·low (bel′ō) *v.i.* **1.** To utter a loud, hollow cry, as a bull. **2.** To roar; shout: to *bellow* with anger. — *v.t.* **3.** To utter with a loud, roaring voice. — *n.* A loud, hollow cry or roar. [ME *belwen*, ? < OE *bylgian*] — **bel′low·er** *n.*

bel·lows (bel′ōz, *earlier* bel′əs) *n.pl.* (construed as sing. or pl.) **1.** An instrument with an air chamber and flexible sides, for drawing in air and expelling it under strong pressure through a nozzle or tube, used for blowing fires, filling the pipes of an organ, etc. **2.** The expansible portion of a camera. **3.** The lungs. [OE *belg, belig* bag]

bell·weth·er (bel′weth′ər) *n.* **1.** A ram with a bell about its neck, that leads a flock of sheep. **2.** One who leads a group, esp. a thoughtless, sheeplike group.

bel·ly (bel′ē) *n. pl.* **·lies 1.** The abdomen in vertebrates, or the underpart of other animals. **2.** The stomach. **3.** The protuberance of a bulging muscle. **4.** Any curved or protrusive line or surface: the *belly* of a sail. **5.** The front or underpart of anything. **6.** A deep, interior cavity: the *belly* of a ship. **7.** The curved front piece, containing the sound holes, of a violin, viola, etc. — *v.t. & v.i.* **·lied, ·ly·ing** To swell out or fill, as a sail. [OE *belg, belig* bag]

bel·ly·ache (bel′ē-āk′) *n.* A pain in the stomach or bowels. — *v.i.* **·ached, ·ach·ing** *Slang* To complain sullenly.

bel·ly·band (bel′ē-band′) *n.* A strap passing around the belly, as of a draft animal, to hold the shafts.

bel·ly·but·ton (bel′ē·but′n) *n. Informal* The navel.

bel·ly·ful (bel′ē-fŏŏl′) *n.* **1.** All that the stomach will hold. **2.** *Slang* All that one wants, or can endure.

be·long (bi-lông′, -long′) *v.i.* **1.** To be the property of someone: with *to*. **2.** To be a part of or an appurtenance to something: with *to*. **3.** To have a proper place; be suitable. **4.** To have relation or be a member. [ME < *be-* completely + *longen* to go along with]

be·long·ing (bi-lông′ing, -long′-) *n.* **1.** That which belongs to a person or thing. **2.** *pl.* Possessions; effects.

be·lov·ed (bi-luv′id, -luvd′) *adj.* Greatly loved. — *n.* One greatly loved. [Orig. pp. of obs. *belove* love dearly]

be·low (bi-lō′) *adv.* **1.** In or to a lower place. **2.** On or to a lower floor or deck. **3.** Farther down on a page or farther on in a list, book, etc. **4.** On earth, as distinguished from heaven. **5.** In or to Hades. **6.** In a lower rank or authority. — *prep.* **1.** Lower than in place, grade, degree, etc. **2.** Unworthy of. [ME < *bi-* near + *loogh* low]

Bel·shaz·zar (bel-shaz′ər) In the Old Testament, the last ruler of Babylon.

belt (belt) *n.* **1.** A strap or band of leather or other flexible material worn about the waist to support clothing, tools, weapons, etc. **2.** Any band or strip resembling a belt. **3.** *Mech.* An endless band of flexible material for transmitting power from one wheel or shaft to another. **4.** A region or zone exhibiting some specific quality or condition: a storm *belt*. **5.** *Slang* A blow, as with the fist. — **below the belt** In violation of the rules; unfair. — **to tighten one's belt** To practice thrift. — *v.t.* **1.** To gird with or as with a belt. **2.** To fasten with a belt. **3.** To mark with belts or bands. **4.** To strike with a belt. **5.** *Informal* To give a blow to; strike. [OE < L *balteus* girdle]

be·lu·ga (bə-lōō′gə) *n.* A dolphin of Arctic and sub-Arctic seas: also called *white whale*. [< Russian *byelukha*]

bel·ve·dere (bel′və-dir′) *n. Archit.* A building, or an upper story of a building, that commands a view.

be·mire (bi-mīr′) *v.t.* **·mired, ·mir·ing 1.** To soil with mud or mire. **2.** To sink or stall in mud.

be·moan (bi-mōn′) *v.t.* **1.** To lament, as a loss. **2.** To express sympathy or pity for. — *v.i.* **3.** To mourn or lament. [OE *bemænan*] — **be·moan′a·ble** *adj.*

be·muse (bi-myōōz′) *v.t.* **·mused, ·mus·ing** To stupefy or preoccupy. — **be·mused′** *adj.*

bench (bench) *n.* **1.** A long seat of wood, marble, etc., with or without a back. **2.** A table for mechanical work. **3.** A seat or thwart in a boat. **4.** The seat for judges in a court. **5.** The judge, or the judges collectively. **6.** The office or dignity of a judge. **7.** A seat for persons sitting in an official capacity. **8.** Level, elevated ground along a shore or coast, or on a slope. — **on the bench** In sports, not participating. — *v.t.* **1.** To furnish with benches. **2.** To seat on a bench. **3.** In sports, to remove (a player) from a game. [OE *benc*]

bench mark A permanent mark, of known position and elevation, for use as a reference point in surveys, etc.

bench warrant *Law* A warrant issued by a judge, directing that an offender be brought into court.

bend¹ (bend) *v.* **bent** (*Archaic* **bend·ed**), **bend·ing** *v.t.* **1.** To cause to take the form of a curve; crook; bow. **2.** To direct or turn, as one's course, in a certain direction; deflect. **3.** To subdue or cause to yield. **4.** To apply closely; concentrate. **5.** *Naut.* To make fast, as a rope or sail. — *v.i.* **6.** To assume the form of a curve. **7.** To take a certain direction. **8.** To bow in submission or respect. **9.** To apply one's energies: with *to.* — *n.* **1.** An act of bending, or the state of being bent. **2.** Something curved or bent; a curve or crook. **3.** *Naut.* A knot by which a rope is fastened to something else. [OE *bendan*]

bend² (bend) *n. Heraldry* A diagonal band across a shield from the upper left to the lower right. [OE *bend* strap]

bend·er (ben′dər) *n.* **1.** One who or that which bends. **2.** *U.S. Slang* A drinking spree. **3.** *Brit. Slang* A sixpence.

bends (bendz) *n.pl. Informal* Caisson disease.

bend sinister *Heraldry* A band drawn diagonally from the upper right to the lower left, used to indicate bastardy.

be·neath (bi-nēth′) *adv.* **1.** In a lower place; below. **2.** underneath; directly below. — *prep.* **1.** Under; underneath; below. **2.** On the underside of; covered by. **3.** Under the power or sway of; subdued by. **4.** Lower in rank or station. **5.** Unworthy of; unbefitting. [OE *beneothan*]

ben·e·dic·i·te (ben′ə-dis′ə-tē) *n.* A blessing; grace or thanksgiving, esp. at table. — *interj.* Bless you!

Ben·e·dic·tine (ben′ə-dik′tin, -tēn; *for n. def. 3*, -tēn) *adj.* Pertaining to St. Benedict or his order. — *n.* **1.** A monk of the order established by St. Benedict at Subiaco, in Italy, about 530. **2.** A nun following the Benedictine rule. **3.** A brandy liqueur formerly made by French Benedictines.

ben·e·dic·tion (ben′ə-dik′shən) *n.* **1.** The act of blessing. **2.** The invocation of divine favor upon a person. [< LL < *benedicere* to bless] — **ben′e·dic′tive, ben·e·dic·to·ry** (ben′ə-dik′tər·ē) *adj.*

Ben·e·dic·tus (ben′ə-dik′təs) *n.* **1.** Either of two canticles *Luke* i 68–71, and *Matt.* xxi 9: so called from their first word in Latin. **2.** A musical setting of either canticle.

ben·e·fac·tion (ben′ə-fak′shən) *n.* **1.** The act of giving help or conferring a benefit. **2.** A charitable deed; generous act. [< LL < *benefacere* to do well]

ben·e·fac·tor (ben′ə-fak′tər, ben′ə-fak′-) *n.* One who gives help or confers a benefit. — **ben′e·fac′tress** *n. fem.*

ben·e·fice (ben′ə-fis) *n. Brit. Eccl.* **1.** A church office endowed with funds or property; a living. **2.** The revenue of such an office. — *v.t.* **·ficed, ·fic·ing** To invest with a benefice. [< OF < L *beneficium* favor] — **ben′e·ficed** *adj.*

be·nef·i·cence (bə-nef′ə-səns) *n.* **1.** The quality of being beneficent. **2.** A beneficent act or gift.

be·nef·i·cent (bə-nef′ə-sənt) *adj.* **1.** Bringing about or doing good. **2.** Resulting in benefit. — **be·nef′i·cent·ly** *adv.*

ben·e·fi·cial (ben′ə-fish′əl) *adj.* Producing benefit; advantageous; helpful. [< F *bénéficial* < LL < L *beneficium* favor] — **ben′e·fi′cial·ly** *adv.* — **ben′e·fi′cial·ness** *n.*

ben·e·fi·ci·ar·y (ben′ə-fish′ē-er′ē, -fish′ər·ē) *n. pl.* **·ar·ies** **1.** One who receives benefits or advantages. **2.** *Eccl.* The holder of a benefice. **3.** *Law* One entitled to the proceeds of property held in trust, or to whom an insurance policy or annuity is payable. [< L < *beneficium* favor]

ben·e·fit (ben′ə-fit) *n.* **1.** That which is helpful; advantage; profit. **2.** An act of kindness; charitable deed. **3.** A theatrical or musical performance given to raise funds for a worthy cause. **4.** *Often pl.* Payments made by an insurance company, etc — *v.* **·fit·ed, ·fit·ing** *v.t.* **1.** To be helpful or useful to. — *v.i.* **2.** To profit; gain advantage. [< OF < L *benefacere* to do well]

benefit of clergy. **1.** Churchly approval or sanction. **2.** Formerly, the privilege accorded to the clergy of demanding trial by an ecclesiastical rather than a secular court.

Ben·e·lux (ben′ə-luks) *n.* The economic union of Belgium, the Netherlands, and Luxembourg. [< BE(LGIUM) + NE(THERLANDS) + LUX(EMBOURG)]

be·nev·o·lence (bə-nev′ə-ləns) *n.* **1.** Disposition to do good; kindliness. **2.** Any act of kindness.

be·nev·o·lent (bə-nev′ə-lənt) *adj.* Disposed to do good; kindly. [< OF < L < *bene* well + *volens*, ppr. of *velle* to wish] — **be·nev′o·lent·ly** *adv.*

Ben·ga·li (ben-gô′lē, beng-) *adj.* Of or pertaining to Bengal. — *n.* **1.** A native of Bengal. **2.** The modern vernacular Indic language of Bengal.

ben·ga·line (beng′gə-lēn, beng′gə-lēn′) *n.* A corded silk, wool, or rayon fabric of fine weave. [< BENGAL]

be·night·ed (bi-nī′tid) *adj.* **1.** Ignorant; unenlightened. **2.** Overtaken by night. — **be·night′ed·ness** *n.*

be·nign (bi-nīn′) *adj.* **1.** Of a kind disposition; kindly. **2.** Gentle; mild. **3.** Favorable. **4.** *Med.* Favorable for recovery. [< OF < L *benignus* kindly] — **be·nign′ly** *adv.*

be·nig·nant (bi-nig′nənt) *adj.* **1.** Kind; gracious, esp. to inferiors. **2.** Favorable; benign. — **be·nig′nant·ly** *adv.*

be·nig·ni·ty (bi-nig′nə·tē) *n. pl.* **·ties 1.** The quality of being benign. Also **be·nig·nan·cy** (bi-nig′nən·sē). **2.** A gracious action or influence.

ben·i·son (ben′ə-zən, -sən) *n.* A benediction; blessing. [< OF < LL *benedictio, -onis* benediction]

Ben·ja·min (ben′jə-mən) In the Old Testament, the youngest son of Jacob and Rachel. *Gen* xxxv 18. — *n.* The tribe of Israel descended from him.

benne (ben′ē) *n.* The sesame. [< Malay *bijen* seed]

bent¹ (bent) Past tense and past participle of BEND¹. — *adj.* **1.** Not straight; crooked. **2.** Set in a course; resolved. — *n.* **1.** State of being bent or turned. **2.** A personal inclination or penchant. **3.** Limit of endurance or capacity: usually in the phrase **to the top of** (**one's**) **bent.**

bent² (bent) *n.* **1.** A stiff, wiry grass. Also **bent grass.** **2.** The stiff flower stalk of various grasses. [OE *beonet*]

Ben·tham·ism (ben′thəm-iz′əm, -təm-) *n.* The philosophy of Jeremy Bentham, maintaining that the happiness of the greatest number is the supreme goal of society. — **Ben′tham·ite** (-īt) *n.*

be·numb (bi-num′) *v.t.* **1.** To make numb; deaden. **2.** To stupefy. [OE *benumen* pp. of *beniman* to deprive.] — **be·numbed** (bi-numd′) *adj.* — **be·numb′ment** *n.*

Ben·ze·drine (ben′zə-drēn, -drin) *n.* Proprietary name of a brand of amphetamine. Also **ben′ze·drine.**

ben·zene (ben′zēn, ben·zēn′) *n. Chem.* A colorless, volatile, flammable, liquid hydrocarbon, C_6H_6, obtained chiefly from coal tar, used as a solvent and in organic synthesis.

ben·zine (ben′zēn, ben·zēn′) *n.* A colorless, flammable liquid derived from crude petroleum and consisting of various hydrocarbons, used as a solvent, cleaner, and motor fuel. Also **ben′zin** (-zin), **ben·zo·line** (ben′zə-lēn).

ben·zo·ate (ben′zō·it, -āt) *n. Chem.* A salt of benzoic acid.

ben·zo·ic (ben-zō′ik) *adj.* **1.** Pertaining to or derived from benzoin. **2.** Pertaining to benzoic acid.

benzoic acid *Chem.* An aromatic compound, $C_7H_6O_2$, used as a food preservative and in medicine.

ben·zo·in (ben′zō·in, -zoin) *n.* **1.** A gum resin from various East Indian plants, used in medicine and as a perfume. [< F < Pg. or Ital. < Arabic *lubān jāwī* incense of Java]

ben·zol (ben′zōl, -zol) *n.* A grade of crude benzene.

Be·o·wulf (bā′ə-wŏŏlf) The princely hero of an Anglo-Saxon epic poem of the eighth century; also, the poem.

be·queath (bi-kwēth′, -kwēth′) *v.t.* **1.** *Law* To give (property) by will. **2.** To hand down. [OE *becwethan*]

be·quest (bi-kwest′) *n.* The act of bequeathing, or that which is bequeathed. [ME *biqueste*]

be·rate (bi-rāt′) *v.t.* **·rat·ed, ·rat·ing** To scold severely.

Ber·ber (bûr′bər) *n.* **1.** One who belongs to a group of Moslem tribes, esp. the Kabyles, inhabiting northern Africa. **2.** The Hamitic language of the Berbers. — *adj.* Of or pertaining to the Berbers or their language.

ber·ceuse (ber-sœz′) *n. pl.* **·ceuses** (-sœz′) A lullaby. [< F]

be·reave (bi-rēv′) *v.t.* **·reaved** or **·reft** (-reft′), **·reav·ing 1.** To deprive, as of hope or happiness. **2.** To leave saddened through death. [OE *berēafian*] — **be·reave′ment** *n.*

be·reft (bi-reft′) Alternative past tense and past participle of BEREAVE. — *adj.* Deprived; bereft of all hope.

be·ret (bə-rā′, ber′ā) *n.* A soft, flat cap, usu. of wool, originating in the Basque regions of France and Spain. [< F]

berg (bûrg) *n.* An iceberg.

ber·ga·mot¹ (bûr′gə-mot) *n.* **1.** A small tree whose fruit furnishes a fragrant essential oil. **2.** The oil itself. **3.** Any of several plants of the mint family. [? after *Bergamo*, Italy]

ber·ga·mot² (bûr′gə-mot) *n.* A minor variety of pear. [< F < Ital. < Turkish *beg-armūdi* prince's pear]

Berg·son·ism (berg′sən-iz′əm) *n.* The philosophy of Henri Bergson. — **Berg·so·ni·an** (berg·sō′nē·ən) *adj. & n.*

be·rhyme (bi-rīm′) *v.t.* **·rhymed, ·rhym·ing 1.** To celebrate in rhyme. **2.** To compose in rhyme. Also **be·rime′.**

ber·i·ber·i (ber′ē·ber′ē) *n. Pathol.* A disease of the peripheral nerves resulting from the absence of B vitamins in the diet. [< Singhalese *beri* weakness] — **ber′i·ber′ic** *adj.*

berke·li·um (bûrk′lē-əm) *n.* The unstable radioactive element of atomic number 97 (symbol Bk), obtained by bombarding americium with alpha particles. [after *Berkeley*, California, location of the University of California]

Berk·shire (bûrk′shir, -shər) *n.* One of a breed of black and white swine originating in Berkshire, England.

berm (bûrm) *n.* A narrow ledge, shelf, or shoulder, as on a slope or at the side of a road: also **berme.** [< F *berme*]

Ber·mu·da shorts (bər-myōō′də) Knee-length shorts.

ber·ret·ta (bə-ret′ə) *n.* A biretta.

ber·ry (ber′ē) *n. pl.* **·ries 1.** Any small, succulent fruit: often used in combination: *strawberry.* **2.** *Bot.* A simple fruit with the seeds in a juicy pulp, as the grape. **3.** The dry kernel of various grains, or the fruit of certain plants, as a coffee bean, etc. — *v.i.* **·ried, ·ry·ing 1.** To form or bear berries. **2.** To gather berries. [OE *berie*]

ber·serk (bər-sûrk′, bûr′sûrk) *adj.* Violently or frenetically destructive. — **to go** (or **run**) **berserk** To have a fit of destructive rage. — *n.* A berserker. [< ON *berserkr*]

ber·serk·er (bûr'sûr'kər) *n.* In Norse legend, a warrior who fought with frenzied fury.

berth (bûrth) *n.* **1.** A bunk or bed in a vessel, sleeping car, etc. **2.** *Naut.* Any place in which a vessel may lie at anchor or at a dock. **3.** Situation or employment on a vessel. **4.** Office or employment in general. **— to give a wide berth to** To avoid; keep out of the way of. **—** *v.t.* **1.** *Naut.* To bring to a berth. **2.** To provide with a berth. **—** *v.i.* **3.** *Naut.* To come to a berth. [< Origin uncertain.]

ber·tha (bûr'thə) *n.* A deep collar worn by women, falling over the shoulders from a low neckline. [< F *berthe*]

Ber·til·lon system (bûr'tə·lon, *Fr.* ber·tē·yôn') A system of coded physical measurements, used as a means of identification, esp. of criminals. [after Alphonse *Bertillon*, 1853–1914, French anthropologist]

ber·yl (ber'əl) *n.* A vitreous, green, light blue, yellow, pink, or white silicate of aluminum and beryllium, of which the aquamarine and emerald are varieties used as gems. [< OF < L < Gk. *bēryllos* beryl] **— ber·yl·line** (ber'ə·lin, -lin) *adj.*

be·ryl·li·um (bə·ril'ē·əm) *n.* A hard, grayish black, noncorrosive metallic element (symbol Be), used in copper and aluminum alloys and for windows of X-ray tubes. See ELEMENT. [< NL < L *beryllus* beryl]

be·seech (bi·sēch') *v.t.* **·sought**, **·seech·ing** **1.** To entreat earnestly; implore. **2.** To beg for earnestly; crave. [ME < *bi-* greatly + *sēcan* to seek] **— be·seech'er** *n.*

be·seem (bi·sēm') *v.i.* To be fitting or appropriate: It ill *beseems* you to speak thus. **— be·seem'ing** *adj.*

be·set (bi·set') *v.t.* **·set**, **·set·ting** **1.** To attack on all sides; harass. **2.** To hem in; encircle. **3.** To set or stud, as with gems. [OE *besettan*] **— be·set'ment** *n.*

be·set·ting (bi·set'ing) *adj.* Constantly attacking or troubling.

be·side (bi·sīd') *prep.* **1.** At the side of; in proximity to. **2.** In comparison with. **3.** Away or apart from: This discussion is *beside* the point. **4.** Other than; over and above. **— beside oneself** Out of one's senses, as from anger, fear, etc. **—** *adv.* In addition; besides. [OE *be sīdan* by the side (of)]

be·sides (bi·sīdz') *adv.* **1.** In addition; as well. **2.** Moreover; furthermore. **3.** Apart from that mentioned; otherwise; else. **—** *prep.* **1.** In addition to; other than. **2.** Beyond; apart from: I care for nothing *besides* this.

be·siege (bi·sēj') *v.t.* **·sieged**, **·sieg·ing** **1.** To lay siege to, as a castle. **2.** To crowd around. **3.** To overwhelm, as with gifts. **— be·siege'ment** *n.* **— be·sieg'er** *n.*

be·smear (bi·smir') *v.t.* To smear over; sully.

be·smirch (bi·smûrch') *v.t.* **1.** To soil; stain. **2.** To sully; dim the luster of. **— be·smirch'er** *n.* **— be·smirch'ment** *n.*

be·som (bē'zəm) *n.* **1.** A bundle of twigs used as a broom. **2.** Broom (def. 2). [OE *besma* broom]

be·sot (bi·sot') *v.t.* **·sot·ted**, **·sot·ting** **1.** To stupefy, as with drink. **2.** To make foolish or stupid. **3.** To infatuate.

be·sought (bi·sôt') Past tense and past participle of BE-SEECH.

be·span·gle (bi·spang'gəl) *v.t.* **·gled**, **·gling** To decorate with or as with spangles.

be·spat·ter (bi·spat'ər) *v.t.* **1.** To cover or soil by spattering, as with mud. **2.** To sully; slander.

be·speak (bi·spēk') *v.t.* **·spoke** (*Archaic* **·spake**), **·spo·ken** or **·spoke**, **·speak·ing** **1.** To ask or arrange for in advance. **2.** To give evidence of. **3.** To foretell. [OE *bisprecan*]

be·spec·ta·cled (bi·spek'tə·kəld) *adj.* Wearing spectacles.

be·spoke (bi·spōk') Past tense and alternative past participle of BESPEAK.

be·spread (bi·spred') *v.t.* **·spread**, **·spread·ing** To cover or spread over thickly.

Bes·se·mer converter (bes'ə·mər) *Metall.* A large, pear-shaped vessel for containing the molten iron to be converted into steel by the Bessemer process.

Bessemer process *Metall.* A process for eliminating impurities from pig iron by forcing a blast of air through the molten metal before its conversion into steel or ingot iron.

BESSEMER CONVERTER

a, b Exhaust gases. *c* Silica refractory lining. *d* Flames. *e* Steel shell. *f* Compressed air. *g* Molten iron.

best (best) *adj.* Superlative of GOOD, WELL². **—** *adj.* **1.** Excelling all others; of the highest quality. **2.** Most advantageous, desirable, or serviceable. **3.** Most; largest: the *best* part of an hour. **—** *adv.* **1.** In the most excellent way; most advantageously. **2.** To the utmost degree; most thoroughly. **—** *n.* **1.** The best thing, part, etc. **2.** Best condition or quality; utmost: Be at your *best*; Do your *best*. **3.** One's best clothes. **— at best** Under the most favorable circumstances. **— to get (or have) the best of** To defeat or outwit. **— to make the best of** To adapt oneself to the disadvantages of. **—** *v.t.* To defeat; surpass. [OE *betst*]

be·stead (bi·sted') *v.t.* To be of service to; help; avail.

bes·tial (bes'chəl, best'yəl) *adj.* **1.** Of or pertaining to beasts. **2.** Brutish; depraved. [< OF < L < *bestia* beast] **— bes·ti·al·i·ty** (bes'chē·al'ə·tē, -tē·al'-) *n.* **— bes'tial·ly** *adv.*

bes·tial·ize (bes'chəl·īz, best'yəl-) *v.t.* **·ized**, **·iz·ing** To brutalize.

be·stir (bi·stûr') *v.t.* **·stirred**, **·stir·ring** To rouse to activity.

best man The chief attendant of a bridegroom at a wedding.

be·stow (bi·stō') *v.t.* **1.** To present as a gift; with *on* or *upon*. **2.** To apply; expend, as time. **3.** To give in marriage. **— be·stow'a·ble** *adj.* **— be·stow'al**, **be·stow'ment** *n.*

be·strad·dle (bi·strad'l) *v.t.* **·dled**, **·dling** To bestride.

be·strew (bi·strō̄') *v.t.* **·strewed**, **·strewed** or **·strewn**, **·strew·ing** **1.** To cover or strew (a surface). **2.** To scatter about. **3.** To lie scattered over. Also **be·strow** (bi·strō').

be·stride (bi·strīd') *v.t.* **·strode**, **·strid·den**, **·strid·ing** **1.** To mount; sit or stand astride of; straddle. **2.** To stride across.

best seller A book, phonograph record, etc., that sells or has sold in large numbers.

bet (bet) *n.* **1.** An agreement to risk something of one's own in return for the chance of winning something belonging to another or others. **2.** That which is risked in a bet, as a sum of money; a stake. **3.** The subject or event about which a bet is made. Also called *wager*. **—** *v.* **bet** or (less commonly) **bet·ted**, **bet·ting** *v.t.* **1.** To stake or pledge (money, etc.) in a bet. **2.** To declare as in a bet: I *bet* he doesn't come. **—** *v.i.* **3.** To place a bet. Also *wager*. **— you bet** *U.S. Slang* Certainly. [Origin uncertain]

be·ta (bā'tə, bē'-) *n.* **1.** The second letter of the Greek alphabet (B, β), corresponding to English *b*. See ALPHABET. **2.** The second object in any series, etc. [< Gk.]

be·take (bi·tāk') *v.t.* **·took**, **·tak·en**, **·tak·ing** **1.** To undertake: used reflexively: She *betook* herself to prayer. **2.** To go; take (oneself): He *betook* himself to an inn. [ME *bitaken*]

beta particle An electron.

beta rays *Physics* A stream of electrons projected by radioactive substances.

be·ta·tron (bā'tə·tron) *n. Physics* An accelerator that uses a magnetic field to increase the velocity of electrons.

be·tel (bēt'l) *n.* A climbing plant of Asia, the leaves of which are chewed by the natives of Malaya and other Asian countries. [< Pg. < Malay *vettila*]

Be·tel·geuse (bēt'l·jōoz, bet'l·jœz) *n.* A giant red star, one of the 20 brightest, 1.2 magnitude; Alpha in the constellation Orion. Also **Be'tel·geux**. [< F *Bételgeuse* < Arabic *bat al-jauza*, ? shoulder of the giant]

be·tel·nut (bēt'l·nut') *n.* The astringent seed of an East Indian palm, the **betel palm** (*Areca catechu*), used for chewing with betel leaves and lime.

bête noire (bāt'nwär', *Fr.* bet nwâr') Anything that is an object of hate or dread; a bugaboo. [< F, black beast]

Beth·a·ny (beth'ə·nē) In the New Testament, a village near Jerusalem: the home of Lazarus, Martha, and Mary.

beth·el (beth'əl) *n.* **1.** A hallowed place. *Gen.* xxviii 19. **2.** A seamen's church. [< Hebrew *bēth-el* house of God]

be·think (bi·thingk') *v.* **·thought**, **·think·ing** *v.t.* To bear in mind; consider: generally used reflexively.

be·thought (bi·thot') Past tense and past participle of BE-THINK.

be·tide (be·tīd') *v.t. & v.i.* **·tid·ed**, **·tid·ing** To happen (to) or befall. [ME *bitiden*]

be·times (bi·tīmz') *adv.* In good time; early; also, soon. [ME *betymes* in time, seasonably]

be·to·ken (bi·tō'kən) *v.t.* **1.** To be a sign of; presage. **2.** To give evidence of. [ME *bitacnien*] **— be·to'ken·er** *n.*

be·took (bi·tŏŏk') Past tense of BETAKE.

be·tray (bi·trā') *v.t.* **1.** To aid an enemy of; be a traitor to. **2.** To prove faithless to. **3.** To disclose, as secret information. **4.** To reveal unwittingly. **5.** To seduce and desert. **6.** To indicate; show: The smoke *betrays* a fire. [ME *bitraien*] **— be·tray'al**, **be·tray'ment** *n.* **— be·tray'er** *n.*

be·troth (bi·trôth', -trōth') *v.t.* To engage to marry; affiance. [ME < *bi-* to + *treuthe* truth]

be·troth·al (bi·trō'thəl, -trôth'əl) *n.* The act of betrothing; engagement or contract to marry. Also **be·troth'ment**.

be·trothed (bi·trōthd', -trôtht') *adj.* Engaged to be married; affianced. **—** *n.* A person engaged to be married.

bet·ter¹ (bet'ər) Comparative of GOOD, WELL². **—** *adj.* **1.** Superior in quality. **2.** More advantageous, desirable, or serviceable. **3.** Larger; greater: the *better* part of the cake. **4.** Improved in health; convalescent. **—** *adv.* **1.** More advantageously. **2.** To a larger degree; more thoroughly. **3.** More: *better* than a week. **— better off** In a better condition or improved circumstances. **—** *v.t.* **1.** To make better; improve. **2.** To surpass; excel. **—** *v.i.* **3.** To become better. **—** *n.* **1.** That which is better. **2.** *Usu. pl.* One's superiors, as in ability, rank, etc. **3.** Advantage. [OE *betera*]

bet·ter² (bet'ər) *n.* One who lays bets. Also **bet'tor**.

bet·ter·ment (bet'ər·mənt) *n.* **1.** Improvement. **2.** *Law* An improvement adding to the value of real property.

be·tween (bi·twēn') *prep.* **1.** In the space that separates (two places or objects).   **2.** Intermediate in relation to, as times, qualities, etc.   **3.** From one to another of; connecting.   **4.** Involving reciprocal action among.   **5.** By the joint action of: *Between* them, they killed three deer.   **6.** In the joint possession of: not a cent *between* them.   **7.** Being one alternative over another: to judge *between* right and wrong. — **between you and me** Confidentially. — *adv.* In intervening time, space, position, or relation: few and far *between.* — **in between** In an intermediate position or state; undecided.   [Fusion of OE *bitwēonum* and *bitwēon* < *bi-* by + *-twēonum* and *-tweon*, both < *twā* two]

be·twixt (bi·twikst′) *adv. & prep. Archaic* Between. — **betwixt and between** In an intermediate or indecisive state.   [OE *betweonæ* twofold < *be-* by + *-tweons* < *twā* two]

bev·el (bev′əl) *n.* **1.** Any inclination of two surfaces other than 90°, as at the edge of a timber, etc.   **2.** An adjustable instrument for measuring angles: also **bevel square.** — *adj.* Oblique; slanting. — *v.* **bev·eled** or **·elled, bev·el·ing** or **·el·ling** *v.t.* **1.** To cut or bring to a bevel. — *v.i.* **2.** To slant.   [? < OF. Cf. F *beveau* bevel (n. def. 2).]

bevel gear *Mech.* A gear having beveled teeth, as for transmitting rotary motion at an angle. For illus. see GEAR.

bev·er·age (bev′rij, bev′ər·ij) *n.* That which is drunk; any drink.   [< OF < L *bibere* to drink]

bev·y (bev′ē) *n. pl.* **bev·ies 1.** A group, esp. of girls or women.   **2.** A flock, esp. of quail, grouse, or larks. — *Syn.* See FLOCK.   [ME *bevey*; origin uncertain]

be·wail (bi·wāl′) *v.t. & v.i.* To lament. — *Syn.* See MOURN.

be·ware (bi·wâr′) *v.t. & v.i.* **·wared, ·war·ing** To look out (for); be cautious or wary (of).   [OE *wær* cautious]

be·wil·der (bi·wil′dər) *v.t.* To confuse utterly; perplex. — **be·wil′dered** *adj.* — **be·wil′dered·ly** *adv.* — **be·wil′der·ment** *n.*

be·witch (bi·wich′) *v.t.* **1.** To gain power over by charms or incantations.   **2.** To attract irresistibly; charm; fascinate.   [ME < *bi-* completely + *wicchen* to enchant] — **be·witch′er** *n.*   **be·witch′ment, be·witch′er·y** *n.*

be·witch·ing (bi·wich′ing) *adj.* Charming; captivating. — **be·witch′ing·ly** *adv.*

bey (bā) *n.* **1.** The governor of a minor Turkish province or district.   **2.** A Turkish title of respect.   [< Turkish *beg* lord]

be·yond (bi·yond′) *prep.* **1.** On or to the far side of; farther on than.   **2.** Later than.   **3.** Outside the reach or scope of: *beyond* help.   **4.** Surpassing; superior to: lovely *beyond* description.   **5.** More than; over and above. — *adv.* Farther on or away; at a distance. — **the (great) beyond** Whatever comes after death.   [OE < *be-* near + *geondan* yonder]

bez·el (bez′əl) *n.* **1.** A bevel on the edge of a cutting tool.   **2.** The upper part of a cut gem, including the table and surrounding facets.   [? < OF. Cf. F *biseau* bias.]

be·zique (bə·zēk′) *n.* A game of cards resembling pinochle, played with a deck of 64 cards.   [Alter. of F *bésique*]

bhang (bang) *n.* **1.** Hemp (def. 1).   **2.** Hashish. Also spelled *bang.*   [< Hind. < Skt. *bhangā* hemp]

Bhu·tan·ese (bōō′tən·ēz′, -ēs′) *n. pl.* **·ese 1.** A native of Bhutan.   **2.** The Sino-Tibetan language of Bhutan. — *adj.* Of or pertaining to Bhutan, its people, or their language.

bi- *prefix* **1.** Twice; doubly; two; especially, occurring twice or having two: *biangular.*   **2.** *Chem.* **a** Indicating the doubling of a radical, etc., in an organic compound. **b** Having double the proportion of the substance named: *bicarbonate.* Also: *bin-* before a vowel, as in *binaural; bis-* before *c, s,* as in *bissextile.*   [< L *bi-* < *bis* twice]

bi·an·gu·lar (bī·ang′gyə·lər) *adj.* Having two angles.

bi·an·nu·al (bī·an′yōō·əl) *adj.* Occurring twice a year; semiannual. Compare BIENNIAL. — **bi·an′nu·al·ly** *adv.*

bi·as (bī′əs) *n. pl.* **bi·as·es 1.** A line running obliquely across a fabric: to cut on the *bias.*   **2.** A mental tendency, preference, or prejudice. — *Syn.* See PREJUDICE. — *adj.* Cut, running, set, or folded diagonally; slanting. — *adv.* Slantingly; diagonally. — *v.t.* **bi·ased** or **·assed, bi·as·ing** or **·as·sing** To influence or affect unduly or unfairly.   [< MF *biais* oblique]

bi·ax·i·al (bī·ak′sē·əl) *adj.* Having two axes, as a crystal. Also **bi·ax·al** (bī·ak′səl). — **bi·ax′i·al·ly** *adv.*

bib (bib) *n.* **1.** A cloth worn under a child's chin at meals to protect the clothing.   **2.** The upper front part of an apron or of overalls.   [? < L *bibere* to drink]

bib and tucker *Informal* Clothes.

bib·ber (bib′ər) *n.* A habitual drinker; tippler.

bib·cock (bib′kok′) *n.* A faucet having the nozzle bent downward.

bibe·lot (bib′lō, *Fr.* bēb·lō′) *n.* A small, decorative and often rare object or trinket.   [< F]

Bi·ble (bī′bəl) *n.* **1.** In Christianity, the Old Testament and the New Testament.   **2.** In Judaism, the Old Testament.   **3.** The sacred book or writings of any religion.   [< OF < L < Gk., pl. of *biblion* book]

Bib·li·cal (bib′li·kəl) *adj.* **1.** Of or in the Bible.   **2.** In harmony with the Bible. Also **bib′li·cal.** — **Bib′li·cal·ly** *adv.*

Bib·li·cist (bib′lə·sist) *n.* **1.** One versed in the Bible.   **2.** One who adheres to the letter of the Bible.

biblio- *combining form* Pertaining to books, or to the Bible: *bibliophile.*   [< Gk. *biblion* book]

bib·li·og·ra·phy (bib′lē·og′rə·fē) *n. pl.* **·phies 1.** A list of the works of an author, or of the literature bearing on a subject.   **2.** A list of books or other sources mentioned or consulted by an author, usu. appended to the end of his text.   **3.** The description and history of books, including details of authorship, editions, dates, etc. — **bib′li·og′ra·pher** *n.* — **bib·li·o·graph·ic** (bib′lē·ə·graf′ik) or **·i·cal** *adj.*

bib·li·o·ma·ni·a (bib′lē·ō·mā′nē·ə) *n.* A passion for collecting books. — **bib·li·o·ma′ni·ac** (-ak) *n. & adj.*

bib·li·o·phile (bib′lē·ə·fīl′, -fil′) *n.* One who loves books. Also **bib′li·o·phil′** (-fil′), **bib·li·oph·i·list** (bib′lē·of′ə·list). — **bib′li·oph′i·lism** *n.* — **bib′li·oph′i·lis′tic** *adj.*

bib·u·lous (bib′yə·ləs) *adj.* **1.** Given to drink; fond of drinking.   **2.** Absorbent.   [< L *bibere* to drink]

bi·cam·er·al (bī·kam′ər·əl) *adj.* Consisting of two chambers, houses, or branches.   [< BI- + L *camera* chamber]

bi·car·bo·nate (bī·kär′bə·nit, -nāt) *n. Chem.* A salt of carbonic acid in which one of the hydrogen atoms of the acid is replaced by a metal: sodium *bicarbonate.*

bicarbonate of soda Sodium bicarbonate.

bi·cen·ten·ni·al (bī′sen·ten′ē·əl) *adj.* **1.** Occurring once in 200 years.   **2.** Lasting or consisting of 200 years. — *n.* A 200th anniversary. Also **bi·cen·te·nar·y** (bī·sen′tə·ner′ē, bī′·sen·ten′ər·ē).

bi·ceps (bī′seps) *n. pl.* **bi·ceps** *Anat.* **1.** The large front muscle of the upper arm.   **2.** The large flexor muscle at the back of the thigh.   [< L < *bis* twofold + *caput* head]

bi·chlo·ride (bī·klôr′īd, -id, -klō′rīd, -rid) *n. Chem.* **1.** A salt having two atoms of chlorine.   **2.** Bichloride of mercury.

bi·chro·mate (bī·krō′māt, -mit) *n. Chem.* Dichromate.

bick·er (bik′ər) *v.i.* **1.** To dispute petulantly; wrangle.   **2.** To flicker, as a flame; twinkle. — *n.* A petty altercation. — *Syn.* See QUARREL¹.   [ME *bikeren*] — **bick′er·er** *n.*

bi·col·or (bī′kul′ər) *adj.* Two-colored. Also **bi′col′ored.**

bi·con·cave (bī·kon′kāv, -kong′-, bī′kon·kāv′) *adj.* Concave on both sides, as a lens.

bi·con·vex (bī·kon′veks, bī′kon·veks′) *adj.* Convex on both sides, as a lens.

bi·cus·pid (bī·kus′pid) *adj.* Having two cusps or points. Also **bi·cus′pi·dal** (-dəl), **bi·cus′pi·date** (-dāt). — *n.* A premolar tooth. For illus. see TOOTH.   [< BI- + L *cuspis,* point]

bi·cy·cle (bī′sik·əl) *n.* A vehicle consisting of a metal frame mounted on two wheels, one in back of the other, having a saddle, handlebars, and pedals. — *v.i.* **·cled, ·cling** To ride a bicycle.   [< F < *bi-* two + Gk. *kyklos* wheel] — **bi′cy·cler, bi′cy·clist** *n.*

bid (bid) *n.* **1.** An offer to pay a price; also, the amount offered.   **2.** In card games, the number of tricks or points that a player engages to make; also, a player's turn to bid.   **3.** An effort to acquire, win, or attain: a *bid* for the governorship.   **4.** *Informal* An invitation. — *v.* **bade** for defs. *3, 4, 6,* or **bid** for defs. *1, 2, 5, 7,* **bid·den** or **bid, bid·ding** *v.t.* **1.** To make an offer of (a price).   **2.** In card games, to declare (the number of tricks or points one will engage to make).   **3.** To command; order.   **4.** To say to, as a greeting or farewell. — *v.i.* **5.** To make a bid. — **to bid fair** To seem probable. — **to bid in** At an auction, to outbid a prospective purchaser on behalf of the owner, when the price offered is too low. — **to bid up** To increase the price by offering higher bids.   [Fusion of OE *biddan* to ask, demand and *bēodan* to proclaim] — **bid′da·ble** *adj.* — **bid′der** *n.*

bid·ding (bid′ing) *n.* **1.** A command.   **2.** An invitation or summons.   **3.** Bids, or the making of a bid or bids.

bid·dy (bid′ē) *n. pl.* **·dies** A hen.   [Origin uncertain]

bide (bīd) *v.* **bid·ed** (*Archaic* **bode**), **bid·ing** *v.t.* **1.** To endure; withstand.   **2.** *Archaic* To tolerate; submit to. — *v.i.* **3.** To dwell; abide; stay. — **to bide one's time** To await the best opportunity.   [OE *bīdan*]

bi·en·ni·al (bī·en′ē·əl) *adj.* **1.** Occurring every second year.   **2.** Lasting or living for two years. — *n.* **1.** *Bot.* A plant that produces flowers and fruit in its second year, then dies.   **2.** An event occurring once in two years.   [< L < *bis* twofold + *annus* year] — **bi·en′ni·al·ly** *adv.*

bien·ve·nue (byañ·və·nü′) *n. French* A welcome.

bier (bir) *n.* A framework for carrying a corpse to the grave; also, a coffin.   [OE *bær*]

biest·ings (bēs′tingz) See BEESTINGS.

biff (bif) *U.S. Slang v.t.* To strike; hit. — *n.* A blow.   [Imit.]

bi·fid (bī′fid) *adj.* Cleft; forked.   [< L < *bis* twofold + *findere* to split] — **bi·fid′i·ty** *n.* — **bi′fid·ly** *adv.*

bi·fo·cal (bī·fō′kəl) *adj. Optics* Having two foci: said of a lens ground for both near and far vision.

---

bi·fo·cals (bī·fō′kəlz, bī′fō·kəlz) *n.pl.* Eyeglasses with bifocal lenses.
bi·fur·cate (bī′fər·kāt, bī·fûr′kāt; *adj. also* bī·fûr′kit) *v.t. & v.i.* **·cat·ed, ·cat·ing** To divide into two branches or stems; fork. — *adj.* Forked: also **bi′fur·cat′ed** (-kā′tid), **bi·fur·cous** (bī·fûr′kəs). [< L *bi-* two + *furca* fork] — **bi·fur·cate·ly** (bī′fər·kit·lē, bī·fûr′kit·lē) *adv.* — **bi′fur·ca′tion** *n.*
big (big) *adj.* **big·ger, big·gest** 1. Of great size, extent, etc. 2. Pregnant: usu. with *with.* 3. Grown. 4. Pompous; pretentious. 5. Important; prominent. 6. Loud. 7. Generous; magnanimous. — *adv. Informal* Pompously; extravagantly: to talk *big.* [ME; origin uncertain] — **big′gish** *adj.* — **big′ly** *adv.* — **big′ness** *n.*
big·a·my (big′ə·mē) *n. Law* The criminal offense of marrying any other person while having a legal spouse living. [< OF < LL < L *bis* twice + Gk. *gamos* wedding] — **big′a·mist** *n.* — **big′a·mous** *adj.* — **big′a·mous·ly** *adv.*
big-bang theory *Astron.* A theory that the universe began with an explosion of matter and is endlessly expanding. Compare OSCILLATING UNIVERSE, STEADY-STATE THEORY.
Big Ben 1. A bell in the Westminster clock in the tower of the House of Parliament, London. 2. The clock itself.
Big Dipper The constellation Ursa Major.
big-heart·ed (big′här′tid) *adj.* Generous; charitable.
big·horn (big′hôrn) *n.* *pl.* **·horns** or **·horn** The Rocky Mountain sheep, remarkable for its large curved horns.
bight (bīt) *n.* 1. The loop, or middle part, of a rope. 2. A bend or curve in a shoreline, a river, etc. 3. A bay bounded by such a bend. — *v.t.* To secure with a bight. [OE *byht*]
big·no·ni·a (big·nō′nē·ə) *n.* A climbing plant having clusters of large, trumpet-shaped flowers. [after Abbé *Bignon*, 1711–1772, librarian to Louis XV]
big·ot (big′ət) *n.* One whose attitude or behavior expresses intolerance, as because of race, religion, politics, etc. [< F; ult. origin unknown] — **big′ot·ed** *adj.* — **big′ot·ed·ly** *adv.*
big·ot·ry (big′ə·trē) *n.* *pl.* **·ries** Attitudes, beliefs, or actions characteristic of a bigot; intolerance.
big shot *Slang* Someone of importance. Also **big wheel.**
big top *U.S. Informal* The main tent of a circus.
big·wig (big′wig′) *n. Informal* Someone of importance.
bi·jou (bē′zhōō, bē·zhōō′) *n.* *pl.* **bi·joux** (bē′zhōōz, bē·zhōō′) A jewel, or a finely wrought trinket. [< MF]
bi·ju·gate (bē′jōō·gāt, bī·jōō′git) *adj. Bot.* Two-paired, as leaves. Also **bi·ju·gous** (bī′jōō·gəs).
bike (bīk) *n. Informal* A bicycle. [Alter. of BICYCLE]
bi·ki·ni (bi·kē′nē) *n.* A type of very scanty bathing suit.
bi·la·bi·al (bī·lā′bē·əl) *adj.* 1. *Phonet.* Articulated with both lips, as certain consonants. 2. Having two lips. — *n.* *Phonet.* A bilabial speech sound, as (b), (p), (m), and (w).
bi·la·bi·ate (bī·lā′bē·āt, -it) *adj. Bot.* Two-lipped: said of a corolla.
bi·lat·er·al (bī·lat′ər·əl) *adj.* 1. Pertaining to or having two sides; two-sided. 2. On two sides. 3. Mutually binding. — **bi·lat′er·al·ly** *adv.* — **bi·lat′er·al·ness** *n.*
bil·ber·ry (bil′ber′ē, -bər·ē) *n.* *pl.* **·ries** The whortleberry.
bil·bo (bil′bō) *n.* *pl.* **·boes** A fetter consisting of two sliding shackles attached to an iron bar. [after *Bilbao*]
bile (bīl) *n.* 1. *Physiol.* A bitter yellow or greenish liquid secreted by the liver and serving to promote digestion. 2. Anger; peevishness. [< F < L *bilis* bile, anger]
bile ducts *Physiol.* The excretory ducts of the gall bladder.
bilge (bilj) *n.* 1. *Naut.* The rounded part of a ship's bottom. 2. The bulge of a barrel. 3. Bilge water. 4. *Slang* Stupid or trivial talk or writing. — *v.t. & v.i.* **bilged, bilg·ing** 1. To break open in the bilge: said of a ship. 2. To bulge. [Var. of BULGE] — **bilg′y** *adj.*
bilge water Foul water that collects in the bilge of a ship.
bi·lin·gual (bī·ling′gwəl) *adj.* 1. Written or expressed in or using two languages. 2. Able to speak two languages, often with equal skill. — *n.* A bilingual person. [< L *bilinguis*] — **bi·lin′gual·ism** *n.* — **bi·lin′gual·ly** *adv.*
bil·ious (bil′yəs) *adj.* 1. Affected or caused by an excess of bile. 2. Of or containing bile. 3. Ill-tempered. 4. Of a sickly color. [< F < L *biliosus*] — **bil′ious·ly** *adv.* — **bil′ious·ness** *n.*
-bility *suffix* Forming nouns from adjectives ending in *-ble: probability* from *probable.* [< L < L *-bilitas, -tatis*]
bilk (bilk) *v.t.* 1. To cheat; deceive. 2. To evade payment of. 3. To balk. — *n.* 1. A swindler; cheat. 2. A hoax. [Origin unknown] — **bilk′er** *n.*
bill[1] (bil) *n.* 1. A statement listing charges for goods delivered or services rendered. 2. A statement of particulars; itemized list. 3. *U.S.* A piece of paper money; a bank note. 4. A bill of exchange; also, loosely, a promissory note. 5. A draft of a proposed law. 6. A handbill or advertising poster. 7. The program of a theatrical performance. 8. *Law* A formal statement of a case, a complaint, a petition for relief, etc. — *v.t.* 1. To enter in a bill or list. 2. To present a bill to. 3. To advertise by bills or placards. [< LL *billa*, var of L *bulla* edict, document] — **bill′a·ble** *adj.*
bill[2] (bil) *n.* A beak, as of a bird. — *v.i.* To join bills, as

doves; caress. — **to bill and coo** To caress lovingly and speak in soft, murmuring tones. [OE *bile*]
bill[3] (bil) *n.* 1. A hook-shaped instrument used in pruning, etc.: also **bill′hook′.** 2. An ancient weapon with a hook-shaped blade; a halberd. [OE]
bil·la·bong (bil′ə·bong) *n. Austral.* A stagnant backwater. [< native Australian < *billa* water + *bong* dead]
bill·board (bil′bôrd′, -bōrd′) *n.* A panel, usu. outdoors, for notices or advertisements.
bil·let[1] (bil′it) *n.* 1. Lodging for troops in private or nonmilitary buildings. 2. An order for such lodging. 3. A place assigned, as for a sailor to sling his hammock; quarters. 4. A job; berth. — *v.t.* To lodge (soldiers, etc.) in a private house by billet. [< OF < L *billa* seal, document]
bil·let[2] (bil′it) *n.* 1. A short, thick stick, as of firewood. 2. *Metall.* A mass of iron or steel drawn into a small bar. [< OF *billette*, dim. of *bille* log]
bil·let-doux (bil′ā·dōō′, *Fr.* bē·yä·dōō′) *n.* *pl.* **bil·lets-doux** (bil′ā·dōōz′, *Fr.* bē·yä·dōō′) A love letter. [<F]
bill·fold (bil′fōld′) *n.* A wallet.
bill·head (bil′hed′) *n.* A heading on paper used for making out bills; also, a blank with such a heading.
bil·liard (bil′yərd) *n. U.S. Informal* A carom. — *adj.* Of or pertaining to billiards: *billiard* player.
bil·liards (bil′yərdz) *n.pl.* (*construed as sing.*) Any of various games played with hard balls (**billiard balls**) hit by cues on an oblong, cloth-covered table (**billiard table**) having cushioned edges. [< F < OF *billart* cue] — **bil′liard·ist** *n.*
bill·ing (bil′ing) *n.* The relative eminence given to an actor or an act on a theater marquee, playbill, etc.
bil·lings·gate (bil′ingz·gāt) *n.* Vulgar or abusive language. [after *Billingsgate* fish market, London]
bil·lion (bil′yən) *n.* 1. *U.S.* A thousand millions, written as 1,000,000,000: called a *milliard* in Great Britain. 2. *Brit.* A million millions, written as 1,000,000,000,000: called a *trillion* in the U.S. [< F < bi- two + (mi)llion million] — **bil′lionth** *n. & adj.*
bil·lion·aire (bil′yən·âr′) *n.* One who owns a billion of money. [< BILLION, on analogy with *millionaire*]
bill of exchange A written order for the payment of a given sum to a designated person.
bill of fare A list of the dishes provided at a meal; menu.
bill of health An official certificate of the crew's health issued to a ship's master on departure from a port. — **a clean bill of health** *Informal* A good record; favorable report.
bill of lading A written acknowledgment of goods received for transportation.
bill of rights 1. A formal summary and declaration of the fundamental principles and rights of individuals. 2. *Often cap.* The first ten amendments to the U.S. Constitution.
bill of sale An instrument attesting the transfer of property.
bil·low (bil′ō) *n.* 1. A great wave or swell of the sea. 2. Any wave or surge, as of sound. — **Syn.** See WAVE. — *v.t.* To rise or roll in billows; surge; swell. [< ON *bylgja*]
bil·low·y (bil′ō·ē) *adj.* **low·i·er, low·i·est** Of, full of, or resembling billows; surging; swelling. — **bil′low·i·ness** *n.*
bill·post·er (bil′pōs′tər) *n.* A person who posts bills, notices, or advertisements on walls, fences, etc. Also **bill′·stick′er.** — **bill′post′ing** *n.*
bil·ly (bil′ē) *n.* *pl.* **·lies** A short bludgeon, as a policeman's club. [< *Billy*, a nickname for William]
billy goat *Informal* A male goat.
bi·lo·bate (bī·lō′bāt) *adj* Divided into or having two lobes. Also **bi·lo′bat·ed.**
Bi·lox·i (bi·lok′sē) *n.* One of a tribe of North American Indians of Siouan stock.
bi·man·u·al (bī·man′yōō·əl) *adj.* Employing or involving both hands. — **bi·man′u·al·ly** *adv.*
bi·met·al·ism (bī·met′l·iz′əm) *n.* The concurrent use of both gold and silver as the standard of currency and value. Also **bi·met′al·ism.** — **bi·met′al·ist** or **bi·met′al·list** *n.*
bi·me·tal·lic (bī′mə·tal′ik) *adj.* 1. Consisting of or relating to two metals. 2. Of or using bimetalism.
bi·month·ly (bī·munth′lē) *adj.* 1. Occurring once every two months. 2. Occurring twice a month; semimonthly. — *n.* A bimonthly publication. — *adv.* 1. Once in two months. 2. Twice a month.
bin (bin) *n.* An enclosed place or large receptacle for holding meal, coal, etc. — *v.t.* **binned, bin·ning** To store or deposit in a bin. [OE *binn* basket, crib < Celtic]
bin- Var. of BI-.
bi·na·ry (bī′nər·ē) *adj.* Pertaining to, characterized by, or made up of two; double; paired. — *n.* *pl.* **·ries** 1. A combination of two things. 2. *Astron.* A binary star. [< L *binarius* < *bini* two, double]
binary star *Astron.* A pair of stars revolving about a common center of gravity.
bi·nate (bī′nāt) *adj. Bot.* Being or growing in pairs, as leaves. [< NL < L *bini* double, two] — **bi′nate·ly** *adv.*
bin·au·ral (bin·ôr′əl) *adj.* 1. Hearing with both ears. 2. *Electronics* Stereophonic.

bind (bīnd) *v.* **bound, bind·ing** *v.t.* **1.** To tie or fasten with a band, cord, etc. **2.** To fasten around; encircle; gird. **3.** To bandage; swathe: often with *up*. **4.** To constrain or obligate, as by moral authority. **5.** *Law* To subject to a definite legal obligation. **6.** To enclose between covers, as a book. **7.** To provide with a border for reinforcement or decoration. **8.** To cause to cohere; cement. **9.** To constipate. **10.** To make irrevocable; seal, as a bargain. **11.** To apprentice or indenture: often with *out* or *over*. — *v.i.* **12.** To tie up anything. **13.** To cohere; stick together. **14.** To have binding force; be obligatory. **15.** To become stiff or hard, as cement; jam, as gears. **16.** That which binds. [OE *bindan*]
bind·er (bīn′dər) *n.* **1.** One who binds; esp., a bookbinder. **2.** Anything used to bind or tie, as a cord or band, or to cause cohesion, as tar, glue, etc. **3.** A cover in which sheets of paper may be fastened.   **4.** *Law* A written statement binding parties to an agreement pending preparation of a contract. **5.** *Agric.* A machine that cuts and ties grain.
bind·er·y (bīn′dər·ē) *n.* *pl.* **·er·ies** A place where books are bound.
bind·ing (bīn′ding) *n.* **1.** The act of one who binds. **2.** Anything that binds; binder. **3.** The cover holding together and enclosing the leaves of a book. **4.** A strip sewed over an edge for protection. — *adj.* **1.** Tying; restraining. **2.** Obligatory. — **bind′ing·ly** *adv.* — **bind′ing·ness** *n.*
bind·weed (bīnd′wēd′) *n.* Any strongly twining plant.
binge (binj) *n.* *Slang* A drunken carousal; spree. [? < dial. E *binge* to soak]
bin·go (bing′gō) *n.* A gambling game resembling lotto, usu. played in large groups. [Origin unknown]
bin·na·cle (bin′ə·kəl) *n.* *Naut.* A stand or case for a ship's compass, usu. placed before the steering wheel. [Earlier *bittacle* < Pg. < L *habitaculum* little house]
bin·oc·u·lar (bə·nok′yə·lər, bī-) *adj.* Pertaining to, using, or intended for both eyes at once. — *n.* Often *pl.* A telescope, opera glass, etc., adapted for use by both eyes. [< L *bini* two, double + *ocularis* of the eyes < *oculus* eye]
bi·no·mi·al (bī·nō′mē·əl) *adj.* Consisting of two names or terms. — *n.* *Math.* An algebraic expression consisting of two terms joined by a plus or minus sign. [< LL *binominus* having two names] — **bi·no′mi·al·ly** *adv.*
bio- *combining form* Life: *biology.* [< Gk. *bios* life]
bi·o·chem·is·try (bī′ō·kem′is·trē) *n.* The branch of chemistry relating to the processes and physical properties of living organisms. — **bi′o·chem′i·cal** or **bi′o·chem′ic** *adj.* — **bi′o·chem′i·cal·ly** *adv.* — **bi′o·chem′ist** *n.*
bi·o·de·grad·a·ble (bī′ō·di·grā′də·bəl) *adj.* Capable of quick decomposition, as by bacteria, into ecologically harmless products. [< BIO- + DEGRAD(E) + -ABLE]
bi·o·feed·back (bī′ō·fēd′bak) *n.* Voluntary control by feedback of involuntary functions, as heart rate.
bi·o·gen·e·sis (bī′ō·jen′ə·sis) *n.* The doctrine that life is generated from living organisms only. Also **bi·og·e·ny** (bī·oj′ə·nē). — **bi·o·ge·net·ic** (bī′ō·jə·net′ik) or **·i·cal** *adj.* — **bi′o·ge·net′i·cal·ly** *adv.*
bi·og·ra·pher (bī·og′rə·fər, bē-) *n.* A writer of biography.
bi·o·graph·i·cal (bī′ə·graf′i·kəl) *adj.* **1.** Of or concerning a person's life. **2.** Pertaining to biography. Also **bi′o·graph′·ic.** — **bi′o·graph′i·cal·ly** *adv.*
bi·og·ra·phy (bī·og′rə·fē, bē-) *n.* *pl.* **·phies** An account of a person's life; also, such accounts as a form of literature. [< LGk. < Gk. *bios* life + *graphein* to write]
bi·o·log·i·cal (bī′ə·loj′i·kəl) *adj.* **1.** Of or pertaining to biology. **2.** Used for or produced by biological research or practice. Also **bi·o·log′ic.** — **bi′o·log′i·cal·ly** *adv.*
biological clock A hypothetical natural timing mechanism in organisms that controls certain behavior, as the migration, nesting, and mating of birds.
biological warfare Warfare that employs bacteria, viruses, and other biological agents noxious to or destructive of life.
bi·ol·o·gy (bī·ol′ə·jē) *n.* The science of life in all its manifestations, and of the origin, structure, reproduction, growth, and development of living organisms collectively. Its two main divisions are botany and zoology. — **bi·ol′o·gist** *n.*
bi·om·e·try (bī·om′ə·trē) *n.* The statistical analysis of biological observations: also **bi·o·met·rics** (bī′ə·met′riks).
bi·on·ics (bī·on′iks) *n.pl.* (*construed as sing.*) The science that applies knowledge of biological systems to engineering problems. — **bi·on′ic** *adj.*
bi·o·phys·ics (bī′ō·fiz′iks) *n.pl.* (*construed as sing.*) The study of biological phenomena using the methods of physics. — **bi′o·phys′i·cal** *adj.* — **bi′o·phys′i·cist** *n.*
bi·op·sy (bī′op·sē) *n.* *pl.* **·sies** *Med.* The examination of tissue from a living subject. — **bi·op·sic** (bī·op′sik) *adj.*
bi·o·rhythm (bī′ō·rith′əm) *n.* Theoretical cyclical patterns in biological activity or behavior. — **bi′o·ryth′mi·cal** *adj.*
-biosis *combining form* Manner of living: *symbiosis.* [<

Gk. *biōsis* < *bios* life]
bi·o·tin (bī′ə·tin) *n.* *Biochem.* A crystalline acid, $C_{10}H_{16}O_3$-N_2S, forming part of the vitamin B complex. [< Gk. *biotos* life + -IN]
bi·par·ti·san (bī·pär′tə·zən) *adj.* Advocated by or consisting of members of two parties. — **bi·par′ti·san·ship** *n.*
bi·par·tite (bī·pär′tīt) *adj.* **1.** Consisting of two parts, esp. two corresponding parts. **2.** *Bot.* Divided into two parts almost to the base, as certain leaves. Also **bi·part′ed.** [< L *bipartire* to divide] — **bi·par′tite·ly** *adv.* — **bi·par·ti·tion** (bī′pär·tish′ən) *n.*
bi·ped (bī′ped) *n.* An animal having two feet. — *adj.* Two-footed: also **bi·pe·dal** (bī′pə·dəl, bip′ə-). [< L *bipes, bipedis*]
bi·pin·nate (bī·pin′āt) *adj.* *Bot.* Twice or doubly pinnate, as a leaf. Also **bi·pin′nat·ed.** — **bi·pin′nate·ly** *adv.*
bi·plane (bī′plān′) *n.* A type of airplane having two wings, one above the other.
bi·po·lar (bī·pō′lər) *adj.* **1.** Relating to or possessing two poles. **2.** Denoting or belonging to both polar regions. **3.** Containing two contradictory qualities, opinions, etc. — **bi·po·lar·i·ty** (bī′pō·lar′ə·tē) *n.*
birch (bûrch) *n.* **1.** A tree or shrub having the outer bark separable in thin layers; esp. the **canoe** or **paper birch** of North America: also called *white birch.* **2.** A rod from this tree, used as a whip. **3.** The tough, close-grained hardwood of the birch. — *v.t.* To whip with a birch rod. [OE *birce*]
bird (bûrd) *n.* **1.** A warm-blooded, feathered, egg-laying vertebrate having the forelimbs modified as wings. ◆ Collateral adjective: *avian.* **2.** A game bird. **3.** A shuttlecock. **4.** A clay pigeon. **5.** *Slang* A person, esp. one who is peculiar or remarkable. **6.** *Slang* A hiss or jeer. [OE *bridd*]
bird·call (bûrd′kôl′) *n.* **1.** A bird's note in calling. **2.** A sound imitating this, or an instrument for producing it.
bird dog A dog used in hunting game birds.
bird·ie (bûr′dē) *n.* **1.** *Informal* A small bird. **2.** In golf, one stroke less than par on a given hole.
bird·lime (bûrd′līm′) *n.* A sticky substance made from holly or mistletoe and smeared on twigs to catch small birds.
bird·man (bûrd′man′, -mən) *n.* *pl.* **·men** (-men′, -mən) **1.** *Informal* An aviator. **2.** A fowler. **3.** An ornithologist.
bird of paradise A tropical bird noted for the beauty of the plumage in the male.
bird of passage A migratory bird.
bird of prey A predatory bird, as an eagle, hawk, etc.
bird's-eye (bûrdz′ī′) *adj.* **1.** Marked with spots resembling birds' eyes: *bird's-eye* maple. **2.** Seen from above or from afar: a *bird's-eye* view. — *n.* **1.** A pattern woven with small, eyelike indentations. **2.** Any of various fabrics having such a pattern. Also **birds′eye′.**
bird watcher One who observes or identifies wild birds in their natural habitats as a pastime. — **bird watching**
bi·ret·ta (bi·ret′ə) *n.* A stiff, square cap with three or four upright projections on the crown, worn by clerics of the Roman Catholic church: also called *berretta.* [< Ital.]
birl (bûrl) *v.t. & v.i.* **1.** To rotate (a floating log). **2.** To whirl. — *n.* A droning noise.
birth (bûrth) *n.* **1.** The fact or act of being born. **2.** The bringing forth of offspring. **3.** Beginning; origin. **4.** Ancestry or descent. **5.** Noble lineage; good family. **6.** Natural or inherited tendency.
birth control The regulation of conception by preventive methods or devices.
birth·day (bûrth′dā) *n.* The day of one's birth or its anniversary.
birth·mark (bûrth′märk′) *n.* A mark or stain existing on the body from birth; nevus.
birth·place (bûrth′plās′) *n.* **1.** Place of birth. Abbr. *bp.* **2.** Place where something originates.
birth rate The number of births per a given number of individuals (usually 1,000), in a specified district and in a specified period of time.
birth·right (bûrth′rīt′) *n.* A privilege or possession into which one is born.
birth·stone (bûrth′stōn′) *n.* A jewel identified with the month of one's birth.
bis (bis) *adv.* Twice: used to denote repetition. [< L]
bis- Var. of BI-.
bis·cuit (bis′kit) *n.* **1.** *U.S.* A kind of shortened bread baked in small cakes, raised with baking powder or soda. **2.** *Brit.* A thin, crisp wafer. **3.** A light brown color. **4.** In ceramics, pottery baked once but not glazed. [< OF < L < *bis* twice + *coctus*, pp. of *coquere* to cook]
bi·sect (bī·sekt′) *v.t.* **1.** To cut into two parts; halve. **2.** *Geom.* To divide into two parts of equal size. — *v.i.* **3.** To fork, as a road. [< BI- + L *sectus*, pp. of *secare* to cut] — **bi·sec′tion** *n.* — **bi·sec′tion·al** *adj.* — **bi·sec′tion·al·ly** *adv.*
bi·sec·tor (bī·sek′tər) *n.* **1.** That which bisects. **2.** *Geom.* A line or plane that bisects an angle or another line.

---

bi·sex·u·al (bī-sek′shōō-əl) *adj.* **1.** Of both sexes. **2.** Having the organs of both sexes; hermaphrodite. **3.** Sexually attracted to both sexes. — *n.* **1.** A hermaphrodite. **2.** A bisexual person. — **bi·sex′u·al·ism, bi·sex·u·al′i·ty** (bī-sek′-shōō-al′ə-tē) *n.* — **bi·sex′u·al·ly** *adv.*

bish·op (bish′əp) *n.* **1.** A prelate in the Christian church; esp., the head of a diocese. **2.** A miter-shaped chess piece that may be moved only diagonally. [OE *biscop*]

bish·op·ric (bish′əp·rik) *n.* The office or the diocese of a bishop.

bis·muth (biz′məth) *n.* A lustrous, reddish white metallic element (symbol Bi) occurring native as well as in combination, used in medicine, in the manufacture of cosmetics, etc. See ELEMENT. [< G] — **bis·muth·al** (biz′məth·əl) *adj.*

bi·son (bī′sən, -zən) *n. pl.* **bi·son** A bovine ruminant, closely related to the true ox; esp., the North American buffalo. [< L *bison* wild ox, ult. < Gmc.]

bisque (bisk) *n.* **1.** A thick, rich soup made from meat or fish, esp. shellfish. **2.** Any thickened, creamy soup. **3.** A kind of ice cream containing crushed macaroons or nuts. [< F]

NORTH
AMERICAN BISON
(5 to 6 feet
high at
shoulder)

bis·ter (bis′tər) *n.* **1.** A yellowish brown pigment made from soot, used chiefly as a watercolor wash. **2.** A dark brown color. Also **bis′tre.** [< F *bistre* dark brown] — **bis′tered** *adj.*

bis·tro (bis′trō, Fr. bē·strō′) *n. Informal* A small bar, tavern or night club. [< F]

bi·sul·fate (bī·sul′fāt) *n. Chem.* An acid sulfate containing the radical HSO₄; also called *disulfate.* Also **bi·sul′phate.**

bi·sul·fide (bī·sul′fīd) *n. Chem.* A disulfide. Also **bi·sul′phide.**

bit¹ (bit) *n.* **1.** A small piece, portion, or quantity. **2.** A short time. **3.** A small part, as in a play or movie. **4.** *U.S.* The Spanish real, worth 12½ cents: now used chiefly in the expression *two bits.* — **to do one's bit** To make one's contribution; do one's share. — *adj.* Small; insignificant; minor. [OE *bita* < *bītan* to bite]

bit² (bit) *n.* **1.** A sharp-edged tool for boring or drilling, having a shank for attachment to a brace, drill press, etc. **2.** The sharp or cutting part of a tool. **3.** The metallic mouthpiece of a bridle. **4.** Anything that controls or restrains. **5.** The part of a key that turns a lock. — *v.t.* **bit·ted, bit·ting** **1.** To put a bit in the mouth of (a horse). **2.** To curb; restrain. [OE *bite* a biting < *bītan* to bite]

bit³ (bit) Past tense and alternative past participle of BITE.

bit⁴ (bit) *n.* A unit of information, expressed as a choice between two equally probable alternative messages or symbols, as a "yes" and a "no" or a dot and a dash. [< b(*inary*) (*dig*)*it*]

bitch (bich) *n.* **1.** The female of the dog or other canine animal **2.** *Slang* A malicious or promiscuous woman: an abusive term. — *v.i. Slang* To complain. — **to bitch up** *Slang* To botch. [< OE *bicce*] — **bitch′y** *adj.*

bite (bīt) *v.* **bit, bit·ten** or **bit, bit·ing** *v.t.* **1.** To seize, tear, or wound with the teeth. **2.** To cut or tear off with or as with the teeth: usually with *off.* **3.** To puncture the skin of with a sting or fangs. **4.** To cut or pierce. **5.** To cause to sting or smart. **6.** To eat into; corrode. **7.** To grip; take hold of. **8.** To cheat; deceive: usually passive. — *v.i.* **9.** To seize or cut into something with the teeth. **10.** To have the effect of biting, as mustard; sting. **11.** To take firm hold; grip. **12.** To take as bait, as fish. **13.** To be tricked. — **to bite off more than one can chew** To attempt something beyond one's capabilities. — *n.* **1.** The act of biting. **2.** A wound inflicted by biting. **3.** A painful sensation; smart; sting. **4.** A morsel of food; mouthful. **5.** *Informal* A light meal; snack. **6.** The grip or hold taken by a tool, etc. [OE *bītan*] — **bit′a·ble** or **bite′a·ble** *adj.* — **bit′er** *n.*

bit·ing (bī′ting) *adj.* **1.** Sharp; stinging. **2.** Sarcastic; caustic. — **bit′ing·ly** *adv.* — **bit′ing·ness** *n.*

bit·stock (bit′stok′) *n.* A brace for a bit. For illus. see BIT².

bitt (bit) *Naut. n.* A post or vertical timber on a ship's deck, to which cables, etc., are made fast, usually in pairs. — *v.t.* To wind (a cable) around a bitt. [? < ON *biti* beam]

bit·ten (bit′n) Past participle of BITE.

bit·ter (bit′ər) *adj.* **1.** Having an acrid, disagreeable taste. **2.** Unpleasant to accept; distasteful. **3.** Painful to body or mind; harsh. **4.** Feeling or showing intense animosity. **5.** Stinging; sharp. — **Syn.** See SOUR. — *n.* That which

BITS AND BRACE
a Brace (or bitstock). Bits: *b* Screwdriver, *c* Drill, *d* Ship auger, *e* Auger, *f* Expanding, *g* Chuck (cross-section).

is bitter. — *v.t. & v.i.* To make or become bitter. [OE *biter* < *bītan* to bite] — **bit′ter·ly** *adv.* — **bit′ter·ness** *n.*

bit·tern (bit′ərn) *n.* Any of various wading birds related to the heron. [< OF *butor*, ? < L *butio*, *-onis* bittern]

bit·ter·root (bit′ər·rōōt′, -rŏŏt′) *n.* An herb with nutritious roots and pink or white flowers.

bit·ters (bit′ərz) *n.pl.* A liquor, usu. spirituous, prepared with an infusion of bitter herbs, etc.

bitter·sweet (bit′ər·swēt′) *n.* A shrubby or climbing plant having green flowers succeeded by orange pods. — *adj.* **1.** Bitter and sweet. **2.** Pleasant and unpleasant.

bi·tu·men (bi·tōō′mən, -tyōō′-, bich′ŏŏ·mən) *n.* **1.** Any natural mixture of solid and semisolid hydrocarbons, as asphalt. **2.** A brown paint made by mixing asphalt with a drying oil. [< L] — **bi·tu·mi·noid** (bi·tōō′mə·noid) *adj.*

bi·tu·mi·nize (bi·tōō′mə·nīz, -tyōō′-) *v.t.* **·nized, ·niz·ing** To render bituminous. — **bi·tu′mi·ni·za′tion** *n.*

bi·tu·mi·nous (bi·tōō′mə·nəs, -tyōō′-, bī-) *adj.* **1.** Of, pertaining to, or containing bitumen. **2.** Containing many volatile hydrocarbons, as shale. [< F *bitumineux*]

bituminous coal A mineral coal low in carbon and burning with a yellow, smoky flame: also called *soft coal.*

bi·va·lent (bī-vā′lənt, biv′ə-) *adj. Chem.* **a** Having a valence of two. **b** Having two valences. Also *divalent.* — **bi·va·lence** (bī-vā′ləns, biv′ə-), **bi·va′len·cy** (-vā′lən·sē) *n.*

bi·valve (bī′valv′) *n. Zool.* A mollusk having a shell of two lateral valves hinged together, as the oyster or clam. — *adj.* Having two valves or parts: also **bi′valved′, bi·val·vous** (bī·val′vəs), **bi·val·vu·lar** (bī·val′vyə·lər).

biv·ou·ac (biv′ŏŏ·ak, biv′wak) *n.* A temporary encampment, esp. for soldiers in the field. — *v.i.* **·acked, ·ack·ing** To encamp in a bivouac. [< F < G *beiwacht* guard]

bi·week·ly (bī·wēk′lē) *adj.* **1.** Occurring once every two weeks. **2.** Occurring twice a week; semiweekly. — *n.* A biweekly publication. — *adv.* **1.** Once in two weeks. **2.** Twice a week.

bi·year·ly (bī·yir′lē) *adj. & adv.* **1.** Occurring twice yearly. **2.** Biennial. — *adv.* Twice a year.

bi·zarre (bi·zär′) *adj.* Singular or eccentric in style, manner, etc.; odd; fantastic; grotesque. [< F, ? ult. < Basque] — **bi·zarre′ly** *adv.* — **bi·zarre′ness** *n.*

blab (blab) *v.t. & v.i.* **blabbed, blab·bing** **1.** To disclose indiscreetly. **2.** To prattle. — *n.* **1.** One who blabs. **2.** Idle chatter. Also **blab′ber.** [ME *blabbe* idle talker]

blab·ber·mouth (blab′ər·mouth′) *n.* One who talks too much and can't be trusted to keep secrets.

black (blak) *adj.* **1.** Having no brightness or color; reflecting no light. **2.** Destitute of light. **3.** Gloomy; dismal; forbidding. **4.** *Sometimes cap.* Belonging to a dark-skinned, esp. the Negro, race. **5.** *Sometimes cap.* Of or pertaining to black, esp. Negro, people. **6.** Soiled; stained. **7.** Indicating disgrace or censure. **8.** Angry; threatening. **9.** Evil; wicked; malignant. **10.** Wearing black garments. **11.** Of coffee, without cream. — *n.* **1.** The absence of light; the darkest of all colors. **2.** Something black, as soot. **3.** A Negro. — *v.t.* **1.** To make black; blacken. **2.** To put blacking on and polish (shoes). — *v.i.* **3.** To become black. — **to black out** **1.** To delete by scoring through. **2.** To suffer a temporary loss of vision or consciousness. **3.** To extinguish or screen all lights. [OE *blæc* dark] — **black′ness** *n.*

black Africa Those states or parts of Africa whose inhabitants are mainly dark-skinned, esp. Negro. Also **Black Africa.** — **black African, Black African.**

black-and-blue (blak′ən·blōō′) *adj.* Discolored: said of skin that has been bruised.

black and white **1.** Writing or print. **2.** A sketch or picture in various shades of black and white.

black art Necromancy; magic.

black·ball (blak′bôl′) *n.* A negative vote. — *v.t.* **1.** To vote against. **2.** To ostracize; exclude. — **black′ball′er** *n.*

black bass A fresh-water game fish of the eastern U.S. and Canada.

black bear The common North American bear, having fur that varies from glossy black to cinnamon brown.

black·ber·ry (blak′ber′ē, -bər·ē) *n. pl.* **·ries. 1.** The black, edible fruit of certain shrubs of the rose family. **2.** Any of the plants producing it.

black·bird (blak′bûrd′) *n.* A common European thrush, the male of which is black with a yellow bill.

black·board (blak′bôrd′, -bōrd′) *n.* A blackened surface, often of slate, for drawing and writing upon with chalk.

Black Death An exceptionally virulent plague, epidemic in Asia and Europe during the 14th century: also called *plague.*

black·en (blak′ən) *v.* **·ened, ·en·ing** **1.** To make black or dark. **2.** To slander; defame. — *v.i.* **3.** To become black; darken. [ME *blaknen* < *blak* black] — **black′en·er** *n.*

black eye **1.** An eye with a black iris. **2.** An eye having the adjacent surface discolored by a blow or bruise. **3.** *Informal* A cause of discredit; blot. — **black′-eyed′** *adj.*

black-eyed Susan One of the coneflowers, with black-centered yellow flowers: also called *yellow daisy.*

black·face (blak'fās') *n.* **1.** An entertainer with exaggerated Negro make-up, esp. a minstrel comedian. **2.** The make-up worn by such an entertainer.

black flag The Jolly Roger.

Black·foot (blak'foŏt') *n. pl.* **·feet** (-fēt') A member of any of the tribes of Algonquian North American Indians living in Alberta and Montana. — *adj.* Of the Blackfeet.

black·guard (blag'ərd, -ärd) *n.* An unprincipled scoundrel; a rogue. — *v.t.* **1.** To revile; vilify. — *v.i.* **2.** To act like a blackguard. — *adj.* Of or like a blackguard; base; vile: also **black'guard·ly.** [< *black guard*] — **black'guard·ism** *n.*

black·head (blak'hed') *n.* **1.** A bird having a black head, as the American scaup duck. **2.** *Vet.* A disease of turkeys. **3.** A plug of dried, fatty matter in a pore of the skin.

black-heart·ed (blak'här'tid) *adj.* Evil; wicked.

black hole *Astron.* A theoretical entity formed by the death and contraction of a large star, having a small, dense mass and gravity so powerful that no light can escape.

black·ing (blak'ing) *n.* A preparation used to give blackness or luster to shoes, stoves, etc.

black·jack (blak'jak') *n.* **1.** A small bludgeon with a flexible handle. **2.** A pirate's flag. **3.** A small oak of the SE U.S. having black bark. **4.** Twenty-one, a card game. **5.** A large drinking cup. — *v.t.* **1.** To strike with a blackjack. **2.** To coerce by threat.

black lead Graphite.

black letter *Printing* A type face characterized by heavy black letters resembling those of early **This line is in black letter.** printed works: also called *gothic, Old English.* — **black·let·ter** (blak'let'ər) *adj.*

black·list (blak'list') *n.* A list of persons or organizations under suspicion or censure, or refused approval or employment for any cause. — *v.t.* To place on a blacklist.

black·ly (blak'lē) *adv.* Darkly, gloomily, or threateningly.

black magic Witchcraft.

black·mail (blak'māl') *n.* Extortion by threats of public accusation or of exposure; also, that which is so extorted, as money. — *v.t.* **1.** To levy blackmail upon. **2.** To force (to do something), as by threats: with *into.* [< BLACK + MAIL³] — **black'mail'er** *n.*

Black Ma·ri·a (mə·rī'ə) *Informal* A patrol wagon.

black mark A mark of censure, failure, etc.

black market A market where goods are sold in violation of official prices, quotas, etc.

Black Muslim A member of a sect (the **Nation of Islam**) of Negroes in the U.S., which follows the practices of Islam and rejects integration with the white race.

black·out (blak'out') *n.* **1.** The extinguishing or screening of all lights, esp. as a precaution against air raids. **2.** *Physiol.* Partial or complete loss of vision and sometimes of consciousness, as experienced by airplane pilots during rapid changes in velocity. **3.** In the theater, the extinguishing of the lights on a stage. **4.** A ban, as on news. **5.** Widespread loss of light caused by electric power failure.

black sheep One regarded as a disgrace by his family.

black·smith (blak'smith') *n.* **1.** One who shoes horses. **2.** One who works iron on an anvil and uses a forge.

black·snake (blak'snāk') *n.* **1.** Any of various agile, nonvenomous snakes of the eastern U.S., having smooth, black scales. **2.** *U.S.* A heavy, pliant whip of braided leather.

black·thorn (blak'thôrn') *n.* **1.** A thorny European shrub of the rose family. **2.** Its small, plumlike, astringent fruit. Also called *sloe.* **3.** A cane made from its wood.

black tie **1.** A black bow tie. **2.** A tuxedo and its correct accessories.

black widow The venomous female of a North American spider: so called from its color and its eating of its mate.

blad·der (blad'ər) *n.* **1.** *Anat.* A distensible membranous sac in the anterior part of the pelvic cavity, for the temporary retention of urine. ◆ Collateral adjective: *vesical.* **2.** An inflatable object resembling a bladder: the *bladder* of a basketball. [OE *blædre*] — **blad'der·y** *adj.*

blad·der·wort (blad'ər·wûrt') *n.* An aquatic herb having little bladders on the leaves in which minute organisms are trapped for nutriment.

blade (blād) *n.* **1.** The flat, cutting part of any edged tool or weapon. **2.** The thin, flat part of an oar, plow, etc. **3.** The leaf of grasses or other plants. **4.** A sword. **5.** A dashing or reckless young man. **6.** *Phonet.* The upper surface of the tongue behind the tip. **7.** *Bot.* The broad, flat part of a leaf, petal, etc. [OE *blæd*] — **blad'ed** *adj.*

blah (blä) *n. U.S. Slang* Nonsense.

blain (blān) *n. Pathol.* A pustule; blister. [OE *blegen*]

blam·a·ble (blā'mə·bəl) *adj.* Deserving blame; culpable. Also **blame·a·ble.** — **blam'a·ble·ness** *n.* — **blam'a·bly** *adv.*

blame (blām) *v.t.* **blamed, blam·ing** **1.** To hold responsible; accuse. **2.** To find fault with; reproach. **3.** To place the responsibility for (an action or error). — **to be to blame** To be at fault. — *n.* **1.** Expression of censure; reproof. **2.** Responsibility for something wrong; culpability. [< OF < LL *blasphemare* to revile, reproach] — **blame'ful** *adj.* — **blame'ful·ly** *adv.* — **blame'ful·ness** *n.* — **blame'·less** *adj.* — **blame'less·ly** *adv.* — **blame'less·ness** *n.*

blame·wor·thy (blām'wûr'thē) *adj.* Deserving of blame. — **blame'wor'thi·ness** *n.*

blanch (blanch, blänch) *v.t.* **1.** To remove the color from; bleach. **2.** To cause to turn pale. **3.** To remove the skin of or whiten. — *v.i.* **4.** To turn or become white or pale. — **Syn.** See WHITEN. [< F *blanc* white] — **blanch'er** *n.*

blanc·mange (blə·mänzh') *n.* A whitish, jellylike preparation of milk, eggs, sugar, cornstarch, flavoring, etc., used chiefly for desserts. [< OF *blanc-manger*, lit., white food]

bland (bland) *adj.* **1.** Gentle and soothing; suave. **2.** Not stimulating or irritating; mild. [< L *blandus* mild] — **bland'ly** *adv.* — **bland'ness** *n.*

blan·dish (blan'dish) *v.t.* To wheedle; flatter. [< OF < L *blandus* mild] — **blan'dish·er** *n.* — **blan'dish·ment** *n.*

blank (blangk) *adj.* **1.** Free from writing or print. **2.** Not completed or filled out, as a check. **3.** Showing no expression or interest; vacant. **4.** Lacking variety or interest. **5.** Disconcerted; bewildered. **6.** Utter; complete: *blank* dismay. **7.** Empty or void; also, fruitless. — *n.* **1.** An empty space; void. **2.** A blank space in a printed document, to be filled in. **3.** A paper or document with such spaces. **4.** A lottery ticket that has drawn no prize. **5.** A partially prepared piece, as of metal, ready for forming into a finished object, as a key. **6.** A cartridge filled with powder but having no bullets: also **blank cartridge.** — *v.t.* **1.** To delete; invalidate: often with *out.* **2.** In games, to prevent (an opponent) from scoring. [< OF *blanc* white] — **blank'·ly** *adv.* — **blank'ness** *n.*

blank check *Informal* **1.** A check bearing a signature but no specified amount. **2.** Unlimited authority or freedom.

blan·ket (blang'kit) *n.* **1.** A large piece of woolen or other soft, warm fabric, used as a covering in bed, as a robe, etc. **2.** Anything that covers, conceals, or protects: a *blanket* of fog. — *adj.* Covering a wide range of conditions, items, or the like: a *blanket* indictment. — *v.t.* **1.** To cover with or as with a blanket. **2.** To cover or apply to uniformly. **3.** To obscure or suppress; interfere with. [< OF *blankete*, dim. of *blanc* white; orig. a white or undyed woolen cloth]

blank verse Verse without rhyme; esp., iambic pentameter verse, used in English epic and dramatic poetry.

blare (blâr) *v.t. & v.i.* **blared, blar·ing** **1.** To sound loudly, as a trumpet. **2.** To exclaim noisily. — *n.* **1.** A loud brazen sound. **2.** Brightness or glare, as of color. [Prob. imit.]

blar·ney (blär'nē) *n.* Wheedling flattery; cajolery. — *v.t. & v.i.* To flatter, cajole, or wheedle. [< BLARNEY STONE]

Blarney Stone A stone in a castle in Blarney, Ireland, that reputedly endows one who kisses it with skill in flattery.

bla·sé (blä·zā', blä'zā) *adj.* Wearied or bored, as from overindulgence in pleasure. [< F *blaser* to satiate]

blas·pheme (blas·fēm') *v.* **·phemed, ·phem·ing** *v.t.* **1.** To speak in an impious manner of (God or sacred things). **2.** To speak ill of; malign. — *v.i.* **3.** To utter blasphemy. [< OF < LL < Gk. *blasphēmos* evil-speaking]

blas·phe·mous (blas'fə·məs) *adj.* Expressing blasphemy. — **blas'phe·mous·ly** *adv.* — **blas'phe·mous·ness** *n.*

blas·phe·my (blas'fə·mē) *n. pl.* **·mies** Impious or profane speaking of God, or of sacred persons or things. — **Syn.** See PROFANITY. [< OF < LL < Gk. *blasphēmia*]

blast (blast, bläst) *v.t.* **1.** To rend in pieces by or as by explosion. **2.** To cause to wither or shrivel; destroy. — **to blast off** *Aerospace* To begin an ascent by means of rocket or jet propulsion. — *n.* **1.** A strong wind; gust. **2.** A loud, sudden sound, as of a trumpet. **3.** A rush of air, as from the mouth. **4.** A strong, artificial current of air, steam, etc. **5.** An explosion of dynamite, etc.; also, the charge set off. **6.** A blight. — **at full blast** At capacity operation or maximum speed. [OE *blæst*] — **blast'er** *n.*

blast·ed (blas'tid, bläs'-) *adj.* **1.** Withered or destroyed; blighted. **2.** Damned: a euphemism.

blast furnace *Metall.* A smelting furnace in which the fire is intensified by an air blast.

blasto- *combining form Biol.* Growth; sprout. Also, before vowels, **blast-.** [< Gk. *blastos* sprout]

blast·off (blast'ôf', -of', bläst'-) *n. Aerospace* The series of events immediately before and after a rocket leaves its launching pad; also the moment of leaving.

blas·tu·la (blas'chŏŏ·lə) *n. pl.* **·lae** (-lē) *Biol.* The stage of the embryo just preceding the formation of the gastrula; a hollow sphere of one layer of cells. [< NL < Gk. *blastos* sprout] — **blas'tu·lar** *adj.*

blat (blat) *v.* **blat·ted, blat·ting** *v.t.* **1.** *Informal* To blurt out. — *v.i.* **2.** To bleat, as a sheep. [Var. of BLEAT]

bla·tant (blā/tənt) *adj.* **1.** Offensively loud or noisy; clamorous. **2.** Obvious; obtrusive: *blatant* stupidity. [Coined by Edmund Spenser] — **bla/tan·cy** *n.* — **bla/tant·ly** *adv.*

blath·er (blath/ər) *v.t. & v.i.* To speak or utter foolishly; babble. — *n.* Foolish talk. [< ON *blathr* nonsense]

blath·er·skite (blath/ər·skīt) *n.* **1.** A blustering, talkative person. **2.** Foolish talk.

blaze[1] (blāz) *v.* **blazed, blaz·ing** *v.i.* **1.** To burn brightly. **2.** To burn as with emotion. **3.** To shine; be resplendent. — *n.* **1.** A vivid glowing flame; fire. **2.** Brilliance; glow. **3.** Sudden activity; outburst, as of anger. [OE *blæse*]

blaze[2] (blāz) *v.t.* **blazed, blaz·ing** **1.** To mark (a tree) by chipping off a piece of bark. **2.** To indicate (a trail) by marking trees in this way. — *n.* **1.** A white spot on the face of a horse, etc. **2.** A mark chipped on a tree to indicate a trail. [Akin to ON *blesi* white spot on a horse's face]

blaz·er (blā/zər) *n.* A lightweight, often striped, jacket for informal wear. [< BLAZE[1]]

bla·zon (blā/zən) *v.t.* **1.** To inscribe or adorn, as with names or symbols. **2.** To describe or depict (coats of arms) in technical detail. **3.** To proclaim; publish. — *n.* **1.** A coat of arms. **2.** A technical description of armorial bearings. **3.** Ostentatious display. [< OF *blason* coat of arms, shield] — **bla/zon·er** *n.* — **bla/zon·ment** *n.* — **bla/zon·ry** *n.*

-ble See -ABLE.

bleach (blēch) *v.t. & v.i.* To make or become colorless or white; whiten. — **Syn.** See WHITEN. — *n.* **1.** The act of bleaching. **2.** The degree of bleaching obtained. **3.** A fluid or powder used as a bleaching agent. [OE *blæcean*]

bleach·er (blē/chər) *n.* **1.** One who or that which bleaches. **2.** *pl. U.S.* Unroofed outdoor seats for spectators.

bleak (blēk) *adj.* **1.** Exposed to wind and weather; bare; barren. **2.** Cold; cutting. **3.** Cheerless; dreary. [? < ON *bleikr* pale] — **bleak/ly** *adv.* — **bleak/ness** *n.*

blear (blir) *v.t.* **1.** To dim (the eyes) with or as with tears. **2.** To blur or make dim. — *adj.* Bleary. [ME *blere*]

blear-eyed (blir/īd/) *adj.* **1.** Having eyes bleared by tears, old age, etc. **2.** Dull of perception.

blear·y (blir/ē) *adj.* **·i·er, ·i·est** **1.** Made dim, as by tears. **2.** Blurred; dim. — **blear/i·ly** *adv.* — **blear/i·ness** *n.*

bleat (blēt) *v.i.* **1.** To utter the cry of a sheep, goat, or calf. **2.** To speak or complain with a similar sound. — *v.t.* **3.** To utter with a bleat. **4.** To babble; prate. — *n.* The act or sound of bleating. [OE *blætan*] — **bleat/er** *n.*

bleed (blēd) *v.* **bled, bleed·ing** *v.i.* **1.** To lose or shed blood. **2.** To suffer wounds or die. **3.** To feel grief, sympathy, or anguish. **4.** To exude sap or other fluid. **5.** *Printing* To extend to or beyond the edge of a page, as an illustration. — *v.t.* **6.** To draw blood from; leech. **7.** To exude, as sap, blood, etc. **8.** *Printing* To print (an illustration, etc.) so that it will bleed. [OE *blēdan*]

bleed·er (blē/dər) *n.* **1.** One who bleeds profusely, even from a slight wound. **2.** A hemophiliac.

bleeding heart A plant having racemes of pink, drooping flowers.

blem·ish (blem/ish) *v.t.* **1.** To mar the perfection of; sully. — *n.* **1.** A disfiguring defect, esp. of the skin. **2.** A moral fault or stain. [< OF *blemir* to make livid] — **blem/ish·er** *n.*

blench[1] (blench) *v.i.* To shrink back; flinch. [OE *blencan* to deceive] — **blench/er** *n.*

blench[2] (blench) *v.t. & v.i.* To make or become pale; blanch. [Var. of BLANCH[1]]

BLEEDING HEART
(1 to 3 feet high)

blend (blend) *v.* **blend·ed** or (less commonly) **blent, blend·ing** *v.t.* **1.** To mingle and combine so as to obscure or harmonize the varying components. **2.** To mix so as to obtain a uniform product: to *blend* paints. — *v.i.* **3.** To mix; intermingle. **4.** To pass or shade imperceptibly into each other, as colors. **5.** To harmonize. — *n.* The act or result of mixing. [Prob. < ON *blanda* to mix] — **blend/er** *n.*

blende (blend) *n. Mineral.* One of a number of rather bright minerals combining sulfur with a metallic element. [< G *blendendes erz* deceptive ore]

blended whisky *U.S.* Whisky that has been blended with other whisky or neutral spirits.

blen·ny (blen/ē) *n. pl.* **·nies** A small marine fish having an elongated body. [< L < Gk. *blennos* slime]

bless (bles) *v.t.* **blessed** or **blest, bless·ing** **1.** To consecrate; make holy by religious rite. **2.** To honor and exalt; glorify. **3.** To make the sign of the cross over, as for sanctification or protection. **4.** To invoke God's favor upon (a person or thing). **5.** To bestow prosperity upon; make happy. **6.** To endow, as with a gift: She was *blessed* with a beautiful face. **7.** To guard; protect: *Bless* me! [OE *blēdsian* to consecrate (with blood) < *blōd* blood] — **bless/er** *n.*

bless·ed (bles/id, blest) *adj.* **1.** Made holy by a religious rite; consecrated. **2.** Enjoying the happiness of heaven; beatified. **3.** Blissful; happy. **4.** Causing happiness. Also spelled **blest.** — **bless/ed·ly** *adv.* — **bless/ed·ness** *n.*

bless·ed event (bles/id) *Informal* The birth of a baby.

Blessed Virgin The Virgin Mary.

bless·ing (bles/ing) *n.* **1.** An invocation or benediction; grace. **2.** The bestowal of divine favor. **3.** That which makes happy or prosperous. **4.** Grateful adoration.

blest (blest) Alternative past participle of BLESS. — *adj.* Blessed.

blew (bloo) Past tense of BLOW.

blight (blīt) *n.* **1.** Any of a number of destructive plant diseases, as mildew, rust, smut, etc. **2.** Anything causing such a disease. **3.** Anything that withers hopes, destroys prospects, or impairs growth. **4.** The state of being blighted. — *v.t.* **1.** To cause to decay; blast. **2.** To ruin; frustrate. — *v.i.* **3.** To suffer blight. [Origin unknown]

blimp (blimp) *n. Informal* A nonrigid dirigible. [< Type *B-Limp*, a kind of British dirigible]

blind (blīnd) *adj.* **1.** Unable to see. **2.** Lacking in perception or judgment. **3.** Acting or done without intelligent control; random. **4.** Unreasoning; heedless: *blind* prejudice. **5.** Concealed: a *blind* ditch. **6.** Closed at one end: a *blind* alley. **7.** Having no opening or outlet: a *blind* wall. **8.** Insensible. **9.** Done without the aid of visual reference: *blind* flying. **10.** Of or for blind persons. — *n.* **1.** Something that obstructs vision or shuts off light; esp., a window shade. **2.** A hiding place, as for a hunter; ambush. **3.** Something intended to deceive. — *adv.* **1.** Blindly. **2.** Without the aid of visual reference: to fly *blind.* — *v.t.* **1.** To make blind. **2.** To dazzle. **3.** To deprive of judgment or discernment. **4.** To darken; obscure. **5.** To eclipse. [OE] — **blind/ing** *adj.* — **blind/ing·ly** *adv.* — **blind/ly** *adv.* — **blind/ness** *n.*

blind alley **1.** An alley, road, etc., open at one end only. **2.** Any search, pursuit, etc., in which progress is blocked.

blind date *Informal* A date with a person of the opposite sex whom one has not previously met.

blind·er (blīn/dər) *n.* **1.** One who or that which blinds. **2.** *U.S.* A flap on the side of a horse's bridle, serving to obstruct sideways vision, also called *blinker.*

blind·fold (blīnd/fōld/) *v.t.* **1.** To cover or bandage the eyes of. **2.** To hoodwink; mislead. — *n.* A bandage over the eyes. — *adj.* **1.** Having the eyes bandaged. **2.** Reckless; rash. [ME < *blind* blind + *fellen* to strike]

blind·man's buff (blīnd/manz/) A game in which one player is blindfolded and must catch and identify another player.

blind spot **1.** *Anat.* A small area on the retina of the eye that is insensible to light because of the entrance of the optic nerve. **2.** A subject about which one is ignorant, or incapable of objective thought.

blink (blingk) *v.i.* **1.** To wink rapidly. **2.** To squint, as in sunlight. **3.** To twinkle; also, to flash on and off. **4.** To look indifferently or evasively: with *at.* — *v.t.* **5.** To cause to wink. **6.** To shut the eyes to; evade. — *n.* **1.** A blinking; wink. **2.** A gleam. **3.** A glance or glimpse. [< Du. *blinken*; ult. origin uncertain]

blink·er (blingk/ər) *n.* **1.** A light that blinks, as in warning or for sending messages. **2.** *pl.* Goggles. **3.** Blinder (def. 2).

blint·ze (blint/sə) *n.* A thin pancake folded about a filling of cottage cheese, potato, fruit, etc., and usu. eaten with sour cream or jam. Also **blintz.** [< Yiddish]

blip (blip) *n. Telecom.* One of the luminous signals recorded on a radarscope. [? Var. of *flip*]

bliss (blis) *n.* **1.** Gladness; joy. **2.** A cause of delight or happiness. [OE *blithe* joyous] — **bliss/ful** *adj.* — **bliss/·ful·ly** *adv.* — **bliss/ful·ness** *n.*

blis·ter (blis/tər) *n.* **1.** A thin vesicle, esp. on the skin, containing watery matter, as from rubbing, a burn, etc. **2.** A similar swelling on various other surfaces. — *v.t.* **1.** To produce a blister or blisters upon. **2.** To rebuke severely. — *v.i.* **3.** To become blistered. [< OF < ON *blāstr* swelling] — **blis/ter·y** *adj.*

blister beetle The Spanish fly.

blithe (blīth, blīth) *adj.* **1.** Cheerful; gay. **2.** Casual or airy in manner. [OE] — **blithe/ly** *adv.* — **blithe/ness** *n.*

blithe·some (blīth/səm, blīth/-) *adj.* Showing or imparting gladness. — **blithe/some·ly** *adv.* — **blithe/some·ness** *n.*

blitz (blits) *Informal n.* A sudden attack; blitzkrieg. — *v.t.* To subject to a blitzkrieg.

blitz·krieg (blits/krēg) *n.* **1.** *Mil.* A swift, sudden attack by tanks, aircraft, etc.; also, warfare so waged. **2.** Any sudden attack or assault. [< G < *blitz* lightning + *krieg* war]

bliz·zard (bliz/ərd) *n.* A severe snowstorm, often with high, cold winds. [< dial. E *blizzer* sudden blow]

bloat (blōt) *v.t.* **1.** To cause to swell, as with fluid. **2.** To puff up; make proud or vain. — *v.i.* **3.** To swell; become puffed up. [ME, ? < ON *blautr* soft, soaked]

bloat·er (blō/tər) *n.* **1.** A smoked herring. **2.** A whitefish of the Great Lakes of North America.

blob (blob) *n.* **1.** A soft, globular mass; a drop, as of viscous liquid. **2.** A daub or spot, as of color. — *v.t.* **blobbed, blob·bing** To mark with ink or color; blot. [Origin unknown]

bloc (blok) *n.* A group, as of politicians, nations, etc., combined to foster special interests. — **Syn.** See FACTION. [< F]

block¹ (blok) *n.* **1.** A solid piece of wood, metal, etc., usu. with one or more flat surfaces. **2.** Such a piece on which cutting or chopping is done. **3.** A support or form on which something is shaped or displayed: a hat *block*. **4.** A stand from which articles are sold at auction. **5.** A small cube used by children for building.

BLOCKS¹ (*def.* 13)
a Tackle. *b* Dock, with attaching screw. *c* Snatch. *d* Triple-sheave steel. *e* Gin. *f* Square-cheeked.

6. A set or section, as of tickets, etc., handled as a unit. **7.** A section of railroad controlled by signals. **8.** *U.S.* An area bounded, usu. on four sides, by streets; also, one side of such an area. **9.** *U.S. & Canadian* An office building. **10.** *Canadian* A group of townships in the midst of unsurveyed land. **11.** A pulley, or set of pulleys, in a frame with a hook or the like at one end. **12.** A piece of wood prepared for engraving. — *v.t.* **1.** To shape into blocks. **2.** To shape, with a block, as a hat. **3.** To secure or strengthen with blocks. — **to block out** To plan broadly without details. [< F *bloc*, ult. < Gmc.] — **block′er** *n.*
block² (blok) *n.* **1.** An obstacle or hindrance. **2.** The act of obstructing, or the state of being obstructed. **3.** In sports, interference with an opponent's actions. **4.** *Med. & Pathol.* **a** An obstruction, as of a nerve or blood vessel. **b** Anesthesia of a specific region: saddle *block*. **5.** *Psychol.* The inability to think or act in certain situations. — *v.t.* **1.** To obstruct. **2.** In sports, to hinder the movements of (an opposing player); also, to stop (a ball), as with the body. **3.** *Med. & Pathol.* To stop (a nerve) from functioning, as with an anesthetic. — *v.i.* **4.** To obstruct an opponent's actions. — **to block out** To obscure from view. — **to block up** To fill (an area or space) so as to prevent movement into or through. [< MF *bloquer* to obstruct] — **block′age** *n.* — **block′er** *n.*
block·ade (blo-kād′) *n.* **1.** The closing by hostile ships or forces of a coast, city, etc., to traffic or communication. **2.** The ships or forces used for this. **3.** An obstruction to action or passage. — **to run the blockade** To elude a blockade. — *v.t.* **·ad·ed, ·ad·ing** To subject to a blockade; obstruct. — **block·ad′er** *n.*
block and tackle A set of pulley blocks and ropes for pulling or hoisting.
block·bust·er (blok′bus′tər) *n. Informal* An aerial bomb, capable of demolishing a large area.
block·head (blok′hed′) *n.* A stupid person; dolt.
block·house (blok′hous′) *n.* **1.** A fortification, formerly of logs and heavy timbers, having loopholes from which to fire. **2.** *U.S.* A house made of hewn logs set square.
block·ish (blok′ish) *adj.* Like a block; stupid; dull. Also **block′like′.** — **block′ish·ly** *adv.* — **block′ish·ness** *n.*
block letter **1.** Printing type cut from wood. **2.** A style of letters without serifs. — **block-let·ter** (blok′let′ər) *adj.*
block·y (blok′ē) *adj.* **block·i·er, block·i·est** **1.** Unequally shaded, as if printed in blocks. **2.** Short and stout; stocky.
bloke (blōk) *n. Brit. Slang* A fellow; guy.
blond (blond) *adj.* **1.** Having fair hair with light eyes and skin. **2.** Flaxen or golden, as hair. — *n.* A blond person. [< F < Med.L *blondus*, prob. < Gmc.]
blonde (blond) *adj.* Blond: feminine form. — *n.* A blonde woman or girl.
blood (blud) *n.* **1.** *Physiol.* The typically red fluid that circulates through the heart, arteries, and veins of animals and delivers oxygen and nutrients to the cells and tissues of the body. ◆ Collateral adjective: *hemal.* **2.** A liquid or juice resembling this in some way, as the sap of plants. **3.** The shedding of blood; slaughter; murder. **4.** Disposition of mind; temperament: hot *blood.* **5.** The principle of life; vitality; lifeblood. **6.** Descent from a common ancestor; kinship. **7.** Noble descent. **8.** Racial or national extraction. **9.** A dashing young man; also, a rake. — **in cold blood** **1.** Deliberately; without passion. **2.** Cruelly; without mercy. — **to make one's blood boil** (or **run cold**) To make one angry (or frightened). [OE *blōd*]
blood bank A place where blood is stored, either in liquid form or as dried plasma, for use in transfusion.
blood bath Wanton killing; a massacre.
blood count *Med.* A measure of the number and proportion of red and white cells in a given sample of blood.
blood·cur·dling (blud′kûrd′ling) *adj.* Terrifying.
blood·ed (blud′id) *adj.* **1.** Having blood or temper of a specified character: cold-*blooded.* **2.** Thoroughbred.
blood group *Physiol.* One of the classes into which blood may be divided on the basis of specific differences in its composition: also called *blood type.*

blood·hound (blud′hound′) *n.* **1.** A large, smooth-coated hound remarkable for its keen sense of smell, and often used to track fugitives. **2.** *Informal* Any persistent pursuer.
blood·less (blud′lis) *adj.* **1.** Devoid of blood; pale. **2.** Without bloodshed. **3.** Lacking vigor; listless. **4.** Cold-hearted. — **blood′less·ly** *adv.* — **blood′less·ness** *n.*
blood·let·ting (blud′let′ing) *n.* **1.** Bleeding for a therapeutic purpose. **2.** Bloodshed.
blood money **1.** *Informal* Money obtained at the cost of another's life, welfare, etc. **2.** Money paid to a hired murderer. **3.** Compensation paid to the kin of a murdered man.
blood plasma *Physiol.* The liquid part of the blood, without its cellular components.
blood platelet *Physiol.* One of the minute bodies found in the blood of higher vertebrates, essential to coagulation.
blood poisoning *Pathol.* Deterioration of the blood caused by bacterial substances: also called *toxemia.*
blood pressure *Physiol.* The pressure of the blood on the walls of the arteries, varying with the force of the heart action, with age, general condition, etc.
blood relation One who is related by birth; kinsman.
blood·root (blud′root′, -root′) *n.* A perennial North American herb having a fleshy rootstalk with deep red sap.
blood·shed (blud′shed′) *n.* The shedding of blood; slaughter; carnage. Also **blood′shed′ding.** — **blood′shed′der** *n.*
blood·shot (blud′shot′) *adj.* Suffused or shot with blood; red and inflamed or irritated: said of the eye.
blood·stain (blud′stān′) *n.* A spot produced by blood. — *v.t.* To stain with blood. — **blood′stained′** *adj.*
blood·stone (blud′stōn′) *n.* A stone of green chalcedony flecked with particles of red jasper: also called *heliotrope.*
blood stream The blood coursing through a living body.
blood·suck·er (blud′suk′ər) *n.* **1.** An animal that sucks blood, as a leech. **2.** *Informal* One who extorts or sponges.
blood·thirst·y (blud′thûrs′tē) *adj.* Thirsting for blood; cruel. — **blood′thirst′i·ly** *adv.* — **blood′thirst′i·ness** *n.*
blood transfusion *Med.* The transfer of blood from one person or animal into another.
blood type Blood group.
blood vessel Any tubular canal, as an artery, vein, or capillary, through which the blood circulates.
blood·y (blud′ē) *adj.* **blood·i·er, blood·i·est** **1.** Stained with blood. **2.** Of, like, or containing blood. **3.** Involving bloodshed. **4.** Bloodthirsty. **5.** Deep red. **6.** *Brit. Slang* Damned: a vulgarism. — *v.t.* **blood·ied, blood·y·ing** To stain with blood. — *adv. Brit. Slang* Very: a vulgarism. [OE *blōdig*] — **blood′i·ly** *adv.* — **blood′i·ness** *n.*
bloom (bloom) *n.* **1.** The flower of a plant; blossom. **2.** The state of being in flower. **3.** A growing or flourishing condition; freshness. **4.** The rosy tint of the cheeks or skin; glow. **5.** *Bot.* The powdery, waxy substance on certain fruits and leaves. **6.** Any of various earthy minerals found as a powdery incrustation on certain ores. — *v.i.* **1.** To bear flowers; blossom. **2.** To glow with health; flourish. **3.** To glow with a warm color. — *v.t.* **4.** To bring into bloom; cause to flourish. **5.** To give a bloom to. [< ON *blōm* blossom] — **bloom′y** *adj.*
bloom·ers (bloo′mərz) *n.pl.* **1.** Loose, wide trousers gathered at the knee, worn by women as a gymnasium costume. **2.** A woman's undergarment resembling these.
bloom·ing (bloo′ming) *adj.* **1.** In flower; blossoming. **2.** Flourishing. — **bloom′ing·ly** *adv.* — **bloom′ing·ness** *n.*
blos·som (blos′əm) *n.* **1.** A flower, esp. one of a plant yielding edible fruit. **2.** The state or period of flowering; bloom. — *v.i.* **1.** To come into blossom. **2.** To prosper; thrive. [OE *blōstm*] — **blos′som·less** *adj.* — **blos′som·y** *adj.*
blot (blot) *n.* **1.** A spot or stain, as of ink. **2.** A stain on reputation or character; blemish. **3.** A detraction from beauty, excellence, etc. **4.** An erasure. — *v.* **blot·ted, blot·ting** *v.t.* **1.** To spot, as with ink; stain. **2.** To disgrace; sully. **3.** To mark over or obliterate, as writing: often with *out.* **4.** To obscure: usually with *out.* **5.** To dry, as with blotting paper. **6.** To paint roughly; daub. — *v.i.* **7.** To spread in a blot or blots, as ink. **8.** To become blotted; stain. **9.** To absorb. [ME *blotte*]
blotch (bloch) *n.* **1.** A spot or blot. **2.** An eruption on the skin. — *v.t.* **1.** To mark or cover with blotches. — *v.i.* **2.** To become blotched. [Blend of BLOT and BOTCH] — **blotch′i·ness** *n.* — **blotch′y** *adj.*
blot·ter (blot′ər) *n.* **1.** A sheet or pad of blotting paper. **2.** The daily record of arrests in a police station.
blotting paper Unsized paper for absorbing excess ink.
blouse (blous, blouz) *n.* **1.** A woman's garment extending from the neck to the waist or just below. **2.** A loose, knee-length smock, usu. belted at the waist, worn chiefly by European workmen. **3.** The service coat of the U.S. Army uniform. — *v.t. & v.i.* **bloused** (bloust, blouzd), **blous·ing** To drape loosely or fully. [< F] — **blouse′like′** *adj.*

blow¹ (blō) *v.* **blew, blown, blow·ing** *v.i.* **1.** To be in motion: said of wind or air. **2.** To move in a current of air. **3.** To emit a current or jet of air, steam, etc., as from the mouth. **4.** To produce sound by blowing or being blown, as a trumpet. **5.** To pant; gasp for breath. **6.** To spout air and water before breathing, as a whale. **7.** To fail or become useless, as a fuse, tire, etc.: often with *out*. **8.** *Informal* To brag. **9.** *U.S. Slang* To depart; go. — *v.t.* **10.** To drive or impel by a current of air. **11.** To direct a current of air upon, as from the mouth. **12.** To sound by blowing into, as a bugle. **13.** To sound (a signal): to *blow* taps. **14.** To emit, as air or smoke, from the mouth. **15.** To clear by forcing air into or through. **16.** To put out of breath, as a horse. **17.** To form by inflating a material: to *blow* bubbles. **18.** To break, shatter, or destroy by explosion: usu. with *up, down*, etc. **19.** *Informal* To melt (a fuse). **20.** *U.S. Slang* To spend (money) lavishly; also, to treat or entertain. **21.** *U.S. Slang* To depart from; leave. — **to blow hot and cold** *Informal* To vacillate; be uncertain. — **to blow off 1.** To let off, as steam from a boiler. **2.** *Slang* To speak in anger. — **to blow out 1.** To extinguish by blowing. **2.** To burst, as a tire. **3.** To melt, as a fuse. — **to blow over 1.** To pass, as a storm; subside. **2.** To pass without bad result. — **to blow up 1.** To inflate. **2.** To make an enlargement of (a photograph). **3.** To explode. **4.** *Informal* To lose one's temper. **5.** To arise; become intense, as a storm. — *n.* **1.** A blowing, as of wind. **2.** A storm or gale. [OE *blāwan*]

blow² (blō) *n.* **1.** A sudden stroke dealt with the fist, a weapon, etc. **2.** A sudden disaster. **3.** A hostile act; assault. — **Syn.** See MISFORTUNE. — **to come to blows** To start fighting. [ME *blaw*]

blow³ (blō) *Archaic & Poetic v.* **blew, blown, blow·ing** *v.i.* **1.** To bloom; blossom. — *v.t.* **2.** To cause to bloom. — *n.* A display, as of blossoms. [OE *blōwan* to blossom]

blow·er (blō′ər) *n.* **1.** One who or that which blows. **2.** A device for forcing air through a building, furnace, etc.

blow·fly (blō′flī′) *n. pl.* **·flies** A blue or green fly whose larvae live in carrion or in living flesh: also called *bluebottle*.

blow·gun (blō′gun′) *n.* A long tube through which a missile, as a dart, may be blown by the breath.

blow·hole (blō′hōl′) *n.* **1.** *Zool.* The nasal openings in the heads of certain whales or other cetaceans. **2.** A vent for gas and bad air, as in mines. **3.** A hole in the ice to which seals, etc., come to breathe.

blown (blōn) Past participle of BLOW¹. — *adj.* **1.** Out of breath, as from overexertion. **2.** Inflated; swollen, esp. with gas. **3.** Made with a blowtube, blowpipe, etc.

blow·out (blō′out′) *n.* **1.** A bursting, as of a tire, or the hole so made. **2.** The melting of a fuse. **3.** *Slang* An elaborate meal or party. **4.** A flameout.

blow·pipe (blō′pīp′) *n.* **1.** A tube for blowing air or gas through a flame to direct and intensify its heat. **2.** A blowgun.

blow·torch (blō′tôrch′) *n.* An apparatus for vaporizing a combustible fluid under pressure and expelling it from a nozzle as a long, intensely hot flame, used for soldering, etc.

blow·up (blō′up′) *n.* **1.** An explosion. **2.** *Informal* A loss of self-control; outburst; also, a fight; quarrel. **3.** An enlargement, as of a photograph.

blow·y (blō′ē) *adj.* **blow·i·er, blow·i·est** Windy.

blowz·y (blou′zē) *adj.* **blowz·i·er, blowz·i·est** **1.** Disheveled; slovenly. **2.** Fat and red-faced. Also **blowzed** (blouzd). [< earlier *blowse* a fat, ruddy woman; origin uncertain]

blub·ber (blub′ər) *v.i.* **1.** To weep and sob noisily. — *v.t.* **2.** To utter with sobs. — *n.* **1.** *Zool.* The layer of fat beneath the skin of a whale or other cetacean, used as a source of oil. **2.** The act of blubbering; weeping. — *adj.* Swollen; protruding. [ME *blubren*; imit.] — **blub′ber·er** *n.* — **blub′ber·ing·ly** *adv.* — **blub′ber·y** *adj.*

blu·cher (blōō′chər, -kər) *n.* A shoe in which there is no front seam, the upper meeting above in two projecting flaps. [after G. L. *Blücher*, 1742–1819, Prussian field marshal]

bludg·eon (bluj′ən) *n.* A short club, commonly loaded at one end, used as a weapon. — *v.t.* **1.** To strike with or as with a bludgeon. **2.** To coerce; bully. [Origin unknown]

blue (blōō) *adj.* **blu·er, blu·est** **1.** Having the color of the clear sky seen in daylight. **2.** Livid, as the skin from bruising or cold. **3.** Depressed in spirits; melancholy. **4.** Dismal; dreary. **5.** Puritanical; strict. — **once in a blue moon** Very seldom. — *n.* **1.** The color of the clear sky; azure. **2.** Any pigment or dye used to impart a blue color. **3.** Bluing. **4.** *Sometimes cap.* One who wears a blue uniform. — **out of the blue** From an unsuspected source. — **the blue 1.** The sky. **2.** The sea. — *v.t.* **blued, blu·ing 1.** To make blue. **2.** To treat with bluing. [< OF *bleu*, ult. < Gmc.] — **blue′ly** *adv.* — **blue′ness** *n.*

blue baby An infant born with cyanosis resulting from a congenital heart lesion or from defective lungs.

Blue·beard (blōō′bird′) In folklore, a man who married and then murdered six women in succession.

blue·bell (blōō′bel′) *n.* Any one of various plants that bear blue, bell-shaped flowers.

blue·ber·ry (blōō′ber′ē, -bər·ē) *n. pl.* **·ries 1.** An edible, blue or black American berry. **2.** The plant that bears it.

blue·bird (blōō′bûrd′) *n.* A small American passerine bird with predominantly blue plumage.

blue blood 1. Aristocratic blood or descent. **2.** One of aristocratic family: also **blue·blood** (blōō′blud′). — **blue′-blood′ed** *adj.* — **blue′blood′ed·ness** *n.*

blue·bon·net (blōō′bon′it) *n.* **1.** The cornflower. **2.** An annual leguminous herb with blue flowers.

blue book 1. A register of persons employed by the U.S. government. **2.** A register of socially prominent people. Also **blue·book** (blōō′book′).

blue·bot·tle (blōō′bot′l) *n.* **1.** A blowfly. **2.** Any of various flowers with tubular, usu. blue florets.

blue cheese A type of cheese resembling Roquefort.

blue chip 1. In finance, the stock of a well-known company with a good sustained record of dividends, earnings, etc. **2.** A gambling chip of the highest value.

blue·coat (blōō′kōt′) *n.* A policeman.

blue devils 1. Despondency. **2.** Delirium tremens.

blue·fish (blōō′fish′) *n. pl.* **·fish** or **·fish·es** A voracious food fish common along the Atlantic coast of the U.S.

blue fox A small fox of arctic regions whose pelt acquires a bluish color in summer; also, its fur.

blue·grass (blōō′gras′, -gräs′) *n.* One of various grasses; esp., the **Kentucky bluegrass.**

Bluegrass State Nickname of Kentucky.

blue·gum (blōō′gum′) *n.* Any of several eucalyptus trees.

blue·ing (blōō′ing), **blue·ish** (blōō′ish) See BLUING, etc.

blue·jack·et (blōō′jak′it) *n.* An enlisted man in the United States or British navy.

blue jay A crested, corvine bird of North America. Also **blue·jay** (blōō′jā′).

blue law *Often pl. U.S.* A puritanical law, esp. one prohibiting entertainment on Sunday.

blue·nose (blōō′nōz′) *n. Informal* A puritanical person.

blue-pen·cil (blōō′pen′səl) *v.t.* **·ciled** or **·cilled, ·cil·ing** or **·cil·ing** To edit or cancel with or as with a blue pencil.

blue point An oyster found off the shore of Long Island.

blue·print (blōō′print′) *n.* **1.** A plan or drawing made by printing on sensitized paper, the drawing showing in white lines on a blue ground. **2.** Any detailed plan. — *v.t.* To make a blueprint of.

blue ribbon The highest award or distinction; first prize.

blues (blōōz) *n.pl.* **1.** Depression of spirits; melancholy. **2.** *Music* A style using deliberately mistuned scale degrees (**blue notes**), often in 4/4 meter with 12-measure phrases; also, the often mournful songs sung to this music.

blue·stock·ing (blōō′stok′ing) *n.* A learned, pedantic, or literary woman. [from the informal blue stockings worn by a leading literary figure in 18th-century London]

blu·et (blōō′it) *n.* **1.** One of various plants having blue flowers. **2.** A delicate meadow flower of the madder family.

bluff¹ (bluf) *v.t. & v.i.* **1.** To deceive by putting on a bold front. **2.** To frighten with empty threats. — **to bluff one's way** To obtain an object by bluffing. — *n.* **1.** The act of bluffing. **2.** One who bluffs. [? < Du. *bluffen* to deceive, mislead] — **bluff′er** *n.*

bluff² (bluf) *n.* **1.** A steep headland or bank. **2.** *Canadian* A clump of trees on a prairie. — *adj.* **1.** Rough and hearty in manner. **2.** Having a broad, steep appearance. [? < Du. *blaf* flat] — **bluff′ly** *adv.* — **bluff′ness** *n.*

blu·ing (blōō′ing) *n.* A blue coloring matter used in laundry work to counteract yellowing in linen: also spelled *blueing*.

blu·ish (blōō′ish) *adj.* Somewhat blue: also spelled *blueish*. — **blu′ish·ness** *n.*

blun·der (blun′dər) *n.* A stupid mistake; error. — *v.i.* **1.** To act or move awkwardly; stumble. **2.** To make a stupid mistake. — *v.t.* **3.** To utter stupidly or confusedly: often with *out*. **4.** To bungle. [ME *blondren* to mix up, confuse] — **blun′der·er** *n.* — **blun′der·ing·ly** *adv.*

blun·der·buss (blun′dər·bus) *n.* **1.** An old-fashioned, short gun with large bore and flaring mouth, used for scattering shot at close range. **2.** A stupid, blustering person. [Blend of BLUNDER and Du. *donderbus* thunder box]

BLUNDERBUSS (def. 1)

blunt (blunt) *adj.* **1.** Having a dull end or edge. **2.** Abrupt in manner; brusque. **3.** Slow of wit; dull. — *v.t. & v.i.* To make or become dull or less hurtful. [ME; origin unknown] — **blunt′ly** *adv.* — **blunt′ness** *n.*

— **Syn.** (adj.) **1.** dull, round, smooth. **2.** *Blunt* suggests an unpleasant frankness and *abrupt* a disconcerting directness: a *blunt* opinion, an *abrupt* departure. *Brusque* implies ungraciousness, while *curt* connotes undue brevity, and often intentional rudeness: a *brusque* handshake, a *curt* rejoinder.

blur (blûr) *v.t. & v.i.* **blurred, blur·ring** **1.** To make or become vague and indistinct in outline. **2.** To dim. **3.** To smear; smudge. — *n.* **1.** A smear; smudge. **2.** Something indistinct. — **blur/ry** *adj.*

blurb (blûrb) *n.* A brief and highly commendatory description or advertisement, esp. one on a book jacket. [Coined by Gelett Burgess, 1866–1951, U.S. humorist]

blurt (blûrt) *v.t.* To utter abruptly or impulsively: often with *out.* [? Blend of BLOW and SPURT]

blush (blush) *v.i.* **1.** To become red in the face from modesty or confusion; flush. **2.** To become red or rosy, as flowers. **3.** To feel shame or regret: usually with *at* or *for.* — *v.t.* **4.** To make red. — *n.* **1.** A reddening of the face from modesty, etc. **2.** A red or rosy tint. **3.** A glance; glimpse: now only in the phrase **at** or **on first blush** — *adj.* Reddish. [OE *blyscan* to redden] — **blush/er** *n.* — **blush/ful** *adj.* — **blush/ing·ly** *adv.*

blus·ter (blus/tər) *v.i.* **1.** To blow gustily and with violence and noise, as the wind. **2.** To utter threats. — *v.t.* **3.** To utter noisily and boisterously. **4.** To force or bully by blustering. — *n.* **1.** Boisterous talk or swagger. **2.** Fitful and noisy blowing of the wind; blast. — **blus/ter·er** *n.* — **blus/ter·ing·ly** *adv.* — **blus/ter·y, blus/ter·ous** *adj.*

bo·a (bō/ə) *n.* *pl.* **bo·as** **1.** Any of several nonvenomous serpents notable for the crushing power of their coils, as the anaconda and python; esp. the **boa constrictor** of South America. **2.** A long feather or fur scarf for women. [< L]

boar (bôr, bōr) *n.* *pl.* **boars** or **boar.** **1.** An uncastrated male swine. **2.** The wild boar. [OE *bār*]

board (bôrd, bōrd) *n.* **1.** A flat, thin slab of sawed wood much longer than it is wide. **2.** A thin slab of wood or the like for a specific purpose: an ironing *board.* **3.** One of the pasteboard covers of a book. **4.** A table set for serving food. **5.** Food or meals; esp., meals furnished for pay, and sometimes including lodging. **6.** An organized official body. **7.** A table at which meetings are held. — **across the board** *Informal* **1.** Designating a racing bet whereby equal sums are wagered on a single horse, etc., to win, place, and show. **2.** Affecting all members or categories in the same degree: said of changes in salary, taxes, etc. — **by the board** Overboard. — **on board** On or in a vessel or other conveyance. — **the boards** The stage. — **to go by the board** To fall into ruin, disuse, etc. — *v.t.* **1.** To cover or enclose with boards: often with *up.* **2.** To furnish with meals, or meals and lodging, for pay. **3.** To place (someone) where meals are provided, as in a boarding school. **4.** To enter, as a ship or train. **5.** *Naut.* To come alongside or go on board of (a ship), as to attack. — *v.i.* **6.** To take meals, or meals and lodging. [OE *bord* board, side of a ship, table]

board·er (bôr/dər, bōr/-) *n.* **1.** One who receives regular meals, or meals and lodging, for pay. **2.** One who is detailed to board an enemy's ship.

board foot *pl.* **board feet** The contents of a board 1 foot square and 1 inch thick; the common unit of measure for logs and lumber in the U.S., equal to 144 cubic inches or 2359.8 cubic centimeters. Abbr. *bd. ft.*

boarding house A house where meals, or meals and lodging, can be had regularly for pay. Also **board·ing·house** (bôr/ding·hous/, bōr/-).

boarding school A school in which pupils are boarded.

board measure A cubic measure applied to boards, the unit of which is the board foot. Abbr. *b.m.*

board·walk (bôrd/wôk/, bōrd/-) *n.* **1.** A promenade along a beach, usually of boards. **2.** A walk made of planks.

boast (bōst) *v.i.* **1.** To talk in a vain or bragging manner. **2.** To speak or possess with pride: used with *of.* — *v.t.* **3.** To brag about; extol. **4.** To be proud to possess; take pride in. — *n.* **1.** A boastful speech. **2.** That which is boasted about. [ME *bosten*] — **boast/er** *n.* — **boast/ing·ly** *adv.*

boast·ful (bōst/fəl) *adj.* Characterized by or addicted to boasting. — **boast/ful·ly** *adv.* — **boast/ful·ness** *n.*

boat (bōt) *n.* **1.** A small, open watercraft propelled by oars, sails, or an engine. **2.** *Informal* Any watercraft of any size, from a rowboat to an ocean liner. **3.** A boat-shaped object, as a dish. — **in the same boat** In the same situation or condition; equally involved. — *v.i.* **1.** To travel by boat. **2.** To go boating for pleasure. — *v.t.* **3.** To transport or place in a boat: to boat oars. [OE *bāt*]

boat·house (bōt/hous/) *n.* A building for storing boats.

boat·ing (bō/ting) *n.* The act or sport of one who boats.

boat·load (bōt/lōd/) *n.* **1.** The amount that a boat can hold. **2.** The load carried by a boat.

boat·man (bōt/mən) *n.* *pl.* **·men** (-mən) **1.** A man who deals in or works on boats. **2.** An aquatic insect.

boat·swain (bō/sən, *rarely* bōt/swān/) *n.* A warrant officer of a naval ship, or a subordinate officer of a merchantman who is in charge of the rigging, anchors, etc. Also spelled *bosun, bo's'n.* [OE *bātswegen*]

bob¹ (bob) *v.* **bobbed, bob·bing** *v.i.* **1.** To move up and down with an irregular motion. **2.** To curtsy. — *v.t.* **3.** To move up and down. — **to bob up** To appear or emerge suddenly. — *n.* **1.** A short, jerky movement: a *bob* of the head. **2.** A quick bow or curtsy. **3.** In fishing, a float or cork. [ME; origin uncertain] — **bob/ber** *n.*

bob² (bob) *n.* **1.** A short haircut for a woman or child. **2.** The docked tail of a horse. **3.** A small, pendant object, as the weight on a plumb line. For illus. see PLUMB BOB. **4.** In fishing, a large, ball-shaped bait made of worms, rags, etc. — *v.* **bobbed, bob·bing** *v.t.* **1.** To cut short, as hair. — *v.i.* **2.** To fish with a bob. [ME *bobbe*] — **bob/ber** *n.*

bob³ (bob) *n.* *pl.* **bob** *Brit. Informal* A shilling. [< *Bob*, a nickname for *Robert*, a personal name]

bob·bin (bob/in) *n.* A spool or reel holding thread for spinning, weaving, or machine sewing. [< F *bobine*]

bob·by (bob/ē) *n.* *pl.* **·bies** *Brit. Informal* A policeman. [after Sir Robert Peel, 1788–1850, who introduced police reforms]

bobby pin A metal hairpin shaped so as to clasp and hold the hair tightly. Also **bob/bie pin.**

bobby socks *Informal* Short socks worn by girls.

bob·by·sox·er (bob/ē·sok/sər) *U.S. Informal* A young girl who follows fads and fashions current among adolescents.

bob·cat (bob/kat/) *n.* The American lynx.

bob·o·link (bob/ə·lingk) *n.* A thrushlike singing bird of North America. [Imit.; from its call]

bob·sled (bob/sled/) *n.* **1.** A racing sled steered by a steering wheel controlling the front runners. **2.** Either of two short sleds connected in tandem; also, the vehicle so formed. — *v.i.* **·sled·ded, ·sled·ding** To go coasting on a bobsled. Also **bob/sleigh/** (-slā/). [Origin unknown]

bob·tail (bob/tāl/) *n.* **1.** A short tail or a tail cut short. **2.** An animal with such a tail. — *adj.* **1.** Having the tail docked. **2.** Cut short; incomplete. — *v.t.* **1.** To cut the tail of; dock. **2.** To cut short. — **bob/tailed/** *adj.*

bob·white (bob/hwīt/) *n.* A quail of North America having brownish, mottled plumage. [Imit.; from its call]

bock beer (bok) A dark, strong beer brewed in the winter and served in early spring. Also **bock.** [< G *bockbier*]

bode¹ (bōd) Archaic past tense and past participle of BIDE.

bode² (bōd) *v.* **bod·ed, bod·ing** *v.t.* **1.** To be a foretoken of; presage. — *v.i.* **2.** To presage good or ill. [OE *bodian* to announce] — **bode/ment** *n.*

bod·ice (bod/is) *n.* **1.** The upper portion of a woman's dress. **2.** A woman's ornamental vest. [Var. of *bodies*]

bod·ied (bod/ēd) *adj.* **1.** Having a body. **2.** Having a (specified kind of) body: used in combination: *full-bodied.*

bod·i·less (bod/i·lis) *adj.* Having no body; incorporeal.

bod·i·ly (bod/ə·lē) *adj.* **1.** Of or pertaining to the body. **2.** Physical, as opposed to mental: *bodily* illness. — *adv.* **1.** In the flesh; in person. **2.** All together; completely.

bod·kin (bod/kin) *n.* **1.** A pointed instrument for piercing holes in cloth, etc. **2.** A blunt needle for drawing tape through a hem. **3.** A long pin for fastening the hair. [ME *boydekin* dagger; origin unknown]

bod·y (bod/ē) *n.* *pl.* **bod·ies** **1.** The entire physical part of a human being, animal, or plant. **2.** A corpse; carcass. **3.** The torso of a human being or animal; the trunk. **4.** The principal part or mass of anything. **5.** A collection of persons or things taken as a whole. **6.** A distinct mass or portion of matter: a *body* of clear water. **7.** Density or consistency; substance: a wine with *body.* **8.** That part of a garment that covers the body or the upper body. **9.** *Informal* A person. — *v.t.* **bod·ied, bod·y·ing** **1.** To furnish with or as with a body. **2.** To exhibit in bodily form; represent: usually with *forth.* [OE *bodig*]

bod·y·guard (bod/ē·gärd/) *n.* **1.** A guard responsible for the physical safety of an individual. **2.** A retinue; escort.

body politic The state or nation as an organized political entity; the people collectively.

body snatcher One who steals bodies from graves.

Boe·o·tia (bē·ō/shə, -shē·o) A state of ancient Greece; capital Thebes.

Boe·o·tian (bē·ō/shən) *adj.* **1.** Of or pertaining to Boeotia. **2.** Dull; clownish. — *n.* **1.** A native of Boeotia. **2.** A stupid, doltish person.

Boer (bôr, bōr, boor) *n.* A Dutch colonist, or person of Dutch descent, in South Africa. — *adj.* Of or pertaining to the Boers. [< Du., farmer]

bog (bog, bôg) *n.* Wet and spongy ground; marsh; morass. — *v.t. & v.i.* **bogged, bog·ging** To sink or be impeded in or as in a bog: often with *down.* [< Irish < *bog* soft] — **bog/gish** *adj.* — **bog/gish·ness** *n.*

bo·gey¹ (bō/gē) *n.* *pl.* **·geys** In golf: **a** An estimated standard score. **b** One stroke over par on a hole. Also **bo/gie.** [after Col *Bogey,* an imaginary faultless golfer]

bo·gey² (bō/gē) See BOGY.

bog·gle (bog′əl) v. **·gled, ·gling** v.i. 1. To hesitate, as from doubt or scruples; shrink back: often with at. 2. To start with fright, as a horse. 3. To equivocate; dissemble. 4. To work clumsily; fumble. — v.t. 5. To make a botch of; bungle. — n. 1. The act of boggling. 2. A scruple; objection. 3. Informal A botch. [< Scot. bogle a hobgoblin]

bog·gy (bog′ē, bôg′ē) adj. **·gi·er, ·gi·est** Swampy; miry.

bo·gie (bō′gē) See BOGY.

bo·gus (bō′gəs) adj. U.S. Counterfeit; spurious; fake.

bo·gy (bō′gē) n. pl. **·gies** A goblin; bugbear: also spelled bogey, bogie. [? Akin to BUG²] — **bo′gy·ism** n.

Bo·he·mi·an (bō·hē′mē·ən) adj. 1. Of or pertaining to Bohemia. 2. Leading the life of a Bohemian; unconventional. — n. 1. An inhabitant of Bohemia. 2. A gypsy. 3. A person, usu. of artistic or literary tastes, who lives in an unconventional manner. Also (for adj. def. 2, n. def. 3) bo·he′mi·an. 4. A former name for the Czech dialect of Czechoslovakian. — **Bo·he′mi·an·ism** n.

boil¹ (boil) v.i. 1. To be agitated by escaping gaseous bubbles, usu. from the effect of heat: said of liquids. 2. To reach the boiling point. 3. To undergo the action of a boiling liquid. 4. To be agitated like boiling water; seethe. 5. To be stirred by rage or passion. — v.t. 6. To bring to the boiling point. 7. To cook or cleanse by boiling. 8. To separate by means of evaporation caused by boiling. — to **boil away** To evaporate in boiling. — to **boil down** 1. To reduce in bulk by boiling. 2. To condense; summarize. — to **boil over** 1. To overflow while boiling. 2. To give vent to one's rage or passion. — n. The act or state of boiling. [< OE bullire to boil]

boil² (boil) n. Pathol. A painful purulent nodule of bacterial origin beneath the skin: also called furuncle. [OE bȳl]

boil·er (boil′ər) n. 1. A closed vessel containing a system of tubes, used for generating steam, as for heating or power. 2. A container in which something is boiled. 3. A tank for hot water.

boiling point The temperature at which a liquid boils; at normal atmospheric pressure the boiling point of water is 212° F. or 100° C.

bois·ter·ous (bois′ter·əs, -trəs) adj. 1. Noisy and unrestrained; uproarious. 2. Stormy; violent, as the weather. [ME boistous] — **bois′ter·ous·ly** adv. — **bois′ter·ous·ness** n.

bo·la (bō′lə) n. A throwing weapon, consisting of balls fastened to cords. Also **bo·las** (bō′ləs) [< Sp., a ball]

bold (bōld) adj. 1. Having courage; fearless. 2. Showing or requiring courage; daring. 3. Presuming unduly; brazen; forward. 4. Vigorous in conception or expression; unconventional. 5. Abrupt; steep, as a cliff. — **to make bold** To venture. [OE bald] — **bold′ly** adv. — **bold′ness** n.

bold·face (bōld′fās′) n. Printing A type in which the lines have been thickened to give a very black impression.

bole (bōl) n. The trunk of a tree. [< ON bolr]

bo·le·ro (bō·lâr′ō) n. pl. **·ros** 1. A short jacket open at the front. 2. A Spanish dance, usu. accompanied by castanets. 3. The music for this dance. [< Sp.]

bol·i·var (bol′ə·vər, -vär; Sp. bō·lē′vär) n. pl. **bol·i·vars**, Sp. **bo·li·va·res** (bō·lē·vä′rās) The monetary unit of Venezuela. [after Simón Bolívar]

bo·li·via·no (bō·lē′vyä′nō) n. pl. **·nos** (-nōs) The monetary unit of Bolivia.

boll (bōl) n. A round pod or seed capsule, as of flax or cotton. — v.i. To form pods.

bol·lix (bol′iks) v.t. **·lixed, ·lix·ing** Slang To bungle; botch: often with up. [Alter. of ballocks testicles]

boll weevil A beetle that destroys cotton bolls.

boll·worm (bōl′wûrm′) n. The very destructive larva of a dark brown moth that feeds on cotton bolls.

bo·lo (bō′lō) n. pl. **·los** (-lōz) A large, single-edged knife used by natives of the Philippines. [< Sp. < Visayan]

Bo·lo·gna sausage (bə·lō′nə, -lōn′yə, -lōn′ə) A highly seasoned sausage of mixed meats: also baloney, boloney.

bo·lo·ney (bə·lō′nē) See BALONEY.

Bol·she·vik (bōl′shə·vik, bol′-) n. pl. **Bol·she·viks** or **Bol·she·vi·ki** (bōl′shə·vē′kē, bol′-) 1. A member of the dominant branch of the Russian Social Democratic Party or, since 1918, of the Russian Communist Party. 2. A member of any Communist party. 3. Loosely, any radical. Also **bol′she·vik.** [< Russian bolshe the majority]

Bol·she·vism (bōl′shə·viz′əm, bol′-) n. The Marxian doctrines and policies of the Bolsheviks; also, any practice, government, etc., based on them. Also **bol′she·vism.**

Bol·she·vist (bōl′shə·vist, bol′-) n. A Bolshevik. Also **bol′she·vist.** — **Bol′she·vis′tic** adj.

bol·ster (bōl′stər) n. 1. A narrow pillow as long as a bed's width. 2. A pad used as a support or for protection. 3. Anything shaped like a bolster or used as a support. — v.t. To prop or reinforce, as something ready to fall: with up. [OE] — **bol′ster·er** n.

bolt¹ (bōlt) n. 1. A sliding bar or piece for fastening a door, etc. 2. A pin or rod for holding something in place, usu. having a head at one end, and threaded at the other. 3. The

part of a lock that is shot or withdrawn by turning the key. 4. A sliding mechanism that closes the breech of some small firearms. 5. An arrow, esp. for a crossbow. 6. A stroke of lightning; thunderbolt. 7. Anything that comes suddenly or unexpectedly: a bolt of bad luck. 8. A sudden start or spring: He made a bolt for the door. 9. U.S. A desertion of one's party, its candidate, etc. 10. A roll of cloth, wallpaper, etc. — **a bolt from the blue** 1. A thunderbolt on a clear day. 2. A sudden and wholly unexpected event. — **to shoot one's bolt** To do one's utmost. — v.i. 1. To move, go, or spring suddenly: He bolted from the room. 2. U.S. To break away, as from a political party; refuse to support party policy. — v.t. 3. To fasten or lock with or as with a bolt or bolts. 4. U.S. To break away from, as a political party. 5. To gulp, as food. 6. To arrange into bolts, as cloth. 7. To blurt out. — adv. Like an arrow; suddenly. — **bolt upright** Stiffly erect. [OE, arrow for a crossbow]

bolt² (bōlt) v.t. 1. To sift. 2. To examine as by sifting. [< OF bulter to sift] — **bolt′er** n.

bo·lus (bō′ləs) n. pl. **·lus·es** 1. A large pill. 2. Any rounded lump or mass. [< Med.L < Gk. bōlos a lump]

bomb (bom) n. 1. Mil. A hollow projectile containing explosive, incendiary, or chemical material to be discharged by concussion or by a time fuse. 2. Any sudden or unexpected event. 3. U.S. Slang A complete failure. — v.t. 1. To attack with or as with bombs. — v.i. 2. U.S. Slang To fail utterly. [< F < Sp. < L < Gk. bombos hollow noise]

bom·bard (v. bom·bärd′) v.t. 1. To attack with bombs or shells. 2. To attack as with bombs. [< MF < OF < L < Gk. bombos hollow noise] — **bom·bard′er** n. — **bom·bard′ment** n.

bom·bar·dier (bom′bər·dir′) n. 1. Mil. The member of the crew of a bomber who operates the bombsight and releases bombs. 2. Brit. & Canadian An artillery corporal. [< F]

bom·bast (bom′bast) n. Grandiloquent or pompous language. [< OF < LL bombax, -acis cotton]

bom·bas·tic (bom·bas′tik) adj. High-flown; grandiloquent. Also **bom·bas′ti·cal.** — **bom·bas′ti·cal·ly** adv.

bom·ba·zine (bom′bə·zēn′, bom′bə·zēn) n. A twilled fabric usu. with silk warp and worsted filling. Also **bom′ba·sine′.** [< F < LL bombax cotton]

bomb bay A compartment in military aircraft in which bombs are carried and from which they are dropped.

bombed (bombd) adj. U.S. Slang Drunk.

bomb·er (bom′ər) n. 1. An airplane designed to carry and drop bombs. 2. One who bombs.

bomb·shell (bom′shel′) n. 1. A bomb. 2. A surprise.

bomb·sight (bom′sīt′) n. Mil. An instrument on an aircraft that enables the bombardier to aim accurately.

bo·na fide (bō′nə·fīd′, -fī′dē) adj. Being, acting, or carried out in good faith; authentic; genuine. [< L]

bo·nan·za (bə·nan′zə) n. U.S. 1. A rich mine or find of ore. 2. A source of great wealth. [< Sp. < L bonus good]

bon·bon (bon′bon′, Fr. bôn·bôn′) n. A sugared candy. [< F < bon good]

bond (bond) n. 1. That which binds or holds together; a band; tie. 2. A uniting force or influence. 3. A voluntary obligation. 4. A substance that cements or unites; also, the union itself. 5. Law An obligation in writing under seal. 6. In finance, an interest-bearing certificate of debt, usu. issued by a government or corporation, obligating the issuer to pay the principal at a specified time. 7. In insurance, a policy covering losses suffered through the acts of an employee. 8. In commerce, the condition of goods stored in a bonded warehouse until duties are paid. 9. A bondsman; also, bail; surety. 10. Chem. A unit of combining power between the atoms of a molecule. — **Syn.** See SECURITY. — **bottled in bond** U.S. Bottled under government supervision and stored in a warehouse for a stated period, as certain whiskies. — v.t. 1. To put a certified debt upon; mortgage. 2. To furnish bond for; be surety for (someone). 3. To place, as goods or an employee, under bond. 4. To unite, as with glue, etc. 5. To lay (bricks, etc.) in interlocking patterns for strength. — v.i. 6. To interlock or cohere. — adj. In bondage; enslaved. [Var. of BAND¹] — **bond′er** n.

bond·age (bon′dij) n. 1. Involuntary servitude; slavery; serfdom. 2. Subjection to any influence or domination. [< Med.L < OE < ON bōnde peasant]

bond·ed (bon′did) adj. 1. Secured or pledged by a bond or bonds. 2. Stored in a warehouse; placed in bond.

bond·hold·er (bond′hōl′dər) n. One owning or holding bonds. — **bond′hold′ing** adj. & n.

bond·man (bond′mən) n. pl. **·men** (-mən) 1. A slave or serf. 2. A man bound to serve without wages. — **bond′maid, bond′wom′an, bonds′wom′an** n. fem.

bond paper A strong grade of paper, used for documents.

bond·ser·vant (bond′sûr′vənt) n. 1. A person bound to serve without wages. 2. A slave; serf: also **bond′slave′.**

bonds·man (bondz′mən) n. pl. **·men** (-mən) 1. One who provides bond for another. 2. A bondman.

bone (bōn) n. 1. Anat. a A hard, dense porous material

forming the skeleton of vertebrate animals. **b** A piece of this material. ◆ Collateral adjectives: *osseous, osteal*. **2.** *pl.* The skeleton as a whole. **3.** A substance resembling bone. **4.** Something made of bone or similar material. **5.** *pl. Informal* Dice. **6.** A strip of whalebone. **— to feel in (one's) bones** To be sure of; have an intuition of. **— to have a bone to pick** To have grounds for complaint or dispute. **— to make no bones about** To be direct or straightforward about or with. **—** *v.* **boned, bon·ing** *v.t.* **1.** To remove the bones from. **2.** To stiffen with whalebone. **—** *v.i.* **3.** *Slang* To study intensely and quickly: often with *up*. [OE *bān*]

bone·black (bōn′blak′) *n.* A black pigment made by calcining bones in airtight containers. Also **bone black**.

bone·head (bōn′hed′) *n. Informal* A stupid person.

bone meal Pulverized bone, used as feed and fertilizer.

bone of contention A cause or subject of disagreement.

bon·er (bō′nər) *n. Slang* An error; blunder.

bone·set (bōn′set′) *n.* A composite herb, formerly used in medicine as a tonic.

bon·fire (bon′fīr′) *n.* **1.** A large fire built in the open air. **2.** Formerly, a fire for burning corpses. [< BONE + FIRE]

bon·go drums (bong′gō) A pair of connected drums played with the hands, originally from Africa. Also **bon′gos**.

bon·ho·mie (bon′ə-mē′, *Fr.* bô-nô-mē′) *n.* Good nature; genial disposition. Also **bon′hom·mie′**. [< F]

bo·ni·to (bə-nē′tō) *n. pl.* **·to** or **·toes** A large mackerellike marine food fish: also called *skipjack*. [< Sp.]

bon jour (bôn zhoor′) *French* Good day; good morning.

bon mot (bôn mō′) *pl.* **bons mots** (bôn mōz′, *Fr.* mō′) A clever saying; terse witticism. [< F]

bon·net (bon′it) *n.* **1.** An outdoor headdress for women or children, typically held in place by ribbons tied under the chin. **2.** *Chiefly Scot.* A cap for men and boys. **3.** An American Indian headdress of feathers. **—** *v.t.* To cover with a bonnet. [< OF < Med.L *bonetus*]

bon·ny (bon′ē) *adj.* **·ni·er, ·ni·est 1.** Having beauty; comely. **2.** Fine; good. **3.** Robust; healthy. Also **bon′nie**. [< F *bon* good] **— bon′ni·ly** *adv.* **— bon′ni·ness** *n.*

bon·sai (bon′sī′) *n. pl.* **·sai 1.** A dwarfed tree or shrub trained, as by pruning, into a pleasing design. **2.** The art of creating such trees or shrubs. [< Japanese]

bon soir (bôn swàr′) *French* Good evening; good night.

bo·nus (bō′nəs) *n. pl.* **bo·nus·es** Something paid or given in addition to a usual or stipulated amount. [< L, good]

bon vi·vant (bôn vē-vän′) *pl.* **bons vi·vants** (bôn vē-vän′) *French* One who enjoys luxurious living; an epicure.

bon vo·yage (bôn vwä-yäzh′) *French* Pleasant trip.

bon·y (bō′nē) *adj.* **bon·i·er, bon·i·est 1.** Of, like, pertaining to, or consisting of bone or bones. **2.** Having prominent bones; thin; gaunt. **— bon·i·ness** *n.*

boo (boo) *n. & interj.* A vocal sound made to indicate contempt or to frighten. **—** *v.* **booed, boo·ing** *v.i.* **1.** To utter "boo." **—** *v.t.* **2.** To shout "boo" at. [Imit.]

boob (boob) *n. Slang* A simpleton; booby.

boo-boo (boo′boo′) *n. pl.* **·boos** *Slang* An embarrassing error; blunder. Also **boo′-boo′**. [Origin uncertain]

boo·by (boo′bē) *n. pl.* **·bies 1.** A stupid person; dunce. **2.** In some games, the person who makes the poorest score. **3.** Any of several gannets of tropical America. [< Sp. *bobo* fool]

booby hatch 1. *Naut.* A raised hood over a small hatchway. **2.** *U.S. Slang* A hospital for the mentally ill.

booby prize A mock award for a worst score or performance.

booby trap 1. A concealed bomb, mine, etc., placed so as to be detonated by casual or careless movements of the victim. **2.** Any device for taking someone unawares.

boo·dle (boo′dl) *U.S. Slang n.* **1.** Bribery money; graft. **2.** Loot; plunder. **3.** A mob. **—** *v.i.* **·dled, ·dling** To receive money corruptly. [Cf. Du. *boedel* property]

boog·ie-woog·ie (boog′ē-woog′ē) *n.* A style of jazz piano playing marked by repetition of bass rhythms and melodic variations in the treble. [Origin uncertain]

boo·hoo (boo′hoo′) *v.i.* **·hooed, ·hoo·ing** To weep loudly. **—** *n. pl.* **·hoos** Noisy sobbing. [Imit.]

book (book) *n.* **1.** A bound set of printed sheets of paper, usually between covers. **2.** A literary composition of some length, written or printed. **3.** A ledger, register, etc. **4.** A main division of a literary composition: a *book* of the Bible. **5.** A libretto. **6.** The script of a play. **7.** A booklike packet, as of matches. **8.** Something regarded as a source of instruction: the *book* of experience. **9.** A record of bets, especially on a horse race. **10.** A specific number of tricks or cards won. **— by the book** According to rule. **— like a book** Thoroughly. **— on the books 1.** Recorded. **2.** Enrolled. **— to make book** *U.S. Slang* To bet or accept bets. **—** *v.t.* **1.** To enter or list in a book. **2.** To arrange for beforehand, as accommodations or seats. **3.** To engage, as actors for a play, for performance. **4.** To make a record of charges against (someone) on a police blotter. [OE]

book·bind·er (book′bīn′dər) *n.* One whose trade is the binding of books. **— book′bind′er·y** *n.* **— book′bind′ing** *n.*

book·case (book′kās′) *n.* A case with shelves for books.

book club 1. An organization that sells books at reduced rates to members who agree to buy a certain number. **2.** A club given over to the reading and discussion of books.

book end A support or prop used to hold books upright.

book·ie (book′ē) *n. Informal* A bookmaker (def. 2).

book·ing (book′ing) *n.* An engagement to perform, etc.

book·ish (book′ish) *adj.* **1.** Fond of books; studious. **2.** Knowing only what has been read in books; pedantic. **3.** Of books. **— book′ish·ly** *adv.* **— book′ish·ness** *n.*

book jacket A dust jacket.

book·keep·ing (book′kē′ping) *n.* The practice of recording business transactions systematically. **— book′keep′er** *n.*

book learning Knowledge obtained from books rather than from experience. **— book-learn·ed** (book′lûr′nid) *adj.*

book·let (book′lit) *n.* A small book or pamphlet.

book·mak·er (book′mā′kər) *n.* **1.** One who compiles, prints, or binds books. **2.** One who makes a business of accepting bets, as in horse racing.

book·mark (book′märk′) *n.* **1.** Any object, as a ribbon, inserted in a book to mark a place. **2.** A bookplate.

book·mo·bile (book′mə·bēl′) *n.* A motor truck equipped to serve as a traveling library.

Book of Common Prayer The book of ritual used in the Anglican church.

book·rack (book′rak′) *n.* **1.** A frame to hold an open book. Also **book′rest′**. **2.** A rack to hold books.

book review An article or essay discussing or critically examining a book, esp. a recently published book.

book·sell·er (book′sel′ər) *n.* One who sells books.

book·stack (book′stak′) *n.* A tall rack containing shelves for books, as in a library.

book·stall (book′stôl′) *n.* **1.** A stall or stand where books are sold. **2.** *Brit.* A newsstand.

book·store (book′stôr′, -stōr′) *n.* A store where books are sold. Also **book′shop′**.

book·worm (book′wûrm′) *n.* **1.** One excessively devoted to books and study. **2.** Any insect destructive to books.

boom[1] (boom) *v.i.* **1.** To emit a deep, resonant sound. **2.** *U.S.* To grow rapidly; flourish. **—** *v.t.* **3.** To utter or sound in a deep resonant tone: often with *out*. **4.** *U.S.* To praise or advertise vigorously. **5.** *U.S.* To cause to flourish. **—** *n.* **1.** A deep, reverberating sound, as of a supersonic aircraft, of waves, etc. **2.** *U.S.* A sudden increase, as in growth; spurt. **—** *adj. U.S.* Caused or maintained by a boom: *boom* prices. [Imit.]

boom[2] (boom) *n.* **1.** *Naut.* A long spar or pole used to hold or extend the bottom of certain sails. **2.** A long pole or beam extending upward at an angle from the foot of the mast of a derrick, and from which are suspended the objects to be lifted. **3.** *U.S.* A floating chain of connected logs used to enclose other floating logs, to retard the advance of a vessel, etc. **—** *v.t.* **1.** To extend (a sail) by means of a boom: with *out*. **2.** To shove off or away, as a vessel from a wharf: with *off*. [< Du. *boom* tree, beam]

BOOM[2]
(def. 2)

boom·e·rang (boo′mə·rang) *n.* **1.** A curved, wooden missile originated in Australia, one form of which will return to the thrower. **2.** A plan, statement, etc., that recoils upon the originator. **—** *v.i.* To react harmfully on the originator. [< native Australian name]

boom town A town showing sudden development or prosperity, as from a discovery of gold.

boon[1] (boon) *n.* **1.** A good thing bestowed; blessing. **2.** *Archaic* A request. [< ON *bōn* petition]

boon[2] (boon) *adj.* Convivial; merry: now only in the phrase **boon companion**. [< F < L *bonus* good]

boon·docks (boon′doks′) *n.pl. U.S. Slang* An uncivilized or backwoods area: with *the*. [< Tagalog *bundok* mountain]

boon·dog·gle (boon′dog′əl, -dôg′əl) *U.S. Informal v.i.* **·gled, ·gling** To work on wasteful or unnecessary projects. **—** *n.* Unnecessary work. [Origin uncertain] **— boon′dog′gler** *n.*

boor (boor) *n.* An awkward, rude, or ill-mannered person. [< Du. *boer* farmer, rustic] **— boor′ish** *adj.* **— boor′ish·ly** *adv.* **— boor′ish·ness** *n.*

boost (boost) *U.S. v.t.* **1.** To raise by pushing from beneath or behind. **2.** To increase: to *boost* prices. **3.** To advance by speaking well of; promote or extol vigorously. **—** *n.* **1.** A lift; help. **2.** An increase. [Origin uncertain]

boost·er (boos′tər) *U.S. n.* **1.** Any device or substance for increasing power. **2.** *Informal* One who gives enthusiastic support to a person, cause, etc.

boot[1] (boot) *n.* **1.** A covering, usu. of leather, for the foot and part or most of the leg. **2.** A flap on an open vehicle for shielding the driver against rain or mud. **3.** A thick patch for the inside of a tire casing. **4.** A kick. **5.** In U.S. Navy and Marine Corps slang, a recent recruit. **— too big for one's boots** U.S. Proud; conceited. **— the boot** Slang Dismissal; discharge. **— to die with one's boots on** To die fighting or working. **— v.t. 1.** To put boots on. **2.** To kick or to punt. **3.** Slang To dismiss; fire. [< OF bote]

boot² (boot) Obs. n. Advantage. **— to boot** In addition; over and above. [ME < OE bōt profit]

boot·black (boot′blak′) n. One whose business is shining boots and shoes.

boo·tee (boo·tē′, boo′tē) n. **1.** A baby's knitted woolen boot. **2.** A light half boot for women. Also **boo·tie** (boo′tē).

Bo·ö·tes (bō·ō′tēz) n. A constellation, the Bear Keeper: also called Herdsman. [< L < Gk. boōtēs plowman]

booth (booth, booth) n. **1.** A small compartment or cubicle for privacy or for keeping out sound, etc. **2.** A seating compartment, as in a restaurant. **3.** A small stall for the display or sale of goods. [ME bothe < Scand.]

boot·jack (boot′jak′) n. A forked device for holding a boot while the foot is withdrawn.

boot·leg (boot′leg′) U.S. v.t. & v.i. **·legged, ·leg·ging** To make, sell, or carry for sale (liquor, etc.) illegally; smuggle. **— adj.** Unlawful: bootleg whisky. **— n. 1.** The part of a boot above the instep. **2.** Bootleg liquor or other merchandise. [With ref. to the smuggling of liquor in bootlegs] **— boot′leg′ger** n. **— boot′leg′ging** n.

boot·less (boot′lis) adj. Profitless; useless; unavailing. **— boot′less·ly** adv. **— boot′less·ness** n.

boot·lick (boot′lik′) U.S. Slang v.t. & v.i. To flatter servilely; toady. **— boot′lick′er** n. **— boot′lick′ing** n. & adj.

boo·ty (boo′tē) n. pl. **·ties 1.** The spoil of war; plunder. **2.** Goods taken by violence. **3.** Any prize or gain. [< F butin < MLG; infl. by obs. boot advantage]

booze (booz) Informal n. **1.** Alcoholic drink. **2.** A drunken spree. **— v.i. boozed, booz·ing** To drink to excess; tipple. [< MDu. busen to drink, tipple] **— booz′er** n.

booz·y (boo′zē) adj. Informal Drunken; alcoholic. **— booz′i·ly** adv. **— booz′i·ness** n.

bop¹ (bop) v.t. **bopped, bop·ping** Slang To hit. [Imit.]

bop² (bop) n. A variety of jazz.

bo·rac·ic (bə·ras′ik) adj. Chem. Boric.

bor·age (bûr′ij, bôr′-, bor′-) n. A European herb having blue flowers and hairy leaves, used medicinally and in salads. [< Med.L borra, burra rough hair]

bo·rate (bôr′āt, bō′rāt) n. Chem. A salt of boric acid. **— bo′rat·ed** adj.

bo·rax (bôr′aks, bō′raks) n. A white crystalline compound, $Na_2B_4O_7 \cdot 10H_2O$, found native and used in medicine, industry, etc. [< OF < Med.L < Arabic < Persian būrah]

bo·ra·zon (bôr′ə·zon, bō′rə-) n. Chem. A crystalline compound of boron and nitrogen, BN, equaling the diamond in hardness but with a much higher melting point.

Bor·deaux (bôr·dō′) n. A white or red wine produced in the vicinity of Bordeaux, France. Red Bordeaux is called claret.

bor·der (bôr′dər) n. **1.** A margin or edge. **2.** The frontier line or district of a country or state; boundary. **3.** A design or stripe in the margins of a page of a book, etc. **4.** A decorative edging or margin. **— adj.** Of, on, or forming the border. **— v.t. 1.** To put a border or edging on. **2.** To lie along the border of; bound. **— to border on** (or **upon**) **1.** To lie adjacent to. **2.** To approach; verge on: That act borders on piracy. [< OF < bord edge] **— bor′der·er** n.

bor·der·land (bôr′dər·land′) n. **1.** Land on or near the border of two adjoining countries. **2.** Debatable or indeterminate ground: the borderland between love and hate.

bor·der·line (bôr′dər·līn′) n. A line of demarcation. Also **border line. — adj.** Difficult to classify; doubtful.

bore¹ (bôr, bōr) v. **bored, bor·ing 1.** To make a hole in or through, as with a drill. **2.** To make (a tunnel, etc.) by or as by drilling. **3.** To force (one's way). **4.** To weary by being dull, long-winded, etc.; tire. **— v.i. 5.** To make a hole, etc., by or as by drilling. **6.** To force one's way. **— n. 1.** A hole made by or as if by boring. **2.** The interior diameter of a firearm or cylinder; caliber. **3.** One who or that which is tiresome. [OE bor auger]

bore² (bôr, bōr) n. A high, crested wave caused by the rush of a flood tide, as in the Amazon. [< ON bāra billow]

bore³ (bôr, bōr) Past tense of BEAR¹.

bo·re·al (bôr′ē·əl, bō′rē-) adj. Of the north or the north wind. [< LL < L Boreas, the north wind]

Bo·re·as (bôr′ē·əs, bō′rē-) In Greek mythology, the god of the north wind. [< L < Gk.]

bore·dom (bôr′dəm, bōr′-) n. The condition of being bored.

bor·er (bôr′ər, bō′rər) n. **1.** A tool used for boring. **2.** A beetle, moth, or worm that burrows in plants, wood, etc.

bo·ric (bôr′ik, bō′rik) adj. Chem. Of, pertaining to, or derived from boron: also boracic.

boric acid Chem. A white crystalline compound, H_3BO_3, used as a preservative and as a mild antiseptic.

born (bôrn) adj. **1.** Brought forth, as offspring. **2.** Natural; by birth: a born musician. [OE beran to bear]

borne (bôrn, bōrn) Past participle of BEAR¹.

bo·ron (bôr′on, bō′ron) n. A nonmetallic element (symbol B) found only in combination. See ELEMENT.

bor·ough (bûr′ō, -ə) n. **1.** An incorporated village or town. **2.** One of the five administrative divisions of New York, N.Y. **3.** Brit. **a** A town with a municipal corporation and certain privileges granted by royal charter: also **municipal borough. b** A town entitled to representation in Parliament: also **parliamentary borough.** [OE burg, burh fort, town]

bor·row (bôr′ō, bor′ō) v.t. **1.** To take or obtain (something) with the promise or understanding that one will return it. **2.** To adopt for one's own use, as ideas. **3.** In arithmetical subtraction, to withdraw (a unit of ten) from any figure of the minuend in order to add it to the next lower denomination. **— v.i. 4.** To borrow something. [OE borg pledge] **— bor′row·er** n.

borscht (bôrsht) n. A Russian beet soup, eaten hot or cold. Also **borsch** (bôrsh). [< Russian borshch]

bort (bôrt) n. An impure diamond, used only for cutting and polishing. Also **bortz** (bôrts). [? < OF bort bastard]

bor·zoi (bôr′zoi) n. A breed of Russian hounds, resembling the greyhound but larger, and having a long, silky coat: also called Russian wolfhound. [< Russian, swift]

bosh (bosh) n. Informal Empty words; nonsense. [< Turkish, empty, worthless]

bo's'n (bō′sən) See BOATSWAIN.

Bos·ni·an (boz′nē·ən) adj. Of or pertaining to Bosnia. Also **Bos·ni·ac** (boz′nē·ak). **— n. 1.** A native or inhabitant of Bosnia. **2.** The Serbo-Croatian language of the Bosnians.

bos·om (booz′əm, boo′zəm) n. **1.** The breast of a human being, esp. of a woman. **2.** The breast as the seat of thought and emotion. **3.** Something suggesting the human breast. **4.** Inner circle; midst: in the bosom of the church. **— adj. 1.** Close; intimate: a bosom friend. **2.** Of or pertaining to the bosom. **— v.t. 1.** To have or cherish in the bosom; embrace. **2.** To hide; conceal. [OE bōsm]

boss¹ (bôs, bos) U.S. Informal n. **1.** A superintendent or employer of workmen. **2.** A professional politician who controls a political organization. **— v.t. 1.** To supervise; direct. **2.** To order in a highhanded manner. **— v.i. 3.** To act as boss. **— adj.** Head; chief. [< Du. baas master]

boss² (bôs, bos) n. **1.** A circular prominence; a knob or projecting ornament. **2.** Mech. An enlarged part of a shaft, coupling with a wheel or another shaft. **— v.t. 1.** To ornament with bosses. **2.** To emboss. [< OF boce bump, knob]

boss·ism (bôs′iz·əm, bos′-) n. U.S. Control by political bosses.

boss·y¹ (bôs′ē, bos′ē) adj. **boss·i·er, boss·i·est** U.S. Informal Tending to boss; domineering.

boss·y² (bôs′ē, bos′ē) n. U.S. Informal A cow or a calf.

Boston terrier A small terrier having a short, smooth, brindled coat with white markings. Also **Boston bull.**

bo·sun (bō′sən) See BOATSWAIN.

bot (bot) n. The larva of a botfly: also spelled **bott.** [Origin unknown]

bo·tan·i·cal (bə·tan′i·kəl) adj. Of or pertaining to botany or to plants. Also **bo·tan′ic. — n.** A drug derived from the leaves, roots, stems, etc., of a plant. [< F < Gk. botanē plant, pasture] **— bo·tan′i·cal·ly** adv. **— bot′a·nist** n.

bot·a·nize (bot′ə·nīz) v. **·nized, ·niz·ing 1.** To study botanical specimens. **2.** To gather plants for study. **— v.t. 3.** To search for botanical specimens. **— bot′a·niz′er** n.

bot·a·ny (bot′ə·nē) n. **1.** The division of biology that treats of plants, their structure, functions, classification, etc. **2.** The total plant life of a region, country, etc. **3.** The characteristics of a group of plants treated collectively.

botch (boch) v.t. **1.** To bungle. **2.** To patch or mend clumsily. **— n. 1.** A bungled piece of work. **2.** A clumsy patch. [ME bocchen; origin unknown] **— botch′er** n. **— botch′er·y** n. **— botch′i·ly** adv. **— botch′y** adj.

bot·fly (bot′flī′) n. A fly of which the larvae are parasitic in vertebrates; esp., the horse botfly.

both (bōth) adj. & pron. The two together: Both girls laughed. **— conj. & adv.** Equally; alike; as well: with and. [< ON bādhar]

both·er (both′ər) v.t. **1.** To pester; give trouble to. **2.** To confuse; fluster. **— v.i. 3.** To trouble or concern oneself. **— n. 1.** A source or state of annoyance; vexation; trouble. **2.** One who or that which bothers. [? dial. E (Irish)]

both·er·some (both′ər·səm) adj. Causing bother.

bott (bot) See BOT.

bot·tle (bot′l) n. **1.** A vessel, usu. of glass, for holding liquids, having a neck and a narrow mouth that can be stopped. **2.** As much as a bottle will hold: also **bot′tle·ful′. — to hit the bottle** U.S. Slang To drink liquor to excess. **— v.t. ·tled, ·tling 1.** To put into a bottle or bottles. **2.** To restrain: often with up or in. [< LL buticula flask] **— bot′tler** n.

bottle green A dark, dull green.

bot·tle·neck (bot′l·nek′) n. **1.** A narrow or congested passageway. **2.** Anything that retards progress; hindrance.

bot·tle·nose (bot′l·nōz′) n. A variety of dolphin.

bottom   73   bowline

bot·tom (bot′əm) *n.* **1.** The lowest part of anything. **2.** The underside or undersurface. **3.** The ground beneath a body of water. **4.** Source or foundation. **5.** *Often pl.* Bottom land. **6.** *Naut.* The part of a vessel below the water line. **7.** *Informal* The buttocks. **8.** The seat of a chair. **9.** Staying power; stamina. **— at bottom** Fundamentally. **— bottoms up!** *Informal* Empty your glass! *— adj.* Lowest; fundamental; basal. *— v.t.* **1.** To provide with a bottom. **2.** To base or found: with *on* or *upon.* **3.** To fathom; comprehend. *— v.i.* **4.** To be founded; rest. **5.** To touch or rest on the bottom. [OE]
bottom land Lowland along a river.
bot·tom·less (bot′əm·lis) *adj.* **1.** Having no bottom. **2.** Unfathomable; limitless; endless. **— the bottomless pit** Hell.
bot·tom·ry (bot′əm·rē) *n.* A contract whereby the owner of a vessel borrows money, pledging the vessel as security.
bot·u·lism (boch′oŏ·liz′əm) *n.* Poisoning caused by a toxin produced by a bacillus sometimes present in improperly preserved food. [< G < L *botulus* sausage]
bou·clé (boō·klā′) *n.* A woven or knitted fabric with a looped or knotted surface; also, the yarn from which this is made. [< F, pp. of *boucler* to buckle, curl]
bou·doir (boō′dwär, boō·dwär′) *n.* A lady's private sitting room or bedroom. [< F, lit., pouting room]
bouf·fant (boō·fänt′) *adj.* Puffed-out; flaring, as a skirt. [< F, ppr. of *bouffer* to swell]
bough (bou) *n.* A large branch of a tree. [OE *bōg* shoulder.]
bought (bôt) Past tense and past participle of BUY.
bouil·la·baisse (boōl′yə·bās′, *Fr.* boō·yà·bes′) *n.* A chowder made of several varieties of fish. [< F < Provençal < *boui* boil + *abaisso* to settle, go down]
bouil·lon (boōl′yon, -yən; *Fr.* boō·yôn′) *n.* Clear soup from beef or other meats. [< F < *bouillir* to boil]
boul·der (bōl′dər) *n.* A large, rounded rock that has been detached: also spelled *bowlder.* [ME *bulderston*]
boul·e·vard (boōl′ə·värd, boō′lə-) *n.* **1.** A broad avenue, often lined with trees. **2.** *Chiefly Canadian* The grass between sidewalk and street; also, the center strip of a divided highway. *Abbr. blvd.* [< F < G *bollwerk* fortification]
bounce (bouns) *v.* **bounced, bounc·ing** *v.i.* **1.** To move with a bound or bounds, as a ball; rebound. **2.** To move suddenly and violently; spring. **3.** *U.S. Slang* To be returned by a bank as worthless: said of a check. *— v.t.* **4.** To cause to bounce. **5.** *Slang* To eject (a person) forcibly; also, to discharge from employment. *— n.* **1.** A bound or rebound. **2.** A sudden spring or leap. **3.** Ability or capacity to bounce or spring. **4.** *Informal* Vivacity; verve; spirit. [ME *bunsen* to thump < MLG] **— bounc′y** *adj.*
bounc·er (boun′sər) *n.* *U.S. Slang* One employed in a bar, night club, etc., to eject disorderly persons.
bounc·ing (boun′sing) *adj.* Strong and active; strapping.
bound¹ (bound) *v.i.* **1.** To strike and spring back from a surface, as a ball. **2.** To leap; move by a series of leaps. *— v.t.* **3.** To cause to bound. *— n.* A leap or spring; also, a rebound. [< MF *bondir* to resound, rebound]
bound² (bound) *n.* **1.** *Usu. pl.* A boundary; limit: out of *bounds.* **2.** *pl.* The area near or within a boundary. *— v.t.* **1.** To set limits to; restrict. **2.** To form the boundary of. **3.** To name the boundaries of. *— v.i.* **4.** To adjoin; abut. [< OE < LL *bodina* limit.]
bound³ (bound) Past tense and past participle of BIND. *adj.* **1.** Made fast; tied with bonds. **2.** Having a cover or binding. **3.** Morally or legally obligated. **4.** Certain; sure: It's *bound* to rain. **5.** *U.S. Informal* Determined; resolved. **— bound up in** (or **with**) **1.** Inseparably connected with. **2.** Devotedly attached to.
bound⁴ (bound) *adj.* Having one's course directed; on the way: *bound* for home. [< ON < *būa* to prepare]
bound·a·ry (boun′də·rē, -drē) *n. pl.* **·ries** Anything indicating a limit or confine.
bound·en (boun′dən) *adj.* **1.** Obligatory: our *bounden* duty. **2.** Under obligations; obliged.
bound·er (boun′dər) *n. Chiefly Brit. Informal* An offensive, ill-mannered person; a cad.
bound·less (bound′lis) *adj.* Having no limit; vast. **— bound′less·ly** *adv.* **— bound′less·ness** *n.*
boun·te·ous (boun′tē·əs) *adj.* **1.** Generous; beneficent. **2.** Marked by abundance; plentiful. [ME < OF < *bonté* goodness] **— boun′te·ous·ly** *adv.* **— boun′te·ous·ness** *n.*
boun·ti·ful (boun′tə·fəl) *adj.* **1.** Free and generous in bestowing gifts. **2.** Showing abundance; plentiful. **— boun′ti·ful·ly** *adv.* **— boun′ti·ful·ness** *n.*
boun·ty (boun′tē) *n. pl.* **·ties** **1.** Liberality in giving. **2.** Gifts or favors generously bestowed. **3.** A reward from a government, as for the killing of predatory animals, etc. [< OF < L *bonitas, -tatis* goodness]
bou·quet (bō·kā′, boō·kā′ *for def.1*; boō·kā′ *for def.* 2) *n.* **1.**

A bunch of flowers. **2.** Delicate odor; esp. the distinctive aroma of a wine. [< F < OF *boschet*]
bour·bon (bûr′bən) *n.* A whiskey distilled from a fermented mash containing at least 51 per cent corn. Also **bourbon whiskey.** [after *Bourbon* County, Ky., where first made]
Bour·bon (boōr′bən) *n.* **1.** A dynasty that reigned over France, 1589–1792, 1815–48, or a related branch that ruled Spain, 1700–1931. **2.** One who is stubbornly conservative in politics. **— Bour′bon·ism** *n.* **— Bour′bon·ist** *n.*
bour·geois¹ (boōr′zhwä, boōr·zhwä′) *n. pl.* **·geois 1.** A member of the middle class; a tradesman. **2.** *pl.* The middle class. **3.** In Marxism, a member of the class in conflict with the working class. *— adj.* Of or characteristic of the middle class: often used disparagingly. [< F < OF < LL < *burgus* town] **— bour·geoise** (boōr·zhwäz′) *n. & adj. fem.*
bour·geois² (bər·jois′) *n.* A size of type, about 9-point. [? after a French printer]
bour·geoi·sie (boōr′zhwä·zē′) *n.* **1.** The middle class of society, esp. in France. **2.** In Marxism, that social class opposed in the class struggle to the proletariat or working class.
bour·geon (bûr′jən) See BURGEON.
Bourse (boōrs) *n.* An exchange or money market; esp., the Paris stock exchange. [< F, purse < LL *bursa* bag]
bout (bout) *n.* **1.** A contest; trial. **2.** A fit or spell, as of drinking or illness. [Var. of ME *bought* bending, turn]
bou·tique (boō·tēk′) *n. French* A small retail shop.
bou·ton·niere (boō′tən·yâr′) *n.* A bouquet or flower worn in the buttonhole. Also **bou′ton·nière.** [< F]
bo·vine (bō′vīn, -vin) *adj.* **1.** Of or pertaining to oxen, cows, etc. **2.** Stolid; null. *— n.* A bovine animal. [< LL < L *bos, bovis* ox]
bow¹ (bou) *n.* **1.** *Naut.* The forward part of a ship, boat, etc. **2.** The forward oarsman of a boat. *— adj.* Of or at the bow. [< LG or Scand.]
bow² (bou) *v.* **bowed, bow·ing** *v.i.* **1.** To bend the body or head, as in salutation, worship, or assent. **2.** To bend or incline downward. **3.** To submit; yield. *— v.t.* **4.** To bend (the body, head, etc.) in reverence, courtesy, or submission. **5.** To express by bowing. **6.** To escort with bows. **7.** To cause to yield; subdue. **8.** To cause to bend or stoop. **— to bow out** To withdraw; resign. *— n.* An inclination of the body or head. [OE *būgan* to bend]
bow³ (bō) *n.* **1.** A weapon made from a strip of elastic wood or other pliable material, bent by a string and used to project an arrow. **2.** An archer. **3.** Something bent or curved; a bend. **4.** A knot with a loop or loops, as of ribbon, etc. **5.** *Music* **a** A rod with hairs stretched between raised ends, used for playing a violin or related stringed instrument. **b** A stroke with a bow. *— adj.* Bent; curved; bowed. *— v.t. & v.i.* **bowed, bow·ing 1.** To bend into the shape of a bow. **2.** *Music* To play (a stringed instrument) with a bow. **— Syn.** See BEND¹. [OE *boga*]
bowd·ler·ize (boud′lər·īz) *v.t.* **ized, ·iz·ing** To expurgate or edit prudishly. [after Dr. Thomas *Bowdler's* "family" edition of Shakespeare (1818)] **— bowd′ler·ism** *n.* **— bowd′·ler·i·za′tion** *n.*
bow·el (bou′əl, boul) *n.* **1.** An intestine. **2.** *pl.* The inner part of anything: the *bowels* of the earth. *— v.t.* **bow·eled** or **·elled, bow·el·ing** or **·el·ling** To disembowel. [< OF < L *botellus,* dim. of *botulus* sausage]
bow·er (bou′ər) *n.* A shaded recess. *— v.t.* To enclose in or as in a bower. [OE *būr* chamber] **— bow′er·y** *adj.*
Bow·er·y (bou′ər·ē) A street in New York City noted for its saloons, shabby hotels, etc.: often preceded by *the.*
bow·ie knife (bō′ē, boō′ē) A strong, single-edged hunting knife. [after James *Bowie,* 1799–1836, its reputed inventor]
bow·knot (bō′not′) *n.* An ornamental slipknot made with one or more loops. For illus. see KNOT.

BOWIE KNIFE

bowl¹ (bōl) *n.* **1.** A deep, round dish. **2.** The amount a bowl will hold. **3.** A large goblet. **4.** Convivial drinking. **5.** An amphitheater. **6.** Something shaped like a bowl: the *bowl* of a pipe. [OE *bolla*]
bowl² (bōl) *n.* **1.** A large ball for bowls or tenpins. **2.** A throw of the ball in bowling. *— v.i.* **1.** To play at bowls, tenpins, etc. **2.** To roll a ball or rounded object. **3.** To move smoothly and swiftly: usually with *along.* *— v.t.* **4.** To roll or throw, as a ball. **5.** To carry or transport on or as on wheels. **— to bowl over 1.** To cause to be confused or helpless. **2.** To knock down. [< F *boule* ball] **— bowl′er** *n.*
bowl·der (bōl′dər) See BOULDER.
bow·leg (bō′leg′) *n.* A leg with an outward curvature at or below the knee. **— bow·leg·ged** (bō′leg′id, -legd′) *adj.*
bowl·er (bō′lər) *n. Brit.* A derby. [< BOWL²]
bow·line (bō′lin, -līn′) *n.* **1.** A knot tied so as to form a loop. Also **bowline knot.** **2.** *Naut.* A rope to keep a sail taut when sailing close-hauled.

PRONUNCIATION KEY: add, āce, câre, pälm; end, ēven; it, īce; odd, ōpen, ôrder; toŏk, poōl; up, bûrn; ə = a in *above,* e in *sicken,* i in *flexible,* o in *melon,* u in *focus;* yoō = u in *fuse;* oil; pout; check; go; ring; thin; this; zh, vision. For å, œ, ü, kh, ṅ, see inside front cover.

bowl·ing (bō'ling) *n.* The game of bowls or of tenpins.

bowling alley A long, narrow space for playing tenpins, or the building containing it.

bowling green A smooth lawn for playing at bowls.

bowls (bōlz) *n.pl.* **1.** *Brit.* An outdoor game played by rolling slightly flattened or weighted balls at a stationary ball. **2.** Tenpins, ninepins, or skittles.

bow·man (bō'mən) *n. pl.* **·men** (-mən) An archer.

bow·shot (bō'shot') *n.* The distance to which an arrow may be sent from the bow.

bow·sprit (bou'sprit', bō'-) *n. Naut.* A spar projecting forward from the bow of a vessel. [? < M.Du. < *boeg* bow of a ship + *spriet* spear]

bow·string (bō'string') *n.* The string of a bow, which projects the arrow.

bow tie A necktie worn in a bowknot.

bow window (bō) A projecting, usually curved window built up from the ground level.

box¹ (boks) *n.* **1.** A receptacle or case of wood, metal, etc., in many sizes and shapes and usu. having a lid. **2.** The quantity contained in a box. **3.** Something resembling a box in form or use. **4.** A small booth for a sentry, watchman, etc. **5.** The raised driver's seat of a coach. **6.** A space partitioned off for seating, as in a theater, courtroom, stadium, etc. **7.** In baseball, any of several designated spaces, as for the pitcher, batter, coach, etc. **8.** *Mech.* An axle bearing, casing, or other enclosed cavity. **9.** An enclosed space on a page of a newspaper, magazine, etc. — *v.t.* **1.** To place in a box. **2.** To furnish with a bushing or box. — **to box in 1.** In racing, to block (another contestant) so that he is unable to get ahead. **2.** To box up. — **to box the compass 1.** To recite in order the 32 points of the compass. **2.** To make a complete revolution or turn. — **to box up** To confine in, or as in, a small space. [OE < Med.L < Gk. *pyxos* boxwood] — **box′er** *n.*

box² (boks) *v.t.* **1.** To strike or buffet with the hand; cuff. **2.** To fight (another) in a boxing match. — *v.i.* **3.** To fight with one's fists; be a boxer. — *n.* A blow on the ear or cheek; cuff. [ME]

box³ (boks) *n.* **1.** Any of a small family of evergreen herbs, shrubs, and trees, used as borders and hedges. **2.** The hard wood of these plants. [OE < L < Gk. *pyxos* boxwood]

box·car (boks'kär') *n.* A roofed, enclosed freight car.

box elder A North American tree of the maple family, having compound leaflets: also called *Manitoba maple.*

box·er¹ (bok'sər) *n.* One who fights with his fists; pugilist.

box·er² (bok'sər) *n.* A breed of dog, related to the bulldog, having a sturdy body, smooth fawn coat, and a black mask.

Box·er (bok'sər) *n.* A member of a Chinese secret society, active in 1900, that aimed to rid China of foreigners by force.

box·ing (bok'sing) *n.* The art or practice of fighting with the fists, esp. when gloved; pugilism.

boxing glove A padded mitten used for prizefighting.

box office 1. The ticket office of a theater, etc. **2.** *Informal* Receipts at the box office, as a measure of success.

box seat A seat in a box of a theater, stadium, etc.

box spring A mattress foundation consisting of an upholstered frame set with coil springs to provide resiliency.

box·wood (boks'wōōd') *n.* **1.** The hard, close-grained, durable wood of box. **2.** The shrub.

boy (boi) *n.* **1.** A male child; lad; youth. **2.** A man; fellow: a familiar use. **3.** A male servant. [ME *boi*] — **boy′ish** *adj.* — **boy′ish·ly** *adv.* — **boy′ish·ness** *n.*

boy·cott (boi'kot) *v.t.* **1.** To combine together in refusing to deal or associate with, so as to punish or coerce. **2.** To refuse to use or buy. — *n.* The act or practice of boycotting. [after Capt. C. *Boycott*, 1832–97, Irish landlord's agent, who was the first victim] — **boy′cott·er** *n.*

boy friend 1. *Informal* A preferred male companion or intimate friend of a girl or woman. **2.** A male friend.

boy·hood (boi'hōōd') *n.* **1.** The state or period of being a boy. **2.** Boys collectively.

boy scout A member of the **Boy Scouts,** an organization for boys, stressing self-reliance and good citizenship.

boy·sen·ber·ry (boi'zən·ber'ē) *n. pl.* **·ries** The edible fruit obtained by crossing the blackberry, raspberry, and loganberry. [after Rudolph *Boysen*, 20th c. U.S. horticulturist]

bra (brä) *n. U.S. Informal* A brassiere.

brace (brās) *v.* **braced, brac·ing** *v.t.* **1.** To make firm or steady; strengthen by or as by braces. **2.** To make ready to withstand pressure, impact, assault, etc. **3.** To increase the tension of; strain. **4.** To tie or fasten firmly, as with straps. **5.** To stimulate; enliven. — *v.i.* **6.** To strain against pressure. — **to brace up** *Informal* To rouse one's courage or resolution. — *n.* **1.** A support, as of wood or metal, used to strengthen something or hold it in place. **2.** A clasp or clamp for fastening, connecting, etc. **3.** A cranklike handle for holding and turning a bit or other boring tool. **4.** A pair; couple. **5.** *Printing* A doubly curved line, { or }, used to connect words, lines, staves of music, etc. **6.** *pl. Brit.* Suspenders. **7.** *Often pl. Dent.* A wire or wires fastened on ir-

regular teeth and gradually tightened to align them. **8.** *Med.* Any of various devices for supporting a joint, limb, or other part. [< OF < L *brachia*, pl. of *brachium* arm]

brace·let (brās'lit) *n.* **1.** An ornamental band worn around the wrist or arm. **2.** *Informal* A handcuff. [< OF, dim. of *bracel* < L *brachiale* bracelet]

brac·er (brā'sər) *n.* **1.** One who or that which braces or steadies. **2.** *U.S. Informal* A stimulating drink.

bra·chi·al (brā'kē·əl, brak'ē-) *adj.* Of or pertaining to the arm or to armlike appendages. [< L < *brachium* arm]

brachio- *combining form* Arm; of the arm: *brachiopod.* Also, before vowels, **brachi-.** [< Gk. *brachiōn* arm]

bra·chi·o·pod (brā'kē·ə·pod', brak'ē-) *n. Zool.* One of a phylum or class of marine animals having a bivalve shell and a pair of armlike parts on the sides of the mouth. [< NL]

bra·chi·um (brā'kē·əm, brak'ē-) *n. pl.* **bra·chi·a** (brā'kē·ə, brak'ē-) **1.** *Anat.* The arm, esp. that part above the elbow. **2.** Any armlike process or appendage. [< L]

brachy- *combining form* Short. [< Gk. *brachys* short]

brach·y·ce·phal·ic (brak'i·sə·fal'ik) *adj.* Having a short, broad skull; short-headed. Also **brach·y·ceph·a·lous** (brak'-i·sef'ə·ləs). [< NL < Gk. < *brachys* short + *kephalē* head] — **brach′y·ceph′a·lism, brach′y·ceph′a·ly** *n.*

brac·ing (brā'sing) *adj.* Strengthening; invigorating. — *n.* A brace or system of braces, as in bridge building.

brack·en (brak'ən) *n.* **1.** A coarse, hardy fern with very large fronds: also called **brake. 2.** A clump of such ferns. [ME *braken* < Scand.]

brack·et (brak'it) *n.* **1.** A piece of wood, metal, stone, etc., projecting from a wall, used to support a shelf or other weight. **2.** A brace used to strengthen an angle. **3.** A projecting wall fixture for a gaslight, electric lamp, etc. **4.** A classification according to income for tax purposes: the high-income *bracket.* **5.** *Printing* One of two marks [ ] used to enclose any part of a text. — *v.t.* **1.** To provide or support with a bracket or brackets. **2.** To enclose within brackets. **3.** To group or categorize together. [< Sp. < L *bracae*, pl., breeches]

brack·ish (brak'ish) *adj.* **1.** Somewhat saline; briny. **2.** Distasteful. [< Du. *brak* salty] — **brack′ish·ness** *n.*

bract (brakt) *n. Bot.* A modified leaf situated at the base of a flower. [< L *bractea* thin metal plate] — **brac·te·al** (brak'tē·əl) *adj.* — **brac·te·ate** (brak'tē·it, -āt) *adj.*

brad (brad) *n.* A small, slender nail with a small head. [< ON *broddr* spike]

brad·awl (brad'ôl') *n.* A short awl for making holes in wood, as for brads or screws.

brady- *combining form* Slow. [< Gk. *bradys* slow]

brae (brā) *n. Scot.* A bank; hillside; slope.

brag (brag) *v.* **bragged, brag·ging** *v.i.* **1.** To boast about oneself or one's deeds or abilities. — *v.t.* **2.** To declare or assert boastfully; boast of. — *n.* **1.** Boastful language; boasting. **2.** A boast. **3.** One who brags. [Origin uncertain] — **brag′ger** *n.*

brag·ga·do·ci·o (brag'ə·dō'shē·ō) *n. pl.* **·ci·os 1.** Pretentious boasting. **2.** One who boasts; a swaggerer. [after *Braggadochio*, a boastful character in Spenser's *Faerie Queene*]

brag·gart (brag'ərt) *n.* A bragger. — *adj.* Boastful. [< MF < *braguer* to brag] — **brag′gart·ism** *n.*

brah·ma (brä'mə, brā'-) *n. Often cap.* A large breed of domestic fowl developed in Asia. [after *Brahmaputra*]

Brah·ma (brä'mə) *n.* **1.** In Hindu religion, the supreme soul of the universe. **2.** God, comprising the Hindu trinity Brahma, Vishnu, and Siva; esp. the first of the trinity as supreme creator. [< Skt. *Brahmā*]

Brah·man (brä'mən) *n. pl.* **·mans 1.** A member of the highest Hindu caste, the sacerdotal caste: also spelled *Brahmin.* **2.** A breed of cattle originating in India. [< Skt. *brāhmana* < *brahman* praise, worship] — **Brah·man·i** (brä'mən·ē) *n.fem.* — **Brah·man·ic** (brä·man'ik) *adj.*

Brah·man·ism (brä'mən·iz'əm) *n.* The religious and social system of the Brahmans: also **Brah′min·ism** (brä'min-).

Brah·min (brä'min) *n.* **1.** A Brahman. **2.** A highly cultured or aristocratic person, esp. an ultraconservative or snobbish one.

braid (brād) *v.t.* **1.** To weave or intertwine several strands of hair, etc. **2.** To bind or ornament (the hair) with ribbons, etc. **3.** To form by braiding. **4.** To ornament (garments) with braid. — *n.* **1.** A narrow, flat tape or strip for binding or ornamenting fabrics. **2.** Any thing braided or plaited. **3.** A string or band used in arranging the hair. [OE *bregdan* to brandish, weave, braid] — **braid′er** *n.* — **braid′ing** *n.*

Braille (brāl) *n.* A system of printing or writing for the blind in which the characters consist of raised dots to be read by the fingers; also, the characters themselves. Also **braille.** [after Louis *Braille*, 1809–52, French educator, the inventor]

brain (brān) *n.* **1.** *Anat.* The enlarged and greatly modified part of the central nervous system contained in the cranium of vertebrates. **2.** *Often pl.* Mind; intellect. — **to have on**

BRACTS
(Around a composite flower)

the brain To be obsessed by. — *v.t.* 1. To dash out the brains of. 2. *Slang* To hit on the head. [OE *brægen*]

brain child *Informal* That which one has created or originated, as an idea, technique, device, etc.

brain·less (brān′lis) *adj.* Lacking intelligence; senseless; stupid. — **brain′less·ly** *adv.* — **brain′less·ness** *n.*

brain·pan (brān′pan′) *n.* The cranium; skull.

brain·sick (brān′sik′) *adj.* Affected with mental disorder.

brain·storm (brān′stôrm′) *n. Informal* A sudden inspiration. Also **brain storm.**

brain trust A group of experts who act as consultants on matters of policy, etc. — **brain truster**

brain·wash (brān′wosh, -wôsh′) *v.t.* To alter the convictions, beliefs, etc., of by means of intensive, coercive indoctrination. — **brain′wash′ing** *n.*

brain wave *Physiol.* A rhythmical fluctuation of electrical potential in the brain.

brain·y (brā′nē) *adj.* **brain·i·er, brain·i·est** *Informal* Intelligent; smart. — **brain′i·ly** *adv.* — **brain′i·ness** *n.*

braise (brāz) *v.t.* **braised, brais·ing** To cook (meat) by searing till brown and then simmering in a covered pan. [< F < *braise* charcoal]

brake[1] (brāk) *n.* 1. A device for slowing or stopping a vehicle or wheel, esp. by friction. 2. An instrument for separating the fiber of flax, hemp, etc., by bruising or crushing. — *v.* **braked, brak·ing** *v.t.* 1. To apply a brake to. 2. To bruise and crush, as flax. — *v.i.* 3. To operate a brake or brakes. [< MDu. *braeke* brake for flax] — **brake′age** *n.*

brake[2] (brāk) *n.* Bracken, a kind of fern. [ME]

brake[3] (brāk) *n.* An area covered with brushwood, briers, cane, etc.; thicket.

brake·man (brāk′mən) *n. pl.* **·men** (-mən) One who tends brakes on a railroad car or assists in operating a train.

brake shoe A rigid metal casting shaped to press against a wheel or brake when braking action is applied.

bram·ble (bram′bəl) *n.* 1. A plant of the rose family, esp. the blackberry of Europe. 2. Any prickly plant. Also **bram′ble-bush** (-boosh′). [OE *bræmble*] — **bram′bly** *adj.*

bran (bran) *n.* 1. The coarse, outer coat of cereals, as separated from the flour by sifting or bolting. 2. Grain by-products used as feed. [< OF *bran, bren*] — **bran′ny** *adj.*

branch (branch, bränch) *n.* 1. A woody outgrowth from the trunk of a tree or other large plant; limb. 2. A part analogous to a branch; an offshoot, as of a deer's antlers. 3. Any separate part or division of a system, subject, etc.; department. 4. A subordinate or local store, office, etc. 5. A division of a family, tribe, nation, etc., having or thought to have a common ancestor. 6. A tributary stream of a river. 7. Any small stream or brook. — *v.i.* 1. To put forth branches. 2. To separate into branches or subdivisions. — *v.t.* 3. To divide into branches. — **to branch off** 1. To separate into branches; fork, as a road. 2. To diverge; go off on a tangent. — **to branch out** To extend or expand, as one's business. [< OF < LL *branca* paw]

bran·chi·ae (brang′ki·ē) *n. pl.* of **bran·chi·a** (brang′kē·ə) *Zool.* Gills, the respiratory organs of fish. [< L < Gk. *branchia*, pl., gills] — **bran′chi·al** *adj.*

bran·chi·ate (brang′kē·it, -āt) *adj.* Having gills.

brand (brand) *n.* 1. A distinctive name or trademark identifying the product of a manufacturer. 2. The kind or make of a product: a good *brand* of coffee. 3. A mark made with a hot iron, as on cattle, to indicate ownership. 4. Formerly, a mark burned on criminals. 5. Any mark of disgrace; stigma. 6. A branding iron. 7. A burning piece of wood; also, a torch. — *v.t.* 1. To mark with a brand. 2. To stigmatize. [OE, torch, sword.] — **brand′er** *n.*

bran·died (bran′dēd) *adj.* Mixed, flavored with, or preserved in brandy: *brandied* cherries.

branding iron An iron for burning in a brand.

bran·dish (bran′dish) *v.t.* To wave or flourish triumphantly, menacingly, or defiantly. — *n.* A flourish, as with a weapon. [< OF *brandir*] — **bran′dish·er** *n.*

brand-new (brand′nōō′, -nyōō′, bran′-) *adj.* Very new; fresh and bright. Also **bran′-new′** (bran′-).

bran·dy (bran′dē) *n. pl.* **·dies** An alcoholic liquor distilled from wine or other fermented fruit juices. — *v.t.* **·died, ·dy·ing** To mix, flavor, strengthen, or preserve with brandy. [< Du. *brandewijn*, lit., distilled (burned) wine]

brant (brant) *n. pl.* **brants** or **brant** A small, black-necked wild goose of Europe and North America. Also **brant goose.**

brash[1] (brash) *adj. U.S.* 1. Acting hastily; rash; impetuous. 2. Impudent; saucy; pert. [Cf. G *barsch* harsh and Sw. *barsk* impetuous] — **brash′ly** *adv.* — **brash′ness** *n.*

brash[2] (brash) *n. Brit.* A shower of rain. [? Blend of *break* and *crash, dash*, etc.] — **brash′i·ness** *n.* — **brash′y** *adj.*

bra·sier (brā′zhər) See BRAZIER.

brass (bras, bräs) *n.* 1. An alloy essentially of copper and zinc, harder than copper, and both ductile and malleable.

2. Formerly, any alloy of copper, esp. one with tin. 3. *Usu. pl.* Ornaments or utensils of brass. 4. *Sometimes pl. Music* The brass instruments of an orchestra or band collectively: also *Rare* **brass winds.** 5. *Informal* Effrontery. 6. *U.S. Informal* High-ranking military officers; any high officials. — *adj.* Made of brass; brazen. [OE *bræs*]

bras·sard (bras′ärd, brə·särd′) *n.* 1. A band worn on the upper arm as a badge or insignia. 2. A piece of armor for the arm. Also **bras·sart** (bras′ərt). [< F < *bras* arm]

brass band *Music* A band using mostly brass instruments.

brass hat *Informal* A high-ranking military officer.

brass·ie (bras′ē, bräs′ē) *n.* A wooden golf club with a brass plate on the sole. Also **brass′y.**

bras·siere (brə·zir′) *n.* A woman's undergarment to support or shape the breasts. Also **bras·sière′.** [< F]

brass knuckles A metal device that fits over the knuckles of a closed fist, used in rough fighting: also called *knuckledusters.* Also **brass knucks** (nuks).

brass tacks *Informal* Basic facts; essentials: usu. in the phrase **to get** (or **come**) **down to brass tacks.**

brass·y (bras′ē, bräs′ē) *adj.* **brass·i·er, brass·i·est** 1. Of or ornamented with brass. 2. Like brass, as in sound or color. 3. Cheap and showy. 4. *Informal* Insolent; brazen. — **brass′i·ly** *adv.* — **brass′i·ness** *n.*

brat (brat) *n.* A nasty child.

bra·va·do (brə·vä′dō) *n. pl.* **·does** or **·dos** Boastful defiance; affectation of bravery. [< Sp. < *bravo* brave]

brave (brāv) *adj.* **brav·er, brav·est** 1. Having or showing courage; intrepid. 2. Making a fine display; elegant. — *v.* **braved, brav·ing** *v.t.* 1. To meet with courage and fortitude. 2. To defy; challenge. — *n.* 1. A man of courage. 2. A North American Indian warrior. [< F < Ital. *bravo*] — **brave′ly** *adv.* — **brave′ness** *n.*

brav·er·y (brā′vər·ē) *n. pl.* **·er·ies** 1. The quality of being brave; valor; heroism. 2. Elegance of attire; show; splendor.

bra·vo (brä′vō) *interj.* Good! well done! — *n. pl.* **·vos** A shout of "bravo!" [< Ital.]

bra·vu·ra (brə·vyŏor′ə, *Ital.* brä·vōō′rä) *n.* 1. *Music* A passage requiring dashing and brilliant execution; also, a brilliant style of execution. 2. Any brilliant or daring performance. [< Ital., dash, daring < *bravo*.]

brawl (brôl) *n.* 1. A noisy quarrel; fight. 2. *U.S. Slang* An uproarious party. — *v.i.* 1. To quarrel noisily; fight. 2. To move noisily, as water. [ME *braulen*, ? < LG] — **brawl′er** *n.* — **brawl′ing·ly** *adv.*

brawn (brôn) *n.* 1. Firm or well-developed muscles. 2. Muscular power. [< OF *braon* slice of flesh, ult. < Gmc.]

brawn·y (brô′nē) *adj.* **brawn·i·er, brawn·i·est** Muscular; strong. — **brawn′i·ness** *n.*

bray (brā) *v.i.* 1. To utter a loud, harsh cry, as an ass. 2. To sound harshly, as a trumpet. — *v.t.* 3. To utter loudly and harshly. — *n.* 1. The cry of an ass, mule, etc. 2. Any loud, harsh sound. [< OF *braire* to cry out] — **bray′er** *n.*

braze[1] (brāz) *v.t.* **brazed, braz·ing** 1. To make of brass. 2. To make like brass in hardness or appearance. 3. To ornament with or as with brass. [OE < *bræs* brass]

braze[2] (brāz) *v.t.* **brazed, braz·ing** *Metall.* To join the surfaces of (similar or dissimilar metals) with a layer of a soldering alloy applied under very high temperature. [< F *braser* solder < OF, burn, ult. < Gmc.] — **braz′er** *n.*

bra·zen (brā′zən) *adj.* 1. Made of brass. 2. Resembling brass in hardness, color, etc. 3. Impudent; shameless. — *v.t.* 1. To face with effrontery or impudence: with *out.* 2. To make bold or reckless. [OE < *bræs* brass] — **bra′zen·ly** *adv.* — **bra′zen·ness** *n.*

bra·zen·face (brā′zən·fās′) *n.* An impudent, shameless person. — **bra′zen·faced′** *adj.*

bra·zier[1] (brā′zhər) *n.* A worker in brass. [ME *brasiere*]

bra·zier[2] (brā′zhər) *n.* An open pan for holding live coals: also spelled *brasier.* [< F < *braise* hot coals]

Bra·zil·ian (brə·zil′yən) *adj.* Of or pertaining to Brazil or its people. — *n.* A citizen or native of Brazil.

Brazil nut The edible seed of a South American tree.

breach (brēch) *n.* 1. The act of breaking, or the state of being broken; infraction. 2. Violation of a legal obligation, promise, etc. 3. A gap or break in a dike, wall, etc. 4. A breaking up of friendly relations; estrangement. — *v.t.* To break through. [OE *bryce*]

bread (bred) *n.* 1. A food made with flour or meal, commonly leavened with yeast and baked. 2. Food in general. 3. The necessities of life. — *v.t.* To roll in bread crumbs before cooking. [OE *brēad* bit, crumb] — **bread′ed** *adj.*

bread-and-but·ter (bred′n-but′ər) *adj.* Expressing gratitude for hospitality: a *bread-and-butter* letter.

bread and butter *Informal* Subsistence; livelihood.

bread·bas·ket (bred′bas′kit, -bäs′-) *n. Slang* The stomach.

bread·fruit (bred′frōōt′) *n.* 1. The fruit of a tree native to the South Sea Islands. 2. The tree.

bread line A line of persons waiting to be given bread or other food as charity.

bread·stuff (bred'stuf') n. 1. Material for bread; grain, meal, or flour. 2. Bread.

breadth (bredth, bretth) n. 1. Measure or distance from side to side, as distinguished from length and thickness; width. 2. Freedom from narrowness; liberality. 3. That which is measured by its width, or which has a definite width: a *breadth* of cloth. [OE < *brād* broad]

breadth·wise (bredth'wīz', bretth'-) adv. In the direction of the breadth. Also **breadth/ways** (-wāz/).

bread·win·ner (bred'win'ər) n. One who supports himself and others by his earnings.

break (brāk) v. **broke** (*Archaic* **brake**), **bro·ken** (*Archaic* **broke**), **break·ing** v.t. 1. To separate into pieces or fragments, as by a blow; shatter. 2. To crack. 3. To part the surface of; pierce: to *break* ground. 4. To burst or cause to discharge, as an abscess. 5. To disable; render useless. 6. To destroy the order, continuity, or completeness of: to *break* ranks. 7. To diminish the force or effect of: to *break* a fall. 8. To overcome by opposing; end: to *break* a strike. 9. To interrupt the course of, as a journey. 10. To violate: to *break* one's promise. 11. To reduce in spirit or health, as by toil. 12. To tame, as a horse. 13. To demote. 14. To give or obtain smaller units for: to *break* a dollar. 15. To make bankrupt or short of money. 16. To force (a way), as through a barrier. 17. To escape from. 18. To surpass; excel: to *break* a record. 19. To make known; tell, as news. 20. To cause to discontinue a habit. 21. *Law* To invalidate (a will) by court action. — v.i. 22. To become separated into pieces or fragments. 23. To give way; become unusable: His pencil *broke*. 24. To dissolve and disperse: The clouds *broke*. 25. To come into being or evidence: The storm *broke* suddenly. 26. To appear above the surface. 27. To start or move suddenly: He *broke* from the crowd. 28. To become overwhelmed with grief: His heart *broke*. 29. To fall off abruptly: The fever *broke*. 30. To change tone, as a boy's voice. 31. In baseball, to curve at or near the plate: said of a pitch. — **to break bread** To take or share a meal. — **to break down 1.** To undergo mechanical failure. 2. To suffer physical or mental collapse. 3. To yield, especially to grief or strong feelings. 4. To cause to yield. 5. To analyze or be analyzed. 6. To decompose. — **to break in** To cause to obey; train; adapt. — **to break into** (or **in**) 1. To interrupt or intervene. 2. To enter by force. — **to break in on** (or **upon**) To interrupt. — **to break off 1.** To stop or cease, as from speaking. 2. To sever (relations); discontinue. 3. To become separate or detached. — **to break out 1.** To start unexpectedly or suddenly, as a fire or plague. 2. To have an eruption or rash, as the skin. 3. To escape, as from prison. — **to break out into** (or **forth in, into,** etc.) To begin to do or perform: The birds *broke out into song*. — **to break up 1.** To disperse; scatter: The meeting *broke up*. 2. To dismantle. 3. To put an end to. 4. *Informal* To distress: The loss *broke up* the old man. 5. *Informal* To sever relations. — **to break with** To sever relations with. — n. 1. The act or result of breaking; fracture; rupture. 2. A starting or opening: the *break* of day. 3. *U.S.* A dash or run; especially, an attempt to escape: to make a *break* for the door. 4. A breach of continuity, as a pause from work or an interruption in a discourse. 5. *U.S. Informal* A chance or opportunity. 6. *Electr.* The opening of a circuit; interruption of current. 7. A rupture in friendship; quarrel. 8. In prosody, a caesura. 9. A sudden decline, as in prices, temperature, etc. 10. *Music* a The point where one register or quality of a voice changes to another in singing. b In jazz, a syncopated cadenza bridging two phrases or choruses. 11. In baseball or cricket, the swerving of a ball from a straight course when thrown. — **break/a·ble** adj. — **break/a·ble·ness** n.

break·age (brā'kij) n. 1. A breaking, or being broken. 2. Articles broken. 3. Compensation for articles broken.

break·down (brāk'doun') n. 1. A collapse or failure, as of a machine, one's health, etc. 2. An analysis or summary.

break·er (brā'kər) n. 1. One who or that which breaks. 2. A wave of the sea that breaks on rocks, a reef, etc.

break·fast (brek'fəst) n. The morning meal. — v.t. 1. To furnish with a breakfast. — v.i. 2. To eat breakfast.

break·neck (brāk'nek') adj. Likely to break the neck; dangrous: *breakneck* speed.

break·through (brāk'thrōo') n. 1. *Mil.* An attack that penetrates through an enemy's defenses into the rear area. 2. Any sudden, important success, as in scientific research.

break·up (brāk'up') n. 1. A breaking up or separation; dissolution; disruption. 2. An ending.

break·wa·ter (brāk'wô'tər, -wot'ər) n. A barrier for protecting a harbor or beach from the force of waves.

bream (brēm) n. pl. **breams** or **bream** 1. Any of several fresh-water fishes with deep, compressed bodies. 2. Any of various fresh-water sunfishes. [OF *bresme*]

breast (brest) n. 1. *Anat.* The front of the chest from the

neck to the abdomen. 2. One of the mammary glands. 3. That part of a garment that covers the breast. 4. The breast as the seat of the emotions. 5. Anything likened to the human or animal breast. — **to make a clean breast of** To confess. — v.t. To meet boldly. [OE *brēost*]

breast·bone (brest'bōn') n. *Anat.* The sternum.

breast-feed (brest'fēd') v.t. & v.i. **-fed, -feed·ing** To suckle.

breast·pin (brest'pin') n. A pin worn at the breast.

breast·plate (brest'plāt') n. Plate armor for the breast.

breast stroke In swimming, a stroke made by thrusting the arms forward simultaneously from the breast.

breast·work (brest'wûrk') n. A low, temporary defensive work, usu. breast-high.

breath (breth) n. 1. Air inhaled and exhaled in respiration. 2. Power or ability to breathe. 3. The act of breathing; also, life; existence: while *breath* remains. 4. A single respiration. 5. The time of a single respiration; instant. 6. A slight delay. 7. A slight movement of air. 8. Anything slight; trifle. 9. A murmur; whisper. 10. Moisture from exhaled air, when visible in cold air. 11. *Phonet.* An exhalation of air without vibration of the vocal cords, as in the production of (p) and (f). — **in the same breath** At the same moment; without a pause or break. — **out of breath** Breathless; gasping. — **to take one's breath away** To awe or produce sudden emotion in. — **under one's breath** In a whisper or mutter. [OE *brǣth* vapor, odor]

breathe (brēth) v. **breathed** (brēthd), **breath·ing** v.i. 1. To inhale and exhale air. 2. To be alive; live. 3. To pause for breath; rest. 4. To murmur; whisper. 5. To move gently, as breezes. 6. To be exhaled, as fragrance. — v.t. 7. To inhale and expel from the lungs, as air; respire. 8. To inject or infuse: to *breathe* life into a statue. 9. To express; manifest: to *breathe* confidence. 10. To exhale. 11. To allow a rest to, as for breath. 12. *Phonet.* To utter with the breath only. [ME *breth* breath] — **breath/a·ble** adj.

breath·er (brē'thər) n. *Informal* A brief rest period.

breath·ing (brē'thing) adj. Respiring; living. — n. 1. The act of respiration; also, a single breath. 2. A gentle breeze. 3. Words spoken; utterance. 4. Aspiration; longing. 5. Time to breathe. 6. *Phonet.* An aspiration; aspirate.

breath·less (breth'lis) adj. 1. Out of breath. 2. Holding the breath from fear, excitement, etc. 3. That takes the breath away: *breathless* speed. 4. Devoid of breath; dead. 5. Motionless. — **breath/less·ly** adv. — **breath/less·ness** n.

breath·tak·ing (breth'tā'king) adj. Thrilling; overawing.

breath·y (breth'ē) adj. Characterized by audible breathing.

brec·ci·a (brech'ē-ə, bresh'-) n. *Geol.* A rock made up of angular fragments. [< Ital., grave] — **brec·ci·at·ed** (brech'ē-ā'tid, bresh'-) adj.

bred (bred) Past tense and past participle of BREED.

breech (brēch; *for v. def. 1, also* brich) n. 1. The posterior and lower part of the body; the buttocks. 2. The part of a gun, cannon, etc., that is behind the bore or barrel. 3. The lower part of something, as of a pulley. — v.t. 1. To clothe with breeches. 2. To provide with a breech. [OE *brēc*]

breech·cloth (brēch'klōth', -kloth') n. A loincloth. Also **breech·clout** (-klout').

breech·es (brich'iz) n.pl. 1. A man's garment covering the hips and thighs. 2. Trousers. [OE *brēc*]

breeches buoy *Naut.* A lifesaving apparatus consisting of canvas breeches attached to a life buoy and run on a rope from one vessel to another or to the shore.

breech·ing (brich'ing, brē'ching) n. A harness strap passing behind a horse's haunches.

breech·load·er (brēch'lō'dər) n. A firearm loaded at the breech. — **breech·load/ing** adj.

BREECHES BUOY
A Mast. *B* Traveling block. *C* Hawser. *D* Fixed block. *E* Hauling line. *F* Breeches buoy.

breed (brēd) v. **bred, breed·ing** v.t. 1. To produce (offspring). 2. To cause: Familiarity *breeds* contempt. 3. To raise: to *breed* horses. 4. To bring up; train. — v.i. 5. To procreate. 6. To originate or be caused: Militarism *breeds* in armies. — n. 1. A race or strain of animals. 2. A sort or kind. [OE *brōd* brood] n.

breed·ing (brē'ding) n. 1. The act of bearing young. 2. The rearing of the young. 3. Good manners. 4. The scientific production of improved varieties of plants, animals, etc.

breeze (brēz) n. 1. *Meteorol.* A moderate current of air; a gentle wind. 2. *Brit. Informal* A flutter of excitement. — **in a breeze** *Slang* Without difficulty; easily. — v.i. **breezed**, **breez·ing** *Slang* To go quickly and blithely. [< Sp. and Pg. *brisa, briza* northeast wind]

breeze·way (brēz'wā') n. A roofed, open passageway between two structures, as a house and garage.

breez·y (brē'zē) adj. **breez·i·er, breez·i·est** 1. Having breezes; windy. 2. Brisk or carefree; sprightly. — **breeze/i·ly** adv. — **breez/i·ness** n.

breth·ren (breth′rən) *n.pl.* **1.** Brothers. **2.** Members of a brotherhood. [ME]

Bret·on (bret′n) *adj.* Of or pertaining to Brittany, its inhabitants, or their language. — *n.* **1.** A native of Brittany. **2.** The Celtic language of the Bretons.

breve (brev, brēv) *n.* **1.** A mark (˘) placed over a vowel to indicate that it has a short sound, as *a* in *hat*. **2.** In prosody, a similar mark (˘) indicating a short or unstressed syllable. **3.** *Music* A note equivalent to two whole notes, or the symbol for it. [< Ital. < L *brevis* short]

bre·vet (brə·vet′, *esp. Brit.* brev′it) *n. Mil.* A commission advancing an officer in honorary rank without advance in pay or in command. — *v.t.* **bre·vet·ted** (brə·vet′id) or **brev·et·ed** (brev′it·id), **bre·vet·ting** (brə·vet′ing) or **brev·et·ing** (brev′it·ing) To raise in rank by brevet. — *adj.* Held or conferred by brevet. [< OF *bref* letter, document] — **bre·vet·cy** (brə·vet′sē) *n.*

brevi- *combining form* Short. [< L *brevis* short]

bre·vi·ar·y (brē′vē·er′ē, brev′ē-) *n. pl.* **·ar·ies** *Eccl.* In the Roman Catholic and Eastern Orthodox churches, a book of daily prayers for the canonical hours. [< L *brevis* short]

bre·vier (brə·vir′) *n. Printing* A size of type, about 8-point. [? < G. *breviary;* because once used in breviaries]

brev·i·ty (brev′ə·tē) *n.* **1.** Shortness of time. **2.** Condensation of language; conciseness. [< L *brevis* short]

brew (broo) *v.t.* **1.** To make, as beer or ale, by steeping, boiling, and fermenting malt, hops, etc. **2.** To prepare (any beverage) as by boiling or mixing. **3.** To plot; devise. — *v.i.* **4.** To make ale, beer, or the like. **5.** To commence to form, as a storm. — *n.* **1.** Something brewed. **2.** The amount brewed. [OE *brēowan*] — **brew′er** *n.*

brew·er·y (broo′ər·ē) *n. pl.* **·er·ies** An establishment for brewing; also, the apparatus used in brewing.

brew·ing (broo′ing) *n.* **1.** The process of making a brew. **2.** The amount brewed at one time.

bri·ar (brī′ər) See BRIER.

bri·ar·root (brī′ər·root′, -root′) See BRIERROOT.

bri·ar·wood (brī′ər·wood′) *n.* Brierroot.

bribe (brīb) *n.* **1.** Any gift or emolument used corruptly to influence a person. **2.** Anything that seduces or allures. — *v.* **bribed, brib·ing** *v.t.* **1.** To offer or give a bribe to. **2.** To gain or influence by means of bribery. — *v.i.* **3.** To give bribes. [< OF, piece of bread given a beggar] — **brib′a·ble** *adj.* — **brib′er** *n.*

brib·er·y (brī′bər·ē) *n. pl.* **·er·ies** The giving, offering, or accepting of a bribe.

bric-a-brac (brik′ə·brak) *n.* Small objects of curiosity or decoration; antiques; knickknacks. [< F]

brick (brik) *n.* **1.** A molded block of clay, baked in various shapes and sizes, used for building, etc. **2.** Bricks collectively. **3.** Any object shaped like a brick. **4.** *Informal* An admirable fellow. — *v.t.* **1.** To build or line with bricks. **2.** To cover with bricks: with *up* or *in.* — *adj.* **1.** Of brick. **2.** Brick-red. [< MF *brique* fragment]

brick·bat (brik′bat′) *n.* **1.** A piece of a brick, esp. when used as a missile. **2.** *Informal* An insulting remark.

brick·kiln (brik′kil′, -kiln′) *n.* A structure in which bricks are burned or baked.

brick·lay·er (brik′lā′ər) *n.* One who builds with bricks. — **brick′lay′ing** *n.*

brick red Dull yellowish or brownish red.

brick·work (brik′wûrk′) *n.* Construction of or with bricks.

brick·yard (brik′yärd′) *n.* A place where bricks are made.

bri·dal (brīd′l) *adj.* Pertaining to a bride or a wedding; nuptial. — *n.* A wedding. [OE *brȳdealo* wedding feast]

bridal wreath A flowering shrub of the rose family, with small white flowers.

bride (brīd) *n.* A newly married woman, or a woman about to be married. [OE *brȳd*]

bride·groom (brīd′groom′, -groom′) *n.* A man newly married or about to be married. [OE < *brȳd* bride + *guma* man]

brides·maid (brīdz′mād′) *n.* A young, usu. unmarried woman who attends a bride at her wedding.

bridge¹ (brij) *n.* **1.** A structure erected across a waterway, ravine, road, etc., to afford passage. **2.** An observation platform built athwart the forward part of a ship for the officers, pilot, etc. **3.** The upper bony ridge of the nose. **4.** The central part of a pair of spectacles that rests on the nose. **5.** In some string instruments, a thin piece of wood that raises the strings above the soundboard. For illus. see VIOLIN. **6.** *Music* A transitional passage connecting two sections of a composition. **7.** *Dent.* A mounting for false teeth, attached on each side to a natural tooth. — **to burn one's bridges (behind one)** To cut off all means of retreat. — *v.t.* **bridged, bridg·ing 1.** To construct a bridge or bridges over. **2.** To make a passage over. [OE *brycg*] — **bridge′a·ble** *adj.*

bridge² (brij) *n.* A card game, derived from whist, in which the trump suit (or the fact that there will be no trumps) is determined by the side proposing to take the higher number of tricks. See AUCTION BRIDGE, CONTRACT BRIDGE.

bridge·head (brij′hed′) *n. Mil.* A position on the hostile side of a river or defile, established by advance troops.

bridge·work (brij′wûrk′) *n.* **1.** *Dent.* A dental bridge. **2.** The construction of bridges.

bri·dle (brīd′l) *n.* **1.** The head harness, including bit and reins, used to guide or restrain a horse. **2.** Anything that restrains or limits. — *v.* **·dled, ·dling** *v.t.* **1.** To put a bridle on. **2.** To check or control with or as with a bridle. — *v.i.* **3.** To raise the head and draw in the chin through resentment, pride, etc. [OE *brīdel*] — **bri′dler** *n.*

bridle path A path for saddle horses or pack animals only.

brief (brēf) *adj.* **1.** Short in time or extent; quickly ending. **2.** Of few words; concise. **3.** Curt or abrupt. — *n.* **1.** A short or abridged statement; summary. **2.** *Law* A memorandum of the material facts, points of law, precedents, etc., of a case. **3.** *pl.* Short underpants. — **in brief** In short; briefly. — **to hold a brief for** To be on the side of. — *v.t.* **1.** To make a summary of; epitomize. **2.** To give a briefing to. **3.** *Brit.* To inform by a legal brief. **4.** *Brit.* To retain as counsel. [< OF < L *brevis* short] — **brief′ly** *adv.* — **brief′ness** *n.*

brief·case (brēf′kās′) *n.* A flexible, rectangular case, usually of leather, for carrying documents, papers, books, etc.

brief·ing (brē′fing) *n.* A short lecture setting forth the details of an operation or procedure.

bri·er¹ (brī′ər) *n.* **1.** A prickly bush or shrub, esp. one of the rose family, as the sweetbrier. **2.** A growth of such prickly bushes. **3.** A thorny or prickly twig. Also spelled *briar.* [OE *brær, brēr*] — **bri′er·y** *adj.*

bri·er² (brī′ər) *n.* **1.** The tree heath of southern Europe. **2.** A pipe made of brierroot. [< F *bruyère* heath]

bri·er·root (brī′ər·root′, -root′) *n.* **1.** The root of the brier or tree heath, used in making tobacco pipes. **2.** A pipe made from this wood. Also **bri·er·wood** (brī′ər·wood′).

brig¹ (brig) *n. Naut.* A two-masted ship, square-rigged on both masts. [Short for BRIGANTINE]

brig² (brig) *n.* A place of confinement on shipboard. [Origin unknown]

bri·gade (bri·gād′) *n.* **1.** *Mil.* A unit of two or more groups or regiments. **2.** Any considerable body of persons more or less organized: a fire *brigade.* — *v.t.* **·gad·ed, ·gad·ing 1.** To form into a brigade. **2.** To classify or combine. [< MF < Ital. *brigare* to brawl, fight]

brig·a·dier (brig′ə·dir′) *n.* **1.** *Mil.* A brigadier general. **2.** In the British, Canadian, and other Commonwealth armies, an office ranking next below a major general. See table at GRADE.

BRIG

brigadier general *Mil.* An officer ranking next above a colonel and next below a major general. See table at GRADE.

brig·and (brig′ənd) *n.* A robber, esp. in a band of outlaws. [< MF < Ital. *brigare* to brawl, fight] — **brig′and·ish** *adj.*

brig·an·tine (brig′ən·tēn, -tīn) *n. Naut.* A two-masted vessel, square-rigged on the foremast, and fore-and-aft rigged on the mainmast: also called *hermaphrodite brig.* [< MF < Ital. *brigare* to fight]

bright (brīt) *adj.* **1.** Emitting or reflecting much light; full of light; shining. **2.** Of brilliant color; vivid. **3.** Glorious; illustrious. **4.** Having or showing high intelligence; quick-witted. **5.** Lively; vivacious. **6.** Hopeful; auspicious. — *adv.* In a bright manner; brightly. [OE *beorht, bryht*] — **bright·ly** *adv.* — **bright′ness** *n.*

bright·en (brīt′n) *v.t. & v.i.* To make or become bright or brighter. — **bright′en·er** *n.*

Bright's disease (brīts) A disease marked by degeneration of the kidneys and imperfect elimination of uric acid. [after Richard Bright, 1789–1858, English physician]

bril·liance (bril′yəns) *n.* **1.** Intense brightness or luster. **2.** Great talent or intellect. **3.** Excellence; preeminence. **4.** *Music* Clarity of sound; vivid tone. Also **bril′lian·cy.**

bril·liant (bril′yənt) *adj.* **1.** Sparkling or glowing with light; very bright. **2.** Splendid; illustrious. **3.** Having great intellect or talent. **4.** *Music* Clear; vivid; intense. — *n.* **1.** A diamond of the finest cut, having as many as 58 facets above and below the girdle. **2.** *Printing* A very small size of type, about 3½-point. [< F *briller* to sparkle] — **bril′liant·ly** *adv.* — **bril′liant·ness** *n.*

bril·lian·tine (bril′yən·tēn) *n.* An oily hairdressing. [< F]

brim (brim) *n.* **1.** The rim or upper edge of a cup, bowl, etc. **2.** A projecting rim, as of a hat. **3.** An edge or margin. — *v.t. & v.i.* **brimmed, brim·ming** To fill or be full to the brim. — **to brim over** To overflow. [OE *brim* seashore]

brim·ful (brim′fool′, brim′fool′) *adj.* Full to the brim.

brim·stone (brim′stōn′) *n.* Sulfur. [OE *bryn-* burning + *stān* stone] — **brim′ston′y** *adj.*

brin·dle (brin′dəl) *adj.* Brindled. — *n.* A brindled color, or a brindled animal.

brin·dled (brin′dəld) *adj.* Tawny or grayish with irregular streaks or spots; barred; streaked.

brine (brīn) *n.* 1. Water saturated with salt. 2. The water of the sea; the ocean. — *v.t.* **brined, brin·ing** To treat with or steep in brine. [OE *brȳne*] — **brin′ish** *adj.*

bring (bring) *v.t.* **brought, bring·ing** 1. To convey or cause (a person or thing) to come with oneself to or toward a place. 2. To cause to come about; involve as a consequence: War *brings* destruction. 3. To introduce into the mind. 4. To cause (a person or oneself) to adopt or admit, as a course of action. 5. To sell for: The house *brought* a good price. 6. *Law* **a** To prefer, as a charge. **b** To institute: to *bring* suit. **c** To set forth, as evidence or an argument. — **to bring about** 1. To accomplish; cause to happen. 2. *Naut.* To reverse; turn, as a ship. — **to bring around** (or **round**) 1. To cause to adopt or admit, as an opinion. 2. To revive; restore to consciousness. — **to bring down the house** To evoke wild applause. — **to bring forth** 1. To give birth or produce. 2. To give rise to. — **to bring forward** 1. To adduce, as an argument. 2. In bookkeeping, to carry, as a sum, from one page or column to another. — **to bring in** 1. To import. 2. To render or submit (a verdict). 3. To yield or produce, as profits. — **to bring off** To do successfully. — **to bring on** 1. To cause; lead to. 2. To produce; cause to appear: *Bring on* the actors. — **to bring out** 1. To reveal; cause to be evident. 2. To publish or produce. 3. To introduce, as a young girl to society. — **to bring to** 1. To revive; restore to consciousness. 2. *Naut.* To cause (a ship) to come up into the wind and lie to. — **to bring up** 1. To rear; educate. 2. To suggest or call attention to, as a subject. 3. To cough or vomit up. [OE *bringan*]

bring·ing-up (bring′ing-up′) *n.* Care, training, and education of a person in childhood; upbringing.

brink (bringk) *n.* 1. The edge or verge, as of a steep place. 2. The shore of a river, etc. [ME < Scand.]

brink·man·ship (bringk′mən-ship) *n.* The willingness to take major risks in order to achieve some end. [< BRINK + *manship*, on analogy with *showmanship*, etc.]

brin·y (brī′nē) *adj.* **brin·i·er, brin·i·est** Of the nature of or like brine. — **the briny** *Slang* The sea. — **brin′i·ness** *n.*

bri·oche (brē′ōsh, -osh; *Fr.* brē-ôsh′) *n.* A soft roll. [< F]

bri·quette (bri-ket′) *n.* A block of compressed coal dust, used for fuel. Also **bri·quet′**. [< F *brique* brick]

brisk (brisk) *adj.* 1. Moving, acting, or taking place quickly; lively; energetic. 2. Sharp or stimulating. [Cf. F *brusque* abrupt, sudden] — **brisk′ly** *adv.* — **brisk′ness** *n.*

bris·ket (bris′kit) *n.* The breast of an animal, esp. of one used as food. [< OF *bruschet*]

bris·tle (bris′əl) *n.* 1. One of the coarse, stiff hairs of swine, used in making brushes. 2. Any similar hair. — *v.* **·tled, ·tling** *v.i.* 1. To erect the bristles in anger or excitement. 2. To show anger or irritation. 3. To stand or become erect, like bristles. 4. To be thickly set as if with bristles. — *v.t.* 5. To erect as or like bristles. 6. To ruffle or agitate. [ME < OE *byrst*] — **bris′tly** *adj.*

Bri·tan·ni·a (bri-tan′ē-ə, -tan′yə) 1. The ancient Roman name for Great Britain. 2. The British Empire.

Bri·tan·nic (bri-tan′ik) *adj.* British. [< L *Britannicus*]

Brit·i·cism (brit′ə-siz′əm) *n.* An idiom or turn of phrase peculiar to the British.

Brit·ish (brit′ish) *adj.* Pertaining to Great Britain or the United Kingdom. — *n.* 1. The people of Great Britain or of the British Empire: preceded by *the*. 2. British English. [OE *Bretisc < Bret* a Briton]

British America 1. Canada. 2. British possessions in or adjacent to North America. Also **British North America**.

British Commonwealth of Nations A political association comprising the United Kingdom, Canada, Australia, New Zealand, Ghana, India, Pakistan, Ceylon, Malaysia, Nigeria, Nyasaland, Cyprus, Sierra Leone, Tanganyika, Trinidad, and Tobago, Jamaica, Uganda, Western Samoa, Kenya, and Zanzibar, and including the dependencies of member nations: officially *The Commonwealth.* Also *Commonwealth of Nations.*

British Empire The sovereign states under the British Crown, comprising those in the British Commonwealth of Nations with their dependencies.

Brit·ish·er (brit′ish-ər) *n.* A native or subject of Great Britain, esp. an Englishman.

British Isles Great Britain, Ireland, the Isle of Man, and the Channel Islands.

British thermal unit *Physics* The quantity of heat required to raise the temperature of one pound of water one degree Fahrenheit.

Brit·on (brit′n) *n.* 1. A member of a Celtic people inhabiting ancient Britain, conquered by the Romans. 2. A Britisher. [< OF < L *Britto* < Celtic]

brit·tle (brit′l) *adj.* Liable to break or snap; fragile. — *Syn.* See FRAGILE. [ME *britil*] **brit′tle·ness** *n.*

broach (brōch) *v.t.* 1. To mention or suggest for the first time; introduce. 2. To pierce so as to withdraw a liquid. — *n.* 1. *Mech.* A pointed, tapering tool for boring; a reamer. 2. A spit for roasting. [< OF < Med.L *brocca* spike, spit] — **broach′er** *n.*

broad (brôd) *adj.* 1. Extended from side to side; wide. 2. Of great extent; vast or spacious. 3. Fully diffused; open and clear: *broad* daylight. 4. Of wide scope or application; extensive. 5. Liberal in spirit; tolerant. 6. Not detailed; general. 7. Obvious; clear: a *broad* hint. 8. Vulgar and indelicate; unrefined. 9. Outspoken or unrestrained. 10. Strongly dialectal: a *broad* pronunciation. 11. *Phonet.* Formed with the oral passage open wide and the tongue low and flat, as the *a* in *calm.* — *n.* 1. The broad part of anything. 2. *Slang* A woman or girl. — *adv.* Completely; fully. [OE *brād*] — **broad′ly** *adv.* — **broad′ness** *n.*

broad·ax (brôd′aks′) *n.* An ax with a broad edge and a short handle. Also **broad′axe′**.

broad·cast (brôd′kast′, -käst′) *v.* **·cast** or (*esp. for defs. 1, 4*) **·cast·ed, ·cast·ing** *v.t.* 1. To send or transmit (music, newscasts, etc.) by radio or television. 2. To scatter, as seed, over a wide area. 3. To disseminate; make public. — *v.i.* 4. To make a radio or television broadcast. — *n.* 1. The act of broadcasting. 2. A radio or television program. — *adj.* 1. By or for radio or television transmission. 2. Scattered far and wide. — *adv.* So as to be scattered over a wide area. — **broad′cast′er** *n.*

broad·cloth (brôd′klôth′, -kloth′) *n.* 1. A fine woolen cloth used for suits, skirts, etc. 2. A closely woven fabric of silk, cotton, etc., used for shirts, dresses, etc.

broad·en (brôd′n) *v.t. & v.i.* To make or become broad.

broad-gauge (brôd′gāj′) *adj.* Having a width of railroad track greater than the standard gauge of 56½ inches. Also **broad′gage′, broad′-gaged′, broad-gauged′.**

broad jump A jump or jumping contest for distance.

broad·loom (brôd′lōōm′) *n.* Carpet woven in widths of from 6 to 18 feet. Also **broadloom carpet.**

broad-mind·ed (brôd′mīn′did) *adj.* Liberal and tolerant; free from bigotry and prejudice. — **broad′-mind′ed·ly** *adv.* — **broad′-mind′ed·ness** *n.*

broad·side (brôd′sīd′) *n.* 1. All the guns on one side of a man-of-war, or their simultaneous discharge. 2. A volley of abuse or denunciation. 3. *Naut.* A vessel's side above the water line. 4. A large sheet of paper, printed on one side: also **broad′sheet′**. — *adv.* With the broadside exposed.

broad·sword (brôd′sôrd′, -sōrd′) *n.* A sword with a broad cutting blade.

broad·tail (brôd′tāl′) *n.* The lustrous black fur obtained from lambs of the karakul sheep.

Broad·way (brôd′wā) A street in New York City, noted for its theatres and entertainment district.

bro·cade (brō-kād′) *n.* A rich fabric interwoven with a raised design, as in silken or gold or silver threads. — *v.t.* **·cad·ed, ·cad·ing** To weave (a cloth) with a raised design or figure. [< Sp. < Med.L *broccare* to embroider]

broc·co·li (brok′ə·lē) *n.* A variety of cauliflower. [< Ital., pl. of *broccolo* cabbage sprout]

bro·chure (brō-shōōr′) *n.* A pamphlet or similar publication. [< F, lit., a stitched book < *brocher* to stitch]

bro·gan (brō′gən) *n.* A coarse, heavy shoe. [< Irish *brógan*, dim. of *bróg* shoe]

brogue[1] (brōg) *n.* An Irish accent in the pronunciation of English. [< Irish *barróg* defect of speech]

brogue[2] (brōg) *n.* 1. A heavy oxford shoe, decorated with perforations. 2. A shoe of untanned hide worn formerly in Ireland and the Scottish Highlands. [< Irish *bróg* a shoe]

broil[1] (broil) *v.t.* 1. To cook, as meat, by subjecting to direct heat. 2. To expose to great heat; scorch. — *v.i.* 3. To be exposed to great heat; cook. — *n.* 1. Something broiled. 2. A broiling heat. [< OF *bruller, bruillir* to burn]

broil[2] (broil) *n.* A turmoil; noisy quarrel; brawl. — *v.i.* To engage in a broil; brawl. [< F *brouiller* to confuse]

broil·er (broi′lər) *n.* 1. A device for broiling. 2. A young, tender chicken suitable for broiling.

broke (brōk) Past tense and archaic past participle of BREAK. — *adj. Informal* Having no money; bankrupt.

bro·ken (brō′kən) Past participle of BREAK. — *adj.* 1. Forcibly separated into pieces; fractured. 2. Violated; transgressed: *broken* vows. 3. Interrupted; disturbed. 4. Incomplete; fragmentary. 5. Rough; uneven, as terrain. 6. In disorder; scattered, as troops. 7. Humbled; crushed. 8. Weakened or infirm. 9. Bankrupt. 10. Trained in procedure; adapted: often with *in.* 11. Imperfectly spoken; disjointed. — **bro′ken·ly** *adv.* — **bro′ken·ness** *n.*

bro·ken-down (brō′kən-doun′) *adj.* 1. Incapable of functioning; out of repair. 2. Ruined; decayed.

bro·ken-heart·ed (brō′kən-här′tid) *adj.* Overwhelmed or crushed in spirit, as by grief.

bro·ker (brō′kər) *n.* One who buys and sells for another, arranges contracts, etc; esp., a stockbroker. [< AF < OF *brochier* to tap, broach (a wine cask)]

bro·ker·age (brō'kər·ij) *n.* The business or commission of a broker. Also **bro'kage.**

bro·mide[1] (brō'mīd, -mid) *n. Chem.* A compound of bromine with an element or an organic radical. Also **bro'mid** (-mid).

bro·mide[2] (brō'mīd, -mid) *n. Informal* A platitude.

bro·mid·ic (brō·mid'ik) *adj. Informal* Commonplace; trite.

bro·mine (brō'mēn, -min) *n.* A dark reddish brown, non-metallic, fuming liquid element (symbol Br) with a suffocating odor. Also **bro'min** (-min). See ELEMENT. [< F *brome* (< Gk. *brōmos* stench) + -INE[2]]

bromo- *combining form* Used to indicate bromine in chemical compounds. Also, before vowels, **brom-.**

bron·chi (brong'kī) *n.* Plural of BRONCHUS.

bron·chi·a (brong'kē·ə) *n.pl. Anat.* The bronchial tubes. [< LL < Gk. *bronchia*]

bron·chi·al (brong'kē·əl) *adj. Anat.* Of or pertaining to the chief air passages of the lungs.

bronchial tube *Anat.* Any of the subdivisions of the trachea conveying air into the lungs.

bron·chi·tis (brong·kī'tis) *n. Pathol.* Inflammation of the bronchial tubes. — **bron·chit·ic** (brong·kit'ik) *adj.*

broncho- *combining form* Windpipe. Also, before vowels, **bronch-.** [< Gk. *bronchos*]

bron·cho·scope (brong'kə·skōp) *n. Med.* An instrument for inspecting or treating the interior of the bronchi.

bron·chus (brong'kəs) *n. pl. ·chi* (-kī) *Anat.* One of the two forked branches of the trachea. For illus. see LUNG. [< NL < Gk. *bronchos* windpipe]

bron·co (brong'kō) *n. pl. ·cos* 1. *U.S.* A small, wild or partly broken horse of the West. 2. *Canadian* An Englishman. Also **bronc, bron'cho.** [< Sp. *bronco* rough]

bron·co·bust·er (brong'kō·bus'tər) *n. U.S. Informal* One who breaks a bronco to the saddle. Also **bron'cho·bust'er.**

bron·to·sau·rus (bron'tə·sôr'əs) *n. pl. ·rus·es Paleontol.* A huge, herbivorous dinosaur of the Jurassic period. Also **bron'to·saur.** [< Gk. *brontē* thunder + *sauros* lizard]

Bronx cheer *U.S. Slang* A noisy fluttering of the lips to show contempt or derision: also called *raspberry, razzberry.*

BRONTOSAURUS
(To 70 feet long; about 20 tons)

bronze (bronz) *n.* 1. *Metall.* **a** A reddish brown alloy essentially of copper and tin. **b** A similar alloy of copper and some other metal, as aluminum. 2. A pigment of the color of bronze. 3. A reddish brown color similar to bronze. 4. A statue, bust, etc., done in bronze. — *v.* **bronzed, bronz·ing** *v.t.* 1. To color like bronze. — *v.i.* 2. To become brown or tan. [< MF < Ital. *bronzo, bronzino*] — **bronz'y** *adj.*

Bronze Age *Archeol.* A stage of prehistory following the Stone Age and preceding the Iron Age, during which weapons and implements were made of bronze.

Bronze Star A U.S. military decoration, awarded for heroism or exemplary conduct in ground combat.

brooch (brōch, brōōch) *n.* An ornamental pin with a clasp for wearing on the breast or shoulder. [Var. of BROACH]

brood (brōōd) *n.* 1. The young of animals, esp. of birds, produced at one time. 2. All the young of the same mother. 3. Kind or species. — *v.i.* 1. To meditate moodily and deeply: usu. with *on* or *over*. 2. To sit on eggs. — *v.t.* 3. To sit upon or incubate (eggs). 4. To protect (young) by covering with the wings. [OE *brōd*]

brood·er (brōō'dər) *n.* 1. A warmed structure for artificially rearing young fowl. 2. One who or that which broods.

brood·y (brōō'dē) *adj.* **brood·i·er, brood·i·est** 1. Meditative; moody. 2. Inclined to sit on eggs: said of hens.

brook[1] (brōōk) *n.* A natural stream, smaller than a river or creek; a rivulet. [OE *brōc*]

brook[2] (brōōk) *v.t.* To put up with; tolerate: usu. with the negative: I cannot *brook* such conduct. [OE *brūcan* to use]

brook·let (brōōk'lit) *n.* A little brook.

brook trout The speckled trout of eastern North America.

broom (brōōm, brōōm) *n.* 1. A brush attached to a long handle for sweeping, formerly made from twigs of broom. 2. Any of various shrubs with yellow flowers and stiff green branches: also called *besom.* — *v.t.* To sweep. [OE *brōm*]

broom·corn (brōōm'kôrn', brōōm'-) *n.* A canelike grass of which brooms are made.

broom·stick (brōōm'stik', brōōm'-) *n.* The handle of a broom.

broth (brôth, broth) *n.* A soup made by boiling meat, vegetables, etc., in water; a thin or strained soup. [OE]

broth·el (broth'əl, broth'-, brôth'əl, brôth'-) *n.* A house of prostitution. [ME, a worthless person]

broth·er (bruth'ər) *n. pl.* **broth·ers** (*Archaic* **breth·ren**) 1. A male individual having the same parents as another or others of either sex. 2. A kinsman, or one of the same tribe, etc. 3. A fellow member, as of an organization. 4. A comrade. 5. One of a male religious order who is not a priest. — *v.t.* To treat or address as a brother. [OE *brōthor*]

broth·er·hood (bruth'ər·hōōd) *n.* 1. The relationship of or state of being brothers, esp. by blood. 2. A society, fraternity, guild, etc. 3. All the persons engaged in an enterprise, profession, etc.

broth·er·in·law (bruth'ər·in·lô') *n. pl.* **broth·ers·in·law** 1. A brother of one's husband or wife. 2. The husband of one's sister. 3. The husband of one's spouse's sister.

broth·er·ly (bruth'ər·lē) *adj.* Pertaining to or characteristic of a brother; fraternal; affectionate. — *adv.* As a brother; kindly. — **broth'er·li·ness** *n.*

brougham (brōōm, brōō'əm, brō'əm) *n.* 1. A closed, four-wheeled carriage having a high, uncovered driver's seat. 2. A limousine with the driver's seat outside. [after Lord Henry *Brougham*, 1778–1868, British statesman]

brought (brôt) Past tense and past participle of BRING.

brow (brou) *n.* 1. The front upper part of the head; forehead. 2. The eyebrow. 3. The countenance in general. 4. The upper edge of a steep place: the *brow* of a hill. [OE *brū*]

brow·beat (brou'bēt') *v.t.* **·beat, ·beat·en, ·beat·ing** To intimidate; bully.

brown (broun) *adj.* 1. Of a dark color combining red, yellow, and black. 2. Dark-complexioned; tanned. — **to do up brown** *Informal* To do thoroughly. — *n.* 1. A brown color. 2. A brown pigment or dye. — *v.t. & v.i.* To make or become brown. [OE *brūn*] — **brown'ness** *n.*

brown bear 1. The black bear. 2. One of several very large bears of North America and Europe, with fur varying from yellowish to dark brown.

brown Bet·ty (bet'ē) Baked pudding made of bread crumbs, apples, sugar, and spices. Also **brown bet'ty.**

brown bread Any bread made of a dark-colored flour.

Brown·i·an movement (brou'nē·ən) *Physics* The rapid oscillatory movement of small particles when suspended in fluids. Also **Brownian motion.** [after Robert *Brown*, 1773–1858, Scottish botanist, who discovered it]

brown·ie (brou'nē) *n.* 1. In folklore, a goblin or sprite, supposed to do useful work at night. 2. *U.S.* A small, flat chocolate cake with nuts. [< BROWN; from its color]

Brown·ie (brou'nē) *n.* A junior girl scout of the age group seven through nine.

brown·out (broun'out') *n.* A partial diminishing of lights either as a defensive measure or to save fuel.

brown rice Unpolished rice grains.

Brown Shirt 1. A storm trooper. 2. A Nazi.

brown·stone (broun'stōn') *n.* A brownish red sandstone used for building; also, a house with a front of brownstone.

brown study A state of absent-mindedness; reverie.

brown sugar Sugar that is unrefined or partly refined.

browse (brouz) *v.* **browsed, brows·ing** *v.i.* 1. To feed on leaves, shoots, etc. 2. To glance through a book or books or look over merchandise casually. — *v.t.* 3. To nibble at; crop; also, to graze on. — *n.* Growing shoots or twigs used as fodder. [< MF *broust* bud, sprout] — **brows'er** *n.*

bru·cel·lo·sis (brōō'sə·lō'sis) *n. Pathol.* Undulant fever. [after Sir David *Bruce*, 1855–1931, English physician]

bru·in (brōō'in) *n.* A bear; esp., a brown bear. [< MDu.]

bruise (brōōz) *v.* **bruised, bruis·ing** *v.t.* 1. To injure, as by a blow, without breaking the surface of the skin; contuse. 2. To dent or mar the surface of. 3. To hurt or offend slightly, as feelings. 4. To crush; pound small, as in a mortar. — *v.i.* 5. To become discolored as from a blow. — *n.* An injury caused by bruising; contusion. [Fusion of OE *brȳsan* to crush and OF *bruisier* to break, shatter]

bruis·er (brōō'zər) *n.* 1. A professional boxer. 2. *Informal* A bully.

bruit (brōōt) *v.t.* To noise abroad; talk about: usu. in the passive. [< F < *bruire* to roar, ? < L *rugire*] — **bruit'er** *n.*

brunch (brunch) *n. U.S. Informal* A late morning meal combining breakfast and lunch. [< BR(EAKFAST) + (L)UNCH]

bru·net (brōō·net') *adj.* Dark-hued; having dark complexion, hair, and eyes. — *n.* A brunet man or boy. [< F]

bru·nette (brōō·net') *adj.* Brunet: feminine form. — *n.* A brunette woman or girl. [< F]

Brun·hild (brōōn'hild, *Ger.* brōōn'hilt) In the *Nibelungenlied*, a queen of Iceland. Compare BRÜNNHILDE.

Brünn·hil·de (brün·hil'də) In Wagner's *Ring of the Nibelung*, a Valkyrie put in a trance and encircled by flames, but eventually released by Siegfried.

brunt (brunt) *n.* The main force or strain of a blow, attack, etc. [? < ON *bruna* to advance quickly, as a fire]

brush[1] (brush) *n.* **1.** An implement having bristles, wires, or other flexible fibrous material, fixed in a handle or a back, and used for sweeping, painting, smoothing the hair, etc. **2.** The act of brushing. **3.** A light, grazing touch. **4.** A brief encounter, esp. a skirmish. **5.** Brushwork. **6.** *Electr.* A conductor, resting on the commutator cylinder of a dynamo, for carrying off the current or for an external current through a motor. — *v.t.* **1.** To use a brush on; sweep, paint, etc., with a brush. **2.** To remove with or as with a brush. **3.** To touch lightly in passing. — *v.i.* **4.** To move lightly and quickly. — **to brush aside** To deny consideration to. — **to brush off** *U.S. Slang* To dismiss or refuse abruptly. — **to brush up** **1.** To refresh one's knowledge of. **2.** To renovate. [< OF *brosse*, ? < Gmc.]

brush[2] (brush) *n.* **1.** A growth of small trees and shrubs. **2.** Wooded country sparsely settled; backwoods. **3.** Brushwood. [< OF *broche, brosse*, ? < Gmc.] — **brush/y** *adj.*

brush-off (brush/ôf′, -of′) *n.* *U.S. Slang* An abrupt refusal or dismissal.

brush-wood (brush/wŏŏd′) *n.* **1.** Bushes or branches cut or broken off. **2.** A thicket of small trees or shrubs.

brusque (brusk, *esp. Brit.* brŏŏsk) *adj.* Rude or curt; blunt. Also **brusk**. — **Syn.** See BLUNT. [< MF < Ital. *brusco* rude, rough] — **brusque/ly** *adv.* — **brusque/ness** *n.*

Brussels sprouts **1.** A variety of cabbage having stems covered with heads like little cabbages. **2.** The small, edible heads of this plant.

brut (brüt, brŏŏt) *adj.* Dry: said of wines, esp. champagne. [< F, lit., rough < L *brutus*]

bru-tal (brŏŏt/l) *adj.* **1.** Characteristic of or like a brute; cruel; savage. **2.** Unfeeling; rude; coarse. [< L *brutus* stupid, rough] — **bru/tal-ly** *adv.*

bru-tal-i-ty (brŏŏ-tal′ə-tē) *n. pl.* **-ties** **1.** The state or quality of being brutal; cruelty. **2.** A brutal act.

bru-tal-ize (brŏŏt/l-īz) *v.t. & v.i.* **-ized, -iz-ing** To make or become brutal. — **bru/tal-i-za/tion** *n.*

brute (brŏŏt) *n.* **1.** Any animal other than man. **2.** A brutal person. — *adj.* **1.** Incapable of reasoning; merely animal. **2.** Like a brute or animal; unintelligent. **3.** Dominated by appetite; gross; sensual. [< F < L *brutus* stupid]

bru-ti-fy (brŏŏ/tə-fī) *v.t. & v.i.* **-fied, -fy-ing** To brutalize.

brut-ish (brŏŏ/tish) *adj.* Of, relating to, or charactistic of a brute or brutes; stupid; gross; sensual. — **brut/ish-ly** *adv.* — **brut/ish-ness, brut/ism** *n.*

Bryn-hild (brün/hilt) In the *Volsunga Saga*, a Valkyrie awakened by Sigurd from an enchanted sleep. Compare BRUNHILD, BRÜNHILDE.

bry-ol-o-gy (brī-ol/ə-jē) *n.* The branch of botany that treats of mosses. [< Gk. *bryon* moss + -LOGY] — **bry-o-log-i-cal** (brī′ə-loj/i-kəl) *adj.* — **bry-ol/o-gist** *n.*

bry-o-ny (brī/ə-nē) *n.* A common English herb of the gourd family, with white or yellowish flowers. [< L < Gk. *bryōnia*]

bry-o-phyte (brī/ə-fīt) *n. Bot.* Any moss or liverwort. [< Gk. *bryon* moss + -PHYTE] — **bry/o-phyt/ic** (-fit/ik) *adj.*

Bry-thon-ic (bri-thon/ik) *n.* The branch of the Celtic languages that includes Welsh, Breton, and the extinct Cornish; Cymric: distinguished from *Goidelic*.

bub-ble (bub/əl) *n.* **1.** A liquid globule filled with air or other gas. **2.** A globule of air or other gas confined in a liquid or solid substance. **3.** Anything unsubstantial; a delusion; fraud. **4.** The process or sound of bubbling. **5.** A glass or plastic dome. — *v.* **-bled, -bling** *v.i.* **1.** To form or emit bubbles; rise in bubbles. **2.** To move or flow with a gurgling sound. **3.** To express joy, delight, exultation, etc., in an irrepressible manner. — *v.t.* **4.** To cause to bubble. [ME *buble*] — **bub/bly** *adj.*

bu-bo (byŏŏ/bō) *n. pl.* **bu-boes** *Pathol.* An inflammatory swelling of a lymph gland in the groin or armpit. [< LL < Gk. *boubōn* groin] — **bu-bon-ic** (byŏŏ-bon/ik) *adj.*

bubonic plague *Pathol.* A contagious, epidemic disease, usually fatal, characterized by fever and buboes and transmitted to man by fleas from infected rats.

buc-cal (buk/əl) *adj. Anat.* **1.** Of or pertaining to the cheek. **2.** Pertaining to the mouth. [< L *bucca* cheek]

buc-ca-neer (buk/ə-nir′) *n.* A pirate or freebooter, esp. one who preyed along the Spanish coasts of America. [< F < Tupi *boucan* a frame for smoking and curing meat]

buck[1] (buk) *n.* **1.** The male of certain animals, as of antelopes, deer, goats, rabbits, and rats. **2.** A dandy; fop. **3.** *Informal* A young man. — *v.i.* **1.** To leap upward suddenly, as a horse or pack animal, in an attempt to dislodge rider or burden. **2.** *U.S. Informal* To resist stubbornly; object. **3.** *U.S. Informal* To move with jerks and jolts. — *v.t.* **4.** To throw by bucking. **5.** *U.S. Dial.* To butt with the head. **6.** *U.S. Informal* To resist stubbornly; oppose. **7.** In football, to charge into (the opponent's line) with the ball. — **to buck for** *U.S. Informal* To try hard to obtain (a promotion, raise, etc.). — **to buck up** *Informal* To encourage or take courage. [OE *bucca* he-goat]

buck[2] (buk) *n.* **1.** A sawhorse. **2.** A padded frame like a sawhorse, used for vaulting. [< Du. *zaagbok* sawbuck]

buck[3] (buk) *n.* In poker, a marker put into a jackpot, indicating that he who receives it must order another jackpot when it is his deal. — **to pass the buck** *U.S. Informal* To shift responsibility, blame, etc., to someone else.

buck and wing An intricate, fast tap dance.

buck-a-roo (buk/ə-rŏŏ, buk/ə-rŏŏ′) *n. U.S.* A cowboy. Also **buck-ay-ro** (buk-â/rō). [Alter. of Sp. *vaquero* cowboy]

buck-board (buk/bôrd′, -bōrd′) *n.* A light, four-wheeled, open carriage having a long, flexible board in place of body and springs.

buck-et (buk/it) *n.* **1.** A deep cylindrical vessel, with a rounded handle, used for carrying water, coal, etc.; a pail. **2.** As much as a bucket will hold: also **buck/et-ful/**. — *v.t. & v.i.* To draw or carry in a bucket. [? < OF *buket* tub]

buck-eye (buk/ī′) *n. Chiefly U.S.* **1.** The horse chestnut. **2.** The glossy brown seed or nut of this tree.

Buck-eye (buk/ī′) *n.* A native or inhabitant of Ohio.

Buckeye State Nickname of Ohio.

Buck-ing-ham Palace (buk/ing-əm) The official London residence of the British sovereign.

buck-le[1] (buk/əl) *n.* **1.** A device for fastening together two loose ends, as of a strap. **2.** An ornament for shoes, etc., resembling a buckle. — *v.* **-led, -ling** *v.t.* **1.** To fasten or attach with or as with a buckle. — *v.i.* **2.** To be fastened or joined by a buckle. — **to buckle down** To apply oneself vigorously. [< F *boucle* cheekstrap, boss of a shield]

buck-le[2] (buk/əl) *v.t. & v.i.* **-led, -ling** To bend under pressure; warp, curl, or crumple. — *n.* A bend, bulge, kink, or twist. [< F *boucler* to bulge]

buck-ler (buk/lər) *n.* **1.** A small, round shield. **2.** A means of defense. [< OF *boucler* having a boss]

buck-o (buk/ō) *n. pl.* **buck-oes** A bully.

buck private *U.S. Slang* A private in the U.S. Army.

buck-ram (buk/rəm) *n.* A coarse cotton fabric sized with glue, used for stiffening garments, in bookbinding, etc. — *v.t.* To stiffen with or as with buckram. [OF *boquerant* coarse cloth < *Bokhara*, Persia, where first made]

buck-saw (buk/sô′) *n.* A wood-cutting saw set in an adjustable H-shaped frame.

buck-shot (buk/shot′) *n.* Shot of a large size, used in hunting deer and other large game.

buck-skin (buk/skin′) *n.* **1.** The skin of a buck. **2.** A soft, strong, grayish yellow leather, formerly made from deerskins, now chiefly from sheepskins. **3.** *pl.* Breeches or clothing made of such skin.

buck-thorn (buk/thôrn′) *n.* A shrub or small tree having veined leaves and axillary flowers.

buck-tooth (buk/tŏŏth′) *n. pl.* **-teeth** A projecting tooth. — **buck/toothed/** *adj.*

buck-wheat (buk/hwēt′) *n.* **1.** A plant yielding triangular seeds used as fodder and for flour. **2.** Its seeds. **3.** The flour. [OE *bōc* beech + WHEAT]

bu-col-ic (byŏŏ-kol/ik) *adj.* Pertaining to or characteristic of shepherds or herdsmen; pastoral; rustic. — **Syn.** See RURAL. — *n.* **1.** A pastoral poem. **2.** A rustic; farmer. [< L < Gk. < *boukolos* herdsman] — **bu-col/i-cal-ly** *adv.*

bud (bud) *n.* **1.** *Bot.* **a** An undeveloped stem, branch, or shoot of a plant, with rudimentary leaves or unexpanded flowers. **b** The act or stage of budding. **2.** *Zool.* A budlike projection or part, as in some lower animals. **3.** Any immature person or thing. — **to nip in the bud** To stop in the initial stage. — *v.* **bud-ded, bud-ding** *v.i.* **1.** To put forth buds. **2.** To begin to grow or develop. — *v.t.* **3.** To cause to bud. **4.** To graft to another type of tree or plant. [ME *budde*; origin uncertain] — **bud/der** *n.*

Bud-dhism (bŏŏd/iz-əm, bŏŏ/diz-) *n.* A mystical and ascetic religious faith of eastern Asia, founded in northern India by Buddha in the sixth century B.C., and teaching that the ideal state of nirvana is reached by right living and believing, and peace of mind through meditation. — **Bud/dhist** *adj. & n.* — **Bud-dhis/tic** or **-ti-cal** *adj.*

bud-ding (bud/ing) *adj.* Just beginning; incipient.

bud-dy (bud/ē) *n. pl.* **-dies** *U.S. Informal* Pal; chum.

budge (buj) *v.t. & v.i.* **budged, budg-ing** To move or stir slightly. [< F *bouger* to stir, move]

budg-et (buj/it) *n.* **1.** A plan for adjusting expenditures to income. **2.** A collection or stock. — *v.t.* **1.** To determine in advance the expenditure of (time, money, etc.). **2.** To provide for or plan according to a budget. [< F < L *bulga* leather bag] — **budg-et-ar-y** (buj/ə-ter/ē) *adj.*

buff[1] (buf) *n.* **1.** A thick, soft, flexible leather made from the skins of buffalo, elk, oxen, etc. **2.** Its color, a light brownish yellow. **3.** A military coat made of buff leather. **4.** *Informal* The bare skin; the nude. **5.** A stick or wheel covered with leather, velvet, etc., and used for polishing. — *adj.* **1.** Made of buff. **2.** Light, brownish yellow. — *v.t.* To clean or polish with or as with a buff. [< F *buffle* buffalo] — **buff/y** *adj.*

buff[2] (buf) *v.t.* To deaden the shock of. — *n.* A blow; buffet: now only in *blindman's buff*. [< OF *buffe* blow]

buff[3] (buf) *n.* An enthusiast or devotee. [Origin uncertain]

buf·fa·lo (buf′ə·lō) *n. pl.* **·loes** or **·los** 1. Any of various large Old World oxen, as the **Cape buffalo** of Africa, and the water buffalo. 2. The North American bison. — *v.t.* **·loed**, **·lo ing** *U.S. Slang* To overawe; intimidate; hoodwink. [< Ital. < LL < Gk. *boubalos* buffalo]

CAPE BUFFALO
(About 5 feet high at shoulder)

buffalo grass A low, creeping grass covering prairies east of the Rocky Mountains.
buff·er¹ (buf′ər) *n.* One who or that which buffs or polishes. [< BUFF¹, v.]
buff·er² (buf′ər) *n.* 1. A shock absorber. 2. One who or that which diminishes shock of any kind.
buffer state A small country situated between two larger rival powers and regarded as lessening the danger of conflict between them.
buf·fet¹ (boo·fā′, *Brit.* buf′it) *n.* 1. A sideboard for china, glassware, etc. 2. A counter for serving meals or refreshments, or a restaurant with such a counter. 3. A light meal at which the guests serve themselves. [< F]
buf·fet² (buf′it) *v.t.* 1. To strike or cuff, as with the hand. 2. To strike repeatedly; knock about. — *v.i.* 3. To fight; struggle. — *n.* A blow or cuff, as with the hand. [< OF *buffet*, dim. of *buffe* a blow, slap] — **buf′fet·er** *n.*
buf·foon (bu·foon′) *n.* 1. A clown. 2. One given to jokes, coarse pranks, etc. [< F < Ital. clown < *buffa* jest] — **buf·foon′er·y** *n.* — **buf·foon′ish** *adj.*
bug (bug) *n.* 1. Any crawling insect with sucking mouth parts, wingless or with two pairs of wings. 2. Loosely, any insect or small arthropod. 3. *Brit.* A bedbug. 4. *Informal* A microorganism; germ. 5. *Slang* An enthusiast; monomaniac. 6. *U.S. Slang* A minor defect, as in a machine. 7. *U.S. Slang* A miniature electronic microphone, used in wiretapping, etc. 8. *Informal* A pathogenic microorganism. — *v.* **bugged**, **bug·ging** *v.i.* 1. To stare; stick out: said of eyes. — *v.t. U.S. Slang* 2. To annoy; pester. 3. To fit (a room, telephone circuit, etc.) with a concealed listening device. — **to bug off** *U.S. Slang* Go away! Get lost! — **to bug out** *U.S. Slang* To quit, especially hastily or ignominiously. [Origin unknown]
bug·bear (bug′bâr′) *n.* 1. A real or imaginary object of dread. 2. A hobgoblin. Also **bug·a·boo** (bug′ə·boo).
bug-eyed (bug′īd′) *adj. Slang* With the eyes bulging.
bug·gy¹ (bug′ē) *n. pl.* **·gies** 1. A light, four-wheeled carriage. 2. A baby carriage. [Origin uncertain]
bug·gy² (bug′ē) *adj.* **·gi·er**, **·gi·est** 1. Infested with bugs. 2. *U.S. Slang* Crazy. — **bug′gi·ness** *n.*
bu·gle¹ (byoo′gəl) *n.* 1. A brass wind instrument resembling a trumpet, usu. without keys or valves. 2. A huntsman's horn. — *v.* **·gled**, **·gling** *v.t.* 1. To summon with a bugle. — *v.i.* 2. To sound a bugle. [< OF < L *buculus*, dim. of *bos* ox] — **bu′gler** *n.*
bu·gle² (byoo′gəl) *n.* A tube-shaped glass bead used for ornamenting garments. — **bu′gled** *adj.*
buhl (bool) *n.* Decoration of furniture with inlaid tortoise shell, ivory, etc.; also a piece so decorated. Also **buhl′work′**. [after A. C. *Boulle*, 1642–1732, French cabinetmaker]
build (bild) *v.* **built** (*Archaic* **build·ed**), **build·ing** *v.t.* 1. To construct, erect, or make by assembling separate parts or materials. 2. To establish and increase. 3. To found; make a basis for. — *v.i.* 4. To construct or erect a house, etc. 5. To base or develop an idea, theory, etc.: with *on* or *upon*. — **to build up** 1. To create or build by degrees. 2. To renew or strengthen; also, to increase. — *n.* The manner or style in which anything is constructed; form; figure. [OE *byldan* < *bold* house] — **build′er** *n.*
build·ing (bil′ding) *n.* 1. A structure; edifice, as a house or barn. 2. The occupation, act, or art of constructing.
build-up (bild′up′) *n.* 1. The act of increasing or strengthening. 2. *Informal* Extravagant publicity or praise.
built-in (bilt′in′) *adj.* Built as a part of the structure.
bulb (bulb) *n.* 1. *Bot.* A leaf bud comprising a cluster of thickened, scalelike leaves growing usu. underground and sending forth roots, as the onion or lily. 2. Any plant growing from a bulb. 3. A rounded protuberance, as at the end of a tube. 4. An incandescent lamp. [< L < Gk. *bolbos* bulbous root] — **bulb·ar** (bul′bər) *adj.*
bul·bous (bul′bəs) *adj.* 1. Of, producing, or growing from bulbs. 2. Shaped like a bulb; swollen.
Bul·gar·i·an (bul·gâr′ē·ən, bool-) *adj.* Of Bulgaria, the Bulgarians, or their language. — *n.* 1. A native or citizen of Bulgaria. 2. The Slavic language of the Bulgarians.
bulge (bulj, boolj) *n.* A protuberant, rounded part. — *v.t. & v.i.* **bulged**, **bulg·ing** To swell out. [< OF < L *bulga*]
bulk (bulk, boolk) *n.* 1. Magnitude, volume, or size. 2. The greater or principal part; main body. 3. A large body

or mass. — **in bulk** 1. Not packaged; loose. 2. In large quantities. — *v.i.* 1. To appear large or important; loom. 2. To increase in magnitude; grow: with *up*. — *v.t.* 3. To cause to expand or grow large: with *out*. [Cf. ON *bulki* heap, cargo, and Dan. *bulk* rump]
bulk·head (bulk′hed′) *n.* 1. *Naut.* An upright partition in a vessel, separating compartments. 2. A partition or wall to keep back earth, gas, etc. 3. A small structure built on a roof to cover an elevator shaft.
bulk·y (bul′kē, bool′kē) *adj.* **bulk·i·er**, **bulk·i·est** Of great size; massive; also, large and unwieldy. — **bulk′i·ly** *adv.* — **bulk′i·ness** *n.*
bull¹ (bool) *n.* 1. The uncastrated male of a bovine animal, esp. of the domesticated types. ◆ Collateral adjective: *taurine*. 2. The male of some other animals, as of the elephant, whale, etc. 3. One likened to a bull, as in strength or manner. 4. A speculator who buys so as to profit from a rise in prices he anticipates or hopes to cause: opposed to *bear²*. 5. *U.S. Slang* A policeman or detective. 6. *U.S. Slang* Empty talk; nonsense. — *v.t.* 1. To speculate for a rise in price of or in. 2. To push or force (a way). — *v.i.* 3. To go up in price. 4. To go or push ahead. — *adj.* 1. Male; masculine. 2. Like a bull; large. 3. Marked by rising prices: a *bull* market. [ME *bule*]
bull² (bool) *n.* An official and authoritative document issued by the Pope. [< L *bulla* edict, seal]
bull·dog (bool′dôg′, -dog′) *n.* A medium-sized, short-haired, powerful dog, with strong jaws. — *adj.* Resembling a bulldog; courageous; tenacious. — *v.t.* **·dogged**, **·dog·ging** *U.S. Informal* To throw (a steer) by gripping its horns and twisting its neck.
bull·doze (bool′dōz′) *v.t.* **·dozed**, **·doz·ing** 1. *U.S. Slang* To intimidate; bully. 2. To clear, dig, scrape, etc., with a bulldozer. [? < BULL¹, adj. + DOSE, with ref. to the violent or excessive treatment given to the victim]
bull·doz·er (bool′dō′zər) *n.* 1. A tractor equipped with a heavy steel blade, used for moving earth, clearing wooded areas, etc. 2. *U.S. Slang* One who intimidates.
bul·let (bool′it) *n.* 1. A small projectile for a firearm. 2. Any small ball. [< F *boulette*, dim. of *boule* ball]
bul·le·tin (bool′ə·tən, -tin) *n.* 1. A brief account of news, as in a newspaper or on radio. 2. A periodical publication, as of the proceedings of a society. — *v.t.* To make public by bulletin. [< F < Ital. *bulletino* < L]
bulletin board A board on which bulletins, etc., are posted.
bul·let·proof (bool′it·proof′) *adj.* Not penetrable by bullets.
bull·fight (bool′fīt′) *n.* A combat in an arena between men and a bull or bulls, popular among the Spanish and Spanish Americans. — **bull′fight·er** *n.* — **bull′fight·ing** *n.*
bull·finch (bool′finch′) *n.* A European songbird having a short bill and red breast.
bull·frog (bool′frog′, -frôg′) *n.* A large frog with a deep bass croak. [< BULL¹, adj. + FROG]
bull·head (bool′hed′) *n.* A fresh-water catfish.
bull·head·ed (bool′hed′id) *adj.* Stubborn; headstrong.
bull·horn (bool′hôrn′) *n.* An electrical, hand-held voice amplifier resembling a megaphone.
bul·lion (bool′yən) *n.* Gold or silver uncoined or in mass, as in bars, plates, etc. [< AF, OF < *bouillir* to boil]
bull·ish (bool′ish) *adj.* 1. Bull-like. 2. Tending to cause prices to rise; also, marked by rising prices. 3. Bullheaded. — **bull′ish·ly** *adv.* — **bull′ish·ness** *n.*
bul·lock (bool′ək) *n.* A gelded bull; a steer or ox. [OE *bulluc*]
bull·pen (bool′pen′) *n. U.S.* 1. An enclosure for bulls. 2. *Informal* A place for temporary detention of prisoners. 3. In baseball, a place where pitchers practice during a game.
bull·ring (bool′ring′) *n.* A circular enclosure for bullfights.
bull session *U.S. Informal* An informal discussion.
bull's-eye (boolz′ī′) *n.* 1. The central colored disk on a target; also, a shot that hits this disk. 2. A thick disk of glass set in a pavement, deck, etc., to admit light. 3. A convex lens. 4. A lantern with such a lens.
bull terrier A white terrier having a long head and stiff coat, originally bred from a bulldog and a white terrier.
bull·whip (bool′hwip′) *n.* A long, heavy whip. — *v.t.* **·whipped**, **·whip·ping** To strike with a bullwhip.
bul·ly¹ (bool′ē) *n. pl.* **·lies** A swaggering, quarrelsome, usu. cowardly person who terrorizes weaker people. — *v.* **·lied**, **·ly·ing** *v.t.* 1. To intimidate or coerce by threats. — *v.i.* 2. To act the bully. — *adj.* 1. *U.S. Informal* Excellent; admirable. 2. Jolly; dashing; gallant. — *interj. U.S. Informal* Well done! [Cf. Du. *boel* friend, lover]
bul·ly² (bool′ē) *n.* Canned or pickled beef. Also **bully beef**. [Prob. < F *bouillir* to boil]
bul·ly·rag (bool′ē·rag′) *v.t.* **·ragged**, **·rag·ging** To bully; intimidate. [? < BULLY, v. + RAG¹]
bul·rush (bool′rush′) *n.* 1. A tall, rushlike plant growing

in water or damp ground. **2.** In the Bible, papyrus. *Ex.*
ii 3. [< BULL[1], adj. + RUSH[2]]

bul·wark (bŏŏl·wərk) *n.* **1.** A defensive wall or rampart;
fortification. **2.** Any safeguard or defense. **3.** *Usu. pl.*
Naut. The raised side of a ship, above the upper deck. — *v.t.*
To surround and fortify with a bulwark. [< MHG *bolwerc*]

bum (bum) *U.S. Slang n.* A worthless or dissolute loafer;
tramp. **— on the bum.** **1.** Out of order; broken. **2.** Living
as a vagrant. **— the bum's rush** Forcible ejection. — *adj.*
Bad; inferior. — *v.* **bummed, bum·ming** *v.i.* **1.** To live by
sponging on others. **2.** To live idly and in dissipation. —
v.t. **3.** To get by begging: to *bum* a ride. [Short for *bummer*,
alter. of G *bummler* loafer, dawdler] **— bum'mer** *n.*

bum·ble (bum'bəl) *v.t. & v.i.* **·bled, ·bling** To bungle, esp.
in an officious manner. [? Imit.] **— bum'bling** *adj. & n.*

bum·ble·bee (bum'bəl·bē') *n.* Any of various large, hairy,
bees. [< dial. E *bumble* to hum + BEE[1]]

bump (bump) *v.t.* **1.** To come into contact with; knock into.
2. To cause to knock into or against. **3.** *U.S. Slang* To
displace, as from a position or seat. — *v.i.* **4.** To strike
heavily or with force: often with *into* or *against.* **5.** To
move with jerks and jolts. **— to bump off** *Slang* To kill,
esp. with a gun. — *n.* **1.** An impact or collision; a blow;
jolt. **2.** A protuberance or uneven place. [Imit.]

bump·er[1] (bum'pər) *n.* The horizontal bar at the front or
rear of an automobile to absorb the shock of collision.

bump·er[2] (bum'pər) *n.* A cup or glass filled to the brim. —
adj. Unusually full or large: a *bumper* crop. [? Alter. of F
bombarde large cup; infl. in form by *bump*]

bump·kin (bump'kin) *n.* An awkward rustic; a lout. [? <
Du. *boomkin* little tree, block]

bump·tious (bump'shəs) *adj.* Aggressively self-assertive.
[Appar. < BUMP] **— bump'tious·ly** *adv.* **— bump'tious·**
ness *n.*

bump·y (bum'pē) *adj.* **bump·i·er, bump·i·est** **1.** Having
bumps. **2.** Jolting. **— bump'i·ly** *adv.* **— bump'i·ness** *n.*

bun (bun) *n.* **1.** A small bread roll, sometimes sweetened or
spiced. **2.** A roll of hair shaped like a bun. [ME *bunne*]

bu·na (bŏŏ'nə, byŏŏ'-) *n.* *Chem.* A synthetic rubber made
by the polymerization of butadiene with certain other substances. [< BU(TADIENE) + NA(TRIUM)]

bunch (bunch) *n.* **1.** A number of things of the same kind
growing, occurring, or fastened together; a cluster. **2.** *In-*
formal A group: a *bunch* of boys. **3.** *Rare* A hump; protuberance. — *v.t. & v.i.* **1.** To form bunches or groups. **2.**
To gather, as in folds. [ME *bunche*] **— bunch'y** *adj.*

bun·co (bung'kō) *U.S. Informal n.* A swindle; confidence
game. — *v.t.* **·coed, ·co·ing** To swindle or rob. Also spelled
bunko. [Prob. < Sp. *banco*, a card game]

bun·combe (bung'kəm) *n.* *U.S. Informal* **1.** Empty
speechmaking for political effect or to please constituents.
2. Empty talk; humbug. Also spelled *bunkum.* [from *Bun-*
combe County, N.C., whose congressman (1919–21) insisted
on making unimportant speeches "for Buncombe"]

bund (bŏŏnd, *Ger.* bŏŏnt) *n.* A league; society. [< G]

bun·dle (bun'dəl) *n.* **1.** A number of things or a quantity
of anything bound together. **2.** Anything folded or wrapped
and tied up; a package. **3.** A group; collection. ◆ Collateral adjective: *fascicular.* — *v.* **·dled, ·dling** *v.t.* **1.** To
tie, roll, or otherwise secure in a bundle. **2.** To send or put
hastily and unceremoniously: with *away, off, out,* or *into.*
— *v.i* **3.** To go hastily; hustle. **4.** To lie or sleep in the
same bed without undressing, formerly a courting custom
in Wales and New England. **— to bundle up** To dress
warmly. [< MDu. *bond* group] **— bun'dler** *n.*

bung (bung) *n.* **1.** A stopper for the hole through which a
cask is filled. **2.** Bunghole. — *v.t.* **1.** To close with or as
with a bung: often with *up* or *down.* **2.** *Slang* To damage;
maul: usually with *up.* [< MDu. *bonghe*]

bun·ga·low (bung'gə·lō) *n.* A small house or cottage,
usually with one or one and a half stories. [< Hind. *banglā,*
lit., Bengalese (house) < *Banga* Bengal]

bung·hole (bung'hōl') *n.* A hole in a keg or barrel from
which liquid is tapped. [< BUNG + HOLE]

bun·gle (bung'gəl) *v.t. & v.i.* **·gled, ·gling** To work, make,
or do (something) clumsily. — *n.* A clumsy job or performance; botch. **— bun'gler** *n.* **— bun'gling·ly** *adv.*

bun·ion (bun'yən) *n.* A painful swelling of the foot, usually
at the base of the great toe. [< OF *bugne* swelling]

bunk[1] (bungk) *n.* **1.** A narrow, built-in bed or shelf for
sleeping; a berth. **2.** *Informal* A bed. — *v.i.* *Informal* **1.** To
sleep in a bunk. **2.** To go to bed. [Cf. MDu. *banc* bench]

bunk[2] (bungk) *n.* *U.S. Slang* Empty talk; buncombe.

bun·ker (bung'kər) *n.* **1.** A large bin, as for coal on a ship.
2. In golf, a mound of earth serving as an obstacle. **3.** *Mil.*
A steel and concrete fortification. [Cf. OSw. *bunke* hold of a
ship and BANK[3] rowers' bench]

bun·ko (bung'kō) See BUNCO.

bun·kum (bung'kəm) See BUNCOMBE.

bun·ny (bun'ē) *n. pl* **·nies** A rabbit: a pet name. [Dim.
of dial. E *bun* a rabbit; ult. origin unknown]

Bun·sen burner (bun'sən) A type of gas burner in which a
mixture of gas and air is burned at the top of a short metal
tube, producing a very hot flame. [after R. W. *Bunsen,*
1811–1899, German chemist]

bunt (bunt) *v.t. & v.i.* **1.** To strike or push as with horns;
butt. **2.** In baseball, to bat (the ball) lightly into the infield, without swinging the bat. — *n.* **1.** A push or shove;
a butt. **2.** In baseball: **a** The act of bunting. **b** A ball that
has been bunted. [Nasalized var. of BUTT[1]]

bunt·ing[1] (bun'ting) *n.* **1.** A light woolen stuff or cotton
fabric used for flags, etc. **2.** Flags, banners, etc., collectively.
3. A type of sleeping bag for infants. [? ME *bonten* to sift]

bunt·ing[2] (bun'ting) *n.* One of various birds related to the
finches and sparrows. [ME *bountyng*; origin unknown]

bunt·line (bunt'lin, -lin') *n.* *Naut.* A rope used in hauling
a square sail up to the yard for furling.

Bun·yan (bun'yən), **Paul** See PAUL BUNYAN.

buoy (boi, bŏŏ'ē) *n.* **1.** *Naut.* A warning float moored on a
dangerous rock or shoal or at the ends of a channel. **2.** A
device for keeping a person afloat; a life buoy. — *v.t.*
1. To keep from sinking in a liquid; keep afloat. **2.** To
sustain the courage or heart of; encourage: usu. with *up.*
3. *Naut.* To mark with buoys. [< MDu. or OF < L *boia*
fetter; because it is chained to one spot]

buoy·an·cy (boi'ən·sē, bŏŏ'yən·sē) *n.* **1.** The tendency or
ability to keep afloat. **2.** The power of a fluid to keep an
object afloat. **3.** Cheerfulness. Also **buoy'ance.**

buoy·ant (boi'ənt, bŏŏ'yənt) *adj.* Having buoyancy.
[Prob. < Sp. < *boyar* to float] **— buoy'ant·ly** *adv.*

bur[1] (bûr) *n.* **1.** *Bot.* A rough or prickly flower head or seedcase. **2.** A plant that bears burs. **3.** A person or thing
that clings like a bur. — *v.t.* **burred, bur·ring** To remove
burs from. Also spelled *burr.* [< Scand.]

bur[2] (bûr) See BURR[2].

bur·ble (bûr'bəl) *v.i.* **·bled, ·bling** **1.** To bubble; gurgle. **2.**
To talk excitedly and confusedly. [ME; imit.]

bur·bot (bûr'bət) *n. pl.* **·bot** A fresh-water fish with barbels
on the chin. [< F, ult. < L *barbata* bearded]

bur·den[1] (bûr'dən) *n.* **1.** Something carried; a load. **2.**
Something that weighs heavily, as responsibility or anxiety.
3. *Naut.* **a** The carrying capacity of a vessel. **b** The weight
of the cargo. **4.** The carrying of loads: beasts of *burden.* —
v.t. To load or overload. [OE *byrthen* load]

bur·den[2] (bûr'dən) *n.* **1.** Something often repeated or dwelt
upon; the prevailing idea. **2.** A refrain of a song. [< F
< LL *burdo* drone]

burden of proof The obligation to prove a point.

bur·den·some (bûr'dən·səm) *adj.* Hard or heavy to bear;
oppressive. **— bur'den·some·ly** *adv.* **— bur'den·some·ness** *n.*

bur·dock (bûr'dok) *n.* A coarse weed of the composite
family having prickly burs. [< BUR[1] + DOCK[4]]

bu·reau (byŏŏr'ō) *n. pl.* **bu·reaus** or **bu·reaux** (byŏŏr'ōz)
1. *U.S.* A chest of drawers for clothing, etc., usu. with a
mirror. **2.** A government department, or a division thereof.
3. An office for transacting business. **4.** *Brit.* A writing
desk or table with drawers. [< F, a desk]

bu·reauc·ra·cy (byŏŏ·rok'rə·sē) *n. pl.* **·cies** **1.** Government
by bureaus; also, the group of officials so governing. **2.** The
undue extension of bureaus in the departments of a government. **3.** Rigid adherence to administrative routine. [< F
< *bureau* office, bureau + Gk. *kratia* power, rule]

bu·reau·crat (byŏŏr'ə·krat) *n.* **1.** A member of a bureauc-
racy. **2.** An official who narrowly adheres to a rigid routine.
— bu'reau·crat'ic or **-i·cal** *adj.* **— bu'reau·crat'i·cal·ly** *adv.*

bu·rette (byŏŏ·ret') *n.* *Chem.* A finely graduated glass tube
with a stopcock at the bottom. Also **bu·ret'.** [< F, dim. of
buire a vase, vial]

burg (bûrg) *n.* *U.S. Informal* A town; esp., a rural town.
[OE *burg*]

bur·geon (bûr'jən) *v.i.* **1.** To flourish; grow. **2.** To bud;
sprout. — *v.t.* **3.** To put forth (buds, etc.). — *n.* A bud;
sprout. Also spelled *bourgeon.* [< OF *burjon*]

bur·gess (bûr'jis) *n.* **1.** A citizen or officer of a borough.
2. In colonial times, a member of the lower house (**House of**
Burgesses) of the legislature of Virginia. [< OF *burgeis*]

burgh (bûrg, *Scot.* bûr'ō, -ə) *n.* In Scottish law, a chartered
town. [Var. of BOROUGH] **— burgh·al** (bûr'gəl) *adj.*

burgh·er (bûr'gər) *n.* A citizen of a burgh, town, or city.

bur·glar (bûr'glər) *n.* One who commits burglary. [<
Med.L < OF < *bourg* dwelling + *laire* robbery]

bur·glar·ize (bûr'glə·rīz) *v.t.* **·ized, ·iz·ing** To commit
burglary upon.

bur·gla·ry (bûr'glər·ē) *n. pl.* **·ries** *Law* The breaking and
entering of a dwelling at night, with intent to commit a
crime. **— Syn.** See THEFT.

bur·gle (bûr'gəl) *v.t. & v.i.* **·gled, ·gling** *Informal* To commit burglary (upon).

bur·go·mas·ter (bûr'gə·mas'tər, -mäs'-) *n.* A Dutch,
Flemish, or German mayor. [< Du. *burgemeester*]

Bur·gun·dy (bûr'gən·dē) *n. pl.* **·dies** A kind of red or white
wine originally made in Burgundy.

bur·i·al (ber′ē-əl) n. The burying of a dead body; interment. —adj. Of or pertaining to burial. [ME buryel, biriel < biriels (mistaken as plural) < OE brygels tomb]

bu·rin (byŏŏr′in) n. A steel tool with a lozenge-shaped point for engraving or carving.

burl (bûrl) n. 1. A knot or lump in wool, cloth, or thread. 2. A large wartlike excrescence formed on the trunks of trees. —v.t. To dress (cloth) by removing burls. [< OF < LL burra shaggy hair] —burled adj. —burl′er n.

bur·lap (bûr′lap) n. A coarse fabric made of jute or hemp, used for wrapping, bagging, etc. [Origin uncertain]

bur·lesque (bər·lesk′) n. 1. A satire or ludicrous imitation, usually of a serious, dignified subject; parody. 2. U.S. A theatrical entertainment marked by low comedy, striptease, etc. —adj. 1. Marked by ridiculous incongruity or broad caricature. 2. U.S. Of or pertaining to theatrical burlesque. —v. ·lesqued, ·les·quing v.t. 1. To represent laughably; satirize. —v.i. 2. To use broad caricature. [< F < Ital. < burla joke]

bur·ley (bûr′lē) n. A fine, light tobacco grown principally in Kentucky. Also **Bur′ley**. [? after Burley, a grower]

bur·ly (bûr′lē) adj. ·li·er, ·li·est Large of body; bulky; stout; lusty. [ME borlich] —bur′li·ly adv. —bur′li·ness n.

Bur·mese (bər·mēz′, -mēs′) adj. Of or pertaining to Burma, its inhabitants, or their language. Also **Bur′man** (-mən). —n. pl. ·mese 1. A native or inhabitant of Burma. 2. The Sino-Tibetan language of Burma.

burn (bûrn) v. burned or burnt, burn·ing v.t. 1. To destroy or consume by fire. 2. To set afire; ignite. 3. To injure or kill by fire; execute by fire. 4. To injure or damage by friction, heat, steam, etc.; scale; wither. 5. To produce by fire. 6. To brand; also, to cauterize. 7. To finish or harden by intense heat; fire. 8. To use or employ, so as to give off light, heat, etc. 9. To cause a feeling of heat in. 10. To sunburn. 11. Chem. To cause to undergo combustion. 12. U.S. Slang To electrocute. —v.i. 13. To be on fire; blaze. 14. To be destroyed or scorched by fire. 15. To give off light, heat, etc.; shine. 16. To die by fire. 17. To appear or feel hot: He burns with fever. 18. To be eager, excited, or inflamed. 19. Chem. To oxidize; undergo combustion. 20. U.S. Slang To be electrocuted. —to burn down To raze or be razed by fire. —to burn out 1. To become extinguished through lack of fuel. 2. To destroy or wear out by heat, friction, etc. 3. To burn up the house, store, or property of. 4. To drive out by heat. —to burn up 1. To consume by fire. 2. Slang To make or become irritated or enraged. —n. 1. A burned place. 2. Pathol. A lesion caused by heat, extreme cold, corrosive chemicals, gases, electricity, radiation, etc. [Fusion of OE beornan to be on fire, and OE bærnan to set afire]

burn·er (bûr′nər) n. 1. One who or that which burns. 2. That part of a stove, lamp, etc., from which the flame comes.

burn·ing (bûr′ning) adj. 1. Consuming or being consumed by or as if by fire. 2. Causing intense feeling; urgent.

burning glass A convex lens for concentrating the sun's rays upon an object so as to heat or ignite it.

bur·nish (bûr′nish) v.t. & v.i. To polish by friction; make or become shiny. —n. Polish; luster. [< OF burnir to polish] —bur′nish·er n. —bur′nish·ment n.

bur·noose (bər·nōōs′, bûr′nōōs) n. An Arab hooded cloak. Also **bur·nous′**. [< F < Arabic burnus]

burn·out (bûrn′out′) n. 1. A destruction or failure due to burning or to excessive heat. 2. Aerospace The cessation of burning in a jet or rocket engine, esp. when caused by stoppage or exhaustion of fuel.

burn·sides (bûrn′sīdz) n.pl. Side whiskers and mustache: also called sideburns. [after A. E. Burnside, 1824–81, Union general in the Civil War]

burnt (bûrnt) Alternative past tense and past participle of BURN.

burnt ocher A permanent, brick red pigment.

burnt offering An animal, food, etc., burned upon an altar as a sacrifice or offering to a god.

burnt sienna A dark brown pigment.

burnt umber A reddish brown pigment.

burp (bûrp) U.S. Informal n. A belch. —v.i. To belch. —v.t. To cause to belch: to burp a baby. [Imit.]

burr[1] (bûr) n. 1. A roughness or rough edge, esp. one left on metal in casting or cutting. 2. Any of several tools for cutting, reaming, etc. 3. A dentist's drill with a rough head. 4. A protuberant knot on a tree. —v.t. 1. To form a rough edge on. 2. To remove a rough edge from. Also spelled bur. [Var. of BUR[1]] —bur′ry adj.

burr[2] (bûr) n. 1. A rough guttural sound of r produced by vibration of the uvula against the back of the tongue. 2. Any rough, dialectal pronunciation: the Scottish burr. 3. A buzz. —v.t. 1. To pronounce with a rough or guttural articulation. —v.i. 2. To speak with a burr. [Imit.]

bur·ro (bûr′ō, bŏŏr′ō) n. pl. ·ros A small donkey. [< Sp.]

bur·row (bûr′ō) n. 1. A hole made in the ground, as by a rabbit. 2. Any similar place of refuge. —v.i. 1. To live or hide in a burrow. 2. To dig a burrow or burrows. 3. To dig into, under, or through something. —v.t. 4. To dig a burrow or burrows in. 5. To make by burrowing. 6. To hide (oneself) in a burrow. [ME borow] —bur′row·er n.

bur·sa (bûr′sə) n. pl. ·sae (-sē) or ·sas Anat. A pouch or saclike cavity; esp. one containing synovia and located at points of friction in the bodies of vertebrates. [< Med.L, sac, pouch] —bur′sal adj.

bur·sar (bûr′sər, -sär) n. A treasurer, as of a college. [< Med.L bursa bag, purse] —bur·sar·i·al (bər·sâr′ē·əl) adj.

bur·sa·ry (bûr′sər·ē) n. pl. ·ries The treasury of a public institution or a religious order.

bur·si·tis (bər·sī′tis) n. Pathol. Inflammation of a bursa.

burst (bûrst) n. burst, burst·ing v.i. 1. To break open or apart suddenly and violently. 2. To be full to the point of breaking open; bulge. 3. To appear or enter suddenly or violently. 4. To become audible or evident. 5. To give sudden expression to passion, grief, etc. —v.t. 6. To cause to break open suddenly or violently; force open; puncture. 7. To cause to swell to the point of breaking open. —n. 1. A sudden exploding or breaking forth. 2. A sudden effort or spurt; rush. 3. A crack or break. [OE berstan] —burst′er n.

bur·y (ber′ē) v.t. bur·ied, bur·y·ing 1. To put (a dead body) in a grave, tomb, or the sea; perform burial rites for; inter. 2. To put underground; to conceal, as by covering. 3. To embed; sink: to bury a nail in a wall. 4. To end; put out of mind: to bury a friendship. 5. To occupy deeply; engross: He buried himself in study. [OE byrgan]

burying ground A cemetery.

bus (bus) n. pl. bus·es or bus·ses 1. A large passenger vehicle usu. following a prescribed route. 2. Informal An automobile. —v.t. bused or bussed, bus·ing or bus·sing 1. To transport by bus. —v.i. 2. To go by bus. 3. Informal To work as a bus boy. [Short form of OMNIBUS]

bus boy An employee in a restaurant who clears tables of soiled dishes, assists the waiters, etc.

bus·by (buz′bē) n. pl. ·bies A tall fur cap worn by British hussars, artillerymen, and engineers. [Origin uncertain]

bush[1] (bŏŏsh) n. 1. A low, treelike or thickly branching shrub. 2. A clump of shrubs; thicket; undergrowth. 3. Wild, uncleared land covered with scrub; also, any rural or unsettled area. 4. A fox's tail. 5. Canadian Wood lot. —v.i. 1. To grow or branch like a bush. 2. To be or become bushy. —v.t. 3. To decorate or support with bushes. [< ON buskr]

bush[2] (bŏŏsh) v.t. To put a bushing in, as a bearing. —n. A bushing. [< MDu. busse box]

BUSBY

bushed (bŏŏsht) adj. Informal 1. U.S. & Canadian Exhausted. 2. Odd from living in isolation. [< BUSH[1]]

bush·el[1] (bŏŏsh′əl) n. 1. A unit of dry measure. 2. A container holding this amount. See table inside back cover. [< OF boissiel, dim. of boisse box]

bush·el[2] (bŏŏsh′əl) v.t. & v.i. bush·eled or ·elled, bush·el·ing or ·el·ling U.S. To repair and restore (a garment). [Cf. G bosseln to do small jobs] —bush′el·er or bush′el·ler n.

bu·shi·do (bōō′shē·dō) n. The chivalric code of the feudal Samurai. Also **Bu′shi·do**. [< Japanese, way of the warrior]

bush·ing (bŏŏsh′ing) n. 1. Mech. A metallic lining for a hole, as in the hub of a wheel, designed to insulate or to prevent abrasion between parts. 2. Electr. A lining inserted in a socket to insulate an electric current. [< BUSH[2]]

bush league In baseball slang, an obscure minor league.

bush leaguer 1. In baseball slang, a player in a bush league. 2. U.S. Slang A mediocre person.

bush·man (bŏŏsh′mən) n. pl. ·men (-mən) Austral. A dweller or farmer in the bush.

Bush·man (bŏŏsh′mən) n. pl. ·men (-mən) 1. One of a nomadic people of South Africa. 2. The language of the Bushmen. [Trans. of Du. boschjesman]

bush·mas·ter (bŏŏsh′mas′tər, -mäs′) n. A venomous pit viper of Central and South America.

bush·whack (bŏŏsh′hwak′) U.S. v.t. 1. To attack or fire upon from hiding; ambush. —v.i. 2. To fight as a guerrilla. [< Du. boschwachter forest keeper; infl. by whack] —bush′whack′er n. —bush′whack′ing n.

bush·y (bŏŏsh′ē) adj. bush·i·er, bush·i·est 1. Covered with bushes. 2. Shaggy. —bush′i·ly adv. —bush′i·ness n.

bus·ied (biz′ēd) Past tense and past participle of BUSY.

bus·i·ly (biz′ə·lē) adv. In a busy manner; industriously.

busi·ness (biz′nis) n. 1. An occupation, trade, or profession. 2. Any of the various operations or details of trade or industry. 3. A commercial enterprise or establishment;

a firm, factory, store, etc. **4.** The amount or volume of trade. **5.** A proper interest or concern; responsibility; duty. **6.** A matter or affair. **7.** In the theater, the movements, facial expressions, etc., apart from dialogue, by which actors interpret a part. — Syn. See OCCUPATION. — **to give (someone) the business** *Slang* **1.** To deal with harshly or summarily. **2.** To beat severely or kill. **3.** To cheat or defraud. — **to have no business** To have no right (to do something). — **to mean business** *Informal* To have a serious intention. [OE *bysignis*]

business college A school that gives training in clerical and secretarial skills for positions in commerce and industry.

busi·ness·like (biz′nis·līk′) *adj.* Methodical; systematic.

busi·ness·man (biz′nis·man′) *n. pl.* **·men** (-men′) One engaged in commercial or industrial activity. — **busi′ness·wom′an** (-wŏm′ən) *n.fem.*

bus·kin (bus′kin) *n.* **1.** A boot reaching halfway to the knee, and strapped or laced to the ankle. **2.** A laced half boot, worn by Greek and Roman tragic actors. **3.** Tragedy. [Origin uncertain] — **bus′kined** *adj.*

bus·man (bus′mən) *n. pl.* **men** (-mən) A bus driver.

busman's holiday A holiday spent by choice in activity similar to one's regular work.

buss (bus) *Archaic & Dial. n.* A kiss; smack. — *v.t. & v.i.* To kiss heartily. [Imit.]

bus·ses (bus′iz) Alternative plural of BUS.

bust¹ (bust) *n.* **1.** The human breast, esp. the bosom of a woman. **2.** A piece of statuary representing the human head, shoulders, and breast. [< F < Ital. *busto*]

bust² (bust) *Slang v.t.* **1.** To burst. **2.** To tame; train, as a horse. **3.** To make bankrupt or short of funds. **4.** To reduce in rank; demote. **5.** To hit; strike. — *v.i.* **6.** To burst. **7.** To become bankrupt or short of funds. — *n.* **1.** Failure; bankruptcy. **2.** A spree. **3.** A blow. [Alter. of BURST]

bus·tard (bus′tərd) *n.* A large Old World game bird related to the plovers and cranes. [< OF *bistarde, oustarde* < L *avis tarda*, lit., slow bird]

bust·er (bus′tər) *n. U.S. Slang* One who breaks or breaks up: trust *buster*.

bus·tle¹ (bus′əl) *n.* Excited activity; noisy stir; fuss. — *v.* **·tled, ·tling** *v.i.* **1.** To move noisily or energetically; hurry. — *v.t.* **2.** To cause to hurry. [? Akin to BUSK²]

bus·tle² (bus′əl) *n.* A frame or pad formerly worn by women on the back of the body below the waist to distend the skirt. [? < BUSTLE¹]

bus·tling (bus′ling) *adj.* Active; busy. — **bus′tling·ly** *adv.*

bus·y (biz′ē) *adj.* **bus·i·er, bus·i·est** **1.** Actively engaged in something; occupied. **2.** Filled with activity; never still. **3.** Officiously active; meddling; prying. **4.** Temporarily engaged, as a telephone line. — *v.t.* **bus·ied, bus·y·ing** To make busy. [OE *bysig* active] — **bus′y·ness** *n.*

bus·y·bod·y (biz′ē·bod′ē) *n. pl.* **·bodies** One who officiously meddles in the affairs of others.

busy signal In a dial telephone, a recurrent buzzing tone indicating that the number called is already connected.

but (but, *unstressed* bət) *conj.* **1.** On the other hand; yet. **2.** Without the result that: It never rains *but* it pours. **3.** Other than; otherwise than. **4.** Except: anything *but* that. **5.** With the exception that: often with *that*: Nothing will do *but* I must leave. **6.** That: We don't doubt *but* he is there. **7.** That ... not: He is not so ill *but* exercise will benefit him. **8.** Who ... not; which ... not: Few sought his advice *but* were helped by it. — *prep.* With the exception of; save: owning nothing *but* his clothes. — *adv.* Only; just: She is *but* a child. — **all but** Almost; nearly. — **but for** Were it not for. — *n.* An objection or condition; exception: no ifs or *buts*. [OE < *be* by + *ūtan* outside]
— **Syn.** (conj.) **1.** *But* ranges in meaning from faintest contrast to absolute negation. *However* suggests a moderate concession or a second point to be considered. *Nevertheless* emphasizes direct opposition, and *yet* serves to introduce a mildly inconsequential outcome.

bu·ta·di·ene (byōō′tə·dī′ēn, -dī·ēn′) *n. Chem.* A hydrocarbon, C₄H₆, similar to isoprene, used in the manufacture of synthetic rubber. [< BUTA(NE) + DI-² (def. 2) + -ENE]

bu·tane (byōō′tān, byōō·tān′) *n. Chem.* A colorless, flammable, gaseous hydrocarbon, C₄H₁₀, of the methane series. [< L *but(yrum)* butter + -ANE²]

butch·er (bōōch′ər) *n.* **1.** One who slaughters or dresses animals for market; also, a dealer in meats. **2.** One guilty of needless bloodshed. **3.** *U.S.* A vendor of candy, etc., on trains. **4.** A botcher. — *v.t.* **1.** To slaughter or dress for market. **2.** To kill cruelly or indiscriminately. **3.** To botch. [< OF *bouchier* slaughterer of bucks] — **butch′er·er** *n.*

butch·er·bird (bōōch′ər·bûrd′) *n.* The shrike, a bird.

butch·er's-broom (bōōch′ərz·brōōm′, -brōōm′) *n.* A low, evergreen shrub with leathery, leaflike branches bearing scarlet berries. Also **butch′er·broom′.**

butch·er·y (bōōch′ər·ē) *n. pl.* **·er·ies** **1.** Wanton slaughter. **2.** A slaughterhouse. **3.** The butcher's trade.

but·ler (but′lər) *n.* A manservant in charge of the dining

room, wine, etc., usu. the head servant in a household. [< AF, OF < Med.L < *buticula* bottle] — **but′ler·ship** *n.*

butler's pantry A room between the kitchen and the dining room, suitable for storage, serving, etc.

butt¹ (but) *v.t.* **1.** To strike with the head or horns; ram. **2.** To drive, push, or bump as with the head. — *v.i.* **3.** To strike or attempt to strike something with the head or horns. **4.** To move or drive head foremost. **5.** To project; jut. — **to butt in** *Informal* To interrupt; intrude. — *n.* **1.** A blow or push with the head. **2.** A thrust in fencing. [< OF *buter* to strike, push, project] — **butt′er** *n.*

butt² (but) *n.* **1.** A person or thing subjected to jokes, ridicule, criticism, etc. **2.** A target, as on a rifle range. **3.** *pl.* A target range. **4.** An embankment or wall behind a target to stop the shot. [< OF *but* end, goal]

butt³ (but) *n.* **1.** The larger or thicker end of anything. **2.** An end or extremity. **3.** An unused end, as of a cigar or cigarette; stub; stump. **4.** The thick part of a tanned hide. **5.** *U.S. Informal* The buttocks. [Akin to Dan. *but* blunt]

butt⁴ (but) *n.* **1.** A large cask. **2.** A measure of wine, 126 U.S. gallons. [< OF *boute*]

butte (byōōt) *n. U.S. & Canadian* A conspicuous hill, esp. one with steep sides and a flattened top. [< F]

but·ter (but′ər) *n.* **1.** The fatty constituent of milk churned and prepared for cooking and table use. **2.** A substance having the consistency or some of the qualities of butter. **3.** Any of several food preparations of semisolid consistency: apple *butter*. **4.** *Informal* Flattery. — *v.t.* **1.** To put butter on. **2.** *Informal* To flatter: usu. with *up*. — **to know which side one's bread is buttered on** To be aware of the true sources of one's fortune or security. [OE < L < Gk. < *bous* cow + *tyros* cheese]

butter bean **1.** The wax bean. **2.** In the southern U.S., the lima bean.

but·ter·cup (but′ər·kup′) *n.* A plant of the crowfoot family, with yellow, cup-shaped flowers.

but·ter·fat (but′ər·fat′) *n.* The fatty substance of milk, from which butter is made.

but·ter·fin·gers (but′ər·fing′gərz) *n. Informal* One who drops things easily or often. — **but′ter·fin′gered** *adj.*

but·ter·fish (but′ər·fish′) *n. pl.* **·fish** or **·fishes** A silvery, laterally compressed fish common along the Atlantic coast.

but·ter·fly (but′ər·flī′) *n. pl.* **·flies** **1.** An insect with large, often brightly colored wings, club-shaped antennae, and slender body. **2.** A frivolous person. [OE *buttorflēoge*]

butter knife A small, blunt-edged knife for cutting or spreading butter.

but·ter·milk (but′ər·milk′) *n.* The sour liquid left after the butterfat has been separated from milk or cream.

but·ter·nut (but′ər·nut′) *n.* **1.** The oily, edible nut of a walnut of North America. **2.** The tree or its cathartic inner bark. **3.** A yellowish brown.

but·ter·scotch (but′ər·skoch′) *n.* **1.** Hard, sticky candy made with brown sugar, butter, and flavoring. **2.** A syrup or flavoring consisting of similar ingredients. — *adj.* Made of or flavored with butterscotch.

but·ter·y¹ (but′ər·ē) *adj.* **1.** Containing, like, or smeared with butter. **2.** *Informal* Grossly flattering; adulatory.

but·ter·y² (but′ər·ē, but′rē) *n. pl.* **·ter·ies** *Chiefly Brit.* A pantry or wine cellar. [< OF < LL *butta* bottle]

but·tock (but′ək) *n.* **1.** *Anat.* Either of the two fleshy prominences that form the rump. **2.** *pl.* The rump. [Dim. of BUTT³]

but·ton (but′n) *n.* **1.** A knob or disk sewn to a garment, etc., serving as a fastening or for ornamentation. **2.** Anything resembling a button, as the knob for operating an electric bell or an electric lamp. **3.** *Slang* The point of the chin. — **on the button** *Informal* Exactly; precisely. — *v.t.* **1.** To fasten or provide with a button or buttons. — *v.i.* **2.** To be capable of being fastened with or as with buttons. [< OF *boton* button, bud] — **but′ton·er** *n.*

but·ton·hole (but′n·hōl′) *n.* A slit or loop to receive and hold a button. — *v.t.* **·holed, ·hol·ing** **1.** To work buttonholes in. **2.** To seize as by the buttonhole so as to detain.

but·tons (but′nz) *n.pl.* (*construed as sing.*) *Brit. Informal* A bellboy; page.

but·ton·wood (but′n·wŏŏd′) *n.* **1.** A plane tree of North America, yielding a wood used for furniture, etc. Also **but·ton·ball′** (-bôl′). **2.** The wood of this tree.

but·ton·y (but′n·ē) *adj.* Of, having, or like a button.

but·tress (but′tris) *n.* **1.** *Archit.* A structure built against a wall to strengthen it. **2.** Any support or prop. **3.** Something suggesting a buttress, as a projecting rock or hillside. — *v.t.* **1.** To support with a buttress. **2.** To prop up; sustain. [< OF *bouter, buter* to push, thrust]

bu·tyl (byōō′til) *n. Chem.* A univalent hydrocarbon radical, C₄H₉, from butane. [< BUT(YRIC) + -YL]

butyl alcohols *Chem.* A group of three isomeric alcohols having the formula C₄H₉OH.

bu·ty·lene (byōō′tə·lēn) *n. Chem.* A gaseous hydrocarbon, C₄H₈, an ingredient of synthetic rubber.

bu·tyr·ic (byōō·tir′ik) *adj.* Of or derived from butter.
bux·om (buk′səm) *adj.* Characterized by health and vigor; plump; comely: said of women. [ME *buhsum* pliant] — **bux′om·ly** *adv.* — **bux′om·ness** *n.*
buy (bī) *v.* **bought, buying** *v.t.* 1. To acquire with money; purchase. 2. To obtain by some exchange or sacrifice: to *buy* wisdom with experience. 3. To bribe; corrupt: He was *bought* cheap. — *v.i.* 4. To make purchases; be a purchaser. — **to buy in** 1. To buy back for the owner, as at an auction when the bids are too low. 2. To buy stock in a company. 3. *Slang* To pay money as a price for joining. — **to buy off** To bribe. — **to buy out** To purchase the stock, interests, etc., of. — **to buy over** To win over to one's interest by a bribe. — **to buy up** To purchase the entire supply of. — *n. Informal* 1. Anything bought or about to be bought. 2. A bargain. [OE *bycgan*] — **buy′a·ble** *adj.*
buy·er (bī′ər) *n.* 1. One who makes purchases. 2. A purchasing agent, as for a department store.
buzz (buz) *v.i.* 1. To make the humming, vibrating sound of the bee. 2. To talk or gossip excitedly. 3. To go busily or hastily. — *v.t.* 4. To cause to buzz. 5. To spread by buzzing. 6. To signal with a buzz. 7. *Informal* To fly an airplane low over. 8. *Informal* To call by telephone. — *n.* 1. A vibrating hum. 2. A low murmur, as of many voices. 3. *Informal* A phone call. [Imit.]
buz·zard (buz′ərd) *n.* 1. One of several large, slow-flying hawks. 2. A turkey buzzard. [< OF *busart*]
buzz bomb A robot bomb.
buzz·er (buz′ər) *n.* An electric signal making a buzzing sound, as on a telephone switchboard.
buzz saw A circular saw, so called from the sound it emits.
by (bī) *prep.* 1. Next to; near: the house *by* the river. 2. Past and beyond: The train roared *by* us. 3. Through the agency of or by means of: to hang *by* a rope; to travel *by* plane. 4. By way of: Come *by* the nearest road. 5. On the part of: a loss felt *by* all. 6. According to: *by* law. 7. In the course of; during: to travel *by* night. 8. Not later than: Be here *by* noon. 9. After: day *by* day. 10. According to as a standard: to work *by* the day. 11. To the extent or amount of: insects *by* the thousands. 12. In multiplication or measurement with: Multiply 6 *by* 8. 13. With reference to: to do well *by* one's friends. 14. In the name of: *by* all that's holy. — **by the way** (or **by the by, bye the bye**) Incidentally. — *adv.* 1. At hand; near. 2. Up to and beyond something; past: The years go *by*. 3. Apart; aside: to lay something *by*. — **by and by** After a time; before long. — **by and large** On the whole; generally. — *adj. & n.* See BYE. [OE *bī* near, about]
by- *combining form* 1. Secondary; incidental: *by-product*. 2. Near; close: *bystander*. 3. Aside; out of the way: *byway*.
by-and-by (bī′ən·bī′) *n.* Future time; hereafter.
bye (bī) *n.* 1. Something of minor or secondary importance. 2. The position of one who, assigned no opponent, automatically advances to the next round, as in a tennis tournament. 3. In golf, any hole remaining unplayed when the match ends. — *adj.* Secondary. Also spelled *by*. [< BY]

bye-bye (bī′bī′) *interj.* Good-by.
by-e·lec·tion (bī′i·lek′shən) *n. Brit.* A parliamentary election between general elections, held to fill a vacancy.
Bye·lo·rus·sian (bye′lə·rush′ən) *adj.* Of or pertaining to the Byelorussian S.S.R., its people, or their language. — *n.* 1. A native or inhabitant of the Byelorussian S.S.R. 2. The language of the Byelorussians. Also *White Russian.*
by·gone (bī′gôn′, -gon′) *adj.* Gone by; past. — *n. Often pl.* Something past. — **to let bygones be bygones** To let disagreements and difficulties in the past be overlooked.
by·law (bī′lô′) *n.* 1. A law adopted by a corporation, etc., and subordinate to a constitution or charter. 2. A secondary law. [ME < *by, bi* village + *lawe* law]
by-line (bī′līn′) *n.* The line at the head of an article in a newspaper, etc., giving the name of the writer.
by-pass (bī′pas′, -päs′) *n.* 1. Any road, path, or route connecting two points in a course other than that normally used; a detour. 2. *Electr.* A shunt. — *v.t.* 1. To go around or avoid (an obstacle). 2. To provide with a by-pass.
by-path (bī′path′, -päth′) *n.* A secluded or indirect path.
by-play (bī′plā′) *n.* Action or speech apart from the main action, especially in a play.
by-prod·uct (bī′prod′əkt) *n.* A secondary product or result.
by·road (bī′rōd′) *n.* A back or side road.
by·stand·er (bī′stan′dər) *n.* One present but not taking part; an onlooker.
byte (bīt) *n.* A group of binary digits, usu. eight, which a computer stores and treats as a unit.
by·way (bī′wā′) *n.* A branch or side road.
by·word (bī′wûrd′) *n.* 1. A proverbial saying; also, a pet phrase. 2. A person, institution, etc., that proverbially represents a type, usually an object of scorn.
Byz·an·tine (biz′ən·tēn, -tīn, bi·zan′tin) *adj.* 1. Of or pertaining to Byzantium or its civilization. 2. Pertaining to the style of architecture developed in Byzantium during the fifth and sixth centuries, using rounded arches, centralized plans surmounted by large domes, and lavishness of mosaic and other decoration. — *n.* A native or inhabitant of Byzantium. Also **By·zan·ti·an** (bi·zan′shē·ən, -shən). [< L *Byzantinus* < *Byzantium*]

BYZANTINE ARCHITECTURE
(Santa Sophia, Constantinople, A.D. 538)

Byzantine Empire The eastern part of the later Roman Empire (395–1453); capital, Constantinople: also, *Byzantium, Eastern Roman Empire.*
By·zan·ti·um (bi·zan′shē·əm, -tē·əm) 1. An ancient city on the Bosporus, later Constantinople. 2. The Byzantine Empire.

C

c, C (sē) *n. pl.* **c's** or **cs, C's** or **Cs, cees** (sēz) 1. The third letter of the English alphabet. 2. Any sound represented by the letter *c.* — *symbol* 1. The Roman numeral for 100. 2. *Chem.* Carbon (symbol C). 3. *Music* **a** The tonic note of the natural scale; do. **b** A written note representing it. **c** The scale built upon C. 4. The third in sequence or class.
Caa·ba (kä′bə, kä′ə·bə) See KAABA.
cab (kab) *n.* 1. A taxicab. 2. A one-horse carriage for hire. 3. A covered compartment of a locomotive, motor truck, etc., for the operator. [Short form of CABRIOLET]
ca·bal (kə·bal′) *n.* 1. A number of persons secretly united for some private purpose. 2. An intrigue; plot. — *v.i.* ·**balled**, ·**bal·ling** To form a cabal; plot. [< MF *cabale*]
cab·a·la (kab′ə·lə, kə·bä′lə) *n.* 1. *Often cap.* An occult system originating in a mystical interpretation of the Scriptures among certain Jewish rabbis. 2. Any secret, occult, or mystic system. Also spelled *kabala, kabbala.* [< Hebrew *qābal* to receive] — **cab′a·lism** *n.* — **cab′a·list** *n. & adj.*

cab·a·lis·tic (kab′ə·lis′tik) *adj.* 1. Pertaining to the cabala. 2. Having a mystic meaning; mysterious. Also **ca·bal·ic** (kə·bal′ik), **cab′a·lis′ti·cal.** — **cab′a·lis′ti·cal·ly** *adv.*
cab·al·le·ro (kab′əl·yâr′ō) *n. pl.* ·**ros.** 1. A Spanish cavalier. 2. *SW U.S.* A horseman. [< Sp. < L *caballus* horse]
ca·ban·a (kə·ban′ə, -bä′nə) *n.* 1. A small cabin. 2. A beach bathhouse. Also **ca·ba·ña** (kə·bän′yə, -bän′-). [< Sp.]
cab·a·ret (kab′ə·rā′) *n.* 1. A restaurant that provides singing, dancing, etc. 2. Entertainment of this type. [< F]
cab·bage (kab′ij) *n.* The close-leaved edible head of a plant of the mustard family. — *v.i.* ·**baged**, ·**bag·ing** To form a head, as cabbage. [< OF, ult. < L *caput* head]
cabbage palm A palm with a terminal leaf bud used as a vegetable.
cab·by (kab′ē) *n. pl.* ·**bies** *Informal* The driver of a cab.
cab·in (kab′in) *n.* 1. A small, rude house; a hut. 2. In the U.S. Navy, the quarters of the captain. 3. *Naut.* On passenger vessels, the living quarters for passengers and officers.

4. *Aeron.* The enclosed space in an aircraft for the crew, passengers, or cargo. — *v.t. & v.i.* To confine or dwell in or as in a cabin. [< F < LL *capanna* cabin]

cabin boy A boy who waits on the officers and passengers of a ship.

cabin class A class of accommodations for steamship passengers, higher than tourist class, lower than first class.

cabin cruiser A cruiser (def. 3).

cab·i·net (kab′ə·nit) *n.* **1.** A piece of furniture fitted with shelves and drawers; a cupboard. **2.** A council, or the chamber in which it meets. **3.** *Often cap.* The body of official advisers and executive chiefs serving a head of state. — *adj.* **1.** Of or suitable for a cabinet. **2.** Secret; confidential. [< F < Ital. *gabinetto* closet, chest of drawers]

cab·i·net·mak·er (kab′ə·nit·mā′kər) *n.* One who does fine woodworking, as for cabinets, furniture, etc.

cab·i·net·work (kab′ə·nit·wûrk′) *n.* Expert woodwork.

ca·ble (kā′bəl) *n.* **1.** A heavy rope, now usu. of steel wire. **2.** A cable's length. **3.** *Electr.* **a** An insulated electrical conductor or group of conductors. **b** An underwater telegraph line. **4.** A cablegram. — *v.* ·**bled, ·bling** *v.t.* **1.** To make fast by a cable. **2.** To signal by underwater telegraph. — *v.i.* **3.** To send a message by underwater telegraph. [< LL < L *capere* to take, grasp]

cable car A car pulled by a moving cable.

ca·ble·gram (kā′bəl·gram) *n.* A telegraphic message sent by underwater cable.

cable's length A unit of nautical measure, in the United States 720 feet, in England 608 feet.

cab·man (kab′mən) *n.* *pl.* ·**men** (-mən) A cab driver.

ca·boo·dle (kə·bōō′dl) *n.* *Informal* Collection; lot: usu. in the phrase **the whole (kit and) caboodle.**

ca·boose (kə·bōōs′) *n.* **1.** *U.S.* A car, usu. at the rear of a freight or work train, for use by the train crew. **2.** *Brit.* The galley of a ship. [< MDu. *cabuse* galley]

cab·ri·o·let (kab′rē·ə·lā′, -let′) *n.* **1.** A light, one-horse carriage with two seats and a folding top. **2.** An automobile of the coupé type. [< MF *cabriole* leap, caper]

ca·ca·o (kə·kā′ō, -kä′ō) *n.* *pl.* ·**ca·os 1.** A small, evergreen tree of tropical America. **2.** The large, nutritive seeds of this tree, used in making cocoa and chocolate. [< Sp. < Nahuatl *cacauatl* cacao seed]

cacao butter Cocoa butter.

cach·a·lot (kash′ə·lot, -lō) *n.* The sperm whale. [< F]

cache (kash) *v.t.* **cached, cach·ing** To conceal or store, as in the earth. — *n.* A place for hiding or storing things; also, the things stored or hidden. [< F *cacher* to hide]

ca·chet (ka·shā′, kash′ā) *n.* **1.** A seal, as for a letter. **2.** A distinctive mark; stamp of individuality. **3.** A mark, slogan, etc., printed on mail. [< F *cacher* to hide]

cach·in·nate (kak′ə·nāt) *v.i.* ·**nat·ed, ·nat·ing** To laugh immoderately or noisily. [< L *cachinnare* to laugh loudly]

ca·cique (kə·sēk′) *n.* A chief among the Indians of the West Indies, Mexico, etc. [< Sp. < native Haitian word]

cack·le (kak′əl) *v.* ·**led, ·ling** *v.i.* **1.** To make a shrill, broken cry, as a hen that has laid an egg. **2.** To laugh or talk with a similar sound. — *v.t.* **3.** To utter in a cackling manner. — *n.* **1.** The shrill, broken cry of a hen or goose. **2.** Idle talk; chatter. **3.** A short, shrill laugh. [Imit.] — **cack′ler** *n.*

caco- *combining form* Bad; vile. [< Gk. *kakos* bad, evil]

ca·cog·ra·phy (kə·kog′rə·fē) *n.* Bad handwriting or spelling. — **ca·cog′ra·pher** *n.* — **cac·o·graph·ic** (kak′ə·graf′ik) or **·i·cal** *adj.*

ca·coph·o·nous (kə·kof′ə·nəs) *adj.* Having a harsh, disagreeable sound; discordant. Also **cac·o·phon·ic** (kak′ə·fon′ik) or **·i·cal.** — **ca·coph′o·nous·ly, cac′o·phon′i·cal·ly** *adv.*

ca·coph·o·ny (kə·kof′ə·nē) *n.* Disagreeable or discordant sound. [< F < Gk. < *kakos* bad + *phōneein* to sound]

cac·tus (kak′təs) *n.* *pl.* ·**tus·es** or ·**ti** (-tī) Any of various green, fleshy, mostly leafless and spiny plants, often having showy flowers, and native in arid regions of America. [< L < Gk. *kaktos*, prickly plant]

cad (kad) *n.* An ungentlemanly or despicable fellow. — **cad′dish** *adj.* — **cad′dish·ly** *adv.* — **cad′dish·ness** *n.*

ca·dav·er (kə·dav′ər, -dā′vər) *n.* A dead body; esp., a human body for dissection; a corpse. [< L]

ca·dav·er·ous (kə·dav′ər·əs) *adj.* Resembling or characteristic of a corpse; pale; ghastly; gaunt. Also **ca·dav′er·ic.** — **ca·dav′er·ous·ly** *adv.* — **ca·dav′er·ous·ness** *n.*

cad·die (kad′ē) *n.* One paid to carry clubs for golf players. — *v.i.* ·**died, ·dy·ing** To act as a caddie. Also spelled *caddy.*

cad·dis fly (kad′is) Any of certain four-winged insects whose aquatic larvae (**caddis worms**) construct cylindrical cases covered with sand, gravel, etc. [Origin uncertain]

cad·dy¹ (kad′ē) *n.* *pl.* ·**dies** A small box or case, as for tea. [< Malay *kaātī*, a measure of weight]

cad·dy² (kad′ē) *n.* *pl.* ·**dies** A caddie.

ca·dence (kād′ns) *n.* **1.** Rhythmic or measured flow, as of poetry. **2.** The measure or beat of music, marching, etc. **3.** Modulation, as of the voice; intonation. **4.** *Music* A melodic, harmonic, or rhythmic formula ending a phrase,

movement, etc. Also **ca′den·cy.** [< F < Ital. < LL < L *cadere* to fall] — **ca′denced** *adj.*

ca·dent (kād′nt) *adj.* Having cadence or rhythm.

ca·den·za (kə·den′zə, *Ital.* kä·dent′sä) *n.* *Music* A flourish or thematic ornamentation, often improvised, for displaying the virtuosity of a solo performer, usu. introduced just before the end of a composition or movement. [< Ital.]

ca·det (kə·det′) *n.* **1.** A student at a military or naval school, esp. one in training for commissioning as an officer. **2.** A younger son or brother. [< F, ult. < L *caput* head, chief] — **ca·det′ship** *n.*

cadge (kaj) *v.* **cadged, cadg·ing** *v.t.* **1.** *Informal* To get by begging. — *v.i.* **2.** *Dial.* To go begging. — **cadg′er** *n.*

cad·mi·um (kad′mē·əm) *n.* A bluish white metallic element (symbol Cd), occurring in small quantities in zinc ores, and used in the manufacture of fusible alloys, in electroplating, and in the control of atomic fission. See ELEMENT. [< NL < L < Gk. *kadmeia* calamine]

Cad·mus (kad′məs) In Greek mythology, a Phoenician prince who killed a dragon and sowed its teeth, from which sprang armed men who fought one another.

cad·re (kad′rē, *Fr.* kä′dr′) *n.* **1.** *Mil.* The nucleus of officers and men needed to train a new military unit. **2.** A framework; nucleus; core. [< F, frame of a picture]

ca·du·ce·us (kə·dōō′sē·əs, -dyōō′-) *n.* *pl.* ·**ce·i** (-sē·ī) **1.** In ancient Greece and Rome, a herald's wand or staff; esp., the staff of Mercury. **2.** A similar staff used as the emblem of a medical corps or of the medical profession. [< L < Gk. (Doric) *karykion* herald's staff] — **ca·du′ce·an** *adj.*

cae- For those words not entered below, see under CE-.

cae·cum (sē′kəm) See CECUM.

Cae·sar (sē′zər) *n.* **1.** The title of the Roman emperors from Augustus to Hadrian. **2.** Any despot.

CADUCEUS

cae·sar·e·an (si·zâr′ē·ən), **cae·sar·i·an,** See CESAREAN, etc.

Cae·sar·e·an (si·zâr′ē·ən) *adj.* Pertaining to Caesar. — *n.* Loosely, a cesarean section. Also **Cae·sar′i·an.**

cae·si·um (sē′zē·əm) See CESIUM.

caes·tus (ses′təs) See CESTUS.

cae·su·ra (si·zhōōr′ə, -zyōōr′ə) *n.* *pl.* ·**su·ras** or ·**su·rae** (-zhōōr′ē, -zyōōr′ē) **1.** In Greek and Latin prosody, a break occurring when a word ends within a foot. **2.** In modern prosody, a pause usu. near the middle of a line. Caesura is indicated by two vertical lines (‖). **3.** *Music* A pause indicating a rhythmic division point. Also spelled *cesura.* [< L *caedere* to cut] — **cae·su′ral** *adj.*

ca·fé (ka·fā′, kə-) *n.* **1.** A coffee house; restaurant. **2.** A barroom. **3.** Coffee. Also *esp. U.S.* **ca·fe′.** [< F]

ca·fé au lait (kà·fā′ ō lā′) *French* **1.** Coffee with scalded milk. **2.** A light brown.

ca·fé noir (kà·fā′ nwár′) *French* Black coffee.

caf·e·te·ri·a (kaf′ə·tir′ē·ə) *n.* A restaurant where the patrons wait upon themselves. [< Am. Sp., coffee store],

caf·feine (kaf′ēn, *in technical usage* kaf′ē·in) *n.* *Chem.* A slightly bitter alkaloid, $C_8H_{10}O_2N_4$, obtained from the leaves and berries of coffee, used as a stimulant and diuretic. Also **caf′fein.** [< F *café* coffee]

caf·tan (kaf′tən, käf·tän′) *n.* An undercoat having long sleeves and a sash, worn in eastern Mediterranean countries: also spelled *kaftan.* [< F < Turkish *qaftān*]

cage (kāj) *n.* **1.** A boxlike structure with openwork of wires or bars, for confining birds or beasts. **2.** Any cagelike structure or framework. **3.** In baseball, a movable backstop for batting practice. **4.** In hockey, the frame and net used as the goal. **5.** In basketball, the basket. — *v.t.* **caged, cag·ing** To shut up in a cage; confine; imprison. [< OF, ult. < L *cavus* empty, hollow]

cage·ling (kāj′ling) *n.* A caged bird.

cage·y (kāj′jē) *adj.* **cag·i·er, cag·i·est** *Informal* Wary of being duped; shrewd and careful. Also **cag′y.** [Origin uncertain] — **cag′i·ly** *adv.* — **cag′i·ness** *n.*

ca·hier (kä·yā′) *n.* **1.** A number of sheets, as of printed matter, loosely bound together. **2.** A report, as of proceedings, etc. [< F < OF, ult. < L *quaterni* a set of four]

ca·hoots (kə·hōōts′) *n.pl. U.S. Slang* Affiliation; partnership, as in the phrase **in cahoots.** [? < F *cahute* cabin]

cai·man (kā′mən) See CAYMAN.

Cain (kān) The eldest son of Adam, who slew his brother Abel. *Gen.* iv. — *n.* A murderer. — **to raise Cain** *U.S. Slang* To cause a disturbance.

ca·ique (kä·ēk′) *n.* A long, narrow skiff used on the Bosporus. [< F < Ital. < Turkish *kāyik*]

cairn (kârn) *n.* A mound or heap of stones set up as a memorial or a marker. [< Scottish Gaelic *carn* heap of stones]

cais·son (kā′sən, -son) *n.* **1.** A large watertight chamber within which work is done under water, as on a bridge pier. **2.** *Naut.* A watertight device used to raise sunken ships. **3.** A two-wheeled vehicle carrying a chest of ammunition to serve a gun. [< F, aug. of *caisse* box, chest]

caisson disease *Pathol.* A painful, paralyzing, sometimes fatal disease caused by too rapid a transition from the compressed air of caissons, diving bells, etc., while the system still contains an excess of nitrogen.

ca·jole (kə·jōl′) *v.t. & v.i.* **·joled, ·jol·ing** To coax with flattery or false promises; wheedle. [< F *cajoler*] —**ca·jole′·ment** *n.* —**ca·jol′er** *n.* —**ca·jol′ing·ly** *adv.*

ca·jol·er·y (kə·jō′lər·ē) *n. pl.* **·er·ies** The act or practice of cajoling or wheedling; artful persuasion; coaxing.

Ca·jun (kā′jən) *n.* A reputed descendant of the Acadian French in Louisiana. [Alter. of ACADIAN]

cake (kāk) *n.* **1.** A mixture of flour, milk, sugar, etc., baked in various forms and generally sweeter and richer than bread. **2.** A small, usu. thin mass of dough, or other food, baked or fried: fish *cake.* **3.** A mass of matter compressed or hardened into a compact form: a *cake* of soap. —**to take the cake** *Informal* To take or deserve a prize; excel: often used sarcastically. —*v.t. & v.i.* **caked, cak·ing** To form into a hardened mass. [< ON *kaka*]

cakes and ale Pleasures of life; easy living.

cake·walk (kāk′wôk′) *n.* Formerly, a dance which American Negroes performed, a cake being awarded for the most original steps. —*v.i.* To do a cakewalk strut.

cal·a·bash (kal′ə·bash) *n.* **1.** The calabash tree. **2.** A gourd from this tree, used for making pipes, bowls, etc. [< F < Sp. *calabaza* pumpkin]

calabash tree **1.** A tropical American tree of the gourd family, bearing a hard-shelled fruit. **2.** A tropical American tree of the bignonia family, with a gourdlike fruit.

cal·a·boose (kal′ə·bōōs) *n. U.S. Informal* A jail; lockup. [< Sp. *calabozo*]

ca·la·di·um (kə·lā′dē·əm) *n.* A tuberous tropical American herb of the arum family. [< NL < Malay *kelǎdy*]

cal·a·mine (kal′ə·mīn, -min) *n.* A vitreous zinc carbonate, $ZnCO_3$, used in the form of a lotion or ointment for the treatment of skin ailments. —*v.t.* **·mined, ·min·ing** To apply calamine to. [< F < LL < L < Gk. *kadmeia* calamine]

ca·lam·i·tous (kə·lam′ə·təs) *adj.* Causing or resulting in a calamity; disastrous. —**ca·lam′i·tous·ly** *adv.*

ca·lam·i·ty (kə·lam′ə·tē) *n. pl.* **·ties** **1.** A disaster. **2.** A state of great distress. [< F < L *calamitas, -tatis*]

cal·a·mus (kal′ə·məs *n. pl.* **·mi** (-mī) **1.** The sweet flag, a plant. **2.** The quill of a feather. [< Gk. *kalamos* reed]

ca·lash (kə·lash′) *n.* **1.** A low-wheeled light carriage with folding top. **2.** A folding carriage top; also **calash top.** **3.** A folding bonnet of the 18th century. [< F *calèche*]

cal·ca·ne·us (kal·kā′nē·əs) *n. pl.* **·ne·i** (-nē·ī) *Anat.* The large bone at the back of the foot: also called **heel bone.** Also **cal·ca′ne·um.** [< L (*os*) *calcaneum* heel bone < *calx* heel]

cal·car·e·ous (kal·kâr′ē·əs) *adj.* **1.** Composed of, containing, or like limestone or calcium carbonate. **2.** Containing calcium. [< L *calcarius* of lime < *calx, calcis* lime]

cal·ces (kal′sēz) Alternative plural of CALX.

calci- *combining form* Lime. [< L *calx, calcis* lime]

cal·cif·er·ol (kal·sif′ər·ōl, -ol) *n. Biochem.* The antirachitic vitamin D_2, a white, crystalline compound, $C_{28}H_{44}O$. [< CALCIFER(OUS) + (ERGOSTER)OL]

cal·cif·er·ous (kal·sif′ər·əs) *adj.* Yielding or containing calcium carbonate, as rocks.

cal·ci·fy (kal′sə·fī) *v.t. & v.i.* **·fied, ·fy·ing** To make or become stony by the deposit of lime salts. —**cal·ci·fi·ca·tion** (kal′sə·fi·kā′shən) *n.*

cal·ci·mine (kal′sə·mīn, -min) *n.* A white or tinted wash for ceilings, walls, etc. —*v.t.* **·mined, ·min·ing** To apply calcimine to. Also, *Brit., distemper:* also spelled *kalsomine.* [< L *calx, calcis* lime; orig. a trade name]

cal·cin·a·to·ry (kal·sin′ə·tôr′ē, -tō′rē) *adj.* For calcining. —*n. pl.* **·ries** An apparatus for calcining, as a furnace.

cal·cine (kal′sīn, -sin) *v.* **·cined, ·cin·ing** *v.t.* **1.** To render (a substance) friable by the expulsion of its volatile content through heat. **2.** To reduce to a calx by subjecting to heat. —*v.i.* **3.** To become changed by dry heat into a friable powder. Also **cal′cin·ize.** [< F < Med.L *calcinare* < L *calx* lime] —**cal·ci·na·tion** (kal′sə·nā′shən) *n.*

cal·cite (kal′sīt) *n.* A widely distributed calcium carbonate mineral, white or variously tinted, including chalk, limestone, marble, etc. —**cal·cit·ic** (kal·sit′ik) *adj.*

cal·ci·um (kal′sē·əm) *n.* A silver-white, malleable, metallic element (symbol Ca), widely distributed in combination, as in chalk, gypsum, and limestone. See ELEMENT. [< NL < L *calx, calcis* lime]

calcium carbide *Chem.* A compound, CaC_2, made from quicklime and carbon and used to make acetylene.

calcium carbonate *Chem.* A compound, $CaCO_3$, forming the principal constituent of certain rocks and minerals, as limestone, aragonite, and calcite, and used in the preparation of lime and as the basis of dentifrices.

calcium chloride *Chem.* A white salt, $CaCl_2$, used as a drying agent, preservative, refrigerant, and dust preventer.

calcium hydroxide *Chem.* Slaked lime, $Ca(OH)_2$: when used in solution called *limewater.*

calc·spar (kalk′spär′) *n.* Crystallized carbonate of lime.

cal·cu·la·ble (kal′kyə·lə·bəl) *adj.* **1.** Capable of being calculated. **2.** Reliable; dependable. —**cal′cu·la·bly** *adv.*

cal·cu·late (kal′kyə·lāt) *v.* **·lat·ed, ·lat·ing** *v.t.* **1.** To determine by computation; arrive at by arithmetical means. **2.** To ascertain beforehand; form an estimate of. **3.** To plan or design: used chiefly in the passive: *calculated* to carry two tons. **4.** *U.S. Dial.* To think; expect. —*v.i.* **5.** To compute. —**to calculate on** To depend or rely on. [< L < *calculus* pebble; with ref. to the use of pebbles in counting]

cal·cu·lat·ing (kal′kyə·lā′ting) *adj.* Inclined to reckon or estimate, esp. for one's own interests; scheming.

cal·cu·la·tion (kal′kyə·lā′shən) *n.* **1.** The act, process, or result of computing. **2.** An estimate; forecast. **3.** Forethought; prudence. —**cal′cu·la·tive** *adj.*

cal·cu·la·tor (kal′kyə·lā′tər) *n.* **1.** One who calculates. **2.** A keyboard machine that adds, subtracts, multiplies, and divides: also **calculating machine.**

cal·cu·lous (kal′kyə·ləs) *adj. Pathol.* Pertaining to or affected with a calculus or calculi. [< L *calculosus* pebbly]

cal·cu·lus (kal′kyə·ləs) *n. pl.* **·li** (-lī) or **·lus·es 1.** *Pathol.* A stonelike mass, as in the bladder. **2.** *Math.* A method of calculating by the use of a highly specialized system of algebraic symbols. —**differential calculus** The branch of analysis that investigates the infinitesimal changes of constantly varying quantities when the relations between the quantities are given. —**integral calculus** The branch of analysis that, from the relations among the infinitesimal changes or variations of quantities, deduces relations among the quantities themselves. [< L, a pebble (used in counting)]

cal·dron (kôl′drən) See CAULDRON.

ca·lèche (kȧ·lesh′) *n.* A calash.

Cal·e·do·ni·a (kal′ə·dō′nē·ə, -dōn′yə) *Poetic* Scotland. [< L] —**Cal′e·do′ni·an** *adj. & n.*

cal·e·fa·cient (kal′ə·fā′shənt) *adj.* Causing heat or warmth. —*n. Med.* A remedy that produces heat. [< L < *calere* to be warm + *facere* to make, cause]

cal·en·dar (kal′ən·dər) *n.* **1.** Any of various systems of fixing the order, length, and subdivisions of the years and months. **2.** A table showing the days, weeks, and months of a year. **3.** A schedule or list, esp. one arranged in chronological order: a court *calendar.* —*v.t.* To place in a calendar; schedule. [< L < *calendae* calends]

—**Gregorian calendar** The calendar now in general use in most parts of the world; first prescribed in 1582 by Pope Gregory XIII to correct the Julian year to the astronomical year, the first being the **Old Style** (*O.S.*) date and the second being the **New Style** (*N.S.*).

—**Hebrew (or Jewish) calendar** A calendar used by the Jews, based on the lunar month and reckoning the year of creation as 3761 B.C. Since the Hebrew months are mostly shorter, they do not coincide in any systematic manner with those of the Gregorian calendar except by approximation.

	Months	Number of days	Approximate month in Gregorian calendar
1	Tishri	30	October
2	Heshwan	29 or 30	November
3	Kislew	29 or 30	December
4	Tebet	29	January
5	Shebat	30	February
6	Adar	29 or 30	March
–	Veadar[1]	29	
7	Nisan	30	April
8	Iyyar	29	May
9	Sivan	30	June
10	Tammuz	29	July
11	Ab	30	August
12	Elul	29	September

[1]The additional intercalary month.

—**Julian calendar** The calendar prescribed by Julius Caesar, in which the ordinary year had 365 days and every fourth year 366 (leap year). It is now replaced by the Gregorian calendar.

—**Moslem (or Mohammedan) calendar** The calendar generally used in all Moslem countries, reckoning time from July 16 A.D. 622, the day following Mohammed's flight from Mecca to Medina, and consisting of 12 lunar months.

—**Republican (or Revolutionary) calendar** The calendar instituted on Oct. 5, 1793, by the first French republic, and abolished Dec. 31, 1805. It divided the year into 12 months of 30 days each, with five (in leap years six) supplementary days (*sansculottides*) at the end of the last month.

—**Roman calendar** A lunar calendar, attributed to Numa.

PRONUNCIATION KEY: add, āce, cȧre, pälm; end, ēven; it, īce; odd, ōpen, ôrder; tŏŏk, pōōl; up, bûrn; ə = a in *above*, e in *sicken*, i in *flexible*, o in *melon*, u in *focus*; yōō = u in *fuse*; oil; pout; check; go; ring; thin; this; zh, vision. For ȧ, œ, ü, kh, ṅ, see inside front cover.

The day of the new moon was the *calends*, and the day of the full moon the *ides* (the 13th or 15th of the month).

cal·en·dar year The 365, or, in leap year, 366 days from midnight of December 31 to the same hour twelve months thereafter.

cal·en·der (kal′ən·dər) *n.* A machine for giving a gloss to cloth, paper, etc., by pressing between rollers. — *v.t.* To press in a calender. [< F < L < Gk. *kylindros* roller]

cal·ends (kal′əndz) *n.pl.* The first day of the Roman month: also spelled *kalends*. [< L *calendae*]

ca·len·du·la (kə·len′jŏŏ·lə) *n.* An annual or perennial herb of the composite family, having bright orange or yellow flowers. [< NL, dim. of L *calendae* calends]

ca·les·cence (kə·les′əns) *n.* The condition of growing warm. [< L *calescere* to grow warm] — **ca·les′cent** *adj.*

calf[1] (kaf, käf) *n. pl.* **calves** (kavz, kävz) **1.** The young of the cow or various other bovine animals. **2.** The young of various mammals, as the elephant, whale, etc. **3.** Calfskin. **4.** *Informal* A gawky, witless young man. [OE *cealf*]

calf[2] (kaf, käf) *n. pl.* **calves** (kavz, kävz) The muscular rear part of the human leg below the knee. [< ON *kálfi*]

calf love *Informal* Adolescent infatuation; puppy love.

calf·skin (kaf′skin′, käf′-) *n.* **1.** The skin or hide of a calf. **2.** Leather made from this.

Cal·i·ban (kal′ə·ban) In Shakespeare's *Tempest*, a deformed, savage slave of Prospero.

cal·i·ber (kal′ə·bər) *n.* **1.** The internal diameter of a tube. **2.** *Mil.* **a** The internal diameter of the barrel of a gun, cannon, etc. **b** The diameter of a bullet, shell, etc. **3.** Degree of personal excellence. Also *Brit.* **cal·i·bre.** [< F *calibre*]

cal·i·brate (kal′ə·brāt) *v.t.* **·brat·ed, ·brat·ing 1.** To graduate, correct, or adjust the scale of (a measuring instrument) into appropriate units. **2.** To determine the reading of (such an instrument). **3.** To ascertain the caliber of. [Cf. F *calibrer*] — **cal′i·bra′tion** *n.* — **cal′i·bra′tor** *n.*

cal·i·ces (kal′ə·sēz) Plural of CALIX.

cal·i·co (kal′i·kō) *n. pl.* **·coes** or **·cos** Cheap cotton cloth printed in a figured pattern of bright colors. — *adj.* **1.** Made of calico. **2.** Resembling printed calico; dappled or streaked: a *calico* cat. [after *Calicut*, where first obtained]

California poppy A plant of the poppy family having showy yellow flowers: the State flower of California.

cal·i·for·ni·um (kal′ə·fôr′nē·əm) *n.* An unstable radioactive element (symbol Cf), artificially produced by bombardment of curium with alpha particles. See ELEMENT. [after the University of *California* where first produced]

ca·lig·ra·phy (kə·lig′rə·fē) See CALLIGRAPHY.

cal·i·per (kal′ə·pər) *n. Usu. pl.* An instrument resembling a pair of compasses, usu. with curved legs, used for measuring diameters. Also **caliper compass.** — *v.t. & v.i.* To measure by using calipers. Also *caliper.* [< CALIBER]

ca·liph (kā′lif, kal′if) *n.* The spiritual and civil head of a Moslem state: also spelled *calif, kalif, kaliph, khalif.* [< F < Arabic *khalifah* successor (to Mohammed)]

cal·i·phate (kal′ə·fāt, -fit) *n.* The office, dominion, or reign of a caliph.

cal·is·then·ics (kal′is·then′iks) *n.pl.* (*construed as sing. def. 2*) **1.** Light gymnastics to promote grace and health. **2.** The science of such exercises. [< Gk. *kalli-* beautiful + *sthenos* strength] — **cal′is·then′ic** or **·i·cal** *adj.*

calk[1] (kôk) See CAULK.

calk[2] (kôk) *n.* **1.** A spur on a horse's shoe to prevent slipping. **2.** *U.S.* A plate with sharp points worn on the sole of a boot or shoe to prevent slipping. Also **calk′er.** — *v.t.* To furnish with calks. [Prob. < L *calx* heel]

call (kôl) *v.t.* **1.** To say in a loud voice; shout; proclaim. **2.** To summon. **3.** To convoke; convene: to *call* a meeting. **4.** To invoke solemnly. **5.** To summon to a specific work: to *call* someone to the ministry. **6.** To arouse, as from sleep. **7.** To telephone to. **8.** To summon or lure (birds or animals) by imitating their cry, whistling, etc. **9.** To name. **10.** To designate or characterize in any way. **11.** To estimate loosely; consider: I *call* it 10 pounds. **12.** To bring to action or consideration: to *call* a case to court. **13.** To insist upon payment of, as by written notice. **14.** In baseball: **a** To stop or suspend (a game). **b** To designate a pitch as (a ball or strike). **c** To declare (a player) out, safe, etc. **15.** In poker, to demand a show of hands by a bet equal to that of (another). **16.** In pool, etc., to predict (a shot) before making the play. — *v.i.* **17.** To raise one's voice; speak loudly. **18.** To make a brief visit, stop, or stay: with *at, on,* or *upon.* **19.** To communicate by telephone. **20.** In poker, to demand a show of hands. **21.** In some card games, to make a demand or signal, as for trumps. — **to call back 1.** To summon back; recall. **2.** To call in return, as by telephone. — **to call down 1.** To invoke from heaven. **2.** *Informal* To rebuke; reprimand. — **to call for 1.** To stop so as to obtain. **2.** To require; need. — **to call forth** To summon into action; draw out. — **to call in 1.** To collect, as debts. **2.** To retire, as currency, from circulation. **3.** To summon, as for consultation. — **to call off 1.** To summon

away. **2.** To say or read aloud. **3.** To cancel. — **to call out** To shout. — **to call up 1.** To recollect. **2.** To summon. **3.** To telephone. — *n.* **1.** A shout or cry. **2.** A summons or invitation. **3.** A signal, as on a bell or horn. **4.** A demand; claim: the *call* of duty. **5.** A communication by telephone. **6.** A roll call. **7.** An inward urge to a religious vocation. **8.** A brief, often formal, visit. **9.** The cry of an animal, esp. of a bird. **10.** A whistle, etc., with which to imitate such a cry. **11.** A need; occasion: You've no *call* to do that. **12.** A request for payment. — **on call 1.** Payable on demand. **2.** Available when sent for. [< ON *kalla*]

cal·la (kal′ə) *n.* **1.** A plant of the arum family having a large white leaf that resembles a flower. Also **calla lily.** **2.** A marsh plant bearing red berries in dense clusters. [< L]

call·board (kôl′bôrd′, -bōrd′) *n.* A theater bulletin board for posting notices of rehearsals, instructions, etc.

call·boy (kôl′boi′) *n.* **1.** A boy who calls actors to go on stage. **2.** A bellboy.

call·er (kô′lər) *n.* **1.** One who or that which calls. **2.** One making a brief visit.

calli- For words not found here, see under CALI-.

cal·lig·ra·phy (kə·lig′rə·fē) *n.* **1.** Beautiful penmanship. **2.** Handwriting in general. Also spelled *caligraphy.* [< Gk. < *kalos* beautiful + *graphein* to write] — **cal·lig′ra·pher, cal·lig′ra·phist** *n.* — **cal·li·graph′ic** *adj.*

call·ing (kô′ling) *n.* **1.** A speaking or crying aloud. **2.** A convocation or summons. **3.** A vocation or profession.

calling card A small card, printed or engraved with one's name, used to announce a visit or call: also *visiting card.*

cal·li·o·pe (kə·lī′ə·pē, kal′ē·ōp) *n.* A musical instrument consisting of a series of steam whistles played by means of a keyboard: also called *steam organ.* [after *Calliope*]

Cal·li·o·pe (kə·lī′ə·pē) The Muse of eloquence and epic poetry. [< L < Gk. < *kalos* beautiful + *ops* voice]

cal·lis·then·ics (kal′is·then′iks) See CALISTHENICS.

call letters The code letters identifying a radio or television transmitting station. Also **call sign.**

call loan A loan of money to be repaid on demand.

call money Money borrowed as a call loan.

call number A classifying number employed by libraries to indicate the subject of a book and its place on the shelves.

cal·los·i·ty (kə·los′ə·tē) *n. pl.* **·ties 1.** *Physiol.* A callus. **2.** Callousness of feelings; insensibility.

cal·lous (kal′əs) *adj.* **1.** Thickened and hardened, as a callus. **2.** Hardened in feelings; insensible. — *v.t. & v.i.* To make or become callous. [< L < *callus* hard skin] — **cal′lous·ly** *adv.* — **cal′lous·ness** *n.*

cal·low (kal′ō) *adj.* **1.** Inexperienced; immature. **2.** Unfledged, as a bird. [OE *calu* bare, bald]

cal·lus (kal′əs) *n. pl.* **·lus·es 1.** *Physiol.* A thickened, hardened part of the skin: also called *callosity.* **2.** *Anat.* The new bony tissue between and around the fractured ends of a broken bone in the process of reuniting. **3.** *Bot.* The tissue that forms over a cut on a stem and protects the exposed wood. — *v.i.* To form a callus. [< L, hard skin]

calm (käm) *adj.* **1.** Free from agitation; still or nearly still. **2.** Not excited by passion or emotion; peaceful. — *n.* **1.** Lack of wind or motion; stillness. **2.** Serenity. — *v.t. & v.i.* To make or become quiet or calm: often with *down.* [< MF < Ital. < LL < Gk. *kauma* heat; with ref. to the midday siesta] — **calm′ly** *adv.* — **calm′ness** *n.*

  — **Syn.** (adj.) *Calm* describes a state that may be transient; *tranquil* suggests a more enduring condition: a *calm* sea, a *tranquil* life. A *placid* person is regarded as temperamentally stolid; a *placid* lake is always peaceful. Things elevated above earthly turmoil are *serene*: a *serene* sky, a *serene* smile. *Quiet* and *still* imply absence of noise as well as of bustle.

cal·o·mel (kal′ə·mel, -məl) *n. Med.* Mercurous chloride, HgCl, a heavy, white, tasteless compound, used as a purgative, etc. [< F < Gk. *kalos* beautiful + *melas* black]

ca·lor·ic (kə·lôr′ik, -lor′-) *adj.* Of or pertaining to heat. — *n.* Heat. [< F < L *calor* heat] — **cal·o·ric·i·ty** (kal′ə·ris′ə·tē) *n.*

cal·o·rie (kal′ə·rē) *n.* **1.** One of two recognized units of heat. The **large** or **great calorie** is the amount of heat required to raise the temperature of one kilogram of water 1° C. The **small calorie** is the amount of heat required to raise one gram of water 1° C. **2.** *Physiol.* The large calorie, a measure of the energy value of foods or the heat output of organisms. Also **cal·o·ry.** [< F < L *calor* heat]

cal·o·rif·ic (kal′ə·rif′ik) *adj.* Pertaining to or producing heat. [< F < L *calorificus*]

cal·o·rim·e·ter (kal′ə·rim′ə·tər) *n.* Any apparatus for measuring the quantity of heat generated by friction, combustion, or chemical change.

cal·o·rim·e·try (kal′ə·rim′ə·trē) *n.* The measurement of heat. — **ca·lor·i·met·ric** (kə·lôr′ə·met′rik, -lor′-) or **·met·ri·cal** *adj.*

ca·lotte (kə·lot′) *n.* A skullcap. [< F]

cal·u·met (kal′yə·met, kal′yə·met′) *n.* A tobacco pipe with a long, ornamented stem, used by American Indians in ceremonies, to ratify treaties, etc.: also called *peace pipe.* [< dial. F, pipe stem < L *calamus* reed]

ca·lum·ni·ate (kə·lum′nē·āt) *v.t. & v.i.* **·at·ed, ·at·ing** To accuse falsely; defame; slander. [< L *calumnia* slander] — **ca·lum′ni·a′tion** *n.* — **ca·lum′ni·a′tor** *n.*

ca·lum·ni·ous (kə·lum′nē·əs) *adj.* Slanderous. Also **ca·lum′ni·a·to·ry** (-tôr′ē, -tōr′ē). — **ca·lum′ni·ous·ly** *adv.*

cal·um·ny (kal′əm·nē) *n. pl.* **·nies** 1. A false and malicious accusation or report, made to injure another. 2. Defamation; slander. [< MF < L *calumnia* slander]

Cal·va·ry (kal′və·rē) The place, near the site of ancient Jerusalem, where Christ was crucified; Golgotha. *Luke* xxiii 33. [< L *calvaria* skull, trans. of Aramaic *golgothā*]

calve (kav, käv) *v.t. & v.i.* **calved, calv·ing** To bring forth (a calf). [OE *cealfian* < *cealf* calf]

calves (kavz, kävz) Plural of CALF.

Cal·vin·ism (kal′vin·iz′əm) *n. Theol.* The system or doctrines of John Calvin, emphasizing the depravity and helplessness of man, the sovereignty of God, and predestination, and characterized by an austere moral code. — **Cal′vin·ist** *n.* — **Cal′vin·is′tic** or **·ti·cal** *adj.* — **Cal′vin·is′ti·cal·ly** *adv.*

calx (kalks) *n. pl.* **calx·es** or **cal·ces** (kal′sēz) The residue from the calcination of minerals. [< L]

cal·y·ces (kal′ə·sēz, kā′lə-) Alternative plural of CALYX.

ca·lyp·so (kə·lip′sō) *n.* An improvised song, originally Trinidadian, dealing with news, love, etc. [Origin uncertain]

Ca·lyp·so (kə·lip′sō) In the *Odyssey,* a nymph who kept Odysseus for seven years on her island.

ca·lyx (kā′liks, kal′iks) *n. pl.* **ca·lyx·es** or **cal·y·ces** (kal′ə·sēz, kā′lə-) *Bot.* The outermost series of leaflike parts of a flower; the sepals. [< L < Gk. *kalyx,* husk, pod]

cam (kam) *n. Mech.* An irregularly shaped piece or projection, as on a wheel or rotating shaft, that imparts reciprocating or variable motion to another piece bearing on it. [< Du., tooth, cog of a wheel]

ca·ma·ra·de·rie (kä′mə·rä′dər·ē) *n.* Comradeship. [< F]

cam·a·ril·la (kam′ə·ril′ə, *Sp.* kä·mä·rē′lyä) *n.* A clique; cabal. [< Sp., dim. of *camara* chamber]

cam·ass (kam′əs) *n.* An herb of the lily family having an edible bulb. Also **cam′as.** [< Chinook jargon]

cam·ber (kam′bər) *v.t.* 1. To cut or bend to a slight upward convex form. — *v.i.* 2. To have or assume a slight upward curve, as a ship's deck. — *n.* A slight upward bend, as of a timber. [< ME < L < *camera* curved roof, vault]

cam·bi·um (kam′bē·əm) *n. Bot.* A layer of tissue in exogenous plants, from which new wood and bark are formed. [< LL, exchange]

Cam·bri·a (kam′brē·ə) Medieval Latin name for WALES.

Cam·bri·an (kam′brē·ən) *adj.* 1. Of or pertaining to Cambria; Welsh. 2. *Geol.* Denoting or of the earliest of the periods of the Paleozoic era. See chart under GEOLOGY. — *n.* 1. The Cambrian strata or period. 2. A Welshman.

cam·bric (kām′brik) *n.* A fine white linen, or a similar fabric of cotton. [< Flemish *Kameryk* Cambrai]

cambric tea A drink made of sweetened hot water and milk, sometimes flavored with a little tea.

came (kām) Past tense of COME.

cam·el (kam′əl) *n.* A large Asian or African ruminant with a humped back, used in the desert as a beast of burden. The **Arabian camel,** or **dromedary,** has one hump, and the **Bactrian camel** has two. [OE < L < Gk. *kamēlos* < Semitic]

cam·el·hair (kam′əl·hâr′) *n.* Camel's hair.

ca·mel·lia (kə·mēl′yə, -mel′ē·ə) *n.* A tropical Asian tree or shrub with glossy leaves and white, pink, red, or variegated flowers: also called *japonica.* [< NL, after G. J. *Kamel,* 1661–1706, Jesuit traveler]

Cam·e·lot (kam′ə·lot) In Arthurian legend, the seat of King Arthur's court.

camel's hair 1. The hair of the camel. 2. A soft, warm, usually tan cloth made of camel's hair, sometimes mixed with wool or other fibers. — **camel's-hair** *adj.*

Cam·em·bert (kam′əm·bâr, *Fr.* kȧ·män·bâr′) *n.* A rich, creamy, soft cheese. [after *Camembert,* town in NW France]

cam·e·o (kam′ē·ō) *n. pl.* **·os** 1. A gem of differently colored layers, having a design carved in relief on one with the other layer or layers serving as background. 2. Carving done in this manner. [< Ital. *cammeo;* ult. origin unknown]

cam·er·a (kam′ər·ə, kam′rə) *n. pl.* **·er·as** for defs. 1 and 2, **·er·ae** (-ə·rē) for def. 3 1. A lightproof chamber or box for taking photographs and consisting of a sensitized plate or film on which light rays are projected through a lens. 2. *Telecom.* An enclosed unit containing the light-sensitive elec-

tron tube that converts optical images into electrical impulses for television transmission. 3. A chamber; esp. a judge's private room. — **in camera** *Law* Not in public court; privately. [< L, vaulted room < Gk. *kamara*]

cam·er·a·man (kam′ər·ə·man′, kam′rə-) *n. pl.* **·men** (-men′) The operator of a camera, esp. a motion-picture camera.

cam·i·sole (kam′ə·sōl) *n.* 1. A woman's fancy underwaist, worn with a sheer bodice. 2. A brief negligée. 3. A type of straitjacket. [< F < Sp. *camisola,* dim. of *camisa* shirt]

cam·o·mile (kam′ə·mīl) *n.* A strongly scented, bitter herb whose aromatic flowers and leaves are used in medicine. [< F < L < Gk. < *chamai* on the ground + *mēlon* apple]

cam·ou·flage (kam′ə·fläzh, -fläj) *n.* 1. *Mil.* Measures or material used to conceal or misrepresent the identity of installations, ships, etc. 2. Any disguise or pretense. — *v.t. & v.i.* **·flaged, ·flag·ing** To hide or obscure, as with disguises. [< F < *camoufler* to disguise] — **cam′ou·flag′er** *n.*

camp[1] (kamp) *n.* 1. A group of tents or other temporary shelters, as for soldiers, hunters, or vacationers. Also, the ground or area so employed. 2. The persons occupying a group of tents, etc. 3. *U.S.* A town hastily constructed near a mine. 4. Military life. 5. A body of persons supporting a policy, theory, or doctrine; also, the position so upheld. — *v.i.* 1. To set up or live in a camp; encamp. 2. To hold stubbornly to a position. — *v.t.* 3. To shelter or station in a camp. — **to camp out** To sleep in a tent; live in the open. [< MF < Ital. < L *campus* level plain]

camp[2] (kamp) *n.* A comical style or quality perceived in theatrical or flamboyant gestures, literary works, etc. [? < dial. E *camp* or *kemp* bold, impetuous fellow]

cam·paign (kam·pān′) *n.* 1. A series of connected military operations conducted for a common objective, in a particular area, etc. 2. An organized series of activities designed to obtain a definite result. — *v.i.* To serve in, conduct, or go on a campaign. [< F < Ital. *campagna*] — **cam·paign′er** *n.*

cam·pa·ni·le (kam′pə·nē′lē, *Ital.* käm′pä·nē′lä) *n. pl.* **·les** or **·li** (-lē) A bell tower. [< Ital. < LL *campana* bell]

cam·pan·u·la (kam·pan′yə·lə) *n.* A plant having bell-shaped flowers. [< NL, dim. of LL *campana* bell]

camp chair A light, folding chair.

camp·er (kamp′ər) *n.* 1. One who camps out or is a member of a camp, as a children's summer camp. 2. A vehicle affording shelter and usu. sleeping facilities: also **camper wagon.**

cam·pes·tral (kam·pes′trəl) *adj.* Growing in or pertaining to fields or open country. [< L *campus* field]

camp·fire (kamp′fīr′) *n.* 1. A fire in an outdoor camp, for cooking, warmth, etc. 2. A gathering around a campfire.

campfire girl A girl between seven and eighteen years of age, belonging to the **Camp Fire Girls of America.**

camp·ground (kamp′ground′) *n.* An area used for a camp or a camp meeting.

cam·phor (kam′fər) *n.* A white, volatile, translucent crystalline compound, $C_{10}H_{16}O$, with a penetrating odor, obtained from the camphor tree, used in medicine, etc. [< Malay *kāpūr*] — **cam·phor·ic** (kam·fôr′ik, -for′-) *adj.*

cam·phor·ate (kam′fə·rāt) *v.t.* **·at·ed, ·at·ing** To treat or saturate with camphor.

camphor ball A moth ball.

camphor ice A mixture of camphor, white wax, spermaceti, and castor oil, used for chapped skin, etc.

camphor tree A large evergreen tree of eastern Asia yielding the camphor of commerce.

camp·ing (kamp′ing) *n.* The act or practice of living outdoors, as in tents or without shelter, esp. for recreation.

cam·pi·on (kam′pē·ən) *n.* One of various herbs of the pink family, as the rose campion.

camp meeting A series of religious meetings held in a grove or field, usu. in a tent; also, one such meeting.

camp·stool (kamp′stool′) *n.* A light, folding stool.

cam·pus (kam′pəs) *n. U.S.* The grounds of a school or college, or the court enclosed by the buildings. [< L, field]

cam·shaft (kam′shaft′, -shäft′) *n.* A shaft having one or more cams on it.

can[1] (kan, *unstressed* kən) *v.* Present *3rd person sing.* **can**; past **could** A defective verb now used only in the present and past tenses as an auxiliary and having the following senses: 1. To be able to. 2. To know how to. 3. To have the right to. 4. *Informal* To be permitted to; may. [OE *cunnan*] ◆ **can, may** In informal speech and writing, *can* is now acceptable in the sense of *may,* to express permission, esp. in questions or negative statements: *Can* I leave now? You *cannot.* At the formal level, the distinction between *can* and *may* is still observed: *can,* to express ability to perform, either mentally or physically; *may,* to denote permission.

can[2] (kan) *n.* 1. A vessel, can, or tin, for holding or carrying liquids, garbage, etc. 2. *U.S.* A container in which fruits, tobacco, etc., are hermetically sealed. 3. *U.S.* The contents of a sealed tin container. 4. *U.S. Slang* a Jail. b A toilet. **c** The buttocks. — *v.t.* **canned, can·ning 1.** To put up in cans, jars, etc.; preserve. **2.** *Slang* To record for sound or film reproduction. **3.** *U.S. Slang* **a** To dismiss. **b** To cease: *Can it!* [OE *canne* cup] — **can'ner** *n.*

Ca·naan (kā'nən) The Promised Land of the Israelites.

Ca·naan·ite (kā'nən·īt) *n.* A dweller in Canaan prior to the Israelite conquest.

Canada balsam A yellowish turpentine derived from the balsam fir, used as a mounting cement in microscopy.

Canada goose The common wild goose of North America, brownish gray with black neck and head.

Canada jay A sooty gray bird of the crow family, native in Canada and the NE United States.

Canada sparrow A tree sparrow.

Ca·na·di·an (kə·nā'dē·ən) *adj.* Of or pertaining to Canada or its people. — *n.* A native or inhabitant of Canada.

CANADA GOOSE
(To 43 inches long)

Canadian English The English language as spoken and written in Canada.

Canadian French The French language as spoken and written in Canada.

Ca·na·di·an·ism (kə·nā'dē·ən·iz'əm) *n.* **1.** A trait, custom, or tradition characteristic of the people of Canada or some of them. **2.** A word, phrase, etc. characteristic of Canadian English or French.

ca·naille (kə·nāl', *Fr.* kà·nä'y') *n.* The rabble; mob. [< F < Ital. *canaglia* pack of dogs < L *canis* dog]

ca·nal (kə·nal') *n.* **1.** An artificial waterway for inland navigation, irrigation, etc. **2.** *Anat.* A passage or duct; tube: the *auditory canal.* **3.** *Astron.* One of the faint, linear markings visible on Mars. — *v.t.* **ca·nalled** or **·naled, ca·nal·ling** or **·nal·ing** To dig a canal through, or provide with canals. [< MF < L *canalis* groove]

canal boat A long barge, used on canals.

can·a·lic·u·late (kan'ə·lik'yə·lit, -lāt) *adj.* Channeled or grooved. Also **can'a·lic'u·lar** (-lər), **can'a·lic'u·lat'ed.**

can·a·lic·u·lus (kan'ə·lik'yə·ləs) *n. pl.* **·li** (-lī) *Anat.* A small tube or canal, as in a bone. [< L *canalis* groove]

ca·nal·i·za·tion (kə·nal'ə·zā'shən, kan'əl·ə-) *n.* **1.** The act of making canals. **2.** A system of canals.

ca·nal·ize (kə·nal'īz, kan'əl·īz) *v.t.* **·ized, ·iz·ing 1.** To convert into a canal. **2.** To furnish with a canal, or a system of canals. **3.** To furnish with an outlet.

can·a·pé (kan'ə·pē, -pā, *Fr.* kà·nà·pā') *n.* A thin piece of toast or a cracker spread with cheese, caviar, etc. [< F]

ca·nard (kə·närd', *Fr.* kà·när') *n.* A false or absurd story or rumor; a hoax. [< F, duck]

ca·nar·y (kə·nâr'ē) *n. pl.* **·nar·ies 1.** A small finch having generally yellow plumage, popular as a cage bird. **2.** A bright yellow color. Also **canary yellow. 3.** A sweet, white wine from the Canary Islands. [< F < Sp. < L *Canaria* (*Insula*) Dog (Island)]

ca·nas·ta (kə·nas'tə) *n.* A card game for two to six players, based on rummy. [< Sp., basket]

can·can (kan'kan', *Fr.* kän·kän') *n.* A fast dance with much high kicking and wild movements. [< MF, noise]

can·cel (kan'səl) *v.* **can·celed** or **·celled, can·cel·ing** or **·cel·ling** *v.t.* **1.** To mark out or off, as by drawing lines through. **2.** To render null and void; annul. **3.** To delete or withdraw; call off. **4.** To mark or otherwise deface, as a postage stamp. **5.** To make up for; neutralize. **6.** *Math.* To eliminate (a common factor) from the numerator and denominator of a fraction, or from both sides of an equation. — *v.i.* **7.** To cancel one another: with *out.* — **Syn.** See ANNUL. — *n.* A cancellation. [< MF < L *cancellare* to cross out] — **can'cel·a·ble** or **can'cel·la·ble** *adj.* — **can'cel·er** or **can'cel·ler** *n.*

can·cel·la·tion (kan'sə·lā'shən) *n.* **1.** The act of canceling or rendering void. **2.** The marks used in canceling. **3.** That which is canceled. Also **can'ce·la'tion.**

can·cer (kan'sər) *n.* **1.** Any of a group of often fatal diseases characterized by abnormal cellular growth and by malignancy. **2.** A malignant tumor. **3.** Any dangerous and spreading evil. [< L, crab] — **can'cer·ous** *adj.*

Can·cer (kan'sər) *n.* A constellation, the Crab; also, the fourth sign of the zodiac. See ZODIAC.

can·de·la·brum (kan'də·lä'brəm, -lā'-) *n. pl.* **·bra** (-brə) or **·brums** A large, branched candlestick. Also **can'de·la'bra** (-brə) *pl.* **·bras.** [< L < *candela* candle]

can·des·cence (kan·des'əns) *n.* Incandescence. [< L *candere* to gleam] — **can·des'cent** *adj.* — **can·des'cent·ly** *adv.*

can·did (kan'did) *adj.* **1.** Honest and open; sincere; frank. **2.** Impartial; fair. [< MF < L *candere* to gleam] — **can'did·ly** *adv.* — **can'did·ness** *n.*

can·di·da·cy (kan'də·də·sē) *n. pl.* **·cies** The state or position of being a candidate. Also **can·di·da·ture** (kan'də·də·chŏŏr, -dā'chər), **can'di·date·ship'** (-dit·ship').

can·di·date (kan'də·dāt, -dit) *n.* One who seeks, or is nominated for, an office, honor, or privilege. [< L *candidus* white; because office seekers in Rome wore white togas]

candid camera A small camera with a fast lens, used for taking informal, unposed pictures.

can·died (kan'dēd) *adj.* **1.** Cooked with or in sugar. **2.** Crystallized or granulated. **3.** Flattering; honeyed.

can·dle (kan'dəl) *n.* **1.** A cylinder of tallow, wax, or other solid fat, containing a wick, that gives light when burning. **2.** Anything like a candle in shape or purpose. **3.** *Physics* A unit of luminous intensity now equal to that of ⅟₆₀ square centimeter of a black body operating at the temperature of solidification of platinum: also called *standard candle.* — **to hold a candle to** To compare with favorably: usually used in the negative. — *v.t.* **·dled, ·dling** To test, as eggs, by holding between the eye and a light. [OE < L *candere* to gleam]

can·dle·ber·ry (kan'dəl·ber'ē) *n. pl.* **·ries 1.** The wax myrtle. **2.** Its fruit.

can·dle·light (kan'dəl·līt') *n.* Light given by a candle; artificial light. **2.** Twilight.

Can·dle·mas (kan'dəl·məs) *n.* February 2, the feast of the Purification, or of the Presentation of Christ in the temple.

can·dle·pow·er (kan'dəl·pou'ər) *n.* The illuminating power of a standard candle, used as a measure.

can·dle·stick (kan'dəl·stik') *n.* A holder with sockets or spikes for a candle or candles.

can·dle·wick (kan'dəl·wik') *n.* The wick of a candle.

can·dor (kan'dər) *n.* **1.** Openness; frankness. **2.** Impartiality; fairness. Also *Brit.* **can'dour.** [< L, sincerity]

can·dy (kan'dē) *n. pl.* **·dies** Any of numerous confections consisting chiefly of sugar or syrup, usu. with chocolate, nuts, fruits, etc., added; also, such confections collectively: usu. called *sweets* in Great Britain. — *v.* **·died, ·dy·ing** *v.t.* **1.** To cause to form into crystals of sugar. **2.** To preserve by boiling or coating with sugar. **3.** To render pleasant; sweeten. — *v.i.* **4.** To become covered with sugar. [< Arabic *qandī* made of sugar < *qand* sugar, ult. < Skt.]

cane (kān) *n.* **1.** A walking stick. **2.** The jointed, woody stem of the bamboo, rattan, and certain palm trees, used as a weaving material in chairs, etc. **3.** Sugar cane. **4.** The stem of a raspberry or allied plant. **5.** Any rod, especially one used for flogging. — *v.t.* **caned, can·ing 1.** To strike or beat with a cane. **2.** To make or repair with cane, as a chair. [< OF < L < Gk. *kanna* reed] — **can'er** *n.*

cane·brake (kān'brāk') *n.* A thick growth of cane.

cane sugar Sucrose obtained from the sugar cane.

ca·nine (kā'nīn) *adj.* **1.** Of or like a dog. **2.** *Zool.* Of the dog family. **3.** Of or pertaining to a canine tooth. — *n.* **1.** A dog or other canine animal. **2.** *Anat.* One of the four pointed teeth situated one on either side of the upper and lower incisors. For illus. see TOOTH. [< L *canis* dog]

Ca·nis Ma·jor (kā'nis mā'jər) A constellation containing the bright star Sirius. [< L, greater dog]

Canis Mi·nor (mī'nər) A constellation containing the bright star Procyon. [< L, lesser dog]

can·is·ter (kan'is·ter) *n.* **1.** A container, usu. metal, for tea, spices, etc. **2.** Formerly, fragments in a metallic cylinder, to be fired from a cannon: also **canister shot.** [< L *canistrum* basket]

can·ker (kang'kər) *n.* **1.** *Pathol.* An ulceration, chiefly of the mouth and lips. **2.** Anything that causes corruption, evil, decay, etc. **3.** A disease of trees, causing decay of the bark and wood. — *v.t.* **1.** To affect with canker. **2.** To eat away like a canker. — *v.i.* **3.** To become infected with canker. [< AF < L *cancer* crab] — **can'ker·ous** *adj.*

can·ker·worm (kang'kər·wûrm') *n.* Any of several insect larvae that destroy fruit and shade trees.

can·na (kan'ə) *n.* An erect, mostly tropical American plant with red or yellow irregular flowers. [< L < Gk. *kanna* reed] — **can·na·ceous** (kə·nā'shəs) *adj.*

canned (kand) *adj.* **1.** Preserved in a can or jar. **2.** *Slang* Recorded: *canned* music.

can·nel (kan'əl) *n.* A bituminous coal with low heating power. Also **cannel coal.**

can·ner·y (kan'ər·ē) *n. pl.* **·ner·ies** A place where foods are canned.

can·ni·bal (kan'ə·bəl) *n.* **1.** One who eats human flesh. **2.** An animal that devours its own species. — *adj.* Of or like cannibals. [< Sp. *Canibales,* var. of *Caribes* Caribs]

can·ni·bal·ism (kan'ə·bəl·iz'əm) *n.* **1.** The act or practice of eating the flesh of one's own kind. **2.** Inhuman cruelty. — **can'ni·bal·is'tic** *adj.* — **can'ni·bal·is'ti·cal·ly** *adv.*

can·ni·bal·ize (kan'ə·bəl·īz') *v.t.* **·ized, ·iz·ing** *Mil.* To take parts from (damaged tanks, etc.) in order to repair others.

can·ni·kin (kan'ə·kin) *n.* **1.** A small can. **2.** A wooden pail.

can·ning (kan'ing) *n.* The act, process, or business of preserving foods in hermetically sealed tin cans, glass jars, etc.

can·non (kan'ən) *n. pl.* **·nons** or **·non 1.** *Mil.* A large tubular weapon, usu. mounted on a fixed or mobile carriage, that discharges a projectile by the use of an explosive. **2.** The large bone between the fetlock and knee or hock of the horse and allied animals. Also **cannon bone. 3.** *Brit.* A carom. — *v.i.* **1.** To fire cannon. **2.** *Brit.* To carom. — *v.t.* **3.** To attack with cannon shot. **4.** *Brit.* To cause to carom. [< OF < Ital. *canna* tube, pipe]

can·non·ade (kan'ən-ād') *v.* **-ad·ed, -ad·ing** *v.t.* **1.** To attack with cannon shot. — *v.i.* **2.** To fire cannon repeatedly. — *n.* A continued discharge of or attack with cannon.

cannon ball A spherical solid shot fired from a cannon.

can·non·eer (kan'ən-ir') *n.* An artillery gunner.

cannon fodder Soldiers considered as that which is consumed by war.

can·not (kan'ot, ka-not') The negative of the auxiliary verb CAN: written *can not* for emphasis. — **cannot but** Have no alternative except to.

can·ny (kan'ē) *adj.* Originally Scot. **·ni·er, ·ni·est 1.** Cautiously shrewd. **2.** Frugal; thrifty. **3.** Skillful. — *adv.* In a canny manner. — **can'ni·ly** *adv.* — **can'ni·ness** *n.*

ca·noe (kə-nōō') *n.* A small, long, narrow boat, pointed at both ends, and propelled by paddles. — *v.* **·noed, ·noe·ing** *v.t.* **1.** To convey by canoe. — *v.i.* **2.** To paddle, sail, or travel in a canoe. [< Sp. *canoa*] — **ca·noe'ist** *n.*

can·on¹ (kan'ən) *n.* **1.** A rule or law; esp., a rule or body of rules of faith and practice enacted by a church council. **2.** An established rule; principle. **3.** A standard for judgment; criterion. **4.** The books of the Bible. **5.** The sacred books of any sect or religion. **6.** A list, as of the recognized works of an author. **7.** The list of canonized saints. **8.** *Often cap. Eccl.* The portion of the Mass between the Sanctus and the Lord's Prayer. **9.** *Music* A composition or passage in which one or more voices follow and imitate the melody of the first voice. [OE < L < Gk. *kanōn* rule, straight rod]

can·on² (kan'ən) *n.* A member of the chapter of a cathedral or collegiate church. [See CANON¹.]

ca·ñon (kan'yən, *Sp.* känyōn') See CANYON.

can·on·ess (kan'ən-is) *n.* A member of a religious community of women living under a rule but not under vows.

ca·non·i·cal (kə-non'i-kəl) *adj.* **1.** Relating or conforming to or prescribed by, a canon or canons. **2.** Of or contained in the canon of Scripture. **3.** Authoritative; recognized. Also **ca·non'ic. — ca·non'i·cal·ly** *adv.*

canonical hours *Eccl.* The seven daily periods, fixed by canon, for prayer and devotion: also called *Divine Office.*

ca·non·i·cals (kə-non'i-kəlz) *n.pl.* The habits or robes prescribed by canon to be worn by the clergy when officiating.

can·on·ist (kan'ən-ist) *n.* One skilled in canon law. — **can'on·is'tic** or **·ti·cal** *adj.*

can·on·ize (kan'ən-īz) *v.t.* **·ized, ·iz·ing 1.** To declare (a deceased person) to be a saint. **2.** To recognize as part of the canon of Scripture. **3.** To sanction as being conformable to church canons. **4.** To glorify. — **can'on·i·za'tion** *n.*

canon law The ecclesiastical laws of a Christian church.

can·on·ry (kan'ən-rē) *n. pl.* **·ries 1.** The office, dignity, or benefice of a canon. **2.** Canons collectively. Also **can'on·ship.**

Ca·no·pus (kə-nō'pəs) *n.* One of the 20 brightest stars, 0.86 magnitude; Alpha in the constellation Carina. [< L]

can·o·py (kan'ə-pē) *n. pl.* **·pies 1.** A covering suspended over a throne, bed, shrine, etc., or held over a person. **2.** Any covering overhead, as the sky. **3.** *Archit.* An ornamental covering over a niche, altar, or tomb. **4.** *Aeron.* The main lifting surface of a parachute. — *v.t.* **·pied, ·py·ing** To cover with or as with a canopy. [< MF < L < Gk. *kōnōpeion* bed with mosquito net]

canst (kanst) Archaic second person singular, present tense of CAN¹: used with *thou.*

cant¹ (kant) *n.* **1.** An inclination from the vertical or horizontal; a slope or tilt. **2.** A sudden motion that tilts or overturns. **3.** An outer corner or angle. **4.** A slant surface, as one produced by cutting off a corner or edge. — *v.t.* **1.** To set (something); tilt. **2.** To give a bevel to. **3.** To throw out or off; jerk; toss. — *v.i.* **4.** To tilt; slant. — *adj.* **1.** Oblique; slanting. **2.** Having canted sides or corners. [Prob. < OF < Med.L *cantus* corner, side]

cant² (kant) *n.* **1.** Insincere religious or moralistic talk. **2.** Phraseology used merely for effect; stock phrases. **3.** Words or phraseology peculiar to a sect, class, or calling: legal *cant.* **4.** The secret jargon of thieves, gypsies, etc.; argot. **5.** Whining speech, esp. of beggars. — *v.i.* To use cant. — *adj.* Having the character of cant; hypocritical. [< AF — L < *canere* to sing] — **cant'er** *n.*

can't (kant, känt) Cannot.

can·ta·bi·le (kän-tä'bē-lā) *Music adj.* Melodious; flowing. — *n.* Music characterized by flowing melody. [< Ital.]

Can·ta·brig·i·an (kan'tə-brij'ē-ən) *adj.* Of or pertaining to Cambridge, England, or Cambridge University. — *n.* A resident of Cambridge, England; also, a student or graduate of Cambridge University. [< LL *Cantabrigia* Cambridge]

can·ta·loupe (kan'tə-lōp) *n.* A muskmelon having a ribbed, warty rind and sweet, orange flesh. Also **can'ta·loup.** [< F, after *Cantalupo*, Italian castle where first grown]

can·tank·er·ous (kan-tang'kər-əs) *adj.* Quarrelsome; ill

natured; perverse. [Prob. akin to ME *contak* strife] — **can·tank'er·ous·ly** *adv.* — **can·tank'er·ous·ness** *n.*

can·ta·ta (kən-tä'tə) *n. Music* A vocal composition in the style of a drama, to be sung but not acted. [< Ital.]

can·teen (kan-tēn') *n.* **1.** A small, usu. metal flask for carrying water or other liquids. **2.** A shop at a military camp where soldiers can buy provisions, refreshments, etc. **3.** A place for refreshments. [< F < Ital. *cantina* cellar]

can·ter (kan'tər) *n.* A moderate, easy gallop. — *v.t. & v.i.* To ride or go at a canter. [Short for *Canterbury gallop*; with ref. to the pace of pilgrims riding to Canterbury]

Canterbury bell One of various cultivated bellflowers.

Canterbury Tales An uncompleted work (1387–1400) by Chaucer, consisting of a series of tales, largely in verse, told by a group of pilgrims on their way to Canterbury.

cant hook A lever equipped with an adjustable hook for handling logs. Also **cant-dog** (kant'dôg', -dog').

can·thus (kan'thəs) *n. pl.* **·thi** (-thī) *Anat.* The angle at the junction of the eyelids. [< Gk. *kanthos*]

can·ti·cle (kan'ti-kəl) *n.* A nonmetrical hymn, said or chanted, in church. [< L *canticum* song]

Canticle of Can·ti·cles (kan'ti-kəlz) In the Bible, the Song of Solomon.

can·ti·lev·er (kan'tə-lev'ər, -lē'vər) *n.* **1.** *Engin.* A long structural member, as a truss, beam, or slab, lying across a support with the projecting arms in balance. **2.** *Archit.* Any structural part projecting horizontally and anchored at one end only. — *v.t. & v.i.* To project (a building member) outward and in balance beyond the base. [Origin uncertain]

CANTILEVER BRIDGE
(Section of Queensboro Bridge, New York City)

cantilever bridge A bridge formed by the meeting of two freely projecting beams, trusses, etc.

can·tle (kan'təl) *n.* The hind part of a saddle, projecting upward. [< AF < Med.L *cantus* corner]

can·to (kan'tō) *n. pl.* **·tos** A division of an extended poem. [< Ital. < L *cantus* song]

can·ton (kan'tən, -ton, kan-ton'; *for v. def. 2* kan-ton', -tōn', -tōōn') *n.* A district; esp., one of the states of Switzerland, or a subdivision of an arondissement in France. — *v.t.* **1.** To divide into cantons or districts. **2.** To assign quarters to, as troops. [< OF] — **can·ton·al** (kan'tə-nəl) *adj.*

Can·ton·ese (kan'tən-ēz', -ēs') *n. pl.* **·ese 1.** A native of Canton, China. **2.** The Chinese language spoken in parts of southern China.

Canton flannel (kan'tən) A heavy cotton flannel.

can·ton·ment (kan-ton'mənt, -tōn'-, -tōōn'-, kan'tən-mənt) *n.* The assignment of troops to temporary quarters; also, such quarters. [< F *cantonner* to quarter]

can·tor (kan'tər, -tôr) *n.* **1.** The chief liturgical singer in a synagogue. **2.** A precentor, or chief singer. [< L]

can·vas (kan'vəs) *n.* **1.** A heavy, closely woven cloth of hemp, flax, or cotton, used for sails, tents, etc. **2.** A piece of such material on which to paint, esp. in oils. **3.** A painting on canvas. **4.** Sailcloth. **5.** Sails collectively. **6.** A tent, esp. a circus tent. — **under canvas 1.** With sails set. **2.** In tents. [< AF, ult. < L *cannabis* hemp]

can·vas·back (kan'vəs-bak') *n.* A sea duck of North America, having a grayish white back.

can·vass (kan'vəs) *v.t.* **1.** To go about (a region) or among (persons) to solicit votes, opinions, etc. **2.** To scrutinize. — *v.i.* **3.** To go about seeking votes, opinions, etc. — *n.* **1.** A solicitation of votes, orders, etc., often to determine the public's attitude toward a candidate, a product, etc. **2.** A detailed examination or discussion. [< CANVAS; with ref. to its early use for sifting] — **can'vass·er** *n.*

can·yon (kan'yən) *n.* A deep gorge or ravine, with steep sides: also spelled *cañon.* [< Sp. *cañón*]

caout·chouc (kōō'chŏŏk, kou-chōōk') *n.* Rubber; esp., crude rubber. [< F < Tupi *cahuchu*]

cap (kap) *n.* **1.** A covering for the head, usu. snug, brimless, and of soft material. **2.** Any headgear designed to denote rank, function, membership, etc. **3.** Something suggesting a cap in form, function, or position. **4.** A primer, as of a cartridge. — **to set one's cap for** To try to win as a suitor or husband. — *v.t.* **capped, cap·ping 1.** To put a cap on; cover. **2.** To serve as a cap or cover to; lie on top of. **3.** To add the final touch to. **4.** To excel. — **to cap the climax** To surpass the climax. [OE < ML, prob. < L *caput* head]

ca·pa·bil·i·ty (kā'pə-bil'ə-tē) *n. pl.* **·ties 1.** The quality of being capable; capacity or ability. **2.** *Usu. pl.* Qualities that may be used or developed; potentialities.

ca·pa·ble (kā′pə·bəl) *adj.* Having ability; competent. — **capable of** 1. Having the capacity or qualities needed for. 2. Susceptible to. [< F < LL < L *capere* to take] — **ca′· pa·ble·ness** *n.* — **ca′pa·bly** *adv.*

ca·pa·cious (kə·pā′shəs) *adj.* Able to contain much; roomy. [< L < *capere* to take] — **ca·pa′cious·ly** *adv.* — **ca·pa′- cious·ness** *n.*

ca·pac·i·tance (kə·pas′ə·təns) *n. Electr.* The property of a circuit or body that permits it to store an electrical charge. — **ca·pac′i·tive** (-tiv) *adj.*

ca·pac·i·tate (kə·pas′ə·tāt) *v.t.* **·tat·ed, ·tat·ing** 1. To render capable. 2. To qualify according to law.

ca·pac·i·tor (kə·pas′ə·tər) *n. Electr.* A device consisting of conductors isolated in a dielectric medium, with each of them attached to only one side of a circuit, used to increase the capacitance to a desired value; also called *condenser.*

ca·pac·i·ty (kə·pas′ə·tē) *n. pl.* **·ties** 1. Ability to receive, contain, or absorb. 2. Maximum ability to hold, contain, etc. 3. Adequate mental power to receive, understand, etc. 4. The ability or aptitude to do something: with *for, of,* or the infinitive. 5. Specific position or office. 6. Legal qualification. 7. Maximum output or production. 8. *Electr.* Capacitance. [< MF < L < *capax* able to hold]

cap and bells A jester's cap ornamented with little bells.

cap and gown Ceremonial academic garb consisting of a cap or mortarboard and a characteristic robe or gown.

cap·a·pie (kap′ə·pē′) *adv.* From head to foot. Also **cap′- à·pie′.** [< OF]

ca·par·i·son (kə·par′ə·sən) *n.* 1. An ornamental covering for a horse. 2. Rich apparel or trappings. — *v.t.* To clothe richly. [< OF < Sp., ult. < LL *cappa* cape]

cape¹ (kāp) *n.* A point of land extending into the sea or a lake. [< F *cap,* ult. < L *caput* head]

cape² (kāp) *n.* A sleeveless garment fastened at the neck and hanging loosely from the shoulders. [< F < LL *cappa*]

cap·e·lin (kap′ə·lin) *n. pl.* **·lin** or **·lins** *U.S. & Canadian* A small, edible fish of northern seas, much used as bait. Also **cap′e·lan.** [< dial. F (Canadian) *capelan* < F]

Ca·pel·la (kə·pel′ə) *n.* One of the 20 brightest stars, 0.21 magnitude, in the constellation Auriga. [< L, she-goat]

ca·per¹ (kā′pər) *n.* 1. A playful leap; a skip. 2. A wild prank; antic. — **to cut a caper** (or **capers**) To caper; frolic. — *v.i.* To leap playfully. [Short for CAPRIOLE] — **ca′- per·er** *n.*

ca·per² (kā′pər) *n.* 1. The flower bud of a low shrub of Mediterranean countries, pickled and used as a condiment. 2. The shrub itself. [< L < Gk. *kapparis*]

cap·er·cail·lie (kap′ər·kāl′yē) *n.* A large, black European grouse. Also **cap′er·cail′zie** (-yē, -zē). [Alter. of Gaelic *capulcoille,* lit., horse of the wood]

Ca·pe·tian (kə·pē′shən) *adj.* Of or belonging to the dynasty (987–1328) founded in France by Hugh Capet.

ca·pi·as (kā′pē·əs, kap′ē·əs) *n. pl.* **·as·es** *Law* A judicial writ commanding an officer to take and hold in custody the person named therein. [< L, you may take]

cap·il·lar·i·ty (kap′ə·lar′ə·tē) *n. pl.* **·ties** 1. The state of being capillary. 2. *Physics* A form of surface tension between the molecules of a liquid and those of a solid. When the adhesive force is stronger (**capillary attraction**) the liquid will tend to rise in a capillary tube; when cohesion dominates (**capillary repulsion**), the liquid tends to fall. [< F]

cap·il·lar·y (kap′ə·ler′ē) *adj.* 1. Of, pertaining to, or like hair; fine. 2. Having a hairlike bore, as a tube or vessel. — *n. pl.* **·lar·ies** 1. *Anat.* A minute vessel, as those connecting the arteries and veins. 2. Any tube with a fine bore. [< L *capillus* hair]

cap·i·ta (kap′ə·tə) Plural of CAPUT.

cap·i·tal¹ (kap′ə·təl) *n.* 1. The city or town that is the seat of government of a country, state, etc. 2. A capital letter. 3. The total amount of money or property owned or used by an individual or corporation. 4. Wealth in any form employed in or available for the production of more wealth. 5. In accounting, the net worth of a business after the deduction of all liabilities. 6. Possessors of wealth as a class. — **to make capital of** To turn to advantage. — *adj.* 1. Chief, as comprising the seat of government. 2. Standing at the head; principal. 3. Of or pertaining to funds or capital. 4. Of the first quality. 5. Punishable by or involving the death penalty. 6. Very injurious; grave. [< OF < L < *caput* head]

cap·i·tal² (kap′ə·təl) *n. Archit.* The upper member of a column or pillar. [< L *caput* head]

capital expenditure Expenditure for permanent additions or improvements to property.

capital gain Profit from the sale of capital investments, such as stocks, real estate, etc.

cap·i·tal·ism (kap′ə·təl·iz′əm) *n.* 1. An economic system in which the means of production and distribution are mostly privately owned and operated for private profit. 2. The possession of private capital and its resulting power.

cap·i·tal·ist (kap′ə·təl·ist) *n.* 1. An owner of capital; esp.

one who has large means employed in productive enterprise. 2. Loosely, any person of wealth. 3. A supporter of capitalism. — **cap′i·tal·is′tic** *adj.* — **cap′i·tal·is′ti·cal·ly** *adv.*

cap·i·tal·i·za·tion (kap′ə·təl·ə·zā′shən, -ī·zā′-) *n.* 1. The act or process of capitalizing. 2. A sum arrived at by capitalizing. 3. The total capital employed in a business.

cap·i·tal·ize (kap′ə·təl·īz′) *v.* **·ized, ·iz·ing** *v.t.* 1. To begin with capital letters, or print or write in capital letters. 2. To convert into capital. 3. To provide capital for; organize on a basis of capital. 4. To estimate the worth of (a business or stock) from earnings or potential earnings. 5. In accounting, to record (expenses) as assets. — *v.i.* 6. To acquire an advantage; profit: with *on* or *by.* 7. To accumulate capital.

capital letter The form of a letter used at the beginning of a sentence, with proper names, etc., as the A in Africa.

cap·i·tal·ly (kap′ə·təl·ē) *adv.* In a capital or excellent way.

capital punishment The death penalty for a crime.

capital ship A warship of large size, as a battleship or aircraft carrier, carrying guns of over 8-inch caliber.

capital stock 1. The amount of stock a corporation is authorized to issue. 2. The total face value of such stock.

cap·i·ta·tion (kap′ə·tā′shən) *n.* An assessment on each person (or head); poll tax. [< LL < L *caput* head]

cap·i·tol (kap′ə·təl) *n.* The building in which a State legislature convenes; a statehouse.

Cap·i·tol (kap′ə·təl) 1. The official building of the U.S. Congress in Washington, D.C. 2. The temple of Jupiter Capitolinus in ancient Rome. [< L *Capitolium* the Capitoline]

ca·pit·u·lar (kə·pich′oo·lər) *adj.* Of or pertaining to an ecclesiastical chapter. [< Med.L *capitulum* chapter]

ca·pit·u·late (kə·pich′oo·lāt) *v.i.* **·lat·ed, ·lat·ing** 1. To surrender on stipulated terms. 2. To surrender. [< L *capitulare* to draw up in chapters] — **ca·pit′u·la′tor** *n.*

ca·pit·u·la·tion (kə·pich′oo·lā′shən) *n.* 1. The act of surrendering conditionally; also, the instrument containing the terms of surrender. 2. A surrender or giving up; yielding. 3. A summary of a subject. — **ca·pit·u·la·to·ry** (kə·pich′oo· lə·tôr′ē, -tō′rē) *adj.*

cap·lin (kap′lin) See CAPELIN.

ca·pon (kā′pon, -pən) *n.* A rooster gelded to improve the flesh for eating. [OE < L *capo, -onis*]

ca·pote (kə·pōt′) *n.* 1. A hooded cloak or overcoat. 2. A bonnet worn by women. [< F, dim. of *cape* hood]

ca·pric·ci·o (kə·prē′chē·ō, *Ital.* kä·prēt′chō) *n. pl.* **·ci·os** or *Ital.* **ca·pric·ci** (kä·prēt′chē) 1. *Music* A composition of lively and spirited mood, fancifully irregular in form. 2. A prank; also, a caprice. [< Ital., whim < *capro* goat < L *caper*]

ca·price (kə·prēs′) *n.* 1. A sudden change of mind or action without adequate motive; a whim. 2. A tendency to make such changes; capriciousness. 3. *Music* A capriccio. [< F < Ital. *capriccio* whim]

ca·pri·cious (kə·prish′əs) *adj.* Characterized by or resulting from caprice; fickle; whimsical. — **ca·pri′cious·ly** *adv.* — **ca·pri′cious·ness** *n.*

Cap·ri·corn (kap′rə·kôrn) *n.* A constellation, the Goat; also, the tenth sign of the zodiac. See ZODIAC. Also **Cap′ri· cor′nus** (-kôr′nəs). [< L < *caper* goat + *cornu* horn]

cap·ri·ole (kap′rē·ōl) *n.* 1. A leap made by a trained horse, with all feet off the ground and no forward motion. 2. A leap. — *v.i.* **·oled, ·ol·ing** To perform a capriole. [< F, leap]

caps or **caps.** *Printing* Capital letters.

cap·si·cum (kap′si·kəm) *n.* 1. An herb or shrub of the nightshade family, producing pods prepared as condiments or gastric stimulants. 2. The fruit of these plants; red pepper. [< L *capsa* box (from the shape of the fruit)]

cap·size (kap·sīz′, kap′sīz) *v.t. & v.i.* **·sized, ·siz·ing** To upset or overturn. [? < Sp. *capuzar* to sink a ship by the head]

cap·stan (kap′stən) *n. Naut.* A drumlike apparatus, turned by bars or levers, for hoisting anchors by exerting traction upon a cable. [< F *cabestan,* ult. < L *capere* to hold]

capstan bar A lever used in turning a capstan.

cap·stone (kap′stōn′) *n.* Copestone.

cap·su·late (kap′sə·lāt, -syoo-) *adj.* In or formed into a capsule. Also **cap′su·lat′ed.** — **cap′su·la′tion** *n.*

cap·sule (kap′səl, -syool) *n.* 1. A small container, usu. made of gelatin, for a dose of medicine. 2. A detachable part of an airplane, rocket, etc., containing the pilot, instruments, etc. 3. A thin covering or seal, as over the cork of a bottle. 4. *Bot.* A dry seed vessel made up of more than one carpel. **b** The spore case of a cryptogam. 5. *Anat.* A fibrous or membranous structure that envelops some part of the body. — *adj.* In concise form; condensed. [< F < L *capsula,* dim. of *capsa* box] — **cap′su·lar** *adj.*

cap·tain (kap′tən, -tin) *n.* 1. One at the head or in command; a chief; leader. 2. The master or commander of a vessel. 3. *Mil.* A commissioned officer ranking below a major. See tables at GRADE. 4. *Naval* A commissioned officer ranking below a commodore or rear admiral. See tables at GRADE. 5. A member of a team designated as its leader. — *v.t.* To act as captain to; command; lead. [< OF < LL < L *caput* head] — **cap′tain·cy, cap′tain·ship** *n.*

captain's walk A widow's walk.

cap·tion (kap′shən) *n.* **1.** A heading, as of a chapter, document, or newspaper article. **2.** The title and descriptive matter for an illustration. **3.** A subtitle in a motion picture. — *v.t.* To provide a caption for. [< L *capere* to take]

cap·tious (kap′shəs) *adj.* **1.** Apt to find fault; disposed to criticize. **2.** Designed to ensnare or perplex: a *captious* question. [< L *captiosus* fallacious] — **cap′tious·ly** *adv.* — **cap′tious·ness** *n.*

cap·ti·vate (kap′tə·vāt) *v.t.* **·vat·ed, ·vat·ing** To enthrall; fascinate; charm. [< LL *captivare* to capture] — **cap′ti·va′tion** *n.* — **cap′ti·va′tor** *n.*

cap·tive (kap′tiv) *n.* **1.** One who or that which is captured and held in confinement; a prisoner. **2.** One enthralled by beauty, passion, etc. — *adj.* **1.** Taken or held prisoner, as in war. **2.** Held in restraint; confined: a *captive* balloon. **3.** Captivated. **4.** Of or pertaining to a captive or captivity. [< F < L *capere* to take]

captive audience *U.S.* A group of people forced by circumstances to listen to something.

cap·tiv·i·ty (kap·tiv′ə·tē) *n.* *pl.* **·ties** The state of being held captive; thralldom.

cap·tor (kap′tər) *n.* One who takes or holds captive.

cap·ture (kap′chər) *v.t.* **·tured, ·tur·ing 1.** To take by force, stratagem, etc., as in war. **2.** To gain or win, as in competition. — *n.* **1.** The act of capturing; seizure. **2.** The person or thing captured. [< MF < L *capere* to take]

cap·u·chin (kap′yŏŏ·chin, -shin) *n.* **1.** A woman's hooded cloak. **2.** A long-tailed South American monkey whose head is covered with a cowl-like growth of hair. [< MF <I tal. *cappa* head]

Cap·u·chin (kap′yŏŏ·chin, -shin) *n.* A member of a branch of the Franciscan order.

ca·put (kā′pət, kap′ət) *n.* *pl.* **cap·i·ta** (kap′ə·tə) A head or headlike part. [< L]

car (kär) *n.* **1.** An automobile. **2.** A vehicle for use on rails. **3.** *Brit.* Any of various wheeled vehicles. **4.** *Poetic* A chariot. **5.** *U.S.* The enclosed platform of an elevator. [< AF < LL < L *carrus* wagon]

ca·ra·ba·o (kä′rä·bä′ō) *n.* *pl.* **·ba·os** or **·ba·o** In the Philippines, the water buffalo. [< Sp. < Malay *karbau*]

car·a·bin (kar′ə·bin), **car·a·bine** (-bīn) See CARBINE.

car·a·bin·eer (kar′ə·bin·ir′), **car·a·bin·ier** See CARBINEER.

ca·ra·ca·ra (kä′rä·kä′rä) A large, vulturelike hawk found in South America and southern U.S. [< Sp. *caracará*]

car·rack (kar′ak) See CARRACK.

car·a·cole (kar′ə·kōl) *n.* A half turn to the right or left made by a horseman's mount in riding. — *v.i.* **·coled, ·col·ing** To perform caracoles; wheel. Also **car′a·col** (-kol). [< F < Ital. < Sp. *caracol* snail shell]

car·a·cul (kar′ə·kəl) See KARAKUL.

ca·rafe (kə·raf′, -räf′) *n.* A glass water bottle. [< F]

car·a·mel (kar′ə·məl, -mel, kär′məl) *n.* **1.** A chewy confection composed of sugar, butter, milk, etc. **2.** Burnt sugar, used to flavor foods. [< OF < Med.L *canna mellis* sugar cane]

car·a·mel·ize (kar′ə·məl·īz′, kär′məl-) *v.t.* & *v.i.* **·ized, ·iz·ing** To convert into caramel. — **car′a·mel·i·za′tion** *n.*

car·a·pace (kar′ə·pās) *n.* *Zool.* A hard, bony, or chitinous outer case or covering, as of a turtle or lobster. Also **car′a·pax** (-paks). [< F < Sp. *carapacho*]

car·at (kar′ət) *n.* **1.** A unit of weight for gems, one metric carat being 200 milligrams, or 3.086 grains. **2.** Loosely, a karat. [< F < Ital. < Arabic < Gk. *keration* seed]

car·a·van (kar′ə·van) *n.* **1.** A company of traders, pilgrims, or the like, traveling together, esp. across deserts. **2.** A number of vehicles traveling together. **3.** A large, covered vehicle; a van. [< F < Persian *kārwān* caravan]

car·a·van·sa·ry (kar′ə·van′sə·rē) *n.* *pl.* **·ries 1.** In Oriental countries, an inn enclosing a court for sheltering caravans. **2.** Any hostelry or inn. Also **car′a·van′se·rai** (-rī, -rā). [< F < Persian *kārwān* caravan + *sarāī* inn]

car·a·vel (kar′ə·vel) *n.* A small ship of the 15th and 16th centuries, used esp. by the Portuguese and Spanish. Also **car′a·velle.** [< MF < Sp. *caraba* boat]

car·a·way (kar′ə·wā) *n.* An herb of the parsley family having small, spicy seeds (**caraway seeds**), used for flavoring. [< Sp. < Arabic *karwiyā* caraway]

car·bide (kär′bīd, -bid) *n.* *Chem.* A compound of carbon with a more electropositive element.

car·bine (kär′bīn, -bēn) *n.* **1.** A light, short-barreled rifle originally devised for mounted troops: also *carabin, carabine.* **2.** *U.S. Mil.* A semi-automatic and now automatic, gas-operated, .30-caliber rifle. [Earlier *carabine* < F]

car·bi·neer (kär′bə·nir′) *n.* A soldier armed with a carbine: also *carabineer, carabinier.*

carbo- combining form Carbon: *carbohydrate.* Also, before vowels, **carb-.** [< L *carbo* coal]

car·bo·hy·drate (kär′bō·hī′drāt) *n.* *Biochem.* Any of a group of compounds containing carbon combined with hydrogen and oxygen, and including sugars, starches, and cellulose.

car·bo·lat·ed (kär′bə·lā′tid) *adj.* Containing carbolic acid.

carbolic acid (kär·bol′ik) *Chem.* Phenol.

car·bo·lize (kär′bə·līz) *v.t.* **·lized, ·liz·ing** *Chem.* To treat or impregnate with carbolic acid.

car·bon (kär′bən) *n.* **1.** A nonmetallic element (symbol C) found in all organic substances and in some inorganic substances, as diamonds, graphite, coal, charcoal, lampblack, etc. See ELEMENT. **2.** *Electr.* **a** A rod of carbon, used as an electrode in an arc light. **b** The negative electrode of a primary cell. **3.** A piece of carbon paper. **4.** A carbon copy. — *adj.* **1.** Of, pertaining to, or like carbon. **2.** Treated with carbon. [< F < L *carbo, -onis* coal]

carbon 14 *Physics* Radiocarbon.

car·bo·na·ceous (kär′bə·nā′shəs) *adj.* Of, pertaining to, or yielding carbon.

car·bon·ate (kär′bə·nāt; *for n., also* kär′bə·nit) *Chem.* *v.t.* **·at·ed, ·at·ing 1.** To impregnate or charge with carbon dioxide. **2.** To carbonize. — *n.* A salt or ester of carbonic acid. [< F] — **car′bon·a′tion** *n.*

carbon copy 1. A copy of a letter, etc., made by means of carbon paper. **2.** An exact or close replica; duplicate.

carbon dioxide *Chem.* A heavy, odorless, incombustible gas, CO_2, taken from the atmosphere in the photosynthesis of plants and returned to it by the respiration of both plants and animals.

carboni- combining form Carbon; coal. [< L *carbo, -onis* coal]

car·bon·ic (kär·bon′ik) *adj.* Of, pertaining to, or obtained from carbon.

carbonic acid *Chem.* A weak, unstable acid, H_2CO_3, existing only in solution.

car·bon·if·er·ous (kär′bə·nif′ər·əs) *adj.* Of, pertaining to, containing, or yielding carbon or coal.

Car·bon·if·er·ous (kär′bə·nif′ər·əs) *adj.* *Geol.* Of or pertaining to a period of the Paleozoic era characterized by the formation of extensive coal beds. — *n.* The Carboniferous period or system of rocks. See chart under GEOLOGY.

car·bon·ize (kär′bən·īz) *v.t.* **·ized, ·iz·ing 1.** To reduce to carbon. **2.** To coat with carbon, as paper. **3.** To charge with carbon. — **car′bon·i·za′tion** *n.* — **car′bon·iz′er** *n.*

carbon monoxide *Chem.* A colorless, odorless gas, CO, formed by the incomplete oxidation of carbon, burning with a blue flame and highly poisonous when inhaled.

carbon paper Thin paper coated with carbon or the like, placed between two sheets of paper to reproduce on the bottom sheet what is written or typed on the upper sheet.

carbon tetrachloride *Chem.* A colorless, nonflammable liquid, CCl_4, used as a solvent, cleaning fluid, etc.

Car·bo·run·dum (kär′bə·run′dəm) *n.* An abrasive of silicon carbide: a trade name. Also **car′bo·run′dum.**

car·box·yl (kär·bok′sil) *n.* *Chem.* A univalent acid radical, COOH, the characteristic group of most organic acids.

car·boy (kär′boi) *n.* A large glass bottle enclosed in a box or in wickerwork, used as a container for, corrosive acids, etc. [Alter. of Persian *qarābah* demijohn]

car·bun·cle (kär′bung·kəl) *n.* **1.** *Pathol.* An inflammation of the subcutaneous tissue, resembling a boil but larger. **2.** A red garnet cut without facets. [< AF < L *carbo, -onis* coal] — **car·bun·cu·lar** (kär·bung′kyə·lər) *adj.*

car·bu·ret (kär′bə·rāt, -byə·ret) *v.t.* **·ret·ed** or **·ret·ted, ·ret·ing** or **·ret·ting** To combine chemically with carbon; esp. to charge (air or gas) with carbon compounds. — **car·bu·re·tion** (kär′bə·rā′shən, -byə·resh′ən) *n.*

car·bu·re·tor (kär′bə·rā′tər, -byə·ret′ər) *n.* An apparatus used to charge air or gas with volatile hydrocarbons to give it illuminative or explosive power. Also *Brit.* **car·bu·ret·tor** (kär′byə·ret′ər) or **car′bu·ret′ter.**

car·bu·rize (kär′bə·rīz, -byə-) *v.t.* **·rized, ·riz·ing 1.** To carburet. **2.** *Metall.* To impregnate the surface layer of (low-carbon steel) with carbon, a stage in casehardening.

car·ca·jou (kär′kə·jōō, -zhōō) *n.* *Canadian* The wolverine. [< dial. F (Canadian) < native Algonquian name]

car·cass (kär′kəs) *n.* **1.** The dead body of an animal. **2.** The human body, living or dead: a contemptuous or humorous use. **3.** Something from which the life or essence is gone; shell. **4.** A framework or skeleton. Also **car′case.** [< AF < Med.L *carcasium*]

car·cin·o·gen (kär·sin′ə·jən) *n.* *Pathol.* A substance that causes cancer. — **car·ci·no·gen·ic** (kär·sə·nō·jen′ik) *adj.*

car·ci·no·ma (kär′sə·nō′mə) *n.* *pl.* **·mas** or **·ma·ta** (-mə·tə) *Pathol.* A malignant epithelial tumor; cancer. Also **car·ci·nus** (kär′sə·nəs). [< L < Gk. *karkinos* cancer] — **car·ci·nom·a·tous** (kär′sə·nom′ə·təs, -nō′mə-) *adj.*

card[1] (kärd) *n.* **1.** A small, usu. rectangular piece of thin pasteboard or stiff paper, used for a variety of purposes. **2.**

One of a pack of such pieces with figures, numbers, or other symbols, used for various games. **3.** *pl.* Games played with playing cards. **4.** A greeting card. **5.** A card certifying the identity of its owner or bearer: library *card.* **6.** A program or form of events, as at the races. **7.** *Naut.* The dial of a compass. **8.** An advertisement or public announcement printed on a card. **9.** *Informal* A person manifesting some peculiarity: a queer *card.* **10.** *Informal* A witty person. — **in the cards** Likely to happen; possible. — **to put one's cards on the table** To reveal one's intentions with complete frankness. — *v.t.* **1.** To fasten or write upon a card or cards. **2.** To provide with a card. [< MF < Ital. < L < Gk. *chartēs* leaf of paper]

card² (kärd) *n.* **1.** A wire-toothed brush for combing and cleansing wool, etc. **2.** A similar instrument for raising a nap. — *v.t. & v.i.* To comb, dress, or cleanse with a card. [< MF < Ital. < Med.L < L *carduus* thistle] — **card′er** *n.*

car·da·mom (kär′də·məm) *n.* **1.** The aromatic seeds of either of two Asian plants of the ginger family. **2.** One of the plants yielding these seeds. Also **car′da·mon** (-mən), **car′da·mum.** [< L < Gk. *kardamon* cress + *amōmon* spice]

card·board (kärd′bôrd′, -bōrd′) *n.* A thin, stiff pasteboard used for making cards, boxes, etc.

card catalogue A catalogue made out on cards, esp. one showing the books in a library.

cardi- Var. of CARDIO-.

car·di·ac (kär′dē·ak) *Med. adj.* **1.** Pertaining to, situated near, or affecting the heart. **2.** Of or pertaining to the upper orifice of the stomach. Also **car·di·a·cal** (kär·dī′ə·kəl). — *n.* **1.** One suffering from a heart disease. **2.** A cardiac remedy or stimulant. [< F < L < Gk. *kardia* heart]

car·di·gan (kär′də·gən) *n.* A jacket or sweater opening down the front. Also **cardigan jacket, cardigan sweater.** [after the seventh Earl of *Cardigan,* 1797–1868]

car·di·nal (kär′də·nəl, kärd′nəl) *adj.* **1.** Of prime importance; chief; principal. **2.** Of a deep scarlet color. **3.** Of or relating to a cardinal or cardinals. — *n.* **1.** In the Roman Catholic Church, a member of the College of Cardinals, or Sacred College. **2.** A bright red, crested finch of the eastern United States: also called *redbird:* also **cardinal bird, cardinal grosbeak. 3.** A deep scarlet. **4.** A cardinal number. [< F < L *cardo, cardinis* hinge, that on which something turns or depends] — **car′di·nal·ly** *adv.*

car·di·nal·ate (kär′də·nəl·āt, kärd′nəl·āt) *n.* The rank, dignity, or term of office of a cardinal. Also **car′di·nal·ship′.**

cardinal flower An herb of North America having large red flowers.

cardinal number *Math.* Any number that expresses the number of objects or units under consideration, as 1, 2, 3, etc.: distinguished from *ordinal number.*

cardinal point Any of the four main points of the compass.

cardinal sins The seven deadly sins.

cardinal virtues Justice, prudence, temperance, and fortitude, classified by Plato as the four types of moral excellence.

card·ing (kär′ding) *n.* **1.** The cleansing and combing of wool, flax, etc., before spinning. **2.** Carded fibers.

cardio- *combining form* Heart: *cardiogram.* Also, before vowels, *cardi-.* [< Gk. *kardia* heart]

car·di·o·gram (kär′dē·ə·gram′) *n.* The graphic record of heart movements produced by the cardiograph.

car·di·o·graph (kär′dē·ə·graf′, -gräf′) *n.* An instrument for tracing and recording the force and character of the heart movements. — **car′di·o·graph′ic** *adj.* — **car·di·og·ra·phy** (kär′dē·og′rə·fē) *n.*

car·di·tis (kär·dī′tis) *n. Pathol.* Inflammation of the heart.

cards (kärdz) *n.pl.* (*construed as sing.*) **1.** Any game played with playing cards. **2.** The playing of card games.

card·sharp (kärd′shärp′) *n.* One who cheats at cards, esp. as a livelihood. Also **card′sharp′er.**

care (kâr) *n.* **1.** A feeling of anxiety or concern; worry. **2.** A cause of worry or anxiety. **3.** Watchful regard or attention; heed. **4.** Charge or guardianship; custody; supervision. **5.** An object of solicitude or attention. — *v.i.* **cared, car·ing. 1.** To have or show regard, interest, or concern. **2.** To be inclined; desire: with *to.* **3.** To mind or be concerned: I don't *care* if it rains. — **to care for 1.** To look after or provide for. **2.** To feel interest concerning; also, to have a fondness for; like. **3.** To want; desire. [OE *caru, cearu*]

ca·reen (kə·rēn′) *v.i.* **1.** *U.S.* To lurch or twist from side to side while moving. **2.** To lean sideways. **3.** To clean a ship when it is on one side. — *v.t.* **4.** To turn (a ship, etc.) on one side; tip. **5.** To clean, repair, or caulk (a careened ship). — *n.* **1.** The act of careening a vessel. **2.** The position of a ship careened or heeled over. [< F < L *carina* keel of a ship] — **ca·reen′er** *n.*

ca·reer (kə·rir′) *n.* **1.** The course or progress of a person's life: a remarkable *career.* **2.** One's lifework; profession. **3.** Successful pursuit of an occupation. **4.** Speed; full speed. — *adj. U.S.* Making one's profession a lifework: *career* diplomat. — *v.i.* To move with a swift, free motion. [< F < LL < L *carrus* wagon] — **ca·reer′er** *n.*

ca·reer·ist (kə·rir′ist) *n.* A person chiefly concerned with advancing himself professionally. — **ca·reer′ism** *n.*

care-free (kâr′frē′) *adj.* Free of troubles or anxiety.

care·ful (kâr′fəl) *adj.* **1.** Exercising care in one's work; painstaking. **2.** Done with care: a *careful* job. **3.** Watchful; cautious. — **care′ful·ly** *adv.* — **care′ful·ness** *n.*

care·less (kâr′lis) *adj.* **1.** Not attentive; reckless: a *careless* worker. **2.** Not done with care; neglectful. **3.** Without care or concern; indifferent: with *about, in,* or *of.* **4.** Artless; unstudied: *careless* elegance. **5.** Carefree: a *careless* life. — **care′less·ly** *adv.* — **care′less·ness** *n.*

ca·ress (kə·res′) *n.* An affectionate touch or gesture, as an embrace, pat, etc. — *v.t.* To touch or treat lovingly; fondle. [< MF < Ital. < L *carus* dear] — **ca·ress′er** *n.* — **ca·ress′ing·ly** *adv.* — **ca·res′sive** *adj.* — **ca·res′sive·ly** *adv.*

car·et (kar′ət) *n.* A sign (∧) placed below a line to indicate where something should be inserted. [< L, it is missing]

care·tak·er (kâr′tā′kər) *n.* One who takes care of a place, thing, or person; a custodian.

care·worn (kâr′wôrn′, -wōrn′) *adj.* Showing the effects of care and anxiety; haggard; weary.

car·fare (kär′fâr′) *n.* The fare for a ride on a bus, etc.

car·go (kär′gō) *n. pl.* **·goes** or **·gos** Goods and merchandise carried by a vessel, aircraft, etc.; freight; load. [< Sp. < LL < L *carrus* wagon]

car·hop (kär′hop′) *n. U.S. Informal* A waiter or waitress at a drive-in restaurant.

Car·ib (kar′ib) *n.* **1.** One of a tribe of Indians now surviving on the coasts of Guiana, Venezuela, Dominica, Honduras, Guatemala, and Nicaragua. **2.** The family of languages spoken by these Indians. [< Sp. < Cariban *caribe* brave] — **Car′ib·an** *adj. & n.*

Car·ib·be·an (kar′ə·bē′ən, kə·rib′ē·ən) *n.* **1.** The Caribbean Sea. **2.** A Carib. — *adj.* **1.** Of or pertaining to the Caribbean Sea. **2.** Of or pertaining to the Caribs, their language, or their culture.

car·i·bou (kar′ə·boo) *n. pl.* **·bou** or **·bous** A North American reindeer found from Maine to the Arctic. [< dial. F (Canadian) < Alonquian *khalibu* pawer]

car·i·ca·ture (kar′i·kə·choor, -chər) *n.* **1.** A picture or description in which features are exaggerated or distorted so as to produce an absurd effect. **2.** The act or art of caricaturing. **3.** A poor imitation. — *v.t.* **·tured, ·tur·ing** To represent so as to make ridiculous; burlesque. [< F < Ital. *caricare* to load, exaggerate] — **car′i·ca·tur′al** *adj.* — **car′i·ca·tur′ist** *n.*

CARIBOU
(4 feet high at shoulder; 6 feet long; tail 4 inches)

car·ies (kâr′ēz, -i·ēz) *n. Pathol.* Decay of a bone or of a tooth. [< L]

car·il·lon (kar′ə·lon, kə·ril′yən) *n.* **1.** A set of stationary bells rung by hammers operated from a keyboard or by a mechanism. **2.** A melody rung on a carillon. **3.** An organ stop imitating bells. — *v.i.* **·lonned, ·lon·ning** To play a carillon. [< F < Med.L *quadrilio,* -*onis* set of four bells]

car·il·lon·neur (kar′ə·lə·nûr′) *n.* One who plays a carillon.

car·i·o·ca (kar′ē·ō′kə) *n.* A type of South American dance, or the music for it. [after Sierra de *Carioca,* a mountain range near Rio de Janeiro]

car·i·ole (kar′ē·ōl) *n.* **1.** A small, open carriage. **2.** A light cart. **3.** *Canadian* A dog sled for one person lying down. Also spelled **carriole.** [< F < Ital. *carra* cart, wagon]

car·i·ous (kâr′ē·əs) *adj.* Affected with caries; decayed. Also **car·ied** (kâr′ēd) — **car′i·os·i·ty** (-os′ə·tē), **car′i·ous·ness** *n.*

carl (kärl) *n.* **1.** *Archaic* A countryman; peasant. **2.** *Scot.* A churl. Also **carle.** [< ON *karl* man, freeman]

car·load (kär′lōd′) *n.* **1.** The load carried in a car. **2.** The minimum load required to ship at the **carload rate,** a rate lower than that for smaller loads.

carload lot A freight shipment meeting the official minimum weight for a carload rate.

car·ma·gnole (kär′mən·yōl′, *Fr.* kàr·mà·nyôl′) *n.* **1.** A wild dance and song of the French revolutionists of 1789. **2.** The costume of the French revolutionists. [< F, after *Carmagnola,* a town in Piedmont]

car·man (kär′mən) *n. pl.* **·men** (-mən) **1.** The driver, or one of the crew, of a streetcar, etc. **2.** One who drives a cart.

Car·mel·ite (kär′məl·īt) *n.* A monk or nun of the order of Our Lady of Mt. Carmel. — *adj.* Of or relating to the Carmelites.

car·min·a·tive (kär·min′ə·tiv, kär′mə·nā′tiv) *Med. adj.* Tending to, or used to, relieve flatulence. — *n.* A remedy for flatulence. [< L *carminare* to cleanse]

car·mine (kär′min, -mīn) *n.* **1.** A deep red or purplish red color. **2.** A crimson pigment obtained from cochineal; rouge. — *adj.* Deep red or purplish red. [< F < Med.L < O Sp. *carmesin* crimson]

car·nage (kär′nij) *n.* Extensive and bloody slaughter, as in war; massacre. — **Syn.** See MASSACRE. [< MF < Ital. < LL < L *caro, carnis* flesh, meat]

car·nal (kär′nəl) *adj.* **1.** Relating to bodily appetites; sensual. **2.** Sexual. **3.** Not spiritual; worldly. [< LL < L *caro, carnis* flesh] — **car′nal·ist** *n.* — **car·nal·i·ty** (kär·nal′ə·tē) *n.* — **car′nal·ly** *adv.*

car·na·tion (kär·nā′shən) *n.* **1.** The perennial, herbaceous, fragrant flower of any of the many varieties of the pink family. **2.** A light pink, bright rose, or scarlet color. [< F < L *caro, carnis* flesh]

car·nel·ian (kär·nēl′yən) *n.* A clear red chalcedony, used as a gem: also *cornelian.* [< L *carnis* flesh]

car·ni·fy (kär′nə·fī) *v.t. & v.i.* **·fied, ·fy·ing** To form into flesh or a fleshlike consistency. [< L < *carnis* flesh + *facere* to make] — **car·ni·fi·ca′tion** *n.*

car·ni·val (kär′nə·vəl) *n.* **1.** An amusement show with merry-go-round, Ferris wheel, side shows, etc. **2.** Any gay festival, wild revel, or merrymaking. **3.** A period of festivity immediately preceding Lent. [< Ital. < Med.L < L *carn⁴ⁱ³* flesh + *levare* to remove]

car·ni·vore (kär′nə·vôr, -vōr) *n.* A flesh-eating mammal, as a cat, dog, etc.

car·niv·o·rous (kär·niv′ə·rəs) *adj.* **1.** Eating or living on flesh. **2.** Of or pertaining to carnivores. [< L < *carnis* flesh + *vorare* to eat, devour] — **car·niv′o·rous·ly** *adv.* — **car·niv′o·rous·ness** *n.*

car·ol (kar′əl) *n.* A song of joy or praise; esp., a Christmas song. — *v.* **car·oled** or **·olled, car·ol·ing** or **·ol·ling** *v.i.* **1.** To sing, esp. in a joyous strain. — *v.t.* **2.** To utter or praise in song. [< OF < L < Gk. < *choros* a dance + *auleein* to play the flute] — **car′ol·er** or **car′ol·ler** *n.*

Car·o·li·nas (kar′ə·lī′nəz), **the** North and South Carolina.

Car·o·lin·gi·an (kar′ə·lin′jē·ən) *adj.* Of or pertaining to the dynasty of Charlemagne.

Car·o·lin·i·an (kar′ə·lin′ē·ən) *adj.* **1.** Of or pertaining to North or South Carolina. **2.** Carolingian. — *n.* A native or inhabitant of North or South Carolina.

car·om (kar′əm) *n.* **1.** In billiards, a shot in which the cue ball strikes against two other balls in succession: in England, called a *cannon.* Also called *billiard.* **2.** Any impact followed by a rebound. — *v.i.* **1.** To hit and rebound. — *v.t.* **2.** To cause to make a carom. [Earlier *carambole* < F]

car·o·tene (kar′ə·tēn) *n. Biochem.* A deep yellow or red crystalline hydrocarbon, $C_{40}H_{56}$, found in carrots, etc., and changed in the body to vitamin A. Also **car′o·tin** (-tin). [< L *carota* carrot + -ENE]

ca·rot·e·noid (kə·rot′ə·noid) *n. Biochem.* One of a large variety of pigments found in plant and animal tissues. — *adj.* Of carotene or carotenoids. Also **ca·rot′i·noid.**

ca·rot·id (kə·rot′id) *adj. Anat.* Of, pertaining to, or near one of the two major arteries on each side of the neck. Also **ca·rot′i·dal.** [< Gk. *karos* stupor]

ca·rou·sal (kə·rou′zəl) *n.* A feast or banquet.

ca·rouse (kə·rouz′) *v.i.* **·roused, ·rous·ing** To drink freely and boisterously. — *n.* A carousal. [< G *gar aus (trinken)* (to drink) all out] — **ca·rous′er** *n.*

car·ou·sel (kar′ə·sel′, -zel′) *n.* **1.** A merry-go-round (def. 1). **2.** A tournament in which horsemen perform. Also spelled *carrousel.* [< F < Ital. *carosello* tournament]

carp¹ (kärp) *v.i.* To find fault unreasonably; complain; cavil. [< ON *karpa* to boast] — **carp′er** *n.*

carp² (kärp) *n. pl.* **carp** or **carps 1.** A fresh-water food fish widely distributed in Europe and America. **2.** Any of various related fishes, as goldfish. [< OF < LL *carpa*]

-carp *combining form* Fruit; fruit (or seed) vessel: *pericarp.* [< Gk. *karpos* fruit]

car·pal (kär′pəl) *Anat. adj.* Of, pertaining to, or near the wrist. — *n.* A carpale. [< NL < L < Gk. *karpos* wrist]

car·pa·le (kär·pā′lē) *n. pl.* **·li·a** (-lē·ə) *Anat.* A bone of the carpus or wrist. [See CARPAL.]

car·pe di·em (kär′pē dī′em) *Latin* Enjoy the present; seize today's opportunities; literally, seize the day.

car·pel (kär′pəl) *n. Bot.* A simple pistil or seed vessel. [< NL < Gk. *karpos* fruit] — **car·pel·lar·y** (kär′pə·ler′ē) *adj.*

car·pen·ter (kär′pən·tər) *n.* A workman who builds and repairs wooden structures, as houses, ships, etc. — *v.i.* **1.** To work as a carpenter. — *v.t.* **2.** To make or build as a carpenter. [< AF < LL < L *carpentum* two-wheeled carriage] — **car′pen·ter·ing** *n.* — **car′pen·try** *n.*

car·pet (kär′pit) *n.* **1.** A heavy covering for floors; also, the fabric used for it. **2.** A surface or covering suggesting this. — **on the carpet 1.** Subjected to reproof or reprimand. **2.** Under consideration or discussion. — *v.t.* To cover with or as with a carpet. [< OF < LL < L *carpere* to pluck, card wool]

car·pet·bag (kär′pit·bag′) *n.* An old type of traveling bag, made of carpeting.

car·pet·bag·ger (kär′pit·bag′ər) *n. U.S.* One of the Northern adventurers who sought to gain advantages in the South from the unsettled conditions after the Civil War.

carpet beetle A beetle whose larvae feed on carpets, fur, etc. Also **carpet bug.**

car·pet·ing (kär′pit·ing) *n.* Carpets or carpet fabric.

carpet sweeper A hand-operated apparatus for sweeping carpets, combining a revolving brush and closed dustpan.

carp·ing (kär′ping) *adj. & n.* Faultfinding. — **carp′ing·ly** *adv.*

carpo- *combining form* Fruit. [< Gk. *karpos* fruit]

car·port (kär′pôrt′, -pōrt′) *n. U.S.* A shelter for an automobile, usu. a roof projecting from the side of a building.

-carpous *combining form* Having a certain kind or number of fruits. Also **-carpic.** [< Gk. *karpos* fruit]

car·pus (kär′pəs) *n. pl.* **·pi** (-pī) *Anat.* The wrist, or the wrist bones collectively. [< NL < Gk. *karpos* wrist]

car·rack (kar′ək) *n.* A galleon: also spelled *carack.* [< OF < Med.L, ? < Arabic *qorqūr* merchant ship]

car·ra·geen (kar′ə·gēn) *n.* An edible seaweed known commercially as Irish moss and used in medicine. Also **car′ra·gheen.** [after *Carragheen*, Ireland, where it grows]

car·rel (kar′əl) *n.* A small space, as among the stacks in a library, for solitary study. Also **car′rell.** [Var. of CAROL]

car·riage (kar′ij; *for def. 7, also* kar′ē·ij) *n.* **1.** A wheeled, usu. horse-drawn vehicle for carrying persons. **2.** *Brit.* A railroad passenger car. **3.** Manner of carrying the head and limbs; bearing. **4.** A moving portion of a machine carrying another part: the *carriage* of a lathe. **5.** A wheeled frame for carrying something heavy. **6.** The act of carrying; transportation. **7.** The cost of transportation.

carriage trade The wealthy patrons of a restaurant, theater, etc., so called because they came in private carriages.

car·ried (kar′ēd) Past tense and past participle of CARRY.

car·ri·er (kar′ē·ər) *n.* **1.** One who or that which carries. **2.** A person or company that carries persons or goods for hire. **3.** *Med.* A person who is immune to a disease but transmits it to others.

carrier pigeon A homing pigeon.

carrier wave *Telecom.* The radio-frequency wave that is varied in some respect in order to transmit intelligence.

car·ri·ole (kar′ē·ōl) See CARIOLE.

car·ri·on (kar′ē·ən) *n.* Dead and putrefying flesh. — *adj.* **1.** Feeding on carrion. **2.** Like or pertaining to carrion; putrefying. [< AF < L *caro, carnis* flesh]

carrion crow The common crow of Europe.

car·rom (kar′əm) See CAROM.

car·rot (kar′ət) *n.* **1.** The long, reddish yellow, edible root of an umbelliferous plant. **2.** The plant itself. [< F < L < Gk. *karōton* carrot]

car·rot·y (kar′ət·ē) *adj.* **1.** Like a carrot, esp. in color. **2.** Having red hair.

car·rou·sel (kar′ə·sel′, -zel′) See CAROUSEL.

car·ry (kar′ē) *v.* **·ried, ·ry·ing** *v.t.* **1.** To bear from one place to another; transport; convey. **2.** To serve as a medium of conveyance for; transmit. **3.** To have or bear upon or about one's person. **4.** To bear the weight, burden, or responsibility of. **5.** To give support to; confirm. **6.** To bear as a mark or attribute: Her words *carried* conviction. **7.** To be pregnant with. **8.** To bear (the body, or a part of it) in a specified manner. **9.** To conduct or comport (oneself). **10.** To take by force or effort; capture; win. **11.** To win the support or interest of. **12.** To gain victory or acceptance for; also, to achieve success in. **13.** To cause to go or come; urge. **14.** To extend; continue. **15.** To have or keep for sale. **16.** To transfer, as a number or figure, to another column. **17.** To maintain on one's account books for a future settlement. **18.** *U.S.* To sing or play (a part or melody). **19.** *Southern U.S.* To escort. — *v.i.* **20.** To act as bearer or carrier. **21.** To have or exert propelling or projecting power: The rifle *carries* well. **22.** To hold the neck and head in a particular manner. **23.** To gain victory or acceptance: The motion *carried.* — **to carry all before one** To meet with uniform success. — **to carry arms 1.** To belong to the army. **2.** To bear weapons. **3.** To hold a weapon in a prescribed position against the shoulder. — **to carry away** To move the feelings greatly; enchant. — **to carry forward 1.** To progress or proceed with. **2.** In bookkeeping, to transfer (an item, etc.) to the next column or page. — **to carry off 1.** To cause to die. **2.** To win, as a prize or honor. **3.** To face consequences boldly; brazen out. **4.** To abduct. — **to carry on 1.** To keep up; keep going; continue. **2.** To behave in a wild, excited, or foolish manner. **3.** To engage in. — **to carry out** To accomplish; bring to completion. — **to carry over 1.** In bookkeeping, to repeat (an item, etc.) on another page or in another column. **2.** To postpone; put off. — **to carry through 1.** To carry to completion or success. **2.** To sustain or support to the end. — *n. pl.* **·ries 1.** Range, as of a gun; also, the distance covered by a projectile, golf ball, etc. **2.** *U.S.* A portage, as between streams. **3.** The act of carrying. [< L *carrus* cart]

car·ry·all[1] (kar′ē·ôl′)   *n.*   A light, four-wheeled covered vehicle having room for several people.

car·ry·all[2] (kar′ē·ôl′)   *n.*   A large basket or bag.

carrying charge   In installment buying, the interest charged on the unpaid balance.

carrying place   *Canadian*   A portage (def. 2).

car·ry·o·ver (kar′ē·ō′vər)   *n.*   1. Something left over or kept until later.   2. In bookkeeping, a sum carried forward.

car·sick (kär′sik′)   *adj.*   Nauseated from riding in a car.

cart (kärt)   *n.*   1. A two-wheeled vehicle, for carrying loads.   2. A light, two-wheeled vehicle with springs, used for business or pleasure.   — *v.t.*   1. To carry in or as in a cart.   — *v.i.*   2. To drive or use a cart.   [ON *kartr*]   — **cart′er** *n.*

cart·age (kär′tij)   *n.*   The act of or charge for carting.

carte blanche (kärt′ blänsh′, *Fr.* kärt blänsh′)   *pl.* **cartes blanches** (kärts′ blänsh′, *Fr.* kärt blänsh′)   1. A signed paper granting its possessor the freedom to write his own conditions.   2. Unrestricted authority.   [< F, white card]

car·tel (kär·tel′, kär′təl)   *n.*   1. An international trust that aims at monopolistic control of a particular market.   2. An official agreement between governments, esp. for the exchange of prisoners.   3. A challenge to single combat.   [< F < Ital. *carta* paper]

Car·te·sian·ism (kär·tē′zhən·iz′əm)   *n.*   The philosophy of Descartes who defended complete dualism between thought (or mind) and extension (the subject matter of physical science).   [< NL *Cartesius*, Latinized form of *Descartes*]   — **Car·te′sian** *n. & adj.*

Car·thage (kär′thij)   An ancient city state in North Africa; destroyed by the Romans in 146 B.C.   Ancient **Car·tha·go** (kär·thā′gō).   — **Car·tha·gin·i·an** (kär·thə·jin′ē·ən)   *adj. & n.*

Car·thu·sian (kär·thōō′zhən)   *n.*   A monk or nun of a contemplative order founded at Chartreuse in the French Alps by St. Bruno in 1084.   — *adj.* Of or pertaining to the Carthusians.   [< Med.L *Carturissium* Chartreuse]

car·ti·lage (kär′tə·lij)   *n.*   *Zool.*   1. A tough, elastic form of connective tissue in man and animals; gristle.   2. A part consisting of cartilage.   [< MF < L *cartilago* gristle]

car·ti·lag·i·nous (kär′tə·laj′ə·nəs)   *adj.*   1. Of or like cartilage; gristly.   2. Having a gristly skeleton, as sharks.

cart·load (kärt′lōd′)   *n.*   As much as a cart can hold.

car·tog·ra·phy (kär·tog′rə·fē)   *n.*   The art of making maps or charts.   [< L *carta* map + -GRAPHY]   — **car·tog′ra·pher** *n.*   — **car·to·graph·ic** (kär′tə·graf′ik) or **-i·cal** *adj.*

car·ton (kär′tən)   *n.*   1. A cardboard box.   2. A paper or plastic container for liquids.   [< F, pasteboard]

car·toon (kär·tōōn′)   *n.*   1. A drawing or caricature depicting a humorous or satirical person or situation.   2. A comic strip.   3. A motion-picture film (**animated cartoon**) produced by photographing a series of action drawings.   4. A full-size sketch for a fresco, mosaic, etc.   — *v.t.* 1. To make a caricature or cartoon of.   — *v.i.* 2. To make cartoons.   [< F < L *charta* paper]   — **car·toon′ist** *n.*

car·tridge (kär′trij)   *n.*   1. A casing of metal, pasteboard, or the like, containing a charge of powder for a firearm and, usu., the projectile or shot and the primer.   2. Any small similar container, as the removable case in a tone arm of a record player.   3. *Photog.* A roll of protected sensitized film.   [< F < Ital. *cartoccio* < L *charta* paper]

cartridge clip   A metal container holding cartridges for a rapid-fire gun, as an automatic rifle.

cart·wheel (kärt′hwēl′)   *n.*   1. A sideways handspring.   2. *U.S. Informal* A large coin, esp. a silver dollar.

carve (kärv)   *v.* **carved, carv·ing**   *v.t.*   1. To make by cutting, or as if by cutting.   2. To create, design, or fashion by cutting.   3. To cut up, as cooked meat; divide.   — *v.i.*   4. To make carved work.   5. To cut up meat.   — *n.* A cut or stroke in carving.   [OE *ceorfan*]   — **carv′er** *n.*

carv·en (kär′vən)   *adj.*   *Poetic or Archaic*   Carved.

carv·ing (kär′ving)   *n.*   1. The act of one who carves.   2. Carved work; a carved figure or design.

car·y·at·id (kar′ē·at′id)   *n.*   *pl.* **·at·ids** or **·at·i·des** (-at′ə·dēz)   *Archit.* A supporting column in the form of a sculptured female figure.   [< L < Gk. *Karyatis* a Greek priestess]

caryo-   See KARYO-.

car·y·o·tin (kar′ē·ō′tin)   See KARYOTIN.

ca·sa·ba (kə·sä′bə)   *n.*   A winter variety of muskmelon with sweet white flesh and yellow rind: also spelled *cassaba*. Also **casaba melon**.   [after *Kasaba*, a town in western Turkey]

ca·sa·va (kə·sä′və)   See CASSAVA.

Cas·bah (käz′bä)   The native quarter of Algiers or of other cities with a large Arab population: also *Kasbah*.

cas·cade (kas·kād′)   *n.*   1. A fall of water over steep rocks, or one of a series of such falls.   2. Anything resembling a waterfall.   — *v.i.* **·cad·ed, ·cad·ing**   To fall in the form of a waterfall.   [< F < Ital. < L *cadere* to fall]

cas·car·a (kas·kâr′ə)   *n.*   A buckthorn of the NW United States, yielding cascara sagrada. Also **cascara buckthorn**.   [< Sp. *cáscara* bark]

cascara sa·gra·da (sə·grä′də)   A laxative obtained from the bark of the cascara.

case[1] (kās)   *n.*   1. A particular instance or occurrence: a *case* of mistaken identity.   2. The actual circumstance or state of affairs: Such is not the *case*.   3. An instance of disease or injury; also, a patient.   4. A set of arguments, reasons, etc.: the *case* for capital punishment.   5. A question or problem: a *case* of conscience.   6. *Law* a An action or suit at law. b The set of facts offered in support of a claim.   7. Condition or situation; plight.   8. *Informal* A peculiar or exceptional person.   9. *Gram.* The syntactical relationship of a noun, pronoun, or adjective to other words in a sentence.   — **in any case** No matter what; regardless.   — **in case** In the event that; if.   — **in case of** In the event of: *in case of* fire.   — *v.t.* **cased, cas·ing**   *U.S. Slang*   To look over carefully, especially with intent to rob.   [< OF < L *casus* event]

case[2] (kās)   *n.*   1. A box, sheath, bag, etc., for containing something.   2. A box and its contents.   3. A set or pair.   4. *Printing* A tray with compartments for holding type, called *upper case* for capital letters, and *lower case* for small letters.   5. The covers and spine in which a book, when sewed, is bound.   6. An outer or protective part, as of a watch.   7. A frame or casing, as for a door.   — *v.t.* **cased, cas·ing**   To put into or cover with a case; incase.   [< AF < L *capsa* box]

ca·se·fy (kā′sə·fī)   *v.t. & v.i.* **·fied, ·fy·ing**   To make or become like cheese.   [< L *caseus* cheese + -FY]

case·hard·en (kās′här′dən)   *v.t.*   1. *Metall.* To harden the surface of (low-carbon steel).   2. To make callous, esp. in feelings.

case history   A record of an individual or a family unit, in which salient facts are collected for use in medical, psychiatric, sociological, or similar studies. Also **case study**.

ca·se·in (kā′sē·in, -sēn)   *n.*   *Biochem.* A protein found esp. in milk and constituting the principal ingredient in cheese.   [< L *caseus* cheese]   — **ca·se·ic** (kā′sē·ik) *adj.*

case knife   1. A knife kept in a sheath.   2. A table knife.

case law   Law based on judicial decisions, as distinguished from that based on statute or other sources of law.

case·mate (kās′māt)   *n.*   A bombproof shelter in a fortification, or an armored compartment on a warship, for a gun and crew.   [< MF < Ital. *casamatta*]   — **case′mat·ed** *adj.*

case·ment (kās′mənt)   *n.*   1. The sash of a window that opens on hinges at the side, or a window having such sashes.   2. A case; covering.   — **case′ment·ed** *adj.*

ca·se·ous (kā′sē·əs)   *adj.*   Of or like cheese; cheesy.

ca·sern (kə·zûrn′)   *n.*   A barrack for soldiers. Also **ca·serne′**.   [< F < Sp. *caserna* small hut < L *quaterna* four each]

case·work (kās′wûrk′)   *n.*   The investigation and guidance by a social worker of maladjusted individuals and families.   — **case·work′er** *n.*

cash[1] (kash)   *n.*   1. Current money in hand or readily available.   2. Money paid down; immediate payment.   — *v.t.*   To convert into ready money, as a check.   — **to cash in**   1. In gambling, to turn in one's chips and receive cash.   2. *U.S. Slang* To die.   — **to cash in on**   *U.S. Informal* 1. To make a profit from.   2. To turn to advantage.   [< F < Ital.< L *capsa* box]   — **cash′a·ble** *adj.*

cash[2] (kash)   *n.*   *pl.* **cash**   Coins of low value of the East Indies and China.   [< Pg. < Tamil *kāsu* small coin]

cash-and-car·ry (kash′ən·kar′ē)   *adj.*   Operated on a system of cash purchase and no delivery.

cash·book (kash′bŏōk′)   *n.*   A book in which a record is kept of money taken in and paid out.

cash discount   A discount from the purchase price allowed the buyer if he pays within a stipulated period.

cash·ew (kash′ōō, kə·shōō′)   *n.*   1. A tropical American tree of the sumac family that yields a gum.   2. Its small, edible fruit: also **cashew nut**.   [< F < Pg. < Tupi *acajoba*]

cash·ier[1] (ka·shir′)   *n.*   1. One employed to collect cash payments, as in a restaurant.   2. A bank officer responsible for the bank's assets.   [< F < Ital. < L *capsa* box]

cash·ier[2] (ka·shir′)   *v.t.*   1. To dismiss in disgrace, as a military officer.   2. To discard.   [< Du. < F < LL *cassare* to annul and L *quassare* to destroy]

cash·mere (kash′mir, kazh′-)   *n.*   1. A fine wool obtained from Kashmir goats.   2. A soft fabric made from this.   3. Something made of cashmere.   [after *Kashmir*, India]

cash register   A device usu. with a money drawer, that records, adds, and displays the amount of cash received.

cas·ing (kā′sing)   *n.*   1. A protective case or covering.   2. A framework, as about a door.   3. *U.S.* The shoe of a tire.

ca·si·no (kə·sē′nō)   *n.*   *pl.* **·nos**   1. A place for dancing, gambling, etc.   2. Cassino.   [< Ital., dim. of *casa* house]

cask (kask, käsk)   *n.*   1. A barrel-shaped wooden vessel, made of staves, hoops, and flat heads.   2. The quantity a cask will hold.   [< Sp. *casco* skull, potsherd, cask]

cas·ket (kas′kit, käs′-)   *n.*   1. *U.S.* A coffin.   2. A small box or chest.   — *v.t.*   To enclose in a casket.   [Orig. uncertain]

casque (kask)   *n.*   A helmet.   [< F, ult. < L *quassare*. Related to CASK.]   — **casqued** (kaskt) *adj.*

cas·sa·ba (kə·sä′bə)   See CASABA.

Cas·san·dra (kə·san′drə)   In Greek mythology, a daughter of Priam whose prophecies were fated by Apollo to be true but never believed. **— n.** Anyone who utters unheeded prophecies of disaster.

cas·sa·va (kə·sä′və) *n.* **1.** A tropical American shrub or herb, cultivated for the edible roots. **2.** A starch made from these roots, the source of tapioca. [< F < Taino *casavi*]

cas·se·role (kas′ə·rōl) *n.* **1.** An earthenware or glass dish in which food is baked and served. **2.** Any food so prepared and served. **3.** *Brit.* A saucepan. [< F]

cas·sette (kə·set′) *n.* **1.** *Photog.* A lightproof magazine for film. **2.** *Electronics* A cartridge containing magnetic tape, used in tape recorders. [< F, lit., small box]

cas·sia (kash′ə, kas′ē·ə) *n.* **1.** A variety of cinnamon obtained from the bark (**cassia bark**) of a tree native in China. **2.** The tree itself. **3.** Any shrub, herb, or tree of tropical regions whose dried pods (**cassia pods**) yield a mild laxative. [< L < Gk. < Hebrew *qātsa′* to strip off bark]

cas·si·no (kə·sē′nō) *n.* A card game for two to four players.

cas·si·o·ber·ry (kas′ē·ō·ber′ē) *n. pl.* **·ries** The shining black edible drupe of a North American shrub. [< N. Am. Ind.]

Cas·si·o·pe·ia (kas′ē·ə·pē′ə) In Greek mythology, the mother of Andromeda. **— n.** A constellation: also **Cassiopeia's Chair.**

cas·sock (kas′ək) *n. Eccl.* A close-fitting vestment, usu. black, reaching to the feet, and worn by clergymen, choir singers, etc. [< MF < Ital. *casacca* greatcoat]

cas·so·war·y (kas′ə·wer′ē) *n. pl.* **·war·ies** A large, three-toed, flightless bird of Australia and New Guinea, related to the emu. [< Malay *kasuārī*]

cast (kast, käst) *v.* **cast, cast·ing** *v.t.* **1.** To throw or hurl with force; fling. **2.** To put with violence or force. **3.** To throw down. **4.** To cause to fall upon or over or in a particular direction: to *cast* a shadow. **5.** To direct, as a glance of the eyes. **6.** To let down; drop: to *cast* anchor. **7.** To throw forth or out. **8.** To throw off; lose; also, to shed; molt. **9.** To throw aside; reject or dismiss. **10.** To give birth to, esp. prematurely. **11.** To deposit; give: He *cast* his vote. **12.** To throw, as dice. **13.** In the theater, movies, etc., to assign the parts of (a play) or a part in a play to (an actor). **14.** To throw up, as with a shovel: to *cast* a mound of earth. **15.** To calculate; add. **16.** To compute astrologically: to *cast* a horoscope. **17.** To arrange by some system. **18.** To contrive; devise. **19.** *Metall.* To shape in a mold. **20.** *Printing* To stereotype or electroplate. **21.** To twist; warp. **22.** *Naut.* To turn (a ship); tack. **— v.i. 23.** To make a throw, as with dice, a fishing line, etc. **24.** To deliberate mentally; also, to scheme. **25.** To conjecture; forecast. **26.** To make arithmetical calculations; add. **27.** *Metall.* To take shape in a mold. **28.** To warp, as timber. **29.** *Naut.* To veer; fall off; also, to tack. **— to cast about** To consider ways and means; scheme. **— to cast away 1.** To discard. **2.** To shipwreck or maroon. **— to cast down 1.** To overthrow; destroy. **2.** To discourage; depress. **— to cast off 1.** To reject or discard. **2.** To let go, as a ship from a dock. **3.** *Printing* To estimate the number of pages, columns, etc., a manuscript will yield. **— to cast up 1.** To eject; vomit. **2.** To compute; add. **3.** To drive ashore. **4.** To direct upward. **— n. 1.** The act of casting or throwing. **2.** The distance to which a thing may be thrown. **3.** The throwing of a line or fishing net into the water. **4.** A throw of dice; also, the number thrown. **5.** Anything thrown out, off, or away. **6.** *Pathol.* A plastic substance formed in and often taking the shape of diseased cavities and organs: a renal *cast.* **7.** *Surg.* A rigid dressing or bandage, usu. made of plaster of Paris, for preventing movement of fractured bones. **8.** The actors who portray the characters in a play, movie, etc. **9.** The act of casting or founding. **10.** An impression made of anything; a mold. **11.** Something shaped or formed in a mold; a casting. **12.** The material poured into molds at one operation. **13.** Kind; sort; type. **14.** The appearance or form of something. **15.** A tinge; shade. **16.** A twist to one side; squint. **17.** A glance; look. **18.** A warp. **19.** A stroke of fortune. [< ON *kasta* to throw]

cas·ta·net (kas′tə·net′) *n.* One of a pair of small concave disks of wood or ivory, clapped together with the fingers, as a rhythmical accompaniment to song or dance. [< Sp. < L *castanea* chestnut]

cast·a·way (kast′ə·wā′, käst′-) *adj.* **1.** Adrift; shipwrecked. **2.** Thrown away. **— n. 1.** One who is shipwrecked. **2.** An outcast.

caste (kast, käst) *n.* **1.** In India, one of the hereditary social classes into which Hindus are divided. **2.** Any rigid social class. **3.** The system or principles of such class divisions. **4.** The position conferred by such a system. [< Pg. < L *castus* pure]

CASTANETS
a Outer and inner sides. *b* Position in use.

cas·tel·lat·ed (kas′tə·lā′tid) *adj.* Having battlements and turrets. [< Med.L < L *castellum* castle] **— cas′tel·la′tion** *n.*

cast·er (kas′tər, käs′-) *n.* **1.** One who or that which casts. **2.** One of a set of small, swiveling wheels or rollers, fastened under articles of furniture, or the like, to allow them to be moved about. **3.** A cruet for condiments; also, a stand for such cruets. Also (for defs. 2 and 3) *castor.*

cas·ti·gate (kas′tə·gāt) *v.t.* **·gat·ed, ·gat·ing** To rebuke or chastise severely; criticize. **— Syn.** See CHASTEN. [< L *castigare* to chasten] **— cas′ti·ga′tion** *n.* **— cas′ti·ga′tor** *n.*

Cas·tile soap (kas′tēl, kas·tēl′) A hard, white, odorless soap made with olive oil and soda. Also **cas′tile soap.** [after *Castile*, where first made]

Cas·til·ian (kas·til′yən) *n.* **1.** A native or citizen of Castile. **2.** The standard form of Spanish as spoken in Spain, originally the dialect of Castile. **— adj.** Of or pertaining to Castile, its people, language, or culture.

cast·ing (kas′ting, käs′-) *n.* **1.** The act of one who or that which casts. **2.** That which is cast or formed in a mold.

casting vote A deciding vote, given by the chairman of an assembly in cases where the votes of the members tie.

cast-i·ron (kast′ī′ərn, käst′-) *adj.* **1.** Made of cast iron. **2.** Like cast iron; rigid or strong; unyielding.

cast iron Iron having a high carbon content, and usu. hard, brittle, and not malleable.

cas·tle (kas′əl, käs′-) *n.* **1.** In feudal times, the fortified dwelling of a prince or noble. **2.** Any large, imposing house. **3.** A place of refuge; stronghold. **4.** In chess, a rook. **— v. ·tled, ·tling** *v.t. & v.i.* In chess, to move (the king) two squares to the right or left and place the rook from that side on the square over which the king has passed. [Ult. < L *castrum* camp, fort]

castle in the air A fanciful, impractical scheme; daydream.

cast-off (kast′ôf′, -of′, käst′-) *adj.* Thrown or laid aside. **— n.** One who or that which is no longer wanted or used.

cas·tor¹ (kas′tər, käs′-) *n.* **1.** An oily, odorous secretion of beavers, used in medicine and perfumery: also **cas·to·re·um** (kas·tôr′ē·əm, -tō′rē·əm) **2.** A hat of beaver or other fur. [< L < Gk. *kastōr* beaver]

cas·tor² (kas′tər, käs′-) See CASTER (defs. 2 and 3).

Cas·tor and Pol·lux (kas′tər, käs′-; pol′əks) **1.** In Greek mythology, twin brothers sent by Zeus among the stars. **2.** *Astron.* The two brightest stars in the constellation Gemini.

castor bean The seed of the castor-oil plant.

castor oil A viscid oil extracted from castor beans and used as a cathartic and lubricant.

cas·tor-oil plant (kas′tər-oil′, käs′-) A plant native in India, yielding the castor bean.

cas·trate (kas′trāt) *v.t.* **·trat·ed, ·trat·ing 1.** To remove the testicles from; emasculate; geld. **2.** To remove the ovaries from; spay. [< L *castrare*] **— cas·tra′tion** *n.*

cas·u·al (kazh′ō̄·əl) *adj.* **1.** Occurring by chance; accidental. **2.** Irregular; occasional: *casual* visits. **3.** Without intention or plan; offhand: a *casual* question. **4.** Negligent; nonchalant: a *casual* manner. **5.** Designed for informal wear: *casual* clothes. **6.** *Med.* Pertaining to accidental injuries. **— n. 1.** One who is employed at irregular intervals. **2.** An occasional visitor. **3.** *Mil.* A soldier temporarily attached to a unit. [< MF < L *casus* accident < *cadere* to fall] **— cas′u·al·ly** *adv.* **— cas′u·al·ness** *n.*

cas·u·al·ty (kazh′ō̄·əl·tē) *n. pl.* **·ties 1.** One who or that which is destroyed, injured, or otherwise made ineffective by an accident. **2.** *Mil.* A soldier who is killed, wounded, captured, or otherwise lost to his command through combat action. **3.** An accident, esp. a fatal or serious one.

cas·u·ist (kazh′ō̄·ist) *n.* One who studies or resolves ethical problems: often used for one who rationalizes about such matters. [< F < L *casus* event, case] **— cas′u·is′tic** or **·ti·cal** *adj.* **— cas′u·is′ti·cal·ly** *adv.*

cas·u·ist·ry (kazh′ō̄·is·trē) *n. pl.* **·ries 1.** The science that treats of or solves ambiguous cases of conscience or questions of right and wrong. **2.** Sophistical or equivocal reasoning, esp. in cases of conscience.

ca·sus bel·li (kā′səs bel′ī) *Latin* A cause justifying war.

cat (kat) *n.* **1.** A domesticated carnivorous mammal having retractile claws, and valued because it kills mice and rats. **2.** Any other animal of the cat family, as a lion, tiger, lynx, ocelot, etc. ◆ Collateral adjective: *feline.* **3.** A gossiping or backbiting woman. **4.** *Naut.* A tackle for hoisting an anchor to the cathead. **5.** A catboat. **6.** A cat-o′-nine-tails. **7.** A catfish. **8.** *U.S. Slang* A man; guy. **9.** *U.S. & Canadian* A caterpillar tractor. **— to let the cat out of the bag** To divulge a secret. **— v.t.** **cat·ted, cat·ting 1.** To hoist and fasten at the cathead. **2.** To flog. [OE *cat, catte*]

cata- *prefix* **1.** Down; against; upon. **2.** Back; over. Also, before vowels, **cat-:** also **cath-.** Also spelled **kata-.** [< Gk. *kata* down, against, back]

ca·tab·o·lism (kə·tab′ə·liz′əm) *n. Biol.* The process by which living tissue breaks down into simpler and more stable substances; destructive metabolism: opposed to *anab-*

olism. [< Gk. < *kata-* down + *ballein* to throw] — **cat·a·bol·ic** (kat/ə·bol/ik) *adj.* — **cat/a·bol/i·cal·ly** *adv.*
cat·a·clysm (kat/ə·kliz/əm) *n.* 1. Any violent upheaval or change, as a war, revolution, etc. 2. Any violent disturbance. 3. A deluge. [< MF < Gk. < *kata-* down + *klyzein* to wash] — **cat/a·clys/mic, cat·a·clys/mal** (-məl) *adj.*
cat·a·comb (kat/ə·kōm) *n. Usu. pl.* An underground place of burial, consisting of passages and small rooms with excavations in their sides for tombs. [< F < LL *catacumbas*]
cat·a·falque (kat/ə·falk) *n.* A structure supporting a coffin during a funeral. Also **cat/a·fal/co.** [< F < Ital. *catafalco*]
Cat·a·lan (kat/ə·lan, -lən) *adj.* Of or pertaining to Catalonia, its people, or their language. — *n.* 1. A native or citizen of Catalonia. 2. The Romance language of Catalonia and Valencia, closely related to Provencal.
cat·a·lep·sy (kat/ə·lep/sē) *n. Psychiatry* An abnormal maintenance of physical postures, accompanied by intense muscular rigidity. [< Med.L < Gk. < *kata-* upon + *lēpsis* seizure] — **cat/a·lep/tic** (-lep/tik) *adj. & n.*
cat·a·log (kat/ə·lôg, -log) *n., v.t., & v.i.* ·loged, ·log·ing Catalogue. — **cat/a·log/er, cat/a·log/ist** *n.*
cat·a·logue (kat/ə·lôg, -log) *n.* 1. A list or enumeration of names, objects, etc., usu. in alphabetical order. 2. A publication containing such a list, as of articles for sale. 3. A card catalogue (which see). Abbr. *cat.* — *v.t. & v.i.* ·logued, ·logu·ing To make a catalogue (of); enter (items) in a catalogue. [< F < LL < Gk. < *kata-* down + *legein* to select, choose] — **cat/a·logu/er, cat/a·logu/ist** *n.*
cat·al·pa (kə·tal/pə) *n.* A tree of China, Japan, and North America, having large, ovate leaves, fragrant flowers, and long, slender pods. [< N. Am. Ind.]
ca·tal·y·sis (kə·tal/ə·sis) *n. pl.* ·ses (-sēz) *Chem.* An increase in the rate of a chemical reaction, caused by the addition of a substance that is not permanently altered by the reaction: also spelled *katalysis*. [< Gk. < *kata-* wholly, completely + *lyein* to loosen] — **cat·a·lyt·ic** (kat/ə·lit/ik) *adj. & n.* — **cat/a·lyt/i·cal·ly** *adv.*
cat·a·lyst (kat/ə·list) *n. Chem.* Any substance that causes catalysis. Also **cat/a·lyz/er.**
cat·a·lyze (kat/ə·līz) *v.t.* ·lyzed, ·lyz·ing To submit to or decompose by catalysis.
cat·a·ma·ran (kat/ə·mə·ran/) *n. Naut.* 1. A long, narrow raft of logs, often with an outrigger. 2. A boat having twin hulls. 3. *Canadian* In Newfoundland, a heavy-duty wooden sled. [< Tamil *kattamaran* tied wood]
cat·a·mount (kat/ə·mount) *n. U.S.* The puma; also, the lynx. [Short form of *cat of the mountain*]
cat·a·pult (kat/ə·pult) *n.* 1. An ancient military device for throwing stones, arrows, etc. 2. *Aeron.* A device for launching an airplane at flight speed, as from the deck of a ship. 3. A slingshot. — *v.t.* 1. To hurl from or as from a catapult. — *v.i.* 2. To hurtle through the air. [< L < Gk. < *kata-* down + *pallein* to brandish, hurl]

CATAMARAN (def. 2) (Tahitian war canoe)

cat·a·ract (kat/ə·rakt) *n.* 1. A waterfall. 2. A downpour. 3. *Pathol.* **a** Opacity of the lens of the eye, causing partial or total blindness. **b** The opaque area. [< MF *cataracte* < L < Gk. < *kata-* down + *arassein* to fall headlong]
ca·tarrh (kə·tär/) *n. Pathol.* Inflammation of the mucous membrane of the air passages in the throat and head, with excessive secretion of mucus. [< MF < L < Gk. < *kata-* down + *rheein* to flow] — **ca·tarrh/al, ca·tarrh/ous** *adj.*
ca·tas·tro·phe (kə·tas/trə·fē) *n.* 1. A great and sudden disaster; calamity. 2. A sudden, violent change or upheaval. 3. In a drama, the conclusion of the plot; dénouement. [< Gk. < *kata-* over, down + *strephein* to turn] — **cat·a·stroph/ic** *adj.* — **cat/a·stroph/i·cal·ly** *adv.*
Ca·taw·ba (kə·tô/bə) *n.* An American red grape; also, a dry white wine made from it.
cat·bird (kat/bûrd/) *n.* A small, slate-colored North American songbird, having a catlike cry.
cat·boat (kat/bōt/) *n. Naut.* A small sailboat, having its mast well forward and carrying a single fore-and-aft sail.
cat·call (kat/kôl/) *n.* A shrill, discordant call or whistle expressing impatience or derision. — *v.t.* 1. To deride or show contempt for with catcalls. — *v.i.* 2. To utter catcalls.
catch (kach) *v.* caught, catch·ing *v.t.* 1. To take, seize, or come upon. 2. To take by trapping; ensnare. 3. To surprise in the act. 4. To take hold of suddenly so as to detain. 5. To grip; entangle. 6. To grasp and retain: to *catch* rain water in a barrel. 7. To overtake: We were *caught* by the storm. 8. To reach in time: to *catch* a train. 9. To strike. 10. To check (oneself) in speaking. 11. To become affected with, as by contagion: to *catch* cold. 12. To take; get: to *catch* fire. 13. To apprehend or perceive; also, to reproduce accurately: The artist has not *caught* her expression. 14. To captivate, as an audience. 15. To seize (the senses, etc.) suddenly or momentarily. 16. *U.S. Informal* To see (a motion picture, television program, etc.). — *v.i.* 17. To make a movement of grasping or seizing. 18. In baseball, to act as catcher. 19. To become entangled or fastened. 20. To be communicated or communicable, as a disease. 21. To take fire; kindle; ignite. — **to catch it** *Informal* To receive a reprimand, scolding, etc. — **to catch on** *Informal* 1. To understand. 2. To become popular or fashionable. — **to catch one's breath** 1. To check the breath suddenly, as in fear. 2. To draw a breath; to rest. — **to catch one's eye** To meet one's glance. — **to catch up** 1. To snatch or pick up suddenly. 2. To raise by attaching something; loop up. 3. To regain lost ground. 4. To discover (someone) in error. 5. To absorb: *caught up* in one's work. — **to catch up with** (or **up to**) To overtake. — *n.* 1. The act of catching; a grasping and holding. 2. That which catches; a fastening. 3. That which is caught; a quantity taken, as of fish. 4. *Informal* One who is worth catching, as in marriage. 5. *Informal* An artful or hidden condition; trick: What's the *catch?* 6. In sports, the catching of a thrown or batted ball before it touches the ground. 7. A scrap or fragment: *catches* of song. 8. A stoppage; break, as in the voice. — *adj.* 1. Attracting or meant to attract attention: a *catch* phrase. 2. Tricky. [< AF < LL < L *capere* to take, hold]
catch·all (kach/ôl/) *n.* 1. A bag or the like to hold odds and ends. 2. Anything that covers a wide range of situations, etc., as a phrase or doctrine.
catch basin A filter at the entrance to a drain or sewer.
catch·er (kach/ər) *n.* 1. One who or that which catches. 2. In baseball, the player stationed behind home plate to catch balls that pass the batter.
catch·ing (kach/ing) *adj.* 1. Infectious. 2. Attractive.
catch·pen·ny (kach/pen/ē) *adj.* Designed merely to sell; cheap and showy. — *n. pl.* ·nies A catchpenny article.
catch·up (kach/əp, kech/-) See KETCHUP.
catch·word (kach/wûrd/) *n.* 1. A word or phrase taken up and often repeated, esp. as a political slogan. Also **catch phrase.** 2. A word at the head of a page or column, identifying the first or last item on the page.
catch·y (kach/ē) *adj.* catch·i·er, catch·i·est 1. Attractive; catching the fancy; also, easily remembered: *catchy* tunes. 2. Deceptive; tricky. 3. Fitful: *catchy* winds.
cat·e·chet·ic (kat/ə·ket/ik) *adj.* Pertaining to oral instruction by question and answer. Also **cat/e·chet/i·cal.**
cat·e·chism (kat/ə·kiz/əm) *n.* 1. A short manual giving, in the form of questions and answers, an outline of the principles of a religious creed. 2. Any similar manual giving instructions. 3. Examination by questions and answers. [< Med.L < Gk. *katēchizein* to instruct]
cat·e·chist (kat/ə·kist) *n.* One who catechizes; esp., an instructor of catechumens. Also **cat/e·chiz/er, cat/e·chis/er.** — **cat/e·chis/tic** or ·ti·cal *adj.*
cat·e·chize (kat/ə·kīz) *v.t.* ·chized, ·chiz·ing 1. To instruct, esp. in the principles of Christianity, by asking questions and discussing the answers. 2. To question searchingly and at length. Also **cat/e·chise.** [< L < Gk. *katēchizein* to instruct] — **cat/e·chi·za/tion** *n.*
cat·e·chu·men (kat/ə·kyōō/mən) *n.* 1. One who is under instruction in the elements of Christianity. 2. One undergoing elementary instruction in any subject. — **cat/e·chu/me·nal, cat·e·chu·men·i·cal** (kat/ə·kyōō·men/i·kəl) *adj.*
cat·e·gor·i·cal (kat/ə·gôr/i·kəl, -gor/-) *adj.* 1. Without qualification; absolute; unequivocal. 2. Of, pertaining to, or included in a category. — **cat/e·gor/i·cal·ly** *adv.*
cat·e·go·rize (kat/ə·gə·rīz/) *v.t.* ·rized, ·riz·ing To put into a category; classify.
cat·e·go·ry (kat/ə·gôr/ē, -gō/rē) *n. pl.* ·ries 1. A division in any system of classification; a class: Drama is a *category* of literature. 2. *Logic* Any of the fundamental concepts or classifications into which all knowledge can be placed. [< L < Gk. *katēgoreein* to allege, predicate]
cat·e·nate (kat/ə·nāt) *v.t.* ·nat·ed, ·nat·ing To connect like the links of a chain. [< L *catena* chain] — **cat/e·na/tion** *n.*
ca·ter (kā/tər) *v.i.* 1. To furnish food or entertainment. 2. To provide for the gratification of any need or taste. — *v.t.* 3. To furnish food for: to *cater* a party. [< AF < LL < L *ad-* toward + *captare* to grasp, seize]
cat·er-cor·nered (kat/ər·kôr/nərd) *adj.* Diagonal. — *adv.* Diagonally. Also *catty-cornered, kitty-cornered.* Also **cat/er·cor/ner.** [< dial. E < F < L *quattuor* four + CORNERED]
ca·ter·er (kā/tər·ər) *n.* One who caters; esp., one who provides food and services for social functions.
cat·er·pil·lar (kat/ər·pil/ər) *n.* The larva of a butterfly or moth, or of certain other insects, as the sawfly. — *adj.* Moving or fitted with treads mounted on endless belts. [< AF < L < *catta* cat + *pilosus* < *pilum* hair]
Cat·er·pil·lar (kat/ər·pil/ər) *n.* A tractor that moves by means of two endless metal tracks running along each side: a trade name. Also **cat/er·pil/lar, caterpillar tractor.**
cat·er·waul (kat/ər·wôl) *v.i.* 1. To utter the discordant

cry of cats at mating time.   2. To make any discordant screeching. — *n.* Such a sound. [ME < *cater* cat + *wawen* to wail, howl]

cat·fish (kat/fish/)   *n.*   *pl.* **·fish** or **·fish·es** Any of numerous scaleless fishes having sensitive barbels around the mouth.

cat·gut (kat/gut/)   *n.* A very tough cord made from the intestines of certain animals, as sheep, and used for stringing musical instruments, making surgical ligatures, etc.

cath- Var. of CATA-.

ca·thar·sis (kə·thär/sis)   *n.*   1. *Med.* Purgation, esp. of the alimentary canal.   2. A purifying or purging of the emotions through the effect of art.   3. *Psychoanal.* A method of psychotherapy that induces the discharge of repressed emotions. Also spelled *katharsis.* [< Gk. *katharos* pure]

ca·thar·tic (kə·thär/tik)   *adj.* Purgative; purifying. Also **ca·thar/ti·cal.** — *n.* A laxative. [< Gk. *katharos* pure]

Ca·thay (ka·thā/)   *Poetic* or *Archaic* China.

cat·head (kat/hed/)   *n.* *Naut.* A beam projecting over the bow, by which the anchor is supported clear of the ship.

ca·the·dra (kə·thē/drə, kath/ə-)   *n.*   1. A bishop's seat or throne in the cathedral of his diocese.   2. The see or office of a bishop.   [< L < Gk. < *kata-* down + *hedra* seat]

ca·the·dral (kə·thē/drəl)   *n.*   1. The church containing the official chair of a bishop.   2. Loosely, any large or important church.   — *adj.*   1. Pertaining to or containing a bishop's chair or see.   2. Authoritative; dogmatic.   3. Of, pertaining to, or resembling a cathedral.

cath·e·ter (kath/ə·tər)   *n.*   *Med.* A slender, flexible tube introduced into body cavities for drainage, esp. one to draw urine from the bladder.   [< L < Gk. *kata-* down + *hienai* to send, let go]

cath·e·ter·ize (kath/ə·tə·rīz/)   *v.t.* **·ized, ·iz·ing** To introduce a catheter into.

cath·ode (kath/ōd)   *n.*   *Electr.* The negatively charged electrode that receives cations during electrolysis. Also spelled *kathode.*   [< Gk. < *kata-* down + *hodos* road, way] — **ca·thod·ic** (kə·thod/ik) or **·i·cal** *adj.*

cathode rays *Physics* A stream of electrons that pass from a cathode to the opposite wall of an evacuated electron tube when it is excited by a current of electricity.

cathode-ray tube *Electronics* A special type of electron tube in which a beam of electrons is focused by an electric or magnetic field and deflected so as to impinge upon a sensitized screen, forming an image, as on a television receiver.

cath·o·lic (kath/ə·lik, kath/lik)   *adj.*   1. Broad-minded, as in belief or tastes; liberal; comprehensive; large.   2. Universal in reach; general.   [< L < Gk. < *kata-* thoroughly + *holos* whole] — **ca·thol·i·cal·ly** (kə·thol/ik·lē) *adv.*

Cath·o·lic (kath/ə·lik, kath/lik)   *adj.*   1. Since the Reformation: **a** Of or pertaining to the Roman Catholic Church. **b** Designating those churches that claim to have the apostolic doctrine and sacraments of the ancient, undivided church, and including the Anglican, Old Catholic, Orthodox, and Roman Catholic churches.   2. Of the ancient, undivided Christian church.   — *n.* A member of any Catholic church.

Catholic Church The Roman Catholic Church.

Ca·thol·i·cism (kə·thol/ə·siz/əm)   *n.* The doctrine, system, and practice of a Catholic church, esp. the Roman Catholic Church. Also **Cath·o·lic·i·ty** (kath/ə·lis/ə·tē).

cath·o·lic·i·ty (kath/ə·lis/ə·tē)   *n.*   1. Freedom from narrowness; liberality.   2. Universality.

ca·thol·i·cize (kə·thol/ə·sīz)   *v.t.* & *v.i.* **·cized, ·ciz·ing** To make or become catholic or Catholic.

cat·i·on (kat/ī·on)   *n.* *Chem.* The electropositive ion of an electrolyte, that moves toward the cathode in electrolysis: opposed to *anion*: also spelled *kation.*   [< Gk. < *kata-* down + *ienai* to go] — **cat·i·on·ic** (-i·on/ik) *adj.*

cat·kin (kat/kin)   *n.* *Bot.* A deciduous, scaly spike of flowers, as in the willow.   [MDu. *katteken*, dim. of *katte* cat]

cat nap A short, light nap; doze.

cat·nip (kat/nip/)   *n.* An aromatic herb of the mint family, of which cats are fond. Also *Brit.* **cat/mint/.**   [< CAT + dial. E *nep* catnip]

cat-o'-nine-tails (kat/ə·nīn/tālz/)   *n.* A whip with nine knotted lines fastened to a handle.

cat rig The rig of a catboat, consisting of one sail on a mast far forward.   — **cat-rigged** (kat/rigd/) *adj.*

cat's cradle A game played with a loop of string stretched in an intricate arrangement over the fingers.

cat's-eye (kats/ī/)   *n.*   1. A gemstone, usually chrysoberyl or quartz, that shows a line of light across the dome when cut.   2. A small metal or glass reflector.

cat's-paw (kats/pô/)   *n.*   1. A person used as a tool or dupe.   2. A light wind that ruffles the water. Also **cats/paw/.**

cat·sup (kat/səp, kech/əp) See KETCHUP.

cat·tail (kat/tāl/)   *n.* A marsh plant having flowers in cylindrical terminal spikes and long leaves used for making mats, chair seats, etc.

cat·tle (kat/l)   *n.*   1. Domesticated bovine animals, as cows, bulls, and steers.   2. Formerly, all livestock, as horses, sheep, etc.   3. Human beings: a contemptuous term.   [< AF < LL < L *capitale* capital, wealth]

cat·tle·man (kat/l·mən)   *n.*   *pl.* **·men** (-mən) One who raises or tends cattle.

cat·ty (kat/ē)   *adj.* **·ti·er, ·ti·est**   1. Like or pertaining to cats.   2. Slyly malicious; spiteful.   — **cat/ti·ly** *adv.* — **cat/ti·ness** *n.*

cat·ty-cor·nered (kat/ē·kôr/nərd)   *adj.* Cater-cornered.

cat·walk (kat/wôk/)   *n.* Any narrow walking space, as at the side of a bridge.

Cau·ca·sian (kô·kā/zhən, -shən, -kash/ən)   *adj.*   1. Of or pertaining to the Caucasus region, its people, and their languages.   2. Of or belonging to a major ethnic division of the human species loosely called the white race. Also **Cau·cas·ic** (kô·kas/ik).   — *n.*   1. A native of the Caucasus region.   2. A member of the Caucasian division of the human race.

cau·cus (kô/kəs)   *n.* A meeting of members of a political party to select candidates, plan a campaign, etc.   — *v.i.* **cau·cused** or **·cussed, cau·cus·ing** or **·cus·sing** To meet in or hold a caucus.   [after the 18th c. *Caucus* Club, Boston, Mass.]

cau·dal (kôd/l)   *adj.* *Zool.*   1. Of, pertaining to, or near the tail or posterior part of the body.   2. Taillike.   [< NL < L *cauda* tail]   — **cau/dal·ly** *adv.*

cau·date (kô/dāt)   *adj.* *Zool.* Having a tail or taillike appendage. Also **cau/dat·ed.**   [< L *caudatus* < *cauda* tail]

cau·dle (kôd/l)   *n.* A warm drink of gruel with wine, eggs, sugar, etc., for invalids.   [< AF < Med.L < L *caldus* warm]

caught (kôt, kot) Past tense and past participle of CATCH.

caul (kôl)   *n.* The part of the prenatal sac that sometimes envelops the head of a child at birth.   [< OF *cale* cap]

caul·dron (kôl/drən)   *n.* A large kettle or boiler: also spelled *caldron.*   [< AF < L *calidus* hot]

cau·li·flow·er (kô/lə·flou/ər, kol/i-)   *n.*   1. The fleshy, edible head of a variety of cabbage.   2. The plant bearing this.   [Alter. of NL *cauliflora* a flowering cabbage]

cauliflower ear An ear that has been deformed by blows.

cau·lis (kô/lis)   *n.*   *pl.* **·les** (-lēz)   *Bot.* The stem of a plant.   [< L < Gk. *kaulos*]   — **cau·line** (kô/lin, -līn) *adj.*

caulk (kôk)   *v.t.*   1. To make tight, as a boat's seams, window frame, etc., by plugging with soft material, such as oakum or tar. Also spelled *calk.*   [< OF < L *calcare* to tread]   — **caulk/er** *n.* — **caulk/ing** *n.*

cau·sal (kô/zəl)   *adj.* Pertaining to, constituting, involving, or expressing a cause.   — *n. Gram.* A form expressing cause or reason, as *therefore.*   [< L *causa* cause]   — **caus/al·ly** *adv.*

cau·sal·i·ty (kô·zal/ə·tē)   *n.*   *pl.* **·ties**   1. The relation of cause and effect.   2. Causal character or agency.

cau·sa·tion (kô·zā/shən)   *n.*   1. The act of causing.   2. That which produces an effect; cause.   3. The relation of cause and effect.   [< Med.L < L *causa* cause]

caus·a·tive (kô/zə·tiv)   *adj.*   1. Effective as a cause.   2. *Gram.* Expressing cause or agency: *to lay* (to cause to lie) is a *causative* verb.   — *n. Gram.* A form that expresses or suggests causation.   [< MF < L *causa* cause]   — **caus/a·tive·ly** *adv.* — **caus/a·tive·ness** *n.*

cause (kôz)   *n.*   1. The agent or force producing an effect or a result.   2. A ground for choice or action: *cause* for complaint.   3. Sufficient ground; good reason: no *cause* to strike.   4. An aim, object, or principle advocated and supported by an individual or group.   5. *Law* A matter to be decided in court.   6. A matter under discussion or in dispute.   — *v.t.* **caused, caus·ing** To be the cause of; produce; effect.   [< MF < L *causa* cause, legal case]   — **caus/a·ble** *adj.* — **cause/less** *adj.* — **caus/er** *n.*

cause cé·lè·bre (kōz sā·leb/r')   *French*   1. A famous legal case.   2. Any well-known controversial issue.

cau·se·rie (kō/zə·rē/, *Fr.* kōz·rē/)   *n.*   1. An informal conversation; a chat.   2. A short, chatty piece of writing.   [< F]

cause·way (kôz/wā/)   *n.*   1. A raised road or way, as over marshy ground.   2. A paved way; a highway.   — *v.t.* To make a causeway for or through, as a marshy tract.   [Earlier *causeyway* < AF < LL < L *calx, calcis* heel + WAY]

caus·tic (kôs/tik)   *adj.*   1. Capable of corroding or eating away tissues; burning; corrosive.   2. Sarcastic; biting: *caustic* wit.   — *n.* A caustic substance.   [< L < Gk. *kaiein* to burn]   — **caus/ti·cal·ly** *adv.* — **caus·tic·i·ty** (kôs·tis/ə·tē) *n.*

caustic potash Potassium hydroxide.

caustic soda Sodium hydroxide.

cau·ter·ize (kô/tə·rīz)   *v.t.* **·ized, ·iz·ing** To sear with a caustic agent or heated iron.   — **cau/ter·i·za/tion** *n.*

cau·ter·y (kô/tər·ē)   *n.*   *pl.* **·ter·ies** *Med.*   1. The destruction of tissue by the application of a caustic substance or a searing iron.   2. A cauterizing agent.   [< L < Gk. *kauterion* < *kaiein* to burn]

cau·tion (kô/shən)   *n.*   1. Care to avoid injury or misfortune; prudence; wariness; discretion.   2. An admonition or warning.   3. *Informal* One who or that which alarms, astonishes,

---

etc. — *v.t.* To advise to be prudent; warn. [< OF < L *cautio, -onis* < *cavere* to beware]

cau·tion·ar·y (kô′shən·er′ē) *adj.* Urging caution.

cau·tious (kô′shəs) *adj.* Using great care or prudence; wary. — **cau′tious·ly** *adv.* — **cau′tious·ness** *n.*

cav·al·cade (kav′əl·kād′, kav′əl·kād) *n.* **1.** A company of horsemen on the march or in procession. **2.** A procession; parade. [< MF < Ital. < LL < L *caballus* horse]

cav·a·lier (kav′ə·lir′) *n.* **1.** A horseman; knight. **2.** A courtly or dashing gentleman; a gallant; also, a lady's escort. — *adj.* **1.** Haughty; supercilious. **2.** Free and easy; offhand. — *v.i.* To behave in a cavalier fashion; show arrogance. [< MF < Ital. < LL < L *caballus* horse, nag] — **cav·a·lier′ly** *adj. & adv.*

Cav·a·lier (kav′ə·lir′) *n.* A supporter of Charles I of England; a Royalist. — *adj.* Pertaining to the Cavaliers.

cav·al·ry (kav′əl·rē) *n. pl.* **·ries** Troops trained to maneuver and fight on horseback or, more recently, in armored motor vehicles. *Abbr. cav.* [< MF < Ital. < LL < L *caballus* horse] — **cav′al·ry·man** (-mən) *n.*

cave (kāv) *n.* A chamber beneath the earth, in a mountain or mountainside, etc. ◆ Collateral adjective: *spelean.* — *v.* **caved, cav·ing** *v.t.* **1.** To hollow out. — *v.i.* **2.** *Informal* To fall in or down; give way. — **to cave in 1.** To fall in or down, as when undermined; cause to fall in. **2.** *Informal* To yield utterly; give in. [< OF < L *cavus* hollow]

ca·ve·at (kā′vē·at) *n.* **1.** *Law* A formal notification given by an interested party to a court or officer not to do a certain act. **2.** A caution or warning, esp. to avoid misinterpretation. [< L, let him beware]

ca·ve·at emp·tor (kā′vē·at emp′tôr) *Latin* Let the buyer beware, implying that the purchase is made at his own risk.

ca·ve·a·tor (kā′vē·ā′tər) *n.* One who enters a caveat.

cave-in (kāv′in′) *n.* A collapse or falling in, as of a mine.

cave man 1. A Paleolithic man; prehistoric cave dweller; troglodyte (def. 1). **2.** *Informal* A man who is rough and brutal, esp. in his approach to women.

cav·ern (kav′ərn) *n.* A cave, esp. one that is large or extensive. — *v.t.* **1.** To shut in or as in a cavern. **2.** To hollow out. [< MF < L *cavus* hollow]

cav·ern·ous (kav′ər·nəs) *adj.* **1.** Full of caverns. **2.** Characteristic of a cavern. **3.** Hollow. — **cav′ern·ous·ly** *adv.*

cav·i·ar (kav′ē·är, kä′vē-) *n.* The salted roe of sturgeon or other fish, used as a relish. Also **cav′i·are.** [< F < Turkish *khāvyār*]

cav·il (kav′əl) *v.* **cav·iled** or **·illed, cav·il·ing** or **·il·ling** *v.i.* **1.** To raise trivial objections; argue captiously; carp: with *at* or *about.* — *v.t.* **2.** To find fault with. — *n.* A captious objection. [< MF < L *cavilla* a jeering, a scoffing] — **cav′il·er** or **cav′il·ler** *n.* — **cav′il·ing·ness** or **cav′il·ling·ness** *n.* — **cav′il·ing·ly** or **cav′il·ling·ly** *adv.*

cav·i·ty (kav′ə·tē) *n. pl.* **·ties 1.** A hollow or sunken space; hole. **2.** A natural hollow in the body. **3.** A decayed place in a tooth. [< MF < LL < L *cavus* hollow]

ca·vort (kə·vôrt′) *v.i. U.S.* To prance about; caper; frisk.

ca·vy (kā′vē) *n. pl.* **·vies** A small South American rodent with the tail absent or rudimentary, as the guinea pig. [< NL *Cavia* < Carib]

caw (kô) *v.i.* To make the high harsh sound of a crow, rook, etc. — *n.* The cry of a crow, raven, etc. [Imit.]

cay (kā, kē) *n.* A coastal reef or sandy islet, as in the Gulf of Mexico. See KEY². [< Sp. *cayo* shoal]

cay·enne pepper (kī·en′, kā-) Red pepper. Also **cay·enne′.**

cay·man (kā′mən) *n. pl.* **·mans** A tropical American crocodilian related to the alligator. [< Sp. *caiman* < Carib]

Ca·yu·ga (kā·yōō′gə, kī-) *n. pl.* **·ga** or **·gas** One of a tribe of Iroquois Indians formerly living near Cayuga Lake, N.Y.

cay·use (kī·yōōs′) *n. U.S.* An Indian pony.

Cay·use (kī·yōōs′) *n.* A member of a tribe of North American Indians formerly inhabiting Oregon.

cease (sēs) *v.* **ceased, ceas·ing** *v.t.* **1.** To leave off or discontinue, as one's own actions. — *v.i.* **2.** To come to an end; stop; desist. — *n.* End; stopping: now only in the phrase **without cease.** [< MF < L *cedere* to withdraw, yield] — **cease′less** *adj.* — **cease′less·ly** *adv.*

cease-fire (sēs′fīr′) *n.* An armistice; truce.

ce·cro·pi·a moth (si·krō′pē·ə) A large, strikingly marked moth common in the eastern U.S.

ce·cum (sē′kəm) *n. pl.* **·ca** (sē′kə) *Anat.* A pouch, or cavity, open at one end, esp. that situated between the large and small intestine: also spelled *caecum.* For illus. see INTESTINE. [< L *caecus* blind] — **ce′cal** *adj.*

ce·dar (sē′dər) *n.* **1.** A large tree of the pine family, having evergreen leaves and fragrant wood. **2.** The red cedar (def. 1). **3.** The wood of these and related trees. — *adj.* Pertaining to or made of cedar. [< OF < L < Gk. *kedros*]

ce·dar·bird (sē′dər·bûrd′) *n.* The cedar waxwing. See under WAXWING.

cede (sēd) *v.t.* **ced·ed, ced·ing 1.** To yield or give up. **2.** To surrender title to; transfer: to *cede* land. [< MF *céder* < L *cedere* to withdraw, yield]

ce·dil·la (si·dil′ə) *n.* A mark put under the letter *c* (ç) before *a, o,* or *u* in some French words, as in *français,* to indicate that it is to be sounded as (s). [< Sp. < Gk. *zēta* letter *z*]

ceil (sēl) *v.t.* To furnish with a ceiling. [< F < L *caelum* heaven, sky]

ceil·ing (sē′ling) *n.* **1.** The overhead covering or lining of a room. **2.** An upper limit; maximum, as one set on prices or wages. **3.** *Aeron.* The maximum height to which a given aircraft can be flown under specified conditions.

cel·an·dine (sel′ən·dīn) *n.* **1.** A plant of the poppy family, with yellow flowers. **2.** A crowfoot having tuberous roots and yellow flowers. [< OF < L < Gk. *chelidōn* a swallow]

-cele¹ *combining form* Tumor or hernia. [< Gk. *kēlē* tumor]

-cele² *combining form* Cavity; hollow space: *blastocele:* also spelled *-coele.* [< Gk. *koilos* hollow]

cel·e·brant (sel′ə·brənt) *n.* **1.** One who participates in a celebration. **2.** The officiating priest at the Eucharist.

cel·e·brate (sel′ə·brāt) *v.* **·brat·ed, ·brat·ing** *v.t.* **1.** To observe, as a festival, with rejoicing. **2.** To make known or famous; extol. **3.** To perform (a ceremony) publicly and as ordained. — *v.i.* **4.** To observe or commemorate a day or event. **5.** To perform a religious ceremony. [< L *celeber* famous] — **cel′e·bra′tor** *n.*

— **Syn. 1.** *Celebrate* is used for joyous occasions: to *celebrate* a holiday or birthday. *Commemorate* refers to the solemnity of an event, as does *solemnize,* but *commemorate* looks to the past, often with sorrow, while *solemnize* refers to a present occasion: to *commemorate* a great man's death, to *solemnize* a marriage.

cel·e·brat·ed (sel′ə·brā′tid) *adj.* Well-known; much publicized: a *celebrated* murder trial.

cel·e·bra·tion (sel′ə·brā′shən) *n.* **1.** The act of celebrating. **2.** That which is done in commemoration of any event.

ce·leb·ri·ty (sə·leb′rə·tē) *n. pl.* **·ties 1.** A famous or celebrated person. **2.** Fame or renown. [< L *celeber* famous]

ce·ler·i·ty (sə·ler′ə·tē) *n.* Quickness of motion; speed; rapidity. [< F < L *celer* swift]

cel·er·y (sel′ər·ē, sel′rē) *n.* A biennial herb whose stems are used as a vegetable or salad. [< F < dial. Ital. < *selinon* parsley < Gk.]

ce·les·ta (sə·les′tə) *n.* A musical instrument having a keyboard and steel plates struck by hammers. [< F *célesta*]

ce·les·tial (sə·les′chəl) *adj.* **1.** Of or pertaining to the sky or heavens. **2.** Of heaven; divine. **3.** *Often cap.* Chinese. — *n.* **1.** A heavenly being. **2.** *Often cap.* A Chinese. [< OF < L *caelum* sky, heaven] — **ce·les′tial·ly** *adv.*

Celestial Empire The former Chinese Empire.

celestial equator *Astron.* The great circle in which the plane of the earth's equator cuts the celestial sphere.

celestial sphere *Astron.* The imaginary spherical surface on which the heavenly bodies seem to lie, commonly conceived as of infinite diameter and enclosing the universe.

ce·li·ac (sē′lē·ak) *adj.* Of or pertaining to the abdomen. Also spelled *coeliac.* [< L *coeliacus* < Gk. *koilos* hollow]

cel·i·ba·cy (sel′ə·bə·sē) *n.* The state of being unmarried, esp. in accordance with religious vows. [< L *caelebs* unmarried]

cel·i·bate (sel′ə·bit, -bāt) *n.* One who remains unmarried, esp. by vow. — *adj.* Unmarried, esp. by vow.

cell (sel) *n.* **1.** A small room, as for a prisoner or monk. **2.** A small compartment, receptacle, or cavity. **3.** A body of persons forming a single unit in an organization of similar groups. **4.** *Biol.* The fundamental structural unit of plant and animal life, consisting of a small mass of cytoplasm and usu. enclosing a central nucleus and surrounded by a membrane (animal) or a rigid cell wall (plant). **5.** A single

True wall
Plasma membrane
Cortical layer
Mitochondria
Plastids
Golgi bodies
Centrosome
Nucleolus
Chromosomes — Nucleus
Nuclear membrane
Vacuoles
Metaplastic bodies or inclusions

GENERALIZED CELL

compartment of a honeycomb. **6.** *Bot.* The seed-bearing cavity of an ovary or pericarp. **7.** *Electr.* The unit composing all or part of a battery, consisting of electrodes in contact with an electrolyte and in which a current is generated by means of chemical action. — **dry cell** *Electr.* A primary cell with its electrolyte distributed in some porous substance. [< OF < L *cella* cell, small room]

cel·lar (sel′ər) *n.* **1.** A space wholly or partly underground and usu. beneath a building, used for storage, etc. **2.** A wine cellar; also, a stock of wines. — *v.t.* To put or keep in a cellar. [< AF, OF < L *cella* cell, small room]

cel·lar·age (sel'ər·ij) *n.* **1.** Space in or for a cellar. **2.** The charge for storing goods in a cellar.

cel·lar·er (sel'ər·ər) *n.* The keeper of a cellar, as the steward in a monastery.

cel·lar·et (sel'ə·ret') *n.* A case or small cabinet for wine and liquor bottles, decanters, glasses, etc. Also **cel'lar·ette'.**

cell-block (sel'blok') *n.* In prisons, a unit of cells.

cel·lo (chel'ō) *n. pl.* **·los** A bass instrument of the violin family, tuned an octave lower than the viola, and held between the performer's knees: also **'cel·lo.** [Short for VIOLONCELLO] — **cel'list** or **'cel'list** *n.*

cel·lo·phane (sel'ə·fān) *n.* A treated cellulose that has been processed in thin, transparent strips or sheets.

cel·lu·lar (sel'yə·lər) *adj.* **1.** Of or like a cell or cells. **2.** Consisting of cells. [See CELLULE.]

cel·lule (sel'yōōl) *n.* A small cell. [< L *cellula,* dim. of *cella* cell, small room]

Cel·lu·loid (sel'yə·loid) *n.* A hard, elastic, flammable plastic, made from guncotton mixed with camphor and other substances: a trade name. Also **cel'lu·loid.**

cel·lu·lose (sel'yə·lōs) *n. Biochem.* An amorphous white carbohydrate, insoluble in all ordinary solvents, and forming the fundamental material of the structure of plants. [< L *cellula.* See CELLULE.]

cellulose acetate *Chem.* **1.** A derivative of cellulose, used in making synthetic yarns and fabrics. **2.** Acetate rayon.

ce·lom (sē'ləm) See COELOM.

Cel·o·tex (sel'ə·teks) *n.* A composition board used for insulation: a trade name. Also **cel'o·tex.**

Cel·si·us scale (sel'sē·əs) A temperature scale in which the freezing point of water at normal atmospheric pressure is 0° and the boiling point is 100°; the centigrade scale. [after Anders *Celsius,* 1701–44, Swedish astronomer]

Celt (selt, kelt) *n.* A person of Celtic linguistic stock, now represented by the Irish, Welsh, Highland Scots, and Bretons, formerly by the Gauls and Britons. Also spelled *Kelt.*

Celt·ic (sel'tik, kel'-) *n.* A subfamily of the Indo-European family of languages, including ancient Gaulish, the Brythonic or Cymric branch (Cornish, Welsh, Breton), and the Goidelic or Gaelic branch (Irish, Scottish Gaelic, Manx). — *adj.* Of or pertaining to the Celtic peoples, their languages, or culture. Also spelled *Keltic.*

Celtic cross An upright cross having a circle behind the crossbeam.

ce·ment (si·ment') *n.* **1.** A mixture, usu. of burned limestone and clay, that is applied as a mortar or used for pavements and other smooth surfaces. **Portland cement** is made by calcining limestone with chalk, mud, etc. **2.** Any material, as glue, that, when hardened, will bind objects together. **3.** Something that unites. **4.** An adhesive material used in filling teeth and in other dental work. **5.** *Anat.* Cementum. — *v.t.* **1.** To unite or join with or as with cement. **2.** To cover or coat with cement. — *v.i.* **3.** To become united by means of cement; cohere. [< OF *ciment* < L *caedere* to cut] — **ce·men·ta·tion** (sē'mən·tā'shən, sem'ən-) *n.* — **ce·ment'er** *n.*

ce·men·tum (si·men'təm) *n. Anat.* The layer of bony tissue developed over the roots of the teeth: also called *cement.* For illus. see TOOTH. [< L]

cem·e·ter·y (sem'ə·ter'ē) *n. pl.* **·ter·ies** A place for burying the dead; graveyard. [< L *coemeterium* < Gk. *koimaein* to put to sleep]

-cene *combining form Geol.* Recent; new: used in the names of geological periods: *Pliocene.* [< Gk. *kainos* new]

ceno- *combining form* Common. Also spelled *coeno-:* also, before vowels, **cen-.** [< Gk. *koinos* common]

cen·o·bite (sen'ə·bīt, sē'nə-) *n.* A member of a religious community: also spelled *coenobite.* [< LL *coenobita* < Gk. < *koinos* common + *bios* life] — **cen'o·bit'ic** (-bit'ik) or **·i·cal** *adj.* — **cen'o·bit·ism** (sen'ə·bīt·iz'əm, sē'nə-) *n.*

cen·o·taph (sen'ə·taf, -täf) *n.* A monument erected to the dead but not containing the remains. [< MF < L < Gk. < *kenos* empty + *taphos* tomb] — **cen'o·taph'ic** *adj.*

Ce·no·zo·ic (sē'nə·zō'ik, sen'ə-) *Geol. adj.* Of or pertaining to the fourth and latest of the eras of geologic time, following the Mesozoic, and extending to and including the present. See chart for GEOLOGY. — *n.* The Cenozoic period. [< Gk. *kainos* new + *zōē* life]

cen·ser (sen'sər) *n.* A vessel for burning incense: also called *thurible.* [< OF *censier* < Med.L *incensum* incense]

cen·sor (sen'sər) *n.* **1.** An official examiner of manuscripts, plays, etc., empowered to suppress them, wholly or in part, if objectionable. **2.** An official who examines dispatches, letters, etc., in time of war. **3.** Anyone who censures or arraigns. **4.** In ancient Rome, one of two magistrates who drew up the census and supervised public morals. — *v.t.*

To act as censor of. [< L < *censere* to judge] — **cen·so·ri·al** (sen·sôr'ē·əl, -sō'rē-) *adj.*

cen·so·ri·ous (sen·sôr'ē·əs, -sō'rē-) *adj.* Given to censure; judging severely; faultfinding. — **cen·so'ri·ous·ly** *adv.* — **cen·so'ri·ous·ness** *n.*

cen·sor·ship (sen'sər·ship) *n.* **1.** The action of censoring. **2.** The office or power of a censor. **3.** A system of censoring.

cen·sur·a·ble (sen'shər·ə·bəl) *adj.* Deserving censure. — **cen'sur·a·bly** *adv.* — **cen'sur·a·bly** *adv.*

cen·sure (sen'shər) *n.* The expression of disapproval or blame; adverse or hostile criticism; reprimand. — **Syn.** See REPROOF. — *v.* **·sured, ·sur·ing** *v.t.* **1.** To express disapproval of; condemn; blame. — *v.i.* **2.** To express disapproval. [< F < L < *censere* to judge] — **cen'sur·er** *n.*

cen·sus (sen'səs) *n. pl.* **·sus·es** **1.** An official count of the people of a country or district, with statistics as to age, sex, employment, etc. **2.** In ancient Rome, a similar enumeration to determine taxation. [< L *censere* to assess] — **cen·su·al** (sen'shōō·əl) *adj.*

cent (sent) *n.* **1.** The hundredth part of a dollar; also, a coin of this value: symbol ¢. **2.** A hundred: used only in *percent, per cent.* [< F < L *centum* hundred]

cen·tare (sen'târ, *Fr.* sän·târ') *n.* A measure of land area, equal to one square meter: also *centiare.* See table inside back cover. [< F *centi-* hundredth (< L *centum* hundred) + *are.* See ARE².]

cen·taur (sen'tôr) *n.* In Greek mythology, one of a race of monsters, having the head, arms, and torso of a man united to the body and legs of a horse. [< L < Gk. *Kentauros*]

CENTAUR

cen·ta·vo (sen·tä'vō) *n. pl.* **·vos** (-vōz, *Sp.* -vōs) **1.** A small coin of the Philippines and various Spanish-American countries, equal to one hundredth of the peso. **2.** A similar coin of Portugal and of Brazil. [< Sp.]

cen·te·nar·i·an (sen'tə·nâr'ē·ən) *n.* One who is 100 years old. — *adj.* **1.** Of the age of 100 years. **2.** Pertaining to a period of 100 years.

cen·te·nar·y (sen'tə·ner'ē, sen·ten'ə·rē) *adj.* **1.** Of or pertaining to 100 or 100 years. **2.** Occurring every 100 years. — *n. pl.* **·nar·ies** **1.** A period of 100 years. **2.** A centennial. [< L *centum* hundred]

cen·ten·ni·al (sen·ten'ē·əl) *adj.* **1.** Of an age or duration of 100 years. **2.** Of or marking a period of 100 years or its completion. **3.** Occurring every 100 years. — *n.* A 100th anniversary or its celebration. [< L *centum* hundred + *annus* year] — **cen·ten'ni·al·ly** *adv.*

Centennial State Nickname of Colorado.

cen·ter (sen'tər) *n.* **1.** The point or place equally distant from the extremities or sides of anything. **2.** *Geom.* The point within a circle or sphere equidistant from every point on the circumference or surface. **3.** A point about which a thing revolves. **4.** A place or point at which activity is concentrated or toward which people seem to converge. **5.** A point from which effects, influences, etc., proceed; source. **6.** *Mil.* The part of an army occupying the front between the wings. **7.** *Often cap.* A group, party, etc., having moderate views or tendencies. **8.** In football, basketball, etc., a player who occupies a middle position, as in the forward line. — *v.t.* **1.** To place in or at the center. **2.** To direct toward one place; concentrate. **3.** To determine or mark the center of. — *v.i.* **4.** To be at the center of. — *adj.* Central; middle. Also, *Brit.,* **centre.** [< L *centrum* < Gk. *kentron* point]

cen·ter·board (sen'tər·bôrd', -bōrd') *n.* A board so hung that it can be lowered below the bottom of a sailboat through a slot to prevent leeway. Also *Brit.* **cen'tre·board'.**

center of gravity *Physics* The point about which a body acted upon by gravity is in equilibrium in all positions.

cen·ter·piece (sen'tər·pēs') *n.* A piece at the center of anything; esp., an ornament in the center of a table.

cen·tes·i·mal (sen·tes'ə·məl) *adj.* **1.** Hundredth. **2.** Pertaining to or divided into hundredths. [< L *centesimus* hundredth] — **cen·tes'i·mal·ly** *adv.*

centi- *combining form* **1.** Hundred: *centipede.* **2.** In the metric system and in technical usage, one hundredth of (a specified unit): *centiliter.* [< L *centum* hundred]

cen·ti·are (sen'tē·âr) See CENTARE.

cen·ti·grade (sen'tə·grād) *adj.* Graduated to a scale of a hundred. [< F < L *centum* hundred + *gradus* step, degree]

centigrade scale A temperature scale in which the freezing point of water at normal atmospheric pressure is 0° and the boiling point is 100°: also called *Celsius scale.*

cen·ti·gram (sen'tə·gram) *n.* In the metric system, the hundredth part of a gram. Also **cen'ti·gramme.** See table inside back cover.

cen·ti·li·ter (sen'tə·lē'tər) *n.* In the metric system, the hundredth part of a liter. Also *esp. Brit.* **cen'ti·li'tre.** See table inside back cover.

cen·time (sän'tēm, *Fr.* sän·têm') *n.* A small coin, the hundredth part of a franc. [< F < OF < L *centesimus* hundredth]

cen·ti·me·ter (sen'tə·mē'tər) *n.* In the metric system, the hundredth part of a meter. Also *esp. Brit.* **cen'ti·me·tre.** See table inside back cover.

cen·ti·me·ter-gram-sec·ond (sen'tə·mē'tər·gram'sek'ənd) *adj.* See CGS.

cen·ti·pede (sen'tə·pēd) *n.* A wormlike animal having many pairs of legs. [< F < L < *centum* hundred + *pes, pedis* foot]

cen·ti·stere (sen'tə·stir) *n.* A hundredth of a stere. See table inside back cover. [< F *centistère*]

cen·tral (sen'trəl) *adj.* **1.** At, in, or near the center. **2.** Of or constituting the center. **3.** That exercises a controlling influence; dominant. **4.** Most important; principal; chief. [< L < *centrum* center] — **cen'tral·ly** *adv.*

cen·tral·ism (sen'trəl·iz'əm) *n.* A centralizing tendency or system; concentration of control in a central authority. — **cen'tral·ist** *n. & adj.* — **cen'tral·is'tic** *adj.*

cen·tral·i·ty (sen·tral'ə·tē) *n.* **1.** The state of being central. **2.** Tendency toward or situation at a center.

cen·tral·ize (sen'trəl·īz) *v.* **·ized, ·iz·ing** *v.t.* **1.** To bring to a center; make central; especially, to bring under a central authority. — *v.i.* **2.** To come to a center; concentrate. — **cen'tral·i·za'tion** *n.* — **cen'tral·iz'er** *n.*

central nervous system *Anat.* That part of the nervous system consisting of the brain and spinal cord.

cen·tre (sen'tər) *n., adj., v.t. & v.i.* **·tred, ·tring** *Brit.* Center.

centri- *combining form* Center: used in words of Latin origin. Compare CENTRO-. [< L *centrum* center]

cen·tric (sen'trik) *adj.* At, relating to, or having a center. Also **cen'tri·cal.** [< Gk. *kentrikos* < *kentron* center] — **cen'tri·cal·ly** *adv.* — **cen·tric·i·ty** (sen·tris'ə·tē) *n.*

cen·trif·u·gal (sen·trif'yə·gəl, -trif'ə·gəl) *adj.* **1.** Directed or tending away from a center; radiating: opposed to *centripetal.* **2.** Employing centrifugal force: a *centrifugal* pump. — *n.* A centrifuge. [< NL < L *centrum* center + *fugere* to flee] — **cen·trif'u·gal·ly** *adv.*

centrifugal force *Physics* The inertial reaction by which a body tends to move away from the center of rotation.

cen·tri·fuge (sen'trə·fyōōj) *n.* A rotary machine for the separation of substances having different densities. — *v.t.* **·fuged, ·fug·ing** To subject to the action of a centrifuge. [< F'] — **cen·trif·u·ga·tion** (sen·trif'yə·gā'shən, -ə·gā') *n.*

cen·trip·e·tal (sen·trip'ə·tal) *adj.* **1.** Directed, tending, or drawing toward a center: opposed to *centrifugal.* **2.** Acting by drawing toward a center. [< NL < L *centrum* center + *petere* to seek] — **cen·trip'e·tal·ly** *adv.*

centripetal force *Physics* A force attracting a body toward a center around which it revolves.

cen·trist (sen'trist) *n.* One who takes a moderate position in politics.

centro- *combining form* Center: used in words of Greek origin, as in *centrosphere.* Also, before vowels, **centr-.** [< Gk. *kentron* center]

cen·tro·some (sen'trə·sōm) *n. Biol.* The small area of protoplasm external to the nucleus of the cell. — **cen'tro·som'ic** (-som'ik) *adj.* For illus. see CELL.

cen·tro·sphere (sen'trə·sfir') *n. Biol.* In living cells, the sphere that surrounds the centrosome. For illus. see CELL.

cen·tu·ple (sen'tə·pəl, sen·tōō'pəl, -tyōō'-) *v.t.* **·pled, ·pling** To increase a hundredfold. — *adj.* Increased a hundredfold. [< F < LL *centuplus* hundredfold]

cen·tu·pli·cate (*v.* sen·tōō'plə·kāt, -tyōō'-; *adj. & n.* sen·tōō'plə·kit, -tyōō'-) *v.t.* **·cat·ed, ·cat·ing** To multiply by a hundred; centuple. — *adj. & n.* Hundredfold. [< LL < L *centuplex* hundredfold] — **cen·tu·pli·ca'tion** *n.*

cen·tu·ri·on (sen·tŏŏr'ē·ən, -tyŏŏr'-) *n.* In the ancient Roman army, a captain of a century. [< L *centurio, -onis*]

cen·tu·ry (sen'chə·rē) *n. pl.* **·ries 1.** A period of 100 years in any system of chronology, esp. in reckoning from the first year of the Christian era. **2.** In ancient Rome: **a** A body of foot soldiers, originally of 100 men. **b** One of 193 electoral divisions. **3.** A group or series of a hundred. [< L *centuria* < *centum* hundred] — **cen·tu·ri·al** (sen·tŏŏr'ē·əl) *adj.*

century plant A succulent plant of the amaryllis family, flowering in twenty to thirty years and then dying, popularly supposed to bloom once in a century.

ce·phal·ic (sə·fal'ik) *adj.* **1.** Of or pertaining to the head. **2.** At, on, in, or near the head. [< F < Gk. *kephalē* head] **-cephalic** *combining form* Head; skull: *brachycephalic.*

cephalic index *Anat.* The ratio of the greatest breadth of the human head from side to side, multiplied by 100, to the greatest length.

cephalo- *combining form* Head. Also, before vowels, **cephal-.** [< Gk. *kephale* head]

ceph·a·lo·pod (sef'ə·lə·pod') *Zool. n.* Any of a class of marine mollusks having a clearly defined head and eyes, ink sac, and tentacles or arms around the mouth, as squids and octopuses. — *adj.* Of or pertaining to cephalopods: also **ceph'·**

a·lo·pod'ic, ceph·a·lop·o·dous (sef'ə·lop'ə·dəs). — **ceph·a·lop·o·dan** (sef'ə·lop'ə·dən) *n. & adj.*

ceph·a·lo·tho·rax (sef'ə·lō·thōr'aks, -thō'raks) *n. Zool.* The anterior portion of certain crustaceans and arachnids, consisting of the united head and thorax. For illus. see SHRIMP. — **ceph'a·lo·tho·rac'ic** (-thə·ras'ik) *adj.*

ceph·a·lous (sef'ə·ləs) *adj.* Having a head.

-cephalous *combining form* Headed: *hydrocephalous.* [< Gk. *kephalē* head]

cer- Var. of CERO-.

ce·ram·ic (sə·ram'ik) *adj.* Pertaining to articles made of fired and baked clay. [< Gk. *keramos* potter's clay]

ce·ram·ics (sə·ram'iks) *n.pl.* (construed as *sing* in def. 1.) **1.** The art of modeling and baking in clay. **2.** Objects made of fired and baked clay. — **ce·ram'ist** *n.*

Cer·ber·us (sûr'bər·əs) In classical mythology, the three-headed dog guarding the portals of Hades. — **Cer·be·re·an** (sər·bir'ē·ən) *adj.*

cere[1] (sir) *v.t.* **cered, cer·ing** To wrap in cerecloth. [< MF < L *cera* wax]

cere[2] (sir) *n. Ornithol.* In parrots and birds of prey, a wax-like area about the bill. [< F < L *cera* wax]

ce·re·al (sir'ē·əl) *n.* **1.** An edible, starchy grain yielded by certain plants of the grass family, as rice, wheat, rye, oats, etc. **2.** Any of such plants. **3.** A breakfast food made from a cereal grain. [< L *Ceres,* goddess of grain]

cer·e·bel·lum (ser'ə·bel'əm) *n. pl.* **·bel·lums** or **·bel·la** (-bel'ə) *Anat.* The part of the brain below and behind the cerebrum serving as the coordination center of voluntary movements, posture, and equilibrium. [< L, dim. of *cerebrum* brain] — **cer'e·bel'lar** *adj.*

cer·e·bral (ser'ə·brəl, sə·rē'-) *adj.* **1.** Of or pertaining to the cerebrum or the brain. **2.** Appealing to or involving the intellect; intellectual. [< F < L *cerebrum* brain]

cerebral palsy *Pathol.* Any paralysis affecting the ability to control movement and caused by brain lesions resulting from prenatal defect or birth injury.

cer·e·brate (ser'ə·brāt) **·brat·ed, ·brat·ing** *v.i.* **1.** To have or manifest brain action. **2.** To think. [< L *cerebrum* brain] — **cer'e·bra'tion** *n.*

cerebro- *combining form* Brain: *cerebrospinal.* Also, before vowels, **cerebr-.** [< L *cerebrum* brain]

cer·e·bro·spi·nal (ser'ə·brō·spi'nəl) *adj. Anat.* Of or affecting the brain and the spinal cord.

cer·e·brum (ser'ə·brəm, sə·rē'brəm) *n. pl.* **·bra** (-brə) *Anat.* The upper anterior part of the brain, consisting of two hemispherical masses enclosed within the cortex and constituting the seat of conscious processes. [< L] — **cer·e·bric** (ser'ə·brik, sə·rē'-) *adj.*

cere·cloth (sir'klôth', -kloth') *n.* Cloth treated with wax, used to wrap the dead. [Orig. *cered cloth* < L *cera* wax]

cere·ment (sir'mənt) *n. Usu. pl.* **1.** A cerecloth. **2.** A shroud. [< F < MF < L *cera* wax]

cer·e·mo·ni·al (ser'ə·mō'nē·əl) *adj.* Of, pertaining to, or characterized by ceremony; ritual; formal. — *n.* **1.** A prescribed set of ceremonies for some particular occasion; ritual. **2.** A rite; ceremony. — **cer'e·mo'ni·al·ism** *n.* — **cer'e·mo'ni·al·ist** *n.* — **cer'e·mo'ni·al·ly** *adv.*

cer·e·mo·ni·ous (ser'ə·mō'nē·əs) *adj.* **1.** Studiously or overly polite. **2.** Characterized by ceremony; formal. — **cer'e·mo'ni·ous·ly** *adv.* — **cer'e·mo'ni·ous·ness** *n.*

cer·e·mo·ny (ser'ə·mō'nē) *n. pl.* **·nies 1.** A formal act or ritual, or a series of them, performed in a prescribed manner. **2.** Formal observances collectively; ritual. **3.** An empty ritual. **4.** Adherence to ritual forms; formality. **5.** An act of formal courtesy. — **to stand on** (or upon) **ceremony** To insist upon formalities. [< OF < L *caerimonia* awe]

Ce·res (sir'ēz) In Roman mythology, the goddess of grain and harvests: identified with the Greek *Demeter.*

cer·iph (ser'if) See SERIF.

ce·rise (sə·rēz', -rēs') *n. & adj.* Vivid red. [< F, cherry]

ce·ri·um (sir'ē·əm) *n.* A silver-white, ductile, highly reactive and electropositive element (symbol Ce) of the lanthanide series. See ELEMENT. [after the asteroid *Ceres*]

cero- *combining form* Wax: *cerotype.* Also, before vowels, **cer-.** [< L *cera* or Gk. *kēros* wax]

ce·ro·plas·tic (sir'ə·plas'tik) *adj.* **1.** Pertaining to wax modeling. **2.** Modeled in wax. [< Gk. < *kēros* wax + *plassein* to mold]

cer·tain (sûr'tən) *adj.* **1.** Absolutely confident; convinced. **2.** Sure; destined. **3.** Beyond doubt; indisputable. **4.** Sure in its workings or results; dependable; also, unerring. **5.** Fixed; determined. **6.** Not explicitly stated or identified: *certain* persons. **7.** Some, or some at least: some improvement. — *n.* An indefinite number or quantity: *Certain* of the students were absent. — **for certain** Without doubt; surely. [< OF, ult. < L *cernere* to determine]

cer·tain·ly (sûr'tən·lē) *adv.* Without doubt: surely.

cer·tain·ty (sûr'tən·tē) *n. pl.* **·ties 1.** The state, quality, or fact of being certain. **2.** A known fact.

cer·tif·i·cate (*n.* sər·tif'ə·kit; *v.* sər·tif'ə·kāt) *n.* An official or sworn document stating something to be a fact. — *v.t.* **·cat·ed, ·cat·ing** To furnish with or attest by a certificate. [< Med.L < L < *certus* certain + *facere* to make] — **cer·tif′i·ca·tor** (-kā′tər) *n.* — **cer·tif′i·ca·to′ry** *adj.*

cer·ti·fi·ca·tion (sûr′tə·fi·kā′shən) *n.* **1.** The act of certifying or guaranteeing. **2.** The state of being certified. **3.** That which guarantees or vouches for. **4.** A certificate.

cer·ti·fied (sûr′tə·fīd) *adj.* **1.** Vouched for in writing; endorsed. **2.** Affirmed or guaranteed by a certificate. **3.** Legally committed to a mental institution.

certified check A check issued by a bank that guarantees that it is drawn on an account having sufficient funds.

cer·ti·fy (sûr′tə·fī) *v.* **·fied, ·fy·ing** *v.t.* **1.** To give certain information of; attest. **2.** To testify to in writing; vouch for. **3.** To endorse as meeting set standards or requirements. **4.** To guarantee in writing on the face of (a check) that the account drawn on has sufficient funds for payment: said of banks. **5.** To make certain; assure. **6.** To commit to a mental institution. — *v.i.* **7.** To make attestation; vouch (*for*) or testify (*to*). [< OF < Med.L < L < *certus* certain + *facere* to make] — **cer′ti·fi′a·ble** *adj.* — **cer′ti·fi′er** *n.*

cer·ti·o·ra·ri (sûr′shē·ə·râr′ē, -râr′ī) *n. Law* A writ from a superior to an inferior court, directing that a record of a designated case be sent up for review. [< LL, to be certified]

cer·ti·tude (sûr′tə·tōōd, -tyōōd) *n.* Complete confidence. [< MF < LL < L < *certus* certain + *facere* to make]

ce·ru·le·an (sə·rōō′lē·ən, -lyən) *adj. & n.* Sky blue; vivid blue. [< L *caeruleus* dark blue]

ce·ru·men (sə·rōō′mən) *n.* Earwax. [< NL < L *cera* wax]

cer·vi·cal (sûr′vi·kəl) *adj. Anat.* Of, pertaining to, in, or near the neck of the cervix uteri. [< L *cervix* neck]

cer·vine (sûr′vīn, -vin) *adj.* **1.** Deerlike. **2.** Of or pertaining to deer. [< L *cervinus* < *cervus* deer]

cer·vix (sûr′viks) *n. pl.* **cer·vix·es** or **cer·vi·ces** (sər·vī′sēz, sûs′və·sēz) *Anat.* **1.** The neck. **2.** The cervix uteri. **3.** A necklike part. [< L] — **cer·vi·cal** (sûr′vi·kəl) *adj.*

cervix u·ter·i (yōō′tə·rī) *Anat.* The constricted neck of the uterus that distends during parturition. [< L]

ce·sar·e·an (si·zâr′ē·ən) *Surg. n.* A cesarean section. — *adj.* Of or pertaining to a cesarean section. Also **ce·sar′i·an.**

Ce·sar·e·an (si·zâr′ē·ən), **Ce·sar·i·an** See CAESAREAN.

cesarean section *Surg.* The birth of a child by section of the abdominal walls and the uterus. Also **cesarean operation.** [< L *sectio caesarea* < *caedere* to cut]

ce·si·um (sē′zē·əm) *n.* A ductile metallic element (symbol Cs) of the alkali group: also spelled *caesium.* See ELEMENT. [< NL < L *caesius* bluish gray]

ces·sa·tion (se·sā′shən) *n.* A ceasing; stop; pause. [< L *cessatio, -onis* < *cessare* to stop]

ces·sion (sesh′ən) *n.* The act of ceding; a giving up, as of territory or rights, to another. [< L pp. of *cedere* to yield]

cess·pool (ses′pōōl′) *n.* **1.** A covered well or pit for the drainage from sinks, toilets, etc. **2.** Any repository of filth. Also **cess′pit′.** [Origin uncertain]

c'est la guerre (se là gâr′) *French* That's war.

c'est la vie (se là vē′) *French* That's life.

ces·tus (ses′təs) *n. pl.* **·tus** A wrapping of thongs, often weighted, worn about the hands by boxers in ancient Rome: also spelled *caestus.* [< L *caedere* to kill]

ce·su·ra (si·zhōōr′ə, -zyōōr′ə) See CAESURA.

ce·ta·cean (si·tā′shən) *adj.* Of or belonging to the aquatic mammals, including the whales, dolphins, and porpoises. Also **ce·ta′ceous.** — *n.* A cetacean animal. [< NL < L < Gk. *kētos* whale]

CESTUS[1]

ce·tane (sē′tān) *n. Chem.* A saturated hydrocarbon of the methane series, $C_{16}H_{34}$, used as fuel for diesel engines. [< L *cetus* whale + -ANE[2]]

Cey·lon·ese (sēl′ən·ēz, -ēs) *adj.* Of or pertaining to Ceylon or to its people. — *n.* A native or resident of Ceylon.

cgs The centimeter-gram-second system of measurement in which the unit of length is the centimeter, the unit of mass is the gram, and the unit of time is one second. Also **c.g.s., CGS, C.G.S.**

Cha·blis (shä·blē′) *n.* A dry, white, Burgundy wine made in the region of Chablis, a town in north central France.

cha·conne (shä·kôn′) *n.* A musical form, important in the Baroque period, usu. in slow triple meter, probably derived from a 16th century Spanish colonial dance: often called *passacaglia.* [< F < Sp. *chacona*]

chaeto- *combining form* Hair. Also, before vowels, **chaet-.** [< Gk. *chaitē* hair, bristle]

chafe (chāf) *v.* **chafed, chaf·ing** *v.t.* **1.** To abrade or make sore by rubbing. **2.** To make warm by rubbing. **3.** To irritate; annoy. — *v.i.* **4.** To rub. **5.** To be irritated; fret; fume: used to *chafe* under the abuse. — **to chafe at the bit** To be

impatient and irritable because of delay. — *n.* **1.** Soreness or wear from rubbing; friction. **2.** Irritation·or vexation. [< OF < L < *calere* to be warm + *facere* to make]

chaf·er (chā′fər) *n.* The cockchafer or other scarabaeid beetle. Also **chaf·fer** (chaf′ər). [OE *ceafor*]

chaff[1] (chaf, chäf) *n.* **1.** The husks of grain. **2.** Any trivial or worthless matter. [OE *ceaf*] — **chaff′y** *adj.*

chaff[2] (chaf, chäff) *v.t. & v.i.* To poke fun (at). — *n.* Good-natured raillery. [Origin uncertain] — **chaff′er** *n.*

chaf·fer (chaf′ər) *v.i.* To haggle about price; bargain. — *n.* A haggling about terms; bargaining. [ME < OE *cēap* bargain + *faru* going] — **chaf′fer·er** *n.*

chaf·finch (chaf′inch) *n.* A song finch of Europe.

chafing dish A vessel with a heating apparatus beneath it, to cook or keep food warm at the table.

cha·grin (shə·grin′) *n.* Distress or vexation caused by disappointment, failure, etc.; mortification. — *v.t.* To humiliate; mortify: used in the passive. [< F]

chain (chān) *n.* **1.** A series of connected rings or links, usu. of metal, serving to bind, drag, hold, or ornament. **2.** *pl.* Anything that confines or restrains; shackles; bonds. **3.** *pl.* Bondage. **4.** Any connected series; a succession. **5.** A series of chain stores. **6.** *Chem.* A series of atoms or radicals of the same or different kinds, linked together and acting as a unit. — *v.t.* **1.** To fasten or connect with a chain. **2.** To fetter; bind. [< OF < L *catena*] — **chain′less** *adj.*

chain gang A gang of convicts chained together while doing hard labor.

chain letter A letter intended to be sent on from one to another in a series of recipients.

chain mail Flexible armor consisting of interlinked metal chains, rings, or scales.

chain reaction **1.** *Physics* The self-sustaining fission of atomic nuclei, in which neutrons released by one fission induce fission in neighboring nuclei, as in a nuclear reactor. **2.** Any series of reactions or events, each of which develops from the preceding one.

chain stitch An ornamental stitch resembling a chain, used in sewing, crocheting, etc.

chain store *U.S.* One of a number of retail stores under the same ownership and selling similar merchandise.

chair (châr) *n.* **1.** A seat, usu. having four legs and a back, for one person. **2.** A seat of office, authority, etc., as that of a professor or bishop. **3.** The office or dignity of one who presides or is in authority. **4.** A presiding officer; chairman. **5.** The electric chair; also, execution in the electric chair. — **to take the chair** To preside at or open a meeting. — *v.t.* **1.** To seat in a chair. **2.** To install in office. **3.** To preside over (a meeting). [< OF *chaiere* < L *cathedra.*]

chair car A parlor car.

chair·man (châr′mən) *n. pl.* **·men** (-mən) One who presides over an assembly, committee, etc. — **chair·wom·an** (châr′wōōm′ən) *n.fem.*

chaise (shāz) *n.* **1.** A two-wheeled, one-horse vehicle for two persons, having a calash top. **2.** A similar carriage with four wheels. Also, *Dial., shay.* [< F, var. of *chaire* chair]

chaise longue (shāz′ lông′, *Fr.* shez lông′) A couchlike chair having the seat prolonged to support the sitter's outstretched legs. [< F, lit., long chair]

cha·la·za (kə·lā′zə) *n. pl.* **·zas** or **·zae** (-zē) *Biol.* One of the two threads attached to each end of the lining membrane of an egg. [< NL < Gk., hailstone, small lump]

chal·ced·o·ny (kal·sed′ə·nē, kal′sə·dō′nē) *n. pl.* **·nies** A waxy, translucent variety of quartz, often of a pale blue or grayish color: also spelled *calcedony.* [after *Chalcedon,* an ancient Greek port]

Chal·de·a (kal·dē′ə) In Biblical times, the southernmost Tigris and Euphrates valley, sometimes including Babylonia. Also **Chal·dae′a.** — **Chal·de′an** *adj. & n.*

cha·let (sha·lā′, shal′ā) *n.* **1.** A Swiss cottage with a gently sloping, projecting roof; also, any cottage built in this style. **2.** A herdsman's hut of the Alpine regions of Europe. [< F]

chal·ice (chal′is) *n.* **1.** A drinking cup or goblet. **2.** *Eccl.* In the Eucharist, a cup in which the wine is consecrated. **3.** A cup-shaped flower. [< OF < L *calix, calicis* cup]

chalk (chôk) *n.* **1.** A soft, grayish white or yellowish compact limestone, largely composed of the shells of marine animals. **2.** A piece of limestone or similar material, frequently colored, used for marking, etc. **3.** A score, tally, or notation of credit given. — *v.t.* **1.** To mark, write, or draw with chalk. **2.** To treat or dress with chalk. **3.** To make pale. — **to chalk up** To score; credit. — *adj.* Made with chalk. [OE < L *calx* limestone] — **chalk′i·ness** *n.* — **chalk′y** *adj.*

chal·lenge (chal′ənj) *v.* **·lenged, ·leng·ing** *v.t.* **1.** To demand a contest with. **2.** To demand defiantly. **3.** To call in question; dispute. **4.** *Law* To object to. **5.** To claim as due; demand. **6.** *Mil.* To stop and demand the countersign from. **7.** *U.S.* To claim that (a person) is not qualified to vote, or that (a vote) is invalid. —*v.i.* **8.** To make a challenge. —*n.* **1.** An invitation or dare to participate in a contest. **2.** *Mil.* A sentry's call, requiring one to halt and give the countersign. **3.** A calling in question; dispute. **4.** *U.S.* A claim that a voter is not qualified, or that a vote is not valid. **5.** *Law* A formal objection, as to a juror. **6.** *Telecom.* An electromagnetic signal requesting identification, as in radar communication. [< OF < L *calumnia* slander] — **chal·lenge·a·ble** *adj.* — **chal'leng·er** *n.*

chal·lis (shal/ē) *n.* A light fabric, usu. of printed wool, rayon, etc. Also **chal'lie.** [Origin uncertain]

cha·lyb·e·ate (kə·lib/ē·āt, -it) *adj.* **1.** Impregnated with compounds of iron, as mineral waters. **2.** Tasting of iron. —*n.* A medicine or water containing iron in solution. [< NL < L, ult. < Gk. *chalyps, chalybos* steel]

cham·ber (chām/bər) *n.* **1.** A room in a house; esp., a bedroom. **2.** An office or suite of rooms, as of a judge. **3.** *pl. Brit.* A set of rooms for one living alone. **4.** A hall where an assembly meets; also, the assembly itself. **5.** A council; board. **6.** An enclosed space or cavity, as in a gun. —*v.t.* **1.** To provide with a chamber. **2.** To fit into or as into a chamber. [< F < L *camera* vaulted room]

chamber concert A concert of chamber music.

cham·ber·lain (chām/bər·lin) *n.* **1.** An official charged with the domestic affairs of a monarch or lord. **2.** A high officer of a royal court. **3.** A treasurer. [< OF < OHG < L *camera* vaulted room] — **cham'ber·lain·ship/** *n.*

cham·ber·maid (chām/bər·mād/) *n.* A female servant who cleans and tends bedrooms in a house, hotel, etc.

chamber music Music composed for a small group of instruments, as for a quartet.

chamber of commerce An association of merchants and businessmen for the regulation and promotion of business in a city or locality.

chamber pot A portable vessel used as a toilet.

cham·bray (sham/brā) *n.* A cotton fabric woven with colored warp and white filling. [after *Cambrai*, France]

cha·me·le·on (kə·mē/lē·ən, -mēl/yən) *n.* **1.** A lizard capable of changing color. **2.** A person of changeable disposition or habits. [< L < Gk. *chamai* on the ground + *leōn* lion]

cham·fer (cham/fər) *v.t.* **1.** To cut away the corner of. **2.** To cut a furrow in; flute. —*n.* A surface produced by chamfering. [< F < OF *chanfraindre* to cut off an edge]

cham·ois (sham/ē, *Fr.* shà·mwà/) *n. pl.* **·ois 1.** A mountain antelope of Europe and western Asia. **2.** A soft leather prepared from the skin of the chamois, sheep, goats, deer, etc.: also spelled *shammy, shamois*: also **cham'·my. 3.** The color of this leather, a yellowish beige. —*v.t.* To dress (leather or skin) like chamois. [< MF]

cham·o·mile (kam/ə·mīl) See CAMOMILE.

champ¹ (champ) *v.t.* **1.** To crush and chew noisily; munch. **2.** To bite upon restlessly. —*v.i.* **3.** To make a biting or chewing movement with the jaws. —*n.* The action of chewing or biting. [Prob. imit.]

champ² (champ) *n. Slang* Champion.

cham·pagne (sham·pān/) *n.* **1.** A sparkling white wine made in the area of Champagne, France; also, any wine made in imitation of this. **2.** A pale or greenish yellow. —*adj.* Pertaining to champagne.

cham·paign (sham·pān/) *n.* Flat and open country. —*adj.* Flat and open. [< OF < LL < L *campus* field]

cham·pi·on (cham/pē·ən) *n.* **1.** One who has defeated all opponents and is ranked first, esp. in a sport. **2.** Anything awarded first place. **3.** One who fights for another or defends a principle or cause. —*adj.* Having won first prize or rank; superior to all others. —*v.t.* To fight in behalf of; defend; support. [< OF < LL *campio, -onis* fighter]

cham·pi·on·ship (cham/pē·ən·ship/) *n.* **1.** The state of being a champion. **2.** The position or honor of a champion. **3.** The act of championing; advocacy; defense.

Champs É·ly·sées (shän zā·lē·zā/) A fashionable avenue in Paris. [< F, lit., Elysian fields]

chance (chans, chäns) *n.* **1.** The unknown or undefined cause of events; fortune; luck. **2.** An unusual and unexplained event. **3.** The probability of anything happening; possibility. **4.** An opportunity: Now is your *chance.* **5.** A risk or gamble; hazard. **6.** A ticket in a lottery. —*v.* **chanced, chanc·ing** *v.i.* **1.** To occur accidentally; happen. —*v.t.* **2.** To take the chance of; risk: I'll *chance* it. — **to chance upon** (or **on**) To find or meet unexpectedly. —*adj.* Occurring by chance. [< OF < LL *cadentia* a falling]

chan·cel (chan/səl, chän/-) *n.* The space near the altar of a church for the clergy and choir, often set apart by a screen or railing. [< OF < LL < L *cancelli*, pl., lattice, railing]

chan·cel·ler·y (chan/sə·lər·ē, -slər·ē, chän/-) *n. pl.* **·ler·ies 1.** The office or dignity of a chancellor. **2.** The building or

room in which a chancellor has his office. **3.** The office of an embassy or legation. Also **chan·cel·ry** (chan/səl·rē, chän/-).

chan·cel·lor (chan/sə·lər, -slər, chän/-) *n.* **1.** In some European countries, a chief minister of state. **2.** The chief secretary of an embassy. **3.** A secretary, as of a nobleman or ruler. **4.** The head of some universities. **5.** *U.S.* A judge of a court of chancery or equity. Also **chan'cel·or.** — **Lord High Chancellor** *Brit.* The highest judicial officer of the crown: also **Lord Chancellor.** [< OF < LL *cancellarius* one who stands at the bar in a court] — **chan'cel·lor·ship/** *n.*

Chancellor of the Exchequer The minister of finance in the British cabinet.

chance-med·ley (chans/med/lē, chäns/-) *n.* **1.** *Law* Unpremeditated homicide in self-defense. **2.** Inadvertent or random action. [< OF < *chance* chance + *medlee* mixed]

chan·cer·y (chan/sər·ē, chän/-) *n. pl.* **·cer·ies 1.** In the United States: **a** A court of equity. Also **court of chancery. b** Equity, or proceedings in equity. **2.** *Brit.* One of the five divisions of the High Court of Justice. **3.** A chancellery. **4.** A court of records; archives. — **in chancery 1.** *Law* Pending in a court of chancery; in litigation. **2.** In wrestling, with the head caught and held under an opponent's arm. **3.** In a hopeless predicament. [See CHANCELLOR.]

chan·cre (shang/kər) *n. Pathol.* A primary syphilitic lesion resembling a sore with a hard base. [< F < L *cancer* crab, ulcer] — **chan·crous** (shang/krəs) *adj.*

chan·croid (shang/kroid) *n. Pathol.* A nonsyphilitic, localized venereal lesion.

chanc·y (chan/sē, chän/-) *adj.* **chanc·i·er, chanc·i·est** *Informal* Subject to chance; risky. — **chan/ci·ly** *adv.*

chan·de·lier (shan/də·lir/) *n.* A branched support for a number of lights, suspended from a ceiling. [< F < Med.L < L *candela* candle]

chan·dler (chan/dlər, chän/-) *n.* **1.** A trader; dealer: ship *chandler.* **2.** One who makes or sells ca:dles. **3.** *Brit.* A shopkeeper. [< OF *chandelier* chandler, candlestick]

change (chānj) *v.* **changed, chang·ing** *v.t.* **1.** To make different; alter. **2.** To exchange: to *change* places. **3.** To give or obtain the equivalent of. **4.** To put other garments, coverings, etc., on: to *change* the bed. —*v.i.* **5.** To become different. **6.** To make a change or exchange. **7.** To transfer from one train, etc., to another. **8.** To put on other garments, etc. — **to change color 1.** To blush. **2.** To turn pale. — **to change hands** To pass from one possessor to another. —*n.* **1.** The act or fact of changing. **2.** A substitution of one thing for another. **3.** Something new or different; variety. **4.** A clean or different set of clothes. **5.** The amount returned when a coin or bill of greater value than the sum due has been tendered. **6.** Money of lower denomination given in exchange for higher. **7.** Small coins. **8.** *Usu. pl.* Any order in which a peal of bells may be struck. **9.** A place for transacting business; an exchange: also **'change.** — **to ring the changes 1.** To operate a chime of bells in every possible order. **2.** To repeat something with every possible variation. [< OF < LL *cambiare* to exchange] — **chang'er** *n.*

change·a·ble (chān/jə·bəl) *adj.* **1.** Likely to change or vary; inconstant; fickle. **2.** Capable of being changed. **3.** Reflecting light so as to appear of different color from different points of view. — **change·a·bil·i·ty** (chān/jə·bil/ə·tē,) **change/a·ble·ness** *n.* — **change/a·bly** *adv.*

change·ful (chānj/fəl) *adj.* Full of or given to change; variable. — **change/ful·ly** *adv.* — **change/ful·ness** *n.*

change·less (chānj/lis) *adj.* Free from change; enduring; unchanging. — **change/less·ly** *adv.* — **change/less·ness** *n.*

change·ling (chānj/ling) *n.* A child secretly left in place of another.

change of life The menopause.

change ringing The production of every possible variation in the ringing of a set of bells.

chan·nel (chan/əl) *n.* **1.** The bed of a stream. **2.** A wide strait: the English *Channel.* **3.** *Naut.* The deep part of a river, harbor, etc. **4.** A tubular passage, as for liquids. **5.** The course through which anything moves or passes. **6.** *pl.* The official or proper routes of communication: to put a request through *channels.* **7.** *Telecom.* **a** A path for the transmission of telegraph, telephone, or radio communications. **b** A range of frequencies assigned for television transmission. **8.** A groove or furrow. —*v.t.* **chan·neled** or **·nelled, chan·nel·ing** or **·nel·ling 1.** To cut or wear channels in. **2.** To direct or convey through or as through a channel. [< OF < L *canalis* groove]

chan·son (chan/sən, *Fr.* shäṅ·sôṅ/) *n.* A song. [< F < L *canere* to sing]

chant (chant, chänt) *n.* **1.** A simple melody in which a varying number of syllables are sung or intoned on each note. **2.** A psalm or canticle so sung or intoned. **3.** A song; melody. **4.** Any monotonous singing or shouting of words, as from a mob. **5.** A singing intonation in speech. —*v.t.* **1.** To sing to a chant. **2.** To celebrate in song. **3.** To recite or say in the manner of a chant. —*v.t.* **4.** To sing

CHAMOIS
(2 feet high at shoulder; 45 inches long)

chants. **5.** To make melody; sing. **6.** To talk monotonously. [< OF < L *canere* to sing] — **chant′er** *n.*

chan·teuse (shän·tœz′) *n. French* A woman singer.

chant·ey (shan′tē, chan′-) *n. pl.* **·eys** A rhythmical working song of sailors: also spelled *shantey, shanty.* Also **chan′ty.** [Alter. of F *chantez,* imperative of *chanter* to sing]

chan·ti·cleer (chan′tə·klir) *n.* A cock. [< OF < *chanter* to sing, crow + *cler* aloud]

chan·try (chan′trē, chän′-) *n., pl.* **·tries** An endowment for the daily masses or special prayers; also, a chapel or altar so endowed. [< OF < L *canere* to sing]

Cha·nu·kah (khä′noo·kə) See HANUKKAH.

cha·os (kā′os) *n.* **1.** Utter disorder and confusion. **2.** The supposed unformed original state of the universe. [< L < Gk., abyss]

cha·ot·ic (kā·ot′ik) *adj.* Utterly disordered and confused. Also **cha·ot′i·cal.** — **cha·ot′i·cal·ly** *adv.*

chap[1] (chap) *n. Informal* A fellow; lad.

chap[2] (chap) *v.* **chapped** or **chapt, chap·ping** *v.t.* **1.** To cause to split, crack, or become rough: The cold has *chapped* my hands. — *v.i.* **2.** To split, crack, or redden. — *n.* A crack or roughened place in the skin. [ME *chappen*]

chap[3] (chap, chop) *n.* **1.** A jaw. **2.** *pl.* The mouth and cheeks. Also spelled *chop.* [Cf. ME *chaft* jaw]

chap·ar·ral (chap′ə·ral′) *n.* A thicket of dwarf oak, low thorny shrubs, etc. [< Sp. < *chaparra* evergreen oak]

chap·book (chap′book′) *n.* A small book containing tales, ballads, etc.

cha·peau (sha·pō′, *Fr.* shà·pō′) *n. pl.* **·peaux** (-pōz′, *Fr.* -pō′) or **·peaus** (-pōz′) A hat. [< F]

chap·el (chap′əl) *n.* **1.** A place of worship smaller than a church. **2.** A recess or enclosed part of a church, for small or special services. **3.** *Brit.* A place of worship not connected with the established church. **4.** A building or room in a college, school, etc., for religious services; also, the services. [< OF < Med.L *cappa* cloak; orig., a sanctuary where the cloak of St. Martin was kept as a relic]

chap·er·on (shap′ə·rōn) *n.* An older person who accompanies and supervises a group of young people. — *v.t.* To act as chaperon to. Also **chap′er·one.** [< F, hood < *chape* cape] — **chap·er·on·age** (shap′ə·rōn′nij) *n.*

chap·fall·en (chap′fô′lən, chop′-) *adj.* Dejected; crestfallen. Also **chopfallen.**

chap·lain (chap′lin) *n.* A clergyman who conducts religious services in a legislative assembly, for a military unit, etc. [< OF < Med.L *cappa* cloak] — **chap′lain·cy, chap′·lain·ship** *n.*

chap·let (chap′lit) *n.* **1.** A wreath or garland for the head. **2.** A rosary, or, more strictly, one third of a rosary. **3.** A string of beads, or anything resembling it. [< OF < LL *cappa* hooded cape]

chap·man (chap′mən) *n. pl.* **·men** (-mən) *Brit.* A peddler; hawker. [OE < *cēap* business + *man* man]

chaps (chaps, shaps) *n.pl. U.S.* Leather overalls without a seat, worn over trousers by cowboys to protect the legs.

chap·ter (chap′tər) *n.* **1.** A main division of a book or treatise, usually numbered. **2.** A branch of a society or fraternity. **3.** *Eccl.* An assembly of the canons of a cathedral or collegiate church; also, the canons collectively. **4.** A meeting of any order or society. **5.** A period of time: an important *chapter* in history. — *v.t.* To divide into chapters, as a book. [< F < OF < L *caput* head, capital]

chapter house 1. A place of assembly for a cathedral or monastery chapter. **2.** The house of a fraternity or sorority.

char[1] (chär) *v.* **charred, char·ring** *v.t.* **1.** To burn or scorch the surface of, as timber. **2.** To convert into charcoal by incomplete combustion. — *v.i.* **3.** To become charred. — *n.* Charcoal. [? < CHARCOAL]

char[2] (chär) *n. pl.* **chars** or **char** Any of various fishes allied to the lake trout. [< Scottish Gaelic *ceara* blood red]

char[3] (chär) *Brit. n.* **1.** A chore; esp., a household task: also called *chare.* **2.** A charwoman. — *v.i.* **charred, char·ring** To work as a charwoman. [OE *cerr* turn of work]

char·a·banc (shar′ə·bangk, -bang) *n. pl.* **·bancs** *Brit.* A long, open vehicle with rows of seats facing forward. Also **char′a·banc.** [< F *char à bancs* car with benches]

char·ac·ter (kar′ik·tər) *n.* **1.** The combination of qualities or traits that distinguishes an individual or group; personality. **2.** Any distinguishing attribute; characteristic; property. **3.** Moral force; integrity. **4.** A good reputation. **5.** Status; capacity: in his *character* as president. **6.** A personage. **7.** A person in a play, novel, etc. **8.** *Informal* An eccentric or humorous person. **9.** A figure engraved, written, or printed; mark; sign; letter. **10.** *Genetics* Any structural or functional trait in a plant or animal resulting from the interaction of genes and regarded as hereditary in origin. — **in** (or **out of**) **character** In keeping (or not in keeping) with the general character or role. — *v.t.* To

write, print, or engrave. [< MF < L < Gk. < *charassein* to sharpen, engrave, carve, scratch] — **char′ac·ter·less** *adj.*

character actor An actor who portrays characters markedly different from himself in age, temperament, etc.

char·ac·ter·is·tic (kar′ik·tə·ris′tik) *adj.* Indicating or constituting the distinctive quality, character, or disposition; typical: a *characteristic* gesture. — *n.* **1.** A distinctive feature or trait. **2.** *Math.* The integral part of a logarithm; index. — **char′ac·ter·is′ti·cal·ly** *adv.*

— **Syn.** (noun) A *characteristic* is that by which we recognize something for what it is; a hump is one of a camel's *characteristics.* A *peculiarity* is a *characteristic* that distinguishes one individual or kind from another. We speak of the qualities of persons as *traits,* and of the qualities of objects or substances as *properties.*

char·ac·ter·ize (kar′ik·tə·rīz′) *v.t.* **·ized, ·iz·ing 1.** To describe by qualities or peculiarities; designate. **2.** To be a mark or peculiarity of; distinguish. **3.** To give character to, as in writing or acting. — **char·ac·ter·i·za·tion** (kar′ik·tər·ə·zā′shən) *n.* — **char′ac·ter·iz′er** *n.*

cha·rades (shə·rādz′, *Brit.* shə·rädz′) *n.pl. (construed as sing.)* A game in which words and phrases are to be guessed, sometimes syllable by syllable, from their representation in pantomime. [< F < Provençal < *charra* to chatter, prattle]

char·coal (chär′kōl′) *n.* **1.** A black, porous substance obtained by the imperfect combustion of organic matter, as wood, used as a fuel, adsorbent, filter, etc. **2.** A drawing pencil made of charcoal dust. **3.** A drawing made with such a pencil. — *v.t.* To write, draw, mark, or blacken with charcoal. [ME *charcole*; origin unknown]

chard (chärd) *n.* A variety of edible white beet cultivated for its large leaves and leafstalks. [< F < L *carduus* thistle]

charge (chärj) *v.* **charged, charg·ing** *v.t.* **1.** To place a load upon. **2.** To place in or on (a thing) what it is intended or able to receive: to *charge* a furnace with ore. **3.** To load (a firearm). **4.** To diffuse something throughout, as water with carbon dioxide. **5.** To fill as if with electricity; make vibrant. **6.** To supply (a storage battery) with a quantity of electricity. **7.** To accuse; impute something to. **8.** To command; enjoin. **9.** To instruct, exhort: to *charge* a jury. **10.** To entrust with a duty, responsibility, etc.; burden, as with care. **11.** To set or state as a price: to *charge* a dollar. **12.** To make financially liable. **13.** To set down or record as a debt to be paid: to *charge* a purchase. **14.** To attack forcefully: to *charge* a fort. **15.** To place (a weapon) in position for use. — *v.i.* **16.** To make an onset; rush violently. **17.** To demand or fix a price. — **Syn.** See ACCUSE. — **to charge off** To regard as a loss. — *n.* **1.** A load or burden. **2.** The quantity of anything that an apparatus or receptacle can hold at one time. **3.** The amount of explosive to be detonated at one time. **4.** The quantity of static electricity present in or on an apparatus, as a storage battery. **5.** Care and custody; superintendence. **6.** A person or thing entrusted to one's care. **7.** A responsibility or duty. **8.** An accusation; allegation. **9.** An address of instruction or admonition given by a judge to a jury at the close of a trial. **10.** An order or injunction; command. **11.** The expense or cost of something; price. **12.** Any pecuniary burden; tax; lien; expense. **13.** A debt or charged purchase, or an entry recording it. **14.** An onslaught or attack; also, the signal for this. **15.** *Physics* The energy present in an atomic particle. — **in charge of** Having responsibility for or control of. [< OF < LL < L *carrus* cart]

charge·a·ble (chär′jə·bəl) *adj.* **1.** That may be or is liable to be charged. **2.** Liable to become a public charge.

charge account A retail credit account to which purchases or services may be charged for future payment.

char·gé d'af·faires (shär·zhā′ də·fâr′, *Fr.* shär·zhā′ dà·fâr′) *pl.* **char·gés d'af·faires** (shär·zhāz′ də·fâr′, *Fr.* shär·zhā′ dà·fâr′) **1.** One who temporarily heads a diplomatic mission in the absence of the ambassador or minister. **2.** A diplomatic of lower rank than an ambassador. Also **char·gé′.**

charg·er (chär′jər) *n.* **1.** One who or that which charges. **2.** A horse trained for use in battle; a war horse. **3.** An apparatus for charging storage batteries.

char·i·ly (châr′ə·lē) *adv.* In a chary manner; carefully.

char·i·ness (châr′ē·nis) *n.* The quality of being chary.

char·i·ot (char′ē·ət) *n.* An ancient two-wheeled vehicle used in war, racing, etc. — *v.t. & v.i.* To convey, ride, or drive in a chariot. [< OF < L *carrus* cart, wagon]

char·i·o·teer (char′ē·ə·tir′) *n.* One who drives a chariot.

cha·ris·ma (kə·riz′mə) *n.* **1.** *Theol.* An extraordinary spiritual grace that benefits others. **2.** Extraordinary personal power or charm. [< Gk., grace, favor]

char·is·mat·ic (kar′iz·mat′ik) *adj.* Possessing charisma.

char·i·ta·ble (char′ə·tə·bəl) *adj.* **1.** Generous in giving gifts to the poor; beneficent. **2.** Inclined to judge others leniently. **3.** Of or concerned with charity: a *charitable* enterprise. — **char′i·ta·ble·ness** *n.* — **char′i·ta·bly** *adv.*

---

char·i·ty (char/ə·tē) *n. pl.* ·ties 1. The providing of help to the poor. 2. That which is given to help the needy; alms. 3. An institution, organization, or fund to aid those in need. 4. Tolerance; leniency. 5. An act of good will. 6. Brotherly love. [< OF < L *carus* dear]

cha·riv·a·ri (shə·riv/ə·rē/, shiv/ə·rē/, shä/rē·vä/rē) *n. pl.* ·ris A mock serenade, as to a newly married couple, performed with tin pans, horns, etc.: also *chivaree, shivaree*. [< MF]

char·la·tan (shär/lə·tən) *n.* One who makes claim to skill and knowledge he does not possess; an impostor; quack. [< F < Ital. *ciarla* chat, idle talk] — **char/la·tan/ic** (-tan/ik) *adj.* — **char/la·tan·ism, char/la·tan·ry** *n.*

Charles's Wain The constellation Ursa Major.

Charles·ton (chärl/stən) *n.* A fast dance in ¼ time, popular in the 1920's. [after *Charleston*, S.C.]

char·ley horse (chär/lē) *U.S. Informal* A muscular cramp in the arm or leg, caused by strain. [Origin unknown]

char·lock (chär/lək) *n.* Any of several herbs of the mustard family having yellow flowers. [OE *cerlic*]

char·lotte russe (shär/lət rōōs) A small sponge cake with a filling of whipped cream or custard. [< F, Russian charlotte]

charm (chärm) *n.* 1. The power to allure or delight; fascination. 2. Any fascinating quality or feature. 3. A small ornament worn on a necklace, bracelet, etc. 4. Something worn to ward off evil or ensure good luck; an amulet. 5. Any formula or action supposed to have magic power. 6. *Physics* A property of matter observable in collisions between subatomic particles. — *v.t.* 1. To delight; fascinate. 2. To influence by or as if by a spell; bewitch. 3. To protect by or as by magic power. — *v.i.* 4. To be pleasing or fascinating. [< F < L *carmen* song] — **charm/er** *n.*

charm·ing (chär/ming) *adj.* 1. Delightful; very attractive. 2. Magically powerful. — **charm/ing·ly** *adv.*

char·nel (chär/nəl) *n.* A charnel house. — *adj.* Suggesting or fit for receiving the dead; sepulchral; ghastly. [< OF < LL < L *caro. carnis* flesh]

charnel house A room or vault where bones or bodies of the dead are placed.

Char·on (kâr/ən, kar/-) In Greek mythology, the ferryman who carried the dead over the river Styx to Hades. — *n.* A ferryman: a humorous use.

chart (chärt) *n.* 1. A map, esp. one for the use of mariners. 2. An outline map on which climatic data, military operations, etc., can be shown. 3. A sheet showing facts graphically or in tabular form. 4. A graph showing changes and variation of temperature, population, prices, wages, etc. — *v.t.* To lay out on a chart; map out. [< OF < L < Gk. *chartēs* leaf of paper] — **chart/less** *adj.*

char·ter (chär/tər) *n.* 1. A document of incorporation of a municipality, institution, or the like, specifying its privileges and purposes. 2. A formal document by which a sovereign or government grants special rights or privileges to a person, company, or the people. 3. An authorization to establish a branch or chapter of some larger organization. 4. A contract for the lease of a vessel, bus, airplane, etc. — *v.t.* 1. To hire (an airplane, train, etc.). 2. To give a charter to. [< OF < L *chartula*, dim. of *charta* paper] — **char/ter·age** *n.* — **char/ter·er** *n.*

charter member An original member of a corporation, order, or society.

char·treuse (shar·trœz/; *for def. 2,* also shär·trōōz/) *n.* 1. A yellow, pale green, or white liqueur made by the Carthusian monks. 2. A pale, yellowish green color. — *adj.* Of the color chartreuse. [< F < *La Grande Chartreuse*, chief Carthusian monastery in France]

char·wom·an (chär/wŏŏm/ən) *n. pl.* ·wom·en (-wim/ən) *Brit.* A woman employed to do housework, or cleaning and scrubbing, as in office buildings.

char·y (châr/ē) *adj.* **char·i·er, char·i·est** 1. Cautious; wary. 2. Fastidious; particular. 3. Sparing; frugal; stingy. [OE *cearig* sorrowful, sad < *cearu* care]

Cha·ryb·dis (kə·rib/dis) In Greek mythology, a monster dwelling in a whirlpool on the Sicilian coast opposite the cave of Scylla; also, the whirlpool. See SCYLLA.

chase¹ (chās) *v.* **chased, chas·ing** *v.t.* 1. To pursue with intent to catch or harm. 2. To follow persistently; run after. 3. To put to flight; drive. — *v.i.* 4. To follow in pursuit. 5. *Informal* To rush; go hurriedly. — *n.* 1. The act of chasing or pursuing. 2. The sport of hunting: preceded by *the*. 3. That which is pursued; prey; quarry. — **to give chase** To pursue. [< OF < LL < L *capere* to take]

chase² (chās) *n.* 1. *Printing* A rectangular metal frame into which pages of type are fastened for printing or platemaking. 2. A groove or slot; hollow; trench. — *v.t.* **chased, chas·ing** 1. To indent or groove. 2. To ornament by embossing; engrave. [Fusion of F *chasse* and *chas*, both ult. < L *capsa* box; *v.* def. 2 < ENCHASE] — **chas/er** *n.*

chas·er (chā/sər) *n.* 1. One who chases or pursues. 2. *U.S. Informal* Water, etc. taken after strong liquor.

chasm (kaz/əm) *n.* 1. A yawning crack in the earth's sur-

face; a gorge. 2. An abrupt interruption; a gap or void. 3. Any great difference of opinion, sentiment, loyalty, etc. [< Gk. *chainein* to gape] — **chas·mal** (kaz/məl) *adj.*

chas·seur (sha·sûr/) *n.* 1. One of a body of light cavalry or infantry trained for rapid maneuvers, as in the French army. 2. A liveried servant. 3. A huntsman. [< F, hunter]

Chas·si·dim (khä·sē/dim) *n. pl. of* **Chas·sid** (khä/sid) A sect of Jewish mystics: also spelled *Hasidim*. [< Hebrew, pious] — **Chas·si·dic** (khä·sē/dik) *adj.*

chas·sis (shas/ē, chas/ē) *n. pl.* **chas·sis** (shas/ēz, chas/ēz) 1. The flat, rectangular frame that supports the body of a motor vehicle and includes the wheels, springs, motor, etc. 2. *Aeron.* The landing gear of an aircraft. 3. *Telecom.* The metal framework to which the tubes and other components of a radio receiver, amplifier, etc., are attached. 4. A movable frame on which the top carriage of a gun moves backward and forward. [< F *chassis* < *chas*. See CHASE².]

chaste (chāst) *adj.* 1. Not guilty of unlawful sexual intercourse; virtuous. 2. Pure in character or conduct; not indecent. 3. Pure in artistic or literary style; simple. [< OF < L *castus* pure] — **chaste/ly** *adv.* — **chaste/ness** *n.*

chas·ten (chā/sən) *v.t.* 1. To discipline by punishment or affliction; chastise. 2. To moderate; soften; temper. [< OF < L *castigare* to correct] — **chast/en·er** *n.* — **Syn. 1.** *Chasten* is a general term to cover mild or severe punishment, whether physical or moral. *Correct* suggests mild punishment or sometimes mere verbal reproof. *Discipline*, like *correct*, looks to future conduct, and stresses training rather than punishment. *Chastise* and *castigate* refer to corporal punishment for past misconduct rather than as a corrective measure.

chas·tise (chas·tīz/) *v.t.* ·tised, ·tis·ing To punish, esp. by beating. — **Syn.** See CHASTEN. [ME *chastisen*] — **chas·tis/a·ble** *adj.* — **chas·tise·ment** (chas/tiz·mənt, chas·tīz/-) *n.* — **chas·tis/er** *n.*

chas·ti·ty (chas/tə·tē) *n.* 1. The state or quality of being chaste. 2. Virginity or celibacy. [< OF < L < *castus* pure]

chas·u·ble (chaz/yə·bəl, chas/-) *n.* A long, sleeveless vestment worn over the alb by a priest when celebrating the Eucharist. [< F < Med.L < L, dim. of *casa* house]

chat (chat) *v.i.* **chat·ted, chat·ting** To converse in an easy or gossipy manner; talk familiarly. — *n.* 1. Easy, informal conversation. 2. Any of several singing birds: so called from their notes. [Short for CHATTER]

cha·teau (sha·tō/, *Fr.* shä·tō/) *n. pl.* ·teaux (-tōz/, *Fr.* -tō/) 1. A French castle. 2. A house on a country estate. Also *French* **châ·teau**. [< F < L *castrum* camp, fort]

chat·e·laine (shat/ə·lān) *n.* 1. A chain hanging from a woman's belt to hold small articles, as keys; also, a clasp to hold a watch or purse. 2. The mistress of a chateau, castle, or any fashionable household. [< F *châtelaine*]

chat·tel (chat/l) *n. Law* An article of personal property; a movable, as distinguished from real property. [< OF *chatel* < L *caput* head]

chattel mortgage A mortgage on personal property.

chat·ter (chat/ər) *v.i.* 1. To click together rapidly, as the teeth in shivering. 2. To talk rapidly and trivially. 3. To utter a rapid series of short, inarticulate sounds, as a squirrel. — *v.t.* 4. To utter in a trivial or chattering manner. — *n.* 1. Idle or foolish talk; prattle. 2. Jabbering, as of a monkey. 3. A rattling of the teeth. [Imit.] — **chat/ter·er** *n.*

chat·ter·box (chat/ər·boks/) *n.* An incessant talker.

chat·ty (chat/ē) *adj.* ·ti·er, ·ti·est 1. Given to chat; loquacious. 2. Easy and familiar; informal: a *chatty* style of writing. — **chat/ti·ly** *adv.* — **chat/ti·ness** *n.*

Chau·ce·ri·an (chô·sir/ē·ən) *adj.* Of or like the writings of Chaucer. — *n.* A specialist in Chaucer's works.

chauf·feur (shō/fər, shō/fûr/) *n.* One who is employed as the driver of an automobile. — *v.t.* To serve as driver for. [< F, stoker < *chauffer* to warm]

chaul·moo·gra (chôl·mōō/grə) *n.* An East Indian and Malayan tree whose seeds yield **chaulmoogra oil**, formerly used in treating leprosy. [< Bengali *cáulmugrá*]

chau·vin·ism (shō/vən·iz/əm) *n.* 1. Militant and vainglorious patriotism. 2. Unreasoning attachment to one's race, group, etc. [after Nicholas *Chauvin*, a soldier and overzealous supporter of Napoleon Bonaparte] — **chau/vin·ist** *n.* — **chau/vin·is/tic** *adj.* — **chau/vin·is/ti·cal·ly** *adv.*

cheap (chēp) *adj.* 1. Bringing a low price; inexpensive. 2. Charging low prices, as a store. 3. Obtainable at a low price in proportion to its value. 4. Easily obtained; costing little trouble. 5. Being of little value; poor; inferior. 6. Not esteemed. 7. Vulgar; mean: a *cheap* person. — *adv.* At a low price; cheaply. [Earlier *good cheap* a bargain < OE *cēap* business, trade] — **cheap/ly** *adv.* — **cheap/ness** *n.*

cheap·en (chē/pən) *v.i. & v.i.* To make or become cheap or cheaper. — **cheap/en·er** *n.*

cheap·skate (chēp/skāt/) *n. U.S. Slang* A miserly person.

cheat (chēt) *v.t.* 1. To swindle or defraud. 2. To mislead or delude; trick. 3. To elude or escape; foil. — *v.i.* 4. To practice fraud or act dishonestly. 5. *U.S. Slang* To be sexually unfaithful. — *n.* 1. A fraud; swindle. 2. One who cheats or defrauds. [ME *chete*, short for *achete* to confiscate, deprive] — **cheat′er** *n.* — **cheat′ing·ly** *adv.*

check (chek) *n.* **1.** A break in progress or advance; a stopping; rebuff; delay. **2.** One who or that which stops or controls. **3.** Control maintained to secure accuracy, honesty etc.; supervision. **4.** A test, examination, or comparison. **5.** A mark to show that something has been verified or investigated. **6.** An order, in writing, upon a bank or banker to pay a designated sum: also, *Brit. cheque.* **7.** *U.S.* A tag, slip, or the like, issued for identification: a baggage *check.* **8.** *U.S.* A slip listing the amount one owes, as in a restaurant. **9.** A counter used in various games; a chip. **10.** A square in a checkered surface, as on a chessboard. **11.** A fabric having a checkered pattern. **12.** In chess, the condition of a king that is subject to capture on the next opposing move. **13.** A crack, as in timber or steel. — **in check** Under control or restraint. — *v.t.* **1.** To bring to a stop suddenly or sharply; halt. **2.** To hold back; curb; restrain. **3.** To test or verify as to accuracy, completeness, etc.; also, to investigate. **4.** To mark with a check, as to indicate correctness. **5.** To mark with squares or crossed lines; checker. **6.** To deposit or accept for temporary safekeeping: to *check* luggage. **7.** In chess, to put (an opponent's king) in check. **8.** To cause to crack. — *v.i.* **9.** To come to a stop; pause. **10.** *U.S.* To agree item for item; correspond accurately. **11.** In chess, to put an opponent's king in check. **12.** *U.S.* To draw on a checking account. **13.** To crack, as paint. — **to check in** *U.S.* To register as a guest at a hotel, etc. — **to check on** (or **up on**) *U.S.* To inquire into; investigate. — **to check out** **1.** *U.S.* To pay one's bill and leave, as from a hotel. **2.** To investigate or confirm. **3.** To be true or as expected, upon investigation. **4.** *Slang* To die. — *interj.* In chess, an exclamation proclaiming that an opponent's king is in check. — *adj.* **1.** *Chiefly Brit.* Formed or marked in a pattern of checks. **2.** Serving to verify or check. [< OF *eschec* defeat, check] — **check′a·ble** *adj.*

check·book (chek′bŏok′) *n.* A book of blank bank checks.

checked (chekt) *adj.* **1.** Marked with squares: *checked* gingham. **2.** Kept in check; restrained. **3.** Stopped.

check·er (chek′ər) *n.* **1.** A piece used in the game of checkers, usually a small disk. **2.** One of the squares in a checkered surface; also, a pattern of such squares. **3.** One who checks; esp., one who inspects, counts, or supervises the disposal of merchandise. — *v.t.* **1.** To mark with squares or crossed lines. **2.** To fill with variations or vicissitudes. Also, *Brit., chequer.* [< ME < OF *eschec* defeat, check]

check·er·board (chek′ər·bôrd′, -bōrd′) *n.* A board divided into 64 squares, used in playing checkers or chess.

check·ered (chek′ərd) *adj.* **1.** Divided into squares. **2.** Marked by light and dark patches. **3.** Marked by alternations; eventful: a *checkered* career.

check·ers (chek′ərz) *n.pl.* (construed as *sing.*) A game played by two persons on a checkerboard, each player starting with twelve pieces: in England usu. called *draughts.*

check·ing account (chek′ing) A bank account against which a depositor may draw checks.

check list A list of items to be checked.

check·mate (chek′māt) *v.t.* **·mat·ed**, **·mat·ing** **1.** In chess, to put (an opponent's king) in check from which no escape is possible, thus winning the game. **2.** To defeat by a skillful maneuver. — *n.* **1.** In chess: **a** The move that checkmates a king. **b** The condition of a king when checkmated. **2.** Utter defeat. Also *mate.* [< OF < Arabic *shāh māt* the king is dead < Persian]

check·off (chek′ôf′, -of′) *n.* The collection of trade-union dues by deduction from the pay of each employee.

check·out (chek′out′) *n.* **1.** The procedure or time of checking out of a hotel. **2.** The itemization of goods and payment for purchases, as at a supermarket: often used attributively: a *check-out* counter. Also **check′out′.**

check·rein (chek′rān′) *n.* A rein from the bit to the saddle of a harness to keep a horse's head up.

check·room (chek′rōōm′, -rŏŏm′) *n.* A room in which packages, coats, etc., may be left temporarily.

check·up (chek′up′) *n.* An examining or searching.

Ched·dar (ched′ər) *n.* Any of several types of white to yellow, hard, smooth cheese. Also **ched′dar, Cheddar cheese.** [after *Cheddar*, Somerset, England, where originally made]

cheek (chēk) *n.* **1.** Either side of the face below the eye and above the mouth. ◆ Collateral adjective: *buccal.* **2.** A side or part analogous to the side of the face. **3.** *Informal* Impudent self-assurance. [OE *cēce, cēace*]

cheek·bone (chēk′bōn′) *n.* Either of two bony prominences of the cheek below the eye socket.

cheek by jowl Side by side; in close intimacy.

cheek·y (chē′kē) *adj.* **cheek·i·er, cheek·i·est** *Informal* Impudent; brazen. — **cheek′i·ly** *adv.* — **cheek′i·ness** *n.*

cheep (chēp) *v.t.* & *v.i.* To make, or utter with, a faint, shrill sound, as a young bird. — *n.* A weak chirp or squeak. [Imit.] — **cheep′er** *n.*

cheer (chir) *n.* **1.** A shout of acclamation or encouragement. **2.** Gladness or gaiety. **3.** State of mind; mood. **4.** That which promotes happiness or joy; encouragement. — *v.t.* **1.** To make cheerful; gladden: often with *up.* **2.** To acclaim with cheers. **3.** To urge; incite: often with *on.* — *v.i.* **4.** To become cheerful or glad: often with *up.* **5.** To utter cries of encouragement, approval, etc. [< OF *chiere, chere* face] — **cheer′er** *n.* — **cheer′ing·ly** *adv.*

cheer·ful (chir′fəl) *adj.* **1.** In good spirits; joyous; lively. **2.** Pleasant: a *cheerful* color. **3.** Willing; ungrudging: a *cheerful* giver. — **cheer′ful·ly** *adv.* — **cheer′ful·ness** *n.*

cheer·i·o (chir′ē·ō) *interj.* & *n. pl.* **cheer·i·os** *Brit. Informal* **1.** Hello. **2.** Good-by. Also **cheer′o.**

cheer·lead·er (chir′lē′dər) *n.* A person who leads organized cheering at an athletic event. Also **cheer leader.**

cheer·less (chir′lis) *adj.* Destitute of cheer; gloomy. — **cheer′less·ly** *adv.* — **cheer′less·ness** *n.*

cheer·y (chir′ē) *adj.* **cheer·i·er, cheer·i·est** Abounding in cheerfulness; gay. — **cheer′i·ly** *adv.* — **cheer′i·ness** *n.*

cheese¹ (chēz) *n.* **1.** The pressed curd of milk, variously prepared and flavored. **2.** Any of various substances like cheese in consistency or shape. [OE *cēse* < L *caseus* cheese]

cheese² (chēz) *v.t.* **cheesed, chees·ing** *Slang* To stop: esp. in the phrase **cheese it!** Look out! Run! [< CEASE]

cheese³ (chēz) *n.* *Slang* Personage: a big *cheese.* [? < Urdu *chīz* thing]

cheese·cake (chēz′kāk′) *n.* **1.** A cake containing sweetened curds, eggs, milk, etc.: also **cheese cake.** **2.** *Slang* A photograph featuring a pretty girl's legs and figure.

cheese·cloth (chēz′klôth′, -kloth′) *n.* A thin, loosely woven cotton fabric, originally used for wrapping cheese.

chees·y (chē′zē) *adj.* **chees·i·er, chees·i·est** **1.** Of or like cheese. **2.** *U.S. Slang* Inferior. — **chees′i·ness** *n.*

chee·tah (chē′ta) *n.* An animal of the cat family, resembling the leopard, native to SW Asia and northern Africa. [< Hind. *chītā* leopard < Skt. *chitraka* speckled]

chef (shef) *n.* A head cook; also, any cook. [< F *chef* (de *cuisine*) head (of the kitchen) < OF]

cheg·oe (cheg′ō) *n.* The chigoe (def. 1).

cheilo- See CHILO-.

cheiro- See CHIRO-.

che·la (kē′lə) *n. pl.* **·lae** (-lē) *Zool.* A pincerlike claw in crustaceans and arachnids. [< NL < Gk. *chēlē* claw] — **che·late** (kē′lāt) *adj.*

chem·i·cal (kem′i·kəl) *adj.* Of or pertaining to chemistry or its phenomena, laws, operations, or results. — *n.* A substance obtained by or used in a chemical process. [< F < Med.L *alchimicus* of alchemy] — **chem′i·cal·ly** *adv.*

chemical warfare The technique of using smoke screens, gases, incendiary materials, etc., in warfare.

che·mise (sha·mēz′) *n.* **1.** A woman's loose undergarment resembling a short slip. **2.** A dress hanging straight from the shoulders. [< OF < LL *camisia* shirt]

chem·ist (kem′ist) *n.* **1.** One versed in chemistry. **2.** *Brit.* A druggist. [< ALCHEMIST]

chem·is·try (kem′is·trē) *n. pl.* **·tries** **1.** The science that treats of the structure, composition, and properties of substances and of their transformations. **2.** Chemical composition or processes.

chemo- *combining form* Chemical; of or with chemicals or chemical reactions. Also **chemi-.** Also, before vowels, **chem-.**

chem·o·ther·a·py (kem′ō·ther′ə·pē, kē′mō-) *n. Med.* The treatment of infections by the use of chemically synthesized drugs. Also **chem′o·ther′a·peu′tics.** — **chem′o·ther′a·peu′tic** *adj.* — **chem′o·ther′a·pist** *n.*

chem·ur·gy (kem′ər·jē) *n.* The chemical exploitation of organic raw materials, esp. agricultural products, in the industrial development of new products. — **chem·ur·gic** (kem·ûr′jik) or **·gi·cal** *adj.*

che·nille (sha·nēl′) *n.* **1.** A soft, fuzzy cord, used for embroidery, fringes, etc. **2.** A fabric made with filling of this cord, used for rugs, bedspreads, or the like. [< F < L *canicula*, dim. of *canis* dog]

cheque (chek) *n. Brit.* A check (def. 6).

chequer (chek′ər) *n. Brit.* A checker.

cher·ish (cher′ish) *v.t.* **1.** To hold dear; treat with tenderness; foster. **2.** To entertain fondly, as a hope or an idea to. [< OF *cheriss-*, stem of *cherir* to hold dear < L *carus*] — **cher′ish·er** *n.* — **cher′ish·ing·ly** *adv.*

Cher·o·kee (cher′ə·kē, cher′ə·kē′) *n. pl.* **·kee** or **·kees** **1.** One of a great tribe of Iroquoian Indians formerly occupying northern Georgia and North Carolina, now dwelling in Oklahoma. **2.** The Iroquoian language of this tribe.

Cherokee rose A trailing shrub having large, solitary white flowers: the State flower of Georgia.

---

che·root (shə·rōōt') *n.* A cigar cut square at both ends: also spelled *sheroot.* [< F < Tamil *shuruttu* roll, cigar]

cher·ry (cher'ē) *n. pl.* **·ries** 1. Any of various trees of the rose family, related to the plum and the peach and bearing small, round or heart-shaped drupes enclosing a smooth pit. 2. The wood or fruit of a cherry tree. 3. A bright red color resembling that of certain cherries: also **cherry red.** — *adj.* 1. Bright red. 2. Made of or with cherries. 3. Made of cherry wood. [ME *chery* < L *cerasus* cherry tree]

cher·ub (cher'əb) *n. pl.* **cher·ubs** or **cher·u·bim** (cher'ə-bim, -yə-bim) *for def. 1,* **cherubs** *for def. 2,* **cherubim** *for def. 3* 1. A representation of a beautiful winged child, the accepted type of the angelic cherub. 2. A beautiful child; also, a chubby, innocent-looking adult. 3. In Scripture, a celestial being. [< LL < Hebrew *kerūb,* an angelic being] — **che·ru·bic** (chə·rōō'bik) *adj.* — **che·ru'bi·cal·ly** *adv.*

cher·vil (chûr'vəl) *n.* A garden herb of the parsley family, the young leaves of which are used for soups, salads, etc. [OE < L < Gk. *chairephyllon*]

cher·vo·nets (cher·vô'nets) *n. pl.* **·vont·si** (-vônt'sē) A former gold monetary unit of the U.S.S.R. [< Russian]

Chesh·ire cat (chesh'ər, -ir) In Lewis Carroll's *Alice's Adventures in Wonderland,* a grinning cat that gradually faded away until only its grin remained.

chess (ches) *n.* A game of skill played on a chessboard by two persons, with 16 pieces on each side. The aim of each player is to checkmate his opponent's king. [< OF *esches,* pl. of *eschec* < Arabic *shāh* king < Persian]

chess·board (ches'bôrd', -bōrd') *n.* A board divided into 64 alternately colored squares, used in playing chess.

chess·man (ches'man', -mən) *n. pl.* **·men** (men', -mən) Any of the pieces used in playing chess.

chest (chest) *n.* 1. The part of the body enclosed by the ribs; thorax. ◆ Collateral adjective: *pectoral.* 2. A box, usu. with a hinged lid, for storing or protecting articles, as tools, jewelry, etc. 3. The treasury of a public institution; also, the funds contained there. 4. A chest of drawers. [< OE < L < Gk. *kistē* basket, box]

ches·ter·field (ches'tər·fēld') *n.* 1. A single-breasted topcoat, generally with concealed buttons. 2. *Chiefly Canadian* A sofa. [after a 19th c. Earl of *Chesterfield*]

Ches·ter·field·i·an (ches'tər·fēl'dē·ən) *adj.* 1. Of or pertaining to Lord Chesterfield. 2. Suave; polished; elegant.

chest·nut (ches'nut', -nət) *n.* 1. The edible nut of various trees of the beech family, growing in a prickly bur; also, a tree that bears this nut. 2. One of certain similar trees, or their fruit, as the horse chestnut. 3. A reddish brown color. 4. A horse of this color. 5. *Informal* **a** A stale joke. **b** Anything trite, as a story, song, etc. — *adj.* Reddish brown. [ME < OF < L < Gk. *kastanea* + NUT]

chest of drawers A piece of furniture containing a set of drawers for storing linens, clothing, etc.

chest·y (ches'tē) *adj.* **chest·i·er, chest·i·est** *Informal* 1. Self-assertive; proud. 2. Large in the chest.

che·val-de-frise (shə·val'də·frēz') *n. pl.* **che·vaux-de-frise** (shə·vō'-) A protecting line, as of broken glass or spikes, on top of a wall. [< F, lit., horse of Friesland]

che·val glass (shə·val') A long mirror mounted on horizontal pivots in a frame.

chev·a·lier (shev'ə·lir') *n.* 1. A member of certain orders of knighthood or honor, as of the French Legion of Honor. 2. A knight or cavalier. 3. A chivalrous man; a gallant. [< OF *chevalier* < LL < L *caballus* horse]

chev·i·ot (shev'ē·ət) *n.* A rough cloth of twill weave, used for suits, overcoats, etc., originally made from Cheviot wool.

Chev·i·ot (chev'ē·ət, chē'vē-) *n.* One of a breed of large sheep, originating in the Cheviot Hills, esteemed for their wool (Cheviot wool).

chev·ron (shev'rən) *n.* An emblem or insignia usu. consisting of stripes meeting at an angle, worn on a uniform sleeve to indicate rank, length of service, etc., used by military, naval, and police forces. [< OF, chevron, rafter]

chev·y (chev'ē) *n. pl.* **chev·ies** *Brit.* A hunt, or a shout in hunting. — *v.* **chev·ied, chev·y·ing** *v.t.* 1. To chase about; hunt. 2. To harass; worry. — *v.i.* 3. To race; scamper. Also *chivy, chivvy.* [Prob. < *Chevy* Chase]

chew (chōō) *v.t. & v.i.* 1. To crush or grind with the teeth; masticate. 2. To meditate upon; consider carefully. — **to chew out** *U.S. Slang* To reprimand severely; berate. — *n.* 1. The act of chewing. 2. That which is chewed; a quid; cut. [OE *cēowan*] — **chew'er** *n.*

chew·ing gum (chōō'ing) A preparation of some natural gum, usu. chicle, flavored for chewing.

che·wink (chi·wingk') *n.* The towhee, a bird. [Imit.]

chew·y (chōō'ē) *adj.* **chew·i·er, chew·i·est** Relatively soft and requiring chewing: Caramels are *chewy.*

Chey·enne (chī·en') *n. pl.* **·enne** or **·ennes** One of a tribe of North American Indians now inhabiting Montana and Oklahoma.

chi (kī) *n.* The twenty-second letter in the Greek alphabet (X, χ), transliterated as *ch.* See ALPHABET. [< Gk.]

chi·an·ti (kē·an'tē, *Ital.* kyän'tē) *n.* A dry, red, Italian wine; also, any similar wine. [after Monti *Chianti,* a region in Italy]

chi·a·ro·scu·ro (kē·är'ə·skyōōr'ō) *n. pl.* **·ros** 1. The distribution and treatment of light and shade in a picture. 2. A kind of painting or drawing using only light and shade. 3. An artist's treatment of light and shade. Also **chi·a·ro·scu·ro** (kē·är'ə·ō·skyōōr'ō). < Ital. < L < *clarus* clear + *obscurus* dark] — **chi·a·ro·scu'rist** *n.*

chic (shēk. shik) *adj.* Smart; stylish; elegant. — *n.* Originality, elegance, and taste, esp. in dress. [< F]

chi·cane (shi·kān') *v.* **·caned, ·can·ing** *v.t.* 1. To deceive by chicanery; trick. 2. To quibble about. — *v.i.* 3. To resort to chicanery; use tricks. — *n.* Chicanery. [< F *chicaner*]

chi·can·er·y (shi·kā'nər·ē) *n. pl.* **·er·ies** 1. Trickery and subterfuge; sophistry; quibbling. 2. A trick; quibble.

Chi·ca·no (chi·kä'nō) *n. pl.* **·nos** *U.S.* A Mexican-American.

chic·co·ry (chik'ər·ē) See CHICORY.

chi·chi (shē'shē) *adj. Informal* Ostentatiously stylish or elegant. [< F, frill]

chick (chik) *n.* 1. A young chicken. 2. Any young bird. 3. A child. 4. *U.S. Slang* A girl. [Short for CHICKEN]

chick·a·dee (chik'ə·dē) *n.* An American titmouse with the top of the head and the throat black or dark colored. [Imit. of its cry]

chick·a·ree (chik'ə·rē) *n.* The red squirrel. See under SQUIRREL. [Imit. of its cry]

Chick·a·saw (chik'ə·sô) *n. pl.* **·saw** or **·saws** One of a tribe of Muskhogean North American Indians now living in Oklahoma.

chick·en (chik'ən) *n.* 1. The young of domestic fowl. 2. A cock or hen of any age. 3. The flesh of the chicken, used as food. 4. *Informal* A child or a young person: now chiefly in the phrase **no chicken,** one no longer young. — *adj. U.S. Slang* Afraid, cowardly. — *v.i. U.S. Slang* To lose one's nerve: often with *out.* [OE *cicen*]

CHICKADEE (5¾ inches long; tail 2¾ inches; wingspread 8½ inches)

chicken feed *Slang* 1. Small change, as pennies, nickels, dimes, etc. 2. Food for chickens.

chicken hawk Any of various hawks that prey on poultry.

chick·en-heart·ed (chik'ən·här'tid) *adj.* Cowardly.

chicken pox *Pathol.* A contagious disease, principally of children, characterized by skin eruptions and a slight fever.

chick·pea (chik'pē') *n.* 1. A plant of Mediterranean regions and central Asia. 2. Its seed, widely used as a food. [ME *chichpease*]

chick·weed (chik'wēd) *n.* Any of various weeds having seeds and leaves that birds eat.

chic·le (chik'əl) *n.* The milky juice or latex of the sapodilla, used as the basic principle of chewing gum. Also **chicle gum.** [< Sp. < Nahuatl *chicili*]

chic·o·ry (chik'ər·ē) *n. pl.* **·ries** 1. A perennial herb, having usu. blue flowers and used as a salad plant. 2. Its dried, roasted, and ground roots, used for mixing with coffee or as a coffee substitute. [< MF < L < Gk. *kichora*]

chide (chīd) *v.t. & v.i.* **chid·ed** or **chid** (chid), **chid·ed** or **chid** or **chid·den** (chid'n), **chid·ing** To speak reprovingly (to); scold. [OE *cīdan*] — **chid'er** *n.* — **chid'ing·ly** *adv.*

chief (chēf) *n.* 1. *Often cap.* The person highest in rank or authority, as the leader or head of a tribe, band, police force, government bureau, etc. 2. *Usu. cap.* A ship's chief engineer; also, a chief petty officer. 3. *Slang* A boss. — **in chief** Having the highest authority: commander *in chief.* — *adj.* 1. Highest in rank or authority. 2. Most important or eminent; leading. [< OF *chef, chief* < L *caput* head]

chief justice The presiding judge of a court composed of several justices.

chief·ly (chēf'lē) *adv.* 1. Most of all; above all; especially. 2. Principally; mainly. — *adj.* Of or like a chief.

chief of staff *U.S.* The principal staff officer of a division or a higher level.

Chief of Staff *U.S.* The ranking officer in the Army or Air Force, responsible to the Secretary of his department.

chief·tain (chēf'tən) *n.* 1. The head of a clan or tribe. 2. Any chief; leader. [< OF < LL < L *caput* head] — **chief'tain·cy, chief'tain·ship** *n.*

chif·fon (shi·fon', shif'on) *n.* 1. A sheer silk or rayon fabric. 2. *pl.* Ornamental adjuncts of feminine attire, as ribbons or lace. — *adj.* 1. Of or pertaining to chiffon. 2. In cooking, having a fluffy texture. [< F, dim. of *chiffe* rag]

chif·fo·nier (shif'ə·nir') *n.* A high chest of drawers, often with a mirror at the top. Also **chif·fon·nier'.** [< F < *chiffon*]

chig·ger (chig'ər) *n.* 1. The larva of various mites of the southern U.S., that attaches itself to the skin, causing intense itching. 2. The chigoe (def. 1). [Alter. of CHIGOE]

chi·gnon (shēn'yon, *Fr.* shē·nyôn') *n.* A knot or roll of hair worn at the back of the head by women. [< F]

chig·oe (chig'ō) *n.* 1. A flea of the West Indies and South America. 2. A chigger (def. 1) [< Carib]

Chi·hua·hua (chi-wä′wä) *n.* One of an ancient breed of very small, smooth-coated dogs with large, pointed ears, originally native to Mexico. [after *Chihuahua*, Mexico]

chil- Var. of CHILO-.

chil·blain (chil′blān) *n. Pathol.* An inflammation of the hands or feet caused by exposure to cold.

child (chīld) *n. pl.* **chil·dren** 1. An offspring of human parents. 2. A boy or girl, most commonly one between infancy and youth. 3. A descendant. 4. A childish person. 5. A product of a specified condition, quality, etc.: a *child* of joy. **— with child** Pregnant. [OE *cild*] **— child′less** *adj.*

child·bear·ing (chīld′bâr′ing) *n.* The bringing forth of children.

child·bed (chīld′bed′) *n.* The state of a woman giving birth to a child.

child·birth (chīld′bûrth′) *n.* Parturition.

child·hood (chīld′hood) *n.* The state or time of being a child. [OE *cildhād*]

child·ish (chīl′dish) *adj.* 1. Of, like, or proper to a child. 2. Unduly like a child; immature; puerile; weak. [OE *cildisc*] **— child′ish·ly** *adv.* **— child′ish·ness** *n.*

child·like (chīld′līk′) *adj.* Like, characteristic of, or appropriate to a child; artless, docile, etc. **— child′like′ness** *n.*

chil·dren (chil′dren) Plural of CHILD.

child's play Something easy to do.

chil·i (chil′ē) *n. pl.* **chil·ies** 1. The acrid pod or fruit of the red pepper, used as a seasoning. 2. Chile con carne. Also **chil′e, chil′li.** [< Sp. < Nahuatl *chilli*]

chile con car·ne (kon kär′nē) A highly seasoned dish made with meat, chili, and often beans. [< Sp., chili with meat]

chili sauce A spiced tomato sauce made with chili.

chill (chil) *n.* 1. A sensation of cold, often with shivering. 2. A moderate degree of coldness. 3. A check to enthusiasm, joy, etc. 4. A numbing sensation of dread or anxiety. **— v.t.** 1. To reduce to a low temperature. 2. To affect with cold; seize with a chill. 3. To check, as ardor; dispirit. 4. To harden the surface of (metal) by sudden cooling. **— v.i.** 5. To become cold. 6. To be stricken with a chill. 7. To become hard by sudden cooling, as metal. **— adj.** 1. Moderately or unpleasantly cold. 2. Affected by or shivering with cold. 3. Cold in manner; distant. 4. Discouraging. [OE *ciele*] **— chill′ing·ly** *adv.* **— chill′ness** *n.*

chill·er (chil′ər) *n.* 1. That which chills. 2. A horror story or movie.

chill·y (chil′ē) *adj.* **chill·i·er, chill·i·est** 1. Causing chill; cold or chilling. 2. Feeling cold; affected by chill. 3. Disheartening; unfriendly. **— chill′i·ly** *adv.* **— chill′i·ness** *n.*

chilo- *combining form* Lip. Also spelled *cheilo-*: also, before vowels, *chil-.* [< Gk. *cheilos* lip]

chime¹ (chīm) *n.* 1. *Often pl.* A set of bells, as in a bell tower, tuned to a scale. 2. A single bell: the *chime* of a clock. 3. *Often pl.* The sounds or music produced by a chime. 4. Agreement; accord. **— v.** **— chimed, chim·ing** *v.t.* 1. To cause to sound musically by striking; ring. 2. To announce (the hour) by the sound of bells. 3. To summon, welcome, or send by chimes. 4. To say rhythmically; prate. **— v.i.** 5. To sound musically. 6. To ring chimes. 7. To harmonize; agree: with *with.* **— to chime in** 1. To join in harmoniously. 2. To join, and so interrupt, a conversation. [ME < L *cymbalum* cymbal] **— chim′er** *n.*

chime² (chīm) *n.* The rim of a cask, barrel, etc. Also **chimb** (chīm). [OE *cimb-* edge, as in *cimbing* joint]

chi·me·ra (kə-mir′ə, kī-) *n.* 1. An absurd creation of the imagination. 2. In painting, sculpture, etc., an imaginary, grotesque monster. [< L < Gk. *chimaira* she-goat]

chi·mer·i·cal (kə-mer′i·kəl, kī-) *adj.* 1. Of the nature of a chimera; fantastic; imaginary. 2. Given to fanciful dreams; visionary. Also **chi·mer′ic.** **— chi·mer′i·cal·ly** *adv.*

chim·ney (chim′nē) *n.* 1. A flue to conduct gases and smoke from a fire to the outer air. 2. A structure containing such a flue, usually vertical and rising above the roof of a building. 3. A smokestack; funnel. 4. A tube, usually of glass, for enclosing the flame of a lamp. 5. A vent of a volcano. [< OF *cheminee* < LL < L < Gk. *kaminos*]

chimney corner 1. The space between the jamb or side of a large fireplace and the fire. 2. The fireside.

chimney piece A mantel.

chimney pot A pipe placed on the top of a chimney to improve the draft and prevent smoking.

chimney sweep One whose occupation is the cleaning of soot from inside chimneys. Also **chimney sweeper.**

chim·pan·zee (chim′pan-zē′, chim·pan′zē) *n.* An arboreal anthropoid ape of equatorial Africa, having large ears and dark brown hair, and smaller and more intelligent than the gorilla. [< native West African name]

chin (chin) *n.* 1. The lower part of the face, between the mouth and the neck. 2. *Anat.* The central and anterior part of the lower jaw. **— v. chinned, chin·ning** *v.t.* 1. To

lift (oneself) while grasping an overhead bar until the chin is level with the hands. **— v.i.** 2. *U.S. Informal* To talk idly. 3. To chin oneself. [OE *cin*]

chi·na (chī′nə) *n.* 1. Fine porcelain or ceramic ware, originally made in China. 2. Any crockery. Also **chi′na·ware′.**

chi·na·ber·ry (chī′nə·ber′ē) *n. pl.* **·ries** 1. Either of two trees of the soapberry family, found in Mexico and the SW U.S. Also **China tree.** 2. Its berrylike fruit.

Chi·na·man (chī′nə·mən) *n. pl.* **·men** (mən) A Chinese: an offensive term.

Chi·na·town (chī′nə·toun′) The Chinese quarter of any city outside China.

chin·ca·pin (ching′kə·pin) See CHINQUAPIN.

chinch (chinch) *n.* 1. A small, brown and black hemipterous insect destructive to grain. Also **chinch bug.** 2. The bedbug. [< Sp. *chinche* < L *cimex* bug]

chin·chil·la (chin-chil′ə) *n.* 1. A small rodent native in the Andes. 2. The soft, valuable, pearl gray fur of the chinchilla. 3. A closely woven, twilled fabric having a tufted surface. [< Sp., ? alter. of Quechua *sinchi* strong]

chine¹ (chīn) *n.* 1. The spine, backbone, or back. 2. A piece of meat including all or part of the backbone. [< OF *eschine* backbone < Gmc.]

chine² (chīn) *n.* Chime².

Chi·nese (chī-nēz′, nēs) *adj.* Of or pertaining to China, its people, or their languages. **— n. pl. ·nese** 1. A native of China, or a person of Chinese ancestry. 2. The standard language of China.

Chinese lantern A collapsible lantern made of thin paper.

Chinese puzzle 1. An intricate puzzle originally made by the Chinese. 2. Any problem difficult to solve.

chink¹ (chingk) *n.* A small, narrow cleft; crevice. **— v.t.** 1. To make cracks or fissures in. 2. To fill the cracks of, as a wall; plug up. [ME *chynke*] **— chink′y** *adj.*

chink² (chingk) *n.* 1. A short, sharp, metallic sound. 2. *Slang* Coin; cash. **— v.t. & v.i.** To make or cause to make a sharp, clinking sound. [Imit.]

chi·no (chē′nō) *n.* 1. A strong cotton fabric with a twilled weave. 2. *pl.* Boys' or men's trousers of this material. [< Sp., toasted; ref. to the original tan color]

Chino- *combining form* Connected with China.

chi·nook (chi-nook′, -nook′) *n. U.S. & Canadian* 1. A warm wind of the Oregon and Washington coasts. 2. A warm, dry wind that blows off the eastern slopes of the Rocky Mountains in the NW U.S. and western Canada. [after *Chinook*]

Chi·nook (chi-nook′, -nook′) *n. pl.* **·nook** or **·nooks** 1. One of a tribe of North American Indians formerly occupying the region of the Columbia River, Oregon. 2. The language of this tribe. **— Chi·nook′an** *adj. & n.*

Chinook jargon A pidgin language comprising words from Chinook, mixed with English, French, etc.

Chinook salmon A salmon of North Pacific coastal waters.

chin·qua·pin (ching′kə·pin) *n.* 1. Any of several trees of North America. 2. A related tree of the Pacific coast. 3. The edible nut of these trees. Also **chin′ka·pin.** [< N. Am. Ind.]

chintz (chints) *n.* A cotton fabric usu. glazed and printed in bright colors. Also **chints.** [< Skt. *chitra* variegated]

chip (chip) *n.* 1. A small piece cut or broken off. 2. A small disk or counter used in certain games, as in poker. 3. A crack or imperfection caused by chipping. 4. A thinly sliced morsel: potato *chips.* 5. *pl. Brit.* French fried potatoes. 6. *Usu. pl.* Dried animal droppings used as fuel. 7. Anything of little or no value. 8. Wood, palm leaves, etc., cut into strips for weaving. **— a chip off (or of) the old block** One who resembles either of his parents in behavior, appearance, etc. **— a chip on one's shoulder** A willingness to take offense; belligerent manner. **— in the chips** *Slang* Possessing money; affluent. **— v. chipped, chip·ping** *v.t.* 1. To break off small pieces of, as china. **— v.i.** 2. To become chipped. **— to chip in** *Informal* To contribute, as to a fund. [ME *chippe*]

Chip·e·wy·an (chip-ə-wī′ən) *n.* 1. One of a tribe of Indians living in NW Canada. 2. The language of this tribe.

chip·munk (chip′mungk) *n.* Any of various striped North American rodents of the squirrel family: also called *ground squirrel.* Also **chip·muck** (chip′muk). [< N. Am. Ind.]

chipped beef (chipt) Beef smoked and sliced thin.

Chip·pen·dale (chip′ən·dāl) *adj.* Designating or in the style of a graceful, rococo type of furniture made in 18th-century England. [after Thomas *Chippendale*, 1718–79, English cabinetmaker.]

chip·per (chip′ər) *adj. U.S. Informal* 1. Brisk; cheerful. 2. Smartly dressed; spruce. [< Brit. Dial. *kipper* frisky]

CHIPMUNK
(About 6½ inches long; tail 4½ inches)

Chip·pe·wa (chip′ə·wä, -wā, -wə) *n. pl.* **·wa** or **·was** Ojibwa. Also **Chip·pe·way** (chip′ə·wā).

chip·py (chip′ē) *n. pl.* **·pies** 1. A chipmunk. 2. *Slang* A young woman of easy morals; also, a prostitute.

chip shot In golf, a short, lofted shot made in approaching the green.

chiro- *combining form* Hand; of or with the hand: *chirography.* Also spelled *cheiro-.* Also, before vowels, **chir-.** [< Gk. *cheir, cheiros* hand]

chi·rog·ra·phy (kī·rog′rə·fē) *n.* The art, style, or character of handwriting. — **chi·rog′ra·pher** *n.* — **chi·ro·graph·ic** (kī′rə·graf′ik) or **·i·cal** *adj.*

chi·ro·man·cy (kī′rə·man′sē) *n.* Palmistry. [< F < Gk. < *cheir* hand + *manteia* divination] — **chi′ro·man′cer** *n.*

chi·rop·o·dy (kə·rop′ə·dē, kī-) *n.* The branch of medicine that deals with ailments of the foot: also called *pedicure, podiatry.* [< CHIRO- + Gk. *podos* foot] — **chi·rop′o·dist** *n.*

chi·ro·prac·tic (kī′rə·prak′tik) *n.* A medical therapy based on the manipulation of bodily structures, esp. the spinal column. [< CHIRO- + Gk. *praktikos* effective] — **chi·ro·prac·tor** (kī′rə·prak′tər) *n.*

chirp (chûrp) *v.i.* 1. To give a short, acute cry, as a sparrow or locust; cheep, as a young bird. 2. To talk in a quick and shrill manner. — *v.t.* 3. To utter with a quick, sharp sound. — *n.* The sound of chirping. [Var. of CHIRK] — **chirp′er** *n.*

chirr (chûr) *v.i.* To make a sharp trilling sound, as that of the grasshopper, cicada, and some birds. — *n.* The trilling sound of crickets, locusts, etc. Also **chirre.** [Imit.]

chir·rup (chir′əp) *v.i.* 1. To chirp continuously or repeatedly, as a bird. 2. To chirp with the lips, as in urging a horse. — *v.t.* 3. To utter with chirps. — *n.* A sound of chirruping. [< CHIRP] — **chir′rup·y** *adj.*

chis·el (chiz′əl) *n.* A cutting tool with a beveled edge, used for cutting, engraving, or mortising metal, stone, or wood. — *v.t. & v.i.* **chis·eled** or **·elled, chis·el·ing** or **·el·ling** 1. To cut, engrave, or carve with or as with a chisel. 2. *Slang* To cheat; swindle; also, to obtain by dishonest methods. [< AF < L *caedere* to cut] — **chis′el·er** or **chis′el·ler** *n.*

chit[1] (chit) *n.* 1. A voucher of a sum owed, as for food. 2. *Brit.* A memorandum: also **chit′ty.** [< Hind. *chitthī* note]

chit[2] (chit) *n.* A pert girl. [ME *chit*]

chit·chat (chit′chat′) *n.* 1. Small talk. 2. Gossip.

chi·tin (kī′tin) *n. Biochem.* A horny substance forming the hard outer covering of insects and crustaceans. [< F < Gk. *chitōn* tunic]. — **chi′tin·ous** *adj.*

chit·ter·lings (chit′ər·lingz) *n.pl.* The small intestines of pigs, esp. as used for food; also **chit′lin** (chit′lin), **chit′·ling.** [Cf. G. *kutteln* entrails]

chiv·al·ric (shiv′əl·rik, shi·val′rik) *adj.* Chivalrous.

chiv·al·rous (shiv′əl·rəs) *adj.* 1. Having the qualities of the ideal knight; gallant, courteous, generous, etc. 2. Pertaining to chivalry. [< OF < *chevalier* knight] — **chiv′al·rous·ly** *adv.* — **chiv′al·rous·ness** *n.*

chiv·al·ry (shiv′əl·rē) *n.* 1. The feudal system of knighthood. 2. The spirit or principles of this system; knighterrantry. 3. The ideal qualities of knighthood, as courtesy, valor, skill in arms, etc. 4. A body of knights, gallant gentlemen, etc. [< OF < LL *caballarius* cavalier]

chiv·a·ree (shiv′ə·rē′) See CHARIVARI.

chive (chīv) *n.* A perennial herb allied to the leek and onion, used as a flavoring in cooking. [< AF < L *cepa* onion]

chiv·y (chiv′ē), **chiv·vy** See CHEVY (def. 1).

chlor- Var. of CHLORO-.

chlo·ral (klôr′əl, klō′rəl) *n. Chem.* 1. A colorless, oily, liquid compound, CCl_3CHO, with a penetrating odor. 2. A white, crystalline, pungent compound, $CCl_3CHO·H_2O$, used medicinally as a hypnotic: also **chloral hydrate.** [< CHLOR(INE) + AL(COHOL)]

chlo·ram·phen·i·col (klôr′am·fen′i·kōl, -kol, klō′ram-) *n. Chem.* A crystalline nitrogenous compound, $C_{11}H_{12}Cl_2O_5N_2$, used as an antibiotic.

chlo·rate (klôr′āt, klō′rāt) *n. Chem.* A salt of chloric acid.

chlor·dane (klôr′dān, klō′r-) *n. Chem.* A toxic compound of chlorine, $C_{10}H_6Cl_8$ used as a fumigant and insecticide.

chlo·ric (klôr′ik, klō′rik) *adj. Chem.* Of, pertaining to, or combined with chlorine in its higher valence.

chlo·ride (klôr′īd, klō′rīd, -rid) *n. Chem.* A compound of chlorine with a more positive element or radical. Also **chlo·rid** (klôr′id, klō′rid). — **chlo·rid·ic** (klə·rid′ik) *adj.*

chloride of lime *Chem.* A disinfecting and bleaching agent made by the action of chlorine on slaked lime.

chlo·rin·ate (klôr′ə·nāt, klō′rə-) *v.t.* **·at·ed, ·at·ing** *Chem.* To treat or cause to combine with chlorine, as in purifying water, whitening fabrics, etc. — **chlo·rin·a′tion** *n.*

chlo·rine (klôr′ēn, -in, klō′rēn, -rin) *n.* A greenish yellow, poisonous, gaseous element (symbol Cl), with a suffocating odor, widely used as a bleach and disinfectant. Also **chlo·rin** (klôr′in, klō′rin). See ELEMENT. [< Gk. *chlōros* green]

chloro- *combining form* 1. Light green: *chlorophyll.* 2. Chlorine. Also, before vowels, **chlor-.** [< Gk. *chlōros* green]

chlo·ro·form (klôr′ə·fôrm, klō′rə-) *n. Chem.* A colorless, volatile, sweetish liquid compound, $CHCl_3$, used as an anesthetic and solvent. — *v.t.* 1. To administer chloroform to. 2. To anesthetize or kill with chloroform.

Chlo·ro·my·ce·tin (klôr′ə·mī·sē′tən, klō′rə-) *n.* Proprietary name for a brand of chloramphenicol, used as an antibiotic: also **chlo′ro·my·ce′tin.**

chlo·ro·phyll (klôr′ə·fil, klō′rə-) *n. Biochem.* The green nitrogenous coloring matter contained in the chloroplasts of plants, essential to the production of carbohydrates by photosynthesis. Also **chlo′ro·phyl.** [< CHLORO- + Gk. *phyllon* leaf] — **chlo·ro·phyl·la·ceous** (klôr′ə·fi·lā′shəs, klō′rə-), **chlo′ro·phyl′lose** (-fil′ōs), **chlo′ro·phyl′lous** (-fil′əs) *adj.*

chlo·ro·plast (klôr′ə·plast, klō′rə-) *n. Bot.* One of the flattened bodies containing chlorophyll. Also **chlo′ro·plas′tid.**

chlor·pro·ma·zine (klôr·prō′mə·zēn, -zin, klôr-) *n.* A synthetic tranquilizing drug used to control severe excitement in certain mental disorders.

chock (chok) *n.* 1. A block or wedge, so placed as to prevent or limit motion. 2. *Naut.* **a** A heavy piece of metal or wood fastened to a deck, etc., and having jaws through which a rope or cable may pass. **b** A block or support on which to rest a boat, etc. — *v.t.* 1. To make fast or fit with a chock or chocks. 2. To place on chocks, as a boat. — *adv.* As far or as close as possible. [< AF *choque* log]

chock-a-block (chok′ə·blok′) *adj.* 1. Drawn to the limit, with blocks touching: said of a tackle. 2. Close together; jammed. — *adv.* Close; very near.

chock-full (chok′fool′) *adj.* Completely full; stuffed: also *choke-full, chuck-full.* [ME *chokke-fulle*]

choc·o·late (chôk′lit, chôk′ə·lit, chok′-) *n.* 1. A preparation of cacao nuts roasted and ground and usu. sweetened. 2. A beverage or confection made from this. 3. A dark brown color. — *adj.* Flavored with or made with chocolate. [< Sp. < Nahuatl *chocolatl*] — **choc′o·lat·y** *adj.*

Choc·taw (chok′tô) *n. pl.* **·taw** or **·taws** 1. A member of a tribe of North American Indians of Muskhogean stock, now living in Oklahoma. 2. The language of this tribe.

choice (chois) *n.* 1. The act of choosing; selection. 2. The right or privilege of choosing; option. 3. The person or thing chosen. 4. A number or variety from which to choose: a great *choice* of dishes. 5. A well-selected supply. 6. An alternative: He had no *choice.* 7. The best or preferred part of anything. 8. Excellence: wine of *choice.* — *adj.* **choic·er, choic·est** 1. Select; excellent. 2. Chosen with care. [< OF < *choisir* to choose] — **choice′ly** *adv.* — **choice′ness** *n.*

choir (kwīr) *n.* 1. An organized body of singers, esp. in a church. 2. The part of a church occupied by such singers; chancel. — *v.i.* 1. To sing, as in a choir. — *v.t.* 2. To sing or utter in chorus. [< OF *cuer* < L *chorus*]

choke (chōk) *v.* **choked, chok·ing** *v.t.* 1. To stop the breathing of by obstructing the windpipe; strangle. 2. To keep back; suppress. 3. To obstruct or close up by filling; clog. 4. To retard the progress, growth, or action of. 5. To lessen the air intake of the carburetor in order to enrich the fuel mixture of (a gasoline engine). — *v.i.* 6. To become suffocated or stifled. 7. To become clogged, fouled, or obstructed. — **to choke up** 1. To be overcome by emotion, tears, etc. 2. To perform poorly because of tension, agitation, etc. — *n.* 1. The act or sound of choking. 2. *Mech.* A device to control the flow of air, as to a gasoline engine. [OE *acēocian*]

choke·bore (chōk′bôr′, -bōr′) *n.* In shotguns, a bore narrowed at the muzzle to concentrate the shot; also, a shotgun with such a bore.

choke·cher·ry (chōk′cher′ē) *n. pl.* **·ries** A wild cherry of North America, or its sour fruit.

choke·damp (chōk′damp′) *n.* Any condition of the atmosphere resulting in choking or suffocation.

choke-full (chōk′fool′) See CHOCK-FULL.

chok·er (chōk′kər) *n.* 1. One who or that which chokes. 2. *Informal* A neckcloth or necklace worn high around the throat; also, a high, tight collar. 3. A small fur neckpiece.

chok·y (chō′kē) *adj.* **chok·i·er, chok·i·est** 1. Causing one to choke. 2. Somewhat choked. Also **chok′ey.**

chole- *combining form* Bile; gall: *cholesterol.* Also **cholo-:** also, before vowels, **chol-.** [< Gk. *cholē* bile]

chol·er (kol′ər) *n.* Anger; hastiness of temper, formerly thought to be caused by an excess of bile. [< OF < L < Gk. *cholē* bile] — **chol′er·ic** *adj.*

chol·er·a (kol′ər·ə) *n. Pathol.* An acute, infectious, epidemic disease characterized principally by serious intestinal disorders. In its more malignant forms, as **Asiatic cholera,** it is usu. fatal. [< L < Gk. *cholē* bile]

cho·les·ter·ol (kə·les′tə·rōl, -rol) *n. Biochem.* A fatty, crystalline alcohol, $C_{27}H_{45}OH$, derived principally from bile, present in most gallstones, and very widely distributed in animal fats and tissues. Also **cho·les′ter·in** (-in). [< CHOLE- + Gk. *stereos* solid + -OL[2]]

chondro- *combining form* Cartilage. Also, before vowels, **chondr-.** [< Gk. *chondros* cartilage]

choose (chooz) *v.* **chose, cho·sen, choos·ing** *v.t.* **1.** To select as most desirable; take by preference. **2.** To desire or have a preference for. **3.** To prefer (to do something): He has *chosen* to remain. — *v.i.* **4.** To make a choice. — **cannot choose but** Must. [OE *cēosan*] — **choos′er** *n.*

choos·y (choo′zē) *adj.* **choos·i·er, choos·i·est** *Informal* Particular or fussy in one's choices. Also **choos′ey.**

chop¹ (chop) *v.* **chopped, chop·ping** *v.t.* **1.** To cut or make by strokes of a sharp tool: to *chop* a hole. **2.** To cut up in small pieces. **3.** To utter jerkily. **4.** To make a cutting, downward stroke at (the ball), as in tennis. — *v.i.* **5.** To make cutting strokes. **6.** To go, come, or move with sudden or violent motion. — *n.* **1.** The act of chopping. **2.** A piece chopped off; esp. a cut of meat, usu. lamb, pork, or veal. **3.** A sharp, downward blow or stroke, as in boxing, tennis, etc. **4.** A quick, broken motion of waves. **5.** A cleft or fissure. [ME *choppen*]

chop² (chop) *v.* **chopped, chop·ping** *v.i.* To veer suddenly; shift, as the wind.

chop³ (chop) *n.* **1.** *Usually pl.* A jaw; also the part of the face around the mouth or jaws. **2.** A sudden bite or snap. — *v.t.* **chopped, chop·ping** **1.** To utter in a quick, abrupt manner. **2.** To seize with the jaws; snap.

chop chop (chop′chop′) In Pidgin English, quickly!

chop·fal·len (chop′fô′lən) *adj.* Chapfallen.

chop·house (chop′hous′) *n.* An eating house specializing in chops and steaks.

chop·per (chop′ər) *n.* **1.** One who or that which chops, esp. a device that chops food. **2.** *pl. Slang* Teeth. **3.** *Slang* A helicopter.

chop·py¹ (chop′ē) *adj.* **·pi·er, ·pi·est 1.** Full of short, rough waves. **2.** Full of cracks or fissures. [< CHOP¹, *n.*]

chop·py² (chop′ē) *adj.* **·pi·er, ·pi·est** Variable, shifting, as wind. [< CHOP²]

chop·sticks (chop′stiks′) *n.pl.* Slender rods of ivory or wood, used in pairs by the Chinese, Japanese, etc., to convey food to the mouth. [< Pidgin English *chop* quick + STICK]

chop su·ey (soo′ē) A Chinese-American dish consisting of bits of meat or chicken, bean sprouts, onions, etc., served with rice. [< Chinese *tsa-sui*, lit., mixed pieces]

cho·ral (kôr′əl, kō′rəl) *adj.* Pertaining to, written for, or sung by a chorus or choir. — **cho′ral·ly** *adv.*

cho·rale (kô·ral′, kə-) *n.* A hymn marked by a simple melody, often sung in unison. Also **cho·ral′.** [< G *choral*]

chord¹ (kôrd) *n. Music* A combination of three or more tones sounded together. [Earlier *cord*, short for ACCORD]

chord² (kôrd) *n.* **1.** A string of a musical instrument. **2.** An emotional response or reaction. **3.** *Geom.* **a** A straight line connecting the extremities of an arc. **b** The portion of a straight line contained by its intersections with a curve. **4.** *Engin.* One of the principal members of a bridge truss. [< L < Gk. *chordē* string of a musical instrument] — **chord′al** *adj.*

CHORD
(def. 3)
Lines *cb* and *ab* are chords respectively of arcs *cab* and *ab*.

chor·date (kôr′dāt) *Zool. n.* Any of a large phylum of the animal kingdom that includes the vertebrates and whose members are characterized by an internal skeleton (in primitive forms a notochord) and a dorsally located central nervous system. — *adj.* Of, pertaining to, or belonging to this phylum or to a chordate. [< NL < L < Gk. *chordē*.]

chore (chôr, chōr) *n. U.S.* **1.** A small or minor job. **2.** An unpleasant or hard task. Also, *Brit.*, **char, chare.**

cho·re·a (kô·rē′ə, kō-) *n. Pathol.* An acute nervous disease characterized by involuntary and uncontrollable muscular twitching: also called *St. Vitus' dance.* [< NL < Gk. *choreia* dance] — **cho·re′al, cho·re′ic** *adj.*

choreo- *combining form* Dance. Also **choro-.** [< Gk. *choreia* dance]

cho·re·og·ra·pher (kôr′ē·og′rə·fər, kō′rē-) *n.* One who devises ballet and other dance compositions.

cho·re·og·ra·phy (kôr′ē·og′rə·fē, kō′rē-) *n.* **1.** The devising of ballets and incidental dances, esp. for the stage. **2.** The written representation of figures and steps of dancing. **3.** The art of dancing; ballet. Also **cho·reg·ra·phy** (kə·reg′rə·fē). — **cho·re·o·graph·ic** (kôr′ē·ə·graf′ik, kō′rē-) *adj.*

cho·ric (kôr′ik, kō′rik) *adj.* Of or like a chorus (defs. 7–9).

chor·is·ter (kôr′is·tər, kor′-) *n.* **1.** A member of a choir; esp., a choirboy. **2.** A leader of a choir. [< AF < L *chorus*]

cho·roid (kôr′oid, kō′roid) *Anat. adj.* Pertaining to or designating a highly vascular membrane. — *n.* The vascular tunic of the eyeball, between the sclera and the retina. For illus. see EYE. Also **cho·ri·oid** (kôr′ē·oid, kō′rē-).

chor·tle (chôr′təl) *v.t. & v.i.* **·tled, ·tling** To utter or utter with chuckles of glee. — *n.* A chuckle; joyful vocal sound. [Blend of CHUCKLE and SNORT; coined by Lewis Carroll]

cho·rus (kôr′əs, kō′rəs) *n.* **1.** A musical composition, usu. in parts, to be sung by a large group. **2.** A group of singers who perform such works. **3.** A body of singers and dancers who perform together in opera, musical comedy, etc. **4.** A group of persons singing or speaking something simultaneously. **5.** A simultaneous utterance of words, cries, etc., by many individuals. **6.** A refrain, as of a song. **7.** In ancient Greece, a ceremonial dance, usu. religious, accompanied by the singing of odes. **8.** In Greek drama, a body of actors who comment upon and sometimes take part in the main action of a play. **9.** The part of a drama performed by a chorus. — *v.t. & v.i.* **cho·rused** or **·russed, cho·rus·ing** or **·rus·sing** To sing or speak all together in unison. [< L < Gk. *choros* dance]

chorus girl A woman in the chorus of a musical comedy, etc. — **chorus boy** *masc.*

chose (chōz) Past tense of CHOOSE.

cho·sen (chō′zən) Past participle of CHOOSE. — *adj.* **1.** Made an object of choice; selected. **2.** *Theol.* Elect.

chow (chou) *n.* **1.** A medium-sized dog having a thick, brown or black coat: also **chow-chow.** **2.** *Slang* Food.

chow-chow (chou′chou′) *n.* **1.** A relish of chopped mixed vegetables pickled in mustard. **2.** Chow¹ (def. 1). [< Pidgin English]

chow·der (chou′dər) *n.* A dish usu. made of clams or fish stewed with vegetables, often in milk. [< F *chaudière* kettle < *calidus* hot]

chow·mein (chou′mān′) A Chinese-American dish made of shredded meat, onions, celery, etc., stewed and served with fried noodles. [< Chinese *ch'ao* to fry + *mein* flour]

chrism (kriz′əm) *n. Eccl.* **1.** Consecrated oil used for anointing at baptism, confirmation, unction, etc. **2.** Any sacramental anointing. [OE < LL < Gk. *chriein* to anoint]

Christ (krīst) *n.* **1.** The Anointed; the Messiah: the deliverer of Israel foretold by the Hebrew prophets. **2.** Jesus of Nazareth, regarded as fulfilling this prophecy: at first a title (*Jesus the Christ*), later a proper name (*Jesus Christ*). [OE < L < Gk. *Christos* (< *chriein* to anoint); trans. of Hebrew *māshīah* anointed] — **Christ′li·ness** *n.* — **Christ′ly** *adv.*

chris·ten (kris′ən) *v.t.* **1.** To name in baptism. **2.** To administer Christian baptism to. **3.** To give a name to. **4.** *Informal* To use for the first time. [See CHRIST.]

Chris·ten·dom (kris′ən·dəm) *n.* **1.** Christian lands. **2.** Christians collectively.

chris·ten·ing (kris′ən·ing) *n.* A Christian baptismal ceremony, esp. the baptizing of an infant.

Chris·tian (kris′chən) *adj.* **1.** Professing or following the religion of Christ; esp., affirming the divinity of Christ. **2.** Relating to or derived from Christ or his doctrine. **3.** Characteristic of Christianity or Christendom. **4.** *Informal* Human; civilized; decent. — *n.* **1.** One who believes in or professes belief in Jesus as the Christ; a member of any of the Christian churches. **2.** *Informal* A civilized, decent, or respectable person. — **Chris′tian·ly** *adv.*

Christian era The era beginning at the approximate date of Christ's birth, but now considered four to six years too late. Dates in this era are denoted A.D., those before it, B.C.

Chris·ti·an·i·ty (kris′chē·an′ə·tē) *n.* **1.** The Christian religion. **2.** Christians collectively. **3.** The state of being a Christian.

Chris·tian·ize (kris′chən·īz) *v.* **·ized, ·iz·ing** *v.t.* **1.** To convert to Christianity. **2.** To imbue with Christian principles, etc. — **Chris′tian·i·za′tion** *n.* — **Chris′tian·iz′er** *n.*

Christian name A baptismal name.

Christian Science A religion and system of healing, founded in 1866 by Mary Baker Eddy: officially called the **Church of Christ, Scientist.** — **Christian Scientist**

Christ·like (krīst′līk′) *adj.* Resembling Christ; having the spirit of Christ. — **Christ′like′ness** *n.*

Christ·mas (kris′məs) *n.* December 25, held as the anniversary of the birth of Jesus Christ and widely observed as a holy day or a holiday. Also **Christmas Day.**

Christmas Eve The evening before Christmas Day.

Christ·mas·tide (kris′mas·tīd′) *n.* The season of Christmas extending from Christmas Eve to Epiphany (Jan. 6).

Christmas tree An evergreen tree decorated with ornaments and lights at Christmas.

chrom- Var. of CHROMO-.

chro·mate (krō′māt) *n. Chem.* A salt of chromic acid.

chro·mat·ic (krō·mat′ik) *adj.* **1.** Pertaining to color or colors. **2.** *Music* Of or pertaining to a chromatic scale, or to an instrument that can play such a scale. — **chro·mat′i·cal·ly** *adv.*

chro·mat·ics (krō·mat′iks) *n.pl.* (construed as *sing.*) The science of colors.

chromatic scale *Music* A scale proceeding by semitones.

chro·ma·tin (krō′mə·tin) *n. Biol.* The readily stainable substance in the protoplasm of the cell nucleus, developing into chromosomes during mitosis. For illus. see CELL.

chromato- *combining form* Color; coloring or pigmentation. Also, before vowels, **chromat-**. [< Gk. *chrōma*, *-atos* color]

chro·ma·tog·ra·phy (krō/mə·tog/rə·fē) *n. Chem.* A method for the analysis of mixtures, in which a solution is passed through a column of powder that selectively adsorbs the constituents in one or more sharply defined, often colored bands. — **chro·mat·o·graph·ic** (krō·mat/ə·graf/ik) *adj.*

chrome (krōm) *n.* 1. Chrome yellow. 2. Chromium. — *v.t.* **chromed, chrom·ing** To plate with chromium. [< F < Gk. *chrōma* color]

-chrome *combining form* 1. Color; colored. 2. *Chem.* Chromium. [< Gk. *chrōma* color]

chrome steel *Metall.* A very hard steel alloyed with chromium. Also **chromium steel.**

chro·mic (krō/mik) *adj. Chem.* 1. Of, from, or pertaining to chromium. 2. Pertaining to compounds of chromium in its higher valence.

chromic acid *Chem.* An acid, H_2CrO_4, existing only in solution and forming chromates.

chro·mi·um (krō/mē·əm) *n.* A grayish white, very hard metallic element (symbol Cr) used in making alloys and pigments. See ELEMENT. [< NL < F < Gk. *chrōma* color; so called from its many brightly colored, poisonous compounds]

chro·mo (krō/mō) *n. pl.* **·mos** A chromolithograph.

chromo- *combining form* 1. Color; in or with color. 2. *Chem.* Chromium. Also, before vowels, **chrom-**. [< Gk. *chrōma* color]

chro·mo·li·thog·ra·phy (krō/mō·li·thog/rə·fē) *n.* The process of reproducing a color print by lithography. — **chro/mo·lith/o·graph** *n.* — **chro/mo·li·thog/ra·pher** *n.* — **chro·mo·lith/o·graph·ic** (krō/mō·lith/ə·graf/ik) *adj.*

chro·mo·some (krō/mə·sōm) *n. Biol.* One of the deeply staining, rod- or loop-shaped bodies into which the chromatin of the cell nucleus divides during cell division, and in which the genes are located.

chro·mo·sphere (krō/mə·sfir/) *n. Astron.* 1. An incandescent, gaseous envelope, consisting mostly of hydrogen and helium, that surrounds the sun beyond the photosphere. 2. A similar envelope surrounding a star. — **chro/mo·spher/ic** (-sfir/ik, -sfer/-) *adj.*

chro·mous (krō/məs) *adj. Chem.* Of or pertaining to chromium in its lower valence.

chron·ic (kron/ik) *adj.* 1. Continuing for a long period; constant. 2. Prolonged; lingering; also, recurrent: said of a disease: opposed to *acute.* 3. Long affected by a disease, or given to a habit; confirmed. [< F < L < Gk. *chronos* time] — **chron/i·cal·ly** *adv.*

chron·i·cle (kron/i·kəl) *n.* A register of events in the order in which they occurred. — *v.t.* **·cled, ·cling** To record in, or in the manner of, a chronicle. [< AF < L < Gk. *chronos* time] — **chron/i·cler** *n.*

Chron·i·cles (kron/i·kəlz) *n.pl.* Either of two historical books, I and II Chronicles, of the Old Testament: also, in the Douai Bible, called *I* and *II Paralipomenon.*

chrono- *combining form* Time: chronometer. Also, before vowels, **chron-**. [< Gk. *chronos* time]

chron·o·log·i·cal (kron/ə·loj/i·kəl) *adj.* 1. Arranged according to sequence in time. 2. Pertaining to chronology. Also **chron/o·log/ic.** — **chron/o·log/i·cal·ly** *adv.*

chro·nol·o·gy (krə·nol/ə·jē) *n. pl.* **·gies** 1. The science of determining the proper sequence of historical events. 2. Arrangement or relationship according to order of occurrence. 3. A chronological list or table. [< NL < Gk. *chronos* time + *-logia* study] — **chro·nol/o·ger, chro·nol/o·gist** *n.*

chro·nom·e·ter (krə·nom/ə·tər) *n.* A timekeeping instrument of high precision. — **chron·o·met·ric** (kron/ə·met/rik) or **·ri·cal** *adj.* — **chron/o·met/ri·cal·ly** *adv.*

chro·nom·e·try (krə·nom/ə·trē) *n.* The science or method of measuring time or periods of time.

-chrous *combining form* Having (a certain) color. [< Gk. *chrōs, chroos* color]

chrys·a·lid (kris/ə·lid) *Entomol. n.* A chrysalis. — *adj.* Of or like a chrysalis: also **chrys·al·i·dal** (kri·sal/ə·dəl) *adj.*

chrys·a·lis (kris/ə·lis) *n. pl.* **chrys·a·lis·es** or **chrys·al·i·des** (kri·sal/ə·dēz) 1. *Entomol.* The capsule-enclosed pupa from which the butterfly or moth develops. 2. Anything in an undeveloped stage. [< L < Gk. *chrysos* gold]

chrys·an·the·mum (kri·san/thə·məm) *n.* 1. Any of a number of cultivated varieties of plants of the genus *Chrysanthemum*, with large heads of showy flowers. 2. The flower. [< L < Gk. *chrysanthemon* golden flower]

chryso- *combining form* Gold; of a golden color. Also, before vowels, **chrys-**. [< Gk. *chrysos* gold]

chrys·o·lite (kris/ə·līt) *n.* A variety of olivine. [< OF < Med.L < L < Gk. < *chrysos* gold + *lithos* stone]

chrys·o·prase (kris/ə·prāz) *n.* A semiprecious, apple-green variety of chalcedony, used as a gem. [< OF < L < Gk. < *chrysos* gold + *prason* leek]

chub (chub) *n. pl.* **chubs** or **chub** 1. A carplike fish common in European rivers. 2. Any of various other unrelated fishes. [ME *chubbe*]

chub·by (chub/ē) *adj.* **·bi·er, ·bi·est** Plump; rounded. — **chub/bi·ness** *n.*

chuck¹ (chuk) *v.t.* 1. To pat or tap affectionately, esp. under the chin. 2. To throw or pitch. 3. *Informal* To throw away; discard. 4. *Informal* To eject forcibly: with *out.* 5. *Slang* To quit. — *n.* 1. A playful pat under the chin. 2. A throw; toss. [Cf. F *choquer* shake, jolt]

chuck² (chuk) *n.* 1. The cut of beef extending from the neck to the shoulder blade. 2. *Mech.* A clamp, chock, or wedge used to hold a tool or work in a machine, as in a lathe.

chuck-full (chuk/fŏŏl/) *adj.* Chockfull.

chuck·le (chuk/əl) *v.i.* **·led, ·ling** 1. To laugh quietly and with satisfaction. 2. To cluck, as a hen. — *n.* A low, mildly amused laugh. [Freq. of CLUCK] — **chuck/ler** *n.*

chuck·le·head (chuk/əl·hed/) *n. Informal* A stupid fellow; blockhead. — **chuck/le·head/ed** *adj.*

chuck wagon *U.S.* A wagon fitted with cooking equipment and provisions for cowboys, harvest hands, etc.

chug (chug) *n.* A dull, explosive sound, as of the exhaust of an engine. — *v.i.* **chugged, chug·ging** To move or operate with a series of such sounds. [Imit.]

chuk·ker (chuk/ər) *n.* In polo, one of the eight periods of continuous play, lasting 7½ minutes. Also **chuk/kar.** [< Hind. < Skt. *chakra* wheel]

chum (chum) *n.* 1. An intimate companion. 2. Originally, a roommate. — *v.i.* **chummed, chum·ming** 1. To associate very closely with another. 2. To share the same room. [? Short for *chamber fellow*]

chum·my (chum/ē) *adj.* **·mi·er, ·mi·est** *Informal* Friendly; intimate. — **chum/mi·ly** *adv.*

chump¹ (chump) *n.* 1. *Informal* A stupid or foolish person. 2. A chunk of wood. 3. The thick end of anything, as of a loin of mutton. 4. *Slang* The head. [? Var. of CHUNK]

chump² (chump) *v.t. & v.i.* To chew; munch. [< CHAMP¹]

chunk (chungk) *n.* 1. A thick mass or piece of anything, as of wood. 2. A considerable quantity of something. 3. *U.S. Informal* A strong, stocky person or animal. [Var. of CHUCK²]

chunk·y (chung/kē) *adj.* **chunk·i·er, chunk·i·est** 1. Short and thickset; stocky. 2. In chunks. — **chunk/i·ness** *n.*

church (chûrch) *n.* 1. A building for Christian worship. 2. Regular religious services; public worship. 3. A congregation of Christians. 4. *Usu. cap.* A distinct body of Christians having a common faith and discipline; a denomination. Abbr. *c., C., ch., Ch.* 5. All Christian believers collectively. 6. Ecclesiastical organization and authority: the separation of *church* and state. 7. The clerical profession. — *v.t.* 1. To subject to church discipline. 2. To conduct a religious service for (a person, esp. a woman after childbirth). [OE *circe,* ult. < Gk. *kyrios* Lord]

church·go·er (chûrch/gō/ər) *n.* One who goes regularly to church. — **church/go/ing** *adj. & n.*

church·ly (chûrch/lē) *adj.* Of, pertaining to, or suitable to a church. — **church/li·ness** *n.*

church·man (chûrch/mən) *n. pl.* **·men** (-mən) 1. A member of a church. 2. A clergyman. — **church/man·ly** *adj.* — **church/man·ship** *n.* — **church/wom/an** *n.fem.*

church mouse A mouse that lives in a church: usually in the phrase *poor as a church mouse,* very poor.

Church of Christ, Scientist See CHRISTIAN SCIENCE.

Church of England The national church of England, established by law in the 16th century, claiming to be an independent branch of the ancient Catholic church, and repudiating papal authority: also called *Anglican Church.*

Church of Jesus Christ of Latter-day Saints The Mormon Church: its official name.

church·war·den (chûrch/wôr/dən) *n.* 1. In the Church of England, an elected lay officer who assists in the administration of a parish. 2. In the Protestant Episcopal Church, one of two elected lay officers of a vestry. 3. A long-stemmed clay pipe. Also **church warden.**

church·yard (chûrch/yärd/) *n.* The ground surrounding or adjoining a church, often used as a cemetery.

churl (chûrl) *n.* 1. A rude or surly person. 2. A stingy person. 3. A rustic; countryman. [OE *ceorl*] — **churl/ish** *adj.* — **churl/ish·ly** *adv.* — **churl/ish·ness** *n.*

churn (chûrn) *n.* 1. A vessel in which milk or cream is agitated to separate the oily globules and gather them as butter. 2. A state of unrest or agitation. — *v.t.* 1. To stir or agitate (cream or milk), as in a churn. 2. To make in a churn, as butter. 3. To agitate violently: The oars *churned* the water. — *v.i.* 4. To work a churn. 5. To move with violent agitation; seethe. [OE *cyrin*] — **churn/er** *n.*

chute (shōōt) *n.* 1. An inclined trough or vertical passage down which water, coal, etc., may pass. 2. A steep, narrow watercourse; a rapid; shoot. 3. A narrow pen for branding or controlling cattle. 4. A slide, as for toboggans. 5. *Informal* A parachute. [Fusion of F *chute* a fall and SHOOT, n.]

chut·ney (chut/nē) *n.* A piquant relish of fruit, spices, etc. Also **chut/nee.** [< Hind. *chatnī*]

chutz·pah (hŏŏts/pə, khŏŏts/-) *n. U.S. Slang* Brazen effrontery; gall. [< Yiddish < Hebrew]

chyle (kīl) *n. Physiol.* The milky emulsion of lymph and fat taken up from the small intestine during digestion and passed from the thoracic duct into the veins. [< F < L < Gk. *chylos* juice] — **chy·la·ceous** (kī·lā′shəs), **chy·lous** (kī′ləs) *adj.*

chyme (kīm) *n. Physiol.* The partly digested food in semi-liquid form as it passes from the stomach into the small intestine. [< L < Gk. *chymos* juice] — **chy·mous** (kī′məs) *adj.*

ci·bo·ri·um (si·bôr′ē·əm, -bō′rē-) *n. pl.* **·bo·ri·a** (-bôr′ē·ə, -bō′rē·ə) **1.** An arched canopy over an altar, esp. a permanent one. **2.** A covered receptacle for the consecrated bread of the Eucharist. [< Med.L < Gk. *kibōrion* cup]

ci·ca·da (si·kā′də, -kä′-) *n. pl.* **·das** or **·dae** (-dē) A large winged insect, the male of which is equipped with vibrating membranes that produce a loud, shrill sound: often called *locust.* [< L]

CICADA (1 to 1¼ inches long)

cic·a·trix (sik′ə·triks) *n. pl.* **cic·a·tri·ces** (sik′ə·trī′sēz) **1.** *Med.* A scar or seam of new tissue remaining after the healing of wounded or ulcerous parts. **2.** *Biol.* A scar left by the healing of a wound, the fall of a leaf, etc. Also **cic·a·trice** (sik′ə·tris). [< L] — **cic·a·tri·cial** (sik′ə·trish′əl), **ci·cat·ri·cose** (si·kat′ri·kōs) *adj.*

cic·a·trize (sik′ə·trīz) *v.t. & v.i.* **·trized, ·triz·ing** To heal by the formation of a scar. — **cic′a·tri·za′tion** *n.*

cic·e·ro·ne (sis′ə·rō′nē, *Ital.* chē′chä·rō′nä) *n. pl.* **·nes,** *Ital.* **·ni** (-nē) A guide for tourists. [< Ital., Cicero]

Cic·e·ro·ni·an (sis′ə·rō′nē·ən) *adj.* Of or pertaining to Cicero, or to his rhetorical style; eloquent.

-cidal *combining form* Killing; able to kill: *homicidal.* [< L *caedere* to kill]

-cide *combining form* **1.** Killer or destroyer of: *regicide.* **2.** Murder or killing of: *parricide.* [def. 1 < L *-cida* killer < *caedere* to kill; def. 2 < L *-cidium* slaughter < *caedere*]

ci·der (sī′dər) *n.* The expressed juice of apples used to make vinegar, and as a beverage before fermentation (**sweet cider**), or after fermentation (**hard cider**). [< OF < LL < Hebrew *shēkār* strong drink]

ci·gar (si·gär′) *n.* A small roll of tobacco leaves prepared and shaped for smoking. [< Sp. *cigarro*]

cig·a·rette (sig′ə·ret′, sig′ə·ret) *n.* A small roll of finely cut tobacco for smoking, usu. enclosed in thin paper. Also *U.S.* **cig′a·ret′.** [< F, dim. of *cigare* cigar]

cil·i·a (sil′ē·ə) Plural of CILIUM. [< L *cilium* eyelid]

cil·i·ar·y (sil′ē·er′ē) *adj. Biol.* Of, pertaining to, or like cilia.

cil·i·ate (sil′ē·it, -āt) *adj. Biol.* Having cilia. Also **cil′i·at′ed.**

cil·i·um (sil′ē·əm) *n. pl.* **cil·i·a** (sil′ē·ə) **1.** *Biol.* A vibratile, microscopic, hairlike process on the surface of a cell, organ, plant, etc. **2.** An eyelash. [< L, eyelid]

Cim·me·ri·an (si·mir′ē·ən) *adj.* **1.** Of or pertaining to the Cimmerians, a mythical people mentioned by Homer as living in perpetual darkness. **2.** Densely dark; gloomy.

cinch (sinch) *n. U.S.* **1.** A pack or saddle girth. **2.** *Informal* A tight grip. **3.** *Slang* Something easy or sure. — *v.t.* **1.** To fasten a saddle girth around. **2.** *Slang* To get a tight hold upon. **3.** *Slang* To make sure of. — *v.i.* **4.** To tighten a saddle girth. [< Sp. < L *cingere* to bind]

cin·cho·na (sin·kō′nə) *n.* **1.** A tropical tree or shrub of the madder family, widely cultivated as a source of quinine and related alkaloids. **2.** The bark of any of these trees: also called *Peruvian bark.* [after the Countess of *Chinchón,* 1576–1639] — **cin·chon·ic** (sin·kon′ik) *adj.*

cin·cho·nize (sin′kə·nīz) *v.t.* **·nized, ·niz·ing** To treat with cinchona or quinine. — **cin′cho·ni·za′tion** *n.*

cinc·ture (singk′chər) *n.* **1.** A belt, cord, etc., put around the waist. **2.** The act of girding or surrounding. — *v.t.* **·tured, ·tur·ing** To encircle with or as with a cincture. [< L *cingere* to bind, gird]

cin·der (sin′dər) *n.* **1.** Any partly burned substance, not reduced to ashes; esp. a tiny particle of such a substance. **2.** A bit of wood, coal, etc., that can burn but without flame. **3.** *pl.* Ashes. — *v.t.* To burn or reduce to a cinder. [OE *sinder*] — **cin′der·y** *adj.*

Cin·der·el·la (sin′də·rel′ə) *n.* **1.** The heroine of a popular fairy tale, who is treated as a drudge, but eventually marries a prince. **2.** Any girl who achieves happiness or success after a period of neglect.

cine- *combining form* Cinema. [< CINEMA]

cin·e·ma (sin′ə·mə) *n.* **1.** A motion picture (def. 2). **2.** A motion-picture theater. — **the cinema** Motion pictures collectively; also, the art or business of making motion pictures. [Short for CINEMATOGRAPH] — **cin·e·mat·ic** (sin′ə·mat′ik) *adj.* — **cin′e·mat′i·cal·ly** *adv.*

cin·e·mat·o·graph (sin′ə·mat′ə·graf, -gräf) *n.* A motion-picture camera or projector. — *v.t. & v.i.* To take photographs (of) with a motion-picture camera: also **cin·e·ma·tize**

(sin′ə·mə·tīz). Also *kinematograph.* [< Gk. *kinēma, -atos* movement + -GRAPH]

cin·e·ma·tog·ra·phy (sin′ə·mə·tog′rə·fē) *n.* The art and process of making motion pictures. — **cin·e·ma·tog′ra·pher** *n.* — **cin·e·mat·o·graph·ic** (sin′ə·mat′ə·graf′ik) *adj.* — **cin′·e·mat′o·graph′i·cal·ly** *adv.*

cin·e·rar·i·a (sin′ə·râr′ē·ə) *n.* A cultivated plant having heart-shaped leaves and white, red, or purple flowers. [< NL < L, fem. of *cinerarius* ashy]

cin·e·rar·i·um (sin′ə·râr′ē·əm) *n. pl.* **·rar·i·a** (-râr′ē·ə) A place for keeping the ashes of a cremated body. [< L] — **cin·er·ar·y** (sin′ə·rer′ē) *adj.*

cin·er·a·tor (sin′ə·rā′tər) *n.* A furnace for cremating dead bodies; crematory. [Short for INCINERATOR]

cin·na·bar (sin′ə·bär) *n.* **1.** A heavy, crystallized red mercuric sulfide, HgS, the chief ore of mercury. **2.** Vermilion. [< L < Gk. < Persian *zanjifrah*]

cin·na·mon (sin′ə·mən) *n.* **1.** The aromatic inner bark of any of several tropical trees of the laurel family, used as a spice. **2.** Any tree that yields this bark. **3.** A shade of light reddish brown. [< L < Gk. < Hebrew *quinnāmōn*]

cinque·foil (singk′foil) *n.* **1.** *Archit.* A five-cusped ornament or window. **2.** Any of several plants of the rose family, with five-lobed leaves: also called *five-fingers.* [< F < L < *quinque* five + *folium* leaf]

ci·on (sī′ən) *n.* See SCION.

-cion Var. of -TION.

Ci·pan·go (si·pang′gō) *Poetic* Japan.

ci·pher (sī′fər) *n.* **1.** The figure 0, the symbol of the absence of quantity; zero. **2.** A person or thing of no value or importance. **3.** Any system of secret writing that uses a prearranged scheme or key. **4.** A message in cipher; also, its key. **5.** A monogram. **6.** Any Arabic number. — *v.t.* **1.** To calculate arithmetically. **2.** To write in characters of hidden meaning. — *v.i.* **3.** To work out arithmetical examples. **4.** To sound continuously, as an organ pipe. Also spelled *cypher.* [< OF < Arabic *sifr* nothing]

CINQUE-FOIL

cir·ca (sûr′kə) *prep. Latin* About; around; used before approximate date or figures.

cir·ca·di·an (sûr·kā′dē·ən) *adj.* Of a biorhythm occurring at intervals of about 24 hours. [< CIRCA + L *dies* day]

Cir·cas·sian (sər·kash′ən, -kash′ē·ən) *n.* **1.** A member of a group of tribes of the Caucasus region. **2.** The language of these tribes. — *adj.* Of or pertaining to Circassia, its people, or their language: also **Cir·cas·sic** (sər·kas′ik).

Cir·ce (sûr′sē) In the *Odyssey,* an enchantress who changed Odysseus's companions into swine by a magic drink.

Cir·ce·an (sər·sē′ən) *adj.* **1.** Of, pertaining to, or characteristic of Circe. **2.** Bewitching and degrading.

cir·cle (sûr′kəl) *n.* **1.** A plane figure bounded by a curved line every point of which is equally distant from the center. **2.** The circumference of such a figure. **3.** Something like a circle, as a crown, halo, or ring. **4.** A round or spherical body; an orb. **5.** A group of persons united by some common interest or pursuit; a set; coterie. **6.** The domain or scope of a special influence or action. **7.** A gallery or tier of seats in a theater: the family *circle.* **8.** A series or process that finishes at its starting point or that repeats itself without end: the *circle* of the seasons. **9.** *Astron.* The orbit of a heavenly body. — *v.* **·cled, ·cling** *v.t.* **1.** To enclose in a circle; encompass. **2.** To move around, as in a circle. — *v.i.* **3.** To move in a circle. [< L *circus* ring] — **cir′cler** *n.*

cir·clet (sûr′klit) *n.* A small ring or ring-shaped object, especially one worn as an ornament. [< F *cercle* ring]

cir·cuit (sûr′kit) *n.* **1.** A moving or traveling round; a circular route or course. **2.** A periodic journey from place to place, as by a judge or minister. **3.** The route traversed, or the district visited, in such a journey. **4.** A group of associated theaters presenting plays, films, etc., in turn. **5.** The line or distance around an area; circumference; also, the area enclosed. **6.** *Electr.* The entire course traversed by an electric current. **7.** *Telecom.* A transmission and reception system. — *v.t. & v.i.* To go or move (about) in a circuit. [< F < L *circum-* around + *ire* to go]

circuit breaker *Electr.* A switch or relay for breaking a circuit under specified or abnormal conditions of current flow.

circuit court A court of law that sits in various counties or districts over which its jurisdiction extends.

circuit judge A judge of a circuit court.

cir·cu·i·tous (sər·kyoo′ə·təs) *adj.* Roundabout; indirect. — **cir·cu′i·tous·ly** *adv.* — **cir·cu′i·tous·ness** *n.*

circuit rider A minister who preaches at churches on a circuit or district route.

cir·cuit·ry (sûr′kit·rē) *n. Electr.* The design and arrangement of circuits in any device, instrument, or system.

cir·cu·i·ty (sər·kyoo′ə·tē) *n. pl.* **·ties** Roundabout procedure or speech; indirectness.

cir·cu·lar (sûr′kyə·lər) *adj.* **1.** Shaped like a circle; round. **2.** Moving in a circle. **3.** Of or referring to a circle. **4.** Roundabout; indirect; devious. **5.** Addressed to several persons, or intended for general circulation. — *n.* A statement, notice, or advertisement printed for general distribution. [See CIRCLE.] — **cir·cu·lar·i·ty** (sûr′kyə·lar′ə·tē), cir′·cu·lar·ness *n.* — **cir′cu·lar·ly** *adv.*

cir·cu·lar·ize (sûr′kyə·lə·rīz′) *v.t.* ·ized, ·iz·ing **1.** To make circular. **2.** To make into a circular. **3.** To distribute circulars to. — **cir·cu·lar·i·za·tion** *n.* — **cir′cu·lar·iz′er** *n.*

circular saw A disk-shaped saw having a toothed edge, rotated at high speed by a motor.

cir·cu·late (sûr′kyə·lāt) *v.* ·lat·ed, ·lat·ing *v.i.* **1.** To move by a circuitous course back to the starting point, as the blood. **2.** To pass from place to place or person to person: Rumors *circulate* quickly. **3.** To be in free motion, as air. — *v.t.* **4.** To cause to circulate. [See CIRCLE.] — **cir·cu·la·tive** (sûr′kyə·lā′tiv) *adj.* — **cir′cu·la′tor** *n.*

circulating library A library from which books may be borrowed or rented: also called *lending library.*

cir·cu·la·tion (sûr′kyə·lā′shən) *n.* **1.** A moving around or through something back to the starting point. **2.** The motion of the blood from and to the heart through the arteries and veins. **3.** A transmission or spreading from one person or place to another; dissemination. **4.** The extent or amount of distribution of a periodical; also, the number of copies distributed. **5.** A current medium of exchange, as coin.

cir·cu·la·to·ry (sûr′kyə·lə·tôr′ē, -tō′rē) *adj.* Of, pertaining to or affecting circulation: a *circulatory* disorder.

circum- *prefix* **1.** About; around; on all sides; surrounding. **2.** Revolving around. [< L *circum-* around, about]

cir·cum·am·bi·ent (sûr′kəm·am′bē·ənt) *adj.* Encompassing; surrounding. — **cir′cum·am′bi·ence, cir′cum·am′bi·en·cy** *n.*

cir·cum·cise (sûr′kəm·sīz) *v.t.* ·cised, ·cis·ing To cut off all or part of the prepuce (of a male) or the clitoris (of a female). [< OF < L < *circum-* around + *caedere* to cut] — **cir′cum·cis′er** *n.* — **cir·cum·ci·sion** (sûr′kəm·sizh′ən) *n.*

cir·cum·fer·ence (sər·kum′fər·əns) *n.* **1.** The boundary line of any area; esp., the boundary of a circle. **2.** The length of such a line. [< L < *circum-* around + *ferre* to bear] — **cir·cum·fer·en·tial** (sər·kum′fə·ren′shəl) *adj.* — **cir·cum′fer·en′tial·ly** *adv.*

cir·cum·flex (sûr′kəm·fleks) *n.* A mark (ˆ, ˆ, ˇ) written over certain letters in ancient Greek, and later, in other languages, to mark a long vowel, contraction, etc., or used as a diacritical mark in phonetic transcription. — *adj.* **1.** Pronounced or marked with the circumflex accent. **2.** *Physiol.* Bent or curving around, as certain nerves. — *v.t.* **1.** To pronounce or mark with a circumflex. **2.** To wind around. [< L < *circum-* around + *flectere* to bend] — **cir·cum·flex·ion** (sûr′kəm·flek′shən) *n.*

cir·cum·flu·ous (sər·kum′flōō·əs) *adj.* Flowing around; surrounding. Also **cir·cum·flu·ent** (sər·kum′flōō·ənt). [< L < *circum-* around + *fluere* to flow]

cir·cum·fuse (sûr′kəm·fyōōz′) *v.t.* ·fused, ·fus·ing **1.** To pour, scatter, or spread about. **2.** To surround, as with a liquid. [< L < *circum-* around + *fundere* to pour] — **cir·cum·fu·sion** (sûr′kəm·fyōō′zhən) *n.*

cir·cum·lo·cu·tion (sûr′kəm·lō·kyōō′shən) *n.* An indirect lengthy way of expressing something; also, an example of this. [< L < *circum-* around + *loqui* to speak] — **cir·cum·loc·u·to·ry** (sûr′kəm·lok′yə·tôr′ē, -tō′rē) *adj.*

cir·cum·nav·i·gate (sûr′kəm·nav′ə·gāt) *v.t.* ·gat·ed, ·gat·ing To sail around. [< L < *circum-* around + *navigare* to sail] — **cir·cum·nav·i·ga·ble** (sûr′kəm·nav′ə·gə·bəl) *adj.* — **cir′cum·nav′i·ga′tion** *n.* — **cir′cum·nav′i·ga′tor** *n.*

cir·cum·scribe (sûr′kəm·skrīb′) *v.t.* ·scribed, ·scrib·ing **1.** To mark out the limits of; define. **2.** To draw a line or figure around. **3.** *Geom.* **a** To draw (a figure) about another figure so that it touches at every possible point without intersecting. **b** To surround (another figure) in this way. [< L < *circum-* around + *scribere* to write] — **cir′cum·scrib′a·ble** *adj.* — **cir′cum·scrib′er** *n.*

cir·cum·scrip·tion (sûr′kəm·skrip′shən) *n.* **1.** The act of circumscribing, or the state of being circumscribed. **2.** Anything that limits or encloses. **3.** The periphery of an object. **4.** A space marked out or bounded. **5.** An inscription around a coin, medallion, etc. — **cir′cum·scrip′tive** *adj.*

cir·cum·spect (sûr′kəm·spekt) *adj.* Attentive to everything; watchful; cautious; wary. Also **cir′cum·spec′tive** *adj.* [< L < *circum-* around + *specere* to look] — **cir′cum·spec′tion, cir′cum·spect′ness** *n.* — **cir′cum·spect′ly** *adv.*

cir·cum·stance (sûr′kəm·stans) *n.* **1.** A factor connected with an act, event, or condition, either as an accessory or as a determining element. **2.** *Often pl.* The conditions, influences, etc., affecting persons or actions. **3.** *pl.* Financial condition in life: in poor *circumstances.* **4.** An occurrence: a happy *circumstance.* **5.** Detail, especially superfluous detail, as in narrative. **6.** Formal display: pomp and *circumstance.* — **under no circumstances** Never; under no conditions. —

under the circumstances Since such is (or was) the case. — *v.t.* **stanced, ·stanc·ing** To place in or under limiting circumstances or conditions. [< OF < L < *circum-* around + *stare* to stand] — **cir′cum·stanced** *adj.*

cir·cum·stan·tial (sûr′kəm·stan′shəl) *adj.* **1.** Pertaining to or dependent on circumstances. **2.** Incidental; not essential. **3.** Full of details. — **cir′cum·stan′tial·ly** *adv.*

circumstantial evidence *Law* Evidence that furnishes reasonable ground for inferring the existence of a fact.

cir·cum·stan·ti·al·i·ty (sûr′kəm·stan′shē·al′ə·tē) *n. pl.* ·ties **1.** The quality of being particular, detailed, or minute. **2.** A particular matter; detail.

cir·cum·stan·ti·ate (sûr′kəm·stan′shē·āt) *v.t.* ·at·ed, ·at·ing To set forth or establish by circumstances or in detail. — **cir′cum·stan′ti·a′tion** *n.*

cir·cum·val·late (sûr′kəm·val′āt) *v.t.* ·lat·ed, ·lat·ing To surround with a rampart or a trench. — *adj.* Enclosed by or as by a wall. [< L < *circum-* around + *vallare* to fortify] — **cir′cum·val·la′tion** *n.*

cir·cum·vent (sûr′kəm·vent′) *v.t.* **1.** To surround or entrap, as an enemy, by stratagem. **2.** To gain an advantage over; outwit. **3.** To go around or avoid. [< L < *circum-* around + *venire* to come] — **cir′cum·vent′er** or **cir′cum·vent′or** *n.* — **cir′cum·ven′tive** *adj.* — **cir′cum·ven′tion** *n.*

cir·cus (sûr′kəs) *n.* **1.** A traveling show of acrobats, clowns, etc.; also, a performance of such a show. **2.** A circular, usu. tented area used for such shows. **3.** In ancient Rome, an oblong enclosure with tiers of seats around three sides, used for races, games, etc. **4.** *Brit.* An open, usu. circular junction of several streets. **5.** *U.S. Informal* Something or someone uproariously entertaining. [< L, a ring, racecourse]

cir·rho·sis (si·rō′sis) *n. Pathol.* A disease of the liver, characterized by an abnormal formation of connective tissue with progressive cellular breakdown. [< NL < Gk. *kirrhos* tawny; with ref. to the color of the cirrhotic liver] — **cir·rhot·ic** (si·rot′ik) *adj.*

cir·ri (sir′ī) Plural of CIRRUS.

cirro- *combining form* Cirrus. Also **cirri-**. [< L *cirrus* curl]

cir·ro·cu·mu·lus (sir′ō·kyōōm′yə·ləs) *n. Meteorol.* A mass of fleecy, globular cloudlets (Symbol Cc) in contact with one another; mackerel sky.

cir·ro·stra·tus (sir′ō·strā′təs) *n. Meteorol.* A fine, whitish veil of cloud (Symbol Cs).

cir·rous (sir′əs) *adj.* **1.** Having or like cirri. **2.** Of or pertaining to a cirrus cloud. Also **cir·rose** (sir′ōs).

cir·rus (sir′əs) *n. pl.* **cir·ri** (sir′ī) **1.** *Meteorol.* A type of white, wispy cloud (Symbol Ci), usually consisting of ice crystals and seen in tufts or feathery bands across the sky. **2.** *Bot.* A tendril. **3.** *Zool.* A threadlike appendage serving as an organ of touch. [< L, ringlet, curl]

cis- *prefix* **1.** On this side of. **2.** Since; following: *cis-Elizabethan.* [< L *cis* on this side]

cis·al·pine (sis·al′pīn, -pin) *adj.* On the Roman side of the Alps. [< L < *cis* on this side + *Alpes* the Alps]

cis·co (sis′kō) *n. pl.* **·coes** or **·cos** *U.S. & Canadian* A whitefish of North America. [? < N. Am. Ind.]

cis·tern (sis′tərn) *n.* **1.** An artificial reservoir, as a tank, for holding water or other liquids. **2.** *Anat.* A large lymph space; a sac. [< OF < L *cista* chest]

cit·a·del (sit′ə·dəl, -del) *n.* **1.** A fortress commanding a city. **2.** Any fortress or stronghold. **3.** The heavily plated casemate in a war vessel. [< MF < Ital. *città* city]

ci·ta·tion (sī·tā′shən) *n.* **1.** A citing or quoting; also, a passage or authority so cited. **2.** A public commendation for outstanding achievement. **3.** A summons, as to appear in court. [See CITE.] — **ci·ta·to·ry** (sī′tə·tôr′ē, -tō′rē) *adj.*

cite (sīt) *v.t.* **cit·ed, cit·ing** **1.** To quote as authority or illustration. **2.** To bring forward or refer to as proof or support. **3.** *Mil.* To mention in a report, esp. for bravery. **4.** To mention or enumerate. **5.** To summon to appear in court. **6.** To summon to action; rouse. [< F < L *citare* < *ciere* to set in motion] — **cit′a·ble** or **cite′a·ble** *adj.*

cith·a·ra (sith′ə·ra) *n.* An ancient Greek stringed instrument resembling a lyre. [< L < Gk. *kithara*]

cith·er (sith′ər) *n.* **1.** A zither. **2.** A cittern. Also **cith·ern** (sith′ərn). — *n.* A cithara.

cit·i·fied (sit′i·fīd) *adj.* Having the ways, habits, fashions, etc., of city life.

cit·i·zen (sit′ə·zən) *n.* **1.** A native or naturalized person owing allegiance to, and entitled to protection from, a government. **2.** A resident of a city or town. **3.** A civilian, as distinguished from a public officer, soldier, etc. [< AF < L *civis* citizen] — **cit′i·zen·ess** *n.fem.*

cit·i·zen·ry (sit′ə·zən·rē) *n. pl.* **·ries** Citizens collectively.

citizen's band A range of radio frequencies allocated for two-way communication between private individuals by low-powered radio sets. Abbr. *CB* — **cit·i·zen's-band** (sit′ə·zənz·band′) *adj.*

cit·i·zen·ship (sit′ə·zən·ship′) *n.* The status of a citizen, with its rights, privileges, and duties.

citra- *prefix* On this side; cis-. [< L]

cit·rate (sit′rāt, -rit, sī′trāt) *n. Chem.* A salt of citric acid.

cit·ric (sit′rik) *adj.* Of or derived from citrus fruits.

citric acid *Chem.* A white, crystalline, sharply sour compound, $C_6H_8O_7$, contained in various fruits, and also made synthetically.

cit·rine (sit′rin) *adj.* Lemon yellow. — *n.* 1. Citrine color. 2. A light yellow variety of quartz. [< F *citrin*]

cit·ron (sit′rən) *n.* 1. A fruit like a lemon, but larger and less acid. 2. The tree producing this fruit. 3. A watermelon with a small, hard-fleshed fruit. Also **citron melon.** 4. The rind of either of these fruits, preserved and used in confections. [< MF < Ital. < L *citrus* citrus tree]

cit·ron·el·la (sit′rə·nel′ə) *n.* A grass cultivated in Ceylon, yielding **citronella oil,** used in perfumery, in cooking, and as protection against mosquitoes. Also **citronella grass.** [< NL < CITRON; so called from its odor]

cit·rus (sit′rəs) *adj.* Of or pertaining to trees bearing oranges, lemons, etc. Also **cit′rous.** [< L, citron tree]

cit·tern (sit′ərn) *n.* Any of a group of old stringed instruments resembling a lute or guitar. [< L < Gk. *kithara*]

cit·y (sit′ē) *n. pl.* **cit·ies** 1. A place inhabited by a large, permanent community. 2. In the United States, a municipality of the first class with definite boundaries and various legal powers. 3. In Canada, a municipality of high rank. 4. In Great Britain, a large incorporated town. 5. The people of a city, collectively. [< OF < L *civis* citizen]

cit·y-bred (sit′ē·bred′) *adj.* Brought up in a city.

city desk A department in a newspaper office where local news is received, rewritten, and edited.

city father One who directs the public affairs of a city.

city manager An administrator not publicly elected but appointed by a city council to manage the city.

city planning Public control of the physical development of a city, as by regulation of the size and use of buildings, etc.

cit·y-state (sit′ē·stāt′) *n.* A state consisting of a city and its contiguous territories, as ancient Athens.

civ·et (siv′it) *n.* 1. A substance of musklike odor, secreted by the genital glands of the civet cat, used in perfumery. 2. The civet cat or its fur. [< MF *civette*]

civet cat A feline carnivore of Africa.

civ·ic (siv′ik) *adj.* Of or pertaining to a city, a citizen, or citizenship; civil. [< L < *civis* citizen]

civ·ics (siv′iks) *n.pl.* (construed as *sing.*) The division of political science dealing with citizenship and civic affairs.

civ·il (siv′əl) *adj.* 1. Of or pertaining to community life rather than military or ecclesiastical affairs. 2. Of or pertaining to citizens and their government: *civil* affairs. 3. Occurring within the state; domestic: *civil* war. 4. Of, proper to, or befitting a citizen. 5. Civilized. 6. Proper; polite. 7. *Law* Related to the rights of citizens and to legal proceedings involving such rights. — **Syn.** See POLITE. [< MF < L *civis* citizen] — **civ′il·ly** *adv.*

civil defense A civilian program for the maintenance of essential services in wartime.

civil disobedience A refusal to comply with certain civil laws, usually done by means of passive resistance.

civil engineer A professional engineer trained to design, build, and maintain public works, as roads, bridges, etc.

ci·vil·ian (sə·vil′yən) *n.* One who is not in the military or naval service. — *adj.* Of or pertaining to a civilian.

ci·vil·i·ty (sə·vil′ə·tē) *n. pl.* **·ties** 1. The quality of being civil; courtesy; politeness. 2. A polite act or speech.

civ·i·li·za·tion (siv′ə·lə·zā′shən, -lī·zā′-) *n.* 1. A state of human society characterized by a high level of intellectual, social, and cultural development. 2. The countries and peoples considered to have reached this stage. 3. The cultural development of a specific people, country, or region. 4. The act of civilizing, or the process of becoming civilized.

civ·i·lize (siv′ə·līz) *v.t.* **·lized, ·liz·ing** To bring into a state of civilization; bring out of savagery; refine; enlighten. Also *Brit.* **civ′i·lise.** [< MF < Med.L < L *civis* citizen] — **civ′i·liz′a·ble** *adj.* — **civ′i·liz′er** *n.*

civil law The body of laws having to do with the rights and privileges of private citizens.

civil liberty A liberty guaranteed to the individual by the laws of a government.

civil marriage A marriage solemnized by a civil or government official rather than by a clergyman.

civil rights Private, nonpolitical privileges; esp., exemption from involuntary servitude, as established by the 13th and 14th amendments to the U.S. Constitution.

civil service 1. The branches of governmental service that are not military, naval, legislative, or judicial. 2. The persons employed in these branches. — **civil servant**

civil war War between parties or sections of the same country.

Civil War See table for WAR.

civ·vies (siv′ēz) *n.pl. Informal* Civilian clothes, as distinguished from military dress; mufti.

clab·ber (klab′ər) *n.* Milk curdled by souring. — *v.t. & v.i.* To curdle, as milk. [< Irish *bainne clabair*]

clack (klak) *v.i.* 1. To make a sharp, dry sound. 2. To chatter heedlessly. 3. To cluck, as a hen. — *v.t.* 4. To cause to clack. 5. To babble. — *n.* 1. A short, sharp sound. 2. Something that makes a clack. 3. Chatter. [Imit.] — **clack′er** *n.*

clad (klad) Alternative past tense and past participle of CLOTHE.

claim (klām) *v.t.* 1. To demand as one's right or due; assert ownership or title to. 2. To hold to be true; assert. 3. To require or deserve: The problem *claims* our attention. — *n.* 1. A demand or an assertion of a right. 2. An assertion of something as true. 3. A ground for claiming something. 4. That which is claimed, as a piece of land. [< OF < L *clamere* to declare] — **claim′a·ble** *adj.* — **claim′er** *n.*

claim·ant (klā′mənt) *n.* One who makes a claim.

clair·voy·ance (klâr·voi′əns) *n.* 1. The alleged ability to perceive distant or hidden objects. 2. Knowledge of things beyond the area of normal perception. [< MF]

clair·voy·ant (klâr·voi′ənt) *adj.* Having clairvoyance or second sight. — *n.* A clairvoyant person.

clam¹ (klam) *n.* 1. Any of various bivalve mollusks, as the quahog. 2. *Informal* A close-mouthed person. — *v.i.* **clammed, clam·ming** To hunt for or dig clams. — **to clam up** *U.S. Slang* To become or keep silent. [< obs. *clam* a clamp]

clam·bake (klam′bāk′) *n. U.S.* 1. A picnic where clams and other foods are baked. 2. Any noisy gathering.

clam·ber (klam′bər, -ər) *v.t. & v.i.* To climb by using the hands and feet; mount or descend with difficulty. — *n.* The act of clambering. [Akin to CLIMB] — **clam′ber·er** *n.*

clam·my (klam′ē) *adj.* **·mi·er, ·mi·est** Stickily soft and damp, and usually cold. [< Du. *klam* sticky] — **clam′mi·ly** *adv.* — **clam′mi·ness** *n.*

clam·or (klam′ər) *n.* 1. A loud, repeated outcry. 2. A vehement protest or demand. 3. Any loud and continuous noise; din. — *v.i.* 1. To make loud outcries, demands, or complaints. — *v.t.* 2. To utter with clamor. 3. To move or drive by clamor. Also *Brit.* **clam′our.** [< OF < L *clamare* to cry out] — **clam′or·er** *n.*

clam·or·ous (klam′ər·əs) *adj.* Making, or made with, a clamor; noisy. — **clam′or·ous·ly** *adv.* — **clam′or·ous·ness** *n.*

clamp (klamp) *n.* Any of a number of devices for holding objects together, securing a piece in position, etc.; esp. one having two opposite parts that can be brought together by a screw or spring action. — *v.t.* To hold or bind with or as with a clamp. — **to clamp down** *U.S. Informal* To become more strict. [Cf. OE *clamm*, M.Du *klampe*]

clan (klan) *n.* 1. A united group of relatives, or families, claiming a common ancestor and having the same surname. 2. A clique; fraternity; club. [< Scottish Gaelic *clann*]

clan·des·tine (klan·des′tin) *adj.* Kept secret for a purpose, usually for something evil or illicit; surreptitious; furtive; — **Syn.** See STEALTHY. [< F < L *clandestinus* < *clam* in secret] — **clan·des′tine·ly** *adv.* — **clan·des′tine·ness** *n.*

clang (klang) *v.t. & v.i.* 1. To make or cause to make a loud, ringing, metallic sound; ring loudly. — *n.* A ringing sound.

clan·gor (klang′gər, klang′ər) *n.* Repeated clanging; clamor; din. — *v.i.* To ring noisily; clang. Also *Brit.* **clan′gour.** [< L < *clangere* to clang] — **clan′gor·ous** *adj.* — **clan′gor·ous·ly** *adv.*

clank (klangk) *n.* A short, harsh, metallic sound. — *v.t. & v.i.* To emit, or cause to emit, a clank. [Imit.]

clan·nish (klan′ish) *adj.* 1. Of or characteristic of a clan. 2. Disposed to cling together, or bound by family prejudices, traditions, etc. — **clan′nish·ly** *adv.* — **clan′nish·ness** *n.*

clans·man (klanz′mən) *n. pl.* **·men** (-mən) A member of a clan. — **clans′wom′an** *n.fem.*

clap (klap) *v.* **clapped, clap·ping** *v.i.* 1. To strike the hands together, as in applauding. 2. To make a sound, as of two boards striking together. — *v.t.* 3. To bring (the hands) together sharply and with an explosive sound. 4. To strike with the open hand, as in greeting. 5. To applaud (someone or something) by clapping. 6. To put, place, or fling quickly or suddenly: They *clapped* him into jail. 7. To flap, as the wings. — *n.* 1. The act or sound of clapping the hands. 2. A loud, explosive sound, esp. of thunder. 3. A blow with the open hand. [OE *clæppan*]

clap·board (klab′ərd, klap′bôrd′, -bôrd′) *n.* A narrow board having one edge thinner than the other, nailed overlapping as siding on frame buildings: sometimes called **weatherboard.** — *v.t.* To cover with clapboards. [Partial trans. of M.Du. *klapholt* barrel stave]

clap·per (klap′ər) *n.* 1. The tongue of a bell. 2. One who or that which claps.

clap·trap (klap'trap) *n.* Pretentious language; cheap, sensational artifice. [< CLAP[1], n. + TRAP[1], n.]

claque (klak) *n.* 1. A group of hired applauders in a theater. 2. Any set of persons who praise or applaud from interested motives. [< F < *claquer* to clap]

clar·et (klar'ət) *n.* 1. Any dry red wine, esp. red Bordeaux. 2. Ruby to deep purplish red. [< OF < L *clarus* bright]

clar·i·fy (klar'ə·fī) *v.t. & v.i.* **·fied, ·fy·ing** 1. To make or become clear or free from impurities. 2. To make or become understandable; explain. [< OF < LL < L *clarus* clear + *facere* to make] — **clar·i·fi·ca·tion** *n.* — **clar·i·fi·er** *n.*

clar·i·net (klar'ə·net') *n.* A cylindrical woodwind instrument having a single-reed mouthpiece, finger holes, and keys. Also *Rare* **clar·i·o·net** (klar'ē·ə·net'). [< F < Ital. *clarinetto*] — **clar·i·net·ist** or **clar·i·net·tist** *n.*

clar·i·on (klar'ē·ən) *n.* 1. An obsolete kind of trumpet having a shrill tone. 2. The sound of a clarion. — *v.t. & v.i.* To proclaim as with a clarion. — *adj.* Clear and resounding. [< OF < L *clarus* clear]

clar·i·ty (klar'ə·tē) *n.* Clearness; lucidity.

clash (klash) *v.t.* 1. To strike or dash together with a harsh, metallic sound. — *v.i.* 2. To collide with loud and confused noise. 3. To conflict; be in opposition. — *n.* 1. A resounding, metallic noise. 2. A conflict or opposition. [Imit.]

clasp (klasp, kläsp) *n.* 1. A fastening, as a hook, by which things or parts are held together. 2. A firm grasp of the hand or embrace. — *v.t.* 1. To embrace. 2. To fasten with or as with a clasp. 3. To grasp firmly in or with the hand. [ME *claspe*] — **clasp·er** *n.*

class (klas, kläs) *n.* 1. A body of persons considered to have certain social or other characteristics in common. 2. The division of society by relative standing; social rank, caste. 3. A category of objects, persons, etc., based on quality or rank: of the first *class.* 4. A number of things grouped together as having common properties; a category. 5. A group of students under one teacher, or pursuing a study together; also, a meeting of such a group. 6. *U.S.* A group of students in a school or college graduating together. 7. *Biol.* A group of plants or animals standing below a phylum and above an order. 8. *Slang* Superiority; elegance. — *v.t.* 1. To assign to a class; classify. — *v.i.* 2. *Rare* To be placed or ranked, as in a class. [< MF < L *classis* class]

class consciousness Awareness of the nature, interest, and unity of one's social group. — **class'-con'scious** *adj.*

clas·sic (klas'ik) *adj.* 1. Belonging to the first class or highest rank; approved as a model. 2. Of or characteristic of ancient Greece and Rome, their literature or art. 3. In the style of ancient Greek and Roman authors and artists; balanced; formal; austere. — *n.* 1. An author, artist, or work generally recognized as a standard of excellence. 2. *Informal* Any well-known event thought of as being typical or traditional. — **the classics** Ancient Greek and Roman literature. [< L *classis* order, class]

clas·si·cal (klas'i·kəl) *adj.* 1. Classic. 2. Generally accepted as being standard and authoritative; not new or experimental: *classical* economic theory. 3. Of ancient Greece and Rome: *classical* civilization. 4. Versed in the Greek and Roman classics: a *classical* scholar. 5. Consisting of or pertaining to studies based on Greek and Roman language, literature, and thought: a *classical* curriculum. 6. *Music* Loosely, of a serious nature, as distinguished from jazz or popular music. — **clas·si·cal·ly** *adv.* — **clas·si·cal·i·ty** *n.*

clas·si·cal·ism (klas'i·kəl·iz'əm) *n.* Classicism. — **clas'·si·cal·ist** *n.*

clas·si·cism (klas'ə·siz'əm) *n.* 1. A group of esthetic principles (simplicity, restraint, balance, dignity, etc.) as manifested in ancient Greek and Roman art and literature: distinguished from *romanticism.* 2. Adherence to these principles. 3. The style of ancient Greek and Roman literature, architecture, etc. 4. Classical scholarship. 5. A Greek or Latin idiom or form.

clas·si·cist (klas'ə·sist) *n.* 1. One versed in the classics. 2. An adherent or imitator of classic style. 3. One who actively supports the study of the classics.

clas·si·fi·ca·tion (klas'ə·fə·kā'shən) *n.* The act, process, or result of classifying. — **clas·si·fi·ca·to·ry** (klas'ə·fə·kā'tər·ē, klə·sif'ə·kə·tôr'ē, -tō'rē) *adj.*

classified advertisement An advertisement under any of various subject headings. Also **classified ad.**

clas·si·fy (klas'ə·fī) *v.t.* **·fied, ·fy·ing** 1. To arrange or put in a class or classes on the basis of resemblances or differences. 2. To designate as of aid to an enemy and restrict as to circulation or use, as a government document. [< L *classis* class + -FY] — **clas·si·fi·a·ble** *adj.* — **clas·si·fi·er** *n.*

class·mate (klas'māt, kläs'-) *n.* A member of the same class in school or college.

class·room (klas'rōōm', -rōōm', kläs'-) *n.* A room in a school or college in which classes are held.

class struggle 1. The conflict between classes in society. 2. In Marxist theory, the economic and political struggle for power between the dominant class and the rising class.

class·y (klas'ē) *adj.* **class·i·er, class·i·est** *Slang* Elegant.

clat·ter (klat'ər) *v.i.* 1. To make a rattling noise; give out short, sharp noises rapidly or repeatedly. 2. To move with a rattling noise. 3. To talk noisily; chatter. — *v.t.* 2. To cause to clatter. — *n.* 1. A rattling or clattering sound. 2. A disturbance or commotion. 3. Noisy talk; chatter. [OE *clatrunge* a clattering noise] — **clat'ter·er** *n.*

clause (klôz) *n.* 1. A distinct part of a composition, as an article in a statute, will, treaty, etc. 2. *Gram.* A group of words containing a subject and a predicate: distinguished from *phrase.* Abbr. *cl.* — **dependent clause** A clause that functions as a subject or complement (noun clause) or as a modifier (adjective or adverb clause) within a sentence: also called *subordinate clause.* — **independent clause** A clause that can stand alone as a simple sentence, or combine with other clauses to form compound or complex sentences: also called *main clause, principal clause.* [< OF < Med.L < L *clausus,* pp. of *claudere* to close] — **claus'al** *adj.*

claus·tro·pho·bi·a (klôs'trə·fō'bē·ə) *n. Psychiatry* Morbid fear of enclosed or confined places. [< L *claustrum* a closed place + -PHOBIA] — **claus'tro·pho'bic** *adj.*

cla·vate (klā'vāt) *adj.* Club-shaped. [< L *clava* a club]

clave (klāv) Archaic past tense of CLEAVE[1] and CLEAVE[2].

clav·i·chord (klav'ə·kôrd) *n.* A keyboard musical instrument that is a forerunner of the piano. [< Med.L < L *clavis* key + *chorda* string]

clav·i·cle (klav'ə·kəl) *n. Anat.* The bone connecting the shoulder blade and breastbone: also called *collarbone.* For illus. see SKELETON. [< L *clavis* key] — **cla·vic·u·lar** (klə·vik'yə·lər) *adj.*

clav·i·er (klə·vir'; for defs. 1 and 3, also klav'ē·ər) *n.* 1. A keyboard. 2. Any keyboard stringed instrument, as a harpsichord, piano, etc. 3. A dummy keyboard for silent practicing. [< F, keyboard < L *clavis* key]

claw (klô) *n.* 1. A sharp, usu. curved, horny nail on the toe of a bird, mammal, or reptile. 2. A chela or pincer of certain insects and crustaceans. 3. Anything sharp and hooked, as the cleft part of a hammerhead. — *v.t. & v.i.* To tear, scratch, dig, pull, etc., with or as with claws. [OE *clawu*]

claw hammer A hammer with one end of its head forked and curved like a claw for drawing nails.

clay (klā) *n.* 1. A fine-grained, variously colored earth, plastic when wet, used in the making of bricks, tiles, pottery, etc. 2. Earth. 3. The human body. — *v.t.* To mix or treat with clay. [OE *clǣg*] — **clay'ey** *adj.* — **clay'ish** *adj.*

clay·more (klā'môr, -mōr) *n.* A double-edged broadsword formerly used by the Scottish Highlanders. [< Scottish Gaelic *claidheamh* sword + *mor* great]

clay pigeon In trapshooting, a saucer-shaped disk, as of baked clay, projected from a trap as a flying target.

-cle *suffix of nouns* Small; minute; *particle, corpuscle.* [< F < L *-culus,* dim. suffix]

clean (klēn) *adj.* 1. Free from dirt or stain; unsoiled. 2. Morally pure; wholesome. 3. Without obstructions, encumbrances, or restrictions: a *clean* title to land. 4. Thorough; complete: a *clean* getaway. 5. Clever; dexterous: a *clean* jump. 6. Well-proportioned; trim; shapely. 7. Neat in habits. 8. Producing an explosion relatively free of radioactive fallout: said of an atomic or thermonuclear bomb. — *v.t.* 1. To render free of dirt or other impurities. 2. To prepare (fowl, game, etc.) for cooking. — *v.i.* 3. To undergo or perform the act of cleaning. — **to clean out** 1. To clear of trash or rubbish. 2. To empty (a place) of contents or occupants. 3. *Informal* To leave without money: The depression *cleaned* him *out.* — **to clean up** 1. To clean completely and thoroughly. 2. *Slang* To make a large profit. 3. *Informal* To finish: to *clean up* one's work. — *adv.* 1. In a clean manner; cleanly. 2. Wholly; completely. [OE *clǣne* clear, pure] — **clean'a·ble** *adj.* — **clean'ness** *n.*

clean-cut (klēn'kut') *adj.* 1. Cut with smooth edge or surface; well-made. 2. Sharply defined; clear. 3. Pleasing in appearance; wholesome; neat: a *clean-cut* young man.

clean·er (klē'nər) *n.* 1. A person whose work is cleaning, esp. clothing. 2. Any substance or device that cleans.

clean·ly (adj. klēn'lē; adv. klēn'lē) *adj.* Habitually and carefully clean; neat; tidy. — *adv.* In a clean manner. — **clean·li·ly** (klēn'lə·lē) *adv.* — **clean·li·ness** (klēn'lē·nis) *n.*

cleanse (klenz) *v.t.* **cleansed, cleans·ing** To free from dirt or defilement; clean; purge. [OE *clǣnsian* < *clǣne* clean]

cleans·er (klenz'ər) *n.* One who or that which cleanses; esp., a soap, detergent, etc., used for cleansing.

clean·up (klēn'up') *n.* 1. A complete cleaning. 2. *Slang* A large profit; gain.

clear (klir) *adj.* 1. Bright; unclouded. 2. Without impurity or blemish. 3. Of great transparency. 4. Free from obstructions: a *clear* road. 5. Understandable; plain to the mind. 6. Plain to the eye, ear, etc. 7. Able to discern; keen: a *clear* mind. 8. Free from uncertainty; sure: Are you *clear* on that point? 9. Free from guilt or blame. 10. Not in contact: usu. with *of:* to stand *clear* of a fire. 11. Emptied of cargo. 12. Without deductions; net: a *clear* $5,000.

— *adv.* **1.** In a clear manner. **2.** *Informal* All the way: *clear* through the day. — *v.t.* **1.** To make clear; brighten. **2.** To free from foreign matter, impurities, or obstructions. **3.** To remove (obstacles, etc.) in making something clear. **4.** To free from blame or guilt. **5.** To make plain. **6.** To pass or get under or over without touching: to *clear* a fence. **7.** To free from debt by payment. **8.** To settle (a debt). **9.** To obtain or give clearance for. **10.** To gain over and above expenses. **11.** To pass (a check) through a clearing-house. — *v.i.* **12.** To become free from fog, rain, etc.; become fair. **13.** To pass away, as mist or clouds. **14.** To settle accounts by exchange of bills and checks, as in a clearing-house. **15.** To obtain clearance. **— to clear away** (or **off**) **1.** To remove out of the way. **2.** To go away; disappear. **— to clear out 1.** *Informal* To go away. **2.** To empty of contents. **— to clear the air** To dispel tensions; settle differences. **— to clear up 1.** To make clear. **2.** To grow fair, as the weather. **3.** To free from confusion or mystery. **4.** To put in order; tidy. **— n.** An unobstructed space. **2.** Clearance. **— in the clear 1.** Free from limitations or obstructions. **2.** *Informal* Free from guilt or blame. [< OF < L *clarus* clear, bright] **— clear′a·ble** *adj.* **— clear′ly** *adv.* **— clear′ness** *n.*
— Syn. (adj.) 1, 3. A thing is *clear* when it presents no obstructions to the sight. We see objects clearly through something *transparent*; that which is *translucent* allows the passage of light, but may obscure form and color.

clear·ance (klir′əns) *n.* **1.** The act or instance of clearing. **2.** A space cleared. **3.** The space by which a moving object clears something. **4.** Permission for a ship, airplane, truck, etc., to proceed, as after a check of its load. **5.** The passage of checks, bank drafts, etc. through a clearing-house.

clear-cut (klir′kut′) *adj.* **1.** Distinctly and sharply outlined. **2.** Plain; evident; obvious.

clear-head·ed (klir′hed′id) *adj.* Not mentally confused; clear in thought; sensible. **— clear′-head′ed·ness** *n.*

clear·ing (klir′ing) *n.* **1.** A making or becoming clear. **2.** That which is clear or cleared, as a tract of land. **3.** In banking, clearance.

clear·ing-house (klir′ing·hous′) *n.* An office where bankers exchange drafts and checks and adjust balances. Also **clear′ing·house′.**

clear-sight·ed (klir′sī′tid) *adj.* **1.** Having accurate perception and good judgment; discerning. **2.** Having keen vision. **— clear′-sight′ed·ly** *adv.* **— clear′-sight′ed·ness** *n.*

clear-sto·ry (klir′stôr′ē, -stō′rē) See CLERESTORY.

cleat (klēt) *n.* **1.** A strip of wood or iron fastened across a surface to strengthen or support. **2.** A piece of metal or wood with arms on which to wind or secure a rope. — *v.t.* **1.** To furnish or strengthen with a cleat or cleats. **2.** *Naut.* To fasten (rope, etc.) to or with a cleat. [ME *clete*]

cleav·age (klē′vij) *n.* **1.** A cleaving or being cleft. **2.** A split or cleft. **3.** *Mineral.* A tendency in certain rocks or crystals to split in certain directions.

cleave¹ (klēv) *v.* **cleft** or **cleaved** or **clove** (*Archaic* **clave**), **cleft** or **cleaved** or **clo·ven, cleav·ing** *v.t.* **1.** To split or sunder, as with an ax or wedge. **2.** To make or achieve by cutting: to *cleave* a path. **3.** To pass through; penetrate: to *cleave* the air. — *v.i.* **4.** To part or divide along natural lines of separation. **5.** To make one's way; pass: with *through.* [OE *clēofan*] **— cleav′a·ble** *adj.*

cleave² (klēv) *v.i.* **cleaved** (*Archaic* **clave, clove**), **cleaved, cleav·ing 1.** To stick fast; adhere: with *to.* **2.** To be faithful: with *to.* [Fusion of OE *clifan* and *clifian*]

cleav·er (klē′vər) *n.* **1.** One who or that which cleaves. **2.** A butcher's heavy, axlike knife. [< CLEAVE¹]

clef (klef) *n. Music* A symbol placed on the staff to show the pitch of the notes. [< MF < L *clavis* key]

cleft (kleft) Past tense and past participle of CLEAVE¹. — *adj.* Divided partially or completely. — *n.* A fissure; crevice; rift. [ME *clift*]

cleft palate A congenital longitudinal fissure in the roof of the mouth.

clem·a·tis (klem′ə·tis) *n.* A perennial shrub or vine of the crowfoot family. [< Gk. *klēmatis*]

clem·en·cy (klem′ən·sē) *n. pl.* **·cies 1.** Leniency; mercy. **2.** An act of mercy or leniency. **3.** Mildness of weather, etc. **— Syn.** See MERCY. [< L *clemens* mild]

clem·ent (klem′ənt) *adj.* **1.** Lenient or merciful in temperament; compassionate. **2.** Mild: said of weather. [< L *clemens, -entis* mild, merciful] **— clem′ent·ly** *adv.*

clench (klench) *v.t.* **1.** To grasp or grip firmly. **2.** To close tightly or lock, as the fist or teeth. **3.** To clinch, as a nail. — *n.* **1.** A tight grip. **2.** A device that clenches or grips. [OE *-clenc(e)an* in *beclencan* to hold fast]

clere·sto·ry (klir′stôr′ē, -stō′rē) *n. pl.* **·ries 1.** *Archit.* The highest story of the nave and choir of a church, with windows opening above the aisle roofs, etc. **2.** A similar part in other structures. Also spelled **clearstory.** Also **clere′sto′rey.** [< earlier *clere* clear + STORY]

cler·gy (klûr′jē) *n. pl.* **·gies** The whole body of men set apart by ordination for religious service. [< OF < LL < Gk. *klēros* lot, portion]

cler·gy·man (klûr′jē·mən) *n. pl.* **·men** (-mən) One of the clergy; an ordained minister. *Abbr. cl.*

cler·ic (kler′ik) *adj.* Clerical. — *n.* A member of the clergy.

cler·i·cal (kler′i·kəl) *adj.* **1.** Of or related to clerks or office workers or their work. **2.** Belonging to or characteristic of the clergy. **3.** Advocating great political influence for the clergy. — *n.* **1.** A clergyman. **2.** *pl.* The distinctive dress of a clergyman. **— cler′i·cal·ly** *adv.*

cler·i·cal·ism (kler′i·kəl·iz′əm) *n.* Excessive clerical influence in politics. **— cler′i·cal·ist** *n.*

clerk (klûrk, *Brit.* klärk) *n.* **1.** A worker in an office who keeps records or accounts, attends to correspondence, etc. **2.** An official or employee of a court, legislative body, or the like, charged with the care of records, etc. **3.** *U.S.* A salesperson. — *v.i.* To work or act as clerk. [OE < LL < Gk. *klēros* lot, portion] **— clerk′ly** *adj. & adv.*

clev·er (klev′ər) *adj.* **1.** Mentally keen; intelligent; quick-witted. **2.** Physically adroit, esp. with the hands; dexterous. **3.** Ingeniously made, said, done, etc. [Cf. ME *cliver* adroit] **— clev′er·ly** *adv.* **— clev′er·ness** *n.*

clev·is (klev′is) *n.* A U-shaped metal fastening pierced for a bolt, used to attach chains, cables, etc. [Akin to CLEAVE¹]

clew (kloō) *n.* **1.** In legends, a ball of thread that guides through a maze. **2.** Something that serves as a guide in solving a problem or mystery: usu. spelled *clue.* **3.** *Naut.* A lower corner of a square sail or the lower aft corner of a fore-and-aft sail; also, a loop at the corner. — *v.t.* **1.** To coil into a ball. **2.** To guide or track by or as by a clew. **3.** *Naut.* To raise the clews of (a square sail): with *up.* [OE *cliwen*]

cli·ché (klē·shā′) *n.* A trite or hackneyed expression, action, etc. [< F, pp. of *clicher* to stereotype]

click (klik) *n.* **1.** A short, sharp, nonresonant metallic sound, as that made by a latch. **2.** *Phonet.* A speech sound made by clicking the tongue, characteristic of certain African languages: also called *suction stop.* — *v.t.* **1.** To cause to make a click or clicks. — *v.i.* **2.** To produce a click or clicks. **3.** *Slang* To succeed. [Imit.] **— click′er** *n.*

cli·ent (klī′ənt) *n.* **1.** One in whose interest a lawyer acts. **2.** One who engages the services of any professional adviser. **3.** A customer. [< L *cliens, -entis* follower]

cli·en·tele (klī′ən·tel′) *n.* A body of clients, patients, customers, etc. Also **cli·ent·age** (klī′ən·tij). [< F]

cliff (klif) *n.* A high steep face of rock; a precipice. [OE]

cliff·hang·er (klif′hang′ər) *n.* **1.** A situation marked by suspense or uncertainty of outcome. **2.** A serialized drama marked by suspense at the end of each episode. Also **cliff′-hang′er. — cliff′hang′ing** *adj. & n.*

cliff swallow A North American swallow that builds mud nests under eaves or against cliffs.

cliff·y (klif′ē) *adj.* Abounding in or resembling cliffs.

cli·mac·ter·ic (klī·mak′tər·ik, klī′mak·ter′ik) *n.* **1.** An age or period of life characterized by marked physiological change, as the menopause. **2.** Any critical year or period. — *adj.* Pertaining to a critical year or period: also **cli·mac·ter·i·cal** (klī·mak·ter′i·kəl). [< L < Gk. *klimaktēr* rung of a ladder]

cli·mac·tic (klī·mak′tik) *adj.* Pertaining to or constituting a climax. Also **cli·mac′ti·cal.**

cli·mate (klī′mit) *n.* **1.** The temperature, precipitation, winds, etc., characteristic of a region. **2.** A region in reference to its characteristic weather. **3.** A prevailing trend or condition in human affairs: the *climate* of opinion. [< OF < LL < Gk. *klima, -atos* region, zone] **— cli·mat·ic** (klī·mat′ik) or **cli·mat′i·cal** *adj.* **— cli·mat′i·cal·ly** *adv.*

climato- *combining form* Climate; pertaining to climate or climatic conditions: *climatology.* Also, before vowels, **climat-.** [< Gk. *klima, -atos* region]

cli·ma·tol·o·gy (klī′mə·tol′ə·jē) *n.* The branch of science dealing with the phenomena of climate. **— cli·ma·to·log·ic** (klī′mə·tə·loj′ik) or **·i·cal** *adj.* **— cli·ma·tol′o·gist** *n.*

cli·max (klī′maks) *n.* **1.** The point of greatest intensity or fullest development; culmination; acme. **2.** In drama, fiction, etc., the scene or moment of action that determines the dénouement. — *v.t. & v.i.* To reach or bring to a climax. [< L < Gk. *klimax* ladder]

climb (klīm) *v.* **climbed, climb·ing** *v.t.* **1.** To ascend or mount (something), by means of the hands and feet. — *v.i.* **2.** To rise or advance in status, rank, etc. **3.** To incline or slope upward. **4.** To rise during growth, as certain vines, by entwining a support. **— to climb down** To descend, esp. by using the hands and feet. — *n.* **1.** The act or process of climbing; ascent. **2.** A place ascended by climbing. [OE *climban*] **— climb′a·ble** *adj.* **— climb′er** *n.*

clinch (klinch) *v.t.* **1.** To secure, as a driven nail or staple, by bending down the protruding point. **2.** To fasten together by this means. **3.** To make sure; settle. — *v.i.* **4.** To grapple, as combatants. **5.** *Slang* To embrace, as lovers. — *n.* **1.** The act of clinching. **2.** That which clinches; a clamp. **3.** A grip or struggle at close quarters, as in boxing. **4.** *Slang* A close embrace. [Var. of CLENCH]

clinch·er (klin'chər) *n.* **1.** One who or that which clinches. **2.** A nail made for clinching. **3.** *Informal* A deciding statement, point, etc.

cling (kling) *v.i.* **clung, cling·ing** **1.** To hold fast, as by grasping, sticking, or winding round. **2.** To resist separation: with *together*. [OE *clingan*] — **cling'er** *n.*

clinging vine *Informal* A woman who displays extreme dependence on a man.

cling·stone (kling'stōn') *n.* A variety of peach in which the pulp adheres to the stone.

clin·ic (klin'ik) *n.* **1.** An infirmary, usu. connected with a hospital or medical school, for the treatment of nonresident patients. **2.** The teaching of medicine by treating patients in the presence of a class; also, a class receiving such instruction. **3.** A place where patients are studied and treated by specialists. **4.** An organization that offers advice on specific problems. [< F < Gk. *klinein* to recline]

clin·i·cal (klin'i·kəl) *adj.* **1.** Of or pertaining to a clinic. **2.** Concerned with the observation and treatment of patients in clinics, as distinguished from laboratory experimentation. **3.** Coldly scientific or detached. — **clin'i·cal·ly** *adv.*

clinical thermometer An accurately calibrated thermometer used for determining body temperature.

cli·ni·cian (kli·nish'ən) *n.* A physician trained in clinical methods, or one who gives instruction in clinics.

clink[1] (klingk) *v.t. & v.i.* To make or cause to make a short, slight, ringing sound. — *n.* A slight tinkling sound. [Imit.]

clink[2] (klingk) *n. Slang* A prison. [? after *Clink* prison in London]

clink·er (kling'kər) *n.* **1.** The fused residue left by coal, etc., in burning. **2.** A very hard brick. — *v.i.* To form clinkers, as coal in burning. [< Du. *klinckaerd* brick]

clino- *combining form* Bend; slope; incline: *clinometer*. [< Gk. *klinein* to bend]

cli·nom·e·ter (kli·nom'ə·tər, klī-) *n.* An instrument for determining angular inclination, as of guns, slopes, etc. — **cli·no·met·ric** (klī'nə·met'rik) or **·ri·cal** *adj.*

Cli·o (klī'ō) The Muse of history.

clip[1] (klip) *n.* A device that clasps, grips, or holds articles together, as letters or papers. — *v.t.* **clipped, clip·ping** To fasten with or as with a clip. [OE *clyppan* to clasp]

clip[2] (klip) *v.* **clipped, clip·ping** *v.t.* **1.** To cut with shears or scissors, as hair or fleece; trim. **2.** To cut short; curtail: to *clip* the ends of words. **3.** *Informal* To strike with a sharp blow. **4.** *U.S. Slang* To cheat or defraud. — *v.i.* **5.** To cut or trim. **6.** *Informal* To run or move swiftly. — **to clip the wings of** To check the aspirations or ambitions of. — *n.* **1.** The act of clipping, or that which is clipped off. **2.** The wool yielded at one shearing or during one season. **3.** A sharp blow; punch. **4.** *Informal* A quick pace. [< ON *klippa*]

clip·board (klip'bôrd', -bōrd') *n.* A board providing a writing surface, with a spring clip for holding paper.

clipped form A shortened form of a polysyllabic word, as *bus* for *omnibus*. Also **clipped word.**

clip·per (klip'ər) *n.* **1.** *pl.* An instrument or tool for clipping or cutting. **2.** A sailing vessel of the mid-19th century, built for speed: also **clipper ship.** **3.** One who clips.

clip·ping (klip'ing) *n.* **1.** The act of one who or that which clips. **2.** *Chiefly U.S.* That which is cut off or out by clipping: a newspaper *clipping*. — *adj.* That cuts or clips.

clique (klēk, klik) *n.* An exclusive or clannish group of people. — *v.i.* **cliqued, cli·quing** To unite in a clique. [< MF < *cliquer* to click, clap] — **cli'quish** *adj.*

cli·to·ris (klī'tə·ris, klit'ə-) *n. Anat.* A small erectile organ at the upper part of the vulva, homologous to the penis. [< NL < Gk. *kleitoris*] — **clit·o·ral** (-rəl) *adj.*

clo·a·ca (klō·ā'kə) *n. pl.* **·cae** (-sē) *Zool.* The common cavity into which the various ducts of the body open in certain fishes, reptiles, birds, and some mammals. **2.** A sewer or a privy. [< L, a drain] — **clo·a'cal** *adj.*

cloak (klōk) *n.* **1.** A loose outer garment, usu. without sleeves. **2.** Something that covers or hides. — *v.t.* **1.** To cover with a cloak. **2.** To conceal; disguise. [< OF < Med.L *cloca* bell, cape; so called from its bell-like shape]

cloak·room (klōk'rōōm', -rŏŏm') *n.* A room where hats, coats, luggage, etc., are left temporarily, as in a theater.

clob·ber (klob'ər) *v.t. U.S. Slang* **1.** To beat severely; trounce; maul. **2.** To defeat utterly. [? Freq. of CLUB[1], v.]

cloche (klōsh, *Fr.* klôsh) *n.* A woman's close-fitting, bell-shaped hat. [< F, bell]

clock[1] (klok) *n.* An instrument for measuring time; esp., a sizable mechanism having pointers that move over a dial marked off in hours. — *v.t.* To ascertain the speed or the time of with a stopwatch. [< MDu. < OF < Med.L *cloca*]

clock[2] (klok) *n.* An embroidered or woven ornament on the side of a stocking or sock at the ankle. [Origin uncertain]

clock·wise (klok'wīz') *adj. & adv.* Going in the direction traveled by the hands of a clock.

clock·work (klok'wûrk') *n.* The machinery of a clock, or any similar mechanism, usu. driven by a spring. — **like clockwork** With regularity and precision.

clod (klod) *n.* **1.** A lump of earth, clay, etc. **2.** Earth. **3.** A dull, stupid person. [Var. of CLOT] — **clod'dish** *adj.*

clod·hop·per (klod'hop'ər) *n.* **1.** *Informal* A rustic; hick; lout. **2.** *pl.* Large, heavy shoes.

clog (klog) *n.* **1.** Anything that impedes motion; an obstruction; hindrance. **2.** A block or weight attached, as to a horse, to hinder movement. **3.** A wooden-soled shoe. **4.** A clog dance. — *v.* **clogged, clog·ging** *v.t.* **1.** To choke up or obstruct. **2.** To impede; hinder. **3.** To fasten a clog to; hobble. — *v.i.* **4.** To become clogged or choked. **5.** To adhere in a mass; coagulate. **6.** To perform a clog dance. [ME *clogge* block of wood] — **clog'gi·ness** *n.* — **clog'gy** *adj.*

cloi·son·né (kloi'zə·nā') *n.* **1.** Enamel work made by laying out the pattern with metal strips and filling the interstices with enamel. **2.** The ware so produced. — *adj.* Of, pertaining to, or made by this method. [< F, partitioned]

clois·ter (klois'tər) *n.* **1.** A covered walk along the inside walls of buildings in a quadrangle, as in a monastery or college. **2.** A monastery; convent. **3.** Any place of quiet seclusion. **4.** Monastic life. — *v.t.* To seclude; confine, as in a cloister. [OF < L *claustrum* enclosed place] — **clois'·tered** *adj.* — **clois'tral** *adj.*

— **Syn.** (noun) **2.** *Cloister* refers to a retreat for either sex, and stresses loneliness. *Convent* was originally a general term, but is now usually restricted to a retreat for women, replacing the former *nunnery*. *Monasteries* are *cloisters* for men.

clone (klōn) *n.* A group of organisms derived from a single individual by asexual means. — *v.t.* **cloned, clon·ing** To produce in the form of a clone. [< Gk. *klōn* sprout, twig]

clon·ing (klōn'ing) *n.* The production of progeny genetically identical with a single progenitor.

clo·nus (klō'nəs) *n. Pathol.* A succession of muscle spasms. [< NL < Gk. *klonos* motion, turmoil] — **clon·ic** (klon'ik) *adj.* — **clo·nic·i·ty** (klō·nis'ə·tē) *n.* — **clo'nism** *n.*

close (*adj., adv., n. defs. 4 and 5* klōs; *v., n. def. 2* klōz) *adj.* **clos·er, clos·est** **1.** Near or near together in space, time, etc. **2.** Dense; compact: a *close* weave. **3.** Near to the surface; short: a *close* haircut. **4.** Near to the mark: a *close* shot. **5.** Nearly even or equal: said of contests. **6.** Fitting tightly. **7.** Conforming to an original: a *close* resemblance. **8.** Logically exact: *close* reasoning. **9.** Thorough; rigorous: *close* attention. **10.** Bound by strong affection, loyalty, etc.: a *close* friend. **11.** Shut in or about; not open. **12.** Confined in space; cramped: *close* quarters. **13.** Open only to a few; restricted. **14.** Strictly guarded: a *close* secret. **15.** Concealing one's thoughts or feelings; reticent. **16.** Hidden; secluded. **17.** Close-fisted; stingy. **18.** Difficult to obtain: said of money or credit. **19.** Stifling and humid; stuffy. **20.** *Phonet.* Of vowels, pronounced with a part of the tongue relatively close to the palate, as (ē): opposed to *open*. — *v.* **closed, clos·ing** *v.t.* **1.** To shut. **2.** To obstruct, as an opening or passage. **3.** To bring to an end; terminate. — *v.i.* **4.** To become shut or closed. **5.** To come to an end. **6.** To grapple; come to close quarters. **7.** To come to an agreement. **8.** To be worth at the end of a business day: stocks *closed* three points higher. — **to close down** To cease operations, as a factory. — **to close in** To advance from all sides so as to prevent escape. — **to close out** *U.S.* To sell all of, usu. at reduced prices. — **to close up** **1.** To close completely. **2.** To come nearer together, as troops. — *n.* **1.** The end; conclusion. **2.** An enclosed place, esp. about a cathedral or building. — *adv.* In a close manner; nearly; closely. [< OF < L *claudere* to close] — **close·ly** (klōs'lē) *adv.* — **close·ness** (klōs'nis) *n.* — **clos·er** (klō'zər) *n.*

close call (klōs) *U.S. Informal* A narrow escape.

closed circuit (klōzd) *Telecom.* A form of television in which broadcasts are transmitted by cable to a restricted number of receivers.

closed shop An establishment where only union members are hired, by agreement with the union.

close-fist·ed (klōs'fis'tid) *adj.* Stingy; miserly. — **close'-fist'ed·ness** *n.*

close-fit·ting (klōs'fit'ing) *adj.* Fitting snugly.

close-hauled (klōs'hôld') *adj. & adv. Naut.* With sails set for sailing as close to the wind as possible.

close-mouthed (klōs'mouthd', -moutht') *adj.* Not given to speaking; taciturn; uncommunicative.

close quarters (klōs) **1.** In fighting, an encounter at close range or hand-to-hand. **2.** A small, confined space.

close shave (klōs) *U.S. Informal* A narrow escape.

clos·et (kloz'it) *n.* **1.** *Chiefly U.S.* A small room or recess for storing clothes, linen, etc. **2.** A small, private room. **3.** A ruler's council chamber. — *v.t.* To shut up or conceal in or as in a closet: usu. reflexive. — *adj.* **1.** Private; confidential. 2. Based on theory rather than practice: *closet* strategy. [< OF, dim. of *clos* < L *claudere* to close]

close-up (klōs'up') *n.* 1. A picture taken at close range, or with a telescopic lens. 2. A close look or view.

clo·sure (klō'zhər) *n.* 1. A closing or shutting up. 2. That which closes or shuts. 3. An end; conclusion. 4. Cloture. —*v.t. & v.i.* **·sured, ·sur·ing** To cloture. [< OF < L *claudere* to close]

clot (klot) *n.* A thick, viscid, or coagulated mass, as of blood. —*v.t. & v.i.* **clot·ted, clot·ting** To form into clots; coagulate. [OE *clott* lump, mass] —**clot'ty** *adj.*

cloth (klôth, kloth) *n.* *pl.* **cloths** (klôthz, klothz, klôths, kloths) 1. A woven, knitted, or felted fabric of wool, cotton, rayon, etc.; also, a piece of such fabric. 2. A piece of cloth for a special use, as a tablecloth. 3. Professional attire, esp. of the clergy. —**the cloth** The clergy. [OE *clāth*]

clothe (klōth) *v.t.* **clothed** or **clad, cloth·ing** 1. To cover or provide with clothes; dress. 2. To cover as if with clothing; invest. [Fusion of OE *clāthian* and *clǣthan*]

clothes (klōz, klōthz) *n.pl.* 1. Garments; clothing. 2. Bedclothes. [OE *clāthas*, pl. of *clāth* cloth]

clothes·horse (klōz'hôrs', klōthz'-) *n.* 1. A frame on which to hang or dry clothes. 2. *U.S. Slang* A person regarded as excessively concerned with dress.

clothes·line (klōz'līn, klōthz'-) *n.* A cord, rope, or wire on which to hang clothes to dry.

clothes·pin (klōz'pin', klōthz'-) *n.* A forked peg or clamp with which to fasten clothes on a line.

clothes·press (klōz'pres', klōthz'-) *n.* A closet; wardrobe.

cloth·ier (klōth'yər) *n.* One who makes or sells cloth or clothing.

cloth·ing (klō'thing) *n.* 1. Dress; apparel. 2. A covering.

Clo·tho (klō'thō) One of the three Fates.

clot·ty (klot'ē) *adj.* 1. Full of clots. 2. Tending to clot.

clo·ture (klō'chər) *n.* A parliamentary device to stop debate in a legislative body in order to secure a vote. —*v.t.* To stop (debate) by cloture. Also *closure.* [< F *clôture*]

cloud (kloud) *n.* 1. A mass of visible vapor or an aggregation of watery or icy particles floating in the atmosphere. 2. Any visible collection of particles in the air, as steam, smoke, or dust. 3. A cloudlike mass of things in motion, esp. in flight: a *cloud* of gnats. 4. Something that darkens, obscures, or threatens. 5. A dimness or milkiness, as in glass or liquids. —**in the clouds** 1. In the realm of the unreal or fanciful. 2. Impractical. —**under a cloud** 1. Overshadowed by reproach or distrust. 2. Troubled or depressed. —*v.t.* 1. To cover with or as with clouds; dim; obscure. 2. To render gloomy or troubled. 3. To disgrace; sully, as a reputation. 4. To mark with different colors; variegate. —*v.i.* 5. To become overcast: often with *up* or *over.* [OE *clūd* rocky mass, hill] —**cloud'less** *adj.*

cloud·burst (kloud'bûrst') *n.* A sudden, heavy downpour.

cloud chamber *Physics* An enclosed receptacle containing air or gas saturated with water vapor whose sudden cooling indicates the presence of ions by the tracks of water droplets they produce: also called *fog chamber, Wilson Cloud Chamber.*

cloud·y (klou'dē) *adj.* **cloud·i·er, cloud·i·est** 1. Overspread with clouds. 2. Of or like a cloud or clouds. 3. Marked with cloudlike spots. 4. Not limpid or clear. 5. Obscure; vague; confused: *cloudy* thinking. 6. Full of foreboding; gloomy. [OE *clūdig*] —**cloud'i·ly** *adv.* —**cloud'i·ness** *n.*

clout (klout) *n.* 1. *Informal* A heavy blow or cuff with the hand. 2. *U.S. Slang* Influence or power; esp., political weight. 3. In baseball slang, a long hit. 4. In archery, the center of a target, or a shot that strikes it. 5. A type of flat-headed nail: also **clout nail.** —*v.t. Informal* To hit or strike, as with the hand. [OE *clūt*]

clove (klōv) *n.* A dried flower bud of a tree of the myrtle family, used as a spice. [OE < L *clavus* nail]

clove hitch *Naut.* A knot consisting of two half hitches, with the ends of the rope going in opposite directions, used for fastening a rope around a spar. For illustration see HITCH.

clo·ven (klō'vən) Alternative past participle of CLEAVE[1]. —*adj.* Parted; split.

cloven-hoofed (klō'vən·hōoft', -hōoft') *adj.* 1. Having the foot cleft, as cattle. 2. Satanic. Also **clo'ven-foot'ed.**

clo·ver (klō'vər) *n.* Any of several plants having dense flower heads and trifoliolate leaves; esp., the red clover, used for forage and adopted as the State flower of Vermont. —**in clover** In a prosperous condition. [OE *clāfre* trefoil]

clo·ver·leaf (klō'vər·lēf') *n. pl.* **·leafs** A type of intersection resembling a four-leaf clover, in which two highways crossing at different levels are connected by curving ramps.

clown (kloun) *n.* 1. A professional buffoon in a play or circus, who entertains by jokes, tricks, etc.; a zany; jester. 2. A coarse or vulgar person; boor. —*v.i.* To behave like a clown. [Earlier *cloune* < MLG] —**clown'er·y** *n.* —**clown'ish** *adj.* —**clown'ish·ly** *adv.* —**clown'ish·ness** *n.*

cloy (kloi) *v.t.* 1. To gratify beyond desire; surfeit. —*v.i.* 2. To cause a feeling of surfeit. [< OF < LL < L *clavus* a nail] —**cloy'ing·ly** *adv.* —**cloy'ing·ness** *n.*

club[1] (klub) *n.* 1. A stout stick or staff; a cudgel. 2. A stick or bat used in games to strike a ball; esp., a stick with a curved head used in golf. 3. In card games: **a** A black marking on a playing card, shaped like a three-leaf clover. **b** A card so marked. **c** *pl.* The suit so marked. —*v.* **clubbed, club·bing** *v.t.* To beat, as with a club. [< ON *klubba*]

club[2] (klub) *n.* 1. A group of persons organized for some mutual aim or pursuit, esp. a group that meets regularly. 2. A house or room reserved for the meetings of such an organization. —*v.* **clubbed, club·bing** *v.t.* 1. To contribute for a common purpose: to *club* resources. —*v.i.* 2. To combine or unite: often with *together.* [Special use of CLUB[1]]

club car A railroad passenger car furnished with easy chairs, tables, a buffet or bar, etc.

club·foot (klub'fōot') *n. pl.* **·feet** *Pathol.* 1. Congenital distortion of the foot: also called *talipes.* 2. A foot so affected. —**club'foot'ed** *adj.*

club·house (klub'hous') *n.* 1. The building occupied by a club. 2. Dressing rooms for an athletic team.

club moss A perennial evergreen herb allied to the ferns.

club sandwich A sandwich consisting of three slices of toast and layers of various meats, lettuce, tomatoes, etc.

club steak A small beefsteak cut from the loin.

club topsail *Naut.* A gaff topsail, extended at its foot by a small spar. For illus. see SCHOONER.

cluck (kluk) *v.i.* 1. To give the low, guttural cry of a hen calling her chicks. 2. To utter any similar sound, as in urging a horse. —*v.t.* 3. To call by clucking. 4. To express with a like sound: to *cluck* disapproval. —*n.* The sound of clucking. [OE *cloccian*; imit.]

clue (klōo) *n.* Something that leads to the solution of a problem or mystery. —*v.t.* **clued, clu·ing** 1. To clew. 2. *U.S. Informal* To give (someone) information. [Var. of CLEW]

clump (klump) *n.* 1. A thick cluster: a *clump* of bushes. 2. A heavy, dull sound, as of tramping. 3. An irregular mass; a lump. —*v.i.* 1. To walk clumsily and noisily. 2. To form clumps. —*v.t.* 3. To place or plant in a clump. [Var. of CLUB[1]] —**clump'y, clump'ish** *adj.*

clum·sy (klum'zē) *adj.* **·si·er, ·si·est** 1. Lacking dexterity, ease, or grace. 2. Ungainly or unwieldy. 3. Ill-contrived: a *clumsy* excuse. [< obs. *clumse* to be numb with cold] —**clum'si·ly** *adv.* —**clum'si·ness** *n.*

clung (klung) Past tense and past participle of CLING.

clus·ter (klus'tər) *n.* 1. A collection of objects of the same kind growing or fastened together. 2. A number of persons or things close together; group. —*v.t. & v.i.* To grow or form into a cluster or clusters. [OE *clyster*] —**clus'tered** *adj.* —**clus'ter·y** *adj.*

clutch[1] (kluch) *v.t.* 1. To snatch, as with hands or talons. 2. To grasp and hold firmly. —*v.i.* 3. To attempt to seize, snatch, or reach: with *at*: He *clutched* at her hand. —*n.* 1. A tight grip; grasp. 2. *pl.* Power or control: in the *clutches* of the police. 3. *Mech.* **a** Any of a number of devices for coupling two working parts, as the engine and driveshaft of an automobile. **b** A lever or pedal for operating such a device. 4. A contrivance for gripping and holding. [ME *clucchen*]

CLUTCH
(n. def. 4)
a Fixed member.
b Movable and splined member.
c Collar. *d* Fork. *e* Lever.

clutch[2] (kluch) *n.* 1. The number of eggs laid at one time. 2. A brood of chickens. —*v.t.* To hatch. [< ON *klekja* hatch]

clut·ter (klut'ər) *n.* 1. A disordered state or collection; litter. 2. A clatter. —*v.t.* 1. To litter, heap, or pile in a confused manner. —*v.i.* 2. To make a clatter. [Var. of earlier *clotter*]

Clydes·dale (klīdz'dāl) *n.* A breed of draft horses originating in the valley of the Clyde, Scotland.

clyp·e·ate (klip'ē·āt) *adj.* Shield-shaped. Also **clyp·e·i·form** (klip'ē·ə·fôrm'). —**clyp'e·at'ed.**

clys·ter (klis'tər) *n. Med.* An enema. [< OF < Gk. *klyster* < *klyzein* to wash out, rinse]

Cly·tem·nes·tra (klī'təm·nes'trə) The wife of Agamemnon, daughter of Leda. See ORESTES. Also **Cly·taem·nes'tra.**

co-[1] *prefix* With; together; joint or jointly; equally: used with verbs, nouns, adjectives, and adverbs. [< L *co-* var. of *com-* before *gn, h,* and vowels < *cum* with]
Following is a list of self-explanatory words containing the prefix *co-*:

coadminister	codefendant	co-owner
coadministrator	coeditor	copartner
coambassador	coheir	copassionate
coarrange	coinvolve	copatron
coauthor	co-oblige	coreign

co-² *prefix* **1.** *Math.* Of the complement: *cosine.* **2.** *Astron.* Complement of. [< L *complementum* complement]

coach (kōch) *n.* **1.** A large, four-wheeled closed carriage. **2.** A passenger bus. **3.** Air coach (which see). **4.** A railroad passenger car; esp., one having only seats and offering the cheapest travel. **5.** A private tutor. **6.** A trainer or director in athletics, dramatics, etc. — *v.t.* **1.** To tutor or train; act as coach to. — *v.i.* **2.** To study with or be trained by a coach. **3.** To act as coach. **4.** To ride or drive in a coach. [< MF < Hung. *kocsi* (*szeker*) (wagon) of Kocs, the village where first used]

coach-and-four (kōch′ən-fôr′, -fōr′) *n.* A coach drawn by four horses.

coach dog A Dalmatian.

coach·man (kōch′mən) *n. pl.* **·men** (-mən) One who drives a coach.

co·ad·ju·tant (kō-aj′ŏŏ-tənt) *adj.* Cooperating. — *n.* An assistant or co-worker. [< co-¹ + L *adjutare* to help]

co·ad·ju·tor (kō-aj′ŏŏ-tər, kō′ə-jŏŏ′tər) *n.* **1.** An assistant or co-worker. **2.** A bishop who assists a diocesan bishop.

co·ae·val (kō-ē′vəl) See COEVAL.

co·ag·u·la·ble (kō-ag′yə-lə-bəl) *adj.* Capable of being coagulated. — **co·ag′u·la·bil′i·ty** *n.*

co·ag·u·lant (kō-ag′yə-lənt) *n.* A coagulating agent, as rennet. [< L *coagulare* to curdle]

co·ag·u·late (kō-ag′yə-lāt) *v.t. & v.i.* **·lat·ed, ·lat·ing** To change from a liquid into a clot or jelly, as blood. [< L *coagulare* to curdle] — **co·ag′u·la′tion** *n.* — **co·ag′u·la′tive** *adj.* — **co·ag′u·la′tor** *n.*

coal (kōl) *n.* **1.** A dark brown to black, combustible mineral produced by the carbonization of prehistoric vegetation, found in beds or veins in the earth and used as fuel and a source of hydrocarbons. **2.** A piece of coal. **3.** A glowing or charred fragment of wood or other fuel; an ember. — **to carry coals to Newcastle** To provide something already in abundant supply. — **to haul (rake,** etc.**) over the coals** To criticize severely; reprimand. — *v.t.* **1.** To supply with coal. — *v.i.* **2.** To take on coal. [OE *col*]

Coal may appear as a combining form or as the first element in two-word phrases as in: **coalbin, coal-burning, coal dust, coal mine, coal-producing.**

co·a·lesce (kō′ə-les′) *v.i.* **·lesced, ·lesc·ing** To grow or come together into one; blend. [< L < co- together + *alescere* to grow up] — **co′a·les′cence** *n.* — **co′a·les′cent** *adj.*

coal gas 1. The poisonous gas produced by the combustion of coal. **2.** A gas used for illuminating and heating, produced by the distillation of bituminous coal.

co·a·li·tion (kō′ə-lish′ən) *n.* **1.** An alliance of persons, parties, or states. **2.** A fusion into one mass. [< L < co- together + *alescere* to grow up] — **co′a·li′tion·ist** *n.*

coal oil 1. Kerosene. **2.** Crude petroleum.

coal·scut·tle (kōl′skut′l) *n.* A bucketlike container in which coal may be kept or carried. Also **coal hod.**

coal tar A black, viscid liquid produced in the distillation of bituminous coal, yielding a variety of compounds used in making dyestuffs, drugs, plastics, etc. — **coal′-tar′** *adj.*

coam·ing (kō′ming) *n.* A curb about a hatchway or skylight, to keep water from entering. [Origin unknown]

coarse (kôrs, kōrs) *adj.* **1.** Lacking refinement; vulgar; low. **2.** Inferior; base; common. **3.** Composed of large parts or particles; not fine in texture. [Adjectival use of COURSE, meaning usual, ordinary] — **coarse′ly** *adv.* — **coarse′ness** *n.*

coarse-grained (kôrs′grānd′, kōrs′-) *adj.* **1.** Having a coarse grain or texture. **2.** Not delicate or refined; crude.

coars·en (kôr′sən, kōr′-) *v.t. & v.i.* To make or become coarse.

coast (kōst) *n.* **1.** The land next to the sea; the seashore. **2.** A slope suitable for sliding, as on a sled; also, a slide down it. — **Syn.** See SHORE¹. — **the Coast** *U.S.* That part of the United States bordering on the Pacific Ocean. — **the coast is clear** There is no danger or difficulty now. — *v.i.* **1.** To slide down a slope by force of gravity alone, as on a sled. **2.** To continue moving on acquired momentum alone. **3.** To sail along a coast. — *v.t.* **4.** To sail along, as a coast; skirt. [< OF < L *costa* rib, flank] — **coast′al** *adj.*

coast·er (kōs′tər) *n.* **1.** One who or that which coasts, as a person or vessel engaged in the coasting trade. **2.** A sled or toboggan. **3.** A small disk of glass, metal, etc., set under a drinking glass to protect the surface beneath.

coaster brake A clutchlike brake on a bicycle, operated by reversing the pressure on the pedals.

coast guard Naval or military coastal patrol and police. — **United States Coast Guard** A force set up to protect life and property at sea and to enforce customs, immigration, and navigation laws, operating under the Department of the Treasury.

coast·line (kōst′līn′) *n.* The contour or boundary of a coast.

coast·ward (kōst′wərd) *adj.* Directed or facing toward the coast. — *adv.* Toward the coast: also **coast′wards.**

coast·wise (kōst′wīz′) *adj.* Following, or along the coast. — *adv.* Along the coast: also **coast′ways** (-wāz′).

coat (kōt) *n.* **1.** A sleeved outer garment, as the jacket of a suit, or an overcoat or topcoat. **2.** A natural covering or integument, as the fur of an animal, the rind of a melon, etc. **3.** Any layer covering a surface, as paint, ice, etc. — *v.t.* **1.** To cover with a surface layer, as of paint. **2.** To provide with a coat. [< OF *cote*] — **coat′ed** *adj.* — **coat′less** *adj.*

co·a·ti (kō-ä′tē) *n. pl.* **·tis** (-tēz) A small, carnivorous, raccoonlike mammal of tropical America, with a mobile snout and plantigrade feet. Also **co·a′ti·mon′di** (-mun′dē), **co·a′ti·mun′di** (-mun′dē). [< Tupi]

coat·ing (kō′ting) *n.* **1.** A covering layer; coat. **2.** Cloth for coats.

coat of arms 1. A shield marked with the insignia of a person or family. **2.** A representation of such insignia.

coat of mail *pl.* **coats of mail** A defensive garment made of chain mail; a hauberk.

coat·tail (kōt′tāl′) *n.* The loose, back part of a coat below the waist; also, either half of this in a coat split at the back.

coax (kōks) *v.t.* **1.** To persuade or seek to persuade by gentleness, tact, flattery, etc.; wheedle. **2.** To obtain by coaxing: to *coax* a promise from someone. — *v.i.* **3.** To use persuasion or cajolery. — *n.* One who coaxes. [< earlier *cokes* a fool, dupe] — **coax′er** *n.* — **coax′ing·ly** *adv.*

co·ax·i·al (kō-ak′sē-əl) *adj.* **1.** Having a common axis or coincident axes. Also **co·ax·al** (kō-ak′səl). **2.** Describing a cable consisting of two or more insulated conductors capable of transmitting radio or television signals or multiple telegraph or telephone messages.

cob (kob) *n.* **1.** A corncob. **2.** A male swan. **3.** A thickset horse with short legs. **4.** A lump. [ME *cobbe*]

co·balt (kō′bôlt) *n.* A tough, lustrous, pinkish gray, metallic element (symbol Co), used as an alloy and in pigments. See ELEMENT. [< G *kobalt,* var. of *kobold* goblin] — **co·bal′tic** *adj.* — **co·bal′tous** *adj.*

cobalt blue 1. A permanent, deep blue pigment, made from oxides of cobalt and aluminum. **2.** An intense blue.

cob·ble¹ (kob′əl) *n.* A cobblestone. — *v.t.* **·bled, ·bling** To pave with cobblestones. [Akin to COB¹]

cob·ble² (kob′əl) *v.t.* **·bled, ·bling 1.** To repair, as shoes. **2.** To put together roughly. [Origin uncertain]

cob·bler¹ (kob′lər) *n.* One who patches boots and shoes.

cob·bler² (kob′lər) *n.* **1.** An iced drink made of wine, sugar, fruit juices, etc. **2.** *U.S.* A deep-dish fruit pie with no bottom crust. [Origin unknown]

cob·ble·stone (kob′əl·stōn′) *n.* A naturally rounded stone, formerly used for paving.

cob coal Coal in large, round lumps.

co·bel·lig·er·ent (kō′bə·lij′ər·ənt) *n.* A country waging war in cooperation with another or others.

co·bra (kō′brə) *n.* A venomous snake of Asia and Africa that when excited can dilate its neck into a broad hood; esp., the **spectacled cobra** of India, and the **king cobra.** [< Pg. < L *colubra* snake]

cob·web (kob′web′) *n.* **1.** The network of fine thread spun by a spider; also, a single thread of this. **2.** Something like a cobweb in flimsiness, or in its ability to ensnare. — *v.t.* **·webbed, ·web·bing** To cover with or as with cobwebs. [ME *coppeweb* < *coppe* spider + WEB] — **cob′web′by** *adj.*

co·ca (kō′kə) *n.* **1.** The dried leaves of a South American shrub, yielding cocaine and other alkaloids. **2.** The shrub itself. [< Sp. < Quechua]

co·caine (kō·kān′, kō′kān; *in technical usage* kō′kə·ēn) *n.* A bitter, crystalline alkaloid, $C_{17}H_{21}NO_4$, contained in coca leaves, used as a local anesthetic and as a narcotic. Also **co·cain′, co·cain′.** [< COCA + -INE²]

COBRA
a Indian or spectacled cobra.
b Markings or "spectacles" on back of head. (To 6 feet long)

cocci- *combining form* Berry; berry-shaped. [< Gk. *kokkos* berry, seed]

coc·coid (kok′oid) *adj. Bacteriol.* Like a coccus, as certain forms of bacteria.

coc·cus (kok′əs) *n. pl.* **coc·ci** (kok′sī) *Bacteriol.* One of the principal forms of bacteria, characterized by an ovoid or spherical shape. [< NL < Gk. *kokkos* berry]

-coccus *combining form* Berry-shaped. [< Gk. *kokkos* berry, seed]

coc·cyx (kok′siks) *n. pl.* **coc·cy·ges** (kok-sī′jēz) *Anat.* The small triangular bone consisting of four or five rudimentary vertebrae at the caudal end of the spine. For illus. see PELVIS. [< L < Gk. *kokkyx* cuckoo; from a fancied resemblance to a cuckoo's bill] — **coc·cyg·e·al** (kok-sij′ē-əl) *adj.*

coch·i·neal (koch′ə·nēl′, koch′ə·nēl) *n.* A brilliant scarlet dye prepared from the dried bodies of the female of a scale insect of tropical America and Java. [< F < Sp. < L < Gk. *kokkos*]

coch·le·a (kok′lē·ə) *n. pl.* **·le·ae** (-lī·ē) *Anat.* A spirally wound tube in the internal ear, forming an essential part of the mechanism of hearing. For illus. see EAR. [< L, snail] — **coch′le·ar** *adj.*

coch·le·ate (kok′lē·āt) *adj.* Spirally twisted like a snail shell. Also **coch′le·at′ed.**

cock¹ (kok) *n.* **1.** A full-grown male of the domestic fowl; a rooster. **2.** Any male bird. **3.** A leader; champion. **4.** A faucet, often with the nozzle bent downward. **5.** In a firearm, the hammer; also, the condition of readiness for firing. **6.** A significant jaunty tip or upward turn, as of a hat brim. — *v.t.* **1.** To set the mechanism of (a firearm) so as to be ready for firing. **2.** To turn up or to one side alertly, jauntily, or inquiringly, as the head, eye, ears, etc. **3.** To bring to a position of readiness. — *v.i.* **4.** To cock a firearm. **5.** To stick up prominently. — *adj.* Male. [OE *cocc*]

cock² (kok) *n.* A conical pile of straw or hay. — *v.t.* To arrange in piles or cocks, as hay. [< ON *kökkr* lump, heap]

cock·ade (kok·ād′) *n.* A knot of ribbon, or the like, worn on the hat as a badge. [< MF *coq* cock] — **cock·ad′ed** *adj.*

Cockade State Nickname of Maryland.

cock·a·too (kok′ə·tōō′, kok′ə·tōō) *n. pl.* **·toos** Any of various brightly colored, crested parrots of the East Indies or Australia. [< Du. < Malay *kakatūa*]

cock·a·trice (kok′ə·tris) *n.* A fabulous serpent, said to be hatched from a cock's egg, deadly to those who felt its breath or met its glance. [< OF *cocatris* (infl. by *coq* cock)]

cock·boat (kok′bōt) *n.* A ship's small rowboat: also called **cockle boat.** [< obs. *cock* (< MF *coque* small boat) + BOAT]

cock·chaf·er (kok′chā′fər) *n.* A large European beetle destructive to vegetation. [< COCK¹ (def. 3) + CHAFER]

cock·crow (kok′krō′) *n.* Early morning. Also **cock′crow′·ing.**

cocked hat (kokt) A hat with the brim turned up, esp. in three places; a tricorn. — **to knock into a cocked hat** To demolish; ruin.

cock·er·el (kok′ər·əl) *n.* A cock less than a year old.

cock·er spaniel (kok′ər) A small, sturdy spaniel of solid or variegated coloring, used for hunting and as a house pet. Also **cocker.** [? Because used in hunting woodcock]

cock·eye (kok′ī) *n.* A squinting eye.

cock·eyed (kok′īd′) *adj.* **1.** Cross-eyed. **2.** *Slang* Off center; askew. **3.** *Slang* Absurd; ridiculous. **4.** *Slang* Drunk.

cock·fight (kok′fīt′) *n.* A fight between gamecocks that are usually fitted with steel spurs. — **cock′fight′ing** *adj. & n.*

cock·horse (kok′hôrs′) *n.* A rocking horse or hobbyhorse.

cock·le¹ (kok′əl) *n.* **1.** A European bivalve mollusk, esp. an edible species, with ridged, somewhat heart-shaped shells. **2.** Any of various similar mollusks. **3.** A cockleshell. **4.** A wrinkle; pucker. — **the cockles of one's heart** The depths of one's heart or feelings. — *v.t. & v.i.* **·led, ·ling** To wrinkle; pucker. [< F < L < Gk. *konchē* a shell, mussel]

cock·le² (kok′əl) *n.* A weed that grows among grain, as the darnel. [OE *coccel*]

cock·le·bur (kok′əl·bûr′) *n.* **1.** A coarse, branching weed having burs about an inch long. **2.** The burdock.

cock·le·shell (kok′əl·shel′) *n.* **1.** The shell of a cockle. **2.** A scallop shell. **3.** A frail, light boat. [< COCKLE¹ + SHELL]

cock·ney (kok′nē) *n.* **1.** *Often cap.* A resident of the East End of London. **2.** The dialect or accent of East End Londoners: also **cock′ney·ese′** (-ēz′, -ēs′). — *adj.* Of or like cockneys or their speech. [ME *cokeney*, lit., a pampered child, a soft person, a city man] — **cock′ney·ish** *adj.*

cock·ney·ism (kok′nē·iz′əm) *n.* A mannerism, idiom, or way of speaking peculiar to cockneys.

cock·pit (kok′pit′) *n.* **1.** A compartment in the fuselage of some small airplanes, where the pilot and copilot sit. **2.** A pit or ring for cockfighting. **3.** *Naut.* In small vessels, a space toward the stern lower than the rest of the deck.

cock·roach (kok′rōch′) *n.* Any of a large group of swift-running, chiefly nocturnal insects, many of which are household pests. [< Sp. *cucaracha*]

cocks·comb (koks′kōm′) *n.* **1.** The comb of a cock. **2.** A plant with showy red or yellowish flowers. **3.** A coxcomb.

cock·spur (kok′spûr′) *n.* **1.** A spur on the leg of a cock. **2.** A kind of hawthorn with long thorns.

cock·sure (kok′shŏŏr′) *adj.* **1.** Absolutely sure. **2.** Overly self-confident; presumptuously sure. — **cock′sure′ness** *n.*

cock·swain (kok′sən, -swān′) See COXSWAIN.

cock·tail (kok′tāl′) *n.* **1.** Any of various chilled alcoholic drinks, consisting usu. of brandy, whisky, gin, etc., mixed with other liquors, fruit juice, etc. **2.** An appetizer, as chilled diced fruits, fruit juices, or seafood seasoned with sauce. [? Alter. of F *coquetel*]

cock·y (kok′ē) *adj.* **cock·i·er, cock·i·est** *Informal* Pertly or swaggeringly self-confident; conceited. — **cock′i·ly** *adv.* — **cock′i·ness** *n.*

co·co (kō′kō) *n. pl.* **·cos** **1.** The coconut palm. **2.** The fruit of the coconut palm. — *adj.* Made of the fiber of the coconut. [< Pg., grinning face]

co·coa (kō′kō) *n.* **1.** A powder made from the roasted, husked seed kernels of the cacao; chocolate. **2.** A beverage made from this. **3.** A reddish brown color. [Alter. of CACAO]

cocoa butter A fatty substance obtained from cacao seeds, used for making soap, cosmetics, etc.: also called *cacao butter.*

co·co·nut (kō′kə·nut′, -nət) *n.* The fruit of the coconut palm, having white meat enclosed in a hard shell, and containing a milky liquid. Also **co′coa·nut′.**

coconut milk The milky fluid within the fresh coconut.

coconut oil The oil derived from the dried meat of the coconut, used in soaps, foodstuffs, etc.

coconut palm A tropical palm tree bearing coconuts. Also **coco palm, coconut tree.**

co·coon (kə·kōōn′) *n.* The envelope spun by the larvae of certain insects, in which they are enclosed in the pupal or chrysalis state. [< F *coque* shell]

cod (kod) *n. pl.* **cod** or **cods** An important food fish of the North Atlantic. [Origin unknown]

co·da (kō′də) *n. Music* A passage at the end of a composition or movement that brings it to a formal, complete close. [< Ital. < L *cauda* tail]

cod·dle (kod′l) *v.t.* **·dled, ·dling** **1.** To boil gently; simmer in water. **2.** To treat as a baby or an invalid; pamper. [? Akin to CAUDLE] — **cod′dler** *n.*

code (kōd) *n.* **1.** A systematized body of law. **2.** Any system of principles or regulations. **3.** A set of signals, characters, or symbols used in communication. **4.** A set of words, letters, or numerals, used for secrecy or brevity in transmitting messages. — *v.t.* **cod·ed, cod·ing** **1.** To systematize; as laws; make a digest of. **2.** To put into the symbols of a code. [< F < L *codex* writing tablet]

co·deine (kō′dēn, kō′di·ēn) *n. Chem.* A white crystalline alkaloid, $C_{18}H_{21}NO_3$, derived from morphine and used in medicine as a mild narcotic. Also **co·de·in** (kō′dē·in, kō′dēn), **co·de·ia** (kō·dē′ə). [< Gk. *kōdeia* head of a poppy + -INE²]

co·dex (kō′deks) *n. pl.* **·di·ces** (kō′də·sēz, kod′ə-) An ancient manuscript volume, as of Scripture. [< L, tablet]

codg·er (koj′ər) *n. Informal* An eccentric or testy man, esp. an old one. [Prob. var. of *cadger*]

cod·i·cil (kod′ə·səl) *n.* **1.** *Law* A supplement to a will, changing or explaining something in it. **2.** An appendix; addition. [< L *codex* writing tablet] — **cod·i·cil·la·ry** (kod′ə·sil′ər·ē) *adj.*

cod·i·fy (kod′ə·fī, kō′də-) *v.t.* **·fied, ·fy·ing** To systematize, as laws. [< F *code* system, code] — **cod′i·fi·ca′tion** *n.* — **cod′i·fi′er** *n.*

cod·ling¹ (kod′ling) *n. pl.* **·lings** (*Rare* **·ling**) **1.** A young cod. **2.** Any of certain related fishes. [Dim. of COD¹]

cod·ling² (kod′ling) *n.* **1.** One of a variety of elongated tapering cooking apples. **2.** Any hard, unripe apple for stewing. Also **cod·lin** (kod′lin). [ME *querdling*]

codling moth A moth whose larvae feed on apples, pears, quinces, etc. Also **codlin moth.**

cod-liver oil (kod′liv′ər, kod′liv′ər) Oil from the livers of cod, used in medicine as a source of vitamins A and D.

co·ed (kō′ed′) *Informal n.* A woman student at a coeducational institution. — *adj.* Coeducational. Also **co-ed′.**

co·ed·u·ca·tion (kō′ej·ŏŏ·kā′shən) *n.* The education of both sexes in the same school. — **co′ed·u·ca′tion·al** *adj.*

co·ef·fi·cient (kō′ə·fish′ənt) *n.* **1.** *Math.* A number or letter put before an algebraic expression and multiplying it. **2.** *Physics* A number indicating the kind and amount of change in a substance, body, or process under given conditions. — *adj.* Acting together.

coe·la·canth (sē′lə·kanth) *n. Zool.* A large-bodied, hollow-spined fish, extinct except for one species. [< COEL(O)- + Gk. *akantha* spine]

-coele Var. of -CELE².

coe·len·ter·ate (si·len′tə·rāt) *Zool. n.* Any of a phylum of invertebrate animals having a large body cavity that functions as a vascular as well as a digestive system, including sea anemones, corals, jellyfish, and hydras. — *adj.* Belonging or pertaining to this phylum. [< COEL(O)- + Gk. *enteron* intestine] — **coe·len·ter·ic** (sē′len·ter′ik) *adj.*

COELACANTH
(4 to 5½ feet long)

coe·li·ac (sē′lē·ak) See CELIAC.

coelo- *combining form* Cavity; cavity of the body, or of an organ. Also, before vowels, **coel-.** [< Gk. *koilos* hollow]

coe·lom (sē′ləm) *n. Zool.* The body cavity of a metazoan, between the viscera and the body wall: also spelled *celom.* Also **coe·lome** (sē′lōm). [< Gk. *koilōma* cavity]

coeno- See CENO-.

coe·no·bite (sen′ə·bīt, sē′nə-) See CENOBITE.

co·e·qual (kō·ē′kwəl) *adj.* Of the same value, age, size, etc. — *n.* The equal of another or others.

co·erce (kō·ûrs′) *v.t.* ·erced, ·erc·ing 1. To compel by force, law, authority, or fear. 2. To restrain or repress by superior force. 3. To bring about by forcible measures: to *coerce* compliance. [< L < *co-* together + *arcere* to shut up, restrain] — co·er′cer *n.* — co·er′ci·ble *adj.*

co·er·cion (kō·ûr′shən) *n.* 1. Forcible constraint or restraint, moral or physical. 2. Government by force. — co·er·cion·ar·y (kō·ûr′shən·er′ē) *adj.* — co·er′cion·ist *n.*

co·er·cive (kō·ûr′siv) *adj.* Serving or tending to coerce. — co·er′cive·ly *adv.* — co·er′cive·ness *n.*

co·e·val (kō·ē′vəl) *adj.* 1. Of or belonging to the same age, time, or duration. 2. Contemporary. — *n.* 1. One of the same age. 2. A contemporary. Also spelled *coaeval.* [< L < *co-* together + *aevum* age] — co·e′val·ly *adv.*

co·ex·ist (kō′ig·zist′) *v.i.* To exist together, in or at the same place or time. — co′ex·ist′ence *n.* — co′ex·ist′ent *adj.*

co·ex·tend (kō′ik·stend′) *v.t. & v.i.* To extend through the same space or time. [< CO-¹ + EXTEND] — co′ex·ten′sion *n.* — co′ex·ten′sive *adj.* — co′ex·ten′sive·ly *adv.*

cof·fee (kôf′ē, kof′ē) *n.* 1. A beverage made from the roasted and ground beans of a tropical evergreen shrub. 2. The seeds or beans of this shrub: also **coffee beans.** 3. The shrub itself, native to Asia and Africa and widely grown in Brazil. 4. The brown color of coffee with cream. [< Ital. < Turkish < Arabic *qahwah*]

coffee break *U.S.* A short recess from work during which coffee or other refreshments are taken.

coffee cake A kind of cake to be eaten with coffee, often containing raisins or nuts and topped with sugar or icing.

coffee house A public room where coffee is the main beverage. Also **cof·fee·house** (kôf′ē·hous′, kof′ē-).

coffee shop A restaurant or public room where coffee and food are served. Also **coffee room.**

coffee table A low table, generally placed in front of a sofa, for serving refreshments, etc.

cof·fer (kôf′ər, kof′-) *n.* 1. A chest or box, esp. one for valuables. 2. *pl.* Financial resources; a treasury. 3. A decorative, sunken panel in a ceiling, dome, etc. 4. A lock in a canal. 5. A cofferdam. — *v.t.* 1. To place in a coffer. 2. To adorn with coffers. [< F < L < Gk. *kophinos* basket]

cof·fer·dam (kôf′ər·dam, kof′-) *n.* 1. A temporary enclosure built in the water and pumped dry to permit work on bridge piers and the like. 2. A watertight structure attached to a ship's side for repairs made below the water line.

cof·fin (kôf′in, kof′-) *n.* A box or case in which a corpse is buried. — *v.t.* To put into or as into a coffin. [< OF < L < Gk. *kophinos* basket]

cog (kog) *n.* 1. *Mech.* A tooth or one of a series of teeth projecting from the surface of a wheel or gear to impart or receive motion. 2. One who plays a minor but necessary part in a large or complex process. 3. A projecting part on the end of a timber, used for forming a joint; tenon. [ME *cogge* < Scand.] — cogged *adj.*

co·gent (kō′jənt) *adj.* Compelling belief, assent, or action; forcible; convincing. [< L < *cogere* to compel] — co′gen·cy *n.* — co′gent·ly *adv.*

cog·i·tate (koj′ə·tāt) *v.t. & v.i.* ·tat·ed, ·tat·ing To give careful thought (to); ponder; meditate. [< L < *co-* together + *agitare* to consider] — cog·i·ta·ble (koj′ə·tə·bəl) *adj.* — cog′i·ta·tor *n.*
— **Syn.** think, deliberate, reflect, reason, cerebrate.

cog·i·ta·tion (koj′ə·tā′shən) *n.* Careful consideration; reflection; thought.

cog·i·ta·tive (koj′ə·tā′tiv) *adj.* Capable of or given to cogitation. — cog′i·ta·tive·ly *adv.* — cog′i·ta·tive·ness *n.*

co·gnac (kōn′yak, kon′-) *n.* 1. Brandy produced in the Cognac region of western France. 2. Any brandy. [< F]

cog·nate (kog′nāt) *adj.* 1. Allied by blood; kindred. 2. Allied by derivation from the same source; belonging to the same stock or root: English "cold" and Latin "gelidus" are *cognate* words. 3. Allied in characteristics; similar. — *n.* A cognate person or thing. [< L < *co-* together + pp. of (*g*)*nasci* to be born] — cog·na′tion *n.*

cog·ni·tion (kog·nish′ən) *n.* 1. The act or faculty of knowing or perceiving. 2. A thing known; a perception. — **Syn.** See KNOWLEDGE. [< L < *co-* together + (*g*)*noscere* to know] — cog·ni′tion·al *adj.* — cog′ni·tive *adj.*

cog·ni·za·ble (kog′nə·zə·bəl, kon′ə-, kog·nī′zə·bəl) *adj.* 1. Capable of being known. 2. Capable of being tried or examined by a court. — cog′ni·za·bly *adv.*

cog·ni·zance (kog′nə·zəns, kon′ə-) *n.* 1. Apprehension or perception of fact; knowledge; notice. 2. *Law* a The hearing of a case by a court. b The right of a court to hear a case. 3. Range or sphere of what can be known. — **to take cognizance of** To acknowledge; recognize; notice. [< OF < L < *co-* together + pp. of (*g*)*nasci* to be born]

cog·ni·zant (kog′nə·zənt, kon′ə-) *adj.* Having knowledge; aware: with *of.*

cog·nize (kog′nīz) *v.t.* ·nized, ·niz·ing To know, perceive, or recognize. Also *Brit.* **cog′nise.**

cog·no·men (kog·nō′mən) *n.* *pl.* ·no·mens or ·nom·i·na (-nom′ə·nə) 1. A surname. 2. In ancient Rome, the last of a citizen's three names. 3. Loosely, any name, nickname, or appellation. [< L < *co-* together + (*g*)*nomen* name] — cog·nom·i·nal (kog·nom′ə·nəl) *adj.*

cog·wheel (kog′hwēl′) *n.* A wheel with cogs, used to transmit or receive motion: also called *gearwheel.*

co·hab·it (kō·hab′it) *v.i.* To live together as husband and wife, esp. illegally. [< LL < L < *co-* together + *habitare* to live] — co·hab′i·tant, co·hab′it·er *n.* — co·hab′i·ta′tion *n.*

co·here (kō·hir′) *v.i.* ·hered, ·her·ing 1. To stick or hold firmly together. 2. To be logically connected, as the parts of a story. [< L < *co-* together + *haerere* to stick]

co·her·ence (kō·hir′əns) *n.* 1. A sticking together; conjunction; cohesion. 2. Logical connection or consistency; congruity: the *coherence* of his thoughts. Also **co·her′en·cy.**

co·her·ent (kō·hir′ənt) *adj.* 1. Sticking together, as particles of the same substance. 2. Observing logical order and connection; consistent. 3. Intelligible or articulate, as speech. — co·her′ent·ly *adv.*

co·he·sion (kō·hē′zhən) *n.* 1. The act or state of cohering. 2. *Physics* That force by which molecules of the same kind or the same body are held together.

co·he·sive (kō·hē′siv) *adj.* Having or exhibiting cohesion. — co·he′sive·ly *adv.* — co·he′sive·ness *n.*

co·hort (kō′hôrt) *n.* 1. The tenth of an ancient Roman legion, 300 to 600 men. 2. A band or group, esp. of warriors. 3. A companion or follower. [< L *cohors, cohortis*]

coif (koif) *n.* A close-fitting cap or hood, as that worn by nuns under the veil. — *v.t.* To cover with or as with a coif. [< OF < LL *cofea* < Gmc.]

coif·feur (kwä·fœr′) *n.* *French* A hairdresser.

coif·fure (kwä·fyoor′, *Fr.* kwà·für′) *n.* 1. A style of arranging or dressing the hair. 2. A headdress. — *v.t.* To dress (the hair). Also **coif** (kwäf). [< F < OF *coife.* See COIF.]

coign (koin) *n.* A projecting angle or stone; a corner. Also **coigne.** [Var. of QUOIN.]

coil (koil) *n.* 1. A series of concentric rings or spirals, as that formed by winding a rope. 2. A single ring or spiral of such a series. 3. A spiral pipe, or series of pipes, forming a continuous conduit, as in a radiator. 4. *Electr.* a A conductor consisting of a number of turns of wire wound on an insulating coil. b An induction coil. 5. *Canadian* A small stack of hay. — *v.t.* 1. To wind spirally or in rings. — *v.i.* 2. To form rings or coils. [< OF < L < *com-* together + *legere* to choose] — coil′er *n.*

coin (koin) *n.* 1. A piece of metal stamped by government authority for use as money. 2. Metal currency collectively. 3. *Archit.* A corner or angle of a building; quoin. — *v.t.* 1. To stamp (coins) from metal. 2. To make into coins. 3. To originate or invent, as a word or phrase. — **to coin money** *Informal* To make money rapidly. [< F, wedge, die < L *cuneus* wedge] — coin′a·ble *adj.* — coin′er *n.*

coin·age (koi′nij) *n.* 1. The act or right of making coins. 2. The coins made; metal money. 3. The system of coins of a country; currency. 4. The act of fabricating or inventing anything, esp. a word or phrase. 5. Something fabricated, as an artificially created word.

co·in·cide (kō′in·sīd′) *v.i.* ·cid·ed, ·cid·ing 1. To have the same dimensions and position in space. 2. To occur at the same time. 3. To agree exactly; accord. [< MF < Med.L < L *co-* together + *incidere* to happen]

co·in·ci·dence (kō·in′sə·dəns) *n.* 1. The fact or condition of coinciding; correspondence. 2. A remarkable concurrence of events, ideas, etc., apparently by mere chance.

co·in·ci·dent (kō·in′sə·dənt) *adj.* 1. Having the same position and extent. 2. Occurring at the same time. 3. In exact agreement; consonant: with *with.* — co·in′ci·dent·ly *adv.*

co·in·ci·den·tal (kō·in′sə·den′tal) *adj.* Characterized by or involving coincidence. — co·in′ci·den′tal·ly *adv.*

coir (koir) *n.* Coconut-husk fiber, used in making ropes, matting, etc.: also called *kyar.* [< Malay *kāyar* rope]

co·i·tion (kō·ish′ən) *n.* Sexual intercourse. Also **co·i·tus** (kō′i·təs). [< L < *co-* together + *ire* to go]

coke (kōk) *n.* A solid, carbonaceous fuel obtained by heating coal in ovens or retorts to remove its gases. — *v.t. & v.i.* coked, cok·ing To change into coke. [? ME *colke.*]

col-¹ Var. of COM-.

col-² Var. of COLO-.

co·la (kō′lə) A small tropical tree bearing cola nuts: also spelled *kolo.* [< *kola* native African name]

cola nut The seed of the cola, yielding an extract used in the manufacture of soft drinks: also spelled *kola nut.*

col·an·der (kul′ən·dər, kol′-) *n.* A perforated vessel for draining off liquids: also *cullender.* [< L *colare* to strain]

cold (kōld) *adj.* 1. Having a relatively low temperature; having little or no perceptible heat: a *cold* night. 2. Having a relatively low temperature as compared with a normal body temperature: *cold* hands. 3. Feeling no or insufficient warmth; chilled. 4. Without vital heat; dead. 5. Detached; objective: *cold* reason. 6. Lacking in affection. 7.

Lacking in sexual desire; frigid. **8.** Unfriendly. **9.** Chilling to the spirit; depressing. **10.** *U.S. Informal* Unconscious, as from a blow. **11.** Lacking freshness; stale; old: a *cold* trail. **12.** *Informal* Distant from the object sought: said of a seeker in a game, etc. **13.** In art, bluish in tone. **— cold feet** *Informal* Loss of courage; timidity. **— to throw cold water on** To discourage by being unenthusiastic or indifferent (about something). **—** *adv. U.S. Slang* Thoroughly; with certainty: to know it *cold*. **—** *n.* **1.** The comparative lack of heat. **2.** The sensation caused by loss or lack of heat. **3.** An acute infection of the mucous membranes of the upper respiratory tract, caused by a virus, and characterized by sneezing, coughing, etc. **— out in the cold** Ignored; neglected. **— to catch (or take) cold** To become affected with a cold. [OE *cald*] **— cold′ly** *adv.* **— cold′ness** *n.*
cold-blood·ed (kōld′blud′id) *adj.* **1.** Unsympathetic; heartless. **2.** Sensitive to cold. **3.** *Zool.* Having a blood temperature that varies with the environments, as in reptiles. **— cold′-blood′ed·ly** *adv.* **— cold′-blood′ed·ness** *n.*
cold chisel A chisel of tempered steel for cutting cold metal.
cold cream A cleansing and soothing ointment for the skin.
cold front *Meteorol.* The irregular, forward edge of a cold air mass advancing beneath and against a warmer mass.
cold·heart·ed (kōld′här′tid) *adj.* Without sympathy; unkind. **— cold′heart′ed·ly** *adv.* **— cold′heart′ed·ness** *n.*
cold shoulder *Informal* A deliberate slight.
cold sore An eruption about the mouth or nostrils, often accompanying a cold or fever.
cold turkey *U.S. Slang* **1.** The abrupt and total deprivation of a substance, as a narcotic drug, from one addicted to its use. **2.** Blunt talk, often unwelcome to the listener.
cold war An intense rivalry between nations, as in diplomatic strategy, falling just short of armed conflict.
cold wave *Meteorol.* An unusual drop in temperature; a spell of cold weather, usu. moving along a specified course.
cole (kōl) *n.* A plant related to the cabbage, esp. rape. Also **cole′wort′** (-wûrt). [OE *cāl, cāwl* < L *caulis* cabbage]
co·le·op·ter·ous (kō′lē·op′tər·əs, kol′ē-) *adj.* Belonging to a large order of insects, including the beetles and weevils, having horny front wings that fit as cases over the hind wings. [< NL < Gk. *koleos* sheath + *pteron* wing]
cole·slaw (kōl′slô′) *n.* A salad of shredded raw cabbage. Also **cole slaw.** [< Du *kool sla* cabbage salad]
col·ic (kol′ik) *n.* Acute abdominal pain resulting from muscular spasms. **—** *adj.* Pertaining to, near, or affecting the colon. [< F < L < Gk. *kolon* colon] **— col′ick·y** *adj.*
-coline Var. of -COLOUS.
col·i·se·um (kol′ə·sē′əm) *n.* A large building or stadium for exhibitions, sports events, etc.: also spelled *colosseum.*
Col·i·se·um (kol′ə·sē′əm) See COLOSSEUM.
co·li·tis (kə·lī′tis) *n. Pathol.* Inflammation of the colon.
col·lab·o·rate (kə·lab′ə·rāt) *v.i.* **·rat·ed, ·rat·ing 1.** To work or cooperate with another, esp. in literary or scientific pursuits. **2.** To be a collaborationist. [< LL < L *com-* with + *laborare* to work] **— col′la·bo·ra′tion** *n.* **— col·lab′o·ra′tive** *adj.* **— col·lab′o·ra′tor** *n.*
col·lab·o·ra·tion·ist (kə·lab′ə·rā′shən·ist) *n.* A citizen of an occupied country who cooperates with the enemy.
col·lage (kə·läzh′) *n.* An artistic composition consisting of or including flat materials pasted on a picture surface; also, the technique of making such compositions. Compare ASSEMBLAGE (def. 4). [< F, pasting < *colle* glue]
col·lapse (kə·laps′) *v.* **·lapsed, ·laps·ing** *v.i.* **1.** To give way; cave in. **2.** To fail utterly; come to naught. **3.** To assume a more compact form by being folded. **4.** To lose health, strength, etc., suddenly. **5.** To lose all or part of its air content, as a lung. **—** *v.t.* **6.** To cause to collapse. **—** *n.* **1.** The act or process of collapsing. **2.** Extreme prostration. **3.** Utter failure; ruin. [< L < *com-* together + *labi* to fall] **— col·laps′i·ble** or **col·laps′a·ble** *adj.* **— col·laps′i·bil′i·ty** *n.*
col·lar (kol′ər) *n.* **1.** The part of a garment at the neck, often folded over. **2.** A band of leather or metal for the neck of an animal. **3.** A cushion placed around the neck of a draft animal to bear most of the strain of the pull. **4.** *Mech.* Any of various devices encircling a rod or shaft, to form a connection, etc. **—** *v.t.* **1.** To provide with a collar. **2.** To grasp by the collar; capture. [< OF, AF < L *collum* neck]
col·lar·bone (kol′ər·bōn′) *n.* The clavicle.
col·lard (kol′ərd) *n. Usu. pl.* A variety of cabbage that does not form a head. [Alter. of *colewort.* See COLE.]
col·late (kə·lāt′, kol′āt) *v.t.* **·lat·ed, ·lat·ing 1.** To compare critically, as writings or facts. **2.** In bookbinding, to examine (the gathered sheets to be bound) in order to verify and correct their arrangement. [< L < *com-* together + *ferre* to bear, carry] **— col·la′tor** (kə·lā′tər, kol′ā·tər) *n.*
col·lat·er·al (kə·lat′ər·əl) *adj.* **1.** Lying or running side by side; parallel. **2.** Concomitant. **3.** Tending to the same conclusion; corroborative. **4.** Subordinate; secondary. **5.**

Guaranteed by stocks, bonds, property, etc.: a *collateral* loan. **6.** Descended from a common ancestor, but in a different line. **—** *n.* **1.** *U.S.* Security pledge for a loan or obligation. **2.** A collateral kinsman. [< Med.L < L *com-* together + *lateralis* lateral] **— col·lat′er·al·ly** *adv.*
collateral adjective An adjective closely related to a given noun in meaning, but not in immediate origin, as *brachial* is to *arm.*
col·la·tion (kə·lā′shən) *n.* **1.** The act or process of collating. **2.** Any light, informal meal. [See COLLATE.]
col·league (kol′ēg) *n.* A fellow member of a profession, official body, etc.; an associate. [< F < L < *com-* together + *legere* to choose] **— col′league·ship** *n.*
col·lect¹ (kə·lekt′) *v.t.* **1.** To gather together; assemble. **2.** To bring together as a hobby: to *collect* stamps. **3.** To request and obtain (payments of money). **4.** To regain control: to *collect* one's wits. **—** *v.i.* **5.** To assemble or congregate, as people. **6.** To accumulate, as sand or dust. **7.** To gather payments or donations. **—** *adj. & adv.* To be paid for by the receiver: Send it *collect*; a *collect* call. [< L *collectus*, pp. of *colligere* < *com-* together + *legere* to choose] **— col·lect′a·ble** or **col·lect′i·ble** *adj.*
col·lect² (kol′ekt) *n. Eccl.* A short, formal prayer used in several Western liturgies. [See COLLECT¹.]
col·lect·ed (kə·lek′tid) *adj.* Composed; self-possessed. **— col·lect′ed·ly** *adv.* **— col·lect′ed·ness** *n.*
col·lec·tion (kə·lek′shən) *n.* **1.** The act or process of collecting. **2.** That which is collected. **3.** That which has accumulated: a *collection* of dirt. **4.** A soliciting of money, as for church expenses; also, the money.
col·lec·tive (kə·lek′tiv) *adj.* **1.** Formed or gathered together by collecting. **2.** Of, relating to, or proceeding from a number of persons or things together. **3.** *Gram.* Denoting in the singular number a collection or aggregate of individuals: a *collective* noun. **—** *n.* **1.** A collective enterprise or body, as a farm. **2.** The individuals comprising such a body or enterprise. **— col·lec′tive·ly** *adv.* **— col·lec′tive·ness, col·lec·tiv·i·ty** (kol′ek·tiv′ə·tē) *n.*
collective bargaining Negotiation between organized workers and employers on wages, hours, etc.
collective noun *Gram.* A singular noun naming a collection or group. It takes either a singular or a plural verb, depending upon whether it refers to the objects composing it as one aggregate or as separate individuals: The audience *was* large; The audience *were* divided in opinion.
col·lec·tiv·ism (kə·lek′tiv·iz′əm) *n.* A system in which the people as a whole, or the state, own and control the material and means of production and distribution. **— col·lec′tiv·ist** *adj. & n.* **— col·lec′tiv·is′tic** *adj.*
col·lec·tiv·ize (kə·lek′tiv·īz) *v.t.* **·ized, ·iz·ing** To organize (an agricultural settlement, industry, economy, etc.) on a collectivist basis. **— col·lec′tiv·i·za′tion** *n.*
col·lec·tor (kə·lek′tər) *n.* **1.** One who or that which collects. **2.** One who collects taxes, duties, debts, etc.
col·leen (kol′ēn, kə·lēn′) *n. Irish* A girl. [< Irish *cailín*]
col·lege (kol′ij) *n.* **1.** A school of higher learning that grants a bachelor's degree at the completion of a course of study. **2.** Any of the undergraduate divisions or schools of a university. **3.** A school for instruction in a special field or a profession. **4.** A building or buildings used by a college or university. **5.** A body of associates engaged in a common task and having certain rights: the electoral *college.* [< OF < L *collegium* body of associates]
College of Cardinals In the Roman Catholic Church, the body of cardinals who elect and advise the Pope, and, in his absence, administer the Holy See: also called *Sacred College.*
col·le·gian (kə·lē′jən, -jē·ən) *n.* A college student.
col·le·giate (kə·lē′jit, -jē·it) *adj.* Of, like, or intended for a college or for college students.
col·lide (kə·līd′) *v.i.* **·lid·ed, ·lid·ing 1.** To come together with violent impact; crash. **2.** To come into conflict; clash. [< L < *com-* together + *laedere* to strike]
col·lie (kol′ē) *n.* A large sheep dog of Scottish breed, characterized by a long, narrow head and full, long-haired coat. [Prob. < Scottish Gaelic *cuilean* puppy]
col·lier (kol′yər) *n.* **1.** *Chiefly Brit.* A coal miner. **2.** A vessel for carrying coal. [OE *col* coal + -IER]
col·lier·y (kol′yər·ē) *n. pl.* **·lier·ies** A coal mine.
col·li·mate (kol′ə·māt) *v.t.* **·mat·ed, ·mat·ing 1.** To bring into line or make parallel, as refracted rays of light. **2.** To adjust the line of sight of (a telescope, etc.). [< L < *com-* together + *lineare* to align] **— col′li·ma′tion** *n.*
col·li·ma·tor (kol′ə·mā′tər) *n. Optics.* A device used to obtain parallel rays of light, as a fixed telescope or the convex lens in a spectroscope. For illus. see SPECTROSCOPE.
col·li·sion (kə·lizh′ən) *n.* **1.** The act of colliding; a violent striking together. **2.** A clash of views or interests; conflict.
col·lo·cate (kol′ō·kāt) *v.t.* **·cat·ed, ·cat·ing** To place to-

gether or in relation; arrange. [< L < *com-* together + *locare* to place] — **col′lo·ca′tion** *n.*

col·lo·di·on (kə·lō′dē·ən) *n.* A flammable solution used as a coating for wounds and formerly for photographic plates. Also **col·lo·di·um** (kə·lō′dē·əm). [< Gk. < *kolla* glue]

col·loid (kol′oid) *n.* **1.** Any gluelike or jellylike substance, as gelatin, starch, raw egg white, etc., that diffuses not at all or very slowly through vegetable and animal membranes. **2.** *Chem.* A state of matter in which finely divided particles of one substance are suspended in another in such manner that the electrical and surface properties acquire special importance. — *adj.* Of or pertaining to a colloid or the colloid state: also **col·loi·dal** (kə·loid′l). [< Gk. *kolla* glue + -OID] — **col·loi·dal·i·ty** (kol/oi·dal/ə·tē) *n.*

col·lo·qui·al (kə·lō′kwē·əl) *adj.* **1.** Denoting a manner of speaking or writing that is characteristic of familiar conversation; informal. **2.** Conversational. — **col·lo′qui·al·ly** *adv.* — **col·lo′qui·al·ness** *n.*

col·lo·qui·al·ism (kə·lō′kwē·əl·iz′əm) *n.* **1.** An expression or form of speech of the type used in informal conversation. **2.** Informal, conversational style.

col·lo·quy (kol′ə·kwē) *n.* *pl.* **·quies** A conversation or conference, esp. a formal one. [< L < *com-* together + *loqui* to speak] — **col′lo·quist** *n.*

col·lude (kə·lōōd′) *v.i.* **·lud·ed, ·lud·ing** To cooperate secretly; conspire; connive. [< L < *com-* together + *ludere* to play, trick] — **col·lud′er** *n.*

col·lu·sion (kə·lōō′zhən) *n.* A secret agreement for a wrongful purpose; conspiracy. [See COLLUDE.]

col·lu·sive (kə·lōō′siv) *adj.* Secretly arranged to defraud another or to circumvent the law. — **col·lu′sive·ly** *adv.* — **col·lu′sive·ness** *n.*

colo- *combining form Anat.* Colon. Also, before vowels, **col-**. [< Gk. *kolon* colon]

co·logne (kə·lōn′) *n.* A toilet water consisting of alcohol scented with aromatic oils: also called *eau de Cologne.* Also **Cologne water.** [after *Cologne*]

co·lon¹ (kō′lən) *n. pl.* **co·lons** A punctuation mark (:), used as a sign of apposition or equality to connect one clause with another that explains it, after a word introducing a quotation, citation, etc., after the salutation in a formal letter, in expressing clock time, and in mathematical proportions. [< L < Gk. *kōlon* member, limb, clause]

co·lon² (kō′lən) *n. pl.* **co·lons** or **co·la** (kō′lə) *Anat.* The portion of the large intestine between the cecum and the rectum. For illus. see INTESTINE. [< L < Gk. *kolon*] — **co·lon·ic** (kə·lon′ik) *adj.*

co·lon³ (kō·lōn′) *n. pl.* **co·lons** (kō·lōnz′), *Sp.* **co·lo·nes** (kō·lō′näs) The monetary unit of Costa Rica and El Salvador.

colo·nel (kûr′nəl) *n. Mil.* A commissioned officer ranking next above a lieutenant colonel and next below a brigadier or brigadier general. See tables at GRADE. Abbr. *Col.* [< MF < Ital. *colonna* column of soldiers] — **colo′nel·cy, colo′nel·ship** *n.*

co·lo·ni·al (kə·lō′nē·əl) *adj.* **1.** Of, pertaining to, or living in a colony or colonies. **2.** Of or referring to the thirteen original colonies of the U.S. **3.** Describing a style of architecture that originated in the American colonies. — *n.* A citizen or inhabitant of a colony. — **co·lo′ni·al·ly** *adv.*

co·lo·ni·al·ism (kə·lō′nē·əl·iz′əm) *n.* The policy of a nation seeking to acquire, extend, or retain overseas dependencies.

col·o·nist (kol′ə·nist) *n.* **1.** A member or inhabitant of a colony. **2.** A settler or founder of a colony.

col·o·nize (kol′ə·nīz) *v.* **·nized, ·niz·ing** *v.t.* **1.** To set up a colony in; settle. **2.** To establish as colonists. — *v.i.* **3.** To establish or unite in a colony or colonies. Also *Brit.* **col′o·nise.** — **col′o·ni·za′tion** *n.* — **col′o·niz′er** *n.*

col·on·nade (kol′ə·nād′) *n. Archit.* A series of regularly spaced columns, usually supporting an entablature. [< F < *colonne* column] — **col′on·nad′ed** *adj.*

col·o·ny (kol′ə·nē) *n. pl.* **·nies 1.** A body of emigrants living in a land apart from, but under the control of, the parent country. **2.** The region thus settled. **3.** Any territory politically controlled by a distant state. **4.** A group of individuals from the same country, of the same occupation, etc., living in a particular part of a city, state, or country: a Chinese *colony.* **5.** The region or quarter occupied by such a group. **6.** *Biol.* A group of organisms of the same species functioning in close association as certain bacteria. **7.** *Ecol.* A group of similar plants or animals living in a particular locality. — **the Colonies** The British colonies that became the original thirteen States of the United States: New Hampshire, Massachusetts, Rhode Island, Connecticut, New York, New Jersey, Pennsylvania, Delaware, Maryland, Virginia, North Carolina, South Carolina, and Georgia. [< L *colonus* farmer]

col·o·phon (kol′ə·fon, -fən) *n.* An emblematic device adopted by a publisher, usu. printed on the title page of his books. [< LL < Gk. *kolophōn* summit, finishing touch]

col·or (kul′ər) *n.* **1.** A visual attribute of bodies or substances that depends upon the spectral composition of the wavelengths stimulating the retina and its associated neural structures. Colors are classified as *achromatic* (black and white and the grays), and *chromatic* (green, blue, red, etc.). **2.** A paint, dyestuff, or pigment. **3.** Complexion; hue of the skin. **4.** Ruddy complexion; also, a blush. **5.** The complexion of those peoples not classed as Caucasians, esp. of Negroes. **6.** *pl.* The ensign or flag of a nation, military or naval unit, etc. **7.** A color, ribbon, badge, etc., used for identification: college *colors.* **8.** *pl.* The side, or the opinions, arguments, etc., one upholds: Stick to your *colors.* **9.** Outward appearance; semblance; aspect: a *color* of reason. **10.** A false appearance; pretext; disguise: under *color* of religion. **11.** General character; sort; kind. **12.** Liveliness or vividness, esp. in literary work. **13.** In art and literature, the use of characteristic details to produce a realistic effect: local *color.* **14.** In art, the total effect of the colors in a painting. **15.** *Music* Timbre. **16.** *pl.* In the U.S. Navy, the salute made when the national flag is hoisted in the morning or lowered in the evening. — **to change color 1.** To turn pale. **2.** To blush. — **to lose color** To turn pale. — **to show one's (true) colors** To show one's real nature, beliefs, etc. — *v.t.* **1.** To apply or give color to, as by painting, staining, or dyeing. **2.** To misrepresent by distortion or exaggeration. **3.** To modify, influence, or change in nature or character. — *v.t.* **4.** To take on or change color, as ripening fruit. **5.** To blush. Also *Brit.* **col′our.** [< OF < L *color*] — **col′or·er** *n.*

col·or·a·ble (kul′ər·ə·bəl) *adj.* **1.** That may be colored. **2.** Capable of appearing true or right. **3.** Specious but apparently plausible; deceptive. Also *Brit.* **col′our·a·ble.** — **col′or·a·bil′i·ty, col′or·a·ble·ness** *n.* — **col′or·a·bly** *adv.*

col·o·ra·do (kol′ə·rä′dō) *adj.* Having medium strength and color: said of cigars. [< Sp., colored, red]

col·or·a·tion (kul′ə·rā′shən) *n.* Arrangement of colors, as in an animal or plant; coloring.

col·or·a·tu·ra (kul′ər·ə·tŏŏr′ə, -tyŏŏr′ə) *n.* **1.** In vocal music, runs, trills, or other florid decoration. **2.** Music characterized by this. **3.** A coloratura soprano. — *adj.* Characterized by or suitable for coloratura. [< Ital., coloration]

coloratura soprano A soprano voice or a singer able to sing coloratura.

color blindness The inability to preceive chromatic color, or, more commonly, to distinguish one of the three primary colors. — **col·or·blind** (kul′ər·blīnd′) *adj.*

col·or·cast (kul′ər·kast′, -käst′) *n.* A television broadcast in color. — *v.t. & v.i.* In television, to broadcast in color.

col·ored (kul′ərd) *adj.* **1.** Having color. **2.** Of a race other than the Caucasoid; especially, wholly or partially Negro. **3.** Of or relating to Negroes. **4.** Influenced or distorted; biased; tainted. **5.** False or misleading; specious.

Col·ored (kul′ərd) *n. pl.* **Col·ored** In South Africa, a person of mixed African and European or Asian parentage.

col·or·fast (kul′ər·fast′, -fäst′) *adj.* Resistant to fading or running: *colorfast* fabrics.

col·or·ful (kul′ər·fəl) *adj.* **1.** Full of colors, especially contrasting colors. **2.** Full of variety; vivid; picturesque: a *colorful* story. — **col′or·ful·ly** *adv.* — **col′or·ful·ness** *n.*

color guard Those who conduct the colors in a ceremony.

col·or·im·e·ter (kul′ə·rim′ə·tər) *n.* An apparatus for determining the hue, purity, and brightness of a color.

col·or·ing (kul′ər·ing) *n.* **1.** The act or manner of applying colors. **2.** A substance used to impart color. **3.** Appearance of anything as to color. **4.** False appearance.

col·or·ist (kul′ər·ist) *n.* **1.** One who uses color. **2.** An artist who uses colors skillfully. — **col′or·is′tic** *adj.*

col·or·less (kul′ər·lis) *adj.* **1.** Without color. **2.** Weak in color; pallid. **3.** Lacking vividness or variety; dull.

color line A social, political, and economic distinction drawn between the white and other races.

co·los·sal (kə·los′əl) *adj.* **1.** Of immense size or extent; enormous; huge. **2.** *Informal* Beyond belief or understanding: *colossal* pride. [< COLOSSUS] — **co·los′sal·ly** *adv.*

col·os·se·um (kol′ə·sē′əm) See COLISEUM.

Col·os·se·um (kol′ə·sē′əm) An amphitheater in Rome built by Vespasian and Titus in A.D. 75–80: also *Coliseum.*

Co·los·sian (kə·losh′ən) *n.* **1.** A native or inhabitant of Colossae. **2.** *pl.* (*construed as sing.*) A book of the New Testament, Saint Paul's epistle to the Colossians.

co·los·sus (kə·los′əs) *n. pl.* **co·los·si** (kə·los′ī) or **co·los·sus·es 1.** A gigantic statue. **2.** Something of great size or stature. [< L < Gk. *kolossos* gigantic statue]

Colossus of Rhodes A gigantic bronze statue of Apollo at the entrance to the harbor of ancient Rhodes about 285 B.C.

col·our (kul′ər) See COLOR.

-colous *combining form* Dwelling in or inhabiting. Also *-coline.* [< L *colere* to dwell, inhabit]

colt (kōlt) *n.* **1.** A young horse, donkey, etc.; esp., a young male horse. **2.** A young or inexperienced person. [OE] — **colt′ish** *adj.*

col·ter (kōl′tər) *n.* A blade or disk on a plow that cuts the sod: also spelled *coulter.* [OE < L *culter* knife]

col·u·brine (kol′yə·brīn, -brĭn) *adj.* **1.** Of or like a snake. **2.** Of or pertaining to a family of snakes that includes the garter snake, blacksnake, etc. [< L *coluber* snake]

col·um·bar·i·um (kol′əm·bâr′ē·əm) *n. pl.* **·bar·i·a** (-bâr′ē·ə) A dovecote; also, a pigeonhole in a dovecote. Also **col·um·bar·y** (kol′əm·ber′ē). [< L *columba* dove]

Co·lum·bi·a (kə·lum′bē·ə) *n. Poetic* The personification of the United States of America. [after Christopher *Columbus*] — **Co·lum′bi·an** *adj.*

col·um·bine (kol′əm·bīn) *n.* A herbaceous plant with variously colored flowers of five petals; esp., the **Colorado columbine**, State flower of Colorado. — *adj.* Dovelike. [< F < L *columba* dove]

Col·um·bine (kol′əm·bīn) A stock character in pantomimes, the daughter of Pantaloon and sweetheart of Harlequin.

co·lum·bi·um (kə·lum′bē·əm) *n.* Former name for the element niobium. [< NL < *Columbia*, the United States]

Columbus Day October 12, a holiday in most of the U.S. commemorating the discovery of America by Columbus.

col·umn (kol′əm) *n.* **1.** *Archit.* A post or pillar; esp., such a member consisting of base, shaft, and capital, serving as support or ornament. **2.** Something suggesting a column: the spinal *column.* **3.** *Printing* A section of printed matter on a page, usu. narrow and enclosed by a rule or blank space. **4.** An entertaining or instructive feature article that appears regularly in a newspaper or periodical. **5.** *Mil. & Naval* A formation in which elements of troops, vehicles, ships, or aircraft are placed one behind another. [< L *columna*] — **co·lum·nar** (kə·lum′nər), **col·umned** (kol′əmd) *adj.*

co·lum·ni·a·tion (kə·lum′nē·ā′shən) *n. Arch.* The use or grouping of columns.

col·um·nist (kol′əm·nist, -əm·ist) *n.* One who writes or conducts a special column in a newspaper or periodical.

col·za (kol′zə) *n.* The summer rape whose seeds produce rape oil. [< F < Du. *kool* cabbage + *zaad* seed]

colza oil Rape oil.

com- *prefix* With; together: *combine, compare.* Also: *co-* before *gn, h* and vowels; *col-* before *l,* as in *collide; con-* before *c, d, f, g, j, n, q, s, t, v,* as in *concur, confluence, connect, conspire; cor-* before *r,* as in *correspond.* [< L *com- < cum* with]

co·ma[1] (kō′mə) *n. pl.* **·mas 1.** *Pathol.* A condition of profound unconsciousness caused by disease, poison, or severe physical or nervous injury. **2.** Stupor. [< Gk. *kōma* deep sleep]

co·ma[2] (kō′mə) *n. pl.* **·mae** (-mē) **1.** *Astron.* A luminous, gaseous envelope around the nucleus of a comet. **2.** *Bot.* A tuft of silky hairs, as at the end of certain seeds. [< L, hair < Gk. *komē*] — **co′mal** *adj.*

Co·man·che (kō·man′chē, kə-) *n. pl.* **·ches 1.** An Indian of Shoshonean stock, ranging between Kansas and northern Mexico, now in Oklahoma. **2.** The language of this tribe.

co·ma·tose (kō′mə·tōs, kom′ə-) *adj.* **1.** Relating to or affected with coma or unconsciousness. **2.** Lethargic; torpid. [< COMA[1]] — **co′ma·tose·ly** *adv.*

comb (kōm) *n.* **1.** A toothed strip of hard, often flexible material, used for smoothing, dressing, or fastening the hair. **2.** A thing resembling this, as a card for dressing wool or flax. **3.** The fleshy crest on the head of a fowl. **4.** Honeycomb. — *v.t.* **1.** To dress or smooth with or as with a comb. **2.** To card, as wool or flax. **3.** To search carefully. — *v.i.* **4.** To crest and break: said of waves. [OE *camb*]

com·bat (*n.* kom′bat, kum′-; *v.* kəm·bat′) *n.* A battle or fight; struggle. — **close combat** Hand-to-hand fighting. — **single combat** A fight between two persons. — *v.* **·bat·ed** or **·bat·ted, ·bat·ing** or **·bat·ting** *v.t.* **1.** To fight or contend with; oppose in battle. **2.** To resist. — *v.i.* **3.** To do battle; struggle: with *with* or *against.* [< F < L *com-* + *batuere* to fight, beat] — **com·bat·a·ble** (kəm·bat′ə·bəl, kom′bat·ə·bəl, kum′-) *adj.* — **com·bat·er** (kom′bat·ər, kum′-, kəm·bat′ər) *n.*

com·bat·ant (kəm·bat′nt, kom′bə·tənt, kum′-) *n.* One engaged in or prepared for combat or hostilities. — *adj.* **1.** Fighting; battling. **2.** Ready or disposed to fight.

combat fatigue *Psychiatry* A psychoneurotic disorder characterized by anxiety, depression, loss of control, etc., associated with the stresses of modern warfare: formerly called *shell shock:* also called *battle fatigue.*

com·bat·ive (kəm·bat′iv, kom′bə·tiv, kum′-) *adj.* Apt or eager to fight. — **com·bat′ive·ly** *adv.* — **com·bat′ive·ness** *n.*

comb·er kō′mər) *n.* **1.** One who or that which combs wool, flax, etc. **2.** A long, crested wave.

com·bi·na·tion (kom′bə·nā′shən) *n.* **1.** The act of joining together or the state of being joined; union. **2.** That which is formed by combining. **3.** An alliance, as of persons, to further a common interest, activity, etc. **4.** The series of numbers or letters forming the key to a combination lock; also, the mechanism of such a lock. **5.** Underwear consisting of an undershirt and underpants made in one piece. **6.** *Math.* Any selection of a group of units such that the order of selection is immaterial, as 123, 321, and 213. — **com′bi·na′tion·al, com′bi·na′tive** *adj.*

combination lock A lock that can be opened only by moving a dial in a set sequence of turns.

com·bine (*v.* kəm·bīn′; *n.* kom′bīn) *v.* **·bined, ·bin·ing** *v.t.* **1.** To bring together into close union; blend; merge; unite. **2.** To possess in union. — *v.i.* **3.** To become one, or parts of a whole. **4.** To associate for a purpose. **5.** *Chem.* To enter into combination. — *n.* **1.** A combination. **2.** *U.S. Informal* A group of persons united in pursuit of selfish commercial or political ends; a trust; ring. **3.** *Agric.* A machine that reaps, threshes, and cleans grain while harvesting it. [< LL < L *com-* together + *bini* two by two] — **com·bin′a·ble** *adj.* — **com·bin′er** *n.*

combining form The stem of a word, usu. of Greek or Latin origin, as *tele-* and *-phone* in *telephone,* or an English word unchanged, as *over* in *overeat,* used in combination with other forms to create compounds.

com·bo (kom′bō) *n.* **1.** Combination. **2.** A small jazz or dance band, usually three or four musicians.

com·bus·ti·ble (kəm·bus′tə·bəl) *adj.* **1.** Capable of burning easily. **2.** Easily excited; fiery. — *n.* Any substance that will readily burn, as paper or wood. — **com·bus′ti·ble·ness, com·bus′ti·bil·i·ty** *n.* — **com·bus′ti·bly** *adv.*

com·bus·tion (kəm·bus′chən) *n.* **1.** The action or operation of burning. **2.** *Chem.* **a** Oxidation of a substance, accompanied by the generation of heat and sometimes light. **b** Slow oxidation, as of food in the body. **3.** Violent disturbance; tumult. [< LL < L *comburere* to burn up] — **com·bus′tive** *adj.*

come (kum) *v.i.* **came, come, com·ing 1.** To move to or toward the speaker; approach. **2.** To arrive as the result of motion or progress. **3.** To advance or move into view. **4.** To arrive in due course or in orderly progression: when your turn comes. **5.** To occur in time: Labor Day came late that year. **6.** To reach or extend. **7.** To arrive at some state or condition: to come to harm. **8.** To happen; occur: come what may. **9.** To exist as an effect or result: This comes of trifling. **10.** To emanate or proceed; be derived. **11.** To become: The wheel came loose. **12.** To turn out or prove to be: His prediction came true. **13.** To be offered, obtainable, or produced: The car comes in many colors. **14.** To act as the speaker wishes: used in the imperative and expressing impatience, anger, protest, etc. — **to come about 1.** To take place; happen. **2.** *Naut.* To turn to the opposite tack. — **to come across 1.** To meet with or find by chance. **2.** *Slang* To give or do what is requested. — **to come around** (or **round**) **1.** To recover or revive. **2.** To change or turn, as in direction or opinion. **3.** *Informal* To pay a visit. — **to come at 1.** To reach. **2.** To attain. **3.** To attack. — **to come back 1.** To return. **2.** *Informal* To regain former status; make a comeback. **3.** *Slang* To reply sharply. — **to come by 1.** To pass near. **2.** To acquire; get. — **to come down 1.** To lose status, wealth, etc. **2.** To descend as by inheritance. — **to come in 1.** To enter. **2.** To arrive. **3.** To be brought into use. — **to come in for** *Informal* **1.** To be eligible to receive. **2.** To acquire; get. — **to come into 1.** To inherit. **2.** To enter into; join. — **to come of 1.** To be descended from. **2.** To result from. — **to come off 1.** To become detached. **2.** To happen; occur. **3.** To emerge from action or trial; acquit oneself. — **to come on 1.** To meet by chance. **2.** To make progress; develop. **3.** To enter, as on stage. — **to come out 1.** To be made public; be published. **2.** To make one's debut. **3.** To speak frankly; declare oneself. **4.** To result; end. — **to come out with 1.** To declare openly. **2.** To offer; publish. — **to come through 1.** To be successful (in). **2.** To survive. **3.** To wear through. **4.** *Informal* To give or do what is required. — **to come to 1.** To recover; revive. **2.** To amount to. **3.** To result in. **4.** *Naut.* **a** To turn close to the wind. **b** To anchor. — **to come up 1.** To arise; appear. **2.** *Naut.* **a** To come closer to the wind. **b** To slacken. — **to come up to 1.** To equal; rival. **2.** To reach. — **to come up with** *U.S. Informal* **1.** To propose or produce: *to come up with* an idea. **2.** To overtake. [OE *cuman*]

come·back (kum′bak′) *n.* **1.** *Informal* A return, as to health or lost position. **2.** *Slang* A smart retort.

co·me·di·an (kə·mē′dē·ən) *n.* **1.** An actor in comedies. **2.** An entertainer specializing in jokes, comic skits, and the like. **3.** One who continually tries to be funny. **4.** A person who writes comedy. [< F *comédien*]

co·me·di·enne (kə·mē′dē·en′) *n.* A female comedian. [< F]

come·down (kum′doun′) *n.* A descent to a lower condition or position; a humiliating or disappointing setback.

com·e·dy (kom′ə·dē) *n. pl.* **·dies** **1.** A play, motion picture, etc., dealing with human folly in a light and humorous manner, and having a happy ending. **2.** The branch of drama treating of such themes. **3.** The art or theory of composing comedy. **4.** An incident, situation, etc., resembling comedy. [< MF < L < Gk. < *kōmos* revel + *aeidein* to sing] — **co·me·dic** (kə·mē′dik, -med′ik) *adj.* — **co·me′di·cal·ly** *adv.*

comedy of manners A satiric comedy portraying the manners, customs, and foibles of the fashionable world.

come·ly (kum′lē) *adj.* **·li·er**, **·li·est** **1.** Pleasing in person; handsome; graceful. **2.** Suitable; becoming. [OE *cȳmlic* < *cȳme* fine] — **come′li·ly** *adv.* — **come′li·ness** *n.*

come-on (kum′on′, -ôn′) *n. U.S. Slang* **1.** Someone or something that lures. **2.** A beckoning look or gesture.

com·er (kum′ər) *n.* **1.** One who comes or arrives. **2.** *Informal* One who or that which shows great promise.

co·mes·ti·ble (kə·mes′tə·bəl) *Rare adj.* Edible. — *n. Usu. pl.* Food. [< MF < LL < L *comedere* to eat up]

com·et (kom′it) *n. Astron.* A celestial body moving in an orbit about the sun and consisting of a nucleus of more or less condensed material, accompanied by a tenuous coma pointing away from the sun. [OE < L < Gk. *komētēs* long-haired] — **com·et·ar·y**, **co·met·ic** (kə·met′ik) *adj.*

come-up·pance (kum′up′əns) *n. U.S. Informal* The punishment one deserves; just deserts. Also **come′up′ance.**

com·fit (kum′fit, kom′-) *n.* A sweetmeat; confection. [< OF < L *confectus.* Related to CONFECT.]

com·fort (kum′fərt) *n.* **1.** A state of mental or physical ease. **2.** Relief from sorrow, distress, etc. **3.** One who or that which brings ease or consolation. **4.** Help or support: aid and *comfort.* **5.** *U.S.* A bed comforter. — *v.t.* **1.** To cheer in time of grief or trouble; solace; console. **2.** *Law* To aid; help. [< OF < LL < L *com-* with + *fortis* strong] — **com′fort·ing** *adj.* — **com′fort·ing·ly** *adv.*

com·fort·a·ble (kum′fər·tə·bəl, kumf′tə·bəl, -tər-) *adj.* **1.** Imparting comfort and satisfaction. **2.** Free from physical or mental distress; content; at ease. **3.** *Informal* Moderate; adequate: a *comfortable* income. — **com′fort·a·ble·ness** *n.* — **com′fort·a·bly** *adv.*

com·fort·er (kum′fər·tər) *n.* **1.** One who comforts. **2.** *U.S.* A thick, quilted bedcover: also called *comfort.*

comfort station A public toilet or rest room.

com·ic (kom′ik) *adj.* **1.** Of or pertaining to comedy. **2.** Provoking mirth; funny; ludicrous. — *n.* **1.** A comic actor or entertainer. **2.** The humorous element in art, life, etc. **3.** *pl. Informal* Comic strips or a book of comic strips. [< L < Gk. *kōmos* revelry]

com·i·cal (kom′i·kəl) *adj.* Causing merriment; funny; ludicrous. — **Syn.** See HUMOROUS. — **com·i·cal·i·ty** (kom′ə·kal′ə·tē), **com′i·cal·ness** *n.* — **com′i·cal·ly** *adv.*

comic opera An opera or operetta having a humorous plot and spoken dialogue.

comic strip A strip of cartoons printed in a newspaper, etc.

Com·in·form (kom′in·fôrm) *n.* The Communist Information Bureau, established in 1947 and dissolved in 1956. [< COM(MUNIST) INFORM(ATION)]

com·ing (kum′ing) *adj.* **1.** Approaching, esp. in time: the *coming* year. **2.** On the way to fame or distinction. — *n.* The act of approaching; arrival; advent.

com·ing-out (kum′ing·out′) *n. Informal* Debut into society.

Com·in·tern (kom′in·tûrn) *n.* An international organization formed in 1919 for extending the scope of Marxist socialism, and dissolved in 1943: also called *Third International.* [< COM(MUNIST) INTERN(ATIONAL)]

com·i·ty (kom′ə·tē) *n. pl.* **·ties** Courtesy; civility. [< L *comitas, -tatis* courtesy]

comity of nations The courteous recognition that one nation accords to the laws and usages of another.

com·ma (kom′ə) *n.* **1.** A punctuation mark (,) indicating a slight separation in ideas or in grammatical construction within a sentence. **2.** Any pause or separation. [< L < Gk. *komma* short phrase]

comma bacillus *Bacteriol.* A bacillus shaped like a comma and causing Asiatic cholera.

com·mand (kə·mand′, -mänd′) *v.t.* **1.** To order, require, or enjoin with authority. **2.** To control or direct authoritatively; rule; have at one's disposal or use. **3.** To overlook, as from a height. **4.** To exact as being due or proper: to *command* respect. — *v.i.* **5.** To be in authority; rule. **6.** To overlook something from a superior position. — *n.* **1.** The act of commanding; bidding. **2.** The authority to command. **3.** That which is commanded; an order. **4.** Dominating power as achieved through superior position.

5. Ability to control; mastery: *command* of one's emotions. **6.** *Mil. & Naval* The unit or units under the command of one person; also, the base of operations of such a unit. [< OF < LL < L *com-* thoroughly + *mandare* to order]

com·man·dant (kom′ən·dant′, -dänt′) *n.* A commanding officer, as of a service school, military district, etc.

com·man·deer (kom′ən·dir′) *v.t.* **1.** To force into military service. **2.** To seize for public use, especially under military necessity. **3.** *Informal* To take by force or constraint.

com·mand·er (kə·man′dər, -män′-) *n.* **1.** One who commands or is in command. **2.** *Mil.* The commissioned officer in command of a force or post. **3.** *Naval* A commissioned officer ranking next above a lieutenant commander and next below a captain. See table at GRADE. — **com·mand′er·ship** *n.*

commander in chief *pl.* **commanders in chief** **1.** *Often cap.* One holding supreme command of the armed forces of a nation: in the U.S., the President. **2.** The officer commanding a fleet, major force, etc.

com·mand·ing (kə·man′ding, -män′-) *adj.* **1.** Exercising command. **2.** Impressive; imperious. **3.** Dominating, as from a height. — **com·mand′ing·ly** *adv.*

commanding officer In the Royal, Royal Canadian, and other Commonwealth navies, a commissioned officer. See table at GRADE.

com·mand·ment (kə·mand′mənt, -mänd′-) *n.* **1.** An authoritative mandate; edict; order; law. **2.** *Sometimes cap.* One of the Ten Commandments.

com·man·do (kə·man′dō, -män′-) *n. pl.* **·dos** or **·does** **1.** A special fighting force trained for quick, destructive raids into enemy territory. **2.** A member of such a unit. **3.** In South Africa, especially in the Boer War, a force of militia; also, a raid. [< Afrikaans < Pg., a group commanded]

command post The field headquarters of a military unit.

com·mem·o·rate (kə·mem′ə·rāt) *v.t.* **·rat·ed**, **·rat·ing** To celebrate the memory of. Also **com·mem′o·rize** (-ə·rīz). — **Syn.** See CELEBRATE. [< L < *com-* together + *memorare* to remember] — **com·mem′o·ra′tor** *n.*

com·mem·o·ra·tion (kə·mem′ə·rā′shən) *n.* **1.** The act of commemorating, or that which commemorates. **2.** A commemorative observance. — **com·mem′o·ra′tion·al** *adj.*

com·mem·o·ra·tive (kə·mem′ə·rā′tiv, -rə·tiv) *adj.* Serving to commemorate. Also **com·mem′o·ra·to·ry** (kə·mem′ər·ə·tôr′ē, -tō′rē). — *n.* Anything that commemorates.

com·mence (kə·mens′) *v.t. & v.i.* **·menced**, **·menc·ing** To start; begin; originate. [< OF < L *com-* thoroughly + *initiare* to begin] — **com·menc′er** *n.*

com·mence·ment (kə·mens′mənt) *n.* **1.** A beginning; origin. **2.** The ceremony at a college or school during which degrees are conferred; also, the day such a ceremony is held.

com·mend (kə·mend′) *v.t.* **1.** To express a favorable opinion of; praise. **2.** To recommend. **3.** To present the regards of. **4.** To commit with confidence. [< L < *com-* thoroughly + *mandare* to order] — **com·mend′a·ble** *adj.* — **com·mend′a·ble·ness** *n.* — **com·mend′a·bly** *adv.*

com·men·da·tion (kom′ən·dā′shən) *n.* **1.** The act of commending; approbation. **2.** Something that commends.

Commendation Ribbon A U.S. military decoration consisting of a ribbon and medallion. See DECORATION.

com·mend·a·to·ry (kə·men′də·tôr′ē, -tō′rē) *adj.* Serving to commend; expressing commendation.

com·men·sal (kə·men′səl) *adj.* **1.** Eating together. **2.** *Zool.* Associated with another in close but nonparasitic relationship. [< OF < L *com-* together + *mensa* table] — **com·men′sal·ly** *adv.*

com·men·su·ra·ble (kə·men′shər·ə·bəl, -sər·ə-) *adj.* **1.** Capable of being measured by a common standard or unit. **2.** Fitting as to proportion; proportionate. [< LL < L *com-* together + *mensurabilis* measurable] — **com·men′su·ra·bil′i·ty** *n.* — **com·men′su·ra·bly** *adv.*

com·men·su·rate (kə·men′shə·rit, -sə·rit) *adj.* **1.** Having the same measure or extent. **2.** In proper proportion; adequate. **3.** Commensurable. [< LL < L *com-* together + *mensurare* to measure] — **com·men′su·rate·ly** *adv.* — **com·men′su·rate·ness** *n.* — **com·men′su·ra′tion** *n.*

com·ment (kom′ent) *n.* **1.** A written note of explanation, illustration, or criticism, as of a literary passage. **2.** A remark made in observation or criticism. **3.** Talk; conversation. — *v.i.* **1.** To make a comment or comments. — *v.t.* **2.** To make comments on. [< OF < L *comminisci* to contrive] — **com′ment·er** *n.*

com·men·tar·y (kom′ən·ter′ē) *n. pl.* **·ries** **1.** A series of illustrative or explanatory notes. **2.** A comment. **3.** A series of remarks. **4.** *Usu. pl.* A historical narrative or memoir. [< L *comminisci* to contrive, devise] — **com·men·tar·i·al** (kom′ən·târ′ē·əl) *adj.*

com·men·ta·tor (kom′ən·tā′tər) *n.* **1.** One who writes commentaries. **2.** One who discusses or analyzes news events.

com·merce (kom′ərs) *n.* **1.** The exchange of materials, products, etc., esp. on a large scale between states or nations; extended trade. **2.** Social intercourse. **3.** Sexual intercourse. — **Department of Commerce** An executive department of the U.S. government headed by the Secretary of Commerce, that supervises transportation and shipping, the census, and food and drug laws. [< F < L < *com-* together + *merx, mercis* wares]

com·mer·cial (kə-mûr′shəl) *adj.* **1.** Of, relating to, or engaged in commerce; mercantile. **2.** Produced in large quantities. **3.** Having financial gain as an object. — *n.* In radio and television, an advertisement. — **com·mer·ci·al·i·ty** (kə-mûr′shē·al′ə·tē) *n.* — **com·mer′cial·ly** *adv.*

com·mer·cial·ism (kə-mûr′shəl·iz′əm) *n.* **1.** The spirit or methods of commerce. **2.** Commercial practices or customs. — **com·mer′cial·ist** *n.* — **com·mer′cial·is′tic** *adj.*

com·mer·cial·ize (kə-mûr′shəl·īz) *v.t.* **·ized, ·iz·ing** To put on a commercial basis; make a matter of business or profit. — **com·mer′cial·i·za′tion** *n.*

commercial paper Any of various short-term negotiable papers, as drafts, bills of exchange, promissory notes, etc.

com·mie (kom′ē) *n. Often cap. Informal* A Communist.

com·min·gle (kə-ming′gəl) *v.t. & v.i.* **·gled, ·gling** To mix together; mingle. [< COM- + MINGLE]

com·mi·nute (kom′ə-noōt, -nyoōt) *v.t.* **·nut·ed, ·nut·ing** To reduce to minute particles; pulverize. [< L < *com-* thoroughly + *minuere* to lessen] — **com′mi·nu′tion** *n.*

com·mis·er·ate (kə-miz′ə·rāt) *v.* **·at·ed, ·at·ing** *v.t.* **1.** To feel or express sympathy for; pity. — *v.i.* **2.** To express sympathy; condole: used with *with*. [< L < *com-* with + *miserari* to feel pity] — **com·mis′er·a′tive** *adj.* — **com·mis′er·a′tive·ly** *adv.* — **com·mis′er·a′tor** *n.*

com·mis·er·a·tion (kə-miz′ə·rā′shən) *n.* A feeling or expression of sympathy; compassion.

com·mis·sar (kom′ə·sär, kom′ə·sär′) *n.* Formerly, an official in charge of a commissariat of the Soviet government. [< Russ. *komissar*]

com·mis·sar·i·at (kom′ə·sâr′ē·ət) *n.* **1.** The department of an army charged with providing food and daily necessities; also, the officers or supplies of such a department. **2.** Formerly, any major department of the Soviet government.

com·mis·sar·y (kom′ə·ser′ē) *n. pl.* **·sar·ies** **1.** A store selling food, equipment, etc., as at a camp or military post. **2.** An authority delegated for a special duty. **3.** In the Soviet Union, a commissar. [See COMMISSAR.] — **com·mis·sar·i·al** (kom′ə·sâr′ē·əl) *adj.* — **com′mis·sar′y·ship** *n.*

com·mis·sion (kə-mish′ən) *n.* **1.** The act of committing to the charge of another; an entrusting. **2.** The matter or trust so committed; a charge. **3.** Authorization or command to act as specified. **4.** A written warrant conferring a particular authority or power. **5.** *Mil.* **a** An official document conferring rank and authority. **b** The rank or authority conferred. **6.** A body of persons acting under lawful authority to perform certain duties. **7.** The fee or percentage given an agent or salesman for his services. **8.** The condition of being authorized or delegated. **9.** The act of committing; also, the act itself. — **in commission** In active service or use; usable. — **out of commission** Not in active service or use; laid up for repairs, etc. — *v.t.* **1.** To give rank or authority to. **2.** *Naval* To put into active service under a commander, as a ship. **3.** To appoint; delegate. [< OF < L *committere*. See COMMIT.]

com·mis·sion·er (kə-mish′ən·ər) *n.* **1.** One who holds a commission. **2.** A member of a commission. **3.** A public official in charge of a department: fire *commissioner*. **4.** In baseball, etc., an official selected as supreme authority.

com·mit (kə-mit′) *v.t.* **·mit·ted, ·mit·ting** **1.** To do; perpetrate. **2.** To place in trust or charge; consign. **3.** To consign for preservation: *commit* a speech to memory. **4.** To devote (oneself) unreservedly. **5.** To refer, as to a committee for consideration. [< L *committere* to join, entrust < *com-* together + *mittere* to send] — **com·mit′ta·ble** *adj.*

com·mit·ment (kə-mit′mənt) *n.* **1.** The act or process of entrusting or consigning. **2.** The state of being committed. **3.** An engagement or pledge to do something. **4.** A consignment to a prison, mental institution, etc.

com·mit·tal (kə-mit′l) *n.* Commitment (defs. 1 and 3).

com·mit·tee (kə-mit′ē) *n.* **1.** A group of people chosen to investigate, report, or act on a matter. **2.** *Law* One appointed by a court to care for the person or property of another. — **in committee** Under consideration by a committee. [< AF *committre* to entrust]

com·mit·tee·man (kə-mit′ē·mən) *n. pl.* **·men** (-mən) A member of a committee. — **com·mit′tee·wom′an** *n.fem.*

com·mode (kə-mōd′) *n.* **1.** A low chest of drawers. **2.** A covered washstand. **3.** A woman's high headdress, worn about 1700. **4.** A toilet. [< MF < L *commodus* convenient]

com·mo·di·ous (kə-mō′dē·əs) *adj.* Containing ample room; spacious. [See COMMODE.] — **com·mo′di·ous·ly** *adv.* — **com·mo′di·ous·ness** *n.*

com·mod·i·ty (kə-mod′ə·tē) *n. pl.* **·ties** **1.** Something

bought and sold. **2.** Anything of use or profit. [< MF < L *commoditas, -tatis* convenience]

com·mo·dore (kom′ə·dôr, -dōr) *n.* **1.** In the U.S. Navy, an officer next above a captain and next below a rear admiral: a rank last used during World War II. **2.** In the Royal, Royal Canadian, and other Commonwealth navies, an officer ranking next below a rear-admiral. See table at GRADE. **3.** A title given to the presiding officer of a yacht club. [Earlier *commandore,* ? < Du. *kommandeur*]

com·mon (kom′ən) *adj.* **1.** Frequent or usual; unexceptional. **2.** Widespread; general. **3.** Shared equally by two or more, or by all. **4.** Pertaining to the entire community; public. **5.** Habitual; notorious: a *common* thief. **6.** Of low rank; ordinary. **7.** Vulgar; low; coarse. **8.** *Gram.* **a** Of gender, applied to either sex, as *parent, spouse, cat.* **b** Of a noun, applicable to any individual of a class of similar objects; not proper or personal, as *dog.* **9.** *Math.* Referring to a number or quantity belonging equally to two or more quantities: a *common* denominator. — *n.* **1.** A tract of land considered as the property of the community, open to the use of all. **2.** *Sometimes cap. Eccl.* An office or service used for any of certain classes of feast. — **in common** Equally with another or others; jointly. [< OF < L *communis* common] — **com′mon·ly** *adv.* — **com′mon·ness** *n.*

com·mon·al·ty (kom′ən·əl·tē) *n. pl.* **·ties** **1.** The common people, as opposed to the nobility. **2.** A body corporate, or its members. **3.** The entire mass; whole.

common carrier An individual or company that, for a fee, provides public transportation for goods or persons.

com·mon·er (kom′ən·ər) *n.* One of the common people.

common fraction *Math.* A fraction expressed by two numbers, a denominator and a numerator.

common law A system of jurisprudence based on custom, traditional usage, and precedent, as that of England.

com·mon-law marriage (kom′ən-lô′) A marriage in which both members consent to live as man and wife without undergoing a religious or civil ceremony.

Common Market Any of several customs unions, esp. the European Economic Community.

common noun *Gram.* A noun that names any member of a class of things, as *man, boat:* distinguished from *proper noun.*

com·mon·place (kom′ən·plās′) *adj.* Not remarkable or interesting; ordinary. — *n.* **1.** A trite or obvious remark. **2.** Something common. — **com′mon·place′ness** *n.*

Common Prayer The public worship of the Anglican Church, as contained in the Book of Common Prayer.

com·mons (kom′ənz) *n.pl. Chiefly Brit.* **1.** The common people. **2.** (*construed as sing.*) Food provided for a common table, as in a college. **3.** Rations; fare. **4.** (*construed as sing.*) The dining hall of a college.

Com·mons (kom′ənz) *n.pl.* The House of Commons.

common sense Practical understanding; sound judgment. — **com′mon-sense′** *adj.*

common stock Corporation stock the ownership of which entitles the holder to dividends or a share in the profits only after other obligations have been met.

common time *Music* Meter in which there are four quarter notes to a measure: also **common measure.**

com·mon·weal (kom′ən·wēl′) *n.* The general welfare; common good. Also **common weal.**

com·mon·wealth (kom′ən·welth′) *n.* **1.** The whole people of a state or nation. **2.** A state or republic in which the sovereignty is vested in the people; loosely, any of the United States. — **The Commonwealth** The official name of the British Commonwealth of Nations.

Commonwealth of England The English government from 1649 to 1660.

Commonwealth of Nations See BRITISH COMMONWEALTH OF NATIONS.

com·mo·tion (kə-mō′shən) *n.* **1.** A violent agitation; excitement. **2.** Popular tumult; social disorder; insurrection. [< L < *com-* thoroughly + *movere* to move]

com·mu·nal (kom′yə-nəl, kə-myoō′nəl) *adj.* **1.** Of or pertaining to a commune. **2.** Of or belonging to a community; common; public. — **com′mu·nal·ly** *adv.*

com·mu·nal·ism (kom′yə-nəl·iz′əm, kə-myoō′nəl-) *n.* A theory or system of government in which the state exists merely as a federation of virtually self-governing communes. — **com′mu·nal·ist** *n.* — **com′mu·nal·is′tic** *adj.*

com·mu·nal·ize (kom′yə-nəl·īz, kə-myoō′nəl·īz) *v.t.* **·ized, ·iz·ing** To render communal. — **com′mu·nal·i·za′tion** *n.*

com·mune¹ (*v.* kə-myoōn′; *n.* kom′yoōn) *v.i.* **·muned, ·mun·ing** **1.** To converse intimately. **2.** To partake of the Eucharist. — *n.* Intimate conversation. [< OF *comuner* to share]

com·mune² (kom′yoōn) *n.* **1.** The smallest political division of France, Belgium, Italy, etc.; also, the people of such a district. **2.** Any community. — **the Commune or the**

Commune of Paris 1. The revolutionary government of Paris between 1789 and 1794. 2. The revolutionary government of Paris in 1871. [< L *communa* community]

com·mu·ni·ca·ble (kə·myōō′ni·kə·bəl) *adj.* Capable of being communicated, as a disease. — **com·mu·ni·ca·bil′i·ty**, **com·mu′ni·ca·ble·ness** *n.* — **com·mu′ni·ca·bly** *adv.*

com·mu·ni·cant (kə·myōō′nə·kənt) *n.* 1. One who communicates. 2. One who partakes or has a right to partake of the Eucharist. — *adj.* Communicating.

com·mu·ni·cate (kə·myōō′nə·kāt) *v.* **·cat·ed, ·cat·ing** *v.t.* 1. To cause another or others to partake of or share in; impart. 2. To transmit, as a disease. — *v.i.* 3. To transmit or exchange thought or knowledge. 4. To be connected. 5. To partake of the Eucharist. [< L *communicare* to share <*communis* common] — **com·mu′ni·ca′tor** *n.*

com·mu·ni·ca·tion (kə·myōō′nə·kā′shən) *n.* 1. The act of imparting or transmitting. 2. The transmission of ideas, information, etc., as by speech or writing. 3. A message. 4. A means of passage or of transmitting messages between places or persons. 5. *pl.* The science of communicating.

com·mu·ni·ca·tive (kə·myōō′nə·kā′tiv, -kə·tiv) *adj.* 1. Talkative. 2. Of or pertaining to communication. — **com·mu′ni·ca′tive·ly** *adv.* — **com·mu′ni·ca′tive·ness** *n.*

com·mun·ion (kə·myōōn′yən) *n.* 1. A having or sharing in common; mutual participation. 2. A mutual sharing of thoughts, feelings, etc. 3. Religious fellowship, as between members of a church; also, a religious denomination. 4. *Usu. cap.* The Eucharist. [< OF < L *communis* common]

com·mu·ni·qué (kə·myōō′nə·kā′, kə·myōō′nə·kā) *n.* An official announcement or bulletin. [< F]

com·mu·nism (kom′yə·niz′əm) *n.* 1. A social system characterized by the communal sharing of goods and services. 2. A theory of social change advocating a classless society, public ownership of almost all productive property, and the sharing of the products of labor. 3. *Often cap.* The system in force in any state based on this theory. [< F *commun* common, shared equally + -ISM]

com·mu·nist (kom′yə·nist) *n.* 1. *Often cap.* A member of a Communist party. 2. One who advocates communism. — *adj.* Pertaining to communism and communists.

com·mu·nis·tic (kom′yə·nis′tik) *adj.* 1. Of, or of the nature of, communism. 2. Tending to or in accordance with communism. — **com′mu·nis′ti·cal·ly** *adv.*

Communist Party 1. The dominant party in Russia since 1917, previously called the Bolshevik Party. 2. Any political party advocating communism.

com·mu·ni·ty (kə·myōō′nə·tē) *n. pl.* **·ties** 1. A group of people living together or in one locality and subject to the same laws, having common interests, etc. 2. The district or area in which they live. 3. The public; society in general. 4. Common ownership or participation. 5. Identity or likeness: *community* of interests. 6. *Ecol.* A group of plants or animals living under relatively similar conditions in a definite area. [< L *communitas, -tatis* fellowship]

community center A building or grounds used by a community for social and recreational activities.

community chest A welfare fund of contributions drawn upon by various charitable organizations.

com·mu·nize (kom′yə·nīz) *v.t.* **·nized, ·niz·ing** To make public property or cause to become communistic. — **com′mu·ni·za′tion** *n.*

com·mu·tate (kom′yə·tāt) *v.t.* **·tat·ed, ·tat·ing** *Electr.* To alter or reverse the direction of (a current).

com·mu·ta·tion (kom′yə·tā′shən) *n.* 1. A substitution or interchange, as of one kind of payment for another. 2. A payment or service substituted. 3. *U.S.* Regular travel to and from work. 4. *Electr.* The reversing of the direction of current. 5. *Law* A reduction of a judicial penalty or sentence. [< L *com-* thoroughly + *mutare* change]

commutation ticket *U.S.* A railroad or other ticket issued at a reduced rate and good for a specified number of trips, or for a specified period, over a given route.

com·mu·ta·tor (kom′yə·tā′tər) *n. Electr.* 1. Any contrivance for reversing the direction of current. 2. A part within a dynamo or generator, serving to collect and transmit the induced current.

com·mute (kə·myōōt′) *v.* **·mut·ed, ·mut·ing** *v.t.* 1. To exchange reciprocally; interchange. 2. To exchange for something less severe. 3. To pay in gross at a reduced rate. — *v.i.* 4. To serve as a substitute. 5. *U.S.* To make regular trips of some distance to and from work. — **com·mut′a·ble** *adj.* — **com·mut′a·ble·ness, com·mut·a·bil′i·ty** *n.* — **com·mut′er** *n.*

com·pact¹ (*adj.* kəm·pakt′, kom′pakt; *v.* kəm·pakt′; *n.* kom′pakt) *adj.* 1. Closely and firmly united; pressed together. 2. Brief and to the point; terse. 3. Packed into a small space. 4. Composed; made up: with *of*. — *v.t.* To pack or press closely; compress. — *n.* A small, hinged box with a mirror, in which a woman carries face powder. [< L *com-* together + *pangere* to fasten] — **com·pact′ly** *adv.* — **com·pact′ness** *n.*

com·pact² (kom′pakt) *n.* A covenant, agreement, or contract. [< L < *com-* together + *pacisci* to agree]

com·pan·ion¹ (kəm·pan′yən) *n.* 1. A comrade; associate. 2. A person employed to live with, accompany, or assist another. 3. One of a pair; a mate. — *v.t.* To be a companion to. [< OF < LL *com-* together + *panis* bread]

com·pan·ion² (kəm·pan′yən) *n. Naut.* A companionway; also, the hood or covering over a companionway. [< Du. *kampanje* quarter-deck, storeroom]

com·pan·ion·a·ble (kəm·pan′yən·ə·bəl) *adj.* Fitted for companionship; friendly; sociable. — **com·pan′ion·a·bil′i·ty** *n.* — **com·pan′ion·a·bly** *adv.*

com·pan·ion·ate (kəm·pan′yən·it) *adj.* 1. Of or characteristic of companions. 2. Agreed upon; shared.

com·pan·ion·ship (kəm·pam′yən·ship) *n.* Fellowship.

com·pan·ion·way (kəm·pan′yən·wā′) *n. Naut.* A staircase leading below from a ship's deck; also, the space it occupies.

com·pa·ny (kum′pə·nē) *n. pl.* **·nies** 1. A group of people. 2. A gathering of persons for social purposes; society. 3. A guest or guests; visitors. 4. Companionship; society. 5. A number of persons associated for some common purpose, as in business. 6. A partner or partners not named in the title of a firm. 7. A body of actors and actresses; troupe. 8. *Mil.* A body of men commanded by a captain, larger than a platoon and smaller than a battalion. 9. *Naut.* The entire crew of a ship, including the officers. — **to keep company** (**with**) 1. To associate (with). 2. To court, as lovers; go together. — **to part company** (**with**) To end friendship or association (with). — *v.t. & v.i.* **·nied, ·ny·ing** *Archaic* To keep or go in company (with). [See COMPANION¹.]

com·pa·ra·ble (kom′pər·ə·bəl) *adj.* 1. Capable of comparison. 2. Worthy of comparison. — **com′pa·ra·ble·ness, com′pa·ra·bil′i·ty** *n.* — **com′pa·ra·bly** *adv.*

com·par·a·tive (kəm·par′ə·tiv) *adj.* 1. Pertaining to, resulting from, or making use of comparison: *comparative* anatomy. 2. Not positive or absolute; relative. 3. *Gram.* Expressing a degree of an adjective or adverb higher than the positive and lower than the superlative. — *n. Gram.* The comparative degree, or a word or form by which it is expressed: "Better" is the *comparative* of "good." — **com·par′a·tive·ly** *adv.*

com·pare (kəm·pâr′) *v.* **·pared, ·par·ing** *v.t.* 1. To represent or speak of as similar or equal: with *to.* 2. To examine so as to perceive similarity or dissimilarity: with *with.* 3. *Gram.* To form or state the degrees of comparison of (an adjective or adverb). — *v.i.* 4. To be worthy of comparison: with *with.* 5. To vie or compete. — *n.* Comparison: usually in the phrase **beyond compare.** [< MF < L < *com-* together + *par* equal]

com·par·i·son (kəm·par′ə·sən) *n.* 1. A comparing or being compared; a statement of relative likeness or unlikeness. 2. Similarity. 3. *Gram.* That inflection of adjectives or adverbs that indicates the three differences of degree, the positive, comparative, and superlative, as *short, shorter, shortest.*

com·part·ment (kəm·pärt′mənt) *n.* 1. One of the parts into which an enclosed space is subdivided. 2. Any separate section. [< F < L < *com-* together + *partiri* to share]

com·pass (kum′pəs, kom′-) *n.* 1. An instrument for determining direction, consisting essentially of a freely suspended magnetic needle that points toward the magnetic north. 2. The reach or extent of something; area or range; scope. 3. An enclosing line or boundary; circumference. 4. *Sometimes pl.* An instrument having two usually pointed legs hinged at one end, used for taking measurements, describing circles, etc.: also **pair of compasses.** — *v.t.* 1. To go round. 2. To surround; encompass. 3. To comprehend. 4. To attain or accomplish. 5. To plot; devise. [< OF < L *com-* together + *passus* step] — **com′pass·a·ble** *adj.*

compass card The circular card or dial resting on the pivot of a mariner's compass, on which the 32 points and 360 degrees of the circle are marked.

com·pas·sion (kəm·pash′ən) *n.* Pity for the suffering or distress of another, with the desire to help or spare. — Syn. See PITY. [< MF < LL < L *com-* together + *pati* to feel, suffer]

com·pas·sion·ate (*adj.* kəm·pash′ən·it; *v.* kəm·pash′ən·āt) *adj.* Feeling compassion or pity; merciful; sympathetic. — *v.t.* **·at·ed, ·at·ing** To

COMPASS CARD

have compassion for; pity; sympathize. **—com·pas′sion·ate·ly** adv. **—com·pas′sion·ate·ness** n.

com·pat·i·ble (kəm·pat′ə·bəl) adj. 1. Capable of existing together; congruous; congenial: usu. with *with*. 2. In television capable of being received in black and white on sets not adapted for color reception. [< MF < Med.L < L com- together + pati to feel, suffer] **—com·pat′i·bil′i·ty, com·pat′i·ble·ness** n. **—com·pat′i·bly** adv.

com·pa·tri·ot (kəm·pā′trē·ət, -pat′rē·ət) n. A fellow countryman. **.—** adj. Of the same country. [< F < LL < L com- together + patriota countryman]

com·peer (kəm·pir′, kom′pir) n. 1. One of equal rank; a peer. 2. A comrade. [< OF < L < com- with + par equal]

com·pel (kəm·pel′) v.t. ·pelled, ·pel·ling 1. To urge irresistibly; constrain. 2. To obtain by force; exact. 3. To force to yield; overpower. [OF < L < com- together + pellere to drive] **—com·pel′la·ble** adj. **—com·pel′la·bly** adv. **—com·pel′ler** n.

com·pen·di·ous (kəm·pen′dē·əs) adj. Stating briefly and succinctly the substance of something; concise. **—com·pend′i·ous·ly** adv. **—com·pen′di·ous·ness** n.

com·pen·di·um (kəm·pen′dē·əm) n. pl. ·di·ums or ·di·a (-dē·ə) A brief, comprehensive summary; an abridgment. [< L < com- together + pendere to weigh]

com·pen·sa·ble (kəm·pen′sə·bəl) adj. That may be compensated. **—com·pen′sa·bil′i·ty** n.

com·pen·sate (kom′pən·sāt) v. ·sat·ed, ·sat·ing v.t. 1. To make suitable amends to or for; requite; remunerate; pay; reimburse. 2. To counterbalance or make up for; offset. **—v.i.** 3. To make returns or amends: often with *for*. [< L < com- together + pendere to weigh] **—com′pen·sa′tor** n. **—com·pen·sa·tive** (kom′pən·sā′tiv, kəm·pen′sə·tiv) adj. **—com·pen·sa·to·ry** (kəm·pen′sə·tôr′ē) adj.

com·pen·sa·tion (kom′pən·sā′shən) n. 1. The act of compensating, or that which compensates; payment; amends. 2. *Biol.* The offsetting of defects of an organ or part by the development of another organ. **—com′pen·sa′tion·al** adj.

com·pete (kəm·pēt′) v.i. ·pet·ed, ·pet·ing To contend with another or others; engage in a contest or competition; vie. [< L < com- together + petere to seek]

com·pe·tence (kom′pə·təns) n. 1. The state of being competent; ability. 2. Sufficient means for comfortable living. 3. *Law* Legal authority, qualification, or jurisdiction. Also **com′pe·ten·cy.**

com·pe·tent (kom′pə·tənt) adj. 1. Having sufficient ability; capable. 2. Sufficient; adequate. 3. *Law* Having legal qualification. [< MF < L < com- together + petere to go, seek] **—com′pe·tent·ly** adv. **—com′pe·tent·ness** n.

com·pe·ti·tion (kom′pə·tish′ən) n. 1. A striving against another or others for some object, as a prize, or for superiority. 2. A trial of skill or ability; a contest. 3. Business rivalry between persons or firms striving for the same market.

com·pet·i·tive (kəm·pet′ə·tiv) adj. Of, pertaining to, or characterized by competition. Also **com·pet·i·to·ry** (kəm·pet′ə·tôr′ē, -tō′rē) **—com·pet′i·tive·ly** adv. **—com·pet′i·tive·ness** n.

com·pet·i·tor (kəm·pet′ə·tər) n. One who competes, as in games or in business.

com·pile (kəm·pīl′) v.t. ·piled, ·pil·ing 1. To put together from materials collected from other sources. 2. To gather (various materials) into a volume. 3. To amass; collect. [< L < com- thoroughly + pilare to strip, plunder] **—com·pi·la·tion** (kom′pə·lā′shən) n. **—com·pil′er** n.

com·pla·cen·cy (kəm·plā′sən·sē) n. pl. ·cies Self-satisfaction; smugness. Also **com·pla′cence.**

com·pla·cent (kəm·plā′sənt) adj. 1. Smug; self-satisfied. 2. Complaisant. [< L < com- thoroughly + placere to please] **—com·pla·cent·ly** adv.

com·plain (kəm·plān′) v.i. 1. To express feelings of dissatisfaction, resentment, pain, etc.; grumble. 2. To describe one's pains or ills. 3. To make a formal accusation; present a complaint. [< OF < LL < L com- thoroughly + plangere to beat (the breast in grief)] **—com·plain′er** n.

com·plain·ant (kəm·plā′nənt) n. One who enters a complaint, as before a magistrate.

com·plaint (kəm·plānt′) n. 1. An expression of pain, grief, or dissatisfaction. 2. A cause for complaining; grievance. 3. An ailment; disorder. 4. *Law* A formal charge.

com·plai·sant (kəm·plā′zənt, kom′plə·zant) adj. Showing a desire to please; yielding; compliant. [< MF < L com- placere] **—com·plai·sance′** n. **—com·plai·sant·ly** adv.

com·ple·ment (n. kom′plə·mənt; v. kom′plə·ment) n. 1. That which fills up or completes a thing. 2. Full or complete number, allowance, or amount: The vessel has her *complement* of men. 3. One of two parts that mutually complete each other. 4. *Geom.* An angle that when added to another angle equals 90°. 5. *Gram.* A word or phrase used after a verb to complete predication. A **subjective comple-**

ment describes the subject, as *happy* in *She is happy.* An **objective complement** describes or identifies the direct object, as *happy* in *It made her happy.* **—v.t.** To make complete. [< L < com- thoroughly + plere to fill]

com·ple·men·tal (kom′plə·men′təl) adj. Complementary.

com·ple·men·ta·ry (kom′plə·men′tər·ē, -trē) adj. 1. Serving as a complement; completing. 2. Mutually providing each other's needs.

complementary color Either of a pair of spectrum colors that when combined give a white or nearly white light.

com·plete (kəm·plēt′) adj. 1. Having all needed or normal parts; lacking nothing; entire; full. 2. Wholly finished; ended; concluded. 3. Perfect in quality or nature. **—v.t.** ·plet·ed, ·plet·ing 1. To make entire or perfect. 2. To finish; end. [< L < com- thoroughly + plere to fill] **—com·plete′ly** adv. **—com·plete′ness** n.

com·ple·tion (kəm·plē′shən) n. The act of completing, or the state of being completed.

com·plex (adj. kəm·pleks′, kom′pleks; n. kom′pleks) adj. 1. Consisting of various connected or interwoven parts; composite. 2. Complicated, as in structure; involved; intricate. **—n.** 1. A whole made up of interwoven or connected parts. 2. *Psychoanal.* A group of interrelated feelings, desires, memories, and ideas, that function as a unit to dominate the personality, and which, when repressed, often lead to abnormal patterns of behavior. 3. Loosely, an excessive concern or fear; an obsession. [< L < com- together + plectere to twist] **—com·plex′ly** adv. **—com·plex′ness** n.

complex fraction *Math.* A fraction in which either the numerator or the denominator is a fraction.

com·plex·ion (kəm·plek′shən) n. 1. The color and appearance of the skin, esp. of the face. 2. General aspect or appearance; quality; character. [< F < L < complecti to put together] **—com·plex′ion·al** adj.

com·plex·ioned (kəm·plek′shənd) adj. Of a certain complexion: used in compounds: light-*complexioned.*

com·plex·i·ty (kəm·plek′sə·tē) n. pl. ·ties 1. The state of being complex. 2. Something complex.

complex sentence. See under SENTENCE.

com·pli·a·ble (kəm·plī′ə·bəl) adj. Compliant. **—com·pli′a·ble·ness** n. **—com·pli′a·bly** adv.

com·pli·ance (kəm·plī′əns) n. 1. The act of complying or yielding. 2. A disposition to comply; complaisance. Also **com·pli′an·cy. —in compliance with** In agreement with.

com·pli·ant (kəm·plī′ənt) adj. Complying; yielding. **—com·pli′ant·ly** adv.

com·pli·cate (v. kom′plə·kāt; adj. kom′plə·kit) v. ·cat·ed, ·cat·ing v.t. 1. To make complex, difficult, or perplexing. 2. To twist or wind around; intertwine. **—v.i.** 3. To become complex or difficult. **—adj.** Complicated; complex. [< L < com- together + plicare to fold]

com·pli·cat·ed (kom′plə·kā′tid) adj. Difficult to separate, analyze, or understand; intricate; involved. **—com′pli·cat·ed·ly** adv. **—com′pli·cat·ed·ness** n.

com·pli·ca·tion (kom′plə·kā′shən) n. 1. The act of complicating. 2. An intricate or perplexing structure, condition, or relationship. 3. Anything that complicates.

com·plic·i·ty (kəm·plis′ə·tē) n. pl. ·ties 1. The state of being an accomplice, as in a wrong act. 2. Complexity.

com·pli·ment (n. kom′plə·mənt; v. kom′plə·ment) n. 1. An expression of admiration, praise, or congratulation. 2. Usu. pl. A formal greeting or remembrance. **—v.t.** 1. To pay a compliment to. 2. To show regard for, as by a gift. [< MF < Ital. < L complementum]

com·pli·men·ta·ry (kom′plə·men′tər·ē, -trē) adj. 1. Conveying, using, or like a compliment. 2. Given free: a *complimentary* copy of a book. **—com·pli·men·ta·ri·ly** adv.

com·plin (kom′plin) n. Often cap. *Eccl.* Prescribed prayers constituting the last of the seven canonical hours. Also **com·pline** (kom′plin, -plīn) [< OF < L com- thoroughly + plere to fill]

com·ply (kəm·plī′) v.i. ·plied, ·ply·ing 1. To act in conformity; consent; obey: with *with*. [< Ital. complire < Sp. < L < com- thoroughly + plere to fill] **—com·pli′er** n.

com·po·nent (kəm·pō′nənt) n. A constituent element or part. **—adj.** Forming a part or ingredient; constituent. [< L < com- together + ponere to pull]

com·port (kəm·pôrt′, -pōrt′) v.t. 1. To conduct or behave (oneself). **—v.i.** 2. To be compatible; agree: with *with*. [< F < L < com- together + portare to carry] **—com·port′ment** n.

com·pose (kəm·pōz′) v. ·posed, ·pos·ing v.t. 1. To constitute; form. 2. To make of elements or parts; fashion. 3. To create (a literary or musical work). 4. To make calm or tranquil; quiet. 5. To reconcile or settle, as differences. 6. *Printing* To arrange (type) in lines; set. **—v.i.** 7. To engage in composition, as of musical works. 8. *Printing* To set type. [< MF < com- together + poser to place]

com·posed (kəm·pōzd′) *adj.* Free from agitation; calm. — **com·pos·ed·ly** (kəm·pō′zid·lē) *adv.* — **com·pos′ed·ness** *n.*

com·pos·er (kəm·pō′zər) *n.* One who composes; esp., one who writes music.

com·pos·ite (kəm·poz′it) *adj.* 1. Made up of separate parts or elements; combined or compounded. 2. *Bot.* Characteristic of or pertaining to a family of plants, as the dandelion, chrysanthemum, etc., the flowers usu. occurring in dense clusters. — *n.* 1. That which is composed or made up of parts. 2. *Bot.* A composite plant. [< L < com- together + ponere to put] — **com·pos′ite·ly** *adv.* — **com·pos′ite·ness** *n.*

com·po·si·tion (kom′pə·zish′ən) *n.* 1. A putting together of parts, ingredients, etc., to form a whole. 2. That which is so formed. 3. Constitution; make-up. 4. The act or art of creating a literary, musical, or artistic work. 5. The work so created, or its general structure. 6. A short essay written as an exercise for school. 7. An agreement or settlement, esp. by compromise. 8. *Printing* The setting of type.

com·pos·i·tor (kəm·poz′ə·tər) *n.* One who sets type.

com·pos men·tis (kom′pəs men′tis) *Latin* Of sound mind.

com·post (kom′pōst) *n.* 1. A fertilizing mixture of decomposed vegetable matter. 2. A compound. [< OF, mixture]

com·po·sure (kəm·pō′zhər) *n.* Tranquillity, as of mind; calmness; serenity.

com·pote (kom′pōt, *Fr.* kôṅ·pôt′) *n.* 1. Fruit stewed or preserved in syrup. 2. A dish for holding fruits, etc. [< F < OF composte]

com·pound[1] (*n.* kom′pound; *v.* kom·pound′, kəm-; *adj.* kom′pound, kom·pound′) *n.* 1. A combination of two or more elements or parts. 2. *Gram.* A word composed of two or more words joined with a hyphen or written in solid form, as *fly-by-night, shoestring.* 3. *Chem.* A definite substance resulting from the combination of specific elements or radicals in fixed proportions: distinguished from *mixture.* — *v.t.* 1. To make by combining various elements or ingredients. 2. To mix (elements or parts). 3. To compute (interest) on both the principal and whatever interest has accrued. 4. To settle for less than the sum due, as a debt; compromise. — *adj.* Composed of two or more elements or parts. [< OF < L < com- together + ponere to put] — **com·pound′a·ble** *adj.* — **com·pound′er** *n.*

com·pound[2] (kom′pound) *n.* 1. In the Orient, an enclosure containing a building, esp. one occupied by Europeans. 2. Any similar enclosed place. [< Malay *kampong*]

compound fraction *Math.* A complex fraction.

compound interest Interest computed on the original principal together with its accrued interest.

compound leaf *Bot.* A leaf having several distinct blades on a common leafstalk.

compound number *Math.* A quantity containing more than one unit or denomination, as 6 feet 3 inches.

compound sentence See under SENTENCE.

com·pre·hend (kom′pri·hend′) *v.t.* 1. To grasp mentally; understand fully. 2. To take in or embrace; include. — *v.i.* 3. To understand. — *Syn.* See APPREHEND. [< L < com- together + prehendere to grasp, seize]

com·pre·hen·si·ble (kom′pri·hen′sə·bəl) *adj.* Capable of being comprehended; understandable; intelligible. Also **com′pre·hend′i·ble.** — **com′pre·hen·si·bil′i·ty, com′pre·hen′si·ble·ness** *n.* — **com′pre·hen′si·bly** *adv.*

com·pre·hen·sion (kom′pri·hen′shən) *n.* 1. The mental grasping of ideas, facts, etc., or the power of so doing; understanding. 2. An including or taking in; comprehensiveness. — *Syn.* See KNOWLEDGE.

com·pre·hen·sive (kom′pri·hen′siv) *adj.* 1. Large in scope or content; broad. 2. Understanding or comprehending. — **com′pre·hen′sive·ly** *adv.* — **com′pre·hen′sive·ness** *n.*

com·press (*v.* kəm·pres′; *n.* kom′pres) *v.t.* To press together or into smaller space; condense; compact. — *n.* 1. *Med.* A cloth or pad, sometimes medicated, for applying moisture, cold, heat, or pressure to a part of the body. 2. An apparatus for compressing bales of cotton, etc. [< OF < LL < L < com- together + premere to press] — **com·pressed′** *adj.* — **com·press′i·bil′i·ty, com·press′i·ble·ness** *n.* — **com·press′i·ble** *adj.* — **com·pres′sive** *adj.*

com·pres·sion (kəm·presh′ən) *n.* 1. The act of compressing or the state of being compressed. Also **com·pres·sure** (kəm·presh′ər). 2. The process by which a confined gas is reduced in volume through the application of pressure, as in the cylinder of an internal-combustion engine.

com·pres·sor (kəm·pres′ər) *n.* 1. One who or that which compresses. 2. *Anat.* A muscle that compresses a part. 3. *Mech.* A power-driven machine for compressing a gas in order to utilize its expansion, as for refrigeration.

com·prise (kəm·prīz′) *v.t.* **·prised, ·pris·ing** To consist of or contain; include. [< MF < L < com- together + premere to press] — **com·pris′a·ble** *adj.* — **com·pri′sal** *n.*

com·pro·mise (kom′prə·mīz) *n.* 1. An adjustment or settlement by which each side makes concessions. 2. The result of such concessions. 3. Something lying midway be-

tween, or combining the qualities of, two different things. 4. An imperiling, as of character or reputation. — *v.* **·mised, ·mis·ing** *v.t.* 1. To adjust by concessions. 2. To expose to risk, suspicion, or disrepute; imperil. — *v.i.* 3. To make a compromise. [< MF < L < com- together + promittere to promise] — **com′pro·mis′er** *n.*

compte ren·du (kôṅt′ räṅ·dü′) *French* An official report; literally, account rendered.

Comp·tom·e·ter (komp·tom′ə·tər) *n.* A high-speed calculating machine: a trade name. Also **comp·tom′e·ter.**

comp·trol·ler (kən·trō′lər) See CONTROLLER (def. 2).

com·pul·sion (kəm·pul′shən) *n.* 1. The act of compelling; coercion. 2. The state of being compelled. 3. *Psychol.* An irresistible impulse or tendency to perform an act. [< MF < L < com- together + pellere to drive]

com·pul·sive (kəm·pul′siv) *adj.* Compelling; compulsory. — **com·pul′sive·ly** *adv.* — **com·pul′sive·ness** *n.*

com·pul·so·ry (kəm·pul′sər·ē) *adj.* 1. Employing compulsion; coercive. 2. Required; obligatory: *compulsory education.* — **com·pul′so·ri·ly** *adv.* — **com·pul′so·ri·ness** *n.*

com·punc·tion (kəm·pungk′shən) *n.* 1. An uneasiness of mind arising from wrongdoing; a sense of guilt or remorse. 2. A feeling of slight regret or pity. [< OF < LL < L com-greatly + pungere to prick, sting] — **com·punc′tious** *adj.* — **com·punc′tious·ly** *adv.*

com·pu·ta·tion (kom′pyə·tā′shən) *n.* 1. The act or method of computing. 2. A computed amount or number.

com·pute (kəm·pyōōt′) *v.t. & v.i.* **·put·ed, ·put·ing** To ascertain (an amount or number) by calculation; reckon. — *n.* Computation. [< MF < L < com- together + putare to reckon.] — **com·put′a·bil′i·ty** *n.* — **com·put′a·ble** *adj.*

com·put·er (kəm·pyōō′tər) *n.* 1. One who or that which computes. 2. An electronic machine for the high-speed performance of mathematical and logical operations, or for the processing of large masses of coded information.

com·rade (kom′rad, -rid, kum′-) *n.* 1. An intimate companion or friend. 2. A person who shares one's own occupation, interests, etc. [< MF camarade < Sp. < L camera room] — **com′rade·ship** *n.*

Com·tism (kom′tiz·əm, kôṅ′-) *n.* The philosophy of Comte; positivism. — **Com·ti·an** (kom′tē·ən, kôṅ′-) *adj.*

con[1] (kon) *v.t.* **conned, con·ning** To study; peruse carefully; commit to memory. [Var. of CAN[1]] — **con′ner** *n.*

con[2] (kon) *Naut. v.t.* **conned, con·ning** To direct the steering of (a vessel). — *n.* The act of conning. Also **conn.** [Earlier cond < F < L < com- together + ducere to lead]

con[3] (kon) *U.S. Slang adj.* Confidence: *con man; con game.* — *v.t.* **conned, con·ning** To defraud; dupe; swindle. [< CONFIDENCE]

con- Var. of COM-.

con·cat·e·nate (kon·kat′ə·nāt) *v.t.* **·nat·ed, ·nat·ing** To join or link together; connect in a series. — *adj.* Connected in a series. [< L < com- together + catena chain]

con·cat·e·na·tion (kon·kat′ə·nā′shən) *n.* 1. The act of linking together. 2. A chainlike series, as of events, etc.

con·cave (*adj.* kon·kāv′, kon′kāv, kong′-; *n.* kon′kāv, kong′-; *v.* kon·kāv′) *adj.* Hollow and curving inward, as the interior of a sphere or bowl: opposed to *convex.* — *n.* A concave surface; vault. — *v.t.* **·caved, ·cav·ing** To make concave. [< MF < L < com- thoroughly + cavus hollow] — **con·cave′ly** *adv.* — **con·cave′ness** *n.*

con·cav·i·ty (kon·kav′ə·tē) *n. pl.* **·ties** 1. The state of being concave. 2. A concave surface; a hollow.

con·ca·vo-con·cave (kon·kā′vō·kon·kāv′) *adj.* Biconcave.

con·ca·vo-con·vex (kon·kā′vō·kon·veks′) *adj.* Concave on one side and convex on the other, as a lens.

con·ceal (kən·sēl′) *v.t.* To keep from sight, discovery, or knowledge; hide; secrete. — *Syn.* See HIDE. [< OF < L < com- thoroughly + celare to hide] — **con·ceal′a·ble** *adj.* — **con·ceal′er** *n.* — **con·ceal′ment** *n.*

con·cede (kən·sēd′) *v.* **·ced·ed, ·ced·ing** *v.t.* 1. To acknowledge as true, correct, or proper; admit. 2. To grant; yield, as a right or privilege. — *v.i.* 3. To make a concession; yield. — *Syn.* See CONFESS. [< L < com- thoroughly + cedere to yield, go away] — **con·ced′er** *n.*

con·ceit (kən·sēt′) *n.* 1. Overweening self-esteem. 2. An ingenious, fanciful thought or expression. 3. In poetry, an elaborate, extended metaphor. 4. Imagination; fancy. — *Syn.* See PRIDE. [< CONCEIVE]

con·ceit·ed (kən·sē′tid) *adj.* Having an excessively high opinion of oneself; vain. — **con·ceit′ed·ly** *adv.* — **con·ceit′ed·ness** *n.*

con·ceive (kən·sēv′) *v.* **·ceived, ·ceiv·ing** *v.t.* 1. To become pregnant with. 2. To form a concept or notion of; imagine: *to conceive the perfect man.* 3. To understand; grasp. 4. To express in a particular way. — *v.i.* 5. To form a mental image; think: with *of.* 6. To become pregnant. [< OF < L < com- thoroughly + capere to grasp, take] — **con·ceiv′a·ble** *adj.* — **con·ceiv′a·bil′i·ty, con·ceiv′a·ble·ness** *n.* — **con·ceiv′a·bly** *adv.* — **con·ceiv′er** *n.*

con·cen·ter (kon·sen′tər) *v.t. & v.i.* To direct or come to a common point or center; focus. Also *Brit.* con·cen′tre. [< F < L < *com-* together + *centrum* center]

con·cen·trate (kon′sən·trāt) v. ·trat·ed, ·trat·ing v.t. 1. To draw or direct to a common point; focus: to *concentrate* troops. 2. To intensify or purify by removing certain constituents; condense. — v.i. 3. To converge toward a center. 4. To become compacted, intensified, or more pure. 5. To direct one's entire attention: often with *on* or *upon*. — n. A product of concentration, as in chemistry or metallurgy. — adj. Concentrated. — **con·cen·tra′tor** n.

con·cen·tra·tion (kon′sən·trā′shən) n. 1. The act of concentrating, or the state of being concentrated. 2. That which is concentrated, as a solution. 3. Complete attention to some single problem, task, etc.

concentration camp An enclosed camp for the confinement of prisoners of war, political prisoners, aliens, etc.

con·cen·tra·tive (kon′sən·trā′tiv, kən·sen′trə·tiv) adj. Tending to concentrate, or characterized by concentration. — **con′cen·tra·tive·ly** adv. — **con′cen·tra′tive·ness** n.

con·cen·tric (kən·sen′trik) adj. Having a common center, as circles: opposed to *eccentric*. Also **con·cen′tri·cal.** — **con·cen′tri·cal·ly** adv. — **con·cen·tric·i·ty** (kon′sen·tris′ə·tē) n.

con·cept (kon′sept) n. A mental image; esp., a generalized idea formed by combining the elements of a class into the notion of one object; also, a thought or opinion. — Syn. See IDEA. [< L *conceptus* a conceiving]

con·cep·tion (kən·sep′shən) n. 1. A conceiving, or a being conceived, in the womb. 2. An embryo or fetus. 3. A beginning; commencement. 4. The act of forming concepts or ideas. 5. A concept, idea, plan, or design. — **con·cep′tion·al** adj. — **con·cep′tive** adj.

con·cep·tu·al (kən·sep′chōō·əl) adj. Of or pertaining to conception or concepts. — **con·cep′tu·al·ly** adv.

con·cern (kən·sûrn′) v.t. 1. To be of interest or importance to. 2. To occupy the attention or mind of; engage; involve: used as a reflexive or in the passive. 3. To affect with anxiety; trouble: often in the passive. — n. 1. That which concerns or affects one; affair; business. 2. Anxiety or interest; solicitous regard; care. 3. Relation or bearing. 4. A business enterprise; a firm. [< MF < Med.L < com- thoroughly + *cernere* to see, discern] — **con·cerned′** adj.

con·cern·ing (kən·sûr′ning) prep. In relation to; regarding; about.

con·cern·ment (kən·sûrn′mənt) n. 1. Importance. 2. Concern; anxiety. 3. Anything that relates to one; affair.

con·cert (n. kon′sûrt; v. kən·sûrt′) n. 1. A musical performance by singers or instrumentalists. 2. Agreement; harmony. — **in concert** In unison; all together. — adj. Of or for concerts. [< MF < Ital. < *concertare* to agree]

con·cert·ed (kən·sûr′tid) adj. 1. Arranged, agreed upon, or done together; combined. 2. *Music* Arranged in parts for voices or instruments. — **con·cert′ed·ly** adv.

con·cer·ti·na (kon′sər·tē′nə) n. A small bellowslike musical instrument with buttons for keys and handles on each of the two hexagonal ends. [< CONCERT + -INA]

con·cert·mas·ter (kon′sərt·mas′tər, -mäs′-) n. The leader of the first violin section of an orchestra, who acts as assistant to the conductor. Also **con′cert·meis′ter** (mīs′-)

con·cer·to (kən·cher′tō) n. pl. ·tos, Ital. ·ti (-tē) *Music* A composition, usu. of three movements, for performance by a solo instrument or instruments accompanied by an orchestra. Abbr. *con.* [< Ital. See CONCERT.]

concerto gros·so (grō′sō) pl. **concerti gros·si** (grō′sē) A concerto for a group of solo instruments and an orchestra. [< Ital., lit., big concerto]

con·ces·sion (kən·sesh′ən) n. 1. The act of conceding. 2. Anything so yielded. 3. A right or privilege granted by a government. 4. *U.S.* The right to operate a subsidiary business on certain premises. 5. *Canadian* In Ontario and Quebec, a subdivision of land in township surveys. — **con·ces′sive** adj.

con·ces·sion·aire (kən·sesh′ən·âr′) n. One who holds or operates a concession. Also **con·ces′sion·er** [< F]

con·ces·sion·ar·y (kən·sesh′ən·er′ē) adj. Of or pertaining to a concession. — n. pl. ·ar·ies A concessionaire.

concession road *Canadian* A road following a survey line.

conch (kongk, konch) n. pl. **conchs** (kongks) or **conch·es** (kon′chiz) 1. Any of various marine mollusks having large, spiral, univalve shells. 2. Such a shell. [< L < Gk. *konchē* shell]

con·chol·o·gy (kong·kol′ə·jē) n. The study of shells and mollusks. [< L *concha* shell + -LOGY] — **con·cho·log·i·cal** (kong′kə·loj′i·kəl) adj. — **con·chol′o·gist** n.

con·cierge (kon′sē·ûrzh′, Fr. kôn·syârzh′) n. An attendant or doorkeeper of a building, esp. in France, who performs custodial services. [< F]

CONCH SHELL

con·cil·i·ate (kən·sil′ē·āt) v.t. ·at·ed, ·at·ing 1. To win over; placate; appease. 2. To secure or attract by favorable measures; win. 3. To make consistent. [< L < *concilium* council] — **con·cil′i·a·ble** (kən·sil′ē·ə·bəl) adj. — **con·cil′i·a′tion** n. — **con·cil′i·a′tor** n.

con·cil·i·a·to·ry (kən·sil′ē·ə·tôr′ē, -tō′rē) adj. Tending to reconcile or conciliate. Also **con·cil′i·a′tive.** — **con·cil′i·a·to′ri·ly** adv. — **con·cil′i·a·to′ri·ness** n.

con·cise (kən·sīs′) adj. Expressing much in brief form; compact. — Syn. See TERSE. [< L < com- thoroughly + *caedere* to cut] — **con·cise′ly** adv. — **con·cise′ness** n.

con·clave (kon′klāv, kong′-) n. 1. A private or secret meeting. 2. The private chambers in which the College of Cardinals meets to elect a pope; also, the meeting. [< F < L < com- together + *clavis* key] — **con′clav·ist** n.

con·clude (kən·klōōd′) v. ·clud·ed, ·clud·ing v.t. 1. To bring to an end; terminate. 2. To arrange or settle finally; effect. 3. To form an opinion or judgment about; decide. 4. To resolve (to do); determine. — v.i. 5. To come to an end. 6. To come to a decision or agreement. [< L < com- thoroughly + *claudere* to close, shut off] — **con·clud′er** n.

con·clu·sion (kən·klōō′zhən) n. 1. The end or termination of something. 2. A closing part, as of a speech. 3. The result of an act or process; outcome. 4. A judgment or opinion obtained by reasoning. 5. A final decision; resolve. 6. A final arranging; settlement, as of a treaty. — **in conclusion** As a final statement or summing up.

con·clu·sive (kən·klōō′siv) adj. Putting an end to a question; decisive. — **con·clu′sive·ly** adv. — **con·clu′sive·ness** n.

con·coct (kon·kokt′, kən-) v.t. 1. To make by mixing ingredients, as food, a drink, etc. 2. To make up; devise: to *concoct* a plan. [< L < com- together + *coquere* to cook, boil] — **con·coct′er** or **con·coc′tor** n. — **con·coc′tive** adj.

con·coc·tion (kon·kok′shən, kən-) n. 1. The act of concocting. 2. Something concocted.

con·com·i·tance (kon·kom′ə·təns, kən-) n. Existence or occurrence together; accompaniment. Also **con·com′i·tan·cy.**

con·com·i·tant (kon·kom′ə·tənt, kən-) adj. Existing or occurring together; attendant. — n. An attendant circumstance, state, or thing. [< L < com- with + *comitari* to accompany] — **con·com′i·tant·ly** adv.

con·cord (kon′kôrd, kong′-) n. 1. Unity of feeling or interest; agreement; accord. 2. Peace; friendly relations. 3. A treaty establishing this. 4. *Music* Consonance. — Syn. See HARMONY. [< MF < L < com- together + *cor, cordis* heart]

con·cor·dance (kon·kôr′dəns, kən-) n. 1. Agreement; concord. 2. An alphabetical index of the important words in a book as they occur in context: a *concordance* of the Bible.

con·cor·dant (kon·kôr′dənt, kən-) adj. Existing in concord; agreeing; harmonious. — **con·cor′dant·ly** adv.

con·cor·dat (kon·kôr′dat) n. 1. An agreement between the papacy and a government on church affairs. 2. Any official agreement or pact.

con·course (kon′kôrs, -kōrs, kong′-) n. 1. A coming together; confluence. 2. A crowd; throng. 3. A large place for the assembling or passage of crowds. [< MF < L < com- together + *currere* to run]

con·crete (kon′krēt; for adj., n., & v. def. 3, also kon·krēt′) adj. 1. Specific, as opposed to general: a *concrete* example. 2. Physically perceptible; objectively real. 3. *Gram.* Naming a specific thing or class of things, rather than an abstract quality or state. 4. Constituting a composite mass or substance; solid. 5. Made of concrete. — n. 1. A building material of sand and gravel or broken rock united by cement, used for roadways, bridges, walls, etc. 2. That which is concrete: often preceded by *the.* — v. ·cret·ed, ·cret·ing v.t. 1. To bring together in one mass or body; cause to coalesce. 2. To cover with concrete. — v.i. 3. To coalesce; solidify. [< L < com- together + *crescere* to grow] — **con·crete′ly** adv. — **con·crete′ness** n.

con·cre·tion (kon·krē′shən) n. 1. The act or process of growing or coming together; a solidifying. 2. A concrete mass. — **con·cre′tive** adj. — **con·cre′tive·ly** adv.

con·cre·tize (kon′kri·tīz) v.t. ·tized, ·tiz·ing To render concrete; make specific.

con·cu·bine (kong′kyə·bīn, kon′-) n. 1. A woman who cohabits with a man without being married to him. 2. In certain polygamous societies, a secondary wife. [< F < L < com- with + *cumbere* to lie] — **con·cu·bi·nage** (kon·kyōō′bə·nij) n. — **con·cu′bi·nar·y** adj.

con·cu·pis·cence (kon·kyōō′pə·səns) n. 1. Sexual desire; lust. 2. Any immoderate desire. [< L < com- thoroughly + *cupere* to desire] — **con·cu′pis·cent** adj.

con·cur (kən·kûr′) v.i. ·curred, ·cur·ring 1. To agree or approve, as in opinion or action. 2. To cooperate or combine. 3. To happen at the same time. 4. To converge to a point, as lines. [< L < com- together + *currere* to run]

con·cur·rence (kən·kûr'əns) *n.* **1.** The act of concurring. **2.** Cooperation or combination to effect some purpose or end. **3.** Agreement in mind or opinion; assent; consent. **4.** Simultaneous occurrence; coincidence. **5.** *Geom.* The point where three or more lines meet. Also **con·cur'ren·cy.**

con·cur·rent (kən·kûr'ənt) *adj.* **1.** Occurring together at the same time. **2.** United in action or application; cooperating; coordinate. **3.** *Law* Having the same authority or jurisdiction. **4.** Meeting at or going toward the same point. **5.** In agreement or accordance. **— con·cur'rent·ly** *adv.*

con·cus·sion (kən·kush'ən) *n.* **1.** A violent shaking; jar. **2.** *Pathol.* A violent shock to some organ, esp. to the brain, by a fall, sudden blow, or blast. [< L < *com-* together + *quatere* to strike, beat] **— con·cus·sive** (kən·kus'iv) *adj.*

con·demn (kən·dem') *v.t.* **1.** To hold to be wrong; censure. **2.** To pronounce judicial sentence against. **3.** To show the guilt of; convict. **4.** To pronounce or declare to be unfit for use, usually by official order. **5.** *U.S.* To appropriate for public use by judicial decree; declare forfeited. [< L < *com-* thoroughly + *damnare* to condemn] **— con·dem·na·ble** (kən·dem'nə·bəl) *adj.* **— con·demn·er** (kən·dem'ər) *n.*

con·dem·na·tion (kon'dem·nā'shən) *n.* **1.** The act of condemning, or the state of being condemned. **2.** A cause or occasion for condemning. **— con·dem·na·to·ry** (kən·dem'nə·tô'rē, -tō'rē) *adj.*

con·den·sa·tion (kon'den·sā'shən) *n.* **1.** The act of condensing, or the state of being condensed. **2.** Any product of condensing.

con·dense (kən·dens') *v.* **·densed, ·dens·ing** *v.t.* **1.** To compress or make dense; consolidate. **2.** To abridge or make concise, as an essay. **3.** To change from the gaseous to the liquid state, or from the liquid to the solid state, as by cooling or compression. **— v.i. 4.** To become condensed. [< L < *com-* together + *densus* crowded, close] **— con·den·sa·bil·i·ty** or **con·den·si·bil·i·ty** *n.* **— con·den·sa·ble** or **con·den·si·ble** *adj.*

condensed milk Cow's milk, sweetened with sugar, and thickened by evaporation of its water content.

con·dens·er (kən·den·sər) *n.* **1.** One who or that which condenses. **2.** Any device for reducing a vapor to liquid or solid form. **3.** *Electr.* A capacitor. **4.** *Optics* A combination of lenses for effectively focusing light rays.

con·de·scend (kon'di·send') *v.i.* **1.** To lower oneself (to do something); deign. **2.** To behave in a patronizing manner. [< MF < LL < L *com-* together + *descendere* to stoop] **— con'de·scen·sion, con'de·scen'dence** *n.*

con·de·scend·ing (kon'di·sen'ding) *adj.* Showing conscious courtesy toward inferiors; esp., making a display of such courtesy; patronizing. **— con'de·scend'ing·ly** *adv.*

con·di·ment (kon'də·mənt) *n.* A sauce, relish, spice, etc., used to season food. [< L *condire* to pickle]

con·di·tion (kən·dish'ən) *n.* **1.** The state or mode of existence of a person or thing. **2.** State of health; esp., a healthful state. **3.** *Informal* An ailment: a heart *condition*. **4.** An event, fact, or circumstance necessary to the occurrence of some other; a prerequisite: Hard work is the *condition* of success. **5.** *Usu. pl.* The circumstances affecting an activity or a mode of existence: poor living *conditions*. **6.** Social status. **7.** In a will, contract, etc., a provision allowing for modification upon the occurrence of some uncertain future event. **— in** (or **out of**) **condition** Fit (or unfit) for proper performance, esp. of some physical activity. **— on condition that** Provided that; if. **— v.t. 1.** To be a condition or prerequisite of. **2.** To specify as a condition; stipulate. **3.** To render fit or in good condition. **4.** *Psychol.* To train to a behavior pattern or conditioned response. **5.** To accustom (someone) to. **— v.i. 6.** To bargain; stipulate. [< OF < L < *com-* together + *dicere* to say] **— con·di'tion·er** *n.*

con·di·tion·al (kən·dish'ən·əl) *adj.* **1.** Not absolute; tentative. **2.** *Gram.* Expressing or implying a condition. **— n.** *Gram.* A conditional word, tense, clause, or mood. **— con·di'tion·al'i·ty** (-al'ə·tē) *n.* **— con·di'tion·al·ly** *adv.*

con·di·tioned response (kən·dish'ənd) *Psychol.* A learned response to a previously neutral stimulus, made directly effective by its repeated association with a stimulus normally evoking the response. Also **conditioned reflex.**

con·dole (kən·dōl') *v.* **·doled, ·dol·ing** To grieve or express sympathy with one in affliction: with *with.* [< LL < L *com-* together + *dolere* to grieve] **— con·do·la·to·ry** (kən·dō'lə·tôr'ē, -tō'rē) *adj.* **— con·dol'er** *n.*

con·do·lence (kən·dō'ləns, *occasionally* kon'də·ləns) *n.* Expression of sympathy with a person in pain or sorrow. Also **con·dole·ment** (kən·dōl'mənt).

con·dom (kon'dəm, kun'-) *n.* A sheath for the penis, usu. made of rubber and having an antivenereal or contraceptive function. [? Alter. of *Conton,* 18th c. English physician]

con·do·min·i·um (kon'də·min'ē·əm) *n.* **1.** Joint sovereignty or ownership. **2.** *U.S.* An apartment house in which the units are owned separately; also, an apartment in such a house. [< NL < L *com-* together + *dominium* rule]

con·done (kən·dōn') *v.t.* **·doned, ·don·ing** To treat (an of-

fense) as overlooked or as if it had not been committed. [< L < *com-* thoroughly + *donare* to give] **— con'do·na'tion** *n.* **— con·don'er** *n.*

con·dor (kon'dôr, -dər) *n.* A vulture of the high Andes, one of the largest flying birds, having a bare head and a white, downy neck. [< Sp. < Quechua *cuntur*]

con·duce (kən·dōōs', -dyōōs') *v.i.* **·duced, ·duc·ing** To help or tend toward a result; contribute: with *to.* [< L *conducere* to bring together]

con·du·cive (kən·dōō'siv, -dyōō'-) *adj.* Contributive or promotive; leading; helping: with *to.* Also **con·du·cent** (kən·dōō'sənt, -dyōō'-). **— con·du'cive·ness** *n.*

con·duct (*v.* kən·dukt'; *n.* kon'dukt) *v.t.* **1.** To accompany and show the way; guide; escort. **2.** To manage or control. **3.** To direct and lead the performance of, as an orchestra, opera, etc. **4.** To serve as a medium of transmission for; convey; transmit. **5.** To act or behave: use reflexively. **— v.i. 6.** To serve as a conductor. **7.** To direct or lead. **— n. 1.** The way a person acts; behavior. **2.** Management; control. **3.** The act of guiding or leading. [< L < *com-* together + *ducere* to lead] **— con·duct'i·bil'i·ty** *n.* **— con·duct'i·ble** *adj.* **— con·duc·tive** (kən·duk'tiv) *adj.*

con·duc·tance (kən·duk'təns) *n.* *Electr.* The ability of a body to pass a current: the reciprocal of *resistance.*

con·duc·tion (kən·duk'shən) *n.* **1.** *Physics* The transmission of heat, sound, or electricity through matter without motion of the conducting body as a whole. **2.** *Physiol.* The transference of a stimulus along nerve fibers.

con·duc·tiv·i·ty (kon'duk·tiv'ə·tē) *n.* *Physics* The capacity to transmit sound, heat, or electricity.

con·duc·tor (kən·duk'tər) *n.* **1.** One who conducts or leads. **2.** *Chiefly U.S.* One who has charge of a railroad car, bus, etc. **3.** The director of an orchestra or chorus. **4.** Any substance, material, or medium that conducts electricity, heat, etc. **— con·duc'tor·ship** *n.* **— con·duc'tress** *n.fem.*

con·duit (kon'dit, -dōō·it) *n.* **1.** A channel or pipe for conveying water or other liquid; a canal; aqueduct. **2.** A covered passage or tube for electric wires. [< MF < L < *com-* together + *ducere* to lead]

cone (kōn) *n.* **1.** *Geom.* **a** A surface generated by a straight line passing through all the points of a fixed closed curve and a fixed point (the vertex) outside the plane of the curve. **b** A solid bounded by such a surface. **2.** A thing that tapers uniformly from a circular part to a point, as a machine part or the pastry shell used to hold ice cream. **3.** *Bot.* A dry multiple fruit, as of the pine, composed of scales arranged symmetrically around an axis and enclosing seeds. **— v.t. coned, con·ing** To shape conically. [< L < Gk. *kōnos*]

con·el·rad (kon'əl·rad) *n.* A technique for controlling radio signals from stations so as to prevent enemy aircraft from using the signals for navigation or information. [< CON(TROL OF) EL(ECTROMAGNETIC) RAD(IATION)]

Con·es·to·ga wagon (kon'is·tō'gə) *U.S.* A type of covered wagon with broad wheels, used by American pioneers for westward travel over the prairies. [after *Conestoga,* Pa., where first made]

CONESTOGA WAGON

co·ney (kō'nē, kun'ē) See CONY.

con·fab (kon'fab) *Informal v.i.* **·fabbed, ·fab·bing** To converse. **— n.** A conversation. [Short for CONFABULATION]

con·fab·u·late (kən·fab'yə·lāt) *v.i.* **·lat·ed, ·lat·ing** To chat; gossip; converse. [< L < *com-* together + *fabulari* to chat] **— con·fab'u·la'tion** *n.* **— con·fab·u·la·to·ry** (kən·fab'yə·lə·tôr'ē, -tō'rē) *adj.*

con·fec·tion (kən·fek'shən) *n.* **1.** The act or process of mixing or compounding. **2.** Any of various sweet preparations, as candy or preserves. **— con·fec'tion·ar·y** *adj. & n.*

con·fec·tion·er (kən·fek'shən·ər) *n.* One who makes or deals in confectionery.

confectioner's sugar A finely ground powdered sugar, used in icings, confections, etc.

con·fec·tion·er·y (kən·fek'shən·er'ē) *n. pl.* **·er·ies 1.** Sweetmeats collectively. **2.** A confectioner's shop, or the business of a confectioner.

con·fed·er·a·cy (kən·fed'ər·ə·sē) *n. pl.* **·cies 1.** A union of states or persons for mutual support or action; a league; alliance. **2.** An unlawful combination; conspiracy. **— the Confederacy** The Confederate States of America: also **Southern Confederacy.**

con·fed·er·ate (*n., adj.* kən·fed'ər·it; *v.* kən·fed'ə·rāt) *n.* One who takes part in a league or plot; an associate; accomplice. **— adj.** Associated in a confederacy. **— v.t. & v.i. ·at·ed, ·at·ing** To form or join in a confederacy. [< LL < L *com-* together + *foedus* league] **— con·fed'er·a'tive** *adj.*

Con·fed·er·ate (kən·fed'ər·it) *adj.* Pertaining to the Confederate States of America. **— n.** An adherent of the Confederate States of America. *Abbr. Confed.*

Confederate States of America A league of eleven southern States that seceded from the United States during the period from December, 1860 to May, 1861.

con·fed·er·a·tion (kən·fed′ə·rā′shən) *n.* **1.** The act of confederating, or the state of being confederated. **2.** An association of states usu. less permanent than a federation.

Con·fed·er·a·tion (kən·fed′ə·rā′shən) *n.* **1.** The federation formed by Ontario, Quebec, Nova Scotia, and New Brunswick in 1867, now including ten provinces. **2.** The union of the American colonies, 1781–89, under the Articles of Confederation.

con·fer (kən·fûr′) *v.* **·ferred, ·fer·ring** *v.t.* **1.** To grant as a gift or benefit; bestow. Abbr. *cf.* — *v.i.* **2.** To hold a conference; consult together; take counsel. [< L < *com-* together + *ferre* to bring, carry] — **con·fer′ment** *n.* — **con·fer′ra·ble** *adj.* — **con·fer′rer** *n.*

con·fer·ee (kon′fə·rē′) *n.* One who takes part in conference or a conference. Also **con′fer·ree′.**

con·fer·ence (kon′fər·əns, -frəns) *n.* **1.** A discussion or consultation on some important matter; also, a formal meeting for this. **2.** A league or association, as of athletic teams, schools, churches, etc. — **con′fer·en′tial** (-fə·ren′shəl) *adj.*

con·fess (kən·fes′) *v.t.* **1.** To acknowledge or admit, as a fault, guilt, or sin. **2.** To concede or admit to be true. **3.** To acknowledge belief or faith in. **4.** *Eccl.* **a** To admit or make known (one's sins), esp. to a priest, in order to obtain absolution. **b** To hear the confession of: said of a priest. — *v.i.* **5.** To make acknowledgment, as of fault or crime: with *to.* **6.** To make confession to a priest. [< MF < L < *com-* thoroughly + *fateri* to own, declare] — **con·fess′ed·ly** *adv.*

— **Syn. 1.** *Confess* is now generally restricted to the sense of making known to others one's own error or wrongdoing: to *confess* a robbery. We *acknowledge* that for which we are responsible, often with no bad implication: to *acknowledge* one's signature. *Admit* and *concede* indicate a yielding to the assertion or wish of another; we *admit* the truth of an allegation; we *concede* a demand, claim, opposing view, etc. — **Ant.** deny, disavow, repudiate.

con·fes·sion (kən·fesh′ən) *n.* **1.** The act of confessing; acknowledgment; admission, esp. of guilt. **2.** That which is confessed. **3.** A statement, esp. a formal document, in which something is confessed. **4.** *Eccl.* The contrite acknowledgment of one's sins to a priest in order to obtain absolution. **5.** A body of doctrine put forth as the belief of a church: also **confession of faith. 6.** A church holding a particular confession of faith.

con·fes·sion·al (kən·fesh′ən·əl) *adj.* Of, pertaining to, or like confession. — *n.* A small enclosure or stall where a priest hears confessions. Also *Rare* **con·fes′sion·ar′y** (-er′ē).

con·fes·sor (kən·fes′ər) *n.* **1.** A priest who hears confessions. **2.** One who confesses. Also **con·fess′er.** Abbr. *conf.*

con·fet·ti (kən·fet′ē) *n.pl.* **1.** (*construed as sing.*) Small pieces of colored paper thrown at carnivals, weddings, etc. **2.** Bonbons. [< Ital., pl. of *confetto* confection]

con·fi·dant (kon′fə·dant′, -dänt′, kon′fə·dant, -dänt) *n.* A person to whom secrets are confided. — **con′fi·dante′** *n.fem.*

con·fide (kən·fīd′) *v.* **·fid·ed, ·fid·ing** *v.t.* **1.** To reveal in trust or confidence. **2.** To put into another's trust or keeping. — *v.i.* **3.** To have trust; impart secrets trustingly: with *in.* [< L < *com-* thoroughly + *fidere* to trust] — **con·fid′er** *n.*

con·fi·dence (kon′fə·dəns) *n.* **1.** A feeling of trust in a person or thing; reliance; faith. **2.** A relationship of trustful intimacy. **3.** Self-assurance; also, fearlessness. **4.** Excessive self-assurance. **5.** A feeling of certainty. **6.** A secret. — **to take into one's confidence** To trust with one's secrets.

confidence game A swindle in which the victim is defrauded after his confidence has been won: also, *U.S. Slang,* **con game.** Also **confidence trick.**

confidence man A swindler in a confidence game.

con·fi·dent (kon′fə·dənt) *adj.* **1.** Having confidence; assured: *confident* of success. **2.** Self-assured; also, bold; presumptuous. — *n.* A confidant. — **con′fi·dent·ly** *adv.*

con·fi·den·tial (kon′fə·den′shəl) *adj.* **1.** Secret: *confidential* information. **2.** Enjoying another's confidence; trusted. **3.** Denoting the confiding of secrets: a *confidential* manner. — **con·fi·den·ti·al·i·ty** (kon′fə·den′shē·al′ə·tē), **con′fi·den′tial·ness** *n.* — **con′fi·den′tial·ly** *adv.*

con·fid·ing (kən·fī′ding) *adj.* That trusts or confides; unsuspicious. — **con·fid′ing·ly** *adv.* — **con·fid′ing·ness** *n.*

con·fig·u·ra·tion (kən·fig′yə·rā′shən) *n.* **1.** The arrangement of the parts of a thing, or the form resulting therefrom; conformation; contour. **2.** *Psychol.* A gestalt. [< LL < L *com-* together + *figurare* to shape, fashion] — **con·fig′u·ra′tion·al, con·fig′u·ra·tive** (kən·fig′yər·ə·tiv, -yə·rā′tiv) *adj.*

con·fine (*v.* kən·fīn′; *n.* kon′fīn) *v.* **·fined, ·fin·ing** *v.t.* **1.** To shut within an enclosure; imprison. **2.** To restrain or oblige to stay within doors. **3.** To hold within limits; restrict: to *confine* remarks. — *n.* Usu. pl. A boundary or border. [< MF < Ital. < L *com-* together + *finis* border] — **con·fin′a·ble** or **con·fine′a·ble** *adj.* — **con·fin′er** *n.*

con·fine·ment (kən·fīn′mənt) *n.* **1.** The act of confining, or the state of being confined. **2.** Childbirth.

con·firm (kən·fûrm′) *v.t.* **1.** To assure the validity of; verify. **2.** To add firmness to; strengthen. **3.** To render valid and binding by formal approval. **4.** To receive into the church by confirmation. [< OF < L < *com-* thoroughly + *firmus* strong] — **con·firm′a·ble** *adj.* — **con·firm′er, Law** **con·firm·or** (kən·fər·môr′, kən·fûr′mər) *n.*

con·fir·ma·tion (kon′fər·mā′shən) *n.* **1.** The act of confirming. **2.** That which confirms; proof. **3.** A religious rite in which a person is admitted to all the privileges of a church.

con·firm·a·to·ry (kən·fûr′mə·tôr′ē, -tō′rē) *adj.* Confirming.

con·firmed (kən·fûrmd′) *adj.* **1.** Firmly established; ratified. **2.** Inveterate; chronic; habitual: a *confirmed* skeptic. **3.** Having received the rites of religious confirmation.

con·fis·cate (kon′fis·kāt′) *v.t.* **·cat·ed, ·cat·ing 1.** To seize or appropriate for the public use or treasury, usu. as a penalty. **2.** To appropriate by or as by authority. — *adj.* **1.** Appropriated or forfeited. **2.** Deprived of property through confiscation. [< L < *com-* together + *fiscus* chest, treasury] — **con·fis·ca·tion** *n.* — **con·fis·ca·tor** *n.* — **con·fis·ca·to·ry** (kən·fis′kə·tôr′ē, -tō′rē) *adj.*

con·fla·gra·tion (kon′flə·grā′shən) *n.* A great or extensive fire. [< L < *com-* thoroughly + *flagare* to burn]

con·flict (*n.* kon′flikt; *v.* kən·flikt′) *n.* **1.** A struggle; battle. **2.** Mutual antagonism, as of ideas, interests, etc. **3.** A clash between contradictory impulses within an individual. — *v.i.* **1.** To come into collision; be in mutual opposition; clash. **2.** To engage in battle; struggle. [< L < *com-* together + *fligere* to strike] — **con·flic′tive** *adj.*

con·flu·ence (kon′floo·əns) *n.* **1.** A flowing together of streams; also, the place where they meet. **2.** The body or stream of water so formed. **3.** A flocking together; crowd. Also **con·flux** (kon′fluks). [< L < *com-* together + *fluere* to flow] — **con′flu·ent** *adj.* — **con′flu·ent·ly** *adv.*

con·form (kən·fôrm′) *v.i.* **1.** To show identity or resemblance; correspond: with *to*: to *conform* to specification. **2.** To adhere to conventional behavior. — *v.t.* **3.** To make the same or similar: with *to.* **4.** To bring (oneself) into harmony or agreement: with *to.* [< F < L < *com-* together + *formare* to shape] — **con·form′er** *n.*

con·form·a·ble (kən·fôr′mə·bəl) *adj.* **1.** In agreement; harmonious. **2.** Corresponding in form, character, or use; similar. **3.** Compliant or obedient; submissive. — **con·form′a·bil′i·ty, con·form′a·ble·ness** *n.* — **con·form′a·bly** *adv.*

con·form·ance (kən·fôr′məns) *n.* Conformity.

con·for·ma·tion (kon′fôr·mā′shən) *n.* **1.** The manner in which a thing is formed; structure or outline. **2.** The symmetrical arrangement and shaping of parts. **3.** The act of conforming, or the state of being conformed.

con·form·ist (kən·fôr′mist) *n.* One who conforms.

con·form·i·ty (kən·fôr′mə·tē) *n.* *pl.* **·ties 1.** Correspondence in form, manner, or use; agreement; harmony; congruity. **2.** The act or habit of conforming; acquiescence.

con·found (kon·found′, kən-; *for def. 4* kon′found′) *v.t.* **1.** To confuse, amaze, or bewilder. **2.** To confuse with something else; fail to distinguish. **3.** To confuse or mingle indistinguishably. **4.** To damn: used as an oath. [< AF, OF < L < *com-* together + *fundere* to pour] — **con·found′er** *n.*

— **Syn. 1.** puzzle, perplex, dumfound, mystify.

con·found·ed (kon·foun′did, kən-) *adj.* **1.** Confused or abashed. **2.** *Informal* Damned; detestable: a *confounded* cheat. — **con·found′ed·ly** *adv.*

con·frere (kon′frâr) *n.* A fellow member; a colleague. [< MF < L *com-* with + *frater* brother]

con·front (kən·frunt′) *v.t.* **1.** To stand face to face with; face defiantly. **2.** To put face to face: to *confront* a liar with the truth. [< F < L *com-* together + *frons, frontis* face, forehead] — **con·front′ment** *n.* — **con·front′er** *n.*

con·fron·ta·tion (kon′frən·tā′shən) *n.* **1.** The act of confronting, or the state of being confronted. **2.** The provocation of conflict as a means of effecting political change; also, a crisis or conflict so caused.

Con·fu·cian·ism (kən·fyoo′shən·iz′əm) *n.* The ethical system taught by Confucius, emphasizing ancestor worship, devotion to family and friends, and the maintenance of justice and peace. — **Con·fu′cian·ist** *n.* — **Con·fu′cian** *n. & adj.*

con·fuse (kən·fyooz′) *v.t.* **·fused, ·fus·ing 1.** To perplex or perturb; confound; bewilder. **2.** To mix indiscriminately; jumble. **3.** To mistake one for the other. [< L < *com-* together + *fundere* to pour] — **con·fus·ed·ly** (kən·fyoo′zid·lē) *adv.* — **con·fus′ed·ness** *n.* — **con·fus′ing·ly** *adv.*

con·fu·sion (kən·fyoo′zhən) *n.* **1.** The act of confusing, or the state of being confused. **2.** Disarray; disorder. **3.** Perplexity of mind. **4.** Embarrassment. — **con·fu′sion·al** *adj.*

con·fute (kən·fyoot′) *v.t.* **·fut·ed, ·fut·ing 1.** To prove to be wrong, false, or invalid; refute successfully. **2.** To overwhelm with proofs or disproofs; prove (a person) to be in the wrong. **3.** To bring to naught; confound. — **Syn.** See REFUTE. [< L *confutare* to check, restrain] — **con·fu·ta·tion** (kon/fyŏŏ·tā/shən) *n.* — **con·fut/er** *n.*

con·ga (kong/gə) *n.* **1.** A dance of Latin American origin in which the dancers form a winding line. **2.** The music for this dance, in fast 4/4 time. [< Am. Sp.]

con game *U.S. Slang* A confidence game.

con·gé (kon/zhā, *Fr.* kôn·zhā/) *n.* **1.** A formal leave-taking. **2.** Dismissal. [< F < L < *com-* thoroughly + *ire* to go]

con·geal (kən·jēl/) *v.t. & v.i.* **1.** To change from a fluid to a solid condition, as by freezing or curdling. **2.** To clot or coagulate, as blood. [< MF < L < *com-* together + *gelare* to freeze] — **con·geal/a·ble** *adj.* — **con·geal/er** *n.* — **con·geal/ment** *n.*

con·gen·ial (kən·jēn/yəl) *adj.* **1.** Having similar character or tastes; sympathetic. **2.** Suited to one's disposition; agreeable: a *congenial* job. — **con·ge·ni·al·i·ty** (kən·jē/nē·al/ə·tē) *n.* — **con·gen/ial·ly** *adv.*

con·gen·i·tal (kən·jen/ə·təl) *adj.* **1.** Existing prior to or at birth: a *congenital* defect. **2.** Loosely, disposed as if by birth: a *congenital* liar. [< L < *com-* together + *genitus,* pp. of *gignere* to bear] — **con·gen/i·tal·ly** *adv.*

con·ger (kong/gər) *n.* A marine eel, used as a food fish. Also **conger eel.** [< OF < L < Gk. *gongros*]

con·ge·ries (kon/jə·rēz, kon·jir/ēz) *n.pl.* (*usu. construed as sing.*) A collection of things; a mass; heap. [< L < *con·gerere* to bring together]

con·gest (kən·jest/) *v.t.* **1.** To collect or crowd together; overcrowd. **2.** *Pathol.* To surcharge (an organ or part) with an excess of blood. — *v.i.* **3.** To become congested. [< L < *com-* together + *gerere* to bear, carry] — **con·ges/tion** *n.* — **con·ges/tive** *adj.*

con·glom·er·ate (*adj., n.* kən·glom/ər·it; *v.* kən·glom/ə·rāt) *adj.* **1.** Massed or clustered. **2.** *Geol.* Consisting of loosely cemented heterogeneous material: *conglomerate* clay. — *n.* **1.** A heterogeneous collection; cluster. **2.** A large corporation formed by merging a number of separate companies, often in unrelated fields. **3.** *Geol.* A rock composed of pebbles, etc., loosely cemented together. — *v.t. & v.i.* **·at·ed, ·at·ing** To gather into a cohering mass. [< L < *com-* together + *glomus, glomeris* ball] — **con·glom/er·a/tion** *n.*

con·glu·ti·nate (kən·glōō/tə·nāt) *v.t. & v.i.* **·nat·ed, ·nat·ing** To glue or stick together; adhere. — *adj.* Glued together; united by adhesion. [< L < *com-* together + *glutinare* to stick] — **con·glu/ti·na/tion** *n.* — **con·glu/ti·na/tive** *adj.*

congo snake A tailed aquatic salamander of the SE U.S. Also **congo eel.**

con·grat·u·late (kən·grach/ŏŏ·lāt) *v.t.* **·lat·ed, ·lat·ing** To express pleasure in or otherwise acknowledge the achievement or good fortune of (another); felicitate. [< L < *com-* together + *gratulari* to rejoice] — **con·grat/u·lant** *adj. & n.* — **con·grat/u·la/tor** *n.* — **con·grat/u·la·to/ry** *adj.*

con·grat·u·la·tion (kən·grach/ŏŏ·lā/shən) *n.* **1.** The act of congratulating. **2.** *pl.* Expressions of pleasure and good wishes on another's fortune or success.

con·gre·gate (*v.* kong/grə·gāt; *adj.* kong/grə·git) *v.t. & v.i.* **·gat·ed, ·gat·ing** To bring or come together into a crowd; assemble. — *adj.* **1.** Relating to a congregation. **2.** Gathered together; collected. [< L < *com-* together + *gregare* to collect] — **con/gre·ga/tive** *adj.* — **con/gre·ga/tor** *n.*

con·gre·ga·tion (kong/grə·gā/shən) *n.* **1.** The act of congregating; a collecting into one mass, body, or assembly. **2.** An assemblage of people or things. **3.** A group of people met together for worship; also, the body of persons who worship in a local church; a parish. — **con/gre·ga/tion·al** *adj.*

con·gre·ga·tion·al·ism (kong/grə·gā/shən·əl·iz/əm) *n.* A form of church government in which each local congregation is autonomous in all church matters.

Con·gre·ga·tion·al·ism (kong/grə·gā/shən·əl·iz/əm) *n.* The type of organization and system of beliefs of an evangelical Protestant denomination (**Congregational Christian Churches**) practicing congregationalism. — **Con/gre·ga/tion·al** *adj.* — **Con/gre·ga/tion·al·ist** *n.*

con·gress (kong/gris) *n.* **1.** An assembly or conference. **2.** A coming together; meeting. **3.** The legislature of various nations, esp. of a republic. — *v.i.* To meet at a congress. [< L < *com-* together + *gradi* to walk]

Con·gress (kong/gris) *n.* The legislative body of the U.S., consisting of the Senate and the House of Representatives; also, this body during one of the two-year periods between elections to the House of Representatives.

con·gres·sion·al (kən·gresh/ən·əl) *adj.* Often *cap. U.S.* Pertaining to a congress, esp. to the U.S. Congress.

Congressional district *U.S.* A division of a State, entitled to one representative in Congress.

Congressional Medal of Honor See MEDAL OF HONOR.

Congressional Record *U.S.* An official publication containing the debates and proceedings of Congress.

con·gress·man (kong/gris·mən) *n.* *pl.* **·men** (-mən) Often *cap.* A member of the U.S. Congress, esp. of the House of Representatives. — **con/gress·wom/an** *n.fem.*

con·gru·ence (kong/grŏŏ·əns) *n.* Conformity; agreement.

con·gru·ent (kong/grŏŏ·ənt) *adj.* **1.** Agreeing or conforming; congruous. **2.** *Geom.* Exactly coinciding when superimposed. [< L *congruere* to agree] — **con/gru·en·cy** *n.* — **con/gru·ent·ly** *adv.*

con·gru·i·ty (kən·grŏŏ/ə·tē) *n.* *pl.* **·ties** **1.** The state or quality of being congruous; agreement or fitness. **2.** An example of agreement. **3.** *Geom.* Exact correspondence when superimposed. — **Syn.** See HARMONY.

con·gru·ous (kong/grŏŏ·əs) *adj.* **1.** Agreeing in nature or qualities; harmonious. **2.** Appropriate; fit. **3.** *Geom.* Congruent. — **con/gru·ous·ly** *adv.* — **con/gru·ous·ness** *n.*

con·ic (kon/ik) *adj.* **1.** Cone-shaped. **2.** Of or formed by or upon a cone. Also **con/i·cal.** — *n. Math.* A conic section. [< Gk. *kōnos* cone] — **con/i·cal·ly** *adv.*

conic section *Math.* A curve formed by the intersection of a plane with a cone having a circular base, being an ellipse, parabola, or hyperbola, according to the inclination of the cutting plane to the axis.

CONIC SECTIONS
a Circle. *b* Parabola. *c* Hyperbola. *d* Ellipse. *e* Right-line.

co·nid·i·um (kō·nid/ē·əm) *n.* *pl.* **·nid·i·a** (-nid/ē·ə) *Bot.* An asexual propagative spore of many species of fungi. Also **co·nid·i·o·spore** (kō·nid/ē·ə·spôr/, -spōr/). [< NL < Gk. *konis* dust] — **co·nid/i·al** *adj.*

con·i·fer (kon/ə·fər, kō/nə-) *n.* Any of a large and widely distributed family of evergreen shrubs and trees, as the pines, spruces, firs, and junipers. [< L < *conus* cone + *ferre* to bear] — **co·nif·er·ous** (kō·nif/ər·əs) *adj.*

con·jec·tur·al (kən·jek/chər·əl) *adj.* **1.** Involving or dependent upon conjecture. **2.** Given to conjecture. — **con·jec/tur·al·ly** *adv.*

con·jec·ture (kən·jek/chər) *v.* **·tured, ·tur·ing** *v.t.* **1.** To conclude from incomplete evidence; guess; infer. — *v.i.* **2.** To make a conjecture. — **Syn.** See SUPPOSE. — *n.* **1.** Inference from incomplete evidence. **2.** A conclusion based on this; a guess; surmise. — **Syn.** See HYPOTHESIS. [< L < *com-* together + *jacere* to throw] — **con·jec/tur·a·ble** *adj.* — **con·jec/tur·a·bly** *adv.* — **con·jec/tur·er** *n.*

con·join (kən·join/) *v.t. & v.i.* To join together; associate; connect; unite. [< MF < L < *com-* together + *jungere* to join] — **con·join/er** *n.*

con·joint (kən·joint/) *adj.* **1.** Associated; conjoined. **2.** Joint. — **con·joint/ly** *adv.*

con·ju·gal (kon/jŏŏ·gəl, -jə-) *adj.* Pertaining to marriage or to the relation of husband and wife; connubial. [< F < L *conjungere* to join in marriage] — **con·ju·gal·i·ty** (kon/jŏŏ·gal/ə·tē) *n.* — **con/ju·gal·ly** *adv.*

con·ju·gate (kon/jŏŏ·gāt, -jə-; *for adj., n., also* kon/jŏŏ·git, -jə-) *v.* **·gat·ed, ·gat·ing** *v.t.* **1.** *Gram.* To give the inflections of (a verb) for person, number, tense, mood, and voice. — *v.i.* **2.** *Biol.* To unite in conjugation. — *adj.* **1.** Joined in pairs; coupled. **2.** Kindred in origin and, usually, meaning: said of words. — *n.* **1.** A conjugate word. **2.** A member of any conjugate pair. [< L < *com-* together + *jugare* to join] — **con/ju·ga/tive** *adj.* — **con/ju·ga/tor** *n.*

con·ju·ga·tion (kon/jŏŏ·gā/shən, -jə-) *n.* **1.** A joining or being joined together. **2.** *Gram.* **a** The inflection of verbs. **b** A schematic presentation of the entire inflection of a verb. **c** A class of verbs that are inflected in the same manner. — **con/ju·ga/tion·al** *adj.* — **con/ju·ga/tion·al·ly** *adv.*

con·junct (kən·jungkt/, kon/jungkt) *adj.* Joined together; conjoined. [See CONJOIN.] — **con·junct/ly** *adv.*

con·junc·tion (kən·jungk/shən) *n.* **1.** The act of joining together, or the state of being so joined. **2.** A coincidence. **3.** *Astron.* **a** The position of two celestial bodies when they are in the same celestial longitude. **b** The position of a planet when it is on a direct line with the earth and the sun. **4.** *Gram.* A word used to connect words, phrases, clauses, or sentences; one of the eight traditional parts of speech. — **coordinate conjunction** A conjunction, as *and, but,* or, that joins words or groups of words of equal rank. — **subordinate conjunction** A conjunction, as *as, because, if, that, though,* that joins clauses of minor rank to principal clauses. — **con·junc/tion·al** *adj.* — **con·junc/tion·al·ly** *adv.*

con·junc·ti·va (kon/jungk/tī·və, kən·jungk/ti·və) *n.* *pl.* **·vas** or **·vae** (-vē) *Anat.* The mucous membrane lining the eyelids and covering the front part of the eyeball. For illus. see EYE. [< NL (*membrana*) *conjunctiva* connective (membrane)] — **con/junc·ti/val** *adj.*

con·junc·tive (kən·jungk/tiv) *adj.* **1.** Joining; connective. **2.** Joined together. **3.** *Gram.* **a** Serving as a conjunction. **b** Of an adverb, serving to unite sentences in larger units, as *furthermore, nevertheless,* etc. — *n. Gram.* A conjunctive word. [See CONJOIN.] — **con·junc/tive·ly** *adv.*

con·junc·ti·vi·tis (kən·jungk/tə·vī/tis) *n. Pathol.* Inflammation of the conjunctiva.

con·junc·ture (kən·jungk/chər) *n.* **1.** A combination of circumstances or events; juncture. **2.** A critical situation; crisis. **3.** Conjunction; union.

con·ju·ra·tion (kon′jōō·rā′shən) *n.* 1. The doing of something by magic. 2. A magic spell or expression.

con·jure (*v. def. 1* kən·jōōr′; *v. defs. 2–5, adj.* kon′jər, kun′-) *v.* **·jured, ·jur·ing** *v.t.* 1. To call on or appeal to solemnly; adjure. 2. To summon by incantation or spell, as a devil. 3. To accomplish by or as by magic. — *v.i.* 4. To practice magic, especially legerdemain. 5. To summon a devil or spirit by incantation. — *adj. U.S. Dial.* Practicing magic. [< OF < L *com-* together + *jurare* to swear]

con·jur·er (kon′jər·ər, kun′- *for def. 1*; kən·jōōr′ər *for def. 2*) *n.* 1. One who practices magic; a sorcerer or magician. 2. One who appeals solemnly. Also **con′jur·or.**

conk (kongk) *n. Slang* 1. *U.S.* The head. 2. The nose. — *v.t. U.S. Slang* To hit on the head. — **to conk out** 1. *Informal* To stall or fail: said of engines. 2. *U.S. Slang* To become suddenly weak and tired. [? < CONCH]

con man (kon) *U.S. Slang* A confidence man.

conn (kon) See CON².

con·nect (kə·nekt′) *v.t.* 1. To join or fasten together; link. 2. To associate by some relation, as in thought or action. — *v.i.* 3. To join or fit. 4. To meet so that passengers can transfer from one route to another: said of trains, buses, etc. [< L < *com-* together + *nectere* to bind] — **con·nec′tor** or **con·nect′er** *n.*

connecting rod *Mech.* A rod joining a piston with the crankshaft in an engine, pump, etc.: also called *piston rod.*

con·nec·tion (kə·nek′shən) *n.* 1. The act of connecting, or the state of being connected. 2. That which joins or relates; a bond; link. 3. Logical sequence of words or ideas; coherence. 4. Context. 5. Family relationship. 6. A religious sect. 7. *Usually pl.* A group of friends or associates, often considered as influential in some way. 8. *Often pl.* A transfer or continuation from one route or vehicle to another. Also *Brit.* **con·nex′ion.** — **con·nec′tion·al** *adj.*

con·nec·tive (kə·nek′tiv) *adj.* Capable of connecting, or serving to connect. — *n.* 1. That which connects. *Gram.* A connecting word or particle, as a conjunction. — **con·nec′tive·ly** *adv.* — **con·nec·tiv′i·ty** (kon′ek·tiv′ə·tē) *n.*

connective tissue *Anat.* The fibrous tissue that serves to unite and support the various organs and tissues of the body.

conning tower 1. The armored pilothouse of a warship. 2. In submarines, an observation tower.

con·nip·tion (kə·nip′shən) *n. U.S. Informal* A fit of hysteria, rage, etc. [Cf. dial. E *canapshus* ill-tempered]

con·niv·ance (kə·nī′vəns) *n.* The act or fact of conniving; silent assent, esp. to wrongdoing. Also **con·niv′ence.**

con·nive (kə·nīv′) *v.i.* **·nived, ·niv·ing** 1. To encourage or assent to a wrong by silence or feigned ignorance: with *at.* 2. To be in collusion: with *with.* [< L *conivere* to wink, shut the eyes] — **con·niv′er** *n.*

con·nois·seur (kon′ə·sûr′) *n.* One competent to judge critically because of thorough knowledge, esp. in matters of art and taste. — **Syn.** See AMATEUR. [< F, ult. < L *cognoscere* to know, understand] — **con′nois·seur′ship** *n.*

con·no·ta·tion (kon′ə·tā′shən) *n.* 1. The suggestive or associative significance of an expression, additional to the literal meaning. Compare DENOTATION. 2. The act of connoting. — **con′no·ta′tive·ly** *adv.*

con·no·ta·tive (kon′ə·tā′tiv, kə·nō′tə·tiv) *adj.* Having or of the nature of connotation. — **con′no·ta′tive·ly** *adv.*

con·note (kə·nōt′) *v.t.* **·not·ed, ·not·ing** To suggest or imply along with the literal meaning. [< Med.L < L *com-* together + *notare* to mark]

con·nu·bi·al (kə·nōō′bē·əl, -nyōō′-) *adj.* Pertaining to marriage or to the married state. [< L < *com-* together + *nubere* to marry] — **con·nu′bi·al′i·ty** *n.* — **con·nu′bi·al·ly** *adv.*

co·noid (kō′noid) *adj.* Cone-shaped. Also **co·noi′dal.** — *n.* Something cone-shaped. [< Gk. *kōnoeidēs* conical]

con·quer (kong′kər) *v.t.* 1. To overcome or subdue by force, as in war; vanquish. 2. To overcome by mental or moral force; surmount. — *v.i.* 3. To be victorious. [< OF < *com-* thoroughly + *quaerere* to search for, procure] — **con′quer·or** *n.* — **con′quer·a·ble** *adj.*

con·quest (kon′kwest, kong′-) *n.* 1. The act of conquering. 2. The thing conquered. 3. A winning of another's favor or love. 4. One whose favor or love has been won.

con·quis·ta·dor (kon·kwis′tə·dôr, -kis′-; *Sp.* kōng·kēs′tä·thōr′) *n. pl.* **·dors,** *Sp.* **·do·res** (-thō′rās) A conqueror; esp., any of the Spanish conquerors of Mexico and Peru in the 16th century. [< Sp. < *conquistar* to conquer]

con·san·guin·e·ous (kon′sang·gwin′ē·əs) *adj.* Of the same blood or ancestry; akin. Also **con·san·guine** (kon·sang′gwin). [< L < *com-* together + *sanguis* blood] — **con·san·guin′e·ous·ly** *adv.*

con·san·guin·i·ty (kon′sang·gwin′ə·tē) *n.* 1. Relationship resulting from common ancestry; blood relationship. 2. Any close affinity or connection. — **Syn.** See RELATIONSHIP.

con·science (kon′shəns) *n.* 1. The faculty by which distinctions are made between moral right and wrong. 2. Con-

formity in conduct to the prescribed moral standard. — **in (all) conscience** 1. In truth; in reason and honesty. 2. Certainly; assuredly. [< OF < L *conscire* to know inwardly] — **con′science·less** *adj.*

con·sci·en·tious (kon′shē·en′shəs, kon′sē-) *adj.* 1. Governed by or done in accordance with conscience; scrupulous. 2. Careful and thorough; painstaking. — **con′sci·en′tious·ly** *adv.* — **con′sci·en′tious·ness** *n.*

conscientious objector One who, on grounds of religious or moral convictions, refuses to perform military service.

con·scion·a·ble (kon′shən·ə·bəl) *adj. Rare* Conformable to conscience or right; just. — **con′scion·a·bly** *adv.*

con·scious (kon′shəs) *adj.* 1. Aware of one's own existence or of external objects and conditions. 2. Aware of some object or fact; *conscious* of one's shortcomings. 3. Felt by oneself; internally known: *conscious* superiority. 4. Overly aware of oneself; self-conscious. 5. Deliberate; intentional. — *n.* That part of mental life of which an individual is aware. [< L *conscius* knowing inwardly < *com-* together + *scire* to know] — **con′scious·ly** *adv.*

con·scious·ness (kon′shəs·nis) *n.* 1. The state of being conscious; awareness of oneself and one's surroundings. 2. Awareness of some object, influence, etc. 3. The mental and emotional awareness of an individual, or of a group.

con·script (*n., adj.* kon′skript; *v.* kən·skript′) *n.* One who is compulsorily enrolled for some service or job. — *adj.* Enlisted by compulsion; conscripted. — *v.t.* To force into military, naval, or other service. [< L < *com-* together + *scribere* to write] — **con·scrip′tion** *n.*

conscript fathers (kon′skript) 1. The senators of ancient Rome. 2. The members of any legislative body.

con·se·crate (kon′sə·krāt) *v.t.* **·crat·ed, ·crat·ing** 1. To set apart as sacred; dedicate to sacred uses. 2. To dedicate; devote: He *consecrated* his life to the cause. 3. To make revered; hallow: *consecrated* by time. [< L < *com-* thoroughly + *sacer* holy] — **con′se·cra′tion** *n.* — **con′se·cra′tor** *n.* — **con·se·cra·to·ry** (kon′sə·krə·tôr′ē, -tō′rē) *adj.*

con·sec·u·tive (kən·sek′yə·tiv) *adj.* 1. Following in uninterrupted succession; successive. 2. Characterized by logical sequence. — **con·sec′u·tive·ly** *adv.* — **con·sec′u·tive·ness** *n.*

con·sen·sus (kən·sen′səs) *n.* A collective opinion; general agreement. ◆ The phrase **consensus of opinion,** although redundant, is now widely used. [< L < *com-* together + *sentire* to feel, think]

con·sent (kən·sent′) *v.i.* To give assent; agree or acquiesce. — *n.* 1. A voluntary yielding; compliance. 2. Agreement; harmony; concord. [See CONSENSUS.] — **con·sent′er** *n.*

con·se·quence (kon′sə·kwens, -kwəns) *n.* 1. That which naturally follows from a preceding action or condition; result. 2. A logical conclusion. 3. Distinction: a man of *consequence.* 4. Importance: an event of no *consequence.*

con·se·quent (kon′sə·kwent, -kwənt) *adj.* 1. Following as a natural result, or as a logical conclusion. 2. Characterized by correctness of reasoning; logical. — *n.* 1. That which follows something else, as in time. 2. An outcome; result. [< L < *com-* together + *sequi* to follow]

con·se·quen·tial (kon′sə·kwen′shəl) *adj.* 1. Following as an effect or conclusion. 2. Of consequence; important. 3. Having or showing self-importance. — **con′se·quen′ti·al′i·ty** **con′se·quen′tial·ness** *n.* — **con′se·quen′tial·ly** *adv.*

con·se·quent·ly (kon′sə·kwent′lē, -kwənt·lē) *adv.* As a result; therefore.

con·ser·va·tion (kon′sər·vā′shən) *n.* 1. The act of keeping or protecting from loss or injury. 2. The preservation of natural resources, as forests, fisheries, etc., for economic or recreational use; also, an area so preserved. [See CONSERVE] — **con′ser·va′tion·al** *adj.* — **con′ser·va′tion·ist** *n.*

conservation of energy *Physics* The principle that in any closed material system the total amount of energy remains constant, though it may assume different forms successively.

con·ser·va·tism (kən·sûr′və·tiz′əm) *n.* 1. Devotion to the existing order of things; opposition to change. 2. The principles of people or groups so devoted.

Con·ser·va·tism (kən·sûr′və·tiz′əm) *n.* The doctrines and policies of the Conservative Party.

con·ser·va·tive (kən·sûr′və·tiv) *adj.* 1. Inclined to preserve the existing order of things; opposed to change. 2. Moderate; cautious: a *conservative* estimate. 3. Conserving; preservative. — *n.* 1. A conservative person. 2. A preservative. — **con·ser′va·tively** *adv.* — **con·ser′va·tive·ness** *n.*

Con·ser·va·tive (kən·sûr′və·tiv) *adj.* Of or pertaining to the Conservative Party. — *n.* 1. A member of this party. 2. A member of the Progressive-Conservative Party in Canada. *Abbr. C.*

Conservative Judaism That branch of Judaism that accepts as binding the Mosaic Laws, but allows some adjustments to the changed conditions of today.

Conservative Party In Great Britain, the principal right-wing party. See TORY.

con·ser·va·to·ry (kən·sûr′və·tôr′ē, -tō′rē) n. pl. ·ries 1. A small greenhouse or glass-enclosed room in which plants are grown and displayed. 2. A school of music. Also **con·ser·va·toire** (kən·sûr′və·twär′). — adj. Adapted to preserve.

con·serve (kən·sûrv′; for n., also kon′sûrv) v.t. ·served, ·serv·ing 1. To keep from loss, decay, or depletion; maintain. 2. To preserve with sugar. — n. Often pl. A kind of jam made of several fruits stewed together in sugar, often with nuts, raisins, etc. [< MF < L < com- thoroughly + servare to keep] — **con·serv′a·ble** adj. — **con·serv′er** n.

con·sid·er (kən·sid′ər) v.t. 1. To think about or deliberate upon; examine mentally; weigh. 2. To look upon or regard (as); think (to be). 3. To hold as an opinion; believe. 4. To take into account; have regard for: to consider the feelings of others. — v.i. 5. To think carefully; deliberate. [< MF < L considerare to observe]

con·sid·er·a·ble (kən·sid′ər·ə·bəl) adj. 1. Somewhat large in amount, extent, etc.; much; considerable trouble. 2. Worthy of consideration. — **con·sid′er·a·bly** adv.

con·sid·er·ate (kən·sid′ər·it) adj. 1. Thoughtful of others; kind. 2. Deliberate; considered. — **con·sid′er·ate·ly** adv. — **con·sid′er·ate·ness** n.

con·sid·er·a·tion (kən·sid′ə·rā′shən) n. 1. The act of considering; deliberation. 2. A circumstance to be taken into account, as in forming an opinion. 3. Thoughtful or kindly feeling or treatment; solicitude. 4. A thought or reflection; opinion. 5. Something given for a service; fee; recompense. 6. Claim to be considered; importance. 7. High regard; esteem. — **in consideration of** In view of, or in return for. — **under consideration** Being thought about or discussed.

con·sid·er·ing (kən·sid′ər·ing) prep. In view of; taking into account. — adv. Informal Taking all the facts into account.

con·sign (kən·sīn′) v.t. 1. To entrust or commit to the care of another. 2. To give up or turn over. 3. To forward or deliver, as merchandise. 4. To set apart or devote, as for a specific use. [< MF < L < com- with + signum a seal] — **con·sign′a·ble** adj. — **con·sig·na·tion** (kon′sig·nā′shən) n.

con·sign·ee (kon′sī·nē′) n. One to whom goods are consigned.

con·sign·ment (kən·sīn′mənt) n. 1. A consigning of something, esp. of goods, for sale or disposal. 2. That which is consigned. — **on consignment** Of goods, paid for by the retailer only after they have been sold.

con·sign·or (kən·sī′nər, kon′sī·nôr′) n. One who consigns, esp. goods for sale. Also **con·sign′er.**

con·sist (kən·sist′) v.i. 1. To be made up or constituted: with of. 2. To have as source or basis; exist; inhere: with in. 3. To be compatible; harmonize: with with. [< L < com- together + sistere to stand]

con·sis·ten·cy (kən·sis′tən·sē) n. pl. ·cies 1. Agreement between things, acts, or statements; logical connection. 2. Agreement with previous acts, statements, or decisions. 3. Firmness, nearness, or density. 4. Degree of firmness, thickness, or density. Also **con·sis′tence.**

con·sis·tent (kən·sis′tənt) adj. 1. Not contradictory or self-contradictory; compatible; harmonious. 2. Conforming to a single set of principles, or to previous action or belief. [See CONSIST.] — **con·sis′tent·ly** adv.

con·sis·to·ry (kən·sis′tər·ē) n. pl. ·ries 1. Eccl. The highest council of the Roman Catholic Church, composed of all the cardinals, and usually presided over by the Pope. 2. The place where any such body meets, or the meeting itself. [< AF < Med.L consistere to stand still, wait] — **con·sis·to·ri·al** (kon′sis·tôr′ē·əl, -tō′rē-), **con′sis·to′ri·an** adj.

con·so·la·tion (kon′sə·lā′shən) n. 1. A consoling or being consoled. 2. One who or that which consoles.

con·sol·a·to·ry (kən·sol′ə·tôr′ē, -tō′rē) adj. Consoling.

con·sole¹ (kən·sōl′) v.t. ·soled, ·sol·ing To comfort (a person) in grief or sorrow; cheer. [< MF < L < com- together + solari to solace] — **con·sol′a·ble** adj.

— **Syn.** We console a person by soothing or sustaining his fallen spirits, or comfort him by any act that brings relief to his mind or body. Solace stresses the feeling of relief that results from our actions. — **Ant.** distress, grieve, sadden.

con·sole² (kon′sōl) n. 1. A bracket, especially one used to support a cornice or ornamental fixture. 2. A console table. 3. The portion of an organ containing the manuals and stops. 4. A cabinet for a radio, phonograph, or television set, designed to rest on the floor. [< MF, a bracket]

console table A table supported by consoles.

con·sol·i·date (kən·sol′ə·dāt) v. ·dat·ed, ·dat·ing v.t. 1. To make solid, firm, or coherent; strengthen. 2. To combine in one; form a union of. — v.i. 3. To become united, solid, or firm. — adj. Consolidated. [< L < com- together + solidus solid] — **con·sol′i·da′tion** n. — **con·sol′i·da′tor** n. — **Syn.** (verb) 1. solidify. 2. merge, unite. 3. unify.

consolidated school U.S. & Canadian A school, usu. rural, for pupils from more than one district.

con·som·mé (kon′sə·mā′, Fr. kôn·sô·mā′) n. A clear soup made of meat and sometimes vegetables boiled in water. [< F, consommer to complete, finish]

con·so·nance (kon′sə·nəns) n. 1. Agreement; accord. 2. Correspondence of sounds; esp. resemblance of consonants but not of vowels. 3. Music A combination of tones regarded as stable and not requiring resolution: also concord. Also **con·so·nan·cy.** — **Syn.** See HARMONY.

con·so·nant (kon′sə·nənt) adj. 1. Being in agreement; consistent. 2. Corresponding in sound; having consonance. 3. Consonantal. — n. 1. Phonet. A sound produced by contact or constriction of the speech organs resulting in complete or partial blockage of the breath stream, as the sounds of b, f, k, s, t, etc. 2. A letter or written symbol representing such a sound. [< MF < L < com- together + sonare to sound] — **con′so·nant·ly** adv.

con·so·nan·tal (kon′sə·nan′təl) adj. 1. Of the nature of a consonant. 2. Having a consonant or consonants.

con·sort (n. kon′sôrt; v. kən·sôrt′) n. 1. A husband or wife; spouse. 2. A companion or partner; mate. 3. Naut. A vessel sailing with another. — v.i. 1. To keep company; associate. 2. To be in agreement; harmonize. — v.t. 3. To join; associate. [< MF < L < com- together + sors share, lot]

con·sor·ti·um (kən·sôr′shē·əm) n. pl. ·ti·a (-shē·ə) A coalition, as of banks or corporations for a venture requiring vast resources. [< L, fellowship]

con·spec·tus (kən·spek′təs) n. pl. ·tus·es 1. A general view of a subject. 2. A summary. [See CONSPICUOUS.]

con·spic·u·ous (kən·spik′yoo·əs) adj. 1. Clearly visible; easy to be seen. 2. Readily attracting attention; striking. [< L < com- together + specere to look at] — **con·spic′u·ous·ly** adv. — **con·spic′u·ous·ness** n.

con·spir·a·cy (kən·spir′ə·sē) n. pl. ·cies 1. The planning of two or more persons to do an evil act; also, the plan so made. 2. An acting together: a conspiracy of the elements.

con·spir·a·tor (kən·spir′ə·tər) n. One who is involved in a conspiracy. [See CONSPIRE.]

con·spir·a·to·ri·al (kən·spir′ə·tôr′ē·əl, -tō′rē-) adj. Of, pertaining to, or like conspiracy or conspirators.

con·spire (kən·spīr′) v. ·spired, ·spir·ing v.i. 1. To combine secretly in an evil or unlawful enterprise. 2. To act together: The winds conspire against us. — v.t. 3. To plan secretly; plot. [< MF < L < com- together + spirare to breathe] — **con·spir′er** n.

con·sta·ble (kon′stə·bəl, kun′-) n. A peace officer who arrests offenders, serves writs, executes warrants, etc. [< OF < LL comes stabuli chief groom] — **con′sta·ble·ship′** n.

con·stab·u·lar·y (kən·stab′yə·ler′ē) n. pl. ·lar·ies 1. The body of constables of a city, etc. 2. The district of a constable. 3. A police force organized in a military fashion. — adj. Pertaining to constables or their functions.

con·stan·cy (kon′stən·sē) n. 1. Steadiness or faithfulness in purpose, action, affections, etc. 2. Unchanging quality.

con·stant (kon′stənt) adj. 1. Long-continuing, or continually recurring; persistent. 2. Unchanging; invariable. 3. Steady in purpose, action, affection, etc.; persevering; faithful. — n. 1. That which is permanent or invariable. 2. Math. A quantity that retains a fixed value throughout a given discussion. 3. In the sciences, any characteristic of a substance, event, etc., numerically determined, that remains the same under specified conditions. [< MF < L < com- thoroughly + stare to stand] — **con′stant·ly** adv.

con·stel·late (kon′stə·lāt) v.t. & v.i. ·lat·ed, ·lat·ing To group in constellations.

con·stel·la·tion (kon′stə·lā′shən) n. 1. Astron. Any of various groups of stars imagined to represent the outline of a being or thing, usu. mythological, and named accordingly. 2. Any brilliant group of persons or things. 3. In astrology, the aspect of the planets at the time of one's birth. 4. Psychol. A group of associated emotions, ideas, etc., centering upon a dominant element. [< LL < L com- together + stella star] — **con·stel·la·to·ry** (kən·stel′ə·tôr′ē·əl, -tō′rē) adj.

con·ster·nate (kon′stər·nāt) v.t. ·nat·ed, ·nat·ing To overwhelm with terror and confusion; dismay. [< L < com- thoroughly + sternere to cast down, prostrate]

con·ster·na·tion (kon′stər·nā′shən) n. Sudden, paralyzing fear or amazement; panic. — **Syn.** See ALARM.

con·sti·pate (kon′stə·pāt) v.t. ·pat·ed, ·pat·ing To cause constipation in. [< L < com- together + stipare to press, crowd] — **con′sti·pat′ed** adj.

con·sti·pa·tion (kon′stə·pā′shən) n. A condition of the bowels characterized by suppressed or difficult evacuation.

con·stit·u·en·cy (kən·stich′oo·ən·sē) n. pl. ·cies 1. A body of voters who elect a representative to a legislative body; also, the district thus represented. 2. Any body of supporters.

con·stit·u·ent (kən·stich′oo·ənt) adj. 1. Serving to form or compose; constituting. 2. Entitled to elect a representative. 3. Having the power to frame or modify a constitution. — n. 1. One represented politically or in business; a voter or client. 2. A necessary part or element.

con·sti·tute (kon′stə·toot, -tyoot) v.t. ·tut·ed, ·tut·ing 1.

To be the substance or elements of; make up; compose. **2.** To enact (a law, etc.). **3.** To found, as a school; establish, as an assembly, in legal form. **4.** To empower; appoint: I *constitute* you my spokesman. **5.** To make by combining elements or parts; frame. [< L < *com-* together + *statuere* to place, station] — **con'sti·tut'er** or **con'sti·tu'tor** *n.*

con·sti·tu·tion (kon'stə·tōō'shən, -tyōō'-) *n.* **1.** The act of constituting; a setting up or appointing. **2.** The composition or make-up of a thing; esp., physical make-up: a weak *constitution.* **3.** The fundamental laws and principles that normally govern the operation of a state or association; also, a document recording such laws and principles. — **the Constitution** The Constitution of the U.S., framed and adopted in 1787 and put into effect March 4, 1789.

con·sti·tu·tion·al (kon'stə·tōō'shən·əl, -tyōō'-) *adj.* **1.** Of or inherent in the constitution of a person or thing; essential: a *constitutional* weakness. **2.** Consistent with or pertaining to the constitution of a state; lawful. **3.** Acting under and controlled by a constitution: a *constitutional* monarchy. **4.** Loyal to the constitution. **5.** Benefiting one's health. — *n.* Exercise taken for one's health. — **con·sti·tu·tion·al·i·ty** (kon'sti·tōō'shən·al'ə·tē) *n.* — **con'sti·tu'tion·al·ly** *adv.*

Constitutional amendment A legal alteration of the U.S. Constitution, ratified by three fourths of the States.

Constitution State Nickname of CONNECTICUT.

con·sti·tu·tive (kon'stə·tōō'tiv, -tyōō'-) *adj.* **1.** Forming an essential element of something; basic. **2.** Having power to enact, institute, or establish. — **con'sti·tu'tive·ly** *adv.*

con·strain (kən·strān') *v.t.* **1.** To compel by physical or moral means; coerce. **2.** To confine, as by bonds. **3.** To restrain; compel to inaction. [< OF < L < *com-* together + *stringere* to bind] — **con·strain'a·ble** *adj.* — **con·strain'er** *n.*

con·strained (kən·strānd') *adj.* Forced; unnatural: a *constrained* smile. — **con·strain·ed·ly** (kən·strā'nid·lē) *adv.*

con·straint (kən·strānt') *n.* **1.** The use of force; coercion. **2.** Confinement; restriction. **3.** Unnaturalness of manner; awkwardness. **4.** A constraining or being constrained.

con·strict (kən·strikt') *v.t.* To draw together by force; cause to shrink or contract; bind; cramp. [< L < *com-* together + *stringere* to bind]

con·stric·tion (kən·strik'shən) *n.* **1.** The act of constricting, or the state of being constricted. **2.** A feeling of tightness. **3.** That which constricts or is constricted. — **con·stric'tive** *adj.*

con·stric·tor (kən·strik'tər) *n.* **1.** That which constricts. **2.** *Anat.* A muscle that contracts an organ of the body. **3.** A serpent that coils about and crushes its prey.

con·struct (*v.* kən·strukt'; *n.* kon'strukt) *v.t.* **1.** To form by combining materials or parts; build; erect. **2.** To form mentally; devise. **3.** To form (anything) systematically. — *n.* Something constructed. [< L < *com-* together + *struere* to build] — **con·struct'er** or **con·struc'tor** *n.*

con·struc·tion (kən·struk'shən) *n.* **1.** The act of constructing; also, the business of building. **2.** Something constructed; a structure or building. **3.** The way in which a thing is put together. **4.** Interpretation given a statement, law, etc.; explanation. **5.** *Gram.* The arrangement of forms syntactically, as in sentences. — **con·struc'tion·al** *adj.*

con·struc·tive (kən·struk'tiv) *adj.* **1.** Tending to build, improve, or advance; resulting in positive conclusions. **2.** Pertaining to construction; structural. **3.** Assumed by interpretation; inferred though not expressly stated. — **con·struc'tive·ly** *adv.* — **con·struc'tive·ness** *n.*

con·strue (*v.* kən·strōō'; *n.* kon'strōō) *v.* **·strued, ·stru·ing** *v.t.* **1.** To analyze the grammatical structure of (a clause or sentence); parse. **2.** To interpret; explain; also, to deduce by inference. **3.** To translate orally. **4.** *Gram.* To use syntactically: The noun "aerodynamics" is *construed* as a singular. — *v.i.* **5.** To determine grammatical structure. **6.** To infer; deduce. **7.** To admit of grammatical analysis. — *n.* An act of construing. [< L < *com-* together + *struere* to build] — **con·stru'a·ble** *adj.* — **con·stru'er** *n.*

con·sul (kon'səl) *n.* **1.** An officer residing in a foreign city to protect his country's commercial interests and the welfare of its citizens. **2.** Either of the two chief magistrates ruling conjointly in the Roman republic. **3.** Any of the three chief magistrates of the French republic, 1799–1804. [< L] — **con'su·lar** (-sə·lər, -syə·lər) *adj.*

con·su·late (kon'sə·lit, -syə-) *n.* **1.** The office or term of office of a consul. Also **con'sul·ship.** **2.** The official place of business of a consul. **3.** Government by consuls. — **the Consulate** The government of France from 1799 to 1804. [< L *consulatus* < *consul* consul]

consul general A consular officer of the highest rank stationed in an important foreign commercial city, who supervises the other consuls in his district.

con·sult (kən·sult') *v.t.* **1.** To ask the advice of; go to for counsel; refer to. **2.** To have regard to in deciding or acting;

consider: to *consult* one's best interests. — *v.i.* **3.** To ask advice. **4.** To compare views; take counsel: with *with.* **5.** To give professional advice. [< L *consultare,* freq. of *consulere* to seek advice] — **con·sult'er** or **con·sul·tor** *n.*

con·sult·ant (kən·sul'tənt) *n.* **1.** A person referred to for expert or professional advice. **2.** One who consults.

con·sul·ta·tion (kon'səl·tā'shən) *n.* **1.** The act or practice of consulting. **2.** A meeting of consultants. — **con·sult·a·tive** (kən·sul'tə·tiv), **con·sult'a·to'ry** (-tôr'ē, -tō'rē) *adj.*

con·sume (kən·sōōm') *v.* **·sumed, ·sum·ing** *v.t.* **1.** To destroy, as by burning. **2.** To eat, drink, or use up. **3.** To squander, as money or time. **4.** To engross or absorb. — *v.i.* **5.** To be wasted or destroyed. [< L < *com-* thoroughly + *sumere* to take up, use] — **con·sum'a·ble** *adj.*

con·sum·ed·ly (kən·sōō'mid·lē) *adv.* Excessively.

con·sum·er (kən·sōō'mər) *n.* **1.** One who or that which consumes. **2.** One who uses an article or service, as distinguished from a producer; one of the buying public.

con·sum·er·ism (kən·sōō'mər·iz'əm) *n.* The policy or program of protecting the interests of the consumer.

con·sum·mate (*v.* kon'sə·māt; *adj.* k n·sum'it) *v.t.* **·mat·ed, ·mat·ing** **1.** To bring to completion or perfection. **2.** To fulfill (a marriage) by sexual intercourse. — *adj.* Of the highest degree; perfect; complete. [< L < *com-* together + *summa* sum, total] — **con·sum'mate·ly** *adv.* — **con'sum·ma'tion** *n.* — **con'sum·ma'tive** *adj.* — **con'sum·ma'tor** *n.*

con·sump·tion (kən·sump'shən) *n.* **1.** The act or process of consuming; destruction, as by burning, use, etc. **2.** The amount consumed. **3.** *Econ.* The using up of goods and services. **4.** *Pathol.* Pulmonary tuberculosis.

con·sump·tive (kən·sump'tiv) *adj. Pathol.* Pertaining to, affected with, or disposed to pulmonary tuberculosis. — *n.* A person affected with pulmonary tuberculosis. — **con·sump'tive·ly** *adv.* — **con·sump'tive·ness** *n.*

con·tact (kon'takt) *n.* **1.** A coming together or touching. **2.** A potentially helpful acquaintance: He has many *contacts.* **3.** *Electr.* The touching or joining of conductors, permitting the flow of a current; also, a conducting part for completing or breaking a circuit. **4.** *Med.* One who has been exposed to a contagious disease. — *v.t.* **1.** To bring or place in contact; touch. **2.** *Informal* To get in touch with (someone). — *v.i.* **3.** To be or come in contact; touch: with *with.* [< L < *com-* together + *tangere* to touch]

contact lens *Optics* A thin lens of glass or plastic ground to optical prescription and worn directly on the eyeball.

con·ta·gion (kən·tā'jən) *n.* **1.** The communication of disease by contact. **2.** A disease that is or may be communicated. **3.** The medium of transmission of disease. **4.** The communication of mental states, of ideas, etc., as by association. [< MF < L < *con-* together + *tangere* to touch]

con·ta·gious (kən·tā'jəs) *adj.* **1.** Transmissible by contact, as a disease. **2.** Spreading contagion. **3.** Exciting or tending to excite similar feelings, etc., in others; spreading; catching. — **con·ta'gious·ly** *adv.* — **con·ta'gious·ness** *n.*

con·tain (kən·tān') *v.t.* **1.** To hold or enclose. **2.** To include or comprise. **3.** To be capable of containing; be able to hold. **4.** To keep within bounds; restrain, as oneself or one's feelings. **5.** *Math.* To be exactly divisible by. [< OF < L < *com-* together + *tenere* to hold] — **con·tain'a·ble** *adj.*

con·tain·er (kən·tā'nər) *n.* Something that contains, as a box, can, etc.

con·tain·ment (kən·tān'mənt) *n.* The prevention of territorial or ideological expansion on the part of another power.

con·tam·i·nate (kən·tam'ə·nāt) *v.t.* **·nat·ed, ·nat·ing** To make impure by contact or admixture; taint; defile; pollute. [< L < *contamen* pollution] — **con·tam'i·na·tion** *n.* — **con·tam'i·na'tive** *adj.* — **con·tam'i·na'tor** *n.*

con·temn (kən·tem') *v.t.* To despise; scorn. [< OF < L < *com-* thoroughly + *temnere* to slight, scorn] — **con·temn·er** (kən·tem'ər, -tem'nər) or **con·tem·nor** (kən·tem'nər) *n.*

con·tem·plate (kon'təm·plāt) *v.* **·plat·ed, ·plat·ing** *v.t.* **1.** To look at attentively; gaze at. **2.** To consider thoughtfully; meditate upon. **3.** To intend or plan: to *contemplate* marriage. — *v.i.* **4.** To meditate; muse. [< L < *com-* together + *templum* temple; with ref. to divination] — **con·tem·pla·tion** (kon'təm·plā'shən) *n.* — **con'tem·pla'tor** *n.*

con·tem·pla·tive (kən·tem'plə·tiv, kon'təm·plā'tiv) *adj.* Of or given to contemplation; meditative. — *n.* A member of a religious order devoted to prayer and penance. — **con·tem'pla·tive·ly** *adv.* — **con·tem'pla·tive·ness** *n.*

con·tem·po·ra·ne·ous (kən·tem'pə·rā'nē·əs) *adj.* Living or occurring at the same time: also *cotemporaneous.* [< L < *com-* together + *tempus, -oris* time] — **con·tem·po·ra·ne·i·ty** (kən·tem'pə·rə·nē'ə·tē), **con·tem'po·ra'ne·ous·ness** *n.* — **con·tem·po·ra'ne·ous·ly** *adv.*

con·tem·po·rar·y (kən·tem'pə·rer'ē) *adj.* **1.** Belonging to the same age; living or occurring at the same time. **2.** Of the same age. **3.** Current; modern. — *n. pl.* **·rar·ies** A contemporary person or thing. Also *cotemporary*. [< L *com-* together + *tempus, -oris* time]

con·tempt (kən·tempt′) *n.* **1.** The feeling of one who views something as mean, vile, and worthless; disdain; scorn. **2.** The state of being despised. **3.** *Law* Willful disregard or disrepect of authority, as of a court. [< L < *com-* thoroughly + *temnere* to scorn]

con·tempt·i·ble (kən·temp′tə·bəl) *adj.* Deserving of contempt; despicable. —**con·tempt′i·bil′i·ty, con·tempt′i·ble·ness** *n.* —**con·tempt′i·bly** *adv.*

con·temp·tu·ous (kən·temp′chōō·əs) *adj.* Showing or feeling contempt; scornful. —**con·temp′tu·ous·ly** *adv.* —**con·temp′tu·ous·ness** *n.*

con·tend (kən·tend′) *v.i.* **1.** To strive in competition or rivalry; vie: to *contend* for a prize. **2.** To argue; dispute. **3.** To struggle; fight. —*v.t.* **4.** To assert; affirm. [< L < *com-* together + *tendere* to strive, strain] —**con·tend′er** *n.*

con·tent¹ (kon′tent) *n.* **1.** *Usu. pl.* That which a thing contains: the *contents* of a box. **2.** Subject matter, as of a document. **3.** Ability to contain; capacity. **4.** Extent or size. **5.** The quantity of a specified part. [See CONTAIN.]

con·tent² (kən·tent′) *adj.* **1.** Satisfied with what one has. **2.** Resigned; accepting. —*n.* Ease of mind; satisfaction. —*v.t.* To satisfy. [See CONTAIN.] —**con·tent′ment** *n.*

con·tent·ed (kən·ten′tid) *adj.* Satisfied with things as they are; content. —**con·tent′ed·ly** *adv.* —**con·tent′ed·ness** *n.*

con·ten·tion (kən·ten′shən) *n.* **1.** Controversy; argument. **2.** Competition; rivalry. **3.** A point asserted in argument. —**in contention** Being contended over. [See CONTEND.]

con·ten·tious (kən·ten′shəs) *adj.* **1.** Given to contention; quarrelsome. **2.** Involving or characterized by contention. —**con·ten′tious·ly** *adv.* —**con·ten′tious·ness** *n.*

con·ter·mi·nous (kən·tûr′mə·nəs) *adj.* **1.** Having a common boundary line. **2.** Contained within the same limits. Also *coterminous*: also **con·ter′mi·nal.** [< L < *com-* together + *terminus* limit] —**con·ter′mi·nous·ly** *adv.*

con·test (*n.* kon′test; *v.* kən·test′) *n.* **1.** A struggling against one another; conflict; strife. **2.** Verbal controversy; dispute. **3.** A competition, game, match, etc. —*v.t.* **1.** To fight for; strive to keep or win. **2.** To call in question; challenge: to *contest* a decision. —*v.i.* **3.** To struggle or dispute; contend: with *with* or *against*. [< F < L < *com-* together + *testari* to bear witness] —**con·test′a·ble** *adj.* —**con·tes·ta·tion** (kon′tes·tā′shən) *n.* —**con·test′er** *n.*

con·test·ant (kən·tes′tənt) *n.* **1.** One who enters a contest; a competitor. **2.** One who contests; a litigant.

con·text (kon′tekst) *n.* **1.** Any phrase, sentence, or passage so closely connected to a word or words as to affect their meaning. **2.** Something that surrounds and influences, as environment or circumstances. [< L < *com-* together + *texere* to weave] —**con·tex·tu·al** (kən·teks′chōō·əl) *adj.* —**con·tex′tu·al·ly** *adv.*

con·ti·gu·i·ty (kon′tə·gyōō′ə·tē) *n.* *pl.* **·ties** The state of being contiguous or in actual contact; nearness.

con·tig·u·ous (kən·tig′yōō·əs) *adj.* **1.** Touching at the edge or boundary. **2.** Close, but not touching; adjacent. [See CONTACT.] —**con·tig′u·ous·ly** *adv.* —**con·tig′u·ous·ness** *n.*

con·ti·nence (kon′tə·nəns) *n.* Self-restraint, esp. abstinence from sexual intercourse. Also **con′ti·nen·cy.**

con·ti·nent (kon′tə·nənt) *n.* One of the large land masses of the earth: Africa, Australia, Europe and Asia (the conventional divisions of the Eurasian land mass), North America, South America, and, usually, Antarctica. —**the Continent** Europe, as distinct from the British Isles. —*adj.* **1.** Self-restrained; moderate. **2.** Abstinent, esp. sexually; chaste. [See CONTAIN.] —**con′ti·nent·ly** *adv.*

con·ti·nen·tal (kon′tə·nen′təl) *adj.* **1.** Of, or of the proportions of, a continent. **2.** *Often cap.* Pertaining to the European continent; European. —*n.* **1.** *Usu. cap.* An inhabitant of the European continent; a European. **2.** A note of the money issued by the Continental Congress.

Con·ti·nen·tal (kon′tə·nen′təl) *adj.* Pertaining to the thirteen American colonies during and just after the Revolution. —*n.* A regular soldier in the Continental army.

Continental Congress The legislative and governing body of the Revolutionary American colonies, that convened in 1774, 1775–76, and 1776–81. It was de facto united 1781 when it became de jure the **Congress of the Confederation.**

con·tin·gen·cy (kən·tin′jən·sē) *n.* *pl.* **·cies** **1.** Uncertainty of occurrence; the condition of being subject to chance or accident. **2.** An unforeseen but possible occurrence. **3.** Something incidental; an adjunct. Also **con·tin′gence.**

con·tin·gent (kən·tin′jənt) *adj.* **1.** Liable, but not certain, to happen; possible. **2.** Occurring by chance; accidental. **3.** Dependent upon an uncertain event or condition: with *on* or *upon*. —*n.* **1.** An accidental or possible occurrence: contingency. **2.** A proportionate share or quota of something to be furnished, as of troops. **3.** A representative group in an assemblage. [< L < *com-* together + *tangere* to touch] —**con·tin′gent·ly** *adv.*

con·tin·u·al (kən·tin′yōō·əl) *adj.* **1.** Renewed frequently;

often repeated. **2.** Continuous (in time). [< OF < L *continuus* hanging together] —**con·tin′u·al·ly** *adv.*

con·tin·u·ance (kən·tin′yōō·əns) *n.* **1.** A continuing of something, as an action or condition, or a remaining in something, as in a place or state. **2.** Continuation, as of a novel. **3.** Duration: a disease of long *continuance*. **4.** *Law* Adjournment to a future time.

con·tin·u·a·tion (kən·tin′yōō·ā′shən) *n.* **1.** The act of continuing or the state of being continued. **2.** The extension or a carrying to a further point: the *continuation* of a history. **3.** Addition; sequel.

con·tin·ue (kən·tin′yōō) *v.* **·tin·ued, ·tin·u·ing** *v.i.* **1.** To go on in some action or condition; persist. **2.** To resume after an interruption. **3.** To remain in the same place, condition, or capacity. **4.** To last; endure. —*v.t.* **5.** To persevere or persist in; carry forward. **6.** To take up again after interruption. **7.** To extend or prolong in space, time, or development. **8.** To cause to last or endure; also, to keep on; retain, as in office. **9.** *Law* To postpone; grant a continuance of. [< OF < L < *com-* together + *tenere* to hold] —**con·tin′u·a·ble** *adj.* —**con·tin′u·er** *n.*

con·ti·nu·i·ty (kon′tə·nōō′ə·tē, -nyōō′-) *n.* *pl.* **·ties 1.** The state or quality of being continuous. **2.** An unbroken series; succession. **3.** In motion pictures, television, etc., a scenario outlining the sequence of scenes; also, the script.

con·tin·u·ous (kən·tin′yōō·əs) *adj.* Extended or prolonged without break; uninterrupted. —**con·tin′u·ous·ly** *adv.* —**con·tin′u·ous·ness** *n.*

con·tin·u·um (kən·tin′yōō·əm) *n.* *pl.* **·tin·u·a** (-tin′yōō·ə) Something that is continuous, of which no separate parts are discernible. [< L, neut. of *continuus* continuous]

con·tort (kən·tôrt′) *v.t.* & *v.i.* To twist violently; wrench out of shape or place. [< L < *com-* together + *torquere* to twist] —**con·tor′tion** *n.* —**con·tor′tive** *adj.*

con·tor·tion·ist (kən·tôr′shən·ist) *n.* A performer trained to twist his limbs and body into unnatural positions.

con·tour (kon′tŏŏr) *n.* **1.** The outline of a figure or body, or a line representing it. —*v.t.* To draw the contour lines of. —*adj.* **1.** *Agric.* Following the contours of land in such a way in plowing as to minimize erosion. **2.** Shaped to fit the outline or contour of something: *contour* sheets. [< F < LL *com-* together + *tornare* to make round]

contour map A map showing topographic configuration by lines (**contour lines**) that connect the points of a surface having similar elevation.

contra- *prefix* Against; opposite. [< L < *contra* against]

con·tra·band (kon′trə·band) *n.* **1.** Goods that, by law or treaty, may not be imported or exported. **2.** Smuggled goods. **3.** Goods that, by international law, a neutral may not furnish to a belligerent, and which are subject to seizure: in full **contraband of war.** —*adj.* Prohibited by law from being imported or exported. [< Sp. < Ital. < *contra* against + *bando* < LL *bannum* law] —**con′tra·ban′dist** *n.*

con·tra·bass (kon′trə·bās) *Music n.* The member of a family of instruments whose range is below the bass; esp., the double bass. Also **con′tra·bas′so** (-bä′sō). —*adj.* Pitched lower than the normal bass: the *contrabass* clarinet. [< Ital. *contrabasso*] —**con′tra·bass·ist** (kon′trə·bā′sist) *n.*

con·tra·bas·soon (kon′trə·bə·sōōn′) *n.* The double bassoon.

con·tra·cep·tion (kon′trə·sep′shən) *n.* The deliberate prevention of fertilization of the human ovum. [< CONTRA- + (CON)CEPTION] —**con′tra·cep′tive** *n.* & *adj.*

con·tra·clock·wise (kon′trə·klok′wīz′) *adj.* & *adv.* Counterclockwise.

con·tract (*v.* kən·trakt′; *for v. def. 2, also* kon′trakt; *n.* kon′trakt) *v.t.* **1.** To cause to draw together; reduce in size. **2.** To enter upon or settle by contract. **3.** To acquire or become affected with, as a disease or habit. **4.** *Gram.* To shorten, as a word, by omitting or combining medial letters or sounds. —*v.i.* **5.** To become smaller, shrink. **6.** To make a contract. —*n.* **1.** A formal agreement between two or more parties, esp. one that is legally binding. **2.** The paper or writing containing such an agreement. **3.** The department of law dealing with contracts. **4.** A betrothal or marriage. **5.** In bridge: **a** The highest and final bid of a hand, stating a denomination and the number of tricks to be made. **b** Contract bridge. *Abbr.* **cont.,** *contr.* [< L < *com-* together + *trahere* to pull, draw] —**con·tract′i·bil′i·ty, con·tract′i·ble·ness** *n.* —**con·tract′i·ble** *adj.*

contract bridge A variety of the game of bridge in which tricks made by the declarer in excess of the contract do not count toward game.

con·trac·tile (kən·trak′təl) *adj.* Able to contract or to induce contraction. —**con·trac·til·i·ty** (kon′trak·til′ə·tē) *n.*

con·trac·tion (kən·trak′shən) *n.* **1.** The act of contracting, or the state of being contracted. **2.** *Gram.* The shortening of a word or phrase by the omission of medial letters or sounds, as in *don't* for *do not*; also, the new word formed. —**Syn.** See ABBREVIATION. —**con·trac′tive** *adj.*

con·trac·tor (kən·trak′tər; *for def. 1, also* kon′trak·tər) *n.* **1.**

One who agrees to supply materals or perform services for a sum, esp. for the construction of buildings. **2.** That which contracts, as a muscle.

con·trac·tu·al (kən·trak'chŏō·əl) *adj.* Connected with or implying a contract.

con·tra·dance (kon'trə·dans', -däns'), **con·tra·danse** See CONTREDANSE.

con·tra·dict (kon'trə·dikt') *v.t.* **1.** To maintain or assert the opposite of (a statement). **2.** To deny a statement of (a person). **3.** To be contrary to or inconsistent with. — *v.i.* **4.** To utter a contradiction. [< L *contra* against + *dicere* to say, speak] — **con'tra·dict'a·ble** *adj.* — **con'tra·dict'er** or **con'tra·dic'tor** *n.*

con·tra·dic·tion (kon'trə·dik'shən) *n.* **1.** Assertion of the opposite of a statement; denial. **2.** A statement that denies the validity of another. **3.** Obvious inconsistency, as between two statements; discrepancy.

con·tra·dic·to·ry (kon'trə·dik'tər·ē) *adj.* **1.** Involving or of the nature of a contradiction; inconsistent; contrary. **2.** Given to contradicting. — *n.* *pl.* **·ries** *Logic* Either of two statements so related that if one is true the other must be false. — **con'tra·dic'to·ri·ly** *adv.* — **con'tra·dic'to·ri·ness** *n.*

con·tra·dis·tinc·tion (kon'trə·dis·tingk'shən) *n.* Distinction by contrast or by contrasting qualities. — **con'tra·dis·tinct', con'tra·dis·tinc'tive** *adj.*

con·trail (kon'trāl) *n.* *Aeron.* A trail of condensed water vapor created by an airplane or rocket flying through super-cooled air. [< (con)densation trail]

con·tra·in·di·cate (kon'trə·in'də·kāt) *v.t.* *Med.* To indicate the danger or undesirability of (a given drug or treatment). — **con'tra·in'di·cant** *n.* — **con'tra·in'di·ca'tion** *n.*

con·tral·to (kən·tral'tō) *n.* *pl.* **·tos** or **·ti** (-tē) **1.** The lowest female voice, intermediate between soprano and tenor. **2.** One having such a voice. — *adj.* Of or pertaining to the contralto or its range. Abbr. *contr.* [< Ital.]

con·trap·tion (kən·trap'shən) *n.* *Informal* A contrivance or gadget. [? < CONTRIVE]

con·tra·pun·tal (kon'trə·pun'təl) *adj.* *Music* **1.** Of or pertaining to counterpoint. **2.** According with the principles of counterpoint. [< Ital. *contrapunto* counterpoint] — **con'·tra·pun'tal·ly** *adv.* — **con'tra·pun'tist, con'tra·pun'tal·ist** *n.*

con·tra·ri·e·ty (kon'trə·rī'ə·tē) *n.* *pl.* **·ties 1.** The quality or state of being contrary. **2.** An inconsistency. [< OF < LL < L *contrarius* opposite]

con·trar·i·wise (kon'trer·ē·wīz'; *for def. 3, also* kən·trâr'ē·wīz') *adv.* **1.** On the contrary; on the other hand. **2.** In the reverse order; conversely. **3.** Contrarily; perversely.

con·trar·y (kon'trer·ē; *for adj. def. 4, also* kən·trâr'ē) *adj.* **1.** Opposed in essence, purpose, aim, etc. **2.** Opposite as to position or direction. **3.** Adverse; unfavorable: *contrary* winds. **4.** Inclined to oppose and contradict; perverse. — *n.* *pl.* **·trar·ies 1.** One of two contrary things. **2.** The opposite: the *contrary* is true. **3.** *Logic* A statement the truth of which is undetermined by the falsity of another, but which cannot be true if the latter is true. — **on the contrary** On the other hand; conversely. — **to the contrary** To the opposite effect. — *adv.* In a contrary manner. [< AF < L *contra* against] — **con'trar·i·ly** *adv.* — **con'trar·i·ness** *n.* — **Syn.** (adj.) **1.** contradictory, opposed, opposite, antithetical.

con·trast (*v.* kən·trast'; *n.* kon'trast) *v.t.* **1.** To place in opposition so as to set off differences or discrepancies. **2.** To set (one another) off by opposition, difference, etc. — *v.i.* **3.** To reveal differences when set in opposition. — *n.* **1.** The act of contrasting, or the state of being contrasted. **2.** A dissimilarity revealed by contrasting. **3.** One who or that which shows unlikeness to another. [< OF to oppose < LL < L *contra-* against + *stare* to stand] — **con·trast'able** *adj.*

con·tra·vene (kon'trə·vēn') *v.t.* **·vened, ·ven·ing 1.** To come into conflict with; run counter to; infringe; transgress: to *contravene* a law. **2.** To oppose or contradict. [< F < L *contra-* against + *venire* to come] — **con'tra·ven'er** *n.* — **con·tra·ven·tion** (kon'trə·ven'shən) *n.*

contre- *prefix* Counter; against; in opposition to. [< F < L *contra*. See CONTRA-.]

con·tre·danse (kôn'trə·däns') *n.* A country-dance: also *contradance, contradanse.* Also **con·tre·dance** (kôn'trə·dans', -däns'). [< F, alter. of COUNTRY-DANCE]

con·tre·temps (kôn'trə·tän') *n.* *pl.* **·temps** (-tänz', *Fr.* -täṅ') An embarrassing or awkward occurrence. [< F]

con·trib·ute (kən·trib'yoot) *v.* **·ut·ed, ·ut·ing 1.** To give with others for a common purpose. **2.** To furnish (an article, story, etc.) to a publication. — *v.i.* **3.** To share in effecting a result: These causes *contributed* to the king's downfall. **4.** To make a contribution. [< L < com- together + *tribuere* to grant, allot] — **con·trib'ut·a·ble** *adj.* — **con·trib'u·tive** *adj.* — **con·trib'u·tive·ly** *adv.* — **con·trib'u·tive·ness** *n.* — **con·trib'u·tor** *n.*

con·tri·bu·tion (kon'trə·byoō'shən) *n.* **1.** The act of con-

tributing. **2.** Something contributed. **3.** An article, story, etc., furnished to a periodical. **4.** A tax or levy.

con·trib·u·to·ry (kən·trib'yə·tôr'ē, -tō'rē) *adj.* **1.** Contributing, as money or aid. **2.** That forms a contribution. — *n.* *pl.* **·ries** One who or that which contributes.

con·trite (kən·trīt', kon'trīt) *adj.* **1.** Deeply and humbly sorry for one's sins; penitent. **2.** Resulting from remorse. [< OF < L < com- together + *terere* to rub] — **con·trite'ly** *adv.* — **con·trite'ness, con·tri'tion** (-trish'ən) *n.*

con·triv·ance (kən·trī'vəns) *n.* **1.** The act or manner of contriving; also, the ability to do this. **2.** A device or mechanical apparatus. **3.** An ingenious plan.

con·trive (kən·trīv') *v.* **·trived, ·triv·ing** *v.t.* **1.** To plan, scheme, or plot. **2.** To improvise; invent. **3.** To manage, as by some scheme. — *v.i.* **4.** To plan, scheme, or plot. [OF < L com- together + *turbare* to stir up, disclose, find] — **con·triv'a·ble** *adj.* — **con·triv'er** *n.*

con·trol (kən·trōl') *v.t.* **·trolled, ·trol·ling 1.** To exercise authority over. **2.** To restrain; curb. **3.** To regulate or verify, as an experiment. **4.** To check, as an account, by means of a duplicate register; verify or rectify. — *n.* **1.** Power to regulate and direct. **2.** A restraining influence; check. **3.** A standard of comparison against which to check the results of a scientific experiment. **4.** *Often pl. Mech.* A device used for operating a machine, airplane, automobile, etc. [< MF < OF < Med.L < L *contra-* against + *rotulus* list] — **con·trol'la·bil'i·ty, con·trol'la·ble·ness** *n.* — **con·trol'la·ble** *adj.*

con·trol·ler (kən·trō'lər) *n.* **1.** One who controls, regulates, or directs. **2.** An officer appointed to examine and verify accounts: also spelled *comptroller.* **3.** A mechanism that regulates the speed of a machine, etc. — **con·trol'ler·ship** *n.*

control tower A specially equipped structure at an airfield, from which aircraft traffic is directed.

con·tro·ver·sial (kon'trə·vûr'shəl) *adj.* **1.** Subject to or characterized by controversy. **2.** Given to controversy; disputatious. — **con'tro·ver'sial·ist** *n.* — **con'tro·ver'sial·ly** *adv.*

con·tro·ver·sy (kon'trə·vûr'sē) *n.* *pl.* **·sies 1.** Dispute regarding a matter on which opinions differ. **2.** A dispute. [< L < *contra-* against + *versus,* pp. of *vertere* to turn]

con·tro·vert (kon'trə·vûrt, kon'trə·vûrt') *v.t.* **1.** To argue against; contradict; dispute. **2.** To argue about. — **con'tro·vert'er** *n.* — **con'tro·vert'i·ble** *adj.* — **con'tro·vert'i·bly** *adv.*

con·tu·ma·cious (kon'too·mā'shəs, -tyoō-) *adj.* Stubbornly disobedient. — **con'tu·ma'cious·ly** *adv.* — **con'tu·ma'cious·ness** *n.*

con·tu·ma·cy (kon'too·mə·sē, -tyoō-) *n.* *pl.* **·cies** Contemptuous disobedience of authority; insolent defiance; insubordination. [< L < *contumax, -acis* stubborn]

con·tu·me·ly (kon'too·mə·lē, -tyoō-, -mē'lē; kən·too'mə·lē, -tyoō'-) *n.* *pl.* **·lies 1.** Insulting rudeness in speech or manner; insolence. **2.** An insult. [< OF < L *contumelia* reproach] — **con'tu·me'li·ous** (kon'too·mē'lē·əs, -tyoō-) *adj.* — **con'tu·me'li·ous·ly** *adv.* — **con'tu·me'li·ous·ness** *n.*

con·tuse (kən·toōz', -tyoōz') *v.t.* **·tused, ·tus·ing** To bruise by a blow. [< L < com- together + *tundere* to beat]

con·tu·sion (kən·too'zhən, -tyoō'-) *n.* A bruise.

co·nun·drum (kə·nun'drəm) *n.* **1.** A riddle of which the answer depends on a pun. **2.** Any problem or puzzle. — **Syn.** See PUZZLE. [Origin unknown]

con·va·lesce (kon'və·les') *v.i.* **·lesced, ·lesc·ing** To recover after illness; regain good health. [< L < com- thoroughly + *valescere,* inceptive of *valere* to be strong]

con·va·les·cence (kon'və·les'əns) *n.* **1.** Gradual recovery from illness. **2.** The period of such recovery. — **con'va·les'cent** *adj. & n.*

con·vec·tion (kən·vek'shən) *n.* **1.** *Physics* The transference of heat in a gas or liquid by currents resulting from unequal temperature and the consequent unequal densities. **2.** The act of conveying. [< L < com- together + *vehere* to carry] — **con·vec'tion·al** *adj.* — **con·vec'tive** *adj.* — **con·vec'tive·ly** *adv.*

con·vene (kən·vēn') *v.* **·vened, ·ven·ing** *v.t.* **1.** To cause to assemble; convoke. **2.** To summon to appear, as by judicial authority. — *v.i.* **3.** To come together; assemble. [< MF < com- together + *venire* to come] — **con·ven'a·ble** *adj.* — **con·ven'er** *n.*

con·ven·ience (kən·vēn'yəns) *n.* **1.** The quality of being convenient; suitability. **2.** Personal comfort; ease. **3.** Anything that increases comfort or saves work. Also *Rare* **con·ven'ien·cy.** — **at one's convenience** At a time or occasion suiting one's needs or preference.

con·ven·ient (kən·vēn'yənt) *adj.* **1.** Well suited to one's purpose or needs; conducive to ease or comfort. **2.** Within easy reach; handy. [See CONVENE.] — **con·ven'ient·ly** *adv.*

con·vent (kon'vent, -vənt) *n.* **1.** A religious community, esp. of nuns, living according to an established rule. **2.** The building or buildings of such a community. — **Syn.** See CLOISTER. [< AF, OF < L *conventus* meeting, assembly]

con·ven·ti·cle (kən·ven'ti·kəl) *n.* **1.** A meeting for religious worship, esp. a secret one. **2.** The meeting place of such an assembly. [See CONVENE.] — **con·ven'ti·cler** *n.*

con·ven·tion (kən·ven'shən) *n.* **1.** A formal meeting of delegates or members, as for political or professional purposes. **2.** The persons attending such a meeting. **3.** A rule or approved technique in conduct or art; a custom or usage. **4.** Conventionality. **5.** An agreement or contract.

con·ven·tion·al (kən·ven'shən·əl) *adj.* **1.** Growing out of· or established by convention or custom. **2.** Following or conforming to approved or established practice. **3.** Formal; stylized. **4.** In art, simplified or abstracted. **5.** Established by general agreement or acceptance: a *conventional* symbol. **6.** Of or pertaining to a convention. — **con·ven'tion·al·ist** *n.* — **con·ven'tion·al·ly** *adv.*

con·ven·tion·al·ism (kən·ven'shən·əl·iz'əm) *n.* **1.** Regard for or adherence to custom. **2.** Anything conventional.

con·ven·tion·al·i·ty (kən·ven'shən·al'ə·tē) *n.* *pl.* **·ties** **1.** The state or quality of being in accord with convention; adherence to established forms, customs, or usages. **2.** A conventional act, principle, custom, etc.

con·ven·tion·al·ize (kən·ven'shən·əl·īz') *v.t.* **·ized**, **·iz·ing** **1.** To make conventional. **2.** To represent in a conventional manner. — **con·ven'tion·al·i·za'tion** *n.*

con·ven·tu·al (kən·ven'chōō·əl) *adj.* Belonging or pertaining to a convent. — *n.* One who belongs to a convent.

con·verge (kən·vûrj') *v.* **·verged**, **·verg·ing** *v.i.* **1.** To move toward one point; come together gradually. — *v.t.* **2.** To cause to tend toward one point. [< LL < L *com-* together + *vergere* to bend]

con·ver·gence (kən·vûr'jəns) *n.* **1.** The act, fact, or state of converging. **2.** The degree or point of converging. Also **con·ver'gen·cy.**

con·vers·a·ble (kən·vûr'sə·bəl) *adj.* **1.** Approachable in conversation; affable. **2.** Fond of talking. ·•· **con·vers'a·ble·ness** *n.* — **con·vers'a·bly** *adv.*

con·ver·sant (kon'vər·sənt, kən·vûr'sənt) *adj.* Well acquainted or familiar, as by study. [See CONVERSE¹.] — **con·ver·sance** (kon'vər·səns, kən·vûr'səns), **con'ver·san·cy** *n.* — **con'ver·sant·ly** *adv.*

con·ver·sa·tion (kon'vər·sā'shən) *n.* **1.** An informal talk with another or others. **2.** Intimate association or social intercourse. **3.** Sexual intercourse. [See CONVERSE¹.]

con·ver·sa·tion·al (kon'vər·sā'shən·əl) *adj.* **1.** Of or characteristic of conversation. **2.** Disposed to or adept at conversation. — **con'ver·sa'tion·al·ly** *adv.*

con·ver·sa·tion·al·ist (kon'vər·sā'shən·əl·ist) *n.* One who enjoys or excels in conversation. Also **con'ver·sa'tion·ist.**

conversation piece Something, as a piece of furniture, that arouses comment.

con·verse¹ (*v.* kən·vûrs'; *n.* kon'vûrs) *v.i.* **·versed**, **·vers·ing** To speak together informally; engage in conversation. — *n.* **1.** Conversation. **2.** Social fellowship. [< OF *converser* to live with < L < *com-* together + *vertere* to turn] — **con·vers'er** *n.*

con·verse² (kon'vûrs; *for adj.,* also kən·vûrs') *adj.* Turned about so that two parts are interchanged; reversed; contrary. — *n.* That which exists in a converse relation; opposite. [< L < *com-* thoroughly + *vertere* to turn] — **con·verse·ly** (kən·vûrs'lē, kon'vûrs·lē) *adv.*

con·ver·sion (kən·vûr'zhən, -shən) *n.* **1.** The act of converting, or the state of being converted. **2.** A change in which one comes to adopt new opinions, esp. a spiritual turning to righteousness and faith. — **con·ver'sion·al, con·ver·sion·ar·y** (kən·vûr'zhən·er'ē, -shən-) *adj.*

con·vert (*v.* kən·vûrt'; *n.* kon'vûrt) *v.t.* **1.** To change into another state, form, or substance; transform. **2.** To apply or adapt to a new or different purpose or use. **3.** To change from one belief, religion, or course of action to another. **4.** To exchange for an equivalent value, as goods for money. **5.** To exchange for value of another form, as preferred for common stock. **6.** To change chemically. **7.** *Law* To assume possession of illegally. — *v.i.* **8.** To become changed in character. **9.** In football, to score an extra point after the touchdown — *n.* A person who has been converted, as from one religion to another. [See CONVERSE²]

con·vert·er (kən·vûr'tər) *n.* **1.** One who or that which converts. **2.** A Bessemer converter. **3.** *Electr.* An apparatus for converting direct into alternating current, or vice versa. Also **con·ver'tor.**

con·vert·i·ble (kən·vûr'tə·bəl) *adj.* Capable of being converted. — *n.* **1.** A convertible thing. **2.** An automobile with a top that folds back. — **con·vert'i·bil'i·ty, con·vert'i·ble·ness** *n.* — **con·vert'i·bly** *adv.*

con·vex (kon'veks; *for adj.,* also kon·veks') *adj.* Curving outward, as the exterior of a globe: opposed to *concave.* — *n.* A convex surface or body; convexity. [< L *convexus* vaulted, curved] — **con·vex'i·ty** *n.* — **con·vex'ly** *adv.*

con·vex·o·con·cave (kon·vek'sō·kon·kāv') *adj.* Convex on one side and concave on the other, as a·lense.

con·vey (kən·vā') *v.t.* **1.** To carry from one place to another; transport. **2.** To serve as a medium or path for; transmit. **3.** To make known; impart; communicate. **4.** To transfer ownership of, as real estate. [< AF < L *com-* together + *via* road, way] — **con·vey'a·ble** *adj.*

con·vey·ance (kən·vā'əns) *n.* **1.** The act of conveying; communication; transportation. **2.** Something used for conveying, as a truck or bus. **3.** *Law* The transfer of title to property; also, the document whereby title is transferred.

con·vey·anc·ing (kən·vā'ən·sing) *n.* The business of preparing conveyances of property. — **con·vey'anc·er** *n.*

con·vey·er (kən·vā'ər) *n.* **1.** One who or that which conveys, transports, or transfers. **2.** Any mechanical contrivance for conveying articles or materials, as an endless belt, a series of rollers, etc. Also (*esp. for def. 2*) **con·vey'or.**

con·vict (*v. adj.* kən·vikt'; *n.* kon'vikt) *v.t.* To prove guilty; find guilty after a judicial trial. — *n.* **1.** One serving a sentence in prison. **2.** One found guilty of a crime. [See CONVINCE.]

con·vic·tion (kən·vik'shən) *n.* **1.** The state of being convinced; firm belief. **2.** A firm belief. **3.** A convincing, as of a truth. **4.** A pronouncing or being guilty. — **Syn.** See BELIEF. — **con·vic'tion·al, con·vic'tive** *adj.*

con·vince (kən·vins') *v.t.* **·vinced**, **·vinc·ing** To cause to believe something, as by proof; bring to belief: often with *of.* [< L < *com-* thoroughly + *vincere* to conquer] — **con·vince'ment** *n.* — **con·vinc'er** *n.* — **con·vin'ci·ble** *adj.*

— **Syn. 1.** *Convince* and *persuade* agree in the sense of making one's view or will prevail over another's. A man is *convinced* by argument or evidence; he is *persuaded* by appeals to his affections. We *convince* a man of a truth, but *persuade* him to act.

con·vinc·ing (kən·vin'sing) *adj.* **1.** Satisfying by evidence: *convincing* testimony. **2.** Credible or believable: a *convincing* act. — **con·vinc'ing·ly** *adv.* — **con·vinc'ing·ness** *n.*

con·viv·i·al (kən·viv'ē·əl) *adj.* **1.** Fond of feasting and good fellowship; jovial. **2.** Of or befitting a feast; festive. [< L *convivium* a feast, banquet < *com-* together + *vivere* to live] — **con·viv'i·al·ist** *n.* — **con·viv'i·al·i·ty** (kən·viv'ē·al'ə·tē) *n.* — **con·viv'i·al·ly** *adv.*

con·vo·ca·tion (kon'vō·kā'shən) *n.* **1.** A calling together; a summoning to assemble. **2.** A meeting, esp. an ecclesiastical one. — **con'vo·ca'tion·al** *adj.* — **con'vo·ca'tor** *n.*

con·voke (kən·vōk') *v.t.* **·voked**, **·vok·ing** To call together; summon to meet. [< F < L < *com-* together + *vocare* to call, summon] — **con·vok'er** *n.*

con·vo·lute (kon'və·lōōt) *adj.* Rolled one part over another or inward from one side. — *v.t. & v.i.* **·lut·ed**, **·lut·ing** To coil up. [See CONVOLVE.] — **con'vo·lute'ly** *adv.*

con·vo·lu·tion (kon'və·lōō'shən) *n.* **1.** A coiled or convoluted state. **2.** A fold or twist in something convoluted. **3.** *Anat.* One of the folds of the cortex of the brain.

con·volve (kon·volv') *v.t. & v.i.* **·volved**, **·volv·ing** To coil up, wind, or twist together. [< L < *com-* together + *volvere* to spin, twist]

con·vol·vu·lus (kən·vol'vyə·ləs) *n.* A twining herb with large flowers, esp. the morning-glory. [< L, bindweed]

con·voy (kon'voi; *for v.,* also kən·voi') *n.* **1.** A protecting escort, as for ships at sea. **2.** A formation of ships, military vehicles, etc., traveling together. **3.** The act of convoying, or the state of being convoyed. — *v.t.* To act as convoy to; escort. [< MF < L *com-* together + *via* road]

con·vulse (kən·vuls') *v.t.* **·vulsed**, **·vuls·ing** **1.** To effect with violent movements; agitate or shake. **2.** To throw into convulsions. **3.** To cause to laugh violently. [< L < *com-* together + *vellere* to pull]

con·vul·sion (kən·vul'shən) *n.* **1.** *Often pl. Pathol.* A violent and involuntary contraction or series of contractions of the voluntary muscles. **2.** Any violent commotion or disturbance, as an earthquake. **3.** A violent fit of laughter. — **con·vul'sion·ar·y** *adj. & n.*

con·vul·sive (kən·vul'siv) *adj.* Producing, characterized by, or of the nature of convulsions: *convulsive* anger. — **con·vul'sive·ly** *adv.* — **con·vul'sive·ness** *n.*

co·ny (kō'nē, kun'ē) *n.* *pl.* **·nies** **1.** A rabbit. **2.** Rabbit fur. Also spelled *coney.* [< OF < L *cuniculus* rabbit]

coo (kōō) *v.* **cooed**, **coo·ing** *v.i.* **1.** To utter the murmuring note of a dove. **2.** To talk amorously or tenderly: to bill and coo. — *v.t.* **3.** To utter with a coo. — *n.* A murmuring sound, as of a dove. [Imit.] — **coo'er** *n.* — **coo'ing·ly** *adv.*

cook (kŏŏk) *v.t.* **1.** To prepare (food) for eating by the action of heat. **2.** *Informal* To tamper with. **3.** *Slang* To ruin. — *v.i.* **4.** To act as a cook. **5.** To undergo cooking. — **to cook up** *Informal* To invent; concoct: to *cook up* a scandal. — *n.* One who prepares food for eating. [OE < LL < L *coquus* a cook] — **cook'er** *n.*

cook·book (kŏŏk'bŏŏk') *n.* A book containing recipes and other information about cooking.

cook·er·y (kŏŏk'ər·ē) *n.* *pl.* **·er·ies** **1.** The art or practice of cooking. **2.** A place for cooking.

cook·out (kŏok′out′) *n. U.S. Informal* A meal cooked outdoors.

cook·y (kŏok′ē) *n. pl.* **cook·ies** *U.S.* A small, thin, dry cake, usu. sweetened. Also **cook′ey, cook′ie.** [< Du. *koekje,* dim. of *koek* cake]

cool (kōōl) *adj.* **1.** Moderately cold; lacking warmth. **2.** Producing a feeling of coolness: a *cool* suit. **3.** Calm in action or thought; composed. **4.** Not cordial; chilling: a *cool* reception. **5.** Suggesting coolness: said of colors. **6.** *U.S. Informal* Not exaggerated; actual: a *cool* million. **7.** *U.S. Slang* Excellent. — *adv. U.S. Informal* Coolly. — *v.t. & v.i.* **1.** To make or become less warm. **2.** To make or become less angry, ardent, or zealous. — *n.* A cool time, thing, place, etc. [OE *cōl*] — **cool′ly** *adv.* — **cool′ness** *n.*

cool·er (kōō′lər) *n.* **1.** A vessel or apparatus that serves to cool something or to keep it cool. **2.** *Slang* A jail.

cool-head·ed (kōōl′hed′id) *adj.* Not readily excited; calm.

coo·lie (kōō′lē) *n.* An unskilled Oriental laborer. Also **coo′·ly.** [Prob. < *Kuli,* an aboriginal Indian tribe]

coon (kōōn) *n.* **1.** A raccoon. **2.** *Slang* A Negro: an offensive term. [Short for RACCOON]

coop (kōōp, kŏop) *n.* **1.** An enclosure or box, as for fowls. **2.** *Slang* A jail. — **to fly the coop** *Slang* To escape from prison, etc. — *v.t.* To put into a coop.

co-op (kō′op, kō-op′) *n. Informal* A cooperative.

coop·er (kōō′pər, kŏop′ər) *n.* One who makes and repairs casks, barrels, etc. — *v.t. & v.i.* To make or mend (casks, barrels, etc.). [ME < LG. Cf. MDu. *kupe* cask.]

coop·er·age (kōō′pər·ij, kŏop′ər-) *n.* **1.** The work or workshop of a cooper. Also **coop′er·y. 2.** A cooper's fee.

co·op·er·ate (kō-op′ə·rāt) *v.i.* **·at·ed, ·at·ing** To work together for a common objective; act in combination. Also **co-op′er·ate, co·öp′er·ate.** [< L < *co-* together + *operari* to work] — **co·op′er·a′tor** *n.*

co·op·er·a·tion (kō-op′ə·rā′shən) *n.* **1.** A working together toward a common end. **2.** The association of laborers, farmers, small capitalists, etc., for mutual economic benefit. Also **co·op′er·a′tion, co·öp′er·a′tion.** — **co·op′er·a′tion·ist** *n.*

co·op·er·a·tive (kō-op′ər·tiv, -ə·rā′tiv) *adj.* **1.** Cooperating or willing to cooperate. **2.** Of or organized for economic cooperation. — *n.* A business enterprise, association, or property organized or owned by a group for its common economic benefit. Also **co-op′er·a·tive, co·öp′er·a·tive.** — **co·op′er·a·tive·ly** *adv.* — **co·op′er·a·tive·ness** *n.*

Cooperative Commonwealth Federation *Canadian* Former name of the NEW DEMOCRATIC PARTY.

co-opt (kō-opt′) *v.t.* **1.** To elect as a fellow member of a committee, etc. **2.** To appoint. **3.** To make ineffectual as an instrument for radical change by incorporating within the established order. [< L < *co-* together + *optare* to choose] — **co′-op·ta′tion, co-op′tion** *n.* — **co-op·ta·tive** (kō′op′tə·tiv) *adj.*

co·or·di·nate (kō-ôr′də·nāt; *for adj., n.,* also kō-ôr′də·nit) *adj.* **1.** Of equal importance or rank; not subordinate. **2.** Of or pertaining to coordinates or coordination. — *n.* **1.** One who or that which is of the same order, rank, power, etc. **2.** *Math.* Any of a set of magnitudes by means of which the position of a point, line, or angle is determined with reference to fixed elements. — *v.* **·nat·ed, ·nat·ing** *v.t.* **1.** To put in the same rank, class, or order. **2.** To bring into harmonious relation or action; adjust. — *v.i.* **3.** To become coordinate. **4.** To act in harmonious or reciprocal relation. Also **co-or′di·nate.** [< Med.L < L *co-* together + *ordinare* to set in order] — **co·or′di·nate·ly** *adv.* — **co·or′di·nate·ness** *n.* — **co·or′di·na′tive** *adj.* — **co·or′di·na′tor** *n.*

co·or·di·na·tion (kō-ôr′də·nā′shən) *n.* **1.** The act of coordinating, or the state of being coordinated. **2.** Harmonious, integrated action or interaction. Also **co-or′di·na′tion.**

coot (kōōt) *n.* **1.** A short-winged aquatic bird resembling the rail. **2.** *Informal* A simpleton. [ME *cote* < LG]

coot·ie (kōō′tē) *n. Slang* A louse. [? < Indonesian *kutu,* a parasitic insect; orig. nautical slang]

cop (kop) *n. Informal* A policeman. — *v.t.* **copped, cop·ping** *Slang* **1.** To steal. **2.** To catch. — **to cop out** *U.S. Slang* To back down; renege. [? Var. of *cap* to catch, take]

co·pa·cet·ic (kō′pə·set′ik) See COPESETIC.

co·pal (kō′pəl) *n.* A hard resin of various tropical trees, used in varnishes. [< Sp. < Nahuatl *copalli* incense]

cope¹ (kōp) *v.* **coped, cop·ing** *v.i.* To contend or strive, esp. successfully: often with *with.* [< OF *coup* blow]

cope² (kōp) *n.* **1.** A semicircular mantle worn by priests on ceremonial occasions. **2.** Something that arches overhead; a vault: the *cope* of heaven. — *v.t.* **coped, cop·ing** To dress or cover in or as in a cope. [See CAP¹.]

co·peck (kō′pek) See KOPECK.

Co·per·ni·can system (kō-pûr′nə·kən) *Astron.* The theory of the solar system of Copernicus that the earth and other planets revolve about the sun.

co·pe·set·ic (kō′pə·set′ik) *adj. U.S. Slang* Fine; excellent: also spelled *copacetic.* Also **co′pa·set′ic, co′pe·set′ic.** [< Creole *coupesètique* able to be coped with]

cope·stone (kōp′stōn) *n.* **1.** One of the stones of a coping. **2.** The final stroke. Also called *capstone.*

cop·i·er (kop′ē·ər) *n.* **1.** An imitator. **2.** A copyist.

co·pi·lot (kō′pī′lət) *n.* The assistant pilot of an aircraft.

cop·ing (kō′ping) *n.* The top course of a wall, roof, etc., usually sloping to shed water. [< COPE², v.]

coping saw A narrow-bladed saw set in a recessed frame and used for cutting curved pieces from wood.

co·pi·ous (kō′pē·əs) *adj.* **1.** Abundant; plentiful. **2.** Diffuse; wordy. [< L *copia* abundance] — **co′pi·ous·ly** *adv.* — **co′pi·ous·ness** *n.*

cop-out (kop′out′) *n. U.S. Slang* **1.** A way of avoiding responsibility; evasion. **2.** One who cops out.

cop·per¹ (kop′ər) *n.* **1.** A reddish, ductile, metallic element (symbol Cu) that is one of the best conductors of heat and electricity. See ELEMENT. **2.** A large pot. **3.** A coin of copper, or of bronze. **4.** A lustrous, reddish brown. — *v.t.* **1.** To cover or coat with copper. **2.** *U.S. Slang* To bet against (another bet). — *adj.* Of, or of the color of, copper. [OE < LL < L < Gk. *Kypros* Cyprus where copper abounded] — **cop′per·y** *adj.*

cop·per² (kop′ər) *n. Slang* A policeman. [< COP¹]

cop·per·as (kop′ər·əs) *n.* A green, crystalline, astringent ferrous sulfate, FeSO₄·7H₂O, used in dyeing, inkmaking, etc. [< MF < Med.L < *(aqua) cuprosa* copper (water)]

cop·per·head (kop′ər·hed′) *n.* A venomous North American snake having reddish brown markings.

Cop·per·head (kop′ər·hed′) *n. U.S.* During the Civil War, a Northerner who sympathized with the South.

cop·per·plate (kop′ər·plāt′) *n.* **1.** An engraved or etched plate of copper. **2.** A print or engraving from such a plate.

cop·per·smith (kop′ər·smith′) *n.* One who works in copper.

copper sulfate A deep blue, crystalline substance, CuSO₄·5H₂O, used in electric batteries, etc.

cop·pice (kop′is) *n.* A copse. [Alter. of COPSE]

cop·ra (kop′rə, kō′prə) *n.* The dried kernel of the coconut, yielding coconut oil. Also **cop·prah** (kop′ər·ə), **cop′rah, cop′pra.** [< Pg. < Malayalam *koppara*]

copse (kops) *n.* A thicket of bushes or small trees: also called *coppice.* [Earlier *coppice* < OF *copeiz* < *coper* to cut]

Copt (kopt) *n.* **1.** A native Egyptian of ancient Egyptian stock. **2.** A member of the Coptic Church. [< Med.L < Arabic < Coptic < Gk. *Aigyptios* Egyptian]

Cop·tic (kop′tik) *adj.* Of or pertaining to the Copts, or to their language. — *n.* The Hamitic language of the Copts.

Coptic Church The principal Christian sect of Egypt.

cop·u·la (kop′yə·lə) *n. pl.* **·las** or **·lae** (-lē) *Gram.* A linking verb. [< L, a link, band] — **cop′u·lar** *adj.*

cop·u·late (kop′yə·lāt) *v.i.* **·lat·ed, ·lat·ing** To unite in sexual intercourse. [< L *copula* a link] — **cop′u·la′tion** *n.*

cop·u·la·tive (kop′yə·lā′tiv, -lə·tiv) *adj.* **1.** Serving to join. **2.** *Gram.* **a** Serving as a copula. **b** Connecting words or clauses in a coordinate relationship. **3.** Copulatory. — *n. Gram.* A copulative word. — **cop′u·la·tive·ly** *adv.*

cop·y (kop′ē) *n. pl.* **cop·ies 1.** A reproduction or imitation of an original; duplicate. **2.** A single specimen of a book, print, etc. **3.** Written matter as distinct from graphic matter, as in advertising, etc. **4.** Something to be reproduced or imitated. **5.** *Printing* Manuscript or other matter to be reproduced in type. **6.** In journalism, subject matter for an article, etc.: The president is good *copy.* Abbr. *c., C.* — *v.* **cop·ied, cop·y·ing** *v.t.* **1.** To make a copy of; reproduce or transcribe. **2.** To follow as a model; imitate. — *v.i.* **3.** To make a copy. [< MF < Med.L *copia* transcript]

cop·y·book (kop′ē·bŏok′) *n.* A book containing copies to be imitated in penmanship. — *adj.* Ordinary; trite.

copy boy An errand boy in a newspaper office.

cop·y·cat (kop′ē·kat′) *n.* An imitator: a child's term.

copy desk A desk in a newspaper office where copy is edited and prepared for the typesetters.

cop·y·ist (kop′ē·ist) *n.* **1.** One who makes copies, esp. of documents. **2.** One who imitates or copies.

cop·y·read·er (kop′ē·rē′dər) *n.* A person who edits work intended for publication.

cop·y·right (kop′ē·rīt) *n.* The exclusive statutory right of authors, composers, playwrights, artists, publishers, and distributors to publish and dispose of their works for a specified period of time. In the U.S. this period is 28 years, with the privilege of one renewal. — *v.t.* To secure copyright for. — *adj.* Of or protected by copyright. — **cop′y·right′a·ble** *adj.* — **cop′y·right′er** *n.*

cop·y·writ·er (kop′ē·rī′tər) *n.* One who writes copy for advertisements.

co·quet (kō·ket′) *v.* **·quet·ted, ·quet·ting** *v.i.* To flirt. [< F *coq* a cock; with ref. to its strutting] — **co·quet′ry** *n.*

co·quette (kō·ket′) *n.* A woman who tries to attract men merely to gratify her vanity; a flirt. — *v.t. & v.i.* **·quet·ted, ·quet·ting** To coquet. — **co·quet′tish** *adj.* — **co·quet′tish·ly** *adv.* — **co·quet′tish·ness** *n.*

co·qui·na (kō·kē′nə) *n.* A soft, highly porous limestone used as building material. [< Sp., shell, ult. < L *concha*]

cor- Var. of COM-.

cor·a·cle (kôr′ə·kəl, kor′-) *n.* A small, rounded boat of hide or oilcloth on a wicker frame. [< Welsh *corwg* boat]

cor·al (kôr′əl, kor′-) *n.* 1. The calcareous skeleton secreted in or by the tissues of various marine coelenterates, deposited in many forms and colors. 2. A mass of these skeletons forming an island, reef, etc. 3. An animal of this type. 4. A pinkish or yellowish red. 5. An object, as a jewel, made of coral. — *adj.* Of, relating to, or of the color of coral. [< OF < L < Gk. *korallion* red coral]

CORAL
a Reef. *b* Mushroom. *c* Bud. *d* Red. *e* Brain.

coral reef A reef, often of great extent, formed by the gradual deposit of coral skeletons.

coral snake A venomous snake of tropical America and the southern U.S., noted for its red, black, and yellow rings.

cor·bel (kôr′bəl, -bel) *n. Archit.* 1. A projection from the face of a wall to support an overhanging weight. 2. A short timber placed under a girder to increase its bearing. — *v.t.* **cor·beled** or **·belled, cor·bel·ing** or **·bel·ling** To support by or furnish with corbels. [< OF < L *corvus* crow]

cor·bel·ing (kôr′bəl·ing) *n. Archit.* An arrangement of stones or bricks in which each successive course projects beyond the one below it. Also **cor′bel·ling.**

cor·bie (kôr′bē) *n. Scot.* A crow or raven. Also **cor′by.**

cord (kôrd) *n.* 1. A string or small rope; twine. 2. A flexible, insulated electric wire, usu. with a plug at one end. 3. A measure for wood, usu. for firewood, equaling a pile 4 × 4 × 8 feet, or 128 cubic feet. See table inside back cover. 4. An influence that draws or restrains. 5. A raised rib in fabric; also, fabric with such ribs. 6. *pl.* Corduroy trousers. 7. *Anat.* A cordlike structure: spinal *cord.* — *v.t.* 1. To bind with cord. 2. To furnish or ornament with cords. 3. To pile (firewood) by the cord. [< MF < L < Gk. *chordē* string of a musical instrument] — **cord′er** *n.*

cord·age (kôr′dij) *n.* 1. Ropes and cords collectively, especially in a ship's rigging. 2. The amount of wood, in cords.

cor·date (kôr′dāt) *adj. Bot.* Heart-shaped, as a leaf. [< L *cordis* heart] — **cor′date·ly** *adv.*

cord·ed (kôr′did) *adj.* 1. Bound or fastened with cord. 2. Ribbed with cords: a *corded* fabric. 3. Piled in cords.

cor·dial (kôr′jəl, *esp. Brit.* -dyəl) *adj.* 1. Warm and hearty; sincere. 2. Giving heart; invigorating. — *n.* 1. A liqueur. 2. Something that invigorates, as a medical stimulant. [< L *cor, cordis* heart] — **cor′dial·ly** *adv.* — **cor′dial·ness** *n.*

cor·di·al·i·ty (kôr·jal′ə·tē, -jē·al′-, *esp. Brit.* -dē·al′-) *n. pl.* **·ties** Cordial quality; sincerity of feeling; warmth.

cor·dil·le·ra (kôr·dil·yâr′ə, kôr·dil′ər·ə) *n. Geog.* An entire system of mountain ranges continuous within a great land mass. [< Sp. < OSp. *cordilla,* dim. of *cuerda* rope] — **cor·dil·ler·an** (kôr·dil·yâr′an, kôr·dil′ər·ən) *adj.*

cord·ite (kôr′dīt) *n.* A smokeless explosive consisting of cellulose nitrate or guncotton, nitroglycerin, and a mineral jelly. [< CORD; with ref. to its appearance]

cor·don (kôr′dən) *n.* 1. A line, as of men or ships, stationed so as to guard or enclose an area. 2. A ribbon or cord worn as an insignia of honor. [< F < *corde* cord]

cor·do·van (kôr′də·vən) *n.* A fine leather first made at Córdoba, Spain, originally of goatskin, but now usu. of split horsehide. Also **cordovan leather.** — *adj.* Made of cordovan. [< OSp. *cordovan* of Córdoba]

cor·du·roy (kôr′də·roi, kôr′də·roi′) *n.* 1. A durable fabric, usu. of cotton, having a ribbed pile. 2. *pl.* Trousers made of corduroy. — *adj.* Made of corduroy. [? < *cord* (ribbed fabric) + obs. *duroy* coarse woolen cloth; prob. < F *corde du roi* king's cord]

corduroy road A road formed from logs laid transversely.

cord·wood (kôrd′wo͝od′) *n.* Firewood or pulpwood cut for stacking in a cord or sold by the cord.

core (kôr, kōr) *n.* 1. The central or innermost part of a thing. 2. The fibrous central part of a fruit, containing the seeds. 3. A cylindrical mass of rock. 4. *Electr.* The central iron mass of an induction coil, armature, or electromagnet. — *v.t.* **cored, cor·ing** To remove the core of. [ME; orig'n uncertain] — **core′less** *adj.* — **cor′er** *n.*

co·re·la·tion (kō′ri·lā′shən) See CORRELATION.

co·re·lig·ion·ist (kō′ri·lij′ən·ist) *n.* An adherent of the same religion, church, or sect as another.

co·re·op·sis (kôr′ē·op′sis, kō′rē-) *n.* A plant of the composite family, with yellow or reddish flowers. [< NL < Gk. *koris* bug + -OPSIS; with ref. to the shape of the seed]

co·re·spon·dent (kō′ri·spon′dənt) *n. Law* In a suit for divorce, one charged with having committed adultery with the husband or wife. — **co′re·spon′den·cy** *n.*

co·ri·an·der (kôr′ē·an′dər, kō′rē-) *n.* 1. A plant of the parsley family, bearing aromatic seeds used for seasoning and in medicine. 2. The seeds of this plant. [< MF < L < Gk. *koriannon*]

Cor·inth (kôr′inth, kor′-) An ancient city in Argolis, Greece.

Co·rin·thi·an (kə·rin′thē·ən) *adj.* 1. Of or pertaining to ancient Corinth, noted for its luxury, licentiousness, and ornate art. 2. Given to luxury and dissipation. 3. *Archit.* Of or pertaining to an order of Greek architecture characterized by ornate, bell-shaped capitals decorated with simulated acanthus leaves. — *n.* A native or inhabitant of Corinth. — **Epistle to the Corinthians** Either of two letters addressed by Saint Paul to the Christians at Corinth, each forming a book of the New Testament. Also **Corinthians.**

co·ri·um (kôr′ē·əm, kō′rē-) *n. Anat.* The dermis. [< L]

cork (kôrk) *n.* 1. The light, porous, elastic outer bark of the cork oak, widely used in industry and the arts. 2. Something made of cork, esp. when used as a bottle stopper; also, a stopper made of other material. — *v.t.* 1. To stop with a cork. 2. To restrain; check. 3. *U.S.* To blacken with burnt cork. [Appar. < OSp. < Arabic ? < L *quercus* oak]

cork·er (kôr′kər) *n.* 1. One who or that which corks. 2. *Slang* Something outstanding or astonishing. 3. An argument, remark, etc., that puts an end to discussion.

cork·ing (kôr′king) *Slang adj.* Excellent; splendid.

cork oak An evergreen oak of southern Europe and North Africa, from whose bark cork is produced.

cork·screw (kôrk′skro͞o′) *n.* An instrument for drawing corks from bottles. — *v.t. & v.i.* To move or twist spirally. — *adj.* Shaped like a corkscrew; twisted; spiral.

cork·y (kôr′kē) *adj.* **cork·i·er, cork·i·est** 1. Of or resembling cork. 2. Tasting of cork, as wine. — **cork′i·ness** *n.*

corm (kôrm) *n. Bot.* A bulblike enlargement of the underground stem in certain plants, as the gladiolus. [< NL *cormus* < Gk. *kormos* tree trunk]

cor·mo·rant (kôr′mər·ənt) *n.* 1. A large, web-footed aquatic bird having a hooked bill and a pouch under the beak. 2. A greedy or voracious person. — *adj.* Greedy; rapacious. [< MF < L *corvus marinus* sea crow]

corn[1] (kôrn) *n.* 1. *U.S.* A tall, extensively cultivated cereal plant bearing seeds on a large ear or cob; also, the seeds of this plant: also called *Indian corn, maize.* 2. *Brit.* In England, wheat. 3. In Scotland and Ireland, oats. 4. A single seed of a cereal plant; kernel; grain. 5. *U.S. Informal* Corn whisky. 6. *U.S. Slang* Anything trite or sentimental. — *v.t.* To preserve in coarse salt or in brine. [OE]

corn[2] (kôrn) *n.* A horny thickening of the skin, commonly on a toe. [< OF < L *cornu*]

Corn Belt *U.S.* The chief corn-growing States, Illinois, Indiana, Iowa, Kansas, Missouri, Nebraska, and Ohio.

corn borer The larva of a moth that feeds on the ears and stalks of corn.

corn·bread (kôrn′bred′) *n.* Bread made from cornmeal.

corn·cob (kôrn′kob′) *n. U.S.* The woody spike of corn around which the kernels grow.

corncob pipe A pipe whose bowl is cut from a corncob.

corn·cock·le (kôrn′kok′əl) *n.* A tall weed of the pink family, with purple flowers.

cor·ne·a (kôr′nē·ə) *n. Anat.* The transparent part of the coat of the eyeball, continuous with the sclera. For illus. see EYE. [< Med.L < L *cornu* horn] — **cor′ne·al** *adj.*

corned (kôrnd) *adj.* Preserved in salt or brine, as beef.

cor·nel (kôr′nəl) *n.* A shrub or small tree with hard wood, as the dogwood. [< MF < L *cornus* cornel]

cor·nel·ian (kôr·nēl′yən) *n.* Carnelian.

cor·ne·ous (kôr′nē·əs) *adj.* Consisting of horn; of a hornlike texture; horny. [< L < *cornu* horn]

cor·ner (kôr′nər) *n.* 1. The point formed by the meeting of two lines or surfaces. 2. The place where two streets meet. 3. A threatening or embarrassing position. 4. A region or place: in every *corner* of the land. 5. A piece for forming, ornamenting, or guarding a corner, as of a book. 6. *Econ.* An operation in which a commodity or security is bought up by an individual or group of individuals with a view to forcing higher prices. — **to cut corners** To economize; reduce expenditures. — *v.t.* 1. To force into a corner; place in a dangerous or embarrassing position. 2. To form a corner in (a stock or commodity). 3. To furnish with corners. 4. To place in a corner. — *v.i.* 5. To form a corner in a stock or commodity. 6. *U.S.* To come together or be located on or at a corner. — *adj.* 1. Located on a corner. 2. Designed for a corner. [< OF < L *cornu* horn] — **cor′nered** *adj.*

cor·ner·stone (kôr′nər·stōn′) *n.* 1. A stone uniting two walls at the corner of a building. **2.** Such a stone ceremonially laid into the foundation of a building under construction. **3.** Something of primary importance.

cor·ner·wise (kôr′nər-wīz′) *adv.* **1.** With the corner in front. **2.** Diagonally. Also **cor′ner·ways′.**

cor·net (kôr·net′) *n.* **1.** A small wind instrument of the trumpet class, with a somewhat wider bore. **2.** A cone-shaped paper wrapper, as for candy, nuts, etc. [< OF < L *cornu* horn] — **cor·net′tist, cor·net′ist** *n.*

corn·flow·er (kôrn′flou′ər) *n.* A hardy annual plant of the composite family, with heads of blue, purple, pink, or white flowers: also called *bachelor's-button, bluebonnet, bluebottle.*

corn·husk (kôrn′husk′) *n. U.S.* The leaves or husk enclosing an ear of corn: also called *corn shuck.*

Corn·husk·er State (kôrn′husk′ər) Nickname of Nebraska.

corn·husk·ing (kôrn′hus′king) *n. U.S.* A social gathering for husking corn, usu. followed by refreshments, dancing, etc.: also called *husking bee.* — **corn′husk′er** *n.*

cor·nice (kôr′nis) *n.* **1.** *Archit.* **a** The horizontal molded projection at the top of a building. **b** The uppermost member of an entablature. **2.** A molding around the walls of a room, close to the ceiling. — *v.t.* **·niced, ·nic·ing** To adorn with a cornice. [< Ital., ? < L < Gk. *korōnis* wreath]

Cor·nish (kôr′nish) *adj.* Pertaining to Cornwall, England, or its people. — *n.* The former language of Cornwall, belonging to the Brythonic branch of the Celtic languages. — **Cor′nish·man** (-mən) *n.*

corn·meal (kôrn′mēl′) *n.* **1.** Meal made from corn: also called *Indian meal.* **2.** *Scot.* Oatmeal. Also **corn meal.**

corn pone *Southern U.S.* Bread made of cornmeal, water, and salt, usu. without milk or eggs.

corn silk The soft, silky styles on an ear of corn.

corn·stalk (kôrn′stôk′) *n.* A stalk of corn. Also **corn stalk.**

corn·starch (kôrn′stärch′) *n.* **1.** Starch made from corn. **2.** A purified starchy cornmeal used in making puddings.

corn syrup Syrup extracted from corn grains, containing glucose mixed with dextrine and maltose.

cor·nu·co·pi·a (kôr′nə-kō′pē-ə) *n.* **1.** A symbol of prosperity, represented as a curved horn overflowing with fruit, vegetables, grains, etc. **2.** A great abundance. Also called *horn of plenty.* [< LL < L *cornu copiae* horn of plenty] — **cor′nu·co′pi·an** *adj.*

corn whisky Whisky distilled from corn.

corn·y (kôr′nē) *adj.* **corn·i·er, corn·i·est 1.** *Slang* Trite, banal, or sentimental. **2.** Of or producing corn.

co·rol·la (kə-rol′ə) *n. Bot.* The circle of flower leaves, usu. colored, forming the inner floral envelope; the petals of a flower. [< L, dim. of *corona* crown] — **cor·ol·la·ceous** (kôr′ə-lā′shəs, kor′-) *adj.* — **cor·ol·late** (kôr′ə-lāt, kor′-) *adj.*

cor·ol·lar·y (kôr′ə-ler′ē, kor′-; *Brit.* kə·rol′ər-ē) *n. pl.* **·lar·ies 1.** A proposition following so obviously from another that it requires little or no proof. **2.** An inference or deduction. **3.** A natural consequence; result. — *adj.* Like a corollary; consequent. [< L *corolla* garland]

co·ro·na (kə-rō′nə) *n. pl.* **·nas** or **·nae** (-nē) **1.** A crownlike structure or part, as the top of the head, the upper part of a tooth, etc. **2.** *Astron.* **a** A luminous circle around one of the heavenly bodies, as when seen through cloud or mist. **b** The luminous envelope of ionized gases visible during a total eclipse of the sun. **3.** Anything resembling a corona or halo. **4.** *Bot.* A crownlike process at the top of the tube of a corolla, as in jonquils. **5.** *Electr.* The luminous discharge appearing at the surface or between the terminals of an electrical conductor under high voltage. [< L, crown] — **co·ro′nal** *adj.*

cor·o·nar·y (kôr′ə-ner′ē, kor′-) *adj.* **1.** Pertaining to or like a crown. **2.** *Anat.* Designating either of two arteries rising from the aorta and supplying blood to the heart muscle. For illus. see HEART. — *n.* Coronary thrombosis. [< L *corona* crown]

coronary thrombosis *Pathol.* The formation of a thrombus, or blood clot, in one of the coronary arteries, resulting in interruption of blood supply to the heart muscle.

cor·o·na·tion (kôr′ə-nā′shən, kor′-) *n.* The act or ceremony of crowning a monarch. [< MF, ult. < L < *corona* crown]

cor·o·ner (kôr′ə-nər, kor′-) *n.* A public officer whose principal duty is the investigation, with the aid of a jury (**coroner's jury**), of the cause of deaths not clearly due to natural causes. [< AF < L *corona*] **cor′o·ner·ship′** *n.*

cor·o·net (kôr′ə-net, -nit, kor′-) *n.* **1.** A small crown, denoting noble rank less than sovereign. **2.** A headband ornamented with jewels, etc. [< OF < L *corona*] — **cor′o·net′ed** *adj.*

cor·po·ra (kôr′pər-ə) Plural of CORPUS.

cor·po·ral[1] (kôr′pər-əl) *adj.* **1.** Belonging or related to the body: *corporal* punishment. **2.** Personal: *corporal* possession. [< L *corpus, -oris* body] — **cor·po·ral·i·ty** (kôr′pə-ral′ə-tē) *n.* — **cor′po·ral·ly** *adv.*

cor·po·ral[2] (kôr′pər-əl, -prəl) *n. Mil.* A noncommissioned

officer of the lowest rank. See tables at GRADE. [< MF < Ital. < L *caput*]

corporal punishment Physical punishment given an offender, as flogging.

cor·po·rate (kôr′pər-it) *adj.* **1.** Of or related to a corporation; incorporated. **2.** Combined as a whole; collective. [< L *corpus, -oris* body] — **cor′po·rate·ly** *adv.*

cor·po·ra·tion (kôr′pə-rā′shən) *n.* **1.** A body of persons recognized by law as an individual person or entity having its own name and identity, and with rights, privileges, and liabilities distinct from those of its members. **2.** Any group of persons acting as one body. **3.** *Informal* A bulging abdomen; paunch. — **cor′po·ra′tive** *adj.* — **cor′po·ra′tor** *n.*

cor·po·re·al (kôr-pôr′ē-əl, -pō′rē-əl) *adj.* **1.** Of, or of the nature of, the body; bodily; mortal. **2.** Of a material nature; physical. — **cor·po·re·al·i·ty** (kôr-pôr′ē-al′ə-tē, -pō′rē-) *n.* — **cor·po′re·al·ly** *adv.* — **cor·po′re·al·ness** *n.*

cor·po·re·i·ty (kôr′pə-rē′ə-tē) *n.* Bodily or material existence. [< Med.L < L *corpus, -oris* body]

corps (kôr, kōr) *n. pl.* **corps** (kōrz, kōrz) **1.** *Mil.* **a** A tactical unit, intermediate between a division and an army, consisting of two or more divisions and auxiliary arms and services. **b** A special department: the Transportation *Corps.* **2.** A number of persons acting together. [See CORPSE.]

corps de bal·let (kôr′ de ba·lā′, *Fr.* bå·le′) The ballet dancers who perform as a group and have no solo parts. [< F]

corpse (kôrps) *n.* A dead body, usu. of a human being. [ME < OF < L *corpus* body]

corps·man (kôr′mən, kōr′-) *n. pl.* **·men** (-mən) **1.** In the U.S. Navy, an enlisted man trained as a pharmacist or hospital assistant. **2.** In the U.S. Army, an enlisted man in the Medical Corps assigned to a combat area.

cor·pu·lence (kôr′pyə-ləns) *n.* An excess accumulation of fat in the body; obesity. Also **cor′pu·len·cy.** [< F < L < *corpus* body] — **cor′pu·lent** *adj.* — **cor′pu·lent·ly** *adv.*

cor·pus (kôr′pəs) *n. pl.* **·po·ra** (-pər-ə) **1.** A human or animal body. **2.** A collection of writings, generally on one subject or by one author. **3.** The main part or mass of anything. [< L]

Cor·pus Chris·ti (kôr′pəs kris′tē, -tī) In the Roman Catholic Church, a festival honoring the Eucharist on the first Thursday after Trinity Sunday. [< L, body of Christ]

cor·pus·cle (kôr′pəs-əl, -pus-əl) *n.* **1.** *Biol.* Any protoplasmic granule of distinct shape or characteristic function, esp. one of the particles forming part of the blood of vertebrates. **2.** A minute particle of matter, as a molecule, atom, or electron. Also **cor·pus·cule** (kôr′pus·kyōol). [< L *corpus, -oris* body] — **cor·pus·cu·lar** (kôr·pus′kyə·lər) *adj.*

cor·pus de·lic·ti (kôr′pəs di·lik′tī) **1.** *Law* The essential fact of the commission of a crime, as, in a case of murder, the finding of the body of the victim. **2.** Loosely, the victim's body in a murder case. [< L, the body of the offense]

corpus ju·ris (jŏŏr′is) *Latin* The body of law.

cor·ral (kə-ral′) *n.* An enclosed space or pen for livestock. — *v.t.* **·ralled, ·ral·ling 1.** To drive into and enclose in a corral. **2.** *U.S. Informal* To seize or capture; secure. [< Sp.]

cor·rect (kə-rekt′) *v.t.* **1.** To make free from error or mistake; set right: to *correct* false notions. **2.** To remedy or counteract; rectify. **3.** To mark the errors of: to *correct* proofs. **4.** To punish or rebuke so as to improve. **5.** To adjust, as to a standard: to *correct* a lens. — *adj.* **1.** Free from fault or mistake; true or exact; accurate. **2.** Conforming to custom or other standard; proper: *correct* behavior. [< L < *com-* together + *regere* to make straight] — **cor·rect′a·ble** or **cor·rect′i·ble** *adj.* — **cor·rect′ly** *adv.* — **cor·rect′ness** *n.* — **cor·rec′tor** *n.*

cor·rec·tion (kə-rek′shən) *n.* **1.** The act of correcting. **2.** That which is offered or used as an improvement; an emendation. **3.** The act or process of disciplining or chastening; punishment. **4.** A quantity added or subtracted for correcting: chronometer *corrections.* — **cor·rec′tion·al** *adj.*

cor·rec·tive (kə-rek′tiv) *adj.* Tending or intended to set right. — *n.* That which corrects. — **cor·rec′tive·ly** *adv.*

cor·re·late (kôr′ə-lāt, kor′-) *v.* **·lat·ed, ·lat·ing** *v.t.* **1.** To place or put in reciprocal relation: to *correlate* literature and philosophy. — *v.i.* **2.** To be mutually or reciprocally related. — *adj.* Having a mutual or reciprocal relation. — *n.* Either of two things mutually related.

cor·re·la·tion (kôr′ə-lā′shən, kor′-) *n.* **1.** Mutual or reciprocal relation. **2.** The act of correlating. — **cor·re·la′tion·al** *adj.*

cor·rel·a·tive (kə-rel′ə-tiv) *adj.* **1.** Having correlation or mutual relation. **2.** Mutually related in grammatical or logical significance: *Either ... or* are *correlative* conjunctions. — *n.* **1.** A correlate. **2.** A correlative term. — **cor·rel′a·tive·ly** *adv.* — **cor·rel′a·tive·ness, cor·rel′a·tiv′i·ty** *n.*

cor·re·spond (kôr′ə-spond′, kor′-) *v.i.* **1.** To conform in fitness or appropriateness; be in agreement; suit: often with

with or *to.* **2.** To be similar in character or function: with *to.* **3.** To hold communication by means of letters. [< Med.L < L *com-* together + *respondere* to answer]

cor·re·spon·dence (kôr′ə·spon′dəns, kor′-) *n.* **1.** The act or state of corresponding; agreement; congruity; also, analogy; similarity. Also **cor′re·spon′den·cy. 2.** Communication by letters; also, the letters written.

correspondence school A school that offers courses of study by mail.

cor·re·spon·dent (kôr′ə·spon′dənt, kor′-) *n.* **1.** One who communicates by means of letters. **2.** A person employed to report news, etc., from a distant place. **3.** A thing that corresponds; a correlative. — *adj.* Corresponding.

cor·re·spond·ing (kôr′ə·spon′ding, kor′-) *adj.* **1.** That corresponds in character or place; similar or equivalent. **2.** Handling correspondence. — **cor′re·spond′ing·ly** *adv.*

cor·ri·dor (kôr′ə·dər, -dôr, kor′-) *n.* **1.** A gallery or passageway, usu. having rooms opening upon it. **2.** A strip of land across a foreign country, as one affording a landlocked nation access to the sea. **3.** A relatively long, narrow, densely-populated region joining two or more major cities. [< MF < Ital. < L *currere* to run]

cor·ri·gen·dum (kôr′ə·jen′dəm, kor′-) *n.* *pl.* **·da** (-də) Something to be corrected, as a printer's error. [< L, gerundive of *corrigere* < *com-* together + *regere* to make straight]

cor·ri·gi·ble (kôr′ə·jə·bəl, kor′-) *adj.* **1.** Capable of being corrected or reformed **2.** Submissive to correction. [See CORRECT.] — **cor′ri·gi·bil′i·ty** *n.* — **cor′ri·gi·bly** *adv.*

cor·rob·o·rate (kə·rob′ə·rāt) *v.t.* **·rat·ed, ·rat·ing** To strengthen or support, as conviction; confirm. [< L < *com-* together + *robur, -oris* strength] — **cor·rob′o·ra′tion** *n.* — **cor·rob′o·ra′tor** *n.*

cor·rob·o·ra·tive (kə·rob′ə·rā′tiv, -ər·ə·tiv) *adj.* Tending to strengthen or confirm. Also **cor·rob·o·ra·to·ry** (kə·rob′-ər·ə·tôr′ē, -tō′rē). — **cor·rob′o·ra′tive·ly** *adv.*

cor·rode (kə·rōd′) *v.* **·rod·ed, ·rod·ing** *v.t.* **1.** To eat away or destroy gradually, as by chemical action. **2.** To destroy, consume, or impair (character, strength, etc.). — *v.i.* **3.** To be eaten away. [< L < *com-* thoroughly + *rodere* to gnaw] — **cor·rod′i·ble** or **cor·ro·si·ble** (kə·rō′sə·bəl) *adj.*

cor·ro·sion (kə·rō′zhən) *n.* **1.** An eating or wearing away. **2.** A product of corrosive action, as rust.

cor·ro·sive (kə·rō′siv) *adj.* Having the power of corroding or eating away. — *n.* A corroding substance. — **cor·ro′-sive·ly** *adv.* — **cor·ro′sive·ness** *n.*

corrosive sublimate *Chem.* Mercuric chloride.

cor·ru·gate (kôr′ə·gāt, -yə-, kor′-) *v.t. & v.i.* **·gat·ed, ·gat·ing** To contract into alternate ridges and furrows; wrinkle. — *adj.* Contracted into ridges or folds; wrinkled, furrowed: also **cor′ru·gat′ed.** [< L *com-* thoroughly + *rugare* to wrinkle] — **cor′ru·ga′tion** *n.*

cor·rupt (kə·rupt′) *adj.* **1.** Open to bribery; dishonest. **2.** Immoral or perverted. **3.** Rotting; putrid. **4.** Debased by changes or errors; altered, as a text. — *v.t. & v.i.* To make or become corrupt. [< OF < L < *com-* thoroughly + *rumpere* to break] — **cor·rupt′er** or **cor·rup′tor** *n.* — **cor·rupt′ly** *adv.* — **cor·rupt′ness** *n.*

cor·rupt·i·ble (kə·rup′tə·bəl) *adj.* Capable of being corrupted. — **cor·rupt′i·bil′i·ty, cor·rupt′i·ble·ness** *n.* — **cor·rupt′i·bly** *adv.*

cor·rup·tion (kə·rup′shən) *n.* **1.** The act of corrupting, or the state of being corrupt. **2.** Dishonesty and lack of integrity; also, bribery. **3.** Moral deterioration. **4.** Physical decay; rot. **5.** Any corrupting influence.

cor·sage (kôr·säzh′) *n.* **1.** A small bouquet of flowers for a woman to wear, as at the waist or shoulder. **2.** The bodice or waist of a woman's dress. [< OF < *cors* body]

cor·sair (kôr′sâr) *n.* **1.** A privateer. **2.** A pirate. **3.** A corsair's vessel. [< MF < Med.L < L *currere* to run]

corse·let (kôrs′lit) **1.** Body armor; also, a breastplate. Also **cors′let. 2.** A light corset, usu. without stays. [< MF, double dim. of OF *cors* body]

cor·set (kôr′sit) *n.* **1.** A close-fitting undergarment, usu. tightened with laces and reinforced by stays, worn chiefly by women to give support or desired shape to the body. **2.** A close-fitting medieval garment. — *v.t.* To enclose or dress in a corset. [< OF, dim. of *cors* body]

cor·tege (kôr·tezh′, -tāzh′) *n.* **1.** A train of attendants. **2.** A ceremonial procession. Also *Chiefly Brit.* **cor·tège** (-tezh′). [< F < Ital. *corteggio* < *corte* court]

cor·tex (kôr′teks) *n.* *pl.* **·ti·ces** (-tə·sēz) **1.** *Bot.* The bark of trees or the rind of fruits. **2.** *Anat.* The external layer of various organs, esp. the gray matter covering the brain. [< L, bark] — **cor′ti·cal** *adj.* — **cor′ti·cal·ly** *adv.*

cor·ti·cate (kôr′ti·kit, -kāt) *adj.* Sheathed in bark or in a cortex. Also **cor′ti·cat′ed.** [< L *cortex* bark]

cor·ti·sone (kôr′tə·sōn, -zōn) *n.* A powerful hormone extracted from the cortex of the adrenal gland and also made synthetically, used in the treatment of rheumatoid arthritis and certain other diseases. [Short for *corticosterone*]

co·run·dum (kə·run′dəm) *n.* An aluminum oxide, Al_2O_3,

used as an abrasive, varieties of which include the ruby and sapphire. [< Tamil *kurundam*]

cor·us·cate (kôr′ə·skāt, kor′-) *v.i.* **·cat·ed, ·cat·ing** To sparkle. [< L *coruscare* to glitter] — **cor′us·ca′tion** *n.*

cor·vette (kôr·vet′) *n.* **1.** A small, swift warship, used chiefly as an antisubmarine escort vessel. **2.** Formerly, a warship equipped with sails and a single tier of guns, smaller than a frigate. Also **cor·vet** (kôr·vet′, kôr′vet). [< F < Pg. < L *corbita* (*navis*) cargo (ship)]

cor·vine (kôr′vīn, -vin) *adj.* Of or pertaining to a crow; crowlike. [< L *corvinus* < *corvus* crow]

cor·ymb (kôr′imb, -im, kor′-) *n.* *Bot.* A flat-topped or convex open flower cluster. [< F < L < Gk. *korymbos* flower cluster] — **co·rym·bose** (kə·rim′bōs) *adj.* — **co·rym′bose·ly** *adv.* — **co·rym·bous** (kə·rim′bəs) *adj.*

co·ry·za (kə·rī′zə) *n.* *Pathol.* A cold in the head. [< L < Gk. *koryza* catarrh]

co·se·cant (kō·sē′kant) *n.* *Trig.* The secant of the complement of an acute angle. [< CO-² + SECANT]

co·sig·na·to·ry (kō·sig′nə·tôr′ē, -tō′rē) *adj.* Signing together or jointly. — *n.* *pl.* **·ries** One of the joint signers of a document: also called *cosigner.*

co·sign·er (kō′sī′nər) *n.* **1.** One who endorses the signature of another, as for a loan. **2.** A cosignatory.

co·sine (kō′sīn) *n.* *Trig.* The sine of the complement of an acute angle.

cos·met·ic (koz·met′ik) *adj.* Used to beautify, esp. the complexion. Also **cos·met′i·cal.** — *n.* A cosmetic preparation. [< Gk. < *kosmos* order] — **cos·met′i·cal·ly** *adv.*

cos·mic (koz′mik) *adj.* **1.** Of or relating to the universe or cosmos. **2.** Limitless; vast. Also **cos′mi·cal.** [< Gk. < *kosmos* order, the universe] — **cos′mi·cal·ly** *adv.*

cosmic dust Fine particles of matter collected by the earth from outer space.

cosmic rays *Physics* Radiation of intense penetrating power and high frequency, emanating from outer space and consisting principally of high-energy rays formed from many types of atomic particles, positive and negative in charge.

cosmo- *combining form* The universe. Also, before vowels, **cosm-.** [< Gk. *kosmos* the universe]

cos·mog·o·ny (koz·mog′ə·nē) *n.* *pl.* **·nies 1.** A theory concerning the origin of the material universe. **2.** The creation of the universe. [< Gk. < *kosmos* the universe + *-gonia* < *-gon,* stem of *gignesthai* to be born] — **cos·mo·gon·ic** (koz′-mə·gon′ik) or **·i·cal, cos·mog′o·nal** *adj.* — **cos·mog′o·nist** *n.*

cos·mog·ra·phy (koz·mog′rə·fē) *n.* *pl.* **·phies** The science that describes the universe, including astronomy, geology, and geography. [< Gk. < *kosmos* the universe + *graphein* to write] — **cos·mog′ra·pher, cos·mog′ra·phist** *n.* — **cos·mo·graph·ic** (koz′mə·graf′ik) or **·i·cal** *adj.*

cos·mol·o·gy (koz·mol′ə·jē) *n.* *pl.* **·gies** The general philosophy of the universe considered as a totality of parts and phenomena subject to laws. [< NL < Gk. *kosmos* the universe + *-logia* study] — **cos·mo·log·i·cal** (koz′mə·loj′i·kəl) or **cos′mo·log′ic** *adj.* — **cos·mol′o·gist** *n.*

cos·mo·naut (koz′mə·nôt) *n.* An astronaut.

cos·mo·pol·i·tan (koz′mə·pol′ə·tən) *adj.* **1.** Common to all the world; not local or limited. **2.** At home in all parts of the world; free from local attachments or prejudices. — *n.* A cosmopolitan person. — **cos′mo·pol′i·tan·ism, cos·mop·o·lit·ism** (koz·mop′ə·līt·īz′əm) *n.*

cos·mop·o·lite (koz·mop′ə·līt) *n.* **1.** A cosmopolitan person. **2.** A plant or animal widely distributed over the world. [< Gk. < *kosmos* world + *politēs* citizen < *polis* city]

cos·mos (koz′məs, -mos) *n.* **1.** The world or universe considered as an ordered system. **2.** Any complete system. **3.** *Bot.* A plant related to the dahlia. [< Gk. *kosmos* order]

Cos·sack (kos′ak, -ək) *n.* One of a people of the southern U.S.S.R., famous as cavalrymen. [< Russ. *kazak* < Turkic *quzzāq* guerrilla, freebooter]

cos·set (kos′it) *v.t.* To pamper; pet. — *n.* **1.** A pet lamb. **2.** Any pet. [? OE *cot-sǣta* dweller in a cottage]

cost (kôst) *v.* **cost** (for def. 3, also **cost·ed**), **cost·ing** *v.i.* **1.** To be acquirable for or have the value of a price, sum, consideration, etc. **2.** To be gained by the expenditure of a specified thing, as health, pain, effort, etc. — *v.t.* **3.** To estimate the amount spent for the production of. — *n.* **1.** The price paid for anything. **2.** Loss; suffering; detriment. **3.** *pl. Law* The expenses of a lawsuit in court. — **at all costs** (or **at any cost**) Regardless of cost; by all means. [< OF < *com-* together + *stare* to stand]

cost accountant One who keeps track of the costs incurred in production and distribution. — **cost accounting**

cos·tal (kos′tal) *adj.* Of, on, or near a rib or the ribs.

cos·ter·mon·ger (kos′tər·mung′gər, -mong′-, kôs′-) *n. Brit.* A street hawker of vegetables, fruits, etc. Also **cos′ter.** [< *costard* a variety of apple + MONGER]

cos·tive (kos′tiv, kôs′-) *adj.* Constipated. [< OF *costivé*] — **cos′tive·ly** *adv.* — **cos′tive·ness** *n.*

cost·ly (kôst′lē, kost′-) *adj.* **·li·er, ·li·est 1.** Costing very much; expensive. **2.** Sumptuous. — **cost′li·ness** *n.*

costo- *combining form* Rib: used in anatomical and surgical terms. Also, before vowels, **cost-.** [< L *costa* rib]

cost of living The average cost, as to an individual or family, of food, clothing, shelter, etc.

cos·tume (*n.* kos′tōōm, -tyōōm; *v.* kos·tōōm′, -tyōōm′) *n.* **1.** The mode of dress, including ornaments and hair style, of a given region, time, or class. **2.** Such dress as worn by actors, dancers, etc. **3.** A set of garments for some occasion or activity: summer *costume.* **4.** Garb; apparel, esp. that of a woman. —*v.t.* **·tumed, ·tum·ing** To furnish with costumes. [< F < Ital. < L *consuetudo* custom]

cos·tum·er (kos·tōō′mər, -tyōō′-) *n.* One who makes or furnishes costumes. Also **cos·tum·ier** (kos·tōōm′yər, -tyōōm′-; *Fr.* kôs·tü·myā′).

cot¹ (kot) *n.* A light, narrow bed, commonly of canvas stretched on a folding frame. [< Hind. *khāṭ* < Skt. *khaṭvā*]

cot² (kot) *n.* **1.** A small house; cottage. **2.** A cote. **3.** A protective covering for an injured finger. [OE]

co·tan·gent (kō·tan′jənt) *n. Trig.* The tangent of the complement of an acute angle. —**co·tan·gen·tial** (kō′tan·jen′shəl) *adj.*

cote (kōt) *n.* **1.** A small shelter for sheep or birds. **2.** *Dial.* A little house; hut. [OE. Akin to COT².]

co·tem·po·ra·ne·ous (kō·tem′pə·rā′nē·əs), **co·tem·po·rar·y** (kō·tem′pə·rer′ē), etc. See CONTEMPORANEOUS, etc.

co·ten·ant (kō·ten′ənt) *n.* One of several tenants holding the same property. —**co·ten′an·cy** *n.*

co·te·rie (kō′tə·rē) *n.* A small, exclusive group of persons who share certain interests or pursuits. [< F]

co·ter·mi·nous (kō·tûr′mə·nəs) See CONTERMINOUS.

co·til·lion (kō·til′yən, kə-) *n.* **1.** *U.S.* An elaborate dance marked by frequent change of partners: also called *german.* **2.** *U.S.* A formal ball at which young ladies are presented to society. **3.** A lively, quick dance. **4.** The music for this dance. Also **co·til·lon** (kō·til′yən, kə-; *Fr.* kô·tē·yôn′). [< F *cotillon* petticoat]

cot·tage (kot′ij) *n.* **1.** A small house in the suburbs or the country. **2.** *U.S.* A temporary home at a resort. [< COT²]

cottage cheese A soft, white cheese made of milk curds.

cottage pudding Plain cake covered with a sweet sauce.

cot·tag·er (kot′ij·ər) *n.* **1.** One who lives in a cottage. **2.** *Brit.* A rural laborer. **3.** *Canadian* A summer resident.

cotter pin A key, wedge, pin, etc., that is split lengthwise so that the ends may be spread apart to hold parts of machinery together.

cot·ton (kot′n) *n.* **1.** The soft, fibrous, white or yellowish material, of high cellulose content, attached to the seeds of the cotton plant and widely used as a textile. **2.** The plant itself. **3.** Cotton plants collectively. **4.** Cotton cloth or thread. —*adj.* Woven or composed of cotton cloth or thread. —**to cotton to** Informal **1.** To become friendly with. **2.** To take a liking to. —**to cotton up to** Informal To attempt to please by friendly overtures or flattery. [< F *coton* < OSp. < Arabic *qutun*] —**cot′ton·y** *adj.*

COTTON
a Boll ready for picking.

cotton belt *U.S.* The region of the southern U.S. in which cotton is the chief crop.

cotton flannel A soft, warm cotton fabric, napped on one or both sides.

cotton gin A machine used to separate the seeds from the fiber of cotton.

cot·ton·mouth (kot′n·mouth′) *n.* The water moccasin, a snake.

cotton picker A machine designed to remove the ripe cotton from standing cotton plants.

cot·ton·seed (kot′n·sēd′) *n.* The seed of the cotton plant.

cottonseed oil A pale yellow, viscid oil pressed from cottonseeds, used in cooking, paints, and as a lubricant.

cot·ton·tail (kot′n·tāl′) *n.* The American gray rabbit.

cot·ton·wood (kot′n·wood′) *n.* An American poplar tree whose seeds discharge a cottony substance.

cotton wool **1.** Raw cotton. **2.** *Brit.* Absorbent cotton.

cot·y·le·don (kot′ə·lēd′n) *n. Bot.* A seed leaf, or one of a pair of the first leaves from a sprouting seed. [< L < Gk. < *kotylē* a cavity] —**cot′y·le′do·nous, cot′y·le′do·nal** *adj.*

couch (kouch) *n.* A piece of furniture, usu. upholstered and having a back, on which several may sit or one may recline; also, a bed, or any place of repose. —*v.t.* **1.** To phrase; put into words. **2.** To cause to recline, as on a bed. **3.** To bend or bring down; lower, as a spear for attack. —*v.i.* **4.** To lie down; recline. **5.** To lie in ambush. [< OF < *coucher* to put to bed] —**couch′er** *n.*

couch·ant (kou′chənt) *adj.* Lying down. [See COUCH.]

couch grass A perennial grass multiplying injuriously in cultivated grounds by its long rootstocks: also called *quitch grass.* [Var. of QUITCH (GRASS)]

cou·gar (kōō′gər) *n.* The puma. [< F < Tupi]

cough (kôf, kof) *v.i.* **1.** To expel air from the lungs in a noisy or spasmodic manner. —*v.t.* **2.** To expel by a cough. —**to cough up 1.** To expel by coughing. **2.** *Slang* To surrender; hand over, as money. —*n.* **1.** A sudden, harsh expulsion of breath. **2.** An illness in which there is frequent coughing. [ME *cozen, couzen*] —**cough′er** *n.*

cough drop A medicated lozenge to relieve coughing, etc.

could (kood) Past tense of CAN¹. [ME *coude*, OE *cuthe* knew how; *l* inserted on analogy with *should* and *would*]

could·n't (kood′nt) Could not.

cou·lee (kōō′lē) *n.* **1.** *U.S.* A deep gulch cut by rainstorms or melting snow. **2.** *Geol.* A sheet of solidified lava. Also French **cou·lée** (kōō·lā′). [< F *couler* to flow]

cou·lomb (kōō·lom′) *n.* The practical unit of quantity in measuring electricity; the amount conveyed by one ampere in one second. [after C. A. de *Coulomb*, 1736–1806, French physicist]

coul·ter (kōl′tər) See COLTER.

coun·cil (koun′səl) *n.* **1.** An assembly of persons convened for consultation or deliberation. **2.** A body of men elected or appointed to act in an administrative, legislative, or advisory capacity in a government. **3.** The deliberation that takes place in a council chamber. [< AF, OF < L < *com-* together + *calare* to call]

coun·cil·man (koun′səl·mən) *n. pl.* **·men** (-mən) A member of a council, esp. the governing council of a city.

coun·cil·or (koun′səl·ər, -slər) *n.* A member of a council. Also *Brit.* **coun′cil·lor.** —**coun′cil·or·ship′** *n.*

coun·sel (koun′səl) *n.* **1.** Mutual exchange of advice, opinions, etc.; consultation. **2.** Advice; guidance. **3.** A deliberate purpose; plan. **4.** A secret intent or opinion: obsolete except in **to keep one's own counsel. 5.** A lawyer or lawyers. —*v.* **coun·seled** or **·selled, coun·sel·ing** or **·sel·ling** *v.t.* **1.** To give advice to; advise. **2.** To advise in favor of; recommend. —*v.i.* **3.** To give or take counsel. [< AF, OF < L *consulere* to deliberate]

coun·sel·or (koun′səl·ər, -slər) *n.* **1.** One who gives counsel; an adviser. **2.** An attorney at law. **3.** A supervisor at a children's camp. Also **coun′sel·lor.**

count¹ (kount) *v.t.* **1.** To list or call off one by one to ascertain the total. **2.** To list numerals in a progressive sequence up to: to *count* ten. **3.** To consider to be; judge. **4.** To take note of; include in a reckoning. **5.** To list numbers in sequence. **6.** To have worth; be of importance. **7.** To be accounted or included. —**to count in** To include. —**to count on** (or **upon**) To rely on. —**to count out 1.** In boxing, to reach a count of ten over (a downed boxer), thus declaring him defeated. **2.** To omit or exclude; disregard. —*n.* **1.** The act of counting. **2.** The number arrived at by counting; total. **3.** An accounting or reckoning. **4.** *Law* A separate and distinct charge, as in an indictment. **5.** In boxing, the ten seconds given a contestant to get up or lose the fight. [< OF < L < *com-* together + *putare* to reckon] —**count′a·ble** *adj.*

count² (kount) *n.* In some European countries, a nobleman having a rank corresponding to that of an earl in England. [< AF *counte*, OF *coute* < L *comes* an associate]

count·down (kount′doun′) *n.* A reverse counting of time units, reaching zero at the instant when an operation, as a rocket launching, nuclear blast, etc., is to be executed.

coun·te·nance (koun′tə·nəns) *n.* **1.** The face or features. **2.** Facial expression. **3.** An encouraging look; also, approval; support. **4.** Self-control; composure. —**out of countenance** Disconcerted; embarrassed; abashed. —*v.t.* **·nanced, ·nanc·ing** To approve; encourage. [< OF < L *continere* to hang together] —**coun′te·nanc·er** *n.*

coun·ter¹ (koun′tər) *n.* **1.** An opposite or contrary. **2.** In boxing, a blow given while receiving or parrying another. **3.** In fencing, a parry in which one foil follows another. **4.** A piece encircling the heel of a shoe. **5.** *Naut.* The curved part of a vessel's stern extending from the water line to the point of fullest outward swell. —*v.t.* **1.** To return, as a blow, by another blow. **2.** To oppose; contradict; controvert. **3.** To put a new counter on (a shoe, etc.). —*v.i.* **4.** To give a blow while receiving or parrying one. **5.** To make a counter-move. —*adj.* Opposing; opposite; contrary. —*adv.* Contrary. [< F < L *contra* against]

coun·ter² (koun′tər) *n.* **1.** A board, table, or the like, on which to expose goods for sale, transact business, or serve refreshments or meals. **2.** A piece of wood, ivory, etc., used in counting, as in billiards. **3.** A piece in chess, checkers, etc. **4.** An imitation coin. [< AF < Med.L < L *computare* to compute]

counter- *combining form* **1.** Opposing; contrary; acting in opposition or response to the action of the main element; as in:

counteraccusation   **counterblow**   **countercharge**

PRONUNCIATION KEY: add, āce, cāre, pälm; end, ēven; it, īce; odd, ōpen, ôrder; tōōk, pōōl; up, bûrn; ə = a in *above*, e in *sicken*, i in *flexible*, o in *melon*, u in *focus*; yōō = u in *fuse*; oil; pout; check; go; ring; thin; this; zh, vision. For à, œ, ü, kh, ń, see inside front cover.

counterdemand counterpropaganda counterstatement
counterforce counterproposal countertheory
counterinfluence counterreform counterthreat
countermeasure counterresolution counterthrust
2. Done or acting in reciprocal or exchange; as in:
counteroffer counterquestion
3. Complementing or corresponding; denoting the duplicate or parallel; as in:
countercheck counterfugue countersecurity
4. Opposite in direction or position; as in:
countercurrent counterflow counterpressure
counterflight counterposition counterturn
[< F < L *contra-* against]

coun·ter·act (koun/tər·akt/) *v.t.* To act in opposition to; check. — **coun/ter·ac/tion** *n.* — **coun/ter·ac/tive** *adj.*

coun·ter·at·tack (*n.* koun/tər·ə·tak/; *v.* koun/tər·ə·tak/) *n.* An attack designed to counter another attack. — *v.t. & v.i.* To make a counterattack (against).

coun·ter·bal·ance (*v.* koun/tər·bal/əns; *n.* koun/tər·bal/əns) *v.t.* -anced, -anc·ing To oppose with an equal weight or force; offset. — *n.* **1.** Any power equally opposing another. **2.** A weight that balances another; counterpoise.

coun·ter·claim (*n.* koun/tər·klām/; *v.* koun/tər·klām/) *n.* A claim that opposes another claim. — *v.t. & v.i.* To make or plead (as) a counterclaim. — **coun/ter·claim/ant** *n.*

coun·ter·clock·wise (koun/tər·klok/wīz/) *adj. & adv.* Opposite to the direction taken by the hands of a clock.

coun·ter·es·pi·o·nage (koun/tər·es·pē·ə·näzh/, -nij) *n.* Measures intended to counteract enemy spying.

coun·ter·feit (koun/tər·fit) *v.t.* **1.** To make an imitation of, as money or stamps, with the intent to defraud. **2.** To copy; imitate; also, to feign; dissemble: to *counterfeit* sorrow. — *v.i.* **3.** To practice deception; feign. **4.** To make counterfeits. — *adj.* **1.** Made to resemble some genuine thing with the intent to defraud. **2.** Pretended; feigned; deceitful. — *n.* **1.** Something made fraudulently to resemble the genuine. **2.** Any imitation of copy. [< OF < L *contra-* against + *facere* to make] — **coun/ter·feit/er** *n.*

coun·ter·in·sur·gen·cy (koun/tər·in·sûr/jən·sē) *n.* Measures to combat revolutionary guerrilla warfare.

coun·ter·in·tel·li·gence (koun/tər·in·tel/ə·jəns) *n.* Activities to oppose espionage, subversion, and sabotage.

coun·ter·ir·ri·tant (koun/tər·ir/ə·tənt) *n.* Anything used to excite irritation in one place so as to counteract more serious irritation elsewhere.

coun·ter·man (koun/tər·mən) *n.* A man who serves at a lunch counter.

coun·ter·mand (*v.* koun/tər·mand/, -mänd/; *n.* koun/tər·mand, -mänd) *v.t.* **1.** To revoke or reverse (a command, order, etc.). **2.** To recall or order back by a contrary command. — *n.* An order contrary to or revoking one previously issued. [< OF < L *contra-* against + *mandare* to order]

coun·ter·march (*n.* koun/tər·märch/; *v.* koun/tər·märch/) *n.* **1.** A return march. **2.** *Mil.* A reversal of direction while marching, keeping the same order. — *v.t. & v.i.* To execute or cause to execute a countermarch.

coun·ter·move (*n.* koun/tər·mōōv/; *v.* koun/tər·mōōv/) *n.* A move designed to counter another move. — *v.t. & v.i.* -moved, -mov·ing To move in opposition (to).

coun·ter·of·fen·sive (koun/tər·ə·fen/siv, koun/tər·ə·fen/siv) *n.* A large-scale attack designed to stop the offensive of an enemy and to seize the initiative along an extended front.

coun·ter·pane (koun/tər·pān/) *n.* A coverlet for a bed. [< F *pan* quilt]

coun·ter·part (koun/tər·pärt/) *n.* **1.** Someone or something resembling another. **2.** One who or that which supplements or completes another.

coun·ter·plot (*n.* koun/tər·plot/; *v.* koun/tər·plot/) *n.* A plot designed to foil another plot. — *v.t. & v.i.* -plot·ted, -plot·ting To oppose (a plot) by another plot.

coun·ter·point (koun/tər·point/) *n. Music* **1.** The technique or practice of composing two or more melodic parts to be heard simultaneously; also, the arrangement of parts so composed. **2.** Any of such parts in relation to the principal part. [< MF < Med.L < L *contra-* against + *punctus* point, note]

coun·ter·poise (*v.* koun/tər·poiz/; *n.* koun/tər·poiz/) *v.t.* -poised, -pois·ing To bring to a balance by opposing with an equal weight, power, or force; counterbalance. — *n.* **1.** A counterbalancing weight, force, power, or influence. **2.** A state of equilibrium. [< OF < L *contra-* against + *pensare* to weigh]

Counter Reformation The reform movement within the Roman Catholic Church in the 16th century in reaction to the Protestant Reformation.

coun·ter·rev·o·lu·tion (koun/tər·rev/ə·lōō/shən) *n.* A revolution designed to counteract a previous revolution and to reverse its effects. — **coun/ter·rev/o·lu/tion·ar/y** *adj. & n.* — **coun/ter·rev/o·lu/tion·ist** *n.*

coun·ter·shaft (koun/tər·shaft/, -shäft/) *n. Mech.* An intermediate shaft driven by a main shaft.

coun·ter·sign (*v.* koun/tər·sīn/, koun/tər·sīn/; *n.* koun/tər·sīn/) *v.t.* To sign (a document already signed by another), as in authenticating. — *n. Mil.* A password. [< OF *contresigner*] — **coun/ter·sig/na·ture** *n.*

coun·ter·sink (*v.* koun/tər·singk/, koun/tər·singk/; *n.* koun/tər·singk/) *v.t.* **sank** or **sunk**, **sunk** (*Obs.* **sunk·en**), **sink·ing 1.** To cut the edges of (a hole) so that a screw, bolthead, etc., will lie flush with or below the surface. **2.** To sink, as a bolt or screw, into such a depression. — *n.* **1.** A tool for countersinking. **2.** A countersunk hole.

coun·ter·ten·or (koun/tər·ten/ər) *n.* An adult male singing voice higher than the tenor. [< MF *contreteneur*]

coun·ter·vail (koun/tər·vāl/, koun/tər·vāl) *v.t.* **1.** To oppose with equal force or effect; counteract. **2.** To compensate or make up for; offset. — *v.i.* **3.** To be of avail: with *against*. [< AF < L *contra valere* to avail against]

coun·ter·weigh (koun/tər·wā/) *v.t. & v.i.* To counterbalance.

coun·ter·weight (koun/tər·wāt/) *n.* Any counterbalancing weight, force, or influence. — **coun/ter·weight/ed** *adj.*

counter word A word widely used without regard to its exact meaning, as *nice, awful, fix.*

count·ess (koun/tis) *n.* **1.** The wife or widow of a count, or, in Great Britain, of an earl. **2.** A woman equal in rank to a count or earl. [See COUNT².]

count·ing house (koun/ting) A building or office in which a mercantile or other firm carries on bookkeeping, correspondence, etc. Also **count/ing·house/, counting room.**

count·less (kount/lis) *adj.* That cannot be counted; innumerable. — **Syn.** See INFINITE.

coun·tri·fied (kun/tri·fīd) *adj.* Having the appearance, manner, etc., associated with the country or with country people; rural; rustic. Also **coun/try·fied.**

coun·try (kun/trē) *n. pl.* **·tries 1.** A land under a particular government, inhabited by a certain people, or within definite geographical limits. **2.** The land of one's birth or allegiance. **3.** The district outside cities and towns; rural areas. **4.** A region of a specified character: sheep *country*. **5.** The people of a nation. — **Syn.** See NATION. — *adj.* Rustic. [< OF < LL < L *contra* on the opposite side]

country club A club in the outskirts of a town or city, with a clubhouse, grounds, and facilities for outdoor sports.

coun·try-dance (kun/trē-dans/, -däns/) *n.* A folk dance of English origin, in which the partners are in opposite lines.

country gentleman A landed proprietor who lives on his country estate.

coun·try·man (kun/trē·mən) *n. pl.* **·men** (-mən) **1.** A man of the same country as another. **2.** A native of a particular country. **3.** A rustic. — **coun/try·wom/an** *n.fem.*

coun·try·seat (kun/trē·sēt/) *n.* A country estate.

coun·try·side (kun/trē·sīd/) *n.* A rural district, or its inhabitants.

coun·ty (koun/tē) *n. pl.* **·ties 1.** An administrative division of a state or kingdom. In the United States, it is the division next below a State. In England a county is sometimes called a *shire*. **2.** The people of a county. [< AF, OF < L *comes* count, companion]

county seat The seat of government of a county.

coup (kōō) *n. pl.* **coups** (kōōz, *Fr.* kōō) A sudden, telling blow; a masterstroke; brilliant stratagem. [< F < L < Gk. *kolaphos* a blow with the fist]

coup de grâce (kōō/ də gräs/) *French* **1.** The mortal stroke, as delivered to a wounded enemy. **2.** Any finishing stroke.

coup d'é·tat (kōō/dā·tä/) *French* An unexpected stroke of policy; esp., a sudden seizure of government.

coupe (kōōp, kōō·pā/) *n.* A closed automobile with two doors, seating two to six persons: also *coupé*. [< COUPÉ]

cou·pé (kōō·pā/) *n.* **1.** A low, four-wheeled, closed carriage with a seat for two and an outside seat for the driver. **2.** A coupe. [< F, pp. of *couper* to cut]

cou·ple (kup/əl) *n.* **1.** Two of a kind; a pair. **2.** Two persons of opposite sex, wedded or otherwise paired, as in dances, games, etc. **3.** *Informal* A few: a *couple* of hours. **4.** Something joining two things together. — *v.* **·led, ·ling** *v.t.* **1.** To join, as one thing to another; link. **2.** To join in wedlock; marry. — *v.i.* **3.** To pair. [< OF < L *copula* bond]

cou·pler (kup/lər) *n.* **1.** One who or that which couples. **2.** A device that connects objects; esp.: **a** A contrivance for linking railroad cars. **b** A device enabling two or more organ keys or keyboards to play together.

cou·plet (kup/lit) *n.* **1.** Two successive lines of verse, usu. rhymed and in the same meter. **2.** A pair.

cou·pling (kup/ling) *n.* **1.** The act of one who or that which couples. **2.** A linking device, as for joining railroad cars.

cou·pon (kōō/pon, kyōō/-) *n.* **1.** One of a number of dated certificates attached to a bond, representing interest accrued. **2.** A section of a ticket, advertisement, etc., entitling the holder to something in exchange. [< F *couper* to cut]

cour·age (kûr/ij) *n.* That quality of mind or spirit enabling one to meet danger or opposition with fearlessness. [< OF *corage*, ult. < L *cor* heart]

cou·ra·geous (kə·rā′jəs) *adj.* Possessing or characterized by courage; brave; daring: *courageous* words. — **cou·ra′·geous·ly** *adv.* — **cou·ra′geous·ness** *n.*

cou·ri·er (kōōr′ē·ər, kûr′-) *n.* **1.** A messenger, esp. one traveling in haste or on official diplomatic business. **2.** One who arranges a journey. [< OF < L *currere* to run]

course (kōrs, kôrs) *n.* **1.** Onward movement in a certain direction; progress. **2.** The path or ground passed over. **3.** Direction: to take an eastward *course*. **4.** Passage or duration in time. **5.** Advance; progression: the *course* of evolution. **6.** Natural or usual development: to run its *course*. **7.** A series of actions, events, etc., constituting a unit. **8.** Line of conduct: a wise *course*. **9.** A prescribed curriculum of studies leading to a degree: a liberal arts *course*; also, any unit of study in a school curriculum: a history *course*. **10.** A portion of a meal served at one time. **11.** A horizontal row or layer, as of stones in a wall. — **in due course** In the proper sequence; at the right time. — **of course** **1.** As might be expected; naturally. **2.** Certainly. — *v.* **coursed**, **cours·ing** *v.t.* **1.** To run through or over. **2.** To pursue. **3.** To cause (hounds) to chase game. — *v.i.* **4.** To race. **5.** To hunt game with hounds. [< L *currere* to run]

cours·er (kōr′sər, kôr′-) *n. Poetic* A fleet, spirited horse. [< F < OF < L *currere* to run]

court (kôrt, kōrt) *n.* **1.** A courtyard. **2.** A short street enclosed by buildings on three sides. **3.** The residence of a sovereign; palace. **4.** A sovereign together with his council and retinue. **5.** A formal assembly held by a sovereign. **6.** A place where justice is judicially administered; also, those judges who administer justice. **7.** The regular session of a judicial tribunal. **8.** A level space laid out for tennis, basketball, squash, or similar games; also, a subdivision of such a space. **9.** Flattering attention paid another to win favor; homage. **10.** Wooing; courtship. — **out of court** **1.** Without a trial. **2.** Without claim to a hearing. — *v.t.* **1.** To try to gain the favor of. **2.** To seek the love of; woo. **3.** To attempt to gain: to *court* applause. **4.** To invite: to *court* disaster. — *v.i.* **5.** To engage in courtship. — *adj.* Of or pertaining to a court. [< OF < L *cohors, cohortis* yard]

Court of Common Pleas A common-law court having original jurisdiction over civil and criminal matters.

cour·te·ous (kûr′tē·əs) *adj.* Showing courtesy; polite. — Syn. See POLITE. [< OF *corteis* befitting a court] — **cour′te·ous·ly** *adv.* — **cour′te·ous·ness** *n.*

cour·te·san (kôr′tə·zən, kōr′-, kûr′-) *n.* A prostitute. Also **cour′te·zan**. [< MF < Ital. *cortigiana* court lady]

cour·te·sy (kûr′tə·sē) *n. pl.* **·sies** **1.** Habitual politeness; good manners. **2.** A courteous favor or act. **3.** Common consent or allowance, as opposed to right: an aunt by *courtesy*. **4.** A curtsy. [< OF *corteis* courteous]

court·house (kôrt′hous′, kōrt′-) *n.* A public building occupied by judicial courts and other administrative offices.

court·i·er (kôr′tē·ər, -tyər, kōr′-) *n.* **1.** A member of a sovereign's court. **2.** One who seeks favor by flattery.

court·ly (kôrt′lē, kōrt′-) *adj.* **·li·er, ·li·est** **1.** Pertaining to or befitting a court. **2.** Elegant in manners. — *adv.* In a courtly manner. — **court′li·ness** *n.*

court-mar·tial (kôrt′mär′shəl, kōrt′-) *n. pl.* **courts-mar·tial** **1.** A military court to try persons subject to military law. **2.** A trial by such a court. — *v.t.* **-mar·tialed** or **·tialled, -mar·tial·ing** or **·tial·ling** To try by court-martial.

court plaster Adhesive tape.

court·room (kôrt′rōōm′, -rŏŏm′, kōrt′-) *n.* A room in which judicial proceedings are held.

court·ship (kôrt′ship, kōrt′-) *n.* The act or period of courting and wooing.

court·yard (kôrt′yärd′, kōrt′-) *n.* An enclosed yard adjoining a building or surrounded by buildings or walls; a court.

cous·in (kuz′ən) *n.* **1.** One collaterally related by descent from a common ancestor, but not a brother or sister. Children of brothers and sisters are **first** or **full cousins** to each other; children of first cousins are **second cousins** to each other. **2.** One of a kindred group or nation: our English *cousins*. **3.** A title of address used by a sovereign to a noble or a fellow sovereign. [< OF < L *consobrinus* child of a maternal aunt] — **cous′in·hood, cous′in·ship** *n.* — **cous′in·ly** *adj. & adv.*

cous·in-ger·man (kuz′ən·jûr′mən) *n. pl.* **cous·ins-ger·man** A first or full cousin. [< F *cousin germain*]

cous·in·ry (kuz′ən·rē) *n. pl.* **·ries** Cousins collectively.

cou·tu·ri·er (kōō·tü·ryā′) *n.* A male dress designer. [< F] — **cou·tu·ri·ère** (kōō·tü·ryâr′) *n. fem.*

co·va·lence (kō′vā′ləns) *n. Chem.* A bond formed by the sharing of electrons between the atoms of a compound. — **co′va′lent** *adj.*

cove¹ (kōv) *n.* **1.** A small bay or baylike recess in a shoreline. **2.** A recess among hills, in a wood, etc. **3.** *Archit.* **a** A concave vault. For illus. see VAULT. **b** A concave molding. **c**

A concave curved portion where a ceiling meets a wall. — *v.t.* **coved, cov·ing** To curve over or inward. [OE *cofa* cave]

cove² (kōv) *n. Brit. Slang* A boy or man; fellow. [< Romany *covo* that man]

cov·e·nant (kuv′ə·nənt) *n.* **1.** An agreement entered into by two or more persons or parties; a compact. **2.** *Theol.* The promise of God to bless those who obey him or fulfill some other condition. **3.** *Law* A written agreement, as a contract, under seal. — **Covenant of the League of Nations** The first twenty-six articles of the Treaty of Versailles. — *v.t. & v.i.* To promise by or in a covenant. [< OF, < L *convenire* to meet together, agree]

cov·er (kuv′ər) *v.t.* **1.** To place something over or upon, as to protect or conceal. **2.** To provide with a cover or covering; clothe. **3.** To invest as if with a covering: *covered* with confusion. **4.** To hide; conceal: often with *up*. **5.** To provide shelter or protection for. **6.** To occupy the surface of: Snow *covered* the house. **7.** To treat of; include: His speech *covered* the tax problem. **8.** To be sufficient to pay, defray, or offset. **9.** To protect or guarantee (life, property, etc.) with insurance. **10.** To incubate or sit on, as eggs. **11.** To travel over: to *cover* 200 miles. **12.** To aim directly at, as with a firearm. **13.** *Mil.* To provide protective fire for (another person, unit, etc.). **14.** In journalism, to report the details of. **15.** In sports, to guard the activity of (an opponent); also, to protect (an area or position). **16.** To match; equal, as the wager of an opponent. **17.** In card games, to play a higher card than (the one previously played). — *v.i.* **18.** To spread over so as to overlay something. **19.** To put on a hat, cap, or the like. — *n.* **1.** That which covers or is laid over something else. **2.** Shelter; protection; concealment, as from enemy fire. **3.** Shrubbery, underbrush, etc. **4.** A pretense or pretext. **5.** In stamp collecting, an envelope or wrapper that bears a postmark. **6.** The table articles, as plate, silverware, napkin, etc., for one person. — **to break cover** To come from hiding. — **under cover** **1.** Protected. **2.** Secret or secretly. [< OF < L *co-* thoroughly + *operire* to hide] — **cov′er·er** *n.*

cov·er·age (kuv′ər·ij) *n.* **1.** The extent to which anything is covered, included, or reported. **2.** The protection afforded by an insurance policy.

cov·er·alls (kuv′ər·ôlz) *n.pl.* A one-piece work garment with sleeves, worn to protect the clothes. Also **cov′er·all**.

cover charge A fixed charge added to the bill at cabarets, hotels, etc., for entertainment or service.

cover crop *Agric.* A crop sown to protect the ground through winter and to enrich it when plowed under in the spring.

covered wagon *U.S.* A large wagon covered with canvas stretched over hoops, used esp. by American pioneers.

cover girl A female model who poses for magazine covers.

cov·er·ing (kuv′ər·ing) *n.* That which covers, protects, etc.

cov·er·let (kuv′ər·lit) *n.* A bedspread. Also **cov′er·lid**.

cov·ert (kuv′ərt, kō′vərt) *adj.* Concealed; secret; sheltered. — *n.* **1.** A covering. **2.** A shelter or hiding place, esp. for game. **3.** *pl. Ornithol.* Small feathers overlying the bases of tail and wing quills. [See COVER.] — **cov′ert·ly** *adv.*

covert cloth (kō′vərt, kuv′ərt) A twilled, chiefly woolen cloth of speckled appearance, used for suits, overcoats, etc.

cov·er-up (kuv′ər·up′) *n.* **1.** An act or effort designed to prevent facts or the truth from becoming known. **2.** A means of covering up or concealing something.

cov·et (kuv′it) *v.t.* **1.** To long for, esp. for something belonging to another. — *v.i.* **2.** To feel desire. [< OF < L *cupere* to desire] — **cov′et·a·ble** *adj.* — **cov′et·er** *n.*

cov·et·ous (kuv′ə·təs) *adj.* Excessively desirous (of something); avaricious; greedy. [< OF *coveitus*] — **cov′et·ous·ly** *adv.* — **cov′et·ous·ness** *n.*

cov·ey (kuv′ē) *n. pl.* **·eys** **1.** A flock of quails or partridges. **2.** A company; set. — Syn. See FLOCK¹. [< OF < L *cubare* to lie down]

cow¹ (kou) *n. pl.* **cows** (*Archaic* **kine**) **1.** The mature female of a bovine animal, esp. of the domesticated species. **2.** The mature female of some other animals, as of the whale, elephant, moose, etc. [OE *cū*]

cow² (kou) *v.t.* To overawe; intimidate; daunt. [< ON *kūga* to tyrannize over]

cow·ard (kou′ərd) *n.* One who yields unworthily to fear of pain or harm. — *adj.* Cowardly. [< OF < L *cauda* tail]

cow·ard·ice (kou′ər·dis) *n.* Lack of courage in the face of danger, pain, opposition, etc.; unworthy timidity.

cow·ard·ly (kou′ərd·lē) *adj.* **1.** Lacking courage; ignobly fearful. **2.** Befitting a coward: a *cowardly* lie. — *adv.* Like a coward; meanly. — **cow′ard·li·ness** *n.* — Syn. (adj.) **1.** craven, pusillanimous, spineless, yellow.

cow·bell (kou′bel) *n.* A bell hung around a cow's neck to indicate her whereabouts.

cow·ber·ry (kou′ber′ē, -bər·ē) *n. pl.* **·ries** A trailing evergreen shrub of the heath family, bearing red berries.

cow·bird (kou'bûrd') *n.* An American blackbird, often found with cattle. Also **cow blackbird.**

cow·boy (kou'boi') *n. U.S.* A man, usu. working on horseback, who herds and tends cattle on a ranch.

cow·catch·er (kou'kach'ər) *n.* An iron frame on the front of a locomotive or streetcar for clearing the track.

cow·er (kou'ər) *v.i.* To crouch, as in fear; tremble; quail. [ME *couren*, prob. < Scand.]

cow·fish (kou'fish) *n. pl.* **·fish** or **·fish·es** 1. Any of various small cetaceans, as the grampus, dolphin, etc. 2. A sirenian.

cow·girl (kou'gûrl') *n.* A girl who helps to herd and tend cattle or who dresses like a cowboy.

cow·hand (kou'hand') *n.* A cowboy.

cow·herd (kou'hûrd') *n.* One who herds cattle.

cow·hide (kou'hīd') *n.* 1. The skin of a cow, either before or after tanning. 2. A heavy, flexible leather whip. — *v.t.* **·hid·ed, ·hid·ing** To whip as with a cowhide.

cow killer A large, antlike wasp of the SW U.S.

cowl (koul) *n.* 1. A monk's hood; also, a hooded cloak. 2. A hood-shaped top for a chimney, to increase the draft. 3. *Aeron.* A cowling. 4. The part of an automobile body to which the windshield, instrument board, and the rear end of the hood are attached. — *v.t.* To cover with or as with a cowl. [OE < LL < L *cucullus* hood]

cowled (kould) *adj.* 1. Wearing a cowl. 2. Like a cowl.

cow·lick (kou'lik') *n.* A tuft of hair turned up.

cowl·ing (kou'ling) *n. Aeron.* The covering over or around the engine or any component of an aircraft. [< COWL]

cow·man (kou'mən) *n. pl.* **·men** (-mən) A rancher.

co-work·er (kō'wûr'kər) *n.* A fellow worker.

cow·pea (kou'pē') *n.* 1. A twining herb of the bean family, cultivated in the southern U.S. 2. The edible pea of this herb: also called *black-eyed pea.*

cow pony *U.S.* A small horse used in herding cattle.

cow·pox (kou'poks') *n. Vet.* An acute contagious disease of cows, forming pustules containing a virus that is used in making smallpox vaccine: also called *vaccinia.*

cow·punch·er (kou'pun'chər) *n. U.S. Informal* A cowboy. Also **cow'poke'.**

cow·ry (kou'rē) *n. pl.* **·ries** A glossy seashell of warm seas; esp. one used as money in Africa and southern Asia. Also **cow'rie.** [< Hind. *kaurī*]

cow·slip (kou'slip') *n.* 1. An English wildflower of the primrose family. 2. The marsh marigold of the U.S. [OE < *cū* cow + *slyppe* dung]

cox (koks) *n. Informal* Coxswain. — *v.t. & v.i.* To act as coxswain to (a boat).

cox·a (kok'sə) *n. pl.* **cox·ae** (kok'sē) *Anat.* The hip or hip joint. [< L, hip] — **cox'al** *adj.*

cox·comb (koks'kōm') *n.* 1. A pretentious and conceited young man. 2. A cockscomb. [Var. of *cockscomb*] — **cox·comb'i·cal** (koks·kom'i·kəl, -kō'mi-) *adj.*

cox·comb·ry (koks'kōm'rē) *adj. pl.* **·ries** Vain, foppish behavior; silly conceit; also, an instance of this.

cox·swain (kok'sən, kok'swān') *n.* One who steers or has charge of a small boat or a racing shell: also spelled *cockswain.* [< *cock* (see COCKBOAT) + SWAIN]

coy (koi) *adj.* 1. Shy and retiring. 2. Feigning shyness to attract attention. [< MF < OF < L *quietus* rest] — **coy'ish** *adj.* — **coy'ly** *adv.* — **coy'ness** *n.*

coy·o·te (kī·ō'tē, kī'ōt) *n.* A small wolf of western North America: also called *prairie wolf.* [< Am. Sp. < Nahuatl]

Coyote State Nickname of South Dakota.

coy·pu (koi'pōō) *n. pl.* **·pus** or **·pu** A South American rodent that yields a beaverlike fur known as nutria. Also **coy'pou.** [< native name]

coz (kuz) *n. Informal* A cousin.

coz·en (kuz'ən) *v.t. & v.i.* To cheat, esp. in a petty way; deceive. [< F *cousiner* to deceive by claiming kinship < *cousin.* See COUSIN.] — **coz'en·age** *n.* — **coz'en·er** *n.*

co·zy (kō'zē) *adj.* **·zi·er, ·zi·est** Snugly comfortable. — *n.* A padded cover for a teapot to keep it hot: also called *tea cozy.* [< dial. E *cosie*] — **co'zi·ly** *adv.* — **co'zi·ness** *n.*

crab¹ (krab) *n.* 1. A ten-footed crustacean having four pairs of legs, a pair of pincers, and a flattened carapace. 2. The hermit crab. 3. The horseshoe crab. — *v.* **crabbed, crab·bing** *v.t.* 1. To take or hunt crabs. 2. *U.S. Informal* To back out. [OE *crabba*]

crab² (krab) *n.* 1. The crab apple or crab tree. 2. An ill-tempered person. — *v.* **crabbed, crab·bing** *v.i.* 1. *Informal* To find fault; complain. — *v.t.* 2. *Informal* To spoil or ruin. 3. *Informal* To criticize; disparage. [? < Scand.]

crab apple 1. A kind of small, sour apple: also called *crab.* 2. A tree bearing crab apples.

crab·bed (krab'id) *adj.* 1. Sour-tempered; surly. 2. Hard to understand; abstruse. 3. Irregular in form; cramped. [< CRAB²] — **crab'bed·ly** *adv.* — **crab'bed·ness** *n.*

crab·ber (krab'ər) *n.* 1. One who fishes for crabs. 2. A boat used for crab fishing.

crab·by (krab'ē) *adj.* **·bi·er, ·bi·est** Ill-tempered; peevish.

crab grass A low-growing grass, a lawn pest.

crack (krak) *v.i.* 1. To break without separation of parts; also, to break apart or to pieces. 2. To make a sharp snapping sound, as in breaking. 3. To change tone abruptly to a higher register: said of the voice. 4. *Informal* To break down; fail. 5. *Slang* To speak flippantly; make remarks. — *v.t.* 6. To break partially or completely. 7. To cause to give forth a short, sharp sound: to *crack* a whip. 8. *Informal* To break into; open: to *crack* a safe. 9. *Informal* To find the solution of. 10. To cause (the voice) to crack. 11. *Informal* To strike sharply or with a sharp sound. 12. *Slang* To tell (a joke). 13. To break mentally; derange. 14. To reduce by distillation, as petroleum. — **to crack a book** *U.S. Slang* To open, as a textbook, and read or study. — **to crack a smile** *Slang* To smile. — **to crack down** *U.S. Informal* To take severe repressive measures: with *on.* — **to crack up** *Informal* 1. To crash or be in a crash. 2. To have a breakdown, nervous or physical. 3. *U.S. Slang* To become convulsed with laughter. — **to crack wise** *U.S. Slang* To wisecrack. — *n.* 1. A partial break, in which parts are not completely separated; a fissure. 2. A narrow space: Open the door a *crack.* 3. A sudden sharp sound, as of a rifle discharging. 4. *Informal* A resounding blow. 5. A defect; flaw. 6. A cracked tone of the voice. 7. *Informal* A try. 8. *Informal* A witty or sarcastic remark. — *adj. Informal* Of superior excellence: a *crack* shot. [OE *cracian*]

crack·brain (krak'brān') *n.* A weak-minded person.

crack·brained (krak'brānd') *adj.* Foolish; crazy.

cracked (krakt) *adj.* 1. Having a crack or cracks. 2. Broken to pieces. 3. Damaged or blemished. 4. *Informal* Mentally deranged. 5. Uneven in tone: said of the voice.

crack·er (krak'ər) *n.* 1. *U.S.* A thin, crisp biscuit. 2. *U.S.* A firecracker. 3. *U.S.* A cylindrical paper roll containing candy, etc., and a weak explosive set off by pulling strips of paper at either end: also **cracker bonbon.** 4. An impoverished white person of parts of the SE United States: a contemptuous term.

crack·er-bar·rel (krak'ər-bar'əl) *adj.* Characteristic of the informal, rambling discussions of those habitually gathered in a country store: *cracker-barrel* philosophy.

crack·er·jack (krak'ər-jak') *Slang adj.* Of exceptional quality; excellent. — *n.* A person or thing of exceptional merit or skill. Also **crack'a·jack'.**

Cracker State Nickname of Georgia.

crack·ing (krak'ing) *n. Chem.* A process by which the molecular structure of petroleum is changed under pressure by heat, etc., so that nonvolatile fractions are broken down to volatile fractions to produce high-octane gasoline.

crack·le (krak'əl) *v.* **·led, ·ling** *v.i.* 1. To make a succession of light, sharp sounds. — *v.t.* 2. To crush with such sounds. 3. To cover, as china, with a delicate network of cracks. — *n.* 1. A sound of crackling. 2. A network of fine cracks produced in the glaze of china, porcelain, etc. 3. Ware having such an appearance: also **crack'le·ware'** (-wâr').

crack·ling (krak'ling) *n.* 1. The giving forth of small sharp sounds. 2. The crisp browned skin of roasted pork. 3. *pl.* The crisp remains of fat after rendering.

crack·ly (krak'lē) *adj.* Likely to crackle; brittle.

crack·pot (krak'pot') *Slang n.* A weak-minded or eccentric person; a crank. — *adj.* Eccentric; foolish; insane.

crack·up (krak'up') *n.* 1. A crash, as of an airplane or automobile. 2. *Informal* A physical or mental breakdown.

-cracy *combining form* Government or authority: *democracy.* [< Gk. *-krateia* power < *krateein* to rule]

cra·dle (krād'l) *n.* 1. A small bed for an infant, usu. on rockers. 2. A place of origin. 3. A framework for supporting something under construction or repair. 4. A frame to protect an injured limb. 5. The holder for the receiver or handset of a telephone. 6. A frame attached to a scythe to catch the cut grain; also, such a scythe. 7. A low frame on casters for a mechanic to lie on while working under an automobile. — **to rob the cradle** *Informal* To marry or take as a sweetheart one much younger than oneself. — *v.* **·dled, ·dling** *v.t.* 1. To put into or rock in or as in a cradle; soothe. 2. To nurse in infancy; nurture. 3. To cut (grain) with a cradle. 4. To place or support in a cradle, as a ship. 5. *Mining* To wash, as gold-bearing gravel, in a cradle. — *v.i.* 6. To lie in or as in a cradle. 7. To cut or reap. [OE *cradol*]

cra·dle·song (krād'l·sông', -song') *n.* A lullaby (def. 1).

craft (kraft, kräft) *n.* 1. Skill or proficiency, esp. in hand work; loosely, art. 2. Skill in deception. 3. An occupation or trade, usually one calling for manual skill. 4. The membership of a particular trade. 5. A vessel or an aircraft: also used collectively. — **Syn.** See OCCUPATION. [OE *cræft* skill, art, strength, courage]

-craft *combining form* Skill; trade; art of: *woodcraft.*

crafts·man (krafts'mən, kräfts'-) *n. pl.* **·men** (-mən) One skilled in a craft or art. — **crafts'man·ship** *n.*

craft union A labor union limited to workers who perform the same type of work: also called *horizontal union.*

craft·y (kraf'tē, kräf'-) *adj.* **craft·i·er, craft·i·est** Skillful in deceiving; cunning. — **craft'i·ly** *adv.* — **craft'i·ness** *n.*

crag (krag) *n.* A rough, steep, or prominently projecting rock. [ME *cragg* < Celtic]

crag·gy (krag′ē) *adj.* **·gi·er, ·gi·est** Having numerous crags. Also **crag′ged** (krag′id). — **crag′gi·ness** *n.*

crake (krāk) *n.* Any of various small, harsh-voiced birds of the rail family. [< ON *kraka* crow]

cram (kram) *v.* **crammed, cram·ming** *v.t.* **1.** To force into an inadequate space; stuff. **2.** To fill or pack tightly. **3.** To feed to excess. **4.** To force (information) into the mind, or to fill (a person or his mind) with information, as in intensive study. — *v.i.* **5.** To eat greedily; stuff oneself with food. **6.** To engage in intensive, hurried study. — *n.* **1.** The act or process of cramming. **2.** A crowded condition; a crush. [OE *crammian* to stuff] — **cram′mer** *n.*

cramp¹ (kramp) *n.* **1.** An involuntary, sudden, painful muscular contraction. **2.** A paralysis of local muscles caused by overexertion. **3.** *pl.* Acute abdominal pains. — *v.t.* To affect with a cramp. [< OF *crampe*]

cramp² (kramp) *n.* **1.** An iron bar bent at both ends, used to bind two stones, timbers, etc., together. **2.** An adjustable frame in which pieces may be held together; a clamp. **3.** Anything that presses or confines. — *v.t.* **1.** To fasten with a cramp. **2.** To restrain or confine; hamper. **3.** To steer; also, to jam (a wheel) by turning too short. — **to cramp one's style** *Slang* To hamper one's customary skill or self-confidence. — *adj.* **1.** Narrowed; contracted. **2.** Difficult to read or make out. [ME < MDu. *krampe* hook.]

cramp·fish (kramp′fish′) *n. pl.* **·fish** or **·fish·es** The electric ray.

cram·pon (kram′pən) *n.* **1.** A pair of hooked pieces of iron for raising heavy stones, etc. **2.** *Usu. pl.* An iron attachment for the shoe to aid in walking on ice or in climbing. Also **cram·poon** (kram-pōōn′). [< MF *crampe* hook]

CRAMPON
(def. 2)

cran·ber·ry (kran′ber′ē, -bər·ē) *n. pl.* **·ries 1.** The edible, scarlet, acid berry of a plant growing in marshy land. **2.** The plant itself.

crane (krān) *n.* **1.** One of a family of large, long-necked, long-legged birds, as the rare **whooping crane** of North America. **2.** Loosely, any of various herons or cormorants. **3.** A hoisting machine, usually having a projecting movable arm, by which a heavy object can be raised and moved. **4.** Any arm swinging horizontally, by which something is suspended. — *v.* **craned, cran·ing** *v.t. & v.i.* **1.** To stretch out one's neck, as a crane does. **2.** To lift or move by or as if by a crane. [OE *cran*]

crane·bill (krān′bil′) *n.* Any species of geranium. Also **cranes′bill** (krānz′bil′), **crane′s-bill′**.

crane fly A fly with very long, slender legs.

cranio- *combining form* Cranium; cranial. Also, before vowels, **crani-**. [< Med.L *cranium* skull]

cra·ni·ol·o·gy (krā′nē·ol′ə·jē) *n.* The branch of anatomy that treats of skulls. — **cra·ni·o·log·i·cal** (krā′nē·ə·loj′i·kəl) *adj.* — **cra′ni·ol′o·gist** *n.*

cra·ni·om·e·ter (krā′nē·om′ə·tər) *n.* An instrument for measuring skulls. — **cra′ni·o·met′ric** (-ə·met′rik) or **·ri·cal** *adj.* — **cra′ni·o·met′ri·cal·ly** *adv.* — **cra·ni·om′e·try** *n.*

cra·ni·um (krā′nē·əm) *n. pl.* **·ni·ums** or **·ni·a** (-nē·ə) The skull, esp. the part enclosing the brain. [< Med.L < Gk. *kranion* skull] — **cra′ni·al** *adj.*

crank (krangk) *n.* **1.** A device for transmitting motion, usu. a handle attached at right angles to a shaft. **2.** *Informal* One given to eccentric or hostile behavior. **3.** *Informal* A grouchy person. **4.** A fantastic turn of speech; conceit. **5.** A perverse notion or action; whim. — *v.t.* **1.** To bend into the shape of a crank. **2.** To furnish with a crank. **3.** To start or operate by a crank. — *v.i.* **4.** To turn a crank. [OE *cranc*]

crank·case (krangk′kās′) *n. Mech.* The case enclosing an engine crankshaft, as of an automobile.

cran·kle (krang′kəl) *n.* A bend; crinkle. — *v.t. & v.i.* **·kled, ·kling** To bend; crinkle. [Dim. of CRANK]

crank·shaft (krangk′shaft′, -shäft′) *n. Mech.* A shaft driven by or driving a crank.

crank·y (krang′kē) *adj.* **crank·i·er, crank·i·est 1.** Irritable; peevish. **2.** Eccentric; queer. **3.** Loose and rickety; shaky. **4.** *Naut.* Liable to heel; top-heavy: also **crank**. [< CRANK] — **crank′i·ly** *adv.* — **crank′i·ness** *n.*

cran·ny (kran′ē) *n. pl.* **·nies** A narrow crevice or chink, as in a wall. [? < OF *cran, cren* notch] — **cran′nied** *adj.*

crap (krap) *U.S. n.* **1.** The game of craps. **2.** A losing throw in craps. **3.** *Slang* Statements that lie, mislead, or exaggerate. **4.** *Slang* Anything worthless. [See CRAPS]

crape (krāp) See CREPE.

crap·pie (krap′ē) *n. pl.* **·pies** or **·pie** An edible fresh-water fish of the central U.S.

craps (kraps) *n.pl.* (construed as sing.) *U.S.* A game of chance, played with two dice. [< F < E *crabs*, the lowest throw (two aces) in hazard]

crap-shoot·er (krap′shōō′tər) *n. U.S.* One who plays the game of craps.

crap·u·lent (krap′yōō·lənt) *adj.* **1.** Grossly intemperate in eating or drinking. **2.** Sick from eating or drinking too much. Also **crap′u·lous.** [< LL < L < Gk. *kraipalē* drunken headache] — **crap′u·lence** *n.*

crash¹ (krash) *v.i.* **1.** To break to pieces with a loud noise. **2.** To suffer damage or destruction, as by falling or striking something. **3.** To make a loud, sharp noise of breaking. **4.** To move with such a noise. **5.** To fail or come to ruin. — *v.t.* **6.** To dash violently to pieces; smash. **7.** To force or drive with a sound of crashing. **8.** To cause (an airplane, automobile, etc.) to crash. **9.** *Informal* To enter without invitation or without paying admission. — *n.* **1.** A loud noise, as of things being violently broken. **2.** A sudden collapse, as of a business enterprise. **3.** The act of crashing, as of an airplane, automobile, etc. — *adj. U.S. Informal* Of, pertaining to, or resembling a crash program. [Imit.]

crash² (krash) *n.* A coarse fabric woven of thick, uneven yarns, used for towels, etc. [? < Russian *krashenina*]

crash dive *Naval* The quick submergence of a submarine.

crash helmet A heavy, padded helmet.

crash landing An emergency landing of an airplane.

crash program *U.S. Informal* An intensive emergency undertaking in government, science, etc., having priority over all others. Also **crash project**.

crass (kras) *adj.* **1.** Grossly vulgar or stupid. **2.** Coarse or thick. [< L *crassus* thick] — **crass′ly** *adv.* — **crass′ness** *n.*

-crat *combining form* A supporter or member of a social class or of a type of government: *democrat, aristocrat.* [< F *-crate* < Gk. *-kratēs* < *kratein* to rule, govern]

crate (krāt) *n.* **1.** A protective case or framework of slats in which to pack something for shipment. **2.** *Slang* A decrepit vehicle or airplane. — *v.t.* **crat·ed, crat·ing** To pack in a crate. [Prob. < L *cratis* wickerwork] — **crat′er** *n.*

cra·ter (krā′tər) *n.* **1.** A bowl-shaped depression at the outlet of a volcano. **2.** Any similar cavity, as one resulting from the explosion of a bomb. [< L < Gk. *kratēr* bowl]

cra·vat (krə·vat′) *n.* **1.** A necktie. **2.** A scarf. [< F *Cravate* a Croatian; with ref. to the neckcloths worn by Croatian soldiers]

crave (krāv) *v.* **craved, crav·ing** *v.t.* **1.** To long for; desire greatly. **2.** To be in need of; require. **3.** To ask for earnestly; beg. — *v.i.* **4.** To desire or long: with *for* or *after.* [OE *crafian*] — **crav′er** *n.*

cra·ven (krā′vən) *adj.* Conspicuously lacking in courage; cowardly. — *n.* A base coward. [? < OF < L *crepare* to creak, break] — **cra′ven·ly** *adv.* — **cra′ven·ness** *n.*

craw (krô) *n.* **1.** The crop of a bird. **2.** The stomach of any animal. — **to stick in one's craw** To be displeasing or unacceptable. [ME *crawe.* Akin to Du. *kraag* neck.]

craw·fish (krô′fish′) *n. pl.* **·fish** or **·fish·es** A crayfish.

crawl¹ (krôl) *v.i.* **1.** To move along slowly with the body on or close to the ground. **2.** To move slowly, feebly, or cautiously. **3.** To be covered with things that crawl. **4.** To feel as if covered with crawling things. **5.** To behave with servility. — *n.* **1.** The act of crawling. **2.** An overarm swimming stroke performed face down, combined with a flutter kick. [Prob. < ON *krafla* to paw] — **crawl′er** *n.* — **crawl′ing·ly** *adv.*

crawl² (krôl) *n.* A pen in shallow water for confining fish, turtles, etc. [See KRAAL.]

crawl·y (krô′lē) *adj.* **crawl·i·er, crawl·i·est** *Informal* Creepy.

cray·fish (krā′fish′) *n. pl.* **·fish** or **·fish·es 1.** A fresh-water crustacean resembling the lobster. **2.** Loosely, the spiny lobster. Also *crawfish.* [Earlier *crevice* < OF < OHG *krebiz*]

cray·on (krā′ən, -on) *n.* **1.** A stick of colored wax, chalk, etc., for use in drawing. **2.** A drawing made with crayons. — *v.t. & v.i.* To sketch or draw with crayons. [< F, pencil]

craze (krāz) *v.* **crazed, craz·ing** *v.t.* **1.** To render insane or demented. **2.** To make full of minute cracks, as the glaze of pottery. — *v.i.* **3.** To become insane. **4.** To become full of minute cracks. — *n.* **1.** A brief fashion or fad; rage. **2.** An extravagant liking or enthusiasm. **3.** Mental disorder; insanity. **4.** A minute flaw in the glaze of pottery, etc. [ME *crasen* to crack] — **crazed** *adj.*

cra·zy (krā′zē) *adj.* **·zi·er, ·zi·est 1.** Disordered in mind; insane; demented; mad; maniacal. **2.** *Informal* Very enthusiastic or excited. **3.** *Informal* Unpredictable or inexplicable: *a crazy driver.* **4.** Dilapidated; rickety; unsound. — **cra′zi·ly** *adv.* — **cra′zi·ness** *n.*

crazy bone The funny bone.

crazy quilt A patchwork quilt made of pieces of various sizes, shapes, and colors.

creak (krēk) *n.* A sharp, squeaking sound, as from friction. — *v.t. & v.i.* To produce or cause to produce a creak. [Imit.]

creak·y (krē′kē) *adj.* **·i·er, ·i·est 1.** Creaking. **2.** Likely to creak: a *creaky* step. — **creak′i·ly** *adv.* — **creak′i·ness** *n.*

cream (krēm) *n.* **1.** An oily, yellowish substance contained in milk. **2.** The best part. **3.** The yellowish white color of cream. **4.** A food or delicacy made with or resembling cream. **5.** Something resembling cream. **6.** A soft, oily cosmetic for cleansing or protecting the skin. — *v.t.* **1.** To skim cream from. **2.** To take the best part from. **3.** To add cream to, as coffee. **4.** To permit (milk) to form cream. **5.** To beat, as butter and sugar, to a creamy consistency. **6.** *U.S. Slang* To defeat decisively. — *v.i.* **7.** To froth or foam. **8.** To form cream. [< OF < LL *chrisma* chrism]

cream cheese Soft, white cheese made of cream or a mixture of cream and milk.

cream·er (krē′mər) *n.* **1.** A small pitcher used for serving cream. **2.** Any device in which cream is separated.

cream·er·y (krē′mər·ē) *n.* *pl.* **·er·ies 1.** A place where milk products are prepared or sold.

cream of tartar Potassium bitartrate.

cream puff A shell of pastry filled with whipped cream or custard. **2.** *Slang* A sissy; weakling.

cream·y (krē′mē) *adj.* **cream·i·er, cream·i·est 1.** Containing cream. **2.** Resembling cream. — **cream′i·ness** *n.*

crease¹ (krēs) *n.* A mark or line made by folding or wrinkling. — *v.* **creased, creas·ing** *v.t.* **1.** To make a crease, line, or fold in; wrinkle. **2.** To graze with a bullet. — *v.i.* **3.** To become wrinkled. [ME *creaste*, ? var. of *creste* crest, ridge]

crease² (krēs) See KRIS.

creas·y (krē′sē) *adj.* **creas·i·er, creas·i·est** Creased.

cre·ate (krē·āt′) *v.t.* **·at·ed, ·at·ing 1.** To cause to come into existence; originate. **2.** To be the cause of; occasion: To *create* interest. **3.** To produce (a work of art, etc.). **4.** To be the first to portray, as a character or part. **5.** To invest with new office, rank, etc.; appoint. [< L *creare* to produce, create]

cre·a·tion (krē·ā′shən) *n.* **1.** The act of creating, or the fact of being created. **2.** Anything created. **3.** *Usu. cap.* God's bringing of the universe into existence. **4.** The universe; also, all living creatures. — **cre·a′tion·al** *adj.*

cre·a·tive (krē·ā′tiv) *adj.* **1.** Having the power or ability to create. **2.** Characterized by originality of thought and execution. **3.** Productive: with *of*. — **cre·a′tive·ly** *adv.* — **cre·a′tive·ness, cre·a·tiv·i·ty** (krē′ā·tiv′ə·tē, ə·tiv′-) *n.*

cre·a·tor (krē·ā′tər) *n.* One who or that which creates. — **the Creator** God. — **cre·a′tor·ship** *n.*

crea·ture (krē′chər) *n.* **1.** A living being; especially, an animal. **2.** A person. **3.** That which has been created. **4.** One who is dependent upon, influenced by, or subordinate to something or someone; puppet; tool. **5.** *U.S.* A domestic animal. [< OF < LL < L *creare* to produce]

crèche (kresh, krāsh) *n.* **1.** A group of figures representing the scene in the stable at the Nativity. **2.** A foundling asylum. **3.** *Brit.* A public day nursery. [< F, crib, cradle]

cre·dence (krēd′ns) *n.* Belief, esp. as based upon the evidence of others. [< MF < L *credere* to believe]

cre·den·tial (kri·den′shəl) *n.* **1.** That which entitles one to authority or confidence. **2.** *Usually pl.* A certificate or letter giving evidence of one's authority or identity. [< Med.L *credentia* belief + -AL¹]

cre·den·za (kri·den′zə) *n.* A sideboard or buffet. [< Ital. < Med.L < L *credere* to believe.]

credibility gap A situation in which claims or promises are unlikely to be believed; lack of trust.

cred·i·ble (kred′ə·bəl) *adj.* **1.** Capable of being believed. **2.** Worthy of confidence; reliable. [< L < *credere* to believe] — **cred′i·bil′i·ty, cred′i·ble·ness** *n.* — **cred′i·bly** *adv.*

cred·it (kred′it) *n.* **1.** Belief in the genuineness or truth of something; trust; faith. **2.** The quality of being trustworthy. **3.** A good reputation. **4.** A source of honor or good repute: a *credit* to one's family. **5.** Approval for some action or quality. **6.** Influence derived from the good opinion of others. **7.** *Usu. pl.* Acknowledgment of a book, motion picture, play, etc. **8.** Confidence in the ability of an individual, firm, etc., to fulfill financial obligations: to buy on *credit*. **9.** Reputation for commercial integrity. **10.** The time extended for payment of a liability. **11.** In bookkeeping: **a** The entry of any amount paid by a debtor, or the amount entered. **b** The right-hand side of an account, where values received are entered. **12.** In an account, the balance in one's favor. **13.** *U.S.* Official certification that a student has passed a course of study; also, a unit of academic study. — *v.t.* **1.** To accept as true. **2.** To ascribe, as intelligence or honor, to: with *with*. **3.** In bookkeeping, to give credit for or enter as credit to. **4.** *U.S.* to give educational credits to (a student). [< MF < L *credere* to believe, trust]

cred·it·a·ble (kred′it·ə·bəl) *adj.* Deserving credit or esteem; praiseworthy. — **cred′it·a·bil′i·ty, cred′it·a·ble·ness** *n.* — **cred′it·a·bly** *adv.*

credit card A card entitling its holder to buy on credit.

cred·i·tor (kred′i·tər) *n.* One to whom money is owed. [< AF < L < *credere* to believe, trust]

credit rating An estimate or rating of the solvency or commercial integrity of a person or business.

credit union A cooperative group for making loans to its members at low rates of interest.

cre·do (krē′dō, krā′-) *n.* *pl.* **·dos 1.** A set of beliefs; a creed. **2.** *Often cap.* The Apostles' Creed or the Nicene Creed; also, a musical setting for this. [< L, I believe]

cre·du·li·ty (krə·dōō′lə·tē, -dyōō′-) *n.* Readiness to believe on slight evidence; gullibility.

cred·u·lous (krej′ōō·ləs) *adj.* **1.** Disposed to believe on slight evidence. **2.** Arising from credulity. [< L < *credere* to believe] — **cred′u·lous·ly** *adv.* — **cred′u·lous·ness** *n.*

Cree (krē) *n.* *pl.* **Cree** or **Crees 1.** One of an Algonquian tribe of North American Indians formerly dwelling in Manitoba and Saskatchewan. **2.** The language of this tribe.

creed (krēd) *n.* **1.** A formal statement of religious belief or doctrine. **2.** Any organized system or statement of beliefs, principles, etc. — **Syn.** See DOCTRINE. — **the Creed** The Apostles' Creed. [OE < L *credo* I believe.]

creek (krēk, krik) *n.* *U.S.* A stream intermediate in size between a brook and a river. **2.** *Chiefly Brit.* A narrow inlet or cove in a shoreline. [ME *creke, crike* < Scand.]

Creek (krēk) *n.* **1.** A member of one of various tribes of North American Indians, once occupying parts of Georgia, Alabama, and Florida. **2.** Their Muskhogean language.

creel (krēl) *n.* An angler's wicker basket for carrying fish. [Appar. related to OF *greille* grating]

creep (krēp) *v.i.* **crept, creep·ing 1.** To move with the body close to or touching the ground; crawl. **2.** To move imperceptibly, stealthily, or timidly. **3.** To act servilely; cringe. **4.** To grow along a surface or support, as a vine. **5.** To have a sensation of being covered with creeping things. **6.** To slip out of position. — *n.* **1.** The act of creeping. **2.** *pl. Informal* A feeling of apprehension. [OE *crēopan*]

creep·er (krē′pər) *n.* **1.** One who or that which creeps. **2.** *Bot.* A plant growing along or across a surface by sending out short stems. **3.** *pl.* A baby's garment resembling overalls.

creep·y (krē′pē) *adj.* **creep·i·er, creep·i·est 1.** Having or producing a feeling of fear or repugnance. **2.** Characterized by a creeping motion. — **creep′i·ly** *adv.* — **creep′i·ness** *n.*

creese (krēs) See KRIS.

cre·mate (krē′māt, kri·māt′) *v.t.* **·mat·ed, ·mat·ing** To burn (a dead body) to ashes. [< L *cremare* to burn to ashes] — **cre·ma·tion** (kri·mā′shən) *n.* — **cre′ma·tor** *n.*

cre·ma·to·ry (krē′mə·tôr′ē, -tō′rē, krem′ə-) *adj.* Related to cremation. — *n.* *pl.* **·ries** A furnace or establishment for cremating dead bodies: also **cre′ma·to′ri·um**.

crème (krem) *n.* *French* Cream: used in names of sauces and liqueurs.

crème de ca·ca·o (də kə·kā′ō, -kā′ō) *French* A sweet, chocolate-flavored liqueur.

crème de menthe (də mänt) *French* A sweet, green or white cordial with a strong flavor of mint.

Cre·mo·na (kri·mō′nə, *Ital.* krā·mō′nä) *n.* Any violin made at Cremona, Italy, from the 16th to the 18th century, by the Amati family, by Antonio Stradivari, and others.

cre·nate (krē′nāt) *adj. Bot.* Scalloped or toothed with even, rounded notches, as a leaf or margin. Also **cre′nat·ed**. [< NL < *crena* notch] — **cre′nate·ly** *adv.* — **cre·na′tion** *n.*

cren·el (kren′əl) *n.* One of the embrasures, or indentations, of a battlement. — *v.t.* **cren·eled** or **·elled, cren·el·ing** or **·el·ling** To crenelate. [< OF, dim. of *cren* notch]

cren·el·ate (kren′ə·lāt) *v.t.* **·lat·ed, ·lat·ing** To provide with battlements or crenels. Also *Brit.* **cren′el·late.** — **cren′el·a′tion, cren′el·la′tion** *n.*

Cre·ole (krē′ōl) *n.* **1.** A native of Spanish America or the West Indies but of European descent. **2.** A descendant of the original French settlers of the southern U.S., esp. of Louisiana. **3.** The French patois spoken by the Louisiana Creoles. — *adj.* Of, relating to, or peculiar to the Creoles. [< F *créole* < Sp. < L *creare* to create]

Creole State Nickname of Louisiana.

cre·o·sol (krē′ə·sōl, -sol) *n. Chem.* A colorless, aromatic, oily liquid compound, $C_8H_{10}O_2$, derived from beechwood tar by distillation. [< CREOS(OTE) + -OL²]

cre·o·sote (krē′ə·sōt) *n. Chem.* An oily liquid obtained by the distillation of wood tar and coal tar, used as an antiseptic and preservative. — *v.t.* **·sot·ed, ·sot·ing** To treat or impregnate with creosote, as shingles, etc. [< Gk. *kreas* flesh + *sōtēr* preserver < *sōzein* to save]

crepe (krāp) *n.* **1.** A thin fabric of silk, cotton, wool, or synthetic fiber, having a crinkled surface. **2.** Black crepe used as a sign of mourning, as in an armband: in this sense usu. *crape*. **3.** Tissue paper resembling crepe: also **crepe paper**. Also spelled *crape*: also **crêpe**. [< F (*tissu*) *crêpe* crinkled (cloth) < L *crispus* curled]

crêpes su·zette (krep′ sōō·zet′) Thin egg pancakes usu. served aflame in cognac or curacao.

crep·i·tate (krep′ə·tāt) *v.i.* **·tat·ed, ·tat·ing** To crackle; rattle. [< L *crepitare*, freq. of *crepare* to creak] — **crep′i·tant** *adj.* — **crep′i·ta′tion** *n.*

crept (krept) Past tense of CREEP.

cre·pus·cu·lar (kri·pus′kya·lər) *adj.* 1. Dim; obscure. 2. *Zool.* Appearing or flying in the twilight.

cres·cen·do (krə·shen′dō, -sen′-) *Music n. pl.* **·dos** A gradual increase in volume: expressed by the sign ——: opposed to *diminuendo.* — *v.i.* **·doed, ·do·ing** To produce a crescendo. [< Ital., ppr. of *crescere* to increase < L]

cres·cent (kres′ənt) *n.* 1. The visible part of the moon in its first or last quarter, having one concave edge and one convex edge. 2. Something crescent-shaped. 3. The device on the Turkish standard. — **the Crescent** Turkish or Moslem power. — *adj.* 1. Increasing: said of the moon in its first quarter. 2. Shaped like the moon in its first quarter. [< L *crescens, -entis,* ppr. of *crescere* to increase]

cre·sol (krē′sōl, -sol) *n. Chem.* A liquid or crystalline compound, C₇H₈O, obtained by the destructive distillation of coal tar, used as an antiseptic. [Var. of CREOSOL]

cress (kres) *n.* One of various plants of the mustard family, as watercress, pungent to taste, used in salads. [OE *cresse*]

cres·set (kres′it) *n.* A metal holder for burning oil, wood, etc., for illumination. [< OF *craicet, craisset*]

crest (krest) *n.* 1. A comb, tuft, or projection on the head of an animal, esp. of birds. 2. The top of a wave. 3. The highest point or stage: the *crest* of a flood. 4. The projection on the top of a helmet; a plume. — *v.t.* 1. To furnish with a crest. 2. To reach the crest of. — *v.i.* 3. To come to a crest, as a wave. [< OF < L *crista* tuft] — **crest′ed** *adj.* — **crest′less** *adj.*

crest·fall·en (krest′fô′lən) *adj.* 1. Depressed; dispirited; dejected. 2. Having a fallen or drooping crest.

cre·ta·ceous (kri·tā′shəs) *adj.* Consisting of, containing, or resembling chalk. [< L *creta* chalk]

Cre·ta·ceous (kri·tā′shəs) *Geol. adj.* Of or pertaining to the third geologic period of the Mesozoic era. — *n.* The system of rocks deposited during this period. See chart under GEOLOGY.

cre·tin (krē′tin, krēt′n) *n.* A person afflicted with cretinism. [< F *crétin,* var. of *chrétien* Christian, human being, i.e., not an animal] — **cre′tin·ous** *adj.*

cre·tin·ism (krē′tən·iz′əm) *n. Pathol.* A congenital condition associated with thyroid deficiency, marked by arrested physical development, goiter, and mental retardation.

cre·tonne (kri·ton′, krē′ton) *n.* A heavy, unglazed cotton, linen, or rayon fabric printed in colored patterns, used esp. for draperies. [after *Creton,* a village in Normandy]

cre·vasse (krə·vas′) *n.* 1. A deep fissure or chasm, as in a glacier. 2. *U.S.* A breach in a levee. — *v.t.* **·vassed, ·vass·ing** To split with crevasses. [See CREVICE.]

crev·ice (krev′is) *n.* A fissure or crack on or through the surface of something; cleft; chink. [< OF *crevace* < LL < L *crepare* to crack, creak] — **crev′iced** *adj.*

crew¹ (kroō) *n.* 1. The company of men belonging to one ship, aircraft, etc. 2. A body of men organized or detailed for a particular job: a repair *crew.* 3. A group trained to handle a racing shell. 4. A company of people; crowd; gang. [< OF < L *crescere* to increase]

crew² (kroō) Past tense of CROW.

crew cut *U.S.* A closely cropped haircut.

crew·el (kroō′əl) *n.* A slackly twisted worsted yarn, used in fancywork. [Origin uncertain] — **crew′el·work′** *n.*

crib (krib) *n.* 1. A child's bed, with side railings. 2. A box, bin, or small building for grain, having slat or openwork sides. 3. A rack or manger for fodder. 4. A stall for cattle. 5. A small house, cottage, or room. 6. A framework of wood or metal, used to retain or support something, as in mines. 7. *Informal* A plagiarism. 8. *Informal* A translation or other unauthorized aid employed by students. — *v.* **cribbed, crib·bing** *v.t.* 1: To enclose in or as in a crib. 2. To line or bolster, as the walls of a pit, with timbers or planking. 3. *Informal* To plagiarize. — *v.i.* 4. *Informal* To use a crib in translating. [OE *cribb*] — **crib′ber** *n.*

crib·bage (krib′ij) *n.* A game of cards for two, three, or four players, the score being kept on a pegboard.

crib death The sudden death, usu. during sleep, of an apparently healthy baby for unknown reasons. Also *sudden infant death syndrome.*

crick (krik) *n.* A painful spasm of the muscles, as of the neck; a cramp. — *v.t.* To turn or twist so as to produce a crick. [Origin uncertain]

crick·et¹ (krik′it) *n.* A leaping insect having long antennae, the male of which makes a chirping sound by friction of the forewings. [< OF < LG; orig. imit.]

crick·et² (krik′it) *n.* 1. An outdoor game played with bats, a ball, and wickets, between two sides of eleven each, popular in England. 2. *Informal* Fair play; sportsmanship. — *v.i.* To play cricket. [< F] — **crick′et·er** *n.*

crick·et³ (krik′it) *n.* A footstool. [Origin unknown]

cried (krīd) Past tense and past participle of CRY.

cri·er (krī′ər) *n.* 1. One who cries. 2. One who makes public announcements, as of sales, news, etc. 3. A hawker.

crime (krīm) *n.* 1. *Law* An act or omission in violation of public law, esp. a felony. 2. Any grave offense against morality or social order. 3. *Informal* Any apparent injustice; a shame. [< OF < L *crimen* accusation]

Crimean War See table for WAR.

crim·i·nal (krim′ə·nəl) *adj.* 1. Implying or involving crime. 2. *Law* Pertaining to the administration of penal as opposed to civil law: a *criminal* court. 3. Guilty of crime. — *n.* One who has committed a crime. [< OF < L < *crimen* charge] — **crim′i·nal·ly** *adv.* — **crim′i·nal′i·ty** *n.*

crim·i·nol·o·gy (krim′ə·nol′ə·jē) *n.* The scientific study and investigation of crime and the behavior of criminals. [< L *crimen, criminis* crime + -LOGY] — **crim·i·no·log·i·cal** (krim′ə·nə·loj′i·kəl) *adj.* — **crim′i·nol·o·gist** *n.*

crimp¹ (krimp) *v.t.* 1. To bend or press into ridges or folds. 2. To curl or wave. — *n.* Something that has been crimped. — **to put a crimp in** *Informal* To hinder or obstruct. [< MDu. *crimpen* to wrinkle] — **crimp′er** *n.* — **crimp′y** *adj.*

crimp² (krimp) *n.* One who gets sailors, soldiers, etc., to serve by decoying or entrapping them. — *v.t.* To decoy or entrap into forced military service. [Origin uncertain]

crim·son (krim′zən) *n.* A deep red color. — *adj.* 1. Of a deep red color. 2. Bloody. — *v.t. & v.i.* To make or become crimson. [ME < Sp. < Arabic < *qirmiz* insect]

cringe (krinj) *v.i.* **cringed, cring·ing** 1. To shrink or crouch in fear or cowardice. 2. To fawn. — *n.* A servile crouching. [ME *cringen, crengen*] — **cring′er** *n.*

crin·gle (kring′gəl) *n. Naut.* A small loop or grommet of rope or metal, attached to the edge of a sail. [Appar. < LG]

crin·kle (kring′kəl) *v.t. & v.i.* **·kled, ·kling** 1. To form or cause to form wrinkles, turns, etc. 2. To rustle or crackle. — *n.* A wrinkle or fold. [ME *crenklen* to curl up] — **crin′kly** *adj.*

cri·noid (krī′noid, krin′oid) *adj.* 1. *Zool.* Of or pertaining to animals having jointed stems attached by stalks to the sea bottom, and radial arms. 2. Lilylike. — *n.* A crinoid animal. [< NL < Gk. < *krinon* lily + *eidos* form]

crin·o·line (krin′ə·lin, -lēn) *n.* 1. A stiff fabric, used in puffed sleeves, hems, interlinings, etc., originally made of horsehair and linen. 2. A petticoat of this fabric. 3. A hoop skirt. [< F < L *crinis* hair + *linum* linen]

crip·ple (krip′əl) *n.* A lame or disabled person or animal; one lacking the natural use of a limb or the body. — *v.t.* **·pled, ·pling** 1. To make lame. 2. To impair or disable. [OE *crypel*] — **crip′pler** *n.*

cri·sis (krī′sis) *n. pl.* **·ses** (-sēz) 1. A crucial turning point in an affair or of a series of events. 2. A critical moment. 3. *Pathol.* Any decisive change in the course of a disease, favorable or unfavorable. [< L < Gk. < *krinein* to decide]

crisp (krisp) *adj.* 1. Brittle; easily crumbled. 2. Fresh and firm: *crisp* vegetables. 3. Brisk; invigorating: a *crisp* breeze. 4. Stimulating; lively: a *crisp* conversation. 5. Terse or pithy; curt: a *crisp* retort. 6. Having tight curls or waves, as hair. — *v.t. & v.i.* To make or become crisp. [OE < L *crispus* curled] — **crisp′ly** *adv.* — **crisp′ness** *n.*

crisp·y (kris′pē) *adj.* **crisp·i·er, crisp·i·est** Crisp.

criss·cross (kris′krôs′, -kros′) *v.t.* 1. To cross with interlacing lines. — *v.i.* 2. To move in crisscrosses. — *adj.* Marked by crossings. — *n.* 1. The cross of one who cannot write. 2. A group of intersecting lines. — *adv.* Crosswise [Alter. of *Christcross*]

cri·te·ri·on (krī·tir′ē·ən) *n. pl.* **·te·ri·a** (-tir′ē·ə) or **·te·ri·ons** A standard or rule by which a judgment can be made; a model, test, or measure. [< Gk. < *krinein* to decide]

crit·ic (krit′ik) *n.* 1. One who judges the merits of anything by some standard or criterion. 2. A skilled judge of literary, theatrical, or other artistic creations. 3. One who judges severely. [< L < Gk. < *kritēs* judge]

crit·i·cal (krit′i·kəl) *adj.* 1. Given to faultfinding or severe judgments; carping. 2. Exhibiting careful, precise judgments; analytical: a *critical* report. 3. Of or characteristic of a critic or criticism. 4. Of the nature of a crisis or turning point; crucial; decisive. 5. Attended with danger; risky; perilous. 6. Necessary for the prosecution of a war: *critical* materiel. 7. *Physics* Indicating a decisive change in a specified condition. — **crit′i·cal·ly** *adv.* — **crit′i·cal·ness** *n.*

crit·i·cism (krit′ə·siz′əm) *n.* 1. The act of criticizing, esp. disapprovingly. 2. A severe or unfavorable judgment. 3. The art of making informed and discriminating judgments. 4. The occupation or profession of a critic. 5. A review, article, or commentary expressing a critical judgment.

crit·i·cize (krit′ə·sīz) *v.t. & v.i.* **·cized, ·ciz·ing** 1. To judge severely; censure. 2. To pass judgment on the merits or faults of. Also *Brit.* **crit′i·cise.** — **crit′i·ciz′a·ble** *adj.* — **crit′i·ciz′er** *n.*

cri·tique (kri·tēk′) *n.* 1. A critical review, esp. of a work of art or literature. 2. The art of criticism. [< F]

crit·ter (krit′ər) *n.* *U.S. Dial.* A creature.

croak (krōk) *v.i.* 1. To utter a hoarse, low-pitched cry, as a frog or crow. 2. To speak in a low, hoarse voice. 3. To talk in a doleful tone; grumble. 4. *Slang* To die. —*v.t.* 5. To utter with a croak. 6. *Slang* To kill. —*n.* A hoarse vocal sound, as of a frog. [Imit.] —**croak′y** *adj.*

croak·er (krō′kər) *n.* 1. Any of various animals that croak, as the grunt, a fish. 2. One who speaks dolefully.

Cro·at (krō′at, -at) *n.* 1. A Slavic native of Croatia. 2. The Croatian language.

Cro·a·tian (krō·ā′shən) *adj.* Pertaining to Croatia or the Croats. —*n.* 1. A Croat. 2. The South Slavic language of the Croats; Serbo-Croatian.

cro·chet (krō·shā′) *v.t. & v.i.* **·cheted** (-shād′) **·chet·ing** (-shā′ing) To form or ornament (a fabric) by interlacing thread with a hooked needle. —*n.* A kind of fancywork produced by crocheting. [< F, dim., of *croche* hook]

crock (krok) *n.* An earthenware pot or jar. [OE *croc*]

crocked (krokt) *adj.* *U.S. Slang* Drunk.

crock·er·y (krok′ər·ē) *n.* Earthen vessels collectively.

croc·o·dile (krok′ə·dīl) *n.* 1. A large lizardlike, amphibious reptile of tropical regions, with long jaws and armored skin. 2. A gavial. [< OF < Med.L < Gk. *krokodilos* lizard, crocodile]

CROCODILE
(To 18 feet long)

crocodile tears False weeping; hypocritical grief.

croc·o·dil·i·an (krok′ə·dil′ē·ən) *adj.* 1. Of or like a crocodile. 2. Belonging to an order of reptiles that includes crocodiles, alligators, and caymans. —*n.* A crocodilian reptile. Also **croc′o·dil′e·an.**

cro·cus (krō′kəs) *n.* *pl.* **·cus·es** or **·ci** (krō′sī) 1. A plant of the iris family, with long grasslike leaves and large flowers. 2. A deep orange yellow. [< L < Gk. *krokos*]

Croe·sus (krē′səs) Sixth-century B.C. Lydian king, noted for his wealth. —*n.* Any very wealthy man.

croft (krôft, kroft) *n.* *Brit.* 1. A small field near a house. 2. A small tenant farm. [OE, field] —**croft′er** *n.*

Croix de Guerre (krwä də gâr′) A French military decoration for bravery; literally, cross of war.

Cro-Mag·non (krō·mag′non, *Fr.* krō·mà·nyôṅ′) *Anthropol. n.* A member of a prehistoric European race considered to be a forerunner of modern man. —*adj.* Pertaining to or belonging to the Cro-Magnon race. [after the cave in France where their remains have been found]

crom·lech (krom′lek) *n.* 1. An ancient monument of large standing stones arranged roughly in a circle. 2. A dolmen. [< Welsh < *crom* bent + *llech* flat stone]

crone (krōn) *n.* A withered old woman. [Prob. < OF *carogne* carcass]

Cro·nus (krō′nəs) In Greek mythology, the youngest of the Titans, who deposed his father Uranus and was himself overcome by his son Zeus: identified with the Roman Saturn: also spelled *Kronos.*

cro·ny (krō′nē) *n.* *pl.* **·nies** A friend. [Orig. university slang < Gk. *chronios* contemporary]

crook (krŏŏk) *n.* 1. A bend or curve. 2. The curved or bent part of a thing. 3. Something with a crook in it, as a shepherd's staff. 4. *Informal* A thief. —*v.t.* 1. To bend; make crooked. —*v.i.* 2. To grow crooked. [< ON *krókr*]

crook·ed (krŏŏk′id) *adj.* 1. Bent; not straight. 2. Tricky; dishonest. —**crook′ed·ly** *adv.* —**crook′ed·ness** *n.*

crook·neck (krŏŏk′nek′) *n.* Any of several varieties of squash with a long, curved neck.

croon (krōōn) *v.t. & v.i.* 1. To sing or hum in a low tone. 2. To sing (popular songs) in a soft and sentimental manner. —*n.* A low, mournful humming or singing. [< MDu. *kronen* to sing softly, lament] —**croon′er** *n.*

crop (krop) *n.* 1. The cultivated produce of the land, as grain or vegetables. 2. The product of a particular kind, place, or season. 3. A collection or quantity of anything. 4. A cropping, esp. of the hair. 5. An earmark, as on cattle. 6. An enlargement of the gullet, as in birds; the craw. 7. The handle of a whip. 8. A whip having a leather loop for a lash. —*v.* **cropped, crop·ping** *v.t.* 1. To cut or eat off the stems of, as grass. 2. To reap. 3. To trim or clip (the hair, ears, tail, etc.) of. 4. To raise a crop or crops on. —*v.i.* 5. To bear or yield a crop or crops. —**crop up** (or **out**) 1. To appear above the surface; sprout. 2. To develop or happen unexpectedly. [OE]

crop·per¹ (krop′ər) *n.* 1. One who or that which crops. 2. *U.S.* One who cultivates another's land for part of the crop.

crop·per² (krop′ər) *n.* A bad fall, as when one is thrown over a horse's head. —**to come a cropper** 1. To fall headlong. 2. To fail. [? < dial. *neck and crop* completely]

cro·quet (krō·kā′) *n.* An outdoor game played by driving wooden balls through a series of wire arches by means of long-handled mallets. [Var. of *crochet.* See CROCHET.]

cro·quette (krō·ket′) *n.* A ball or cake of minced food fried brown in deep fat. [< F < *croquer* to crunch]

cro·sier (krō′zhər) *n.* A staff surmounted by a crook or cross, borne by or before a bishop or archbishop on occasions of ceremony. [< OF < Med.L < *crocia* bishop's crook]

cross (krôs, kros) *n.* 1. An ancient instrument of execution, an upright with a transverse piece near the top, upon which the condemned persons were fastened. 2. The emblem of Christianity, a representation of the cross upon which Christ died. 3. Any severe trial, affliction, or suffering: to bear one's *cross.* 4. The sign of the cross, made with the right hand as a devotional act. 5. A monument, staff, or other structure in the form of a cross. 6. The mark of one who cannot write. 7. Anything that resembles or is intermediate between two other things: a *cross* between poetry and prose. 8. A mixture of varieties or breeds of plants or animals; a hybrid. —**the Cross** 1. The cross on which Christ was crucified. 2. Christianity. —*v.t.* 1. To move or pass from one side to the other side of; go across; traverse. 2. To extend from side to side of; span: An overpass *crosses* a highway. 3. To pass across or intersect, as streets or lines. 4. To transport or convey across. 5. To make the sign of the cross upon or over. 6. To draw or put a line across: to *cross* a *t.* 7. To lay or place across or over: to *cross* the legs, fingers, etc. 8. To meet and pass: Your ship *crossed* mine. 9. To obstruct or hinder; thwart. 10. *Biol.* To crossbreed (plants or animals). —*v.i.* 11. To pass, move, or extend from side to side. 12. To intersect; lie athwart. 13. To meet and pass: Our paths *crossed.* 14. *Biol.* To crossbreed. —**to cross one's mind** To occur to one. —**to cross up** *Informal* To betray. —*adj.* 1. Peevish; ill-humored. 2. Lying across each other: *cross* streets. 3. Embodying interchange; reciprocal. 4. Contrary; adverse: at *cross* purposes. 5. Hybrid. —*adv.* 1. Across; crosswise; transversely. 2. Adversely; contrarily. [< OE < ON < L *crux*] —**cross′ly** *adv.* —**cross′ness** *n.*

cross·bar (krôs′bär′, kros′-) *n.* A transverse bar or line. —*v.t.* **·barred, ·bar·ring** To secure or mark with crossbars.

cross·beam (krôs′bēm′, kros′-) *n.* 1. A large beam or girder going from wall to wall. 2. Any beam that crosses another.

cross·bill (krôs′bil′, kros′-) *n.* A finchlike bird having points on its mandibles that cross each other.

cross·bones (krôs′bōnz′, kros′-) *n.* A representation of two bones crossing each other, usu. surmounted by a skull, and used as a symbol of death.

cross·bow (krôs′bō′, kros′-) *n.* A medieval weapon consisting of a bow fixed transversely on a grooved stock along which arrows or stones are released. —**cross′bow′man** *n.*

cross·breed (krôs′brēd′, kros′-) *v.t. & v.i.* **·bred, ·breed·ing** *Biol.* To produce (a strain or animal) by interbreeding or blending two varieties. —*n.* A strain or animal produced by crossbreeding; a hybrid.

cross·check (krôs′chek′) *v.t. & v.i.* To confirm or make certain by using parallel or additional data.

cross·coun·try (krôs′kun′trē, kros′-) *adj. & adv.* Across open country and disregarding roads, lanes, etc.

cross·cur·rent (krôs′kûr′ənt, kros′-) *n.* 1. A current flowing across another. 2. A contradictory tendency.

cross·cut (krôs′kut′, kros′-) *v.t. & v.i.* **·cut, ·cut·ting** To cut crosswise or through. —*adj.* 1. Used or made for the purpose of crosscutting. 2. Cut across or on the bias: *crosscut* silk. —*n.* 1. A cut across or a shortcut. 2. *Mining* A cutting that intersects the lode or the main workings.

cross·ex·am·ine (krôs′ig·zam′in, kros′-) *v.t. & v.i.* **·ined, ·in·ing** 1. To question anew (a witness called by the opposing party) for the purpose of testing the reliability of his previous testimony. 2. To question carefully. —**cross′ex·am′i·na′tion** *n.* —**cross′-ex·am′in·er** *n.*

cross·eye (krôs′ī′, kros′-) *n.* Strabismus in which one or both eyes are turned inward. —**cross′-eyed** *adj.*

cross·fer·ti·li·za·tion (krôs′fûr′tə·lə·zā′shən, kros′-) *n.* 1. *Biol.* The fertilization of an organism by sexually differentiated reproductive cells. 2. *Bot.* The fertilization of one plant or flower by the pollen from another.

cross·fer·ti·lize (krôs′fûr′tə·līz, kros′-) *v.t.* **·lized, ·liz·ing** To fertilize (a plant or animal) by cross-fertilization.

cross·grained (krôs′grānd′, kros′-) *adj.* 1. Having the grain running transversely: a *cross-grained* board. 2. Stubborn; perverse: a *cross-grained* man.

cross·hatch (krôs′hach′, kros′-) *v.t.* To shade, as a picture, by crossed lines. —**cross′hatch′ing** *n.*

cross·in·dex (krôs′in′deks, kros′-) *v.t. & v.i.* To insert cross-references in (an index, etc.).

cross·ing (krôs′ing, kros′-) *n.* 1. The act of going across, hindering, etc. 2. The place where something, as a road, may be crossed. 3. Intersection, as of roads.

cross·patch (krôs′pach′, kros′-) *n.* *Informal* A cranky, ill-tempered person.

cross·piece (krôs'pēs', kros'-) *n.* Any piece of material that crosses another.

cross·pol·li·nate (krôs'pol'ə-nāt, kros'-) *v.t.* **·nat·ed, ·nat·ing** To cross-fertilize (a plant). — **cross'-pol'li·na'tion** *n.*

cross·pur·pose (krôs'pûr'pəs, kros'-) *n.* A purpose or aim in conflict with another. — **to be at cross-purposes** To misunderstand or act counter to each other's purposes.

cross·ques·tion (krôs'kwes'chən, kros'-) *v.t.* To cross-examine. — *n.* A question asked in a cross-examination.

cross·re·fer (krôs'ri-fûr', kros'-) *v.* **·ferred, ·fer·ring** *v.t.* **1.** To refer to another passage or part. — *v.i.* **2.** To make a cross-reference.

cross·ref·er·ence (krôs'ref'rəns, kros'-) *n.* A note or statement directing a reader from one part of a book, index, etc., to another part.

cross·road (krôs'rōd', kros'-) *n.* **1.** A road that intersects another. **2.** A road connecting one road to another.

cross·roads (krôs'rōdz', kros'-) *n.pl.* (construed as *sing.*) **1.** The place where roads meet: in rural areas, often a settlement. **2.** The meeting place of different cultures. — **at the crossroads** At any critical point or moment.

cross·ruff (krôs'ruf', kros'-) *n.* In cards, a play in which each of two partners alternately trumps the other's lead.

cross section **1.** A plane section of any object cut at right angles to its length. **2.** A sampling meant to be characteristic or typical of the whole: a *cross section* of opinion. **3.** A cutting through anything at right angles.

cross·stitch (krôs'stich', kros'-) *n.* **1.** A double stitch in the form of an *x*. **2.** Needlework made with this stitch. — *v.t.* To make or mark with a cross-stitch.

cross·tie (krôs'tī', kros'-) *n.* Chiefly *U.S.* A beam or tie laid crosswise under railroad tracks to support them.

cross·town (krôs'toun', kros'-) *adj.* Going across a town or city: a *cross-town* bus. — *adv.* Across a town or city.

cross·tree (krôs'trē', kros'-) *n.* Usu. *pl. Naut.* Pieces of wood or metal set crosswise at the head of a mast to sustain the top or to extend the topgallant shrouds.

cross·walk (krôs'wôk', kros'-) *n.* A lane marked off for use by pedestrians in crossing a street.

cross·way (krôs'wā', kros'-) *n.* A crossroad.

cross·wise (krôs'wīz', kros'-) *adv.* **1.** Across. **2.** In the form of a cross. **3.** Contrarily. Also **cross'ways'** (-wāz').

cross·word puzzle (krôs'wûrd', kros'-) A puzzle worked on a pattern of white and black space, of which the white spaces are to be filled with letters that form words to agree with numbered definitions or similar clues.

crotch (kroch) *n.* **1.** The fork or angle formed by two diverging parts, as by the branches of a tree. **2.** The region of the human body where the legs separate from the pelvis. **3.** A forked pole, support, etc. [? < AF *croche* crook]

crotched (krocht) *adj.* Having a crotch; forked.

crotch·et (kroch'it) *n.* **1.** A whimsical or perverse notion or whim; an eccentricity. **2.** A small hook or hooklike instrument. **3.** *Entomol.* A hooklike process. **4.** *Music* Chiefly *Brit.* A quarter note. [< F *croche* hook]

crotch·et·y (kroch'ə-tē) *adj.* **1.** Full of eccentric or stubborn notions; perverse; contrary. **2.** Like a crotchet. — **crotch'et·i·ness** *n.*

cro·ton (krōt'n) *n.* **1.** A tree or shrub of the spurge family, often used medicinally. **2.** An ornamental tropical shrub. [< NL < Gk. *krotón* a tick]

Cro·ton bug (krōt'n) A small, light-colored cockroach. [after *Croton* Aqueduct; the first infestation in New York City occurred after this aqueduct was opened in 1842]

crouch (krouch) *v.i.* **1.** To stoop or bend low, as an animal ready to spring. **2.** To cringe; abase oneself; cower. — *v.t.* **3.** To bend low. — *n.* A crouching or crouching position. [? < OF *crochir* to be bent]

croup[1] (krōōp) *n.* *Pathol.* **1.** A disease of the throat characterized by hoarse coughing, laryngeal spasm, and difficult breathing. **2.** Loosely, inflammation of the larynx. [Imit.]

croup[2] (krōōp) *n.* The rump of certain animals, esp. of a horse. Also **croupe.** [< OF *crope*]

crou·pi·er (krōō'pē-ər, *Fr.* krōō-pyā') *n.* One who collects the stakes lost and pays out those won at a gaming table. [< F, lit., one who rides on the croup]

croup·y (krōō'pē) *adj.* **1.** Of or indicating croup. **2.** Having croup. Also **croup'ous.** — **crou'pi·ness** *n.*

crou·ton (krōō'ton, krōō-ton'; *Fr.* krōō-tôn') *n.* A small piece of toasted bread used in soups. [< F]

crow[1] (krō) *n.* **1.** An omnivorous, raucous bird having glossy black plumage. **2.** Loosely, the rook or raven. ♦ Collateral adjective: *corvine.* **3.** A crowbar. — **as the crow flies** In a straight line. — **to eat crow** *Informal* To recant a statement; back down; humiliate oneself. [OE *crāwe*]

crow[2] (krō) *v.i.* **crowed** or (for def. 1) **crew, crowed, crow·ing** **1.** To utter the shrill cry of a cock. **2.** To exult; boast. **3.** To utter sounds expressive of delight, as an infant. — *n.*

1. The cry of a cock. **2.** Any shrill, inarticulate sound resembling this, as an infant's cry of pleasure. [OE *crāwan*]

Crow (krō) *n.* **1.** A North American Indian of a Siouan tribe formerly inhabiting the region between the Platte and Yellowstone rivers. **2.** The language of this tribe.

crow·bar (krō'bär') *n.* A straight iron or steel bar with a flattened point often set at an angle, used as a lever.

crowd (kroud) *n.* **1.** A large number of persons gathered closely together. **2.** The populace in general; mob. **3.** *Informal* A particular set of people; a clique. — *v.t.* **1.** To shove or push. **2.** To fill to overflowing. **3.** To cram together; force into a confined space. **4.** *Informal* To put pressure on, esp. for payment. — *v.i.* **5.** To gather in large numbers. **6.** To force one's way. **7.** To shove or push. [OE *crūdan*] — **crowd'ed** *adj.* — **crowd'er** *n.*

crow·foot (krō'fŏŏt') *n. pl.* **·foots** **1.** Any of a genus of plants that includes the buttercup, columbine, etc. **2.** A plant having leaves, etc., suggestive of a bird's foot.

crown (kroun) *n.* **1.** A circlet, often of precious metal set with jewels, worn on the head as a mark of sovereign power. **2.** A decorative covering for the head. **3.** Anything shaped like a crown. **4.** A coin stamped with a crown or a crowned head, esp. the English crown, worth five shillings. **5.** The top part of a hat. **6.** The head itself. **7.** The upper part of a hat. **8.** The top or summit of something. **9.** The most perfect or complete state or type. **10.** A reward or prize for achievement. **11.** *Dent.* The part of a tooth that is covered with enamel or an artificial substitute for it. **12.** *Naut.* The lowest point of junction of the two arms of an anchor. — **the Crown 1.** The sovereign ruler; monarch. **2.** The power or the empire of a monarch. — *v.t.* **1.** To place a crown or garland on the head of. **2.** To make a monarch of. **3.** To endow with honor or dignity. **4.** To form the crown, ornament, or top to. **5.** To finish or make complete. **6.** *Informal* To strike on the head. **7.** In checkers, to make (a piece) into a king by placing another piece upon it. [< AF, OF < L *corona*] — **crown'er** *n.*

crown colony A colony of Great Britain in which the Crown retains control of legislation.

crown glass Hard optical glass of low refraction.

crown prince The male heir apparent to a throne.

crown princess **1.** The wife of a crown prince. **2.** The female heir apparent to a throne.

crow's-foot (krōz'fŏŏt') *n. pl.* **-feet** One of the wrinkles diverging from the outer corner of the eye.

crow's-nest (krōz'nest') *n.* **1.** *Naut.* An observation platform near the top of a ship's mast. **2.** Any similar platform.

cro·zier (krō'zhər) See CROSIER.

cru·ces (krōō'sēz) Alternative plural of CRUX.

cruci- combining form Cross. [< L *crux, crucis* cross]

cru·cial (krōō'shəl) *adj.* **1.** Of a critical or decisive nature. **2.** Involving difficulties; severe. [< MF < L *crux, crucis* cross, torture] — **cru'cial·ly** *adv.*

cru·ci·ble (krōō'sə-bəl) *n.* **1.** A heat-resistant vessel for melting metals or minerals. **2.** A severely trying test or experience. [< Med.L *crucibulum* earthen pot, lamp]

cru·ci·fix (krōō'sə-fiks) *n.* **1.** A cross bearing an effigy of Christ crucified. **2.** The cross as a Christian emblem. [< OF < L *cruci fixus* one hanged on a cross]

cru·ci·fix·ion (krōō'sə-fik'shən) *n.* **1.** The act of crucifying, or the state of being crucified. **2.** A painting, etc., that represents Christ's death on the cross. — **the Crucifixion** The execution of Jesus Christ on the cross.

cru·ci·form (krōō'sə-fôrm) *adj.* Cross-shaped.

cru·ci·fy (krōō'sə-fī) *v.t.* **·fied, ·fy·ing** **1.** To put to death by nailing or fastening the hands and feet to a cross. **2.** To torture; torment. [< OF < L *cruci figere* to fasten to a cross] — **cru'ci·fi'er** *n.*

crude (krōōd) *adj.* **crud·er, crud·est** **1.** In an unrefined or unprepared state; raw: *crude* oil. **2.** Immature; unripe. **3.** Showing a lack of skill or knowledge. **4.** Roughly made; unfinished. **5.** Lacking tact, refinement, or taste. [< L *crudus* rough] — **crude'ly** *adv.* — **crude'ness** *n.*

cru·di·ty (krōō'də-tē) *n. pl.* **·ties** **1.** The state or quality of being crude. **2.** A crude act, remark, etc.

cru·el (krōō'əl) *adj.* **cru·el·er** or **·el·ler, cru·el·est** or **·el·lest** **1.** Indifferent to or enjoying the suffering of others. **2.** Causing or inflicting mental or physical suffering. [< OF < L *crudelis* severe] — **cru'el·ly** *adv.* — **cru'el·ness** *n.*

cru·el·ty (krōō'əl-tē) *n. pl.* **·ties** **1.** The quality or condition of being cruel; mercilessness; inhumanity. **2.** That which causes suffering; an inhuman act; brutal treatment.

cru·et (krōō'it) *n.* A small glass bottle for vinegar, oil, etc. [< AF, dim. of OF *crue* pot]

cruise (krōōz) *v.* **cruised, cruis·ing** *v.i.* **1.** To sail about with no fixed destination, as for pleasure. **2.** To travel about at a moderate speed, as a police squad car. **3.** To move at the optimum speed for sustained travel: said of aircraft, etc. — *v.t.* **4.** To cruise over. — *n.* A cruising trip, esp. a voyage at sea. [< Du. *kruisen* to cross, traverse]

cruis·er (kroō′zər) *n.* **1.** One who or that which cruises. **2.** A fast, maneuverable warship, having medium tonnage and armament. **3.** A small power vessel equipped with living facilities: also called *cabin cruiser.*

crul·ler (krul′ər) *n.* A small cake of sweetened dough, fried in deep fat. [< Du. < *krullen* to curl]

crumb (krum) *n.* **1.** A tiny fragment of bread, cake, or the like. **2.** A bit or scrap of anything: *crumbs* of information. **3.** The soft inner part of bread, as distinguished from the crust. **4.** *U.S. Slang* A contemptible person. — *v.t.* **1.** To break into small pieces; crumble. **2.** In cooking, to dress or cover with bread crumbs. [OE *cruma*]

crum·ble (krum′bəl) *v.* **·bled, ·bling** *v.t.* **1.** To cause to break into tiny parts. — *v.i.* **2.** To fall to small pieces; disintegrate. [ME < OE *cruma* crumb]

crum·bly (krum′blē) *adj.* **·bli·er, ·bli·est** Apt to crumble; friable. — **crum′bli·ness** *n.*

crumb·y (krum′ē) *adj.* **crumb·i·er, crumb·i·est** **1.** Full of crumbs. **2.** Soft, like the inner part of bread.

crum·my (krum′ē) *adj.* **crum·mi·er, crum·mi·est** *U.S. Slang* Inferior; cheap; shabby.

crum·pet (krum′pit) *n.* A thin, leavened batter cake baked on a gridiron, then usu. toasted. [< ME *crompen* to curl up]

crum·ple (krum′pəl) *v.* **·pled, ·pling** *v.t.* **1.** To press into wrinkles; rumple. — *v.i.* **2.** To become wrinkled; shrivel. **3.** *Informal* To collapse. — *n.* Anything crumpled; a wrinkle. [Freq. of obs. *crump,* var. of CRIMP]

crunch (krunch) *v.t. & v.i.* **1.** To chew with a crushing or crackling sound. **2.** To move, press, or advance with a crushing sound. — *n.* A crunching, or its sound. [Imit.]

crup·per (krup′ər) *n.* **1.** The strap that goes under a horse's tail. **2.** The rump of a horse. [< OF *crope* croup²]

cru·sade (kroō·sād′) *n.* **1.** *Usu. cap.* Any of the military expeditions undertaken by Christians to recover the Holy Land from the Moslems. **2.** Any expedition under papal sanction against heathens or heretics. **3.** Any vigorous concerted movement or cause, esp. a reform movement. — *v.i.* **·sad·ed, ·sad·ing** To engage in a crusade. [< Sp. < Med.L *cruciare* to mark with a cross] — **cru·sad′er** *n.*

crush (krush) *v.t.* **1.** To press or squeeze out of shape; mash. **2.** To smash or grind into fine particles. **3.** To obtain or extract by pressure. **4.** To crowd. **5.** To subdue; conquer. — *v.i.* **6.** To become broken or misshapen by pressure. **7.** To move ahead by crushing or pressing. — *n.* **1.** The act of crushing. **2.** The state of being crushed. **3.** A crowd or throng; jam. **4.** A substance obtained by crushing: orange *crush.* **5.** *Informal* An infatuation. [< OF < MHG *krosen* to crush] — **crush′a·ble** *adj.* — **crush′er** *n.*

crust (krust) *n.* **1.** The hard outer part of bread. **2.** A piece of bread consisting mostly of crust (def. 1); also, any dry, hard piece of bread. **3.** The pastry shell of a pie, tart, etc. **4.** Any hard, crisp surface, as of snow. **5.** *Slang* Insolence; impertinence. **6.** *Geol.* The exterior shell of the earth. — *v.t. & v.i.* **1.** To cover with or acquire a crust. **2.** To form into a crust. [< OF < L *crusta*] — **crus′tal** *adj.*

crus·ta·cean (krus·tā′shən) *n.* One of a class of arthropods having crustlike shells, and generally aquatic, including lobsters, crabs, shrimps, etc. — *adj.* Of or pertaining to this class of arthropods. [< NL *Crustacea* < L *crusta* crust] — **crus·ta′ceous** *adj.*

crust·y (krus′tē) *adj.* **crust·i·er, crust·i·est** **1.** Like of having a crust. **2.** Harshly curt in manner or speech; surly. — **crust′i·ly** *adv.* — **crust′i·ness** *n.*

crutch (kruch) *n.* **1.** A staff used by the lame as a support in walking, esp. one having a crosspiece to fit under the armpit and a grip for the hand. **2.** Anything that gives support. **3.** Any of various devices resembling a crutch. — *v.t.* To prop up or support, as on crutches. [OE *crycc*]

crux (kruks) *n. pl.* **crux·es** or **cru·ces** (kroō′sēz) **1.** A pivotal, fundamental, or vital point. **2.** A cross. **3.** A tormenting or baffling problem. [< L, cross]

Crux (kruks) *n.* A constellation, the Southern Cross, containing the bright star Acrux.

cry (krī) *v.* **cried, cry·ing** *v.i.* **1.** To utter sobbing sounds of grief, pain, fear, etc., usu. accompanied by tears. **2.** To call out or appeal loudly; shout: often with *out.* **3.** To make characteristic calls: said of animals. — *v.t.* **4.** To utter loudly or shout out; exclaim. **5.** To affect (oneself) by weeping: to *cry* oneself to sleep. **6.** To beg for. — **to cry down 1.** To belittle; disparage. **2.** To silence or put down by cries. — **to cry up** To praise highly. — *n. pl.* **cries 1.** A loud or emotional utterance; shout; call. **2.** A fit of weeping. **3.** An appeal; entreaty. **4.** Advertisement by outcry. **5.** General report or rumor. **6.** A rallying call; battle cry. **7.** A catchword. **8.** A demand; clamor. **9.** The characteristic call of a bird or animal. **10.** A pack of hounds. — **a far cry 1.** A long distance away. **2.** Something very unlike. — **in full cry** In full pursuit, as a pack of hounds. [< OF < L *quiritare* to call out]

cry·ba·by (krī′bā′bē) *n. pl.* **·bies** A person, esp. a child, given to crying or complaining.

cry·ing (krī′ing) *adj.* **1.** That cries: a *crying* child. **2.** Calling for immediate action or remedy: a *crying* shame.

cryo- *combining form* Cold; frost. [< Gk. *kryos* frost]

cry·o·gen·ics (krī′ə·jen′iks) *n.pl.* (*construed as sing.*) The branch of physics dealing with very low temperatures.

cry·o·lite (krī′ə·līt) *n.* A fluoride of sodium and aluminum, used in the production of aluminum, soda, and glass.

cry·on·ics (krī·on′iks) *n.pl.* (*construed as sing.*) The practice of freezing the bodies of the dead, in hopes of reviving them when cures for their illnesses are found.

crypt (kript) *n.* A chamber or vault, esp. one beneath a church, used as a place of burial. [< L < Gk. *kryptos* hidden]

cryp·tan·al·y·sis (krip′tə·nal′ə·sis) *n. pl.* **·ses** (-sēz) The scientific study of cryptograms, ciphers, codes, etc., to which the key is not known. — **cryp·tan·a·lyst** (krip·tan′ə·list) *n.* — **cryp·tan·a·lyt·ic** *adj.*

cryp·tic (krip′tik) *adj.* **1.** Secret or hidden; occult. **2.** Puzzling; mystifying. [< LL < Gk. *kryptos* hidden]

crypto- *combining form* Hidden; secret. Also, before vowels, **crypt-.** [< Gk. *kryptos* hidden]

cryp·to·gam (krip′tə·gam) *n. Bot.* Any of a former division of plants that have no seeds or flowers, but propagate by spores, as algae, fungi, ferns, and mosses. [< F < Gk. *kryptos* hidden + *gamos* marriage] — **cryp′to·gam′ic,** **cryp·tog·a·mous** (krip·tog′ə·məs) *adj.*

cryp·to·gram (krip′tə·gram) *n.* A message written in code or cipher. — **cryp′to·gram′ic** *adj.*

cryp·tog·ra·phy (krip·tog′rə·fē) *n.* **1.** The art or process of writing in or reconverting cipher. **2.** Any system of writing in secret characters. — **cryp·tog′ra·pher, cryp·tog′ra·phist** *n.* — **cryp·to·graph·ic** (krip′tə·graf′ik) *adj.*

crys·tal (kris′təl) *n.* **1.** Colorless transparent quartz, or rock crystal. **2.** *Physics* A homogeneous solid body, exhibiting a symmetrical structure, with geometrically arranged planes and faces that assume any of various patterns associated with peculiarities of atomic structure. **3.** Flint glass, or any fine clear glass; also, articles made of such glass, as bowls, etc. **4.** Anything transparent and colorless. **5.** A glass or plastic covering over the face of a watch. — *adj.* **1.** Composed of crystal. **2.** Like crystal; extremely clear; limpid. [< OF < L < Gk. *krystallos* ice, crystal]

crystal ball A ball of crystal or glass used in crystal gazing.

crystal detector *Telecom.* A device consisting of metal electrodes in contact with suitable crystal materials, used to rectify incoming radio signals.

crystal gazing The act of looking into a crystal ball in order to induce a vision of distant objects or future events; also, the alleged ability to do this. — **crys·tal·gaz·er** (kris′təl·gā′zər) *n.*

CRYSTALS
a Tetragonal pyramid.
b Tetragonal prism.
c Dodecahedron.
d Deltahedron.

crys·tal·line (kris′tə·lin, -lēn) *adj.* **1.** Of, pertaining to, like, or made of crystal or crystals. **2.** Transparent; clear.

crys·tal·lize (kris′tə·līz) *v.* **·lized, ·liz·ing** *v.t.* **1.** To cause to form crystals or become crystalline. **2.** To bring to definite and permanent form. **3.** To coat with sugar. — *v.i.* **4.** To assume the form of crystals. **5.** To assume definite and permanent form. Also **crys′ta·lize.** — **crys′tal·liz′a·ble** *adj.* — **crys′tal·li·za′tion** *n.*

crystallo- *combining form* Crystal. Also, before vowels, **crystall-.** [< Gk. *krystallos* crystal]

crys·tal·log·ra·phy (kris′tə·log′rə·fē) *n.* The science and study of crystals. — **crys·tal·log′ra·pher** *n.*

crys·tal·loid (kris′tə·loid) *adj.* Like or having the nature of a crystal or a crystalloid. Also **crys′tal·loi′dal.** — *n. Chem.* One of a class of substances, usu. crystallizable, whose solutions pass easily through membranes. [< Gk. *krystalloeidēs* like crystal]

crystal pickup A pickup that utilizes a piezoelectric crystal to transform mechanical motion into sound, etc., often used in electric record players.

crystal set A radio receiving set operating with a crystal detector but without electron tubes.

cub (kub) *n.* **1.** The young of the bear, fox, wolf, and certain other carnivores; a whelp. **2.** An awkward youth. **3.** A beginner or learner. [Origin uncertain]

cub·by·hole (kub′ē·hōl′) *n.* A small, enclosed space. Also **cub′by.** [< *cubby,* dim. of dial. E *cub* shed + HOLE]

cube (kyoōb) *n.* **1.** A solid bounded by six equal squares and having all its angles right angles. **2.** *Math.* The third power of a quantity: the *cube* of 3 is 27, or $3^3 = 3 \times 3 \times 3 = 27$. — *v.t.* **cubed, cub·ing 1.** To raise (a number or quantity) to the third power. **2.** To find the cubic capacity of. **3.** To form or cut into cubes or cubelike shapes; dice: to *cube* potatoes. [< OF < L < Gk. *kybos* cube]

cu·beb (kyōō′beb) *n.* A berry of an East Indian shrub of the pepper family, often smoked in the form of cigarettes to treat catarrh. [< OF < Arabic *kabābah*]

cube root The number that, taken three times as a factor, produces a number called its cube: 4 is the *cube root* of 64.

cu·bic (kyōō′bik) *adj.* **1.** Shaped like a cube. **2.** Having three dimensions, or pertaining to three-dimensional content: a *cubic* foot. **3.** *Math.* Of the third power or degree.

cu·bi·cal (kyōō′bi·kəl) *adj.* Shaped like a cube. **— cu′bi·cal·ly** *adv.* **— cu′bi·cal·ness** *n.*

cu·bi·cle (kyōō′bi·kəl) *n.* **1.** A bedroom, esp. a partially enclosed section in a dormitory. **2.** Any small partitioned area, as a carrell. [< L *cubiculum* bedroom]

cubic measure A unit or system of units for measuring volume, or the amount of space occupied in three dimensions. See table inside back cover.

cu·bism (kyōō′biz·əm) *n.* A movement in modern art concerned with the abstract and geometric interpretation of form, rather than with a realistic representation of nature. **— cu′bist** *adj. & n.* **— cu·bis′tic** *adj.*

cu·bit (kyōō′bit) *n.* An ancient measure of length, usu. about 18 to 20 inches. [< L *cubitum* elbow]

cu·boid (kyōō′boid) *adj.* Shaped like a cube. Also **cu·boi′dal.** — *n. Geom.* A rectangular parallelepiped.

cub reporter A young, inexperienced newspaper reporter.

cub scout A member of a subdivision of the Boy Scouts, comprising boys eight to ten years of age.

cuck·old (kuk′əld) *n.* The husband of an unfaithful wife. **— v.t.** To make a cuckold of. [< OF *cucu* cuckoo]

cuck·old·ry (kuk′əl·drē) *n.* The cuckolding of a husband.

cuck·oo (kōōk′ōō; *for adj., also* kōō′kōō) *n.* **1.** A bird, as the common European cuckoo, that deposits its eggs in the nests of other birds. **2.** A simpleton; fool. **3.** A cuckoo's cry. **— v.t. ·ooed, ·oo·ing** *v.t.* **1.** To repeat without cessation. **— v.i. 2.** To utter or imitate the cry of the cuckoo. — *adj. Slang* Crazy; silly. [< OF *cucu, coucou;* imit.]

cuckoo clock A clock in which a mechanical cuckoo announces the hours.

cuckoo spit **1.** A frothy secretion exuded upon plants by certain insect larvae. **2.** An insect that secretes such froth.

cu·cul·late (kyōō′kə·lāt, kyōō·kul′āt) *adj. Bot.* Shaped like a hood as certain leaves. [< LL < L *cucullus* hood]

cu·cum·ber (kyōō′kum·bər) *n.* **1.** The cylindrical, hard-rinded fruit of a plant of the gourd family, cultivated as a vegetable. **2.** The plant. [< OF < L *cucumis, -eris*]

cud (kud) *n.* Food forced up into the mouth from the first stomach of a ruminant and chewed over again. [OE *cwidu*]

cud·dle (kud′l) *v.* **·dled, ·dling** *v.t.* **1.** To caress fondly within a close embrace; fondle. **— v.i. 2.** To lie close; nestle together. **— n.** An embrace or caress; a hug. [? < dial. E *couth* snug] **— cud′dle·some** (səm) *adj.* **— cud′dly** *adj.*

cud·dy (kud′ē) *n. pl.* **·dies** *Naut.* A small cabin or galley.

cudg·el (kuj′əl) *n.* A short, thick club. **— to take up the cudgels** To enter into a contest or controversy. **— v.t.** **cudg·eled** *or* **·elled, cudg·el·ing** *or* **·el·ling** To beat with a cudgel. **— to cudgel one's brains** To think hard; puzzle. [OE *cycgel*] **— cudg′el·er** *or* **cudg′el·ler** *n.*

cue¹ (kyōō) *n.* **1.** A long, tapering rod, used to strike the cue ball. **2.** A queue of hair. **3.** A queue of persons. **— v.t. cued, cu·ing 1.** To braid, or tie into a cue. **2.** In billiards, etc., to hit with a cue. [< F *queue* tail]

cue² (kyōō) *n.* **1.** In plays, movies, etc., any action or sound that signals the start of another action, speech, etc. **2.** Anything that serves as a signal to begin. **3.** A hint or suggestion. **4.** State of mind; mood. **— v.t. cued, cu·ing** To call a cue to (an actor); prompt. [Earlier *Q, qu,* supposedly an abbreviation of L *quando* when]

cue ball The ball struck by the cue in billiards or pool.

cuff¹ (kuf) *n.* **1.** A band or fold at the lower end of a sleeve. **2.** *U.S.* The turned-up fold on the bottom of a trouser leg. **3.** A detachable band of fabric worn about the wrist. **4.** A handcuff. **— off the cuff** *U.S. Slang* Spontaneously. **— on the cuff** *U.S. Slang* On credit. [ME *cuffe, coffe*]

cuff² (kuf) *v.t.* **1.** To strike, as with the open hand; buffet. **— v.i. 2.** To scuffle or fight; box. **— n.** A blow, esp. with the open hand. [? < Scand.]

cuff links Linked buttons or the like, used to fasten shirt cuffs.

cui bo·no (kwē′ bō′nō, kī′) *Latin* For whose benefit? Also, inaccurately, for what purpose?

cui·rass (kwi·ras′) *n.* A piece of armor consisting of a breastplate and backplate; also, the breastplate alone. **— v.t.** To equip with a cuirass. [< MF, ult. < L *corium* leather]

cui·ras·sier (kwi′rə·sir′) *n.* A mounted soldier wearing a cuirass.

cui·sine (kwi·zēn′) *n.* **1.** The style or quality of cooking. **2.** The food prepared. [< F < L < *coquere* to cook]

cuisse (kwis) *n.* A piece of plate armor for the thigh. Also **cuish** (kwish). [< OF < *cuisse* thigh < L *coxa* hip]

cul-de-sac (kul′də·sak′, kōōl′-; *Fr.* kü′də·säk′) *n. pl.* **culs-de-sacs,** *Fr.* **culs-de-sac** (kü′-) A passage open only at one end; blind alley; trap. [< F, bottom of the bag]

-cule *suffix of nouns* Small; little; *animalcule.* [< F < L *-culus,* dim. suffix]

cu·li·nar·y (kyōō′lə·ner′ē, kul′-) *adj.* Of or pertaining to cookery or the kitchen. [< L < *culina* kitchen]

cull (kul) *v.t.* **1.** To pick or sort out; select. **2.** To gather. **3.** To pick over and divide as to quality. **— n.** Something picked or sorted out, esp. something rejected as inferior. [< OF < L *colligere* to collect] **— cull′er** *n.*

culm¹ (kulm) *n. Bot.* The jointed, usu. hollow, stem or straw of grasses. **— v.i.** To form a culm. [< L *culmus* stalk] **— cul·mif·er·ous** (kul·mif′ər·əs) *adj.*

culm² (kulm) *n.* **1.** Coal refuse or dust. **2.** An inferior anthracite coal. [Var. of dial. *coom* soot]

cul·mi·nate (kul′min·āt) *v.i.* **·nat·ed, ·nat·ing 1.** To reach the highest point or degree; come to a final result: with *in.* **2.** *Astron.* To reach the meridian. [< LL < L *culmen,* highest point] **— cul′mi·nant** *adj.*

cul·mi·na·tion (kul′mə·nā′shən) *n.* **1.** The act of culminating. **2.** The highest point, condition, or degree.

cu·lottes (kyōō·lots′, kōō-; *Fr.* kü·lôt′) *n.pl.* A woman's trouserlike garment cut to resemble a skirt. [< F]

cul·pa·ble (kul′pə·bəl) *adj.* Deserving of blame or censure. [< OF < L *culpa* fault] **— cul′pa·bil′i·ty, cul′pa·ble·ness** *n.* **— cul′pa·bly** *adv.*

cul·prit (kul′prit) *n.* **1.** One guilty of some offense or crime. **2.** One charged with or arraigned for a crime. [< AF *cul prit,* short for *culpable* guilty + *prit* ready for trial]

cult (kult) *n.* **1.** A system of religious rites and observances. **2.** Zealous devotion to a person, ideal, or thing. **3.** The object of this devotion. **4.** The followers of a cult. [< F < L < *colere* to cultivate, worship]

cul·ti·va·ble (kul′tə·və·bəl) *adj.* Capable of cultivation. Also **cul′ti·vat′a·ble** (-vā′tə·bəl). **— cul′ti·va·bil′i·ty** *n.*

cul·ti·vate (kul′tə·vāt) *v.t.* **·vat·ed, ·vat·ing 1.** To make fit for raising crops, as by plowing, fertilizing, etc.; till. **2.** To care for (plants, etc.) so as to promote growth and abundance. **3.** To raise from seeds, bulbs, etc., for later planting. **4.** To produce or improve (plants, etc.) by selective breeding or other techniques. **5.** To improve or develop by study, or training; refine: to *cultivate* one's mind. **6.** To give one's attention to in order to acquire: to *cultivate* a habit, good manners, etc. **7.** To promote the development or advancement of. **8.** To court the friendship of. [< Med.L < L *cultus,* pp. of *colere* to care for, cherish] **— cul′ti·vat·ed** *adj.*

cul·ti·va·tion (kul′tə·vā′shən) *n.* **1.** The act of cultivating the ground, plants, etc. **2.** The improvement or development of anything through study and effort. **3.** Culture; refinement. **— Syn.** See REFINEMENT.

cul·ti·va·tor (kul′tə·vā′tər) *n.* **1.** One who cultivates. **2.** *Agric.* A machine for cultivating, commonly having several blades that loosen the ground and destroy weeds.

cul·tur·al (kul′chər·əl) *adj.* **1.** Of, pertaining to, or developing culture: *cultural* studies. **2.** Produced by breeding, as certain varieties of fruits or plants. **— cul′tur·al·ly** *adv.*

cul·ture (kul′chər) *n.* **1.** The cultivation of plants or animals, esp. to improve the breed. **2.** The development, and refinement of mind, morals, or taste. **3.** The condition thus produced; refinement. **4.** A specific stage in the development of a civilization. **5.** Cultivation of the soil. **6.** *Anthropol.* The sum total of the attainments and learned behavior patterns of any specific period, race, or people. **7.** *Biol.* **a** The development of microorganisms in artificial media. **b** The organisms so developed. **— Syn.** See REFINEMENT. **— v.t. ·tured, ·tur·ing 1.** To cultivate (plants or animals). **2.** *Biol.* **a** To develop or grow (microorganisms) in an artificial medium. **b** To inoculate with a prepared culture. [< F < L < *colere* to care for] **— cul′tur·ist** *n.*

cul·tured (kul′chərd) *adj.* **1.** Possessing or manifesting culture. **2.** Created or grown by cultivation.

cul·tus (kul′təs) *n. pl.* **·tuses** *or* **·ti** (-tī) A cult.

cul·ver·in (kul′vər·in) *n.* **1.** A long cannon used in the 16th and 17th centuries. **2.** An early form of musket. [< F < *couleuvre* serpent]

cul·vert (kul′vərt) *n.* An artificial, covered channel for water, as under a road. [Origin uncertain]

cum·ber (kum′bər) *v.t.* **1.** To hinder; obstruct; hamper. **2.** To weigh down; burden. **— n.** A hindrance or encumbrance. [Cf. OF *encombrer* to hinder]

cum·ber·some (kum′bər·səm) *adj.* **1.** Unwieldy; clumsy. **2.** Vexatious; burdensome. **— cum′ber·some·ly** *adv.* **— cum′ber·some·ness** *n.*

cum·brance (kum'brəns) *n.* An encumbrance.

cum·brous (kum'brəs) *adj.* Cumbersome. **—cum'brous·ly** *adv.* **—cum'brous·ness** *n.*

cum·in (kum'in) *n.* 1. An annual of the parsley family. 2. Its seeds, used as a condiment. Also **cum'min.** [OE < L < Gk. *kyminon* < Semitic]

cum lau·de (kum lô'dē, kŏŏm lou'de) *Latin* With praise: used on diplomas to denote the special merit of the recipient's work. **—magna cum laude** With high praise. **—summa cum laude** With highest praise.

cum·mer·bund (kum'ər·bund) *n.* A broad sash worn as a waistband. [< Persian < *kamar* loin + *band* band]

cu·mu·late (kyŏŏm'yə·lāt; *for adj., also* kyŏŏm'yə·lit) *v.t. & v.i.* **·lat·ed, ·lat·ing** To collect into a heap; accumulate. **—** *adj.* Massed; accumulated. [< L < *cumulus* a heap] **—cu·mu·la'tion** *n.*

cu·mu·la·tive (kyŏŏm'yə·lā'tiv, -lə·tiv) *adj.* 1. Gathering volume, strength, or value. 2. Gained by accumulation: *cumulative* knowledge. 3. Increasing or accruing, as unpaid interest or dividends. **—cu'mu·la'tive·ly** *adv.*

cu·mu·lo·cir·rus (kyŏŏm'yə·lō·sir'əs) *n. Meteorol.* Altocumulus.

cu·mu·lo·nim·bus (kyŏŏm'yə·lō·nim'bəs) *n. Meteorol.* A massive cloud formation (Symbol Cb) in the shape of mountains, and producing thunder and showers.

cu·mu·lo·stra·tus (kyŏŏm'yə·lō·strā'təs) *n. Meteorol.* Stratocumulus.

cu·mu·lus (kyŏŏm'yə·ləs) *n. pl.* **·li** (-lī) 1. A mass; pile. 2. *Meteorol.* A dense, usu. white cloud formation (Symbol Cu) with dome-shaped upper surfaces and horizontal bases, seen in fair weather. [< L] **—cu'mu·lous** *adj.*

cu·ne·ate (kyŏŏ'nē·it, -āt) *adj.* Wedge-shaped: said esp. of leaves. Also **cu'ne·at'ed, cu·ne·at·ic** (kyŏŏ'nē·at'ik). [< L < *cuneus* wedge] **—cu'ne·ate·ly** *adv.*

cu·ne·i·form (kyŏŏ·nē'ə·fôrm, kyŏŏ'nē·ə·fôrm') *adj.* 1. Wedge-shaped, as the characters in some ancient Sumerian, Assyrian, Babylonian, and Persian inscriptions. 2. *Anat.* Designating a wedge-shaped bone in the wrist, or one of three in the human foot. **—** *n.* Cuneiform writing. Also **cu·ni·form** (kyŏŏ'nə·fôrm). [< L *cuneus* wedge + -FORM]

CUNEIFORM
a Earth. *b* Woman. *c* Man. *d* Food.

cun·ning (kun'ing) *n.* 1. Skill in deception; craftiness. 2. Knowledge combined with manual skill; dexterity. **—** *adj.* 1. Crafty or shrewd. 2. Executed with skill; ingenious. 3. *U.S.* Innocently amusing; cute. [OE < *cunnan* to know, be able] **—cun'ning·ly** *adv.* **—cun'ning·ness** *n.*

cup (kup) *n.* 1. A small, open vessel, often with a handle, used chiefly for drinking from. 2. The contents of a cup; a cupful: as a measure, equal to 8 ounces or half a pint. 3. The bowl of a drinking vessel that has a stem and base. 4. In the Eucharist, the chalice, or its contents. 5. One's lot in life: the bitter *cup* of exile. 6. Intoxicating drink, or the habit of drinking. 7. An alcoholic beverage, usu. chilled and served with herbs, fruits, etc. 8. A cup-shaped object or part, as of a flower. 9. A cup-shaped vessel given as a prize, esp. in sports. 10. In golf, a hole, or the metal receptacle within it. **—in one's cups** Drunk. **—** *v.t.* **cupped, cup·ping** 1. To shape like a cup. 2. To place in or as in a cup. 3. *Med.* To perform cupping on. [OE < L *cupa* tub]

cup·bear·er (kup'bâr'ər) *n.* One who serves drinks.

cup·board (kub'ərd) *n.* 1. A closet or cabinet with shelves, as for dishes. 2. Any small cabinet or closet.

cup·cake (kup'kāk') *n.* A small individual cake.

cup·ful (kup'fŏŏl') *n. pl.* **·fuls** The quantity held by a cup.

Cu·pid (kyŏŏ'pid) In Roman mythology, the god of love: identified with the Greek *Eros*. **—** *n.* 1. A representation of the god of love as a naked, winged boy with a bow and arrow. 2. One who helps to arrange meetings between lovers; chiefly in the phrase **to play Cupid.** [< L *cupido* desire]

cu·pid·i·ty (kyŏŏ·pid'ə·tē) *n.* Eager desire for possession, esp. of wealth; avarice; greed. [< L *cupiditas, -tatis*]

cup of tea *Informal* A favorite object, activity, etc.

cu·po·la (kyŏŏ'pə·lə) *n.* 1. *Archit.* **a** A rounded roof; dome. **b** A small, vaulted structure, usu. hemispherical, rising above a roof. 2. Any of various dome-shaped structures, organs, etc. **—** *v.t.* **·laed, ·la·ing** To provide with or shape like a cupola. [< Ital. < LL < L *cupa* tub]

cup·ping (kup'ing) *n. Med.* The process of drawing blood to the surface of the skin by creating a vacuum at that point.

cupping glass *Med.* A cup used for cupping.

cu·pre·ous (kyŏŏ'prē·əs) *adj.* Of, pertaining to, containing, or resembling copper. [< LL < L *cuprum* copper]

cu·pric (kyŏŏ'prik) *adj. Chem.* Of or pertaining to copper, esp. in its highest valence: *cupric* oxide, CuO.

cupro- *combining form* Copper. Also, before vowels, **cupri-.**

cu·prous (kyŏŏ'prəs) *adj. Chem.* Of or pertaining to copper, esp. in its lowest valence: *cuprous* oxide, Cu₂O.

cu·prum (kyŏŏ'prəm) *n.* Copper. [< L]

cur (kûr) *n.* 1. A mongrel dog. 2. A mean or despicable person. [Short for earlier *kur-dogge*]

cur·a·ble (kyŏŏr'ə·bəl) *adj.* Capable of being cured. **—cur'a·bil·i·ty, cur'a·ble·ness** *n.* **—cur'a·bly** *adv.*

cu·ra·çao (kyŏŏr'ə·sō', kŏŏ'rä·sou') *n.* A liqueur made by distilling spirits with the peel of the sour orange. Also **cu'ra·çoa'** (-sō'). [after *Curaçao*]

cu·ra·cy (kyŏŏr'ə·sē) *n. pl.* **·cies** The position, duties, or term of office of a curate.

cu·ra·re (kyŏŏ·rä'rē) *n.* 1. A blackish, resinous extract of certain South American trees, that, when introduced into the blood stream, paralyzes the motor nerves; used as an arrow poison and in general anesthesia. 2. A plant from which this is extracted. Also called *oorali, urare, urari, woorali:* also **cu·ra·ra** (kyŏŏ·rä'rə), **cu·ra'ri.** [< Sp. < Tupi]

cu·rate (kyŏŏr'it) *n.* A clergyman assisting a parish priest, rector, or vicar. [< Med.L < L *cura* care, cure]

cur·a·tive (kyŏŏr'ə·tiv) *adj.* Having the power to cure. **—** *n.* A remedy. **—cur'a·tive·ly** *adv.* **—cur'a·tive·ness** *n.*

cu·ra·tor (kyŏŏ·rā'tər) *n.* A person in charge of a museum or similar institution. [< L < *cura* care] **—cu·ra·to·ri·al** (kyŏŏr'ə·tôr'ē·əl, -tō'rē-) *adj.* **—cu·ra'tor·ship** *n.*

curb (kûrb) *n.* 1. Anything that restrains or controls: a *curb* on inflation. 2. A border of concrete or stone along the edge of a street: also, *Brit.,* **kerb.** 3. A chain or strap bracing a bit against the lower jaw of a horse, used to check the horse. 4. An enclosing or confining framework, margin, etc. **—** *v.t.* 1. To control, as with reins and curb. 2. To provide with a curb. 3. To lead (a dog) off a curb for defecation in the street. [< F *courbe,* orig. adj., curved < L *curvus*]

curb·ing (kûr'bing) *n.* Material forming a curb.

curb roof *Archit.* A roof consisting of two slopes of varying pitch; a mansard or gambrel roof.

curb·stone (kûrb'stōn') *n.* A stone, row of stones, etc., on the outer edge of a sidewalk. Also, *Brit.,* **kerbstone.**

cur·cu·li·o (kûr·kyŏŏ'lē·ō) *n. pl.* **·os** Any of various long-snouted weevils, injurious to fruits and nuts. [< L, weevil]

curd (kûrd) *n. Often pl.* The coagulated portion of milk, of which cheese is made, as distinct from the watery whey. **—** *v.t. & v.i.* To form into or become curd. [Metathetic var. of CRUD] **—curd'y** *adj.*

cur·dle (kûr'dəl) *v.t. & v.i.* **·dled, ·dling** To change or turn to curd; coagulate; congeal; thicken. [Freq. of CURD]

cure (kyŏŏr) *n.* 1. A restoration to a sound or healthy condition. 2. That which restores health or removes an evil. 3. A special method or course of remedial or medicinal treatment. 4. Spiritual care, esp. of a clergyman for his congregation: also **cure of souls.** 5. A process of preserving food or other products. **—** *v.* **cured, cur·ing** *v.t.* 1. To restore to a healthy or sound condition. 2. To remedy or eradicate: to *cure* a bad habit. 3. To preserve, as by salting, smoking, or aging. **—** *v.i.* 4. To bring about recovery. 5. To be or become cured by a preserving process. [< OF < L *cura* care] **—cure'less** *adj.* **—cur'er** *n.*

cu·ré (kyŏŏ·rā') *n.* A parish priest, esp. in France. [< F]

cure-all (kyŏŏr'ôl') *n.* A cure for all ills; panacea.

cur·few (kûr'fyŏŏ) *n.* 1. A police or military regulation requiring persons to keep off the streets after a designated hour; also, a similar order applying to children. 2. A medieval regulation requiring fires to be put out at the tolling of a bell. 3. The bell itself. 4. The hour of ringing such a bell, or the ringing itself. [< OF *covrir* to cover + *feu* fire]

cu·ri·a (kyŏŏr'ē·ə) *n. pl.* **cu·ri·ae** (kyŏŏr'ē·ē) 1. A court of justice. 2. *Often cap.* The collective body of officials of the papal government: also **Cu'ri·a Ro·ma·na** (rō·mä'nə). [< L] **—cu'ri·al** *adj.*

cu·rie (kyŏŏr'ē, kyŏŏ·rē') *n. Physics* The unit of radioactivity, equal to 3.70×10^{10} nuclear disintegrations per second. [after Marie *Curie*]

cu·ri·o (kyŏŏr'ē·ō) *n. pl.* **·os** A rare or curious art object, piece of bric-a-brac, etc. [Short for CURIOSITY]

cu·ri·os·i·ty (kyŏŏr'ē·os'ə·tē) *n. pl.* **·ties** 1. Eager desire for knowledge of something, esp. of something novel or unusual. 2. Interest in the private affairs of others. 3. That which excites interest by its strangeness or rarity.

cu·ri·ous (kyŏŏr'ē·əs) *adj.* 1. Eager for information or knowledge. 2. Given to prying or meddling. 3. Attracting interest because of novelty or unusualness; odd; strange. 4. Executed with ingenuity or skill. [< OF < L *curiosus* < *cura* care] **—cu'ri·ous·ly** *adv.* **—cu'ri·ous·ness** *n.*

cu·ri·um (kyŏŏr'ē·əm) *n.* An unstable radioactive element (symbol Cm), produced originally by the bombardment of uranium and plutonium with alpha particles. See ELEMENT. [after Marie and Pierre *Curie*]

curl (kûrl) *v.t.* 1. To twist into ringlets or curves, as the hair. 2. To form into a curved or spiral shape. **—** *v.i.* 3. To form ringlets, as the hair. 4. To become curved; take a spiral shape. 5. To play at the game of curling. **—to curl up** 1. To assume a position with the back curved and the legs drawn close to the body. 2. To form into a curved or spiral shape. **—** *n.* 1. Something coiled or spiral, as a ringlet of hair. **2.** A curled or circular shape or mark. **3.** The act of curling, or the state of being curled. [Metathetic var. of ME *crollid, crulled* curled < *crull* curly < MLG]

curl·er (kûr′lər) *n.* **1.** One who or that which curls. **2.** One who plays the game of curling.

cur·lew (kûr′lōō) *n.* A shore bird with a long bill and long legs. [< OF *corlieu, courlieus;* orig. imit.]

curl·i·cue (kûr′li·kyōō) *n.* Any fancy curl or twist, as a flourish with a pen. Also **curl′y·cue.**

curl·ing (kûr′ling) *n.* A game played on ice in which the opposing players slide heavy, smooth, circular stones (**curling stones**) toward a goal or tee at either end.

curling iron An implement of metal, used when heated for curling or waving the hair. Also **curling irons.**

curl·y (kûr′lē) *adj.* **1.** Having curls. **2.** Tending to curl. **3.** Containing curllike marks: *curly* maple. — **curl′i·ness** *n.*

cur·mudg·eon (kər·muj′ən) *n.* A gruff or irritable person, esp. an elderly man. [Origin unknown]

cur·rant (kûr′ənt) *n.* **1.** A small, round, acid berry, used for making jelly. **2.** The bush producing this berry. **3.** A small seedless raisin of the Levant. [Back formation < AF *(raisins de) Corauntz* (raisins from) Corinth]

cur·ren·cy (kûr′ən·sē) *n. pl.* **·cies 1.** The current medium of exchange; money. **2.** General acceptance or circulation. **3.** The time during which something is current.

cur·rent (kûr′ənt) *adj.* **1.** Belonging to the immediate present: the *current* year. **2.** Passing from person to person; circulating, as money or news. **3.** Generally accepted; prevalent. — *n.* **1.** A continuous onward movement, as of water. **2.** The part of any body of water or air that has a more or less steady flow in a definite direction: an ocean *current.* **3.** Any perceptible course or trend. **4.** *Electr.* **a** A movement or flow of electricity passing through a conductor. **b** The rate at which it flows. — **alternating current** *Electr.* A current that periodically reverses its direction of flow, each complete cycle having the same value. Abbr. AC, a.c., A.C. — **direct current** *Electr.* A current flowing in one direction. Abbr. DC, d.c., D.C. [< OF < L *currere* to run] — **cur′rent·ly** *adv.* — **cur′rent·ness** *n.*

cur·ric·u·lum (kə·rik′yə·ləm) *n. pl.* **·lums** or **·la** (-lə) **1.** All the courses of study offered at a university or school. **2.** A regular or particular course of study. [< L, a race < *currere* to run] — **cur·ric′u·lar** *adj.*

cur·ry[1] (kûr′ē) *v.t.* **·ried, ·ry·ing 1.** To rub down and clean with a currycomb. **2.** To dress (tanned hides) by soaking, smoothing, etc. — **to curry favor** To seek favor by flattery, etc. [< OF *correier, conreder* to prepare]

cur·ry[2] (kûr′ē) *n. pl.* **·ries 1.** A pungent sauce of East Indian origin. **2.** A dish of meat, fish, etc., cooked with this sauce. **3.** Curry powder. — *v.t.* **·ried, ·ry·ing** To flavor with curry. [< Tamil *kari* sauce]

cur·ry·comb (kûr′ē·kōm′) *n.* A comb consisting of a series of teeth or upright serrated ridges, for grooming horses, etc. — *v.t.* To comb with a currycomb.

curry powder A condiment prepared from pungent spices, turmeric, etc., used in making curry and curried dishes.

curse (kûrs) *n.* **1.** An appeal for evil or injury to befall another, as through the intercession of God or gods. **2.** The evil or injury so invoked. **3.** Any profane oath; imprecation. **4.** A source of calamity or evil. **5.** Something cursed. — *v.* **cursed** (kûrst) or **curst, curs·ing** *v.t.* **1.** To invoke evil or injury upon; damn. **2.** To swear at. **3.** To cause evil or injury to; afflict. — *v.i.* **4.** To utter curses; swear. [OE < OIrish *cursagim* to blame]

curs·ed (kûrst; *for adj., also* kûr′sid) A past tense and past participle of CURSE. — *adj.* **1.** Under a curse. **2.** Deserving a curse; wicked. Also **curst.** — **curs′ed·ly** *adv.* — **curs′ed·ness** *n.*

cur·sive (kûr′siv) *adj.* Running; flowing: said of writing in which the letters are joined. — *n.* **1.** A cursive character. **2.** *Printing* A typeface resembling handwriting. [< Med.L < L *currere* to run] — **cur′sive·ly** *adv.*

cur·so·ry (kûr′sər·ē) *adj.* Rapid and superficial. [< LL < L *currere* to run] — **cur′so·ri·ly** *adv.* — **cur′so·ri·ness** *n.*

curt (kûrt) *adj.* **1.** Brief and abrupt; esp., rudely brief: a *curt* nod. **2.** Short or shortened. — **Syn.** See BLUNT. [< L *curtus* shortened] — **curt′ly** *adv.* — **curt′ness** *n.*

cur·tail (kər·tāl′) *v.t.* To cut off or cut short; reduce. [< obs. *curtal* cut short] — **cur·tail′er** *n.* — **cur·tail′ment** *n.*

cur·tain (kûr′tən) *n.* **1.** A piece or pieces of cloth, etc. hanging in a window or opening, usu. capable of being drawn to the sides or raised. **2.** Something that conceals or separates like a curtain: the *curtain* of darkness. **3.** *pl. Slang* Ruin; death. — *v.t.* To provide, shut off, or conceal with or as with a curtain. [< OF < LL *cortina*]

curtain call Prolonged applause of an audience at the end of a play, scene, etc., as a call for the performers to reappear and acknowledge it; also, their reappearance.

curtain raiser 1. A short play or sketch presented before a longer or more important play. **2.** Any introductory event.

curtain wall *Archit.* An outside wall providing enclosure but giving no structural support.

curt·sy (kûrt′sē) *n. pl.* **·sies** A bending of the knees and lowering of the body as a gesture of civility or respect, performed by women: sometimes spelled *courtesy.* — *v.i.* **·sied, ·sy·ing** To make a curtsy. Also **curt′sey.** [Var. of COURTESY]

cur·va·ceous (kûr·vā′shəs) *adj. U.S. Informal* Having voluptuous curves; shapely: said of a woman.

cur·va·ture (kûr′və·chər) *n.* **1.** The act of curving, or the state of being curved. **2.** *Physiol.* A curving, esp. when abnormal: *curvature* of the spine. [< L *curvare* to bend]

curve (kûrv) *n.* **1.** A line continuously bent, as the arc of a circle. **2.** A curving, or something curved. **3.** An instrument for drawing curves. **4.** *Math.* The locus of a point moving in such a way that its course can be defined by an equation. **5.** In baseball, a ball pitched with a spin that causes it to veer to one side. **6.** A grading system based upon a theoretical frequency distribution. — *v.* **curved, curv·ing** *v.t.* **1.** To cause to assume the form of or move in the path of a curve. — *v.i.* **2.** To assume the form of a curve. **3.** To move in a curve. — *adj.* Curved. [< L *curvus* bent] — **curv′ed·ly** *adv.* — **curv′ed·ness** *n.*

cur·vet (*n.* kûr′vit; *v.* kər·vet′, kûr′vit) *n.* A light, low leap of a horse, made so that all four legs are off the ground at one time. — *v.* **cur·vet·ted** or **·vet·ed, cur·vet·ting** or **·vet·ing** *v.i.* **1.** To make a curvet. **2.** To prance; frisk. — *v.t.* **3.** To cause to curvet. [< Ital. < L *curvus* bent]

curvi- *combining form* Curved. [< L *curvus* curved]

cur·vi·lin·e·ar (kûr′və·lin′ē·ər) *adj.* Formed or enclosed by curved lines. Also **cur′vi·lin′e·al.**

cush·ion (kŏosh′ən) *n.* **1.** A flexible bag or casing filled with some soft or elastic material, as feathers, air, etc., used for lying or resting on. **2.** Anything resembling a cushion in appearance or use; esp., any device to deaden the jar or impact of parts, as padding, etc. **3.** The elastic rim of a billiard table. **4.** *Canadian* The ice of a hockey rink. — *v.t.* **1.** To seat or arrange on or as on a cushion. **2.** To provide with a cushion. **3.** To absorb the shock or effect of. [< F *coussin,* ult. < L *coxa* hip, thigh] — **cush′ion·y** *adj.*

Cush·it·ic (kŏosh·it′ik) *n.* A group of Hamitic languages spoken in Ethiopia and Somaliland. — *adj.* Pertaining to this group of languages. Also spelled *Kushitic.*

cush·y (kŏosh′ē) *adj. Slang* **cush·i·er, cush·i·est** Comfortable; agreeable; easy. [< CUSHION; orig. Brit. slang]

cusp (kusp) *n.* **1.** A point or pointed end. **2.** Either point of a crescent moon. **3.** *Geom.* A point at which two branches of a curve meet and end, with a common tangent. [< L *cuspis, -idis* a point] — **cus·pate** (kus′pāt), **cus′pated, cusped** (kuspt) *adj.*

cus·pid (kus′pid) *n.* A canine tooth.

cus·pi·date (kus′pə·dāt) *adj.* Having a cusp or cusps. Also **cus·pi·dal** (kus′pə·dəl), **cus′pi·dat′ed.**

cus·pi·dor (kus′pə·dôr) *n.* A spittoon. [< Pg. < L < *com-* thoroughly + *spuere* to spit]

cuss (kus) *U.S. Informal v.t. & v.i.* To curse. — *n.* **1.** A curse. **2.** A perverse person or animal. [Var. of CURSE] — **cuss·ed** (kus′id) *adj.* — **cuss′ed·ly** *adv.* — **cuss′ed·ness** *n.*

cus·tard (kus′tərd) *n.* A mixture of milk, eggs, sugar, and flavoring, either boiled or baked. [< F < L *crusta* crust]

cus·to·di·an (kus·tō′dē·ən) *n.* A guardian; caretaker. — **cus·to′di·an·ship** *n.*

cus·to·dy (kus′tə·dē) *n. pl.* **·dies 1.** A keeping; guardianship. **2.** The state of being held in keeping or under guard. [< L < *custos* guardian] — **cus·to·di·al** (kus·tō′dē·əl) *adj.*

cus·tom (kus′təm) *n.* **1.** The habitual practice of a community or a people. **2.** An ordinary or usual manner of doing or acting; habit. **3.** *Law* An old and general usage that has obtained the force of law. **4.** Habitual patronage, as of a hotel, store, etc. **5.** *pl.* A tariff or duty upon imported or, rarely, exported goods; also, the agency of the government that collects such duties. — *adj.* **1.** Made to order. **2.** Specializing in made-to-order goods. [< OF < L < *com-* thoroughly + *suescere* to become used to]

cus·tom·ar·y (kus′tə·mer′ē) *adj.* **1.** Conforming to or established by custom; usual; habitual. **2.** *Law* Holding or held by custom, as a feudal estate. — *n. pl.* **·ar·ies** A written statement of laws and customs. [See CUSTOM.] — **cus·tom·ar·i·ly** (kus′tə·mer′ə·lē, kus′tə·mer′ə·lē) *adv.*

cus·tom-built (kus′təm·bilt′) *adj.* Built to order or to individual specifications: a *custom-built* boat.

cus·tom·er (kus′təm·ər) *n.* **1.** One who buys something; esp., one who deals regularly at a given establishment. **2.** *Informal* One to be dealt with: a queer *customer.*

cus·tom·house (kus′təm·hous′) *n.* The government office where duties are collected and vessels cleared for entering or leaving. Also **custom house.**

cus·tom-made (kus′təm-mād′) *adj.* Made to order.
cus·toms union (kus′təmz) An association of nations that remove tariff restrictions among themselves and have a common tariff policy toward other nations: also *common market.*
cut (kut) *v.* **cut, cut·ting** *v.t.* **1.** To open or penetrate with a sharp edge; gash; pierce. **2.** To divide with a sharp edge into parts or segments. **3.** To make or shape by cutting, as gems. **4.** To fell or hew: often with *down.* **5.** To strike sharply, as with a whip. **6.** To hurt the feelings of. **7.** *Informal* To pretend not to know; snub. **8.** *Informal* To absent oneself from: to *cut* a class. **9.** To cross or intersect. **10.** To shorten or trim, as hair, grass, etc. **11.** To shorten or edit by removing parts. **12.** To mow or reap (wheat, etc.) **13.** To reduce or lessen: to *cut* prices. **14.** To dilute or weaken, as whisky. **15.** To dissolve or break down: to *cut* grease. **16.** To have (a new tooth) grow through the gum. **17.** In certain games, to strike the ball so as to deflect it to one side. **18.** To divide (a pack of cards), as before dealing. — *v.i.* **19.** To make an incision. **20.** To act as a sharp edge. **21.** To penetrate like a knife. **22.** To veer sharply in one's course. **23.** To go by the shortest and most direct route: with *across, through,* etc. **24.** In certain sports and games, to deflect the ball. **25.** To grow through the gum: said of teeth. **26.** To divide a pack of cards, as before dealing. **— to cut back 1.** To shorten by removing the end. **2.** To reduce or curtail. **3.** To reverse one's direction. **— to cut down 1.** To reduce; curtail. **2.** To kill, as with a sword. **— to cut in 1.** To move into a line or queue abruptly or out of turn. **2.** To interrupt a dancing couple so as to take the place of one partner. **3.** To break in, as on a conversation; interrupt. **— to cut off 1.** To remove or detach by cutting. **2.** To put an end to; stop. **3.** To interrupt. **4.** To intercept. **5.** To disinherit. **— to cut out 1.** To remove by cutting; excise. **2.** To shape by cutting. **3.** To be suited for: He's not *cut out* for the work. **4.** To move sharply from one's course, as in traffic. **5.** To oust and supplant, as a rival. **6.** *Slang* To stop doing; cease. **— to cut up 1.** To cut in pieces. **2.** To affect deeply; distress. **3.** *Informal* To behave in an unruly manner. — *n.* **1.** A severing, slashing, or piercing stroke: a clean *cut.* **2.** The opening or sound made by such a stroke; gash; cleft. **3.** A part cut off; esp. the part of a meat animal. **4.** A deletion or excision of a part. **5.** A passage or channel that has been cut or dug out. **6.** A direct route: a short *cut.* **7.** Something that hurts the feelings, as an insult. **8.** *Informal* A refusal to recognize an acquaintance. **9.** The manner in which a thing is cut; fashion; style: the *cut* of a suit. **10.** A reduction in prices, wages, etc. **11.** *U.S. Slang* A share or commission. **12.** *Informal* An absence from a class at school. **13.** *Printing* An engraved block or plate; also, an impression made from this. **14.** A stroke imparting spin to a ball, as in tennis, billiards, etc. **15.** A cutting of a deck of cards. **16.** *Chem.* A fraction, as of petroleum, obtained in distillation. **— a cut above** A degree better than. — *adj.* **1.** That has been cut off, into, or through: a *cut* finger. **2.** Dressed or finished by a tool, as stone or glass. **3.** Reduced, as rates or prices. **4.** Diluted, as whisky. **— cut and dried 1.** Prepared or arranged beforehand. **2.** Lacking interest or suspense. [ME < Scand.]
cu·ta·ne·ous (kyoo·tā′nē·əs) *adj.* Of, pertaining to, affecting, or like skin. [< Med.L < L *cutis* skin]
cut·a·way (kut′ə·wā′) *n.* A man's formal daytime coat, having the front corners cut slopingly away from the waist down to the tails at the back: also **cutaway coat.**
cut·back (kut′bak′) *n.* **1.** A sharp reduction, as in personnel or scheduled production. **2.** A reduction.
cute (kyoot) *adj.* **cut·er, cut·est** *U.S. Informal* Pretty, dainty, or attractive. [Var. of ACUTE] **— cute′ly** *adv.* **— cute′ness** *n.*
cut glass Glass that has been shaped or ornamented by cutting on a wheel of stone, iron, copper, etc.
cu·ti·cle (kyoo′ti·kəl) *n.* **1.** *Anat.* The epidermis. **2.** Any superficial covering. **3.** The crescent of toughened skin around the base of a fingernail or toenail. [< L *cuticula,* dim. of *cutis* skin] **— cu·tic′u·lar** *adj.*
cu·tin (kyoo′tin) *n. Bot.* A fatty or waxy protective cuticle of leaves, stems, etc., of plants. [< L *cutis* skin + -IN]
cu·tin·i·za·tion (kyoo′tən·ə·zā′shən, -ī·zā′-) *n. Bot.* The modification of cell walls by the presence of cutin, making them waterproof.
cu·tin·ize (kyoo′tən·īz) *v.t. & v.i.* **·ized, ·iz·ing** To undergo or cause to undergo cutinization.
cut·lass (kut′ləs) *n.* A short, swordlike weapon, often curved. Also **cut′las.** [< F < L *culter* knife]
cut·ler (kut′lər) *n.* One who makes repairs, or deals in cutlery. [< OF < Med.L < L *cultellus,* dim. of *culter* knife]
cut·ler·y (kut′lər·ē) *n.* **1.** Cutting instruments collectively, esp. those for use at the dinner table. **2.** The occupation of a cutler.
cut·let (kut′lit) *n.* **1.** A thin piece of meat for frying or broiling, usu. veal or mutton. **2.** A flat croquette of chopped meat, fish, etc. [< F < L *costa* rib]

cut·off (kut′ôf′, -of′) *n.* **1.** The prescribed termination or limit of a process or series. **2.** *U.S.* A shorter route; short cut. **3.** *Mech.* **a** A cutting off of the flow of something, as fluid or steam. **b** The mechanism that does this.
cut·out (kut′out′) *n.* **1.** Something cut out or intended to be cut out. **2.** *Electr.* A device that cuts off the current when the flow reaches an unsafe level. **3.** A device to let the exhaust gases from an internal-combustion engine pass directly to the air without going through the muffler.
cut·o·ver (kut′ō′vər) *adj.* Cleared of timber, as land.
cut·purse (kut′pûrs′) *n.* A pickpocket; formerly, one who cut away purses that were attached to a girdle or belt.
cut-rate (kut′rāt′) *adj.* Sold or selling at reduced prices.
cut·ter (kut′ər) *n.* **1.** One who cuts, esp. one who shapes, fits, decorates, or edits by cutting. **2.** A device that cuts. **3.** *Naut.* **a** A single-masted, fast-sailing vessel of narrow beam and deep draft, and normally spreading no more than four sails. **b** A small, swift, armed, and engined vessel, as used by the Coast Guard for coastal patrol, etc. **c** A small to medium-sized boat either employed by or carried on a larger vessel (such as a warship) and used to discharge passengers, transport stores, etc. **4.** A small sleigh.
cut·throat (kut′thrōt′) *adj.* **1.** Bloodthirsty; murderous. **2.** Ruinous; merciless. — *n.* A murderer.
cut·ting (kut′ing) *adj.* **1.** Adapted to cut; edged. **2.** Sharp; chilling. **3.** Unkind; sarcastic. — *n.* **1.** The act of one who or that which cuts. **2.** Something obtained or made by cutting. **3.** *Brit.* A newspaper clipping.
cut·tle·bone (kut′l·bōn′) *n.* The internal calcareous plate of a cuttlefish, used as a dietary supplement for birds and, when powdered, as a polishing agent.
cut·tle·fish (kut′l·fish′) *n. pl.* **·fish** or **·fish·es** A sea mollusk having lateral fins, ten sucker-bearing arms, a hard inner shell, and concealing itself by ejecting an inky fluid.
cut-up (kut′up′) *n. Informal* A person who tries to seem funny, as a practical joker.
cut·wa·ter (kut′wô′tər, -wot′ər) *n.* The forward part of the prow of a vessel.
cut·work (kut′wûrk′) *n.* Openwork embroidery with cut-out edges.
cut·worm (kut′wûrm′) *n.* Any of several nocturnal caterpillars that cut off plants at the surface of the ground.
-cy *suffix* Forming nouns: **1.** (*from adjectives*) Quality, state, or condition of: *secrecy, bankruptcy.* **2.** (*from nouns*) Rank or condition of: *chaplaincy.* [< F *-cie* < L *-cia* < Gk. *-kia*]
cyan- Var. of CYANO-.
cy·an·ic (sī·an′ik) *adj.* **1.** Of, pertaining to, or containing cyanogen. **2.** Blue.
cy·a·nide (sī′ə·nīd) *n. Chem.* A compound of cyanogen with a metallic element or radical. Also **cy′a·nid** (-nid). — *v.t.* **·nid·ed, ·nid·ing** *Metall.* To subject to the action of cyanide: to extract gold by *cyaniding* the ore. **— cy·a·ni·da′tion** *n.*
cyano- *combining form* **1.** Characterized by bluish coloring: *cyanosis.* **2.** *Chem.* Cyanide. Also, before vowels, **cyan-.** [< Gk. *kyanos* dark blue]
cy·an·o·gen (sī·an′ə·jən) *n. Chem.* **1.** A colorless, flammable, poisonous, liquefiable gas, C_2N_2, having an almondlike odor. **2.** The univalent radical CN. [< F *cyanogène*]
cy·a·no·sis (sī′ə·nō′sis) *n. Pathol.* A disordered condition due to inadequate oxygenation of the blood, causing the skin to look blue. **— cy·a·not·ic** (sī′ə·not′ik) *adj.*
cy·ber·net·ics (sī′bər·net′iks) *n.pl.* (*construed as sing.*) The science that treats of the principles of control and communication as they apply both to the operation of complex machines and the functions of organisms. [< Gk. *kybernetēs* steersman + -ICS] **— cy·ber·net′ic** *adj.*
cy·cad (sī′kad) *n.* Any of a family of primitive, seed-bearing, mostly tropical plants of fernlike or palmlike appearance. [< Gk. *kykas,* erroneous pl. of *koïx* a palm tree] **— cyc·a·da·ceous** (sik′ə·dā′shəs) *adj.*
cyc·la·men (sik′lə·mən, -men) *n.* An Old World bulbous flowering herb of the primrose family, with white, pink, or crimson flowers. [< NL < L < Gk. *kyklaminos, kyklamis*]
cy·cle (sī′kəl) *n.* **1.** A recurring period within which certain events or phenomena occur in a definite sequence. **2.** A completed round of events or phenomena in which there is a final return to the original state. **3.** A pattern of regularly recurring events. **4.** A vast period of time; an eon. **5.** A body of poems or stories relating to the same character or subject. **6.** A bicycle, tricycle, etc. — *v.i.* **·cled, ·cling 1.** To pass through cycles. **2.** To ride a bicycle, tricycle, etc. [< OF < LL < Gk. *kyklos* circle]
cy·clic (sī′klik, sik′lik) *adj.* **1.** Pertaining to or characterized by cycles; recurring in cycles. **2.** *Chem.* Arranged in a closed chain or ring formation, as the atoms of benzene, naphthalene, etc. Also **cy′cli·cal.**
cy·clist (sī′klist) *n.* One who rides a bicycle, tricycle, etc.
cyclo- *combining form* **1.** Circular. **2.** *Chem.* A cyclic compound. Also, before vowels, **cycl-.** [< Gk. *kyklos* circle]
cy·cloid (sī′kloid) *adj.* Resembling a circle or somewhat circular. — *n. Geom.* The curve described by a point on the

circumference of a circle rolling along a straight line in a single plane. [< Gk. *kykloeidēs* circular] — **cy·cloi′dal** *adj.*

cy·clom·e·ter (sī·klom′ə·tər) *n.* An instrument for recording the rotations of a wheel to show speed and distance.

cy·clone (sī′klōn) *n.* **1.** *Meteorol.* A system of winds circulating about a center of relatively low barometric pressure, and advancing at the earth's surface with clockwise rotation in the Southern Hemisphere, counterclockwise in the Northern. **2.** Loosely, any violent storm. [< Gk. < *kyklos* circle] — **cy·clon·ic** (sī·klon′ik) or **·i·cal** *adj.* — **cy·clon′i·cal·ly** *adv.*

cy·clo·pe·an (sī′klə·pē′ən) *adj.* **1.** *Usu. cap.* Of or pertaining to the Cyclopes. **2.** Gigantic: a *cyclopean* task.

cy·clo·pe·di·a (sī′klə·pē′dē·ə) *n.* An encyclopedia (which see). Also **cy′clo·pae′di·a.** — **cy′clo·pe′dic** or **cy′clo·pe′di·cal·ly** *adv.* — **cy′clo·pe′dist,** or **cy′clo·pae′dist** *n.*

cy·clo·pro·pane (sī′klə·prō′pān) *n. Chem.* A colorless, pungent, inflammable gas, C_3H_6, used as an anesthetic.

Cy·clops (sī′klops) *n.* *pl.* **Cy·clo·pes** (sī·klō′pēz) In Homeric legend, any of a race of one-eyed giants of Sicily.

cy·clo·ram·a (sī′klə·ram′ə, -rä′mə) *n.* **1.** A series of pictures on the interior of a cylindrical surface, appearing in natural perspective to a spectator standing in the center. **2.** A backdrop curtain, often concave, used on theater stages. [< CYCLO- + Gk. *horama* a view] — **cy′clo·ram′ic** *adj.*

cy·clo·tron (sī′klə·tron) *n. Physics* An accelerator that obtains high-energy electrified particles by whirling them at very high speeds in a strong magnetic field.

cyg·net (sig′nit) *n.* A young swan. [< MF *cygne* a swan]

Cyg·nus (cig′nəs) A constellation, the Swan, containing the bright star Deneb: also called *Northern Cross.* [< L]

cyl·in·der (sil′in·dər) *n.* **1.** *Geom.* A solid figure generated by one side of a rectangle rotated about the opposite fixed side, the ends of the figure being equal, parallel circles. **2.** Any object or container resembling a cylinder in form. **3.** *Mech.* In a reciprocating engine, the chamber in which the pistons move. **4.** In a revolver, the rotating part that holds the cartridges. — *v.t.* To press or fit with a cylinder. [< L < Gk. < *kylindein* to roll]

cy·lin·dri·cal (si·lin′dri·kəl) *adj.* **1.** Of a cylinder. **2.** Shaped like a cylinder. Also **cy·lin′dric.** *Abbr. cyl.* — **cy·lin·dri·cal·i·ty** (si·lin′dri·kal′ə·tē) *n.* — **cy·lin′dri·cal·ly** *adv.*

cym·bal (sim′bəl) *n.* One of a pair of concave metal plates clashed to produce a musical ringing sound. [OE and OF < L < Gk. *kymbē* cup, hollow of a vessel] — **cym′bal·ist** *n.*

cyme (sīm) *n. Bot* A flat-topped flower cluster in which the central flowers bloom first. [< F < L < Gk *kyma*] — **cy·mose** (sī′mōs, sī·mōs′) *adj.*

cymo- *combining form* Wave. [< Gk. *kymo-* < *kyma* wave]

Cym·ric (kim′rik, sim′-) *adj.* Of or pertaining to the Cymry; Brythonic. — *n.* **1.** The Welsh language. **2.** The Brythonic branch of the Celtic languages.

Cym·ry (kim′rē, sim′-) *n.* A collective name for the Welsh and their Cornish and Breton kin: also *Kymry.* Also **Cym′ri.**

cyn·ic (sin′ik) *n.* A sneering, faultfinding person; esp., one who believes that all men are motivated by selfishness. — *adj.* Cynical. [< L < Gk < *kyōn, kynos* dog]

Cyn·ic (sin′ik) *n.* One of a sect of Greek philosophers of the fifth and fourth centuries B.C., who held that virtue was the goal of life. Their doctrine eventually came to represent insolent self-righteousness. — *adj.* Pertaining to or characteristic of the Cynics: also **Cyn′i·cal.**

cyn·i·cal (sin′i·kəl, -ə-) *adj.* Distrusting or contemptuous of virtue in others; sneering; sarcastic. — **cyn′i·cal·ly** *adv.*

cyn·i·cism (sin′ə·siz′əm, -i-) *n.* **1.** Cynical character or attitude; contempt for or disbelief in the virtues of others. **2.** A cynical remark, action, etc. Also **cyn′i·cal·ness.**

cy·no·sure (sī′nə·shŏŏr, sin′ə-) *n.* **1.** A person or object that attracts notice and admiration. **2.** Something that guides. [< MF < L < Gk. < *kyōn, kynos* dog + *oura* tail]

Cy·no·sure (sī′nə·shŏŏr, sin′ə-) *n.* **1.** The constellation Ursa Minor, containing the polestar. **2.** Polaris.

Cyn·thi·a (sin′thē·ə) Artemis. — *n. Poetic* The moon.

cy·pher (sī′fər) See CIPHER.

cy·press¹ (sī′prəs) *n.* **1.** An evergreen tree of the pine family, having flat, scalelike foliage. **2.** A related tree. **3.** The wood of these trees. [< OF < LL < Gk. *kyparissos*]

Cyp·ri·an (sip′rē·ən) *adj.* Of or pertaining to Cyprus. — *n.* A Cypriote.

cyp·ri·noid (sip′rə·noid, si·prī′-) *adj.* Of or pertaining to the carp family of fishes. Also **cy·pri·nid** (si·prī′nid, sip′rə·nid). [< Gk. *kyprinos* carp + -OID]

Cyp·ri·ote (sip′rē·ōt) *n.* **1.** A native or inhabitant of Cyprus. **2.** The ancient or modern Greek dialect of Cyprus. — *adj.* Of or pertaining to Cyprus. Also **Cyp·ri·ot** (sip′rē·ət). [< F *cypriote*]

Cy·ril·lic alphabet (si·ril′ik) A Slavic alphabet based mainly on that of the Greeks, ascribed traditionally to Saint Cyril, used for Russian, Bulgarian, Serbo-Croatian, Ukrainian, Byelorussian, and Macedonian. See ALPHABET.

cyst (sist) *n.* **1.** *Pathol.* Any abnormal sac or vesicle in which matter may collect and be retained. **2.** *Biol.* Any saclike organ in plants or animals. [< Med.L < Gk. *kyein* to contain] — **cys′tic, cys′toid** *adj.*

cys·ti·tis (sis·tī′tis) *n. Pathol.* Inflammation of the bladder.

cysto- *combining form* Bladder; cyst. Also, before vowels, **cyst-:** also **cysti-.** [< Gk. *kystis* bladder]

cys·to·scope (sis′tə·skōp) *n. Med.* A device for examining the interior of the urinary bladder. — **cys·to·scop·ic** (sis′tə·skop′ik) *adj.*

-cyte *combining form* Cell: *phagocyte.* [< Gk. *kytos* hollow vessel]

Cyth·e·re·a (sith′ə·rē′ə) Aphrodite. — **Cyth′e·re′an** *adj.*

cyto- *combining form* Cell. Also, before vowels, **cyt-.** [< Gk. *kytos* hollow vessel < *kyein* to contain, be pregnant with]

cy·to·ge·net·ics (sī′tō·jə·net′iks) *n.pl.* (*construed as sing.*) The study of the role of cells in heredity.

cy·tol·o·gy (sī·tol′ə·jē) *n.* The study of the structure, organization, and function of cells. — **cy·to·log·ic** (sī′tə·loj′ik) or **·i·cal** *adj.* — **cy·to·log′i·cal·ly** *adv.* — **cy·tol′o·gist** *n.*

cy·to·plasm (sī′tə·plaz′əm) *n. Biol.* All the protoplasm of a cell except that in the nucleus. Also **cy′to·plast.**

czar (zär) *n.* **1.** An emperor or king; one of the former emperors of Russia. **2.** An absolute ruler; despot. Also *tsar, tzar.* [< Russ. *tsar'*, ult. < L *Caesar* Caesar] — **czar′dom** *n.* — **czar′ism** *n.* — **czar′ist** *adj.* & *n.*

czar·e·vitch (zär′ə·vich) *n.* The eldest son of a czar: also *tsarevitch, tzarevitch.* [< Russ. *tsarevich*]

cza·rev·na (zä·rev′nə) *n.* **1.** The wife of the czarevitch. **2.** Formerly, the title of any daughter of the czar. Also *tsarevna, tzarevna.* [< Russ. *tsarevna*]

cza·ri·na (zä·rē′nə) *n.* The wife of a czar; an empress of Russia: also *tsarina, tzarina.* Also **cza·rit·za** (zä·rit′sə) [< G *czarin*, for Russ. *tzaritsa*]

Czech (chek) *n.* **1.** A member of the western branch of Slavs, including the peoples of Bohemia and Moravia. **2.** The West Slavic language of the Czechs, formerly called Bohemian. — *adj.* Relating to Czechoslovakia, the Czechs, or their language: also **Czech′ic, Czech′ish.**

Czech·o·slo·vak (chek′ə·slō′vak, -väk) *n.* A Czech or Slovak inhabiting Czechoslovakia. — *adj.* Of or pertaining to the Czechoslovaks. Also **Czech·o·slo·va·ki·an** (chek′ə·slō·väk′ē·ən, -vak′ē·ən).

D

d, D (dē) *n.* *pl.* **d's** or **ds, D's** or **Ds, dees** (dēz) **1.** The fourth letter of the English alphabet. **2.** The sound represented by the letter *d.* **3.** Anything shaped like the letter D. — *symbol* **1.** The Roman numeral for 500. **2.** *Music* **a** The second tone in the natural scale of C; re. **b** A written note representing it. **c** The scale built upon D. **3.** *Math.* Differential. **4.** The fourth in a series or group. **5.** Pence **6.** *Chem.* Deuterium (symbol D). **7.** *Physics* Density.

dab¹ (dab) *n.* **1.** Any of various flounders. **2.** Any flatfish.

dab² (dab) *n.* **1.** A gentle pat. **2.** A soft, moist patch: a *dab* of paint. **3.** A little bit. — *v.t. & v.i.* **dabbed, dab·bing 1.** To strike softly; tap. **2.** To peck. **3.** To pat with something soft and damp. **4.** To apply (paint, etc.) with light strokes. [ME *dabben*] — **dab′ber** *n.*

dab·chick (dab′chik) *n.* A small grebe of Europe, or the pied-billed grebe of North America.

dab·ble (dab'əl) v. **·bled**, **·bling** v.i. 1. To play in a liquid, as with the hands; splash gently. 2. To engage oneself slightly or superficially: to *dabble* in art. — v.t. 3. To wet slightly; bespatter. [Freq. of DAB[2], v.] — **dab'bler** n.

da ca·po (dä kä'pō) *Music* From the beginning: a direction to repeat the opening section of a piece.

dace (dās) n. pl. **dac·es** or **dace** A small fresh-water fish of the carp family. [< OF *dars*, a small fish, lit., dart]

dachs·hund (däks'hŏont/, daks'hŏond/, dash'-) n. A breed of dog native to Germany, having a long, compact body, short legs, and a short coat, usu. of red, tan, or black and tan. [< G < *dachs* badger + *hund* dog]

Da·cron (dā'kron, dak'ron) n. A synthetic polyester textile fiber of high tensile strength, having great resistance to stretching and wrinkling: a trade name. Also **da'cron**.

DACHSHUND
(7 to 9 inches high at shoulder)

dac·tyl (dak'təl) n. In prosody, a metrical foot consisting of one long or accented syllable followed by two short or unaccented ones (—◡◡). [< L < Gk. *daktylos* finger, dactyl] — **dac·tyl·ic** (dak·til'ik) adj. & n.

dactylo- *combining form* Finger; toe. Also, before vowels, **dactyl-**. [< L < Gk. *daktylos* finger]

dad (dad) n. *Informal* Father. Also **dad·dy** (dad'ē). [Origin unknown]

da·da (dä'dä, -də) n. *Often cap.* A movement in art and literature, occurring esp. in France, Germany, and Switzerland about 1916–20, that protested against civilization and violently satirized all previous art. Also **da'da·ism**. [< F *dada*, a nonsense word] — **da·da·ist** n. — **da·da·ist'ic** adj.

dad·dle (dad'l) v.t. & v.i. **·dled**, **·dling** Diddle[1].

dad·dy-long·legs (dad'ē·lông'legz/, -long'-) n. pl. **legs** A longlegged insect resembling a spider: also called *harvestman*.

da·do (dā'dō) n. pl. **·does** 1. *Archit.* The part of a pedestal between the base and the cornice; the die. 2. The lower part of an interior wall, often ornamented. [< Ital., a cube]

Daed·a·lus (ded'ə·ləs, *Brit.* dē'də-) In Greek mythology, an Athenian architect who devised the Cretan Labyrinth in which he was later imprisoned with his son Icarus, and from which they escaped by artificial wings.

daf·fo·dil (daf'ə·dil) n. A plant of the amaryllis family, with solitary yellow flowers. Also *Dial.* or *Poetic* **daf·fa·dil·ly** (daf'ə·dil'ē), **daf·fa·down·dil·ly** (daf'ə·doun·dil'ē), **daf·fy·down·dil·ly** (daf'ē-). [< ME *affodile*]

daf·fy (daf'ē) adj. **daf·fi·er**, **daf·fi·est** *Informal* Crazy; silly; zany. [< DAFF[2]]

daft (daft, däft) adj. 1. *Chiefly Brit.* Of weak mind; insane. 2. *Chiefly Brit.* Foolish; silly. [OE *gedæfte* mild, meek] — **daft'ly** adv. — **daft'ness** n.

dag·ger (dag'ər) n. 1. A short, pointed and edged weapon for stabbing. 2. *Printing* A reference mark (†). — **double dagger** *Printing* A reference mark (‡); a diesis. — **to look daggers (at)** To glare or scowl (at). — v.t. 1. To stab. 2. *Printing* To mark with a dagger. [? ME *dag* to stab]

da·go (dā'gō) n. pl. **·gos** or **·goes** *U.S. Slang* An Italian, or less commonly, a Spaniard or Portuguese: an offensive term. [Alter. of Sp. *Diego*, a personal name]

da·guerre·o·type (də·ger'ə·tīp/, -ē·ə·tīp/) n. 1. An early photographic process using silver-coated metallic plates that were sensitive to light. 2. A picture made by this process. [after Louis Jacques Mandé *Daguerre*, 1789–1851, French inventor] — **da·guerre·o·typ'er**, **da·guerre·o·typ'ist** n. — **da·guerre·o·typ'y** n.

dahl·ia (dal'yə, däl'-, dāl'-) n. A tender perennial plant of the composite family, having tuberous roots and showy red, purple, yellow, or white flowers; also, the flowers. [after Anders *Dahl*, 18th c. botanist]

Dail Ei·reann (dô·əl âr'ən) The lower house of the legislature of Ireland.

dai·ly (dā'lē) adj. Of, occurring, or appearing every day or every weekday. — n. pl. **·lies** A daily publication. — adv. Day after day; on every day. [OE *dæg* day]

dain·ty (dān'tē) adj. **·ti·er**, **·ti·est** 1. Delicately pretty or graceful. 2. Of pleasing taste; delicious. 3. Of fine sensibilities; fastidious; also, too fastidious; overnice. — n. pl. **·ties** Something tasty or delicious; a delicacy. [< OF < L *dignitas* worth, dignity] — **dain'ti·ly** adv. — **dain'ti·ness** n.

dai·qui·ri (dī'kər·ē, dak'ər·ē) n. A cocktail made of rum, lime or lemon juice, and sugar. [*Daiquiri*, Cuba]

dair·y (dâr'ē) n. pl. **·ies** 1. A commercial establishment that sells milk products. 2. A room or building on a farm where milk and cream are kept and processed. 3. A dairy farm or dairy cattle. 4. Dairying. [ME *deie* dairymaid]

dairy cattle Cows of a breed adapted for milk production.

dairy farm A farm for producing dairy products.

dair·y·ing (dâr'ē·ing) n. The business of a dairy.

dair·y·maid (dâr'ē·mād/) n. A female worker in a dairy.

dair·y·man (dâr'ē·mən) n. pl. **·men** (-mən) A man who works in or owns a dairy.

da·is (dā'is, dās) n. A raised platform in a room or hall on which a speaker, eminent guests, etc., may sit or stand. [< OF *deis* < LL *discus* table]

dai·sy (dā'zē) n. pl. **·sies** 1. Any of various plants of the composite family; esp., the **oxeye daisy**, of the U.S., having a yellow disk and white rays, and the **English daisy**, having a small yellow disk and numerous white or rose rays. 2. *Slang* Something excellent or exceptional. [OE *dægas ēage* day's eye] — **dai'sied** adj.

Da·ko·ta (də·kō'tə) n. 1. A member of the largest division of the Siouan stock of North American Plains Indians, now on reservations in North and South Dakota, Minnesota, and Montana. 2. The Siouan language of the Dakotas. 3. A Sioux Indian. — **Da·ko'tan** adj. & n.

Da·lai La·ma (dä·lī' lä'mə) The pontiff of the principal Buddhist faith in Tibet, and traditional chief of state.

dale (dāl) n. A small valley. [OE *dæl*]

dal·li·ance (dal'ē·əns) n. 1. Amorous play, flirting, or fondling. 2. Idle wasting of time; trifling.

dal·ly (dal'ē) v. **·lied**, **·ly·ing** v.i. 1. To make love sportively; frolic. 2. To play; trifle. 3. To waste time. — v.t. 4. To waste (time): with *away*. [< OF *dalier* to converse, chat] — **dal'li·er** n.

Dal·ma·tian (dal·mā'shən) n. 1. A large, short-haired dog, white with black spots: also called *coach dog*. 2. One of the Slavic people of Dalmatia. — adj. Of or pertaining to Dalmatia or its people.

dal·mat·ic (dal·mat'ik) n. *Eccl.* A wide-sleeved vestment worn by a deacon over the alb, as at High Mass. [< OF < L *dalmatica* (*vestis*) Dalmatian (robe)]

dal se·gno (däl sā'nyō) *Music* From the sign: a direction to repeat from the sign :S: to the end. [< Ital.]

dam[1] (dam) n. 1. A barrier to obstruct or control the flow of water. 2. The water held back by such a barrier. 3. Any obstruction. — v.t. **dammed**, **dam·ming** 1. To erect a dam in; obstruct or confine by a dam. 2. To keep back; restrain: with *up* or *in*. [ME. Akin to OE *demman* to block.]

dam[2] (dam) n. A female parent: said of animals. [< DAME]

dam·age (dam'ij) n. 1. Injury to person or property. 2. pl. *Law* Money to compensate for an injury or wrong. 3. *Sometimes pl. Informal* Price or expense. — v. **·aged**, **·ag·ing** v.t. 1. To cause damage to. — v.i. 2. To be susceptible to damage. [< OF < L *damnum* loss] — **dam'age·a·ble** adj.

dam·as·cene (dam'ə·sēn, dam'ə·sēn') v.t. **·cened**, **·cen·ing** To ornament (iron, steel, etc.) with wavy patterns or by inlaying or etching. Also **dam·as·keen** (dam'ə·skēn, dam'ə·skēn'). — adj. Relating to damascening or to damask. — n. Work ornamented by damascening.

Damascus steel A steel with wavy markings, formerly used in swords made at Damascus. Also **damask steel**.

dam·ask (dam'əsk) n. 1. A rich, reversible, elaborately patterned fabric, originally made of silk. 2. A fine, twilled table linen. 3. Damascus steel, or the wavy pattern on such steel. 4. A deep pink or rose color. — adj. 1. Of or from Damascus. 2. Made of Damascus steel or of damask. 3. Deep pink or rose-colored. — v.t. 1. To damascene. 2. To weave or ornament with rich patterns. [after *Damascus*]

damask rose A large, fragrant, pink rose of the Near East.

dame (dām) n. 1. A mature woman; matron. 2. *U.S. Slang* A woman. 3. In Great Britain: **a** A title of the Order of the British Empire conferred on women, equivalent to that of knight. **b** The legal title of the wife of a knight or baronet. [< OF < L *domina* lady]

damn (dam) v.t. 1. To pronounce worthless, bad, a failure, etc. 2. To curse or swear at. 3. *Theol.* To condemn to eternal punishment. 4. To pronounce guilty; bring ruin upon. — v.i. 5. To swear; curse. — **to damn with faint praise** To praise so reluctantly as to imply adverse criticism. — n. 1. The saying of "damn" as an oath. 2. The smallest, most contemptible bit. — *interj.* An oath expressive of irritation, disappointment, etc. — adj. & adv. *Informal* Damned. [< OF < L *damnare* to condemn to punishment]

dam·na·ble (dam'nə·bəl) adj. Meriting damnation; detestable; outrageous. [< OF < L *damnare* to condemn] — **dam'na·ble·ness** n. — **dam'na·bly** adv.

dam·na·tion (dam·nā'shən) n. 1. The act of damning, or the state of being damned. 2. *Theol.* Condemnation to eternal punishment; also, eternal punishment. — *interj.* Damn. — **dam·na·to·ry** (dam'nə·tôr'ē, -tō'rē) adj.

damn·dest (dam'dist) *Informal* adj. 1. Most detestable or outrageous: the *damndest* lie. 2. Most extraordinary. — n. The utmost: Do your *damndest*. Also **damned'est**.

damned (damd, *poetic or rhetorical* dam'nid) adj. 1. Doomed; condemned, esp. to eternal punishment. 2. Deserving damnation. — adv. *Informal* Very: *damned* funny.

damn·ing (dam'ing, dam'ning) adj. That damns or condemns; inculpating: *damning* evidence. — **damn'ing·ly** adv.

Dam·o·cles (dam'ə·klēz) In Greek legend, a courtier who was forced to sit at a banquet under a sword suspended by a hair that he might learn the perilous nature of a ruler's life. — **sword of Damocles** Any impending calamity.

Da·mon and Pyth·i·as (dā′mən; pith′ē·əs) In Roman legend, two devoted friends.
damp (damp) *adj.* Somewhat wet; moist. — *n.* 1. Moisture or moistness; vapor; mist. 2. Foul air or poisonous gas, especially in a mine. 3. Depression of spirits. — *v.t.* 1. To make damp; moisten. 2. To discourage or dull (energy, ardor, etc.). 3. To stifle, check, reduce, etc. 4. *Physics* To reduce the amplitude of (a series of waves). [< MDu., vapor, steam] — **damp′ly** *adv.* — **damp′ness** *n.*
damp·en (dam′pən) *v.t.* 1. To make damp; moisten. 2. To check; depress, as ardor or spirits. — *v.i.* 3. To become damp. — **damp′en·er** *n.*
damp·er (dam′pər) *n.* 1. One who or that which damps, depresses, or checks. 2. A flat plate in the flue of a stove, furnace, etc., for controlling the draft. 3. *Music* **a** A mechanism for stopping the vibrations of the strings in a piano. **b** In brass instruments, a mute.
damp·ish (dam′pish) *adj.* Slightly damp.
dam·sel (dam′zəl) *n.* A young unmarried woman; maiden. Also, *Archaic,* **dam′o·sel.** [< OF *dameisele* gentlewoman]
dam·son (dam′zən, -sən) *n.* 1. An oval purple plum. 2. The tree producing it. Also **damson plum.** [ME < L *Damascenum* from Damascus]
Dan (dan) In the Old Testament, a son of Jacob and Bilhah. *Gen.* xxx 6. — *n.* The tribe of Israel descended from him.
Dan (dan) In the Bible, a city at the north end of Palestine.
Dan·a·id (dan′ē·id) *n.* One of the Danaides.
Da·na·i·des (də·nā′ə·dēz) *n.pl.* In Greek mythology, the forty-nine daughters of a King of Argos who murdered their husbands on their bridal night and who were punished by having to draw water in a sieve forever.
dance (dans, däns) *v.* **danced, danc·ing** *v.i.* 1. To move the body and feet rhythmically, esp. to music. 2. To move about lightly or excitedly; leap about. 3. To move up and down jerkily; bob. — *v.t.* 4. To perform the steps of (a waltz, tango, etc.). 5. To cause to dance. — **to dance attendance** To wait upon another constantly. — *n.* 1. A series of regular rhythmic steps or movements, usually performed to music. 2. An act or instance of dancing. 3. A musical composition for dancing. 4. A gathering of people for dancing; a ball. [< OF *danser*] — **danc′er** *n.*
dan·de·li·on (dan′də·lī′ən, -dē-) *n.* A widespread plant having yellow flowers and toothed, edible leaves. [< F *dent de lion* lion's tooth; with ref. to the shape of the leaves]
dan·der (dan′dər) *n.* U.S. Informal Ruffled temper; anger. — **to get one's dander up** To become angry. [? Var. of Scottish *dunder* to ferment]
dan·di·fy (dan′də·fī) *v.t.* **·fied, ·fy·ing** To cause to resemble a dandy or fop. — **dan′di·fi·ca′tion** *n.*
dan·dle (dan′dəl) *v.t.* **·dled, ·dling** 1. To move up and down lightly on the knees or in the arms, as an infant or child. 2. To fondle; caress. [< Ital. *dandolare*] — **dan′dler** *n.*
dan·druff (dan′drəf) *n.* A fine scurf that forms on the scalp and comes off in small scales. [Origin unknown]
dan·dy (dan′dē) *n. pl.* **·dies** 1. A man who is excessively interested in fine clothes and elegant appearance; a fop. 2. *Informal* A particularly fine specimen of its kind. — *adj.* 1. Like a dandy; foppish. 2. *U.S. Informal* Excellent; very fine. [Alter. of *Andy,* a personal name] — **dan′dy·ish** *adj.*
Dane (dān) *n.* A native or inhabitant of Denmark, or a person of Danish descent. [< ON *Danir* the Danes]
Dane·law (dān′lô′) *n.* A ninth-century code of laws established by Danish settlers in NE England; also, the region of England under these laws. Also **Dane′lagh′** (-lô′). [OE]
dan·ger (dān′jər) *n.* 1. Exposure to evil, injury, or loss; peril; risk. 2. A cause or instance of peril or risk. [< OF, power to harm]
dan·ger·ous (dān′jər·əs) *adj.* Attended with danger; perilous; unsafe. — **dan′ger·ous·ly** *adv.* — **dan′ger·ous·ness** *n.*
dan·gle (dang′gəl) *v.* **·gled, ·gling** *v.i.* 1. To hang loosely; swing to and fro. 2. To follow or hover near someone as a suitor or hanger-on. — *v.t.* 3. To hold so as to swing loosely. — *n.* 1. Manner or act of dangling. 2. Something that dangles. [< Scand. Cf. Dan. *dangle.*] — **dan′gler** *n.*
Dan·iel (dan′yəl) In the Bible, a young Hebrew prophet, captive in Babylon. *Dan.* i 3–6. — *n.* A book of the Old Testament, containing the story and prophecies of Daniel.
Dan·ish (dā′nish) *adj.* Of or pertaining to Denmark, the Danes, or their language. — *n.* The North Germanic language of the Danes. Abbr. *Dan.* [OE *Denisc*]
dank (dangk) *adj.* Unpleasantly damp; cold and wet. [ME *danke*] — **dank′ly** *adv.* — **dank′ness** *n.*
dan·seuse (dän·sœz′) *n. pl.* **·seus·es** (-sœ′ziz, Fr. -sœz′) A female ballet dancer. [< F, fem. of *danseur*]
Dan·tesque (dan·tesk′) *adj.* Pertaining to or in the style of Dante Alighieri. Also **Dan·te·an** (dan′tē·ən, dan·tē′ən).
Daph·ne (daf′nē) In Greek mythology, a nymph changed into a laurel tree to escape the pursuit of Apollo.

dap·per (dap′ər) *adj.* 1. Smartly dressed; trim; natty. 2. Small and active. [< MDu., strong]
dap·ple (dap′əl) *v.t.* **·pled, ·pling** To make spotted or variegated in color. — *adj.* Spotted; variegated: also **dap′pled.** — *n.* 1. A spot or dot, as on the skin of a horse. 2. An animal marked with spots. [Origin uncertain]
dap·ple-gray (dap′əl·grā′) *adj.* Gray with a pattern of variegated rounded markings: usu. said of horses.
dare (dâr) *v.* **dared, dar·ing** *v.t.* 1. To have the courage or boldness to undertake; venture on. 2. To challenge (someone) to attempt something as proof of courage, etc. 3. To oppose and challenge; defy. — *v.i.* 4. To have the courage or boldness to do or attempt something; venture. — **I dare say** I believe (it): also **I dare·say** (dâr′sā). — *n.* A challenge; taunt. [OE *durran*] — **dar′er** *n.*
dare·dev·il (dâr′dev′əl) *n.* One who is recklessly bold. — *adj.* Rash; reckless. — **dare′dev′il·ry, dare′dev′il·try** *n.*
dar·ing (dâr′ing) *adj.* 1. Brave and adventurous; bold; fearless. 2. Audacious; presuming. — *n.* Adventurous courage; bravery. — **dar′ing·ly** *adv.* — **dar′ing·ness** *n.*
dark (därk) *adj.* 1. Having little or no light; dim: a *dark* cave. 2. Giving off or reflecting little light; gloomy: a *dark* day. 3. Of a deep shade; black, or almost black: a *dark* color. 4. Brunet in complexion. 5. Cheerless or disheartening. 6. Sullen in disposition or appearance; frowning; dour. 7. Unenlightened in mind or spirit; ignorant. 8. Evil or sinister; wicked; atrocious: a *dark* deed. 9. Not understandable; mysterious: a *dark* saying. 10. Not known; secret. — *n.* 1. Lack of light. 2. A place or condition of little or no light. 3. Night. 4. Obscurity; secrecy. 5. Ignorance. 6. A dark shadow or color. — **in the dark** 1. In secret. 2. Ignorant; uninformed. [OE *deorc*] — **dark′ness** *n.*
Dark Ages The period in European history between the fall of the Western Roman Empire (A.D. 476) and the Italian Renaissance; the Middle Ages, esp. the early part.
Dark Continent Africa: so called because little was known about it until the 19th century.
dark·en (där′kən) *v.t.* 1. To make dark or darker; deprive of light. 2. To make dark in color; make black. 3. To fill with gloom; sadden. 4. To obscure; confuse. 5. To blind. — *v.i.* 6. To grow dark or darker; become obscure. 7. To grow clouded or flushed. 8. To become blind. — **dark′en·er** *n.*
dark horse One who unexpectedly wins a race, contest, nomination, etc.
dark lantern A lantern having a case with one transparent side that can be covered by a shield to hide the light.
dark·ling (därk′ling) *Poetic adj.* Occurring or being in the dark; dim. — *adv.* In the dark. [< DARK + -LING²]
dark·ly (därk′lē) *adv.* 1. Obscurely. 2. Mysteriously.
dark·room (därk′rōōm′, -rŏŏm′) *n. Photog.* A room equipped to exclude actinic rays, for treating plates, films, etc.
dark star *Astron.* An invisible or dimly shining star, known only through spectrum analysis, gravitational effect, etc.
dar·ling (där′ling) *n.* 1. A person tenderly loved: often a term of address. 2. A person in great favor. — *adj.* Beloved; very dear. [OE *dēorling,* dim. of *dēor* dear]
darn¹ (därn) *v.t. & v.i.* To repair (a garment or a hole) by filling the gap with interlacing stitches. — *n.* 1. A place mended by darning. 2. The act of darning. [? OE *dernan* to conceal < *derne* hidden] — **darn′er** *n.*
darn² (därn) *v.t., adj., n., & interj. U.S. Informal* Damn: a euphemism. [Alter. of DAMN]
dar·nel (där′nəl) *n.* An annual grass often found in grain fields: also called *cockle, ryegrass.* [< dial. F *darnelle*]
darn·ing needle (där′ning) 1. A large-eyed needle used in darning. 2. A dragonfly.
dart (därt) *n.* 1. A thin, pointed weapon to be thrown or shot. 2. Anything like a dart in appearance. 3. A sudden, rapid motion. 4. The stinger of an insect. 5. A tapering tuck made in a garment to make it fit. — *v.i.* 1. To move suddenly like a dart; rush. — *v.t.* 2. To throw or emit suddenly or swiftly. [< OF < Gmc.]
dart·er (där′tər) *n.* 1. One who or that which darts. 2. A small American percoid fish.
dar·tle (där′təl) *v.t. & v.i.* **·tled, ·tling** To dart or shoot out repeatedly.
darts (därts) *n.pl.* (construed as sing.) A game of skill in which small darts are thrown at a bull's-eye target.
Dar·win·i·an (där·win′ē·ən) *adj.* Pertaining to Charles Darwin, or to Darwinism. — *n.* An advocate of Darwinism: also **Dar′win·ite** (-īt).
Dar·win·ism (där′win·iz′əm) *n.* The biological doctrine of the origin of species through descent by natural selection with variation, advocated by Charles Darwin. — **Dar′win·ist** *n. & adj.* — **Dar′win·is′tic** *adj.*
dash (dash) *v.t.* 1. To strike with violence, esp. so as to break or shatter. 2. To throw, thrust, or knock suddenly

and violently: usually with *away, out, down*, etc. **3.** To bespatter. **4.** To do, write, etc., hastily: with *off* or *down*. **5.** To frustrate; confound: to *dash* hopes. **6.** To daunt or discourage. **7.** To put to shame; abash. **8.** To adulterate; mix: with *with*: to *dash* with salt. —*v.i.* **9.** To strike; hit: The waves *dashed* against the shore. **10.** To rush or move impetuously. —*n.* **1.** A collision; impact. **2.** The splashing of water or other liquid against an object. **3.** A small addition of some other ingredient: a *dash* of bitters. **4.** A hasty stroke, as with a pen or brush. **5.** A check or hindrance. **6.** A sudden advance or onset; a short rush. **7.** A short race run at full speed: the 100-yard *dash*. **8.** Spirited action. **9.** Vigor of style; verve. **10.** A horizontal line (—) used as a mark of punctuation to set off words or phrases in a sentence, to indicate an abrupt breaking off, to mark omissions of words or letters, etc. **11.** *Telecom.* The long sound in the Morse or similar code, used in combination with the dot to represent letters or numbers. [ME *daschen* < Scand.]

dash·board (dash'bôrd', -bōrd') *n.* **1.** The instrument panel of an automobile. **2.** An upright screen on the front of a vehicle to intercept mud, spray, etc.

dash·er (dash'ər) *n.* **1.** One who or that which dashes. **2.** A lively or showy person. **3.** The plunger of a churn.

dash·ing (dash'ing) *adj.* **1.** Spirited; bold; impetuous. **2.** Ostentatiously showy or gay. —**dash'ing·ly** *adv.*

dash·y (dash'ē) *adj.* **dash·i·er, dash·i·est** Stylish; showy.

das·tard (das'tərd) *n.* A base coward; a sneak. —*adj.* Dastardly. [? ME *dased, dast*, pp. of *dasen* to daze + -ARD]

das·tard·ly (das'tərd·lē) *adj.* Base; cowardly. —**das'tard·li·ness** *n.*

da·ta (dā'tə, dat'ə, dä'tə) *n. orig. pl. of* **datum** Facts or figures from which conclusions may be drawn. ◆ Those who continue to regard data as a Latin plural use it with a plural verb (These data *are* new), but its use with a singular verb (This data *is* new) is widespread. [< L, neut. pl. of *datus*, pp. of *dare* to give]

data processing The operations involved in handling and storing information, using computers and other machines.

date¹ (dāt) *n.* **1.** A particular point of time; esp., the time of the occurrence of an event. **2.** The part of a writing, coin, statue, etc., that tells when, or where and when, it was written or made. **3.** The age or period to which a thing belongs: a town of ancient *date*. **4.** The term or duration of a thing. **5.** The day of the month. **6.** *Informal* A social appointment or engagement for a specified time. **7.** *Informal* A person of the opposite sex with whom such an appointment is made. —**to date** Up to and including the present day; till now. —*v.* **dat·ed, dat·ing** *v.t.* **1.** To furnish or mark with a date. **2.** To ascertain the time or era of; assign a date to. **3.** *U.S. Informal* To make an appointment with (a member of the opposite sex). —*v.i.* **4.** To have origin in an era or time: usually with *from*: This coin *dates* from the Renaissance. **5.** To reckon time. **6.** *Informal* To have appointments with members of the opposite sex. [< F < L *data*, fem. pp. of *dure* to give] —**dat'a·ble** *adj.* —**dat'er** *n.*

date² (dāt) *n.* **1.** The sweet fruit of a palm, enclosing a single hard seed. **2.** A palm bearing this fruit: also **date palm**. [< OF < L < Gk. *daktylos* finger]

dat·ed (dā'tid) *adj.* **1.** Marked with a date. **2.** Antiquated; old-fashioned.

date·less (dāt'lis) *adj.* **1.** Bearing no date. **2.** Without end or limit. **3.** Immemorial. **4.** Of permanent interest.

date line **1.** The line containing the date of publication of a periodical or of any contribution printed in it. **2.** An imaginary line roughly corresponding to 180° longitude from Greenwich, internationally agreed upon as determining those points on the earth's surface where a day is dropped on crossing it from west to east and added crossing east to west.

da·tive (dā'tiv) *n. Gram.* **1.** In inflected Indo-European languages, the case of a noun, pronoun, or adjective denoting the indirect object. It is expressed in English by *to* or *for* with the objective or by word order, as in *I told the story to him; I told him the story.* **2.** A word in this case. —*adj. Gram.* Pertaining to or designating the dative case or a word in this case: also **da·ti·val** (dā·tī'vəl). [< L *dativus*, trans. of Gk. (*ptōsis*) *dotikē* (the case) of giving] —**da'tive·ly** *adv.*

da·tum (dā'təm, dat'əm, dä'təm) Singular of DATA.

daub (dôb) *v.t. & v.i.* **1.** To smear or coat (something), as with plaster, grease, etc. **2.** To paint without skill. —*n.* **1.** Any sticky application, as of mud, plaster, clay, etc. **2.** A smear or spot. **3.** A poor painting. **4.** An instance or act of daubing. [< OF < L *dealbare* to whitewash] —**daub'er** *n.* —**daub'y** *adj.*

daugh·ter (dô'tər) *n.* **1.** A female child, considered in relationship to either or both of her parents. **2.** A female descendant. **3.** A woman or girl considered to be in a relationship like that of a daughter: a *daughter* of nobility. **4.** Anything regarded as a female descendant. [OE *dohtor*] —**daugh'ter·ly** *adj.* —**daugh'ter·li·ness** *n.*

daugh·ter-in-law (dô'tər·in·lô') *n. pl.* **daugh·ters-in-law** The wife of one's son.

daunt (dônt, dänt) *v.t.* To dishearten or intimidate; cow. [< OF < L *domare* to tame]

daunt·less (dônt'lis, dänt'-) *adj.* Fearless; intrepid. —**daunt'less·ly** *adv.* —**daunt'less·ness** *n.*

dau·phin (dô'fin, *Fr.* dō·faɴ') *n.* The eldest son of a king of France, a title used from 1349 to 1830. [< F, a dolphin]

dav·en·port (dav'ən·pôrt, -pōrt) *n. U.S.* A large, upholstered sofa, often usable as a bed. [Prob. from the name of the first manufacturer]

Da·vid (dā'vid), 1040?–970? B.C., second king of Judah and Israel 1010?–970? B.C., succeeded Solomon. —**Da·vid·ic** (də·vid'ik) *adj.*

dav·it (dav'it, dā'vit) *n. Naut.* One of a pair of small cranes on a ship's side for hoisting its boats, stores, etc. [Appar. from *David*, proper name]

da·vy (dā'vē) *n. pl.* **·vies** A safety lamp (def. 1). [after Sir Humphry *Davy*, who invented it] Also **Davy lamp.**

Da·vy Jones (dā'vē jōnz') The spirit of the sea.

Davy Jones's locker The bottom of the ocean, esp. as the grave of the drowned.

daw·dle (dôd'l) *v.t. & v.i.* **·dled, ·dling** To waste (time) in slow trifling; loiter: often with *away*. [? Var. of DADDLE] —**daw'dler** *n.*

DAVIT
a Position on deck.
b Position when lowering lifeboat.

dawn (dôn) *n.* **1.** Daybreak. ◆ Collateral adjective: *auroral.* **2.** A beginning or unfolding. —*v.i.* **1.** To begin to grow light in the morning. **2.** To begin to be understood: with *on* or *upon*. **3.** To begin to expand or develop. [ME *dawenyng* daybreak < Scand.]

day (dā) *n.* **1.** The period of light from dawn to dark; daylight. **2.** The interval represented by one rotation of the earth upon its axis; twenty-four hours. ◆ Collateral adjective: *diurnal.* **3.** A portion of a day spent in a particular way or place: a shopping *day*; a *day* outdoors. **4.** The hours of a day devoted to work: a seven-hour *day*. **5.** A time or period; age; epoch: in Caesar's *day*. **6.** *Usu. cap.* A particular day: Labor *Day*. **7.** *Often pl.* A lifetime: in my *day*. **8.** A period of success, influence, accomplishment, etc.: Your *day* will come. **9.** The contest or battle of the day: to win the *day*. —**day after day** Every day. —**day by day** Each day. —**day in, day out** Every day. —**(from) day to day** From one day to the next. [OE *dæg*]

day bed A lounge or couch that can be converted into a bed.

day·book (dā'bŏŏk') *n.* **1.** In bookkeeping, the book in which transactions are recorded in the order of their occurrence. **2.** A diary or journal.

day·break (dā'brāk') *n.* The time each morning when daylight replaces darkness.

day camp A camp where children spend the day in supervised activities, returning home each evening.

day coach A railroad car without special accommodations, as distinguished from a sleeping car, dining car, etc.

day·dream (dā'drēm') *n.* A dreamlike thought, as of a future or desired event, situation, etc.; reverie. —*v.i.* To have daydreams. —**day'dream'er** *n.*

day·fly (dā'flī') *n.* A May fly.

day laborer One who works for pay by the day, esp. at unskilled manual tasks.

day letter A long telegram, slower and cheaper than a regular telegram, sent during the day.

day·light (dā'līt') *n.* **1.** The light received from the sun; the light of day. **2.** Insight into or understanding of something formerly puzzling. **3.** Exposure to view; publicity. **4.** The period of light during the day.

day·light-sav·ing time (dā'līt'sā'ving) Time in which more daylight is obtained at the end of each working day by setting clocks one or more hours ahead of standard time, esp. during the summer months.

day·long (dā'lông', -long') *adj.* Lasting all day. —*adv.* Through the entire day.

day nursery A place for the care of small children, esp. those of working mothers, during the day.

Day of Atonement Yom Kippur.

Day of Judgment *Theol.* Judgment Day.

day school **1.** A school that holds classes only during the daytime. **2.** A private school for pupils who live at home.

day·time (dā'tīm') *n.* The time of daylight.

daze (dāz) *v.t.* **dazed, daz·ing** To stupefy or bewilder; stun. —*n.* The state of being dazed. [ME *dasen*] —**daz·ed·ly** (dā'zid·lē) *adv.*

daz·zle (daz'əl) *v.* **·zled, ·zling** *v.t.* **1.** To blind or dim the vision of by excess of light. **2.** To bewilder or charm, as with brilliant display. —*v.i.* **3.** To be blinded by lights or glare. **4.** To excite admiration. —*n.* **1.** The act of dazzling; dazzled condition. **2.** Something that dazzles; brightness. [Freq. of DAZE] —**daz'zling·ly** *adv.*

D-day (dē′dā′) *n.* In military operations, the unspecified date of the launching of an attack; especially, June 6, 1944, the day on which the Allies invaded France in World War II.

DDT A powerful insecticide effective on contact. [< D(I-CHLORO)D(IPHENYL)T(RICHLOROETHANE)]

de- *prefix* **1.** Away; off: *deflect, decapitate.* **2.** Down: *decline, descend.* **3.** Completely; utterly: *derelict, denude.* **4.** The undoing, reversing, or ridding of (the action, condition or substance expressed by the main element: *decode, decentralization, decarbonization.* [< L *de* from, away, down; also < F *dé-* < L *de-,* or < OF *des-* < L *dis-* (see DIS-¹)]

dea·con (dē′kən) *n.* **1.** A lay church officer or subordinate minister. **2.** In the Anglican, Eastern Orthodox, and Roman Catholic churches, a clergyman ranking next below a priest. [OE < L < Gk. *diakonos* servant, minister] — **dea·con·ry** (dē′kən·rē), **dea′con·ship** *n.*

dea·con·ess (dē′kən·is) *n.* A woman appointed or chosen as a lay church worker or officer.

de·ac·ti·vate (dē·ak′tə·vāt) *v.t.* **·vat·ed, ·vat·ing** **1.** To render inactive or ineffective, as an explosive, chemical, etc. **2.** *Mil.* To release (a military unit, ship, etc.) from active duty; demobilize. — **de·ac′ti·va′tion** *n.*

dead (ded) *adj.* **1.** Having ceased to live; lifeless. **2.** Deathlike: a *dead* faint. **3.** Inanimate. **4.** Insensible: with *to:* *dead* to pity. **5.** Lacking sensation; numb. **6.** Extinct: a *dead* language. **7.** No longer in force: a *dead* law. **8.** Not productively used: *dead* capital. **9.** *Informal* Very tired. **10.** Lacking activity, excitement, etc.: a *dead* town. **11.** Extinguished: a *dead* fire. **12.** Dull: said of colors. **13.** Muffled: said of sounds. **14.** Without elasticity. **15.** Complete; utter: *dead* silence. **16.** Having no outlet or opening: a *dead* end. **17.** Perfect; exact: a *dead* center. **18.** Unerring; sure: a *dead* shot. **19.** In certain games, out of play: said of the ball. — *n.* **1.** A dead person, or dead persons collectively: preceded by *the.* **2.** The coldest, darkest, or most intense part: the *dead* of winter. — *adv.* **1.** Completely: to stop *dead.* **2.** Directly: *dead* ahead. [OE *dēad*] — **dead′ness** *n.*

dead·beat (ded′bēt′) *n.* *U.S. Slang* **1.** One who avoids paying his bills. **2.** A sponger.

dead center *Mech.* One of two points in the motion of a crank and connecting rod when they are in alignment and the connecting rod has no power to turn the crank.

dead·en (ded′n) *v.t.* **1.** To diminish the sensitivity, force, or intensity of. **2.** To impede the velocity of; retard. **3.** To render soundproof. **4.** To make dull or less brilliant in color. — *v.i.* **5.** To become dead. — **dead′en·er** *n.*

dead end **1.** A passage, street, etc., having no outlet. **2.** A point from which no progress can be made.

dead·eye (ded′ī′) *n.* *Naut.* A wooden disk pierced by holes through which lanyards are passed, and having a grooved circumference, used to set up shrouds, stays, etc.

dead·fall (ded′fôl′) *n.* A trap operated by a weight that falls upon and kills or holds an animal.

dead·head (ded′hed′) *Informal n.* **1.** One who is admitted, entertained, or accommodated free of charge. **2.** A dull, stupid person. — *v.t. & v.i.* To treat or go as a deadhead. — *adj.* Traveling without passengers or freight.

dead heat A race in which two or more competitors tie.

dead letter **1.** A letter that is unclaimed, or cannot be delivered because of a faulty address. **2.** A law, issue, etc., no longer valid or enforced, though still formally in effect.

dead·line (ded′līn′) *n.* **1.** A time limit, as for the completion of newspaper copy, payment of debts, etc. **2.** Originally, a boundary line that prisoners might not cross.

dead·lock (ded′lok′) *n.* A standstill or stoppage of activity resulting from the unrelenting opposition of equally powerful forces. — *v.t. & v.i.* To cause or come to a deadlock.

dead·ly (ded′lē) *adj.* **·li·er, ·li·est** **1.** Likely or certain to cause death. **2.** Implacable; mortal: a *deadly* enemy. **3.** Resembling death: *deadly* pallor. **4.** *Theol.* Causing spiritual death: a *deadly* sin. **5.** Excessive. — *adv.* **1.** As in death; deathly. **2.** *Informal* Very. — **dead′li·ness** *n.*

deadly nightshade Belladonna.

dead pan *U.S. Slang* A completely expressionless face. — **dead·pan** (ded′pan′) *adj. & adv.*

dead reckoning *Naut.* The computation of a vessel's position by log and compass without astronomical observations.

Dead Sea Scrolls A number of scrolls of parchment, leather, or copper, dating from about 100 B.C. to A.D. 100, containing Hebrew and Aramaic texts of Biblical works, found in 1947 and after in caves near the Dead Sea.

dead weight **1.** A heavy weight or load, as of something inert. **2.** In transportation, the weight of a vehicle as distinguished from its load.

dead·wood (ded′wŏod′) *n.* **1.** Wood dead on the tree. **2.** *U.S.* Worthless material; a useless person or thing.

deaf (def) *adj.* **1.** Partly or completely lacking the power to

hear. **2.** Determined not to hear; unwilling to listen. [OE *dēaf*] — **deaf′ly** *adv.* — **deaf′ness** *n.*

deaf-and-dumb alphabet (def′ən-dum′) Manual alphabet (which see).

deaf·en (def′ən) *v.t.* **1.** To make deaf. **2.** To confuse, stupefy, or overwhelm, as with noise. **3.** To drown (a sound) by a louder sound. **4.** To make soundproof.

deaf-mute (def′myōōt′) *n.* A deaf person who cannot speak, usu. because of deafness from early life. Also **deaf mute.**

deal¹ (dēl) *v.* **dealt** (delt), **deal·ing** *v.t.* **1.** To distribute or portion out, as playing cards. **2.** To apportion to (one person) as his or her share. **3.** To deliver or inflict, as a blow. — *v.i.* **4.** To conduct oneself; behave toward: with *with.* **5.** To be concerned or occupied: with *in* or *with:* to *deal* in facts. **6.** To consider, discuss, or take action: with *with.* **7.** To do business: with *in, with,* or *at.* **8.** In card games, to act as dealer. — *n.* **1.** The act of dealing. **2.** In card games: **a** The distribution of the cards to the players. **b** The right or turn to distribute the cards. **c** The cards distributed to a player; a hand. **d** A single round of play. **3.** An indefinite amount, degree, extent, etc.: a great *deal* of time. **4.** *Informal* A business transaction. **5.** *Informal* A secret arrangement, as in politics. **6.** *Informal* A plan, agreement, or treatment: a rough *deal.* [OE *dǣlan.*]

deal² (dēl) *n.* **1.** A fir or pine plank. **2.** Such planks collectively. — *adj.* Made of deal. [< MDu. *dele* plank]

deal·er (dē′lər) *n.* **1.** One engaged in a specified business; a trader. **2.** In card games, one who distributes the cards.

deal·ing (dē′ling) *n.* **1.** The act of distributing. **2.** *Usu. pl.* Transactions or relations with others. **3.** Method or manner of treatment: honest *dealing.*

dealt (delt) Past tense and past participle of DEAL.

dean (dēn) *n.* **1.** An officer of a college or university, having jurisdiction over a particular group of students, area of study, or acting as head of a faculty. **2.** The senior member, in length of service, of a group of men. **3.** The chief ecclesiastical officer of a cathedral or of a collegiate church. [< OF < LL < L *decem* ten] — **dean′ship** *n.*

dean·er·y (dē′nər·ē) *n. pl.* **·er·ies** The office, revenue, jurisdiction, or place of residence of a dean.

dear (dir) *adj.* **1.** Beloved; precious. **2.** Highly esteemed: used in letter salutations. **3.** Expensive; costly. **4.** Characterized by high prices. **5.** Intense; earnest: our *dearest* wish. — *n.* One who is much beloved; a darling. — *adv.* Dearly. — *interj.* An exclamation of regret, surprise, etc. [OE *dēore*] — **dear′ly** *adv.* — **dear′ness** *n.*

dearth (dúrth) *n.* Scarcity; lack; famine. [ME *derthe*]

dear·y (dir′ē) *n. pl.* **dear·ies** *Informal* Darling; dear. Also **dear′ie.**

death (deth) *n.* **1.** The permanent cessation of all vital functions in an animal or plant. **2.** The condition of being dead. **3.** *Usu. cap.* A personification of death, usu. a skeleton holding a scythe. **4.** The extinction of anything; destruction. **5.** The cause of dying. **6.** The time or manner of dying: to meet a tyrant's *death.* **7.** Something considered as terrible as death. ◆ Collateral adjectives: *lethal, mortal.* — **to death** Very much: He frightened me *to death.* — **to put to death** To kill; execute. [OE *dēath*]

death·bed (deth′bed′) *n.* **1.** The bed on which a person dies or died. **2.** The last hours of life.

death·blow (deth′blō′) *n.* That which causes the death or the end of a person or thing.

death·cup (deth′kup′) *n.* A poisonous mushroom having a usu. white, olive, or umber cap.

death house That part of a prison, as a block of cells, in which prisoners condemned to death are confined.

death·less (deth′lis) *adj.* Not liable to die; perpetual; immortal. — **death′less·ly** *adv.* — **death′less·ness** *n.*

death·ly (deth′lē) *adj.* **1.** Resembling or suggesting death. Also **death′like.** **2.** Causing death; fatal. — *adv.* **1.** In a deathlike manner. **2.** Extremely: *deathly* ill.

death mask A cast of the face taken just after death.

death rate The number of persons per thousand of population who die within a given time.

death rattle The rattling sound caused by the breath passing through mucus in the throat of one dying.

death's-head (deths′hed′) *n.* A human skull, or a representation of it, as a symbol of death.

death trap (deth′trap′) *n.* **1.** An unsafe building or structure. **2.** Any very dangerous situation.

death warrant **1.** *Law* An official order for the execution of a person. **2.** Anything that destroys hope, happiness, etc.

death·watch (deth′woch′, -wôch′) *n.* **1.** A vigil kept at the side of one who is dying or has recently died. **2.** A guard set over a condemned man before his execution.

de·ba·cle (dā-bäk′əl, -bak′əl, di-) *n.* **1.** A sudden and disastrous breakdown or collapse. **2.** The breaking up of ice in a river. **3.** A violent flood. [< F < *débâcler* to unbar]

de·bar (di·bär′) v.t. **·barred**, **·bar·ring** 1. To bar or shut out: usu. with *from*. 2. To hinder. [< F < *dé-* away + *barrer* to bar] — **de·bar′ment** n.

de·bark (di·bärk′) v.t. & v.i. To put or go ashore from a ship. [< F < *dé-* away + *barque* ship] — **de·bar·ka·tion** (dē′bär·kā′shən) n.

de·base (di·bās′) v.t. **·based**, **·bas·ing** To lower in character or worth; degrade. [< DE- + obs. *base*] — **de·base′ment** n. — **de·bas′er** n.

de·bate (di·bāt′) n. 1. A discussion of any question; argument; dispute. 2. A formal contest in argumentation conducted between persons taking opposite sides of a question. — v. **·bat·ed**, **·bat·ing** v.t. 1. To argue about; discuss, as in a public meeting. 2. To deliberate upon; consider, as alternatives. 3. To discuss in formal debate. — v.i. 4. To engage in argument; discuss a question. 5. To take part in a formal debate. 6. To deliberate; ponder. [< OF < *de-* down + *batre* to strike] — **de·bat′a·ble** adj. — **de·bat′er** n.

de·bauch (di·bôch′) v.t. 1. To corrupt in morals; seduce; deprave. — v.i. 2. To indulge in debauchery; dissipate. — n. 1. An act or period of debauchery. 2. Debauchery. [< F < OF *desbaucher* to lure from work] — **de·bauch·ed·ly** (di·bô′chid·lē) adv. — **de·bauch′er** n. — **de·bauch′ment** n.

deb·au·chee (deb′ô·chē′, -shē′) n. One habitually profligate, drunken, or lewd; a libertine.

de·bauch·er·y (di·bô′chər·ē) n. pl. **·er·ies** Gross indulgence of one's sensual appetites.

de·ben·ture (di·ben′chər) n. 1. A certificate given as acknowledgment of debt. 2. A bond, usu. without security, issued by a corporation and often convertible into common stock. Also **debenture bond**. [< L *debere* to owe]

de·bil·i·tate (di·bil′ə·tāt) v.t. **·tat·ed**, **·tat·ing** To make feeble or languid; weaken. [< L *debilitare* < *debilis* weak] — **de·bil′i·ta′tion** n. — **de·bil′i·ta′tive** adj.

de·bil·i·ty (di·bil′ə·tē) n. pl. **·ties** Abnormal weakness; languor; feebleness. [< F < L < *debilis* weak]

deb·it (deb′it) n. 1. An item of debt recorded in an account. 2. An entry of debt in an account, or the sum of such entries. 3. The left-hand side of an account, where debts are recorded. — v.t. 1. To enter (a debt) in an account. 2. To charge (someone) with a debt. [< L *debere* to owe]

deb·o·nair (deb′ə·nâr′) adj. 1. Urbane; nonchalant. 2. Pleasantly gracious. 3. Cheerful; lively; gay. Also **deb′o·naire′**, **deb′on·naire′**. [< OF *de bon aire* of good mien] — **deb′o·nair′ly** adv. — **deb′o·nair′ness** n.

de·bouch (di·boōsh′) v.i. 1. *Mil.* To march from a narrow passage, wood, etc., into the open. 2. To come forth; emerge; issue. — v.t. 3. To cause to emerge. [< F < *dé-* from + *bouche* a mouth] — **de·bouch′ment** n.

de·bris (da·brē′, dā′brē; *Brit.* deb′rē) n. 1. Fragments, or scattered remains, as of something destroyed; ruins; rubble. 2. *Geol.* An accumulation of detached fragments of rocks. Also **dé·bris′**. [< F < OF *debrisier* to break away]

debt (det) n. 1. That which one owes, as money, goods, or services. 2. The obligation to pay or render something to another. 3. The condition of owing something. 4. *Theol.* A sin. [< OF < L *debere* to owe]

debt of honor A gambling debt.

debt·or (det′ər) n. One who owes a debt.

de·bunk (di·bungk′) v.t. *Informal* To expose or deride the sham, false pretensions, etc., of. [< BUNK²]

de·but (di·byoō′, dā-, dā′byoō) n. 1. A first public appearance. 2. A formal introduction to society. 3. The beginning, as of a career. — v.i. To make a debut. Also **dé·but′**. [< F < *débuter* to begin]

deb·u·tante (deb′yoō·tänt, -yə-, *Fr.* deb′ü·tänt′) n. fem. A young woman making a debut in society. Also **dé′bu·tante′**.

deca- *combining form* 1. Ten. 2. In the metric system, deka-. Also, before vowels, **dec-**.

dec·ade (dek′ād, de·kād′) n. 1. A period of ten years. 2. A group or set of ten. [< MF < L < Gk. < *deka* ten]

de·ca·dence (di·kād′ns, dek′ə·dəns) n. 1. A process of deterioration; decay. 2. A condition or period of decline, as in morals. [< F < Med.L < L < *de-* down + *cadere* to fall]

dec·a·dent (dek′ə·dənt, di·kād′nt) adj. Falling into, or characteristic of, decay and decline. — n. A decadent person, esp. an artist or writer. — **dec·a′dent·ly** adv.

dec·a·gon (dek′ə·gon) n. *Geom.* A polygon with ten sides and ten angles. [< Gk. < *deka* ten + *gōnia* angle] — **de·cag·o·nal** (di·kag′ə·nəl) adj. — **de·cag′o·nal·ly** adv.

dec·a·gram (dek′ə·gram) See DEKAGRAM.

dec·a·he·dron (dek′ə·hē′drən) n. pl. **·drons** or **·dra** (-drə) *Geom.* A polyhedron bounded by ten plane faces. [< DECA- + Gk. *hedra* seat] — **dec′a·he′dral** adj.

de·cal (dē′kal, di·kal′) n. A decalcomania.

de·cal·ci·fy (dē·kal′sə·fī) v.t. **·fied**, **·fy·ing** To remove lime or calcareous matter from (bones, teeth, etc.). — **de·cal′ci·fi·ca′tion** n.

de·cal·co·ma·ni·a (di·kal′kə·mā′nē·ə, -män′yə) n. 1. A process of transferring prints, designs, etc., from specially prepared paper to glass, porcelain, or other material. 2. The design or print to be transferred. [< F < *décalquer* to transfer a tracing + *-manie* -mania]

DECA-
HEDRON

dec·a·li·ter (dek′ə·lē′tər) See DEKALITER.

Dec·a·logue (dek′ə·lôg, -log) n. The Ten Commandments. Also **Dec′a·log**. [< Gk. < *deka* ten + *logos* word]

dec·a·me·ter (dek′ə·mē′tər) See DEKAMETER.

de·camp (di·kamp′) v.i. 1. To break camp. 2. To leave suddenly or secretly; run away. — **de·camp′ment** n.

de·cant (di·kant′) v.t. 1. To pour off (a liquid) without disturbing its sediment. 2. To pour from one container into another. [< F < Med.L < *de-* from + *canthus* lip of a jug] — **de·can·ta·tion** (dē′kan·tā′shən) n.

de·cant·er (di·kan′tər) n. A vessel for decanting; esp. a decorative, stoppered bottle for serving wine, etc.

de·cap·i·tate (di·kap′ə·tāt) v.t. **·tat·ed**, **·tat·ing** To cut off the head of; behead. [< Med.L < *de-* off + *caput* head] — **de·cap′i·ta′tion** n. — **de·cap′i·ta′tor** n.

dec·a·pod (dek′ə·pod) adj. Ten-footed or ten-armed. — n. *Zool.* 1. A crustacean having five pairs of legs, including the crabs, lobsters, shrimps, etc. 2. Any ten-armed cephalopod, as a cuttlefish or squid. [< Gk. < *deka* ten + *pous* foot] — **de·cap·o·dal** (di·kap′ə·dəl), **de·cap′o·dous** adj.

de·car·bon·ate (dē·kär′bə·nāt) v.t. **·at·ed**, **·at·ing** To free from carbon dioxide. — **de·car′bon·a′tor** n.

de·car·bon·ize (dē·kär′bən·īz) v.t. **·ized**, **·iz·ing** To decarburize. — **de·car′bon·i·za′tion** n. — **de·car′bon·iz′er** n.

de·car·bu·rize (dē·kär′byə·rīz) v.t. **·rized**, **·riz·ing** To remove carbon from (molten steel or the cylinders of an internal-combustion engine). — **de·car′bu·ri·za′tion** n.

dec·are (dek′âr, dek·âr′) See DEKARE.

dec·a·stere (dek′ə·stir) See DEKASTERE.

dec·a·syl·la·ble (dek′ə·sil′ə·bəl) n. A line of verse having ten syllables. — **dec·a·syl·lab·ic** (dek′ə·si·lab′ik) adj.

de·cath·lon (di·kath′lon) n. An athletic contest consisting of ten different track and field events in all of which each contestant participates. [< DEC(A)- + Gk. *athlon* a contest]

de·cay (di·kā′) v.i. 1. To fail slowly in health, beauty, quality, or any form of excellence. 2. To decompose; rot. — v.t. 3. To cause to decay. — n. 1. A falling into a ruined or reduced condition. 2. Decomposition, as of a dead organism. 3. Rottenness. [< OF < L < *de-* down + *cadere* to fall] — **Syn.** (verb) 2. Dead organic matter *decays* by the action of bacteria; also, a great mind may *decay* with age. *Putrefy* is used only of animal matter, as is also the strong, direct *rot*. *Spoil* suggests mild decay or taint; food *spoils* if not refrigerated.

de·cease (di·sēs′) v.i. **·ceased**, **·ceas·ing** To die. — n. Death. [< OF < L < *de-* away + *cedere* to go]

de·ceased (di·sēst′) adj. Dead. — **the deceased** The dead person or persons.

de·ce·dent (di·sēd′nt) n. *Law* A person deceased.

de·ceit (di·sēt′) n. 1. The act of deceiving. 2. An instance of deception or a device that deceives; a trick. 3. The quality of being deceptive; falseness. [See DECEIVE.]

de·ceit·ful (di·sēt′fəl) adj. 1. Given to deceiving; lying or treacherous. 2. Tending to deceive; false. — **Syn.** See DECEPTIVE. — **de·ceit′ful·ly** adv. — **de·ceit′ful·ness** n.

de·ceive (di·sēv′) v. **·ceived**, **·ceiv·ing** v.t. 1. To mislead by falsehood; lead into error; delude. — v.i. 2. To practice deceit. [< OF < L < *de-* away, down + *capere* to take] — **de·ceiv′er** n. — **de·ceiv′ing·ly** adv.

de·cel·er·ate (dē·sel′ə·rāt) v.t. & v.i. **·at·ed**, **·at·ing** To diminish in velocity. [< DE- + L *celarare* to hasten] — **de·cel′er·a′tion** n. — **de·cel′er·a′tor** n.

De·cem·ber (di·sem′bər) n. The twelfth month of the year, having 31 days. [< L < *decem* ten; December was the tenth month in the old Roman calendar]

de·cem·vir (di·sem′vər) n. pl. **·virs** or **·vi·ri** (-və·rī) A member of any body of ten magistrates; esp. one in ancient Rome. [< L < *decem* ten + *vir* man] — **de·cem′vi·ral** adj.

de·cem·vi·rate (di·sem′və·rit, -rāt) n. 1. A body of ten men in authority. 2. The government of such a body.

de·cen·cy (dē′sən·sē) n. pl. **·cies** 1. The quality or state of being decent; propriety in conduct, speech, or dress. 2. *Usu. pl.* Those things that are proper or decent. 3. pl. The requirements for a proper manner of life.

de·cen·ni·al (di·sen′ē·əl) adj. 1. Of or continuing for ten years. 2. Occurring every ten years. — n. An anniversary observed every ten years. — **de·cen′ni·al·ly** adv.

de·cent (dē′sənt) adj. 1. Characterized by propriety of conduct, speech, or dress; proper; respectable. 2. Free of coarseness or indelicacy; modest; chaste. 3. Adequate; satisfactory. 4. Generous; kind. *Informal* Adequately or properly clothed. [< L *decere* to be fitting, proper] — **de′cent·ly** adv. — **de′cent·ness** n.

de·cen·tral·ize (dē·sen′trəl·īz) v.t. **·ized**, **·iz·ing** To undo the centralization of; reorganize into smaller and more dispersed parts. — **de·cen′tral·i·za′tion** n.

de·cep·tion (di·sep′shən) n. 1. The act of deceiving; deceit. 2. The state of being deceived. 3. Anything that deceives or is meant to deceive; a delusion. [See DECEIVE.]

de·cep·tive (di-sep/tiv) *adj.* Having power or tendency to deceive. **—de·cep/tive·ly** *adv.* **—de·cep/tive·ness** *n.*

deci- *combining form* In the metric system, one tenth of (a specified unit): *decimeter.* [< L *decimus* tenth < *decem* ten]

dec·i·are (des/ē-âr) *n.* In the metric system, one tenth of an are. Abbr. *da.* [< F *déciare*]

dec·i·bel (des/a-bal) *n. Physics* One tenth of a bel: a measure of sound intensity.

de·cide (di-sīd/) *v.* **·cid·ed, cid·ing** *v.t.* **1.** To determine; settle, as a controversy, contest, etc. **2.** To determine the issue or conclusion of: *The charge decided the battle.* **3.** To bring (someone) to a decision. **—** *v.i.* **4.** To give a decision or verdict. **5.** To make a decision. [< MF < L < *de-* down, away + *caedere* to cut] **—de·cid/a·ble** *adj.*

de·cid·ed (di-sī/did) *adj.* **1.** Free from uncertainty; definite. **2.** Exhibiting determination; resolute; emphatic. **—de·cid/ed·ly** *adv.* **—de·cid/ed·ness** *n.*

de·cid·u·ous (di-sij/ōō-as) *adj.* **1.** *Biol.* Falling off or shed at maturity or at specific seasons, as petals, fruit, leaves, antlers, etc. **2.** Characterized by such a falling off: distinguished from *evergreen.* [< L < *de-* down, away + *cadere* to fall] **—de·cid/u·ous·ly** *adv.* **—de·cid/u·ous·ness** *n.*

dec·i·gram (des/a-gram) *n.* In the metric system, the tenth part of a gram. Also **dec/i·gramme.** See table inside back cover.

dec·i·li·ter (des/a-lē/tar) *n.* In the metric system, the tenth part of a liter. Also *esp. Brit.* **dec/i·li/tre.** Abbr. *dl, dl.* See table inside back cover.

de·cil·lion (di-sil/yan) *n.* **1.** *U.S.* A thousand nonillions, written as 1 followed by thirty-three zeros: a cardinal number. **2.** *Brit.* A million nonillions (def. 2), written as 1 followed by sixty zeros: a cardinal number. **—** *adj.* Being a decillion. [< DEC(A)- + (M)ILLION] **—de·cil/lionth** *adj.*

dec·i·mal (des/a-mal) *adj.* **1.** Pertaining to or founded on the number 10. **2.** Proceeding by tens. **—** *n.* A decimal fraction or one of its digits. [< Med.L < L *decem* ten]

decimal fraction *Math.* A fraction whose denominator is any power of 10 and which may be expressed in decimal form, as 7/10 (0.7), 3/100 (0.03), etc.

decimal point A dot used before a decimal fraction.

decimal system A system of reckoning by tens or tenths.

dec·i·mate (des/a-māt) *v.t.* **·mat·ed, ·mat·ing** **1.** To destroy or kill a large proportion of. **2.** To select by lot and kill one out of every ten of. [< L *decimare* to take a tenth part from] **—dec/i·ma/tion** *n.* **—dec/i·ma/tor** *n.*

dec·i·me·ter (des/a-mē/tar) *n.* In the metric system, the tenth part of a meter. Also *esp. Brit.* **dec/i·me/tre.** Abbr. *dec., decim., dm, dm.* See table inside back cover.

de·ci·pher (di-sī/far) *v.t.* **1.** To determine the meaning of (something obscure, illegible, etc.). **2.** To translate from cipher or code into plain text; decode. **—de·ci/pher·a·ble** *adj.* **—de·ci/pher·er** *n.* **—de·ci/pher·ment** *n.*

de·ci·sion (di-sizh/an) *n.* **1.** The act of deciding (an issue, question, etc.). **2.** A conclusion or judgment reached by deciding. **3.** The making up of one's mind. **4.** Firmness in judgment, action, or character. **5.** In boxing, a victory decided when there has not been a knockout. [See DECIDE.]

de·ci·sive (di-sī/siv) *adj.* **1.** Ending uncertainty or dispute; conclusive. **2.** Characterized by decision and firmness; determined. **3.** Unquestionable; unmistakable. **—deci·sive·ly** *adv.* **—de·ci/sive·ness** *n.*

dec·i·stere (des/a-stir) *n.* In the metric system, a cubic decimeter, or the tenth part of a stere. Abbr. *ds.*

deck (dek) *n.* **1.** *Naut.* **a** A platform covering or extending horizontally across a vessel, and serving as both floor and roof. **b** The space between two such platforms. **2.** Any similar flat surface. **3.** *U.S.* A pack of playing cards. **—to hit the deck** *Slang* **1.** To rise from bed; get up. **2.** To prepare for action. **—on deck** *Slang* Present and ready for action. **—** *v.t.* **1.** To dress or decorate elegantly; adorn. **2.** *Naut.* To furnish with a deck. [< MDu. *dek* roof, covering]

deck·er (dek/ar) *n.* Something with one or more decks, layers, levels, etc.: usu. in combination: *a double-decker.*

deck hand A common sailor employed on deck.

deck·le (dek/al) *n.* **1.** In making paper by hand, a frame that limits the size of the sheet. **2.** The ragged edge of handmade paper: also **deckle edge.** Also **deck/el.** [< G *deckel* cover] **—deck/le-edged/** *adj.*

de·claim (di-klām/) *v.i.* **1.** To speak loudly and rhetorically. **2.** To give a formal, set speech. **3.** To attack verbally and vehemently: with *against.* **—** *v.i.* **4.** To utter rhetorically. [< L < *de-* completely + *clamare* to shout] **—de·claim/er** *n.* **—dec·la·ma·tion** (dek/la-mā/shan) *n.*

de·clam·a·to·ry (di-klam/a-tôr/ē, -tō/rē) *adj.* Of, like, or pertaining to declamation. **—de·clam/a·to/ri·ly** *adv.*

dec·la·ra·tion (dek/la-rā/shan) *n.* **1.** The act of declaring or proclaiming. **2.** That which is declared. **3.** A statement of goods liable to taxation. **4.** In bridge, a contract.

Declaration of Independence The manifesto that formally declared the political independence of the American colonies from Britain. It was written by Thomas Jefferson and adopted July 4, 1776.

de·clar·a·tive (di-klar/a-tiv) *adj.* Making a declaration or statement. Also **de·clar·a·to·ry** (di-klar/a-tôr/ē, -tō/rē).

de·clare (di-klâr/) *v.* **·clared, ·clar·ing** *v.t.* **1.** To make known or clear; esp. to announce formally; proclaim. **2.** To say emphatically; assert; avow. **3.** To reveal; prove. **4.** To make full statement of, as goods liable to duty. **5.** In bridge, to make a final bid designating (a trump suit or no-trump). **—** *v.i.* **6.** To make a declaration. **7.** To proclaim a choice or opinion: with *for* or *against.* [< L < *de-* completely + *clarare* to make clear] **—de·clar/er** *n.*

dé·clas·sé (dā-klá-sā/) *adj. French* Fallen or lowered in social status, class, rank, etc.

de·clen·sion (di-klen/shan) *n.* **1.** *Gram.* **a** The inflection of nouns, pronouns, and adjectives according to case, number, and gender. **b** A class of words similarly inflected. **2.** A sloping downward; descent. **3.** A decline. **4.** Deviation, as from a belief. [See DECLINE.] **—de·clen/sion·al** *adj.*

dec·li·na·tion (dek/la-nā/shan) *n.* **1.** The act of inclining or bending downward. **2.** Deviation, as in direction or conduct. **3.** The angle formed between the direction of a compass needle and true north. **4.** *Astron.* The angular distance of a heavenly body north or south from the celestial equator. **5.** A polite refusal.

de·cline (di-klīn/) *v.* **·clined, ·clin·ing** *v.i.* **1.** To refuse politely to accept, comply with, or do something. **2.** To lessen or fail gradually, as in health. **3.** To draw to an end. **4.** To lower oneself, as to a mean action. **5.** To bend or incline downward or aside. **—** *v.t.* **6.** To refuse politely to accept, comply with, or do. **7.** To cause to bend or incline downward or aside. **8.** *Gram.* To give the inflected forms of (a noun, pronoun, or adjective). **—** *n.* **1.** The act or result of declining; deterioration. **2.** A period of declining. **3.** A condition in which one's mental or physical faculties weaken or deteriorate. **4.** A downward slope. [< OF < L *declinare* to lean down] **—de·clin/a·ble** *adj.* **—de·clin/er** *n.*

de·cliv·i·ty (di-kliv/a-tē) *n. pl.* **·ties** A downward slope or surface: opposed to *acclivity.* [< L < *de-* down + *clivus* hill, slope] **—de·cliv/i·tous, de·cli/vous** (-klī/vas) *adj.*

de·coct (di-kokt/) *v.t.* To extract by boiling; condense. [< L < *de-* down + *coquere* to cook] **—de·coc/tion** *n.*

de·code (dē-kōd/) *v.t.* **·cod·ed, ·cod·ing** To convert from code into plain language. **—de·cod/er** *n.*

dé·col·le·té (dā/kol-tā/, *Fr.* dā-kôl-tā/) *adj.* **1.** Cut low in the neck, as a gown. **2.** Wearing a low-necked gown. [< F]

de·com·mis·sion (dē/ka-mish/an) *v.t.* To take out of active service, as a ship; retire from use.

de·com·pose (dē/kam-pōz/) *v.t. & v.i.* **·posed, ·pos·ing** **1.** To separate into constituent parts. **2.** To decay. **—de/com·pos/a·ble** *adj.* **—de/com·pos/er** *n.*

de·com·po·si·tion (dē/kom-pa-zish/an) *n.* The act, process, or result of decomposing.

de·com·press (dē/kam-pres/) *v.t.* **1.** To free of pressure. **2.** To remove the pressure on (divers, caisson workers, etc.). **—de/com·pres/sion** *n.*

decompression sickness Caisson disease.

de·con·tam·i·nate (dē/kan-tam/a-nāt) *v.t.* **·nat·ed, ·nat·ing** To make a (contaminated object or area) safe by destroying or neutralizing poisonous chemicals, radioactivity, etc.

de·con·trol (dē/kan-trōl/) *v.t.* **·trolled, ·trol·ling** To remove from control. **—** *n.* The removal of controls.

dé·cor (dā/kôr, dā-kôr/) *n.* **1.** The scheme or style of decoration in a room, home, club, etc. **2.** In the theater, the scenery. Also **de/cor.** [< F < *décorer* to decorate]

dec·o·rate (dek/a-rāt) *v.t.* **·rat·ed, ·rat·ing** **1.** To embellish or furnish with things beautiful; adorn. **2.** To confer a decoration or medal upon. [< L *decus, decoris* grace, embellishment] **—dec/o·ra/tor** *n.*

dec·o·ra·tion (dek/a-rā/shan) *n.* **1.** The act, process, or art of decorating. **2.** A thing or group of things that decorate; ornamentation. **3.** A badge or emblem; medal. ◆ The U.S. military decorations in order of precedence are: Medal of Honor, Distinguished Service Cross or Navy Cross (Navy and Marine Corps), Distinguished Service Medal, Silver Star, Legion of Merit, Distinguished Flying Cross, Soldier's Medal, Bronze Star, Air Medal, Commendation Ribbon, and Purple Heart.

Decoration Day Memorial Day.

dec·o·ra·tive (dek/a-rā/tiv, dek/ra-tiv, dek/a-rā/tiv) *adj.* Of, pertaining to, or suitable for decoration; ornamental. **—dec/o·ra·tive·ly** *adv.* **—dec/o·ra·tive·ness** *n.*

dec·o·rous (dek/ar-as, di-kôr/as, -kō/ras) *adj.* Marked by decorum; seemly; proper. [< L *decus, decoris* grace] **—dec/o·rous·ly** *adv.* **—dec/o·rous·ness** *n.*

de·co·rum (di-kôr/am, -kō/ram) *n.* **1.** Conformity to the requirements of good taste or social convention; propriety in behavior, dress, etc.; seemliness. 2. *Usu. pl.* The proprieties. [See DECOROUS.]

de·coy (*n.* di·koi′, dē′koi; *v.* di·koi′) *n.* 1. A person or thing that lures into danger, deception, etc. 2. A bird or animal, or the likeness of one, used to lure game. 3. An enclosed place into which game may be lured. — *v.t. & v.i.* To lure or be lured into danger or a trap. [Earlier *coy* < Du. *kooi* a cage] — **de·coy′er** *n.*

DECOY (def. 2)

de·crease (*v.* di·krēs′; *n.* dē′krēs, di·krēs′) *v.t. & v.i.* **·creased, ·creas·ing** To grow, or cause to grow, gradually less or smaller; diminish. — *n.* 1. The act, process, or state of decreasing. 2. The amount or degree of decreasing. [< OF < L < *de-* down + *crescere* to grow] — **de·creas′ing·ly** *adv.*

— Syn. *Decrease* is applied to amount, *lessen* to number, *dwindle* to size, and *abate* to force. To *diminish* is to grow smaller by the removal of a part. *Reduce* is used in all the foregoing senses, but is usually transitive: *to reduce the temperature of a room.*

de·cree (di·krē′) *n.* 1. A formal and authoritative order or decision. 2. A foreordained and eternal purpose. — *v.* **·creed, ·cree·ing** *v.t.* 1. To order, adjudge, ordain, or appoint by law or edict. — *v.i.* 2. To issue an edict or decree. [< Of < L < *de-* down + *cernere* to decide]

dec·re·ment (dek′rə·mənt) *n.* 1. The act or process of decreasing. 2. The amount lost by decrease.

de·crep·it (di·krep′it) *adj.* Enfeebled or worn out by old age or excessive use. [< L < *de-* completely + *crepare* to creak] — **de·crep′it·ly** *adv.*

de·crep·i·tude (di·krep′ə·tood, -tyood) *n.* A decrepit or enfeebled condition, as from infirmity or old age.

de·cre·tal (di·krēt′l) *n.* A decree; esp. a papal decree.

de·cry (di·krī′) *v.t.* **·cried, ·cry·ing** 1. To condemn or disparage openly. 2. To depreciate, as foreign coins. [< F < *dé-* down + *crier* to cry] — **de·cri′al** *n.* — **de·cri′er** *n.*

de·cum·bent (di·kum′bənt) *adj.* 1. Lying down. 2. *Bot.* Prostrate: said of stems, shoots, etc., growing along the ground. [< L < *de-* down + *cumbere* to lie, recline] — **de·cum′bence, de·cum′ben·cy** *n.*

de·cus·sate (di·kus′āt, -it) *adj. Bot.* Having each pair of leaves at right angles with the pair below or above. [< L *decussare* to mark with an X] — **de·cus′sate·ly** *adv.* — **de·cus·sa·tion** (dē′kə·sā′shən, dek′ə-) *n.*

ded·i·cate (ded′ə·kāt, -it) *v.t.* **·cat·ed, ·cat·ing** 1. To set apart for sacred uses. 2. To set apart for any special use, duty, or purpose. 3. To inscribe (a work of literature, etc.) to someone. 4. To commit (oneself) to a certain course of action or thought. 5. To open or unveil (a bridge, statue, etc.) to the public. [< L < *de-* down + *dicare* to proclaim]

ded·i·ca·tion (ded′ə·kā′shən, -i-) *n.* 1. The act of dedicating or the state of being dedicated. 2. An inscription dedicating a literary work, etc. to someone or something.

ded·i·ca·tive (ded′ə·kā′tiv, -i-) *adj.* That dedicates.

ded·i·ca·to·ry (ded′ə·kə·tôr′ē, -tō′rē, -i-) *adj.* Constituting, containing, or serving as a dedication: a *dedicatory* preface.

de·duce (di·dōōs′, -dyōōs′) *v.t.* **·duced, ·duc·ing** 1. To derive as a conclusion by reasoning. 2. To trace, as origin. [< L < *de-* down + *ducere* to lead] — **de·duc′i·ble** *adj.*

de·duct (di·dukt′) *v.t.* To take away or subtract. [See DEDUCE.] — **de·duct′i·ble** *adj.*

de·duc·tion (di·duk′shən) *n.* 1. The act of deducing. 2. *Logic* Reasoning from the general to the particular; also, reasoning from stated premises to logical conclusions. 3. The act of deducting; also, the amount deducted. — **de·duc′tive** *adj.* — **de·duc′tive·ly** *adv.*

deed (dēd) *n.* 1. Anything done; an act. 2. A notable achievement; feat. 3. Action in general, as opposed to words. 4. *Law* Any written, sealed instrument of bond, contract, transfer, etc., especially of real estate conveyance. — Syn. See ACT. — **in deed** In fact; in truth; actually. — *v.t.* To transfer by deed. [OE *dǣd*] — **deed′less** *adj.*

deem (dēm) *v.t. & v.i.* To judge; think; believe. [OE *dēman* to judge]

deep (dēp) *adj.* 1. Extending or situated far below a surface. 2. Extending far inward or backward, or to either side. 3. Having a (specified) depth or dimension: six feet *deep.* 4. Rising to the level of: used in combination: *knee-deep.* 5. Coming from or penetrating to a depth: a *deep* sigh. 6. Difficult to understand. 7. Learned and penetrating; wise. 8. Of great intensity; extreme: *deep* sorrow. 9. Of intense or dark hue. 10. Of low, sonorous tone. 11. Absorbed: *deep* in thought. 12. Artful; cunning. — **to go off the deep end** *Informal* To become excited or hysterical. — *n.* 1. A place or thing of great depth; an abyss. 2. The most intense or profound part. 3. *Naut.* The interval between two successive marked fathoms. — **the deep** *Poetic* The sea or ocean. — *adv.* 1. Deeply. 2. Far along in time. [OE *dēop*] — **deep′ly** *adv.* — **deep′ness** *n.*

deep-dyed (dēp′dīd′) *adj.* Thoroughgoing; absolute.

deep·en (dē′pən) *v.t. & v.i.* To make or become deep or deeper.

deep-freeze (dēp′frēz′) *n.* 1. A refrigerator for freezing and storing foods for long periods of time at temperatures approximating 0° F. 2. Storage, esp. of long duration. — *v.t.* **·froze** or **·freezed, ·fro·zen** or **·freezed, ·freez·ing** To place or store in or as in a deepfreeze.

deep-fry (dēp′frī) *v.t.* **·fried, ·fry·ing** To fry in deep fat.

deep-root·ed (dēp′rōō′tid, -rŏŏt′id) *adj.* 1. Having roots far below the surface. 2. Firmly held: said of beliefs, etc.

deep-seat·ed (dēp′sē′tid) *adj.* Established far within; difficult to remove, as a fear or disease.

deep-set (dēp′set′) *adj.* Deeply placed, as eyes.

deer (dir) *n. pl.* **deer** A ruminant animal having deciduous antlers, usu. in the male only, as the moose, elk, and reindeer. ◆ Collateral adjective: *cervine.* [OE *dēor* beast]

deer·hound (dir′hound′) *n.* A breed of hunting dog, having a shaggy, dark gray or brindle coat: also called *staghound.*

deer·skin (dir′skin′) *n.* A deer's hide, or leather made from it.

de·es·ca·late (dē·es′kə·lāt) *v.t. & v.i.* **·lat·ed, ·lat·ing** To decrease or be decreased gradually, as in scope, effect, or intensity: to *de-escalate* a war. — **de·es·ca·la′tion** *n.*

de·face (di·fās′) *v.t.* **·faced, ·fac·ing** To mar the surface or appearance of; disfigure. [< F < OF < *des-* down, away + *face* face] — **de·fac′a·ble** *adj.* — **de·face′ment** *n.*

de fac·to (dē fak′tō) Actually or really existing. [< L]

de·fal·cate (di·fal′kāt) *v.i.* **·cat·ed, ·cat·ing** To embezzle. [< Med.L < L *de-* down, away + *falx* scythe] — **de·fal·ca·tion** (dē′fal·kā′shən) *n.* — **de·fal′ca·tor** *n.*

de·fam·a·to·ry (di·fam′ə·tôr′ē, -tō′rē) *adj.* Slanderous.

de·fame (di·fām′) *v.t.* **·famed, ·fam·ing** To attack the good name or reputation of; slander; libel. [< L < *dis-* away, from + *fama* a report, reputation] — **def·a·ma·tion** (def′ə·mā′shən) *n.* — **de·fam′er** *n.*

de·fault (di·fôlt′) *n.* A failure or neglect to fulfill an obligation or requirement, as to pay money due, to appear in court, or to appear for or finish a contest. — **in default of** Owing to lack or failure of. — *v.i.* 1. To fail to do or fulfill something required. 2. To fail to meet financial obligations. 3. *Law* To fail to appear in court. 4. In sports, to fail to compete or to complete a game, etc. — *v.t.* 5. To fail to perform or pay. 6. In sports, to fail to compete in, as a game; also, to forfeit by default. [< OF < L *de-* down + *fallere* to deceive] — **de·fault′er** *n.*

de·feat (di·fēt′) *v.t.* 1. To overcome in any conflict or competition; vanquish. 2. To prevent the successful outcome of; baffle; frustrate. 3. *Law* To make void; annul. — *n.* 1. The act or result of defeating; an overthrow; failure. 2. Frustration; bafflement. 3. *Law* An annulment. [< OF < *des-* not + *faire* to do]

de·feat·ism (di·fē′tiz·əm) *n.* The practice of those who accept defeat as inevitable. — **de·feat′ist** *n. & adj.*

def·e·cate (def′ə·kāt) *v.* **·cat·ed, ·cat·ing** *v.i.* 1. To discharge excrement. 2. To become free of dregs. — *v.t.* 3. To refine; purify. [< L < *de-* down, away + *faex* dregs] — **def·e·ca′tion** *n.* — **def′e·ca′tor** *n.*

de·fect (*n.* di·fekt′, dē′fekt; *v.* di·fekt′) *n.* 1. Lack of something necessary for perfection or completeness. 2. A blemish; failing; fault. — *v.i.* To desert. [< L < *de-* not + *facere* to do] — **de·fec′tion** *n.*

de·fec·tive (di·fek′tiv) *adj.* 1. Having a defect; imperfect; faulty. 2. *Gram.* Lacking one or more of the inflected forms normal for its class: *Can* is a *defective* verb. 3. *Psychol.* Having less than normal intelligence. — *n.* One who or that which is imperfect; esp., a mentally defective person. — **de·fec′tive·ly** *adv.* — **de·fec′tive·ness** *n.*

de·fec·tor (di·fek′tər) *n.* One who deserts.

de·fend (di·fend′) *v.t.* 1. To shield from danger, attack, or injury; protect. 2. To justify or vindicate; support. 3. *Law* **a** To act in behalf of (an accused). **b** To contest (a claim, charge, or suit). — *v.i.* 4. To make a defense. [< L < *de-* down, away + *fendere* to strike] — **de·fend′a·ble** *adj.* — **de·fend′er** *n.*

de·fen·dant (di·fen′dənt) *n. Law* One against whom an action is brought: opposed to *plaintiff.* — *adj.* Defending.

de·fense (di·fens′) *n.* 1. The act of defending against danger or attack. 2. Anything that defends or serves to defend. 3. A plea or argument in justification or support of something. 4. *Law* **a** The defendant's denial of the truth of a complaint; also, whatever is alleged in such denial. **b** A defendant and his legal counsel, collectively. 5. The act or science of protecting oneself or a goal, as in sports. Also, *Brit.,* **defence.** — **Department of Defense** An executive department of the U.S. government (established 1949), headed by the Secretary of Defense, that supervises military and civil defense operations. [See DEFEND.] — **de·fense′less** *adj.* — **de·fense′less·ly** *adv.* — **de·fense′less·ness** *n.*

defense mechanism *Psychoanal.* An unconscious adjustment of behavior or mental attitude directed toward shutting out painful emotions and unacceptable impulses.

de·fen·si·ble (di·fen′sə·bəl) *adj.* Capable of being defended, maintained, or justified. **—de·fen′si·bil′i·ty, de·fen′si·ble·ness** *n.* **—de·fen′si·bly** *adv.*

de·fen·sive (di·fen′siv) *adj.* 1. Intended or suitable for defense. 2. Carried on for the purpose of defense: distinguished from *offensive.* 3. Having an attitude of defense. **—** *n.* 1. An attitude or position of defense. 2. A means of defense. **—de·fen′sive·ly** *adv.* **—de·fen′sive·ness** *n.*

de·fer¹ (di·fûr′) *v.t. & v.i.* **·ferred, ·fer·ring** To delay or put off to some other time; postpone. [See DIFFER.] **—de·fer′·ra·ble** *adj.* **—de·fer′ment, de·fer′ral** *n.*

de·fer² (di·fûr′) *v.i.* **·ferred, ·fer·ring** To yield to the opinions or decisions of another: with *to.* [< MF < L < *de-* down + *ferre* to bear, carry] **—de·fer′rer** *n.*

def·er·ence (def′ər·əns) *n.* 1. Submission or yielding to the will, opinions, etc., of another. 2. Respectful regard.

def·er·ent (def′ər·ənt) *adj.* Deferential; respectful.

def·er·en·tial (def′ə·ren′shəl) *adj.* Marked by deference; respectful; courteous. **—def·er·en′tial·ly** *adv.*

de·ferred (di·fûrd′) *adj.* 1. Postponed. 2. With benefits or payments held back for a specific time: *deferred* stock. 3. Temporarily exempted from military draft.

de·fi·ance (di·fī′əns) *n.* 1. Bold opposition; disposition to oppose or resist. 2. A challenge to meet in combat. **—de·fi′ant** *adj.* **—de·fi′ant·ly** *adv.*

de·fi·cien·cy (di·fish′ən·sē) *n.* *pl.* **·cies** 1. The state of being deficient. 2. A lack; insufficiency.

de·fi·cient (di·fish′ənt) *adj.* 1. Lacking an adequate or proper supply. 2. Lacking some essential; incomplete. [See DEFECT.] **—de·fi′cient·ly** *adv.*

def·i·cit (def′ə·sit) *n.* The amount by which an expected or required sum of money falls short. [< L, it is lacking]

de·fi·er (di·fī′ər) *n.* One who defies.

de·file¹ (di·fīl′) *v.t.* **·filed, ·fil·ing** 1. To make foul or dirty. 2. To tarnish the brightness of; corrupt the purity of. 3. To sully or profane (a name, reputation, etc.). 4. To violate the chastity of. [< OF < *de-* down + *fouler* to trample] **—de·file′ment** *n.* **—de·fil′er** *n.*

de·file² (di·fīl′, dē′fīl) *v.i.* **·filed, ·fil·ing** To march in a line. **—** *n.* 1. A long, narrow pass, as between mountains. 2. A marching in file. [< MF < *de-* down + *file* row]

de·fine (di·fīn′) *v.t.* **·fined, ·fin·ing** 1. To state precisely the meaning of (a word, etc.). 2. To describe the nature or properties of; explain. 3. To determine the boundary or extent of. 4. To bring out the outline of; show clearly. 5. To fix with precision; specify, as the limits of power. **—** *v.i.* 6. To make definitions. [< OF < L *de-* down + *finire* to finish] **—de·fin′a·ble** *adj.* **—de·fin′er** *n.*

def·i·nite (def′ə·nit) *adj.* 1. Having precise limits, quantity, etc.: a *definite* sum. 2. Known for certain; positive: It is *definite* that he won. 3. Clearly defined; explicit; precise. 4. *Gram.* Limiting; particularizing. [< L. See DEFINE.] **—def′i·nite·ly** *adv.* **—def′i·nite·ness** *n.*

definite article *Gram.* In English, the article *the*, which limits or particularizes the noun before which it stands.

def·i·ni·tion (def′ə·nish′ən) *n.* 1. The act of stating what a word, phrase, set of terms, etc., means or signifies. 2. A statement of the meaning of a word, phrase, etc. 3. The determining of the outline or limits of anything. 4. The state of being clearly outlined or determined. 5. *Optics* The power of a lens to give a distinct image. 6. *Telecom.* The clarity of detail in a televised image, or of sounds received in a radio set. **—Syn.** See EXPLANATION.

de·fin·i·tive (di·fin′ə·tiv) *adj.* 1. Sharply defining or limiting; explicit. 2. Conclusive and unalterable; final. 3. Most nearly accurate and complete: a *definitive* edition of Chaucer. **—** *n. Gram.* A word that defines or limits, as the definite article. **—de·fin′i·tive·ly** *adv.* **—de·fin′i·tive·ness** *n.*

de·flate (di·flāt′) *v.* **·flat·ed, ·flat·ing** *v.t.* 1. To cause to collapse by removing air or gas. 2. To take the conceit or self-esteem out of. 3. *Econ.* To reduce or restrict (money or spending) so that prices decline. **—** *v.i.* 4. To become deflated. [< L < *de-* down + *flare* to blow] **—de·fla′tor** *n.*

de·fla·tion (di·flā′shən) *n.* 1. The act of deflating, or the state of being deflated. 2. *Econ.* A decline in prices caused by a decrease in money supply or spending. **—de·fla′tion·ar′y** (-er′ē) *adj.* **—de·fla′tion·ist** *n. & adj.*

de·flect (di·flekt′) *v.t. & v.i.* To turn aside; swerve or cause to swerve from a course. [< L *de-* down + *flectere* to bend] **—de·flec′tive** *adj.* **—de·flec′tor** *n.*

de·flec·tion (di·flek′shən) *n.* 1. The act of deflecting, or the state of being deflected. 2. The amount of deviation. Also *Brit.* **de·flex′ion.**

de·flow·er (di·flou′ər) *v.t.* 1. To despoil of flowers. 2. To deprive (a woman) of virginity. 3. To violate; rob of beauty, charm, etc. Also **de·flo·rate** (di·flôr′āte, -flō′rāte). [< LL < L *de-* down, away + *flos, floris* flower; infl. in form by *flower*] **—def·lo·ra·tion** (def′lə·rā′shən) *n.*

de·for·est (dē·fôr′ist, -for′-) *v.t.* To clear of forests or trees. **—de·for′es·ta′tion** *n.* **—de·for′est·er** *n.*

de·form (di·fôrm′) *v.t.* 1. To distort the form of; render misshapen. 2. To mar the beauty or excellence of. **—** *v.i.* 3. To become deformed. [< L < *de-* away, down + *forma* form] **—de·form′a·bil′i·ty** *n.* **—de·form′a·ble** *adj.* **—de·form′er** *n.*

de·form·a·tion (dē′fôr·mā′shən, def′ər-) *n.* 1. The act of deforming, or the state of being deformed. 2. A change in form or condition for the worse. 3. An altered form.

de·formed (di·fôrmd′) *adj.* 1. Marred in form; misshapen. 2. Morally distorted; perverted; warped. **—de·form·ed·ly** (di·fôr′mid·lē) *adv.* **—de·form′ed·ness** *n.*

de·form·i·ty (di·fôr′mə·tē) *n. pl.* **·ties** 1. A deformed condition. 2. An abnormally shaped part, as of the body. 3. A deformed person or thing. 4. Moral defect; also, depravity. [< OF < L *de-* away, down + *forma* figure, form]

de·fraud (di·frôd′) *v.t.* To take or withhold from by fraud; cheat; swindle. [< L < *de-* completely + *fraus, fraudis* cheat] **—de·fraud·a·tion** (dē′frô·dā′shən), **de·fraud′ment** *n.* **—de·fraud′er** *n.*

de·fray (di·frā′) *v.t.* To pay (the costs, expenses, etc.). [< F < OF < *de-* away + *fraier* to spend] **—de·fray′a·ble** *adj.* **—de·fray′al, de·fray′ment** *n.* **—de·fray′er** *n.*

de·frock (dē·frok′) *v.t.* To unfrock.

de·frost (dē·frôst′, -frost′) *v.t.* To remove ice or frost from.

de·frost·er (dē·frôs′tər, -fros′-) *n.* A device for removing ice or frost, or for preventing their formation.

deft (deft) *adj.* Neat and skillful in action; adroit. [OE *gedǣfte* meek, gentle] **—deft′ly** *adv.* **—deft′ness** *n.*

de·funct (di·fungkt′) *adj.* Dead; deceased. **—the defunct** The dead person. [< L < *de-* not + *fungi* to perform]

de·fy (*v.* di·fī′; *n.* dē′fī) *v.t.* **·fied, ·fy·ing** 1. To resist or confront openly and boldly. 2. To resist or withstand successfully. 3. To challenge (someone) to do something; dare. **—** *n. pl.* **·fies** *U.S.* A challenge; defiance. [< OF < Med.L < L *di-* not + *fidare* to be faithful]

de·gen·er·a·cy (di·jen′ər·ə·sē) *n.* 1. The process of degenerating; deterioration. 2. The state of being degenerate.

de·gen·er·ate (*v.* di·jen′ə·rat; *adj., n.* di·jen′ər·it) *v.i.* **·at·ed, ·at·ing** 1. To become worse, or more debased. 2. *Biol.* To revert to a lower type; deteriorate. **—Syn.** See RETROGRESS. **—** *adj.* Having become worse; degraded. **—** *n.* 1. A deteriorated or degraded animal or human. 2. A morally degraded person. [< L < *de-* down + *generare* to create] **—de·gen′er·ate·ly** *adv.* **—de·gen′er·ate·ness** *n.* **—de·gen′er·a·tive** (di·jen′ə·rā′tiv, -ər·ə·tiv) *adj.*

de·gen·er·a·tion (di·jen′ə·rā′shən) *n.* 1. The process of degenerating. 2. A degenerate condition. 3. *Biol.* The reversion of a group of organisms into a less complex type. 4. *Pathol.* Progressive deterioration of an organ or part.

deg·ra·da·tion (deg′rə·dā′shən) *n.* 1. The act of degrading. 2. The state of being reduced in rank, honor, quality, etc.

de·grade (di·grād′) *v.t.* **·grad·ed, ·grad·ing** 1. To debase or lower in character, morals, etc. 2. To bring into contempt; dishonor. 3. To reduce in rank; remove from office, dignity, etc. 4. To reduce in quality, intensity, etc. 5. *Geol.* To reduce the height of by erosion. [< OF < LL < L *de-* down + *gradi* to step] **—de·grad′ed** *adj.* **—de·grad′ed·ly** *adv.* **—de·grad′ed·ness** *n.*

de·grad·ing (di·grā′ding) *adj.* Debasing; humiliating. **—de·grad′ing·ly** *adv.* **—de·grad′ing·ness** *n.*

de·gree (di·grē′) *n.* 1. One of a succession of steps or stages. 2. Relative extent, amount, or intensity. 3. Relative dignity or rank, or position. 4. Relative condition, manner, or respect. 5. An academic title conferred by an institution of learning upon the completion of a course of study, or as an honorary distinction. 6. A division or unit of a scale, as of a thermometer. 7. A step in a line of genealogical descent. 8. *Law* Measure of culpability: murder in the first *degree.* 9. *Geom.* One 360th of the circumference of a circle. 10. *Math* **a** The sum of the exponents of the unknowns of an algebraic term: x^3 and xy^2 are both of the third *degree.* **b** The exponent of the highest degree term in a polynomial or equation: $x^4 + 2x^2$ is of the fourth *degree.* 11. *Geog.* A line or point of the earth's surface defined by its angular distance east or west of a standard meridian, or north or south of the equator. 12. *Gram.* One of the forms of comparison (positive, comparative, or superlative) of an adjective or adverb. 13. *Music* **a** The interval between consecutive tones of a scale. **b** A line or space in a staff. **—by degrees** Little by little; gradually. **—to a degree** 1. Somewhat. 2. Greatly. [< OF < *de-* down + *gre* < L *gradus* a step]

de·hisce (di·his′) *v.i.* **·hisced, ·hisc·ing** To split open, as the capsule of a plant. [< L < *de-* down + *hiscere,* inceptive of *hiare* to gape] **—de·his′cence** *n.* **—de·his′cent** *adj.*

de·horn (dē·hôrn′) *v.t.* To remove the horns of (cattle).

de·hu·man·ize (dē·hyōō′mən·īz) *v.t.* **·ized, ·iz·ing** 1. To deprive of human qualities or attributes. **2.** To make mechanical, abstract, or artificial. —**de·hu′man·i·za′tion** n.

de·hu·mid·i·fi·er (dē′hyōō·mid′ə·fī′ər) n. An apparatus by which moisture is removed from the air.

de·hu·mid·i·fy (dē′hyōō·mid′ə·fī) v.t. ·fied, ·fy·ing To render less humid. —**de·hu·mid′i·fi·ca′tion** n.

de·hy·drate (dē·hī′drāt) v. ·drat·ed, ·drat·ing v.t. **1.** To deprive of water, as a chemical compound, vegetables, etc. —v.i. **2.** To suffer loss of water. —**de′hy·dra′tion** n.

de·ice (dē·īs′) v.t. ·iced, ·ic·ing To free from ice.

de·ic·er (dē·ī′sər) n. A mechanical or thermal device that breaks up formations of ice, as on an airplane wing.

de·if·ic (dē·if′ik) adj. **1.** Making, or tending to make, divine. **2.** Divine. Also **de·if′i·cal.**

de·i·fy (dē′ə·fī) v.t. ·fied, ·fy·ing **1.** To make a god of. **2.** To regard or worship as a god. **3.** To glorify or idealize. [< F < LL < L deus god + facere to make] —**de′i·fi·ca′tion** n. —**de′i·fi′er** n.

deign (dān) v.i. **1.** To think it befitting oneself (to do something); condescend. —v.t. **2.** To condescend to grant or allow: He deigned no reply. [< OF < L dignus worthy]

De·i gra·ti·a (dē′ī grā′shē·ə, dā′ē grä′tē·ä) Latin By the grace of God. Abbr. D.G.

de·ism (dē′iz·əm) n. **1.** Belief in the existence of a personal God, based solely on the testimony of reason. **2.** Belief that God created the world subject to natural laws, but takes no interest in it. [< L deus a god + -ISM] —**de′ist** n. —**de·is′tic** or ·ti·cal adj. —**de·is′ti·cal·ly** adv.

de·i·ty (dē′ə·tē) n. pl. ·ties **1.** A god, goddess, or divine person. **2.** Divine nature or status; godhead; divinity. — **the Deity** God. [< F < LL < L deus a god]

de·ject (di·jekt′) v.t. To depress in spirit; dishearten. [< L de- down + jacere to throw]

de·ject·ed (di·jek′tid) adj. Depressed in spirits; disheartened. —**de·ject′ed·ly** adv. —**de·ject′ed·ness** n.

de·jec·tion (di·jek′shən) n. A state or condition of being dejected; lowness of spirits; depression; melancholy.

dé·jeu·ner (dā·zhœ·nā′) n. **1.** A late breakfast. **2.** Luncheon. [< F < dé- away + jeun fasting < L jejunus empty]

de ju·re (dē jŏŏr′ē) Latin By right; rightfully or legally: distinguished from de facto.

deka- combining form In the metric system, ten times (a specified unit). Also, before vowels, **dek-**. [< Gk. deka ten]

dek·a·gram (dek′ə·gram) n. In the metric system, a measure of weight equal to 10 grams: also spelled decagram. Also **dek′a·gramme.** See table inside back cover.

dek·a·li·ter (dek′ə·lē′tər) n. In the metric system, a measure of capacity equal to 10 liters: also spelled decaliter. Also esp. Brit. **dek′a·li′tre.** See table inside back cover.

dek·a·me·ter (dek′ə·mē′tər) n. In the metric system, a measure of length equal to 10 meters: also spelled decameter. Also esp. Brit. **dek′a·me′tre.** See table inside back cover.

dek·are (dek′âr) n. In the metric system, a thousand square meters or 10 ares: also spelled decare.

dek·a·stere (dek′ə·stir) n. In the metric system, a measure of volume equal to 10 steres: also spelled decastere.

Del·a·ware (del′ə·wâr) n. **1.** A confederacy of Algonquian tribes of North American Indians, formerly occupying the whole Delaware River valley. **2.** The language of these people. Also called Lenape, Leni-Lenape, Lenni-Lenape.

de·lay (di·lā′) v.t. **1.** To put off to a future time; postpone; defer. **2.** To cause to be late; detain. —v.i. **3.** To linger; procrastinate. —n. **1.** The act of delaying. **2.** The fact or condition of being delayed. [< OF delaier] —**de·lay′er** n.

de·le (dē′lē) v.t. ·led, ·le·ing Printing To take out; delete: usu. an imperative represented by a sign (ϑ). Compare STET. [< L, imperative of delere to erase]

de·lec·ta·ble (di·lek′tə·bəl) adj. Giving great pleasure; delightful. [< OF < L delectare. See DELIGHT.] —**de·lec′ta·ble·ness, de·lec′ta·bil′i·ty** n. —**de·lec′ta·bly** adv.

de·lec·ta·tion (dē′lek·tā′shən) n. Delight, enjoyment.

del·e·ga·cy (del′ə·gə·sē) n. pl. ·cies **1.** The act of delegating, or the state of being delegated. **2.** The office or authority given a delegate. **3.** A body of delegates.

del·e·gate (n. del′ə·gāt, -git; v. del′ə·gāt) n. **1.** A person sent with authority to represent or act for another or others. **2.** U.S. **a** A person elected or appointed to represent a Territory in the House of Representatives, where he may speak but not vote. **b** A member of the lower house (**House of Delegates**) of the legislature in Maryland, Virginia, and West Virginia. —v.t. ·gat·ed, ·gat·ing **1.** To send as a representative, with authority to act. **2.** To commit or entrust (powers, authority, etc.) to another as an agent. **3.** To assign (a debtor of one's own) to one's creditor to satisfy a claim. [< L < de- down + legare to send]

del·e·ga·tion (del′ə·gā′shən) n. **1.** The act of delegating, or the state of being delegated; deputation. **2.** A person or persons appointed to represent others; delegates collectively.

de·lete (di·lēt′) v.t. ·let·ed, ·let·ing To take out (written or printed matter); cancel. [< L deletus, pp. of delere to erase, destroy] —**de·le′tion** n.

del·e·te·ri·ous (del′ə·tir′ē·əs) adj. Causing moral or physical injury. —**Syn.** See PERNICIOUS. [< NL < Gk. dēlētērios harmful] —**del′e·te·ri·ous·ly** adv. —**del′e·te·ri·ous·ness** n.

Del·fi (del′fī) See DELPHI.

delft (delft) n. **1.** A glazed earthenware, usu. white or blue, first made at Delft, Holland, about 1310. **2.** Any tableware resembling this. Also **delf** (delf), **delft′ware′.**

del·i (del′ē) n. pl. **del·is** U.S. Colloq. A delicatessen.

de·lib·er·ate (v. di·lib′ə·rāt; adj. di·lib′ər·it) v. ·at·ed, ·at·ing v.i. **1.** To consider carefully and at length. **2.** To take counsel together so as to reach a decision. —v.t. **3.** To think about or consider carefully; weigh. —adj. **1.** Carefully thought out; intentional. **2.** Slow and cautious in determining or deciding. **3.** Leisurely in movement or manner. [< L de- completely + librare to weigh] —**de·lib′er·ate·ly** adv. —**de·lib′er·ate·ness** n.

de·lib·er·a·tion (di·lib′ə·rā′shən) n. **1.** Careful and prolonged consideration. **1.** Often pl. Examination and discussion of the arguments for and against a measure. **3.** Slowness and care in decision or action.

de·lib·er·a·tive (di·lib′ə·rā′tiv, -rə·tiv) adj. Involved in or characterized by deliberation: a deliberative body.

del·i·ca·cy (del′ə·kə·sē) n. pl. ·cies **1.** The quality of being delicate. **2.** Frailty or weakness of body or health. **3.** Refinement of feeling, appreciation, etc. **4.** Consideration for the feelings of others. **5.** Nicety of touch or execution. **6.** Sensitivity in reaction, as of instruments. **7.** Need of cautious, tactful treatment: a subject of great delicacy. **8.** Something choice and dainty, as an item of food.

del·i·cate (del′ə·kit) adj. **1.** Exquisite and fine in workmanship, texture, etc. **2.** Daintily pleasing, as in taste, aroma, or color. **3.** Easily injured or destroyed; frail. **4.** Requiring tactful treatment. **5.** Gentle and skilled: a delicate touch. **6.** Sensitive and subtle in feeling, perception, or expression: a delicate eye for color. **7.** Showing a fine appreciation for what is proper and becoming. **8.** Considerate of the feelings of others. **9.** Sensitively accurate: a delicate thermometer. **10.** Subtle: a delicate distinction. [< L delicatus pleasing] —**del′i·cate·ly** adv. —**del′i·cate·ness** n.

del·i·ca·tes·sen (del′ə·kə·tes′ən) n.pl. **1.** (often construed as sing.) Cooked or preserved foods, as cooked meats, cheeses, pickles, etc. **2.** (construed as sing.) A store that sells such foods. [< G, pl. of delicatesse delicacy]

de·li·cious (di·lish′əs) adj. Extremely pleasant or enjoyable, esp. to the taste. [< OF < LL < L delicia delight] —**de·li′cious·ly** adv. —**de·li′cious·ness** n.

De·li·cious (di·lish′əs) n. A variety of sweet, red apple.

de·light (di·līt′) n. **1.** Great pleasure; gratification; joy. **2.** That which gives extreme pleasure. **3.** Poetic The quality of delighting; charm. —v.i. **1.** To take great pleasure; rejoice: with in or the infinitive. **2.** To give great enjoyment. —v.t. **3.** To please or gratify highly. [< OF < L delectare, freq. of delicere < de- away + lacere to entice] —**de·light′ed** adj. —**de·light′ed·ly** adv.

de·light·ful (di·līt′fəl) adj. Affording delight; extremely pleasing. —**de·light′ful·ly** adv. —**de·light′ful·ness** n.

De·li·lah (di·lī′lə) A Philistine woman, the mistress of Samson, who betrayed him to the Philistines by cutting off his hair, thus depriving him of his strength. Judg. xvi 4-20. —n. A voluptuous but treacherous woman.

de·lim·it (di·lim′it) v.t. To prescribe the limits of. Also **de·lim′i·tate.** [< F < L de- completely + limitare bound] —**de·lim′i·ta′tion** n. —**de·lim′i·ta·tive** adj.

de·lin·e·ate (di·lin′ē·āt) v.t. ·at·ed, ·at·ing **1.** To draw in outline. **2.** To represent by a drawing. **3.** To portray verbally; describe. [< L < de- completely + lineare to draw a line] —**de·lin′e·a′tion** n.

de·lin·quen·cy (di·ling′kwən·sē) n. pl. ·cies **1.** Neglect of duty. **2.** A fault; offense. **3.** Juvenile delinquency.

de·lin·quent (di·ling′kwənt) adj. **1.** Neglectful of or failing in duty or obligation; guilty of an offense. **2.** Due and unpaid, as taxes. —n. **1.** One who fails to perform a duty or commits a fault. **2.** A juvenile delinquent. [< L de- down, away + linquere to leave] —**de·lin′quent·ly** adv.

del·i·quesce (del′ə·kwes′) v.i. ·quesced, ·quesc·ing **1.** To melt or pass away gradually. **2.** To become liquid by absorption of moisture from the air, as certain salts. [< L < de- completely + liquescere to melt] —**del′i·ques′cence** n. —**del′i·ques′cent** adj.

de·lir·i·ous (di·lir′ē·əs) adj. **1.** Suffering from delirium. **2.** Characteristic of delirium: delirious dreams. **3.** Wildly excited. —**de·lir′i·ous·ly** adv. —**de·lir′i·ous·ness** n.

de·lir·i·um (di·lir′ē·əm) n. **1.** A sporadic or temporary mental disturbance associated with fever, intoxication, etc., and marked by excitement, hallucinations, and general incoherence. **2.** Wild emotion or excitement. [< L < de- down, away + lira furrow, track]

delirium tre·mens (trē′mənz) A violent delirium caused esp. by excessive use of alcoholic liquors.

de·liv·er (di·liv′ər) v.t. **1.** To hand over; surrender. **2.** To carry and distribute: to *deliver* newspapers. **3.** To give forth; send forth: to *deliver* a blow. **4.** To give forth in words; utter. **5.** To throw or pitch, as a ball. **6.** To free from restraint, evil, danger, etc. **7.** To assist in the birth of (offspring). **— to be delivered of** To give birth. **— to deliver oneself of** To put into words; express. [< OF < LL < L *de-* down, away + *liberare* to set free] **— de·liv·er·a·ble** *adj.* **— de·liv'er·er** *n.*

de·liv·er·ance (di·liv'ər·əns) *n.* **1.** The act of delivering, or the state of being delivered. **2.** An expression of opinion.

de·liv·er·y (di·liv'ər·ē) *n. pl.* **·er·ies 1.** The act of delivering or distributing something. **2.** That which is distributed, as mail. **3.** The act of liberating; release. **4.** A transferring or handing over. **5.** The bringing forth of offspring. **6.** Manner of utterance, as in public speaking. **7.** The act or manner of giving forth or discharging a ball, a blow, etc.

dell (del) *n.* A small, secluded, usu. wooded valley. [ME]

de·louse (dē·lous') *v.t.* **·loused, ·lous·ing** To remove lice or other insect vermin from.

Del·phi (del'fī) An ancient city in Phocis, Greece; famous for its oracle: also *Delfi.* **— Del·phi·an** (del'fē·ən) *adj. & n.*

Del·phic (del'fik) *adj.* **1.** Relating to Delphi or to Apollo's oracle there. **2.** Oracular.

del·phin·i·um (del·fin'ē·əm) *n.* Any of a genus of perennial plants of the crowfoot family, having large, spurred flowers, usu. blue; the larkspur. [< NL < Gk. *delphis* dolphin; so called from the shape of the nectary]

del·ta (del'tə) *n.* **1.** The fourth letter in the Greek alphabet (Δ, δ), corresponding to English *d*. See ALPHABET. **2.** *Geog.* An alluvial, typically triangular-shaped, silt deposit at or in the mouth of a river. **3.** Anything triangular. [< Gk.]

del·ta·he·dron (del'tə·hē'drən) *n. pl.* **·dra** (-drə) *Crystall.* A crystal form having twelve equal, trapezoidal faces. Also **del'to·he'dron.** For illus. see CRYSTAL.

del·toid (del'toid) *n. Anat.* A triangular muscle covering the shoulder joint. **—** *adj.* Shaped like a delta; triangular. [< Gk. < *delta* the letter Δ + *eidos* form]

de·lude (di·lōōd') *v.t.* **·lud·ed, ·lud·ing** To mislead the mind or judgment of; deceive. [< L < *de-* from, away + *ludere* to play] **— de·lud'er** *n.* **— de·lud'ing·ly** *adv.*

del·uge (del'yōōj) *v.t.* **·uged, ·ug·ing 1.** To flood with water. **2.** To overwhelm; destroy. **—** *n.* **1.** A great flood or inundation. **2.** Something that overwhelms or engulfs: a *deluge* of tears. **— the Deluge** The flood in the time of Noah. *Gen.* vii. [< OF < L < *dis-* away + *luere* to wash]

de·lu·sion (di·lōō'zhən) *n.* **1.** The act of deluding. **2.** The state of being deluded. **3.** A false, fixed belief, held in spite of evidence to the contrary. **— de·lu'sion·al** *adj.*

de·lu·sive (di·lōō'siv) *adj.* Tending to delude; misleading. Also **de·lu·so·ry** (di·lōō'sər·ē). **— de·lu'sive·ly** *adv.* **— de·lu'sive·ness** *n.*

de luxe (di lōōks', di luks'; *Fr.* də lüks') Elegant and expensive; of superfine quality. [< F, lit., of luxury]

delve (delv) *v.* **delved, delv·ing** *v.i.* To make careful investigation; search for information. [OE *delfan*] **— delv'er** *n.*

de·mag·net·ize (dē·mag'nə·tīz) *v.t.* **·ized, ·iz·ing** To deprive (a substance) of magnetism. **— de·mag'net·i·za'tion** *n.* **— de·mag'net·iz'er** *n.*

dem·a·gog·ic (dem'ə·goj'ik, -gog'ik) *adj.* Of or like a demagogue. Also **dem·a·gog'i·cal.** **— dem·a·gog'i·cal·ly** *adv.*

dem·a·gogue (dem'ə·gôg, -gog) *n.* One who leads the populace by appealing to prejudices and emotions. Also **dem'a·gog.** [< Gk. < *dēmos* people + *agein* to lead]

dem·a·gogu·er·y (dem'ə·gôg'ər·ē, -gog'ər·ē) *n.* The spirit, method, or conduct of a demagogue. Also **dem'a·gog·ism.**

dem·a·go·gy (dem'ə·gō'jē, -gôg'ē, -gog'ē) *n.* **1.** Demagoguery. **2.** The rule of a demagogue. **3.** Demagogues collectively.

de·mand (di·mand', -mänd') *v.t.* **1.** To ask for boldly or preemptorily. **2.** To claim as due. **3.** To inquire formally. **4.** To have need for; require. **5.** *Law* a To summon to court. b To make formal claim to (property). **—** *v.i.* **6.** To make a demand. **—** *n.* **1.** The act of demanding. **2.** That which is demanded. **3.** A claim or requirement: the *demands* on one's time. **4.** An inquiry. **5.** *Law* A request or claim. **6.** *Econ.* a The desire to possess combined with the ability to purchase. b The potential amount of certain goods that will be purchased at a given time for a given price. **— in demand** Desired; sought after. **— on demand** On presentation: a note payable *on demand.* [< F < L < *de-* down, away + *mandare* to command, order] **— de·mand'a·ble** *adj.* **— de·mand'er** *n.*

de·mar·cate (di·mär'kāt, dē'mär·kāt) *v.t.* **·cat·ed, ·cat·ing 1.** To mark the limits of. **2.** To differentiate; separate.

de·mar·ca·tion (dē'mär·kā'shən) *n.* **1.** The fixing or marking of boundaries or limits. **2.** The limits or boundaries fixed. **3.** A limiting or separating. [< Sp. < *de-* down (< L *de-*) + *marcar* to mark a boundary]

dé·marche (dā·märsh') *n. French* **1.** A mode of procedure. **2.** In diplomacy, a change in policy.

de·mean¹ (di·mēn') *v.t.* To behave or conduct (oneself) in a particular way. [< OF < *de-* down (< L *de-*) + *mener* to lead < LL *minare* to threaten, drive]

de·mean² (di·mēn') *v.t.* To lower in dignity or reputation; debase; degrade. **— Syn.** See ABASE.

de·mean·or (di·mē'nər) *n.* The manner in which one behaves or bears oneself. Also, *Brit.*, **de·mean'our.**

de·ment·ed (di·men'tid) *adj.* Mentally ill; insane. **— de·ment'ed·ly** *adv.* **— de·ment'ed·ness** *n.*

de·men·tia (di·men'shə, -shē·ə) *n.* Loss or serious impairment of mental powers. [< L, madness]

dementia pre·cox (prē'koks) *Psychiatry* Schizophrenia: a former name. Also **de·men'tia prae'cox.**

de·mer·it (di·mer'it) *n.* **1.** A defect; fault. **2.** In schools, etc., a mark for failure or misconduct. [< Med.L < L < *de-* down, away + *merere* to deserve]

de·mesne (di·mān', -mēn') *n.* **1.** In law, lands held in one's own power. **2.** A manor house and the adjoining lands. **3.** A region; domain. [< OF *demeine, demaine*]

De·me·ter (di·mē'tər) The Greek goddess of agriculture, marriage, and fertility: identified with *Ceres.*

demi- *prefix* **1.** Half; intermediate. **2.** Inferior or less in size, quality, etc.; partial. [< F < L < *dis-* from, apart + *medius* middle]

dem·i·god (dem'ē·god') *n.* **1.** An inferior diety. **2.** A man with the attributes of a god. **— dem'i·god'dess** *n.fem.*

dem·i·john (dem'ē·jon') *n.* A narrow-necked jug, often enclosed in wickerwork. [< F *dame-jeanne,* lit., Lady Jane]

de·mil·i·ta·rize (dē·mil'ə·tə·rīz') *v.t.* **·rized, ·riz·ing** To remove military characteristics from; free from militarism.

dem·i·mon·daine (dem'ē·mon·dān') *n.* A woman of the demimonde. Also **dem·i·rep** (dem'ē·rep'). [< F]

dem·i·monde (dem'ē·mond, dem'ē·mond') *n.* The class of women who have lost social position because of their scandalous behavior. [< F < *demi-* half, partial + *monde* world]

de·mise (di·mīz') *n.* **1.** Death. **2.** *Law* A transfer of rights or an estate. **—** *v.* **·mised, ·mis·ing** *v.t.* **1.** To bestow (royal power) by death or abdication. **2.** *Law* To lease or transfer (an estate). **—** *v.i.* **3.** To pass by will or inheritance. [< OF < L < *de-* down, away + *mittere* to send]

dem·i·sem·i·qua·ver (dem'ē·sem'ē·kwā'vər) *n. Music* *Chiefly Brit.* A thirty-second note.

dem·i·tasse (dem'ē·tas', -täs') *n.* **1.** A small cup in which after-dinner coffee is served. **2.** Coffee served in such a cup. [< F, a half cup]

demo- *combining form* People. [< Gk. *dēmos* people]

de·mo·bi·lize (dē·mō'bə·līz') *v.t.* **·lized, ·liz·ing** To disband (an army or troops). **— de·mo·bi·li·za'tion** *n.*

de·moc·ra·cy (di·mok'rə·sē) *n. pl.* **·cies 1.** A form of government in which political power resides in all the people and is exercised by them directly or is given to elected representatives. **2.** A state so governed. **3.** The spirit or practice of political, legal, or social equality. [< F < Med.L < Gk. < *dēmos* people + *krateein* to rule]

dem·o·crat (dem'ə·krat) *n.* **1.** One who favors a democracy. **2.** One who believes in political and social equality.

Dem·o·crat (dem'ə·krat) *n.* A member of the Democratic Party in the United States. Abbr. *D., Dem.*

dem·o·crat·ic (dem'ə·krat'ik) *adj.* **1.** Of, pertaining to, or characterized by the principles of democracy. **2.** Existing or provided for the benefit or enjoyment of all. **3.** Practicing social equality. **— dem'o·crat'i·cal·ly** *adv.*

Dem·o·crat·ic (dem'ə·krat'ik) *adj.* Of, pertaining to, or characteristic of the Democratic Party.

Democratic Party One of the two major political parties in the United States, dating from 1828.

de·moc·ra·tize (di·mok'rə·tīz) *v.t. & v.i.* **·tized, ·tiz·ing** To make or become democratic. **— de·moc·ra·ti·za'tion** *n.*

de·mog·ra·phy (di·mog'rə·fē) *n.* The statistical study of population, esp. its size and distribution. [< DEMO- + -GRAPHY] **— de·mog'ra·pher** *n.* **— dem·o·graph·ic** (dem'ə·graf'ik) *adj.*

de·mol·ish (di·mol'ish) *v.t.* **1.** To tear down, as a building. **2.** To destroy utterly; ruin. [< F < L < *de-* down + *moliri* to build] **— de·mol'ish·er** *n.* **— de·mol'ish·ment** *n.* **— Syn.** A building is *demolished* if smashed to fragments, and *razed* if leveled to the ground. It is *ruined* if made unfit for habitation or use, though much of its structure may remain. *Destroy* is a very general term, covering all these senses.

dem·o·li·tion (dem'ə·lish'ən) *n.* The act or result of demolishing; destruction. **— dem·o·li'tion·ist** *n.*

de·mon (dē'mən) *n.* **1.** An evil spirit; devil. **2.** A very wicked or cruel person. **3.** *Informal* A person of great skill or zeal: a *demon* with a gun. [< L < Gk. *daimōn*]

de·mon·e·tize (dē·mon'ə·tīz) *v.t.* **·tized, ·tiz·ing 1.** To deprive (currency) of standard value. **2.** To withdraw from use, as currency. **— de·mon'e·ti·za'tion** *n.*

de·mo·ni·ac (di·mō′nē·ak) *adj.* **1.** Of, like, or befitting a demon. **2.** Influenced or possessed by or as by demons; frenzied. Also **de·mo·ni·a·cal** (dē′ma·nī′a·kəl). — *n.* One supposedly possessed of a demon. — **de′mo·ni′a·cal·ly** *adv.*

de·mon·ic (di·mon′ik) *adj.* **1.** Of or like a demon. Also **de·mo·ni·an** (di·mō′nē·ən). **2.** Inspired, as by a demon.

de·mon·ism (dē′mən·iz′əm) *n.* **1.** Belief in demons. **2.** Demonolatry. **3.** Demonology. — **de′mon·ist** *n.*

demono- *combining form* Demon. Also, before vowels, **demon-.** [< Gk. *daimōn* spirit, god]

de·mon·ol·a·try (dē′mən·ol′ə·trē) *n.* The worship of demons. [< DEMONO- + Gk. *latreia* worship] — **de′mon·ol′a·ter** *n.*

de·mon·ol·o·gy (dē′mən·ol′ə·jē) *n.* The study of demons or of belief in demons. — **de′mon·ol′o·gist** *n.*

de·mon·stra·ble (di·mon′strə·bəl, dem′ən-) *adj.* Capable of being demonstrated or proved. — **de·mon′stra·bil′i·ty, de·mon′stra·ble·ness** *n.* — **de·mon′stra·bly** *adv.*

dem·on·strate (dem′ən·strāt) *v.* **strat·ed, ·strat·ing** *v.t.* **1.** To explain or describe by use of experiments, examples, etc. **2.** To prove or show by reasoning; make evident. **3.** To show feelings clearly. — *v.i.* **4.** To take part in a public demonstration. **5.** To make a show of military force. [< L < *de-* completely + *monstrare* to show, point out]

dem·on·stra·tion (dem′ən·strā′shən) *n.* **1.** The act of making known or evident. **2.** Undeniable proof or evidence. **3.** An explanation or showing of how something works, as a product. **4.** A show or expression: a *demonstration* of love. **5.** A display of public feeling, as a mass meeting or parade. **6.** A show of military force or maneuver.

de·mon·stra·tive (di·mon′strə·tiv) *adj.* **1.** Serving to demonstrate or point out. **2.** Able to prove beyond doubt; convincing and conclusive. **3.** Inclined to strong expression. **4.** *Gram.* Indicating the person or object referred to. — *n. Gram.* A demonstrative pronoun. — **de·mon′stra·tive·ly** *adv.* — **de·mon′stra·tive·ness** *n.*

demonstrative pronoun *Gram.* A pronoun that directly points out its antecedents, as *this, those.*

dem·on·stra·tor (dem′ən·strā′tər) *n.* One who or that which demonstrates.

de·mor·al·ize (di·môr′əl·īz, -mor′-) *v.t.* **ized, ·iz·ing 1.** To corrupt or deprave. **2.** To lower the morale of. **3.** To throw into disorder. — **de·mor′al·i·za′tion** *n.* — **de·mor′al·iz′er** *n.*

de·mote (di·mōt′) *v.t.* **·mot·ed, ·mot·ing** To reduce to a lower grade or rank. — **de·mo′tion** *n.*

de·mul·cent (di·mul′sənt) *adj.* Soothing. — *n. Med.* A soothing substance. [< L < *de-* down + *mulcere* to soothe]

de·mur (di·mûr′) *v.i.* **murred, ·mur·ring 1.** To offer objections; take exception. **2.** To delay; hesitate. **3.** *Law* To interpose a demurrer. — *n.* **1.** The act of demurring. **2.** An objection, as to proposed action. **3.** A delay. [< OF < L < *de-* completely + *morari* to delay]

de·mure (di·myŏŏr′) *adj.* **·mur·er, ·mur·est 1.** Grave; reserved. **2.** Prim; coy. [ME < OF < L *maturus* mature, discreet] — **de·mure′ly** *adv.* — **de·mure′ness** *n.*

de·mur·rage (di·mûr′ij) *n.* **1.** The detention of a vessel, railway freight car, or other commercial conveyance, beyond the specified time for departure, as a result of loading, unloading, etc. **2.** Compensation for such delay.

de·mur·rer (di·mûr′ər) *n.* **1.** *Law* A pleading that allows the truth of the facts stated by the opposite party, but denies that they are sufficient to constitute a good cause of action or defense in law. **2.** Any objection or exception taken. **3.** One who demurs. [< AF]

den (den) *n.* **1.** The cave or retreat of a wild animal; a lair. **2.** A site or dwelling: used pejoratively: a *den* of thieves. **3.** A small, private room for relaxation or study. — *v.i.* **denned, den·ning** To dwell in or as in a den. [OE *denn*]

de·nar·i·us (di·nâr′ē·əs) *n. pl.* **nar·i·i** (-nâr′ē·ī). **1.** A silver coin of ancient Rome; the penny of the New Testament. **2.** A gold coin of ancient Rome. [< L < *decem* ten]

de·na·tion·al·ize (dē·nash′ən·əl·īz′) *v.t.* **ized, ·iz·ing** To deprive of national character, status, or rights. Also *Brit.* **de·na′tion·al·ise′.** — **de·na′tion·al·i·za′tion** *n.*

de·nat·u·ral·ize (dē·nach′ər·əl·īz′) *v.t.* **ized, ·iz·ing 1.** To render unnatural. **2.** To deprive of citizenship. Also *Brit.* **de·nat′u·ral·ise′.** — **de·nat′u·ral·i·za′tion** *n.*

de·na·ture (dē·nā′chər) *v.t.* **tured, ·tur·ing 1.** To change the nature of. **2.** To adulterate (alcohol, fat, etc.) so as to make unfit for drinking or eating without destroying other useful properties. Also **de·na′tur·ize.** — **de·na′tur·ant** *n.*

den·drite (den′drīt) *n. Physiol.* A threadlike, branching process of a nerve cell that conducts impulses toward the cell body. [< Gk. < *dendron* tree] — **den·drit′ic** (-drit′ik) or **·i·cal** *adj.* — **den·drit′i·cal·ly** *adv.*

dendro- *combining form* Tree. Also **dendr-** (before vowels), **dendri-.** [< Gk. *dendron* tree]

-dendron *combining form* Tree. [< Gk. *dendron* tree]

Den·eb (den′eb) *n.* One of the 20 brightest stars, 1.33 magnitude; Alpha in the constellation Cygnus.

den·gue (deng′gē, -gā) *n. Pathol.* An acute, tropical, virus disease transmitted by the bite of a mosquito and characterized by fever, eruptions, and severe pains in the joints. [< Sp., ult. < Swahili]

de·ni·a·ble (di·nī′ə·bəl) *adj.* That can be denied. — **de·ni′a·bly** *adv.*

de·ni·al (di·nī′əl) *n.* **1.** A contradiction, as of a statement. **2.** Refusal to believe a doctrine, etc. **3.** A disowning or disavowal. **4.** Refusal to grant, give, or allow.

de·nic·o·tin·ize (dē·nik′ə·tin·īz′) *v.t.* **ized, ·iz·ing** To remove nicotine from (tobacco). Also **de·nic′o·tine.**

de·ni·er[1] (di·nī′ər) *n.* One who makes denial.

den·ier[2] (den′yər, də·nir′) *n.* A unit of weight for denoting the coarseness or fineness of rayon, nylon, or silk yarns. [See DENARIUS.]

den·im (den′əm) *n.* **1.** A strong, twilled cotton used for overalls, uniforms, etc.; also, a finer grade of this fabric used for hangings, upholstery, etc. **2.** *pl.* Garments made of this material. [< F (*serge*) *de Nîmes* (serge) of Nîmes]

den·i·zen (den′ə·zən) *n.* **1.** An inhabitant. **2.** A person, animal, or thing at home or naturalized in a region or condition not native to it. — *v.t.* To make (someone or something) a denizen. [< AF < *deinz* inside < *de intus* from within] — **den′i·zen·a′tion** *n.*

de·nom·i·nate (*v.* di·nom′ə·nāt; *adj.* di·nom′ə·nit) *v.t.* **nat·ed, ·nat·ing** To give a name to; call. — *adj.* Having a specific name. [< L < *de-* down + *nomen* name]

de·nom·i·na·tion (di·nom′ə·nā′shən) *n.* **1.** The act of naming or calling by name. **2.** A name. **3.** Any specifically named class or group of things or people: There were many *denominations* of criminals. **4.** A religious group; a sect.

de·nom·i·na·tion·al (di·nom′ə·nā′shən·əl) *adj.* Of, pertaining to, or supported by a religious denomination or sect; sectarian. — **de·nom′i·na′tion·al·ly** *adv.*

de·nom·i·na·tion·al·ism (di·nom′ə·nā′shən·əl·iz′əm) *n.* **1.** A disposition to divide into or form denominations. **2.** Rigid adherence or devotion to a denomination or sect; sectarianism. — **de·nom′i·na′tion·al·ist** *n. & adj.*

de·nom·i·na·tive (di·nom′ə·nā′tiv, -nə·tiv) *adj.* **1.** That gives or constitutes a name; appellative. **2.** *Gram.* Derived from a noun or adjective, as the verb *to garden.* — *n. Gram.* A denominative word. — **de·nom′i·na·tive·ly** *adv.*

de·nom·i·na·tor (di·nom′ə·nā′tər) *n. Math.* The term of a fraction below the line indicating the number of equal parts into which the unit is divided.

de·no·ta·tion (dē′nō·tā′shən) *n.* **1.** The specific meaning of, or the object or objects designated by, a word. **2.** The act of denoting. **3.** That which indicates, as a sign.

de·note (di·nōt′) *v.t.* **not·ed ·not·ing 1.** To point out or make known; mark. **2.** To signify; indicate. **3.** To designate; mean: said of words, symbols, etc. [< L < *de-* down + *notare* to mark] — **de·not′a·ble** *adj.* — **de·no·ta·tive** (di·nō′tə·tiv, dē′nō·tā′tiv) *adj.*

dé·noue·ment (dā·nōō·män′) *n.* **1.** The final solution of the plot of a play, novel, etc. **2.** Any final outcome. [< OF < *des-* away (< L *dis-*) + *nouer* to knot]

de·nounce (di·nouns′) *v.t.* **nounced, ·nounc·ing 1.** To attack or condemn openly and vehemently; inveigh against. **2.** To inform against; accuse. **3.** To announce as a threat. **4.** To give formal notice of the termination of (a treaty, etc.). [< OF < L < *de-* down + *nuntiare* to announce] — **de·nounce′ment** *n.* — **de·nounc′er** *n.*

dense (dens) *adj.* **dens·er, dens·est 1.** Compact; thick; close. **2.** Hard to penetrate. **3.** Stupid. [< L *densus*] — **dense′ly** *adv.* — **dense′ness** *n.*

den·si·ty (den′sə·tē) *n. pl.* **·ties 1.** The state or quality of being dense; closeness of parts; compactness. **2.** Stupidity. **3.** *Physics* The mass of a substance per unit of its volume. **4.** *Sociol.* The number of specified units, as persons, families, or dwellings, per unit of area. [< MF < L *densus* thick]

dent (dent) *n.* A small depression made by striking or pressing. — *v.t.* **1.** To make a dent in. — *v.i.* **2.** To become dented. [Var. of DINT]

den·tal (den′təl) *adj.* **1.** Of or pertaining to the teeth. **2.** Of or pertaining to dentistry. **3.** *Phonet.* Produced with the tip of the tongue against or near the upper front teeth. — *n. Phonet.* A dental consonant. [< NL < L *dens,* tooth]

dental plate A denture.

den·tate (den′tāt) *adj.* Having teeth or toothlike processes; toothed; notched. [< L *dentatus* having teeth] — **den′tate·ly** *adv.* — **den′ta·tion** *n.*

denti- *combining form* Tooth. Also, before vowels, **dent-.**

den·ti·frice (den′tə·fris) *n.* A preparation, as a powder or paste, for cleaning the teeth. [< MF < L < *dens, dentis* tooth + *fricare* to rub]

den·tine (den′tēn, -tin) *n. Anat.* The hard, calcified substance forming the body of a tooth, situated just beneath the enamel and cementum. Also **den′tin** (-tin). For illus. see TOOTH. — **den′tin·al** *adj.*

den·tist (den′tist) *n.* One who practices dentistry. [< F *dentiste* < *dent* a tooth]

den·tist·ry (den′tis·trē) *n.* 1. The branch of medicine concerned with the diagnosis, prevention, and treatment of diseases affecting the teeth. 2. The work of a dentist.

den·ti·tion (den·tish′ən) *n.* 1. The process or period of cutting teeth; teething. 2. The kind, number, and arrangement of teeth in man and other animals.

den·ture (den′chər) *n.* 1. A set of teeth. 2. A set of artificial teeth, either partial or full: also called *dental plate.* [< F < *dent* tooth] —**den′tur·al** *adj.*

de·nu·date (di·nōō′dāt, -nyōō′-, den′yōō·dāt) *adj.* Stripped of foliage or other covering; naked. —*v.t.* ·dat·ed, ·dat·ing To denude. [< L *denudatus,* pp. of *denudare.* See DENUDE.]

de·nude (di·nōōd′, -nyōōd′) *v.t.* ·nud·ed, ·nud·ing 1. To strip the covering from; make naked. 2. *Geol.* To expose to view by erosion. [< L < *de-* down, completely + *nudare* to strip] —**den·u·da·tion** (den′yōō·dā′shən, dē′nōō-, -nyōō-) *n.*

de·nun·ci·ate (di·nun′sē·āt, -shē-) *v.t. & v.i.* ·at·ed, ·at·ing To denounce. [< L < *de-* down + *nuntiare* to announce]

de·nun·ci·a·tion (di·nun′sē·ā′shən, -shē-) *n.* 1. Open disapproval or condemnation of a person or action. 2. An accusation. 3. A threat or warning. 4. Formal notice that a treaty is to be terminated.

de·nun·ci·a·to·ry (di·nun′sē·ə·tôr′ē, -tō′rē, -shē-) *adj.* Of the nature of or containing denunciation; accusing.

de·ny (di·nī′) *v.t.* ·nied, ·ny·ing 1. To declare to be untrue; contradict. 2. To refuse to believe; declare to be false or invalid, as a doctrine. 3. To refuse to give; withhold. 4. To refuse (someone) a request. 5. To refuse to acknowledge; disown; repudiate. 6. To refuse access to. —**to deny oneself** To refuse oneself something desired; practice self-denial. [< OF < L *de-* completely + *negare* to say no, refuse]

de·o·dar (dē′ə·där) *n.* The East Indian cedar, prized for its durable, light red wood. [< Skt. < *deva* god + *dāru* wood]

de·o·dor·ant (dē·ō′dər·ənt) *adj.* Destroying, absorbing, or disguising bad odors. —*n.* A deodorant substance.

de·o·dor·ize (dē·ō′dər·īz) *v.t.* ·ized, ·iz·ing To modify, destroy, or disguise the odor of. —**de·o′dor·i·za′tion** *n.* —**de·o′dor·iz′er** *n.*

de·ox·i·dize (dē·ok′sə·dīz) *v.t.* ·dized, ·diz·ing 1. To remove oxygen from. 2. To reduce from the state of an oxide. —**de·ox′i·di·za′tion** *n.* —**de·ox′i·diz′er** *n.*

de·ox·y- *combining form* Containing less oxygen than. Also **desoxy-.**

de·ox·y·ri·bo·nu·cle·ic acid (dē·ok′sē·rī′bō·nōō·klē′ik, -nyōō′-) *Biochem.* A nucleic acid forming a principal constituent of the genes and known to play an important role in the genetic action of the chromosomes. *Abbr.* DNA.

de·part (di·pärt′) *v.i.* 1. To go away; leave. 2. To deviate; differ; vary: with *from:* to *depart* from tradition. 3. To die. —*v.t.* 4. To leave: now archaic except in the phrase **to depart this life.** [< OF < *de-* away + *partir* to divide]

de·part·ed (di·pär′tid) *adj.* 1. Gone; past. 2. Dead. —**the departed** The dead person, or the dead collectively.

de·part·ment (di·pärt′mənt) *n.* 1. A distinct part or division of something, as of a business or college: the English *department.* 2. *Usu. cap. U.S.* An executive division of the government, headed by a cabinet officer. 3. In France, an administrative district. [See DEPART.] —**de·part·men·tal** (dē′pärt·men′təl) *adj.* —**de·part·men′tal·ly** *adv.*

de·part·men·tal·ize (dē′pärt·men′təl·īz) *v.t. & v.i.* ·ized, ·iz·ing To divide into departments.

department store A large retail establishment selling various types of merchandise and service.

de·par·ture (di·pär′chər) *n.* 1. The act of going away or taking leave. 2. Deviation from an accepted or ordinary method, course, etc. 3. *Archaic* Death.

de·pend (di·pend′) *v.i.* 1. To rely; trust: with *on* or *upon.* 2. To be conditioned or determined; be contingent: with *on* or *upon.* 3. To rely for maintenance, etc.: with *on* or *upon.* 4. To hang down: with *from.* [< OF < L *de-* down + *pendere* to hang]

de·pend·a·ble (di·pen′də·bəl) *adj.* That can be depended upon; trustworthy. —**de·pend′a·bil′i·ty, de·pend′a·ble·ness** *n.* —**de·pend′a·bly** *adv.*

de·pen·dence (di·pen′dəns) *n.* 1. The state of relying on something or someone. 2. Reliance or trust. 3. The state of being contingent on or determined by something else. 4. Subjection to the control or guidance of another. 5. The object of one's reliance. Also **de·pen′dance.**

de·pen·den·cy (di·pen′dən·sē) *n. pl.* ·cies 1. The state of being dependent; dependence. 2. That which is dependent or subordinate. 3. A territory or state separate from but subject to another state or country. Also **de·pen′dan·cy.**

de·pen·dent (di·pen′dənt) *adj.* 1. Conditioned by or contingent upon something else. 2. Subordinate. 3. Relying on someone or something for support. 4. Hanging down. —*n.* One who depends on another. Also **de·pen′dant.**

dependent clause *Gram.* See under CLAUSE.

de·pict (di·pikt′) *v.t.* 1. To portray or represent by or as by drawing, etc. 2. To portray in words. [< L < *de-* down + *pingere* to paint] —**de·pic′tion** *n.*

dep·i·late (dep′ə·lāt) *v.t.* ·lat·ed, ·lat·ing To remove hair from. [< L < *de-* away + *pilus* hair] —**dep′i·la′tion** *n.* **dep′i·la′tor** *n.*

de·pil·a·to·ry (di·pil′ə·tôr′ē, -tō′rē) *adj.* Having the power to remove hair. —*n. pl.* ·ries A depilatory agent.

de·plane (dē·plān′) *v.i.* ·planed, ·plan·ing To alight from an airplane: to *deplane* in Boston.

de·plete (di·plēt′) *v.t.* ·plet·ed, ·plet·ing 1. To reduce or lessen, as by use, exhaustion, or waste. 2. To empty completely or partially. [< L < *de-* not + *plere* to fill] —**de·ple′tion** *n.* —**de·ple′tive** *adj. & n.*

de·plor·a·ble (di·plôr′ə·bəl, -plō′rə-) *adj.* 1. To be deplored; lamentable. 2. Wretched; sad. —**de·plor′a·ble·ness, de·plor′a·bil′i·ty** *n.* —**de·plor′a·bly** *adv.*

de·plore (di·plôr′, -plōr′) *v.t.* ·plored, ·plor·ing To have or show regret or sadness over; lament. —**Syn.** See MOURN. [< L < *de-* completely + *plorare* to bewail]

de·ploy (di·ploi′) *v.t. & v.i.* To place or position (forces, people, etc.) according to a plan. [< F < OF < LL < L *dis-* from + *plicare* to fold] —**de·ploy′ment** *n.*

de·po·nent (di·pō′nənt) *adj.* In Latin and Greek grammar, denoting a verb that has the form of the passive but is active in meaning. —*n.* 1. A deponent verb. 2. *Law* One who gives sworn testimony, especially in writing.

de·pop·u·late (dē·pop′yə·lāt) *v.t.* ·lat·ed, ·lat·ing To remove the inhabitants from, as by massacre, famine, eviction, etc. [< L < *de-* down + *populari* to lay waste] —**de·pop′u·la′tion** *n.* —**de·pop′u·la′tor** *n.*

de·port (di·pôrt′, -pōrt′) *v.t.* 1. To expel from a country. 2. To behave or conduct (oneself). [< OF < L *de-* away + *portare* to carry] —**de′por·ta′tion** *n.*

de·port·ment (di·pôrt′mənt, -pōrt′-) *n.* Conduct or behavior; demeanor; bearing.

de·pose (di·pōz′) *v.* ·posed, ·pos·ing *v.t.* 1. To deprive of rank or office; oust. 2. *Law* To declare under oath. —*v.i.* 3. *Law* To give testimony under oath. [< OF < *de-* down + *poser* to put down] —**de·pos′a·ble** *adj.* —**de·pos′al** *n.*

de·pos·it (di·poz′it) *v.t.* 1. To set down; place; put. 2. To put down in the form of a layer, as silt. 3. To entrust (money, valuables, etc.) for safekeeping, as in a bank. 4. To give as partial payment or security. —*v.i.* 5. To be collected or precipitated: Sediments *deposit* in layers. —*n.* 1. Something entrusted for safekeeping, especially money placed in a bank. 2. The state of being placed for safekeeping: chiefly in the phrase **on deposit.** 3. Anything given as partial payment or security. 4. That which is or has been deposited, as sediment. 5. *Geol.* A mass of iron, coal, oil, etc. [< OF < L *de-* down + *ponere* to place]

de·pos·i·tar·y (di·poz′ə·ter′ē) *n. pl.* ·tar·ies 1. One entrusted with anything for safekeeping. 2. A depository.

dep·o·si·tion (dep′ə·zish′ən, dē′pə-) *n.* 1. The act of deposing, as from an office. 2. The act of depositing; also, that which is deposited. 3. *Law* The written testimony of a witness who is under oath. —**Syn.** See TESTIMONY.

de·pos·i·tor (di·poz′ə·tər) *n.* One who makes a deposit.

de·pos·i·to·ry (di·poz′ə·tôr′ē, -tō′rē) *n. pl.* ·ries 1. A place where anything is deposited. 2. A depositary.

de·pot (dē′pō, *Mil. & Brit.* dep′ō) *n.* 1. A warehouse or storehouse. 2. *U.S.* A railroad station. 3. *Mil.* **a** An installation that manufactures, procures, stores, or repairs military materiel. **b** An installation for assembling and processing personnel. —**Syn.** See STATION. [See DEPOSIT.]

de·prave (di·prāv′) *v.t.* ·praved, ·prav·ing To render bad or worse, especially in morals; corrupt; pervert. [< L < *de-* completely + *pravus* corrupt, wicked] —**dep·ra·va·tion** (dep′rə·vā′shən) *n.* —**de·prav′er** *n.*

de·prav·i·ty (di·prav′ə·tē) *n. pl.* ·ties 1. The state of being depraved; wickedness. 2. A depraved act or habit.

dep·re·cate (dep′rə·kāt) *v.t.* ·cat·ed, ·cat·ing 1. To express disapproval of or regret for. 2. To disparage or belittle. [< L < *de-* away + *precari* to pray] —**dep′re·cat′ing·ly** *adv.* —**dep′re·ca′tion** *n.* —**dep′re·ca′tor** *n.*

dep·re·ca·to·ry (dep′rə·kə·tôr′ē, -tō′rē) *adj.* Expressing deprecation. Also **dep′re·ca′tive.**

de·pre·ci·ate (di·prē′shē·āt) *v.* ·at·ed, ·at·ing *v.t.* 1. To lessen the value of; lower the price or rate of. 2. To disparage; belittle. —*v.i.* 3. To become less in value, etc. [< L < *de-* down + *pretium* price] —**de·pre′ci·a′tor** *n.* —**de·pre′ci·a·to′ry, de·pre′ci·a·to′ry** *adj.*

de·pre·ci·a·tion (di·prē′shē·ā′shən) *n.* 1. A loss in value or efficiency resulting from usage, age, etc. 2. A decline in the purchasing value of money. 3. A disparagement.

dep·re·date (dep′rə·dāt) *v.t. & v.i.* ·dat·ed, ·dat·ing To prey upon; pillage; plunder. [< LL < L *de-* completely +

praeda booty, prey] **—dep·re·da·tion** (dep′rə·dā′shən) *n.* **—dep′re·da′tor** *n.* **—dep·re·da·to·ry** (dep′rə·dā′tər·ē, di·pred′ə·tôr′ē, -tō′rē) *adj.*

de·press (di·pres′) *v.t.* **1.** To lower the spirits of; make gloomy; sadden. **2.** To lessen in vigor, force, or energy. **3.** To lower in price or value. **4.** To press or push down. [< OF < L < *de*- down + *primere* to press]

de·pres·sant (di·pres′ənt) *Med. adj.* Tending to lessen nervous or functional activity. **—** *n.* A sedative.

de·pressed (di·prest′) *adj.* **1.** Sad; dejected. **2.** Pressed down; flattened. **3.** Lowered or sunk even with or below the surface. **4.** Reduced in power, amount, value, etc.

depressed area A region characterized by unemployment.

de·pres·sion (di·presh′ən) *n.* **1.** The act of depressing, or the state of being depressed. **2.** Low spirits or vitality. **3.** A low or depressed place or surface. **4.** A severe decline in business, accompanied by increasing unemployment, falling prices, etc. **5.** *Psychiatry* Deep dejection characterized by withdrawal, lack of response to stimulation, etc. **—de·pres′sive** *adj.* **—de·pres′sive·ly** *adv.*

de·pres·sor (di·pres′ər) *n.* **1.** One who or that which depresses. **2.** *Physiol.* An afferent nerve connected with the heart, controlling heart rate and blood pressure.

dep·ri·va·tion (dep′rə·vā′shən) *n.* The act of depriving, or the state of being deprived. Also **de·priv·al** (di·prī′vəl).

de·prive (di·prīv′) *v.t.* **·prived, ·priv·ing** **1.** To take something away from; divest. **2.** To keep from acquiring, using, or enjoying something. [< OF < L *de*- completely + *privare* to strip, remove] **—de·priv′a·ble** *adj.*

depth (depth) *n.* **1.** The state or degree of being deep; deepness. **2.** Extent or distance downward, inward, or backward. **3.** Profundity of thought or feeling. **4.** *Usu. pl.* An extremely remote, deep, or distant part. **5.** *Usu. pl.* An intense state of being or feeling. **6.** The most intense part or stage: the *depth* of night. **7.** Richness or intensity of color, sound, etc. **8.** Lowness of pitch. [ME *depthe*]

depth charge A drum-shaped bomb that explodes under water at a desired depth. Also **depth bomb.**

dep·u·ta·tion (dep′yə·tā′shən) *n.* **1.** A person or persons acting for another or others; a delegation. **2.** The act of deputing, or the state of being deputed.

de·pute (di·pyoot′) *v.t.* **·put·ed, ·put·ing** **1.** To appoint as an agent, deputy, etc. **2.** To transfer (authority, etc.) to another. [< OF < LL < L *de*- away + *putare* to think]

dep·u·tize (dep′yə·tīz) *v.* **·tized, ·tiz·ing** *v.t.* To appoint as a deputy. **—** *v.i.* To act as a deputy.

dep·u·ty (dep′yə·tē) *n. pl.* **·ties** **1.** One appointed to act for another: a sheriff's *deputy.* **2.** A member of a legislative assembly in certain countries. **—** *adj.* Acting as deputy.

de·rail (dē·rāl′) *v.t.* **1.** To cause (a train, etc.) to run off the rails. **—** *v.i.* **2.** To run off the rails. [< F *dé*- from + *rail* rail] **—de·rail′ment** *n.*

de·range (di·rānj′) *v.t.* **·ranged, ·rang·ing** **1.** To disturb the arrangement, working, or order of. **2.** To unbalance the reason of; render insane. [< F < *dé*- away + *ranger* to set in line] **—de·ranged′** *adj.* **—de·range′ment** *n.*

der·by (dûr′bē) *n. pl.* **·bies** A stiff felt hat with a curved, narrow brim and round crown: also, *Brit.,* **bowler.** [< DERBY]

Der·by (dûr′bē, *Brit.* där′bē) *n.* **1.** An annual horse race for three-year-olds run at Epsom Downs in Surrey, England, since 1780. **2.** Any similar horse race, as the Kentucky Derby. [after the 12th Earl of *Derby,* the founder]

der·e·lict (der′ə·likt) *adj.* **1.** Neglectful of obligation; remiss. **2.** Deserted or abandoned. **—** *n.* **1.** That which is deserted or abandoned, as a ship at sea. **2.** A social outcast, etc. [< L *de*- completely + *relinquere* to abandon]

der·e·lic·tion (der′ə·lik′shən) *n.* **1.** Neglect of or failure in duty. **2.** Voluntary abandonment of something. **3.** The state or fact of being abandoned.

de·ride (di·rīd′) *v.t.* **·rid·ed, ·rid·ing** To treat with scornful mirth; ridicule. [< L < *de*- completely + *ridere* to laugh, mock] **—de·rid′er** *n.* **—de·rid′ing·ly** *adv.*

de ri·gueur (də rē·gœr′) *French* Necessary according to etiquette; required by good form.

de·ri·sion (di·rizh′ən) *n.* **1.** The act of deriding; ridicule; mockery. **2.** An object of ridicule or scorn.

de·ri·sive (di·rī′siv) *adj.* Expressive of or characterized by derision; mocking. Also **de·ri·so·ry** (di·rī′sər·ē). **—de·ri′sive·ly** *adv.* **—de·ri′sive·ness** *n.*

der·i·va·tion (der′ə·vā′shən) *n.* **1.** The act of deriving, or the condition of being derived. **2.** That which is derived; a derivative. **3.** Origin or descent. **4.** The tracing of a word from its original form and meaning; also, a statement of this; an etymology. **—der′i·va′tion·al** *adj.*

de·riv·a·tive (di·riv′ə·tiv) *adj.* **1.** Resulting from or characterized by derivation. **2.** Not original or primary; based on other sources. **—** *n.* **1.** That which is derived. **2.** *Gram.* A word developed from another, as by the addition of affixes. **3.** *Chem.* A compound formed or regarded as being formed from a specified substance, usu. by partial substitution: a benzene *derivative.* **—de·riv′a·tive·ly** *adv.*

de·rive (di·rīv′) *v.* **·rived, ·riv·ing** *v.t.* **1.** To draw or receive, as from a source or principle. **2.** To deduce, as from a premise. **3.** To trace the source of (a word, etc.). **4.** *Chem.* To obtain (a compound) from another, as by partial substitution. **—** *v.i.* **5.** To originate; proceed. [< L < *de*- from + *rivus* stream] **—de·riv′a·ble** *adj.* **—de·riv′er** *n.*

derm- Var. of DERMO-.

-derm *suffix* Skin. [< Gk. *derma* skin]

der·ma (dûr′mə) *n. Anat.* The dermis. [< Gk., skin] **—der′mal** *adj.*

dermato- *combining form* Skin. Also, before vowels, **der·mat-.** [< Gk. *derma, dermatos* skin]

der·ma·tol·o·gy (dûr′mə·tol′ə·jē) *n.* The branch of medical science that relates to the skin and its diseases. **—der·ma·to·log·i·cal** (dûr′mə·tə·loj′i·kəl) *adj.* **—der′ma·tol′o·gist** *n.*

der·mis (dûr′mis) *n. Anat.* **1.** The sensitive, vascular portion of the skin below the epidermis: also called *corium, derma.* **2.** The skin. [< LL < Gk. *derma* skin]

dermo- *combining form* Skin. Also, before vowels, **derm-.**

der·o·gate (der′ə·gāt) **·gat·ed, ·gat·ing** *v.t. & v.i.* **1.** To take or cause to take away; detract: with *from.* **2.** To become or cause to become inferior: with *from.* [< L < *de*- away + *rogare* to ask] **—der′o·ga′tion** *n.*

de·rog·a·tive (di·rog′ə·tiv) *adj.* Tending to derogate or detract; derogatory. **—de·rog′a·tive·ly** *adv.*

de·rog·a·to·ry (di·rog′ə·tôr′ē, -tō′rē) *adj.* Having the effect of lessening or detracting; belittling; disparaging. **—de·rog′a·to′ri·ly** *adv.* **—de·rog′a·to′ri·ness** *n.*

der·rick (der′ik) *n.* **1.** An apparatus for hoisting and swinging heavy weights, usu. consisting of a tackle at the end of a boom or mast. **2.** The framework over the mouth of an oil well. [after *Derrick,* 17th c. London hangman]

DERRICKS
a Hoisting.
b Oil-well.

der·ring-do (der′ing·doo′) *n.* Courageous or daring action. [ME *dorrying don* daring to do]

der·rin·ger (der′in·jər) *n.* A pistol having a short barrel and a large bore. [after Henry *Deringer,* 19th c. U.S. gunsmith]

der·vish (dûr′vish) *n.* A member of any of various Moslem orders, some of whom express their devotion in whirling, howling, etc. [< Turkish < Persian *darvēsh*]

de·salt (dē·sôlt′) *v.t.* To remove the salt from, as sea water, to make potable. **—de·salt′er** *n.* **—de·salt′ing** *n.*

des·cant (*n.* des′kant; *v.* des·kant′, dis-) *n.* **1.** A discussion or a series of remarks. **2.** *Music* **a** A varied melody or song. **b** A counterpoint above the basic melody. **c** The upper part in part music. **—** *v.i.* **1.** To discourse at length: with *on* or *upon.* **2.** *Music* **a** To make or perform a descant. **b** To sing. [< AF < Med.L < L *dis*- away + *cantus* a song]

de·scend (di·send′) *v.i.* **1.** To move from a higher to a lower point. **2.** To slope downward, as a path. **3.** To lower oneself; stoop: to *descend* to begging. **4.** To come by inheritance; be inherited. **5.** *Biol.* To be derived by heredity. **6.** To pass from the general to the specific. **7.** To arrive or come in great numbers. **8.** *Astron.* To move toward the horizon. **—** *v.t.* **9.** To move from an upper to a lower part of; go down, as stairs. [< OF < L < *de*- down + *scandere* to climb] **—de·scend′er** *n.*

de·scen·dant (di·sen′dənt) *n.* One who is descended lineally from another; offspring.

de·scen·dent (di·sen′dənt) *adj.* Proceeding downward.

de·scent (di·sent′) *n.* **1.** The act of descending. **2.** A decline or deterioration. **3.** A declivity; slope. **4.** Ancestral derivation; lineage. **5.** In genealogy, a generation. **6.** *Law* The succession of property or title by inheritance.

de·scribe (di·skrīb′) *v.t.* **·scribed, ·scrib·ing** **1.** To present in spoken or written words. **2.** To give a picture or idea of by means of words; depict. **3.** To draw the figure of; trace; outline. [< L < *de*- down + *scribere* to write] **—de·scrib′a·ble** *adj.* **—de·scrib′er** *n.*

de·scrip·tion (di·skrip′shən) *n.* **1.** The act or technique of describing. **2.** An account that describes. **3.** A drawing or tracing, as of an arc. **4.** Sort, kind, or variety: birds of every description. **—Syn.** See EXPLANATION.

de·scrip·tive (di·skrip′tiv) *adj.* Characterized by or containing description; serving to describe. **—de·scrip′tive·ly** *adv.* **—de·scrip′tive·ness** *n.*

de·scry (di·skrī′) *v.t.* **·scried, ·scry·ing** **1.** To discover with the eye, as something distant. **2.** To discover by observation. [< OF < L < *des*- away + *crier* to cry]

des·e·crate (des′ə·krāt) *v.t.* **·crat·ed, ·crat·ing** To divert from a sacred to a common use; treat sacrilegiously; profane. [< DE- + L *sacrare* to make holy] **—des′e·crat′er** or **des′e·cra′tor** *n.* **—des′e·cra′tion** *n.*

de·seg·re·gate (dē·seg′rə·gāt) *v.t.* **·gat·ed, ·gat·ing** To eliminate racial segregation in. **—de′seg·re·ga′tion** *n.*

de·sen·si·tize (dē·sen′sə·tīz) *v.t.* **·tized, ·tiz·ing** To make less sensitive, esp. in medicine, to lessen or eliminate the sensitiveness of (an individual, organ, tissue, etc.), as to an allergen. **—de·sen′si·ti·za′tion** *n.* **—de·sen′si·tiz′er** *n.*

des·ert¹ (dez′ərt) *n.* **1.** A region greatly lacking in rainfall, moisture, and vegetation. **2.** Any region that is uncultivated and desolate. **—adj.** Of or like a desert; uninhabited. [< OF < LL < L *deserere* < *de-* away + *serere* to join]

de·sert² (di·zûrt′) *v.t.* **1.** To forsake or abandon. **2.** To forsake in violation of one's oath or orders, as a service, post, etc. **—v.i. 3.** To abandon one's post, duty, etc. **4.** *Mil.* To be absent without leave with the intention of not returning.

de·sert³ (di·zûrt′) *n.* **1.** *Often pl.* That which is deserved or merited: to get one's just *deserts*. **2.** The state of deserving reward or punishment. [See DESERVE.]

de·sert·er (di·zûr′tər) *n.* One who forsakes a duty, friends, etc.; esp., one who deserts from a military service.

de·ser·tion (di·zûr′shən) *n.* **1.** The act of deserting. **2.** The state of being deserted; desolation. **3.** *Law* The willful abandonment of one's spouse or children, or both.

de·serve (di·zûrv′) *v.* **·served, ·serv·ing** *v.t.* **1.** To be entitled to or worthy of. **—v.i. 2.** To be worthy. [< OF < L < *de-* completely + *servire* to serve] **—de·serv′er** *n.*

de·served (di·zûrvd′) *adj.* Earned or merited. **—de·serv′ed·ly** (di·zûr′vid·lē) *adv.* **—de·serv′ed·ness** *n.*

de·serv·ing (di·zûr′ving) *adj.* Worthy; meritorious: *deserving* of praise. **—de·serv′ing·ly** *adv.* **—de·serv′ing·ness** *n.*

des·ha·bille (dez′ə·bēl′) *n.* Dishabille.

des·ic·cant (des′ə·kənt) *adj.* Producing dryness; desiccating, as a medicine. **—n.** A drying agent or substance.

des·ic·cate (des′ə·kāt) *v.* **·cat·ed, ·cat·ing** *v.t.* **1.** To dry thoroughly. **2.** To preserve (foods) by drying. **—v.i. 3.** To become dry. [< L < *de-* completely + *siccare* to dry out] **—des′ic·ca′tion** *n.* **—des·ic·ca′tive** *adj.* & *n.*

de·sid·er·a·tum (di·sid′ə·rā′təm) *n.* *pl.* **·ta** (-tə) Something needed or regarded as desirable. [< L]

de·sign (di·zīn′) *v.t* **1.** To draw or prepare preliminary plans or sketches of. **2.** To plan and make with skill, as a work of art. **3.** To form or make (plans, schemes, etc.) in the mind; conceive; invent. **4.** To intend; purpose. **—v.i. 5.** To be a designer. **6.** To plan; conceive. **—n. 1.** A preliminary sketch or outline; pattern. **2.** The arrangement and coordination of the parts or details of any object: the *design* of a jet airplane. **3.** A piece of artistic or decorative work. **4.** The art of making designs. **5.** A visual pattern or composition. **6.** A plan or project. **7.** An object or purpose. **8.** *Often pl.* A sinister scheme or plot. **9.** Intelligent, purposeful, or discoverable pattern, as opposed to chaos. [See DESIGNATE.] **—de·sig′na·ble** *adj.*

des·ig·nate (*v.* dez′ig·nāt; *for adj., also* dez′ig·nit) *v.t.* **·nat·ed, ·nat·ing 1.** To indicate or specify. **2.** To name or entitle; characterize. **3.** To select or appoint for a specific purpose, duty, etc. **—adj.** Designated; selected. [< L < *de-* completely + *signare* to mark] **—des′ig·na·tive** (-nā′tiv) *adj.* **—des′ig·na′tor** *n.*

des·ig·na·tion (dez′ig·nā′shən) *n.* **1.** A distinctive mark or title. **2.** The act of pointing out something. **3.** Appointment or nomination.

de·sign·ed·ly (di·zī′nid·lē) *adv.* By design; intentionally.

des·ig·nee (dez′ig·nē′) *n.* A person designated.

de·sign·er (di·zī′nər) *n.* **1.** One who creates designs, as for dresses, machinery, etc. **2.** A schemer; contriver.

de·sign·ing (di·zī′ning) *n.* **1.** The act or art of making designs. **2.** The act of plotting or scheming. **—adj. 1.** Scheming. **2.** Exercising foresight. **—de·sign′ing·ly** *adv.*

de·sir·a·ble (di·zīr′ə·bəl) *adj.* Worthy of or exciting desire. **—de·sir′a·bil′i·ty, de·sir′a·ble·ness** *n.* **—de·sir′a·bly** *adv.*

de·sire (di·zīr′) *v.t.* **·sired, ·sir·ing 1.** To wish or long for; crave. **2.** To ask for; request. **—n, 1.** A longing or craving. **2.** A request or wish. **3.** An object desired. **4.** Sexual appetite; passion; lust. [< OF < L < *de-* from + *sidus, sideris* star; with ref. to astrology] **—de·sir′er** *n.*

de·sir·ous (di·zīr′əs) *adj.* Having a desire or craving.

de·sist (di·zist′) *v.i.* To cease, as from an action. [< L < *de-* from + *sistere* to stop] **—de·sis′tance,** or **de·sis′tence** *n.*

desk (desk) *n.* **1.** A table or case adapted for writing or studying, usu. having compartments or drawers. **2.** A table or stand to hold reading matter; also, a pulpit. **3.** A division or post in an organization: the service *desk.* **4.** *U.S.* A department in a newspaper office: the copy *desk.* **5.** *Music* An orchestral music stand. [< Med.L < LL *discus* table]

des·o·late (*adj.* des′ə·lit; *v.* des′ə·lāt) *adj.* **1.** Destitute of inhabitants or dwellings; deserted. **2.** Made unfit for habitation. **3.** Gloomy; dreary. **4.** Without friends; forlorn. **—v.t. ·lat·ed, ·lat·ing 1.** To deprive of inhabitants. **2.** To lay waste; devastate. **3.** To make sorrowful or forlorn. **4.** To forsake; abandon. [< L < *de-* completely + *solus* alone] **—des′o·late·ly** *adv.* **—des′o·late·ness** *n.*

des·o·la·tion (des′ə·lā′shən) *n.* **1.** The act of making desolate; a laying waste. **2.** The condition of being ruined or deserted. **3.** Loneliness. **4.** A desolate region; waste.

des·ox·y- Var. of DEOXY-.

de·spair (di·spâr′) *v.i.* To lose or abandon hope; be or become hopeless: with *of.* **—n. 1.** Utter hopelessness and discouragement. **2.** That which causes despair. [< OF < L < *de-* away + *sperare* to hope] **—de·spair′ing** *adj.* **—de·spair′ing·ly** *adv.*

—Syn. (noun) **1.** *Despair* is the utter abandonment of hope that leaves the mind apathetic or numb. *Desperation* is energized *despair,* vigorous in action and reckless of consequences. *Despondency* is paralyzing *despair* coupled with deep sorrow. The mere absence of hope is *hopelessness* and is often used to characterize circumstances. **—Ant.** hope, expectation, confidence.

des·per·a·do (des′pə·rā′dō, -rā′dō) *n.* *pl.* **·does** or **·dos** A desperate or violent criminal. [< OSp. See DESPAIR.]

des·per·ate (des′pər·it) *adj.* **1.** Without care for danger; reckless, as from despair. **2.** Resorted to in desperation. **3.** Regarded as almost hopeless; critical. **4.** Extreme; very great. **—des′per·ate·ly** *adv.* **—des′per·ate·ness** *n.*

des·per·a·tion (des′pə·rā′shən) *n.* The state of being desperate; also, the recklessness growing out of despair.

des·pi·ca·ble (des′pi·kə·bəl, di·spik′ə·bəl) *adj.* That is to be despised; contemptible; vile. [See DESPISE.] **—des′pi·ca·bil′i·ty, des′pi·ca·ble·ness** *n.* **—des′pi·ca·bly** *adv.*

de·spise (di·spīz′) *v.t.* **·spised, ·spis·ing** To regard as contemptible or worthless; disdain; scorn. [< OF < L < *de-* down + *specere* to look at] **—de·spis′er** *n.*

de·spite (di·spīt′) *prep.* In spite of; notwithstanding. **—n. 1.** Contemptuous defiance. **2.** An act of defiance, malice, or injury. **—in despite of** In spite of. [See DESPISE.]

de·spoil (di·spoil′) *v.t.* To deprive of possessions; rob. [< OF < L < *de-* completely + *spoliare* to rob] **—de·spoil′er** *n.* **—de·spoil′ment, de·spo·li·a·tion** (di·spō′lē·ā′shən) *n.*

de·spond (di·spond′) *v.i.* To lose spirit, courage, or hope. **—n.** *Archaic* Despondency. [< L < *de-* away + *spondere* to promise] **—de·spond′ing·ly** *adv.*

de·spon·den·cy (di·spon′dən·sē) *n.* Dejection of spirits from loss of hope or courage. Also **de·spon′dence.**

de·spon·dent (di·spon′dənt) *adj.* Dejected in spirit; disheartened. **—de·spon′dent·ly** *adv.*

des·pot (des′pət, -pot) *n.* **1.** An absolute monarch; autocrat. **2.** A tyrant. [< OF < Gk. *despotēs* master]

des·pot·ic (di·spot′ik) *adj.* Of or like a despot; tyrannical; autocratic. **—des·pot′i·cal·ly** *adv.*

des·pot·ism (des′pə·tiz′əm) *n.* **1.** Unlimited authority; absolute power. **2.** A state ruled by a despot.

des·sert (di·zûrt′) *n.* **1.** *U.S.* A serving of pastry, ice cream, etc., as the last course of a meal. **2.** *Brit.* Fruits, nuts, etc., served after a dinner. [< F < *desservir* to clear a table]

des·ti·na·tion (des′tə·nā′shən) *n.* **1.** The point or place set for a journey's end, or to which something is directed. **2.** The purpose or end for which anything is created or intended. **3.** The act of designating or appointing.

des·tine (des′tin) *v.t.* **·tined, ·tin·ing 1.** To design for or appoint to a distinct purpose. **2.** To determine the future of, as by destiny. [< OF < L *destinare* to make fast, ult. < *de-* completely + *stare* to stand] **—des′tined** *adj.*

des·ti·ny (des′tə·nē) *n.* *pl.* **·nies 1.** The fate to which a person or thing is destined. **2.** The preordained or predetermined ordering of events. **3.** The power that is thought to predetermine the course of events. [See DESTINE.]

des·ti·tute (des′tə·tōōt, -tyōōt) *adj.* **1.** Not having; entirely lacking: with *of.* **2.** Extremely poor. [< L < *de-* down + *statuere* to set]

des·ti·tu·tion (des′tə·tōō′shən, -tyōō′-) *n.* **1.** Extreme poverty. **2.** Deficiency; lack.

de·stroy (di·stroi′) *v.t.* **1.** To ruin utterly; consume. **2.** To tear down; demolish. **3.** To put an end to. **4.** To kill. **5.** To make ineffective or useless. **—Syn.** See DEMOLISH. [< OF, ult. < L < *de-* down + *struere* to construct]

de·stroy·er (di·stroi′ər) *n.* **1.** One who or that which destroys. **2.** A speedy war vessel, smaller than a cruiser.

de·struct (di·strukt′) *n.* *Aerospace* The act of destroying a defective or dangerous missile or rocket after launch.

de·struc·ti·ble (di·struk′tə·bəl) *adj.* Capable of being destroyed. **—de·struc′ti·bil′i·ty, de·struc′ti·ble·ness** *n.*

de·struc·tion (di·struk′shən) *n.* **1.** The act of destroying, or the state of being destroyed; demolition; ruin. **2.** That which destroys, or is a means of destroying.

de·struc·tive (di·struk′tiv) *adj.* **1.** Causing destruction; tending to destroy; ruinous: with *of* or *to.* **2.** Tending to tear down or discredit. **—de·struc′tive·ly** *adv.* **—de·struc′tive·ness, de·struc·tiv·i·ty** (dē′struk·tiv′ə·tē) *n.*

destructive distillation *Chem.* The distillation of organic substances, as wood and coal, in such a way as to decompose them chemically: also called *dry distillation.*

des·ue·tude (des'wə-tōōd, -tyōōd) *n.* A condition of disuse. [< MF < L < *de-* away + *suescere* to be used to]

de·sul·fur·ize (dē-sul'fə-rīz) *v.t.* ·ized, ·iz·ing To remove sulfur from. Also **de·sul·fur, de·sul·fur·ate, de·sul·phur·ize.** — **de·sul·fur·i·za·tion** *n.* — **de·sul·fur·iz·er** *n.*

des·ul·to·ry (des'əl-tôr'ē, -tō'rē) *adj.* 1. Passing abruptly from one thing to another; unmethodical. 2. Occurring by chance. [< L < *de-* down + *sultus,* pp. of *salire* to leap] — **des'ul·to'ri·ly** *adv.* — **des'ul·to'ri·ness** *n.*

de·tach (di-tach') *v.t.* 1. To unfasten and separate; disconnect. 2. To send off for special duty, as a regiment or a ship. [< F < *de-* away + OF *tache* nail] — **de·tach'a·bil'i·ty** *n.* — **de·tach'a·ble** *adj.* — **de·tach'er** *n.*

de·tached (di-tacht') *adj.* 1. Separated from others; disconnected. 2. Unconcerned; impartial.

detached retina *Pathol.* A disconnection of the inner layers of the retina from the pigment layer.

de·tach·ment (di-tach'mənt) *n.* 1. The act of detaching or separating. 2. The state of being detached. 3. Dissociation from surroundings or worldly affairs. 4. Absence of prejudice or partiality. 5. *Mil.* **a** A part of a unit separated from its parent organization for duty. **b** A permanent unit organized for a specific purpose.

de·tail (*n.* di-tāl', dē'tāl; *v.* di-tāl'; *Mil.* dē'tāl) *n.* 1. A separately considered part or item; particular. 2. A dealing with particulars: to go into *detail.* 3. A narrative account giving particulars. 4. In art, architecture, etc., a minor or secondary part. 5. *Mil.* A small detachment designated for a particular task. — **in detail** Item by item. — *v.t.* 1. To report or narrate minutely. 2. *Mil.* To select and send off for a special service, duty, etc. [< F < *dé-* completely + *tailler* to cut up]

de·tain (di-tān') *v.t.* 1. To keep from proceeding; stop; delay. 2. To withhold (what belongs to another). 3. To hold in custody; confine. [< OF < L < *de-* away + *tenere* to hold] — **de·tain'ment** *n.*

de·tect (di-tekt') *v.t.* 1. To perceive or find, as something obscure: to *detect* an error in spelling. 2. To expose or uncover, as a crime. 3. *Telecom.* To recover the (signal, audio component, etc.) from a modulated carrier wave. [< L < *de-* away, off + *tegere* to cover] — **de·tect'a·ble** or **de·tect'i·ble** *adj.* — **de·tect'er** *n.*

de·tec·tion (di-tek'shən) *n.* 1. The act of detecting, or the fact of being detected. 2. *Telecom.* Any method of operating on a modulated signal wave so as to obtain the signal imparted to it; demodulation of incoming electrical signals.

de·tec·tive (di-tek'tiv) *n.* A person, often a policeman, whose work is to investigate crimes, discover evidence, capture criminals, etc. — *adj.* 1. Belonging or pertaining to detectives or their work. 2. Fitted for or used in detection.

de·tec·tor (di-tek'tər) *n.* 1. One who or that which detects. 2. *Telecom.* A device for obtaining the signal from a modulated carrier.

dé·tente (dā-tänt') *n.* An easing, as of discord between nations. [< F]

de·ten·tion (di-ten'shən) *n.* 1. The act of detaining; a restraining. 2. The state of being detained. [See DETAIN.]

de·ter (di-tûr') *v.t.* ·terred, ·ter·ring To prevent or discourage (someone) from acting by arousing fear, uncertainty, etc. [< L < *de-* away + *terrere* to frighten] — **de·ter'ment** *n.*

de·terge (di-tûrj') *v.t.* ·terged, ·terg·ing 1. To cleanse, as a wound. 2. To wipe off. [< L < *de-* away + *tergere* to wipe]

de·ter·gent (di-tûr'jənt) *adj.* Having cleansing or purging qualities. — *n.* A cleansing agent. — **de·ter'gen·cy, de·ter'gence** *n.*

de·te·ri·o·rate (di-tir'ē-ə-rāt') *v.t. & v.i.* ·rat·ed, ·rat·ing To make or become worse; depreciate. [< L < *deterior* worse] — **de·te'ri·o·ra'tion** *n.* — **de·te'ri·o·ra'tive** *adj.*

de·ter·mi·na·ble (di-tûr'mi·nə·bəl) *adj.* 1. That may be found out, settled, or decided. 2. *Law* Liable to be ended.

de·ter·mi·nant (di-tûr'mə-nənt) *adj.* Determinative. — *n.* That which influences or determines.

de·ter·mi·nate (di-tûr'mə-nit) *adj.* 1. Definitely limited or fixed; specific; distinct. 2. Settled and conclusive; decided; final. 3. Fixed in purpose; resolute. 4. *Bot.* Terminating in a flower or bud, as each axis of an inflorescence. — **de·ter'mi·nate·ly** *adv.* — **de·ter'mi·nate·ness** *n.*

de·ter·mi·na·tion (di-tûr'mə-nā'shən) *n.* 1. The act of reaching a decision; also, the decision reached. 2. The quality of being firm in purpose or action; resoluteness. 3. The determining or fixing of the quality, degree, etc., of anything; also, the result of this. 4. A decisive tendency or movement toward some object or end.

de·ter·mi·na·tive (di-tûr'mə-nā'tiv, -mə-nə-tiv) *adj.* Tending or having power to determine. — *n.* That which determines.

de·ter·mine (di-tûr'min) *v.* ·mined, ·min·ing *v.t.* 1. To settle or decide, as an argument, question, or debate. 2. To ascertain or fix. 3. To cause to reach a decision. 4. To fix or give definite form to; influence. 5. To give purpose or direction to. 6. To set bounds to; limit. 7. *Law* To limit: terminate: to *determine* a contract. — *v.i.* 8. To come to a decision; resolve. 9. *Law* To come to an end. [< OF < L < *de-* completely + *terminare* to end] — **de·ter'min·er** *n.*

de·ter·mined (di-tûr'mind) *adj.* Having or showing fixed purpose; resolute; firm. — **de·ter·mined·ly** (di-tûr'mind-lē, -min-id-lē) *adv.* — **de·ter'mined·ness** *n.*

de·ter·min·ism (di-tûr'mə-niz'əm) *n. Philos.* The doctrine that every event is the inevitable result of antecedent conditions, and that human beings do not have free will.

de·ter·rent (di-tûr'ənt) *adj.* Tending or serving to deter. — *n.* Something that deters. — **de·ter'rence** *n.*

de·test (di-test') *v.t.* To dislike with intensity; hate; abhor. [< MF < L *detestari* to denounce < *de-* away + *testis* a witness] — **de·test'er** *n.*

de·test·a·ble (di-tes'tə-bəl) *adj.* Deserving to be detested; extremely hateful; abominable. — **de·test'a·bil'i·ty, de·test'a·ble·ness** *n.* — **de·test'a·bly** *adv.*

de·tes·ta·tion (dē'tes-tā'shən) *n.* 1. Extreme dislike; hatred; abhorrence. 2. One who or that which is detested.

de·throne (dē-thrōn') *v.t.* ·throned, ·thron·ing To remove from the throne. — **de·throne'ment** *n.* — **de·thron'er** *n.*

det·o·nate (det'ə-nāt, dē'tə-) *v.* ·nat·ed, ·nat·ing *v.t.* 1. To cause to explode suddenly and with violence. — *v.i.* 2. To explode suddenly with a loud report. [< L < *de-* down + *tonare* to thunder] — **det'o·na'tion** *n.* — **det'o·na'tor** *n.*

de·tour (dē'tŏŏr, di-tŏŏr') *n.* A deviation from a direct route or course of action; esp., a byroad used when a main road is impassable. — *v.t. & v.i.* To go or cause to go by a roundabout way. [< F < *dé-* away + *tourner* to turn]

de·tract (di-trakt') *v.i.* 1. To take away a part; diminish: with *from.* — *v.t.* 2. To take away (a part). 3. To distract; divert. [< L < *de-* away + *trahere* to pull] — **de·trac'tion** *n.* — **de·trac'tor** *n.*

de·train (dē-trān') *v.t. & v.i. Chiefly Brit.* To leave or cause to leave a railroad train. — **de·train'ment** *n.*

det·ri·ment (det'rə-mənt) *n.* 1. Damage or loss. 2. Something that impairs, injures, or causes loss. [< L < *de-* away + *terere* to rub]

det·ri·men·tal (det'rə-men'təl) *adj.* Causing damage or loss. — **Syn.** See PERNICIOUS. — **det'ri·men'tal·ly** *adv.*

de·tri·tus (di-trī'təs) *n.* 1. Loose fragments or particles separated from masses of rock by erosion, glacial action, or other forces. 2. Debris. [See DETRIMENT.]

de trop (də trō') *French* Too much; superfluous.

deuce¹ (dōōs, dyōōs) *n.* 1. Two; esp., a card or side of a die having two spots. 2. In tennis, a score tied at 40 or at five or more games each, requiring either side to win two successive points for the game or two successive games for the set. [< F < OF < L *duos,* accusative of *duo* two]

deuce² (dōōs, dyōōs) *n. Informal* The devil; bad luck: a mild oath. [< LG *de duus* the deuce (throw at dice)]

deu·ced (dōō'sid, dyōō'-, -dōōst, -dyōōst) *Informal adj.* Confounded; excessive. — *adv.* Devilishly. — **deu'ced·ly** *adv.*

De·us (dē'əs, dā'ōōs) *n. Latin* God.

deu·te·ri·um (dōō·tir'ē·əm, dyōō-) *n.* The isotope of hydrogen having the atomic weight 2.01 (symbol, D or H²): also called *heavy hydrogen.* [< NL < Gk. *deuteros* second]

deuterium oxide Heavy water.

deutero- *combining form* Second; secondary. Also, **deuter-** (before vowels), **deuto-.** [< Gk. *deuteros* second]

deu·ter·on (dōō'tə-ron, dyōō'-) *n. Physics* The nucleus of a deuterium atom. [< NL < Gk. *deuteros* second]

Deu·ter·on·o·my (dōō'tə-ron'ə-mē, dyōō'-) The fifth book of the Old Testament, containing a second statement of the Mosaic law. [< Gk. < *deuteros* second + *nomos* law]

deut·sche·mark (doi'chə-märk') *n.* 1. The standard monetary unit of West Germany, equivalent to 100 pfennigs; in 1960 worth about 24 U.S. cents. 2. The standard monetary unit of East Germany. Also **deutsche mark.**

de·val·u·ate (dē-val'yōō-āt) *v.t.* ·at·ed, ·at·ing To reduce the value or worth of. Also **de·val'ue.** — **de·val'u·a'tion** *n.*

dev·as·tate (dev'ə-stāt) *v.t.* ·tat·ed, ·tat·ing 1. To lay waste, as by war, fire, etc. 2. *Informal* To confound; crush. [< L < *de-* completely + *vastare* to lay waste] — **dev'as·tat'ing·ly** *adv.* — **dev·as·ta'tion** *n.* — **dev'as·ta'tor** *n.*

de·vel·op (di-vel'əp) *v.t.* 1. To expand or bring out the potentialities, capabilities, etc., of. 2. To work out in detail; enlarge upon: to *develop* an idea. 3. To reveal or unfold gradually: to *develop* a plot. 4. To bring into active existence: to *develop* patience. 5. *Photog.* **a** To make visible (the hidden image) upon a sensitized plate that has been exposed to the action of light. **b** To subject (a plate or film) to a developer. 6. *Music* To elaborate on (a theme). — *v.i.* 7. To increase in capabilities, maturity, etc. 8. To advance from a lower to a higher stage; evolve. 9. To be disclosed; as events, a plot, etc. 10. To come into existence: Some tastes *develop* slowly. [< F < *dé-* away + OF *voluper* to fold, wrap up] — **de·vel'op·a·ble** *adj.*

de·vel·op·er (di-vel'əp-ər) *n.* 1. One who or that which develops. 2. *Photog.* A solution for developing photographs.

de·vel·op·ment (di·vel′əp·mənt) n. **1.** The act of developing. **2.** The state or condition of that which has been developed. **3.** A result or product of developing. **4.** An event or occurrence: a political *development*.

de·vel·op·men·tal (di·vel′əp·men′təl) adj. Of or pertaining to development; evolutionary. — **de·vel′op·men′tal·ly** adv.

de·vi·ate (n. dē′vē·it; v. dē′vē·āt) — n. One whose actions and beliefs differ considerably from the standards of his society. Also **de·vi·ant** (dē′vē·ənt). — v. **·at·ed, ·at·ing** v.i. **1.** To turn aside from a straight or appointed way or course. **2.** To differ, as in belief. — v.t. **3.** To cause to turn aside. [< LL < L *de-* from + *via* road] — **de′vi·a′tor** n.

de·vi·a·tion (dē′vē·ā′shən) n. **1.** The act of deviating, or its result. **2.** *Stat.* The difference between one value in a series of observations and the arithmetic mean of the series.

de·vice (di·vīs′) n. **1.** Something devised or constructed for a specific purpose. **2.** A scheme or plan, esp. a crafty or evil one. **3.** An ornamental design, as in embroidery. **4.** An emblem in a coat of arms; also, any emblem or motto. — **to leave (someone) to his own devices** To allow (someone) to do as he wishes. [< OF < L *dividere* to divide]

dev·il (dev′əl) n. **1.** *Sometimes cap.* In Jewish and Christian theology, the prince and ruler of the kingdom of evil; Satan. **2.** Any subordinate evil sprit; a demon. **3.** A wicked or malicious person. **4.** A wretched fellow: poor *devil*. **5.** A person of great energy or daring. **6.** A machine for any of various purposes, as for cutting or tearing up rags. **7.** A printer's apprentice: also called *printer's devil*. — **between the devil and the deep blue sea** Between equally bad alternatives. — **the devil** An exclamation of anger, surprise, etc. — **the devil to pay** Trouble to be expected as a consequence. — **to give the devil his due** To acknowledge the ability or success of even a disliked person, antagonist, etc. — v.t. dev·iled or ·illed, dev·il·ing or ·il·ling **1.** To prepare for eating by seasoning highly. **2.** To cut up (cloth, etc.) in a devil. **3.** To annoy or harass. [OE < LL < Gk. *diabolos* slanderer]

dev·il·fish (dev′əl·fish′) n. pl. **·fish** or **·fish·es 1.** The manta. **2.** Any of various large cephalopods, as the octopus.

dev·il·ish (dev′əl·ish, dev′lish) adj. **1.** Having the qualities of the devil; diabolical. **2.** *Informal* Excessive. — adv. *Informal* Excessively. — **dev′il·ish·ly** adv. — **dev′il·ish·ness** n.

dev·il-may-care (dev′əl·mā·kâr′) adj. Careless; reckless.

dev·il·ment (dev′əl·mənt) n. Impish conduct; mischief.

devil's advocate (dev′əlz) **1.** In the Roman Catholic Church, an official appointed to argue against a candidate for canonization. **2.** One who argues perversely.

dev·il's-food cake (dev′əlz·food′) A chocolate cake.

dev·il·try (dev′əl·trē) n. pl. **·tries 1.** Wanton or malicious mischief. **2.** Wickedness or cruelty. Also *Brit.* **dev′il·ry**.

de·vi·ous (dē′vē·əs) adj. **1.** Winding or leading away from the regular, straight, or direct course; rambling; swerving. **2.** Straying from the proper way; erring. [< L < *de-* from + *via* way] — **de′vi·ous·ly** adv. — **de′vi·ous·ness** n.

de·vis·al (di·vī′zəl) n. A contriving or bequeathing.

de·vise (di·vīz′) v. **·vised, ·vis·ing** v.t. **1.** To form in the mind; invent; contrive; plan. **2.** *Law* To transmit (real estate) by will. — v.i. **3.** To form a plan. — n. *Law* **1.** The act of bequeathing lands. **2.** A gift of lands by will. **3.** A will, or clause in a will, conveying real estate. [< OF < L *dividere* to separate] — **de·vis′a·ble** adj. — **de·vis′er** n.

de·vi·see (di·vī′zē′, dev′ə·zē′) n. *Law* The person to whom a devise is made.

de·vi·sor (di·vī′zər, -zôr) n. *Law* One who devises property.

de·vi·tal·ize (dē·vīt′l·īz) v.t. **·ized, ·iz·ing** To destroy the vitality of; make weak. — **de·vi′tal·i·za′tion** n.

de·void (di·void′) adj. Not possessing; destitute; empty: with *of*. [ME *devoided*, pp. of obs. *devoid* to empty out]

de·voir (də·vwär′, dev′wär) n. **1.** *Usu. pl.* Courteous attentions; respects. **2.** Duty. [< OF < L *debere* to owe]

dev·o·lu·tion (dev′ə·loo′shən) n. **1.** A passing down from one stage to another. **2.** The passing of authority, property, etc., to a successor. [See DEVOLVE.]

de·volve (di·volv′) v. **·volved, ·volv·ing** v.t. **1.** To cause (authority, duty, etc.) to pass to a successor. — v.i. **2.** To pass to a successor or substitute: with *on, upon,* or *to*. [< L < *de-* down + *volvere* to roll] — **devolve′ment** n.

De·vo·ni·an (di·vō′nē·ən) adj. **1.** Of or pertaining to Devon in England. **2.** *Geol.* Of or pertaining to the period in the Paleozoic era following the Silurian. See chart for GEOLOGY. — n. *Geol.* The Devonian period or its rock system. [after *Devon*, England; with ref. to rocks found there]

de·vote (di·vōt′) v.t. **·vot·ed, ·vot·ing 1.** To apply (attention, time, or oneself) completely to some activity, purpose, etc. **2.** To dedicate. [< OF < L < *de-* completely + *vovere* to vow] — **de·vote′ment** n.

de·vot·ed (di·vō′tid) adj. **1.** Feeling or showing devotion; devout. **2.** Set apart, as by a vow; consecrated. — **de·vot′ed·ly** adv. — **de·vot′ed·ness** n.

dev·o·tee (dev′ə·tē′) n. **1.** One who is deeply devoted to anything. **2.** One who is marked by religious ardor.

de·vo·tion (di·vō′shən) n. **1.** Strong attachment or affection, as to a person or cause. **2.** Ardor or zeal in the performance of religious acts or duties. **3.** *Usu. pl.* An act of worship or prayer. **4.** The act of devoting, or the state of being devoted. — **de·vo′tion·al** adj. — **de·vo′tion·al·ly** adv.

de·vour (di·vour′) v.t. **1.** To eat up greedily. **2.** To destroy; waste. **3.** To take in greedily with the senses or the intellect. **4.** To engross the attention of. **5.** To engulf; absorb. [< OF < L < *de-* down + *vorare* to gulp, swallow] — **de·vour′er** n. — **de·vour′ing·ly** adv.

de·vout (di·vout′) adj. **1.** Earnestly religious; pious. **2.** Heartfelt; sincere. **3.** Containing or expressing devotion. [See DEVOTE.] — **de·vout′ly** adv. — **de·vout′ness** n.

dew (doo, dyoo) n. **1.** Moisture condensed from the atmosphere in small drops upon cool surfaces. **2.** Anything moist, pure, or refreshing as dew. **3.** Moisture generally, esp. that which appears in minute drops, as perspiration, tears, etc. — v.t. To wet with or as with dew. [OE *dēaw*]

dew·ber·ry (doo′ber′ē, -bər·ē, dyoo′-) n. pl. **·ries** The fruit of several species of trailing blackberry; also, the plant.

dew·claw (doo′klô′, dyoo′-) n. **1.** A rudimentary toe in some dogs and other mammals. **2.** The false hoof above the true hoof of hogs, deer, etc. — **dew′clawed′** adj.

dew·drop (doo′drop′, dyoo′-) n. A drop of dew.

dew·lap (doo′lap′, dyoo′-) n. The pendulous skin under the throat of cattle, certain dogs, etc. [ME < *dew*, origin uncertain + *lappe* pendulous piece, lobe] — **dew′lapped′** adj.

DEW line A chain of radar stations in North America, maintained by the United States in cooperation with Canada. [< D(*istant*) E(*arly*) W(*arning*)]

dew point The temperature at which dew forms or condensation of vapor occurs.

dew·y (doo′ē, dyoo′ē) adj. **dew·i·er, dew·i·est 1.** Moist. **2.** Of, resembling, or forming dew. — **dew′i·ness** n.

dex·ter (dek′stər) adj. **1.** Of or situated on the right side. **2.** *Heraldry* Being on the wearer's right, and thus on the observer's left: opposed to *sinister*. [< L, right]

dex·ter·i·ty (dek·ster′ə·tē) n. **1.** Skill in using the hands or body. **2.** Mental adroitness. [< L *dexter* on the right] — **Syn.** Both *dexterity* and *adroitness* are, literally, "right-handedness," or proficiency in manual tasks. In extended use, *dexterity* is applied to technical proficiency in the use of tools, methods, etc.: the *dexterity* of a magician. *Adroitness* has become cleverness in dealing with people or in handling situations. *Handiness* applies chiefly to manual work; *skill* is acquired, at least in part and sometimes wholly, by mental training.

dex·ter·ous (dek′strəs, -stər·əs) adj. **1.** Possessing dexterity; adroit. **2.** Done with dexterity. Also **dex·trous** (dek′strəs) — **dex′ter·ous·ly** adv. — **dex′ter·ous·ness** n.

dex·tral (dek′strəl) adj. **1.** Of or pertaining to, or turned toward the right side; right-hand. **2.** Right-handed. — **dex·tral·i·ty** (dek·stral′ə·tē) n. — **dex′tral·ly** adv.

dex·trin (dek′strin) n. *Biochem.* A gummy, water-soluble substance formed from starch, and used as a substitute for gum arabic. Also **dex·trine** (dek′strin, -strēn).

dextro- combining form Turned or turning to the right, or clockwise; used esp. in chemistry and physics. Also, before vowels, **dextr-**. [< L *dexter* right]

dex·trorse (dek′strôrs, dek·strôrs′) adj. *Bot.* Twining spirally toward the right, as certain climbing plants: opposed to *sinistrorse*. Also **dex·tror′sal**. [< L < *dexter* right + *vertere* to turn] — **dex′trorse·ly** adv.

dex·trose (dek′strōs) n. *Biochem.* A sugar occurring in plants. Also **dex·tro·glu·cose** (dek′·strō·gloo′kōs).

di-¹ Var. of DIS-¹.

di-² prefix **1.** Twice; double. **2.** *Chem.* Containing two atoms, molecules, radicals, etc. Also, before *s*, dis-. [< Gk. *di-* < *dis* twice]

di-³ Var. of DIA-.

dia- prefix **1.** Through; across; between; apart. **2.** Thoroughly. Also, before vowels, di-. [< Gk. *dia-* through]

di·a·be·tes (dī′ə·bē′tis, -tēz) n. *Pathol.* A disease, **diabetes mel·li·tus** (mə·lī′təs), associated with deficient insulin secretion, leading to excess sugar in the blood and urine, extreme hunger and thirst, and metabolic failure. [< NL < Gk. < *dia-* through + *bainein* to go]

di·a·bet·ic (dī′ə·bet′ik, -bē′tik) *Med.* adj. Of, pertaining to, or affected with diabetes. — n. One who has diabetes.

di·a·bol·ic (dī′ə·bol′ik) adj. **1.** Of, belonging to, or proceeding from the devil; satanic; infernal. **2.** Atrociously wicked or inhuman. Also **di′a·bol′i·cal**. [< OF < LL < Gk. < *diabolos*] — **di′a·bol′i·cal·ly** adv. — **di′a·bol′i·cal·ness** n.

di·ac·o·nal (dī·ak′ə·nəl) adj. Of, pertaining to, or befitting a deacon or the diaconate. [< LL *diaconus* deacon]

di·ac·o·nate (dī·ak′ə·nit, -nāt) n. **1.** The office or rank of a deacon. **2.** Deacons collectively.

di·a·crit·ic (dī′ə·krit′ik) *n.* A diacritical mark. — *adj.* Diacritical. [< Gk. < *dia*- between + *krinein* to distinguish]
di·a·crit·i·cal (dī′ə·krit′i·kəl) *adj.* Serving to mark a distinction, as between phonetic values assigned to a letter; distinguishing. — **di′a·crit′i·cal·ly** *adv.*
diacritical mark A mark, point, or sign attached to a letter to indicate its phonetic value, or to distinguish it from another letter: also called *diacritic.*
di·a·dem (dī′ə·dem) *n.* **1.** A crown or headband worn as a symbol of royalty or honor. **2.** Regal power. — *v.t.* To crown. [< OF < L < Gk. < *dia*- across + *deein* to bind]
di·aer·e·sis (dī·er′ə·sis) See DIERESIS.
di·ag·nose (dī′əg·nōs′, -nōz′) *v.t. & v.i.* ·nosed, ·nos·ing To make a diagnosis.
di·ag·no·sis (dī′əg·nō′sis) *n. pl.* ·ses (-sēz) **1.** *Med.* **a** The act or process of recognizing diseases by their characteristic symptoms. **b** The conclusion arrived at. **2.** Any similar examination, summary, and conclusion. [< NL < Gk. < *dia*- between + *gignōskein* to know] — **di·ag·nos·tic** (dī′əg·nos′tik) *adj.* — **di′ag·nos′ti·cal·ly** *adv.*
di·ag·nos·ti·cian (dī′əg·nos·tish′ən) *n.* One who is versed in diagnosis.
di·ag·o·nal (dī·ag′ə·nəl) *adj.* **1.** Having an oblique direction from corner to corner or from side to side. **2.** Marked by oblique lines, ridges, etc. — *n.* **1.** *Geom.* A diagonal line or plane. **2.** Anything running diagonally. [< L < Gk. < *dia*- across + *gōnia* angle] — **di·ag′o·nal·ly** *adv.*
di·a·gram (dī′ə·gram) *n.* **1.** An outline figure or scheme of lines, spaces, points, etc., intended to demonstrate a geometrical proposition, represent an object or area, show the relation between parts or places, etc. **2.** A graph or chart. — *v.t.* **di·a·gramed** or ·**grammed**, **di·a·gram·ing** or ·**gram·ming** To represent or illustrate by a diagram. [< Gk. < *dia*- across + *graphein* to write] — **di·a·gram·mat·ic** (dī′ə·grə·mat′ik) or ·**i·cal** *adj.* — **di′a·gram·mat′i·cal·ly** *adv.*
di·al (dī′əl, dīl) *n.* **1.** Any graduated circular plate or face upon which pressure, temperature, etc., is indicated by means of a pointer or needle. **2.** The face of a watch or clock; also, a sundial. **3.** A knob or disk on a radio or television set, used to tune in stations. **4.** A rotating disk used to make connections in an automatic telephone system. — *v.* **di·aled** or ·**alled**, **di·al·ing** or ·**al·ling** *v.t.* **1.** To measure with a dial. **2.** To turn to or indicate by means of a dial. **3.** To call by means of a dial telephone. **4.** To adjust a radio or television set to (a station, program, etc.). — *v.i.* **5.** To use a dial, as in telephoning. [< Med.L *dialis* daily < L *dies* day] — **di′al·er** or **di′al·ler** *n.*
di·a·lect (dī′ə·lekt) *n.* **1.** A variety of speech distinguished from the standard language by variations of idiom, vocabulary, pronunciation, etc.: the Yorkshire *dialect* of England. **2.** Any of the regional forms of the standard language: the Southern *dialect* of American English. **3.** A manner of speech characteristic of the members of a particular class, trade, or profession. **4.** A language developed from an earlier language; a linguistic branch. [< MF < L < Gk. < *dia*- across + *legein* to speak]
di·a·lec·tal (dī′ə·lek′təl) *adj.* Of or characteristic of a dialect. — **di′a·lec′tal·ly** *adv.*
di·a·lec·tic (dī′ə·lek′tik) *n.* **1.** *Often pl.* The art or practice of examining statements logically, as by question and answer, to establish validity. **2.** A specific logical mode of argument: Hegel's *dialectic.* **3.** Formerly, logic. — *adj.* **1.** Pertaining to or using dialectic. **2.** Dialectal. [< OF < L < Gk. < *dia*- across + *legein* to speak]
di·a·lec·ti·cal (dī′ə·lek′ti·kəl) *adj.* Dialectic. — **di′a·lec′ti·cal·ly** *adv.*
dialectical materialism *Philos.* The doctrine of Karl Marx and Friedrich Engels.
di·a·lec·ti·cian (dī′ə·lek·tish′ən) *n.* **1.** A logician. **2.** One who specializes in the study of dialects.
di·a·logue (dī′ə·lôg, -log) *n.* **1.** A conversation in which two or more take part. **2.** The conversation in a play, novel, etc. **3.** A literary work in which two or more characters are represented as conversing: a Platonic *dialogue.* **4.** An exchange of opinions or ideas; discussion. — *v.* ·**logued**, ·**logu·ing** *v.t.* **1.** To express in dialogue form. — *v.i.* **2.** To carry on a dialogue. Also **di′a·log.** [< F < L < Gk. < *dia*- *legesthai* to converse] — **di′a·log′uer** or **di′a·log′er** *n.*
di·al·y·sis (dī·al′ə·sis) *n. pl.* ·ses (-sēz) **1.** Separation of parts previously or normally joined together. **2.** *Chem.* The separating of solutions of unequal diffusibility by means of moist membranes; esp., the separation of a colloid from a crystalloid. [< Gk. < *dia*- completely + *lyein* to loosen] — **di·a·lyt·ic** (dī′ə·lit′ik) *adj.* — **di′a·lyt′i·cal·ly** *adv.*
di·a·mag·net·ic (dī′ə·mag·net′ik) *Physics adj.* Pertaining to or designating the property of substances that tend to lie at right angles to the poles of a magnet. — **di′a·mag·net′i·cal·ly** *adv.* — **di′a·mag′net·ism** *n.*
di·am·e·ter (dī·am′ə·tər) *n. Math.* **1.** A straight line passing through the center of a circle or sphere and terminating at the circumference or surface. **2.** The length of such a line.

3. *Optics* A unit used to measure the magnifying power of binoculars, microscopes, etc. [< OF < L < Gk. < *dia*- through + *metron* measure]
di·a·met·ri·cal (dī′ə·met′ri·kəl) *adj.* **1.** Of, pertaining to, or coinciding with a diameter. Also **di·am·e·tral** (dī·am′ə·trəl). **2.** Directly opposite; as far removed as possible: *diametrical* motives. Also **di·a·met′ric.** — **di′a·met′ri·cal·ly** *adv.*
di·am·ine (dī·am′ēn, -in, dī′ə·mēn, -min) *n. Chem.* Any of a group of compounds containing two amino (NH_2) radicals; a double amine. Also **di·am·in** (dī·am′in, dī′ə·min).
di·a·mond (dī′mənd, dī′ə-) *n.* **1.** A mineral of great hardness and refractive power, consisting of carbon crystallized under great pressure and temperature; also, this mineral when used as a gem. **2.** The uncut face of this stone, used in cutting glass, etc. **3.** A figure bounded by four equal straight lines, having two of the angles acute and two obtuse; a lozenge. **4.** In card games: **a** A red, lozenge-shaped spot on a playing card. **b** A card with such a mark. **c** *pl.* A suit of cards so marked. **5.** In baseball, the infield of a baseball field; also, the entire field. **6.** *Printing* A size of type next above brilliant, 4- or 4½-point. — *adj.* Made of or like diamonds. — *v.t.* To adorn with or as with diamonds. [< OF < LL < L < Gk. *adamas* adamantine] — **di′a·mond·ed** *adj.*
diamond anniversary A 60th or 75th anniversary.
di·a·mond·back (dī′mənd·bak′, dī′ə-) *n.* **1.** An edible turtle of the southern U.S., having diamond-shaped markings on the shell. Also **diamondback terrapin.** **2.** A large rattlesnake of the SE U.S., having diamond-shaped markings on the back: also **dia′mond-rat′tler** (-rat′lər).

DIAMONDBACK TERRAPIN
(Upper shell 5 to 7½ inches long)

Diamond State Nickname of Delaware.
Di·an·a (dī·an′ə) In Roman mythology, goddess of the hunt, virginity, and the moon.
di·a·pa·son (dī′ə·pā′sən, -zən) *n.* **1.** In a pipe organ, either of two principal stops (the **open diapason** and the **stopped diapason**) that extend throughout the entire compass of the instrument and produce its fundamental tone. **2.** The entire compass of an instrument or voice. [< L < Gk. *dia pasōn* (*chordōn*) through all (the notes)]
di·a·per (dī′ə·pər; *for n. def. 1, v. def. 1, also* dī′pər) *n.* **1.** A folded piece of soft fabric used as a baby's breechcloth. **2.** A decorative pattern consisting of a system of repeated figures or designs. — *v.t.* **1.** To put a diaper on (a baby). **2.** To decorate with a repeated figure or similar figures. [< OF < Med.Gk. < *dia*- completely + *aspros* white]
di·aph·a·nous (dī·af′ə·nəs) *adj.* Showing light through its substance; transparent; translucent. [< Med.L < Gk. < *dia*- through + *phainein* to show] — **di·aph′a·nous·ly** *adv.* — **di·aph′a·nous·ness** *n.*
di·a·pho·re·sis (dī′ə·fə·rē′sis) *n. Med.* Copious perspiration, esp. when produced artificially. [< LL < Gk. < *dia*- across + *phoreein* to carry] — **di′a·pho·ret′ic** *adj. & n.*
di·a·phragm (dī′ə·fram) *n.* **1.** *Anat.* A muscular wall separating the thoracic and abdominal cavities in mammals. **2.** Any membrane or partition that separates. **3.** Any device resembling a diaphragm in appearance or elasticity, as the thin vibrating disk of a telephone. **4.** *Optics* A disk with an adjustable aperture that can control the amount of light passing through the lens of a camera, telescope, etc. — *v.t.* To act upon or furnish with a diaphragm. [< LL < Gk. < *dia*- across + *phragma* fence]
di·a·phrag·mat·ic (dī′ə·frag·mat′ik) *adj.* Of, pertaining to, or like a diaphragm. — **di′a·phrag·mat′i·cal·ly** *adv.*
di·ar·rhe·a (dī′ə·rē′ə) *n. Pathol.* A disorder of the intestine marked by abnormally frequent and fluid evacuation of the bowels. Also **di′ar·rhoe·a.** [< L < Gk. < *dia*- through + *rheein* to flow] — **di′ar·rhe′al** or ·**rhoe′al, di′ar·rhe′ic** or ·**rhoe′ic, di′ar·rhet′ic** or ·**rhoet′ic** (-ret′ik) *adj.*
di·a·ry (dī′ə·rē, dī′rē) *n. pl.* ·ries. **1.** A record of daily events; esp., a personal record of one's activities, experiences, or observations; journal. **2.** A book for keeping such a record. [< L < *dies* day] — **di′a·rist** *n.*
Di·as·po·ra (dī·as′pər·ə) *n.* The dispersion of the Jews among the Gentiles after the Babylonian captivity. [< Gk., dispersion < *dia*- completely + *speirein* to sow, scatter]
di·a·stase (dī′ə·stās) *n. Biochem.* An enzyme that converts starch and glycogen into dextrin and maltose. [< F < Gk. < *dia*- apart + *histanai* to set, cause to stand] — **di′a·sta′sic, di′a·stat′ic** (-stat′ik) *adj.*
di·as·to·le (dī·as′tə·lē) *n.* **1.** *Physiol.* The usual rhythmic dilatation of the heart, esp. of the ventricles, after each contraction. Compare SYSTOLE. **2.** In classical prosody, the lengthening of a syllable. [< LL < Gk. < *dia*- apart + *stellein* to send, put] — **di·as·tol·ic** (dī′ə·stol′ik) *adj.*
di·as·tro·phism (dī·as′trə·fiz′əm) *n. Geol.* **1.** Any of the processes through which the earth's crust is deformed, producing continents, mountains, etc. **2.** Any deformation resulting from this. [< Gk. < *dia*- apart + *strephein* to turn] — **di·a·stroph·ic** (dī′ə·strof′ik) *adj.*

di·a·ther·my (dī'ə·thûr'mē) *n. pl.* **·mies** *Med.* **1.** The generation of heat in the body tissues through their resistance to the passage of high-frequency electric currents. **2.** The apparatus used. Also **di·a·ther·mi·a** (dī'ə·thûr'mē·ə). [< NL < Gk. *dia-* through + *thermē* heat]

di·a·tom (dī'ə·tom, -təm) *n.* Any of various marine and fresh-water plankton, unicellular or colonial whose walls contain silica. [< NL < Gk. *dia-* through + *temnein* to cut]

di·a·ton·ic (dī'ə·ton'ik) *adj. Music* Pertaining to the order of intervals in a major or minor scale of eight tones without the chromatic intervals. [< MF < LL < Gk. < *dia-* through, at the interval of + *tenein* to stretch] — **di'a·ton'·i·cal·ly** *adv.* — **di·a·ton·i·cism** (dī'ə·ton'i·siz'əm) *n.*

di·a·tribe (dī'ə·trīb) *n.* A bitter or malicious denunciation. [< MF < L < Gk. < *dia-* thoroughly + *tribein* to rub]

di·ba·sic (dī·bā'sik) *adj. Chem.* **1.** Of an acid, containing two atoms of hydrogen replaceable by a base or basic radical, as sulfuric acid. **2.** Of or derived from such an acid: said of salts. Also **bibasic.** — **di·ba·sic·i·ty** (dī'bā·sis'ə·tē) *n.*

dib·ble (dib'əl) *n.* A gardener's pointed tool for planting seeds, setting slips, etc. Also **dib·ber** (dib'ər). — *v.t.* **·bled, ·bling** To make holes for seeds or plants in (soil) with a dibble. [ME, ? < *dib,* var. of DAB³] — **dib'bler** *n.*

dice (dīs) *n. pl. of* **die 1.** Small cubes of bone, ivory, etc., having the sides marked with spots from one to six. **2.** A game of chance played with such cubes. — *v.* **diced, dic·ing** *v.t.* **1.** To cut into small cubes. **2.** To gamble away or win with dice. — *v.i.* **3.** To play at dice. [See DIE²] — **dic'er** *n.*

di·chlo·ro·di·phen·yl·tri·chlor·o·eth·ane (dī·klôr'ō·dī·fen'əl·trī·klôr'ō·eth'ān, -klō'rō-) *n.* DDT.

dicho- *combining form* In two; in pairs. Also, before vowels, **dich-.** [< Gk. *dicha* in two < *dis* twice]

di·chot·o·my (dī·kot'ə·mē) *n. pl.* **·mies 1.** Division into two parts or by pairs; a cutting in two. **2.** *Logic* The division of a class into two mutually exclusive subclasses, as minerals into gold and not-gold. **3.** *Bot.* A system of branching in which each successive axis forks into two equally developed branches. [< Gk. < *dich-* in two + *temnein* to cut] — **di·chot'o·mous** *adj.* — **di·chot'o·mous·ly** *adv.*

di·chro·mat·ic (dī'krō·mat'ik) *adj.* **1.** Having two colors. **2.** *Zool.* Having two color phases within the species apart from changes due to age or sex. **3.** *Pathol.* Able to see only two of the three primary colors. Also **dichromic.**

di·chro·ma·tism (dī·krō'mə·tiz'əm) *n.* The state of being dichromatic, esp. with reference to color blindness.

di·chro·mic (dī·krō'mik) *adj.* **1.** Containing two atoms of chromium or their equivalents. **2.** Dichromatic.

dick·er (dik'ər) *U.S. v.i.* **1.** To make a petty trade; haggle. **2.** In politics, to work toward a deal; bargain. — *v.t.* **3.** To barter; exchange. — *n.* The act of dickering; also, a petty trade; a bargain. [ME *dyker* lot of ten, esp. skins or hides]

dick·ey (dik'ē) *n. pl.* **·eys 1.** A blouse front worn by women under a jacket or low-necked dress. **2.** A detachable shirt front for a man. **3.** Any small bird. Also **dick'ey·bird', dick'y·bird'** (-bûrd') **4.** A driver's outside seat on a carriage; also, a seat for servants in the rear. Also **dick'y.** [< *Dicky,* double dim. of *Richard,* a personal name]

di·cot·y·le·don (dī·kot·ə·lēd'n, dī·kot'-) *n. Bot.* A plant having two seed leaves. — **di'cot·y·le'do·nous** *adj.*

dic·ta (dik'tə) Plural of DICTUM.

Dic·ta·phone (dik'tə·fōn) *n.* A type of phonographic instrument that records and reproduces speech, as for dictation to a stenographer: a trade name. Also **dic'ta·phone.**

dic·tate (dik'tāt; *for v.,* also dik·tāt') *v.* **tat·ed, ·tat·ing** *v.t.* **1.** To utter or read aloud (something) to be recorded by another. **2.** To prescribe authoritatively, as commands, terms, rules, etc. — *v.i.* **3.** To utter aloud something to be recorded by another. **4.** To give orders. — *n.* An authoritative suggestion, rule, or command: the *dictates* of reason. [< L, pp. of *dictare,* freq. of *dicere* to say, speak]

dic·ta·tion (dik·tā'shən) *n.* **1.** The act of dictating material to a copyist. **2.** That which is dictated. **3.** Authoritative direction. — **dic·ta'tion·al** *adj.*

dic·ta·tor (dik'tā·tər, dik·tā'tər) *n.* **1.** A person having absolute powers of government, esp. one considered to be an oppressor. **2.** A person who rules, prescribes, or suggests authoritatively: a *dictator* of fashion. **3.** One who dictates words to be written down.

dic·ta·to·ri·al (dik'tə·tôr'ē·əl, -tō'rē-) *adj.* **1.** Given to dictating; overbearing. **2.** Of or pertaining to a dictator; autocratic. — **dic'ta·to'ri·al·ly** *adv.* — **dic'ta·to'ri·al·ness** *n.*

dic·ta·tor·ship (dik'tā·tər·ship', dik·tā'tər·ship') *n.* **1.** The office or term of office of a dictator. **2.** A state under the rule of a dictator. **3.** Supreme or despotic control.

dic·tion (dik'shən) *n.* **1.** The use, choice, and arrangement of words in writing and speaking. **2.** The manner of uttering speech sounds; enunciation. [< L < *dicere* to say, speak]

dic·tion·ar·y (dik'shən·er'ē) *n. pl.* **·ar·ies 1.** A reference work containing alphabetically arranged words together with their definitions, pronunciations, etymologies, etc.; a lexicon. **2.** A lexicon whose words are given in one language together with their equivalents in another. **3.** A reference work containing information relating to a special branch of knowledge and arranged alphabetically. [< Med.L *dictionarium* a collection of words and phrases < L *dicere* to speak.]

Dic·to·graph (dik'tə·graf, -gräf) *n.* A telephonic device capable of reproducing or recording sounds made at a considerable distance from the transmitter, used to transmit or overhear conversations: a trade name. Also **dic'to·graph.**

dic·tum (dik'təm) *n. pl.* **·ta** (-tə) **1.** An authoritative, dogmatic, or positive utterance; pronouncement. **2.** A popular saying; maxim. [< L < *dicere* to say]

did (did) Past tense of DO¹.

di·dac·tic (dī·dak'tik, di-) *adj.* **1.** Intended to instruct. **2.** Morally instructive; preceptive. **3.** Overly inclined to teach or moralize; pedantic. Also **di·dac'ti·cal.** [< Gk. < *didaskein* to teach] — **di·dac'ti·cal·ly** *adv.* — **di·dac'ti·cism** (-siz·əm) *n.*

di·dac·tics (dī·dak'tiks, di-) *n.pl.* (*construed as sing.*) The science or art of instruction or education.

did·dle¹ (did'l) *v.* **·dled, ·dling** *Informal v.t.* **1.** To cheat. — *v.i.* **2.** To dawdle; pass time idly. Also *daddle.* [? < DIDDLE²] — **did'dler** *n.*

did·dle² (did'l) *v.t. & v.i.* **·dled, ·dling** To jerk up and down or back and forth; jiggle. [? Var. of dial. *didder,* ME *diddiren* to quiver, shake, tremble]

did·n't (did'nt) Did not.

di·do (dī'dō) *n. pl.* **·dos** or **·does** *Informal* A caper; antic. [Origin unknown]

Di·do (dī'dō) In the *Aeneid,* the queen of Carthage in love with Aeneas.

didst (didst) Archaic second person singular past tense of DO¹: used with *thou.*

di·dym·i·um (dī·dim'ē·əm, di-) *n.* A mixture of the elements neodymium and praseodymium, formerly regarded as one of the elements. [< NL < Gk. *didymos* double]

die¹ (dī) *v.i.* **died, dy·ing 1.** To suffer death; expire. **2.** To suffer the pains of death: The coward *dies* many times. **3.** To pass gradually: with *away, down,* or *out.* **4.** To cease to exist; fade away: The smile *died* on his lips. **5.** To become extinct: often with *out* or *of.* **6.** *Informal* To desire exceedingly. **7.** To stop functioning, as an engine. **8.** To faint. **9.** *Theol.* To suffer spiritual death. — **to die hard** To resist death or defeat to the end. — **to die off** To be removed one after another by death. [< ON *deyja*]

die² (dī) *n. pl.* **dies** *for def.* 1; **dice** *for defs.* 2 *and* 3. **1.** *Mech.* Any of various hard metal devices for stamping, shaping, or cutting out some object. **2.** A small marked cube. See DICE. **3.** A cast, as in playing dice; stake; hazard. — **the die is cast** The choice or course of action is irrevocable. — *v.t.* **died, die·ing** To cut, stamp, or shape with or as with a die. [< OF *de* < L *datum* something given]

die casting *Metall.* **1.** The process of giving a metal or alloy a desired shape by forcing the molten material into a mold under pressure. **2.** A metal object so made.

di·e·cious (dī·ē'shəs), etc. See DIOECIOUS, etc.

die-hard (dī'härd') *n.* One who obstinately refuses to abandon or modify his views; esp., a political conservative. — *adj.* Characterized by obstinate resistance. Also **die'hard'.**

di·e·lec·tric (dī'ə·lek'trik) *Electr. adj.* **1.** Nonconducting. **2.** Capable of sustaining an electric field, as by induction. Also **di'e·lec'tri·cal.** — *n.* A dielectric substance, medium, or material. — **di'e·lec'tri·cal·ly** *adv.*

di·en·ceph·a·lon (dī'en·sef'ə·lon) *n. Anat.* That part of the brain forming the posterior part of the forebrain. [< NL < Gk. *di(a)-* between + *enkephalos* brain]

-diene *suffix Chem.* Denoting an open-chain unsaturated hydrocarbon compound having two double bonds: *butadiene.*

di·er·e·sis (dī·er'ə·sis) *n. pl.* **·ses** (-sēz) Two dots (¨) placed over the second of two adjacent letters to indicate that two separate vowel sounds are to be pronounced, as in *Noël.* Also spelled *diaeresis.* [< LL < Gk. < *dia-* apart + *hairein* to take, seize] — **di·e·ret·ic** (dī'ə·ret'ik) *adj.*

die·sel engine (dē'zəl) An internal-combustion engine in which fuel oil is sprayed directly into the cylinder, where it is ignited by the high temperature of the air held within the cylinder at a constant pressure. Also **Diesel engine.** [after Rudolf *Diesel,* 1858–1913, German inventor]

die·sink·er (dī'singk'ər) *n.* One who engraves metal dies.

Di·es I·rae (dī'ēz ī'rē) The name of a medieval Latin hymn on the Day of Judgment, used in masses for the dead: so called from its opening words. [< L, day of wrath]

di·e·sis (dī'ə·sis) *n. pl.* **·ses** (-sēz) *Printing* The double dagger (‡). [< L < Gk. < *dia-* through + *hienai* to send]

die·stock (dī'stok') *n. Mech.* A device for holding dies that are used to cut threads on screws, bolts, etc.

di·et¹ (dī'ət) *n.* **1.** A regulated course of eating and drinking, esp. one followed for medical or hygienic reasons. **2.** The daily fare. **3.** Food, as regards its nutritive value. — *v.t.* **1.** To regulate the food and drink of. — *v.i.* **2.** To take food and drink according to a regimen. [< OF < L < Gk. *diaita* way of living] — **di'et·er** *n.*

di·et² (dī'ət) *n.* A legislative assembly. [< Med.L < L *dies* a day]

Di·et (dī'ət) *n.* **1.** The legislature of certain countries, as Japan. **2.** The semiannual meeting of the estates of the Holy Roman Empire.

di·e·tar·y (dī'ə·ter'ē) *adj.* Pertaining to diet. — *n. pl.* **·tar·ies 1.** A system or regimen of dieting. **2.** A standard or regulated allowance of food.

di·e·tet·ic (dī'ə·tet'ik) *adj.* Relating to diet or the regulation of diet. Also **di·e·tet'i·cal.** — **di·e·tet'i·cal·ly** *adv.*

di·e·tet·ics (dī'ə·tet'iks) *n.pl.* (construed as sing.) The branch of hygiene that treats of diet and dieting.

di·e·ti·tian (dī'ə·tish'ən) *n.* One skilled in the principles of dietetics. Also **di·e·tet·ist** (dī'ə·tet'ist), **di·e·ti·cian.**

dif- Assimilated var. of DIS-.

dif·fer (dif'ər) *v.i.* **1.** To be unlike in quality, degree, etc.: often with *from.* **2.** To disagree: often with *with.* **3.** To quarrel. [< OF < L < *dis-* apart + *ferre* to carry]

dif·fer·ence (dif'ər·əns, dif'rəns) *n.* **1.** The state, quality, or degree of being unlike or different. **2.** A specific instance of such unlikeness. **3.** A distinguishing characteristic or peculiarity. **4.** A disagreement or controversy; dispute. **5.** A discrimination: She makes no *difference* between truth and falsehood. **6.** *Math.* The amount by which one quantity differs from another. — **to make a difference 1.** To affect or change the case or situation. **2.** To distinguish between. — *v.t.* **·enced, ·enc·ing** To make or mark as different.

dif·fer·ent (dif'ər·ənt, dif'rənt) *adj.* **1.** Marked by a difference; unlike. **2.** Not the same; separate; other: There is a *different* clerk there now. **3.** Differing from the ordinary; unusual. — **dif'fer·ent·ly** *adv.* — **dif'fer·ent·ness** *n.*

♦ **different from, than** In American usage, *from* is established as the idiomatic preposition to follow *different*; when, however, a clause follows the connective, *than* is gaining increasing acceptance.

dif·fer·en·ti·a (dif'ə·ren'shē·ə) *n. pl.* **·ti·ae** (shi·ē) *Logic* A specific difference; a characteristic attribute distinguishing a species from others of the same genus. [< L]

dif·fer·en·tial (dif'ə·ren'shəl) *adj.* **1.** Relating to, indicating, or exhibiting a difference or differences. **2.** Constituting or creating a difference. **3.** Based on a difference or distinction. **4.** *Math.* Pertaining to or involving differentials or differentiation. **5.** *Mech.* Of or having a construction in which a movement is obtained by the difference in two motions in the same direction. — *n.* **1.** *Math.* An infinitesimal increment of a quantity: symbol *d.* **2.** *Mech.* A differential gear. **3.** *Electr.* One of two resistance coils, the current of which flows in a direction opposite to that of the other. **4.** In commerce, a difference in rates charged. — **dif'fer·en'tial·ly** *adv.*

differential gear or **gearing** *Mech.* A coupling consisting of a train of gears used to connect two or more shafts so that the wheels can move at different speeds on curves.

differential windlass *Mech.* A windlass having two drums of different diameters on the same axis, the power being increased in inverse proportion to the difference between the diameters.

DIFFERENTIAL GEAR
a Drive shaft. *b* Drive-shaft gear. *c* Axles. *d* Ring gear. *e* Epicyclic train of gears.

dif·fer·en·ti·ate (dif'ə·ren'shē·āt) *v.* **·at·ed, ·at·ing** *v.t.* **1.** To constitute the difference between. **2.** To perceive and indicate the differences in or between. **3.** *Biol.* To develop differences in, as a species. **4.** *Math.* To find the derivative of (a function): opposed to *integrate.* — *v.i.* **5.** To acquire a distinct character; become specialized. **6.** To discriminate. **7.** *Biol.* Of cells during embryological growth, to diversify and develop into specialized organs and tissues. — **dif'fer·en'ti·a'tion** *n.*

dif·fi·cult (dif'ə·kult, -kəlt) *adj.* **1.** Hard to do, accomplish, or deal with; demanding effort or great care. **2.** Not easy to understand; perplexing. **3.** Hard to please: a *difficult* customer. **4.** Hard to persuade; stubborn. — **dif'fi·cult·ly** *adv.*

dif·fi·cul·ty (dif'ə·kul'tē, -kəl-) *n. pl.* **·ties 1.** The state, fact, or quality of being difficult. **2.** That which is difficult to do, overcome, or understand. **3.** *Usu. pl.* A troublesome state of affairs, especially financial embarrassment. **4.** A dispute. **5.** Reluctance or objection. **6.** A trouble; worry. [< L < *dis-* away, not + *facilis* easy < *facere* to do, make]

dif·fi·dent (dif'ə·dənt) *adj.* Lacking confidence in oneself; timid. [< L *diffidens, -entis,* ppr. of *diffidere* < *dis-* away + *fidere* to trust] — **dif'fi·dence** *n.* — **dif'fi·dent·ly** *adv.*

dif·fract (di·frakt') *v.t.* **1.** To separate into parts. **2.** To subject to diffraction. [< L < *dis-* away + *frangere* to break] — **dif·frac'tive** *adj.* — **dif·frac'tive·ly** *adv.* — **dif·frac'tive·ness** *n.*

dif·frac·tion (di·frak'shən) *n. Physics* **1.** A modification of light rays when partially cut off by any obstacle or passing near the edges of an opening, or through a minute hole, generally accompanied by light and dark, or colored, bands due to interference. **2.** An analogous modification of other kinds of wave motion, as of sound, electricity, X-rays, etc.

dif·fuse (*v.* di·fyōoz'; *adj.* di·fyōos') *v.t. & v.i.* **·fused, ·fus·ing 1.** To pour or send out so as to spread in all directions; permeate. **2.** To subject to or spread by diffusion. — *adj.* **1.** Characterized by the excessive use of words. **2.** Widely spread out; dispersed. [< L < *dis-* from + *fundere* to pour] — **dif·fuse'ly** (di·fyōos'lē) *adv.* — **dif·fuse'ness** (di·fyōos'nis) *n.* — **dif·fus'er** or **dif·fus'or** *n.*

dif·fus·i·ble (di·fyōo'zə·bəl) *adj.* Capable of being diffused. — **dif·fus'i·bil'i·ty, dif·fus'i·ble·ness** *n.*

dif·fu·sion (di·fyōo'zhən) *n.* **1.** The act or process of diffusing, or the state of being diffused. **2.** Imprecision of verbal expression; verbosity. **3.** *Physics* **a** The intermingling by thermal agitation of the molecules of two fluids, as of gases. **b** The scattering and crisscrossing of light rays, producing general illumination rather than direct radiation.

dif·fu·sive (di·fyōo'siv) *adj.* Tending to diffuse; marked by diffusion. — **dif·fu'sive·ly** *adv.* — **dif·fu'sive·ness** *n.*

dig (dig) *v.* **dug, dig·ging** *v.t.* **1.** To break up, turn up, or remove (earth, etc.), as with a spade, claws, or the hands. **2.** To make or form by or as by digging. **3.** To take out or obtain by digging: to *dig* clams. **4.** To thrust or force into or against, as a heel. **5.** To discover or bring out by careful effort or study: often with *up* or *out.* **6.** *U.S. Slang* To understand or like. — *v.i.* **7.** To break or turn up earth, etc. **8.** To force or make a way by or as by digging. **9.** *U.S. Informal* To study hard; plod. — **to dig in 1.** To dig trenches. **2.** *U.S. Informal* To entrench (oneself). **3.** *U.S. Informal* To begin to work intensively. — *n. Informal* **1.** A thrust; poke. **2.** A sarcastic remark; slur. [< MF *diguer*]

di·gest (*v.* di·jest', dī-; *n.* dī'jest) *v.t.* **1.** *Physiol.* To change (food) chemically in the alimentary canal into material suitable for assimilation by the body. **2.** To take in or assimilate mentally. **3.** To arrange in systematic form, usu. by condensing. **4.** To tolerate patiently; endure. **5.** *Chem.* **a** To soften or decompose with heat or moisture. **b** To treat, as wood, with chemical agents under pressure so as to obtain a desired result. — *v.i.* **6.** To be assimilated, as food. **7.** To assimilate food. **8.** To be subjected to heat, moisture, chemical agents, or pressure. — *n.* A systematically arranged collection or summary of literary, scientific, legal, or other material; a synopsis. — **Syn.** See ABRIDGEMENT. [< L < *dis-* away + *gerere* to carry] — **di·gest'er** *n.*

di·ges·tant (di·jes'tənt, dī-) *n. Med.* Any agent that assists digestion. — *adj.* Digestive.

di·gest·i·ble (di·jes'tə·bəl, dī-) *adj.* Capable of being digested. — **di·gest'i·bil'i·ty, di·gest'i·ble·ness** *n.* — **di·gest'i·bly** *adv.*

di·ges·tion (di·jes'chən, dī-) *n.* **1.** *Physiol.* The act, process, or function of digesting; also, the resulting condition or state of this process. **2.** Mental reception and assimilation.

di·ges·tive (di·jes'tiv, dī-) *adj.* Pertaining to or promoting digestion: *digestive* tract. — *n.* A medicine to aid digestion.

dig·ger (dig'ər) *n.* **1.** One who digs. **2.** Any implement or part of a machine for digging.

dig·gings (dig'ingz) *n.pl.* **1.** A place of excavation; esp., a mining region. **2.** The materials dug out of such a region. **3.** *Informal* One's lodgings.

dig·it (dij'it) *n.* **1.** A finger or toe. **2.** Any one of the ten Arabic numeral symbols, 0 to 9. **3.** *Electronics* One of a set of characters by which, a digital computer provides required information. [< L *digitus* finger]

dig·i·tal (dij'ə·təl) *adj.* **1.** Of, pertaining to, or like the fingers or digits. **2.** Having digits. **3.** Digitate. — *n.* A key on a piano, organ, etc. — **dig'i·tal·ly** *adv.*

digital computer A computing machine that receives problems and processes the answers in digital form. Compare ANALOG COMPUTER.

dig·i·tal·is (dij'ə·tal'is, -tā'lis) *n.* **1.** Any of a genus of herbs of the figwort family, as the foxglove. **2.** The dried leaves of foxglove, containing several substances, that are used as a heart stimulant. [< NL < L *digitus* finger]

dig·i·tate (dij'ə·tāt) *adj. Bot.* Having parts, as leaflets, arranged like the fingers of a hand. Also **dig'i·tat·ed.** [< L < *digitus* finger] — **dig'i·tate·ly** *adv.*

digiti- *combining form* Finger; toe. [< L *digitus* finger, toe]

dig·i·ti·grade (dij'ə·tə·grād') *Zool. adj.* Walking on the toes, without resting on the whole sole of the foot. See PLANTIGRADE. [< DIGITI- + L *gradus* a step, going]

dig·ni·fied (dig'nə·fīd) *adj.* Characterized by or invested with dignity; stately. — **dig'ni·fied·ly** *adv.*

dig·ni·fy (dig'nə·fī) *v.t.* **fied, ·fy·ing 1.** To impart or add

dignity to. **2.** To give a high-sounding name to. [< OF < Med.L < L *dignus* worthy + *facere* to make]

dig·ni·tar·y (dig′nə·ter′ē) *n. pl.* **·tar·ies** One having high official position, as in the government or church.

dig·ni·ty (dig′nə·tē) *n. pl.* **·ties 1.** Stateliness and nobility of manner; gravity. **2.** The state or quality of being excellent, worthy, or honorable. **3.** Relative importance or position. **4.** A high rank, title, or office, esp. in the church. **5.** A dignitary. **6.** Persons of high rank or position collectively: preceded by *the*. [< OF < L *dignus* worthy]

di·graph (dī′graf, -gräf) *n.* A combination of two characters representing a single sound, as *oa* in *boat*, *sh* in *she*.

di·gress (di·gres′, dī-) *v.i.* **1.** To turn aside from the main subject. **2.** To ramble; wander. [< L < *di-* away, apart + *gradi* to go, step] — **di·gres′sion** *n.* — **di·gres′sion·al** *adj.*

di·gres·sive (di·gres′iv, dī-) *adj.* Given to or marked by digression. — **di·gres′sive·ly** *adv.* — **di·gres′sive·ness** *n.*

di·he·dral (dī·hē′drəl) *adj.* **1.** Two-sided; formed by or having two plane faces. **2.** Pertaining to or having a dihedral angle. — *n. Aeron.* The upward or downward inclination of an airplane's supporting surfaces. [< DI-² + Gk. *hedra* base, face of a regular solid]

dihedral angle *Geom.* The angle formed by two intersecting planes.

dik·dik (dik′dik′) *n.* A NE African antelope about a foot tall. [< native East African name]

dike (dīk) *n.* **1.** An embankment to protect low land from being flooded. **2.** A bank formed by earth thrown up during the excavation of a ditch. **3.** A ditch. **4.** A causeway. **5.** A barrier or obstruction. **6.** *Geol.* A mass of igneous rock intruded into a fissure in other rocks. — *v.t.* **diked, dik·ing 1.** To surround or furnish with a dike. **2.** To drain by ditching. Also, *Chiefly Brit.*, **dyke**. [OE *dīc*] — **dik′er** *n.*

di·lap·i·date (di·lap′ə·dāt) *v.t. & v.i.* **·dat·ed, ·dat·ing** To fall or cause to fall into partial ruin or decay. [< L < *dis-* away + *lapidare* to throw stones] — **di·lap′i·da′tion** *n.*

di·la·tate (dī·lā′tāt, dī′lə·tāt) *adj.* Dilated.

dil·a·ta·tion (dil′ə·tā′shən, dī′lə-) *n.* **1.** The process of dilating, or the state of being dilated. **2.** That which is dilated. **3.** *Pathol.* An excessive enlargement of an organ, etc.

di·late (dī·lāt′, di-) *v.* **·lat·ed, ·lat·ing** *v.t.* **1.** To make wider or larger; cause to expand. — *v.i.* **2.** To become larger or wider. **3.** To speak or write diffusely; enlarge; expatiate: with *on* or *upon*. [< F < L < *dis-* apart + *latus* wide] — **di·lat′a·ble** *adj.* — **di·lat′a·bil′i·ty, di·lat′a·ble·ness** *n.* — **di·lat′a·bly** *adv.* — **di·la′tive** *adj.*

di·la·tion (dī·lā′shən, di-) *n.* **1.** Dilatation. **2.** *Med.* The expanding of an abnormally small canal or orifice.

di·la·tor (dī·lā′tər, di-) *n.* **1.** One who or that which dilates. **2.** *Med.* An instrument for expanding a wound, aperture, or cavity. Also **di·la·ta·tor** (dī′lə·tā′tər, dil′ə-), **di·lat′er.**

dil·a·to·ry (dil′ə·tôr′ē, -tō′rē) *adj.* **1.** Given to or characterized by delay; tardy; slow. **2.** Tending to cause delay. [< LL < L *dilatus*, pp. of *differe* to delay] — **dil′a·to′ri·ly** *adv.* — **dil′a·to′ri·ness** *n.*

di·lem·ma (di·lem′ə) *n.* **1.** A situation requiring a choice between equally undesirable alternatives. **2.** *Logic* An argument that presents an antagonist with alternatives that are equally conclusive against him. — **the horns of a dilemma** The equal and usu. undesirable alternatives between which a choice must be made. [< LL < Gk. < *di-* two + *lēmma* a premise] — **dil·em·mat·ic** (dil′ə·mat′ik) *adj.*

dil·et·tan·te (dil′ə·tan′tē, dil′ə·tänt′) *n. pl.* **·ti** (-tē) or **·tes 1.** One who interests himself in a subject superficially or merely for amusement; a dabbler. **2.** One who loves the fine arts. — **Syn.** See AMATEUR. — *adj.* Pertaining to or like a dilettante. [< Ital., ppr. of *dilettare* to delight < L < *de-* away + *lacio* to allure] — **dil′et·tan′tish** or **dil′et·tan′te·ish** *adj.* — **dil′et·tan′tism** or **dil′et·tan′te·ism** *n.*

dil·i·gence¹ (dil′ə·jəns) *n.* **1.** Persistent application to one's work or duty; persevering effort. **2.** Proper heed; care.

dil·i·gence² (dil′ə·jəns, *Fr.* dē·lē·zhäns′) *n.* A public stagecoach used in the 18th century in Europe, esp. France. Also **dil·ly** (dil′ē). [< F (*carrosse de*) *diligence* fast coach]

dil·i·gent (dil′ə·jənt) *adj.* **1.** Showing perseverance and application in whatever is undertaken; industrious. **2.** Pursued with painstaking effort: a *diligent* search. [< OF < L *diligere* to care for] — **dil′i·gent·ly** *adv.*

dill (dil) *n.* **1.** An Old World annual of the parsley family, with aromatic seeds, used medicinally and for flavoring. **2.** The seeds or leaves of this plant. [OE *dile*]

dill pickle A pickle flavored with dill.

dil·ly-dal·ly (dil′ē·dal′ē) *v.i.* **·dal·lied, ·dal·ly·ing** To waste time, esp. in indecision. [Varied reduplication of DALLY]

dil·u·ent (dil′yōō·ənt) *adj.* Serving to dilute. — *n.* A diluent agent.

di·lute (di·lōōt′, dī-; *for adj., also* dī′lōōt) *v.t.* **·lut·ed, ·lut·ing 1.** To make weaker or more fluid by adding a liquid, as

water. **2.** To weaken or reduce the intensity, strength, or purity of. — *adj.* Weak; diluted. [< L *dilutus*, pp. of *diluere* < *dis-* away + *luere* to wash] — **di·lu′tion** *n.*

di·lu·vi·al (di·lōō′vē·əl) *adj.* **1.** Of or pertaining to a flood, esp. the Deluge. **2.** *Geol.* **a** Produced by a deluge or by floods. **b** Made of or related to diluvium. Also **di·lu′vi·an.**

di·lu·vi·um (di·lōō′vē·əm) *n. Geol.* Coarse rock deposited by glaciers; glacial drift. [< NL < L, a flood]

dim (dim) *adj.* **dim·mer, dim·mest 1.** Obscured or darkened from faintness of light. **2.** Not clearly seen or recognized; indistinct: a *dim* figure. **3.** Not clear to the understanding or memory; vague. **4.** Not perceiving clearly; obtuse. **5.** Not seeing clearly: said of the eye. **6.** Lacking luster or brilliance. **7.** Faint: a *dim* sound. **8.** Discouraging; pessimistic. — *v.t. & v.i.* **dimmed, dim·ming** To render or grow dim. [OE *dimm*, *dim*] — **dim′·ly** *adv.* — **dim′ness** *n.*

dime (dim) *n.* A silver coin of the United States and Canada, equal to ten cents or one tenth of a dollar. [< OF < L *decima*, fem. of *decimus* a tenth part]

dime novel *Chiefly U.S.* **1.** A cheap, sensational novel, originally costing a dime. **2.** Any trashy novel.

di·men·sion (di·men′shən) *n.* **1.** Any measurable extent, as length, breadth, or thickness. **2.** *Usu. pl.* Extent or magnitude: the *dimensions* of the case. [< MF < L *-onis* < *dis-* apart + *metiri* to measure] — **di·men′sion·al** *adj.*

dime store A five-and-ten-cent store.

di·min·ish (di·min′ish) *v.t.* **1.** To make smaller or less; decrease, as in size, amount, or degree. **2.** To reduce in rank, power, or authority. — *v.i.* **3.** To dwindle; decrease. — **Syn.** See DECREASE. [Fusion of ME *diminuen* to lessen and OF *menusier* to make small] — **di·min′ish·a·ble** *adj.*

di·min·ished (di·min′isht) *adj. Music* **1.** One semitone smaller than the corresponding minor or perfect interval. **2.** Denoting a theme that has been subjected to diminution.

di·min·u·en·do (di·min′yōō·en′dō) *Music n. pl.* **·dos** A gradual lessening in volume: expressed by the sign ⎯⎯ : opposed to *crescendo*. — *v.i.* **·doed, ·do·ing** To produce a diminuendo. [< Ital., ppr. of *diminuire* to lessen]

dim·i·nu·tion (dim′ə·nōō′shən, -nyōō′-) *n.* The act of diminishing or the condition of being diminished; decrease.

di·min·u·tive (di·min′yə·tiv) *adj.* **1.** Of relatively small size. **2.** Diminishing or tending to diminish. **3.** *Gram.* Expressing diminished size: said of certain suffixes. — *n.* **1.** *Gram.* A word formed from another to express diminished size, familiarity, affection, etc. **2.** Anything very small. — **dim·in′u·tive·ly** *adv.*

dim·i·ty (dim′ə·tē) *n. pl.* **·ties** A sheer cotton fabric woven with stripes, cords, or checks, used for dresses, curtains, etc. [< Ital. < ML < Gk. < *di-* two + *mitos* thread]

dim·mer (dim′ər) *n.* A rheostat used for varying the intensity of illumination, as in a theater lighting system.

di·mor·phism (dī·môr′fiz·əm) *n.* The existence of two distinct forms of the same organ or substance. [< Gk. < *di-* two + *morphē* form] — **di·mor′phic, di·mor′phous** *adj.*

dim-out (dim′out′) *n.* A form of modified lighting in a city, etc., used as a precautionary measure against aerial attack.

dim·ple (dim′pəl) *n.* **1.** A slight depression in the surface of the human body, esp. one made visible in the cheek by smiling. **2.** A similar depression in any smooth surface. — *v.t. & v.i.* **·pled, ·pling** To mark with or form dimples. [ME *dympull*] — **dim′ply** *adj.*

dim·wit (dim′wit′) *n. Slang* A stupid or simple-minded person. — **dim′wit′ted** *adj.* — **dim′wit′ted·ly** *adv.*

din (din) *n.* A loud, continuous noise or clamor; a rattling or clattering sound. — *v.* **dinned, din·ning** *v.t.* **1.** To assail with confusing noise. **2.** To urge or press with repetition or insistence. — *v.i.* **3.** To make a din. [OE *dyne*]

dine (din) *v.* **dined, din·ing** *v.i.* **1.** To eat dinner. **2.** To eat; feed: with *on* or *upon*. — *v.t.* **3.** To entertain at dinner. [< F < OF, prob. < L *dis-* away + *jejunus* fast]

din·er (dī′nər) *n.* **1.** One who dines. **2.** A dining car. **3.** A restaurant resembling a railroad car.

di·nette (dī·net′) *n.* An alcove or small room used as a dining room.

ding (ding) *v.t.* **1.** To sound, as a bell; ring. **2.** *Informal* To instill by constant repetition; din. — *v.i.* **3.** To ring or sound. **4.** *Informal* To speak with constant repetition. — *n.* The sound of a bell, or a sound resembling this. [Imit.]

ding-dong (ding′dông′, -dong′) *n.* **1.** The peal of a bell. **2.** Any monotonous repetition. — *adj. Informal* Energetically and closely contested, as a fight. [Imit.]

din·ghy (ding′gē, ding′ē) *n. pl.* **·ghies** Any of various kinds of small rowing boats. Also **din′gey, din′gy.** [< Hind. *dīngī*]

din·go (ding′gō) *n. pl.* **·goes** The native wild dog of Australia. [< native name]

din·gus (ding′əs) *n. Informal* A thing or device of which the name is unknown or forgotten; a gadget or thingamabob. [< Afrikaans < Du. *ding* thing]

din·gy (din′jē) *adj.* **·gi·er, ·gi·est** Darkened or discolored, as if soiled; dull; grimy; shabby. [Origin unknown] — **din′gi·ly** *adv.* — **din′gi·ness** *n.*

dining car A railway car in which meals are served en route.

dining room A room in which meals are served, esp. dinner.

dink·y (dĭng′kē) *adj.* **dink·i·er, dink·i·est** *Informal* **1.** *U.S.* Small; insignificant. **2.** *Brit.* Little; cute; neat. — *n. pl.* **din·kies** A dinkey. [< Scot. *dink* neat, tidy]

din·ner (din′ər) *n.* **1.** The principal meal of the day, taken usu. at some hour between noon and nine P.M. **2.** A banquet in honor of a person or event. [< F *dîner* to dine]

dinner coat or **jacket** A tuxedo jacket.

din·ner·ware (din′ər-wâr′) *n.* Dishes, etc., used for meals.

di·no·saur (dī′nə-sôr′) *n. Paleontol.* One of a group of extinct reptiles, widely distributed during the Mesozoic period and including the largest known land animals. [< DINO- + Gk. *sauros* lizard] — **di′no·sau′ri·an** *adj. & n.*

dint (dint) *n.* **1.** Active agency; means; force: to win by *dint* of effort. **2.** A dent. — *v.t.* **1.** To make a dent in. **2.** To drive in forcibly. [OE *dynt* a blow]

di·oc·e·san (dī-os′ə-sən, dī′ə-sē′sən) *adj.* Of or pertaining to a diocese. — *n.* A bishop in charge of a diocese.

di·o·cese (dī′ə-sēs, -sis) *n.* The territory or the churches under a bishop's jurisdiction. [< OF < Med.L < L < Gk. < *dia-* completely + *oikeein* to dwell, manage]

di·ode (dī′ōd) *n. Electronics* An electron tube that permits electrons to pass in one direction only, used as a rectifier.

di·oe·cious (dī-ē′shəs) *adj. Bot.* Having the male and female organs borne by different plants; unisexual: also spelled *diecious.* [< DI-² + Gk. *oikia* house, dwelling]

Di·o·nys·ian (dī′ə-nish′ən, -nis′ē-ən) *adj.* Of or characteristic of Dionysius. Also **Di·o·nys·i·ac** (dī′ə-nis′ē-ak).

Di·o·ny·sus (dī′ə-nī′səs) In Greek mythology, the god of wine, fertility, etc., worshiped with orgiastic rites: identified with the Roman *Bacchus.* Also **Di′o·ny′sos.**

di·op·ter (dī-op′tər) *n. Optics* The unit for measuring the refractive power of a lens, expressed as the reciprocal of its focal length in meters. Also **di·op′tre.** [< MF < L < Gk., optical instrument]

di·op·tric (dī-op′trik) *adj. Optics* **1.** Aiding the vision by refraction, as a lens. **2.** Of or pertaining to dioptrics. **3.** Of or pertaining to a diopter. Also **di·op′tri·cal.**

di·op·trics (dī-op′triks) *n.pl.* (*construed as sing.*) The branch of optics treating of light refraction by transparent media.

di·o·ra·ma (dī′ə-rä′mə, -ram′ə) *n.* **1.** An exhibit consisting of modeled figures, etc., set in a naturalistic foreground. **2.** A picture that changes by means of cloth transparencies, etc. [< Gk. *dia-* through + *horama* a sight] — **di·o·ram·ic** (dī′ə-ram′ik) *adj.*

di·ox·ide (dī-ok′sīd, -sid) *n. Chem.* An oxide containing two atoms of oxygen to the molecule. Also **di·ox·id** (dī-ok′sid).

dip (dip) *v.* **dipped, dip·ping** *v.t.* **1.** To put or let down into a liquid momentarily. **2.** To obtain or lift up and out by scooping, bailing, etc. **3.** To lower and then raise, as a flag in salute. **4.** To baptize by immersion. **5.** To plunge (animals) into a disinfectant. **6.** To dye by immersion. **7.** To make (candles) by repeatedly immersing wicks in wax or tallow. — *v.i.* **8.** To plunge into and quickly come out of water or other liquid. **9.** To plunge one's hand or a receptacle into water, etc., or into a container, especially so as to take something out. **10.** To sink or go down suddenly. **11.** To incline downward; go down; decline. **12.** *Geol.* To lie at an angle to the horizon, as rock strata. **13.** *Aeron.* To drop rapidly and then climb. **14.** To engage in or read something slightly or superficially. — *n.* **1.** An act of dipping; a brief immersion or plunge. **2.** A liquid sauce, etc., into which something is to be dipped. **3.** The quantity of something taken up at a dipping; also, the object used for dipping. **4.** A candle made by dipping. **5.** A sloping downward; also, the degree of such a sloping. **6.** A hollow or depression. **7.** The angle that a magnetic needle makes with the horizon. **8.** *Aeron.* A rapid drop of an airplane followed by a climb. **9.** *Slang* A pickpocket. [OE *dyppan*]

diph·the·ri·a (dif-thir′ē-ə, dip-) *n. Pathol.* An acute contagious disease, caused by a bacillus and characterized by the formation of a false membrane in the air passages, fever, and weakness. [< F < Gk. *diphthera* leather, membrane] — **diph·the·ri·al** (dif-thir′ē-əl, dip-) *adj.* Of, pertaining to, or having diphtheria. Also **diph·the·ri·an, diph·the·ric** (dif-thir′ik, dip-), **diph·the·rit·ic** (dif′thə-rit′ik, dip-).

diph·thong (dif′thông, -thong, dip′-) *n. Phonet.* A blend of two vowel sounds in one syllable, as *oi* in *coil,* or as *i* in *fine.* [< F < LL < Gk. < *di-* two + *phthongos* sound] — **diph·thon′gal** *adj.*

diph·thong·ize (dif′thông-īz, -thong-, dip′-) *v.* **·ized, ·iz·ing** *v.t.* **1.** To make a diphthong of; pronounce as a diphthong. — *v.i.* **2.** To become a diphthong. — **diph′thong·i·za′tion** *n.*

diplo- *combining form* Double. Also, before vowels, **dipl-.** [< Gk. *diploos* double]

dip·loid (dip′loid) *adj. Biol.* Having two sets of chromosomes.

di·plo·ma (di-plō′mə) *n.* **1.** A certificate given by a school, college, or university testifying that a student has earned a degree or completed a course of study. **2.** A certificate conferring some honor or privilege. [< L < Gk. *diplōma* paper folded double, a letter]

di·plo·ma·cy (di-plō′mə-sē) *n. pl.* **·cies 1.** The art, science, or practice of conducting negotiations between nations. **2.** Skill or tact in dealing with others, etc.

dip·lo·mat (dip′lə-mat) *n.* **1.** One engaged in diplomacy. **2.** Any individual possessing skill or tact in dealing with others. [See DIPLOMA.]

dip·lo·mat·ic (dip′lə-mat′ik) *adj.* **1.** Of or pertaining to diplomacy. **2.** Tactful and skillful in dealing with people. Also **dip′lo·mat′i·cal.** — **dip′lo·mat′i·cal·ly** *adv.*

diplomatic corps The corps of officials, as ambassadors and envoys, who are assigned to represent their country in another country. Also **diplomatic body.**

diplomatic immunity Exemption of the members of a diplomatic corps from the ordinary processes of local law.

di·plo·ma·tist (di-plō′mə-tist) *n. Brit.* A diplomat.

dip·per (dip′ər) *n.* **1.** One who dips. **2.** A long-handled cup used to dip liquids. **3.** Any of several American birds that are quick divers; esp. the water ouzel.

Dip·per (dip′ər) *n.* Either of two northern constellations, the Big Dipper or the Little Dipper.

dip·so·ma·ni·a (dip′sə-mā′nē-ə) *n.* Uncontrollable craving for alcoholic drink. [< Gk. *dipsa* thirst + -MANIA]

dip·so·ma·ni·ac (dip′sə-mā′nē-ak) *n.* A person affected with dipsomania. — *adj.* Pertaining to or affected with dipsomania: also **dip·so·ma·ni·a·cal** (dip′sə-mə-nī′ə-kal).

dip·ter·ous (dip′tər-əs) *adj.* **1.** *Entomol.* Of or pertaining to insects having a single pair of wings, including the flies, gnats, mosquitoes, etc. **2.** Two-winged, as a seed or fruit. [< Gk. < *di-* twice + *pteron* wing]

dip·tych (dip′tik) *n.* **1.** An ancient Greek or Roman hinged double writing tablet. **2.** A double picture or carving, often of a religious subject. [< LL < Gk., pair of tablets]

dire (dīr) *adj.* **dir·er, dir·est** Calamitous; dreadful; terrible. [< L *dirus* awful] — **dire′ly** *adv.* — **dire′ness** *n.*

di·rect (di-rekt′, dī-) *v.t.* **1.** To control or conduct the affairs of; manage. **2.** To order or instruct with authority; command. **3.** *Music* To lead as a conductor. **4.** To tell (someone) the way. **5.** To cause to move or face in a desired direction: to *direct* one's gaze. **6.** To indicate the destination of, as a letter. **7.** To intend, as remarks or insults, to be heard by a person; address. **8.** To guide or supervise (the performance of a play, film, etc.). — *v.i.* **9.** To give commands or guidance. **10.** To guide the production or interpretation of a play, film, etc. — *adj.* **1.** Having or being the straightest course; shortest; nearest. **2.** Free from intervening agencies or conditions. **3.** Straightforward; candid; plain. **4.** Complete; absolute: the *direct* antithesis. **5.** In a continuous line of descent; lineal. **6.** In the exact words of the speaker or writer: a *direct* quote. **7.** *Govt.* By the efforts of the people through referendum, etc., without the intervention of delegates or representatives. **8.** *Electr.* Continuous as opposed to alternating, as a current. — *adv.* In a direct line or manner; directly. [< L < *dis-* apart + *regere* to guide, conduct] — **di·rect′ness** *n.*

di·rec·tion (di-rek′shən, dī-) *n.* **1.** The act of directing. **2.** The course or position of an object or point in relation to another object or point: in the *direction* of Chicago. **3.** *Usu. pl.* Instructions about how to do or use something. **4.** An order, command, or regulation. **5.** Management, control, or administration. **6.** Supervision and organization of a play, film, etc. **7.** Tendency or movement. **8.** The address on a letter, parcel, etc., that indicates the intended recipient.

di·rec·tion·al (di-rek′shən-əl, dī-) *adj.* **1.** Pertaining to direction in space. **2.** *Telecom.* **a** Adapted for indicating from which of several directions signals are received. **b** Describing an antenna that radiates or receives radio waves more effectively in or from some directions than from others.

direction finder *Telecom.* A receiving device with which the direction of incoming radio signals may be determined.

di·rec·tive (di-rek′tiv, dī-) *n.* An order or regulation; esp., a governmental or military pronouncement. — *adj.* That directs or points out, rules, or governs.

di·rect·ly (di-rekt′lē, dī-) *adv.* **1.** In a direct line or manner. **2.** Without medium, agent, or go-between. **3.** As soon as possible; immediately. **4.** Exactly; precisely. — *conj. Brit.* As soon as.

di·rec·tor (di-rek′tər, dī-) *n.* **1.** One who directs, as the head member of a corporation, the conductor of an orchestra, etc. **2.** *Mil.* An apparatus that computes firing data for use against moving targets. — **di·rec′tress** *n.fem.*

di·rec·tor·ate (di-rek′tər-it, dī-) *n.* **1.** A body of directors. **2.** The office or power of a director: also **di·rec′tor·ship.**

di·rec·to·ri·al (di-rek′tôr′ē-əl, -tō′rē-) *adj.* **1.** That directs; directive. **2.** Pertaining to a director or directorate.

di·rec·to·ry (di-rek′tər-ē, dī-) *n. pl.* **·ries 1.** An alphabetical or classified list, as of the names and addresses of the inhabitants or businesses of a city. **2.** A collection of rules. **3.** A directorate. — *adj.* Serving to direct.

direct primary *Govt.* A preliminary election in which a party chooses its candidates for public office by direct vote.

direct tax A tax charged directly to the taxpayer.

dire·ful (dīr′fŏŏl, -fəl) *adj.* Dreadful; terrible; dire. — **dire′ful·ly** *adv.* — **dire′ful·ness** *n.*

dirge (dûrj) *n.* **1.** A song or melody expressing mourning. **2.** A funeral hymn. [< L *dirige* (imperative of *dirigere* to direct), the first word of the antiphon (*Ps.* v 8) of matins]

dir·i·gi·ble (dir′ə·jə·bəl) *n.* A lighter-than-air aircraft that may be steered by means of its own motive power. — *adj.* That can be steered. [< L *dirigere* to direct]

dirk (dûrk) *n.* A dagger. [Origin uncertain]

dirn·dl (dûrn′dəl) *n.* **1.** A woman's dress with a full skirt gathered to a tight bodice. **2.** The skirt of such a dress: also **dirndl skirt.** [< G *dirndl,* dim. of *dirne* girl]

dirt (dûrt) *n.* **1.** Any foul or filthy substance, as mud, dust, excrement, etc. **2.** Loose earth or soil; loam. **3.** Something contemptible, mean, or of small worth. **4.** Obscene speech, pictures, or writing. **5.** Rude language. **6.** Gossip. **7.** *Mining* Washed-down earth, broken ore or rock, etc., containing precious metal. — *adj.* Made of earth: a *dirt* road. [ME *drit* < ON, dirt, bird droppings]

dirt-cheap (dûrt′chēp′) *adj.* Very inexpensive. — *adv.* At a very low price.

dirt farmer *U.S. Informal* A farmer who does his own work.

dirt·y (dûr′tē) *adj.* **dirt·i·er, dirt·i·est 1.** Soiled with or as with dirt; unclean; filthy. **2.** Imparting dirt; making filthy. **3.** Indecent; obscene. **4.** Despicable; mean. **5.** Lacking brightness or clarity: said of colors. **6.** Stormy: *dirty* weather. **7.** Having excessive radioactive fallout: a *dirty* atomic bomb. — *v.t. & v.i.* **dirt·ied, dirt·y·ing** To make or become dirty. — **dirt′i·ly** *adv.* — **dirt′i·ness** *n.*

dis-¹ *prefix* **1.** Away from; apart: *disembody.* **2.** The reverse of or the undoing of (what is expressed in the rest of the word): *disconnect.* **3.** Deprivation of some quality, power, rank, etc.: *disable.* **4.** Not: *disloyal.* **5.** Completely; thoroughly (with an already negative word): *disannul.* Also: *di-* before *b, d, l, m, n, r, s, v,* and usu. before *g,* as in *digress, direct, diverge;* *dif-* before *f,* as in *differ.* The living English prefix is always in the form *dis-.* [< L *dis-,* sometimes replacing OF *des-* (see DE-), ult. < *duo* two]

dis-² *prefix* Var. of DI-². [< MF, ult. < Gk. *dis* twice]

Dis (dis) In Roman mythology: **a** God of the lower world: identified with *Pluto.* **b** The kingdom of the dead.

dis·a·bil·i·ty (dis′ə·bil′ə·tē) *n. pl.* **·ties 1.** That which disables. **2.** Lack of ability. **3.** Legal incapacity to act.

dis·a·ble (dis·ā′bəl) *v.t.* **·bled, ·bling 1.** To render incapable; cripple. **2.** To render legally incapable. — **dis·a′ble·ment** *n.*

dis·a·buse (dis′ə·byōōz′) *v.t.* **·bused, ·bus·ing** To free from false or mistaken ideas; undeceive.

dis·ad·van·tage (dis′əd·van′tij, -vän′-) *n.* **1.** An unfavorable condition or situation. **2.** That which produces an unfavorable condition or situation; drawback; handicap. **3.** Loss, injury, or detriment. — **at a disadvantage** In an unfavorable condition or situation. — *v.t.* **·taged, ·tag·ing** To subject to a disadvantage.

dis·ad·van·taged (dis′əd·van′tijd, -vän′-) *adj.* Having less money, social status, etc., than is needed for decent living.

dis·ad·van·ta·geous (dis·ad′vən·tā′jəs) *adj.* Attended with disadvantage; detrimental; inconvenient. — **dis·ad′van·ta′geous·ly** *adv.* — **dis·ad′van·ta′geous·ness** *n.*

dis·af·fect (dis′ə·fekt′) *v.t.* To destroy or weaken the affection or loyalty of; alienate; estrange. — **dis′af·fec′tion** *n.*

dis·af·fect·ed (dis′ə·fek′tid) *adj.* Alienated in feeling or loyalty; estranged; unfriendly. — **dis′af·fect′ed·ly** *adv.*

dis·a·gree (dis′ə·grē′) *v.i.* **·greed, ·gree·ing 1.** To vary in opinion; differ; dissent. **2.** To quarrel; argue. **3.** To fail to agree or harmonize, as facts. **4.** To be unacceptable or unfavorable: with *with:* Heat *disagreed* with him.

dis·a·gree·a·ble (dis′ə·grē′ə·bəl) *adj.* **1.** Repugnant or offensive; not agreeable. **2.** Of unpleasant disposition; quarrelsome; bad-tempered. — **dis′a·gree′a·bil′i·ty, dis′a·gree′a·ble·ness** *n.* — **dis′a·gree′a·bly** *adv.*

dis·a·gree·ment (dis′ə·grē′mənt) *n.* **1.** Failure to agree. **2.** Dissimilarity; inconsistency; discrepancy. **3.** Difference in views; dissent. **4.** A quarrel; dispute.

dis·al·low (dis′ə·lou′) *v.t.* **1.** To refuse to allow. **2.** To reject as untrue or invalid. — **dis′al·low′ance** *n.*

dis·ap·pear (dis′ə·pir′) *v.i.* **1.** To pass from sight; fade away; vanish. **2.** To cease to exist. — **dis′ap·pear′ance** *n.*

dis·ap·point (dis′ə·point′) *v.t.* **1.** To fail to fulfill the expectation, hope, or desire of (a person). **2.** To prevent the fulfillment of (a hope or plan). — **dis′ap·point′ing·ly** *adv.*

dis·ap·point·ed (dis′ə·poin′tid) *adj.* Frustrated in one's expectations or hopes.

dis·ap·point·ment (dis′ə·point′mənt) *n.* **1.** The act of disappointing. **2.** The feeling of being disappointed. **3.** One who or that which disappoints.

dis·ap·pro·ba·tion (dis′ap·rə·bā′shən) *n.* Disapproval.

dis·ap·pro·val (dis′ə·prōō′vəl) *n.* The act of disapproving; the withholding of approval; censure.

dis·ap·prove (dis′ə·prōōv′) *v.* **·proved, ·prov·ing** *v.t.* **1.** To regard with disfavor or censure; condemn. **2.** To refuse to approve. — *v.i.* **3.** To have or express an unfavorable opinion: often with *of.* — **dis′ap·prov′ing·ly** *adv.*

dis·arm (dis·ärm′) *v.t.* **1.** To deprive of weapons or of any means of attack or defense. **2.** To overcome the suspicion, antagonism, etc., of. **3.** To allay or reduce (suspicion, antagonism, etc.). — *v.i.* **4.** To lay down arms. **5.** To reduce or eliminate one's military forces, equipment, etc.

dis·ar·ma·ment (dis·är′mə·mənt) *n.* The act of disarming; esp., the elimination, reduction, or limitation of armed forces, military equipment, or weapons of war.

dis·arm·ing (dis·är′ming) *adj.* Tending to overcome suspicion, etc.: a *disarming* smile. — **dis·arm′ing·ly** *adv.*

dis·ar·range (dis′ə·rānj′) *v.t.* **·ranged, ·rang·ing** To disturb the arrangement of; disorder. — **dis′ar·range′ment** *n.*

dis·ar·ray (dis′ə·rā′) *n.* **1.** Disorder; confusion. **2.** Disorder of clothing. — *v.t.* To throw into disarray.

dis·as·sem·ble (dis′ə·sem′bəl) *v.t.* **·bled, ·bling** To take apart. — **dis·as·sem′bly** *n.*

dis·as·so·ci·ate (dis′ə·sō′shē·āt) *v.t.* **·at·ed, ·at·ing** To dissociate. — **dis′as·so′ci·a′tion** *n.*

dis·as·ter (di·zas′tər, -zäs′-) *n.* An event causing great distress or ruin; sudden and crushing misfortune. [< MF < *des-* away + *astre* a star]

dis·as·trous (di·zas′trəs, -zäs′-) *adj.* Causing or accompanied by disaster; calamitous. — **dis·as′trous·ly** *adv.* — **dis·as′trous·ness** *n.*

dis·a·vow (dis′ə·vou′) *v.t.* To disclaim responsibility for or approval of; refuse to acknowledge. — **dis′a·vow′al** *n.*

dis·band (dis·band′) *v.t.* **1.** To break up the organization of; dissolve; especially, to break up (an army or similar unit) by dismissing the members. — *v.i.* **2.** To become disbanded. — **dis·band′ment** *n.*

dis·bar (dis·bär′) *v.t.* **·barred, ·bar·ring** To expel officially from the legal profession. — **dis·bar′ment** *n.*

dis·be·lief (dis′bi·lēf′) *n.* Lack of belief.

dis·be·lieve (dis′bi·lēv′) *v.t. & v.i.* **·lieved, ·liev·ing** To withhold belief (from); reject. — **dis·be·liev′er** *n.*

dis·bur·den (dis·bûr′dən) *v.t.* **1.** To relieve of a burden. **2.** To get rid of (a burden). — *v.i.* **3.** To put off a burden.

dis·burse (dis·bûrs′) *v.t.* **·bursed, ·burs·ing** To pay out; expend. [< OF < *des-* away + *bourse* a purse] — **dis·burs′a·ble** *adj.* — **dis·burse′ment** *n.* — **dis·burs′er** *n.*

disc (disk) *n.* **1.** See DISK. **2.** *Anat.* Any approximately flat, circular outgrowth, organ, or structure, as of cartilage between the joints of certain bones. [Var. of DISK]

dis·calced (dis·kalst′) *adj.* Barefooted, as certain orders of monks [< dis- not + *calceatus* a shoe]

dis·cant (dis′kant, dis·kant′) *n. & v.i.* Descant.

dis·card (*v.* dis·kärd′; *n.* dis′kärd) *v.t.* **1.** To cast aside as useless or undesirable; reject; dismiss. **2.** In card games, to throw out (a card or cards) from one's hand; also, to play (a card, other than a trump, not of the suit led). — *v.i.* **3.** In card games, to throw out a card or cards. — *n.* **1.** The act of discarding, or the state of being discarded. **2.** A card or cards discarded. **3.** One who or that which is discarded.

dis·cern (di·sûrn′, di·zûrn′) *v.t.* **1.** To perceive, as with sight or mind. **2.** To recognize as separate and different. — *v.i.* **3.** To distinguish or discriminate something. [< OF < L < *dis-* apart + *cernere* to separate] — **dis·cern′er** *n.* — **dis·cern′i·ble** *adj.* — **dis·cern′i·bly** *adv.*

dis·cern·ing (di·sûr′ning, -zûr′-) *adj.* Quick to discern; discriminating; penetrating. — **dis·cern′ing·ly** *adv.*

dis·cern·ment (di·sûrn′mənt, -zûrn′-) *n.* **1.** The act or process of discerning. **2.** Keenness of judgment; insight.

dis·charge (dis·chärj′; *n. also* dis′chärj) *v.* **·charged, ·charg·ing** *v.t.* **1.** To remove the contents of; unload. **2.** To remove by unloading. **3.** To emit (fluid). **4.** To shoot or fire, as a gun. **5.** To dismiss from office or employment. **6.** To set at liberty, as a prisoner. **7.** To relieve of duty or obligation. **8.** To perform the duties of (a trust, office, etc.). **9.** To pay (a debt) or meet and satisfy (an obligation or duty). **10.** To set aside legally; annul. **11.** *Electr.* To free of an electrical charge. — *v.i.* **12.** To get rid of a load, burden, etc. **13.** To go off, as a cannon. **14.** To give or send forth contents. **15.** *Electr.* To lose a charge of electricity. — *n.* **1.** The act of discharging or the state of being discharged. **2.** The firing of a weapon or missile. **3.** An issuing forth; emission. **4.** That which is discharged, as pus. **5.** Release or dismissal from service, employment, or custody. **6.** Something that discharges, as a certificate separating one from military service. **7.** *Electr.* The flow of electricity between the terminals of a condenser when placed in very near contact. [< OF *deschargier* < *des-* away (< L *dis-*) + *chargier* to carry] — **dis·charge/a·ble** *adj.* — **dis·charg/er** *n.*

dis·ci·ple (di·si/pəl) *n.* **1.** One who accepts and follows a teacher or a doctrine. **2.** One of the twelve chosen companions and apostles of Jesus Christ. — **Syn.** See ADHERENT. [OE < L *discere* to learn] — **dis·ci/ple·ship** *n.*

dis·ci·pli·nar·i·an (dis/ə·plə·nâr/ē·ən) *n.* One who administers or advocates discipline. — *adj.* Disciplinary.

dis·ci·pli·nar·y (dis/ə·plə·ner/ē) *adj.* Of, relating to, or of the nature of discipline; used for discipline.

dis·ci·pline (dis/ə·plin) *n.* **1.** Training of the mental, moral, and physical powers by instruction, control, and exercise. **2.** The state or condition resulting from such training. **3.** Subjection to rule and authority. **4.** Punishment or disciplinary action for the sake of training. **5.** A system of rules, or method of practice, as of a church. **6.** A branch of knowledge or instruction. **7.** A penitential instrument; a scourge. — *v.t.* **·plined, ·plin·ing 1.** To train to obedience or subjection. **2.** To drill; educate. **3.** To punish. — **Syn.** See CHASTEN, TEACH. [< OF < L *disciplina* instruction] — **dis·ci·plin/a·ble** *adj.* — **dis/ci·plin·er** *n.*

disc jockey See DISK JOCKEY.

dis·claim (dis·klām/) *v.t.* **1.** To disavow any claim to, or responsibility for. **2.** To reject or deny the authority of. — *v.i.* **3.** *Law* To renounce a legal claim. — **dis·cla·ma·tion** (dis/klə·mā/shən) *n.*

dis·claim·er (dis·klā/mər) *n.* **1.** One who disclaims. **2.** A disclaiming act, notice, or instrument.

dis·close (dis·klōz/) *v.t.* **·closed, ·clos·ing 1.** To expose to view; uncover. **2.** To make known. — **dis·clos/er** *n.*

dis·clo·sure (dis·klō/zhər) *n.* **1.** The act or process of disclosing. **2.** That which is disclosed.

dis·coid (dis/koid) *adj.* Having the form of a disk. Also **dis·coi/dal.** — *n.* A disk or disklike object. [< L < Gk. *diskos* discus < *eidos* form]

dis·col·or (dis·kul/ər) *v.t.* **1.** To change or destroy the color of; stain. — *v.i.* **2.** To become discolored. Also *Brit.* **dis·col/our.** — **dis·col/or·a/tion, dis·col/or·ment** *n.*

dis·com·bob·u·late (dis/kəm·bob/yə·lāt) *v.t.* **·lat·ed, ·lat·ing** *U.S. Slang* To throw into confusion. [Origin uncertain]

dis·com·fit (dis·kum/fit) *v.t.* **1.** To defeat the plans or purposes of; frustrate. **2.** To throw into confusion. **3.** To vanquish. [< OF < *des-* away + *confire* to prepare]

dis·com·fi·ture (dis·kum/fi·chər) *n.* The act of discomfiting, or the state of being discomfited; defeat; frustration.

dis·com·fort (dis·kum/fərt) *n.* **1.** Lack of ease or comfort; disquietude. **2.** That which interferes with comfort. — *v.t.* To make uneasy; distress.

dis·com·mode (dis/kə·mōd/) *v.t.* **·mod·ed, ·mod·ing** To cause inconvenience to; trouble; disturb. [< DIS-¹ + L *commodus* fit, suitable, convenient]

dis·com·pose (dis/kəm·pōz/) *v.t.* **·posed, ·pos·ing 1.** To disturb the calm of; make uneasy. **2.** To disorder or disarrange. — **dis/com·pos/ed·ly** *adv.* — **dis/com·pos/ing·ly** *adv.*

dis·com·po·sure (dis/kəm·pō/zhər) *n.* The state of being discomposed; agitation; perturbation.

dis·con·cert (dis/kən·sûrt/) *v.t.* **1.** To disturb the composure of; confuse; upset. **2.** To frustrate, as a plan. [< MF < *dis-* apart + *concerter* to agree] — **dis/con·cert/ed** *adj.* — **dis/con·cert/ed·ly** *adv.* — **dis/con·cert/ed·ness** *n.* — **dis/con·cert/ing·ly** *adv.*

dis·con·form·i·ty (dis/kən·fôr/mə·tē) *n. pl.* **·ties** Lack of conformity; nonconformity.

dis·con·nect (dis/kə·nekt/) *v.t.* To break the connection of or between. — **dis/con·nec/tion** *n.*

dis·con·nect·ed (dis/kə·nek/tid) *adj.* **1.** Not connected; disjointed. **2.** Incoherent; rambling. — **dis/con·nect/ed·ly** *adv.* — **dis/con·nect/ed·ness** *n.*

dis·con·so·late (dis·kon/sə·lit) *adj.* **1.** Not to be consoled; inconsolable; dejected. **2.** Producing or marked by gloominess; cheerless. [< Med.L < L *dis-* not + *consolari* to cheer, console] — **dis/con/so·late·ly** *adv.* — **dis/con/so·late·ness, dis·con/so·la/tion** *n.*

dis·con·tent (dis/kən·tent/) *adj.* Discontented. — *n.* Lack of contentment; dissatisfaction; uneasiness: also **dis/con·tent/ment.** — *v.t.* To make discontent.

dis·con·tent·ed (dis/kən·ten/tid) *adj.* Restless; uneasy in mind, as through frustration; dissatisfied. — **dis/con·tent/ed·ly** *adv.* — **dis/con·tent/ed·ness** *n.*

dis·con·tin·ue (dis/kən·tin/yōō) *v.* **·tin·ued, ·tin·u·ing** *v.t.* **1.** To break off or cease from; stop. **2.** To cease using, receiving, etc. — *v.i.* **3.** To come to an end; cease. — **dis/con·tin/u·ance, dis/con·tin/u·a/tion** *n.* — **dis/con·tin/u·er** *n.*

dis·con·ti·nu·i·ty (dis/kon·tə·nōō/ə·tē, ·nyōō/-) *n. pl.* **·ties 1.** Lack of continuity. **2.** A gap or break.

dis·con·tin·u·ous (dis/kən·tin/yōō·əs) *adj.* Not continuous; characterized by interruptions or breaks. — **dis/con·tin/u·ous·ly** *adv.* — **dis/con·tin/u·ous·ness** *n.*

dis·cord (*n.* dis/kôrd; *v.* dis·kôrd/) *n.* **1.** Lack of agreement or concord; contention; conflict; strife. **2.** A harsh or disagreeable mingling of noises; din. **3.** *Music* Dissonance. — *v.i.* To be out of accord or harmony; clash. [< OF < L < *dis-* apart + *cor, cordis* heart]

dis·cor·dant (dis·kôr/dənt) *adj.* **1.** Characterized by lack of agreement or concord; differing; clashing. **2.** Dissonant, harsh, or disagreeable in sound. [See DISCORD.] — **dis·cor/dance, dis·cor/dan·cy** *n.* — **dis·cor/dant·ly** *adv.*

dis·co·thèque (dis·kə·tek/) *n.* A night club offering recorded music for dancing instead of music played by a band of live musicians. [< F, lit., record library]

dis·count (*v.* dis/kount, dis·kount/; *n.* dis/kount) *v.t.* **1.** To deduct (an indicated sum or percent) from the full amount that would otherwise be charged or owed. **2.** To buy or sell (a bill, note, or other negotiable paper), less the amount of interest to be accumulated before maturity. **3.** To lend money on (negotiable notes, etc., not immediately payable), deducting the interest. **4.** To reduce the cost or value of: to *discount* merchandise. **5.** To take little or no account of; disregard: *Discount* what she says. **6.** To allow for exaggeration, prejudice, etc., in; accept with reservation: to *discount* stories of great heroism. **7.** To take into account in advance and so lessen the full intensity or effect of. — *v.i.* **8.** To lend money, deducting the interest beforehand. — *n.* **1.** A deduction of a particular sum or percent, as one made for immediate cash payment. **2.** The interest deducted beforehand in buying, selling, or lending money on negotiable notes, etc. **3.** The rate of interest so deducted: also **discount rate. 4.** The act of discounting. — **at a discount 1.** Below the amount regularly charged; at less than face value. **2.** In little demand and of little value. [< MF < OF < Med.L < L *dis-* away + *computare*. See COMPUTE.] — **dis/count·a·ble** *adj.* — **dis/count·er** *n.*

dis·coun·te·nance (dis·koun/tə·nəns) *v.t.* **·nanced, ·nanc·ing 1.** To disapprove of. **2.** To abash; disconcert.

dis·cour·age (dis·kûr/ij) *v.t.* **·aged, ·ag·ing 1.** To weaken the courage or lessen the confidence of; dishearten. **2.** To deter or dissuade: with *from.* **3.** To obstruct; hinder. **4.** To attempt to repress or prevent by disapproval. [< OF < *des-* away + *corage* courage] — **dis·cour/ag·er** *n.* — **dis·cour/ag·ing·ly** *adv.* — **dis·cour/age·ment** *n.*

dis·course (*n.* dis/kôrs, -kōrs, dis·kôrs/, -kōrs/; *v.* dis·kôrs/, -kōrs/) *n.* **1.** Communication, as in conversation or writing. **2.** A formal, extensive, oral or written treatment of a subject. — *v.* **·coursed, ·cours·ing** *v.i.* **1.** To set forth one's ideas concerning a subject: with *on* or *upon.* **2.** To converse; confer. [< F < L < *dis-* apart + *cursus* a running, pp. of *currere* to run] — **dis·cours/er** *n.*

dis·cour·te·ous (dis·kûr/tē·əs) *adj.* Not courteous; impolite. — **dis·cour/te·ous·ly** *adv.* — **dis·cour/te·ous·ness** *n.*

dis·cour·te·sy (dis·kûr/tə·sē) *n. pl.* **·sies 1.** Lack of courtesy; rudeness. **2.** A discourteous act.

dis·cov·er (dis·kuv/ər) *v.t.* To find out, get knowledge of, or come upon, esp. for the first time. [< OF < *des-* away + *covrir* to cover] — **dis·cov/er·a·ble** *adj.* — **dis·cov/er·er** *n.*

dis·cov·er·y (dis·kuv/ər·ē) *n. pl.* **·er·ies 1.** The act of discovering. **2.** Something discovered.

dis·cred·it (dis·kred/it) *v.t.* **1.** To harm the credit or reputation of; bring into disrepute. **2.** To cause to be doubted, disbelieved, or distrusted. **3.** To refuse to believe (something asserted). — *n.* **1.** The state of being discredited; as: **a** Lack or loss of credit, reputation, or general esteem. **b** Doubt; disbelief; distrust. **2.** Something that discredits. — **dis·cred/it·a·ble** *adj.* — **dis·cred/it·a·bly** *adv.*

dis·creet (dis·krēt/) *adj.* Tactful and judicious, esp. in dealing with others. [< OF < LL *discretus*, orig. pp. of L *discernere* to discern] — **dis·creet/ly** *adv.* — **dis·creet/ness** *n.*

dis·crep·an·cy (dis·krep/ən·sē) *n. pl.* **·cies 1.** Lack of agreement or consistency; contradiction. **2.** An instance of this. Also **dis·crep/ance.** [< OF < L *dis-* apart + *crepare* to creak] — **dis·crep/ant** *adj.* — **dis·crep/ant·ly** *adv.*

dis·crete (dis·krēt/) *adj.* **1.** Distinct or separate. **2.** Made up of distinct parts. [Var. of DISCREET] — **dis·crete/ly** *adv.* — **dis·crete/ness** *n.*

dis·cre·tion (dis·kresh/ən) *n.* **1.** The quality of being discreet; tactfulness; prudence. **2.** Freedom or power to make one's own judgments. — **at one's discretion** According to one's own judgment. [< OF < L < *discernere* to discern]

dis·cre·tion·ar·y (dis·kresh/ən·er/ē) *adj.* Left to or determined by one's discretion. Also **dis·cre/tion·al.**

dis·crim·i·nate (*v.* dis·krim/ə·nāt; *adj.* dis·krim/ə·nit) *v.* **·nat·ed, ·nat·ing** *v.i.* **1.** To act toward someone or something with partiality or prejudice: to *discriminate* against a minority. **2.** To draw a clear distinction; distinguish: to *discriminate* between good and evil. — *v.t.* **3.** To draw or constitute a clear distinction between: differentiate: to *discriminate* good and evil. **4.** To recognize as being different. — *adj.* Discriminating. [< L < *dis-* apart + *crimen* judgment] — **dis·crim/i·nate·ly** *adv.* — **dis·crim/i·nat·ing** *adj.* — **dis·crim/i·nat·ing·ly** *adv.* — **dis·crim/i·na/tion** *n.* — **dis·crim/i·na/tor** *n.*

dis·crim·i·na·to·ry (dis-krim′ə-nə-tôr′ē, -tō′rē) *adj.* Showing prejudice or bias: *discriminatory* practices.

dis·cur·sive (dis-kûr′siv) *adj.* Passing quickly or disjointedly from one subject to another digressive. [See DIS-COURSE.] **— dis·cur′sive·ly** *adv.* **— dis·cur′sive·ness** *n.*

dis·cus (dis′kəs) *n. pl.* **dis·cus·es** or **dis·ci** (dis′ī) 1. A flat, heavy disk, as of metal or stone, hurled for distance in athletic contests. 2. Such a contest. [< L < Gk. *diskos*]

dis·cuss (dis-kus′) *v.t.* To have as the subject of conversation or writing; treat or consider formally. [< L, pp. of *discutere* to discuss < *dis-* apart + *quatere* to shake] **— dis·cuss′er** *n.* **— dis·cus′si·ble** *adj.*

dis·cus·sion (dis-kush′ən) *n.* The act of discussing; examination or consideration of a subject in speech or writing.

dis·dain (dis-dān′) *v.t.* 1. To consider unworthy of one's regard or notice: to *disdain* a coward. 2. To refuse scornfully: to *disdain* to beg for food. **—** *n.* A feeling or attitude of superiority and dislike. [< OF < L < *dis-* away + *dignare* to deign] **— dis·dain′ful** *adj.* **— dis·dain′ful·ly** *adv.* **— dis·dain′ful·ness** *n.*

dis·ease (di-zēz′) *n.* 1. A condition of ill health or malfunctioning in a living organism, esp. one having particular symptoms. 2. Any disordered or unwholesome condition. **—** *v.t.* **eased, eas·ing** To cause disease in; make unhealthy; corrupt. [< AF *desaise.* See EASE.] **— dis·eased′** *adj.*

dis·em·bark (dis′em-bärk′) *v.t. & v.i.* To put or go ashore from a ship; land; unload. **— dis·em·bar·ka′tion** *n.*

dis·em·bar·rass (dis′em-bar′əs) *v.t.* To free from embarrassment, entanglement, etc. **— dis′em·bar′rass·ment** *n.*

dis·em·bod·y (dis′em-bod′ē) *v.t.* **·bod·ied, ·bod·y·ing** To free from the body or from physical existence: a *disembodied* spirit. **— dis′em·bod′i·ment** *n.*

dis·em·bow·el (dis′em-bou′əl, -boul′) *v.t.* **·bow·eled** or **·elled, ·bow·el·ing** or **·el·ling** To take out the bowels or entrails of; eviscerate. **— dis′em·bow′el·ment** *n.*

dis·en·chant (dis′en-chant′, -chänt′) *v.t.* To free from enchantment; disillusion. **— dis′en·chant′er** *n.* **— dis′en·chant′ment** *n.*

dis·en·cum·ber (dis′en-kum′bər) *v.t.* To free from encumbrance.

dis·en·fran·chise (dis′en-fran′chīz) *v.t.* **·chised, ·chis·ing** To disfranchise. **— dis′en·fran′chise·ment** (-chiz-mənt, -chīz-) *n.*

dis·en·gage (dis′en-gāj′) *v.* **·gaged, ·gag·ing** *v.t.* 1. To free from entanglement, obligation, occupation, etc.; set free. **—** *v.i.* 2. To free oneself; get loose. **— dis′en·gage′ment** *n.*

dis·en·tan·gle (dis′en-tang′gəl) *v.* **·gled, ·gling** *v.t.* 1. To free or relieve of entanglement, confusion, etc. **—** *v.i.* 2. To become disentangled. **— dis′en·tan′gle·ment** *n.*

dis·en·twine (dis′en-twīn′) *v.t. & v.i.* **·twined, ·twin·ing** To untwine; disentangle.

dis·es·tab·lish (dis′es-tab′lish) *v.t.* 1. To deprive of fixed or established status or character. 2. To take away government support from (a state church). **— dis′es·tab′lish·ment** *n.*

dis·es·teem (dis′es-tēm′) *v.t.* To regard with little esteem; have a low opinion of. **—** *n.* Lack of esteem.

di·seuse (dē-zœz′) *n. French* A woman entertainer who performs dramatic impersonations, monologues, etc.

dis·fa·vor (dis-fā′vər) *n.* 1. Lack of favor; disapproval; dislike. 2. The state of being frowned upon or disliked. **—** *v.t.* To treat or regard disapprovingly. Also *Brit.* **dis·fa′vour.**

dis·fig·ure (dis-fig′yər) *v.t.* **·ured, ·ur·ing** To mar or destroy the appearance or form of; make unsightly; deform. **— dis·fig′ur·er** *n.* **— dis·fig′ure·ment** *n.*

dis·fran·chise (dis-fran′chīz) *v.t.* **·chised, ·chis·ing** 1. To deprive (a citizen) of a right or privilege, esp. of the ballot. 2. To deprive of a franchise, privilege, or right, as a corporation. Also *disenfranchise.* **— dis·fran′chise·ment** (-chiz·mənt, -chīz-) *n.* **— dis·fran′chis·er** *n.*

dis·gorge (dis-gôrj′) *v.t.* **·gorged, ·gorg·ing** 1. To throw out, as from the throat or stomach; eject; vomit. 2. To give up unwillingly. **—** *v.i.* 3. To disgorge something. [< OF < *des-* from + *gorge* throat]

dis·grace (dis-grās′) *n.* 1. A condition of shame, dishonor, or infamy; ignominy. 2. Anything that brings about dishonor or shame. 3. A state of being out of favor: in *disgrace* at court. **—** *v.t.* **·graced, ·grac·ing** 1. To bring reproach or shame upon. 2. To treat with dishonor. [< MF < Ital. < *dis-* away + *grazia* favor] **— dis·grac′er** *n.*

dis·grace·ful (dis-grās′fəl) *adj.* Characterized by or causing disgrace; shameful; disreputable. **— dis·grace′ful·ly** *adv.* **— dis·grace′ful·ness** *n.*

dis·grun·tle (dis-grun′təl) *v.t.* **·tled, ·tling** To make dissatisfied or sulky; put out of humor.

dis·guise (dis-gīz′) *v.t.* **·guised, ·guis·ing** 1. To alter the appearance of so as to make unrecognizable. 2. To conceal the actual nature of: to *disguise* the facts. **—** *n.* 1. The act of disguising or the state of being disguised. 2. Something

that disguises, as a mask or costume. [< OF < *des-* down + *guise.* See GUISE.] **— dis·guis′er** *n.*

dis·gust (dis-gust′) *v.t.* 1. To affect with nausea or loathing. 2. To offend the sensibilities, moral values, or good taste of; sicken. **—** *n.* Strong aversion aroused by something offensive. [< MF < *des-* not + *gouster* to taste] **— dis·gust′ed** *adj.* **— dis·gust′ed·ly** *adv.*

dis·gust·ing (dis-gus′ting) *adj.* Provoking disgust; repugnant; revolting; offensive. **— dis·gust′ing·ly** *adv.*

dish (dish) *n.* 1. An open, concave, usu. shallow container, as of china or glass, typically used for holding or serving food. 2. A particular kind or preparation of food: a delicious *dish.* 3. A dishful. 4. A hollow or depression like that in a dish. **—** *v.t.* 1. To put (food, etc.) into a dish; serve: usu. with *up* or *out.* 2. To hollow out (a surface). **— to dish it out** *Slang* 1. To administer severe punishment or reproof. 2. To talk glibly. [OE < L *discus* disk] **— dish′like′** *adj.*

dis·ha·bille (dis′ə-bēl′) *n.* 1. A state of being partially or negligently dressed. 2. The garments worn in this state. Also *deshabille.* [< F < *des-* away + *habiller* to dress]

dis·har·mo·ny (dis-här′mə-nē) *n. pl.* **·nies** Lack of harmony or agreement; discord. **— dis′har·mo′ni·ous** *adj.* **— dis′har·mo′ni·ous·ly** *adv.*

dish·cloth (dish′klôth′, -kloth′) *n.* A cloth used in washing dishes: also called *dishrag.*

dis·heart·en (dis-här′tən) *v.t.* To discourage. **— dis·heart′en·ing·ly** *adv.* **— dis·heart′en·ment** *n.*

di·shev·el (di-shev′əl) *v.t.* **di·shev·eled** or **·elled, di·shev·el·ing** or **·el·ling** 1. To muss up, disarrange, or rumple (the hair or clothing). 2. To disorder the hair or clothing of. [< MF < *des-* away + *chevel* hair] **— di·shev′el·ment** *n.*

di·shev·eled (di-shev′əld) *adj.* 1. Tousled or rumpled. 2. Untidy; unkempt. Also **di·shev′elled.**

dish·ful (dish′fŏŏl′) *n.* As much as a dish holds.

dis·hon·est (dis-on′ist) *adj.* 1. Not honest; not trustworthy. 2. Marked by a lack of honesty. [< OF < LL *dis-* away + *honestus* honest] **— dis·hon′est·ly** *adv.*

dis·hon·es·ty (dis-on′is-tē) *n. pl.* **·ties** 1. Lack of honesty or integrity. 2. A dishonest act or statement.

dis·hon·or (dis-on′ər) *v.t.* 1. To deprive of honor; disgrace; insult. 2. To decline or fail to pay, as a note. **—** *n.* 1. Lack or loss of honor or of honorable character. 2. An insult, indignity, taint, etc. 3. Refusal or failure to pay a note, etc., when due. Also *Brit.* **dis·hon′our. — dis·hon′or·er** *n.*

dis·hon·or·a·ble (dis-on′ər-ə-bəl) *adj.* 1. Characterized by or bringing dishonor; discreditable: a *dishonorable* act. 2. Lacking honor or honorableness: a *dishonorable* lawyer. **— dis·hon′or·a·ble·ness** *n.* **— dis·hon′or·a·bly** *adv.*

dish·rag (dish′rag′) *n.* A dishcloth.

dis·il·lu·sion (dis′i-loo′zhən) *v.t.* To free from illusion; disenchant. **—** *n.* The state or process of being disillusioned; also **dis′il·lu′sion·ment.**

dis·in·cli·na·tion (dis-in′klə-nā′shən) *n.* Distaste; aversion; unwillingness.

dis·in·cline (dis′in-klīn′) *v.t. & v.i.* **·clined, ·clin·ing** To make or be unwilling or averse.

dis·in·fect (dis′in-fekt′) *v.t.* To cleanse of disease germs; sterilize. **— dis′in·fec′tion** *n.* **— dis′in·fec′tor** *n.*

dis·in·fec·tant (dis′in-fek′tənt) *n.* A substance or agent used to disinfect. **—** *adj.* Capable of disinfecting.

dis·in·gen·u·ous (dis′in-jen′yŏŏ-əs) *adj.* Lacking simplicity, frankness, or sincerity; not straightforward; crafty. **— dis′in·gen′u·ous·ly** *adv.* **— dis′in·gen′u·ous·ness** *n.*

dis·in·her·it (dis′in-her′it) *v.t.* To deprive of an inheritance. **— dis′in·her′i·tance** *n.*

dis·in·te·grate (dis-in′tə-grāt) *v.* **·grat·ed, ·grat·ing** *v.t.* 1. To break or reduce into component parts or particles; destroy the wholeness of. **—** *v.i.* 2. To become reduced to fragments or particles; crumble. **— dis·in′te·gra·ble** (-grə-bəl) *adj.* **— dis·in′te·gra′tion** *n.* **— dis·in′te·gra′tor** *n.*

dis·in·ter (dis′in-tûr′) *v.t.* **·terred, ·ter·ring** 1. To dig up, as from a grave; exhume. 2. To bring to light or life as if from a grave. **— dis′in·ter′ment** *n.*

dis·in·ter·est (dis-in′tər·ist, -trist) *n.* 1. Freedom from self-seeking and personal bias; impartiality. 2. Loosely, lack of interest; indifference. **— dis·in′ter·est·ed** *adj.* **— dis·in′ter·est·ed·ly** *adv.* **— dis·in′ter·est·ed·ness** *n.*

dis·join (dis-join′) *v.t.* 1. To undo or prevent the joining of; separate. **—** *v.i.* 2. To become divided or separated.

dis·joint (dis-joint′) *v.t.* 1. To take apart at the joints; dismember. 2. To put out of joint; dislocate. 3. To separate forcibly; disunite. 4. To upset or destroy the coherence, connection, or sequence of. **—** *v.i.* 5. To come apart at the joints; fall apart. 6. To get out of joint. **— dis·joint′ed** *adj.* **— dis·joint′ed·ly** *adv.* **— dis·joint′ed·ness** *n.*

dis·junct (dis-jungkt′) *adj.* Not connected; detached. [< L < *dis-* not + *jungere* to join] **— dis·junc′tion** *n.*

dis·junc·tive (dis-jungk′tiv) *adj.* 1. Serving to disconnect or separate; dividing. **2.** *Gram.* Indicating alternation or opposition, as *either* or *or* in *either you or I.* **3.** *Logic* Involving choice between two or more predicates in a proposition. — **n. 1.** *Gram.* A disjunctive conjunction. **2.** *Logic* A disjunctive proposition. — **dis·junc′tive·ly** *adv.*

disk (disk) *n.* **1.** A fairly flat, circular plate. **2.** *Biol.* A disc. **3.** A phonograph record. **4.** A discus. — *v.t. & v.i.* To break up or plow (land) with a disk harrow. Also, *esp. Brit., disc.* [< L *discus* < Gk. *diskos* disk, platter]

disk harrow A harrow consisting of a series of rolling saucer-shaped disks set on edge and at an angle along one or more axles, used for pulverizing the soil, covering seeds, etc.

DISK HARROW

disk jockey *U.S. Informal* An announcer and commentator on a radio program presenting recorded music.

dis·like (dis·līk′) *v.t.* **·liked, ·lik·ing** To regard with aversion; feel repugnance for; consider disagreeable. — *n.* A feeling of repugnance or distaste. — **dis·lik′a·ble** *adj.*

dis·lo·cate (dis′lō·kāt, dis·lō′kāt) *v.t.* **·cat·ed, ·cat·ing 1.** To put out of proper place or order. **2.** *Med.* To displace an organ or part, esp. a bone from a joint. — **dis′lo·ca′tion** *n.*

dis·lodge (dis·loj′) *v.* **·lodged, ·lodg·ing** *v.t.* **1.** To remove or drive out, as from an abode, hiding place, or firm position. — *v.i.* **2.** To leave a place of abode; move. — **dis·lodg′ment,** or **dis·lodge′ment** *n.*

dis·loy·al (dis·loi′əl) *adj.* Not loyal; false to one's allegiance or obligations; faithless. — **dis·loy′al·ly** *adv.*

dis·loy·al·ty (dis·loi′əl·tē) *n. pl.* **·ties 1.** The quality of being disloyal; unfaithfulness. **2.** A disloyal action.

dis·mal (diz′məl) *adj.* **1.** Cheerless and depressing; dark and gloomy: a *dismal* day. **2.** Devoid of joy; bleak: to feel *dismal.* [ult. < L *dies mali* evil or unpropitious days] — **dis′mal·ly** *adv.* — **dis′mal·ness** *n.*

dis·man·tle (dis·man′təl) *v.t.* **·tled, ·tling 1.** To strip of furniture or equipment. **2.** To raze. **3.** To take apart. [< MF < *des-* away + *manteller* to cover with a cloak] — **dis·man′tle·ment** *n.*

dis·may (dis·mā′) *v.t.* To fill with consternation or apprehension; dishearten and depress. — *n.* An onrush of consternation or downheartedness. [ME *dismayen*]

dis·mem·ber (dis·mem′bər) *v.t.* **1.** To cut off or pull off the limbs or members of; tear asunder. **2.** To divide forcibly into pieces; mangle. [< OF < L *dis-* apart + *membrum* limb, member] — **dis·mem′ber·ment** *n.*

dis·miss (dis·mis′) *v.t.* **1.** To discharge, as from a job. **2.** To tell or allow to go or disperse. **3.** To get rid of: to *dismiss* all fear. **4.** To have done with quickly: He *dismissed* the matter in a few words. **5.** *Law* To put out of court without further hearing. [< LL < L *dimissus,* pp. of *dimittere* to send away] — **dis·miss′al** *n.* — **dis·miss′i·ble** *adj.*

dis·mount (dis·mount′) *v.i.* **1.** To get off, as from a horse; alight. — *v.t.* **2.** To remove from a setting, support, etc. **3.** To disassemble. **4.** To knock off or throw down, as from a horse; unseat. — **dis·mount′a·ble** *adj.*

dis·o·be·di·ence (dis′ə·bē′dē·əns) *n.* Refusal or failure to obey; lack of obedience; insubordination. — **dis′o·be′di·ent** *adj.* — **dis′o·be′di·ent·ly** *adv.*

dis·o·bey (dis′ə·bā′) *v.t. & v.i.* To refuse or fail to obey. — **dis′o·bey′er** *n.*

dis·o·blige (dis′ə·blīj′) *v.t.* **·bliged, ·blig·ing 1.** To act contrary to the wishes of. **2.** To slight; affront. — **dis′o·blig′ing** *adj.* — **dis′o·blig′ing·ly** *adv.*

dis·or·der (dis·ôr′dər) *n.* **1.** Lack of good order; disarrangement or confusion. **2.** Disturbance of proper civic order; tumult; riot. **3.** A sickness; ailment. **4.** An act, occurrence, or condition marked by disorder. — *v.t.* **1.** To put out of order; throw into disorder; disarrange. **2.** To disturb or upset the normal health or functions of. — **dis·or′dered** *adj.*

dis·or·der·ly (dis·ôr′dər·lē) *adj.* **1.** Devoid of good order or arrangement; full of disorder. **2.** Devoid of method; unsystematic. **3.** Undisciplined and unruly; tumultuous: a *disorderly* mob. **4.** Violating public order or decency. — *adv.* In a disorderly manner. — **dis·or′der·li·ness** *n.*

dis·or·gan·ize (dis·ôr′gən·īz) *v.t.* **·ized, ·iz·ing 1.** To destroy the organization of; break up the systematic arrangement or unity of. **2.** To throw into confusion; disorder. — **dis·or′gan·i·za′tion** *n.* — **dis·or′gan·iz′er** *n.*

dis·o·ri·ent (dis·ôr′ē·ent′, -ō′rē-) *v.t.* To mix up; confuse; esp., to cause to lose one's sense of direction, perspective, or time. — **dis·o′ri·en·ta′tion** *n.*

dis·own (dis·ōn′) *v.t.* To refuse to acknowledge or to admit responsibility for or connection with; deny; repudiate.

dis·par·age (dis·par′ij) *v.t.* **·aged, ·ag·ing 1.** To treat or speak of with disrespect or contempt; belittle. **2.** To bring discredit upon; cause to have less esteem. [< OF < *des-* down, away + *parage* equality of rank] — **dis·par′age·ment** *n.* — **dis·par′ag·er** *n.* — **dis·par′ag·ing·ly** *adv.*

dis·pa·rate (dis′pər·it) *adj.* Essentially different; altogether

dissimilar. [< L < *dis-* apart + *parare* to make ready] — **dis′pa·rate·ly** *adv.* — **dis′pa·rate·ness** *n.*

dis·par·i·ty (dis·par′ə·tē) *n. pl.* **·ties 1.** Lack of equality, as in age or rank. **2.** Dissimilarity. **3.** An instance of inequality. [< MF < L *dis-* apart + *paritas* equality]

dis·pas·sion (dis·pash′ən) *n.* Freedom from passion or bias.

dis·pas·sion·ate (dis·pash′ən·it) *adj.* Free from passion or bias. — **dis·pas′sion·ate·ly** *adv.* — **dis·pas′sion·ate·ness** *n.*

dis·patch (dis·pach′) *v.t.* **1.** To send off, as a messenger, telegram, or vehicle, to a particular destination. **2.** To dispose of quickly, as a business matter. **3.** To kill summarily. — *n.* **1.** The act of dispatching. **2.** Efficient quickness; promptness: to finish a job with *dispatch.* **3.** A message, usu. in writing, sent with speed; esp., an official communication, as a military report. **4.** A news story sent to a newspaper. [< Ital. *dispacciare* or Sp. *despachar*]

dis·patch·er (dis·pach′ər) *n.* **1.** One who dispatches. **2.** One who sends out trains, buses, etc., on schedule.

dis·pel (dis·pel′) *v.t.* **·pelled, ·pel·ling** To drive away by or as by scattering; disperse: to *dispel* fear, rumors, etc. [< L < *dis-* away, apart + *pellere* to drive]

dis·pen·sa·ble (dis·pen′sə·bəl) *adj.* **1.** That can be relinquished or dispensed with. **2.** That can be removed by dispensation. — **dis·pen′sa·bil′i·ty, dis·pen′sa·ble·ness** *n.*

dis·pen·sa·ry (dis·pen′sər·ē) *n. pl.* **·ries** A place where medicines and medical advice are given out.

dis·pen·sa·tion (dis′pən·sā′shən) *n.* **1.** The act of dispensing; a dealing out; distribution. **2.** That which is dispensed or distributed. **3.** A specific plan, order, or system of dispensing or administering. **4.** A special exemption from something, as from a law or obligation; esp., an exemption by ecclesiastical authority from an obligation or from church law. **5.** *Theol.* **a** The arrangement or ordering of events, as by a divine Providence. **b** A religious or moral system: the Mosaic *dispensation.* — **dis′pen·sa′tion·al** *adj.*

dis·pen·sa·to·ry (dis·pen′sə·tôr′ē, -tō′rē) *adj.* Of or pertaining to dispensation. — *n. pl.* **·ries** A book in which medicinal substances are described; a pharmacopoeia.

dis·pense (dis·pens′) *v.* **·pensed, ·pens·ing** *v.t.* **1.** To give or deal out in portions: to *dispense* patronage. **2.** To compound and give out (medicines). **3.** To administer, as laws. **4.** To excuse or exempt, as from an obligation, esp., a religious obligation. — *v.i.* **5.** To grant dispensation. — **to dispense with 1.** To get along without. **2.** To dispose of. [< OF < L < *dis-* away + *pendere* to weigh]

dis·pens·er (dis·pen′sər) *n.* One who or that which dispenses, manages, or administers: a soap *dispenser.*

dis·perse (dis·pûrs′) *v.* **·persed, ·pers·ing** *v.t.* **1.** To cause to scatter in various directions. **2.** To drive away; dispel: The sun *dispersed* the mists. **3.** To spread abroad; diffuse. **4.** To separate (light) into a spectrum. — *v.i.* **5.** To scatter in various directions. [< MF < L < *dis-* away + *spargere* to scatter] — **dis·per′sal** *n.* — **dis·pers′ed·ly** *adv.* — **dis·pers′er** *n.* — **dis·pers′i·ble** *adj.*

dis·per·sion (dis·pûr′zhən, -shən) *n.* **1.** The act of dispersing, or the state of being dispersed. **2.** *Mil.* The pattern of hits made, as by bombs. **3.** *Physics* The separation of white or complex light into different colors by passing it through a prism. **4.** *Stat.* The arrangement of a series of values around the median or mean of a distribution.

dis·per·sive (dis·pûr′siv) *adj.* Tending to disperse.

dis·pir·it (dis·pir′it) *v.t.* To make downhearted or depressed. — **dis·pir′it·ed** *adj.* — **dis·pir′it·ed·ly** *adv.*

dis·place (dis·plās′) *v.t.* **·placed, ·plac·ing 1.** To remove or shift from the usual or proper place. **2.** To take the place of; supplant. **3.** To remove from a position or office; discharge. [< OF < *des-* away (< L *dis-*) + *placer* to place]

displaced person A person made homeless by war and forced to live in a foreign country.

dis·place·ment (dis·plās′mənt) *n.* **1.** The act of displacing, or the state of being displaced. **2.** *Astron.* An apparent change of position, as of a star. **3.** *Physics* The weight of a fluid displaced by a floating body, being equal to the weight of the body.

dis·play (dis·plā′) *v.t.* **1.** To make evident or noticeable; reveal: to *display* ignorance. **2.** To expose to the sight; exhibit. **3.** To make a prominent or ostentatious show of. **4.** *Printing* To make (printed matter) stand out prominently, as by the use of large type or wide spacing. — *n.* **1.** The act of displaying; exhibition. **2.** That which is displayed. **3.** Ostentatious show. **4.** *Printing* A style or arrangement of type designed to make printed matter stand out prominently. [< OF < LL < *dis-* apart + *plicare* to fold, add]

dis·please (dis·plēz′) *v.* **·pleased, ·pleas·ing** *v.t.* **1.** To cause displeasure in or annoyance to; vex; offend. — *v.i.* **2.** To cause displeasure or annoyance. [< OF, ult. < L < *dis-* not + *placere* to please] — **dis·pleas′ing·ly** *adv.*

dis·pleas·ure (dis·plezh′ər) *n.* The state of being displeased.

dis·port (dis·pôrt′, -pōrt′) *v.t.* **1.** To divert or amuse (oneself). — *v.i.* **2.** To frisk about playfully. — *n.* Diversion; sport. [< OF < L *dis-* away + *portare* to carry]

dis·pos·a·ble (dis·pō′zə·bəl) *adj.* **1.** Capable of being disposed of; esp., designed to be discarded after use. **2.** Free to be used as occasion may require: *disposable* funds.

dis·po·sal (dis·pō′zəl) *n.* **1.** A particular ordering or arrangement; disposition. **2.** A particular way of attending to or settling something, as business affairs. **3.** Transfer, as by gift or sale. **4.** A getting rid of something. **5.** Liberty to deal with or dispose of in any way.

dis·pose (dis·pōz′) *v.* **·posed, ·pos·ing** *v.t.* **1.** To put into a receptive frame of mind for. **2.** To condition toward something; esp., to make susceptible. **3.** To put or set in a particular arrangement or position. **4.** To put into proper, definitive, or final shape; settle. —*v.i.* **5.** To control the course of events. — **to dispose of 1.** To attend to; deal with. **2.** To finish up with; settle. **3.** To transfer to another, as by gift or sale. **4.** To throw away. [< OF < *dis-* apart + *poser* to place] — **dis·pos′er** *n.*

dis·posed (dis·pōzd′) *adj.* Having a particular inclination, frame of mind, or mood: *disposed* to take offense.

dis·po·si·tion (dis′pə·zish′ən) *n.* **1.** One's usual frame of mind; temperament. **2.** Acquired tendency or inclination, esp. when habitual: a *disposition* to drink. **3.** Natural organic tendency or inclination. **4.** A particular ordering, arrangement, or distribution, as of troops. **5.** Management, as of business affairs. **6.** Transfer, as by gift or sale. **7.** A getting rid of something, as by throwing away. **8.** Liberty to deal with or dispose of in any way.

dis·pos·sess (dis′pə·zes′) *v.t.* To deprive of possession of something, as a house or land; oust. — **dis′pos·ses′sion** (-zesh′ən) *n.* — **dis′pos·ses′sor** *n.*

dis·praise (dis·prāz′) *v.t.* **·praised, ·prais·ing** To express disapproval of; disparage. —*n.* Disparagement; censure. — **dis·prais′er** *n.* — **dis·prais′ing·ly** *adv.*

dis·proof (dis·prōōf′) *n.* **1.** The act of disproving. **2.** Something that disproves, as evidence.

dis·pro·por·tion (dis′prə·pôr′shən, -pōr′-) *n.* **1.** Lack of proportion or symmetry; disparity. **2.** An instance of this. —*v.t.* To make disproportionate. — **dis′pro·por′tion·al** *adj.* — **dis′pro·por′tion·al·ly** *adv.*

dis·pro·por·tion·ate (dis′prə·pôr′shən·it, -pōr′-) *adj.* Out of proportion, as in size, form, or value. — **dis′pro·por′tion·ate·ly** *adv.* — **dis′pro·por′tion·ate·ness** *n.*

dis·prove (dis·prōōv′) *v.t.* **·proved, ·proved** or **·prov·en, ·prov·ing** To prove to be false, invalid, or erroneous. — **Syn.** See REFUTE. [< OF < *des-* not + *prouver* to prove] — **dis·prov′a·ble** *adj.* — **dis·prov′al** *n.*

dis·put·a·ble (dis·pyōō′tə·bəl, dis·pyōō′tə·bəl) *adj.* Open to being disputed or called into question; arguable; debatable. — **dis·put′a·bil′i·ty** *n.* — **dis·put′a·bly** *adv.*

dis·pu·tant (dis′pyōō·tənt, dis·pyōō′tənt) *adj.* Engaged in controversy; disputing. —*n.* One who disputes; a debater.

dis·pu·ta·tion (dis′pyōō·tā′shən) *n.* **1.** The act of disputing; argumentation; controversy. **2.** A formal debate; esp., formal argumentation in philosophy or theology.

dis·pu·ta·tious (dis′pyōō·tā′shəs) *adj.* Given to disputing; argumentative. Also **dis·pu·ta·tive** (dis·pyōō′tə·tiv). — **dis′pu·ta′tious·ly** *adv.* — **dis′pu·ta′tious·ness** *n.*

dis·pute (dis·pyōōt′) *v.* **·put·ed, ·put·ing** *v.t.* **1.** To argue about. **2.** To question the validity, genuineness, etc., of. **3.** To strive or contest for, as a prize. **4.** To resist; oppose. —*v.i.* **5.** To argue. **6.** To quarrel. —*n.* **1.** A discussion; debate. **2.** A quarrel. [< OF < L < *dis-* away + *putare* to think] — **dis·put′er** *n.*

dis·qual·i·fy (dis·kwol′ə·fī) *v.t.* **·fied, ·fy·ing 1.** To make unqualified or unfit; incapacitate. **2.** To pronounce unqualified or ineligible. **3.** In sports, to bar from competition because of rule infractions, etc. — **dis·qual′i·fi·ca′tion** *n.*

dis·qui·et (dis·kwī′ət) *n.* An unsettled or disturbed condition. —*v.t.* To make anxious or uneasy. — **dis·qui′et·ly** *adv.*

dis·qui·e·tude (dis·kwī′ə·tōōd, -tyōōd) *n.* Uneasiness.

dis·qui·si·tion (dis′kwi·zish′ən) *n.* A formal treatise or discourse. [< L < *dis-* thoroughly + *quaerere* to seek]

dis·re·gard (dis′ri·gärd′) *v.t.* **1.** To pay no attention to; ignore. **2.** To treat as undeserving of consideration. —*n.* Lack of notice or due regard, esp. when deliberate. — **dis′·re·gard′ful** *adj.*

dis·re·pair (dis′ri·pâr′) *n.* The state of being out of repair.

dis·rep·u·ta·ble (dis·rep′yə·tə·bəl) *adj.* **1.** Not in good repute; not esteemed. **2.** Not respectable: a *disreputable* tavern. — **dis·rep′u·ta·ble·ness** *n.* — **dis·rep′u·ta·bly** *adv.*

dis·re·spect (dis′ri·spekt′) *n.* Lack of courtesy or respect. —*v.t.* To treat without respect. — **dis′re·spect′ful** *adj.* — **dis′re·spect′ful·ly** *adv.* — **dis′re·spect′ful·ness** *n.*

dis·robe (dis·rōb′) *v.t. & v.i.* **·robed, ·rob·ing** To undress.

dis·rupt (dis·rupt′) *v.t.* **1.** To throw into disorder; upset. **2.** To halt or impede the movement of, procedure of, etc. **3.** To break or burst apart. —*v.i.* **4.** To break; burst. [< L < *dis-* apart + *rumpere* to burst] — **dis·rupt′er** or **dis·rup′·**

tor *n.* — **dis·rup′tion** *n.* — **dis·rup′tive** *adj.* — **dis·rup′·tive·ly** *adv.*

dis·sat·is·fac·tion (dis′sat·is·fak′shən) *n.* **1.** A dissatisfied state or feeling; discontent. **2.** That which dissatisfies.

dis·sat·is·fac·to·ry (dis′sat·is·fak′tər·ē) *adj.* Causing dissatisfaction; unsatisfactory.

dis·sat·is·fy (dis·sat′is·fī) *v.t.* **·fied, ·fy·ing** To fail to satisfy; disappoint; displease. — **dis·sat′is·fied** *adj.*

dis·sect (di·sekt′, dī-) *v.t.* **1.** To cut apart or divide, as an animal body or a plant, in order to examine the structure; anatomize. **2.** To analyze in detail. [< L < *dis-* apart + *secare* to cut] — **dis·sec′tion** *n.* — **dis·sec′tor** *n.*

dis·sect·ed (di·sek′tid, dī-) *adj.* **1.** Cut in pieces; separated at the joints. **2.** *Geol.* Cut into ridges, as a plateau. **3.** *Bot.* Deeply cut into lobes or segments, as a leaf.

dis·sem·blance (di·sem′bləns) *n.* **1.** The act of dissembling; dissimulation. **2.** Lack of resemblance; dissimilarity.

dis·sem·ble (di·sem′bəl) *v.* **·bled, ·bling** *v.t.* **1.** To conceal or disguise the actual nature of (intentions, feelings, etc.). **2.** To make a false show of; feign. —*v.i.* **3.** To conceal one's true nature, intentions, etc.; act hypocritically. [Var. of earlier *dissimule* < OF < L < *dis-* apart + *similis* alike] — **dis·sem′bler** *n.* — **dis·sem′bling·ly** *adv.*

dis·sem·i·nate (di·sem′ə·nāt) *v.t.* **·nat·ed, ·nat·ing** To scatter, as if sowing: to *disseminate* knowledge. [< L < *dis-* away + *seminare* to sow] — **dis·sem′i·na′tion** *n.* — **dis·sem′i·na·tive** *adj.* — **dis·sem′i·na′tor** *n.*

dis·sen·sion (di·sen′shən) *n.* **1.** Difference of opinion, esp. arising from dissatisfaction or anger; discord; strife. **2.** A heated quarrel or disagreement.

dis·sent (di·sent′) *v.i.* **1.** To differ in thought or opinion: with *from.* **2.** To withhold approval or consent. **3.** To refuse adherence to an established church. —*n.* **1.** Difference of opinion. **2.** Refusal to conform to an established church. [< L < *dis-* apart + *sentire* to think, feel]

dis·sent·er (di·sen′tər) *n.* One who dissents or disagrees.

dis·sen·tient (di·sen′shənt) *adj.* Dissenting. —*n.* A dissenter. — **dis·sen′tience** *n.*

dis·sent·ing (di·sen′ting) *adj.* Expressing disagreement: a *dissenting* opinion. — **dis·sent′ing·ly** *adv.*

dis·sen·tious (di·sen′shəs) *adj.* Quarrelsome; disputatious.

dis·ser·ta·tion (dis′ər·tā′shən) *n.* An extended formal treatise or discourse; esp., a written treatise required of a doctoral candidate. [< L < *dis-* apart + *serere* to join]

dis·serve (dis·sûrv′) *v.t.* **·served, ·serv·ing** To serve poorly or treat badly; do an ill turn to.

dis·ser·vice (dis·sûr′vis) *n.* Ill service; an ill turn; injury.

dis·sev·er (di·sev′ər) *v.t.* **1.** To divide; separate. **2.** To separate into parts. —*v.i.* **3.** To become separated. — **dis·sev′er·ance, dis·sev′er·ment** *n.*

dis·si·dent (dis′ə·dənt) *adj.* Dissenting; differing. —*n.* A dissenter. [< L < *dis-* apart + *sedere* to sit] — **dis′si·dence** *n.*

dis·sim·i·lar (di·sim′ə·lər) *adj.* Not similar; unlike; different: sometimes with *to.* — **dis·sim′i·lar·ly** *adv.*

dis·sim·i·lar·i·ty (di·sim′ə·lar′ə·tē) *n. pl.* **·ties 1.** Lack of similarity; unlikeness; difference. **2.** An example of this.

dis·sim·i·late (di·sim′ə·lāt) *v.t. & v.i.* **·lat·ed, ·lat·ing 1.** To make or become unlike. **2.** *Phonet.* To undergo or cause to undergo dissimilation. [< DIS-¹ + L *similis* alike]

dis·sim·i·la·tion (di·sim′ə·lā′shən) *n.* **1.** The act or process of making or becoming dissimilar. **2.** *Phonet.* The process whereby one of two or more similar sounds in a word is omitted, as in the pronunciation (lī′bər·ē) for *library*, or replaced by another sound, as *turtle* from Latin *turtur.*

dis·si·mil·i·tude (dis′si·mil′ə·tōōd, tyōōd) *n.* **1.** Lack of resemblance; unlikeness. **2.** An instance of this.

dis·sim·u·late (di·sim′yə·lāt) *v.t. & v.i.* **·lat·ed, ·lat·ing** To conceal (intentions, feelings, etc.) by pretense. — **dis·sim′u·la′tion** *n.* — **dis·sim′u·la′tive** *adj.* — **dis·sim′u·la′tor** *n.*

dis·si·pate (dis′ə·pāt) *v.* **·pat·ed, ·pat·ing** *v.t.* **1.** To disperse or drive away; dispel. **2.** To squander. —*v.i.* **3.** To become dispersed. **4.** To engage in excessive or dissolute pleasures. [< L < *dis-* away + *supare* to scatter] — **dis′si·pat′er** or **dis′si·pa′tor** *n.* — **dis′si·pa′tive** *adj.*

dis·si·pat·ed (dis′ə·pā′tid) *adj.* **1.** Wasted; scattered. **2.** Pursuing pleasure to excess; dissolute. — **dis′si·pat′ed·ly** *adv.* — **dis′si·pat′ed·ness** *n.*

dis·si·pa·tion (dis′ə·pā′shən) *n.* **1.** The act of dissipating, or the state of being dissipated; dispersion; scattering. **2.** Excessive indulgence, esp. in dissolute pleasures. **3.** Distraction or diversion, as of the mind.

dis·so·ci·ate (di·sō′shē·āt, -sē-) *v.* **·at·ed, ·at·ing** *v.t.* **1.** To break the association of; disconnect; separate. **2.** To regard as separate in concept or nature. **3.** To subject to dissociation. —*v.i.* **4.** To break an association. **5.** To undergo dissociation. Also *disassociate.* [< L < *dis-* apart + *sociare* to join together] — **dis·so′ci·a′tive** *adj.*

dis·so·ci·a·tion (di·sō'sē·ā'shən, -shē·ā'-) *n.* **1.** The act of dissociating, or the state of being dissociated. **2.** *Chem.* a The resolution of a compound into simpler constituents by a change in physical state, as by heat or pressure.

dis·sol·u·ble (di·sol'yə·bəl) *adj.* Capable of being dissolved or decomposed. — **dis·sol·u·bil'i·ty, dis·sol'u·ble·ness** *n.*

dis·so·lute (dis'ə·lōōt) *adj.* Not governed by moral restraints. — **dis'so·lute·ly** *adv.* — **dis'so·lute·ness** *n.*

dis·so·lu·tion (dis'ə·lōō'shən) *n.* **1.** Separation into parts; disintegration. **2.** Change from a solid to a fluid form; liquefaction. **3.** The breaking up or liquidation of a formal or legal union, bond, or tie. **4.** Dismissal of a meeting or assembly. **5.** Termination or destruction. **6.** Separation of soul and body; death. — **dis'so·lu'tive** *adj.*

dis·solve (di·zolv') *v.* **·solved, ·solv·ing** *v.t.* **1.** To cause to pass into solution. **2.** To overcome, as by emotion. **3.** To disintegrate. **4.** To put an end to: to *dissolve* a partnership. **5.** To dismiss (a meeting or assembly). — *v.i.* **6.** To pass into solution. **7.** To be overcome: to *dissolve* in tears. **8.** To come to an end; break up. **9.** To dwindle or fade away. **10.** In motion pictures and television, to change gradually from one scene to another by overlapping two shots. — *n.* A lap dissolve. [< L < *dis-* apart + *solvere* to loosen] — **dis·solv'a·ble** *adj.* — **dis·solv'er** *n.*

dis·so·nance (dis'ə·nəns) *n.* **1.** A discordant mingling of sounds; discord. **2.** Harsh disagreement; incongruity. **3.** *Music* A simultaneous combination of tones that seem to clash and require resolution. Also **dis'so·nan·cy.**

dis·so·nant (dis'ə·nənt) *adj.* **1.** Harsh in sound; inharmonious. **2.** Naturally hostile; incongruous. **3.** *Music* Consisting of or containing a dissonance. [< L < *dis-* away + *sonare* to sound] — **dis'so·nant·ly** *adv.*

dis·suade (di·swād') *v.t.* **·suad·ed, ·suad·ing** To alter the plans or intentions of (someone) by persuasion or advice: with *from.* [< L < *dis-* away + *suadere* to persuade] — **dis·suad'er** *n.* — **dis·sua'sion** *n.* — **dis·sua'sive** *adj.*

dis·syl·la·ble (di·sil'ə·bəl, dis'sil'ə·bəl) *n.* A word of two syllables: also spelled *disyllable.* [< F < L < Gk. < *di-* two + *syllabē* syllable] — **dis'syl·lab'ic** *adj.*

dis·taff (dis'taf, -täf) *n. pl.* **·taffs** or *Rare* **·taves** (-tāvz) **1.** A rotating vertical staff that holds a bunch of flax or wool for spinning by hand. **2.** Women in general. **3.** Woman's work or domain. [OE < *dis* bundle of flax + *stæf* staff]

distaff side The maternal branch or female line of a family.

dis·tal (dis'təl) *adj. Anat.* Relatively remote from the center of the body or point of attachment. — **dis'tal·ly** *adv.*

dis·tance (dis'təns) *n.* **1.** The extent of spatial separation between things, places, or locations. **2.** The extent of separation between points of time; interval. **3.** The state or fact of being separated from something else, esp. to a notable extent, in space, time, or condition. **4.** A gap, as in relationship or rank, between persons or things. **5.** Remoteness; esp., reserve or aloofness: to keep one's *distance.* **6.** A point or location removed from another, esp. to a notable extent. **7.** *Music* The interval between two tones. — *v.t.* **·tanced, ·tanc·ing 1.** To leave behind; outdo. **2.** To cause to appear distant. **3.** To hold off or place at some distance.

dis·tant (dis'tənt) *adj.* **1.** Separated or apart by a specified amount of space or time; away: often with *from.* **2.** Remote in time or space. **3.** At, from, or to a distance: a *distant* journey. **4.** Not closely related; remote, as to similarity, kinship, etc. **5.** Reserved or unapproachable. [< F < L < *dis-* apart + *stare* to stand] — **dis'tant·ly** *adv.*

dis·taste (dis·tāst') *n.* Dislike; aversion: a *distaste* for work.

dis·taste·ful (dis·tāst'fəl) *adj.* Causing dislike; offensive; disagreeable. — **dis·taste'ful·ly** *adv.* — **dis·taste'ful·ness** *n.*

dis·tem·per¹ (dis·tem'pər) *n.* **1.** *Vet.* Any of several infectious diseases of animals; esp., a catarrhal disease of puppies. **2.** A disorder of the mind or body; illness. **3.** Political or civil disturbance. — *v.t.* **1.** To derange the faculties or functions of. **2.** To ruffle; disturb. [< Med.L < L *dis-* away + *temperare* to regulate, mix]

dis·tem·per² (dis·tem'pər) *n.* **1.** Tempera. **2.** A painting medium in which size is the only agent used to bind the pigments. **3.** The art or method of using this medium. **4.** A painting done in distemper. **5.** *Brit.* Calcimine. — *v.t.* **1.** To mix (colors or pigments) with a binding medium, such as casein. **2.** To paint in distemper. [< OF < Med.L < L *dis-* apart + *temperare* to mix, soak]

dis·tend (dis·tend') *v.t.* & *v.i.* **1.** To expand by or as by pressure from within. **2.** To stretch out; swell. [< L < *dis-* apart + *tendere* to stretch] — **dis·ten'si·ble** *adj.* — **dis·ten'tion, dis·ten'sion** *n.*

dis·tich (dis'tik) *n.* In prosody, a couplet. [< Gk. < *di-* two + *stichos* a row, line]

dis·till (dis·til') *v.* **·tilled, ·till·ing** *v.t.* **1.** To subject to distillation so as to purify or produce, concentrate, or refine. **2.** To extract by distillation. **3.** To give forth or send down in drops. — *v.i.* **4.** To undergo distillation. **5.** To exude in drops. Also *Brit.* **dis·til'.** [< L < *de-* down + *stillare* to drop, trickle] — **dis·till'a·ble** *adj.*

dis·til·late (dis'tə·lit, -lāt) *n.* The condensed product separated by distillation: also called *distillation.*

dis·til·la·tion (dis'tə·lā'shən) *n.* **1.** The act or process of separating the more volatile parts of a substance from those less volatile by heating in a retort or still and then condensing the vapor thus produced by cooling. **2.** The purification or rectification of a substance by this process. **3.** A distillate. **4.** The essential or abstract quality of anything. Also **dis·till·ment** (dis·til'mənt), *Brit.* **dis·til'ment.**

dis·til·ler (dis·til'ər) *n.* **1.** One who distills; esp., a maker of distilled liquors. **2.** A condenser for distilling.

dis·til·ler·y (dis·til'ər·ē) *n. pl.* **·ler·ies** An establishment for distilling, esp. alcoholic liquors.

dis·tinct (dis·tingkt') *adj.* **1.** Recognizably not the same; clearly different. **2.** Differentiated by individualizing features. **3.** Sharp and clear to the senses or mind; definite. **4.** Undeniably such: a *distinct* step forward. [< L *distinguere* to separate] — **dis·tinct'ly** *adv.* — **dis·tinct'ness** *n.*

dis·tinc·tion (dis·tingk'shən) *n.* **1.** The act of distinguishing; discrimination. **2.** A difference that may be distinguished: the *distinction* between thrift and avarice. **3.** The state of being different or distinguishable. **4.** A characteristic difference or distinctive quality. **5.** A mark of honor. **6.** A distinguishing superiority or preeminence.

dis·tinc·tive (dis·tingk'tiv) *adj.* Serving to distinguish; characteristic. — **dis·tinc'tive·ly** *adv.* — **dis·tinc'tive·ness** *n.*

dis·tin·gué (dis'tang·gā', Fr. dēs·taṅ·gā') *adj.* Eminently well-bred and dignified. [< F] — **dis·tin·gué'e** *adj.fem.*

dis·tin·guish (dis·ting'gwish) *v.t.* **1.** To indicate the differences of or between. **2.** To be an outstanding or individualizing characteristic of: Honesty *distinguished* his career. **3.** To classify. **4.** To bring fame or credit upon. **5.** To perceive with the senses. — *v.i.* **6.** To make or discern differences; discriminate: often with *among* or *between.* [< MF < L *distinguere* to separate] — **dis·tin'guish·a·ble** *adj.* — **dis·tin'guish·a·bly** *adv.* — **dis·tin'guish·er** *n.*

dis·tin·guished (dis·ting'gwisht) *adj.* **1.** Conspicuous for qualities of excellence; celebrated; eminent; famous. **2.** Having an air of distinction; distingué.

Distinguished Flying Cross A U.S. military decoration awarded for heroism or exceptional achievement in aerial flight. See DECORATION.

Distinguished Service Cross A U.S. military decoration awarded for heroism in combat. See DECORATION.

Distinguished Service Medal A U.S. military decoration awarded for meritorious service in a duty of great responsibility. See DECORATION.

dis·tort (dis·tôrt') *v.t.* **1.** To twist or bend out of shape; make misshapen. **2.** To twist the meaning of; misrepresent; pervert. [< L < *dis-* apart + *torquere* to twist] — **dis·tort'ed** *adj.* — **dis·tort'ed·ly** *adv.* — **dis·tort'ed·ness** *n.* — **dis·tort'er** *n.*

dis·tor·tion (dis·tôr'shən) *n.* **1.** The act of distorting. **2.** The condition of being distorted; deformity. **3.** That which is distorted, as a misleading statement. **4.** *Telecom.* A change in the wave form of a signal caused by nonuniform transmission at different frequencies. — **dis·tor'tion·al** *adj.*

dis·tract (dis·trakt') *v.t.* **1.** To draw or divert (the mind, etc.) from something claiming attention. **2.** To bewilder; confuse. **3.** To make frantic; craze. [< L < *dis-* away + *trahere* to draw] — **dis·tract'er** *n.* — **dis·trac'tion** *n.*

dis·tract·ed (dis·trak'tid) *adj.* **1.** Bewildered or harassed. **2.** Mentally deranged; mad. — **dis·tract'ed·ly** *adv.*

dis·sract·ing (dis·trak'ting) *adj.* Serving or tending to distract. Also **dis·tract'ing·ly** *adv.*

dis·train (dis·trān') *Law v.t.* & *v.i.* To seize and detain (personal property) as security for a debt, claim, etc. [< OF < L *distringere* to detain, hinder] — **dis·train'a·ble** *adj.* — **dis·train'or** or **dis·train'er** *n.* — **dis·traint'** *n.*

dis·trait (dis·trā', Fr. dēs·tre') *adj.* Absent-minded. [< F. See DISTRACT.]

dis·traught (dis·trôt') *adj.* **1.** Deeply agitated in mind; worried, tense, and bewildered. **2.** Driven insane; crazed. [Var. of earlier *distract,* pp. of DISTRACT]

dis·tress (dis·tres') *v.t.* To inflict suffering upon; cause agony or worry to; afflict; harass. — *n.* **1.** Acute or extreme suffering or its cause; pain; trouble. **2.** A state of extreme need: a ship in *distress.* **3.** *Law* a The act of distraining. b The goods distrained. — Syn. See SUFFERING. [< OF < LL < L *distringere* to detain, hinder] — **dis·tress'ful** *adj.* — **dis·tress'ful·ly** *adv.* — **dis·tress'ful·ness** *n.* — **dis·tress'ing** *adj.* — **dis·tress'ing·ly** *adv.*

dis·trib·u·tar·y (dis'trib'yōō·ter'ē) *n. pl.* **·tar·ies** A river branch flowing away from the main branch.

dis·trib·ute (dis·trib'yōōt) *v.t.* **·ut·ed, ·ut·ing 1.** To divide and deal out in shares; apportion; allot. **2.** To divide and classify; arrange. **3.** To scatter or spread out, as over a surface. [< L < *dis-* away, apart + *tribuere* to give, allot] — **dis·trib'ut·a·ble** *adj.*

dis·tri·bu·tion (dis'trə·byōō'shən) *n.* **1.** The act of distributing or the state of being distributed. **2.** The manner in which something is distributed: random *distribution*. **3.** That which is distributed. **4.** In commerce, the system of distributing goods among consumers. **5.** *Stat.* Frequency: symbolized by *t*. — **dis·tri·bu′tion·al** *adj.*

dis·trib·u·tive (dis-trib′yə-tiv)   *adj.* **1.** Pertaining to or caused by distribution. **2.** Serving or tending to distribute. **3.** *Gram.* Singling out the separate individuals of a group: *Each* and *every* are *distributive* adjectives. — *n. Gram.* A distributive word or expression. — **dis·trib′u·tive·ly** *adv.* — **dis·trib′u·tive·ness** *n.*

dis·trib·u·tor (dis-trib′yə-tər, -tôr)   *n.* **1.** One who or that which distributes or sells merchandise. **2.** In a gasoline engine, a device that directs the electrical current to the spark plugs. Also **dis·trib′ut·er** (-yə-tər).

dis·trict (dis′trikt)   *n.* A particular region or locality; esp., an area, as within a city or state, set off for administrative or judicial purposes. — *v.t.* To divide into districts. [< MF < Med.L *districtus* jurisdiction]

district attorney   The prosecuting officer of a Federal or State judicial district.

dis·trust (dis-trust′)   *v.t.* To doubt; suspect. — *n.* Doubt; suspicion. — **dis·trust′ful** *adj.* — **dis·trust′ful·ly** *adv.*

dis·turb (dis-tûrb′)   *v.t.* **1.** To destroy the repose, tranquillity, or peace of. **2.** To agitate the mind of; trouble. **3.** To upset the order, system, or progression of. **4.** To interrupt; break in on. **5.** To inconvenience. [< OF < L < *dis-* completely + *turbare* to disorder] — **dis·turb′er** *n.*

dis·tur·bance (dis-tûr′bəns)   *n.* **1.** The act of disturbing, or the state of being disturbed. **2.** Something that disturbs. **3.** A tumult or commotion; especially, a public disorder.

dis·turbed (dis-tûrbd′)   *adj.* **1.** Characterized by disturbance. **2.** Troubled emotionally or mentally; neurotic.

di·sul·fate (dī-sul′fāt)   *n. Chem.* A bisulfate. Also **di·sul′phate.**

di·sul·fide (dī-sul′fīd)   *n. Chem.* A sulfide containing two atoms of sulfur to the molecule: also called *bisulfide*. Also **di·sul′fid** (-fid), **di·sul′phide.**

dis·un·ion (dis-yōōn′yən)   *n.* **1.** The state of being disunited; severance; rupture. **2.** A condition of disagreement.

dis·u·nite (dis′yōō-nīt′)   *v.* **·nit·ed, ·nit·ing** *v.t.* **1.** To break the union of; separate; part. **2.** To alienate; estrange. — *v.i.* **3.** To come apart. — **dis·u′ni·ty** *n.*

dis·use (*n.* dis·yōōs′; *v.* dis-yōōz′)   *n.* The state of not being used; out of use. — *v.t.* **used, ·us·ing** To stop using.

ditch (dich)   *n.* A long, narrow trench or channel dug in the ground, typically used for irrigation or drainage. — *v.t.* **1.** To make a ditch in. **2.** To surround with a ditch. **3.** To throw into or as into a ditch. **4.** *U.S. Slang* To get rid of. — *v.i.* **5.** To make a ditch. [OE *dīc*] — **ditch′er** *n.*

dith·er (dith′ər)   *n.* A state of nervous excitement or anxiety, or of trembling agitation. — *v.i.* To be in a dither. [Var. of earlier *didder* to tremble, shake; origin uncertain]

dith·y·ramb (dith′ə-ram, -ramb)   *n.* **1.** In ancient Greece, a wild, passionate choric hymn in honor of Dionysus. **2.** A highly emotional speech or piece of writing. [< L < Gk. *dithyrambos*] — **dith′y·ram′bic** *adj. & n.*

dit·to (dit′ō)   *n. pl.* **·tos 1.** The same thing (as something written above or mentioned or done before), usually symbolized by ditto marks. **2.** A duplicate or copy of something. **3.** Ditto marks. — *adv.* As written above or as mentioned before. — *interj. Informal* I agree. — *v.t.* **·toed, ·to·ing 1.** To repeat. **2.** To duplicate. [< Ital. < L *dicere* to say]

ditto marks   Two small marks (″) placed beneath an item to indicate that it is to be repeated. Also **ditto mark.**

dit·ty (dit′ē)   *n. pl.* **·ties** A short, simple song. [< OF *dittie, ditie* < L *distatum* a thing said]

ditty bag   A sailor's bag for needles, thread, personal belongings, etc. Also **ditty box.** [Origin uncertain]

di·u·ret·ic (dī′yŏŏ-ret′ik)   *adj.* Increasing the secretion of urine. — *n.* A diuretic medicine.

di·ur·nal (dī-ûr′nəl)   *adj.* **1.** Of, belonging to, or occurring each day; daily. **2.** Of or occurring during the daytime; not nocturnal. [< L *diurnus* daily] — **di·ur′nal·ly** *adv.*

di·va (dē′və)   *n. pl.* **·vas** *or* **·ve** (-vā)   A celebrated female operatic singer; a prima donna. [< Ital., fem of *divo* divine]

di·va·gate (dī′və-gāt)   *v.i.* **·gat·ed, ·gat·ing 1.** To wander or stray aimlessly. **2.** To digress. [< L < *dis-* about + *vagari* to wander] — **di′va·ga′tion** *n.*

di·va·lent (dī-vā′lent, dīv′ə-)   *adj. Chem.* Bivalent.

di·van (di-van′, dī′van)   *n.* **1.** A sofa or couch, usu. without arm rests or back. **2.** A room for smoking or drinking. [< Turkish *divan* < Persian *dēvān* council, chamber]

dive (dīv)   *v.* **dived** *or* **dove, dived, div·ing** *v.i.* **1.** To plunge, esp. headfirst, as into water. **2.** To go underwater or to the bottom; submerge. **3.** To plunge downward at a sharp angle. **4.** To dart away or leap into something. **5.** To rush into and become deeply engrossed in something. **6.** To reach into something eagerly. — *v.t.* **7.** To cause to plunge,

especially, to cause (an airplane) to move swiftly downward at a sharp angle. — *n.* **1.** A plunge, as into water. **2.** A sharp, swift descent, as of an airplane. **3.** *Informal* A cheap, disreputable place, as a saloon, etc. — **to take a dive** *U.S. Slang* In boxing, to allow an opponent to win by prearrangement. [Blend of OE *dūfan* to dive and *dyfan* to immerse]

dive bomber   An airplane designed to bomb a target while in a steep dive.

div·er (dī′vər)   *n.* **1.** One who dives, esp. one who dives to salvage sunken cargo, etc. **2.** A bird that dives, as a loon.

di·verge (di-vûrj′, dī-)   *v.* **·verged, ·verg·ing** *v.i.* **1.** To move or extend in different directions from a common point or from each other. **2.** To deviate. **3.** To differ. — *v.t.* **4.** To cause to diverge. [< NL < L *dis-* apart + *vergere* to incline]

di·ver·gence (di-vûr′jəns, dī-)   *n.* **1.** The act of diverging, or the state of being divergent. **2.** Deviation or difference, as of opinion. Also **di·ver′gen·cy.** — **di·ver′gent** *adj.* — **di·ver′gent·ly** *adv.*

di·vers (dī′vərz)   *adj.* **1.** Several. **2.** Various. [< OF < L *diversus* different]

di·verse (di-vûrs′, dī-, dī′vûrs)   *adj.* **1.** Marked by distinct differences; not alike. **2.** Varied in kind or form; diversified. [See DIVERS.] — **di·verse′ly** *adv.* — **di·verse′ness** *n.*

di·ver·si·fy (di-vûr′sə-fī, dī-)   *v.t.* **·fied, ·fy·ing 1.** To make diverse; give variety to; vary. **2.** To make or distribute (investments) among different types of securities so as to minimize risk. — **di·ver·si·fi·ca·tion** (di-vûr′sə-fə-kā′shən, dī-) *n.*

di·ver·sion (di-vûr′zhən, -shən, dī-)   *n.* **1.** The act of diverting or turning aside, as from a course. **2.** A drawing away of the attention from something. **3.** An amusement.

di·ver·sion·ar·y (di-vûr′zhən·er′ē, -shən, dī-)   *adj.* Designed to distract the enemy from the point of operation.

di·ver·si·ty (di-vûr′sə-tē, dī-)   *n. pl.* **·ties 1.** Unlikeness; difference. **2.** Variety; multiplicity.

di·vert (di-vûrt′, dī-)   *v.t.* **1.** To turn aside, as from a set course; deflect. **2.** To distract the attention of. **3.** To amuse; entertain. [< L < *dis-* apart + *vertere* to turn] — **di·vert′ing** *adj.* — **di·vert′ing·ly** *adv.*

di·ver·ti·men·to (di·ver′ti·men′tō)   *n. pl.* **·ti** (-tē) *Music* A light instrumental composition in several movements. [< Ital., diversion]

di·ver·tisse·ment (də-vûr′təs·mənt, dē-ver·tēs·män′)   *n.* **1.** A diversion; amusement. **2.** *Music* A divertimento. **3.** A short ballet, etc. performed during or between the parts of an opera or play. [< MF]

di·vest (di-vest′, dī-)   *v.t.* **1.** To strip, as of clothes. **2.** To deprive, as of rights or possessions. [See DEVEST.]

di·vest·i·ture (di-ves′tə·chər, dī-)   *n.* The act of divesting, or the state of being divested. Also **di·vest′ment, di·ves′ture.**

di·vide (di-vīd′)   *v.* **·vid·ed, ·vid·ing** *v.t.* **1.** To separate into pieces or portions, as by cutting. **2.** To distribute the pieces or portions of. **3.** To separate into sections. **4.** To separate into groups; classify. **5.** To split up into opposed sides; cause dissent in. **6.** To cause to be apart. **7.** *Math.* **a** To subject to the process of division. **b** To be an exact divisor of. **8.** *Mech.* To graduate; calibrate. — *v.i.* **9.** To become separated into parts; diverge. **10.** To be at variance. **11.** *Brit.* In Parliament and other legislative bodies, to separate into two groups in order to vote. **12.** To share. **13.** To perform mathematical division. — *n.* A mountain range separating one drainage system from another; watershed. [< L *dividere* to separate, divide] — **di·vid′a·ble** *adj.*

di·vid·ed (di-vī′did)   *adj.* **1.** Separated into parts; parted. **2.** Disunited. **3.** *Bot.* Having incisions or indentations.

div·i·dend (div′ə·dend)   *n.* **1.** *Math.* A quantity divided into equal parts. **2.** A sum of money to be distributed to stockholders, etc. **3.** The portion of such a sum given to each individual. [< L *dividendum* thing to be divided]

di·vid·er (di-vī′dər)   *n.* **1.** One who or that which divides, separates, or apportions. **2.** *pl.* A pair of compasses typically used for measuring or marking off short intervals.

div·i·na·tion (div′ə·nā′shən)   *n.* **1.** The act or art of knowing the future or that which is hidden or unknown. **2.** A prophecy. **3.** A clever guess. — **di·vin·a·to·ry** (div·in′ə·tôr′ē, -tō′rē) *adj.*

di·vine (di·vīn′)   *adj.* **1.** Of or pertaining to God or a god. **2.** Given by or derived from God or a god. **3.** Directed or devoted to God or a god; sacred. **4.** Like a god. **5.** Extraordinarily perfect. **6.** *Informal* Altogether delightful. — *n.* **1.** A clergyman. **2.** A theologian. — *v.* **·vined, ·vin·ing** *v.t.* **1.** To foretell or find out by occult means. **2.** To locate (water, etc.) by means of a divining rod. **3.** To conjecture or surmise by instinct. — *v.i.* **4.** To practice divination. **5.** To guess. [< OF < L *deus* god] — **di·vine′ly** *adv.* — **di·vine′ness** *n.* — **di·vin′er** *n.*

Divine Comedy   A narrative poem by Dante Alighieri.

Divine Office   The canonical hours.

diving bell A large, hollow, inverted vessel supplied with air under pressure, in which men may work under water.

diving board A flexible board upon which divers jump to gain impetus for the dive: also called *springboard*.

diving suit A waterproof garment with detachable helmet that is supplied with air through a hose, worn by divers.

divining rod A forked branch popularly asserted to indicate underground water or metal: also called *dowsing rod*.

di·vin·i·ty (di·vin′ə·tē) *n. pl.* **·ties** 1. The state or quality of being divine. 2. A godlike character or attribute. 3. A deity. 4. *Theology*. 5. A soft, creamy candy. — **the Divinity** God. [< OF < L *divinitas* godhead, deity]

di·vis·i·ble (di·viz′ə·bəl) *adj.* 1. Capable of being divided. 2. *Math*. That can be divided and leave no remainder. — **di·vis·i·bil′i·ty, di·vis/i·ble·ness** *n.* — **di·vis/i·bly** *adv.*

di·vi·sion (di·vizh′ən) *n.* 1. The act of dividing; separation. 2. The state of being divided. 3. One of the parts into which a thing is divided. 4. A part or section of a country, government, etc., that has been divided for administrative, political, or other reasons. 5. Something that divides or separates. 6. Disagreement; discord. 7. *Math*. The operation of finding how many times a number or quantity (the *divisor*) is contained in another number or quantity (the *dividend*), the number or quantity found being called the *quotient*. 8. A voting of a legislative body. 9. *Mil*. A major administrative and tactical unit that is larger than a regiment and smaller than a corps. 10. In the U.S. Navy, a number of ships grouped for operational command. 11. In the U.S. Air Force, an air combat organization with appropriate service units. [< OF < L *dividere* to divide] — **di·vi/sion·al** *adj.*

division sign *Math*. The symbol (÷) that denotes a first number is to be divided by a second, as $6 ÷ 2 = 3$.

di·vi·sive (di·vī′siv) *adj.* 1. Causing or expressing division or distribution. 2. Creating division, dissension, or strife.

di·vi·sor (di·vī′zər) *n. Math.* 1. A number by which another number is divided. 2. A common divisor.

di·vorce (di·vôrs′, -vōrs′) *n.* 1. Dissolution of a marriage bond by legal process or by accepted custom. 2. Any radical or complete separation. Also **di·vorce/ment.** — *v.* **·vorced, ·vorc·ing** *v.t.* 1. To dissolve the marriage of. 2. To free oneself from (one's husband or wife) by divorce. 3. To separate; cut off; disunite. — *v.i.* 4. To get a divorce. [< MF < L *divertere* to divert]

di·vor·cé (di·vôr′sā′, -vōr′-, di·vôr′sā, -vōr′-) *n.* A divorced man. [< F, pp. of *divorcer* to divorce] — **di·vor/cée** *n.fem.*

di·vor·cee (di·vôr′sē′, -vōr′-) *n.* A divorced person.

div·ot (div′ət) *n.* A piece of turf torn by a golf club.

di·vulge (di·vulj′) *v.t.* **·vulged, ·vulg·ing** To tell, as a secret; disclose; reveal. [< L < *dis-* away + *vulgare* to make public] — **di·vulge/ment, di·vul/gence** *n.* — **di·vulg/er** *n.*

div·vy (div′ē) *Slang n. pl.* **·vies** A share; portion. — *v.t.* **·vied, ·vy·ing** To divide: often with *up*. [Short for DIVIDE]

Dix·ie (dik′sē) 1. Traditionally, those States that comprised the Confederacy during the Civil War. Also **Dixie Land.** 2. A Confederate marching song.

Dix·ie·land (dik′sē·land′) *n.* A style of jazz in two-beat or four-beat rhythm, originally played in New Orleans.

diz·en (diz′ən, dī′zən) *v.t.* To dress in finery; deck out. [< M.Du. *disen* to put flax on a distaff] — **diz/en·ment** *n.*

diz·zy (diz′ē) *adj.* **·zi·er, ·zi·est** 1. Having a feeling of whirling or unsteadiness. 2. Causing giddiness. 3. *Informal* Silly; stupid. — *v.t* **·zied, ·zy·ing** To make giddy; confuse. [OE *dysig* foolish, stupid] — **diz/zi·ly** *adv.* — **diz/zi·ness** *n.*

djin·ni (ji·nē′) See JINNI.

DNA *Biochem.* Deoxyribonucleic acid.

do¹ (dōō) *v.* **did, done, do·ing** Present: *sing.* **do, do** (*Archaic* **thou do·est** or **dost**), **does** (*Archaic* **do·eth** or **doth**), *pl.* **do;** past: **did** (*Archaic* **thou didst**); pp. **done;** ppr. **do·ing** *v.t.* 1. To perform, as an action; produce, as a piece of work. 2. To fulfill; complete; accomplish. 3. To cause; bring about: to *do* no wrong. 4. To put forth: He *did* his best. 5. To render: to *do* homage. 6. To work at. 7. To work out; solve. 8. To translate. 9. To present (a play, reading, etc.). 10. To enact the part of. 11. To cover (a distance); travel. 12. To make a tour of; visit. 13. To be sufficient for. 14. *Informal* To serve, as a term in prison. 15. *Informal* To cheat; swindle. — *v.i.* 16. To exert oneself; be active: to *do* or die. 17. To conduct oneself. 18. To fare; get along. 19. To serve the purpose; suffice. — **to do away with** 1. To throw away. 2. To kill; destroy. — **to do by** To act toward. — **to do for** 1. To provide for; care for. 2. *Informal* To ruin; kill. — **to do in** *Slang* To kill. — **to do over** *Informal* To redecorate. — **to do up** 1. To wrap or tie up. 2. To roll up or arrange. 3. To clean; repair. 4. To tire out. — **to do without** To get along without. — **to have to do with** To be involved with. — *auxiliary* As an auxiliary, *do* is used: 1. Without specific meaning in negative, interrogative, and inverted constructions: I *do* not want it; *Do* you want to leave? 2. To add force to impera-

tives: *Do* hurry. 3. To express emphasis: I *do* believe you. 4. As a substitute for another verb to avoid repetition: I will not affirm, as some *do.* — *n. pl.* **do's** or **dos** 1. *Informal* A trick; cheat. 2. Deed; duty: chiefly in the phrase **to do one's do.** 3. *Informal* Festivity; celebration. 4. *pl.* That which ought to be done: used chiefly in the expression **do's and don'ts.** [OE *dōn*]

do² (dō) *n. Music* The keynote syllable of a major scale; also, the tone C. [< Ital.]

do·a·ble (dōō′ə·bəl) *adj.* Capable of being done.

do-all (dōō′ôl′) *n.* A general helper; factotum.

dob·bin (dob′in) *n.* A horse, esp. a plodding one. [after *Dobbin*, var. of *Robin* < *Robert*, a personal name]

Do·ber·man pinscher (dō′bər·mən) A breed of large, short-haired dogs originally developed in Germany. [after Ludwig *Dobermann*, its first breeder]

doc·ile (dos′əl, *Brit.* dō′sīl) *adj.* 1. Amenable to training; easy to manage; tractable. 2. Easily worked or handled. [< MF < L *docilis* able to be taught] — **doc/ile·ly** *adv.* — **do·cil·i·ty** (do·sil′ə·tē, dō-) *n.*

dock¹ (dok) *n.* 1. The water space between two adjoining piers or wharves where ships can remain for loading, unloading, or repair. 2. A wharf or pier. 3. *Often pl.* A group of wharves or piers. 4. A shipping or loading platform, as for trucks, trains, etc. — **Syn.** See WHARF. — *v.t.* 1. To bring (a vessel, truck, etc.) into or next to a dock. — *v.i.* 2. To come into a dock. [< MDu. *docke*]

dock² (dok) *n.* 1. The fleshy part of an animal's tail. 2. The stump of a tail that remains after clipping. — *v.t.* 1. To cut off the end of (a tail, etc.), or clip short the tail of. 2. To take a part from (wages, etc.). 3. To take from the wages, etc. of. [Cf. ME *docken* to cut short] — **dock/er** *n.*

dock³ (dok) *n.* An enclosed space for the defendant in a criminal court. [< Flemish *dok* cage]

dock⁴ (dok) *n.* Any of various plants of the buckwheat family, as the sour dock. [OE *docce*]

dock·age¹ (dok′ij) *n.* 1. A charge for docking (a ship, etc.). 2. Facilities for docking a vessel. 3. The act of docking.

dock·age² (dok′ij) *n.* 1. Curtailment, as of wages; deduction. 2. Waste matter in grain, easily separated by cleaning.

dock·et (dok′it) *n.* 1. A written summary or abstract. 2. *Law* **a** A record of court judgments. **b** The book in which such a record is kept. **c** A court calendar of the cases still pending. 3. Any calendar of things to be done. 4. A tag or label attached to a parcel, listing contents, directions, etc. — *v.t.* 1. To enter in a docket. 2. To put a tag or label on (a parcel, etc.). [ME; origin uncertain]

dock·yard (dok′yärd′) *n.* 1. An area of docks, etc., where ships are built, repaired, etc. 2. *Brit.* A navy yard.

doc·tor (dok′tər) *n.* 1. A licensed practitioner of medicine, surgery, or any of certain other healing arts, as a dentist, veterinarian, etc. 2. A person who has received a diploma of the highest degree, as in law, literature, etc. 3. A medicine man. 4. *Informal* One who or that which removes defects, mends broken parts, etc. — *v.t. Informal* 1. To prescribe for or treat medically. 2. To repair. 3. To falsify or alter, as evidence. — *v.i. Informal* 4. To practice medicine. 5. To undergo medical treatment. [< L *docere* to teach] — **doc/tor·al** *adj.*

doc·tor·ate (dok′tər·it) *n.* The degree or status of a doctor.

doc·tri·naire (dok′trə·nâr′) *adj.* Theoretical; visionary. — *n.* One whose views are derived from theories rather than from facts; an impractical theorist. — **doc/tri·nair/ism** *n.*

doc·trine (dok′trin) *n.* 1. That which is presented for acceptance or belief; teachings, as of a religious group. 2. A particular principle or tenet that is taught. [< OF < L *docere* to teach] — **doc/tri·nal** *adj.* — **doc/tri·nal·ly** *adv.* — **Syn.** *Doctrine* primarily signifies a principle that is taught. A *theory* is a proposition regarded as susceptible of verification, and thus is usually scientific. A *dogma* rests on authority, such as the decision of a church council. Any *doctrine* is a *belief* on the part of those who accept it, but *belief* more often suggests matters of faith rather than of reason. A *creed* is the list of *doctrines* or *dogmas* of a religion or church; any single item of such a list is a *tenet*.

doc·u·ment (*n.* dok′yə·mənt; *v.* dok′yə·ment) *n.* Something written or printed that furnishes conclusive information or evidence, as an official paper or record. — *v.t.* 1. To furnish with documents. 2. To support by conclusive information or evidence. 3. To supply (a book, etc.) with citations that prove what is stated. [< OF < L *docere* to teach] — **doc/u·men·ta/tion** *n.*

doc·u·men·ta·ry (dok′yə·men′tər·ē) *adj.* 1. Pertaining to, consisting of, or based upon documents. 2. That presents factual material objectively without fictionalizing. Also **doc/u·men·tal.** — *n. pl.* **·ries** A motion picture dealing with events, circumstances, etc., in a factual way.

dod·der (dod′ər) *v.i.* To tremble or totter, as from age. [Cf. ME *didder* to tremble] — **dod/der·ing** *adj.*

dodeca- *combining form* Twelve; of or having twelve. Also before vowels, **dodec-.** [< Gk. *dōdeka* twelve]

do·dec·a·gon (dō·dek′ə·gon) *n. Geom.* A polygon having

twelve sides and twelve angles. [< Gk. *dōdekagōnon*] — **do·de·cag·o·nal** (dō/de·kag/ə·nəl) *adj.*

do·dec·a·he·dron (dō/dek·ə·hē/drən) *n. pl.* **·drons** or **·dra** (-drə) *Geom.* A polyhedron bounded by twelve plane faces. For illus. see CRYSTAL. — **do/dec·a·he/dral** *adj.*

dodge (doj) *v.* **dodged, dodg·ing** *v.t.* 1. To avoid, as a blow, by a sudden turn or twist. 2. To evade, as a duty or issue. — *v.i.* 3. To move suddenly, as to avoid a blow. 4. To practice trickery. — *n.* 1. An act of dodging. 2. A trick to deceive or cheat. [Origin unknown]

dodg·er (doj/ər) *n.* 1. One who dodges; a tricky fellow. 2. *U.S.* A small handbill. 3. *U.S.* A cake of Indian meal.

do·do (dō/dō) *n. pl.* **·does** or **·dos** 1. An extinct bird about the size of a turkey, with rudimentary, functionless wings. 2. *Informal* One who is slow or dull. [< Pg. *doudo*]

doe (dō) *n.* 1. The female of the deer, antelope, rabbit, kangaroo, and certain other animals. 2. Loosely, the female of the moose or elk (properly called *cow*). [OE *dā*]

do·er (dōo/ər) *n.* One who acts, does, or performs; an agent.

does (duz) Present tense, third person singular, of DO[1].

doe·skin (dō/skin/) *n.* 1. The skin of the female deer. 2. Leather made from this, used especially for gloves. 3. A heavy, short-napped, woolen or cotton fabric.

does·n't (duz/ənt) Does not. ◆ See note at DON'T.

doff (dof, dôf) *v.t.* 1. To take off, as a hat or clothing. 2. To discard. [Contraction of *do off*] — **doff/er** *n.*

dog (dôg, dog) *n.* 1. A domesticated, carnivorous mammal of many varieties. ◆ Collateral adjective: *canine.* 2. Any of various other species of this family, as wolves, foxes, etc. 3. The male of any of these species. 4. One of various animals having an appearance suggestive of a dog, as a prairie dog. 5. A despicable person. 6. *Informal* A man or boy; fellow. 7. An andiron. 8. *Mech.* One of several devices for gripping or holding logs, etc. 9. *pl. U.S. Slang* The feet. — **to go to the dogs** *Informal* To go to ruin. — **to put on the dog.** *U.S. Informal* To make a pretentious display. — *adv.* Very; utterly: used in combination: *dog-tired.* — *v.t.* **dogged, dog·ging** 1. To pursue persistently; hound. 2. *Mech.* To grip or fasten (a log, etc.) with a dog. [OE *docga*] **Dog** (dôg, dog) *n.* Either of two constellations, Canis Major (the Greater Dog) or Canis Minor (the Little Dog).

dog·bane (dôg/bān/, dog/-) *n.* A smooth, reddish-stemmed herb having a milky juice.

dog biscuit A hard biscuit made with meat scraps, ground bones, etc., for feeding dogs.

dog·cart (dôg/kärt/, dog/-) *n.* 1. A one-horse vehicle, usu. two-wheeled, with two seats set back to back. 2. A cart hauled by one or more dogs.

dog·catch·er (dôg/kach/ər, dog/-) *n. U.S.* A person employed or elected to pick up and impound stray dogs.

dog days The hot, sultry days of July and early August.

doge (dōj) *n.* The elective chief magistrate in the former republics of Venice and Genoa. [< Ital. < L *dux, ducis* chief]

dog·ear (dôg/ir/, dog/-) *n.* A turned-down corner of a book page. — *v.t.* To turn down the corner of (a page). Also *dog's-ear.* — **dog/-eared** *adj.*

dog·face (dôg/fās/, dog/-) *n. U.S. Slang* A soldier in the U.S. Army; esp., an infantryman.

dog·fight (dôg/fīt/, dog/-) *n.* 1. A fight between or as between dogs. 2. *Mil.* An aerial battle between planes.

dog·fish (dôg/fish/, dog/-) *n. pl.* **·fish** or **·fish·es** One of various small, littoral sharks of North American waters.

dog·ged (dôg/id, dog/-) *adj.* Stubborn; obdurate. — **dog/ged·ly** *adv.* — **dog/ged·ness** *n.*

dog·ger·el (dôg/ər·əl, dog/-) *n.* Trivial, awkwardly written verse, usu. comic or burlesque. — *adj.* Of or composed of such verse. Also **dog/grel.** [ME; origin unknown]

dog·gish (dôg/ish, dog/-) *adj.* 1. Relating to or suggestive of a dog. 2. Bad-tempered; snappish. 3. *U.S. Informal* Pretentiously stylish. — **dog/gish·ly** *adv.* — **dog/gish·ness** *n.*

dog·gone (dôg/gôn/, dog/gon/) *Informal interj.* Damn!; darn! — *v.t.* **goned, ·gon·ing** To damn.

dog·gy (dôg/ē, dog/ē) *n. pl.* **·gies** A dog; esp., a small dog. Also **dog/gie.** — *adj.* **dog·gi·er, dog·gi·est** 1. Of or like a dog: *doggy* odor. 2. *U.S. Informal* Showily fashionable.

dog·house (dôg/hous/, dog/-) *n.* A small house for a dog. — **in the doghouse** *U.S. Informal* In disfavor with someone.

do·gie (dō/gē) *n.* In the western U.S., a stray or motherless calf: also spelled *dogy.* [Origin unknown]

dog·ma (dôg/mə, dog/-) *n. pl.* **·mas** or **·ma·ta** (-mə·tə) 1. *Theol.* A doctrine or system of doctrine maintained by a religious body as true and necessary of belief. 2. A belief, principle, or tenet. 3. A system of such beliefs or principles. — Syn. See DOCTRINE. [< L < Gk. *dogma* opinion]

dog·mat·ic (dôg·mat/ik, dog-) *adj.* 1. Of, like, or pertaining to dogma. 2. Marked by authoritative, often arrogant, assertion of opinions or beliefs. Also **dog·mat/i·cal.** — **dog/mat/i·cal·ly** *adv.*

dog·ma·tism (dôg/mə·tiz/əm, dog/-) *n.* Positive or arrogant assertion, as of opinions or beliefs. — **dog/ma·tist** *n.*

dog·ma·tize (dôg/mə·tīz, dog/-) *v.* **·tized, ·tiz·ing** *v.i.* 1. To express oneself dogmatically. — *v.t.* 2. To declare or assert as a dogma. — **dog/ma·ti·za/tion** *n.* — **dog/ma·tiz/er** *n.*

do-good·er (dōo/good/ər) *n. Informal* An idealistic philanthropist or reformer: a derisive term.

dog's-ear (dôgz/ir/, dogz/-) *n.* Dog-ear.

dog sled A sled drawn by one or more dogs. Also **dog sledge.**

Dog Star 1. The star Sirius. 2. Procyon.

dog tag 1. A small metal plate on the collar of a dog, usu. indicating ownership. 2. *U.S. Informal* A soldier's identification tag, worn on a chain around the neck.

dog·tooth (dôg/tooth/, dog/-) *n.* A canine tooth.

dogtooth violet 1. A European herb of the lily family: also called *adder's tongue.* 2. One of various American plants, bearing yellow or pinkish flowers. Also **dog's-tooth violet.**

dog·trot (dôg/trot/, dog/-) *n.* A regular and easy trot.

dog·watch (dôg/woch/, dog/-) *n. Naut.* Either of two short watches aboard ship, from 4 to 6 or 6 to 8 P.M.

dog·wood (dôg/wood/, dog/-) *n.* Any of certain trees or shrubs, esp. the **flowering dogwood** or **Virginia dogwood** of the U.S., with white or pink flowers. Also called *cornel.*

do·gy (dō/gē) See DOGIE.

doi·ly (doi/lē) *n. pl.* **·lies** A small, ornamental piece of lace, etc., used to protect surfaces. Also spelled *doyley, doyly.* [after *Doily* or *Doyley,* 17th c. English draper]

do·ings (dōo/ingz) *n.pl.* 1. Activities or proceedings. 2. Behavior; conduct.

do-it-your·self (dōo/it·yoor·self/) *adj. U.S. Informal* Designed to be used or done without special or hired help.

Dol·by (dôl/bē, dōl/bē) *adj.* Designating electronic devices that eliminate noise from recorded sound: a trade name.

Dol·by·ized (dôl/bē·īzd, dōl/-) *adj.* Equipped with or recorded using a Dolby device.

dol·drums (dôl/drəmz, dōl/-) *n.pl.* 1. Those parts of the ocean near the equator where calms or baffling winds prevail. 2. A becalmed state. 3. A dull, depressed, or bored condition of mind; the dumps. [Cf. OE *dol* dull, stupid]

dole (dōl) *n.* 1. That which, as food or money, is distributed, esp. in charity. 2. A giving out of something. 3. A sum of money paid to an unemployed person. — **on the dole** Receiving relief payments from the government. — *v.t.* **doled, dol·ing** To dispense in small quantities; distribute: usually with *out.* [OE *dāl*]

dole·ful (dōl/fəl) *adj.* Melancholy. [< OF < LL < *dolere* to feel pain] — **dole/ful·ly** *adv.* — **dole/ful·ness** *n.*

dol·i·cho·ce·phal·ic (dol/i·kō·sə·fal/ik) *adj.* Having a long skull; longheaded. Also **dol/i·cho·ceph/a·lous** (-sef/ə·ləs). [< Gk. *dolichos* long + *kephalē* head] — **dol/i·cho·ceph/a·lism, dol/i·cho·ceph/a·ly** *n.*

doll (dol) *n.* 1. A child's toy made to resemble the human figure. 2. A pretty but superficial woman. 3. A pretty or lovable child. 4. *Slang* An attractive or charming person of either sex. — *v.t. & v.i. Informal* To adorn or dress smartly: with *up.* [from *Doll,* nickname for *Dorothy*]

dol·lar (dol/ər) *n.* 1. The standard monetary unit of the United States, equivalent to 100 cents. 2. The standard monetary unit of Canada, China, various British colonies, etc. 3. A coin or a piece of paper currently worth one dollar. 4. Loosely, a Mexican peso. 5. Any of various coins or currency originally issued for trade. Symbol $ or $. [< earlier *daler* < LG < G *taler, thaler,* short for *Joachimstaler,* a coin of *Joachimstal,* a village in Bohemia]

dol·lar-a-year (dol/ər·ə·yir/) *adj. U.S.* Designating a government employee, job, etc., having only token pay.

dollar diplomacy A practice or policy whereby a government uses public or private funds to advance its own interests abroad.

dol·lop (dol/əp) *n. Informal* A portion, serving, etc., of indefinite form or amount, as of a soft substance or liquid.

dol·ly (dol/ē) *n. pl.* **·lies** 1. A doll: a child's term. 2. A low, flat frame set on small wheels or rollers, used for moving heavy loads, cameras, etc. 3. A wooden instrument for beating or stirring clothes, etc. — *v.i.* **·lied, ·ly·ing** To move a motion-picture or television camera toward or away from the action.

dol·man (dol/mən) *n.* A woman's coat with dolman sleeves or capelike arm pieces. [< F < Turkish *dōlāmān* long robe]

dolman sleeve A sleeve tapering from a wide opening at the armhole to a narrow one at the wrist.

dol·men (dol/mən) *n.* A prehistoric monument made of a huge stone set on upright stones. [< F]

dol·o·mite (dol/ə·mīt) *n.* A marblelike rock consisting principally of a brittle calcium and magnesium carbonate. [after D. de *Dolomieu,* 1750–1801, French geologist]

do·lor (dō/lər) *n. Poetic* Sorrow; anguish. Also *Brit.* **do/lour.** [< OF < L, pain]

do·lor·ous (dŏ′lər·əs, dol′ər-) *adj.* **1.** Sad; mournful. **2.** Painful. — **do′lor·ous·ly** *adv.* — **do′lor·ous·ness** *n.*

dol·phin (dol′fin) *n.* **1.** Any of various cetaceans with beaklike snouts; esp. the **common dolphin** of the Mediterranean and Atlantic. **2.** *Naut.* A buoy or post to which a boat can be moored. [< OF *daulphin* < L *delphinus* < Gk. *delphis*, *-inos*]

DOLPHIN (*def.* 1)
(To 8 feet long)

dolt (dōlt) *n.* A stupid person. [ME *dold* stupid] — **dolt′ish** *adj.* — **dolt′ish·ly** *adv.* — **dolt′ish·ness** *n.*

-dom *suffix of nouns* **1.** State or condition of being: *freedom.* **2.** Domain of: *kingdom.* **3.** Rank of: *earldom.* **4.** The totality of those having a certain rank, state, or condition: *Christendom.* [OE *-dōm* < *dōm* state, condition]

do·main (dō·mān′) *n.* **1.** A territory under a sovereign or one government. **2.** A sphere or field of action, knowledge, etc. **3.** A landed estate. [< MF < OF < L *dominus* lord]

dome (dōm) *n.* **1.** A roof resembling an inverted cup or hemisphere. **2.** Something shaped like this. **3.** *Slang* The head. — *v.* domed, dom·ing *v.t.* **1.** To furnish or cover with a dome. **2.** To shape like a dome. — *v.i.* **3.** To rise or swell upward like a dome. [< MF < Ital. < L *domus* house]

domes·day (dōōmz′dā′) *n.* See DOOMSDAY.

do·mes·tic (də·mes′tik) *adj.* **1.** Of or pertaining to the home or family. **2.** Given to or fond of things concerning the home or family. **3.** Tame; domesticated: *domestic* animals. **4.** Of, produced, or pertaining to one's own country. — *n.* **1.** A household servant. **2.** *pl.* Native products. [< MF < L *domus* house] — **do·mes′ti·cal·ly** *adv.*

do·mes·ti·cate (də·mes′tə·kāt) *v.* ·cat·ed, ·cat·ing *v.t.* **1.** To tame. **2.** To civilize. **3.** To cause to feel at ease or at home. — *v.i.* **4.** To become domestic. Also **do·mes′ti·cize.** [< Med.L < L *domesti·ca′tion n.*

do·mes·tic·i·ty (dō′mes·tis′ə·tē) *n. pl.* ·ties **1.** Life at home or with one's family. **2.** Devotion to home and family. **3.** *pl.* Domestic matters.

domestic science Home economics.

dom·i·cile (dom′ə·səl, -sīl) *n.* **1.** A home, house, or dwelling. **2.** The place of one's legal abode. — *v.* ·ciled, ·cil·ing *v.t.* **1.** To establish in a place of abode. — *v.i.* **2.** To dwell. [< MF < L *domus* house] — **dom·i·cil·i·ar·y** (dom′ə·sil′ē·er′ē) *adj.*

dom·i·nance (dom′ə·nəns) *n.* The state or fact of being dominant; control; ascendancy. Also **dom′i·nan·cy.**

dom·i·nant (dom′ə·nənt) *adj.* **1.** Dominating; ruling; governing. **2.** Conspicuously prominent, as in position. **3.** *Genetics* Designating one of a pair of hereditary characters that, appearing in hybrid offspring, masks a contrasting character: opposed to *recessive.* **4.** *Music* Of or based upon the dominant. — *n.* **1.** *Genetics* A dominant character. **2.** *Music* The fifth tone of a diatonic scale, a perfect fifth above the tonic. [See DOMINATE.] — **dom′i·nant·ly** *adv.*

dom·i·nate (dom′ə·nāt) *v.* ·nat·ed, ·nat·ing *v.t.* **1.** To exercise control over; govern. **2.** To tower above; loom over. — *v.i.* **3.** To be dominant, as in power. [< L *dominari* to rule, dominate] — **dom′i·na·tive** *adj.* — **dom′i·na·tor** *n.*

dom·i·na·tion (dom′ə·nā′shən) *n.* **1.** The act of dominating, or the state of being dominated. **2.** Control; authority.

dom·i·neer (dom′ə·nir′) *v.t. & v.i.* To rule arrogantly or insolently. [< Du. < F < L *dominus* lord] — **dom′i·neer′ing** *adj.* — **dom′i·neer′ing·ly** *adv.*

Do·min·i·can (də·min′i·kən) *adj.* **1.** Of or pertaining to St. Dominic or to his monastic order. **2.** Of the Dominican Republic. — *n.* **1.** A member of the monastic order founded by St. Dominic. **2.** A native of the Dominican Republic.

do·min·ion (də·min′yən) *n.* **1.** Sovereign or supreme authority. **2.** A country under a particular government. **3.** A self-governing member of the British Commonwealth of Nations. [< F < L *dominus* lord]

Dominion Day In Canada, July 1, the anniversary of Canada's federation into a dominion, 1867: a legal holiday.

dom·i·no[1] (dom′ə·nō) *n. pl.* ·noes or ·nos **1.** A small mask for the eyes. For illus. see MASK[1]. **2.** A loose robe, hood, and mask worn at masquerades. **3.** A person wearing this. [< MF, hood worn by clerics]

dom·i·no[2] (dom′ə·nō) *n. pl.* ·noes or ·nos **1.** A small, oblong piece of wood, plastic, etc., with the upper side marked with dots. **2.** *pl.* (construed as *sing.*) A game usu. played with a set of 28 of these pieces. [? < DOMINO[1]]

don[1] (don) *n.* **1.** A Spanish gentleman or nobleman. **2.** An important personage. **3.** *Brit. Informal* A head, fellow, or tutor of a college. [< Sp. < L *dominus* lord]

don[2] (don) *v.t.* donned, don·ning To put on, as a garment. [Contraction of *do on*]

Don (don) *n.* Sir: a title of respect or address, used with the given name in Spanish-speaking countries.

Do·ña (dō′nyä) *n.* Lady; Madam: a title of respect or address used with the given name in Spanish-speaking countries.

do·nate (dō′nāt, dō·nāt′) *v.t.* nat·ed, nat·ing *Chiefly U.S.* To give, as to a charitable organization; contribute. [Back formation < DONATION] — **do′na·tor** *n.*

do·na·tion (dō·nā′shən) *n.* **1.** The act of giving. **2.** A gift. [< F < L *donare* to give]

done (dun) Past participle of DO[1]. — *adj.* **1.** Completed; finished; ended; agreed. **2.** Cooked sufficiently.

do·nee (dō·nē′) *n.* One who receives a gift.

done for *U.S. Informal* **1.** Ruined; finished; exhausted. **2.** Dead or about to die.

done in *U.S. Informal* **1.** Utterly exhausted; worn out with fatigue. Also **done up. 2.** Killed; destroyed.

don·jon (dun′jən, don′-) *n.* The main tower or keep of a castle. [< OF, the lord's tower]

Don Juan (don wän′) **1.** A legendary Spanish nobleman and seducer of women. **2.** Any rake or seducer.

don·key (dong′kē, dung′-) *n.* **1.** The ass. **2.** A stupid or stubborn person. [? after *Duncan*, a personal name]

Don·na (don′ə, *Ital.* dôn′nä) *n.* Lady; Madam, a title of respect or address in Italian-speaking countries.

don·nish (don′ish) *adj.* **1.** Of or suggestive of a university don. **2.** Formal; pedantic. — **don′nish·ness** *n.*

don·ny·brook (don′ē·brŏŏk′) *n.* A brawl marked by roughness and abusive lamguage; free-for-all. [after *Donnybrook Fair*, an event known for its brawls, held in Ireland]

do·nor (dō′nər) *n.* **1.** One who gives. **2.** *Med.* One who furnishes blood, skin, etc. [< AF < L *donare* to give]

Don Quix·ote (don kwik′sət, kē·hō′tē; *Sp.* dôn kē·hō′tä) **1.** A satirical novel by Cervantes. **2.** The hero of this novel, a naive, dreamy, befuddled idealist.

don't (dōnt) **1.** Do not. **2.** Does not: now nonstandard in general American speech.

doo·dad (dōō′dad) *n. Informal* **1.** A small ornament; bauble. **2.** A doohickey. [Humorous coinage; extension of DO]

doo·dle (dōōd′l) *Informal v.t. & v.i.* ·dled, ·dling To draw or scribble in an aimless, preoccupied way. — *n.* A design so made. [Cf. dial. E *doodle* to be idle, trifle]

doo·dle·bug (dōōd′l·bug′) *n.* **1.** *U.S. Dial.* The larva of several insects. **2.** Loosely, the tumblebug. [? < dial. E *doodle* idler, fool + BUG]

doo·hick·ey (dōō′hik′ē) *n. pl.* ·eys *U.S. Informal* A small object whose exact name is not known or remembered. [Humorous coinage; extension of DO]

doom (dōōm) *v.t.* **1.** To pronounce judgment or sentence upon; condemn. **2.** To destine to an unhappy fate. — *n.* **1.** An unhappy fate. **2.** An adverse judicial sentence. **3.** Death or ruin. **4.** The Last Judgment. [OE *dōm*]

dooms·day (dōōmz′dā′) *n.* **1.** The day of the Last Judgment; the end of the world. **2.** Any day of final judgment. Also spelled *domesday.* [OE *dōm* doom + *dæg* day]

door (dôr, dōr) *n.* **1.** A hinged, sliding, folding, or rotating structure, as of wood, used for closing or opening an entrance to a house, vehicle, etc. **2.** A doorway, often representing an entire building or room: to live six *doors* away. **3.** Any means of entrance or exit. — **Syn.** See ENTRANCE[1]. [Fusion of OE *duru* pair of doors and *dor* gate]

door·bell (dôr′bel′, dōr′-) *n.* A bell at a doorway.

door·jamb (dôr′jam′, dōr′-) *n.* A vertical piece at the side of a doorway supporting the lintel.

door·keep·er (dôr′kē′pər, dōr′-) *n.* A guardian or keeper of a doorway.

door·knob (dôr′nob′, dōr′-) *n.* A handle to open a door.

door·man (dôr′man′, -mən, dōr′-) *n. pl.* ·men (′men′, -mən) An attendant at the door of a hotel, apartment house, etc., who assists persons entering and leaving the building.

door mat A mat placed at an entrance for wiping the shoes.

door·nail (dôr′nāl′, dōr′-) *n.* A large-headed nail, formerly used in the construction and ornamentation of doors. — **dead as a doornail** Unquestionably dead.

door·plate (dôr′plāt′, dōr′-) *n.* A metal plate on a door, with the occupant's name, street number, etc.

door·post (dôr′pōst′, dōr′-) *n.* A doorjamb.

door·sill (dôr′sil′, dōr′-) *n.* The sill or threshold of a door.

door·step (dôr′step′, dōr′-) *n.* A step or one of a series of steps leading to a door.

door·stop (dôr′stop′, dōr′-) *n.* A device to keep a door open.

door·way (dôr′wā′, dōr′-) *n.* The passage for entrance and exit into and out of a building, room, etc. — **Syn.** See ENTRANCE[1].

door·yard (dôr′yärd′, dōr′-) *n.* A yard around, or esp. in front of, a house.

dope (dōp) *n.* **1.** A viscid substance or unusually thick liquid used as a lubricant. **2.** A filler, varnish, or similar preparation used for protecting and making taut the fabric of airplane wings, etc. **3.** *Photog.* A developer. **4.** *Slang* A drug or narcotic. **5.** *Slang* A dull-witted or incapable individual. **6.** *Slang* Inside information. — *v.t.* doped, dop·ing **1.** To apply dope to. **2.** To adulterate or treat (a substance) with another. **3.** *Slang* To give drugs to; drug;

often with *up*. **4.** *Slang* To plan or solve: usu. with *out*. [Orig. U.S., prob. < Du. *doop* a dipping, sauce]

do·pey (dō′pē) *adj.* **·pi·er**, **·pi·est** *Slang* **1.** Lethargic from or as from narcotics. **2.** Stupid. Also **do′py**.

Doppler effect *Physics* The change in the frequency of a sound, light, or other wave caused by movement of its source relative to the observer. Also **Doppler shift**. [after C. J. *Doppler*, 1803–53, German physicist and mathematician]

Dor·ic (dôr′ik, dor′-) *adj. Archit.* Of or pertaining to the simplest of the three orders of Greek architecture characterized by heavy, fluted columns and unadorned capitals.

dorm (dôrm) *n. Informal* A dormitory.

dor·mant (dôr′mənt) *adj.* **1.** Asleep or as if asleep; motionless through sleep or torpidity. **2.** Not active; inoperative. **3.** *Biol.* Marked by partial suspension of vital processes, as many animals and plants in winter. [< OF < L *dormire* to sleep] — **dor′man·cy** *n.*

dor·mer (dôr′mər) *n.* **1.** A vertical window set in a small gable that projects from a sloping roof. Also **dormer window**. **2.** The roofed projection or gable itself. [< OF *dormeor* < L < *dormire* to sleep]

DORMER WINDOW

dor·mi·to·ry (dôr′mə·tôr′ē, -tō′rē) *n. pl.* **·ries** **1.** A large room with sleeping accommodations for many persons. **2.** A building providing sleeping and living accommodations, esp. at a school, college, or resort. [< L < *dormire* to sleep]

dor·mouse (dôr′mous′) *n. pl.* **·mice** A small, arboreal European rodent. [ME ? dial. E *dorm* to doze + MOUSE]

dor·sal (dôr′səl) *adj. Anat.* Of, pertaining to, on or near the back. [< L *dorsum* back] — **dor′sal·ly** *adv.*

dorsi- *combining form* **1.** On, to, or of the back. **2.** Dorso-. [< L *dorsum* back]

dorso- *combining form* Dorsal. [< L *dorsum* back]

do·ry (dôr′ē, dō′rē) *n. pl.* **·ries** A deep, flat-bottomed rowboat with a sharp prow, used esp. by North Atlantic fishermen. [< native Honduran name]

dos·age (dō′sij) *n.* **1.** The administering of medicine in prescribed quantity. **2.** The amount of medicine to be given.

dose (dōs) *n.* **1.** A particular quantity of medicine given or prescribed to be given at one time. **2.** *Informal* A particular amount of something usually disagreeable or painful. — *v.* **dosed**, **dos·ing** *v.t.* **1.** To give medicine, etc., to in doses. **2.** To give, as medicine or drugs, in doses. — *v.i.* **3.** To take medicines. [< MF < Med.L < Gk. *dosis* gift]

do·sim·e·ter (dō·sim′ə·tər) *n. Med.* An instrument for measuring the total amount of radiation absorbed in a given time. [< Gk. *dosis* dose + -METER]

dos·si·er (dos′ē·ā, dos′ē·ər; *Fr.* dô·syā′) *n.* A collection of papers, documents, etc., relating to a particular matter or person. [< F, bundle of papers]

dost (dust) Do: archaic or poetic second person singular, present tense of DO¹: used with *thou*.

dot¹ (dot) *n.* **1.** A tiny, usu. round, mark; a speck, spot, or point. **2.** A small amount. **3.** In writing and printing, a point used as a part of a letter, in punctuation, etc. **4.** *Music* **a** A point written after a note or rest that increases its time value by half. **b** A point placed over a note to indicate staccato treatment. **5.** A signal in Morse code that is of shorter duration than the dash. — *v.* **dot·ted**, **dot·ting** *v.t.* **1.** To mark with a dot or dots. **2.** To make by means of dots; stud. **3.** To be scattered thickly over or about. — *v.i.* **4.** To make a dot or dots. — **to dot one's i's and cross one's t's** To be exact or correct. [OE *dott* head of a boil] — **dot′ter** *n.*

dot² (dot, *Fr.* dō) *n.* A woman's marriage portion; dowry. [< F < L *dos*, *dotis*] — **do·tal** (dōt′l) *adj.*

do·tage (dō′tij) *n.* **1.** Feebleness of mind as a result of old age; senility. **2.** Foolish and excessive affection.

do·tard (dō′tərd) *n.* A foolish old person.

dote (dōt) *v.i.* **dot·ed**, **dot·ing** **1.** To lavish extreme fondness: with *on* or *upon*. **2.** To be feeble-minded as a result of old age. [ME *doten*] — **dot′er** *n.*

doth (duth) Does: archaic or poetic third person singular, present tense of DO¹.

dot·ing (dō′ting) *adj.* **1.** Extravagantly or foolishly fond. **2.** Feeble-minded; senile. — **dot′ing·ly** *adv.*

dot·ter·el (dot′ər·əl) *n.* A migratory plover of northern Europe and Asia. Also **dot′trel** (-rəl). [ME *dotrelle*]

dot·tle (dot′l) *n.* The plug of tobacco ash left in a pipe after smoking. Also **dot′tel**. [? Dim. of DOT¹]

dot·ty (dot′ē) *adj.* **·ti·er**, **·ti·est** **1.** Consisting of or marked with dots. **2.** *Informal* Of unsteady or feeble gait. **3.** *Informal* Slightly demented; mentally weak.

Douai Bible An English translation of the Vulgate Bible made by Roman Catholic scholars at Reims and Douai and completed in 1610. A revision of the New Testament was published in 1941. Also **Douay Bible** or **Version**.

doub·le (dub′əl) *adj.* **1.** Combined with another usu. identical one: a *double* consonant. **2.** Two together: *double* lines. **3.** Twofold; duple. **4.** More than one; not single; dual: a *double* role. **5.** Consisting of two layers. **6.** Made for two: a *double* bed. **7.** Twice as great, as large, as many, etc.: *double* fare. **8.** Extra heavy, large, wide, etc.: a *double* blanket. **9.** Marked by duplicity; two-faced: a *double* life. **10.** *Music* Producing tones one octave lower than the notes indicated on a score: said of an instrument. **11.** *Bot.* Having the petals increased in number. — *n.* **1.** Something that is twice as much. **2.** A duplicate. **3.** A player or singer who can substitute for another; understudy. **4.** A sharp or backward turn, as of a hunted fox. **5.** A trick or stratagem. **6.** A fold or pleat. **7.** *pl.* In tennis, etc., a game having two players on each side. **8.** In baseball, a fair hit that enables the batter to reach second base. **9.** In bridge, the act of challenging an opponent's bid by increasing its value and thus the penalty if the contract is not fulfilled; also, a hand warranting such an act. — **on** (or at) **the double 1.** In double time. **2.** *Informal* Quickly. — *v.* **led**, **ling** *v.t.* **1.** To make twice as great in number, size, value, force, etc. **2.** To be twice the quantity or number of. **3.** To fold or bend one part of upon another: usu. with *over*, *up*, *back*. **4.** To clench (the fist): often with *up*. **5.** *Naut.* To sail around: to *double* a cape. **6.** *Music* To duplicate a voice or part in unison or in another octave. **7.** In baseball, to advance (a base runner) by making a two-base hit: He *doubled* him home. **8.** In bridge, to challenge (an opponent) by announcing a double. — *v.i.* **9.** To become double; increase by an equal amount. **10.** To turn and go back on a course: often with *back*. **11.** To act or perform in two capacities. **12.** To serve as a double: to *double* for an actress. **13.** In baseball, to make a two-base hit. **14.** In bridge, to announce a double. — **to double in brass** *U.S. Slang* **1.** To be useful or adept in another capacity apart from one's (or its) specialty. **2.** Originally, of musicians, to play a second instrument in addition to the regular one. — **to double back 1.** To fold back. **2.** To turn and go back on the same or a parallel course. — **to double up 1.** To bend over or cause to bend over, as from pain or laughter. **2.** *U.S. Informal* To share one's quarters, bed, etc., with another. — *adv.* In pairs; twofold; doubly. [< OF < L *duplus* double]

doub·le-bar·reled (dub′əl·bar′əld) *adj.* **1.** Having two barrels, as a shotgun. **2.** Ambiguous, as a remark.

double bass **1.** The largest and deepest-toned of the stringed instruments played with a bow: also called *bass viol*. **2.** The contrabass.

double bassoon A double-reed instrument pitched an octave below the ordinary bassoon: also called *contrabassoon*.

double bed A bed wide enough for two people.

double boiler A cooking utensil consisting of two pots, one fitting into the other. Food in the upper pot is cooked by the heat from water boiling in the lower pot.

dou·ble-breast·ed (dub′əl·bres′tid) *adj.* Having two rows of buttons and fastening so as to provide a double thickness of cloth across the breast: said of a coat or vest.

double chin A fat, fleshy fold under the chin.

doub·le-cross (*v.* dub′əl·krôs′, -kros′; *n.* dub′əl·krôs′, -kros′) *Slang v.t.* To betray by failing to act as promised. — *n.* A betrayal; a treacherous act. — **doub′le-cross′er** *n.*

doub·le-date (dub′əl·dāt′) *v.i.* **·dat·ed**, **·dat·ing** *U.S. Informal* To make or go out on a social engagement of two couples. — **double date**

doub·le-deal·ing (dub′əl·dē′ling) *adj.* Treacherous; deceitful. — *n.* Treachery; duplicity. — **doub′le-deal′er** *n.*

doub·le-deck·er (dub′əl·dek′ər) *n.* **1.** A ship, vehicle, etc., having two levels. **2.** *U.S. Informal* A sandwich made with three slices of bread and two layers of filling.

doub·le-edged (dub′əl·ejd′) *adj.* **1.** Having two cutting edges. **2.** Applicable both ways, as an argument.

dou·ble-en·ten·dre (dōō-blän-tän′dr) *n.* A word or phrase of double meaning. [Alter. of F *double entente*]

double entry A method of bookkeeping in which every transaction is made to appear as both a debit and a credit.

double exposure *Photog.* The act of exposing the same film or plate twice, as in making a composite photograph; also, a print developed from a film or plate so exposed.

doub·le-faced (dub′əl·fāst′) *adj.* **1.** Having two faces. **2.** Deceitful; hypocritical; two-faced.

double feature A program of two motion pictures.

doub·le-head·er (dub′əl·hed′ər) *n.* **1.** In baseball, two games played in succession on the same day by the same two teams. **2.** A train pulled by two locomotives.

double indemnity A clause in a life insurance policy by which a payment of double the face value of the policy is made in the event of accidental death.

double jeopardy The peril under which a defendant is placed when he is tried more than once for the same offense.

doub·le-joint·ed (dub'əl-join'tid) *adj.* Having very flexible joints that allow limbs, fingers, etc., to be bent at unusual angles.

doub·le·ness (dub'əl-nis) *n.* **1.** The state or quality of being double. **2.** Duplicity; deceitfulness.

doub·le-park (dub'əl-pärk') *v.t. & v.i.* To park (a motor vehicle) alongside another already parked at the curb.

double play In baseball, a play in which two base runners are put out during one continuous play of the ball.

double pneumonia Pneumonia affecting both lungs.

dou·ble-reed (dub'əl-rēd') *adj. Music* Designating a group of wind instruments having two reeds united at the lower end and separated at the upper, as the oboe and bassoon.

double standard A moral standard that permits men greater freedom than women, esp. in sexual behavior.

doub·let (dub'lit) *n.* **1.** A short, close-fitting outer garment, with or without sleeves, worn by men during the Renaissance. **2.** A pair of like things; a couple. **3.** *Ling.* One of a pair of words derived from the same original but entering a language through different routes, as *regal* and *royal*. [< OF, something folded, orig. dim. of *double*]

double take Delayed reaction to a joke or unusual situation, characterized by blank acceptance initially and then sudden, startled realization of the actual significance.

double talk **1.** A rapid flow of actual words mixed with meaningless syllables, made to sound like talk. **2.** Ambiguous talk meant to deceive.

double time **1.** In the U.S. Army, a fast marching step at the rate of 180 three-foot steps per minute. **2.** A wage rate that is twice one's normal pay.

doub·le·tree (dub'əl-trē') *n. U.S.* A crossbar on a wagon, carriage or plow.

doub·loon (du-bloon') *n.* A former Spanish gold coin, originally worth about 16 dollars. [< Sp. *doble* double]

doub·ly (dub'lē) *adv.* **1.** In twofold degree; twice. **2.** In pairs. **3.** In twice the quantity.

doubt (dout) *v.t.* **1.** To hold the truth, validity, or reliability of as uncertain; hesitate to believe or accept. — *v.i.* **2.** To be unconvinced or mistrustful. — *n.* **1.** Lack of certainty about the truth or fact of something. **2.** A condition or state of affairs giving rise to uncertainty: Their fate was in *doubt*. **3.** An unresolved point or matter. — **beyond doubt** Unquestionably; certainly. — **no doubt 1.** Certainly. **2.** Most likely; probably. — **without doubt** Certainly. [< OF < L *dubitare*] — **doubt'er** *n.*

doubt·ful (dout'fəl) *adj.* **1.** Subject to or causing doubt; uncertain; unsettled. **2.** Having or experiencing doubt; undecided. **3.** Indistinct or obscure in appearance, meaning, etc.; vague; ambiguous. **4.** Of questionable character: a *doubtful* reputation. — **doubt'ful·ly** *adv.* — **doubt'ful·ness** *n.*

doubt·less (dout'lis) *adv.* **1.** Unquestionably. **2.** Probably. Also **doubt'less·ly.** — *adj.* Free from uncertainty.

douche (doosh) *n.* **1.** A jet of water, etc., directed into or onto some part of the body. **2.** A cleansing or medicinal treatment of this kind. **3.** A syringe or other device for administering a douche. — *v.* **douched, douch·ing** *v.t.* **1.** To cleanse or treat medicinally with a douche. — *v.i.* **2.** To administer a douche. [< F < Ital. < L *ducere* to lead]

dough (dō) *n.* **1.** A soft mass of moistened flour or meal and other ingredients, mixed for making bread, pastry, etc. **2.** Any soft, pasty mass. **3.** *Slang* Money. [OE *dāh*]

dough·nut (dō'nut') *n.* A small cake of usu. leavened and sweetened dough, cooked by frying in deep fat.

dough·ty (dou'tē) *adj.* **·ti·er, ·ti·est** Valiant; brave: chiefly humorous. — [OE *dyhtig, dohtig*] — **dough'ti·ly** *adv.* — **dough'ti·ness** *n.*

dough·y (dō'ē) *adj.* **dough·i·er, dough·i·est** Resembling dough in consistency or appearance; soft, pasty, pale, etc.

Douglas fir A large timber tree of the pine family, growing on the Pacific coast of the U.S.: often called *red fir, Nootka fir.* Also **Douglas hemlock, Douglas pine, Douglas spruce.** [after David *Douglas*, 1798–1834, Scottish botanist]

dour (door, dour) *adj.* Forbidding and surly; morosely stern; ill-tempered. [< OF < L *durus* hard] — **dour'ly** *adv.* — **dour'ness** *n.*

dou·ra (door'ə) See DURRA.

douse[1] (dous) *v.* **doused, dous·ing** *v.t.* **1.** To plunge into water or other liquid; dip suddenly; duck. **2.** To drench with liquid. — *v.i.* **3.** To become drenched or immersed. — *n.* A ducking or drenching. [Origin unknown]

douse[2] (dous) *v.t.* **doused, dous·ing** **1.** *Informal* To put out; extinguish. **2.** *Informal* To take off, as clothes. **3.** *Naut.* To take in or haul down quickly, esp. a sail. [Cf. MDu. *dossen* to beat, strike]

dove[1] (duv) *n.* **1.** Any bird of the pigeon family, esp. the mourning dove, turtle dove, etc. **2.** *Usu. cap.* A symbol of the Holy Ghost. **3.** A symbol of peace. **4.** A gentle, innocent, tender person. [ME *duve*]

dove[2] (dōv) *Informal* Alternative past tense of DIVE.

dove·cote (duv'kōt', -kot') *n.* A box set on a pole or on a building, used for breeding pigeons. Also **dove'cot'** (-kot').

dove·tail (duv'tāl') *n.* **1.** A tenon shaped like a wedge and designed to interlock with a mortise of similar shape. **2.** A joint thus formed. — *v.t. & v.i.* **1.** To join by dovetails. **2.** To fit together closely or harmoniously.

DOVETAIL
JOINT
a Before joining.
b Joined.

dow·a·ger (dou'ə-jər) *n.* **1.** In English law, a widow holding property or title derived from her deceased husband. **2.** *Informal* An elderly woman of dignified bearing. [< OF *douaigiere*, ult. < L *dotare* to give]

dow·dy (dou'dē) *adj.* **·di·er, ·di·est** Notably devoid of smartness in dress; frumpish. — *n.* *pl.* **·dies** A dowdy woman. [ME *doude* slut] — **dow'di·ly** *adv.* — **dow'di·ness** *n.*

dow·el (dou'əl) *n.* A pin or peg fitted tightly into adjacent holes of two pieces so as to hold them together. Also **dowel pin.** — *v.t.* **dow·eled** or **·elled, dow·el·ing** or **·el·ling** To furnish or fasten with dowels. [ME, ? < MLG *dovel* plug]

dow·er (dou'ər) *n.* **1.** The part of a deceased man's estate that is assigned by law to his widow for life. **2.** A natural talent or endowment. **3.** A dowry. — *v.t.* **1.** To provide with a dower. **2.** To endow, as with a talent or quality. [< OF < LL < L *dos, dotis* dowry]

dow·er·y (dou'ər-ē) See DOWRY.

DOWELS

down[1] (doun) *adv.* **1.** From a higher to a lower place. **2.** In or on a lower place, level, etc. **3.** On or to the ground. **4.** To or toward the south. **5.** To or in a place regarded as distant or outlying: *down* on the farm. **6.** Below the surface or horizon. **7.** From an upright to a prone or prostrate position: to knock a man *down*. **8.** To lesser bulk, heavier consistency, etc.: The mixture boiled *down*. **9.** To less activity, intensity, etc.: Things quieted *down*. **10.** To a lower amount, rate, etc.: Prices have gone *down*. **11.** In or into subjection or control: to put the rebels *down*. **12.** In or into a depressed or prostrate physical or mental state. **13.** Completely; fully: loaded *down* with honors. **14.** From an earlier time or individual. **15.** In cash as partial payment: five dollars *down*. **16.** In writing: Take *down* his name. — **down with** (Let us) do away with or overthrow. — *adj.* **1.** Directed downward: a *down* curve. **2.** *Informal* Downcast; depressed. **3.** Given in cash as a partial amount: a *down* payment. **4.** In games, behind an opponent by a specified number of points, strokes, etc. **5.** In football, not in play: said of the ball. — **down and out** In a completely miserable state, as of poverty or desolation. — **down on** *Informal* Annoyed with or hostile to. — *prep.* **1.** In a descending direction along, upon, or in. **2.** During the course of: *down* the years. — *v.t.* **1.** To knock, throw, or put down. **2.** *Informal* To swallow quickly; gulp. — *n.* **1.** A downward movement; descent. **2.** A reverse of fortune: chiefly in the phrase **ups and downs. 3.** In football, any of the four consecutive plays during which a team must advance the ball at least ten yards to keep possession of it; also, the declaring of the ball as out of play. [OE *dūne* < *of dūne* from the hill]

down[2] (doun) *n.* **1.** The fine, soft plumage of birds under the feathers, esp. that on the breast of water birds. **2.** Any feathery, fluffy substance. [< ON *dūnn*]

down[3] (doun) *n.* **1.** *pl.* Turf-covered, undulating tracts of upland, esp. in southern and SE England. **2.** A hill, esp. of sand; dune. [OE *dūn.* Akin to DUNE.]

down·cast (doun'kast', -käst') *adj.* **1.** Directed downward: *downcast* eyes. **2.** Low in spirits; dejected; depressed.

Down East *Informal* New England, esp. Maine. — **down·east** (doun'ēst') *adj.* — **down'east'er** *n.*

down·er (doun'ər) *n.* *Slang* Any of various drugs that depress the central nervous system, as barbiturates.

down·fall (doun'fôl') *n.* **1.** A sudden descent, as in reputation or fortune; collapse; ruin. **2.** A sudden, heavy fall of rain, etc. **3.** A deadfall (def. 1). — **down'fall·en** *adj.*

down·grade (doun'grād') *n.* A descending slope, as of a hill or road. — **on the downgrade** Declining in health, reputation, status, etc. — *adj.* Downhill. — *v.t.* **·grad·ed, ·grad·ing** To reduce in status, salary, etc.

down·heart·ed (doun'här'tid) *adj.* Dejected; discouraged. — **down'heart'ed·ly** *adv.* — **down'heart'ed·ness** *n.*

down·hill (*adv.* doun'hil'; *adj.* doun'hil') *adv.* In a downward direction; toward the bottom of a hill. — **to go downhill** To decline, as in success or health. — *adj.* Descending.

Downing Street (dou'ning) **1.** A street in London; site of many British government offices. **2.** *Informal* The British government.

down payment An initial payment on a purchase.

down·pour (doun'pôr', -pōr') *n.* A heavy fall of rain.

down·right (doun'rīt') *adj.* **1.** Thorough; utter: *downright* nonsense. **2.** Straightforward. — *adv.* Thoroughly; utterly.

down·stairs (*adv.* doun'stârz'; *adj. & n.* doun'stârz') *adv.* **1.** Down the stairs. **2.** On or to a lower floor. — *adj.* Situated on a lower floor: also **down'stair'.** — *n.* The downstairs part of a house or other building.

down·stream (*adv.* doun′strēm′; *adj.* doun′strēm′) *adv.* Down the stream. — *adj.* In the direction of the current.

down·town (*adv.* doun′toun′; *adj.* doun′toun′) *adv.* To, toward, or in the geographically lower section of a town or city. — *adj.* Located in the geographically lower section of a town or city, usu. the chief business section.

down·trod·den (doun′trod′n) *adj.* **1.** Trampled under foot. **2.** Subjugated; oppressed. Also **down′trod′.**

down·ward (doun′wərd) *adv.* **1.** From a higher to a lower level, position, etc. **2.** From an earlier or more remote time, place, etc. Also **down′wards**, occasionally **down′ward·ly.** — *adj.* **1.** Descending from a higher to a lower level. **2.** Descending in course from that which is more remote.

down·y (dou′nē) *adj.* **down·i·er, down·i·est 1.** Of, like, or covered with down. **2.** Soft; quiet. — **down′i·ness** *n.*

dow·ry (dou′rē) *n. pl.* **·ries 1.** The money or property a wife brings to her husband at marriage: also called *portion.* **2.** A natural talent or endowment. [See DOWER]

dowse[1] (dous) See DOUSE[1].

dowse[2] (douz) *v.i.* **dowsed, dows·ing** To search for with a divining rod. [Origin uncertain] — **dows′er** *n.*

dows·ing rod (douz′ing) A divining rod.

dox·ol·o·gy (dok·sol′ə·jē) *n. pl.* **·gies** A hymn or verse of praise to God. — **greater doxology** The Gloria in excelsis Deo. — **lesser doxology** The Gloria Patri. [< Med.L < Gk. < *doxa* praise + *legein* to speak] — **dox·o·log·i·cal** (dok′sə·loj′i·kəl) *adj.* — **dox·o·log′i·cal·ly** *adv.*

doy·ley, doy·ly (doi′lē) See DOILY.

doze (dōz) *v.* **dozed, doz·ing** *v.i.* **1.** To sleep lightly or be drowsy for brief periods of time; nap. — *v.t.* **2.** To spend (time) in napping or in being half asleep. — **to doze off** To fall into a light, brief sleep. — *n.* A light, brief sleep; nap. [< Scand., ? ult. < ON *dūsa* to doze]

doz·en (duz′ən) *n. pl.* **doz·ens**; *when preceded by a number,* **doz·en** A group or set of twelve things. Abbr. *doz, doz., dz.* [< OF < L < *duo* two + *decem* ten]

do·zy (dō′zē) *adj.* **·zi·er, ·zi·est** Drowsy. — **do′zi·ly** *adv.* — **do′zi·ness** *n.*

drab[1] (drab) *adj.* **drab·ber, drab·best 1.** Lacking brightness; dull and monotonous. **2.** Having a dull, yellowish brown color. **3.** Made of a thick, woolen, yellowish brown cloth. — *n.* **1.** A dull, yellowish brown color. **2.** A thick, woolen, yellowish brown cloth. [< F *drap* cloth < LL *drappus,* ? < Celtic] — **drab′ly** *adv.* — **drab′ness** *n.*

drab[2] (drab) *n.* **1.** A slipshod, untidy woman. **2.** A prostitute; slut. — *v.i.* **drabbed, drab·bing 1.** To associate with prostitutes. **2.** To be a prostitute. [? < Celtic]

drachm (dram) *n.* **1.** A dram. **2.** A drachma.

drach·ma (drak′mə) *n. pl.* **·mas** or **·mae** (-mē) **1.** An ancient Greek silver coin. **2.** The standard monetary unit of Greece: in 1960 worth about 3 U.S. cents. **3.** An ancient Greek unit of weight. **4.** Any of several modern weights, as the dram. [< L < Gk. *drachmē* a handful]

draft (draft, dräft) *n.* **1.** The act or process of selecting an individual or individuals for some special duty or purpose; esp., the selection of men for compulsory military service; conscription. **2.** The condition of being selected for some special duty or purpose; also, those selected. **3.** A current of air. **4.** A device for controlling the airflow, as in a furnace. **5.** A written order, as of an individual or bank, directing the payment of money. **6.** A sketch, plan, or design of something to be made. **7.** A preliminary or rough version of a writing. **8.** A quantity of liquid for drinking: a *draft* of ale. **9.** The act of drinking; also, the liquid taken at one drink. **10.** The drawing of liquid from its container. **11.** The act of drawing in a fishnet; also, the amount of fish taken with one drawing of a net. **12.** The act of drawing air, smoke, etc., into the lungs; also, the air, etc., taken in. **13.** The pulling of something, as a loaded wagon; also, the load pulled. **14.** A heavy demand or drain on something. **15.** *pl.* Draughts. **16.** *Naut.* The depth of water required for a ship to float, esp. when loaded. — **on draft** Ready to be drawn, as beer, from a cask, etc. — *v.t.* **1.** To draw up in preliminary form, esp. in writing. **2.** To select and draw off, as for military service. **3.** To draw off or away. **4.** To cut a draft on (a stone). — *adj.* **1.** Suitable to be used for pulling heavy loads: a *draft* animal. **2.** Not bottled, as beer. Also *Brit.* **draught.** [ME < OE *dragan* to draw]

draft board An official board of civilians that selects men for compulsory service in the U.S. armed forces.

draft dodger One who avoids or attempts to avoid conscription into military service.

draft·ee (draf·tē′, dräf-) *n.* A person drafted for service in the armed forces.

drafts·man (drafts′mən, dräfts′-) *n. pl.* **·men** (-mən) **1.** One who draws or prepares designs or plans of buildings, machinery, etc. **2.** One who draws up documents, as deeds. **3.** An artist esp. skilled in drawing.

draft·y (draf′tē, dräf′-) *adj.* **draft·i·er, draft·i·est** Having or exposed to drafts of air: a *drafty* room. Also spelled *draughty.* — **draft′i·ly** *adv.* — **draft′i·ness** *n.*

drag (drag) *v.* **dragged, drag·ging** *v.t.* **1.** To pull along by main force; haul. **2.** To sweep or search the bottom of, as with a net or grapnel; dredge. **3.** To catch or recover, as with a grapnel or net. **4.** To draw along heavily and wearily. **5.** To harrow (land). **6.** To continue tediously: often with *on* or *out.* **7.** To introduce (an irrelevant subject or matter) into a discussion, argument, etc.: usu. with *in.* — *v.i.* **8.** To be pulled or hauled along. **9.** To move heavily or slowly. **10.** To lag behind. **11.** To pass slowly. **12.** To use a grapnel, drag, or dredge. — **to drag one's feet** *U.S. Informal* To act with deliberate slowness. — *n.* **1.** The act of dragging. **2.** The resistance encountered in dragging: a heavy *drag* on the left wheel. **3.** A slow, heavy, usu. impeded motion or movement. **4.** Something that slows down movement, as a clog on a wheel. **5.** Something heavy that is dragged. **6.** A contrivance for dragging through water to find or bring up something. **7.** Anything that hinders. **8.** A stagecoach, with seats inside and on the top. **9.** *U.S. Slang* Influence that brings special favors; pull. **10.** *Slang* A puff on a cigarette, etc. **11.** *U.S. Slang* One who or that which is tedious or colorless. [ME, prob. < OE *dragan*]

drag·gle (drag′əl) *v.* **·gled, ·gling** *v.t.* **1.** To make soiled or wet by dragging in mud or water. — *v.i.* **2.** To become wet or soiled. **3.** To follow slowly; lag. [Freq. of DRAG]

drag·net (drag′net′) *n.* **1.** A net to be drawn along the bottom of the water or along the ground, to find or capture something. **2.** Any device or plan for catching a criminal.

drag·o·man (drag′ə·mən) *n. pl.* **·mans** (-mənz) or **·men** (-mən) An interpreter or guide for travelers in the Near East. [< F < LGk. < Arabic *tarjumān* translator]

drag·on (drag′ən) *n.* **1.** A mythical, serpentlike, winged monster. **2.** A fierce, violent person. **3.** An overbearing, watchful woman. [< OF < L < Gk. *drakōn* serpent]

drag·on·fly (drag′ən·flī′) *n. pl.* **·flies** A predatory insect having a slender body, four wings, and strong jaws.

dra·goon (drə·gōōn′) *n.* In some European armies, a cavalryman. — *v.t.* **1.** To harass by dragoons. **2.** To coerce; browbeat. [< F *dragon,* a type of 17th c. firearm]

drain (drān) *v.t.* **1.** To draw off (water, etc.) gradually. **2.** To draw water, etc., from: to *drain* a swamp. **3.** To empty (a glass, cup, etc.) by drinking. **4.** To use up gradually; exhaust. **5.** To filter. — *v.i.* **6.** To flow off gradually. **7.** To become dry by the flowing off or away of liquid. **8.** To discharge waters contained: said of an area: The region *drains* into the lake. — *n.* **1.** A trench, or similar device for draining. **2.** *Surg.* A substance, or appliance inserted into a wound or cavity to afford a channel for discharge. **3.** A continuous outflow, expenditure, or depletion. **4.** The act of draining. [OE *drēahnian*] — **drain′er** *n.*

drain·age (drā′nij) *n.* **1.** The act or method of draining. **2.** A system of drains. **3.** That which is drained off. **4.** A drainage basin.

drainage basin A large surface area whose waters are drained off into a principal river system.

drain·pipe (drān′pīp′) *n.* A pipe used for draining.

drake (drāk) *n.* A male duck. [ME]

dram (dram) *n.* **1.** An apothecaries' weight equal to 60 grains, 3.89 grams, or one eighth of an ounce. Abbr. *dr.* **2.** An avoirdupois measure equal to 27.34 grains, 1.77 grams, or one sixteenth of an ounce. See table inside back cover. **3.** A fluid dram. **4.** A drink of alcoholic liquor. **5.** A drachma. **6.** A small portion. Also spelled *drachm.* — *v.* **drammed, dram·ming** *v.t.* **1.** To ply with liquor. — *v.i.* **2.** To use intoxicants freely. [< OF < L < Gk. *drachmē* a handful]

dra·ma (drä′mə, dram′ə) *n.* **1.** A literary composition written to be performed upon a stage, telling a story, usu. of human conflicts and emotions; a play. **2.** Stage plays as a branch of literature: the classical *drama.* **3.** The art or profession of writing, acting, or producing plays. **4.** A series of dramatic events. **5.** The quality of being dramatic. [< LL < Gk., action < *draein* to act, do]

Dram·a·mine (dram′ə·mēn) *n.* Proprietary name of a drug for relieving motion sickness. Also **dram′a·mine.**

dra·mat·ic (drə·mat′ik) *adj.* **1.** Of, connected with, or like the drama. **2.** Characterized by the action or spirit of the drama; theatrical. — **dra·mat′i·cal·ly** *adv.*

dra·mat·ics (drə·mat′iks) *n.pl.* (*usu. construed as sing. in def. 2*) **1.** Dramatic performance, esp. by amateurs. **2.** The art of staging or acting plays.

dram·a·tis per·so·nae (dram′ə·tis pər·sō′nē) *Latin* The characters of a play; also, a list of these.

dram·a·tist (dram′ə·tist) *n.* One who writes plays.

dram·a·tize (dram′ə·tīz) *v.* **·tized, ·tiz·ing** *v.t.* **1.** To present in dramatic form; adapt for performance, as a play. **2.** To represent or interpret (events, oneself, etc.) in a theatrical manner. —*v.i.* **3.** To be suitable for dramatizing. Also *Brit.* **dram'a·tise.** —**dram'a·ti·za'tion** *n.*

dram·a·turge (dram'ə·tûrj) *n.* A dramatist. Also **dram'a·tur'gist.** [< F < Gk. < *ergein* to work]

dram·a·tur·gy (dram'ə·tûr'jē) *n.* The art of writing or producing plays, or of acting in them; dramatics. —**dram·a·tur'gic** (dram'ə·tûr'jik) *or* **·gi·cal** *adj.*

drank (drangk) Past tense of DRINK.

drape (drāp) *v.* **draped, drap·ing** *v.t.* **1.** To cover or adorn in a graceful fashion, as with drapery or clothing. **2.** To arrange in graceful folds. **3.** *Informal* To dispose in a leisurely or sloppy manner. **4.** To hang in folds. —*n.* **1.** *U.S. & Canadian Usu. pl.* Drapery. **2.** The way in which cloth hangs, as in clothing. [< F *draper* to weave]

drap·er (drā'pər) *n. Brit.* A dealer in cloth or dry goods.

drap·er·y (drā'pər·ē) *n. pl.* **·er·ies 1.** Loosely hanging attire, esp. on figures in painting, sculpture, etc. **2.** *Often pl.* Hangings or curtains arranged in loose folds. **3.** Cloth.

dras·tic (dras'tik) *adj.* Acting vigorously; extreme. [< Gk. *drastikos* effective < *draein* to act] —**dras'ti·cal·ly** *adv.*

draught (draft, dräft) See DRAFT.

draughts (drafts, dräfts) *n.pl.* (*construed as sing.*) *Brit.* The game of checkers: also spelled *drafts.* [See DRAFT.]

draughts·man (drafts'mən, dräfts'-) *n. pl.* **·men** (-mən) See DRAFTSMAN.

draught·y (draf'tē, dräf'-) See DRAFTY.

Dra·vid·i·an (drə·vid'ē·ən) *n.* **1.** A member of an ancient people of southern India. **2.** A family of languages spoken in southern India and northern Ceylon. —*adj.* Of the Dravidians or their languages: also **Dra·vid'ic.**

draw (drô) *v.* **drew, drawn, draw·ing** *v.t.* **1.** To cause to move toward or to follow behind an agent exerting physical force; pull. **2.** To obtain, as from a receptacle: to *draw* water. **3.** To extract, as a tooth, cork, etc. **4.** To cause to flow forth, as blood. **5.** To bring forth; elicit: to *draw* praise. **6.** To take or pull off, on, or out, as a sword, gloves, etc. **7.** To portray with lines or words; sketch; delineate: to *draw* a portrait. **8.** To deduce or extract by a mental process: to *draw* a conclusion. **9.** To attract; entice: Honey *draws* flies. **10.** To pull tight, as a rope. **11.** To make or manufacture by stretching or hammering, as wire or dies. **12.** To take in, as air or a liquid, by inhaling or sucking. **13.** To close or shut as curtans. **14.** To disembowel. **15.** To cause (an abscess, etc.) to soften and drain by applying a poultice. **16.** To shrink or wrinkle. **17.** To extract (essence) by infusion, distillation, etc.: to *draw* tea. **18.** To select or obtain, as by chance; also, to win (a prize) in a lottery. **19.** To receive; earn, as a salary or interest. **20.** To withdraw, as money from a bank. **21.** To write out; draft (a check). **22.** *Naut.* Of a vessel, to sink to (a specified depth) in floating. **23.** To leave undecided, as a game or contest. —*v.i.* **24.** To practice the art of drawing; sketch. **25.** To exert a pulling or drawing force. **26.** To approach or retreat: to *draw* near or away. **27.** To exert an attracting influence. **28.** To pull out or unsheathe a weapon for action: usu. with *on.* **29.** To shrink or become contracted, as a wound. **30.** To cause redness or irritation of the skin, as a poultice or blister. **31.** To obtain by making an application to some source; with *on* or *upon*: to *draw* on one's credit; to *draw* on one's experience. **32.** To produce a current of air: This chimney *draws* well. **33.** To end a contest without a decision; tie. —**to draw a blank** To be unsuccessful. —**to draw on** To approach: Evening is *drawing* on. —**to draw oneself up** To straighten up or stiffen, as in anger or indignation. —**to draw out 1.** To prolong. **2.** To cause (someone) to talk freely. —**to draw the line** To fix a limit and refuse to go further. —**to draw up 1.** To write out in proper form: to *draw up* a deed. **2.** To bring or come to a standstill, as horses. **3.** To come alongside. —*n.* **1.** The act of drawing. **2.** The act of drawing out a weapon for action. **3.** Something drawn, as a ticket in a lottery. **4.** Something that attracts a large audience. **5.** A stalemate; tie. **6.** *U.S.* A gully or ravine into which water drains. [OE *dragan*]

draw·back (drô'bak') *n.* **1.** Anything that hinders progress, success, etc. **2.** A refund on money paid, esp. on duties for reexported goods or on excess payment for freight.

draw·bridge (drô'brij') *n.* A bridge of which the whole or a part may be raised, let down, or drawn aside.

draw·ee (drô'ē') *n.* One on whom an order for the payment of money is drawn.

draw·er (drô'ər *for def. 1;* drôr *for def. 2*) *n.* **1.** One who draws; as: **a** A draftsman. **b** One who draws a check or money order. **c** One who draws beer, etc. **2.** A sliding receptacle, as in a desk, that can be drawn out.

DRAWBRIDGE

draw·ers (drôrz) *n.pl.* An undergarment covering the lower part of the body, including all or part of each leg.

draw·ing (drô'ing) *n.* **1.** The act of one who or that which draws. **2.** That which is drawn. **3.** The art of representing something, usu. by pen, pencil, or crayon. **4.** The picture, sketch, or design produced by this art. **5.** A lottery.

drawing board A smooth, flat board to which paper, etc., is attached for making drawings.

drawing card Something that attracts a large audience.

drawing room 1. A room in which visitors are received and entertained. **2.** *Chiefly Brit.* A formal reception in a drawing room. **3.** *U.S.* A private compartment in a sleeping car on a train. [Short for WITHDRAWING ROOM]

draw·knife (drô'nif') *n. pl.* **·knives** (-nīvz') A knife with a handle at each end, used for shaving over a surface with a drawing motion. Also **drawing knife.**

drawl (drôl) *v.t. & v.i.* To speak or pronounce slowly, esp. with a drawing out of the vowels. —*n.* The act of drawling. [? Freq. of DRAW] —**drawl'er** *n.* —**drawl'ing·ly** *adv.* —**drawl·y** *adj.*

drawn (drôn) Past participle of DRAW.

drawn butter *U.S.* A sauce of melted butter.

drawn work Ornamental openwork made by pulling out threads of fabric and forming various patterns.

dray (drā) *n.* A low, strong cart with removable sides, for carrying heavy articles. —*v.t.* To transport by dray. [OE < *dragan* to draw] —**dray'man** *n.*

dray·age (drā'ij) *n.* **1.** The act of conveying in a dray. **2.** The charge for draying.

dread (dred) *v.t.* To anticipate with great fear or anxiety. —*adj.* **1.** Causing great fear; terrible. **2.** Exciting awe. —*n.* **1.** A terrifying anticipation, as of evil or danger. **2.** Fear mixed with deep respect; awe. **3.** A person or thing inspiring fear or awe. [ME < OE *ondrædan*]

dread·ful (dred'fəl) *adj.* **1.** Inspiring dread; terrible. **2.** *Informal* Disgusting; shocking; very bad; awful. —**dread'ful·ly** *adv.* —**dread'ful·ness** *n.*

dread·nought (dred'nôt') *n.* Any battleship of great size carrying large-caliber guns. Also **dread'naught'.**

dream (drēm) *n.* **1.** A series of thoughts or images passing through the mind in sleep; also, the mental state in which this occurs. **2.** A daydream; reverie. **3.** A cherished or vain hope or ambition. **4.** Anything of dreamlike quality, esp. of unreal beauty or charm. —*v.* **dreamed** *or* **dreamt** (dremt), **dream·ing** *v.t.* **1.** To see or imagine in a dream. **2.** To imagine, as in a dream. **3.** To spend (time) in idle reverie: with *away.* —*v.i.* **4.** To have a dream or dreams. **5.** To indulge in daydreams. **6.** To consider something as possible: with *of*: I would not *dream* of staying. —**to dream up** *Informal* To concoct or create, as by ingenuity or cleverness. [ME < OE *drēam* joy] —**dream'er** *n.* —**dream'ful** *adj.* —**dream'ful·ly** *adv.* —**dream'ing·ly** *adv.* —**dream'less** *adj.* —**dream'less·ly** *adv.* —**dream'like'** *adj.*

dream·y (drē'mē) *adj.* **dream·i·er, dream·i·est 1.** Of, pertaining to, or causing dreams. **2.** Appropriate to dreams. **3.** Given to dreams; visionary. **4.** Soothing. **5.** *Informal* Wonderful. —**dream'i·ly** *adv.* —**dream'i·ness** *n.*

drear (drir) *adj. Poetic* Dreary.

drear·y (drir'ē) *adj.* **drear·i·er, drear·i·est 1.** Causing or manifesting sadness or gloom. **2.** Dull or monotonous. [OE < *drēor* gore] —**drear'i·ly** *adv.* —**drear'i·ness** *n.*

dredge[1] (drej) *n.* **1.** A large, powerful scoop or suction apparatus for removing mud or gravel from the bottoms of channels, harbors, etc. Also **dredging machine. 2.** Any smaller device for bringing up something from under water. —*v.* **dredged, dredg·ing** *v.t.* **1.** To clear or widen by means of a dredge. **2.** To remove, catch, or gather with a dredge. —*v.i.* **3.** To use a dredge. [ME *dreg*] —**dredg'er** *n.*

dredge[2] (drej) *v.t.* **dredged, dredg·ing** To sprinkle or dust with a powdered substance, esp. flour. [ME < OF < L *tragemata* spices < Gk.]

dregs (dregz) *n.pl.* **1.** The sediment of liquids, esp. of beverages; lees. **2.** Coarse, worthless residue: the *dregs* of society. **3.** (*construed as sing.*) A small amount left over. [ME < ON *dregg*] —**dreg'gy** *adj.* —**dreg'gi·ness** *n.*

drench (drench) *v.t.* **1.** To wet thoroughly; soak. **2.** *Vet.* To administer a potion to by force. —*n.* **1.** *Vet.* A liquid medicine administered by force. **2.** A large quantity of fluid. **3.** A water solution for drenching. **4.** The act of drenching. [OE *drencan* to cause to drink] —**drench'er** *n.*

Dres·den (drez'dən) *n.* A china made in Dresden, Germany.

dress (dres) *v.* **dressed** *or* **drest, dress·ing** *v.t.* **1.** To put clothes on; clothe. **2.** To supply with clothing. **3.** To trim or decorate, as a store window. **4.** To treat medicinally, as a wound. **5.** To comb and arrange (hair). **6.** To curry (a horse). **7.** To prepare (stone, timber, etc.) for use or sale. **8.** To clean (fowl, game, etc.) for cooking. **9.** To till, trim, or prune. **10.** To put in proper alignment, as troops. —*v.i.* **11.** To put on or wear clothing, esp. formal clothing. **12.** To come into proper alignment. —**to dress down** *Informal* To rebuke severely; scold. —**to dress up** To put on or wear formal attire. — *n.* **1.** An outer garment for a woman or child, consisting of a skirt and waist, usu. in one piece. **2.** Clothing collectively. **3.** Formal or fashionable clothing. **4.** External adornment or appearance. — *adj.* **1.** Of, pertaining to, or suitable for a dress. **2.** To be worn on formal occasions: a *dress* suit. [< OF *dresser* to arrange, ult. < L < *dis-* apart + *regere* to guide]

dress circle A section of seats in a theater or concert hall, usu. the first gallery behind and above the orchestra.

dress·er¹ (dres′ər) *n.* **1.** One who dresses something. **2.** One who assists another in dressing. **3.** One who dresses well or in a particular way: a fancy *dresser*. **4.** A tool used in dressing stone, leather, etc. **5.** *Brit.* A surgical assistant.

dress·er² (dres′ər) *n.* **1.** A chest of drawers for articles of clothing, usu. with a mirror. **2.** A piece of furniture for holding dishes, silverware, etc. [< OF *dresser* to dress]

dress·ing (dres′ing) *n.* **1.** The act of one who or that which dresses. **2.** That with which something is dressed, as medicated bandages for a wound, manure for the soil, etc. **3.** A stuffing for poultry or roasts. **4.** A sauce for salads, etc.

dress·ing-down (dres′ing-doun′) *n.* *U.S. Informal* **1.** A severe scolding. **2.** A beating.

dressing gown A loose gown worn while lounging at home.

dressing room A room for dressing, as in a theater.

dressing table A small table or stand with a mirror, used while putting on make-up, grooming the hair, etc.

dress·mak·er (dres′mā′kər) *n.* One who makes women's dresses or other articles of clothing. — *adj.* Not severely tailored; having soft, feminine lines. — **dress′mak′ing** *n.*

dress parade A formal military parade in dress uniform.

dress rehearsal A final rehearsal of a play, done with the costumes, lighting, etc., to be used in the public performance.

dress suit A man's suit for formal evening wear.

dress·y (dres′ē) *adj.* **dress·i·er, dress·i·est** *Informal* **1.** Having or giving an appearance of smart elegance; stylish; chic. **2.** Fond of dressing up. — **dress′i·ness** *n.*

drew (drōō) Past tense of DRAW.

drib (drib) *n.* *Dial.* Driblet. — **dribs and drabs** Small quantities. [Var. of DRIP]

drib·ble (drib′əl) *v.t. & v.i.* **·bled, ·bling 1.** To fall or let fall in drops. **2.** To drool. **3.** In basketball, to propel (the ball) by bouncing. **4.** In soccer, to propel (the ball) by successive kicks. — *n.* **1.** A small quantity of a liquid falling in drops. **2.** The act of dribbling. — **drib′bler** *n.*

drib·let (drib′lit) *n.* **1.** A small drop of water or other liquid. **2.** A tiny quantity of something. Also **drib′blet.**

dried (drīd) Past tense and past participle of DRY.

dri·er (drī′ər) Comparative of DRY. — *n.* **1.** One who or that which dries. **2.** A substance added to paint, etc., to make it dry more quickly. **3.** A mechanical device for drying, as for drying clothes. Also spelled *dryer.*

dri·est (drī′ist) Superlative of DRY: also spelled *dryest.*

drift (drift) *n.* **1.** The act of moving along, or the fact of being carried along, in or as in a current of water, air, etc. **2.** A force or influence that drives something along. **3.** The course along which something is directed; tendency or intent: the *drift* of a conversation. **4.** A usu. slow, broad current of water, as in some parts of an ocean. **5.** The rate at which a current of water moves. **6.** The direction of a current of water. **7.** Something driven along or heaped up by air or water currents: a snow *drift*. **8.** Material carried along from one place to another. **9.** The act of driving something along. **10.** The distance a ship, aircraft, missile, etc., is driven from its direct or intended course by wind, sea, etc. **11.** *Mining* A horizontal passage in a mine. — *v.i.* **1.** To move along in or as in a current. **2.** To become heaped up by air currents or water currents. **3.** To move along aimlessly. — *v.t.* **4.** To cause to drift. [ME < OE *drīfan* to drive] — **drift′er** *n.* — **drift′y** *adj.*

drift·age (drif′tij) *n.* **1.** The act or process of drifting. **2.** Deviation caused by drifting. **3.** Something carried along or deposited by air currents or water currents.

drift·wood (drift′wŏŏd′) *n.* Wood floated or drifted by water; esp., wood washed up on a seashore.

drill¹ (dril) *n.* **1.** A tool used for boring holes in metal, stone, wood, or other hard substances. **2.** A mollusk that kills oysters by drilling holes in their shells. **3.** A process of training marked by fixed procedures and much repetition, as in gymnastics, in arithmetic, etc. **4.** The act of teaching through such training; also, a particular exercise. — **Syn.** See PRACTICE. — *v.t.* **1.** To pierce with or as with a drill. **2.** To make (a hole) with a drill. **3.** To train in military procedures, etc. **4.** To teach by drill. — *v.i.* **5.** To make a hole with or as with a drill. **6.** To take part in a drill. **7.** To train someone by drill. [< Du. *drillen* to bore] — **drill′er** *n.*

drill² (dril) *Agric.* **1.** A machine for planting seeds in rows. **2.** A furrow in which seeds are sown. **3.** A row of seeds so planted. — *v.t. & v.i.* To sow or plant in rows.

drill³ (dril) *n.* Heavy, twilled linen or cotton cloth. Also **drill′ing.** [< G *drillich* cloth with three threads]

drill⁴ (dril) *n.* A baboon of West Africa, similar to the mandrill. [? < native name]

drill·mas·ter (dril′mas′tər, -mäs′-) *n.* One who teaches or trains by drilling; esp., a trainer in military exercises.

drill press A machine tool used in drilling holes.

dri·ly (drī′lē) See DRYLY.

drink (dringk) *v.* **drank** (*Archaic* **drunk**), **drunk** (*Archaic* **drunk·en** or **drank**), **drink·ing** *v.t.* **1.** To take into the mouth and swallow (a liquid). **2.** To soak up or absorb (liquid or moisture). **3.** To receive eagerly through the senses or the mind. **4.** To swallow the contents of (a glass, etc.). — *v.i.* **5.** To swallow a liquid. **6.** To drink alcoholic liquors, especially to excess. **7.** To drink a toast: with *to.* — **to drink the health of** To offer homage or good wishes to by a toast. — *n.* **1.** A drinkable liquid; beverage. **2.** A portion of liquid swallowed. **3.** Alcoholic liquor. **4.** The practice of drinking alcoholic liquor to excess. **5.** *Slang* A body of water. [OE *drincan*] — **drink′a·ble** *adj.* — **drink′er** *n.*

drip (drip) *n.* **1.** The falling of liquids in drops. **2.** Liquid falling in drops; also, the sound so made. **3.** Melted fat exuded from meat being roasted or fried. Also **drip′pings.** **4.** *Archit.* A projecting molding for shedding rain. **5.** *U.S. Slang* A disagreeable, insipid, or inept individual. — *v.t. & v.i.* **dripped** or **dript, drip·ping** To fall or cause to fall in drops. [OE *dryppan*] — **drip′py** *adj.*

drip-dry (drip′drī′) *adj.* Designating or pertaining to a garment or fabric treated to dry quickly and retain its proper shape after being hung while dripping wet. — *v.i.* **-dried, -dry·ing** To dry in such a manner.

drive (drīv) *v.* **drove, driv·en, driv·ing** *v.t.* **1.** To push or propel onward with force. **2.** To force to work or activity. **3.** To goad by force or compulsion: Failure *drove* him to despair. **4.** To cause to penetrate by force. **5.** To produce by penetration: to *drive* a well. **6.** To cause to go rapidly by striking or throwing. **7.** To control the operation of (a vehicle). **8.** To transport in a vehicle. **9.** To provide the motive power for. **10.** To carry through without letup: to *drive* a hard bargain. — *v.i.* **11.** To move along rapidly. **12.** To strike, throw, or impel a ball, etc., with force. **13.** To drive a vehicle. **14.** To be transported in a vehicle. **15.** To work toward a particular objective or meaning: with *at.* — **to drive home 1.** To force in all the way, as a nail. **2.** To make evident with force or emphasis: to *drive home* one's meaning. — **to let drive** To aim or release (a blow, shot, etc.). — *n.* **1.** The act of driving. **2.** A road for driving. **3.** A journey in a vehicle. **4.** Urgent pressure, as of business. **5.** The gathering together of cattle, logs, etc.; also, the cattle, logs, etc., being driven. **6.** An organized campaign: a *drive* for money. **7.** *U.S. Informal* Energy; aggressiveness. **8.** *Psychol.* A strong, motivating power or stimulus: the sex *drive*. **9.** *Mil.* A large-scale, sustained attack. **10.** *Mech.* A means of transmitting power, as from the motor of an automobile to the wheels. **11.** In certain games, as golf, the act of driving the ball. [OE *drīfan*]

drive-in (drīv′in′) *n.* **1.** An outdoor motion-picture theater designed for viewing from parked cars. **2.** A restaurant, shop, etc., serving patrons in their cars.

driv·el (driv′əl) *v.* **driv·eled** or **·elled, driv·el·ing** or **·el·ling** *v.i.* **1.** To let saliva flow from the mouth. **2.** To flow like saliva. **3.** To talk foolishly. — *v.t.* **4.** To let flow from the mouth. **5.** To say in a foolish manner. — *n.* **1.** A flow of saliva from the mouth. **2.** Senseless talk; twaddle. [OE *dreflian*] — **driv′el·er** or **driv′el·ler** *n.*

driv·en (driv′ən) Past participle of DRIVE.

driv·er (drī′vər) *n.* **1.** One who drives a vehicle, animals, logs, etc. **2.** Something used for driving. **3.** In golf, a wooden-headed club with full-length shaft, for driving from the tee. **4.** *Mech.* A part that transmits motion.

drive·way (drīv′wā′) *n.* **1.** A private road providing access to a garage, house, or other building. **2.** A road for driving.

driz·zle (driz′əl) *v.t. & v.i.* **·zled, ·zling** To rain steadily in fine drops. — *n.* A light rain. [? Freq. of ME *dresen,* OE *drēosan* to fall] — **drizz′ly** *adj.*

droll (drōl) *adj.* Humorously odd; comical; funny. — **Syn.** See HUMOROUS. — *n.* A buffoon; clown. — *v.i.* To clown. [< MF < MDu. *drol* a jolly man] — **droll′ly** *adv.*

droll·er·y (drō′lər-ē) *n.* *pl.* **·er·ies 1.** The quality of being droll; humor. **2.** An amusing way of acting or talking. **3.** Something droll, as a funny remark.

-drome *combining form* Place for running; racecourse. [< Gk. < *dramein* to run]

drom·e·dar·y (drom′ə-der′ē, drum′-) *n.* *pl.* **·dar·ies** The swift, one-humped Arabian camel trained for riding. [< OF < LL < L *dromas* a running]

drone¹ (drōn) *v.* **droned, dron·ing** *v.i.* **1.** To make a dull, humming sound. **2.** To speak monotonously. — *v.t.* **3.** To utter in a monotonous tone. — *n.* **1.** A dull humming sound, as of a bee. **2.** One of the single-note pipes of the bagpipe; also, a bagpipe. [ME *drone* male bee]

drone² (drōn) *n.* **1.** The male of the bee, esp. of the honey-bee, having no sting and gathering no honey. **2.** A loafer who lives by the labor of others. **3.** *Aeron.* An unmanned airplane piloted by remote control. — *v.i.* **droned, dron·ing** To live in idleness. [OE *drān*]

drool (drōōl) *v.t. & v.i.* To drivel; slaver. — *n.* **1.** Spittle. **2.** *Informal* Foolish talk; twaddle. [Contraction of DRIVEL]

droop (drōōp) *v.i.* **1.** To sink down; hang downward. **2.** To lose vigor or spirit; languish. — *v.t.* **3.** To let hang or sink down. — *n.* A drooping. [< ON *drūpa*]

droop·y (drōō′pē) *adj.* **droop·i·er, droop·i·est** Tending to droop. — **droop′i·ly** *adv.* — **droop′i·ness** *n.*

drop (drop) *n.* **1.** A small quantity of liquid, shaped like a tiny ball. **2.** A very small amount of anything. **3.** *pl.* A liquid medicine given in drops. **4.** Something resembling a drop in shape, size, etc. **5.** Something designed to fall, slide, or hang down, as a curtain. **6.** A slot or other aperture, as in a mailbox. **7.** A sudden or quick downward movement. **8.** A sudden or quick decrease, as in prices. **9.** The vertical distance from a higher to a lower level. **10.** A falling off or away: a sheer *drop*. **11.** A parachuting of men or supplies. — **at the drop of a hat** With little or no hesitation or provocation; at once. — **to have** (or **get**) **the drop on** To have (or get) the advantage over. — *v.* **dropped** or **dropt, drop·ping** *v.i.* **1.** To fall in drops, as a liquid. **2.** To fall or descend rapidly. **3.** To fall down exhausted, injured, or dead. **4.** To decline or decrease, as in amount. **5.** To crouch, as a hunting dog at the sight of game. **6.** To fall into some state or condition. **7.** To come to an end: to let the matter *drop*. — *v.t.* **8.** To let fall by letting go of. **9.** To let fall in drops. **10.** To give birth to: said of animals. **11.** To utter (a hint, etc.) in a casual way. **12.** To write and send (a note, etc.). **13.** To cause to fall, as by striking, etc. **14.** To have no more to do with. **15.** To let out or deposit at a particular place. **16.** To parachute (soldiers, supplies, etc.). **17.** To omit, as a word, line, or stitch. **18.** *U.S.* To discharge (an employee). **19.** To move down; lower. **20.** *Slang* To lose (money, etc.), as in gambling. **21.** In football, to drop-kick (the ball); also, to score (a goal) by drop-kicking. — **to drop behind** (or **back**) To fall behind or lag behind purposely or by necessity. — **to drop in** To make a casual visit. — **to drop off 1.** To decline or decrease. **2.** To go to sleep. — **to drop out** To withdraw, as from membership. [OE *dropa*]

drop·forge (drop′fôrj′) *v.t.* **·forged, ·forg·ing** To forge (metal) between dies with a drop hammer.

drop hammer A machine for forging, stamping, etc., in which a heavy weight sliding between vertical guides hammers the metal beneath it. Also **drop press.**

drop-kick (drop′kik′) *v.t. & v.i.* To give a drop kick (to).

drop kick In football, a kick given the ball just as it is rebounding after being dropped by the kicker.

drop·let (drop′lit) *n.* A tiny drop.

drop·out (drop′out′) *n. U.S. & Canadian* A child who leaves school as soon as attendance is no longer compulsory.

drop·sy (drop′sē) *n. Pathol.* An abnormal accumulation of serous fluid in body cavities. [< OF < L < Gk. *hydrōps* dropsy] — **drop′si·cal** (-si·kəl), **drop·sied** (-sēd) *adj.*

drosh·ky (drosh′kē, drôsh′-) *n. pl.* **·kies** A light, open, four-wheeled Russian carriage or any similar carriage.

dro·soph·i·la (drō·sof′ə·lə, drə-) *n. pl.* **·lae** (-lē) The fruit fly (def. 2). [< NL < Gk. *drosos* dew + *phileein* to love]

dross (drôs, dros) *n.* **1.** *Metall.* Refuse or impurity in melted metal; slag; cinders. **2.** Waste matter; refuse. [OE *drōs*] — **dross′i·ness** *n.* — **dross′y** *adj.*

drought (drout) *n.* **1.** Long-continued dry weather; lack of rain. **2.** Scarcity; dearth. **3.** *Dial.* Thirst. Also **drouth** (drouth). [OE *drūgath*] — **drought′y** *adj.*

drove¹ (drōv) Past tense of DRIVE.

drove² (drōv) *n.* **1.** A number of animals driven or herded for driving. **2.** A moving crowd of human beings. **3.** A stonemason's broad-edged chisel. Also **drove chisel.** — Syn. See FLOCK. — *v.t.* **droved, drov·ing 1.** To drive (cows, etc.) for some distance. **2.** To dress (stone) with a drove. [OE *drāf*. Akin to DRIVE.] — **drov′er** *n.*

drown (droun) *v.i.* **1.** To die by suffocation with a liquid. — *v.t.* **2.** To kill by suffocation with a liquid. **3.** To cover with or as with a flood; inundate. **4.** To lessen the sound of; muffle. **5.** To lessen or extinguish. [ME *drounen*]

drowse (drouz) *v.* **drowsed, drows·ing** *v.i.* **1.** To be only half awake; doze. — *v.t.* **2.** To make sleepy, dull, or lethargic. **3.** To pass (time) in drowsing. — *n.* The state of being half asleep; doze. [OE *drūsian* to become sluggish]

drow·sy (drou′zē) *adj.* **·si·er, ·si·est 1.** Heavy with sleepiness; dull. **2.** Produced by sleepiness or lethargy. **3.** Making sleepy; soporific. — **drow′si·ly** *adv.* — **drow′si·ness** *n.*

drub (drub) *v.t.* **drubbed, drub·bing 1.** To beat, as with a stick. **2.** To vanquish; overcome. — *n.* A blow; thump. [? < Arabic *darb* a beating] — **drub′ber** *n.*

drudge (druj) *v.i.* **drudged, drudg·ing** To work hard at wearisome or menial tasks. — *n.* One who drudges. [OE *drēogan* work, labor] — **drudg′er** *n.* — **drudg′ing·ly** *adv.*

drudg·er·y (druj′ər·ē) *n. pl.* **·er·ies** Dull, wearisome, or menial work. — Syn. See TOIL¹.

drug (drug) *n.* **1.** Any chemical or biological substance, other than food, intended for use in the treatment, prevention, or diagnosis of disease. **2.** A narcotic. **3.** A commodity that is overabundant: a *drug* on the market. — *v.t.* **drugged, drug·ging 1.** To mix drugs with (food, drink, etc.). **2.** To administer drugs to. **3.** To stupefy or poison with or as with drugs. [ME *drogge*]

drug addict One who uses narcotics habitually.

drug·gist (drug′ist) *n.* **1.** One who compounds prescriptions and sells drugs; a pharmacist. **2.** A dealer in drugs.

drug·store (drug′stôr′, -stōr′) *n. U.S.* A place where prescriptions are compounded, and drugs and miscellaneous merchandise are sold; pharmacy. Also **drug store.**

dru·id (drōō′id) *n.* One of an order of priests or teachers of an ancient Celtic religion. [< MF < L *druides* < Celtic] — **dru·id·ic** (drōō·id′ik) or **·i·cal** *adj.* — **dru′id·ism** *n.*

drum (drum) *n.* **1.** A hollow percussion instrument, typically shaped like a cylinder or hemisphere, having a membrane stretched tightly over one or both ends, and played by beating the membrane with sticks, the hands, etc. **2.** A sound produced by or as by a drum. **3.** Something resembling a drum in shape; as: **a** A metal cylinder around which cable, wire, etc., is wound. **b** A cylindrical metal container, as for oil. **4.** *Anat.* The middle ear, or the tympanic membrane. — *v.* **drummed, drum·ming** *v.i.* **1.** To beat a drum. **2.** To tap or thump continuously, as with the fingers. — *v.t.* **3.** To perform on or as on a drum. **4.** To summon by beating a drum. **5.** To force upon by constant repetition. **6.** To work up (business or trade) by advertising, canvassing, etc.: usually with *up*. **7.** To expel in disgrace: usually with *out*. [Prob. < MDu. *tromme*] — **drum′mer** *n.*

drum·head (drum′hed′) *n.* **1.** The membrane stretched over the end of a drum. **2.** *Naut.* The circular top of a capstan. **3.** *Anat.* The tympanic membrane.

drum major One who instructs or leads a band or drum corps. — **drum ma·jor·ette** (mā′jə·ret′) *fem.*

drum·stick (drum′stik′) *n.* **1.** A stick for beating a drum. **2.** The lower joint of the leg of a cooked fowl.

drunk (drungk) Past participle and archaic past tense of DRINK. — *adj.* **1.** Affected with alcoholic drink; intoxicated; inebriated. **2.** Overwhelmed by some powerful emotion. — *n. Informal* **1.** One who is drunk. **2.** A drunkard. **3.** A bout of drinking; binge.

drunk·ard (drungk′ərd) *n.* One who habitually drinks alcoholic beverages to excess.

drunk·en (drungk′ən) Archaic past participle of DRINK. — *adj.* **1.** Habitually drunk. **2.** Relating to or caused by a drunken state. — **drunk′en·ness** *n.* — **drunk′en·ly** *adv.*

drupe (drōōp) *n. Bot.* A soft, fleshy fruit, as a peach or cherry, enclosing a hard-shelled stone or seed. [< NL < L *drupa* (*oliva*) an overripe (olive)] — **dru·pa′ceous** *adj.*

dry (drī) *adj.* **dri·er** or, occasionally, **dry·er, dri·est** or, occasionally, **dry·est. 1.** Devoid of moisture; not wet or damp. **2.** Marked by little or no rainfall. **3.** Not lying under water: *dry* land. **4.** Parched. **5.** Having all or nearly all the water drained away, exhausted or evaporated: a *dry* stream. **6.** No longer giving milk. **7.** Devoid of tears. **8.** Thirsty. **9.** Eaten or served without butter, jam, etc.: *dry* toast. **10.** Unaccompanied by the discharge of phlegm, etc. **11.** Consisting of or pertaining to commodities, etc., that are not liquids: *dry* provisions. **12.** Lacking sweetness: said of wines. **13.** Plain; unadorned; bare: the *dry* facts. **14.** Dull; boring: a *dry* lecture. **15.** Devoid of warmth, color, or emotion: a *dry* welcome. **16.** Crisp; quietly shrewd: *dry* humor. **17.** *U.S. Informal* Opposing or prohibiting the sale of or indulgence in alcoholic beverages: a *dry* State. — *v.* **dried, dry·ing** *v.t.* **1.** To make dry. **2.** To preserve (meat, fish, etc.) by removing moisture. — *v.i.* **3.** To become dry. — **to dry up 1.** To become thoroughly dry. **2.** To become unproductive. **3.** *Slang* To stop talking. [OE *drȳge*]

dry·ad (drī′ad, -əd) *n.* In classical mythology, a nymph dwelling in or presiding over woods and trees. [< L < Gk. < *drys, dryos* tree] — **dry·ad′ic** *adj.*

dry cell *Electr.* A primary cell containing an electrolyte of liquid and powder combined to form a paste.

dry-clean (drī′klēn′) *v.t.* To clean (clothing, etc.) with solvents other than water, such as carbon tetrachloride. Also **dry′-cleanse′.** — **dry cleaner** — **dry cleaning**

dry distillation *Chem.* Destructive distillation.

dry-dock (drī′dok′) *v.t.* **1.** To put into dry dock. — *v.i.* **2.** To go into dry dock.

dry dock A floating or stationary structure from which water can be removed, used for repairing and cleaning ships.

dry·er (drī′ər) Alternative comparative of DRY. — *n.* A drier.

dry·est (drī′ist) Alternative superlative of DRY.

dry-eyed (drī/īd/) *adj.* Not weeping; tearless.
dry farming In an arid country, the raising of crops without irrigation, mainly by saving the moisture of the soil and by raising drought-resisting crops. — **dry farmer**
dry goods Textile fabrics, as distinguished from groceries, hardware, etc.
dry ice Solid carbon dioxide, having a temperature of about −110° F., and passing directly to the gaseous state, widely used as a refrigerant: also called *carbon dioxide snow.*
dry law *U.S.* A law banning the sale of alcoholic beverages.
dry·ly (drī/lē) *adv.* In a dry manner: also spelled *drily.*
dry measure A unit or system of units for measuring the volume of dry commodities, as fruits or grains. See table inside back cover.
dry·ness (drī/nis) *n.* The state or quality of being dry.
dry nurse A nurse who rears a child without suckling it.
dry point 1. A fine, hard etching needle used to incise fine lines on copperplate without the use of acid. 2. An engraving made by this method.
dry rot 1. A fungous disease of timber, causing it to crumble. 2. A disease of potato tubers and other vegetables.
dry run 1. *Mil.* A practice exercise in combat skills without using live ammunition. 2. Any rehearsal or trial run.
du·al (dōō/əl, dyōō/-) *adj.* 1. Denoting or relating to two. 2. Composed of two; twofold; double; binary. 3. *Gram.* In some languages, as Sanskrit and Greek, of or designating a word form that denotes two: distinguished from *singular, plural.* — *n. Gram.* The dual number, or a word form having this number. [< L *duo* two]
du·al·ism (dōō/əl·iz/əm, dyōō/-) *n.* 1. The state of being twofold; duality. 2. *Philos.* The theory that the universe is composed of two principles, as mind and matter. — **du/al·ist** *n.* — **du/al·is/tic** *adj.* — **du/al·is/ti·cal·ly** *adv.*
du·al·i·ty (dōō·al/ə·tē, dyōō-) *n. pl. ·ties* The state, character, or quality of being two or composed of two.
dub[1] (dub) *v.t.* **dubbed, dub·bing** 1. To confer knighthood upon by tapping on the shoulder with a sword. 2. To name or style. 3. To smooth or rub, as timber. [OE *dubbian*]
dub[2] (dub) *U.S. Informal n.* A clumsy, blundering person. — *v.t.* **dubbed, dub·bing** To bungle. [? < DUB[1]]
dub[3] (dub) *v.t.* **dubbed, dub·bing** 1. To rerecord (a record, tape, etc.) in order to edit or add portions or to change volume, frequency, or tonal quality. 2. To insert a new sound track into (a film) [Short for DOUBLE]
du·bi·e·ty (dōō·bī/ə·tē, dyōō-) *n. pl. ·ties* 1. The state of being dubious. 2. Something doubtful. Also **du·bi·os·i·ty** (dōō/bē·os/ə·tē, dyōō-). [< LL < L *dubius* doubtful]
du·bi·ous (dōō/bē·əs, dyōō/-) *adj.* 1. Unsettled in judgment or opinion; doubtful. 2. Causing doubt; equivocal. 3. Not predictable; uncertain. 4. Open to criticism, objection, or suspicion: a *dubious* reputation. [< L *dubium* doubt] — **du/bi·ous·ly** *adv.* — **du/bi·ous·ness** *n.*
Du·bon·net (dōō/bə·nā/, *Fr.* dü·bô·ne/) *n.* 1. A fortified French wine used as an apéritif: a trade name. 2. A reddish purple, the color of red Dubonnet. Also **du/bon·net/.**
du·cal (dōō/kəl, dyōō/-) *adj.* Pertaining to a duke or a duchy. [< MF < LL < L *dux* leader] — **du/cal·ly** *adv.*
duc·at (duk/ət) *n.* 1. Any of several gold or silver coins, formerly current in Europe. 2. *Slang* A ticket, as to a show. [< MF < Ital. *ducato* a coin with a picture of a duke]
duch·ess (duch/is) *n.* 1. The wife or widow of a duke. 2. The female sovereign of a duchy [< OF < L *dux* leader]
duch·y (duch/ē) *n. pl.* **duch·ies** The territory of a duke or duchess; dukedom.
duck[1] (duk) *n.* 1. Any of various aquatic birds, with webbed feet and broad bills. 2. The female of this bird. The male is called a **drake.** 3. *Chiefly Brit. Informal* A dear; darling. 4. *U.S. Slang* A person; fellow. [OE *dūce* diver]
duck[2] (duk) *v.t.* 1. To thrust suddenly under water. 2. To lower quickly; bob, as the head. 3. *Informal* To dodge; evade (a blow or punishment). 4. *Informal* To avoid (a duty, person, etc.) — *v.i.* 5. To submerge suddenly under water. 6. *Informal* To move quickly and abruptly, as in dodging. — *n.* The act of ducking; esp., a quick plunge under water. [ME *douken, duken* to dive, ult. < Gmc.]
duck[3] (duk) *n.* 1. A strong linen or cotton fabric similar to canvas. 2. *pl.* Trousers made of duck. [< Du. *doek* cloth]
duck·bill (duk/bil/) *n.* A platypus.
duck·ling (duk/ling) *n.* A young duck.
duck·pin (duk/pin/) *n.* 1. A small pin used in a variation of the game of tenpins. 2. *pl.* (construed as sing.) The game played with such pins.
duck·y (duk/ē) *adj.* **duck·i·er, duck·i·est** *Slang* Delightful.
duct (dukt) *n.* 1. Any tube, canal, or passage by which a liquid, gas, etc., is conveyed. 2. *Anat.* A tubular passage by which a secretion is carried away. 3. *Electr.* A tubular channel for carrying telegraph or telephone cables. [< L < *ducere* to lead]

duc·tile (duk/təl, -til) *adj.* 1. Capable of being hammered into thin layers, drawn out into wire, or otherwise subjected to stress without breaking, as certain metals. 2. Easily molded or shaped; plastic. 3. Ready to obey; easily led. [< F < L < *ducere* to lead] — **duc·til·i·ty** (duk·til/ə·tē) *n.*
duct·less gland (dukt/lis) *Physiol.* A gland that has no excretory duct but releases its secretions directly into the blood or lymph, as the thyroid gland, etc.
dud (dud) *n.* 1. *Mil.* A bomb or shell that fails to explode. 2. *Informal* One who or that which proves a failure. [< Du. *dood* dead]
dude (dōōd, dyōōd) *n. U.S.* 1. A man who dresses in a flashy or extremely fastidious manner; dandy; fop. 2. *U.S. Informal* A city person; esp., an Easterner vacationing on a ranch. [Origin unknown] — **dud/ish** *adj.*
dude ranch *U.S.* A ranch operated as a resort for tourists.
dudg·eon (duj/ən) *n.* Sullen displeasure; resentment: to leave in high *dudgeon.* [Origin unknown]
duds (dudz) *n.pl. Informal* 1. Clothing. 2. Belongings in general. [ME *dudde* cloak]
due (dōō, dyōō) *adj.* 1. Subject to demand for payment; esp., payable because of the arrival of a stipulated date. 2. That should be rendered or given; proper: the honor *due.* 3. Adequate; sufficient: *due* cause for alarm. 4. Appointed or expected to arrive, be present, or be ready: The bus is *due.* 5. That may be charged or attributed; ascribable: with *to*: The mistake was *due* to carelessness. — **due to** *Informal* Because of; on account of: widely used but still questioned by some. — *n.* 1. That which is owed or rightfully required; a debt. 2. *pl.* Charge or fee: club *dues.* — *adv.* Directly: *due* east. [< OF *deü,* pp. of *devoir* to owe < L *debere*]
du·el (dōō/əl, dyōō/-) *n.* 1. A prearranged combat between two persons, usu. fought with deadly weapons. 2. A struggle between two contending parties. — *v.t. & v.i.* **du·eled or ·elled, du·el·ing** or **·el·ling** To fight, or fight with, in a duel. [< F < Ital. < L *duellum,* earliest form of *bellum* war] — **du/el·er** or **du/el·ler, du/el·ist** or **du/el·list** *n.*
du·en·na (dōō·en/ə, dyōō-) *n.* 1. In Spain and Portugal, an elderly woman who serves as a companion and protector to a young girl. 2. A chaperon. [< Sp. < L *domina* lady]
du·et (dōō·et/, dyōō-) *n.* A musical composition for two performers. [< Ital. < L *duo* two]
duff (duf) *n.* A thick flour pudding boiled in a cloth bag. [Var. of DOUGH]
duf·fel (duf/əl) *n.* 1. A coarse woolen fabric napped on both sides. 2. Equipment or supplies, esp. for camping. Also **duf/fle.** [after *Duffel,* a town near Antwerp]
duffel bag A sack, usu. of canvas or duck, used to carry clothing and personal possessions. Also **duffle bag.**
dug[1] (dug) Past tense and past participle of DIG.
dug[2] (dug) *n.* A teat or udder. [Cf. Dan. *dægge* to suckle]
du·gong (dōō/gong) *n.* A herbivorous marine mammal of warm seas, having flippers and a paddlelike tail: also called *sea cow.* [< Malay *duyong*]
dug·out (dug/out/) *n.* 1. A canoe made by hollowing out a log. 2. An excavated shelter or dwelling for protection against storms, bombs, etc. 3. In baseball, a structure set back from the diamond, in which team members sit when not at bat or in the field.
duke (dōōk, dyōōk) *n.* 1. In Great Britain and certain other European countries, a nobleman ranking immediately below a prince and above a marquis. 2. A European prince ruling over a duchy. [< OF < L *dux* leader] — **duke/dom** *n.*
dul·cet (dul/sit) *adj.* Pleasing to the ear; melodious; also, soothing; pleasant. [< OF dim. of *douz,* sweet < L *dulcis*]
dul·ci·mer (dul/sə·mər) *n.* A stringed instrument played with two padded hammers or plucked with the fingers. [< OF, ? < LL < *dulcis* sweet + *melos* a song < Gk.]
dull (dul) *adj.* 1. Lacking in intelligence or understanding; stupid. 2. Wanting in perception or responsiveness: a *dull* audience. 3. Not brisk or active: Trade is *dull.* 4. Without spirit; listless. 5. Having a blunt edge or point. 6. Exciting little or no interest: a *dull* book. 7. Not acute or intense: a *dull* pain. 8. Cloudy; gloomy. 9. Not bright, clear, or vivid: a *dull* color. 10. Unclear in sound. — *v.t. & v.i.* To make or become dull. [ME *dul*] — **dull/ish** *adj.* — **dull/ness** or **dul/ness** *n.* — **dul/ly** *adv.*
dul·lard (dul/ərd) *n.* A stupid person; dolt.
dulse (duls) *n.* A reddish brown seaweed sometimes eaten as a vegetable. [< Irish *duileasg*]
du·ly (dōō/lē, dyōō/-) *adv.* 1. In due or proper manner; fitly. 2. At the proper time. 3. To an adequate degree.
dumb (dum) *adj.* 1. Having no power of speech; mute. 2. Temporarily speechless: *dumb* with grief. 3. Not inclined to speak; silent. 4. *U.S. Informal* Stupid; dull-witted. 5. Made or done without speech, as a pantomime. [OE] — **dumb/ly** *adv.* — **dumb/ness** *n.*
dumb·bell (dum/bel/) *n.* 1. A gymnastic hand instrument

---

used for exercising, consisting of a wood or metal handle with a weighted ball at each end. **2.** *U.S. Slang* A stupid person.
dumb·wait·er (dum'wā'tər) *n.* **1.** *U.S.* A small elevator for conveying food, dishes, garbage, etc., between floors. **2.** *Brit.* A movable serving stand placed near a dining table.
dum·dum bullet (dum'dum') A small-arms bullet having a soft point or a jacket cut across at the point so that it will expand on impact and tear a gaping wound. [after *Dum-dum*, a town near Calcutta, India, where first made]
dum·found (dum·found') *v.t.* To strike dumb; confuse; amaze. Also **dumb'found'**. [Blend of DUMB and CONFOUND]
dum·my (dum'ē) *n. pl.* ·**mies 1.** A figure representing the human form, used for displaying clothing, for tackling in football practice, etc. **2.** An imitation object, as a false drawer. **3.** One who is dumb; a mute. **4.** *Slang* A stupid person. **5.** One who seems to be acting for his own interests while secretly representing another. **6.** *Printing* **a** A sample book or magazine, usually blank, used as a model of the final product. **b** A model page form for the printer, made up of proofs pasted into position. **7.** In certain card games, esp. bridge: **a** An exposed hand played in addition to his own by the person sitting opposite it. **b** The inactive player who has exposed such a hand. —*adj.* **1.** Sham; counterfeit. **2.** Silent; mute. **3.** Ostensibly acting for oneself, but actually for another. **4.** Played with a dummy, as in card games.
dump (dump) *v.t.* **1.** To drop or throw down heavily or abruptly. **2.** To empty out, as from a container. **3.** To empty (a container), as by overturning. **4.** To throw away, as rubbish. **5.** To put up (goods) for sale cheaply and in large quantities, esp. in a foreign market. —*v.i.* **6.** To fall or drop suddenly. **7.** To unload. **8.** To offer large quantities of goods for sale at low prices. —*n.* **1.** A dumping area, as for rubbish. **2.** That which is dumped. **3.** *Mil.* A temporary storage place for ammunition and supplies. **4.** *U.S. Slang* A shabby, poorly kept place. [ME < Scand.]
dump·ling (dump'ling) *n.* **1.** A ball of biscuit dough filled with fruit and baked or steamed. **2.** A small mass of dough dropped into boiling soup or stew.
dumps (dumps) *n.pl.* A gloomy state of mind: now only in the phrase **in the dumps**. [Cf. MDu. *domp* haze]
dump truck A truck for hauling gravel, coal, etc., that unloads by tilting back the cargo bin and opening the tailboard.
dump·y[1] (dump'ē) *adj.* **dump·i·er, dump·i·est** Sullen or discontented; sulky. [See DUMPS]
dump·y[2] (dump'ē) *adj.* **dump·i·er, dump·i·est** Short and thick; squat. —**dump'i·ly** *adv.* —**dump'i·ness** *n.*
dun[1] (dun) *v.t. & v.i.* **dunned, dun·ning** To demand (a debtor) for payment; importune; pester. —*n.* **1.** One who duns. **2.** A repeated demand for payment. [Prob. var. of DIN.]
dun[2] (dun) *adj.* Of a grayish brown or reddish brown color. —*n.* **1.** Dun color. **2.** A dun-colored horse. —*v.t.* **dunned, dun·ning** To make dun-colored. [OE *dunn*]
dunce (duns) *n.* A stupid or ignorant person. [Earlier *Dunsman*, a follower of John *Duns* Scotus]
dunce cap A conical cap, formerly placed on the head of a dull student. Also **dunce's cap.**
dun·der·head (dun'dər·hed') *n.* A blockhead; dunce. Also **dun'der·pate'** (-pāt'). [? < dial. E (Scottish) *dunder* thunder, noise + HEAD] —**dun'der·head'ed** *adj.*
dune (dōōn, dyōōn) *n.* A hill of loose sand heaped up by the wind. [< F < MDu.]
dung (dung) *n.* **1.** Animal excrement; manure. **2.** Anything foul. —*v.t.* To cover with or as with dung. [OE]
dun·ga·ree (dung'gə·rē') *n.* **1.** A coarse cotton cloth used for work clothes, tents, sails, etc. **2.** *pl.* Trousers or overalls made of this fabric. [< Hind. *dungrī*]
dung beetle Any of various beetles that breed in dung.
dun·geon (dun'jən) *n.* **1.** A dark confining prison or cell, esp. one underground. **2.** A donjon. [< DONJON]
dung·hill (dung'hil') *n.* **1.** A heap of manure. **2.** A vile thing, abode, or condition.
dunk (dungk) *v.t. & v.i.* To dip (bread, doughnuts, etc.) into tea, coffee, soup, etc. [< G *tunken* to dip] —**dunk'er** *n.*
dun·lin (dun'lin) *n.* A sandpiper having in summer plumage a black belly and a reddish back. [< DUN[2] + -LING[1]]
dun·nage (dun'ij) *n.* **1.** *Naut.* Mats and battens used to protect cargo. **2.** Baggage.
du·o (dōō'ō, dyōō'ō) *n. pl.* **du·os** or **du·i** (-ē) *Music* An instrumental duet. [< Ital. < L *duo* two]
duo- *combining form* Two. [< L *duo* two]
du·o·dec·i·mal (dōō'ō·des'ə·məl, dyōō'-) *adj.* **1.** Pertaining to twelfth or twelfths. **2.** Reckoning by twelves. —*n.* **1.** One of the numbers used in duodecimal arithmetic; a twelfth. **2.** *pl.* A method of computing by twelves instead of by tens. [< L < *duodecim* twelve]
du·o·dec·i·mo (dōō'ō·des'ə·mō, dyōō'-) *adj.* **1.** Having twelve pages to one sheet of printing paper. **2.** Measuring about 5 x 7¾ inches in size: said of a page or book. —*n. pl.* ·**mos** The size of a page folded twelve to a sheet; also, a page or book of this size. Also *twelvemo*. Also written **12 mo., 12°.**
du·o·de·num (dōō'ō·dē'nəm, dyōō'-; dōō·od'ə·nəm) *n. pl.*

·**na** (-nə) *Anat.* The part of the small intestine extending from the stomach to the jejunum. For illus. see INTESTINE. [< Med.L *duodenum* (*digitorum*) of twelve (fingers); with ref. to its length] —**du'o·de'nal** *adj.*
du·o·logue (dōō'ə·lôg, -log, dyōō'-) *n.* **1.** A dramatic piece for two performers. **2.** A dialogue. Also **du'o·log.**
dupe (dōōp, dyōōp) *n.* One who is easily deceived or misled. —*v.t.* **duped, dup·ing** To make a dupe of; deceive. [< OF *huppe* hoopoe < L *upupa*] —**dup'er** *n.* —**dup'er·y** *n.*
du·ple (dōō'pəl, dyōō'-) *adj.* Double. [< L *duplus* double]
du·plex (dōō'pleks, dyōō'-) *adj.* **1.** Having two parts; twofold. **2.** *Mech.* Having two similar parts operating independently or in conjunction within one framework. **3.** *Telecom.* Pertaining to or allowing the transmission of two messages simultaneously over a single wire and in opposite directions. —*n.* A duplex apartment or house. [< L < *duo* two + stem of *plicare* to fold] —**du·plex'i·ty** *n.*
duplex apartment **1.** *U.S.* An apartment having rooms on two floors. **2.** *Canadian* A two-story building having an apartment on each floor.
duplex house *U.S. & Canadian* A house having two one-family units.
du·pli·cate (*adj., n.* dōō'plə·kit, dyōō'-; *v.* dōō'plə·kāt, dyōō'-) *adj.* **1.** Made like or corresponding exactly to an original: a *duplicate* key. **2.** Growing or existing in pairs. **3.** In card-playing, replayed by other players with the same hands as originally dealt. —*n.* **1.** An exact copy. **2.** A double or counterpart. **3.** A duplicate game of cards. —*v.t.* ·**cat·ed, ·cat·ing 1.** To copy exactly; reproduce. **2.** To double. **3.** To do a second time. [< L < *duplex* twofold] —**du'pli·cate·ly** *adv.* —**du'pli·ca'tion** *n.* —**du'pli·ca'tive** *adj.*
du·pli·ca·tor (dōō'plə·kā'tər, dyōō'-) *n.* A mechanical device for making duplicates.
du·plic·i·ty (dōō·plis'ə·tē, dyōō-) *n. pl.* ·**ties** Tricky deceitfulness; double-dealing. [< OF < LL < L *duplex* twofold]
du·ra (dōōr'ə) See DURRA.
du·ra·ble (dōōr'ə·bəl, dyōōr'-) *adj.* **1.** Able to withstand decay or wear. **2.** Not easily changed or upset. [< OF < L *durus* hard] —**du'ra·bil'i·ty, du'ra·ble·ness** *n.*
Du·ral·u·min (dōō·ral'yə·min, dyōō-) *n.* A light, strong alloy of aluminum and copper, with addition of magnesium and manganese: a trade name. Also **du'ral·u·min.**
du·ra ma·ter (dōōr'ə mā'tər, dyōōr'ə) *Anat.* The tough fibrous membrane forming the outermost of the three coverings of the brain and spinal cord. [< Med.L < L *dura* hard + *mater* mother] —**du'ral** *adj.*
du·ra·men (dōō·rā'min, dyōō-) *n. Bot.* The heartwood, or darker central portion, of an exogenous stem or tree trunk. [< L, a ligneous vine branch]
dur·ance (dōōr'əns, dyōōr'-) *n.* Forced confinement or imprisonment. [< OF < L *durare* to endure]
du·ra·tion (dōō·rā'shən, dyōō-) *n.* **1.** The period of time during which anything lasts. **2.** Continuance in time. [< LL < L *durare* to endure, last]
du·ress (dōō·res', dyōō-; dōōr'is, dyōōr'-) *n.* **1.** Constraint by force or fear; compulsion. **2.** *Law* **a** Coercion to do or say something against one's will or judgment. **b** Imprisonment without full legal sanction. [< OF < L *durus* hard]
dur·ing (dōōr'ing, dyōōr'-) *prep.* **1.** Throughout the time, existence, or action of. **2.** In the course of; at some period in. [ME. Orig. ppr. of *duren* to endure]
dur·ra (dōōr'ə) *n.* A variety of sorghum of southern Asia and northern Africa: also spelled *doura, dura.* Also **durr** (dōōr). [< Arabic *dhura*]
du·rum (dōōr'əm, dyōōr'-) *n.* A species of wheat widely grown for macaroni products. [< L *durus* hard]
dusk (dusk) *n.* **1.** The partial darkness between day and night, usu. considered darker than twilight. **2.** Any degree of light or dark resembling this. —*adj.* Somewhat dark or dim; shadowy. —*v.t. & v.i.* To make grow, or appear shadowy or dim; darken. [OE *dox*] —**dusk'ish** *adj.*
dusk·y (dus'kē) *adj.* **dusk·i·er, dusk·i·est 1.** Somewhat dark; dim; obscure. **2.** Rather dark in shade or coloring; swarthy. **3.** Gloomy. —**dusk'i·ly** *adv.* —**dusk'i·ness** *n.*
dust (dust) **1.** Earthy matter reduced to particles so fine as to be easily borne in the air. **2.** Any substance reduced to fine powder. **3.** A cloud of powdered earth or other fine particles. **4.** Confusion; turmoil. **5.** Earth, esp. as the receptacle of the dead. **6.** The disintegrated remains of a human body. **7.** A low or despised condition. **8.** Something worthless. **9.** *Brit.* Sweepings, ashes, or other refuse. **10.** Pollen. **11.** Gold dust. **12.** *Slang* Money. — **to bite the dust** To be killed or injured. — **to lick the dust 1.** To be defeated; grovel. **2.** To be killed or wounded. — **to throw dust in someone's eyes** To deceive. —*v.t.* **1.** To wipe or brush dust from. **2.** To sprinkle with powder, insecticide, etc. **3.** To sprinkle (powder, etc.) over something. **4.** To soil with dust. —*v.i.* **5.** To wipe or brush dust from furniture, etc. **6.** To cover oneself with dust, as a bird. **7.** To become dusty. [OE *dūst*] —**dust'less** *adj.*
dust bowl An area subject to dust storms and drought. —

the Dust Bowl A region in the south central U.S. where the topsoil was blown away by dust storms during 1934–37.

dust·er (dus'tər) *n.* **1.** One who or that which dusts. **2.** A cloth or brush for removing dust. **3.** A device for sprinkling a powder, insecticide, etc., over something. **4.** An outer garment worn to protect clothing from dust.

dust jacket A removable paper cover that protects the binding of a book: also called *book jacket.* Also **dust cover.**

dust·pan (dust'pan') *n.* An implement resembling a short-handled shovel into which dust from a floor is swept.

dust storm A windstorm of arid regions that carries clouds of dust with it.

dust·y (dus'tē) *adj.* **dust·i·er, dust·i·est 1.** Covered with or as with dust. **2.** Like dust; powdery. **3.** Of the color of dust. **4.** Having a grayish or dull cast: *dusty* pink. **— dust'i·ly** *adv.* **— dust'i·ness** *n.*

Dutch (duch) *adj.* **1.** Of or relating to the Netherlands, its people, culture, or language. **2.** Loosely, German. **— n. 1.** The people of the Netherlands: preceded by *the.* **2.** Loosely, the German people: preceded by *the.* **3.** The language of the Netherlands. **4.** Pennsylvania Dutch. **— in Dutch** *U.S. Informal* In trouble or disgrace. **— to beat the Dutch** *U.S. Informal* To be most unusual or surprising. **— to go Dutch** *U.S. Informal* To have each participant in a meal or entertainment pay his own expenses. [< MDu. *dutsch* Germanic]

Dutch door A door divided horizontally in the middle, allowing either half to open individually.

Dutch·man (duch'mən) *n. pl.* **·men** (-mən) **1.** A native of the Netherlands. **2.** Loosely, a German. **3.** A Dutch ship.

dutch·man's-breech·es (duch'mənz-brich'iz) *n. sing. & pl.* A low herb with widely spreading spurs. Also **dutch'mans-breech'es.**

Dutch oven 1. A cast-iron kettle with a tight-fitting cover, used for meats, stews, etc. **2.** A metal box with an open side, set before a fire for cooking.

Dutch treat *U.S. Informal* An entertainment or meal at which each person pays his own bill.

Dutch uncle A very frank and severe critic or adviser.

du·te·ous (dōō'tē-əs, dyōō'-) *adj.* Obedient; dutiful. **— du'te·ous·ly** *adv.* **— du'te·ous·ness** *n.*

du·ti·ful (dōō'ti·fəl, dyōō'-) *adj.* **1.** Performing one's duties; obedient. **2.** Expressive of a sense of duty; respectful: *dutiful* attentions. **— du'ti·ful·ly** *adv.* **— du'ti·ful·ness** *n.*

du·ty (dōō'tē, dyōō'-) *n. pl.* **·ties 1.** That which one is morally or legally bound to do; obligation. **2.** The impelling or controlling force of such obligations: *Duty* calls. **3.** Action or conduct required by one's profession or position. **4.** Specific obligatory service, esp. of military personnel. **5.** A tax on imported or exported goods. **— off duty** Temporarily not at work. [< AF *dû.* See DUE.]

du·ve·tyn (dōō'və·tēn, dōō'və·tēn') *n.* Twill-weave fabric with a napped surface, made of wool, rayon, cotton, or silk. Also **du've·tine, du've·tyne.** [< F *duvet* down]

dwarf (dwôrf) *n.* A human being, animal, or plant that is stunted in its growth and often has abnormal physical proportions. **— v.t. 1.** To prevent the natural development of; stunt. **2.** To cause to appear small or less by comparison. **— v.i. 3.** To become stunted; grow smaller. **— adj.** Diminutive; stunted. [OE *dweorh*] **— dwarf'ish** *adj.* **— dwarf'ish·ly** *adv.* **— dwarf'ish·ness** *n.*

dwarf chestnut The chinquapin.

dwell (dwel) *v.i.* **dwelt** or **dwelled, dwell·ing 1.** To have a fixed abode; reside. **2.** To linger, as on a subject: with *on* or *upon.* **3.** To continue in a state or place. **— Syn.** LIVE. [OE *dwellan* to go astray] **— dwell'er** *n.*

dwell·ing (dwel'ing) *n.* A place of residence; abode; house.

dwin·dle (dwin'dəl) *v.t. & v.i.* **·dled, ·dling** To diminish or become less; make or become smaller. **— Syn.** See DECREASE. [OE *dwīnan* to waste away]

dye (dī) *v.* **dyed, dye·ing** *v.t.* **1.** To fix a color in (cloth, hair, etc.), esp. by soaking in liquid coloring matter. **— v.i. 2.** To take or give color: This cloth *dyes* badly. **— n.** A coloring matter used for dyeing; also, the color so produced. [OE *dēagian* to dye < *dēag* dye] **— dy'er** *n.*

dyed-in-the-wool (dīd'in-thə-wŏŏl') *adj.* **1.** Dyed before being woven. **2.** Thoroughgoing; complete.

dye·ing (dī'ing) *n.* The act of fixing colors in cloth, etc.

dye-stuff (dī'stuf') *n.* Any material used for dyeing.

dy·ing (dī'ing) *adj.* **1.** Near death; expiring. **2.** Coming to a close; destined to end: a *dying* civilization. **3.** Given, uttered, or manifested just before death. **— n.** Death.

dyke (dīk) See DIKE.

dyna- *combining form* Power. Also, before vowels, **dyn-.** [< Gk. *dynamis* power]

dy·nam·ic (dī·nam'ik) *adj.* **1.** Of or pertaining to forces not in equilibrium, or to motion as the result of force: opposed to *static.* **2.** Pertaining to dynamics. **3.** Characterized by energy or forcefulness: a *dynamic* personality. [< Gk. < *dynamis* power] **— dy·nam'i·cal·ly** *adv.*

dy·nam·ics (dī·nam'iks) *n.pl.* (construed as sing. in defs. 1 and 2) **1.** The branch of physics that treats of the motion of bodies and the effects of forces in producing motion, including kinetics. **2.** *Music* **a** Variations in loudness or softness. **b** Symbols in a score indicating these variations.

dy·na·mite (dī'nə·mīt) *n.* **1.** An explosive composed of nitroglycerin held in some absorbent substance. **2.** *Slang* Anything wonderful or spectacular: The news was *dynamite!* **--- v.t.** **·mit·ed, ·mit·ing** To blow up or shatter with or as with dynamite. [< Gk. *dynamis* power] **— dy'na·mit'er** *n.*

dy·na·mo (dī'nə·mō) *n. pl.* **·mos** A generator for the conversion of mechanical energy into electrical energy.

dynamo- *combining form* Force; power. [< Gk. *dynamis* power]

dy·na·mo·e·lec·tric (dī'nə·mō·i·lek'trik) *adj.* Pertaining to the conversion of mechanical energy into electrical energy, or the reverse. Also **dy'na·mo·e·lec'tri·cal.**

dy·na·mom·e·ter (dī'nə·mom'ə·tər) *n.* An instrument for measuring force or power. **— dy·na·mo·met·ric** (dī'nə·mō·met'rik) or **·ri·cal** *adj.* **— dy'na·mom'e·try** *n.*

dy·na·mo·tor (dī'nə·mō'tər) *n.* A dynamoelectric machine having one field magnet, one armature core, and two armature windings, each being insulated from the other.

dy·nast (dī'nast, -nəst; *Brit.* din'əst) *n.* A ruler, esp. a hereditary one. [< L < Gk. < *dynasthai* to be powerful]

dy·nas·ty (dī'nəs·tē, *Brit.* din'əs·tē) *n. pl.* **·ties** A succession of sovereigns in one line of descent; also, the length of time during which one family is in power. **— dy·nas·tic** (dī·nas'tik, di-) or **·ti·cal** *adj.* **— dy·nas'ti·cal·ly** *adv.*

dyne (dīn) *n. Physics* The fundamental unit of force in the cgs system that, if applied to a mass of one gram, would give it an acceleration of one centimeter per second per second. Abbr. *d.,* **D.** [< F < Gk. *dynamis* power]

dys·en·ter·y (dis'ən·ter'ē) *n. Pathol.* A painful inflammation of the large intestine, attended with bloody evacuations and some fever. [< OF < L < Gk. < *dys-* bad + *enteron* intestine] **— dys'en·ter'ic** or **·i·cal** *adj.*

dys·pep·sia (dis·pep'shə, -sē-ə) *n.* Difficult or painful digestion. [< L < Gk. < *dys-* hard + *peptein* to cook, digest]

dys·pep·tic (dis·pep'tik) *adj.* **1.** Relating to or suffering from dyspepsia. **2.** Gloomy; peevish. Also **dys·pep'ti·cal.** **— n.** A dyspeptic person. **— dys·pep'ti·cal·ly** *adv.*

dysp·ne·a (disp·nē'ə) *n. Pathol.* Labored breathing. Also **dysp·noe'a.** [< NL < L < Gk. < *dys-* hard + *pneein* to breathe] **— dysp·ne'al** or **dysp·ne'ic** *adj.*

dys·pro·si·um (dis·prō'sē-əm, -shē-) *n.* A highly magnetic element (symbol Dy) of the lanthanide series. See ELEMENT. [< NL < Gk. < *dys-* hard + *prosienai* to approach]

dys·to·pia (dis·tō'pē·ə) *n.* A place of utter wretchedness. [< Gk. *dys-* hard + *topos* place, after *Utopia*]

E

e, E (ē) *n. pl.* **e's, E's** or **es, Es, ees** (ēz) **1.** The fifth letter of the English alphabet. **2.** Any sound represented by the letter *e.* **— symbol 1.** *Music* **a** The third tone in the natural scale of C, *mi.* **b** A written note representing it. **c** The scale built upon E. **2.** *Math.* The limit of the expression $(1 + 1/n)^n$, as *n* increases without limit: 2.7182818284+: the base to which Napierian logarithms are calculated: written *e.*

e- Reduced var. of EX-.

each (ēch) *adj.* Being one of two or more individuals that together form an aggregate; every. — *pron.* Every one of any number or group considered individually; each one. ◆ The pronoun *each* is usu. treated as a singular, as *Each* did *his* own work. — *adv.* For or to each person, article, etc.; apiece: one dollar *each.* [OE ǣlc < ā ever + gelīc alike]

each other A compound reciprocal pronoun used in oblique cases: They saw *each other*. The possessive is *each other's*.

ea·ger (ē′gər) *adj.* Impatiently desirous of something. [< OF < L *acer* sharp] — **ea′ger·ly** *adv.* — **ea′ger·ness** *n.*

ea·gle (ē′gəl) *n.* 1. A large bird of prey related to the falcon, esp. the **bald** (or **American**) **eagle**, dark brown, with the head, neck, and tail white, the national emblem of the United States; and the **imperial eagle** of Europe. ◆ Collateral adjective: *aquiline.* 2. Any national seal or standard that bears an eagle as symbol. 3. A former gold coin of the U.S. having a value of $10. 4. In golf, a score of two under par on any hole. [< OF *egle, aigle,* < L *aquila*]

ea·gle-eyed (ē′gəl-īd′) *adj.* Having keen sight.

ea·glet (ē′glit) *n.* A young eagle.

ear[1] (ir) *n.* 1. The organ of hearing in its entirety. ◆ Collateral adjective: *aural.* 2. The fleshy or cartilaginous external part of the organ of hearing. 3. The sense of hearing. 4. The ability to perceive the refinements of music, poetry, or the like. 5. Attentive consideration; heed. 6. Something resembling the external ear in shape or position, as a projecting piece on a vase. **— to be all ears** To be eagerly attentive. **— to be up to the ears** To be submerged in work, problems, etc. **— to have an ear to the ground** To listen to or heed current public opinion. **— to lend an ear** To pay attention. [OE *ēare*] **— ear′less** *adj.*

Incus (anvil)   Semicircular canals   Groove for auditory nerves   Malleus (hammer)   Auditory canal to outer ear   Cochlea   Tympanic membrane (eardrum)   Tympanic cavity   Stapes (stirrup)   Eustachian tube

HUMAN EAR, FRONTAL SECTION
(Anatomical nomenclature)

ear[2] (ir) *n.* The fruit-bearing part of a cereal plant; the head. **— in** (or **on**) **the ear** On the cob, as corn; unhusked, as grain. — *v.i.* To form ears, as grain. [OE *ēar*]

ear·ache (ir′āk′) *n.* Pain in the middle or internal ear.

ear·drum (ir′drum′) *n.* The tympanic membrane.

eared (ird) *adj.* Having ears or earlike appendages.

earl (ûrl) *n.* A member of the British nobility next in rank above a viscount and below a marquis. [OE *eorl* nobleman] **— earl′dom** *n.*

ear·lap (ir′lap′) *n.* 1. One of two flaps attached to a cap for protecting the ears from the cold. 2. The ear lobes.

ear lobe The fleshy lower part of the external ear.

ear·ly (ûr′lē) *adj.* **·li·er, ·li·est** 1. Coming near the beginning of any specified period of time or of any series of related things: an *early* Shaw play. 2. Belonging to a distant time or stage of development. 3. Occurring ahead of the usual or arranged time: an *early* dinner. 4. Occurring in the near future: An *early* truce is expected. — *adv.* 1. Near the beginning of any specified period or series of things. 2. Far back in time. 3. Before the usual or arranged time. [OE *līce* < ǣr before + *-līce* -ly] **— ear′li·ness** *n.*

ear·mark (ir′märk′) *n.* 1. A distinctive mark made on an animal's ear to denote ownership. 2. Any mark of identification. — *v.t.* 1. To put an earmark on. 2. To set aside, as money, for a particular purpose.

earn (ûrn) *v.t.* 1. To receive or deserve as recompense for labor, service, or performance. 2. To acquire as a consequence. 3. To produce as profit. [OE *earnian*]

ear·nest[1] (ûr′nist) *adj.* 1. Intent and direct in purpose; zealous: an *earnest* student. 2. Of a serious or important nature. **— in earnest** With serious intent or determination. [OE *eornoste*] **— ear′nest·ly** *adv.* **— ear′nest·ness** *n.*

ear·nest[2] (ûr′nist) *n.* 1. *Law* Money paid in advance to bind a contract. Also **earnest money.** 2. An assurance or token of something to come. [Prob. < OF *erres* < L *arra, arrhabo* < Gk. *arrhabōn* < Hebrew *'ērābōn* pledge]

earn·ings (ûr′ningz) *n.pl.* Wages or profits.

ear·phone (ir′fōn′) *n.* A radio or telephone device held at or inserted into the ear; also, a similar part of a hearing aid.

ear·ring (ir′ring′) *n.* An ornament worn at the ear lobe.

ear·shot (ir′shot′) *n.* The distance at which sounds may be heard.

earth (ûrth) *n.* 1. The dry land surface of the globe, as distinguished from the oceans and sky; ground. 2. Soil; dirt. 3. The planet on which man dwells; also, the people who inhabit it. 4. The abode of mortal man, as opposed to heaven and hell. 5. Worldly or temporal affairs. 6. The mortal body. 7. The hole or lair of a burrowing animal. **— down to earth** Realistic; practical; unaffected. **— to run to earth**

To hunt down and find, as a fox. — *v.t.* 1. To heap up (plants, etc.) with soil for protection. 2. To chase into hiding. — *v.i.* 3. To burrow in the earth. [OE *eorthe*]

Earth (ûrth) *n.* The planet fifth in order of size, having an area of about 196 million square miles and a mass of 6.57 sextillion tons (6.57 × 10²¹). See PLANET. *Abbr. E.*

earth·en (ûr′thən) *adj.* Made of earth or baked clay.

earth·en·ware (ûr′thən-wâr′) *n.* Dishes, pots, and the like, made of a coarse grade of baked clay.

earth·ly (ûrth′lē) *adj.* 1. Of or relating to the earth and its material qualities; worldly; secular. 2. Possible; imaginable: of no *earthly* use. **— earth′li·ness** *n.*

earth·quake (ûrth′kwāk′) *n.* A shaking of the earth's crust, caused by the splitting of a mass of rock or by volcanic disturbances. ◆ Collateral adjective: *seismic.*

earth·ward (ûrth′wərd) *adv.* Toward the earth. Also **earth′wards.** — *adj.* Moving toward the earth.

earth·work (ûrth′wûrk′) *n. Mil.* A fortification made largely or wholly of earth.

earth·worm (ûrth′wûrm′) *n.* Any burrowing worm.

earth·y (ûr′thē) *adj.* **earth·i·er, earth·i·est** 1. Of or like earth. 2. Unrefined; coarse. 3. Natural; robust; lusty. **— earth′i·ness** *n.*

ear·wax (ir′waks′) *n.* A substance secreted by glands lining the passages of the external ear: also called *cerumen.*

ear·wig (ir′wig′) *n.* 1. An insect with horny forewings and a tail pair of forceps, erroneously believed to enter the human ear. 2. *U.S.* A small centipede. — *v.t.* **·wigged, ·wigging** To insinuate against in secret. [OE *ēarwicga*]

ease (ēz) *n.* 1. Freedom from physical discomfort or mental agitation. 2. Freedom from great effort or difficulty. 3. Naturalness; poise. — *v.* **eased, eas·ing** *v.t.* 1. To relieve the mental or physical pain or oppression of; comfort. 2. To make less painful or oppressive; alleviate. 3. To lessen the pressure, weight, tension, etc., of: to *ease* an axle. 4. To make easier; facilitate. 5. To move, lower, or put in place slowly and carefully. — *v.i.* 6. To lessen in severity, tension, speed, etc.: often with *up* or *off.* [< OF < L *adjacens, -entis* close at hand] **— ease′ful** *adj.* **— eas′er** *n.*

ea·sel (ē′zəl) *n.* A folding frame or tripod used to support an artist's canvas, etc. [< Du. *ezel* easel, orig. an ass]

ease·ment (ēz′mənt) *n.* 1. Anything that gives ease or comfort. 2. *Law* The right to use another's property.

eas·i·ly (ē′zə-lē) *adv.* 1. In an easy manner. 2. Beyond question. 3. Very possibly.

eas·i·ness (ē′zi-nis) *n.* The state of being at ease, or of being easy to do.

east (ēst) *n.* 1. The direction of the sun in relation to an observer on earth at sunrise. 2. One of the four cardinal points of the compass, directly opposite *west* and 90° clockwise from *north.* See COMPASS CARD. 3. Any direction near this point. 4. *Sometimes cap.* Any region east of a specified point. **— the East** Asia and its adjacent islands; the Orient. — *adj.* 1. To, toward, facing, or in the east. 2. Coming from the east. — *adv.* In or toward the east. [OE *ēast*]

east·bound (ēst′bound′) *adj.* Going eastward. Also **east′bound′.**

East·er (ēs′tər) *n.* 1. A Christian festival commemorating the resurrection of Christ. 2. The day on which this festival is celebrated, the Sunday immediately after the first full moon that occurs on or after March 21: also **Easter Sunday.** [OE *Eastre* goddess of spring]

east·er·ly (ēs′tər·lē) *adj.* 1. In, of, toward, or pertaining to the east. 2. From the east, as a wind. — *adv.* Toward or from the east. — *n. pl.* **·lies** A wind or storm from the east.

east·ern (ēs′tərn) *adj.* 1. To, toward, or in the east. 2. Native to or inhabiting the east: an *eastern* species. 3. *Sometimes cap.* Of, or like the east or the East.

Eastern Church 1. The church of the Byzantine Empire, including the patriarchates of Constantinople, Alexandria, Antioch, and Jerusalem, that separated from the Western Church in 1054: also called *Greek Church.* 2. The Eastern Orthodox Church. 3. The Uniat Church.

east·ern·er (ēs′tərn·ər) *n. Often cap.* One who is native to or lives in the east, esp. the eastern U.S.

Eastern Orthodox Church The modern churches derived from the medieval Eastern Church, including the Greek and Russian Orthodox churches, that agree in faith and order with the patriarch of Constantinople: also called *Eastern Church, Orthodox Church,* or loosely *Greek Church.*

Eastern Roman Empire The Byzantine Empire.

East·er·tide (ēs′tər·tīd′) *n.* The season of Easter, a period extending in various churches from Easter to Ascension Day, Whitsunday, or Trinity Sunday.

east·ward (ēst′wərd) *adv.* Toward the east. Also **east′wards.** — *adj.* To, toward, facing, or in the east. — *n.* An eastward direction or point; also, an eastern part or region.

east·ward·ly (ēst′wərd·lē) *adj. & adv.* 1. Toward the east. 2. Coming from the east, as a wind.

eas·y (ē′zē) *adj.* **eas·i·er, eas·i·est** **1.** Requiring little work or effort; offering few difficulties: an *easy* task. **2.** Free from discomfort, trouble, or anxiety: an *easy* mind. **3.** Characterized by rest or comfort: an *easy* life. **4.** Not stiff or formal; relaxed: an *easy* manner. **5.** Not strict; lenient; indulgent. **6.** Yielding; credulous: an *easy* victim. **7.** Complacent; easygoing. **8.** Unhurried; gentle: an *easy* trot. **9.** Not burdensome; moderate: to buy on *easy* terms. **10.** Well-to-do; affluent: in *easy* circumstances. **11.** *Econ.* In little demand: said of a commodity. **— to be on easy street** *Informal* To be well-to-do; live in comfort. **— adv.** *Informal* In an easy manner; easily. **— to go easy on** *Slang* **1.** To use with moderation, as liquor. **2.** To be lenient with. **3.** To be tactful about. **— to take it easy** *Informal* **1.** To relax. **2.** To remain calm. [< OF *aiser* to put at ease]

eas·y·go·ing (ē′zē-gō′ing) *adj.* **1.** Not inclined to effort or worry. **2.** Moving at an easy pace, as a horse.

eat (ēt) *v.* **ate** (āt, *Brit.* et) or *Archaic* **eat** (et, ĕt), **eat·en, eat·ing** *v.t.* **1.** To take (food) in the mouth, chew, and swallow. **2.** To consume or destroy. **3.** To wear away or corrode. **4.** To bother: What's *eating* him? **— v.i.** **5.** To have a meal. **— to eat one's words** To retract what one has said. [OE *etan*] **— eat′a·ble** *adj. & n.* **— eat′er** *n.*

eau de Co·logne (ō′ də kə-lōn′) Cologne, a toilet water.

eaves (ēvz) *n.* (*orig. sing., now construed as pl.*) The lower projecting edge of a sloping roof. [OE *efes* edge]

eaves·drop (ēvz′drop′) *v.i.* **·dropped, ·drop·ping** To listen secretly, as to a conversation. **— eaves′drop′per** *n.*

ebb (eb) *v.i.* **1.** To recede, as the tide: opposed to *flow*. **2.** To decline or weaken; fail. **— n.** **1.** The flowing back of tidewater to the ocean: opposed to *flood*. Also **ebb tide**. **2.** A condition or period of decline or decay. [OE *ebbian*]

eb·on·ite (eb′ən-īt) *n.* Vulcanite, a rubber product.

eb·on·y (eb′ən-ē) *n. pl.* **·ies** **1.** A hard, heavy wood, usu. black, used for cabinetwork, etc., furnished by various species of tropical hardwood trees. **2.** Any tree yielding this wood. **— adj.** **1.** Made of ebony. **2.** Like ebony; black. [< L < Gk. < Egyptian *hebni*]

e·bul·lient (i-bul′yənt) *adj.* **1.** Full of enthusiasm; exuberant. **2.** Boiling or bubbling up. [< L < *e-* out + *bullire* to boil] **— e·bul′lient·ly** *adv.* **— e·bul′lience, e·bul′lien·cy** *n.*

eb·ul·li·tion (eb′ə-lish′ən) *n.* **1.** The bubbling of a liquid; boiling. **2.** Any sudden or violent agitation, as of emotions.

ec- Var. or EX-².

ec·cen·tric (ek-sen′trik) *adj.* **1.** Differing conspicuously in behavior, appearance, or opinions. **2.** Not situated in the center, as an axis. **3.** Deviating from a perfect circle: said chiefly of an elliptical orbit. **4.** *Math.* Not having the same center: opposed to *concentric*. **— n.** An odd or erratic individual. [< LL < Gk. < *ek-* out, away + *kentron* center] **— ec·cen′tri·cal·ly** *adv.*

ec·cen·tric·i·ty (ek′sen-tris′ə-tē) *n. pl.* **·ties** **1.** Deviation from what is regular or expected; irregularity. **2.** A peculiarity. **3.** The quality or degree of being eccentric.

Ec·cle·si·as·tes (i-klē′zē-as′tēz) *n.* A book of the Old Testament: also, *Hebrew, Koheleth*. [< Gk. *ekklēsiastēs*, trans. of Hebrew *qōhĕleth* preacher]

ec·cle·si·as·tic (i-klē′zē-as′tik) *adj.* Ecclesiastical. **— n.** One officially in the service of the church; a cleric; churchman. [< Gk. < *ek-* out + *kaleein* to call]

ec·cle·si·as·ti·cal (i-klē′zē-as′ti-kəl) *adj.* Of or pertaining to the church, especially as an organized and governing power. **— ec·cle′si·as′ti·cal·ly** *adv.*

Ec·cle·si·as·ti·cus (i-klē′zē-as′ti-kəs) *n.* One of the didactic books of the Old Testament Apocrypha.

ech·e·lon (esh′ə-lon) *n.* **1.** A troop, fleet, or airplane formation resembling a series of steps, in which each rank, ship, or airplane extends behind and slightly to the right or left of the preceding one. **2.** *Mil.* **a** One of the different fractions of a command arranged from front to rear, to which a particular combat mission is assigned: assault *echelon*; support *echelon*. **b** One of the various subdivisions from front to rear of a military headquarters: forward *echelon*; rear *echelon*. **c** Level of command: command *echelon*. **— v.t. & v.i.** To form in echelon. [< F *échelon* < *échelle* ladder < L *scala*]

e·chid·na (i-kid′nə) *n. pl.* **·nae** (-nē) An egg-laying mammal of Australia, Tasmania, and New Guinea, having strong spines intermixed with fur. [< NL < Gk., viper]

e·chi·no·derm (i-kī′nə-dûrm) *n.* A marine animal having a radial body and a hard, spiny shell, as the starfish.

ech·o (ek′ō) *n. pl.* **ech·oes** **1.** The repetition of a sound by the reflection of sound waves from an opposing surface; also, the sound so produced. **2.** The repetition or reproduction of the views, style, etc., of another. **3.** One who imitates another or repeats his words. **4.** Prompt, sympathetic response. **— v.i.** **1.** To repeat or send back (sound) by echo: The walls *echoed* the shot. **2.** To repeat the words, opinions, etc., of. **3.** To repeat (words, opinions, etc.) in imitation. **— v.i.** **4.** To give back sound. **5.** To be repeated or given back. [< L < Gk. *ēche* sound, noise] **— ech′o·er** *n.* **— e·cho′ic** *adj.*

Ech·o (ek′ō) In Greek mythology, a nymph who, because of love for Narcissus, pined away until only her voice was left.

é·clair (ā-klâr′, i-klâr′) *n.* A small oblong pastry shell filled with custard or whipped cream. [< F, lit., flash of lightning]

é·clat (ā-klä′, i-klä′) *n.* **1.** Brilliance of action or effect; conspicuous success. **2.** Splendor of reputation; renown; also, notoriety. **3.** Acclaim. [< F < *éclater* to burst out]

ec·lec·tic (ek-lek′tik, ik-) *adj.* **1.** Selecting what is considered best from different systems or sources. **2.** Composed of elements selected from diverse sources. **— n.** One favoring no particular belief or practice, as in philosophy or art, but selecting from all schools or methods. [< Gk. < *ek-* out + *legein* to select] **— ec·lec′ti·cal·ly** *adv.* **— ec·lec′ti·cism** *n.*

e·clipse (i-klips′) *n.* **1.** *Astron.* The apparent dimming or elimination of light from one heavenly body by another. A lunar eclipse is caused by the passage of the moon through the earth's shadow; a solar eclipse by the passage of the moon between the sun and the observer. **2.** Any overshadowing or dimming, as of power or reputation. **— v.t.** **e·clipsed, e·clips·ing** **1.** To cause an eclipse of; darken. **2.** To obscure the beauty, fame, worth, etc., of; overshadow; surpass. [< OF < L < Gk. < *ek-* out + *leipein* to leave]

e·clip·tic (i-klip′tik, ē-) *n.* *Astron.* **1.** The plane, passing through the center of the sun, that contains the orbit of the earth: also **plane of the ecliptic**. **2.** The great circle in which this plane intersects the celestial sphere. **— adj.** Pertaining to eclipses or to the ecliptic: also **e·clip′ti·cal.** **— e·clip′ti·cal·ly** *adv.*

ec·logue (ek′lôg, -log) *n.* A short pastoral poem. [< F < L < Gk. < *ek-* out + *legein* to select]

e·col·o·gy (i-kol′ə-jē, ē-) *n.* The division of biology that treats of the relations between organisms and their environment. [< Gk. *oikos* home + -LOGY] **— ec·o·log·ic** (ek′ə-loj′ik) or **·i·cal** *adj.* **— ec′o·log′i·cal·ly** *adv.* **— e·col′o·gist** *n.*

ec·o·nom·ic (ek′ə-nom′ik, ē′kə-) *adj.* **1.** Of or pertaining to the development and management of the material wealth of a government or community: the French *economic* policy. **2.** Relating to the science of economics: *economic* theory. **3.** Of or pertaining to financial matters. **4.** Of practical use.

ec·o·nom·i·cal (ek′ə-nom′i·kəl, ē′kə-) *adj.* **1.** Frugal. **2.** Economic. **— ec′o·nom′i·cal·ly** *adv.*

economic determinism The theory that all human activities and institutions have economic origins.

ec·o·nom·ics (ek′ə-nom′iks, ē′kə-) *n.pl.* **1.** (*construed as sing.*) The science that treats of the production, distribution, and consumption of wealth. **2.** Economic matters.

e·con·o·mist (i-kon′ə-mist) *n.* **1.** One who is proficient in economics. **2.** One who is careful and thrifty.

e·con·o·mize (i-kon′ə-mīz) *v.* **·mized, ·miz·ing** *v.i.* **1.** To be sparing in expenditure; manage thriftily. **— v.t.** **2.** To use sparingly or to best advantage. Also *Brit.* **e·con′o·mise.**

e·con·o·my (i-kon′ə-mē) *n. pl.* **·mies** **1.** Frugal management of money, materials, resources, and the like; also, an example of this. **2.** The practical administration of the material resources of a country, community, or establishment: the national *economy*. **3.** The orderly distribution and interplay of parts in a structure or system: the *economy* of nature. [< L < Gk. < *oikos* house + *nemein* to manage]

e·co·sys·tem (ē′kō·sis′təm, ek′ō-) *n.* A community in nature including all the plants and animals and the environment associated with them. [< Gk. *oikos* home + SYSTEM]

ec·ru (ek′rōō, ā′krōō) *adj.* Of the color of unbleached linen. **— n.** A light, yellowish brown. Also **é·cru.** [< F < OF < L *ex-* thoroughly + *crudus* raw]

ec·sta·sy (ek′stə-sē) *n. pl.* **·sies** **1.** The state of being beside oneself through some overpowering emotion: in an *ecstasy* of anticipation. **2.** Intense delight; rapture. **3.** A trance. [< OF < LL < Gk. < *ek-* out + *histanai* to place]

ec·stat·ic (ek·stat′ik) *adj.* **1.** Pertaining to, of the nature of, or exciting to ecstasy; rapturous. **2.** In a state of ecstasy; transported. Also **ec·stat′i·cal.** **— n.** A person subject to ecstasies or trances. **— ec·stat′i·cal·ly** *adv.*

ecto- combining form Without; outside; external: *ectoderm*. Also-, before vowels, **ect-**. [< Gk. *ekto-* < *ektos* outside]

ec·to·derm (ek′tə-dûrm) *n.* *Biol.* The outermost of the three primary germ layers in the embryo, developing into the skin, sense organs, and nervous system. **— ec′to·der′mal,** or **ec·to·der′mic** *adj.*

ec·to·mor·phic (ek′tō-môr′fik) *adj.* Of human body types, characterized by a lean body structure. **— ec′to·morph** *n.*

-ectomy combining form Removal of a part by cutting out: used in surgical terms to indicate certain kinds of operations: *appendectomy*. [< Gk. < *ek-* out + *temnein* to cut]

ec·to·plasm (ek′tə-plaz′əm) *n.* *Biol.* The firm outer layer of the cytoplasm of a unicellular organism or of a plant cell.

2. The substance alleged to emanate from the body of a spiritualist medium during a trance. — **ec'to·plas'mic** adj.

ec·u·men·i·cal (ek'yōō·men'i·kəl) adj. World-wide in scope, esp. of the Christian church: an ecumenical council. Also **ec'u·men'ic.** [< LL < Gk. oikeein to inhabit]

ec·u·men·ism (ek'yōō·men'iz·əm) n. The movement for world-wide unity and cooperation among all Christian churches. Also **ec'u·men'i·cal·ism, ec'u·men'i·cism.**

ec·ze·ma (ek'sə·mə, eg'zə·mə, eg·zē'mə) n. Pathol. An inflammatory disease of the skin attended by itching, watery discharge, and the appearance of lesions. [< Gk. < ek- out + zeein to boil] — **ec·zem·a·tous** (eg·zem'ə·təs) adj.

-ed¹ suffix Forming the past tense of regular verbs: walked, killed, played. [OE -ede, -ode, -ade]

-ed² suffix 1. Forming the past participle of regular verbs: washed. 2. Forming adjectives from adjectives in -ate, with the same general meaning: bipinnated. [OE -ed, -ad, -od]

-ed³ suffix Forming adjectives from nouns with the senses: 1. Having; possessing; characterized by: toothed, green-eyed. 2. Like; resembling: bigoted. [OE -ede]

ed·dy (ed'ē) n. pl. **·dies** A backward-circling current of water or air; whirlpool. — v.t. & v.i. **·died, ·dy·ing** To move, or cause to move, in or as in an eddy. [Prob. < ON idha]

e·del·weiss (ā'dəl·vīs) n. A small, perennial herb growing chiefly in the Alps, with white, woolly leaves suggesting a flower. [< G edel noble + weiss white]

e·de·ma (i·dē'mə) n. pl. **·ma·ta** (-mə·tə) Pathol. An abnormal accumulation of serous fluid in various organs, cavities, or tissues of the body; swelling: also spelled oedema. [< NL < Gk. oidein to swell] — **e·dem·a·tous** (i·dem'ə·təs), EDELWEISS **e·dem'a·tose** (-tōs) adj. (To 4 inches high)

E·den (ēd'n) n. 1. In the Bible, the garden that was the first home of Adam and Eve: often called Paradise. 2. Any delightful place or condition. [< Hebrew ēden delight]

e·den·tate (ē·den'tāt, i·den'-) adj. 1. Of or pertaining to an order of mammals, some of which lack teeth, including sloths, anteaters, and armadillos. 2. Toothless. — n. An edentate mammal. [< L < e- without + dens, dentis tooth]

edge (ej) n. 1. A bounding or dividing line; also, the part along a boundary; border; margin: the edge of a lawn. 2. A verge or brink; rim: the edge of a cliff. 3. The line where two surfaces of a solid meet: the edge of a cube. 4. The thin, sharp, cutting side of a blade. 5. Sharpness; keenness. 6. U.S. Informal Advantage; superiority. — **on edge** 1. Keenly sensitive; tense; irritable. 2. Eager; impatient. — v. **edged, edg·ing** v.t. 1. To sharpen. 2. To furnish with an edge or border. 3. To push sidewise or by degrees. — v.i. 4. To move sidewise or by degrees. [OE ecg]

edge·wise (ej'wīz') adv. 1. With the edge forward. 2. On, by, with, or toward the edge. Also **edge'ways'** (-wāz').

edg·ing (ej'ing) n. A trimming; border.

edg·y (ej'ē) adj. **edg·i·er, edg·i·est** 1. Tense, nervous, or irritable. 2. Having an edge or edges. — **edg'i·ness** n.

ed·i·ble (ed'ə·bəl) adj. Fit to eat. — n. Usu. pl. Something fit to eat. [< LL < L edere to eat]

e·dict (ē'dikt) n. An official decree publicly proclaimed. [< L < e- out + dicere to say] — **e·dic·tal** (ē·dik'təl) adj.

ed·i·fi·ca·tion (ed'ə·fə·kā'shən) n. Intellectual or moral enlightenment and improvement.

ed·i·fice (ed'ə·fis) n. A building or other structure, esp. one that is large and imposing. [< F < L < aedes building + facere to make] — **ed·i·fi·cial** (ed'ə·fish'əl) adj.

ed·i·fy (ed'ə·fi) v.t. **·fied, ·fy·ing** To enlighten and benefit, esp. morally or spiritually. [< OF < L < aedes building + facere to make] — **ed'i·fi'er** n.

ed·it (ed'it) v.t. 1. To correct and prepare for publication: to edit a manuscript. 2. To compile, arrange, and emend for publication: to edit a collection of poems. 3. To direct the preparation, publication, and editorial policies of (a newspaper, magazine, etc.). [Back formation < EDITOR]

e·di·tion (i·dish'ən) n. 1. The form in which a book is published: a three-volume edition. 2. The total number of copies of a publication issued at any one time; also, such a copy. [< F < L < e- out + dare to give]

ed·i·tor (ed'i·tər) n. 1. One who edits. 2. A writer of editorials. [< L] — **ed'i·tor·ship'** n.

ed·i·to·ri·al (ed'i·tôr'ē·əl, -tō'rē-) n. An article in a newspaper, magazine, or the like, published as the periodical's official expression of opinion on some issue. — adj. Of, pertaining to, or written by an editor. — **ed'i·to'ri·al·ly** adv.

ed·i·to·ri·al·ize (ed'i·tôr'ē·əl·iz', -tō'rē-) v.t. & v.i. **·ized, ·iz·ing** 1. To express opinions (on a subject) editorially. 2. To insert editorial opinions (into a news item, etc.).

editor in chief pl. **editors in chief** The chief editor of a publication, who establishes its policy and supervises operations.

ed·u·cate (ej'ōō·kāt) v.t. **cat·ed, ·cat·ing** 1. To develop or train the mind, capabilities, or character of by instruction or study; teach. 2. To train for some special purpose. 3. To develop or train (taste, special ability, etc.). 4. To provide schooling for. [< L < e- out + ducere to lead] — **ed'u·ca·ble** adj. — **ed'u·ca'tor** n.

ed·u·cat·ed (ej'ōō·kā'tid) adj. 1. Developed and informed by education; instructed; trained. 2. Having a cultivated mind, speech, manner, etc.

ed·u·ca·tion (ej'ōō·kā'shən) n. 1. The act of educating; systematic development or training of the mind, capabilities, or character through instruction or study. 2. Acquisition of knowledge or skills; esp., formal schooling in an institution of learning. 3. Knowledge, skills, or cultivation acquired through instruction or study. 4. The study of teaching methods and problems, the learning process, and other matters related to the classroom; pedagogy.

ed·u·ca·tion·al (ej'ōō·kā'shən·əl) adj. Of, pertaining to, or imparting education: an educational trip. — **ed'u·ca'tion·al·ly** adv.

ed·u·ca·tive (ej'ōō·kā'tiv) adj. 1. That educates or tends to educate; educational. 2. Of or relating to education.

e·duce (i·dōōs', i·dyōōs') v.t. **e·duced, e·duc·ing** 1. To call forth; bring out; elicit. 2. To infer or develop from data; deduce. [< L < e- out + ducere to lead] — **e·duc'i·ble** adj. — **e·duc·tion** (i·duk'shən) n. — **e·duc'tive** adj.

-ee suffix of nouns 1. One who undergoes, or benefits from, some action: used esp. in legal terms, and opposed to -er, -or, as in grantor, grantee. 2. One who is described by the main element: absentee. [< AF -é, suffix of pp. < L -atus]

eel (ēl) n. pl. **eels** or **eel** A fish having a snakelike body, usu. without scales or pelvic fins, and of both marine and fresh-water habitat. [OE æl] — **eel'y** adj.

e'en¹ (ēn) adv. Poetic Even.

e'en² (ēn) n. Poetic & Dial. Evening.

e'er (âr) adv. Poetic Ever.

-eer suffix of nouns and verbs 1. One who is concerned with, works with, or makes something indicated: engineer. 2. Be concerned with; work at: electioneer. [< F -ier < L -arius]

ee·rie (ir'ē, ē'rē) adj. 1. Inspiring fear; weird; ghostly. 2. Affected by superstitious fear. Also **ee'ry.** [ME eri timid, var. of erg < OE earg] — **ee'ri·ly** adv. — **ee'ri·ness** n.

ef·face (i·fās') v.t. **·faced, ·fac·ing** 1. To rub out, as written characters; erase. 2. To obliterate, as a memory. 3. To make (oneself) insignificant. [< F < L ex- out + facies face] — **ef·face'ment** n. — **ef·fac'er** n.

ef·fect (i·fekt') n. 1. Something brought about by some cause or agency; result; consequence. 2. Capacity to produce some result; efficacy. 3. The condition or fact of being in active force: to put a law into effect. 4. The state of being actually accomplished or realized: to carry plans into effect. 5. The particular way in which something affects or influences something else. 6. The overall reaction or impression produced by something seen, heard, or done. 7. A technique used in art, literature, music, etc., to achieve a certain result or produce a distinctive impression. 8. The actual or basic meaning intended or conveyed; purport: usu. with to: She said something to that effect. 9. pl. Movable goods; belongings. — **in effect** 1. In actual fact. 2. For all practical purposes; virtually. 3. In active force or operation. — **to take effect** To begin to act upon something; be or become operative. — v.t. To bring about; cause; esp., to accomplish; achieve: to effect an escape. [< L < ex- out + facere to do, make] — **ef·fect'er** n. — **ef·fect'i·ble** adj.

ef·fec·tive (i·fek'tiv) adj. 1. Producing or adapted to produce the proper result. 2. Being in force, as a law. 3. Producing a striking impression, as a speaker. 4. Ready for action, as an army. — n. 1. One who is fit for duty. 2. The number of men available for military service. — **ef·fec'tive·ly** adv. — **ef·fec'tive·ness** n.

ef·fec·tu·al (i·fek'chōō·əl) adj. 1. Producing or having adequate power to produce an intended effect. 2. Legally valid or binding. — **ef·fec'tu·al·ly** adv. — **ef·fec'tu·al·ness, ef·fec·tu·al·i·ty** (-al'ə·tē) n.

ef·fec·tu·ate (i·fek'chōō·āt) v.t. **·at·ed, ·at·ing** To bring about; accomplish; effect. — **ef·fec'tu·a'tion** n.

ef·fem·i·nate (i·fem'ə·nit) adj. 1. Having womanlike traits or qualities to a degree unbefitting a man; womanish; unmanly. 2. Characterized by weakness or self-indulgence. [< L < ex- out + femina a woman] — **ef·fem'i·na·cy** (-nə·sē) n. — **ef·fem'i·nate·ly** adv. — **ef·fem'i·nate·ness** n.

ef·fer·ent (ef'ər·ənt) adj. Physiol. Carrying or carried outward: said esp. of impulses transmitted from the central nervous system to muscles, etc.; opposed to afferent. — n. Physiol. An efferent duct, vessel, or nerve. [< L < ex- out + ferre to carry]

ef·fer·vesce (ef'ər·ves') v.i. **·vesced, ·vesc·ing** 1. To give off bubbles of gas, as water charged with carbon dioxide. 2. To issue out in bubbles, as a gas. 3. To show exhilaration or lively spirits. [< L < ex- out + fervescere to boil] — **ef'fer·ves'cence** n. — **ef'fer·ves'cent** adj.

ef·fete (i·fēt') adj. 1. Having lost strength or virility. 2. Incapable of further production; barren. [< L < ex- out + fetus a breeding] — **ef·fete'ly** adv. — **ef·fete'ness** n.

ef·fi·ca·cious (ef′ə·kā′shəs) *adj.* Producing or capable of producing an intended effect. [See EFFECT.] — **ef′fi·ca′cious·ly** *adv.* — **ef′fi·ca′cious·ness** *n.*

ef·fi·ca·cy (ef′ə·kə·sē) *n. pl.* **·cies** Power to produce a desired or intended result.

ef·fi·cien·cy (i·fish′ən·sē) *n. pl.* **·cies** 1. The quality of being efficient. 2. The ratio of work done or energy expended to the energy supplied in the form of food or fuel.

ef·fi·cient (i·fish′ənt) *adj.* 1. Productive of results with a minimum of wasted effort. 2. Producing an effect. [See EFFECT.] — **ef·fi′cient·ly** *adv.*

ef·fi·gy (ef′ə·jē) *n. pl.* **·gies** 1. A likeness or representation; esp., a sculptured portrait. 2. A crude image of a disliked person. [< F < L < *ex-* out + *fingere* to fashion]

ef·flo·resce (ef′lôr·es′, -lō·res′) *v.i.* **·resced**, **·resc·ing** 1. To blossom, bloom, or flower. 2. *Chem.* **a** To become powdery, wholly or in part, and lose crystalline structure through evaporation of water. **b** To become covered with a crust of saline particles left by evaporation or by chemical change. [< L < *ex-* thoroughly + *florescere* to bloom]

ef·flo·res·cence (ef′lôr·es′əns, -lō·res′-) *n.* 1. The act or season of flowering. 2. *Chem.* The act or process of efflorescing. 3. *Pathol.* A rash. — **ef′flo·res′cent** *adj.*

ef·flu·ent (ef′lōō·ənt) *adj.* Flowing out. — *n.* An outflow, as of water from a lake, industrial sewage, etc. [< L < *ex-* out + *fluere* to flow] — **ef′flu·ence** *n.*

ef·flu·vi·um (i·flōō′vē·əm) *n. pl.* **·vi·a** (-vē·ə) or **·vi·ums** 1. An invisible emanation; esp., a foul-smelling exhalation, as from decaying matter. 2. A supposed imponderable agent formerly regarded as the source of electric and magnetic forces. [< L, a flowing out] — **ef·flu′vi·al** *adj.*

ef·flux (ef′luks) *n.* 1. A flowing out. 2. That which flows forth; emanation. [< L < *ex-* out + *fluere* to flow]

ef·fort (ef′ərt) *n.* 1. Expenditure of physical, mechanical, or mental energy to get something done; exertion. 2. Something produced by exertion: a new theatrical *effort*. [< F < OF < L *ex-* thoroughly + *fortis* strong] — **ef′fort·less** *adj.* — **ef′fort·less·ly** *adv.*

ef·front·er·y (i·frun′tər·ē) *n. pl.* **·ies** Shameless or insolent boldness; audacity. [< F < L < *ex-* out + *frontis* face]

ef·fulge (i·fulj′) *v.t. & v.i.* **·fulged**, **·fulg·ing** To shine forth; radiate. [< L < *ex-* out + *fulgere* to shine]

ef·ful·gent (i·ful′jənt) *adj.* Shining brilliantly; radiant; splendid. — **ef·ful′gence** *n.* — **ef·ful′gent·ly** *adv.*

ef·fuse (*adj.* i·fyōōs′; *v.* i·fyōōz′) *adj.* 1. *Bot.* Spreading out loosely or flat. 2. *Zool.* Having the lips separated by a groove, as certain shells. — *v.* **·fused**, **·fus·ing** *v.t.* 1. To pour forth; shed. — *v.i.* 2. To emanate; exude. [< L < *ex-* out + *fundere* to pour] — **ef·fu′sion** *n.*

ef·fu·sive (i·fyōō′siv) *adj.* 1. Overflowing with sentiment; demonstrative; gushing. 2. Pouring forth; overflowing. — **ef·fu′sive·ly** *adv.* — **ef·fu′sive·ness** *n.*

e·gad (ē·gad′, ē·gad′) *interj.* By God!: a mild oath.

e·gal·i·tar·i·an (i·gal′ə·târ′ē·ən) *adj.* Of, relating to, or believing in political and social equality. — *n.* One who believes in or advocated political and social equality. Also **equalitarian.** [< F *égalitaire*] — **e·gal′i·tar′i·an·ism** *n.*

egg¹ (eg) *n.* 1. The round or oval reproductive body produced by female birds, insects, and most reptiles and fishes, consisting of the germ and a nutritive yolk enclosed in a shell or membrane. 2. *Biol.* The reproductive cell of female animals; ovum: also **egg cell.** 3. The hen's egg as a food. 4. Something oval like a hen's egg. 5. *U.S. Slang* Person: He's a good *egg.* — **to lay an egg** *U.S. Slang* To fail completely. — **to put all one's eggs in one basket** To risk all in a single venture. — *v.t.* 1. To cover with beaten egg before cooking. 2. *U.S. Informal* To pelt with eggs. [< ON]

egg² (eg) *v.t.* To incite; urge: usu. with *on.* [< ON *eggja*]

egg·head (eg′hed′) *n. U.S. Slang* An intellectual; highbrow: often derisive.

egg·nog (eg′nog′) *n.* A drink made of beaten eggs and milk with sugar and nutmeg and sometimes with liquor.

egg·plant (eg′plant′, -plänt′) *n.* 1. A widely cultivated herb with large, egg-shaped, usu. purple-skinned fruit. 2. The fruit of this plant, used as a vegetable.

egg·shell (eg′shel′) *n.* The hard, brittle covering of a bird's egg. — *adj.* 1. Thin and fragile. 2. Pale yellow or ivory.

egg white The uncooked albumen of an egg.

e·gis (ē′jis) See AEGIS.

eg·lan·tine (eg′lən·tīn, -tēn) *n.* Any of various fragrant wild roses. [< F < OF, ult. < L *acus* needle]

e·go (ē′gō, eg′ō) *n. pl.* **e·gos** 1. The thinking, feeling, and acting self that is conscious of itself and aware of its distinction from the objects of its thought and perceptions. 2. *Psychoanal.* The conscious aspect of the psyche that develops through contact with the external world and resolves conflicts between the id and the superego. 3. *Informal* Self-centeredness; conceit. [< L, I]

e·go·cen·tric (ē′gō·sen′trik, eg′ō-) *adj.* Regarding oneself as the object of all experience and acts. — *n.* An egocentric person. — **e′go·cen·tric′i·ty** (-sen·tris′ə·tē) *n.*

e·go·ism (ē′gō·iz′əm, eg′ō-) *n.* 1. Inordinate concern for one's own welfare and interests. 2. Self-conceit; egotism.

e·go·ist (ē′gō·ist, eg′ō-) *n.* 1. One who is completely devoted to his own interests. 2. A conceited person; egotist. — **e′go·is′tic** or **·ti′cal** *adj.* — **e′go·is′ti·cal·ly** *adv.*

e·go·ma·ni·a (ē′gō·mā′nē·ə, -mãn′yə, eg′ō-) *n.* Abnormal or excessive egotism. — **e′go·ma′ni·ac** (-ak) *n.*

e·go·tism (ē′gō·tiz′əm, eg′ə-) *n.* 1. Excessive reference to oneself in speech or writing; self-conceit. 2. Selfishness; egoism. — **e′go·tist** *n.* — **e′go·tis′tic** or **·ti·cal** *adj.* — **e′go·tis′ti·cal·ly** *adv.*

e·gre·gious (i·grē′jəs, -jē·əs) *adj.* Conspicuously bad; glaring; flagrant. [< L < *e-* out + *grex, gregis* herd] — **e·gre′gious·ly** *adv.* — **e·gre′gious·ness** *n.*

e·gress (ē′gres) *n.* 1. A going out, as from a building; emergence; also, the right of going out. Also **e·gres′sion.** 2. A place of exit. [< L < *e-* out + *gradi* to walk]

e·gret (ē′grit, eg′rit) *n.* 1. One of various herons characterized in the breeding season by long and loose plumes drooping over the tail. 2. Aigrette (def. 1). [Var. of AIGRETTE]

E·gyp·tian (i·jip′shən) *adj.* Of or pertaining to Egypt, its people, or their culture. — *n.* 1. One of the people of Egypt. 2. The ancient Hamitic language of Egypt.

E·gyp·tol·o·gy (ē′jip·tol′ə·jē) *n.* The study of the antiquities of Egypt. — **E′gyp·tol′o·gist** *n.*

eh (ā, e) *interj.* What: used to express uncertainty: surprise, etc.

ei·der (ī′dər) *n.* A large sea duck of northern regions. [< ON *ædhr-* in *ædhar-dūn* eiderdown]

ei·der·down (ī′dər·doun′) *n.* The down of the eider used for stuffing pillows and quilts; such also, a quilt.

eight (āt) *n.* 1. The sum of seven and one: a cardinal number. 2. Any symbol of this number, as 8, viii, VIII. 3. Anything consisting of eight units. — *adj.* Being one more than seven. [OE *eahta*] — **eighth** (ātth, āth) *adj. & n.*

eight·een (ā′tēn′) *n.* 1. The sum of seventeen and one: a cardinal number. 2. Any symbol of this number, as 18, xviii, XVIII. 3. Anything consisting of or representing eighteen units. — *adj.* Being one more than seventeen. [OE *eahtatiene*] — **eight·eenth′** *adj. & n.*

eight·een·mo (ā′tēn′mō′) *adj. & n.* Octodecimo.

eighth note *Music* A note having one eighth the time value of a whole note: also, *Chiefly Brit.,* quaver.

eight·vo (āt′vō) *adj. & n.* Octavo.

eight·y (ā′tē) *n. pl.* **·ies** 1. The sum of seventy and ten: a cardinal number. 2. Any symbol of this number, as 80, lxxx, LXXX. 3. Anything consisting of or representing eighty units. — *adj.* Being ten more than seventy. [OE *eahtatig*] — **eight′i·eth** *adj. & n.*

-ein Var. of -IN.

ein·stein·i·um (īn·stī′nē·əm) *n.* A radioactive element (symbol Es), originally detected in the debris of a thermonuclear explosion and artificially produced by the irradiation of plutonium. See ELEMENT. [after Albert *Einstein*]

ei·ther (ē′thər, ī′thər) *adj.* 1. One or the other of two: Use *either* foot. 2. Each of two; one and the other: They sat on *either* side of him. — *pron.* One or the other: Choose *either.* — *conj.* In one of two or more cases, indeterminately or indifferently: a disjunctive correlative used with *or:* *Either* I shall go or he will come. — *adv.* Any more so: used after the denial of an alternative, or to emphasize a preceding negative: He could not speak, and I could not *either;* I shall leave, and you can't stop me *either.* [OE *ægther*]

◆ **either, neither** *Either,* like *neither,* is singular and in formal writing takes a singular verb: *Either* of them *is* suitable. In informal speech and writing, however, a plural verb is commonly used: *Are either* of you going to the party? When there are two subjects of differing number, the verb agrees with the nearer: *Neither* he nor *they are* ever there.

e·jac·u·late (i·jak′yə·lāt) *v.* **·lat·ed**, **·lat·ing** *v.t.* 1. To utter suddenly, as a brief exclamation. 2. To discharge suddenly and quickly, as seminal fluid. — *v.i.* 3. To ejaculate something. — *n.* That which is ejaculated. — **Syn.** See EXCLAIM. [< L < *e-* out + *jaculari* to throw] — **e·jac′u·la′tion** *n.* — **e·jac′u·la′tive** (-lā′tiv, -lə·tiv) *adj.* — **e·jac′u·la·tor** *n.* — **e·jac′u·la·to′ry** *adj.*

e·ject (i·jekt′) *v.t.* 1. To throw out with sudden force. 2. To put forcibly outside; expel: to *eject* an intruder. 3. *Law* To dispossess; evict. [< L < *e-* out + *jacere* to throw] — **e·jec′tion** *n.* — **e·jec′tive** *adj.* — **e·ject′ment** *n.* — **e·jec′tor** *n.*

eke (ēk) *v.t.* **eked**, **ek·ing** 1. To piece out; supplement: usually with *out.* 2. To make a (living) with difficulty: usually with *out.* [Var. of obs. *eche* to increase]

el- Assimilated var. of EN-².

---

e·lab·o·rate (*adj.* i·lab′ər·it; *v.* i·lab′ə·rāt) *adj.* Worked out with great thoroughness or exactness; developed in minute detail: *elaborate* precautions. — *v.* ·rat·ed, ·rat·ing *v.t.* 1. To work out in detail; develop carefully and thoroughly. 2. To produce by labor. — *v.i.* 3. To add details or embellishments: with *on* or *upon*: to *elaborate* on a subject. [< L < *e*- out + *laborare* to work] — **e·lab′o·rate·ly** *adv.* — **e·lab′o·rate·ness** *n.* — **e·lab′o·ra′tion** *n.* — **e·lab′o·ra′tive** *adj.* — **e·lab′o·ra′tor** *n.*

E·lam (ē′ləm) An ancient country of SW Asia between the Persian Gulf and the Caspian Sea. *Gen.* xiv 1. — **E′lam·ite** (-īt) *adj. & n.* — **E′lam·it′ic** (-lə·mit′ik) *adj. & n.*

é·lan (ā·län′) *n.* Enthusiasm; dash; vivacity. [< F]

e·land (ē′land) *n.* A large, oxlike African antelope with twisted horns. [< Du., elk]

e·lapse (i·laps′) *v.i.* **e·lapsed**, **e·laps·ing** To slip by; pass away: said of time. [< L < *e*- out, away + *labi* to glide]

e·las·mo·branch (i·las′mō·brangk, i·laz′-) *n. Zool.* One of a class or subclass of sharks, rays, etc., having cartilaginous skeletons, and lacking air bladders. [< NL < Gk. *elasmos* metal plate + *branchia* gills]

e·las·tic (i·las′tik) *adj.* 1. Spontaneously regaining former size, shape, or bulk after compression, extension, or other distortion. 2. Adjusting readily to fit the circumstances; flexible. 3. Recovering quickly, as from emotional or physical distress; resilient. 4. Marked by a springy motion. — *n.* 1. Fabric made stretchable by interwoven threads of rubber. 2. An article manufactured of this fabric, as a garter. 3. A rubber band. [< NL < Gk. < *elaunein* to drive] — **e·las′ti·cal·ly** *adv.*

e·las·tic·i·ty (i·las′tis′ə·tē, ē′las-) *n. pl.* ·ties The property or quality of being elastic; flexibility; resilience.

e·late (i·lāt′) *v.t.* **e·lat·ed**, **e·lat·ing** To raise the spirits of; stimulate; excite. [< L < *ex*- out + *ferre* to bear]

e·lat·ed (i·lā′tid) *adj.* Filled with joy or triumph, as over good fortune. — **e·lat′ed·ly** *adv.* — **e·lat′ed·ness** *n.*

e·la·tion (i·lā′shən) *n.* Exalted feeling, as from success.

E layer The Heaviside layer.

el·bow (el′bō) *n.* 1. The joint at the bend of the arm between the forearm and the upper arm; esp., the projecting outer side of this joint. 2. The joint corresponding to an elbow in the shoulder or hock of a quadruped. 3. Something having an angle or bend like an elbow. — **at one's elbow** Within easy reach. — **out at the elbows** Shabby; impoverished. — **to rub elbows with** To associate closely with (celebrities, etc.). — **up to the elbows** (in) Deeply immersed (in). — *v.t.* 1. To push or jostle with or as with the elbows. 2. To make (one's way) by such pushing. — *v.i.* 3. To push one's way along. [OE *elnboga*]

el·der[1] (el′dər) *adj.* 1. Of earlier birth; older; senior. 2. Superior or prior in rank, office, etc. 3. Pertaining to a previous time; earlier; former. — *n.* 1. *Often pl.* An older person; also, a forefather or predecessor. 2. An influential senior member of a family, community, etc. 3. *Eccl.* A governing or counseling officer in certain Christian churches. 4. An aged person. [OE *eldra*] — **eld′er·ship** *n.*

el·der[2] (el′dər) *n.* 1. A shrub of the honeysuckle family, with white flowers and purple-black or red berries. 2. Any trees or plants resembling this shrub. [OE *ellæn*]

el·der·ber·ry (el′dər·ber′ē, -bər·ē) *n. pl.* ·ber·ries 1. The berry of the elder, used to make wine. 2. The elder.

eld·er·ly (el′dər·lē) *adj.* Rather advanced in age; approaching old age; quite old. — **Syn.** See OLD.

eld·est (el′dist) *adj.* Alternative superlative of OLD.

e·lect (i·lekt′) *v.t.* 1. To choose (a person or persons) for an office by vote. 2. To pick out; select. 3. *Theol.* To set aside by divine will for salvation: used in the passive voice. — *v.i.* 4. To make a choice. — *adj.* 1. Chosen; selected. 2. Elected to office, but not yet inducted: used in compounds: president-*elect*. — *n.* An elect person or group. [< L < *e*- out + *legere* to choose]

e·lec·tion (i·lek′shən) *n.* 1. The formal choice of a person or persons for any position or dignity, usu. by ballot. 2. A popular vote upon any question officially proposed. 3. In Calvinism, the predestination of individuals to salvation.

e·lec·tion·eer (i·lek′shən·ir′) *v.i.* To work for votes for a particular candidate or political party.

e·lec·tive (i·lek′tiv) *adj.* 1. Of or pertaining to a choice by vote. 2. Obtained or settled by election. 3. Having the power to elect. 4. Subject to choice; optional. — *n. U.S.* An optional subject in a school or college curriculum.

e·lec·tor (i·lek′tər) *n.* 1. One who elects; a person qualified to vote. 2. *U.S.* A member of the electoral college. 3. *Usu. cap.* One of the German princes who formerly elected the Holy Roman emperor. — **e·lec′tor·al** *adj.*

electoral college A body of electors, chosen by the voters in the States and the District of Columbia, which formally elects the president and vice president of the United States.

e·lec·tor·ate (i·lek′tər·it) *n.* 1. The whole body of voters. 2. A district of voters. 3. The rank or territory of an elector.

E·lec·tra (i·lek′trə) In Greek legend, the sister of Orestes.

She persuaded him to kill their mother and their mother's lover to avenge their father's murder. Also *Elektra*.

e·lec·tric (i·lek′trik) *adj.* 1. Relating to, produced by, or operated by electricity. 2. Producing or carrying electricity: an *electric* cable. 3. Thrillingly exciting or magnetic: an *electric* personality. — *n.* A vehicle run by electricity. [< NL < L < Gk. *ēlektron* amber]

e·lec·tri·cal (i·lek′tri·kəl) *adj.* 1. Electric. 2. Concerned with the use of electricity. — **e·lec′tri·cal·ly** *adv.*

electrical transcription *Telecom.* A transcription.

electric eel An eellike, fresh-water fish of tropical America, that is capable of delivering powerful electric shocks.

electric eye A photoelectric cell.

electric field A field of force surrounding a charged object or a moving magnet.

e·lec·tri·cian (i·lek′trish′ən, ē′lek-) *n.* A technician who designs, installs, operates, or repairs electrical apparatus.

e·lec·tric·i·ty (i·lek′tris′ə·tē, ē′lek-) *n.* 1. A fundamental property of matter, associated with atomic particles whose movements develop fields of force and generate kinetic or potential energy. 2. A current or charge of energy so generated. 3. The science that deals with the laws, theory, and application of electric energy. 4. The property of many substances to attract or repel each other when subjected to friction. 5. A state of great tension or excitement.

electric motor A machine for transforming electric energy into mechanical power: distinguished from *generator*.

electric needle A high-frequency, needle-shaped electrode used in surgery for simultaneous cutting and cautery.

electric ray A fish having muscles that store and discharge electricity: also called *crampfish, torpedo*.

e·lec·tri·fy (i·lek′trə·fī) *v.t.* ·fied, ·fy·ing 1. To charge with or subject to electricity. 2. To equip or adapt for operation by electric power, as a railroad, house, etc. 3. To arouse; startle. — **e·lec′tri·fi′a·ble** *adj.* — **e·lec′tri·fi·ca′tion** *n.*

electro- *combining form* 1. Electric; by, with, or of electricity. 2. Electrolytic. Also, before vowels, sometimes **electr-**. [< Gk. *ēlektron* amber]

e·lec·tro·car·di·o·gram (i·lek′trō·kär′dē·ə·gram′) *n. Med.* The record made by an electrocardiograph.

e·lec·tro·car·di·o·graph (i·lek′trō·kär′dē·ə·graf′, ·gräf′) *n. Med.* An instrument for recording the electric current produced by the action of the heart muscle, used in the diagnosis of diseases affecting the heart.

e·lec·tro·chem·is·try (i·lek′trō·kem′is·trē) *n.* The study of electricity as active in effecting chemical change. — **e·lec′tro·chem′i·cal** *adj.* — **e·lec′tro·chem′i·cal·ly** *adv.*

e·lec·tro·cute (i·lek′trə·kyōōt) *v.t.* ·cut·ed, ·cut·ing 1. To execute in the electric chair. 2. To kill by electricity. — **e·lec′tro·cu′tion** *n.*

e·lec·trode (i·lek′trōd) *n. Electr.* 1. Any terminal connecting a conductor, as copper wire, with an electrolyte. 2. Any of the elements in an electron tube, transistor, etc., that emit, collect, or control the movement of electrons.

e·lec·tro·de·pos·it (i·lek′trō·di·poz′it) *v.t.* To precipitate metal from an electrolyte containing it in ionic form. — *n.* That which is precipitated by electrolysis. — **e·lec′tro·dep′o·si′tion** (-dep′ə·zish′ən, -dē′pə-) *n.*

e·lec·tro·dy·nam·ics (i·lek′trō·dī·nam′iks) *n.pl.* (*construed as sing.*) The branch of physics that deals with the forces of electrical attraction and repulsion and with the energy transformations of magnetic fields and electric currents. — **e·lec′tro·dy·nam′ic** or ·i·cal *adj.*

e·lec·tro·en·ceph·a·lo·gram (i·lek′trō·en·sef′ə·lə·gram′) *n. Med.* The record made by an electroencephalograph.

e·lec·tro·en·ceph·a·lo·graph (i·lek′trō·en·sef′ə·lə·graf′, -gräf′) *n. Med.* An instrument for recording the strength and character of electrical impulses in the brain used in the diagnosis of brain disorders. — **e·lec′tro·en·ceph′a·lo·graph′ic** *adj.*

e·lec·tro·lu·mi·nes·cence (i·lek′trō·lōō′mə·nes′əns) *n.* The emission of light from a specially coated surface subjected to the action of an alternating current.

e·lec·trol·y·sis (i·lek′trol′ə·sis) *n.* 1. The application of a direct current to an electrolyte so as to attract its positive ions to the cathode and its negative ions to the anode. 2. The removal of hair by treating the follicle with an electrically charged needle.

e·lec·tro·lyte (i·lek′trə·līt) *n.* 1. *Chem.* A compound that when in solution or a fluid state conducts electricity by the dissociation of its constituents into free ions. 2. A solution that conducts electricity; esp., the solution used in a cell or battery. — **e·lec′tro·lyt′ic** (i·lek′trə·lit′ik) or ·i·cal *adj.* — **e·lec′tro·lyt′i·cal·ly** *adv.*

e·lec·tro·lyze (i·lek′trə·līz) *v.t.* ·lyzed, ·lyz·ing To decompose by electric current. — **e·lec′tro·ly·za′tion** *n.*

e·lec·tro·mag·net (i·lek′trō·mag′nit) *n.* A core of soft iron that temporarily becomes a magnet when an electric current passes through a coil of wire surrounding it.

e·lec·tro·mag·net·ism (i·lek′trō·mag′nə·tiz′əm) *n.* 1. Magnetism developed by electricity. 2. The science that treats of the relations between electricity and magnetism and the resulting phenomena. — **e·lec′tro·mag·net′ic** (-mag-net′ik) *adj.* — **e·lec′tro·mag·net′i·cal·ly** *adv.*

electromagnetic wave *Physics* Any of a class of waves propagated by a system of electric and magnetic fields and including all forms of radiant energy from radio and light waves to gamma and cosmic rays.

e·lec·trom·e·ter (i·lek′trom′ə·tər, ē′lek-) *n.* An instrument for measuring the voltage of an electric current.

e·lec·trom·e·try (i·lek′trom′ə·trē, ē′lek-) *n.* The science of making electrical measurements. — **e·lec·tro·met·ric** (i·lek′trō·met′rik) or **·ri·cal** *adj.*

e·lec·tro·mo·tive (i·lek′trə·mō′tiv) *adj.* Producing, or tending to produce, a flow of electric current.

electromotive force 1. That which tends to produce a flow of electricity from one point to another. **2.** Difference of electrical potential between two points in a circuit, a battery, etc.; voltage. Abbr. *emf., e.m.f., E.M.F.*

e·lec·tron (i·lek′tron) *n.* An atomic particle carrying a unit charge of negative electricity, and having a mass approximately one eighteen-hundredth of that of the proton. [< Gk. *ēlektron* amber]

e·lec·tro·neg·a·tive (i·lek′trō·neg′ə·tiv) *adj.* **1.** Appearing at the positive electrode in electrolysis. **2.** Having the property of becoming negatively electrified by contact or chemical action. **3.** Nonmetallic.

e·lec·tron·ic (i·lek′tron′ik, ē′lek-) *adj.* **1.** Of or pertaining to electrons. **2.** Operating or produced by the movement of free electrons, as in radio and radar. **3.** Pertaining to electronics. — **e·lec·tron′i·cal·ly** *adv.*

e·lec·tron·ics (i·lek′tron′iks, ē′lek-) *n.pl. (construed as sing.)* The study of the properties and behavior of electrons under all conditions, esp. with reference to technical and industrial applications.

electron microscope A powerful microscope that projects a greatly enlarged image of an object held in the path of a sharply focused electron beam.

electron tube A device in which a stream of electrons is conducted through a vacuum or a rarefied gas and usu. controlled by a grid: also called *vacuum tube.*

electron volt The energy acquired by an electron that passes through a potential difference of one volt.

e·lec·tro·pho·re·sis (i·lek′trō·fə·rē′sis) *n. Chem.* The movement of the electrically charged colloidal particles in a fluid, when under the influence of an electric field.

e·lec·troph·o·rus (i·lek′trof′ər·əs, ē′lek-) *n. pl.* **·ri** (-rī) An instrument for generating static electricity by induction. Also **e·lec·tro·phore** (i·lek′trə·fôr, -fōr).

e·lec·tro·plate (i·lek′trə·plāt′) *v.t.* **·plat·ed, ·plat·ing** To coat (an object) with metal by electrodeposition. — *n.* An electroplated article. — **e·lec′tro·plat′er** *n.*

e·lec·tro·pos·i·tive (i·lek′trō·poz′ə·tiv) *adj.* **1.** Appearing at the negative electrode in electrolysis. **2.** Having the property of becoming positively electrified by contact or chemical action. **3.** Basic; not acid.

e·lec·tro·scope (i·lek′trə·skōp) *n.* An instrument for detecting the presence of an electric charge upon a conductor by the attraction or repulsion of pith balls or strips of gold leaf. — **e·lec′tro·scop′ic** (-skop′ik) *adj.*

e·lec·tro·stat·ics (i·lek′trō·stat′iks) *n.pl. (construed as sing.)* A branch of physics that deals primarily with electric charges, fields, induction in conductors, and polarization in dielectrics. — **e·lec′tro·stat′ic** or **·i·cal** *adj.* — **e·lec′tro·stat′i·cal·ly** *adv.*

e·lec·tro·ther·a·peu·tics (i·lek′trō·ther′ə·pyōō′tiks) *n.pl. (construed as sing.)* **1.** The treatment of disease by electricity. **2.** The principles of such treatment. Also **e·lec′tro·ther′a·py.** — **e·lec′tro·ther′a·peu′tic** or **·ti·cal** *adj.*

e·lec·tro·type (i·lek′trə·tīp′) *n.* **1.** A metallic copy, made by electrodeposition, of any surface, esp. of a page of type for printing. **2.** An impression from an electrotype. — *v.t.* **·typed, ·typ·ing** To make an electrotype of. — **e·lec′tro·typ′er, e·lec′tro·typ′ist** *n.* — **e·lec′tro·typ′ic** *adj.* — **e·lec′tro·typ′ing** *n.*

e·lec·trum (i·lek′trəm) *n.* An alloy of native gold and silver. [< L < Gk. *ēlektron* amber]

el·ee·mos·y·nar·y (el′ə·mos′ə·ner′ē, el′ē·ə-) *adj.* **1.** Of or pertaining to charity or alms. **2.** Aided by or dependent upon charity. **3.** Done as a charitable act. [See ALMS.]

el·e·gance (el′ə·gəns) *n.* **1.** The state or quality of being elegant or refined; tasteful opulence. **2.** Something elegant, as a fastidiously chosen word or phrase. Also **el′e·gan·cy.**

el·e·gant (el′ə·gənt) *adj.* **1.** Tastefully ornate in dress, furnishings, etc. **2.** Marked by grace and refinement, as in style, manners, etc. **3.** Marked by ingenuity and simplicity. **4.** *Informal* Excellent; first-rate. [< F < L < *e-* out + *legare* to choose] — **el′e·gant·ly** *adv.*

el·e·gi·ac (el′ə·jī′ək, i·lē′jē·ak) *adj.* **1.** Pertaining to ele-

gies. **2.** Like an elegy; sad; lamenting. — *n. Usu. pl.* Verse composed in elegiac form.

el·e·gize (el′ə·jīz) *v.* **·gized, ·giz·ing** *v.i.* **1.** To write elegiac verse. — *v.t.* **2.** To lament or commemorate in elegy.

el·e·gy (el′ə·jē) *n. pl.* **·gies 1.** In classical prosody, a poem written in elegiac verse. **2.** Any meditative poem of lamentation. **3.** *Music* A work of lamentation or mourning. [< F < L < Gk. *elegos* a song of lament] — **el′e·gist** *n.*

E·lek·tra (i·lek′trə) See ELECTRA.

el·e·ment (el′ə·mənt) *n.* **1.** A relatively simple constituent that is a basic part of a whole; an essential, principle, fact, etc.: the *elements* of poetry. **2.** A group or class of people belonging to a larger group but distinguished from it by belief, behavior, etc.: a rowdy *element* in a crowd; the conservative *element.* **3.** One of four substances (earth, air, fire, water) anciently viewed as composing the physical universe. **4.** The surrounding conditions best suited to some person or thing. **5.** *pl.* Atmospheric powers or forces: the fury of the *elements.* **6.** *Physics & Chem.* One of a limited number of substances, as gold or carbon, each of which is composed entirely of atoms having the same atomic number, and none of which may be decomposed by ordinary chemical means. See table below. **7.** *Mil.* A subdivision of an organization or formation: a command *element.* **8.** *Eccl.* The bread or wine of the Eucharist. [< L *elementum* first principle]

TABLE OF ELEMENTS

NAME	Symbol	Atomic No.	Atomic Wt.
Actinium	Ac	89	227
Aluminum	Al	13	26.9815
Americium	Am	95	243
Antimony (*stibium*)	Sb	51	121.75
Argon	Ar	18	39.948
Arsenic	As	33	74.9216
Astatine	At	85	210
Barium	Ba	56	137.34
Berkelium	Bk	97	249
Beryllium	Be	4	9.0122
Bismuth	Bi	83	208.98
Boron	B	5	10.811
Bromine	Br	35	79.909
Cadmium	Cd	48	112.40
Calcium	Ca	20	40.08
Californium	Cf	98	251
Carbon	C	6	12.01115
Cerium	Ce	58	140.12
Cesium	Cs	55	132.905
Chlorine	Cl	17	35.453
Chromium	Cr	24	51.996
Cobalt	Co	27	58.9332
Columbium	(Cb)		
See NIOBIUM			
Copper (*cuprum*)	Cu	29	63.54
Curium	Cm	96	247
Dysprosium	Dy	66	162.50
Einsteinium	Es	99	254
Erbium	Er	68	167.26
Europium	Eu	63	151.96
Fermium	Fm	100	253
Fluorine	F	9	18.9984
Francium	Fr	87	223
Gadolinium	Gd	64	157.25
Gallium	Ga	31	69.72
Germanium	Ge	32	72.59
Glucinum			
See BERYLLIUM			
Gold (*aurum*)	Au	79	196.967
Hafnium	Hf	72	178.44
Helium	He	2	4.0026
Holmium	Ho	67	164.93
Hydrogen	H	1	1.00797
Indium	In	49	114.82
Iodine	I	53	126.9044
Iridium	Ir	77	192.2
Iron (*ferrum*)	Fe	26	55.847
Krypton	Kr	36	83.80
Lanthanum	La	57	138.91
Lawrencium	Lw	103	257?
Lead (*plumbum*)	Pb	82	207.19
Lithium	Li	3	6.939
Lutetium	Lu	71	174.97
Magnesium	Mg	12	24.312
Manganese	Mn	25	54.938
Mendelevium	Md	101	256
Mercury (*hydrargyrum*)	Hg	80	200.59
Molybdenum	Mo	42	95.94
Neodymium	Nd	60	144.24
Neon	Ne	10	20.183
Neoytterbium			
See YTTERBIUM			
Neptunium	Np	93	237
Nickel	Ni	28	58.71
Niobium	Nb	41	92.906

(continued)

NAME	Symbol	Atomic No.	Atomic Wt.
Niton	See RADON		
Nitrogen	N	7	14.0067
Nobelium	No	102	253
Osmium	Os	76	190.2
Oxygen	O	8	15.9994
Palladium	Pd	46	106.4
Phosphorus	P	15	30.9738
Platinum	Pt	78	195.09
Plutonium	Pu	94	242
Polonium	Po	84	210
Potassium (kalium)	K	19	39.102
Praseodymium	Pr	59	140.90
Promethium	Pm	61	147
Proctactinium	Pa	91	231
Radium	Ra	88	226.05
Radon	Rn	86	222
Rhenium	Re	75	186.20
Rhodium	Rh	45	102.905
Rubidium	Rb	37	85.47
Ruthenium	Ru	44	101.07
Samarium	Sm	62	150.35
Scandium	Sc	21	44.956
Selenium	Se	34	78.96
Silicon	Si	14	28.086
Silver (argentum)	Ag	47	107.87
Sodium (natrium)	Na	11	22.9898
Strontium	Sr	38	87.62
Sulfur	S	16	32.064
Tantalum	Ta	73	180.948
Technetium	Tc	43	99
Tellurium	Te	52	127.60
Terbium	Tb	65	158.924
Thallium	Tl	81	204.37
Thorium	Th	90	232.038
Thulium	Tm	69	168.934
Tin (stannum)	Sn	50	118.69
Titanium	Ti	22	47.90
Tungsten	W	74	183.85
Uranium	U	92	238.03
Vanadium	V	23	50.942
Wolfram	See TUNGSTEN		
Xenon	Xe	54	131.30
Ytterbium	Yb	70	173.04
Yttrium	Y	39	88.90
Zinc	Zn	30	65.37
Zirconium	Zr	40	91.22

el·e·men·tal (el′ə-men′təl) *adj.* **1.** Of or relating to an element or elements. **2.** Fundamental and relatively simple; basic. **3.** Relating to first principles; rudimentary. **4.** Of or suggestive of the powerful forces at work in nature or in man. **5.** Chemically uncombined. — **el′e·men′tal·ly** *adv.*

el·e·men·ta·ry (el′ə-men′tər-ē, -men′trē) *adj.* **1.** Elemental. **2.** Fundamental; basic. **3.** Simple and rudimentary. — **el′e·men·ta′ri·ly** *adv.* — **el′e·men·ta·ri·ness** *n.*

elementary school A school giving a course of education of from six to eight years, pupils usu. entering at about six years of age: also called *grade school, grammar school.*

el·e·phant (el′ə-fənt) *n.* A massively built, almost hairless mammal of Asia and Africa, having a flexible trunk, and the upper incisors developed as tusks, which are the chief source of ivory. The **Asian elephant** has relatively small ears, and the **African elephant** has large, flapping ears. [< OF < L < Gk. *elephas, -antos* ivory]

el·e·phan·ti·a·sis (el′ə-fən-tī′ə-sis) *n. Pathol.* A disease caused by a parasitic worm, characterized by a hardening of the skin, and an enormous enlargement of the part affected. [< L < Gk. < *elephas* elephant]

el·e·phan·tine (el′ə-fən′tin, -tēn, -tīn) *adj.* **1.** Of or pertaining to an elephant. **2.** Enormous; unwieldy; ponderous.

El·eu·sin·i·an (el′yōō-sin′ē-ən) **mysteries** The secret religious rites originated in ancient Greece at Eleusis.

el·e·vate (el′ə-vāt) *v.t.* ·**vat·ed**, ·**vat·ing 1.** To lift up; raise. **2.** To raise in rank, status, etc. **3.** To raise the spirits of; cheer; elate. **4.** To raise the pitch or loudness of (the voice). **5.** To raise the moral character or intellectual level of. [< L < *e-* out + *levare* to lighten, raise]

el·e·vat·ed (el′ə-vā′tid) *adj.* **1.** Raised up; high. **2.** Lofty in character; sublime. **3.** In high spirits; elated. — *n. U.S. Informal* An overhead railroad.

el·e·va·tion (el′ə-vā′shən) *n.* **1.** The act of elevating, or the state of being elevated. **2.** An elevated place. **3.** Height above sea level. **4.** Loftiness of thought, feeling, station, etc. **5.** In dancing, the ability to leap. **6.** *Often cap. Eccl.* The raising of the eucharistic elements for adoration during the Mass. **7.** *Astron.* The angular distance of a celestial body above the horizon. **8.** In drafting, a side, front, or rear view of a machine or other structure.

el·e·va·tor (el′ə-vā′tər) *n.* **1.** One who or that which elevates. **2.** A mechanism for hoisting grain. **3.** *U.S.* A granary. **4.** *U.S.* A movable platform or car that carries passengers or freight up and down.

e·lev·en (i-lev′ən) *n.* **1.** The sum of ten and one: a cardinal number. **2.** Any symbol of this number, as 11, xi, XI. **3.** Anything consisting of or representing eleven units. — *adj.* Being one more than ten. [OE *endleofan* one left over (after ten)] — **e·lev′enth** *adj. & n.*

elf (elf) *n. pl.* **elves** (elvz) **1.** In folklore, a dwarfish sprite with magical powers, usu. intent upon playful mischief. **2.** Any mischievous creature. **3.** A tiny person. [OE *ælf*] — **elf′ish** *adj.* — **elf′ish·ly** *adv.* — **elf′ish·ness** *n.*

elf·in (el′fin) *adj.* Elfish. — *n.* An elf.

elf·lock (elf′lok′) *n.* A lock of hair tangled as if by elves.

e·lic·it (i-lis′it) *v.t.* **1.** To draw out or forth; evoke: to *elicit* a reply. **2.** To bring to light: to *elicit* the truth. [< L < *e-* out + *lacere* to entice] — **e·lic′i·ta′tion** *n.* — **e·lic′i·tor** *n.*

e·lide (i-līd′) *v.t.* **e·lid·ed, e·lid·ing 1.** To omit (a vowel or syllable) in pronunciation. **2.** To suppress; omit; ignore. [< L < *e-* out + *laedere* to strike] — **e·lid′i·ble** *adj.*

el·i·gi·bil·i·ty (el′ə-jə-bil′ə-tē) *n. pl.* ·**ties 1.** The quality of being eligible; suitableness. **2.** *pl.* Qualities that make a person or thing eligible.

el·i·gi·ble (el′ə-jə-bəl) *adj.* **1.** Capable of and qualified for an office, position, function, etc. **2.** Fit for or worthy of choice or adoption. **3.** Agreeable to have; suitable. — *n.* An eligible person. [See ELECT.] — **el′i·gi·bly** *adv.*

E·li·jah (i-lī′jə) Ninth-century B.C. Hebrew prophet: also **E·li·as** (i-lī′əs). [< Hebrew, Jehovah is my God]

e·lim·i·nate (i-lim′ə-nāt) *v.t.* ·**nat·ed, ·nat·ing 1.** To get rid of. **2.** To ignore. **3.** To remove (a contestant, team, etc.) from further competition by defeating. **4.** *Physiol.* To void; excrete. **5.** *Math.* To remove (a quantity) from a system of algebraic equations. [< L < *e-* out + *limen* threshold] — **e·lim′i·na′tion** *n.* — **e·lim′i·na′tor** *n.* — **e·lim′i·na′tive, e·lim′i·na·to·ry** (-nə-tôr′ē, -tō′rē) *adj.*

E·li·sha (i-lī′shə) Ninth-century B.C. Hebrew prophet, successor of Elijah. [< Hebrew, God is Salvation]

e·li·sion (i-lizh′ən) *n.* Omission of a vowel or syllable, as in "th′ imperial towers." [See ELIDE.]

e·lite (ā-lēt′) *n.* **1.** The choicest part, as of a social group. **2.** A size of typewriter type, equivalent to 10-point, with 12 characters to the inch. *Also U.S.* **e·lite′.** [See ELECT.]

e·lix·ir (i-lik′sər) *n.* **1.** A sweetened alcoholic medicinal preparation. **2.** In ancient philosophy, a substance sought by alchemists for changing base metals into gold, or for prolonging life: also **elixir vi·tae** (vī′tē). **3.** The essential principle of anything. **4.** A cure-all. [< Med.L < Arabic *al-iksīr* < Gk. *zērion* medicated powder]

E·liz·a·be·than (i-liz′ə-bē′thən, -beth′ən) *adj.* Of or pertaining to Elizabeth I of England, or to her era. — *n.* An Englishman living during the reign of Elizabeth I.

Elizabethan sonnet A Shakespearean sonnet.

elk (elk) *n. pl.* **elks** or **elk 1.** A large deer of northern Europe and Asia. **2.** The wapiti. **3.** A pliant, tanned leather of calfskin, horsehide, etc. [ME < OE *elh*]

ell[1] (el) *n.* A measure of length now rarely used: in England, 45 inches or 1.114 meters. [OE *eln* an arm's length]

ell[2] (el) *n.* Anything shaped like the letter L.

el·lipse (i-lips′) *n. Geom.* A plane curve such that the sum of the distances from any point of the curve to two fixed points, called *foci*, is a constant; a conic section. [< L *ellipsis.* See ELLIPSIS.]

el·lip·sis (i-lip′sis) *n. pl.* ·**ses** (-sēz) **1.** *Gram.* The omission of a word or words necessary for the complete grammatical construction of a sentence, but not required for the understanding of it. **2.** Marks (... or ***) indicating omission. [< L < Gk. < *en-* in + *leipsis* a leaving < *leipein* to leave]

ELLIPSE
AA′ Major axis. BB′ Minor axis. F, F′ Foci. P, P′ Points on curve.
(FP + F′P = FP′ + F′P′)

el·lip·tic (i-lip′tik) *adj.* **1.** Of, pertaining to, or shaped like an ellipse. **2.** *Gram.* Characterized by ellipsis; shortened. *Also* **el·lip′ti·cal.** — **el·lip′ti·cal·ly** *adv.*

elm (elm) *n.* **1.** A shade tree of America, Europe, and Asia, having a broad, spreading, or overarching top. **2.** The wood of this tree. [OE] — **elm′y** *adj.*

el·o·cu·tion (el′ə-kyōō′shən) *n.* **1.** The art of public speaking, including vocal delivery and gesture. **2.** Manner of speaking. [< L < *e-* out + *loqui* to speak] — **el′o·cu′tion·ar′y** *adj.* — **el′o·cu′tion·ist** *n.*

E·lo·him (e·lō′him′, e·lō′him) God: Hebrew name used in the Old Testament. [< Hebrew ′*Elōhīm*, pl. of ′*Elōah* God]

e·lon·gate (i·lông′gāt, i·long′-) *v.t. & v.i.* ·**gat·ed, ·gat·ing** To increase in length; stretch. — *adj.* Drawn out; lengthened. [< LL < L < *e-* out + *longe* far off] — **e′lon·ga′tion** *n.*

e·lope (i·lōp′) *v.i.* **e·loped, e·lop·ing 1.** To run away with a lover, usu. to get married. **2.** To abscond. [< AF *aloper.*] — **e·lope′ment** *n.* — **e·lop′er** *n.*

el·o·quence (el′ə-kwəns) *n.* **1.** Fluent, polished, and effective use of language, esp. in public speaking. **2.** The quality of being moving, forceful, or persuasive.

el·o·quent (el'ə·kwənt) *adj.* **1.** Possessed of or manifesting eloquence. **2.** Visibly expressive of emotion: *eloquent* tears. [< L < e- out + *loqui* to speak] — **el'o·quent·ly** *adv.*

else (els) *adv.* **1.** In a different place, time, or way; instead: Where *else*? How *else*? **2.** If the case or facts were different; otherwise: Hurry, or *else* you will be caught. — *adj.* Additional; different: somebody *else*. [OE *elles.* Akin to L *alius*.]

else·where (els'hwâr') *adv.* In or to another place or places; somewhere or anywhere else.

e·lu·ci·date (i·lōō'sə·dāt) *v.* **·dat·ed, ·dat·ing** *v.t.* **1.** To make clear; explain. — *v.i.* **2.** To clarify something. [< LL < L e- out + *lucidus* clear] — **e·lu'ci·da'tion** *n.* — **e·lu'ci·da'tive** *adj.* — **e·lu'ci·da'tor** *n.*

e·lude (i·lōōd') *v.t.* **e·lud·ed, e·lud·ing** **1.** To avoid or escape from by dexterity or artifice; evade. **2.** To escape the notice or understanding of: The meaning *eludes* me. [< L < e- out + *ludere* to play]

E·lul (e·lōōl', el'ōōl) *n.* The twelfth month of the Hebrew year. See (Hebrew) CALENDAR.

e·lu·sive (i·lōō'siv) *adj.* Tending to slip away; hard to grasp or perceive: an *elusive* fragrance. Also **e·lu'so·ry** (-sər·ē). — **e·lu'sive·ly** *adv.* — **e·lu'sive·ness** *n.*

elves (elvz) Plural of ELF.

elv·ish (el'vish) *adj.* Elfish. — **elv'ish·ly** *adv.*

E·ly·si·um (i·lizh'ē·əm, i·liz'-) **1.** In Greek mythology, the land of the blessed dead. Also **Elysian Fields. 2.** A place or condition of supreme delight; paradise. [< L < Gk. *Elysion (pedion)* the Elysian (field)] — **E·ly·sian** (i·lizh'ən, -ē·ən) *adj.*

em (em) *n. Printing* The square of the body size of a type; esp., a pica em, about ⅙ of an inch, used as a standard unit of measurement: originally, the size of the letter M.

em-¹ Var. of EN-¹.

em-² Var. of EN-².

'em (em, m) *pron. Informal* Them.

e·ma·ci·ate (i·mā'shē·āt) *v.t.* **·at·ed, ·at·ing** To make abnormally lean; cause to lose flesh. [< L *macies* leanness] — **e·ma'ci·at'ed** *adj.* — **e·ma'ci·a'tion** *n.*

em·a·nate (em'ə·nāt) *v.i.* **·nat·ed, ·nat·ing** To flow forth from a source; issue. [< L < e- out + *manare* to flow]

em·a·na·tion (em'ə·nā'shən) *n.* **1.** The act of emanating. **2.** Something that emanates; efflux; effluence. **3.** *Physics* A gaseous product of disintegration in certain radioactive substances, as radon and thoron. — **em'a·na'tive** *adj.*

e·man·ci·pate (i·man'sə·pāt) *v.t.* **·pat·ed, ·pat·ing** **1.** To release from bondage, oppression, or authority; set free. **2.** *Law* To free (a child) from paternal control. [< L < e- out + *manus* hand + *capere* to take] — **e·man'ci·pa'tive** *adj.* — **e·man'ci·pa'tion** *n.* — **e·man'ci·pa'tor** *n.*

Emancipation Proclamation A proclamation issued by President Abraham Lincoln on January 1, 1863, declaring free all Negro slaves in all States.

e·mas·cu·late (*v.* i·mas'kyə·lāt; *adj.* i·mas'kyə·lit) *v.t.* **·lat·ed, ·lat·ing 1.** To deprive of procreative power; castrate; geld. **2.** To deprive of strength and·vigor; weaken. — *adj.* Emasculated; effeminate; weakened. [< L *emasculare* < e- away + *masculus* male] — **e·mas'cu·la'tion** *n.* — **e·mas'cu·la'tor** *n.* — **e·mas·cu·la·to·ry** (i·mas'kyə·lə·tôr'ē, -tō'rē), **e·mas'cu·la·tive** *adj.*

em·balm (im·bäm') *v.t.* **1.** To preserve (a dead body) from decay by treatment with chemicals, etc. **2.** To preserve or keep in memory. [< F *embaumer*] — **em·balm'er** *n.*

em·bank·ment (im·bangk'mənt) *n.* A mound or bank raised to hold back water, support a roadway, etc.

em·bar·go (im·bär'gō) *n. pl.* **·goes 1.** An order by a government restraining merchant vessels from leaving or entering its ports. **2.** Authoritative stoppage of foreign commerce or of any special trade. **3.** A restraint or prohibition. — *v.t.* **·goes, ·go·ing** To lay an embargo upon. [< Sp. < *embargar,* ult. < LL *barra* bar]

em·bark (im·bärk') *v.t.* **1.** To put or take aboard a vessel. **2.** To invest (money) or involve (a person) in a venture. — *v.i.* **3.** To go aboard a vessel for a voyage. **4.** To engage in a venture. [< F < LL < *in-* in + *barca* boat] — **em·bar·ka·tion, em·bar·ca·tion** (em'bär·kā'shən) *n.* — **em·bark'ment** *n.*

em·bar·rass (im·bar'əs) *v.t.* **1.** To make self-conscious and uncomfortable; abash; disconcert. **2.** To involve in financial difficulties. **3.** To hamper; impede. **4.** To render difficult; complicate. [< F < em- in + *barre* < OF] — **em·bar'rass·ing** *adj.* — **em·bar'rass·ing·ly** *adv.* — **em·bar'rass·ment** *n.*

em·bas·sy (em'bə·sē) *n. pl.* **·sies 1.** An ambassador together with his staff. **2.** The mission, function, or position of an ambassador. **3.** The official residence or headquarters of an ambassador. [< OF < Med.L < L *ambactus* servant]

em·bat·tle (em·bat'l) *v.t.* **·tled, ·tling** To form in line of battle; prepare or equip for battle. [< OF < em¹- in + *bataille* < L *battuere* to beat]

em·bed (im·bed') *v.t.* **bed·ded, ·bed·ding 1.** To set firmly in surrounding matter. **2.** To place in or as in a bed. — **em·bed'ment** *n.*

em·bel·lish (im·bel'ish) *v.t.* **1.** To beautify by adding ornamental features; decorate. **2.** To heighten the interest of (a narrative) by adding fictitious details. [< OF < em- in + *bel* beautiful] — **em·bel'lish·er** *n.* — **em·bel'lish·ment** *n.*

em·ber (em'bər) *n.* **1.** A live coal or unextinguished brand. **2.** *pl.* A dying fire. [OE *æmerge*]

em·bez·zle (im·bez'əl) *v.t.* **·zled, ·zling** To appropriate fraudulently to one's own use, as money or securities entrusted to one's care. [< AF < em- in + *besiler* to destroy] — **em·bez'zle·ment** *n.* — **em·bez'zler** *n.*

em·bit·ter (im·bit'ər) *v.t.* To make bitter, unhappy, or resentful. — **em·bit'ter·ment** *n.*

em·bla·zon (im·blā'zən) *v.t.* **1.** To adorn magnificently, esp. with heraldic devices. **2.** To extol; celebrate. — **em·bla'zon·er** *n.* — **em·bla'zon·ment** *n.* — **em·bla'zon·ry** *n.*

em·blem (em'bləm) *n.* **1.** An object or pictorial device that serves to represent something more or less abstract; symbol. **2.** A distinctive badge or figured object. [< L < Gk. < em- in + *ballein* to throw]

em·blem·at·ic (em'blə·mat'ik) *adj.* Of, pertaining to, or serving as an emblem; symbolic. Also **em'blem·at'i·cal.** — **em'blem·at'i·cal·ly** *adv.*

em·bod·i·ment (im·bod'i·mənt) *n.* **1.** The act of embodying, or the state of being embodied. **2.** That which embodies, or in which something is embodied.

em·bod·y (im·bod'ē) *v.t.* **·bod·ied, ·bod·y·ing 1.** To invest with or as with a body; put into visible or concrete form: to *embody* ideals in action. **2.** To collect into, or make part of, an organized whole; incorporate.

em·bold·en (im·bōl'dən) *v.t.* To give courage to.

em·bo·lism (em'bə·liz'əm) *n. Pathol.* The stopping up of a vein or artery by an embolus.

em·bo·lus (em'bə·ləs) *n. pl.* **·li** (-lī) *Pathol.* A foreign body that forms an obstruction in a blood vessel, as a piece of fibrin, a blood clot, or an air bubble. [< L < Gk. < en- in + *ballein* to throw] — **em·bol·ic** (em·bol'ik) *adj.*

em·bos·om (em·bŏŏz'əm, -bōō'zəm) *v.t.* **1.** To embrace. **2.** To cherish. **3.** To enclose protectively; shelter.

em·boss (im·bôs', -bos') *v.t.* **1.** To cover or adorn (a surface) with raised figures, designs, etc. **2.** To raise or represent (designs, figures, etc.) from or upon a surface. **3.** To decorate sumptuously. [Origin unknown] — **em·boss'er** *n.* — **em·boss'ment** *n.*

em·bou·chure (äm·bŏŏ·shŏŏr', Fr. än·bōō·shür') *n.* **1.** The mouth of a river. **2.** The opening out of a river valley into flat land. **3.** *Music* **a** The mouthpiece of a wind instrument. **b** The position or application of the lips and tongue in playing a wind instrument. [< F < em- in + *bouche* mouth]

em·bow·er (em·bou'ər) *v.t. & v.i.* To cover or shelter in or as in a bower.

em·brace (im·brās') *v.* **braced, brac·ing** *v.t.* **1.** To clasp or infold in the arms; hug. **2.** To accept willingly; adopt, as a religion or doctrine. **3.** To avail oneself of: to *embrace* an offer. **4.** To surround; encircle. **5.** To include; contain. **6.** To take in visually or mentally. **7.** To have sexual intercourse with. — *v.i.* **8.** To hug each other. — *n.* The act of embracing. [< OF *embracer,* ult. < L in- in + *bracchium* arm] — **em·brace'ment** *n.* — **em·brac'er** *n.*

em·bra·sure (em·brā'zhər) *n.* **1.** *Archit.* An opening in a wall, as for a window or door, sloped or beveled so as to enlarge its interior outline. **2.** An opening that enlarges inwardly or outwardly in a parapet, battlement, or wall. [< F < *embraser (ébraser)* to widen (an opening)]

em·broi·der (im·broi'dər) *v.t.* **1.** To ornament (cloth) with designs in needlework. **2.** To execute (a design) in needlework. **3.** To exaggerate. — *v.i.* **4.** To make embroidery. [< MF *broder* to stitch] — **em·broi'der·er** *n.*

em·broi·der·y (im·broi'dər·ē) *n. pl.* **·der·ies 1.** Ornamental needlework. **2.** Any elaborate ornamentation.

em·broil (em·broil') *v.t.* **1.** To involve in dissension or strife. **2.** To complicate or confuse. [< F < em- + *brouiller* to confuse] — **em·broil'ment** *n.*

em·bry·o (em'brē·ō) *n. pl.* **·os 1.** *Biol.* The earliest stages in the development of an organism, before it has assumed its distinctive form, in the human species, the first eight weeks. **2.** *Bot.* The rudimentary plant within the seed. **3.** The rudimentary stage of anything. Also **em'bry·on.** — *adj.* Rudimentary. [< Gk. < en- in + *bryein* to swell]

embryo- *combining form* Embryo; embryonic. Also, before vowels, **embry-.** [< Gk. *embryon* embryo]

em·bry·ol·o·gy (em'brē·ol'ə·jē) *n.* The science that deals with the origin, structure, and development of the embryo.

—**em·bry·o·log·i·cal** (em'brē·ə·loj'i·kəl) or **em'bry·o·log'ic** *adj.* —**em'bry·o·log'i·cal·ly** *adv.* —**em'bry·ol'o·gist** *n.*

em·bry·on·ic (em'brē·on'ik) *adj.* Of, pertaining to, or in the state of an embryo; rudimentary; immature; undeveloped.

em·cee (em'sē') *Informal n.* Master of ceremonies. —*v.t. & v.i.* **·ceed, ·cee·ing** To act as master of ceremonies.

e·meer (ə·mir') See EMIR.

e·mend (i·mend') *v.t.* **1.** To make corrections or changes in (a literary work, etc.), esp. after scholarly study. **2.** To free from faults. [< L < e- out + *menda* fault] —**e·mend'a·ble** *adj.* —**e·mend'er** *n.*

e·men·date (ē'men·dāt) *v.t.* **·dat·ed, ·dat·ing** To emend (a text). —**e·men·da·tion** (ē'men·dā'shən, em'en-) *n.* —**e'men·da'tor** *n.* —**e·mend·a·to·ry** (i·men'də·tôr'ē) *adj.*

em·er·ald (em'ər·əld, em'rəld) *n.* **1.** A bright green variety of beryl, valued as a jewel. **2.** A rich green. —*adj.* **1.** Of, pertaining to, or like the emerald. **2.** Of a rich green color. [< OF *emeraude, esmeralde* < L < Gk. *smaragdos*]

Emerald Isle Ireland: so called from its green landscape.

e·merge (i·mûrj') *v.i.* **·merged, ·merg·ing 1.** To come forth as from water, a hiding place, etc. **2.** To come to light; become apparent. [< L < e- out + *mergere* to dip] —**e·mer'gence** *n.* —**e·mer'gent** *adj.*

e·mer·gen·cy (i·mûr'jən·sē) *n.* *pl.* **·cies** A sudden and unexpected turn of events calling for immediate action.

e·mer·i·tus (i·mer'ə·təs) *adj.* Retired from active service, usu. because of age, but retained in an honorary position: professor emeritus. —*n.* *pl.* **·ti** (-tī) One who is emeritus. [< L, pp. of *emerere* < e- out + *merere* to earn]

e·mer·sion (ē·mûr'shən, -zhən) *n.* An emerging.

em·er·y (em'ər·ē, em'rē) *n.* A very hard, black or grayish black variety of corundum mixed with magnesite and other minerals, used as an abrasive. [F < OF < LL < Gk. *smēris* emery powder]

e·met·ic (i·met'ik) *adj.* Tending to produce vomiting. —*n.* An emetic agent. [< Gk. < *emeein* to vomit]

-emia *combining form Med.* Blood; condition of the blood: used in names of diseases: *leukemia.* Also spelled *-aemia, -haemia, -hemia.* [< Gk. *haima* blood]

em·i·grant (em'ə·grənt) *adj.* Moving from one place or country to settle in another. —*n.* A person who emigrates.

em·i·grate (em'ə·grāt) *v.i.* **·grat·ed, ·grat·ing** To move away from one country, or section of a country, to settle in another. —Syn. See MIGRATE. [< L < e- out + *migrare* to move] —**em'i·gra'tion** *n.*

é·mi·gré (em'ə·grā, *Fr.* ā·mē·grā') An emigrant; esp. one who fled to escape the French or Russian revolution.

em·i·nence (em'ə·nəns) *n.* **1.** Superiority in rank, power, achievement, etc. **2.** A high place or elevation, as a hill. Also **em'i·nen·cy.** [< L < e- out + *minere* to jut out]

Em·i·nence (em'ə·nəns) *n.* A title for cardinals.

em·i·nent (em'ə·nənt) *adj.* **1.** High in station, merit, or esteem; distinguished: an *eminent* scholar. **2.** Noteworthy; conspicuous: *eminent* valor. **3.** High; lofty: an *eminent* tower. [< L *eminere* to stand out] —**em'i·nent·ly** *adv.*

eminent domain *Law* The right or power of the state to take or control private property for public use.

e·mir (ə·mir') *n.* **1.** A Moslem prince or commander. **2.** A descendant of Mohammed. **3.** A high Turkish official. Also spelled *emeer.* [< Arabic *amīr* ruler] —**e·mir'ate** *n.*

em·is·sar·y (em'ə·ser'ē) *n.* *pl.* **·sar·ies 1.** A person sent on a mission as an agent or representative of a government. **2.** A secret agent; spy. —*adj.* Of, pertaining to, or serving as an emissary. [< L *emissarius* < *emittere* to send out]

e·mis·sion (i·mish'ən) *n.* **1.** The act of emitting. **2.** That which is emitted. **3.** The issuance of currency, notes, shares, etc. [< L *emissio, -onis* < -e out + *mittere* to send]

e·mis·sive (i·mis'iv) *adj.* Sending or sent forth; emitting.

e·mit (i·mit') *v.t.* **e·mit·ted, e·mit·ting 1.** To send forth or give off (light, heat, sound, etc.); discharge. **2.** To give expression to; utter, as an opinion. **3.** To issue authoritatively, as an edict. **4.** To put into circulation, as money. [< L < e- out + *mittere* to send] —**e·mit'ter** *n.*

Em·man·u·el (i·man'yoo·əl) See IMMANUEL.

e·mol·li·ent (i·mol'yənt, -ē·ənt) *adj.* Softening or relaxing; soothing, esp. to the skin. —*n. Med.* A softening or soothing medicament. [< L < e- thoroughly + *mollire* to soften]

e·mol·u·ment (i·mol'yə·mənt) *n.* A salary or fee as for a service. [< L < e- out + *molere* to grind]

e·mote (i·mōt') *v.i.* **e·mot·ed, e·mot·ing** *Informal* To exhibit an exaggerated emotion, as in acting. [< EMOTION]

e·mo·tion (i·mō'shən) *n.* **1.** A strong surge of feeling marked by an impulse to outward expression and often accompanied by complex bodily reactions; any strong feeling, as love, hate, or joy. **2.** The power of feeling; sensibility. [< L *emotio, -onis* < e- out + *movere* to move]

e·mo·tion·al (i·mō'shən·əl) *adj.* **1.** Of, pertaining to, or expressive of emotion. **2.** Easily or excessively affected by emotion. **3.** Arousing the emotions. —**e·mo'tion·al·ist** *n.* —**e·mo'tion·al'i·ty** *n.* —**e·mo'tion·al·ly** *adv.*

e·mo·tion·al·ism (i·mō'shən·əl·iz'əm) *n.* **1.** The tendency

to overindulge the emotions or to be too much affected by them. **2.** A display of emotion. **3.** Appeal to the emotions.

e·mo·tion·al·ize (i·mō'shən·əl·īz') *v.t.* **·ized, ·iz·ing** To treat in an emotional manner. —**e·mo'tion·al·i·za'tion** *n.*

e·mo·tive (i·mō'tiv) *adj.* Characterized by, expressing, or tending to excite emotion: *emotive* eloquence. —**e·mo'tive·ly** *adv.* —**e·mo'tive·ness, e·mo·tiv'i·ty** (ē'mō·tiv'ə·tē) *n.*

em·pan·el (im·pan'əl) See IMPANEL.

em·pa·thize (em'pə·thīz) *v.t. & v.i.* **·thized, ·thiz·ing** To regard with or feel empathy.

em·pa·thy (em'pə·thē) *n. Psychol.* Intellectual or imaginative apprehension of another's condition or state of mind. —**em·path·ic** (em·path'ik) *adj.* —**em·path'i·cal·ly** *adv.*

em·per·or (em'pər·ər) *n.* The sovereign of an empire. [< OF < L *imperator* commander] —**em'per·or·ship'** *n.*

em·pha·sis (em'fə·sis) *n.* *pl.* **·ses** (-sēz) **1.** Special significance or importance assigned to something. **2.** Stress given by voice or rhetorical contrivance to a particular syllable, word, or phrase. **3.** Force or intensity of meaning, action, etc. [< L < Gk. < en- in + *phainein* to show]

em·pha·size (em'fə·sīz) *v.t.* **·sized, ·siz·ing** To give emphasis to; make specially prominent or important; stress.

em·phat·ic (em·fat'ik) *adj.* **1.** Spoken or done with emphasis; forcibly expressive. **2.** Characterized by forcefulness or intensity. **3.** Striking; decisive. —**em·phat'i·cal·ly** *adv.*

em·phy·se·ma (em'fə·sē'mə) *n. Pathol.* A lung condition marked by loss of elasticity of the air sacs, causing difficulty in breathing. [< NL < Gk. *emphysēma* inflation]

em·pire (em'pīr) *n.* **1.** A state, or union of states, governed by an emperor; also, the historical period of such government. **2.** A union of dispersed states and unrelated peoples under one rule. **3.** Wide and supreme dominion. [< F < L *imperium* rule, authority]

Empire State Nickname of New York.

em·pir·i·cal (em·pir'i·kəl) *adj.* **1.** Relating to or based upon direct experience or observation alone: *empirical* knowledge. **2.** Relying on practical experience without benefit of scientific knowledge or theory. Also **em·pir'ic.** [< L < Gk. < en- in + *peira* trial] —**em·pir'i·cal·ly** *adv.*

em·pir·i·cism (em·pir'ə·siz'əm) *n.* **1.** Empirical method or practice. **2.** *Philos.* The doctrine that all knowledge is derived from sensory experience. **3.** Reliance on sensory observation and experiment as the bases of knowledge. **4.** Quackery. —**em·pir'i·cist** *n.*

em·place·ment (im·plās'mənt) *n.* **1.** The position assigned to guns or to a battery within a fortification; also, a gun platform, the parapet, or the like. **2.** A setting in place; location. [< F < *emplacer* to put into position]

em·ploy (im·ploi') *v.t.* **1.** To engage the services of; hire. **2.** To provide work and livelihood for. **3.** To make use of as a means or instrument: to *employ* cunning. **4.** To devote or apply: to *employ* one's energies in research. —*n.* The state of being employed; service. [< F *employer* < L *in-* in + *plicare* to fold] —**em·ploy'a·ble** *adj.* —**em·ploy'ment** *n.*

em·ploy·ee (im·ploi'ē, em'ploi·ē') *n.* One who works for another in return for salary. Also **em·ploy'e, em·ploy'é.**

em·ploy·er (im·ploi'ər) *n.* **1.** One who employs. **2.** A person or business firm that employs persons for wages or salary.

em·po·ri·um (em·pôr'ē·əm, -pō'rē-) *n.* *pl.* **·po·ri·ums** or **·po·ri·a** (-pôr'ē·ə, -pō'rē·ə) **1.** A store carrying general merchandise. **2.** A trading or market center. [< L < Gk. *emporion* market < en- in + *poros* way]

em·pow·er (im·pou'ər) *v.t.* **1.** To authorize; delegate authority to. **2.** To enable; permit.

em·press (em'pris) *n.* **1.** A woman who rules an empire. **2.** The wife or widow of an emperor.

emp·ty (emp'tē) *adj.* **·ti·er, ·ti·est 1.** Containing nothing; void; vacant: an *empty* pitcher; an *empty* room. **2.** Without significance; unsubstantial; hollow: *empty* promises. **3.** Carrying nothing: *empty* hands. **4.** Destitute or devoid: with of: *empty* of compassion. **5.** *Informal* Hungry. —*v.* **·tied, ·ty·ing** *v.t.* **1.** To remove the contents of. **2.** To transfer the contents of (a container): to *empty* a bucket onto a fire. **3.** To pour out or draw off (the contents of something). **4.** To unburden; clear: with of. —*v.i.* **5.** To become empty. **6.** To discharge itself or its contents. —*n.* *pl.* **·ties** An empty container, vehicle, etc. [OE *æmetig* < *æmetta* leisure] —**emp'ti·ly** *adv.* —**emp'ti·ness** *n.*

emp·ty-hand·ed (emp'tē·han'did) *adj.* Carrying nothing.

em·pyr·e·al (em·pir'ē·əl, em'pə·rē'əl, -pī-) *adj.* **1.** Of or pertaining to the highest region of heaven. **2.** Of pure fire; fiery. [< Med.L < Gk. < en- in + *pyr* fire]

em·py·re·an (em'pə·rē'ən, -pī-) *n.* **1.** The highest heaven; the abode of God and the angels, anciently conceived as a region of pure fire. **2.** The firmament. —*adj.* Empyreal.

e·mu (ē'myoo) *n.* A flightless, three-toed Australian bird related to the ostrich. [Prob. < Pg. *ema* ostrich]

em·u·late (em'yə·lāt) *v.t.* **·lat·ed, ·lat·ing 1.** To try to equal or surpass. **2.** To rival or vie with successfully. [< L < *aemulus* jealous] —**em'u·la·tive** *adj.* —**em'u·la'tion** *n.* —**em'u·la·tive·ly** *adv.* —**em'u·la'tor** *n.*

em·u·lous (em′yə·ləs) *adj.* **1.** Eager to equal or excel another; competitive. **2.** Pertaining to or arising from emulation. — **em′u·lous·ly** *adv.* — **em′u·lous·ness** *n.*

e·mul·si·fy (i·mul′sə·fī) *v.t.* **·fied, ·fy·ing** To make into an emulsion. — **e·mul′si·fi·ca′tion** *n.* — **e·mul′si·fi′er** *n.*

e·mul·sion (i·mul′shən) *n.* **1.** A liquid mixture in which a fatty or resinous substance is suspended in minute globules, as butter in milk. **2.** Any milky liquid. **3.** *Photog.* A light-sensitive coating for film, plates, papers, etc. [< LL < L < e- out + *mulgere* to milk] — **e·mul′sive** *adj.*

en (en) *n. Printing* A space half the width of an em.

en-¹ *prefix* Forming transitive verbs: **1.** (from nouns) To cover or surround with; place into or upon: *encircle*. **2.** (from adjectives and nouns) To make; cause to be or to resemble: *enable, enfeeble*. **3.** (from verbs) Often with simple intensive force, or used to form transitive verbs from intransitives: *enact*. Also *em-* before *b*, *p*, and sometimes *m*, as in *embark*. Many words in *en-* or *em-* have variant forms in *in-* or *im-* respectively. [< OF < L *in-* < *in*, into]

en-² *prefix* In; into; on: *endemic*. Also *el-* before *l*, as in *ellipse*; *em-* before *b*, *m*, *p*, *ph*, as in *embolism, empathy*; *er-* before *r*, as in *errhine*. [< Gk. *en-* < *en* in, into]

-en¹ *suffix* Forming verbs: **1.** (from adjectives) Cause to be; become: *deepen, harden*. **2.** (from nouns) Cause to have; gain: *hearten, strengthen*. [OE *-nian*]

-en² *suffix of adjectives* Made of; resembling: *woolen*. [OE]

-en³ *suffix* Used in the past participles of many strong verbs: *broken, beaten*. [OE]

-en⁴ *suffix* Used in the plurals of certain nouns: *oxen, children*. [OE *-an*, plural ending of the weak declension]

-en⁵ *suffix* Small; little: *chicken, kitten*. [OE]

en·a·ble (in·ā′bəl) *v.t.* **·bled, ·bling 1.** To supply with adequate power or opportunity; make able. **2.** To make possible or practicable.

en·act (in·akt′) *v.t.* **1.** To make into a law; decree. **2.** To carry on in action; perform. **3.** To represent in or as in a play; act the part of. — **en·act′a·ble** *adj.* — **en·ac′tor** *n.*

en·act·ment (in·akt′mənt) *n.* **1.** The act of enacting, or the state of being enacted. **2.** That which is enacted; a law.

en·am·el (in·am′əl) *n.* **1.** A vitreous, usu. opaque material applied by fusion to surfaces of metal, glass, or porcelain as a decoration or a protective surface. **2.** A piece executed in enamel. **3.** A paint, varnish, or lacquer that dries to form a hard, glossy surface. **4.** Any coating resembling enamel. **5.** *Anat.* The hard, glossy, calcareous outer layer of the teeth. For illus. see TOOTH. — *v.t.* **en·am·eled** or **·elled, en·am·el·ing** or **·el·ling 1.** To cover or inlay with enamel. **2.** To surface with or as with enamel. **3.** To adorn with different colors. [< AF < *en-* on + *amayl*, OF *esmail* enamel] — **en·am′el·er** or **en·am′el·ler, en·am′el·ist** or **en·am′el·list** *n.*

en·am·el·ware (in·am′əl·wâr′) *n.* Enameled kitchenware.

en·am·or (in·am′ər) *v.t.* To inflame with love; also, to charm; fascinate: chiefly in the passive, followed by *of*: He is *enamored* of his cousin. *Brit.* **en·am′our.** [< OF < *en-* in + *amour* love] — **en·am′ored** *adj.*

en·camp (in·kamp′) *v.i.* **1.** To go into camp; live in a camp. — *v.t.* **2.** To place in a camp. — **en·camp′ment** *n.*

en·case (in·kās′) See INCASE.

en·caus·tic (en·kôs′tik) *adj.* Having the pigments burned in: *encaustic* tile. [< L < Gk. < *en-* in + *kaiein* to burn]

-ence *suffix of nouns* Forming nouns of action, quality, or condition from adjectives in *-ent*, as *prominence*. Compare *-ENCY*. See note under *-ANCE*. [< F < L *-entia*, suffix used to form nouns from present participles]

en·ce·phal·ic (en′sə·fal′ik) *adj.* **1.** Of or pertaining to the brain. **2.** Situated within the cranial cavity.

en·ceph·a·li·tis (en′sef·ə·lī′tis, en·sef′-) *n. Pathol.* Inflammation of the brain. — **en′ceph·a·lit′ic** (-lit′ik) *adj.*

encephalitis le·thar·gi·ca (li·thär′ji·kə) *Pathol.* An acute virus form of encephalitis, affecting the central nervous system and accompanied by fever, lethargy, and sensory disturbances: also called *sleeping sickness*.

encephalo- *combining form* The brain. Also, before vowels, **encephal-.** [< Gk. < *en-* in + *kephalē* head]

en·ceph·a·lon (en·sef′ə·lon) *n. pl.* **·la** (-lə) *Anat.* The brain. [< NL < Gk. *enkephalos*] — **en·ceph′a·lous** *adj.*

en·chain (in·chān′) *v.t.* **1.** To bind with or as with a chain. **2.** To hold fast or captive, as attention. — **en·chain′ment** *n.*

en·chant (in·chant′, -chänt′) *v.t.* **1.** To put a spell upon; bewitch. **2.** To charm completely; delight. [< F < L *in-* in + *cantare* to sing] — **en·chant′er** *n.* — **en·chant′ment** *n.* — **en·chant′ress** *n. fem.*

en·chant·ing (in·chan′ting, -chän′-) *adj.* Having power to enchant; charming; fascinating. — **en·chant′ing·ly** *adv.*

en·ci·pher (en·sī′fər) *v.t.* To convert (a message, report, etc.) from plain text into cipher.

en·cir·cle (en·sûr′kəl) *v.t.* **·cled, ·cling 1.** To form a circle around. **2.** To go around. — **en·cir′cle·ment** *n.*

en·clave (en′klāv) *n.* **1.** A territory completely or partially enclosed by the territory of a power to which it is not politically subject, as San Marino and Vatican City in Italy. **2.** A district, as in a city, inhabited by a minority group. [< F < LL < L *in-* in + *clavis* key]

en·clit·ic (en·klit′ik) *adj.* Having no independent accent, but pronounced as part of a preceding word, as English *is* in *Tom′s going*, French *je* in *ai-je*. — *n. Gram.* An enclitic form. [< LL < Gk. < *en-* on + *klinein* to lean]

en·close (in·klōz′) *v.t.* **·closed, ·clos·ing 1.** To close in on all sides; surround. **2.** To transmit within the cover of a letter. **3.** To contain. Also spelled *inclose*.

en·clo·sure (in·klō′zhər) *n.* **1.** The act of enclosing, or the state of being enclosed. **2.** An enclosed object or area. **3.** That which encloses, as a wall. Also spelled *inclosure*.

en·code (en·kōd′) *v.t.* **·cod·ed, ·cod·ing** To convert (a message, document, etc.) from plain text into code.

en·co·mi·um (en·kō′mē·əm) *n. pl.* **·mi·ums** or **·mi·a** (-mē·ə) A formal expression of praise; eulogy. [< L < Gk. *enkōmion* eulogy]

en·com·pass (in·kum′pəs) *v.t.* **1.** To form a circle around; surround. **2.** To enclose; contain. — **en·com′pass·ment** *n.*

en·core (äng′kôr, -kōr, än′-) *interj.* Again! once more! — *n.* The call by an audience, as by prolonged applause, for repetition of a performance or for an additional performance; also, that which is performed in response to this call. — *v.t.* **·cored, ·cor·ing** To call for a repetition of (a performance) or by (a performer). [< F]

en·coun·ter (in·koun′tər) *n.* **1.** A meeting with a person or thing, esp. when casual or unexpected. **2.** A hostile meeting; contest. — *v.t.* **1.** To meet, esp. casually or unexpectedly. **2.** To meet in battle. **3.** To be faced with or contend against (opposition, difficulties, etc.). — *v.i.* **4.** To meet each other unexpectedly or in conflict. [< OF < LL < L *in-* in + *contra* against]

en·cour·age (in·kûr′ij) *v.t.* **·aged, ·ag·ing 1.** To inspire with courage, hope, or resolution. **2.** To help or foster. [< OF < *en-* in + *corage* courage] — **en·cour′age·ment** *n.*

en·cour·ag·ing (in·kûr′ij·ing) *adj.* Giving, or tending to give, courage or confidence. — **en·cour′ag·ing·ly** *adv.*

en·croach (in·krōch′) *v.i.* **1.** To intrude stealthily or gradually upon the possessions or rights of another: with *on* or *upon*. **2.** To advance beyond the proper or usual limits. [< OF < *en-* in + *croc* hook] — **en·croach′ment** *n.*

en·crust (in·krust′), etc. See INCRUST, etc.

en·cum·ber (in·kum′bər) *v.t.* **1.** To hinder in action or motion, as with a burden; impede. **2.** To block up; crowd, as with obstacles or useless additions. **3.** To weigh down, as with debts. Also spelled *incumber*. [< OF < LL < *in-* in + *combrus* obstacle]

en·cum·brance (in·kum′brəns) *n.* **1.** That which encumbers; a hindrance. **2.** A dependent, esp. a child. **3.** *Law* A lien attached to real property. Also spelled *incumbrance*.

-ency *suffix of nouns* A variant of *-ENCE*, as in *decency*, used to form words expressing quality or condition, the earlier form being used largely for nouns of action. [< L *-entia*]

en·cyc·li·cal (en·sik′li·kəl, -sī′kli-) *adj.* Intended for general circulation; circular: said of letters. Also **en·cyc′lic.** — *n.* A circular letter addressed by the Pope to the bishops of the world. [< LL < Gk. < *en-* in + *kyklos* circle]

en·cy·clo·pe·di·a (en·sī′klə·pē′dē·ə) *n.* **1.** A comprehensive work made up of systematically arranged articles broadly covering the whole range of knowledge or treating of one particular field. **2.** The entire circle of knowledge. Also **en·cy·clo·pae′di·a.** [< NL < Gk. < *enkyklios paideia* a general education] — **en·cy·clo·pe′dic** or **·di·cal, en·cy·clo·pae′dic** *adj.* — **en·cy·clo·pe′di·cal·ly** *adv.*

en·cy·clo·pe·dist (en·sī′klə·pē′dist) *n.* A writer for or compiler of an encyclopedia. Also **en·cy·clo·pae′dist.**

en·cyst (en·sist′) *v.t. & v.i. Biol.* To enclose or become enclosed in a cyst or sac. — **en·cyst′ment, en′cys·ta′tion** *n.*

end (end) *n.* **1.** The terminal point or part of anything that has length: the *end* of a street. **2.** The extreme limit of the space occupied by any extended object; boundary: the *ends* of the earth. **3.** The point in time at which something ceases. **4.** The purpose of an action. **5.** An inevitable or natural consequence. **6.** Ultimate state. **7.** The termination of existence; death. **8.** Fragment; remnant: odds and *ends*. **9.** In football, the outermost player at each side of the line of scrimmage; also, the position of this player. — **to make (both) ends meet** To live within one's income. — *v.t.* **1.** To bring to a finish or termination. **2.** To be the end of. **3.** To cause the death of. — *v.i.* **4.** To come to an end. **5.** To die. [OE *ende*]

en·da·me·ba (en′də·mē′bə) *n.* A parasitic ameba; esp. one causing dysentery and liver abscess. Also **en′da·moe′ba.**

en·dan·ger (in·dān′jər) *v.t.* To expose to danger; imperil.

en·dear (in·dir′) *v.t.* To make dear or beloved.

en·dear·ing (in·dîr′ing) *adj.* **1.** Making dear or beloved. **2.** Manifesting affection; caressing. **— en·dear′ing·ly** *adv.*

en·dear·ment (in·dîr′mənt) *n.* **1.** The act of endearing, or the state of being endeared. **2.** A loving word, act, etc.

en·deav·or (in·dev′ər) *n.* An attempt or effort to do or attain something. **—** *v.t.* **1.** To make an effort to do or effect; try: usu. with an infinitive as object. **—** *v.i.* **2.** To strive. Also *Brit.* **en·deav′our.** [ME < EN-¹ + DEVOIR]

en·dem·ic (en·dem′ik) *adj.* **1.** Peculiar to a particular country or people. **2.** *Med.* Confined to or characteristic of a given locality: said of a disease. Also **en·dem′i·cal.** — **Syn.** See NATIVE. [< Gk. < *en-* in + *dēmos* people]

end·ing (en′ding) *n.* **1.** The act of bringing or coming to an end. **2.** The concluding or final part; end; extremity. **3.** One or more concluding letters or syllables added to the base of a word, esp. to indicate an inflection.

en·dive (en′dīv, än′dēv) *n.* An herb whose blanched leaves are used as a salad. [< F < L *intibus* endive]

end·less (end′lis) *adj.* **1.** Enduring forever; eternal. **2.** Having no end in space; infinite. **3.** Continually recurring; incessant. **4.** Forming a closed loop or circle. **— end′less·ly** *adv.* **— end′less·ness** *n.*

end·most (end′mōst′) *adj.* Most remote; farthest.

endo- *combining form* Within; inside. Also, before vowels, **end-.** [< Gk. < *endon* within]

en·do·blast (en′dō·blast) *n. Biol.* The endoderm. **— en′do·blas′tic** *adj.*

en·do·carp (en′dō·kärp) *n. Bot.* The inner layer of a ripened fruit, as of a cherry stone.

en·do·crine (en′dō·krin, -krēn, -krīn) *Physiol. adj.* **1.** Secreting internally. **2.** Of or pertaining to an endocrine gland or its secretion. Also **en′do·cri′nal** (-krī′nəl), **en′do·crin′ic** (-krin′ik), **en·doc·ri·nous** (en·dok′rə·nəs) *adj.* [< ENDO- + Gk. *krinein* to separate]

endocrine gland One of several ductless glands, as the thyroid, pituitary, and suprarenal glands, whose secretions, released directly into the blood or lymph, have a critical importance in many phases of physiological activity.

en·do·cri·nol·o·gy (en′dō·krī·nol′ə·jē, -krī-) *n.* The branch of medicine dealing with the endocrine glands and the various internal secretions. **— en′do·cri·nol′o·gist** *n.*

en·do·derm (en′dō·dûrm) *n. Biol.* The innermost of the three germ layers of the embryo, developing into the digestive and respiratory systems: also called *endoblast, entoblast, entoderm.* **— en′do·der′mal, en·do·der′mic** *adj.*

en·dog·a·my (en·dog′ə·mē) *n. Anthropol.* Marriage within the group, class, caste, or tribe. **— en·dog′a·mous** *adj.*

en·dog·e·nous (en·doj′ə·nəs) *adj. Biol.* Originating or growing from within, as cells within the wall of the parent cell. **— en·dog′e·nous·ly** *adv.* **— en·dog′e·ny** *n.*

en·do·mor·phic (en′dō·môr′fik) *adj.* Of human body types, characterized by a heavy body structure. **— en′do·morph** *n.* **— en′do·mor′phy** *n.*

en·do·plasm (en′dō·plaz′əm) *n. Biol.* The inner granular portion of the cytoplasm of the cell, enclosing the nucleus. Also **en·do·sarc** (en′dō·särk). **— en′do·plas′mic** *adj.*

end organ *Physiol.* Any organ adapted for the reception or delivery of nervous stimuli.

en·dorse (in·dôrs′) *v.t.* **dorsed, dors·ing** **1.** To write on the back of (a paper); esp., to transfer ownership or assign payment of (a check, note, etc.) by signing on the reverse side. **2.** To give sanction or support to. Also spelled *indorse.* [< OF < Med.L < L *in-* on + *dorsum* back] **— en·dors′a·ble** *adj.* **— en·dors′er** or **en·dor′sor** *n.*

en·dor·see (en′dôr·sē′, in·dôr′sē) *n.* One to whom transference by endorsement is made.

en·dorse·ment (in·dôrs′mənt) *n.* **1.** The act of endorsing. **2.** That which endorses, as a signature. **3.** Confirmation; approval. Also spelled *indorsement.*

en·do·skel·e·ton (en′dō·skel′ə·tən) *n. Anat.* The internal supporting structure of an animal, as in all vertebrates. **— en′do·skel′e·tal** *adj.*

en·do·sperm (en′dō·spûrm) *n. Bot.* The nutritive substance with the embryo sac of an ovule.

en·do·ther·mic (en′dō·thûr′mik) *adj. Chem.* Pertaining to, attended by, or produced from the absorption of heat. Also **en′do·ther′mal.** [< ENDO- + Gk. *thermē* heat]

en·dow (in·dou′) *v.t.* **1.** To bestow a permanent fund or income upon. **2.** To furnish or equip, as with talents or natural gifts: usu. with *with.* [< OF < *en-* in + L *dotare* to give]

en·dow·ment (in·dou′mənt) *n.* **1.** Money or property given for the permanent use of an institution, person, etc. **2.** Any natural gift, as talent or beauty. **3.** The act of endowing.

end table *U.S.* A small table beside a chair, sofa, etc.

en·due (in·dōō′, -dyōō′) *v.t.* **dued, du·ing** **1.** To endow with some quality, power, etc. **2.** To put on. **3.** To clothe. [Fusion of OF *enduire* to introduce and *enduire* to clothe]

en·dur·ance (in·dōōr′əns, -dyōōr′-) *n.* **1.** The act or capacity of bearing up, as under hardship or prolonged stress. **2.** Duration. **3.** That which is endured.

en·dure (in·dōōr′, -dyōōr′) *v.* **dured, dur·ing** *v.t.* **1.** To

bear up under: to *endure* hardships. **2.** To put up with; tolerate. **—** *v.i.* **3.** To continue to be; last. **4.** To suffer without yielding. [< OF < L *in-* in + *durare* to harden] **— en·dur′a·ble** *adj.* **— en·dur′a·bly** *adv.*

en·dur·ing (in·dōōr′ing, -dyōōr′-) *adj.* **1.** Lasting; permanent. **2.** Long-suffering. **— en·dur′ing·ly** *adv.* **— en·dur′ing·ness** *n.*

end·wise (end′wīz′) *adv.* **1.** With the end foremost or uppermost. **2.** On end. **3.** Lengthwise. **4.** End to end. Also **end′ways′** (-wāz′).

En·dym·i·on (en·dim′ē·ən) In Greek mythology, a beautiful youth loved by Selene and granted eternal youth.

-ene *suffix Chem.* **1.** Denoting a hydrocarbon compound having one double bond: *ethylene.* **2.** Denoting a compound of the benzene series.

en·e·ma (en′ə·mə) *n. pl.* **en·e·mas** or **e·nem·a·ta** (e·nem′ə·tə) *Med.* **1.** A liquid injected into the rectum for cleansing, diagnostic, or nutritive purposes. **2.** The injection of such a liquid. [< Gk. < *en-* in + *hienai* to send]

en·e·my (en′ə·mē) *n. pl.* **mies** **1.** One who harbors hatred or malicious intent toward another; also, one who or that which opposes a person, cause, etc. **2.** A hostile power or military force; also, a member of a hostile force. **— adj.** Of or pertaining to a hostile army or power. [< OF < L < *in-* not + *amicus* friend]

— Syn. (noun) An *enemy* is one who manifests ill will, or broadly anyone on the opposite side in a struggle. An *opponent* may vie with one in a friendly contest, while an *antagonist* is always hostile and unfriendly. *Adversary* is a general word and may be applied to a friendly *opponent* or to the most implacable *enemy.*

en·er·get·ic (en′ər·jet′ik) *adj.* Having or displaying energy; forceful and efficient. **— en′er·get′i·cal·ly** *adv.*

en·er·gize (en′ər·jīz) *v.* **gized, giz·ing** *v.t.* **1.** To give energy, force, or strength to; activate. **—** *v.i.* **2.** To be in operation; be active. **— en′er·giz′er** *n.*

en·er·gy (en′ər·jē) *n. pl.* **gies** **1.** Vigor or intensity of action, expression, or utterance. **2.** Capacity or tendency for vigorous action. **3.** Inherent power to produce an effect. **4.** *Often pl.* Power forcefully and effectively exercised. **5.** *Physics* The capacity for doing work and for overcoming inertia. **Potential energy** is due to the position of one body relative to another, and **kinetic energy** is manifested by bodies in motion. [< LL < Gk. < *en-* + *ergon* work]

en·er·vate (*v.* en′ər·vāt; *adj.* i·nûr′vit) *v.t.* **vat·ed, vat·ing** To sap the strength or vitality of; weaken in body or will. **— adj.** Weakened; devitalized. [< L < *e-* out + *nervus* sinew] **— en′er·va′tion** *n.* **— en′er·va′tor** *n.*

en·fee·ble (en·fē′bəl) *v.t.* **bled, bling** To make feeble. **— en·fee′ble·ment** *n.* **— en·fee′bler** *n.*

en·fi·lade (en′fə·lād′) *Mil. v.t.* **lad·ed, lad·ing** To fire or be in a position to fire down the length of, as a column of troops. **—** *n.* **1.** Gunfire that can rake lengthwise a line of troops, etc. **2.** A position exposed to such fire. [< F < *en-* in + *fil* thread]

en·fold (in·fōld′) See INFOLD.

en·force (in·fôrs′, -fōrs′) *v.t.* **forced, forc·ing** **1.** To compel observance of (a law, etc.). **2.** To impose (obedience, etc.) by force. **3.** To lay stress upon; emphasize. [< OF < LL < L *in-* in + *fortis* strong] **— en·force′a·ble** *adj.* **— en·force′ment** *n.* **— en·forc′er** *n.*

en·fran·chise (in·fran′chīz) *v.t.* **chised, chis·ing** **1.** To endow with a franchise, as with the right to vote. **2.** To set free, as from bondage or legal liabilities. [< OF < *en-* in + *franc* free] **— en·fran′chise·ment** (-chiz·mənt) *n.*

en·gage (in·gāj′) *v.* **gaged, gag·ing** *v.t.* **1.** To hire or employ (a person); also, to secure or contract for (professional services, assistance, etc.). **2.** To reserve the use of, as lodgings. **3.** To hold the interest or attention of; engross. **4.** To occupy; keep busy: to *engage* one's time in revelry. **5.** To bind by a pledge, contract, etc. **6.** To betroth: usu. in the passive. **7.** To enter into conflict with: to *engage* the enemy. **8.** *Mech.* To mesh or interlock with. **—** *v.i.* **9.** To occupy oneself in an undertaking. **10.** To pledge oneself; warrant. **11.** To enter into combat. **12.** *Mech.* To mesh. [< F < *en-* in + *gager* to pledge]

en·gaged (in·gājd′) *adj.* **1.** Occupied or busy. **2.** Betrothed. **3.** Involved in conflict. **4.** *Mech.* Geared together. **5.** *Archit.* Partially sunk into another part of a structure.

en·gage·ment (in·gāj′mənt) *n.* **1.** The act of engaging, or the state of being engaged. **2.** Something that engages or binds, as an obligation. **3.** Betrothal. **4.** A business appointment. **5.** A salaried position, esp. for a limited period. **6.** A hostile encounter. **7.** *Mech.* The state of being in gear. **8.** *pl.* Financial obligations. **— Syn.** See BATTLE.

en·gag·ing (in·gāj′ing) *adj.* Attracting interest or affection; winning; pleasing. **— en·gag′ing·ly** *adv.*

en garde (än gärd′) *French* On guard: a fencing position.

en·gen·der (in·jen′dər) *v.t.* **1.** To cause to exist; produce. **2.** *Rare* To beget. **—** *v.i.* **3.** To come into being. [< OF < L *ingenerare* to create < *in-* in + *genus, generis* race]

en·gine (en′jən) *n.* **1.** A machine that converts heat energy into mechanical work. **2.** A locomotive. **3.** An apparatus or mechanical contrivance for producing some effect. **4.** Any agency, means, or instrument. [< OF < L *in-* in + *gen-*, root of *gignere* to beget]

en·gi·neer (en/jə·nir/) *n.* **1.** One versed in or practicing any branch of engineering. **2.** One who operates an engine. **3.** *Mil.* A member of a corps of men engaged in constructing forts and bridges, clearing and building roads, etc. —*v.t.* **1.** To put through or manage by contrivance: to *engineer* a scheme. **2.** To plan and superintend as engineer.

en·gi·neer·ing (en/jə·nir/ing) *n.* **1.** The art and science of designing, constructing, and operating roads, bridges, buildings, etc. **2.** Clever planning or maneuvering.

Eng·lish (ing/glish) *adj.* **1.** Of, pertaining to, or derived from England or its people. **2.** Expressed in or belonging to the English language. —*n.* **1.** The people of England collectively: with *the.* **2.** The language spoken by the people of the British Isles and most of the British Commonwealth, and of the United States, its territories, and possessions. — **Old English** or **Anglo-Saxon** The English language from about A.D. 450 to 1050, consisting of a basically Germanic vocabulary. — **Middle English** The language of England after the Norman Conquest, from about 1050 to 1475, represented by the works of Chaucer and having extensive borrowings from Latin, French, and the Low German languages. — **Modern English** The English language since 1475. **3.** *U.S.* In billiards, a horizontal twist or spin given to the cue ball by striking it on one side. —*v.t.* **1.** To translate into English. **2.** To Anglicize, as a foreign word. **3.** *U.S.* In billiards, to apply English to. [OE *Engle* the Angles]

English horn A double-reed instrument having a pitch a fifth lower than an oboe.

Eng·lish·man (ing/glish·mən) *n. pl.* **·men** (-mən) **1.** A native or citizen of England. **2.** An English ship.

English muffin A round, flat muffin made with little shortening, and usu. eaten toasted.

English sonnet The Shakespearean sonnet.

Eng·lish·wom·an (ing/glish·wŏŏm/ən) *n. pl.* **·wom·en** (-wim/in) A woman who is a native or citizen of England.

en·gorge (en·gôrj/) *v.t.* **·gorged, ·gorg·ing 1.** To fill with blood, as an artery. **2.** To devour or swallow greedily. [< F < *en-* in + *gorge* throat] —**en·gorge/ment** *n.*

en·graft (en·graft/, -gräft/) *v.t.* **1.** *Bot.* To graft. **2.** To set firmly; implant.

en·gram (en/gram) *n.* A permanently altered state in the protoplasm of animal cells assumed to result from the temporary excitation of certain stimuli.

en·grave (en·grāv/) *v.t.* **·graved, ·grav·ing 1.** To carve or etch figures, letters, etc., into (a surface). **2.** To impress deeply on the mind. **3.** To cut (pictures, lettering, etc.) into metal, stone, or wood, for printing. **4.** To print from plates so made. [< EN-¹ + *grave* to carve] —**en·grav/er** *n.*

en·grav·ing (en·grā/ving) *n.* **1.** The act or art of cutting designs, etc., into a surface. **2.** An engraved design; plate. **3.** An impression printed from an engraved plate; print.

en·gross (en·grōs/) *v.t.* **1.** To occupy completely; absorb. **2.** To copy legibly in a large hand, as a document. **3.** In business, to monopolize (goods already on the market). [< AF < LL *ingrossare* to write large] —**en·gross/ment** *n.*

en·gross·ing (en·grō/sing) *adj.* Holding the attention or interest completely; absorbing. —**en·gross/ing·ly** *adv.*

en·gulf (en·gulf/) *v.t.* To swallow up in or as in a gulf; bury or overwhelm completely.

en·hance (en·hans/, -häns/) *v.t.* **·hanced, ·hanc·ing** To heighten or increase, as in reputation, cost, beauty, quality, etc. [< AF < *en-* in, on + *haucer* to lift] —**en·hanc/er** *n.* —**en·hance/ment** *n.*

en·har·mon·ic (en/här·mon/ik) *adj. Music* Of or relating to tones, as C♯ and D♭, having different notation but the same pitch. [< L < *en-* in + *harmonia* harmony]

e·nig·ma (i·nig/mə) *n.* **1.** An obscure or ambiguous saying. **2.** Anything that puzzles or baffles. —**Syn.** See PUZZLE. [< L < Gk. *ainissesthai* to speak in riddles]

en·ig·mat·ic (en/ig·mat/ik, ē/nig-) *adj.* Of or like an enigma; puzzling. Also **en·ig·mat/i·cal.** —**en·ig·mat/i·cal·ly** *adv.*

en·join (en·join/) *v.t.* **1.** To order or command (a person or group). **2.** To impose (a condition, course of action, etc.) on a person or group. **3.** To forbid or prohibit, especially by judicial order. [< OF < L *in-* on + *jungere* to join] —**en·join/er** *n.* —**en·join/ment** *n.*

en·joy (en·joi/) *v.t.* **1.** To experience joy or pleasure in. **2.** To have the use or benefit of. [< OF < *en-* in + *joir* to rejoice] —**en·joy/a·ble** *adj.* —**en·joy/a·ble·ness** *n.* —**en·joy/a·bly** *adv.* —**en·joy/er** *n.* —**en·joy/ment** *n.*

en·kin·dle (en·kin/dəl) *v.t.* **·dled, ·dling 1.** To set on fire; kindle. **2.** To stir to action; excite. —**en·kin/dler** *n.*

en·large (en·lärj/) *v.* **·larged, ·larg·ing** —*v.t.* **1.** To make larger. —*v.i.* **2.** To become larger. **3.** To express oneself in greater detail or at greater length: with *on* or *upon.* — **Syn.** See INCREASE. —**en·large/ment** *n.* —**en·larg/er** *n.*

en·light·en (en·līt/n) *v.t.* To give revealing or broadening knowledge to; cause to know. —**en·light/en·er** *n.*

en·light·en·ment (en·līt/n·mənt) *n.* The act of enlightening, or the state of being enlightened. — **the Enlightenment** A philosophical movement of the 18th century, characterized by rationalistic methods.

en·list (en·list/) *v.t.* **1.** To engage (someone) for the armed forces. **2.** To secure the active aid or participation of (a person, etc.). —*v.i.* **3.** To enter military service without being drafted. **4.** To join some venture, cause, etc.: with *in.*

en·list·ed man (en·lis/tid) Any male member of the armed forces who is not a commissioned officer or warrant officer.

en·list·ment (en·list/mənt) *n.* **1.** An enlisting or being enlisted. **2.** The term for which one enlists.

en·li·ven (en·lī/vən) *v.t.* **1.** To make lively, cheerful, or sprightly. **2.** To make active or vigorous; stimulate. — **en·li/ven·er** *n.* —**en·li/ven·ment** *n.*

en masse (en mas/, *Fr.* än mäs/) All together. [< F]

en·mesh (en·mesh/) *v.t.* To ensnare in or as in a net.

en·mi·ty (en/mə·tē) *n. pl.* **·ties** Deep-seated unfriendliness; hostility. [< OF < L < *in-* not + *amicus* friend]

en·no·ble (i·nō/bəl, en-) *v.t.* **·bled, ·bling 1.** To make honorable or noble in nature, quality, etc.; dignify. **2.** To confer a title of nobility upon. —**en·no/ble·ment** *n.* —**en·no/bler** *n.*

en·nui (än·nwē/, än/wē, *Fr.* än·nwē/) *n.* A feeling of listless weariness and boredom. [< F < L *in odio* in hatred]

e·nor·mi·ty (i·nôr/mə·tē) *n. pl.* **·ties 1.** The quality of being outrageous; heinousness. **2.** An outrageous offense; atrocity. [See ENORMOUS.]

e·nor·mous (i·nôr/məs) *adj.* Far exceeding the usual size, amount, degree, etc. [< L *enormis* < *e-* out + *norma* rule] —**e·nor/mous·ly** *adv.* —**e·nor/mous·ness** *n.*

e·nough (i·nuf/) *adj.* Adequate for any demand or need; sufficient. —*n.* An ample supply; a sufficiency. —*adv.* **1.** So as to be sufficient. **2.** Quite; very. **3.** Adequately; fairly; tolerably. —*interj.* That's enough! [OE *genōh, genōg*]

en·plane (en·plān/) *v.i.* **·planed, ·plan·ing** To board an airplane.

en·quire (in·kwīr/), **en·quir·y** (in·kwīr/ē, in/kwər·ē) See INQUIRE, INQUIRY.

en·rage (in·rāj/) *v.t.* **·raged, ·rag·ing** To throw into a rage.

en rap·port (än rá·pôr/) *French* In sympathy; in accord.

en·rapt (in·rapt/) *adj.* Rapt; enraptured.

en·rap·ture (in·rap/chər) *v.t.* **·tured, ·tur·ing** To bring into a state of rapture; delight extravagantly.

en·rich (in·rich/) *v.t.* **1.** To make rich or increase the wealth of. **2.** To make more productive, as soil. **3.** To add attractive or desirable elements to; make better, more interesting, etc., by adding. **4.** To increase the food value of. —**en·rich/er** *n.* —**en·rich/ment** *n.*

en·roll (in·rōl/) *v.t.* **1.** To write or record (a name) in a roll; register; list. **2.** To enlist. **3.** To place on record; record, as a document or decree. **4.** To roll up; wrap. —*v.i.* **5.** To place one's name on a list; register oneself. Also *Brit.* **en·rol/.**

en·roll·ment (in·rōl/mənt) *n.* **1.** An enrolling or being enrolled. **2.** A record of persons or things enrolled. **3.** The number of persons or things enrolled. Also **en·rol/ment.**

en route (än·rōōt/, en-, *Fr.* än·rōōt/) On the way.

en·sconce (en·skons/) *v.t.* **·sconced, ·sconc·ing 1.** To fix securely or comfortably in some place. **2.** To shelter; hide.

en·sem·ble (än·säm/bəl, *Fr.* än·sän/bl/) *n.* **1.** All the parts of a thing viewed as a whole. **2.** An individual's entire costume, including accessories. **3.** The over-all effect of something. **4.** The entire cast of a play, ballet, etc. **5.** *Music* **a** The degree of precision, balance, and unification achieved by a group of performers. **b** A group of players or singers performing together. [< F < L < *in-* in + *simul* at the same time]

en·shrine (in·shrīn/) *v.t.* **·shrined, ·shrin·ing 1.** To place in or as in a shrine. **2.** To cherish devoutly; hold sacred. Also spelled *inshrine.* —**en·shrine/ment** *n.*

en·shroud (in·shroud/) *v.t.* To shroud; conceal.

en·sign (en/sīn; *also, and always for def. 2,* en/sən) *n.* **1.** A flag or banner. **2.** In the U.S. Navy or Coast Guard, a commissioned officer of the lowest grade. See table at GRADE. **3.** A badge, symbol, or distinguishing mark. [< OF < L < *in-* in + *signum* mark] —**en/sign·ship, en/sign·cy** *n.*

en·si·lage (en/sə·lij) *n.* **1.** The process of preserving green fodder in closed pits or silos. **2.** Fodder preserved in silos: also called *silage.* —*v.t.* **·laged, ·lag·ing** To store in a silo for preservation: also **en·sile** (en·sīl/). [< F]

en·slave (in·slāv/) *v.t.* **·slaved, ·slav·ing 1.** To make a slave of. **2.** To dominate; control. —**en·slave/ment** *n.*

en·snare (en·snâr/) *v.t.* **·snared, ·snar·ing** To catch in a snare; trick: also *insnare.* —**en·snare/ment** *n.*

en·sue (en·sōō/) *v.i.* **·sued, ·su·ing 1.** To follow subsequently; occur afterward.   **2.** To follow as a consequence; result. [< OF < L < *in-* on, in + *sequi* to follow]

en·sure (in·shoor′)   *v.t.* **·sured, ·sur·ing 1.** To make sure or certain: to *ensure* victory.   **2.** To make safe or secure: with *from* or *against*: to *ensure* liberty against tyranny.   **3.** To insure (life, etc.).   [< OF < *en-* in + *seur* sure]

-ent *suffix of nouns and adjectives* **1.** Having the quality, or performing the action of (the main element); *dependent.*   **2.** One who or that which performs the action of (the main element); *superintendent.* Compare -ANT.   [< F *-ent* < L *-ens, -entis,* suffix of present participle]

ent- See ENTO-.

en·ta·bla·ture (en·tab′lə·chər)   *n. Archit.* **1.** The uppermost member of a classical order or columnar system, consisting of the architrave, frieze, and cornice.   **2.** Any projecting frieze or cornice of several members.   [< MF < Ital. < *in-* in + *tavola* base, table]

en·tail (in·tāl′)   *v.t.* **1.** To impose, involve, or result in by necessity.   **2.** *Law* To restrict or leave the inheritance of (real property) to an unalterable succession of heirs.   — *n.* **1.** The act of entailing, or the state of being entailed.   **2.** Something entailed, as an inherited estate.   **3.** A restricted line of succession or inheritance.   [< OF < *en-* + *taillier* to cut]   **— en·tail′ment** *n.*

en·ta·me·ba (en′tə·mē′bə)   *n.* Endameba.

en·tan·gle (in·tang′gəl)   *v.t.* **·gled, ·gling 1.** To catch in or as in a snare; hamper.   **2.** To make tangled; snarl.   **3.** To involve in difficulties; perplex; embarrass.   **— en·tan′gle·ment** *n.* **— en·tan′gler** *n.*

en·tente (än·tänt′, *Fr.* än·tänt′)   *n.* A mutual agreement; also, the parties entering into a mutual agreement.   [< F]

entente cor·diale (kôr·dyäl′)   Cordial understanding, as between governments; friendly agreement.   [< F]

en·ter (en′tər)   *v.t.* **1.** To come or go into.   **2.** To penetrate; pierce.   **3.** To set in; insert.   **4.** To become a member of; join.   **5.** To start out upon; embark on.   **6.** To obtain admission to (a school, etc.).   **7.** To cause to be admitted to; enroll in.   **8.** To write down, as in a list.   **9.** To file notice of (goods, a ship, etc.) at a custom house.   **10.** *Law* **a** To place (a plea, evidence, etc.) on the records of a court. **b** To file a claim to (public lands).   — *v.i.* **11.** To come or go into a particular place.   **12.** To begin to sing, play an instrument, etc.   **— to enter into 1.** To start out; embark on.   **2.** To engage in.   **3.** To form a part or constituent of.   **4.** To consider or discuss.   **— to enter on** (or **upon**) **1.** To start out on.   **2.** To start to have or use.   [< OF < L *intra* within]

en·ter·ic (en·ter′ik)   *adj.* Intestinal.   [< Gk. *enteron* intestine]

en·ter·i·tis (en′tə·rī′tis)   *n. Pathol.* Inflammation of the intestines, chiefly the small intestine.

en·te·ro- *combining form* Intestine. Also, before vowels, **enter-.**   [< Gk. *enteron* intestine]

en·ter·prise (en′tər·prīz)   *n.* **1.** Any project, undertaking, or task, especially when difficult, demanding, or of major importance.   **2.** Boldness, energy, and venturesomeness in practical affairs.   **3.** Active engagement in projects.   [< OF < *entre-* between + *prendre* to take]

en·ter·pris·ing (en′tər·prī′zing)   *adj.* Energetic, bold, and full of initiative; venturesome.   **— en′ter·pris′ing·ly** *adv.*

en·ter·tain (en′tər·tān′)   *v.t.* **1.** To amuse; divert.   **2.** To extend hospitality to; receive as a guest.   **3.** To take into consideration, as a proposal.   **4.** To keep or bear in mind: to *entertain* a grudge.   — *v.i.* **5.** To receive and care for guests.   [< F < *entre-* between + *tenir* to hold]   **— en′ter·tain′er** *n.*

en·ter·tain·ing (en′tər·tā′ning)   *adj.* That entertains; amusing; diverting.   **— en′ter·tain′ing·ly** *adv.*

en·ter·tain·ment (en′tər·tān′mənt)   *n.* **1.** The act of entertaining, or the state of being entertained.   **2.** Something that entertains, as a play.   **3.** The care of guests.

en·thrall (in·thrôl′)   *v.t.* **1.** To keep spellbound; fascinate; charm.   **2.** To enslave. Also **en·thral′.**   **— en·thrall′ment** or **en·thral′ment** *n.*

en·throne (in·thrōn′)   *v.t.* **·throned, ·thron·ing 1.** To put upon a throne.   **2.** To invest with authority.   **3.** To exalt; revere.   **— en·throne′ment** *n.*

en·thuse (in·thōōz′)   *v.* **·thused, ·thus·ing** *U.S. Informal v.t.* **1.** To make enthusiastic.   — *v.i.* **2.** To become enthusiastic.

en·thu·si·asm (in·thōō′zē·az′əm)   *n.* **1.** Keen, animated interest in and preoccupation with something; ardor; zeal.   **2.** A cause or object of intense, lively interest.   [< LL < Gk. < *entheos, enthous* inspired, possessed]

en·thu·si·ast (in·thōō′zē·ast, -ist)   *n.* **1.** One given to or moved by enthusiasm.   **2.** A religious fanatic.

en·thu·si·as·tic (in·thōō′zē·as′tik)   *adj.* Full of or marked by enthusiasm; ardent.   **— en·thu′si·as′ti·cal·ly** *adv.*

en·tice (in·tīs′)   *v.t.* **·ticed, ·tic·ing** To lead on or attract by arousing hope of pleasure, profit, etc.; allure.   [< OF *enticier* to set afire]   **— en·tice′ment** *n.* **— en·tic′ing·ly** *adv.*

en·tire (in·tīr′)   *adj.* **1.** Having no part missing; whole; complete.   **2.** Not broken; intact.   **3.** Not lessened; full; total.   **4.** Consisting wholly of one piece; not divided into sections.   — *n.* The whole of something; total.   [< OF < L *integer* whole]   **— en·tire′ly** *adv.* **— en·tire′ness** *n.*

en·tire·ty (in·tī′rə·tē)   *n.* *pl.* **·ties 1.** The state or condition of being entire; completeness.   **2.** That which is entire.

en·ti·tle (in·tīt′l)   *v.t.* **·tled, ·tling 1.** To give (a person or thing) the right to receive, demand, or do something.   **2.** To give a name or designation to.   **3.** To give (a person) a title designating rank, honor, etc.

en·ti·ty (en′tə·tē)   *n.* *pl.* **·ties 1.** Something existing objectively or in the mind; an actual or conceivable being.   **2.** Existence as opposed to nonexistence.   **3.** Essence; substance.   [< L ppr. of *esse* to be]

ento- *combining form* Interior. Also, before vowels, **ent-.**

en·to·blast (en′tō·blast)   *n. Biol.* The endoderm.   **— en′to·blas′tic** *adj.*

en·to·derm (en′tō·dûrm)   *n.* Endoderm.

en·tomb (in·tōōm′)   *v.t.* **1.** To place in or as in a tomb; bury.   **2.** To serve as a tomb for. Also spelled *intomb.*   [< OF < *en-* in + *tombe* tomb]   **— en·tomb′ment** *n.*

en·to·mo- *combining form* Insect. Also, before vowels, **en·tom-.**   [< Gk. *entoma* insects]

en·to·mol·o·gy (en′tə·mol′ə·jē)   *n.* The branch of zoology that treats of insects.   **— en′to·mo·log′i·cal** or **en′to·mo·log′ic** *adj.*   **— en′to·mo·log′i·cal·ly** *adv.* **— en′to·mol′o·gist** *n.*

en·tou·rage (än′tōō·räzh′, *Fr.* än·tōō·räzh′)   *n.* **1.** A group of followers, retainers, or attendants; retinue.   **2.** Environment.   [< F < *entourer* to surround]

en·tr'acte (än·trakt′, *Fr.* än·träkt′)   *n.* **1.** The interval between the acts of a play, opera, etc.   **2.** A musical interlude, dance, or the like, performed between acts.   [< F]

en·trails (en′trālz, -trəlz)   *n.pl.* **1.** The internal parts of a man or animal; esp., the intestines; bowels; guts.   **2.** The internal parts of anything.   [< OF < LL *intralia* intestines]

en·train (en·trān′)   *v.i.* **1.** To board a train.   — *v.t.* **2.** To put aboard a train.   **— en·train′ment** *n.*

en·trance[1] (en′trəns)   *n.* **1.** The act of entering.   **2.** A passage, opening, or the like, affording a means of entering.   **3.** The right or power of entering; admittance.   **4.** The point in a play, ballet, etc., at which a performer is cued to enter.

en·trance[2] (in·trans′, -träns′)   *v.t.* **·tranced, ·tranc·ing 1.** To fill with rapture or wonder; delight; charm.   **2.** To put into a trance.   **— en·trance′ment** *n.* **— en·tranc′ing·ly** *adv.*

en·trance·way (en′trəns·wā′)   *n.* A means of entrance.

en·trant (en′trənt)   *n.* **1.** One who enters; a beginner.   **2.** One who competes in a contest.

en·trap (in·trap′)   *v.t.* **·trapped, ·trap·ping 1.** To catch in or as in a trap.   **2.** To trick into danger of difficulty; deceive; ensnare.   **— en·trap′ment** *n.*

en·treat (in·trēt′)   *v.t.* **1.** To beseech with great intensity; implore; beg.   **2.** To make an earnest request of or for; petition.   — *v.i.* **3.** To ask earnestly.   [< OF < *en-* in + *traitier* to treat]   **— en·treat′ing·ly** *adv.* **— en·treat′ment** *n.*

en·treat·y (in·trē′tē)   *n.* *pl.* **·ies** An earnest request.

en·tre·chat (än·trə·shä′)   *n. French* In ballet, a leap upward in which the dancer repeatedly crosses his feet.

en·trée (än′trā, *Fr.* än·trā′)   *n.* **1.** The act or privilege of entering; entrance; admission.   **2.** The principal course at a meal.   **3.** In lavish or formal dinners, a dish served between the fish and meat courses or directly before the main course. Also *U.S.* **en′tree.**   [< F, orig. pp. of *entrer.* See ENTER.]

en·trench (in·trench′)   *v.t.* **1.** To fortify or protect with or as with a trench or trenches.   **2.** To establish firmly: The idea was *entrenched* in his mind.   — *v.i.* **3.** To encroach or trespass: with *on* or *upon.*   **— en·trench′ment** *n.*

en·tre·pre·neur (än′trə·prə·nûr′, *Fr.* än·trə·prə·nœr′)   *n.* One who undertakes to start and conduct an enterprise or business.   [< F < *entreprendre.* See ENTERPRISE.]

en·tro·py (en′trə·pē)   *n. Physics* **1.** A mathematical expression of the degree to which the energy of a thermodynamic system is unavailable for conversion into work.   **2.** The irreversible tendency of a system, including the universe, toward increasing disorder; also, the final state predictable from this.   [< Gk. < *en-* in + *trepein* to turn]

en·trust (in·trust′)   *v.t.* **1.** To give over (something) for care, safekeeping, or performance.   **2.** To place something in the care or trust of. Also spelled *intrust.*

en·try (en′trē)   *n.* *pl.* **·tries 1.** The act of coming in; entrance.   **2.** A place of entrance; a small hallway or vestibule.   **3.** The act of entering anything in a register, list, etc.; also, the item entered.   **4.** The act of reporting at a customhouse the arrival of a ship in port and the nature of her cargo.   **5.** The act of assuming possession of lands or tenements by entering upon them.   **6.** A contestant listed for a race, competition, etc.   **7.** In bridge and whist, a card that will win a trick and place the lead in a specified hand: also *reentry.*

en·twine (in·twīn′)   *v.t. & v.i.* **·twined, ·twin·ing** To twine around; twine or twist together. Also spelled *intwine.*

e·nu·mer·ate (i·nōō′mə·rāt, -nyōō′-)   *v.t.* **·at·ed, ·at·ing 1.** To name one by one; list.   **2.** To ascertain the number of.   [< L < *e-* out + *numerare* to count]   **— e·nu′mer·a′tion** *n.*   **— e·nu′mer·a′tive** *adj.* **— e·nu′mer·a′tor** *n.*

e·nun·ci·ate (i·nun/sē·āt, -shē-) *v.* **·at·ed, ·at·ing** *v.t.* **1.** To articulate (speech sounds), esp. in a clear and distinct manner. **2.** To state with exactness, as a theory or dogma. **3.** To announce or proclaim. — *v.i.* **4.** To pronounce words, esp. with distinct articulation. [< L < *e-* out + *nuntiare* to announce] — **e·nun·ci·a·ble** (i·nun/sē·ə·bəl, -shē-) *adj.* — **e·nun·ci·a/tive, e·nun·ci·a·to/ry** (-sē·ə·tôr/ē, -tō/rē) *adj.* — **e·nun/ci·a/tive·ly** *adv.* — **e·nun/ci·a/tor** *n.*

e·nun·ci·a·tion (i·nun/sē·ā/shən, -shē-) *n.* **1.** The utterance or mode of utterance of speech sounds. **2.** A declaration.

en·u·re·sis (en/yə·rē/sis) *n. Pathol.* Involuntary urination. [< NL < Gk. < *en-* in + *oureein* to urinate]

en·vel·op (in·vel/əp) *v.t.* **·oped, ·op·ing 1.** To wrap; enclose. **2.** To hide; conceal. **3.** To surround. [< OF < *en-* in + *voluper* to wrap] — **en·vel/op·er** *n.*

en·ve·lope (en/və·lōp, än/-) *n.* **1.** A paper case or wrapper for enclosing a letter or the like, usu. having a gummed flap for sealing. **2.** Any enveloping cover or wrapper. **3.** *Aeron.* The outer fabric covering of a dirigible, balloon, etc.

en·vel·op·ment (in·vel/əp·mənt) *n.* **1.** The act of enveloping, or the state of being enveloped. **2.** A covering.

en·ven·om (en·ven/əm) *v.t.* **1.** To impregnate with venom; poison. **2.** To make vindictive; embitter.

en·vi·a·ble (en/vē·ə·bəl) *adj.* So admirable or desirable as to arouse envy. — **en/vi·a·bly** *adv.*

en·vi·ous (en/vē·əs) *adj.* Full of, characterized by, or expressing envy. — **en/vi·ous·ly** *adv.* — **en/vi·ous·ness** *n.*

en·vi·ron (in·vī/rən) *v.t.* To extend around; encircle; surround. [< F < *environ* around]

en·vi·ron·ment (in·vī/rən·mənt, -vī/ərn-) *n.* **1.** The external circumstances, conditions, and things that affect the existence and development of an individual, organism, or group. **2.** The act of surrounding or being surrounded. **3.** Surroundings. — **en·vi/ron·men/tal** *adj.*

en·vi·ron·ment·al·ist (in·vī/rən·men/tal·ist) *n.* **1.** One who advocates preservation of the environment. **2.** One who attaches more importance to environment than to heredity in the development of a person. — **en·vi/ron·men/tal·ism** *n.*

en·vi·rons (in·vī/rənz) *n.pl.* A surrounding, outlying area, as about a city; outskirts; suburbs.

en·vis·age (en·viz/ij) *v.t.* **·aged, ·ag·ing 1.** To form a mental image of; visualize. **2.** To conceive of in advance; contemplate. [< EN- + VISAGE] — **en·vis/age·ment** *n.*

en·vi·sion (en·vizh/ən) *v.t.* To see or foresee in the mind.

en·voy¹ (en/voi, än/-) *n.* **1.** A diplomatic representative of the second class ranking next below an ambassador. **2.** A diplomat on a special mission. **3.** Anyone entrusted with a mission. [< F *envoyé* < OF < L *in-* + *via* way, road]

en·voy² (en/voi, än/-) *n.* The closing lines of a poem or prose work, often in the form of a dedication: also *l'envoie*, *l'envoy*. Also **envoi**. [See ENVOY¹.]

en·vy (en/vē) *n. pl.* **·vies 1.** A feeling of resentment or discontent over another's superior attainments, endowments, or possessions. **2.** A desire to possess the goods of another. **3.** Any object of envy. — *v.* **·vied, ·vy·ing** *v.t.* **1.** To regard with envy; feel envy because of: I *envy* you your calm. — *v.i.* **2.** To feel or show envy. [< OF < L *in-* on + *videre* to see, look] — **en/vi·er** *n.* — **en/vy·ing·ly** *adv.*

en·zyme (en/zīm, -zim) *n. Biochem.* A protein able to initiate or accelerate specific chemical reactions in the metabolism of plants and animals; an organic catalyst. Also **en/zym** (-zim). [< L < Gk. < *en-* in + *zymē* leaven] — **en·zy·mat·ic** (en/zī·mat/ik, -zi-) *adj.*

eo- *combining form* Earliest; early part or early representative of. [< Gk. *ēos* dawn, daybreak]

E·o·cene (ē/ə·sēn) *Geol. adj.* Of, pertaining to, or existing in the Early Tertiary period of the Cenozoic era. — *n.* The second epoch of the Cenozoic era. See chart for GEOLOGY. [< EO- + Gk. *kainos* new]

e·o·lith (ē/ə·lith) *n.* A stone tool of the earliest form; celt. [< EO- + Gk. *lithos* stone]

E·o·lith·ic (ē/ə·lith/ik) *adj. Anthropol.* Of or pertaining to a period of early human culture, known only by the rudest implements of bone and chipped stone.

e·on (ē/on, ē/ən) *n.* **1.** An incalculable period of time; an age; eternity. **2.** *Geol.* A time interval including two or more eras. Also spelled **aeon**. [< L *aeon* < Gk. *aiōn* age]

E·os (ē/əs) In Greek mythology, the goddess of the dawn, daughter of Hyperion; identified with the Roman *Aurora*.

e·o·sin (ē/ə·sin) *n. Chem.* A reddish coloring matter, $C_{20}H_8Br_4O_5$, derived from coal tar, used for dyeing and as a stain in microscopy. Also **e/o·sine** (-sin, -sēn). [< Gk. *ēos* morning red, dawn + -IN] — **e/o·sin/ic** *adj.*

-eous *suffix* Of the nature of. [< L *-eus*]

E·o·zo·ic (ē/ə·zō/ik) *adj. Geol.* Of or pertaining to the portion of Pre-Cambrian time immediately before the Paleozoic era and showing the first signs of invertebrate life. [< EO- + Gk. *zōē* life]

ep- Var. of EPI-.

ep·au·let (ep/ə·let) *n. Mil.* A shoulder ornament, as on military and naval uniforms. Also **ep/au·lette**. [< F *épaulette* < OF < LL < L < Gk. *spathē* blade]

é·pée (ā·pā/) *n.* A dueling sword with a sharp point and no cutting edge. [< F < OF < L] — **é·pée·ist** *n.*

eph- Var. of EPI-.

e·phed·rine (i·fed/rin, ef/ə·drēn) *n. Chem.* An alkaloid, $C_{10}H_{15}ON$, used for relief of asthma, hay fever, nasal congestion, etc. Also **e·phed·rin** (i·fed/rin, ef/ə·drin). [< NL *Ephedra*, a genus of plants + -INE²]

e·phem·er·a (i·fem/ər·ə) *n. pl.* **·er·as** or **·er·ae** (-ə·rē) **1.** An ephemerid or May fly. **2.** Anything of very short life or duration. [< Gk. < *epi-* on + *hēmera* day]

e·phem·er·al (i·fem/ər·əl) *adj.* **1.** Lasting but a short time. **2.** Living one day only, as certain insects. — *n.* Anything lasting for a very short time. — **e·phem/er·al·ly** *adv.*

e·phem·er·id (i·fem/ər·id) *n.* A May fly.

E·phe·sian (i·fē/zhən) *adj.* Of or pertaining to Ephesus. — *n.* A citizen of Ephesus.

E·phe·sians (i·fē/zhənz) *n.pl.* (*construed as sing.*) A book of the New Testament, consisting of St. Paul's epistle to the church at Ephesus.

E·phra·im (ē/frē·əm, ē/frəm) In the Old Testament, Joseph's younger son, who obtained the birthright. *Gen.* xlvi 20. — *n.* **1.** The tribe of Israel descended from this son. *Josh.* xiv 4. **2.** The kingdom of Israel. — **E/phra·im·ite** (-īt) *n.*

epi- *prefix* **1.** Upon; above; among; outside: *epidermis.* **2.** Besides; over; in addition to: *epilogue.* **3.** Near; close to; beside. Also: *ep-*, before vowels, as in *eponym*; *eph-*, before an aspirate, as in *ephemeral*. [< Gk. *epi* upon, on, besides]

ep·ic (ep/ik) *n.* **1.** A long, formal, narrative poem in elevated style, typically having as its subject heroic exploits and achievements or grandiose events. **2.** A novel, drama, etc., that in scale or subject resembles such a poem. — *adj.* **1.** Of, pertaining to, or suitable as a theme for an epic. **2.** Heroic; grandiose. Also **ep/i·cal** *adj.* [< L *epicus* < Gk. *epikos* < *epos* word, tale, song] — **ep/i·cal·ly** *adv.*

ep·i·ca·lyx (ep/ə·kā/liks, -kal/iks) *n. pl.* **·ca·lyx·es** or **·ca·ly·ces** (-kā/lə·sēz, -kal/ə-) *Bot.* An involucre resembling an accessory calyx and lying outside the true calyx of a flower.

ep·i·can·thus (ep/ə·kan/thəs) *n. pl.* **·thi** (-thī) A small fold of skin over the inner corner of the eye, typical of Mongoloid peoples. Also **epicanthic fold.** [< NL < Gk. *epi-* upon + *kanthos* corner of the eye] — **ep/i·can/thic** *adj.*

ep·i·car·di·um (ep/ə·kär/dē·əm) *n. pl.* **·di·a** (-dē·ə) *Anat.* The inner portion of the pericardium that is directly united with the substance of the heart. [< NL < Gk. *epi-* upon + *kardia* heart] — **ep/i·car/di·ac** (-ak), **ep/i·car/di·al** *adj.*

ep·i·carp (ep/ə·kärp) *n. Bot.* The outer layer of a pericarp.

ep·i·cene (ep/ə·sēn) *adj.* Belonging to or partaking of the characteristics of both sexes; hermaphrodite. — *n.* An epicene person. [< L < Gk. < *epi-* upon + *koinos* common]

ep·i·cen·ter (ep/ə·sen/tər) *n. Geol.* The point or area on the earth's surface directly above the focus of an earthquake.

ep·i·cure (ep/ə·kyŏŏr) *n.* One given to luxurious living and discriminating gratification of the senses; a sensualist; esp., a fastidious devotee of good food and drink; a gourmet. [after *Epicurus*, Greek philosopher] — **ep/i·cu·re/an** *adj. & n.*

Ep·i·cu·re·an·ism (ep/ə·kyŏŏ·rē/ən·iz/əm) *n.* The doctrines of Epicurus, Greek philosopher, who taught that the chief aims of life are pleasure regulated by temperance, peace of mind, and cultural pursuits. Also **Ep/i·cur·ism.** — **Ep/i·cu·re/an** *adj. & n.*

ep·i·dem·ic (ep/ə·dem/ik) *adj.* Breaking out suddenly in a particular area so as to affect many individuals at the same time: used esp. of contagious diseases. Also **ep/i·dem/i·cal.** — *n.* **1.** An epidemic disease. **2.** Anything temporarily widespread, as a fad. [< F < LL < Gk. < *epi-* among + *dēmos* people] — **ep/i·dem/i·cal·ly** *adv.*

ep·i·der·mis (ep/ə·dûr/mis) *n.* **1.** *Anat.* The outer, nonvascular covering of the skin: also called *cuticle.* **2.** Any of various other outer coverings. **3.** *Bot.* The outermost layer of cells covering the surface of a plant when there are several layers of tissue. Also **ep/i·derm.** [< NL < Gk. < *epi-* upon + *derma* skin] — **ep/i·der/mal, ep/i·der/mic** *adj.*

ep·i·der·moid (ep/ə·dûr/moid) *adj.* Of the nature of epidermis. Also **ep/i·der·moi/dal.**

ep·i·glot·tis (ep/ə·glot/is) *n. Anat.* A leaf-shaped, cartilaginous lid at the base of the tongue that covers the windpipe during the act of swallowing. [< NL < Gk. < *epi-* upon + *glōtta* tongue] — **ep/i·glot/tal** *adj.*

ep·i·gram (ep/ə·gram) *n.* **1.** A brief, clever, pointed remark or observation typically marked by antithesis. **2.** A short, pithy piece of verse with a witty, often satirical point. **3.** Epigrammatic expression. [< L < Gk. < *epi-* upon + *graphein* to write] — **ep/i·gram·mat/ic** (ep/i·grə·mat/ik) *adj.* — **ep/i·gram·mat/i·cal·ly** *adv.* — **ep/i·gram/ma·tist** *n.*

ep·i·graph (ep′ə-graf, -gräf) *n.* **1.** An inscription on a monument, tomb, etc. **2.** A quotation or motto prefixed to a book, etc. [< Gk. < *epi*- upon + *graphein* to write]

ep·i·graph·ic (ep′ə-graf′ik) *adj.* Of epigraphs or epigraphy. Also **ep′i·graph′i·cal.** — **ep′i·graph′i·cal·ly** *adv.*

e·pig·ra·phy (i-pig′rə-fē) *n.* **1.** The science that treats of the study, interpretation, etc., of inscriptions. **2.** Epigraphs collectively. — **e·pig′ra·pher, e·pig′ra·phist** *n.*

ep·i·lep·sy (ep′ə-lep′sē) *n. Pathol.* A disorder of cerebral function marked by attacks of unconsciousness with or without convulsions. See GRAND MAL, PETIT MAL. [< OF < LL < Gk. < *epi*- upon + *lambanein* to seize]

ep·i·lep·tic (ep′ə-lep′tik) *adj.* **1.** Of, relating to, or resembling epilepsy. **2.** Affected with epilepsy. — *n.* One affected with epilepsy. — **ep′i·lep′ti·cal·ly** *adv.*

ep·i·logue (ep′ə-lôg, -log) *n.* **1.** A short section appended to a novel, poem, etc., by way of commentary. **2.** A short speech appended to a play. Also **ep′i·log.** [< F < L < Gk. < *epi*- in addition + *legein* to say]

ep·i·neph·rine (ep′ə-nef′rin, -rēn) *n. Chem.* The active principle of the medullary portion of the adrenal glands, $C_9H_{13}O_3N$, used as a heart stimulant: also called *adrenalin.* Also **ep′i·neph′rin** (-rin). [< EPI- + Gk. *nephros* kidney]

E·piph·a·ny (i-pif′ə-nē) *n. Eccl.* A festival, held on January 6, commemorating the manifestation of Christ to the Gentiles as represented by the Magi: also called *Twelfth day.*

ep·i·phyte (ep′ə-fīt) *n. Bot.* A plant growing upon, but not receiving its nourishment from, another plant, as an orchid, moss, or lichen. — **ep′i·phyt′ic** (-fit′ik) or **·i·cal** *adj.*

ep·is·co·pa·cy (i-pis′kə-pə-sē) *n. pl.* **·cies 1.** Government of a church by bishops. **2.** The rank, office, or incumbency of a bishop; episcopate. **3.** Bishops, collectively. [< LL < Gk. < *epi*- over + *scopein* to look]

ep·is·co·pal (i-pis′kə-pəl) *adj.* **1.** Of, pertaining to, or governed by bishops. **2.** Advocating episcopacy. [< LL *episcopalis* < *episcopus*] — **e·pis′co·pal·ly** *adv.*

Episcopal Church The Protestant Episcopal Church.

E·pis·co·pa·li·an (i-pis′kə-pā′lē-ən, -pāl′yən) *n.* A member of the Protestant Episcopal Church. — *adj.* Belonging to the Protestant Episcopal Church, etc.; Episcopal.

e·pis·co·pate (i-pis′kə-pit, -pāt) *n.* **1.** The office, dignity, or term of office of a bishop. **2.** Bishops collectively.

ep·i·sode (ep′ə-sōd) *n.* **1.** A section of a novel, poem, etc., complete in itself. **2.** A part of a serialized story or play; installment. [< Gk. < *epi*- beside + *eisodos* entrance]

ep·i·sod·ic (ep′ə-sod′ik) *adj.* **1.** Of, relating to, or resembling an episode. **2.** Broken up into episodes; esp., disjointed. Also **ep′i·sod′i·cal.** — **ep′i·sod′i·cal·ly** *adv.*

e·pis·te·mol·o·gy (i-pis′tə-mol′ə-jē) *n. pl.* **·gies** The branch of philosophy that investigates the nature, limits, criteria, or validity of human knowledge; also, a particular theory of cognition. [< Gk. *epistēmē* knowledge + -LOGY] — **e·pis′te·mo·log′i·cal** (i-pis′tə-mə-loj′i-kəl) *adj.* — **e·pis′te·mo·log′i·cal·ly** *adv.* — **e·pis′te·mol′o·gist** *n.*

e·pis·tle (i-pis′əl) *n.* **1.** A letter, esp. when long or formal. **2.** *Usu. cap. Eccl.* **a** One of the letters written by an apostle. **b** A selection taken from one of these letters and read as part of a service. [OE < L < Gk. < *epi*- to + *stellein* to send]

e·pis·to·lar·y (i-pis′tə-ler′ē) *adj.* **1.** Of or relating to a letter or an Epistle. **2.** Included in or maintained by a letter.

ep·i·taph (ep′ə-taf, -täf) *n.* An inscription on a tomb or monument in memory of the dead. [< L < Gk. < *epi*- upon, at + *taphos* a tomb] — **ep′i·taph′ic** (-taf′ik) *adj.*

ep·i·the·li·um (ep′ə-thē′lē-əm) *n. pl.* **·li·ums** or **·li·a** (-lē-ə) *Biol.* A membranous tissue consisting of one or more layers of cells, serving to line the cavities and ducts of the body. [< NL < Gk. *epi*- upon + *thēlē* nipple] — **ep′i·the′li·al** *adj.*

ep·i·thet (ep′ə-thet) *n.* **1.** A descriptive word or phrase qualifying or used in place of the usual name of a person or thing. **2.** Loosely, any disparaging name. [< L < Gk. < *epi*- upon + *tithenai* to place] — **ep′i·thet′ic** or **·i·cal** *adj.*

e·pit·o·me (i-pit′ə-mē) *n.* **1.** A typical or extreme example; embodiment: the *epitome* of arrogance. **2.** A concise summary; abridgement. [< L < Gk. < *epi*- upon + *temnein* to cut]

e·pit·o·mize (i-pit′ə-mīz) *v.t.* **·mized, ·miz·ing** To make or be an epitome of. Also *Brit.* **e·pit′o·mise.** — **e·pit′o·miz′er** *n.*

ep·i·zo·ot·ic (ep′ə-zō-ot′ik) *adj.* Affecting many animals within a wide area: said esp. of diseases. — *n.* An epizootic disease: also **ep′i·zo′o·ty** (-zō′ə-tē).

e plu·ri·bus u·num (ē plŏŏr′ə-bəs yōō′nəm) *Latin* One out of many: motto of the U.S.

ep·och (ep′ək, *Brit.* ē′pok) *n.* **1.** A point in time marked by the beginning of a new development or state of things. **2.** An interval of time memorable for extraordinary events, important influences, unusual circumstances, etc. **3.** *Geol.* A minor subdivision of time; a time interval less than a period. See chart for GEOLOGY. **4.** *Astron.* A moment of time when a planet reaches a certain known position in relation to the sun, selected arbitrarily and thereafter used as a reference point. [< Gk. < *epi*- upon + *echein* to hold] — **ep′och·al** *adj.* — **ep′och·al·ly** *adv.*

ep·o·nym (ep′ə-nim) *n.* A real or legendary personage from whom a nation, city, epoch, theory, etc., is reputed to derive its name. [< Gk. < *epi*- upon + *onyma* name] — **e·pon′y·mous** *adj.* — **e·pon′y·my** *n.*

ep·ox·y (e-pok′sē) *n. Chem.* The radical -O-, esp. as bonded to different atoms already joined in different ways, to form the durable, thermosetting **epoxy resins** much used for varnishes and adhesives. [< EP(I)- + OXY-²]

ep·si·lon (ep′sə-lon) *n.* The fifth letter and second vowel in the Greek alphabet (E, ε), corresponding to English short *e.* See ALPHABET. [< Gk. *epsilon* < *e e* + *psilon* simple]

Epsom salts A hydrous magnesium sulfate, used as a purge or to reduce inflammation. Also **Epsom salt.**

eq·ua·ble (ek′wə-bəl, ē′kwə-) *adj.* **1.** Not changing or varying greatly; even. **2.** Not easily upset; tranquil. **3.** Evenly proportioned; uniform. [< L *aequare* to make equal] — **eq′ua·bil′i·ty, eq′ua·ble·ness** *n.* — **eq′ua·bly** *adv.*

e·qual (ē′kwəl) *adj.* **1.** Identical in size, extent, etc. **2.** Having the same rights, rank, etc. **3.** Having the same abilities, degree of excellence, etc. **4.** Evenly proportioned; balanced. **5.** Affecting or shared by all alike: *equal* rights. **6.** Having the requisite ability, power, etc.: with *to*: *equal* to the task. — *v.t.* **e·qualed** or **e·qualled, e·qual·ing** or **e·qual·ling 1.** To be equal to; match. **2.** To do or produce something equal to. **3.** To recompense in full. — *n.* A person or thing equal to another. [< L *aequus* even] — **e′qual·ly** *adv.*

e·qual·i·tar·i·an (i-kwol′ə-târ′ē-ən) *adj. & n.* Egalitarian. — **e·qual′i·tar′i·an·ism** *n.*

e·qual·i·ty (i-kwol′ə-tē) *n. pl.* **·ties** The state or quality of being equal; also an instance of this.

e·qual·ize (ē′kwəl-īz) *v.t.* **·ized, ·iz·ing** To make equal or uniform. — **e′qual·iz′er** *n.* — **e′qual·i·za′tion** *n.*

equal sign A sign (=) denoting numbers, quantities, etc., equal to one another.

e·qua·nim·i·ty (ē′kwə-nim′ə-tē, ek′wə-) *n.* Evenness of mind or temper. [< L < *aequus* even + *animus* mind]

e·quate (i-kwāt′) *v.t.* **e·quat·ed, e·quat·ing 1.** To make equal; treat or consider as equivalent. **2.** To reduce to a common standard. **3.** *Math.* To indicate the equality of; express as an equation. [< L *aequus* even]

e·qua·tion (i-kwā′zhən, -shən) *n.* **1.** The process or act of making equal. **2.** The state of being equal. **3.** *Math.* A statement expressing (usu. by =) the equality of two quantities. **4.** *Chem.* A symbolic representation of a chemical reaction, as $Na_2CO_3 + H_2SO_4 \rightarrow Na_2SO_4 + CO_2 + H_2O$.

e·qua·tor (i-kwā′tər) *n.* **1.** The great circle of the earth, a line lying in a plane perpendicular to the earth's polar axis. **2.** Any similar circle, as of the sun. **3.** *Astron.* The celestial equator. [< LL (*circulus*) *aequator* equalizer (circle)]

e·qua·to·ri·al (ē′kwə-tôr′ē-əl, -tō′rē) *adj.* **1.** Of, pertaining to, or like the equator. **2.** Relating to conditions prevailing at the earth's equator.

eq·uer·ry (ek′wər-ē) *n. pl.* **·ries 1.** An officer in charge of the horses of a prince or nobleman. **2.** A personal attendant on a member of the royal household of England. [Confusion, of F *écurie* stable (< OF *escuerie*) with OF *escuier* esquire]

e·ques·tri·an (i-kwes′trē-ən) *adj.* **1.** Pertaining to horses or horsemanship. **2.** Mounted on horseback; also, representing someone as being on horseback: an *equestrian* portrait. — *n.* A rider on horseback, esp. when skilled. [< L *equus* horse] — **e·ques′tri·enne′** *n.fem.*

equi- *combining form* Equal; equally. [< L *aequus* equal]

e·qui·dis·tant (ē′kwə-dis′tənt) *adj.* Equally distant. — **e′qui·dis′tance** *n.* — **e′qui·dis′tant·ly** *adv.*

e·qui·lat·er·al (ē′kwə-lat′ər-əl) *n.* **1.** A side of equal length with another. **2.** A geometric figure with equal sides. — *adj.* Having all the sides equal. — **e′qui·lat′er·al·ly** *adv.*

e·qui·li·brate (ē′kwə-lī′brāt, i-kwil′ə-brāt) *v.t. & v.i.* **·brat·ed, ·brat·ing 1.** To bring into or be in a state of equilibrium. **2.** To counterpoise. — **e′qui·li·bra′tion** *n.*

e·qui·lib·ri·um (ē′kwə-lib′rē-əm) *n.* **1.** *Physics* A state of balance between two or more forces acting within or upon a body such that there is no change in the state of rest or motion of the body. **2.** Any state of balance, compromise, or adjustment. [< L *aequus* equal + *libra* balance]

e·quine (ē′kwīn) *adj.* Of, pertaining to, or like a horse. — *n.* A horse. [< L < *equus* horse]

e·qui·noc·tial (ē′kwə-nok′shəl) *adj.* **1.** Occurring at or near the time of the equinox. **2.** Of or pertaining to the equinox. — *n. Meteorol.* A severe storm occurring usu. at or near the time of the equinox.

equinoctial line *Astron.* The celestial equator.

e·qui·nox (ē′kwə-noks) *n.* One of two opposite points at which the sun crosses the celestial equator, when the days and nights are equal; also, the time of this crossing (about March 21, the **vernal** or **spring equinox**, and Sept. 21, the **autumnal equinox**). [< F < L *aequus* equal + *nox* night]

e·quip (i-kwip′) *v.t.* **e·quipped, e·quip·ping 1.** To furnish or fit out with whatever is needed for any purpose or undertaking. **2.** To dress or attire. [< F < OF, prob. ∨ ON *skipa* to outfit a vessel]

eq·ui·page (ek′wə·pij) *n.* **1.** The equipment for a camp, army, etc. **2.** A horse-drawn carriage and its attendants.

e·quip·ment (i·kwip′mənt) *n.* **1.** The act of equipping, or the state of being equipped. **2.** Material with which a person or organization is provided for some special purpose.

e·qui·poise (ē′kwə·poiz, ek′wə-) *n.* **1.** Equality of weight; equal balance. **2.** A counterpoise.

eq·ui·ta·ble (ek′wə·tə·bəl) *adj.* **1.** Marked by equity; impartially just, fair, and reasonable. **2.** *Law* Of, relating to, or valid in equity as distinguished from statute law and common law. — **eq′ui·ta·ble·ness** *n.* — **eq′ui·ta·bly** *adv.*

eq·ui·ty (ek′wə·tē) *n. pl.* **·ties 1.** Fairness or impartiality. **2.** Something that is fair or equitable. **3.** *Law* a Justice based on the concepts of ethics and fairness. **b** A system of jurisprudence administered by courts of equity and designed primarily to mitigate the rigors of common law. **4.** In business or property, the value remaining in excess of any liability or mortgage. [< F < L *aequus* equal]

e·quiv·a·lent (i·kwiv′ə·lənt) *adj.* **1.** Equal in value, force, meaning, effect, etc. **2.** *Geom.* Equal in area, but not identical or congruent. **3.** *Chem.* Having the same valence or the same combining weight. — *n.* **1.** That which is equivalent. **2.** *Chem.* The weight of an element that combines with or displaces 1.008 grams of hydrogen. [< LL < L *aequus* equal + *valere* to be worth] — **e·quiv′a·lence, e·quiv′a·len·cy** *n.*

e·quiv·o·cal (i·kwiv′ə·kəl) *adj.* **1.** Having a doubtful meaning; ambiguous. **2.** Of uncertain origin, character, value, etc.; dubious. **3.** Questionable or suspicious: *equivocal kindness.* [< LL < L *aequus* equal + *vox, vocis* voice] — **e·quiv′o·cal·ly** *adv.* — **e·quiv′o·cal·ness** *n.*

e·quiv·o·cate (i·kwiv′ə·kāt) *v.i.* **·cat·ed, ·cat·ing** To use ambiguous language with intent to mislead or deceive. — **e·quiv′o·ca′tion** *n.* — **e·quiv′o·ca′tor** *n.*

er- Assimilated var. of EN-².

-er¹ *suffix of nouns* **1.** A person or thing that performs the action of the root verb: *maker, reaper.* See -EE (def. 1). **2.** A person concerned with or practicing a trade or profession: *geographer, hatter.* **3.** One who lives in or comes from: *New Yorker, southerner.* **4.** A person, thing, or action related to or characterized by: *three-decker.* ◆ Nouns of agency are generally formed in English by adding -er to a verb, as in *leader,* but some such nouns have the suffix -or, as in *creditor, elevator.* [OE < L *-arius, -arium*]

-er² *suffix of nouns* A person or thing connected with: *grocer, jailer.* [< AF, OF < L *-arius, -arium*]

-er³ *suffix* Forming the comparative degree of adjectives and adverbs: *harder, later.* [OE *-ra, -or*]

-er⁴ *suffix* Repeatedly: used in frequentative verbs: *stutter.* [OE *-rian*]

-er⁵ *suffix of nouns* Denoting the action expressed by the root word: *rejoinder, waiver.* [< F *-er,* infinitive ending]

e·ra (ir′ə, ē′rə) *n.* **1.** An extended period of time, esp. one reckoned from some fixed point in the past and characterized by certain events, conditions, influences, etc.: the Christian *era.* **2.** An epoch. **3.** *Geol.* A division of geological history of highest rank. See chart for GEOLOGY. [< LL *aera* counters, orig. pl. of L *aes* brass, money]

e·ra·di·ate (i·rā′dē·āt) *v.t. & v.i.* **·at·ed, ·at·ing** To radiate. — **e·ra′di·a′tion** *n.*

e·rad·i·cate (i·rad′ə·kāt) *v.t.* **·cat·ed, ·cat·ing 1.** To pull up by the roots. **2.** To destroy utterly. [< L < e- out + *radix, -icis* a root] — **e·rad′i·ca·ble** (-kə·bəl) *adj.* — **e·rad′i·ca′tion** *n.* — **e·rad′i·ca′tor** *n.* One who or that which eradicates; esp., a preparation for removing ink, etc.

e·rase (i·rās′) *v.t.* **e·rased, e·ras·ing 1.** To obliterate, as by scraping or rubbing out; efface. **2.** *U.S. Slang* To kill. [< L < e- out + *radere* to scrape] — **e·ras′a·ble** *adj.*

e·ras·er (i·rā′sər) *n.* Something used for erasing, as a piece of rubber, felt, etc.

e·ra·sure (i·rā′shər, -zhər) *n.* **1.** The act of erasing, or the state of being erased. **2.** That which is erased.

Er·a·to (er′ə·tō) The Muse of lyric and love poetry.

er·bi·um (ûr′bē·əm) *n.* A metallic element (symbol Er) of the lanthanide series, found in gadolinite. See ELEMENT. [< NL < (*Ytt*)*erby,* town in Sweden where first found]

ere (âr) *Archaic & Poetic prep.* Prior to; before in time. — *conj.* **1.** Before. **2.** Sooner than; rather than. [OE *ǣr*]

Er·e·bus (er′ə·bəs) In Greek mythology, a dark region through which the dead pass on their way to Hades.

e·rect (i·rekt′) *v.t.* **1.** To put up (a building, etc.). **2.** To assemble the parts of; set up. **3.** To set upright; raise. **4.** To establish or found, as an empire. **5.** To work out or formulate, as a theory or system. **6.** To make into; form: with *into.* — *v.i.* **7.** *Physiol.* To become rigidly upright, as through an influx of blood. — *adj.* **1.** Marked by a vertical position or posture; upright. **2.** Directed or pointed upward. [< L < e- out + *regere* to direct] — **e·rect′ly** *adv.*

— **e·rect′ness** *n.* — **e·rec′tion** *n.*

e·rec·tile (i·rek′təl, -til) *adj.* Capable of becoming erected.

e·rec·tor (i·rek′tər) *n.* **1.** One who or that which erects. **2.** *Anat.* Any of various muscles that stiffen or hold up a part of the body. Also **e·rec′ter.**

erg (ûrg) *n. Physics* In the cgs system, the unit of work and of energy, being the work done in moving a body one centimeter against the force of one dyne. [< Gk. *ergon* work]

er·go (ûr′gō) *conj. & adv. Latin* Hence; therefore. [< L]

er·got (ûr′gət) *n.* **1.** A fungus sometimes replacing the grain in rye and other cereal grasses. **2.** The disease caused by this fungus growth. **3.** A medicine derived from rye ergot. [< F < OF *argot* spur of a cock]

E·rid·a·nus (i·rid′ə·nəs) *n.* A constellation, the River. [< L, the Po river]

E·rie (ir′ē) *n. pl.* **E·rie** or **E·ries** One of a tribe of North American Indians of Iroquoian stock, formerly inhabiting the southern shores of Lake Erie.

Er·in (âr′in, ir′in) *Chiefly Poetic* Ireland.

erl·king (ûrl′king′) *n.* In Germanic folklore, an evil spirit, malicious toward children. [< G *erlkönig,* wrong trans. of Dan. *ellerkonge, elverkonge* king of the elves]

er·mine (ûr′min) *n.* **1.** One of several weasels of the northern hemisphere, having brown fur that in winter turns white with a black tip on the tail. **2.** The white fur of the ermine, used in Europe for the facings of the official robes of judges, etc. **3.** The rank or functions of a judge. [< OF (*h*)*ermine,* ? < Gmc.] — **er′mined** *adj.*

ERMINE (def. 1)
(Body 9 to 12 inches long; tail 3 to 3½ inches)

erne (ûrn) *n.* A sea eagle. Also **ern.** [OE *earn*]

e·rode (i·rōd′) *v.* **e·rod·ed, e·rod·ing** *v.t.* **1.** To wear away gradually by constant friction; wear down by scraping, rubbing, etc. **2.** To eat into; corrode. **3.** To make (a channel, gully, etc.) by wearing away or eating into. — *v.i.* **4.** To become eroded. [< L < e- off + *rodere* to gnaw]

e·rog·e·nous (i·roj′ə·nəs) *adj.* **1.** Sexually sensitive, as an area of the body. **2.** Exciting or tending to excite sexual desire. [< Gk. *eros* love + -GENOUS]

Er·os (ir′os, er′os) In Greek mythology, the god of love, son of Aphrodite: identified with the Roman *Cupid.*

e·ro·sion (i·rō′zhən) *n.* **1.** The act of eroding, or the state of being eroded. **2.** *Geol.* The wearing away of the earth's surface by the action of wind, water, glaciers, etc.

e·ro·sive (i·rō′siv) *adj.* **1.** Eroding or tending to erode. **2.** Caustic or corrosive. Also **e·ro·dent** (i·rōd′nt).

e·rot·ic (i·rot′ik) *adj.* **1.** Of, pertaining to, or concerned with sexual love; amatory. **2.** Designed to arouse sexual desire. **3.** Strongly moved by sexual desire. — *n.* **1.** An erotic person. **2.** An erotic poem. [< Gk. < *erōs, -erōtos* love] — **e·rot′i·cal·ly** *adv.* — **e·rot′i·cism** *n.*

e·rot·i·ca (i·rot′i·kə) *n.pl.* Erotic pictures, books, etc.

e·ro·to·gen·ic (i·rō′tə·jen′ik, i·rō′tō-) *adj.* Erogenous.

err (ûr, er) *v.i.* **erred, err·ing 1.** To make a mistake. **2.** To go astray morally. [< OF < L *errare* to wander] — **err′ing** *adj.* — **err′ing·ly** *adv.*

er·rand (er′ənd) *n.* **1.** A trip made to carry a message or perform some task, usu. for someone else. **2.** The business or purpose of such a trip. [OE *ǣrende* message, news]

er·rant (er′ənt) *adj.* **1.** Roving or wandering, esp. in search of adventure. **2.** Straying from the proper course or standard. [< OF < L *iter* journey] — **er′rant·ly** *adv.*

er·rat·ic (i·rat′ik) *adj.* **1.** Not conforming to usual standards; eccentric. **2.** Lacking a fixed or certain course; straying. **3.** *Geol.* Transported from the original site by glaciers, currents, etc. — *n.* An erratic person or thing. [< L < *errare* to wander] — **er·rat′i·cal·ly** *adv.*

er·ra·tum (i·rä′təm, i·rā′təm) *n. pl.* **·ra·ta** (-rä′tə, -rā′tə) An error, as in writing or printing. [< L]

er·ro·ne·ous (ə·rō′nē·əs, e·rō′-) *adj.* Marked by error; incorrect. — **er·ro′ne·ous·ly** *adv.* — **er·ro′ne·ous·ness** *n.*

er·ror (er′ər) *n.* **1.** Something done, said, or believed incorrectly; a mistake. **2.** The condition of deviating from what is correct or true in judgment, belief, or action. **3.** An offense against morals; sin. **4.** In baseball, a misplay by a member of the team not batting. **5.** *Math.* **a** The difference between the observed value of a magnitude and the true or mean value. **b** Any deviation from the true or mean value not due to gross blunders of observation or measurement.

er·satz (er·zäts′, er′zäts) *adj.* Substitute, and usu. inferior. — *n.* A usu. inferior substitute. [< G]

Erse (ûrs) *n.* **1.** Scottish Gaelic. **2.** Irish Gaelic. — *adj.* Of or pertaining to the Celts of Ireland or Scotland or their language. [Var. of IRISH]

erst (ûrst) *Archaic adv.* **1.** Formerly; long ago. **2.** In the beginning. — *First.* [OE *ǣrest,* superl. of *ǣr* before]

erst·while (ûrst′hwīl′) *adj.* Former: an *erstwhile* colleague.

e·ruct (i·rukt′) *v.t. & v.i.* To belch. Also **e·ruc′tate.** [< L < *e-* out + *ructare* to belch] — **e·ruc′ta′tion** *n.* — **e·ruc′ta·tive** *adj.*

er·u·dite (er′yŏŏ·dīt, er′ŏŏ-) *adj.* Very learned; scholarly. [< L < *e-* out + *rudis* untrained] — **er′u·dite·ly** *adv.* — **er′u·dite·ness** *n.*

er·u·di·tion (er′yŏŏ·dish′ən, er′ŏŏ-) *n.* Great learning.

e·rupt (i·rupt′) *v.i.* **1.** To cast forth lava, steam, etc., as a volcano or geyser. **2.** To be cast forth from a volcano, geyser, etc. **3.** To burst forth suddenly and violently. **4.** To show a rash or become covered with pimples, etc. **5.** Of new teeth, to break through the gums. — *v.t.* **6.** To make erupt. **7.** To cast forth (lava, etc.). [< L < *e-* out + *rumpere* to burst] — **e·rup′tion** *n.* — **e·rup′tive** *adj.*

-ery *suffix of nouns* **1.** A business, place of business, or place where something is done: *brewery.* **2.** A place or residence for: *nunnery.* **3.** A collection of things: *finery.* **4.** The qualities, principles, or practices of: *snobbery.* **5.** An art, trade, or profession: *cookery.* **6.** A state, or condition of being: *slavery.* Also *-ry,* as in *jewelry.* [< OF < *-ier* (< L *-arius*) + *-ie* < L *-ia*]

erythro- *combining form* Red. Also, before vowels, **erythr-.** [< Gk. *erythros* red]

e·ryth·ro·cyte (i·rith′rō·sīt) *n. Anat.* A disk-shaped red blood cell formed in bone marrow; it contains hemoglobin and transports oxygen to all tissues of the body. — **e·ryth′ro·cyt′ic** (-sit′ik) *adj.*

es- *prefix* Out: used in words borrowed from Old French: *escape, escheat.* [< OF < L *ex* from, out of]

-es[1] An inflectional ending used to form the plural of nouns ending in a sibilant (*fuses, fishes*), an affricate (*witches*), or, in some cases, a vowel. Compare -s[1]. [OE *-as*]

-es[2] An inflectional ending used to form the third person singular present indicative of verbs ending in a sibilant, affricate, or vowel: *goes, poaches.* Compare -s[2]. [ME *-es*]

E·sau (ē′sô) The eldest son of Isaac, who sold his birthright to his brother Jacob. *Gen.* xxv 25. [< Hebrew '*ēsāw* hairy]

es·ca·drille (es′kə·dril′, *Fr.* es·kȧ·drē′y) *n.* **1.** In France, a unit of military airplanes. **2.** A squadron of naval vessels. [< F, dim. of *escadre* squadron]

es·ca·late (es′kə·lāt) *v.t. & v.i.* **·lat·ed, ·lat·ing** **1.** To increase or be increased gradually: to *escalate* a war. **2.** To ascend on an escalator. [Back formation < ESCALATOR] — **es′ca·la′tion** *n.*

es·ca·la·tor (es′kə·lā′tər) *n.* A moving stairway built on the conveyor-belt principle.

es·cal·lop (e·skol′əp, e·skal′-) *n.* Scallop. — *v.t.* To scallop.

es·ca·pade (es′kə·pād) *n.* **1.** A brief piece of reckless behavior or prankish disregard of convention; fling; spree. **2.** An act of getting away from rigid restraint or confinement. [< F < Sp. < *escapar* to escape]

es·cape (ə·skāp′, e·skāp′) *v.* **·caped, ·cap·ing** *v.i.* **1.** To get free from confinement, restraint, or capture. **2.** To manage to avoid some danger or evil. **3.** To come out gradually from a container or enclosure, as by seeping, leaking, etc. **4.** To fade away and disappear; vanish. — *v.t.* **5.** To get away from (prison, captors, etc.). **6.** To succeed in avoiding (capture, harm, etc.). **7.** To get away from the notice or recollection of: No detail *escaped* him. **8.** To slip out from unintentionally: A cry *escaped* his lips. — *n.* **1.** The act of escaping, or the fact of having escaped. **2.** A means of escaping something: Drinking is an *escape* for him. **3.** A gradual leaking or seeping. — *adj.* **1.** That provides a means of getting away from reality, etc.; escapist: *escape literature.* **2.** That provides a means of lessening or avoiding liability, etc.: an *escape* clause in a contract. [< AF < L *ex-* out + *cappa* cloak] — **es·cap′a·ble** *adj.*

es·cap·ee (es′kā·pē′, ə·skā′pē, e·skā′pē) *n.* One who has escaped, as from prison.

es·cape·ment (ə·skāp′mənt, e·skāp′-) *n.* **1.** *Mech.* A device used in timepieces for securing a uniform movement, consisting of a notched escape wheel that is released one tooth at a time by a small lock. **2.** A typewriter mechanism controlling the horizontal movement of the carriage.

escape velocity *Physics* The minimum velocity a body must attain to escape a gravitational field: on the earth this velocity is approximately 7 miles per second.

escape wheel *Mech.* A notched wheel in an escapement.

es·cap·ism (ə·skā′piz·əm, e·skā′-) *n.* A desire or tendency to escape unpleasant reality by resorting to diversions, or by indulging in daydreaming.

es·cap·ist (ə·skā′pist, e·skā′-) *adj.* Catering to or providing a means of indulging in escapism: *escapist* literature. — *n.* One given to escapism.

es·ca·role (es′kə·rōl) *n.* A variety of endive whose leaves are used for salads. [< F < ML *escarius* fit for eating]

es·carp·ment (es·kärp′mənt) *n.* **1.** A precipitous artificial slope about a fortification or position. **2.** A steep slope or drop; esp., the precipitous face of a line of cliffs.

-esce *suffix of verbs* To become or grow; begin to be or do

(what is indicated by the main element): *phosphoresce.* [< L *-escere,* suffix of inceptive verbs]

-escence *suffix of nouns* Forming nouns of state or quality corresponding to adjectives in *-escent.* [< L *-escentia*]

-escent *suffix of adjectives* Beginning to be, have, or do (what is indicated by the main element): *effervescent.* [< L *-escens, -escentis,* suffix of ppr. of inceptive verbs]

es·cheat (es·chēt′) *Law n.* **1.** Reversion of property to the state or to the crown in default of legal heirs or other qualified claimants. **2.** Property entering possession of the state, etc., by this process. — *v.i. & v.t.* To revert or cause to revert to the state, etc., by escheat. [< OF < *es-* out + *cheoir* to fall] — **es·cheat′a·ble** *adj.*

es·chew (es·chōō′) *v.t.* To shun, as something unworthy or injurious. [< OF *eschiver*] — **es·chew′al** *n.*

es·cort (*n.* es′kôrt; *v.* es·kôrt′) *n.* **1.** An individual or group of individuals accompanying another so as to give protection or guidance. **2.** A male who takes a girl or woman to a dance, party, etc. **3.** One or more planes, ships, cars, etc., moving along with another so as to give protection, guidance, etc. — *v.t.* To accompany in the capacity of an escort. [< F < Ital. *scorgere* to lead]

es·cri·toire (es′kri·twär′) *n.* A writing desk; secretary. [< OF < LL *scriptorium* place for writing]

es·crow (es′krō, es·krō′) *n. Law* **1.** A written deed, contract, etc., placed in the custody of a third party and effective upon fulfillment of a stipulated condition. **2.** The condition of being an escrow: a bond in *escrow.* [< AF *escrowe,* OF *escroe* scroll]

es·cu·do (es·kōō′dō; *Pg.* ish·kōō′thōō; *Sp.* es·kōō′thō) *n. pl.* **·dos** (-dōz; *Pg.* -thōōs; *Sp.* -thōs) The monetary unit of Portugal, containing 100 centavos: in 1960 worth about 4 U.S. cents. [< Pg. & Sp. < L *scutum* shield]

es·cu·lent (es′kyə·lənt) *adj.* Edible. — *n.* Anything edible, esp. a plant. [< L *esca* food]

es·cutch·eon (i·skuch′ən) *n. Heraldry* A usu. shield-shaped surface carrying armorial bearings. Also *scutcheon.* [< AF < L *scutum* shield]

Es·dras (ez′drəs) The Douai Bible name for EZRA. — *n.* In the Douai Bible, either of two books of the Old Testament. I Esdras corresponds to the book of Ezra, and II Esdras corresponds to the book of Nehemiah. [< Gk.]

-ese *suffix of nouns and adjectives* **1.** A native or inhabitant of: *Milanese.* **2.** The language or dialect of: *Chinese.* **3.** Originating in: *Tirolese.* **4.** In the manner or style of: *journalese.* [< OF *-eis, -ese* < L *-ensis*]

Es·ki·mo (es′kə·mō) *n. pl.* **·mos** or **·mo** **1.** One of a Mongoloid people indigenous to the Arctic coasts of North America, Greenland, and NE Siberia. **2.** The language of the Eskimos. — *adj.* Of or relating to the Eskimos, their language, or their culture. Also spelled *Esquimau.* [< Dan. (< F *Esquimaux*) < N. Am. Ind., eaters of raw flesh]

Es·ki·mo·an (es′kə·mō′ən) *adj.* Eskimo. Also **Es′ki·mau′an.**

Eskimo dog One of a breed of large, sturdy, broad-chested dogs used by the Eskimos to draw sledges.

e·soph·a·gus (i·sof′ə·gəs) *n. pl.* **·gi** (-jī) *Anat.* The tube through which food passes from the mouth to the stomach; gullet: also spelled *oesophagus.* For illus. see MOUTH, THROAT. [< NL < Gk. *oisophagos*] — **e·so·phag·e·al** (ē′sō·faj′ē·əl, i·sof′ə·jē′əl) or **e·soph′a·gal** (-ə·gəl) *adj.*

es·o·ter·ic (es′ə·ter′ik) *adj.* **1.** Understood by or meant for only a few specially instructed or initiated individuals: *esoteric* doctrine. **2.** Confidential; kept secret: an *esoteric* motive. — **Syn.** See MYSTERIOUS. [< Gk. *esōterikos* inner] — **es·o·ter′i·cal·ly** *adv.*

ESP Extrasensory perception.

es·pal·ier (es·pal′yər) *n.* **1.** A trellis or other flat framework on which small trees, shrubs, etc., are trained to grow. **2.** A tree or row of plants so trained. — *v.t.* To furnish with an espalier. [< F < Ital. < L *spatula* shoulder]

es·pe·cial (es·pesh′əl) *adj.* Preeminent in place or degree; very special. [< OF < L *species* kind, type]

es·pe·cial·ly (es·pesh′əl·ē) *adv.* To a very special extent or degree; particularly: *especially* frequent; *especially* good.

Es·pe·ran·to (es′pə·rän′tō, -ran′tō) *n.* An artificial language having a vocabulary based on words in the major European languages. [after pseudonym of the inventor]

es·pi·al (es·pī′əl) *n.* **1.** The act of noticing something, or the fact of being noticed. **2.** The act of spying upon. [< OF *espier* to look]

es·pi·o·nage (es′pē·ə·nij′, -näzh′; *Fr.* es·pyô·näzh′) *n.* **1.** The practice of spying. **2.** The work of spies; esp., the securing of secret information. [< F *espier* to espy]

es·pla·nade (es′plə·nād′, -näd′) *n.* A level, open stretch of land, as along a shore, used as a roadway or public walk. **2.** An open embankment or level area before a fortress. [< F < Sp. < L *ex-* out + *planus* level]

es·pou·sal (es·pou′zəl) *n.* **1.** Adoption or support, as of a cause. **2.** A betrothal. **3.** *Often pl.* A marriage ceremony.

es·pouse (es·pouz′) *v.t.* **·poused, ·pous·ing** **1.** To make one's own; support, as a cause or doctrine. **2.** To take as a spouse; marry. **3.** To give in marriage. [< OF < L *spondere* to promise] **—es·pous′er** *n.*

es·pres·so (es·pres′ō) *n. pl.* **·sos** Coffee brewed from darkly roasted beans by steam pressure. [< Ital. *espresso*]

es·prit (es·prē′) *n.* Spirit; wit. [< F < L *spiritus*]

esprit de corps (də kôr′) *French* A spirit of enthusiastic devotedness to and support of the common goals of a group.

es·py (es·pī′) *v.t.* **·pied, ·py·ing** To catch sight of (something); see; descry. [< OF *espier* to look, spy]

-esque *suffix of adjectives* Having the manner or style of; resembling; like: *picturesque.* [< F < Ital. *-iscus*]

Es·qui·mau (es′kə·mō) *n. pl.* **·maux** (-mōz) See ESKIMO.

es·quire (es·kwīr′; *for n., also* es′kwīr) *n.* **1.** *Usu. cap.* A title of courtesy or respect sometimes written abbreviated after a man's surname: John Smith, *Esq.* **2.** In England, a man ranking just below a knight. **3.** A squire or young candidate for knighthood. [< OF < LL *scutarius* shield-bearer]

-ess *suffix* Used to form the feminine of many nouns: *goddess, lioness.* [< F *-esse* < LL *-issa* < Gk.]

es·say (*n. def. 1* es′ā; *n. defs. 2 and 3* es′ā, e·sā′; *v.* e·sā′) *n.* **1.** A short composition dealing with a single topic and typically personal in approach. **2.** An attempt; endeavor. **—***v.t.* **1.** To attempt to do or accomplish; try. **2.** To test the nature, etc., of. [< OF *essai* trial] **—es·say′er** *n.*

es·say·ist (es′ā·ist) *n.* A writer of essays.

es·sence (es′əns) *n.* **1.** That in which the real nature of a thing consists; intrinsic or fundamental nature. **2.** The distinctive quality of something. **3.** *Philos.* A real or true substance. **4.** An immaterial being; spirit. **5.** An extract, as of a plant or food, containing the distinctive properties of the plant; also, an alcoholic solution of such an extract. **6.** A perfume. [< F < L *esse* to be]

es·sen·tial (ə·sen′shəl) *adj.* **1.** Of, belonging to, or constituting the intrinsic nature of something. **2.** Extremely important; vital; indispensable. **3.** Derived from the extract of a plant, etc.: an *essential* oil. **4.** Complete, total, or absolute. **—***n.* Something fundamental, indispensable, or extremely important. **—es·sen′tial·ly** *adv.*

es·sen·ti·al·i·ty (ə·sen′shē·al′ə·tē) *n. pl.* **·ties 1.** The state or quality of being essential. **2.** Something essential.

essential oil Any of a group of volatile oils that give to plants their characteristic odors, flavors, etc.

-est¹ *suffix* Forming the superlative degree of adjectives and adverbs: *hardest, latest.* [OE *-ast, -est, -ost*]

-est² An archaic inflectional ending used in the second person singular present and past indicative, with *thou: eatest, walkest.* Also, in contracted forms, *-st,* as in *hast, didst.* [OE *-est, -ast*]

es·tab·lish (ə·stab′lish) *v.t.* **1.** To make secure, stable, or permanent. **2.** To set up, found, or institute: to *establish* a government. **3.** To install: to *establish* oneself in a new home. **4.** To initiate and cause to last: to *establish* a precedent. **5.** To cause to be recognized and accepted: to *establish* oneself as a writer. **6.** To clear from doubt; demonstrate; prove. **8.** To cause to be the official church of a state. [< OF < L *stabilis* stable] **—es·tab′lish·er** *n.*

established church A church recognized by a government and supported in part by public funds.

es·tab·lish·ment (ə·stab′lish·mənt) *n.* **1.** The act of establishing, or the state or fact of being established. **2.** Something established, as a business, residence, etc. **—the Establishment** Those collectively who occupy positions of influence and status in a society.

es·tate (ə·stāt′) *n.* **1.** A usu. extensive piece of landed property or the residence built on it. **2.** One's entire property and possessions. **3.** A particular condition or state: to rise to high *estate;* man's *estate.* **4.** A particular class of persons with distinct political or social status, rights, and powers. **5.** *Law* The degree, nature, and extent of ownership or use of property. [< OF < L *status* a state]

es·teem (ə·stēm′) *v.t.* **1.** To have a high opinion of; value greatly. **2.** To think of as; rate. **—***n.* **1.** High regard or respect. **2.** Judgment. [< F < L *aestimare* to value]

es·ter (es′tər) *n. Chem.* Any of a class of organic compounds formed by the reaction of an acid with an alcohol. [Coined by Leopold Gmelin, 1788–1853, German chemist]

Es·ther (es′tər) In the Old Testament, the Jewish queen, wife of King Ahasuerus (Xerxes) of Persia, who saved her people from massacre. **—***n.* A book of the Old Testament containing her story. [< Hebrew *ester,* ? < Babylonian]

es·thete (es′thēt) *n.* **1.** One who is very responsive to beauty in art, nature, etc. **2.** One who cultivates an extravagant, usu. artificial admiration for beauty and art. Also *Brit.,* aesthete. [< Gk. *aisthētēs* one who perceives]

es·thet·ic (es·thet′ik) *adj.* **1.** Of or relating to esthetics. **2.** Of or relating to the beauty in art, nature, etc. **3.** Keenly responsive to beauty in art, nature, etc. Also spelled *aesthetic:* also **es·thet′i·cal. —es·thet′i·cal·ly** *adv.*

es·thet·i·cism (es·thet′ə·siz′əm) *n.* **1.** A particular theory or outlook relating to the nature, forms, and importance of beauty. **2.** Keen responsiveness to and appreciation of beauty in art, etc. Also spelled *aestheticism.*

es·thet·ics (es·thet′iks) *n.pl.* (*construed as sing.*) **1.** A branch of philosophy relating to the nature and forms of beauty. **2.** Study of the mental and emotional responses to the beauty in art, etc. Also spelled *aesthetics.*

es·ti·ma·ble (es′tə·mə·bəl) *adj.* **1.** Worthy of respect or admiration. **2.** That may be estimated or calculated. **—es′ti·ma·ble·ness** *n.* **—es′ti·ma·bly** *adv.*

es·ti·mate (*v.* es′tə·māt; *n.* es′tə·mit) *v.* **·mat·ed, ·mat·ing** *v.t.* **1.** To form an approximate opinion of (size, amount, number, etc.). **2.** To form an opinion about; judge. **—***v.i.* **3.** To make or submit an estimate. **—***n.* **1.** A rough calculation based on incomplete data. **2.** A preliminary statement of the approximate cost for certain work. **3.** A judgment or opinion. [< L *aestimare* to value] **—es′ti·ma′tive** *adj.* **—es′ti·ma′tor** *n.*

es·ti·ma·tion (es′tə·mā′shən) *n.* **1.** The act of estimating. **2.** A conclusion arrived at by estimating. **3.** Esteem; regard: I hold him in high *estimation.*

es·ti·val (es′tə·val, es·tī′-) *adj.* Of or pertaining to summer.

es·ti·vate (es′tə·vāt) *v.i.* **·vat·ed, ·vat·ing** To pass the summer in a dormant state. [< L *aestivare* to spend the summer] **—es′ti·va′tion** *n.* **—es′ti·va′tor** *n.*

Es·to·ni·an (es·tō′nē·ən) *adj.* Of or pertaining to Estonia. **—***n.* **1.** One of a people inhabiting Estonia and part of Livonia. **2.** The Finno-Ugric language of this people.

es·trange (es·trānj′) *v.t.* **·tranged, ·trang·ing 1.** To make (someone previously friendly or affectionate) indifferent or hostile; alienate. **2.** To remove or dossociate (oneself, etc.). [< OF < L *extraneus* foreign] **—es·trange′ment** *n.*

es·tro·gen (es′trə·jən) *n. Biochem.* Any of various substances that influence estrus or produce changes in the sexual characteristics of female mammals: also spelled *oestrogen.* **—es′tro·gen′ic** (-jen′ik) *adj.*

es·trus (es′trəs, ēs′-) *n.* **1.** *Biol.* **a** The entire cycle of physiological changes in female mammals, preparing the generative organs for their fertile period. **b** The peak of the sexual cycle, culminating in ovulation; heat. Also called *oestru m:* also spelled *oestrus.* Also **es′trum** (-trum). [< L *oestrus* frenzy, passion < Gk. *oistros* gadfly]

es·tu·ar·y (es′chŏō·er′ē) *n. pl.* **·ar·ies 1.** A wide mouth of a river where its current meets the sea and is influenced by the tides. **2.** An inlet or arm of the sea. [< L < *aestus* tide] **—es′tu·ar′i·al** (-âr′ē·əl) *adj.*

-et *suffix* Small; little: *islet:* often without appreciable force, as in *sonnet.* [< F]

e·ta (ā′tə, ē′-) *n.* The seventh letter and third vowel in the Greek alphabet (H, η), corresponding to English long *e.* See ALPHABET. [< Gk. *ēta* < Phoenician *hēth*]

et cet·er·a (et set′ər·ə, set′rə) And other things; and the rest; and so forth. Also **et caet′er·a.** Abbr. *etc., &c.* [< L]

etch (ech) *v.t.* **1.** To engrave by means of acid or other corrosive fluid, esp. in making a design on a plate for printing. **2.** To outline or sketch by scratching lines with a pointed instrument. **—***v.i.* **3.** To engage in etching. [< Du. *etsen* < G *ätzen* < OHG *azzon* to corrode] **—etch′er** *n.*

etch·ing (ech′ing) *n.* **1.** A process of engraving in which lines are scratched with a needle on a plate covered with wax or other coating, and the parts exposed are subjected to the corrosive action of an acid. **2.** A figure or design formed by etching. **3.** An impression from an etched plate.

e·ter·nal (i·tûr′nəl) *adj.* **1.** Existing without beginning or end; forever existent. **2.** Unending: *eternal* happiness. **3.** Valid and true for and beyond all time. **4.** Seemingly endless. **—the Eternal** God. [< OF < LL < L *aevum* age] **—e·ter′nal·ly** *adv.* **—e·ter′nal·ness** *n.*

Eternal City Rome.

e·ter·ni·ty (i·tûr′nə·tē) *n. pl.* **·ties 1.** Existence without beginning or end; endless duration. **2.** An immeasurable extent of time. **3.** The endless time following death.

e·ter·nize (i·tûr′nīz) *v.t.* **·nized, ·niz·ing 1.** To make eternal. **2.** To perpetuate the fame of; immortalize. Also **e·ter′nal·ize** (-nəl·īz). **—e·ter′ni·za′tion** *n.*

eth (eth) See EDH.

-eth¹ An archaic inflectional ending used in the third person singular present indicative of some verbs: *eateth, drinketh.* Also, in contracted forms, *-th,* as in *hath, doth.* [OE *-eth, -ath*]

-eth² *suffix* Var. of -TH².

eth·ane (eth′ān) *n. Chem.* A colorless, odorless, gaseous hydrocarbon, C_2H_6, of the methane series contained in crude petroleum and in illuminating gas. [< ETHER]

eth·a·nol (eth′ə·nōl, -nol) *n. Chem.* An alcohol, C_2H_5OH, obtained by the distillation of certain fermented sugars or starches, the intoxicant in liquors, wines, and beers: also called *ethyl alcohol, grain alcohol.* [< ETHANE + -OL¹]

---

e·ther (ē'thər) *n*. **1.** Ethyl ether. **2.** *Chem.* Any of a group of organic compounds in which an oxygen atom is joined with two organic radicals. **3.** A solid or semisolid medium formerly assumed to pervade all of space: also spelled *aether*. **4.** The clear, upper regions of space: also spelled *aether*. [< L *aether* sky]

e·the·re·al (i·thir'ē·əl) *adj*. **1.** Resembling ether or air; airy. **2.** Delicate or exquisite in line, feature, etc.: an *ethereal* face. **3.** Spiritual; celestial. **4.** Of or existing in the upper regions. **5.** *Chem.* Of or pertaining to ether. — **e·the're·al·ly** *adv*. — **e·the're·al·i·ty** (-əl/ə·tē), **e·the're·al·ness** *n*.

e·the·re·al·ize (i·thir'ē·əl·īz') *v.t.* **·ized, ·iz·ing** To make ethereal; spiritualize. — **e·the're·al·i·za'tion** *n*.

e·ther·ize (ē'thə·rīz) *v.t.* **·ized, ·iz·ing** To subject to the fumes of ether; anesthetize. — **e'ther·i·za'tion** *n*.

eth·ic (eth'ik) *n*. A philosophy or system of morals; ethics. — *adj*. Ethical; moral. [< L < Gk. *ēthos* character]

eth·i·cal (eth'i·kəl) *adj*. **1.** Pertaining to or treating of ethics and morality. **2.** Conforming to right principles of conduct as accepted by a specific profession, etc. — **eth'i·cal·ly** *adv*. — **eth'i·cal·ness, eth'i·cal'i·ty** (-kal'ə·tē) *n*.

eth·ics (eth'iks) *n.pl.* (*construed as sing. in defs. 1 and 3*) **1.** The study and philosophy of human conduct, with emphasis on the determination of right and wrong. **2.** The principles of right conduct with reference to a specific profession, mode of life, etc. **3.** A treatise on morals.

E·thi·o·pi·an (ē'thē·ō'pē·ən) *adj*. Of or pertaining to Ethiopia, its people, or their language. — *n*. A native or inhabitant of Ethiopia.

E·thi·op·ic (ē'thē·op'ik, -ō'pik) *n*. A Semitic language of ancient Ethiopia. — *adj*. Ethiopian.

eth·nic (eth'nik) *adj*. **1.** Of, belonging to, or distinctive of a particular racial, cultural, or language division of mankind. **2.** Of or belonging to a people neither Jewish nor Christian; heathen. Also **eth'ni·cal.** [< Gk. < *ethnos* nation] — **eth'ni·cal·ly** *adv*.

ethno- *combining form* Race; nation; peoples. Also, before vowels, **ethn-.**

eth·nog·ra·phy (eth·nog'rə·fē) *n*. *pl.* **·phies 1.** The branch of anthropology concerned with the classification and description of regional, chiefly primitive human cultures. **2.** Loosely, ethnology. — **eth·nog'ra·pher** *n*. — **eth·no·graph·ic** (eth'nə·graf'ik) or **·i·cal** *adj*. — **eth'no·graph'i·cal·ly** *adv*.

eth·nol·o·gy (eth·nol'ə·jē) *n*. *pl.* **·gies 1.** The branch of anthropology concerned with the study of racial and ethnic groups in their origins, distribution, and cultures. **2.** Loosely, ethnography. — **eth·nol'o·gist** *n*. — **eth·no·log·ic** (eth'nə·loj'ik) or **·i·cal** *adj*. — **eth'no·log'i·cal·ly** *adv*.

eth·yl (eth'əl) *n*. *Chem.* **1.** A univalent hydrocarbon radical, C_2H_5. **2.** Any gasoline treated with tetraethyl lead to reduce knock. [< ETH(ER) + -YL] — **e·thyl·ic** (i·thil'ik) *adj*.

ethyl alcohol Ethanol.

eth·yl·ene (eth'ə·lēn) *n*. *Chem.* A colorless, flammable, gaseous hydrocarbon, C_2H_4, contained in coal gas, used as an anesthetic and in organic syntheses.

ethylene glycol *Chem.* A colorless, sweetish alcohol, $C_2H_4(OH)_2$, formed by decomposing certain ethylene compounds and used as an antifreeze, solvent, and lubricant.

ethyl ether *Chem.* A colorless, volatile, flammable liquid compound, $(C_2H_5)_2O$, having a characteristic odor, used as an anesthetic and solvent: also called *ether*.

e·ti·ol·o·gy (ē'tē·ol'ə·jē) *n*. *pl.* **·gies 1.** The science of causes or reasons. **2.** *Med.* A theory of the cause of a particular disease. **3.** The giving of a cause or reason for anything; also, the reason given. Also spelled *aetiology*. [< LL < Gk. < *aitia* cause + *logos* word, study] — **e·ti·o·log·i·cal** *adj*. — **e'ti·o·log'i·cal·ly** *adv*. — **e'ti·ol'o·gist** *n*.

et·i·quette (et'ə·ket) *n*. The rules conventionally established for behavior in polite society or in official or professional life. [< F < OF *estiquette*; orig., label]

Eton College A public school for boys in Eton, England.

E·to·ni·an (i·tō'nē·ən) *n*. One who is or has been a student at Eton College. — *adj*. Of or relating to Eton College.

Eton jacket A short jacket cut off square at the hips and generally worn with a wide, overlapping, stiff collar (the **Eton collar**), originally worn at Eton College.

E·trus·can (i·trus'kən) *adj*. Of or relating to Etruria, its people, or language. Also **E·tru'ri·an.** — *n*. **1.** One of the people of Etruria. **2.** The extinct Etruscan language.

-ette *suffix of nouns* **1.** Little; small: *kitchenette*. **2.** Resembling; imitating: *leatherette*. **3.** Feminine: *farmerette*. [< F *-ette*, fem. of *-et*, dim. suffix]

é·tude (ā'tōōd, -tyōōd; *Fr.* ā·tüd') *n*. *Music* An exercise for solo instrument or voice, designed to perfect some phase of technique. [< F. See STUDY.]

et·y·mol·o·gize (et'ə·mol'ə·jīz) *v.* **·gized, ·giz·ing** *v.t.* **1.** To give the etymology of. — *v.i.* **2.** To give an etymology.

et·y·mol·o·gy (et'ə·mol'ə·jē) *n*. *pl.* **·gies 1.** The history of a word as shown by breaking it down into basic elements or by tracing it back to the earliest known form and indicating its changes in form and meaning; also, a statement of this. **2.** The study of the derivation of words. [< F < L < Gk. < *etymon* true meaning + *logos* word, study] — **et·y·mo·log·i·cal** (et'ə·mə·loj'i·kəl) or **et'y·mo·log'ic** *adj*. — **et'y·mo·log'i·cal·ly** *adv*. — **et'y·mol'o·gist** *n*.

eu- *prefix* Good; well; easy; agreeable: *euphony*. [< Gk. *eu*]

eu·ca·lyp·tus (yōō'kə·lip'təs) *n*. *pl.* **·tus·es** or **·ti** (-tī) Any of a genus of large, chiefly Australian evergreen trees, widely used as timber and yielding a volatile, pungent oil (**oil of eucalyptus**) used in medicine. [< NL < Gk. *eu*- well + *kalyptos* covered, from the covering of the buds]

Eu·char·ist (yōō'kə·rist) *n*. **1.** A Christian sacrament in which bread and wine are consecrated and received in commemoration of the passion and death of Christ: also called *Communion, Holy Communion*. **2.** The consecrated bread and wine of this sacrament. [< OF < LL < Gk. < *eu*- well + *charizesthai* to show favor] — **Eu'cha·ris'tic** or **·ti·cal** *adj*.

eu·chre (yōō'kər) *n*. **1.** A card game for two to four players, played with 32 cards. **2.** An instance of euchring an opponent. — *v.t.* **·chred** (-kərd), **·chring 1.** In the game of euchre, to defeat (the trump-making side) by taking three tricks. **2.** *Informal* To outwit or defeat. [Origin uncertain]

Eu·clid·e·an (yōō·klid'ē·ən) *adj*. Of or relating to the geometric principles of Euclid. Also **Eu·clid'i·an.**

eu·gen·ic (yōō·jen'ik) *adj*. Of or pertaining to eugenics. Also **eu·gen'i·cal.** [< Gk. < *eu*- well + *genēs* born) + -IC] — **eu·gen'i·cal·ly** *adv*.

eu·gen·i·cist (yōō·jen'ə·sist) *n*. A specialist in or a student of eugenics. Also **eu·ge·nist** (yōō'jə·nist, yōō·jen'ist).

eu·gen·ics (yōō·jen'iks) *n.pl.* (*construed as sing.*) The science of improving the physical and mental qualities of human beings through control of the factors influencing heredity.

eu·lo·gist (yōō'lə·jist) *n*. One who eulogizes.

eu·lo·gis·tic (yōō'lə·jis'tik) *adj*. Relating to or having the nature of eulogy; laudatory. Also **eu·lo·gis'ti·cal.** — **eu'lo·gis'ti·cal·ly** *adv*.

eu·lo·gize (yōō'lə·jīz) *v.t.* **·gized, ·giz·ing** To speak or write a eulogy about; praise highly; extol. — **eu'lo·giz'er** *n*.

eu·lo·gy (yōō'lə·jē) *n*. *pl.* **·gies 1.** A spoken or written piece of high praise, esp. when delivered publicly. **2.** Great praise. [< Gk. < *eu*- well + *legein* to speak]

Eu·men·i·des (yōō·men'ə·dēz) *n.pl.* The Furies. [< Gk., the kind ones: a euphemistic name]

eu·nuch (yōō'nək) *n*. A castrated man, esp. one employed as a harem attendant or as an Oriental palace official. [< L < Gk. < *eunē* bed + *echein* to keep, guard]

eu·phe·mism (yōō'fə·miz'əm) *n*. **1.** Substitution of a mild or roundabout word or expression for another felt to be too blunt or painful. **2.** A word or expression so substituted, as "the departed" for "the dead." [< Gk. < *eu*- well + *phēmizein* < *phanai* to speak] — **eu'phe·mist** *n*. — **eu'phe·mis'tic** or **·ti·cal** *adj*. — **eu'phe·mis'ti·cal·ly** *adv*.

eu·phe·mize (yōō'fə·mīz) *v.* **·mized, ·miz·ing** *v.t. & v.i.* To speak or write of (something) by using a euphemism.

eu·phon·ic (yōō·fon'ik) *adj*. **1.** Of or relating to euphony. **2.** Agreeable in sound; euphonious. — **eu·phon'i·cal·ly** *adv*.

eu·pho·ni·ous (yōō·fō'nē·əs) *adj*. Marked by euphony; agreeable and pleasant in sound. — **eu·pho'ni·ous·ly** *adv*.

eu·pho·ni·um (yōō·fō'nē·əm) *n*. A brass instrument having a tone resembling that of a tuba but slightly higher in range.

eu·pho·ny (yōō'fə·nē) *n*. *pl.* **·nies 1.** The quality of being pleasant and agreeable in sound, as in speech or music. **2.** Progressive change in speech sounds through assimilation, allowing greater ease of pronunciation. [< Gk. < *eu*- good + *phōnē* sound]

eu·phor·bi·a (yōō·fôr'bē·ə) *n*. An herb having a milky juice and various medicinal properties: also called *spurge*. [< NL < L < Gk. *euphorbion*] — **eu·phor'bi·al** *adj*.

eu·pho·ri·a (yōō·fôr'ē·ə, -fō'rē-) *n*. A feeling of wellbeing, relaxation, and happiness. [< NL < Gk. *eu*- well + *pherein* to bear] — **eu·phor'ic** *adj*.

eu·phu·ism (yōō'fyōō·iz'əm) *n*. **1.** An artificially elegant style of speech or writing, characterized by strained similes, excessive use of alliteration and antithesis, etc. **2.** An expression or rhetorical device typical of such a style. [after *Euphues*, character created by John Lyly, English writer, 1554?-1606 < Gk. < *eu*- well + *phyein* to grow, form] — **eu'phu·ist** *n*. — **eu'phu·is·tic** *adj*. — **eu'phu·is'ti·cal·ly** *adv*.

Eur·a·sian (yōō·rā'zhən, -shən) *adj*. **1.** Pertaining to Eurasia. **2.** Of European and Asian descent. — *n*. A person of mixed European and Asian parentage.

eu·re·ka (yōō·rē'kə) *interj*. I have found (it): an exclamation of triumph or achievement. [< Gk. *heurēka*]

Eu·ro·pa (yōō·rō'pə) In Greek mythology, a Phoenician princess abducted by Zeus, in the guise of a bull, to Crete.

Eu·ro·pe·an (yōōr'ə·pē'ən) *adj*. Relating to or derived from Europe or its inhabitants. — *n*. **1.** A native or inhabitant of Europe. **2.** A person of European descent.

European Economic Community A customs union of

France, Italy, West Germany, and the Benelux nations: also called *Common Market.* Also **European Common Market.**
Eu·ro·pe·an·ize (yŏŏr′ə·pē′ən·īz) v.t. **·ized, ·iz·ing** To make European, as in culture. — **Eu/ro·pe/an·i·za/tion** n.
European plan At a hotel, the system of paying for room and service separately from the charge for meals.
eu·ro·pi·um (yŏŏ·rō′pē·əm) n. A steel-gray, malleable metallic element (symbol Eu) of the lanthanide series. See ELEMENT. [< NL < L *Europa* Europe]
eury- *combining form* broad. [< Gk. *eurys* wide]
Eu·ryd·i·ce (yŏŏ·rid′ə·sē) In Greek mythology, the wife of Orpheus. See ORPHEUS.
eu·ryth·mics (yŏŏ·rith′miks) n.pl. (*construed as sing.*) A system for developing grace and rhythm through bodily movements made in response to music: also **eu·rhyth′mics.** [< L < Gk. < *eu-* good + *rhythmos* symmetry] — **eu·ryth/mic** or **·mi·cal** adj.
Eu·sta·chi·an tube (yŏŏ·stā/kē·ən, -shē·ən, -shən) *Anat.* A passage between the pharynx and the middle ear, serving to equalize air pressure between the tympanic cavity and the atmosphere: also called *syrinx.* For illus. see EAR. [after Bartolomeo *Eustachio,* died 1574, Italian anatomist]
Eu·ter·pe (yŏŏ·tûr′pē) The Muse of lyric song and music.
eu·tha·na·si·a (yŏŏ′thə·nā′zhə, -zhē·ə) n. 1. Painless, peaceful death. 2. The deliberate putting to death painlessly of a person suffering from an incurable disease: also called *mercy killing.* [< Gk. < *eu-* easy + *thanatos* death]
eu·then·ics (yŏŏ·then′iks) n.pl. (*construed as sing.*) The science of improving the physical and mental qualities of human beings, through control of environmental factors. [< Gk. *euthenein* to thrive]
e·vac·u·ant (i·vak′yŏŏ·ənt) *Med. adj.* Cathartic or emetic. — n. An evacuant medicine, drug, etc.
e·vac·u·ate (i·vak′yŏŏ·āt) v. **·at·ed, ·at·ing** v.t. 1. *Mil.* **a** To give up or abandon possession of, as a fortress or city. **b** To move out or withdraw (troops, inhabitants, etc.) from a threatened area or place. 2. To depart from and leave vacant; vacate. 3. To remove the contents of. 4. *Physiol.* To discharge or eject, as from the bowels. — v.i. 5. To withdraw, as from a threatened area [< L < *e-* out + *vacuare* to make empty] — **e·vac/u·a/tion** n. — **e·vac/u·a/tor** n.
e·vac·u·ee (i·vak′yŏŏ·ē′) n. A person moved out or withdrawn from a destroyed or threatened area. [See EVACUATE]
e·vade (i·vād′) v. **e·vad·ed, e·vad·ing** v.t. 1. To get away from by tricks or cleverness: to *evade* pursuers. 2. To get out of or avoid: to *evade* a question. 3. To baffle; elude: The facts *evade* explanation. — v.i. 4. To dodge a question, responsibility, etc. [< L < *e-* out + *vadere* to go] — **e·vad/a·ble** or **e·vad/i·ble** adj. — **e·vad/er** n.
e·val·u·ate (i·val′yŏŏ·āt) v.t. **·at·ed, ·at·ing** To find or determine the amount, worth, etc., of. [< F < OF *valoir* to be worth] — **e·val/u·a/tion** n.
ev·a·nesce (ev′ə·nes′) v.i. **·nesced, ·nesc·ing** To disappear by degrees; vanish gradually. [< L < *e-* out + *vanescere* to vanish] — **ev/a·nes/cence** n.
ev·a·nes·cent (ev′ə·nes′ənt) adj. Passing away, or liable to pass away, gradually or imperceptibly; fleeting. — **ev/a·nes/cent·ly** adv.
e·van·gel (i·van′jəl) n. 1. The gospel. 2. *Usu. cap.* One of the four Gospels. 3. Any good news or glad tidings. [< OF < LL < Gk. < *eu-* good + *angellein* to announce]
e·van·gel·i·cal (ē′van·jel′i·kəl, ev′ən-) adj. 1. Of, relating to, or contained in the New Testament, esp. the Gospels. 2. Of, relating to, or maintaining the doctrine that the Bible is the only rule of faith. 3. Evangelistic. — n. A member of an evangelical church. Also **e·van·gel/ic.** — **e/van·gel/i·cal·ism** n. — **e/van·gel/i·cal·ly** adv.
e·van·gel·ism (i·van′jə·liz′əm) n. The zealous preaching or speaking of the gospel.
e·van·gel·ist (i·van′jə·list) n. 1. *Usu. cap.* One of the four writers of the New Testament Gospels: Matthew, Mark, Luke, or John. 2. An itinerant or missionary preacher. — **e·van/gel·is/tic** adj. — **e·van/gel·is/ti·cal·ly** adv.
e·van·gel·ize (i·van′jəl·īz) v. **·ized, ·iz·ing** v.t. 1. To preach the gospel to. 2. To convert to Christianity. — v.i. 3. To preach or act as an evangelist. — **e·van/gel·i·za/tion** n.
e·vap·o·rate (i·vap′ə·rāt) v. **·rat·ed, ·rat·ing** v.t. 1. To convert into vapor; vaporize. 2. To remove moisture or liquid from (milk, fruit, etc.) so as to dry or concentrate. — v.i. 3. To become vapor. 4. To yield vapor. 5. To vanish; disappear. [< L < *e-* out, away + *vaporare* to emit vapor] — **e·vap/o·ra·ble** adj. — **e·vap/o·ra/tive** adj. — **e·vap/o·ra/·tion** n. — **e·vap/o·ra/tor** n.
evaporated milk Unsweetened canned milk slightly thickened by removal of some of the water.
e·va·sion (i·vā′zhən) n. 1. The act of evading; esp., the act of dodging something difficult or distasteful. 2. A piece of trickery or shrewdness used in dodging a question, etc.

e·va·sive (i·vā′siv) adj. 1. Given to or characterized by evasion; not direct and frank: an *evasive* person; *evasive* promises. 2. Elusive. — **e·va/sive·ly** adv. — **e·va/sive·ness** n.
eve (ēv) n. 1. The evening before a holiday: Christmas *Eve.* 2. The time immediately preceding some event. 3. *Poetic* Evening. [Var. of EVEN²]
Eve (ēv) The first woman; wife of Adam and mother of the human race. *Gen.* iii 20. [< Hebrew *hawwah* life]
e·ven¹ (ē′vən) adj. 1. Flat and smooth; level: an *even* surface. 2. Extending to the same height or depth: a tree *even* with the housetop. 3. Extending along; parallel to: a bookcase *even* with the wall. 4. Equally distributed; uniform: an *even* coat of paint. 5. Calm and controlled: an *even* disposition. 6. Equally matched: an *even* struggle. 7. Being about the same for any one of several alternatives: The chances for success or failure are *even.* 8. Being the same (score) for each side or competitor. 9. Having accomplished exact settlement of a debt. 10. Identical in quantity, number, measure, etc.: *even* portions. 11. Exactly divisible by 2: an *even* number: opposed to *odd.* — **to break even** *Informal* To end up with neither profit nor loss, as in a business deal. — **to get even** To exact one's full measure of revenge. — adv. 1. To all the greater extent or degree; still: an *even* better plan. 2. During the very same moment: with *as: Even* as they watched, the ship sank. 3. In exactly the same way; precisely; just: with *as:* Do *even* as I do. 4. In very fact; indeed; actually: to feel glad, *even* delighted. 5. Unlikely or inconceivable as it may seem: He was kind *even* to his enemies. 6. All the way; as far as: faithful *even* to death. 7. All the same; nevertheless; notwithstanding: *Even* with that handicap, he managed to win. 8. Not otherwise than; right: It is happening *even* now. 9. *Informal* In a smooth manner; evenly: to keep things running *even.* — **even if** Although; notwithstanding. — v.t. 1. To make even: often with *up* or *off:* to *even* up accounts. — v.i. 2. To become even: often with *up* or *off.* [OE *efen*] — **e/ven·ly** adv. — **e/ven·ness** n.
e·ven² (ē′vən) n. *Archaic* Evening. [OE *æfen*]
e·ven·fall (ē′vən·fôl′) n. Early evening; twilight; dusk.
e·ven·hand·ed (ē′vən·han′did) adj. Treating all alike; impartial. — **e/ven·hand/ed·ly** adv. — **e/ven·hand/ed·ness** n.
eve·ning (ēv′ning) n. 1. The latter part of day and the first part of night. ◆ Collateral adjective: *vesperal.* 2. An evening's entertainment or activity. 3. The declining years of life, a career, etc. [OE *æfnian* to approach evening]
evening dress Formal evening wear. Also **evening clothes.**
evening gown A woman's formal dress for evening wear.
evening primrose An erect American biennial herb with conspicuous yellow flowers that open in the evening.
evening star A bright planet visible in the west just after sunset, especially Venus. Also called *Hesperus, Vesper.*
e·vent (i·vent′) n. 1. Something that takes place; a happening or an incident: the *events* of that period. 2. An actual or possible set of circumstances; a real or contingent situation: in the *event* of failure. 3. Final outcome: In the *event,* she decided not to go. 4. One of the items forming part of a variegated program of sports: the skating exhibition and other *events.* — **in any event** or **at all events** Regardless of what happens. [< OF < L < *e-* out + *venire* to come]
e·vent·ful (i·vent′fəl) adj. 1. Marked by important events: an *eventful* era. 2. Having important consequences: an *eventful* decision. — **e·vent/ful·ly** adv. — **e·vent/ful·ness** n.
e·ven·tide (ē′vən·tīd′) n. *Poetic* Evening.
e·ven·tu·al (i·ven′chŏŏ·əl) adj. Occurring or resulting in due course of time. — **e·ven/tu·al·ly** adv.
e·ven·tu·al·i·ty (i·ven′chŏŏ·al′ə·tē) n. *pl.* **·ties** A likely or possible occurrence; a conceivable outcome.
e·ven·tu·ate (i·ven′chŏŏ·āt) v.i. **·at·ed, ·at·ing** To result ultimately: His efforts *eventuated* in success.
ev·er (ev′ər) adv. 1. At any time; on any occasion: Did you *ever* see it? 2. By any possible chance: If the sun *ever* comes out, the fog will disappear. 3. In any possible or conceivable way: Do it as fast as *ever* you can. 4. At all times; invariably: They remained *ever* on guard. 5. Throughout the entire course of time; always; forever: now usually followed by *since, after,* or *afterward.* ◆ In informal speech, *ever* is often used merely to add force. Was I *ever* glad! — **ever so** *Informal* To an extremely great extent or degree: It was *ever* so pleasant. — **ever so often** *Informal* 1. Extremely often; repeatedly. 2. Now and then; every so often. — **for ever and ever** Forever: an intensive form. [OE *æfre*]
ev·er·glade (ev′ər·glād) n. A tract of low swampy land.
Everglade State Nickname of Florida.
ev·er·green (ev′ər·grēn′) adj. Having foliage that remains green until the formation of new foliage: distinguished from *deciduous.* — n. 1. An evergreen tree or plant. 2. *pl.* Evergreen branches or twigs, esp. as used for decorations.
Evergreen State Nickname of Washington.
ev·er·last·ing (ev′ər·las′ting, -läs′-) adj. 1. Existing or

lasting forever; eternal: belief in an *everlasting* God. **2.** Continuing for an indefinitely long period; perpetual: *everlasting* happiness. **3.** Incessant; interminable: her *everlasting* chatter. — *n.* **1.** Endless duration; eternity: to love for *everlasting*. **2.** One of several plants, chiefly of the aster family, whose flowers keep their form and color when dried: also called *immortelle*. — **the Everlasting** God. [ME] — **ev′·er·last′ing·ly** *adv.* — **ev′er·last′ing·ness** *n.*

ev·er·more (ev′ər·môr′, -mōr′) *adv.* *Poetic* For and at all time to come; always. — **for evermore** Forever.

e·ver·sion (i·vûr′zhən) *n.* The act of everting, or the condition of being everted. — **e·ver′si·ble** (-sə·bəl) *adj.*

e·vert (i·vûrt′) *v.t.* To turn outward or inside out. [< L < *e*- out + *vertere* to turn]

ev·er·y (ev′rē, ev′ər·ē) *adj.* **1.** Each without excepting any of all those that together form an aggregate. **2.** Each (member or unit singled out in some way) of a series: *every* tenth man. **3.** The utmost; all possible: Show him *every* consideration. — **every bit** *Informal* In all respects: He is *every bit* as good as you. — **every now and then** From time to time; occasionally. Also **every now and again**, **every once in a while**. — **every other** Each alternate (specified thing). — **every so often** *Informal* Every now and then. — **every which way** *Informal* In every way or direction and with little or no order. [ME < OE *ǣfre* ever + *ǣlc* each]₁

ev·er·y·bod·y (ev′rē·bod′ē, -bud′ē) *pron.* Every person.

eve·ry·day (ev′rē·dā′, -dā′) *adj.* **1.** Happening every day; daily. **2.** Suitable for ordinary days: *everyday* clothes. **3.** Commonplace; ordinary: *everyday* folks.

eve·ry·one (ev′rē·wun′, -wən) *pron.* Everybody.

every one Each individual person or thing out of the whole number, excepting none: *Every one* of the men is ill.

eve·ry·thing (ev′rē·thing′) *pron.* **1.** Whatever exists; all things whatsoever. **2.** Whatever is relevant, needed, or important: I have *everything*. **3.** The only thing that really matters; the essential thing: Happiness is *everything*.

eve·ry·where (ev′rē·hwâr′) *adv.* At, in, or to every place.

e·vict (i·vikt′) *v.t.* **1.** To expel (a tenant) by legal process; dispossess; put out. **2.** To recover (property, etc.) by legal process or superior claim. — **Syn.** See EXPEL. [< L < *e*- out + *vincere* to conquer] — **e·vic′tion** *n.* — **e·vic′tor** *n.*

ev·i·dence (ev′ə·dəns) *n.* **1.** That which serves to prove or disprove something; support; proof. **2.** That which serves as a ground for knowing something with certainty or for believing something with conviction; corroboration. **3.** An outward indication of the existence or fact of something: Her paleness was *evidence* of her distress. **4.** *Law* That which is properly presented before a court as a means of establishing or disproving something alleged or presumed, as the statements of witnesses. — **in evidence** In the condition of being readily seen or perceived; esp., conspicuously present. — **to turn state's evidence** To testify in court against one's accomplices. — *v.t.* **·denced**, **·denc·ing** **1.** To show unmistakably. **2.** To support by oral testimony.

ev·i·dent (ev′ə·dənt) *adj.* Easily perceived or recognized; clearly perceptible; plain. [< L < *e*- out + *videre* to see]

ev·i·den·tial (ev′ə·den′shəl) *adj.* Relating to, serving as, or based on evidence. — **ev′i·den′tial·ly** *adv.*

ev·i·dent·ly (ev′ə·dənt·lē, -dent′-, ev′ə·dent′lē) *adv.* **1.** To all appearances; apparently. **2.** Quite clearly; obviously.

e·vil (ē′vəl) *adj.* **1.** Morally bad; wicked. **2.** Causing injury or any other undesirable result. **3.** Marked by or threatening misfortune or distress: an *evil* omen. **4.** Low in public esteem: an *evil* reputation. — **the Evil One** Satan. — *n.* **1.** That which is evil; as: **a** That which is morally bad. **b** That which is injurious. **c** That which causes suffering or misfortune. **2.** Some particular act, characteristic, etc. that is evil: one of the *evils* of that political system. — *adv.* In an evil manner; badly: now chiefly in combinations: an *evil*-smelling plant. [OE *yfel*] — **e′vil·ly** *adv.* — **e′vil·ness** *n.*

e·vil-do·er (ē′vəl·dōō′ər) *n.* One who does evil. — **e′vil·do′ing** *n.*

evil eye A glance superstitiously supposed capable of inflicting misfortune or injury.

e·vil-mind·ed (ē′vəl·mīn′did) *adj.* Obsessed with vicious or depraved thoughts; esp., sexually indecent thoughts. — **e′vil-mind′ed·ly** *adv.* — **e′vil-mind′ed·ness** *n.*

e·vince (i·vins′) *v.t.* **e·vinced**, **e·vinc·ing** **1.** To indicate clearly; demonstrate convincingly. **2.** To give an outward sign of having (a quality, feeling, etc.). [< L < *e*- out + *vincere* to conquer] — **e·vin′ci·ble** *adj.* — **e·vin′cive** *adj.*

e·vis·cer·ate (*v.* i·vis′ə·rāt; *adj.* i·vis′ər·it) *v.t.* **·at·ed**, **·at·ing** **1.** To disembowel. **2.** To remove the vital part of. — *adj.* *Surg.* Disemboweled: an *eviscerate* abdomen. [< L < *e*- out + *viscera* entrails] — **e·vis′cer·a′tion** *n.*

ev·o·ca·tion (ev′ə·kā′shən) *n.* The act of evoking; a summoning, as of memories.

e·voc·a·tive (i·vok′ə·tiv, -vō′kə-) *adj.* Tending to evoke.

e·voke (i·vōk′) *v.t.* **e·voked**, **e·vok·ing** **1.** To call or summon forth, as memories. **2.** To draw forth or produce (a response, reaction, etc.). **3.** To summon up (spirits) by or as

by incantations. [< L < *e*- out + *vocare* to call] — **ev·o·ca·ble** (ev′ə·kə·bəl, i·vō′kə·bəl) *adj.*

ev·o·lu·tion (ev′ə·lōō′shən) *n.* **1.** The process of unfolding, growing, or developing, usu. by slow stages. **2.** Anything developed by such a process. **3.** *Biol.* **a** The theory that all forms of life originated by descent from earlier forms. **b** The series of changes, as by natural selection, mutation, etc., through which a given type of organism has acquired its present characteristics. **4.** One of a series of complex movements. **5.** A movement or maneuver of troops, ships, etc. **6.** The process of giving off gas, heat, sound, etc. — **ev′o·lu′tion·al**, **ev′o·lu′tion·ar·y** *adj.* — **ev′o·lu′tion·al·ly** *adv.*

ev·o·lu·tion·ist (ev′ə·lōō′shən·ist) *n.* **1.** A proponent of the theory of biological evolution. **2.** One who advocates progress through gradual stages, as in political structure. — *adj.* **1.** Evolutionary. **2.** Of or relating to evolutionists. — **ev′o·lu′tion·ism** *n.*

e·volve (i·volv′) *v.* **e·volved**, **e·volv·ing** *v.t.* **1.** To work out; develop gradually. **2.** *Biol.* To develop, as by a differentiation of parts or functions, to a more highly organized state: usu. in the passive. **3.** To give or throw off (vapor, heat, etc.). **4.** To unfold or expand. — *v.i.* **5.** To undergo the process of evolution. **6.** To develop. [< L < *e*- out + *volvere* to roll] — **e·volv′a·ble** *adj.* — **e·volve′ment** *n.*

ewe (yōō, *Dial.* yō) *n.* A female sheep. [OE *eowu*]

ew·er (yōō′ər) *n.* A large, wide-mouthed jug or pitcher for water. [ME < AF, OF < L *aqua* water]

ex (eks) *prep.* In finance, without the right to have or participate in: *ex* dividend. [< L *ex* out]

ex-¹ *prefix* **1.** Out of: *exit*, *exhale*. **2.** Thoroughly; *exasperate*. **3.** Not having; lacking. **4.** Being formerly: attached with a hyphen to the word it qualifies: *ex-president*. Also: *e*- before consonants except *c*, *f*, *p*, *q*, *s*, *t*; *ef*- before *f*. [< L *ex* from, out of]

ex-² *prefix* Out of; from; forth: *exodus*. Also, before consonants, *ec*-, as in *eclipse*. [< Gk. *ex* out]

ex-³ *Var.* of EXO-.

ex·ac·er·bate (ig·zas′ər·bāt) *v.t.* **·bat·ed**, **·bat·ing** **1.** To make more sharp or severe; aggravate (feelings, a disease, pain, etc.). **2.** To embitter or irritate (someone). [< L < *ex*- very + *acerbus* bitter, harsh] — **ex·ac′er·ba′tion** *n.*

ex·act (ig·zakt′) *adj.* **1.** Perfectly clear and complete in every detail; precise. **2.** Altogether accurate: to ask for an *exact* answer. **3.** Being precisely (what is specified): the *exact* amount necessary. **4.** Corresponding in every detail with something taken as a model. **5.** Free from vagueness; clear: *exact* thinking. **6.** Extremely careful about detail and accuracy: an *exact* editor. **7.** Designed for use where the utmost precision is required: an *exact* scientific instrument. **8.** Rigorously demanding: an *exact* schoolmaster. — *v.t.* **1.** To demand rigorously the full payment of: to *exact* full compensation for an injury. **2.** To force unjustly the payment of. **3.** To obtain by or as if by forcing out: to *exact* a full reply. **4.** To insist upon the performance or yielding of as a strict right or obligation: to *exact* obedience. **5.** To require: The situation *exacted* quick thinking. [< L < *ex*- out + *agere* to drive] — **ex·act′ness**, **ex·act′i·tude** (-i·tōōd, -i·tyōōd) *n.* — **ex·ac′tor** or **ex·act′er** *n.* — **ex·ac′tion** *n.*

ex·act·ing (ig·zak′ting) *adj.* **1.** Making rigorous demands; severe. **2.** Involving constant hard work, attention, etc. — **ex·act′ing·ly** *adv.* — **ex·act′ing·ness** *n.*

ex·act·ly (ig·zakt′lē) *adv.* **1.** In an exact manner; with great precision or accuracy. **2.** Precisely right; just so.

ex·ag·ger·ate (ig·zaj′ə·rāt) *v.* **·at·ed**, **·at·ing** *v.t.* **1.** To represent or look upon as greater than is actually the case: to *exaggerate* one's troubles. **2.** To make greater in size, intensity, etc., than what would be normal or expected. — *v.i.* **3.** To overstate or overemphasize something. [< L < *ex*- out + *agger* heap] — **ex·ag′ger·at′ed** *adj.* — **ex·ag′ger·a′tion** *n.* — **ex·ag′ger·a′tive** *adj.* — **ex·ag′ger·a′tor** *n.*

ex·alt (ig·zôlt′) *v.t.* **1.** To raise in rank, character, honor, etc. **2.** To glorify or praise. **3.** To fill with delight, pride, etc.; elate. **4.** To increase the intensity of, as colors; heighten. [< L < *ex*- out + *altus* high] — **ex·alt′ed** *adj.* — **ex·alt′ed·ly** *adv.* — **ex·alt′er** *n.*

ex·al·ta·tion (eg′zôl·tā′shən) *n.* **1.** The act of exalting, or the state of being exalted. **2.** A state or feeling of great, often extreme, exhilaration and well-being; ecstasy.

ex·am (ig·zam′) *n.* *Informal* An examination.

ex·am·i·na·tion (ig·zam′ə·nā′shən) *n.* **1.** The act of examining, or the state of being examined. **2.** Medical scrutiny and testing. **3.** A formal test of knowledge or skills; also, the questions or problems posed. — **ex·am′i·na′tion·al** *adj.*

ex·am·ine (ig·zam′in) *v.t.* **·ined**, **·in·ing** **1.** To inspect or scrutinize with care; inquire into. **2.** To subject (a person, organ, etc.) to medical scrutiny and testing. **3.** To test by questions or exercises as to qualifications, fitness, etc. **4.** To question formally in order to elicit facts, etc. [< OF < L < *ex*- out + *ag*-, root of *agere* to drive] — **ex·am′in·a·ble** *adj.* — **ex·am′in·er** *n.*

ex·am·ple (ig·zam′pəl, -zäm′-) *n.* **1.** A particular thing that belongs to and is typical of a group of things and that is singled out as a representative specimen. **2.** Something deserving imitation; model. **3.** An instance or object of punishment, reprimand, etc., designed to warn or deter others. **4.** A previous case or instance identical with or similar to something under consideration. **5.** A particular problem or exercise in arithmetic, algebra, etc. — **for example** By way of illustration. — **to set an example** To act in such a way as to arouse others to imitation. — *v.t.* **·pled, ·pling** To present an example of; exemplify: now only in the passive. [< OF < L < *ex-* out + *emere* to buy, take]

ex·as·per·ate (ig·zas′pə·rāt) *v.t.* **·at·ed, ·at·ing 1.** To make very annoyed or angry; infuriate. **2.** To make (a disagreeable condition, feeling, etc.) still worse; aggravate. — **Syn.** See OFFEND. [< L < *ex-* out + *asper* rough] — **ex·as′per·at′er** *n.* — **ex·as′per·at·ing** *adj.* — **ex·as′per·a′tion** *n.*

ex ca·the·dra (eks kə·thē′drə, kath′i-) *Latin* With authority; in one's official capacity; literally, from the chair.

ex·ca·vate (eks′kə·vāt) *v.t.* **·vat·ed, ·vat·ing 1.** To make a hole or cavity in. **2.** To form or make (a hole, tunnel, etc.) by hollowing, digging out, or scooping. **3.** To remove by digging or scooping out, as soil. **4.** To uncover by digging, as ruins; unearth. [< L < *ex-* out + *cavus* hollow] — **ex′·ca·va′tion** *n.* — **ex′ca·va′tor** *n.*

ex·ceed (ik·sēd′) *v.t.* **1.** To surpass, as in quantity or quality. **2.** To go beyond the limit or extent of: to *exceed* one's income. — *v.i.* **3.** To be superior; surpass others. [< F < L < *ex-* out, beyond + *cedere* to go]

ex·ceed·ing (ik·sē′ding) *adj.* Greater than usual. — *adv.* *Archaic* Extremely. — **ex·ceed′ing·ly** *adv.*

ex·cel (ik·sel′) *v.* **·celled, ·cel·ling** *v.t.* **1.** To surpass, usu. in some good quality or action; be better than; outstrip: to *excel* all rivals. — *v.i.* **2.** To surpass others; be outstanding. [< OF < L *excellere* to rise]

ex·cel·lence (ek′sə·ləns) *n.* **1.** The state or quality of excelling; superiority. **2.** That in which someone or something excels; a superior trait or quality. Also **ex′cel·len·cy.**

Ex·cel·len·cy (ek′sə·lən·sē) *n. pl.* **·cies** An honorary title or form of address for certain dignitaries: often preceded by *His, Her, Your,* etc.

ex·cel·lent (ek′sə·lənt) *adj.* Being of the very best quality; exceptionally good. — **ex′cel·lent·ly** *adv.*

ex·cel·si·or (ik·sel′sē·ər) *n. U.S.* Long, fine wood shavings used as stuffing or as packing material.

ex·cept (ik·sept′) *prep.* With the exclusion or omission of; aside from. — *conj.* **1.** Aside from the fact that. Also **except that.** **2.** Otherwise than. ◆ In this sense, *except* may also be construed as a preposition governing the following adverb, phrase, or clause. — **except for** If it were not for. — *v.t.* **1.** To exclude from consideration, enumeration, etc.; leave deliberately out of account. — *v.i.* **2.** To raise an objection, esp. a formal objection: now usu. with *to:* to *except* to an accusation. [< F < L < *ex-* out + *capere* to take]

ex·cept·ing (ik·sep′ting) *prep.* Barring; except.

ex·cep·tion (ik·sep′shən) *n.* **1.** The act of excepting, or the state of being excepted. **2.** Something excluded from or not conforming to a general class, principle, rule, etc. **3.** An objection or complaint; adverse criticism. **4.** *Law* A formal objection to the decision of a court during trial. — **to take exception 1.** To express disagreement. **2.** To feel resentful.

ex·cep·tion·a·ble (ik·sep′shən·ə·bəl) *adj.* Open to exception or objection. — **ex·cep′tion·a·bly** *adv.*

ex·cep·tion·al (ik·sep′shən·əl) *adj.* Being an exception; unusual or extraordinary. — **ex·cep′tion·al·ly** *adv.*

ex·cerpt (*n.* ek′sûrpt; *v.* ik·sûrpt′) *n.* An extract from a book, speech, etc. — *v.t.* To pick out and cite (a passage from a book, etc.). [< L < *ex-* out + *carpere* to pluck]

ex·cess (*n.* ik·ses′, ek′ses; *adj.* ek′ses, ik·ses′) *n.* **1.** The condition or fact of going beyond what is usual, necessary, proper, etc. **2.** An overabundance. **3.** The quantity, extent, or degree by which one thing is over and above another thing. **4.** Overindulgence, as in food or drink; intemperance. — *adj.* **1.** Being over and above what is expected or usual. **2.** Immoderate. [See EXCEED.]

ex·ces·sive (ik·ses′iv) *adj.* Going beyond what is usual, necessary, proper, etc.; extreme. — **ex·ces′sive·ly** *adv.*

excess profits Net profits exceeding the normal average for a specified period of years.

ex·change (iks·chānj′) *v.* **·changed, ·chang·ing** *v.t.* **1.** To give and receive reciprocally. **2.** To give up for something taken as a replacement. **3.** To return as unsatisfactory and get a replacement for. **4.** To transfer to another in return for the equivalent in goods or money; trade. — *v.i.* **5.** To exchange something. **6.** To be exchanged: money that *exchanges* at face value. — *n.* **1.** The act of giving or receiving one thing as equivalent for another. **2.** A giving and receiving in turn: an *exchange* of compliments. **3.** The substitution of one thing for another. **4.** That which is given or re-

ceived in trade or substitution. **5.** A place where brokers, etc., meet to buy, sell, or trade commodities or securities: stock *exchange.* **6.** A central telephone system in a part of a city or in a town. **7.** A bill of exchange; also, the system of using a bill of exchange, or the fee for it. **8.** Rate of exchange. **9.** The mutual giving and receiving of equal sums of money, as between two countries using different currencies, and allowing for differences in value. **10.** *pl.* Bills, drafts, etc., presented to a clearing-house for exchange or settlement. [< AF < LL < L *ex-* out + *cambiare* to exchange] — **ex·change′a·ble** *adj.* — **ex·change′a·bil′i·ty** *n.*

ex·cheq·uer (iks·chek′ər, eks′chek·ər) *n.* **1.** The treasury of a state, organization, etc. **2.** *Informal* One's total financial resources. [ME < OF *eschaquier* chessboard, then table marked in squares for keeping of accounts]

Ex·cheq·uer (iks·chek′ər, eks′chek·ər) *n.* The department of the British government managing the public revenue.

ex·cise¹ (*n.* ek′sīz, ik·sīz′; *v.* ik·sīz′) *n.* **1.** An indirect tax on such commodities as liquor, tobacco, etc., produced, sold, used, or transported within a country. Also **excise tax. 2.** A license fee charged for various sports, trades, etc. — *v.t.* **·cised, ·cis·ing** To levy an excise upon. [< MDu. < OF < L *ad-* to + *census* tax] — **ex·cis′a·ble** *adj.*

ex·cise² (ik·sīz′) *v.t.* **·cised, ·cis·ing 1.** To cut out, as a growth. **2.** To delete (a word, passage, etc.). [< L < *ex-* out + *caedere* to cut] — **ex·ci·sion** (ik·sizh′ən) *n.*

ex·cise·man (ik·sīz′mən) *n. pl.* **·men** (-mən) *Brit.* An officer who collects excise duties.

ex·cit·a·ble (ik·sī′tə·bəl) *adj.* **1.** Easily excited; highstrung. **2.** *Physiol.* Susceptible to stimuli. — **ex·cit′a·bil′i·ty** *n.* — **ex·cit′a·ble·ness** *n.* — **ex·cit′a·bly** *adv.*

ex·ci·tant (ik·sī′tənt, ek′sə·tənt) *n.* Something that excites or stimulates. — *adj.* Tending to excite or stimulate; stimulating: also **ex·ci′ta·tive, ex·ci′ta·to′ry** (-tôr′ē, -tō′rē).

ex·ci·ta·tion (ek′sī·tā′shən) *n.* The act of exciting, or the state of being excited; disturbance; agitation.

ex·cite (ik·sīt′) *v.t.* **·cit·ed, ·cit·ing 1.** To arouse (a feeling, reaction, etc.) into being or activity. **2.** To arouse strong feeling in; stimulate the emotions of. **3.** To provoke action in; rouse: to *excite* someone to greater endeavor. **4.** To bring about; stir up: to *excite* a riot. [< OF < L < *ex-* out + *ciere* to arouse] — **ex·cit′ed** *adj.* — **ex·cit′ed·ly** *adv.*

ex·cite·ment (ik·sīt′mənt) *n.* **1.** The state of being excited; agitation. **2.** That which excites.

ex·cit·ing (ik·sī′ting) *adj.* Causing excitement; stirring; rousing; thrilling. — **ex·cit′ing·ly** *adv.*

ex·claim (iks·klām′) *v.t. & v.i.* To cry out abruptly; speak vehemently, as in surprise or anger. [< F < L < *ex-* out + *clamare* to cry] — **ex·claim′er** *n.*

— **Syn.** *Exclaim* and *ejaculate* mean to say forcefully. *Exclaim* suggests merely vehement feeling; *ejaculate* adds a note of explosive utterance and incoherence.

ex·cla·ma·tion (eks′klə·mā′shən) *n.* **1.** The act of exclaiming. **2.** An abrupt or emphatic utterance, outcry, etc. — **ex·clam·a·to·ry** (iks·klam′ə·tôr′ē, -tō′rē) *adj.*

exclamation mark A mark (!) used in punctuation to indicate that the immediately preceding word, phrase, or sentence is an exclamation. Also **exclamation point.**

ex·clude (iks·klood′) *v.t.* **·clud·ed, ·clud·ing 1.** To keep from entering; bar. **2.** To refuse to notice, consider, or allow for; leave out. **3.** To put out; eject. [< L < *ex-* out + *claudere* to close] — **ex·clud′a·ble** *adj.* — **ex·clud′er** *n.*

ex·clu·sion (iks·kloo′zhən) *n.* **1.** The act of excluding, or the state of being excluded. **2.** That which is excluded.

ex·clu·sive (iks·kloo′siv) *adj.* **1.** Intended for or possessed by a single individual or group. **2.** Belonging to or found in a single source: an *exclusive* news story. **3.** Having no duplicate; altogether original: an *exclusive* design. **4.** Admitting or catering to only a very select group. **5.** Concentrated upon only one individual, thing, or group; complete and undivided: one's *exclusive* attention. **6.** Excluding the other or others by reason of being completely opposed or unrelated: mutually *exclusive* doctrines. **7.** Being the only one: the *exclusive* owner. **8.** Not including; not comprising: usu. with *of:* the expense *exclusive* of fees. **9.** Not including the items, dates, figures, etc., that are specified as the limits: from 1 to 10 *exclusive* (1 and 10 are not included). — **ex·clu′sive·ly** *adv.* — **ex·clu′sive·ness** *n.*

ex·cog·i·tate (iks·koj′ə·tāt) *v.t.* **·tat·ed, ·tat·ing** To think out carefully; think up; devise. [< L < *ex-* out + *cogitare* to think] — **ex·cog′i·ta′tion** *n.* — **ex·cog′i·ta′tive** *adj.*

ex·com·mu·ni·cate (*v.* eks′kə·myoo′nə·kāt; *adj. & n.* eks′kə·myoo′nə·kət) *v.t.* **·cat·ed, ·cat·ing** *Eccl.* To cut off by ecclesiastical authority from sharing in the sacraments, worship, privileges, or fellowship of a church. — *adj.* Excommunicated. — *n.* An excommunicated person. [< LL < *ex-* out + *communicare* to share] — **ex·com·mu′ni·ca·ble** *adj.* — **ex·com′mu·ni·ca′tion** *n.* — **ex·com′mu·ni·ca′tor** *n.*

ex·com·mu·ni·ca·tive (eks/kə-myōō/nə-kā/tiv, -kə-tiv) *adj.* Relating to, favoring, or effecting excommunication. Also **ex·com·mu·ni·ca·to·ry** (eks/kə-myōō/nə-kə-tôr/ē, -tō/rē).

ex·co·ri·ate (ik-skôr/ē-āt, -skŏr/ē-) *v.t.* **·at·ed, ·at·ing** 1. To tear, chafe, or burn away strips of (skin, bark, etc.). 2. To upbraid or denounce scathingly. [< L < *ex-* out, off + *corium* skin] **— ex·co/ri·a/tion** *n.*

ex·cre·ment (eks/krə-mənt) *n.* Refuse matter expelled from the body; esp., feces. **— ex·cre·men/tal** *adj.*

ex·cres·cence (iks-kres/əns) *n.* 1. An unnatural or disfiguring outgrowth, as a wart. 2. Any unnatural addition or outgrowth. 3. A natural outgrowth, as hair. [< L < *ex-* out + *crescere* to grow] **— ex·cres/cen·cy** *n.* **— ex·cres/cent** *adj.*

ex·cre·ta (iks-krē/tə) *n.pl.* Excretions, as sweat, urine, etc.

ex·crete (iks-krēt/) *v.t.* **·cret·ed, ·cret·ing** To throw off or eliminate (waste matter) by normal discharge. [< L < *ex-* out + *cernere* to separate] **— ex·cre/tion** *n.*

ex·cre·to·ry (eks/krə-tôr/ē, -tō/rē, iks-krē/tər-ē) *adj.* Relating to or adapted for excretion. Also **ex·cre·tive** (iks-krē/tiv).

ex·cru·ci·ate (iks-krōō/shē-āt) *v.t.* **·at·ed, ·at·ing** To inflict extreme pain or agony upon; rack with pain. [< L < *ex-* completely + *cruciare* to torture] **— ex·cru/ci·at·ing·ly** *adv.* **— ex·cru/ci·a/tion** *n.*

ex·cul·pate (eks/kul-pāt, ik-skul/-) *v.t.* **·pat·ed, ·pat·ing** To free from blame or prove innocent of guilt. [< EX-¹ + L *culpare* to blame] **— ex·culp·a·ble** (ik-skul/pə-bəl) *adj.* **— ex/cul·pa/tion** *n.* **— ex·cul/pa·to·ry** *adj.*

ex·cur·sion (ik-skûr/zhən, -shən) *n.* 1. A short trip, as for relaxation, sightseeing, etc. 2. A short trip on ⸰ train, etc., that is available at reduced rates. 3. A group of people making such a trip. 4. *Physics* An oscillating movement between two points; also, half of this total distance. [< L < *ex-* + *currere* to run] **— ex·cur/sion·ist** *n.*

ex·cur·sive (ik-skûr/siv) *adj.* Going in one direction and then another; rambling; discursive; digressive. **— ex·cur/sive·ly** *adv.* **— ex·cur/sive·ness** *n.*

ex·cuse (*v.* ik-skyōōz/; *n.* ik-skyōōs/) *v.t.* **·cused, ·cus·ing** 1. To ask pardon or forgiveness for (oneself). 2. To grant pardon or forgiveness to. 3. To accept or overlook: to *excuse* a child's mistakes. 4. To free from censure or blame; extenuate. 5. To release or exempt, as from a duty. 6. To allow to leave. **— to excuse oneself** 1. To ask forgiveness for oneself. 2. To ask that one be released from some duty, etc. 3. To ask for permission to leave. **— n.** 1. A statement made or a reason given as a ground for being excused. 2. A cause, factor, or circumstance that frees from blame, etc. [< OF < L < *ex-* out, away + *causa* charge, accusation] **— ex·cus/a·ble** *adj.* **— ex·cus/a·bly** *adv.*

ex·e·cra·ble (ek/sə-krə-bəl) *adj.* 1. Detestable and revolting. 2. Extremely bad. **— ex/e·cra·bly** *adv.*

ex·e·crate (ek/sə-krāt) *v.* **·crat·ed, ·crat·ing** *v.t.* 1. To call down evil upon; curse. 2. To detest; abhor. **— v.i.** 3. To utter curses. [< L < *ex-* out + *sacrare* to devote to good or evil] **— ex/e·cra/tion** *n.* **— ex/e·cra·tive, ex/e·cra·to/re** (-krə-tôr/ē, -tō/rē) *adj.* **— ex/e·cra/tor** *n.*

ex·ec·u·tant (ig-zek/yə-tənt) *n.* One who carries into effect something to be done; also, one who gives a performance.

ex·e·cute (ek/sə-kyōōt) *v.t.* **·cut·ed, ·cut·ing** 1. To follow or carry out fully. 2. To put into force, as a law. 3. To put to death legally. 4. To make (a will, deed, etc.) legal or valid. 5. To perform (something demanding skill). 6. To produce or fashion. **— Syn.** See KILL. [< L < *ex-* throughout + *sequi* to follow] **— ex/e·cut/a·ble** *adj.* **— ex/e·cut/er** *n.*

ex·e·cu·tion (ek/sə-kyōō/shən) *n.* 1. The act of executing, or the fact or condition of being executed. 2. The particular way in which something is done or performed; style or technique. 3. *Law* A judicial writ for carrying into effect a judgment or decree of a court.

ex·e·cu·tion·er (ek/sə-kyōō/shən-ər) *n.* One who executes a death sentence.

ex·e·cu·tive (ig-zek/yə-tiv) *adj.* 1. Relating or adapted to the putting into effect of plans, projects, work programs, etc. 2. Relating or adapted to the execution of laws and the administration of judgments, decrees, etc. **— n.** 1. An individual or a group managing the administrative affairs of a nation, state, or other political division. 2. An individual responsible for the management of a business, etc.

executive officer *U.S.* The principal staff officer assisting a commanding officer in units smaller than a division.

ex·e·cu·tor (ek/sə-kyōō/tər *for def. 1,* ig-zek/yə-tər *for def. 2*) *n.* 1. One who carries plans, etc., into effect. 2. *Law* One who is appointed by a testator to carry out the terms of the will. **— ex·e·cu·to·ri·al** (ig-zek/yə-tôr/ē-əl, -tō/rē-) *adj.*

ex·ec·u·to·ry (ig-zek/yə-tôr/ē, -tō/rē] *adj.* 1. Executive.

ex·ec·u·trix (ig-zek/yə-triks) *n.* *pl.* **·trix·es** or **·tri·ces** (-trī/sēz) *Law* A female executor.

ex·e·ge·sis (ek/sə-jē/sis) *n.* *pl.* **·ses** (-sēz) Critical explanation of the meaning of words and passages in a literary or Biblical work. [< Gk. *exēgeesthai* to explain] **— ex/e·get/ic** (-jet/ik) *adj.* **— ex/e·get/i·cal·ly** *adv.*

ex·e·gete (ek/sə-jēt) *n.* One skilled in critical explanation, as of the Bible. Also **ex·e·ge·tist** (ek/sə-jē/tist).

ex·em·plar (ig-zem/plər, -plär) *n.* 1. A model, pattern, or original. 2. A typical example or specimen. [< OF < LL *exemplum* a pattern]

ex·em·pla·ry (ig-zem/plər-ē) *adj.* 1. Serving as a worthy model or example. 2. Serving as a warning: *exemplary* punishment. **— ex·em/pla·ri·ly** *adv.* **— ex·em/pla·ri·ness** *n.*

ex·em·pli·fy (ig-zem/plə-fī) *v.t.* **·fied, ·fy·ing** 1. To show by example; illustrate. 2. *Law* To make an authenticated copy from. [< Med.L < L *exemplum* copy + *facere* to make] **— ex·em/pli·fi·ca/tion** *n.* **— ex·em/pli·fi·ca·tive** (-fə-kā/tiv) *adj.*

ex·empt (ig-zempt/) *v.t.* To free or excuse from some obligation to which others are subject. **— adj.** Free, clear, or excused, as from some duty, etc. **— n.** A person who is exempted. [< L < *ex-* out + *emere* to buy, take] **— ex·empt/i·ble** *adj.* **— ex·emp/tion** *n.*

ex·er·cise (ek/sər-sīz) *v.* **·cised, ·cis·ing** *v.t.* 1. To subject to drills, etc., so as to train or develop. 2. To make use of; employ. 3. To perform, as duties. 4. To exert, as influence or authority. 5. To occupy the mind or; especially, to make anxious or fretful. **— v.i.** 6. To perform exercises. **— n.** 1. A putting into use: an *exercise* of patience. 2. Activity performed for physical conditioning, etc. 3. A lesson, problem, etc., designed to train some particular function or skill. 4. *Usu. pl.* A ceremony, etc., as at a graduation. **— Syn.** See PRACTICE. [< OF < L *exercere* to practice] **— ex/er·cis/er** *n.* **— ex/er·cis/a·ble** *adj.*

ex·ert (ig-zûrt/) *v.t.* To put forth or into action, as force or influence. [< L *exserere* to thrust out] **— ex·er/tive** *adj.*

ex·er·tion (ig-zûr/shən) *n.* 1. The act of exerting some power, faculty, etc. 2. Strong action or effort; labor. [< L]

ex·e·unt (ek/sē-ənt, -sē-ōōnt) They go out: a stage direc ⸰

ex·fo·li·ate (eks-fō/lē-āt) *v.t. & v.i.* **·at·ed, ·at·ing** To separate or peel off in scales, layers, flakes, etc., as skin, bark, rock, etc. [< LL < L *ex-* off + *folium* leaf] **— ex·fo/li·a/tion** *n.* **— ex·fo/li·a·tive** *adj.*

ex·ha·la·tion (eks/hə-lā/shən, eg/zə-) *n.* 1. The act of exhaling. 2. That which is exhaled, as air.

ex·hale (eks-hāl/, ig-zāl/) *v.* **·haled, ·hal·ing** *v.i.* 1. To expel air or vapor; breathe out. 2. To pass off or rise as a vapor or emanation. **— v.t.** 3. To breathe forth or give off, as air, vapor, or an aroma. 4. To draw off; cause to evaporate. [< F < L < *ex-* out + *halare* to breathe] **— ex·hal/a·ble** *adj.*

ex·haust (ig-zôst/) *v.t.* 1. To make extremely tired. 2. ʼᴏ drain of resources, strength, etc. 3. To draw off, as gas, steam, etc., from or as from a container. 4. To empty (a container) of contents; drain. 5. To study, treat of, or develop thoroughly. **— v.i.** 6. To escape, as a waste gas, steam, etc. **— n.** 1. The escape or discharge of waste gases, working fluid, etc.; also, the waste gases, etc., that escape. 2. A pipe or other engine part through which waste gases, etc., escape. 3. Creation of a partial vacuum to suck out stale air, dust, etc., as from a room; also, a device to do this. [< L < *ex-* out + *haurire* to draw] **— ex·haust/i·ble** *adj.* **— ex·haust/i·bil/i·ty** *n.*

ex·haust·ed (ig-zôs/tid) *adj.* 1. Entirely used up; drained; spent. 2. Extremely tired. **— ex·haust/ed·ly** *adv.*

ex·haust·ing (ig-zôs/ting) *adj.* Extremely tiring; most fatiguing; wearying. **— ex·haust/ing·ly** *adv.*

ex·haus·tion (ig-zôs/chən) *n.* 1. Extreme fatigue; utter weariness. 2. The condition of being completely used up.

ex·haus·tive (ig-zôs/tiv) *adj.* 1. That exhausts or tends to exhaust; exhausting. 2. Thoroughly; comprehensive. **— ex·haus/tive·ly** *adv.* **— ex·haus/tive·ness** *n.*

ex·hib·it (ig-zib/it) *v.t.* 1. To put on view, esp. publicly. 2. To make evident; reveal. 3. *Law* To submit (evidence, etc.) formally or officially to a court or officer. **— v.i.** 4. To put something on display. **— n.** 1. A putting on view; display. 2. An object or objects displayed, as at a fair. 3. *Law* An object submitted as a piece of evidence. [< L < *ex-* out + *habere* to hold, have] **— ex·hib/i·tive, ex·hib/i·to/ry** *adj.* **— ex·hib/i·tor, ex·hib/it·er** *n.*

ex·hi·bi·tion (ek/sə-bish/ən) *n.* 1. The act of exhibiting. 2. That which is exhibited. 3. A public display of art works.

ex·hi·bi·tion·ism (ek/sə-bish/ən-iz/əm) *n.* 1. A tendency to attract attention to oneself. 2. *Psychiatry* The tendency to obtain sexual gratification by public exposure of one's body or genitalia. **— ex/hi·bi/tion·ist** *n.*

ex·hil·a·rant (ig-zil/ər-ənt) *adj.* Causing exhilaration. **— n.** Something that exhilarates.

ex·hil·a·rate (ig-zil/ə-rāt) *v.t.* **·rat·ed, ·rat·ing** To set aglow with happiness or elation; make cheerful. [< L < *ex-* completely + *hilarare* to gladden] **— ex·hil/a·ra/tion** *n.* **— ex·hil/a·ra/tor** *n.* **— ex·hil/a·ra/tive** *adj.*

ex·hort (ig-zôrt/) *v.t.* 1. To urge by earnest appeal or argument; advise or recommend strongly. **— v.i.** 2. To utter or give exhortation. [< L < *ex-* completely + *hortari* to urge] **— ex·hor·ta·tion** (eg/zôr·tā/shən, ek/sôr-) *n.* **— ex·hor/ta·tive** (-tə-tiv), **ex·hor/ta·to·ry** (-tôr/ē) *adj.* **— ex·hort/er** *n.*

ex·hume (ig·zyōōm′, iks·hyōōm′) v.t. **·humed, ·hum·ing** 1. To dig up; disinter. 2. To bring to light; reveal. [< F < L ex- out + humus ground] — **ex·hu·ma·tion** (eks′hyŏŏ·mā′·shən) n. — **ex·hum′er** n.

ex·i·gen·cy (ek′sə·jən·sē) n. pl. **·cies** 1. Urgency. 2. A situation that requires immediate attention. 3. Usu. pl. A pressing need or necessity. Also **ex′i·gence.**

ex·i·gent (ek′sə·jənt) adj. 1. Urgent. 2. Requiring or exacting a great deal; unreasonably demanding. [< L < ex- out + agere to drive] — **ex′i·gent·ly** adv.

ex·ig·u·ous (ig·zig′yŏŏ·əs, ik·sig′-) adj. Small; scanty. [< L exiguus scanty] — **ex·i·gu·i·ty** (ek′sə·gyŏŏ′ə·tē) n.

ex·ile (eg′zīl, ek′sīl) n. 1. Separation by necessity or choice from one's native country, home, etc. 2. One who is separated from his native country, home, etc. — v.t. **·iled, ·il·ing** To cause (a person) to leave and stay away from (the person's) native country, home, etc. [< OF < L exsilium]

ex·ist (ig·zist′) v.i. 1. To have actual being or reality; be. 2. To continue to live or be. 3. To be present; occur. [< F < L < ex- out + sistere to be located] — **ex·is′tent** adj. & n.

ex·is·tence (ig·zis′təns) n. 1. The state or fact of being or continuing to be. 2. Possession or continuance of animate being; life. 3. Way or mode of living. 4. Presence; occurrence. 5. Anything or all that exists. — **ex′is·ten′tial** (-ten′shəl) adj. — **ex′is·ten′tial·ly** adv.

ex·is·ten·tial·ism (eg′zis·ten′shəl·iz′əm) n. A philosophy that stresses the active role of the will rather than of reason in confronting problems posed by a hostile universe. — **ex′·is·ten′tial·ist** adj. & n.

ex·it (eg′zit, ek′sit) n. 1. A way or passage out; egress. 2. The departure of an actor from the stage. 3. Any departure. — v.i. To go out; depart. [< L < ex- out + ire to go]

ex li·bris (eks lī′bris, lē′-) Latin. 1. From the books (of): used as an inscription on a book. 2. A bookplate.

exo- combining form Out; outside; external: exocarp. Also, before vowels, **ex-.** [< Gk. exo-, ex- < exō outside]

ex·o·carp (ek′sō·kärp) n. Bot. The epicarp.

ex·o·derm (ek′sō·dûrm) See ECTODERM.

ex·o·dus (ek′sə·dəs) n. A going forth. — **the Exodus** The departure of the Israelites from Egypt under the guidance of Moses, described in **Exodus**, the second book of the Old Testament. [< L < Gk. < ex- out + hodos way]

ex of·fi·ci·o (eks ə·fish′ē·ō) Latin. By virtue of or because of office or position.

ex·og·a·my (eks·og′ə·mē) n. The custom of marriage outside the tribe, family, clan, etc. — **ex·og′a·mous** adj.

ex·o·gen (ek′sō·jen) n. Bot. A plant that increases in size by successive concentric additions beneath the bark. [< EXO- + -GEN] — **ex·og·e·nous** (eks·oj′ə·nəs) adj.

ex·on·er·ate (ig·zon′ə·rāt) v.t. **·at·ed, ·at·ing** 1. To free from accusation or blame. 2. To relieve or free from a responsibility or the like. [< L < ex- out, away + onus, oneris burden] — **ex·on′er·a′tion** n. — **ex·on′er·a′tive** adj.

ex·oph·thal·mos (ek′sof·thal′məs) n. Pathol. Abnormal protrusion of the eyeball. Also **ex′oph·thal′mi·a** (-mē·ə), **ex′oph·thal′mus.** [< NL < Gk. < ex- out + ophthalmos eye] — **ex′oph·thal′mic** adj.

ex·or·bi·tant (ig·zôr′bə·tənt) adj. Going beyond usual and proper limits, as in price or demand; excessive; extravagant. [< LL exorbitare to go astray] — **ex·or′bi·tance, ex·or′bi·tan·cy** n. — **ex·or′bi·tant·ly** adv.

ex·or·cise (ek′sôr·sīz) v.t. **·cised, ·cis·ing** 1. To cast out (an evil spirit) by prayers or incantations. 2. To free (a person, place, etc.) of an evil spirit. Also **ex′or·cize.** [< OF < LL < Gk. < ex- out + horkos oath] — **ex′or·cis′er, ex′or·cist** n. — **ex·or·cism** (ek′sôr·siz′əm) n.

ex·or·di·um (ig·zôr′dē·əm, ik·sôr′-) n. pl. **·di·ums** or **·di·a** (-dē·ə) The beginning or introductory part of anything, esp. of a discourse, treatise, etc. [< L < ex- out + ordiri to begin] — **ex·or′di·al** adj.

ex·o·sphere (ek′sō·sfir) n. Meteorol. The region of the earth's atmosphere beginning at about 400 miles up.

ex·ot·ic (ig·zot′ik) adj. 1. Belonging by nature or origin to another part of the world; not native. 2. Strangely different and fascinating. — n. Something exotic. [< L < Gk. exōtikos foreign] — **ex·ot′i·cal·ly** adv. — **ex·ot′i·cism** n.

ex·pand (ik·spand′) v.t. 1. To increase the range, scope, volume, size, etc. 2. To spread out by unfolding; open. 3. To develop more fully the details or form of. — v.i. 4. To grow larger, wider, etc. [< L < ex- out + pandere to spread] — **ex·pand′er** n.

ex·panse (ik·spans′) n. 1. A wide, continuous area or stretch. 2. Expansion. [See EXPAND.]

ex·pan·si·ble (ik·span′sə·bəl) adj. Capable of being expanded. — **ex·pan′si·bil′i·ty** n.

ex·pan·sion (ik·span′shən) n. 1. The act of expanding, or the state of being expanded. 2. The amount of increase in size, range, volume, etc. 3. That which is expanded.

ex·pan·sive (ik·span′siv) adj. 1. Capable of expanding or tending to expand. 2. Characterized by expansion; broad; extensive. 3. Open and effusive; outgoing. — **ex·pan′sive·ly** adv. — **ex·pan′sive·ness** n.

ex·pa·ti·ate (ik·spā′shē·āt) v.i. **·at·ed, ·at·ing** To speak or write at length; elaborate: with on. [< L < ex- out + spatiari to walk] — **ex·pa′ti·a′tion** n. — **ex·pa′ti·a′tor** n.

ex·pa·tri·ate (v. eks·pā′trē·āt; n. & adj. eks·pā′trē·it, -āt) v.t. **·at·ed, ·at·ing** To exile; banish. — n. An expatriated person. — adj. Banished; expatriated. [< Med.L < L ex- out + patria native land] — **ex·pa′tri·a′tion** n.

ex·pect (ik·spekt′) v.t. 1. To look forward to as certain or probable. 2. To look for as right, proper, or necessary. 3. Informal To presume; suppose. [< L < ex- out + spectare to look at] — **ex·pec′ta·ble** adj.

ex·pec·tan·cy (ik·spek′tən·sē) n. pl. **·cies** 1. The action or state of expecting. 2. An object of expectation.

ex·pec·tant (ik·spek′tənt) adj. 1. Having expectations. 2. Awaiting the birth of a child. — **ex·pec′tant·ly** adv.

ex·pec·ta·tion (ek′spek·tā′shən) n. 1. The action of expecting, or the state of mind of one who expects; anticipation. 2. The state of being expected: preceded by in. 3. Something expected or looked forward to.

ex·pect·ing (ik·spek′ting) adj. Pregnant; also, due to give birth: She is expecting?; She is expecting in July.

ex·pec·to·rant (ik·spek′tər·ənt) adj. Promoting expectoration. — n. A medicine used to promote expectoration.

ex·pec·to·rate (ik·spek′tə·rāt) v.t. & v.i. **·rat·ed, ·rat·ing** 1. To discharge (phlegm, etc.) by spitting. 2. To spit. [< L < ex- out + pectus, -oris breast] — **ex·pec′to·ra′tion** n.

ex·pe·di·en·cy (ik·spē′dē·ən·sē) n. pl. **·cies** 1. The state or quality of being expedient. 2. That which is expedient. 3. Adherence to what is opportune or politic, not for what is just or right. Also **ex·pe′di·ence.**

ex·pe·di·ent (ik·spē′dē·ənt) adj. 1. Serving to promote a desired end; suitable, advisable, or proper. 2. Pertaining to or prompted by utility, interest, or advantage rather than by what is right. — n. 1. Something expedient. 2. A device; shift. [< OF < L expedire to free the feet from fetters]

ex·pe·dite (ek′spə·dīt) v.t. **·dit·ed, ·dit·ing** 1. To speed up the process or progress of; facilitate. 2. To do with quick efficiency. [< L expedire to free the feet from fetters]

ex·pe·dit·er (ek′spə·dī′tər) n. One who facilitates the delivery of needed material. Also **ex′pe·di′tor.**

ex·pe·di·tion (ek′spə·dish′ən) n. 1. A journey or march for a definite purpose. 2. The body of persons engaged in such a journey, together with their equipment. 3. Speed.

ex·pe·di·tion·ar·y (ek′spə·dish′ən·er′ē) adj. Relating to, designed for, or constituting an expedition.

ex·pe·di·tious (ek′spə·dish′əs) adj. Quick; speedy. — **ex′·pe·di′tious·ly** adv. — **ex′pe·di′tious·ness** n.

ex·pel (ik·spel′) v.t. **·pelled, ·pel·ling** 1. To drive out by force. 2. To force to end attendance at a school, terminate membership, etc.: oust. [< L < ex- out + pellere to drive, thrust] — **ex·pel′la·ble** adj.

— **Syn.** A school expels an unruly pupil; water in the lungs must be promptly expelled. A rifle ejects a shell automatically; a squid ejects an inky fluid. To dislodge is to move something heavy from its place; an avalanche may dislodge a large boulder. A man is evicted from his house; an official is ousted from office; an employee is dismissed from his job.

ex·pend (ik·spend′) v.t. To pay out or spend; use up. [< L < ex- out + pendere to weigh, pay]

ex·pend·a·ble (ik·spen′də·bəl) adj. 1. Available for spending. 2. Mil. Denoting supplies or equipment that can be sacrificed. — **ex·pend′a·bil′i·ty** n.

ex·pen·di·ture (ik·spen′də·chər) n. 1. The act of expending; outlay. 2. That which is expended; expense.

ex·pense (ik·spens′) n. 1. Outlay or consumption of money. 2. The amount of money required to buy or do something. 3. Something that requires or involves the spending of money. 4. pl. Funds allotted or spent to cover incidental costs. 5. Loss or injury involved in doing something: preceded by at. [See EXPEND.]

ex·pen·sive (ik·spen′siv) adj. Involving much expense; costly. — **ex·pen′sive·ly** adv. — **ex·pen′sive·ness** n.

ex·pe·ri·ence (ik·spir′ē·əns) n. 1. Actual participation in or direct contact with something. 2. A particular activity or occurrence actually participated in. 3. Knowledge or skill derived from actual participation or training. 4. The period of such activity. 5. The totality of one's judgments or reactions. 6. The accumulated variety of whatever has been actually met with or engaged in: the entire experience of mankind. — v.t. **·enced, ·enc·ing** To be personally involved in; undergo. [< OF < L < experiri to try out]

ex·pe·ri·enced (ik·spir′ē·ənst) adj. 1. Having had considerable experience. 2. Made skillful or proficient through actual practice, etc.

ex·pe·ri·en·tial (ik·spir′ē·en′shəl) *adj.* Pertaining to or acquired by experience; empirical. — **ex·pe′ri·en′tial·ly** *adv.*

ex·per·i·ment (ik·sper′ə·mənt, -ment) *n.* **1.** An act or operation designed to discover, test, or illustrate a truth, principle, or effect. **2.** The conducting of such operations. — *v.i.* To make experiments; make a test or trial. [< OF < L *experiri* to try out] — **ex·per′i·ment′er** *n.*

ex·per·i·men·tal (ik·sper′ə·men′təl) *adj.* **1.** Pertaining to, resulting from, or known by experiment. **2.** Growing out of or based on experience; empirical. **3.** Having the nature of an experiment; provisional; tentative. — **ex·per′i·men′tal·ism** *n.* — **ex·per′i·men′tal·ist** *n.* — **ex·per′i·men′tal·ly** *adv.*

ex·per·i·men·ta·tion (ik·sper′ə·men·tā′shən) *n.* The act or practice of experimenting.

ex·pert (*n.* ek′spûrt; *for adj. also* ik·spûrt′) *n.* One who has special skill or knowledge; a specialist. — *adj.* **1.** Skillful as the result of training or experience. **2.** Characteristic of or produced by an expert. [< OF < L *expertus*, pp. of *experiri* to try out] — **ex·pert′ly** *adv.* — **ex·pert′ness** *n.*

ex·pi·ate (ek′spē·āt) *v.t.* **·at·ed, ·at·ing** To atone for; make amends for. [< L < *ex-* completely + *piare* to appease] — **ex′pi·a·ble** *adj.* — **ex′pi·a′tion** *n.* — **ex′pi·a′tor** *n.*

ex·pi·a·to·ry (eks′pē·ə·tôr′ē, -tō′rē) *adj.* Having the power or character of an expiation; offered in atonement.

ex·pi·ra·tion (ek′spə·rā′shən) *n.* **1.** The termination of anything; close. **2.** The act of breathing out air from the lungs.

ex·pire (ik·spīr′) *v.* **·pired, ·pir·ing** *v.i.* **1.** To come to an end, as a contract. **2.** To breathe out air from the lungs; exhale. **3.** To breathe one's last breath; die. **4.** To die out, as embers. — *v.t.* **5.** To breathe out from the lungs. [< F < L < *ex-* out + *spirare* to breathe] — **ex·pir′a·to·ry** *adj.*

ex·plain (ik·splān′) *v.t.* **1.** To make plain or understandable. **2.** To give the meaning of; interpret; expound. **3.** To give reasons for; account for. — *v.i.* **4.** To give an explanation. [< L < *ex-* out + *planare* to make level] — **ex·plain′a·ble** *adj.*

ex·pla·na·tion (ek′splə·nā′shən) *n.* **1.** The act or process of explaining. **2.** A statement that clarifies or accounts for something. **3.** The meaning assigned or adduced to explain something; sense; significance.

ex·plan·a·to·ry (ek·splan′ə·tôr′ē, -tō′rē) *adj.* Serving to explain. Also **ex·plan′a·tive.** — **ex·plan′a·to′ri·ly** *adv.*

ex·ple·tive (eks′plə·tiv) *n.* **1.** An exclamation, often profane. **2.** A word or syllable added solely for the completion of a syntactic pattern. — *adj.* Added merely to fill out a sentence, complete a rhythm, etc.: also **ex′ple·to′ry** (-tôr′ē, -tō′rē). [< LL < L < *ex-* completely + *plere* to fill]

ex·pli·ca·ble (eks′pli·kə·bəl, ik·splik′ə·bəl) *adj.* Capable of explanation.

ex·pli·cate (eks′plə·kāt) *v.t.* **·cat·ed, ·cat·ing** To clear from obscurity; explain. [< L < *ex-* out + *plicare* to fold] — **ex′pli·ca′tion** *n.* — **ex′pli·ca′tor** *n.*

ex·pli·ca·tive (eks′plə·kā′tiv, ik·splik′ə·tiv) *adj.* Serving to interpret or explain. Also **ex′pli·ca·to′ry** (-kə·tôr′ē).

ex·plic·it (ik·splis′it) *adj.* **1.** Plainly expressed; clear. **2.** Unreserved in expression; straightforward. [See EXPLICATE.] — **ex·plic′it·ly** *adv.* — **ex·plic′it·ness** *n.*

ex·plode (ik·splōd′) *v.* **·plod·ed, ·plod·ing** *v.t.* **1.** To cause to burst or blow up violently and with noise; detonate. **2.** To disprove utterly; refute. **3.** To cause to expand violently or pass suddenly from a solid to a gaseous state. — *v.i.* **4.** To burst into pieces or fragments; blow up. **5.** To make a noise as if bursting: to *explode* with laughter. **6.** To be exploded, as gunpowder. [< L < *ex-* out + *plaudere* to clap]

ex·ploit (*n.* eks′ploit, ik·sploit′; *v.* ik·sploit′) *n.* A deed or act, esp. one marked by heroism or daring; feat. — *v.t.* **1.** To use meanly for one's own gain or advantage: to *exploit* workers. **2.** To utilize for profitable ends: to *exploit* water power. [See EXPLICATE.] — **ex·ploit′a·ble** *adj.* — **ex′ploi·ta′tion** *n.* — **ex·ploit′a·tive** *n.* — **ex·ploi′ter** *n.*

ex·plo·ra·tion (eks′plə·rā′shən) *n.* The act of exploring; esp., the exploring of unfamiliar or unknown regions.

ex·plor·a·to·ry (ik·splôr′ə·tôr′ē, ik·splō′rə·tō′rē) *adj.* Of, for, or relating to exploration. Also **ex·plor′a·tive.**

ex·plore (ik·splôr′, -splōr′) *v.* **·plored, ·plor·ing** *v.t.* **1.** To subject to a close search or examination; scrutinize carefully. **2.** To travel through (unfamiliar territory, etc.). — *v.i.* **3.** To make an exploration. [< L < *ex-* out + *plorare* to cry out] — **ex·plor′er** *n.*

ex·plo·sion (ik·splō′zhən) *n.* **1.** The act of exploding. **2.** The sudden, loud noise produced by exploding. **3.** A sudden, violent outbreak of feeling: an *explosion* of laughter.

ex·plo·sive (ik·splō′siv) *adj.* **1.** Pertaining to or marked by explosion. **2.** Liable to explode or to cause explosion. — *n.* Any substance or mixture of substances that, on impact or by ignition, reacts by a violent expansion of gases and the liberation of relatively large amounts of thermal energy. — **ex·plo′sive·ly** *adv.* — **ex·plo′sive·ness** *n.*

ex·po·nent (ik·spō′nənt; *for def. 3, also* ek′spō·nənt) *n.* **1.** One who or that which explains or expounds. **2.** One who or that which represents or symbolizes something: an *expo-*

nent of fair play. **3.** *Math.* A number or symbol placed as a superscript to the right of a quantity to indicate a power or the reciprocal or root of a power: 2 is an *exponent* in 3^2. [< L < *ex-* out + *ponere* to place]

ex·port (*v.* ik·spôrt′, -spōrt′, eks′pôrt, -pōrt; *n. & adj.* eks′-pôrt, -pōrt) *v.t.* To carry or send, as merchandise or raw materials, to other countries for sale or trade. — *n.* **1.** The act of exporting. **2.** That which is exported, as a commodity. — *adj.* Of or pertaining to exports or exportation. [< L < *ex-* out + *portare* to carry] — **ex·port′a·ble** *adj.* — **ex·port′a·bil′i·ty** *n.* — **ex′por·ta′tion** *n.* — **ex·port′er** *n.*

ex·pose (ik·spōz′) *v.t.* **·posed, ·pos·ing 1.** To lay open to criticism, ridicule, etc.: to *expose* oneself to scorn. **2.** To lay open to some force, influence, etc.: to *expose* a mixture to heat. **3.** To present to view by baring: to *expose* one's shoulders. **4.** To reveal (something evil, disgraceful, etc.): to *expose* a crime. **5.** To reveal the identity of (an evildoer, criminal, etc.); unmask. **6.** To place so as to cause the death of by cold, starvation, etc. **7.** *Photog.* To admit light to (a sensitized film or plate). [< MF < *ex-* out + *poser.* See POSE¹.] — **ex·pos′er** *n.*

ex·po·sé (ek′spō·zā′) *n.* A making known publicly of something evil or disgraceful. [< F, pp. of *exposer*]

ex·po·si·tion (eks′pə·zish′ən) *n.* **1.** The act of presenting, explaining, or expounding facts or ideas. **2.** A detailed presentation of subject matter; also, a commentary or interpretation. **3.** A large public display or show.

ex·pos·i·tor (ik·spoz′ə·tər) *n.* One who expounds.

ex·pos·i·to·ry (ik·spoz′ə·tôr′ē, -tō′rē) *adj.* Of or pertaining to exposition; explanatory. Also **ex·pos′i·tive.**

ex post fac·to (eks pōst fak′tō) *Latin* Arising or enacted after some act, occurrence, etc., and having retroactive effect: said esp. of a law.

ex·pos·tu·late (ik·spos′chŏŏ·lāt) *v.i.* **·lat·ed, ·lat·ing** To reason earnestly with a person concerning the inadvisability of his actions, etc.; remonstrate: usu. with *with.* [< L < *ex-* out + *postulare* to demand] — **ex·pos′tu·la′tion** *n.* — **ex·pos′tu·la′tor** *n.* — **ex·pos′tu·la·to′ry** (-lə·tôr′ē, -tō′rē), **ex·pos′tu·la′tive** *adj.*

ex·po·sure (ik·spō′zhər) *n.* **1.** The act of exposing, or the state of being exposed. **2.** Situation in relation to the sun, elements, or points of the compass: a room with southern *exposure.* **3.** *Photog.* **a** The act of subjecting a sensitized plate or film to the action of actinic rays. **b** The time required for this. **c** A single film or plate so acted upon.

ex·pound (ik·spound′) *v.t.* **1.** To set forth in detail; state; declare. **2.** To explain the meaning of; interpret. [< OF < L < *ex-* out + *ponere* to place] — **ex·pound′er** *n.*

ex·press (ik·spres′) *v.t.* **1.** To formulate in words; verbalize; state: to *express* an idea. **2.** To give an outward indication of; reveal: to *express* anger by frowning. **3.** To communicate through some medium other than words or signs. **4.** To indicate by means of a symbol, formula, etc., as in mathematics or chemistry. **5.** To squeeze out (a liquid, juice, etc.); press out. **6.** *U.S.* To send (goods, etc.) by special messenger or a system of rapid delivery. — **to express oneself 1.** To communicate one's thoughts. **2.** To give vent to one's feelings, desires, etc., through creative activity. — *adj.* **1.** Communicated or indicated in a clear and unmistakable way; explicit. **2.** Made or intended for a precise purpose. **3.** Designed for or operating at high speed: an *express* highway; an *express* train. **4.** Of or relating to a system of rapid delivery of goods, etc., as by railway: to send something by *express* delivery. **5.** Exact; precise. — *adv.* By rapid delivery: to send something *express.* — *n.* **1.** A system designed to convey goods, parcels, money, etc., rapidly from one point to another. **2.** Goods, parcels, etc., conveyed by this system. **3.** Any means of rapid conveyance. **4.** A company specializing in the rapid conveyance of goods, parcels, etc. **5.** A train or other conveyance operating at high speed and making few stops. **6.** A message sent with speed. [< OF < L < *ex-* out + *pressare* to press] — **ex·press′er** *n.* — **ex·press′i·ble** *adj.*

ex·press·age (ik·spres′ij) *n.* **1.** The transportation of goods by express. **2.** The charge for this.

ex·pres·sion (ik·spresh′ən) *n.* **1.** Communication of thought, opinion, etc. **2.** Outward indication or manifestation of some feeling, condition, quality, etc. **3.** A conventional sign or set of signs used to indicate something; symbolization. **4.** A particular cast of the features that expresses a feeling, meaning, etc. **5.** The particular way in which one expresses oneself. **6.** The quality of expressing oneself with understanding, insight, sensitivity, etc. **7.** A particular word, phrase, etc., used in communication. **8.** The kind of language used in communication: poetic *expression.* **9.** The action of pressing or squeezing out juice, etc.

ex·pres·sion·ism (ik·spresh′ən·iz′əm) *n.* An early 20th-century movement in the arts, originating in Europe, that had as its object the free expression of the inner experience of the artist rather than realistic representation. — **ex·pres′sion·ist** *n. & adj.* — **ex·pres′sion·is′tic** *adj.*

ex·pres·sive (ik-spres′iv) *adj.* **1.** Of or characterized by expression. **2.** Serving to express or indicate: a manner *expressive* of contempt. **3.** Significant: an *expressive* sigh. — **ex·pres′sive·ly** *adv.* — **ex·pres′sive·ness** *n.*

ex·press·ly (ik-spres′lē) *adv.* **1.** With definitely stated intent or application. **2.** Exactly and unmistakably; plainly.

ex·press·way (ik-spres′wā′) *n.* A road for rapid travel.

ex·pro·pri·ate (eks-prō′prē-āt) *v.t.* **·at·ed, ·at·ing 1.** To take or transfer (property) from the owner, esp. for public use. **2.** To deprive (a person) of ownership or property. [< LL < L *ex-* out + *proprium* property < *proprius* one's own] — **ex·pro′pri·a′tion** *n.* — **ex·pro′pri·a′tor** *n.* — **ex·pro′pri·a·to′ry** (-ə-tôr′ē, -tō′rē) *adj.*

ex·pul·sion (ik-spul′shən) *n.* **1.** The act of expelling. **2.** The state or fact of being expelled. — **ex·pul′sive** *adj.*

ex·punge (ik-spunj′) *v.t.* **·punged, ·pung·ing** To erase or wipe out. [< L < *ex-* out + *pungere* to prick]

ex·pur·gate (eks′pər-gāt, ik-spûr′gāt) *v.t.* **·gat·ed, ·gat·ing 1.** To take out obscene or otherwise objectionable material from: to *expurgate* a novel. **2.** To remove or omit (objectionable words, lines, etc.). [< L < *ex-* out + *purgare* to cleanse] — **ex′pur·ga′tion** *n.* — **ex′pur·ga′tor** *n.* — **ex·pur′ga·to′ry** *adj.*

ex·qui·site (eks′kwi·zit, ik·skwiz′it) *adj.* **1.** Marked by rare and delicate beauty, craftsmanship, etc. **2.** Being of a high degree of excellence; consummate; admirable: an *exquisite* skill. **3.** Highly sensitive to sounds, colors, forms, etc.; discriminating: an *exquisite* eye for design. **4.** Extremely refined; very fastidious. **5.** Intensely keen or acute, as pleasure or pain. — *n.* A person, usu. a man, who is overelegant in dress, manners, etc. [< L < *ex-* out + *quaerere* to seek] — **ex′qui·site·ly** *adv.* — **ex′qui·site·ness** *n.*

ex·tant (ek′stənt, ik·stant′) *adj.* Still existing; not lost nor destroyed; surviving. [< L < *ex-* out + *stare* to stand]

ex·tem·po·ra·ne·ous (ik·stem′pə·rā′nē·əs) *adj.* **1.** Uttered, performed, or composed with little or no advance preparation: an *extemporaneous* talk. **2.** Prepared with regard to content but not read or memorized word for word: an *extemporaneous* political speech. **3.** Made with anything immediately available; improvised to meet circumstances. [< LL < L *ex-* out + *tempus, temporis* time] — **ex·tem′po·ra·ne·ous·ly** *adv.* — **ex·tem′po·ra·ne·ous·ness** *n.*

ex·tem·po·rar·y (ik·stem′pə·rer′ē) *adj.* Extemporaneous. — **ex·tem′po·rar′i·ly** *adv.* — **ex·tem′po·rar′i·ness** *n.*

ex·tem·po·re (ik·stem′pə·rē) *adj.* Extemporaneous. — *adv.* With little or no advance preparation; extemporaneously. [< L *ex tempore* out of the time]

ex·tem·po·rize (ik·stem′pə·rīz) *v.t.* & *v.i.* **·rized, ·riz·ing** To do, make or perform with little or no advance preparation. — **ex·tem′po·ri·za′tion** *n.* — **ex·tem′po·riz′er** *n.*

ex·tend (ik·stend′) *v.t.* **1.** To open or stretch to full length. **2.** To make longer. **3.** To prolong; continue. **4.** To spread out; expand. **5.** To hold out or put forth, as the hand. **6.** To give or offer to give: to *extend* hospitality. — *v.i.* **7.** To be extended; stretch. — **Syn.** See INCREASE. [< L < *ex-* out + *tendere* to stretch] — **ex·tend′ed** *adj.* — **ex·tend′i·bil′i·ty** *n.* — **ex·tend′i·ble** *adj.*

ex·ten·si·ble (ik·sten′sə·bəl) *adj.* Capable of being extended. — **ex·ten′si·bil′i·ty** *n.*

ex·ten·sion (ik·sten′shən) *n.* **1.** The act of extending, or the state of being extended. **2.** An extended part; addition. **3.** Range; extent. **4.** An agreement by which a creditor allows a debtor further time in which to pay a debt. **5.** *Physics* That property of matter by virtue of which it occupies space. — **ex·ten′sion·al** *adj.*

ex·ten·sive (ik·sten′siv) *adj.* **1.** Large in area: an *extensive* farm. **2.** Having a wide range; broad in scope: *extensive* experience. **3.** Widespread; far-reaching: *extensive* damage. — **ex·ten′sive·ly** *adv.* — **ex·ten′sive·ness** *n.*

ex·ten·sor (ik·sten′sər, -sôr) *n. Anat.* A muscle that straightens out a limb.

ex·tent (ik·stent′) *n.* **1.** The dimension, degree, or limit to which anything is extended; compass; reach; size. **2.** Size within given bounds; limits; scope: the *extent* of his powers. **3.** A vast area. [< L < *ex-* out + *tendere* to stretch]

ex·ten·u·ate (ik·sten′yōō·āt) *v.t.* **·at·ed, ·at·ing 1.** To represent (a fault, crime, etc.) as less blameworthy; make excuses for. **2.** To belittle the importance of. [< L < *ex-* out + *tenuis* thin] — **ex·ten′u·a′tion** *n.* — **ex·ten′u·a′tor** *n.*

ex·ten·u·at·ing (ik·sten′yōō·ā′ting) *adj.* Serving to lessen the odiousness, as of a crime: *extenuating* circumstances.

ex·te·ri·or (ik·stir′ē·ər) *adj.* **1.** Of, pertaining to, or situated on the outside; external; outer. **2.** Coming or acting from without: *exterior* influences. **3.** Pertaining to foreign countries; foreign. — *n.* **1.** That which is outside, as an external surface. **2.** Outside appearance or demeanor. [< L *exterus* outside] — **ex·te′ri·or·ly** *adv.*

exterior angle *Geom.* **1.** Any of four angles formed on the outside of two nonintersecting straight lines cut by a third line. **2.** The angle formed between any side of a polygon and the extension of an adjacent side.

ex·ter·mi·nate (ik·stûr′mə·nāt) *v.t.* **·nat·ed, ·nat·ing** To destroy (living things) entirely; annihilate. [< L < *ex-* out + *terminus* boundary] — **ex·ter′mi·na·to′ry** (-nə·tôr′ē, -tō′rē) *adj.* — **ex·ter′mi·na·to·ry** (-nə·tôr′ē, -tō′rē) *adj.*

ex·ter·mi·na·tor (ik·stûr′mə·nā′tər) *n.* One who or that which exterminates.

ex·ter·nal (ik·stûr′nəl) *adj.* **1.** Of, pertaining to, or situated on the outside; outer; exterior. **2.** Belonging to or derived from the outside; extrinsic: an *external* factor. **3.** Pertaining to the outer self; superficial. **4.** Pertaining to foreign countries: *external* affairs. **5.** Relating to, affecting, or meant for the outside of the body: *external* medication. — *n.* **1.** The outside; exterior. **2.** *Usu. pl.* Outward or superficial aspects, circumstances, etc. [< L *externus* outer] — **ex·ter·nal·i·ty** (ek′stər·nal′ə·tē) *n.* — **ex·ter′nal·ly** *adv.*

ex·ter·nal·ize (ik·stûr′nəl·īz) *v.t.* **·ized, ·iz·ing 1.** To give external shape to; make external. **2.** To make outwardly real. — **ex·ter′nal·i·za′tion** *n.*

ex·tinct (ik·stingkt′) *adj.* **1.** Extinguished; inactive, as a volcano. **2.** No longer existing: an *extinct* animal. **3.** Void. [< L < *ex-* completely + *stinguere* to quench]

ex·tinc·tion (ik·stingk′shən) *n.* **1.** The act of extinguishing, or the state of being extinguished. **2.** The process or condition of becoming extinct; a dying out. **3.** Annihilation. — **ex·tinc′tive** *adj.*

ex·tin·guish (ik·sting′gwish, -wish) *v.t.* **1.** To put out or quench, as a fire. **2.** To make extinct; wipe out. **3.** To obscure; eclipse. [< L < *ex-* completely + *stinguere* to quench] — **ex·tin′guish·a·ble** *adj.* — **ex·tin′guish·er** *n.*

ex·tir·pate (ek′stər·pāt, ik·stûr′-) *v.t.* **·pat·ed, ·pat·ing** To root out or up; destroy wholly. [< L < *ex-* out + *stirps, stirpis* stem, root] — **ex′tir·pa′tion** *n.* — **ex′tir·pa′tive** *adj.* — **ex′tir·pa′tor** *n.*

ex·tol (ik·stōl′, -stol′) *v.t.* **·tolled, ·tol·ling** To praise in the highest terms; exalt; laud. — **Syn.** See PRAISE. Also **ex·toll′**. [< L < *ex-* out, up + *tollere* to raise] — **ex·tol′ler** *n.* — **ex·tol′ment** or **ex·toll′ment** *n.*

ex·tort (ik·stôrt′) *v.t.* To obtain (money, etc.) from a person by threat, oppression, or abuse of authority. [< L < *ex-* out + *torquere* to twist] — **ex·tor′tive** *adj.*

ex·tor·tion (ik·stôr′shən) *n.* **1.** The act or practice of extorting. **2.** The act of exacting an exorbitant price for something. **3.** That which has been extorted. — **ex·tor′tion·ar·y, ex·tor′tion·ate** *adj.* — **ex·tor′tion·er** *n.*

ex·tor·tion·ist (ik·stôr′shən·ist) *n.* One guilty of extortion.

ex·tra (eks′trə) *adj.* **1.** Over and above what is normal, required, expected, etc.; additional. **2.** Larger or of better quality than usual. — *n.* **1.** Something beyond what is usual or required. **2.** A copy or an edition of a newspaper issued to cover news of special importance. **3.** Something for which a special charge is made: Meals are an *extra*. **4.** Something of special quality. **5.** In motion pictures, a person hired for a small part, as in a mob scene. — *adv.* Unusually: *extra* good. [< L, outside, beyond]

extra- *prefix* Beyond or outside the scope, area, or limits of: used chiefly in forming adjectives and usu. written without a hypen (*extracurricular, extragovernmental, extraterritorial*) except before words beginning with *a* (*extra-atmospheric*) or with a capital letter (*extra-Scriptural*).

ex·tract (*v.* ik·strakt′; *n.* eks′trakt) *v.t.* **1.** To draw or pull out by force. **2.** To derive (happiness, instruction, etc.) from some source. **3.** To draw out or formulate (a principle, doctrine, etc.); deduce. **4.** To obtain by force or contrivance: to *extract* money. **5.** To obtain from a substance as by pressure, distillation, etc.: to *extract* juice. **6.** To select or copy out (a passage, word, or the like), as for quotation. **7.** *Math.* To calculate (the root of a number). — *n.* Something extracted as: **a** A concentrated form of a food, drug, etc. **b** A passage selected from a book. [< L < *ex-* out + *trahere* to draw, pull] — **ex·trac′tive** *adj.* & *n.* — **ex·trac′tor** *n.* — **ex·tract′a·ble** or **ex·tract′i·ble** *adj.*

ex·trac·tion (ik·strak′shən) *n.* **1.** The act of extracting, or the state of being extracted. **2.** That which is extracted. **3.** Lineage; descent: of European *extraction*.

ex·tra·cur·ric·u·lar (eks′trə·kə·rik′yə·lər) *adj.* Of or pertaining to those activities not a direct part of the curriculum of school or college life, as athletics, fraternities, etc.

ex·tra·dite (eks′trə·dīt′) *v.t.* **·dit·ed, ·dit·ing 1.** To deliver up (an accused individual, prisoner, or fugitive) to the jurisdiction of some other state, country, etc. **2.** To obtain the extradition of. — **ex′tra·dit′a·ble** *adj.*

ex·tra·di·tion (eks′trə·dish′ən) *n.* The surrender of an accused individual, prisoner, or fugitive by one state, etc., to another. [< F < L < *ex-* out + *traditio* surrender]

ex·tra·mu·ral (eks′trə·myōōr′əl) *adj.* **1.** Situated without or beyond the walls, as of a fortified city. 2. Taking place outside of an educational institution: *extramural* games.

ex·tra·ne·ous (ik-strā′nē-əs) *adj.* 1. Coming from without; foreign: *extraneous* rock. 2. Unrelated to the matter at hand. [< L *extraneus* foreign, external < *extra*] — **ex·tra′ne·ous·ly** *adv.* — **ex·tra′ne·ous·ness** *n.*

ex·traor·di·nar·y (ik-strôr′də-ner′ē; *esp. for def. 3* eks′trə-ôr′də-ner′ē) *adj.* 1. Being beyond or out of the common order, course, or method. 2. Far exceeding the usual; exceptional; remarkable. 3. Employed on an exceptional occasion; special: an envoy *extraordinary*. [< L < *extra* beyond + *ordo, ordinis* order] — **ex·traor′di·nar′i·ly** *adv.*

ex·trap·o·late (eks·trap′ə-lāt) *v.t. & v.i.* **·lat·ed, ·lat·ing** 1. *Math.* To project (those values of a magnitude or function that lie beyond the range of known values) on the basis of values that have already been determined: distinguished from *interpolate*. 2. To infer (a possibility) beyond the strict evidence of a series of facts, events, observations, etc. [< EXTRA- + (INTER)POLATE] — **ex·trap′o·la′tion** *n.* — **ex·trap′o·la′tive** *adj.*

ex·tra·sen·so·ry (eks′trə-sen′sər-ē) *adj.* Beyond the range of normal sensory perception.

ex·trav·a·gance (ik-strav′ə-gəns) *n.* 1. Wasteful expenditure of money. 2. Extreme lack of moderation in behavior or speech. 3. An instance of wastefulness or excess. [< F] Also **ex·trav′a·gan·cy.**

ex·trav·a·gant (ik-strav′ə-gənt) *adj.* 1. Overly lavish in expenditure; wasteful. 2. Exceeding reasonable limits; immoderate; unrestrained: *extravagant* praise. 3. Flagrantly high; exorbitant: *extravagant* prices. [< MF < L *extra* outside + *vagari* to wander] — **ex·trav′a·gant·ly** *adv.*

ex·trav·a·gan·za (ik-strav′ə-gan′zə) *n.* A lavish, spectacular theatrical production. [< Ital. *estravaganza* extravagance.]

ex·treme (ik-strēm′) *adj.* 1. Exceedingly great or severe: *extreme* danger; *extreme* weakness. 2. Going far beyond the bounds of moderation; exceeding what is considered reasonable; immoderate; radical: an *extreme* fashion; an *extreme* reactionary; also, very strict or drastic: *extreme* measures. 3. Outermost: the *extreme* border of a country. 4. Last; final: *extreme* unction. — *n.* 1. The highest degree; utmost point or verge: the *extreme* of cruelty. 2. One of the two ends or farthest limits of anything: the *extremes* of joy and sorrow. 3. *pl.* A condition of great danger or difficulty: He is constantly in *extremes*. 4. *Math.* The first or last term of a proportion or series. — **in the extreme** To the greatest or highest degree. — **to go to extremes** To carry something to excess. [< OF < L *extremus*, superl. of *exterus* outside] — **ex·treme′ly** (ik-strēm′lē) *adv.* Exceedingly; very.

extreme unction Unction (def. 2b).

ex·trem·ist (ik-strē′mist) *n.* 1. One who advocates extreme measures or holds extreme views. 2. One who carries something to excess. — *adj.* Of or pertaining to extreme measures or views. — **ex·trem′ism** *n.*

ex·trem·i·ty (ik-strem′ə-tē) *n., pl.* **·ties** 1. The utmost or farthest point; termination, end, or edge: the *extremity* of a line. 2. The greatest degree: the *extremity* of grief. 3. One's dying moments. 4. *pl.* Extreme measures: to resort to *extremities*. 5. A limb or appendage of the body; esp., the hands or feet.

ex·tri·ca·ble (eks′tri-kə-bəl) *adj.* That can be extricated.

ex·tri·cate (eks′trə-kāt) *v.t.* **·cat·ed, ·cat·ing** 1. To free from entanglement, hindrance, or difficulties; disentangle. 2. To cause to be given off; emit, as gas or moisture. [< L < *ex*- out + *tricae* trifles, troubles] — **ex′tri·ca′tion** *n.*

ex·trin·sic (ek-strin′sik) *adj.* 1. Being outside the nature of something; not inherent: opposed to *intrinsic*. 2. Derived or acting from without; extraneous. Also **ex·trin′si·cal.** [< F < LL < *exter* outside + *secus* besides < *sequi* to follow] — **ex·trin′si·cal·ly** *adv.* — **ex·trin′si·cal·ness** *n.*

ex·tro·ver·sion (eks′trə-vûr′zhən, -shən) *n. Psychol.* The turning of one's interest toward objects and actions outside the self rather than toward one's own thoughts or feelings. [< *extro*- outwards + L *versio, -onis* a turning]

ex·tro·vert (eks′trə-vûrt) *n. Psychol.* 1. A person characterized by extroversion. 2. Loosely, one who is gregarious, exuberant, etc. — *adj.* Characterized by extroversion.

ex·trude (ik-strōōd′) *v.* **·trud·ed, ·trud·ing** *v.t.* 1. To force, thrust, or push out. 2. To shape (plastic, metal, etc.) by forcing through dies under pressure. — *v.i.* 3. To protrude. [< L < *ex*- out + *trudere* to thrust] — **ex·tru·sion** (ik-strōō′zhən) *n.* — **ex·tru′sive** *adj.*

ex·u·ber·ance (ig-zōō′bər-əns) *n.* 1. The quality of being exuberant. 2. An instance of this. Also **ex·u·ber·an·cy.**

ex·u·ber·ant (ig-zōō′bər-ənt) *adj.* 1. Abounding in high spirits and vitality; full of joy and vigor. 2. Overflowing; lavish; effusive: *exuberant* praise. 3. Growing luxuriantly: *exuberant* foliage. [< L < *ex*- completely + *uberare* to be fruitful] — **ex·u′ber·ant·ly** *adv.*

ex·ude (ig-zōōd′, -zyōōd′, ik-sōōd′, -syōōd′) *v.* **·ud·ed, ·ud·ing** *v.i.* 1. To ooze or trickle forth, as sweat, gum, etc. — *v.t.*

2. To discharge gradually in this manner. 3. To manifest; display: to *exude* confidence. [< L < *ex*- out + *sudare* to sweat] — **ex·u·da·tion** (eks′yōō-dā′shən) *n.*

ex·ult (ig-zult′) *v.i.* To rejoice greatly, as in triumph; be jubilant. [< F < L < *ex*- out + *salire* to leap] — **ex·ul·ta·tion** (eg′zul-tā′shən, ek′sul-) — **ex·ult′ing·ly** *adv.*

ex·ul·tant (ig-zul′tənt) *adj.* Jubilant; triumphant; elated. — **ex·ul′tant·ly** *adv.*

ex·urb (eks′ûrb′) *n.* A usu. affluent residential area outside a city beyond the suburbs. [< EX- + -URB (on analogy with *suburb*)] — **ex·urb·an** (eks-ûr′bən) *adj.* — **ex·ur′ban·ite** *n.*

ex·ur·bi·a (eks-ûr′bē-ə) *n.* Exurbs collectively.

-ey Var. of -Y¹.

eye (ī) *n.* 1. The organ of vision in animals; in man, a nearly spherical mass set in the skull and consisting of the cornea, iris, pupil, retina, and lens, and protected by the eyelids, eyelashes, and eyebrows. 2. The area around the eye. 3. The iris, in regard to its color. 4. A look; gaze. 5. Attentive observation. 6. Sight; view: in the public *eye*. 7. Capacity to see or discern with discrimination. 8. *Often pl.* Judgment; opinion. 9. *Meteorol.* The calm central area of a hurricane or cyclone. 10. Anything resembling the human eye: the *eye* of a needle. — **eye of the wind** *Naut.* The direction from which the wind blows. — **to catch one's eye** To get one's attention. — **to give (someone) the eye** *Slang* To look at (someone) admiringly or invitingly. — **to keep an eye out (or peeled)** To watch for something; keep alert. — **to lay (or set) eyes on** To catch sight of. — **to make eyes at** To look at amorously or covetously. — **with an eye to** With a view to; looking to. — *v.* **eyed, ey·ing or eye·ing** *v.t.* 1. To look at carefully. 2. To make a hole in (a needle, etc.). [OE *ēage*]

EYE (Anatomical nomenclature)

eye·ball (ī′bôl′) *n.* The globe or ball of the eye.

eye·brow (ī′brou′) *n.* 1. The bony ridge over the eyes. 2. The arch of small hairs growing on this ridge.

eye·cup (ī′kup′) *n.* A small cup with a rim curved to fit the eye, used in applying lotions.

eyed (īd) *adj.* Having an eye or eyes: *brown-eyed*; *one-eyed*.

eye·ful (ī′fool′) *n.* 1. An amount of something in the eye. 2. *Slang* A strikingly beautiful person.

eye·glass (ī′glas′, ī′gläs′) *n.* 1. *pl.* A pair of corrective glass lenses mounted in a frame: also called *glasses*, *spectacles*. 2. Any lens used to assist vision. 3. An eyepiece.

eye·hole (ī′hōl′) *n.* 1. An opening through which to pass a pin, hook, rope, etc. 2. A peephole. 3. The eye's socket.

eye·lash (ī′lash′) *n.* One of the stiff, curved hairs growing from the edge of the eyelids. ♦ Collateral adjective: *ciliary*.

eye·less (ī′lis) *adj.* Lacking eyes; blind.

eye·let (ī′lit) *n.* 1. A small hole or opening. 2. A hole made in leather, canvas, etc., and lined with metal. 3. A metal ring for lining such a hole. 4. In embroidery, a small hole edged with ornamental stitches. — *v.t.* **·let·ed, ·let·ting** To make eyelets in. [< F *œillet*, dim. of *œil* eye]

eye·lid (ī′lid′) *n.* Either of the movable folds of skin by which the eyes are opened or closed.

eye opener *U.S.* 1. That which opens the eyes or enlightens, as startling news, revelatory behavior, etc. 2. *Informal* A drink of liquor, especially one taken early in the morning.

eye·piece (ī′pēs′) *n.* The lens or combination of lenses nearest the eye in a telescope, microscope, etc.

eye shadow A cosmetic preparation, tinted blue, green, gray, etc., applied to the eyelids.

eye·shot (ī′shot′) *n.* The range or scope of one's sight.

eye·sight (ī′sīt′) *n.* 1. The power or faculty of sight. 2. Extent or range of vision; view.

eye·sore (ī′sôr′, ī′sōr′) *n.* Something that offends the sight.

eye·strain (ī′strān′) *n.* Weariness or discomfort of the eyes caused by excessive or improper use.

eye·tooth (ī′tōōth′) *n. pl.* **·teeth** (-tēth′) One of the upper canine teeth.

eye·wash (ī′wosh′, ī′wôsh′) *n.* 1. A medicinal wash for the eye. 2. *U.S. Slang* Nonsense; bunk; flattery.

eye·wink (ī′wingk′) *n.* 1. A wink or glance. 2. An instant.

eye·wit·ness (ī′wit′nis) *n.* One who has seen something happen and can give testimony about it. — *adj.* Of or by an eyewitness: an *eyewitness* account.

ey·rie (âr′ē, ir′ē) *n. & v.i. -ry* See AERIE.

E·ze·ki·el (i-zē′kē-əl, -kyəl) Sixth-century B.C. Hebrew prophet. — *n.* A book of the Old Testament written by him. Also, in the Douai Bible, **E·ze′chi·el.**

Ez·ra (ez′rə) Fifth-century B.C. Hebrew high priest. — *n.* A book of the Old Testament written in part by him. Also, in the Douai Bible, *Esdras.* [< Hebrew, help]

F

f, F (ef) *n. pl.* **f's** or **fs, F's** or **Fs, effs** (efs) **1.** The sixth letter of the English alphabet. **2.** The sound represented by the letter *f.* — *symbol* **1.** *Music* **a** The fourth tone in the musical scale of C. **b** A note representing it. **c** The scale built upon F. **d** The bass clef in musical notation. **e** Forte. **2.** *Chem.* Fluorine (symbol F). **3.** *Genetics* A filial generation, usu. followed by a subscript numeral, as F_1, F_2, for each successive filial generation offspring of a given mating.

fa (fä) *n. Music* The fourth syllable used in solmization; the fourth degree of a major scale; also, the tone F.

Fa·bi·an (fā/bē·ən) *adj.* Characterized by or practicing a policy of deliberate delay. — *n.* A member of the Fabian Society. [after *Fabius* Maximus, Roman general, died 203 B.C.] — **Fa/bi·an·ism** *n.* — **Fa/bi·an·ist** *n. & adj.*

Fabian Society An association formed in Great Britain in 1884, aiming at the gradual achievement of socialism.

fa·ble (fā/bəl) *n.* **1.** A brief tale embodying a moral and using persons, animals, or inanimate things as characters. **2.** A legend or myth. **3.** A foolish or improbable story. — *v.t. & v.i.* **·bled, ·bling** To invent or tell (fables or stories). [< OF < L *fari* to say, speak] — **fa/bled** *adj.* — **fa/bler** *n.* — **fab·u·list** (fab/yə·list) *n.*

fab·ric (fab/rik) *n.* **1.** A woven, felted, or knitted material, as cloth, felt, or lace. **2.** The texture or workmanship of such material. **3.** Structure or framework: the social *fabric.* [< F < L *faber* workman]

fab·ri·cate (fab/rə·kāt) *v.t.* **·cat·ed, ·cat·ing** **1.** To make or manufacture; build. **2.** To make by combining parts. **3.** To make up or invent, as a lie or story. [< L *fabricare* to construct] — **fab/ri·ca/tion** *n.* — **fab/ri·ca/tor** *n.*

fab·u·lous (fab/ye·ləs) *adj.* **1.** Passing the limits of belief; incredible; astounding. **2.** Of, like, or recorded in fable; fictitious; mythical. — **fab/u·lous·ly** *adv.* — **fab/u·lous·ness** *n.*

fa·çade (fə·säd/) *n.* **1.** *Archit.* The front or principal face of a building. **2.** A front or a false appearance: a *façade* of respectability. Also **fa·cade₁** [< F < Ital <LL < L *facies* face]

face (fās) *n.* **1.** The front portion of the head; countenance. **2.** The expression of the countenance. **3.** A grimacing expression. **4.** External aspect or appearance; look. **5.** *Informal* Effrontery; audacity. **6.** The value as written on the printed surface of a bond, note, etc. **7.** The front, principal, finished, or working surface of anything: the *face* of a clock, of a fabric, a golf club, etc. **8.** The surface of a coin. **9.** The side or surface of a solid. **10.** One of the sides of any military formation. **11.** The land surface or the geographical features of a region. **12.** *Printing* **a** The surface of a type body or printing plate that makes the impression. **b** The size or style of the letter or character on the type. **c** The letter or character itself: also *type face.* **13.** *Mining* The end of a drift or excavation. — **face to face** **1.** In each other's immediate presence. **2.** Confronting; followed by *with.* — **in the face of** **1.** Confronting. **2.** In spite of; notwithstanding. — **on the face of it** Judging by all appearances; apparently. — **to fly in the face of** To act in open defiance of. — **to lose face** To lose dignity or reputation. — **to one's face** Openly; frankly. — **to save face** To save oneself from embarrassment or disgrace; preserve one's dignity or reputation. — **to show one's face** To put in an appearance. — *v.* **faced, fac·ing** *v.t.* **1.** To bear or turn the face toward. **2.** To cause to turn in a given direction, as soldiers. **3.** To meet face to face; confront. **4.** To realize or be aware of. **5.** To cover with a layer or surface of another material. **6.** To make smooth the surface of. **7.** To turn face upward, as a playing card. — *v.i.* **8.** To turn or be turned with the face in a given direction. — **to face down** To disconcert or prevail over by a bold, fixed gaze or an audacious denial or assertion. — **to face out** To see to completion. — **to face the music** *U.S. Slang* To accept the consequences. — **to face up to** To meet with courage. [< F, ult.< L *facies* face] — **face/a·ble** *adj.*

face card In playing cards, a king, queen, or jack.

fac·et (fas/it) *n.* **1.** One of the small plane surfaces cut upon a gem. **2.** A phase, side, or aspect of a subject or person. — **Syn.** See PHASE. — *v.t.* **fac·et·ed** or **·et·ted, fac·et·ing** or **·et·ting** To cut or work facets upon. [< F *facette,* dim. of *face* face]

fa·ce·tious (fə·sē/shəs) *adj.* Given to or marked by levity or flippant humor. [< F < L *facetiae* jests] — **fa·ce/tious·ly** *adv.* — **fa·ce/tious·ness** *n.*

face value **1.** The value stated on the face of a bond, coin, note, etc. **2.** Apparent value: at *face value.*

fa·cial (fā/shəl) *adj.* Of, near, or for the face. — *n. Informal* A massage or other treatment for the face.

facient *suffix* Causing; making: *sorbefacient.* [< L *faciens, -entis,* ppr. of *facere* to do]

fac·ile (fas/əl, -il) *adj.* **1.** Requiring little effort; easily achieved or performed; also, superficial: a *facile* prose style. **2.** Ready or quick in performance; also, smooth; glib. **3.** Easily moved or persuaded; affable; agreeable. [< F < L *facilis* easy to do] — **fac/ile·ly** *adv.* — **fac/ile·ness** *n.*

fa·cil·i·tate (fə·sil/ə·tāt) *v.t.* **·tat·ed, ·tat·ing** To make easier or more convenient. — **fa·cil/i·ta/tion** *n.*

fa·cil·i·ty (fə·sil/ə·tē) *n. pl.* **·ties** **1.** Ease of performance or action. **2.** Ready skill or ability. **3.** *Usu. pl.* Something that makes an action or operation easier: *facilities* for research. **4.** Readiness to comply. [See FACILE.]

fac·ing (fā/sing) *n.* **1.** A lining or covering of a garment, often sewn on parts exposed by being turned back. **2.** A fabric used for this. **3.** Any covering, as on a building, that protects or is ornamental.

fac·sim·i·le (fak·sim/ə·lē) *n.* **1.** An exact copy. **2.** *Telecom.* A method of transmitting messages, drawings, or the like, by means of radio, telegraph, etc. — *adj.* Of or like a facsimile. [< L *fac simile* make like]

fact (fakt) *n.* **1.** Something that actually exists or has occurred. **2.** Something asserted to be true or to have happened. **3.** Reality or actuality. **4.** A criminal deed: now only in the legal phrases **before** (or **after**) **the fact, to deny the fact,** etc. — **as a matter of fact,** in fact, in point of fact In reality; actually. [< L *factum* < *facere* to do]

fac·tion (fak/shən) *n.* **1.** A group of people operating within, and often in opposition to, a larger group. **2.** Party strife; internal dissension. [< F < L *facere* to do] — **fac/tion·al** *adj.* — **fac/tion·al·ism** *n.* — **fac/tion·ist** *n.*
— **Syn. 1.** *Faction, wing,* and *bloc* refer to subgroups, especially within political parties. *Faction* is often applied to a disruptive subgroup: *wing* refers to either of two directly opposed groups: the liberal and conservative *wings* of the Republican party. A *bloc* is a coalition that cuts across party lines: the farm *bloc.*

fac·tious (fak/shəs) *adj.* Given to dissension.

fac·ti·tious (fak·tish/əs) *adj.* **1.** Not spontaneous; affected: *factitious* enthusiasm. **2.** Produced by artificial conditions or standards: a *factitious* demand. [< L *factitius* artificial] — **fac·ti/tious·ly** *adv.* — **fac·ti/tious·ness** *n.*

fac·tor (fak/tər) *n.* **1.** One of the elements or causes that contribute to produce a result. **2.** *Math.* One of two or more quantities that, when multiplied together, produce a given quantity. **3.** *Biol.* A gene. **4.** One who transacts business for another on a commission basis. — *v.t. Math.* To resolve into factors. [< L, maker] — **fac/tor·ship** *n.*

fac·tor·age (fak/tər·ij) *n.* **1.** A factor's commission. **2.** The business of a factor.

fac·to·ri·al (fak·tôr/ē·əl, -tō/rē-) *n. Math.* The product of a series of consecutive positive integers from 1 to a given number. The *factorial* of four (written 4!) = $1 \times 2 \times 3 \times 4 = 24.$ — *adj.* Pertaining to a factor or a factorial.

fac·tor·ize (fak/tə·rīz) *v.t.* **·ized, ·iz·ing** *Math.* To resolve into factors. — **fac/tor·i·za/tion** *n.*

fac·to·ry (fak/tər·ē) *n. pl.* **·ries** An establishment for the manufacture or assembly of goods. [< L *facere* to make]

fac·to·tum (fak·tō/təm) *n.* A man of all work. [< Med.L < L *fac,* sing. imperative of *facere* to do + *totum* everything]

fac·tu·al (fak/chōō·əl) *adj.* Pertaining to, containing, or consisting of facts; literal and exact. — **fac/tu·al·ly** *adv.*

fac·ul·ty (fak/əl·tē) *n. pl.* **·ties** **1.** A natural or acquired power or ability. **2.** One of the inherent powers or capabilities of the body or mind. **3.** *U.S.* The entire teaching staff at an educational institution. **4.** A department of learning at a university: the English *faculty.* **5.** The members of a learned profession collectively. **6.** Conferred power or privilege. **7.** *Eccl.* The right to perform certain ecclesiastical functions. [< OF < L < *facilis* easy to do]

fad (fad) *n.* A temporary style, amusement, fashion, etc. [Origin unknown] — **fad/dish** *adj.* — **fad/dist** *n.*

fade (fād) *v.* **fad·ed, fad·ing** *v.i.* **1.** To lose brightness or clearness. **2.** To vanish slowly. **3.** To lose freshness, vigor, youth, etc. — *v.t.* **4.** To cause to fade. **5.** *U.S. Slang* In dice, to cover the bet of. — **to fade in** or **out** In television, motion pictures, and radio, to come into or depart from perception gradually. [< OF *fade* pale, insipid]

fae·ces (fē/sēz), **fae·cal** (fē/kəl) See FECES, FECAL.

fag¹ (fag) *v.* **fagged, fag·ging** *v.t.* **1.** To exhaust by hard work: usu. with *out.* **2.** *Brit.* To make a fag of. — *v.i.* **3.** To weary oneself by working. **4.** *Brit.* To serve as a fag. — *n.* **1.** *Brit.* In English public schools, a boy who does menial service for one in a higher class. **2.** *U.S. Slang* A homosexual: also **fag·got** (fag/ət). [Origin unknown]

fag² (fag) *n. Slang* A cigarette. [< FAG END]

fag end 1. The frayed end, as of a rope. **2.** A remnant or last part, usually of slight utility. [< FAG¹]

fag·ot (fag/ət) *n.* **1.** A bundle of sticks, twigs, or branches, used for fuel, etc. **2.** A bundle of pieces of wrought iron or steel for working into bars, etc. — *v.t.* **1.** To make a fagot of. **2.** To ornament by fagoting. Also **fag/got.** [< OF]

fag·ot·ing (fag/ət·ing) *n.* **1.** A mode of ornamenting textile fabrics in which a number of threads of a material are drawn out and the cross threads tied together in the middle. **2.** A kind of criss-cross hemstitch. Also **fag/got·ing.**

FAGOTING.
a Hemstitch.
b Drawn work.

Fahr·en·heit scale (far/ən·hīt, *Ger.* fär/ən·hīt) A temperature scale in which the freezing point of water is 32° and the boiling point 212°, under standard atmospheric pressure. [after Gabriel Daniel *Fahrenheit*, 1686–1736, German physicist]

fail (fāl) *v.i.* **1.** To turn out to be deficient or wanting, as in ability, quality, etc. **2.** To miss doing or accomplishing something: He *failed* to make himself clear. **3.** To prove inadequate; fall short; give out. **4.** To decline in health or strength. **5.** To go bankrupt. **6.** In education, to receive a grade of failure. — *v.t.* **7.** To prove of no help to; desert: His friends *failed* him. **8.** In education: **a** To receive a grade of failure in (a course or examination). **b** To assign a grade of failure to (a student). — *n.* Failure: in the phrase *without fail.* [< OF < L *fallere* to deceive]

fail·ing (fā/ling) *n.* **1.** A minor fault; defect. **2.** The act of one who or that which fails. — **Syn.** See FOIBLE. — *prep.* In default of; lacking. — **fail/ing·ly** *adv.*

faille (fāl, fīl; *Fr.* fä/y') *n.* An untwilled silk dress fabric having a light grain or cord. [< F]

fail-safe (fāl/sāf') *adj.* Designating any of various systems designed to prevent equipment failure from causing operational failure, esp. such a system that makes the carrying out of a nuclear bombing automatically contingent upon a specific confirming order.

fail·ure (fāl/yər) *n.* **1.** A turning out to be unsuccessful, disappointing, or lacking. **2.** A breaking down in health, strength, action, efficiency, etc. **3.** Nonperformance; neglect: *failure* to obey the law. **4.** A becoming insolvent or bankrupt. **5.** One who or that which fails. **6.** In education, a failing to pass, or the grade indicating this.

fain (fān) *adv. Archaic & Poetic* Gladly; preferably: He would *fain* depart. — *adj.* **1.** *Archaic & Poetic* Glad; rejoiced. **2.** *Archaic & Poetic* Eager. [OE *fægen*]

faint (fānt) *v.i.* To lose consciousness; swoon. — *adj.* **1.** Feeble; weak. **2.** Lacking in distinctness, brightness, etc. **3.** Dizzy; weak. **4.** Lacking courage; timid. — *n.* A sudden, temporary loss of consciousness; swoon. [< OF, pp. of *faindre* to shape] — **faint/ly** *adv.* — **faint/ness** *n.*

faint·heart·ed (fānt/här/tid) *adj.* Cowardly; timorous; timid. — **faint/heart/ed·ly** *adv.* — **faint/heart/ed·ness** *n.*

fair¹ (fâr) *adj.* **1.** Light in coloring; not dark or sallow. **2.** Pleasing to the eye; beautiful. **3.** Free from blemish or imperfection: a *fair* name. **4.** Having no aspect of rain, snow, or hail. **5.** Just; upright. **6.** According to rules, principles, etc.; legitimate: a *fair* win. **7.** Properly open to attack: He is *fair* game. **8.** Moderately good or large: a *fair* crop. **9.** Likely; promising. **10.** Gracious or courteous; pleasant. **11.** In baseball, situated, falling or remaining in the area bounded by the foul lines; not foul. — *adv.* **1.** In a fair manner. **2.** Squarely; directly. — **to bid fair** To seem probable or favorable. — *n. Archaic* **1.** A fair woman. **2.** Beauty. — **for fair** For sure. [OE *fæger*]

fair² (fâr) *n.* **1.** A periodic and usually competitive exhibit of agricultural products, livestock, machinery, etc. **2.** A large exhibition or show of products, etc.: a world's *fair.*

3. An exhibit and sale of fancywork. **4.** A gathering of buyers and sellers. [< OF < L *feria* holiday]

fair-haired (fâr/hârd/) *adj.* **1.** Having blond hair. **2.** Favorite: the teacher's *fair-haired* boy.

fair·ing (fâr/ing) *n. Aeron.* In airplanes, an auxiliary structure or surface to reduce drag or resistance.

fair·ish (fâr/ish) *adj.* Moderately good, well, or large.

fair·ly (fâr/lē) *adv.* **1.** In a just manner; equitably. **2.** Moderately; somewhat. **3.** Positively; completely: The crowd *fairly* roared. **4.** Clearly; distinctly.

fair-mind·ed (fâr/mīn/did) *adj.* Free from bias or bigotry; open to reason; unprejudiced. — **fair/-mind/ed·ness** *n.*

fair-trade (fâr/trād/) *v.t.* **-trad·ed, -trad·ing** To set a price no less than the manufacturer's minimum price on (a branded or trademarked product). — *adj.* Of or pertaining to such a price.

fair·way (fâr/wā/) *n.* **1.** That part of a golf course, between the tees and putting greens, where the grass is kept short. **2.** *Naut.* The navigable or usual course through a channel or harbor.

fair-weath·er (fâr/weth/ər) *adj.* **1.** Suitable for fair weather, as a racetrack. **2.** Not helpful in adversity.

fair·y (fâr/ē) *n. pl.* **fair·ies 1.** An imaginary being, ordinarily small and capable of working good or ill. **2.** *Slang* A male homosexual. — *adj.* **1.** Of or pertaining to fairies. **2.** Resembling a fairy. [< OF *faerie* fairyland]

fair·y·land (fâr/ē·land/) *n.* **1.** The fancied abode of the fairies. **2.** Any delightful, enchanting place.

fairy tale 1. A tale about fairies. **2.** An incredible or highly imaginative story or statement.

fait ac·com·pli (fe·tà·kòṅ·plē/) *French* A thing done beyond recall or opposition; literally, an accomplished fact.

faith (fāth) *n.* **1.** Confidence in or dependence on a person, statement, or thing as trustworthy. **2.** Belief without need of certain proof. **3.** Belief in God or in the Scriptures or other religious writings. **4.** A system of religious belief. **5.** Anything given adherence or credence. **6.** Allegiance. — **Syn.** See BELIEF. — **bad faith** Deceit; dishonesty. — **in faith** Indeed; truly. — **in good faith** With honorable intentions. — **to break faith 1.** To betray one's principles or beliefs. **2.** To fail to keep a promise. — **to keep faith 1.** To adhere to one's principles or beliefs. **2.** To keep a promise. — *interj.* Indeed. [< OF < L *fidere* to trust]

faith·ful (fāth/fəl) *adj.* **1.** True or trustworthy in the performance of duty, the fulfillment of promises or obligations, etc.; loyal. **2.** Worthy of belief or confidence; truthful: a *faithful* saying. **3.** True in detail or accurate in description: a *faithful* copy. — **the faithful 1.** The followers of a religious faith. **2.** The loyal members of any group. — **faith/ful·ly** *adv.* — **faith/ful·ness** *n.*

faith·less (fāth/lis) *adj.* **1.** Untrue to promise or obligation; unfaithful. **2.** Not dependable or trustworthy. **3.** Devoid of faith. — **faith/less·ly** *adv.* — **faith/less·ness** *n.*

fake (fāk) *Informal n.* Any person or thing not genuine. — *adj.* Not genuine; spurious. — *v.* **faked, fak·ing** *v.t.* **1.** To make up and attempt to pass off as genuine: to *fake* a pedigree. **2.** To stimulate; feign. **3.** To improvise, as in music or a play. — *v.i.* **4.** To practice faking. [? Var. of obs. *feague, feak* < G *fegen* to sweep] — **fak/er** *n.*

fa·kir (fə·kir/, fā/kər) *n.* **1.** A Moslem ascetic or religious mendicant. **2.** Loosely, any Hindu yogi or religious devotee. Also **fa·keer** (fə·kir/). [< Arabic *faqīr* poor]

fal·chion (fôl/chən, -shən) *n.* **1.** A sword of the Middle Ages. **2.** *Poetic* Any sword. [< OF, ult. < L *falx* sickle]

fal·con (fal/kən, fôl-, fô/-) *n.* **1.** A bird of prey noted for its powerful wings, keen vision, and swiftness of attack upon its quarry. **2.** Any other birds of the same family, having long, pointed wings, a notched bill, and strong talons. [< OF < LL < L *falx, falcis* sickle, because of its curved beak]

fal·con·ry (fôl/kən·rē, fô/-, fal/-) *n.* **1.** The art of training falcons to hunt other birds and game. **2.** The sport of hunting with falcons: also called *hawking.* — **fal/con·er** *n.*

fal·de·ral (fal/də·ral) *n.* **1.** Any foolish nonsense or fancy. **2.** A trifling ornament. **3.** A meaningless refrain used in old songs. Also **fal·de·rol** (fal/də·rol).

fall (fôl) *v.* **fell, fall·en, fall·ing** *v.i.* **1.** To drop from a higher to a lower place or position because of removal of support or loss of hold or attachment. **2.** To drop suddenly from an erect position, striking the ground with some part of the body. **3.** To collapse. **4.** To become less in number, intensity, value, etc.: Prices *fell.* **5.** To become less in rank, importance, etc. **6.** To drop wounded or slain. **7.** To be overthrown, as a government. **8.** To be captured: The fort *fell.* **9.** To yield to temptation; sin. **10.** To hit; land: The bombs *fell* on target. **11.** To slope downward: The road *falls* into the valley. **12.** To hang down; droop. **13.** To come as though descending: Night *fell.* **14.** To pass into some specified condition: to *fall* asleep. **15.** To experience or show dejection: His face *fell.* **16.** To be cast down: His eyes *fell.* **17.** To come or happen by chance or lot: to *fall* among thieves. **18.** To happen; occur at a specified time or place. **19.** To pass by right or inheritance. **20.** To be uttered as if accidentally: An oath *fell* from his lips. **21.** To be classified or divided: with *into*. **22.** To be born: said of animals. — *v.t.* **23.** *U.S.* To fell or cut down, as a tree. — **to fall away 1.** To become lean or emaciated. **2.** To die; decline. — **to fall away from** To renounce allegiance to. — **to fall back** To recede; retreat. — **to fall back on** (or **upon**) **1.** To resort to; have recourse to. **2.** To retreat to. — **to fall behind 1.** To lose ground. **2.** To be in arrears. — **to fall down on** *U.S. Informal* To fail in. — **to fall flat** To fail to produce the intended effect or result. — **to fall for** *U.S. Informal* **1.** To be deceived by. **2.** To fall in love with. — **to fall in** *Mil.* To take proper place in a formation or group. — **to fall in with 1.** To meet and accompany. **2.** To agree with. — **to fall off 1.** To leave or withdraw. **2.** To become less. — **to fall on** (or **upon**) **1.** To attack. **2.** To discover. **3.** To light upon: said of the eyes, the glance, etc. — **to fall out 1.** To quarrel. **2.** To happen; result. **3.** *Mil.* To leave ranks. — **to fall short 1.** To fail to meet a standard, reach a particular place, etc.: with *of*. **2.** To be or prove deficient. — **to fall through** To come to nothing; fail. — **to fall to 1.** To set about; begin. **2.** To begin fighting. **3.** To begin eating. **4.** To come or drop into position. — **to fall under 1.** To be classified as or included in. **2.** To come under (a spell, power, etc.). — *n.* **1.** The act of falling; a descending. **2.** That which falls. **3.** The amount that falls. **4.** The distance through which anything falls. **5.** A more or less sudden descent from a vertical or erect position. **6.** A hanging down. **7.** A downward direction or slope. **8.** *Usu. pl.* A waterfall; cascade. **9.** A loss or reduction in value, price, reputation, etc. **10.** A moral lapse. **11.** A surrender, as of a city or fort. **12.** *Often cap. Chiefly U.S.* Autumn. **13.** In wrestling: **a** The throwing of an opponent to his back. **b** The method used. **c** A wrestling match or part thereof. — **the fall of man** *Theol.* The disobedience of Adam and Eve that resulted in original sin. [OE *feallan*]

fal·la·cious (fə-lā′shəs) *adj.* **1.** Deceptive or misleading. **2.** Containing or involving a fallacy. **3.** Delusive: a *fallacious* hope. — **fal·la′cious·ly** *adv.* — **fal·la′cious·ness** *n.*

fal·la·cy (fal′ə-sē) *n. pl.* **·cies 1.** An erroneous or misleading notion. **2.** Unsoundness or incorrectness, as of belief, judgment, etc. **3.** Deceptive quality. **4.** Any reasoning contrary to the rules of logic. [< L *fallere* to deceive]

fall·en (fô′lən) Past participle of FALL. — *adj.* **1.** Having come down by falling. **2.** Brought down. **3.** Overthrown; vanquished. **4.** Disgraced; ruined. **5.** Slain.

fall guy *U.S. Slang* One who is left to receive the blame or penalties; a dupe; scapegoat.

fal·li·ble (fal′ə-bəl) *adj.* **1.** Liable to err. **2.** Liable to be misled or deceived. **3.** Liable to be erroneous or false. [< Med.L < L *fallere* to deceive] — **fal′li·bil′i·ty, fal′li·ble·ness** *n.* — **fal′li·bly** *adv.*

Fal·lo·pi·an tube (fə-lō′pē-ən) *Anat.* One of a pair of long, slender ducts serving as a passage for the ovum from the ovary to the uterus: also called *oviduct*. [after Gabriello *Fallopio*, 1523–62, Italian anatomist]

fall·out (fôl′out′) *n. Physics* **1.** The descent of minute particles of radioactive material resulting from the explosion of an atomic or thermonuclear bomb. **2.** The particles themselves. **3.** *Informal* A by-product. Also **fall′-out′**.

fal·low[1] (fal′ō) *adj.* Left unseeded after being plowed; uncultivated. — **to lie fallow** To remain unused, idle, dormant, etc. — *n.* **1.** Land left unseeded after plowing. **2.** The process of plowing or working land and leaving it unseeded for a time. — *v.t. & v.i.* To make, keep, or become fallow. [OE *fealging* fallow land] — **fal′low·ness** *n.*

fal·low[2] (fal′ō) *adj.* Light yellowish brown. [OE *fealu*]

fallow deer A European deer about 3 feet high at the shoulders and spotted white in the summer

FALLOW DEER

false (fôls) *adj.* **1.** Contrary to truth or fact. **2.** Incorrect: *false* reasoning. **3.** Not genuine; artificial. **4.** Deceptive or misleading: a *false* impression. **5.** Given to lying. **6.** Wanting in fidelity; faithless. **7.** Supplementary; substitutive. **8.** *Music* Not correct in pitch. — *adv.* In a false manner. [< OF < L *falsus*, orig. pp. of *fallere* to deceive] — **false′ly** *adv.* — **false′ness** *n.*

false face A mask.

false-heart·ed (fôls′här′tid) *adj.* Treacherous; deceitful.

false·hood (fôls′hŏŏd) *n.* **1.** Lack of accord to fact or truth. **2.** An intentional untruth; lie. — **Syn.** See LIE[2].

false ribs *Anat.* Ribs that do not unite directly with the sternum. In man there are five on each side.

fal·set·to (fôl·set′ō) *n. pl.* **·tos 1.** The higher, less colorful register of a voice, esp. of an adult male voice: also called *head voice*. **2.** A man who sings or speaks in this register: also **fal·set′tist**. — *adj.* Having the quality of falsetto; shrill. — *adv.* In falsetto. [< Ital., dim. of *falso* false]

fal·si·fy (fôl′sə·fī) *v.* **·fied, ·fy·ing** *v.t.* **1.** To tell lies about; misrepresent. **2.** To alter or tamper with, esp. in order to deceive. **3.** To prove to be false. — *v.i.* **4.** To tell lies. — **Syn.** See PERVERT. [< F < LL < L < *falsus* false + *facere* to make] — **fal′si·fi·ca′tion** *n.* — **fal′si·fi′er** *n.*

fal·si·ty (fôl′sə·tē) *n. pl.* **·ties 1.** The quality of being false. **2.** That which is false. — **Syn.** See ERROR.

Fal·staff (fôl′staf, -stäf), **Sir John** A fat, fun-loving old knight in Shakespeare's *Henry IV* and *The Merry Wives of Windsor*. — **Fal·staff′i·an** *adj.*

fal·ter (fôl′tər) *v.i.* **1.** To be hesitant or uncertain; waver. **2.** To move unsteadily. **3.** To speak haltingly. — *v.t.* **4.** To utter haltingly. — **Syn.** See VACILLATE. — *n.* **1.** An uncertainty or hesitation in voice or action. **2.** A quavering sound. [? < ON *faltrask* to be encumbered] — **fal′ter·er** *n.* — **fal′ter·ing** *adj.* — **fal′ter·ing·ly** *adv.*

fame (fām) *n.* **1.** Widespread and illustrious reputation; renown. **2.** Public reputation or estimation. — *v.t.* **famed, fam·ing** *Archaic* To speak of widely; celebrate. [< F < L *fama* report, reputation]

fa·mil·ial (fə·mil′yəl) *adj.* Of, pertaining to, associated with, or transmitted within the family.

fa·mil·iar (fə·mil′yər) *adj.* **1.** Having thorough knowledge of something; well-acquainted: followed by *with*. **2.** Well-known; customary. **3.** Intimate; close. **4.** Unduly intimate; forward. **5.** Informal or unconstrained. **6.** Domesticated: said of animals. — *n.* **1.** A friend or close associate. **2.** A spirit serving a witch, usu. in animal form. [< OF < L *familia* family] — **fa·mil′iar·ly** *adv.*

fa·mil·i·ar·i·ty (fə·mil′ē·ar′ə·tē, -mil′yar′-) *n. pl.* **·ties 1.** Thorough knowledge of or acquaintance with something. **2.** Friendly closeness; intimacy. **3.** Offensively familiar conduct; unwarranted intimacy. **4.** *Often pl.* An action warranted only by intimate acquaintance.

fa·mil·iar·ize (fə·mil′yə·rīz) *v.t.* **·ized, ·iz·ing 1.** To make (oneself or someone) familiar with something. **2.** To cause (something) to be familiar. — **fa·mil′iar·i·za′tion** *n.*

fam·i·ly (fam′ə·lē, fam′lē) *n. pl.* **·lies 1.** Parents and their children. **2.** The children as distinguished from the parents. **3.** A group of persons connected by blood or marriage. **4.** A succession of persons connected by blood, name, etc.; a house; clan. **5.** Distinguished or ancient lineage or descent. **6.** A household. **7.** Any class or group of like or related things. **8.** *Biol.* A taxonomic category higher than a genus and below an order. **9.** *Ling.* A grouping of languages assumed to be descended from a common parent, as the Indo-European family. — *adj.* Of, belonging to, or suitable for a family. [< L < *famulus* servant]

family name A surname.

family tree 1. A diagram showing family descent. **2.** The ancestors and descendants of a family, collectively.

fam·ine (fam′in) *n.* **1.** A widespread scarcity of food. **2.** A great scarcity of anything; dearth: a water *famine*. **3.** Starvation. [< OF < L *fames* hunger]

fam·ish (fam′ish) *v.t. & v.i.* To suffer or die, or to cause to suffer or die, from starvation. [Earlier *fame* < F *afamer* to starve] — **fam′ished** *adj.* — **fam′ish·ment** *n.*

fa·mous (fā′məs) *adj.* **1.** Celebrated in history or public report; well-known; renowned. **2.** *Informal* Excellent; admirable. — **fa′mous·ly** *adv.* — **fa′mous·ness** *n.*

fan[1] (fan) *n.* **1.** A device for putting the air into motion; esp., a light, flat implement, often collapsible and opening into a wedgelike shape, a circle, etc. **2.** Anything shaped like a fan. **3.** A machine fitted with blades that revolve rapidly about a central hub, for stirring air, etc. **4.** A machine for blowing away chaff. — *v.* **fanned, fan·ning** *v.t.* **1.** To move or stir (air) with or as with a fan. **2.** To direct air upon; cool or refresh with or as with a fan. **3.** To move or stir to action; excite: to *fan* someone's rage. **4.** To winnow (grain or chaff). **5.** To spread like a fan. **6.** In baseball, to cause (a batter) to strike out. — *v.i.* **7.** To spread out like a fan. **8.** In baseball, to strike out. [OE < L *vannus* winnowing basket] — **fan′ner** *n.*

fan[2] (fan) *n. Informal* An enthusiastic devotee or admirer of a sport, diversion, celebrity, etc. [? < FANATIC]

fa·nat·ic (fə·nat′ik) *n.* A person who is moved by a frenzy of enthusiasm or zeal; esp., a religious zealot. [< L *fanum* temple] — **fa·nat′i·cal** *adj.* — **fa·nat′i·cal·ly** *adv.* — **fa·nat′i·cism** (-siz′əm) *n.*

fan·cied (fan′sēd) *adj.* Imaginary: *fancied* insults.

fan·ci·er (fan′sē·ər) *n.* **1.** One having a special taste for or interest in something. **2.** A breeder of animals.

fan·ci·ful (fan′si·fəl) *adj.* **1.** Produced by or existing only in the fancy: *fanciful* schemes. **2.** Marked by fancy in design: a *fanciful* costume. 3. Indulging in fancies: a *fanciful* mind. — **fan'ci·ful·ly** *adv.* — **fan'ci·ful·ness** *n.*

fan·cy (fan'sē) *n. pl.* **·cies** 1. Imagination of a capricious or whimsical sort. 2. An extravagant, odd, or whimsical invention or image. 3. An idea or notion not based on fact or evidence. 4. A caprice or whim. 5. A liking or inclination, as if resulting from caprice. 6. Taste or judgment in art, style, etc. — *adj.* **·ci·er, ·ci·est** 1. Adapted to please the fancy; ornamental. 2. Coming from the fancy; imaginary. 3. Capricious; whimsical. 4. Of higher grade than the average: *fancy* fruits. 5. Exorbitant: *fancy* prices. 6. Performed with exceptional grace and skill. 7. Selectively bred for certain points, as an animal: also **fan'cy-bred** — *v.t.* **·cied, ·cy·ing** 1. To imagine; picture: *Fancy* that! 2. To take a fancy to. 3. To believe without proof or conviction; suppose. 4. To breed, as animals, for conventional points of symmetry or beauty. — *interj.* An exclamation of surprise. [Contr. of FANTASY]

fan·cy·work (fan'sē·wûrk') *n.* Ornamental needlework.

fan·dan·go (fan·dang'gō) *n. pl.* **·gos** 1. A Spanish dance in triple time. 2. The music for this dance. [< Sp.]

fan·fare (fan'fâr') *n.* 1. A short, lively passage, as of trumpets. 2. A noisy or showy parade. [< F]

fang (fang) *n.* 1. A long, pointed tooth or tusk by which an animal seizes or tears at its prey. 2. One of the long, hollow or grooved, usu. erectile teeth with which a venomous serpent injects its poison into its victim. [OE, a seizing] — **fanged** *adj.* — **fang'less** *adj.* — **fang'like'** *adj.*

fan·light (fan'līt') *n. Archit.* 1. A semicircular window containing a sash with bars radiating from the middle of its base: also called *fan window.* 2. *Brit.* A transom.

fan·ny (fan'ē) *n. pl.* **·nies** *U.S. Slang* The buttocks.

fan·tail (fan'tāl') *n.* 1. A variety of domestic pigeon having fanlike tail feathers. 2. Any fan-shaped end or tail.

fan·tan (fan'tan') *n.* 1. A Chinese gambling game. 2. A game of cards played in sequence. [< Chinese *fan t'an*]

fan·ta·si·a (fan·tā'zhə, -zhē·ə, fan'tə·zē'ə) *n. Music* 1. A fanciful composition observing no strict musical form. 2. A medley of various themes. [< Ital., a fancy]

fan·ta·size (fan'tə·sīz) *v.i.* **·sized, ·siz·ing** To create mental fantasies.

fan·tas·tic (fan·tas'tik) *adj.* 1. Odd, grotesque, or whimsical in appearance, construction, etc.: a *fantastic* room. 2. Wildly fanciful or exaggerated. 3. Capricious or impulsive, as moods, actions, etc. 4. Coming from the imagination or fancy. — *n. Archaic* One who is fantastic. [< Med.L < Gk. < *phantastēs* a boaster]

fan·tas·ti·cal (fan·tas'ti·kəl) *adj.* 1. Extremely capricious, odd, or eccentric. 2. Extravagantly fanciful, imaginative or grotesque. — **fan·tas'ti·cal'i·ty** (-kal'ə·tē), **fan·tas'ti·cal·ness** *n.* — **fan·tas'ti·cal·ly** *adv.*

fan·ta·sy (fan'tə·sē, -zē) *n. pl.* **·sies** 1. Imagination unrestrained by reality; wild fancy. 2. An odd, unreal, or grotesque mental image. 3. An odd or whimsical notion. 4. A capricious mood. 5. An ingenious or highly imaginative creation. 6. *Psychol.* A sequence of more or less pleasant mental images, usu. fulfilling a need not gratified in the real world. 7. *Music* A fantasia. — *v.t. & v.i.* **·sied, ·sy·ing** To envision; imagine. [< OF < L < Gk. *phainein* to show]

fan·tom (fan'təm) See PHANTOM.

fan window *Archit.* A fanlight.

far (fär) *adv.* 1. At, to, or from a great distance. 2. To or at a particular distance, point, or degree. 3. To a great degree; very much: *far* wiser. 4. Very remotely in time, degree, quality, etc.: *far* from pleasant. — **as far as** To the distance, extent, or degree that. — **by far** In a great degree; very much. — **far and away** Very much; decidedly. — **far and wide** Distantly and extensively; everywhere. Also **far and near.** — **far be it from me** I have not the audacity or desire. — **how far** To what extent, distance, or degree. — **in so far as** To the extent that. — **so far** 1. To that extent; up to that point. 2. Up to now. — **so far as** To the extent that. — **so far so good** Up to now everything is all right. — **to go far** 1. To accomplish much; have success. 2. To last a long time or cover a great extent. 3. To tend strongly. — *adj.* **far·ther** or **fur·ther, far·thest** or **fur·thest** (See note under FARTHER). 1. Very remote in space or time. 2. Extending widely or at length. 3. More distant: the *far* end of the garden. [OE *feor*]

far·ad (far'əd, -ad) *n. Electr.* The unit of capacitance; the capacitance of a condenser that retains one coulomb of charge with one volt difference of potential. [after Michael Faraday]

far·a·way (fär'ə·wā') *adj.* 1. Distant: a *faraway* town. 2. Absent-minded; abstracted: a *faraway* look.

farce (färs) *n.* 1. A comedy employing ludicrous or exaggerated situations. 2. A ridiculous action or situation. — *v.t.* **farced, farc·ing** To fill out with witticisms, jibes, etc., as a play. [< F < L *farcire* to stuff]

far·ci·cal (fär'si·kəl) *adj.* Of, belonging to, or resembling farce. — **far'ci·cal·ly** *adv.* — **far'ci·cal'i·ty, far'ci·cal·ness** *n.*

far cry A long way.

fare (fâr) *v.i.* **fared, far·ing** 1. To be in a specified state; get on: He *fares* poorly. 2. To turn out: It *fared* well with him. 3. To be supplied with food and drink. — *n.* 1. The fee for conveyance in a vehicle, etc. 2. A passenger carried for hire. 3. Food and drink; diet. [OE *faran* to go, travel]

Far East The countries of eastern Asia, including China, Japan, Korea, Manchuria, and adjacent islands.

fare·well (*n.* fâr'wel'; *interj.* fâr'wel') *adj.* fâr'wel') *n.* 1. A parting salutation; a good-by. 2. Leave-taking. — *interj.* Good-by. — *adj.* Parting; closing. [Earlier *fare well*]

far-fetched (fär'fecht') *adj.* Neither natural nor obvious; forced; strained: a *far-fetched* joke.

far-flung (fär'flung') *adj.* Extending over great distances.

fa·ri·na (fə·rē'nə) *n.* 1. A meal or flour obtained chiefly from cereals, nuts, potatoes, or Indian corn, and used as a breakfast food. 2. Starch. [< L < *far* spelt]

far·i·na·ceous (far'ə·nā'shəs) *adj.* 1. Consisting or made of farina. 2. Containing or yielding starch. 3. Mealy.

far·kle·ber·ry (fär'kəl·ber'ē) *n. pl.* **·ries** A shrub or small tree with edible black berries. [Origin unknown]

farm (färm) *n.* 1. A tract of land forming a single property and devoted to agriculture. 2. A tract of water used for the cultivation of marine life. 3. In baseball, a minor-league club used by a major-league club for training its recruits. — *v.t.* 1. To cultivate (land). 2. To take a lease of, as the use of a business or the collection of taxes, for a fixed rental, retaining the profits. 3. To let at a fixed rental, as the authority to collect taxes, etc.: usu. with *out.* 4. To let out the services of (a person) for hire. 5. To arrange for (work) to be performed by persons or a firm not in the main organization: with *out.* 6. In baseball, to place (a player) with a minor-league team for training: often with *out.* — *v.i.* 7. To practice farming. [< F < Med.L < L *firmare* to fix]

farm·er (fär'mər) *n.* 1. One who operates a farm. 2. One who pays for the privilege of collecting taxes, etc.

farm hand One who works on a farm, esp. for hire.

farm·house (färm'hous') *n.* The homestead on a farm.

farm·ing (fär'ming) *n.* 1. The business of operating a farm; agriculture. 2. The leasing of the authority to collect taxes, etc. — *adj.* Engaged in, suitable for, or used for agriculture.

farm·stead (färm'sted) *n.* A farm and the buildings on it.

farm·yard (färm'yärd') *n.* A space surrounded by farm buildings, and enclosed for confining stock, etc.

far·o (fâr'ō) *n.* A game of cards in which the players bet against the dealer as to the order in which certain cards will appear. [Alter. of *Pharaoh*]

Far·o·ese (fâr'ō·ēz', -ēs') *n. pl.* **·ese** A native or inhabitant of the Faeroe Islands. 2. The North Germanic language spoken in these islands, closely resembling Icelandic.

far-off (fär'ôf', -of') *adj.* Distant; remote.

far-out (fär'out') *adj.* **far·ther-out, far·thest-out** *Slang* Advanced, unconventional, or avant-garde.

far·ra·go (fə·rā'gō, -rä'-) *n. pl.* **·goes** A confused mixture; medley. [< L *far* spelt]

far-reach·ing (fär'rē'ching) *adj.* Having wide influence, range, or effect.

far·row (far'ō) *n.* A litter of pigs. — *v.t. & v.i.* To give birth to (young): said of swine. [OE *fearh* young pig]

far·see·ing (fär'sē'ing) *adj.* 1. Having foresight; prudent; wise. 2. Able to see distant objects clearly.

far·sight·ed (fär'sī'tid) *adj.* 1. Able to see things at a distance more clearly than things at hand. 2. Having foresight. — **far'sight'ed·ly** *adv.* — **far'sight'ed·ness** *n.*

far·ther (fär'thər) Comparative of FAR. — *adv.* To or at a more advanced point in space or, less often, time. — *adj.* 1. More distant or remote. 2. Additional: in this sense usu. *further.* [ME *ferther*; var. of FURTHER]

far·ther·most (fär'thər·mōst') *adj.* Most distant; farthest.

far·thest (fär'thist) Superlative of FAR. — *adv.* To or at the greatest distance. — *adj.* 1. Most distant or remote. 2. Longest or most extended: the *farthest* way around.

far·thing (fär'thing) *n.* 1. A small, bronze, English coin, formerly worth one fourth of a penny. 2. Something of no value; a trifle. [OE < *fēortha* a fourth]

far·thin·gale (fär'thing·gāl) *n.* A woman's hoop skirt of the 16th and 17th centuries. [< OF *verdugale*, alter. of Sp. *verdugado* < *verdugo* rod, hoop]

fas·ces (fas'ēz) *n.pl.* In ancient Rome, a bundle of rods enclosing an ax, used as a symbol of power. [< L, pl. of *fascis* bundle] — **fas·ci·al** (fash'ē·əl) *adj.*

fas·ci·a (fash'ē·ə) *n. pl.* **fas·ci·ae** (fash'ī·ē) 1. *Anat.* Fibrous connective tissue for enclosing or connecting muscles or internal organs. 2. Something that binds together, as a fillet; a band. [< L, band] — **fas·ci·al** *adj.*

fas·ci·cle (fas'i·kəl) *n.* 1. A small bundle or cluster, as of leaves, flowers, etc. 2. One of the sections of a book that is published in installments. [< L *fascis* bundle] — **fas'ci·cled** (-kəld) *adj.* — **fas·cic·u·lar** (fə·sik'yə·lər) *adj.*

fas·ci·nate (fas'ə·nāt) *v.* **·nat·ed, ·nat·ing** *v.t.* 1. To attract irresistibly, as by beauty or other qualities; captivate. 2.

To hold spellbound, as by terror or awe. — *v.i.* **3.** To be fascinating. [< L *fascinum* spell] — **fas′ci·nat′ing** *adj.* — **fas′ci·nat′ing·ly** *adv.* — **fas′ci·na′tor** *n.*

fas·ci·na·tion (fas′ə·nā′shən) *n.* **1.** The act of fascinating, or the state of being fascinated. **2.** A fascinating attraction, influence, or quality; enchantment; charm.

fas·cism (fash′iz·əm) *n.* A one-party system of government in which the individual is subordinated to the state and control is maintained by military force, secret police, rigid censorship, and governmental regimentation of industry and finance. [See FASCISTI.]

fas·cist (fash′ist) *n.* **1.** An advocate of fascism. **2.** A member of a fascist party. — *adj.* Of, advocating, or practicing fascism: a *fascist* state: also **fa·scis·tic** (fə·shis′tik).

fash·ion (fash′ən) *n.* **1.** The mode of dress, manners, living, etc., prevailing in society, esp. in high society; also, good form or style. **2.** A current practice or usage. **3.** An object of enthusiasm among fashionable people. **4.** Fashionable people collectively; the élite. **5.** Manner: He walks in a peculiar *fashion*. **6.** Kind; sort. — **after a fashion** To a limited extent. — *v.t.* **1.** To give shape or form to; mold. **2.** To adapt, as to the occasion. [< AF, OF < L *factio*, *-onis* a (special) way of making] — **fash′ion·er** *n.*

fash·ion·a·ble (fash′ən·ə·bəl) *adj.* **1.** Conforming to the current fashion. **2.** Associated with, characteristic of, or patronized by persons of fashion. — *n.* A person of fashion. — **fash′ion·a·ble·ness** *n.* — **fash′ion·a·bly** *adv.*

fash·ioned (fash′ənd) *adj.* **1.** Made; shaped; formed. **2.** Of a certain style or fashion: *old-fashioned*.

fashion plate 1. One who dresses in the latest fashion. **2.** A picture representing the prevailing fashions in dress.

fast¹ (fast, fäst) *adj.* **1.** Firm in place; not easily moved. **2.** Firmly secured. **3.** Constant; steadfast: *fast* friends. **4.** Not liable to fade: said of colors. **5.** Resistant: *acid-fast.* **6.** Sound or deep, as sleep. **7.** Acting or moving quickly. **8.** Performed quickly: *fast* work. **9.** Permitting or suitable for quick movement: a *fast* track. **10.** Requiring rapidity of action or motion: a *fast* schedule. **11.** In advance of the true time. **12.** Characterized by or given to dissipation or moral laxity. **13.** *Photog.* Intended for short exposure, as a high-velocity shutter or a highly sensitive film. — **to play fast and loose** To act in a tricky or untrustworthy fashion. — *adv.* **1.** Firmly; securely. **2.** Soundly: *fast* asleep. **3.** Quickly. **4.** Dissipatedly: to live *fast.* [OE *fæst*]

fast² (fast, fäst) *v.i.* To abstain from food; esp., to eat sparingly or abstain from certain foods, as in observance of a religious duty. — *n.* **1.** Abstinence from food or from prescribed kinds of food, particularly as a religious duty. **2.** A period prescribed for fasting. [OE *fæstan*]

fas·ten (fas′ən, fäs′-) *v.t.* **1.** To attach to something else; connect. **2.** To make fast; secure. **3.** To direct (the attention, eyes, etc.) steadily. **4.** To impute or attribute. — *v.i.* **5.** To take fast hold; cling: usu. with *on.* **6.** To become firm or attached. [OE *fæst* fixed] — **fas′ten·er** *n.*

fas·ten·ing (fas′ən·ing, fäs′-) *n.* **1.** The act of making fast. **2.** That which fastens, as a bolt.

fas·tid·i·ous (fas·tid′ē·əs, fəs-) *adj.* Hard to please in matters of taste; exceedingly delicate or refined; overnice; squeamish. — **Syn.** See METICULOUS. [< L *fastidium* disgust] — **fas·tid′i·ous·ly** *adv.* — **fas·tid′i·ous·ness** *n.*

fast·ness (fast′nis, fäst′-) *n.* **1.** A fortress; stronghold. **2.** The state of being firm or fixed. **3.** Swiftness.

fat (fat) *adj.* **fat·ter, fat·test 1.** Having superfluous flesh or fat; obese; plump. **2.** Containing much fat, oil, etc. **3.** Rich or fertile, as land. **4.** Abundant; plentiful: a *fat* profit. **5.** Profitable: a *fat* job. **6.** Thick; broad. — **a fat chance** *Slang* Very little chance; no chance at all. — *n.* **1.** *Biochem.* Any of a large class of yellowish to white, greasy, solid or liquid substances widely distributed in plant and animal tissues. They are compounds of various fatty acids and glycerol, and are generally odorless, tasteless, and colorless. **2.** Animal tissue containing large quantities of such compounds. **3.** Any vegetable or animal fat or oil used in cooking. **4.** Plumpness; corpulence. **5.** The richest or most desirable part of anything. — **the fat is in the fire** The mischief is done. — **to chew the fat** *Slang* To talk. — *v.t.* & *v.i.* **fat·ted, fat·ting** To make or become fat. [OE *fæt*] — **fat′ly** *adv.* — **fat′ness** *n.* — **fat′tish** *adj.*

fa·tal (fāt′l) *adj.* **1.** Resulting in or capable of causing death. **2.** Bringing ruin or disaster; destructive. **3.** Highly significant or decisive; fateful: the *fatal* hour. **4.** Decreed or brought about by fate; destined; inevitable. [< L *fatum.* See FATE.] — **fa′tal·ly** *adv.*

fa·tal·ism (fāt′l·iz′əm) *n.* **1.** The doctrine that all events are predetermined and thus unalterable. **2.** A disposition to accept every event or condition as inevitable. — **fa′tal·ist** *n.* — **fa′tal·is′tic** *adj.* — **fa′tal·is′ti·cal·ly** *adv.*

fa·tal·i·ty (fā·tal′ə·tē, fə-) *n.* *pl.* **·ties 1.** A death brought

about through some disaster or calamity. **2.** The capability of causing death or disaster. **3.** The state or quality of being subject to or determined by fate. **4.** A decree of fate.

fat·back (fat′bak′) *n.* Unsmoked salt pork.

fate (fāt) *n.* **1.** A force viewed as unalterably determining events in advance; destiny. **2.** That which inevitably happens as though determined by this force. **3.** Final result or outcome. **4.** An evil destiny; esp., death or destruction. — *v.t.* **fat·ed, fat·ing** To predestine: obsolete except in the passive. [< L *fatus,* pp. of *fari* to speak]

fat·ed (fā′tid) *adj.* **1.** Controlled by or subject to fate; destined. **2.** Condemned to ruin or destruction; doomed.

fate·ful (fāt′fəl) *adj.* **1.** Determining destiny; momentous. **2.** Brought about by or as if by fate. **3.** Bringing death or disaster; fatal. **4.** Ominously prophetic; portentous. — **fate′ful·ly** *adv.* — **fate′ful·ness** *n.*

Fates (fāts) In classical mythology, the three goddesses who control human destiny (Atropos, Clotho, and Lachesis).

fat·head (fat′hed′) *n.* A stupid person. — **fat′head′ed** *adj.*

fa·ther (fä′thər) *n.* **1.** A male parent. **2.** A male who adopts a child or who otherwise holds a paternal relationship toward another. **3.** Any male ancestor; forefather. **4.** A male who founds or establishes something. **5.** Any elderly man: a title of respect. **6.** One of the orthodox writers of the early Christian church. **7.** A leader or elder of a council, assembly, etc. **8.** A member of the ancient Roman senate. **9.** *Eccl.* **a** *Usu. cap.* A priest or other church dignitary, as in the Roman Catholic or Anglican church: often used as a title of respect. **b** A confessor. — *v.t.* **1.** To beget. **2.** To act as a father toward. **3.** To found or make. [OE *fæder*] — **fa′ther·less** *adj.*

fa·ther-in-law (fä′thər·in·lô′) *n.* *pl.* **fa·thers-in-law 1.** The father of one's husband or wife. **2.** *Rare* A stepfather.

fa·ther·land (fä′thər·land′) *n.* **1.** The land of one's birth. **2.** The native country of one's forebears.

fa·ther·ly (fä′thər·lē) *adj.* **1.** Of or like a father. **2.** Showing the affection of a father. — **fa′ther·li·ness** *n.*

Father's Day The third Sunday in June.

fath·om (fath′əm) *n.* *pl.* **·oms** or **·om** A measure of length, 6 feet or 1.829 meters, used principally in marine and mining measurements. See table inside back cover. — *v.t.* **1.** To find the depth of; sound. **2.** To understand; interpret; puzzle out. [OE *fæthm* the span of two arms outstretched] — **fath′om·a·ble** *adj.* — **fath′om·less** *adj.*

fa·tigue (fə·tēg′) *n.* **1.** The condition of being very tired as a result of physical or mental exertion. **2.** *Mech.* Structural weakness or loss of resiliency in metals or other materials, produced by excessive subjection to strain. **3.** *Mil.* **a** A special work assignment done by soldiers in training: also **fatigue duty. b** *pl.* Strong, durable clothes worn on fatigue duty: also **fatigue clothes.** — *v.t.* & *v.i.* **·tigued, ·ti·guing 1.** To tire out; weary. **2.** To weaken, as metal. [< F < L *fatigare* to tire] — **fat′i·ga·ble** (fat′ə·gə·bəl) *adj.*

fat·ling (fat′ling) *n.* A young animal fattened for slaughter.

fat·ten (fat′n) *v.t.* **1.** To cause to become fat. **2.** To make (land) rich by fertilizing. **3.** To add to (a sum of money, etc.) so as to make larger and more attractive. — *v.i.* **4.** To grow fatter, heavier, etc. — **fat′ten·er** *n.*

fat·ten·ing (fat′n·ing) *adj.* That fattens: a *fattening* food.

fat·ty (fat′ē) *adj.* **·ti·er, ·ti·est 1.** Containing, possessing, or made of fat. **2.** Having the properties of fat; greasy; oily. — **fat′ti·ly** *adv.* — **fat′ti·ness** *n.*

fatty acid *Chem.* Any of a class of organic acids derived from hydrocarbons, and occurring in plant and animal fats.

fa·tu·i·ty (fə·tōō′ə·tē, -tyōō′-) *n.* *pl.* **·ties 1.** Smug stupidity; asininity. **2.** An utterly stupid action, remark, etc.

fat·u·ous (fach′ōō·əs) *adj.* **1.** Foolish and silly in a self-satisfied way; inane. **2.** Stupid: a *fatuous* grin. [< L *fatuus* foolish] — **fat′u·ous·ly** *adv.* — **fat′u·ous·ness** *n.*

fau·ces (fô′sēz) *n.pl. Anat.* The passage from the back of the mouth to the pharynx, formed by the membranous, muscular arches extending downward from each side of the soft palate. [< L] — **fau′cal** (-kəl), **fau′cial** (-shəl) *adj.*

fau·cet (fô′sit) *n.* A fixture with an adjustable valve that controls the flow of liquids from a pipe, vat, etc.; tap. [< OF, prob. < *fausser* to break into, create a fault]

faugh (fô) *interj.* An exclamation of disgust, contempt, etc.

fault (fôlt) *n.* **1.** Whatever impairs excellence; a flaw. **2.** A mistake or blunder. **3.** A slight offense; misdeed. **4.** Responsibility for some mishap, blunder, etc.; blame. **5.** *Geol.* A break in the continuity of rock strata or veins of ore. **6.** In tennis, squash, etc., failure to serve the ball into the prescribed area of the opponent's court; also, a ball that is improperly served according to rule. — **at fault 1.** Open to blame; in the wrong; culpable. **2.** At a loss; perplexed; astray.

FAULT (*def.* 5)

3. Off the scent. — **to a fault** Immoderately; excessively. — **to find fault** To seek out and complain about some imperfection, error, misdeed, etc.: often with *with.* — *v.t.* **1.** *Geol.* To cause a fault in. **2.** To find fault with; blame. — *v.i.* **3.** *Geol.* To crack. [< OF, ult. < L *fallere* to deceive]

fault·find·ing (fôlt′fīn′ding) *n.* The act of one who finds fault. — *adj.* Inclined to find fault; critical; carping. — **fault′find′er** *n.*

fault·less (fôlt′lis) *adj.* Free from faults; flawless; perfect. — **fault′less·ly** *adv.* — **fault′less·ness** *n.*

fault·y (fôl′tē) *adj.* **fault·i·er, fault·i·est** Having faults; defective; imperfect. — **fault′i·ly** *adv.* — **fault′i·ness** *n.*

faun (fôn) *n.* In Roman mythology, a woodland deity typically represented as a man having the ears, horns, tail, and hind legs of a goat; satyr. [< L *Faunus,* a rural god]

fau·na (fô′nə) *n.* *pl.* **·nas** or **·nae** (-nē) The animals living within a given area or environment or during a stated period. [< NL, after L *Fauna,* a rural goddess] — **fau′nal** *adj.*

Faust (foust) In medieval legend, drama, etc., a philosopher who sells his soul to a devil, Mephistopheles, for wisdom.

faux pas (fō pä′) *pl.* **faux pas** (fō päz′, *Fr.* fō pä′) A false step; esp., a breach of etiquette. [< F, lit., false step]

fa·vor (fā′vər) *n.* **1.** A helpful or considerate act. **2.** An attitude of friendliness or approbation. **3.** The condition of being looked upon with liking or approval. **4.** Unfair discrimination; narrow partiality: to show *favor.* **5.** The condition of leading one's opponent in the score of a game. **6.** A small gift presented to each guest on some festive occasion, as at a birthday party. **7.** *pl.* Consent to sexual intimacy. — **in favor** Having approval or support: a style much *in favor.* — **in favor of 1.** On the side of. **2.** To the furtherance or advantage of. **3.** Made out to the benefit of. — **in one's favor** Of such a kind as to help one or promote one's interests. — **out of favor** Lacking approval or support; not liked. — **to find favor** To come to be looked upon with approval or liking; gain acceptance. — *v.t.* **1.** To do a favor for; oblige. **2.** To look upon with approval or liking. **3.** To show special consideration to, often in an unfair way. **4.** To increase the chances of success of. **5.** *Informal* To show a resemblance to in features. **6.** To be careful of. Also *Brit.* **fa′vour.** [< OF < L < *favere* to favor] — **fa′vor·er** *n.*

fa·vor·a·ble (fā′vər·ə·bəl) *adj.* **1.** Granting something requested or hoped for. **2.** Building up hope or confidence. **3.** Boding well; promising; approving. **4.** Well-disposed or indulgent; friendly. Also *Brit.* **fa′vour·a·ble.** — **fa′vor·a·ble·ness** *n.* — **fa′vor·a·bly** *adv.*

fa·vored (fā′vərd) *adj.* **1.** Treated with or looked upon with friendliness, liking, or approbation. **2.** Endowed with esp. good qualities. **3.** Having an (indicated) aspect or appearance: an *ill-favored* countenance. Also *Brit.* **fa′voured.**

fa·vor·ite (fā′vər·it) *adj.* Regarded with special favor; preferred. — *n.* **1.** A person or thing greatly liked or preferred. **2.** A person granted special privileges by a high official, etc. **3.** In sports, the contestant considered to have the best chance of winning. Also *Brit.* **fa′vour·ite.**

fa·vor·it·ism (fā′vər·ə·tiz′əm) *n.* **1.** Preferential treatment, esp. when unjust or narrowly discriminating. **2.** The condition of being a favorite. Also *Brit.* **fa′vour·it·ism.**

fawn¹ (fôn) *v.i.* **1.** To show cringing fondness, as a dog: often with *on* or *upon.* **2.** To show affection or seek favor by or as by cringing. [OE *fahnian,* var. of *fægnian* to rejoice] — **fawn′er** *n.* — **fawn′ing·ly** *adv.*

fawn² (fôn) *n.* **1.** A young deer, esp. in its first year. **2.** The light yellowish brown color of a young deer. — *adj.* Light yellowish brown. [< OF < L *fetus* offspring]

fay (fā) *n.* A fairy. [< OF < L *fatum* fate]

faze (fāz) *v.t.* **fazed, faz·ing** *U.S. Informal* To worry; disconcert. [Var. of dial. E *feaze,* OE *fēsian* to frighten]

fe·al·ty (fē′əl·tē) *n.* *pl.* **·ties 1.** The obligation of fidelity owed to a feudal lord by his vassal or tenant. **2.** Faithfulness; loyalty. [< OF < L *fidelitas*]

fear (fir) *n.* **1.** An agitated feeling aroused by awareness of actual or threatening danger, trouble, etc.; dread; terror. **2.** An uneasy feeling that something may happen contrary to one's desires. **3.** A feeling of deep, reverential awe and dread. **4.** A continuing state or attitude of fright, dread, or alarmed concern: to live in *fear.* **5.** The possibility that something dreaded or unwanted may occur: There is no *fear* that such a thing will happen. — **for fear of** So as to avoid or keep from happening. — **for fear that** (or **lest**) So that ... not: He held her hand *for fear that* she would fall. — *v.t.* **1.** To be frightened of. **2.** To be uneasy or apprehensive over (an unwanted or unpleasant possibility). **3.** To have a deep, reverential awe of. — *v.i.* **4.** To feel dread or terror. **5.** To feel uneasy. [OE *fǣr* peril] — **fear′er** *n.*

fear·ful (fir′fəl) *adj.* **1.** Filled with dread or terror. **2.** Filled with uneasiness; apprehensive. **3.** Filled with deep, reverential awe. **4.** Causing dread or terror; terrifying; frightening. **5.** Showing fear; moved by fear: a *fearful* look. **6.** *Informal* Extremely bad. **6.** Going to extremes: a *fearful* drinker. — **fear′ful·ly** *adv.* — **fear′ful·ness** *n.*

fear·less (fir′lis) *adj.* Devoid of fear; not at all afraid. — **fear′less·ly** *adv.* — **fear′less·ness** *n.*

fear·some (fir′səm) *adj.* **1.** Causing fear; alarming. **2.** Timid; frightened. — **fear′some·ly** *adv.* — **fear′some·ness** *n.*

fea·sance (fē′zəns) *n.* *Law* Fulfillment of a condition, obligation, etc. [< AF < F < L *facere* to do]

fea·si·ble (fē′zə·bəl) *adj.* **1.** Capable of being put into effect or accomplished; practicable: a *feasible* project. **2.** Capable of being successfully utilized; suitable. **3.** Fairly probable; likely: a *feasible* explanation. [< OF < F < L *facere*] — **fea′si·bil′i·ty, fea′si·ble·ness** *n.* — **fea′si·bly** *adv.*

feast (fēst) *n.* **1.** A sumptuous meal. **2.** Something affording great pleasure to the senses or intellect. **3.** An elaborate banquet for many persons. **4.** A day or days of celebration regularly set aside for a religious purpose or in honor of some person, event, or thing; also **feast day.** — *v.t.* **1.** To give a feast for; entertain lavishly. **2.** To delight; gratify. — *v.i.* **3.** To partake of a feast; eat heartily. **4.** To dwell delightedly, as on a painting. [< OF < L *festa,* neut. pl. of *festus* joyful < *feriae* holidays] — **feast′er** *n.*

feat (fēt) *n.* A notable act, as one displaying skill or daring. — **Syn.** See ACT. [< OF *fait* < L *factum.* See FACT.]

feath·er (feth′ər) *n.* **1.** Any of the horny, elongated structures that form the plumage of birds and much of the wing surface. **2.** *pl.* Plumage. **3.** *pl.* Dress; attire. **4.** A lock or tuft of hair resembling a feather. **5.** The hairy fringe on the legs and tails of some dogs. **6.** A feather or feathers fastened to the shaft of an arrow to guide its flight. **7.** Something resembling a bird's feather, as a key, wedge, etc. **8.** Class or species; kind: birds of a *feather.* **9.** The act of feathering (an oar blade or propeller). — **a feather in one's cap** An achievement to be proud of. — **in full feather** In full force; fully equipped. — **in high, fine, or good feather** In good spirits or health. — *v.t.* **1.** To fit with a feather, as an arrow. **2.** To cover, adorne, line, or fringe with feathers. **3.** To join by a tongue-and-groove joint. **4.** In rowing, to turn (the oar blade) following each stroke so that the blade is more or less horizontal as it is carried back to the position for reentering the water. **5.** *Aeron.* To change the pitch of (a propeller) so that the blades are parallel with the line of flight. — *v.i.* **6.** To grow feathers or become covered with feathers. **7.** To move, spread, or expand like feathers. **8.** To feather an oar or propeller blade. — **to feather one's nest** To grow prosperous. [OE *fether*] — **feath′ered** *adj.*

feather bed A mattress stuffed with feathers or down.

feath·er·bed·ding (feth′ər·bed′ing) *n.* The practice of requiring the employment of more workers than are needed so as to create more jobs and prevent unemployment.

feath·er·brain (feth′ər·brān′) *n.* A flighty, stupid, or mentally unbalanced individual. — **feath′er·brained** *adj.*

feath·er·edge (feth′ər·ej′) *n.* A very thin, tapering edge, as of a planed board. — **feath′er·edged** *adj.*

feath·er·stitch (feth′ər·stich′) *n.* An embroidery stitch resembling a feather, made by taking one or more short stitches alternately on either side of a straight line. — *v.t.* & *v.i.* To embroider with such a stitch.

feath·er·weight (feth′ər·wāt′) *n.* **1.** A boxer or wrestler weighing between 118 pounds and 127 pounds. **2.** Any person or thing relatively light in weight or size. — *adj.* **1.** Of or like a featherweight. **2.** Insignificant; trivial.

feath·er·y (feth′ər·ē) *adj.* **1.** Provided with or as if with feathers; feathered. **2.** Suggestive of feathers in lightness, etc. — **feath′er·i·ness** *n.*

fea·ture (fē′chər) *n.* **1.** A distinctive part of the face, as the eyes, nose, or mouth. **2.** *Usu. pl.* The overall appearance or structure of a face. **3.** A distinguishing mark, part, or quality. **4.** A full-length motion picture, esp. a principal attraction. **5.** Anything given special prominence: as: **a** A special article, department, etc., in a magazine or newspaper. **b** An item publicized, as during a sale. **c** A special attraction, as on a program, etc. — *v.t.* **·tured, ·tur·ing 1.** To give special prominence to. **2.** To be a distinctive characteristic of. **3.** *Slang* To form an idea of; imagine. [< OF < L *facere* to do] — **fea′ture·less** *adj.*

fea·tured (fē′chərd) *adj.* **1.** Having (specified) facial characteristics: *hard-featured.* **2.** Presented as a special or central attraction.

febri- *combining form* Fever. Also, before vowels, **febr-.** [< L *febris* fever]

fe·brif·ic (fə·brif′ik) *adj.* **1.** Causing fever. **2.** Feverish.

feb·ri·fuge (feb′rə·fyooj) *n.* A medicine efficacious in reducing or removing fever. — *adj.* Reducing or removing fever. [< F < L *febris* + *fugare* to drive away]

fe·brile (fē′brəl, feb′rəl) *adj.* Feverish.

Feb·ru·ar·y (feb′roo·er′ē) *n.* *pl.* **·ar·ies** or **·ar·ys** The second month of the year, having twenty-eight, or, in leap years, twenty-nine days. *Abbr. F., Feb, Feb.* [< L *februa,* a Roman purificatory festival celebrated on Feb. 15]

fe·ces (fē′sēz) *n.pl.* **1.** Animal excrement; ordure. **2.** Any foul refuse matter or sediment. Also spelled **faeces.** [< L < *faex, faecis* sediment] — **fe′cal** (-kəl) *adj.*

feck·less (fek′lis) *adj.* **1.** Devoid of energy or effectiveness; feeble. **2.** Devoid of vitality; listless. **3.** Careless and irresponsible. **—feck′less·ly** *adv.* **—feck′less·ness** *n.*

fec·u·lent (fek′yə·lənt) *adj.* Turbid or foul with impurities; filthy. [< L *faex* dregs] **—fec′u·lence, fec′u·len·cy** *n.*

fe·cund (fē′kənd, fek′ənd) *adj.* Fruitful; prolific. [< OF < L *fecundus* fruitful] **—fe·cun·di·ty** (fi·kun′də·tē) *n.*

fe·cun·date (fē′kən·dāt, fek′ən-) *v.t.* **·dat·ed, ·dat·ing** **1.** To make fruitful. **2.** To fertilize. **—fe′cun·da′tion** *n.*

fed (fed) Past tense and past participle of FEED. **—fed up** *Slang* Surfeited with something to an extreme degree.

fed·er·al (fed′ər·əl) *adj.* **1.** Of, relating to, or formed by an agreement among two or more states, groups, etc., to merge into a union in which control of common affairs is granted to a central authority, with each member retaining jurisdiction over its own internal affairs; also, of, relating to, or supporting such a union or central government. **2.** Of or pertaining to a confederacy (def. 1). **—** *n.* An advocate or supporter of a federal union or federal government. [< F < L *foedus*, *-eris* compact, league] **—fed′er·al·ly** *adv.*

Fed·er·al (fed′ər·əl) *adj.* **1.** Of, relating to, or supporting the central government of a specific country, as of the U.S. **2.** Of, relating to, or loyal to the Union cause in the American Civil War. **3.** Of, relating to, or supporting the Federalist Party. **—** *n.* **1.** One who favored the Union cause in the Civil War. **2.** A Federalist. **—Fed′er·al·ly** *adv.*

Federal Bureau of Investigation An agency of the U.S. government that investigates violations of Federal laws.

fed·er·al·ism (fed′ər·əl·iz′əm) *n.* The doctrine, system, or principle of federal union or federal government; also, advocacy or support of this doctrine, system, or principle.

fed·er·al·ist (fed′ər·əl·ist) *n.* An advocate or supporter of federalism. **—** *adj.* Of or relating to federalism or federalists: also **fed′er·al·is′tic.**

Fed·er·al·ist (fed′ər·əl·ist) *n.* **1.** One who supported the federal union of the American colonies and the adoption of the Constitution of the United States. **2.** A member of the Federalist Party. **—Fed′er·al·ism** *n.* **—** *adj.* Of or relating to the Federalist Party or Federalists: also **Fed′er·al·is′tic.**

Federalist Party A political party (1787–1830) that advocated the adoption of the U.S. Constitution and the formation of a strong national government. Also **Federal Party.**

fed·er·al·ize (fed′ər·əl·īz′) *v.t.* **·ized, ·iz·ing** To unite in a federal union; federate.

fed·er·ate (*v.* fed′ə·rāt; *adj.* fed′ə·rit) *v.t. & v.i.* **·at·ed, ·at·ing** To unite in a federal union. [See FEDERAL.]

fed·er·a·tion (fed′ə·rā′shən) *n.* **1.** The joining together of two or more states, groups, etc., into a federal union or a confederacy. **2.** A league or confederacy.

fe·do·ra (fə·dôr′ə, -dō′rə) *n.* A soft hat, usu. of felt, with a curved brim and a crown creased lengthwise. [after *Fédora*, a play by V. Sardou, French dramatist]

fee (fē) *n.* **1.** A charge, compensation, or payment for something, as: **a** A sum charged for professional services: medical *fee.* **b** A sum charged for some privilege: membership *fee.* **c** A sum charged for admission: an entrance *fee.* **d** A gratuity or tip. **— to hold in fee** To have full and absolute possession of. **—** *v.t.* **feed, fee·ing** To pay a fee to. [< AF, var. of OF *fé, fief* < Med.L *feudum* fief, property, money]

fee·ble (fē′bəl) *adj.* **·bler, ·blest 1.** Lacking strength; very weak. **2.** Lacking energy, direction, or effectiveness: *feeble* efforts. **3.** Lacking point or substance: a *feeble* joke. **4.** Indistinct; faint: a *feeble* light. [< OF < L *flebilis* lamentable < *flere* to weep] **—fee′ble·ness** *n.* **—fee′bly** *adv.*

fee·ble-mind·ed (fē′bəl·mīn′did) *adj.* Mentally deficient. **—fee′ble-mind′ed·ly** *adv.* **—fee′ble-mind′ed·ness** *n.*

feed (fēd) *v.* **fed, feed·ing** *v.t.* **1.** To supply with food: to *feed* a hungry family. **2.** To give (something) as food or nourishment to: to *feed* carrots to rabbits. **3.** To serve as food or nourishment for; also, to produce food for: acreage that will *feed* many. **4.** To keep supplied, as with fuel: to *feed* a fire; also, to keep supplying: to *feed* data into a computing machine. **5.** To keep or make more intense or greater: to *feed* suspicions. **6.** To gratify; feast: to *feed* one's eyes on beauty. **—** *v.i.* **7.** To eat: said chiefly of animals. **— to feed on** (or **upon**) **1.** To consume (something) as food; use as food: said chiefly of animals. **2.** To draw support, encouragement, etc., from: to *feed on* hope. **—** *n.* **1.** Food given to animals. **2.** The amount of fodder, etc., given at one time. **3.** Material supplied, as to a machine. **4.** The supplying of such material. **5.** A mechanical part, as of a sewing machine, that keeps supplying material to be worked on, etc. **6.** *Informal* A meal. **— off one's feed** *Slang* Having little appetite. [OE *fēdan* < *fōda* food] **—feed′er** *n.*

feed·back (fēd′bak′) *n.* The return of part of the output of a system into the input for purposes of modification and control of the output, as in electronic amplifiers, automatic machines, certain biological and psychological processes, etc.

feel (fēl) *v.* **felt, feel·ing** *v.t.* **1.** To examine or explore with the hands, fingers, etc. **2.** To be aware of touch: to *feel* drops of sweat on one's forehead. **3.** To experience consciously (an emotion, pain, etc.): to *feel* joy. **4.** To be emotionally affected by: to *feel* disgrace deeply. **5.** To perceive or be aware of through thought: to *feel* the need for reform. **6.** To think; suppose; judge: I *feel* that you should do this. **7.** To have one's whole being respond to through understanding, etc. **8.** To experience the force or impact of: to *feel* the full weight of an attack. **—** *v.i.* **9.** To have physical sensation. **10.** To produce a sensory impression of being hard, soft, cold, hot, etc. **11.** To experience consciously the sensation or condition of being: He *feels* cold; to *feel* joyful. **12.** To produce an indicated overall condition, impression, or reaction: It *feels* good to be home. **13.** To experience compassion or pity: with *for:* I *feel* for you. **14.** To have convictions or opinions: to *feel* strongly about an issue. **15.** To search for by touching; grope: to *feel* around a darkened room. **— to feel like** *Informal* To have a desire or inclination for. **— to feel out 1.** To try to learn indirectly and cautiously the viewpoint, opinions, etc., of (a person); sound out. **2.** To explore the nature of (a situation, etc.) in a cautious way. **— to feel up to** To seem to oneself to be capable of or ready for. **—** *n.* **1.** Perception by touch or contact. **2.** The quality of something as perceived by touch. **3.** A sensation or impression. **4.** The act of feeling. [OE *fēlan*]

feel·er (fē′lər) *n.* **1.** One who or that which feels. **2.** Any action, hint, proposal, etc., intended to draw out the views or intentions of another. **3.** *Zool.* An organ of touch.

feel·ing (fē′ling) *n.* **1.** The faculty by which one perceives sensations of pain, pressure, heat, etc. **2.** Any particular sensation of this sort: a *feeling* of warmth. **3.** An emotion: a *feeling* of joy, sadness, etc. **4.** A sensation or awareness of something: a *feeling* of insecurity. **5.** A capacity to feel deeply: a woman of *feeling.* **6.** *pl.* Sensibilities; sensitivities: His *feelings* are easily hurt. **7.** A generous, sympathetic attitude; compassion. **8.** An impression produced upon a person by an object, place, etc. **9.** An opinion or sentiment; also, a foreboding. **—** *adj.* **1.** Having sensation; sentient. **2.** Having warm emotions; sympathetic: a *feeling* heart. **3.** Marked by or indicating emotion. **—feel′ing·ly** *adv.*

feet (fēt) Plural of FOOT. **— on one's** (or **its**) **feet 1.** In or into a condition of stability; well-established: to get a business *on its feet.* **2.** In or into a condition of restored health: to get a patient *on his feet.* **3.** Standing or walking.

feign (fān) *v.t.* **1.** To make a false show of; sham: to *feign* madness. **2.** To think up (a false story, a lying excuse, etc.) and give out as true; fabricate. **3.** To imitate so as to deceive. **—** *v.i.* **4.** To make pretense of something. [< OF < L *fingere* to shape] **—feigned** *adj.* **—feign′er** *n.*

feint (fānt) *n.* **1.** A deceptive appearance or movement; a ruse or pretense. **2.** An apparent or pretended blow or attack meant to divert attention. **—** *v.i.* To make a feint. [< F *feinte*, pp. of *feindre* < L *fingere* to shape]

feld·spar (feld′spär, fel′spär) *n.* Any one of a group of crystalline materials largely made up of silicates of aluminum: sometimes spelled *felspar.* Also **feld′spath** (-spath). [Partial trans. of G < *feld* field + *spat* spar] **—feld·spath′ic, feld·spath′ose** (-ōs) *adj.*

fe·lic·i·tate (fə·lis′ə·tāt) *v.t.* **·tat·ed, ·tat·ing** To congratulate. [< L < *felix, -icis* happy] **—fe·lic′i·ta′tion** *n.*

fe·lic·i·tous (fə·lis′ə·təs) *adj.* **1.** Most appropriate; apt. **2.** Using an agreeably pertinent or effective manner or style. **—fe·lic′i·tous·ly** *adv.* **—fe·lic′i·tous·ness** *n.*

fe·lic·i·ty (fə·lis′ə·tē) *n.* *pl.* **·ties 1.** Happiness; bliss. **2.** An instance of happiness. **3.** A source of happiness. **4.** An agreeably pertinent or effective manner or style. **5.** A pleasantly appropriate remark. [< OF < L *felix* happy]

fe·line (fē′līn) *adj.* **1.** Of or relating to a cat, as the domestic cat or lions, tigers, and leopards. **2.** Resembling a cat, as in stealthiness. **—** *n.* An animal of the cat family: also **fe·lid** (fē′lid). [< L < *felis* cat] **—fe′line·ly** *adv.* **—fe′line·ness, fe·lin·i·ty** (fə·lin′ə·tē) *n.*

fell¹ (fel) Past tense of FALL.

fell² (fel) *v.t.* **felled, fell·ing 1.** To strike and cause to fall down. **2.** To cut down (timber). **3.** In sewing, to finish (a seam) with a flat, smooth strip made by joining edges, folding them under, and stitching flat. **—** *n.* **1.** The timber cut down during one season. **2.** In sewing, a felled seam. [OE *fellan*, causative of *feallan* to fall] **—fell′a·ble** *adj.*

fell³ (fel) *adj.* Cruel; vicious; inhuman. [< OF *fel* cruel]

fell⁴ (fel) *n.* The skin of an animal, esp. as covered with its natural hair, wool, etc. [OE *hide*]

fel·lah (fel′ə) *n. pl.* **fel·lahs** or *Arabic* **fel·la·hin, fel·la·heen** (fel′ə·hēn′) In Arabic-speaking countries, a peasant or laborer. [< Arabic *fellāh*]

fell·er (fel′ər) *n.* **1.** One who or that which fells. **2.** A sewing-machine attachment for the felling of seams.

fel·low (fel′ō) *n.* **1.** A man or boy: often in informal address. **2.** *U.S. Informal* The sweetheart of a woman or girl. **3.** A person in general; anybody; one. **4.** A comrade or companion. **5.** A person viewed as being of little importance or worth. **6.** A partner or accomplice: *fellows* in crime. **7.** An individual belonging to the same kind, class, or group as oneself. **8.** Either one of a pair; mate. **9.** A member of one of several learned societies. **10.** A graduate student of a university or college who, in recognition of merit, is granted financial assistance to pursue further study. — *adj.* Joined through some common occupation, interests, objectives, etc.: *fellow* citizens. [OE *fēolaga* business partner]

fel·low·ship (fel′ō-ship) *n.* **1.** Companionship; association. **2.** The condition or fact of having common interests, ideals, experiences, etc. **3.** A body of individuals joined together through similar interests, beliefs, etc.; brotherhood. **4.** The status of being a fellow at a university or college; also, the financial grant made to a fellow. — *v* ·shiped or ·shipped, ·ship·ing or ·ship·ping *Rare v.t.* **1.** To grant fellowship to. — *v.i.* **2.** To join in fellowship with others.

fellow traveler One who favors the ideology or program of a particular group without being a member.

fel·ly (fel′ē) *n. pl.* ·lies A segment of or the entire rim of a wooden wheel, in which the spokes are inserted. [OE *felg*]

fel·on[1] (fel′ən) *n. Law* One who has committed a felony. — *adj. Poetic* Wicked, or cruel. [< OF *felon* base]

fel·on[2] (fel′ən) *n. Pathol.* An inflammation of a finger or toe in the terminal joint or at the cuticle. [? < FELON[1]]

fe·lo·ni·ous (fə-lō′nē-əs) *adj.* **1.** *Law* **a** Of, relating to, or involving a felony: *felonious* intent. **b** Constituting, resembling, or having the nature of a felony: *felonious* assault. **2.** *Poetic* Wicked. — **fe·lo′ni·ous·ly** *adv.* — **fe·lo′ni·ous·ness** *n.*

fel·o·ny (fel′ə-nē) *n. pl.* ·nies *Law* Any of several grave crimes, as murder, rape, arson, or burglary, for which a punishment greater than that for a misdemeanor is provided.

fel·spar (fel′spär) See FELDSPAR.

felt[1] (felt) Past tense and past participle of FEEL.

felt[2] (felt) *n.* **1.** An unwoven fabric made by matting together fibers of wool, fur, or hair through pressure and the use of heat, chemicals, etc. **2.** Something made of felt, as a hat. — *adj.* Relating to, made of, or resembling felt. — *v.t.* **1.** To make into felt. **2.** To overlay with felt. — *v.i.* **3.** To become matted together like felt. [OE]

fe·luc·ca (fə-luk′ə, fe-) *n.* A small, swift vessel propelled by lateen sails and by oars. [< Ital. < Arabic *fulk* ship]

FELUCCA

fe·male (fē′māl) *adj.* **1.** Of or pertaining to the sex that brings forth young or produces ova. **2.** Typical of or suitable to this sex; feminine. **3.** Made up of women and girls: the *female* portion of the population. **4.** *Bot.* Designating a plant that has a pistil but no stamen and that is capable of being fertilized and of producing fruit. **5.** *Mech.* Denoting or having a bore or slot designed to receive a correlated inserted part, called *male*, as some electric plugs. — *n.* **1.** A human being of the female sex. **2.** A female animal or plant. [< OF < L *femina* woman]

fem·i·nine (fem′ə-nin) *adj.* **1.** Of or pertaining to the female sex; female. **2.** Of or pertaining to women and girls; typical of or appropriate to women and girls: *feminine* gentleness. **3.** Lacking manly qualities; effeminate. **4.** *Gram.* Applicable to females only or to persons or things classified, as in declension, as female. — *n. Gram.* **1.** The feminine gender. **2.** A word or form belonging to the feminine gender. — **fem′i·nine·ly** *adv.* — **fem′i·nine·ness** *n.*

feminine rhyme Rhyme in which the primary stress falls upon the next to the last syllable, as in *clever, never.*

fem·i·nin·i·ty (fem′ə-nin′ə-tē) *n. pl.* ·ties **1.** The quality or state of being feminine. **2.** A feminine trait.

fem·i·nism (fem′ə-niz′əm) *n.* **1.** A doctrine advocating the granting of the same social, political, and economic rights to women as the ones granted to men; also, a movement to win these. **2.** *Med.* The existence of female characteristics in the male. — **fem′i·nist** *n. & adj.* — **fem′i·nis′tic** *adj.*

fem·i·nize (fem′ə-niz) *v.t. & v.i.* ·nized, ·niz·ing To make or become feminine or effeminate. — **fem′i·ni·za′tion** *n.*

femme (fåm) *n. French* Woman; wife.

femme fa·tale (få-tål′) *French* A seductive woman.

fe·mur (fē′mər) *n. pl.* fe·murs or fem·o·ra (fem′ər·ə) *Anat.* The long bone extending from the pelvis to the knee. Also called *thighbone.* For illustration see PELVIS. [< L, thigh] — **fem·o·ral** (fem′ər·əl) *adj.*

fen (fen) *n.* A marsh; bog. [OE *fenn*]

fence (fens) *n.* **1.** A structure of rails, stakes, strung wire, etc., erected as an enclosure, barrier, or boundary. **2.** Fencing. **3.** Skill at making quick, effective remarks or retorts, as in a discussion or debate. **4.** A dealer in stolen goods. —

on the fence Unwilling or unable to commit oneself one way or the other. — *v.* fenced, fenc·ing *v.t.* **1.** To enclose with or as with a fence. **2.** To cause to be separated by or as by a fence. — *v.i.* **3.** To practice the art of fencing. **4.** To avoid giving direct answers. **5.** To deal in stolen goods. [Aphetic var. of DEFENCE] — **fence′less** *adj.* — **fenc′er** *n.*

fenc·ing (fen′sing) *n.* **1.** The art or practice of using a foil, sword, or similar weapon. **2.** The art or practice of making quick, effective remarks or retorts, as in a debate. **3.** Material used in making fences; also, fences collectively.

fend (fend) *v.t.* **1.** To ward off; parry: usu. with *off.* — *v.i.* **2.** To offer resistance; parry. **3.** *Informal* To provide; shift: with *for:* to *fend* for oneself. [Aphetic var. of DEFEND]

fend·er (fen′dər) *n.* **1.** One who or that which fends or wards off. **2.** *U.S.* A part projecting over each wheel of a car or other vehicle, designed to keep water, mud, dirt, etc., from being thrown upwards. **3.** A metal guard set before an open fire. **4.** A part projecting from the front of a locomotive or streetcar, designed to push obstructions from the tracks.

Fe·ni·an (fē′nē·ən, fēn′yən) *n.* A member of an organization founded in New York about 1857 to seek independence for Ireland. — *adj.* Of Fenians. [< OIrish *fene* Irishman]

fen·nel (fen′əl) *n.* **1.** A tall herb of the parsley family that produces aromatic seeds used in cookery and pharmacy. **2.** The seeds of this plant. [OE < L *faeniculum* fennel]

feod (fyōod) See FEUD[2].

feoff (*v.* fef, fēf; *n.* fēf) *Law v.t.* **feoffed, feoff·ing** To give or grant a fief to. — *n.* A fief. [See FIEF.] — **feof′fer** *n.* — **feoff′ment** *n.*

-fer *combining form* One who or that which bears: *conifer.* [< L < *ferre* to bear]

fe·ral (fir′əl) *adj.* **1.** Not tame nor domesticated; wild. **2.** Of, relating to, or typical of a wild beast; savage. [< LL *feralis* < L *fera* wild beast]

fer-de-lance (fâr′də·läns′) *n.* A large, venomous snake of tropical South America and Martinique. [< F, lance iron]

fer·ment (*n.* fûr′mənt; *v.* fər·ment′) *n.* **1.** Any substance or agent producing fermentation, as enzymes, yeast, certain bacteria, etc. **2.** Fermentation. **3.** Excitement or agitation. — *v.t.* **1.** To produce fermentation in. **2.** To excite with emotion or passion; agitate. — *v.i.* **3.** To undergo fermentation; work. **4.** To be agitated, as with emotion; seethe. [< F < L *fervere* to boil] — **fer·ment′a·ble** *adj.* — **fer·ment′a·bil′i·ty** *n.* — **fer·ment′a·tive** *adj.*

fer·men·ta·tion (fûr′mən·tā′shən) *n.* **1.** *Chem.* The gradual decomposition of organic compounds induced by the action of various ferments; specifically, the conversion of glucose into ethyl alcohol through the action of zymase. **2.** Commotion, agitation, or excitement.

fer·mi (fer′mē, fûr′-) *n. Physics* A unit for the measurement of the radii of nuclear atomic particles, equal to 10^{-13} centimeter. [after E. *Fermi*]

fer·mi·um (fer′mē·əm, fûr′-) *n.* A radioactive element (symbol Fm), artificially produced by the bombardment of einsteinium with alpha particles. See ELEMENT. [after E. *Fermi*]

fern (fûrn) *n.* A plant that bears no flowers or seeds, having roots, stems, and large, feathery fronds, and reproducing by means of asexual spores. [OE *fearn*] — **fern′y** *adj.*

fern·er·y (fûr′nər·ē) *n. pl.* ·er·ies **1.** A place in which ferns are grown. **2.** A standing growth or bed of ferns.

fe·ro·cious (fə·rō′shəs) *adj.* **1.** Extremely savage, fierce, bloodthirsty, or cruel. **2.** *Informal* Very intense: *ferocious* heat. [< L *ferox, ferocis* fierce + -OUS] — **fe·ro′cious·ly** *adv.* — **fe·ro′cious·ness** *n.*

fe·roc·i·ty (fə·ros′ə·tē) *n. pl.* ·ties The state or quality of being ferocious. [< F < L *ferox* fierce]

-ferous *combining form* Bearing or producing: *coniferous.* [< -FER + -OUS]

fer·rate (fer′āt) *n. Chem.* A salt of ferric acid. [< L *ferrum* iron + -ATE[2]]

fer·ret (fer′it) *n.* A small, red-eyed polecat of Europe, often domesticated and used in hunting rodents and other vermin. — *v.t.* **1.** To search out by careful investigation: with *out.* **2.** To drive out of hiding or hunt with a ferret. — *v.i.* **3.** To search. **4.** To hunt by means of ferrets. [< OF < LL < L *fur* thief] — **fer′ret·er** *n.* — **fer′ret·y** *adj.*

FERRET
(Body about 14 inches long; tail 5 inches)

ferri- *combining form Chem.* Containing iron in the ferric condition. [Var. of FERRO-]

fer·ric (fer′ik) *adj. Chem.* **1.** Pertaining to iron. **2.** Pertaining to or designating compounds of iron in its higher valence. [< L *ferrum* iron + -IC]

Fer·ris wheel (fer′is) *U.S.* A giant, vertical, power-driven wheel that revolves on a stationary axle and has hanging seats in which passengers ride for amusement. Also **ferris wheel.** [after G. W. G. Ferris, 1859–96, U.S. engineer]

fer·rite (fer′it) *n.* **1.** *Geol.* A substance of uncertain composition that is found in igneous rocks and apparently contains iron. **2.** *Chem.* One of several compounds, often magnetic, containing ferric oxide. **3.** *Metall.* The pure metallic constituent in iron and steel. [< L *ferrum* iron + -ITE]

ferro- *combining form* **1.** Derived from, containing, or alloyed with iron. **2.** *Chem.* Containing iron in the ferrous condition. [< L *ferrum* iron]

fer·ro·con·crete (fer′ō-kon′krēt, -kon·krēt′) *n.* Reinforced concrete.

fer·ro·mag·net·ic (fer′ō-mag·net′ik) *adj. Physics* Highly magnetic, as is iron. — **fer′ro·mag′ne·tism** *n.*

fer·ro·man·ga·nese (fer′ō-mang′gə-nēs, -nēz) *n.* An alloy of iron rich in manganese, used in making tough steel.

fer·rous (fer′əs) *adj. Chem.* Of or pertaining to iron, esp. bivalent iron, where its combining value is lowest: *ferrous chloride,* FeCl₂. [< L *ferrum* iron + -OUS]

fer·ru·gi·nous (fə-rōō′jə-nəs) *adj.* **1.** Of or like iron. **2.** Rust-colored. [< L < *ferrum* iron]

fer·rule (fer′əl, -ōol) *n.* A metal ring or cap used on or near the end of a stick, as of a cane or a tool handle, to protect the end or reinforce the stick. — *v.t.* **·ruled, ·rul·ing** To equip with a ferrule. [< OF < L *viriae* bracelets]

fer·rum (fer′əm) *n.* Iron. [< L]

fer·ry (fer′ē) *n. pl.* **·ries** **1.** A boat or other craft used in conveying people, cars, or merchandise across a river or other narrow extent of water. **2.** Delivery of a boat or other craft to a user under its own motive power. — *v.* **·ried, ·ry·ing** *v.t.* **1.** To convey across a river, etc., by a boat or other craft. **2.** To cross (a river, etc.) in a boat or other craft. **3.** To deliver by ferry (def. 2). — *v.i.* **4.** To cross a river, etc., by or as by a ferry. [OE *ferian* to carry, convey]

fer·ry·boat (fer′ē-bōt) *n.* A boat used as a ferry.

fer·tile (fûr′təl, *esp. Brit.* -til) *adj.* **1.** Yielding or capable of producing abundant crops or vegetation: *fertile* land. **2.** Reproducing or able to reproduce. **3.** Inventive or productive: *a fertile* talent. [< OF < L *fertilis* < *ferre* to bear] — **fer′tile·ly** *adv.* — **fer′tile·ness** *n.*

fer·til·i·ty (fər-til′ə-tē) *n.* The state or quality of being fertile; productiveness.

fer·til·ize (fûr′təl-īz) *v.t.* **·ized, ·iz·ing** **1.** To make fertile; cause to be productive or fruitful. **2.** To cause (a female reproductive cell to begin development of a new individual. **3.** To spread manure, nitrates, or other enriching material on (land). *adj.* — **fer′til·i·za′tion** (-təl-ə-zā′shən) *n.*

fer·til·iz·er (fûr′təl-ī′zər) *n.* That which fertilizes; esp., a material, as manure or nitrates, used to enrich land.

fer·ule (fer′əl, -ōol) *n.* A flat stick or ruler sometimes used for punishing children. — *v.t.* **·uled, ·ul·ing** To punish with a ferule. [< L *ferula* whip, rod]

fer·vent (fûr′vənt) *adj.* **1.** Moved by or showing great warmth or intensity, as of emotion or enthusiasm; ardent. **2.** *Poetic* Very hot; burning. [< L *fervere* to boil] — **fer′vent·ly** *adv.* — **fer′ven·cy, fer′vent·ness** *n.*

fer·vid (fûr′vid) *adj.* **1.** Fervent, esp. to an extreme degree; most impassioned. **2.** *Poetic* Very hot; burning. [< L *fervere* to boil] — **fer′vid·ly** *adv.* — **fer′vid·ness** *n.*

fer·vor (fûr′vər) *n.* **1.** Great warmth or intensity, as of emotion; fervency; ardor. **2.** Heat; warmth. Also *Brit.* **fer′vour.** [< OF < L, violent heat, ardor]

fes·cue (fes′kyōō) *n.* Any of a genus of tough grasses, used for pasturage. [< OF < L *festuca* stalk, straw]

fess (fes) *n. Heraldry* A horizontal band across the middle of an escutcheon. Also **fesse.** [< OF < L *fascia* band]

-fest *combining form Slang* Bout; session: *gabfest.* [< G. *fest* festival]

fes·tal (fes′təl) *adj.* Pertaining to or typical of a festival, feast, or holiday. [< OF < L *festum* feast] — **fes′tal·ly** *adv.*

fes·ter (fes′tər) *v.i.* **1.** To develop pus; ulcerate. **2.** To be or become rotten and foul. **3.** To be a constant source of vexation or irritation; rankle. — *v.i.* **4.** To cause to fester. — *n.* A small, ulcerous sore. [< OF < L *fistula* ulcer]

fes·ti·val (fes′tə-vəl) *n.* **1.** A particular feast, holiday, or celebration. **2.** Any occasion for rejoicing or feasting. **3.** A special series of performances, exhibitions, etc.: a Shakespeare *festival.* — *adj.* Festive. [See FESTIVE.]

fes·tive (fes′tiv) *adj.* Of, relating to, or suitable for a feast or other celebration. [< L *festum* feast < *festus* joyful] — **fes′tive·ly** *adv.* — **fes′tive·ness** *n.*

fes·tiv·i·ty (fes-tiv′ə-tē) *n. pl.* **·ties** **1.** A festival. **2.** Gladness and rejoicing. **3.** *pl.* Festive merrymaking.

fes·toon (fes-tōōn′) *n.* **1.** Flowers or leaves, or colored paper, ribbon, etc., hanging in loops between two points. **2.** An ornamental carving, sculpture, etc., representing this. — *v.t.* To decorate, fashion into, or link together by festoons. [< F < Ital. *festa* feast] — **fes·toon′er·y** *n.*

fe·tal (fēt′l) *adj.* Of or typical of a fetus: also spelled *foetal.*

fetch (fech) *v.t.* **1.** To go after and bring back. **2.** To draw forth; elicit. **3.** To draw in (breath); also, to give forth (a sigh, groan, etc.); heave. **4.** To infer. **5.** To cost or sell for.

6. *Informal* To attract or delight. **7.** *Informal* To give or deal (a blow, slap, etc.). **8.** *Naut.* To arrive at (a port, etc.). — *v.i.* **9.** To go after something and bring it back. **10.** *Naut.* To hold to a particular course; also, to swing around; veer. — *n.* **1.** The act of fetching. **2.** A trick; stratagem. [OE *feccan*] — **fetch′er** *n.*

fetch·ing (fech′ing) *adj. Informal* Very attractive or pleasing; charming. — **fetch′ing·ly** *adv.*

fete (fāt) *n.* **1.** A festival. **2.** An outdoor celebration; esp. a dinner, bazaar, etc. — *v.t.* **fet·ed, fet·ing** To honor with festivities. Also *Brit.* **fête.** [< F *fête*]

fet·id (fet′id) *adj.* Having a foul odor; stinking. [< L *fetere* to stink] — **fet′id·ly** *adv.* — **fet′id·ness** *n.*

fet·ish (fet′ish, fē′tish) *n.* **1.** An object regarded as having magical powers. **2.** Something to which one is devoted excessively or irrationally. **3.** *Psychiatry* Some object not in itself erotic but which is sexually stimulating to certain individuals. Also **fetich.** [< F < Pg. *feitiço* charm]

fet·ish·ism (fet′ish-iz′əm, fē′tish-) *n.* **1.** Superstitious belief in or worship of fetishes. **2.** Excessive or irrational devotion to something. **3.** *Psychiatry* Sexual stimulation produced by an object that is not in itself erotic. Also **fet′ich·ism.** — **fet′ish·ist** *n.* — **fet′ish·is′tic** *adj.*

fet·lock (fet′lok′) *n.* **1.** A tuft of hair growing at the back of the leg of a horse just above the hoof. **2.** The joint of the leg from which this tuft grows: also **fetlock joint.** [ME *fitlock, fetlak,* prob. < LG]

fet·ter (fet′ər) *n.* **1.** A chain or other bond put about the ankles to restrain movement or prevent escape. **2.** *Usu. pl.* Anything checking freedom of movement or expression. — *v.t.* **1.** To put fetters upon. **2.** To prevent the free movement or expression of. [OE *feter, fetor*]

fet·tle (fet′l) *v.t.* **·tled, ·tling** To put in proper order; attend to; arrange. — *n.* Proper condition of health or spirits: in fine *fettle.* [ME *fetlen* to prepare, lit., to gird up]

fe·tus (fē′təs) *n. pl.* **·tus·es** The individual unborn organism carried within the womb in the later stages of its development. Also spelled *foetus.* [< L, a bringing forth]

feud¹ (fyōōd) *n.* A state of bitter hostility existing between two or more individuals, families, etc., usu. lasting over a long period of time. — *v.i.* To take part in a feud. [ME < OF < OHG *fehida* hatred, revenge] — **feud′ist** *n.*

feud² (fyōōd) *n.* In feudal law, a fief: also spelled *feod.* [< Med.L *feudum* fief]

feu·dal (fyōōd′l) *adj.* **1.** Of, relating to, or typical of the feudal system. **2.** Of or relating to a fief. — **feu′dal·ly** *adv.*

feu·dal·ism (fyōōd′l-iz′əm) *n.* The mode of life produced by the feudal system. — **feu′dal·ist** *n.* — **feu′dal·is′tic** *adj.*

feudal system A social, political, and economic system in medieval Europe in which vassals were granted land holdings by their lords in return for military service or the performance of other duties.

feu·da·to·ry (fyōō′də-tôr′ē, -tō′rē) *n. pl.* **·ries** A vassal holding a fief; also, the fief held. — *adj.* **1.** Of or typical of a feudal relationship. **2.** Subject to a feudal lord.

fe·ver (fē′vər) *n.* **1.** A disorder marked by unduly high body temperature, rapid pulse, often delirium, etc. **2.** Any of several diseases that produce this symptom. **3.** Emotional excitement or restless eagerness. ◆ Collateral adjective: *febrile.* — *v.t.* To affect with fever. [OE *fēfer* < L *febris*] — **fe′vered** *adj.*

fever blister A cold sore. Also **fever sore.**

fe·ver·few (fē′vər-fyōō′) *n.* A plant bearing white flowers.

fe·ver·ish (fē′vər·ish) *adj.* **1.** Having a fever, esp. a low fever. **2.** Of or resembling a fever. **3.** Tending to produce fever. **4.** Agitated, uneasy, or restless. Also **fe′ver·ous.** — **fe′ver·ish·ly** *adv.* — **fe′ver·ish·ness** *n.*

fe·ver·wort (fē′vər·wûrt′) *n.* **1.** A perennial herb with brownish purple flowers and a root used medicinally. Also **fe′ver·root′** (-rōōt′, -rŏŏt′). **2.** Boneset, an herb.

few (fyōō) *adj.* Small in number; not very many. — *pron. & n.* A small number; not very many. — **quite a few** A considerable number. — **the few** The minority. [OE *fēa* little]

fey (fā) *adj.* **1.** Acting as if enchanted or under a spell. **2.** Suggestive of a sprite. [< F < OF *fae* fairy]

fez (fez) *n. pl.* **fez·zes** A brimless, tapering, felt cap, usu. red and having a black tassel, often worn by Egyptian men. [after *Fez,* a city in Morocco]

fi·a·cre (fē·ä′kər, *Fr.* fyȧ′kr′) *n.* A small hackney coach. [after Hotel *St. Fiacre* in Paris, where they were first hired]

fi·an·cé (fē′än-sā′, fē·än′sā; *Fr.* fē·äṅ-sā′) *n.* A man to whom a woman is engaged to be married. [< F]

fi·an·cée (fē′än-sā′, fē·än′sā; *Fr.* fē·äṅ-sā′) *n.* A woman to whom a man is engaged to be married. [< F]

fi·as·co (fē·as′ko) *n. pl.* **·coes** or **·cos** A complete or humiliating failure. [< Ital., flask]

fi·at (fī′at, -ət) *n.* **1.** A positive and authoritative order or decree. **2.** Authorization. [< L, let it be done]

fiat money Paper money made legal tender by decree, as of a government, and not based on gold or silver reserves.
fib (fib) *n.* A lie about something unimportant. —*v.i.* **fibbed, fib·bing** To tell a fib. [? Alter. of FABLE] —**fib′ber** *n.*
fi·ber (fī′bər) *n.* **1.** A fine, relatively long, continuous piece of something, suggestive of a thread, as a filament of asbestos, spun glass, textile or fabric. **2.** *Biol.* One of similar filaments that together form animal or plant tissue or parts: a nerve *fiber*. **3.** A material made up of fine filaments; also, collectively, the filaments themselves. **4.** The particular composition or structure of something. **5.** Character: to lack moral *fiber*. Also *Brit.* **fi′bre.** [< F < L *fibra*]
fi·ber·board (fī′bər·bôrd′, -bōrd′) *n.* **1.** A tough, pliable building material made of wood fiber or other plant fiber.
Fi·ber·glas (fī′bər·glas′, -gläs′) *n.* A flexible, nonflammable material of glass spun into filaments, used for textiles, insulation, etc.: a trade name. Also **fi′ber·glas′, fi′ber·glass′.**
fibr- See FIBRO-
fi·bril (fī′brəl) *n.* **1.** A minute fiber. **2.** *Bot.* A root hair. [< NL < L *fibra* fiber] —**fi·bril·lar** (fī′brə·lər) *adj.*
fi·bril·la·tion (fī′brə·lā′shən) *n.* **1.** The formation of fibers. **2.** *Pathol.* Rapid contraction of muscle fibers of the heart.
fi·brin (fī′brin) *n.* *Biochem.* An insoluble protein that promotes the clotting of blood. —**fi·bri·nous** (fī′brə·nəs) *adj.*
fi·brin·o·gen (fī·brin′ə·jən) *n.* *Biochem.* A complex protein occurring in the formation of fibrin.
fibro- *combining form* Pertaining to or composed of fibrous tissue. Also, before vowels, **fibr-.** [< L *fibra* fiber]
fi·broid (fī′broid) *adj.* Made up of or resembling fibrous tissue.
fi·brous (fī′brəs) *adj.* Made up of, having, or resembling fiber: *fibrous* tissue.
fib·u·la (fib′yŏŏ·lə) *n.* *pl.* **·lae** (-lē) or **·las 1.** *Anat.* The outer and smaller of the two bones forming the lower part of the human leg from the knee to the ankle. **2.** *Zool.* In animals, a similar bone of the hind leg. **3.** An ancient ornamental brooch. [< L, a clasp] —**fib′u·lar** *adj.*
-fic *suffix* Making, rendering, or causing: *beatific*. [< L *-ficus* < *facere* to make, render]
-fication *suffix* A causing to be (something indicated): *beatification*. [< L *facere* to make, render]
fiche (fēsh) *n.* A microfiche (which see).
fi·chu (fik′ŏŏ, *Fr.* fē·shö′) *n.* A capelike piece of light material worn about the neck. [< F *ficher* to put on hastily]
fick·le (fik′əl) *adj.* Inconstant in feeling or purpose; changeful; capricious. [OE *ficol* crafty] —**fick′le·ness** *n.*
fic·tile (fik′til) *adj.* Produced by molding or able to be molded. [< L *fingere* to form]
fic·tion (fik′shən) *n.* **1.** Prose works in narrative form, the characters and incidents of which are wholly or partly imaginary; also, such works collectively. **2.** Something imagined or deliberately falsified. **3.** The action of arbitrarily making up an explanation, etc. [< F < L *fictio* a making < *fingere* to form] —**fic′tion·al** *adj.* —**fic′tion·al·ly** *adv.*
fic·ti·tious (fik·tish′əs) *adj.* **1.** Not corresponding to actual fact; artificially invented. **2.** Not genuine; not real; false. **3.** Fictional. —**fic·ti′tious·ly** *adv.* —**fic·ti′tious·ness** *n.*
fic·tive (fik′tiv) *adj.* **1.** Fictitious. **2.** Relating to the creation of fiction:·*fictive* ability. —**fic′tive·ly** *adv.*
fid (fid) *n.* *Naut.* **1.** A supporting bar or crosspiece to hold a topmast in place. **2.** A large, tapering wooden pin used for opening ropes when splicing, etc. [Origin uncertain]
-fid *combining form* **1.** Divided (into an indicated number of parts. **2.** Separated into lobes (of an indicated kind). [< L *-fidus* < *findere* to split]
fid·dle (fid′l) *n.* **1.** A violin; also, any other instrument of the violin or viol family. **2.** *Naut.* A rack used at table to prevent things from sliding off. —**fit as a fiddle** Enjoying perfect health. —**to play second fiddle** To have a position subordinate to that of another. —*v.* **·dled ·dling** *v.i.* **1.** *Informal* To play a violin. **2.** To make nervous or restless movements; fidget. —*v.t.* **3.** To spend (time) in a careless way: usu. with *away*. [OE *fithele* < ML *fidula, fidella,* dim. of L *fides* lyre] —**fid′dler** *n.*
fid·dle-de-dee (fid′l-dē′dē′) *n. & interj.* Nonsense.
fid·dle-fad·dle (fid′l·fad′l) *n. & interj.* Nonsense. —*v.i.* **·dled, ·dling** To occupy oneself with unimportant things.
fiddler crab A small burrowing crab found chiefly off the Atlantic coast of the U.S., one of whose claws is, in the male, much larger than the other.
fid·dle·stick (fid′l·stik′) *n.* **1.** A bow used on a violin, etc. **2.** Something trifling.
fid·dle·sticks (fid′l·stiks′) *interj.* Nonsense!

FIDDLER CRAB
(Carapace ¼ to 1 inch wide)

fi·del·i·ty (fī·del′ə·tē, fə-) *n. pl.* **·ties 1.** Faithfulness to duties, obligations, vows, truth, etc. **2.** Exactness of reproductive detail. **3.** *Electronics* The extent to which a phonograph, tape recorder, etc., receives and transmits input signals without distortion <F < L *fides* faith]

fidg·et (fij′it) *v.i.* **1.** To make nervous or restless movements. —*v.i.* **2.** To cause to fidget. —*n.* **1.** *Usu. pl.* The condition of being restless or nervous. **2.** One who fidgets. [ME *fiken* to fidget]
fi·du·cial (fi·dōō′shəl, -dyōō′-) *adj.* **1.** Fiduciary. **2.** Based on trust or faith. **3.** *Physics* Fixed as a basis of measurement. [< L *fidere* to trust] —**fi·du′cial·ly** *adv.*
fi·du·ci·ar·y (fi·dōō′shē·er′ē, -shər·ē, -dyōō′-) *adj.* **1.** Of, pertaining to, or acting as a trustee. **2.** Held in trust. **3.** Consisting of fiat money. —*n. pl.* **·ar·ies** One who holds something in trust. [< L *fidere* to trust]
fie (fī) *interj.* An expression of impatience or disapproval. [< OF *fi, fy* < L *fi,* an expression of disgust]
fief (fēf) *n.* A landed estate held under feudal tenure. [< OF < Med.L *feudum*]
field (fēld) *n.* **1.** A piece of land with few or no trees, covered with grass, weeds, or similar vegetation. ◆ Collateral adjective: *campestral*. **2.** A piece of land set aside for use as pasture or for crops. **3.** A large expanse of open country; also, any wide expanse. **4.** An area in which a natural resource is found: an oil *field*. **5.** An airport. **6.** The whole extent or a particular division of knowledge, research, study, etc.: the *field* of chemistry. **7.** In sports and athletics: **a** The bounded area where a game is played or where athletic contests, exhibitions, etc., are held: a football *field*. **b** The members of a team, etc., actually engaged in active play. **c** The competitors in a race or other contest. **8.** *Mil.* A region of active operations or maneuvers. **9.** In business, the area away from the home office. **10.** *Physics* An extent of space within which lines of magnetic or electric force are in operation: also called *field of force*. **11.** *Optics* The area within which objects are seen in a telescope, etc. **12.** The part of a painting canvas, flag, coin, etc., used for background. —**to leave the field** *U.S. Informal* To back out of a contest, struggle, dispute, etc —**to play the field** *U.S. Informal* To give one's energies, interest, or attention to the entire range of something. —**to take the field** To begin a game, military campaign, struggle, etc. —*v.t.* **1.** In baseball, cricket, etc.: **a** To catch or pick up (a ball) and return to the inner field. **b** To send (a player) to a field position. —*v.i.* **2.** In baseball, cricket, etc., to play in a field position. —*adj.* **1.** Of, pertaining to, or growing in fields. **2.** Used or designed for use in fields. **3.** Played or held on an open field. [OE *feld*]
field artillery Artillery so mounted as to be freely movable, and suitable for use with troops in the field.
field day 1. A day of military maneuvers, athletic contests, etc. **2.** A gala day full of pleasurable activities, etc.
field·er (fēl′dər) *n.* In baseball, etc., a player in the field.
field events The events at an athletic meet other than races.
field glass A compact, portable, binocular telescope. Also **field glasses.**
field goal 1. In football, a goal scored by a drop kick or a place kick, counting three points. **2.** In basketball, a goal scored while the ball is in active play, counting two points.
field hospital A military hospital near a combat zone.
field magnet The magnet that produces the magnetic field in a generator or electric motor.
field marshal In the armies of several European nations, an officer just below the commander in chief.
Field-Mar·shal (fēld′mär′shəl) *n.* In the British and Canadian armies, an officer of the highest rank. See table at GRADE.
field officer *Mil.* A colonel, lieutenant colonel, or major.
field of force *Physics* Field (def. 10).
field sports Athletic events, as jumping and pole-vaulting, held on the field, as opposed to races held on the track.
field·stone (fēld′stōn′) *n.* Loose stone found near a construction site and used in building. —*adj.* Consisting of or having the appearance of fieldstone: a *fieldstone* house.
field·work (fēld′wûrk′) *n.* A temporary fortification.
field work Observations and investigations made in the field, as by a scientist. —**field worker**
fiend (fēnd) *n.* **1.** An evil spirit; devil; demon. **2.** An intensely wicked or cruel person. **3.** *Informal* One who is highly skilled in a game, etc.: a bridge *fiend*. **4.** *Informal* One addicted to an injurious habit. —**the Fiend** Satan; the devil. [OE *fēond* enemy, devil] —**fiend′like** *adj.*
fiend·ish (fēn′dish) *adj.* Exceedingly cruel or malicious; diabolical. —**fiend′ish·ly** *adv.* —**fiend′ish·ness** *n.*
fierce (firs) *adj.* **1.** Having a violent and cruel nature. **2.** Violent in action or force. **3.** Vehement; intense: *fierce* anger. **4.** *Slang* Very disagreeable, bad, etc. [< OF < L *ferus* wild] —**fierce′ly** *adv.* —**fierce′ness** *n.*
fiery (fīr′ē, fī′ər·ē) *adj.* **fier·i·er, fier·i·est 1.** Like, containing, or composed of fire. **2.** Brightly glowing; blazing. **3.** Passionate; impetuous. **4.** Inflamed, as a boil. —**fier′i·ly** *adv.* —**fier′i·ness** *n.*
fi·es·ta (fē·es′tə, *Sp.* fyes′tä) *n.* **1.** A religious festival. **2.** Any holiday or celebration. [< Sp. < L *festa*]
fife (fīf) *n.* A small, shrill-toned flute used chiefly for mili-

tary music. **—v.t. & v.i. fifed, fif·ing** To play on a fife. [< G < LL < L *pipare* to peep, chirp] **—fif'er** *n.*

fif·teen (fif'tēn') *n.* **1.** The sum of fourteen and one: a cardinal number. **2.** Any symbol of this number, as 15, xv, XV. **3.** Anything consisting of or representing fifteen units, as an organization, game token, etc. **— adj.** Being one more than fourteen. [OE *fíftēne*] **—fif'teenth** *n. & adj.*

fifth (fifth) *adj.* **1.** Next after the fourth: the ordinal of *five.* **2.** Being one of five equal parts. **— n. 1.** One of five equal parts. **2.** That which follows the fourth. **3.** *Music* **a** The interval between a tone and another tone five steps from it. **b** One of these tones, esp. the one higher in pitch. **c** The fifth above the tonic: the dominant. **4.** One fifth of a U.S. gallon, used as a measure of liquors. **— adv.** In the fifth order, place, or rank: also, in formal discourse, **fifth'ly.** [OE *fífta*]

Fifth Amendment An amendment to the Constitution of the U.S. guaranteeing due process of law and that no person "shall be compelled to be a witness against himself".

fifth column In wartime, the civilians within defense lines who secretly assist the enemy. **— fifth columnist**

fifth wheel A superfluous person or thing.

fif·ty (fif'tē) *n. pl.* **·ties 1.** The sum of forty and ten: a cardinal number. **2.** Any symbol of this number, as 50, l, L. **3.** Anything consisting of or representing fifty units, as an organization, bill, etc. **— adj.** Being ten more than forty. [OE *fíftig*] **—fif'ti·eth** *n. & adj.*

fifty-fifty (fif'tē-fif'tē) *Informal adj.* Sharing equally, as in benefits: *fifty-fifty* partners. **— adv.** Equally.

fig (fig) *n.* **1.** The small, edible, pear-shaped fruit of a tree, cultivated in warm climates. **2.** The tree that bears this fruit. [< OF < L *ficus*]

fight (fīt) *v.* **fought, fight·ing** *v.t.* **1.** To struggle against in battle or physical combat. **2.** To struggle against in any manner. **3.** To carry on or engage in (a duel, court action, etc.) **4.** To make (one's way) by struggling. **5.** To manage the fighting of, as boxers or gamecocks. **— v.i. 6.** To take part in combat. **7.** To struggle in any manner. **— to fight it out** To fight until a final decision is reached. **— to fight shy of** To avoid meeting (an opponent or an issue) squarely; dodge. **— n. 1.** Strife or struggle; battle; conflict; combat. **2.** Power or disposition to fight; pugnacity. [OE *feohtan*]

fight·er (fī'tər) *n.* **1.** One who fights. **2.** *Mil.* A fast, highly maneuverable airplane for aerial fighting: formerly called *pursuit plane:* also **fighter plane.**

fig·ment (fig'mənt) *n.* A capricious product of the mind; a fiction; fabrication. [< L *figmentum* anything made]

fig·u·ra·tion (fig'yə·rā'shən) *n.* **1.** The act of shaping something. **2.** Form, shape, or outline. **3.** The act of representing figuratively. **4.** *Music* Ornamentation.

fig·ur·a·tive (fig'yər·ə·tiv) *adj.* **1.** Based on, like, or containing a figure or figures of speech; metaphorical. **2.** Representing by means of a form or figure. **3.** Pertaining to pictorial or sculptural representation. **—fig'ur·a·tive·ly** *adv.*

fig·ure (fig'yər, *Brit.* fig'ər) *n.* **1.** A character or symbol representing a number: the *figure* 5. **2.** *pl.* The use of such characters in calculating. **3.** An amount stated in numbers, as of price, etc. **4.** The visible form of anything; shape; outline. **5.** The human form or body. **6.** A personage or character, esp. a prominent one. **7.** The appearance or impression that a person makes. **8.** A representation or likeness, as in painting or sculpture. **9.** A pattern or design, as in a fabric. **10.** A printed illustration; a cut. **11.** One who or that which represents or symbolizes something: a *figure* of wisdom. **12.** A figure of speech. **13.** A movement or series of movements, as in a dance. **14.** *Geom.* A surface enclosed by lines, as a square or a space enclosed by planes, as a cube. **15.** *Music* Any short succession of notes that produces a single and distinct impression. **— v. ·ured, ·ur·ing** *v.t.* **1.** To compute numerically; calculate. **2.** To make an image or other representation of; depict. **3.** To ornament with a design. **4.** To picture mentally; imagine. **5.** To express by a figure of speech; symbolize. **6.** *Informal* To believe; predict. **7.** *Music* To mark with figures above or below the bass notes, indicating accompanying chords. **— v.i. 8.** To appear prominently; be conspicuous. **9.** To compute; reckon. **— to figure on** (or **upon**) *U.S. Informal* **1.** To count on; rely on. **2.** To plan on. **— to figure out 1.** To solve; compute. **2.** To make out; understand. [< F < L *fingere* to form] **—fig'ur·er** *n.*

fig·ured (fig'yərd) *adj.* **1.** Adorned or marked with figures or designs: *figured* cottons. **2.** Represented by figures.

figured bass *Music* A bass part with numerals, etc., indicating chords: also called *thorough bass.*

figure eight 1. A maneuver in ice skating that consists in tracing the figure 8. **2.** A style of knot: for illus. see KNOT.

fig·ure·head (fig'yər·hed') *n.* **1.** A person having nominal leadership but no real power. **2.** A carved or ornamental figure on the prow of a vessel.

figure of speech An expression that intentionally deviates from the literal meanings of words so as to create a more vivid effect, as in simile, metaphor, etc.

figure skating The art or sport of skating in prescribed dancelike patterns. **— figure skater**

fig·u·rine (fig'yə·rēn') *n.* A small, molded or carved figure; statuette. [< F < Ital. *figurina*]

fig·wort (fig'wûrt') *n.* A plant with small, dark flowers, formerly supposed to cure scrofula.

Fi·ji (fē'jē) *n.* **1.** One of the native people of the Fiji Islands. **2.** The Melanesian language of the Fijis.

Fi·ji·an (fē'jē·ən, fi·jē'ən) *adj.* Of Fiji, its people, or their language. **— n.** A Fiji.

fil·a·gree (fil'ə·grē) See FILIGREE.

fil·a·ment (fil'ə·mənt) *n.* **1.** A fine thread, fiber, or fibril; also, any threadlike structure or appendage. **2.** *Bot.* The stalk or support of an anther. For illus. see FLOWER. **3.** *Electr.* The slender wire of tungsten, carbon, etc., which, when heated by an electric current in a vacuum produces light. **4.** A similar wire that forms or heats the cathode of an electron tube. [< F < L *filum* thread] **—fil'a·men·ta·ry** (-men'tər·ē), **fil·a·men'tous** (-men'təs) *adj.*

fi·lar·i·a (fi·lâr'ē·ə) *n. pl.* **·lar·i·ae** (-lâr'i·ē) A worm parasitic in the blood and intestines of vertebrates. [< NL < L *filum* thread] **— fi·lar'i·al** (-əl), **fi·lar'i·an** (-ən) *adj.*

fil·bert (fil'bərt) *n.* The edible nut of the hazel or the tree it grows on: also called *hazelnut.* [after St. *Philibert,* because these nuts ripen about the time of his feast day (Aug. 22)]

filch (filch) *v.t.* To steal slyly and in small amounts; pilfer. [Origin uncertain] **—filch'er** *n.*

file[1] (fīl) *n.* **1.** Any device in which papers are systematically arranged for quick reference, as a folder, drawer, or cabinet. **2.** A collection of papers thus arranged. **3.** A line of persons, animals, or things placed one behind another. **— on file** Stored in systematic order for quick reference; in a file. **— single file** An arrangement of persons or things one behind another in a single line: also *Indian file.* **— v. filed, fil·ing** *v.t.* **1.** To store (papers, etc.) in systematic order. **— v.i. 2.** To march in file, as soldiers. **3.** To make an application, as for a job. [< L *filum* thread] **—fil'er** *n.*

file[2] (fīl) *n.* A hard steel instrument with ridged cutting surfaces, used to abrade, smooth, or polish. **— v.t. filed, fil·ing 1.** To cut, smooth, or sharpen with or as with a file. **2.** To remove with a file. [OE *fíl*] **— fil'er** *n.*

fi·let (fi·lā', fil'ā; *Fr.* fē·le') *n.* **1.** Net lace having a square mesh. **2.** Fillet (def. 2). **— v.t. ·leted** (fi·lād', fil'ād) **fi·let·ing** (fi·lā'ing, fil'ā·ing) To fillet (def. 2). [< F]

fi·let mi·gnon (fi·lā' min·yon', *Fr.* fē·le' mē·nyôn') A small, choice, boneless cut of beef from the inside of the loin. [< F]

fil·i·al (fil'ē·əl, fil'yəl) *adj.* **1.** Of, pertaining to, or befitting a son or daughter: *filial* devotion. **2.** *Genetics* Pertaining to a generation following the parental. [< LL < L *filius* son] **—fil'i·al·ly** *adv.*

fil·i·bus·ter (fil'ə·bus'tər) *n.* **1.** *U.S.* In a legislative body, an instance of the use of delaying tactics, esp. the making of time-consuming speeches; also, a legislator who makes such speeches: also **fil'i·bus'ter·er. 2.** An adventurer who takes part in an unlawful military expedition. **— v.i. 1.** *U.S.* To obstruct legislation by long speeches and delay. **2.** To act as an adventurer. **— v.t. 3.** *U.S.* To block passage of (legislation) by dilatory tactics. [< Sp. *filibustero* < Du. *vrijbuiter* freebooter] **—fil'i·bus'trous** *adj.*

fil·i·form (fil'ə·fôrm) *adj.* Threadlike.

fil·i·gree (fil'ə·grē) *n.* **1.** Delicate ornamental work formed of intertwisted gold or silver wire. **2.** Anything fanciful and delicate. **— adj.** Resembling, made of, or adorned with filigree; fanciful; ornate. **— v.t. ·greed, ·gree·ing** To adorn with or work in filigree. Sometimes spelled *filagree* or *fillagree.* [< Ital. < L *filum* thread + *granum* grain]

fil·ings (fī'lingz) *n.pl.* Particles removed by a file.

Fil·i·pi·no (fil'ə·pē'nō) *n. pl.* **·nos** A native or inhabitant of the Philippine Islands. **— adj.** Of or pertaining to the Philippine Islands or their inhabitants.

fill (fil) *v.t.* **1.** To supply (a container, space, etc.) with as much of something as can be contained. **2.** To supply fully, as with food. **3.** To occupy or pervade the whole of. **4.** To stop up; plug: to *fill* a tooth. **5.** To put together or make up what is indicated in (an order, prescription, etc.). **6.** To satisfy or meet (a need, requirements, etc.). **7.** To occupy (an office or position). **8.** To level out (an embankment, ravine, etc.) by adding fill. **— v.i. 9.** To become full. **— to fill away** *Naut.* To trim the yards so that the sails will catch the wind. **— to fill in 1.** To fill completely, as an excavation. **2.** To insert (something): to *fill in* one's name. **3.** To complete by inserting something; to *fill in* as an application. **4.** To be a substitute. **— to fill (someone) in on** *Informal* To give (someone) additional facts or details about. **— to fill out 1.** To make or become fuller or more rounded.

2. To make complete, as an application. **— to fill the bill** *U.S. Informal* To do or be what is wanted or needed. **— to fill up** To make or become full. *— n.* **1.** That which fills or is sufficient to fill. **2.** An embankment built up by filling in with stone, gravel, etc. [OE *fyllan* fill]

fil·la·gree (fil′ə·grē) See FILIGREE.

fill·er (fil′ər) *n.* **1.** One who fills. **2.** That which fills; as: **a** A substance added to increase bulk, weight, etc. **b** A composition for filling pores or holes in wood. **c** Tobacco used for the inside of cigars. **d** A piece of writing used to fill space.

fil·let (fil′it; *for n. def. 2 and v., also* fil′ā, fi·lā′) *n.* **1.** A narrow band or ribbon for binding the hair. **2.** A strip of boneless meat or fish. **3.** A narrow band of any material. *— v.t.* To slice into fillets. [< F < L *filum* thread]

fill-in (fil′in′) *n.* **1.** A person or thing included to fill a gap or omission. **2.** *Informal* A summary of facts.

fill·ing (fil′ing) *n.* **1.** That which is used to fill something; esp. the material put into a prepared cavity in a tooth. **2.** The act of becoming full. **3.** In weaving, the weft.

filling station *U.S.* A retail station for supplying gasoline, oil, etc., to motor vehicles: also called *gas station.*

fil·lip (fil′əp) *n.* **1.** The snap of a finger that has been pressed down by the thumb and suddenly released. **2.** Something that serves to excite or stimulate. *— v.t.* **1.** To strike with a fillip. **2.** To project by or as by a fillip. **3.** To stimulate; arouse. *— v.i.* **4.** To make a fillip. [Var. of FLIP]

fil·ly (fil′ē) *n. pl.* ·**lies 1.** A young mare. **2.** *Informal* A spirited young girl. [< ON *fylja* < *foli* foal]

film (film) *n.* **1.** A thin covering, layer, or membrane. **2.** A thin haze or blur. **3.** *Photog.* A sheet, roll, or strip of transparent material coated with a light-sensitive emulsion and used for making photographs. **4.** In motion pictures: **a** The film containing the pictures projected on the screen. **b** The motion picture itself. **c** *pl.* Motion pictures collectively. *— v.t.* **1.** To cover or obscure by or as by a film. **2.** To photograph on a film. **3.** To make a motion picture of: to *film* a play. *— v.i.* **4.** To become covered or obscured by a film. **5.** To make a motion picture. **6.** To be adaptable for filming. [OE *filmen* membrane]

film·strip (film′strip′) *n.* A length of processed film containing frames of still pictures that are projected on a screen.

film·y (fil′mē) *adj.* **film·i·er, film·i·est 1.** Composed of or like film; gauzy. **2.** Covered with or as with a film; hazy; dim. **— film′i·ly** *adv.* **— film′i·ness** *n.*

fil·ter (fil′tər) *n.* **1.** Any device, as paper, cloth, or charcoal, used as a strainer for clearing or purifying liquids, air, etc. **2.** *Physics* A device that permits the passage of waves and currents of certain frequencies and limits the flow of certain others. **3.** *Photog.* A colored screen that controls the kind and intensity of light waves in an exposure. *— v.t.* **1.** To pass (liquids, air, etc.) through a filter; strain. **2.** To separate or remove (impurities, etc.) by or as by a filter. **3.** To act as a filter for. *— v.i.* **4.** To pass through a filter. **5.** To leak out, as news. [< OF < Med.L *feltrum* felt (used as a filter)] **— fil′ter·er** *n.*

fil·ter·a·ble (fil′tər·ə·bəl) *adj.* **1.** Capable of being filtered. **2.** Capable of passing through a filter. Also **fil·tra·ble** (fil′trəb·əl) **— fil·ter·a·bil′i·ty** *n.*

filterable virus Virus (def. 1).

filth (filth) *n.* **1.** Anything that is foul or dirty. **2.** A foul condition. **3.** Moral defilement; obscenity. [OE *fylth*]

filth·y (fil′thē) *adj.* **filth·i·er, filth·i·est 1.** Of the nature of or containing filth. **2.** Morally foul; obscene. **3.** Highly unpleasant. **— filth′i·ly** *adv.* **— filth′i·ness** *n.*

fil·trate (fil′trāt) *v.t.* ·**trat·ed, ·trat·ing** To filter. *— n.* The liquid that has been separated by filtration. [< NL < Med.L *filtrum* a filter] **— fil·tra′tion** *n.*

fin (fin) *n.* **1.** A membranous extension from the body of a fish or other aquatic animal, serving to propel, balance, or steer it in the water. **2.** Any finlike or projecting part, appendage, or attachment. **3.** A flipper (def. 3). **4.** *Slang* The hand. *— v.* **finned, fin·ning** *v.t.* **1.** To cut up or trim off the fins of (a fish). *— v.i.* **2.** To beat the water with the fins, as a whale when dying. [OE *finn*] **— fin′less** *adj.*

fin² (fin) *n. U.S. Slang* A five-dollar bill. [< Yiddish *finf* five]

fi·na·gle (fi·nā′gəl) *v.* ·**gled, ·gling** *Informal v.t.* **1.** To get (something) by trickery or deceit. **2.** To cheat or trick (someone). *— v.i.* **3.** To use trickery or deceit; be sly. [Origin uncertain] **— fi·na′gler** *n.*

fi·nal (fī′nəl) *adj.* **1.** Pertaining to, or coming at the end; ultimate; last. **2.** Precluding further action or controversy; conclusive. **3.** Relating to or consisting in the end or purpose aimed at: a *final* cause. *— n.* **1.** Something that is terminal or last. **2.** *Often pl.* Something decisively final, as the last match in a tournament. [< F < L *finis* end]

fi·na·le (fi·nä′lē, ·nal′ē; *Ital.* fē·nä′lā) *n.* The last part, as the final scene in a play or the concluding section of a musical composition. [< Ital., final]

fi·nal·ist (fī′nəl·ist) *n.* In games, contests, etc., a contestant who takes part in the final matches.

fi·nal·i·ty (fī·nal′ə·tē) *n. pl.* ·**ties 1.** The state or quality of being final or settled. **2.** A final act, offer, etc.

fi·nal·ize (fī′nəl·īz) *v.t.* ·**ized, ·iz·ing** To put into final or complete form; bring to completion.

fi·nal·ly (fī′nəl·ē) *adv.* **1.** At or in the end; in conclusion; lastly. **2.** Completely; irrecoverably; decisively.

fi·nance (fi·nans′, fī′nans) *n.* **1.** The science of monetary affairs. **2.** *pl.* Monetary affairs; funds; revenue; income. *— v.t.* ·**nanced, ·nanc·ing 1.** To supply the money for. **2.** To manage the finances of. [< OF, payment]

fi·nan·cial (fi·nan′shəl, fī-) *adj.* **1.** Of or pertaining to finance or finances. **2.** Of or pertaining to those dealing with money and credit. **— fi·nan′cial·ly** *adv.*

fin·an·cier (fin′ən·sir′) *n.* One engaged or skilled in financial operations. *— v.t.* To finance.

fin·back (fin′bak′) *n.* A rorqual. Also **finback whale.**

finch (finch) *n.* A small, seed-eating bird, as the bunting, sparrow, bullfinch, goldfinch, or canary. [OE *finc*]

find (fīnd) *v.* **found, find·ing** *v.t.* **1.** To come upon unexpectedly. **2.** To discover after search, experience, or effort. **3.** To recover (something lost). **4.** To arrive at; reach. **5.** To gain or recover the use of: He *found* his tongue. **6.** To determine by legal inquiry and declare. *— v.i.* **7.** To express a decision after legal inquiry: to *find* for the plaintiff. **— to find oneself** To discover one's special abilities or one's proper vocation. **— to find out 1.** To learn; discover. **2.** To detect the identity or the true nature of. *— n.* **1.** The act of finding. **2.** Something found or discovered; esp., a valuable discovery. [OE *findan*]

find·er (fīn′dər) *n.* **1.** One who or that which finds. **2.** *Astron.* A small telescope by the side of a large one, used to locate a particular object. **3.** *Photog.* A camera attachment that shows the scene as it will appear in the photograph.

fin de siè·cle (faṅ də sye′kl′) *French* End of the century; esp. the close of the 19th century.

find·ing (fīn′ding) *n.* **1.** The act of one who finds. **2.** That which is found; a discovery or conclusion.

fine¹ (fīn) *adj.* **fin·er, fin·est 1.** Superior in quality; excellent. **2.** Highly satisfactory; very good. **3.** Light or delicate in texture, workmanship, structure, etc. **4.** Composed of very small particles: *fine* powder. **5.** Very thin: *fine* thread. **6.** Keen; sharp: a *fine* edge. **7.** Possessing superior ability or skill. **8.** Subtle; nice: a *fine* point. **9.** Discriminating: a *fine* ear for music. **10.** Elegant; polished; also, overelegant; showy; affected. **11.** Handsome; good-looking. **12.** Cloudless; clear: *fine* weather. **13.** Free from impurities. **14.** Containing a given proportion of pure metal: gold 18 karats *fine.* *— adv. Informal* Very well: It suits me *fine.* *— v.t. & v.i.* To make or become fine or finer. [< OF *fin* finished, perfected] **— fine′ly** *adv.* **— fine′ness** *n.*

fine² (fīn) *n.* A sum of money required as the penalty for an offense. **— in fine** Finally; in short. *— v.t.* **fined, fin·ing** To punish by fine. [< OF *fin* settlement]

fi·ne³ (fē′nā) *n. Music* The end; finis. [< Ital.]

fine arts The arts of painting, drawing, sculpture, and architecture, and sometimes including literature, music, drama, and the dance.

fine-drawn (fīn′drôn′) *adj.* Drawn out to extreme fineness or subtlety: a *fine-drawn* distinction.

fin·er·y (fī′nər·ē) *n. pl.* ·**er·ies** Elaborate adornment; showy or fine clothes or decorations.

fine-spun (fīn′spun′) *adj.* **1.** Drawn or spun out to an extreme degree of fineness. **2.** Excessively subtle.

fi·nesse (fi·nes′) *n.* **1.** Highly refined skill; subtlety of style or performance. **2.** Smoothness and tact, as in handling a delicate situation; also, artful strategy; cunning. **3.** In bridge and other card games an attempt to take a trick with the lower of two nonsequential cards in the hope that the hand yet to play does not hold an intervening card. *— v.* ·**nessed, ·ness·ing** *v.t.* **1.** To change or bring about by finesse. **2.** In card games, to play as a finesse. *— v.i.* **3.** To use finesse. **4.** In card games, to make a finesse. [< F < *fin.* See FINE¹.]

fine-toothed comb (fīn′tootht′) A comb with fine teeth set very close together. Also **fine′-tooth′ comb.** **— to go over with a fine-toothed comb** To examine minutely.

fin·ger (fing′gər) *n.* **1.** One of the terminating members of the hand, usu. excluding the thumb. **2.** That part of a glove made to fit the finger. **3.** Anything that resembles or serves as a finger. **4.** A unit of measure based on the width of a finger (from ¾ inch to one inch); or on the length of the middle finger (about 4 to 4½ inches). **— to burn one's fingers** To suffer the consequences of meddling or interfering. **— to have (or put) a finger in the pie** To take part in some matter. **2.** To meddle. **— to put one's finger on** To identify or indicate correctly. **— to put the finger on** *U.S. Slang* **1.** To betray as, to the police. **2.** To point out (the victim of a planned crime). **— to twist around one's (little) finger** To influence or control with little or no effort. *— v.t.* **1.** To touch or handle with the fingers; toy with. **2.** To steal; pilfer. **3.** *Music* **a** To play (an instrument) with the fingers. **b** To mark the fingering of (music). **4.** *U.S. Slang* To betray, as to the police. — *v.i.* **5.** To touch or feel anything with the fingers. [OE] — **fin′ger·er** *n.*

finger board In stringed instruments, as the violin, guitar, etc., the strip of wood upon which the strings are pressed by the fingers of the player. For illus. see VIOLIN.

finger bowl A bowl containing water for cleansing the fingers at the table after eating.

fin·gered (fing′gərd) *adj.* **1.** Having fingers. **2.** *Music* Having the fingering marked. **3.** Marked by fingers.

fin·ger·ing (fing′gər·ing) *n.* **1.** The act of touching or feeling with the fingers. **2.** *Music* **a** The action or technique of using the fingers in playing an instrument. **b** The notation indicating what fingers are to be used.

fin·ger·ling (fing′gər·ling) *n.* A young, small fish.

fin·ger·nail (fing′gər·nāl′) *n.* The horny substance along the upper surface of the end of a finger.

fin·ger·print (fing′gər·print′) *n.* An impression of the skin pattern on the inner surface of a finger tip, used for purposes of identification. — *v.t.* To take the fingerprints of.

finger tip The extreme end of a finger. — **to have at one's finger tips** To have ready and available knowledge of or access to.

fin·i·al (fin′ē·əl) *n. Archit.* An ornament at the apex of a spire, pinnacle, or the like. [< L *finis* end + -IAL]

fin·i·cal (fin′i·kəl) *adj.* Finicky. — **fin′i·cal·ly** *adv.* — **fin′i·cal·ness, fin′i·cal′i·ty** (-kal′ə·tē) *n.*

fin·ick·ing (fin′i·king) *adj.* Finicky.

fin·ick·y (fin′i·kē) *adj.* Excessively fastidious or precise; fussy; exacting. [< FINE¹ + -ICAL]

fin·is (fin′is, fī′nis) *n. pl.* **fin·is·es** The end. [< L]

FINIAL

fin·ish (fin′ish) *v.t.* **1.** To complete or bring to an end. **2.** To use up completely. **3.** To perfect (a person) in social graces, education, etc. **4.** To give (fabric, wood, etc.) a particular surface quality. **5.** *Informal* To kill, destroy, or defeat. — *v.i.* **6.** To reach or come to an end; stop. — *n.* **1.** The conclusion or last stage of anything. **2.** Something that finishes, completes, or perfects. **3.** Completeness and perfection of detail. **4.** Perfection or polish in speech, manners, education, etc. **5.** The surface quality or appearance of textiles, paint, etc.: a glossy *finish.* [< OF < L *finis* end] — **fin′ish·er** *n.*

fin·ished (fin′isht) *adj.* **1.** Ended; completed. **2.** Perfected to a high degree; polished. **3.** Highly accomplished.

fin·ish·ing school (fin′ish·ing) A school that prepares girls for entrance into society.

fi·nite (fī′nīt) *adj.* **1.** Having bounds, ends, or limits. **2.** That may be determined, counted, or measured. **3.** Subject to human or natural limitations: our *finite* minds. — *n.* Finite things collectively, or that which is finite. [< L *finitus* limited] — **fi′nite·ly** *adv.* — **fi′nite·ness** *n.*

finite verb *Gram.* A verb form that is limited as to person, number, tense, and mood, and that can serve as a predicate.

fin·i·tude (fin′ə·tōōd, -tyōōd, fī′nə-) *n.* The state of being finite.

fink (fingk) *n. U.S. Slang* **1.** A strikebreaker. **2.** An unsavory person. [? < FINGER, v. (def. 4)]

Finn (fin) *n.* **1.** A native or inhabitant of Finland. **2.** One whose native language is Finnish. [OE *Finnas* Finns]

fin·nan had·die (fin′ən had′ē) Smoked haddock Also **fin′·nan had·dock** (had′ək) [*Findhorn haddock,* after *Findhorn,* a Scottish fishing port where originally prepared]

finned (find) *adj.* Having fins or finlike extensions.

Finn·ish (fin′ish) *adj.* Of Finland, the Finns, or their language. — *n.* The Uralic language of the Finns.

Fin·no-U·gric (fin′ō-ōō′grik, -yōō′grik) *n.* A subfamily of the Uralic languages, including Finnish, Estonian, Lapp, Magyar, etc. Also **Fin′no-U′gri·an.**

fin·ny (fin′ē) *adj.* **1.** Having fins. **2.** Resembling a fin. **3.** Of or pertaining to fish. **4.** Abounding in fish.

fiord (fyôrd, fyōrd) *n.* A long and narrow arm of the sea running between high, rocky cliffs or banks: also spelled *fjord.* [< Norw. *fjord*]

fip·ple (fip′əl) *n.* A plug of wood at the mouth of certain wind instruments, as recorders. [? < ON *flipi* lip of a horse]

fir (fûr) *n.* **1.** Any of several trees of the pine family. **2.** The wood of these trees. [OE *fyrh*] — **fir′ry** *adj.*

fire (fīr) *n.* **1.** The visible, active phase of combustion, manifested in light and heat. **2.** A burning mass of fuel, as in a fireplace. **3.** A destructive burning, as of a building. **4.** A substance or device that produces fire or a firelike display: Greek *fire.* **5.** A flash or spark: to strike *fire.* **6.** A discharge of firearms: Cease *fire.* **7.** A rapid volley: a *fire* of questions. **8.** Flashing brightness; brilliance: the *fire* of a diamond. **9.** Intensity of spirit or feeling; ardor; passion. **10.** Vividness of imagination. **11.** Warmth or heat, as of

liquor. **12.** Fever or inflammation. **13.** An affliction or grievous trial. — **between two fires** Under attack or criticism from both sides. — **on fire** **1.** Burning; ablaze. **2.** Ardent; zealous. — **to catch fire.** To start to burn. — **to go through fire and water** To experience great afflictions. — **to hang fire** **1.** To fail to fire promptly, as a firearm. **2.** To be delayed or undecided. — **to lay a fire** To arrange fuel for igniting. — **to miss fire** **1.** To fail to discharge: said of firearms. **2.** To be unsuccessful; fail. — **to open fire** **1.** To begin to shoot. **2.** To commence. — **to play with fire** To do something rash or dangerous. — **to set fire to** or **to set on fire** **1.** To make burn. **2.** To inflame or excite. — **to set the world on fire** To gain great success or fame. — **to strike fire** **1.** To create a fire, as with flint. **2.** To get a reaction. — **to take fire** **1.** To start to burn. **2.** To become excited, angry, or enthusiastic. — **under fire** **1.** Exposed to gunshot or artillery fire. **2.** Subjected to severe criticism. — *v.* **fired, fir·ing** *v.t.* **1.** To set on fire. **2.** To tend the fire of. **3.** To subject to the heat of fire. **4.** To set off, as explosives. **5.** To set off explosives within or near: to *fire* an oil well. **6.** To discharge, as a gun or bullet. **7.** *Informal* To hurl: to *fire* questions. **8.** *Informal* To dismiss from employment. **9.** To bake, as pottery, in a kiln. **10.** To cure by heat. **11.** To cause to glow or shine. **12.** To inspire; excite. **13.** *Vet.* To cauterize. — *v.i.* **14.** To take fire; become ignited. **15.** To go off, as a gun. **16.** To set off firearms, a rocket, etc. **17.** *Informal* To hurl a missile. **18.** To tend a fire. — **to fire away** To start off and proceed energetically, esp. in asking questions. [OE *fȳr*]

fire-arm (fīr′ärm′) *n.* Any weapon, usu. small, from which a missile, as a bullet, is hurled by an explosive.

fire-ball (fīr′bôl′) *n.* **1.** A luminous meteor. **2.** Ball-shaped lightning. **3.** A hot, incandescent sphere of air and vaporized debris, formed around the center of a nuclear explosion. **4.** *U.S. Slang* A remarkably energetic person or thing.

fire-boat (fīr′bōt′) *n.* A boat equipped for fighting fires.

fire-box (fīr′boks′) *n.* The chamber in which the fuel of a locomotive, furnace, etc., is burned.

fire-brand (fīr′brand′) *n.* **1.** A piece of burning or glowing wood. **2.** One who stirs up trouble or dissension.

fire-break (fīr′brāk′) *n. U.S.* A strip of land that has been plowed or cleared to prevent the spread of fire.

fire-brick (fīr′brik′) *n.* A brick made of fire clay, used for lining furnaces.

fire-bug (fīr′bug′) *n. U.S. Informal* One who enjoys setting fire to buildings, etc.; a pyromaniac.

fire clay A refractory material, used to make crucibles, furnace linings, and the like.

fire control *Mil.* The control of the delivery of gunfire or of guided missiles by the use of special equipment.

fire-crack-er (fīr′krak′ər) *n.* A small paper cylinder charged with an explosive, used as a noisemaker.

fire-damp (fīr′damp′) *n.* **1.** A combustible gas, chiefly methane, that enters mines from coal seams. **2.** The explosive mixture formed by this gas and air.

fire-dog (fīr′dôg′, -dog′) *n.* An andiron.

fire-eat-er (fīr′ē′tər) *n.* **1.** A performer who pretends to eat fire. **2.** A hot-headed person eager to fight or quarrel.

fire engine A motor truck equipped to fight fires.

fire escape A metal stairway usu. attached to the outside of a building and furnishing a means of escape in case of fire.

fire extinguisher A portable apparatus containing fire-extinguishing chemicals ejected through a short hose.

fire-fly (fīr′flī′) *n. pl.* **·flies** A night-flying beetle emitting a phosphorescent light from an abdominal organ.

fire-house (fīr′hous′) *n. U.S.* A building housing fire-fighting equipment and personnel.

fire-light (fīr′līt′) *n.* Light from a fire, as from a campfire.

fire-man (fīr′mən) *n. pl.* **·men** (-mən) **1.** A man employed to prevent or extinguish fires. **2.** One who tends fires.

fire opal A variety of opal having translucent orange-yellow to red colors suggesting streaks of flame.

fire-place (fīr′plās′) *n.* A recess or structure in which a fire is built; esp., the part of a chimney opening into a room.

fire-plug (fīr′plug′) *n.* A hydrant for supplying water in case of fire.

fire-pow-er (fīr′pou′ər) *n. Mil.* **1.** Capacity for delivering fire, as from the guns of a ship, battery, etc. **2.** The amount or effectiveness of fire delivered by a given weapon or unit.

fire-proof (fīr′prōōf′) *adj.* Resistant to fire; relatively incombustible. — *v.t.* To make resistant to fire.

fire sale *U.S.* A sale of goods damaged by fire.

fire-side (fīr′sīd′) *n.* **1.** The hearth or space before the fireplace. **2.** Home or home life.

fire station A firehouse.

fire-trap (fīr′trap′) *n.* A building notoriously flammable.

fire-wa-ter (fīr′wô′tər, -wot′ər) *n.* Whiskey: term first used by the North American Indian.

fire·weed (fīr′wēd′) *n.* The willow herb.

fire·work (fīr′wûrk′) *n.* **1.** *Usu. pl.* A device containing combustibles or explosives that, when ignited, produce brilliant light or a loud noise. **2.** *pl.* A pyrotechnic display.

firing line 1. In combat, the front line from which gunfire is delivered. **2.** The foremost position in any activity.

firing pin The part of a firearm that strikes the primer or detonator, igniting the charge of the projectile.

firing squad 1. A military or naval detachment assigned to execute, by shooting, a person condemned to death. **2.** A similar squad to honor a deceased person with a salvo.

fir·kin (fûr′kən) *n.* **1.** A wooden vessel for butter, lard, etc. **2.** A measure of capacity, usu. equal to one fourth of a barrel. [ME < MDu. *vierde* fourth + -KIN]

firm[1] (fûrm) *adj.* **1.** Relatively solid, compact, or unyielding to touch or pressure. **2.** Difficult to move, loosen, etc. **3.** Fixedly settled and established. **4.** Constant and steadfast. **5.** Full of or indicating strength; vigorous; steady. **6.** Not fluctuating widely, as prices. — *v.t. & v.i.* To make or become firm. — *adv.* Solidly; resolutely; fixedly. [< L *firmus*] — **firm′ly** *adv.* — **firm′ness** *n.*

firm[2] (fûrm) *n.* A partnership of two or more persons for conducting business. [< Ital. < L < *firmus* firm]

fir·ma·ment (fûr′mə·mənt) *n.* The expanse of the heavens; sky. [< L *firmare* to make firm] — **fir′ma·men′tal** *adj.*

first (fûrst) *adj.* **1.** Preceding all others in the order of numbering: the ordinal of *one.* **2.** Prior to all others in time; earliest. **3.** Nearest or foremost in place. **4.** Highest or foremost in character, rank, etc.; chief. **5.** *Music* Designating one of two parts for like instruments or voices, usu. the one higher in pitch or the principal one. — **in the first place** To start with. — *n.* **1.** One who or that which is first in time, rank, order, or position. **2.** The beginning: from *first* to last. **3.** The winning position in a race or contest. **4.** *Music* One of two parts for like instruments or voices, usu. the one higher in pitch or the principal one. **5.** In English universities, the highest rank in examinations for honors; also, one winning this rank. **6.** *pl.* The best grade of certain merchandise, as of lumber, hosiery, etc. — **at first** At the beginning. — *adv.* **1.** Before all others in order, time, place, rank, etc.; also (more formally) *firstly.* **2.** For the first time. **3.** In preference to anything else: He would die *first.* [OE *fyrst*, superl. of *fore* before]

first aid Treatment given in an emergency before full medical care can be obtained. — **first-aid** (fûrst′ād′) *adj.*

First Amendment An amendment to the Constitution of the United States forbidding Congress to interfere with religion, free speech, a free press, the right to assemble peaceably, or the right to petition the government: ratified 1791.

first base In baseball, the base first reached by the runner, at the right-hand angle of the infield. — **first base′man**

first-born (fûrst′bôrn′) *adj.* First brought forth; eldest. — *n.* The first-born child.

first-class (fûrst′klas′, -kläs′) *adj.* **1.** Of highest rank or best quality. **2.** *U.S.* Of a class of sealed mail consisting wholly or partly of written matter. **3.** Of the most luxurious accommodations on a ship, plane, etc. — *adv.* By first-class mail or conveyance.

first-hand (fûrst′hand′) *adj.* Direct from the original source or producer. — *adv.* From the original source.

first lady The wife of the president of the U.S.

first lieutenant *Mil.* A commissioned officer ranking next above a second lieutenant and next below a captain.

first·ling (fûrst′ling) *n.* The first of a kind.

first·ly (fûrst′lē) *adv.* In the first place.

first mate A ship's officer ranking next below the captain.

first mortgage A mortgage having priority over all others.

first night The opening performance of a play, opera, etc. — **first-night** (fûrst′nīt′) *adj.* — **first′-night′er** *n.*

first papers Documents filed by an alien, declaring intention to be naturalized as a citizen of the U.S.

first-rate (fûrst′rāt′) *adj.* Of the finest class or quality; excellent. — *adv. Informal* Excellently.

firth (fûrth) *n. Scot.* An arm of the sea: also spelled *frith.*

fis·cal (fis′kəl) *adj.* Of or pertaining to the treasury or finances of a government; financial. [< F < L *fiscus* purse]

fiscal year Any twelve-month period at the end of which accounts are balanced.

fish (fish) *n. pl.* **fish** or (with reference to different species) **fish·es 1.** A vertebrate, cold-blooded aquatic animal with permanent gills, having a typically elongate, tapering body, usu. covered with scales and provided with fins for locomotion. ◆ Collateral adjective: *piscine.* **2.** Loosely, any animal habitually living in water. **3.** The flesh of fish used as food. — **like a fish out of water** Not comfortable or at ease. — *v.t.* **1.** To catch or try to catch fish in (a body of water). **2.** To catch or try to catch (fish, eels, etc.). **3.** To grope for and bring out: with *out* or *up*: to *fish* money out of one's pocket. — *v.i.* **4.** To catch or try to catch fish. **5.** To try to get something in an artful or indirect manner: with *for.* [OE *fisc*] — **fish′a·ble** *adj.* — **fish′like′** *adj.*

fish·bowl (fish′bōl′) *n.* A bowl, usu. of glass, serving as a small aquarium for fish.

fish cake A fried ball or cake of chopped fish, usu. salt codfish mixed with mashed potatoes. Also **fish ball.**

fish·er (fish′ər) *n.* **1.** A fisherman. **2.** A weasellike carnivore of eastern North America; also, its fur.

fish·er·man (fish′ər·mən) *n. pl.* **·men** (-mən) **1.** One who fishes as an occupation or for sport. **2.** A fishing boat.

fish·er·y (fish′ər·ē) *n. pl.* **·er·ies 1.** The operation or business of catching fish or other aquatic animals. **2.** The place for such an operation; a fishing ground. **3.** A fish hatchery.

fish hatchery A place designed for the artificial propagation, hatching, and nurture of fish.

fish hawk The osprey.

fish·hook (fish′hŏŏk′) *n.* A hook, usu. barbed, for fishing.

fishing rod A slender pole with a line and usu. a reel.

fishing tackle Equipment for fishing, as a rod, reel, etc.

fish·meal (fish′mēl′) *n.* Ground dried fish, used as fertilizer and feed for animals.

fish·mon·ger (fish′mung′gər, -mong′-) *n.* A dealer in fish.

fish stick *U.S. & Canadian* A frozen fish filet in bar form.

fish story *Informal* An extravagant or incredible narrative.

fish·tail (fish′tāl′) *adj.* Resembling the tail of a fish.

fish·wife (fish′wīf′) *n. pl.* **·wives** (-wīvz′) **1.** A woman who sells fish. **2.** A coarse, abusive woman.

fish·y (fish′ē) *adj.* **fish·i·er, fish·i·est 1.** Of or like fish. **2.** Abounding in fish. **3.** *Informal* Improbable. **4.** Vacant of expression. — **fish′i·ly** *adv.* — **fish′i·ness** *n.*

fissi- *combining form* Split; cleft. Also, before vowels, **fiss-.** [< L *fissus*, pp. of *findere* to split]

fis·sile (fis′əl) *adj.* **1.** Capable of being split or separated into layers. **2.** Tending to split. [< L *fissilis* < *findere* to split] — **fis·sil·i·ty** (fi·sil′ə·tē) *n.*

fis·sion (fish′ən) *n.* **1.** The act of splitting or breaking apart. **2.** *Biol.* Spontaneous division of a cell or organism into new cells or organisms, esp. as a mode of reproduction. **3.** *Physics* The disintegration of the nucleus of an atom, leading to the formation of more stable atoms and the release of energy. [< L *findere* to split] — **fis′sion·a·ble** *adj.*

fis·sure (fish′ər) *n.* **1.** A narrow opening, cleft or furrow. **2.** The act of cleaving, or the state of being cleft. **3.** *Anat.* Any cleft or furrow of the body, as on the surface of the brain. — *v.t. & v.i.* **·sured, ·sur·ing** To crack; split; cleave. [< L *fissura* < *findere* to split]

fist (fist) *n.* **1.** The hand closed tightly, as for striking; also, grip; clutch. **2.** *Informal* The hand. **3.** *Informal* Handwriting. **4.** *Printing* The index mark ☞. — *v.t.* To strike with the fist. [OE *fȳst*]

fist·ful (fist′fŏŏl) *n. pl.* **·fuls** *Informal* A handful.

fist·ic (fis′tik) *adj.* Of or pertaining to boxing; pugilistic.

fist·i·cuff (fis′ti·kuf′) *n.* **1.** *pl.* A fight with the fists. **2.** *pl.* The science of boxing. **3.** A blow with the fist. — *v.t. & v.i.* To fight with the fists. — **fist′i·cuff′er** *n.*

fis·tu·la (fis′chŏŏ·lə) *n. pl.* **·las** or **·lae** (-lē) *Pathol.* A duct or canal formed by the imperfect closing of a wound, abscess, or the like, and leading either to the body surface or from one cavity or hollow organ to another. [< L, a pipe]

fis·tu·lous (fis′chŏŏ·ləs) *adj.* **1.** Of, pertaining to, or like a fistula. **2.** Cylindrical and hollow like a reed. **3.** Having or consisting of cylindrical, hollow parts. Also **fis′tu·lar** (-lər).

fit[1] (fit) *adj.* **fit·ter, fit·test 1.** Adapted to an end, aim, or design; suited. **2.** Proper or appropriate; becoming. **3.** Possessing the proper qualifications; competent. **4.** In a state of preparation; ready. **5.** In good physical condition; healthy. — *v.* **fit·ted** or **fit, fit·ting** *v.t.* **1.** To be suitable or proper for. **2.** To be of the right size and shape for. **3.** To prepare, make or alter to the proper size or purpose. **4.** To provide with what is suitable or necessary; equip. **5.** To put in place carefully or exactly. — *v.i.* **6.** To be suitable or proper. **7.** To be of the proper size, shape, etc. — **to fit out** (or **up**) To supply with what is necessary; outfit. — *n.* **1.** Condition or manner of fitting. **2.** Something that fits. **3.** The act of fitting. [ME *fyt*] — **fit′ness** *n.*

fit[2] (fit) *n.* **1.** A sudden onset of an organic or functional disorder, often attended by convulsions; spasm. **2.** A sudden overmastering emotion or feeling. **3.** Impulsive and irregular exertion or action. — **by fits** or **by fits and starts** Spasmodically; irregularly. [OE *fitt* struggle]

fitch (fich) *n.* The polecat of Europe or its fur. Also **fitch′et** (-it), **fitch′ew** (-ōō) [< MDu. *vitsche* polecat]

fit·ful (fit′fəl) *adj.* Characterized by irregular actions, moods; capricious. — **fit′ful·ly** *adv.* — **fit′ful·ness** *n.*

fit·ly (fit′lē) *adv.* In a fit manner, place, or time; properly.

fit·ter (fit′ər) *n.* One who or that which fits.

fit·ting (fit′ing) *adj.* Fit; suitable; proper; appropriate. — *n.* **1.** The act of one who fits. **2.** A piece of equipment or an appliance used in an adjustment. **3.** *pl.* Furnishings, fixtures, or decorations. — **fit′ting·ly** *adv.* — **fit′ting·ness** *n.*

Fitz- *prefix* Son of: formerly used in forming the surnames of illegitimate children of royalty. [< OF < L *filius* son]

five (fīv) *n.* **1.** The sum of four and one: a cardinal number.

2. Any symbol of this number, as 5, v, V. **3.** Anything having five units, as a team, playing card, etc. — *adj.* Being one more than four. [OE fīf]

five-and-ten-cent store (fīv′ən·ten′sent′) **1.** Originally, a store selling miscellaneous articles priced at five and ten cents. **2.** A store selling articles priced from a few cents to one dollar or more. Also called *dime store, ten-cent store.* Also **five′-and-ten′, five-and-dime** (fīv′ən·dīm′).

five iron In golf, an iron with a moderately sloping face, used in lofting the ball: also called *mashie.*

Five Nations A confederacy of five tribes of Iroquois Indians, the Mohawks, Oneidas, Onondagas, Cayugas, and Senecas, within New York State.

fiv·er (fī′vər) *n. Informal* **1.** A five-dollar bill or a five-pound note. **2.** Anything counting as five.

Five-Year Plan (fīv′yir′) A plan for national economic development: a term first used by the Soviet Union.

fix (fiks) *v.t.* **1.** To make firm or secure; fasten so as to be immovable. **2.** To set or place permanently. **3.** To render unchangeable: to *fix* color. **4.** To hold or direct (the attention, gaze, etc.) steadily. **5.** To look at steadily or piercingly. **6.** To settle or decide (something); to determine or establish. **7.** To place (blame or responsibility) on a person. **8.** *U.S.* To put in order; adjust. **9.** To repair or mend. **10.** *U.S.* To prepare (food or a meal). **11.** *U.S. Informal* To prearrange or influence the outcome, etc., of (a race, game, jury, etc.) as by bribery. **12.** *U.S. Informal* To chastise or discipline. **13.** To prepare (specimens) for microscopic study. **14.** *Chem.* To cause to form a nonvolatile or solid compound. **15.** *Photog.* To bathe (a film or plate) in chemicals to remove light-sensitive substances and prevent fading. **16.** *Informal* To castrate or spay (a dog, cat, etc.) — *v.i.* **17.** To become firm or stable. — *n.* **1.** *Informal* A difficult situation; predicament. **2.** The position of a ship or aircraft as determined by fixed points on shore, astronomical observations, or bearings. **3.** *U.S. Slang* A decision or outcome prearranged by bribery or other corrupt means. **4.** *U.S. Slang* An injection of heroin or other narcotic. [< Med.L < L *fixus,* pp. of *figere* to fasten] — **fix′a·ble** *adj.* — **fix′er** *n.*

fix·a·tion (fik·sā′shən) *n.* **1.** The act of fixing, or the state of being fixed. **2.** *Chem.* The conversion of free nitrogen from the air into useful compounds; also, any similar process applied to an oil or a gas. **3.** *Psychoanal.* An arrested excessive attachment of the libido in a developmental stage. **4.** Loosely, a preoccupation or obsession.

fix·a·tive (fik′sə·tiv) *n.* That which serves to render permanent or fixed, as certain substances used on paintings.

fixed (fikst) *adj.* **1.** Placed or fastened securely; made firm in position. **2.** Steadily or intently directed; set. **3.** Stationary or unchanging in relative position. **4.** Definite and unalterable. **5.** Permanent. **6.** *U.S. Informal* Prearranged as to outcome or decision. **7.** *Chem.* a Formed into or forming part of a compound. b Not volatile. **8.** *Biol.* Sessile. — **fix·ed·ly** (fik′sid·lē) *adv.* — **fix′ed·ness** *n.*

fixed charge *Econ.* A charge that cannot be changed or avoided, esp. one payable at fixed intervals, as rent; taxes.

fixed idea *Psychiatry* An obsessional, delusional idea that influences a person's attitude or thinking: also *idée fixe.*

fixed star *Astron.* A star that seems to preserve the same position with respect to the stars around it.

fix·ings (fik′singz) *n.pl. U.S. Informal* Trimmings.

fix·i·ty (fik′sə·tē) *n. pl.* **·ties** **1.** The state or quality of being fixed; stability; permanence. **2.** That which is fixed.

fix·ture (fiks′chər) *n.* **1.** Anything securely fixed or fastened into position; esp., a permanent part or appendage of a house. **2.** A person or thing regarded as fixed in a particular place or job. **3.** *Law* a Any chattel or article of personal property affixed to reality to become a part thereof and thereafter governed by the law of real property. b Such chattel of a tenant, that can be removed without injury to the premises. [< FIXURE; infl. in form by *mixture*]

fizz (fiz) *v.i.* To make a hissing or sputtering noise. — *n.* **1.** A hissing sound. **2.** An effervescent beverage made with soda water, liquor, flavoring, etc.: a gin *fizz.*

fiz·zle (fiz′əl) *v.i.* **·zled, ·zling** **1.** To make a hissing or sputtering sound. **2.** *Informal* To fail, esp. after a good start. — *n.* **1.** Hissing. **2.** *Informal* A failure. [Freq. of obs. *fise* to fart]

fizz·y (fiz′ē) *adj.* **fizz·i·er, fizz·i·est** Fizzing; effervescent.

fjord (fyôrd) See FIORD.

flab·ber·gast (flab′ər·gast) *v.t. Informal* To astound.

flab·by (flab′ē) *adj.* **·bi·er, ·bi·est** **1.** Lacking strength or firmness; soft. **2.** Lacking vigor or force; weak, as language. — **flab′bi·ly** *adv.* — **flab′bi·ness** *n.*

flac·cid (flak′sid) *adj.* Lacking firmness or elasticity; limp; flabby. [< F < L *flaccus* limp] — **flac′cid·ly** *adv.* — **flac·cid′i·ty, flac′cid·ness** *n.*

fla·con (flå·kôn′) *n. French* A stoppered bottle or flask.

flag¹ (flag) *n.* **1.** A piece of cloth or bunting, usu. oblong, bearing devices and colors to designate a nation, state, organization, etc. **2.** The bushy part of the tail of a dog. **3.** The tail of a deer. **4.** *pl. Ornithol.* The long leg- or wing-feathers of a hawk or bird of prey. **5.** *Music* A hook. — *v.t.* **flagged, flag·ging** **1.** To mark out or adorn with flags. **2.** To signal as with a flag. **3.** To send (information) by signals. **4.** To decoy (deer, etc.), as by waving a flag. — **to flag down** To cause to stop, as a train, by signaling.

flag² (flag) *n.* **1.** Any of various irises having sword-shaped leaves and growing in moist places. **2.** The leaf of a flag.

flag³ (flag) *v.i.* **flagged, flag·ging** **1.** To grow tired or weak. **2.** To become limp. [? < obs. *flack* flutter]

flag⁴ (flag) *n.* A flagstone. — *v.i.* **flagged, flag·ging** To pave with flags. [< ON *flaga* slab of stone]

Flag Day June 14, the anniversary of the day in 1777 on which Congress proclaimed the Stars and Stripes the national standard of the United States.

flag·el·lant (flaj′ə·lənt, flə·jel′ənt) *n.* One who whips; esp., one who whips himself or has himself whipped from religious motives or for sexual excitement. Also **flag′el·la·tor** (flaj′ə·lā′tər). [< L *flagellum* whip] — **flag′el·la′tion** (-shən) *n.*

flag·el·late (flaj′ə·lāt) *v.t.* **·lat·ed, ·lat·ing** To whip; scourge. — *adj. Biol.* **1.** Having or producing whiplike processes or branches. **2.** Shaped like a flagellum. Also **flag′el·lat′ed.**

fla·gel·lum (flə·jel′əm) *n. pl.* **·la** (-ə) **1.** *Biol.* A lashlike appendage, as of a protozoan. **2.** A whip. [< L, whip]

flag·eo·let (flaj′ə·let′) *n.* A flutelike musical instrument blown at the end and having six finger holes. [< OF *flageol*]

flag·ging¹ (flag′ing) *adj.* Growing weak; failing; drooping.

flag·ging² (flag′ing) *n.* **1.** A pavement of flagstones; also, flagstones collectively. **2.** The act of paving with flagstones.

fla·gi·tious (flə·jish′əs) *adj.* Flagrantly wicked. [< L *flagitium* disgraceful act] — **fla·gi′tious·ly** *adv.*

flag·man (flag′mən) *n. pl.* **·men** (-mən) **1.** One who carries a flag. **2.** One who signals with a flag, as on a railway.

flag officer In the U.S. Navy, an officer above the rank of captain entitled to display a flag indicating his rank.

flag·on (flag′ən) *n.* A vessel with a handle, spout, and often a hinged lid, used to serve liquids. [< OF < Med.L *flasco*]

flag·pole (flag′pōl′) *n.* A pole on which a flag is displayed.

fla·grant (flā′grənt) *adj.* Openly disgraceful; notorious; heinous. [< L *flagrare* to blaze, burn] — **fla′gran·cy, fla′grance** *n.* — **fla′grant·ly** *adv.*

fla·gran·te de·lic·to (flə·gran′tē di·lik′tō) In the very act of committing a crime: literally, while the crime is blazing.

flag·ship (flag′ship′) *n.* The ship in a naval formation that carries a flag officer and displays his flag.

flag·staff (flag′staf′, -stäf′) *n. pl.* **·staffs** or **·staves** (-stāvz′) A staff on which a flag is hung or displayed.

flag·stone (flag′stōn′) *n.* A broad, flat stone for pavements.

flail (flāl) *n.* An implement for threshing grain by hand. — *v.t. & v.i.* To beat as with a flail. [OE *flygel,* prob. < L *flagellum* whip]

flair (flâr) *n.* **1.** A talent or aptitude. **2.** Instinctive perceptiveness; discernment. **3.** *Informal* A showy or dashing style. [< OF *flairer* to scent out]

flak (flak) *n.* Antiaircraft fire. [< G *fl(ieger)* aircraft + *a(bwehr)* defense + *k(anone)* gun]

flake (flāk) *n.* **1.** A small, thin piece peeled or split off from a surface. **2.** A small piece of light substance: a *flake* of snow. **3.** A stratum, layer, or lamina. — *v.t. & v.i.* **flaked, flak·ing** **1.** To peel off in flakes. **2.** To form into flakes. [ME < Scand.] — **flak′er** *n.*

flak·y (flā′kē) *adj.* **flak·i·er, flak·i·est** **1.** Resembling or consisting of flakes. **2.** Splitting off or easily separated into flakes. — **flak′i·ly** *adv.* — **flak′i·ness** *n.*

flam·beau (flam′bō) *n. pl.* **·beaux** (-bōz) or **·beaus** **1.** A burning torch. **2.** A large candlestick. [< F < OF *flamme*]

flam·boy·ant (flam′boi′ənt) *adj.* **1.** Extravagantly ornate; florid; showy. **2.** Brilliant in color; resplendent. **3.** *Archit.* Pertaining to a highly decorative style of architecture. [< F < OF *flambeier*] — **flam·boy′ance, flam·boy′an·cy** *n.* — **flam·boy′ant·ly** *adv.*

flame (flām) *n.* **1.** A mass of burning vapor or gas rising from a fire in streams or darting tongues of light. **2.** A single tongue of flame. **3.** *Often pl.* A state of bright, intensely active combustion. **4.** Something resembling a flame in brilliance, shape. **5.** Intense passion or emotion; ardor. **6.** *Informal* A sweetheart. **7.** A bright, red-yellow color. — *Syn.* See FIRE. — *v.* **flamed, flam·ing** *v.i.* **1.** To give out flame; blaze; burn. **2.** To light up or glow as if on fire; flash. **3.** To become enraged or excited. — *v.t.* **4.** To subject to heat or fire. [< OF < L *flamma* flame]

fla·men·co (flə·meng′kō, -men′-, flä-) *n.* **1.** A fiery, percussive style of singing and dancing practiced esp. by the Gypsies of Andalusia. **2.** A song or dance in this style. [< Sp.]

flame·out (flām′out′) n. Burnout, esp. of a jet engine.

flame thrower *Mil.* A weapon that throws a stream of burning napalm or other gasoline mixture.

flam·ing (flā′ming) adj. 1. In flames; blazing; fiery. 2. Brilliant. 3. Ardent. 4. Flagrant. — **flam′ing·ly** adv.

fla·min·go (flə-ming′gō) n. pl. ·gos or ·goes A long-necked wading bird of a pink or red color, having very long legs. [< Pg. or Sp. < L *flamma* flame + -ING³]

flam·ma·ble (flam′ə-bəl) adj. Capable of catching fire easily; combustible; inflammable. — **flam′ma·bil′i·ty** n.

flange (flanj) n. 1. A projecting rim or collar on a wheel, designed to keep it on a fixed track. 2. A similar projecting part of a beam, pipe, etc., designed to aid attachment or to increase stiffness. 3. A tool used to shape flanges. — v.t. & v.i. **flanged, flang·ing** To provide with or take the shape of a flange. [? < OF *flangir* to bend]

flank (flangk) n. 1. The part between the ribs and the hip at either side of the body of an animal or human being; also, a cut of meat from such a part. 2. Loosely, the outside part of the leg between the hip and the knee; thigh. 3. The extreme right or left part of something; side. 4. *Mil.* The right or left section of an army, fleet, fortification, etc. — v.t. 1. To be at the side of. 2. *Mil.* To defend, launch an attack against, or move around the flank of. — v.i. 3. To be located at the side of something. [< F *flanc* < Gmc.] — **flank′er** n.

flan·nel (flan′əl) n. 1. A woven fabric made of wool, or of wool and cotton. 2. A soft fabric made chiefly of cotton, with a nap on one or both sides: also **flan·nel·ette** (flan′əl-et′). 3. pl. A garment or garments made of flannel. [Prob. < Welsh *gwlan* wool] — **flan′nel·ly** adj.

flap (flap) v. **flapped, flap·ping** v.t. 1. To move (wings, the arms, etc.) vigorously up and down, esp. with a muffled slapping sound. 2. To cause to move with an irregular waving or rippling motion, esp. with noise. 3. To strike with something flat or flexible; slap. 4. *Informal* To throw down or close up suddenly or noisily. — v.i. 5. To flap the wings, arms, etc. 6. To have an irregular waving motion, as a flag. 7. *Slang* To lose one's composure. — n. 1. The part of an envelope that is folded down in closing or sealing. 2. A loosely hanging covering over the entrance to a tent, etc. 3. A loose cover over the opening of a pocket; also, a lapel. 4. *Aeron.* A hinged section as on the wings of an airplane, used to increase the lift or decrease speed. 5. *Surg.* A partially detached piece of tissue. 6. *Slang* An agitated or tempestuous reaction.

flap·jack (flap′jak′) n. *U.S.* A griddlecake.

flap·per (flap′ər) n. 1. One who or that which flaps. 2. A broad flipper, as of a seal. 3. A young bird not yet able to fly. 4. *U.S. Informal* A young woman trying to appear sophisticated in dress and behavior: term current in the 1920's.

flare (flâr) v. **flared, flar·ing** v.i. 1. To blaze up or burn with a wavering light, esp. suddenly: often with *up*. 2. To break out in sudden or violent emotion or action: often with *up* or *out*. 3. To spread or gradually open outward, as the sides of a bell. — v.t. 4. To cause to flare. 5. To signal (information) with flares. — n. 1. A bright, flickering light. 2. An outburst, as of emotion. 3. A spreading outward; also, that which so flares. 4. *Photog.* Excess light striking a film. 5. *Mil.* A signal that gives off a bright white or colored light. — Syn. See FIRE. [Origin unknown]

flare-up (flâr′up′) n. 1. A sudden outburst of flame or light. 2. A sudden outbreak of emotion.

flar·ing (flâr′ing) adj. 1. Blazing with a bright, unsteady light. 2. Gaudy. 3. Spreading outward. — **flar′ing·ly** adv.

flash (flash) v.i. 1. To burst forth suddenly or repeatedly into brilliant light or fire. 2. To gleam brightly; glitter. 3. To move suddenly or with lightning speed. — v.t. 4. To cause to shine or glitter brightly. 5. To emit bursts of (light, fire, etc.). 6. To send or communicate with lightning speed. 7. *Informal* To show suddenly or abruptly; also, to make an ostentation display of. 8. To provide (a roof, etc.) with sheet metal or flashing. 9. In glassmaking, to cover (glass) with a thin layer of differently colored glass. — n. 1. A quick blaze of light or fire, lasting an instant. 2. A sudden, brilliant manifestation, as of wit or talent. 3. Vulgar display. 4. An extremely brief space of time; instant. 5. *U.S.* A brief news dispatch sent by radio, etc. 6. A volatile mixture containing metal salts, used in applying a colored glaze to glass, etc. 7. A lock, dam, etc.; also, the sudden flow of water made available by such a device. — **flash in the pan** 1. Explosion of the powder in the pan of a flintlock musket without ignition of the charge. 2. A person, thing, or action that shows promise for a short time and then fails. 4. Done or occurring very quickly. [ME *flaschen*; prob. imit.] — **flash′er** n.

flash·back (flash′bak′) n. A break in the continuity of a novel, drama, motion picture, etc., to give a scene occurring earlier; also, the scene itself.

flash bulb *Photog.* Any of various electrical devices that emit an intense light of brief duration for taking photographs.

flash·cube (flash′kyoōb′) n. A small, rotatable cube containing four flash bulbs for use with a camera.

flash flood A sudden, rushing flood caused by heavy rainfall.

flash gun *Photog.* A device that ignites a flash bulb.

flash·ing (flash′ing) n. Sheet metal or other protective material used to cover joints or angles, as of a roof.

flash·light (flash′līt′) n. *U.S.* A small, portable device that emits a beam of light, usu. powered by dry batteries.

flash point The lowest temperature at which the vapors of combustible liquids, esp. lubricating oils, will ignite.

flash·y (flash′ē) adj. **flash·i·er, flash·i·est** 1. Brilliant for a moment; sparkling; flashing. 2. Showy; cheap. — **flash′i·ly** adv. — **flash′i·ness** n.

flask (flask, fläsk) n. Any of various small containers made of glass, metal, etc., with a narrow neck; as: **a** A flat container, esp. for liquor, to be carried in the pocket. **b** A rounded receptacle with a long neck, for laboratory work. **c** A powder flask. [< F < Med.L *flasca*]

flat¹ (flat) adj. **flat·ter, flat·test** 1. Extended horizontally with little or no slope. 2. Smooth and regular with few or no hollows or projections. 3. Stretched out level or prostrate. 4. Having the front or back in full contact with an even surface. 5. Shallow: a *flat* dish. 6. Absolute and unqualified: a *flat* refusal. 7. Lacking interest or zestfulness; lifeless; dull. 8. Lacking variety or contrast. 9. Deflated: a *flat* tire. 10. *U.S. Informal* Having little or no money: broke. 11. Fixed; uniform: at a *flat* rate. 12. Marked by little or no commercial activity: Trade was *flat*. 13. Exact; precise: in a minute *flat*. 14. *Music* **a** Lowered in pitch by a semitone. **b** Lower than the right, true pitch. **c** Having flats in the key signature. 15. *Phonet.* Designating the vowel sound in *man*, as opposed to the sound in *calm*. — *adv.* 1. In a flat state, position, or manner. 2. Exactly. 3. In finance, without interest. 4. *Music* Below the right, true pitch. — **to fall flat** To fail to achieve a desired effect. — n. 1. The flat, plane surface or part of something. 2. Something that has a flat surface; as: **a** A piece of stage scenery. **b** A railroad flat car. **c** A level area of land. **d** *Usu. pl.* A partially submerged plain or shallow; shoal. 3. *Informal* A tire from which the air has escaped. 4. pl. *Informal* Women's shoes with flat heels. 5. *Music* A sign (♭) placed before a note to indicate it is at a lower semitone in pitch. — v.t. & v.i. **flat·ted, flat·ting** To make or become flat. [< ON *flatr*] — **flat′ly** adv.

flat² (flat) n. A suite of rooms on one floor, used as a residence; apartment. [Var. of obs. *flet* floor, OE *flet*]

flat·car (flat′kär′) n. *U.S.* A railroad car with no sides or roof, used for freight.

flat·fish (flat′fish′) n. pl. ·**fish** or ·**fish·es** One of several fishes, as the halibut, flounder, or sole, having a flat body.

flat·foot (flat′foŏt′) n. 1. *Pathol.* A condition caused by a flattened arch. 2. *Slang* A policeman.

flat·foot·ed (flat′foŏt′id) adj. 1. Having flat feet. 2. *U.S. Informal* Direct and uncompromising; plain and resolute. — **flat′-foot′ed·ly** adv. — **flat′-foot′ed·ness** n.

flat·i·ron (flat′ī′ərn) n. An iron (def. 4).

flat·ten (flat′n) v.t. & v.i. To make or become flat or flatter. — **flat′ten·er** n.

flat·ter (flat′ər) v.t. 1. To praise excessively, esp. without sincerity. 2. To try to gain favor by praising. 3. To play upon the hopes or vanity of; beguile. 4. To make pleased, as by compliments; to pamper. 5. To show as more attractive. — v.i. 6. To flatter someone or something. [< OF *flater* to fawn] — **flat′ter·er** n. — **flat′ter·ing·ly** adv.

flat·ter·y (flat′ər-ē) n. pl. ·**ter·ies** 1. The act of flattering. 2. An overly complimentary remark.

flat·top (flat′top′) n. A *U.S.* naval aircraft carrier.

flat·u·lence (flach′oō-ləns, flat′yoō-) n. 1. Gas in the intestines. 2. Windy boastfulness. Also **flat′u·len·cy.** [< L *flatus* blowing] — **flat′u·lent** adj. — **flat′u·lent·ly** adv.

flat·ware (flat′wâr′) n. 1. Dishes that are flat, as plates and saucers. 2. Table utensils, as knives, forks, and spoons.

flat·work (flat′wûrk′) n. Sheets, tablecloths, etc., that can be ironed in a mangle and do not require hand ironing.

flaunt (flônt) v.i. 1. To make a brazen or gaudy display; parade impudently. 2. To wave freely. — v.t. 3. To display. — n. The act of flaunting. [ME *flant* < Scand.] — **flaunt′er** n. — **flaunt′ing·ly** adv. — **flaunt′y** adj.

flau·tist (flô′tist) n. A flutist.

fla·vin (flā′vən) n. *Biochem.* One of a group of yellow pigments widely distributed in plant and animal tissues and including riboflavin. [< L *flavus* yellow + -IN]

fla·vor (flā′vər) n. 1. Taste; esp., a distinctive element in the overall taste of something. 2. Something added to increase or impart taste; flavoring. 3. A special, subtle quality pervading something. — v.t. To give flavor to. Also *Brit.* **fla′vour.** [< OF < L *flare* to blow] — **fla′vor·er** n.

fla·vor·ful (flā′vər-fəl) adj. Full of flavor; esp., pleasant to the taste. Also **fla′vor·ous, fla′vor·some, fla′vor·y.**

fla·vor·ing (flā′vər-ing) n. Something, as an essence or extract, added to heighten flavor or give a distinctive taste.

flaw[1] (flô) n. 1. Something missing or faulty; defect. 2. Something questionable. 3. A crack or fissure. —v.t. 1. To produce a flaw in. —v.i. 2. To become cracked or torn. [? < ON *flaga* slab of stone] —**flaw′less** adj.

flaw[2] (flô) n. A gust; also, a brief windstorm, often accompanied by precipitation; squall. [Prob. < ON *flaga* gust]

flax (flaks) n. 1. An annual plant that yields the fiber used in making linen. 2. The fiber. [OE *fleax*]

flax·en (flak′sən) 1. Pertaining to or made of flax. 2. Having a light golden color like straw. Also **flax′y**.

flax·seed (flaks′sēd′, flak′sēd′) n. The mucilaginous seed of flax, yielding linseed oil: also called *linseed*.

flay (flā) v.t. 1. To remove the skin, hide, bark, etc., of; esp., to rip off strips of skin from, as by lashing. 2. To attack with scathing criticism. 3. To get the money or goods of by extortion or swindling. [OE *flēan*] —**flay′er** n.

F layer Appleton layer.

flea (flē) n. A small, wingless, parasitic insect that sucks the blood of mammals and birds. [OE *flēa, flēah*]

flea-bit·ten (flē′bit′n) adj. 1. Bitten by fleas; also, covered with fleas. 2. *Informal* Broken-down; decrepit.

fleck (flek) n. 1. A tiny streak or spot. 2. A bit; speck. —v.t. To mark with flecks. [Cf. ON *flekkr* spot]

flec·tion (flek′shən) n. The act of bending, or the state of being bent. [< L *flectere* to bend] —**flec′tion·al** adj.

fled (fled) Past tense and past participle of FLEE.

fledge (flej) v. **fledged, fledg·ing** v.t. 1. To furnish with feathers. 2. To bring up (a young bird). —v.i. 3. To grow enough feathers for flight. [< OE *-flycge* ready to fly]

fledg·ling (flej′ling) n. 1. A fledged bird. 2. A beginner. Also **fledg′ling**.

flee (flē) v. **fled, flee·ing** v.i. 1. To run away, as from danger. 2. To move swiftly; leave abruptly. —v.t. 3. To run away from (a person, place, etc.). [OE *flēon*] —**fle′er** n.

fleece (flēs) n. 1. The coat of wool covering a sheep or similar animal. 2. The quantity of wool sheared from a sheep. 3. Anything resembling fleece. 4. A textile fabric with a soft, silky pile, used for linings, etc.; also, the pile. —v.t. **fleeced, fleec·ing** 1. To shear the fleece from. 2. To swindle; defraud. [OE *flēos*] —**fleec′er** n.

fleec·y (flē′sē) adj. **fleec·i·er, fleec·i·est** Like, covered with, or made of fleece. —**fleec′i·ly** adv. —**fleec′i·ness** n.

fleet[1] (flēt) n. 1. The entire number of ships belonging to one government; navy; also, a number of ships, esp. ships of war, operating together under one command. 2. A group of aircraft, trucks, etc., organized into a unit. [OE *flēot* ship]

fleet[2] (flēt) adj. Swift; quick. —Syn. See SWIFT. —v.i. To move swiftly. [OE *flēotan* to float] —**fleet′ly** adv.

fleet·ing (flē′ting) adj. Passing quickly. —**fleet′ing·ly** adv. —**fleet′ing·ness** n.

Flem·ing (flem′ing) n. 1. A native of Flanders, esp. of Belgian Flanders. 2. A native speaker of Flemish.

Flem·ish (flem′ish) adj. Of or pertaining to Flanders, its people, or their language. —n. 1. Flemings collectively. 2. The language of the Flemings, closely related to Dutch.

flesh (flesh) n. 1. The soft substance of the body of a human being or animal, esp. that consisting of muscle but usu. exclusive of fat. 2. The edible substance of animals, excluding that of fish and sometimes of birds; meat. 3. The soft, pulpy substance of fruits and vegetables. 4. The surface of the body of a human being or animal. 5. The color of the skin of a white person, usu. pink or pale orange-yellow. 6. Plumpness; fatness; weight. 7. The body of man as opposed to the soul or spirit; also, the physical, sensual nature. 8. Mankind; also, living creatures. 9. Kindred; kin. —v.t. 1. To excite the hunting instinct of (dogs, etc.) by feeding with meat. 2. To initiate into fighting, bloodshed, etc. —v.i. 3. To become fat. [OE *flæsc*]

flesh-col·ored (flesh′kul′ərd) adj. Having moderate pink or pale orange-yellow color.

flesh·ly (flesh′lē) adj. **·li·er, ·li·est** 1. Pertaining to the body. 2. Sensuous. 3. Worldly. —**flesh′li·ness** n.

flesh·pot (flesh′pot′) n. Usu. pl. Material advantages or luxuries; also, places for indulgence, as night clubs, etc.

flesh·y (flesh′ē) adj. **flesh·i·er, flesh·i·est** 1. Of or resembling flesh. 2. Plump; fat. 3. Firm and pulpy. —**flesh′i·ness** n.

fleur-de-lis (flœr′də-lē′, -lēs′, flŏŏr′) n. pl. **fleurs-de-lis** (flœr′də-lēz′, flŏŏr′) 1. *Heraldry* A device of three leaves or petals bound near the base. 2. The armorial bearings of the former royal family of France. 3. The iris flower or plant. Also **fleur-de-lys′**. [< F, flower of lily]

flew (flŏŏ) Past tense of FLY[1].

flex (fleks) v.t. & v.i. 1. To bend, as the arm. 2. To contract, as a muscle. [< L *flexus*, pp. of *flectere* to bend]

FLEUR-DE-LIS

flexi- *combining form* Bent. [See FLEX.]

flex·i·ble (flek′sa·bəl) adj. 1. Capable of being bent, twisted, etc.; pliant. 2. Yielding; tractable. 3. Able to adjust; adaptable. Also **flex·ile** (flek′sil). —**flex′i·bil′i·ty, flex′i·ble·ness** n. —**flex′i·bly** adv.

flex·or (flek′sər) n. *Anat.* A muscle that serves to bend a part of the body.

flex·ure (flek′shər) n. 1. The act of bending, or the state of being bent. 2. A turn; curve. [< L *flectere* a bending]

fiib·ber·ti·gib·bet (fiib′ər·tē·jib′it) n. An impulsive, flighty, or gossipy person. [Imit.]

flick[1] (flik) n. 1. A quick, light, snapping movement or blow. 2. A slight, cracking sound made by such a blow. 3. A slight trace of something. —v.t. 1. To strike with a quick, light stroke, as with a whip. 2. To cause to move or snap with a quick movement; also, to remove in such a way. —v.i. 3. To move in a darting manner. 4. To flutter.

flick[2] (flik) n. *Slang* A movie. [Short for FLICKER[1]]

flick·er[1] (flik′ər) v.i. 1. To burn or shine with an unsteady or wavering light. 2. To flash up and die away quickly, as lightning. 3. To flutter or quiver. —v.t. 4. To cause to flicker. —n. 1. A wavering or unsteady light. 2. A quivering or fluttering. 3. A slight stirring, as of emotion. [OE *flicorian* to move the wings]

flick·er[2] (flik′ər) n. A woodpecker of eastern North America.

Flickertail State Nickname of North Dakota.

flied (flīd) Past tense and past participle of FLY[1] (def. 9).

fli·er (flī′ər) n. 1. One who or that which flies, as an aviator. 2. One who or that which moves very fast, as an express train. 3. A big leap or jump. 4. *U.S. Informal* A risky financial investment. 5. *U.S.* A handbill. Also spelled *flyer*.

flight[1] (flīt) n. 1. The act or manner of flying; also, the power of flying. 2. Any swift movement through the air. 3. The distance traveled or the course followed by an airplane, bird, projectile, etc. 4. A journey by airplane; also, a scheduled trip by airplane. 5. A group flying through the air together. 6. In the U.S. Air Force, a tactical formation, usu. of four or more aircraft. 7. A soaring or excursion: a *flight* of imagination. 8. A continuous series of stairs. —v.t. To migrate, as wild fowl. [OE *flyht*]

flight[2] (flīt) n. The act of fleeing or escaping from danger.

flight engineer *Aeron.* The crew member of an airplane in charge of mechanical performance during flight.

flight lieutenant (lef·ten′ənt) In the Commonwealth air forces, a commissioned officer. See table at GRADE.

flight sergeant In the Commonwealth air forces, a non-commissioned officer. See table at GRADE.

flight·y (flī′tē) adj. **flight·i·er, flight·i·est** 1. Moving erratically from one idea or topic to another; unable to concentrate long or well; giddy. 2. Moved by impulse or whim; frivolous; fickle. 3. Not quite sane or clear-headed: a *flighty* old lady. —**flight′i·ly** adv. —**flight′i·ness** n.

flim·flam (flim′flam′) *Informal* v.t. **·flammed, ·flam·ming** To swindle; hoax; trick. —n. 1. Nonsense; silly talk. 2. Petty trickery or deception. [Cf. Norw. *flim* lampoon]

flim·sy (flim′zē) adj. **·si·er, ·si·est** 1. Not strong or solid in structure. 2. Light, thin, and delicate in texture. 3. Lacking real validity or effectiveness: a *flimsy* excuse. —n. pl. **·sies** 1. Thin paper used for carbon copies or transfers. 2. Copy written on this paper. [< FILM, by metathesis] —**flim′si·ly** adv. —**flim′si·ness** n.

finch (flinch) v.i. To shrink back or wince, as from anything threatening or unpleasant. —n. 1. Any act of shrinking back or wincing. 2. A card game. [< OF *flechier* to bend] —**flinch′er** n. —**flinch′ing·ly** adv.

fin·der (flin′dər) n. Usu. pl. Small fragments; splinters; shreds. [Cf. Norw. *flindra* splinter]

fling (fling) v. **flung, fling·ing** v.t. 1. To toss or hurl, esp. with violence. 2. To put abruptly or violently: to *fling* someone into prison. 3. To throw (oneself) into something completely or with energy. 4. To send forth suddenly or rapidly: to *fling* reinforcements into battle. 5. To move (a part of the body) with sudden vigor. 6. To give off or diffuse. —v.i. 7. To move, rush, or flounce, as in anger or contempt. 8. To make abusive remarks; speak harshly: usu. with *out*. —n. 1. The act of casting out, down, or away. 2. A sneering or contemptuous comment. 3. A brief period of self-indulgence, unrestraint, etc. 4. *Informal* An attempt: to have a *fling* at painting. [ME *flingen* < Scand.]

flint (flint) n. 1. A very hard, dull-colored variety of quartz that produces a spark when struck with steel. 2. Anything very hard or cruel. —v.t. To provide with a flint. [OE]

flint glass A hard glass, used for lenses, cut glass, etc.

flint·lock (flint′lok′) n. 1. A gunlock in which a flint is used to ignite the powder in the pan. 2. An obsolete firearm that was equipped with such a gunlock.

flint·y (flin′tē) adj. **flint·i·er, flint·i·est** 1. Made of, containing, or resembling flint. 2. Hard; cruel; obdurate.

flip (flip) v. **flipped, flip·ping** v.t. **1.** To throw or move with a jerk; flick. **2.** To propel, as a coin, by an outward snap of a finger pressed down by the thumb and suddenly released. — v.i. **3.** To move with a jerk. **4.** To strike lightly and quickly. **5.** U.S. Slang To become angry or upset. — n. **1.** A quick, light snapping movement, as of a lash. **2.** A drink made with liquor, as sherry, mixed with egg, sugar, and spices. — adj. Informal Pert; saucy; impertinent. [Imit.]

flip·pan·cy (flip′ən·sē) n. pl. **·cies 1.** Careless disrespect; impertinence; sauciness. **2.** An impertinent act or remark.

flip·pant (flip′ənt) adj. Lacking due respect or seriousness; impertinent; saucy. [< FLIP v. + -ANT] — **flip′pant·ly** adv. — **flip′pant·ness** n.

flip·per (flip′ər) n. **1.** A broad, flat limb adapted for swimming, as in seals, etc. **2.** A rubber, paddlelike shoe used by skin divers and other swimmers. **3.** Slang The hand.

flirt (flûrt) v.i. **1.** To act in a coquettish manner; play at love. **2.** To expose oneself to something carelessly or lightly: to flirt with danger. **3.** To dart; flit. — v.t. **4.** To move abruptly or briskly. **5.** To toss or snap quickly. — n. **1.** One who plays at love. **2.** A sudden movement. [Imit.]

flir·ta·tion (flûr·tā′shən) n. **1.** Coquettish behavior. **2.** A brief, casual love affair. — **flirt′y, flir·ta′tious** adj. — **flir·ta′tious·ly** adv.

flit (flit) v. **flit·ted, flit·ting** v.i. **1.** To move or fly rapidly and lightly; dart; skim. **2.** To pass away quickly. — n. A flitting movement. [< ON flytja to remove, move] — **flit′ter** n.

flitch (flich) n. **1.** A salted and smoked cut of meat from a pig. **2.** A piece of timber cut lengthwise. [OE flicce]

flit·ter (flit′ər) v.t. & v.i. Dial. To flutter. [Freq. of FLIT]

fliv·ver (fliv′ər) n. U.S. Slang **1.** An old, battered car. **2.** Formerly, the Model T Ford car. [Origin unknown]

float (flōt) v.i. **1.** To rest on or at the surface of a liquid. **2.** To remain suspended below the surface of a liquid. **3.** To remain suspended or be carried along in the air or some other gas. **4.** To move lightly and effortlessly. **5.** To go about from one person or thing to another in a random or unstable way. — v.t. **6.** To cause to float. **7.** To put (a stock, bond, etc.) on the market. **8.** To cause (a rumor, report, etc.) to circulate. **9.** To launch (a business venture, scheme, etc.). **10.** To irrigate by flooding. — n. **1.** An object that floats in a liquid or buoys up something in a liquid. **2.** A piece of cork or similar material attached to a fishing line. **3.** A hollow metal ball attached to a lever governing the supply of water in a tank. **4.** An anchored raft. **5.** A tableau or display carried atop a wheeled platform, truck, etc., in parades or pageants. **6.** A soda or milk shake with a ball of ice cream in it. [OE flotian] — **float′a·ble** adj.

float·age (flō′tij), **float·a·tion** (flō·tā′shən) See FLOTAGE, FLOTATION.

float·er (flō′tər) n. **1.** One who or that which floats. **2.** A person who drifts about from one thing to another.

float·ing (flō′ting) adj. **1.** That floats or is able to float. **2.** Moving about or inclined to move about from one place, job, etc., to another. **3.** Pathol. Abnormally movable or detached from the usual position: a floating kidney. **4.** Econ. **a** Due at various times and in various sums: said of a debt. **b** Not assigned to any particular investment: said of capital.

floating dock A type of dry dock that can be raised to leave the ship dry for repairs. Also **floating dry dock.**

floating rib A rib of either of the two lowest pairs of ribs in a human being, not attached to the other ribs or to the sternum.

floc·cu·late (flok′yə·lāt) v.t. & v.i. **·lat·ed, ·lat·ing** To form into small, lumpy masses, as clouds. — **floc′cu·la′tion** n.

floc·cu·lent (flok′yə·lənt) adj. **1.** Having soft, fluffy wool or hair. **2.** Marked by or producing woolly tufts. — **floc′·cu·lence** n. — **floc′cu·lent·ly** adv.

flock¹ (flok) n. **1.** A group of animals of the same kind, esp. sheep, goats, or birds, feeding, living, or kept together. **2.** A group of members of the same church or congregation. **3.** Any group of persons under the care or supervision of someone. **4.** A large number or assemblage of persons or things. — v.i. To come or go in crowds. [OE flocc]
— **Syn.** (noun) **1.** Flock is applied to birds and to small mammals, now usually sheep or goats. Larger animals, as cattle and elephants, form a herd; when gathered together to be driven, they are a drove. Other terms are fairly restricted in application: a bevy of quail, a covey of partridges, a gaggle of geese, a gam of whales, a pack of dogs or wolves, a pride of lions, a swarm of bees.

flock² (flok) n. **1.** Refuse wool, rags, etc., used to stuff furniture. **2.** A tuft of wool, hair, etc. — v.t. To cover or fill with flock. [Prob. < OF < L floccus lock of wool]

floe (flō) n. A large, comparatively level field of floating ice; also, a detached section of such a field. [< ON flō a layer]

flog (flog, flôg) v.t. **flogged, flog·ging** To beat hard with a whip, rod, strap, etc. [? < L flagellare to whip] — **flog′ger** n.

flood (flud) n. **1.** An unusually large flow or rise of water, esp. over land not usu. covered with water; deluge. ◆ Collateral adjective: diluvial. **2.** The coming in of the tide; high tide: opposed to ebb: also **flood tide. 3.** Any copious flow or stream: a flood of words. **4.** Poetic Any great body

of water, as the ocean, a lake, etc. — **the Flood** The Deluge. — v.t. **1.** To cover or inundate with a flood. **2.** To fill or overwhelm as with a flood. **3.** To supply excessively: to flood an engine with gasoline. — v.i. **4.** To rise to a flood; overflow. **5.** To flow in a flood. [OE flōd]

flood control The use of dikes, dams, etc., to regulate and control bodies of water that flood easily.

flood·gate (flud′gāt′) n. **1.** A gate or valve at the head of a water channel, designed to regulate the flow or depth of the water. **2.** Something restraining or checking an outburst.

flood·light (flud′līt′) n. **1.** A lamp that throws a bright, broad beam of light. **2.** The light of this lamp. — v.t. **·light·ed** or **·lit, ·light·ing** To illuminate with a floodlight.

floor (flôr, flōr) n. **1.** The surface in a room or building upon which one stands or walks. **2.** The area between two adjacent levels of a building; story. **3.** The bottom surface of any cavity: the ocean floor. **4.** A level structure or platform for some special purpose: a threshing floor. **5.** The part of a legislative house, stock exchange, etc., where the members gather to conduct business. **6.** In parliamentary procedure, the right to speak to the assembly: to be given the floor. **7.** The lowest or minimum price for anything. **8.** Naut. The more or less horizontal parts of a ship's bottom on each side of the keel. — v.t. **1.** To cover or provide with a floor. **2.** To knock down, as to the floor. **3.** Informal To puzzle or vanquish completely. [OE flōr]

floor·ing (flôr′ing, flō′ring) n. **1.** Material for the making of a floor. **2.** A floor; also, floors collectively.

floor leader A party leader in either house of the U.S. Congress, who directs his party's business on the floor.

floor plan An architectural plan of the rooms and other spaces on one floor of a building.

floor show Entertainment consisting of dancing, singing, etc., presented on the dance floor of a night club or cabaret.

floor·walk·er (flôr′wô′kər, flōr′-) n. In a department store, one who walks about so as to supervise the sales force, give information to customers, etc.: also, Brit., shopwalker.

flooz·y (flōō′zē) n. pl. **flooz·ies** U.S. Slang A loose woman or a prostitute. Also **floos′y.** [Cf. FLOSSY]

flop (flop) v. **flopped, flop·ping** v.i. **1.** To move, flap, or beat about heavily or clumsily. **2.** To fall loosely and heavily. **3.** Informal To be completely unsuccessful. — v.t. **4.** To cause to drop or fall heavily. **5.** To flap in a loose, awkward, or noisy way, as wings. — n. **1.** The act of flopping. **2.** A flopping noise. **3.** Informal A total failure. [Var. of FLAP]

flop·house (flop′hous′) n. A cheap, shabby hotel.

flop·py (flop′ē) adj. **·pi·er, ·pi·est** Informal That flops or tends to flop. — **flop′pi·ly** adv. — **flop′pi·ness** n.

flo·ra (flôr′ə, flō′rə) n. pl. **·ras** or **·rae** (flôr′ē, flō′rē) The aggregate of plants growing in and usu. peculiar to a particular region or period: distinguished from fauna. [< NL, after L Flora, goddess of flowers]

flo·ral (flôr′əl, flō′rəl) adj. Of, like, or pertaining to flowers.

Flor·en·tine (flôr′ən·tēn, -tīn, flor′-) adj. Of or pertaining to Florence, Italy. — n. A native or inhabitant of Florence.

flo·res·cence (flô·res′əns, flō-) n. **1.** The state, period, or process of blossoming. **2.** A state or period of prosperity or success. [< NL < L florere to bloom] — **flo·res′cent** adj.

flo·ret (flôr′it, flō′rit) n. **1.** A little flower. **2.** Bot. One of the small individual flowers that make up the head of a composite flower. [< OF dim. of flor a flower < L flos, floris]

flo·ri·bun·da (flô′rə·bun′də, flōr′ə-) n. A long-flowering variety of rose with large blooms. [< NL, fem. of floribundus flowering freely < flori- + -bundus adj. suffix]

flo·ri·cul·ture (flô′rə·kul′chər, flō′rə-) n. The cultivation of flowers. — **flo′ri·cul′tur·al** adj. — **flo′ri·cul′tur·ist** n.

flor·id (flôr′id, flor′-) adj. **1.** Having a ruddy color, esp. of the type typical of high blood pressure; flushed with redness. **2.** Ornate, esp. to an excessive degree; flowery: a florid style. [< L floridus flowery] — **flor′id·ly** adv.

flo·rid·i·ty (flə·rid′ə·tē) n. pl. **·ties 1.** Ruddiness. **2.** Floweriness. Also **flor′id·ness.**

flor·in (flôr′in, flor′-) n. **1.** A British silver coin, equal to two shillings. **2.** The guilder of the Netherlands. **3.** One of several former European coins. [< OF < Ital. < L flos, floris flower; from the figure of a lily stamped on it]

flo·rist (flôr′ist, flō′rist, flor′ist) n. A dealer in flowers.

-florous combining form Bot. Having (a specified number, kind, etc., of) flowers. [< L flos, floris a flower]

floss (flôs, flos) n. **1.** One of several light, silk or silklike substances or fibers. **2.** Soft fibers produced by some plants, as tassels of corn. **3.** The outside fibers on the cocoon of a silkworm. Also **floss silk.** [< OF flosche] — **floss′y** adj.

flo·ta·tion (flō·tā′shən) n. **1.** The act or state of floating. **2.** The act of financing a business undertaking, as by an issue of stocks or bonds. Also spelled flotation.

flo·til·la (flō·til′ə) n. A fleet of small vessels; also, a numerically small fleet. [< Sp., dim. of flota fleet]

flot·sam (flot′səm) n. Any goods from a wrecked or imperiled ship that are cast or swept into the sea and found floating there. [< AF < OE flotian to float]

flotsam and jetsam 1. Parts of a wrecked ship or its cargo drifting on the water or cast ashore. 2. Worthless or trifling things; oddments. 3. Transients; drifters.

flounce[1] (flouns) *n.* A gathered or pleated strip of material used for trimming skirts, etc. — *v.t.* **flounced, flounc·ing** To furnish with flounces. [Earlier *frounce* < OF *fronce* fold]

flounce[2] (flouns) *v.i.* **flounced, flounc·ing** 1. To move or go with exaggerated tosses of the body, as in anger or petulance. 2. To plunge or flounder: said of animals. — *n.* The act of flouncing. [< Scand.]

floun·der[1] (floun′dər) *v.i.* 1. To struggle clumsily; move awkwardly as if mired. 2. To proceed, as in speech or action, in a stumbling or confused manner. — *n.* A stumbling or struggling motion. [? Blend of FLOUNCE[2] and FOUNDER[2]]

floun·der[2] (floun′dər) *n.* Any of certain flatfish, valued as food. [< AF *floundre,* prob. < Scand.]

flour (flour) *n.* 1. A fine, soft, usu. white powder obtained by sifting and grinding the meal of a grain, esp. wheat. 2. Any finely powdered substance. — *v.t.* 1. To sprinkle or cover with flour. 2. To make into flour by sifting and grinding. [Var. of FLOWER] — **flour′y** *adj.*

flour·ish (flûr′ish) *v.i.* 1. To grow or fare well or prosperously; thrive. 2. To be at the peak of success or development. 3. To move with sweeping motions. 4. To write with sweeping or ornamental strokes. 5. To use elegant, flowery language. 6. *Music* **a** To play or sing a showy passage or in a showy manner. **b** To sound a fanfare. — *v.t.* 7. To wave about or brandish, as a weapon or flag. 8. To display ostentatiously. 9. To embellish, as with ornamental lines, notes, etc. — *n.* 1. A brandishing, as of a sword. 2. A curved or decorative stroke in penmanship. 3. Something done primarily for display. 4. Ornate language. 5. *Music* **a** A fanfare, as of trumpets. **b** A florid passage. [< OF < L *florere* to bloom] — **flour′ish·er** *n.*

flout (flout) *v.t.* 1. To scoff at; defy with open contempt: to *flout* convention. — *v.i.* 2. To express one's contempt. — *n.* A contemptuous act or remark. [Prob. ME *flouten* to play the flute; to deride] — **flout′er** *n.* — **flout′ing·ly** *adv.*

flow (flō) *v.i.* 1. Of fluids, to move steadily and smoothly along, as through a channel or over a surface; also, of electricity or other forms of energy, to pass along or be conveyed. 2. To move along steadily and freely as a fluid. 3. To well out or pour forth. 4. To move steadily in an agreeably effortless or rhythmic way: Conversation *flowed.* 5. To be marked by a satisfying, harmonious continuity: The lines of the statue *flow.* 6. To hang or ripple down in rich profusion, as hair. 7. To be abundant in something; also, to overflow. 8. Of the tide, to rise: opposed to *ebb.* — *v.t.* 9. To cover or flood with some fluid. 10. To cause to flow. — *n.* 1. The act of flowing. 2. Something that flows, as a current or stream. 3. A continuous stream or outpouring, as of words. 4. The amount of that which flows. 5. The manner of flowing. 6. An overflowing. [OE *flōwan*] — **flow′ing** *adj.*

flow chart A schematic diagram showing a sequence of operations, stages, etc., as for an industrial process.

flow·er (flou′ər, flour) *n.* 1. A simple or complex cluster of petals, usu. brightly colored, at or near the tip of a seed-bearing plant or sometimes along the stem, and enclosing the reproductive parts of the plant; blossom. 2. *Bot.* The reproductive structure of any plant. 3. The condition in which the reproductive parts of a plant are mature, esp. when marked by brightly colored, open petals. 4. The condition of having arrived at fullest growth, development, or vigor; prime: usu. preceded by *in.* 5. The finest or choicest part or representative of something: the *flower* of youth. 6. *Usu. pl.* A decorative feature; ornamentation. 7. *pl. Chem.* A powdery substance usu. produced by heating a solid to a gaseous state and condensing the vapors: *flowers* of sulfur. — *v.i.* 1. To produce flowers; bloom. 2. To reach fullest development, or vigor. — *v.t.* 3. To decorate with flowers or floral designs. [< OF < L *flos, floris* flower]

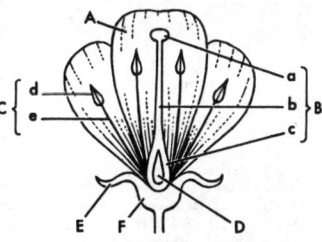

FLOWER

A Petal. *B* Pistil: *a* Stigma, *b* Style, *c* Ovary. *C* Stamen: *d* Anther, *e* Filament. *D* Ovule. *E* Sepal. *F* Receptacle.

flower girl 1. A girl or woman who sells flowers. 2. A young girl who carries flowers in a procession.

flower head *Bot.* A dense cluster of tiny flowers all growing directly from the main stem of a plant.

flow·er·y (flou′ər·ē, flour′ē) *adj.* **·er·i·er, ·er·i·est** 1. Full of or covered with flowers. 2. Using or containing highly embellished language. 3. Having a floral pattern. — **flow′er·i·ly** *adv.* — **flow′er·i·ness** *n.*

flown (flōn) Past participle of FLY[1].

flu (flōō) *n. Informal* Influenza.

flub (flub) *U.S. Informal v.t. & v.i.* **flubbed, flub·bing** To make a mess of (an opportunity, performance, etc.). — *n.* A botch or blunder. [Origin unknown]

fluc·tu·ate (fluk′chōō·āt) *v.* **·at·ed, ·at·ing** *v.i.* 1. To change or vary often and in an irregular manner; waver. 2. To undulate. — *v.t.* 3. To cause to fluctuate. [< L *fluctus* wave] — **fluc′tu·ant** *adj.* — **fluc′tu·a′tion** *n.*

flue (flōō) *n.* 1. A pipe or tube through which smoke, hot air, etc., is drawn off, as from a furnace or stove. 2. A pipe or tube, as of a boiler, through which steam or hot air is carried so as to heat water surrounding the pipe or tube. 3. In an organ, a flue pipe. [Origin uncertain]

flu·ent (flōō′ənt) *adj.* 1. Capable of speaking or writing with effortless ease. 2. Spoken or written with effortless ease. 3. Marked by smoothness, grace, and expressiveness: *fluent* gestures. 4. Running freely, as a stream of water; fluid; also, not stable; changeable. [< L *fluens, -entis,* ppr. of *fluere* to flow] — **flu′en·cy** *n.* — **flu′ent·ly** *adv.*

flue pipe An organ pipe in which the tone is produced by a stream of air passing over the lips of an opening in the side of the pipe rather than by the vibration of a reed.

fluff (fluf) *n.* 1. A soft, light cluster, ball, or tuft of loosely gathered fibers of wool, cotton, etc. 2. A mass of soft, fine feathers; down. 3. *Informal* An error made in reading or speaking lines: said of actors, announcers, etc. — *v.t.* 1. To make (pillows, blankets, etc.) soft and light by patting or shaking. 2. *Informal* To make an error in reading or speaking (lines). — *v.i.* 3. To become soft, light, or feathery. 4. *Informal* To make an error in reading or speaking lines.

fluff·y (fluf′ē) *adj.* **fluff·i·er, fluff·i·est** Of, covered with, or resembling fluff. — **fluff′i·ly** *adv.* — **fluff′i·ness** *n.*

flu·id (flōō′id) *adj.* 1. Capable of flowing; not solid. 2. Consisting of or pertaining to liquids. 3. Readily changing; not fixed: a *fluid* policy. — *n.* A substance capable of flowing; esp., a liquid or gas. [< F < L < *fluere* to flow] — **flu·id′ic** *adj.* — **flu·id′i·ty** *n.* — **flu′id·ly** *adv.*

fluid dram A measure of capacity equal to one eighth of a fluid ounce. Also **fluid drachm.** See table inside back cover.

fluid ounce 1. *U.S.* One sixteenth of a pint. 2. *Brit.* One twentieth of a pint. See table inside back cover.

fluke[1] (flōōk) *n.* 1. One of several parasitic trematode worms. 2. A flatfish or flounder. [OE *flōc*]

fluke[2] (flōōk) *n.* 1. A sharp projection turned backward at an angle from the principal tip or point of an arrow, harpoon, etc.; also, the entire head of an arrow, etc. 2. The triangular head at the end of either arm of an anchor. [? < FLUKE[1]]

fluke[3] (flōōk) *n.* 1. A lucky stroke, as in the game of pool. 2. Any piece of good luck. 3. Anything that happens by chance. — *v.* **fluked, fluk·ing** *v.t.* 1. To get, make, etc., by a fluke. — *v.i.* 2. To make a fluke. [Origin unknown] — **fluk′ey, fluk′y** *adj.*

flume (flōōm) *n.* 1. *U.S.* A narrow gap in a mountain through which a torrent passes. 2. A chute or trough for carrying water, used as a source of water power, to convey logs, etc. — *v.t.* **flumed, flum·ing** 1. To drain away or divert by means of a flume, as in mining. 2. To transport, as logs, by means of a flume. [< OF < L *flumen* river]

flum·mer·y (flum′ər·ē) *n. pl.* **·mer·ies** 1. One of several soft, light, easily digested foods, as a custard. 2. Vapid flattery. 3. Utter nonsense. [< Welsh *llymru*]

flung (flung) Past tense and past participle of FLING.

flunk (flungk) *U.S. Informal v.t.* 1. To fail in (an examination, course, etc.). 2. To give a failing grade to. — *v.i.* 3. To fail, as in an examination. — **to flunk out** To leave or cause to leave a school or college because of failure in studies. — *n.* A failure, as in an examination. [Origin unknown]

flunk·y (flung′kē) *n. pl.* **flunk·ies** 1. An obsequious, servile fellow; toady. 2. A manservant in livery. Also **flunk′ey.** [? Alter. of *flanker* < FLANK, *v.*] — **flunk′y·ism** *n.*

fluo- See FLUORO-.

fluor- Var. of FLUORO-.

flu·o·resce (flōō′ə·res′, flôr·es′) *v.i.* **·resced, ·resc·ing** To become fluorescent. [Back formation < FLUORESCENCE]

flu·o·res·cence (flōō′ə·res′əns, flôr·es′-) *n.* 1. The property possessed by certain substances of absorbing radiation of a particular wavelength and emitting it as light while the stimulus is active. 2. The light so produced. [< FLUOR- (SPAR)] — **flu′o·res′cent** *adj.*

fluorescent lamp A tubular lamp in which ultraviolet light from a low-pressure mercury arc is reradiated as visible light after impact upon a coating of phosphors.

fluor·i·date (flôr′ə·dāt, flōō′ə·ri·dāt) *v.t.* **·dat·ed, ·dat·ing**

To add sodium fluoride to (drinking water), esp. as a means of preventing tooth decay. — **fluor'i·da'tion** *n.*

flu·o·ride (floo'ǝ·rīd, -rid; floor'īd, -id) *n.* A compound of fluorine and another element. Also **flu'o·rid** (-rid).

flu·o·rine (floo'ǝ·rēn, -rin; floor'ēn, -in) *n.* A pale, greenish yellow, pungent, corrosive, and extremely reactive gaseous element (symbol F) belonging to the halogen group. See ELEMENT. Also **flu'o·rin** (-rin).

flu·o·rite (floo'ǝ·rīt, floor'īt) *n.* A cleavable, isometric, variously colored calcium fluoride, CaF$_2$, used as a flux in making steel and glass.

fluoro- *combining form* 1. *Chem.* Indicating the presence of fluorine in a compound. 2. Fluorescence. Also, before vowels, **flour:**, also *fluo-.*

flu·o·ro·car·bon (floo'ǝ·rō·kär'bǝn, floor'ō-) *n. Chem.* Any of a group of very stable compounds of carbon and fluorine used as solvents, lubricants, insulators, and refrigerants.

fluor·o·scope (floor'ǝ·skōp, floo'ǝr·ǝ-) *n.* A device for observing the shadows projected upon a fluorescent screen by objects put between it and a direct beam of X-rays or other radiation. — **fluor'o·scop'ic** (-skop'ik) *adj.* — **fluor·os·co·py** (floor·os'kǝ·pē, floo'ǝ·ros'/-) *n.*

flur·ry (flûr'ē) *v.* **·ried, ·ry·ing** *v.t.* 1. To bewilder or confuse. — *v.i.* 2. To move in a flurry. — *n. pl.* **·ries** 1. A sudden commotion or excitement. 2. A sudden, light gust of wind. 3. A light, brief rain or snowfall, accompanied by small gusts. 4. In the stock exchange, a sudden, short-lived increase in trading. [Blend of FLUTTER and HURRY]

flush¹ (flush) *v.i.* 1. To become red in the face through a rush of blood; blush. 2. To glow or shine with a reddish brightness. 3. To flow or rush suddenly and copiously: Blood *flushed* into his face. 4. To become cleaned or purified through a quick gush of water, etc. — *v.t.* 5. To wash out, purify, etc., as a sewer, with a quick, sudden flow or gush of water. 6. To cause to glow red or blush. 7. To stir up or elate with the warmth of achievement, pride, etc.: usu. in the passive: to be *flushed* with success. — *n.* 1. A heightened, reddish color. 2. A pervasive feeling of being hot. 3. A pervasive, warm feeling of elation, excitement, etc. 4. Glowing bloom or freshness. 5. A sudden gush or flow of water, etc. [? < FLUSH⁴] — **flush'er** *n.*

flush² (flush) *adj.* 1. Even or level with another surface. 2. Of a line of print, even with the margin; not indented. 3. Of the deck of a ship, extending on one plane from stem to stern. 4. Having plenty of money on hand. 5. Of a period or epoch, marked by prosperity: *flush* times. 6. Having a heightened, reddish color: *flush* faces. 7. Of a blow, direct: a *flush* hit. — *adv.* 1. In an even position with another surface; also, — in alignment with a margin. 2. In a direct manner; squarely: hit *flush* on the jaw. — *v.t.* To make even or level, as with another surface. [? < FLUSH¹]

flush³ (flush) *n.* In poker, etc., a hand of cards all of one suit. — **royal flush** In poker, a hand of cards made up of the ace, king, queen, jack, and ten of one suit. — **straight flush** In poker, a hand of cards made up entirely of cards of the same suit and in sequence.

flush⁴ (flush) *v.t.* 1. To drive (an animal) from cover; esp., to startle (birds) from cover. — *v.i.* 2. To rush out or fly from cover. [ME *flusschen*]

flus·ter (flus'tǝr) *v.t. & v.i.* To make or become confused, agitated, or befuddled. — *n.* Confusion or agitation of mind. [Cf. Icel. *flaustr* to hurry] — **flus·tra'tion** *n.*

flute (floot) *n.* 1. A tubular, reedless, woodwind instrument of small diameter, equipped with holes and keys and with a mouthpiece located either along the side or at the end, and producing tones of a high pitch and clear, silvery quality. 2. *Archit.* A groove, usu. of semicircular section, as in a column. 3. A small groove, as in pleated cloth. — *v.* **flut·ed, flut·ing** *v.i.* 1. To play on a flute. 2. To produce a flutelike sound. — *v.t.* 3. To sing, whistle, or utter with flutelike tones. 4. To make flutes in (a column, dress, etc.). [< OF *flaüte*]

flut·ing (floo'ting) *n.* 1. The act of making flutes in a column, frill, etc. 2. Flutes or grooves collectively. 3. Ornamentation with flutes. 4. The act of playing on a flute.

flut·ist (floo'tist) *n.* A flute player: also called *flautist.*

flut·ter (flut'ǝr) *v.i.* 1. To wave or flap rapidly and irregularly. 2. To flap the wings rapidly in or as in erratic flight. 3. To move or proceed with irregular motion. 4. To move about lightly and quickly; flit. 5. To be excited or nervous. 6. To beat rapidly and sometimes unevenly, as the heart. — *v.t.* 7. To cause to flutter; agitate. 8. To excite or confuse; fluster. — *n.* 1. A vibrating or quivering motion. 2. Nervous agitation; dither. 3. Excited interest; commotion. 4. *Aeron.* A periodic oscillation set up in any part of an airplane by mechanical disturbances and maintained by inertia, structural characteristics, etc. 5. *Telecom.* A distortion of sound caused by irregular variation in the frequency of a transmitter signal, message, or recording. 6. *Pathol.* An abnormally rapid contraction of the atria of the heart. [OE *floterian*] — **flut'ter·er** *n.* — **flut'ter·y** *adj.*

flut·y (floo'tē) *adj.* Flutelike in tone; clear and mellow.

flu·vi·al (floo'vē·ǝl) *adj.* Pertaining to, found in, or formed by a river. Also **flu·vi·a·tile** (floo'vē·ǝ·til).

flux (fluks) *n.* 1. A flowing or discharge. 2. Constant movement or change. 3. The flowing in of the tide. 4. *Pathol.* An abnormal discharge of fluid matter from the body. 5. The act or process of melting. 6. *Metall.* A substance that promotes the fusing of metals, as borax, or that serves to purify metals or prevent undue oxidation of metal surfaces. 7. *Physics* The rate of flow of fluids, heat, electricity, light, etc. — **bloody flux** Dysentery. — *v.t.* 1. To make fluid; melt. 2. To treat, as metal, with a flux. [< F < L *fluere* to flow] — **flux·ion** (fluk'shǝn) *n.*

fly¹ (flī) *v.* **flew** or (for def. 9) **flied, flown** or (for def. 9) **flied, fly·ing** *v.i.* 1. To move through the air on wings, as a bird. 2. To move or travel through the air by aircraft. 3. To rush or be propelled through the air, as an arrow. 4. To wave or flutter in the air. 5. To move swiftly or with a rush. 6. To pass swiftly: Time *flies.* 7. To be used up quickly, as money. 8. To flee; escape. 9. In baseball, to bat the ball high over the field. — *v.t.* 10. To cause to fly or float in the air. 11. To operate (an aircraft). 12. To transport by aircraft. 13. To pass over in an aircraft. 14. To flee from. — **to fly at** To attack suddenly or violently. — **to fly in the face of** To defy openly. — **to fly into** To enter suddenly into (an outburst of rage, etc.). — **to fly off** To leave quickly. — **to fly off the handle** To lose one's temper. — **to fly out** In baseball, to be retired by batting a ball high over the field and having it caught by an opposing player. — **to fly the coop** *U.S. Slang* To sneak off; escape. — **to let fly** To utter, throw, or discharge violently, as an oath, a stone, etc. — *n. pl.* **flies** 1. A flap of material concealing the zipper or other fastening in a garment, esp. in a pair of trousers. 2. The flap at the entrance to a tent. 3. The flyleaf of a book. 4. The length of a flag from the staff to its farthest edge; also, the farthest edge. 5. In baseball, a ball batted high over the field. 6. A flywheel. 7. *pl.* In a theater, the space above the stage and behind the proscenium, containing drop curtains, overhead lights, etc. 8. *Brit.* A light hackney coach. — **on the fly** 1. While flying. 2. *U.S. Informal* While in great haste. [OE *flēogan*]

fly² (flī) *n. pl.* **flies** 1. Any of various small, two-winged insects; esp., the common housefly. 2. Any of various other flying insects, as the May fly. 3. A fishhook to which colored bits of material, feathers, etc., are attached to resemble an insect. — **fly in the ointment** Some small thing that detracts from the enjoyment of something. [OE *flyge*]

fly·blow (flī'blō') *n.* The egg or young larva of a blowfly, deposited on food, etc. — *v.t. & v.i.* **·blew, ·blown, ·blow·ing** 1. To taint (food) with flyblows. 2. To spoil.

fly·by (flī'bī') *n. pl.* **·bys** *Aerospace* The passage of a spacecraft relatively near a heavenly body.

fly-by-night (flī'bī·nīt') *adj.* Financially unsound. — *n.* One who cheats a creditor by departing secretly.

fly·catch·er (flī'kach'ǝr) *n.* Any of a large order of passerine birds of limited vocal powers and migratory habits.

fly·er (flī'ǝr) See FLIER.

fly-fish (flī'fish') *v.i.* To fish with artificial flies as bait.

fly·ing (flī'ing) *adj.* 1. Capable of or adapted for flight in the air. 2. Moving or passing quickly, as if in flight. 3. Waving, streaming, or floating in or through the air. 4. Hurried: a *flying* trip. 5. Pertaining to or used in aviation. 6. *Naut.* Pertaining to sails not secured on all sides by stays or spars. — *n.* The act of one who or that which flies.

flying buttress *Archit.* A bracing structure, usu. a band of stone carried by a rampant arch from a wall to a supporting abutment and receiving the outward thrust of the wall.

flying fish A fish with large pectoral fins that enable it to glide through the air for short distances.

flying jib *Naut.* A jib set out beyond the standing jib, on an extended boom called the **flying-jib boom.** For illus. see SCHOONER.

flying officer In the Commonwealth air forces, a commissioned officer. See table at GRADE.

flying saucer Any of various objects of vaguely saucerlike shape, alleged to have been seen flying at high altitudes and great speeds; an unidentified flying object (UFO).

flying squirrel A squirrel having a fold of skin connecting its front and back limbs, enabling it to glide.

flying start 1. In racing, the passing of the starting post at full speed. 2. A speedy, efficient beginning.

fly·leaf (flī'lēf') *n. pl.* **·leaves** (-lēvz') A blank leaf at the beginning or end of a book, pamphlet, etc.

fly·pa·per (flī'pā'pǝr) *n.* A piece of paper coated with a sticky poisonous substance, placed so as to catch or kill flies.

fly·speck (flī'spek') *n.* 1. The dot made by the excrement of a fly. 2. Any slight speck. — *v.t.* To mark with flyspecks.

fly·trap (flī'trap') *n.* 1. A trap for catching flies. 2. A plant, as the Venus's-flytrap, that traps insects.

fly·weight (flī'wāt') *n.* A boxer belonging to the lightest weight class, weighing 112 pounds or less.

fly·wheel (flī'hwēl') *n.* A wheel heavy enough to resist sudden changes of speed, used to secure uniform motion in the working parts of a machine.

F number *Photog.* A number obtained by dividing the focal length of a lens by its effective diameter: the smaller the number, the shorter the exposure required.

foal (fōl) *n.* One of the young of an animal of the horse family. —*v.t. & v.i.* To give birth to (a foal). [OE *fola*]

foam (fōm) *n.* **1.** A frothy mass of bubbles produced on the surface of a liquid by agitation, fermentation, etc. **2.** A frothy mass of saliva, etc. **3.** *Chem.* A colloid system of gas dispersed in a liquid. —*v.i.* **1.** To become foam or become covered with foam. —*v.t.* **2.** To cause to foam. [OE *fām*]

foam rubber A firm, spongy rubber produced by chemical treatment and used esp. in mattresses, cushions, etc.

foam·y (fō′mē) *adj.* **foam·i·er, foam·i·est 1.** Pertaining to, consisting of, or resembling foam. **2.** Producing, covered with, or full of foam. —**foam′i·ly** *adv.* —**foam′i·ness** *n.*

fob¹ (fob) *n.* **1.** A small pocket at the front waistline of trousers or at the front of a vest, designed to hold a watch, a small amount of change, etc. **2.** *U.S.* A short chain or ribbon attached to a watch and worn dangling from such a pocket; also, a small ornament attached to the dangling end of such a chain or ribbon. [Cf. dial. G *fuppe* pocket]

fob² (fob) *v.t.* **fobbed, fob·bing 1.** To dispose of by fraud or trickery: with *off*. **2.** To put off by lies, evasion, etc.; also, to try deceitfully to appease: with *off*. [? < FOB¹]

fo·cal (fō′kəl) *adj.* Of or placed at a focus. —**fo′cal·ly** *adv.*

focal distance *Optics* The distance from the center of a lens or curved mirror to the point where rays from a distant object converge. Also **focal length.**

fo·cal·ize (fō′kəl·īz) *v.t. & v.i.* **·ized, ·iz·ing 1.** To bring to a focus or become focused. **2.** *Med.* To confine or be confined to a localized area of the body. —**fo′cal·i·za′tion** *n.*

fo′c's'le (fōk′səl) See FORECASTLE.

fo·cus (fō′kəs) *n.* *pl.* **·cus·es** or **·ci** (-sī) **1.** *Optics* **a** The point (**real focus**) at which a system of light rays converges after passage through a lens or other optical arrangement or after reflection from a mirror. **b** The point (**virtual focus**) at which such rays appear to diverge and where they would meet if their direction were reversed. **2.** The adjustment of the eye, a camera lens, etc., so that a clear image is produced; also, the position of the viewed object. **3.** Focal distance. **4.** Any central point, as of importance or interest. **5.** *Physics* The meeting point of any system of rays, beams, or waves. **6.** *Geom.* **a** One of two points, the sum or difference of whose distances to a conic section is a constant. **b** A similar point in some other curve. —*v.* **·cused** or **·cussed, ·cus·ing** or **·cus·sing** *v.t.* **1.** To adjust the focus of (the eye, a lens, etc.) to receive a clear image. **2.** To fix; concentrate. —*v.i.* **3.** To become focused. [< L, hearth]

FOCUS

A Biconcave lens: light rays *a, a* refract as at *b, b* and form the virtual focus at *c.*
B Biconvex lens: light rays *d, d* converge to the real focus at *e.*

fod·der (fod′ər) *n.* Coarse feed for horses, cattle, etc., as the stalks and leaves of field corn. —*v.t.* To feed with fodder. [OE *fōdor*]

foe (fō) *n.* An enemy; adversary. [Fusion of OE *fāh* hostile and *gefā* enemy]

foe·man (fō′mən) *n.* *pl.* **·men** (-mən) A foe.

foe·tal (fēt′l), **foe·tus** (fē′təs), etc. See FETAL, FETUS, etc.

fog (fog, fôg) *n.* **1.** A cloud of varying size formed at the surface of the earth by the condensation of atmospheric vapor and interfering to a greater or lesser extent with horizontal visibility. **2.** Any hazy condition of the atmosphere caused by smoke, dust particles, etc. **3.** A state of mental bewilderment or blurred perception. **4.** *Photog.* A dark blur clouding part or all of a developed print or plate. —*v.* **fogged, fog·ging** *v.t.* **1.** To surround with or as with fog. **2.** To confuse or bewilder. **3.** *Photog.* To cloud (a print or plate) with a dark blur. —*v.i.* **4.** To become enveloped by or covered with or as with fog. **5.** To become confused. **6.** *Photog.* Of a print or plate, to become clouded with a dark blur. [Prob. back formation < *foggy*, in the sense "marshy"]

fog bank A mass of fog seen at a distance, esp. at sea.

fog·bound (fog′bound′, fôg′-) *adj.* Prevented from traveling, sailing, flying, etc., because of fog.

fog chamber *Physics* A cloud chamber.

fog·gy (fog′ē, fôg′ē) *adj.* **·gi·er, ·gi·est 1.** Full of or marked by fog. **2.** Resembling fog; cloudy. **3.** Mentally confused; bewildered. —**fog′gi·ly** *adv.* —**fog′gi·ness** *n.*

fog·horn (fog′hôrn′, fôg′-) *n.* **1.** A horn or whistle for sounding a warning during a fog. **2.** A loud, harsh voice.

fo·gy (fō′gē) *n.* *pl.* **·gies** A person of old-fashioned or ultra-conservative notions: usu. preceded by *old.* Also **fo′gey, fo′·gie.** [? < FOGGY] —**fo′gy·ish** *adj.* —**fo′gy·ism** *n.*

foi·ble (foi′bəl) *n.* A personal weakness or failing. [< F, obs. var. of *faible* weak]

foil¹ (foil) *v.t.* **1.** To prevent the success of; thwart. **2.** In hunting, to cross and recross (a scent or trail) to confuse pursuers. —*n.* An animal's trail. [< OF *fouler, fuler* to crush < LL *fullare* to full cloth]

foil² (foil) *n.* **1.** A metal hammered or rolled into thin, pliant sheets. **2.** A leaf of bright metal set beneath an artificial or inferior gem to add brilliance or color. **3.** A person or thing serving by contrast to enhance the qualities of another. **4.** *Archit.* A division, space, or piece of tracery suggestive of a leaf. —*v.t.* **1.** To apply foil to; cover with foil. **2.** To intensify or set off by contrast. **3.** *Archit.* To adorn (windows, etc.) with foils. [< OF < L *folium* leaf]

foil³ (foil) *n.* **1.** A blunted, rapierlike implement sometimes having a button on its end, used in fencing. **2.** *pl.* The art of fencing with a foil. [Origin uncertain]

foist (foist) *v.t.* **1.** To impose (someone or something) slyly or wrongfully; palm off. **2.** To insert or introduce fraudulently. [Prob. < dial. Du. *vuisten* hold in the hand]

fold¹ (fōld) *v.t.* **1.** To turn back or bend over so that one part covers or lies alongside another. **2.** To close or collapse: often with *up.* **3.** To wrap up; enclose. **4.** To place together and interlock: to *fold* one's hands; also, to bring (wings) close to the body. **5.** To embrace; enfold. **6.** To wind; coil: with *about, around,* etc. **7.** In cooking, to mix (beaten egg whites, etc.) into other ingredients by gently turning one part over the other: with *in.* —*v.i.* **8.** To become folded. **9.** *U.S. Slang* **a** To fail financially; close: The show *folded.* **b** To collapse, as from exhaustion. —*n.* **1.** One part folded over another. **2.** The space between two folded parts. **3.** The crease made by folding. **4.** The act of folding. **5.** *Anat.* A thin edge or slip of tissue folded over an organ or part. **6.** *Geol.* A bend in a layer of rock. [OE *fealdan*]

fold² (fōld) *n.* **1.** A pen, as for sheep. **2.** The sheep enclosed in a pen. **3.** A flock of sheep. **4.** A group of people, as the congregation of a church, having a leader, a common purpose, etc. —*v.t.* To shut up in a fold, as sheep. [OE *fald*]

-fold *suffix* **1.** Having (a specified number of) parts: a *three-fold* blessing. **2.** (A specified number of) times as great or as much: to reward *tenfold.* **3.** An amount multiplied by (a specified number): a *hundredfold.* [OE *fealdan* to fold]

fold·er (fōl′dər) *n.* **1.** One who or that which folds. **2.** A road map, timetable, etc., designed to be folded up into a small, compact form. **3.** A large binder for loose papers.

fol·de·rol (fol′də·rol) See FALDERAL.

fo·li·a·ceous (fō′lē·ā′shəs) *adj.* **1.** Of, pertaining to, or resembling the leaf of a plant: also **fo·li·ar** (fō′lē·ər). **2.** Made up of thin, laminated sheets.

fo·li·age (fō′lē·ij) *n.* **1.** The growth of leaves on a tree or other plant; also, leaves collectively. **2.** An ornamental representation of leaves, flowers, and branches. [Earlier *foillage* < F < L *folium* leaf] —**fo′li·aged** *adj.*

fo·li·ate (fō′lē·āt; *for adj., also* fō′lē·it) *adj.* **1.** Having leaves. **2.** Foliaceous. —*v.* **·at·ed, ·at·ing** *v.t.* **1.** To roll or hammer (gold, etc.) into thin plates. —*v.i.* **2.** To split into thin leaves or layers. **3.** To produce leaves, as a tree.

fo·li·a·tion (fō′lē·ā′shən) *n.* **1.** *Bot.* **a** The act of bursting into leaf, or the state of being in leaf. **b** The arrangement or formation of leaves in a bud. **2.** *Geol.* In certain rocks, a crystalline formation into leaflike layers; also, the layers themselves. **3.** The consecutive numbering of the leaves of a book. Also **fo·li·a·ture** (fō′lē·ə·choŏr′).

fo·lic acid (fō′lik) *Biochem.* An orange-yellow crystalline compound, $C_{19}H_{19}N_7O_6$, included in the vitamin-B complex. It is found in green leaves, mushrooms, yeast, and some animal tissues: also *vitamin Bc.*

fo·li·o (fō′lē·ō) *n.* *pl.* **·li·os 1.** A sheet of paper folded once to form four pages (two leaves) of a book, the height of the pages usu. ranging from 13 to 19 inches. **2.** A book, manuscript, etc., having the oversize pages made from such a sheet; also, the size of such a work. **3.** A leaf of a book, manuscript, etc., only one side of which is numbered. **4.** The page number of a book. —*adj.* Of, pertaining to, or being of the size of a folio. —*v.t.* **·li·oed, ·li·o·ing** To number in order the pages of (a book, manuscript, etc.).

fo·li·o·late (fō′lē·ə·lāt′) *adj.* *Bot.* Of, pertaining to, or composed of leaflets. [< L *foliolum*, dim. of *folium* leaf + -ATE¹]

-folious *suffix of adjectives* Leaflike or leafy. [< L *folium* leaf]

folk (fōk) *n.* *pl.* **folk** or **folks 1.** A people; nation. **2.** *Usu. pl.* People of a particular group or class: old *folks.* **3.** *pl. Informal* People in general. **4.** *pl. Informal* One's family, esp. one's parents. —Syn. See PEOPLE. —*adj.* Originating among or characteristic of the common people. [OE *folc*]

folk dance   1. A dance originating among the common people of a district or country.   2. The music for such a dance.

folk etymology   Popular modification of an unfamiliar word, thereby causing the word to correspond with better known forms, as *agnail* (in Middle English, a painful nail) becoming *hangnail*.

folk·lore (fōk′lôr′, -lōr′)   n.   1. The traditions, beliefs, customs, sayings, stories, etc., preserved among the common people.   2. The study of folk cultures.   — **folk′lor·ist** n.

folk music   Music created and perpetuated by the common people.

folk singer   One who sings folk songs.

folk song   1. A song, usu. of unknown authorship, originating among the common people and handed down orally.   2. A song copying the style of such a song.

folk·sy (fōk′sē)   adj.   ·si·er, ·si·est   U.S. Informal   Friendly; sociable; unpretentious.   — **folk′si·ness** n.

folk·ways (fōk′wāz′)   n.pl.   Sociol.   The traditional habits, customs, and behavior of a group, tribe, or nation.

fol·li·cle (fol′i·kəl)   n.   1. Anat. A small cavity or sac in certain parts of the body, having a protective or secretory function.   2. Bot. A dry seed vessel of one carpel.   [< L, dim. of *follis* bag]   — **fol·lic·u·lar** (fə·lik′yə·lər) adj.

fol·lic·u·lat·ed (fə·lik′yə·lā′tid)   adj.   1. Having a follicle.   2. Encased in a cocoon.   Also **fol·lic′u·late** (-lit).

fol·low (fol′ō)   v.t.   1. To go or come after and in the same direction.   2. To succeed in time or order.   3. To pursue.   4. To hold to the course of: to *follow* a road.   5. To conform to: to *follow* the customs of a country.   6. To use or take as a model; imitate.   7. To watch or observe closely.   8. To have an active interest in: to *follow* sports.   9. To understand the course, sequence, or meaning of, as an explanation.   10. To come after as a consequence or result.   11. To work at as a profession or livelihood: men who *follow* the sea.   12. To be under the leadership or authority of.   13. To accompany; attend.   — v.i.   14. To move or come after.   15. To pay attention.   16. To understand.   17. To come as a result or consequence.   — **to follow out** 1. To follow to the end, as an argument.   2. To comply with, as orders or instructions.   — **to follow suit** 1. In card games, to play a card of the suit led.   2. To follow another's example.   — **to follow through** 1. To swing to the full extent of the stroke after having struck the ball, as in tennis or golf.   2. To perform fully.   — **to follow up** 1. To pursue closely.   2. To bring to full completion.   3. To increase the effectiveness of by further action.   — n. The act of following.   [OE *folgian*]

fol·low·er (fol′ō·ər)   n.   One who or that which follows; as: **a** A pursuer.   **b** A disciple or supporter.   **c** A servant or attendant.   — **Syn.** See ADHERENT.   — **fol′low·er·ship′** n.

fol·low·ing (fol′ō·ing)   adj.   That comes next in time or sequence: the *following* week.   — n. A body of adherents, attendants, or disciples.

fol·low-through (fol′ō-thrōō′)   n.   1. In sports, the continuation and full completion of a motion; esp., in tennis and golf, the last part of the stroke after the ball has been hit.   2. Any continuing or completion.

fol·low-up (fol′ō-up′)   n.   1. The act of following up.   2. Something, as an action, procedure, letter, etc., used in following up.   — adj. Designed to follow up: a *follow-up* visit.

fol·ly (fol′ē)   n.   pl. ·lies   1. The condition or state of being foolish; foolishness.   2. A foolish idea or action.   3. A foolish or ruinous undertaking.   [< F < *fol* fool]

Fo·mal·haut (fō′mal·hôt)   n.   One of the 20 brightest stars, 1.29 magnitude; Alpha in the constellation Piscis Austrinus.   [< F < Arabic *fom al-hūt* the whale's mouth]

fo·ment (fō·ment′)   1. To stir up or instigate (rebellion, discord, etc.).   2. To treat with warm water or medicated lotions, as in applying a poultice.   [< F < LL < L *fomentum* poultice]   — **fo′men·ta′tion** n.   — **fo·ment′er** n.

fond (fond)   adj.   1. Having affection (for someone or something specified): with *of*.   2. Loving or deeply affectionate.   3. Unwisely or indulgently affectionate; doting.   4. Affectionately nurtured; cherished.   [ME *fonned*, pp. of *fonnen* to be foolish]   — **fond′ly** adv.

fon·dant (fon′dənt, Fr. fôn·dän′)   n.   A soft, creamy confection.   [< F, orig. ppr. of *fondre* to melt]

fon·dle (fon′dəl)   v.t.   ·dled, ·dling   To handle lovingly; caress.   [Freq. of obs. *fond* to caress]   — **fon′dler** n.

fond·ness (fond′nis)   n.   1. Tender affection; liking.   2. Extravagant or foolish affection.   3. Strong preference.

fon·due (fon·dōō′, Fr. fôn·dü′)   n.   A dish of grated cheese, cooked with eggs, butter, etc.   [< F]

font¹ (font)   n.   1. A basin, often of stone, for the water used in baptism.   2. A receptacle for holy water.   3. Source; origin.   [OE < L *fons, fontis* fountain]   — **font′al** adj.

font² (font)   n.   Printing   A full assortment of type of a particular face and size: also, Brit., **fount**.   [< F *fondre* to melt]

fon·ta·nel (fon′tə·nel′)   n.   Anat.   A soft, pulsating, unossified area in the fetal and infantile skull.   [< F *fontanelle*]

food (fōōd)   n.   1. That which is eaten, drunk, or absorbed by an organism for the maintenance of life and the growth and repair of tissues.   2. Nourishment taken in more or less solid form as opposed to liquid form.   3. A particular kind of nourishment: breakfast *food*.   4. Anything that is used in a manner suggestive of food: intellectual *food*.   [OE *fōda*]

food poi·son·ing (poi′zən·ing)   A gastrointestinal disorder caused by certain bacterial toxins found in rancid or decomposed food: erroneously called *ptomaine poisoning*.

food·stuff (fōōd′stuf′)   n.   1. Any substance suitable for food.   2. Any substance, as fat, protein, etc., that enters into the composition of food.

fool (fōōl)   n.   1. A person lacking understanding, judgment, or common sense.   2. A clown formerly kept by noblemen for household entertainment; jester.   3. One who has been duped or imposed upon.   — **to be nobody's fool** Informal To be shrewd.   — v.i.   1. To act like a fool.   2. To act, speak, etc., in a playful or teasing manner.   — v.t.   3. To make a fool of; deceive.   — **to fool around** or **about** Informal 1. To waste time on trifles; putter.   2. To loiter about idly.   — **to fool with** Informal 1. To meddle with.   2. To play or toy aimlessly with.   — adj. Informal Stupid or silly.   [< F < L *follis* a bellows; later, simpleton]

fool·er·y (fōō′lə·rē)   n.   pl. ·er·ies   Foolish behavior, speech, etc.; also, an instance of this.

fool·har·dy (fōōl′här′dē)   adj.   ·di·er, ·di·est   Bold in a foolish or reckless way.   — **fool′har′di·ly** adv.   — **fool′har′di·ness** n.

fool·ish (fōō′lish)   adj.   1. Marked by or showing a lack of good sense; silly.   2. Resulting from folly or stupidity: *foolish* consequences.   3. Utterly ridiculous; absurd.   4. Archaic Insignificant.   — **fool′ish·ly** adv.   — **fool′ish·ness** n.

fool·proof (fōōl′prōōf′)   adj.   1. So simple and strong as to be incapable of damage or harm even through misuse.   2. Having no weak points; infallible: a *foolproof* plan.

fools·cap (fōōlz′kap)   n.   A writing paper measuring about 13 x 16 inches, usu. folded into a page measuring about 13 x 8 inches, so called from the watermark of a fool's cap.

fool's cap   1. A pointed cap, usu. with bells at its tip, formerly worn by jesters.   2. A dunce cap.

fool's gold   One of several metallic sulfides, as pyrite, resembling gold in color.

foot (fŏŏt)   n.   pl. **feet** (fēt)   1. The terminal section of the limb of a vertebrate animal, upon which it stands or moves.   ◆ Collateral adjective: *pedal*.   2. Any part, as of an invertebrate animal or of a plant, piece of furniture, etc., corresponding in form or position to the foot.   3. The part of a boot or stocking that covers the wearer's foot.   4. The lower part of anything; base; esp.: **a** The base of a hill or mountain.   **b** The part of a bed, grave, etc., where the feet rest.   **c** The bottom of a page, ladder, etc.   **d** Naut. The lower edge of a sail.   5. The last part of a series; end.   6. The inferior part or section: the *foot* of the class.   7. A measure of length, equivalent to 12 inches: symbol (′).   See table inside back cover.   8. In prosody, a group of syllables having a primary stress or accent on one of the syllables and forming a major unit of poetic rhythm.   9. Foot soldiers, collectively; infantry.   10. Step or manner of movement: a light *foot*.   — **on foot** 1. Walking or standing.   2. In progress.   — **to put one's best foot forward** 1. To do one's best.   2. To try to look one's best.   — **to put one's foot down** To act firmly.   — **to put one's foot in it** or **in one's mouth** To make an embarrassing mistake or blunder.   — v.i.   To walk or dance: often with indefinite *it*.   — v.t.   3. To move on or through by foot.   4. To furnish with a foot, as a stocking.   5. Informal To pay, as a bill.   6. To add, as a column of figures: often with *up*.   [OE *fōt*]   — **foot′less** adj.

foot·age (fŏŏt′ij)   n.   The extent of something as measured in linear feet.

foot-and-mouth disease (fŏŏt′ən-mouth′)   Vet.   A contagious virus disease of cattle, swine, etc., marked by fever and blisters about the mouth and hoofs.

foot·ball (fŏŏt′bôl′)   n.   1. U.S. A game played between two teams of eleven men on a field with goals at each end, in which points are made by carrying the ball across the opponent's goal line or by kicking the ball over the opponent's goal posts.   2. The ball used in this game, an inflated, leather-covered ball with an ellipsoidal shape.   3. Canadian A similar game played by teams of twelve men: also called *rugby, rugby football*.   4. In Great Britain: a Rugby football (def. 1); also, the ball.   **b** Soccer; also, the inflated ball.

foot·board (fŏŏt′bôrd′, -bōrd′)   n.   1. A board or small platform on which to prop or rest the feet.   2. An upright piece at the foot of a bedstead.

foot-can·dle (fŏŏt′kan′dəl)   n.   The illumination thrown on one square foot of surface, all points of which are at a distance of one foot from one international candle.

foot·ed (fŏŏt′id)   adj.   1. Having a foot or feet: a *footed* goblet.   2. Having or characterized by a (specified kind of) foot or (a specified number of) feet: *light-footed; four-footed*.

foot·er (fŏŏt′ər)   n.   One who or that which has an indicated number of linear feet in height or length: a *six-footer*.

foot·fall (fŏŏt′fôl′)   n.   The sound of a footstep.

foot·hill (fŏŏt′hil′)   n.   A low hill at the base of a mountain.

foot·hold (fŏŏt/hōld/) *n.* **1.** A place on which the foot can rest securely, as in climbing. **2.** A good, firm position from which one can begin or carry forward some course of action.

foot·ing (fŏŏt/ing) *n.* **1.** A place on which to stand, walk, or climb securely. **2.** A secure support for the foot; foothold. **3.** An established or secure position or foundation. **4.** Social or professional status in relation to others; standing. **5.** The act of adding a foot to something, as a shoe; also, the material used for this. **6.** The adding up of a column of figures; also, the sum obtained. **7.** *Archit.* A base or foundation wider than the structure it supports, as for a pedestal.

foot·lights (fŏŏt/līts/) *n.pl.* **1.** Lights in a row near the front of the stage of a theater, nearly level with the performers' feet. **2.** The profession of acting on the stage.

foot·loose (fŏŏt/lōōs/) *adj.* Free to travel or do as one pleases; unattached.

foot·man (fŏŏt/mən) *n.* *pl.* **·men** (-mən) A male servant in livery who answers the door, waits at table, etc.

foot·note (fŏŏt/nōt/) *n.* An explanatory note, reference, or comment on the text, usu. appearing at the bottom of a page. — *v.t.* **·not·ed, ·not·ing** To furnish with footnotes.

foot·path (fŏŏt/path/, -päth/) *n.* **1.** A path to be used only by persons on foot. **2.** *Brit.* A sidewalk.

foot·pound (fŏŏt/pound/) *n.* *Mech.* A unit of energy, equal to the amount of energy necessary to raise a one-pound mass through one linear foot.

foot·print (fŏŏt/print/) *n.* The outline or impression made by a foot treading on a surface.

foot·rest (fŏŏt/rest/) *n.* Something, as a small stool or platform, on which the feet can be propped or rested.

foot soldier A soldier trained and equipped to fight on foot.

foot·sore (fŏŏt/sôr, -sōr/) *adj.* Having sore or tired feet.

foot·step (fŏŏt/step/) *n.* **1.** The action of taking a step with the foot. **2.** The distance covered by a foot in stepping. **3.** The sound made by a foot in stepping. **4.** A footprint. **5.** A step of a stairway, etc. — **to follow in someone's footsteps** **1.** To repeat or duplicate the work or actions of another. **2.** To succeed to another's position.

foot·stool (fŏŏt/stōōl/) *n.* A low stool on which the feet can be rested while one is sitting.

foot·wear (fŏŏt/wâr/) *n.* Articles worn on the feet, as shoes.

foot·work (fŏŏt/wûrk/) *n.* Use or control of the feet, as in boxing or tennis.

foo·zle (fōō/zəl) *v.t. & v.i.* **·zled, ·zling** To do awkwardly; fumble. — *n.* A misstroke or misplay, esp. in golf. [Cf. dial. G *fuseln* to work badly] — **foo/zler** *n.*

fop (fop) *n.* A man overly fastidious in dress or deportment; a dandy. [Cf. Du. *foppen* to cheat] — **fop/pish** *adj.* **fop/pish·ly** *adv.* — **fop/pish·ness** *n.*

fop·per·y (fop/ər·ē) *n.* *pl.* **·per·ies** **1.** The conduct or ways of a fop. **2.** Something worn by or typical of a fop.

for (fôr, *unstressed* fər) *prep.* **1.** To the extent of: The ground is flat *for* miles. **2.** Through the duration or period of: *for* a week. **3.** To the number or amount of: a check *for* six dollars. **4.** At the cost or payment of: a hat *for* ten dollars. **5.** On account of: He is respected *for* his ability. **6.** In honor of: He is named *for* his grandfather. **7.** Appropriate to: a time *for* work. **8.** In place of: using a book *for* a desk. **9.** In favor, support, or approval of. **10.** In the interest or behalf of. **11.** Directed toward: an eye *for* bargains. **12.** As affecting (in a particular way): good *for* your health. **13.** Sent, given, or assigned to. **14.** In proportion to: big *for* his age. **15.** As the equivalent to or requital of: blow *for* blow. **16.** In spite of. **17.** In order to reach or go toward: He left *for* his office. **18.** In order to find or obtain: looking *for* a hat. **19.** At (a particular time or occasion): to meet *for* the last time. **20.** As being or seeming: We took him *for* an honest man. **21.** In consideration of the usual characteristics of: She is strong *for* a woman. **22.** With the purpose of: walking *for* exercise. — **O for . . . !** Would that I had! — *conj.* Inasmuch as; because. [OE]

for-[1] *prefix* **1.** Away; off (in a privative sense): *forget, forgo.* **2.** Very; extremely: *forlorn.* [OE]

for-[2] See also words beginning FORE-.

for·age (fôr/ij, for/-) *n.* **1.** Food suitable for cattle or other domestic animals; fodder. **2.** A searching about for food or supplies; also, a raid to find or capture provisions. — *v.* **·aged, ·ag·ing** *v.i.* **1.** To search about or rummage around for something, esp. for food or supplies. **2.** To make a raid so as to find or capture supplies. — *v.t.* **3.** To search through for food, supplies, etc. **4.** To obtain by plundering or rummaging about. **5.** To provide with food or supplies. [< F < OF *feurre* fodder] — **for/ag·er** *n.*

fo·ra·men (fō·rā/mən) *n.* *pl.* **·ram·i·na** (-ram/ə·nə) *Biol.* A small opening or hole, usu. natural, as in a bone. [< L < *forare* to bore]

for·a·min·i·fer (fôr/ə·min/ə·fər, for/-) *n.* One of a large order of extremely tiny unicellular marine animals, usu. having bony shells perforated with many minute holes. [< L *foramen, -inis* hole + *-fer* having] — **fo·ram·i·nif·er·al** (fə·ram/ə·nif/ər·əl), **fo·ram·i·nif/er·ous** *adj.*

for·as·much as (fôr/əz·much/) Inasmuch as; since.

for·ay (fôr/ā, for/ā) *n. & v.t. & v.i.* To plunder; raid. — *n.* An expedition or raid, as for plunder. [Prob. back formation < *forayer* raider < OF *feurre* fodder] — **for/ay·er** *n.*

for·bear[1] (fôr·bâr/) *v.* **·bore, ·borne, ·bear·ing** *v.t.* **1.** To refrain or abstain from (some action). **2.** To cease or desist from. — *v.i.* **3.** To abstain. **4.** To be patient. [OE] — **for·bear/er** *n.*

for·bear[2] (fôr/bâr/) See FOREBEAR.

for·bear·ance (fôr·bâr/əns) *n.* **1.** The act of forbearing. **2.** The quality of being forbearing; patience.

for·bear·ing (fôr·bâr/ing) *adj.* Disposed to forbear; patient.

for·bid (fər·bid/, fôr-) *v.t.* **·bade** (-bad/) or **·bad, ·bid·den** (*Archaic* ·bid), **·bid·ding** **1.** To command (a person) not to do something, etc.; prohibit from doing, having, etc. **2.** To prohibit the doing, use, etc., of. **3.** To have the effect of preventing; making impossible, impractical, etc. [OE *forbēodan*] — **for·bid/al, for/bid/dance** *n.*

for·bid·den (fər·bid/n, fôr-) *adj.* Not allowed; prohibited.

for·bid·ding (fər·bid/ing, fôr-) *adj.* **1.** Grim and unfriendly in appearance: a *forbidding* face. **2.** Having a threatening or ominous look: a *forbidding* swamp. — **for·bid/ding·ly** *adv.*

for·bore (fôr·bôr/, -bōr/) Past tense of FORBEAR[1].

for·borne (fôr·bôrn/, -bōrn/) Past participle of FORBEAR[1].

force (fôrs, fōrs) *n.* **1.** Power or energy; strength: the *force* of a gale. **2.** Power exerted on any resisting person or thing; also, the use of such power; coercion. **3.** The quality of anything that tends to produce an effect on the mind or will. **4.** Any moral, social, or political power or influence. **5.** A body of individuals belonging to one of a nation's military, naval, or air divisions: the armed *forces.* **6.** Any body of individuals organized for some specific work: police *force.* **7.** *Law* Binding effect; validity: the *force* of a contract. **8.** *Physics* Anything that changes or tends to change the state of rest or motion in a body. — **in** (**full**) **force** **1.** Still operative or enforceable, as a law. **2.** With no one missing. — *v.t.* **forced, forc·ing** **1.** To compel to do something; coerce. **2.** To get or obtain by or as by force. **3.** To bring forth or about by or as by effort: to *force* a smile. **4.** To drive or move despite resistance. **5.** To assault and capture, as a fortification. **6.** To break open, as a door or lock. **7.** To make, as a passage or way, by force. **8.** To press or impose upon someone as by force. **9.** To exert to the utmost; strain, as the voice. **10.** To rape. **11.** To stimulate the growth of artificially, as plants in a hothouse. **12.** In baseball: **a** To put out (a base runner compelled to leave one base for the next). **b** To cause (the base runner on third base) to score by walking the batter when the bases are full. **c** To allow (a run) in such a manner. **13.** In card games: **a** To compel (a player) to choose between losing a trick or playing a trump from his hand. **b** To play so as to compel (a player) to reveal the strength of a hand held. [< F < L *fortis* brave, strong] — **force/a·ble** *adj.* — **forc/er** *n.*

forced (fôrst, fōrst) *adj.* **1.** Done under force; compulsory: *forced* labor. **2.** Strained; affected: *forced* gaiety. **3.** Done in an emergency: a *forced* landing of an airplane.

force·ful (fôrs/fəl, fōrs/-) *adj.* Full of or done with force; vigorous; effective. — **force/ful·ly** *adv.* — **force/ful·ness** *n.*

force·meat (fôrs/mēt/, fōrs/-) *n.* Finely chopped, seasoned meat served separately or used as stuffing. [< *force*, alter. of FARCE, v. + MEAT]

for·ceps (fôr/səps) *n.* A pair of pincers for grasping and manipulating small or delicate objects, used by surgeons, dentists, etc. [< L < *formus* warm + *capere* to take]

for·ci·ble (fôr/sə·bəl) *adj.* **1.** Accomplished or brought about by force: a *forcible* exit. **2.** Characterized by or having force; vigorous. — **forc/i·ble·ness** *n.* — **for/ci·bly** *adv.*

ford (fôrd, fōrd) *n.* A shallow place in a stream, river, etc., that can be crossed by wading. — *v.t.* To cross (a river, stream, etc.) at a shallow place. [OE] — **ford/a·ble** *adj.*

fore (fôr, fōr) *adj.* Situated at or toward the front in relation to something else: the *fore* and hind legs of a horse. — *n.* **1.** The front part of something. **2.** *Naut.* A foremast; also, the bows of a ship. — **to the fore** **1.** To or at the front part of something. **2.** In or into a prominent or conspicuous position. — *interj.* In golf, a cry made to warn anyone standing in the line of a ball. — *adv.* *Naut.* At or toward the bow of a ship. — *prep. & conj.* *Archaic* or *Dial.* Before: also **'fore.** [OE, adv. & prep.]

fore-[1] *prefix* **1.** Prior in time, place, or rank; as in:

foreacquaint   foreanswer   foreconclude

2. Situated at or near the front; as in:

forebody   forecabin   forecourt

[OE *fore-, for-* before]

fore-[2] See also words beginning FOR-.

fore-and-aft (fôr'ən·aft', fôr'-, -äft') *adj. Naut.* Lying or going in the direction of a ship's length: a *fore-and-aft* sail.
fore and aft *Naut.* **1.** Lengthwise of a boat. **2.** In, at, or toward both the stem and the stern of a boat.
fore·arm¹ (fôr'ärm') *n.* The part of the arm between the elbow and the wrist. ◆ Collateral adjective: *cubital.*
fore·arm² (fôr·ärm', fôr-) *v.t.* To arm beforehand.
fore·bear (fôr'bâr, fôr'-) *n.* An ancestor: also spelled *forbear.* [Earlier *for-be-er*]
fore·bode (fôr·bōd', fôr-) *v.t. & v.i.* **·bod·ed, ·bod·ing 1.** To indicate in advance; portend. **2.** To have a premonition of (something evil or harmful). [< FORE-¹ + BODE²]
fore·brain (fôr'brān', fôr'-) *n. Anat.* The prosencephalon.
fore·cast (fôr'kast', -käst', fôr'-) *v.t.* **·cast** or **·cast·ed, ·cast·ing 1.** To calculate beforehand; especially, to predict (weather conditions). **2.** To foreshadow. **3.** To arrange or plan beforehand. —*n.* **1.** A calculated prediction of weather conditions. **2.** A prediction or prophecy. —**fore'cast'er** *n.*
fore·cas·tle (fōk'səl) *n. Naut.* **1.** That part of the upper deck of a ship located forward of the mast nearest the bow. **2.** A section of a merchant ship near the bow, in which the sailors' living quarters are located. Also spelled *fo'c's'le.*
fore·close (fôr·klōz', fôr-) *v.* **·closed, ·clos·ing** *v.t.* **1.** *Law* **a** To deprive (a mortgager in default) of the right to redeem mortgaged property. **b** To take away the power to redeem (a mortgage or pledge). **2.** To shut out; exclude. —*v.i.* **3.** To foreclose a mortgage. [< OF *forclore* to exclude]
fore·clo·sure (fôr·klō'zhər, fôr-) *n.* The act of foreclosing.
fore·deck (fôr'dek', fôr'-) *n. Naut.* The forward part of a deck, especially of an upper deck.
fore·doom (*v.* fôr·dōōm', fôr-; *n.* fôr'dōōm', fôr'-) *v.t.* To doom or condemn in advance. —*n.* Preordained doom.
fore·fa·ther (fôr'fä'thər, fôr'-) *n.* An ancestor.
fore·fin·ger (fôr'fing'gər, fôr'-) *n.* The finger next to the thumb; index finger.
fore·foot (fôr'fōōt', fôr'-) *n. pl.* **·feet 1.** One of the front feet of an animal, insect, etc. **2.** *Naut.* The part of a boat where the prow and keel meet.
fore·front (fôr'frunt', fôr') *n.* **1.** The very front of something. **2.** The position of most prominence, activity, etc.
fore·gath·er (fôr·gath'ər, fôr-) See FORGATHER.
fore·go¹ (fôr·gō', fôr-) *v.t. & v.i.* **·went, ·gone, ·go·ing** To go before or precede in time, place, etc. [OE *foregān*]
fore·go² (fôr·gō', fôr-) See FORGO.
fore·go·ing (fôr·gō'ing, fôr-; fôr'gō'ing, fôr'-) *adj.* Said, written, or done previously; preceding; antecedent.
fore·gone (fôr·gôn', fôr·gon'; fôr'gôn', fôr'gon') *adj.* Already gone or finished; also, previous or past: *foregone* eras.
foregone conclusion 1. A conclusion determined in advance of the evidence. **2.** A foreseen or inevitable result.
fore·ground (fôr'ground', fôr'-) *n.* **1.** The part of a landscape, picture, etc., nearest or represented as nearest to the spectator. **2.** The position of most prominence or activity.
fore·hand (fôr'hand', fôr'-) *adj.* **1.** Of or pertaining to a stroke in tennis, etc., in which the palm of the hand holding the racket faces the direction of the stroke. **2.** First or foremost; leading. —*n.* **1.** A forehand stroke, as in tennis. **2.** A position of advantage.
fore·hand·ed (fôr'han'did, fôr'-) *adj.* **1.** *U.S.* Prudent; thrifty. **2.** Done in good time. —**fore'hand'ed·ness** *n.*
fore·head (fôr'id, fôr'-; *occasionally* fôr'hed') *n.* **1.** The part of the face from the eyebrows to the hair. ◆ Collateral adjective: *frontal.* **2.** The front part of anything.
for·eign (fôr'in, for'-) *adj.* **1.** Belonging to, located in, characteristic of, or concerned with another country, region, society, etc. **2.** Unfamiliar; strange: Anything mechanical is *foreign* to him. **3.** Having little or no relation; not pertinent. **4.** Occurring in a place or body in which it is not normally found. [< F *forain*, ult. < L *foras* out of doors]
foreign affairs Matters of diplomacy, commerce, etc., in the dealings of one country or nation with another.
for·eign-born (fôr'in·bôrn', fôr'-) *adj.* Born in a foreign country or state; not native to a country or region.
for·eign·er (fôr'in·ər, fôr'-) *n.* A native or citizen of a foreign country or region; alien. —**Syn.** See ALIEN.
foreign office The department of government in charge of foreign affairs.
fore·judge (fôr·juj', fôr-) *v.t. & v.i.* **·judged, ·judg·ing** To judge in advance.
fore·know (fôr·nō', fôr-) *v.t.* **·knew, ·known, ·know·ing** To know beforehand. —**fore·knowl'edge** *n.*
fore·land (fôr'land', fôr'-) *n.* A projecting point of land.
fore·leg (fôr'leg', fôr'-) *n.* One of the front legs of an animal, insect, etc. Also **fore'limb'** (-lim').
fore·lock (fôr'lok', fôr'-) *n.* A lock of hair growing over the forehead.
fore·man (fôr'mən, fôr'-) *n. pl.* **·men** (-mən) **1.** The overseer of a body of workmen. **2.** The chairman and spokesman of a jury. —**fore'man·ship** *n.*
fore·mast (fôr'mast', -mäst', -məst, fôr'-) *n. Naut.* The mast that is closest to the bow of a ship.

fore·most (fôr'mōst, -məst, fôr'-) *adj.* First in place, time, rank, or order; chief. —*adv.* In the chief or principal place, rank, etc. [OE *formest*]
fore·named (fôr'nāmd', fôr'-) *adj.* Previously named or mentioned; aforesaid.
fore·noon (fôr'nōōn', fôr'-; fôr·nōōn', fôr-) *n.* The period of daylight preceding midday, esp. the later business hours; morning. —*adj.* Of or occurring in the forenoon.
fo·ren·sic (fə·ren'sik) *adj.* Relating to, characteristic of, or used in courts of justice or public debate. [< L *forum* market place, forum] —**fo·ren'si·cal·ly** *adv.*
forensic medicine Medical jurisprudence.
fore·or·dain (fôr·ôr·dān', fôr'-) *v.t.* **1.** To decree or appoint in advance. **2.** To fix the fate of in advance. —**fore'or·dain'ment, fore·or·di·na·tion** (fôr·ôr'də·nā'shən, fôr-) *n.*
fore·part (fôr'pärt', fôr'-) *n.* The first part in time, place, or order. Also **fore part.**
fore·quar·ter (fôr'kwôr'tər, fôr'-) *n.* The front portion of a side of beef, etc., including the leg and adjacent parts.
fore·reach (fôr·rēch', fôr-) *v.t.* **1.** To catch up with or get ahead of, as a ship. —*v.i.* **2.** To catch up with or move ahead of a ship, etc.: usu. with *on, upon.*
fore·run (fôr·run', fôr-) *v.t.* **·ran, ·run, ·run·ning 1.** To foreshadow; herald. **2.** To precede. **3.** To forestall.
fore·run·ner (fôr·run'ər, fôr-, fôr'run'ər, fôr'-) *n.* **1.** One who or that which precedes another; also, a forefather or ancestor. **2.** One who proclaims the coming of another. **3.** An advance indication of something; omen.
fore·sail (fôr'sāl', -səl, fôr'sāl, fô'səl) *n. Naut.* **1.** The lowest sail on the foremast of a square-rigged vessel. **2.** The fore-and-aft sail on a schooner's foremast, set on a boom and gaff. For illus. see SCHOONER.
fore·see (fôr·sē', fôr-) *v.t.* **·saw, ·seen, ·see·ing** To see or know in advance. —**fore·see'a·ble** *adj.* —**fore·se'er** *n.*
fore·shad·ow (fôr·shad'ō, fôr-) *v.t.* To give an advance indication or suggestion of; presage. —**fore·shad'ow·er** *n.*
fore·sheet (fôr'shēt', fôr-) *n. Naut.* **1.** A rope holding one of the clews of a foresail. **2.** *pl.* A boat's forward space.
fore·shore (fôr'shôr', fôr'shōr') *n.* That part of a shore uncovered at low tide.
fore·short·en (fôr·shôr'tən, fôr-) *v.t.* In drawing, to shorten parts of the representation of (an object) so as to create the illusion of depth and distance.
fore·sight (fôr'sīt', fôr'-) *n.* **1.** The act or capacity of foreseeing; also, a look directed toward something distant. **2.** Prudent anticipation of the future. —**fore'sight'ed** *adj.* —**fore'sight'ed·ly** *adv.* —**fore'sight'ed·ness** *n.*
fore·skin (fôr'skin', fôr'-) *n. Anat.* The prepuce.
for·est (fôr'ist, for'-) *n.* A large tract of land covered with a growth of trees and underbrush; also, the trees themselves. —*adj.* Of, pertaining to, or inhabiting forests; sylvan. —*v.t.* To plant with trees; make a forest of. [< OF < Med.L (*silva*) *foresta* an unenclosed (wood)]
fore·stall (fôr·stôl', fôr-) *v.t.* **1.** To hinder, prevent, or guard against in advance. **2.** To deal with, think of, or realize beforehand; anticipate. **3.** To buy up (goods) for reselling. —**Syn.** See PREVENT. [OE *foresteall* ambush]
for·est·a·tion (fôr'is·tā'shən, for'-) *n.* **1.** The planting of trees so as to make a forest. **2.** The science of forestry.
fore·stay (fôr·stā', fôr'-) *n. Naut.* A wire or rope running from the head of the foremast to the stem and used primarily to support the mast.
for·est·er (fôr'is·tər, for'-) *n.* **1.** One skilled in forestry or in charge of a forest. **2.** An animal dwelling in a forest.
for·est·ry (fôr'is·trē, for'-) *n.* **1.** The science of planting and managing forests. **2.** Forest land.
fore·taste (*n.* fôr'tāst', fôr'-; *v.* fôr·tāst', fôr-) *n.* An advance experiencing or sampling of something. —*v.t.* To have a foretaste of; taste in advance.
fore·tell (fôr·tel', fôr-) *v.t. & v.i.* **·told, ·tell·ing** To tell of or about in advance; utter a prophecy of; predict. —**Syn.** See PROPHESY. —**fore·tell'er** *n.*
fore·thought (fôr'thôt', fôr'-) *n.* **1.** Advance deliberation or consideration. **2.** Prudence; foresight.
fore·top (fôr'top', fôr'-; *Naut.* fôr'təp, fôr'-) *n. Naut.* A platform at the top of the lower section of a foremast.
fore·top·gal·lant (fôr'tə·gal'ənt, fôr'-) *adj. Naut.* Of, pertaining to, or designating the mast, sail, yard, etc., immediately above the foretopmast.
fore·top·mast (fôr·top'məst, fôr-) *n. Naut.* The section of a mast above the foretop.
fore·top·sail (fôr·top'səl, fôr-) *n. Naut.* The sail set on the foretopmast.
for·ev·er (fôr·ev'ər, fər-) *adv.* **1.** Throughout eternity; to the end of time. **2.** Incessantly; constantly.
for·ev·er·more (fôr·ev'ər·môr', -mōr', fər-) *adv.* Forever: an intensive form. Also **for evermore.**
fore·warn (fôr·wôrn', fôr-) *v.t.* To warn in advance.
fore·word (fôr'wûrd', fôr'-) *n.* A prefatory statement preceding the text of a book.
for·feit (fôr'fit) *n.* **1.** Something taken away or given up

as a penalty for an offense, shortcoming, error, etc.; fine. **2.** The giving up or loss of something as a penalty for an offense, etc. — *v.t.* To incur the deprivation of as a penalty for an offense, mistake, etc. — *adj.* Taken away or lost as a penalty for some offense, etc. [< OF *forfait* misdeed] — **for·feit·a·ble** *adj.* — **for′feit·er** *n.*

for·fei·ture (fôr′fi·chər) *n.* **1.** The giving up or loss of something by way of penalty. **2.** That which is forfeited.

for·gath·er (fôr·gath′ər) *v.i.* **1.** To meet or gather together; assemble. **2.** To meet by chance. **3.** To associate or converse socially. Also spelled *foregather.*

for·gave (fər·gāv′, fôr-) Past tense of FORGIVE.

forge[1] (fôrj, fôrj) *n.* **1.** An apparatus in which intense heat is maintained, used for heating and softening metal to be worked into shape. **2.** A workshop or factory in which such an apparatus is used. **3.** A furnace for melting or refining metals, as in the production of wrought iron. — *v.* **forged**, **forg·ing** *v.t.* **1.** To heat (metal) in a forge and work into shape; also, to produce or form as if by hammering into shape. **2.** To produce, change, or imitate so as to deceive; especially, to counterfeit (a signature, etc.). — *v.i.* **3.** To produce an imitation of something; esp. to counterfeit a signature, etc. **4.** To work at a forge. [< OF, ult. < L *fabrica* fabric] — **forg′er** *n.*

forge[2] (fôrj, fôrj) *v.i.* **forged**, **forg·ing** To move steadily forward in spite of difficulties, etc. [? Alter. of FORCE]

for·ger·y (fôr′jər·ē, fôr′-) *n. pl.* **·ger·ies** **1.** The act of making imitations of works of art, writings, signatures, etc., for fraudulent purposes. **2.** A fraudulent imitation.

for·get (fər·get′, fôr-) *v.* **·got**, **·got·ten** or **·got**, **·get·ting** *v.t.* **1.** To be unable to recall (something previously known). **2.** To neglect (to do or take something). **3.** To lose interest in or regard for. — *v.i.* **4.** To lose remembrance of something. — **to forget oneself** **1.** To be unselfish. **2.** To lose self-control and act in an unbecoming manner. **3.** To be lost in thought. [OE *forgietan*] — **for·get′a·ble** *adj.*

for·get·ful (fər·get′fəl, fôr-) *adj.* **1.** Inclined to forget. **2.** Neglectful; inattentive. **3.** *Poetic* Producing forgetfulness. — **for·get′ful·ly** *adv.* — **for·get′ful·ness** *n.*

for·get-me-not (fər·get′mē·not′) *n.* A small herb having blue or white flowers growing in clusters.

for·give (fər·giv′, fôr-) *v.* **·gave**, **·giv·en**, **·giv·ing** *v.t.* **1.** To grant pardon for or remission of (something). **2.** To cease to blame or feel resentment against. **3.** To remit, as a debt. — *v.i.* **4.** To show forgiveness; grant pardon. [OE *forgiefan*] — **for·giv′a·ble** *adj.* — **for·giv′er** *n.*

for·give·ness (fər·giv′nis, fôr-) *n.* **1.** The act of forgiving, or the state of being forgiven. **2.** A disposition to forgive.

for·giv·ing (fər·giv′ing, fôr-) *adj.* Disposed to forgive; merciful. — **for·giv′ing·ly** *adv.* — **for·giv′ing·ness** *n.*

for·go (fôr·gō′) *v.t.* **·went**, **·gone**, **·go·ing** To give up or refrain from; go without. Also spelled *forego.* [OE *forgān* to pass over] — **for·go′er** *n.*

for·got (fər·got′, fôr-) Past tense and alternative past participle of FORGET.

for·got·ten (fər·got′n, fôr-) Past participle of FORGET.

fork (fôrk) *n.* **1.** An implement consisting of a handle at the end of which are two or more prongs; as: **a** A utensil used at table. **b** An agricultural tool used for digging, lifting, tossing, etc. **2.** The division of something into two or more separately continued parts; also, the point at which this division begins, or any one of the parts. — *v.i.* **1.** To convey, lift, toss, etc., with or as with a fork. **2.** To give the shape of a fork to. — *v.i.* **3.** To branch into two or more separately continued parts. [OE *forca* < L *furca*]

forked (fôrkt, *Poetic* fôr′kid) *adj.* Having a fork or forking parts; also, sharply angled; zigzag.

for·lorn (fôr·lôrn′, fər-) *adj.* **1.** Left in distress; abandoned. **2.** Wretched; cheerless; desolate. **3.** Hopeless. **4.** Bereft: with *of.* [Orig. pp. of obs. *forlese* to lose, abandon] — **for·lorn′ly** *adv.* — **for·lorn′ness** *n.*

form (fôrm) *n.* **1.** The shape or contour of something as distinguished from its substance or color; external structure. **2.** The body of a living being. **3.** A mold, frame, etc., that gives shape to something. **4.** The particular state, character, etc., in which something presents itself: energy in the *form* of light. **5.** A specific type or species: a *form* of government. **6.** The style or manner of a poem, play, picture, etc.: traditional *forms.* **7.** Proper arrangement or order. **8.** The manner in which something is done: diving *form.* **9.** Fitness of mind or body for performance: He is in good *form.* **10.** A document having spaces for the insertion of names, dates, etc.: an application *form.* **11.** An established method of doing something. **12.** Mere outward formality; convention. **13.** A model formula or draft, as of a letter. **14.** A prescribed order of words, as in religious ceremonies, etc. **15.** *Philos.* The intrinsic nature of something; essence. **16.** *Gram.* Any of the various shapes assumed by a word in a

particular context, as *talk, talks, talked, talking.* **17.** *Printing* The body of type and cuts secured in a chase. **18.** *Brit.* A grade or class in school. — *v.t.* **1.** To give shape or form to; mold; fashion. **2.** To construct in the mind; devise: to *form* a plan. **3.** To combine or organize into: to *form* a club. **4.** To develop or acquire, as a habit. **5.** To be an element of. — *v.i.* **6.** To take shape; assume a specific form or arrangement. **7.** To begin to exist. [< OF < L *forma*]

-form *combining form* Like; in the shape of: *cuneiform.* [< L *-formis* -like < *forma* form]

for·mal[1] (fôr′məl) *adj.* **1.** Of, pertaining to, or based on established methods, models, or forms: *formal* procedure. **2.** Marked by and requiring more or less elaborate detail, ceremony, dress, etc.: a *formal* dinner. **3.** Appropriate for elaborate or state occasions: *formal* attire. **4.** Extremely regular and well-proportioned as to form, design, etc.: a *formal* garden. **5.** Adhering to rule, convention, or etiquette. **6.** Of or pertaining to external appearance, manner, or form: the *formal* elements of a poem. **7.** Binding and valid: a *formal* agreement. **8.** Pertaining to study in regular academic institutions or classes: a *formal* education. **9.** Pertaining to or characterized by language of a more complex and elaborate construction and vocabulary than that of informal speech or writing. — *n.* Something formal in character, as an evening gown. — **for′mal·ly** *adv.*

for·mal·de·hyde (fôr·mal′də·hīd) *n. Chem.* A colorless, pungent gas, CH_2O, used in solution as an antiseptic, preservative, etc. [< FORM(IC) + ALDEHYDE]

for·mal·ism (fôr′məl·iz′əm) *n.* Scrupulous observance of prescribed forms, as in religious worship, social life, art, etc. — **for′mal·ist** *n.* — **for′mal·is′tic** *adj.*

for·mal·i·ty (fôr·mal′ə·tē) *n. pl.* **·ties** **1.** The state or quality of being formal. **2.** Adherence to rules, conventions, forms, etc. **3.** Excessive devotion to outward form. **4.** A proper or customary act, method, practice, or observance.

for·mal·ize (fôr′məl·īz) *v.* **·ized**, **·iz·ing** *v.t.* **1.** To make formal. **2.** To give form to. — *v.i.* **3.** To be formal; act formally. — **for′mal·i·za′tion** *n.* — **for′mal·iz′er** *n.*

for·mat (fôr′mat) *n.* **1.** The form, size, type face, margins, and general style of a publication. **2.** The general form or arrangement of anything. [< F < L *formare* to form]

for·ma·tion (fôr·mā′shən) *n.* **1.** The act or process of forming, or the state of being formed. **2.** That which is formed. **3.** The manner in which a thing is shaped or formed. **4.** *Mil.* The disposition of troops, as in a column, line, or square. **5.** *Aeron.* A grouping of aircraft in flight. **6.** *Geol.* Mineral deposits, or rock masses, having common characteristics.

form·a·tive (fôr′mə·tiv) *adj.* **1.** Having power to shape, form, or mold: a *formative* influence. **2.** Of or pertaining to formation or development: *formative* years. — *n. Gram.* **1.** An element added to the base of a word to give it a new and special grammatical form. **2.** A word so formed.

form·er[1] (fôr′mər) *n.* One who or that which forms.

for·mer[2] (fôr′mər) *adj.* **1.** Being the first of two persons or things referred to: often preceded by *the* and used absolutely: opposed to *latter.* **2.** Previous: my *former* colleague. **3.** Earlier: *former* times. [ME *formere*]

for·mer·ly (fôr′mər·lē) *adv.* Some time or a long time ago.

for·mic (fôr′mik) *adj.* **1.** Of or pertaining to ants. **2.** Designating or derived from formic acid. [< L *formica* ant]

formic acid *Chem.* A colorless, corrosive compound, HCOOH, with a penetrating odor, occurring in ants and certain other insects and in some plants.

for·mi·da·ble (fôr′mi·də·bəl) *adj.* **1.** Exciting fear or dread by reason of strength, size, etc. **2.** Extremely difficult. [< MF < L *formidare* to fear] — **for′mi·da·bil′i·ty**, **for′mi·da·ble·ness** *n.* — **for′mi·da·bly** *adv.*

form·less (fôrm′lis) *adj.* Lacking form or structure; shapeless. — **form′less·ly** *adv.* — **form′less·ness** *n.*

form letter One of many reproductions of a letter, etc.

For·mo·san (fôr·mō′sən) *n.* **1.** A native or inhabitant of the island of Formosa (Taiwan). **2.** The Indonesian language of the Malay aborigines of Formosa. — *adj.* Of or pertaining to Formosa, its people, or their language.

for·mu·la (fôr′myə·lə) *n. pl.* **·las** or **·lae** (-lē) **1.** An exact or prescribed method or form for doing something. **2.** A fixed order or form of words. **3.** A prescription or recipe; also, the mixture prepared. **4.** *Math.* A rule or combination expressed in algebraic or symbolic form. **5.** *Chem.* A symbolic representation of the composition of a chemical compound, as H_2SO_4, sulfuric acid. [< L, dim. of *forma* form]

for·mu·lar·ize (fôr′myə·lə·rīz′) *v.t.* **·ized**, **·iz·ing** To formulate. — **for′mu·lar·i·za′tion** *n.*

for·mu·lar·y (fôr′myə·ler′ē) *adj.* Pertaining to, stated in, or resembling a formula. — *n. pl.* **·lar·ies** **1.** A compilation of formulas. **2.** A book listing pharmaceutical substances, their formulas, and preparation. **3.** A church ritual, or a book containing such rituals. **4.** A formula.

---

for·mu·late (fôr′myə·lāt) *v.t.* **·lat·ed**, **·lat·ing** **1.** To express in or as a formula. **2.** To put or state in exact and systematic form. **— for′mu·la′tion** *n.* **— for′mu·la′tor** *n.*

for·mu·lize (fôr′myə·līz) *v.t.* **·lized**, **·liz·ing** To formulate.

for·ni·cate (fôr′nə·kāt) *v.i.* **·cat·ed**, **·cat·ing** To commit fornication. [< L *fornix, -icis* brothel] **— for′ni·ca′tor** *n.*

for·ni·ca·tion (fôr′nə·kā′shən) *n.* Voluntary sexual intercourse between unmarried persons.

for·sake (fôr·sāk′, fər-) *v.t.* **·sook**, **·sak·en**, **·sak·ing** **1.** To renounce or relinquish (an occupation, belief, etc.). **2.** To abandon; desert. [OE *forsacan* to repudiate, deny]

for·sooth (fôr·sōōth′, fər-) *adv.* In truth; certainly. [OE]

for·swear (fôr·swâr′) *v.* **swore**, **sworn**, **swear·ing** *v.t.* **1.** To renounce or abandon emphatically or upon oath. **2.** To deny absolutely or upon oath: to *forswear* a debt. **— v.i. 3.** To swear falsely; commit perjury. **— Syn.** See RENOUNCE. [OE *forswerian* to swear falsely]

for·sworn (fôr·swôrn′, -swōrn′) *adj.* Perjured.

for·syth·i·a (fôr·sith′ē·ə, -sī′thē·ə, fər-) *n.* A shrub of the olive family, cultivated for its bright yellow flowers. [after William *Forsyth*, 1737–1804, British botanist]

fort (fôrt, fōrt) *n.* **1.** A fortified enclosure or structure capable of defense against an enemy. **2.** A permanent U.S. army post. [< F, orig. adj. strong]

forte[1] (fôrt, fōrt, fôr′tā) *n.* That which one does with excellence; strong point. [See FORT.]

for·te[2] (fôr′tā, -tē) *Music adj.* Loud; forceful. **— adv.** Loudly; forcefully. [< Ital.]

forth (fôrth, fōrth) *adv.* **1.** Forward in place, time, or order. **2.** Out, as from seclusion, confinement, or inaction. **3.** Away or out, as from a place of origin; abroad. **— and so forth** And the rest; and so on. [OE]

forth·com·ing (fôrth′kum′ing, fōrth′-) *adj.* **1.** Drawing near in time; approaching. **2.** Ready or about to appear, arrive, etc. **3.** Available or produced when expected or due. **— n.** Arrival or appearance of something due or expected.

forth·right (fôrth′rīt′, fōrth′-) *adj.* **1.** Coming straight to the point; candid; frank. **2.** Going forward in a straight line; direct. **— adv. 1.** In a direct course or straightforward manner. **2.** At once; straightway. **— forth′right′ness** *n.*

forth·with (fôrth′with′, -with′, fōrth′-) *adv.* Immediately.

for·ti·fi·ca·tion (fôr′tə·fə·kā′shən) *n.* **1.** The act, art, or science of fortifying. **2.** That which fortifies, as walls, ditches, etc. **3.** A military place of defense.

for·ti·fy (fôr′tə·fī) *v.* **·fied**, **·fy·ing** *v.t.* **1.** To provide with defensive works; strengthen against attack. **2.** To give physical or moral strength to. **3.** To strengthen the structure of; reinforce. **4.** To confirm. **5.** To strengthen, as wine, by adding alcohol. **6.** To enrich (food) by adding minerals, vitamins, etc. **— v.i. 7.** To raise defensive works. [< F < L *fortis* strong + *facere* to make] **— for′ti·fi′a·ble** *adj.* **— for′ti·fi′er** *n.*

for·tis·si·mo (fôr·tis′ə·mō, *Ital.* fôr·tēs′sē·mō) *adj. & adv. Music* Very loud. **— n.** *pl.* **·mos** A fortissimo note, chord, or passage. [< Ital., superl. of *forte* strong]

for·ti·tude (fôr′tə·tōōd, -tyōōd) *n.* Strength of mind in the face of pain, adversity, or peril; patient courage. **— for′ti·tu′di·nous** (-də·nəs) *adj.*

fort·night (fôrt′nīt′, -nit′) *n.* A period of two weeks; fourteen days. [OE *fēowertēne* fourteen + *niht* nights]

fort·night·ly (fôrt′nīt′lē) *adj.* Occurring, coming, or issued every fortnight. **— adv.** Once a fortnight.

for·tress (fôr′tris) *n.* **1.** A large military stronghold; a fort, a series of forts, or a heavily fortified town. **2.** Any place of security. **— v.t.** To furnish or strengthen with a fortress; fortify. [< OF < L *fortis* strong]

for·tu·i·tous (fôr·tōō′ə·təs, -tyōō′-) *adj.* Occurring by chance rather than by design; casual; accidental. **— Syn.** See ACCIDENTAL. [< L *fors* chance] **— for·tu′i·tous·ly** *adv.* **— for·tu′i·tous·ness** *n.*

for·tu·i·ty (fôr·tōō′ə·tē, -tyōō′-) *n.* *pl.* **·ties** Chance occurrence; also, chance.

for·tu·nate (fôr′chə·nit) *adj.* **1.** Happening by a favorable chance; lucky. **2.** Favored with good fortune. **— for′tu·nate·ly** *adv.* **— for′tu·nate·ness** *n.*

for·tune (fôr′chən) *n.* **1.** That which happens or is to happen to one, whether good or bad. **2.** A power supposed to control one's future; fate; often personified. **3.** Luck or chance, esp. when favorable. **4.** An amount of wealth or possessions. **5.** Great wealth or riches. **6.** A particular condition or state of life, usu. prosperous.

for·tune·tell·er (fôr′chən·tel′ər) *n.* One who claims to foretell events in a person's future. **— for′tune·tell′ing** *n. & adj.*

for·ty (fôr′tē) *n.* *pl.* **·ties 1.** The sum of thirty and ten: a cardinal number. **2.** Any symbol of this number, as 40, xl, XL. **3.** Anything consisting of or representing forty units. **— adj.** Being ten more than thirty. [OE *fēowertig*] **— for′ti·eth** *adj. & n.*

for·ty-nin·er (fôr′tē·nī′nər) *n.* *U.S.* A pioneer who went to California in 1849, the year of the gold rush.

forty winks *Informal* A short nap.

fo·rum (fôr′əm, fō′rəm) *n.* *pl.* **fo·rums** or **fo·ra** (fôr′ə, fō′rə) **1.** The public market place of an ancient Roman city, where popular assemblies met, and most legal and political business was transacted. **2.** A tribunal; court. **3.** An assembly for discussion of public affairs. [< L]

for·ward (fôr′wərd) *adv.* **1.** Toward what is ahead or what is in front; onward. Also **for′wards. 2.** At or in the front part, as of a ship. **3.** Out into a conspicuous position; to the forefront. **— forward of** *U.S.* In front of. **— adj. 1.** Being at or near the front. **2.** Moving or directed toward a point lying ahead. **3.** Overstepping the usual bounds of propriety in an insolent or presumptuous way; bold. **4.** Well-developed; not backward. **5.** Developing or developed earlier than usual; also, precocious. **6.** Extremely progressive or unconventional, as in political opinions. **7.** Ready or prompt. **8.** Made or done in advance: a *forward* contract for goods. **— n. 1.** In football, one of the players in the front lines of attack or defense. **2.** In basketball, hockey, etc., a player who leads the offensive play. **— v.t. 1.** To help onward or ahead. **2.** To send onward; esp., to send (mail) on to a new address. [OE *foreweard*] **— for′ward·er** *n.* **— for′ward·ly** *adv.* **— for′ward·ness** *n.*

forward pass In football, the throwing or passing of the ball toward the opponent's goal.

fos·sa (fos′ə) *n.* *pl.* **fos·sae** (fos′ē) *Anat.* A shallow depression or cavity in the body. [< L. See FOSSE.]

fos·sil (fos′əl) *n.* *Paleontol.* **1.** The remains of plants or animals, preserved in the rocks of the earth's crust. **2.** Some petrified trace of the existence of an early organism, as a petrified footprint. **3.** *Informal* One who or that which is out of date. **— adj. 1.** Of or like a fossil. **2.** Belonging to the past; out-of-date. [< F < L *fodire* to dig]

fos·sil·ize (fos′əl·īz) *v.* **ized**, **iz·ing** *v.t.* **1.** To change into a fossil; petrify. **2.** To make antiquated or out of date. **— v.i. 3.** To become a fossil. **— fos′sil·i·za′tion** *n.*

fos·ter (fôs′tər, fos′-) *v.t.* **1.** To bring up (a child); rear. **2.** To promote the growth or development of: to *foster* genius. **3.** To keep alive (feelings, hopes, etc.) within oneself; cherish. [OE *fōstrian* nourish] **— fos′ter·age** *n.*

foster child A child reared by a foster parent or parents.

foster parent A man or woman rearing a child not his or her own.

fought (fôt) Past tense and past participle of FIGHT.

foul (foul) *adj.* **1.** Offensive or revolting to the senses; disgusting: a *foul* odor. **2.** Full of dirt or impure matter; filthy. **3.** Clogged or packed with dirt, etc. **4.** Spoiled or rotten, as food. **5.** Unfavorable; adverse: *foul* weather. **6.** Obscene; vulgar. **7.** Morally offensive; wicked. **8.** Not according to rule or justice; unfair. **9.** Impeded or entangled: a *foul* anchor. **10.** In baseball, etc., of or pertaining to a foul ball or the foul lines. **11.** *Informal* Very bad; unsatisfactory. **— n. 1.** An act of fouling, colliding, or becoming entangled. **2.** Something foul, as: **a** A foul ball. **b** A breach of rule in various sports. **c** An entanglement or collision, as of ropes, boats, etc. **— v.t. 1.** To make foul or dirty. **2.** To dishonor; disgrace. **3.** To clog or choke, as a drain. **4.** To entangle or snarl, as a rope. **5.** To cover or encumber (a ship's bottom) with barnacles, seaweed, etc. **6.** To collide with. **7.** In sports, to commit a foul against. **8.** In baseball, to bat (the ball) outside of the foul lines. **— v.i. 9.** To become foul or dirty. **10.** To become clogged or encumbered. **11.** To become entangled. **12.** To collide. **13.** In sports, to violate a rule. **14.** In baseball, to bat a foul ball. **— to foul up** *Slang* **1.** To throw into disorder or confusion. **2.** To blunder. [OE *fūl*] **— foul′ly** *adv.* **— foul′ness** *n.*

fou·lard (fōō·lärd′) *n.* **1.** A lightweight, satiny fabric of silk, rayon, cotton, etc., usu. with a printed design. **2.** A scarf, necktie, or other article made of this fabric. [< F < OF < LL *fullare* to full cloth]

foul ball In baseball: **a** A batted ball that first hits the ground outside the foul lines. **b** A batted ball hitting the ground within the foul lines but passing outside the lines before reaching first or third base.

foul line 1. In baseball, either of the two lines extending from home plate past first and third base to the limits of the field. **2.** In basketball, the free-throw line. **3.** In bowling, etc., any line limiting the area of play or action.

foul·mouthed (foul′mouthd′, -mouth′) *adj.* Using abusive, profane, or obscene language.

foul play 1. Unfairness; in games and sports, a violation of rule. **2.** Any unfair or treacherous action, often murder.

found[1] (found) *v.t.* **1.** To give origin to; set up; establish. **2.** To lay the foundation of; establish on a foundation or basis. **— v.i. 3.** To be established or based: with *on, upon.* [< OF < L *fundus* base, bottom]

found[2] (found) *v.t.* **1.** To cast, as iron, by melting and pouring into a mold. **2.** To make by casting molten metal. [< F < L *fundere* to pour]

found[3] (found) Past tense and past participle of FIND. **— adj.** Provided with food, lodging, equipment, etc.

foun·da·tion (foun·dā′shən) *n.* **1.** The act of founding or establishing. **2.** The state of being founded or established. **3.** That on which anything is founded; basis: Equality is the *foundation* of democracy. **4.** A base on which something rests: a machine's *foundation*. **5.** That part of a building or wall, wholly or partly below the surface of the ground, that constitutes a base. **6.** A fund for the maintenance of an institution; an endowment. **7.** An endowed institution, esp. that grants funds for research projects, charities, etc. **8.** A foundation garment. — **foun·da/tion·al** *adj.*

foundation garment *U.S.* A girdle or corset.

found·er¹ (foun/dər) *n.* One who establishes.

found·er² (foun/dər) *n.* One who makes metal castings.

foun·der³ (foun/dər) *v.i.* **1.** To sink after filling with water, as a boat or ship. **2.** To fall or cave in, as land or buildings. **3.** To fail completely; collapse. **4.** To stumble and become lame, as a horse. — *v.t.* **5.** To cause to sink. — *n.* The act of foundering. [< OF < L *fundus* bottom]

found·ling (found/ling) *n.* A deserted infant of unknown parentage. [ME *funde*, pp. of *find* + -LING¹]

foun·dry (foun/drē) *n. pl.* **·dries 1.** An establishment in which metal, etc., is cast; also, an article made by casting. **2.** The act or operation of founding metal, etc.

fount¹ (fount) *n.* **1.** A fountain. **2.** Any source. [< F < L *fons*, *fontis* fountain]

fount² (fount) British spelling of FONT².

foun·tain (foun/tən) *n.* **1.** A spring or jet of water issuing from the earth; esp., the source of a stream. **2.** The origin or source of anything. **3.** A jet or spray of water forced upward artificially, as to provide water for drinking. **4.** A basinlike structure for such a jet to rise and fall in. [< OF < LL *fontana*, orig. fem. singular of L *fontanus* of a spring]

foun·tain·head (foun/tən·hed/) *n.* **1.** A spring from which a stream takes its source. **2.** Any source or origin.

fountain pen A pen having a supply of ink automatically fed to the writing end from a reservoir or cartridge.

four (fôr, fōr) *n.* **1.** The sum of three and one: a cardinal number. **2.** Any symbol of this number, as 4, iv, IV. **3.** Anything consisting of or representing four units. — **on all fours 1.** On hands and knees. **2.** On all four feet. — *adj.* Being one more than three; quaternary. [OE *fēower*] — **fourth** (fôrth, fōrth) *adj. & n.*

four-flush (fôr/flush/, fōr/-) *v.i.* **1.** To bet on a poker hand lacking one card to a flush. **2.** *Slang* To bluff.

four-flush·er (fôr/flush/ər, fōr/-) *n. Slang* A fake or cheat.

four-foot·ed (fôr/fŏŏt/id, fōr/-) *adj.* Having four feet.

four-hand·ed (fôr/han/did, fōr/-) *adj.* **1.** Designed for four players, as certain games. **2.** Designed for performance by two persons on a keyboard instrument, as a piano duet.

four hundred *U.S.* The exclusive social group of a place.

four-in-hand (fôr/in·hand/, fōr/-) *n.* **1.** A four-horse team driven by one person. **2.** A vehicle drawn by such a team. **3.** A necktie tied in a slip knot with the ends hanging.

four-leaf clover (fôr/lēf/, fōr/-) A clover plant having four leaflets, supposed to bring good luck.

four-post·er (fôr/pōs/tər, fōr/-) *n.* A bedstead with four tall posts at the corners and typically with a canopy or curtains.

four·some (fôr/səm, fōr/-) *n.* **1.** A game, esp. of golf, in which four players take part, two on each side; also, the players in such a game. **2.** Any group of four.

four-square (fôr/skwâr/, fōr/-) *adj.* **1.** Having four equal sides; square. **2.** Firm; solid. **3.** Forthright; direct. — *n.* A square. — *adv.* Squarely; bluntly.

four·teen (fôr/tēn/, fōr/-) *n.* **1.** The sum of thirteen and one: a cardinal number. **2.** Any symbol of this number, as 14, xiv, XIV. **3.** Anything consisting of or representing fourteen units. — *adj.* Being one more than thirteen. [OE *fēowertēne*] — **four/teenth** *adj. & n.*

fourth dimension A hypothetical dimension in addition to height, width, and thickness; esp., in the theory of relativity. — **fourth/-di·men/sion·al** *adj.*

fourth estate The public press; journalism.

fourth·ly (fôrth/lē, fōrth/-) *adv.* In the fourth place.

Fourth of July Independence Day.

fowl (foul) *n. pl.* **fowl** or **fowls 1.** The common domestic hen or cock; a chicken. **2.** Any related bird, as the duck, goose, etc. **3.** The flesh of fowl. **4.** Birds collectively. — *v.i.* To catch or hunt wild fowl. [OE *fugol*] — **fowl/er** *n.*

fowl·ing (fou/ling) *n.* The hunting of birds for sport.

fowling piece A light gun used for shooting birds.

fox (foks) *n.* **1.** Any of several small, wild mammals of the dog family, having long, pointed muzzles, bushy tails, and erect ears, esp. the **red fox** of North America, having a reddish brown fur. ◆ Collateral adjective: *vulpine.* **2.** The fur of the fox. **3.** A sly, crafty person. — *v.t.* **1.** To trick; outwit. **2.** To intoxicate. **3.** To stain, as paper or timber, with a reddish color. **4.** To make sour, as beer, in fermenting. **5.** To repair (shoes) with new uppers. —

v.i. **6.** To act slyly and cunningly. **7.** To become sour. **8.** To become stained with red. [OE]

fox·glove (foks/gluv/) *n.* A plant of the figwort family, having flowers in long one-sided racemes.

fox·hole (foks/hōl/) *n.* A shallow pit dug by a combatant as cover against enemy fire.

fox·hound (foks/hound/) *n.* One of a breed of large, strong, very swift dogs trained for fox hunting.

NORTH AMERICAN RED FOX (Body about 2 feet long; tail 16 inches)

fox·tail (foks/tāl/) *n.* **1.** The tail of a fox. **2.** Any of various species of grass bearing a spike of flowers like a fox's tail.

fox terrier A small, white terrier with dark markings, formerly used to bring foxes out of their burrows.

fox-trot (foks/trot/) *v.i.* **·trot·ted, ·trot·ting** To do a fox trot.

fox trot A ballroom dance in 2/4 or 4/4 time, consisting of a variety of rhythmic steps.

fox·y (fok/sē) *adj.* **fox·i·er, fox·i·est 1.** Sly; crafty; sharp. **2.** Reddish brown. **3.** Discolored or stained, as from decay. **4.** Improperly fermented: said of beer, etc. **5.** Defective, esp. from age and damp. — **fox/i·ly** *adv.* — **fox/i·ness** *n.*

foy·er (foi/ər, foi/ā; *Fr.* fwà·yā/) *n.* **1.** A public lobby in a hotel, theater, etc. **2.** An entrance room or hall in a house or apartment. [< F < LL < L *focus* hearth]

fra·cas (frā/kəs, *Brit.* frak/ä) *n.* A noisy disturbance, fight, or dispute; brawl; row. [< F < Ital. *fracassare* to shatter]

frac·tion (frak/shən) *n.* **1.** A disconnected part of anything; small portion; fragment. **2.** *Math.* A quantity less than a whole number, expressed as a decimal (0.3) or with numerator and denominator (3/10). **3.** *Chem.* One of the components separated from a substance by distilling, etc. — **Syn.** See PORTION. [< F < LL < L *fractus*, pp. of *frangere* to break]

frac·tion·al (frak/shən·əl) *adj.* **1.** Pertaining to or constituting a fraction. **2.** Small in size or importance. Also **frac/tion·ar/y** (-er/ē). — **frac/tion·al·ly** *adv.*

frac·tious (frak/shəs) *adj.* **1.** Apt to be unruly or rebellious. **2.** Easily annoyed or angered. [< FRACTION, in obs. sense of discord] — **frac/tious·ly** *adv.* — **frac/tious·ness** *n.*

frac·ture (frak/chər) *n.* **1.** The act of breaking, or the state of being broken. **2.** A break; crack; rupture. **3.** *Med.* The breaking or cracking of a bone; also, sometimes, the tearing of a cartilage. **4.** *Mineral.* The characteristic appearance of the freshly broken surface of a mineral. — **compound (or open) fracture** *Med.* A fracture in which the broken ends of the bone protrude through the skin. — **simple (or closed) fracture** *Med.* A bone fracture in which the skin remains unbroken. — *v.t. & v.i.* **·tured, ·tur·ing** To break or be broken; crack. [< F < L *fractura* a breaking] — **frac/tur·al** *adj.*

frag (frag) *v.t.* **fragged, frag·ging** *Mil. Slang* To kill or attempt to kill (one's superior officer). [< *frag(mentation grenade)*, a weapon so used]

frag·ile (fraj/əl) *adj.* Easily broken or damaged; frail; delicate. [< L *frangere* to break] — **frag/ile·ly** *adv.* — **fra·gil·i·ty** (frə·jil/ə·tē), **frag/ile·ness** *n.*
— **Syn.** That which cannot withstand even mild shocks or jars is *fragile* or, if constructed of parts poorly connected, *frail*: a *fragile* teacup, a *frail* scaffold. *Brittle* is used to describe things that are hard but so rigid or inelastic that they crack under stress.

frag·ment (*n.* frag/mənt; *v.* frag·ment/) *n.* **1.** A part broken off; a small detached portion. **2.** A part or portion of something that has been left unfinished: a *fragment* of a novel. **3.** A separate or isolated bit: He heard *fragments* of their conversation. — *v.t. & v.i.* To break into fragments. [< F < L *fragmentum*] — **frag/ment·ed** *adj.*

frag·men·tar·y (frag/mən·ter/ē) *adj.* Composed of fragments; broken; incomplete. Also **frag·men/tal.** — **frag/men·tar/i·ly** *adv.* — **frag/men·tar/i·ness** *n.*

frag·men·ta·tion (frag/mən·tā/shən) *n.* **1.** A breaking up into fragments. **2.** *Mil.* The scattering in all directions of the fragments of an exploding grenade, shell, or bomb.

frag·ment·ize (frag/mən·tīz) *v.t. & v.i.* **·ized, ·iz·ing** To fragment.

fra·grance (frā/grəns) *n.* **1.** The state or quality of being fragrant. **2.** A pleasant scent; sweet odor. Also *Rare* **fra/gran·cy.** — **Syn.** See SMELL.

fra·grant (frā/grənt) *adj.* Having an agreeable or sweet smell. [< L *fragrare* to smell sweet] — **fra/grant·ly** *adv.*

frail (frāl) *adj.* **1.** Delicately constituted; weak. **2.** Fragile. **3.** Deficient in moral strength. — **Syn.** See FRAGILE. — *n. U.S. Slang* A young woman or girl. [< OF < L *fragilis*] — **frail/ly** *adv.* — **frail/ness** *n.*

frail·ty (frāl/tē) *n. pl.* **·ties 1.** The state or quality of being frail; weakness. **2.** A fault or moral weakness.

frame (frām) *n.* **1.** A case or border made to enclose something, as a picture. **2.** A supporting structure surrounding something, as around a window or door. **3.** A framework; skeleton: the *frame* of a building, ship, etc. **4.** The general

arrangement, structure, or constitution of a thing. **5.** A system or order, as of a government. **6.** Bodily structure or build, esp. of the human body. **7.** A machine built in the form of or utilizing a framework: a silk *frame*. **8.** In pool or billiards: **a** The triangular form for grouping the balls. **b** The balls placed in this form. **c** The time required to pocket all the balls. **9.** In bowling, one of the ten divisions of the game. **10.** *Informal* In baseball, an inning. **11.** One of the individual exposures on a roll of motion-picture film. **12.** *Slang* A frame-up. — **frame of mind** Mental state; mood. — *v.* **framed, fram·ing** *v.t.* **1.** To surround with or put into a frame, as a picture. **2.** To put together: to *frame* a shelter. **3.** To put into words; utter. **4.** To conceive or create (a theory, idea, etc.). **5.** To draw up; devise: to *frame* a law. **6.** To shape or adapt to a purpose: Traffic rules are *framed* for safety. **7.** *Slang* To incriminate falsely. **8.** *Slang* To plan or set up dishonestly in advance, as a race, contest, etc. [OE *framian* to be of service to, provide for] — **fram′er** *n.*
frame house A house built on a wooden framework covered on the outside by shingles, boards, stucco, etc.
frame-up (frām′up′) *n. Slang* **1.** A prearranged plan to bring about a fraudulent outcome, as in a contest. **2.** A conspiracy to convict a person on a false charge.
frame·work (frām′wûrk′) *n.* **1.** A skeleton structure for supporting or enclosing something; also, frames, collectively. **2.** The arrangement of the basic or component parts of something: the *framework* of society.
franc (frangk) *n.* **1.** The standard monetary unit of various countries, equivalent to 100 centimes; esp.: **a** The French franc, in 1960 worth about 20 U.S. cents. **b** The Belgian franc, in 1960 worth about 2 U.S. cents. **c** The Swiss franc, in 1960 worth about 23 U.S. cents. **2.** A coin of this denomination. [< Med.L *Franc(orum rex)* (king of the) Franks, the motto on the earliest of these coins]
fran·chise (fran′chīz) *n.* **1.** The right to vote; suffrage. **2.** A right or privilege granted by a government or sovereign. **3.** A special privilege bestowed upon an individual or a corporate group of individuals by government grant: a *franchise* to operate a bus line. **4.** The territory over which any of the preceding special privileges or dispensations extend. [< OF < *franc, franche* free] — **fran′chised** *adj.*
Fran·cis·can (fran·sis′kən) *n.* A member of the mendicant order, the Gray Friars, founded in 1209 by St. Francis of Assisi. — *adj.* **1.** Of or pertaining to St. Francis. **2.** Belonging to a religious order following his rule.
fran·ci·um (fran′sē·əm) *n.* A radioactive element (symbol Fr), isolated from actinium, and replacing the hypothetical element known as *virginium*. See ELEMENT. [after *France*]
Franco- *combining form* French [< L *Francus* a Frank]
Fran·co·phile (frang′kə·fīl) *n.* An admirer of France or of French customs, etc. — *adj.* Kindly disposed toward France.
Fran·co·phobe (frang′kə·fōb) *n.* A person who fears or dislikes France or French things. — *adj.* Fearful of France.
Fran·co-Prus·sian War (frang′kō·prush′ən) See table for WAR.
fran·gi·ble (fran′jə·bəl) *adj.* Easily broken; brittle. [< L *frangere* to break] — **fran′gi·bil′i·ty, fran′gi·ble·ness** *n.*
fran·gi·pan·i (fran′ji·pan′ē, -pä′nē) *n.* **1.** A perfume derived from or resembling that of the West Indian red jasmine. **2.** The West Indian plant. Also **fran′gi·pane** (-pān). [after Marquis *Frangipani*, the inventor]
frank[1] (frangk) *adj.* **1.** Completely honest and unreserved in speech; candid. **2.** Marked by no effort at concealment or disguise: *frank* hostility. — *v.t.* To mark (a letter, package, etc.) in indication that no charge is to be made for delivery; also, to send (a letter, etc.) without charge by marking in this way. — *n.* **1.** The right to send mail, etc., without charge; also, the mark used to indicate this right. **2.** Mail sent without charge. [< OF *franc* frank, free] — **frank′ly** *adv.* — **frank′ness** *n.*
frank[2] (frangk) *n. Informal* A frankfurter.
Frank (frangk) *n.* **1.** A member of one of the Germanic tribes living on the Rhine early in the Christian era who gave their name to France. **2.** In the Near East, any European. [< L *Francus* a Frank + Gmc., a spear]
Frank·en·stein (frangk′ən·stīn) The hero of Mary Shelley's *Frankenstein*, a medical student who fashions a manlike monster that slays its maker. — *n.* **1.** Loosely, Frankenstein's monster. **2.** Anything that destroys its own creator.
frank·furt·er (frangk′fər·tər) *n.* A smoked sausage made of beef or beef and pork. [after *Frankfurt*, Germany]
frank·in·cense (frangk′in·sens) *n.* An aromatic gum or resin from various trees of East Africa, used as an incense and in medicine. [< OF *franc* pure + *encens* incense]
Frank·ish (frang′kish) *adj.* Of or pertaining to the Franks. — *n.* The West Germanic language of the Franks.
fran·tic (fran′tik) *adj.* **1.** Nearly driven out of one's mind, as with grief, fear, or rage. **2.** Madly excited. [< OF < LL < Gk. *phrenitis* delirium] — **fran′ti·cal·ly, fran′tic·ly** *adv.*
frap·pé (fra·pā′) *U.S. adj.* Iced; chilled. — *n.* **1.** A fruit juice or other beverage frozen to a soft, mushy consistency.

2. A liqueur or other beverage poured over shaved ice. [< F, pp. of *frapper* to chill]
frat (frat) *n. U.S. Informal* A college fraternity.
fra·ter·nal (frə·tûr′nəl) *adj.* **1.** Pertaining to or befitting a brother; brotherly. **2.** Of or pertaining to a fraternal order or society. **3.** *Genetics* Designating either of a pair of twins that develop from separately fertilized ova: distinguished from *identical*. [< L *frater* brother] — **fra·ter′nal·ism** *n.* — **fra·ter′nal·ly** *adv.*
fraternal order A brotherhood of men organized to further their mutual benefit or to attain a common goal.
fra·ter·ni·ty (frə·tûr′nə·tē) *n. pl.* **·ties 1.** The state of being brothers; the spirit of fraternal regard or affection. **2.** In U.S. schools, a society of male students, usu. having a Greek letter name, and represented by chapters in many institutions. **3.** A fraternal order. **4.** A body of people sharing the same interests, profession, etc.
frat·er·nize (frat′ər·nīz) *v.* **·nized, ·niz·ing** *v.i.* **1.** To associate closely with someone in a comradely way. **2.** To mingle intimately with the people of an enemy or conquered country. — **frat′er·ni·za′tion** *n.* — **frat′er·niz′er** *n.*
frat·ri·cide (frat′rə·sīd) *n.* **1.** The killing of one's brother. **2.** One who has killed his brother. [< L < *frater* brother + *caedere* to kill] — **frat′ri·ci′dal** *adj.*
Frau (frou) *n. pl.* **Frau·en** (-ən) *German* A married woman; wife: as a title, the equivalent of *Mrs*.
fraud (frôd) *n.* **1.** Willful deceit; trickery. **2.** An act or instance of this. **3.** *U.S. Informal* One who acts deceitfully; impostor. **4.** A deceptive or spurious thing. [< OF < L *fraus, fraudis* deceit]
fraud·u·lent (frô′jə·lənt) *adj.* **1.** Practicing or given to fraud; dishonest or deceitful. **2.** Proceeding from, obtained by, or characterized by fraud. — **fraud′u·lence, fraud′u·len·cy** *n.* — **fraud′u·lent·ly** *adv.*
fraught (frôt) *adj.* Filled; laden: with *with*: a journey *fraught* with danger. [< MDu. *vrachten* freight]
Fräu·lein (froi′līn) *n. German* An unmarried woman: as a title, the equivalent of *Miss*.
fray[1] (frā) *n.* Conflict; fight; also a noisy, quarrelsome uproar or disturbance. [Aphetic var. of AFFRAY]
fray[2] (frā) *v.t.* **1.** To cause (cloth, rope, etc.) to become worn by friction. **2.** To wear holes in (cloth, etc.) by rubbing or chafing. — *v.i.* **3.** To become frayed. — *n.* A frayed place, as of a sleeve. [< F *frayer* < L *fricare* to rub]
fraz·zle (fraz′əl) *Informal v.t. & v.i.* **·zled, ·zling 1.** To fray or become frayed; make or become tattered. **2.** To tire out; weary. — *n.* The state of being frazzled. — **worn to a frazzle 1.** Worn to shreds. **2.** Tired out; exhausted. [? Blend of FRAY[2] + obs. *fasel* to ravel]
freak (frēk) *n.* **1.** A deformed human being, animal, or plant; monstrosity. **2.** Anything unusual or bizarre. **3.** A sudden whim; caprice. **4.** *Slang* One given to the use of drugs, esp. illegal drugs. **5.** *Slang* An unconventional person. — *adj.* Strange; abnormal. — **to freak out** *Slang* **1.** To experience, often unpleasantly, the effects of psychedelic drugs. **2.** To act as if under the influence of a psychedelic drug. [Cf. OE *frician* to dance] — **freak′ish** *adj.* — **freak′ish·ly** *adv.* — **freak′ish·ness** *n.* — **freak′y** *adj.*
freck·le (frek′əl) *n.* A small brownish or dark-colored spot on the skin. — *v.t. & v.i.* **·led, ·ling** To mark or become marked with freckles. [< ON *freknur* freckles] — **freck′led, freck′ly** *adj.*
free (frē) *adj.* **fre·er, fre·est 1.** Having personal liberty. **2.** Having civil, political, or religious liberty. **3.** Not controlled by a foreign power; autonomous. **4.** Not bound by restrictions or regulations: *free* trade. **5.** Released from legal charge of crime or misdeed; acquitted. **6.** Exempt from certain regulations or impositions, as some taxes. **7.** Cleared or devoid of something: with *from, of*: *free* from scandal. **8.** Allowed or permitted to do something: *free* to go. **9.** Not controlled, restricted, or hampered by external agents or influences. **10.** Released from or not hindered by burdens, debts, discomforts, etc.: with *from, of*: *free* from care. **11.** Not occupied; not busy. **12.** Available to all; open: a *free* port. **13.** Not attached, bound, fixed, or held; loose: the *free* end of a rope. **14.** Not obstructed; easy to pass through or over: The road is now *free*; also, unimpeded; profuse: a *free* flow of water. **15.** Given or provided without charge or cost: *free* seats. **16.** Easy and unconstrained: a *free* stride. **17.** Not adhering to strict form or rule: *free* verse. **18.** Not closely or literally following the original: a *free* translation. **19.** *Informal;* unconventional. **20.** Frank and honest; candid. **21.** Unrestrained by propriety, dignity, or decency. **22.** Generous in giving; liberal: *free* with advice. **23.** *Chem.* Uncombined: *free* hydrogen. **24.** *Physics* Available for work: *free* energy. — **free and clear** *Law* Pertaining to real property held without a mortgage or other encumbrance. — **to set free** To release, as from prison, slavery, or other restraint; disengage. — *adv.* **1.** In a free manner; easily. **2.** Without cost; gratuitously. — **to make free with 1.** To use freely. **2.** To treat with undue famil-

iarity. **—v.t. freed, free·ing 1.** To release from confinement, worry, etc. **2.** To clear or rid of obstruction or hindrance. [OE *frēo*] **—free·ly** *adv.* **—free·ness** *n.*

free association *Psychoanal.* A method of uncovering unconscious conflicts by encouraging spontaneous verbal association of memories, ideas, impressions, etc.

free·board (frē′bôrd′, -bōrd′) *n. Naut.* The side of a vessel between the water line and the main deck or gunwale.

free·boot·er (frē′boo̅′tər) *n.* A pirate or buccaneer. [< MDu. < *vrij* free + *buit* booty]

free·dom (frē′dəm) *n.* **1.** The state or condition of being free; esp., the condition of enjoying civil liberty. **2.** Political autonomy, as of a nation or people. **3.** Liberty from bondage or slavery. **4.** Liberation, as from prison or other confinement. **5.** Liberty to move or act without outside interference, coercion, or restriction. **6.** Liberty of personal choice, action, or thought. **7.** Release or immunity from any stated thing or condition: with *from*: *freedom* from pain. **8.** Exemption or release from obligations, ties, etc. **9.** Facility or ease, as in moving or acting. **10.** Boldness of concept or execution. **11.** Openness or frankness. **12.** Excessive familiarity or candor. [OE *frēodōm*]

freedom of the seas The doctrine that any waters not subject to the territorial jurisdiction of any one country or nation are open to unhampered navigation by any ships or, in war, by the ships of any neutral country or nation.

free enterprise An economic system based upon private ownership and operation of business with little or no governmental control: also called *private enterprise*.

free-for-all (frē′fər-ôl′) *n.* A noisy, generalized fight.

free·hand (frē′hand′) *adj.* Drawn or sketched by hand without the help of rulers, drafting instruments, etc.

free hand Full liberty to act as one sees fit.

free·hand·ed (frē′han′did) *adj.* **1.** Having the hands free. **2.** Openhanded; generous. **—free′hand′ed·ness** *n.*

free·hold (frē′hōld′) *n. Law* **1.** Tenure of an estate, or sometimes of an office or dignity, for life or as something capable of being transferred to another. **2.** The estate, office, or dignity held by such tenure. **—free′hold′er** *n.*

free·lance (frē′lans′, -läns′) *v.i.* **-lanced, -lanc·ing** To work as a free lance. **—***adj.* Working as a free lance.

free lance A writer, artist, etc., whose services are not sold exclusively to any one buyer.

free·man (frē′mən) *n. pl.* **·men,** (-mən) **1.** A person not in bondage of any kind. **2.** One having full political rights.

Free·ma·son (frē′mā′sən) *n.* A member of an extensive secret order or fraternity, the members denoting themselves *Free and Accepted Masons*: also called *Mason.* **—Free·ma·son·ic** (frē′mə·son′ik) *adj.* **—Free′ma′son·ry** *n.*

free on board Delivered, without charge to the buyer, for shipment by a common carrier. *Abbr. f.o.b., F.O.B.*

free·si·a (frē′zhē·ə, -sē·ə, -zhə) *n.* A South African plant having bell-shaped, variously colored, fragrant flowers. [< NL. after E. M. *Fries*, 1794–1878, Swedish botanist]

free silver The free and unlimited coinage of silver, particularly at a fixed ratio to gold.

free-spo·ken (frē′spō′kən) *adj.* Unreserved or frank in speech. **—free-spo′ken·ness** *n.*

Free State 1. Before the Civil War, any State where slavery was forbidden. **2.** The Irish Free State.

free·stone (frē′stōn′) *adj.* Having a pit from which the pulp easily separates, as a peach. **—***n.* **1.** Any stone, as sandstone or limestone, that can be cut in any direction without breaking. **2.** A fruit easily freed from its pit.

free·style (frē′stīl′) *adj.* In swimming, using or permitting any stroke the swimmer desires. **—***n.* The use of freestyle swimming techniques.

free·think·er (frē′thing′kər) *n.* One who forms his own religious beliefs without regard to church authority. **—Syn.** See SKEPTIC. **—free′think′ing** *adj. & n.*

free-throw line (frē′thrō′) In basketball, the line from which a free throw is made: also called *foul line.*

free trade 1. International commerce free from government regulations and from import and export duties. **2.** A trade system where duties are levied only for revenue and not to protect home industries.

free verse Verse marked by an absence or irregularity of rhyme: also, *French, vers libre.*

free·way (frē′wā′) *n.* A wide highway skirting populated areas and passing over or around intersections.

free will 1. The power of personal self-determination. **2.** The doctrine that one's ability to choose between courses of action is not completely determined by circumstances.

free·will (frē′wil′) *adj.* Of one's own free choice; voluntary.

freeze (frēz) *v.* **froze, fro·zen, freez·ing** *v.i.* **1.** To become ice or a similar hard solid through loss of heat. **2.** To become sheeted or filled with ice, as water pipes. **3.** To become stiff or hard with cold, as wet clothes. **4.** To adhere to

something by the formation of ice. **5.** To be extremely cold. **6.** To be damaged or killed by great cold. **7.** To become suddenly motionless, inactive, or rigid, as through fear, shock, etc. **8.** To become icily aloof: often with *up.* **—***v.t.* **9.** To cause to become ice or a similar hard solid through loss of heat. **10.** To cause ice to form on or in. **11.** To make stiff or hard by freezing the moisture of. **12.** To make adhere by the formation of ice. **13.** To make extremely cold. **14.** To damage or kill by great cold. **15.** To make motionless or rigid, as through fear; paralyze. **16.** To make icily aloof, unfriendly, etc.; alienate. **17.** To check abruptly the ardor, enthusiasm, etc., of. **18.** To fix or stabilize (prices, wages, etc.) at a particular level. **19.** To prohibit the continued making, use, or selling of (a raw material). **20.** To make the liquidation, collection, or use of (funds or other assets) contrary to law or edict. **— to freeze one's blood** To fill one with terror. **— to freeze onto** (or **to**) To hold tightly to. **—***n.* **1.** The act of freezing, or the state of being frozen. **2.** Freezing weather. [OE *frēosan*]

freez·er (frē′zər) *n.* **1.** One who or that which freezes. **2.** A refrigerator designed to freeze and preserve food.

freezing point *Physics* The temperature at which a liquid freezes under given pressure. For water at sea level it is 32° F. or 0° C.

freight (frāt) *n.* **1.** In the United States and Canada: **a** The service of transporting commodities by land, air, or water; esp., ordinary transportation as opposed to express. **b** The commodities so transported. **2.** The price paid for the transportation of commodities. **3.** *U.S. & Canadian* A freight train. **—***v.t.* **1.** To load with commodities for transportation. **2.** To load; burden. **3.** To send or transport as or by freight. [< MDu. *vrecht*, var. of *vracht* a load]

freight·age (frā′tij) *n.* **1.** A cargo; freight. **2.** The price charged or paid for carrying goods. **3.** The transportation of merchandise.

freight car A railway car for carrying freight.

freight·er (frā′tər) *n.* A ship used primarily for transporting cargo.

freight train *U.S.* A railroad train of freight cars.

French (french) *adj.* Of, pertaining to, or characteristic of France, its people, or their language; also, in Canada, pertaining to Canadian French persons, their speech, etc. **—***n.* **1.** The people of France collectively: preceded by *the*; also, in Canada, the French-speaking Canadians. **2.** The Romance language of France. **— Old French** The French language from about 850 to 1400, descended from Vulgar Latin as it developed in Gaul. **— Middle French** The French language from about 1400 to 1600. **— Modern French** The language of France after 1600. [OE *Francisc*]

French and Indian War See table for WAR.

French-Ca·na·di·an (french′kə·nā′dē·ən) *n.* A French settler in Canada or a descendant of French settlers. Also **French Canadian. —***adj.* Of or pertaining to the language, culture, etc., of French-speaking people in Canada.

French cuff A cuff of a sleeve turned back and secured with a link.

French doors A pair of doors, usu. with glass panes, attached to opposite doorjambs and opening in the middle.

French dressing A salad dressing consisting of oil, vinegar, and spices.

French fried Cooked by frying crisp in deep fat.

French horn A valved, brass instrument with a long, coiled tube, flaring widely at the end and producing a mellow tone.

French·i·fy (fren′chə·fī) *v.t. & v.i.* **·fied, ·fy·ing** To make or become French in form or characteristics.

French leave An informal, secret, or hurried departure.

French·man (french′mən) *n. pl.* **·men** (-mən) A native or citizen of France. **French·wom·an** (-wŏŏm′ən) *n.fem.*

FRENCH HORN

French pastry A rich, fancy pastry often having a filling of whipped cream, custard, or preserved fruits.

French toast Bread dipped in a batter of beaten eggs and milk and fried in shallow fat.

French window A casement window with adjoining sashes attached to opposite jambs and opening in the middle.

fre·net·ic (frə·net′ik) *adj.* Feverishly excited; frenzied; frantic. Also **fre·net′i·cal. —***n.* A frenetic person. **—fre·net′i·cal·ly** *adv.*

fren·zy (fren′zē) *n. pl.* **·zies** A state of extreme excitement or agitation suggestive of or bordering on delirium or insanity. **—***v.t.* **·zied, ·zy·ing** To make frantic. [< OF < LL < Gk. *phrenitis* delirium] **—fren′zied** *adj.*

fre·quence (frē′kwəns) *n. Rare* Frequency (defs. 1, 2).

fre·quen·cy (frē′kwən·sē) *n. pl.* **·cies 1.** The state or fact of being frequent; repeated occurrence. **2.** The number of times something occurs within a particular extent of time, a particular group, etc. **3.** *Stat.* The number of times a given case, value, or event occurs in relation to the total number of classified cases, values, or events; distribution. **4.** *Physics* The number of occurrences of a periodic phenomenon, as oscillation, per unit time, usu. expressed in cycles per second.

frequency modulation *Telecom.* A type of modulation in which the carrier wave of a transmitter is varied in frequency rather than in amplitude. Abbr. *FM, f-m, f.m., F.M.*

fre·quent (adj. frē′kwənt; v. fri·kwent′, frē′kwənt) *adj.* **1.** Happening time after time; occurring again and again: *frequent relapses.* **2.** Showing up often; appearing repeatedly: *frequent visitors.* —*v.t.* To go to repeatedly; be in or at often: to *frequent* bars. [< L *frequens, -entis* crowded] —**fre·quen·ta′tion** *n.* —**fre·quent′er** *n.* —**fre′quent·ly** *adv.*

fre·quen·ta·tive (fri·kwen′tə·tiv) *Gram. adj.* Denoting repeated or habitual action. —*n.* A frequentative verb.

frère (frâr) *n.* *pl.* **frères** (frâr) *French* **1.** Brother. **2.** Friar; monk.

fres·co (fres′kō) *n.* *pl.* **·coes** or **·cos** **1.** The art of painting on plaster that is still moist. **2.** A picture so painted. —*v.t.* **·coed, ·co·ing** To paint in fresco. [< Ital., fresh]

fresh¹ (fresh) *adj.* **1.** Newly made, obtained, received, etc.: *fresh coffee; fresh* footprints. **2.** New; novel: a *fresh* approach. **3.** Recent; latest: *fresh* news. **4.** Additional; further: *fresh* supplies. **5.** Not smoked, frozen, or otherwise preserved: *fresh* vegetables. **6.** Not spoiled, stale, musty, etc. **7.** Retaining original vividness; not faded or worn, as colors or memories. **8.** Not salt: *fresh* water. **9.** Pure and clear: *fresh* air. **10.** Appearing healthy or youthful. **11.** Not fatigued; energetic. **12.** Vivid; colorful; stimulating. **13.** Inexperienced; untrained: *fresh* recruits. **14.** *Meteorol.* Moderately rapid and strong: esp. designating a breeze or a gale on the Beaufort scale. **15.** Having a renewed supply of milk: said of a cow that has recently calved. [OE *fersc,* infl. by OF *freis,* both ult. < Gmc.] —**fresh′ly** *adv.* —**fresh′ness** *n.*

fresh² (fresh) *adj.* *U.S. Informal* Saucy; impudent; disrespectful. [< G *frech* impudent]

fresh·en (fresh′ən) *v.t. & v.i.* To make or become fresh. —**fresh′en·er** *n.*

fresh·et (fresh′it) *n.* **1.** A sudden rise or overflow of a stream. **2.** A fresh-water stream emptying into the sea.

fresh·man (fresh′mən) *n.* *pl.* **·men** (-mən) **1.** A student during the first year of studies in a high school, college, or university. **2.** A beginner; novice.

fresh-wa·ter (fresh′wô′tər, -wot′ər) *adj.* **1.** Pertaining to or living in fresh water: a *fresh-water* fish. **2.** Not situated on or near the seacoast; inland. **3.** Lacking skill or experience. **4.** *U.S.* Not well known; small: a *fresh-water* college.

fret¹ (fret) *v.* **fret·ted, fret·ting** *v.i.* **1.** To be vexed, annoyed, or troubled. **2.** To become worn, chafed, or corroded. **3.** To bite bit after bit of something with or as with the teeth; gnaw: with *on, upon, into.* **4.** To eat through something by or as if by corrosion. **5.** To rankle; fester. **6.** To become rough or agitated, as water. —*v.t.* **7.** To vex, annoy, or trouble. **8.** To wear away or eat away by or as if by chafing, gnawing, or corrosion; also, to produce (a hole, frayed ends, etc.) in this way. **9.** To roughen or agitate (the surface of water). —*n.* **1.** Vexation. **2.** The act of chafing or gnawing. **3.** A worn spot. [OE *fretan* to devour]

fret² (fret) *n.* One of a series of ridges, as of metal, fixed across the fingerboard of a guitar, ukulele, etc., to guide the fingers in stopping the strings. —*v.t.* **fret·ted, fret·ting** To provide (a guitar, etc.) with frets. [Cf. OF *frete* ring]

FRETS²

fret³ (fret) *n.* An ornamental band or border consisting of angular or sometimes curved lines symmetrically arranged. —*v.t.* **fret·ted, fret·ting** To adorn with a fret. [Prob. < OF *frette* lattice, trellis]

fret·ful (fret′fəl) *adj.* Inclined to fret; peevish or restless. —**fret′ful·ly** *adv.* —**fret′ful·ness** *n.*

— Syn. complaining, impatient, pettish, petulant, restive.

fret·work (fret′wûrk′) *n.* **1.** Ornamental openwork, usu. composed of frets or interlaced parts. **2.** A pattern, as of light and shade, resembling such openwork.

Freu·di·an (froi′dē·ən) *adj.* Of, pertaining to, or conforming to the teachings of Sigmund Freud. —*n.* An adherent of the theories of Freud. —**Freu′di·an·ism** *n.*

fri·a·ble (frī′ə·bəl) *adj.* Easily crumbled or pulverized. [< F < L < *friare* to crumble] —**fri′a·bil′i·ty, fri′a·ble·ness** *n.*

fri·ar (frī′ər) *n.* A man who is a member of one of several religious orders, esp. the mendicant orders, as the Dominicans or Franciscans. [< OF *frere* < L *frater* brother]

fri·ar·y (frī′ər·ē) *n.* *pl.* **·ar·ies** **1.** A monastery, especially of a mendicant order. **2.** A community of friars.

fric·as·see (frik′ə·sē′) *n.* A dish of meat cut small, stewed, and served with gravy. —*v.t.* **·seed, ·see·ing** To make into a fricassee. [< F *fricassé,* orig. pp. of *fricasser* to sauté]

fric·a·tive (frik′ə·tiv) *Phonet. adj.* Of consonants, produced by the passage of breath through a narrow aperture with resultant audible friction, as (f), (v), (th). —*n.* A consonant so produced. [< NL < L *fricare* to rub]

fric·tion (frik′shən) *n.* **1.** The rubbing of one object against another. **2.** Conflict of opinions, differences in temperament, etc. [< F < L *fricare* to rub] —**fric′tion·al** *adj.*

friction tape Cotton tape impregnated with an adhesive, moisture-resisting compound, used in electrical work.

Fri·day (frī′dē, -dā) *n.* The sixth day of the week. [OE *Frīgedæg* Frigg's day]

Fri·day (frī′dē, -dā) In Defoe's *Robinson Crusoe,* Crusoe's native servant and companion. —*n.* Any devoted or faithful attendant or helper: man *Friday;* girl *Friday.*

fried (frīd) Past tense and past participle of FRY.

fried cake A small cake or doughnut fried in deep fat.

friend (frend) *n.* **1.** One who is personally well known by oneself and for whom one has warm regard or affection; intimate. **2.** One with whom one is on speaking terms; an associate or acquaintance. **3.** One who belongs to the same nation, party, etc., as oneself; also, one with whom one is united in some purpose, cause, etc. **4.** A patron or supporter. [OE *frēond*] —**friend′less** *adj.* —**friend′less·ness** *n.*

Friend (frend) *n.* A member of the Society of Friends; Quaker.

friend·ly (frend′lē) *adj.* **·li·er, ·li·est** **1.** Of, pertaining to, or typical of a friend. **2.** Well-disposed; not antagonistic. **3.** Acting as a friend; showing friendship. **4.** Helpful; favorable: a *friendly* wind. —*adv.* In a friendly manner: also **friend′li·ly.** —**friend′li·ness** *n.*

friend·ship (frend′ship) *n.* **1.** The state or fact of being friends. **2.** Mutual liking and esteem.

fri·er (frī′ər) See FRYER.

frieze¹ (frēz) *n.* **1.** The horizontal strip running between a cornice and architrave, either plain or decorated with sculpture, scrolls, etc. **2.** Any decorative horizontal strip, as along the top of a wall in a room. [< F < Med.L *frisium*]

frieze² (frēz) *n.* A coarse, woolen cloth with a shaggy nap. [< MF < *friser* to curl]

frig·ate (frig′it) *n.* A sailing war vessel of medium size, in use from about the 17th to the 19th centuries. [< F < Ital. *fregata*]

frigate bird Either of two large, rapacious, web-footed marine birds having hooked beaks and very long wings: also called *man-of-war bird.*

Frigg (frig) In Norse mythology, the wife of Odin and the goddess of marriage. Also **Frig·ga** (frig′ə).

fright (frīt) *n.* **1.** Sudden, violent alarm or fear. **2.** *Informal* One who or that which is ugly, etc. [OE *fryhto*]

fright·en (frīt′n) *v.t.* **1.** To make suddenly alarmed, fearful, or terrified; scare. **2.** To drive, force, etc., (away, out, into, etc.) by scaring. —*v.i.* **3.** To become afraid. —**fright′en·ing** *adj.* —**fright′en·ing·ly** *adv.*

fright·ful (frīt′fəl) *adj.* **1.** Repulsive, shocking, or contemptible. **2.** *Informal* Most distressing; very bad: a *frightful* headache. **3.** *Informal* Excessively great: a *frightful* number of losses. **4.** Such as fills with fright; alarming or terrifying. —**fright′ful·ly** *adv.* —**fright′ful·ness** *n.*

frig·id (frij′id) *adj.* **1.** Bitterly cold. **2.** Lacking warmth of feeling; formal. **3.** Habitually lacking sexual feeling or response: said of women. [< L *frigere* to be cold] —**frig′id·ly** *adv.* —**fri·gid·i·ty** (fri·jid′ə·tē), **frig′id·ness** *n.*

fri·jol (frē′hōl) *n.* *pl.* **fri·joles** (frē′hōlz, *Sp.* frē·hō′lās) A bean used as food, esp. by Latin-Americans. Also **fri·jole** (frē′hōl, *Sp.* frē·hō′lā). [< Sp.]

frill (fril) *n.* **1.** An ornamental strip of lace, etc., gathered together and attached along one edge and left free along the other; ruffle. **2.** *U.S. Informal* Any showy or superfluous detail of dress, manner, etc. **3.** *Zool.* A ruff of feathers about the neck of some birds or of hair about the neck of some animals. —*v.t.* **1.** To make into a frill. **2.** To put frills on. [Origin uncertain] —**frill′y** *adj.*

frill·ing (fril′ing) *n.* **1.** Frills collectively. **2.** A material or trimming suitable for use in a frill or frills.

fringe (frinj) *n.* **1.** An ornamental border of hanging cords, threads, etc. **2.** Something suggestive of such a border or trimming: a *fringe* of grass along a sidewalk. **3.** The area along the edge of something: the *fringes* of a city. —*v.t.* **fringed, fring·ing** **1.** To provide with or as with a fringe. **2.** To constitute a fringe on or along. —*adj.* Outer; marginal: a *fringe* area. [< OF < L *fimbria* fringe] —**fring′y** *adj.*

fringe benefit Anything of value given an employee in addition to his salary or wages, as insurance, pension, etc.

frin·gil·line (frin·jil′īn, -in) *adj.* Of, pertaining to, or resembling a family of small birds including the finches and sparrows. [< L *fringilla* small bird + -INE¹]

frip·per·y (frip′ər·ē) *n.* *pl.* **·per·ies** **1.** Cheap, flashy dress or ornamentation. **2.** Showiness or affectation in speech, manner, etc. [< F < OF *frepe* rag]

Fris·bee (friz′bē) *n.* A light plastic disk tossed in play from person to person: a trade name. Also **fris′bee.**

Fris·co (fris′kō) *Informal* San Francisco, California.
fri·sé (fri·zā′) *n.* An upholstery or rug fabric faced with a thick pile of uncut loops or of cut and uncut loops in design. [< F, orig. pp. of *friser* to curl]
Fris·ian (frizh′ən, frizh′ē·ən) *adj.* Of or pertaining to the Dutch province of Friesland, its people, or their language. — *n.* 1. A native or inhabitant of Friesland. 2. The Germanic language of the Frisians. Also spelled *Friesian.*
frisk (frisk) *v.i.* 1. To move or leap about playfully; frolic. — *v.t.* 2. To move with quick jerks: a lamb *frisking* its tail. 3. *U.S. Slang* To search (someone) for a concealed weapon, etc., by quickly feeling the pockets and clothing. 4. *Slang* To rob of valuables in this way. — *n.* 1. A playful skipping about. 2. *U.S. Slang* A search of someone for a weapon, etc. [< obs. *frisk* lively < F *frisque*] — **frisk′er** *n.*
frisk·y (fris′kē) *adj.* **frisk·i·er, frisk·i·est** Lively or playful. — **frisk′i·ly** *adv.* — **frisk′i·ness** *n.*
frit (frit) *n.* The material formed by the partial fusion of sand and fluxes in the process of making glass. — *v.t.* To make (a mixture of sand, alkalis, etc.) into frit. Also **fritt.** [< F < Ital. *fritta,* pp. of *friggere* to fry]
frit·ter¹ (frit′ər) *v.t.* To waste or squander little by little, as money, time, etc.: usu. with *away.* [< L *frangere* to break]
frit·ter² (frit′ər) *n.* A small cake made of plain batter or of corn, meat, fruit, etc., covered with batter and fried in deep fat. [< F < L *frigere* to fry]
friv·o·lous (friv′ə·ləs) *adj.* 1. Lacking importance or significance; petty. 2. Inclined to levity; not serious; silly; fickle. [< L *frivolus* silly] — **fri·vol·i·ty** (fri·vol′ə·tē) *n.* — **friv′o·lous·ly** *adv.* — **friv′o·lous·ness** *n.*
frizz (friz) *v.t. & v.i.* 1. To form into tight, crisp curls, as the hair. 2. To make or form into small, tight tufts or knots, as the nap of cloth. — *n.* 1. That which is frizzed, as hair. 2. The condition of being frizzed. Also **friz.** [< F *friser* to curl] — **frizz′er** or **friz′er** *n.*
friz·zle¹ (friz′əl) *v.t. & v.i.* **·zled, ·zling** 1. To fry or cook with a sizzling noise. 2. To make or become curled or crisp, as by frying. [Blend of FRY and SIZZLE; ? infl. by FRIZZLE²]
friz·zle² (friz′əl) *v.t. & v.i.* **·zled, ·zling** To form into tight curls, as the hair; frizz. — *n.* A crisp curl; frizz. [? Freq. of obs. *frieze* produce a nap on < MF *friser* to curl]
friz·zly (friz′lē) *adj.* Having tight, crisp curls.
frizz·y (friz′ē) *adj.* **frizz·i·er, frizz·i·est** Frizzly. — **friz′zi·ly** *adv.* — **friz′zi·ness** *n.*
fro (frō) *adv.* Away from; back: used in the phrase *to and fro.* — *prep. Scot.* From. [< ON *frā* from]
frock (frok) *n.* 1. A long, loose-fitting robe with wide sleeves worn by monks; also, the clerical or priestly state. 2. Any of several types of garments; as: **a** A dress. **b** A workers' smock. **c** A frock coat. — *v.t.* 1. To furnish with or clothe in a frock. 2. To invest with ecclesiastical office. [< OF *froc*]
frock coat A man's dress overcoat, worn esp. in the 19th century, having knee-length skirts and a tight-fitting, double-breasted upper part.
frog (frog, frôg) *n.* 1. One of a genus of small, tailless, web-footed animals with short front legs and large, strong hind legs adapted to leaping. 2. One of several similar amphibians, as a tree frog. 3. A slight irritation, accumulation of phlegm, etc., producing difficulty or hoarseness in speaking: also **frog in the** (or **one's**) **throat.** 4. A triangular prominence in the sole of a horse's foot. 5. A section of intersecting railroad tracks designed to permit wheels to pass over the junction without difficulty. 6. An ornamental braid or cord, as on a jacket, often looped, so as to permit passage of a button. — *v.i.* **frogged, frog·ging** To hunt frogs. [OE *frogga*]

STAGES IN THE DEVELOPMENT OF THE FROG
a Eggs. *b* Embryo. *c–h* Development of the tadpole. *i* Young frog. *j* Adult frog.

frog·man (frog′mən, -man′, frôg′-) *n. pl.* **·men** (-mən, -men′) An underwater reconnaissance and demolition expert, able to swim and operate under water using a scuba.
frol·ic (frol′ik) *n.* 1. Merriment. 2. A gay occasion or diversion. 3. A playful antic. — *v.i.* **·icked, ·ick·ing** 1. To move about or behave in a frisky way. 2. To be prankish. [< Du. < MDu. *vro* glad] — **frol′ick·er** *n.*
frol·ic·some (frol′ik·səm) *adj.* Gay and lighthearted. Also **frol′ick·y.** — **frol′ic·some·ly** *adv.* — **frol′ic·some·ness** *n.*

from (frum, from; *unstressed* frəm) *prep.* 1. Starting at (a particular place or time): the plane *from* New York. 2. With (a particular person, place or thing) as the origin or instrument: a letter *from* your mother. 3. Out of (a holder, container, etc.). 4. Out of the control of: He escaped *from* his captors. 5. Out of the totality of: to subtract 3 *from* 8. 6. At a distance in relation to: far *from* the city. 7. Beyond the possibility of: He kept her *from* falling. 8. By reason of; because of. 9. As being other or another than: He couldn't tell me *from* my brother. [OE *fram, from*]
frond (frond) *n. Bot.* 1. A leaflike expansion in which the functions of stem and leaf are not fully differentiated, as in ferns and seaweeds. 2. A large leaf of tropical plants and trees, as of the palm tree. [< L *frons, frondis* leaf]
front (frunt) *n.* 1. The part or side of an object or body that faces forward or is viewed as facing forward. 2. An area or position located directly ahead or before: He stood in *front* of her. 3. An area or position of principal or most important activity. 4. *Mil.* **a** The lateral space from flank to flank occupied by a unit. **b** The line of contact of two opposing forces. 5. The outer side of a building, usu. the side where the main entrance is. 6. An extent of land lying directly along a lake, road, etc. 7. A group or movement uniting various individuals with a common aim. 8. One chosen to head a group, movement, etc., to give it prestige, often lacking real authority. 9. An apparently respectable person, business, etc., used for cloaking objectionable or illegal activities. 10. One's bearing or attitude in facing a particular situation, problem, etc.: to put on a bold *front.* 11. *Informal* An outward air of pretense of wealth, social importance, etc. 12. A detachable, starched part of a man's formal dress shirt covering the chest. 13. In hotels, the bellhop first in line. 14. *Meteorol.* The fore part of a mass of warm or cold air; also, the line of separation between a mass of warm and cold air. 15. *Phonet.* The part of the tongue immediately behind the blade and directly below the hard palate. — *adj.* 1. Of, pertaining to, or directed toward the front. 2. Located on, in, or at the front. — *v.t.* 1. To face toward. 2. To meet face to face. 3. To provide with a front. 4. To serve as a front for. — *v.i.* 5. To face toward something. [< OF < L *frons, frontis* forehead]
front·age (frun′tij) *n.* 1. The front part of a lot or building; also, the linear extent of this. 2. The direction in which something faces; exposure. 3. Land adjacent to a street, body of water, etc.
front·al (frun′təl) *adj.* 1. Of or pertaining to the front. 2. Of or pertaining to the forehead or to the bone forming the anterior part of the skull. — **fron′tal·ly** *adv.*
fron·tier (frun·tir′) *n.* 1. The part of a nation's territory lying along the border of another country. 2. The part of a settled region lying along the border of an unsettled region. 3. A new or unexplored area of thought or knowledge. — *adj.* Of or pertaining to a frontier. [< OF *front* front]
fron·tiers·man (frun·tirz′mən) *n. pl.* **·men** (-mən) One who lives on the frontier.
fron·tis·piece (frun′tis·pēs′, fron′-) *n.* 1. A picture or drawing on the page facing the title page of a book; also, formerly, the title page itself. 2. *Archit.* **a** A façade; also, a highly decorated section of a façade. **b** A pediment. [< F < Med.L < L *frons, frontis* forehead + *specere* to look at]
front matter *Printing* The pages preceding the actual text of a book or pamphlet.
front-page (frunt′pāj′) *adj.* Appearing on or important enough to appear on the first page of a newspaper.
frosh (frosh) *n. pl.* **frosh** *U.S. Slang* A college freshman.
frost (frôst, frost) *n.* 1. A feathery deposit of ice formed on the ground or on the surface of exposed objects by dew or water vapor that has frozen. 2. Rime. 3. Frozen moisture within a porous substance, as in the ground. 4. Temperature cold enough to freeze. 5. The act of freezing. 6. Coldness of manner. 7. *Slang* A cold reception by the public. — *v.t.* 1. To cover with frost. 2. To damage or kill by frost. 3. To produce a frostlike surface or effect on (glass, etc.). 4. To apply frosting to. [OE] — **frost′less** *adj.*
frost·bite (frôst′bīt′, frost′-) *n.* The condition of having some part of the body partially frozen, often resulting in gangrene. — *v.t.* **·bit, ·bit·ten, ·bit·ing** To injure, as a part of the body, by partial freezing. — **frost′bit·ten** (-bit′n) *adj.*
frost·ed (frôs′tid, fros′-) *adj.* 1. Covered with frost. 2. Covered with frosting, as a cake. 3. Presenting a surface resembling frost, as translucent glass. 4. Frostbitten.
frost·ing (frôs′ting, fros′-) *n.* 1. A mixture of sugar, egg white, butter, etc., cooked or beaten together, and used to cover cakes. 2. The rough or lusterless surface produced on metal, glass, etc., in imitation of frost. 3. Coarsely powdered glass, etc., used for decorative work.
frost·y (frôs′tē, fros′-) *adj.* **frost·i·er, frost·i·est** 1. Attended with frost; freezing: *frosty* weather. 2. Composed of

or covered with frost. **3.** Lacking warmth of manner. **4.** Having white hair; hoary. — **frost′i·ly** *adv.* — **frost′i·ness** *n.*

froth (frôth, froth) *n.* **1.** A mass of bubbles resulting from fermentation or agitation. **2.** Any foamy excretion or exudation, as of saliva. **3.** Any unsubstantial or trivial thing, as a foolish conversation. — *v.t.* **1.** To cause to foam. **2.** To cover with froth. **3.** To give forth in the form of foam. — *v.i.* **1.** To form or give off froth. [< ON *frodha*]

froth·y (frô′thē, froth′ē) *adj.* **froth·i·er, froth·i·est 1.** Consisting of, covered with, or full of froth; foamy. **2.** Unsubstantial or trivial. — **froth′i·ly** *adv.* — **froth′i·ness** *n.*

frou-frou (frōō′frōō′) *n.* **1.** A rustling, as of silk; swish. **2.** *Informal* Affected elegance; fanciness. [< F]

fro·ward (frō′ərd, -wərd) *adj.* Disobedient; intractable. — **fro′ward·ly** *adv.* — **fro′ward·ness** *n.*

frown (froun) *v.i.* **1.** To contract the brow, as in displeasure or concentration; scowl. **2.** To look with distaste: with *on* or *upon.* — *v.t.* **3.** To make known (one's displeasure, disgust, etc.) by contracting one's brow. **4.** To silence, rebuke, etc., by or as by a frown. — *n.* **1.** A wrinkling of the brow, as in displeasure; scowl. **2.** Any showing of displeasure. [< OF *froignier,* prob. < Gmc.] — **frown′ing·ly** *adv.*

frow·zy (frou′zē) *adj.* **·zi·er, ·zi·est 1.** Slovenly in appearance; unkempt. **2.** Having a disagreeable smell; musty. Also **frou′zy, frow′sy.** [Origin uncertain]

froze (frōz) Past tense of FREEZE.

fro·zen (frō′zən) Past participle of FREEZE. — *adj.* **1.** Changed into or covered or clogged with ice, as a river. **2.** Killed or damaged by cold. **3.** Extremely cold, as a climate. **4.** Cold and unfeeling in manner. **5.** Made rigid or immobile: *frozen* with fear. **6.** *Econ.* **a** Arbitrarily maintained at a given level: said of prices, wages, etc. **b** Not readily convertible into cash: *frozen* assets. **7.** Made solid by cold.

fruc·ti·fy (fruk′tə·fī, frōōk′-) *v.* **·fied, ·fy·ing** *v.t.* **1.** To make fruitful; fertilize. — *v.i.* **2.** To bear fruit. [< F < L < *fructus* fruit + *facere* to do, make] — **fruc′ti·fi·ca′tion** *n.*

fruc·tose (fruk′tōs, frōōk′-) *n.* *Biochem.* A very sweet sugar, $C_6H_{12}O_6$, occurring in fruits: also called *fruit sugar, levulose.* [< L *fructus* + -OSE²]

fru·gal (frōō′gəl) *adj.* **1.** Exercising economy; saving. **2.** Costing little money: a *frugal* meal. [< L < *frugi* temperate, orig. dative singular of *frux* food] — **fru·gal′i·ty** (-gal′ə·tē) *n.* — **fru′gal·ly** *adv.*

fru·giv·o·rous (frōō·jiv′ər·əs) *adj.* Fruit-eating. [< L *frux, frugis* fruit + -VOROUS]

fruit (frōōt) *n.* **1.** *Bot.* **a** The pulpy, usu. edible mass covering the seeds of various plants and trees. **b** In flowering plants, the mature seed vessel and its contents. **c** In spore plants, the spores with their enveloping or accessory organs. **2.** Any useful plant product, as cotton or flax. **3.** The outcome, consequence, or result of some action, effort, etc.: the *fruit* of labor. — *v.i. & v.t.* To produce or cause to produce fruit. [< OF < L *fructus* < *frui* to enjoy]

fruit·age (frōō′tij) *n.* **1.** Fruit collectively. **2.** The state, process, or time of producing fruit. **3.** Any result or effect.

fruit·cake (frōōt′kāk′) *n.* A rich, spiced cake containing nuts, raisins, citron, and other dried fruits.

fruit·er (frōō′tər) *n.* **1.** A ship that carries fruit; also, a fruit dealer or grower. **2.** A fruit-bearing tree or plant.

fruit fly 1. Any of various flies whose larvae attack fruit. **2.** A fly whose larvae feed on fruit and which is used in research in genetics: also called *drosophila.*

fruit·ful (frōōt′fəl) *adj.* **1.** Bearing fruit or offspring abundantly. **2.** Producing results: a *fruitful* discussion. — **fruit′ful·ly** *adv.* — **fruit′ful·ness** *n.*

fru·i·tion (frōō·ish′ən) *n.* **1.** The accomplishment or realization of things worked for or hoped for; fulfillment. **2.** The enjoyment of this. **3.** The bearing of fruit. [< OF < LL < L *frui* to enjoy]

fruit·less (frōōt′lis) *adj.* **1.** Yielding no fruit; barren. **2.** Ineffectual; useless; unproductive. — Syn. See FUTILE. — **fruit′less·ly** *adv.* — **fruit′less·ness** *n.*

fruit sugar Fructose.

frump (frump) *n.* A dowdy, sometimes ill-tempered woman. [? < MDu. *frompelen,* var. of *verrompelen* to wrinkle]

frump·ish (frum′pish) *adj.* **1.** Dowdy or old-fashioned in dress. **2.** Ill-tempered; peevish. Also **frump′y.** — **frump′ish·ly** *adv.* — **frump′ish·ness** *n.*

frus·trate (frus′trāt) *v.t.* **·trat·ed, ·trat·ing 1.** To keep (someone) from doing or achieving something; baffle the efforts, hopes, or desires of. **2.** To keep, as plans or schemes, from being fulfilled. [< L *frustrari* to disappoint]

frus·tra·tion (frus·trā′shən) *n.* **1.** The state of being frustrated or thwarted. **2.** Something that frustrates.

frus·tum (frus′təm) *n.* *pl.* **·tums** or **·ta** (-tə) *Geom.* **1.** That which is left of a cone or pyramid after cutting off the upper part along a plane parallel to the base. **2.** That part of a solid included between any two, usu. parallel planes. [< L, fragment]

FRUSTUM OF A PYRAMID

fry¹ (frī) *v.t. & v.i.* **fried, fry·ing** To cook in hot fat, usu. over direct heat. — *n. pl.* **fries 1.** A dish of anything fried. **2.** A social occasion, at which foods are fried and eaten. [< F *frier* < L *frigere*]

fry² (frī) *n. pl.* **fry 1.** Very young fish; also, small adult fish when together in large numbers. **2.** The young of certain animals, as of frogs, when produced in very large quantities. **3.** Young children, etc. See SMALL FRY. [< ON *friō* seed]

fry·er (frī′ər) *n.* **1.** One who or that which fries. **2.** A young chicken suitable for frying. Also spelled *frier.*

fuch·sia (fyōō′shə, -shē·ə) *n.* **1.** Any of various plants of the evening-primrose family, with red, pink, white, or purple, drooping, four-petaled flowers. **2.** A bright bluish red, the typical color of the fuchsia. [after Leonhard *Fuchs,* 1501–66, German botanist]

fuch·sin (fōōk′sin) *n. Chem.* One of two deep red or violet dye compounds obtained from aniline, used as a bacterial stain, dye, etc.: also called *magenta.* Also **fuch·sine** (-sin, -sēn). [< FUCHSIA + -IN]

fud·dle (fud′l) *v.* **·dled, ·dling** *v.t.* **1.** To confuse or make stupid with or as with liquor. — *v.i.* **2.** To tipple. [Cf. dial. G *fuddeln* to swindle]

fud·dy-dud·dy (fud′ē-dud′ē) *n. pl.* **·dud·dies** *Informal* **1.** An old-fashioned person. **2.** A faultfinding, fussy person. [Varied reduplication, ? < dial. E *fud* the buttocks]

fudge (fuj) *n.* **1.** A soft, cooked confection made of butter, sugar, chocolate, etc. **2.** Humbug; nonsense. — *v.t.* **fudged, fudg·ing** To make, adjust, or fit together in a clumsy or dishonest manner. [Origin uncertain]

Fueh·rer (fyōō′ər, *Ger.* fü′rər) See FÜHRER.

fu·el (fyōō′əl) *n.* **1.** Combustible matter used as a source of heat energy or to feed a fire. **2.** Whatever sustains or heightens emotion, etc. — *v.t. & v.i.* **fu·eled** or **·elled, fu·el·ing** or **·el·ling** To supply with or take in fuel. [< OF *fouaille* < LL < L *focus* hearth] — **fu′el·er** or **fu′el·ler** *n.*

fu·gal (fyōō′gəl) *adj. Music* Of or pertaining to a fugue.

fu·gi·tive (fyōō′jə·tiv) *adj.* **1.** Fleeing or having fled, as from pursuit, arrest, etc. **2.** Not fixed or lasting; transient; fleeting. **3.** Treating of subjects of passing interest; occasional. **4.** Wandering about; shifting. — *n.* One who flees, as from pursuit, danger, etc.; runaway. [< F < L < *fugere* to flee] — **fu′gi·tive·ly** *adv.* — **fu′gi·tive·ness** *n.*

fugue (fyōōg) *n. Music* A contrapuntal composition in which a theme is introduced by one part, repeated by other parts, and subjected to complex development. [< F < Ital. *fuga* < L, flight]

Füh·rer (fyōōr′ər, *Ger.* fü′rər) *n. German* Leader: a title applied to Adolf Hitler by his adherents: also spelled *Fuehrer.*

-ful *suffix* **1.** Full of; characterized by: *joyful.* **2.** Able to; tending to: *helpful.* **3.** Having the character of: *manful.* **4.** The quantity or number that will fill: *cupful.* ◆ Nouns ending in *-ful* form the plural by adding *-s,* as in *cupfuls, spoonfuls.* [OE *-full, -ful* < *full* full]

ful·crum (fool′krəm) *n. pl.* **·crums** or **·cra** (-krə) **1.** The support on which a lever rests or about which it turns when raising a weight. For illus. see LEVER. **2.** Any prop or support. [< L, bedpost < *fulcire* to prop up]

ful·fill (fool·fil′) *v.t.* **·filled, ·fill·ing 1.** To bring about the accomplishment of (something promised, hoped for, anticipated, etc.); make an actuality of. **2.** To execute or perform (something commanded or requested). **3.** To come up to or satisfy (something stipulated). **4.** To get through to the end of (a period of time, a task, etc.); finish up. Also *Brit.* **ful·fil′.** [OE *fullfyllan*] — **ful·fill′ment** or **ful·fil′ment** *n.*

full¹ (fool) *adj.* **1.** Filled up with as much or as many as is possible. **2.** Containing an abundant or sufficient supply. **3.** Complete or sufficient in number, quantity, etc.; not deficient: a *full* dozen; also, whole or entire: to pay the *full* price. **4.** Maximum in size, extent, degree, etc.: a *full* load; *full* speed. **5.** Of the tide, risen to its highest level. **6.** Of the moon, having the face wholly illuminated. **7.** Having had ample food or drink. **8.** Of the face, figure, etc., well rounded out; plump. **9.** Engrossed or preoccupied: with *of: full* of plans for the future. **10.** Charged with emotion: a *full* heart. **11.** Having satisfying resonance and volume: *full* tones. **12.** Of garments, cut in ample folds; flowing: a long, *full* cape. — **in full cry** In close pursuit: said esp. of dogs. — **in full view** In a position allowing complete visibility. — *n.* The maximum size, extent, degree, etc. — **in full 1.** To the entire amount: paid *in full.* **2.** Without abridgement, condensation, or abbreviation: to reprint a text *in full.* — **to the full** To the most complete extent: to enjoy something *to the full.* — *adv.* **1.** To a complete degree or extent: now chiefly in compounds: *full-fledged.* **2.** Directly; straight; right: I looked him *full* in the face. — *v.t.* **1.** To gather or pleat (the fabric of a garment). — *v.i.* **2.** To become full: said of the moon. [OE *ful*]

full² (fool) *v.t.* **1.** To make (cloth, yarn, etc.) thicker and more compact, as by moistening and beating or pressing. — *v.i.* **2.** Of cloth, etc., to become thicker and more compact through special treatment. [Back formation < FULLER.]

full·back (fŏŏl/bak/) *n.* In football, a player stationed behind the line of scrimmage, usu. just behind the quarterback and the halfbacks; also, this position.

full-blood·ed (fŏŏl/blud/id) *adj.* Unmixed in race or breed; also, related to another through descent from the same parents: also **full-blood** (fŏŏl/blud/).

full-blown (fŏŏl/blōn/) *adj.* **1.** Blooming fully: a *full-blown* rose. **2.** Fully developed: a *full-blown* genius.

full-bod·ied (fŏŏl/bod/ēd) *adj.* Of beverages, having a satisfying richness and strength.

full-dress (fŏŏl/dres/) *adj.* **1.** Characterized by or requiring full dress; formal: a *full-dress* dinner. **2.** Undertaken or engaged in to the fullest possible extent: a *full-dress* debate.

full dress Formal or ceremonial attire.

full·er (fŏŏl/ər) *n.* One who fulls cloth, etc. [OE *fullere*]

full·er's earth (fŏŏl/ərz) A soft, absorbent material resembling clay, used in removing grease from material to be fulled, and also as a catalyst, and in talcs, poultices, etc.

full-fledged (fŏŏl/flejd/) *adj.* **1.** Having the feathers fully grown. **2.** Completely developed or trained.

full gainer A dive in which one springs forward off the board and makes a complete back somersault.

full-grown (fŏŏl/grōn/) *adj.* Having reached full growth.

full house In poker, a hand made up of three cards of one kind plus two cards of another kind. Also **full hand.**

full-length (fŏŏl/lengkth/) *adj.* **1.** Showing the entire length of an object or figure: a *full-length* portrait. **2.** Being of the original or usual length; not abridged.

full moon 1. The moon when the whole of its face is illuminated. **2.** The time of month when this occurs.

full·ness (fŏŏl/nis) *n.* The state or quality of being full. Also **full/ness.**

full-scale (fŏŏl/skāl/) *adj.* **1.** Scaled to actual size; not reduced: a *full-scale* drawing. **2.** Engaged in or undertaken to the fullest possible extent; all-out: a *full-scale* attack.

full swing 1. The height of activity: a party in *full swing.* **2.** Freedom of activity: to be given *full swing.*

ful·ly (fŏŏl/ē) *adv.* **1.** To the fullest extent or degree; entirely: *fully* convinced. **2.** Adequately; sufficiently: *fully* fed. **3.** At the lowest estimate: *fully* three hundred.

ful·mi·nate (ful/mə·nāt) *v.* **·nat·ed, ·nat·ing** *v.i.* **1.** To make loud or violent denunciations; make scathing verbal attacks; inveigh: to *fulminate* against taxes. **2.** To explode suddenly and violently, as a chemical. — *v.t.* **3.** To issue (decrees, censures, etc.) in scathing rebuke or condemnation. **4.** To cause, as a chemical, to explode with sudden violence. — *n. Chem.* Any explosive compound. [< L *fulmen, fulminis* lightning] — **ful/mi·na/tion** *n.* — **ful/mi·na·to·ry** (ful/mə·nə·tôr/ē, -tō/rē) *adj.* — **ful/mi·na/tor** *n.*

ful·some (fŏŏl/səm, ful/-) *adj.* Distastefully excessive in an insincere way: a *fulsome* compliment. [< FULL, adj. + -SOME; infl. by FOUL] — **ful/some·ly** *adv.* — **ful/some·ness** *n.*

fum·ble (fum/bəl) *v.* **·bled, ·bling** *v.i.* **1.** To try to locate something by groping blindly or clumsily: with *for, after.* **2.** To try awkwardly to do something: with *at.* **3.** In football, etc., to get hold of the ball and then let it slip awkwardly from one's grasp. — *v.t.* **4.** To handle awkwardly or ineffectually; botch. **5.** To drop awkwardly (a ball in one's grasp). — *n.* The act of fumbling. [Prob. < Scand. *famla* to grope] — **fum/bler** *n.*

fume (fyŏŏm) *n.* **1.** A gaseous exhalation or smoke, esp. when acrid or otherwise disagreeable. **2.** A sharply penetrating odor. **3.** Something with no more substance than smoke. **4.** A state of rage: in a *fume.* — *v.* **fumed, fum·ing** *v.i.* **1.** To give off fumes. **2.** To pass off in a mist or vapor. **3.** To be filled with or show rage, irritation, etc. — *v.t.* **4.** To subject to fumes. [< OF < L *fumus* smoke]

fu·mi·gate (fyŏŏ/mə·gāt) *v.t.* **·gat·ed, ·gat·ing** To subject to smoke or fumes, as for disinfection or to kill vermin. [< L < *fumus* smoke + *agere* to drive] — **fu/mi·ga/tion** *n.* — **fu/mi·ga/tor** *n.*

fun (fun) *n.* **1.** Pleasant diversion or amusement. **2.** Lighthearted playfulness; full of *fun.* — *adj. Informal* Full of fun: a *fun* game. — **for** (or **in**) **fun** In jest. — **like fun** *Informal* Absolutely not; by no means. — **to make fun of** To ridicule. — *v.i.* **funned, fun·ning** *Informal* To behave or speak in jest. [< obs. *fonnen* to befool]

func·tion (fungk/shən) *n.* **1.** The specific, natural, or proper action or activity of anything. **2.** The special duties or action required of anyone in an occupation, office, or role. **3.** Any more or less formal or elaborate social gathering or ceremony. **4.** Any fact, quality, or thing depending upon or varying with another. **5.** *Math.* A quantity whose value is dependent on the value of some other quantity. — *v.i.* **1.** To perform as expected or required. **2.** To perform the role of something else. [< OF < L *fungi* to perform]

func·tion·al (fungk/shən·əl) *adj.* **1.** Of or pertaining to a function or functions. **2.** Designed for or suited to a particular operation or use. **3.** Affecting the functions of an organ or part: *functional* disease: distinguished from *organic.* — **func/tion·al·ly** *adv.*

func·tion·al·ism (fungk/shən·əl·iz/əm) *n.* The doctrine that the function or use of an object should determine the form, structure, or material of the object.

func·tion·ar·y (fungk/shən·er/ē) *n. pl.* **·ar·ies** One who serves in a specific capacity; esp., an official.

fund (fund) *n.* **1.** A sum of money, or its equivalent, accumulated or reserved for a specific purpose. **2.** *pl.* Money readily available. **3.** A ready supply: a *fund* of humor. — *v.t. Finance* **1.** To accumulate or furnish a fund for. **2.** To convert into a long-term debt.

fun·da·ment (fun/də·mənt) *n.* The buttocks; also, the anus. [< L *fundus* bottom]

fun·da·men·tal (fun/də·men/təl) *adj.* **1.** Pertaining to or constituting a foundation; basic. **2.** *Music* Of or pertaining to a root. **3.** *Physics* Designating the component of a wave form or other periodic oscillation on which all harmonic frequencies are based. — *n.* **1.** Anything that serves as the basis of a system, as a truth, law, etc. **2.** *Music* A root. **3.** *Physics* That frequency on which a harmonic or group of harmonics is based. — **fun/da·men/tal·ly** *adv.*

fun·da·men·tal·ism (fun/də·men/təl·iz/əm) *n.* **1.** The belief that all statements in the Bible are to be taken literally. **2.** In the U.S., a movement among Protestants holding such a belief. — **fun/da·men/tal·ist** *n. & adj.*

fu·ner·al (fyŏŏ/nər·əl) *n.* The burial, cremation, or other final disposal of the body of a dead person, together with accompanying services and ceremonies. — *adj.* Of, pertaining to, or suitable for a funeral. [< OF < Med.L. < L *funus, funeri* burial rite] — **fu·ner·ar·y** (fyŏŏ/nə·rer/ē) *adj.*

fu·ne·re·al (fyŏŏ·nir/ē·əl) *adj.* **1.** Depressingly sad or gloomy; doleful: a *funereal* countenance. **2.** Pertaining to or suitable for a funeral. — **fu·ne/re·al·ly** *adv.*

fungi- *combining form* Fungus. Also, before vowels, **fung-.** [< L *fungus* mushroom]

fun·gi·cide (fun/jə·sīd, -gə-) *n.* Something, as a chemical compound, used in destroying fungi. — **fun/gi·ci/dal** *adj.*

fun·goid (fung/goid) *adj.* Resembling or typical of fungi. — *n. Pathol.* A fungus-like growth.

fun·gous (fung/gəs) *adj.* Of, pertaining to, or having the nature of a fungus.

fun·gus (fung/gəs) *n. pl.* **fun·gus·es** or **fun·gi** (fun/jī, -gī, -gē) **1.** Any nonflowering plants that have no chlorophyll, usu. reproduce asexually, and grow on dead organic matter or live parasitically, including mushrooms, molds, and mildews. **2.** Something that appears or spreads rapidly. **3.** *Pathol.* A soft, spongy, granular growth of tissue. — *adj.* Fungous. [< L, mushroom.] — **fun/gal** *adj. & n.*

fu·nic·u·lar (fyŏŏ·nik/yə·lər) *adj.* Moved by the pull of a cable, as a streetcar in a hilly section. — *n.* A railway along which cable cars are drawn: also **funicular railway.**

funk (fungk) *Chiefly Brit. Informal n.* **1.** A state of fear or panic: esp. in the phrase **to be in a blue funk. 2.** One who quails with fear. — *v.t.* **1.** To shrink back from (something difficult, etc.). **2.** To cause to quail. — *v.i.* **3.** To be in a funk. [Cf. Flemish *fonck* fear]

funk·y¹ (fung/kē) *adj.* **funk·i·er, funk·i·est** *Informal* Frightened or terrified.

funk·y² (fung/kē) *adj.* **funk·i·er, funk·i·est** *Slang* **1.** Having an odor; foul. **2.** Earthy or powerful; as blues music. **3.** Down-to-earth or plain: *funky* denim overalls. [? < F *funkier* to smoke, stink < L *fumus* smoke]

fun·nel (fun/əl) *n.* **1.** A utensil, usu. conical, with a wide mouth tapering to a small outlet or narrow tube, through which liquids, or other free-running substances are poured into bottles, etc., having narrow necks. **2.** One of the smokestacks of a large ship, locomotive, etc. **3.** Any chimney, flue, or similar shaft or tube. — *v.t. & v.i.* **fun·neled** or **·nelled, fun·nel·ing** or **·nel·ling 1.** To pass through or as through a funnel. **2.** To converge to a particular point, area, etc. [Earlier *fonel*, ult. < L < *in-* into + *fundere* to pour]

fun·nies (fun/ēz) *n.pl. U.S. informal* Comic strips.

fun·ny (fun/ē) *adj.* **·ni·er, ·ni·est 1.** Causing one to laugh or be amused; comical. **2.** *Informal* Peculiar; strange; odd. — **fun/ni·ly** *adv.* — **fun/ni·ness** *n.*

funny bone The part of the elbow where the ulnar nerve joins the humerus and which, when struck, produces an unpleasant, tingling sensation: also called *crazy bone.*

fur (fûr) *n.* **1.** The soft, fine, hairy coat covering the skin of foxes, bears, squirrels, cats, and many other mammals. **2.** An animal skin or a part of an animal skin covered with such a coat, esp. when prepared for use in garments, rugs, etc.; also, such skins collectively. **3.** A layer of foul matter, as on the tongue when the digestive tract is upset. — **to make the fur fly** *U.S. Informal* To stir up a furor, as by making accusations, revealing faults, etc. — *adj.* Made of or lined or trimmed with fur. —*v.t.* **furred, fur·ring 1.** To cover, line, trim, or clothe with fur. **2.** To cover, as the tongue, with a layer of foul matter. **3.** To apply furring. [< OF *forrer* to line with fur < Gmc.]

fur·be·low (fûr′bə·lō) *n.* **1.** A ruffle, frill, or similar piece of ornamentation. **2.** Any showy bit of decoration. —*v.t.* To provide with furbelows. [Var. of obs. *falbala* < F]

fur·bish (fûr′bish) *v.t.* **1.** To make bright by rubbing; burnish. **2.** To restore to brightness or beauty; renovate: often with *up*. [< OF < OHG *furban* to clean] —**fur′bish·er** *n.*

fur·cate (fûr′kāt; *for adj., also* -kit) *v.i.* **·cat·ed, ·cat·ing** To divide into branches. —*adj.* Forked: also **fur′cat·ed** (-kāt·id). [< Med.L < L *furca* fork] —**fur·ca′tion** *n.*

Fu·ries (fyŏŏr′ēz) *n.pl.* In classical mythology, the three goddesses who avenge unpunished crimes: also called *Eumenides*.

fu·ri·ous (fyŏŏr′ē·əs) *adj.* **1.** Extremely angry; raging. **2.** Extremely violent or intense; fierce. **3.** Pushed to the limit; extremely great: a *furious* rate of speed. [< L *furere* to rage] —**fu′ri·ous·ly** *adv.* —**fu′ri·ous·ness** *n.*

furl (fûrl) *v.t.* **1.** To roll up (a sail, flag, etc.) and make secure, as to a mast or staff. —*v.i.* **2.** To become furled. —*n.* **1.** The act of furling, or the state of being furled. **2.** A rolled-up section of a sail, flag, etc. [< F *ferler* < OF < L *firmum* firm + *ligare* to tie]

fur·long (fûr′lông, -long) *n.* A measure of length, equal to ⅛ mile, 220 yards, or 201.168 meters. See table inside back cover. [OE *furlang* < *furh* furrow + *lang* long]

fur·lough (fûr′lō) *n.* Permission to be absent from duty, esp. in the armed services: now called *leave* or *leave of absence*. —*v.t.* To grant a furlough to. [< Du. *verlof*]

fur·nace (fûr′nis) *n.* **1.** A large apparatus with an enclosed chamber designed to produce intense heat for warming a building, melting metal, creating steam power, etc. **2.** Any intensely hot place. [< OF < L < *furnus* oven]

fur·nish (fûr′nish) *v.t.* **1.** To equip, or fit out, as with fittings or furniture. **2.** To supply; provide. [< OF *furnir* < OHG *frumjan* to provide] —**fur′nish·er** *n.*

fur·nish·ings (fûr′nish·ingz) *n.pl.* **1.** Articles of clothing, including accessories. **2.** Articles of furniture and other fixtures for a home, office, etc.

fur·ni·ture (fûr′nə·chər) *n.* **1.** The movable articles used in a home, office, etc., as sofas, chairs, tables, or mirrors. **2.** Any necessary equipment, as for a factory or ship. [< F *fourniture* < OF *furnir* < OHG *frumjan* to provide]

fu·ror (fyŏŏr′ôr) *n.* **1.** A great stir; commotion; rumpus. **2.** A state of intense excitement or enthusiasm. [< L *furor* < *furere* to rage]

furred (fûrd) *adj.* **1.** Having or clad in fur. **2.** Made of or trimmed with fur, as garments. **3.** Coated, as the tongue.

fur·ri·er (fûr′ē·ər, -yər) *n.* **1.** One who deals in, repairs, or stores furs. **2.** One who processes furs for garments, etc.

fur·ring (fûr′ing) *n.* **1.** A trimming or lining of fur. **2.** Furs collectively. **3.** An animal's coat of fur. **4.** A coating of foreign matter, as on the tongue. **5.** Strips of wood, metal, etc., fixed to a wall, floor, etc., so as to make a level surface or create air spaces.

fur·row (fûr′ō) *n.* **1.** A narrow channel made in the ground by or as if by a plow. **2.** Any long, narrow, deep depression, as a groove, rut, or deep wrinkle. —*v.t.* **1.** To make furrows or deep wrinkles in. **2.** To plow. —*v.i.* **3.** To become furrowed or wrinkled. [OE *furh*]

fur·ry (fûr′ē) *adj.* **fur·ri·er, fur·ri·est 1.** Of, pertaining to, or resembling fur. **2.** Covered or provided with fur. **3.** Coated, as the tongue. —**fur′ri·ness** *n.*

fur·ther (fûr′thər) Comparative of FAR. —*adv.* **1.** At or to a more distant or remote point in time or space. **2.** To a greater degree; more. **3.** In addition; besides; moreover. —*adj.* **1.** More distant or advanced in time or degree. **2.** More distant in space; farther. **3.** Additional. —*v.t.* To help forward; promote. [OE *furthra*] —**fur′ther·er** *n.*

fur·ther·ance (fûr′thər·əns) *n.* **1.** The act of furthering; advancement. **2.** That which furthers.

fur·ther·more (fûr′thər·môr′, -mōr′) *adv.* In addition; moreover.

fur·ther·most (fûr′thər·mōst′) *adj.* Furthest.

fur·thest (fûr′thist) Superlative of FAR. —*adv.* **1.** At or to the most remote or distant point in space of time. **2.** To the greatest degree. —*adj.* **1.** Most distant, remote, or advanced in time or degree. **2.** Most distant in space.

fur·tive (fûr′tiv) *adj.* **1.** Done in secret; surreptitious; stealthy. **2.** Evasive; shifty. —**Syn.** See STEALTHY. [< F < L < *fur* thief] —**fur′tive·ly** *adv.* —**fur′tive·ness** *n.*

fu·ry (fyŏŏr′ē) *n.* *pl.* **·ries 1.** Vehement and uncontrolled anger; ungovernable rage. **2.** A fit of such anger or rage. **3.** Violent action or agitation; fierceness: the storm's *fury*. **4.** A person of violent temper, esp. a woman. [< L *furia* < *furere* to rage]

furze (fûrz) *n.* A spiny evergreen shrub of the bean family, having many branches and yellow flowers: also called *gorse, whin*. [OE *fyrs*] —**furz′y** *adj.*

fuse¹ (fyŏŏz) *n.* **1.** A length of combustible material passing into the charge of an explosive, designed to be lit so as to ignite the charge. **2.** *Mil.* Any mechanical or electronic device designed to detonate a bomb, projectile, etc. **3.** *Electr.* A device consisting of a small strip of metal mounted in a casing and completing a circuit when put into position, the metal melting and breaking the circuit if the current becomes excessive. —*v.t.* To attach a fuse to (a rocket, bomb, etc.). Also spelled *fuze*. [< Ital. < L *fusus* spindle]

fuse² (fyŏŏz) *v.t. & v.i.* **fused, fus·ing 1.** To liquefy by heat; melt. **2.** To join by or as if by melting together. [< L *fusus*, pp. of *fundere* to pour]

fu·see (fyŏŏ·zē′) *n.* **1.** A friction match with a large head capable of burning in the wind. **2.** A flare used as a railroad signal. Also spelled *fuzee*. [< F < Med.L < L *fusus* spindle]

fu·se·lage (fyŏŏ′sə·lij, -läzh, -zə-) *n. Aeron.* The body of an airplane, containing the cockpit, cabin, etc. [< F]

fu·sel oil (fyŏŏ′zəl, -səl) A volatile, poisonous, oily liquid, obtained from rectified corn, potato, or grape spirits and used as a solvent in various chemical processes. Also **fu′sel**. [< G *fusel* inferior spirits]

fu·si·ble (fyŏŏ′zə·bəl) *adj.* Capable of being fused. —**fu′si·bil′i·ty** *n.* —**fu′si·ble·ness** *n.* —**fu′si·bly** *adv.*

fu·si·form (fyŏŏ′zə·fôrm) *adj.* Shaped like a spindle.

fu·sil (fyŏŏ′zəl) *n.* A flintlock musket. [< F < OF *foisil* a steel for striking sparks, ult. < L *focus* hearth]

fu·si·lier (fyŏŏ′zə·lir′) *n.* **1.** A soldier armed with a flintlock musket. **2.** *pl.* Soldiers of certain regiments of the British army: used in titles of the regiments. Also **fu′si·leer′**.

fu·sil·lade (fyŏŏ′zə·lād′) *n.* **1.** A simultaneous or quickly repeated discharge of firearms. **2.** Anything resembling this: a *fusillade* of hail. —*v.t.* **·lad·ed, ·lad·ing** To attack or bring down with a fusillade. Also **fu′si·lade′**. [< F < *fusiller* to shoot < *fusil* musket]

fu·sion (fyŏŏ′zhən) *n.* **1.** A melting or blending together. **2.** Something formed by fusing. **3.** In politics, the union of two parties or two factions within a party. **4.** *Physics* A thermonuclear reaction in which the nuclei of a light element undergo transformation into those of a heavier element, with the release of great energy: also called *nuclear fusion*. [< L *fusio, -onis*, < *fundere* to pour]

fuss (fus) *n.* **1.** Nervous activity; bustle; commotion; ado. **2.** One excessively concerned with trifles: also **fuss′er**. —*v.i.* **1.** To be too much concerned with trifles. —*v.t.* **2.** To bother with trifles. [Origin unknown]

fuss·y (fus′ē) *adj.* **fuss·i·er, fuss·i·est 1.** Too much concerned with trifles; finicky. **2.** Fidgety; fretful. **3.** Requiring meticulous attention. **4.** Having elaborate and showy trimmings, as clothing. —**fuss′i·ly** *adv.* —**fuss′i·ness** *n.*

fus·tian (fus′chən) *n.* **1.** Formerly, a kind of stout cloth made of cotton and flax; now, a coarse, twilled cotton fabric, as corduroy. **2.** Pretentious verbiage; bombast. —*adj.* **1.** Made of fustian. **2.** Pompous; bombastic. [< OF < Med.L < L *fustis* cudgel]

fust·y (fus′tē) *adj.* **fust·i·er, fust·i·est 1.** Musty; moldy; rank. **2.** Old-fashioned; fogeyish. [< obs. *fust* moldy odor < OF, wine cask] —**fust′i·ly** *adv.* —**fust′i·ness** *n.*

fu·tile (fyŏŏ′təl, -til; *esp. Brit.* -tīl) *adj.* **1.** Being of no avail; done in vain; useless. **2.** Frivolous; trivial: *futile* chatter. [< F < L *futilis* pouring out easily, useless] —**fu′tile·ly** *adv.* —**fu′tile·ness** *n.* —**fu·til·i·ty** (fyŏŏ·til′ə·tē) *n.* —**Syn. 1.** vain, fruitless, abortive.

fu·ture (fyŏŏ′chər) *n.* **1.** The time yet to come. **2.** What will be in time to come. **3.** A condition, usu. of success or prosperity, in time to come: a man with a *future*. **4.** *Usu. pl.* Any commodity or security sold or bought upon agreement of future delivery. **5.** *Gram.* **a** A verb tense denoting action that will take place at some time to come. **b** A verb in this tense. —*adj.* **1.** Such as will be in time to come. **2.** Pertaining to or expressing time to come. [< OF < L *futurus*, future participle of *esse* to be] —**fu′ture·less** *adj.*

future perfect *Gram.* **1.** The verb tense expressing a future action or state completed before a specified future time: He *will have finished* by tomorrow. **2.** A verb in this tense.

fu·tur·ism (fyŏŏ′chər·iz′əm) *n.* A movement in art, music, and literature during World War I that rejected traditional forms in an effort to portray more vividly the intensity and speed of contemporary life. —**fu′tur·ist** *adj. & n.*

fu·tu·ri·ty (fyŏŏ·tŏŏr′ə·tē, -tyŏŏr′-) *n.* *pl.* **·ties 1.** Time to come; the future. **2.** The state or quality of being future. **3.** A future event or possibility.

fuze (fyŏŏz) See FUSE¹.

fu·zee (fyŏŏ·zē′) See FUSEE.

fuzz (fuz) *n.* **1.** Fine, loose particles, fibers, or hairs. **2.** A fluffy mass of these. —*v.t. & v.i.* To become or cause to become fuzzy. [Origin unknown]

fuzz·y (fuz′ē) *adj.* **fuzz·i·er, fuzz·i·est 1.** Having fuzz. **2.** Resembling fuzz. **3.** Lacking sharp distinctness or clarity; blurred. —**fuzz′i·ly** *adv.* —**fuzz′i·ness** *n.*

-fy *suffix of verbs* **1.** Cause to be or become: *deify*. **2.** Become: *liquefy*. [< OF < L *facere* to do, to make]

G

g, G (jē) *n. pl.* **g's** or **gs, G's** or **Gs, gees** (jēz) **1.** The seventh letter of the English alphabet. Also *gee.* **2.** Any sound represented by the letter *g.* **3.** *Usu. cap. U.S. Slang* One thousand dollars; a grand. — *symbol* **1.** *Music* **a** The fifth tone in the scale of C major or the seventh in the natural scale of A minor. **b** A written note representing this tone. **c** A scale built upon the tone of G. **d** The treble clef. **2.** *Physics* The acceleration of a body due to the earth's gravity, about 32 feet per second per second; also, a unit of acceleration equal to that due to the earth's gravity (symbol g).
gab (gab) *Informal v.i.* **gabbed, gab·bing** To talk, esp. glibly or excessively; chatter; prate. — *n.* Glib or excessive speech. [Prob. < ON *gabba* to mock] — **gab'ber** *n.*
gab·ar·dine (gab'ər·dēn, gab'ər·dēn') *n.* **1.** A firm, twilled, worsted fabric, having a diagonal raised weave, used for coats, suits, etc. **2.** A similar, softer fabric of mercerized cotton. **3.** A gaberdine. [Var. of GABERDINE]
gab·ble (gab'əl) *v.* **·bled, ·bling** *v.i.* **1.** To talk quickly or incoherently. **2.** To utter rapid, cackling sounds, as geese. — *v.t.* **3.** To utter rapidly or incoherently. — *n.* **1.** Glib, incoherent, or foolish talk. **2.** Cackling sounds, as of geese. [Freq. of GAB] — **gab'bler** *n.*
gab·er·dine (gab'ər·dēn, gab'ər·dēn') *n.* **1.** A loose, coarse coat or frock. **2.** A long, loose, coarse cloak worn by Jews in medieval times. **3.** Gabardine. [< Sp. *garbardina*]
ga·bi·on (gā'bē·ən) *n.* **1.** *Mil.* A cylindrical wicker basket filled with earth, stones, etc., used as a defense. **2.** An open cylinder, usu. of metal, filled with stones, etc., and used in the preliminary construction of dams, etc. [< F < Ital. *gabbione,* aug. of *gabbia* cage < L *cavea* cage]
ga·ble (gā'bəl) *n. Archit.* **1.** The outside, usu. triangular section of a wall extending upward from the level of the eaves of a sloped roof to the ridge pole. **2.** The end wall of a building whose upper part is a gable. **3.** Any gablelike feature, as above a door. — *v.t.* **1.** To cause to form a gable: a *gabled* roof. — *v.i.* **2.** To form a gable. [< OF, prob. < ON *gafl* gable]
gable roof A roof that forms a gable.
Ga·bri·el (gā'brē·əl) In the Bible, one of the archangels, chosen as a special messenger of God.
gad¹ (gad) *v.i.* **gad·ded, gad·ding** To roam about restlessly or capriciously; ramble. — *n.* The act of gadding. [? < obs. *gadling* vagabond] — **gad'der** *n.*
gad² (gad) *n.* **1.** In mining, a pointed tool. **2.** A goad. — *v.t.* **gad·ded, gad·ding** To break up (ore) with a gad. [< ON *gaddr* goad]
gad·a·bout (gad'ə·bout') *Informal n.* One who goes about aimlessly, frivolously, etc. — *adj.* Fond of gadding.
gad·fly (gad'flī') *n. pl.* **·flies** **1.** One of various large flies, as a horsefly, that bite cattle, horses, etc. **2.** An irritating, bothersome individual. [< GAD² + FLY]
gadg·et (gaj'it) *n. Informal* **1.** Any small device or contrivance. **2.** Some little thing whose exact name is unknown.
gad·o·lin·i·um (gad'ə·lin'ē·əm) *n.* A metallic element (symbol Gd) of the lanthanide series. See ELEMENT. [after John *Gadolin,* 1760–1852, Finnish chemist]
gad·wall (gad'wôl) *n. pl.* **·walls** or **·wall** A large freshwater duck found in the northern hemisphere.
Gae·a (jē'ə) In Greek mythology, the goddess of earth and mother and wife of Uranus. [< Gk. *Gaia* Earth]
Gael (gāl) *n.* One of the Celts of Ireland or the Scottish Highlands. [< Scottish Gaelic *Gaidheal*]
Gael·ic (gā'lik) *adj.* Belonging or relating to the Gaels or their languages. — *n.* **1.** The languages of the Gaels. **2.** The Goidelic branch of the Celtic languages.
gaff (gaf) *n.* **1.** A sharp iron hook at the end of a pole, for landing a large fish; also, the pole. **2.** *Naut.* A spar for extending the upper edge of a fore-and-aft sail. **3.** *Slang* Loud or annoying talk. — *v.t.* To strike or land with a gaff. — **to stand the gaff** *U.S. Informal* To endure hardship, etc., patiently. [< OF *gaffe,* prob. < Celtic]
gaf·fer (gaf'ər) *n.* An old man. [Alter. of GODFATHER]

gag (gag) *n.* **1.** Something, as a wadded cloth, forced into or over the mouth to prevent a person from speaking or crying out. **2.** Any restraint or suppression of free speech, as by censorship. **3.** A device to keep the jaws open, as in dentistry. **4.** *Slang* A joke or hoax. **5.** *Slang* Something interpolated by an actor into a role, as a topical comment. — **to pull a gag** *U.S. Slang* To perform or perpetrate a practical joke, deception, etc. — *v.* **gagged, gag·ging** *v.t.* **1.** To keep from speaking out by means of a gag. **2.** To keep from speaking or discussing freely, as by force or authority. **3.** To cause nausea in; cause to retch. **4.** To keep (the mouth) open with a gag. — *v.i.* **5.** To heave with nausea; also, to choke on something. [ME *gaggen*] — **gag'ger** *n.*
ga·ga (gä'gä') *adj. Slang* Foolish; crazy. [< F (slang), a foolish old man]
gage¹ (gāj) See GAUGE.
gage² (gāj) *n.* **1.** Something given as security for an action to be performed; pledge. **2.** Anything, as a glove, proffered as a challenge. **3.** Any challenge. [< OF *gage* pledge]
gag·gle (gag'əl) *v.i.* **·gled, ·gling** To cackle; gabble. — *n.* **1.** A flock of geese. **2.** A chattering group of women.
gai·e·ty (gā'ə·tē) *n. pl.* **·ties** **1.** The state of being gay; cheerfulness. **2.** Bright colorfulness or showiness, as of dress. **3.** Fun; merrymaking. Also *gayety.* [< F *gai*]
gail·lar·di·a (gā·lär'dē·ə) *n.* A western American herb with showy yellow or reddish flowers.
gai·ly (gā'lē) *adv.* In a gay manner: also spelled *gayly.*
gain (gān) *v.t.* **1.** To obtain; acquire; get: to *gain* an advantage. **2.** To succeed in winning (a victory, etc.). **3.** To develop an increase of: to *gain* momentum. **4.** To put on (weight). **5.** To earn (a living, etc.). **6.** To arrive at; reach: to *gain* port. — *v.i.* **7.** To grow better: to *gain* in health. **8.** To draw nearer; also, to increase one's lead: usu. with *on* or *upon.* — *n.* **1.** *Often pl.* Something obtained by way of profit, winnings, etc.: small *gains.* **2.** An advantage or lead. **3.** An increase, as in size, amount, etc. **4.** The act of gaining. [< F < OF *gaaignier* < Gmc.]
— *Syn.* (verb) **1.** See GET. **2.** attain, achieve. **7.** prosper, flourish.
gain·er (gā'nər) *n.* **1.** One who or that which gains. **2.** A full gainer. **3.** A half gainer.
gain·ful (gān'fəl) *adj.* Yielding profit; lucrative. — **gain'ful·ly** *adv.* — **gain'ful·ness** *n.*
gain·say (gān'sā') *v.t.* **·said, ·say·ing** **1.** To deny. **2.** To contradict. **3.** To act against; oppose. [OE *gegn-* against + SAY²] — **gain'say'er** *n.*
'gainst (genst, *esp. Brit.* gānst) *prep.* Against.
gait (gāt) *n.* **1.** One's manner of moving along on foot. **2.** One of the ways in which a horse steps or runs. — *v.t.* To train (a horse) to take a gait. [< ON *gata* way]
gai·ter (gā'tər) *n.* **1.** A covering, as of leather or canvas, worn over the leg, as a puttee. **2.** A similar covering for the ankle and instep; a spat. **3.** An old-fashioned shoe with a high top. [< F *guêtre*]
gal (gal) *n. Slang* **1.** A girl. **2.** A girl friend.
ga·la (gā'lə, gal'ə, gä'lə) *adj.* Appropriate to a festive occasion; festive. — *n.* An occasion marked by joyous festivity. [< F < Ital., holiday dress]
galacto- *combining form* Milk; milky. Also, before vowels, **galact-.** [< Gk. *galaktos* milk]
Gal·a·had (gal'ə·had) **1.** In Arthurian legend, the noblest knight of the Round Table, son of Lancelot, who accomplished the quest for the Holy Grail. **2.** Any pure man.
Gal·a·te·a (gal'ə·tē'ə) In Greek mythology, a statue of a maiden brought to life by Aphrodite after its sculptor, Pygmalion, had fallen in love with it.
Ga·la·tia (gə·lā'shə, -shē·ə) An ancient country of Asia Minor, so called from the Gauls who conquered it.
Ga·la·tian (gə·lā'shən) *adj.* Of ancient Galatia. — *n.* A native of Galatia. — **Epistle to the Galatians** A book of the New Testament, a letter written by the apostle Paul.
gal·ax·y (gal'ək·sē) *n. pl.* **·ax·ies** **1.** *Astron.* Any very large system of stars, nebulae, or other celestial bodies. **2.** *Usu. cap.* The Milky Way. **3.** A brilliant group, as of persons. [< F < L < Gk. < *gala* milk]

GABLES

PRONUNCIATION KEY: add, āce, câre, pälm; end, ēven; it, īce; odd, ōpen, ôrder; tŏŏk, pōōl; up, bûrn; ə = a in *above,* e in *sicken,* i in *flexible,* o in *melon,* u in *focus;* yōō = u in *fuse;* oil; pout; check; go; ring; thin; this; zh, vision. For å, œ, ü, kh, ṅ, see inside front cover.

gale (gāl) *n.* **1.** *Meteorol.* A wind stronger than a stiff breeze. **2.** An outburst, as of hilarity. [Origin uncertain]

ga·le·na (gə-lē′nə) *n.* A metallic, dull gray, cleavable, isometric lead sulfide, PbS, one of the principal ores of lead. Also **ga·le·nite** (gə-lē′nīt). [< L, lead ore]

Ga·li·cian (gə-lish′ən) *adj.* **1.** Of Spanish Galicia, its people, or their language. **2.** Of Polish Galicia or its people. — *n.* **1.** A native of Spanish Galicia. **2.** The Portuguese dialect spoken there. **3.** A native of Polish Galicia.

Gal·i·le·an (gal′ə-lē′ən) *adj.* Of Galilee, in ancient northern Palestine. — *n.* **1.** An inhabitant of Galilee. **2.** A Christian. — **the Galilean** Jesus Christ. Also **Gal′i·lae′an.**

Gal·i·le·an (gal′ə-lē′ən) *adj.* Of or pertaining to Galileo.

gall¹ (gôl) *n.* **1.** *Physiol.* The bitter fluid secreted by the liver; bile. **2.** Bitter feeling; rancor. **3.** Something bitter. **4.** *U.S. Slang* Impudence. [OE *gealla*]

gall² (gôl) *n.* **1.** An abrasion or sore produced by friction. **2.** Something that irritates or vexes. **3.** Exasperation. — *v.t.* **1.** To injure (the skin) by friction; chafe. **2.** To vex or irritate. — *v.i.* **3.** To become or be chafed. [Prob. < GALL¹]

gall³ (gôl) *n.* An abnormal plant growth that on certain oaks yields tannin. [< F < L *galla* gallnut]

gal·lant (gal′ənt *for adj. defs.* 1, 4, 5; gə-lant′, gal′ənt *for adj. defs.* 2 & 3; n. gal′ənt, gə-lant′; v. gə-lant′) *adj.* **1.** Possessing spirit and courage; brave: *gallant* soldiers. **2.** Chivalrously attentive to women; also, dashingly amorous. **3.** Stately; imposing. **4.** Showy: *gallant* attire. — *n.* **1.** A brave, spirited man. **2.** A man chivalrously attentive to women or amorous in a courtly way; a paramour. — *v.t.* **1.** To be chivalrously attentive to (a woman). **2.** To escort. — *v.i.* **3.** To be a suitor. [< OF *galer* to rejoice] — **gal′lant·ly** *adv.*

gal·lant·ry (gal′ən-trē) *n. pl.* **·ries** **1.** Nobility and bravery. **2.** Chivalrous or amorous behavior. **3.** An instance of gallant speech or behavior.

gall bladder *Anat.* A small, pear-shaped muscular pouch situated beneath the liver in man and serving as a reservoir for bile conducted through the **gall duct.**

gal·le·on (gal′ē-ən) *n.* A large sailing vessel of the 15th to 17th centuries. [< Sp. < Med.L]

gal·ler·y (gal′ər-ē) *n. pl.* **·ler·ies** **1.** A roofed promenade, esp. an open-sided one extending along an inner or outer wall of a building. **2.** Any similar long, usu. narrow enclosed area, as a hall. **3.** *Southern U.S.* A veranda. **4.** An elevated rear floor section for seating in a theater or other large building, over the back of the main floor. **5.** A group of spectators, as of those in a grandstand. **6.** A part of the general public viewed as shallow, undiscriminating, etc. **7.** A room or building in which statues, paintings, etc., are displayed. **8.** A room or building in which articles are sold to the highest bidder. **9.** An enclosed place, as at a fair, where one shoots at targets for amusement. **10.** A tunnel or underground passage, as in a mine. — **to play to the gallery** To play or cater to the common crowd. — *v.t.* **·ler·ied, ·ler·y·ing** To provide with a gallery. [< F < Med.L *galeria*]

gal·ley (gal′ē) *n. pl.* **·leys** **1.** A long, low vessel used in ancient times, propelled by oars and sails. **2.** A large rowboat. **3.** The kitchen of a ship. **4.** *Printing* **a** A long tray for holding composed type. **b** A galley proof. [< OF < Med.L < LGk. *galaia*]

galley proof *Printing* **1.** A proof taken from type composed in a galley and used for making corrections before page composition. **2.** Two or more such proofs collectively.

galley slave **1.** A slave or convict condemned to row a galley. **2.** One who does monotonous work; drudge.

gall·fly (gôl′flī′) *n. pl.* **·flies** A small insect that deposits eggs in plant tissue, with consequent production of galls.

gal·lic (gal′ik) *adj. Chem.* **1.** Of, pertaining to, or derived from gallium. **2.** Relating to or derived from gallnuts.

gallic acid *Chem.* A white, odorless, crystalline organic compound, $C_7H_6O_5 \cdot H_2O$, found in many plants and used in the making of inks, dyestuffs, paper, etc.

Gal·lic (gal′ik) *adj.* Of or pertaining to ancient Gaul or modern France; French. [< L *Gallus* inhabitant of Gaul]

Gal·li·cism (gal′ə-siz′əm) *n.* An idiom or turn of phrase peculiar to French.

Gal·li·cize (gal′ə-sīz) *v.t. & v.i.* **·cized, ·ciz·ing** To make French in character, language, etc.; Frenchify.

gal·li·na·ceous (gal′ə-nā′shəs) *adj.* Of or pertaining to an order of birds including the common hen, turkeys, partridges, etc. [< L < *gallina* hen] — **gal′li·na′cean** *n.*

gall·ing (gô′ling) *adj.* Very annoying or exasperating.

gal·li·nule (gal′ə-nyōōl, -nōōl) *n.* Any of several cootlike wading birds of the rail family. [< L *gallina* hen]

gal·li·pot (gal′i·pot) *n.* A small earthen jar, as for ointments, used esp. by druggists. [? < GALLEY + POT]

gal·li·um (gal′ē·əm) *n.* A rare, bluish white, metallic element in the aluminum group, having a low melting point (86° F.). See ELEMENT. [< NL < L *gallus* cock, trans. of *Lecoq* de Boisbaudran, 1838–1912, its discoverer]

gal·li·vant (gal′ə-vant, gal′ə-vant′) *v.i.* To roam about capriciously; gad. [? Alter. of GALLANT]

gall·nut (gôl′nut′) *n.* A gall produced on certain oaks or other plants.

Gallo- *combining form* Gaulish or French. [< L *Gallus*]

gal·lon (gal′ən) *n.* **1.** A liquid measure of capacity that by the U.S. standard contains 231 cubic inches or 4 quarts and by the British standard (**imperial gallon**) 277.3 cubic inches or 4 imperial quarts. **2.** A dry measure equivalent to ⅛ bushel. **3.** A container with a capacity of 1 gallon. See table inside back cover. [< AF *galon*, ? < Celtic]

gal·lop (gal′əp) *n.* **1.** The fastest gait of a horse, etc., characterized by regular leaps during which all four feet are off the ground at once. **2.** A ride at a gallop. **3.** Any rapid pace. — *v.i.* **1.** To ride at a gallop. **2.** To go very fast. — *v.t.* **3.** To cause to gallop. [< OF < *galoper* < Gmc.] — **gal′lop·er** *n.*

gal·lows (gal′ōz) *n. pl.* **·lows·es** or **·lows** **1.** A framework of two or more upright beams supporting a crossbeam, used for execution by hanging. **2.** Any similar structure, as a set of crossbars. [OE *galga*]

gallows bird *Informal* One who merits hanging.

gall·stone (gôl′stōn′) *n. Pathol.* A small, stony mass sometimes formed in the gall bladder or bile passages.

gal·op (gal′əp) *n.* **1.** A lively round dance. **2.** Music for this dance, written in duple meter. [< F, gallop]

ga·lore (gə-lôr′, -lōr′) *adv.* In great numbers or abundance: to offer bargains *galore.* [< Irish *go leór* enough]

ga·losh (gə-losh′) *n. Usu. pl.* An overshoe reaching above the ankle and worn in bad weather. [< F *galoche*]

ga·lumph (gə-lumf′) *v.i.* To clump along pompously. [< GAL(LOP) + (TRI)UMPH; coined by Lewis Carroll]

gal·van·ic (gal-van′ik) *adj.* **1.** Of or caused by electricity as produced by chemical action. **2.** Pertaining to a reaction to an electric shock; convulsive. Also **gal·van′i·cal.**

gal·va·nism (gal′və-niz′əm) *n.* **1.** Electricity as produced by chemical action: also called *voltaism.* **2.** *Med.* The therapeutic application of a continuous electric current from voltaic cells. [after Luigi *Galvani* + -ISM]

gal·va·nize (gal′və-nīz) *v.t.* **·nized, ·niz·ing** **1.** To stimulate to muscular action by electricity. **2.** To rouse to action; excite. **3.** To provide steel, etc. with a protective coating of zinc. — **gal′va·ni·za′tion** *n.* — **gal′va·niz′er** *n.*

galvanized iron Iron coated with zinc, as for protection against rust.

galvano- *combining form* Galvanic; galvanism.

gal·va·nom·e·ter (gal′və-nom′ə·tər) *n. Electr.* An apparatus for indicating the presence and determining the strength and direction of an electric current. — **gal·va·no·met·ric** (gal′və-nō-met′rik, gal-van′ō-) or **·ri·cal** *adj.*

gal·va·no·scope (gal′və-nō-skōp′, gal-van′ə-) *n.* An instrument for detecting an electric current and showing its direction. — **gal·va·no·scop·ic** (gal′və-nō-skop′ik, gal-van′ō-) *adj.* — **gal′va·nos′co·py** (-nos′kə-pō) *n.*

gam (gam) *n. Slang* A leg, esp. of a woman. Also **gamb.**

gam·bit (gam′bit) *n.* **1.** In chess, an opening in which a player risks or sacrifices a piece to gain a favorable position. **2.** Any opening move, as one to promote discussion. [< F < OF *gambet*, a tripping up, ult. < LL *gamba* leg]

gam·ble (gam′bəl) *v.* **·bled, ·bling** *v.i.* **1.** To risk or bet something of value on the outcome of a game of chance, etc. **2.** To take a risk to obtain a result. — *v.t.* **3.** To wager or bet (something of value). **4.** To lose by taking risks: usu. with *away.* — *n. Informal* **1.** Any risky venture. **2.** A gambling transaction. [Cf. OE *gamenian* to sport, play] — **gam·bler** (gam′blər) *n.*

gam·boge (gam-bōj′, -bōōzh′) *n.* **1.** A gum resin obtained from a tropical tree, used as a pigment and cathartic. **2.** A bright yellow or orange-yellow color.

gam·bol (gam′bəl) *v.i.* **·boled** or **·bolled, gam·bol·ing** or **·bol·ling** To skip or leap about in play; frolic. — *n.* A skipping about in sport. [< F < Ital. *gamba* leg]

gam·brel (gam′brəl) *n.* **1.** The hock of a horse, etc. **2.** A gambrel roof. [< OF < LL *gamba*]

gambrel roof *Archit.* A ridged roof with the slope broken on each side.

GAMBREL ROOF

game¹ (gām) *n.* **1.** A contest governed by set rules, entered into for amusement, as a test of prowess, or for money or other stakes. **2.** *pl.* Athletic competitions. **3.** A single contest forming part of a fixed series. **4.** The number of points for winning, as in tennis or cards. **5.** The score during a contest: The *game* was 6–6. **6.** The equipment used in playing games, as chess boards and pieces. **7.** The style or prowess in a contest: His *game* of golf is not good. **8.** A form of playful activity: Love is a *game.* **9.** *Informal* Any profession, business, etc.: the teaching *game.* **10.** A plan designed to attain an objective. **11.** Animals, fish, etc., that are hunted or taken; also, the flesh of such animals, etc. **12.** Anything hunted; quarry. **13.** A fit target for ridicule, criticism, etc.: They were fair *game.* —

to make game of To subject to ridicule, etc. **— to play the game 1.** To act with honor, consideration, etc. **2.** To act in accordance with what is expected. **— v. gamed, gam·ing v.i. 1.** To gamble at cards, etc., for money or other stakes. **— v.t. 2.** To lose by gambling: with *away.* **— adj. 1.** Of hunted animals, etc., or their flesh. **2.** Having a fighting spirit; plucky. **3.** *Informal* Ready; willing. [OE *gamen*]

game² (gām) *adj. Informal* Lame: a *game* leg.

game·cock (gām′kok′) *n.* A rooster bred and trained for cockfighting.

game·keep·er (gām′kē′pər) *n.* A person having the care of game, as on an estate.

game·ly (gām′lē) *adv.* In a game manner; pluckily.

game·ness (gām′nis) *n.* Pluck; bravery; endurance.

game·ster (gām′stər) *n.* One who gambles.

gam·ete (gam′ēt, gə-mēt′) *n. Biol.* Either of two mature reproductive cells, an ovum or sperm, that in uniting produce a zygote. [< NL < Gk. *gametē* wife, or *gametēs* husband] **— ga·met·ic** (gə-met′ik) *adj.*

gameto- *combining form* Gamete. [< Gk. < *gamos* marriage]

ga·me·to·phyte (gə-mē′tə-fīt) *n. Bot.* The phase or generation that produces the sexual organs of a plant.

gam·in (gam′in, *Fr.* gå-man′) *n.* A homeless youngster who wanders about the streets of a city or town. [< F]

gam·ma (gam′ə) *n.* The third letter in the Greek alphabet (Γ, γ), corresponding to *g* (as in *go*). See ALPHABET.

gamma globulin *Biochem.* A globulin present in blood plasma and containing antibodies effective against certain pathogenic microorganisms.

gamma rays *Physics* A type of electromagnetic radiation of great penetrating power.

gam·mer (gam′ər) *n.* An old woman: now humorous or contemptuous. Compare GAFFER. [Alter. of GODMOTHER]

gam·mon (gam′ən) *n.* In backgammon, a double victory, in which one player removes all his pieces before the other player removes any. **— v.t.** To obtain a gammon over. [? ME *gamen* game]

gamo- *combining form* **1.** *Biol.* Sexually joined. **2.** *Bot.* Fused; united. [< Gk. *gamos* marriage]

-gamous *combining form* Pertaining to marriage or union for reproduction: used in adjectives corresponding to nouns in *-gamy: polygamous.* [< Gk. *gamos* marriage + -OUS]

gam·ut (gam′ət) *n.* **1.** The whole range of anything: the *gamut* of emotions. **2.** *Music* **a** The entire range or compass of tones used in modern music. **b** The major diatonic scale. [< Med.L *gamma ut* < *gamma,* the first note of the early musical scale + *ut* (later, *do*). The names of the notes of the scale were taken from a medieval Latin hymn: *Ut* queant laxis *R*esonare fibris, *M*ira gestorum *F*amuli tuorum, Solve polluti *L*abii reatum, Sancte Iohannes.]

gam·y (gā′mē) *adj.* **gam·i·er, gam·i·est 1.** Having the flavor or odor of game, esp. game that has been kept raw until somewhat tainted. **2.** Full of pluck; disposed to fight.

-gamy *combining form* Marriage or union for reproduction: *polygamy.* [< Gk. *gamos* marriage]

gan·der (gan′dər) *n.* **1.** A male goose. **2.** *U.S. Slang* A look or glance: to take a *gander.* [OE *gandra*]

gang¹ (gang) *n.* **1.** A group of persons organized or associated together for disreputable or illegal purposes. **2.** A crew of persons who work together. **3.** *Informal* A group of persons associated together for some purpose. **4.** A set of similar tools or other devices designed to operate as a unit. **— v.t. 1.** To unite into or as into a gang. **2.** *Informal* To attack as a group. **— v.i. 3.** To form a gang. [OE *gangan* to go]

gang² (gang) *v.i. Scot.* To go or walk.

gan·gli·at·ed (gang′glē-ā′tid) *adj.* Possessing ganglia. Also **gan′gli·ate** (-it, -āt), **gan·gli·on·at·ed** (gang′glē-ən-ā′tid).

gan·gling (gang′gling) *adj.* Awkwardly tall and lanky. Also **gan′gly.** [Cf. dial. E *gangrel* a lanky person]

ganglio- *combining form* Ganglion. Also, before vowels, **gangli-** or **ganglion-.**

gan·gli·on (gang′glē-ən) *n. pl.* **·gli·ons** or **·gli·a** (glē-ə) **1.** *Physiol.* A collection of nerve cells, outside of the central nervous system. **2.** Any center of energy, activity, or strength. [< LL < Gk. *ganglion* tumor] **— gan·gli·on·ic** (gang′glē-on′ik) *adj.*

gang plank (gang′plangk′) *n.* A temporary bridge for passengers between a vessel and a wharf.

gan·grene (gang′grēn, gang-grēn′) *n. Pathol.* The rotting of tissue in the body, caused by a failure in the circulation of the blood, as from infection, etc. **— v.t. & v.i. ·grened, ·gren·ing** To cause gangrene in or become affected by gangrene. [< L < Gk. *gangraina*] **— gan′gre·nous** (-grə·nəs) *adj.*

gang·ster (gang′stər) *n.* A member of a criminal gang.

gang·way (*n.* gang′wā, *interj.* gang′wā′) *n.* **1.** A passage-

way through, into, or out of any enclosure. **2.** *Naut.* **a** A passage on a ship's upper deck. **b** An opening in a ship's side to give entrance to passengers or freight. **c** A gangplank. **— interj.** Get out of the way! [OE *gangweg*]

gan·net (gan′it) *n.* Any of several large sea birds related to the pelicans and herons. [OE *ganot*]

gan·oid (gan′oid) *adj.* **1.** Pertaining to a large division of fishes, including sturgeons, bowfins, etc. **2.** Having an enamellike appearance, as the scales of such fishes. **— n.** A ganoid fish. [< Gk. *ganos* brightness + -OID]

gant·let¹ (gônt′lit, gant′-) See GAUNTLET¹.

gant·let² (gônt′lit, gant′-) *n.* **1.** A former military punishment in which the offender ran between two lines of men armed with clubs, whips, etc., who struck him as he passed. **2.** An onslaught of difficulties or criticism from all sides. **— to run the gantlet 1.** To be punished by the gantlet. **2.** To be subjected to a fierce onslaught, as of criticism, difficulties, etc. Also spelled *gauntlet.* [Earlier *gantlope,* alter. of Sw. *gatlopp* a running down a lane]

gan·try (gan′trē) *n. pl.* **·tries 1.** A bridgelike framework for holding the rails of a traveling crane or for supporting railway signals. **2.** A gantry scaffold. **3.** A frame to support a barrel in a horizontal position. Also spelled *gauntry.* [< OF < L *canterius* beast of burden, framework]

gantry scaffold *Aerospace* A large mobile scaffolding used to assemble and service a large rocket on its launching pad.

gaol (jāl) *n. Brit.* Jail. [Var. of JAIL] **— gaol′er** *n.*

gap (gap) *n.* **1.** An opening or wide crack, as in a wall. **2.** A deep notch or ravine in a mountain ridge. **3.** A break in continuity; interruption. **4.** A difference, as in character, opinions, etc. **— v.t. gapped, gap·ping** To make or adjust a breach or opening in. [< ON *gap* gap, abyss]

gape (gāp, gap) *v.i.* **gaped, gap·ing 1.** To stare with or as with the mouth wide open. **2.** To open the mouth wide, as in yawning. **3.** To be or become open wide. **— n. 1.** The act of gaping. **2.** A wide opening; gap. **3.** *Zool.* The width of the fully opened mouth, as of birds, fishes, etc. [< ON *gapa*] **— gap′er** *n.*

gap·py (gap′ē) *adj.* **·pi·er, ·pi·est** Having gaps.

gar (gär) *n.* **1.** Any of several fresh-water fishes having a spearlike snout and elongate body. [Short for GARFISH]

ga·rage (gə-räzh, -räj′; *Brit.* gar′ij) *n.* A building in which motor vehicles are stored, serviced, or repaired. **— v.t. ·raged, ·rag·ing** To put or keep in a garage. [< F < *garer* to protect]

Gar·and rifle (gar′ənd, gə-rand′) *U.S. Mil.* The M-1 rifle. [after J. C. Garand, born 1888, U.S. inventor]

garb (gärb) *n.* **1.** Clothes; esp., apparel characteristic of some office, rank, etc. **2.** External appearance, form, or expression. **— v.t.** To clothe; dress. [< MF *garbe* gracefulness]

gar·bage (gär′bij) *n.* **1.** Refuse from a kitchen, etc., consisting of unwanted or unusable pieces of meat, vegetable matter, eggshells, etc. **2.** Anything worthless or offensive. [Prob. < AF. Cf. OF *garbe* sheaf of grain, animal fodder.]

gar·ble (gär′bəl) *v.t.* **·bled, ·bling 1.** To mix up or confuse (a story, facts, etc.) unintentionally. **2.** To change or distort the meaning of (facts, texts, etc.) with intent to mislead or misrepresent. **— n. 1.** The act of garbling. **2.** That which is garbled. [< Ital. < Arabic *gharbala* to sift]

gar·çon (går·sôn′) *n. pl.* **·çons** (-sôn′) *French* **1.** A boy or youth. **2.** A waiter. **3.** A male servant.

gar·den (gär′dən) *n.* **1.** A place for the cultivation of flowers, vegetables, or small plants. **2.** Any territory remarkable for the beauty of its vegetation. **3.** *Often pl.* A piece of ground, commonly used as a place of public resort. **— adj. 1.** Grown or capable of being grown in a garden. **2.** Ordinary; common. **— v.t. 1.** To cultivate as a garden. **— v.i. 2.** To till or work in a garden. [< AF *gardin*] **— gar′den·er** *n.* **— gar′den·ing** *n.*

gar·de·ni·a (gär-dē′nē-ə, -dēn′yə) *n.* Any of mainly tropical shrubs or trees with large, fragrant, yellow or white flowers. [after Alexander *Garden,* 1730–91, U.S. botanist]

Garden State Nickname of New Jersey.

gar·fish (gär′fish′) *n. pl.* **·fish** or **·fish·es** A gar. Also **gar′pike.** [OE *gar* spear + FISH]

Gar·gan·tu·a (gär-gan′chŏō·ə) The peace-loving giant of Rabelais' satirical romance *Gargantua* (1534), noted for his enormous appetite. **— Gar·gan′tu·an** *adj.*

gar·gle (gär′gəl) *v.* **·gled, ·gling** *v.i.* **1.** To rinse the throat with a liquid kept agitated by slowly expelling air through the liquid. **— v.t. 2.** To rinse (the throat and mouth) by gargling. **3.** To utter throatily as if gargling. **— n.** A liquid used for gargling. [< OF *gargouille* throat]

gar·goyle (gär′goil) *n.* A waterspout, usu. made in the form of a grotesque human or animal figure, projecting from the gutter of a building. [< OF *gargouille* throat]

gar·ish (gâr′ish) *adj.* Vulgarly showy or gaudy: Her new dress is very *garish*. [Cf. obs. *gaure* to stare] — **gar′ish·ly** *adv*. — **gar′ish·ness** *n*.

gar·land (gär′lənd) *n*. **1.** A wreath or rope of flowers, leaves, vines, etc. **2.** Anything resembling a garland. **3.** A collection of poems, bits of prose, etc. **4.** *Naut*. A ring of rope, wire, etc., lashed to a spar to aid in hoisting it. — *v.t.* To decorate with or make into a garland. [< OF *garlande*]

gar·lic (gär′lik) *n*. **1.** A hardy bulbous perennial with a compound bulb. **2.** One of the cloves of this perennial, used in cooking and medicine. [OE *gār* spear + *lēac* leek] — **gar′lick·y** *adj*.

gar·ment (gär′mənt) *n*. **1.** An article of clothing, esp. of outer clothing. **2.** *pl*. Clothes. **3.** Outer covering. — *v.t.* To clothe. [< OF *garnir* to garnish]

gar·ner (gär′nər) *v.t.* To gather or store as in a granary; accumulate. — *n*. **1.** A granary. **2.** Any storage place. [< OF < L *granum* grain]

gar·net (gär′nit) *n*. **1.** Any of a group of vitreous silicate minerals varying in color; esp., any of the deep red varieties, used as gems. **2.** A deep red color. [< OF < Med.L *granatum* < L, pomegranate]

gar·nish (gär′nish) *v.t.* **1.** To add something to by way of decoration; embellish. **2.** In cookery, to decorate (a dish) with flavorsome or colorful trimmings. **3.** *Law* To garnishee. — *n*. **1.** Something that garnishes food. **2.** An added decoration; embellishment. [< OF *garnir* to prepare]

gar·nish·ee (gär′nish·ē′) *Law v.t.* **·nish·eed**, **·nish·ee·ing** **1.** To attach (any debt or property in the hands of a third person that is due or belongs to a defendant) with notice that no return or disposal is to be made until a court judgment is issued. **2.** To issue a garnishment to. — *n*. A person who has been garnisheed.

gar·nish·ment (gär′nish·mənt) *n*. **1.** The act of garnishing. **2.** That which garnishes; embellishment. **3.** *Law* **a** A summons to appear in court, issued to one who is not a litigant in the case. **b** A notice to a person holding money or effects belonging to a defendant not to return or dispose of the money or effects pending court judgment.

gar·ni·ture (gär′ni·chər) *n*. Anything used to garnish.

gar·ret (gar′it) *n*. A room or set of rooms in an attic. [< OF *garir* to watch, defend]

gar·ri·son (gar′ə·sən) *n*. **1.** The military force stationed in a fort, town, etc. **2.** The place where such a force is stationed. — *v.t.* **1.** To place troops in, as a fort or town, for defense. **2.** To station (troops) in a fort, town, etc. **3.** To occupy as a garrison. [< OF *garir* to defend]

gar·rote (gə·rot′, -rōt′) *n*. **1.** A former Spanish method of execution with a cord or metal collar tightened by a screwlike device; also, the cord or collar used. **2.** Any similar method of strangulation. — *v.t.* **·rot·ed**, **·rot·ing** **1.** To execute with a garrote. **2.** To throttle in order to rob, silence, etc. Also **ga·rote′**, **ga·rotte′**. [< Sp. *garrote*]

gar·ru·lous (gar′ə·ləs, -yə-) *adj*. **1.** Given to continual or glib talking. **2.** Rambling and wordy. [< L *garrulus* talkative] — **gar′ru·lous·ly** *adv*. — **gar·ru·li·ty** (gə·rōō′lə·tē), **gar′ru·lous·ness** *n*.

gar·ter (gär′tər) *n*. A band worn around the leg or a tab attached to an undergarment to hold a stocking in place. — *v.t.* To support or fasten with a garter. [< AF < OF *garet* bend of the knee < Celtic]

Gar·ter (gär′tər) *n*. **1.** The distinctive badge of the **Order of the Garter**, the highest order of knighthood in Great Britain. **2.** The order itself.

garter snake Any of various small, harmless, viviparous, brightly striped snakes.

gas (gas) *n*. *pl*. **gas·es** or **gas·ses** **1.** A form of matter having extreme molecular mobility and capable of diffusing and expanding rapidly in all directions. **2.** A combustible mixture used for lighting or heating. **3.** A mixture used to produce anesthesia; laughing *gas*. **4.** A chemical or mixture of chemicals designed to stupefy. **5.** An explosive mixture of air and methane, etc., sometimes accumulated in coal mines. **6.** A noxious exhalation given off by improperly digested food in the stomach or intestines. **7.** *U.S. Informal* Gasoline. **8.** *Slang* Long-winded talking. **9.** *Slang* Something very exciting, exciting, etc. — *v.* **gassed**, **gas·sing**; he, she, it **gas·ses** or **gas·es** — *v.t.* **1.** To subject to or affect with gas. **2.** To fill or supply with gas. **3.** *U.S. Slang* To evoke a strong reaction, as of amusement or excitement, from: *His remark gassed them.* — *v.i.* **4.** To give off gas. **5.** *Slang* To talk excessively. [Coined by J. B. van Helmont, 1577–1644, Belgian chemist, either < Du. *geest* spirit or < L < Gk. *chaos* formless mass]

Gas·con (gas′kən) *adj*. Of or pertaining to Gascony or its assertedly boastful people. — *n*. A native of Gascony.

gas·e·ous (gas′ē·əs, -yəs) *adj*. **1.** Of, pertaining to, or resembling gas. **2.** Light and unsubstantial; superficial.

gas fitter One who fits and puts up gas fixtures.

gash (gash) *v.t.* To make a long, deep cut in. — *n*. A long, deep cut or flesh wound. [< OF *garser* to scratch]

gas·ket (gas′kit) *n*. **1.** *Mech*. A ring, disk or plate of packing to make a joint or closure watertight or gastight. **2.** *Naut*. A rope or cord used to confine furled sails to the yard or boom. [Cf. Ital. *gaschetta* end of rope]

gas·light (gas′līt′) *n*. Light produced by the burning of illuminating gas. Also **gas light**.

gas·man (gas′man′) *n*. *pl*. **·men** (-men′) A man employed to read gas meters and note the amount of gas used.

gas mask A protective mask with an air filter worn to prevent poisoning or irritation by noxious gases.

gas meter An apparatus for measuring the quantity of gas that passes through it.

gas·o·hol (gas′ə·hôl, -hol) *n*. A mixture of gasoline and alcohol, used as a motor fuel, esp. in automobiles.

gas·o·line (gas′ə·lēn, gas′ə·lēn′) *n*. *U.S.* A colorless, volatile, flammable liquid hydrocarbon, made by the distillation of crude petroleum and used chiefly as a fuel and as a solvent for fats. Also **gas′o·lene**.

gas·om·e·ter (gas·om′ə·tər) *n*. **1.** An apparatus for measuring gases. **2.** A reservoir for gas. — **gas·om′e·try** *n*.

gasp (gasp, gäsp) *v.i.* **1.** To take in the breath suddenly and sharply, as from fear. **2.** To have great longing or desire: with *for* or *after*. — *v.t.* **3.** To say or utter while gasping. — *n*. **1.** An act of gasping. **2.** An utterance made while gasping. [< ON *geispa* yawn]

gas station *U.S.* A filling station.

gas·sy (gas′ē) *adj*. **·si·er**, **·si·est** **1.** Filled with, containing, or causing the formation of gas. **2.** Resembling or suggestive of gas. **3.** *Informal* Very talkative.

gas·tric (gas′trik) *adj*. Of or pertaining to the stomach.

gastric juice *Biochem*. A fluid secreted by stomach glands, essential to digestion and containing several enzymes.

gastric ulcer *Pathol*. An ulcer formed on the stomach lining, often by excess secretion of gastric juice.

gas·tri·tis (gas·trī′tis) *n*. *Pathol*. Inflammation of the lining of the stomach. — **gas·trit·ic** (gas·trit′ik) *adj*.

gastro- *combining form* **1.** Stomach. **2.** Stomach and. Also **gastero-** or, before vowels, **gastr-**. [< Gk. *gastēr* stomach]

gas·tro·in·tes·ti·nal (gas′trō·in·tes′tə·nəl) *adj*. *Anat*. Of or pertaining to the stomach and intestines.

gas·tro·nome (gas′trə·nōm) *n*. A gourmet. Also **gas·tron′o·mer** (gas·tron′ə·mər), **gas·tron′o·mist**.

gas·tro·nom·ic (gas′trə·nom′ik) *adj*. Of or pertaining to gastronomes or gastronomy. Also **gas′tro·nom′i·cal**.

gas·tron·o·my (gas·tron′ə·mē) *n*. The art of good eating; epicurism. [< F < Gk. < *gastēr* stomach + *nomos* law]

gas·tro·pod (gas′trə·pod) *n*. One of a large class of aquatic and terrestrial mollusks, including snails, slugs, limpets, etc., usu. having a univalve, spiral shell and a muscular creeping organ. — *adj*. Of or pertaining to this class. [< NL < Gk. *gastēr* stomach + *pous, podos* foot] — **gas·trop′o·dan** (gas·trop′ə·dan) *adj*. & *n*. — **gas·trop′o·dous** *adj*.

gas·tru·la (gas′trōō·lə) *n*. *pl*. **·lae** (-lē) *Biol*. An early embryonic form, consisting of a two-layered sac enclosing a central cavity opening to the outside at one end. [< NL, dim. of Gk. *gastēr* stomach] — **gas′tru·lar** *adj*.

gas turbine A turbine engine in which liquid or gaseous fuel is burned and the gases sent through a rotor unit.

gas·works (gas′wûrks′) *n*. *pl*. **·works** An establishment where illuminating gas or heating gas is made.

gat (gat) *n*. *Slang* A pistol. [Short for GATLING GUN]

gate (gāt) *n*. **1.** A movable barrier, commonly swinging on hinges, that closes or opens a passage through a wall, fence, etc. **2.** An opening for exit or entrance through a wall or fence. **3.** The structure on either side of such an opening. **4.** Anything that gives access: the *gate* to success. **5.** A mountain gap or other natural passageway. **6.** A protective barrier capable of being raised or lowered, as at a railroad crossing. **7.** A structure or valvelike device for controlling the supply of water, oil, gas, etc. **8.** The total paid attendance at a sports event, theatrical presentation, etc.; also, the money collected. — **to get the gate** *Slang* To be sent away or be rejected. — **to give the gate to** *Slang* To dismiss, reject, or get rid of. [OE *gatu*, pl. of *geat* opening]

gate·crash·er (gāt′krash′ər) *n*. *Informal* One who gains admittance without paying or being invited.

gate-leg table (gāt′leg′) A table with swinging legs that support drop leaves and fold against the frame when the leaves are let down. Also **gate-legged table** (-legd′).

gate·way (gāt′wā′) *n*. **1.** An entrance that is or may be closed with a gate. **2.** That which is regarded as a means of entry or exit: the *gateway* to the Orient.

gath·er (gath′ər) *v.t.* **1.** To bring together into one place or group. **2.** To bring together from various places, sources, etc. **3.** To harvest or pick, as crops, fruit, etc. **4.** To accumulate or gain more and more of: The storm *gathered* force. **5.** To clasp or enfold. **6.** To wrinkle (the brow). **7.** To draw into folds, as cloth on a thread. **8.** To become aware of; infer. **9.** To summon up or muster, as one's energies. — *v.i.* **10.** To come together or assemble. **11.**

To increase by accumulation. **12.** To become wrinkled or creased, as the brow. **13.** To come to a head, as a boil. — *n. Usu. pl.* A pleat or fold in cloth, held by a thread passing through the folds. [OE *gadrian*] — **gath′er·er** *n.*
gath·er·ing (gath′ər·ing) *n.* **1.** The action of one who or that which gathers. **2.** That which is gathered. **3.** An assemblage of people; group. **4.** A series of gathers in cloth, etc. **5.** An abscess or boil. **6.** In bookbinding, a collection of printed sheets in proper order.
gauche (gōsh) *adj.* Awkward; clumsy; boorish. [< F, left-handed]
gauche·rie (gōsh·rē′) *n.* **1.** An awkward or tactless action, statement, etc. **2.** Clumsiness; tactlessness. [< F]
Gau·cho (gou′chō) *n. pl.* **·chos** A cowboy of the South American pampas. [< Sp.]
gaud·y (gô′dē) *adj.* **gaud·i·er, gaud·i·est** Tastelessly brilliant or showy; garish. — **gaud′i·ly** *adv.* — **gaud′i·ness** *n.*
gauge (gāj) *v.t.* **gauged, gaug·ing 1.** To determine the dimensions, amount, force, etc., of. **2.** To determine the contents or capacity of, as a cask. **3.** To estimate, appraise, or judge. **4.** To make conform to a standard measurement. — *n.* **1.** A standard measurement, dimension, or quantity. **2.** A means or standard of comparing, estimating, or judging; criterion. **3.** Any of various instruments or devices for measuring something. **4.** The distance between rails in a railway. **5.** The distance between wheel treads. **6.** The diameter of the bore of a gun. Also spelled *gage.* [< OF *gauger* to measure]
gaug·er (gā′jər) *n.* One who or that which gauges.
Gaul (gôl) **1.** An ancient name for the territory that is roughly the area of modern France. **2.** A native of ancient Gaul. **3.** A Frenchman.
Gaul·ish (gô′lish) *adj.* Of ancient Gaul, its people, or their Celtic language. — *n.* The extinct Celtic language of Gaul.
gaunt (gônt) *adj.* **1.** Emaciated and hollow-eyed, as from hunger, illness, or age; haggard. **2.** Desolate or gloomy in appearance: a *gaunt* region. [? < OF *gent* elegant] — **gaunt′ly** *adv.* — **gaunt′ness** *n.*
gaunt·let[1] (gônt′lit, gänt′-) *n.* **1.** In medieval armor, a glove covered with metal plates to protect the hand. **2.** Any glove with a long, often flaring extension over the wrist. Sometimes spelled **gantlet.** — **to take up the gauntlet** To accept a challenge. — **to throw** (or **fling**) **down the gauntlet** To challenge to combat. [< OF *gant* mitten]
gaunt·let[2] (gônt′lit, gänt′-) See GANTLET[2].
gaun·try (gôn′trē) See GANTRY.
gauss (gous) *n. Physics* The electromagnetic unit of magnetic induction, equal to 1 maxwell per square centimeter. [after K. F. *Gauss*]
gauze (gôz) *n.* **1.** A lightweight, transparent fabric with an open weave, made of silk, cotton, etc. **2.** Any thin, open-mesh material: wire *gauze.* **3.** A mist or light fog. — *adj.* Resembling or made of gauze. [< MF *gaze,* appar. after *Gaza,* where originally made] — **gauz′y** *adj.* — **gauz′i·ness** *n.*
gave (gāv) Past tense of GIVE.
gav·el (gav′əl) *n.* A mallet used by a presiding officer to call for order or attention. [< OF (Norman) *keville* pin]
ga·vi·al (gā′vē·əl) *n.* A large crocodile of India, having long, slender jaws. [< F < Hind. *ghaṛiyal*]
ga·votte (gə·vot′) *n.* **1.** A dance of French origin, popular in the 17th and 18th centuries and resembling a quick-moving minuet. **2.** Music for this dance, written in duple meter. Also **ga·vot′.** [< F < Provençal *gavoto* Alpine dance]
gawk (gôk) *Informal v.i.* **1.** To stare stupidly; gape. **2.** To move about or behave awkwardly. — *n.* An ungainly, stupid individual. [Cf. dial. E *gawk* lefthanded]
gawk·y (gô′kē) *adj.* **gawk·i·er, gawk·i·est** Awkward or clumsy; ungainly. — *n. pl.* **gawk·ies** An awkward or ungainly person. — **gawk′i·ly** *adv.* — **gawk′i·ness** *n.*
gay (gā) *adj.* **1.** Happy and carefree; merry. **2.** Brightly colorful or ornamental. **3.** Jaunty; sporty. **4.** Full of or given to lighthearted pleasure. **5.** Rakish; libertine. **6.** *Slang* Homosexual. — *n. Slang* A homosexual. [< OF < Gmc.] — **gay′ness** *n.*
gay·e·ty (gā′ə·tē) See GAIETY.
Gay Liberation An organized movement advocating equal rights for homosexuals.
gay·ly (gā′lē) See GAILY.
gaze (gāz) *v.i.* **gazed, gaz·ing** To look steadily or fixedly at something, as in wonder or admiration; stare. — *n.* A steady or fixed look. [ME *gasen* < Scand.] — **gaz′er** *n.*
ga·zelle (gə·zel′) *n.* A small, delicately formed antelope of northern Africa and Arabia, with curved horns and large eyes. [< OF < Arabic *ghazāl*]
ga·zette (gə·zet′) *n.* **1.** A newspaper or similar periodical. **2.** An official publication, as of a government or society; esp.,

one of several publications issued by the British government listing government appointments, public bankruptcies, etc. — *v.t.* **zet·ted, ·zet·ting** To publish or announce in a gazette. [< F < Ital. < dial. Ital. (Venetian) *gazeta* coin]
gaz·et·teer (gaz′ə·tir′) *n.* **1.** A work or section of a work listing countries, cities, rivers, etc., together with their location, size, etc. **2.** A writer for or publisher of a gazette.
gear (gir) *n.* **1.** *Mech.* **a** A mechanical assembly of interacting parts that serves to transmit motion or to change the rate or direction of motion. **b** A related group of parts that work together for a special purpose: steering *gear.* **2.** *Naut.* **a** The ropes, blocks, etc., used in working a spar or sail. **b** A ship's rigging or equipment. **c** The personal baggage or effects of a sailor. **3.** Any equipment, as clothing, tools, etc., used for a special task: a plumber's *gear.* — *v.t.* **1.** *Mech.* **a** To put into gear. **b** To equip with gears. **c** To connect by means of gears. **2.** To regulate so as to match or suit something else: to *gear* production to demand. **3.** To put gear on; dress. — *v.i.* **4.** To come into or be in gear; to mesh. — **out of gear 1.** Not engaged or connected, as one gear with another or with a motor. **2.** Not in working order or not in good condition. [< ON *gervi* equipment]

GEARS

A Spur. B Spur and crown. C Bevel. D Square. E Annular. F Elliptical.

gear·ing (gir′ing) *n.* **1.** *Mech.* Any system of gears or parts that transmit power or motion. **2.** *Naut.* Rope and tackle.
gear·shift (gir′shift′) *n. Mech.* A device for engaging or disengaging the gears in a power-transmission system.
gear·wheel (gir′hwēl′) *n. Mech.* A cogwheel. Also **gear wheel.**
geck·o (gek′ō) *n. pl.* **·os** or **·oes** Any of a family of small lizards having toes with adhesive disks. [< Malay *gēkoq*]
gee[1] (jē) *interj.* A cry used to guide horses, cattle, etc., to the right or (usu. with *up*) to urge them to move forward or faster. — *v.t. & v.i.* **geed, gee·ing 1.** To turn to the right. **2.** To move onward or faster: usu. with *up.* **3.** To evade. Opposed to *haw:* also spelled *jee.* [Origin uncertain]
gee[2] (jē) *interj.* An exclamation expressing mild surprise, sympathy, etc.: a euphemism for *Jesus.* Also **gee whiz.**
gee·zer (gē′zər) *n. Slang* A fellow; guy; esp., an old man.
Ge·hen·na (gi·hen′ə) *n.* **1.** A place of torment. **2.** In the New Testament, hell. [< LL < Gk. < Hebrew *ge hinnom* valley of Hinnom near Jerusalem where refuse was thrown]
Gei·ger counter (gī′gər) *Physics* An instrument for detecting ionizing radiation by means of a sealed tube containing a gas that when struck by ionizing particles conducts an electrical impulse between two electrodes connected to a suitable counting device. Also **Geiger-Müller counter** (mü′lər), **geiger counter.** [after Hans *Geiger* and W. *Müller,* 20th c. German physicists]
gei·sha (gā′shə) *n. pl.* **·sha** or **·shas** A Japanese girl furnishing entertainment by singing, dancing, etc. [< Japanese]
gel (jel) *n. Chem.* A colloidal dispersion of a solid in a liquid, typically having a jellylike consistency, as gelatin, mucilage, uncooked egg white, etc. — *v.t. & v.i.* **gelled, gel·ling** To change into a gel; jellify. [Short for GELATIN]
gel·a·tin (jel′ə·tin) *n.* **1.** An almost tasteless, odorless, dried protein soluble in water and extracted by boiling the bones, tendons, skins, etc., of animals, used in food and drug preparation and in the manufacture of photographic film, plastics, etc. **2.** A jelly made from gelatin. Also **gel′a·tine** (-tin, -tēn). [< F *gélatine,* orig. a soup made from fish]
ge·lat·i·nate (ji·lat′ə·nāt) *v.t. & v.i.* **·nat·ed, ·nat·ing** To change into gelatin or jelly. — **ge·lat′i·na′tion** *n.*
ge·lat·i·nize (ji·lat′ə·nīz) *v.* **·nized, ·niz·ing** *v.t.* **1.** To gelatinate. **2.** To treat or coat with gelatin. — *v.i.* **3.** To be changed into gelatin or jelly. — **ge·lat′i·ni·za′tion** *n.*
ge·lat·i·nous (ji·lat′ə·nəs) *adj.* **1.** Having the nature of or resembling gelatin. **2.** Of or consisting of gelatin. — **ge·lat′i·nous·ly** *adv.* — **ge·lat′i·nous·ness** *n.*
geld (geld) *v.t.* **geld·ed** or **gelt, geld·ing 1.** To castrate or spay. **2.** To deprive of an essential part. [< ON *gelda*]
geld·ing (gel′ding) *n.* A castrated animal, esp. a horse.
gel·id (jel′id) *adj.* Very cold; icy; frozen. [< L *gelidus*] — **ge·lid·i·ty** (ji·lid′ə·tē) *n.* — **gel′id·ly** *adv.*
gem (jem) *n.* **1.** A cut and polished precious or semiprecious stone; jewel. **2.** One who or that which is treasured for having perfect or nearly perfect qualities. **3.** A kind of small, light cake. — *v.t.* **gemmed, gem·ming** To decorate or set with or as with gems. [OE < L *gemma* jewel]

gem·i·nate (jem′ə-nāt) *v.t. & v.i.* **·nat·ed, ·nat·ing** To double or become doubled; form into an identical pair. — *adj.* Formed into or appearing as a pair. [< L *geminus* twin]

Gem·i·ni (jem′ə-nī) *n.pl.* A constellation, the Twins; also, the third sign of the zodiac. See ZODIAC.

gem·ma (jem′ə) *n. pl.* **gem·mae** (jem′ē) *Biol.* **1.** A bud. **2.** A part of a plant or animal that grows outward, detaches, and forms a new individual. Also **gem/mule** (-yōol). [< L]

gem·mate (jem′āt) *adj. Biol.* Bearing or reproducing by gemmae. — *v.i.* **·mat·ed, ·mat·ing** To form or reproduce by gemmae. — **gem·ma′tion** *n.*

gems·bok (gemz′bok) *n. pl.* **·bok** or **·boks** A South African antelope having long, sharp horns and a tufted tail. [< Afrikaans < G *gemse* chamois + *bock* a buck]

Gem State Nickname of Idaho.

gem·stone (jem′stōn′) *n.* A precious or semiprecious stone, esp. before it is cut and polished for use as a gem.

-gen *suffix of nouns* **1.** *Chem.* That which produces: *oxygen.* **2.** *Biol.* That which is produced: *antigen.* [< F < Gk. *gen-*, stem of *gignesthai* to be born, become]

gen·darme (zhän′därm, *Fr.* zhän·därm′) *n. pl.* **·darmes** (-därmz, *Fr.* -därm′) One of a corps of armed police, esp. in France. [< F < *gens d′armes* men-at-arms]

gen·der (jen′dər) *n.* **1.** *Gram.* **a** One of two or more categories of words (esp. nouns and pronouns) or affixes based upon differences of sex or absence of sex or sometimes upon other distinctions (as of animateness or inanimateness), each category having distinctive forms for the words or affixes themselves or for the words modifying them. **b** Such categories collectively, or a system of such categories. **c** The distinctive form or forms used for such categories. **2.** *Informal* The quality of being of the male or female sex: a humorous use. [< OF < L *genus, -eris*]

gene (jēn) *n. Biol.* One of the complex protein molecules associated with the chromosomes of reproductive cells and acting, as a unit or in various biochemically determined combinations, in the transmission of specific hereditary characters from parents to offspring. [< Gk. *genea* breed, kind]

ge·ne·al·o·gist (jē′nē·al′ə·jist, jen′ē-, -nē·ol′-) *n.* One who traces genealogies or who is a student of genealogy.

ge·ne·al·o·gy (jē′nē·al′ə·jē, jen′ē-, -nē·ol′-) *n. pl.* **·gies 1.** A record or table showing the descent of an individual or family from a certain ancestor. **2.** Descent in a direct line from a progenitor; pedigree. **3.** The study of pedigrees. [< Gk. *genea* race + -LOGY] — **ge·ne·a·log·i·cal** (jē′nē·ə·loj′i·kəl, jen′ē-) or **·log·ic** *adj.* — **ge′ne·a·log′i·cal·ly** *adv.*

gen·er·a (jen′ər·ə) Plural of GENUS. [< L]

gen·er·al (jen′ər·əl) *adj.* **1.** Pertaining to, including, or affecting all or the whole; not particular. **2.** Common to or current among the majority: the *general* opinion. **3.** Not restricted in application: a *general* principle. **4.** Not limited to a special class; miscellaneous: a *general* cargo. **5.** Not detailed or precise: a *general* idea. **6.** Usual or customary. **7.** Dealing with all branches of a business or pursuit; not specialized: a *general* practitioner. **8.** Superior in rank: a second element in some titles: attorney *general.* **9.** *Med.* Relating to or affecting the entire body. — *n.* **1.** *Mil.* **a** In the U.S. Army, Air Force, or Marine Corps, a high-ranking officer. **b** In the Canadian Army, an officer ranking just below Field Marshal. **c** An equivalent officer in other armies. Abbr. *Gen.* See tables at GRADE. **2.** A general officer: a shortened form. **3.** The head of a religious order. **4.** A general statement, fact, or principle. — **in general 1.** Without going into detail. **2.** All things considered. **3.** Usually; commonly. [< OF < L *generalis* of a race or king < *genus, generis* kind]

gen·er·al·cy (jen′ər·əl·sē) *n. pl.* **·cies 1.** The rank or office of a general. **2.** The time during which it is held.

general delivery *U.S.* **1.** A building or department of the post office in which an addressee′s mail is kept until called for. **2.** Mail directed to this department.

general election 1. An election in which all the people vote. **2.** An election held to make a final choice for office among candidates selected in a preliminary election.

gen·er·al·is·si·mo (jen′ər·ə·lis′i·mō) *n. pl.* **·mos** In certain countries, the supreme military commander. [< Ital.]

gen·er·al·i·ty (jen′ə·ral′ə·tē) *n. pl.* **·ties 1.** The state or quality of being general. **2.** Something lacking detail or precision, as a statement or idea: a speech filled with *generalities.* **3.** The greater number of a group; mass.

gen·er·al·i·za·tion (jen′ər·əl·i·zā′shən, -ī·zā′-) *n.* **1.** The act of generalizing. **2.** Something, as a broad, overall statement or conclusion, arrived at by generalizing.

gen·er·al·ize (jen′ər·əl·īz′) *v.* **·ized, ·iz·ing** *v.t.* **1.** To make general; as: **a** To make broad in application. **b** To avoid making detailed. **c** To cause to be widespread. **2.** To derive a broad conclusion, principle, etc., from (particular instances, facts, etc.). — *v.i.* **3.** To write or speak without going into details, etc. Also *Brit.* **gen′er·al·ise′.**

gen·er·al·ly (jen′ər·əl·ē) *adv.* **1.** For the most part; ordinarily. **2.** Without going into specific details or instances: *generally* speaking. **3.** Commonly: *generally* believed.

general officer *Mil.* Any officer ranking above a colonel, as a general, lieutenant general, major general, etc.

General of the Air Force The highest-ranking officer of the U.S. Air Force. See table at GRADE.

General of the Army The highest rank in the U.S. Army. See table at GRADE.

general paresis *Pathol.* Chronic paralysis of syphilitic origin, characterized by degeneration of body and brain tissue, and progressive dementia. Also **general paralysis.**

general practitioner A physician whose practice is not limited to a medical specialty.

gen·er·al·ship (jen′ər·əl·ship) *n.* **1.** A general′s office or rank; generalcy. **2.** A general′s military skill or management. **3.** Management or leadership of any sort.

general staff 1. A body of officers who direct the military policy and strategy of a national state. **2.** *Mil.* A group of officers who assist the commander in planning, coordination, and supervision of operations.

gen·er·ate (jen′ə·rāt) *v.t.* **·at·ed, ·at·ing 1.** To produce or cause to be; bring into being. **2.** To beget; procreate. **3.** *Geom.* To trace out by motion: A moving point *generates* a line. [< L *generatus,* pp. of *generare* to generate]

gen·er·a·tion (jen′ə·rā′shən) *n.* **1.** The process of begetting offspring. **2.** A successive step or degree in natural descent. **3.** The average period between any two such successive steps, about 30 years among human beings. **4.** Any group of individuals born at about the same time. **5.** The act or process of generating or being generated.

gen·er·a·tive (jen′ə·rā′tiv) *adj.* **1.** Of or pertaining to generation. **2.** Having the power to produce or originate.

gen·er·a·tor (jen′ə·rā′tər) *n.* **1.** One who or that which generates. **2.** *Chem.* An apparatus designed to generate a gas. **3.** Any of a class of machines for the conversion of mechanical energy into electrical energy.

gen·er·a·trix (jen′ə·rā′triks) *n. pl.* **gen·er·a·tri·ces** (jen′ər·ə·trī′sēz) **1.** *Geom.* A line, point, or figure that generates another figure by its motion. **2.** A female that generates.

ge·ner·ic (ji·ner′ik) *adj.* **1.** Pertaining to a genus or class of related things. **2.** Applicable to every member of a class or genus. **3.** Having a wide, general application. Also **ge·ner′·i·cal.** [< L *genus, -eris* race, kind + -IC]

gen·er·os·i·ty (jen′ə·ros′ə·tē) *n. pl.* **·ties 1.** The quality of being generous. **2.** The quality of being free of pettiness; magnanimity. **3.** A generous act.

gen·er·ous (jen′ər·əs) *adj.* **1.** Marked by or showing great liberality; munificent. **2.** Having gracious or noble qualities: a *generous* nature. **3.** Abundant and overflowing: a *generous* serving. **4.** Stimulating or strong, as wine. **5.** Fertile: *generous* soil. [< F < L *generosus* of noble birth < *genus* race] — **gen′er·ous·ly** *adv.* — **gen′er·ous·ness** *n.*

gen·e·sis (jen′ə·sis) *n. pl.* **·ses** (-sēz) **1.** The act or mode of originating. **2.** Origin. [< L < Gk. *genēsis* origin]

Gen·e·sis (jen′ə·sis) The first book of the Old Testament.

-genesis *combining form* Genesis; evolution: *biogenesis.*

gen·et¹ (jen′it, jə·net′) *n.* A small carnivore related to the civet. Also **ge·nette′.** [< F < Sp. < Arabic *jarnait* genet]

gen·et² (jen′it) *n.* A jennet.

ge·net·ic (jə·net′ik) *adj.* **1.** Of, pertaining to, or based on genetics. **2.** Of, or pertaining to the origin or development of something. Also **ge·net′i·cal.** [< GENESIS; formed on analogy with *synthetic,* etc.] — **ge·net′i·cal·ly** *adv.*

(About 22 inches long; tail about 18 inches)

GENET¹

genetic code The molecular makeup of the chromosomes of cells that determines inherited characteristics, deoxyribonucleic acid being the code-bearing constituent.

ge·net·ics (jə·net′iks) *n.pl.* **1.** (*construed as sing.*) The science dealing with the interaction of the genes in producing similarities and differences between individuals related by descent. **2.** The inherited characteristics of an organism. — **ge·net′i·cist** (-ə·sist) *n.*

Geneva Convention An international agreement signed at Geneva in 1864 governing the war-time treatment of prisoners of war and of the sick and the wounded.

gen·ial (jēn′yəl, jē′nē·al) *adj.* **1.** Kindly, pleasant, or cordial in disposition or manner. **2.** Imparting warmth, comfort, or life. [< L *genius* tutelary spirit] — **ge·ni·al·i·ty** (jē′nē·al′ə·tē) *n.* — **gen′ial·ly** *adv.*

-genic *combining form* Related to generation or production: *biogenic.* [< -GEN + -IC]

ge·nie (jē′nē) See JINNI.

ge·ni·i (jē′nē·ī) Plural of GENIUS (def. 4).

gen·i·tal (jen′ə·təl) *adj.* Of or pertaining to the reproductive organs or the process of reproduction. [< L *genitus,* pp. of *gignere* to beget]

gen·i·tals (jen′ə·təlz) *n.pl.* The external sexual organs. Also **gen·i·ta·li·a** (jen′ə·tā′lē·ə, -tāl′yə).

gen·i·tive (jen′ə·tiv) *adj.* **1.** Indicating source, origin, possession, or the like. **2.** *Gram.* Pertaining to a case in Latin,

Greek, etc., corresponding in part to the English possessive. — *n. Gram.* **1.** The genitive case. **2.** A word in this case. [< L *gignere* to beget] — **gen·i·ti·val** (-tī/vəl) *adj.* — **gen·i·ti·val·ly** *adv.*

genito- *combining form* Genital. [< L *genitus*, pp. of *gignere* to beget]

gen·i·to·u·ri·nar·y (jen/ə·tō·yŏŏr/ə·ner/ē) *adj. Anat.* Of or pertaining to the genital and the urinary organs.

gen·ius (jēn/yəs) *n. pl.* **gen·ius·es** for *defs 1, 2, 3, & 5;* **ge·ni·i** (jē/nē·ī) *for def. 4.* **1.** Extraordinary intelligence surpassing that of most intellectually superior individuals; also, one who possesses such intelligence. **2.** An outstanding gift for some specialized activity; also, one who possesses such a gift. **3.** The essential spirit or distinguishing characteristics of a particular individual, people, era, etc. **4.** In ancient mythology, a supernatural being appointed to guide a person throughout life. **5.** A person who exerts a strong influence over another. [< L *gen-*, stem of *gignere* to beget]

gen·o·cide (jen/ə·sīd) *n.* The systematic extermination or destruction of an entire people or national group. [< Gk. *genos* race, tribe + -CIDE] — **gen/o·ci/dal** *adj.*

Gen·o·ese (jen/ō·ēz/, -ēs/) *adj.* Of or pertaining to Genoa. — *n. pl.* **·ese** A native or citizen of Genoa.

gen·o·type (jen/ə·tīp) *n. Biol.* **1.** The genetic constitution of an organism. **2.** A group of organisms with the same genetic constitution. **3.** A type species. — **gen·o·typ·ic** (jen/ə·tip/ik) or **·i·cal** *adj.* — **gen/o·typ/i·cal·ly** *adv.*

-genous *suffix of adjectives* **1.** Generating; yielding. **2.** Produced or generated by.

gen·re (zhän/rə, *Fr.* zhän/r') *n.* **1.** A particular sort, kind, or category; esp., a category of art or literature characterized by a certain form, style, or subject matter. **2.** A class of painting or other art depicting everyday life. — *adj.* Of or pertaining to genre. [< F < L *genus, -eris* race, kind]

gens (jenz) *n. pl.* **gen·tes** (jen/tēz) **1.** *Anthropol.* In primitive society, a body of blood kindred having a common descent traced through the male line. **2.** In ancient Rome, a clan descended through the male line. [< L]

gent (jent) *n. Slang* A gentleman. [Short for GENTLEMAN]

gen·teel (jen·tēl/) *adj.* **1.** Well-bred or refined; elegant; polite. **2.** Pertaining or appropriate to well-bred persons. **3.** Stylish or fashionable. ◆ This word is now used chiefly in a derogatory or humorous sense. [< MF *gentil*] — **gen·teel/ly** *adv.* — **gen·teel/ness** *n.*

gen·tian (jen/shən) *n.* An annual or perennial herb with showy blue, red, yellow, or white flowers. [< L *gentiana*, appar. after *Gentius*, an Illyrian king]

gen·tian·el·la (jen/shən·el/ə) *n.* **1.** A European alpine gentian having blue flowers. **2.** A bright blue color. [< NL, dim. of L *gentiana.* See GENTIAN.]

gentian violet *Chem.* A purple dye used as an antiseptic.

gen·tile (jen/tīl, -til; *for adj. def. 2* -tīl) *adj.* **1.** Of or pertaining to a gens, tribe, or people. **2.** Of or pertaining to Gentiles. [< L LL *gentilis* foreign]

Gen·tile (jen/tīl) *n.* **1.** Among Jews, one not a Jew. **2.** Among Christians, a heathen or pagan. **3.** Among Mormons, one not a Mormon. — *adj.* Of, pertaining to, or being a Gentile.

gen·til·i·ty (jen·til/ə·tē) *n. pl.* **·ties** **1.** The quality of being genteel; refinement: now often used ironically. **2.** Gentle birth; good extraction. **3.** Well-born or well-bred persons collectively. [< OF < L *gentilis* of good birth]

gen·tle (jen/təl) *adj.* **·tler** (-tlər), **·tlest** (-tlist) **1.** Mild and amiable in nature or disposition. **2.** Not harsh, rough, or loud; mild. **3.** Not steep or abrupt; gradual: a *gentle* ascent. **4.** Easily managed; docile. **5.** Of good family and breeding. **6.** Like or befitting one of good family; polite. **7.** *Meteorol.* Designating a moderate breeze. — *v.t.* **·tled, ·tling** To make easy to control; tame. — *n.* A bluebottle larva used as fish bait. [< OF < L *gentilis* of good birth > *gens, gentis* race, clan] — **gen/tly** (-tlē) *adv.* — **gen/tle·ness** *n.*

gen·tle·folk (jen/təl·fōk/) *n.pl.* Persons of good family and good breeding. Also **gen/tle·folks/**.

gen·tle·man (jen/təl·mən) *n. pl.* **·men** (-mən) **1.** A man of good birth and social position. **2.** A courteous, considerate man. **3.** Any man: in the plural, used as a form of address.

gen·tle·man-at-arms (jen/təl·mən·ət·ärmz/) *n. pl.* **·men** (-mən) *Brit.* One of forty gentlemen who attend the sovereign on various state and solemn occasions.

gen·tle·man-com·mon·er (jen/təl·mən·kom/ən·ər) *n. pl.* **gen·tle·men-com·mon·ers** (jen/təl·mən·kom/ən·ərz) *Brit.* Formerly, a commoner at Oxford and Cambridge Universities, enjoying special privileges.

gen·tle·man-farm·er (jen/təl·mən·fär/mər) *n.* One who owns a farm but hires others to work it.

gentleman in waiting A gentleman of a royal household staff, appointed to attend the sovereign or his son.

gen·tle·man·ly (jen/təl·mən·lē) *adj.* Pertaining to or be-

---

fitting a gentleman; courteous. Also **gen/tle·man·like/** (-līk/).

gentleman of fortune **1.** An adventurer or gambler. **2.** Formerly, a pirate.

gentleman of the road **1.** A highwayman. **2.** *U.S.* A hobo.

gen·tle·man's agreement (jen/təl·mənz) An understanding about something to be done, arrived at by informal mutual agreement and guaranteed solely by the pledged word of the parties involved. Also **gentlemen's agreement**.

gen·tle·man's gentleman (jen/təl·mənz) A valet.

gentle sex Women collectively. Also **gentler sex**.

gen·tle·wom·an (jen/təl·wŏŏm/ən) *n. pl.* **·wom·en** (-wim/in) **1.** A woman of good family or superior social position; lady. **2.** A gracious, well-mannered woman.

gen·try (jen/trē) *n.* **1.** People of good family or superior social background; in England, the upper ranks of the middle class. **2.** Individuals of a particular area, profession, etc.: the local *gentry*: now chiefly a patronizing or humorous term. [< OF *genterise* < *gentil* gentle]

ge·nu (jē/nōō, -nyōō) *n. pl.* **gen·u·a** (jen/yōō·ə) *Anat.* **1.** The knee. **2.** A kneelike structure or part. [< L]

gen·u·flect (jen/yə·flekt) *v.i.* To bend the knee, as in worship. [< Med.L < L *genu* knee + *flectere* to bend] — **gen/u·flec/tion** or **gen/u·flex/ion** *n.*

gen·u·ine (jen/yŏŏ·in) *adj.* **1.** Being actually of the origin, authorship, or character claimed. **2.** Not spurious or counterfeit. **3.** Not affected or hypocritical; sincere. **4.** Being of the original or true stock: a *genuine* Indian. [< L *genuinus* innate] — **gen/u·ine·ly** *adv.* — **gen/u·ine·ness** *n.*

ge·nus (jē/nəs) *n. pl.* **gen·e·ra** (jen/ər·ə) or, less commonly, **ge·nus·es** **1.** *Biol.* A grouping or category of plants and animals ranking next above the species and next below the family or subfamily. **2.** *Logic* A class of things divisible into two or more subordinate classes or species. **3.** A particular sort, kind, or class. [< L, race, kind]

-geny *combining form* Mode of production of; generation or development of: *anthropogeny*. [< F < L < Gk. *gen-*, stem of *gignesthai* to become]

geo- *combining form* Earth; ground; soil.

ge·o·cen·tric (jē/ō·sen/trik) *adj.* **1.** Calculated or viewed with relation to the earth's center. **2.** Formulated on the assumption that the earth is the center of the universe. Also **ge/o·cen/tri·cal** *adj.* — **ge/o·cen/tri·cal·ly** *adv.*

ge·o·chem·is·try (jē/ō·kem/is·trē) *n.* A specialized branch of chemistry dealing with the chemical composition of the earth's crust. — **ge/o·chem/i·cal** *adj.* — **ge/o·chem/ist** *n.*

ge·ode (jē/ōd) *n. Geol.* **1.** A rock, usually globular, having a cavity lined with crystals. **2.** The cavity in such a rock. [< F *géode* < L *geodes*, a precious stone < Gk. *geōdēs* earthy] — **ge·od·ic** (jē·od/ik) *adj.*

ge·o·des·ic (jē/ə·des/ik) *adj.* **1.** Of or pertaining to the geometry of geodesic lines or curved surfaces. **2.** Geodetic. Also **ge/o·des/i·cal.** — *n.* A geodesic line.

geodesic dome *Archit.* A light and strong hemispherical dome made of prefabricated polyhedral or triangular lattice nodules and covered with a thin, strong material.

geodesic line *Math.* The shortest line connecting two points on a given, esp. a curved, surface.

ge·od·e·sist (jē·od/ə·sist) *n.* One who specializes in geodesy.

ge·od·e·sy (jē·od/ə·sē) *n.* The science dealing with the determination of the shape, area, and curvature of the earth, with the precise mapping of continents or other large tracts, or location of specific points. Also **ge·o·det·ics** (jē/ə·det/iks). [< F < NL < Gk. < *gē* earth + *daiein* to divide]

ge·o·det·ic (jē/ə·det/ik) *adj.* **1.** Of or pertaining to geodesy. **2.** Geodesic. Also **ge/o·det/i·cal.** — **ge/o·det/i·cal·ly** *adv.*

ge·o·dy·nam·ics (jē/ō·dī·nam/iks, -di-) *n.pl. (construed as sing.)* The branch of geology concerned with the forces affecting the structure of the earth.

ge·o·graph·i·cal (jē/ə·graf/i·kəl) *adj.* **1.** Of or pertaining to geography. **2.** Relating to topographical facts and influences. Also **ge/o·graph/ic.** — **ge/o·graph/i·cal·ly** *adv.*

geographic determinism *Sociol.* The theory that attributes the forms and characteristics of a given society to geographic factors.

ge·og·ra·phy (jē·og/rə·fē) *n. pl.* **·phies** **1.** The science that describes the surface of the earth and its associated physical, biological, economic, political, and demographic characteristics. **2.** The natural aspect, features, etc., of a place or area: the *geography* of the Arctic. **3.** A particular work on or system of geography. [< L < Gk. < *gē* earth + *graphein* to write, describe] — **ge·og/ra·pher** *n.*

ge·oid (jē/oid) *n.* The earth considered hypothetically as an ellipsoidal solid whose surface coincides with the mean level of the ocean. [< Gk. *geoidēs* earthlike < *gē* earth + *eidos* form]

ge·o·log·ic (jē/ə·loj/ik) *adj.* Of or pertaining to geology. Also **ge/o·log/i·cal.** — **ge/o·log/i·cal·ly** *adv.*

---

ge·ol·o·gy (jē·ol′ə·jē) *n. pl.* **·gies 1.** The science that treats of the origin and structure of the earth, including the physical forces which have shaped it and its physical and organic history, esp. as shown by rocks and rock formations. **2.** The structure of the earth in a given region. — **ge·ol′o·gist** *n.*

ge·o·met·ric (jē′ə·met′rik) *adj.* **1.** Pertaining to or according to the rules and principles of geometry. **2.** Forming, consisting of, or characterized by straight lines, bars, crosses, zigzags, etc., as in painting or sculpture. Also **ge′o·met′ri·cal.** — **ge′o·met′ri·cal·ly** *adv.*

ge·o·pol·i·tics (jē′ō·pol′ə·tiks) *n.pl. (construed as sing.)* **1.** The study of political and economic geography. **2.** A doctrine, of Nazi Germany, advocating aggressive expansion: also German **Ge·o·pol·i·tik** (gä′ō·pôl·ē·tēk′). — **ge′o·po·lit′·i·cal** (-pə·lit′i·kəl), **ge′o·po·lit′ic** *adj.* — **ge′o·po·lit′i·cal·ly** *adv.* — **ge′o·pol′i·ti′cian** (-pol′ə·tish′ən) *n.*

Geor·gian (jôr′jən) *adj.* **1.** Of or pertaining to the reigns or period of the first four Georges in England, 1714–1830, or of George V, 1910–36. **2.** Of or pertaining to Georgia or Georgians. **3.** Of or pertaining to the language of Georgia (def.

GEOLOGICAL TIME SCALE

Read from bottom to top.

ERAS	TIME PERIODS ROCK SYSTEMS	TIME EPOCHS ROCK SERIES	APPROX. DURATION MILLION YEARS	APPROX. PERCENT TOTAL AGE	LIFE FORMS
CENOZOIC	QUATERNARY	RECENT PLEISTOCENE	1		Rise and dominance of Man.
CENOZOIC	UPPER TERTIARY	PLIOCENE MIOCENE		2	Modern animals and plants.
CENOZOIC	LOWER TERTIARY	OLIGOCENE EOCENE PALEOCENE	65		Rapid development of modern mammals, insects, and plants.
MESOZOIC	UPPER CRETACEOUS		75		Primitive mammals; last dinosaurs; last ammonites.
MESOZOIC	LOWER CRETACEOUS				Rise of flowering plants.
MESOZOIC	JURASSIC		45	5	First birds, first mammals. Diversification of reptiles; climax of ammonites; coniferous trees.
MESOZOIC	TRIASSIC		45		Rise of dinosaurs; cycadlike plants; bony fishes.
PALEOZOIC	PERMIAN		45		Rise of reptiles. Modern insects. Last of many plant and animal groups.
PALEOZOIC	PENNSYLVANIAN (CARBONIFEROUS)		75		First reptiles. Amphibians; primitive insects; seed ferns; primitive conifers.
PALEOZOIC	MISSISSIPPIAN (CARBONIFEROUS)			9	Climax of shell-crushing sharks. Primitive ammonites.
PALEOZOIC	DEVONIAN		50		First amphibians, first land snails. Primitive land plants. Climax of brachiopods.
PALEOZOIC	SILURIAN		20		First traces of land life. Scorpions. First lungfishes. Widespread coral reefs.
PALEOZOIC	ORDOVICIAN		70		First fish. Climax of trilobites. First appearance of many marine invertebrates.
PALEOZOIC	CAMBRIAN		50		First marine invertebrates, including trilobites.
PROTEROZOIC (PRE-CAMBRIAN)			About 3000	84	First signs of life. Algae.
ARCHEOZOIC (PRE-CAMBRIAN)					

Age of oldest dated rocks: about 3,500,000,000 years.

ge·om·e·tri·cian (jē·om′ə·trish′ən, jē′ə·mə-) *n.* A specialist in geometry. Also **ge·om′e·ter** (-ə·tər).

geometric progression *Math.* A sequence of terms of which each member is greater than its predecessor by a constant ratio, as 2, 4, 8, 16, 32, 64.

ge·om·e·try (jē·om′ə·trē) *n. pl.* **·tries** The branch of mathematics that treats of space and its relations, esp. as shown in the properties and measurement of points, lines, angles, surfaces, and solids. [< OF < L < Gk. < *gē* earth + *metreein* to measure]

ge·o·phys·ics (jē′ō·fiz′iks) *n.pl. (construed as sing.)* The study of the earth as the product of complex physico-chemical forces acting upon it internally and from outer space, esp. with reference to exploration of its less accessible regions. — **ge′o·phys′i·cal** *adj.* — **ge′o·phys′i·cist** *n.*

2). — *n.* **1.** A native or inhabitant of Georgia. **2.** One of an ancient mountain people native to the Caucasus. **3.** The Caucasian language of the Georgians of the Soviet Union.

ge·o·stat·ics (jē′ō·stat′iks) *n.pl. (construed as sing.)* The statics of rigid bodies in relation to balanced forces on or beneath the earth's surface. — **ge′o·stat′ic** *adj.*

ge·ra·ni·um (ji·rā′nē·əm) *n.* **1.** A plant with showy pink or purple flowers: also called *cranebill*. **2.** A closely related plant, originally from South Africa. **3.** A very deep pink, almost red, color. [< L < Gk. *geranos* crane]

ger·fal·con (jûr′fal′kən, -fôl′-, -fô′-) *n.* A large falcon of the arctic regions, with feathered shanks: also spelled *gyrfalcon.* [< OF < OHG *gir* vulture + OF *faucon* falcon]

ger·i·at·rics (jer′ē·at′riks) *n.pl. (construed as sing.)* **1.** The branch of medicine that deals with the structural changes, physiology, diseases, and hygiene of old age. **2.** Gerontology. [< Gk. *gēras* old age + -IATRICS] — **ger'i·at'ric** *adj.* — **ger'i·a·tri'cian** (-ə·trish'ən), **ger'i·at'rist** *n.*

germ (jûrm) *n.* **1.** A microorganism that causes disease; a microbe. **2.** Something in its essential though rudimentary form: the *germ* of an idea. **3.** That which gives rise to the production or development of something: to sow the *germs* of war. **4.** *Biol.* **a** A reproductive cell. **b** An organism in its embryonic form. [< F < L *germen* sprig]

ger·man¹ (jûr'mən) *n.* A cotillion (def. 1). [Short for *German cotillion*]

ger·man² (jûr'mən) *adj.* **1.** Having the same father and mother as oneself: *sister-german*. **2.** Related to oneself through being the child of one's uncle or aunt: *cousin-german*. **3.** Germane. [< OF < L *germanus* closely related]

Ger·man (jûr'mən) *adj.* Of, pertaining to, or characteristic of Germany, its people, or their language. — *n.* **1.** A native or inhabitant of Germany. **2.** The language of the Germans, belonging to the West Germanic branch. — **High German** The standard literary and spoken language used throughout Germany and Austria and in parts of Switzerland and Alsace: also called *New High German*. — **Low German** Collectively, the languages of the Low Countries, including Dutch, Flemish, and Frisian, and of the northern lowlands of Germany (*Plattdeutsch*). — **Old High German** The language of southern Germany from about 800 to 1100. — **Middle High German** The High German language from 1100 to 1450. — **Middle Low German** The Low German language from 1100 to 1450. [< L *Germanus*, prob. < Celtic]

ger·man·der (jər·man'dər) *n.* An herb of the mint family, with pale purple flowers. [< OF < Med.L < LGk. < Gk. < *chamai* on the ground + *drys* an oak]

ger·mane (jər·mān') *adj.* Related to what is being discussed or considered; pertinent; relevant. [See GERMAN²]

Ger·man·ic (jər·man'ik) *adj.* **1.** Of or pertaining to a group of early Indo-European tribes living in the region between the Rhine, Danube, and Vistula rivers: later including the Germans, English, Dutch, Flemings, Danes, Scandinavians, and German-Swiss. **2.** Relating to the language or customs of any of these people. — *n.* A sub-family of the Indo-European family of languages, divided into **East Germanic**, including Gothic (extinct); **North Germanic** or Scandinavian, including Norwegian, Swedish, Danish, Icelandic, and Faroese; and **West Germanic**, including all the High and Low German languages and dialects.

ger·ma·ni·um (jər·mā'nē·əm) *n.* A grayish white, metallic element (symbol Ge) of the silicon group, used in electronics and optics. See ELEMENT. [< NL < L *Germania* Germany]

German measles *Pathol.* A contagious virus disease accompanied by fever, sore throat, and a skin rash: also called *rubella, rubeola*.

Germano- *combining form* German.

German shepherd A breed of dog with a large, strong body and thick, smooth coat: also called *police dog*.

German silver A white alloy of copper, nickel, and zinc, used in the manufacture of cutlery and as a base for plated ware: also called *nickel silver*.

germ cell *Biol.* A cell specialized for reproduction.

ger·mi·cide (jûr'mə·sīd) *n.* An agent used to destroy disease germs or other microorganisms. — **ger·mi·ci·dal** (jûr'·mə·sī'dəl) *adj.*

ger·mi·nal (jûr'mə·nəl) *adj.* **1.** Of, relating to, or constituting a germ or germ cell. **2.** Pertaining to the earliest stage of development. [< L *germen, -inis* sprig]

ger·mi·nate (jûr'mə·nāt) *v.* **·nat·ed, ·nat·ing** *v.i.* **1.** To begin to grow or develop; sprout. — *v.t.* **2.** To cause to sprout. [< L *germinatus*, pp. of *germinare* to sprout] — **ger·mi·na·ble** (-nə·bəl) *adj.* — **ger'mi·na'tion** *n.* — **ger'mi·na'tive** *adj.* — **ger'mi·na'tor** *n.*

germ plasm *Biol.* The part of the protoplasm of a germ cell that contains the chromosomes and genes.

geronto- *combining form* Old age; pertaining to old people: *gerontology*. Also, before vowels, **geront-**. [< Gk. *gerōn, gerontos* old man]

ger·on·tol·o·gy (jer'on·tol'ə·jē) *n.* **1.** The scientific study of the processes and phenomena of aging. **2.** Geriatrics. — **ger'on·tol'o·gist** *n.*

-gerous *suffix* Bearing or producing. [< L *gerere* to bear + -OUS]

ger·ry·man·der (jer'i·man'dər, ger'-) *v.t.* **1.** To alter (a voting area) so as to advance unfairly the interests of a political party. **2.** To adapt to one's advantage; manipulate. — *n.* The act or result of gerrymandering. [after Elbridge *Gerry*, 1744-1814, + (SALA)MANDER; from the shape of a district formed in Massachusetts while he was governor]

ger·und (jer'ənd) *Gram.* *n.* **1.** A form of a verb used like a noun. **2.** In English, the -*ing* form of a verb, as *doing*, or a compound tense of a verb made with the -*ing* form of an auxiliary, as *having done*, when used as the subject or object of a verb or as the object of a preposition. [< LL < L *gerere* to do] — **ge·run·di·al** (jə·run'dē·əl) *adj.*

ge·run·dive (jə·run'div) *Gram.* *n.* **1.** In Latin, a form of the verb constituting the future passive participle, having the stem of the gerund and expressing obligation, propriety, etc. **2.** In some other languages, a form similar to a gerundive in form or function. — *adj.* Of, pertaining to, or resembling a gerundive, or, sometimes, a gerund.

gest (jest) *n.* *Archaic* **1.** A noteworthy deed; exploit. **2.** A tale of adventure or romance; esp., a metrical romance. Also **geste**. [< OF < L *gesta* deeds < *gerere* to do]

ge·stalt (gə·shtält', -shtôlt') *n.* *pl.* **·stalts** or **·stalt·en** (-shtält'ən, -shtôlt'-) A synthesis of separate elements of emotion, experience, etc., that constitutes more than the mechanical sum of the parts. Also **Ge·stalt'**. [< G, form]

gestalt psychology Psychology based on the theory of the gestalt.

Ge·sta·po (gə·stä'pō, *Ger.* gə·shtä'pō) *n.* The German state secret police under the Nazi regime, noted for their brutality. [< G *Ge*(*heime*) *Sta*(*ats*) *Po*(*lizei*) Secret State Police]

ges·tate (jes'tāt) *v.t.* **·tat·ed, ·tat·ing** To carry in the uterus during pregnancy. [< L *gestare* to carry] — **ges·ta'tion** *n.*

ges·tic·u·late (jes·tik'yə·lāt) *v.* **·lat·ed, ·lat·ing** *v.i.* **1.** To make emphatic or expressive gestures, as in speaking. — *v.t.* **2.** To express by gestures. [< L *gesticulus*, dim. of *gestus* gesture] — **ges·tic'u·la'tive** *adj.* — **ges·tic'u·la'tor** *n.*

ges·tic·u·la·tion (jes·tik'yə·lā'shən) *n.* **1.** The act of gesticulating. **2.** An energetic or expressive gesture.

ges·ture (jes'chər) *n.* **1.** A bodily motion, as of the hands in speaking, used to emphasize or express some idea or emotion. **2.** Such motions collectively. **3.** Something said or done as a mere formality, or for effect. — *v.* **·tured, ·tur·ing** *v.i.* **1.** To make gestures. — *v.t.* **2.** To express by gestures. [< Med.L < L *gerere* to carry on, do] — **ges'tur·er** *n.*

Ge·sund·heit (gə·zŏŏnt'hīt) *interj.* *German* (Your) health: said to someone who has just sneezed.

get (get) *v.* **got, got** or *U.S.* **got·ten, get·ting** *v.t.* **1.** To come into possession of; obtain. **2.** To go for and bring back. **3.** To capture; seize. **4.** To cause to come, go, etc.: to *get* baggage through customs. **5.** To carry away; take: *Get* this out of the house. **6.** To prepare: to *get* lunch. **7.** To bring to a state or condition: to *get* the work done. **8.** To persuade: *Get* her to sign the paper. **9.** To find out or obtain by calculation, experiment, etc.: to add the totals and *get* 100. **10.** To receive (reward or punishment). **11.** To learn or master, as by study or practice: Have you *got* your history lesson? **12.** To become sick with. **13.** To establish contact with: I'll *get* him on the phone. **14.** To catch, as a train; board. **15.** To beget: now said chiefly of animals. **16.** *Informal* To come to an understanding of. **17.** *Informal* To possess: with *have* or *has*: He has *got* quite a temper. **18.** *Informal* To obtain the advantage over: Drink will *get* him. **19.** *Informal* To square accounts with: I'll *get* you yet. **20.** *Informal* To be obliged or forced (to do something specified): with *have* or *has*. **21.** *Informal* To hit: The shrapnel *got* him in the arm. **22.** *Slang* To puzzle or baffle. **23.** *Slang* To please, irritate, etc.: That music *gets* me. **24.** *Slang* To take note of. **25.** To bring to or place in some specified location. — *v.i.* **26.** To arrive: When does the train *get* there? **27.** To come, go, or move: *Get* in here. **28.** To board; enter: with *on, in,* etc. **29.** To become. — **to get about 1.** To become known, as gossip. **2.** To move about. **3.** To be active socially. — **to get across 1.** To make or be convincing or clear, as to an audience. **2.** To be successful, as in projecting one's personality. — **to get ahead** To attain success. — **to get along 1.** To leave; go: *Get along* with you! **2.** To be successful, as in business. **3.** To be friendly or compatible. **4.** To proceed. **5.** To grow old or older. — **to get around 1.** To become known, as gossip. **2.** To move about. **3.** To attend social or public functions, etc. **4.** To flatter, cajole, etc., so as to obtain the favor of. **5.** To dodge; circumvent. — **to get around to** To give attention to after some delay. — **to get at 1.** To arrive at; reach. **2.** To intend; mean: I don't see what you're *getting* at. **3.** To apply oneself to: to *get at* a problem. **4.** *Informal* To prevail upon; influence. — **to get away 1.** To escape. **2.** To leave; go. **3.** To start, as a race horse. — **to get away with** *Slang* To do (something) without discovery, criticism, or punishment. — **to get back** To return to a previous position or state. — **to get back at** *Slang* To revenge oneself on. — **to get by 1.** To pass: This *got by* the censor. **2.** *Informal* To manage to survive. **3.** *Informal* To get away with. — **to get down 1.** To descend, as from a horse or ladder. — **to get down to** (business, facts, etc.) To begin to act on, investigate, or consider. — **to get in 1.** To arrive or enter. **2.** To slip in (a remark, etc.). **3.** To become involved or familiar with. — **to get it** *Informal* **1.** To understand. **2.** To be

punished in some way. **—to get off 1.** To descend from; dismount. **2.** To depart. **3.** To be relieved or freed, as of a duty. **4.** To be released with a lesser penalty, etc., or none at all. **5.** To utter: to *get off* a joke. **—to get on 1.** To mount (a horse, vehicle, etc.). **2.** To get along. **—to get out 1.** To depart or leave. **2.** To escape. **3.** To become known, as a secret. **4.** To publish. **5.** To express or utter with difficulty. **6.** To take out. **—to get out of 1.** To obtain from. **2.** To escape or evade. **3.** To depart from. **—to get over 1.** To recover from (illness, surprise, anger, etc.). **2.** To get across. **—to get there** *Informal* To succeed. **—to get through 1.** To complete. **2.** To survive. **—to get through (to) 1.** To establish communication (with). **2.** To make clear (to). **—to get to 1.** To begin. **2.** To be able to (do something). **3.** To get through to. **—to get together 1.** To assemble. **2.** To come to an agreement. **—to get up 1.** To rise, as from sleep. **2.** To climb. **3.** To devise. **4.** To acquire, develop, or work up. **5.** *Informal* To dress up. [< ON *geta*] **—get′ta·ble** *adj.* **—get′ter** *n.*
—Syn. (verb) **1.** obtain, procure, gain, acquire.
get·a·way (get′ə·wā′) *n.* **1.** An escape, as of a criminal. **2.** The start, as of an automobile, race horse, etc.
get-to·geth·er (get′tə·geth′ər) *n.* *Informal* A gathering.
get-up (get′up′) *n.* *Informal* **1.** Overall arrangement and appearance, esp. of a book or magazine. **2.** The combination of articles of dress worn on a particular occasion. **3.** Vigorous initiative: also **get′-up′-and-go′** (-ən-gō′).
gew·gaw (gyōō′gô) *n.* Some little ornamental article of small value. **—** *adj.* Showy; gaudy. [ME *giue-goue*]
gey·ser (gī′zər, -sər) *n.* A natural hot spring from which intermittent jets of steam, hot water, or mud are ejected in a fountainlike column. [< Icel. *geysan* to gush]
ghast·ly (gast′lē, gäst′-) *adj.* **·li·er, ·li·est 1.** Horrible; terrifying. **2.** Deathlike in appearance; pale; wan. **3.** *Informal* Very bad or unpleasant. **—** *adv.* **1.** Spectral in manner or appearance. **2.** Fearfully; horribly. [ME < OE *gæstan* to terrify + -*lich* -ly¹] **—ghast′li·ness** *n.*
ghat (gôt) *n.* *Anglo-Indian* **1.** A stairway leading down to the edge of a river. **2.** A mountain pass. **3.** A range or chain of mountains. Also **ghaut**. [< Hind. *ghāt*]
ghee (gē) *n.* *Anglo-Indian* A butterlike substance made with the butterfat of buffalo milk. [< Hind. < Skt. *ghrta*]
gher·kin (gûr′kin) *n.* **1.** A very small, prickly cucumber pickled as a relish. **2.** The plant producing it. **3.** Any small, immature cucumber used for pickling. [< Du. *agurk* cucumber < G < Slavic, ult. < LGk. *angourion*]
ghet·to (get′ō) *n.* *pl.* **·tos 1.** An often run-down section of a city inhabited chiefly by a minority group that cannot live elsewhere, as because of racial or social prejudice. **2.** A section of a city in certain European countries in which Jews were formerly required to live. [< Ital.]
ghost (gōst) *n.* **1.** A disembodied spirit; a wraith, specter, or phantom. **2.** The animating spirit or soul: now only in the phrase **to give up the ghost**, to die. **3.** A haunting recollection of something: *ghosts* from the past. **4.** A mere suggestion of something: the *ghost* of a smile. **5.** *Informal* A ghostwriter. **6.** *Optics & Telecom.* An unwanted false or secondary image. **—** *v.t. & v.i.* **1.** To haunt as a ghost. **2.** *Informal* To write as a ghostwriter. [OE *gāst* spirit]
ghost·ly (gōst′lē) *adj.* **·li·er, ·li·est 1.** Of or like an apparition; spectral. **2.** Of religion; spiritual. **—ghost′li·ness** *n.*
ghost town A deserted town, esp. a former boom town.
ghost·write (gōst′rīt′) *v.t. & v.i.* **·wrote, ·writ·ten, ·writ·ing** To write or act as a ghostwriter.
ghost·writ·er (gōst′rī′tər) *n.* One who writes for someone else to whom the authorship is to be attributed.
ghoul (gōōl) *n.* **1.** One who robs graves. **2.** One who takes pleasure in revolting things. **3.** In Moslem legend, an evil spirit who preys on corpses. [< Arabic *ghūl*] **—ghoul′ish** *adj.* **—ghoul′ish·ly** *adv.* **—ghoul′ish·ness** *n.*
GI (jē′ī′) *U.S. Informal n. pl.* **GIs** or **GI's** An enlisted man in the U.S. Army. **—the GIs** (or **GI's**) *Mil. Slang* Diarrhea. **—** *adj.* **1.** Of or characteristic of GIs. **2.** Furnished by the government for the use of the armed forces. **—** *v.t.* **GIed** or **GI'ed, GIing** or **GI'ing** To clean or scrub, as for military inspection. [< G(overnment) I(ssue)]
gi·ant (jī′ənt) *n.* **1.** In legend, a manlike being of supernatural size and strength, as in Greek mythology, one of the race who warred against the gods of Olympus. **2.** Any person or thing of great size, capability, etc. **—** *adj.* **1.** Of or typical of a giant. **2.** Huge; great. [< OF < L < Gk. *gigas, -antos*] **—gi′ant·ess** *n. fem.*
gi·ant·ism (jī′ənt·iz′əm) *n.* Gigantism.
giant panda The panda (def. 2).
gia·our (jour) *n.* Among Moslems, a nonbeliever; esp., a Christian. [< Turkish < Persian *gabr* infidel]
gib·ber (jib′ər, gib′-) *v.i. & v.t.* To talk rapidly and incoherently; jabber. **—** *n.* Gibberish.
gib·ber·ish (jib′ər·ish, gib′-) *n.* **1.** Rapid or unintelligible talk; gabble. **2.** Needlessly difficult or obscure language.
gib·bet (jib′it) *n.* **1.** Formerly, a gallows. **—** *v.t.* **gib·bet·ed** or

·bet·ted, gib·bet·ing or **·bet·ting 1.** To execute by hanging. **2.** To hold up to public contempt. [< OF *gibet* staff]
gib·bon (gib′ən) *n.* A slender, long-armed arboreal anthropoid ape of southern Asia and the East Indies. [< F]
gib·bos·i·ty (gi·bos′ə·tē) *n. pl.* **·ties 1.** The state of being gibbous or convex. **2.** A rounded protuberance; hump.
gib·bous (gib′əs) *adj.* **1.** Irregularly rounded or convex, as the moon when more than half full and less than full. **2.** Hunchbacked. Also **gib·bose** (gib′ōs, gi·bōs′). [< L *gibbus* hump] **—gib′bous·ly** *adv.* **—gib′bous·ness** *n.*
gibe¹ (jīb) *v.* **gibed, gib·ing** *v.i.* **1.** To utter jeers or derisive remarks. **—** *v.t.* **2.** To taunt. **—** *n.* A jeer. [Cf. OF *giber* to treat roughly] **—gib′er** *n.* **—gib′ing·ly** *adv.*
gibe² (jīb) See JIBE¹.
gib·let (jib′lit) *n. Usu. pl.* The heart, liver, gizzard, etc., of a fowl. [< OF *gibelet* stew made from game]
gid·dy (gid′ē) *adj.* **·di·er, ·di·est 1.** Affected by a reeling or whirling sensation; dizzy. **2.** Tending to cause such a sensation. **3.** Rotating rapidly; whirling. **4.** Frivolous; heedless. **—** *v.t. & v.i.* **·died, ·dy·ing** To make or become dizzy. [OE *gydig* insane] **—gid′di·ly** *adv.* **—gid′di·ness** *n.*
gift (gift) *n.* **1.** Something that is given; present. **2.** The action or right of giving. **3.** A natural aptitude; talent. **—to look a gift horse in the mouth** To find fault with a gift or favor. [OE < *gifan* to give]
gift·ed (gif′tid) *adj.* Endowed with talent.
gig¹ (gig) *n.* **1.** A light, two-wheeled vehicle drawn by one horse. **2.** A machine for raising a nap on cloth. **3.** *Naut.* A long ship's boat usu. for the captain; also, a speedy, light rowboat. **—** *v.* **gigged, gig·ging** *v.i.* **1.** To ride in a gig. **—** *v.t.* **2.** To raise the nap on (cloth).
gig² (gig) *n.* An arrangement of fishhooks. **—** *v.t. & v.i.* **gigged, gig·ging** To spear or catch (fish) with a gig. [< FISHGIG]
gig³ (gig) *Slang n.* A demerit, as in the army, school, etc. **—** *v.t.* **gigged, gig·ging 1.** To give a demerit to. **2.** To punish.
gi·ga- *combining form* A billion (10⁹) times (a specified unit).
gi·gan·tic (ji·gan′tik) *adj.* **1.** Of, like, or suited to a giant. **2.** Tremendous; huge. Also **gi·gan·te·an** (jī′gan·tē′ən). [< L *gigas, -antis* giant + -IC] **—gi·gan′ti·cal·ly** *adv.*
gi·gan·tism (jī·gan′tiz·əm) *n.* Abnormal size, esp., excessive growth of the body due to disturbances in the pituitary gland: also called *giantism.*
gig·gle (gig′əl) *v.i.* **·gled, ·gling** To laugh in a high-pitched, silly, or nervous manner. **—** *n.* A titter. **—gig′gler** *n.*
gig·gly (gig′lē) *adj.* **·gli·er, ·gli·est** Tending to giggle.
gig·o·lo (jig′ə·lō, *Fr.* zhē·gô·lô′) *n. pl.* **·los** (-lōz, *Fr.* -lô′) **1.** A professional male dancer who dances with women patrons; also, a woman's paid escort. **2.** A man supported by a woman not his wife. [< F, prob. < *gigolette* prostitute]
gig·ot (jig′ət) *n.* **1.** A leg-of-mutton sleeve. **2.** A cooked haunch of lamb, veal, etc. [< F]
gigue (zhēg) *n.* **1.** A jig (def. 1). **2.** *Music* A lively dance form, often the final movement of a suite.
Gi·la monster (hē′lə) A large, venomous lizard of the N. American desert, having an orange and black body.
gild¹ (gild) *v.t.* **gild·ed** or **gilt, gild·ing 1.** To coat with a layer of gold. **2.** To brighten or adorn. **3.** To gloss over. [OE *gyldan*] **—gild′ing** *n.*
gild² (gild) *n.* A guild.
gild·er¹ (gil′dər) *n.* One who or that which gilds.
gild·er² (gil′dər) *n.* A guilder.
Gil·e·ad (gil′ē·əd) A mountainous region of ancient Palestine east of the Jordan. *Josh.* xii 2.
gill¹ (gil) *n.* **1.** *Zool.* The organ for underwater breathing of fishes, amphibians, and other aquatic vertebrates. **2.** *Usu. pl.* The wattles of a fowl. **3.** *pl. Informal* The face and throat: usu. in the phrase **green around the gills**, Sickly in appearance. **—** *v.t.* **1.** To catch by the gills. **2.** To gut (fish). [ME *gile*]
gill² (jil) *n.* A liquid measure equal to ¼ pint. See table inside back cover. [< OF *gell* measure for wine]
gil·ly·flow·er (jil′ē·flou′ər) *n.* **1.** A plant of the mustard family, as the wallflower. **2.** A plant of the pink family, as the clove pink. Also **gil/li·flow/er.** [Alter. of ME *gilofre*]
gilt (gilt) Alternative past tense and past participle of GILD. **—** *adj.* Gold-colored; gilded. **—** *n.* A material for gilding.
gilt-edged (gilt′ejd′) *adj.* **1.** Having the edges gilded. **2.** Of the best quality: *gilt-edged* securities. Also **gilt′-edge′.**
gim·bals (jim′bəlz, gim′-) *n.pl.* A set of three metal rings so pivoted one within the other that it maintains an object supported by it, as a ship's compass, on a horizontal plane. [OF < L *geminus* twin]
gim·crack (jim′krak) *n.* A useless, gaudy object; knick-knack. **—** *adj.* Cheap and showy. **—gim′crack·er·y** *n.*
gim·let (gim′lit) A small, sharp tool with a bar handle and a pointed, spiral tip for boring holes. **—** *v.t.* To make a hole in with a gimlet. [< OF *guimbelet*]

GIMBALS

gimlet eyes Sharp eyes. — **gim′let-eyed′** adj.
gim·mick (gim′ik) n. U.S. Slang 1. A novel or tricky feature or detail. 2. A hidden or deceptive device, as one used by a magician. 3. Some little gadget of uncertain name. — **gim′mick·ry** n. — **gim′mick·y** adj.
gimp[1] (gimp) n. A narrow piece of fabric, often stiffened with wire, used to trim curtains, etc. [Cf. OF guimpre, a kind of trimming]
gimp[2] (gimp) U.S. Slang n. One who limps; also, a limp.
gin[1] (jin) n. An aromatic alcoholic liquor distilled from various grains, esp. rye, and flavored with juniper berries or sometimes with other flavoring agents. [Short for GENEVA]
gin[2] (jin) n. 1. A cotton gin. 2. A tripodlike machine for hoisting. 3. A type of pulley and block. For illus. see BLOCK. 4. A snare or trap. — v.t. ginned, gin·ning 1. To remove the seeds from (cotton) in a gin. 2. To trap or snare. [Aphetic var. of OF engin ingenuity] — gin′ner n.
gin·ger (jin′jər) n. 1. The pungent, spicy rootstock of a tropical plant, used in medicine and cookery. 2. The plant itself. 3. A tawny, reddish brown color. 4. Informal Pep. — v.t. 1. To spice with ginger. 2. Informal To make lively: often with up. [< OF < LL < Gk. zingiberis, ult. < Skt.]
ginger ale An effervescent soft drink flavored with ginger.
ginger beer An effervescent, nonalcoholic ginger drink.
gin·ger·bread (jin′jər-bred′) n. 1. A dark, ginger-flavored cake or cooky. 2. Gaudy ornamentation, as ornate carvings on furniture, etc. — adj. Cheap and tawdry.
gin·ger·ly (jin′jər-lē) adv. In a cautious manner. — adj. Careful. [Cf. OF gent delicate] — **gin′ger·li·ness** n.
gin·ger·snap (jin′jər-snap′) n. A brittle, ginger cooky.
gin·ger·y (jin′jər-ē) adj. 1. Having the piquantly spicy flavor of ginger. 2. Having the reddish brown color of ginger. 3. Sharply pointed or peppery, as a remark.
ging·ham (ging′əm) n. A cotton fabric, yarn-dyed, woven in solid colors, checks, etc. [< F < Malay gingang striped]
gin·gi·vi·tis (jin′jə-vī′tis) n. Pathol. Inflammation of the gums. [< L gingiva gum]
gink (gingk) n. U.S. Slang A man or boy; fellow; guy.
gink·go (ging′kō, jing′kō) n. pl. ·goes A large tree native to China and cultivated in the U.S., with edible fruits and nuts. Also **ging′ko**. [< Japanese]
gin mill Slang A saloon.
gin rummy A variety of rummy.
gin·seng (jin′seng) n. 1. An herb native to China and North America, having a root of aromatic and stimulant properties. 2. The root of this herb as used in a medicinal preparation. [< Chinese jen shen]
gip·sy (jip′sē), **Gip·sy** See GYPSY, GYPSY.
gi·raffe (jə-raf′, -räf′) n. pl. ·raffes or ·raffe An African ruminant, the tallest of all mammals, having a very long neck and long slender legs. [< F, ult. < Arabic zarāfah]
gird[1] (gûrd) v.t. gird·ed or girt, gird·ing 1. To surround or make fast with a belt or girdle. 2. To encircle; surround. 3. To prepare (oneself) for action. 4. To clothe, equip, or endow, as with some quality or attribute. [OE gyrdan]
gird[2] (gûrd) v.t. & v.i. To attack with sarcasm; gibe. [ME girden; origin unknown]
gird·er (gûr′dər) n. A long heavy beam, as of steel or wood, that supports the joists of a floor, etc.
gir·dle (gûr′dəl) n. 1. A belt or cord worn around the waist; sash. 2. Anything that encircles like a belt. 3. A woman's flexible undergarment worn to give support and shape. 4. An encircling cut made through the bark of a tree trunk or branch. 5. The outer edge of a cut gem. — v.t. ·dled, ·dling 1. To fasten a girdle or belt around. 2. To encircle; encompass. 3. To make an encircling cut through the bark of (a branch or tree). [OE gyrdle] — **gir′dler** n.
girl (gûrl) n. 1. A female infant or child. 2. A young, unmarried woman. 3. A female servant. 4. Informal A sweetheart. 5. Informal Any woman of any age. [ME gurle] — **girl′ish** adj. — **girl′ish·ly** adv. — **girl′ish·ness** n.
girl guide A member of a British and Canadian organization, the **Girl Guides**, resembling the Girl Scouts.
girl scout A member of an organization of girls between the ages of 7 and 17, founded in the U.S. in 1912 to develop health, character, etc.
girt[1] (gûrt) Past tense and past participle of GIRD[1].
girt[2] (gûrt) v.t. & v.i. 1. To gird. 2. To measure in girth. — n. Girth. [< GIRD[1]]
girth (gûrth) n. 1. The circumference of anything. 2. A band passed under the belly of a horse or other animal to make fast a saddle, harness, pack, etc. 3. A girdle or band. — v.t. 1. To bind with a girth. 2. To encircle; girdle. — v.i. 3. To measure in girth. [< ON gjordh]
gis·mo (giz′mō) n. pl. ·mos U.S. Slang A gadget. Also spelled gizmo.
gist (jist) n. The main idea or substance, as of an argument, question, etc. [< OF giste place of rest]

git·tern (git′ərn) n. A cittern. [< OF < L < Gk. kithara]
give (giv) v. gave, giv·en, giv·ing v.t. 1. To transfer freely (what is one's own) to the permanent possession of another without asking anything in return. 2. To put into the hands of another for temporary use; hand over; let have. 3. To put into the grasp of another: Give me your hand. 4. To make available; furnish. 5. To be a source of. 6. To grant or concede, as permission. 7. To impart: to give advice. 8. To administer (a dose of medicine, a treatment, etc.). 9. To assign or allot. 10. To deal, deliver, or inflict (a blow, beating, etc.). 11. To transmit or communicate (a disease, etc.). 12. To perform or do: to give a play. 13. To issue (an order, etc.). 14. To part with; relinquish or yield: to give one's life. 15. To devote, as oneself, to a cause, etc. — v.i. 16. To make donations; make free gifts. 17. To move down, back, etc., as under pressure: The door gave. 18. To be springy, flexible, etc.: The bed gives comfortably. 19. To furnish a view or passage; open: with on or onto. — **to give a good account of** To conduct (oneself) creditably. — **to give and take** To exchange on equal terms. — **to give away** 1. To bestow as a gift. 2. To hand over (the bride) to the bridegroom. 3. Informal To make known, as a secret; reveal. — **to give back** To restore or return. — **to give birth** To bear offspring. — **to give birth to** 1. To bear (offspring). 2. To create or originate, as an idea. 3. To result in. — **to give forth** To discharge; emit. — **to give in** 1. To yield, as to something demanded. 2. To cease opposition; acknowledge oneself vanquished. 3. To deliver or hand in (a report, resignation, etc.). — **to give it to** To administer a scolding, beating, etc., to. — **to give off** To send forth, as odors; emit. — **to give out** 1. To send forth; emit. 2. To hand out or distribute. 3. To make known; publish. 4. To become completely used up or exhausted. — **to give over** 1. To hand over, as to another's care. 2. To cease; desist. — **to give rise to** To cause or produce; result in. — **to give up** 1. To surrender. 2. To stop; cease. 3. To desist from as hopeless. 4. To lose all hope for, as a sick person. 5. To devote wholly: to give oneself up to art. — **to give way** 1. To collapse, bend, fail, etc., as under pressure or force. 2. To draw back. 3. To concede or yield. 4. To abandon oneself, as to despair. — n. 1. The quality of being resilient; elasticity. 2. The act or process of bending or yielding. [Fusion of OE giefan and ON gefa] — **giv′er** n.
give-and-take (giv′ən-tāk′) n. The making of mutual concessions, exchanges, etc.
give·a·way (giv′ə-wā′) Informal n. 1. A disclosure or betrayal, generally unintentional. 2. Something given free or at a greatly reduced price. — adj. Characterized by prizes.
giv·en (giv′ən) adj. 1. Presented; bestowed. 2. Habitually inclined; addicted: with to. 3. Specified; stated: a given date. 4. Issued on an indicated date: said of official documents, etc. 5. Admitted as a fact. — Syn. See ADDICTED.
given name The name bestowed on a person at birth, or shortly thereafter, as distinguished from his surname.
giz·mo (giz′mō) See GISMO.
giz·zard (giz′ərd) n. 1. A second stomach in birds, in which partly digested food is finely ground. 2. Informal The human stomach. [< OF < L gigeria cooked entrails of poultry]
gla·brous (glā′brəs) adj. Biol. 1. Devoid of hair or down. 2. Having a smooth surface. [< L glaber smooth]
gla·cé (gla-sā′) adj. 1. Sugared or candied, as preserved fruits. 2. Having a glossy surface, as certain leathers. 3. Iced; frozen. — v.t. ·céed, ·cé·ing 1. To cover with icing. 2. To make smooth and glossy. [< F glace ice]
gla·cial (glā′shəl) adj. 1. Pertaining to, caused by, or marked by the presence of glaciers. 2. Freezingly cold. 3. Indifferent. [< F < L glacies ice] — **gla·cial·ly** adv.
glacial epoch Geol. Any portion of geological time characterized by ice sheets over much of the earth's surface.
gla·ci·ate (glā′shē-āt) v.t. ·at·ed, ·at·ing To cover with or subject to the action of glaciers. — **gla·ci·a′tion** n.
gla·cier (glā′shər) n. A field of ice, formed in regions of perennial frost from compacted snow, that moves slowly until it either breaks off to form icebergs or melts in warmer regions. [< F < L glacies ice]
glad[1] (glad) adj. glad·der, glad·dest 1. Having a feeling of joy, pleasure, or content; gratified: often with of or at. 2. Showing joy; brightly cheerful: a glad face. 3. Giving reason to rejoice; bringing joy. 4. Very willing: He'd be glad to help. [OE glæd shining, glad]
glad[2] (glad) n. Informal A gladiolus.
glad·den (glad′n) v.t. To make glad. — **glad′den·er** n.
glade (glād) n. 1. A clearing in a wood. 2. U.S. An everglade. [Prob. akin to glad in obs. sense of "bright, sunny"]
glad eye Slang A flirtatious glance: esp. in the phrase **to get** (or **give**) **the glad eye.**
glad hand Slang A display, often insincere, of cordiality.
glad·i·a·tor (glad′ē-ā′tər) n. 1. In ancient Rome, a slave,

captive, or paid freeman who fought other men or animals as public entertainment. **2.** One who engages in any kind of struggle. [< L *gladius* sword] — **glad·i·a·to·ri·al** (glad/ē·ə·tôr/ē·əl, -tō/rē-) *adj.*

glad·i·o·lus (glad/ē·ō/ləs, glə·dī/ə·ləs) *n. pl.* **·lus·es** or **·li** (-lī) A plant of the iris family with fleshy bulbs, sword-shaped leaves, and spikes of colored flowers. Also **glad·i·o/la.**

glad·ly (glad/lē) *adv.* In a glad manner; with joy; willingly.

glad·ness (glad/nis) *n.* The state of being glad; joy.

glad·some (glad/səm) *adj.* Glad. — **glad/some·ly** *adv.* — **glad/some·ness** *n.*

Glad·stone (glad/stōn, -stən) *n.* A suitcase hinged to open flat and form two equal compartments. Also **Gladstone bag.** [after W. E. *Gladstone*, 1809–98, English statesman]

glair (glâr) *n.* **1.** Raw egg white, used in making size or glaze; also, the glaze or size. **2.** Any sticky matter. — *v.t.* To coat with glair. [< F < L *clarus* clear] — **glair/y** *adj.*

glam·or·ize (glam/ər·īz) *v.t.* **·rized**, **·riz·ing** To make glamorous.

glam·or·ous (glam/ər·əs) *adj.* Full of glamour; alluring. — **glam/or·ous·ly** *adv.* — **glam/or·ous·ness** *n.*

glam·our (glam/ər) *n.* Alluring charm or fascination. Also *U.S.* **glam/or.** [< Scot *gramarye* magic power]

glance (glans, gläns) *v.* **glanced**, **glanc·ing** *v.i.* **1.** To take a quick look. **2.** To touch briefly on some matter. **3.** To be deflected at an angle after obliquely striking. **4.** To flash intermittently; glint. — *v.t.* **5.** To cause to strike a surface obliquely. — *n.* **1.** A quick look. **2.** A flash; glint. **3.** Oblique impact and deflection. [< OF *glacier* to slip]

gland (gland) *n. Anat.* Any of various organs by means of which certain constituents are removed from the blood, either for use in the body or for elimination from it. [< F < L *glans*, *glandis* acorn]

glan·ders (glan/dərz) *n. Vet.* A contagious disease of horses and other equines, characterized by nasal discharges and ulcerative lesions of the lungs and other organs. [< OF *glandre* gland] — **glan/dered, glan/der·ous** *adj.*

glan·du·lar (glan/jə·lər) *adj.* **1.** Of, pertaining to, or resembling a gland. **2.** Having glands. Also **glan/du·lous.**

glan·dule (glan/jōōl) *n.* A small gland.

glare¹ (glâr) *v.* **glared**, **glar·ing** *v.i.* **1.** To shine with a steady and dazzling intensity. **2.** To gaze or stare fiercely or in hostility. **3.** To be conspicuous or showy. — *v.t.* **4.** To express or send forth with a glare. — *n.* **1.** A dazzling, steady light or reflection. **2.** An intense, piercing look or gaze, usually hostile. **3.** Gaudy or showy display; vulgar brilliance. [ME *glaren* < LG]

glare² (glâr) *U.S. n.* A glassy, smooth surface, as of ice. — *adj.* Having a glassy, smooth surface. [? < GLARE¹, n.]

glar·ing (glâr/ing) *adj.* **1.** Looking or staring fixedly or with hostility. **2.** Emitting an excessively brilliant light. **3.** Gaudy. **4.** Plainly conspicuous. — **glar/ing·ly** *adv.*

glar·y¹ (glâr/ē) *adj.* **glar·i·er, glar·i·est** Dazzling; glaring.

glar·y² (glâr/ē) *adj. U.S.* Slippery, as ice.

glass (glas, gläs) *n.* **1.** A hard, amorphous, brittle, usu. transparent substance made by fusing one or more of the oxides of silicon, boron, or phosphorus with certain basic oxides, followed by rapid cooling to prevent crystallization. ◆ Collateral adjective: *vitreous.* **2.** Any substance made of or resembling glass. **3.** An article made wholly or partly of glass; as: **a** A windowpane, lens, or mirror, tumbler, etc. **b** *pl.* A pair of eyeglasses; also, binoculars. **4.** Glassware. **5.** The contents of a drinking glass; glassful. — *v.t.* **1.** To put in a glass container. **2.** To enclose in or cover with glass. **3.** To equip with glass parts. **4.** To give a glassy surface or appearance to. — *adj.* **1.** Of, pertaining to, or consisting of glass. **2.** Fitted with glass: a *glass* frame. [OE *glæs*]

glass blowing The art or process of directing a controlled stream of air through a tube into a mass of molten glass at the end of the tube so as to form the glass into various shapes.

glass·ful (glas/fōōl, gläs/-) *n. pl.* **·fuls** The amount contained in a drinking glass.

glass snake A lizard of the southern U.S., having a very brittle tail.

glass·ware (glas/wâr/, gläs/-) *n.* Articles made of glass.

glass wool Fibers of spun glass of woollike appearance, used for insulation, filters, etc.

glass·work (glas/wûrk/, gläs/-) *n.* **1.** The manufacture of glass. **2.** Glass as a material used in glassware, decoration, etc. **3.** Glassware. **4.** The fitting of panes of glass.

glass·works (glas/wûrks/, gläs/-) *n.pl.* (*usu. construed as sing.*) A factory where glass is made.

glass·wort (glas/wûrt, gläs/-) *n.* Any of several seaside herbs: also called *saltwort*.

glass·y (glas/ē, gläs/ē) *adj.* **glass·i·er, glass·i·est 1.** Resembling glass. **2.** Fixed, blank, and uncomprehending: a *glassy* stare. — **glass/i·ly** *adv.* — **glass/i·ness** *n.*

glau·co·ma (glô·kō/mə) *n. Pathol.* A disease of the eye characterized by pressure of fluids within the eyeball with gradual loss of vision. [< L < Gk. *glaukos* bluish gray] — **glau·co·ma·tous** (glô·kō/mə·təs, -kom/ə-) *adj.*

glau·cous (glô/kəs) *adj.* **1.** Yellowish green; also, sea-green. **2.** *Bot.* Covered with a whitish bloom, as grapes. [< L < Gk. *glaukos* bluish gray]

glaze (glāz) *v.* **glazed, glaz·ing** *v.t.* **1.** To fit, as a window, with glass panes; also, to provide (a building, etc.) with windows. **2.** To cover or coat with a thin film; as: **a** To coat (pottery) with a glasslike surface applied by fusing. **b** To cover (foods) with a thin coating of eggs, syrup, etc. **c** To cover (paintings) with a thin, transparent coating to modify the tone. — *v.i.* **3.** To become covered with a thin coating or film. — *n.* **1.** A thin, glossy coating; also, the substance used to make such a coating. **2.** A filmy haze. **3.** *U.S.* A thin coating of ice. [ME *glas* glass] — **glaz/er** *n.*

gla·zier (glā/zhər) *n.* **1.** One who fits windows, doors, etc., with panes of glass. **2.** One who applies glaze to pottery.

gla·zier·y (glā/zhər·ē) *n.* The work of a glazier.

glaz·ing (glā/zing) *n.* **1.** The act of setting glass, as in a window. **2.** The glass used. **3.** A glaze. **4.** The act or art of applying a glaze.

glaz·y (glā/zē) *adj.* **glaz·i·er, glaz·i·est 1.** Covered with or as with a glaze. **2.** Resembling a glaze. — **glaz/i·ness** *n.*

gleam (glēm) *n.* **1.** An intermittent or momentary ray or beam of light. **2.** A soft radiance; glow; also, reflected light. **3.** A brief manifestation, as of humor; a faint trace, as of hope. — *v.i.* **1.** To shine softly; emit gleams. **2.** To appear briefly as in a small burst of light. — *v.t.* **3.** To emit in gleams. — **Syn.** See SHINE. [OE *glæm*] — **gleam/y** *adj.*

glean (glēn) *v.t. & v.i.* **1.** To collect (facts, etc.) by patient effort. **2.** To gather (the leavings) from a field after the crop has been reaped. **3.** To gather the leavings from (a field, etc.). [< OF < LL *glenare* < Celtic] — **glean/er** *n.*

glean·ing (glē/ning) *n. Usu. pl.* That which is gleaned.

glebe (glēb) *n. Brit.* A portion of land attached to a church benefice as part of its endowment. [< OF < L *gleba* clod]

glee (glē) *n.* **1.** Lively, exuberant joy. **2.** A musical composition for male voices, without accompaniment. [OE *glēo*]

glee club A group of singers organized to sing part songs.

glee·ful (glē/fəl) *adj.* Feeling or exhibiting glee; mirthful. Also **glee/some (-səm).** — **glee/ful·ly** *adv.* — **glee/ful·ness** *n.*

glen (glen) *n.* A small, secluded valley. [< Scot. Gael. *glenn*]

Glen·gar·ry (glen·gar/ē) *n.* A Scottish cap having sloping sides and streamers in back. [after a valley in Scotland]

glib (glib) *adj.* **glib·ber, glib·best 1.** Speaking fluently without much thought: a *glib* talker. **2.** More facile than sincere. **3.** Characterized by smoothness, as of manner. [< MLG *glibberich* slippery] — **glib/ly** *adv.* — **glib/ness** *n.*

glide (glīd) *v.* **glid·ed, glid·ing** *v.i.* **1.** To move, slip, or flow smoothly or effortlessly. **2.** To pass unnoticed or imperceptibly, as time: often with *by.* **3.** *Aeron.* To descend along an oblique line gradually without motor power; also, to fly a glider. **4.** *Music & Phonet.* To produce a glide. — *v.t.* **5.** To cause to glide. — *n.* **1.** The act of gliding. **2.** *Phonet.* A transitional sound made in passing from one speech sound to another. [OE *glīdan*] — **glid/ing·ly** *adv.*

glid·er (glī/dər) *n.* **1.** One who or that which glides. **2.** *Aeron.* An engineless airplane, constructed to soar on air currents. **3.** A swing gliding in a metal frame.

glim·mer (glim/ər) *v.i.* **1.** To gleam unsteadily; flicker. **2.** To appear fitfully or faintly. — *n.* **1.** A faint, unsteady light. **2.** A trace; inkling. [ME *glimeren* to shine] — **glim/mer·ing** *n. & adj.* — **glim/mer·ing·ly** *adv.*

glimpse (glimps) *n.* **1.** A momentary view or look. **2.** A faint intimation; inkling. — *v.* **glimpsed, glimps·ing** *v.t.* **1.** To see for an instant; catch a glimpse of. — *v.i.* **2.** To look for an instant: with *at.* [ME *glimsen* to shine faintly]

glint (glint) *v.i.* **1.** To gleam; glitter. **2.** To dart. — *v.t.* **3.** To reflect; shine. — *n.* **1.** A gleam. **2.** A luster, as of metal. [ME *glinten* to shine < Scand.]

glis·sade (gli·säd/, -sād/) *n.* **1.** The act of skillfully sliding down an icy slope. **2.** A gliding dance step. — *v.i.* **·sad·ed, ·sad·ing** To execute a glissade. [< F *glisser* to slip]

glis·san·do (gli·sän/dō) *Music n. pl.* **·di** (-dē) or **·dos 1.** A passing from one tone to another by a continuous change of pitch; also, a rapid succession of tones. **2.** A passage so written or performed. — *adj.* Of a glissando. — *adv.* Like a glissando. [< F *glissant* slipping + Ital. *-ando*]

glis·ten (glis/ən) *v.i.* To shine, as reflected light. — *n.* Brightness; sparkle. [OE *glisnian* to shine]

glit·ter (glit/ər) *v.i.* **1.** To sparkle brightly or brilliantly, as a diamond. **2.** To display striking magnificence; be brilliantly showy. — *n.* Sparkling magnificence; brilliance. [< ON *glitra*] — **glit/ter·ing·ly** *adv.* — **glit/ter·y** *adj.*

gloam·ing (glō/ming) *n.* The dusk of early evening; twilight. [OE *glōming*]

gloat (glōt) *v.i.* To take an intense, often malicious delight: usu. with *over.* [Cf. ON *glotta* to grin] — **gloat/ing** *adj.*

glob (glob) *n.* **1.** A small drop or ball of something. **2.** A rounded, often large mass of something.

glob·al (glō/bəl) *adj.* **1.** Involving the whole world: *global* war. **2.** Spherical. — **glob/al·ly** *adv.*

globe (glōb) *n.* **1.** A perfectly round body; ball; sphere;

also, anything like a sphere, as a fishbowl. 2. The earth. 3. A spherical model of the earth or heavens. 4. A ball, usu. of gold, used as an emblem of authority. — *v.t. & v.i.* **globed, glob·ing** To form into a globe. [< F < L *globus* ball] — **glo·bate** (glō′bāt) *adj.*

globe·fish (glōb′fish) *n. pl.* **·fish** or **·fish·es** Any of various spiny-finned, tropical fishes that inflate their bodies into globular form.

globe·trot·ter (glōb′trot′ər) *n.* One who travels all over the world, esp. for sightseeing. — **globe′trot′ting** *n.*

glo·bin (glō′bin) *n. Biochem.* The protein constituent of hemoglobin. [< L *globus* ball + -IN]

glo·bose (glō′bōs, glō·bōs′) *adj.* Spherical. Also **glo′bous** (-bəs). [< L *globus* ball] — **glo·bos·i·ty** (glō·bos′ə·tē) *n.*

glob·u·lar (glob′yə·lər) *adj.* 1. Spherical. 2. Formed of globules.

glob·ule (glob′yool) *n.* A tiny sphere of matter or drop of liquid. [< F < L *globulus* ball]

glob·u·lin (glob′yə·lin) *n. Biochem.* Any of a group of simple plant and animal proteins, insoluble in water but soluble in dilute saline solutions.

glob·u·lous (glob′yə·ləs) *adj.* 1. Containing or consisting of globules. 2. Spherical; globular. Also **glob′u·lose** (-lōs).

glock·en·spiel (glok′ən·spēl) *n.* A portable musical instrument with a series of chromatically tuned metal bars played by hammers. [< G < *glocken* bells + *spiel* play]

glom·er·ate (glom′ər·āt, -it) *adj.* Gathered or wound into a rounded mass. [< L *glomus* mass] — **glom′er·a′tion** *n.*

gloom (gloom) *n.* 1. Partial or total darkness; heavy shadow. 2. Darkness or depression of the mind or spirits. 3. A dark or gloomy place. — *v.i.* 1. To look sullen or dejected. 2. To be dark or threatening. — *v.t.* 3. To make dark, sad, or sullen. [ME *glom(b)en* to look sad]

gloom·y (gloo′mē) *adj.* **gloom·i·er, gloom·i·est** 1. Dark; dismal. 2. Melancholy; morose. 3. Producing gloom or melancholy. — **gloom′i·ly** *adv.* — **gloom′i·ness** *n.*

Glo·ri·a (glôr′ē·ə, glō′rē·ə) *n. Eccl.* **a** The section of the Mass consisting of the recitation or singing of *Gloria in excelsis Deo.* **b** Its musical setting. [< L, glory]

glo·ri·fi·ca·tion (glôr′ə·fə·kā′shən, glō′rə-) *n.* 1. The act of glorifying or exalting. 2. Invested with glory. 3. *Informal* A glorified form of something.

glo·ri·fy (glôr′ə·fī, glō′rə-) *v.t.* **·fied, ·fy·ing** 1. To make glorious. 2. To honor; worship. 3. To give great praise to; laud. 4. To make seem more splendid than is so. [< OF < L *gloria* glory + *facere* to make] — **glo′ri·fi′er** *n.*

glo·ri·ous (glôr′ē·əs, glō′rē-) *adj.* 1. Full of glory; illustrious. 2. Bringing glory or honor. 3. Resplendent. 4. *Informal* Delightful. — **glo′ri·ous·ly** *adv.* — **glo′ri·ous·ness** *n.*

glo·ry (glôr′ē, glō′rē) *n. pl.* **·ries** 1. Distinguished honor or praise; exalted reputation. 2. Something bringing praise. 3. Worshipful adoration: to give *glory* to God. 4. Magnificence; splendor: the *glory* of Rome. 5. The bliss of heaven. 6. A state of extreme well-being: to be in one's *glory*. 7. A nimbus; halo. — *v.i.* **·ried, ·ry·ing** 1. To take pride: with *in.* 2. To boast; brag. [< OF < L *gloria*]

gloss[1] (glôs, glos) *n.* 1. The luster or sheen of a polished surface. 2. A deceptive or superficial appearance. — *v.t.* 1. To make lustrous, as by polishing. 2. To hide (errors, etc.) by falsehood: usu. with *over.* — *v.i.* 3. To become shiny. [< Scand. Cf. ON *glossi* blaze.] — **gloss′er** *n.*

gloss[2] (glôs, glos) *n.* 1. An explanatory note, esp. marginal or interlinear; a commentary; a translation; a glossary. 2. An artful or deceptive explanation to cover up a fault, etc. — *v.t.* 1. To write glosses for (a text, etc.); annotate. 2. To excuse by false explanations. — *v.i.* 3. To make glosses. [< OF < L < Gk. *glōssa* foreign word] — **gloss′er** *n.*

glos·sa·ry (glos′ə·rē, glôs′-) *n. pl.* **·ries** A lexicon of the technical, obscure, or foreign words of a work or field. [< L < *glossa*] — **glos·sar·i·al** (glo·sâr′ē·əl, glô-) *adj.* — **glos·sar′i·al·ly** *adv.* — **glos·sa·rist** (glos′ə·rist, glôs′-) *n.*

glosso- *combining form* The tongue; speech; language. Also, before vowels, **gloss-.** [< Gk. *glōssa* tongue]

gloss·y (glôs′ē, glos′ē) *adj.* **gloss·i·er, gloss·i·est** 1. Having a bright sheen; lustrous. 2. Made superficially attractive. 3. Specious. — **gloss′i·ly** *adv.* — **gloss′i·ness** *n.*

-glot *combining form* Using or able to use (a number of) languages: *polyglot.* [< Gk. *glōssa* tongue, language]

glot·tal (glot′l) *adj.* Of or articulated in the glottis.

glot·tis (glot′is) *n. pl.* **glot·ti·des** (glot′ə·dēz) or **glot·tis·es** *Anat.* The cleft between the vocal cords at the upper opening of the larynx. [< NL < Gk. < *glōtta* tongue]

glotto- *combining form* Language. [< Gk. *glōtta*]

glove (gluv) *n.* 1. A covering for the hand, having a separate sheath for each finger. 2. In baseball, a large leather mitt for catching the ball. 3. A boxing glove. — **to be hand in glove** (with) To be in close relationship (with). — **to handle with kid gloves** To use great care and tact in dealing

with. — **to put on the gloves** *Informal* To box or spar. — *v.t.* **gloved, glov·ing** 1. To put gloves on. 2. To furnish with gloves. 3. To be a glove for. [OE *glōf*]

glov·er (gluv′ər) *n.* A maker of or dealer in gloves.

glow (glō) *v.i.* 1. To give off light and heat, esp. without flame; be incandescent. 2. To shine but without heat. 3. To be red, as from heat; flush. 4. To be animated, as with emotion, etc. 5. To be very hot; burn. — *n.* 1. The incandescence given off by a heated substance. 2. Vividness. 3. Ruddiness, as from health. 4. Strong emotion; ardor. [OE *glōwan*] — **glow′ing** *adj.* — **glow′ing·ly** *adv.*

glow·er (glou′ər) *v.i.* To stare with an angry frown; scowl sullenly. — *n.* The act of glowering; a fierce stare. [? Obs. *glow* to stare] — **glow′er·ing·ly** *adv.*

glow·worm (glō′wûrm′) *n.* 1. A European beetle, the larva and wingless female of which display phosphorescent light. 2. The firefly.

glox·in·i·a (glok·sin′ē·ə) *n.* A plant with large, bell-shaped flowers. [after *Gloxin*, 18th c. Ger. doctor]

gloze (glōz) *v.* **glozed, gloz·ing** *v.t.* To explain away.

glu·cose (gloo′kōs) *n.* 1. *Chem.* A monosaccharide carbohydrate, $C_6H_{12}O_6$, less sweet than cane sugar, found as dextrose in plants and animals and obtained by hydrolysis. 2. A thick yellowish syrup made from starch and used in candy making, baking, etc. [< F < Gk. *glykys* sweet]

glu·co·side (gloo′kə·sīd) *n. Chem.* Any of a class of carbohydrate compounds that yield glucose or other sugar.

glue (gloo) *n.* 1. An adhesive in the form of a gelatine made from animal substances, as skin, bones, etc. 2. An adhesive or cement made of casein or other synthetics. 3. Any sticky adhesive. — *v.t.* **glued, glu·ing** To stick or fasten with or as with glue. [< OF *glu* birdlime]

glue·y (gloo′ē) *adj.* **glu·i·er, glu·i·est** 1. Having the nature of glue; sticky; viscous. 2. Covered or spread with glue.

glum (glum) *adj.* **glum·mer, glum·mest** Moody and silent; sullen. — **glum′ly** *adv.* — **glum′ness** *n.*

glume (gloom) *n. Bot.* One of the two lowest bracts on the spikelet of certain grassy plants. [< L *gluma* husk]

glu·on (gloo′on) *n. Physics* According to the quantum chromodynamics theory, the carrier of the strong force that keeps nuclear particles from drifting apart.

glut (glut) *v.* **glut·ted, glut·ting** *v.t.* 1. To feed or supply to excess; satiate. 2. To supply (the market) with an excess of goods so that the price falls. — *v.i.* 3. To eat to excess. — *n.* 1. An excessive supply. 2. The act of glutting or being glutted. [< obs. *glut* glutton < OF *gloutir* to swallow]

glu·ten (gloo′tn) *n.* A tough, sticky mixture of proteins obtained by washing out the starch from wheat flour. [< L, glue] — **glu·te·nous** (gloo′tn·əs) *adj.*

glu·te·us (gloo·tē′əs) *n. pl.* **·te·i** (-tē′ī) *Anat.* Any of three muscles of the buttocks. [< NL < Gk. *gloutos* rump] — **glu·te′al** *adj.*

glu·ti·nous (gloo′tn·əs) *adj.* Resembling glue; sticky. — **glu′ti·nous·ly** *adv.* — **glu′ti·nous·ness** *n.*

glut·ton[1] (glut′n) *n.* 1. One who eats to excess. 2. One who has a great appetite or capacity for something. [< OF < L *gluto, -onis* glutton]

glut·ton[2] (glut′n) *n.* A wolverine, esp. of Asia or Europe. [Trans. of G *vielfrass* great eater]

glut·ton·ous (glut′n·əs) *adj.* 1. Given to excess in eating; voracious. 2. Desiring excessively. — **glut′ton·ous·ly** *adv.*

glut·ton·y (glut′n·ē) *n. pl.* **·ton·ies** The act or habit of eating to excess.

glyc·er·ide (glis′ər·īd, -id) *n. Chem.* An ether or ester of glycerol with a fatty acid.

glyc·er·in (glis′ər·in) *n.* Glycerol. Also **glyc′er·ine** (-in, -ēn).

glyc·er·ol (glis′ər·ōl, -ol) *n. Chem.* A sweet, oily, colorless alcohol, $C_3H_8O_3$, formed by decomposition of natural fats with alkalis or superheated steam, used in medicine, industry, and the arts. [< Gk. *glykeros* sweet + -OL²]

glyc·er·yl (glis′ər·il) *n. Chem.* The trivalent glycerol radical C_3H_5.

glyco- *combining form* Sweet. [< Gk. *glykys* sweet]

gly·co·gen (glī′kə·jən) *n. Biochem.* A white, mealy, amorphous polysaccharide, $(C_6H_{10}O_5)_x$, contained principally in the liver and hydrolized into glucose.

gly·col (glī′kōl, -kol) *n. Chem.* 1. One of several alcohols containing two hydroxyl radicals, having the general formula $C_nH_{2n}(OH)_2$. 2. Ethylene glycol.

gly·co·side (glī′kə·sīd) *n. Chem.* Any of a group of carbohydrates that when decomposed yield glucose or other sugar.

G-man (jē′man′) *n. pl.* **-men** (-men′) An agent of the Federal Bureau of Investigation. [< G(OVERNMENT) MAN]

gnarl (närl) *n.* A protuberance on a tree; a tough knot. — *v.t.* To make knotty and twisted like an old tree.

gnarled (närld) *adj.* 1. Having snarls. 2. Weather-beaten and rugged. 3. Of the hands, having prominent knuckles and twisted fingers as from hard work. Also **gnarl′y.**

PRONUNCIATION KEY: add, āce, câre, pälm; end, ēven; it, īce; odd, ōpen, ôrder; took, pool; up, bûrn; ə = a in *above*, e in *sicken*, i in *flexible*, o in *melon*, u in *focus*; yoo = u in *fuse*; oil; pout; check; go; ring; thin; this; zh, vision. For à, œ, ü, kh, ṅ, see inside front cover.

gnash (nash) *v.t.* **1.** To grind or snap (the teeth) together, as in rage. **2.** To bite or chew by grinding the teeth. —*v.i.* **3.** To grind the teeth. —*n.* A bite of the teeth. [< Scand.]

gnat (nat) *n.* Any of various small stinging or biting flies. — **to strain at a gnat** To fuss. [OE *gnæt*]

-gnathous *combining form* Having a jaw of an indicated kind: *prognathous.* [< Gk. *gnathos* jaw + -OUS]

gnaw (nô) *v.t.* **gnawed,** *or sometimes* **gnawn, gnaw·ing 1.** To bite or eat away little by little as with the teeth; to make by gnawing; also, to bite on repeatedly. **2.** To torment or oppress with fear, pain, etc. —*v.i.* **3.** To bite, chew, or corrode persistently. **4.** To cause constant worry, etc. [OE *gnagan*] — **gnaw'er** *n.* — **gnaw'ing·ly** *adv.*

gnaw·ing (nô'ing) *n.* **1.** A dull, persistent sensation of discomfort or distress. **2.** *pl.* Pangs of hunger.

gneiss (nīs) *n.* A coarse-grained, banded rock like granite but having layered components. [< G] — **gneiss'ic** *adj.*

gnome (nōm) *n.* In folklore, one of a group of dwarfish, little old men, living in caves and guarding buried treasure, etc. [< F < NL *gnomus*] — **gnom'ish** *adj.*

gno·mic (nō'mik, nom'ik) *adj.* Consisting of or resembling maxims; aphoristic. Also **gno'mi·cal.** — **gno'mi·cal·ly** *adv.*

gno·mon (nō'mon) *n.* A pointer or similar device used to indicate time by the shadow it casts, as on a sundial. For illus. see SUNDIAL. [< Gk. < *gnō-* stem of *gignōskein* to know] — **gno·mon·ic** (nō-mon'ik) *or* **·i·cal** *adj.*

-gnomy *combining form* Knowledge or art of judging: *physiognomy.* [< Gk. *gnōmē* judgment]

-gnosis *combining form Med.* Knowledge; recognition: *prognosis.* [< Gk. *gnōsis* knowledge]

gnos·tic (nos'tik) *adj.* Of or possessing knowledge, esp. spiritual knowledge or insight. Also **gnos'ti·cal.**

Gnos·ti·cism (nos'tə·siz'əm) *n.* A system of ancient Greek and Oriental philosophy, an attempted synthesis with Christian doctrine, denounced as heretical by the Church. — **Gnos'tic** *adj. & n.*

gnu (nōō, nyōō) *n. pl.* **gnus** *or* **gnu** A South African antelope having an oxlike head with curved horns, a mane, and a long tail: also called *wildebeest.* [< Xhosa *nqu*]

GNU
(To 4 feet high at shoulder)

go[1] (go) *v.* **went, gone, go·ing;** *3rd person sing. present* **goes** *v.i.* **1.** To proceed or pass along; move. **2.** To move from a place; leave; depart: often used as a command or signal, as in a race: *Go!* **3.** To have a scheduled route destination: This train *goes* to Chicago daily. **4.** To be in operation; also, to work or function properly. **5.** To extend or reach: This pipe *goes* to the basement. **6.** To emit a specified sound or act in a certain way: The chain *goes* "clank." **7.** To fail, give away, or collapse; also, to disappear. **8.** To have a specific place: belong: The plates *go* on the shelf. **9.** To be awarded or given; also, to be allotted or applied: This *goes* for rent. **10.** To pass from one person to another. **11.** To pass into a condition; become: to *go* insane. **12.** To be, continue, or appear in a specified state: to *go* unpunished. **13.** To happen or end in a specific manner: The election *went* badly. **14.** To be considered or ranked: good as lunches *go*. **15.** To be suitable; harmonize; fit. **16.** To be phrased; have a certain form: How does the tune *go*? **17.** To have recourse; resort: to *go* to court. **18.** To die. **19.** To pass: said of time. **20.** To be abolished or given up: These expenses must *go*. **21.** To serve, contribute, or help; also, to make up a certain quantity: Two ounces *go* to each serving. **22.** To be sold or bid for: with *at* or *for*: These shoes will *go* at a high price. **23.** To subject oneself; put oneself: He *went* to great pains. **24.** To continue one's actions to or beyond certain limits: He *goes* too far in his criticism. **25.** To endure; last: Can he *go* two more rounds? **26.** To be about to: used in the progressive form and followed by the present infinitive: They are *going* to protest. —*v.t.* **27.** *Informal* To furnish or provide (bail). **28.** *Informal* To risk or bet; wager. **29.** *Informal* To put up with; tolerate: I cannot *go* that music. —*adj. Aerospace* Operating or proceeding as planned. — **to go** *Informal* **1.** Remaining: ten pages *to go*. **2.** Prepared for taking outside: a sandwich *to go*. — **to go about 1.** To be occupied or busy with. **2.** To circulate. **3.** *Naut.* To tack; turn. — **to go after 1.** To try to catch; chase. **2.** To follow in sequence. — **to go against** To be opposed to; act contrary to. — **to go along 1.** To continue; carry on. **2.** To be in accord; agree: often with *with*. **3.** To escort; accompany: with *with*. — **to go around 1.** To move about or circulate. **2.** To enclose; encircle. **3.** To be enough for all to have some. — **to go at** To attack; work at. — **to go back on 1.** To be disloyal to; forsake. **2.** To fail to fulfill. — **to go behind** To inquire or investigate so as to test the validity of. — **to go beyond** To surpass; exceed. — **to go by 1.** To pass. **2.** To conform to or be guided by. **3.** To be known by. — **to go down 1.** To sink or descend. **2.** To experience defeat. **3.** To attain lasting remembrance, as

in history. **4.** To decrease, as prices. — **to go for 1.** To try to get. **2.** To advocate. **3.** *Informal* To attack. **4.** *Informal* To be attracted by. — **to go halves** (or **shares**) *Informal* To share equally. — **to go hard with** To bring trouble to. — **to go in for** *Informal* **1.** To strive for; advocate. **2.** To like or participate in. — **to go into 1.** To investigate. **2.** To take up, as a study. **3.** To be contained in. — **to go in with** To unite or join forces with. — **to go off 1.** To explode or be discharged, as a gun. **2.** To depart; leave. **3.** *Informal* To occur. — **to go on 1.** To act; behave. **2.** To happen: What's *going* on here? **3.** To persevere; endure. **4.** In the theater, to make an entrance. — **to go (someone) better** *Informal* To surpass (someone). — **to go out 1.** To go to social gatherings, etc. **2.** To be extinguished, as a light. **3.** To become outdated, as fashions. **4.** To go on strike. **5.** To sympathize. My heart *goes out* to him. — **to go over 1.** To repeat; also, to rehearse. **2.** To examine carefully. **3.** *Informal* To succeed. **4.** To change sides or allegiance. — **to go through 1.** To search thoroughly. **2.** To undergo; suffer; endure. **3.** To run over, as a role. **4.** To spend. **5.** To be accepted or approved. — **to go through with** To perform to the finish; complete. — **to go together 1.** To be suitable; harmonize. **2.** To be sweethearts. — **to go under 1.** To be overwhelmed. **2.** To fail, as a business. — **to go up** To increase, as prices. — **to go with 1.** To harmonize with. **2.** To accompany. **3.** *Informal* To be sweethearts. — **to go without** To do or be without. — **to go without saying** To be taken for granted. — **to let go 1.** To release one's hold; set free. **2.** To abandon. — **to let oneself go** To be uninhibited. —*n.* **1.** The act of going. **2.** *Informal* The capacity for action; He has plenty of *go*. **3.** *Informal* A try: to have a *go* at something. **4.** *Informal* A success: He made a *go* of it. **5.** *Informal* An agreement; bargain: It's a *go*. — **no go** *Informal* Useless; hopeless. — **on the go** *Informal* In constant motion; very busy. [OE *gān*]

go[2] (go) *n.* A Japanese game resembling chess or checkers.

goad (gōd) *n.* **1.** A stick for urging on oxen, etc. **2.** Something that drives. —*v.t.* To drive; incite. [OE *gād*]

go-a·head (gō'ə·hed') *n.* A signal or permission to move ahead or proceed.

goal (gōl) *n.* **1.** Something toward which effort or movement is directed; an end or objective. **2.** The terminal point of a journey or race. **3.** In some games, the point to which the players try to bring the ball, puck, etc., to score; also, the scoring; also, the score made. [ME *gol*]

goal·ie (gō'lē) *n. Informal* A goalkeeper.

goal·keep·er (gōl'kē'pər) *n.* In hockey, soccer, etc., a player whose function is to prevent the ball or puck from passing over the goal for a score. Also **goal'tend'er.**

goat (gōt) *n.* **1.** A cud-chewing mammal related to the sheep and having hollow horns. **2.** A lecherous man. **3.** *Slang* One who is the butt of a joke; scapegoat. — **to get one's goat** *Slang* To move one to anger or annoyance. [OE *gāt*] — **goat'ish** *adj.* — **goat'ish·ly** *adv.* — **goat'ish·ness** *n.*

Goat (gōt) *n.* The constellation and sign of the zodiac Capricorn.

goat·ee (gō·tē') *n.* A man's short, pointed beard.

goat·herd (gōt'hûrd') *n.* One who tends goats.

goat·skin (gōt'skin') *n.* **1.** The hide of a goat. **2.** Leather made from this hide. **3.** Something made from this leather.

goat·suck·er (gōt'suk'ər) *n.* Any of numerous nocturnal, insectivorous birds, as the whippoorwill.

gob[1] (gob) *n. Informal* **1.** A piece or lump, as of a soft substance. **2.** *pl.* Great quantities. [< OF *gobe* mouthful]

gob[2] (gob) *n. Slang* A sailor of the U.S. Navy.

gob·bet (gob'it) *n.* **1.** A piece or hunk of raw meat. **2.** *Archaic* A large lump of food. [See GOB[1].]

gob·ble[1] (gob'əl) *v.* **bled, ·bling** *v.t.* **1.** To swallow (food) greedily. **2.** *U.S. Slang* To seize in a grasping manner. — *v.i.* **3.** To eat greedily. [< F *gover* to bolt; devour]

gob·ble[2] (gob'əl) *v.i.* **bled, ·bling** To make the throaty sound of a male turkey. —*n.* This sound. [Var. of GABBLE]

gob·ble·dy·gook (gob'əl·dē·gōōk') *n. Informal* Involved, pedantic, repetitious, and pompous jargon. [Coined by M. Maverick, U.S. Congressman, about 1940]

gob·bler (gob'lər) *n.* A male turkey.

Gob·e·lin (gob'ə·lin; *Fr.* gô·be·laɴ') *n.* A rich tapestry made in Paris or Beauvais, France. [after *Gobelin,* name of its first creator]

go-be·tween (gō'bə·twēn') *n.* One who acts as an agent or mediator between other persons.

gob·let (gob'lit) *n.* **1.** A drinking vessel, typically with a base and stem. **2.** A large, festive shallow drinking cup. [< OF *gobel* a drinking cup]

gob·lin (gob'lin) *n.* In folklore, an ugly elf regarded as evil or mischievous. [< OF *gobelin*]

go·bo (gō'bō) *n. pl.* **·bos 1.** A portable shield placed around a microphone to keep out extraneous sounds. **2.** A screen for shielding the lens of a television camera from the direct rays of light. [Origin uncertain]

go·by (gō'bē) *n. pl.* **·by** *or* **·bies** Any of a family of fishes having ventral fins and a funnel-shaped suction disk. [< L < Gk. *kóbios*, a small fish]

go-by (gō′bī′) *n. Informal* An intentional slight.

go-cart (gō′kärt′) *n.* 1. A small wagon for young children. 2. A framework with rollers, designed to support babies learning to walk. 3. A handcart.

god (god) *n.* 1. One of various beings, usu. male, in mythology, primitive religions, etc., conceived of as immortal, as embodying a particular quality or having special powers over some phase of life. 2. A statue, image, or symbol of such a being. 3. Any person or thing much loved. [OE]

God (god) *n.* In monotheism, the ruler of life and the universe.

god-child (god′chīld′) *n. pl.* **-chil-dren** One whom a person sponsors at baptism, circumcision, etc.

god-dam (god′dam′) *interj.* A strong oath used to express anger, annoyance, surprise, etc. Also **God damn.** — *adj. & adv.* Goddamned.

god-damned (god′damd′) *adj.* Utterly detestable or outrageous. — *adv. Informal* To an extreme degree; very.

god-daugh-ter (god′dô′tər) *n.* A female godchild.

god-dess (god′is) 1. A female deity. 2. A woman or girl of extraordinary beauty.

god-fa-ther (god′fä′thər) *n.* A man who sponsors a child at its baptism. — *v.t.* To act as a godfather to.

god-fear-ing (god′fir′ing) *adj.* 1. *Often cap.* Having reverence for God. 2. Pious; devout.

god-for-sak-en (god′fər-sā′kən) *adj.* 1. *Often cap.* Abandoned by God. 2. Totally wicked. 3. Wretched; desolate.

god-head (god′hed′) *n.* Godhood; divinity.

God-head (god′hed′) *n.* The essential nature of God.

god-hood (god′hōōd) *n.* The state or quality of being divine.

Go-di-va (gə-dī′və) A legendary lady who agreed to ride naked through Coventry if her husband would remove oppressive taxes.

god-less (god′lis) *adj.* 1. Having or believing in no god. 2. Wicked. — **god′less-ly** *adv.* — **god′less-ness** *n.*

god-like (god′līk) *adj.* 1. Befitting or like God or a god. 2. Being of supreme excellence, beauty, etc. — **god′like′ness** *n.*

god-ly (god′lē) *adj.* **-li-er, -li-est** Filled with love for God. — **god′li-ness** *n.*

god-moth-er (god′muth′ər) *n.* A woman who sponsors a child at its baptism. — *v.t.* To act as a godmother to.

god-par-ent (god′pâr′ənt) *n.* A godfather or godmother.

God's acre A burying ground.

god-send (god′send′) *n.* Something received or acquired unexpectedly that is just what one needed or wanted.

god-son (god′sun′) *n.* A male godchild.

God-speed (god′spēd′) *n.* Best wishes for someone's journey or venture. [Shortened form of *God speed you*]

god-wit (god′wit) *n.* A shore bird resembling a curlew, with long legs and bill. [Origin uncertain]

go-get-ter (gō′get′ər) *n. U.S. Informal* A hustling, energetic, aggressive person.

gog-gle (gog′əl) *n.* 1. *pl.* Spectacles designed to protect the eyes against dust, sparks, wind, etc. 2. An erratic movement or bulging of the eyes. — *v.* **-gled, -gling** *v.i.* 1. To roll the eyes erratically. 2. Of the eyes, to move erratically, bulge, or be fixed in a stare. — *v.t.* 3. To cause (the eyes) to goggle. 4. Of the eyes, rolling erratically, staring, or bulging. [ME *gogelen* to look aside]

gog-gle-eyed (gog′əl-īd′) *adj.* Having eyes that goggle.

go-go (gō′gō′) *adj.* 1. Of or describing discothèques, the usu. erotic dances performed there, or the women dancers. 2. Lively, modern, glamorous, etc. [< F *à gogo* joyfully]

Goi-del-ic (goi-del′ik) *n.* The branch of the Celtic languages including Irish, the Gaelic of the Scottish Highlands, and Manx; Gaelic: distinguished from *Brythonic.* — *adj.* Of or pertaining to the Gaels or their languages. Also **Goi-dhel′ic.** [< OIrish *Goídel* Gael]

go-ing (gō′ing) *n.* 1. The act of departing or moving; leaving. 2. The condition of ground or roads as affecting walking, riding, racing, etc. 3. *Informal* A condition influencing progress or activity. — **goings on** *Informal* Actions or behavior: used chiefly to express disapproval. — *adj.* 1. That goes, moves, or works. 2. Continuing to function; moving ahead: a *going* concern. 3. In existence; available.

goi-ter (goi′tər) *n. Pathol.* Any abnormal enlargement of the thyroid gland, visible as a swelling in the front of the neck. Also **goi′tre.** [< F, ult. < L *guttur* throat] — **goi-trous** (goi′trəs) *adj.*

gold (gōld) *n.* 1. A precious, yellow, metallic element (symbol Au) that is highly ductile and resistant to oxidation: also called *aurum.* See ELEMENT. 2. Coin made of this metal. 3. Wealth; riches. 4. A bright yellow color. 5. Something valuable, etc.: a heart of *gold.* — *adj.* 1. Pertaining to, made of, containing, or like gold. 2. Based on or redeemable in gold. [OE]

gold-brick (gōld′brik′) *U.S. Slang n.* One who shirks work: said esp. of soldiers. Also **gold′brick′er.** — *v.t. & v.i.* 1. To shirk (work or duty). 2. To cheat or swindle.

gold brick *Informal* Anything deceitfully substituted for an object of value.

gold digger 1. One who or that which digs for gold. 2. *U.S. Slang* A woman who uses feminine wiles to get money.

gold-en (gōl′dən) *adj.* 1. Made of or containing gold. 2. Bright yellow. 3. Resembling gold. 4. Happy, prosperous, etc. — **gold′en-ly** *adv.* — **gold′en-ness** *n.*

golden age 1. In Greek and Roman legend, an early period marked by perfect innocence, peace, and happiness. 2. Any period of prosperity or excellence.

golden anniversary A 50th anniversary.

golden calf 1. A molten image worshiped by the Israelites. *Ex.* xxxii. 2. Riches, as unduly prized.

gold-en-eye (gōl′dən-ī′) *n.* A large diving duck of America and Europe with yellow eyes.

golden glow A tall garden plant having many-rayed yellow flowers.

golden mean Moderation; avoidance of extremes.

gold-en-rod (gōl′dən-rod′) *n.* A widely distributed North American herb of the composite family, having small, usu. yellow flowers: the State flower of Alabama, Kentucky, and Nebraska.

golden rule The rule or principle of treating others as one wants to be treated. *Matt.* vii 12.

Golden State Nickname of California.

golden wedding The 50th anniversary of a marriage.

gold-filled (gōld′fild′) *adj.* Filled with a base metal over which a thick covering of gold is laid.

gold-finch (gōld′finch′) *n.* 1. A European finch having a yellow patch on each wing. 2. An American finch of which the male, in the summer, has a yellow body with black tail.

gold-fish (gōld′fish′) *n. pl.* **-fish** or **-fish-es** A small carp, usu. golden in color, cultivated as an aquarium fish.

gold foil Thin sheets of gold, thicker than gold leaf.

gold leaf Sheets of gold hammered to extreme thinness, used in gilding, etc.

gold mine 1. A mine producing gold ore. 2. *Informal* Any source of great profit, riches, etc.

gold plate Vessels and utensils of gold, collectively.

gold reserve 1. Gold held in reserve by the U.S. Treasury to protect U.S. promissory notes. 2. The quantity of gold bullion or coin owned by the central bank of a country.

gold rush A mass movement of people to an area where gold has been discovered, as that to California in 1849.

gold-smith (gōld′smith′) *n.* One who makes or deals in articles of gold.

gold standard A monetary system based on gold of a specified weight and fineness as the unit of value.

go-lem (gō′lem, -ləm) *n.* In medieval Jewish legend, an automaton made to resemble a human being and given life by a magic incantation. [< Hebrew, embryo, monster]

golf (gôlf, golf) *n.* An outdoor game played on a large course with a small resilient ball and a set of clubs, the object being to direct the ball into a series of variously distributed holes (usually nine or eighteen) in as few strokes as possible. — *v.i.* To play golf. [Cf. dial. E (Scot.) *gowf* strike] — **golf′er** *n.*

golf club 1. One of several slender clubs with wooden or metal heads, used in playing golf. 2. An organization of golfers; also, the building and grounds used by them.

golf course The course over which a game of golf is played. Also **golf links.**

Gol-gi body (gôl′jē) *Biol.* A netlike structure of rod-shaped elements found in the cytoplasm of animal cells. Also **Golgi apparatus.** For illus. see CELL. [after Camillo *Golgi*, 1844–1926, Italian pathologist]

Gol-go-tha (gol′gə-thə) A place near Jerusalem where Jesus was crucified; Calvary. *Matt.* xxvii 33. [< LL < Gk. < Aramaic *gogolthā* skull]

Go-li-ath (gə-lī′əth) In the Bible, a giant Philistine slain by David with a sling. I *Sam.* xvii 4.

gol-li-wog (gol′ē-wog) *n.* 1. A grotesque black doll. 2. A grotesque person. Also **gol-li-wogg.** [after illustrations by Florence Upton (1895) for a series of children's books]

gol-ly (gol′ē) *interj.* An exclamation of mild surprise, impatience, etc. [Euphemistic alter. of GOD]

Go-mor-rah (gə-môr′ə, -mor′ə), **Go-mor-rha** See SODOM.

gon- Var. of GONO-.

-gon *combining form* Having (an indicated number of) angles: *pentagon.* [< Gk. *gōnia* angle]

gon-ad (gō′nad, gon′ad) *n. Anat.* A male or female sex gland, in which the reproductive cells develop; an ovary or testis. — **gon′a-dal, go-na-di-al** (gō-nā′dē-əl), **go-nad-ic** (gō-nad′ik) *adj.*

gon-do-la (gon′də-lə, gon-dō′lə) *n.* 1. A long, narrow, flat-bottomed Venetian boat propelled by one man with an oar at the stern. **2.** *U.S.* A large, flat-bottomed, river boat; also, a gondola car. **3.** *Aeron.* The car attached below a dirigible. [< Ital. < *gondola* to rock]

gon·do·la car *U.S.* A long, shallow, open freight car.

gon·do·lier (gon/də·lir/) *n.* The boatman of a gondola.

gone (gôn, gon) Past participle of GO. — *adj.* **1.** Moved away; left. **2.** Beyond hope; ruined; lost. **3.** Dead; departed. **4.** Ended; past. **5.** Marked by faintness or weakness. **6.** Consumed; spent. — **far gone 1.** Exhausted; wearied. **2.** Almost ended or dead.

gon·er (gôn/ər, gon/-) *n. Informal* A person or thing that is close to death, ruined, or beyond all hope of saving.

gon·fa·lon (gon/fə·lən) *n.* A banner or ensign, usu. cut so as to end in streamers. Also **gon·fa·non** (gon/fə·nən). [< Ital. < OHG *gundfano* war banner]

gong (gông, gong) *n.* **1.** A heavy metal disk giving a deep, resonant tone when struck. **2.** A flat, saucerlike bell struck with a small mechanical hammer. [< Malay]

gonio- *combining form* Angle; corner. [< Gk. *gōnia* angle]

-gonium *combining form* Reproductive cell; seed. [< Gk. *gonos* seed]

gono- *combining form* Procreative; sexual. Also, before vowels, **gon.-** [< Gk. *gonos* seed]

gon·o·coc·cus (gon/ə·kok/əs) *n. pl.* **·coc·ci** (-kok/sī) The bacterium that causes gonorrhea. [< NL]

gon·or·rhe·a (gon/ə·rē/ə) *n. Pathol.* A contagious venereal infection, caused by the gonococcus, in which there is a purulent inflammation of the mucous membranes of the genitourinary tract. Also **gon/or·rhoe/a.** [< LL < Gk. < *gonos* seed + *rheein* to flow] — **gon/or·rhe/al** *adj.*

-gony *combining form* Production of; generation: *cosmogony.* [< L *-gonia* < Gk. < *gonos* seed, reproduction. Cf. -GENY.]

goo (gōō) *n. U.S. Slang* Any sticky substance.

goo·ber (gōō/bər) *n. U.S.* A peanut. Also **goober pea.** [? < Bantu *nguba*]

good (gōōd) *adj.* **bet·ter, best 1.** Morally excellent; virtuous. **2.** Honorable; worthy: a *good* reputation. **3.** Generous; loving; kind. **4.** Well-behaved; tractable. **5.** Proper; desirable: *good* manners. **6.** Favorable: a *good* opinion. **7.** Pleasant; agreeable. **8.** Having beneficial effects; helpful: *good* advice. **9.** Reliable; safe: a *good* investment. **10.** Suitable; qualified: a *good* man for the job. **11.** Skillful; expert: He is *good* at sports. **12.** Genuine; valid: a *good* excuse. **13.** Backed by sufficient funds: a *good* check. **14.** Excellent in quality or degree: *good* literature. **15.** Orthodox; conforming. **16.** Sufficient; ample: a *good* rest. **17.** Unspoiled; fresh: *good* meat. **18.** Healthy: *good* lungs. **19.** Satisfactory or appropriate: *good* weather for flying. **20.** Attractive or striking: She looks *good* in that hat. **21.** Great in amount; also, maximum; full. — **as good as** Practically; virtually: *as good as* done. — **good and** *Informal* Completely; very: *good and* hot. — **good for 1.** Capable of lasting for. **2.** *Informal* Able to pay, give, or produce. — **no good** Worthless. — *n.* **1.** That which is fitting, etc. **2.** Benefit: for the *good* of mankind. **3.** That which is morally or ethically desirable. — **for good (and all)** For the last time; forever. — **to make good 1.** To be successful. **2.** To compensate for. **3.** To fulfill. **4.** To prove; substantiate. — *interj.* An exclamation of satisfaction. — *adv. Informal* Well. ♦ *Good* is gaining acceptance in informal usage as a substitute for *well* when reference is made to the functioning of a machine or the like, as in *This watch runs good.* In other contexts it is usually nonstandard. [OE *gōd*]

good book The Bible. Also **Good Book.**

good-by (gōōd/bī/) *adj., n. & interj. pl.* **-bys** (-bīz/) Farewell. Also **good/-bye/.** [Contraction of *God be with you*]

good-for-noth·ing (gōōd/fər·nuth/ing) *n.* A worthless person. — *adj.* Having no use or worth.

Good Friday The Friday before Easter, a day observed by Christians as a commemoration of the crucifixion of Jesus.

good·heart·ed (gōōd/här/tid) *adj.* Kind; charitable; generous. — **good/heart/ed·ly** *adv.* — **good/heart/ed·ness** *n.*

good-hu·mored (gōōd/hyōō/mərd, -yōō/-) *adj.* Having a cheerful temper or mood. — **good/-hu/mored·ly** *adv.*

good·ish (gōōd/ish) *adj.* **1.** Somewhat good. **2.** Rather big.

good-look·ing (gōōd/lōōk/ing) *adj.* Handsome.

good·ly (gōōd/lē) *adj.* **·li·er, ·li·est 1.** Having a pleasing appearance. **2.** Of fine quality. **3.** Large. — **good/li·ness** *n.*

good-na·tured (gōōd/nā/chərd) *adj.* Having a pleasant disposition; not easily provoked. Also **good-tempered** (gōōd/tem/pərd). — **good/-na/tured·ly** *adv.* — **good/-na/tured·ness** *n.*

good·ness (gōōd/nis) *n.* **1.** The state or quality of being good; esp.: **a** Excellence of character, morals, etc.; virtue. **b.** Generous and kindly feelings; benevolence. **2.** The best part. **3.** God: *Goodness* knows. — **Syn.** See VIRTUE.

goods (gōōdz) *n.pl.* **1.** Merchandise; wares. **2.** Fabric; material. **3.** Property, esp. when personal and movable.

Good Samaritan 1. In a New Testament parable, the only passer-by to aid a man who had been injured and robbed. *Luke* x 30–37. **2.** A humane, compassionate person.

Good Shepherd A name for Jesus. *John* x 11, 12.

good will 1. A desire for the well-being of others; benevolence. **2.** Cheerful, ready consent or willingness. **3.** Intangible assets in terms of prestige and friendly relations. Also **good·will** (gōōd/wil/).

good·y (gōōd/ē) *n. pl.* **good·ies** *Informal* **1.** Something tasty. **2.** A prissy person: also **goody-goody.** — *adj.* Good or pious in a weak, sentimental way: also **goody-goody.** — *interj.* A childish exclamation.

goof (gōōf) *Slang n.* **1.** A dull-witted person; dope. **2.** A mistake; blunder. — *v.i.* **1.** To blunder. — *v.t.* **2.** To make a mess of. — **to goof off** *Slang* To loaf.

goon (gōōn) *n. U.S. Slang* **1.** A thug or hoodlum, esp. one hired to break strikes. **2.** A stupid person. [after a character created by E. C. Segar, 1894–1938, U.S. cartoonist]

goose (gōōs) *n. pl.* **geese** (gēs) **1.** A subfamily of web-footed birds larger than ducks. **2.** The female: distinguished from *gander.* **3.** The flesh as food. **4.** A fool. — **to cook one's goose** *Informal* To spoil one's chances. [OE *gos*]

goose·ber·ry (gōōs/ber/ē, -bər·ē, gōōz/-) *n. pl.* **·ries 1.** The tart berry of a spiny shrub of the saxifrage family, used for jams, pies, etc. **2.** The shrub itself.

goose flesh A taut, prickling sensation in the skin. Also **goose bumps, goose pimples, goose skin.**

goose·foot (gōōs/fōōt/) *n. pl.* **·foots** A plant, having green flowers, as beets and spinach.

goose·neck (gōōs/nek/) *n.* Any of various mechanical devices curved like a goose's neck.

goose-step (gōōs/step/) *v.i.* **-stepped, -step·ping** To march along or mark time kicking stiffly and sharply.

goose step 1. The action of goose-stepping. **2.** The manner of moving the legs in goose-stepping.

go·pher (gō/fər) *n. U.S. & Canadian* **1.** A burrowing American rodent with large cheek pouches. **2.** A North American ground squirrel. [< F *gaufre* honeycomb]

Gor·di·an knot (gôr/dē·ən) **1.** A legendary knot tied by **Gordius,** king of Phrygia, which an oracle predicted would be undone by a ruler of Asia. Alexander the Great cut it. **2.** Any difficulty solved only by drastic measures.

gore[1] (gôr, gōr) *n.* Blood that has been shed; esp., a copious amount of thickened, clotted, or dried blood. [OE *gor* dirt]

gore[2] (gôr, gōr) *v.t.* **gored, gor·ing** To pierce with the horns or tusks. [ME *goren*]

gore[3] (gôr, gōr) *n.* A triangular or tapering section set into a garment, sail, etc., for greater fullness. — *v.t.* **gored, gor·ing 1.** To cut into gore-shaped pieces. **2.** To furnish with gores. [OE *gāra* triangular piece of land]

gorge (gôrj) *n.* **1.** A narrow, deep ravine, esp. with a stream flowing through. **2.** The act of gorging. **3.** That which is gorged, as a greedily swallowed meal. **4.** Deep or violent disgust. **5.** A mass obstructing a passage. — *v.* **gorged, gorg·ing** *v.t.* **1.** To stuff with food. **2.** To swallow gluttonously. — *v.i.* **3.** To stuff oneself with food. [< OF < L *gurges* whirlpool] — **gorg/er** *n.*

gor·geous (gôr/jəs) *adj.* **1.** Dazzlingly colorful; brilliant. **2.** *Informal* Extremely beautiful, etc. [< OF *gorgias* elegant] — **gor/geous·ly** *adv.* — **gor/geous·ness** *n.*

gor·gon (gôr/gən) *n.* A terrifyingly ugly woman.

Gor·gon (gôr/gən) *n.* In Greek mythology, one of three sisters with serpents for hair, so terrifying that the sight of them turned the beholder to stone. [< L < Gk. < *gorgos* terrible] — **Gor·go·ni·an** (gôr·gō/nē·ən) *adj.*

Gor·gon·zo·la (gôr/gən·zō/lə) *n.* A strongly flavored, white Italian cheese. [after *Gorgonzola*, a town]

go·ril·la (gə·ril/ə) *n.* An African jungle ape, the largest and most powerful of the anthropoids, having a massive body, long arms, and tusklike canine teeth. [< NL < Gk., appar. < native name]

gorse (gôrs) *n. Brit.* Furze, a plant. [OE *gors(t)*]

go·ry (gôr/ē, gōr/ē) *adj.* **·ri·er, ·ri·est 1.** Covered, stained with, or resembling gore. **2.** Full of bloodshed: a *gory* battle. — **gor/i·ly** *adv.* — **gor/i·ness** *n.*

gosh (gosh) *interj.* An exclamation. [Euphemism for GOD]

gos·hawk (gos/hôk/, gôs/-) *n.* Any of various large, short-winged hawks formerly used in falconry. [OE *gōshafoc*]

Go·shen (gō/shən) **1.** The region in Egypt inhabited by the Israelites. *Gen.* xlv 10. **2.** Any place of peace or plenty.

gos·ling (goz/ling) *n.* A young goose. [< ON *gæslingr*]

gos·pel (gos/pəl) *n.* **1.** The teachings of the Christian church as originally preached by Jesus Christ and the apostles. **2.** A narrative of Christ's life and teachings, as in the first four books of the New Testament. **3.** Any information accepted as unquestionably true. **4.** A doctrine considered of major importance. [OE *godspell* good news]

Gos·pel (gos/pəl) *n.* Any of the first four books of the New Testament, attributed to Matthew, Mark, Luke, and John.

gos·sa·mer (gos/ə·mər) *n.* **1.** Fine strands of spider's silk, esp. when floating in the air. **2.** Any flimsy, delicate substance, as filmy, gauzelike fabric. — *adj.* Resembling gossamer; flimsy; unsubstantial: also **gos/sa·mer·ry** (-mər·ē) [< ME *gossomer* Indian summer, lit., goose summer]

gos·sip (gos′əp) *n.* **1.** Idle, often malicious talk, esp. about others. **2.** Informal talk or writing, as of personages. **3.** A person, esp. a woman, who indulges in idle talk. — *v.* **·siped** or **·sipped**, **·sip·ing** or **·sip·ping** *v.t. & v.i.* To talk idly; repeat as gossip. [OE *god* + *sibb* a relative] — **gos′sip·er** *n.*

gos·sip·y (gos′əp·ē) *adj.* **1.** Indulging in gossip. **2.** Chatty.

got (got) Past tense and past participle of GET. ◆ See note under GOTTEN.

Goth (goth, gôth) *n.* **1.** A member of a Germanic people that invaded the Roman Empire in the third to fifth centuries: including the Ostrogoths (**East Goths**) and Visigoths (**West Goths**). **2.** A barbarian. [< LL < Gk. *Gothoi* < Gothic]

Goth·am (goth′əm, gō′thəm; *Brit.* got′əm) A nickname for New York City. — **Goth′am·ite** (-īt) *n.*

Goth·ic (goth′ik) *adj.* **1.** Of or pertaining to the Goths or to their language. **2.** Of a style of architecture used in Europe, from about 1200 to 1500, characterized by pointed arches, ribbed vaulting, flying buttresses, etc. **3.** Denoting a literature usu. medieval in setting, and emphasizing the grotesque and the supernatural. **4.** Of the Middle Ages. **5.** Barbarous. — *n.* **1.** The extinct East Germanic language of the Goths. **2.** Gothic architecture or art. Also (for *adj. defs. 3–5*) **goth′ic.** — **Goth′i·cal·ly** *adv.*

GOTHIC ARCHITECTURE
Westminster Abbey, London,
13th–15th century.

goth·ic (goth′ik) *n. Sometimes cap. Printing* **a** *U.S.* Sans serif. **b** *Brit.* Black letter.

got·ten (got′n) Past participle of GET. ◆ *Gotten*, obsolete in British, is current in American English along with *got.*

gouache (gwosh) *n.* **1.** A method of painting using opaque colors mixed with water and gum. **2.** The opaque pigment so used. **3.** A painting done in this medium. [< F < Ital. *guazzo* a spray < L *aqua* water]

Gou·da cheese (gou′də, gōō′-) A mild, yellow cheese similar to Edam cheese. [after *Gouda*, town in the Netherlands]

gouge (gouj) *n.* **1.** A chisel having a scoop-shaped blade, used for woodcarving. **2.** A groove made as by a gouge. **3.** *U.S. Informal* The action of cutting as with a gouge. **4.** *U.S. Informal* The act of cheating. — *v.t.* **gouged**, **goug·ing** **1.** To cut or carve as with a gouge. **2.** To scoop, force, or tear out. **3.** *U.S. Informal* To cheat; esp., to charge exorbitant prices. — **goug′er** *n.*

gou·lash (gōō′läsh, -lash) *n.* A stew made with beef or veal and vegetables, seasoned with paprika, etc.: also called *Hungarian goulash.* [< Hung. *gulyas* (hus) shepherd's (meat)]

gou·ra·mi (gōō·rä′mē, gōōr′ə·mē) *n.* **1.** A large, freshwater fish of SE Asia. **2.** Any of various related fishes frequently kept in home aquariums, as the **dwarf gourami** and the **three-spot gourami.** [< Malay *gurami*]

gourd (gôrd, gōōrd) *n.* **1.** The fruit of any of various plants, having hard, durable shells. **2.** The fruit of the calabash tree. **3.** A utensil, as a ladle, made from the dried shell. [< F *gourde* < L *cucurbita* gourd]

gour·mand (gōōr′mənd, *Fr.* gōōr·män′) *n.* One who takes hearty pleasure in eating. [< F, glutton]

gour·met (gōōr·mā′, *Fr.* gōōr·me′) *n.* A fastidious devotee of good food and drink. [< F < OF, winetaster]

gout (gout) *n. Pathol.* A disease arising from a defect in metabolism and characterized by attacks of painful inflammation of the joints. [< F *goutte* drop < L *guita*]

gout·y (gou′tē) *adj.* **gout·i·er**, **gout·i·est** **1.** Of, from or like gout. **2.** Affected with gout; swollen. — **gout′i·ly** *adv.* — **gout′i·ness** *n.*

gov·ern (guv′ərn) *v.t.* **1.** To rule or direct by right or authority: to *govern* a nation. **2.** To guide or control the action of; influence. **3.** To serve as a rule or deciding factor for. **4.** To keep in check. — *v.i.* **5.** To exercise authority; rule. [< OF < L *gubernare* to steer < Gk.] — **gov′ern·a·ble** *adj.*

gov·ern·ance (guv′ər·nəns) *n.* Exercise of authority.

gov·ern·ess (guv′ər·nis) *n.* A woman employed in a private household to train and instruct children.

gov·ern·ment (guv′ərn·mənt, -ər-) *n.* **1.** The authoritative administration of the affairs of a nation, state, city, etc.; the jurisdiction exercised over the people; rule. **2.** The official governing body of a nation, community, etc. **3.** The system or established form by which a nation, etc., is controlled: democratic *government.* **4.** Any governed territory, district, etc. **5.** Control. — **gov·ern·men·tal** (guv′ərn·men′təl, -ər-) *adj.* — **gov′ern·men′tal·ly** *adv.*

gov·er·nor (guv′ər·nər) *n.* **1.** One who governs; as: **a** The elected chief executive of any State in the U.S. **b** An official appointed to administer a province, territory, etc. **c** *Brit.* The manager of a society, etc. **2.** *Mech.* A device for controlling speed, as of a motor. — **gov′er·nor·ship** *n.*

governor general *pl.* **governors general** **1.** *Often cap. Brit.* The chief representative of the Crown in a dominion or colony. **2.** A governor or governors under his jurisdiction. Also *Brit.* **gov·er·nor-gen′er·al.**

gown (goun) *n.* **1.** A woman's dress, esp. one for formal occasions: evening *gown.* **2.** Any long, loose garment. **3.** A long, loose outer robe worn by certain officials, scholars, clergymen, etc. — *v.t. & v.i.* To dress in a gown. [< OF < Med.L *gunna* a loose robe]

Graaf·i·an follicle (grä′fē·ən) *Anat.* One of the numerous, small, round sacs embedded in the cortex of a mammalian ovary, each of which contains a single ovum. Also **Graafian vesicle.** [after Regnier de *Graaf*, 1641–73, Dutch physician and anatomist]

grab (grab) *v.* **grabbed**, **grab·bing** *v.t.* **1.** To grasp or seize suddenly. **2.** To take possession of by force or by dishonest means. — *v.i.* **3.** To make a sudden grasp. — *n.* **1.** The act of grabbing. **2.** That which is grabbed. **3.** A dishonest acquisition. **4.** A mechanical apparatus used to grasp and lift. [Cf. MDu. *grabben* to grip] — **grab′ber** *n.*

grab bag *U.S.* A bag or other receptacle filled with miscellaneous unidentified articles, from which one draws an object at random.

grab·ble (grab′əl) *v.i.* **·bled**, **·bling** **1.** To feel about with the hands; grope. **2.** To flounder; sprawl. [Cf. Du. *grabbelen*, freq. of *grabben* to grab]

gra·ben (grä′bən) *n. Geol.* A generally elongate depression of the land caused by the downward faulting of a portion of the earth's crust. [< G, ditch]

grace (grās) *n.* **1.** Beauty or harmony of motion, form, or manner. **2.** Any attractive quality. **3.** Service freely rendered; good will. **4.** The act of showing favor. **5.** Clemency; mercy. **6.** The perception of what is appropriate: He had the *grace* to go. **7.** An extension of time granted after a set date, as for paying a debt. **8.** A short prayer at a meal. **9.** *Theol.* **a** The love of God toward man. **b** The divine influence operating in man. **c** The state of being pleasing to God. **d** Any divinely inspired spiritual virtue or excellence. **10.** *Music* A note or notes added as an ornament. — **to be in the good** (or **bad**) **graces of** To be regarded with favor (or disfavor) by. — **with good** (or **bad**) **grace** In a willing (or grudging) manner. — *v.t.* **graced**, **grac·ing** **1.** To add grace and beauty to; adorn. **2.** To dignify; honor. **3.** *Music* To ornament with grace notes. [< OF < L *gratia* favor]

Grace (grās) *n.* A title or form of address for a duke, duchess, archbishop, or bishop: preceded by *Your, His, Her,* etc.

grace·ful (grās′fəl) *adj.* Characterized by grace, elegance, or beauty. — **grace′ful·ly** *adv.* — **grace′ful·ness** *n.*

grace·less (grās′lis) *adj.* **1.** Lacking grace, charm, or elegance. **2.** Having no sense of what is right or decent. — **grace′less·ly** *adv.* — **grace′less·ness** *n.*

grace note *Music* A note written smaller than those of the main text, played or sung as an embellishment.

Grac·es (grā′siz) In Greek mythology, three sister goddesses who confer grace, beauty, and joy. Also **the three Graces.**

gra·cious (grā′shəs) *adj.* **1.** Having or showing kindness, affability, etc. **2.** Condescendingly polite or indulgent. **3.** Full of compassion; merciful. **4.** Refined. — *interj.* An exclamation of mild surprise. [< OF < L *gratia* favor] — **gra′cious·ly** *adv.* — **gra′cious·ness** *n.*

grack·le (grak′əl) *n.* Any of various New World blackbirds having long tails. [< NL < L *graculus* jackdaw]

grad (grad) *n. U.S. Informal* A graduate.

gra·date (grā′dāt) *v.t. & v.i.* **·dat·ed**, **·dat·ing** **1.** To pass or cause to pass imperceptibly from one shade or degree to another, as color. **2.** To arrange or be arranged in grades.

gra·da·tion (grā·dā′shən) *n.* **1.** An orderly and gradual progression or arrangement according to size, quality, rank, etc. **2.** *Usu. pl.* A step, degree, or relative position in such a progression. **3.** The act of arranging in grades. [< F < L *gradus* step] — **gra·da′tion·al** *adj.*

grade (grād) *n.* **1.** A degree or step in any scale, as of quality, merit, rank, etc. **2.** A stage or degree in an orderly progression, classification, or process. **3.** A group or category. **4.** *U.S.* In education: **a** A level of progress in school, generally constituting a year's work. **b** The pupils in such a division. **c** *pl.* Elementary school: preceded by *the*. **5.** *U.S.* A rating or mark indicating the quality of school work done. **6.** In the U.S. armed forces, rank or rating. See below. **7.** The degree of inclination of a road, track, or other surface as compared with the horizontal **8.** A rise or elevation in a road, track, etc. — **to make the grade** *Informal* To succeed in any undertaking. — **up to grade** In accordance with an established standard of quality, progress, etc. — *v.* **grad·ed, grad·ing** *v.t.* **1.** To arrange or classify by grades or degrees; sort according to size, quality, type, etc. **2.** In education, to assign a grade to. **3.** To level or reduce (a road, ground, etc.) to a desirable gradient. **4.** To gradate. — *v.i.* To be of a specific grade or rank. [< F < L *gradus* step]
-grade *combining form* **1.** Progressing or moving: *retrograde*. **2.** *Zool.* Walking in a specified manner. [< L *gradi* to walk]

grade crossing An intersection of two railroads, or a road and a railroad, at the same level: also called *level crossing*.
grad·er (grā/dər) *n.* **1.** One who or that which grades. **2.** *U.S.* A pupil in a specified school grade: a third *grader*.
grade school An elementary school.
gra·di·ent (grā/dē·ənt) *n.* **1.** Degree of inclination, as in a slope; grade. **2.** An incline; ramp. **3.** *Physics* A rate of change in certain variable factors, as pressure, temperature, etc. — *adj.* Rising or descending gradually or by uniform degrees. [< L *gradiens, -entis*, ppr. of *gradi* to walk]
grad·u·al (graj/ōō·əl) *adj.* **1.** Moving, changing, etc., slowly and by degrees. **2.** Having a slight degree of inclination; not abrupt or steep, as a slope. [< Med.L < L *gradus* a step] — **grad·u·al·ly** *adv.* — **grad·u·al·ness** *n.*
grad·u·ate (*v.* graj/ōō·āt; *n. & adj.* graj/ōō·it) *v.* **·at·ed, ·at·ing** *v.i.* **1.** To receive a diploma or degree upon completion of a course of study. **2.** To change gradually or by degrees. — *v.t.* **3.** To grant an academic diploma or degree to (someone). **4.** To arrange or sort according to size, degree, etc. **5.** To mark (a thermometer, scale, etc.) in units or degrees;

TABLE OF COMPARATIVE GRADES (UNITED STATES ARMED SERVICES)

Grade	Army	Air Force	Marine Corps	Navy	Coast Guard
O–11	General of the Army	General of the Air Force	(no equivalent)	Admiral of the Fleet	(no equivalent)
O–10	General	General	General	Admiral	Admiral
O–9	Lieutenant General	Lieutenant General	Lieutenant General	Vice Admiral	Vice Admiral
O–8	Major General	Major General	Major General	Rear Admiral (upper half)	Rear Admiral (upper half)
O–7	Brigadier General	Brigadier General	Brigadier General	Rear Admiral (lower half)	Rear Admiral (lower half)
O–6	Colonel	Colonel	Colonel	Captain	Captain
O–5	Lieutenant Colonel	Lieutenant Colonel	Lieutenant Colonel	Commander	Commander
O–4	Major	Major	Major	Lieutenant Commander	Lieutenant Commander
O–3	Captain	Captain	Captain	Lieutenant	Lieutenant
O–2	1st Lieutenant	1st Lieutenant	1st Lieutenant	Lieutenant (Junior Grade)	Lieutenant (Junior Grade)
O–1	2nd Lieutenant	2nd Lieutenant	2nd Lieutenant	Ensign	Ensign
W–4	Chief Warrant Officer	SAME	SAME	SAME	SAME
W–3	Chief Warrant Officer				
W–2	Chief Warrant Officer				
W–1	Warrant Officer				
E–9	Sergeant Major of the Army				
E–9	Sergeant Major Specialist 9	Chief Master Sergeant	Master Gunnery Sergeant Sergeant Major	Master Chief Petty Officer	Master Chief Petty Officer
E–8	Master Sergeant First Sergeant Specialist 8	Senior Master Sergeant	Master Sergeant First Sergeant	Senior Chief Petty Officer	Senior Chief Petty Officer
E–7	Sergeant First Class Platoon Sergeant Specialist 7	Master Sergeant	Gunnery Sergeant	Chief Petty Officer	Chief Petty Officer
E–6	Staff Sergeant Specialist 6	Technical Sergeant	Staff Sergeant	Petty Officer First Class	Petty Officer First Class
E–5	Sergeant Specialist 5	Staff Sergeant	Sergeant	Petty Officer Second Class	Petty Officer Second Class
E–4	Corporal Specialist 4	Airman First Class	Corporal	Petty Officer Third Class	Petty Officer Third Class
E–3	Private First Class	Airman Second Class	Lance Corporal	Seaman	Seaman
E–2	Private	Airman Third Class	Private First Class	Seaman Apprentice	Seaman Apprentice
E–1	Recruit	Recruit	Private	Seaman Recruit	Seaman Recruit

TABLE OF CANADIAN MILITARY GRADES

At left are ranks in Canada's single service, unified in 1968. The other columns show comparative ranks in the old, separate services·

Canadian Armed Forces	Royal Canadian Navy	Canadian Army	Royal Canadian Air Force
Officers General	Admiral of the Fleet	Field-Marshal	Marshal of the Royal Canadian Air Force
Lieutenant-General	Admiral	General	Air Chief Marshal
Major-General	Vice-Admiral	Lieutenant-General	Air Marshal
Brigadier-General	Rear-Admiral	Major-General	Air Vice-Marshal
Colonel	Commodore	Brigadier	Air Commodore
Lieutenant-Colonel	Captain	Colonel	Group Captain
Major	Commander	Lieutenant-Colonel	Wing Commander
Captain	Lieutenant-Commander	Major	Squadron Leader
Lieutenant	Lieutenant	Captain	Flight Lieutenant
2nd Lieutenant	Sub-Lieutenant	Lieutenant	Flying Officer
Officer Cadet	Acting Sub-Lieutenant	Second Lieutenant	Pilot Officer
	Midshipman		
Men Chief Warrant Officer	Chief Petty Officer, First Class	Warrant Officer, First Class	Warrant Officer, First Class
Master Warrant Officer	Chief Petty Officer, Second Class	Warrant Officer, Second Class	Warrant Officer, Second Class
Warrant Officer	Petty Officer, First Class	Staff Sergeant	Flight Sergeant
Sergeant	Petty Officer, Second Class	Sergeant	Sergeant
Master Corporal	Leading Seaman	Corporal	Corporal
Corporal	Able Seaman	Private	Leading Aircraftman
Private (Career Status)	Ordinary Seaman (trained)	Private (trained)	Aircraftman, First Class
Private	Ordinary Seaman (entry)	Private (entry)	Aircraftman, Second Class
	Ordinary Seaman (under 17 years)	Private (under 17 years)	Aircraftman, Second Class (under 17 years)

calibrate. — *n.* **1.** One who has been granted a diploma or degree by an educational institution. **2.** A beaker or similar vessel marked in units or degrees, used for measuring liquids, etc. — *adj.* **1.** Denoting a graduate student. **2.** Pertaining to or intended for such a student. [< Med.L < L *gradus* step, degree]

graduate student A student who has received a college degree and is working toward a more advanced degree.

grad·u·a·tion (graj/ōō-ā/shən) *n.* **1.** The act of graduating, or the state of being graduated. **2.** The ceremony of granting diplomas or degrees. **3.** A mark or division in a graduated scale; also, such divisions collectively.

Grae·cism (grē/siz-əm) *n.* A Grecism.

Grae·cize (grē/sīz) *v.t. & v.i.* **-cized, -ciz·ing** To Grecize.

Graeco- See GRECO-.

graf·fi·to (grə-fē/tō) *n. pl.* **-ti** (-tē) **1.** *Usu. pl.* Any design or scribble drawn on a wall or other surface. **2.** *Archeol.* A pictograph scratched on an escarpment, etc. [< Ital.]

graft[1] (graft, gräft) *n.* **1.** A shoot (the cion) inserted into a prepared slit in a tree or plant (the stock) so as to become a living part of it. **2.** A plant, fruit, etc., obtained as a result of this operation. **3.** *Surg.* A piece of viable tissue transplanted to another part of the body or to the body of another individual. — *v.t.* **1.** To insert (a cion) into a tree or plant. **2.** To obtain (a plant, fruit, etc.) by grafting. **3.** *Surg.* To transplant (a piece of viable tissue) as a graft. **4.** To attach or incorporate, as by grafting: to *graft* new ideas on outworn concepts. — *v.i.* **5.** To insert or transplant grafts. **6.** To be or become grafted. [< OF < LL < Gk. *graphein* to write] — **graft/age** *n.* — **graft/er** *n.*

graft[2] (graft, gräft) *U.S. n.* **1.** The act of getting personal advantage or profit by dishonest or unfair means, esp. through one's political connections. **2.** Anything thus gained. — *v.t.* **1.** To acquire by graft. — *v.i.* **2.** To practice graft. [Cf. dial. E *graft* work, livelihood] — **graft/er** *n.*

gra·ham (grā/əm) *adj.* Made of unsifted whole-wheat flour. [after Sylvester *Graham*, 1794–1851, U.S. vegetarian]

grail (grāl) *n.* In medieval legend, the cup or dish used at the Last Supper by Jesus Christ, in which some of the blood shed at the Crucifixion was caught. Also called *Holy Grail.* [< OF < Med.L *gradalis*]

grain (grān) *n.* **1.** A hard seed or kernel; esp., that of any of the cereal plants, as wheat, oats, etc. **2.** The harvested seeds of these plants. **3.** These plants collectively. **4.** Any very small, hard mass. **5.** The smallest possible quantity of anything: a *grain* of truth. **6.** The smallest unit of weight used in several systems in the U.S. and Great Britain. Abbr. *g., G., gr.* See table inside back cover. **7.** The direction or arrangement of the fibers or fibrous particles in various kinds of wood; also, the resulting markings or pattern. **8.** The side of a piece of leather from which the hair has been removed; also, the characteristic texture or patterned markings of this side. **9.** A paint, stamp, or pattern used to imitate the characteristic markings of leather, wood, etc. **10.** The comparative size or texture of the particles composing a substance, surface, or pattern: marble of fine *grain.* **11.** The direction of cleavage of a mineral substance, as diamond, coal, etc. **12.** A state of crystallization. **13.** Natural disposition or temperament. — **against the grain** Contrary to one's temperament or inclinations. — *v.t.* **1.** To form into grains; granulate. **2.** To paint or stain in imitation of the grain of wood, marble, etc. **3.** To give a roughened or granular appearance or texture to. **4.** In leathermaking: **a** To scrape the hair from. **b** To soften or raise the grain or pattern of. — *v.i.* **5.** To form grains. [< OF < L *granum* seed] — **grain/er** *n.* — **grain/less** *adj.*

grain alcohol Ethanol.

grain elevator *U.S.* A building designed to store grain.

grain·y (grā/nē) *adj.* **grain·i·er, grain·i·est** **1.** Full of or consisting of grains or kernels. **2.** Having a granular texture. **3.** Resembling the grain in wood. — **grain/i·ness** *n.*

gram (gram) *n.* The unit of mass or weight in the metric system, equivalent to 15.432 grains, or one thousandth of a kilogram. Also **gramme.** Abbr. *g, g., gm., gr.* See table inside back cover. [< F < LL < Gk. *gramma* small weight]

-gram[1] *combining form* Something written or drawn: *telegram.* [< Gk. *gramma* letter, writing < *graphein* to write]

-gram[2] *combining form* A gram: used in the metric system: *kilogram.* [< GRAM]

gram atom *Chem.* The quantity of an element, expressed in grams, that is equal to the atomic weight of that element. Also **gram/-a·tom/ic weight** (-ə·tom/ik).

gram·mar (gram/ər) *n.* **1.** The scientific study and description of the morphology and syntax of a language or dialect. **2.** A system of morphologic and syntactic rules for the regulation of a given language. **3.** A treatise or book dealing with grammatical matters. **4.** Speech or writing considered with regard to current standards of cor-

rectness. **5.** The elements of any science or art, or a book or treatise dealing with them. [< OF < L < Gk. *grammatikē (technē)* literary (art) < *grammata* literature]

gram·mar·i·an (grə-mâr/ē-ən) *n.* A specialist in grammar.

grammar school **1.** An elementary school. **2.** *Brit.* A secondary school.

gram·mat·i·cal (grə-mat/i-kəl) *adj.* **1.** Of or pertaining to grammar. **2.** Conforming to the usage of standard speech or writing. — **gram·mat/i·cal·ly** *adv.* — **gram·mat/i·cal·ness** *n.*

gram molecule *Chem.* The quantity of a compound, expressed in grams, that is equal to the molecular weight of that compound: also called *mole.* Also **gram/-mo·lec/u·lar weight** (-mə·lek/yə·lər).

gram·o·phone (gram/ə·fōn) *n. Chiefly Brit.* A record player. [< *Gramophone,* a trade name]

gram·pus (gram/pəs) *n. pl.* **·pus·es** A large, dolphinlike cetacean of Atlantic and Pacific waters. [Alter. of obs. *grapeys* < OF < Med.L *crassus piscis* fat fish]

gran·a·ry (gran/ər·ē, grā/nər-) *n. pl.* **·ries** **1.** A storehouse for threshed grain. **2.** A region where grain grows in abundance. [< L *granum* grain]

grand (grand) *adj.* **1.** Impressive because of great size, extent, or splendor. **2.** In literature and the arts, lofty or sublime in subject or treatment. **3.** Majestic; stately. **4.** Worthy of respect because of age, experience, or dignity: often with *old*: the *grand* old man of politics. **5.** Of high or highest rank or official position: a *grand* duke; the *grand* jury. **6.** Principal; main: the *grand* ballroom. **7.** Characterized by pomp or luxury. **8.** Conscious of one's wealth or importance. **9.** Comprehensive; all-inclusive: the *grand* total. **10.** Having a family relationship one degree more distant than: used in combination: *grandson.* **11.** *Informal* Highly satisfactory; excellent. — *n.* **1.** A grand piano. **2.** *U.S. Slang* A thousand dollars. [< OF < L *grandis*] — **grand/ly** *adv.* — **grand/ness** *n.*

gran·dam (gran/dam, -dəm) *n. Archaic* A grandmother; an old woman. Also **gran/dame** (-dām, -dəm). [< AF *graund dame*]

grand·aunt (grand/ant/, -änt/) *n.* A great-aunt.

grand·child (grand/chīld/) *n. pl.* **·chil·dren** (-chil/drən) A child of one's son or daughter.

grand·dad (gran/dad/) *n. Informal* Grandfather. Also **grand/dad/dy.**

grand·daugh·ter (gran/dô/tər, grand/-) *n.* A daughter of one's son or daughter.

grand duchess **1.** The wife or widow of a grand duke. **2.** A woman who is sovereign of a grand duchy. **3.** Formerly, in Russia, a daughter of a czar.

grand duchy The territory under the rule of a grand duke or grand duchess.

grand duke **1.** The sovereign of a grand duchy, holding a rank just below king. **2.** Formerly, in Russia, a ruler of a principality; later, a son or grandson of a czar.

gran·dee (gran-dē/) *n.* **1.** A Spanish or Portuguese nobleman of the highest rank. **2.** Any person of high rank or great importance. [< Sp. *grande* great]

gran·deur (gran/jər, -jōōr) *n.* **1.** The quality or condition of being grand; magnificence. **2.** Greatness of character.

grand·fa·ther (grand/fä/thər) *n.* **1.** The father of one's father or mother. **2.** An ancestor. — **grand/fa/ther·ly** *adv.*

grandfather clock A clock having a pendulum and enclosed in a tall cabinet. Also **grandfather's clock.**

gran·dil·o·quent (gran-dil/ə-kwənt) *adj.* Speaking in or characterized by a pompous or bombastic style. [< L *grandis* great + *loqui* to speak] — **gran·dil/o·quence** *n.*

gran·di·ose (gran/dē·ōs, gran/dē·ōs/) *adj.* **1.** Producing an effect of grandeur; imposing. **2.** Pretentiously grand; pompous; bombastic. [< F < Ital. < L *grandis* great] — **gran/di·ose/ly** *adv.* — **gran·di·os·i·ty** (gran/dē·os/ə·tē) *n.*

grand jury A body of persons called to hear complaints of the commission of offenses and to ascertain whether there is prima-facie evidence for an indictment.

Grand Lama The Dalai Lama.

grand·ma (grand/mä, gran/mä/, gram/mä, gram/ə) *n. Informal* Grandmother. Also **grand·ma·ma** (grand/mə·mä, -mä/mə), **grand/mam·ma/.**

grand mal (grän mal/) *Pathol.* A type of epilepsy characterized by severe convulsions and loss of consciousness: distinguished from *petit mal.* [< F, lit., great sickness]

grand·moth·er (grand/muth/ər) *n.* **1.** The mother of one's father or mother. **2.** A female ancestor.

grand·neph·ew (grand/nef/yōō, -nev/-, gran/-) *n.* A son of one's nephew or niece.

grand·niece (grand/nēs/, gran/-) *n.* A daughter of one's nephew or niece.

Grand Old Party In U.S. politics, the Republican Party.

grand opera A form of opera, usu. having a serious and complex plot, in which the entire text is set to music.

grand·pa (grand'pä', gram'pä', gram'pə) *n. Informal* Grandfather. Also **grand'pa·pa'** (-pə·pä', -pä'pə).

grand·par·ent (grand'pâr'ənt, gran'-) *n.* A grandmother or grandfather.

grand piano A large piano having strings arranged horizontally in a curved, wooden case.

grand·sire (grand'sīr', -sər) *n. Archaic* 1. A grandfather. 2. An ancestor. 3. Any venerable old man.

grand slam In bridge, the winning, by the declarer, of all thirteen tricks in a round of play; also, a bid to do so.

grand·son (grand'sun', gran'-) *n.* A son of one's child.

grand·stand (grand'stand', gran'-) *n.* A raised series of seats for spectators at a racetrack, sports stadium, etc. — *v.i.* To act so as to impress others or win applause.

grand tour 1. Formerly, an extended journey through the chief cities of continental Europe. 2. Any extended trip.

grand·un·cle (grand'ung'kəl) *n.* A great-uncle.

grange (grānj) *n.* 1. *Often cap. U.S.* Any subsidiary lodge or branch of the Grange. 2. *Brit.* A farm, with its dwelling house, barns, etc.; esp., the residence of a gentleman farmer. [< AF, OF < Med.L < L *granum* grain]

Grange (grānj) *n.* The order of Patrons of Husbandry, an association of U.S. farmers founded in 1867.

grang·er (grān'jər) *n.* 1. *Often cap. U.S.* A member of a grange. 2. A farmer. — **grang'er·ism** *n.*

gran·ite (gran'it) *n.* 1. A hard, coarse-grained, igneous rock composed principally of quartz, feldspar, and mica, used for building, in sculpture, etc. 2. Firmness or endurance. [< Ital. < L *granum* seed] — **gra·nit·ic** (grə·nit'ik) *adj.*

Granite State Nickname of New Hampshire.

gran·ite·ware (gran'it·wâr') *n.* 1. A variety of ironware coated with hard enamel. 2. A type of fine, hard pottery.

gra·niv·o·rous (grə·niv'ər·əs) *adj.* Feeding on grain.

gran·ny (gran'ē) *n. pl.* **·nies** 1. Grandmother: used familiarly. 2. An old woman. 3. *Informal* A fussy, interfering person. 4. A granny knot. Also **gran'nie.**

granny knot A knot resembling the square knot but crossed in such a way as to form an insecure fastening. For illus. see KNOT. Also **granny's knot, granny's bend.**

gra·no·la (grə·nō'lə) *n.* Any of various cereal foods containing whole grain products, sugar, and dried fruits.

grant (grant, gränt) *v.t.* 1. To confer or bestow, as a privilege, charter, etc. 2. To allow (someone) to have; give, as permission. 3. To accede to; yield to, as a request. 4. To admit as true, as for the sake of argument. 5. To transfer (property), esp. by deed. — *n.* 1. The act of granting. 2. That which is granted, as a piece of property, a sum of money, or a special privilege. — **to take for granted** 1. To assume to be true. 2. To accept as one's due. [< AF, ult. < L *credere* to believe]

gran·tee (gran·tē', grän-) *n.* The recipient of a grant.

grant·or (gran'tər, gran·tôr', grän-) *n.* The person by whom a grant is made.

gran·u·lar (gran'yə·lər) *adj.* 1. Composed of, like, or containing grains or granules. 2. Having a granulated surface. — **gran·u·lar·i·ty** (-lar'ə·tē) *n.* — **gran'u·lar·ly** *adv.*

gran·u·late (gran'yə·lāt) *v.t. & v.i.* **·lat·ed, ·lat·ing** 1. To make or become granular; form into grains. 2. To become or cause to become roughened, as by the formation of granules. — **gran'u·la'tion** *n.* — **gran'u·la·tive** *adj.*

gran·ule (gran'yōōl) *n.* A small grain or particle; tiny pellet. [< LL *granulum,* dim. of L *granum* grain]

grape (grāp) *n.* 1. One of the smooth-skinned, juicy, edible berries borne in clusters by various climbing vines or small shrubs, cultivated in many species as a fruit and for making wine. 2. Any of the vines bearing these berries. 3. A dark, purplish blue color. 4. Grapeshot. [< OF, bunch of grapes]

grape·fruit (grāp'frōōt') *n.* 1. A large, round citrus fruit having a pale yellow rind and tart, juicy pulp. 2. The tree bearing this fruit.

grape·shot (grāp'shot') *n.* A kind of shot consisting of a cluster of iron balls, formerly fired from cannons.

grape sugar Dextrose.

grape·vine (grāp'vīn') *n.* 1. Any of the climbing vines that bear grapes. 2. *U.S.* A secret or unofficial means of relaying information, usu. from person to person.

graph (graf, gräf) *n.* A diagram representing variations in the relationship between two or more factors by means of a series of connected points, or by bars, curves, lines, etc. — *v.t.* To express or represent in the form of a graph.

-graph *combining form* 1. That which writes or records: *seismograph.* 2. A writing or record: *autograph.* [< F < L < Gk. *graphein* to write]

-grapher *combining form* Forming nouns of agency corresponding to words in *-graph* or *-graphy: photographer.*

graph·ic (graf'ik) *adj.* 1. Describing in full detail; vivid. 2. Of, pertaining to, or illustrated by graphs or diagrams. 3. Pertaining to, consisting of, or expressed by writing. 4. Of, pertaining to, or characteristic of the graphic arts. Also **graph'i·cal.** [< L < Gk. *graphē* writing] — **graph'i·cal·ly** or **graph'ic·ly** *adv.*

-graphic *combining form* Forming adjectives corresponding to nouns ending in *-graph: photographic.* Also **-graphical.**

graphic arts 1. Those visual arts involving the use of lines or strokes on a flat surface, as painting, drawing, engraving, etc. 2. In recent usage, those arts that involve impressions or reproductions taken from blocks, plates, type, or the like.

graph·ite (graf'īt) *n.* A soft, black variety of carbon having a metallic luster and a slippery texture, used as a lubricant and in making pencils, etc. Also called *black lead.* [< G < Gk. *graphein* to write + -ITE¹] **gra·phit·ic** (-fit'ik) *adj.*

grapho- *combining form* Of or pertaining to writing. Also, before vowels, **graph-.** [< Gk. *graphein* to write]

graph·ol·o·gy (gra·fol'ə·jē) *n.* The study of handwriting, esp. as a method of estimating the writer's character. — **graph·o·log·i·cal** (graf'ə·loj'i·kəl) *adj.* — **graph·ol'o·gist** *n.*

-graphy *combining form* 1. A writing, recording, or process of representation: *biography, photography.* 2. A descriptive science: *petrography.* [< Gk. *graphein* to write]

grap·nel (grap'nəl) *n.* 1. A small anchor with several flukes at the end of the shank. 2. Any of various devices consisting of a hook or arrangement of hooked parts, used to seize and hold objects. [ME *grapenel,* dim. of OF *grapin* hook]

grap·ple (grap'əl) *v.* **·pled, ·pling** *v.t.* 1. To seize or take hold of with or as with a grapnel. — *v.i.* 2. To struggle in close combat, as in wrestling. 3. To struggle or contend: with *with.* 4. To use a grapnel. — *n.* 1. A grapnel. 2. The act of grappling. 3. A grip or close hold, as in wrestling. [< OF *grappil* grapnel] — **grap'pler** *n.*

grappling iron A grapnel. Also **grappling hook.**

grasp (grasp, gräsp) *v.t.* 1. To seize firmly with or as with the hand; grip. 2. To grab. 3. To comprehend. — *v.i.* 4. To make the motion of grasping or clutching. — **to grasp at** 1. To try to seize. 2. To accept eagerly, as an offer or suggestion. — *n.* 1. The act of grasping; also, a grip of the hand. 2. The power or ability to seize; reach. 3. Absolute domination: the tyrant's *grasp.* 4. Intellectual comprehension or mastery. [ME *graspen,* metathetic var. of *grapsen* < LG] — **grasp'a·ble** *adj.* — **grasp'er** *n.*

grasp·ing (gras'ping, gräs'-) *adj.* 1. Greedy. 2. That grasps. — **grasp'ing·ly** *adv.* — **grasp'ing·ness** *n.*

grass (gras, gräs) *n.* 1. Any plant of a large family having rounded and hollow jointed stems, narrow, sheathing leaves, flowers borne in spikes or panicles, and hard, grainlike seeds. 2. Herbage generally; esp., the herbaceous plants eaten by grazing animals. 3. Any of numerous plants with grasslike foliage. 4. Ground on which grass is growing. 5. Grazing ground; pasture. 6. *pl.* Stalks or sprays of grass. — **to let the grass grow under one's feet** To let opportunity go by. — *v.t.* 1. To cover with grass or turf. 2. To feed with grass. 3. To spread (cloth, etc.) on the grass, for bleaching. — *v.i.* 4. To graze. 5. To become grassy. [OE *græs*]

grass·hop·per (gras'hop'ər, gräs'-) *n.* 1. Any of several insects, as the locust and katydid, with powerful hind legs adapted for leaping, many species of which are destructive to crops and vegetation. 2. *U.S. Slang* Any small, light airplane, used for dusting crops, military observation, etc.

grass·land (gras'land', gräs'-) *n.* 1. Land reserved for pasturage or mowing. 2. Land in which grasses are the predominant vegetation, as the American prairies.

grass·roots (gras'rōōts', -rōōts, gräs'-) *U.S. Informal n.pl.* The common people, thought of as having practical and highly independent views or interests. — *adj.* 1. Coming from, pertaining to, or directed toward such people. 2. Basic. Also **grass'-roots'.**

grass widow A woman who is divorced, separated, or lives apart from her husband.

grass widower A man who is divorced, separated, or lives apart from his wife.

gras·sy (gras'ē, gräs'ē) *adj.* **grass·i·er, grass·i·est** 1. Covered with or abounding in grass. 2. Of or containing grass. 3. Like grass. — **grass'i·ly** *adv.* — **grass'i·ness** *n.*

grate¹ (grāt) *v.* **grat·ed, grat·ing** *v.t.* 1. To reduce to fine pieces or powder by rubbing against a rough or sharp surface. 2. To rub or grind to produce a harsh sound. — *v.i.* 3. To have an irritating effect: with *on* or *upon.* 4. To produce a harsh sound. [< OF *grater* < Gmc.] — **grat'er** *n.*

grate² (grāt) *n.* 1. A framework of crossed or parallel bars placed over a window, drain, etc. 2. A metal framework to hold burning fuel in a furnace, etc. 3. A fireplace. — *v.t.* **grat·ed, grat·ing** To fit with a grate or grates. [< Ital. < L *cratis* lattice]

grate·ful (grāt'fəl) *adj.* 1. Thankful for benefits or kindnesses; appreciative; also, expressing gratitude. 2. Giving pleasure; welcome; agreeable. [< L *gratus* pleasing] — **grate'ful·ly** *adv.* — **grate'ful·ness** *n.*

grat·i·fi·ca·tion (grat'ə·fə·kā'shən) *n.* 1. The act of gratifying, or the state of being gratified. 2. That which gratifies.

grat·i·fy (grat'ə·fī) *v.t.* **·fied, ·fy·ing** 1. To give pleasure or satisfaction to. 2. To satisfy, humor, or indulge. — **Syn.** See SATISFY. [< MF < L *gratus* pleasing + *facere* to make] — **grat'i·fi'er** *n.* — **grat'i·fy'ing** *adj.* — **grat'i·fy'ing·ly** *adv.*

grat·ing¹ (grā/ting) *n.* **1.** An arrangement of bars or slats used as a cover or screen. **2.** *Physics* A diffraction grating.

grat·ing² (grā/ting) *adj.* **1.** Harsh or disagreeable in sound; rasping. **2.** Irritating; annoying. — **grat/ing·ly** *adv.*

gra·tis (grā/tis, grat/is) *adv.* Without requiring payment. — *adj.* Free of charge. [< L, var. of *gratiis* out of kindness]

grat·i·tude (grat/ə-tōod, -tyōod) *n.* Appreciation for favors, kindness, etc. [< F < L *gratus* pleasing]

gra·tu·i·tous (grə-tōo/ə-təs, -tyōo/-) *adj.* **1.** Given or obtained without payment or return; free. **2.** Lacking cause or justification; uncalled-for. [< L *gratuitus*] — **gra·tu/i·tous·ly** *adv.* — **gra·tu/i·tous·ness** *n.*

gra·tu·i·ty (grə-tōo/ə-tē, -tyōo/-) *n. pl.* **·ties** A gift, usu. of money, given in return for services rendered; tip.

gra·va·men (grə-vā/men) *n. pl.* **·vam·i·na** (-vam/ə-nə) **1.** *Law* The burden or gist of a charge. **2.** A grievance. [< LL < L *gravis* heavy]

grave¹ (grāv) *adj.* **1.** Of great importance; weighty: a *grave* responsibility. **2.** Filled with danger; critical: a *grave* situation. **3.** Solemn and dignified; sober. **4.** Somber, as colors. **5.** *Music* Slow and solemn. **6.** *Phonet.* **a** Having the tonal quality indicated by the grave accent; also, marked with this accent. **b** Unaccented, as a syllable. — *n.* A mark (`) used in French to indicate open *e*, or to make a distinction, as in *ou*, *où*: also **grave accent.** [< F < L *gravis* heavy] — **grave/ly** *adv.* — **grave/ness** *n.*

grave² (grāv) *n.* **1.** A burial place for a dead body, usu. a hole in the earth. **2.** A sepulcher; tomb. **3.** Death. **4.** Any place or state regarded as an end or final loss. — **to have one foot in the grave** **1.** To be very old or frail. **2.** To be dangerously ill. — **to turn (over) in one's grave** To be presumably uneasy after one's death because of the behavior of the living. [OE *græf*] — **grave/less** *adj.*

grave³ (grāv) *v.t.* **graved, grav·en, grav·ing** **1.** To carve or sculpt. **2.** To engrave or incise. **3.** To impress firmly, as on the memory. [OE *grafan* to dig] — **grav/er** *n.*

grave-dig·ger (grāv/dig/ər) *n.* One who digs graves.

grav·el (grav/əl) *n.* **1.** A mixture of small, rounded pebbles or fragments of stone, often with sand. **2.** *Pathol.* **a** A deposit of sandlike crystals formed in the kidneys. **b** The disease of which these are characteristic. — *v.t.* **grav·eled** or **·elled, grav·el·ing** or **·el·ling** **1.** To cover or pave with gravel. **2.** To confound; baffle. [< OF *gravele* beach] — **grav/el·ly** *adj.*

grave·stone (grāv/stōn/) *n.* A stone marking a grave.

grave·yard (grāv/yärd/) *n.* A burial place; cemetery.

graveyard shift *U.S. Informal* A work shift during the night, generally beginning at midnight.

grav·i·met·ric (grav/ə-met/rik) *adj. Chem.* **1.** Determined by weight, as the constituents of a compound. **2.** Pertaining to measurement by weight. Also **grav/i·met/ri·cal.** — **grav/i·met/ri·cal·ly** *adv.*

gra·vim·e·try (grə-vim/ə-trē) *n.* The measurement of weight, density, or specific gravity.

grav·i·tate (grav/ə-tāt) *v.i.* **·tat·ed, ·tat·ing** **1.** To move or tend to move as a result of the force of gravity. **2.** To move as though from a force or natural impulse. **3.** To sink or settle to a lower level. [< NL < L *gravis* heavy] — **grav/i·tat·er** *n.* — **grav/i·ta·tive** *adj.*

grav·i·ta·tion (grav/ə-tā/shən) *n.* **1.** *Physics* The force whereby any two bodies attract each other. **2.** The act or process of gravitating. — **grav/i·ta/tion·al** *adj.* — **grav/i·ta/tion·al·ly** *adv.*

grav·i·ty (grav/ə-tē) *n. pl.* **·ties** **1.** *Physics* Gravitation as manifested by the tendency of material bodies to fall toward the center of the earth. **2.** Gravitation in general. **3.** Weight; heaviness. **4.** Great importance; seriousness. **5.** Solemnity; dignified reserve. **6.** Lowness of pitch, as of music. [< F < L *gravitas* heaviness]

gra·vure (grə-vyōor/, grāv/yər) *n.* **1.** A process of printing or engraving by photographically prepared plates. **2.** A plate, usu. copper or wood, used in this process; also, a print made from such a plate. [< F < L *graver* to engrave]

gra·vy (grā/vē) *n. pl.* **·vies** **1.** The juice, exuded by cooking meat; also, a sauce made from it. **2.** *U.S. Slang* Money or profit easily acquired. [ME *gravey*]

gray (grā) *adj.* **1.** Of a color produced by a mixture of black and white. **2.** Dark or dull, as from insufficient light; dismal. **3.** Having gray hair. **4.** Characteristic of old age; old. — *n.* **1.** A color consisting of a mixture of black and white. **2.** Something gray, as an animal. **3.** The state of being unbleached or undyed: said of fabrics. — *v.t. & v.i.* To make or become gray. Also, *esp. Brit.,* **grey.** [OE *græg*] — **gray/ly** *adv.* — **gray/ness** *n.*

gray·beard (grā/bird/) *n.* An old man.

gray·ling (grā/ling) *n. pl.* **·ling** or **·lings** **1.** A troutlike fish having a large, colorful dorsal fin. **2.** Any of several North American butterflies having gray and brown markings.

gray matter **1.** *Anat.* The reddish gray nervous tissue of the brain and spinal cord, composed largely of nerve cells and nerve fibers. **2.** *Informal* Brains; intelligence.

graze¹ (grāz) *v.* **grazed, graz·ing** *v.i.* **1.** To feed upon growing grass or herbage. — *v.t.* **2.** To put (livestock) to feed on grass, pasturage, etc. **3.** To tend at pasture. **4.** To cause (a field, etc.) to be fed on. [OE *græs* grass] — **graz/er** *n.*

graze² (grāz) *v.* **grazed, graz·ing** *v.t.* **1.** To brush against lightly in passing. **2.** To scrape or abrade slightly: The bullet *grazed* his arm. — *v.i.* **3.** To move so as to scrape lightly against something. — *n.* **1.** A grazing. **2.** A scrape made by grazing. — **graz/ing·ly** *adv.*

graz·ing (grā/zing) *n.* Pasturage.

gra·zi·o·so (grä-tsyō/sō) *Music adj.* Graceful; elegant. — *adv.* Gracefully; elegantly. [Ital.]

grease (*n.* grēs; *v.* grēs, grēz) *n.* **1.** Animal fat in a soft state, as after melting or rendering. **2.** Any thick fatty or oily substance, as a lubricant. — *v.t.* **greased, greas/ing** To smear or lubricate with grease or fat. [< OF < L *crassus* fat] — **greas/er** *n.*

grease paint A waxy substance used for theater make-up.

grease·wood (grēs/wood/) *n.* A stunted, prickly shrub of the SW U.S. Also **grease/bush/.**

greas·y (grē/sē, -zē) *adj.* **greas·i·er, greas·i·est** **1.** Smeared or spotted with grease. **2.** Containing grease or fat; oily. **3.** Appearing or feeling like grease; smooth; slick. — **greas/i·ly** *adv.* — **greas/i·ness** *n.*

great (grāt) *adj.* **1.** Very large in bulk, volume, expanse, etc.; immense; big. **2.** Large in quantity or number: a *great* army. **3.** Prolonged in duration or extent; a *great* distance. **4.** More than ordinary; considerable: *great* pain. **5.** Of unusual importance; momentous; also, renowned: a *great* victory. **6.** Marked by nobility of thought, action, etc.: *great* deeds. **7.** Unusual in ability or achievement; highly gifted. **8.** Impressive; remarkable. **9.** Favored; popular. **10.** Absorbed or enthusiastic; also, proficient; skillful. **11.** Being of a relationship more remote by a single generation: used in combination: *great-uncle.* — *n.* **1.** Those who are eminent, powerful, etc.: preceded by *the.* **2.** *Usu. pl. Informal* An outstanding person: one of baseball's *greats.* — *adv. Informal* Very well; splendidly. [OE *great*] — **great/ness** *n.*

great-aunt (grāt/ant/, -änt/) *n.* An aunt of either of one's parents; grandaunt.

Great Bear The constellation Ursa Major.

great circle *Geom.* A circle formed on the surface of a sphere by a plane that passes through the center of the sphere.

Great Dane One of a breed of large, smooth-haired dogs.

great·er (grāt/ər) Comparative of GREAT. — *adj. Usu. cap.* Comprising a (specified) city and suburbs: *Greater* London.

great-grand·child (grāt/grand/child/) *n.* A child of a grandchild.

great-grand·daugh·ter (grāt/gran/dô/tər) *n.* A daughter of a grandchild.

great-grand·fa·ther (grāt/grand/fä/thər) *n.* The father of a grandparent.

great-grand·moth·er (grāt/grand/muth/ər) *n.* The mother of a grandparent.

great-grand·par·ent (grāt/grand/pâr/ənt) *n.* The father or mother of a grandparent.

great-grand·son (grāt/grand/sun/) *n.* A son of a grandchild.

great gross Twelve gross, a unit of quantity.

great-heart·ed (grāt/här/tid) *adj.* **1.** Noble or generous in spirit; magnanimous. **2.** High-spirited; courageous.

great horned owl A large owl having tufts of feathers that resemble horns, found chiefly in North America.

great·ly (grāt/lē) *adv.* **1.** To a great degree; very much. **2.** In a way characteristic of or befitting greatness.

great-neph·ew (grāt/nef/yōo, -nev/-) *n.* A grandnephew.

great-niece (grāt/nēs/) *n.* A grandniece.

Great Rebellion The Civil War in England. See table under WAR.

Great Russian *adj.* Of or pertaining to Great Russia. — *n.* **1.** A native of Great Russia. **2.** The East Slavic language of the Great Russians.

great seal *Often cap.* The chief seal of a government.

great-un·cle (grāt/ung/kəl) *n.* An uncle of either of one's parents; granduncle.

Great White Way The brightly lighted theater district of New York City near Broadway and Times Square.

grebe (grēb) *n.* Any of a family of swimming and diving birds having partially webbed feet and very short tails; esp., the **pied-billed grebe** or **dabchick.** [< F *grèbe*]

Gre·cian (grē/shən) *adj.* Greek. — *n.* **1.** A Greek. **2.** One learned in the language or literature of Greece.

Gre·cism (grē/siz/əm) *n.* **1.** A Greek idiom. **2.** The style or spirit of Greek art, culture, etc. Also spelled *Graecism.*

Gre·cize (grē/sīz) *v.* **·cized, ·ciz·ing** *v.t.* **1.** To make Greek in form, character, etc.; Hellenize. **2.** To translate into Greek. —*v.i.* **3.** To adopt or imitate Greek customs, speech, etc. Also spelled *Graecize.* [< F < L *Graecus* a Greek]

Greco- *combining form* Greek. Also spelled *Graeco-*.

Greco-Persian Wars See table for WAR.

Gre·co-Ro·man (grē′kō-rō′mən) *adj.* Of or pertaining to Greece and Rome together: also *Graeco-Roman.*

greed (grēd) *n.* Selfish and grasping desire for possession, esp. of wealth; avarice, covetousness. [< GREEDY]

greed·y (grē′dē) *adj.* **greed·i·er, greed·i·est 1.** Excessively eager for acquisition or gain; covetous; grasping. **2.** Having an excessive appetite for food and drink; voracious; gluttonous. [OE *grædig*] —**greed′i·ly** *adv.* —**greed′i·ness** *n.*

Greek (grēk) *adj.* **1.** Of or pertaining to Greece, or its people, language, or culture. **2.** Of or pertaining to the Greek Church. —*n.* **1.** One of the people of ancient or modern Greece. **2.** The Indo-European language of ancient or modern Greece. —**Late Greek** The Greek language from about A.D. 200 to 600. —**Medieval Greek** The Greek language of the Byzantine period, from 600 to 1500. —**Modern Greek** The language of Greece since 1500: also called *Romaic*, especially in its spoken form. **3.** Language or information that is unintelligible. **4.** *U.S. Slang* A member of a fraternity. [< L < Gk. *Graikos* Greek]

Greek Catholic 1. A member of the Eastern Orthodox Church. **2.** A member of a Uniat Church.

Greek Church 1. The Eastern Church. **2.** Loosely, the Eastern Orthodox Church.

Greek fire An incendiary substance first used by the Byzantine Greeks in naval warfare.

Greek Orthodox Church The established church of Greece, a branch of the Eastern Orthodox Church.

green (grēn) *adj.* **1.** Of the color between blue and yellow in the spectrum, as in the foliage of growing plants. **2.** Covered with or abounding in grass, growing plants, etc. **3.** Consisting of edible green leaves or plant parts: a *green* salad. **4.** Not fully developed; immature. **5.** Not cured or ready for use. **6.** Lacking training or skill; inexperienced. **7.** Wan. —*n.* **1.** The color between blue and yellow in the spectrum, characteristic of the foliage of growing plants. **2.** A green pigment, dye, or substance. **3.** Green material, clothing, etc. **4.** A smooth grassy area or plot: the village *green*. **5.** In golf, the area of smooth, clipped grass surrounding the hole. **6.** *pl.* Freshly cut leaves, branches, vines, etc. **7.** *pl.* The edible leaves and stems of certain plants, as spinach, beets, etc. —*v.t. & v.i.* To make or become green. [OE *grēne*] —**green′ly** *adv.* —**green′ness** *n.*

green algae A class of algae in which the cells containing chlorophyll are dominant.

green·back (grēn′bak′) *n.* One of a class of U.S. notes used as legal tender.

green bean A string bean.

green·bri·er (grēn′brī′ər) A thorny vine having small, greenish flowers.

green·er·y (grē′nər·ē) *n. pl. ·er·ies* **1.** Green plants; verdure. **2.** A place where plants are grown or kept.

green-eyed (grēn′īd′) *adj.* **1.** Having green eyes. **2.** Jealous.

green·gage (grēn′gāj′) *n.* A variety of sweet plum.

green·gro·cer (grēn′grō′sər) *n. Brit.* A shopkeeper dealing in fresh vegetables, fruit, etc. —**green′gro′cer·y** (-sər·ē) *n.*

green·horn (grēn′hôrn′) *n.* **1.** An inexperienced person; beginner. **2.** One easily imposed upon or duped.

green·house (grēn′hous′) *n.* A heated shed or building constructed chiefly of glass, in which tender or exotic plants are grown or sheltered; hothouse.

green·ing (grē′ning) *n.* One of several varieties of apples having a green skin when ripe.

green·ish (grē′nish) *adj.* Somewhat green.

green light 1. A green signal light indicating that vehicles, pedestrians, etc., may proceed. **2.** *Informal* Approval or authorization to proceed.

Green Mountain State Nickname of Vermont.

green pepper 1. The unripe fruit of the sweet pepper. **2.** The unripe fruit of the red pepper, used in pickling.

green·room (grēn′rōōm′, -rōōm′) *n.* The waiting room in a theater used by performers when they are off-stage.

green soap A soap made from linseed oil and the hydroxides of potassium and sodium, used for skin diseases.

green·sward (grēn′swôrd′) *n.* Turf green with grass.

green tea Tea from tea leaves that have been heated, withered, and rolled without undergoing fermentation.

green thumb A special knack for making plants thrive.

green vitriol Copperas.

Greenwich mean time Time as reckoned from the meridian at Greenwich, England. Also **Greenwich time.**

green·wood (grēn′wood′) *n.* A forest in leaf.

greet (grēt) *v.t.* **1.** To express friendly recognition or courteous respect to, as upon meeting. **2.** To meet or receive in a specified manner. **3.** To present itself to; be evident to:

The warmth of a fire *greeted* us. —*v.i.* **4.** To offer a salutation upon meeting. [OE *grētan*] —**greet′er** *n.*

greet·ing (grē′ting) *n.* **1.** The act of one who greets; salutation; welcome. **2.** A friendly or complimentary message.

gre·gar·i·ous (gri-gâr′ē-əs) *adj.* **1.** Habitually associating with others, as in flocks, herds, or groups. **2.** Enjoying or seeking others; sociable. **3.** Of or characteristic of a flock, crowd, or aggregation. **4.** *Bot.* Growing in compact groups; clustered. [< L *grex, gregis* flock] —**gre·gar′i·ous·ly** *adv.* —**gre·gar′i·ous·ness** *n.*

Gre·go·ri·an (gri-gôr′ē-ən, -gō′rē-) *adj.* Of, pertaining to, or associated with Pope Gregory I or Pope Gregory XIII.

Gregorian Chant The system of plainsong associated with the liturgical reforms made by Pope Gregory I.

grem·lin (grem′lin) *n.* A mischievous, imaginary creature jokingly said to cause mechanical trouble in airplanes; also, any similar gnomelike troublemaker. [Origin uncertain]

gre·nade (gri-nād′) *n.* **1.** A small explosive or incendiary bomb designed either to be thrown by hand or projected from a rifle. **2.** A glass container that shatters and diffuses its volatile contents when thrown. [< F, pomegranate]

gren·a·dier (gren′ə-dir′) *n.* **1.** Formerly, a soldier assigned to throw grenades. **2.** A member of a special corps or regiment, as the British Grenadier Guards. [See GRENADE.]

gren·a·dine¹ (gren′ə-dēn′, gren′ə·dēn) *n.* A silk, wool, or cotton fabric of loose, open weave. [< F, ? after *Granada*]

gren·a·dine² (gren′ə-dēn′, gren′ə·dēn) *n.* A syrup made from pomegranates or red currants, used for flavoring.

Gresh·am's law (gresh′əmz) *Econ.* The principle stating that of two forms of currency, the less valuable form tends to drive the other from circulation, owing to the hoarding of the preferred form. Also **Gresham's theorem.** [after Sir Thomas Gresham, 1519–79, English merchant]

grew (grōō) Past tense of GROW.

grew·some (grōō′səm) See GRUESOME.

grey (grā) See GRAY.

grey·hound (grā′hound′) *n.* **1.** One of a breed of tall, slender, smooth-coated dogs noted for their speed. **2.** A fast ocean vessel. Also, *Rare, grayhound.* [OE *grīghund*]

grid (grid) *n.* **1.** An arrangement of regularly spaced parallel or intersecting bars, wires, etc.; grating; gridiron. **2.** A system of intersecting parallel lines dividing a map, chart, etc., into squares. **3.** A network of high-tension wires transmitting electric power over a wide area. **4.** *Electr.* A perforated or grooved metal plate in a storage cell or battery. **5.** *Electronics* An electrode, between the cathode and anode of an electron tube that controls the flow of electrons. [Back formation < GRIDIRON]

GREYHOUND
(28 inches high
at shoulder)

grid·dle (grid′l) *n.* A flat pan used for cooking pancakes, etc. —*v.t.* **·dled, ·dling** To cook on a griddle. [< AF *gredil*]

grid·dle·cake (grid′l·kāk′) *n.* A pancake baked on a griddle; also, *U.S., flapjack.*

grid·i·ron (grid′ī′ərn) *n.* **1.** A football field. **2.** A metal grating set in a frame, used for broiling meat, fish, etc. **3.** Something resembling a cooking gridiron. [ME *gredire*, var. of *gredile* griddle]

grief (grēf) *n.* **1.** Deep sorrow or mental distress caused by loss, remorse, affliction, etc. **2.** A cause of such sorrow. —**to come to grief** To end badly; meet with disaster; fail.

grief-strick·en (grēf′strik′ən) *adj.* Overwhelmed by grief.

griev·ance (grē′vəns) *n.* **1.** A real or imaginary wrong regarded as cause for complaint or resentment. **2.** A feeling of resentment arising from a sense of having been wronged.

grieve (grēv) *v.* **grieved, griev·ing** *v.t.* **1.** To cause to feel sorrow or grief. —*v.i.* **2.** To feel sorrow or grief. [< OF < L *gravis* heavy] —**griev′er** *n.* —**griev′ing·ly** *adv.*

griev·ous (grē′vəs) *adj.* **1.** Causing grief, sorrow, or misfortune. **2.** Meriting severe punishment or censure: a *grievous* sin. **3.** Expressing grief or sorrow. **4.** Causing physical suffering. —**griev′ous·ly** *adv.* —**griev′ous·ness** *n.*

grif·fin (grif′ən) *n.* In Greek mythology, a creature with the head and wings of an eagle and the body of a lion: also spelled *gryphon.* Also **grif′fon.** [< OF < L < Gk. *gryps*]

grift·er (grif′tər) *n. U.S. Slang* A petty swindler or confidence man; esp., one who operates a dishonest game of chance at a carnival or circus. [? < GRAFTER]

grill (gril) *v.t.* **1.** To cook on a gridiron or similar utensil. **2.** To subject to or torment with extreme heat. **3.** *U.S. Informal* To question or cross-examine persistently and searchingly. —*v.i.* **4.** To undergo grilling. —*n.* **1.** A gridiron or similar cooking utensil. **2.** A meal or portion of grilled food. **3.** A grillroom. **4.** A grille. [< F *gril,* var. of *grille* grating] —**grilled** *adj.* —**grill′er** *n.*

gril·lage (gril′ij) *n.* A framework of crossed timbers or steel beams serving as a foundation, esp. on soft ground.

grille (gril) *n.* A grating, often of decorative, open metalwork, used as a screen, divider, etc.: also spelled *grill.* [< F < OF, ult. < L *craticula,* dim. of *cratis* grating, lattice]

grill·room (gril/rōōm/, -rŏŏm/) *n.* A restaurant or eating place where grilled foods are prepared and served.

grilse (grils) *n. pl.* **grilse** (*Rare* **grils·es**) A young salmon that has returned for the first time from the sea to fresh water. [Origin unknown]

grim (grim) *adj.* **grim·mer, grim·mest** 1. Stern or forbidding in appearance or character. 2. Unyielding; relentless. 3. Sinisterly ironic; ghastly: a *grim* joke. 4. Savagely destructive; fierce. [OE] — **grim/ly** *adv.* — **grim/ness** *n.*

gri·mace (gri·mās/) *n.* A distorted facial expression, usu. indicative of pain, annoyance, disgust, etc. — *v.i.* **·maced, ·mac·ing** To distort the features; make faces. [< MF < Sp. *grimazo*, prob. < Gmc.] — **gri·mac/er** *n.*

gri·mal·kin (gri·mal/kin, -môl/-) *n.* 1. A cat, particularly an old female cat. 2. A shrewish old woman.

grime (grīm) *n.* Dirt, esp. soot, rubbed into or coating a surface. — *v.t.* **grimed, grim·ing** To make dirty; begrime. [< Flemish *grijm*]

grim·y (grī/mē) *adj.* **grim·i·er, grim·i·est** Full of or covered with grime; dirty. — **grim/i·ly** *adv.* — **grim/i·ness** *n.*

grin (grin) *v.* **grinned, grin·ning** *v.i.* 1. To smile broadly. 2. To draw back the lips so as to show the teeth, as in a snarl or a grimace of pain, rage, etc. — *v.t.* 3. To express by grinning. — *n.* 1. The act of grinning. 2. A facial expression produced by grinning, as a broad smile. — **Syn.** See SMILE. [OE *grennian*] — **grin/ner** *n.* — **grin/ning·ly** *adv.*

grind (grīnd) *v.* **ground, grind·ing** *v.t.* 1. To reduce to fine particles, as by crushing; pulverize. 2. To sharpen, polish, or wear down by friction or abrasion. 3. To rub together or press down with a scraping or turning motion: to *grind* the teeth. 4. To oppress; crush. 5. To operate by or as by turning a crank, as a coffee mill. 6. To produce by or as by grinding. 7. To produce mechanically or laboriously: followed by *out.* 8. To teach or instill with great and constant effort: with *into.* — *v.i.* 9. To perform the operation or action of grinding. 10. To undergo grinding. 11. To scrape; grate. 12. *Informal* To study or work steadily and laboriously. — *n.* 1. The act of grinding. 2. The sound made by grinding. 3. A specified state of pulverization, as of coffee. 4. *Informal* Prolonged and laborious work or study. 5. *U.S. Informal* A student who studies constantly. [OE *grindan*] — **grind/ing·ly** *adv.*

grind·er (grīn/dər) *n.* 1. One who grinds; esp., one who sharpens tools, etc. 2. A device used for grinding, as a coffee mill, etc. 3. A molar. 4. *pl. Informal* The teeth.

grind·stone (grīnd/stōn/) *n.* 1. A flat, circular stone rotated on an axle, used for sharpening tools, abrading, polishing, etc. 2. A millstone. — **to keep (or have) one's nose to the grindstone** To work hard and continuously.

grin·go (gring/gō) *n. pl.* **·gos** In Latin America, a foreigner, esp. one from any country where English is the official language: an offensive term. [< Am. Sp., gibberish]

grip¹ (grip) *n.* 1. The act of seizing and holding firmly. 2. The ability to seize or maintain a hold; grasping power. 3. Control; domination. 4. Mental or intellectual grasp. 5. The manner of grasping or holding something, as a tool or implement. 6. A distinctive handclasp, as one used by members of a fraternal organization in greeting one another. 7. The handle of an object. 8. A device or mechanical part that seizes or holds something. 9. The strength of the hand in grasping. 10. *U.S.* A suitcase or valise. 11. *U.S.* A stagehand. — **to come to grips** 1. To struggle in hand-to-hand combat. 2. To deal decisively or energetically, as with a problem. — *v.* **gripped** or **gript, grip·ping** *v.t.* 1. To seize; grasp firmly. 2. To capture, as the mind or imagination; attract and hold the interest of. 3. To join or attach securely with a grip or similar device. — *v.i.* 4. To take firm hold. 5. To capture the imagination or attention. [OE *gripan* to seize] — **grip/per** *n.* — **grip/ping·ly** *adv.*

grip² (grip) *n.* Influenza.

gripe (grīp) *v.* **griped, grip·ing** *v.t.* 1. *U.S. Informal* To annoy; anger. 2. To cause sharp pain or cramps in the bowels of. — *v.i.* 3. *U.S. Informal* To complain; grumble. 4. To cause or experience sharp pains in the bowels. — *n.* 1. *U.S. Informal* A grievance. 2. *Usu. pl.* Spasmodic pain in the bowels. [OE *gripan*] — **grip/er** *n.*

grippe (grip) *n.* Influenza. [< F *gripper* to seize] — **grip/py** *adj.*

grip·sack (grip/sak/) *n. U.S.* A traveling bag; valise.

gris·ly (griz/lē) *adj.* **·li·er, ·li·est** Inspiring horror; gruesome. [OE *grislic*] — **gris/li·ness** *n.*

grist (grist) *n.* 1. Grain that is to be ground; also, a batch of such grain. 2. Ground grain. — **grist for one's mill** Something that can be used to one's advantage. [OE < *grindan* to grind]

gris·tle (gris/əl) *n.* Cartilage, esp. in meat. [OE]

gris·tly (gris/lē) *adj.* 1. Pertaining to or resembling gristle. 2. Consisting of or containing gristle. — **gris/tli·ness** *n.*

grist·mill (grist/mil/) *n.* A mill for grinding grain.

grit (grit) *n.* 1. Small, rough, hard particles, as of sand, stone, etc. 2. A hard, coarse-grained sandstone. 3. Resolute spirit; pluck. — *v.* **grit·ted, grit·ting** *v.t.* 1. To grind or press together, as the teeth. 2. To cover with grit. — *v.i.* 3. To make a grating sound. [OE *grēot*]

grits (grits) *n.pl.* 1. Coarse meal. 2. *U.S.* Coarsely ground hominy: also called *hominy grits.* [OE *grytte*]

grit·ty (grit/ē) *adj.* **·ti·er, ·ti·est** 1. Like, containing, or consisting of grit. 2. Courageous; plucky. — **grit/ti·ly** *adv.* — **grit/ti·ness** *n.*

griz·zle (griz/əl) *v.t. & v.i.* **·zled, ·zling** To become or cause to become gray. — *n.* 1. The color gray, esp. when produced by intermixed hairs, specks, etc., of black and white. 2. Gray or graying hair. — *adj.* Gray. [< OF *gris* gray] — **griz/zled** *adj.*

griz·zly (griz/lē) *adj.* **·zli·er, ·zli·est** Grayish; grizzled. — *n. pl.* **·zlies** A grizzly bear.

grizzly bear A large bear of western North America.

groan (grōn) *v.i.* 1. To utter a low, prolonged sound of or as of pain, disapproval, etc. 2. To make a noise resembling such a sound; creak harshly. 3. To suffer, as from cruel or unfair treatment: usu. with *under* or *beneath.* 4. To be overburdened. — *v.t.* 5. To utter or express with or as with a groan. — *n.* 1. A low moaning or murmuring sound expressing pain, derision, etc. 2. A creaking or roaring sound. [OE *grānian*] — **groan/er** *n.* — **groan/ing·ly** *adv.*

groat (grōt) *n.* 1. A former English silver coin, worth fourpence. 2. A tiny sum. [< MDu. *groot*, orig., large]

groats (grōts) *n.pl.* Hulled, usu. coarsely crushed grain, as barley, oats, or wheat. [OE *grotan*]

gro·cer (grō/sər) *n.* One who deals in foodstuffs and various household supplies. [< OF < Med.L < LL *grossus* gross]

gro·cer·y (grō/sər·ē, grōs/rē) *n. pl.* **·cer·ies** 1. *U.S.* A store in which foodstuffs and household supplies are sold. 2. *pl.* The merchandise sold by a grocer.

grog (grog) *n.* Any alcoholic liquor, esp. rum, mixed with water. [after Old *Grog*, nickname of Admiral E. Vernon, 1684–1757, who first rationed it to English sailors]

grog·gy (grog/ē) *adj.* **·gi·er, ·gi·est** *Informal* 1. Dazed or not fully conscious, as from a blow or exhaustion. 2. Drunk. [< GROG] — **grog/gi·ly** *adv.* — **grog/gi·ness** *n.*

grog·ram (grog/rəm) *n.* A loosely woven, sometimes stiffened, fabric of coarse silk, or silk mixed with mohair or wool. [< F *gros grain* coarse grain]

groin (groin) *n.* 1. *Anat.* The fold or crease formed at the juncture of either of the thighs with the abdomen. 2. *Archit.* The curve formed by the intersection of two vaults. For illus. see VAULT. — *v.t.* To build with or form into groins. [? OE *grynde* abyss, hollow]

groin rib *Archit.* A rib covering a groin.

grom·met (grom/it) *n.* 1. A reinforcing eyelet of metal or other material, through which a rope, cord, or fastening may be passed. 2. *Naut.* A ring of rope or metal used to secure the edge of a sail. [< F < *gourmer* to curb]

GROIN RIBS IN GROIN VAULTING

groom (grōōm, grŏŏm) *n.* 1. A man or boy employed to tend horses; stableman. 2. A bridegroom. 3. One of several honorary functionaries in the British royal household. — *v.t.* 1. To attend to the neatness or appearance of. 2. To take care of (a horse) by cleaning, currying, etc. 3. *U.S.* To prepare by giving special training or attention to, as for a political office. [ME *grom.*]

grooms·man (grōōmz/mən, grŏŏms/-) *n. pl.* **·men** (-mən) The best man at a wedding.

groove (grōōv) *n.* 1. A long, narrow indentation or furrow cut into a surface, esp. by a tool. 2. Any narrow depression, channel, or rut. 3. A fixed, settled routine or habit. 4. *Anat.* Any of various furrows or depressions in an organ or part of the body. — **in the groove** *U.S. Slang* Operating or performing expertly or smoothly. — *v.t.* **grooved, groov·ing** To form a groove in. [< Du. *groeve*]

groov·y (grōō/vē) *adj.* **groov·i·er, groov·i·est** *U.S. Slang* Satisfying; delightful; great: a *groovy* feeling.

grope (grōp) *v.* **groped, grop·ing** *v.i.* 1. To feel about with or as with the hands, as in the dark; feel one's way. 2. To search bewilderedly or uncertainly. — *v.t.* 3. To seek out or find by or as by groping. — *n.* The act of groping. [OE *grāpian*] — **grop/er** *n.* — **grop/ing·ly** *adv.*

gros·beak (grōs/bēk/) *n.* Any of various finchlike birds having a short, stout beak. [< F < *gros* large + *bec* beak]

gros·grain (grō/grān) *n.* A strong, horizontally corded silk or rayon fabric, usu. woven as ribbon.

gross (grōs) *adj.* 1. Undiminished by deductions; total: distinguished from *net: gross* income. 2. Conspicuously bad or wrong: *gross* errors. 3. Excessively fat or large. 4.

Coarse in composition, structure, or texture. **5.** Coarse or obscene in character. **6.** Insensitive; dull. **7.** Dense; thick. **8.** *Anat.* or *Pathol.* Visible without the aid of a microscope: a *gross* lesion. — *n. pl.* **gross** for def. *1*, **gross·es** for def. *2* A unit of quantity comprising twelve dozen. **2.** The entire amount; bulk. — **in the gross. 1.** In bulk; all together. **2.** Wholesale. — *v.t.* To earn or produce as total income or profit, before deductions for expenses. etc. [< OF < LL *grossus* thick] — **gross′ly** *adv.* — **gross′ness** *n.*

gross weight Total weight. Abbr. *gr. wt.*

grosz (grôsh) *n. pl.* **gro·szy** (grôsh′ē) A monetary denomination of Poland, the hundredth part of a zloty.

gro·tesque (grō·tesk′) *adj.* **1.** Distorted, incongruous, or fantastically ugly in appearance or style; outlandish. **2.** Characterized by fantastic combinations of human and animal figures with conventional design forms. — *n.* **1.** One who or that which is grotesque. **2.** Grotesque style or quality. [< F < Ital. *grotta* excavation; from art found in excavations] — **gro·tesque′ly** *adv.* — **gro·tesque′ness** *n.*

grot·to (grot′ō) *n. pl.* **·toes** or **·tos 1.** A cave. **2.** An artificial cavelike structure, as for a recreational retreat, shrine, etc. [< Ital. *grotta* < L *crypta*]

grouch (grouch) *U.S. Informal v.i.* To be surly, grumble. — *n.* **1.** A discontented, grumbling person. **2.** A grumbling, sulky mood. [< OF *groucher* to murmur]

grouch·y (grou′chē) *adj.* **grouch·i·er, grouch·i·est** *U.S. Informal* Ill-humored. — **grouch′i·ly** *adv.* — **grouch′i·ness** *n.*

ground[1] (ground) *n.* **1.** The layer of solid substances constituting the surface of the earth; land. **2.** Soil, sand, etc., at or near the earth's surface. **3.** *Sometimes pl.* An area or tract of land; esp., one reserved or used for a specific purpose: a burial *ground.* **4.** *pl.* Private land, as the surrounding premises of a dwelling, public institution, etc. **5.** *Usu. pl.* The fundamental cause, reason, or motive for an action, belief, etc.: *grounds* for suspicion: when plural, often construed as singular. **6.** A subject; topic. **7.** *Often pl.* A foundation or basis, as for a decision, argument, or relationship; footing: when plural, often construed as singular. **8.** *pl.* Sediment; dregs; esp., the particles remaining after a beverage has been brewed. **9.** The solid bottom of a body of water. **10.** In various arts and crafts, the background against which colors, designs, etc., are placed. **11.** *Electr.* The connection of an electrical current or circuit with the earth through a conductor. **12.** *Music* A ground bass. — **Syn.** See REASON. — **from the ground up** In every detail; thoroughly. — **on home** (or **on one's own**) **ground 1.** In accustomed circumstances or surroundings. **2.** Dealing with a thoroughly familiar subject. — **to break ground 1.** To dig into or cut through the soil, as in plowing, excavating a building site, etc. **2.** To make a start in any undertaking. **3.** *Naut.* To be raised or loosened from the bottom, as an anchor. — **to cover ground 1.** To move or travel, esp. over a considerable distance. **2.** To make progress. — **to gain ground 1.** To advance; make headway. **2.** To increase in favor, influence, etc. — **to give ground** To yield a position or advantage; retreat. — **to hold** (or **stand**) **one's ground** To refuse to yield or retreat. — **to lose ground 1.** To fail to maintain an advantage or gain. **2.** To decline in favor, influence, etc. — **to shift one's ground** To change one's point of view, as in an argument or discussion. — *adj.* Being on, near, or at a level with the ground. **2.** Living, growing, or active on or in the ground. — *v.t.* **1.** To place on the ground. **2.** To base on or as on a foundation; establish; found. **3.** To teach fundamentals to. **4.** *Aeron.* To confine (an aircraft, pilot, etc.) to the ground. **5.** *Electr.* To place in connection with the earth or a ground, as a circuit. **6.** *Naut.* To run (a vessel) aground. **7.** To supply with a ground or background. — *v.i.* **8.** To come or fall to the ground. **9.** In baseball, to hit a ground ball. **10.** *Naut.* To run aground. [OE *grund*]

ground[2] (ground) Past tense and past participle of GRIND.

ground alert *Mil.* A state of preparedness in which airplanes and their crews stand ready for a quick takeoff.

ground ball In baseball, etc., a batted ball that rolls or bounces along the ground. Also **ground·er** (groun′dər).

ground bass *Music* A short melodic phrase in the bass, repeated continually with varied melody and harmony.

ground crew *Aeron.* A group of workers responsible for the servicing and maintenance of aircraft on the ground.

ground floor In a building, the floor that is level or almost level with the ground. — **to get in on the ground floor** *U.S. Informal* To enter upon a project at its beginning.

ground glass 1. Glass of which the surface has been treated so that it is not fully transparent. **2.** Finely powdered glass.

ground hog The woodchuck.

ground-hog day (ground′hôg′, -hog′) February 2, on which, allegedly, if the ground hog sees his shadow, he goes underground again for six more weeks of winter.

ground·less (ground′lis) *adj.* Having no reason or cause; baseless. — **ground′less·ly** *adv.* — **ground′less·ness** *n.*

ground·ling (ground′ling) *n.* **1.** A plant or animal living, growing, or remaining on or close to the ground. **2.** A fish that keeps close to the bottom of the water.

ground·nut (ground′nut′) A plant bearing edible tubers or underground nutlike seed pods, as the peanut.

ground pine Any of various creeping, evergreen plants of the club moss family.

ground plan 1. A diagrammatic plan of any floor of a building. **2.** Any preliminary plan or basic outline.

ground·sel (ground′səl) *n.* A common herb of the composite family having numerous yellow flowers. [OE *gundæswelge,* lit., that swallows pus (with ref. to its use in poultices)]

ground·sill (ground′sil′) *n.* The lowest horizontal timber in a frame building. Also **ground·sel.**

ground squirrel One of several small, terrestrial rodents of the squirrel family, as the gopher or chipmunk.

ground swell A billowing of the ocean in broad, deep waves caused by a prolonged storm, earthquake, etc.

ground water Underground water, accumulating by seepage, and serving as the source of springs, wells, etc.

ground wire *Electr.* The wire connecting an electrical apparatus with the ground or with a grounded object.

ground·work (ground′wûrk′) *n.* A foundation; basis.

ground zero The point on the ground vertically beneath or above the point of detonation of an atomic or thermonuclear bomb: also called *hypocenter.*

group (grōōp) *n.* **1.** A collection or assemblage of persons or things, considered as a unit; aggregation; cluster. **2.** A number of persons or things having in common certain characteristics, interests, etc. **3.** *Biol.* A number of plants or animals considered to be related because of certain common characteristics. **4.** In painting or sculpture, two or more figures or objects forming a harmonious unit or design. **5.** In the U.S. Air Force, a subdivision of a wing, designated for a specific purpose. **6.** *Chem.* An arrangement of atoms constituting part of a molecule; a radical. — *v.t.* **1.** To arrange or classify in a group or groups. — *v.i.* **2.** To form or be part of a group. [< F < Ital. *groppo* knot, lump]

group captain In the Commonwealth air forces, a commissioned officer. See table at GRADE.

group·er (grōō′pər) *n.* A food fish related to the sea basses, esp. the red grouper. [< Pg. *garupa,* appar. < S. Am. Ind.]

group·ie (grōō′pē) *n.* A girl who follows a pop group or singer on tours, usually for sexual reasons.

grouse[1] (grous) *n. pl.* **grouse** Any of a family of game birds characterized by rounded bodies and mottled plumage, as the ruffed grouse. [Origin uncertain]

grouse[2] (grous) *Informal v.i.* **groused, grous·ing** To grumble. — *n.* A complaint. [? < OF *grousser* to murmur]

grove (grōv) *n.* A small wood or group of trees, esp. when cleared of underbrush. [OE *gráf*]

grov·el (gruv′əl, grov′-) *v.i.* **grov·eled** or **·elled, grov·el·ing** or **·el·ling 1.** To lie prostrate or crawl face downward, as in abjection, fear, etc. **2.** To act with abject humility. [Back formation < GROVELING] — **grov′el·er** or **grov′el·ler** *n.*

grov·el·ing (gruv′əl·ing, grov′-) *adj.* **1.** Lying or crawling in an abject, prostrate position. **2.** Abjectly humble. **3.** Low; sordid. Also **grov′el·ling.** [ME *grovelynge,* adv. < *on gruff* face down + -LING[2]] — **grov′el·ing·ly** *adv.*

grow (grō) *v.* **grew, grown, grow·ing** *v.i.* **1.** To increase in size by the assimilation of nutriment; progress toward maturity. **2.** To germinate and develop to maturity, as from a seed or spore; originate, as from a basic source or cause. **3.** To flourish; thrive. **4.** To increase in size, amount, or degree. **5.** To become: She *grew* angry. **6.** To become joined or attached by or as by growth. — *v.t.* **7.** To cause to grow; cultivate. **8.** To produce by a natural process: to *grow* hair. **9.** To cover with a growth: used in the passive. — **to grow on** To become increasingly acceptable, pleasing, or necessary to. — **to grow out of 1.** To outgrow. **2.** To result from. [OE *grōwan*] — **grow′er** *n.*

growl (groul) *v.i.* **1.** To utter a deep, guttural sound, as that made by a hostile or agitated animal. **2.** To speak gruffly and angrily. **3.** To rumble, as distant thunder. — *v.t.* **4.** To utter or express by growling. — *n.* **1.** A deep, sustained, guttural sound uttered by a hostile or agitated animal. **2.** Any sound resembling this. **3.** A gruff, angry utterance. [? < OF *grouler* to mumble < Gmc.] — **growl′er** *n.*

grown (grōn) Past participle of GROW. — *adj.* Arrived at full physical growth or stature; mature; adult.

grown-up (grōn′up′) *n.* A mature person; adult.

grown-up (grōn′up′) *adj.* **1.** Physically or mentally mature; adult. **2.** Characteristic of or appropriate to an adult.

growth (grōth) *n.* **1.** The act or process of growing. **2.** A gradual increase in size, influence, etc. **3.** Something grown or in the process of growing: a *growth* of timber. **4.** Origin; source. **5.** *Pathol.* An abnormal formation of tissue.

grub (grub) *v.* **grubbed, grub·bing** *v.i.* **1.** To dig in the ground. **2.** To lead a dreary or miserable existence; drudge. **3.** To make careful or plodding search; rummage. — *v.t.* **4.** To dig from the ground; root out: often with *up* or *out.* **5.** To clear (ground) of roots, stumps, etc. **6.** *U.S. Slang* To scrounge. — *n.* **1.** The wormlike larva of certain insects, as of the June beetle. **2.** A drudge. **3.** *Slang* Food. [ME *grubben*] **— grub′ber** *n.*

grub·by (grub′ē) *adj.* **·bi·er, ·bi·est 1.** Dirty; sloppy. **2.** Infested with grubs. **— grub′bi·ly** *adv.* **— grub′bi·ness** *n.*

grub·stake (grub′stāk′) *U.S. Informal n.* **1.** Money, supplies, or equipment provided a prospector on condition that he share his finds with the donor. **2.** Money or assistance furnished to advance any venture. **—** *v.t.* **·staked, ·stak·ing** To supply with a grubstake.

grudge (gruj) *n.* A feeling of ill will, rancor, or enmity, harbored for a remembered wrong, etc. **—** *v.* **grudged, grudg·ing** *v.t.* **1.** To be displeased or resentful because of the possessions, good fortune, etc. of (another): They *grudge* him his wealth. **2.** To give or allow unwillingly and resentfully. [< OF *groucher*] **— grudg′er** *n.* **— grudg′ing·ly** *adv.*

gru·el (grōō′əl) *n.* A semiliquid food made by boiling meal in water or milk. **—** *v.t.* **gru·eled** or **·elled, gru·el·ing** or **·el·ling** To disable or exhaust by hard work, punishment, relentless questioning, etc. [< OF, ult. < Med.L *grutum* coarse meal < Gmc.] **— gru′el·er** or **gru′el·ler** *n.*

gru·el·ing (grōō′əl·ing) *adj.* Causing strain or exhaustion. **—** *n.* Any grueling experience. Also **gru′el·ling.**

grue·some (grōō′səm) *adj.* Inspiring repugnance; frightful; also spelled *grewsome.* [< Scot. *grue* to shudder + -SOME[1]] **— grue′some·ly** *adv.* **— grue′some·ness** *n.*

gruff (gruf) *adj.* **1.** Brusque and rough in manner or speech. **2.** Hoarse and guttural; harsh. [< Du. *grof* rough] **— gruff′ly** *adv.* **— gruff′ness** *n.*

grum·ble (grum′bəl) *v.* **·bled, ·bling** *v.i.* **1.** To complain in a surly manner. **2.** To utter low, throaty sounds; growl. **3.** To rumble. **—** *v.t.* **4.** To utter or express by grumbling. **—** *n.* **1.** A low, muttered complaint. **2.** A rumble. [Cf. Du. *grommelen* < *grommen* to growl] **— grum′bler** *n.* **— grum′bling·ly** *adv.* **— grum′bly** *adj.*

grump·y (grum′pē) *adj.* **grump·i·er, grump·i·est** Ill-tempered; cranky; surly. Also **grump′ish.** [? Blend of GRUNT and DUMP] **— grump′i·ly** *adv.* **— grump′i·ness** *n.*

grunt (grunt) *v.i.* **1.** To make the deep, guttural sound of a hog. **2.** To make a similar sound, as in annoyance, assent, effort, etc. **—** *v.t.* **3.** To utter or express by grunting. **—** *n.* **1.** A short, deep, guttural sound, as of a hog. **2.** A food fish of warm American seas. [OE *grunnettan*] **— grunt′er** *n.*

Gru·yère cheese (grē·yâr′, grōō–; *Fr.* grü·yâr′) A light yellow, whole-milk Swiss cheese having a firm texture and few or no holes. [after *Gruyère*, a town in Switzerland]

G-string (jē′string′) *n.* **1.** A narrow loincloth supported by a waistband. **2.** A similar garment worn by stripteasers. **3.** On musical instruments, a string tuned to G.

gua·no (gwä′nō) *n. pl.* **·nos 1.** The excrement of sea birds, found on the Peruvian coast, and used as a fertilizer. **2.** Any similar fertilizer. [< Sp. < Quechua *huanu* dung]

Gua·ra·ni (gwä′rä·nē′) *n. pl.* **·nis** or **·ni 1.** A member of a South American Indian tribe, formerly occupying the valleys of the Paraná and the Uruguay. **2.** The Tupian language of these tribes. [< Tupi, *warrior*]

guar·an·tee (gar′ən·tē′) *n.* **1.** A pledge or formal promise that something will meet stated specifications or that a specified act will be performed or continued: also called *warranty.* **2.** A guaranty (def. 2). **3.** A guarantor. **4.** One who receives a guaranty. **—** *v.t.* **1.** To certify; vouch for: We *guarantee* our work. **2.** To accept responsibility for. **3.** To give security to (a person or thing), as against loss, damage, injury, etc. [Var. of GUARANTY]

guar·an·tor (gar′ən·tər, -tôr′) *n.* One who makes or gives a guaranty.

guar·an·ty (gar′ən·tē) *n. pl.* **·ties 1.** A pledge or promise to be responsible for the contract, debt, or duty of another person in case of his default or miscarriage. **2.** Something given or taken as security. **3.** A guarantor. **—** *v.t.* **·tied, ·ty·ing** To guarantee. [< OF *guarant* warrant < Gmc.]

guard (gärd) *v.t.* **1.** To watch over or care for; protect. **2.** To watch over so as to prevent escape, etc. **3.** To control or prevent exit or entry through. **4.** To maintain cautious control over. **5.** To furnish (something) with a protective device or shield. **—** *v.i.* **6.** To take precautions: followed by *against.* **7.** To serve as a guard. **—** *n.* **1.** One who guards; as: **a** A warder; keeper. **b** One who has control over a point of entry, exit, etc. **2.** A group of persons serving as a ceremonial escort. **3.** The act of guarding. **4.** That which provides protection. **5.** A defensive posture or stance, as in boxing or fencing. **6.** In football, one of two linemen whose position in the front line is usually between one of the tackles and the center. **7.** In basketball, one of two players who direct the offense and are in the front line of defense. **— off (one's) guard** Unprepared. **— on (one's) guard** Watchful, cautious. **— to mount guard** To go on duty as a sentry. **— to stand guard 1.** To maintain a protective watch. **2.** To serve as a sentry. [< OF *guarder*] **— guard′er** *n.*

guard·ed (gär′did) *adj.* **1.** Cautious; prudent; reserved: *guarded* criticism. **2.** Closely defended or kept under surveillance by a guard. **— guard′ed·ly** *adv.* **— guard′ed·ness** *n.*

guard·house (gärd′hous′) *n.* **1.** The quarters and headquarters for military guards. **2.** A jail confining military personnel convicted of minor offenses, etc.

guard·i·an (gär′dē·ən) *n.* **1.** One who guards or watches over something. **2.** One who is legally assigned care of the person, property, etc., esp. of an infant or minor. ◆ Collateral adjective: *custodial.* **—** *adj.* Keeping guard; protecting. **— guard′i·an·ship** *n.*

guard·room (gärd′rōōm′, -rŏŏm′) *n.* A room for the use and accommodation of military or other guards.

guards·man (gärdz′mən) *n. pl.* **·men** (-mən) **1.** A guard. **2.** *U.S.* A member of the National Guard.

gua·va (gwä′və) *n.* **1.** A tree or shrub of the myrtle family, native to tropical America. **2.** Its small, pear-shaped edible fruit. [< Sp. *guayaba.*]

gu·ber·na·to·ri·al (gōō′bər·nə·tôr′ē·əl, -tō′rē, gyōō′-) *adj.* Of or pertaining to a governor. [< L *gubernator* governor]

guck (guk) *n. U.S. & Canadian Slang* Goo; muck.

gudg·eon (guj′ən) *n.* **1.** A small, carplike, fresh-water fish of Europe. **2.** A minnow. **3.** A bait or enticement. **—** *v.t.* To cheat; dupe. [< OF < L *gobio* small fish]

guer·don (gûr′dən) *Poetic n.* Reward; recompense. **—** *v.t.* To reward. [< OF < Med.L < OHG < *widar* in turn + *lōn* reward] **— guer′don·er** *n.*

guern·sey (gûrn′zē) *n. pl.* **·seys** A closely fitting knitted woolen shirt or sweater worn by seamen.

Guern·sey (gûrn′zē) *n. pl.* **·seys** One of a breed of dairy cattle having fawn and white coloration.

guer·ril·la (gə·ril′ə) *n.* One of a combatant band often operating in rear of the enemy. **—** *adj.* Of guerrillas or their warfare. Also **gue·ril′la.** [< Sp., dim. of *guerra* war]

guess (ges) *v.t.* **1.** To form a judgment or opinion of (some quantity, fact, etc.) on uncertain or incomplete knowledge. **2.** To conjecture correctly. **3.** *U.S.* To believe: I *guess* we'll be late. **—** *v.i.* **4.** To form a judgment or opinion on uncertain or incomplete knowledge: often with *at.* **5.** To conjecture correctly: How did you *guess?* **—** *n.* **1.** An opinion or conclusion arrived at by guessing. **2.** The act of guessing. [ME *gessen*] **— guess′er** *n.*

guess·ti·mate (ges′tə·mit) *n. Slang* An estimate that is little better than a guess. [Blend of GUESS and ESTIMATE]

guess·work (ges′wûrk′) *n.* **1.** The process of guessing. **2.** Something based on a guess or guesses, as an opinion.

guest (gest) *n.* **1.** One who is received and entertained by another or others, as at a party or meal, or for a visit, etc. **2.** One who pays for lodging, etc., as at a hotel. **—** *adj.* **1.** Intended for guests. **2.** Acting on invitation. [OE *giest*]

guff (guf) *n. Slang* Empty talk; nonsense; baloney. [Imit.]

guf·faw (gə·fô′) *n.* A loud burst of boisterous laughter. **—** *v.i.* To utter such a laugh. [Imit.]

gui·dance (gīd′ns) *n.* **1.** The act, process, or result of guiding. **2.** Something that guides.

guide (gīd) *v.* **guid·ed, guid·ing** *v.t.* **1.** To lead or direct, as to a destination. **2.** To direct the motion or physical progress of, as a vehicle, tool, animal, etc. **3.** To lead or direct the affairs, standards, opinions, etc., of. **—** *v.i.* **4.** To act as a guide. **—** *n.* **1.** A person who guides; esp., one who conducts others on trips, through museums, on sight-seeing tours, etc. **2.** One who or that which is taken as a model. **3.** A book that guides or explains; esp., a guidebook. **4.** *Mech.* Any device that regulates or controls the operation of a part. [< OF *guider*] **— guid′a·ble** *adj.* **— guid′er** *n.*

guide·book (gīd′bŏŏk′) *n.* A handbook containing directions and other information for tourists, visitors, etc.

guid·ed missile (gī′did) *Mil.* An unmanned aerial missile whose course can be altered during flight by mechanisms that are preset, self-reacting, or actuated by radio signals.

guide·line (gīd′līn′) *n.* **1.** A line, as a rope, for guiding. **2.** Any suggestion, rule, etc., intended as a guide.

guide·post (gīd′pōst′) *n.* **1.** A post on which directions for travelers are given. **2.** A guideline.

gui·don (gī′don, gīd′n) *n. Mil.* A small flag for unit identification. [< F < Ital. *guidone*]

guild (gild) *n.* **1.** In medieval times, an association of artisans or merchants, formed for mutual aid, etc. **2.** Any similar association or fellowship. Also spelled *gild.* [Fusion of OE *gild* payment and *gegyld* association]

guil·der (gil′dər) *n.* The basic monetary unit of the Netherlands: in 1960 worth about 27 U.S. cents. Also called *gulden:* also spelled *gilder.* [< Du. *gulden* golden]

guild·hall (gild′hôl′) *n. Brit.* **1.** The hall where a guild meets. **2.** A town hall.

guilds·man (gildz′mən) *n. pl.* **·men** (-mən) A member of a guild.

guild socialism An English theory of socialism that advo-

cates ownership of all industry by the state with guilds of workers exercising the powers of management and control.
guile (gīl) *n.* Treacherous cunning or craft; deceit. [< OF < Gmc.]
guile·ful (gīl'fəl) *adj.* Full of guile; treacherous; deceitful. — **guile'ful·ly** *adv.* — **guile'ful·ness** *n.*
guile·less (gīl'lis) *adj.* Free from guile; sincere. — **Syn.** See INGENUOUS. — **guile'less·ly** *adv.* — **guile'less·ness** *n.*
guil·le·mot (gil'ə-mot) *n.* Any of several narrow-billed auks found in northern latitudes. [< F, dim. of *Guillaume* William]
guil·lo·tine (*n.* gil'ə-tēn, gē'ə-tēn; *v.* gil'ə-tēn', gil'ə-tēn) *n.* 1. The instrument of capital punishment in France, consisting of a weighted blade that slides down between two vertical guides and beheads the victim. 2. A similar machine for cutting paper, etc. — *v.t.* ·tined, ·tin·ing To behead with the guillotine. [< F, after J. I. *Guillotin*, 1738–1814, French physician who advocated a humane means of execution]
guilt (gilt) *n.* 1. The fact or condition of having committed a legal or moral offense. 2. A feeling of remorse arising from a real or imagined commission of an offense. 3. Guilty conduct. [OE *gylt*]
guilt·less (gilt'lis) *adj.* 1. Free from guilt; innocent. 2. Lacking knowledge or experience: with *of*. — **guilt'less·ly** *adv.* — **guilt'less·ness** *n.*
guilt·y (gil'tē) *adj.* **guilt·i·er, guilt·i·est** 1. Deserving of blame for some offense. 2. Convicted of some offense. 3. Involving, pertaining to, or showing guilt. — **guilt'i·ly** *adv.* — **guilt'i·ness** *n.*
guimpe (gimp, gamp) *n.* A short blouse. [< F]
guin·ea (gin'ē) *n.* 1. Formerly, an English gold coin. 2. A British money of account, equal to 21 shillings. 3. The guinea fowl. 4. *U.S. Slang* A person of Italian descent: an offensive term.
guinea fowl A gallinaceous bird of African origin, having dark gray plumage speckled with white spots, long domesticated in Europe and America. Also **guinea, guinea hen.**
guinea pig 1. A small, domesticated rodent, usu. white, having a short tail and widely used in biological and medical experiments. 2. Any person used in experimentation.
Guinea worm A threadlike aquatic worm of tropical Africa and Asia, whose larvae infect the legs and lower trunk of men and animals.
Guin·e·vere (gwin'ə-vir) In Arthurian legend, Arthur's unfaithful queen and the mistress of Lancelot.
guise (gīz) *n.* 1. External appearance or aspect; semblance. 2. Assumed or false appearance; pretense. [< OF < Gmc.]
gui·tar (gi·tär') *n.* A musical instrument having a fretted fingerboard, a large sound box with indented sides, and strings, usu. six, that are plucked with the fingers or plectrum. [< Sp. *guitarra*] — **gui·tar'ist** *n.*
gu·lar (gōō'lər, gyōō'-) *adj.* Of or pertaining to the throat; pharyngeal. [< L *gula* throat]
gulch (gulch) *n. U.S.* A deep, narrow ravine cut out by a rushing stream. [? < dial. *gulch* to swallow greedily]
gul·den (gōōl'dən) *n.* The guilder. [< Du., lit., golden]
gules (gyōōlz) *n. Heraldry* The tincture red. [< OF *gueules* red-dyed ermine fur]
gulf (gulf) *n.* 1. A large area of ocean or sea partially enclosed by an extended sweep of land. 2. An abyss; chasm; gorge. 3. A wide or impassable separation, as in social position, education, etc. — *v.t.* To swallow up; engulf. [< OF < Ital. < LGk. < Gk. *kolpos* bay]
Gulf Stream A warm ocean current flowing NE along the eastern coast of North America toward Europe.
gulf·weed (gulf'wēd') *n.* Sargasso.
gull¹ (gul) *n.* A long-winged, web-footed sea bird, usu. white and gray, and having the upper mandible hooked. [ME]
gull² (gul) *n. Archaic* A person easily tricked. — *v.t. Archaic* To deceive; swindle; cheat. [? < obs. *gull* swallow]
Gul·lah (gul'ə) *n.* 1. One of a group of Negroes dwelling on a narrow coastal strip of South Carolina, Georgia, and NE Florida, or on islands lying off this coast. 2. The mixed (English and African) language of these people.
gul·let (gul'it) *n.* 1. The passage from the mouth to the stomach; esophagus. 2. The throat; pharynx; also, anything resembling a throat. [< OF < L *gula*]
gul·li·ble (gul'ə-bəl) *adj.* Easily cheated or fooled; credulous. — **gul'li·bil'i·ty** *n.* — **gul'li·bly** *adv.*
Gul·li·ver (gul'ə-vər) Lemuel The hero of Jonathan Swift's satire **Gulliver's Travels** (1726).
gul·ly (gul'ē) *n. pl.* ·lies A channel, ravine, or ditch; esp., a ravine cut in the earth by running water. — *v.t.* ·lied, ·ly·ing To cut or wear a gully in. [Var. of GULLET]
gulp (gulp) *v.t.* 1. To swallow greedily or in large amounts. 2. To choke back or stifle. — *v.i.* 3. To swallow convul-

sively as a sign of surprise, etc. — *n.* 1. The act of gulping. 2. The amount swallowed in gulping. [< Du. *gulpen*] — **gulp'er** *n.* — **gulp'ing·ly** *adv.*
gum¹ (gum) *n.* 1. A sticky, viscid substance exuded from various trees and plants, soluble in water and hardening on exposure to air. 2. Any similar substance, as resin. 3. A preparation made from gum and used in art, industry, etc. 4. Chewing gum. 5. Mucilage; glue. 6. The gum tree. 7. Rubber. 8. *U.S. Dial. pl.* Rubber overshoes. — *v.* **gummed, gum·ming** *v.t.* 1. To smear, stiffen, or clog with gum. 2. To glue or stick together with gum — *v.i.* 3. To exude or form gum. 4. To become sticky or clogged with gum. — **to gum up** *Slang* To bungle. [< OF < L < Gk. *kommi*]
gum² (gum) *n. Often pl.* The fleshy tissue that covers the arches of the jaws and surrounds the necks of the teeth. — *v.t. & v.i.* **gummed, gum·ming** *U.S. Dial.* To chew without teeth. [OE *goma* inside of the mouth]
gum ammoniac Ammoniac².
gum arabic The gum from various species of acacia, used in medicine, candy, ink, etc.
gum·bo (gum'bō) *n. pl.* -bos 1. The okra or its edible, slippery pods. 2. A thick soup or stew containing okra pods. 3. *U.S. & Canadian* In the West, a type of fine, silty soil. Also **gumbo soil.** 4. A patois of French spoken by Negroes in Louisiana. [< Bantu (Angola)]
gum·boil (gum'boil') *n.* A small boil or abscess on the gum.
gum·drop (gum'drop') *n. U.S.* A small, round piece of jellylike candy, usu. colored and coated with sugar.
gum·my (gum'ē) *adj.* ·mi·er, ·mi·est 1. Of or like gum; sticky; viscid. 2. Covered or clogged with gum or a gum-like substance. 3. Exuding gum. — **gum'mi·ness** *n.*
gump·tion (gump'shən) *n. Informal* 1. Bold, energetic initiative. 2. Shrewd common sense. [< dial. E (Scot.)]
gum resin A mixture of gum and resin that exudes as a milky juice from incisions in certain plants.
gum·shoe (gum'shōō') *n. U.S.* 1. A rubber shoe or overshoe. 2. *pl.* Sneakers. 3. *Slang* A detective. — *v.i.* ·shoed, ·shoe·ing *Slang* To go stealthily and noiselessly; sneak.
gum tree Any of various trees that produce gum.
gun (gun) *n.* 1. A weapon or projectile device from which a missile is thrown by the force of an explosive, by compressed air, by a spring, etc. 2. Loosely, any portable firearm. 3. *Mil.* **a** Any of various cannons with a flat trajectory, high muzzle velocity, and a barrel of over .25 caliber: anti-tank *gun.* **b** Any of various automatic weapons: machine *gun.* 4. Any device resembling a gun: grease *gun.* 5. The discharging of a firearm. 6. *U.S. Slang* The throttle controlling an engine. 7. *U.S. Slang* A gunman. — **big gun** *Slang* A person of influence. — **to give it** (or **her**) **the gun** *Slang* 1. To increase sharply the speed of a motor. 2. To give added speed, efficiency, etc., to some action. — **to go great guns** *U.S. Slang* To work or perform with great skill, speed, etc. — **to spike** (**someone's**) **guns** To destroy or make ineffective someone's plans, ideas, etc. — **to stick to one's guns** To continue in one's actions, plans, opinions, etc., in spite of opposition. — *v.* **gunned, gun·ning** *v.i.* 1. To go shooting or hunting with a gun. — *v.t.* 2. *U.S. Slang* To open the throttle of (an engine). 3. To shoot (a person) with a gun. — **to gun for** (or **after**) *U.S. Slang* 1. To seek with intent to injure or kill. 2. To seek out in order to win favor, etc. [ME *gonne, gunne*]
gun·boat (gun'bōt') *n.* A small, armed naval vessel, used for patrolling rivers and coastal waters.
gun carriage The mechanical structure, often wheeled, upon which a cannon is mounted for firing or maneuvering.
gun·cot·ton (gun'kot'n) *n.* A type of cellulose nitrate used as an explosive.
gun·fire (gun'fīr') *n.* 1. The firing of a gun or guns. 2. *Mil.* The use of artillery or small arms in warfare.
gung ho (gung'hō') *U.S. Slang* Eager; enthusiastic; zealous: *gung ho* about army life. [< Chinese]
gun·lock (gun'lok') *n.* The mechanism in certain guns by which the hammer is driven and the charge exploded.
gun·man (gun'mən) *n. pl.* ·men (-mən) 1. A man armed with a gun; esp., an armed criminal. 2. A gunsmith.
gun·met·al (gun'met'l) *adj.* Of the color of gun metal.
gun metal 1. A bronze made of copper, tin, and zinc. 2. Any of various metal alloys of a dark bluish gray color, used for metal novelties. 3. A dark bluish gray color.
gun moll *U.S. Slang* 1. A female associate or accomplice of criminals. 2. A female thief.
gun·nel¹ (gun'əl) See GUNWALE.
gun·nel² (gun'əl) *n. pl.* ·nels or ·nel A fish of the blenny family, found in North Atlantic waters.
gun·ner (gun'ər) *n.* 1. One who operates a gun. 2. In the U.S. Navy and Marine Corps, a warrant officer whose duties were traditionally connected with ordnance. 3. In the U.S. Army, a noncommissioned officer who does the actual firing of a gun. 4. *Brit. Mil.* An artilleryman.
gun·ner·y (gun'ər·ē) *n.* 1. The science and art of constructing and operating guns. 2. Guns collectively.

GUILLOTINE
b Basket for body.
r Receptacle for head.

gun·ny (gun/ē) *n. pl.* **·nies** 1. A coarse, heavy material made of jute or hemp, used for making sacks, etc. 2. A bag or sack made from this material: also **gunny bag, gunny sack.** [< Hind. *goni* gunny sack]

gun·pow·der (gun/pou/dər) *n.* An explosive mixture of potassium nitrate, charcoal, and sulfur, used in blasting and fireworks, and still occasionally as a propellant in guns.

gun·run·ning (gun/run/ing) *n.* The smuggling of guns and ammunition into a country. — **gun/run/ner** *n.*

gun·shot (gun/shot/) *n.* 1. The range or reach of a gun. 2. The shooting of a gun; also, the noise or the shot. — *adj.* Caused by a gunshot.

gun-shy (gun/shī/) *adj.* Afraid of a gun or of its sound.

gun·smith (gun/smith/) *n.* One who makes or repairs guns.

gun·stock (gun/stok/) *n.* The wooden stock of a gun.

gun·wale (gun/əl) *n. Naut.* The upper edge of the side of a boat: also spelled *gunnel.* [< GUN + WALE[1] (plank).]

gup·py (gup/ē) *n. pl.* **·pies** A small, tropical, fresh-water fish, valued as an aquarium fish because of its coloring. [after R. J. L. *Guppy,* British scientist]

gur·gle (gûr/gəl) *v.* **·gled, ·gling** *v.i.* 1. To flow irregularly, with a bubbling sound, as water from a bottle. 2. To make such a sound. — *v.t.* 3. To utter with a gurgling sound. — *n.* The act or sound of gurgling. [Var. of GARGLE]

gur·nard (gûr/nərd) *n. pl.* **·nards** or **·nard** Any of various marine fishes having a spiny head. Also **gur/net** (-nit). [< OF *grognard* grumbler]

gu·ru (gōō/rōō) *n.* 1. In the East, a spiritual teacher or guide. 2. A teacher or leader regarded as having special knowledge, power, etc. [< Hind.]

gush (gush) *v.i.* 1. To pour out in volume and with sudden force. 2. To emit a sudden flow, as of blood, tears, etc. 3. *Informal* To be overly enthusiastic. — *v.t.* 4. To pour forth (blood, tears, words, etc.). — *n.* 1. A sudden flow or outburst. 2. *Informal* An extravagant effusion of emotion, praise, etc. [ME *guschen*] — **gush/ing·ly** *adv.*

gush·er (gush/ər) *n.* 1. One who gushes. 2. An oil well that spurts oil without the need of pumps.

gush·y (gush/ē) *adj.* **gush·i·er, gush·i·est** *Informal* Overly enthusiastic. — **gush/i·ness** *n.*

gus·set (gus/it) *n.* 1. A triangular piece inserted into a garment, glove, shoe, etc., for added strength or roomier fit. 2. A bracket used to strengthen a corner or angle of a structure. — *v.t.* To furnish with a gusset. [< OF *gousse* pod]

gust (gust) *n.* 1. A sudden, violent rush of wind or air. 2. A sudden burst or outpouring of fire, sound, water, etc. 3. A brief outburst of emotion. [< ON *gustr*]

gus·ta·to·ry (gus/tə·tôr/ē, -tō/rē) *adj.* Of or pertaining to the sense of taste or the act of tasting.

gus·to (gus/tō) *n.* 1. Keen enjoyment or enthusiasm; relish. 2. Individual taste or preference. 3. In art, a characteristic style or treatment. [< Ital. < L *gustus* taste]

gust·y (gus/tē) *adj.* **gust·i·er, gust·i·est** 1. Characterized by fitful gusts of wind or rain; blustery. 2. Given to sudden outbursts of feeling, etc. — **gust/i·ly** *adv.* — **gust/i·ness** *n.*

gut (gut) *n.* 1. The alimentary canal or any part of it; esp., the stomach or intestine. 2. *pl.* Bowels; entrails. 3. The specially prepared intestines of certain animals, used as strings for musical instruments, surgical sutures, etc. 4. *pl. Slang* **a** Courage; stamina; grit. **b** Effrontery. 5. A narrow passage, as a strait. — *v.t.* **gut·ted, gut·ting** 1. To take out the intestines of. 2. To plunder. 3. To destroy the contents of. [OE *guttas*]

gut·ta-per·cha (gut/ə·pûr/chə) *n.* A coagulated, rubber-like material, formed from the juice of various Malayan trees, used in electrical insulation, in the arts, as a dental plastic, etc. [< Malay *getah* gum + *percha* gum tree]

gut·ter (gut/ər) *n.* 1. A channel or ditch at the side of a street, for carrying off surface water. 2. A furrow or ditch formed by running water. 3. A trough, fixed below or along the eaves of a house, for carrying off rain water from the roof. 4. A state or condition of life, marked by poverty, filth, etc. 5. Any groove or channel. — *v.t.* 1. To form channels or grooves in. 2. To furnish with gutters, as a house. — *v.i.* 3. To flow in channels, as water. 4. To melt rapidly: said of lighted candles. [< OF < *goute* drop]

gut·ter·snipe (gut/ər·snīp/) *n.* A neglected child, usu. of the slums, who spends much time in the streets.

gut·tur·al (gut/ər·əl) *adj.* 1. Pertaining to the throat. 2. Having a harsh, or muffled, grating quality. 3. *Phonet.* Velar. — *n. Phonet.* A velar sound. [< NL < L *guttur* throat] — **gut/tur·al/i·ty** *n.* — **gut/tur·al·ly** *adv.*

gut·ty (gut/ē) *adj.* **gut·ti·er, gut·ti·est** *Slang* Courageous.

guy[1] (gī) *n.* 1. *Informal* A man or boy; fellow. 2. *Brit.* A person of grotesque appearance. — *v.t.* **guyed, guy·ing** *Informal* To ridicule. [after *Guy* Fawkes, leader of an abortive conspiracy in 1605 to assassinate King James I]

guy[2] (gī) *n.* A rope, cable, wire, etc., used to steady, guide,

or secure something. — *v.t.* To secure, steady, or guide with a guy. [< OF *guider* to guide]

guz·zle (guz/əl) *v.t. & v.i.* **·zled, ·zling** To drink greedily or to excess. [? < OF *gosier* throat] — **guz/zler** *n.*

gym (jim) *n. U.S. Informal* 1. A gymnasium. 2. A course in physical training. [Short for GYMNASIUM]

gym·na·si·um (jim·nā/zē·əm) *n. pl.* **·si·ums** or **·si·a** (-zē·ə) 1. A building or room equipped for certain athletic activities. 2. A place where ancient Greek youths met for physical exercise and discussion. [< L < Gk. *gymnazein* to exercise]

Gym·na·si·um (gim·nä/zē·ōōm) *n.* In Europe, esp. Germany, a secondary school to prepare students for the universities.

gym·nast (jim/nast) *n.* One skilled in gymnastics.

gym·nas·tic (jim·nas/tik) *adj.* Of or pertaining to gymnastics. Also **gym·nas/ti·cal.** — **gym·nas/ti·cal·ly** *adv.*

gym·nas·tics (jim·nas/tiks) *n.pl.* 1. Any physical exercises designed to improve strength, agility, etc. 2. (construed as sing.) The art or practice of such exercises.

gym·no·sperm (jim/nə·spûrm/) *n.* One of a class of plants whose ovules and seeds are not enclosed in a case, as certain evergreens. [< Gk. *gymnos* naked + *sperma* seed] — **gym/no·sper/mous** *adj.*

gyneco- *combining form* Female; pertaining to women. Also, before vowels, **gynec-.** [< Gk. *gynē, gynaikos* woman]

gy·ne·col·o·gy (gī/nə·kol/ə·jē, jī/nə-, jin/ə-) *n.* That branch of medicine dealing with the functions and diseases peculiar to women. — **gy·ne·co·log·i·cal** (gī/nə·kə·loj/i·kəl, jī/nə-, jin/ə-) *adj.* — **gy·ne·col/o·gist** *n.*

gyno- *combining form* 1. Woman; female. 2. *Bot. & Med.* Female reproductive organ; ovary; pistil. Also, before vowels, **gyn-.** [< Gk. *gynē* woman]

gy·noe·ci·um (jī·nē/sē·əm, ji-) *n. pl.* **·ci·a** (-sē·ə) *Bot.* The female parts of a flower collectively; the pistil or pistils taken as a unit. Also **gy·nae/ce·um, gy·nae/ci·um, gy·ne/ci·um.**

-gynous *combining form* 1. Female; of women. 2. *Biol.* Having or pertaining to female organs or pistils: *androgynous.* [< Gk. *gynē* woman]

gyp (jip) *U.S. Informal v.t. & v.i.* **gypped, gyp·ping** To cheat, swindle, or defraud. — *n.* A fraud. [? < GYPSY]

gyp·sum (jip/səm) *n.* A mineral, hydrous calcium sulfate, $CaSO_4 \cdot 2H_2O$, used in plaster of Paris, fertilizer, etc. [< L < Gk. *gypsos* chalk]

gyp·sy (jip/sē) *n. pl.* **·sies** A person who looks like, or leads the life of, a Gypsy. — *adj.* Of, pertaining to, or like a gypsy or the Gypsies. — *v.i.* **·sied, ·sy·ing** To live or wander like a gypsy or the Gypsies. Also spelled *gipsy.*

Gyp·sy (jip/sē) *n. pl.* **·sies** 1. A member of a wandering, dark-haired, dark-skinned Caucasian people believed to have migrated to Europe from India in the 15th century, and known as fortunetellers, musicians, etc. 2. Romany (def. 2). Also spelled *Gipsy.* [Var. of *Egypcyan* Egyptian]

gypsy moth A moth having larvae destructive to foliage.

gy·rate (jī/rāt) *v.i.* **·rat·ed, ·rat·ing** 1. To rotate or revolve, usu. around a fixed point or axis. 2. To turn in a spiral motion. — *adj.* Winding or coiled about; convolute. [< L *gyrare* to gyrate < Gk. *gyros*] — **gy·ra·tor** (jī/rā/tər, jī·rā/-) *n.* — **gy/ra·to/ry** *adj.*

gy·ra·tion (jī·rā/shən) *n.* 1. The act of gyrating; a spiral or whirling motion. 2. A single whorl of a spiral shell.

gyre (jīr) *n.* A spiral or round form, as a ring or vortex; also, whirling motion. [< L < Gk. *gyros* circle] — **gy/ral** *adj.*

gyr·fal·con (jûr/fal/kən, -fôl/-, -fô/-) *n.* See GERFALCON.

gy·ro (jī/rō) *n.* A gyroscope or gyrocompass.

gyro- *combining form* 1. Rotating; gyrating. 2. Spiral. Also, before vowels, **gyr-.** [< Gk. *gyros* circle]

gy·ro·com·pass (jī/rō·kum/pəs, -kom/-) *n.* A compass that employs a motor-driven gyroscope so mounted that its axis of rotation maintains a constant position with reference to the true or geographic north.

gyro pilot *Aeron.* An automatic pilot.

gy·ro·plane (jī/rə·plān/) *n.* An aircraft that obtains its lift from rotating airfoils, as a helicopter.

gy·ro·scope (jī/rə·skōp) *n.* Any of a class of devices consisting essentially of a heavy wheel, so mounted that when set to rotate at high speeds it resists all forces tending to change the angular position of its axis of rotation. [< F] — **gy/ro·scop/ic** (-skop/ik) *adj.*

GYROSCOPE

Showing possible directional movements.

gy·ro·sta·bi·liz·er (jī/rō·stā/bə·lī/zər) *n.* A gyroscopic device designed to reduce the rolling motion of ships.

gy·ro·stat·ics (jī/rō·stat/iks) *n.pl.* (construed as sing.) The branch of physics that investigates the laws governing the rotation of solid bodies. — **gy/ro·stat/ic** *adj.* — **gy/ro·stat/i·cal·ly** *adv.*

H

h, H (āch) *n. pl.* **h's** or **hs, H's** or **Hs, aitch·es** (ā/chiz) **1.** The eighth letter of the English alphabet. **2.** The sound represented by the letter *h*, a voiceless, glottal fricative. In a few English words of French origin, as *heir, honor, hour*, etc., the letter *h* has no phonetic value. **3.** Anything shaped like an H. **4.** *U.S. Slang* Heroin. — *symbol* **1.** *Chem.* Hydrogen. **2.** *Physics* Strength or intensity of magnetic field (symbol H). **3.** *Electr.* Henry (symbol H).

ha (hä) *n. & interj.* An exclamation or sound expressing surprise, discovery, triumph, laughter, etc. Also spelled *hah*.

ha·ba·ne·ra (ä/bä·nā/rä) *n.* **1.** A slow, Cuban dance of African origin. **2.** Music for it. [< Sp., of Havana]

ha·be·as cor·pus (hā/bē·əs kôr/pəs) *Law* A writ commanding a person who detains another to produce the detained person before a court, esp. in order to determine the lawfulness of the detention. [< L, (you) have the body]

hab·er·dash·er (hab/ər·dash/ər) *n. U.S.* A shopkeeper who deals in men's furnishings, as shirts, hats, socks, etc. [Prob. < AF *hapertas*, kind of fabric]

hab·er·dash·er·y (hab/ər·dash/ər·ē) *n. pl.* **·er·ies 1.** The goods sold by haberdashers. **2.** A haberdasher's shop.

ha·bil·i·ment (hə·bil/ə·mənt) *n. Usu. pl.* Clothing; attire. [< OF < L *habilis* fit, apt]

ha·bil·i·tate (hə·bil/ə·tāt) *v.t.* **·tat·ed, ·tat·ing** *U.S.* In the West, to supply (a mine) with money, equipment, etc. [< L *habilis* fit] — **ha·bil/i·ta/tion** *n.*

hab·it (hab/it) *n.* **1.** An act or practice so frequently repeated as to become almost automatic. **2.** A tendency or disposition to act consistently or to repeat. **3.** An addiction: the drug *habit*. **4.** Mental or moral disposition: the scholar's *habit* of mind. **5.** A characteristic appearance or condition of the body. **6.** The clothing associated with a particular profession, etc.: a monk's *habit*. **7.** *Biol.* A characteristic action, aspect, or mode of growth of a plant or animal. — *v.t.* To clothe; dress. [< OF < L *habitus* condition, dress]

hab·it·a·ble (hab/it·ə·bəl) *adj.* Suitable for habitation. [< L *habitare* to inhabit] — **hab/it·a·bil/i·ty, hab/it·a·ble·ness** *n.* — **hab/it·a·bly** *adv.*

hab·i·tant (hab/ə·tənt) *n.* **1.** An inhabitant. **2.** A French farmer in Canada or Louisiana. [< F < L *habitare* to dwell]

hab·i·tat (hab/ə·tat) *n.* **1.** The region or environment where a plant or animal is normally found, as salt water, desert, equatorial forest, etc. **2.** The place where a person or thing usu. resides or is found. [< NL, it dwells]

hab·i·ta·tion (hab/ə·tā/shən) *n.* **1.** A place of abode; residence. **2.** The act of dwelling or inhabiting.

ha·bit·u·al (hə·bich/ōō·əl) *adj.* **1.** Practiced or recurring by habit; customary: *habitual* courtesy; also, occurring constantly. **2.** Given to or addicted to a practice. **3.** Expected from habit or usage: her *habitual* place. [< Med.L < L *habitus*] — **ha·bit/u·al·ly** *adv.* — **ha·bit/u·al·ness** *n.*

hab·it-form·ing (hab/it-fôr/ming) *adj.* Producing or resulting in a habitual practice or addiction.

ha·bit·u·ate (hə·bich/ōō·āt) *v.t.* **·at·ed, ·at·ing** To accustom (oneself, an animal, etc.) to a condition by repetition. [< LL *habituare* to accustom] — **ha·bit/u·a/tion** *n.*

hab·i·tude (hab/ə·tōōd, ·tyōōd) *n.* **1.** Customary or characteristic state of mind or body. **2.** A usual course of action.

ha·bit·u·é (hə·bich/ōō·ā, hə·bich/ōō·ā/; *Fr.* à·bē·tü·ā/) *n.* One who frequents a specific restaurant, club, etc. [< F *habituer* to accustom]

ha·chure (n. ha·shōōr/, hash/ōōr) *n.* One of the short, parallel lines used in drawing and mapmaking. [< F < *hacher*]

ha·ci·en·da (hä/sē·en/də, *Sp.* ä·syen/dä) *n.* In Spanish America: **a** A landed estate; a country house. **b** A farming, mining, or manufacturing establishment in the country. [< Am. Sp. < L *facienda* things to be done]

hack¹ (hak) *v.t.* **1.** To cut or chop crudely or irregularly, as with an ax, cleaver, etc. **2.** In basketball, to strike (an opposing player) on the arm. — *v.i.* **3.** To make cuts or notches with heavy, crude blows. **4.** To emit short, dry coughs. — *n.* **1.** A gash, cut, or nick made as by a sharp instrument. **2.** An ax, hoe, or tool for hacking. **3.** A short, dry cough. [OE *haccian* to cut] — **hack/er** *n.*

hack² (hak) *n.* **1.** A horse for hire, as a saddle horse. **2.** An old, worn-out horse; jade. **3.** A person hired to do routine work, esp. literary work. **4.** *U.S.* A hackney coach. **5.**

U.S. Informal A taxicab. — *v.t.* **1.** To let out for hire, as a horse. **2.** To use or employ as a hack. **3.** To make stale or trite by constant use; hackney. **4.** *U.S. Informal* To drive a taxicab. **5.** To ride on horseback at a jog. — *adj.* **1.** Of or for hack: a *hack* stand. **2.** For hire as a hack: a *hack* writer. **3.** Of a routine, mercenary, or hackneyed nature.

hack³ (hak) *n.* A frame or rack on which to dry bricks, cheese, fish, etc. — *v.t.* To set on hacks to dry.

hack·ber·ry (hak/ber/ē, -bər·ē) *n. pl.* **·ries 1.** An American tree resembling the elm and having small, sweet, edible fruit. **2.** The fruit or wood. [< ON < *neggr* hedge + BERRY]

hack·ie (hak/ē) *n. U.S. Slang* The driver of a taxicab.

hack·le (hak/əl) *n.* **1.** One of the long, narrow feathers on the neck of a rooster, pigeon, etc.; also, such feathers collectively. **2.** In angling: A tuft of these used in a **hack/le fly. 3.** *pl.* The hairs on the neck and back of a dog, that rise in anger, etc. — **to make (someone's) hackles rise** To make angry; infuriate. — *v.t.* **·led, ·ling** To furnish (a fly) with a hackle. [Var. of *hatchel* a comb for flax]

hack·ma·tack (hak/mə·tak) *n. U.S. & Canadian* **1.** The tamarack. **2.** The wood of this tree. [< N. Am. Ind.]

hack·ney (hak/nē) *n. pl.* **·neys 1.** A horse of medium size used for ordinary driving and riding. **2.** A carriage for hire. [< OF *haquenee* horse]

hack·neyed (hak/nēd) *adj.* Made commonplace by frequent use; trite. — **Syn.** See TRITE.

hack·saw (hak/sô/) *n.* A saw with a fine-toothed, narrow blade set in a frame, used for cutting metal. Also **hack saw.** [diagram] **HACKSAW**

had (had) Past tense and past participle of HAVE.

had·dock (had/ək) *n. pl.* **·dock** or **·docks** A food fish of the North Atlantic, allied to but smaller than the cod. [ME]

Ha·des (hā/dēz) **1.** In Greek mythology: **a** The brother of Zeus, god of the underworld, identified with the Greek and Roman *Pluto.* **b** The underground kingdom of the dead. **2.** In the New Testament, the condition or the abode of the dead. [< Gk. *a-* not + *idein* to see]

ha·des (hā/dēz) *n. Often cap. Informal* Hell: a euphemism.

hadj (haj) *n.* The pilgrimage to Mecca required of every Moslem at least once in his life. [< Turkish < Arabic *hājj* pilgrimage. Akin to HEGIRA.]

hadj·i (haj/ē) *n.* A Moslem who has made his hadj: used also as a title. Also **hadj/ee.**

hae (hā, ha) *v.t. Scot.* To have.

haem-, haemo- See HEMO-.

haema- See HEMA-.

haemat-, haemato- See HEMATO-.

-haemia See -EMIA.

haf·ni·um (haf/nē·əm) *n.* A metallic element (symbol Hf) found in zirconium minerals. See ELEMENT. [< NL, from L *Hafnia* Copenhagen]

haft (haft, häft) *n.* A handle of a knife, sword, etc. — *v.t.* To fit with a haft. [OE *hæft* handle]

hag (hag) *n.* **1.** A repulsive, usu. malicious old woman. **2.** A witch; sorceress. [OE *hægtes* witch]

Ha·gar (hā/gər) Abraham's concubine. *Gen.* xvi 1.

hag·fish (hag/fish/) *n. pl.* **·fish** or **·fish·es** A primitive eel-like, marine fish allied to the lamprey, that bores its way into the bodies of living fishes by means of a rasping mouth.

Hag·ga·dah (hə·gä/də, *Hebrew* hä·gô/dô) *n. pl.* **·doth** (-dōth) **1.** The nonlegal elements of Talmudic literature, consisting of fables, proverbs, etc. **2.** The story of the Exodus read at Passover. **3.** A book containing this story. Also **Ha·ga/dah, Hag·ga/da.** [< Hebrew < *higgid* to tell]

Hag·ga·i (hag/ē·ī, hag/ī) Sixth-century B.C. Hebrew prophet. Also, — *n.* A book of the Old Testament written by him. Also, in the Douai Bible, *Aggeus.*

hag·gard (hag/ərd) *adj.* **1.** Having a worn, gaunt, or wild look, as from fatigue, worry, hunger, etc. **2.** Wild or intractable. [< OF *hagard* wild] — **hag/gard·ly** *adv.*

hag·gish (hag/ish) *adj.* Characteristic of a hag; haglike. — **hag/gish·ly** *adv.* — **hag/gish·ness** *n.*

hag·gle (hag/əl) *v.* **·gled, ·gling** *v.i.* **1.** To argue or bargain in a petty, mean way, esp. about price or terms. — *v.t.* **2.** To cut unskillfully; hack; mangle. **3.** To tire or harass, as by wrangling. — *n.* The act of haggling. — **hag/gler** *n.*

hagio- *combining form* Sacred: *hagiography*. Also, before vowels, **hagi-**. [< Gk. *hagios* sacred]

Hag·i·og·ra·pha (hag′ē·og′rə·fə, hä′jē-) *n.pl.* The third of the three ancient divisions of the Old Testament, containing all those books not found in the Pentateuch or the Prophets. The Hagiographa consist of the following books (names in the Douai Bible, when different, are given in parentheses): I Chronicles (I Parlipomenon), II Chronicles (II Paralipomenon), Ruth, Ezra (I Esdras), Nehemiah (II Esdras), Esther, Job, Psalms, Proverbs, Ecclesiastes, Song of Solomon (Canticle of Canticles), Lamentations, Daniel. [< Gk. < *hagios* sacred + *graphein* to write]

hag·i·og·ra·pher (hag′ē·og′rə·fər, hä′jē-) *n.* 1. A writer of or authority on the lives of saints. 2. Any writer on sacred subjects; esp., one of the authors of the Hagiographa.

hag·i·og·ra·phy (hag′ē·og′rə·fē, hä′jē-) *n. pl.* **·phies** 1. The study of the lives of saints. 2. A book of such studies. — **hag·i·o·graph·ic** (hag′ē·ə·graf′ik, hä′jē-) or **·i·cal** *adj.*

hag·i·ol·o·gy (hag′ē·ol′ə·jē, hä′jē-) *n. pl.* **·gies** 1. That part of literature dealing with the lives of the saints. 2. A book on saints' lives. 3. A list of saints. — **hag·i·o·log·ic** (hag′ē·ə·loj′ik, hä′jē-) or **·i·cal** *adj.* — **hag·i·ol·o·gist** *n.*

hah (hä) See HA.

ha-ha (hä′hä′, hä·hä′) *n. & interj.* A sound imitating laughter. — *v.i.* To laugh. Also spelled *haw-haw*. [Imit.]

hai·ku (hī′kōō) *n. pl.* **·ku** A Japanese verse form in three short lines. Also called *hokku.* [< Japanese]

hail¹ (hāl) *n.* 1. Small lumps of ice that fall from the sky during a storm; hailstones. 2. A rapid or heavy showering: a *hail* of blows. — *v.i.* 1. To pour down hail. 2. To fall like hail. — *v.t.* 3. To hurl or pour like hail. [OE *hægel*]

hail² (hāl) *v.t.* 1. To call loudly to in greeting. 2. To call to so as to attract attention. 3. To name as; designate. — *v.i.* 4. To call out to, esp. between ships. — **to hail from** To come from, as a birthplace, residence, etc. — *n.* 1. The act of hailing. 2. A shout, as of greeting or for attention. 3. The distance a shout can be heard; earshot: within *hail.* [ME < ON < *heill* whole, hale] — **hail′er** *n.*

hail fellow A genial companion. Also **hail fellow well met.**

hair (hâr) *n.* 1. One of the fine, threadlike structures that grow from the skin of most mammals. ◆ Collateral adjective: *capillary.* 2. Such structures collectively, esp. those that grow on the human head and on the skin of most mammals. 3. *Bot.* A hairlike outgrowth of the epidermis in plants. 4. Material woven of hair. 5. Any exceedingly minute measure, etc. — **not to turn a hair** To show or reveal no sign of embarrassment, etc. — **to a hair** With the utmost exactness; in minute detail. — **to get in one's hair** *Slang* To vex or annoy one. — **to let one's hair down** *U.S. Slang* To discard one's reserve. — **to make one's hair stand on end** To horrify one. — **to split hairs** To make trivial distinctions. — *adj.* 1. Like, or made of, hair. 2. For the hair: *hair* oil. [OE *hær*] — **hair′less** *adj.*

hair·ball (hâr′bôl′) *n.* A rounded mass of hair often found in stomachs of animals that groom themselves by licking.

hair·breadth (hâr′bredth′, -bretth′) *n.* An extremely small space or margin. — *adj.* Very narrow or close: *hairbreadth* escape. Also **hair′s′-breadth** (hârz′-), **hairs′breadth′.**

hair·brush (hâr′brush′) *n.* A brush for grooming the hair.

hair·cloth (hâr′klôth′, -kloth′) *n.* A stiff fabric of horsehair.

hair·cut (hâr′kut′) *n.* The act of cutting the hair or the style in which it is cut.

hair·do (hâr′dōō′) *n. pl.* **·dos** 1. A style of dressing or arranging a woman's hair. 2. The hair so arranged.

hair·dress·er (hâr′dres′ər) *n.* One who cuts or arranges the hair, esp. women's hair.

hair·dres·sing (hâr′dres′ing) *n.* 1. The act of arranging or dressing the hair. 2. A preparation used in dressing the hair.

haired (hârd) *adj.* Having or characterized by a (specified kind of) hair: used in combination: *gray-haired.*

hair·line (hâr′līn′) *n.* 1. The edge of the growth of hair on the head. 2. A very thin line. 3. *Printing* A very thin line on a type face; also, a style of type.

hair·piece (hâr′pēs′) *n.* A wig, toupee, or switch.

hair·pin (hâr′pin′) *n.* A thin, U-shaped piece of metal, bone, etc., used by women to hold the hair or a headdress in place. — *adj.* Bending sharply in a U: a *hairpin* curve.

hair·rais·er (hâr′rā′zər) *n. Informal* Something that causes excitement or fear. — **hair′-rais′ing** *adj.*

hair shirt A girdle or shirt made of haircloth, worn next to the skin by religious ascetics as a penance or mortification.

hair space *Printing* The thinnest of the metal spaces for separating letters or words.

hair·split·ting (hâr′split′ing) *n.* Insistence upon minute or trivial distinctions. — *adj.* Characterized by petty or overly fine distinctions. — **hair′split′ter** *n.*

hair·spring (hâr′spring′) *n.* The fine spring that regulates the movement of the balance wheel in a watch or clock.

hair trigger A trigger so delicately adjusted that it discharges the firearm at the slightest pressure.

hair-trig·ger (hâr′trig′ər) *adj. Informal* Stimulated or set in operation by the slightest provocation.

hair·y (hâr′ē) *adj.* **hair·i·er, hair·i·est** 1. Covered with or having much hair. 2. Made of hair. — **hair′i·ness** *n.*

Hai·ti·an (hā′tē·ən, -shən) *adj.* Of or pertaining to Haiti, its people, or their culture. — *n.* 1. A native or inhabitant of Haiti. 2. A French patois spoken by the Haitians: also **Haitian Creole.** Also spelled *Haylian.*

hake (hāk) *n. pl.* **hake** or **hakes** 1. A marine food fish related to the cod. 2. The codling¹ (def. 2). [OE *haca* hook]

ha·kim (hä′kēm) *n.* In Moslem countries: 1. A judge or governor. 2. A physician. [< Arabic *hakīm* wise]

hal- Var. of HALO-.

hal·berd (hal′bərd; *earlier* hôl′-, hô′-) *n.* A weapon used in the 15th and 16th centuries, an ax and spear combined. [< OF < MHG *helm* handle + *barte* broadax]

hal·cy·on (hal′sē·ən) *n.* A legendary bird supposed to calm the wind and the sea at the winter solstice so as to be able to breed on the water. — *adj.* 1. Calm; peaceful. 2. Of the halcyon. [< L < Gk. *alkyōn* kingfisher]

halcyon days 1. The seven days before and the seven days after the winter solstice. 2. Any period of peace and quiet.

hale¹ (hāl) *v.t.* **haled, hal·ing** To compel to go: to *hale* into court. [Var. of HAUL] — **hal′er** *n.*

hale² (hāl) *adj.* Having sound and vigorous health; robust. [OE *hāl*] — **hale′ness** *n.*

half (haf, häf) *n. pl.* **halves** (havz, hävz) 1. Either of two equal or approximately equal parts or quantities into which a thing may be divided. 2. In sports: **a** In basketball, football, etc., either of two periods into which a game is divided between which play is suspended. **b** *Informal* In football, a halfback. — **better half** *Informal* One's wife or husband. — *adj.* 1. Being either of two equal parts of a thing, amount, value, etc. 2. Not complete; partial; imperfect. — *adv.* 1. To the extent of half or approximately half. 2. To a considerable extent; very nearly. 3. *Informal* To any extent; at all: used with *not*: not *half* bad. [OE *healf*]

half-and-half (haf′ənd·haf′, häf′ənd·häf′) *n.* 1. A mixture of half one thing and half another. 2. A mixture of two malt liquors, esp. of porter and ale. — *adj.* Half of one thing and half of another. — *adv.* In two equal parts.

half·back (haf′bak′, häf′-) *n.* 1. In football, either of two players who with the quarterback and fullback make up the backfield; also, his position. 2. In other sports, as field hockey and soccer, a player behind the forward line.

half-baked (haf′bākt′, häf′-) *adj.* 1. Incompletely baked; doughy. 2. *Informal* Stupid; half-witted. 3. *Informal* Imperfectly planned or conceived: a *half-baked* venture.

half blood 1. The relationship between persons with one parent in common; also, a person in such a relationship. 2. A half-breed. 3. A half-blooded animal. Also **half-blood** (haf′blud′, häf′-). — **half′-blood′ed** *adj.*

half-breed (haf′brēd′, häf′-) *n.* One having parents of different races; esp., the offspring of a white person and an American Indian. — *adj.* Hybrid: also **half-bred** (-bred′).

half brother A brother related through only one parent.

half-caste (haf′kast′, häf′käst′) *n.* 1. A person having one Asian and one European parent; Eurasian. 2. A half-breed. — *adj.* Of or pertaining to mixed racial stock.

half cock In a firearm, the position of the hammer when raised halfway and so locked. — **to go off at half cock** 1. To discharge too soon. 2. *Informal* To act or speak too hastily. Also **to go off half-cocked** (haf′kokt′, häf′-).

half crown An English silver coin worth 2½ shillings.

half dollar A U.S. silver coin worth fifty cents.

half gainer A dive in which one springs forward off the board, twists about, and plunges into the water head first.

half-heart·ed (haf′här′tid, häf′-) *adj.* Possessing or showing little interest, enthusiasm, etc. — **half′heart′ed·ly** *adv.* — **half′heart′ed·ness** *n.*

half hitch A knot made by passing the end of a rope once around the rope, then through the loop, and then drawing the end tight. For illus. see HITCH.

half-hour (haf′our′, häf′-) *n.* 1. Thirty minutes. 2. Thirty minutes past the beginning of an hour. — *adj.* 1. Lasting for half an hour. 2. Occurring at the half-hour. — **half′-hour′ly** *adj. & adv.*

half life *Physics* The period of time during which half the atoms of a radioactive element or isotope will disintegrate.

half-mast (haf′mast′, häf′mäst′) *n.* The position of a flag flown about halfway up the staff, used in public mourning. — *v.t.* To put (a flag, etc.) at half-mast. Also *half-staff.*

half-moon (haf′mōōn′, häf′-) *n.* 1. The moon when only half its disk is brightly illuminated. 2. Something similar in shape to a half-moon. — *adj.* Shaped like a half-moon.

half nel·son (nel′sən) A wrestling hold in which one arm

G
H

is passed under the opponent's armpit, usu. from behind, and the hand pressed against the back of his neck.

half note *Music* A note having one half the time value of a whole note. Also, *esp. Brit.*, **minim.**

half·pen·ny (hā′pən·ē, hāp′nē) *n. pl.* **half·pence** (hā′pəns) or **half·pen·nies** (hā′pən·ēz, hāp′nēz) **1.** The sum of one half of a penny. **2.** A British bronze coin equivalent to such a sum. — *adj.* **1.** Costing a halfpenny. **2.** Of little value.

half pint 1. A measure of capacity equal to one half of a pint. **2.** *U.S. Slang* A person of short stature.

half sister A sister related through only one parent.

half-sole (haf′sōl′, häf′-) *v.t.* **soled,** **sol·ing** To repair (a shoe, boot, etc.) by attaching a half sole.

half sole The part of the sole of a boot or shoe extending from the shank or arch to the toe.

half step 1. *Music* A semitone. **2.** *Mil.* A step of fifteen inches at quick time; in double time, one of eighteen inches.

half·tone (haf′tōn′, häf′-) *n.* **1.** In photoengraving: **a** A picture whose lights and shadows are composed of minute dots obtained by photographing the original through a finely lined screen. **b** The process by which such pictures are made. **2.** In art, photography, etc., any tone or shading halfway between a highlight and a deep shadow.

half tone *Music* A semitone (which see).

half-track (haf′trak′, häf′-) *n.* A vehicle propelled by caterpillar treads in the rear and wheels in front.

half·way (haf′wā′, häf′-) *adv.* **1.** At or to half the distance. **2.** Incompletely; partially. — *adj.* **1.** Midway between two points. **2.** Partial; inadequate.

half-wit (haf′wit′, häf′-) *n.* A feeble-minded person.

half-wit·ted (haf′wit′id, häf′-) *adj.* **1.** Feeble-minded. **2.** Frivolous. — **half′-wit′ted·ly** *adv.* — **half′-wit′ted·ness** *n.*

hal·i·but (hal′ə·bət, hol′-) *n. pl.* **·but** or **·buts** Either of two large flatfishes of northern seas, much esteemed as food. [ME *halybutte,* OE *halig* holy + BUT²]

hal·ide (hal′īd, -id; hā′līd, -lid) *n. Chem.* Any compound of a halogen with an element or radical. Also **hal·id** (hal′id).

hal·ite (hal′īt, hā′līt) *n.* A massive or granular, white or variously colored sodium chloride: also called *rock salt.*

hal·i·to·sis (hal′ə·tō′sis) *n.* Offensive or foul-smelling breath. [< NL < L *halitus* breath + -OSIS]

hall (hôl) *n.* **1.** A passage or corridor in a building. **2.** A vestibule; lobby. **3.** A large building or room used for public business or entertainment. **4.** In a university or college, a large building used for various purposes, as for dormitories, classrooms, etc. **5.** In British universities: **a** A college dining room; also, the dinner. **b** A building where university students reside. **6.** The main house on an estate. **7.** In medieval times, the large main room of a castle. [OE *heall*]

hal·le·lu·jah (hal′ə·lōō′yə) *interj.* Praise ye the Lord! — *n.* A musical composition of praise. Also **hal·le·lu′iah.** [< Hebrew *hallelū* praise + *yāh* Jehovah]

hal·liard (hal′yərd) See HALYARD.

hall·mark (hôl′märk′) *n.* **1.** An official mark stamped on gold and silver articles in England to guarantee their purity. **2.** Any proof of excellence. — *v.t.* To stamp with a hallmark. [< Goldsmiths' *Hall,* London, where the assaying and stamping were formerly exclusively done + MARK]

hal·loo (hə·lōō′) *interj.* A shout to attract attention, etc. — *n.* A cry of "halloo." — *v.i.* **1.** To shout "halloo"; cry out. — *v.t.* **2.** To incite with shouts. **3.** To shout to; hail. **4.** To shout (something). Also **hal·lo** (hə·lō′), **hal·loa** (hə·lō′), **hal·low** (hə·lō). [< OF *halloer* to pursue noisily]

hal·low (hal′ō) *v.t.* **1.** To make holy; consecrate. **2.** To look upon as holy; reverence. [OE *hālig* holy]

hal·lowed (hal′ōd, *in liturgical use* hal′ō·id) *adj.* **1.** Made holy. **2.** Honored as holy. — **hal′lowed·ness** *n.*

Hal·low·een (hal′ō·ēn′, hol′-) *n.* The evening of Oct. 31, vigil of All Saints' Day, celebrated by children with masquerading. Also **Hal′low·e′en′.** [< (ALL)HALLOW(S)E(V)EN]

hal·lu·ci·nate (hə·lōō′sə·nāt) *v.t.* **nat·ed,** **nat·ing** To affect with hallucinations. [< L *hallucinari* to wander mentally]

hal·lu·ci·na·tion (hə·lōō′sə·nā′shən) *n.* **1.** *Psychol.* Any of numerous auditory, visual, or tactile perceptions that have no external cause or stimulus. **2.** A mistaken notion.

hal·lu·ci·na·to·ry (hə·lōō′sə·nə·tôr′ē, -tō′rē) *adj.* Of, characterized by, or causing hallucination.

hal·lu·ci·no·gen (hə·lōō′sin·ə·jən) *n.* Any drug or chemical capable of inducing hallucinations.

hal·lu·ci·no·gen·ic (hə·lōō′sə·nə·jen′ik) *adj.* **1.** Causing or having to do with hallucinations or with a distortion of perception. **2.** Of or pertaining to hallucinogens.

hall·way (hôl′wā′) *n. U.S.* **1.** A hall or corridor. **2.** A passage or room leading into the main part of a building.

ha·lo (hā′lō) *n. pl.* **·los** or **·loes 1.** In art, a disk or ring of light surrounding the head of a deity or holy person; nimbus. **2.** A splendor investing a person or thing held in reverence, etc. **3.** *Meteorol.* A luminous circle around the sun or moon. — *v.t.* **1.** To enclose with a halo. — *v.t.* **2.** To form a halo. [< L < Gk. *halōs* circular threshing floor]

halo- *combining form* **1.** Of or relating to salt. **2.** Of the

sea. **3.** Related to or containing a halogen. Also, before vowels, **hal-.** [< Gk. *hals, halos* salt, the sea]

hal·o·gen (hal′ə·jən) *n. Chem.* Any of the group of nonmetallic elements, fluorine, chlorine, bromine, iodine, and astatine. [< Gk. *hals* sea, salt + -GEN]

hal·oid (hal′oid, hā′loid) *adj.* Of, like, or derived from a halogen. — *n.* A salt formed from a halogen and a metal.

halt¹ (hôlt) *n.* A complete but temporary stop in any activity or movement. — *v.t. & v.i.* To bring or come to a halt. [< F < G *halten* to stop] — **halt′er** *n.*

halt² (hôlt) *v.i.* **1.** To be imperfect or defective in some way. **2.** To be in doubt; waver. — **the halt** Lame or crippled persons. [OE *healt* lame] — **halt′er** *n.*

hal·ter¹ (hôl′tər) *n.* **1.** A strap or rope to lead or secure a horse, cow, etc. **2.** A woman's upper garment designed to leave the arms and back bare, and held up by a band around the neck. **3.** A rope with a noose for hanging a person. **4.** Death by hanging. — *v.t.* **1.** To secure with a halter. **2.** To hang (someone). [OE *hælftre*]

hal·ter² (hal′tər) *n. pl.* **hal·te·res** (hal·tir′ēz) *Entomol.* One of a pair of appendages on each side of a winged insect, used to give balance in flight. [< NL < Gk. *haltēres* weights used in jumping]

ha·lutz (khä·lōōts′) *n. pl.* **ha·lu·tzim** (khä′lōō·tsēm′) A pioneer Jewish farmer in Palestine or Israel. [< Hebrew]

halve (hav, häv) *v.t.* **halved,** **halv·ing 1.** To divide into two equal parts; share equally. **2.** To lessen by half; take away half of. **3.** In golf, to play (a match or hole) in the same number of strokes as one's opponent. [< HALF]

halves (havz, hävz) Plural of HALF. — **by halves 1.** Imperfectly. **2.** Half-heartedly.

hal·yard (hal′yərd) *n. Naut.* A rope for hoisting or lowering a sail, a yard, or a flag: also spelled *halliard, haulyard.*

ham (ham) *n.* **1.** The thigh of an animal, as of the hog. **2.** The meat of a hog's thigh, used for food. **3.** *pl.* The back of the thigh together with the buttocks. **4.** That part of the leg behind the knee joint. **5.** *Slang* An actor who overacts or exaggerates. **6.** *Informal* An amateur radio operator. — *v.t. & v.i.* **hammed,** **ham·ming** *Slang* To act in an exaggerated manner. [OE *hamm*] — **ham′my** *adj.*

Ha·man (hā′mən) In the Bible, a Persian minister who was hanged when his plot to destroy the Jews was disclosed by Esther to King Ahasuerus (*Esth.* iii-vii).

ham·burg (ham′bûrg) *n.* Hamburger.

ham·burg·er (ham′bûr′gər) *n.* **1.** Ground or chopped beef. Also **hamburger steak. 2.** A sandwich consisting of such meat placed between the halves of a round roll. [after *Hamburg,* Germany]

Ham·ite (ham′īt) *n.* **1.** A descendant of Ham, one of the sons of Noah. **2.** A member of an ethnic group that includes the ancient Egyptians, inhabiting NE Africa.

Ha·mit·ic (ha·mit′ik) *adj.* **1.** Of or pertaining to Ham or the Hamites. **2.** Designating a group of languages spoken by the Hamites. — *n.* A North African subfamily of the Hamito-Semitic family of languages, including ancient Egyptian, the modern Berber dialects, etc.

ham·let (ham′lit) *n.* **1.** A little village. **2.** *Brit.* A village without a church. [< OF < LL *hamellum* village]

Ham·let (ham′lit) In Shakespeare's play of this name, the hero, a Danish prince.

ham·mer (ham′ər) *n.* **1.** A tool usu. consisting of a handle with a metal head set crosswise at one end, used for driving nails, etc. **2.** Any object or machine that serves the same function as or resembles such a tool. **3.** A mechanical part that operates by striking; as: **a** The part of a gunlock that strikes the primer or firing pin. **b** One of the levers that strike the strings of a piano. **c** A piece that strikes a bell or gong. **4.** *Anat.* The malleus, a small bone of the middle ear. For illus. see EAR. **5.** An auctioneer's mallet. **6.** A metal ball attached to a flexible handle, thrown for distance in athletic contests. — **to go** (or **come**) **under the hammer** To be for sale at an auction. — *v.t.* **1.** To strike, beat, or drive with or as with a hammer. **2.** To produce or shape with or as with hammer blows. **3.** To join by hammering, as with nails. **4.** To force, impress, etc., by emphatic repetition. — *v.i.* **5.** To strike blows with or as with a hammer. **6.** To have the sound or feeling of rapid pounding: My heart *hammers.* **7.** To work at persistently: to *hammer* away at a task. [OE *hamer*] — **ham′mer·er** *n.*

ham·mer·head (ham′ər·hed′) *n.* A voracious shark of warm seas, having a transversely elongated head with the eyes at each end.

hammer lock A wrestling hold in which an opponent's arm is twisted behind his back and upward.

ham·mock (ham′ək) *n.* A hanging bed or couch of sturdy cloth or netting, suspended from a support at each end. [< Sp. *hamaca* < native West Indian name]

ham·per¹ (ham′pər) *v.t.* To interfere with the movements of; impede. [ME *hampren*]

ham·per² (ham′pər) *n.* A large, usu. covered basket, often used to store soiled laundry. [< OF *hanapier* a cup case]

ham·ster (ham′stər) *n.* Any of various burrowing rodents, used as a laboratory animal. [< G < OHG *hamastro*]

ham·string (ham′string′) *n.* **1.** One of the tendons at the back of the human knee. **2.** The large sinew at the back of the hock of a quadruped. — *v.t.* **·strung, ·string·ing 1.** To cripple by cutting the hamstring of. **2.** To frustrate.

hand (hand) *n.* **1.** In man and other primates, the end of the forearm beyond the wrist, comprising the palm, fingers, and thumb. ◆ Collateral adjective: *manual.* **2.** In other organisms, a part that serves a similar function. **3.** An action performed by the hand or as by the hand: to die by one's own *hand.* **4.** The use of the hand or hands: to launder by *hand.* **5.** A characteristic mark, or kind of work: the *hand* of a master. **6.** A part or role: We all had a *hand* in it **7.** Assistance: to give a *hand.* **8.** *Usu. pl.* Supervisory care: in God's *hands.* **9.** A pledge or promise, often of marriage. **10.** A position to the side: on the right *hand.* **11.** One of two or more sides, aspects, or viewpoints: usu. with *on:* on the one *hand.* **12.** A source of information, etc.: at second *hand.* **13.** A person, considered as producing something. **14.** A person, considered with reference to his skill. **15.** A manual laborer: a stage *hand.* **16.** Style of handwriting. **17.** A person's signature. **18.** Show of approval by clapping. **19.** Something that resembles a hand in function, as the pointer of a clock. **20.** A unit of measurement four inches long, used to state the height of horses. **21.** In card games: **a** The cards held by a player in one round of a game. **b** The player. **c** The complete playing of all the cards given out at one deal. **— at hand 1.** Near by; readily available. **2.** About to occur. **— at the hand** (or **hands**) **of** By the action of. **— clean hands** Freedom from guilt. **— from hand to hand** Into the possession of one person after another. **— from hand to mouth** Using or spending immediately all of one's income, provisions, etc. **— hand and foot 1.** So as to satisfy all needs or wishes. **2.** So as to be unable to move the hands and feet. **— hand in** (or **and**) **glove** In close alliance or connection. **— hand in hand** Each holding the hand of the other; in close association. **— hands down** With ease; effortlessly. **— Hands off!** A command not to touch or interfere. **— Hands up!** A command to raise the hands, intended to forestall resistance. **— in hand 1.** In one's immediate grasp or possession. **2.** Under control. **3.** In process of execution. **— off one's hands** Out of one's care or responsibility. **— on hand 1.** In one's possession; available for use. **2.** *U.S.* Present. **— on one's hands** In one's care or responsibility. **— out of hand 1.** Unruly; uncontrollable. **2.** Immediately. **3.** Finished and done with. **— to hand 1.** Within reach; readily accessible. **2.** In one's possession. **— to have one's hands full** To be engaged in a great or excessive amount of work. **— to keep one's hand in** To continue an activity or interest so as not to lose skill or knowledge. **— to lay hands on 1.** To do physical harm to. **2.** To bless, consecrate, ordain, etc. **— to show one's hand** To disclose one's involvement or intentions. **— to turn** (or **put**) **one's hand to** To engage in; undertake. **— to throw up one's hands** To give up in despair. **— to wash one's hands of** To refuse further responsibility for. **— upper hand** The controlling advantage. **— with a heavy hand 1.** In a clumsy manner or style. **2.** In an overbearing manner. **— with a high hand** In an arrogant, tyrannical manner. — *v.t.* To give, offer, assist, or transmit with the hand or hands. **— to hand down 1.** To transmit to one's heirs. **2.** To deliver or announce the decision or verdict of a court. **— to hand in** To give to a person or persons in authority; submit. **— to hand it to** *Slang* To give deserved praise or recognition to. **— to hand on** To give to the next in succession. **— to hand out** To distribute. **— to hand over** To give up possession of. *adj.* Of or pertaining to the hand or hands; as: **a** Suitable for carrying in the hand. **b** Operated by hand. **c** Executed by hand: *hand* embroidery. [OE *hand*]

hand·bag (hand′bag′) *n.* **1.** A woman's purse or other bag for carrying small articles. **2.** A small suitcase.

hand·ball (hand′bôl′) *n.* A game in which the players hit a ball with their hand against the wall of a court.

hand·bar·row (hand′bar′ō) *n.* A flat framework for carrying loads, having handles at either end for the bearers.

hand·bill (hand′bil′) *n.* A printed advertisement or notice.

hand·book (hand′bŏŏk′) *n.* **1.** A small guidebook or book of instructions. **2.** *U.S.* A place away from a racetrack where bets are made; also, the record of such bets.

hand·breadth (hand′bredth′, -bretth′) *n.* A unit of measurement, usually 2½ to 4 inches: also *hand's breadth.*

hand·cart (hand′kärt′) *n.* A cart pushed or pulled by hand.

hand·clasp (hand′klasp′, -kläsp′) *n.* The act of clasping a person's hand, as in greeting, an introduction, etc.

hand·cuff (hand′kuf′) *n. Usu. pl.* One of a pair of metal rings joined by a chain, designed to lock around the wrist or wrists; a manacle. — *v.t.* To fetter with handcuffs.

hand·ed (han′did) *adj.* **1.** Characterized by or designed for the use of a (specified). hand: a *left-handed* batter. **2.** Having or characterized by a (specified kind of) hand or (a specified number of) hands: *four-handed; empty-handed.*

hand·ful (hand′fŏŏl) *n. pl.* **·fuls 1.** As much or as many as a hand can hold at once. **2.** A small number or quantity. **3.** *Informal* Something or someone difficult to control.

hand·gun (hand′gun′) *n.* A firearm held and fired in one hand, as a pistol.

hand·i·cap (han′dē·kap) *n.* **1.** A race or contest in which disadvantages are imposed on superior contestants or advantages given to those of inferior ability, so that each may have an equal chance of winning. **2.** One of the conditions stipulated; esp., a disadvantage. **3.** Any disadvantage. — *v.t.* **·capped, ·cap·ping 1.** To serve as a hindrance or disadvantage to. **2.** To assign handicaps in a race. [? < *hand in cap*, a lottery game] **— hand′i·cap·per** *n.*

hand·i·craft (han′dē·kraft′, -kräft′) *n.* **1.** Skill and expertness in working with the hands. **2.** An occupation requiring such skill. Also *U.S.* **hand′craft′.** [OE *handcræft*]

hand·i·ly (han′də·lē) *adv.* **1.** In a handy manner; dexterously; easily. **2.** Conveniently.

hand·i·ness (han′dē·nis) *n.* **1.** Manual skill; expertness. **2.** Convenience. — *Syn.* See DEXTERITY.

hand·i·work (han′dē·wûrk′) *n.* **1.** Work done by the hands; any article or articles made by hand. **2.** The result or product of working or action. [OE *handgeweorc*]

hand·ker·chief (hang′kər·chif) *n.* A piece of cloth, usu. square, used for wiping the nose or face.

han·dle (han′dəl) *v.* **·dled, dling** *v.t.* **1.** To touch, hold, or move with the hand or hands. **2.** To use the hands upon; manipulate: to *handle* clay. **3.** To have control over. **4.** To dispose of; deal with. **5.** To treat of or discuss. **6.** To act or behave toward. **7.** To trade or deal in as a commodity. — *v.i.* **8.** To respond to manipulation or control. — *n.* **1.** That part of an object designed to be grasped in the hand. **2.** Something that resembles or serves as a handle. **3.** That which serves as an opportunity in achieving a desired end. **4.** *Informal* A title added to a person's name. **— to fly off the handle** To become angry. [OE *hand* hand]

han·dle·bar (han′dəl·bär′) *n. Usu. pl.* **1.** The curved steering bar of a bicycle, etc. **2.** *U.S. Informal* A luxuriant mustache resembling handlebars: also **handlebar mustache.**

han·dler (hand′lər) *n.* **1.** One who handles. **2.** In sports, one who trains or manages animals, boxers, etc.

hand·made (hand′mād′) *adj.* Made by hand.

hand·me-down (hand′mē-doun′) *n. Informal* A worn or outgrown garment passed on to another person.

hand organ A large music box played by turning a hand crank; barrel organ.

hand·out (hand′out′) *n.* **1.** Any free ration of food, money, apparel, etc. **2.** A prepared, distributed statement.

hand·pick (hand′pik′) *v.t.* **1.** To gather by hand. **2.** To choose with care. **3.** To select for a particular purpose or job.

hand·rail (hand′rāl′) *n.* A railing of a height for grasping in the hand, used at a staircase, balcony, etc.

hand·saw (hand′sô′) *n.* A saw used with one hand.

hand's breadth A handbreadth.

hand·sel (hand′səl, han′-) *n.* A gift given at the start of a new year, enterprise, or situation in life. — *v.t.* **hand·seled** or **·selled, hand·sel·ing** or **·sel·ling** To give a handsel to. Also spelled *hansel.* [OE *hand* hand + *selen* gift]

hand·set (hand′set′) *n.* A telephone receiver and transmitter combined in a unit that may be held in one hand.

hand·shake (hand′shāk′) *n.* The act of clasping and shaking a person's hand, as in greeting, agreement, parting, etc.

hand·some (han′səm) *adj.* **1.** Pleasing or well-proportioned in appearance, form, feature, etc. **2.** Considerable; ample. **3.** Generous; gracious. [< HAND + -SOME "easy to handle"] **— hand′some·ly** *adv.* **— hand′some·ness** *n.*

hand·spike (hand′spīk′) *n.* A bar used as a lever for moving heavy objects.

hand·spring (hand′spring′) *n.* An acrobatic turn in which the body is supported by one or both hands while the feet are quickly passed in an arc over the head.

hand-to-hand (hand′tə·hand′) *adj.* At close quarters.

hand-to-mouth (hand′tə·mouth′) *adj.* Consuming immediately what is obtained; improvident or impoverished.

hand·work (hand′wûrk′) *n.* Work done by hand.

hand·writ·ing (hand′rī′ting) *n.* **1.** Writing done by hand, as distinct from printing, typing, etc.; calligraphy. **2.** A characteristic style or form of writing. **— to see the handwriting on the wall** To sense or be aware beforehand of impending misfortune, etc.

hand·y (han′dē) *adj.* **hand·i·er, hand·i·est 1.** Ready at hand; available; nearby. **2.** Skillful. **3.** Useful.

hand·y·man (han′dē·man′) *n. pl.* **·men** (-men′) A man employed to perform odd jobs. Also **handy man.**

hang (hang) *v.* **hung** or (*esp. for defs 3, 12*) **hanged, hang-ing** *v.t.* **1.** To fasten, attach, or support from above only. **2.** To attach by means of a hinge, etc. **3.** To put to death on a gallows, cross, etc. **4.** To cause to bend downward; to *hang* one's head. **5.** To decorate or cover with things suspended; also, to fasten (wallpaper) to a wall. **6.** To suspend (pictures, etc.) in a gallery for display. **7.** *U.S.* To cause (a jury, etc.) to be unable to reach a decision. **8.** To damn: used as a mild oath. —*v.i.* **9.** To be suspended from above; dangle. **10.** To be attached so as to swing easily. **11.** To fall, drape, or fit. **12.** To be put to death or to die by hanging. **13.** To bend or project downward; droop. **14.** To keep one's hold; cling: with *on* or *onto*. **15.** To hover; float in the air. **16.** To be imminent; threaten: with *over*. **17.** To depend; be contingent: with *on* or *upon*. **18.** To be in a state of uncertainty or indecision. **19.** To pay close attention: He *hung* on her words. **— to be hung up** *U.S. Slang* To be halted or impeded, usu. temporarily. **— to hang around** (or **about**) *Informal* To loiter or linger about. **— to hang back** To be reluctant or unwilling. **— to hang in the balance** To be undecided or doubtful. **— to hang on** To be tenacious; persist. **— to hang one on** *U.S. Slang* **1.** To get very drunk. **2.** To strike (someone) with the fist. **— to hang out 1.** To lean out, as through a window. **2.** *Slang* To spend one's time. **— to hang together 1.** To remain in close association. **2.** To be coherent or consistent. **— to hang up 1.** *Chiefly U.S.* To end a telephone conversation. **2.** To delay or suspend the progress of. —*n.* **1.** The way in which a thing hangs. **2.** *Informal* A bit; a rap: I don't give a *hang*. **— to get the hang of** *U.S. Informal* **1.** To acquire the knack of. **2.** To understand the basic idea of. [Fusion of ME *hangen* and ME *henge* to cause to hang]

han-gar (hang′ər) *n.* A shelter, esp. one for aircraft. [< F]

hang-dog (hang′dôg′, -dog′) *adj.* Sneaky, furtive, or degraded in manner or appearance. —*n.* A low sneak.

hang-er (hang′ər) *n.* **1.** A device on or from which something may be hung; esp., a hooked frame of shoulder width for garments. **2.** One who hangs something.

hang-er-on (hang′ər·on′, -ôn′) *n.* *pl.* **hang-ers-on** (hang′-ərz-) A clinging or self-seeking follower; parasite.

hang-fire (hang′fīr′) *n.* A delay in the explosion of a propelling charge, igniter, or the like.

hang-ing (hang′ing) *adj.* **1.** Suspended from something. **2.** Leaning or inclining downward. **3.** Lying on a steep slope: a *hanging* meadow. **4.** Worthy of or involving capital punishment. **5.** Undecided: The matter was left *hanging*. —*n.* **1.** The act of suspending, or the state of being suspended. **2.** Execution by being hanged from the neck. **3.** *Usu. pl.* Something hung on a wall, window, etc.

hang-man (hang′mən) *n.* *pl.* **-men** (-mən) A public executioner who hangs condemned persons.

hang-nail (hang′nāl′) *n.* Skin partially torn loose at the side or root of a fingernail.

hang-out (hang′out′) *n.* *Slang* A habitual loitering or dwelling place of some person or group: a thieves' *hangout*.

hang-o-ver (hang′ō′vər) *n.* *U.S. Informal* **1.** The headache following overindulgence in alcoholic liquor. **2.** Something or someone remaining from a past era or regime.

hang-up (hang′up′) *n.* *Slang* **1.** A psychological difficulty, esp. an obsession. **2.** Any block or obstacle to a process.

hank (hangk) *n.* **1.** A skein of yarn or thread. **2.** A measure of yarn or thread. **3.** A loop or curl, as of hair. [ME]

han-ker (hang′kər) *v.i.* To yearn; have desire: with *after, for,* or an infinitive. [Cf. Flemish *hankeren* to long for.]

hank-er-ing (hang′kər·ing) *n.* A yearning; craving.

han-ky-pan-ky (hang′kē-pang′kē) *n.* *Slang* **1.** Deceitful or mischievous behavior. **2.** Foolish talk; blather. [? Formed on analogy with HOCUS-POCUS]

Hanse (hans) *n.* The Hanseatic League.

Han-se-at-ic League (han′sē·at′ik) A medieval league of free towns in northern Germany and neighboring countries for mutual protection and trade advantages.

han-sel (han′səl) See HANDSEL.

Han-sen's disease (han′sənz) Leprosy. [after Gerhart *Hansen,* 1841–1912, Norwegian physician]

han-som (han′səm) *n.* A low, two-wheeled, one-horse carriage, with the driver seated behind and above the cab: also **hansom cab.** [after J. A *Hansom,* 1803–82, English inventor]

Ha-nuk-kah (khä′nŏŏ-kə, hä′-) *n.* A Jewish festival, lasting eight days from Kislev 25 (early December), in memory of the rededication of the temple at Jerusalem under the Maccabees in 164 B.C.: also *Chanukah.* Also **Ha′nu-kah.** [< Hebrew *hanukkah* dedication]

HANSOM

hap-haz-ard (hap′haz′ərd) *adj.* Dependent upon or happening by chance; accidental; random. —*n.* Mere chance; hazard. —*adv.* By chance; at random. —**hap′haz′ard-ly** *adv.* —**hap′haz′ard-ness** *n.*

hap-less (hap′lis) *adj.* Having no luck; unfortunate; unlucky. —**hap′less-ly** *adv.* —**hap′less-ness** *n.*

haplo- *combining form* Simple; single: also, before vowels, **hapl-.** [< Gk. *haploos* simple]

hap-loid (hap′loid) *adj.* *Biol.* Having only one set of unpaired chromosomes, as a germ cell, in contradistinction to the normal diploid number as found in somatic cells. Also **hap-loid′ic.** —*n.* A haploid organism or cell.

hap-pen (hap′ən) *v.i.* **1.** To take place or occur; come to pass. **2.** To occur by chance rather than by design. **3.** To chance: We *happened* to hear him sing. **4.** To come by chance: with *on* or *upon*. **5.** To come or go by chance: with *in, along, by,* etc. **— to happen to 1.** To befall. **2.** To become of: What *happened* to your old friend? [ME *happenen*]

hap-pen-ing (hap′ən·ing) *n.* **1.** An event; occurrence. **2.** A staged event, usu. partly improvised and often spectacular.

hap-pen-stance (hap′ən·stans, -stəns) *n.* *U.S. Informal* A chance occurrence; accident.

hap-py (hap′ē) *adj.* **·pi-er, ·pi-est 1.** Enjoying, showing, or characterized by pleasure; joyous; contented. **2.** Attended with good fortune; lucky. **3.** Produced or uttered with skill and aptness; felicitous: a *happy* phrase. [ME *happi* < *hap* an occurrence] —**hap′pi-ly** *adv.* —**hap′pi-ness** *n.*

hap-py-go-luck-y (hap′ē-gō-luk′ē) *adj.* Trusting habitually to luck; cheerful; unconcerned; easygoing.

ha-ra-ki-ri (har′ə·kir′ē; hä′rä·kē′rē) *n.* Suicide by disembowelment, traditionally practiced by the Japanese Samurai when disgraced: also *hari-kari.* Also **ha′ra-ka′ri** (-kä′·rē). [< Japanese *hara* belly + *kiri* cut]

ha-rangue (hə·rang′) *n.* A lengthy, loud, and vehement speech; tirade. —*v.* **·rangued, ·rangu-ing** *v.t.* **1.** To address in a harangue. —*v.i.* **2.** To deliver a harangue. [< F < Med.L < OHG *hari* army, host + *hringa* ring] —**ha-rangu′er** *n.*

har-ass (har′əs, hə·ras′) *v.t.* **1.** To trouble or pursue relentlessly with cares, annoyances, etc.; torment. **2.** *Mil.* To worry (an enemy) by raids and small attacks. [< OF < *harer* to set dogs on] —**har′ass-er** *n.* —**har′ass-ment** *n.*

har-bin-ger (här′bin·jər) *n.* One who or that which goes before and announces the coming of something; herald. —*v.t.* To act as a harbinger to; presage; herald. [< OF < *herberge* shelter < Gmc.]

har-bor (här′bər) *n.* **1.** A sheltered place, natural or artificial, on the coast of a sea, lake, etc., used to provide protection and anchorage for ships; port. **2.** Any place of refuge or rest. —*v.t.* **1.** To give refuge to; shelter; esp., to conceal or be hospitable to harmful persons or things: to *harbor* thieves. **2.** To entertain in the mind; cherish: to *harbor* a grudge. —*v.i.* **3.** To take shelter in or as in a harbor. Also *Brit.* **har′bour.** [ME < OE *here* army + *beorg* refuge]

har-bor-age (här′bər·ij) *n.* **1.** A port or place of anchorage for ships. **2.** Shelter; lodging; entertainment.

har-bor-mas-ter (här′bər·mas·tər, -mäs′-) *n.* An officer in charge of enforcing the regulations of a harbor.

hard (härd) *adj.* **1.** Resisting indentation or compression; solid; firm; unyielding. **2.** Requiring vigorous mental or physical effort to do, solve, understand, explain, etc.; difficult. **3.** Energetic and steady; industrious: a *hard* worker. **4.** Showing little mercy or feeling; stern: a *hard* judge. **5.** Strict or exacting in terms: a *hard* bargain. **6.** Having force or intensity; severe; violent: a *hard* knock. **7.** Involving or inflicting sorrow, discomfort, pain, poverty, etc.: *hard* times. **8.** *U.S. Informal* Verified and specific: said of facts, information, etc. **9.** Given to shrewdness, practicality, and obstinacy: a *hard* head. **10.** Too harsh, brilliant, or penetrating: a *hard* light. **11.** *U.S. Informal* Menacing, cruel, or disreputable in character or appearance; tough: a *hard* face. **12.** Containing certain mineral salts that interfere with the cleansing action of soap: said of water. **13.** *U.S.* Containing much alcohol; strong: *hard* cider. **14.** *Agric.* High in gluten content: said of wheat. **15.** *Phonet.* Denoting (c) or (g) when articulated as a stop, as in *cod* or *god*, and not as a fricative or affricate. **16.** *Physics* Denoting radiant energy of great penetrating power, as gamma rays. — **hard and fast** Fixed and unalterable. — **hard of hearing** Deaf or partially deaf. — **hard up** *Informal* **1.** Poor; broke. **2.** In need of (something): with *for.* — **to be hard on** To be severe, cruel, or damaging to. —*adv.* **1.** With great energy or force; vigorously: to work *hard.* **2.** Intently; earnestly: to look *hard* for something. **3.** With effort or difficulty: to breathe *hard.* **4.** With resistance; reluctantly: to die *hard.* **5.** Securely; tightly: to hold on *hard.* **6.** So as to become firm or solid: to freeze *hard.* **7.** In close proximity; near: with *after, by,* or *upon.* **8.** *Naut.* To the extreme limit; fully: *Hard* aport. — **to be hard put** To have great difficulty. — **to go hard with** To be very painful and harsh for. [OE *heard*] —**hard′ness** *n.*

hard-bit-ten (härd′bit′n) *adj.* Tough; unyielding.

hard-boiled (härd′boild′) *adj.* **1.** Boiled until cooked through: said of an egg. **2.** *Informal* Callous; tough.

hard cash Actual money; cash on hand.

hard cider Cider that has fermented.

hard coal Anthracite.

hard-core (härd′kôr′, -kōr′) *adj.* 1. Being irreducible. 2. Of or relating to the chronically unemployed. 3. Being explicit and graphic: *hard-core* pornography.

hard·en (här′dən) *v.t. & v.i.* To make or become hard in various senses. — **hard′en·er** *n.*

hard-fist·ed (härd′fis′tid) *adj.* 1. Stingy; miserly. 2. Having hard hands, as a laborer. — **hard′-fist′ed·ness** *n.*

hard·hat (härd′hat′) *n.* 1. A construction worker. 2. A man, esp. a laborer, who holds extremely conservative views. [From the protective helmets worn by construction workers]

hard·head (härd′hed′) *n. pl.* **·heads** 1. A shrewd and practical person. 2. An obstinate person.

hard·head·ed (härd′hed′id) *adj.* 1. Having a shrewd and practical mind. 2. Having a stubborn character; obstinate. — **hard′head′ed·ly** *adv.* — **hard′head′ed·ness** *n.*

hard·heart·ed (härd′här′tid) *adj.* Lacking pity; unfeeling. — **hard′heart′ed·ly** *adv.* — **hard′heart′ed·ness** *n.*

hard labor Compulsory physical labor imposed upon imprisoned criminals as part of their punishment.

hard·ly (härd′lē) *adv.* 1. Scarcely; barely; only just: I *hardly* felt it. 2. Not quite; not: That is *hardly* enough.

hard-nosed (härd′nōzd′) *adj. Slang* Hard-bitten; unyielding.

hard·pan (härd′pan′) *n. U.S.* 1. A layer of very hard, often claylike matter under soft soil. 2. Solid, unbroken ground. 3. The firm foundation of anything.

hard sauce Creamed butter, sugar, and flavorings.

hard-shell (härd′shel′) *adj.* 1. Having a hard shell. 2. *U.S. Informal* Rigidly orthodox; inflexible.

hard·ship (härd′ship) *n.* 1. A difficult, painful condition, as from privation, suffering, etc. 2. An instance of this.

hard·tack (härd′tack′) *n.* Hard, crackerlike biscuit.

hard·top (härd′top′) *n.* An automobile with the body design of a convertible, but with a rigid top.

hard·ware (härd′wâr′) *n.* 1. Manufactured articles of metal, as utensils or tools. 2. Weapons: military *hardware.* 3. Any of the machinery that makes up a digital computer installation: distinguished from *software.*

hard·wood (härd′wŏŏd′) *n.* 1. Wood from deciduous trees, as oak, maple, etc., as distinguished from the wood of coniferous trees. 2. Any hard, compact, heavy wood. 3. A tree yielding such wood.

har·dy¹ (här′dē) *adj.* **·di·er, ·di·est** 1. Able to endure hardship, fatigue, privation, etc.; robust; tough. 2. Having courage and valor. 3. Foolhardy; rash. 4. Able to survive the winter outdoors: said of plants. [< OF < OHG *hartjan* to make hard] — **har′di·ly** *adv.* — **har′di·ness** *n.*

har·dy² (här′dē) *n. pl.* **·dies** A square-shanked chisel or fuller for insertion in a square hole (**hardy hole**) in a blacksmith's anvil.

hare (hâr) *n. pl.* **hares** or **hare** 1. A mammal allied to but larger than the rabbit, having long ears and long hind legs. ◆ Collateral adjective: *leporine.* 2. The common American rabbit. [OE *hara*]

hare·bell (hâr′bel′) *n.* A perennial herb with blue, bell-shaped flowers. Also called *bluebell.*

hare·brained (hâr′brānd′) *adj.* Foolish; flighty; giddy.

hare·lip (hâr′lip′) *n.* A congenital fissure of the upper lip, resembling the cleft lip of a hare. — **hare′lipped′** *adj.*

har·em (hâr′əm, har′-) *n.* 1. The apartments of a Moslem household reserved for females. 2. The women occupying the harem. [< Arabic < *harama* to forbid]

har·i·cot (har′ə·kō) *n.* 1. A stew of meat, esp. mutton, and vegetables; ragout. 2. The kidney bean or its pods. [< F]

ha·ri-ka·ri (har′ē-kar′ē; har′ē-kä′rē) *n.* Hara-kiri.

hark (härk) *v.i.* To listen; harken: usu. in the imperative. — **to hark back** To return to some previous point; revert. — *n.* A cry used to urge on or guide hounds. [ME *herkien*]

hark·en (här′kən) *v.i. Poetic* To listen; give heed. Also spelled *hearken.* [OE *heorcnian*]

har·le·quin (här′lə·kwin, -kin) *n.* A buffoon. — *adj.* 1. Parti-colored; motley, like the dress of a Harlequin. 2. Designating eyeglasses with frames slanting upward like the eyes of a Harlequin's mask. [< MF < Ital. *arlecchino,* prob. akin to OF *Herlequin,* a devil in medieval legend]

Har·le·quin (här′lə·kwin, -kin) *n.* A pantomime character traditionally masked and dressed in parti-colored tights.

har·lot (här′lət) *n.* A prostitute. [< OF, rogue]

har·lot·ry (här′lət-rē) *n. pl.* **·ries** Prostitution.

harm (härm) *n.* 1. Injury; damage; hurt. 2. Wrong; evil. — *v.t.* To do harm to; damage; hurt. [OE *hearm* an insult]

harm·ful (härm′fəl) *adj.* Having power to injure or do harm. — **harm′ful·ly** *adv.* — **harm′ful·ness** *n.*

harm·less (härm′lis) *adj.* Inflicting no injury; not harmful; innocuous. — **harm′less·ly** *adv.* — **harm′less·ness** *n.*

har·mon·ic (här·mon′ik) *adj.* 1. Producing, characterized by, or pertaining to harmony; consonant; harmonious. 2. *Music* **a** Pertaining to harmony in musical sounds. **b** Pertaining to a tone whose rate of vibration is an integral multiple of a given primary tone. 3. *Physics* Designating or characterized by a harmonic. — *n.* 1. *Music* **a** A tone on a stringed instrument produced by touching a string lightly at a point. **b** A partial tone with a vibration rate that is an integral multiple of a given primary tone. 2. *Physics* Any component of a periodic quantity that is an integral multiple of a given fundamental frequency. [< L < Gk. < *harmonia* harmony] — **har·mon′i·cal·ly** *adv.*

har·mon·i·ca (här·mon′i·kə) *n.* 1. A musical instrument consisting of metal reeds fixed in slots in a small oblong frame, and played by blowing and inhaling through the slots: also called *mouth organ.* 2. An instrument composed of glass or metal strips, struck by hammers.

har·mon·ics (här·mon′iks) *n.pl.* (construed as *sing.* in def. 1) 1. The branch of acoustics dealing with musical sounds. 2. *Music* The overtones of a fundamental.

har·mo·ni·ous (här·mō′nē·əs) *adj.* 1. Made up of sounds, colors, or other elements that combine agreeably: a *harmonious* pattern. 2. Manifesting agreement and concord in views, attitudes, feelings, etc. 3. Pleasing to the ear; euphonious. — **har·mo′ni·ous·ly** *adv.* — **har·mo′ni·ous·ness** *n.*

har·mo·ni·um (här·mō′nē·əm) *n.* A type of reed organ in which air is compressed in the bellows, then driven out through the reeds; melodeon. [< F < *harmonia*]

har·mo·nize (här′mə·nīz) *v.t. & v.i.* **·nized, ·niz·ing** 1. To make or become harmonious, suitable, or agreeable. 2. To arrange or sing in musical harmony. 3. To show the harmony or agreement of, as the Gospels. Also *Brit.* **har′mo·nise.** — **har′mo·ni·za′tion** *n.* — **har′mo·niz′er** *n.*

har·mo·ny (här′mə·nē) *n. pl.* **·nies** 1. Accord or agreement in feeling, manner, action, etc.: to live in *harmony.* 2. A state of order, agreement, or esthetically pleasing relationships among the elements of a whole. 3. Pleasing sounds; music. 4. *Music* **a** A simultaneous combination of tones or a group of melodic tones that suggest a simultaneous combination. **b** Musical structure in terms of the relations between successive harmonies. **c** The science or study of this structure. 5. A scholarly work displaying the similarities, etc., of different books or passages: a *harmony* of the Gospels. [< OF < L < Gk. < *harmozein* to join] — **Syn.** 1, 2. Concord, accord, consonance, congruity.

har·ness (här′nis) *n.* 1. The combination of traces, straps, etc., forming the gear of a draft animal and used to attach it to a wheeled vehicle or plow. 2. Any similar arrangement of straps, cords, etc.; esp., one used for attaching something, as a parachute, to the body. — **in harness** Working at one's routine job. — *v.t.* 1. To put harness on (a horse, etc.). 2. To make use of the power or potential of: to *harness* a waterfall. [< OF *harneis*; ult. origin unknown] — **har′ness·er** *n.*

harp (härp) *n.* 1. A stringed musical instrument that in its present form is upright and triangular in shape, and is played by plucking with the fingers. 2. A harplike object or device. — **to harp on** (or **upon**) To talk or write about persistently and vexatiously. [OE *hearpe*] — **harp′er** *n.*

harp·ist (här′pist) *n.* One who plays the harp.

har·poon (här·pŏŏn′) *n.* A barbed missile weapon, carrying a long cord, for striking whales or large fish. — *v.t.* To strike, take, or kill with or as with a harpoon. [< F < *harpe* claw] — **har·poon′er, har·poon·eer′** (ir′) *n.*

harpoon gun A gun that fires a harpoon, used in whaling.

harp·si·chord (härp′sə·kôrd) *n.* A keyboard instrument widely used from the 16th to the 18th century and revived in the 20th, having the strings plucked by quills or leather points instead of struck. [< MF *harpechorde* < Ital. < LL *harpa* harp + L *chorda* string]

har·py (här′pē) *n. pl.* **·pies** 1. A rapacious, predatory person, esp. a woman. 2. A large, crested, voracious tropical American eagle: also **harpy eagle.** [< HARPY]

Har·py (här′pē) *n. pl.* **·pies** In Greek mythology, one of several winged monsters with the head of a woman and the body of a bird, who carried off the souls of the dead, etc. [< F *Harpie* < L < Gk. < *harpazein* to seize]

har·que·bus (här′kwə·bəs) *n.* An early portable firearm, in its later form having a matchlock and fired from a forked rest: also *arquebus.* [< F < MLG *hakebusse* hooked gun]

har·ri·dan (har′ə·dən) *n.* A hateful old woman; vicious hag. [< OF *haridelle* jade]

har·ri·er (har′ē·ər) *n.* 1. A small hound used for hunting hares. 2. A cross-country runner.

har·row (har′ō) *n.* A farm implement set with spikes or disks, for leveling plowed ground, breaking clods, etc. For illus. see DISK HARROW. — *v.t.* 1. To draw a harrow over (a field, etc.). 2. To disturb the mind or feelings of painfully; distress. — *v.i.* 3. To undergo harrowing. [ME *harwe,* prob. < Scand.] — **har′row·er** *n.*

har·row·ing (har′ō·ing) *adj.* Lacerating or tormenting to the feelings. — **har′row·ing·ly** *adv.*

har·ry (har′ē) *v.* **·ried, ·ry·ing** *v.t.* **1.** To lay waste, as in war or invasion; pillage; sack. **2.** To harass in any way. — *v.i.* **3.** To make raids. [OE *hergian* to ravage]

harsh (härsh) *adj.* **1.** Grating, rough, or unpleasant to any of the senses: a *harsh* tone; a *harsh* light. **2.** Unpleasing to the mind or the artistic sense; ungraceful; crude. **3.** Manifesting severity; cruel: a *harsh* punishment. [ME *harsk,* prob. < Scand.] — **harsh′ly** *adv.* — **harsh′ness** *n.*

hart (härt) *n.* The male of the red deer, esp. after it has passed its fifth year. [OE *heort*]

harte·beest (härt′bēst, här′tə-) *n.* A large, grayish brown antelope of Africa. Also **hart′beest.** [< Afrikaans < Du. *hert* hart + *beest* beast]

harts·horn (härts′hôrn′) *n.* **1.** The antler of a hart. **2.** Ammonium carbonate or a preparation made from it.

har·um-scar·um (hâr′əm·skâr′əm) *adj.* Reckless and wild; harebrained; irresponsible. — *adv.* In a wild, unrestrained manner. — *n.* **1.** A reckless person. **2.** Wild and heedless behavior. [prob. < obs. *hare* to frighten + SCARE]

har·vest (här′vist) *n.* **1.** The act of gathering or collecting a ripened crop of grain, fruit, vegetables, etc. **2.** The yield of such a crop; also, the crop itself. **3.** The time of year when such crops are gathered. **4.** The products of any effort. — *v.t. & v.i.* **1.** To gather (a crop). **2.** To gather the crop of (a field, hive, etc.). **3.** To reap or suffer (consequences, etc.). [OE *hærfest* autumn, harvest]

har·vest·er (här′vis·ter) *n.* **1.** One who harvests. **2.** A reaping machine.

har·vest·man (här′vist·mən) *n. pl.* **·men** (-mən) **1.** One who labors in the harvest. **2.** A daddy-longlegs.

harvest moon The full moon that occurs near the autumnal equinox.

has (haz) Present indicative, third person singular, of HAVE.

has-been (haz′bin′) *n. Informal* One who or that which is no longer popular or effective.

ha·sen·pfef·fer (hä′sən·fef′ər) *n.* A highly seasoned dish made of marinated rabbit, braised and simmered. [< G < *hase* rabbit, hare + *pfeffer* pepper]

hash (hash) *n.* **1.** A dish of chopped meat and potatoes or other vegetables, usu. sautéed, then baked or browned. **2.** A mess; jumble; mishmash. **3.** *Slang* Hashish. — **to make a hash of** *Informal* **1.** To bungle; spoil; mess up. **2.** To destroy or overcome (an argument, adversary, etc.). — **to settle** (or **fix**) **one's hash** *Informal* To deal with punitively; to subdue. — *v.t.* **1.** To cut or chop into small pieces; mince. **2.** *U.S. Informal* To discuss at length: often with *over.* [< OF *hacher* to chop]

hash house *U.S. Slang* A cheap restaurant.

hash·ish (häsh′ēsh, -ish) *n.* The tops and sprouts of hemp, used as a narcotic and intoxicant. Also called *bhang.* Also **hash′eesh.** [< Arabic *hashish* hemp]

hash mark *Mil. Slang* A service stripe.

Has·i·dim (has′i·dim, *Hebrew* khä·sē′dim) See CHASSIDIM.

has·n't (haz′ənt) Has not.

hasp (hasp, häsp) *n.* A hinged fastening for a door, lid, etc., esp. one that passes over a staple and is secured by a padlock. — *v.t.* To shut or fasten with or as with a hasp. [OE *hæpse*]

has·sle (has′əl) *n. U.S. Slang* An argument; squabble; fight. Also **has′sel.** [? < HAGGLE + TUSSLE]

has·sock (has′ək) *n.* **1.** An upholstered stool or cushion, used for kneeling or as a footstool. **2.** A rank tuft of coarse or boggy grass. [OE *hassuc* coarse grass, ? < Celtic]

hast (hast) Archaic or poetic second person singular, present tense, of HAVE: used with *thou.*

haste (hāst) *n.* **1.** Swiftness of movement or action; rapidity. **2.** Undue or reckless hurry. **3.** The necessity to act quickly; urgency. — **to make haste** To hurry. — *v.t. & v.i.* **hast·ed, hast·ing** *Poetic* To hasten. [< OF < Gmc.]

has·ten (hā′sən) *v.i.* **1.** To move or act with speed; be quick; hurry. — *v.t.* **2.** To cause to hurry or move quickly; expedite. — **has′ten·er** *n.*

hast·y (hās′tē) *adj.* **hast·i·er, hast·i·est** **1.** Speedy; quick; rapid. **2.** Acting or made with excessive speed; rash. **3.** Manifesting anger: *hasty* words. **4.** Easily excited to anger. — **hast′i·ly** *adv.* — **hast′i·ness** *n.*

hasty pudding **1.** A dish made of meal, seasoning, and boiling water or milk. **2.** *U.S.* A mush made with cornmeal.

hat (hat) *n.* A covering for the head, esp. one with a crown and brim. — **to pass the hat** To solicit and collect contributions of money. — **to talk through one's hat** *Informal* To talk nonsense; also, to bluff. — **to throw** (**toss,** etc.) **one's hat into the ring** To enter a contest or competition, esp. a contest for political office. — **under one's hat** *U.S. Informal* Secret; private. — *v.t.* **hat·ted, hat·ting** To provide or cover with a hat. [OE *hæt*]

hat·band (hat′band′) *n.* A ribbon or band of cloth around a hat just above the brim.

hatch¹ (hach) *n.* **1.** An opening in a floor, deck, etc., giving access to spaces beneath: also called *hatchway.* **2.** A cover

or grating over such an opening: also **hatch cover.** **3.** A door or gate with an opening above; also, the lower half of a door that is divided into two independently swinging parts. **4.** A floodgate (def. 1). — **Down the hatch!** *U.S. Slang* Drink up! [OE *hæcc* grating]

hatch² (hach) *v.t.* **1.** To bring forth (young) from the egg by incubation. **2.** To bring forth young from (the egg). **3.** To devise, as a plan or plot. — *v.i.* **4.** To emerge from the egg. — *n.* **1.** The act of hatching. **2.** The brood hatched at one time. **3.** The result or outcome of any plan. [ME *hacchen*] — **hatch′er** *n.*

hatch³ (hach) *v.t.* To mark with close parallel or crossed lines in order to produce shading effects, etc. — *n.* Any of these lines. [< OF *hache* an ax < Gmc.] — **hatch′ing** *n.*

hatch·er·y (hach′ər·ē) *n. pl.* **·er·ies** A place for hatching eggs, esp. those of poultry or fish.

hatch·et (hach′it) *n.* **1.** A small, short-handled ax, for use with one hand. **2.** A tomahawk. — **to bury the hatchet.** To make peace. [< F, dim. of *hache* an ax]

hatch·way (hach′wā′) *n.* Hatch¹ (def. 1).

hate (hāt) *v.* **hat·ed, hat·ing** *v.t.* **1.** To regard with extreme aversion; detest. **2.** To dislike: I *hate* doing that. — *v.i.* **3.** To feel hatred. — *n.* **1.** An extreme feeling of dislike or animosity; hatred. **2.** A person or thing detested. [OE *hatian*] — **hat′a·ble** or **hate′a·ble** *adj.* — **hat′er** *n.*

— **Syn.** (verb) **1.** *Hate* frequently refers to a deep, personal feeling actuated by enmity or malice; Iago *hated* Othello. *Loathe* and *abhor* both suggest aversion or disgust; *loathe* pictures that which causes a nauseating repugnance, and *abhor,* that from which we turn or shrink away. *Abominate* is used of things *hated* for moral reasons, and often indicates a righteous indignation.

hate·ful (hāt′fəl) *adj.* Arousing or worthy of hatred; detestable. — **hate′ful·ly** *adv.* — **hate′ful·ness** *n.*

hath (hath) Archaic or poetic third person singular, present tense, of HAVE.

ha·tred (hā′trid) *n.* Intense dislike or aversion; animosity; enmity. [ME < *hate* + *-red* < OE *-ræden* state]

haugh·ty (hô′tē) *adj.* **·ti·er, ·ti·est** Exhibiting great disdain for others; supercilious. [< OF *haut* high] — **haugh′ti·ly** *adv.* — **haugh′ti·ness** *n.*

haul (hôl) *v.t.* **1.** To pull or draw strongly; drag; tug. **2.** To transport or carry, as in a truck, car, etc. **3.** *Naut.* To change the course of (a ship), esp. so as to sail closer to the wind. — *v.i.* **4.** To pull or drag; tug. **5.** To change direction: said of the wind. **6.** To change one's views or course of action. **7.** *Naut.* To change course; especially, to steer nearer the wind. — **to haul off** To draw back the arm so as to punch. — **to haul up** **1.** To compel to go: I was *hauled up* before the court. **2.** To come to a stop. **3.** *Naut.* To sail nearer the wind. — *n.* **1.** A strong pull; tug. **2.** That which is caught, won, taken, etc., at one time: a good *haul* of fish. **3.** The distance over which something is hauled. **4.** That which is hauled. [< OF *haler* < Gmc.] — **haul′er** *n.*

haul·age (hô′lij) *n.* **1.** The act or operation of hauling. **2.** A charge for hauling. **3.** Force expended in hauling.

haul·yard (hôl′yərd) See HALYARD.

haunch (hônch, hänch) *n.* **1.** In man and animals, the upper thigh, including the hip and buttock. **2.** The leg and loin of an animal, considered as meat. [< OF *hanche*]

haunch bone The innominate bone.

haunt (hônt, hänt) *v.t.* **1.** To visit or resort to (a person or place) repeatedly; esp., to do so, as a ghost or spirit. **2.** To recur persistently to the mind or memory of: The tune *haunts* me. **3.** To linger about; pervade. — *v.i.* **4.** To appear or recur often, esp. as a ghost. — *n.* A place often visited; resort; habitat. [< OF *hanter*] — **haunt′er** *n.*

haunt·ed (hôn′tid, hän′-) *adj.* Supposedly visited by ghosts.

haunt·ing (hôn′ting, hän′-) *adj.* Recurring to the mind; difficult to forget: a *haunting* tune. — **haunt′ing·ly** *adv.*

haut·boy (hō′boi, ō′-) *n.* An oboe. [< F *haut* high (in tone) + *bois* wood]

hau·teur (hō·tûr′, *Fr.* ō·tœr′) *n.* Haughtiness. [< F]

haut monde (ō mônd′) *French* High society.

have (hav) *v.t.* Present indicative: I, you, we, they **have** (*Archaic* **thou hast**), he, she, it **has** (*Archaic* **hath**); past indicative **had** (*Archaic* **thou hadst**); present subjunctive **have;** past subjunctive **had;** *pp.* **had;** *ppr.* **hav·ing 1.** To possess as property; own. **2.** To be connected with; be possessed of: to *have* a good government. **3.** To bear or possess as an attribute, quality, etc. **4.** To hold in the mind or among the feelings; entertain. **5.** To receive, take, or acquire. **6.** To achieve mastery of: Now I *have* it. **7.** To suffer from: to *have* boils. **8.** To engage in: to *have* a quarrel. **9.** To undergo or experience: to *have* a bad fright. **10.** To plan, arrange, and carry out: to *have* a party. **11.** To give birth to. **12.** To manifest or exercise: to *have* patience. **13.** To cause to, or cause to be: *Have* it cleaned. **14.** To allow; tolerate. **15.** To maintain; declare: So rumor *has* it. **16.** *Informal* To catch (someone) at a disadvantage in a game, etc. **17.** *Informal* To cheat; trick. **18.** *Informal* To perform the sexual act with. **19.** As an auxiliary, *have* is used: **a** With past participles to form perfect tenses expressing completed action: I *have* gone. **b** With the infinitive to express obligation or compulsion: I *have* to go. **— to have at** To attack. **— have done** To stop; desist. **— to have it in for** *Informal* To hold a grudge against. **— to have it out** To continue a fight or discussion to a final settlement. **— to have on** To be dressed in. **— to let someone have it** *Informal* To attack or assault someone. **—** *n.* *Informal* A relatively wealthy person or country: the *haves* and the have-nots. [OE *habban*]

ha·ven (hā′vən) *n.* **1.** A harbor; port. **2.** A refuge; shelter. **—** *v.t.* To shelter in or as in a haven. [OE *hæfen*]

have-not (hav′not′) *n.* *Informal* A person or country relatively lacking in wealth: the haves and *have-nots*.

have·n't (hav′ənt) Have not.

hav·er·sack (hav′ər·sak) *n.* A bag for carrying rations, etc., on a march or hike. [< F < G *habersack* oat sack]

hav·oc (hav′ək) *n.* General carnage or destruction; ruin. **— to cry havoc** To give the signal for pillage and destruction. **— to play havoc with** To ruin; destroy; devastate. [< OF *havot* to plunder < Gmc.]

haw¹ (hô) *v.i.* To hesitate in speaking: to hem and *haw*. **—** *n.* & *interj.* A hesitating sound made by a speaker.

haw² (hô) *n.* The hawthorn or its fruit. [OE *haga*]

haw³ (hô) *n.* & *interj.* An order to turn to the left or near side in driving horses: opposed to *gee*. **—** *v.t.* & *v.i.* To turn to the left. [Origin uncertain]

Ha·wai·ian (hə·wī′yən) *adj.* Of or pertaining to Hawaii, the Hawaiians, or their language. **—** *n.* **1.** A native or inhabitant of Hawaii. **2.** The Polynesian language of Hawaii.

Hawaiian guitar A guitar played horizontally, the chords being selected by a metal bar sliding on the strings.

haw-haw (hô′hô′) See HA-HA.

hawk¹ (hôk) *n.* **1.** Any of a large and widely distributed family of birds of prey, having broad, rounded wings, a long tail, and powerful talons. **2.** Any of various related birds, as the gerfalcon, kestrel, and osprey. **3.** A person who preys on others. **—** *v.i.* **1.** To hunt game with hawks. **2.** To fly in search of prey, as a hawk. [OE *hafoc, hafuc*]

hawk² (hôk) *v.t.* & *v.i.* To cry (goods) for sale in the streets; peddle. [Back formation < HAWKER]

hawk³ (hôk) *v.t.* **1.** To cough up (phlegm). **—** *v.i.* **2.** To clear the throat with a coughing sound. **—** *n.* An effort to clear phlegm from the throat; also, the sound of this. [Imit.]

hawk·er (hô′kər) *n.* One who peddles goods in the street. [< MLG *hoker* peddler, huckster]

Hawk·eye (hôk′ī′) *n.* A native or inhabitant of Iowa.

hawk-eyed (hôk′īd′) *adj.* Having very keen eyesight.

Hawkeye State Nickname of Iowa.

hawk moth A large, stout-bodied moth that flies by twilight and sucks nectar from flowers.

hawks·bill (hôks′bil′) *n.* A tropical turtle that furnishes the best grade of tortoise shell used in commerce. Also **hawk′s-bill′, hawksbill turtle.**

hawk·weed (hôk′wēd′) *n.* A weedy perennial herb having small red, yellow, or orange flowers.

hawse (hôz) *n.* *Naut.* **1.** The part of a ship's bow where the hawseholes are located. **2.** *pl.* Hawseholes. **3.** The space between the bow of a moored ship and her anchor. [< ON *hals* neck, bow of a ship]

hawse·hole (hôz′hōl′) *n.* *Naut.* A hole in the bow of a ship, through which cables and hawsers pass.

haw·ser (hô′zər) *n.* *Naut.* A rope or cable used for mooring, towing, etc. [< OF *haucier* to lift]

haw·thorn (hô′thôrn) *n.* A shrub or tree of the rose family having a white or pink flower and a small pome fruit called *haw*: the State flower of Missouri. [OE *haguthorn*]

hay (hā) *n.* Grass, clover, or the like, cut and dried for fodder. **— not hay** *U.S. Slang* Not a small sum of money. **— to hit the hay** *U.S. Slang* To go to bed. **— to make hay while the sun shines** To take full advantage of an opportunity. **—** *v.i.* **1.** To mow, cure, gather, and store hay. **—** *v.t.* **2.** To make (grass, etc.) into hay. **3.** To feed with hay. **4.** To sow (land, etc.) with hay plants. [OE *hēg*]

hay·cock (hā′kok′) *n.* A dome-shaped pile of hay in the field.

hay fever *Pathol.* An allergic reaction to pollen of certain plants, characterized by sneezing, running nose, etc.

hay·loft (hā′lôft′, -loft′) *n.* An open upper section of a barn or stable, used for storing hay.

hay·mak·er (hā′mā′kər) *n.* **1.** One who makes hay. **2.** *Slang* A powerful punch. **— hay′mak′ing** *n.*

hay·mow (hā′mou′) *n.* **1.** A mass of hay, esp. one stored in a loft or bay. **2.** A hayloft.

hay·rack (hā′rak′) *n.* **1.** A frame or rack mounted on a wagon body, in which hay is hauled; also, a wagon so equipped. **2.** A framework for holding hay to feed livestock.

hay·seed (hā′sēd′) *n.* **1.** Grass seed that has shaken loose from hay. **2.** The chaff, seeds, etc., that fall from hay. **3.** *U.S.* A hick; rustic; yokel.

hay·wire (hā′wīr′) *adj.* *U.S. Slang* **1.** Broken; broken down; dilapidated. **2.** Crazy; nutty.

haz·ard (haz′ərd) *n.* **1.** Danger of loss, injury, etc.; peril. **2.** Chance; accident. **3.** A gambling game played with dice. **4.** An obstacle or trap on a golf course. **5.** In tennis, any of various winning openings. **—** *v.t.* **1.** To put in danger; risk. **2.** To venture (a statement, opinion, etc.). **3.** To gamble on. [< OF < Arabic *al-zahr* a die]

haz·ard·ous (haz′ər·dəs) *adj.* **1.** Exposed to or involving danger, risk, loss, etc. **2.** Dependent on chance; fortuitous. **— haz′ard·ous·ly** *adv.* **— haz′ard·ous·ness** *n.*

haze¹ (hāz) *n.* **1.** A light suspension of water vapor, smoke, dust, etc., in the air. **2.** Mental confusion. [< HAZY]

haze² (hāz) *v.t.* hazed, haz·ing *U.S.* To subject (newcomers or initiates) to pranks and humiliating horseplay. [< OF *haser* to irritate] **— haz′er** *n.* **— haz′ing** *n.*

ha·zel (hā′zəl) *n.* **1.** A bushy shrub or small tree of the birch family; also, the wood of this tree. **2.** The hazelnut. **3.** A medium yellowish brown. **—** *adj.* **1.** Of or pertaining to the hazel. **2.** Of the color hazel. [OE *hæsel*]

ha·zel·nut (hā′zəl·nut′) *n.* The edible nut of the hazel.

haz·y (hā′zē) *adj.* haz·i·er, haz·i·est **1.** Misty. **2.** Lacking clarity; vague. **— haz′i·ly** *adv.* **— haz′i·ness** *n.*

H-bomb (āch′bom′) *n.* A hydrogen bomb.

he (hē) *pron.*, *possessive* **his**, *objective* **him**; *pl. nominative* **they**, *possessive* **their** or **theirs**, *objective* **them** **1.** The nominative singular pronoun of the third person, used of the male person. **2.** That person; anyone; one: *He* who hesitates is lost. **—** *n.*, *pl.* **hes** A male person or animal. [OE *hē*]

he- *combining form* Male; masculine: used in hyphenated compounds: *he-goat.* [< HE]

head (hed) *n.*, *pl.* **heads** or *for def. 15* **head** **1.** The part of a vertebrate animal situated at the top or front of the spinal column, containing the brain, eyes, ears, nose, and mouth. ◆ Collateral adjective: *cephalic.* **2.** The analogous part of other animals and organisms. **3.** A part like a head: the *head* of a pin. **4.** A representation of the head. **5.** A leader or chief person. **6.** The position or rank of a leader. **7.** The front or beginning part of something. **8.** The highest part of something. **9.** The superior part of something. **10.** The source, as of a river. **11.** The part of a bomb or other missile that contains the explosive. **12.** Mind; intelligence. **13.** Self-control; self-possession. **14.** A person: two dollars a *head.* **15.** Of animals, a single specimen. **16.** The length of a head. **17.** A newspaper headline. **18.** A subject: He had much to say on that *head.* **19.** The side of a coin on which a face is struck. **20.** The tip or point of a boil, abscess, etc. **21.** Progress; headway. **22.** A climax, culmination, or crisis. **23.** A compact cluster of leaves or leaf stalks. **24.** The foam on the surface of beer or ale. **25.** An amount of stored-up pressure. **26.** A projecting, usu. high, piece of land on a coast. **27.** The taut, sounding membrane of a drum, tambourine, etc. **28.** The part of a tape recorder that imparts magnetic patterns to the tape or removes them from it. **29.** *Naut.* A toilet. **30.** *Slang* One who habitually uses a drug, especially an illicit one, as LSD or marijuana, that distorts perception. **— head over heels** **1.** End over end. **2.** Rashly; impetuously. **3.** Entirely; totally. **— Heads up!** *U.S. Informal* Watch out! **— one's head off** *Informal* Excessively; vigorously: to yell *one's head off.* **— out of** (or **off**) **one's head** *Informal* **1.** Crazy; deluded. **2.** Delirious. **— over one's head** **1.** Too difficult to understand. **2.** Beyond one's power to cope with or manage. **3.** To a higher authority. **— to come to a head** **1.** Of boils, etc., to form a core or tip of pus. **2.** To reach a crisis. **— to give someone his head** To give someone freedom of action or unrestricted authority. **— to go to one's head** **1.** To decrease one's sobriety, etc. **2.** To make one conceited. **— to have a head** *Informal* To have a bad headache. **— to have rocks** (or **holes**) **in the head** *U.S. Slang* **1.** To be crazy. **2.** To be stupid. **— to keep one's head above water** **1.** To keep afloat. **2.** To manage to exist, keep out of debt, etc. **— to make head or tail of** To understand: usu. used in the negative. **— to take it into one's head** To do or originate something on one's own initiative. **— to turn one's head** To spoil or make vain by praising. **—** *v.t.* **1.** To be first or most prominent on: to *head* the list. **2.** To command; preside over. **3.** To direct the course of. **4.** To furnish with a head. **5.** To cut off the head or top of. **—** *v.i.* **6.** To move in a specified direction or toward a specified point. **7.** To come to or form a head. **8.** To originate: said of streams. **— to head off** To intercept the course of. **—** *adj.* **1.** Principal; chief. **2.** Situated at the front. **3.** Bearing against the front: a *head* wind. [OE *hēafod*]

head·ache (hed′āk′) *n.* **1.** A pain in the head. **2.** *U.S. Informal* A difficulty or vexation. **— head′ach′y** *adj.*

head·board (hed′bôrd′, -bōrd′) *n.* A board at the head end of a bed, grave, etc.

head·cheese (hed′chēz′) *n. U.S.* A cooked and jellied cheeselike meat made of the head and feet of a hog or calf.

head·dress (hed′dress′) *n.* 1. A covering or ornament for the head. 2. The style in which the hair is arranged; coiffure.

head·ed (hed′id) *adj.* 1. Having a head. 2. Having or characterized by a (specified kind of) head or (a specified number of) heads: *clear-headed; two-headed.*

head·er (hed′ər) *n.* 1. One who or that which makes or puts on heads, as of nails, rivets, etc. 2. *Agric.* A harvesting machine that cuts off the ripe ends of the grain. 3. *Informal* A fall or plunge: now only in the phrase **to take a header.**

head·first (hed′fûrst′) *adv.* 1. With the head first. 2. Without deliberation; recklessly. Also **head/fore/most′.**

head·gear (hed′gir′) *n.* 1. A hat, headdress, etc. 2. The parts of the harness placed about the horse's head.

head·hunt·ing (hed′hun′ting) *n.* Among certain savage tribes, the custom of decapitating slain enemies and preserving the heads as trophies. — **head/·hunt′er** *n.*

head·ing (hed′ing) *n.* 1. A caption or title, as of a chapter. 2. A section or division of a subject or discourse. 3. Something serving as the front or top part of anything. 4. *Naut. & Aeron.* Direction; course.

head·land (hed′lənd *for def. 1*; hed′land′ *for def. 2) n.* 1. A cliff projecting into the water. 2. A strip of unplowed land.

head·less (hed′lis) *adj.* 1. Having no head; decapitated. 2. Having no leader. 3. Stupid; erratic; brainless.

head·light (hed′līt′) *n.* A powerful light, as at the front of a locomotive, motor vehicle, etc.

head·line (hed′līn′) *n.* 1. A summarizing word or words set in bold type, as in a newspaper. 2. A line at the head of a page, containing title, page number, etc. — *v.t.* **head·lined, head·lin·ing** 1. To provide with a headline, as a news story. 2. To be a headliner in (a show, etc.).

head·lin·er (hed′lī′nər) *n.* One billed as the main attraction or star of a theatrical performance.

head·long (hed′lông′, -long′) *adv.* 1. Headfirst. 2. Without deliberation; recklessly; rashly. 3. With unbridled speed or force. — *adj.* 1. Made with the head foremost. 2. Advancing impetuously; rash. 3. *Rare* Steep.

head·mas·ter (hed′mas′tər, -mäs′-) *n.* The principal of a school, esp. a private school. Also **head master.**

head·mis·tress (hed′mis′tris) *n.fem.* The female principal of a school. Also **head mistress.**

head·most (hed′mōst′) *adj.* Most advanced; foremost.

head-on (hed′on′, -ôn′) *adj. & adv.* Front end to front end: *a head-on collision; to collide head-on.*

head·phone (hed′fōn′) *n.* An earphone, usu. attached by a band passing over the head.

head·piece (hed′pēs′) *n.* 1. A hat, helmet, or other covering for the head. 2. The head; intelligence. 3. A headset.

head·quar·ters (hed′kwôr′tərz) *n.pl.* (*construed as sing. or pl.*) 1. The place from which a chief or leader directs the operations of a military unit, police force, etc. 2. Any center of operations; also, the persons working there.

head·set (hed′set′) *n.* A pair of headphones.

head·ship (hed′ship) *n.* The position or function of a chief authority; command.

heads·man (hedz′mən) *n. pl.* **·men** (-mən) A public executioner who carries out the death sentence by decapitation.

head·stall (hed′stôl′) *n.* The part of a bridle that fits over the horse's head.

head start An advance start; also, an advantage.

head·stock (hed′stok′) *n. Mech.* One of various machine parts that support or hold some revolving part.

head·stone (hed′stōn′) *n.* 1. The memorial stone at the head of a grave. 2. The cornerstone or keystone of a structure: also **head stone.**

head·strong (hed′strông′, -strong′) *adj.* 1. Stubbornly bent on having one's own way; obstinate; determined. 2. Proceeding from willfulness or obstinacy.

head·wait·er (hed′wā′tər) *n.* A restaurant employee who supervises waiters, seats guests, makes reservations, etc.

head·wa·ters (hed′wô′tərz, -wot′ərz) *n.pl.* The tributaries or other waters that form the source of a river.

head·way (hed′wā′) *n.* 1. Forward motion; progress. 2. The space or time interval between two trains, ships, etc., traveling over the same route. 3. Overhead clearance.

head wind A wind from ahead, blowing directly opposite to the course of a ship, aircraft, etc.

head·y (hed′ē) *adj.* **head·i·er, head·i·est** 1. Tending to affect the senses; intoxicating: a *heady* fragrance. 2. Headstrong; obstinate. — **head/i·ly** *adv.* — **head/i·ness** *n.*

heal (hēl) *v.t.* 1. To restore to health or soundness. 2. To bring about the remedy or cure of. 3. To remedy or mend (a quarrel, breach, etc.). 4. To cleanse of sin, grief, worry, etc. — *v.i.* 5. To become well. 6. To perform a cure or cures. [OE *hǣlan*] — **heal′er** *n.* — **heal′a·ble** *adj.*

health (helth) *n.* 1. Freedom from defect or disease. 2. General condition of body or mind. 3. A toast wishing health or happiness. — *adj.* Of, pertaining to, connected with, or conducive to health. [OE *hǣlth < hāl* whole]

Health, Education and Welfare, Department of An executive department of the U.S. government (established 1953), administering Social Security and other services.

health·ful (helth′fəl) *adj.* 1. Promoting health; salubrious. 2. Having or manifesting health; healthy. — **health/ful·ly** *adv.* — **health/ful·ness** *n.*

health·y (hel′thē) *adj.* **health·i·er, health·i·est** 1. Having good health. 2. Conducive to health. 3. Indicative or characteristic of sound condition. — **health/i·ly** *adv.* — **health/i·ness** *n.*

heap (hēp) *n.* 1. A collection of things piled up; a pile. 2. *Informal* A large number; lot. — *v.t.* 1. To pile into a heap. 2. To fill or pile (a container) full or more than full. 3. To bestow in great quantities: to *heap* insults on someone. — *v.i.* 4. To form or rise in a heap. [OE *hēap* crowd]

hear (hir) *v.* **heard** (hûrd), **hear·ing** *v.t.* 1. To perceive by means of the ear. 2. To listen to; give ear to. 3. To be informed of: to *hear* good news. 4. To attend (an opera, concert, recitation, etc.). 5. To listen officially or judicially: to *hear* a case. 6. To respond or accede to: to *hear* a prayer. — *v.i.* 7. To perceive sound. 8. To be informed or made aware. — **to hear of** To approve of: usu. in the negative: He won't *hear* of it. [OE *hēran*] — **hear′er** *n.*

hear·ing (hir′ing) *n.* 1. The capacity to hear. 2. The act of perceiving sound. 3. Reach or range within which sound may be heard. 4. An opportunity to be heard, as in a court. 5. *Law* **a** The examination of an accused person. **b** A judicial trial, esp. without a jury.

hark·en (här′kən) See HARKEN.

hear·say (hir′sā′) *n.* Common talk; report; rumor.

hearse (hûrs) *n.* A vehicle for conveying a dead person to the place of burial. [< F *herse* harrow]

heart (härt) *n.* 1. *Anat.* The primary organ of the circulatory system of animals, a hollow muscular structure that maintains the circulation of the blood by alternate contraction and dilatation. ◆ Collateral adjective: *cardiac.* 2. The seat of emotion. 3. Tenderness; affection; love. 4. The capacity for kindness. 5. Courage. 6. One's inmost thoughts or feelings. 7. Enthusiasm; energy. 8. State of mind; mood. 9. A person, esp. a dear one. 10. The central or inner part of anything. 11. The vital or essential part. 12. Anything represented as or shaped like a heart. 13. A playing card bearing red, heart-shaped spots. 14. *pl.* The suit of such playing cards. 15. *pl.* A game of cards. — **after one's own heart** Suiting one's taste. — **at heart** In one's deepest thoughts or feelings. — **by heart** By memory. — **from (the bottom of) one's heart** With all sincerity. — **heart and soul** With complete sincerity. — **one's heart of hearts** The deepest and most intimate part of one's being. — **to break the heart of** To cause deep disappointment and sorrow to. — **to eat one's heart out** 1. To endure great remorse or grief. 2. To have a great longing. — **to have a heart** To be sympathetic and generous. — **to have a change of heart** To change one's opinions, attitudes, etc. — **to have one's heart in one's mouth** To be excessively excited or frightened. — **to have the heart** To be callous or cruel enough: usually in the negative. — **to lose heart** To become discouraged. — **to lose one's heart (to)** To fall in love (with). — **to set one's heart on** To long for; crave. — **to take to heart** 1. To consider seriously. 2. To be concerned or anxious about. — **to wear one's heart on one's sleeve** To show one's feelings openly. — **with all one's heart** 1. With great willingness. 2. With great sincerity. [OE *heorte*]

HEART

a Right atrium. *b* Right ventricle. *c* Left ventricle. *d* Aorta. *e* Pulmonary artery. *f* Inferior vena cava. *g* Superior vena cava. *h* Anterior coronary artery. *i* Posterior coronary artery.

heart·ache (härt′āk′) *n.* Mental anguish; grief; sorrow.

heart·beat (härt′bēt′) *n. Physiol.* A pulsation of the heart consisting of one full systole and diastole.

heart·break (härt′brāk′) *n.* Deep grief; overwhelming sorrow. — **heart/break′er** *n.* — **heart/break′ing** *adj. & n.*

heart·bro·ken (härt′brō′kən) *adj.* Overwhelmingly grieved. — **heart/bro′ken·ly** *adv.* — **heart/bro′ken·ness** *n.*

heart·burn (härt′bûrn′) *n. Pathol.* 1. A burning sensation in the esophagus due to acidity. 2. Discontent; jealousy.

heart·burn·ing (härt′bûrn′ing) *n.* Gnawing discontent, as from envy or jealousy. — *adj.* Deeply felt; distressful.

heart·ed (här′tid) *adj.* Having or characterized by a (specified kind of) heart: used in combination: *lighthearted.*

heart·en (här′tən) *v.t.* To give heart or courage to.

heart·felt (härt′felt′) *adj.* Deeply felt; most sincere.

hearth (härth) *n.* 1. The floor of a fireplace, furnace, or the like. 2. The fireside; home. 3. In a blast furnace, the lowest part, through which the melted metal flows. [OE *heorth*]

hearth·stone (härth′stōn′) *n.* 1. A stone forming a hearth. 2. The fireside; home.

heart·i·ly (här′tə·lē) *adv.* **1.** With sincerity or cordiality. **2.** Abundantly and with good appetite. **3.** Completely; thoroughly: to be *heartily* disgusted.

heart·land (härt′land′) *n.* In geopolitics, any central, strategically important area.

heart·less (härt′lis) *adj.* **1.** Having no sympathy or kindness; pitiless. **2.** Having little courage or enthusiasm; dispirited. — **heart′less·ly** *adv.* — **heart′less·ness** *n.*

heart-rend·ing (härt′ren′ding) *adj.* Causing great distress or emotional anguish; grievous.

hearts·ease (härts′ēz′) *n.* Freedom from sorrow or care. Also **heart′s′ease′.**

heart·sick (härt′sik′) *adj.* Deeply disappointed or despondent. Also **heart′sore′** (-sôr′, -sōr′).

heart-strick·en (härt′strik′ən) *adj.* Overwhelmed with grief or fear. Also **heart′-struck′** (-struk′).

heart·strings (härt′stringz′) *n.pl.* The strongest feelings or affections.

heart-to-heart (härt′tə-härt′) *adj.* Marked by frankness, intimacy, and sincerity.

heart·wood (härt′wŏŏd′) *n.* *Bot.* The duramen.

heart·y (här′tē) *adj.* **heart·i·er, heart·i·est** **1.** Full of affectionate warmth or cordiality. **2.** Strongly felt; unrestrained. **3.** Healthy and strong. **4.** Supplying or enjoying abundant nourishment: a *hearty* meal; a *hearty* appetite. — *n.* *pl.* **heart·ies** A hearty fellow. — **heart′i·ness** *n.*

heat (hēt) *n.* **1.** The state or quality of being hot; hotness; also, degree of hotness. **2.** That which raises the temperature; also, the rise itself. **3.** *Physics* A form of energy associated with and proportional to the molecular motions of a substance or body. ◆ Collateral adjective: *thermal.* **4.** The sensation produced by hotness. **5.** Condition, appearance, or color indicating high temperature. **6.** Hot weather or climate. **7.** Warmth supplied for a building, room, etc. **8.** *Metall.* A single heating or smelting operation, as in working iron or steel. **9.** A single effort or trial, esp. in a race. **10.** Great intensity of feeling: the *heat* of debate. **11.** The highest point of excitement or fury: the *heat* of battle. **12.** *Zool.* a Sexual excitement. b The period of sexual excitement. **13.** *U.S. Slang* a Any vigorous activity. b In the underworld, pressure applied to obtain information; also, intensive police action. — *v.t. & v.i.* **1.** To make or become hot or warm. **2.** To excite or become excited. [OE *hātu*] — **heat′ed** *adj.* — **heat′ed·ly** *adv.*

heat·er (hē′tər) *n.* An apparatus for producing heat.

heat exhaustion A mild form of heat stroke.

heath (hēth) *n.* **1.** Any of a large genus of hardy evergreen shrubs, including the arbutus, azalea, and rhododendron. **2.** The common heather. **3.** *Brit.* An area of open land overgrown with heath or coarse herbage. [OE *hǣth*]

hea·then (hē′thən) *n.* *pl.* **·thens** or **·then** **1.** One who has not adopted Christianity, Judaism, or Islam. **2.** In the Old Testament, a non-Jew; Gentile. **3.** Any irreligious or uncultivated person. — *adj.* **1.** Unbelieving; irreligious. **2.** Of or pertaining to heathen peoples. [OE *hǣthen.* Akin to HEATH.] — **hea′then·dom** *n.* — **hea′then·ish** *adj.* — **hea′then·ish·ly** *adv.* — **hea′then·ish·ness** *n.* — **hea′then·ism** *n.*

heath·er (heth′ər) *n.* **1.** A hardy evergreen shrub related to the heath and having pinkish flowers. **2.** A dull, grayish red color. [ME *hadder*] — **heath′er·y** *adj.*

heath grouse A grouse found in Great Britain, the male of which is mostly black: also called *black grouse.* Also **heath·bird** (hēth′bûrd′), **heath cock.**

heat lightning A fitful play of lightning without thunder, sometimes seen near the horizon on hot evenings.

heat prostration Heat exhaustion.

heat stroke A state of exhaustion or collapse, usu. accompanied by fever, caused by excessive heat.

heat wave A period of very hot weather.

heave (hēv) *v.* **heaved** or (*esp. Naut.*) **hove, heav·ing** *v.t.* **1.** To throw or hurl, esp. with great effort. **2.** To raise with effort. **3.** To cause to rise or bulge. **4.** To utter painfully. **5.** *Naut.* a To pull or haul on (a rope, cable, etc.). b To cause (a ship) to move in a specified direction by or as by hauling on cables or ropes. — *v.i.* **6.** To rise or swell up; bulge. **7.** To rise and fall repeatedly. **8.** To vomit; retch. **9.** *Naut.* a To move or proceed: said of ships. b To haul or pull, as on a rope. — **heave, ho!** *Naut.* Pull (or push) hard together! — **to heave in** (or **into**) **sight** To appear to rise into view. — **to heave to** **1.** To bring (a ship) to a standstill by heading into the wind with the sails hauled in or shortened. **2.** To cause a ship to lie to, as in a storm. — *n.* The act or exertion of heaving. [OE *hebban* to lift] — **heav′er** *n.*

heav·en (hev′ən) *n.* **1.** *Theol.* The abode of God and his angels, where virtuous souls receive eternal reward after death. **2.** In various religious systems, any supernatural region inhabited by a deity or deities, slain heroes, etc. **3.** *Usu. pl.* The regions around and above the earth; sky. **4.** Any condition of great happiness. **5.** Any place resembling heaven. [OE *heofon*] — **heav′en·li·ness** *n.*

Heav·en (hev′ən) God or the celestial powers.

heav·en·ly (hev′ən·lē) *adj.* **1.** Of or belonging to the heaven of God. **2.** Of or pertaining to the sky. **3.** Full of the beauty and peace befitting heaven. — **heav′en·li·ness** *n.*

heav·en·ward (hev′ən·wərd) *adv.* Toward heaven. Also **heav′en·wards.** — *adj.* Directed toward heaven.

heav·i·er-than-air (hev′ē·ər-thən-âr′) *adj.* Having a weight greater than that of the air it displaces: said of airplanes, etc.

Heav·i·side layer (hev′i·sīd) The lower region of the ionosphere, about 60 miles above the earth, that reflects radio waves of relatively low frequency back to the earth. [after O. *Heaviside,* 1850–1925, English physicist]

heav·y (hev′ē) *adj.* **heav·i·er, heav·i·est** **1.** Having great weight; hard to move. **2.** Having relatively great weight in relation to size: the *heavy* metals. **3.** Having more than usual quantity, volume, etc.: a *heavy* snowfall. **4.** Practicing or indulging on a large scale: a *heavy* smoker. **5.** Having force and severity: a *heavy* blow. **6.** Exceeding the usual weight: *heavy* woolens. **7.** Having great importance; grave; serious: a *heavy* responsibility. **8.** Hard to do or accomplish: *heavy* labor. **9.** Hard to endure or bear; oppressive: *heavy* taxes. **10.** Of food, not easily digested. **11.** Of bread, pastry, etc., dense in texture; poorly leavened. **12.** Giving an impression of weight or ponderousness; thick: *heavy* lines. **13.** Despondent: a *heavy* heart. **14.** Lacking animation and grace; tedious: a *heavy* prose style. **15.** Lacking precision and delicacy: a *heavy* hand. **16.** Permeating and strong: a *heavy* odor. **17.** Profound; unbroken: a *heavy* silence. **18.** Showing fatigue: *heavy* eyes. **19.** Producing massive or basic goods: *heavy* industry. **20.** Weighted down. **21.** Pregnant. **22.** In the theater, designating a serious or tragic role, or the role of a villain. **23.** *Physics* Designating an isotope having a mass greater than that of others occurring in the same element: *heavy* hydrogen. **24.** *Mil.* a Designating the more massive types of weapons. b Formerly, designating troops or units with relatively massive equipment. — *adv.* Heavily. — **to hang heavy** To drag by tediously, as time. — *n.* *pl.* **heav·ies** **1.** In the theater, the role of a villainous or tragic personage; also, the actor portraying him. **2.** *U.S. Informal* In sports, a heavyweight. [OE *hefig*] — **heav′i·ly** *adv.* — **heav′i·ness** *n.*

heav·y-du·ty (hev′ē·dōō′tē, -dyōō′-) *adj.* Strongly constructed for long strain, hard use, etc.

heav·y-hand·ed (hev′ē·han′did) *adj.* **1.** Bungling; clumsy. **2.** Oppressive; domineering; cruel. — **heav′y-hand′ed·ly** *adv.* — **heav′y-hand′ed·ness** *n.*

heav·y-heart·ed (hev′ē·här′tid) *adj.* Melancholy; sad. — **heav′y-heart′ed·ly** *adv.* — **heav′y-heart′ed·ness** *n.*

heavy hydrogen Deuterium.

heav·y-lad·en (hev′ē·lād′n) *adj.* **1.** Bearing a heavy burden. **2.** Troubled; oppressed.

heavy spar Barite.

heavy water Deuterium oxide, D_2O, the compound of oxygen and the heavy isotope of hydrogen.

heav·y·weight (hev′ē·wāt′) *n.* **1.** A person or animal of much more than average weight. **2.** A boxer or wrestler over 175 pounds in weight. — *adj.* Of more than average weight or thickness.

heb·dom·a·dal (heb·dom′ə·dəl) *adj.* Weekly. Also **heb·dom′a·dar′y** (-der′ē). — **heb·dom′a·dal·ly** *adv.*

He·be (hē′bē) In Greek mythology, the goddess of youth and spring, cupbearer to the gods.

He·bra·ic (hi·brā′ik) *adj.* Relating to or characteristic of the Hebrew people and their culture and language. Also **He·bra′i·cal.** [< LL < Gk. *Hebraios* a Hebrew] — **He·bra′i·cal·ly** *adv.*

He·bra·ism (hē′brā·iz′əm, -brə-) *n.* **1.** A Hebrew idiom. **2.** Hebrew thought; character, practice, etc. **3.** The religion of the Hebrews; Judaism. — **He′bra·ist, He′brew·ist** *n.* — **He′bra·is′tic** or **·ti·cal** *adj.*

He·brew (hē′brōō) *n.* **1.** A member of that group of Semitic peoples claiming descent from the house of Abraham; Israelite; Jew. **2.** The ancient Semitic language of the Israelites as used in much of the Old Testament. **3.** The modern Hebrew language: official language of the republic of Israel. — **Epistle to the Hebrews** A book of the New Testament addressed to Hebrew Christians: also **Hebrews.** — *adj.* Hebraic; Jewish. [< OF < L < Gk. < Hebrew *'ibhri,* lit., one from beyond (Jordan)]

Hebrew calendar See (Hebrew) CALENDAR.

Hec·a·te (hek′ə·tē) In Greek mythology, a goddess of earth, moon, and underworld: also spelled *Hekate.*

heck (hek) *interj.* *Slang* Darn: a euphemism for *hell.*

heck·le (hek′əl) *v.t.* **·led, ·ling** To try to annoy with taunts, questions, etc. [ME *hechelen*] — **heck′ler** *n.*

hec·tare (hek′târ) *n.* A unit of area in the metric system: also spelled *hektare*. Abbr. *ha.* See table inside back cover.

hec·tic (hek′tik) *adj.* 1. Characterized by great excitement, turmoil, haste, etc.: a *hectic* trip. 2. Denoting a condition of body, as in wasting diseases. 3. Designating the fever accompanying wasting diseases. Also **hec′ti·cal.** [< F < LL < Gk. *hektikos* consumptive] — **hec′ti·cal·ly** *adv.*

hecto- *combining form* In the metric system and in technical usage, a hundred times (a specified unit). Also spelled *hekto-*. Also, before vowels, **hect-.** [< F < Gk. *hekaton* hundred]

hec·to·gram (hek′tə·gram) *n.* In the metric system, a measure of weight: also spelled *hektogram.* Also **hec′to·gramme.** Abbr. *hg.* See table inside back cover.

hec·to·graph (hek′tə·graf, -gräf) *n.* A gelatin pad for making multiple copies of a writing or drawing. — *v.t.* To copy by hectograph. — **hec′to·graph′ic** *adj.*

hec·to·li·ter (hek′tə·lē′tər) *n.* In the metric system, a measure of capacity. Also *esp. Brit.* **hec′to·li′tre.** Abbr. *hl, hl.* See table inside back cover.

hec·to·me·ter (hek′tə·mē′tər, hek·tom′ə·tər) *n.* In the metric system, a measure of length. Also *esp. Brit.* **hec′to·me′tre.** Abbr. *hm., hm* See table inside back cover.

hec·tor (hek′tər) *v.t. & v.i.* 1. To bully; bluster; rant. 2. To tease; torment. — *n.* A bully. [after *Hector*]

Hec·tor (hek′tər) In the *Iliad*, a Trojan hero, son of Priam and Hecuba: killed by Achilles.

Hec·u·ba (hek′yŏō·bə) In the *Iliad*, the wife of Priam and mother of Hector, Troilus, Paris, Cassandra, and others.

he'd (hēd) 1. He had. 2. He would.

hedge (hej) *n.* 1. A fence or barrier formed of privet or other bushes set close together; also, any boundary or barrier. 2. The act of hedging a bet, risk, etc.; also, that which is used to hedge. — *v.* **hedged, hedg·ing** *v.t.* 1. To border or separate with a hedge. 2. To set barriers and restrictions to, so as to hinder freedom of movement or action; hem: often with *in* or *about.* 3. To guard against undue loss from (a bet, investment, etc.) by making compensatory bets, etc. — *v.i.* 4. To make compensatory bets, etc., in order to restrict losses. 5. To avoid forthright statement or action. [OE *hegg*] — **hedg′er** *n.* — **hedg′y** *adj.*

hedge·hog (hej′hôg′, -hog′) *n.* 1. A small, nocturnal, insectivorous mammal of Europe, having stout spines on the back and sides. 2. *U.S.* The porcupine. 3. *Mil.* An obstacle made of barbed wire on frames.

EUROPEAN HEDGEHOG
(About 10 inches long)

hedge·hop (hej′hop′) *v.i.* **·hopped, ·hop·ping** To fly close to the ground in an airplane. — **hedge′hop′per** *n.*

hedge·row (hej′rō′) *n.* A dense row of bushes, trees, etc., planted as a hedge.

he·don·ism (hēd′n·iz′əm) *n.* 1. The doctrine that pleasure is the only proper goal of moral endeavor. 2. The pursuit of pleasure. [< Gk. *hēdonē* pleasure] — **he′don·ist** *n.* — **he′don·is′tic** *adj.* — **he·don·is′ti·cal·ly** *adv.*

-hedral *combining form* Having (a specified number of) sides or faces: *octahedral.*

-hedron *combining form* Having (a specified number of) sides or faces: *octahedron.* [< Gk. *hedra* surface]

heed (hēd) *v.t.* 1. To pay attention to; take more than casual notice of. — *v.i.* 2. To pay attention; listen. — *n.* Careful attention. [OE *hēdan*] — **heed′er** *n.*

heed·ful (hēd′fəl) *adj.* Giving heed; attentive; mindful. — **heed′ful·ly** *adv.* — **heed′ful·ness** *n.*

heed·less (hēd′lis) *adj.* Not showing any heed or attention; reckless. — **heed′less·ly** *adv.* — **heed′less·ness** *n.*

hee·haw (hē′hô′) *n.* The braying sound of a donkey. — *v.i.* To bray. [Imit.]

heel¹ (hēl) *n.* 1. In man, the rounded posterior part of the foot under and in back of the ankle; also, the rounded part of the palm of the hand nearest the wrist. 2. The analogous part of the hind foot of an animal. 3. That part of a shoe, stocking, etc., covering the heel. 4. In a shoe or boot, the built-up portion on which the rear of the foot rests. 5. Something analogous to the human heel, as the rounded end of a loaf of bread. 6. *Slang* A habitually dishonorable person; contemptible chiseler. — **at heel** Close behind. — **down at the heel** 1. Having the heels of one's shoes worn down. 2. Shabby; rundown. — **on** (or **upon**) **the heels of** 1. Right behind. 2. Close after; quickly following. — **to cool one's heels** To be kept waiting. — **to heel** 1. To an attendant position close behind one. 2. To submission; under control. — **to kick up one's heels** 1. To have a good time. 2. To let oneself go. — **to take to one's heels** To run away; flee. — *v.t.* 1. To supply with a heel, as a shoe. 2. To pursue closely. 3. *U.S. Slang* To supply with something, esp. with money or a weapon. — *v.i.* 4. To move the heels. 5. To follow at one's heels. [OE *hēla*] — **heel′less** *adj.*

heel² (hēl) *Naut. v.t. & v.i.* To lean or cause to lean to one side; cant, as a ship. — *n.* The act of heeling; a cant; list: also **heel′ing.** [Earlier *heeld*, OE *hieldan*]

heel bone The calcaneus.

heeled (hēld) *adj.* 1. Having heels: *high-heeled.* 2. *U.S. Slang* Supplied with money or a weapon.

heel·er (hē′lər) *n.* 1. One who heels shoes. 2. *U.S. Slang* A ward heeler.

heel·tap (hēl′tap′) *n.* 1. A thickness of leather on the heel of a shoe. 2. A small quantity of liquor left in a glass.

heft (heft) *Informal v.t.* 1. To test or gauge the weight of by lifting. 2. To lift up; heave. — *v.i.* 3. To weigh. — *n.* 1. Weight. 2. *U.S.* The bulk or gist. [Akin to HEAVE]

heft·y (hef′tē) *adj.* **heft·i·er, heft·i·est** *Informal* 1. Heavy; weighty. 2. Big and powerful; muscular.

He·ge·li·an·ism (hə·gā′lē·ən·iz′əm) *n.* The philosophical doctrine of Hegel that dialectic reasoning, a process whereby thought passes repeatedly in ascending stages from thesis to antithesis to synthesis, can unravel the order of development in which human consciousness and reality participate. Also **He·ge′lism** (hā′gəl·iz′əm). — **He·ge′lian** *n. & adj.*

he·gem·o·ny (hə·jem′ə·nē, hej′ə·mō′nē, hē′jə-) *n. pl.* **·nies** Domination or leadership; esp., the predominant influence of one state over others. [< Gk. *hēgeesthai* to lead] — **heg·e·mon·ic** (hej′ə·mon′ik) *adj.*

he·gi·ra (hi·jī′rə, hej′ə·rə) *n.* Any precipitate departure: also spelled *hejira.* [< Med.L < Arabic *hijrah* departure]

He·gi·ra (hi·jī′rə, hej′ə·rə) *n.* 1. The flight of Mohammed from Mecca to Medina in 622, now taken as the beginning of the Moslem era. 2. The Moslem era. Also spelled *Hejira.*

heif·er (hef′ər) *n.* A young cow that has not produced a calf. [OE *heahfore*]

height (hīt) *n.* 1. The state or quality of being high or relatively high. 2. The distance from the base to the top; altitude. 3. The distance above a given level, as the sea or horizon. 4. *Often pl.* A lofty or high place; eminence. 5. The highest part of anything; summit. 6. The highest degree: the *height* of quality. [OE *hīehtho*]

height·en (hīt′n) *v.t. & v.i.* 1. To make or become high or higher; raise or lift. 2. To make or become more in degree, amount, size, etc.; intensify. — **height′en·er** *n.*

heil (hīl) *German interj.* Hail! — *v.t.* To salute with "heil."

hei·nous (hā′nəs) *adj.* Extremely wicked; atrocious; odious. [< OF *haine* hatred < *hair* to hate] — **hei′nous·ly** *adv.* — **hei′nous·ness** *n.*

heir (âr) *n.* 1. Anyone inheriting rank or property from a deceased person; also, anyone likely to inherit upon the death of an incumbent or holder. 2. One who or that which takes over or displays the qualities of some forerunner. [< OF < L *heres*] — **heir′ess** *n.fem.* — **heir′less** *adj.*

heir apparent *pl.* **heirs apparent** *Law* One who must by course of law become the heir if he survives his ancestor.

heir·dom (âr′dəm) *n.* Heirship; inheritance.

heir·loom (âr′lōōm) *n.* 1. Anything that has been handed down in a family for generations. 2. *Law* Those chattels and articles that descend to an heir along with the estate.

heir presumptive *pl.* **heirs presumptive** *Law* An heir whose claim to an estate may become void by the birth of a nearer relative.

heir·ship (âr′ship) *n.* 1. The state or condition of being an heir. 2. The right to inheritance.

heist (hīst) *v.t. U.S. Slang* To steal. [Var. of HOIST]

he·ji·ra (hi·jī′rə, hej′ə·rə) See HEGIRA.

He·ji·ra (hi·jī′rə, hej′ə·rə) See HEGIRA.

Hek·a·te (hek′ə·tē) See HECATE.

hek·tare (hek′târ), **hek·to·gram** (hek′tə·gram), etc. See HECTARE, etc.

hekto- See HECTO-.

held (held) Past tense of HOLD.

Helen of Troy In Greek mythology, the beautiful wife of Menelaus, king of Sparta. Her elopement to Troy with Paris caused the Trojan War.

hel·i·cal (hel′i·kəl) *adj.* Pertaining to or shaped like a helix.

hel·i·ces (hel′ə·sēz) Alternative plural of HELIX.

helico- *combining form* Spiral; helical. Also, before vowels, **helic-.** [< Gk. *helix* spiral]

hel·i·coid (hel′ə·koid) *adj.* Coiled spirally, as certain univalve shells. Also **hel′i·coid′al.** — *n. Geom.* A surface generated by a straight line moving along a fixed helix in such a way as to maintain a constant angle with its axis. [< Gk. *helikoeidēs* spiral-shaped] — **hel′i·coi′dal·ly** *adv.*

hel·i·con (hel′i·kon, -kən) *n. Music* A large, circular tuba. [< HELICON; infl. by HELIX]

Hel·i·con (hel′i·kon, -kən) A mountain in Greece, legendary home of the Muses. — **Hel·i·co·ni·an** (hel′i·kō′nē·ən) *adj.*

hel·i·cop·ter (hel′ə·kop′tər, hē′lə-) *n. Aeron.* A type of aircraft whose aerodynamic support is obtained from engine-driven airfoil blades rotating around a vertical axis, and that is capable of rising and descending vertically. [< F < Gk. *helix, -ikos* spiral + *pteron* wing]

helio- *combining form* Sun; of the sun. Also, before vowels, **heli-.** [< Gk. *hēlios* the sun]

he·li·o·cen·tric (hē′lē·ə·sen′trik) *adj.* Having or regarding the sun as the center. Also **he′li·o·cen′tri·cal.**

he·li·o·graph (hē′lē·ə·graf′, -gräf′) n. 1. Astron. An instrument for taking photographs of the sun. 2. A mirror for signaling by flashes of light. Also **he/li·o** (-lē·ō). — v.t. & v.i. To signal with a heliograph. — **he·li·og·ra·pher** (hē′lē·og′rə·fər) n. — **he/li·o·graph/ic** adj. — **he/li·og/ra·phy** n.

He·li·os (hē′lē·os) In Greek mythology, the sun god.

he·li·o·scope (hē′lē·ə·skōp′) n. Astron. A device within a telescope by which the eyes are protected from pain or injury while observing the sun.

he·li·o·ther·a·py (hē′lē·ō·ther′ə·pē) n. Med. Exposure to the sun for purposes of treatment.

he·li·o·trope (hē′lē·ə·trōp′, hēl′yə-) n. 1. An herb of the borage family, with white or purplish fragrant flowers. 2. Any plant that turns toward the sun. 3. The bloodstone. 4. A soft, rosy purple. [< F < L < Gk. < hēlios sun + trepein to turn]

he·li·ot·ro·pism (hē′lē·ot′rə·piz′əm) n. Biol. The tendency of some organisms to move or turn toward or away from the sun. Also **he/li·ot/ro·py**. — **he·li·o·trop/ic** adj.

hel·i·port (hel′ə·pôrt′, -pōrt′, hē′lə-) n. An airport for helicopters.

he·li·um (hē′lē·əm) n. An inert, odorless, nonflammable, gaseous element (symbol He) that is found chiefly in certain natural gas deposits, used to inflate balloons, dirigibles, etc. See ELEMENT. [< NL < Gk. hēlios sun]

he·lix (hē′liks) n. pl. **he·lix·es** or **hel·i·ces** (hel′ə·sēz) 1. A line, thread, wire, or the like, curved as if wound in a single layer round a cylinder; a form like a screw thread. 2. Any spiral. 3. Anat. The recurved border of the external ear. 4. Archit. A small volute. [< L, spiral < Gk.]

hell (hel) n. 1. Sometimes cap. In various religions, the abode of the dead or the place of punishment for the wicked after death; the abode of evil spirits. 2. Any condition of great mental or physical suffering; also, anything causing such suffering. — **a** (or one) **hell of a** Slang A remarkably bad, good, difficult, etc. (thing). — **like hell** Slang 1. Very much, very fast, very bad, etc.: He ran like hell. 2. Not at all; never. Like hell he will! — **to be hell on** Slang 1. To be damaging or harmful to. 2. To be unpleasant or difficult for. 3. To be very harsh or strict with. — **to catch** (or get) **hell** U.S. Slang To be roundly scolded or punished, as for a misdeed. — **to give** (someone) **hell** Slang To upbraid or punish (someone) severely. — **to raise hell** Slang To create a disturbance. — interj. An exclamation used as an imprecation or an expression of anger or impatience. [OE hel]

he'll (hel) He will.

Hel·las (hel′əs) Ancient or modern Greece. [< Gk.]

hell·bend·er (hel′ben′dər) n. U.S. A large aquatic salamander common to the Ohio River Valley.

hell·bent (hel′bent′) adj. U.S. Slang Determined to have or do; recklessly eager: hell-bent for home.

hell·cat (hel′kat′) n. 1. A shrewish woman. 2. A witch.

hel·le·bore (hel′ə·bôr, -bōr) n. 1. A perennial herb of the crowfoot family, having serrated leaves and large flowers; esp. the black hellebore of Europe, the root of which is a powerful cathartic. [< L < Gk. helleboros]

Hel·lene (hel′ēn) n. A Greek. Also **Hel·le/ni·an**. [< Gk.]

Hel·len·ic (he·len′ik, -lē′nik) adj. Greek; Grecian. — n. A group of Indo-European languages, including Greek.

Hel·len·ism (hel′ə·niz′əm) n. 1. Ancient Greek character, ideals, or civilization. 2. An idiom or turn of phrase peculiar to Greek. 3. Assimilation of Greek speech, ideas, and culture. — **Hel/le·nist** n.

Hel·le·nis·tic (hel′ə·nis′tik) adj. 1. Pertaining to, resembling, or characteristic of the Hellenists or Hellenism. 2. Of or pertaining to the period that began with the conquests of Alexander the Great and ended about 300 years later, characterized by the spread of Greek language and culture throughout the Near East. Also **Hel/le·nis/ti·cal**.

Hel·le·nize (hel′ə·nīz) v.t. & v.i. ·nized, ·niz·ing To make or become Greek; adopt or imbue with Greek language or customs. — **Hel/le·ni·za/tion** n. — **Hel/le·niz/er** n.

Hel·les·pont (hel′əs·pont) The ancient name for the DARDANELLES.

hell·fire (hel′fīr′) n. The flames or the punishment of hell.

hel·lion (hel′yən) n. Informal A person who delights in deviltry; a mischief-maker. [< HELL]

hell·ish (hel′ish) adj. 1. Of, like, or pertaining to hell. 2. Fiendish; horrible. — **hell/ish·ly** adv. — **hell/ish·ness** n.

hel·lo (hə·lō′) interj. 1. An exclamation of greeting, esp. over the telephone. 2. An exclamation used to gain attention. 3. An exclamation of surprise. — n. pl. ·loes The saying or calling of "hello." — v.t. & v.i. ·loed, ·lo·ing To call or say "hello."

helm (helm) n. 1. Naut. The steering apparatus of a vessel, esp. the tiller or wheel. 2. Any place of control or responsibility; administration. — v.t. To manage the helm of; steer; direct. [OE helma rudder]

hel·met (hel′mit) n. 1. Any of a number of protective coverings for the head; as: **a** The topmost piece of a suit of medieval or ancient armor. **b** The metal headguard worn by modern soldiers. **c** The leather or plastic headgear used by football players. **d** A head protector, as worn by firemen, welders, divers, etc. **e** A pith sun hat worn in hot countries. 2. Something resembling a helmet in appearance or position. [< OF, dim. of helme helmet < Gmc.] — **hel/met·ed** adj.

hel·minth (hel′minth) n. A worm; esp., a parasitic intestinal worm. [< Gk. helmins, -inthos worm]

helms·man (helmz′mən) n. pl. ·men (-mən) A steersman; one who guides a ship.

hel·ot (hel′ət, hē′lət) n. 1. A slave; serf. 2. Usu. cap. One of a class of serfs in ancient Sparta. [< L < Gk., appar. < Helos, a Laconian town enslaved by Sparta] — **hel/ot·ry** n.

help (help) v.t. 1. To assist (someone) in doing something; cooperate with. 2. To assist (someone or something) in some action, change, etc.: with onto, into, out of, up, down, etc. 3. To provide aid or relief to. 4. To be or be considered, responsible for: He can't help being lame. 5. To refrain from: I couldn't help laughing. 6. To remedy; alleviate. 7. To contribute to. 8. To serve; wait on, as a salesclerk. — v.i. 9. To give assistance. — **cannot help but** Cannot avoid; be obliged to. — **to help oneself** 1. To serve oneself, as with food. 2. To take without requesting or being offered. — n. 1. The act of helping. 2. Remedy; relief. 3. One who or that which gives assistance. 4. Any hired worker or helper. [OE helpan] — **help/er** n.

help·ful (help′fəl) adj. Affording help; giving service; beneficial. — **help/ful·ly** adv. — **help/ful·ness** n.

help·ing (hel′ping) n. 1. The act of assisting or aiding. 2. A single portion of food served at table.

help·less (help′lis) adj. 1. Unable to help oneself; dependent; feeble. 2. Incompetent; incapable. 3. Without recourse to help. — **help/less·ly** adv. — **help/less·ness** n.

help·mate (help′māt′) n. 1. A helper; partner. 2. A wife. Also **help·meet** (help′mēt′).

hel·ter-skel·ter (hel′tər·skel′tər) adv. In a hurried and confused manner. — adj. Hurried and confused. — n. Disorderly hurry; confused and hasty action. [Imit.]

helve (helv) n. The handle, as of an ax or hatchet. — v.t. **helved, helv·ing** To furnish with a helve. [OE helfe]

Hel·ve·tia (hel·vē′shə) n. 1. A country of Roman times including a large part of what is now Switzerland. 2. The Latin name for SWITZERLAND. — **Hel·ve/tian** adj. & n.

hem¹ (hem) n. 1. A finished edge made on a piece of fabric or a garment by turning the raw edge under and sewing it down. 2. Any similar border or edging. — v.t. **hemmed, hem·ming** 1. To provide with a hem. 2. To shut in; enclose; restrict: usu. with in, about, etc. [OE] — **hem/mer** n.

hem² (hem) interj. A sound made as in clearing the throat to attract attention, cover embarrassment, etc.; ahem. — v.i. **hemmed, hem·ming** 1. To make the sound "hem." 2. To hesitate in speaking. — **to hem and haw** To hesitate in speaking so as to keep from being explicit. [Imit.]

hem- See also words beginning HAEM-.

hem- See HEMO-.

hema- combining form Blood. Also spelled haema-. [< Gk. haima blood]

he·mal (hē′məl) adj. 1. Pertaining to blood or the vascular system. 2. Pertaining to or situated on the side of the body that contains the heart. Also spelled haemal.

he-man (hē′man′) n. pl. ·men (-men′) Informal A virile, muscular man.

hem·a·tite (hem′ə·tīt, hē′mə-) n. Red ferric oxide, Fe_2O_3, an ore of iron, occurring in masses and crystallizing in the hexagonal system: also called ferric oxide. Also spelled haematite. [< L < Gk. < haima blood] — **hem·a·tit·ic** (hem′ə·tit′ik, hē′mə-) adj.

hemato- combining form Blood. Also, before vowels, he-mat-. Also spelled haemato-. [< Gk. haima, haimatos, blood]

he·ma·tol·o·gy (hē′mə·tol′ə·jē, hem′ə-) n. The branch of biology that treats of the blood and its diseases. Also **he/ma·to·log/i·a** (-tə·lōj′ē·ə). — **he/ma·to·log/ist** n.

he·ma·tol·y·sis (hē′mə·tol′ə·sis, hem′ə-) n. Hemolysis.

he·ma·to·ma (hē′mə·tō′mə, hem′ə-) n. pl. ·to·ma·ta (-tō′mə·tə) or ·to·mas Pathol. A tumor or swelling formed by the effusion of blood.

hemi- prefix Half: hemisphere. Also, before vowels, hem-. [< Gk., half]

-hemia See -EMIA.

hem·ic (hē′mik, hem′ik) adj. Of or pertaining to blood.

hem·i·dem·i·sem·i·qua·ver (hem′ē·dem′ē·sem′ē·kwā′vər) n. Music Chiefly Brit. A sixty-fourth note.

hem·i·ple·gi·a (hem′i·plē′jē·ə) n. Pathol. Paralysis of one side of the body. — **hem/i·ple/gic** (-plē′jik, -plej′ik) adj.

he·mip·ter·ous (hi·mip′tər·əs) adj. Of an order of insects generally having sucking mouth parts and four wings, including the cicadas, crickets, etc. [< NL < Gk. *hēmi-* half + *pteron* wing] — **he·mip'ter·an** *adj. & n.*

hem·i·sphere (hem'ə·sfir) *n.* **1.** A half-sphere formed by a plane passing through the center of the sphere. **2.** A half of the terrestrial or celestial globe, or a map or projection of one. The world is usu. divided either at the equator into the **Northern** and **Southern Hemispheres,** or at some meridian between Europe and America into the **Eastern** and **Western Hemispheres.** [< F < L < Gk. *hēmi-* half + *sphaira* sphere] — **hem·is·spher·ic** (hem'ə·sfir'ik, -sfer-) *adj.*

hem·i·stich (hem'i·stik) *n.* Half a line of verse.

hem·line (hem'līn) *n.* The line formed by the lower edge of a garment, as a dress or coat.

hem·lock (hem'lok) *n.* **1.** One of several North American or Asian evergreen trees of the pine family, having coarse, nonresinous wood used for paper pulp. Also **hemlock spruce.** **2.** A large, biennial herb of the parsley family, yielding a poison: also **poison hemlock.** [OE *hymlice*]

hemo- *combining form* Blood. Also, before vowels, **hem-.** Also spelled **haemo-.** [< Gk. *haima* blood]

he·mo·glo·bin (hē'mə·glō'bin, hem'ə-) *n. Biochem.* The respiratory pigment in red blood corpuscles, composed of globin and heme, and serving as a carrier of oxygen.

he·mol·y·sis (hē·mol'ə·sis) *n.* Breakdown of red blood corpuscles with liberation of hemoglobin: also called *hematolysis.* — **he·mo·lyt·ic** (hē'mə·lit'ik, hem'ə-) *adj.*

he·mo·phil·i·a (hē'mə·fil'ē·ə, -fil'yə, hem'ə-) *n. Pathol.* A disorder characterized by immoderate bleeding even from slight injuries. [< NL < Gk. *haima* blood + *philia* fondness] — **he'mo·phil'i·ac, he'mo·phile'** (-fīl, -fil) *n.*

he·mo·phil·ic (hē'mə·fil'ik, hem'ə-) *adj.* **1.** Of hemophilia. **2.** Thriving in blood, as certain bacteria.

hem·or·rhage (hem'ər·ij, hem'rij) *n.* Copious discharge of blood from a ruptured blood vessel. — *v.i.* **·rhaged, ·rhag·ing** To bleed copiously. [< L < Gk. *haima* blood + *rhēgnynai* to burst] — **hem·or·rhag·ic** (hem'ə·raj'ik) *adj.*

hem·or·rhoid (hem'ə·roid) *n. Pathol.* A tumor or dilation of a vein in the anal region, usu. painful: also, in the plural, *piles.* [< F < L < Gk. < *haima* blood + *rheein* to flow] — **hem·or·rhoi·dal** (hem'ə·roid'l) *adj.*

he·mo·stat (hē'mə·stat, hem'ə-) *n. Med.* A device or drug for checking the flow of blood from a ruptured vessel.

he·mo·stat·ic (hē'mə·stat'ik, hem'ə-) *Med. adj.* **1.** Stopping the flow of blood. **2.** Preventive of bleeding.

hemp (hemp) *n.* **1.** A tall, annual herb of the mulberry family, native in Asia but cultivated elsewhere. **2.** The tough, strong fiber from this plant, used for cloth and cordage. **3.** A narcotic prepared from the plant. [OE *henep*]

hemp·en (hem'pən) *adj.* Made of or like hemp.

hem·stitch (hem'stich') *n.* The ornamental finishing of a hem, made by pulling out several threads and drawing the cross threads together in groups. — *v.t.* To embroider with a hemstitch. — **hem'stitch'er** *n.*

hen (hen) *n.* **1.** The mature female of the domestic fowl and related birds. **2.** The female of the lobster. [OE *henn*]

hen·bane (hen'bān) *n.* A poisonous Old World herb of the nightshade family, with sticky, malodorous foliage.

hence (hens) *adv.* **1.** As a consequence; therefore; thus. **2.** From this time or date: a week *hence;* also, ever afterwards; henceforth. **3.** Away from this place. — *interj. Archaic & Poetic* Go! Depart! [ME < OE *heonan* from here]

hence·forth (hens'fôrth', -fôrth'; hens'fôrth', -fôrth') *adv.* From this time on. Also **hence'for'ward** (-fôr'ward).

hench·man (hench'mən) *n. pl.* **·men** (-mən) **1.** A faithful follower. **2.** *U.S.* A political supporter who works chiefly for personal gain. [ME < OE *hengst* horse + *man* groom]

hen·e·quen (hen'ə·kin) *n.* **1.** A tough fiber obtained from the leaves of a Mexican plant. **2.** The plant. Also **hen'e·quin.** [< Sp. < Taino]

hen·na (hen'ə) *n.* **1.** An ornamental Oriental shrub or small tree. **2.** A cosmetic made from its leaves, used for dyeing the hair, fingernails, etc. **3.** A color varying from reddish orange to coppery brown. — *v.* **hen·naed, hen·na·ing** *v.t.* To dye with henna. [< Arabic *henna*]

hen·ner·y (hen'ər·ē) *n. pl.* **·ner·ies** A place where hens are kept.

hen·peck (hen'pek') *v.t.* To domineer over or harass (one's husband) by nagging, ill temper, and petty annoyances. **hen·pecked** (hen'pekt') *adj.* Dominated by one's wife.

hen·ry (hen'rē) *n. pl.* **·ries** or **·rys** *Electr.* The unit equal to the inductance of a circuit in which the variation of a current at the rate of one ampere per second induces an electromotive force of one volt. [after Joseph Henry, 1797–1878, U.S. physicist]

hep·a·rin (hep'ə·rin) *n. Biochem.* A substance found in liver and other tissues, having the power to prevent coagulation of blood, used in medicine. [< Gk. *hēpar* liver]

he·pat·ic (hi·pat'ik) *adj.* **1.** Of or like the liver. **2.** Acting upon the liver. **3.** Liver-colored. — *n.* A drug acting upon the liver. Also **he·pat'i·cal.** [< L < Gk. *hēpar* liver]

he·pat·i·ca (hi·pat'ə·kə) *n. pl.* **·cas** or **·cae** (-sē) A small perennial herb with delicate flowers: also called *liverwort.* [< NL < L *hepaticus* of the liver]

hepatico- *combining form* Hepato-.

hep·a·ti·tis (hep'ə·tī'tis) *n. Pathol.* Inflammation of the liver.

hepato- *combining form* Pertaining to the liver. Also, before vowels, **hepat-.** [< Gk. *hēpar, hēpatos* the liver]

Hep·ple·white (hep'əl·hwīt) *adj.* Denoting an English style of furniture characterized by graceful curves and light, slender woodwork, developed in the reign of George III. [after G. Hepplewhite, died 1786, the designer]

hepta- *combining form* Seven. Also, before vowels, **hept-.** [< Gk. *hepta* seven]

hep·ta·gon (hep'tə·gon) *n.* A polygon having seven sides and seven angles. — **hep·tag·o·nal** (hep·tag'ə·nəl) *adj.*

hep·tam·e·ter (hep·tam'ə·tər) *n.* In prosody, a line of verse consisting of seven metrical feet.

hep·tane (hep'tān) *n. Chem.* A colorless flammable liquid hydrocarbon of the methane series, C_7H_{16}, used as a solvent and in the determination of the octane number of motor fules.

HEPPLEWHITE CHAIR

her (hûr) *pron.* The objective case of the pronoun *she.* — *pronominal adj.* The possessive case of *she.* [OE *hire*]

He·ra (hir'ə) In Greek mythology, the queen of the gods and goddess of women and marriage, sister and wife of Zeus: identified with the Roman *Juno.* Also spelled *Here.*

Her·a·cles (her'ə·klēz) Hercules. Also **Her'a·kles.**

her·ald (her'əld) *n.* **1.** Any bearer of important news; messenger. **2.** One who or that which shows what is to follow; harbinger. **3.** *Brit.* An official whose duty is to grant or record arms, trace genealogies, etc. **4.** Formerly, an officer who carried messages, arranged tournaments, etc. — *v.t.* To announce or proclaim publicly. [< OF < OHG *heren* to call] — **he·ral·dic** (hi·ral'dik) *adj.*

her·ald·ry (her'əl·drē) *n. pl.* **·ries** **1.** The art or science that treats of armorial bearings, genealogies, etc., as in heraldic symbolism. **2.** The office or function of a herald.

herb (ûrb, hûrb) *n.* **1.** A plant without woody tissue, that withers and dies after flowering. **2.** Any such plant as a medicine, seasoning, scent, etc. [< L *herba* grass, herbage]

her·ba·ceous (hûr·bā'shəs) *adj.* **1.** Like herbs. **2.** Having the semblance, color, or structure of a leaf.

herb·age (ûr'bij, hûr'-) *n.* **1.** Herbs collectively, esp. pasturage. **2.** The succulent parts of herbaceous plants.

herb·al (hûr'bəl, ûr'-) *adj.* Of or pertaining to herbs. — *n.* Formerly, a treatise on herbs or plants.

herb·al·ist (hûr'bəl·ist, ûr'-) *n.* A dealer in herbs.

her·bar·i·um (hûr·bâr'ē·əm) *n. pl.* **·bar·i·ums** or **·bar·i·a** (-bâr'ē·ə). **1.** A collection of dried plants scientifically arranged. **2.** A room or building containing such a collection.

her·biv·o·rous (hûr·biv'ər·əs) *adj.* **1.** Feeding on vegetable matter; plant-eating. **2.** Belonging to a group of mammals that feed mainly on herbage, as cows, horses, camels, etc. [< L *herba* grass] — **her·biv'o·rous·ly** *adv.*

her·cu·le·an (hûr·kyōō'lē·ən, hûr'kyə·lē'ən) *adj.* **1.** Having great strength. **2.** Requiring great strength.

Her·cu·le·an (hûr·kyōō'lē·ən, hûr'kyə·lē'ən) *adj.* Of or pertaining to Hercules (Heracles); Heraclean.

Her·cu·les (hûr'kyə·lēz) In classical mythology, the son of Zeus, renowned for his great strength: also called *Heracles.* — *n.* **1.** Any man of great strength. **2.** A constellation.

herd (hûrd) *n.* **1.** A number of cattle or other animals feeding, moving about, or kept together. **2.** A large crowd of people: a contemptuous term. — *v.t. & v.i.* To bring or drive together in a herd. — **Syn.** See FLOCK. [OE *heord*]

-herd *combining form* Herdsman: *swineherd, cowherd,* etc. [OE *hierde* herdsman]

herds·man (hûrdz'mən) *n. pl.* **·men** (-mən) *Brit.* One who owns or tends a herd. Also **herd'er, herd'man.**

here (hir) *adv.* **1.** In, at, or about this place: opposed to *there.* Also used to indicate or emphasize: George *here* is a good swimmer. **2.** To this place; hither. **3.** At this point in time, in an action, etc.: *Here* you begin; *Here* are my reasons. **4.** In the present life: distinguished from *hereafter.* — *interj.* An exclamation used to answer a roll call, attract attention, call an animal, etc. — **here and there 1.** Irregularly scattered. **2.** Hither and thither. — **here goes!** For better or worse, I start now! — **neither here nor there** Beside the point; irrelevant. — *n.* **1.** This place. **2.** This time; this life: the *here* and now. [OE *hēr*]

He·re (hir'ē) See HERA.

here·a·bout (hir'ə·bout') *adv.* About this place; in this vicinity. Also **here'a·bouts'.**

here·af·ter (hir·af'tər, -äf'-) *adv.* **1.** At some future time. **2.** From this time forth. **3.** In the state of life after death. — *n.* A future state or existence. [OE *hēræfter*]

here·at (hir·at') *adv.* **1.** At this time. **2.** Because of this.

here·by (hir·bī′) *adv.* By means or by virtue of this.

he·red·i·ta·ble (hə·red′i·tə·bəl) *adj.* Heritable. [< MF *héréditable*] **— he·red′i·ta·bil′i·ty** *n.* **— he·red′i·ta·bly** *adv.*

her·e·dit·a·ment (her′ə·dit′ə·mənt) *n. Law* Every kind of property capable of being inherited.

he·red·i·tar·y (hə·red′ə·ter′ē) *adj.* **1.** Derived from ancestors; inherited. **2.** Of or pertaining to heredity or inheritance. **3.** *Biol.* Transmitted or transmissible directly from an animal or plant to its offspring: distinguished from *congenital.* **4.** *Law* **a** Passing by inheritance to an heir. **b** Holding possession or title through inheritance. **— he·red′i·tar′i·ly** *adv.* **— he·red′i·tar′i·ness** *n.*

he·red·i·ty (hə·red′ə·tē) *n. pl.* **·ties** *Biol.* **1.** Transmission of characteristics from parents to offspring. **2.** The tendency manifested by an organism to develop in the likeness of a progenitor. **3.** The sum total of an individual's inherited characteristics. [< F < L *hereditas, -tatis* inheritance]

Her·e·ford (her′ə·fərd, *U.S.* hûr′fərd) *n.* One of a breed of beef cattle having a white face and a red and white coat.

here·in (hir·in′) *adv.* **1.** In or into this place; in this. **2.** In this case, circumstance, matter, etc. [OE *hērinne*]

here·in·af·ter (hir′in·af′tər, -äf′-) *adv.* In a subsequent part of this document, deed, contract, etc.

here·in·be·fore (hir′in·bi·fôr′, -fōr′) *adv.* In a preceding part of this document, deed, contract, etc.

here·in·to (hir·in′tōō) *adv.* **1.** Into this place. **2.** Into this case, circumstance, matter, etc.

here·of (hir·uv′, -ov) *adv.* **1.** Of this. **2.** In regard to this.

here·on (hir·on′, -ôn′) *adv.* On this; hereupon.

her·e·sy (her′ə·sē) *n. pl.* **·sies 1.** A belief contrary to the established doctrines of a church or religious system. **2.** Any belief contrary to established doctrine. **3.** The holding of such a belief or opinion. [< OF < Gk. *hairesis* sect]

her·e·tic (her′ə·tik) *n.* **1.** One who holds beliefs or opinions contrary to the established doctrines of his religion. **2.** One who maintains unorthodox opinions on any subject.

he·ret·i·cal (hə·ret′i·kəl) *adj.* Of, pertaining to, or characterized by heresy. **— he·ret′i·cal·ly** *adv.*

here·to (hir·tōō′) *adv.* To this thing, matter, etc.

here·to·fore (hir′tə·fôr′, -fōr′) *adv.* Before now; previously.

here·un·der (hir·un′dər) *adv.* **1.** Under this heading, etc. **2.** Under the terms of this statement, etc.

here·un·to (hir·un·tōō′) *adv.* To this; hereto.

here·up·on (hir′ə·pon′, -pôn′) *adv.* Immediately resulting from or following this; upon this.

here·with (hir·with′, -with′) *adv.* **1.** Along with this. **2.** By means of or through this.

her·i·ta·ble (her′ə·tə·bəl) *adj.* **1.** That can be inherited. **2.** *Rare* Capable of inheriting. [< OF < *heriter* to inherit] **— her′i·ta·bil′i·ty** *n.* **— her′i·ta·bly** *adv.*

her·i·tage (her′ə·tij) *n.* **1.** That which is inherited. **2.** A cultural tradition, body of knowledge, etc., handed down from past times. **3.** *Law* Property that is or can be inherited by descendants. [< OF *heriter* to inherit]

her·i·tor (her′ə·tər) *n.* An inheritor. **— her′e·trix** or **her′i·trix** or **her′i·tress** (-tris) *n.fem.*

her·maph·ro·dite (hûr·maf′rə·dīt) *n.* **1.** An individual having both male and female reproductive organs. **2.** *Bot.* A plant having both stamens and pistils. *— adj.* Hermaphroditic. [after *Hermaphroditus*, son of Hermes, who became united with a nymph in a single body]

hermaphrodite brig *Naut.* A brigantine.

her·maph·ro·dit·ic (hûr·maf′rə·dit′ik) *adj.* Of, pertaining to, or characteristic of a hermaphrodite.

her·maph·ro·dit·ism (hûr·maf′rə·dīt·iz′əm) *n.* The state or condition of being a hermaphrodite.

Her·mes (hûr′mēz) In Greek mythology, the messenger of the gods, usually depicted with winged sandals, a hat, and a caduceus: identified with the Roman *Mercury.*

her·met·ic (hûr·met′ik) *adj.* **1.** Made impervious to air and liquids; airtight. **2.** Of or relating to alchemy; occult; magical. Also **her·met′i·cal.** [< Med.L *hermeticus*] **— her·met′i·cal·ly** *adv.*

her·mit (hûr′mit) *n.* **1.** One who abandons society and lives in seclusion, often for religious reasons. **2.** A molasses cooky. [< OF < LL < Gk. *erēmia* desert] **— her·mit′ic** or **·i·cal** *adj.* **— her·mit′i·cal·ly** *adv.*

her·mit·age (hûr′mə·tij) *n.* **1.** The retreat or dwelling of a hermit. **2.** Any secluded dwelling place.

hermit crab Any of various soft-bodied crustaceans that live in the empty shells of snails, etc.

her·ni·a (hûr′nē·ə) *n. pl.* **·ni·as** or **·ni·ae** (ni·ē) *Pathol.* The protrusion of an organ or part of an organ, as of the intestine, through an opening in the wall surrounding its; rupture. [< L] **— her′ni·al** *adj.*

hernio- *combining form* Hernia.

he·ro (hir′ō, hē′rō) *n. pl.* **·roes 1.** A man distinguished for exceptional courage, fortitude, or bold enterprise. **2.** One

idealized for superior qualities or deeds of any kind. **3.** The principal male character in a drama, fictional work, etc. **4.** In classical mythology and legend, a man of great nobility or physical prowess, often the son of a god and a mortal. **5.** *U.S.* A sandwich made with a loaf of bread cut lengthwise. [< L < Gk. *hērōs*]

He·ro (hir′ō) In Greek legend, a priestess whose lover, Leander, nightly swam the Hellespont to join her. Finding him drowned one night, she cast herself into the sea.

he·ro·ic (hi·rō′ik) *adj.* **1.** Characteristic of or befitting a hero. **2.** Resembling a hero. **3.** Showing great daring or boldness; extreme in action or effect: a *heroic* attempt. **4.** Of or pertaining to the heroes of antiquity. **5.** Relating to or describing a hero or heroic deeds: epic: *heroic* poetry. **6.** Grandiose in style or language. **7.** Of sculpture, considerably larger than life size. Also **he·ro′i·cal.** *— n.* **1.** *Often pl.* Heroic verse. **2.** *pl.* Melodramatic or extravagant language, action, or ideas. **— he·ro′i·cal·ly** *adv.*

heroic couplet An English verse form consisting of two rhyming lines of iambic pentameter.

heroic verse One of several verse forms used especially in epic and dramatic poetry, as the iambic pentameter of the English heroic couplet and blank verse.

her·o·in (her′ō·in) *n.* A white, odorless, crystalline derivative of morphine, $C_{21}H_{23}O_5N$, a powerful, habit-forming narcotic. [< G]

her·o·ine (her′ō·in) *n.fem.* **1.** A girl or woman of heroic character. **2.** The principal female character of a drama, fictional work, etc. [< L < Gk. *hērōinē*]

her·o·ism (her′ō·iz′əm) *n.* **1.** The character or qualities of a hero or heroine. **2.** Heroic behavior.

her·on (her′ən) *n.* **1.** Any of several wading birds, having a long neck, a long, slender bill, and long legs. **2.** Any of various similar or related birds, as the egret or the bittern. [< OF *hairon*, ult. < Gmc.]

her·on·ry (her′ən·rē) *n. pl.* **·ries** A place where herons congregate and breed.

hero worship Enthusiastic or extravagant admiration for heroes or other persons. **— hero worshiper**

her·pes (hûr′pēz) *n. Pathol.* A virus infection of the skin and mucous membranes, characterized by the eruption of blisters. [< L < Gk. *herpein* to creep]

herpes zos·ter (zos′tər) *Pathol.* Shingles. [< L, herpes + *zoster* (< Gk., girdle, belt)]

her·pe·tol·o·gy (hûr′pə·tol′ə·jē) *n.* The branch of zoology that treats of reptiles and amphibians. [< Gk. *herpeton* reptile + -LOGY] **— her·pe·to·log′i·cal** (hûr′pə·tə·loj′i·kəl) *adj.* **— her·pe·tol′o·gist** *n.*

Herr (her) *n. pl.* **Her·ren** (her′ən) *German* A title of address equivalent oo the English *Mister.* Abbr. *Hr.*

her·ring (her′ing) *n. pl.* **·rings** or **·ring 1.** A small food fish frequenting the North Atlantic, the young of which are canned as sardines, and the adults smoked, pickled, or salted. **2.** Any of various fish allied to the herring, as the shad, sardine, etc. [OE *hæring*]

her·ring·bone (her′ing·bōn′) *n.* **1.** A pattern utilizing a design, often repeated, resembling the spinal structure of a herring, in which the ribs form slanting parallel lines on either side of the spine. **2.** Something made in or consisting of such a pattern. *— adj.* Having or forming the pattern of a herringbone. *— v.* **·boned, ·bon·ing** *v.t.* **1.** To ornament with or arrange in a herringbone pattern. *— v.i.* **2.** To produce a herringbone pattern. **3.** In skiing, to walk up an incline with the skis pointed outward.

hers (hûrz) *pron.* **1.** The possessive case of the pronoun *she,* used predicatively: That book is *hers.* **2.** The one or ones belonging to or relating to her. **— of hers** Belonging or relating to her. [OE *hire* + *-s* (after *his*)]

her·self (hər·self′) *pron.* A form of the third person singular feminine pronoun, used: **1.** As a reflexive or as object of a preposition in a reflexive sense: She excused *herself*; She talks to *herself.* **2.** As an emphatic or intensive form of *she*: She *herself* called the police. **3.** As a designation of a normal or usual state: After her illness, she was *herself* again. **4.** *Irish* As a pronoun meaning *she*: How is *herself*?

Hertz·i·an wave (hert′sē·ən, hûrt′-) An electromagnetic wave in the radio and radar range, artificially produced. [after H. R. *Hertz*]

he's (hēz) **1.** He is. **2.** He has.

Hesh·wan (hesh·vän′, hesh′van) *n.* The second month of the Hebrew year. Also **Hesh·van′.** See (Hebrew) CALENDAR.

hes·i·tan·cy (hez′ə·tən·sē) *n. pl.* **·cies** The act or condition of hesitating; hesitation; uncertainty. Also **hes′i·tance.**

hes·i·tant (hes′ə·tənt) *adj.* Lacking certainty or decisiveness; hesitating; irresolute. **— hes′i·tant·ly** *adv.*

GREAT BLUE HERON

(About 4 feet high)

hes·i·tate (hez′ə·tāt) *v.i.* **·tat·ed, ·tat·ing 1.** To be slow or doubtful in acting, making a decision, etc.; be uncertain; waver. **2.** To be reluctant. **3.** To pause or falter. **4.** To falter in speech. [< L *haesitare,* freq. of *haerere* to stick]

hes·i·ta·tion (hez′ə·tā′shən) *n.* **1.** The act of hesitating. **2.** A pause or delay caused by indecision or uncertainty. **3.** A pause or faltering in speech. **— hes′i·ta·tive** *adj.*

Hes·pe·ri·an (hes·pir′ē·ən) *adj.* **1.** *Poetic* In or of the west. **2.** Of the Hesperides. [< L < Gk. *hesperios* western]

Hes·per·i·des (hes·per′ə·dēz) *n.pl.* **1.** In Greek mythology, the daughters of Atlas who, together with a dragon, guarded the golden apples given to Hera. **2.** The garden where these apples grew. [< Gk. *hesperis* western]

Hes·per·us (hes′pər·əs) *n.* The evening star, esp. Venus. Also *Poetic* **Hes′per.** [< L < Gk. *Hesperos*]

Hes·sian (hesh′ən) *n.* **1.** A native of Hesse. **2.** A soldier from Hesse hired by the British to fight in the American Revolution. **— adj.** Of Hesse or its inhabitants.

Hessian fly A small, blackish fly, whose larvae are very destructive to wheat, barley, and rye.

het (het) *Dial.* Past tense and past participle of HEAT. **— het up** Excited; angry.

he·tae·ra (hi·tir′ə, -tī′rə) *n.* *pl.* **·tae·rae** (-tir′ē, -tī′rē) In ancient Greece, a professional courtesan or concubine. Also **he·tae·ra** (hi·tī′rə). [< Gk. *hetaira* companion]

hetero- *combining form* Other; different: opposed to *homo-.* Also, before vowels, **heter-.** [< Gk. *hetero-* < *heteros* other]

het·er·o·cy·clic (het′ər·ə·sī′klik, -sik′lik) *adj. Chem.* Pertaining to or designating an organic ring compound containing atoms of one or more elements other than carbon.

het·er·o·dox (het′ər·ə·doks′) *adj.* **1.** At variance with accepted or established doctrines or beliefs, esp. in religion. **2.** Holding unorthodox beliefs or opinions. [< Gk. *hetero-* other + *doxa* opinion] **— het′er·o·dox′y** *n.*

het·er·o·dyne (het′ər·ə·dīn′) *adj. Telecom.* Denoting a radio circuit, receiver, etc., in which the incoming signal is combined with a signal of fixed frequency and the signal resulting from their beats is used as the amplifier input. **— v.i. ·dyned, ·dyn·ing** To modify a signal in this manner.

het·er·o·ge·ne·i·ty (het′ər·ə·jə·nē′ə·tē) *n.* *pl.* **·ties** The state of being heterogeneous; dissimilarity.

het·er·o·ge·ne·ous (het′ər·ə·jē′nē·əs) *adj.* **1.** Consisting of parts or elements that are dissimilar or unrelated; not homogeneous. **2.** Differing in nature or kind; unlike. [< Med.L < Gk. < *hetero-* other + *genos* kind] **— het′er·o·ge′ne·ous·ly** *adv.* **— het′er·o·ge′ne·ous·ness** *n.*

het·er·og·e·nous (het′ə·roj′ə·nəs) *adj. Biol.* Originating outside the organism.

het·er·o·nym (het′ər·ə·nim′) *n.* A word spelled like another, but having a different sound and meaning, as *bass,* a male voice, and *bass,* a fish. Compare HOMOGRAPH. [< HETER(O)- + Gk. *onyma* name; on analogy with *synonym*] **— het·er·on·y·mous** (het′ə·ron′ə·məs) *adj.*

het·er·op·ter·ous (het′ə·rop′tər·əs) *adj.* Designating a suborder of hemipterous insects that includes the true bugs. [< NL < Gk. *hetero-* other + *pteron* wing]

het·er·o·sex·u·al (het′ər·ə·sek′shōō·əl) *adj.* **1.** Of, or having sexual desire for those of the opposite sex. **2.** *Biol.* Of or pertaining to the opposite sex or to both sexes. **— n.** A heterosexual individual. **— het′er·o·sex′u·al′i·ty** (-al′ə·tē) *n.*

het·er·o·zy·gote (het′ər·ə·zī′gōt, -zig′ōt) *n. Biol.* A hybrid that carries different alleles of the same character and that does not breed true. **— het′er·o·zy′gous** (-zī′gəs) *adj.*

heu·ris·tic (hyōō·ris′tik) *adj.* **1.** Aiding or guiding in discovery. **2.** Designating an educational method by which a pupil is stimulated to make his own investigations and discoveries. [< Gk. *heuriskein* to find out]

hew (hyōō) *v.* **hewed, hewn** or **hewed, hew·ing** *v.t.* **1.** To make or shape with or as with blows of an ax or other cutting tool. **2.** To cut or strike with an ax, sword, etc. **3.** To fell with or as with ax blows. **— v.i. 4.** To make cutting and repeated blows, as with an ax or sword. **5.** To conform, as to a principle. [OE *hēawan*] **— hew′er** *n.*

hex (heks) *U.S. Dial.* or *Informal n.* **1.** An evil spell. **2.** A witch. **— v.t.** To bewitch. [< G *hexe* witch]

hexa- *combining form* Six. Also, before vowels, **hex-.** [< Gk. *hexa-* < *hex* six]

hex·a·gon (hek′sə·gon) *n. Geom.* A polygon having six sides and six angles. [< L < Gk. *hex* six + *gonia* angle] **— hex·ag·o·nal** (hek·sag′ə·nəl) *adj.* **— hex·ag′o·nal·ly** *adv.*

hex·a·gram (hek′sə·gram) *n.* **1.** A six-pointed star made by or as by completing the equilateral triangles based on the sides of a regular hexagon. **2.** Any of various figures formed by six intersecting lines.

HEXAGRAM

hex·am·e·ter (hek·sam′ə·tər) *n.* **1.** In prosody, a line of verse consisting of six metrical feet. **2.** The dactylic verse of Greek and Latin epics. **— adj.** Having six metrical feet. [< L < Gk. *hexametros*] **— hex·a·met·ric** (hek′sə·met′rik), **hex·am′e·tral** (-ə·trəl), **hex′a·met′ri·cal** *adj.*

hex·a·pod (hek′sə·pod) *n.* One of the true or six-legged insects. **— adj.** Having six feet. [< Gk. *hexapous, -podos* six-footed] **— hex·ap·o·dous** (hek·sap′ə·dəs) *adj.*

hex·ose (hek′sōs) *n. Biochem.* Any simple sugar, as glucose or fructose, containing six carbon atoms to the molecule.

hey (hā) *interj.* An exclamation calling for attention or expressing surprise, pleasure, inquiry, etc. [ME *hei*]

hey·day (hā′dā′) *n.* **1.** Period of greatest vigor; height, as of power. **2.** Exuberance; ardor. [Prob. < HIGH DAY]

H-hour (āch′our′) *n.* The hour appointed for a military operation to begin: also called *zero hour.*

hi (hī) *interj.* **1.** *U.S.* An exclamation of greeting. **2.** *Brit.* A call to attract attention. [Var. of HEY]

hi·a·tus (hī·ā′təs) *n.* *pl.* **·tus·es** or **·tus 1.** A gap or space from which something is missing, as in a manuscript; lacuna. **2.** Any break or interruption. **3.** A pause due to the coming together in a word or successive words of two separately pronounced vowels without an intervening consonant. [< L]

Hi·a·wath·a (hī′ə·woth′ə, -wô′thə, hē′ə-) **1.** A Mohawk chief credited with organizing the Five Nations. **2.** The hero of Longfellow's poem *The Song of Hiawatha* (1855).

hi·ba·chi (hi·bä′chē) *n.* *pl.* **·chis** A deep container to hold burning coals, used for heating and cooking. [< Japanese]

hi·ber·nal (hī·bûr′nəl) *adj.* Of or pertaining to winter; wintry. [< L *hibernus* wintry]

hi·ber·nate (hī′bər·nāt) *v.i.* **·nat·ed, ·nat·ing 1.** To pass the winter in a dormant state, as certain animals. **2.** To remain inactive or secluded. [< L *hibernare*] **— hi′ber·na′tion** *n.*

Hi·ber·ni·a (hī·bûr′nē·ə) Latin and poetic name for Ireland. [< L, alter. of *Iverna*] **— Hi·ber′ni·an** *n. & adj.*

hi·bis·cus (hī·bis′kəs, hi-) *n.* A shrub or tree of the mallow family, having large, showy flowers: the state flower of Hawaii. [< L < Gk. *hibiskos* mallow]

hic·cup (hik′əp) *n.* **1.** An involuntary contraction of the diaphragm, causing a sudden, audible inspiration of breath checked by a spasmodic closure of the glottis. **2.** *pl.* A condition characterized by repetition of such spasms. **— v. ·cuped** or **·cupped, ·cup·ing** or **·cup·ping** **— v.i. 1.** To make a sound of or as of a hiccup. **— v.t. 2.** To utter with hiccups. Also **hic·cough** (hik′əp). [Imit.]

hic ja·cet (hik jā′set) *Latin* Here lies: often inscribed on tombstones.

hick (hik) *n. Informal* One having the clumsy, unsophisticated manners, etc. supposedly typical of rural areas; bumpkin. **— adj.** Of or typical of hicks. [Alter. of *Richard*]

hick·ey (hik′ē) *n.* *pl.* **·eys** *U.S. Informal* **1.** Any gadget or contrivance. **2.** A pimple or blemish. [Origin unknown]

hick·o·ry (hik′ər·ē, hik′rē) *n.* *pl.* **·ries 1.** A North American tree of the walnut family, having hard, durable wood and yielding edible nuts. **2.** The wood of such trees. **3.** A switch made of this wood. [< Algonquian *pawcohiccoro*]

hid (hid) Past tense and alternative past participle of HIDE[1].

hi·dal·go (hi·dal′gō, *Sp.* ē·thäl′gō) *n.* *pl.* **·gos** (-gōz, *Sp.* -gōs) A Spanish nobleman of lower rank than a grandee. [< Sp. < *hijo de algo* son of something]

hid·den (hid′n) Past participle of HIDE[1]. **— adj.** Not seen or known; concealed; obscure; mysterious.

hide[1] (hīd) *v.* **hid, hid·den** or **hid, hid·ing** *v.t.* **1.** To put or keep out of sight; conceal. **2.** To keep secret; withhold from knowledge. **3.** To block or obstruct the sight of. **— v.i. 4.** To keep oneself out of sight; remain concealed. **— to hide out** *U.S. Informal* To remain in concealment, esp. as a fugitive. [OE *hȳdan*] **— hid′er** *n.*

— Syn. 1. *Hide, conceal,* and *secrete* mean to put or keep out of sight. We may *hide* without intention, but we *conceal* intentionally. An object is *hidden* or *concealed* when covered from view, when disguised as something else, or when buried out of reach. It is *secreted* when put into some private, secret place.

hide[2] (hīd) *n.* **1.** The skin of an animal, esp. when stripped from the carcass or made into leather. **2.** *Informal* The human skin. **— v.t. hid·ed, hid·ing** *Informal* To flog severely; whip. [OE *hȳd* skin]

hide-and-seek (hīd′n·sēk′) *n.* A children's game in which those who hide are sought by one who is "it." Also **hide′-and-go-seek′.**

hide·a·way (hīd′ə·wā′) *n.* A place of concealment.

hide·bound (hīd′bound′) *adj.* **1.** Obstinately fixed in opinion; narrow-minded; bigoted. **2.** Having the skin too tightly adhering to the back and ribs: said of cattle, etc.

hid·e·ous (hid′ē·əs) *adj.* **1.** Extremely ugly: a *hideous* sight. **2.** Morally odious or detestable; shocking. [< AF < OF *hisde, hide* fright] **— hid′e·ous·ly** *adv.* **— hid′e·ous·ness** *n.*

hide-out (hīd′out′) *n. Informal* A place of concealment or refuge, especially from legal authority. Also **hide′out′.**

hid·ing[1] (hī′ding) *n.* **1.** The act of one who or that which hides. **2.** A state or place of concealment.

hid·ing[2] (hī′ding) *n. Informal* A flogging; whipping.

hie (hī) *v.t. & v.i.* **hied, hie·ing** or **hy·ing** To hasten; hurry: often reflexive: I *hied* myself home. [OE *hīgian*]

hi·er·arch (hī′ə·rärk′) *n.* A high priest or prelate. [< Med.L < Gk. *hierarchēs* sacred + *hieros* ruler]

hi·er·ar·chi·cal (hī′ə·rär′ki·kəl) *adj.* Of, belonging to, or characteristic of a hierarchy. Also **hi′er·ar′chic, hi′er·ar′. chal.** — **hi′er·ar′chi·cal·ly** *adv.*

hi·er·ar·chy (hī′ə·rär′kē) *n. pl.* **·chies 1.** Any group of persons or things arranged in successive orders or classes, each of which is subject to or dependent on the one above it. **2.** A body of ecclesiastics so arranged. **3.** Government or rule by such a body of ecclesiastics. **4.** In science and logic, a series of systematic groupings in graded order.

hi·er·at·ic (hī′ə·rat′ik) *adj.* **1.** Of or pertaining to priests or priestly usage. **2.** Of or pertaining to a shortened form of hieroglyphic writing used by priests in ancient Egypt.

hiero- *combining form* Sacred; divine. Also, before vowels, **hier-.** [< Gk. *hieros* sacred]

hi·er·o·glyph·ic (hī′ər·ə·glif′ik, hī′rə·glif′ik) *n.* **1.** *Usu. pl.* A picture or symbol representing an object, idea, or sound, as in the writing system of the ancient Egyptians. **2.** *pl.* A system of writing using such pictures or symbols. **3.** Any symbol or character having an obscure or hidden meaning. **4.** *pl.* Illegible writing. Also **hi·er·o·glyph** (hī′ər·ə·glif′, hī′rə·glif). — *adj.* **1.** Pertaining to, consisting of, or resembling hieroglyphics. **2.** Written in or inscribed with hieroglyphics. **3.** Difficult to decipher. Also **hi′er·o·glyph′i·cal.** [< LL < Gk. < *hieros* sacred + *glyphein* to carve] — **hi′er·o·glyph′i·cal·ly** *adv.* — **hi·er·og·ly·phist** (hī′ər·og′lə·fist, hī·rog′-) *n.*

hi-fi (hī′fī′) *n.* **1.** High fidelity. **2.** Radio, phonograph, or recording equipment capable of reproducing sound with high fidelity. — *adj.* Of or pertaining to high fidelity.

hig·gle (hig′əl) *v.i.* **·gled, ·gling** To argue over terms, prices, etc.; haggle. [Var. of HAGGLE] — **hig′gler** *n.*

hig·gle·dy-pig·gle·dy (hig′əl·dē-pig′əl·dē) *adj.* Disordered or confused; jumbled; topsy-turvy. — *adv.* In chaotic confusion or disorder. — *n.* Great confusion; muddle. [< obs. *higle-pigle,* a varied reduplication]

high (hī) *adj.* **1.** Reaching or extending upward to some great or considerable distance; lofty; tall. **2.** Having a specified elevation: ten feet *high.* **3.** Located at some distance above the ground or other horizontal. **4.** Reaching to the height of: used in combination: *knee-high.* **5.** Produced or extending to or from a height: a *high* jump. **6.** Greater or more than is usual or normal in degree, amount, etc.: *high* fever; *high* speed. **7.** Superior, lofty, or exalted in quality, rank, kind, etc.: a *high* official. **8.** Most important; main. **9.** Having serious consequences: *high* treason. **10.** Elated; joyful: *high* spirits. **11.** *Informal* Feeling the effects of liquor, drugs, etc.; intoxicated. **12.** Expensive; costly. **13.** Luxurious or fashionable: *high* living. **14.** Advanced to the fullest extent or degree: *high* tide. **15.** Complex; advanced: usu. in the comparative degree: *higher* mathematics. **16.** Strict or extreme in opinion, doctrine, etc.: *high* Tory. **17.** Arrogant; haughty. **18.** Slightly decomposed; gamy: said of meat. **19.** Of sounds, having relatively short wavelengths; shrill. **20.** *Music* **a** Having relatively short wavelengths: said of vocal or instrumental tones. **b** Being above the proper or indicated pitch; sharp. **21.** *Mech.* Denoting a gear arrangement, as in a transmission, yielding the most rapid output speed. **22.** *Phonet.* Of vowel sounds, produced with the tongue raised close to the roof of the mouth, as (ē) in *bead:* opposed to *low.* — **high and dry 1.** Completely above water level. **2.** Stranded; helpless. — **high and mighty** *Informal* Overbearing; haughty. — *adv.* **1.** To or at a high level, position, degree, price, rank, etc. **2.** In a high manner. — **high and low** Everywhere. — *n.* **1.** A high level, position, etc. **2.** *Mech.* A gear arrangement yielding the most rapid output speed. **3.** *Meteorol.* An area of high barometric pressure. [OE *hēah*]

high·ball¹ (hī′bôl′) *n. U.S.* A drink of whisky or other liquor mixed with soda, ginger ale, etc., and served with ice in a tall glass. [Prob. < HIGH + *ball,* obs., a drink of whisky]

high·ball² (hī′bôl′) *n.* A railroad signal to go ahead. — *v.i. U.S. Slang* To go at great speed. [From a large ball once used as a semaphore]

high·born (hī′bôrn′) *adj.* Of noble birth or ancestry.

high·boy (hī′boi′) *n.* A tall chest of drawers, usu. in two sections, the lower one mounted on legs. [Origin unknown]

high·bred (hī′bred′) *adj.* **1.** Descended from fine stock; well-born. **2.** Characteristic of or indicating good breeding.

high·brow (hī′brou′) *Informal n.* One who has or claims to have intellectually superior tastes: sometimes a term of derision. — *adj.* Of, pertaining to, or suitable for a highbrow: also **high′browed′.** — **high′brow′ism** *n.*

high·chair (hī′châr′) *n.* A baby's chair standing on tall legs and equipped with an eating tray. Also **high chair.**

HIERO-
GLYPHICS

High-Church (hī′chûrch′) *adj.* Of or pertaining to a group (High Church) in the Anglican Church that stresses authority and ritual. — **High′-Church′man** *n.*

high-class (hī′klas′, -kläs′) *adj. Slang* High or superior in quality, condition, status, etc.

high comedy Comedy dealing with the world of polite society and relying chiefly on witty dialogue for its effect.

high·er-up (hī′ər-up′) *n. Informal* A person of superior rank or position.

high·fa·lu·tin (hī′fə·loot′n) *adj. Informal* Extravagant, pompous, or high-flown in manner, speech, etc. Also **high′· fa·lu′ting.** [? < HIGH-FLOWN]

high fidelity *Electronics* The reproduction of a signal or sound with a minimum of distortion, esp. by phonographic equipment: also called *hi-fi.*

high-fli·er (hī′flī′ər) *n.* **1.** One who or that which flies high. **2.** *Informal* One having extravagantly pretentious or unrealistic ambitions, opinions, tastes, etc. Also **high′fly′er.**

high-flown (hī′flōn′) *adj.* **1.** Extravagant or bombastic in style, language, etc. **2.** Pretentious: *high-flown* tastes.

high frequency *Telecom.* A radio frequency in the band from 3 to 30 megacycles.

High German See under GERMAN.

high-grade (hī′grād′) *adj.* Of superior quality.

high·hand·ed (hī′han′did) *adj.* Arbitrary and overbearing. — **high′hand′ed·ly** *adv.* — **high′hand′ed·ness** *n.*

high hat A top hat.

high-hat (hī′hat′) *Informal v.t.* **-hat·ted, -hat·ting** To snub. — *adj.* **1.** Snobbish. **2.** Fashionable. — *n.* A snob.

high·jack (hī′jak′) See HIJACK.

high jinks (jingks) Boisterous fun or roughhousing.

high jump In athletics, a jump for height.

high·land (hī′lənd) *n.* **1.** Elevated land, as a plateau or promontory. **2.** *Usu. pl.* A hilly or mountainous region. — *adj.* Of, pertaining to, or of the nature of a highland.

High·land·er (hī′lən·dər) *n.* **1.** A native or inhabitant of the Highlands. **2.** A soldier of a Highlands regiment.

Highland fling A lively Scottish dance.

high·light (hī′līt′) *n.* **1.** An area or point in a painting, photograph, etc., showing or representing a brightly lighted part. **2.** An event, detail, etc., of special importance. — *v.t.* **1.** *Informal* To give special emphasis to; feature. **2.** To provide or emphasize with a highlight or highlights.

high·ly (hī′lē) *adv.* **1.** In or to a high degree; extremely. **2.** With great approval or appreciation. **3.** In a high position or rank. **4.** At a high price or rate.

High Mass *Eccl.* A Mass celebrated with full ceremony, music, incense, etc.

high-mind·ed (hī′mīn′did) *adj.* Possessing or manifesting noble thoughts or sentiments. — **high′-mind′ed·ly** *adv.*

high·ness (hī′nis) *n.* The state or quality of being high.

High·ness (hī′nis) *n.* A title or form of address for persons of royal rank: often preceded by His, Her, Your, etc.

high-pitched (hī′picht′) *adj.* **1.** High in pitch; shrill. **2.** Of a roof, having a steep slope. **3.** Lofty or exalted.

high-pres·sure (hī′presh′ər) *adj.* **1.** Using or sustaining high steam pressure, as an engine. **2.** Having or showing high barometric pressure. **3.** *Informal* Exerting vigorously persuasive methods or tactics. — *v.t.* **·sured, ·sur·ing** *Informal* To persuade by aggressive or insistent methods.

high priest A chief priest.

high-rise (hī′rīz′) *adj.* Describing a relatively tall building or structure. — *n.* A tall building: also **high rise.**

high·road (hī′rōd′) *n.* **1.** A main road. **2.** An easy or sure method or course: the *highroad* to fame.

high school A school following elementary school or junior high school, in the U.S. typically comprising grades 9 to 12.

high seas The open waters of an ocean or sea that are beyond the territorial jurisdiction of any one nation.

high-sound·ing (hī′soun′ding) *adj.* Pretentious or imposing in sound or implication: *high-sounding* praise.

high-spir·it·ed (hī′spir′it·ed) *adj.* Having a courageous, vigorous, or fiery spirit; mettlesome.

high-ten·sion (hī′ten′shən) *adj. Electr.* Pertaining to, characterized by, or operating under very high voltage.

high-test (hī′test′) *adj.* **1.** Designating a substance or product that has passed severe tests for fitness, quality, etc. **2.** Denoting a grade of gasoline with a low boiling point.

high tide 1. The maximum level reached by the incoming tide. **2.** The time that this occurs. **3.** A culminating point.

high time 1. So late as to be almost past the proper time. **2.** *Informal* A hilarious and enjoyable time.

high-toned (hī′tōnd′) *adj.* **1.** *U.S. Informal* Stylish; modish. **2.** Characterized by a lofty character, high principles, etc.: often used ironically. **3.** High in tone or pitch.

high treason Treason against the sovereign or state.

high-up (hī′up′) *Informal adj.* Of high rank or position. — *n.* One who is in a high rank or position.

high water 1. High tide. 2. The condition of a body of water at its time of highest elevation, as during a flood.

high·wa·ter mark (hī′wô′tər, -wot′ər) 1. The highest point reached by a body of water, as during high tide, a flood, etc. 2. A mark left by such waters after receding. 3. A point of highest achievement or development.

high·way (hī′wā′) n. 1. A road or thoroughfare; esp., a main or principal road of some length that is open to the public. 2. A main route on land or water. 3. An ordinary, natural, or direct course of action, progress, etc.

high·way·man (hī′wā′mən) n. pl. **·men** (-mən) Formerly, a robber who waylaid travelers on highways.

hi·jack (hī′jak′) v.t. U.S. Slang 1. To seize illegally while in transit, as cargo, vehicles, etc. 2. To hold up and rob (a truck, etc.). 3. To seize or steal valuables from (a person). 4. To coerce or compel (someone). Also spelled *highjack*. [Orig. from hoboes who hailed their victim with "Hi Jack"]

hike (hīk) v. **hiked, hik·ing** v.i. 1. To walk for a considerable distance, esp. through rugged terrain, woods, etc. 2. To rise or be uneven, as part of a garment: often with *up*. — v.t. 3. *Informal* To raise or lift: usu. with *up*. 4. *Informal* To increase (prices, etc.): usu. with *up*. — n. 1. A long walk or march. 2. *Informal* An increase. [? Var. of HITCH] — **hi′ker** n.

hi·lar·i·ous (hi·lâr′ē-əs, hī-) adj. Boisterously gay or cheerful. — **hi·lar′i·ous·ly** adv. — **hi·lar′i·ous·ness** n.

hi·lar·i·ty (hi·lar′ə·tē, hī-) n. pl. **·ties** Noisy, exuberant gaiety. [< OF < L < Gk. *hilaros* cheerful]

hill (hil) n. 1. A conspicuous, usu. rounded, elevation of the earth's surface, not as high as a mountain. 2. A heap or pile: often used in combination: a *molehill*. 3. A small mound of earth placed over or around certain plants and tubers. 4. A plant or group of plants thus covered. — v.t. 1. To surround or cover with hills, as potatoes. 2. To form a hill or heap of. [OE *hyll*] — **hill′er** n.

hill·bil·ly (hil′bil′ē) n. pl. **·lies** U.S. Informal A person coming from or living in the mountains or a backwoods area, esp. of the southern U.S.: originally a disparaging term.

hill·ock (hil′ək) n. A small hill or mound. — **hill′ock·y** adj.

hill·side (hil′sīd′) n. The side or slope of a hill.

hill·top (hil′top′) n. The summit of a hill.

hill·y (hil′ē) adj. **hill·i·er, hill·i·est** 1. Having many hills. 2. Resembling a hill; steep. — **hill′i·ness** n.

hilt (hilt) n. The handle of a sword, dagger, etc. — **to the hilt** Thoroughly; fully. — v.t. To provide with a hilt. [OE]

hi·lum (hī′ləm) n. pl. **·la** (-lə) Bot. The scar on a seed at the point where it was attached to the placenta. [< L, a trifle]

him (him) pron. The objective case of the pronoun *he*.

him·self (him·self′) pron. A form of the third person singular masculine pronoun, used: 1. As a reflexive or as object of a preposition in a reflexive sense: He cut *himself*. 2. As an intensive form of *he*: He *himself* will do it. 3. As a designation of a normal or usual state: He is not *himself*.

hind[1] (hīnd) adj. **hind·er, hind·most** or **hind·er·most** Situated at or toward the rear part; posterior. [OE *hindan*]

hind[2] (hīnd) n. The female of the red deer, esp. when fully grown. [OE]

hind·brain (hīnd′brān′) n. Anat. The rhombencephalon.

hind·er[1] (hin′dər) v.t. 1. To interfere with the progress of; retard. 2. To prevent from acting or occurring; deter; thwart. — v.i. 3. To be an impediment or obstacle. [OE *hinder* behind] — **hin′der·er** n.

hind·er[2] (hīn′dər) Comparative of HIND[1]. — adj. Pertaining to or situated at the rear or posterior end. [OE]

Hin·di (hin′dē) n. 1. The principal language of northern India, belonging to the Indic branch of the Indo-Iranian languages, usu. divided into **Western Hindi**, of which Hindustani is the major dialect, and **Eastern Hindi**. 2. A form of literary Hindustani used by Hindus. [< Hind. < Persian < OPersian < Skt. *sindhu* river, the Indus]

hind·most (hīnd′mōst′) Superlative of HIND[1]. Also **hind′er·most** (hīn′dər-).

hind·quar·ter (hīnd′kwôr′tər) n. 1. One of the two back quarters of a carcass of beef, lamb, etc. 2. pl. The rump.

hin·drance (hin′drəns) n. 1. The act of hindering. 2. One who or that which hinders.

hind·sight (hīnd′sīt′) n. 1. The understanding of an event after it has happened. 2. The rear sight of a gun, rifle, etc.

Hin·du (hin′dōo) n. 1. A native of India who speaks one of the Indic languages. 2. One whose religion is Hinduism. 3. Loosely, a native of Hindustan. — adj. Of, pertaining to, or characteristic of the Hindus or Hinduism. Also **Hin′doo**.

Hin·du·ism (hin′dōo-iz′əm) n. The religion of the Hindus of India, characterized by worship of Brahma.

Hin·du·sta·ni (hin′dōo-stä′nē, -stan′ē) n. The major dialect of Hindi, the official language and general medium of communication in India. See URDU. — adj. 1. Of or pertaining to Hindustan or its people. 2. Of or pertaining to Hindustani. Abbr. *Hind.*

hinge (hinj) n. 1. A device consisting of two parts, usu.

metal plates, connected by a pin inserted into interlocking grooves, and constituting a movable joint on which a door, gate, lid, etc., swings or turns. 2. A natural movable joint connecting two parts, as the shells of a bivalve. 3. That on which something turns or depends. — v. **hinged, hing·ing** v.t. 1. To attach by or equip with a hinge cr hinges. — v.i. 2. To hang or turn on or as on a hinge. 3. To depend or be contingent: with *on*. [ME, prob. < OE *hengja* to hang]

hin·ny (hin′ē) n. pl. **·nies** The hybrid offspring of a stallion and a she-ass. Compare MULE[1]. [< L < Gk. *ginnos*]

hint (hint) n. 1. An indirect suggestion or implication. 2. A slight indication or trace. — v.t. 1. To suggest indirectly; imply. — v.i. 2. To show one's wishes, intentions, etc., by a hint or hints. 3. To give a slight indication or suggestion: with *at*. [OE *hentan*]

hin·ter·land (hin′tər·land′) n. 1. An inland region immediately adjacent to a coastal area. 2. A region remote from urban areas; back country. 3. An area adjacent to and dependent upon a port or other urban center. [< G]

hip[1] (hip) n. 1. The part of the human body projecting below the waist on either side, formed by the edge of the pelvis and the upper part of the femur. 2. An analogous part in animals. 3. Archit. The angle at the juncture of adjacent sloping sides of a roof. — v.t. **hipped, hip·ping** Archit. To build (a roof) with a hip or hips. [OE *hype*]

hip[2] (hip) n. The ripened fruit of a rose. [OE *hēope*]

hip[3] (hip) adj. U.S. Slang Aware; informed.

hip·bone (hip′bōn′) n. The innominate bone.

hipped[1] (hipt) adj. 1. Having or characterized by (a specified kind of) hips: used in combination: *slim-hipped*. 2. Archit. Having a hip or hips, as a roof.

hipped[2] (hipt) adj. U.S. Slang Fanatically interested or concerned; obsessed: followed by *on*: *hipped on modern art*.

hip·pet·y-hop (hip′ə·tē-hop′) adv. Informal With a jerky gait or motion. Also **hip·pet·y-hop·pet·y** (-hop′ə·tē).

hip·pie (hip′ē) n. One of a group of chiefly young people whose unconventional dress and behavior and use of drugs express withdrawal from middle-class life and indifference to its values. [Var. of HIPSTER]

hip·po (hip′ō) n. pl. **·pos** Informal A hippopotamus.

hippo- combining form Horse. Also, before vowels, **hipp-**. [< Gk. *hippos* horse]

Hip·po·crat·ic oath (hip′ə·crat′ik) An oath, attributed to Hippocrates, incorporating a code of ethics for physicians and administered to those about to receive a medical degree.

hip·po·drome (hip′ə·drōm) n. 1. An arena or similar structure for horse shows, circuses, etc. 2. In ancient Greece and Rome, a course or track for horse races and chariot races. [< F < L < Gk. < *hippos* horse + *dromos* running, course]

hip·po·pot·a·mus (hip′ə·pot′ə·məs) n. pl. **·mus·es** or **·mi** (-mī) A large, chiefly aquatic, herbivorous mammal, native to Africa, and having short legs, a massive, thick-skinned, hairless body, and a very broad muzzle. [< L < Gk. < *hippos* horse + *potamos* river]

-hippus combining form Paleontol. Horse. [< Gk. *hippos* horse]

hip roof Archit. A roof having sloping ends and sides.

hip·ster (hip′stər) n. U.S. Slang One who is hip; esp., one versed in jazz music. [< HIP[3] + -STER]

hire (hīr) v.t. **hired, hir·ing** 1. To obtain the services of (a person) for compensation. 2. To acquire the use of (a thing) for a fee; rent. 3. To grant the use or services of (someone or something) in return for payment: often with *out*. — **to hire out** To provide one's services in return for compensation. — n. 1. Compensation paid for labor, services, etc. 2. The act of hiring, or the condition of being hired. [OE *hȳr*] — **hir′able** or **hire′a·ble** adj. — **hir′er** n.

hire·ling (hīr′ling) n. One who serves for hire; esp., one who does something unpleasant or reprehensible for mercenary motives: usu. a contemptuous term.

hir·sute (hûr′sōot, hûr·sōot′) adj. Covered with hair. [< L *hirsutus* rough] — **hir′sute·ness** n.

his (hiz) pron. 1. The possessive case of the pronoun *he*, used predicatively: This room is *his*. 2. The one or ones belonging or pertaining to him: Her book is better than *his*. — **of his** Belonging or pertaining to him: a double possessive. — pronominal adj. The possessive case of the pronoun *he*, used attributively: *his* book. [OE]

His·pa·ni·a (his·pā′nē·ə, -nyə, -pä′-) 1. The Latin name for the region comprising modern Spain and Portugal. 2. Poetic Spain. — **His·pan·ic** (his·pan′ik) adj.

hiss (his) v.i. 1. To utter or produce a prolonged, sibilant sound, as that of *ss*, of air or steam escaping under pressure, etc. 2. To utter such a sound as an expression of disapproval or derision. — v.t. 3. To utter with a hiss. 4. To e·press disapproval of by hissing. 5. To rout or silence by hissing: with *off, down,* etc. — n. The sound produced by hissing. [ME *hissen*, imit.] — **hiss′er** n.

his·ta·mine (his′tə·mēn, -min) n. Biochem. A white, crystalline substance, $C_5H_9N_3$, found in plant and animal tissues. It reduces blood pressure, has a contracting action on the uterus, and is released in allergic reactions. — **his·ta·min·ic** (his/tə·min/ik) *adj.*

histo- *combining form* Tissue. Also, before vowels, **hist-**. [< Gk *histos* web]

his·tol·o·gy (his·tol/ə·jē) *n. pl.* **·gies** 1. The branch of biology that treats of the microscopic structure of tissues. 2. The tissue structure of an organism, part, etc. — **his·to·log·i·cal** (his/tə·loj/i·kəl) *adj.* — **his·tol·o·gist** *n.*

his·to·ri·an (his·tôr/ē·ən, -tō/rē-) *n.* 1. A writer of or authority on history. 2. A compiler of a record, esp. for a specific group or purpose: the class *historian*.

his·tor·ic (his·tôr/ik, -tor/-) *adj.* 1. Important or famous in history. 2. Memorable; significant. 3. Historical.

his·tor·i·cal (his·tôr/i·kəl, -tor/-) *adj.* 1. Constituting, belonging to, or of the nature of history. 2. Pertaining to, concerned with, or treating of events of history: a *historical* account. 3. Of, pertaining to, or based on known facts as distinct from legendary or fictitious accounts. 4. Serving as a source for knowledge of the past. 5. Historic. — **his·tor/i·cal·ly** *adv.* — **his·tor/i·cal·ness** *n.*

historical present *Gram.* The present tense used to narrate a past event.

his·to·ri·og·ra·pher (his·tôr/ē·og/rə·fər, -tō/rē-) *n.* A historian or chronicler, esp. one officially associated with a group or public institution. — **his·to/ri·og/ra·phy** *n.*

his·to·ry (his/tə·rē, his/trē) *n. pl.* **·ries** 1. That branch of knowledge concerned with past events, esp. those involving human affairs. 2. A record or account, usu. written and in chronological order, of past events, esp. those concerning a particular nation, people, field of knowledge or activity, etc. 3. A connected or related series of facts, events, etc., esp. those concerning a specific group or subject: the *history* of a political party. 4. Past events in general. 5. Something in the past. 6. An unusual or noteworthy past: That house has a *history*. 7. A drama depicting historical events. 8. A long narrative or story. [< L < Gk. *histōr* knowing]

his·tri·on·ic (his/trē·on/ik) *adj.* 1. Of or pertaining to actors or acting. 2. Overly dramatic. Also **his/tri·on/i·cal**. [< L *histrio, -onis* actor] — **his/tri·on/i·cal·ly** *adv.*

his·tri·on·ics (his/trē·on/iks) *n.pl.* (*construed as sing. in def. 1*) 1. Theatrical art or representation; dramatics. 2. Feigned emotional display; affectation in manner, speech, etc.

hit (hit) *v.* **hit, hit·ting** *v.t.* 1. To give a blow to; strike forcibly. 2. To reach or strike with or as with a missile, hurled or falling object, etc. 3. To come forcibly in contact with; collide with. 4. To cause (something) to make forcible contact: often with *on, against,* etc. 5. To inflict (a blow, etc.) on: I *hit* him a tremendous blow. 6. To set in motion or propel by striking. 7. To arrive at, achieve, or discover. 8. To accord with; suit. 9. To affect adversely; cause to suffer. 10. To attack; beset. 11. In baseball, to succeed in making (a specified kind of base hit). 12. *U.S. Informal* To begin to journey on: to *hit* the road. 13. *U.S. Informal* To arrive in or reach (a place). — *v.i.* 14. To deliver a blow; strike. 15. To make forcible contact; bump: often with *against, on,* etc. 16. To come or light; happen: followed by *on* or *upon*: to *hit* on the right answer. — **to hit it off** To be friendly; get along well. — **to hit on** (a specified number of) **cylinders** To function by or as by firing the charge in the cylinders: said originally of an internal-combustion engine. — *n.* 1. A blow, stroke, shot, etc., that reaches the objective aimed at. 2. A forceful impact; collision. 3. A popular or obvious success. 4. A fortunate chance or circumstance. 5. An apt or telling remark, witticism, piece of sarcasm, etc. 6. In baseball, a base hit. [OE < ON *hitta* to come upon] — **hit/ter** *n.*

hit-and-run (hit/n·run/) *adj.* Designating or caused by the driver of a vehicle who illegally continues on his way after hitting a pedestrian or another vehicle.

hitch (hich) *v.t.* 1. To fasten or tie, esp. temporarily, with a knotted rope, strap, etc. 2. To harness to a vehicle: sometimes with *up*. 3. To move, pull, raise, etc., with a jerk: often with *up*: He *hitched* his pants up. 4. *Informal* To marry. 5. *U.S. Slang* To obtain (a ride) by hitchhiking. — *v.i.* 6. To move with a jerk or limp: to *hitch* forward. 7. To become fastened, caught, or entangled. 8. *U.S. Slang* To travel by hitchhiking. — *n.* 1. An obstacle; halt; delay. 2. A sudden, jerking movement; tug. 3. A limp or hobble. 4. A fastening or device used for fastening. 5. Any of various knots used for quick, temporary fastening. 6. *U.S. Informal* A period of enlistment in military service, esp. in the navy. 7. *U.S. Slang* In hitchhiking, a ride. [ME *hicchen*]

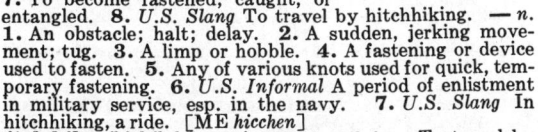

HITCHES
a Half-hitch.
b Clove-hitch.
c Rolling-hitch.

hitch·hike (hich/hīk/) *v.i.* **·hiked, ·hik·ing** To travel by signaling for rides in passing vehicles. — **hitch/hik/er** *n.*

hitch·ing post (hich/ing) A post to which a horse, etc., may be hitched.

hith·er (hith/ər) *adv.* To or toward this place: Come *hither*. — *adj.* Situated toward this side; nearer. [OE *hider*]

hith·er·most (hith/ər·mōst/) *adj.* Nearest to this place.

hith·er·to (hith/ər·tōō/, hith/ər·tōō/) *adv.* Until this time.

hit or miss Without regard for the outcome; at random.

hit-or-miss (hit/ər·mis/) *adj.* Haphazard; careless.

Hit·tite (hit/īt) *n.* 1. One of an ancient people who established a powerful empire in Asia Minor and northern Syria about 2000–1200 B.C. 2. Their language. — *adj.* Of or relating to the Hittites or their language. [< Hebrew *Hittim*]

hive (hīv) *n.* 1. An artificial structure serving as a habitation for honeybees; beehive. 2. A colony of bees inhabiting a hive; swarm. 3. A place astir with industrious activity. 4. A teeming multitude; throng. — *v.* **hived, hiv·ing** *v.t.* 1. To induce (bees) to enter into or collect in a hive. 2. To house or shelter in or as in a hive. 3. To store (honey) in a hive. 4. To store or hoard for future use. — *v.i.* 5. To enter a hive. 6. To dwell in or as in a hive. [OE *hȳf*]

hives (hīvz) *n.* Any of various skin disorders characterized by swellings, itching, etc., as urticaria. [Origin unknown]

ho (hō) *interj.* 1. An exclamation, often repeated, expressing exultation, derision, etc. 2. A call to attract attention.

Ho *Chem.* Holmium.

hoar (hôr, hōr) *adj.* 1. Having white or gray hair. 2. Ancient. 3. White or grayish, as with frost. — *n.* Hoariness. [OE *hār* gray-haired]

hoard (hôrd, hōrd) *n.* An accumulation of something stored away for safekeeping or future use. — *v.t.* 1. To amass and store or hide (money, valuables, etc.). — *v.i.* 2. To amass and store. [OE *hord* treasure] — **hoard/er** *n.*

hoard·ing[1] (hôr/ding, hōr/-) *n.* 1. The act of one who hoards. 2. *Usu. pl.* That which is hoarded.

hoard·ing[2] (hôr/ding, hōr/-) *n. Brit.* 1. A temporary fence. 2. A billboard. [< OF *hourd* palisade]

hoar·frost (hôr/frôst/, -frost/, hōr/-) *n.* Frost whitening the surface on which it is formed.

hoar·hound (hôr/hound/, hōr/-) See HOREHOUND.

hoarse (hôrs, hōrs) *adj.* 1. Deep, harsh, and grating in sound. 2. Having a husky, gruff, or croaking voice. [OE *hā(r)s*] — **hoarse/ly** *adv.* — **hoarse/ness** *n.*

hoars·en (hôr/sən, hōr/-) *v.t. & v.i.* To make or become hoarse.

hoar·y (hôr/ē, hō/rē) *adj.* **hoar·i·er, hoar·i·est** 1. Ancient; aged; venerable. 2. Gray or white with age. 3. White or whitish in color. — **hoar/i·ness** *n.*

hoax (hōks) *n.* A trick or deception, usu. on the public. — *v.t.* To deceive by a hoax. — **hoax/er** *n.*

hob[1] (hob) *n.* A projection at the interior of a fireplace, serving as a shelf on which to keep things warm.

hob[2] (hob) *n.* A hobgoblin or elf. — **to play** (or **raise**) **hob** To cause mischief or confusion. [Orig. a nickname for *Robert, Robin*]

hob·ble (hob/əl) *v.* **·bled, ·bling** *v.i.* 1. To walk with a limp. 2. To progress clumsily or irregularly. — *v.t.* 3. To hamper the free movement of, as a horse, by fettering the legs. 4. To cause to move lamely or awkwardly. — *n.* 1. An awkward or limping gait. 2. A rope, etc., used to hobble the legs of an animal. — **hob/bler** *n.*

hob·ble·de·hoy (hob/əl·dē·hoi/) *n.* An adolescent boy, esp. when awkward and gawky. [Origin uncertain]

hob·by (hob/ē) *n. pl.* **·bies** A pursuit of interest, undertaken for pleasure during one's leisure; avocation. [after *Robin*, a personal name]

hob·by·horse (hob/ē·hôrs/) *n.* 1. A rocking horse. 2. A toy consisting of a stick surmounted by a horse's head.

hob·gob·lin (hob/gob/lin) *n.* 1. An imaginary cause of terror or dread. 2. A mischievous imp.

hob·nail (hob/nāl/) *n.* A nail used to stud the soles of heavy shoes against wear or slipping. — **hob/nailed/** *adj.*

hob·nob (hob/nob/) *v.i.* **·nobbed, ·nob·bing** 1. To associate in a friendly manner; be on intimate terms. 2. To drink together. [OE *habban* to have + *nabban* to have not]

ho·bo (hō/bō) *n. pl.* **·boes** or **·bos** *U.S.* 1. A tramp. 2. An itinerant, usu. unskilled worker. [< *Hey, Bo*, a vagabond's greeting] — **ho/bo·ism** *n.*

Hob·son's choice (hob/sənz) A choice in which one must take what is offered or nothing. [after Thomas *Hobson*, 1544?–1631, English liveryman, who required each customer to take the horse nearest the door]

hock[1] (hok) *n.* 1. The joint of the hind leg in the horse, ox, etc., corresponding to the ankle in man. 2. The corresponding joint in a fowl. — *v.t.* To disable by cutting the tendons of the hock; hamstring. [OE *hōh* heel]

hock[2] (hok) *n.* Any white Rhine wine: originally **Hoch·hei·mer** (hok/hī·mər). [*Hochheim*, a German town]

hock[3] (hok) *U.S. Informal v.t.* To pawn. — *n.* The state of being in pawn. **—in hock** *Informal* **1.** In pawn. **2.** In prison. **3.** In debt. [< Du. *hok* prison, debt]

hock·ey (hok′ē) *n.* **1.** A game played on ice (*ice hockey*), in which players, wearing skates and wielding sticks, try to drive a disk (puck) into the opponent's goal. **2.** A similar game played on a field (*field hockey*), in which a small ball is used instead of a puck. [< *hock* bent stick, var. of HOOK]

hockey stick A stick having a characteristic curve or bend at one end, used to move the ball or puck in hockey.

hock·shop (hok′shop′) *n. U.S. Informal* A pawnshop. Also **hock shop.**

ho·cus (hō′kəs) *v.t.* **·cused** or **·cussed, ·cus·ing** or **·cus·sing 1.** To deceive by a trick; dupe; cheat. **2.** To drug, as a drink. [Abbr. of HOCUS-POCUS]

ho·cus-po·cus (hō′kəs-pō′kəs) *n.* **1.** A verbal formula used in conjuring or sleight of hand. **2.** Deceptive skill. **3.** Any trickery or deception, as misleading gestures. **—** *v.t. & v.i.* **-po·cused** or **·cussed, -po·cus·ing** or **·cus·sing** To trick; cheat. [A sham Latin phrase]

hod (hod) *n.* **1.** A trough rested on the shoulder, to carry bricks, etc. **2.** A coalscuttle. [< OF *hotte* pannier]

hodge·podge (hoj′poj′) *n.* **1.** A jumbled mixture or collection; conglomeration. **2.** A stew. Also *hotchpotch*.

Hodg·kin's disease (hoj′kinz) *Pathol.* A generally fatal disease characterized by progressive enlargement of the lymph nodes, lymphoid tissue, and spleen. [after Dr. Thomas *Hodgkin*, 1798–1866, English physician, who described it]

hoe (hō) *n.* An implement as for weeding, having a flat blade attached to a long handle. **—** *v.t. & v.i.* **hoed, hoe·ing** To dig with a hoe. [< OF < OHG *houwan* to cut]

hoe·cake (hō′kāk′) *n. Southern U.S.* A thin, flat cake made from cornmeal, originally baked on a hoe.

hoe·down (hō′doun′) *n. U.S. Informal* A lively country dance or square dance; also, its music. [Origin uncertain]

hog (hog, hôg) *n.* **1.** A pig, esp. one weighing more than 120 pounds and raised for the market. **2.** An animal related to the pig, as the peccary. **3.** *Informal* A gluttonous or filthy person. **—** *v.* **hogged, hog·ging** *v.t. Slang* To take more than one's share of; grab selfishly. [OE *hog*]

hog·back (hog′bak′, hôg′-) *n. Geol.* A sandy or rocky ridge caused by unequal erosion on the edges of tilted strata.

hog·gish (hog′ish, hôg′-) *adj.* **1.** Of or like a hog. **2.** Greedy or dirty; piggish. **—hog′gish·ly** *adv.*

hog·nose (hog′nōz′, hôg′-) *n.* Any of several American nonvenomous snakes with flat heads and prominent snouts.

hogs·head (hogz′hed′, hôgz′-) *n.* **1.** A large cask, esp. one with a capacity of 63 to 140 gallons. **2.** A liquid measure, esp. one equal to 63 gallons, or 8.42 cubic feet.

hog-tie (hog′tī′, hôg′-) *v.t.* **-tied, -ty·ing** or **-tie·ing 1.** To tie together four feet, or the hands and feet of.. **2.** *Informal* To render (a person) ineffective, as by tying. Also **hog′tie′.**

hog·wash (hog′wosh′, -wôsh′, hôg′-) *n.* **1.** Kitchen refuse, etc., fed hogs. **2.** Any nonsense; insincere talk.

hoicks (hoiks) *interj.* A cry to the hounds in hunting. Also *yoicks*.

hoi pol·loi (hoi′ pə-loi′) The common people; the masses: usu. used contemptuously. [< Gk., the many]

hoist (hoist) *v.t.* To raise, lift, or heave up, esp. by mechanical means. **—** *n.* **1.** Any machine for raising large objects; a lift. **2.** The act of hoisting. [? < Du. *hijschen*]

hoi·ty-toi·ty (hoi′tē-toi′tē) *interj.* An exclamation of disapproval. **—** *adj.* **1.** Self-important; haughty. **2.** Flighty; giddy. **3.** Easily offended. **—** *n. pl.* **-toi·ties 1.** Arrogance. **2.** Flighty behavior. [Obs. *hoit* to romp]

ho·kum (hō′kəm) *n. U.S. Slang* **1.** The devices used by a performer, etc., to get a response. **2.** Meaningless bunk. **3.** Insincere flattery. [Alter. of HOCUS]

hold[1] (hōld) *v.* **held, hold·ing** *v.t.* **1.** To take and keep in the hand, arms, etc.; clasp. **2.** To sustain or keep, as in position; support: to *hold* one's head high. **3.** To contain or enclose: The barrel *holds* ten gallons. **4.** To keep under control; restrain; also, to retain possession of. **5.** To keep in reserve; designate for future use. **6.** To have the benefit or responsibilities of: to *hold* office. **7.** To regard in a specified manner: to *hold* someone dear. **8.** To bind by contract or duty: *Hold* him to his agreement. **9.** *Music* To prolong or sustain (a tone). **10.** *Law* **a** To adjudge; decide. **b** To have title to. **11.** To maintain in the mind; harbor: to *hold* a grudge. **12.** To engage in; carry on: to *hold* a conference. **—** *v.i.* **13.** To maintain a grip or grasp. **14.** To withstand strain or remain unbroken: The rope *holds*. **15.** To continue in a state: the breeze *held*. **16.** To remain true: This decision *holds*. **17.** To adhere, as to a principle or purpose; cling. **—to hold back 1.** To keep in check; restrain. **2.** To refrain. **3.** To retain. **—to hold down 1.** To suppress; keep under control. **2.** *Informal* To be employed at (a job). **—to hold forth** To preach or speak at great length. **—to hold in 1.** To keep in check; curb. **2.** To conceal (one's feelings, etc.). **—to hold off 1.** To keep at a distance, as from attacking. **2.** To refrain from doing something. **—to hold on 1.** To maintain a grip or

hold. **2.** To persist or continue. **3.** *Informal* To stop or wait. **—to hold one's own** To maintain one's position, as in a contest. **—to hold out 1.** To stretch forth; offer. **2.** To last; endure: Our supplies *held out*. **3.** To continue resistance. **4.** *Slang* To refuse something anticipated or due. **—to hold over 1.** To put off to a later time. **2.** To remain or retain beyond the expected limit, as in office. **3.** To use as a means of controlling. **—to hold up 1.** To support; prop. **2.** To exhibit to view. **3.** To delay; stop. **4.** *Informal* To endure; remain firm. **5.** *Informal* To stop so as to rob. **6.** *Informal* To charge too high a price. **—to hold water 1.** To contain without leaking. **2.** *Informal* To be credible or sound, as an argument. **—to hold with** To approve of. **—** *n.* **1.** The act or method of grasping, as with the hands. **2.** Something grasped, held, or seized for support. **3.** A controlling force or influence. **4.** *Law* A holding or tenure: used in combination: *freehold*. **5.** *Music* **a** The holding of a note or rest beyond its time value. **b** The symbol (⌢) indicating this: also called *pause*. [OE *haldan*]

hold[2] (hōld) *n. Naut.* The space below the decks of a vessel, where cargo is stowed. [< HOLE or < MDu. *hol*]

hold·er (hōl′dər) *n.* **1.** One who or that which holds. **2.** An object used as an aid in holding. **3.** An owner; possessor: chiefly in compounds: *householder*. **4.** *Law* One who has a check, etc., for which he is entitled to payment.

hold·ing (hōl′ding) *n.* **1.** The act of one who or that which holds. **2.** A piece of land rented. **3.** *Often pl.* Property held by legal right, esp. stocks or bonds.

holding company A company that invests in the stocks of one or more other corporations, which it may thus control.

hold·o·ver (hōld′ō′vər) *n. Informal* **1.** One who or that which remains from a previous time or situation. **2.** An incumbent continuing in office after his term has expired.

hold·up (hōld′up′) *n.* **1.** Stoppage or delay. **2.** *Informal* A waylaying and robbing.

hole (hōl) *n.* **1.** A cavity in a solid mass or body; pit. **2.** An opening in anything; aperture. **3.** An animal's burrow or enclosed hiding place. **4.** Any small, crowded, squalid place, esp. a dwelling; also, a prison cell. **5.** A defect; fault. **6.** *Informal* An awkward situation. **7.** In golf: **a** A small cavity into which the ball is played. **b** A division of the course, usu. one of nine or eighteen. **8.** *U.S.* A deep, wide place in a creek, etc.; also, a cove. **—hole in one** In golf, the act of sinking the ball into a hole with one drive from the tee. **—in the hole** *Informal* In debt. **—** *v.* **holed, hol·ing** *v.t.* **1.** To make a hole in; perforate. **2.** To drive (a ball, etc.) into a hole. **3.** To dig (a shaft, tunnel, etc.). **—** *v.i.* **4.** To make a hole or holes. **—to hole out** In golf, to hit the ball into a hole. **—to hole up** To hide away; isolate oneself. [OE *hol*] **—hole′y** *adj.*

hol·i·day (hol′ə-dā) *n.* **1.** A day appointed by law for suspension of business in commemoration of some event. **2.** Any day of rest. **3.** A day for special religious observance. **4.** *pl. Chiefly Brit.* A vacation. **—** *v.i. Chiefly Brit.* To spend a holiday or vacation. [OE *hālig dæg* holy day]

ho·li·er-than-thou (hō′lē-ər-than-thou′) *adj. Informal* Affecting an attitude of superior goodness or virtue.

ho·li·ness (hō′lē-nis) *n.* The state or quality of being holy.

Ho·li·ness (hō′lē-nis) *n.* A title or form of address for the Pope: preceded by *His* or *Your*.

ho·lism (hō′liz-əm) *n.* The theory that the whole, esp. a living organism, is more than the sum of its parts. **—ho·lis′tic** *adj.*

hol·lan·daise sauce (hol′ən-dāz′) A creamy sauce of butter, egg yolks, and lemon juice served with vegetables, etc. [< F, fem. of *hollandais* of Holland]

Hol·land·er (hol′ən-dər) *n.* A native or citizen of the Netherlands; a Dutchman.

Hol·lands (hol′əndz) *n.* Gin in which juniper is added to the mash instead of to the spirits. Also **Holland gin.**

hol·ler (hol′ər) *U.S. Informal v.t. & v.i.* To call out loudly; shout; yell. **—** *n.* A loud shout; yell.

hol·low (hol′ō) *adj.* **1.** Having a cavity within; enclosing an empty space. **2.** Having a deep opening; concave. **3.** Sunken; fallen: *hollow* cheeks. **4.** Deep or muffled in tone: a *hollow* groan. **5.** Not genuine; meaningless; empty. **6.** Hungry. **—** *n.* **1.** A cavity or empty space in anything; depression; hole. **2.** A valley. **—** *v.t. & v.i.* To make or become hollow: usu. with *out*. **—** *adv. Informal* Completely: used in the phrase **to beat (all) hollow.** [OE *holh*] **—hol′low·ly** *adv.* **—hol′low·ness** *n.*

hol·low·ware (hol′ō-wâr′) *n.* Utensils, serving dishes, etc., esp. of silver, that are hollow.

hol·ly (hol′ē) *n. pl.* **·lies** A tree or shrub having dark green leaves edged with spines, and scarlet berries. [OE *holen*]

hol·ly·hock (hol′ē-hok) *n.* A tall, cultivated plant of the mallow family, having spikes of showy flowers. [ME *holi* holy + *hoc* mallow]

hol·mi·um (hōl′mē-əm) *n.* A metallic element (symbol Ho) of the lanthanide series, found in gadolinite. See ELEMENT. [after *Holmia*, Latinized name of Stockholm, Sweden]

hol·o·caust (hŏl′ə·kôst) *n.* **1.** Wholesale destruction and loss of life, esp. by fire. **2.** A sacrificial offering that is wholly consumed by fire. — **the Holocaust** The genocidal destruction of Jews by Nazi Germany. [< F < LL < Gk. *holos* whole + *kaustos* burnt]

hol·o·gram (hŏl′ə·gram) *n.* A picture made by holography.

hol·o·graph (hŏl′ə·graf) *n.* A letter, document, etc., in the handwriting of the person whose signature it bears; also, the handwriting itself. — *adj.* Denoting such written material. [< F < Gk. *holos* whole + *graphein* to write]

hol·o·graph·ic (hŏl′ə·graf′ik) *adj.* **1.** Pertaining to holographs. **2.** Pertaining to holograms.

ho·log·ra·phy (hō·lŏg′rə·fē) *n.* A technique of producing a three-dimensional picture on photographic film using laser beams and without the aid of a camera. [< Gk. *holos* whole + -GRAPHY]

Hol·stein (hŏl′stīn, -stēn) *n.* A breed of black-and-white cattle. Also **Hol′stein-Frie′sian** (-frē′zhən).

hol·ster (hōl′stər) *n.* A leather case for a pistol, generally worn on a belt or attached to a saddle. [< Du.]

ho·ly (hō′lē) *adj.* **·li·er, ·li·est 1.** Regarded with or characterized by reverence because associated with God; having a divine origin; sacred. **2.** Having spiritual and moral worth. **3.** Designated for religious worship; consecrated. **4.** Evoking or meriting reverence or awe. — *n., pl.* **·lies** A sacred or holy place. [OE *hālig*] — **ho·li·ly** (hō′lə·lē) *adv.*

Holy Communion The Eucharist.

ho·ly·day (hō′lē·dā′) *n.* A day designated as a religious festival: sometimes called *holiday.* Also **holy day.**

Holy Father A title of the Pope.

Holy Ghost The third person of the Trinity. Also **Holy Spirit.**

Holy Grail The Grail.

Holy Land Palestine.

holy of holies 1. The innermost shrine of the Jewish tabernacle and temple, in which the ark of the covenant was kept. **2.** Any very sacred place. Also called *sanctum sanctorum.*

holy orders *Eccl.* **1.** The rite of admission to the priesthood or ministry; ordination. **2.** The rank of the ministry.

Holy Roman Empire An empire in central and western Europe, 962–1806, regarded as the reestablishment of the Western Roman Empire under the Pope.

ho·ly·stone (hō′lē·stōn′) *n.* A piece of sandstone used to scour the decks of a ship. — *v.t.* **·stoned, ·ston·ing** To scrub with a stone. [Said to be used to clean decks for Sunday]

Holy Week The week before Easter Sunday.

Holy Writ The Scriptures.

hom·age (hom′ij, om′-) *n.* **1.** Respect or honor given or shown, esp. by action. **2.** A payment, etc., indicating allegiance. [< OF < LL *homo* vassal, man]

hom·bre (om′brā, om′brē) *U.S. Slang* Man. [< Sp.]

Hom·burg (hom′bûrg) *n.* A felt hat having a brim slightly turned up at the sides, and the crown indented lengthwise. Also **hom′burg.** [after *Homburg,* Germany]

home (hōm) *n.* **1.** A house or other dwelling where a person or a family lives; residence. **2.** A family or group dwelling together: a happy *home.* **3.** The country, region, city, etc., where one lives. **4.** A birthplace or residence during one's early years. **5.** The place where something originates or is found: New Orleans is the *home* of jazz. **6.** A shelter for care of the orphaned, needy, infirm, etc. **7.** In some games, the goal or base that must be reached in order to win or score. — **at home 1.** In one's own residence, town, country, etc. **2.** At one's ease, as if in one's residence. **3.** Having a knowledge of; conversant: *at home* in the sciences. **4.** Prepared to receive callers. **5.** An informal social gathering at one's home. — *adj.* **1.** Of or pertaining to one's home, country, etc.; domestic. **2.** Being at the base of operations or place of origin: the *home* office. **3.** Going straight to the point; effective. — *adv.* **1.** To or at one's home. **2.** To the place or point intended; to the mark. **3.** Deeply and intimately; to the heart. — *v.* **homed, hom·ing** *v.t.* **1.** To cause (an aircraft or guided missile) to proceed toward a target by means of radio waves, radar, or automatic timing devices. **2.** To furnish with a home. — *v.i.* **3.** To go home; return home. **4.** To be directed toward a target by automatic devices: said of guided missiles: usu. with *in* or *in on.* **5.** To have residence. [OE *hām*] — **home′less** *adj.*

home·bod·y (hōm′bod′ē) *n., pl.* **·ies** One who prefers to stay at home or whose main interest is in the home.

home·brew (hōm′broō′) *n.* An alcoholic beverage made at home, as for home use. — **home′-brewed′** *adj.*

home·com·ing (hōm′kum′ing) *n.* **1.** A return to one's home. **2.** *U.S.* In colleges, an annual alumni celebration.

home economics The science of home management, as of food, clothing, children, budgets, etc.

home·land (hōm′land′) *n.* The country of one's birth or allegiance.

home·ly (hōm′lē) *adj.* **·li·er, ·li·est 1.** Having a familiar, everyday character. **2.** Having plain or ugly features. **3.** Lacking in refinement. — **home′li·ness** *n.*

home·made (hōm′mād′) *adj.* **1.** Made at home. **2.** Simply or crudely fashioned.

home·mak·er (hōm′mā′kər) *n.* One in charge of managing her own home; housewife. — **home′mak′ing** *n.*

homeo- *combining form* Like; similar: *homeomorphism:* also spelled *homoeo-, homoio-.* [< Gk. *homoios* similar]

ho·me·op·a·thist (hō′mē·op′ə·thist, hom′ē-) *n.* One who practices homeopathy. Also **ho·me·o·path** (hō′mē·ə·path′).

ho·me·op·a·thy (hō′mē·op′ə·thē, hom′ē-) *n.* A system of therapy using minute doses of medicines that produce the symptoms of the disease treated. — **ho′me·o·path′ic** *adj.* — **ho′me·o·path′i·cal·ly** *adv.*

ho·me·o·sta·sis (hō′mē·ə·stā′sis, hom′ē-) *n. Biol.* The tendency of an organism to maintain a uniform and beneficial physiological stability within and between its parts; organic equilibrium. — **ho′me·o·stat′ic** (-stat′ik) *adj.*

home plate In baseball, the marker at which a player stands when batting, and to which he returns in scoring a run.

hom·er (hō′mər) *n. U.S. Informal* **1.** In baseball, a home run. **2.** A homing pigeon.

Ho·mer·ic (hō·mer′ik) *adj.* Of, pertaining to, or suggestive of Homer or his epic poetry. Also **Ho·mer′i·cal.**

home rule Self-government in local affairs within the framework of state or national laws. — **home ruler**

home run In baseball, a hit that cannot be fielded, thus permitting the batter to touch all the bases and score a run.

home·sick (hōm′sik′) *adj.* Unhappy or ill through longing for home; nostalgic. — **home′sick′ness** *n.*

home·spun (hōm′spun′) *adj.* **1.** Spun at home. **2.** Plain and simple; unsophisticated. **3.** Made of homespun. — *n.* **1.** Fabric woven at home or by hand. **2.** A rough, loosely woven fabric similar to this.

home·stead (hōm′sted) *n.* **1.** A house and its land, etc. **2.** *U.S.* A tract of land occupied under the Homestead Act. — *v.i.* **1.** *U.S.* To occupy land under the Homestead Act. — *v.t.* **2.** *U.S.* To settle on (land) under the Homestead Act. — **home′stead′er** *n.*

Homestead Act *U.S.* A Congressional enactment of 1862 that provided a settler with 160 acres of free public land for cultivation and eventual ownership.

homestead law *U.S.* A law exempting up to a certain amount a dwelling and its land from certain liabilities incurred by the owner. Also **homestead exemption law.**

home·stretch (hōm′strech′) *n.* **1.** The straight portion of a racetrack forming the final approach to the finish. **2.** The last stage of any journey or endeavor.

home·ward (hōm′wərd) *adv.* Toward home. Also **home′wards** (-wərdz). — *adj.* Directed toward home.

home·work (hōm′wûrk′) *n.* Work done at home, esp. school work.

home·y (hō′mē) *adj.* **hom·i·er, hom·i·est** Suggesting the comforts of home. — **home′y·ness** or **hom′i·ness** *n.*

hom·i·ci·dal (hom′ə·sīd′l, hō′mə-) *adj.* **1.** Of homicide. **2.** Tending to homicide; murderous. — **hom′i·ci′dal·ly** *adv.*

hom·i·cide (hom′ə·sīd, hō′mə-) *n.* **1.** The killing of any human being by another. **2.** A person who has killed another. [< F < L *homo* man + *caedere* to cut, kill]

hom·i·let·ic (hom′ə·let′ik) *adj.* **1.** Pertaining to or having the nature of a sermon or homily. **2.** Of or pertaining to homiletics. Also **hom′i·let′i·cal.** — **hom′i·let′i·cal·ly** *adv.*

hom·i·let·ics (hom′ə·let′iks) *n.pl. (construed as sing.)* The branch of theological study that treats of the art of writing and delivering sermons. [< Gk. *homilētikos* sociable]

hom·i·ly (hom′ə·lē) *n., pl.* **·lies 1.** A sermon, especially one based on a Biblical text. **2.** A solemn discourse or lengthy reproof, especially on morals or conduct. [< OF < LL < Gk. *homilos* assembly] — **hom′i·list** *n.*

hom·ing (hō′ming) *adj.* **1.** Returning home. **2.** Helping or causing an aircraft, missile, etc., to home.

homing pigeon A pigeon capable of making its way home from great distances: also called *carrier pigeon.*

hom·i·noid (hom′ə·noid, hō′mə-) *adj.* Like or related to man. — *n.* An animal resembling man. [< NL < L *homo, hominis* man]

hom·i·ny (hom′ə·nē) *n.* Kernels of dried, hulled white corn, prepared as a food by boiling. [< Algonquian *rockahominie* parched corn]

hominy grits Grits (def. 2).

homo- *combining form* Same; like: opposed to *hetero-.* [< Gk. *homo-* < *homos* same]

homoeo- See HOMEO-.

ho·mo·ge·ne·i·ty (hō′mə·jə·nē′ə·tē, hom′ə-) *n.* The quality or condition of being homogeneous.

ho·mo·ge·ne·ous (hō′mə·jē′nē·əs, hom′ə-) *adj.* **1.** Having the same composition, structure, or character throughout;

uniform. **2.** Similar or identical in nature or form; like. [< Med.L < Gk. < *homos* same + *genos* race] — **ho′mo·ge′ne·ous·ly** *adv.* — **ho′mo·ge′ne·ous·ness** *n.*

ho·mog·en·ize (hə·mŏj′ə·nīz, hō′mə·jə·nīz′) *v.t.* **·ized, ·iz·ing 1.** To make or render homogeneous. **2.** To process, as milk, so as to break up fat globules and disperse them uniformly. — **ho·mog′en·i·za′tion** *n.* — **ho·mog′en·iz′er** *n.*

hom·o·graph (hom′ə·graf, -gräf, hō′mə-) *n.* A word identical with another in spelling, but differing from it in origin and meaning and sometimes in pronunciation, as *wind*, an air current, and *wind*, to coil: also called *homonym.* [< Gk. < *homos* same + *graphein* to write] — **hom·o·graph′ic** *adj.*

ho·mol·o·gize (hō·mŏl′ə·jīz) *v.* **·gized, ·giz·ing** *v.t.* **1.** To make or demonstrate to be homologous. — *v.i.* **2.** To be homologous; have correspondence.

ho·mol·o·gous (hō·mŏl′ə·gəs) *adj.* **1.** Similar or related in structure, position, proportion, value, etc.; corresponding in nature or relationship. **2.** *Biol.* Corresponding in structure or origin, as an organ or part of one animal to a similar organ or part of another: The foreleg of a horse and the wing of a bird are *homologous*: distinguished from *analogous.* [< Gk. < *homos* same + *logos* measure, proportion]

ho·mol·o·gy (hō·mŏl′ə·jē) *n. pl.* **·gies 1.** The state or quality of being homologous. **2.** A homologous relationship.

ho·mo·mor·phism (hō′mə·môr′fiz·əm, hom′ə-) *n. Biol.* Resemblance between unrelated parts or organisms. Also **ho′mo·mor′phy.** — **ho′mo·mor′phic, ho′mo·mor′phous** *adj.*

hom·o·nym (hom′ə·nim, hō′mə-) *n.* A word identical with another in pronunciation but differing from it in origin, spelling, and meaning, as *fair* and *fare, read* and *reed*: also called *homophone.* **2.** A word identical with another in spelling and pronunciation, but differing from it in origin and meaning, as *butter*, the food, and *butter*, one who butts. **3.** A homograph. [< Gk. *homos* same + *onyma* name] — **hom·o·nym·ic** (hom′ə·nim′ik, hō′mə-), **ho·mon·y·mous** (hō·mon′ə·məs) *adj.*

hom·o·phone (hom′ə·fōn, hō′mə-) *n.* A homonym (def. 1). [< Gk. *homos* same + *phōnē* sound]

hom·o·phon·ic (hom′ə·fon′ik, hō′mə-) *adj.* **1.** Of, pertaining to, or having the same sound. **2.** *Music* Having one predominant part carrying the melody, with the other parts used for harmonic effect: opposed to *polyphonic.* — **ho·moph·o·ny** (hō·mof′ə·nē) *n.*

ho·mop·ter·ous (hō·mop′tər·əs) *adj.* Of or pertaining to insects with sucking mouth parts and usu. two pairs of wings. [< NL < Gk. *homos* same + *pteron* wing] — **ho·mop′ter·an** *adj. & n.*

Homo sa·pi·ens (sā′pē·enz) The scientific name for modern man. [< NL < L *homo* man + *sapiens* wise]

ho·mo·sex·u·al (hō′mə·sek′shōō·əl, hom′ə-) *adj.* Of or having sexual desire for persons of the same sex. — *n.* A homosexual individual. — **ho′mo·sex′u·al′i·ty** (-al′ə·tē) *n.*

ho·mun·cu·lus (hō·mung′kyə·ləs) *n. pl.* **·li** (-lī) A midget; dwarf. [< L *homo* man] — **ho·mun′cu·lar** *adj.*

hone (hōn) *n.* A fine, compact whetstone used for sharpening edged tools, razors, etc. — *v.t.* **honed, hon·ing** To sharpen, as a razor, on a hone. [OE *hān* stone]

hon·est (on′ist) *adj.* **1.** Not given to lying, cheating, stealing, etc. **2.** Not characterized by falsehood or intent to mislead: an *honest* statement. **3.** Giving or having full worth or value. **4.** Performed or earned in a conscientious manner. **5.** Sincere; frank. [< OF < L *honos* honor]

hon·est·ly (on′ist·lē) *adv.* **1.** In an honest manner. **2.** Really; truly; indeed: used for emphasis: *Honestly,* I'll go.

hon·es·ty (on′is·tē) *n.* **1.** The state or quality of being honest. **2.** Truthfulness; sincerity; fairness.

hon·ey (hun′ē) *n. pl.* **hon·eys 1.** A sweet, viscous substance made by bees from nectar gathered from flowers. **2.** Anything resembling honey. **3.** Sweetness. **4.** Darling: a term of endearment. **5.** *U.S. Slang* Something regarded as a superior example of its kind: a *honey* of a car. — *v.* **hon·eyed** or **hon·ied, hon·ey·ing** — *v.t.* **1.** To sweeten with or as with honey. **2.** To talk in a loving or flattering manner to. — *adj.* Of or like honey; sweet. [OE *hunig*]

hon·ey·bee (hun′ē·bē′) *n.* A bee that produces honey.

hon·ey·comb (hun′ē·kōm′) *n.* **1.** A structure consisting of series of hexagonal, wax cells, made by bees for the storage of honey, pollen, or their eggs. **2.** Anything like a honeycomb. — *v.t.* **1.** To fill with small holes or cavities; riddle. **2.** To penetrate or pervade so as to undermine or weaken. — *adj.* Like a honeycomb.

hon·ey·dew (hun′ē·dōō′, -dyōō′) *n.* **1.** A sweet fluid exuded by the leaves of various plants during warm weather. **2.** A sweetish substance secreted by certain insects.

honeydew melon A variety of melon having a smooth, white skin and sweet, greenish pulp.

hon·eyed (hun′ēd) *adj.* **1.** Full of, consisting of, or resembling honey. **2.** Sweet, soothing, or flattering.

honey locust A large, thorny North American tree bearing long pods with a sweet pulp between the seeds.

hon·ey·moon (hun′ē·mōōn′) *n.* **1.** A vacation spent by a

---

newly-married couple. **2.** The first, happy period of a marriage. **3.** *U.S. Informal* The early and easy period of any relationship. — *v.i.* To spend one's honeymoon.

hon·ey·suck·le (hun′ē·suk′əl) *n.* **1.** A climbing shrub having white, buff, or crimson flowers. **2.** Any of a number of similar fragrant plants. [OE *hunisūce*]

honk (hôngk, hongk) *n.* **1.** The sound made by a goose. **2.** A sound resembling this, as that of an automobile horn. — *v.i.* **1.** To make the sound of the goose. **2.** To make the sound of an automobile horn. — *v.t.* **3.** To cause (an automobile horn) to sound. [Imit.] — **honk′er** *n.*

hon·ky (hông′kē) *n. pl.* **·kies** *U.S. Slang* A white person: an offensive term. Also **hon·kie.** [? < *hunky* < *Bohunk*, a foreign-born laborer: an offensive term < BO(HEMIAN) + HUNG(ARIAN)]

hon·ky-tonk (hông′kē·tôngk′, hong′kē·tongk′) *n. U.S. Slang* A noisy, squalid barroom or tavern. [Prob. imit.]

hon·or (on′ər) *n.* **1.** High regard, respect, or esteem. **2.** Glory; fame; credit. **3.** *Usu. pl.* An outward token, sign, act, etc., of regard or esteem. **4.** A strong sense of what is right. **5.** A reputation for high standards of conduct. **6.** A cause or source of esteem or pride: to be an *honor* to one's profession. **7.** A privilege or pleasure: May I have the *honor* of this dance? **8.** *Usu. pl.* Special recognition given to a student for superior scholarship, etc. **9.** Chastity in women. **10.** In bridge, one of the five highest cards of a suit. **11.** In golf, the privilege of playing first from the tee. **— to do honor to 1.** To pay homage to. **2.** To bring respect or credit to. **— to do the honors 1.** To act as host or hostess. **2.** To perform any of various social courtesies, as proposing toasts, etc. — *v.t.* **1.** To regard with honor or respect. **2.** To treat with courtesy. **3.** To confer an honor upon; dignify. **4.** To accept or pay, as a check or draft. Also *Brit.* **hon′our.** [< OF < L] — **hon′or·er** *n.*

Hon·or (on′ər) *n.* A title or form of address for a judge, mayor, etc.: preceded by *Your, His,* or *Her.*

hon·or·a·ble (on′ər·ə·bəl) *adj.* **1.** Worthy of honor or respect. **2.** Conferring honor or credit. **3.** Having eminence or high rank. **4.** Possessing or according to high moral principles. **5.** Accompanied by marks of honor. Also *Brit.* **hon′our·a·ble.** — **hon′or·a·ble·ness** *n.* — **hon′or·a·bly** *adv.*

Hon·or·a·ble (on′ər·ə·bəl) *adj.* A formal title of courtesy for certain important officials, as cabinet members, justices of the Supreme Court, etc.: preceded by *The.*

hon·o·rar·i·um (on′ə·râr′ē·əm) *n. pl.* **·rar·i·ums** or **·rar·i·a** (-râr′ē·ə) A payment given, as to a professional man, for services rendered when law or propriety forbids a set fee. [< L *honorarium* honorary]

hon·or·ar·y (on′ə·rer′ē) *adj.* **1.** Designating an office, title, etc., bestowed as an honor, without the customary powers, duties, or salaries. **2.** Having such a title, office, etc.: an *honorary* chairman. **3.** Bringing, conferred in, or denoting honor: an *honorary* membership. [< L *honorarius*]

hon·or·if·ic (on′ə·rif′ik) *adj.* **1.** Conferring or implying honor or respect. **2.** Denoting certain phrases, words, or word elements, as in Oriental languages, used in respectful address. — *n.* Any honorific title, word, phrase, etc. [< L < *honor* honor + *facere* to make] — **hon′or·if′i·cal·ly** *adv.*

honors system In some colleges, a plan for selected students to undertake individual, specialized work.

honor system In some colleges, schools, etc., a system of government without immediate supervision.

hooch (hōōch) *n. U.S. Slang* Alcoholic liquor, esp. illegally distilled whisky. [< *hoochinoo,* alter. of *Hutanuwu,* name of Alaskan Indian tribe that made liquor]

hood[1] (hōōd) *n.* **1.** A covering for the head and back of the neck, sometimes forming part of a garment. **2.** Anything resembling a hood in form or use; as: **a** *U.S.* The movable metal cover protecting the engine of an automobile. **b** A projecting cover for a hearth, ventilator, etc. **3.** In falconry, a cover for the head and eyes of a hawk when it is not hunting. **4.** *Zool.* In certain animals, as the cobra, the folds of skin near the head, capable of expansion. — *v.t.* To cover or furnish with or as with a hood. [OE *hōd*] — **hood′ed** *adj.*

hood[2] (hōōd) *n. U.S. Slang* A hoodlum. [< HOODLUM]

-hood *suffix of nouns* **1.** Condition or quality of; state of being: *babyhood, falsehood.* **2.** Class or totality of those having a certain character: *priesthood.* [OE *hād* state, condition]

hood·lum (hōōd′ləm) *n. U.S.* **1.** A young street rowdy or tough. **2.** A thug or ruffian. [? < dia. G *hodalum* rowdy]

hoo·doo (hōō′dōō) *n.* **1.** Voodoo. **2.** *Informal* One who or that which brings bad luck; a jinx. **3.** *Informal* Bad luck. — *v.t. Informal* To bring bad luck to. [Var. of VOODOO]

hood·wink (hōōd′wingk′) *v.t.* **1.** To blindfold. **2.** To trick; cheat. **3.** To conceal or hide. — **hood′wink′er** *n.*

hoof (hōōf, hŏŏf) *n. pl.* **hoofs** or **hooves** (hōōvz, hŏŏvz) **1.** The horny sheath incasing the foot in various mammals, as horses, cattle, swine, etc. ◆ Collateral adjective: *ungular.* **2.** The entire foot of such an animal. **3.** An animal with hoofs, especially as a unit of a herd. **4.** The human foot: a humorous usage. **— on the hoof** Alive; not butchered: said of cattle. — *v.t. & v.i.* **1.** To trample with the hoofs. **2.** *Informal* To walk or dance: usually with *it*. [OE *hōf*]

hoof·beat (hŏŏf'bēt', hŏŏf'-) *n.* The sound made by a hoofed animal in walking, trotting, etc.

hoof·er (hŏŏf'ər, hŏŏf'ər) *n. U.S. Slang* A professional dancer, esp. a tap dancer.

hoof·print (hŏŏf'print', hŏŏf'-) *n.* One of the tracks left by a hoofed animal.

hook (hŏŏk) *n.* **1.** A curved or bent piece of metal, wood, bone, etc., having one free end that serves to hold up, fasten, or drag something. **2.** A fishhook. **3.** A curved cutting tool. **4.** The fixed half of a hinge from which a door, gate, etc., swings. **5.** Something that ensnares; a trap. **6.** Something resembling a hook; as: **a** A recurved organ or part of an animal or plant. **b** A curved point of land. **c** A bend in a river. **d** A hook-shaped part of a letter. **7.** In baseball, a curve. **8.** In boxing, a short, swinging blow, with the elbow bent. **9.** In golf, a stroke that sends the ball curving to his left. **10.** *Music* One of the lines at the end of the stem of a note, used to indicate the note's value. **11.** *Naut. Slang* An anchor. — **by hook or by crook** In one way or another. — **hook, line, and sinker** *Informal* Entirely; unreservedly. — **off the hook** *Slang* Free from a troublesome situation, obligation, etc. — **on one's own hook** *Informal* By one's own efforts. — *v.t.* **1.** To fasten, attach, or take hold of with or as with a hook. **2.** To catch on a hook, as fish. **3.** To make into the shape of a hook. **4.** To catch on or wound with the horns, as those of a bull. **5.** To make (a rug, mat, etc.) by looping yarn through a backing of canvas or burlap. **6.** In baseball, to pitch (the ball) in a curve. **7.** In boxing, to strike with a short, swinging blow. **8.** In golf, to drive (the ball) to one's left. **9.** In hockey, to check illegally with the stick. **10.** *Informal* To trick; dupe. **11.** *Slang* To pilfer; steal. — *v.i.* **12.** To curve like a hook; bend. **13.** To be fastened or caught with or as with a hook or hooks. — **to hook up 1.** To fasten or attach with a hook or hooks. **2.** To put together or connect. — **to hook up with** *Slang* **1.** To become a companion of. **2.** To marry. [OE *hōc*] — **hook'y** *adj.*

hook·ah (hŏŏk'ə) *n.* An Oriental tobacco pipe having a long, flexible tube that passes through a vessel of water, thus cooling the smoke. Also **hook'a.** [< Arabic *huqqah*]

hook and eye A fastening for clothes, consisting of a small hook that passes through a loop of metal or thread.

hooked (hŏŏkt) *adj.* **1.** Curved like a hook. **2.** Supplied with a hook or hooks. **3.** Made by means of a hook, as a rug. **4.** *Slang* Married. **5.** *Slang* Addicted to a habit or practice, especially a harmful one. — **hook·ed·ness** (hŏŏk'id·nis) *n.*

hooked rug A rug made by looping yarn or strips of cloth with a hooked tool through a backing of burlap or canvas.

hook·nose (hŏŏk'nōz') *n.* A nose with a downward curve; aquiline nose. — **hook'-nosed'** (-nōzd') *adj.*

hook·up (hŏŏk'up') *n.* **1.** *Telecom.* The arrangement of the apparatus and connections used for a radio broadcast or other electrical transmission. **2.** *Informal* A relationship or connection, as between countries, persons, etc.

hook·worm (hŏŏk'wûrm') *n.* A nematode worm with hooked mouth parts, parasitic in the intestines and causing ancylostomiasis in man.

hookworm disease Ancylostomiasis.

hook·y (hŏŏk'ē) *n. U.S. Informal* Absence without leave, as from school: now only in the phrase **to play hooky,** to be a truant. [< HOOK, in dial. sense of "make off"]

hoo·li·gan (hŏŏ'lə·gən) *n. Slang* A young hoodlum; petty gangster. [after *Hooligan,* name of an Irish family]

hoop (hŏŏp, hŏŏp) *n.* **1.** A circular band of metal, wood, etc.; esp., such a band used to confine the staves of a barrel, etc. **2.** A child's toy in the shape of a large ring. **3.** One of the rings of flexible metal, whalebone, etc., used to make a woman's skirt stand out from her body. **4.** The band of a finger ring. — *v.t.* **1.** To surround or fasten with a hoop or hoops. **2.** To encircle. [OE *hōp*]

hoop·er (hŏŏ'pər, hŏŏp'ər) *n.* A cooper.

hoop·la (hŏŏp'lä) *n. U.S. Slang* Noise and excitement.

hoo·poe (hŏŏ'pŏŏ) *n.* An Old World bird having a long bill and an erectile crest. Also **hoo'poo.** [< F < L *upupa*]

hoop skirt **1.** A bell-shaped structure made from several hoops of graduated sizes, used to expand a woman's skirt. **2.** The skirt worn over this.

hoo·ray (hŏŏ·rā', hə-, hŏŏ-) See HURRAH.

hoose·gow (hŏŏs'gou) *n. U.S. Slang* Jail or prison. Also **hoos'gow.** [< Sp. *juzgado* tribunal]

Hoo·sier (hŏŏ'zhər) *n. U.S.* A native or resident of Indiana. [Prob. < dial. *hoosier* mountaineer]

Hoosier State A nickname of Indiana.

HOOPOE
(About 12 inches long; bill 2¼ inches)

hoot¹ (hŏŏt) *n.* **1.** The cry of an owl. **2.** A sound similar to this, as of a train whistle. **3.** A loud, derisive outcry. — *v.i.* **1.** To make the sound of an owl. **2.** To make a sound similar to this. **3.** To jeer, as in contempt. — *v.t.* **4.** To jeer at or mock with derisive cries. **5.** To drive off with hoots. **6.** To express (disapproval, scorn, etc.) by hooting. [< Scand. Cf. Sw. *huta.*]

hoot² (hŏŏt) *n. U.S. Informal* An insignificant amount; bit: commonly in the expression **I don't give a hoot,** I don't care a bit. [Earlier *hooter,* ? alter. of *iota.* Cf. JOT.]

hoot·en·an·ny (hŏŏt'n·an'ē) *n. pl.* **·nies 1.** *U.S.* A gathering of folk singers, especially for a public performance. **2.** *Informal* A gadget; thingamajig. [Origin unknown]

hooves (hŏŏvz, hŏŏvz) Alternative plural of HOOF.

hop¹ (hop) *v.* **hopped, hop·ping** *v.i.* **1.** To move by making short leaps on one foot. **2.** To move in short leaps on both feet or on all four feet. **3.** To limp. **4.** *Informal* To dance. **5.** *Informal* To go, especially by airplane. — *v.t.* **6.** To jump over, as a fence. **7.** *Informal* To get on or board. — **to hop off** To leave the ground in flight, as an airplane. — *n.* **1.** The act of hopping. **2.** *Informal* A dance or dancing party. **3.** *Informal* A trip in an airplane. [OE *hoppian*]

hop² (hop) *n.* **1.** A perennial climbing herb with scaly fruit. **2.** *pl.* The dried cones, used medicinally, and as a flavoring in beer. [< MDu. *hoppe*]

hope (hōp) *v.* **hoped, hop·ing** *v.t.* **1.** To desire with expectation of fulfillment. **2.** To wish; want. — *v.i.* **3.** To have desire or expectation: usually with *for.* — **to hope against hope** To continue hoping even when it may be in vain. — *n.* **1.** Desire accompanied by expectation of fulfillment. **2.** Confident expectation. **3.** That which is desired. **4.** One who or that which is a cause of hopeful expectation. [OE *hopa*]

hope chest A box or chest used by young women to hold linen, clothing, etc., in anticipation of marriage.

hope·ful (hōp'fəl) *adj.* **1.** Full of or manifesting hope: a *hopeful* attitude. **2.** Affording grounds for hope; promising: a *hopeful* situation. — *n.* A young person who seems likely to succeed. — **hope'ful·ness** *n.*

hope·ful·ly (hōp'fə·lē) *adv.* **1.** In a hopeful manner. **2.** It is hoped; one hopes: *Hopefully,* a strike can be averted.

hope·less (hōp'lis) *adj.* **1.** Without hope; despairing: a *hopeless* feeling. **2.** Affording no ground for hope: a *hopeless* predicament. — **hope'less·ly** *adv.* — **hope'less·ness** *n.*

Ho·pi (hō'pē) *n.* **1.** One of a group of North American Pueblo Indians of Shoshonean stock, now on a reservation in NE Arizona. **2.** Their Shoshonean language. [< Hopi *hópitu,* lit., peaceful ones]

hopped-up (hopt'up') *adj. U.S. Slang* **1.** Stimulated by narcotics; drugged. **2.** Supercharged, as an engine.

hop·per (hop'ər) *n.* **1.** One who or that which hops. **2.** A jumping insect or larva. **3.** Any of various funnel-shaped receptacles in which coal, sand, grain, etc., may be kept until ready for discharge through the bottom.

hop·scotch (hop'skoch') *n.* A children's game in which the player hops on one foot over the lines of a diagram, so as to recover a block or pebble.

Ho·ra·tian (hə·rā'shən) *adj.* Of or pertaining to Horace.

horde (hôrd, hōrd) *n.* **1.** A multitude, pack, or swarm, as of people, animals, etc. **2.** A tribe of nomadic Mongols. **3.** Any nomadic tribe. — *v.i.* **hord·ed, hord·ing** To gather in or live in a horde. [< F < G < Polish *horda*]

hore·hound (hôr'hound', hōr'-) *n.* **1.** A whitish, bitter, perennial herb of the mint family. **2.** The juice or extract of this plant. **3.** A candy or cough remedy flavored with this extract. Also spelled *hoarhound.* [OE *hārhūne*]

ho·ri·zon (hə·rī'zən) *n.* **1.** The line of the apparent meeting of the sky with the earth or sea. **2.** The bounds or limits of one's observation, knowledge, or experience. [< OF < L < Gk. *horizein* to bound]

hor·i·zon·tal (hôr'ə·zon'təl, hor'-) *adj.* **1.** Of, pertaining to, or close to the horizon. **2.** Parallel to the horizon; level: opposed to *vertical.* **3.** Equal and uniform: a *horizontal* tariff. — *n.* A line, plane, etc., assumed to be parallel with the horizon. — **Syn.** See LEVEL. — **hor'i·zon'tal·ly** *adv.*

horizontal union A craft union.

hor·mone (hôr'mōn) *n.* **1.** *Physiol.* An internal secretion produced by one of the endocrine glands, as the pituitary, thyroid, adrenals, etc., and carried by the blood stream to other parts of the body where it has a specific effect. **2.** *Bot.* A similar substance in plants. [< Gk. *hormaein* to excite] — **hor·mo·nal** (hôr·mō'nəl), **hor·mon·ic** (hôr·mon'ik) *adj.*

horn (hôrn) *n.* **1.** A hard, bonelike, permanent growth of epidermal tissue, usu. occurring in pairs and projecting from the head in various hoofed animals, as in oxen, sheep, cattle, etc. **2.** Either of the two antlers of a deer, shed annually. **3.** Any outgrowth projecting naturally from the head of an animal. **4.** The substance of which animal horn is made. **5.** The appendage like an animal's horn attributed to demons, deities, etc. **6.** In the Bible, a symbol of glory and power. **7.** *Usu. pl.* The imaginary projections from the forehead of a cuckold. **8.** A vessel or implement formed from or shaped like a horn: a powder *horn.* **9.** One of the extremities of the crescent moon. **10.** The pommel of a saddle. **11.** A device for sounding warning signals: an automobile *horn.* **12.** A cornucopia. **13.** Any pointed or tapering projection, as the point of an anvil. **14.** One of the two or more alternatives of a dilemma. **15.** *Music* **a** Any of the various brass instruments, formerly made from animal horns, in the shape of a long, coiled tube widening out into a bell at one end. **b** The French horn. **16.** *Informal* Any musical wind instrument. **17.** *Electronics* A hollow, tubular device terminating in a cone of varying cross section, for collecting sound waves, as in a loudspeaker. **18.** *Geog.* **a** One of the branches forming the delta of a stream or river. **b** A cape or peninsula. **— to blow one's own horn** To brag. **— to haul** (or **pull or draw**) **in one's horns 1.** To check one's anger, zeal, etc. **2.** To retract or withdraw, as a previous statement. **— adj.** Of or like horn. **— v.t. 1.** To provide with horns. **2.** To shape like a horn. **3.** To attack with the horns; gore. **— to horn in** *Slang* To intrude or enter without being invited. [OE]

horn·bill (hôrn′bil′) *n.* A tropical bird, having a large bill surmounted by a hornlike extension.

horn·blende (hôrn′blend′) *n.* A common variety of amphibole, greenish black or black, containing iron and silicate of magnesium, calcium, and aluminum. **— horn′blend′ic** *adj.*

horn·book (hôrn′bŏŏk′) *n.* **1.** A leaf or page containing a printed alphabet, etc., covered with transparent horn and framed, formerly used in teaching reading to children. **2.** A primer or book of rudimentary knowledge.

horned (hôrnd, *Poetic* hôr′nid) *adj.* **1.** Having a horn or horns. **2.** Having a projection or process resembling a horn.

horned owl Any of various American owls with conspicuous ear tufts; esp. the screech owl.

horned toad A flat-bodied, spiny lizard with a short tail and toadlike appearance, common in semiarid regions of the western U.S. Also **horn toad.**

horned viper A venomous African or Indian viper with a hornlike growth over each eye.

hor·net (hôr′nit) *n.* Any of various wasps capable of inflicting a severe sting. [OE *hyrnet*]

horn of plenty A cornucopia.

horn·pipe (hôrn′pīp′) *n.* **1.** An obsolete musical instrument resembling the clarinet. **2.** A lively English dance for one or more performers. **3.** The music for such a dance.

horn·y (hôr′nē) *adj.* **horn·i·er, horn·i·est 1.** Made of horn or a similar substance. **2.** Having horns or projections resembling horns. **3.** Hard as horn; tough. **— horn′i·ness** *n.*

hor·o·loge (hôr′ə·lŏj, hor′-) *n.* A timepiece, as a watch, clock, etc. [< OF < L < Gk. < *hōra* time + *legein* to tell]

ho·rol·o·ger (hô·rol′ə·jər, hō-) *n.* One skilled in horology; also, one who makes or sells timepieces. Also **ho·rol′o·gist.**

ho·rol·o·gy (hô·rol′ə·jē, hō-) *n.* The science of the measurement of time or of the construction of timepieces. **— hor·o·log·ic** (hôr′ə·loj′ik, hor′-) or **·i·cal** *adj.*

hor·o·scope (hôr′ə·skōp, hor′-) *n.* **1.** In astrology, the aspect of the heavens, with special reference to the positions of the planets at any specific instant, esp. at a person's birth. **2.** The diagram of the twelve divisions or houses of the heavens, used in predicting the future. [< L < Gk. < *hōra* hour + *skopos* watcher] **— hor·o·scop·y** (hô·ros′kə·pē) *n.*

hor·ren·dous (hô·ren′dəs, ho-) *adj.* Horrible; frightful. [< L *horrere* to bristle] **— hor·ren′dous·ly** *adv.*

hor·ri·ble (hôr′ə·bəl, hor′-) *adj.* **1.** Exciting or tending to excite horror; shocking. **2.** *Informal* Inordinate; excessive: a *horrible* liar. **3.** *Informal* Unpleasant; ugly. [< F < L *horrere* to bristle] **— hor′ri·ble·ness** *n.* **— hor′ri·bly** *adj.*

hor·rid (hôr′id, hor′-) *adj.* **1.** Causing great aversion or horror; dreadful. **2.** *Informal* Very objectionable; offensive. **— hor′rid·ly** *adv.* **— hor′rid·ness** *n.*

hor·ri·fy (hôr′ə·fī, hor′-) *v.t.* **·fied, ·fy·ing 1.** To affect or fill with horror. **2.** *Informal* To shock or surprise painfully; startle. **— hor′ri·fi·ca′tion** *n.*

hor·ror (hôr′ər, hor′-) *n.* **1.** A painful, strong emotion caused by extreme fear, dread, repugnance, etc. **2.** One who or that which excites such an emotion. **3.** *Often pl.* A quality that excites horror: the *horrors* of crime. **4.** Great aversion; loathing. **5.** *Informal* Something disagreeable, ugly, etc. [< L]

hors d'oeuvre (ôr dûrv′, *Fr.* ôr dœ′vr′) *Usu. pl.* An appetizer, as olives, celery, etc. [< F]

horse (hôrs) *n. pl.* **hors·es** or **horse 1.** A large, strong, herbivorous mammal with solid hoofs and a long mane and tail, employed in the domestic state as a draft or pack animal or for riding. ◆ Collateral adjective: *equine.* **2.** The full-grown male horse as contrasted with the mare; a gelding or stallion. **3.** Mounted soldiers; cavalry. **4.** A device, generally having four legs, for holding or supporting something: often in combination: *clotheshorse.* **5.** In gymnastics, a wooden leather-covered block on four legs, used for vaulting and

other exercises. **6.** *Informal* In chess, a knight. **— a horse of another** (or **a different**) **color** A completely different matter. **— out of** (or **straight from**) **the horse's mouth** From the most direct and reliable source. **— to be** (or **get**) **on one's high horse** *Informal* To act haughtily or scornfully. **— to hold one's horses** *Slang* To restrain one's impetuosity or impatience. **— To horse!** A command for cavalry troops to mount. **— v. horsed, hors·ing** *v.t.* **1.** To furnish with a horse or horses. **2.** To put on horseback. **3.** *U.S. Slang* To subject to horseplay or ridicule. **— v.i. 4.** To mount or ride on a horse. **5.** *Slang* To engage in horseplay: often with *around.* **— adj. 1.** Of or pertaining to a horse or horses. **2.** Mounted on horses. **3.** Large for its kind. [OE *hors*]

horse·back (hôrs′bak′) *n.* **1.** A horse's back. **2.** A ridge of earth or rock; hogback. **— adv.** On a horse's back.

horse·car (hôrs′kär′) **1.** A tramcar drawn by horses. **2.** A car for transporting horses.

horse chestnut 1. A tree having digitate leaves, clusters of flowers, and chestnutlike fruits. **2.** The fruit of this tree.

horse·flesh (hôrs′flesh′) *n.* Horses collectively.

horse·fly (hôrs′flī′) *n. pl.* **·flies** A large fly, the female of which sucks the blood of horses, cattle, etc.

horse·hair (hôrs′hâr′) *n.* **1.** The hair of horses, esp. that of their manes and tails. **2.** A fabric made of such hair; haircloth. **— adj.** Covered, stuffed, or made of horsehair.

horse·hide (hôrs′hīd′) *n.* **1.** The hide of a horse. **2.** Leather made from a horse's hide.

horse latitudes *Naut.* A belt at about 35° north or south latitude, characterized by calms and light variable winds, with diminishing to prevailing westerlies toward the poles and trade winds toward the equator.

horse·laugh (hôrs′laf′, -läf′) *n.* A loud, scornful laugh.

horse·man (hôrs′mən) *n. pl.* **·men** (-mən) **1.** A man who rides a horse. **2.** A cavalryman. **— horse′man·ship** *n.*

horse pistol A large pistol formerly carried by horsemen.

horse·play (hôrs′plā′) *n.* Rough, boisterous play or fun.

horse·pow·er (hôrs′pou′ər) *n. Mech.* A unit of the rate of work, equal to 550 pounds lifted one foot in one second.

horse·rad·ish (hôrs′rad′ish) *n.* **1.** A garden herb of the mustard family. **2.** A condiment made from its root.

horse sense *Informal* Innate common sense.

horse·shoe (hôr′shōō′, hôrs′-) *n.* **1.** A piece of metal, U-shaped to fit the edge of a horse's hoof, to which it is nailed as a protective device. **2.** Something resembling a horseshoe in shape. **3.** *pl.* A game similar to quoits, in which the object is to throw horseshoes over or near a stake. **— v.t. ·shoed, ·shoe·ing** To furnish with horseshoes.

horseshoe crab A large marine arthropod having a horseshoe-shaped carapace and a long telson: also called *king crab.*

horse·tail (hôrs′tāl′) *n.* **1.** The tail of a horse. **2.** A perennial flowerless plant of wide distribution.

horse·whip (hôrs′hwip′) *n.* A whip for managing horses. **— v.t. ·whipped, ·whip·ping** To flog with a horsewhip.

horse·wom·an (hôrs′wōōm′ən) *n. pl.* **·wom·en** (-wim′in) **1.** A woman who rides on horseback. **2.** A woman who is skilled in riding or managing horses.

hors·y (hôr′sē) *adj.* **hors·i·er, hors·i·est 1.** Pertaining to, suggestive of, or having the nature of a horse or horses. **2.** Associated with or devoted to horses, horseracing, fox hunting, etc. Also **hors′ey. — hors′i·ly** *adv.* **— hors′i·ness** *n.*

hor·ta·to·ry (hôr′tə·tôr′ē, -tō′rē) *adj.* Of, characterized by, or giving exhortation or encouragement. Also **hor′ta·tive.** [< L *hortatorius*] **— hor′ta·tive·ly** *adv.*

hor·ti·cul·ture (hôr′tə·kul′chər) *n.* **1.** The cultivation of a garden. **2.** The art or science of growing garden vegetables, fruits, flowers, etc. [< L *hortus* garden + *cultura* cultivation] **— hor′ti·cul′tur·al** *adj.* **— hor′ti·cul′tur·ist** *n.*

ho·san·na (hō·zan′ə) *interj.* Praised be the Lord. **— n. 1.** A cry of "hosanna." **2.** Any exultant praise. [< LL < Gk. < Hebrew *hōshi āhnnā* save, we pray]

hose (hōz) *n. pl.* **hose** (*Archaic* **hos·en**) for defs. 1, 2; **hos·es** for def. 3 **1.** *pl.* Stockings or socks. **2.** *pl.* Formerly, a garment worn by men for covering the legs and lower part of the body like tight trousers. **3.** A flexible tube of rubber, plastic, etc., for conveying water and other fluids. **— v.t. hosed, hos·ing 1.** To water, drench, or douse with a hose. **2.** *Canadian Slang* To cheat or defeat. [OE *hosa*]

Ho·se·a (hō·zē′ə, -zā′ə) Eighth-century B.C. Hebrew prophet. **— n.** A book of the Old Testament bearing his name: also, in the Douai Bible, *Osee.*

ho·sier·y (hō′zhər·ē) *n.* Stockings and socks of all types.

hos·pice (hos′pis) *n.* A place of rest or shelter, usu. maintained by a religious order for pilgrims, travelers, etc. [< F < L *hospitium* inn, hospitality]

hos·pi·ta·ble (hos′pi·tə·bəl, hos·pit′ə·bəl) *adj.* **1.** Behaving in a kind and generous manner toward guests. **2.** Affording or expressing welcome and generosity toward guests. **3.** Receptive in mind. [< OF < L *hospitare* to entertain] **— hos′pi·ta·ble·ness** *n.* **— hos′pi·ta·bly** *adv.*

hos·pi·tal (hos′pi·təl) *n.* An institution that provides medical, surgical, or psychiatric treatment and nursing care for the ill or injured temporarily lodged there; also, the building used for this purpose. [< OF < L *hospes* guest]

hos·pi·tal·i·ty (hos/pə·tal/ə·tē) *n. pl.* **·ties** The spirit, practice, or act of being hospitable.

hos·pi·tal·ize (hos/pi·təl·īz/) *v.t.* **·ized, ·iz·ing** To put in a hospital for treatment and care.

hos·pi·tal·i·za·tion (hos/pi·təl·ə·zā/shən, -ī·zā/shən) *n.* **1.** The act of hospitalizing. **2.** *U.S.* A form of insurance that guarantees all or partial payment of hospital expenses: also **hospital insurance.**

host¹ (hōst) *n.* **1.** A man who extends hospitality to others, usu. to guests in his own home. **2.** *Biol.* Any living organism from which a parasite obtains nourishment and protection. — *v.t. Informal* To conduct or entertain in the role of host. [< OF < L *hospes* guest, host]

host² (hōst) *n.* **1.** A large number of men or things; a multitude. **2.** An army. [< OF < L *hostis* enemy]

host³ (hōst) *n. Eccl. Sometimes cap.* The Eucharistic bread or wafer. [< OF < L *hostia* sacrificial victim]

hos·tage (hos/tij) *n.* **1.** A person given or held as a pledge until specified conditions are met, as in war. **2.** The state of any person so treated. **3.** A pledge or security. [< OF]

hos·tel (hos/təl) *n.* One of a chain of supervised lodging houses for young people on bicycle or hiking trips.

hos·tel·ry (hos/təl·rē) *n. pl.* **·ries** *Archaic* A lodging place; inn. — **hos/tel·er, hos/tel·ler** *n.*

host·ess (hōs/tis) *n.* **1.** A woman who performs the duties of a host. **2.** A woman employed in a restaurant, etc., to greet and serve guests. **3.** A woman paid to dance with the patrons of a public dance hall. **4.** A female innkeeper.

hos·tile (hos/təl, *esp. Brit.* -tīl) *adj.* **1.** Having or expressing enmity or opposition; unfriendly. **2.** Of, pertaining to, or characteristic of an enemy: *hostile* acts; *hostile* forces. [< F < L *hostilis*] — **hos/tile·ly** *adv.*

hos·til·i·ty (hos·til/ə·tē) *n. pl.* **·ties** **1.** The state of being hostile. **2.** A hostile act. **3.** *pl.* War or acts of war.

hos·tler (hos/lər, os/-) *n.* A stableman; groom: also spelled *ostler.* [< OF *hostelier* innkeeper]

hot (hot) *adj.* **hot·ter, hot·test** **1.** Having or giving off great heat; having a high temperature. **2.** Having a relatively high degree of heat; very warm. **3.** Feeling or showing abnormal bodily warmth. **4.** Giving the sensation of heat or burning to the tongue or skin: *hot* pepper. **5.** Carrying an electric current, esp. one of high voltage. **6.** Dangerously radioactive. **7.** Constantly in action or use: War news kept the wires hot. **8.** In hunting, strong or fresh, as a scent. **9.** Not far behind: in *hot* pursuit. **10.** Marked by or showing strong or violent emotion: *hot* words. **11.** Marked by intense activity; raging; violent: a *hot* battle. **12.** *Slang* Lustful; sexy. **13.** *Slang* Strongly disposed toward; eager: often with *for*. **14.** *Informal* Controversial: a *hot* issue. **15.** *Informal* So new as not to have lost its currency, excitement, etc.: a *hot* item. **16.** *Slang* Excellent, skillful, etc.: He is not so *hot* tonight. **17.** *U.S. Slang* Recently stolen or illegally procured. **18.** *Music Slang* a Designating jazz marked by a fast tempo, heavily accented beat, exciting improvisations, etc. **b** Playing or performing such jazz: a *hot* trumpet. — **in hot water** *Informal* In trouble. — **to make it hot for** *Informal* To make the situation extremely uncomfortable for. — *adv.* In a hot manner. [OE *hāt*] — **hot/ly** *adv.*

hot air *Slang* Empty or pretentious talk; exaggeration.

hot·bed (hot/bed/) *n.* **1.** A bed of rich earth, protected by glass and warmed usu. by fermenting manure, used to promote the growth of plants in advance of their season. **2.** A place or condition favoring rapid growth or great activity.

hot-blood·ed (hot/blud/id) *adj.* Easily moved or excited.

hot cake A pancake or griddlecake. — **to go** (or **sell**) **like hot cakes** *Informal* To be disposed of quickly.

hot cross bun A circular cake or bun marked with a cross of frosting, eaten esp. during Lent.

hot dog *Informal* A cooked frankfurter, usu. grilled, served in a split roll, and garnished with mustard, relish, etc.

ho·tel (hō·tel/) *n.* **1.** An establishment or building providing lodging, food, etc., to travelers and long-term residents. **2.** *Canadian* Beer parlor. [< F < OF *hostel* inn]

hot·foot (hot/foot/) *v.i. Informal* To hurry: often with *it.*

hot·head (hot/hed/) *n.* A hotheaded person.

hot·head·ed (hot/hed/id) *adj.* **1.** Quick-tempered. **2.** Impetuous. — **hot/head/ed·ly** *adv.* — **hot/head/ed·ness** *n.*

hot·house (hot/hous/) *n.* A greenhouse kept warm artificially for the growth of out-of-season or delicate plants.

hot line A direct means of communication, esp. a telephone line for emergency use between Washington, D.C. and Moscow.

hot plate A small portable gas or electric stove.

hot rod *U.S. Slang* An automobile, usu. an older model, modified for high speeds.

hot spring A natural spring emitting waters with a temperature of 98° F. or above: also called *thermal spring.*

Hot·ten·tot (hot/ən·tot) *n.* **1.** A member of a South African people believed to be related to both the Bantus and the Bushmen. **2.** The language of this people. — *adj.* Of or pertaining to the Hottentots or their language.

hou·dah (hou/də) See HOWDAH.

hound (hound) *n.* **1.** A dog of any of several breeds kept for hunting, esp. one that hunts by scent and in a pack. **2.** A dog of any breed. **3.** A mean, detestable man. — **to follow** (or **ride to**) **the hounds** To engage in hunting (a fox, etc.) on horseback and with a pack of hounds. — *v.t.* **1.** To hunt with or as with hounds. **2.** To incite to pursue. **3.** *Informal* To nag persistently; pester. [OE *hund* dog]

hour (our) *n.* **1.** A space of time equal to ¹⁄₂₄ of a day; sixty minutes. ◆ Collateral adjective: horal. **2.** Any one of the twelve points on a timepiece indicating such a space of time. **3.** A definite time of day as shown in hours and minutes by a timepiece: The *hour* is 6:15. **4.** An indefinite, but usu. short, period of time: The happiest *hour* of one's life. **5.** A particular or regularly fixed time for some activity. **6.** *pl.* A set period of time for work or other regular pursuits: school *hours.* **7.** *pl.* One's usual time of rising and of going to bed: to keep regular *hours.* **8.** The present time or current situation. **9.** Distance calculated by the time ordinarily required to cover it: an *hour* away from home. **10.** In education, a single class session or period, usu. 50 minutes long. **11.** *Eccl.* **a** The canonical hours. **b** The office or prayers recited or sung at these hours. **12.** *Astron.* An angular measure of right ascension or longitude, being 15 degrees or the 24th part of a great circle of the sphere. — **the small** (or **wee**) **hours** The early hours of the morning. [< L < Gk. *hōra* time, period]

hour·glass (our/glas/, -gläs/) *n.* An old device for measuring time, consisting of two globular glass vessels connected by a narrow neck through which a quantity of sand, mercury, or water runs from the upper vessel to the lower during a stated interval of time, usu. an hour.

hou·ri (hoo/rē, hour/ē) *n.* In Moslem belief, one of the beautiful virgins allotted to those who attain Paradise. [< F < Persian < Arabic *hūrīyah* black-eyed woman]

HOURGLASS

hour·ly (our/lē) *adj.* **1.** Of, happening, or performed every hour. **2.** Occurring or accomplished in the course of an hour. **3.** Frequent. — *adv.* **1.** At intervals of an hour. **2.** Hour by hour. **3.** Frequently; often.

house (*n.* hous; *v.* houz) *n. pl.* **hous·es** (hou/zəz) **1.** A building intended as a dwelling for human beings, esp. one used as the residence of a family or single tenant. **2.** A household; family. **3.** The abode of a fraternity, religious community, or other group living together as a unit. **4.** A dormitory or resident hall, esp. in a college or university. **5.** *Brit.* A college in a university. **6.** Anything providing shelter or protection to an animal, as the shell of a snail. **7.** A structure for storing or sheltering something, as goods, plants, etc. **8.** A building used for any of various purposes: a *house* of correction. **9.** A place of worship. **10.** A theater or other place of entertainment. **11.** The audience in such a place of entertainment. **12.** *Govt.* **a** A legislative or deliberative body: *House* of Representatives. **b** A quorum of such a body. **c** The chamber or building such a body occupies. **13.** *Often cap.* A line of ancestors and descendants regarded as forming a single family: the *House* of Stuart. **14.** A business firm or establishment: a publishing *house.* **15.** In astrology: **a** One of the twelve divisions of the heavens. **b** A sign of the zodiac considered as the seat of greatest influence of a particular planet. — **like a house on fire** Very quickly and vigorously. — **on the house** At the expense of the proprietor. — **to bring down the house** To receive loud and enthusiastic applause. — **to clean house** *U.S. Slang* To get rid of undesirable conditions or persons, as in an organization. — **to keep house** To manage the affairs or work of a home. — **to put** (or **set**) **one's house in order** To tidy up one's personal or business affairs. — *v.* **housed, hous·ing** *v.t.* **1.** To take or put into a house; lodge. **2.** To store in a house or building. **3.** In carpentry, to fit into a mortise, joint, etc. — *v.i.* **4.** To take shelter or lodgings; dwell. [OE *hūs*] — **house/ful** *n.* — **house/less** *adj.*

house·boat (hous/bōt/) *n.* A barge or flat-bottomed boat fitted out as a dwelling and used in quiet waters.

house·break·ing (hous/brā/king) *n.* The act of breaking into and entering another's home with intent to commit theft or some other felony. — **house/break/er** *n.*

house·bro·ken (hous/brō/kən) *adj.* Trained to urinate and defecate outdoors or in a specific place, as a dog.

house·coat (hous/kōt/) *n.* A woman's garment, usu. long with a loose skirt, for informal wear within the house.

house·dress (hous/dres/) *n.* A dress, usu. of printed cotton fabric, worn esp. during household chores.

PRONUNCIATION KEY: add, āce, câre, pälm; end, ēven; it, īce; odd, ōpen, ôrder; took, pool; up, bûrn; ə = a in *above*, e in *sicken*, i in *flexible*, o in *melon*, u in *focus*; yoo = u in *fuse*; oil; pout; check; go; ring; thin; this; zh, vision. For á, œ, ü, kh, ń, see inside front cover.

house·fly (hous′flī′) *n. pl.* **·flies** The common fly, found in nearly all parts of the world.

house·hold (hous′hōld′) *n.* **1.** A number of persons dwelling as a unit under one roof: esp., a family living together, including servants, etc. **2.** A home or the various domestic affairs of a home. —*adj.* Of or pertaining to the home.

house·hold·er (hous′hōl′dər) *n.* **1.** One who owns or occupies a house. **2.** The head of a family.

household word A person, product, place, etc., that is known or familiar to many people. Also **household name.**

house·keep·er (hous′kē′pər) *n.* **1.** One who performs the tasks of maintaining a home, as a housewife. **2.** A paid manager of a home. —**house′keep′ing** *n.*

house·maid (hous′mād′) *n.* A girl or woman employed to do housework.

housemaid's knee *Pathol.* A chronic inflammation of the bursa in front of the knee, afflicting housemaids, etc.

house·mas·ter (hous′mas′tər, -mäs′-) *n. Chiefly Brit.* A teacher in charge of one of the houses of a boys' school.

house·moth·er (hous′muth′ər) *n.* A woman acting as a supervisor for a group of people living together.

House of Commons 1. The lower house of the British Parliament, the members of which are elected. **2.** The lower house of the Canadian Parliament.

house of correction An institution confining those given short-term sentences for minor offenses and considered to be capable of rehabilitation.

House of Lords The upper and nonelective house of the British Parliament, made up of the peerage and the highest ranking clergy.

House of Representatives 1. The lower, larger branch of the United States Congress, and of many State legislatures, composed of members elected on the basis of population. **2.** A similar legislative body, as in Australia, Mexico, etc.

house organ A publication regularly issued by a business organization for its employees and customers.

house party An entertainment of a group of guests for several days, usu. in a house or a college fraternity.

house physician A physician resident by appointment in a hospital, hotel, or other institution.

house·top (hous′top′) *n.* The roof of a house. —**to shout (or cry) from the housetops** To give wide publicity to.

house·wares (hous′wârz′) *n.* Kitchen utensils, dishes, glassware, and other wares used in the home.

house·warm·ing (hous′wôr′ming) *n.* A party held by or for those who have just moved into new living quarters.

house·wife (hous′wif′ for def. 1, huz′if for def. 2) *n. pl.* **house·wives** (hous′wīvz′) *for def. 1;* **house·wifes** (huz′ifs) or **house·wives** (huz′ivz) *for def. 2* **1.** A married woman who manages her own household and does not work for a living. **2.** *Chiefly Brit.* A kit holding sewing articles. —**house′·wife′ly** *adj. & adv.*

house·wife·ry (hous′wī′fər·ē, -wīf′rē) *n.* The duties of a housewife; housekeeping.

house·work (hous′wûrk′) *n.* The chores involved in keeping house, washing, cooking, etc.

hous·ing[1] (hou′zing) *n.* **1.** The act of providing shelter or lodging; also, the shelter or lodging so provided. **2.** The providing of houses on a large scale. **3.** Houses or dwellings collectively. **4.** That which serves as a shelter, cover, etc.: a bamboo *housing* for plants. **5.** *Mech.* **a** Something that holds part of a machine in place, as a frame or set of brackets. **b** A casing or cover for a machine or part of a machine.

hous·ing[2] (hou′zing) *n,* **1.** An ornamental cover for a horse. **2.** *Usu. pl.* Trappings. [< OF *houce,* prob. < Gmc.]

hove (hōv) Past tense of HEAVE.

hov·el (huv′əl, hov′-) *n.* **1.** A small, wretched dwelling. **2.** A low, open shed for sheltering cattle, tools, etc. —*v.t.* **hov·eled** or **·elled, hov·el·ing** or **·el·ling** To shelter or lodge in a hovel. [? Dim. of OE *hof* building]

hov·er (huv′ər, hov′-) *v.i.* **1.** To remain suspended in or near one place in the air. **2.** To linger or remain nearby, as if watching: with *around, near,* etc. **3.** To remain in an uncertain or irresolute state: with *between.* —*n.* The act or state of hovering. [< obs. *hove* to float] —**hov′er·er** *n.*

Hov·er·craft (huv′ər·kraft′, hov′-, -kräft′) *n.* A vehicle designed to travel just above the surface of land or water on a cushion of air generated by powerful fans: a trade name. Also **hov′er·craft.**

how (hou) *adv.* **1.** In what way or manner. **2.** To what degree, extent, or amount. **3.** In what state, or condition. **4.** For what reason or purpose. **5.** At what price: *How* is the stock selling today? **6.** With what meaning: *How* is that remark to be taken? **7.** By what name or designation. **8.** *Informal* What: *How* about having lunch? —*n.* A manner or means of doing. [OE *hū*]

how·be·it (hou·bē′it) *adv. Archaic* Be that as it may.

how·dah (hou′də) *n.* A seat for riders on an elephant or camel, often fitted with a canopy. [< Hind. *haudah*]

how-do-you-do (hou′də·yə·dōō′) *n. Informal* An embarrassing or difficult situation: usu. preceded by *fine, pretty,* etc.

How do you do? What is the state of your health?: used as a formal greeting when being introduced to a person.

how·dy (hou′dē) *interj. Informal* An expression of greeting.

how·ev·er (hou·ev′ər) *adv.* **1.** In whatever manner; by whatever means. **2.** To whatever degree or extent: Spend *however* much it costs. —*conj.* Nevertheless; in spite of; still; yet. —**Syn.** See BUT[1]. Also **how·e′er′** (-âr′)

how·it·zer (hou′it·sər) *n.* A cannon with a barrel of medium length and operating at a relatively high angle of fire. [< Du. *ult.* < Czechoslovakian *houfnice* catapult]

howl (houl) *v.i.* **1.** To utter the loud, mournful wail of a dog, wolf, or other animal. **2.** To utter such a cry in pain, grief, or rage. **3.** To make a sound similar to this. **4.** To laugh loudly. —*v.t.* **5.** To utter or express with howling. **6.** To condemn, suppress, or drive away by howling: often with *down.* —*n.* **1.** The wailing cry of a wolf, dog, or other animal. **2.** Any howling sound. [ME *houlen*]

howl·er (hou′lər) *n.* **1.** One who or that which howls. **2.** A monkey of Central and South America, having a long, grasping tail and making loud howling sounds. **3.** *Informal* An absurd blunder in speaking or writing.

howl·ing (hou′ling) *adj.* **1.** Producing or uttering howls. **2.** Characterized by or filled with howls: the *howling* wilderness. **3.** *Slang* Very great; tremendous: a *howling* success.

how·so·ev·er (hou′sō·ev′ər) *adv.* **1.** In whatever manner. **2.** To whatever degree or extent.

hoy·den (hoid′n) *n.* A boisterous or ill-mannered girl. —*adj.* Boisterous. —*v.i.* To act like a hoyden. [Origin uncertain] —**hoy′den·ish** *adj.* —**hoy′den·ish·ness** *n.*

Hoyle (hoil) *n.* A book of rules and instructions for indoor games, esp. card games. [after Sir Edmund *Hoyle,* 1672–1769, English writer on card games]

hub (hub) *n.* **1.** The center part of a wheel into which the axle is inserted. **2.** Any center of great activity or interest.

hub·bub (hub′ub) *n.* **1.** A loud, confused noise, as of many voices shouting or talking. **2.** Uproar. [Origin unknown]

huck·le·ber·ry (huk′əl·ber′ē) *n. pl.* **·ries 1.** The edible black or dark blue berry of any of various North American shrubs. **2.** A shrub yielding this berry.

huck·ster (huk′stər) *n.* **1.** A peddler of wares, esp. fruits and vegetables. **2.** A petty, greedy tradesman. **3.** *U.S. Slang* One engaged in the advertising business. —*v.t.* **1.** To sell; peddle. **2.** To haggle. [< MDu. *heuken* to retail]

hud·dle (hud′l) *v.* **·dled, ·dling** *v.i.* **1.** To crowd or nestle together closely, as from fear or cold. **2.** To draw or hunch oneself together. **3.** In football, to gather in a huddle. —*v.t.* **4.** To bring or crowd together closely. **5.** To draw (oneself) together: often with *up.* **6.** To make or do hurriedly or confusedly, as dressing. —*n.* **1.** A number of persons or things crowded together. **2.** A state of confusion or disorder. **3.** In football, the grouping of a team before play. **4.** *U.S. Informal* Any small conference. [Origin uncertain]

hue[1] (hyōō) *n.* **1.** The attribute of a color that determines its position in the spectrum and differentiates it from an achromatic color of the same brightness. **2.** Color: the autumnal *hues.* **3.** A particular tint or shade of color. [OE *hīw* appearance] —**hued** *adj.*

hue[2] (hyōō) *n.* A loud clamor; shouting. —**hue and cry** Any great public stir. [< OF *huer* to shout after]

huff (huf) *n.* A fit of sudden anger or irritation. —*v.t.* **1.** To offend; make angry. —*v.i.* **2.** To take offense. **3.** To puff; blow. —**huff′ish** *adj.*

huf·fy (huf′ē) *adj.* **huff·i·er, huff·i·est 1.** Touchy. **2.** Petulant; sulky. —**huff′i·ly** *adv.* —**huff′i·ness** *n.*

hug (hug) *v.* **hugged, hug·ging** *v.t.* **1.** To take and clasp affectionately within the arms; press in close embrace. **2.** To squeeze between the forepaws, as a bear. **3.** To cherish or cling to, as a belief. **4.** To keep close to. —*v.i.* **5.** To crowd closely together; snuggle. —*n.* **1.** A close, affectionate embrace. **2.** A tight clasp with the arms, as in wrestling. **3.** A bear's grip. [Prob. < ON *hugga* to console]

huge (hyōōj) *adj.* Very great in size, quantity, extent, etc. [< OF *ahuge* high] —**huge′ly** *adv.* —**huge′ness** *n.*

hug·ger·mug·ger (hug′ər·mug′ər) *n.* Disorder; confusion. —*adj.* **1.** Secret; sly. **2.** Disorderly; slovenly.

Hu·gue·not (hyōō′gə·not) *n.* Any French Protestant of the 16th and 17th centuries. [< F < G *eidgenoss* confederate]

huh (hu) *interj.* An exclamation of inquiry, surprise, etc.

hu·la (hōō′lə) *n.* A Hawaiian dance characterized by sinuous arm movements that tell a story in pantomime. Also **hu′la-hu′la.** [< Hawaiian]

hulk (hulk) *n.* **1.** The body of an old, wrecked, or dismantled ship. **2.** *Often pl.* An old ship used for a prison, etc. **3.** Any bulky, unwieldy object or person. —*v.i.* **1.** To rise or loom bulkily: usu. with *up.* **2.** *Dial.* To lounge or slouch about. [OE, prob. < Med.L < Gk. *helkein* to drag]

hulk·ing (hul′king) *adj.* Big and unwieldy, bulky, or clumsy: a great *hulking* fellow. Also **hulk′y.**

hull (hul) *n.* **1.** The outer covering of certain fruits or seeds. **2.** The calyx of some fruits, as the strawberry. **3.** Any outer covering. **4.** *Naut.* The body of a ship, exclusive of the masts, etc. —*v.t.* **1.** To remove the hull of. **2.** To strike or pierce the hull of (a ship). [OE *hulu*]

hul·la·ba·loo (hul′ə·bə·lōō′) *n.* A loud, confused noise; uproar. Also **hul′la·bal·loo′.** [Imit. reduplication of HULLO]

hum¹ (hum) *v.* **hummed, hum·ming** *v.i.* **1.** To make a low, murmuring or droning sound. **2.** To sing with the lips closed. **3.** To give forth an indistinct sound: The streets *hummed* with traffic. **4.** To mumble indistinctly, as from confusion; hem. **5.** *Informal* To be very busy or active: The office *hummed.* —*v.t.* **6.** To sing with closed lips without words. **7.** To put into a state by humming: to *hum* a child to sleep. —*n.* The act or sound of humming. [ME *hummer*] —**hum′mer** *n.*

hum² *interj.* A nasal, murmuring sound made to express mental concentration, deliberation, hesitation, etc.

hu·man (hyōō′mən) *adj.* **1.** Of or characteristic of man. **2.** Having the nature or attributes of a man. **3.** Consisting of a man or men: *human* race. —*n.* A human being. [< OF < L *humanus*] —**hu′man·ness** *n.*

human being A man, woman, or child; a person.

hu·mane (hyōō·mān′) *adj.* **1.** Having kindness, sympathy, etc.; benevolent. **2.** Tending to refine or civilize: *humane* learning. —**hu·mane′ly** *adv.* —**hu·mane′ness** *n.*

hu·man·ism (hyōō′mən·iz′əm) *n.* **1.** The character or quality of being human. **2.** A system or attitude in thought, religion, etc., in which human ideals and the perfection of personality are made central. **3.** The study of the humanities.

Hu·man·ism (hyōō′mən·iz′əm) *n.* The intellectual and literary movement of the Renaissance, characterized by the study of Greek and Roman classics and by an emphasis on human interests rather than on religion.

hu·man·ist (hyōō′mən·ist) *n.* **1.** One learned in or devoted to the study of the humanities; esp., a classical scholar. **2.** One who subscribes to humanism (def. 2). —**hu′man·is′tic** *adj.* —**hu′man·is′ti·cal·ly** *adv.*

hu·man·i·tar·i·an (hyōō·man′ə·târ′ē·ən) *n.* One who seeks to promote the welfare of mankind; philanthropist. —*adj.* Pertaining to humanitarians. —**hu·man′i·tar′i·an·ism** *n.*

hu·man·i·ty (hyōō·man′ə·tē) *n.* *pl.* **·ties 1.** The human race; mankind. **2.** The state of being human; human nature. **3.** The state of being humane; benevolence. —**the humanities 1.** The study of classical Greek and Latin literature. **2.** Literature, philosophy, the fine arts, etc., as distinguished from the sciences. [< OF < L *humanus* humane]

hu·man·ize (hyōō′mən·īz) *v.* **·ized, ·iz·ing** *v.t.* **1.** To make human; give human characteristics to. **2.** To make gentle, kindly, etc. —*v.i.* **3.** To become human or humane. —**hu′man·i·za′tion** (-ə·zā′shən, -ī·zā′-) *n.* —**hu′man·iz′er** *n.*

hu·man·kind (hyōō′mən·kīnd′) *n.* The human race; people.

hu·man·ly (hyōō′mən·lē) *adv.* **1.** In a human manner. **2.** Within human power or ability: Is this *humanly* possible? **3.** In accordance with man's experience or knowledge.

hum·ble (hum′bəl) *adj.* **·bler, ·blest 1.** Free from pride or vanity; modest. **2.** Lowly in station, condition, etc.; unpretentious. **3.** Servile; fawning. **4.** Respectful. —*v.t.* **·bled, ·bling 1.** To reduce the pride of. **2.** To lower in rank or dignity. [< F < L *humus* ground] —**hum′ble·ness** *n.* —**hum′bler** *n.* —**hum′bly** *adv.*

humble pie Formerly, a pie containing the inner and less choice parts (**humbles**) of a deer and given to the servants at hunting feasts: also spelled *umble pie.* —**to eat humble pie** To be forced to apologize. [< OF < LL *lumbus* loin]

hum·bug (hum′bug) *n.* **1.** Anything intended or used to delude; fraud. **2.** One who seeks to deceive others. **3.** The quality or practice of deceiving. —*v.* **·bugged, ·bug·ging** *v.t.* **1.** To delude; trick. —*v.i.* **2.** To practice deception. [Origin unknown] —**hum′bug·ger** *n.* —**hum′bug·ger·y** *n.*

hum·ding·er (hum·ding′ər) *n.* *Slang* One who or that which is remarkable or out of the ordinary.

hum·drum (hum′drum′) *adj.* Lacking interest, variety, or excitement; dull. —*n.* **1.** That which is tedious or dull. **2.** A tiresome person; bore. [Reduplication of HUM]

hu·mer·us (hyōō′mər·əs) *n.* *pl.* **·mer·i** (-mər·ī) *Anat.* The bone of the upper part of the arm, from shoulder to elbow. For illus. see SKELETON. [< L, shoulder] —**hu′mer·al** *adj.*

hu·mid (hyōō′mid) *adj.* Containing vapor or water; moist; damp. [< L *humere* to be moist] —**hu′mid·ly** *adv.*

hu·mid·i·fy (hyōō·mid′ə·fī) *v.t.* **·fied, ·fy·ing** To make moist or humid. —**hu·mid′i·fi·ca′tion** *n.* —**hu·mid′i·fi′er** *n.*

hu·mid·i·ty (hyōō·mid′ə·tē) *n.* Moisture; dampness, esp. of the atmosphere. —**relative humidity** The ratio of the amount of water vapor actually in the air to the total amount it could hold at the same temperature.

hu·mi·dor (hyōō′mə·dôr) *n.* A container in which moisture is retained, used for cigars, etc.

hu·mil·i·ate (hyōō·mil′ē·āt) *v.t.* **·at·ed, ·at·ing** To lower the pride or self-esteem of; mortify. [< L *humilis* lowly] —**hu·mil′i·a·to·ry** (-ə·tôr′ē, -ə·tō′rē) *adj.* —**hu·mil′i·a′tion** *n.*

hu·mil·i·ty (hyōō·mil′ə·tē) *n.* *pl.* **·ties** The state or quality of being humble. [< L *humilitas* lowness]

hum·ming·bird (hum′ing·bûrd′) *n.* Any of a family of very small birds of the New World, having a long, slender bill for sipping nectar from flowers, and rapidly vibrating wings that produce a humming sound during flight.

hum·mock (hum′ək) *n.* **1.** A low mound of earth or rock; hillock. **2.** Wooded land above a marsh. **3.** A ridge or pile in an ice field. [Origin unknown] —**hum′mock·y** *adj.*

hu·mor (hyōō′mər, yōō′-) *n.* **1.** The quality of anything that is funny or appeals to the comic sense. **2.** The ability to appreciate or express what is amusing, comic, etc. **3.** Speech, writing, or actions that are amusing or comic. **4.** A temporary mood: to be in a good *humor.* **5.** Temperament; disposition. **6.** A sudden liking, etc.; whim; caprice. **7.** *Physiol.* **a** A liquid or semiliquid substance of the body, as blood, bile, lymph, etc. **b** The aqueous humor of the eye. **8.** In ancient physiology, one of the four principal bodily fluids (**cardinal humors**), blood, phlegm, choler (yellow bile), and melancholy (black bile), which, according to their proportions in the body, were believed to influence health and temperament. —*v.t.* **1.** To comply with the moods of; indulge. **2.** To adapt oneself to the nature of (something). Also *Brit.* **hu′mour.** [< OF < L *umere* to be moist]

hu·mor·esque (hyōō′mə·resk′, yōō′-) *n.* A playful, lively musical composition; caprice. [< G *humoreske*]

hu·mor·ist (hyōō′mər·ist, yōō′-) *n.* **1.** One who exercises a sense of humor; joker; wag. **2.** A professional writer, entertainer, etc., in humor or jokes. —**hu′mor·is′tic** *adj.*

hu·mor·ous (hyōō′mər·əs, yōō′-) *adj.* **1.** Full of or characterized by humor; laughable; funny. **2.** Displaying or using humor. —**hu′mor·ous·ly** *adv.* —**hu′mor·ous·ness** *n.* —**Syn.** Comical, droll, witty.

hump (hump) *n.* **1.** A rounded protuberance, esp. on the back, as in the camel, bison, etc., or the deformity produced in man by a curvature of the spine. **2.** A low mound; hummock. —**over the hump** Beyond the most critical point. —*v.t.* To round into a hump; hunch. [Akin to LG *hump*]

hump·back (hump′bak′) *n.* **1.** A back with a hump. **2.** A person having a back with a hump; hunchback. **3.** A large whale. —**hump′backed′** *adj.*

humph (humf) *interj.* An exclamation of dissatisfaction.

Hump·ty Dump·ty (hump′tē dump′tē) A character in a nursery rhyme and riddle personifying an egg that fell from a wall and could not be pieced together again.

hump·y (hum′pē) *adj.* **hump·i·er, hump·i·est 1.** Covered with or full of humps. **2.** Like a hump.

hu·mus (hyōō′məs) *n.* The black or brown substance of the soil, formed by the decay of animal and vegetable matter, and providing nutrition for plant life. [< L, ground]

Hun (hun) *n.* **1.** One of a barbarous Asian people who invaded Europe in the fourth and fifth centuries, led by Attila. **2.** Any barbarous or destructive person. [OE < LL *Hunnus*] —**Hun′nish** *adj.* —**Hun′nish·ness** *n.*

hunch (hunch) *n.* **1.** *U.S. Informal* A premonition of some coming event. **2.** A hump. **3.** A lump or hunk. —*v.t.* **1.** To bend or draw up so as to form a hump. —*v.i.* **2.** To move or thrust forward jerkily. [Origin unknown]

hunch·back (hunch′bak′) *n.* **1.** A deformed back with a hump. **2.** A person so deformed. —**hunch′backed′** *adj.*

hun·dred (hun′drid) *n.* **1.** The sum of ninety and ten, written as 100, c, or C: a cardinal number. **2.** Anything consisting of a hundred units. —*adj.* Being ten more than ninety. [OE] —**hun·dredth** (hun′dridth) *adj. & n.*

hun·dred·fold (hun′drid·fōld′) *n.* An amount or number a hundred times as great as a given unit. —*adv.* So as to be a hundred times as many or as great. —*adj.* **1.** Consisting of one hundred parts. **2.** One hundred times as great.

hun·dred·weight (hun′drid·wāt′) *n.* A unit of weight commonly reckoned in the United States at 100 pounds avoirdupois, in England at 112 pounds.

Hundred Years' War See table for WAR.

hung (hung) Past tense and past participle of HANG.

Hun·gar·i·an (hung·gâr′ē·ən) *adj.* Of Hungary, its people, or their language. —*n.* **1.** A native or citizen of Hungary; esp., a Magyar. **2.** The Finno-Ugric language of the Hungarians: also called *Magyar.* [< Med.L *Hungarus*]

hun·ger (hung′gər) *n.* **1.** The state of discomfort or weakness caused by lack of food. **2.** A desire or need for food. **3.** Any strong desire or craving. —*v.i.* **1.** To be hungry. **2.** To have a desire or craving: with *for* or *after.* —*v.t.* **3.** To cause to undergo hunger; starve. [OE *hungor*]

hunger strike A self-imposed fast, as by a prisoner, political or religious leader, etc., as a means of protest.

hun·gry (hung′grē) *adj.* **·gri·er, ·gri·est 1.** Desiring or in need of food. **2.** Eagerly craving: *hungry* for applause. **3.** Indicating hunger: a *hungry* look. **4.** Not fertile. [OE *hungor*] —**hun′gri·ly** *adv.* —**hun′gri·ness** *n.*

---

hunk (hungk) *n. Informal* A large piece or lump; chunk: a *hunk* of meat. [Prob. < Flemish *hunke*]

hun·ky-do·ry (hung/kē-dôr/ē, -dō/rē) *adj. U.S. Slang* Fully satisfactory; all right. Also **hunk/y.**

hunt (hunt) *v.t.* **1.** To pursue (game) for the purpose of killing or catching. **2.** To range over (an area) in search of game. **3.** To use in the chase, as hounds. **4.** To chase, drive away, or pursue with hostility, violence, etc. **5.** To search for eagerly; seek: to *hunt* the truth. **6.** To search (a place) thoroughly. — *v.i.* **7.** To seek or pursue game. **8.** To search or seek: often with *for* or *after.* — **to hunt down 1.** To pursue until caught or killed. **2.** To search for until found. — *n.* **1.** The act of hunting game; chase. **2.** A group of huntsmen. **3.** A search; pursuit. **4.** An area used for hunting. [OE *huntian*]

hunt·er (hun/tər) *n.* **1.** One who hunts. **2.** An animal used in hunting, as a dog or horse.

hunt·ing (hun/ting) *n.* The act of one who or that which hunts. — *adj.* Of or used for hunting.

hunt·ress (hun/tris) *n.* A woman who hunts.

hunts·man (hunts/mən) *n. pl.* **·men** (-mən) **1.** One who hunts game; hunter. **2.** One who directs a hunt, hounds, etc.

Hu·pa (hōō/pə) *n.* **1.** One of a tribe of North American Indians in NW California. **2.** The language of this tribe.

hur·dle (hûr/dəl) *n.* **1.** A light, portable barrier for horses or runners to leap over in races. **2.** *pl.* A race in which such barriers are used: often with *the.* **3.** An obstacle or difficulty to be surmounted. — *v.* **·dled, ·dling** *v.t.* **1.** To leap over (a barrier) in a race. **2.** To make, cover, or enclose with hurdles. **3.** To surmount or overcome (a difficulty, etc.). — *v.i.* **4.** To leap over hurdles, etc. [OE *hyrdel*] — **hur/dler** *n.*

hur·dy-gur·dy (hûr/dē-gûr/dē) *n. pl.* **·dies** Musical instruments played by turning a crank, as the barrel organ.

hurl (hûrl) *v.t.* **1.** To throw, fling, or send with force. **2.** To throw down; overthrow. **3.** To utter with vehemence. — *v.i.* **4.** To throw something. — *n.* The act of hurling; also, a forceful throw. [ME *hurlen*] — **hurl/er** *n.*

hurl·ing (hûr/ling) *n.* An Irish game resembling field hockey. Also **hur/ley.** [< HURL]

hur·ly-bur·ly (hûr/lē-bûr/lē) *n. pl.* **·lies** Tumult; confusion; turmoil. — *adj.* Full of turmoil and confusion; tumultuous. [< earlier *hurling and burling*]

Hu·ron (hyŏŏr/ən, -on) *n.* A member of any of four tribes of North American Indians of Iroquoian stock, formerly between Lakes Huron and Ontario. [< F, ruffian]

hur·rah (hŏŏ-rô/, hə-rä/) *n. & interj.* An exclamation expressing triumph, joy, encouragement, etc. — *v.i.* **1.** To shout a hurrah or hurrahs. — *v.t.* **2.** To cheer with hurrahs. Also spelled *hooray.* Also **hur·ray/** (-rā/). [? < G *hurra*]

hur·ri·cane (hûr/ə-kān) *n.* **1.** *Meteorol.* A tropical cyclone, esp. one originating in the West Indies and often covering a wide area, having a wind velocity exceeding 75 miles per hour. **2.** Anything suggesting a hurricane in violence or speed. [< Sp. *huracán* < Carib]

hurricane deck A light, upper deck on a passenger vessel.

hur·ried (hûr/ēd) *adj.* **1.** Urged or forced to move, act, etc., in haste. **2.** Done or carried on in great or too great haste; a *hurried* decision. — **hur/ried·ly** *adv.* — **hur/ried·ness** *n.*

hur·ry (hûr/ē) *v.* **·ried, ·ry·ing** *v.i.* **1.** To act or move rapidly or in haste; hasten. — *v.t.* **2.** To cause or urge to act or move more rapidly. **3.** To hasten the progress, etc., of, often unduly. — *n. pl.* **·ries 1.** The act of hurrying; haste. **2.** Eagerness to move, act, etc. [ME *horyen*]

hur·ry-scur·ry (hûr/ē-skûr/ē) *n. pl.* **·ries** A hasty, confused bustling about. — *v.i.* **·ried, ·ry·ing** To rush pell-mell. — *adv.* In disorderly haste. — *adj.* Hurried; confused. Also **hur/ry-skur/ry.**

hurt (hûrt) *v.* **hurt, hurt·ing** *v.t.* **1.** To cause physical harm or pain to; injure. **2.** To impair in some way: to *hurt* one's reputation. **3.** To grieve or distress; cause mental suffering to. — *v.i.* **4.** To cause discomfort, suffering, or damage. **5.** To give out a feeling of pain. — *n.* **1.** Any injury, wound, etc. **2.** Damage; impairment. **3.** An injury to the feelings; affront. [< OF *hurter* to hit] — **hurt/er** *n.*

hurt·ful (hûrt/fəl) *adj.* Causing hurt; injurious. — **hurt/ful·ly** *adv.* — **hurt/ful·ness** *n.*

hur·tle (hûr/təl) *v.* **·tled, ·tling** *v.i.* **1.** To collide or strike violently; clash. **2.** To rush headlong or impetuously. **3.** To make a rushing or crashing sound. — *v.t.* **4.** To hurl, throw, or drive violently. [Freq. of ME *hurten* to hit, hurt]

hus·band (huz/bənd) *n.* A man joined to a woman in lawful wedlock. — *v.t.* To use or spend wisely; conserve: to *husband* one's forces. [OE *hūs* house + *bonda* freeholder]

hus·band·ry (huz/bən-drē) *n.* **1.** The occupation or business of farming. **2.** Careful management; economy; thrift. **3.** Management of household affairs, expenditures, etc.

hush (hush) *v.t.* **1.** To make silent; cause to be quiet. **2.** To keep hidden or secret: usu. with *up.* **3.** To soothe or allay, as fears. — *v.i.* **4.** To be or become quiet or still. — *n.* Deep silence; quiet. — *interj.* Be quiet! [Back formation < ME *hussht* quiet]

hush·a·by (hush/ə-bī/) *interj.* Go to sleep.

hush-hush (hush/hush/) *adj. Informal* Done in secrecy.

hush money A bribe to secure silence or secrecy.

hush·pup·py (hush/pup/ē) *n. pl.* **·pies** *Southern U.S.* A small fried ball of cornmeal dough.

husk (husk) *n.* **1.** The outer coating of certain fruits or seeds, esp. of an ear of corn. **2.** Any outer covering, esp. when comparatively worthless. — *v.t.* To remove the husk or outer covering of. [ME, prob. < Du. *huus* house]

husk·ing bee (hus/king) *U.S.* A cornhusking.

husk·y¹ (hus/kē) *adj.* **husk·i·er, husk·i·est 1.** Rough, or coarse in vocal quality. **2.** Full of or made of husks. **3.** Like a husk. [< HUSK] — **husk/i·ly** *adv.* — **husk/i·ness** *n.*

husk·y² (hus/kē) *U.S. Informal adj.* **husk·i·er, husk·i·est** Physically strong; burly. — *n. pl.* **husk·ies** A strong or powerful person. [HUSKY¹, with ref. to toughness of husks]

Hus·ky (hus/kē) *n. pl.* **Husk·ies** *U.S. & Canadian* **1.** A heavily furred Eskimo dog. Also **husk/y.** **2.** An Eskimo. **3.** The Eskimo language. [? Alter. of ESKIMO]

hus·sar (hŏŏ-zär/) *n.* A member of a cavalry regiment found in some European armies and usu. distinguished by brilliant dress uniforms. [< Hungarian < Serbian < Ital. < Med.L *corsarius*]

hus·sy (huz/ē, hus/ē) *n. pl.* **·sies 1.** A woman of questionable behavior or reputation. **2.** A pert or forward girl; minx. [Alter. of HOUSEWIFE]

hust·ings (hus/tingz) *n.pl. (usu. construed as sing.)* **1.** The proceedings at an election. **2.** Any place where political speeches are made. [OE < ON *hūs* house + *thing* assembly]

hus·tle (hus/əl) *v.* **·tled, ·tling** *v.t.* **1.** To push about or crowd roughly; jostle. **2.** To force, push, or thrust hurriedly. **3.** *U.S. Informal* To cause to proceed rapidly or too rapidly; hurry. **4.** *U.S. Slang* To sell or solicit (something) in an aggressive or unethical manner. — *v.i.* **5.** To push or shove; elbow. **6.** *U.S. Informal* To move or work with great energy. **7.** *U.S. Slang* To make money by clever or unscrupulous means. — *n.* **1.** The act of hustling. **2.** *U.S. Informal* Energetic activity; drive; push. [< Du. *hutselen* to shake, toss] — **hus/tler** *n.*

hut (hut) *n.* A small, rude house or cabin; hovel. — *v.t. & v.i.* **hut·ted, hut·ting** To shelter or live in a hut. [< OF < OHG *hutta*]

hutch (huch) *n.* **1.** A coop or pen for small animals: rabbit *hutch.* **2.** A chest, locker, or bin in which to store things; also, a cupboard for dishes. **3.** A small hut or cabin. **4.** A trough, as used by bakers for kneading dough. — *v.t.* To store up or hoard, as in a chest. [< F < LL *hutica*]

hutz·pah (hŏŏts/pə, khŏŏts/-) See CHUTZPAH.

huz·za (hə-zä/) *Archaic n. & interj.* An exclamation of joy, triumph, etc. — *v.* **·zaed, za·ing** *v.i.* **1.** To shout huzzas. — *v.t.* **2.** To cheer with huzzas. [Origin uncertain]

hwan (hwän) *n. pl.* **hwan** The monetary unit of South Korea: in 1960 worth about ⁹⁄₁₀ of a U.S. cent.

hy·a·cinth (hī/ə-sinth) *n.* **1.** A plant of the lily family, having clusters of fragrant, bell-shaped flowers. **2.** The bulb or flower of this plant. **3.** A brownish, reddish, or orange zircon: also called *jacinth.* **4.** In ancient times, a bluish or purplish gem, probably the sapphire or amethyst. **5.** A blue or purplish blue color. [< OF < L < Gk. *hyakinthos.*] — **hy/a·cin/thine** (-thin, -thīn) *adj.*

HYACINTH
(def. 1)

hy·ae·na (hī-ē/nə) See HYENA.

hy·a·line (hī/ə-lin, -līn) *adj.* Resembling glass; transparent. — *n.* Something transparent, like glass. [< L < Gk. *hyalos* glass]

hy·brid (hī/brid) *n.* **1.** An animal or plant produced by a male and female of different species, varieties, or breeds. **2.** Anything of mixed origin. **3.** *Ling.* A word composed of elements from more than one language. — *adj.* Of, pertaining to, or like a hybrid. [< L *hybrida* offspring of tame sow and wild boar] — **hy/brid·ism, hy·brid·i·ty** (hī-brid/ə-tē).

hy·brid·ize (hī/brid-īz) *v.t. & v.i.* **·ized, ·iz·ing** To produce or cause to produce hybrids. Also *Brit.* **hy/brid·ise.** — **hy·brid·i·za·tion** (hī/brid·ə-zā/shən, -ī-zā/-) *n.* — **hy/brid·iz/er** *n.*

hydr- Var. of HYDRO-.

hy·dra (hī/drə) *n. pl.* **·dras** or **·drae** (-drē) **1.** Any of various small, fresh-water polyps characterized by a long, slender body and tentacles. **2.** An evil that persists or reappears.

Hy·dra (hī/drə) *n.* **1.** In Greek mythology, a nine-headed serpent that grew two heads for each cut off. **2.** A constellation, the Hydra. [< L < Gk. *hydra* water serpent]

hy·dran·ge·a (hī/drān/jē·ə, -jə) *n.* A tree or shrub, having large clusters of white, blue, or pink flowers. [< NL < Gk. *hydōr* water + *angeion* vessel]

hy·drant (hī/drənt) *n.* A large, upright pipe connected to a water main, used for firefighting; fireplug. [< Gk. *hydōr* water + -ANT]

hy·drar·gy·rum (hī-drär/jə-rəm) *n. Chem.* Mercury. [< NL < L < Gk. *hydōr* water + *argyros* silver] — **hy/drar·gy/ric** (-jir/ik) *adj.*

hy·drate (hī′drāt) *Chem. n.* Any of a class of compounds associated with water in definite proportions. — *v.t.* **·drat·ed**, **·drat·ing** To form a hydrate. — **hy·dra′tion** *n.*

hy·drau·lic (hī·drô′lik) *adj.* 1. Of or pertaining to hydraulics. 2. Operated by water or other liquid under pressure. 3. Hardening under water: *hydraulic cement.* [< L < Gk. *hydōr* water + *aulos* pipe] — **hy·drau′li·cal·ly** *adv.*

hy·drau·lics (hī·drô′liks) *n.pl. (construed as sing.)* The science of the laws governing the motion of water and other liquids and of their practical applications in engineering.

hy·dra·zine (hī′drə·zēn, -zin) *n. Chem.* A colorless fuming liquid, N_2H_4, used esp. as a rocket or jet fuel.

hy·dric (hī′drik) *adj.* Of or containing hydrogen.

hy·dride (hī′drīd, -drid) *n. Chem.* A compound of hydrogen with another element or radical. Also **hy′drid** (-drid).

hy·dro (hī′drō) *Canadian adj.* Hydroelectric.

hydro- *combining form* 1. Water; of, related to, or resembling water. 2. *Chem.* Denoting a compound of hydrogen. Also, before vowels, **hydr-**. [< Gk. *hydōr* water]

hy·dro·car·bon (hī′drə·kär′bən) *n. Chem.* One of a large and important group of organic compounds that contain hydrogen and carbon only, as benzene, ethylene, methane, etc.

hy·dro·ceph·a·lus (hī′drə·sef′ə·ləs) *n. Pathol.* A condition characterized by the accumulation of fluid within the brain, causing abnormal enlargement of the head. Also **hy′dro·ceph′a·ly**. [< HYDRO- + Gk. *kephalē* head] — **hy′dro·ceph′a·loid** (-loid), **hy′dro·ceph′a·lous** *adj.*

hy·dro·chlo·ric acid (hī′drə·klôr′ik, -klō′rik) *Chem.* An aqueous solution of hydrogen chloride, widely used in industry, medicine, and the arts: also called *muriatic acid.*

hy·dro·chlo·ride (hī′drə·klôr′īd, -klō′rīd) *n. Chem.* A salt of hydrochloric acid with an organic base.

hy·dro·cy·an·ic acid (hī′drō·sī·an′ik) *Chem.* An aqueous solution of hydrogen cyanide, a colorless, volatile, very poisonous liquid with a bitter odor: also called *prussic acid.*

hy·dro·dy·nam·ic (hī′drō·dī·nam′ik) *adj.* 1. Of or pertaining to the force or motion of water and other fluids. 2. Of or pertaining to hydrodynamics. Also **hy′dro·dy·nam′i·cal.**

hy·dro·dy·nam·ics (hī′drō·dī·nam′iks) *n.pl. (construed as sing.)* The branch of dynamics that treats of the motions and forces of liquids, especially water.

hy·dro·e·lec·tric (hī′drō·i·lek′trik) *adj.* Of or pertaining to electricity generated by the energy of water. — **hy·dro·e·lec·tric·i·ty** (hī′drō·i·lek′tris′ə·tē, -ē′lek-) *n.*

hy·dro·flu·or·ic acid (hī′drə·floō·ôr′ik, -or′-, -flôr′ik) *Chem.* An aqueous solution of hydrogen fluoride, used for etching glass, treating metals, etc.

hy·dro·foil (hī′drə·foil) *n.* 1. A streamlined surface designed to provide support in the water through which it moves, as an attachment to a boat. 2. A horizontal rudder used in raising or submerging a submarine.

hy·dro·gen (hī′drə·jən) *n.* The lightest of the elements (symbol H), an odorless, colorless, flammable gas, occurring chiefly in combination. See ELEMENT. [< F < Gk. *hydōr* water + -GEN] — **hy·drog·e·nous** (hī·droj′ə·nəs) *adj.*

hy·dro·gen·ate (hī′drə·jə·nāt′, hī·droj′ə·nāt) *v.t.* **·at·ed**, **·at·ing** *Chem.* To combine with, treat with, or expose to the chemical action of hydrogen. — **hy′dro·gen·a′tion** *n.*

hydrogen bomb A very destructive thermonuclear bomb having no theoretical limit in size and power, releasing energy by the fusion, under extremely high temperatures, of light elements, as hydrogen isotopes: also called *H-bomb.*

hydrogen chloride *Chem.* A corrosive, pungent, gaseous compound of hydrogen and chlorine, HCl.

hydrogen cyanide *Chem.* An unstable, colorless, intensely poisonous gas, HCN, used chiefly as an extermination agent.

hydrogen ion The positively charged ion (H^+) present in all acid solutions.

hydrogen peroxide *Chem.* An unstable, colorless, syrupy liquid, H_2O_2, used for bleaching, etc.

hydrogen sulfide *Chem.* A colorless, gaseous, poisonous compound, H_2S, having a characteristic odor of rotten eggs.

hy·drog·ra·phy (hī·drog′rə·fē) *n.* The science of surveying, describing, and mapping seas, lakes, rivers, etc. — **hy·drog′ra·pher** *n.* — **hy′dro·graph′ic** or **·i·cal** *adj.* — **hy′dro·graph′i·cal·ly** *adv.*

hy·droid (hī′droid) *Zool. adj.* 1. Pertaining or belonging to a group of hydrozoans. 2. Designating a stage in the development of hydrozoans, characterized by the budding of polyps. — *n.* A hydroid coelenterate, esp. a polyp.

hy·dro·ki·net·ics (hī′drō·ki·net′iks) *n.pl. (construed as sing.)* The branch of hydrodynamics dealing with the laws governing fluids in motion. — **hy′dro·ki·net′ic** *adj.*

hy·drol·o·gy (hī·drol′ə·jē) *n.* The branch of physical geography that deals with the waters of the earth, their distribution, characteristics, and effects in relation to human activities. — **hy·dro·log·ic** (hī′drə·loj′ik) or **·i·cal** *adj.* — **hy′dro·log′i·cal·ly** *adv.* — **hy·drol′o·gist** *n.*

hy·drol·y·sis (hī·drol′ə·sis) *n. pl.* **·ses** (-sēz) *Chem.* 1. Action between the ions of water (H^+ and OH^-) and those of a salt to form an acid and a base. 2. The decomposition of a compound by water. — **hy·dro·lyt·ic** (hī′drə·lit′ik) *adj.*

hy·dro·lyte (hī′drə·līt) *n.* Any substance affected by hydrolysis.

hy·dro·lyze (hī′drə·līz) *v.t. & v.i.* **·lyzed**, **·lyz·ing** To undergo or cause to undergo hydrolysis. — **hy′dro·lyz′a·ble** *adj.* — **hy·dro·ly·za·tion** (hī′drə·lə·zā′shən, -lī·zā′-) *n.*

hy·drom·e·ter (hī·drom′ə·tər) *n.* A sealed tube marked with a graduated scale and weighted at one end, that determines the specific gravity or density of a liquid. — **hy·dro·met·ric** (hī′drə·met′rik) or **·ri·cal** *adj.* — **hy·drom′e·try** *n.*

hy·dro·pa·thy (hī·drop′ə·thē) *n.* A treatment that professes to cure diseases by the use of water both internally and externally: also called *water cure.* — **hy·dro·path·ic** (hī′drə·path′ik) or **·i·cal** *adj.* — **hy′dro·path′ist, hy′dro·path** *n.*

hy·dro·pho·bi·a (hī′drə·fō′bē·ə) *n.* 1. Rabies. 2. Any morbid fear of water. [< L < Gk. *hydōr* water + *phobos* fear] — **hy′dro·pho′bic** (hī′drə·fō′bik, -fob′ik) *adj.*

hy·dro·phyte (hī′drə·fīt) *n. Bot.* A plant growing in water or in wet ground. — **hy·dro·phyt·ic** (hī′drə·fit′ik) *adj.*

hy·dro·plane (hī′drə·plān′) *n.* 1. A seaplane. 2. A type of motor boat designed so that its hull is raised partially out of the water when driven at high speeds. 3. A hydrofoil (def. 2). — *v.i.* **·planed**, **·plan·ing** To move at great speed on the water.

hy·dro·pon·ics (hī′drə·pon′iks) *n.pl. (construed as sing.)* The science of growing plants with their roots in nutrient solutions rather than in soil: also called *tank farming.* [< HYDRO- + Gk. *ponos* labor] — **hy′dro·pon′ic** *adj.*

hy·dro·sphere (hī′drə·sfir) *n.* 1. The total water on the surface of the earth. 2. The moisture in the earth's atmosphere. — **hy′dro·spher′ic** (-sfir′ik, -sfer′-) *adj.*

hy·dro·stat (hī′drə·stat) *n.* 1. A device for preventing the explosion of a steam boiler due to lack of water. 2. An electrical device for detecting the presence of water.

hy·dro·stat·ics (hī′drə·stat′iks) *n.pl. (construed as sing.)* The science that deals with the pressure and equilibrium of fluids, especially of liquids. — **hy′dro·stat′ic** or **·i·cal** *adj.* — **hy′dro·stat′i·cal·ly** *adv.*

hy·dro·sul·fide (hī′drə·sul′fīd) *n. Chem.* A compound derived from hydrogen sulfide by replacing one of the hydrogen atoms with a basic radical or a base.

hy·dro·sul·fu·rous acid (hī′drō·sul·fyŏor′əs, hī′drə·sul′fər-əs) Hyposulfurous acid.

hy·dro·ther·a·peu·tics (hī′drō·ther′ə·pyōō′tiks) *n.pl. (construed as sing.)* Hydrotherapy. — **hy′dro·ther′a·peu′tic** *adj.*

hy·dro·ther·a·py (hī′drō·ther′ə·pē) *n. Med.* The scientific use of water in the treatment of various diseases.

hy·drot·ro·pism (hī·drot′rə·piz′əm) *n. Biol.* A tropism in response to water. — **hy·dro·trop·ic** (hī′drə·trop′ik) *adj.*

hy·drous (hī′drəs) *adj.* 1. Watery. 2. *Chem.* Containing water of crystallization or hydration.

hy·drox·ide (hī·drok′sīd) *n. Chem.* A compound containing the hydroxyl ion, which consists of one atom each of oxygen and hydrogen and bears a charge of -1.

hy·dro·zo·an (hī′drə·zō′ən) *adj. Zool.* Pertaining or belonging to a class of freshwater and marine coelenterates, including the hydra, certain jellyfishes and corals, etc. — *n.* A hydrozoan organism.

hy·e·na (hī·ē′nə) *n.* Any of a group of wolflike, carnivorous mammals of Africa and Asia, feeding chiefly on carrion, with short hind legs, a bristly mane, and strong teeth. Also *hyaena.* [< L < Gk. *hyaina* sow]

Hy·ge·ia (hī·jē′ə) In Greek mythology, the goddess of health. [< Gk. *hygieia* health]

hy·giene (hī′jēn, -ji·ēn) *n.* The science of health. [< F < Gk. *hygieinos* healthful]

hy·gi·en·ic (hī′jē·en′ik, hī·jē′nik, -jen′ik) *adj.* 1. Of or pertaining to hygiene. 2. Sanitary. — **hy′gi·en′i·cal·ly** *adv.*

hy·gi·en·ics (hī′jē·en′iks, hī·jē′niks) *n.pl. (construed as sing.)* The science of preserving or promoting health; hygiene.

hy·gi·en·ist (hī′jē·ən·ist) *n.* One who studies or is versed in the principles of hygiene. Also **hy·gi·est** (-jē·ist), **hy′gie·ist.**

hygro- *combining form* Wet; moist. Also, before vowels, **hygr-**. [< Gk. *hygros* wet, moist]

hy·grom·e·ter (hī·grom′ə·tər) *n.* An instrument for measuring the humidity or moisture in the atmosphere. — **hy·gro·met·ric** (hī′grə·met′rik) *adj.*

hy·grom·e·try (hī·grom′ə·trē) *n.* The branch of physics that deals with the measurement of moisture in the air.

hy·gro·scope (hī′grə·skōp) *n.* A device for indicating the approximate humidity of the air.

hy·gro·scop·ic (hī′grə·skop′ik) *adj.* 1. Pertaining to the hygroscope. 2. Absorbing moisture from the air.

hy·la (hī′lə) *n.* Any of a genus of amphibians, esp. the tree frog. [< NL < Gk. *hylē* wood]

---

hy·men (hī'mən) *n. Anat.* A thin mucous membrane partially covering the external entrance of the vagina in a virgin. [< Gk. *hymēn* skin, membrane]

Hy·men (hī'mən) In Greek mythology, the god of marriage.

hy·me·ne·al (hī'mə-nē'əl) *adj.* Of or pertaining to marriage or a wedding. — *n.* A wedding song or poem.

hy·men·op·ter·on (hī'mən-op'tər-on) *n. pl.* **·ter·a** (-tər-ə) A hymenopterous insect. Also **hy'men·op'ter.**

hy·men·op·ter·ous (hī'mən-op'tər-əs) *adj. Entomol.* Of or belonging to an order of insects, typically having four wings, including bees, wasps, sawflies, etc. [< NL < Gk. *hymēn* membrane + *pteron* wing] — **hy·men·op·ter·an** (hī'mən-op'tə-rən) *adj. & n.*

hymn (him) *n.* A song of praise, adoration, thanksgiving, etc., esp. one sung at a religious service. — *v.t.* **1.** To praise or express with a hymn. — *v.i.* **2.** To sing hymns. [< LL < Gk. *hymnos* song, ode] — **hym'nic** (-nik) *adj.*

hym·nal (him'nəl) *n.* A book of hymns. Also *Canadian* **hym'na·ry** (-nə-rē), **hymn'book'** (-bŏŏk'). — *adj.* Of or relating to a hymn or hymns.

hym·nist (him'nist) *n.* A writer of hymns.

hym·nol·o·gy (him-nol'ə-jē) *n.* **1.** The study of hymns. **2.** The writing of hymns. **3.** Hymns collectively. — **hym·no·log·ic** (him'nə-loj'ik) or **·i·cal** *adj.* — **hym·nol'o·gist** *n.*

hy·oid (hī'oid) *n. Anat.* In man, a U-shaped bone at the base of the tongue. Also **hyoid bone.** For illus. see MOUTH. — *adj.* Pertaining to the hyoid bone. [< F *hyoide*]

hype (hīp) *v.t.* **hyped, hyp·ing** *Slang* **1.** To increase artificially: *hype* the profit figure. **2.** To stimulate: often with *up*. **3.** To deceive. **4.** To publicize extravagantly. — *n.* **1.** A narcotics addict. **2.** A deception. **3.** One who or that which is promoted by hype. [< HYP(ODERMIC)]

hyper- *prefix* **1.** Over; above; excessive: *hypercritical*. **2.** *Med.* Denoting an abnormal state of excess: *hypertension*: opposed to *hypo-*. **3.** *Chem.* Denoting the highest in a series of compounds: now generally replaced by *per-*. [< Gk. *hyper* above]

hy·per·a·cid·i·ty (hī'pər-ə-sid'ə-tē) *n. Med.* An excess of acidity, as of the gastric juice.

hy·per·bar·ism (hī-per'bə-riz'əm) *n. Med.* A disturbed condition caused by atmospheric pressure greater than the pressure within the body: opposed to *hypobarism.* [< HYPER- + Gk. *baros* weight] — **hy'per·bar'ic** (-bar'ik) *adj.*

hy·per·bo·la (hī-pûr'bə-lə) *n. Math.* The curve produced by the intersection of a plane with the surface of a cone, the plane intersecting both nappes. [< NL < Gk. *hyperbolē* a throwing beyond, excess]

hy·per·bo·le (hī-pûr'bə-lē) *n.* An exaggeration or overstatement intended to produce an effect without being taken literally, as: *He was centuries old.* [< L < Gk. *hyperbolē* a throwing beyond, excess] — **hy·per'bo·lism** *n.*

hy·per·bol·ic (hī'pər-bol'ik) *adj.* **1.** Of, pertaining to, or using hyperbole. **2.** *Math.* Of or pertaining to the hyperbola. Also **hy'per·bol'i·cal.** — **hy'per·bol'i·cal·ly** *adv.*

hy·per·bo·lize (hī-pûr'bə-līz) *v.t. & v.i.* **·lized, ·liz·ing** To express in or use hyperbole; exaggerate.

hy·per·bo·re·an (hī'pər-bôr'ē-ən, -bō'rē-) *adj.* Of or pertaining to the far north; frigid; arctic.

Hy·per·bo·re·an (hī'pər-bôr'ē-ən, -bō'rē-) *n.* In Greek mythology, one of the people who lived in the far north in a land of everlasting peace and sunshine. [< L < Gk. *hyper-* beyond + *Boreas* north wind]

hy·per·crit·i·cal (hī'pər-krit'i-kəl) *adj.* Excessively critical or carping; faultfinding. — **hy'per·crit'i·cal·ly** *adv.* — **hy'per·crit'i·cism** (-siz'əm) *n.*

hy·per·gol·ic (hī'pər-gol'ik) *adj. Aerospace* Denoting a type of rocket propellant that ignites spontaneously on contact with an oxidizer. [< HYPER- + G *gola*, a code word used in German rocketry]

Hy·pe·ri·on (hī-pir'ē-ən) In Greek mythology: **a** A Titan, the son of Uranus. **b** Helios. **c** In later use, Apollo.

hy·per·me·tro·pi·a (hī'pər-mə-trō'pē-ə) *n. Pathol.* Farsightedness. Also **hy'per·met'ro·py** (-met'rə-pē). [< NL < Gk. *hypermetros* excessive + *ōps* eye] — **hy'per·me·trop'ic** (-mə-trop'ik, -trō'pik) *adj.*

hy·per·on (hī'pər-on) *n. Physics* Any of a class of atomic particles having a mass intermediate between that of a neutron and a deuteron.

hy·per·sen·si·tive (hī'pər-sen'sə-tiv) *adj.* **1.** Excessively sensitive. **2.** Allergic. — **hy'per·sen'si·tive·ness, hy'per·sen'si·tiv'i·ty** (-sen'sə-tiv'ə-tē) *n.*

hy·per·sen·si·tize (hī'pər-sen'sə-tīz) *v.t.* **·tized, ·tiz·ing** *Photog.* To increase the sensitiveness or speed of, as a film.

hy·per·son·ic (hī'pər-son'ik) *adj.* Of, pertaining to, or characterized by supersonic speeds of mach 5 or greater.

hy·per·son·ics (hī'pər-son'iks) *n.pl.* (*construed as sing.*) The branch of dynamics concerned with the design, performance, etc., of objects moving at hypersonic speeds.

hy·per·ten·sion (hī'pər-ten'shən) *n. Pathol.* High blood pressure. — **hy'per·ten'sive** (-siv) *adj.*

hy·per·thy·roid·ism (hī'pər-thī'roid·iz'əm) *n. Pathol.* **1.** Excessive activity of the thyroid gland. **2.** Any disorder caused by this. — **hy'per·thy'roid** *adj. & n.*

hy·per·tro·phy (hī-pûr'trə-fē) *n. Pathol.* **1.** The excessive development of an organ or part. **2.** The enlargement resulting from such a condition. — *v.i. & v.t.* **·phied, ·phy·ing** To grow or cause to grow excessively. — **hy·per·troph·ic** (hī'pər-trof'ik, -trō'fik) or **·i·cal** *adj.*

hy·pha (hī'fə) *n. pl.* **·phae** (-fē) *Bot.* One of the long, threadlike, branching bodies that constitute the mycelium of a fungus. [< NL < Gk. *hyphē* web] — **hy'phal** *adj.*

hy·phen (hī'fən) *n.* A mark (- or - or ·) used to connect the elements of certain compound words or to show division of a word at the end of a line. — *v.t.* To hyphenate. [< LL < Gk. *hyph' hen* under one, together < *hypo-* under + *hen* one]

hy·phen·ate (hī'fən-āt) *v.t.* **·at·ed, ·at·ing** **1.** To connect by a hyphen. **2.** To write with a hyphen. — **hy'phen·a'tion** *n.*

hyp·no- *combining form* Sleep; of or related to sleep. Also, before vowels, **hypn-.** [< Gk. *hypnos* sleep]

hyp·noi·dal (hip-noid'l) *adj. Psychiatry* Resembling light hypnosis. Also **hyp·noid'.**

hyp·no·sis (hip-nō'sis) *n. pl.* **·ses** (-sēz) *Psychol.* A trancelike condition that can be artificially induced, characterized by an increased responsiveness to suggestion.

hyp·no·ther·a·py (hip'nō-ther'ə-pē) *n. Med.* The use of hypnotism in treating disease, esp. mental disease.

hyp·not·ic (hip-not'ik) *adj.* **1.** Pertaining to hypnosis or hypnotism. **2.** Readily hypnotized. **3.** Tending to produce sleep. — *n.* **1.** A drug or other agent producing sleep. **2.** A hypnotized person or one susceptible to hypnosis. [< Gk. *hypnos* sleep] — **hyp·not'i·cal·ly** *adv.*

hyp·no·tism (hip'nə-tiz'əm) *n.* **1.** The act or practice of inducing hypnosis. **2.** The study of the techniques of hypnosis. **3.** Hypnosis. — **hyp'no·tist** *n.*

hyp·no·tize (hip'nə-tīz) *v.t.* **·tized, ·tiz·ing** **1.** To produce hypnosis in. **2.** To fascinate; charm. Also *Brit.* **hyp'no·tise.** — **hyp'no·tiz'a·ble** *adj.* — **hyp·no·ti·za'tion** (-tə-zā'shən, -tī·zā'-) *n.* — **hyp'no·tiz'er** *n.*

hy·po¹ (hī'pō) *n. Photog.* Sodium thiosulfate (formerly called *sodium hyposulfite*), used as a fixing agent.

hy·po² (hī'pō) *n. pl.* **·pos** *Informal* A hypodermic injection.

hy·po³ (hī'pō) *n. pl.* **·pos** *Slang* A hypochondriac.

hypo- *prefix* **1.** Under; beneath. **2.** Less than. **3.** *Med.* Denoting a lack of or deficiency in: opposed to *hyper-*. **4.** *Chem.* Indicating the lowest member in a series of compounds (that is, the lowest degree of oxidation). Also, before vowels, **hyp-.** [< Gk. < *hypo* under]

hy·po·bar·ism (hī'pə-bär'iz·əm) *n. Med.* A condition brought about when the atmospheric pressure is less than that of the gases within the body: opposed to *hyperbarism.* [< HYPO- + Gk. *baros* weight] — **hy'po·bar'ic** *adj.*

hy·po·cen·ter (hī'pə-sen'tər) *n.* Ground zero.

hy·po·chlo·rite (hī'pə-klôr'īt, -klō'rīt) *n. Chem.* A salt of hypochlorous acid.

hy·po chlo·rous acid (hī'pə-klôr'əs, -klō'rəs) *Chem.* An unstable acid, HClO, used in aqueous solution as an oxidizer and bleach.

hy·po·chon·dri·a (hī'pə-kon'drē·ə, hip'ə-) *n.* A persistent anxiety about one's health, often with imagined symptoms of illness. Also **hy·po·chon·dri·a·sis** (hī'pō·kən-drī'ə·sis). [< L, abdomen (once taken to be the seat of this condition)]

hy·po·chon·dri·ac (hī'pə-kon'drē·ak, hip'ə-) *adj.* **1.** Pertaining to or affected with hypochondria. **2.** Of, pertaining to, or situated in the hypochondrium. Also **hy·po·chon·dri·a·cal** (hī'pō·kən-drī'ə·kəl). — *n.* A person subject to or affected with hypochondria. — **hy'po·chon·dri'a·cal·ly** *adv.*

hy·po·chon·dri·um (hī'pə-kon'drē·əm, hip'ə-) *n. pl.* **·dri·a** (-drē·ə) *Anat.* The region of the abdomen situated on either side of the body, under the short ribs. [< NL < Gk.]

hy·po·cot·yl (hī'pə-kot'l) *n. Bot.* The part of the axis of a seedling below the seed leaves or cotyledons. — **hy'po·cot'y·lous** *adj.*

hy·poc·ri·sy (hi-pok'rə-sē) *n. pl.* **·sies** The pretense of having feelings or characteristics one does not possess; esp., the deceitful assumption of virtue. [< OF < L < Gk. *hypokrinesthai* to play a part, act]

hyp·o·crite (hip'ə-krit) *n.* One who practices hypocrisy. — **hyp'o·crit'i·cal** *adj.* — **hyp'o·crit'i·cal·ly** *adv.*

hyp·o·derm (hī'pə-dûrm) *n. Zool.* The layer that secretes the outer skin of an arthropod: also called *hypodermis.*

hy·po·der·ma (hī'pə-dûr'mə) *n. Bot.* The distinct sheath of tissue beneath the epidermis of stems in plants. [< NL < Gk. *hypo-* under + *derma* skin]

hy·po·der·mic (hī'pə-dûr'mik) *adj.* **1.** Of or pertaining to the area under the skin. **2.** Injected under the skin. — *n.* A hypodermic injection or syringe.

hypodermic syringe A syringe having a sharp, hollow needle for injection of substances beneath the skin.

hy·po·der·mis (hī'pə-dûr'mis) *n. Zool.* The hypoderm.

hy·po·gas·tric (hī'pə-gas'trik) *adj.* Pertaining to or situated in the hypogastrium.

hy·po·gas·tri·um (hī'pə-gas'trē·əm) *n. pl.* **·tri·a** (-trē·ə)

Anat. The region at the lower part of the abdomen on the middle line. [< NL < Gk. *hypo-* below + *gastēr* belly]

hy·po·sul·fite (hī'pə·sul'fīt) *n. Chem.* **1.** Sodium thiosulfate. **2.** A salt of hyposulfurous acid.

hy·po·sul·fu·rous acid (hī'pō·sul·fyŏŏr'əs, hī'pə·sul'fər·əs) *Chem.* An unstable acid, $H_2S_2O_4$, of strong reducing and bleaching properties: also called *hydrosulfurous acid.*

hy·pot·e·nuse (hī·pot'ə·nōos, -nyōos, hī-) *n. Geom.* The side of a right triangle opposite the right angle. Also **hy·poth'e·nuse** (-poth'-). [< L < Gk. *hypo-* under + *teinein* to stretch]

hy·po·thal·a·mus (hī'pə·thal'ə·məs, hip'ə-) *n. pl.* **·mi** *Anat.* A group of structures forming part of the diencephalon, controlling visceral activities, regulating body temperature and many metabolic processes, and influencing certain emotional states. — **hy·po·tha·lam·ic** (hī'pə·thə·lam'ik) *adj.*

hy·poth·e·cate (hī·poth'ə·kāt, hi-) *v.t.* **·cat·ed, ·cat·ing** *Law* To pledge (personal property) as security for debt without transfer of possession. [< Med.L < LL *hypotheca* pledge] — **hy·poth'e·ca'tion** *n.* — **hy·poth'e·ca'tor** *n.*

hy·poth·e·sis (hī·poth'ə·sis, hi-) *n. pl.* **·ses** (-sēz) **1.** An unproved scientific conclusion drawn from known facts. **2.** An assumption or set of assumptions provisionally accepted. [< NL < Gk., foundation, supposition]

— **Syn.** In science, a *hypothesis* is a proposition advanced as possibly true, and consistent with known data, but requiring further investigation; a *theory* is a *hypothesis* so well substantiated as to be generally accepted. *Supposition* and *assumption* are propositions accepted with less assurance than a *hypothesis*. A *conjecture* is a conclusion drawn from admittedly insufficient data; it differs from a guess only in not being wholly random and uninformed.

hy·poth·e·size (hī·poth'ə·sīz, hi-) *v.* **·sized, ·siz·ing** *v.t.* **1.** To offer or assume as a hypothesis. — *v.i.* **2.** To make a hypothesis; theorize.

hy·po·thet·i·cal (hī'pə·thet'i·kəl) *adj.* **1.** Pertaining to or of the nature of a hypothesis. **2.** Based on hypothesis; theoretical. **3.** Characterized by the use of hypotheses. **4.** *Logic* Denoting a proposition based on another proposition; conditional. Also **hy'po·thet'ic.** — **hy'po·thet'i·cal·ly** *adv.*

hy·po·thy·roid·ism (hī'pō·thī'roid·iz'əm) *n. Pathol.* **1.** Deficient functioning of the thyroid gland. **2.** A disorder resulting from this, as goiter. — **hy'po·thy'roid** *adj. & n.*

hy·son (hī'sən) *n.* A green tea from China. [< Chinese]

hys·sop (his'əp) *n.* **1.** A bushy, medicinal herb of the mint family, with small clusters of blue flowers. **2.** In the Bible, an unidentified plant furnishing the twigs used in the Mosaic rites, etc. [OE and OF < L < Gk. *hyssōpos*]

hys·ter·ec·to·my (his'tə·rek'tə·mē) *n. pl.* **·mies** *Surg.* Complete removal of part or all of the uterus.

hys·te·ri·a (his·tir'ē·ə, -ter'-) *n.* **1.** Abnormal excitement; wild emotionalism; frenzy. **2.** *Psychiatry* A psychoneurotic condition characterized by violent emotional paroxysms and disturbances in the sensory and motor functions. — **Syn.** See FRENZY. [< NL < Gk. *hystera* the womb]

hys·ter·ic (his·ter'ik) *adj.* Hysterical. — *n.* **1.** One who is subject to hysteria. **2.** *pl.* A fit of hysteria.

hys·ter·i·cal (his·ter'i·kəl) *adj.* **1.** Resembling hysteria; uncontrolled; violent. **2.** Characterized or caused by hysteria. **3.** Inclined to hysteria. — **hys·ter'i·cal·ly** *adv.*

hystero- *combining form* **1.** The womb; uterine. **2.** Hysteria. Also, before vowels, **hyster-.** [< Gk. *hystera* the womb]

hys·ter·ot·o·my (his'tə·rot'ə·mē) *n. pl.* **·mies** *Surg.* **1.** The operation of cutting into the womb. **2.** Cesarean section.

I

i, I (ī) *n. pl.* **i's** or **is, I's** or **Is,** eyes (īz) **1.** The ninth letter of the English alphabet. **2.** Any sound represented by the letter *i.* — **symbol** **1.** The Roman numeral for 1: written I or i. **2.** *Chem.* Iodine (symbol I).

I (ī) *pron., possessive* **my** or **mine,** *objective* **me;** *pl. nominative* **we,** *possessive* **our** or **ours,** *objective* **us** The nominative singular pronoun of the first person, used by a speaker or writer in referring to himself. — *n. pl.* **I's** **1.** The pronoun *I* used as a noun: His talk was full of *I's.* **2.** *Philos.* The ego. [OE *ic*]

-ia[1] *suffix of nouns* Occurring in: **1.** *Geog.* Names of countries: *Australia.* **2.** *Pathol.* Names of diseases and related terms: *hysteria.* **3.** *Bot.* Names of genera: *Lobelia.* **4.** Words borrowed directly from Latin or Greek: *militia.* [< L and Gk. *-ia,* suffix of fem. nouns]

-ia[2] *suffix of nouns* Occurring in: **1.** *Biol.* Names of classes: *Mammalia.* **2.** Names of classical festivals: *Bacchanalia.* **3.** Words, usu. collectives, borrowed from Latin or Greek: *regalia.* [< L and Gk. *-ia,* plural suffix of neut. nouns]

I·a·go (ē·ä'gō) The villain of Shakespeare's *Othello.*

-ial *suffix of adjectives* Var. of -AL[1], with connective *-i-,* as in *filial, nuptial.*

i·amb (ī'amb) *n.* **1.** In prosody, a metrical foot consisting of an unaccented syllable followed by an accented one (˘ ´). **2.** A line of verse made up of such feet: Thĕ bīrd | wăs grēen | ănd gōld | ĕn īn | thĕ sūn. [< L < Gk. *iambos*]

i·am·bic (ī·am'bik) *adj.* Consisting of, using, or like iambs. — *n.* **1.** A foot, line, or stanza consisting of an iamb or iambs. **2.** Iambic verse.

i·am·bus (ī·am'bəs) *n. pl.* **·bi** (-bī) or **·bus·es** An iamb.

-ian *suffix of adjectives and nouns* Var. of -AN, with *-i-* of the stem or as a connective: *amphibian, Bostonian.*

-iana See -ANA.

-iasis *suffix Med.* Denoting a process and its results, esp. in diseased conditions: *psoriasis.* [Var. of -OSIS]

-iatrics *combining form* Medical treatment: *pediatrics.* [< Gk. *iatrikos* pertaining to the art of healing]

iatro- *combining form* Medicine and. [< Gk. *iatros* physician]

i·at·ro·gen·ic (ī·at'rə·jen·ik) *adj.* Caused or aggravated by medical treatment. [< Gk. *iatros* physician + -GENIC]

-iatry *combining form* Medical or curative treatment: *psychiatry.* [< Gk. *iatreia* healing]

I-beam (ī'bēm') *n.* A beam or joist that in cross section has the shape of the letter I.

I·be·ri·an (ī·bir'ē·ən) *adj.* Of, pertaining to, or characteristic of the Iberian Peninsula, its people, or their culture. — *n.* **1.** One of the ancient or modern inhabitants of the Iberian Peninsula. **2.** The unclassified language of the Iberian Peninsula. [< Gk. *Iberes* Spaniards]

i·bex (ī'beks) *n. pl.* **i·bex·es** or **i·bi·ces** (ī'bə·sēz, ib'ə-) One of various wild goats of Europe and Asia, with long, recurved horns.

i·bi·dem (i·bī'dem) *adv. Latin* In the same place; in the work, chapter, etc., just mentioned. Abbr. *ib., ibid.*

i·bis (ī'bis) *n. pl.* **i·bis·es** or **i·bis** One of various wading birds related to the heron. [< Egyptian]

-ible See -ABLE.

-ic *suffix* **1.** Forming adjectives with the meanings: **a** Of, pertaining to, or connected with: *volcanic.* **b** Of the nature of; resembling: *angelic.* **c** Produced by or in the manner of: *Homeric.* **d** Consisting of; containing: *alcoholic.* **e** *Chem.* Having a higher valence than that indicated by *-ous:* said of elements in compounds: *sulfuric* acid. **2.** Forming nouns by the substantive use of adjectives in *-ic: classic, lunatic.* **3.** Occurring in nouns derived from Latin and Greek nouns formed from adjectives: *stoic, music.* See note under -ICS. [< F *-ique* or L *-icus* or Gk. *-ikos*]

-ical *suffix* **1.** Forming parallel adjectives from adjectives in *-ic,* often in the same sense, as *alphabetic, alphabetical,* but sometimes with extended or special senses, as *economic, economical.* **2.** Forming adjectives from nouns in *-ic* or *-ics: musical, mathematical.* [< LL *-icalis* < L *-icus* + *-alis*]

Ic·a·rus (ik'ə·rəs, ī'kə-) In Greek mythology, the son of Daedalus, who, by means of artificial wings, flew so high that the sun melted the wax that fastened the wings and he fell into the sea and drowned.

ice (īs) *n.* **1.** Congealed or frozen water. ◆ Collateral adjective: *glacial.* **2.** The frozen surface of a body of water. **3.** Something resembling ice. **4.** A frozen dessert made without cream. **5.** Icing for cake. **6.** *Slang* A diamond. — **to break the ice 1.** To dispel reserve or formality, esp. at a social gathering. **2.** To make a start. — **to cut no ice** *U.S. Informal* To have no influence. — **on ice** *U.S. Slang* **1.** Set aside; in reserve. **2.** Certain to be achieved or won. **3.** In-

communicado. — *v.* **iced, ic·ing** *v.t.* **1.** To cause to turn to ice; freeze. **2.** To cover or surround with ice. **3.** To chill with ice. **4.** To decorate with icing. **5.** In hockey, to put (a team) on the ice. — *v.i.* **6.** To turn to ice. [OE *īs*]

-ice *suffix of nouns* Condition, quality, or act: *cowardice, notice.* [< OF *-ice* < L *-itius, -itia, -itium*]

ice bag A flexible, waterproof container designed to hold ice, applied to parts of the body: also called *ice pack.*

ice·berg (īs′bûrg′) *n.* A thick mass of ice separated from a glacier and floating in the ocean. [Prob. < Du. *ijsberg*]

ice·boat (īs′bōt′) *n.* **1.** A framework with skatelike runners and sails for sailing over ice. **2.** An icebreaker (def. 1).

ice·bound (īs′bound′) *adj.* Surrounded or obstructed by ice.

ice·box (īs′boks′) *n. U.S.* A cabinet for holding ice, in which food or other perishables are stored.

ice·break·er (īs′brā′kər) *n.* **1.** A vessel used to break up ice in waterways and harbors. **2.** A structure for deflecting floating ice from the base of a bridge, a pier, etc.

ice·cap (īs′kap′) *n.* A covering of ice and snow permanently overlying an extensive tract of land.

ice cream A mixture of cream, butterfat, or milk, flavoring, sweetening, and often egg whites, beaten to a uniform consistency and frozen. [Orig., *iced cream*]

iced (īst) *adj.* **1.** Coated or covered with ice or sleet. **2.** Made cold with ice. **3.** Covered with icing, as a cake.

ice field A large, flat expanse of floating ice. Also **ice floe.**

ice hockey Hockey played by skaters on ice.

ice·house (īs′hous′) *n.* A building in which ice is stored.

Ice·land·er (īs′lan′dər) *n.* A native or citizen of Iceland.

Ice·land·ic (īs·lan′dik) *adj.* Of or pertaining to Iceland, its inhabitants, or their language. — *n.* The North Germanic language of Iceland. — **Old Icelandic** The language of Iceland before the 16th century: sometimes called *Old Norse.*

Iceland spar *Mineral.* A transparent variety of calcite exhibiting double refraction and polarizing light.

ice·man (īs′man′, -mən) *n. pl.* **·men** (men′, -mən) One who supplies or delivers ice to consumers.

ice pack 1. A large expanse of floating ice cakes jammed together and frozen into a single mass. **2.** An ice bag.

ice pick An awllike tool for breaking ice into small pieces.

ich·neu·mon (ik·nōō′mən, -nyōō′-) *n.* **1.** An Egyptian species of mongoose. **2.** An ichneumon fly. [< L < Gk. *ichneumon,* lit., tracker]

ichneumon fly A hymenopterous insect whose larvae feed upon caterpillars or other larvae.

i·chor (ī′kôr, ī′kər) *n.* **1.** In classical mythology, the ethereal fluid supposed to flow in the veins of the gods. **2.** *Pathol.* A watery, acrid fluid discharged from sores. [< Gk. *ichōr*] — **i·chor·ous** (ī′kər·əs) *adj.*

ichthyo- *combining form* Fish. Also, before vowels, **ichthy-.** [< Gk. *ichthys* fish]

ich·thy·ol·o·gy (ik′thē·ol′ə·jē) *n.* The branch of zoology that treats of fishes. — **ich·thy·o·log·ic** (ik′thē·ə·loj′ik) or **·i·cal** *adj.* — **ich·thy·ol′o·gist** *n.*

ich·thy·o·saur (ik′thē·ə·sôr′) *n. Paleontol.* Any of an order of extinct marine reptiles of the Mesozoic era, having a porpoiselike form. [< ICHTHYO- + Gk. *sauros* lizard]

ich·thy·o·sau·rus (ik′thē·ə·sôr′əs) *n. pl.* **·sau·ri** (-sôr′ī) An ichthyosaur.

-ician *suffix of nouns* One skilled in or engaged in some specified field: *musician, beautician.* [< F *-icien*]

i·ci·cle (ī′si·kel) *n.* A hanging, tapering rod of ice formed by dripping water. [OE *īsgicel*] — **i′ci·cled** *adj.*

i·ci·ly (ī′sə·lē) *adv.* In an icy manner.

i·ci·ness (ī′sē·nis) *n.* **1.** The state or quality of being frozen or extremely cold. **2.** Marked aloofness of manner.

ic·ing (ī′sing) *n.* **1.** A coating made of sugar, usu. mixed with egg whites or cream, used to cover cakes, pastry, etc. **2.** The formation of ice on the surface of an aircraft.

i·con (ī′kon) *n. pl.* **i·cons** or **i·co·nes** (ī′kə·nēz) **1.** In the Eastern Orthodox Church, a pictorial representation of Jesus Christ, the Virgin Mary, or some other sacred figure. **2.** An image; likeness; picture. Also spelled *ikon.* [< Gk. *eikōn* image] — **i·con′ic** *adj.*

icono- *combining form* Image. Also, before vowels, **icon-.** [< Gk. *eikōn* image]

i·con·o·clast (ī·kon′ə·klast) *n.* **1.** One who attacks conventional or cherished beliefs and institutions. **2.** One who opposes the ues of religious images. [< LL < G,. *eikōn* image + *-klastēs* breaker] — **i·con′o·clasm′** *n.* — **i·con′o·clas′tik** *adj.*

i·con·o·scope (ī·kon′ə·skōp) *n. Telecom.* The part of a television camera that converts the image to be transmitted into electrical impulses.

-ics *suffix of nouns* **1.** An art or a field of study: *mathematics.* **2.** Methods, practices, or activities: *athletics.* [See -IC]

i·cy (ī′sē) *adj.* **i·ci·er, i·ci·est 1.** Consisting of, containing, or covered with ice. **2.** Resembling or having the characteristics of ice: *icy* tone. **3.** Extremely cold. **4.** Forbiddingly aloof: an *icy* greeting. [OE *īsig*]

id (id) *n. Psychoanal.* The unconscious part of the psyche, but actuated by fundamental impulses toward fulfilling in-

stinctual needs; the reservoir of psychic energy or libido· [< NL < L *id* it, trans. of G *es*]

-id¹ *suffix of nouns* **1.** Offspring of: often occurring in names from classical mythology: *Danaid, Nereid.* **2.** An epic about a specified person or subject: *Aeneid.* **3.** *Zool.* **a** A member of a family: *leporid.* **b** A member of a class: *arachnid.* **4.** *Astron.* A meteor seeming to originate in a specified constellation: *Perseid.* [< L *-is, -idis* < Gk. *-is, -idos,* suffix of patronymics]

-id² *suffix of adjectives* Having a particular quality, or existing in a particular state: *humid, fluid.* [< F *-ide* < L *-idus*; or directly < L]

-id³ *Chem.* Var. of -IDE.

I'd (īd) **1.** I would. **2.** I should. **3.** I had.

-idae *suffix Zool.* Forming the names of families: *Canidae.* [< NL *-idae* < L < Gk. *-idai,* plural patronymic suffix]

-ide *suffix Chem.* Used in the names of compounds, usu. binary, and attached to the electronegative element or radical: *sodium chloride.* Also spelled *-id.* [< F *-ide.* See -ID².]

i·de·a (ī·dē′ə) *n.* **1.** That which is conceived in the mind; a thought. **2.** An impression or notion. **3.** A conviction; opinion; belief. **4.** An intention; plan. **5.** Vague knowledge; inkling: I had an *idea* you might come. **6.** A passing fancy; whim. **7.** *Informal* Significance; meaning: Do you get the *idea?* **8.** *Philos.* The Platonic concept of an archetype or fundamental example, of which an existing thing is but a representation. [< L < Gk. < *ideein* to see] — **Syn.** Concept, conception, thought, notion, image.

i·de·al (ī·dē′əl, ī·dēl′) *n.* **1.** A concept or standard of supreme perfection. **2.** A person or thing taken as a standard of perfection. **3.** A high principle; lofty aim. **4.** That which exists only as a concept of the mind. — *adj.* **1.** Conforming to an absolute standard of excellence. **2.** Completely satisfactory: an *ideal* situation. **3.** Capable of existing as a mental concept only; utopian; imaginary. **4.** Pertaining to or existing in the form of an idea or ideas. **5.** *Philos.* Pertaining to or existing as a Platonic idea. [< F < L *idealis*]

i·de·al·ism (ī·dē′əl·iz′əm) *n.* **1.** The envisioning of things as they should be or are wished to be rather than as they are. **2.** Pursuit of an ideal. **3.** That which is idealized. **4.** In literature and art, the imaginative treatment of subject matter in accordance with preconceived standards of perfection: opposed to *realism.* **5.** *Philos.* Any of several theories that there is no reality, no world of objects or thing in itself apart from a reacting mind or consciousness and therefore that reality is essentially spiritual or mental.

i·de·al·ist (ī·dē′əl·ist) *n.* **1.** One who formulates or attempts to live in accordance with ideals. **2.** An impractical dreamer. **3.** An exponent of idealism in literature, art, or philosophy.

i·de·al·is·tic (ī′dē·əl·is′tik, ī·dē′əl-) *adj.* Of, pertaining to, or characteristic of idealists or idealism. Also **i′de·al·is′ti·cal.** — **i′de·al·is′ti·cal·ly** *adv.*

i·de·al·ize (ī·dē′əl·īz) *v.* **·ized, ·iz·ing** *v.t.* **1.** To consider to be ideal; hold in high esteem. **2.** To glorify. — *v.i.* **3.** To form an ideal or ideals. **4.** To consider or represent things in their ideal form. Also *Brit.* **i·de′al·ise.** — **i·de′al·i·za′tion** *n.* — **i·de′al·iz′er** *n.*

i·de·al·ly (ī·dē′əl·ē, ī·dēl′ē) *adv.* **1.** In conformance with an ideal; perfectly. **2.** As conceived in the mind.

i·de·ate (ī·dē′āt) *v.t. & v.i.* **·at·ed, ·at·ing** To form an idea or ideas of something; think.

i·de·a·tion (ī·dē·ā′shən) *n.* Thinking. — **i′de·a′tion·al** *adj.*

i·dée fixe (ē·dā′ fēks′) *French* A fixed idea; obsession.

i·dem (ī′dem) *pron. & adj. Latin* The same: used as a reference to what has been previously mentioned. Abbr. *id.*

i·den·ti·cal (ī·den′ti·kəl) *adj.* **1.** One and the same; the very same. **2.** Alike in every respect. **3.** *Genetics* Designating human twins that develop from a single fertilized ovum: distinguished from *fraternal.* [< Med.L *idem* the same] — **i·den′ti·cal·ly** *adv.* — **i·den′ti·cal·ness** *n.*

i·den·ti·fi·ca·tion (ī·den′tə·fə·kā′shən) *n.* **1.** The act of identifying, or the state of being identified. **2.** Anything by which identity can be established.

i·den·ti·fy (ī·den′tə·fī) *v.* **·fied, ·fy·ing** *v.t.* **1.** To establish as being a particular person or thing; recognize. **2.** To regard as the same. **3.** To serve as a means of recognizing; be characteristic of. **4.** To associate closely. **5.** To consider (oneself) as one with another person. **6.** *Psychol.* To imagine (oneself) to be thinking or behaving like a person with whom one has formed a strong emotional tie. — *v.i.* **7.** To put oneself in the place of another. [< LL *identificare*] — **i·den′ti·fi′a·ble** *adj.* — **i·den′ti·fi′er** *n.*

i·den·ti·ty (ī·den′tə·tē) *n. pl.* **·ties 1.** The state of being identical. **2.** The state of being a specific person or thing and no other. **3.** The distinctive character belonging to an individual. [< F < LL < L *idem* the same]

ideo- *combining form* Idea. [< Gk. *idea* form, idea]

id·e·o·graph (id′ē·ə·graf′, -gräf′, ī′dē-) *n.* **1.** A pictorial symbol of an object or idea. **2.** A graphic symbol, as +, =, ¶, 4, $. Also **id·e·o·gram** (id′ē·ə·gram′, ī′dē-). — **id′e·o·graph′ic** or **·i·cal** *adj.* — **id′e·o·graph′i·cal·ly** *adv.*

i·de·ol·o·gist (ī/dē·ol/ə·jist, id/ē-) *n.* **1.** One who formulates or supports an ideology. **2.** One who studies or is expert in ideology or ideologies. **3.** A visionary.

i·de·ol·o·gy (ī/dē·ol/ə·jē, id/ē-) *n. pl.* **·gies 1.** The ideas and objectives that influence a whole group or national culture, shaping their political and social procedure. **2.** The science that treats of the origin, evolution, and expression of human ideas. **3.** Fanciful or visionary speculation. — **i·de·o·log·ic** (ī/dē·ə·loj/ik, id/ē-) or **·i·cal** *adj.* — **i/de·o·log/i·cal·ly** *adv.*

ides (īdz) *n.pl.* In the ancient Roman calendar, the 15th of March, May, July, and October, and the 13th of the other months. [< OF < L *idus*]

id est (id est) *Latin* That is. Abbr. *i.e.*

idio- *combining form* One's own; peculiar to a person or thing; individual: *idiosyncrasy.* [< Gk. *idios* own, private]

id·i·o·cy (id/ē·ə·sē) *n. pl.* **·cies 1.** The condition of being an idiot. **2.** Extreme stupidity or foolishness.

id·i·om (id/ē·əm) *n.* **1.** An expression peculiar to a language, not readily understandable from the meaning of its parts, as *to put up with* (tolerate, endure). **2.** The language or dialect of a region or people. **3.** The special terminology of a class, occupational group, etc. **4.** The distinctive character of a specific language. **5.** Typical style, form, or character, as in art, literature or music. [< F < L < Gk. *idios* one's own]

id·i·o·mat·ic (id/ē·ə·mat/ik) *adj.* **1.** Characteristic of a specific language. **2.** Of the nature of an idiom. **3.** Employing many idioms. Also **id/i·o·mat/i·cal.** — **id/i·o·mat/i·cal·ly** *adv.*

id·i·o·mor·phic (id/ē·ō·môr/fik) *adj.* **1.** Having its own distinctive form. **2.** *Mineral.* Possessing crystal faces: said of minerals of a rock. — **id/i·o·mor/phi·cal·ly** *adv.*

id·i·o·syn·cras·y (id/ē·ō·sing/krə·sē) *n. pl.* **·sies 1.** A habit, mannerism, expression, etc., peculiar to an individual; oddity. **2.** The distinctive physical or psychological constitution of an individual. [< Gk. *syn* together + *krasis* mixing] — **id/i·o·syn·crat/ic** (-sin·krat/ik) *adj.* — **id/i·o·syn·crat/i·cal·ly** *adv.*

id·i·ot (id/ē·ət) *n.* **1.** A person exhibiting mental deficiency in its most severe form. **2.** An extremely foolish or stupid person. [< OF < L < Gk. *idios* one's own]
— **Syn. 1.** The *idiot* is incapable of learning, and is completely helpless. An *imbecile* may learn to communicate, but is incapable of earning his own living. A *moron* may take a normal place in society, but needs constant supervision.

id·i·ot·ic (id/ē·ot/ik) *adj.* Of or characteristic of an idiot; senseless; stupid. Also **id/i·ot/i·cal.** — **id/i·ot/i·cal·ly** *adv.*

i·dle (īd/l) *adj.* **i·dler** (īd/lər), **i·dlest** (īd/list) **1.** Not engaged in work. **2.** Not being used; not operating. **3.** Unwilling to work; avoiding effort; lazy. **4.** Spent in inactivity; reserved for leisure: *idle* moments. **5.** Having no effectiveness; fruitless: *idle* threats. **6.** Of little value; frivolous; trifling. **7.** Having no basis; unfounded. — *v.* **i·dled, i·dling** *v.i.* **1.** To be engaged in trivial or useless activities; loaf. **2.** To move or progress lazily or aimlessly; linger. **3.** *Mech.* To operate without transmitting power, usu. at reduced speed: said of motors or machines. — *v.t.* **4.** To spend (time) wastefully; fritter: often with *away.* **5.** *U.S. Informal* To cause to be idle. **6.** To cause to idle, as a motor. [OE *īdel* empty, useless] — **i/dle·ness** *n.* — **i/dly** *adv.*

i·dler (īd/lər) *n.* **1.** One who idles; a lazy person; loafer. **2.** An idle wheel or pulley.

i·dol (īd/l) *n.* **1.** An image representing a god, and worshiped as divine. **2.** In the Christian and Jewish religions, a false or nonexistent god; object of heathen worship. **3.** One who is loved or admired to an excessive degree; object of infatuation. **4.** A false or misleading idea. [< OF < L < Gk. *eidos* form, shape]

i·dol·a·ter (ī·dol/ə·tər) *n.* **1.** One who worships an idol or idols. **2.** A blindly devoted admirer. [< OF < LL < Gk. *eidōlatrēs*] — **i·dol/a·tress** (-tris) *n. fem.*

i·dol·a·trous (ī·dol/ə·trəs) *adj.* **1.** Of or characterized by worship of idols. **2.** Blindly devoted. — **i·dol/a·trous·ly** *adv.* — **i·dol/a·trous·ness** *n.*

i·dol·a·try (ī·dol/ə·trē) *n. pl.* **·tries 1.** The worship of idols. **2.** Excessive admiration or veneration; blind infatuation. [< OF < LL < Gk. < *eidolon* idol + *latreia* worship]

i·dol·ize (īd/l·īz) *v.* **·ized, ·iz·ing** *v.t.* **1.** To love or admire blindly or to excess; adore. **2.** To worship as an idol. — *v.i.* **3.** To worship idols. — **i/dol·i·za/tion** *n.* — **i/dol·iz/er** *n.*

i·dyl (īd/l) *n.* **1.** A poem or prose piece, usu. short, depicting simple scenes of pastoral, domestic, or country life. **2.** An event, scene, etc., suitable for an idyl. Also *Brit.* **i/dyll.** [< L < Gk. *eidyllion* form]

i·dyl·lic (ī·dil/ik) *adj.* **1.** Of or having the qualities of an idyl. **2.** Charmingly simple or picturesque. Also **i·dyl/li·cal.** — **i·dyl/li·cal·ly** *adv.*

-ie *suffix* Little; dear: used affectionately: *birdie.*

-ier *suffix of nouns* One who is concerned with or works with: *cashier.* Also, after *w*, *-yer*, as in *lawyer.* [< F]

if (if) *conj.* **1.** In the event that; in case: We shall turn back *if* it rains. **2.** On condition that; provided that. **3.** Allowing the possibility that; granting that: *If* I am wrong, I'm sorry. ◆ In the preceding senses, *if* is often used in elliptical constructions: I'll do it *if* possible; He's sixty, *if* a day. **4.** Whether: See *if* the mail has come. **5.** Even though; although: Her clothes are neat, *if* not stylish. — *n.* A possibility or condition. [OE *gif*]

ig·loo (ig/lōō) *n. pl.* **·loos** A dome-shaped hut used by Eskimos, usu. built of blocks of snow. [< Eskimo *igdlu* house]

ig·ne·ous (ig/nē·əs) *adj.* **1.** *Geol.* Formed by the action of great heat within the earth, as rocks consolidated from a molten state. **2.** Of or like fire. [< L *ignis* fire]

ig·nis fat·u·us (ig/nis fach/ōō·əs) *pl.* **ig·nes fat·u·i** (ig/nēz fach/ōō·ī) **1.** A flickering, phosphorescent light sometimes seen over marshes, thought to be caused by the spontaneous combustion of marsh gas: also called *will-o'-the-wisp.* **2.** A deceptive attraction. [< Med.L, foolish fire]

ig·nite (ig·nīt/) *v.* **·nit·ed, ·nit·ing** *v.t.* **1.** To set on fire; make burn. **2.** To enkindle; arouse. **3.** *Chem.* To cause to glow with intense heat; bring to combustion. — *v.i.* **4.** To start to burn. [< L *ignire* to burn] — **ig·nit/a·ble** or **ig·nit/i·ble** *adj.* — **ig·nit/a·bil·i·ty** or **ig·nit/i·bil/i·ty** *n.*

ig·nit·er (ig·nī/tər) *n.* **1.** One who or that which ignites. **2.** A detonator (def. 1). Also **ig·ni/tor.**

ig·ni·tion (ig·nish/ən) *n.* **1.** The act of igniting, or the state of being ignited. **2.** The process of igniting the explosive mixture of fuel and air in a cylinder of an internal-combustion engine. **3.** The device or system that fires this mixture. [< Med.L < L *ignire* to burn]

ig·no·ble (ig·nō/bəl) *adj.* **1.** Dishonorable in purpose or character; base. **2.** Not of noble rank. **3.** Of low quality; inferior. [< F < L < *in-* not + *gnobilis* known] — **ig·no·bil·i·ty** (ig/nō·bil/ə·tē), **ig·no/ble·ness** *n.* — **ig·no/bly** *adv.*

ig·no·min·i·ous (ig/nə·min/ē·əs) *adj.* **1.** Marked by or involving dishonor or disgrace; shameful. **2.** Meriting disgrace; despicable. **3.** Tending to diminish one's self-respect. — **ig/no·min/i·ous·ly** *adv.* — **ig/no·min/i·ous·ness** *n.*

ig·no·min·y (ig/nə·min/ē) *n. pl.* **·min·ies 1.** Disgrace; dishonor. **2.** That which causes disgrace; dishonorable conduct. [< L < *in-* not + *gnomen* name, reputation]

ig·no·ra·mus (ig/nə·rā/məs, -ram/əs) *n.* An ignorant person. [< L, we do not know]

ig·no·rance (ig/nər·əns) *n.* The state of being ignorant; lack of knowledge, information, or awareness. [< F < L *ignorantia*]

ig·no·rant (ig/nər·ənt) *adj.* **1.** Having no learning or education; unenlightened. **2.** Lacking awareness: with *of: ignorant* of the facts. **3.** Uninformed; inexperienced: with *in.* [< OF < L *ignorare.* See IGNORE.] — **ig/no·rant·ly** *adv.*

ig·nore (ig·nôr/, -nōr/) *v.t.* **·nored, ·nor·ing 1.** To refuse to notice or recognize; disregard. **2.** *Law* To reject (a bill of indictment) for insufficient evidence. [< L *in-* not + *gnoscere* to know] — **ig·nor/er** *n.* — **ig·nor/a·ble** (-ə-bəl) *adj.*

i·gua·na (i·gwä/nə) *n.* Any of several tropical American lizards that sometimes attain a length of 6 feet. [< Sp. < Carib]

IHS A monogram of the name Jesus, derived from the Greek IH(ΣΟΥ)Σ, Jesus.

i·kon (ī/kon) See ICON.

il- Assimilated var. of IN-¹ and IN-².

-ile *suffix* Found in adjectives derived from French and Latin, and in nouns based on such adjectives: *docile, agile, juvenile.* Also, sometimes, **-il,** as in *civil, fossil.* [< F < L *-ilis,* suffix of adjectives; or directly < L]

il·e·um (il/ē·əm) *n. pl.* **il·e·a** (il/ē·ə) *Anat.* The lowest of the three divisions of the small intestine. For illus. see INTESTINE. [< LL < L *ileum* groin, small intestine] — **il·e·ac** (il/ē·ak) *adj.*

i·lex (ī/leks) *n.* Any tree or shrub of the holly family. [< L, holm oak]

Il·i·ad (il/ē·əd) An ancient Greek epic poem ascribed to Homer, describing the siege of Troy. — *n.* Any similar long narrative poem. [< L < Gk. *Ilion* Ilium (Troy)]

il·i·um (il/ē·əm) *n. pl.* **il·i·a** (il/ē·ə) *Anat.* The large upper portion of bones of the pelvis. For illus. see PELVIS. [< NL < L *ilia* loins, belly] — **il/i·ac** (-ak) *adj.*

Il·i·um (il/ē·əm) See TROY. Also **Il·i·on** (-ən).

ilk (ilk) *n.* Breed; sort; class: Smith and others of his *ilk.* [OE *ilca* same]

ill (il) *adj.* **worse, worst 1.** Not in good health; suffering from a disorder; sick. **2.** Destructive in effect; harmful. **3.** Hostile or malevolent; unfriendly; spiteful. **4.** Portending danger or disaster; unfavorable. **5.** Morally bad; evil. **6.** Contrary to accepted standards; improper. — **Syn.** See SICK¹. — *n.* **1.** Evil; wrong. **2.** Injury; harm: I wish him no *ill.* **3.** A cause of unhappiness, misfortune, etc. **4.** Disaster; trouble: to bode *ill.* **5.** A malady; sickness. — *adv.*

1. Not well; badly. 2. With difficulty; hardly. 3. Unsuitably; poorly. [ME < ON *illr*]

Ill may be used in combination. Such combinations are hyphenated when they appear before the words they modify, as in *ill-concealed* envy, but are not hyphenated when used predicatively, as in: His envy was *ill concealed*.

I'll (il) 1. I will. 2. I shall.

ill-ad·vised (il′əd·vīzd′) *adj.* Undertaken or acting in accordance with poor or insufficient advice; injudicious; rash.

ill-bred (il′bred′) *adj.* Unmannerly; impolite; rude.

ill-con·sid·ered (il′kən·sid′ərd) *adj.* Done with insufficient deliberation or forethought; thoughtless; unwise.

ill-dis·posed (il′dis·pōzd′) *adj.* 1. Having an unpleasant disposition; unfriendly. 2. Disinclined; averse. **—ill′-dis·pos′ed·ly** (-əd·lē) *adv.* **—ill′-dis·pos′ed·ness** (-əd·nes) *n.*

il·le·gal (i·lē′gəl) *adj.* 1. Not legal; contrary to law. 2. Violating official rules. **—il·le′gal·ly** *adv.*

il·le·gal·i·ty (il′ē·gal′ə·tē) *n. pl.* **·ties** 1. The state or quality of being illegal; unlawfulness. 2. An illegal act.

il·leg·i·ble (i·lej′ə·bəl) *adj.* Not legible; incapable of being read. **—il·leg′i·bil′i·ty, il·leg′i·ble·ness** *n.* **—il·leg′i·bly** *adv.*

il·le·git·i·ma·cy (il′i·jit′ə·mə·sē) *n. pl.* **·cies** The state or quality of being illegitimate; esp., the status or condition of a person born out of wedlock.

il·le·git·i·mate (il′i·jit′ə·mit) *adj.* 1. Born out of wedlock. 2. Not according to law; unlawful. 3. Contrary to good usage; incorrect. 4. Contrary to logic; unsound. [< L < *in-* not + *legitimus* lawful] **—il′le·git′i·mate·ly** *adv.*

ill fame Bad repute. **—house of ill fame** A brothel.

ill-fa·vored (il′fā′vərd) *adj.* 1. Unpleasant in appearance; ugly. 2. Objectionable; disagreeable. **—ill′-fa′vored·ly** *adv.* **—ill′-fa′vored·ness** *n.*

ill-found·ed (il′foun′did) *adj.* Based on weak or incorrect evidence or premises; unsupported.

ill-got·ten (il′got′n) *adj.* Obtained illegally or evilly.

ill humor A disagreeable mood; ill temper; sullenness.

ill-hu·mored (il′hyōō′mərd) *adj.* Irritable; cross. **—ill′-hu′mored·ly** *adv.* **—ill′-hu′mored·ness** *n.*

il·lib·er·al (i·lib′ər·əl) *adj.* 1. Not generous in giving; stingy. 2. Narrow-minded; intolerant. 3. Lacking breadth of culture; provincial. **—il·lib′er·al′i·ty** *n.* **—il·lib′er·al·ly** *adv.*

il·lic·it (i·lis′it) *adj.* Not permitted; unlawful; unauthorized. [< L < *in-* not + *licitus*] **—il·lic′it·ly** *adv.* **—il·lic′it·ness** *n.*

il·lim·it·a·ble (i·lim′it·ə·bəl) *adj.* Incapable of being limited; limitless; boundless. **—il·lim′it·a·bil′i·ty, il·lim′it·a·ble·ness** *n.* **—il·lim′it·a·bly** *adv.*

Il·li·nois (il′ə·noi′, -noiz′) *n. pl.* **·nois** A North American Indian of a tribe belonging to a confederacy of Algonquian tribes. [< F < N.Am.Ind.]

il·lit·er·a·cy (i·lit′ər·ə·sē) *n. pl.* **·cies** 1. The state of being illiterate; esp., inability to read and write. 2. An error in speaking or writing indicative of lack of education.

il·lit·er·ate (i·lit′ər·it) *adj.* 1. Lacking education; esp., unable to read and write. 2. Of language, characteristic of the uneducated. **—n.** An illiterate person. [< L *in-* not + *litteratus* lettered] **—il·lit′er·ate·ly** *adv.* **—il·lit′er·ate·ness** *n.*

ill-man·nered (il′man′ərd) *adj.* Characterized by bad manners; discourteous; rude. **—ill-man′nered·ly** *adv.*

ill nature Unpleasant or spiteful disposition; surliness. **—ill′-na′tured** *adj.* **—ill′-na′tured·ly** *adv.*

ill·ness (il′nis) *n.* 1. The state of being in poor health; sickness. 2. An ailment; disease.

il·log·i·cal (i·loj′i·kəl) *adj.* Not logical; neglectful of reason. **—il·log′i·cal′i·ty, il·log′i·cal·ness** *n.* **—il·log′i·cal·ly** *adv.*

ill repute Evil reputation. **—house of ill repute** Brothel.

ill-spent (il′spent′) *adj.* Wasted; misspent.

ill-starred (il′stärd′) *adj.* Unlucky, as if under the influence of an evil star.

ill temper Cross disposition; irritable mood. **—ill′-tem′pered** *adj.* **—ill′-tem′pered·ly** *adv.*

ill-timed (il′tīmd′) *adj.* Occurring at an unsuitable time.

ill-treat (il′trēt′) *v.t.* To act cruelly toward; maltreat.

il·lu·mi·nant (i·lōō′mə·nənt) *n.* Something that gives light. [< L *illuminare* to give light]

il·lu·mi·nate (i·lōō′mə·nāt) *v.* **·nat·ed, ·nat·ing** *v.t.* 1. To give light to; light up. 2. To shed light upon; clarify. 3. To enlighten, as the mind. 4. To make illustrious; glorify. 5. To decorate with lights. 6. To decorate, as a manuscript, with ornamental borders, figures, etc., often of gold. **—v.i.** 7. To shed light; become lighted. [< L < *in-* thoroughly + *luminare* to light] **—il·lu′mi·na′tor** *n.*

il·lu·mi·na·tion (i·lōō′mə·nā′shən) *n.* 1. The act of illuminating, or the state of being illuminated. 2. An amount or source of light. 3. Decoration by means of lighting. 4. Mental or spiritual enlightenment. 5. Embellishment, as of a manuscript, by means of gold or colored decorations, letters, etc.; also, a letter, ornament, etc., so used.

il·lu·mi·na·tive (i·lōō′mə·nā′tiv) *adj.* Capable of illuminating; serving to illuminate.

il·lu·mine (i·lōō′min) *v.t. & v.i.* **·mined, ·min·ing** To illuminate or be illuminated. [< F < L *illuminare* to illuminate]

ill-use (*v.* il′yōōz′; *n.* il′yōōs′) *v.t.* **-used, -us·ing** To treat cruelly or unjustly; abuse. **—n.** Bad or unjust treatment: also **ill′-us′age** (-yōō′sij, -yōō′zij) *n.*

il·lu·sion (i·lōō′zhən) *n.* 1. A false, misleading, or overly optimistic idea: youthful *illusions*. 2. A general impression not consistent with fact: Red gives an *illusion* of heat. 3. A delicate, transparent, netted fabric. [< OF < L *illudere* to make sport of < *in-* toward, against + *ludere* to play] **—il·lu′sion·al** (-əl), **il·lu′sion·ar·y** (-er-ē) *adj.*

il·lu·sive (i·lōō′siv) *adj.* Deceptive; unreal; illusory. **—il·lu′sive·ly** *adv.* **—il·lu′sive·ness** *n.*

il·lu·so·ry (i·lōō′sər·ē) *adj.* Of the nature of illusion; deceptive. **—il·lu′so·ri·ly** *adv.* **—il·lu′so·ri·ness** *n.*

il·lus·trate (il′ə·strāt, i·lus′trāt) *v.t.* **·trat·ed, ·trat·ing** 1. To explain or make clear by means of examples, comparisons, etc. 2. To supply or accompany (a book, etc.) with pictures, as for instruction or decoration. [< L < *in-* thoroughly + *lustrare* to illuminate] **—il′lus·tra′tor** *n.*

il·lus·tra·tion (il′ə·strā′shən) *n.* 1. An example, comparison, anecdote, etc., by which a statement is explained. 2. A print, drawing, or picture in written or printed text. 3. The act or art of illustrating. [< L *illustratio*]

il·lus·tra·tive (i·lus′trə·tiv, il′ə·strā′tiv) *adj.* Serving to illustrate. **—il·lus′tra·tive·ly** *adv.*

il·lus·tri·ous (i·lus′trē·əs) *adj.* 1. Greatly distinguished; renowned. 2. Conferring greatness or glory. [< L < *in-* in + *lustrum* light] **—il·lus′tri·ous·ly** *adv.* **—il·lus′tri·ous·ness** *n.*

ill will Hostile feeling; malevolence.

il·ly (il′lē) *adv.* Not well; badly; ill. ◆ While *illy* is regularly formed from the adjective *ill*, the form *ill* is preferred for the adverb as well.

Il·lyr·i·a (i·lir′ē·ə) An ancient country bordering the east coast of the Adriatic. **—Il·lyr′i·an** *adj.*

im-¹ Var. of EM-¹.

im-² Assimilated var. of IN-¹ and IN-².

I'm (īm) I am.

im·age (im′ij) *n.* 1. A representation or likeness of a real or imaginary person, creature, or object. 2. A mental representation of something not perceived at the moment through the senses; mental picture. 3. The way in which a person or thing is popularly perceived or regarded; public impression: a politician's *image*. 4. A person or thing that closely resembles another. 5. A sculptured likeness, as a statue. 6. A representative example; embodiment. 7. A literary device that evokes a mental picture, as a figure of speech. 8. *Optics* The counterpart of an object produced by reflection, refraction, or the passage of rays through a small aperture. 9. The optical replica of a scene reproduced by a television camera. **—v.t.** **·aged, ·ag·ing** 1. To form a mental picture of. 2. To make a visible representation of; portray. 3. To mirror; reflect. 4. To describe effectively or vividly. 5. To symbolize. [< OF < L *imitari* to imitate]

im·age·ry (im′ij·rē) *n. pl.* **·ries** 1. Mental images collectively. 2. The act or process of forming mental images. 3. The use of vivid descriptions or figures of speech in speaking or writing. 4. Images used in art or decoration.

im·ag·i·nar·y (i·maj′ə·ner′ē) *adj.* Existing in the imagination only; unreal. **—im·ag′i·nar′i·ly** *adv.* **—im·ag′i·nar′i·ness** *n.*

im·ag·i·na·tion (i·maj′ə·nā′shən) *n.* 1. The process of forming mental images of the objects of perception or thought in the absence of the concrete external stimuli. 2. The mental ability to reproduce the images of memory. 3. The mental ability to create original and striking images and concepts; the creative faculty. 4. A creation of the mind; mental image. 5. An absurd fancy. **—im·ag′i·na′tion·al** *adj.*

im·ag·i·na·tive (i·maj′ə·nə·tiv, -nā′tiv) *adj.* 1. Endowed with imagination. 2. Given to flights of fancy. 3. Of or characterized by the creative imagination: *imaginative* poetry. **—im·ag′i·na·tive·ly** *adv.* **—im·ag′i·na·tive·ness** *n.*

im·ag·ine (i·maj′in) *v.* **·ined, ·in·ing** 1. To form a mental picture or idea of. 2. To suppose; guess: I *imagine* he will be elected. **—v.i.** 3. To use the imagination. 4. To suppose; guess. [< L *imago* image] **—im·ag′i·na·ble** *adj.*

im·a·gism (im′ə·jiz′əm) *n.* A movement in poetry characterized by precise images and freedom in form. [< F *Des Imagistes*, the title of the first anthology of imagist poetry] **—im′a·gist** *n. & adj.* **—im′a·gis′tic** *adj.*

i·ma·go (i·mā′gō) *n. pl.* **i·ma·goes** or **i·mag·i·nes** (i·maj′ə·nēz) 1. *Entomol.* An insect in its adult, sexually mature stage. 2. *Psychoanal.* An infantile, unconscious concept of a parent or other loved one persisting in the adult. [< L]

im·bal·ance (im·bal′əns) *n.* 1. The state of being out of balance. 2. *Physiol.* Any defective coordination.

im·be·cile (im′bə·sil) *n.* 1. A person exhibiting a degree of mental deficiency between that of the idiot and the moron. 2. A foolish or stupid person. **—Syn.** See IDIOT. **—adj.** 1. Mentally deficient. 2. Stupid; senseless. [< F < L *imbecillus* weak, feeble] **—im′be·cil′i·ty** *n.*

im·bibe (im·bīb′) *v.* **·bibed, ·bib·ing** *v.t.* 1. To drink. 2.

To suck up; absorb. **3.** To take in mentally: to *imbibe* learning. — *v.i.* **4.** To drink. [< F < L *in-* in + *bibere* to drink] — **im·bib′er** *n.*

im·bri·cate (*adj.* im′brə·kit; *v.* im′brə·kāt) *adj.* **1.** Arranged in a regular pattern with overlapping edges, as shingles on a roof. **2.** Covered or decorated with a design resembling overlapping scales, leaves, etc. Also **im′bri·ca′tive** (-kā′tiv). — *v.t. & v.i.* **·cat·ed, ·cat·ing** To overlap in a regular arrangement. [< L *imbrex* gutter tile < *imber* rain]

im·bro·glio (im·brōl′yō) *n.* *pl.* **·glios 1.** A confused state of affairs. **2.** A confused heap or tangle. [< Ital.]

im·brue (im·brōō′) *v.t.* **·brued, ·bru·ing** To stain or drench, esp. with blood. [< OF < L *in-* in + *bibere* to drink]

im·bue (im·byōō′) *v.t.* **·bued, ·bu·ing 1.** To pervade or permeate (with emotions, ideals, etc.). **2.** To wet thoroughly; saturate, as with color. [< L *imbuere* to wet, soak]

im·i·ta·ble (im′ə·tə·bəl) *adj.* Capable of being imitated.

im·i·tate (im′ə·tāt) *v.t.* **·tat·ed, ·tat·ing 1.** To behave or attempt to behave in the same way as; follow the example of. **2.** To mimic or impersonate. **3.** To make a copy or reproduction of. **4.** To have or take on the appearance of. [< L *imitari* to imitate] — **im′i·ta′tor** *n.*

im·i·ta·tion (im′ə·tā′shən) *n.* **1.** The act of imitating. **2.** That which is done by or results from imitating; copy. **3.** *Biol.* Mimicry. — *adj.* Resembling or made to resemble something superior; not genuine. [< L *imitatio, -onis*]

im·i·ta·tive (im′ə·tā′tiv) *adj.* **1.** Tending to imitate; characterized by imitation. **2.** Patterned after or reproducing the characteristics of an original. **3.** Not genuine; spurious. **4.** *Ling.* Designating words that resemble natural sounds, as *buzz, swish.* — **im′i·ta′tive·ly** *adv.* — **im′i·ta′tive·ness** *n.*

im·mac·u·late (i·mak′yə·lit) *adj.* **1.** Without spot or stain; unsullied. **2.** Without sin; pure. **3.** Without error or blemish; faultless; flawless. [< L < *in-* not + *macula* spot] — **im·mac′u·late·ly** *adv.* — **im·mac′u·late·ness** *n.*

Immaculate Conception *Theol.* The doctrine that the Virgin Mary was conceived without original sin.

im·ma·nent (im′ə·nənt) *adj.* **1.** Existing or remaining within; indwelling. **2.** Of God, pervading all creation. [< L < *in-* in + *manere* to stay] — **im′ma·nence, im′ma·nen·cy** *n.* — **im′ma·nent·ly** *adv.*

Im·man·u·el (i·man′yōō·əl) A name of the Messiah. *Isa.* vii 14; *Matt.* i 23. Also **Emmanuel.**

im·ma·te·ri·al (im′ə·tir′ē·əl) *adj.* **1.** Of little or no importance; inconsequential; irrelevant. **2.** Not consisting of material substance. [< Med.L < *in-* not + *materia* matter] — **im′ma·te′ri·al·ly** *adv.* — **im′ma·te′ri·al·ness** *n.*

im·ma·ture (im′ə·chōōr′, -tyōōr′, -tōōr′) *adj.* **1.** Not mature or ripe. **2.** *Geog.* In an early stage of development. [< L < *in-* not + *maturus* mature] — **im′ma·ture′ly** *adv.* — **im′ma·ture′ness, im′ma·tur′i·ty** *n.*

im·meas·ur·a·ble (i·mezh′ər·ə·bəl) *adj.* Not capable of being measured; without limit; immense. — **im·meas′ur·a·bly** *adv.* — **im·meas′ur·a·bil′i·ty, im·meas′ur·a·ble·ness** *n.*

im·me·di·a·cy (i·mē′dē·ə·sē) *n.* **1.** The state or quality of being immediate; direct relationship. **2.** Intuitive knowledge as distinguished from that arrived at by reasoning.

im·me·di·ate (i·mē′dē·it) *adj.* **1.** Done or occurring without delay or lapse of time; instant. **2.** Pertaining to the present moment: We have no *immediate* vacancies. **3.** Separated by no appreciable interval of time or space: the *immediate* future. **4.** Very close in rank or relationship: the *immediate* family. **5.** Occurring or acting directly or without an intervening agency or cause. [< Med.L < *in-* not + *mediare* to stand between] — **im·me′di·ate·ness** *n.*

im·me·di·ate·ly (i·mē′dē·it·lē) *adv.* **1.** Without lapse of time; instantly; at once. **2.** In direct or close succession. **3.** Without an intervening agency or cause; directly. — *conj.* As soon as; at the instant that.

im·me·mo·ri·al (im′ə·môr′ē·əl, -mō′rē-) *adj.* Reaching back beyond memory; ancient. — **im′me·mo′ri·al·ly** *adv.*

im·mense (i·mens′) *adj.* **1.** Of great size, degree, or extent; huge. **2.** Having no limits; infinite. **3.** *Slang* Excellent; admirable. [< F < L < *in-* not + *mensus,* pp. of *metiri* to measure] — **im·mense′ly** *adv.* — **im·mense′ness** *n.*

im·men·si·ty (i·men′sə·tē) *n.* *pl.* **·ties 1.** The condition or quality of being immense; vastness. **2.** Boundless space.

im·men·sur·a·ble (i·men′shōōr·ə·bəl, -sə·rə-) *adj.* Immeasurable. [< MF < L < *in-* not + *mensurare* to measure] — **im·men′sur·a·bil′i·ty** *n.*

im·merge (i·mûrj′) *v.* **·merged, ·merg·ing** *v.t.* **1.** To immerse. — *v.i.* **2.** To plunge or sink into a liquid. [< L < *in-* in + *mergere* to dip] — **im·mer′gence** *n.*

im·merse (i·mûrs′) *v.t.* **·mersed, ·mers·ing 1.** To plunge or dip into water or other fluid so as to cover completely. **2.** To involve deeply; engross. **3.** To baptize by plunging the entire body under water. [< L *immersus,* pp. of *immergere* to dip] — **im·mer′sion** *n.*

im·mi·grant (im′ə·grənt) *adj.* Coming into a country or region of which one is not a native in order to settle there. Compare EMIGRANT. — *n.* A person who immigrates.

im·mi·grate (im′ə·grāt) *v.* **·grat·ed, ·grat·ing** *v.i.* **1.** To come into a country or region of which one is not a native in order to settle there. — *v.t.* **2.** To bring in as immigrants. — Syn. See MIGRATE. [< L < *in-* in + *migrare* to migrate]

im·mi·gra·tion (im′ə·grā′shən) *n.* **1.** The act of immigrating. **2.** The total number of immigrants entering a country during a stated period. **3.** Immigrants collectively. — **im·mi·gra·to·ry** (im′ə·grə·tôr′ē, -tō′rē) *adj.*

im·mi·nence (im′ə·nəns) *n.* **1.** The state or quality of being imminent. **2.** That which is imminent; esp., impending disaster. Also **im′mi·nen·cy.**

im·mi·nent (im′ə·nənt) *adj.* About to happen; impending; threatening: said esp. of danger or catastrophe. [< L < *in-* on + *-minere* so project] — **im′mi·nent·ly** *adv.*

im·mis·ci·ble (i·mis′ə·bəl) *adj.* Not capable of being mixed, as oil and water. [< L *in-* not + *miscere* to mix] — **im·mis′ci·bil′i·ty** *n.* — **im·mis′ci·bly** *adv.*

im·mo·bile (i·mō′bəl, -bēl) *adj.* **1.** Incapable of being moved. **2.** Not moving; motionless. [< OF < LL < L *in-* not + *movere* to move] — **im′mo·bil′i·ty** *n.*

im·mo·bil·ize (i·mō′bə·līz) *v.t.* **·lized, ·liz·ing 1.** To make immovable; fix in place. **2.** To make unable to move or mobilize, as a body of troops. — **im·mo′bi·li·za′tion** *n.*

im·mod·er·ate (i·mod′ər·it) *adj.* Not moderate; exceeding reasonable or proper bounds. — **im·mod′er·ate·ly** *adv.* — **im·mod′er·a′tion** *n.*

im·mod·est (i·mod′ist) *adj.* **1.** Without sense of decency; improper. **2.** Lacking humility; bold. — **im·mod′est·ly** *adv.* — **im·mod′es·ty** *n.*

im·mo·late (im′ə·lāt) *v.t.* **·lat·ed, ·lat·ing** To sacrifice; esp., to kill as a sacrificial victim. [< L < *in-* on + *mola* meal] — **im′mo·la′tion** *n.* — **im′mo·la′tor** *n.*

im·mor·al (i·môr′əl, i·mor′-) *adj.* **1.** Violating the moral law; contrary to conscience or public morality. **2.** Sexually impure; licentious. — **im·mor′al·ly** *adv.*
— Syn. **1.** The *immoral* person violates moral principles knowingly; he is consciously wicked, dissolute, evil, etc. The *amoral* person lacks the sense of right and wrong, and thus may violate morality without evil intent. *Unmoral* and *nonmoral* mean not within the realm of morality; a baby is *unmoral.*

im·mo·ral·i·ty (im′ə·ral′ə·tē, -ôr·al′-) *n.* *pl.* **·ties 1.** The state or quality of being immoral; wickedness; dissoluteness. **2.** Sexual impurity or misconduct. **3.** An immoral act.

im·mor·tal (i·môr′təl) *adj.* **1.** Not subject to death; living forever; deathless. **2.** Having unending existence; eternal. **3.** Pertaining to immortality or to beings or concepts that are immortal; divine. **4.** Of enduring fame; memorable. — *n.* **1.** An immortal being. **2.** *pl.* The gods of classical mythology. **3.** A person who has gained enduring fame. — **im·mor′tal·ly** *adv.*

im·mor·tal·i·ty (im′ôr·tal′ə·tē) *n.* **1.** Unending existence; eternal life. **2.** Eternal fame.

im·mor·tal·ize (i·môr′təl·īz) *v.t.* **·ized, ·iz·ing** To make immortal; endow with perpetual fame. Also *Brit.* **im·mor′tal·ise.** — **im·mor′tal·i′zer** *n.* — **im·mor′tal·i·za′tion** *n.*

im·mor·telle (im′ôr·tel′) *n.* An everlasting (def. 2). [< F]

im·mov·a·ble (i·mōō′və·bəl) *adj.* **1.** Incapable of being moved; stable. **2.** Unable to move; stationary. **3.** Firm of purpose or opinion; unyielding. **4.** Not easily aroused emotionally; impassive. — *n.pl. Law* Real property. — **im·mov′a·bil′i·ty, im·mov′a·ble·ness** *n.* — **im·mov′a·bly** *adv.*

im·mune (i·myōōn′) *adj.* **1.** Protected against a disease, poison, or the like, as by inoculation. **2.** Not susceptible to harmful influence. **3.** Not subject to obligation, penalty, etc. — *n.* One who is immune, esp. to a disease.

im·mu·ni·ty (i·myōō′nə·tē) *n.* *pl.* **·ties 1.** Protection against or lack of susceptibility to a disease, poison, infection, or the like. **2.** Resistance to harmful influence. **3.** Exemption from civil obligations or jurisdiction. [< OF < L < *in-* not + *munis* serviceable]

im·mu·nize (im′yə·nīz) *v.t.* **·nized, ·niz·ing** To make immune; esp., to protect against a disease by inoculation. — **im′mu·ni·za′tion** *n.*

im·mu·nol·o·gy (im′yə·nol′ə·jē) *n.* The branch of medical science that deals with immunity to disease. — **im·mu·no·log·i·cal** (i·myōō′nə·loj′i·kəl) *adj.* — **im·mu·nol′o·gist** *n.*

im·mure (i·myōōr′) *v.t.* **·mured, ·mur·ing 1.** To enclose within walls; imprison. **2.** To place in seclusion; confine. **3.** To entomb within a wall. [< Med.L < *in-* in + LL *murare* to wall] — **im·mure′ment** *n.*

im·mu·ta·ble (i·myōō′tə·bəl) *adj.* Not mutable; unchanging; unalterable. — **im·mu′ta·bil′i·ty, im·mu′ta·ble·ness** *n.* — **im·mu′ta·bly** *adv.*

imp (imp) *n.* **1.** An evil spirit; small or minor demon. **2.** A mischievous or unruly child. [OE *impian* to ingraft]

im·pact (*n.* im′pakt; *v.* im·pakt′) *n.* **1.** A striking together; collision. **2.** The forcible momentary contact of a moving body with another either moving or at rest. **3.** Strong influence; powerful effect. —*v.t.* To press or drive firmly into something. [< L *impactus*, pp. of *impingere* to impinge]

im·pact·ed (im·pak′tid) *adj.* *Dent.* Denoting a tooth unable to emerge through the gum.

im·pac·tion (im·pak′shən) *n.* **1.** The act of impacting, or the state of being impacted. **2.** *Dent.* An impacted tooth.

im·pair (im·pâr′) *v.t.* To cause to become less in quality, power, or value; make worse. [< OF < LL *in-* thoroughly + *pejorare* to make worse] —**im·pair′ment** *n.*

im·pale (im·pāl′) *v.t.* **·paled**, **·pal·ing 1.** To fix upon a pale or sharp stake. **2.** To torture or put to death by thrusting a sharp stake through the body. **3.** To make helpless as if by fixing upon a stake. [< OF < LL < *in-* + *palus* stake] —**im·pale′ment** *n.* —**im·pal′er** *n.*

im·pal·pa·ble (im·pal′pə·bəl) *adj.* **1.** Not capable of being perceived by the sense of touch. **2.** Not capable of being distinguished by the mind. —**im·pal′pa·bil′i·ty** *n.* —**im·pal′pa·bly** *adv.*

im·pan·el (im·pan′əl) *v.t.* **·pan·eled** or **·elled**, **·pan·el·ing** or **·el·ling 1.** To enroll upon a panel or list, as for jury duty. **2.** To choose (members of a jury, etc.) from such a list. Also spelled *empanel.* —**im·pan′el·ment** *n.*

im·part (im·pärt′) *v.t.* **1.** To make known; disclose. **2.** To bestow a measure or quantity of: to *impart* happiness. [< OF < L < *in-* in + *partire* to share] —**im·par·ta·tion** (im′pär·tā′shən), **im·part′ment** *n.* —**im·part′er** *n.*

im·par·tial (im·pär′shəl) *adj.* Not favoring one above another; free from bias; disinterested. —**im·par′tial·ly** *adv.* —**im·par′tial·ness** *n.*

im·par·ti·al·i·ty (im′pär·shē·al′ə·tē, im·pär′-) *n.* Freedom from bias; fairness.

im·pass·a·ble (im·pas′ə·bəl, -päs′-) *adj.* That cannot be traveled over or through: an *impassable* jungle. —**im·pass′a·bil′i·ty**, **im·pass′a·ble·ness** *n.* —**im·pass′a·bly** *adv.*

im·passe (im′pas, im·pas′; *Fr.* an·päs′) *n.* **1.** A situation in which no further progress is possible; deadlock. **2.** A way or passage open at one end only; blind alley. [< F]

im·pas·si·ble (im·pas′ə·bəl) *adj.* **1.** Incapable of emotion; unfeeling. **2.** Incapable of suffering pain. **3.** Invulnerable. [< OF < Med.L < *in-* not + *pati* to suffer] —**im·pas′si·bil′i·ty**, **im·pas′si·ble·ness** *n.* —**im·pas′si·bly** *adv.*

im·pas·sion (im·pash′ən) *v.t.* To fill with passion; inflame.

im·pas·sioned (im·pash′ənd) *adj.* Filled with passion or strong feeling; fervent. —**im·pas′sioned·ly** *adv.*

im·pas·sive (im·pas′iv) *adj.* **1.** Not feeling emotion; unmoved. **2.** Calm; serene. **3.** Unconscious. —**im·pas′sive·ly** *adv.* —**im·pas′sive·ness**, **im·pas·siv·i·ty** (im/pa·siv′ə·tē) *n.*

im·pa·ti·ens (im·pā′shē·enz) *n.* An herb with stems enlarged at the joints and irregular flowers, as the jewelweed: also called *touch-me-not.* [< L, impatient; because the ripe seed pods burst open at a touch.]

im·pa·tient (im·pā′shənt) *adj.* **1.** Lacking patience; easily annoyed at delay, discomfort, etc.; irritable. **2.** Unwilling to tolerate: with *of.* **3.** Restlessly eager: *impatient* for success. **4.** Exhibiting lack of patience: an *impatient* gesture. —**im·pa′tience** *n.* —**im·pa′tient·ly** *adv.*

im·peach (im·pēch′) *v.t.* **1.** To charge (a high public official) before a legally constituted tribunal with crime or misdemeanor in office. **2.** To challenge or bring discredit upon the honesty or validity of. [< OF < LL < *in-* in + *pedica* fetter] —**im·peach′a·bil′i·ty** *n.* —**im·peach′a·ble** *adj.* —**im·peach′ment** *n.*

im·pec·ca·ble (im·pek′ə·bəl) *adj.* **1.** Free from error, fault, or flaw. **2.** Incapable of doing wrong; unerring. —*n.* An impeccable person. [< LL < L *in-* not + *peccare* to sin] —**im·pec′ca·bil′i·ty** *n.* —**im·pec′ca·bly** *adv.*

im·pe·cu·ni·ous (im′pə·kyoo′nē·əs) *adj.* Having no money; penniless. Also **im·pe·cu·ni·ar·y** (im′pə·kyoo′nē·er′ē). [< F < *in-* not + *pecunia* money] —**im′pe·cu′ni·ous·ly** *adv.* —**im′pe·cu′ni·ous·ness**, **im·pe·cu′ni·os·i·ty** (-os′ə·tē) *n.*

im·ped·ance (im·pēd′ns) *n.* *Electr.* The total opposition to an alternating current presented by a circuit.

im·pede (im·pēd′) *v.t.* **·ped·ed**, **·ped·ing** To retard or hinder in progress or action; put obstacles in the way of. [< L *impedire*, lit., to shackle the feet < *in-* in + *pes, pedis* foot] —**im·ped′er** *n.* —**im·ped′ing·ly** *adv.*

im·pe·di·ent (im·pē′dē·ənt) *adj.* That impedes. —*n.* That which impedes.

im·ped·i·ment (im·ped′ə·mənt) *n.* **1.** That which hinders or obstructs; an obstacle. **2.** A physical handicap, esp. a speech defect. **3.** *Law* a A disability that prevents the making of a valid contract, as infancy, insanity, etc. b A disability that affects the validity of a marriage. —**im·ped′i·men′tal** (-men′təl), **im·ped′i·men′ta·ry** (-men′tər·ē) *adj.*

im·ped·i·men·ta (im·ped′ə·men′tə) *n.pl.* **1.** The baggage, supplies, and equipment carried by an army. **2.** Cumbersome baggage or equipment; also, any drawbacks or burdens. **3.** *Law* Impediments. [< L]

im·pel (im·pel′) *v.t.* **·pelled**, **·pel·ling 1.** To force or drive to an action; move by an impulse; urge on. **2.** To drive or push forward. —**Syn.** See ACTUATE. [< L < *in-* on + *pellere* to drive] —**im·pel′lent** *adj.* & *n.* —**im·pel′ler** *n.*

im·pend (im·pend′) *v.i.* **1.** To be about to occur; be imminent. **2.** To be suspended: with *over.* [< L < *in-* + *pendere* to hang] —**im·pen′dent** *adj.* —**im·pen′dence** *n.*

im·pend·ing (im·pen′ding) *adj.* **1.** About to occur; imminent; threatening. **2.** Overhanging.

im·pen·e·tra·bil·i·ty (im·pen′ə·trə·bil′ə·tē) *n.* **1.** The state or quality of being impenetrable. **2.** *Physics* The property of matter that makes impossible the occupation of the same space by two bodies at the same time.

im·pen·e·tra·ble (im·pen′ə·trə·bəl) *adj.* **1.** Incapable of being penetrated; that cannot be pierced, entered, seen through, etc.; impervious. **2.** Incapable of being understood. **3.** Inaccessible to intellectual or moral influences. **4.** *Physics* Possessing impenetrability. [< OF < L < *in-* not + *penetrare* to put within] —**im·pen′e·tra·bil′i·ty**, **im·pen′e·tra·ble·ness** *n.* —**im·pen′e·tra·bly** *adv.*

im·pen·i·tent (im·pen′ə·tənt) *adj.* Not penitent; obdurate. —**im·pen′i·tence**, **im·pen′i·ten·cy** *n.* —**im·pen′i·tent·ly** *adv.* —**im·pen′i·tent·ness** *n.*

im·per·a·tive (im·per′ə·tiv) *adj.* **1.** Urgently necessary; obligatory. **2.** Having the nature of or expressing a command. **3.** *Gram.* Designating the mood used to express commands, requests, exhortations, etc. —*n.* **1.** That which is imperative. **2.** *Gram.* The mood used to express command, exhortation, etc., or a verb or verb form in this mood. [< LL *imperare* to command] —**im·per′a·tive·ly** *adv.* —**im·per′a·tive·ness** *n.*

im·per·cep·ti·ble (im′pər·sep′tə·bəl) *adj.* **1.** That can barely be perceived, as by reason of smallness, extreme delicacy, subtlety, etc. **2.** Not discernible by the mind or senses. —**im′per·cep′ti·ble·ness**, **im′per·cep′ti·bil′i·ty** *n.* —**im′per·cep′ti·bly** *adv.*

im·per·cep·tive (im′pər·sep′tiv) *adj.* Not perceptive; lacking the power of perception. —**im·per·cep·tiv·i·ty** (im′pər·sep·tiv′ə·tē), **im′per·cep′tive·ness** *n.*

im·per·fect (im·pûr′fikt) *adj.* **1.** Falling short of perfection; faulty: an *imperfect* performance. **2.** Wanting in completeness; deficient. **3.** Denoting a tense that indicates action, usu. past action, as uncompleted, continuing, or synchronous with some other action. —*n.* *Gram.* The imperfect tense, or a verb or verb form in this tense, as *was speaking* in *He was speaking when I entered.* —**im·per′fect·ly** *adv.* —**im·per′fect·ness** *n.*

im·per·fec·tion (im′pər·fek′shən) *n.* **1.** The state or quality of being imperfect. **2.** A defect; flaw. [< OF < LL < L *imperfectus* incomplete.]

im·per·fo·rate (im·pûr′fər·it) *adj.* **1.** Without perforations; not perforated. **2.** Not separated by lines of perforations: said of stamps. Also **im·per′fo·rat′ed** (-rā′tid). —*n.* An imperforated stamp. —**im·per′fo·ra′tion** *n.*

im·pe·ri·al (im·pir′ē·əl) *adj.* **1.** Of or pertaining to an empire. **2.** Designating a nation having sovereign power over colonies or dependencies. **3.** Pertaining to or suitable to the rank of an emperor or supreme ruler. **4.** Possessing commanding power or dignity; majestic; magnificent. **5.** Exercising the authority of or having the manner of a supreme ruler or commander; overbearing. **6.** Superior in size or quality. **7.** Designating or conforming to the legal standards of weights and measures of the United Kingdom. —*n.* **1.** A pointed tuft of hair on the chin. **2.** An article of more than usual size or of superior excellence. **3.** A size of paper: in the U.S. 23 x 31 inches. [< OF < L < *imperium* rule, power] —**im·pe′ri·al·ly** *adv.* —**im·pe′ri·al·ness** *n.*

im·pe·ri·al·ism (im·pir′ē·əl·iz′əm) *n.* **1.** The creation, maintenance, or extension of an empire, comprising many nations and areas, all controlled by a central government. **2.** A system of imperial government. **3.** Imperial character, authority, or spirit. —**im·pe′ri·al·ist** *n.* & *adj.* —**im·pe′ri·al·is′tic** *adj.* —**im·pe′ri·al·is′ti·cal·ly** *adv.*

im·per·il (im·per′il) *v.t.* **·per·iled** or **·illed**, **·per·il·ing** or **·il·ling** To place in peril; endanger.

im·pe·ri·ous (im·pir′ē·əs) *adj.* **1.** Characterized by an attitude of command; domineering; arrogant. **2.** Urgent; imperative. [< L *imperium*] —**im·pe′ri·ous·ly** *adv.* —**im·pe′ri·ous·ness** *n.*

im·per·ish·a·ble (im·per′ish·ə·bəl) *adj.* Not perishable; not subject to decay; enduring; everlasting. —**im·per′ish·a·bil′i·ty**, **im·per′ish·a·ble·ness** *n.* —**im·per′ish·a·bly** *adv.*

im·per·ma·nent (im·pûr′mə·nənt) *adj.* Not permanent; fleeting. —**im·per′ma·nence**, **im·per′ma·nen·cy** *n.*

im·per·me·a·ble (im·pûr′mē·ə·bəl) *adj.* **1.** Not permitting passage or penetration. **2.** Impervious to moisture. —**im·per′me·a·bil′i·ty**, **im·per′me·a·ble·ness** *n.* —**im·per′me·a·bly** *adv.*

im·per·mis·si·ble (im′pər·mis′ə·bəl) *adj.* Not to be permitted. —**im′per·mis′si·bil′i·ty** *n.* —**im′per·mis′si·bly** *adv.*

im·per·son·al (im·pûr′sən·əl) *adj.* **1.** Not personal; objective: an *impersonal* observation. **2.** Not having the characteristics of a person: an *impersonal* deity. **3.** *Gram.* Of a verb, having no specific subject: in English the word *it* is usu. used with such verbs. — *n. Gram.* An impersonal verb. **—im·per′son·al′i·ty** (-al′ə·tē) *n.* **—im·per′son·al·ly** *adv.*

im·per·son·ate (v. im·pûr′sən·āt; adj. im·pûr′sən·it) *v.t.* **·at·ed, ·at·ing 1.** To adopt or mimic the appearance, mannerisms, etc., of. **2.** To act or play the part of. **3.** *Archaic* To represent in human form. — *adj.* Embodied in one person. **—im·per′son·a′tion** *n.* **—im·per′son·a′tor** *n.*

im·per·ti·nence (im·pûr′tə·nəns) *n.* **1.** Deliberate disrespectfulness; rudeness. **2.** Irrelevancy. **3.** Unsuitability; inappropriateness; incongruity. **4.** An impertinent remark, act, etc. Also **im·per′ti·nen·cy.**

im·per·ti·nent (im·pûr′tə·nənt) *adj.* **1.** Deliberately disrespectful or unmannerly; impudent. **2.** Not pertinent; irrelevant. **3.** Not suitable; inappropriate; incongruous. **—im·per′ti·nent·ly** *adv.*

im·per·turb·a·ble (im′pər·tûr′bə·bəl) *adj.* Incapable of being disturbed or agitated; calm. **—im′per·turb′a·bil′i·ty, im′per·turb′a·ble·ness** *n.* **—im′per·turb′a·bly** *adv.*

im·per·vi·ous (im·pûr′vē·əs) *adj.* **1.** Incapable of being passed through, as by moisture or light rays; impermeable. **2.** Not open; unreceptive: a mind *impervious* to reason. Also **im·per′vi·a·ble.** [< L < *in-* not + *per-* through + *via* way, road] **—im·per′vi·ous·ly** *adv.* **—im·per′vi·ous·ness** *n.*

im·pe·ti·go (im′pə·tī′gō) *n. Pathol.* A contagious skin disease marked by pustules. [< L < *impetere* to attack]

im·pet·u·os·i·ty (im·pech′oo̅·os′ə·tē) *n. pl.* **·ties 1.** The quality of being impetuous. **2.** An impetuous action.

im·pet·u·ous im·pech′oo̅·əs) *adj.* **1.** Tending to act on sudden impulse and without forethought. **2.** Resulting from sudden impulse; rashly hasty. **3.** Moving with violent force: an *impetuous* wind. [< MF < L < *impetere* to attack] **—im·pet′u·ous·ly** *adv.* **—im·pet′u·ous·ness** *n.*
— **Syn. 1.** impulsive, reckless, rash. **2.** sudden, spontaneous, precipitate, swift, headlong. **— Ant.** deliberate.

im·pe·tus (im′pə·təs) *n.* **1.** The force that sets a body in motion; also, the energy with which a body moves or is driven. **2.** Any motivating force; stimulus; incentive. [< L < *in-* upon + *petere* to seek]

im·pi·e·ty (im·pī′ə·tē) *n. pl.* **·ties 1.** Lack of reverence for God; ungodliness. **2.** Lack of respect for those to whom respect is due; undutifulness. **3.** An impious act.

im·pinge (im·pinj′) *v.i.* **·pinged, ·ping·ing 1.** To strike; fall: with *on, upon,* or *against.* **2.** To encroach; infringe: with *on* or *upon.* [< L < *in-* against + *pangere* to strike] **— im·pinge′ment** *n.* **—im·ping′er** *n.*

im·pi·ous (im′pē·əs) *adj.* **1.** Lacking in reverence for God; ungodly; blasphemous. **2.** Lacking in due respect, as for one's parents. [< L < *in-* not + *pius* reverent] **—im′pi·ous·ly** *adv.* **—im′pi·ous·ness** *n.*

imp·ish (imp′ish) *adj.* Characteristic of or resembling an imp; mischievous. **—imp′ish·ly** *adv.* **—imp′ish·ness** *n.*

im·pla·ca·ble (im·plā′kə·bəl, -plak′ə-) *adj.* That cannot be appeased or pacified. [< F < L < *in-* not + *placere* to please] **—im·pla′ca·bil′i·ty, im·pla′ca·ble·ness** *n.* **— im·pla′ca·bly** *adv.*

im·plant (v. im·plant′, -plänt′; n. im′plant′, -plänt′) *v.t.* **1.** To fix firmly, as in the ground; plant; embed. **2.** To instill in the mind: to *implant* new ideas; inculcate. **3.** *Med.* To insert or embed in (living tissue). — *n. Med.* **1.** A tissue implanted in the body. **2.** A small tube containing radioactive material, embedded in tissue for therapeutic or remedial purposes. [< F *implanter*] **—im′plan·ta′tion** *n.*

im·plau·si·ble (im·plô′zə·bəl) *adj.* Not plausible; lacking the appearance of truth or trustworthiness. **—im·plau′si·bil′i·ty, im·plau′si·ble·ness** *n.* **—im·plau′si·bly** *adv.*

im·ple·ment (n. im′plə·mənt; v. im′plə·ment) *n.* **1.** A piece of equipment used in some form of work or activity; tool; instrument; utensil. **2.** Any means or agent for the accomplishment of a purpose. — *v.t.* **1.** To provide for the accomplishment or carrying into effect of. **2.** To accomplish; fulfill. **3.** To furnish with implements. [< L < *in-* in + *plere* to fill] **—im′ple·men′tal** *adj.* **—im′ple·men·ta′tion** *n.*

im·pli·cate (im′plə·kāt) *v.t.* **·cat·ed, ·cat·ing 1.** To show to be involved or concerned, as in a plot or crime. **2.** To indicate as something to be inferred; imply. **3.** To twist together. [< L < *in-* in + *plicare* to fold] **— im′pli·ca′tive** *adj.*

im·pli·ca·tion (im′plə·kā′shən) *n.* **1.** The act of involving, or the state of being involved. **2.** The act of implying, or the state of being implied. **3.** That which is implied.

im·plic·it (im·plis′it) *adj.* **1.** Unreserved; absolute. **2.** Implied or understood, but not specifically expressed: *implicit* agreement. **3.** Essentially contained, but not apparent; inherent: with *in:* The man is *implicit* in the child. [< F < L *implicare* to involve] **—im·plic′it·ly** *adv.* **—im·plic′it·ness** *n.*

im·plied (im·plīd′) *adj.* Understood, suggested, or included

without being specifically expressed. **— im·pli′ed·ly** *adv.*

im·plode (im·plōd′) *v.t. & v.i.* **·plod·ed, ·plod·ing** To burst inward. **— im·plo·sion** (im·plō′zhən) *n.* **— im·plo·sive** (im·plō′siv) *adj.* [< IN-² + (EX)PLODE]

im·plore (im·plôr′, -plōr′) *v.* **·plored, ·plor·ing** *v.t.* **1.** To call upon in humble or urgent entreaty; beseech. **2.** To beg for urgently. — *v.i.* **3.** To make urgent supplication. [< L < *in-* thoroughly + *plorare* to cry out] **— im·plo·ra·tion** (im′plə·rā′shən) *n.* **— im·plor′er** *n.* **— im·plor′ing·ly** *adv.*

im·ply (im·plī′) *v.t.* **·plied, ·ply·ing 1.** To involve necessarily as a circumstance, condition, effect, etc.: An action *implies* an agent. **2.** To indicate or suggest without stating; hint at; intimate. **3.** To signify. ◆ See note at INFER. [< OF < L < *in-* in + *plicare* to fold]

im·po·lite (im′pə·līt′) *adj.* Lacking in politeness; discourteous; rude. **— im′po·lite′ly** *adv.* **— im′po·lite′ness** *n.*

im·pol·i·tic (im·pol′ə·tik) *adj.* Not in keeping with good policy; not prudent; inexpedient; injudicious. **— im·pol′i·tic·ly** *adv.* **— im·pol′i·tic·ness** *n.*

im·pon·der·a·ble (im·pon′dər·ə·bəl) *adj.* Incapable of being estimated, calculated, or valued. — *n.* An imponderable factor or circumstance. **— im·pon′der·a·bil′i·ty, im·pon′der·a·ble·ness** *n.* **— im·pon′der·a·bly** *adv.*

im·port¹ (v. im·pôrt′, -pōrt′; im′pôrt, -pōrt; n. im′pôrt, -pōrt) *v.t.* **1.** To bring or cause to be brought into a country from abroad for commercial purposes, as merchandise. **2.** To bring in from an outside source or another relationship; introduce. **3.** To have as its meaning; signify. — *n.* **1.** An imported commodity. **2.** The act of importing. **3.** That which is implied; meaning. [< F < L < *in-* + *portare* to carry] **— im·port′a·ble** *adj.* **— im·port′a·bil′i·ty** *n.*

im·port² (n. im′pôrt, -pōrt; v. im·pôrt′, -pōrt′) *n.* Importance: a matter of no *import.* — *v.i.* To be of consequence; matter. [< F < Ital. < Med.L *importare* to be important]

im·por·tance (im·pôr′təns) *n.* **1.** The quality of being important; consequence; significance. **2.** Worthiness of esteem; standing: a man of *importance.* **3.** Pretentiousness.

im·por·tant (im·pôr′tənt) *adj.* **1.** Having much significance, value, or influence; outstanding; great. **2.** Deserving of special notice or attention; noteworthy. **3.** Having special relevance; mattering greatly: with *to.* **4.** Considering oneself worthy of high esteem or special attention; pompous. **— im·por′tant·ly** *adv.*

im·por·ta·tion (im′pôr·tā′shən, -pōr-) *n.* **1.** The act of importing. **2.** That which is imported.

im·port·er (im·pôr′tər, -pōr′-) *n.* One who is in the business of importing merchandise.

im·por·tu·nate (im·pôr′chə·nit) *adj.* **1.** Urgently or stubbornly persistent in demand; insistent: an *importunate* creditor. **2.** Of a demand or request, repeatedly made; pressing. **— im·por′tu·nate·ly** *adv.* **— im·por′tu·nate·ness** *n.*

im·por·tune (im′pôr·tōōn′, -tyōōn′, im·pôr′chən) *v.* **·tuned, ·tun·ing** *v.t.* **1.** To harass with persistent demands or requests. **2.** To ask or beg for persistently or urgently. — *v.i.* **3.** To make persistent requests or demands. — *adj.* Importunate. [< L < L *importunus* not blowing towards port (of a wind), hence unfavorable] **— im′por·tune′ly** *adv.* **— im′por·tun′er** *n.*

im·por·tu·ni·ty (im′pôr·tōō′nə·tē, -tyōō′-) *n. pl.* **·ties 1.** Persistence in making demands or requests. **2.** *pl.* Repeated demands or requests.

im·pose (im·pōz′) *v.t.* **·posed, ·pos·ing 1.** To establish by authority as an obligation, penalty, etc.: to *impose* a fine. **2.** To inflict or enforce in an arbitrary or authoritarian manner. **3.** To force (oneself, one's company, etc.) upon others. **4.** To palm off as true or genuine; foist. **5.** *Eccl.* To lay on (hands), as in confirmation. **6.** *Printing* To arrange in correct order in a form, as pages of type. **— to impose on** (or **upon**). **1.** To take advantage of; make unwarranted or unfair use of. **2.** To deceive; cheat. [< F *im-* on + *poser* to put down] **— im·pos′a·ble** *adj.* **— im·pos′er** *n.*

im·pos·ing (im·pō′zing) *adj.* Impressive in appearance or manner; grand; stately. **— im·pos′ing·ly** *adv.*

im·po·si·tion (im′pə·zish′ən) *n.* **1.** The act of imposing or imposing on. **2.** That which is imposed, as a tax or an excessive requirement. **3.** An act of trickery or deception. **4.** The laying on of hands, as in the religious ceremonies. [< L *impositio, -onis* < *impositus.* See IMPOST.]

im·pos·si·bil·i·ty (im·pos′ə·bil′ə·tē) *n. pl.* **·ties 1.** The quality of being impossible. **2.** Something impossible.

im·pos·si·ble (im·pos′ə·bəl) *adj.* **1.** Incapable of existing or taking place. **2.** Incapable of being done or put into practice. **3.** Contrary to fact or reality; inconceivable. **4.** Not acceptable; objectionable; intolerable. [< F. See POSSIBLE.] **— im·pos′si·bly** *adv.*

im·post¹ (im′pōst) *n.* A tax or customs duty. — *v.t.* To classify (imported goods) for the purpose of determining customs duties. [< OF < L < *in-* on + *ponere* to lay, place]

im·post¹ (im'pōst) *n. Archit.* The top section of a pillar or wall, serving as support for an arch. [See IMPOST.¹]

im·pos·tor (im·pos'tər) *n.* One who deceives; esp., one who assumes the name of another. [< F < LL *impostor*]

im·pos·ture (im·pos'chər) *n.* Deception by means of false pretenses; esp., the act of posing under a false name.

im·po·tence (im'pə·təns) *n.* The condition or quality of being impotent; esp., an incapacity for sexual intercourse: said of males. Also **im'po·ten·cy.** [< OF < L *impotentia*]

im·po·tent (im'pə·tənt) *adj.* 1. Powerless to act or to accomplish anything. 2. Physically weak. 3. Incapable of sexual intercourse: said of males. —**im'po·tent·ly** *adv.*

im·pound (im·pound') *v.t.* 1. To shut up in a pound, as a stray dog. 2. To place in legal custody. 3. To collect (water) for irrigation. —**im·pound'age** (-poun'dij) *n.*

im·pov·er·ish (im·pov'ər·ish) *v.t.* 1. To reduce to poverty. 2. To exhaust the fertility of, as soil. [< OF < L *pauperare* to impoverish] —**im·pov'er·ish·ment** *n.*

im·pow·er (im·pou'ər) See EMPOWER.

im·prac·ti·ca·ble (im·prak'ti·kə·bəl) *adj.* 1. Incapable of being carried out or put into effect; not feasible. 2. Incapable of being used for an intended purpose. 3. Hard to get on with; intractable. —**im·prac'ti·ca·bil'i·ty, im·prac'ti·ca·ble·ness** *n.* —**im·prac'ti·ca·bly** *adv.*

im·prac·ti·cal (im·prak'ti·kal) *adj.* Not practical. —**im·prac'ti·cal'i·ty** (-kal'ə·tē) *n.*

im·pre·cate (im'prə·kāt) *v.t.* **·cat·ed, ·cat·ing** To invoke or call down (some curse or calamity): to *imprecate* evil upon a person. [< L *in-* on + *precari* to pray] —**im'pre·ca·tor** *n.* —**im'pre·ca·to·ry** (-kə·tôr'ē, -tō'rē) *adj.*

im·pre·ca·tion (im'prə·kā'shən) *n.* 1. The act of imprecating. 2. A malediction; curse.

im·preg·na·ble (im·preg'nə·bəl) *adj.* 1. Incapable of being taken by force. 2. Incapable of being overcome; unyielding. [< OF < *im-* not + *prendre* to take] —**im·preg'na·bil'i·ty** *n.* —**im·preg'na·bly** *adv.*

im·preg·nate (im·preg'nāt) *v.t.* **·nat·ed, ·nat·ing** 1. To make pregnant. 2. To fertilize, as an ovum. 3. To saturate or permeate. 4. To fill or imbue, as with ideas, etc. —*adj.* Made pregnant. [< LL < L *in-* in + *praegnans* pregnant] —**im'preg·na'tion** *n.* —**im'preg·na'tor** *n.*

im·pre·sa·ri·o (im'prə·sä'rē·ō) *n. pl.* **·sa·ri·os** or **·sa·ri** (-sä'rē) One who manages or sponsors performers or performances for entertainment. [< Ital. *impresa* enterprise]

im·press¹ (*v.* im·pres'; *n.* im'pres) *v.t.* 1. To produce a marked effect upon the mind or feelings of; influence. 2. To establish firmly in the mind, as ideas, beliefs, etc. 3. To form or make (an imprint or mark) by pressure; stamp. 4. To form or make an imprint or mark upon. 5. *Electr.* To establish (a voltage) in a conductor or circuit. —*n.* 1. The act or process of impressing. 2. A mark, indentation, or design produced by pressure. 3. Distinctive character or mark; stamp. [< L < *in-* on + *premere* to press] —**im·press'er** *n.*

im·press² (*v.* im·pres'; *n.* im'pres) · *v.t.* 1. To force to enter public service, esp. naval service. 2. To seize (property) for public use. —*n.* The act of impressing; impressment. —**im·press'er** *n.* —**im·press'ment** *n.*

im·press·i·ble (im·pres'ə·bəl) *adj.* Capable of being impressed or of receiving an impression; susceptible. —**im·press'i·bil'i·ty, im·press'i·ble·ness** *n.* —**im·press'i·bly** *adv.*

im·pres·sion (im·presh'ən) *n.* 1. An effect produced on the mind, the senses, or the feelings. 2. A vague remembrance or uncertain belief. 3. A material change produced by any agency. 4. A mark made by pressure. 5. The act or process of impressing. 6. *Printing* a The act or result of pressing type or plates to paper. b The total number of copies of a publication printed at one time; also, a single copy: distinguished from *edition.* [< OF < L *impressio, -onis*]

im·pres·sion·a·ble (im·presh'ən·ə·bəl) *adj.* Highly receptive to impressions; readily influenced or molded; sensitive. [< F] —**im·pres'sion·a·bil'i·ty, im·pres'sion·a·ble·ness** *n.*

im·pres·sion·ism (im·presh'ən·iz'əm) *n.* 1. In art, a theory of painting, developed in the 19th century, that attempted to produce, by simulating the appearance of light, etc., the impressions made by the subject on the artist. 2. In literature, the presenting of the most arresting aspects of character, emotion, etc., with relatively little realistic detail. 3. In music, a style of composition, developed by Debussy and Ravel, that attempted to create impressions or moods. —**im·pres'sion·ist** *n. & adj.* —**im·pres'sion·is'tic** *adj.*

im·pres·sive (im·pres'iv) *adj.* Producing or tending to produce an impression; exciting emotion or admiration. —**im·pres'sive·ly** *adv.* —**im·pres'sive·ness** *n.*

im·pri·ma·tur (im'pri·mā'tər, -mä'-) *n.* 1. Official license or approval for publication of a literary work, esp. that granted by a censor or by the Roman Catholic Church. 2. Authorization in general. [< L, let it be printed.]

im·print (*v.* im·print'; *n.* im'print) *v.t.* 1. To produce (a figure, mark, etc.) by pressure. 2. To mark or produce a mark on, as with a stamp or seal. 3. To fix firmly in the heart, mind, etc. —*n.* 1. A mark or indentation made by

printing, stamping, or pressing. 2. Characteristic effect; impression; stamp. 3. The name of the publisher, place of publication, date of issue, etc., printed in a book usu. on the title page. [< OF < L < *in-* in + *premere* to press]

im·pris·on (im·priz'ən) *v.t.* 1. To put into a prison; hold in confinement. 2. To confine or restrain forcibly, as in a small space, tight garment etc. —**im·pris'on·ment** *n.*

im·prob·a·bil·i·ty (im'prob·ə·bil'ə·tē, im·prob'-) *n. pl.* **·ties** 1. The quality of being improbable; unlikelihood. 2. An unlikely circumstance, event, or result.

im·prob·a·ble (im·prob'ə·bəl) *adj.* Not probable; not likely to be true or not reasonably to be expected. —**im·prob'a·ble·ness** *n.* —**im·prob'a·bly** *adv.*

im·promp·tu (im·promp'tōō, -tyōō) *adj.* Made, done, or uttered on the spur of the moment. —*n.* Anything produced on the impulse of the moment. —*adv.* Without preparation. [< F < L *in promptu* in readiness]

im·prop·er (im·prop'ər) *adj.* 1. Deviating from fact, truth, or established usage. 2. Not conforming to accepted standards of conduct or good taste. 3. Unsuitable. —**im·prop'er·ly** *adv.* —**im·prop'er·ness** *n.*

improper fraction *Math.* A fraction in which the numerator exceeds the denominator.

im·pro·pri·e·ty (im'prə·prī'ə·tē) *n. pl.* **·ties** 1. The quality of being improper. 2. An improper action. 3. An improper usage in speech or writing.

im·prove (im·prōōv') *v.* **proved, ·prov·ing** *v.t.* 1. To raise to a higher or more desirable quality, value, or condition; make better. 2. *U.S.* To increase the value or profit of, as land. 3. To use to good advantage; utilize. —*v.i.* 4. To become better. —**to improve on** (or **upon**) To do or produce something better than. [< AF < OF *en-* into + *prou* profit] —**im·prov'a·bil'i·ty, im·prov'a·ble·ness** *n.* —**im·prov'a·ble** *adj.* —**im·prov'a·bly** *adv.* —**im·prov'er** *n.*

im·prove·ment (im·prōōv'mənt) *n.* 1. The act of making better, or the state of becoming better. 2. A modification or addition by means of which a thing's excellence or value is increased. 3. A person, thing, or process that constitutes an advance in excellence. 4. Advantageous use.

im·prov·i·dent (im·prov'ə·dənt) *adj.* 1. Lacking foresight; incautious; rash. 2. Taking no thought of future needs; thriftless. —**im·prov'i·dence** *n.* —**im·prov'i·dent·ly** *adv.*

im·pro·vi·sa·to·ry (im'prə·vī'zə·tôr'ē, -tō'rē) *adj.* 1. Of or pertaining to an improviser. 2. Of the nature of improvisation. Also **im·prov'i·sa·to'ri·al** (im·prov'ə·zə·tôr'ē·əl, -tō'rē-).

im·pro·vise (im'prə·vīz) *v.* **·vised, ·vis·ing** *v.t.* 1. To produce (music, verse, drama, etc.) without previous thought or preparation. 2. To contrive or construct from whatever comes to hand. —*v.i.* 3. To produce anything extemporaneously. [< F < Ital. < L < *in-* not + *providere* to foresee] —**im·pro·vi·sa·tion** (im'prə·vī·zā'shən, im'prov·ə-) *n.* —**im·pro'vi·sa'tion·al** *adj.* —**im·pro·vis'er, im'prov·i·sa·tor** (im·prov'ə·zā'tər, im·prō'vī-) *n.*

im·pru·dent (im·prōōd'nt) *adj.* Not prudent; lacking discretion; unwise. —**im·pru'dence** *n.*

im·pu·dence (im'pyə·dəns) *n.* 1. The quality of being impudent; offensive boldness. 2. Impudent speech or conduct. Also **im'pu·den·cy.**

im·pu·dent (im'pyə·dənt) *adj.* Offensively bold; insolently assured; saucy; brazen. [< OF < L < *in-* not + *pudens* modest] —**im'pu·dent·ly** *adv.*

im·pugn (im·pyōōn') *v.t.* To attack (a statement, motives, etc.) with criticism or arguments; dispute the truth of. [< OF < L *in-* against + *pugnare* to strike, fight] —**im·pugn'a·ble** *adj.* —**im·pug·na·tion** (im'pəg·nā'shən), **im·pugn'ment** *n.* —**im·pugn'er** (im·pyōō'nər) *n.*

im·pulse (im'puls) *n.* 1. A brief exertion or communication of force tending to produce motion. 2. The motion produced. 3. A sudden, unreasoned inclination to action, often induced by an emotion, etc. 4. *Physiol.* The transference of a stimulus through a nerve fiber. [See IMPEL.]

im·pul·sion (im·pul'shən) *n.* 1. The act of impelling, or the state of being impelled. 2. An impelling force.

im·pul·sive (im·pul'siv) *adj.* 1. Actuated by impulse rather than by reflection. 2. Prompted by impulse; spontaneous; unpremeditated. 3. Having the power of inciting to action. —**im·pul'sive·ly** *adv.* —**im·pul'sive·ness** *n.*

im·pu·ni·ty (im·pyōō'nə·tē) *n. pl.* **·ties** Freedom or exemption from punishment, harm, or unpleasant consequence. [< L *in-* not + *poena* punishment]

im·pure (im·pyōōr') *adj.* 1. Containing something offensive or contaminating. 2. Mixed with an inferior or worthless substance, adulterated. 3. Contrary to moral purity; sinful. 4. Not for religious use. 5. Having the characteristics of more than one style, period, color, language, etc.; mixed. —**im·pure'ly** *adv.* —**im·pure'ness** *n.*

im·pu·ri·ty (im·pyōōr'ə·tē) *n. pl.* **·ties** 1. The state or quality of being impure. 2. That which is impure.

im·put·a·ble (im·pyōō'tə·bəl) *adj.* Capable of being imputed; ascribable; chargeable. —**im·put'a·bil'i·ty, im·put'a·ble·ness** *n.* —**im·put'a·bly** *adv.*

im·pu·ta·tion (im′pyŏŏ·tā/shən) *n.* **1.** The act of imputing; accusation. **2.** That which is imputed or charged.

im·pu·ta·tive (im·pyŏŏ/tə·tiv) *adj.* **1.** Transferred or transmitted by imputation; imputed. **2.** Tending to impute. — **im·pu/ta·tive·ly** *adv.*

im·pute (im·pyŏŏt′) *v.t.* **·put·ed, ·put·ing 1.** To attribute (a fault, crime, etc.) to a person; charge. **2.** To consider as the cause or source of; ascribe: with *to.* — **Syn.** See ATTRIBUTE. [< OF < L < *in-* in + *putare* to reckon]

in (in) *prep.* **1.** Held by or within the confines of; enclosed by: apples *in* a bag. **2.** Surrounded by; amidst: buried *in* the mud. **3.** Within the limits of: sightseeing *in* Paris. **4.** Within the range or scope of: He said it *in* my hearing. **5.** Within the category, class, or number of; included as a member of; belonging to: twelve inches *in* a foot; *in* the best society. **6.** Existing as a part, characteristic, or property of: *in* the works of Shaw. **7.** Affecting: dust *in* one's eye. **8.** Wearing; covered by; decorated with: a man *in* a straw hat. **9.** Made of a specified color, style, or material. **10.** Arranged, disposed, or proceeding so as to form: trees *in* a row. **11.** Engaged at; occupied by: *in* business. **12.** For the purpose of: to run *in* pursuit. **13.** By means of: speaking *in* whispers. **14.** According to: *In* my opinion. **15.** With regard or respect to: Students vary *in* talent. **16.** Affected by; under the influence of: to shout *in* rage. **17.** During: a concert given *in* the evening. — **Syn.** See AT. — **in that** For the reason that; because; since. — *adv.* **1.** To or toward the inside from the outside: Please come *in.* **2.** In one's home, place of business, etc.: We stayed *in* all day. **3.** In or into some activity or office; to join *in.* **4.** Into some place, condition, or position: Tuck the baby *in.* **5.** Into some understood substance, object, etc.: Blend *in* the oil. — **to be in** for *Informal* To be certain to experience (usu. something unpleasant). — **to have it in for** *Informal* To hold a grudge against. — *adj.* **1.** That is in or remains within. **2.** That has gained power or control: the *in* group. **3.** Coming or leading in: the *in* door. — *n.* **1.** A member of the group in power or at an advantage. **2.** *Informal* A means of entrance or access; also, a position of favor or influence: to have an *in.* — **ins and outs** The full complexities or particulars: the *ins and outs* of a business. — *v.t.* **inned, in·ning** To enclose, as land. [OE]

in-¹ *prefix* Not; without; un-; non–. Also: *i-* before *gn*, as in *ignore*; *il-* before *l*, as in *illiterate*; *im-* before *b, m, p*, as in *imbalance, immiscible, impecunious*; *ir-* before *r*, as in *irresistible.* ◆ See note under UN-². [< L]

in-² *prefix* In; into; on; within; toward: *include, incur, invade*: also used intensively, as in *inflame*, or without perceptible force. Also *il-* before *l*, as in *illuminate*; *im-* before *b, m, p*, as in *imbibe, immigrate, impress*; *ir-* before *r*, as in *irradiate.* [< OE *in*; sometimes < L *in-* in, prep.]

-in *suffix Chem.* Occasionally used to denote neutral compounds, as fats, proteins, and glycerides: *stearin, albumin, lecithin*. Also *-ine*. [Var. of *-INE²*]

in·a·bil·i·ty (in′ə·bil/ə·tē) *n.* The state or quality of being unable; lack of the necessary power or means.

in ab·sen·ti·a (in ab·sen/shē·ə, -shə) *Latin* In absence (of the person concerned).

in·ac·ces·si·ble (in′ak·ses/ə·bəl) *adj.* Not accessible; not capable of being reached or closely approached. — **in′ac·ces/si·bil/i·ty, in′ac·ces/i·ble·ness** *n.* — **in′ac·ces/si·bly** *adv.*

in·ac·cu·ra·cy (in·ak/yər·ə·sē) *n. pl.* **·cies 1.** The state or quality of being inaccurate. **2.** An error; mistake.

in·ac·cu·rate (in·ak/yər·it) *adj.* Not accurate; inexact; incorrect. — **in·ac/cu·rate·ly** *adv.* — **in·ac/cu·rate·ness** *n.*

in·ac·tion (in·ak/shən) *n.* Absence of action; idleness.

in·ac·ti·vate (in·ak/tə·vāt) *v.t.* **·vat·ed, ·vat·ing** To make inactive. — **in·ac/ti·va/tion** *n.*

in·ac·tive (in·ak/tiv) *adj.* **1.** Characterized by inaction; idle; inert. **2.** Marked by absence of effort or action; indolent. **3.** *Mil.* Not mobilized. — **in·ac/tive·ly** *adv.* — **in·ac·tiv·i·ty** (in/ak·tiv′ə·tē), **in·ac/tive·ness** *n.*

in·ad·e·qua·cy (in·ad/ə·kwə·sē) *n. pl.* **·cies 1.** The state or quality of being inadequate; insufficiency. **2.** A defect.

in·ad·e·quate (in·ad/ə·kwit) *adj.* Not adequate; not equal to that which is required; insufficient. — **in·ad/e·quate·ly** *adv.* — **in·ad/e·quate·ness** *n.*

in·ad·mis·si·ble (in′ad·mis/ə·bəl) *adj.* Not admissible; not to be considered, approved, or allowed. — **in′ad·mis/si·bil/i·ty** *n.* — **in′ad·mis/si·bly** *adv.*

in·ad·ver·tence (in′əd·vûr/təns) *n.* **1.** The fact or quality of being inadvertent; lack of due care or attention. **2.** A result of inattention; oversight. Also **in′ad·ver/ten·cy.**

in·ad·ver·tent (in′əd·vûr/tənt) *adj.* **1.** Not exercising due care or consideration; negligent. **2.** Resulting from inattention or oversight; unintentional. — **in′ad·ver/tent·ly** *adv.*

in·ad·vis·a·ble (in′əd·vī/zə·bəl) *adj.* Not advisable; injudicious; unwise. — **in′ad·vis/a·bil/i·ty** *n.*

-inae *suffix Zool.* Used in the names of subfamilies: *Cervinae.* [< NL < L, fem. pl. of *-inus*, adj. suffix]

in·al·ien·a·ble (in·āl/yən·ə·bəl) *adj.* Not transferable; that cannot be rightfully taken away. — **in·al/ien·a·bil/i·ty** *n.* — **in·al/ien·a·bly** *adv.*

in·am·o·ra·ta (in·am/ə·rä/tə, in/am-) *n. pl.* **·tas** A woman who is loved or in love. [< Ital. < *in-* in + *amore* love]

in·ane (in·ān′) *adj.* **1.** Lacking in sense; empty-headed; silly. **2.** Empty of meaning; pointless. [< L *inanis* empty] — **in·ane/ly** *adv.*

in·an·i·mate (in·an/ə·mit) *adj.* **1.** Not living or animate. **2.** Lacking animation; torpid; spiritless. — **in·an/i·mate·ly** *adv.* — **in·an/i·mate·ness** *n.*

in·a·ni·tion (in/ə·nish/ən) *n.* **1.** Exhaustion caused by lack of nourishment or inability to assimilate food. **2.** Emptiness. [< F < LL < L *inanire* to empty]

in·an·i·ty (in·an/ə·tē) *n. pl.* **·ties 1.** Lack of sense or meaning; silliness; foolishness. **2.** A foolish remark, action, etc. **3.** Emptiness. [< OF < L *inanis* empty]

in·ap·pli·ca·ble (in·ap/li·kə·bəl) *adj.* Not applicable; irrelevant; unsuitable. — **in·ap/pli·ca·bil/i·ty, in·ap/pli·ca·ble·ness** *n.* — **in·ap/pli·ca·bly** *adv.*

in·ap·po·site (in·ap/ə·zit) *adj.* Not pertinent or suitable. — **in·ap/po·site·ly** *adv.*

in·ap·pre·cia·ble (in/ə·prē/shē·ə·bəl, -shə·bəl) *adj.* Imperceptible; unnoticeable. — **in/ap·pre/ci·a·bly** *adv.*

in·ap·pro·pri·ate (in/ə·prō/prē·it) *adj.* Not appropriate; unsuitable; unfitting. — **in/ap·pro/pri·ate·ly** *adv.* — **in/ap·pro/pri·ate·ness** *n.*

in·apt (in·apt′) *adj.* **1.** Not apt or fit. **2.** Lacking skill or aptitude; inept; clumsy. — **in·apt/ly** *adv.* — **in·apt/ness** *n.*

in·ap·ti·tude (in·ap/tə·tōōd, -tyōōd) *n.* **1.** Lack of skill. **2.** Unsuitability.

in·ar·tic·u·late (in/är·tik/yə·lit) *adj.* **1.** Uttered without the distinct sounds of spoken language: *inarticulate* cries. **2.** Incapable of speech; dumb. **3.** Unable to speak coherently. **4.** Unspoken; unexpressed: *inarticulate* grief. **5.** *Zool.* Not segmented, as certain worms. — **in/ar·tic/u·late·ly** *adv.* — **in/ar·tic/u·late·ness** *n.*

in·ar·tis·tic (in/är·tis/tik) *adj.* **1.** Contrary to the principles of art; made or done without skill or taste. **2.** Lacking in artistic ability. — **in/ar·tis/ti·cal·ly** *adv.*

in·as·much as (in/əz·much′) **1.** Considering the fact that; seeing that; because. **2.** Insofar as; according as.

in·at·ten·tion (in/ə·ten/shən) *n.* Lack of attention.

in·at·ten·tive (in/ə·ten/tiv) *adj.* Not attentive; heedless. — **in/at·ten/tive·ly** *adv.* — **in/at·ten/tive·ness** *n.*

in·au·di·ble (in·ô/də·bəl) *adj.* Incapable of being heard. — **in·au/di·bil/i·ty, in·au/di·ble·ness** *n.* — **in·au/di·bly** *adv.*

in·au·gu·ral (in·ô/gyər·əl) *adj.* Of or pertaining to an inauguration. — *n.* A speech made at an inauguration.

in·au·gu·rate (in·ô/gyə·rāt) *v.t.* **·rat·ed, ·rat·ing 1.** To begin or commence upon formally; initiate. **2.** To induct into office with formal ceremony. **3.** To celebrate the public opening of. [< L *inaugurare* to take omens, consecrate, install] — **in·au/gu·ra/tion** *n.* — **in·au/gu·ra/tor** *n.*

Inauguration Day The day (January 20th) on which the inauguration of the President of the United States takes place.

in·aus·pi·cious (in/ô·spish/əs) *adj.* Not auspicious; ill-omened; unfavorable. — **in/aus·pi/cious·ly** *adv.* — **in/aus·pi/cious·ness** *n.*

in·board (in/bôrd′, -bōrd′) *adj. & adv.* **1.** *Naut.* **a** Inside the hull. **b** Toward the center line of a vessel. **2.** *Aeron.* Inward from the tip of an airfoil; close to the fuselage.

in·born (in/bôrn′) *adj.* Implanted by nature; existing from birth; natural; inherent.

in·bound (in/bound′) *adj.* Approaching a destination.

in·bred (in/bred′; *for def. 2, also* in/bred′) *adj.* **1.** Inborn; innate. **2.** Produced by inbreeding; also, bred in-and-in.

in·breed (in/brēd′, in/brēd′) *v.t.* **·bred, ·breed·ing** To breed by continual mating of closely related stock.

In·ca (ing/kə) *n.* A member of a group of Quechuan Indian tribes dominant in Peru at the time of the Spanish conquest. [< Sp. < Quechua *ynca* royal prince]

in·cal·cu·la·ble (in·kal/kyə·lə·bəl) *adj.* **1.** Incapable of being calculated. **2.** Unpredictable. — **in·cal/cu·la·bil/i·ty** *n.* — **in·cal/cu·la·bly** *adv.*

in cam·er·a (in kam/ər·ə) In closed or secret session; privately. [< L, in a room]

In·can (ing/kən) *adj.* Of or pertaining to the Incas, their culture, or their empire. — *n.* **1.** An Inca. **2.** The language of the Incas; Quechua.

in·can·desce (in/kən·des′) *v.t. & v.i.* **·desced, ·desc·ing** To be or become, or cause to become, luminous with heat.

in·can·des·cent (in/kən·des/ənt) *adj.* **1.** Luminous or glowing with intense heat. **2.** Shining with intense brilliance. — **in/can·des/cence, in/can·des/cen·cy** *n.* — **in/can·des/cent·ly** *adv.*

incandescent lamp A lamp having a filament that is heated to incandescence by an electric current.

in·can·ta·tion (in/kan·tā/shən) *n.* 1. The uttering or intoning of words or syllables supposed to produce magical results. 2. The magic words or formula so uttered. [< F < L *incantare* to make an incantation]

in·ca·pa·ble (in·kā/pə·bəl) *adj.* 1. Lacking in natural ability, power, or capacity; incompetent. 2. *Law* Not legally qualified. — **incapable of** 1. Lacking the necessary ability or fitness for. 2. Of such a nature or condition as not to allow or admit of: *incapable* of deceit. — *n.* A totally incompetent person. — **in·ca/pa·bil/i·ty, in·ca/pa·ble·ness** *n.* — **in·ca/pa·bly** *adv.*

in·ca·pac·i·tate (in/kə·pas/ə·tāt) *v.t.* ·tat·ed, ·tat·ing 1. To disable, as for normal physical activity. 2. *Law* To deprive of legal capacity; disqualify. — **in/ca·pac/i·ta/tion** *n.*

in·ca·pac·i·ty (in/kə·pas/ə·tē) *n. pl.* ·ties 1. Lack of ability, power, or fitness; disability. 2. *Law* A condition or circumstance that legally disqualifies.

in·cap·su·late (in·kap/sə·lāt, -syŏŏ-) *v.t.* ·lat·ed, ·lat·ing To enclose as in a capsule.

in·car·cer·ate (*v.* in·kär/sə·rāt; *adj.* in·kär/sər·it, -sə·rāt) *v.t.* ·at·ed, ·at·ing 1. To put in prison; imprison. 2. To confine; enclose. — *adj.* Imprisoned. [< Med.L < L *in-* in + *carcer* jail] — **in·car/cer·a/tion** *n.* — **in·car/cer·a/tor** *n.*

in·car·na·dine (in·kär/nə·dīn, -din) *adj.* 1. Flesh-colored; pale red; pink. 2. Blood-red; crimson. — *n.* An incarnadine color. — *v.t.* ·dined, ·din·ing To color deep red or flesh-color. [< F < Ital. *incarnato* flesh-colored]

in·car·nate (*adj.* in·kär/nit; *v.* in·kär/nāt) *adj.* 1. Embodied in flesh, esp. in human form: a fiend *incarnate*. 2. Personified; exemplified: cruelty *incarnate*. — *v.t.* ·nat·ed, ·nat·ing 1. To give bodily form to. 2. To invest with concrete shape or form. [< LL < L *in-* in + *caro, carnis* flesh]

in·car·na·tion (in/kär·nā/shən) *n.* 1. The assumption of bodily form, esp. human form. 2. *Often cap.* The assumption by Jesus Christ of the human form and condition. 3. The bodily form assumed by a deity. 4. A person, animal, or thing in which some ideal or quality is incarnated.

in·case (in·kās/) *v.t.* ·cased, ·cas·ing To enclose in or as in a case: also spelled *encase*. — **in·case/ment** *n.*

in·cau·tion (in·kô/shən) *n.* Lack of caution; carelessness.

in·cau·tious (in·kô/shəs) *adj.* Lacking in caution; heedless; imprudent. — **in·cau/tious·ly** *adv.* — **in·cau/tious·ness** *n.*

in·cen·di·ar·y (in·sen/dē·er/ē) *adj.* 1. Of or pertaining to the malicious burning of property. 2. Inciting to riot, rebellion, etc.; inflammatory. 3. Capable of generating intense heat. — *n. pl.* ·ar·ies 1. One who maliciously sets fire to property. 2. One who stirs up mob violence, etc. 3. An incendiary bomb. [< L *incendere* to set on fire] — **in·cen/di·a·rism** (-ə·riz·əm) *n.*

incendiary bomb A bomb designed to start a fire.

in·cense[1] (in·sens/) *v.t.* ·censed, ·cens·ing To inflame with anger; enrage. [< OF < L *incendere* to set on fire]

in·cense[2] (in/sens) *n.* 1. An aromatic substance that gives off an agreeable odor when burned. 2. The odor or smoke produced in burning such a substance. 3. Any pleasant fragrance or aroma. — *v.* ·censed, ·cens·ing *v.t.* 1. To perfume with incense. 2. To burn incense to. — *v.i.* 3. To burn incense. [< OF < L *incendere* to set on fire]

in·cen·tive (in·sen/tiv) *n.* That which incites, or tends to incite, to action; motivating force. — *adj.* Serving to incite to action. [< L *in-* in + *canere* to sing]

in·cep·tion (in·sep/shən) *n.* Beginning, as of an undertaking; start. [< L *incipere* to begin]

in·cep·tive (in·sep/tiv) *adj.* 1. Beginning; incipient; initial. 2. *Gram.* Denoting the beginning of an action, as certain verbs. — *n. Gram.* An inceptive word or construction.

in·cer·ti·tude (in·sûr/tə·tōōd, -tyōōd) *n.* 1. Uncertainty; doubtfulness; indecisiveness. 2. Insecurity.

in·ces·sant (in·ses/ənt) *adj.* Continuing without interruption; never ceasing. [< LL < L *in-* not + *cessare* to cease] — **in·ces/san·cy** *n.* — **in·ces/sant·ly** *adv.*

in·cest (in/sest) *n.* Sexual intercourse between persons so closely related that marriage between them is forbidden by law or taboo. [< L *in-* not + *castus* chaste]

in·ces·tu·ous (in·ses/chōō·əs) *adj.* 1. Guilty of incest. 2. Involving incest. — **in·ces/tu·ous·ly** *adv.*

inch (inch) *n.* 1. A measure of length equal to the twelfth part of a foot: symbol ″. *Abbr.* in. See table inside back cover. 2. *Meteorol.* **a** The amount of rainfall or snowfall capable of covering a level surface to the depth of one inch. **b** A unit of atmospheric pressure expressed by an inch of the mercury column of a barometer. 3. A very small distance, quantity, or degree. — **every inch** In every way; completely. — *v.t. & v.i.* To move or advance by inches or small degrees. [OE < L *uncia* the twelfth part, inch, ounce]

inch·meal (inch/mēl/) *adv.* Inch by inch.

in·cho·ate (in·kō/it) *adj.* 1. In an early or rudimentary stage. 2. Lacking order, form, coherence, etc. [< L *incohare* to begin] — **in·cho/ate·ly** *adv.* — **in·cho/ate·ness** *n.*

in·cho·a·tive (in·kō/ə·tiv) *adj.* 1. *Gram.* Inceptive. 2. *Rare* Inchoate. — *n. Gram.* An inceptive.

inch·worm (inch/wûrm/) *n.* A measuring worm.

in·ci·dence (in/sə·dəns) *n.* 1. The degree of occurrence or effect: a high *incidence* of illiteracy. 2. The act or manner of falling on, impinging upon, or affecting something.

in·ci·dent (in/sə·dənt) *n.* 1. A distinct event or piece of action. 2. A minor episode or event. — *adj.* 1. Naturally or usu. appertaining or attending: with *to*: the dangers *incident* to travel. 2. Attached as a subsidiary. 3. Falling or striking: *incident* rays of light. [< F < L *in-* on + *cadere* to fall]

in·ci·den·tal (in/sə·den/təl) *adj.* 1. Occurring in the course of something. 2. Naturally or usually attending: with *to*: problems *incidental* to adolescence. 3. Minor; secondary: *incidental* expenses. — *n.* 1. An incidental circumstance or event. 2. *pl.* Minor or casual expenses or items.

in·ci·den·tal·ly (in/sə·den/tə·lē; *for def. 2, also* in/sə·dent/lē) *adv.* 1. As a subordinate, casual, or chance occurrence along with something else: The book *incidentally* contains some valuable references. 2. By the by; by the way.

in·cin·er·ate (in·sin/ə·rāt) *v.t.* ·at·ed, ·at·ing To consume with fire; reduce to ashes; cremate. [< Med.L < *in-* in + *cinis, cineris* ashes] — **in·cin/er·a/tion** *n.*

in·cin·er·a·tor (in·sin/ə·rā/tər) *n.* An apparatus for burning refuse or for cremating.

in·cip·i·ent (in·sip/ē·ənt) *adj.* Coming into existence; just beginning to appear. [< L *incipere* to begin] — **in·cip/i·ence, in·cip/i·en·cy** *n.* — **in·cip/i·ent·ly** *adv.*

in·cise (in·sīz/) *v.t.* ·cised, ·cis·ing 1. To cut into, or cut marks upon, with a sharp instrument. 2. To engrave; carve. [< OF < L *in-* in + *caedere* to cut] — **in·cised/** *adj.*

in·ci·sion (in·sizh/ən) *n.* 1. The act of incising. 2. A cut; gash. 3. *Surg.* A cut made in soft tissue. 4. Incisive quality; acuteness. [< OF < L *incisio, -onis*]

in·ci·sive (in·sī/siv) *adj.* 1. Sharp; keen; penetrating: an *incisive* mind. 2. Cutting; biting; sarcastic. [< Med.L *incisivus*] — **in·ci/sive·ly** *adv.* — **in·ci/sive·ness** *n.*

in·ci·sor (in·sī/zər) *n.* A front tooth adapted for cutting; in man, one of eight such teeth, four in each jaw. For illus. see TOOTH. [< NL]

in·cite (in·sīt/) *v.t.* ·cit·ed, ·cit·ing To spur to action; urge on; instigate. [< OF < L < *in-* thoroughly + *citare* to rouse] — **in·ci·ta/tion** *n.* — **in·cit/er** *n.*

in·ci·vil·i·ty (in/sə·vil/ə·tē) *n. pl.* ·ties 1. The state or quality of being uncivil; discourtesy. 2. An uncivil or rude act.

in·clem·ent (in·klem/ənt) *adj.* 1. Of the weather, severe; stormy. 2. Without mercy; harsh. [< L *inclemens, -entis*] — **in·clem/en·cy** (-ən·sē) *n.* — **in·clem/ent·ly** *adv.*

in·cli·na·tion (in/klə·nā/shən) *n.* 1. A personal leaning or bent; liking. 2. A tendency toward a state or condition; trend. 3. An activity, state, etc., toward which one is inclined. 4. The act of inclining, or the state of being inclined. 5. Deviation or degree of deviation from the vertical or horizontal; slope. 6. A sloping surface. 7. *Geom.* The angle formed between two intersecting lines, planes, etc. — **in/cli·na/tion·al, in·cli·na·to·ry** (in·klī/nə·tôr/ē) *adj.*

in·cline (*v.* in·klīn/; *n.* in/klīn, in·klīn/) *v.* ·clined, ·clin·ing *v.i.* 1. To diverge from the horizontal or vertical; slant; slope. 2. To have a bent or preference; be disposed. 3. To tend in some quality or degree: purple *inclining* toward blue. 4. To bend the head or body, as in courtesy; bow. — *v.t.* 5. To cause to bend, lean, or slope. 6. To impart a tendency or leaning to (a person); dispose; influence. 7. To bow or nod, as the head. — *n.* An inclined plane or surface; gradient; slope. [< OF < L < *in-* on + *clinare* to lean] — **in·clin/a·ble** *adj.* — **in·clin/er** *n.*

in·clined (in·klīnd/) *adj.* 1. Having a tendency or inclination; disposed. 2. Sloping; bent. 3. Bending or intersecting so as to form an angle with another line, plane, etc.

inclined plane A plane forming any but a right angle with a horizontal plane.

in·cli·nom·e·ter (in/klə·nom/ə·tər) *n.* An instrument for measuring the attitude or tilt of an aircraft, ship, etc., with relation to the horizontal.

in·close (in·klōz/), **in·clo·sure** (in·klō/zhər) See ENCLOSE, etc.

in·clude (in·klōōd/) *v.t.* ·clud·ed, ·clud·ing 1. To have as a component part or parts; comprise; contain. 2. To place in a general category, group, etc.; consider in a reckoning. 3. To have or involve as a subordinate part, quality, etc.; imply. [< L *in-* in + *claudere* to shut] — **in·clud/a·ble** or **in·clud/i·ble** *adj.*

in·clu·sion (in·klōō/zhən) *n.* 1. The act of including, or the state of being included. 2. That which is included.

in·clu·sive (in·klōō/siv) *adj.* 1. Including: with *of*. 2. Including the limits specified: from 1959 to 1964 *inclusive*. 3. Comprehensive: an *inclusive* report. [< Med.L *inclusivus*] — **in·clu/sive·ly** *adv.* — **in·clu/sive·ness** *n.*

in·cog·ni·to (in·kog/nə·tō, in/kog·nē/tō) *adj. & adv.* Under an assumed name or identity, esp. so as to avoid recognition or attention; in disguise. — *n. pl.* ·tos (-tōz) 1. The state of being incognito.   **2.** The name or disguise assumed by one who is incognito.   **3.** One who takes on an assumed name or identity.   [< Ital. < L < *in-* not + *cognitus*, pp. of *cognoscere* to know]   — in·cog′ni·ta (-tə) *n. & adj. fem.*

in·cog·ni·zant (in·kog′nə·zənt)   *adj.* Not cognizant; unaware; with *of*.   — in·cog′ni·zance *n.*

in·co·her·ence (in′kō·hir′əns)   *n.* **1.** The state of being incoherent.   **2.** That which is incoherent. Also in′co·her′en·cy.

in·co·her·ent (in′kō·hir′ənt)   *adj.* **1.** Lacking in logical connection; confused: an *incoherent* speech.   **2.** Unable to think clearly or express oneself logically.   **3.** Consisting of parts or ingredients that do not stick together; loose: an *incoherent* mass.   **4.** Lacking in agreement or harmony; disorganized.   — in′co·her′ent·ly *adv.*   — in′co·her′ent·ness *n.*

in·com·bus·ti·ble (in′kəm·bus′tə·bəl)   *adj.* Incapable of being burned; not flammable.   — *n.* An incombustible substance or material.   — in′com·bus′ti·bil′i·ty, in′com·bus′ti·ble·ness *n.*   — in′com·bus′ti·bly *adv.*

in·come (in′kum)   *n.* Money, or sometimes its equivalent, received periodically by an individual, a corporation, etc., in return for labor or services rendered, or from property, etc.

income tax   A tax levied on annual income over a specified amount and with certain legally permitted deductions.

in·com·ing (in′kum′ing)   *adj.* Coming in or about to come in: *incoming* profits.   — *n.* The act of coming in.

in·com·men·su·ra·ble (in′kə·men′shər·ə·bəl, -sər·ə-)   *adj.* **1.** Lacking a common measure or standard of comparison.   **2.** *Math.* Not expressible in terms of a common factor or divisor.   **3.** Greatly out of proportion; not in accordance: conclusions *incommensurable* with the facts.   — *n.* That which is incommensurable.   — in′com·men′su·ra·bil′i·ty, in′com·men′su·ra·ble·ness *n.*   — in′com·men′su·ra·bly *adv.*

in·com·men·su·rate (in′kə·men′shər·it)   *adj.* **1.** Inadequate; disproportionate: a salary *incommensurate* with the position.   **2.** Incommensurable.   — in′com·men′su·rate·ly *adv.*   — in′com·men′su·rate·ness *n.*

in·com·mode (in′kə·mōd′)   *v.t.* **·mod·ed, ·mod·ing** To cause inconvenience to; disturb; bother.   [< MF < L < *in-* not + *commodus* convenient]

in·com·mo·di·ous (in′kə·mō′dē·əs)   *adj.* **1.** Uncomfortably small; cramped.   **2.** Causing discomfort; inconvenient.   — in′com·mo′di·ous·ly *adv.*   — in′com·mo′di·ous·ness *n.*

in·com·mu·ni·ca·ble (in′kə·myōō′ni·kə·bəl)   *adj.* Incapable of being communicated.   — in′com·mu′ni·ca·bil′i·ty, in′com·mu′ni·ca·ble·ness *n.*   — in′com·mu′ni·ca·bly *adv.*

in·com·mu·ni·ca·do (in′kə·myōō′nə·kä′dō)   *adj. & adv.* Confined without means of communication.   [< Sp., < L *in-* not + *communicare* to share]

in·com·mu·ni·ca·tive (in′kə·myōō′nə·kā′tiv, -kə·tiv)   *adj.* Not communicative; taciturn; reserved.   — in′com·mu′ni·ca′tive·ly *adv.*   — in′com·mu′ni·ca′tive·ness *n.*

in·com·pa·ra·ble (in·kom′pər·ə·bəl)   *adj.* **1.** Incapable of being equaled or surpassed; matchless.   **2.** Lacking in qualities or characteristics that can be compared.   — in·com′pa·ra·bil′i·ty, in·com′pa·ra·ble·ness *n.*   — in·com′pa·ra·bly *adv.*

in·com·pat·i·ble (in·kəm·pat′ə·bəl)   *adj.* **1.** Incapable of coexisting harmoniously.   **2.** Disagreeing in nature; conflicting.   **3.** Incapable of being held or occupied by one person at the same time, as more than one rank or office.   **4.** *Med.* Having a harmful or undesirable effect when combined or used together.   — *n.pl.* Incompatible persons, drugs, etc.   — in′com·pat′i·bil′i·ty *n.*   — in·com·pat′i·ble·ness *n.*   — in′·com·pat′i·bly *adv.*

in·com·pe·tent (in·kom′pə·tənt)   *adj.* **1.** Lacking in ability or skill; inadequate to the task; unfit.   **2.** Reflecting a lack of ability or skill.   **3.** *Law* Not legally qualified.   — *n.* One who is incompetent.   [< F < L *incompentem*]   — in·com′pe·tence, in·com′pe·ten·cy *n.*   — in·com′pe·tent·ly *adv.*

in·com·plete (in·kəm·plēt′)   *adj.* **1.** Not having all essential elements or parts; unfinished.   **2.** Not fully developed; defective; imperfect: *incomplete* growth.   — in·com·plete′ly *adv.*   — in·com·plete′ness, in·com·ple′tion *n.*

in·com·pre·hen·si·ble (in′kom·pri·hen′sə·bəl, in·kom′-)   *adj.* **1.** Incapable of being understood; unintelligible.   **2.** *Archaic* Boundless.   — in′com·pre·hen′si·bil′i·ty, in′com·pre·hen′si·ble·ness *n.*   — in′com·pre·hen′si·bly *adv.*

in·com·pre·hen·sion (in′kom·pri·hen′shən, in·kom′-)   *n.* Lack of understanding.

in·com·pre·hen·sive (in′kom·pri·hen′siv, in·kom′-)   *adj.* Not comprehensive; limited in scope.

in·com·press·i·ble (in′kəm·pres′ə·bəl)   *adj.* Incapable of being compressed.   — in′com·press′i·bil′i·ty *n.*

in·con·ceiv·a·ble (in′kən·sē′və·bəl)   *adj.* Incapable of being conceived by the mind; unbelievable.   — in′con·ceiv′a·bil′i·ty, in′con·ceiv′a·ble·ness *n.*   — in′con·ceiv′a·bly *adv.*

in·con·clu·sive (in′kən·klōō′siv)   *adj.* **1.** Not leading to an ultimate conclusion; indeterminate; indecisive: *inconclusive* evidence.   **2.** Not achieving a definite result; ineffective.   — in′con·clu′sive·ly *adv.*   — in′con·clu′sive·ness *n.*

in·con·gru·i·ty (in′kong·grōō′ə·tē, in′kən-)   *n.   pl.* **·ties 1.** The state or quality of being incongruous; unsuitableness; inappropriateness.   **2.** That which is incongruous.

in·con·gru·ous (in·kong′grōō·əs)   *adj.* **1.** Not suitable; inappropriate.   **2.** Not corresponding or conforming; at odds: with *with* or *to*.   **3.** Consisting of elements or qualities not properly belonging together.   [< L < *in-* not + *congruus* agreeing]   — in·con′gru·ous·ly *adv.*   — in·con′gru·ous·ness *n.*

in·con·se·quent (in·kon′sə·kwənt)   *adj.* **1.** Not following from the premises; contrary to logical inference.   **2.** Not proceeding according to the usual course; irrelevant; disconnected.   **3.** Illogical in thought or action; eccentric.   — in·con′se·quence *n.*   — in·con′se·quent·ly *adv.*

in·con·se·quen·tial (in′kon·sə·kwen′shəl, in·kon′-)   *adj.* **1.** Having little or no consequence; unimportant; trivial.   **2.** Inconsequent.   — *n.* A thing of no importance.   — in·con′se·quen′ti·al′i·ty (-kwen′shē·al′ə·tē), in·con·se·quen′tial·ness *n.*   — in·con′se·quen′tial·ly *adv.*

in·con·sid·er·a·ble (in′kən·sid′ər·ə·bəl)   *adj.* **1.** Small in quantity, size, or value.   **2.** Not worth considering; trivial.   — in′con·sid′er·a·ble·ness *n.*   — in′con·sid′er·a·bly *adv.*

in·con·sid·er·ate (in′kən·sid′ər·it)   *adj.* **1.** Lacking in concern for the rights or needs of others; thoughtless.   **2.** Not carefully considered or thought out.   — in′con·sid′er·ate·ly *adv.*   — in′con·sid′er·ate·ness, in′con·sid·er·a′tion *n.*

in·con·sis·ten·cy (in′kən·sis′tən·sē)   *n.   pl.* **·cies 1.** The quality of being inconsistent.   **2.** Something that is inconsistent. Also in·con·sis′tence.

in·con·sis·tent (in′kən·sis′tənt)   *adj.* **1.** Lacking in agreement or compatibility; inconsonant; at variance.   **2.** Containing contradictory elements or parts.   **3.** Lacking uniformity in behavior or thought; erratic; changeable.   — in′·con·sis′tent·ly *adv.*

in·con·sol·a·ble (in′kən·sō′lə·bəl)   *adj.* Not to be consoled; disconsolate; dejected.   — in′con·sol′a·bil′i·ty, in′con·sol′a·ble·ness *n.*   — in′con·sol′a·bly *adv.*

in·con·so·nant (in·kon′sə·nənt)   *adj.* Not consonant; not in accord.   — in·con′so·nance *n.*   — in·con′so·nant·ly *adv.*

in·con·spic·u·ous (in′kən·spik′yōō·əs)   *adj.* **1.** Not conspicuous; not prominent or striking.   **2.** Not attracting attention to oneself; shrinking from or not meriting notice.   — in′con·spic′u·ous·ly *adv.*   — in′con·spic′u·ous·ness *n.*

in·con·stant (in·kon′stənt)   *adj.* Not constant; variable; fickle.   — *n.* One who or that which is inconstant.   — in·con′stan·cy *n.*   — in·con′stant·ly *adv.*

in·con·test·a·ble (in′kən·tes′tə·bəl)   *adj.* Not admitting of question; unassailable: *incontestable* evidence.   [< F]   — in′con·test′a·bil′i·ty, in′con·test′a·ble·ness *n.*   — in′con·test′a·bly *adv.*

in·con·ti·nence (in·kon′tə·nəns)   *n.* **1.** The quality or condition of being incontinent.   **2.** An instance of incontinence. Also in·con′ti·nen·cy.

in·con·ti·nent (in·kon′tə·nənt)   *adj.* **1.** Exercising little control or restraint, esp. in sexual desires.   **2.** Incapable of keeping back: often with *of*.   **3.** Unrestrained; unchecked: an *incontinent* flow of abuse.   — in·con′ti·nent·ly *adv.*

in·con·trol·la·ble (in′kən·trō′lə·bəl)   *adj.* Incapable of being controlled; uncontrollable.   — in′con·trol′la·bly *adv.*

in·con·tro·vert·i·ble (in′kon·trə·vûr′tə·bəl)   *adj.* Not admitting of controversy; undeniable.   — in′con·tro·vert′i·bil′i·ty, in′con·tro·vert′i·ble·ness *n.*   — in′con·tro·vert′i·bly *adv.*

in·con·ven·ience (in′kən·vēn′yəns)   *n.* **1.** The state or quality of being inconvenient.   **2.** Something that is inconvenient.   — *v.t.* **·ienced, ·ienc·ing** To cause inconvenience to.

in·con·ven·ient (in′kən·vēn′yənt)   *adj.* Causing or lending itself to discomfort and difficulty; troublesome; awkward.   — in′con·ven′ient·ly *adv.*

in·con·ver·sant (in·kon′vər·sənt, in′kən·vûr′sənt)   *adj.* Not conversant or familiar: with *in* or *with*.

in·con·vert·i·ble (in′kən·vûr′tə·bəl)   *adj.* Incapable of being changed, exchanged, or converted; esp., of paper money, not exchangeable for specie.   — in′con·vert′i·bil′i·ty, in′con·vert′i·ble·ness *n.*   — in′con·vert′i·bly *adv.*

in·con·vin·ci·ble (in′kən·vin′sə·bəl)   *adj.* Not to be convinced; not convincible.   — in′con·vin′ci·bil′i·ty, in′con·vin′ci·ble·ness *n.*   — in′con·vin′ci·bly *adv.*

in·co·or·di·nate (in′kō·ôr′də·nit, -nāt)   *adj.* Not coordinated. Also in·co·or′di·nat′ed (-nā′tid).

in·cor·po·rate (*v.* in·kôr′pə·rāt; *adj.* in·kôr′pə·rit)   *v.* **·rat·ed, ·rat·ing** *v.i.* **1.** To form a legal corporation or other association capable of acting as an individual.   **2.** To become combined or merged as one body or whole.   — *v.t.* **3.** To take in or include as part of a whole.   **4.** To add or inject (an ingredient, certain elements, etc.).   **5.** To form (persons, groups, etc.) into a legal corporation or other association.   **6.** To combine or merge into a whole.   — **Syn.** See ENROLL, MIX, UNITE.   — *adj.* **1.** Joined or combined into a single unit or whole; closely blended.   **2.** Legally incorporated.

[< LL < *in-* in + *corporare* to form into a body] —**in·cor/po·ra/tive** *n.* —**in·cor/po·ra/tor** *n.*

in·cor·po·rat·ed (in·kôr/pə·rā/tid) *adj.* **1.** Forming one body or whole; combined. **2.** Organized into a legal corporation. Abbr. (def. 2) *inc., incor., incorp.*

in·cor·po·ra·tion (in·kôr/pə·rā/shən) *n.* **1.** The act or process of incorporating. **2.** A corporation.

in·cor·po·re·al (in/kôr·pôr/ē·əl, -pō/rē-) *adj.* **1.** Not consisting of matter; insubstantial. **2.** Of or pertaining to nonmaterial things; spiritual. **3.** *Law* Having no material existence, but regarded as existing by the law: *incorporeal* rights. [< *in-* not + *corpus, -oris* body] —**in·cor·po/re·al/i·ty** (-al/ə·tē) *n.* —**in/cor·po/re·al·ly** *adv.*

in·cor·rect (in/kə·rekt/) *adj.* **1.** Inaccurate or untrue as to fact or usage; wrong. **2.** Not proper or fitting; unsuitable: *incorrect* behavior. **3.** Not conforming to known or accepted standards; faulty: an *incorrect* idea. [< L *incorrectus*] —**in/cor·rect/ly** *adv.* —**in/cor·rect/ness** *n.*

in·cor·ri·gi·ble (in·kôr/ə·jə·bəl, -kor/-) *adj.* **1.** Incapable of being reformed or chastened. **2.** Firmly implanted; ineradicable, as a bad habit. **3.** Incapable of being corrected or amended. —*n.* One who is incorrigible. —**in·cor/ri·gi·bil/i·ty, in/cor/ri·gi·ble·ness** *n.* —**in·cor/ri·gi·bly** *adv.*

in·cor·rupt (in/kə·rupt/) *adj.* **1.** Not morally corrupt; esp., not susceptible to bribery; honest; upright. **2.** Not marred by decay or spoilage; untainted; fresh. **3.** Free from errors or alterations, as language, a literary text, etc. Also **in/cor·rupt/ed.** —**in/cor·rupt/ly** *adv.* —**in/cor·rupt/ness** *n.*

in·cor·rupt·i·ble (in/kə·rup/tə·bəl) *adj.* **1.** Not accessible to bribery; steadfastly honest. **2.** Incapable of corruption; not subject to decay or spoilage. —**in/cor·rupt/i·bil/i·ty, in/cor·rupt/i·ble·ness** *n.* —**in/cor·rupt/i·bly** *adv.*

in·crease (v. in·krēs/, n. in/krēs) *v.* **·creased, ·creas·ing** *v.i.* **1.** To become greater, as in amount, size, degree, etc.; grow. **2.** To grow in number, esp. by reproduction; multiply. —*v.t.* **3.** To make greater, as in amount, size, degree, etc.; augment; enlarge. —*n.* **1.** A growing or becoming greater, as in size, quantity, etc. **2.** The amount of growth or augmentation; that which is added; increment. [< OF < L < *in-* in + *crescere* to grow] —**in·creas/a·ble** *adj.* —**in·creas/er** *n.* —**in·creas/ing·ly** *adv.*

—**Syn.** (verb) augment, enlarge, extend, multiply.

in·cred·i·ble (in·kred/ə·bəl) *adj.* **1.** Not credible; impossible to believe; unbelievable. —**in·cred/i·bil/i·ty, in·cred/i·ble·ness** *n.* —**in·cred/i·bly** *adv.* **2.** Amazing; wonderful.

in·cre·du·li·ty (in/krə·dōō/lə·tē, -dyōō/-) *n.* The quality or state of being incredulous; disbelief; skepticism.

in·cred·u·lous (in·krej/ə·ləs) *adj.* **1.** Not willing or not disposed to believe; skeptical. **2.** Characterized by or showing disbelief. [< L < *in-* not + *credulus* < *credere* to believe] —**in·cred/u·lous·ly** *adv.* —**in·cred/u·lous·ness** *n.*

in·cre·ment (in/krə·mənt) *n.* **1.** A quantity added to another quantity. **2.** The act of increasing; enlargement. [< L *increscere* to increase] —**in/cre·men/tal** *adj.*

in·crim·i·nate (in·krim/ə·nāt) *v.t.* **·nat·ed, ·nat·ing** **1.** To imply the wrongdoing or guilt of (a person, etc.). **2.** To charge with a crime or fault. —**Syn.** See ACCUSE. [< Med.L < *in-* in + *criminare* to accuse one of a crime] —**in·crim/i·na/tion** *n.* —**in·crim/i·na·to/ry** (-nə·tôr/ē) *adj.*

in·crust (in·krust/) *v.t.* **1.** To cover with or as with a crust or hard coating; form a crust on. **2.** To decorate lavishly, as with jewels. Also **encrust.** [< OF < L < *in-* on + *crustare* to form a crust] —**in·crus·ta/tion** *n.*

in·cu·bate (in/kyə·bāt, ing/-) *v.* **·bat·ed, ·bat·ing** *v.t.* **1.** To sit upon (eggs) in order to hatch them; brood. **2.** To hatch (eggs) in this manner or by artificial heat. **3.** To maintain under conditions favoring optimum growth or development, as bacterial cultures. —*v.i.* **4.** To sit on eggs; brood. **5.** To undergo incubation. [< L < *in-* on + *cubare* to lie] —**in/cu·ba/tive** *adj.*

in·cu·ba·tion (in/kyə·bā/shən, ing/-) *n.* **1.** The act of incubating, or the state of being incubated. **2.** *Med.* The period between the time of exposure to an infectious disease and the appearance of the symptoms. [< L *incubatio, -onis*]

in·cu·ba·tor (in/kyə·bā/tər, ing/-) *n.* **1.** An apparatus kept at a uniform warmth for artificial hatching of eggs. **2.** *Bacteriol.* A device for the artificial development of microorganisms. **3.** An apparatus for keeping warm a prematurely born baby. [< L, a hatcher]

in·cu·bus (in/kyə·bəs, ing/-) *n.* *pl.* **·bus·es** or **·bi** (-bī) **1.** Anything that tends to oppress or discourage. **2.** A nightmare. **3.** In folklore, a male demon that has sexual intercourse with sleeping women. [< Med.L < LL, nightmare < L *incubare* to lie on]

in·cul·cate (in·kul/kāt, in/kul-) *v.t.* **·cat·ed, ·cat·ing** To impress upon the mind by frequent repetition or forceful admonition; instill. [< L < *in-* on + *calcare* to tread] —**in/cul·ca/tion** *n.* —**in/cul·ca/tor** *n.*

in·cul·pate (in·kul/pāt, in/kul-) *v.t.* **·pat·ed, ·pat·ing** To involve in an accusation; incriminate. [< Med.L < *in-* in + *culpa* fault] —**in/cul·pa/tion** *n.*

in·cum·ben·cy (in·kum/bən·sē) *n. pl.* **·cies** **1.** The state or quality of being incumbent. **2.** That which is incumbent. **3.** The holding of an office or the period in which it is held.

in·cum·bent (in·kum/bənt) *adj.* **1.** Resting upon one as a moral obligation, or as necessary under the circumstances; obligatory. **2.** Resting, leaning, or weighing wholly or partly upon something. —*n.* One who holds an office or performs official duties. [< L < *in-* on + *cubare* to lie] —**in·cum/bent·ly** *adv.*

in·cum·ber (in·kum/bər), **in·cum·brance** (in·kum/brəns), etc. See ENCUMBER, etc.

in·cu·nab·u·la (in/kyōō·nab/yə·lə) *n. pl.* of **in·cu·nab·u·lum** (-ləm) **1.** Specimens of early European printing from movable type; esp., books printed before A.D. 1500. **2.** The earliest stages of development; beginnings. [< L < *in-* in + *cunabula*, dim. of *cunae* cradle] —**in/cu·nab/u·lar** *adj.*

in·cur (in·kûr/) *v.t.* **·curred, ·cur·ring** To become subject to (unpleasant consequences); bring on oneself. [< L < *in-* in + *currere* to run] —**in·cur/rence** *n.*

in·cur·a·ble (in·kyŏŏr/ə·bəl) *adj.* Not curable or remediable. —*n.* One suffering from an incurable disease. —**in·cur/a·bil/i·ty, in·cur/a·ble·ness** *n.* —**in·cur/a·bly** *adv.*

in·cur·sion (in·kûr/zhən, -shən) *n.* **1.** A hostile, often sudden entrance into a territory; an invasion; raid. **2.** A running in or running against; encroachment. [< L < *in-* + *currere* to run] —**in·cur/sive** *adj.*

in·curve (v. in·kûrv/; n. in/kûrv) *v.i. & v.t.* To curve inward. —*n.* In baseball, a pitch that curves toward the batter.

in·cus (ing/kəs) *n. pl.* **in·cu·des** (in·kyōō/dēz) *Anat.* The anvil-shaped central bone of the group of three bones in the middle ear of mammals: also called *anvil*. [< L, anvil]

in·debt·ed (in·det/id) *adj.* **1.** Legally obligated to pay for value received; in debt. **2.** Morally obligated to acknowledge benefits or favors. [< OF < *en-* in + *dette* debt]

in·debt·ed·ness (in·det/id·nis) *n.* **1.** The state of being indebted. **2.** The amount of one's debts.

in·de·cen·cy (in·dē/sən·sē) *n. pl.* **·cies** **1.** The quality or condition of being indecent. **2.** An indecent act, speech, etc.

in·de·cent (in·dē/sənt) *adj.* **1.** Offensive to one's moral sense or modesty; immodest. **2.** Contrary to propriety or good taste; indelicate; vulgar. —**in·de/cent·ly** *adv.*

in·de·ci·pher·a·ble (in/di·sī/fər·ə·bəl) *adj.* Not decipherable; unreadable. —**in/de·ci/pher·a·bil/i·ty** *n.*

in·de·ci·sion (in/di·sizh/ən) *n.* Inability to make decisions.

in·de·ci·sive (in/di·sī/siv) *adj.* **1.** Not bringing about a definite conclusion, solution, etc. **2.** Incapable of making decisions. —**in/de·ci/sive·ly** *adv.* —**in/de·ci/sive·ness** *n.*

in·dec·o·rous (in·dek/ər·əs, in/di·kôr/əs) *adj.* Not decorous; unseemly. —**in·dec/o·rous·ly** *adv.* —**in·dec/o·rous·ness** *n.*

in·de·cor·um (in/di·kôr/əm, -kō/rəm) *n.* Lack of propriety.

in·deed (in·dēd/) *adv.* In fact; in truth: used to emphasize an affirmation, to mark a qualifying word or clause, or to denote a concession. —*interj.* Is that true?

in·de·fat·i·ga·ble (in/də·fat/ə·gə·bəl) *adj.* Not yielding readily to fatigue; tireless; unflagging. [< MF < L < *in-* not + *de-*, intens. + *fatigare* to tire out] —**in/de·fat/i·ga·bil/i·ty, in/de·fat/i·ga·ble·ness** *n.* —**in/de·fat/i·ga·bly** *adv.*

in·de·fea·si·ble (in/də·fē/zə·bəl) *adj.* Incapable of being annulled, set aside, or made void. —**in/de·fea/si·bil/i·ty** *n.* —**in/de·fea/si·bly** *adv.*

in·de·fen·si·ble (in/di·fen/sə·bəl) *adj.* **1.** Incapable of being justified. **2.** Incapable of being defended. —**in/de·fen/si·bil/i·ty, in/de·fen/si·ble·ness** *n.* —**in/de·fen/si·bly** *adv.*

in·de·fin·a·ble (in/di·fī/nə·bəl) *adj.* Incapable of being defined or described; vague; subtle; ineffable. —**in/de·fin/a·ble·ness** *n.* —**in/de·fin/a·bly** *adv.*

in·def·i·nite (in·def/ə·nit) *adj.* **1.** Not definite or precise; vague. **2.** Without a fixed number; indeterminate. **3.** *Gram.* Not definite or determining, as the *indefinite* article. —**in·def/i·nite·ly** *adv.* —**in·def/i·nite·ness** *n.*

indefinite pronoun *Gram.* A pronoun that represents an object indefinitely or generally, as *each, none, another.*

in·de·his·cent (in/di·his/ənt) *adj. Bot.* Not opening spontaneously when ripe, as certain grains and fruits. —**in/de·his/cence** *n.*

in·del·i·ble (in·del/ə·bəl) *adj.* **1.** Incapable of being blotted out or effaced. **2.** Leaving a mark or stain not easily erased. [< L < *in-* not + *delibilis* perishable] —**in·del/i·bil/i·ty, in·del/i·ble·ness** *n.* —**in·del/i·bly** *adv.*

in·del·i·ca·cy (in·del/ə·kə·sē) *n. pl.* **·cies** **1.** The quality of being indelicate; coarseness. **2.** An indelicate thing, act, etc.

in·del·i·cate (in·del/ə·kit) *adj.* **1.** Lacking or offending a sense of delicacy or good taste; crude. **2.** Unconcerned about the feelings of others; tactless. —**in·del/i·cate·ly** *adv.*

in·dem·ni·fy (in·dem/nə·fī) *v.t.* **·fied, ·fy·ing** **1.** To compensate (a person, etc.) for loss or damage sustained. **2.** To make good (a loss). **3.** To give security against future loss or punishment. [< L *indemnis* unhurt (< *in-* not + *damnum* harm) + -FY] —**in·dem/ni·fi·ca/tion** *n.*

in·dem·ni·ty (in·dem/nə·tē) *n. pl.* **·ties** **1.** That which is given as compensation for a loss or for damage. **2.** An agreement to remunerate another for loss or protect him against liability. **3.** Exemption from penalties or liabilities.

in·dent¹ (in·dent'; *for n., also* in'dent) *v.t.* **1.** To set in from the margin, as the first line of a paragraph. **2.** To cut or mark the edge or border of with toothlike notches; serrate. **3.** To indenture, as an apprentice. — *v.i.* **4.** To be notched or cut; form a recess. **5.** To set a line, paragraph, etc., in from the margin. — *n.* **1.** A cut or notch on the edge of a thing. **2.** A space before the first word of a paragraph; indention. [< OF < Med.L < *in-* in + *dentis* tooth]

in·dent² (in·dent'; *for n., also* in'dent) *v.t.* **1.** To press or push in so as to form a dent or depression; impress. **2.** To make a dent in. — *n.* A dent or depression; indentation.

in·den·ta·tion (in'den·tā'shən) *n.* **1.** A notch or series of notches in an edge or border. **2.** The act of notching, or the condition of being notched. **3.** A dent. **4.** An indention.

in·den·tion (in·den'shən) *n.* **1.** *Printing* **a** The setting in of a line or body of type at the left side. **b** The space thus left blank. **2.** A dent; indentation.

in·den·ture (in·den'chər) *n.* **1.** *Law* A deed or contract made between two or more parties. **2.** *Usu. pl.* Such a contract between master and apprentice. **3.** The act of indenting, or the state of being indented. **4.** Indentation. — *v.t.* **·tured, ·tur·ing** **1.** To bind by indenture. **2.** To make an indentation in.

in·de·pen·dence (in'di·pen'dəns) *n.* **1.** The quality or condition of being independent. **2.** Sufficient income for one's needs; a competence.

Independence Day July 4, a holiday in the U.S. commemorating the adoption of the Declaration of Independence, July 4, 1776.

in·de·pen·den·cy (in'di·pen'dən·sē) *n. pl.* **·cies** **1.** Independence. **2.** An independent state or territory.

in·de·pen·dent (in'di·pen'dənt) *adj.* **1.** Not subject to the authority of another; autonomous. **2.** Not dependent on or part of some larger group, system, etc.: an *independent* union. **3.** Not an adherent of a party or faction: an *independent* voter. **4.** Not influenced or guided by others. **5.** Acting so as to manage one's own affairs; self-reliant. **6.** Self-supporting. **7.** Having a competence; also, constituting a competence: *independent* means. **8.** *Gram.* Constituting or capable of constituting a complete sentence: said of clauses. — *n.* One who or that which is independent, esp. one not an adherent of a party or faction. — **in'de·pen'dent·ly** *adv.*

independent clause *Gram.* A clause constituting or capable of constituting a sentence.

in·de·scrib·a·ble (in'di·skrī'bə·bəl) *adj.* Incapable of being described; esp., too complex, extreme, etc., to be described; ineffable. — **in'de·scrib'a·bil'i·ty, in'de·scrib'a·ble·ness** *n.* — **in'de·scrib'a·bly** *adv.*

in·de·struc·ti·ble (in'di·struk'tə·bəl) *adj.* Incapable of being destroyed; very tough and durable. — **in'de·struc'ti·bil'i·ty, in'de·struc'ti·ble·ness** *n.* — **in'de·struc'ti·bly** *adv.*

in·de·ter·mi·na·ble (in'di·tûr'mi·nə·bəl) *adj.* **1.** Incapable of being ascertained. **2.** Incapable of being decided. — **in'·de·ter'mi·na·ble·ness** *n.* — **in'de·ter'mi·na·bly** *adv.*

in·de·ter·mi·na·cy (in'di·tûr'mə·nə·sē) *n.* The state or quality of being indeterminate.

in·de·ter·mi·nate (in'di·tûr'mə·nit) *adj.* **1.** Not definite in extent, amount, or nature. **2.** Not clear or precise; vague. **3.** Not decided; unsettled. **4.** Not fixed; inconclusive. — **in'de·ter'mi·nate·ly** *adv.* — **in'de·ter'mi·nate·ness** *n.*

in·de·ter·mi·na·tion (in'di·tûr'mə·nā'shən) *n.* **1.** Lack of determination. **2.** The condition of being indeterminate.

in·dex (in'deks) *n. pl.* **·dex·es** *or* **·di·ces** (-də·sēz) **1.** An alphabetical list, as at the end of a book or similar publication, of topics, names, etc., and the numbers of the pages where they occur in the text. **2.** A descriptive list, as of items in a collection. **3.** Anything that serves as an indicator, as the needle on the dial of scientific instruments. **4.** The index finger. **5.** Anything that indicates or gives evidence of; sign: Alertness is an *index* of intelligence. **6.** *Printing* A mark (☞) used to direct attention to a specific word, passage, etc.: also called *fist, hand.* **7.** A numerical expression of the ratio between one dimension or magnitude and another: the cephalic *index.* **8.** *Math.* A subscript or superscript. — *v.t.* **1.** To provide with an index, as a book. **2.** To enter in an index, as a subject. **3.** To indicate. [< L, forefinger, sign] — **in'dex·er** *n.* — **in·dex'i·cal** *adj.*

In·dex (in'deks) *n.* A list of books the Roman Catholic Church forbids its members to read except with special permission.

index finger The finger next to the thumb: also called *forefinger.*

index number *Stat.* A figure indicating the relative changes in costs, production, etc., at a given period of time, as compared with those of a specific period in the past represented by the number 100 and used as an arbitrary base.

India ink **1.** A black pigment composed of lampblack

mixed with a binding material and molded in sticks or cakes. **2.** A liquid ink made from this pigment.

In·di·an (in'dē·ən) *n.* **1.** A citizen of the Republic of India. **2.** A native of India or the East Indies. **3.** A member of the aboriginal races of North America, South America, and the West Indies. **4.** Loosely, any of the languages of the American Indian. — *adj.* **1.** Of or pertaining to India and the East Indies and their peoples. **2.** Of or pertaining to the aborigines of North America, South America, and the West Indies. **3.** Made by or used by Indians. [< L *India*]

Indian club A bottle-shaped wooden club used in gymnastics, usu. in pairs.

Indian corn Corn (def. 1).

Indian file Single file.

Indian giver *U.S. Informal* One who gives a present and then wants it back.

Indian hemp **1.** Hemp (def. 1). **2.** A perennial American herb of the dogbane family.

Indian meal Cornmeal.

Indian pipe An herb with one pipe-shaped white flower.

Indian pudding A pudding of cornmeal, milk, and molasses.

Indian summer A period of mild, warm weather occurring in late autumn, often after the first frost.

India paper A thin, yellowish, absorbent printing paper, used in taking the finest proofs from engraved plates.

India rubber Rubber (def. 1).

In·dic (in'dik) *adj.* Pertaining to India, its peoples, languages, and culture; Indian. — *n.* A branch of the Indo-Iranian subfamily of Indo-European languages, including Sanskrit, Hindi, etc.

in·di·cate (in'də·kāt) *v.t.* **·cat·ed, ·cat·ing** **1.** To be or give a sign of; signify. **2.** To direct attention to; point out. **3.** To express or make known. [< L < *in-* in + *dicare* to point out, proclaim]

in·di·ca·tion (in'də·kā'shən) *n.* **1.** The act of indicating. **2.** That which indicates; sign. **3.** A degree or quantity shown on a measuring instrument.

in·dic·a·tive (in·dik'ə·tiv) *adj.* **1.** Suggestive of; pointing out. **2.** *Gram.* Pertaining to or denoting a mood in which an act or condition is stated or questioned as an actual fact. — *n.* *Gram.* **a** The indicative mood. **b** A verb in this mood. — **in·dic'a·tive·ly** *adv.*

in·di·ca·tor (in'də·kā'tər) *n.* **1.** One who or that which indicates or points out. **2.** An instrument or device that measures or shows position; also, its pointer or needle.

in·di·ces (in'də·sēz) Alternative plural of INDEX.

in·dict (in·dīt') *v.t.* **1.** *Law* To prefer an indictment against. **2.** To charge with a crime or offense. — **Syn.** See ACCUSE. [< AF *enditer* to make known, inform; later infl. in form by Med.L *dictare* to accuse] — **in·dict'a·ble** *adj.* — **in·dict·ee** (in·dī·tē') *n.* — **in·dict'er, in·dict'or** *n.*

in·dict·ment (in·dīt'mənt) *n.* **1.** The act of indicting, or the state of being indicted. **2.** *Law* A formal written charge of crime, presented by a grand jury on oath to the court, as the basis for trial of the accused. [< AF *enditement*]

in·dif·fer·ence (in·dif'ər·əns) *n.* **1.** The state or quality of being indifferent. **2.** Unimportance; insignificance. **3.** Mediocrity. — **Syn.** See APATHY. Also **in·dif'fer·en·cy.**

in·dif·fer·ent (in·dif'ər·ənt) *adj.* **1.** Having no interest or feeling; unconcerned. **2.** Lacking in distinction; mediocre. **3.** Only average in size, amount, etc. **4.** Having little importance or significance. **5.** Showing no preference; unbiased. **6.** Not active; inert: said of chemical compounds, electrical or magnetic properties, etc. [< OF < L *indifferens*] — **in·dif'fer·ent·ly** *adv.*

in·di·gence (in'də·jəns) *n.* The state of being indigent; poverty. Also **in'di·gen·cy.**

in·dig·e·nous (in·dij'ə·nəs) *adj.* **1.** Originating or occurring naturally in the place specified; native. **2.** Innate; inherent. — **Syn.** See NATIVE. [< L *indu-* within + *gignere* to be born] — **in·dig'e·nous·ly** *adv.*

in·di·gent (in'də·jənt) *adj.* Lacking means of subsistence; poor. [< F < L *indu-* within + *egere* to need] — **in'di·gent·ly** *adv.*

in·di·gest·i·ble (in'də·jes'tə·bəl) *adj.* Difficult to digest; not digestible. — **in'di·gest'i·bil'i·ty, in'di·gest'i·ble·ness** *n.* — **in'di·gest'i·bly** *adv.*

in·di·ges·tion (in'də·jes'chən) *n.* Difficulty in digesting food. [< F]

in·dig·nant (in·dig'nənt) *adj.* Feeling or showing indignation. — **in·dig'nant·ly** *adv.*

in·dig·na·tion (in'dig·nā'shən) *n.* Anger aroused by injustice or baseness. [< OF < L < *in-* not + *dignus* worthy]

in·dig·ni·ty (in·dig'nə·tē) *n. pl.* **·ties** An act that humiliates, degrades, or injures self-respect.

in·di·go (in'də·gō) *n. pl.* **·gos** *or* **·goes** **1.** A blue coloring substance obtained from certain plants of the pea family or made synthetically. **2.** A deep violet blue. Also **indigo blue.** **3.** A plant yielding a blue dyestuff. — *adj.* Deep violet blue. [< Sp. < L < Gk. *Indikon* (*pharmakon*) Indian (dye)]

in·di·go bunting A finch of North America, the male of which is a brilliant indigo. Also **indigo bird.**

in·di·rect (in′də·rekt′) *adj.* **1.** Not following a direct line or path. **2.** Not straightforward or open; underhand. **3.** Not coming as an immediate result: *indirect* benefits. **4.** Not aimed directly: an *indirect* proof. **5.** Not proceeding through a direct line of succession, as an inheritance. **6.** *Gram.* Not expressed in the exact words of the source: an *indirect* question. — **in′di·rect′ly** *adv.* — **in′di·rect′ness** *n.*

in·di·rec·tion (in′də·rek′shən) *n.* **1.** Indirect method or practice. **2.** Dishonest dealing; deceit.

indirect lighting Lighting that is reflected, as from a white ceiling, or diffused to give a minimum of glare and shadow.

indirect tax A tax, the burden of which is ultimately passed on to another, as in the form of higher market prices.

in·dis·cern·i·ble (in′di·sûr′nə·bəl, -zûr′-) *adj.* Incapable of being discerned; imperceptible. — **in′dis·cern′i·ble·ness** *n.* — **in′dis·cern′i·bly** *adv.*

in·dis·cov·er·a·ble (in′dis·kuv′ər·ə·bəl) *adj.* Incapable of being discovered. — **in′dis·cov′er·a·bil′i·ty** *n.*

in·dis·creet (in′dis·krēt′) *adj.* Lacking discretion; imprudent. — **in′dis·creet′ly** *adv.* — **in′dis·creet′ness** *n.*

in·dis·crete (in′dis·krēt′) *adj.* Not discrete; not separated; unified. — **in′dis·crete′ly** *adv.* — **in′dis·crete′ness** *n.*

in·dis·cre·tion (in′dis·kresh′ən) *n.* **1.** The state or quality of being indiscreet. **2.** An indiscreet act, speech, etc.

in·dis·crim·i·nate (in′dis·krim′ə·nit) *adj.* **1.** Showing no discrimination; not perceiving differences. **2.** Confused; chaotic. — **in′dis·crim′i·nate·ly** *adv.* — **in′dis·crim′i·nate·ness** *n.* — **in′dis·crim′i·nat′ing** *adj.* — **in′dis·crim′i·na′tion** *n.* — **in′dis·crim′i·na′tive** *adj.*

in·dis·pen·sa·ble (in′dis·pen′sə·bəl) *adj.* **1.** Not to be dispensed with; essential. **2.** Not to be ignored: an *indispensable* responsibility. — *n.* An indispensable person or thing. — **in′dis·pen′sa·bil′i·ty, in′dis·pen′sa·ble·ness** *n.* — **in′dis·pen′sa·bly** *adv.*

in·dis·pose (in′dis·pōz′) *v.t.* **·posed, ·pos·ing** **1.** To render unwilling; disincline. **2.** To render unfit. **3.** To make slightly ill or ailing. — **in′dis·po·si′tion** *n.*

in·dis·posed (in′dis·pōzd′) *adj.* **1.** Mildly ill; unwell. **2.** Disinclined; not willing. — **Syn.** See SICK.

in·dis·put·a·ble (in′dis·pyoo′tə·bəl, in·dis′pyoo·tə·bəl) *adj.* Incapable of being disputed. — **in′dis·put·a·bil′i·ty, in′dis·put′a·ble·ness** *n.* — **in′dis·put′a·bly** *adv.*

in·dis·sol·u·ble (in′di·sol′yə·bəl, in·dis′ə·lyə·bəl) *adj.* **1.** Incapable of being dissolved, separated into its elements, or destroyed. **2.** Binding; extremely durable. — **in′dis·sol′u·bil′i·ty, in′dis·sol′u·ble·ness** *n.* — **in′dis·sol′u·bly** *adv.*

in·dis·tinct (in′dis·tingkt′) *adj.* **1.** Not clearly perceptible; blurred. **2.** Not readily distinguishable from something else; confused. **3.** Not producing clear impressions, images, etc. — **in′dis·tinct′ly** *adv.* — **in′dis·tinct′ness** *n.*

in·dis·tin·guish·a·ble (in′dis·ting′gwish·ə·bəl) *adj.* Incapable of being perceived. — **in′dis·tin′guish·a·ble·ness, in′dis·tin′guish·a·bil′i·ty** *n.* — **in′dis·tin′guish·a·bly** *adv.*

in·di·um (in′dē·əm) *n.* A soft, malleable, silver-white metallic element (symbol In). See ELEMENT. [< NL < *indicum* indigo; with ref. to its spectrum color]

in·di·vid·u·al (in′də·vij′oo·əl) *adj.* **1.** Existing as a unit; single. **2.** Separate, as distinguished from others of the same kind. **3.** Pertaining to or meant for a single person, animal, etc.: an *individual* serving. **4.** Differentiated from others by distinctive characteristics. — *n.* **1.** A single human being as distinct from others. **2.** A person. [< Med.L < L < *in-* not + *dividere* to divide] — **in′di·vid′u·al·ly** *adv.*

in·di·vid·u·al·ism (in′də·vij′oo·əl·iz′əm) *n.* **1.** Personal independence in action, thought, etc. **2.** The state of being individual. **3.** Self-interest; egoism. **4.** The social theory that emphasizes the importance of the individual.

in·di·vid·u·al·ist (in′də·vij′oo·əl·ist) *n.* **1.** One who is independent in character, action, thought, etc. **2.** One who advocates individualism. — **in′di·vid′u·al·is′tic** *adj.*

in·di·vid·u·al·i·ty (in′də·vij′oo·al′ə·tē) *n.* pl. **·ties** **1.** A quality or trait that distinguishes one person or thing from others. **2.** Strikingly distinctive character or personality. **3.** The state of having separate, independent existence.

in·di·vid·u·al·ize (in′də·vij′oo·əl·īz′) *v.t.* **ized, ·iz·ing** **1.** To make individual; distinguish. **2.** To treat, mention, or consider individually. — **in′di·vid′u·al·i·za′tion** *n.*

in·di·vis·i·ble (in′də·viz′ə·bəl) *adj.* Not divisible; incapable of being divided. — *n.* Something that is indivisible. — **in′di·vis′i·ble·ness, in′di·vis′i·bil′i·ty** *n.* — **in′di·vis′i·bly** *adv.*

Indo- *combining form* Indian. [< Gk. *Indos* Indian]

In·do·chi·nese (in′dō·chī·nēz′, -nēs′) *adj.* Of or pertaining to Indochina, its inhabitants, or their language. — *n.* pl. **·nese** **1.** A member of one of the Mongoloid peoples of Indochina. **2.** The Sino-Tibetan family of languages.

in·doc·tri·nate (in·dok′trə·nāt) *v.t.* **·nat·ed, ·nat·ing** To instruct in doctrines; esp., to teach partisan or sectarian dogmas. [< Med.L *in-* into + *doctrinare* to teach < L *docere* to teach] — **in·doc′tri·na′tion** *n.*

In·do-Eu·ro·pe·an (in′dō·yoor′ə·pē′ən) *n.* The largest family of languages in the world, comprising most of the languages of Europe and many languages of India and SW Asia, and including as subfamilies Hellenic, Italic, Celtic, Germanic, Indo-Iranian, Armenian, Albanian, and Balto-Slavic. — *adj.* Of or pertaining to the Indo-European family of languages, or to the peoples speaking them.

In·do-I·ra·ni·an (in′dō·i·rā′nē·ən) *n.* A subfamily of the Indo-European family of languages, consisting of Indic and Iranian branches. — *adj.* Of or pertaining to this subfamily.

in·do·lent (in′də·lənt) *adj.* Averse to exertion or work; lazy. [< LL *in-* not + *dolere* to feel pain] — **in′do·lence** *n.* — **in′do·lent·ly** *adv.*

in·dom·i·ta·ble (in·dom′i·tə·bəl) *adj.* Not easily defeated or subdued. [< LL < L < *in-* not + *domitare* to tame] — **in·dom′i·ta·bly** *adv.*

In·do·ne·sian (in′dō·nē′zhən, -shən) *n.* **1.** A citizen of Indonesia. **2.** One of a small, light-brown-skinned people native throughout the Malay Peninsula and Archipelago, the Philippines, Sumatra, Java, etc. **3.** The languages spoken by these people, including Malay, Tagalog, etc.: also called *Malayan.* — *adj.* Of or pertaining to Indonesia, its peoples, or their languages.

in·door (in′dôr′, -dōr′) *adj.* **1.** Pertaining to or meant for the interior of a house or building. **2.** Located or performed within a house or building. [Earlier *within-door*]

in·doors (in′dôrz′, -dōrz′) *adv.* Inside or toward the inside of a building.

in·dorse (in·dôrs′), etc. See ENDORSE, etc.

in·du·bi·ta·ble (in·doo′bə·tə·bəl, -dyoo′-) *adj.* Not to be doubted. — **in·du′bi·ta·ble·ness** *n.* — **in·du′bi·ta·bly** *adv.*

in·duce (in·doos′, -dyoos′) *v.t.* **·duced, ·duc·ing** **1.** To cause to act, speak, etc., by convincing or other influence; persuade. **2.** To bring on; cause. **3.** To reach, as a conclusion, by inductive reasoning. [< L *in-* in + *ducere* to lead] — **in·duc′er** *n.* — **in·duc′i·ble** *adj.*

in·duce·ment (in·doos′mənt, -dyoos′-) *n.* **1.** That which induces; incentive. **2.** The act of inducing.

in·duct (in·dukt′) *v.t.* **1.** *U.S.* To bring (a draftee) into military service. **2.** To install formally in an office, etc. **3.** To initiate in knowledge, experience, etc.: with *to.* **4.** *Physics* To produce by induction. [See INDUCE.]

in·duc·tance (in·duk′təns) *n.* *Electr.* The ability of a circuit to produce induction.

in·duc·tee (in′duk·tē′) *n.* One inducted or being inducted.

in·duc·tile (in·duk′təl, -til) *adj.* **1.** Not ductile; not malleable. **2.** Not submissive; unyielding. — **in·duc·til′i·ty** *n.*

in·duc·tion (in·duk′shən) *n.* **1.** The act of inducting, or state of being inducted. **2.** The act of inducing or causing. **3.** The bringing forward of separate facts as evidence in order to prove a general statement; also, the resulting statement. **4.** *Electr.* The production of magnetization or electrification in a body by the mere proximity of a magnetic field or electric charge, or of an electric current in a conductor by the variation of the magnetic field in its vicinity. [< OF < L *inductio, -onis*] — **in·duc′tion·al** *adj.*

induction coil *Electr.* A device that changes a low steady voltage into a high intermittent alternating voltage by electromagnetic induction.

in·duc·tive (in·duk′tiv) *adj.* **1.** Pertaining to or resulting from induction: *inductive* reasoning. **2.** *Electr.* Produced by or causing induction or inductance. [< LL *inductivus*] — **in·duc′tive·ly** *adv.* — **in·duc′tive·ness** *n.*

in·duc·tiv·i·ty (in′duk·tiv′ə·tē) *n.* *Electr.* **1.** Specific capability for induction. **2.** Inductance.

in·duc·tor (in·duk′tər) *n.* **1.** One who or that which inducts. **2.** *Electr.* Any part of an electrical apparatus that acts inductively upon another.

in·dulge (in·dulj′) *v.* **·dulged, ·dulg·ing** *v.t.* **1.** To yield to or gratify, as desires or whims. **2.** To yield to or gratify the desires, whims, etc., of; humor. **3.** In business, to grant more time (to someone) for payment of a bill. — *v.i.* **4.** To gratify one's own desire. — **Syn.** See PAMPER. [< L *indulgere* to be kind to] — **in·dulg′er** *n.*

in·dul·gence (in·dul′jəns) *n.* **1.** The act of indulging, or state of being indulgent. **2.** That which is indulged in. **3.** Something granted as a favor. **4.** In business, permission to defer paying a bill, etc. **5.** In the Roman Catholic Church, remission of temporal punishment due for a sin after it has been forgiven through sacramental absolution. Also **in·dul′gen·cy.** [< OF < L *indulgentia*]

in·dul·gent (in·dul′jənt) *adj.* Prone to indulge; lenient. — **in·dul′gent·ly** *adv.*

in·du·rate (*v.* in′doo·rāt, -dyoo-; *adj.* in′doo·rit, -dyoo-) *v.t. & v.i.* **·rat·ed, ·rat·ing** **1.** To make or become hard or unfeeling. **2.** To make or become hardy. — *adj.* Hard; unfeeling: also **in′du·rat′ed.** [< L *indurare* to make hard] — **in′du·ra′tion** *n.* — **in′du·ra′tive** *adj.*

in·dus·tri·al (in·dus′trē·əl) *adj.* **1.** Of, characteristic of, or resulting from industry. **2.** Engaged in industry. **3.** Having many industries: an *industrial* area. **4.** Intended for use in industry. **5.** Relating to, affecting, or benefiting workers in industry. —*n. pl.* Stocks or securities of industrial enterprises. [< F *industriel* and Med.L *industrialis*] —**in·dus′tri·al·ly** *adv.*

industrial arts The technical skills used in industry, esp. as subjects of study in schools.

industrial design. The esthetic and practical design of industrial products; also, the study of such design.

industrial engineer An engineer who supervises production in factories, lays out machinery, etc.

in·dus·tri·al·ism (in·dus′trē·al·iz′əm) *n.* An economic system based chiefly on large-scale industries and production of goods rather than on agriculture, foreign trade, etc.

in·dus·tri·al·ist (in·dus′trē·al·ist) *n.* A person important in the ownership or management of industry.

in·dus·tri·al·ize (in·dus′trē·al·īz′) *v.t.* **·ized, ·iz·ing 1.** To establish large-scale industries in. **2.** To make or form into an industry. —**in·dus′tri·al·i·za′tion** *n.*

industrial relations The relations between management and employees in industrial concerns.

industrial union A labor union to which all workers in a particular industry may belong: also called *vertical union.*

in·dus·tri·ous (in·dus′trē·əs) *adj.* Hard-working. —**in·dus′tri·ous·ly** *adv.* —**in·dus′tri·ous·ness** *n.*

in·dus·try (in′dəs·trē) *n. pl.* **·tries 1.** Any specific branch of production or manufacture. **2.** Manufacturing and productive interests collectively. **3.** Diligent and regular application to work or tasks. [< MF < L *industrius* diligent]

in·dwell (in′dwel′) *v.* **·dwelt, ·dwell·ing** *v.t.* **1.** To dwell in. —*v.i.* **2.** To dwell. —**in′dwell′er** *n.* —**in′dwell′ing** *n.*

-ine¹ *suffix* Like; pertaining to; of the nature of: *marine, canine.* [< L *-inus,* adj. suffix]

-ine² *suffix* **1.** *Chem.* **a** Used in the names of halogens: *bromine.* **b** Used to indicate an alkaloid or basic substance: *morphine.* **c** Var. of **-IN. 2.** Used in names of commercial products: *brilliantine.* [Special use of -INE¹]

-ine³ *suffix* **1.** Used to form feminine words, names, and titles: *heroine.* **2.** Used to form originally feminine abstract nouns: *medicine, doctrine.* [< F < L *-ina,* suffix of fem. nouns < Gk. *-inē;* or directly < L or < Gk.]

-ine⁴ *suffix* Like; resembling: *crystalline.* [< L < Gk. *-inos*]

in·e·bri·ate (*v.* in·ē′brē·āt; *n. & adj.* in·ē′brē·it, ·āt) *v.t.* **·at·ed, ·at·ing 1.** To make drunk; intoxicate. **2.** To exhilarate; excite. —*n.* A habitual drunkard. —*adj.* Intoxicated. [< L < *in-* thoroughly + *ebriare* to make drunk] —**in·e′bri·a′ted** *adj.* —**in·e′bri·a′tion** *n.*

in·ed·i·ble (in·ed′ə·bəl) *adj.* Not eatable. —**in·ed′i·bil′i·ty** *n.*

in·ef·fa·ble (in·ef′ə·bəl) *adj.* **1.** Too overpowering to be expressed in words. **2.** Too lofty or sacred to be uttered. **3.** Indescribable; indefinable. [< MF < L < *in-* not + *effabilis* utterable] —**in·ef′fa·bil′i·ty, in·ef′fa·ble·ness** *n.* —**in·ef′fa·bly** *adv.*

in·ef·fec·tive (in′i·fek′tiv) *adj.* **1.** Not effective. **2.** Incompetent. —**in′ef·fec′tive·ly** *adv.* —**in′ef·fec′tive·ness** *n.*

in·ef·fec·tu·al (in′i·fek′chōō·əl) *adj.* **1.** Not effectual. **2.** Unsuccessful; fruitless. —**in′ef·fec′tu·al′i·ty, in′ef·fec′tu·al·ness** *n.* —**in′ef·fec′tu·al·ly** *adv.*

in·ef·fi·ca·cious (in′ef·ə·kā′shəs) *adj.* Not producing the effect desired or intended, as a medicine. —**in′ef·fi·ca′cious·ly** *adv.* —**in′ef·fi·ca′cious·ness** *n.*

in·ef·fi·ca·cy (in·ef′ə·kə·sē) *n.* The state of being inefficacious.

in·ef·fi·cient (in′i·fish′ənt) *adj.* **1.** Not efficient; not performing a function economically; wasteful. **2.** Incompetent. —**in′ef·fi′cien·cy** *n.* —**in′ef·fi′cient·ly** *adv.*

in·e·las·tic (in′i·las′tik) *adj.* Not elastic; inflexible; unadaptable. —**in·e·las·tic·i·ty** (in′i·las·tis′ə·tē) *n.*

in·el·e·gance (in·el′ə·gəns) *n.* **1.** The quality of being inelegant. **2.** Something inelegant. —**in·el′e·gant·ly** *adv.*

in·el·e·gan·cy (in·el′ə·gən·sē) *n. pl.* **·cies** Inelegance.

in·el·e·gant (in·el′ə·gənt) *adj.* **1.** Not elegant. **2.** Coarse; crude. —**in·el′e·gant·ly** *adv.*

in·el·i·gi·ble (in·el′ə·jə·bəl) *adj.* Not eligible; not qualified or suitable. —*n.* One who is not eligible. —**in·el′i·gi·bil′i·ty** *n.* —**in·el′i·gi·bly** *adv.*

in·e·luc·ta·ble (in′i·luk′tə·bəl) *adj.* Not to be escaped from or avoided; inevitable. [< L < *in-* not + *eluctabilis* resistible] —**in′e·luc′ta·bil′i·ty** *n.* —**in′e·luc′ta·bly** *adv.*

in·ept (in·ept′) *adj.* **1.** Not suitable or appropriate. **2.** Clumsy; awkward. [< L < *in-* not + *aptus* fit] —**in·ept′ly** *adv.* —**in·ept′ness** *n.*

in·ep·ti·tude (in·ep′tə·tōōd, ·tyōōd) *n.* **1.** The state or quality of being inept. **2.** An inept act or remark.

in·e·qual·i·ty (in′i·kwol′ə·tē) *n. pl.* **·ties 1.** The state of being unequal. **2.** An instance of this. **3.** Lack of evenness of proportion; variableness. **4.** Disparity of social position, opportunity, justice, etc. [< OF < L *inaequalitas*]

in·eq·ui·ta·ble (in·ek′wə·tə·bəl) *adj.* Not equitable; unfair. —**in·eq′ui·ta·bly** *adv.*

in·eq·ui·ty (in·ek′wə·tē) *n. pl.* **·ties 1.** Lack of equity; injustice. **2.** An unfair act or course of action.

in·e·rad·i·ca·ble (in′i·rad′ə·kə·bəl) *adj.* Not eradicable; impossible to remove or root out. —**in′e·rad′i·ca·bly** *adv.*

in·e·ras·a·ble (in′i·rā′sə·bəl) *adj.* Not erasable; impossible to erase or rub out. —**in′e·ras′a·bly** *adv.*

in·ert (in·ûrt′) *adj.* **1.** Lacking independent power to move or to resist applied force. **2.** Disinclined to move or act; sluggish. **3.** *Chem.* Devoid of active properties. [< L < *in-* not + *ars* art] —**in·ert′ly** *adv.* —**in·ert′ness** *n.*

in·er·tia (in·ûr′shə) *n.* **1.** The state of being inert; inactivity. **2.** *Physics* The property of matter by virtue of which any physical body persists in its state of rest or of uniform motion until acted upon by some external force. [< L, idleness] —**in·er′tial** *adj.*

in·es·cap·a·ble (in′ə·skā′pə·bəl) *adj.* Impossible to escape; unavoidable. —**in′es·cap′a·bly** *adv.*

in·es·ti·ma·ble (in·es′tə·mə·bəl) *adj.* **1.** Not to be estimated. **2.** Having great value. —**in·es′ti·ma·bly** *adv.*

in·ev·i·ta·ble (in·ev′ə·tə·bəl) *adj.* That cannot be avoided or prevented from happening. —*n.* Something inevitable. [< L < *in-* not + *evitare* to avoid] —**in·ev′i·ta·bil′i·ty, in·ev′i·ta·ble·ness** *n.* —**in·ev′i·ta·bly** *adv.*

in·ex·act (in′ig·zakt′) *adj.* Not exact; not completely accurate or true. —**in′ex·act′ly** *adv.* —**in′ex·act′ness** *n.*

in·ex·cus·a·ble (in′ik·skyōō′zə·bəl) *adj.* Not excusable; impossible to excuse or justify. —**in′ex·cus′a·bil′i·ty, in′ex·cus′a·ble·ness** *n.* —**in′ex·cus′a·bly** *adv.*

in·ex·haust·i·ble (in′ig·zôs′tə·bəl) *adj.* **1.** Incapable of being exhausted or used up. **2.** Incapable of fatigue; tireless. —**in′ex·haust′i·bil′i·ty, in′ex·haust′i·ble·ness** *n.* —**in′ex·haust′i·bly** *adv.*

in·ex·o·ra·ble (in·ek′sər·ə·bəl) *adj.* **1.** Not to be moved by entreaty or persuasion; unyielding. **2.** Unalterable; relentless. [< L *inexorabilis*] —**in·ex′o·ra·bil′i·ty, in·ex′o·ra·ble·ness** *n.* —**in·ex′o·ra·bly** *adv.*

in·ex·pe·di·ent (in′ik·spē′dē·ənt) *adj.* Not expedient; unsuited to a particular purpose; inadvisable. —**in′ex·pe′di·ence, in′ex·pe′di·en·cy** *n.* —**in′ex·pe′di·ent·ly** *adv.*

in·ex·pen·sive (in′ik·spen′siv) *adj.* Not expensive; costing little. —**in′ex·pen′sive·ly** *adv.* —**in′ex·pen′sive·ness** *n.*

in·ex·pe·ri·ence (in′ik·spir′ē·əns) *n.* Lack of experience.

in·ex·pe·ri·enced (in′ik·spir′ē·ənst) *adj.* Not experienced.

in·ex·pert (in·ek′spûrt) *adj.* Not expert; unskilled; inept. —**in·ex′pert·ly** *adv.* —**in·ex′pert·ness** *n.*

in·ex·pi·a·ble (in·ek′spē·ə·bəl) *adj.* Incapable of being expiated or atoned for; unpardonable.

in·ex·pli·ca·ble (in·eks′pli·kə·bəl, in′iks·plik′ə·bəl) *adj.* Not explicable; impossible to explain. —**in·ex′pli·ca·bil′i·ty, in·ex′pli·ca·ble·ness** *n.* —**in·ex′pli·ca·bly** *adv.*

in·ex·press·i·ble (in′ik·spres′ə·bəl) *adj.* Incapable of being expressed or put into words. —**in′ex·press′i·bil′i·ty, in′ex·press′i·ble·ness** *n.* —**in′ex·press′i·bly** *adv.*

in·ex·tin·guish·a·ble (in′ik·sting′gwish·ə·bəl) *adj.* Incapable of being extinguished; unquenchable. —**in′ex·tin′guish·a·ble·ness** *n.* —**in′ex·tin′guish·a·bly** *adv.*

in ex·tre·mis (in·iks·trē′mis) *Latin* At the point of death.

in·ex·tri·ca·ble (in·eks′tri·kə·bəl) *adj.* **1.** Impossible to extricate oneself from. **2.** Impossible to disentangle or undo. **3.** Too intricate to be solved. —**in·ex′tri·ca·bil′i·ty, in·ex′tri·ca·ble·ness** *n.* —**in·ex′tri·ca·bly** *adv.*

in·fal·li·ble (in·fal′ə·bəl) *adj.* **1.** Exempt from fallacy or error of judgment. **2.** Not liable to fail; sure: an *infallible* remedy. **3.** In Roman Catholic doctrine, incapable of error in matters of faith and morals. —*n.* One who or that which is infallible. —**in·fal′li·bil′i·ty** *n.* —**in·fal′li·bly** *adv.*

in·fa·mous (in′fə·məs) *adj.* **1.** Having a vile reputation. **2.** Deserving or producing infamy; odious. [< Med.L < L < *in-* not + *fama* fame] —**in′fa·mous·ly** *adv.* —**in′fa·mous·ness** *n.*

in·fa·my (in′fə·mē) *n. pl.* **·mies 1.** Dishonor; disgrace. **2.** The state of being infamous. **3.** An infamous act.

in·fan·cy (in′fən·sē) *n. pl.* **·cies 1.** The state or period of being an infant; babyhood. **2.** The beginnings of anything. **3.** *Law* The years before attaining the age of legal majority.

in·fant (in′fənt) *n.* **1.** A child in the earliest stages of life; baby. **2.** *Law* One who has not attained the age of legal majority, usu. 21; a minor. —*adj.* **1.** Of or typical of infancy or infants. **2.** Beginning to exist or develop. [< OF < L < *in-* not + *fari* to speak.] —**in′fant·hood** *n.*

in·fan·ta (in·fän′tə) *n.* A daughter of a Spanish or Portuguese king. [< Sp., infant (fem.)]

in·fan·te (in·fän′tā) *n.* A son, except the eldest, of a Spanish or Portuguese king. [< Sp., infant (masc.)]

in·fan·ti·cide (in-fan′tə-sīd) n. 1. The killing of an infant, esp. at birth. 2. One who has killed an infant. [< F < LL < L *infans* child + *caedere* to kill]

in·fan·tile (in′fən-tīl, -til) adj. 1. Of infancy or infants. 2. Like or characteristic of infancy or infants; babyish. 3. Being at the earliest stage of development. Also **in′fan·tine** (-tīn, -tin). [< LL *infantilis*]

infantile paralysis Poliomyelitis.

in·fan·til·ism (in-fan′tə-liz-em) n. Abnormal persistence of infantile mental and physical characteristics into adult life.

in·fan·try (in′fən-trē) n. pl. ·tries Soldiers, units, or a branch of an army trained and equipped to fight on foot. [< F < Ital. < L *infans, infantis* child]

in·fan·try·man (in′fən-trē-mən) n. pl. ·men (-mən) A soldier of the infantry.

in·fat·u·ate (v. in-fach′ōō-āt; for adj., also in-fach′ōō-it) v.t. ·at·ed, ·at·ing 1. To inspire with a foolish and unreasoning love or passion. 2. To make foolish or fatuous. —adj. Infatuated. [< L *infatuare* to make a fool of] —in·fat′u·a′tion n.

in·fat·u·at·ed (in-fach′ōō-ā-tid) adj. 1. Possessed by a foolish passion, esp. for another person. 2. Made fatuous. —in·fat′u·at·ed·ly adv.

in·fect (in-fekt′) v.t. 1. To affect or infuse with disease-producing organisms, as a wound. 2. To cause (a person, etc.) to contract a communicable disease. 3. To contaminate with impurities; pollute. 4. To affect or inspire, as with attitudes or beliefs, esp. harmfully. [< L *inficere* to dip into, stain] —in·fec′tor or in·fect′er n.

in·fec·tion (in-fek′shən) n. 1. An injurious invasion of body tissue by disease-producing organisms. 2. A disease or other harmful condition resulting from an invasion by injurious organisms. 3. The communication or transference of a disease, idea, mood, etc. [< OF]

in·fec·tious (in-fek′shəs) adj. 1. Liable to produce infection. 2. Denoting diseases communicable by infection. 3. Tending to excite similar reactions: *infectious* laughter. —in·fec′tious·ly adv. —in·fec′tious·ness n.

infectious mononucleosis Pathol. An acute communicable disease marked by fever, sore throat, a swelling of the lymph nodes and an increase in mononuclear cells.

in·fec·tive (in-fek′tiv) adj. Liable to produce infection.

in·fe·lic·i·tous (in′fə-lis′ə-təs) adj. Not felicitous or suitable. —in′fe·lic′i·tous·ly adv. —in′fe·lic′i·tous·ness n.

in·fe·lic·i·ty (in′fə-lis′ə-tē) n. pl. ·ties 1. The state of being infelicitous. 2. That which is infelicitous, as an inappropriate remark, etc. [< L *infelicitas*]

in·fer (in-fûr′) v. ·ferred, ·fer·ring v.t. 1. To derive by reasoning; conclude or accept from evidence or premises. 2. To involve or imply as a conclusion: said of facts, statements, etc. —v.i. 3. To draw an inference. [< L < *in-* in + *ferre* to bring, carry] —in·fer′a·ble adj. —in·fer′a·bly adv.

◆ **infer, imply** *Infer* means to derive or conclude by reasoning: I *inferred* from the noise that you were at home. *Imply* means to suggest implicitly something that might be *inferred* by an observer: The noise *implied* that you were at home. *Infer* stresses the use of reason, whereas *imply*, the more general term, may be applied also to conclusions that are suggested or presumed.

in·fer·ence (in′fər-əns) n. 1. That which is inferred; a conclusion. 2. The act or process of inferring.

in·fer·en·tial (in′fə-ren′shəl) adj. Deducible by inference. —in′fer·en′tial·ly adv.

in·fe·ri·or (in-fir′ē-ər) adj. 1. Lower in quality, worth, or adequacy. 2. Lower in rank or importance. 3. Mediocre; ordinary: an *inferior* wine. 4. Astron. a Between the earth and the sun: an *inferior* planet. b Below the horizon. —n. A person inferior in rank or in attainments. [< L, lower]

in·fe·ri·or·i·ty (in-fir′ē-ôr′ə-tē, -or′-) n. pl. ·ties The state or quality of being inferior.

in·fer·nal (in-fûr′nəl) adj. 1. Of or pertaining to the mythological world of the dead, or to hell. 2. Diabolical; hellish. 3. *Informal* Damnable; hateful. [< OF < L *infernus* situated below] —in·fer′nal·ly adv.

in·fer·no (in-fûr′nō) n. pl. ·nos 1. The infernal regions; hell. 2. Any place comparable to hell. [< Ital.]

in·fer·tile (in-fûr′til) adj. Not fertile or productive; sterile.

in·fest (in-fest′) v.t. To overrun or occur in large numbers so as to be annoying or dangerous. [< MF *infester* or L *infestare* to assail] —in′fes·ta′tion n. —in·fest′er n.

in·fi·del (in′fi-dəl) n. 1. One who rejects all religious belief; unbeliever. 2. Among Christians, one who is not a Christian. 3. Among Moslems, one who is not a Moslem. —adj. 1. Having no religious belief. 2. Rejecting a particular faith, esp. Christianity or Islam. 3. Of or relating to infidels or unbelief. [< MF < L < *in-* not + *fidelis* faithful]

in·fi·del·i·ty (in′fi-del′ə-tē) n. pl. ·ties 1. Lack of fidelity. 2. A disloyal act. 3. Adultery. 4. Lack of belief in a particular religion, esp. Christianity or Islam.

in·field (in′fēld′) n. In baseball: a The space within the

base lines of the field, and some adjacent space beyond the second and third base lines. b The infielders collectively.

in·field·er (in′fēld′ər) n. In baseball, either the first baseman, second baseman, shortstop, or third baseman, or the pitcher or catcher considered as a fielder.

in·fil·trate (in-fil′trāt, in′fil-trāt) v. ·trat·ed, ·trat·ing v.t. 1. To gain or seek control of (an organization, etc.) by secretly occupying positions of power. 2. To cause (a liquid or gas) to pass into or through pores. 3. To filter or move through or into. —v.i. 4. To pass into or through a substance. —n. That which infiltrates. —in′fil·tra′tion n.

in·fi·nite (in′fə-nit) adj. 1. Having no boundaries or limits; extending without end. 2. Very numerous or great; vast. 3. All-embracing; perfect: *infinite* wisdom. 4. Math. Of or designating a quantity conceived as always exceeding any other quantity in value. —n. 1. That which is infinite. 2. Math. An infinite quantity. —the Infinite God. [< OF < L < *in-* not + *finitus* finite] —in′fi·nite·ly adv. —in′fi·nite·ness n.

—Syn. (adj.) 1. *Infinite* is applied to those things which we believe to have no bounds. *Measureless, numberless, countless,* and *innumerable* often mean merely vast in dimension or number. *Eternal* means *infinite* in time, but is also used to mean continued for a very long time.

in·fin·i·tes·i·mal (in′fin-ə-tes′ə-məl) adj. 1. Infinitely small. 2. So small as to be incalculable. —n. An infinitesimal quantity. [< NL < *infinitus* infinite + *-esimus* (after *centesimus* hundredth)] —in′fin·i·tes′i·mal·ly adv.

in·fin·i·tive (in-fin′ə-tiv) Gram. adj. 1. Without limitation of person or number. 2. Of or pertaining to the infinitive. —n. A verb form generally used either as the principal verb of a verb phrase, most often without *to,* or as a noun, most often with *to.* [< Med.L *infinitivus*]

in·fin·i·tude (in-fin′ə-tōōd, -tyōōd) n. 1. The quality of being infinite or boundless. 2. An unlimited quantity.

in·fin·i·ty (in-fin′ə-tē) n. pl. ·ties 1. The state of being infinite. 2. Something considered infinite, as space or time. 3. A very large amount or number. [< OF < L < *in-* not + *finitus* finite]

in·firm (in-fûrm′) adj. 1. Feeble or weak, as from old age. 2. Lacking firmness of purpose. [< OF < L *infirmus* < *in-* not + *firmus* firm] —in·firm′ly adv. —in·firm′ness n.

in·fir·ma·ry (in-fûr′mər-ē) n. pl. ·ries A place for the treatment of the sick, esp. in a school, etc. [< Med.L < L *infirmus* infirm, indisposed]

in·fir·mi·ty (in-fûr′mə-tē) n. pl. ·ties 1. The state of being infirm. 2. A physical or mental defect.

in·fix (in-fiks′) v.t. 1. To set firmly or insert in. 2. To implant (an idea, fact, etc.) in the mind. 3. Gram. To insert (an infix) within a word. —n. Gram. A modifying addition inserted in the body of a word. —in·fix′ion n.

in·flame (in-flām′) v. ·flamed, ·flam·ing v.t. 1. To set on fire; kindle. 2. To excite to violent emotion or activity. 3. To increase or make more intense, as anger, passion, etc. 4. To produce heat, swelling, and soreness in. —v.i. 5. To catch fire. 6. To become excited or aroused. 7. To become inflamed. [< OF < L < *in-* in + *flamma* flame]

in·flam·ma·ble (in-flam′ə-bəl) adj. 1. Flammable. 2. Easily excited or aroused. —n. A flammable thing or substance. —in·flam′ma·bil′i·ty, in·flam′ma·ble·ness n. —in·flam′ma·bly adv.

in·flam·ma·tion (in′flə-mā′shən) n. 1. The act of inflaming, or the state of being inflamed. 2. Pathol. A diseased condition characterized by redness, swelling, and pain.

in·flam·ma·to·ry (in-flam′ə-tôr′ē, -tō′rē) adj. 1. Tending to arouse excitement, anger, etc. 2. Med. Characterized by or causing inflammation.

in·flat·a·ble (in-flā′tə-bəl) adj. Capable of being inflated.

in·flate (in-flāt′) v. ·flat·ed, ·flat·ing v.t. 1. To cause to expand by filling with or as with gas or air. 2. To enlarge excessively; puff up: to *inflate* one's ego. 3. Econ. To increase (prices, credit, etc.) in excess of usual or prior levels. —v.i. 4. To become inflated. [< L < *in-* in + *flare* to blow] —in·flat′er or in·flat′or n.

in·fla·tion (in-flā′shən) n. 1. The act of inflating, or the state of being inflated. 2. Econ. An unstable rise in price levels due to an increase in currency and a mounting demand for goods. —in·fla′tion·ar′y adj.

in·flect (in-flekt′) v.t. 1. To vary the tone or pitch of (the voice) modulate. 2. To turn from a straight or usual course; bend. 3. Gram. To give the inflections of (a word) by conjugating or declining. [< L < *in-* in + *flectere* to bend]

in·flec·tion (in-flek′shən) n. 1. The act of inflecting, or the state of being inflected. 2. An angle or bend. 3. Modulation of the voice. 4. Gram. a A change in form undergone by words to express grammatical and syntactical relations, as of case, number, tense, etc. The inflection of nouns, pronouns, and adjectives is called *declension;* that of verbs, *conjugation.* b An inflected form. —in·flec′tion·al adj.

in·flex·i·ble (in-flek′sə-bəl) adj. 1. Incapable of being bent; rigid. 2. Unyielding; stubborn. 3. That cannot be altered;

fixed: the *inflexible* laws of nature. [< L *inflexibilis*] — **in·flex'i·bil'i·ty, in·flex'i·ble·ness** *n.* — **in·flex'i·bly** *adv.*

in·flict (in-flikt') *v.t.* 1. To deal; lay on: to *inflict* a blow. 2. To impose. [< L < *in-* on + *fligere* to strike] — **in·flict'er** or **in·flic'tor** *n.* — **in·flic'tive** *adj.*

in·flic·tion (in-flik'shən) *n.* 1. The act of inflicting. 2. That which is inflicted, as pain, punishment, etc.

in·flo·res·cence (in'flə-res'əns) *n.* 1. A flowering; flourishing. 2. *Bot.* **a** The mode of arrangement of flowers in relation to the stem or axis. **b** A cluster of flowers. **c** A single flower. [< NL < LL *inflorescere* to come into flower] — **in'flo·res'cent** *adj.*

in·flow (in'flō') *n.* 1. The act of flowing in. 2. That which flows in.

in·flu·ence (in'flōō-əns) *n.* 1. The power of persons or things to produce effects on others, esp. by indirect means. 2. Power resulting from social position, wealth, etc. 3. One who or that which possesses the power to affect others. — *v.t.* **·enced, ·enc·ing** 1. To produce an effect upon the actions or thought of. 2. To have an effect upon. [< OF < LL < L < *in-* in + *fluere* to flow] — **in'flu·enc·er** *n.*

in·flu·en·tial (in'flōō-en'shəl) *adj.* 1. Having or exercising influence. 2. Wielding influence. — **in'flu·en'tial·ly** *adv.*

in·flu·en·za (in'flōō-en'zə) *n.* *Pathol.* A contagious, infectious virus disease characterized by respiratory inflammation and fever: also called *flu, grip, grippe*. [< Ital., (illness due to) the influence (of the stars)]

in·flux (in'fluks') *n.* 1. A flowing in, as of a fluid. 2. A continuous coming, as of people. 3. The mouth of a river. [< MF < LL *influere* to flow in]

in·fold (in-fōld') *v.t.* 1. To wrap in folds. 2. To embrace. 3. To turn or fold inward. Also spelled *enfold*.

in·form (in-fôrm') *v.t.* 1. To notify. 2. To give character to: with *with* or *by.* — *v.i.* 3. To disclose information. [< OF < L *informare* to give form to]

in·for·mal (in-fôr'məl) *adj.* 1. Not in the usual or prescribed form; unofficial. 2. Without formality; relaxed; casual. 3. Not requiring formal attire. 4. Characteristic of or suitable to the language of ordinary conversation or familiar writing. ◆ Informal language is widely used by educated people and is not to be confused with nonstandard usage or slang. — **in·for'mal·ly** *adv.*

in·for·mal·i·ty (in'fôr·mal'ə·tē) *n. pl.* **·ties** 1. The state of being informal. 2. An informal act or proceeding.

in·form·ant (in-fôr'mənt) *n.* One who gives information.

in·for·ma·tion (in'fər-mā'shən) *n.* 1. Knowledge acquired or derived; facts. 2. Timely knowledge; news. 3. The act of informing, or the state of being informed. 4. A service or facility for providing facts: Call *information.* [< F < L *informatio, -onis*] — **in'for·ma'tion·al** *adj.*

in·form·a·tive (in-fôr'mə·tiv) *adj.* Affording information; instructive. Also **in·form'a·to·ry** (-tôr'ē, -tō'rē).

in·formed (in-fôrmd') *adj.* Having a high degree of knowledge, information, or education.

in·form·er (in-fôr'mər) *n.* 1. One who informs against others; stool pigeon; tattletale. 2. An informant.

in·fra- *prefix* Below; beneath; on the lower part. [< L]

in·frac·tion (in-frak'shən) *n.* The act of breaking or violating (a pledge, law, etc.); infringement. [< L *infractio, -onis*]

in·fran·gi·ble (in-fran'jə·bəl) *adj.* 1. Not breakable or capable of being broken into parts. 2. Inviolable. — **in·fran'gi·bil'i·ty, in·fran'gi·ble·ness** *n.* — **in·fran'gi·bly** *adv.*

in·fra·red (in'frə·red') *adj. Physics* Having a wavelength greater than that of visible red light, and radiating heat.

in·fre·quent (in-frē'kwənt) *adj.* Present or occurring at widely separated intervals; uncommon. — **in·fre'quence** *n.*, **in·fre'quen·cy** *n.* — **in·fre'quent·ly** *adv.*

in·fringe (in-frinj') *v.t.* **fringed, fring·ing** To break or disregard the terms of, as a law; violate. — **to infringe on** (or **upon**) To transgress or trespass on rights or privileges. [< L < *in-* in + *frangere* to break] — **in·fring'er** *n.*

in·fringe·ment (in-frinj'mənt) *n.* 1. The act of infringing. 2. Any violation of a right, privilege, regulation, etc.

in·fu·ri·ate (*v.* in-fyŏŏr'ē·āt) *v.t.* **·at·ed, ·at·ing** To make furious or very angry; enrage. [< Med.L *infuriare* to madden] — **in·fu'ri·ate·ly** *adv.* — **in·fu'ri·at'ing·ly** *adv.*

in·fuse (in-fyŏōz') *v.t.* **·fused, ·fus·ing** 1. To instill or inculcate, as principles. 2. To inspire; imbue: with *with.* 3. To pour in. [< L < *in-* in + *fundere* to pour] — **in·fus'er** *n.*

in·fus·i·ble[1] (in-fyŏō'zə·bəl) *adj.* Incapable of or resisting fusion or melting. — **in·fus'i·bil'i·ty, in·fus'i·ble·ness** *n.*

in·fus·i·ble[2] (in-fyŏō'zə·bəl) *adj.* Capable of being infused or poured in. — **in·fus'i·bil'i·ty, in·fus'i·ble·ness** *n.*

in·fu·sion (in-fyŏō'zhən) *n.* 1. The act of infusing. 2. That which is infused. 3. A liquid extract obtained by soaking a substance in water. [< OF < L *infusio, -onis*]

in·fu·so·ri·an (in'fyŏō·sôr'ē·ən, -sō'rē-) *n.* One of a class of one-celled animals. [< NL < L *infundere* to pour into]

-ing[1] *suffix* 1. The act or art of doing the action expressed in the root verb: *hunting.* 2. The product or result of an action: a *painting.* 3. Material for: *flooring.* 4. That which performs the action of the root verb: a *covering.* ◆ In formal writing when the *-ing* form of the verb (see *gerund*) is modified by a noun or pronoun the modifier appears in the possessive. Thus, "We objected to *his* leaving" is preferred to "We objected to *him* leaving." [OE, *-ung, -ing*]

-ing[2] *suffix* Used in the present participle of verbs and in participial adjectives: He is *talking*; an *eating* apple. [ME < OE *-ende*]

-ing[3] *suffix of nouns* 1. One having the quality of: *sweeting.* 2. Descendant of: *Browning.* 3. Small; little. [OE]

in·gen·ious (in·jēn'yəs) *adj.* 1. Showing ingenuity; cleverly conceived. 2. Having inventive and adaptive ability; clever. [< MF < L < *in-* in + *gignere* to beget] — **in·gen'ious·ly** *adv.* — **in·gen'ious·ness** *n.*

in·gé·nue (an'zhə·nōō', *Fr.* añ·zhā·nü') *n. pl.* **·nues** (-nōōz', *Fr.* -nü') The role of a young girl in a play, film, etc.; also, an actress who plays such roles. [< F]

in·ge·nu·i·ty (in'jə·nōō'ə·tē, -nyōō'-) *n. pl.* **·ties** 1. Imaginative resources; inventiveness. 2. Originality of design or execution. 3. A cleverly conceived act, device, etc.

in·gen·u·ous (in·jen'yŏō·əs) *adj.* 1. Straightforward; candid; frank. 2. Innocent and simple; naive. [< L *ingenuus* inborn, natural < *in-* in + *genus* birth, origin] — **in·gen'u·ous·ly** *adv.* — **in·gen'u·ous·ness** *n.*

in·gest (in·jest') *v.t.* To take or put (food, etc.) into the body by or as by swallowing. [< L *ingerere* < *in-* in + *gerere* to carry] — **in·ges'tion** *n.* — **in·ges'tive** *adj.*

in·glo·ri·ous (in·glôr'ē·əs, -glō'rē-) *adj.* Not reflecting honor or courage; disgraceful. — **in·glo'ri·ous·ly** *adv.*

in·go·ing (in'gō'ing) *adj.* Entering; going in.

in·got (ing'gət) *n.* A mass of cast metal from the crucible or mold. [? ME < OE *in-* in + *geotan* to pour]

in·grain (*v.* in·grān') *v.t.* To impress firmly on the mind.

in·grained (in·grānd') *adj.* 1. Worked into the inmost texture; deep-rooted. 2. Thorough; inveterate.

in·grate (in'grāt) *n.* An ungrateful person. [< OF < L < *in-* not + *gratus* pleasing]

in·gra·ti·ate (in·grā'shē·āt) *v.t.* **·at·ed, ·at·ing** To bring (oneself) deliberately into the favor or confidence of others. — **in·gra'ti·at'ing·ly** *adv.* — **in·gra'ti·a'tion** *n.* — **in·gra'ti·a·to·ry** (-ə·tôr'ē, -tō'rē) *adj.* [< L *in-* in + *gratia* favor]

in·grat·i·tude (in·grat'ə·tōōd, -tyōōd) *n.* Lack of gratitude; insensibility to kindness; thanklessness.

in·gre·di·ent (in·grē'dē·ənt) *n.* 1. Anything that enters into the composition of a mixture. 2. A component of anything. [< F < L < *in-* in + *gradi* to walk]

in·gress (in'gres) *n.* 1. A going in, as into a building. Also **in·gres·sion** (in·gresh'ən). 2. A place of entrance. [< L *ingredi* to enter] — **in·gres'sive** *adj.*

in-group (in'grōōp') *n. Sociol.* Any group with strong feelings of mutual cohesiveness and identification.

in·grow·ing (in'grō'ing) *adj.* 1. Growing into the flesh: an *ingrowing* hair. 2. Growing within or into.

in·grown (in'grōn') *adj.* 1. Grown into the flesh, as a toenail. 2. Grown within; innate: *ingrown* vice.

in·gui·nal (ing'gwə·nəl) *adj. Anat.* Of, pertaining to, or located in the groin. [< L *inguen, -inis* groin]

inguino- *combining form* In or related to the groin. Also, before vowels, **inguin-.** [< L *inguen, -inis* groin]

in·hab·it (in·hab'it) *v.t.* To live in; occupy as a home. [< OF < L < *in-* in + *habitare* to dwell] — **in·hab'it·a·bil'i·ty** *n.* — **in·hab'it·a·ble** *adj.* — **in·hab'it·er** *n.* — **in·hab'i·ta'tion** *n.*

in·hab·i·tant (in·hab'ə·tənt) *n.* One who or that which dwells permanently, as distinguished from a visitor.

in·ha·la·tion (in'hə·lā'shən) *n.* 1. The act of inhaling. 2. That which is inhaled.

in·ha·la·tor in'hə·lā'tər) *n.* A device for enabling one to inhale air, medicinal vapors, anesthetics, etc.

in·hale (in·hāl') *v.* **·haled, ·hal·ing** *v.t.* 1. To draw into the lungs, as breath, tobacco smoke, etc.; breathe in. — *v.i.* 2. To draw breath, tobacco smoke, etc., into the lungs. Opposed to *exhale.* [< L < *in-* in + *halare* to breathe]

in·hal·er (in·hāl'ər) *n.* 1. One who inhales. 2. *Med.* An inhalator. 3. A respirator.

in·har·mo·ni·ous (in'här·mō'nē·əs) *adj.* Lacking harmony; discordant. Also **in'har·mon'ic** (-mon'ik), **in'har·mon'i·cal.** — **in'har·mo'ni·ous·ly** *adv.* — **in'har·mo'ni·ous·ness** *n.*

in·here (in·hir') *v.i.* **·hered, ·her·ing** To be a permanent or essential part: with *in.* [< L < *in-* to + *haerere* to stick] — **in·her'ence, in·her'en·cy** *n.*

in·her·ent (in·hir'ənt, -her'-) *adj.* Forming an essential element or quality of something. — **in·her'ent·ly** *adv.*

in·her·it (in·her'it) *v.t.* 1. To receive (property, title, etc.) by legal succession or will. 2. To derive (traits, qualities, etc.) from one's parents or ancestors. **3.** To receive from one's predecessors. — *v.i.* **4.** To take possession of an inheritance. [< OF < LL *inhereditare* to appoint an heir]

in·her·it·a·ble (in·her′ə·tə·bəl) *adj.* **1.** Capable of being inherited. **2.** Entitled to inherit. — **in·her′it·a·bil′i·ty, in·her′it·a·bly** *adv.*

in·her·i·tance (in·her′ə·təns) *n.* **1.** The act of inheriting. **2.** That which is legally transmissible to an heir; legacy. **3.** Derivation of qualities from one's forebears. **4.** A property, quality, etc., derived from predecessors. **5.** Hereditary right. [< OF *enheritance*]

inheritance tax A tax imposed on an inherited estate.

in·her·i·tor (in·her′ə·tər) *n.* An heir. — **in·her′i·tress** (-tris), **in·her′i·trix** (-triks) *n.fem.*

in·hib·it (in·hib′it) *v.t.* To restrain or check (an impulse, action, etc.) [< L < *in-* + *habere* to have, hold] — **in·hib′it·er** or **in·hib′i·tor** *n.* — **in·hib′it·a·ble** *adj.* — **in·hib′i·tive, in·hib′i·to·ry** (-tôr′ē, -tō′rē) *adj.*

in·hi·bi·tion (in′hi·bish′ən, in′i-) *n.* **1.** A checking or re. straining; esp., a self-imposed restriction on one's behavior. **2.** *Psychol.* The blocking of one impulse or by another.

in·hos·pi·ta·ble (in·hos′pi·tə·bəl, in′hos·pit′ə·bəl) *adj.* **1.** Not hospitable. **2.** Not affording shelter, comfort, etc. — **in·hos·pi·ta·ble·ness** (in·hos′pi·tə·bəl·nis, in′hos·pit′-) *n.* — **in·hos·pi·ta·bly** (in·hos′pi·tə·blē, in′hos·pit′-) *adv.* — **in·hos′pi·tal′i·ty** (-tal′ə·tē) *n.*

in·hu·man (in·hyōō′mən) *adj.* **1.** Not befitting human nature; bestial. **2.** Not of the ordinary human type.

in·hu·mane (in′hyōō·mān′) *adj.* Not humane; cruel.

in·hu·man·i·ty (in′hyōō·man′ə·tē) *n. pl.* **·ties** **1.** Lack of human or humane qualities. **2.** A cruel act, word, etc.

in·im·i·cal (in·im′i·kəl) *adj.* **1.** Characterized by harmful opposition; antagonistic. **2.** Behaving as an enemy; hostile. [< LL < L < *in-* not + *amicus* friend] — **in·im′i·cal′i·ty** (-kal′ə·tē) *n.* — **in·im′i·cal·ly** *adv.*

in·im·i·ta·ble (in·im′ə·tə·bəl) *adj.* Matchless; unique. — **in·im′i·ta·bil′i·ty, in·im′i·ta·ble·ness** — **in·im′i·ta·bly** *adv.*

in·iq·ui·tous (in·ik′wə·təs) *adj.* Characterized by iniquity; unjust. — **in·iq′ui·tous·ly** *adv.* — **in·iq′ui·tous·ness** *n.*

in·iq·ui·ty (in·ik′wə·tē) *n. pl.* **·ties** **1.** Grievous violation of right or justice; wickedness. **2.** A wrongful act; sin. [< OF < L < *in-* not + *aequus* equal]

in·i·tial (in·ish′əl) *adj.* **1.** Standing at the beginning. **2.** Of or pertaining to the beginning; first. — *n.* **1.** *pl.* The first letters of one's proper name. **2.** The first letter of a word, name, etc. — *v.t.* **·tialed** or **·tialled, ·tial·ing** or **·tial·ling** To mark or sign with initials. [< L *initialis* < *initium* beginning] — **in·i′tial·ly** *adv.*

Initial Teaching Alphabet An alphabet representing the sounds of English, used in teaching children to read: also called *Augmented Roman.* *Abbr. I.T.A.*

in·i·ti·ate (in·ish′ē·āt; *for adj. & n., also* in·ish′ē·it) *v.t.* **·at·ed, ·at·ing** **1.** To begin; commence; originate. **2.** To admit to membership in an organization, fraternity, cult, etc. **3.** To instruct in fundamentals. — *adj.* Initiated. — *n.* One who has been ritually admitted to an organization, cult, etc. [< L *initiare* to begin] — **in·i′ti·a·tor** *n.*

in·i·ti·a·tion (in·ish′ē·ā′shən) *n.* **1.** The act of initiating, or the state of being initiated. **2.** The rites admitting one to some position, society, knowledge, etc.

in·i·ti·a·tive (in·ish′ē·ə·tiv, -ē·ā′tiv, -ish′ə·tiv) *n.* **1.** The power or right to take the first step or the next step in some action. **2.** The action of commencing or originating. **3.** The spirit needed to originate action. **4.** In government: **a** The right or power to propose legislative measures. **b** The process by which the electorate acts to originate legislation. — **on one's own initiative** Without instruction or compulsion; freely. — *adj.* **1.** Of or pertaining to initiation. **2.** Serving to initiate. [< MF] — **in·i′ti·a·tive·ly** *adv.*

in·ject (in·jekt′) *v.t.* **1.** To drive (a fluid, drug, etc.) into a bodily cavity, blood vessel, etc. by means of a syringe, needle, etc. **2.** To introduce (some new element): with *into.* **3.** To throw in or introduce abruptly (a comment, etc.). [< L < *in-* + *jacere* to throw] — **in·jec′tion** *n.*

in·ju·di·cious (in′jōō·dish′əs) *adj.* Not judicious; imprudent. — **in′ju·di′cious·ly** *adv.* — **in′ju·di′cious·ness** *n.*

in·junc·tion (in·jungk′shən) *n.* **1.** The act of enjoining. **2.** An authoritative order. **3.** *Law* A judicial order requiring the party to do or refrain from some specified action. [< LL *injungere* to join to, enjoin] — **in·junc′tive** *adj.*

in·jure (in′jər) *v.t.* **·jured, ·jur·ing** **1.** To harm, damage, or impair, especially physically; hurt. **2.** To wrong or offend. [Back formation < INJURY] — **in′jur·er** *n.*

in·ju·ri·ous (in·jŏŏr′ē·əs) *adj.* **1.** Causing damage or hurt; harmful. **2.** Slanderous; abusive. — **in·ju′ri·ous·ly** *adv.* — **in·ju′ri·ous·ness** *n.*

in·ju·ry (in′jər·ē) *n. pl.* **·ries** **1.** Harm, damage, or grievous distress inflicted or suffered. **2.** A particular instance of such harm. [< OF < L < *in-* not + *jus, juris* right]

in·jus·tice (in·jus′tis) *n.* **1.** The fact or quality of being unjust. **2.** An unjust act; wrong. [< OF < L *injustus* unjust]

ink (ingk) *n.* **1.** Any of various colored substances used in a fluid or viscous consistency for writing, drawing, and printing. **2.** The dark fluid ejected by cuttlefish, etc. — *v.t.* To spread ink upon; stain or color with ink. [< OF < LL *encaustum* purple ink] — **ink′er** *n.*

ink·horn (ingk′hôrn′) *n.* A small container for ink.

inkhorn term A bookish, pedantic word.

ink·ling (ingk′ling) *n.* **1.** A slight suggestion or hint. **2.** A vague idea or notion. [ME < OE *inca* suspicion]

ink·stand (ingk′stand′) *n.* **1.** A rack or device for holding ink, pens, etc. **2.** An inkwell.

ink·well (ingk′wel′) *n.* A container for ink.

ink·y (ing′kē) *adj.* **ink·i·er, ink·i·est** **1.** Resembling ink in color; dark; black. **2.** Of, pertaining to, or containing ink. **3.** Smeared or stained with ink. — **ink′i·ness** *n.*

in·laid (in′lād, in·lād′) *adj.* **1.** Decorated with wood, ivory, or other material embedded flush with the surface. **2.** Inserted to form a flush embedded pattern.

in·land (in′lənd; *for n. and adv., also* in′land′) *adj.* **1.** Remote from the sea or the border. **2.** Pertaining to or located in the interior of a country: *inland* population. **3.** Not foreign; domestic: *inland* trade. — *n.* The interior of a country. — *adv.* In or towards the interior of a land.

in·land·er (in′lən·der, -land′ər) *n.* One who lives inland.

in·law (in′lô′) *n. Informal* A close relative by marriage.

in·lay (*v.* in·lā′, in′lā′; *n.* in′lā′) *v.t.* **·laid, ·lay·ing** **1.** To set or embed (ivory, gold, etc.) flush into a surface so as to form a pattern. **2.** To decorate by inserting such designs. — *n.* **1.** That which is inlaid. **2.** A pattern or design so produced. **3.** *Dent.* A filling for a tooth. — **in′lay·er** *n.*

in·let (*n.* in′let, -lit; *v.* in·let′) *n.* **1.** A relatively narrow channel of water: as: **a** A stream or bay leading into land. **b** A passage between nearby islands, floes, etc. **c** An entry from one body of water into another. **2.** An opening.

in lo·co pa·ren·tis (in lō′kō pə·ren′tis) *Latin* In the place of a parent.

in·mate (in′māt′) *n.* **1.** One who is lodged or confined in a prison, asylum, hospital, etc. **2.** An inhabitant. **3.** One who dwells with another or others. [? < INN + MATE]

in me·di·as res (in mē′dē·əs rēz) *Latin* In the midst of things; in the middle of events and not at the beginning.

in me·mo·ri·am (in mə·môr′ē·əm, -mō′rē) *Latin* In memory (of); as a memorial (to).

in·most (in′mōst′, -məst) *adj.* **1.** Located farthest from the outside. **2.** Most private or intimate. [OE *innemest*]

inn (in) *n.* A hotel, etc., where travelers may obtain meals or lodging. [OE *inn* room, house]

in·nards (in′ərdz) *n.pl. Dial. & Informal* The internal organs or parts of the body, a machine, etc.; insides.

in·nate (i·nāt′, in′āt) *adj.* Inherent in one's nature; inborn; not acquired. [< L *in-* + *nasci* to be born] — **in·nate′ly** *adv.* — **in·nate′ness** *n.*

in·ner (in′ər) *adj.* **1.** Located or occurring farther inside; internal; interior. **2.** Pertaining to the mind or spirit; subjective. **3.** More obscure; hidden; esoteric. [OE *innera*, compar. of *inne* in (adv.)] — **in′ner·ly** *adv.* — **in′ner·ness** *n.*

inner city A central part of a large city, usu. characterized by poverty and often populated by minority groups.

in·ner·most (in′ər·mōst′) *adj.* Inmost; farthest within.

inner tube A flexible, inflatable tube, usu. of rubber, used inside a pneumatic tire.

in·ning (in′ing) *n.* **1.** In baseball, a division of the game during which each team has a turn to bat. **2.** *pl.* In cricket, the period during which one side bats. **3.** *Often pl.* A chance for action. [OE *innung*, gerund of *innian* to put in]

inn·keep·er (in′kē′pər) *n.* The proprietor or host of an inn.

in·no·cence (in′ə·səns) *n.* The fact of being innocent.

in·no·cent (in′ə·sənt) *adj.* **1.** Not tainted with sin, evil, or moral wrong; pure. **2.** Free from blame or guilt, especially legally. **3.** Not tending to harm or injure: *innocent* pastimes. **4.** Not maliciously intended: an *innocent* lie. **5.** Lacking in worldly knowledge; naive. **6.** Devoid of, entirely lacking in: with *of: innocent* of grammar. — *n.* **1.** One who is free from evil or sin. **2.** A simple or unsuspecting person. [< OF < L < *in-* not + *nocere* to harm] — **in′no·cent·ly** *adv.*

in·noc·u·ous (i·nok′yōō·əs) *adj.* Having no harmful qualities or effects; harmless. [< L < *in-* not + *nocuus* harmful] — **in·noc′u·ous·ly** *adv.* — **in·noc′u·ous·ness** *n.*

in·nom·i·nate bone (i·nom′ə·nit) *Anat.* One of two large, irregular bones that form the sides of the pelvis.

in·no·vate (in′ə·vāt) *v.* **·vat·ed, ·vat·ing** *v.t.* **1.** To introduce or bring in (something new). — *v.i.* **2.** To bring in new ideas, methods, etc. [< L *in-* in + *novare* to make new] — **in′no·va′tive** *adj.* — **in′no·va′tor** *n.*

in·no·va·tion (in′ə·vā′shən) *n.* **1.** Something newly introduced. **2.** The act of introducing something new. — **in′no·va′tion·al** *adj.* — **in′no·va′tion·ist** *n.*

in·nu·en·do (in′yōō·en′dō) *n. pl.* **·does** An oblique comment, hint, or suggestion, usu. derogatory. [< L < *in-* to + *-nuere* to nod]

in·nu·mer·a·ble (i·nōō′mər·ə·bəl, i·nyōō′-) *adj.* Too numerous to be counted; numberless. Also **in·nu′mer·ous.** — **Syn.** See INFINITE. — **in·nu′mer·a·bil′i·ty, in·nu′mer·a·ble·ness** *n.* — **in·nu′mer·a·bly** *adv.*

in·oc·u·late (in·ok′yə·lāt) *v.* **·lat·ed, ·lat·ing** *v.t.* **1.** To communicate a mild form of a disease to (a person, animal, etc.) so as to produce immunity; also, to implant (a disease, bacteria, etc.). **2.** To inject immunizing serums, vaccines, etc. into. **3.** To implant ideas, opinions, etc., in the mind of. — *v.i.* **4.** To perform inoculation. [< L *inoculare* to put an eye or bud into] — **in·oc′u·la′tion** *n.* — **in·oc′u·la′tive** (-lā′tiv) *adj.* — **in·oc′u·la′tor** (-lā′tər) *n.*

in·of·fen·sive (in′ə·fen′siv) *adj.* Giving no offense; innocuous. — **in′of·fen′sive·ly** *adv.* — **in′of·fen′sive·ness** *n.*

in·op·er·a·ble (in·op′ər·ə·bəl) *adj.* **1.** Incapable of being cured or improved by surgical operation: *inoperable cancer.* **2.** Not practicable; unworkable. — **in·op′er·a·bil′i·ty, in·op′er·a·ble·ness** *n.* — **in·op′er·a·bly** *adv.*

in·op·er·a·tive (in·op′ər·ə·tiv) *adj.* **1.** Not functioning. **2.** Not effectual or in effect. — **in·op′er·a·tive·ness** *n.*

in·op·por·tune (in·op′ər·tōōn′, -tyōōn′) *adj.* Untimely or inappropriate; unsuitable. — **in·op′por·tune′ly** *adv.*

in·or·di·nate (in·ôr′də·nit) *adj.* **1.** Exceeding proper limits; immoderate; excessive. **2.** Unrestrained: *inordinate passion.* — **in·or′di·na·cy** (-nə·sē), **in·or′di·nate·ness** *n.* — **in·or′di·nate·ly** *adv.*

in·or·gan·ic (in′ôr·gan′ik) *adj.* **1.** Not having the organized structure of animal or vegetable life; not living; inanimate. **2.** Not characterized by life processes. **3.** *Chem.* Of, pertaining to, or designating the branch of chemistry dealing with compounds lacking carbon or containing it only in the form of carbonates, carbides, and most cyanides.

in·pa·tient (in′pā′shənt) *n.* A patient who is lodged and fed as well as medically treated in a hospital, clinic, or the like.

in·put (in′pŏŏt′) *n.* **1.** The amount of energy delivered to a machine, storage battery, etc. **2.** *Electr.* The voltage, current, power, etc., delivered to a circuit. **3.** *Electronics* Information placed in an electronic computer for later use.

in·quest (in′kwest) *n.* **1.** A legal investigation into a special matter; esp., one undertaken before a jury or by a coroner. **2.** The body of men chosen to make such an inquiry; also, its findings. [See INQUIRE.]

in·qui·e·tude (in·kwī′ə·tōōd, -tyōōd) *n.* **1.** A state of restlessness; uneasiness. **2.** *pl.* Anxieties; disquieting thoughts. — **in·qui′et** *adj.* — **in·qui′et·ly** *adv.*

in·quire (in·kwīr′) *v.* **·quired, ·quir·ing** *v.i.* **1.** To seek information by asking questions; ask. **2.** To make an investigation: with *into.* — *v.t.* **3.** To ask information about: They *inquired* the way. Also spelled *enquire.* — **Syn.** See ASK. [< OF < L < *in-* into + *quaerere* to seek] — **in·quir′er** *n.* — **in·quir′ing·ly** *adv.*

in·quir·y (in·kwīr′ē, in′kwər·ē) *n. pl.* **·quir·ies 1.** The act of inquiring or seeking. **2.** Investigation; research. **3.** A question; query. Also spelled *enquiry.* [ME *enquery*]

in·qui·si·tion (in′kwə·zish′ən) *n.* **1.** An investigation of the beliefs and activities of individuals, political groups, etc., for the ultimate purpose of enforcing orthodoxy. **2.** The act of inquiring or searching out. **3.** An inquest. — **in′·qui·si′tion·ist, in·quis′i·tor** (in·kwiz′ə·tər) *n.*

In·qui·si·tion (in′kwə·zish′ən) *n.* A former judicial system of the Roman Catholic Church for the discovery, examination, and punishment of heretics: also called *Holy Office.*

in·qui·si·tion·al (in′kwə·zish′ən·əl) *adj.* **1.** Of or pertaining to an inquisition or the Inquisition. **2.** Characterized by questioning, prying, etc. — **in′qui·si′tion·al·ly** *adv.*

in·quis·i·tive (in·kwiz′ə·tiv) *adj.* **1.** Somewhat too curious; unduly questioning; prying. **2.** Eager for knowledge or learning. [< OF < LL *inquisitivus*] — **in·quis′i·tive·ly** *adv.* — **in·quis′i·tive·ness** *n.*

in·quis·i·tor (in·kwiz′ə·tər) *n.* **1.** One who inquires, investigates, or examines. **2.** A member of the Inquisition. [< OF < L *inquisitor*]

in·quis·i·to·ri·al (in·kwiz′ə·tôr′ē·əl, -tō′rē, in′kwiz-) *adj.* **1.** Of, pertaining to, or resembling an inquisitor or inquisition; offensively curious. **2.** Acting as an inquisitor. — **in·quis′i·to′ri·al·ly** *adv.* — **in·quis′i·to′ri·al·ness** *n.*

in re (in rē′) *Law* In the matter (of); concerning. [< L]

I.N.R.I. Jesus of Nazareth, King of the Jews (L *Iesus Nazarenus, Rex Iudaeorum*).

in·road (in′rōd′) *n.* **1.** *Usu. pl.* A serious encroachment; harmful trespass: with *on* or *upon*: *inroads* on one's happiness. **2.** A hostile raid or foray. [< IN-[2] + *obs. road* riding]

in·rush (in′rush′) *n.* A sudden rushing in; invasion.

in·sa·lu·bri·ous (in′sə·lōō′brē·əs) *adj.* Not wholesome; not healthful. [< L *insalubris*] — **in′sa·lu′bri·ous·ly** *adv.*

in·sane (in·sān′) *adj.* **1.** Not sane; mentally deranged or unsound. **2.** Characteristic of one who is not sane. **3.** Extremely foolish; hare-brained. **4.** Set apart for demented persons: *insane* asylum. [< L *in-* not + *sanus* whole] — **in·sane′ly** *adv.* — **in·sane′ness** *n.*

in·san·i·tar·y (in·san′ə·ter·ē) *adj.* Not sanitary; dangerous to health; unhygienic. — **in·san′i·ta′tion** *n.*

in·san·i·ty (in·san′ə·tē) *n. pl.* **·ties 1.** The state of being insane: not a technical term in medicine or psychiatry. **2.** *Law* A defect or weakness of mind that releases a person from legal responsibility. **3.** Extreme folly.

in·sa·tia·ble (in·sā′shə·bəl, -shē·ə·bəl) *adj.* Incapable of being sated or satisfied; extremely greedy. Also **in·sa′ti·ate** (in·sā′shē·it). — **in·sa′tia·bil′i·ty, in·sa′tia·ble·ness** *n.* — **in·sa′tia·bly, in·sa′ti·ate·ly** *adv.* — **in·sa′ti·ate·ness** *n.*

in·scribe (in·skrīb′) *v.t.* **·scribed, ·scrib·ing 1.** To write, mark, or engrave (words, names, characters, etc.). **2.** To mark (a document, tablet, etc.) with writing or engraving. **3.** To enter (a name) on a formal or official list. **4.** To sign or dedicate (a book, photograph, etc.) for presentation. **5.** *Geom.* To draw (one figure) in another so that the latter circumscribes the former. [< L < *in-* on, in + *scribere* to write] — **in·scrib′er** *n.*

in·scrip·tion (in·skrip′shən) *n.* **1.** That which is inscribed; also, the act of inscribing. **2.** A durable marking or engraving on a solid object. **3.** An informal written dedication. — **in·scrip′tion·al, in·scrip′tive** *adj.*

in·scru·ta·ble (in·skrōō′tə·bəl) *adj.* That cannot be searched into or understood; incomprehensible. — **Syn.** See MYSTERIOUS. [< LL < *in-* not + *scrutare* to explore] — **in·scru′ta·bil′i·ty, in·scru′ta·ble·ness** *n.* — **in·scru′ta·bly** *adv.*

in·sect (in′sekt) *n.* **1.** *Zool.* Any of a large, cosmopolitan class of small to minute air-breathing invertebrate animals, usu. having six legs, a body divided into a head, thorax, and abdomen, and one or two pairs of wings or none. **2.** Loosely, any small, air-breathing invertebrate resembling an insect, as spiders, centipedes, ticks, etc. [< L (*animal*) *insectum* (animal) notched, alluding totheir segmented bodies]

in·sec·ti·cide (in·sek′tə·sīd) *n.* A substance used or prepared for killing insects.

in·sec·ti·val (in′sek·tī′vəl, in·sek′tə-) *adj.* Of, pertaining to, or resembling an insect.

in·sec·tiv·o·rous (in′sek·tiv′ər·əs) *adj.* Feeding or subsisting upon insects, as shrews, moles, hedgehogs, etc.

in·se·cure (in′sə·kyŏŏr′) *adj.* **1.** Liable to break, fail, collapse, etc.; unsafe. **2.** Troubled by anxiety and apprehensiveness; threatened. [< Med.L *insecurus*] — **in′se·cure′·ly** *adv.* — **in′se·cure′ness** *n.*

in·se·cu·ri·ty (in′sə·kyŏŏr′ə·tē) *n. pl.* **·ties 1.** The state or quality of being unsafe or liable to injury, failure, loss, etc. **2.** A condition of anxiety and apprehensiveness; sense of being unsafe and threatened. **3.** *Often pl.* An instance of insecurity. [< Med.L *insecuritas*]

in·sem·i·nate (in·sem′ə·nāt) *v.t.* **·nat·ed, ·nat·ing 1.** To make pregnant; inject semen into the vagina of. **2.** To sow (seed); also, to implant (ideas, etc.). **3.** To sow seed in; implant in. [< L < *in-* in + *seminare* to sow] — **in·sem′i·na′tion** *n.*

in·sen·sate (in·sen′sāt, -sit) *adj.* **1.** Showing a lack of humane feeling; unmoved; brutish. **2.** Stupid; foolish. **3.** Lacking physical sensation; inanimate. [< LL *insensatus*] — **in·sen′sate·ly** *adv.* — **in·sen′sate·ness** *n.*

in·sen·si·ble (in·sen′sə·bəl) *adj.* **1.** Deprived of consciousness; unconscious. **2.** Incapable of feeling or perceiving; indifferent: *insensible* to pain. **3.** So slight or gradual as to escape notice; imperceptible. [< LL *insensibilis*] — **in·sen′si·bil′i·ty** *n.* — **in·sen′si·bly** *adv.*

in·sen·si·tive (in·sen′sə·tiv) *adj.* **1.** Not keenly responsive in feeling or reaction. **2.** Without physical feeling or sensation. **3.** Not affected by physical agencies: *insensitive* to light. — **in·sen′si·tiv′i·ty, in·sen′si·tive·ness** *n.* — **in·sen′si·tive·ly** *adv.*

in·sen·ti·ent (in·sen′shē·ənt, -shənt) *adj.* Lacking senses or consciousness; inanimate. — **in·sen′ti·ence** *n.*

in·sep·a·ra·ble (in·sep′ər·ə·bəl) *adj.* Incapable of being separated or parted. — *n. Usu. pl.* Persons or things that are always together. — **in·sep′a·ra·bil′i·ty, in·sep′a·ra·ble·ness** *n.* — **in·sep′a·ra·bly** *adv.*

in·sert (*v.* in·sûrt′; *n.* in′sûrt) *v.t.* **1.** To put in; place; set. **2.** To introduce into a body of printed matter. — *n.* **1.** That which is inserted. **2.** In bookbinding, illustrations, maps, etc., not part of the printed text, bound into the finished book: also called *inset.* **3.** *U.S.* A circular, pamphlet, etc., set within a newspaper, magazine, or book for mailing. [< L *in-* in + *serere* to sow, plant] — **in·sert′er** *n.*

in·ser·tion (in·sûr′shən) *n.* **1.** The act of inserting. **2.** That which is inserted; as: **a** A word, sentence, etc. **b** A strip of lace or embroidery sewn into plain cloth. **c** Each appearance of an advertisement, as in a newspaper.

in·set (*v.* in·set′; *n.* in′set) *v.t.* **·set, ·set·ting** To set in; insert; implant. — *n.* **1.** In bookbinding, an inset. **2.** A small diagram, map, etc., inserted in the border of a larger one. **3.** A piece of material let or set into a garment.

in·sheathe (in-shēth′) *v.t.* **sheathed**, **sheath·ing** To place in or as in a sheath.

in·shore (in′shôr′, -shōr′) *adj.* Near or coming toward the shore. — *adv.* Toward the shore.

in·shrine (in-shrīn′) See ENSHRINE.

in·side (*n.* & *adj.* in′sīd′, -sīd′; *adv.* & *prep.* in′sīd′) *n.* **1.** The part, surface, space, etc., that lies within; interior. **2.** The internal nature or workings that are concealed. **3.** *pl. Informal* The inner parts of the body or a machine; innards. — **inside out** Reversed so that the inside is exposed. — *adj.* **1.** Situated within; inner; internal; interior. **2.** Restricted to a few; confidential. **3.** In baseball, passing too close to the batter: said of pitches. **4.** Suitable for, used, or working indoors; indoor. — *adv.* **1.** In or into the interior; within. **2.** Indoors. — *prep.* In or into the interior of. — **inside of** *Informal* **1.** Within; enclosed by. **2.** Within the time or distance specified: *inside of* a year.

in·sid·er (in′sī′dər) *n.* **1.** A member of a given group, club, etc. **2.** One close to a source, as of knowledge or influence.

inside track 1. The shortest path around a race track. **2.** *Informal* A position of special advantage.

in·sid·i·ous (in-sid′ē-əs) *adj.* **1.** Subtly cunning or deceitful; treacherous; wily. **2.** Progressing imperceptibly but harmfully: *insidious* disease. [< L *insidere* to sit in, lie in wait] — **in·sid′i·ous·ly** *adv.* — **in·sid′i·ous·ness** *n.*

in·sight (in′sīt′) *n.* Perception into the inner nature or real character of a thing. — *Syn.* See ACUMEN.

in·sig·ni·a (in-sig′nē-ə) *n. pl. of* **sig·ne** (in-sig′nē) **1.** Badges, emblems, brassards, and the like, used as marks of membership, office, or honor: the royal *insignia*. **2.** Marks betokening anything: the *insignia* of grief. [< L]

in·sig·nif·i·cance (in′sig-nif′ə-kəns) *n.* The quality or state of being insignificant; unimportance.

in·sig·nif·i·can·cy (in′sig-nif′ə-kən-sē) *n. pl.* **·cies 1.** Insignificance. **2.** An insignificant person or thing.

in·sig·nif·i·cant (in′sig-nif′ə-kənt) *adj.* **1.** Having no importance; trivial; trifling. **2.** Meaningless. **3.** Lacking size or quantity. **4.** Of persons, lacking distinction, character, etc. — **in′sig·nif′i·cant·ly** *adv.*

in·sin·cere (in′sin-sir′) *adj.* Not sincere; hypocritical. — **in′sin·cere′ly** *adv.* — **in′sin·cer′i·ty** (-ser′ə-tē) *n.*

in·sin·u·ate (in-sin′yoo-āt) *v.* **·at·ed**, **·at·ing** *v.t.* **1.** To suggest by innuendo; hint. **2.** To introduce subtly and gradually. — *v.i.* **3.** To give sly and indirect intimations. [< L < *in-* in + *sinuare* to curve] — **in·sin′u·at′ing·ly** *adv.* — **in·sin′u·a′tive** *adj.* — **in·sin′u·a′tor** *n.*

in·sin·u·a·tion (in-sin′yoo-ā′shən) *n.* **1.** That which is insinuated; a sly hint. **2.** The act of insinuating.

in·sip·id (in-sip′id) *adj.* **1.** Lacking spirit and vivacity; vapid; dull. **2.** Lacking flavor or savor; tasteless; flat; bland. [< L < *in-* not + *sapidus* savory] — **in·si·pid·i·ty** (in′si·pid′ə·tē), **in·sip′id·ness** *n.* — **in·sip′id·ly** *adv.*

in·sist (in-sist′) *v.i.* **1.** To demand or assert firmly and forcefully: with *on* or *upon*. **2.** To dwell on or repeatedly emphasize something: with *on* or *upon*. — *v.t.* **3.** To demand or maintain forcefully: with a noun clause as object: He *insisted* that the gate be opened. [< OF < L *insistere* to stand on, tread on] — **in·sis′tence, in·sis′ten·cy** *n.*

in·sis·tent (in-sis′tənt) *adj.* **1.** Insisting; persistent; urgent. **2.** Demanding attention. — **in·sis′tent·ly** *adv.*

in·snare (in-snâr′) See ENSNARE.

in·so·bri·e·ty (in′sə·brī′ə·tē) *n. pl.* **·ties** Lack of sobriety; intemperance, esp. in drinking.

in·so·far (in′sō·fär′) *adv.* To such an extent; in such measure: followed by *as*. Also **in so far.**

in·sole (in′sōl′) *n.* **1.** The fixed inner sole of a shoe or boot. **2.** A removable inner sole placed in a shoe to improve its fit or to protect against dampness.

in·so·lence (in′sə·ləns) *n.* **1.** The character or quality of being insolent. **2.** An insult.

in·so·lent (in′sə·lənt) *adj.* Overbearing or offensively impertinent in conduct or speech; insulting; disrespectful. — *n.* An insolent person. [< L *insolens, -entis* unusual, haughty] — **in′so·lent·ly** *adv.*

in·sol·u·ble (in·sol′yə·bəl) *adj.* **1.** Not soluble; incapable of being dissolved. **2.** Not solvable; incapable of being solved. — **in·sol′u·bil′i·ty, in·sol′u·ble·ness** *n.* — **in·sol′u·bly** *adv.*

in·solv·a·ble (in·sol′və·bəl) *adj.* Not solvable.

in·sol·ven·cy (in·sol′vən·sē) *n. pl.* **·cies** The state of being insolvent; bankruptcy.

in·sol·vent (in·sol′vənt) *adj. Law* **1.** Unable to meet the claims of creditors; bankrupt. **2.** Insufficient for the payment of debts. **3.** Of insolvency. — *n.* An insolvent person.

in·som·ni·a (in·som′nē·ə) *n.* Chronic inability to sleep. [< L < *in-* without + *somnus* sleep] — **in·som′ni·ac** *n.* — **in·som′ni·ous** *adj.*

in·so·much (in′sō·much′) *adv.* **1.** To such a degree: with *that* or *as.* **2.** Inasmuch: with *as.*

in·sou·ci·ant (in·sōō′sē·ənt, *Fr.* aṅ·sōō·syäṅ′) *adj.* Light-

hearted; carefree; unconcerned. [< F] — **in·sou′ci·ance** *n.* — **in·sou·ci·ant·ly** (in·sōō′sē·ənt·lē) *adv.*

in·spect (in-spekt′) *v.t.* **1.** To look at or examine carefully; esp., to examine for faults or defects. **2.** To examine or review officially and with ceremony, as troops. [< L < *in-* into + *specere* to look]

in·spec·tion (in-spek′shən) *n.* **1.** The act of inspecting; careful or critical examination. **2.** An official examination, check, or review, as of troops. — **in·spec′tion·al** *adj.*

in·spec·tor (in-spek′tər) *n.* **1.** One who inspects. **2.** An official examiner or checker. **3.** An officer of police usu. ranking next below the superintendent. [< L] — **in·spec′to·ral, in·spec·to·ri·al** (-tôr′ē·əl, -tō′rē·əl) *adj.* — **in·spec′tor·ate, in·spec′tor·ship** *n.*

in·spi·ra·tion (in′spə·rā′shən) *n.* **1.** The infusion or arousal within the mind of some idea, feeling, or impulse, esp. one that leads to creative action. **2.** The state or quality of being inspired. **3.** One who or that which acts as an inspiring influence. **4.** Something that results from being inspired, as an idea, etc. **5.** *Theol.* Divine influence exerted upon the mind or spirit. **6.** The act of drawing in the breath; inhalation. — **in′spi·ra′tion·al** *adj.* — **in′spi·ra′tion·al·ly** *adv.*

in·spire (in-spīr′) *v.* **spired, spir·ing** *v.t.* **1.** To exert an invigorative influence upon (a person); animate; stir. **2.** To move (a person) to a particular feeling, idea, etc.: It *inspires* me with hope. **3.** To arouse or create (a feeling, idea, etc.); generate: to *inspire* fear. **4.** To direct or guide, as by special divine influence. **5.** To breathe in; inhale: opposed to *expire.* — *v.i.* **6.** To inhale. **7.** To give or provide inspiration. [< OF < L < *in-* into + *spirare* to breathe] — **in·spir′a·ble** *adj.* — **in·spir′er** *n.*

in·spir·it (in-spir′it) *v.t.* To fill with renewed spirit or life; animate; exhilarate; enliven. — **in·spir′it·ing·ly** *adv.*

in·spis·sate (in·spis′āt) *v.t. & v.i.* **·sat·ed, ·sat·ing** To thicken, as by evaporation. [< L < *in-* thoroughly + *spissare* to thicken] — **in·spis·sa′tion** (in′spi·sā′shən) *n.* — **in·spis′sa·tor** (in′spi·sā′tər) *n.*

in·sta·bil·i·ty (in′stə·bil′ə·tē) *n. pl.* **·ties 1.** Lack of stability. **2.** Unsteadiness of character; unreliability.

in·sta·ble (in·stā′bəl) *adj.* Unstable.

in·stall (in-stôl′) *v.t.* **1.** To fix in position and adjust for service or use: to *install* a hot-water system. **2.** To place in any office, rank, etc. **3.** To establish in a place or position; settle. Also *Chiefly Brit.* **in·stal′.** [< MF < Med.L < *in-* in + *stallum* seat < OHG *stal* seat] — **in·stall′er** *n.*

in·stal·la·tion (in′stə·lā′shən) *n.* **1.** Any device or system, esp. mechanical, set in place and readied for use. **2.** The act of installing, or the state of being installed. **3.** *Mil.* Any large, fixed base or facility of the armed service.

in·stall·ment[1] (in-stôl′mənt) *n.* **1.** A portion of a debt or sum of money made payable in specified amounts at specified intervals. **2.** One of several parts, as of a serial in a newspaper or magazine. Also *Brit.* **in·stal′ment.**

in·stall·ment[2] (in-stôl′mənt) *n.* Installation.

installment plan A system of paying for goods or services by fixed, periodic amounts.

in·stance (in′stəns) *n.* **1.** A case or example. **2.** A step in proceedings: in the first *instance.* — **at the instance of** At the request or urging of. — **for instance** For example. — *v.t.* **stanced, stanc·ing** To cite as an example. [< OF < L *instantia* presence, urgent pleading]

in·stant (in′stənt) *n.* **1.** A very short time; moment; twinkling. **2.** A specific point in time: at the same *instant.* — *adj.* **1.** Instantaneous; immediate: *instant* recognition. **2.** Pressing; urgent. **3.** Prepared quickly by the addition of water, milk, etc.: *instant* coffee. — *adv. Poetic* Instantaneously; instantly. [< OF < L < *in-* upon + *stare* to stand]

in·stan·ta·ne·ous (in′stən·tā′nē·əs) *adj.* **1.** Happening with no delay; immediate. **2.** Acting or completed within a moment. [< INSTANT, on analogy with *simultaneous*] — **in′stan·ta′ne·ous·ly** *adv.* — **in′stan·ta′ne·ous·ness** *n.*

in·stant·er (in-stan′tər) *adv.* Immediately; at once. [< L]

in·stant·ly (in′stənt·lē) *adv.* **1.** Without delay; at once. **2.** *Archaic* With urgency. — *conj.* As soon as.

in·stead (in-sted′) *adv.* **1.** In place or lieu; rather than: with *of*: a friend *instead* of an enemy. **2.** In the place of that just mentioned: to look for silver and find gold *instead.*

in·step (in′step′) *n.* **1.** *Anat.* The arched upper part of the human foot, extending from the toes to the ankle. **2.** The part of a shoe or stocking covering this.

in·sti·gate (in′stə·gāt) *v.t.* **·gat·ed, ·gat·ing 1.** To spur on or goad to some drastic course or deed; incite. **2.** To bring about by inciting; foment; provoke: to *instigate* treason. [< L < *in-* against + the root *-stig-* to prick, goad] — **in′sti·ga′tion** *n.* — **in′sti·ga′tive** *adj.* — **in′sti·ga′tor** *n.*

in·still (in-stil′) *v.t.* **1.** To introduce (a quality, feeling, idea, etc.) gradually or by degrees: to *instill* courage. **2.** To pour in gradually by drops. Also *esp. Brit.* **in·stil′.** [< L < *in-* + *stillare* to drop] — **in·stil·la·tion** (in′stə·lā′shən) *n.* — **in·still′er** *n.* — **in·still′ment** or **in·stil′ment** *n.*

in·stinct (*n.* in′stingkt; *adj.* in·stingkt′) *n.* **1.** *Biol. & Psy-*

chol. An innate tendency or response of a given species to act in ways that are essential to its existence, development, and preservation. **2.** A natural aptitude; knack. — *adj.* Animated from within; alive: usu. with *with.* [< L *instinctus,* pp. of *instinguere* to impel] — **in·stinc′tu·al** (-chōō-əl) *adj.*

in·stinc·tive (in·stingk′tiv) *adj.* **1.** Arising from or as from instinct: an *instinctive* fear. **2.** Of or pertaining to instinct. — **in·stinc′tive·ly** *adv.*

in·sti·tute (in′stə·tōōt, -tyōōt) *v.t.* **·tut·ed, ·tut·ing 1.** To set up or establish; found. **2.** To set in operation; initiate; start. **3.** *Eccl.* To place (a clergyman) in spiritual charge of a parish: with *in* or *into.* — *n.* **1.** A group or society devoted to the promotion of some particular field, often of a learned nature: an art *institute.* **2.** In education: **a** *Usu. cap.* A college for specialized instruction, often technical. **b** A center for postgraduate study and research. **3.** Something instituted, as an established principle, rule, or order. [< L < *in-* in, on + *statuere* to set up] — **in′sti·tut′er, in′sti·tu′tor** *n.*

in·sti·tu·tion (in′stə·tōō′shən, -tyōō′-) *n.* **1.** A principle, custom, etc., that forms part of a society or civilization: the *institution* of slavery. **2.** A corporate body organized to perform some particular function, often in education, research, charity, etc.; also, the building or buildings housing such a body. **3.** A mental hospital, prison, or other place of confinement: a euphemistic use. **4.** *Informal* A familiar and characteristic object, custom, or person. **5.** The act of instituting, establishing, or setting in operation.

in·sti·tu·tion·al (in′stə·tōō′shən·əl, -tyōō′-) *adj.* **1.** Of, pertaining to, or characteristic of an institution. **2.** Designating a form of advertising intended to promote good will and prestige. — **in′sti·tu′tion·al·ly** *adv.*

in·sti·tu·tion·al·ize (in′stə·tōō′shən·əl·īz′, -tyōō′-) *v.t.* **·ized, ·iz·ing 1.** To make institutional. **2.** To turn into or regard as an institution. **3.** *U.S. Informal* To put (someone) in an institution, as for the aged. — **in′sti·tu′tion·al·i·za′tion** *n.*

in·struct (in·strukt′) *v.t.* **1.** To impart knowledge or skill to, esp. by systematic method; educate; teach. **2.** To give specific orders or directions to; order — **Syn.** See TEACH. [< L < *in-* in + *struere* to build]

in·struc·tion (in·struk′shən) *n.* **1.** The act of instructing or teaching. **2.** Knowledge or factual matter imparted; also, an item of such knowledge taught, as a rule, precept, or lesson. **3.** *pl.* Directions; orders. — **in·struc′tion·al** *adj.*

in·struc·tive (in·struk′tiv) *adj.* Serving to instruct; informative. — **in·struc′tive·ly** *adv.* — **in·struc′tive·ness** *n.*

in·struc·tor (in·struk′tər) *n.* **1.** One who instructs; teacher. **2.** *U.S.* A college teacher not having professorial rank. [< L] — **in·struc′tor·ship** *n.* — **in·struc·tress** *n. fem.*

in·stru·ment (*n.* in′strə·mənt; *v.* in′strə·ment) *n.* **1.** A tool or implement, esp. one used for exacting work: a surgical *instrument.* **2.** A device for producing musical sounds. **3.** An apparatus for measuring or recording; as: **a** A gauge or device for indicating engine performance, etc., in aircraft, refineries, and other complex systems. **b** A system or device used for navigation and control in aircraft, ships, rockets, etc. **4.** Anything serving to accomplish a purpose; means; agency. **5.** A person doing the will of another; dupe. **6.** *Law* A formal legal document, as a contract, deed, etc. — **on instruments** *Aeron.* Flying, landing, or navigating by means of instruments rather than by visual observation of the horizon, ground objects, etc. — **Syn.** See TOOL. — *v.t.* To provide instrumentation for (an aircraft, missile, or other apparatus). [See INSTRUCT]

in·stru·men·tal (in′strə·men′təl) *adj.* **1.** Serving as a means or instrument; useful; helpful. **2.** Of or pertaining to an instrument or tool. **3.** Of, pertaining to, composed for, or performed on musical instruments. — **in′stru·men′tal·ly** *adv.* [< Med.L *instrumentum*]

in·stru·men·tal·ist (in′strə·men′təl·ist) *n.* One who plays a musical instrument.

in·stru·men·tal·i·ty (in′strə·men·tal′ə·tē) *n. pl.* **·ties 1.** Anything serving to accomplish a purpose; means; agency. **2.** The condition of being instrumental.

in·stru·men·ta·tion (in′strə·men·tā′shən) *n.* **1.** The use of instruments; work performed with instruments. **2.** *Music* **a** The study of the characteristics and groupings of instruments. **b** Loosely, orchestration. **3.** A branch of engineering concerned with the use of instruments in military, technical, and scientific operations; also, an assembly of instruments, considered as a unit. **4.** Instrumentally.

instrument panel The panel holding the gauges and other indicators of performance in an automobile, airplane, engine room, etc. Also **instrument board.**

in·sub·or·di·nate (in′sə·bôr′də·nit) *adj.* Not subordinate or obedient; rebellious. — *n.* An insubordinate person. — **in′sub·or′di·nate·ly** *adv.* — **in′sub·or′di·na′tion** *n.*

in·sub·stan·tial (in′səb·stan′shəl) *adj.* **1.** Not real; imagi-

nary; illusive. **2.** Not substantial, solid, or firm; flimsy. — **in′sub·stan′ti·al′i·ty** (-shē·al′ə·tē) *n.*

in·suf·fer·a·ble (in·suf′ər·ə·bəl) *adj.* Not to be endured; intolerable. — **in·suf′fer·a·ble·ness** *n.* — **in·suf′fer·a·bly** *adv.*

in·suf·fi·cien·cy (in′sə·fish′ən·sē) *n. pl.* **·cies** Lack of adequate effectiveness, amount, quality, etc.; inadequacy.

in·suf·fi·cient (in′sə·fish′ənt) *adj.* Not enough; inadequate; deficient. — **in′suf·fi′cient·ly** *adv.*

in·su·lar (in′sə·lər, -syə-) *adj.* **1.** Of or like an island. **2.** Dwelling or situated on an island. **3.** Composing or forming an island. **4.** Narrow or limited in customs, opinions, etc.; provincial. — *n.* An islander. [< L *insula* island] — **in′su·lar·ism, in·su·lar′i·ty** (in′sə·lar′ə·tē, -syə-) *n.*

in·su·late (in′sə·lāt, -syə-) *v.t.* **·lat·ed, ·lat·ing 1.** To surround or separate with nonconducting material in order to prevent or lessen the leakage of electricity, heat, sound, radiation, etc. **2.** To isolate. [< L *insula* island]

in·su·la·tion (in′sə·lā′shən, -syə-) *n.* **1.** Nonconducting material used for insulating. **2.** The act of insulating, or the state of being insulated.

in·su·la·tor (in′sə·lā′tər, -syə-) *n.* **1.** *Electr.* A device made of dielectric material, as glass, and used to insulate and support a conductor. **2.** One who or that which insulates.

in·su·lin (in′sə·lin, -syə-) *n.* *Biochem.* **1.** A hormone secreted by the pancreas, essential in regulating the metabolism of sugar. **2.** A preparation of this hormone, used in treating diabetes. [< L *insula* island (of Langerhans) + -IN]

in·sult (*v.* in·sult′; *n.* in′sult) *v.t.* To treat with insolence or contempt; disparage; abuse; affront. — **Syn.** See OFFEND. — *n.* An act, remark, etc., that offends or affronts. [< MF < L < *in-* on + *salire* to leap] — **in·sult′er** *n.* — **in·sult′ing** *adj.* — **in·sult′ing·ly** *adv.*

in·su·per·a·ble (in·sōō′pər·ə·bəl) *adj.* Not to be surmounted or overcome. [< L *insuperabilis*] — **in·su′per·a·bil′i·ty, in·su′per·a·ble·ness** *n.* — **in·su′per·a·bly** *adv.*

in·sup·port·a·ble (in′sə·pôr′tə·bəl, -pōr′-) *adj.* **1.** Not bearable; insufferable. **2.** Having no grounds; unjustifiable. — **in′sup·port′a·ble·ness** *n.* — **in′sup·port′a·bly** *adv.*

in·sur·ance (in·shoor′əns) *n.* **1.** Protection against risk, loss, or ruin, by a contract in which an insurer or underwriter guarantees to pay a sum of money to the insured or the beneficiary in the event of death, accident, fire, etc., in return for the payment of premiums; also, the business of providing this protection. **2.** A contract guaranteeing such protection. Also **insurance policy. 3.** The payment made by the insured party. **4.** The amount for which anything is insured. **5.** Any safeguard against risk or harm.

in·sure (in·shoor′) *v.* **·sured, ·sur·ing** *v.t.* **1.** To guarantee against loss of (life, property, etc.) with insurance. **2.** To ensure. — *v.i.* **3.** To issue or buy insurance. [< AF < *en-* in + *seur* sure] — **in·sur′a·bil′i·ty** *n.* — **in·sur′a·ble** *adj.*

in·sured (in·shoord′) *n.* The person protected by insurance.

in·sur·er (in·shoor′ər) *n.* A person or company that insures against specified loss or damage.

in·sur·gence (in·sûr′jəns) *n.* The act of rising in insurrection; revolt; uprising. Also **in·sur′gen·cy.**

in·sur·gent (in·sûr′jənt) *adj.* Rising in revolt against established authority; rebellious. — *n.* An insurgent person. [< L < *in-* against + *surgere* to rise]

in·sur·mount·a·ble (in′sər·moun′tə·bəl) *adj.* Incapable of being surmounted or overcome. — **in′sur·mount′a·bly** *adv.*

in·sur·rec·tion (in′sə·rek′shən) *n.* An organized resistance to established government. [< F < LL < L *insurrectus,* pp. of *insurgere* to rise up against] — **in′sur·rec′tion·al** *adj.* — **in′sur·rec′tion·ar′y** *adj. & n.* — **in′sur·rec′tion·ist** *n.*

in·sus·cep·ti·ble (in′sə·sep′tə·bəl) *adj.* Incapable of being affected or infected; immune. — **in′sus·cep′ti·bil′i·ty** *n.*

in·tact (in·takt′) *adj.* Remaining whole, unchanged, and undamaged; unimpaired. [< L < *in-* not + *tactus,* pp. of *tangere* to touch] — **in·tact′ness** *n.*

in·ta·glio (in·tal′yō, *Ital.* ēn·tä′lyō) *n. pl.* **·glios** or **·gli** (-lyē) **1.** Incised carving; a sunken design. **2.** The art of making such designs. **3.** A work, esp. a gem, with incised carving. [< Ital. < *in-* in + *tagliare* to cut]

in·take (in′tāk′) *n.* **1.** The act of taking in or absorbing. **2.** That which is taken in: the annual *intake.* **3.** The amount or quantity absorbed. **4.** The place where water is drawn into a pipe, channel, or conduit.

in·tan·gi·ble (in·tan′jə·bəl) *adj.* **1.** Incapable of being perceived by touch; impalpable. **2.** Indefinite or vague to the mind. — *n.* That which is intangible; esp., any incorporeal asset, as good will. [< Med.L *intangibilis*] — **in·tan′gi·bil′i·ty, in·tan′gi·ble·ness** *n.* — **in·tan′gi·bly** *adv.*

in·te·ger (in′tə·jər) *n.* **1.** Any of the numbers 1, 2, 3, etc., as distinguished from a fraction or mixed number: also called *whole number.* **2.** A whole entity. [< L, untouched < *in-* not + root *tag-,* of *tangere* to touch]

in·te·gral (in′tə·grəl) *adj.* **1.** Being an indispensable part of a whole; essential; constituent. **2.** Formed of parts that together constitute a unity: an *integral* whole. **3.** Whole; entire; complete. **4.** *Math.* **a** Pertaining to an integer. **b** Produced by integration. — *n.* **1.** An entire thing; a whole. **2.** *Math.* The result of integration. [< LL *integralis*] **—in·te·gral·i·ty** (-grăl/ə-tē) *n.* **—in·te·gral·ly** *adv.*

in·te·grate (in/tə-grāt) *v.* **·grat·ed, ·grat·ing** *v.t.* **1.** To bring together into a whole; unify. **2.** *U.S.* To make the use or occupancy of (a school, neighborhood, etc.) available to persons of all races. **3.** To make whole or complete by the addition of necessary parts. **4.** *Math.* To determine a function from its derivatives: opposed to *differentiate.* — *v.i.* **5.** *U.S.* To become available to persons of all races, as a school, etc. [< *integratus*, pp. of *integrare* to make whole, renew] **—in/te·gra/tion** *n.* **—in/te·gra/tor** *n.*

in·teg·ri·ty (in-teg/rə-tē) *n.* *pl.* **·ties** **1.** Uprightness of character; honesty. **2.** The condition or quality of being unimpaired or sound. **3.** The state of being complete or undivided. [< L *integer* untouched]

in·teg·u·ment (in-teg/yə-mənt) *n.* A covering or outer coating; esp., a natural covering or envelope, as the skin of an animal, coat of a seed, etc. [< L < *in-* thoroughly + *tegere* to cover] **—in·teg/u·men/ta·ry** *adj.*

in·tel·lect (in/tə-lekt) *n.* **1.** The power of the mind to grasp ideas and relations, and to exercise dispassionate reason and rational judgment; reason. **2.** A mind or intelligence, especially a strong or brilliant one. **3.** An intelligent person. **4.** Mental power collectively: the *intellect* of the nation. [< L *intellectus,* pp. of < *intelligere* to understand]
— **Syn. 1.** *Intellect* refers to the powers of knowing and thinking, as distinguished from those of feeling and willing, while *mind* is the sum of all these powers or faculties. *Reason* is the ability to think, or at its simplest the ability to elaborate sense impressions into concepts. *Intelligence* is chiefly used to mean the capacity to learn or to deal with new situations.

in·tel·lec·tu·al (in/tə-lek/chōō-əl) *adj.* **1.** Of or pertaining to the intellect; mental. **2.** Engaging, or requiring the use of, the intellect. **3.** Possessing or showing intellect, esp. of a high order. — *n.* **1.** One who pursues and enjoys matters of the intellect and of refined taste. **2.** One whose work requires primarily the use of the intellect. [< L *intellectualis*] **—in/tel·lec/tu·al/i·ty** *n.* **—in/tel·lec/tu·al·ly** *adv.*

in·tel·lec·tu·al·ism (in/tə-lek/chōō-əl-iz/əm) *n.* **1.** Devotion to intellectual interests. **2.** The exercise of the intellect. **—in/tel·lec/tu·al·ist** *n.* **—in/tel·lec/tu·al·is/tic** *adj.*

in·tel·lec·tu·al·ize (in/tə-lek/chōō-əl-īz) *v.* **·ized, ·iz·ing** *v.t.* **1.** To make intellectual; view or express intellectually. — *v.i.* **2.** To think; reason.

in·tel·li·gence (in-tel/ə-jəns) *n.* **1.** The faculty of perceiving and comprehending meaning; active intellect; understanding. **2.** The ability to adapt to new situations. **3.** The collection of secret information, as by police or military authorities. **4.** Information that has been so collected; also, the persons so occupied. **— Syn.** See INTELLECT.

intelligence quotient *Psychol.* A number indicating the level of a person's mental development, obtained by multiplying his mental age by 100, and dividing by his chronological age.

intelligence test *Psychol.* Any standardized test, or series of tests, designed to determine relative mental capacity.

in·tel·li·gent (in-tel/ə-jənt) *adj.* **1.** Having an active, discerning mind; acute: an *intelligent* reader. **2.** Marked or characterized by intelligence. **3.** Endowed with intellect or understanding; reasoning. [< L < *inter-* between + *legere* to choose] **—in·tel/li·gent·ly** *adv.*

in·tel·li·gent·si·a (in-tel/ə-jent/sē-ə, -gent/-) *n.pl.* Intellectual or educated people collectively, esp. those with a broad and informed point of view. [< Russian, ? < Ital. < L *intelligentia*]

in·tel·li·gi·ble (in-tel/ə-jə-bəl) *adj.* Capable of being understood. [< L *intelligibilis*] **—in·tel/li·gi·bil/i·ty** *n.* **—in·tel/li·gi·bly** *adv.*

in·tem·per·ance (in-tem/pər-əns) *n.* Lack of temperance or moderation; esp., excessive use of alcoholic drinks.

in·tem·per·ate (in-tem/pər-it) *adj.* **1.** Lacking moderation; unrestrained. **2.** Given to excessive use of alcoholic drinks. **3.** Excessive or extreme, as climate or the weather. **—in·tem/per·ate·ly** *adv.* **—in·tem/per·ate·ness** *n.*

in·tend (in-tend/) *v.t.* **1.** To have as a specific aim or purpose; plan. **2.** To make, design, or destine for a purpose, use, etc.: a dress *intended* for summer. **3.** To mean or signify; indicate. — *v.i.* **4.** To have a purpose or plan. [< OF < L < *in-* in, at + *tendere* to stretch]

in·ten·dan·cy (in-ten/dən-sē) *n.* *pl.* **·cies** The office or work of an intendant; intendants collectively.

in·ten·dant (in-ten/dənt) *n.* A superintendent; provincial administrator, as under the Bourbons in France. [< F]

in·tend·ed (in-ten/did) *adj.* **1.** Planned; proposed: the *intended* results. **2.** Prospective: one's *intended* wife. — *n. Informal* Prospective husband or wife.

in·tense (in-tens/) *adj.* **1.** Having great force; overpower-ing: *intense* feelings. **2.** Performed strenuously and steadily: *intense* study. **3.** Expressing strong emotion: an *intense* look; also, characterized by strong and earnest feelings: an *intense* person. **4.** Having its quality strongly concentrated. [< OF < L *intensus*, pp. of *intendere* to stretch out] **—in·tense/ly** *adv.* **—in·tense/ness** *n.*

in·ten·si·fy (in-ten/sə-fī) *v.* **·fied, ·fy·ing** *v.t.* **1.** To make more intense or acute; aggravate; also, to make intense. **2.** *Photog.* To increase the contrast of (a negative or print). — *v.i.* **3.** To become more intense; become intense. **—in·ten/si·fi·ca/tion, in·ten/si·fi/er** *n.*

in·ten·si·ty (in-ten/sə-tē) *n.* *pl.* **·ties** **1.** The state or quality of being intense; extreme force, brightness, concentration, etc. **2.** The strength or degree of some action, quality, feeling, etc.: pain of low *intensity*. **3.** Power and vehemence of thought or feeling; also, extreme effort and concentration.

in·ten·sive (in-ten/siv) *adj.* **1.** Of, pertaining to, or marked by intensity. **2.** Intensifying. **3.** *Agric.* Pertaining to a method of farming whereby much capital and labor are expended upon making a small area highly productive. **4.** *Gram.* Adding emphasis or force. — *n.* **1.** That which gives intensity or emphasis. **2.** *Gram.* An intensive particle, word, or phrase. [< F < Med.L *intensivus*] **—in·ten/sive·ly** *adv.* **—in·ten/sive·ness** *n.*

in·tent (in-tent/) *n.* **1.** Purpose; aim; goal; design. **2.** The act of intending. **3.** *Law* The state of mind in which or the purpose with which one does an act; also, the character that the law imputes to an act. — *adj.* **1.** Firmly directed or fixed: an *intent* stare. **2.** Directing one's mind or efforts steadfastly: with *on* or *upon*. [< OF < L *intendere* to stretch out, endeavor] **—in·tent/ly** *adv.* **—in·tent/ness** *n.*

in·ten·tion (in-ten/shən) *n.* **1.** Purpose, either ultimate or immediate; aim; goal. **2.** The act of intending. **3.** *pl. Informal* Purpose with regard to marriage.

in·ten·tion·al (in-ten/shən-əl) *adj.* Resulting from purpose; deliberate; intended. **—in·ten/tion·al·ly** *adv.*

in·ten·tioned (in-ten/shənd) *adj.* Having or characterized by (a specified kind of) intention or intentions: used in combination: *well-intentioned.*

in·ter (in-tûr/) *v.t.* **·terred, ·ter·ring** To place in a grave; bury. [< OF < LL < *in-* in + *terra* earth]

inter- *prefix* **1.** With each other; together: *intertwine.* **2.** Mutual; mutually: *intercommunicate.* **3.** Between (the units signified): *intercollegiate.* **4.** Occurring or situated between: *interlinear.* [< L *inter-* < *inter* between, among]

in·ter·act (in/tər-akt/) *v.i.* To act on each other. **—in/ter·ac/tion** *n.* **—in/ter·ac/tive** *adj.* **—in/ter·ac·tiv/i·ty** *n.*

in·ter·brain (in/tər-brān/) *n. Anat.* The diencephalon.

in·ter·breed (in/tər-brēd/) *v.* **·bred, ·breed·ing** *v.t.* **1.** To breed (different stocks) together; crossbreed. **2.** To produce (offspring) by crossbreeding. — *v.i.* **3.** To breed genetically dissimilar stocks or individuals.

in·ter·ca·lar·y (in-tûr/kə-ler/ē) *adj.* **1.** Added to the calendar. **2.** Having an added day or month. **3.** Interpolated.

in·ter·ca·late (in-tûr/kə-lāt) *v.t.* **·lat·ed, ·lat·ing** **1.** To insert or interpolate. **2.** To insert, as an additional day or month, into the calendar. [< L < *inter-* between + *calare* to proclaim, call] **—in·ter/ca·la/tion** *n.*

in·ter·cede (in/tər-sēd/) *v.i.* **·ced·ed, ·ced·ing** **1.** To plead or petition in behalf of another or others. **2.** To come between parties in a dispute; mediate. [< L < *inter-* between + *cedere* to pass, go] **—in/ter·ced/er** *n.*

in·ter·cel·lu·lar (in/tər-sel/yə-lər) *adj. Biol.* Situated between or among cells.

in·ter·cept (*v.* in/tər-sept/; *n.* in/tər-sept) *v.t.* **1.** To seize or stop on the way; prevent from reaching the destination. **2.** To meet, as a moving person, ship, etc. **3.** To interrupt the course of; obstruct: to *intercept* the light. **4.** *Math.* To mark off or bound a line, plane, surface, or solid. — *n.* **1.** In the U.S. Air Force, an act or instance of interception. **2.** *Math.* **a** An intercepted part. **b** A point of interception. [< L < *inter-* between + *capere* to seize] **—in/ter·cep/tion** *n.* **—in/ter·cep/tive** *adj.*

in·ter·cep·tor (in/tər·sep/tər) *n.* **1.** One who or that which intercepts. **2.** An airplane designed for the pursuit and interception of enemy aircraft. Also **in/ter·cept/er.** [< L]

in·ter·ces·sion (in/tər-sesh/ən) *n.* The act of interceding; entreaty or prayer in behalf of others. [< L < *intercessus,* pp. of *intercedere* to come between] **—in/ter·ces/sion·al** *adj.*

in·ter·ces·sor (in/tər-ses/ər) *n.* One who intercedes; a mediator. [< L] **—in/ter·ces/so·ry** *adj.*

in·ter·change (in/tər-chānj/) *v.* **·changed, ·chang·ing** *v.t.* **1.** To put each of (two things) in the place of the other. **2.** To cause to alternate. **3.** To give and receive in return, as gifts. — *v.i.* **4.** To change places one with the other. — *n.* **1.** A reciprocal giving in exchange. **2.** An exchanging of places. **3.** Alternation. **4.** An intersection of a superhighway with another highway, so designed that vehicles may enter or turn off without obstructing traffic. [< OF < *entre-* between + *changier* to exchange] **—in/ter·chang/er** *n.*

in·ter·change·a·ble (in/tər-chān/jə-bəl) *adj.* Capable of being interchanged or substituted one for the other; permitting transposition. — **in'ter·change'a·bil'i·ty, in'ter·change'a·ble·ness** n. — **in'ter·change'a·bly** adv.

in·ter·col·le·giate (in'tər·kə·lē'jit, -jē·it) adj. Pertaining to or involving two or more colleges: *intercollegiate* sports.

in·ter·com (in'tər·kom') n. *Informal* A telephone or radio system for intercommunication.

in·ter·com·mu·ni·cate (in'tər·kə·myōō'nə·kāt) v.i. ·cat·ed, ·cat·ing To communicate with one another; esp., by a telephone system. — **in'ter·com·mu'ni·ca'tion** n. — **in'ter·com·mu'ni·ca'tive** adj. — **in'ter·com·mu'ni·ca'tor** n.

in·ter·con·nect (in'tər·kə·nekt') v.t. & v.i. To connect or be connected one with the other. — **in'ter·con·nec'tion** n.

in·ter·con·ti·nen·tal (in'tər·kon'tə·nen'təl) adj. Reaching or capable of reaching from one continent to another; also, pertaining to or involving two or more continents.

in·ter·cos·tal (in'tər·kos'təl) adj. *Anat.* Situated or occurring between the ribs. [< NL < L *inter-* between + *costa* rib] — **in'ter·cos'tal·ly** adv.

in·ter·course (in'tər·kôrs, -kōrs) n. 1. Mutual exchange; commerce. 2. The interchange of ideas. 3. Sexual connection; coitus. [< OF < L *inter-* between + *currere* to run]

in·ter·de·nom·i·na·tion·al (in'tər·di·nom'ə·nā'shən·əl) adj. Of or pertaining to two or more religious denominations.

in·ter·de·pen·dent (in'tər·di·pen'dənt) adj. Dependent one on another; reciprocally dependent. — **in'ter·de·pend'·ence, in'ter·de·pend'en·cy** n. — **in'ter·de·pend'ent·ly** adv.

in·ter·dict (in'tər·dikt') v.t. 1. To prohibit or debar (some action, right of use, etc.) authoritatively; also, to forbid (a person or persons) to have or do something. 2. *Eccl.* To exclude (a place or certain persons) from participation in rites and services. — n. In the Roman Catholic Church, a ban forbidding the sacraments and solemn services to a place or to certain church members, but not imposing excommunication. [< OF < L *inter-* between + *dicere* to say] — **in'·ter·dic'tion** n. — **in'ter·dic'tive, in'ter·dic'to·ry** (-tə·rē) adj. — **in'ter·dic'tive·ly** adv. — **in'ter·dic'tor** n.

in·ter·est (in'tər·ist, -trist) n. 1. A feeling of curiosity or attentiveness. 2. The power to arouse curiosity or attentiveness; also, something that has such power: Tennis is his chief *interest.* 3. That which is of advantage; benefit. 4. Involvement or concern in something; also, selfish concern. 5. Payment for the use of money or credit, usu. expressed as a percentage of the amount owed or used, and depending also on the duration of the debt. 6. Something added in making a return: to give back a blow with *interest.* 7. Legal or financial right, claim, or share, as in a business or estate; also, that in which one has such a right, claim, or share. 8. *Usu. pl.* A group of persons involved in a particular business, cause, etc.: the dairy *interests.* — **in the interest** (or **interests) of** In behalf of. — v.t. 1. To excite or hold the curiosity or attention of. 2. To cause to be concerned in; involve: with *in.* [< OF < L *inter-* between + *esse* to be]

in·ter·est·ed (in'tər·is·tid, -tris-, -tə·res'-) adj. 1. Having or displaying curiosity; having the attention involved. 2. Having a concern or wish for something. 3. Having a right or share in. 4. Seeking personal advantage; biased. — **in'ter·est·ed·ly** adv. — **in'ter·est·ed·ness** n.

in·ter·est·ing (in'tər·is·ting, -tris-, -tə·res'-) adj. Exciting interest, attention, or curiosity; attractive. — **in'ter·est·ing·ly** adv. — **in'ter·est·ing·ness** n.

in·ter·fere (in'tər·fir') v.i. ·fered, ·fer·ing 1. To get in the way; be an obstacle or obstruction; impede: often with *with.* 2. To intervene and take part in the affairs of others; esp., to interpose oneself without invitation or warrant; meddle. 3. In sports, to obstruct the play of an opponent illegally. 4. *Physics* To cause interference. [< OF < L *inter-* between + *ferire* to strike] — **in'ter·fer'er** n. — **in'ter·fer'ing·ly** adv.

in·ter·fer·ence (in'tər·fir'əns) n. 1. The act of interfering. 2. In sports, illegal obstruction of the play of an opponent. 3. In football, the protection given the ball carrier from opposing tacklers. 4. *Physics* The effect produced by two or more sets of waves, as of light or sound, that on meeting tend to neutralize or augment each other by a combination of dissimilar or like phases. 5. *Telecom.* A disturbance in the reception of radio, etc., due to reception with undesired signals.

in·ter·fold (in'tər·fōld') v.t. & v.i. To fold together or one within another.

in·ter·fuse (in'tər·fyōōz') v. ·fused, ·fus·ing v.t. 1. To cause to permeate or spread throughout, as a fluid. 2. To spread through or permeate with something. 3. To intermix. — v.i. 4. To become intermixed. — **in'ter·fu'sion** n.

in·ter·im (in'tər·im) n. A time between periods or events; an intervening time. — adj. For an intervening period of time; temporary. [< L, meanwhile]

in·te·ri·or (in·tir'ē·ər) adj. 1. Of or situated on the inside; inner. 2. Remote from the coast or border; inland. 3. Pertaining to the internal affairs of a country. 4. Not exposed

to view; private. — n. 1. The internal part; the inside. 2. The inland region of a country, continent, etc. 3. The domestic affairs of a country. 4. The inner nature of a person or thing. 5. A representation of the inside of a building or room. — **Department of the Interior** An executive department of the U.S. government (established 1849), headed by the Secretary of the Interior, that controls Indian affairs and conservation of natural resources. [< OF < L *interior,* compar. of *inter* within] — **in·te'ri·or'i·ty** (-ôr'ə·tē, -or'-) n. — **in·te'ri·or·ly** adv.

interior decoration The decorating and furnishing of interiors, as homes, offices, etc.; also, this occupation.

in·ter·ject (in'tər·jekt') v.t. To throw in between other things: to *interject* a comment. [< L < *inter-* between + *jacere* to throw]

in·ter·jec·tion (in'tər·jek'shən) n. 1. The act of interjecting. 2. That which is interjected. 3. *Gram.* An exclamation lacking any grammatical connection, as *Oh!, Alas!* — **in'ter·jec'tion·al** adj. — **in'ter·jec'tion·al·ly** adv.

in·ter·lace (in'tər·lās') v. ·laced, ·lac·ing v.t. 1. To join by or as by weaving together; intertwine. 2. To blend; combine. 3. To vary or relieve the sameness of. — v.i. 4. To interlock or alternate with one another. [< OF *entrelacier*]

in·ter·lard (in'tər·lärd') v.t. 1. To vary by interjecting something different: to *interlard* speech with profanity. 2. To occur frequently in. [< MF *entrelar der* to lard]

in·ter·lay (in'tər·lā') v.t. ·laid, ·lay·ing 1. To place between. 2. To decorate with something put or laid between.

in·ter·leaf (in'tər·lēf') n. pl. ·leaves (-lēvz') An extra leaf. usu. blank, inserted between the regular leaves of a book.

in·ter·leave (in'tər·lēv') v.t. ·leaved, ·leaving To insert interleaves into (a book).

in·ter·line[1] (in'tər·līn') v.t. ·lined, ·lin·ing 1. To insert (words, phrases, etc.) between written or printed lines. 2. To annotate between the lines. [< OF < Med.L < L *inter-* between + *linea* line] — **in'ter·lin'er** n.

in·ter·line[2] (in'tər·līn') v.t. ·lined, ·lin·ing To put a lining between the usual lining and the outer fabric of (a garment).

in·ter·lin·e·ar (in'tər·lin'ē·ər) adj. 1. Situated or written between the lines. 2. Having lines inserted between the lines. Also **in'ter·lin'e·al.** [< Med.L *interlinearis*]

in·ter·lin·ing (in'tər·lī'ning) n. 1. An intermediate lining placed between the usual lining and the outer fabric of a garment. 2. The material of which such a lining is made.

in·ter·lock (v. in'tər·lok') v.t. & v.i. To join firmly. — **in'·ter·lock'er** n.

interlocking directorates *Econ.* Boards of directors that control separate corporations by overlapping membership.

in·ter·loc·u·tor (in'tər·lok'yə·tər) n. One who takes part in a conversation. [< L *interloqui* to speak between, converse] — **in'ter·loc'u·tress** (-tris) n.fem.

in·ter·loc·u·to·ry (in'tər·lok'yə·tôr'ē, -tō'rē) adj. 1. Pertaining to or having the nature of dialogue. 2. Interposed, as in a conversation. 3. *Law* Pronounced while a suit is pending; provisional.

in·ter·lope (in'tər·lōp') v.i. To intrude in the affairs of others; meddle. [< INTER- + *lope* < Du. *loopen* to run] — **in'ter·lo'per** n.

in·ter·lude (in'tər·lōōd) n. 1. A period that occurs in and divides some longer process. 2. In English drama, a separate episode, usu. light or humorous, introduced between the acts or parts of a longer performance. 3. A short passage of instrumental music played between the stanzas of a hymn, etc. [< Med.L < L *inter-* between + *ludus* game, play]

in·ter·lu·nar (in'tər·lōō'nər) adj. *Astron.* Pertaining to the period between old and new moon, during which the moon is invisible. Also **in·ter·lu'na·ry.**

in·ter·mar·ry (in'tər·mar'ē) v.i. ·ried, ·ry·ing 1. To marry someone not a member of one's own religion, race, class, etc. 2. To become connected through the marriage of members: said of different families. — **in'ter·mar'riage** n.

in·ter·me·di·ar·y (in'tər·mē'dē·er'ē) adj. 1. Situated, acting, or coming between; intermediate. 2. Acting as a mediator. — n. pl. ·ar·ies 1. One who acts as a mediator; go-between. 2. An intermediate form, stage, or product.

in·ter·me·di·ate[1] (in'tər·mē'dē·it) adj. Situated or occurring between two points, places, levels, etc. — n. Something intermediate. [< L < *inter-* between + *medius* middle] — **in'ter·me'di·ate·ly** adv. — **in'ter·me'di·ateness** n.

in·ter·me·di·ate[2] (in'tər·mē'dē·āt) v.i. ·at·ed, ·at·ing To act as an intermediary; mediate. — **in'ter·me'di·a'tion** n. — **in'ter·me'di·a'tor** n.

in·ter·ment (in·tur'mənt) n. The act of interring; burial.

in·ter·mez·zo (in'tər·met'sō, -med'zō) n. pl. ·zos or ·zi (-sē, -zē) 1. A short musical offering given between the acts of a play or opera. 2. *Music* A short movement connecting the main divisions of a large musical composition. [< Ital. < L *intermedius* intermediate]

in·ter·mi·na·ble (in-tûr′mə-nə-bəl) *adj.* Having no apparent end or limit; continuing for a very long time; endless. [< OF] **—in·ter′mi·na·bly** *adv.*

in·ter·min·gle (in′tər-ming′gəl) *v.t. & v.i.* **·gled, ·gling** To mingle together; mix.

in·ter·mis·sion (in′tər-mish′ən) *n.* **1.** An interval of time between events or activities; recess. **2.** The act of intermitting, or the state of being intermitted. **3.** *U.S.* The time between acts of a play, opera, etc. **—in·ter·mis′sive** *adj.*

in·ter·mit (in′tər-mit′) *v.t. & v.i.* **·mit·ted, ·mit·ting** To stop temporarily or at intervals; pause. [< L < *inter-* between + *mittere* to send, put] **—in·ter·mit′tence** *n.*

in·ter·mit·tent (in′tər-mit′ənt) *adj.* Ceasing from time to time; coming at intervals. **—in·ter·mit′tent·ly** *adv.*

in·ter·mix (in′tər-miks′) *v.t. & v.i.* To mix together. **in′·ter·mix′ture** *n.*

in·tern (*n.* in′tûrn; *v.* in·tûrn′) *n.* **1.** A medical graduate serving in and living at a hospital for clinical training before being licensed to practice medicine. **2.** One who is interned; internee. Also spelled *interne.* **—v.t.** **1.** To confine or detain during wartime. **—v.i.** **2.** To serve as an intern. [< F < L *internus* internal] **—in·tern′ment** *n.*

in·ter·nal (in·tûr′nəl) *adj.* **1.** Of or situated on the inside; inner. **2.** Belonging to or derived from the inside: *internal* evidence. **3.** Pertaining to the inner self or the mind. **4.** Pertaining to the domestic affairs of a country: *internal* revenue. **5.** Relating to or affecting the inside of the body. **6.** Intended to be taken or applied inwardly, as medication. **7.** *Anat.* Situated relatively nearer to the axis of the body. [< LL *internus*] **—in·ter′nal·ly** *adv.*

in·ter·nal-com·bus·tion (in·tûr′nəl-kəm·bus′chən) *adj.* Designating a heat engine in which the fuel burns inside the engine itself, most often in a cylinder.

internal medicine The branch of medicine that is concerned with the diseases of the internal organs.

internal revenue Revenue (def. 1).

in·ter·na·tion·al (in′tər·nash′ən·əl) *adj.* **1.** Existing or conducted among nations. **2.** Of or affecting various nations and their peoples. **—n.** A person having ties with more than one nation. **—in·ter·na′tion·al·ly** *adv.*

In·ter·na·tion·al (in′tər·nash′ən·əl) *n.* Any of several international socialistic organizations of the late 19th and early 20th centuries. **— First International** A federation of trade unions founded in London in 1864 by Karl Marx and Friedrich Engels. **— Second International** An organization formed at Paris in 1889 to unite Socialist Party groups. **— Third International** The Comintern.

International Court of Justice The principal judicial organ of the United Nations. Also called *World Court.*

International Date Line See DATE LINE (def. 2).

in·ter·na·tion·al·ism (in′tər·nash′ən·əl·iz′əm) *n.* **1.** The belief that cooperation among nations will advance the common welfare. **2.** The state of being international. **—in′·ter·na′tion·al·ist** *n.* **—in·ter·na′tion·al·i·ty** *n.*

in·ter·na·tion·al·ize (in′tər·nash′ən·əl·īz′) *v.t.* **·ized, ·iz·ing** To place under international control; make international.

International Phonetic Alphabet An alphabet in which each symbol represents a specific sound defined as to place and manner of articulation.

in·terne (in′tûrn) See INTERN.

in·ter·ne·cine (in′tər·nē′sin, -sīn) *adj.* **1.** Destructive to both sides. **2.** Involving great slaughter. [< L < *inter-* among + *necare* to kill]

in·tern·ee (in′tûr·nē′) *n.* An interned person.

in·ter·nist (in·tûr′nist) *n.* A specialist in internal medicine.

in·ter·pel·late (in′tər·pel′āt, in·tûr′pə·lāt) *v.t.* **·lat·ed, ·lat·ing** To subject (a member of the government) to a demand for an explanation of an official act or policy. [< L < *inter-* between + *pellere* to drive] **—in′ter·pel·la′tion** *n.*

in·ter·pen·e·trate (in′tər·pen′ə·trāt) *v.* **·trat·ed, ·trat·ing** *v.t.* **1.** To penetrate thoroughly or mutually. **—v.i.** **2.** To penetrate each other. **—in′ter·pen′e·tra′tion** *n.* **—in′ter·pen′e·tra′tive** *adj.*

in·ter·plan·e·tar·y (in′tər·plan′ə·ter′ē) *adj.* **1.** Between or among planets. **2.** Situated or occurring in the solar system, but not within the atmosphere of the sun or any other planet.

in·ter·play (in′tər·plā′) *n.* Reciprocal action, movement, or influence. **—v.i.** To act on each other; interact.

in·ter·po·late (in·tûr′pə·lāt) *v.* **·lat·ed, ·lat·ing** *v.t.* **1.** To introduce (additions, comments, etc.) into a discourse, process, or series. **2.** To interrupt with additions. **3.** *Math.* **a** To compute intermediate values in (a series): distinguished from *extrapolate.* **b** To insert (intermediate values) into a series. **—v.i.** **4.** To make additions, insertions, interruptions, etc. [< L < *inter-* between + root of *polire* to polish] **—in·ter′po·la′tion** *n.* **—in·ter′po·la′tor** *n.*

in·ter·pose (in′tər·pōz′) *v.* **·posed, ·pos·ing** *v.t.* **1.** To put between other things, esp. as a separation or barrier. **2.** To put in or inject (a comment, etc.) in the course of speech or argument. **3.** To exercise (authority, action, etc.) in order to intervene. **—v.i.** **4.** To come between; intervene. **5.**

To put in a remark. [< F *interposer* to place between] **—in′ter·po′sal** *n.* **—in′ter·pos′er** *n.* **—in·ter·po·si′tion** *n.*

in·ter·pret (in·tûr′prit) *v.* **·pret·ed, ·pret·ing** *v.t.* **1.** To give the meaning of; explain. **2.** To judge (persons, events, etc.) in a personal way. **3.** To convey the meaning of (an experience, a play, etc.) by artistic representation or performance. **—v.i.** **4.** To explain or construe. **5.** To restate orally in one language what is said in another. [< F < L *interpres* agent, interpreter] **—in·ter′pret·a·ble** *adj.* **—in·ter′pret·a·bil′i·ty, in·ter′pret·a·ble·ness** *n.*

in·ter·pre·ta·tion (in·tûr′prə·tā′shən) *n.* **1.** The process of interpreting. **2.** The sense arrived at in interpreting; the explanation given. **3.** The meaning assigned to actions, intentions, works of art, etc. **—in·ter′pre·ta′tion·al** *adj.*

in·ter·pre·ta·tive (in·tûr′prə·tā′tiv) *adj.* **1.** Of or pertaining to interpretation. **2.** Providing an interpretation; explanatory. Also **in·ter′pre·tive. —in·ter′pre·ta′tive·ly** *adv.*

in·ter·pret·er (in·tûr′prit·ər) *n.* One who interprets; esp., one who serves as oral translator between people speaking different languages.

in·ter·ra·cial (in′tər·rā′shəl) *adj.* **1.** Of or for members of different races. **2.** Between, among, or affecting different races, or persons of different races.

in·ter·reg·num (in′tər·reg′nəm) *n.* **1.** An interval between the end of a sovereign's reign and the accession of his lawful successor. **2.** Any suspension of the usual ruling powers of a state. **3.** Any break in continuity. [< L < *inter-*between + *regnum* reign]

in·ter·re·lat·ed (in′tər·ri·lā′tid) *adj.* Reciprocally related.

in·ter·re·la·tion (in′tər·ri·lā′shən) *n.* Mutual or reciprocal relation. **—in′ter·re·la′tion·ship** *n.*

in·ter·ro·gate (in·ter′ə·gāt) *v.* **·gat·ed, ·gat·ing** *v.t.* **1.** To examine formally by questioning. **—v.i.** **2.** To ask questions. **— Syn.** See ASK. [< L *inter-* between + *rogare* to ask] **—in·ter′ro·ga′tor** *n.*

in·ter·ro·ga·tion (in·ter′ə·gā′shən) *n.* **1.** The act of interrogating or questioning. **2.** A question; query.

interrogation point A question mark (?). Also **interrogation mark.**

in·ter·rog·a·tive (in′tə·rog′ə·tiv) *adj.* **1.** Asking or having the nature of a question. **2.** *Gram.* Used to ask or indicate a question. **—n.** *Gram.* An interrogative word, phrase, etc. [< L *interrogativus*] **—in′ter·rog′a·tive·ly** *adv.*

interrogative pronoun *Gram.* A pronoun that is used to introduce a question, as *which, whose, what.*

in·ter·rog·a·to·ry (in′tə·rog′ə·tôr′ē, -tō′rē) *adj.* Of, expressing, or implying a question. **—n.** *pl.* **·ries** A question. **—in·ter·rog′a·to′ri·ly** (-tôr′ə·lē, -tō′rə-) *adv.*

in·ter·rupt (in′tə·rupt′) *v.t.* **1.** To break the continuity or regularity of. **2.** To hinder or stop (someone talking, working, etc.) by intervening. **—v.i.** **3.** To intervene abruptly. [< L *inter-* between + *rumpere* to break] **—in′ter·rup′tive** *adj.* **—in′ter·rup′tive·ly** *adv.*

in·ter·rupt·ed (in′tə·rup′tid) *adj.* **1.** Lacking continuity. **2.** *Bot.* Exhibiting an abrupt change, as the alternation of leaflets with larger leaves. **—in′ter·rupt′ed·ly** *adv.*

in·ter·rup·tion (in′tə·rup′shən) *n.* **1.** The act of interrupting, or the state of being interrupted. **2.** That which interrupts. **3.** A temporary cessation; intermission; interval.

in·ter·scho·las·tic (in′tər·skə·las′tik) *adj.* Between or among schools, esp. elementary and secondary schools.

in·ter·sect (in′tər·sekt′) *v.t.* **1.** To divide by cutting or passing across. **—v.i.** **2.** To cross each other. [< L < *inter-*between + *secare* to cut]

in·ter·sec·tion (in′tər·sek′shən) *n.* **1.** A place of crossing; esp., a place where streets or roads cross. **2.** The act of intersecting, or the state of being intersected.

in·ter·sperse (in′tər·spûrs′) *v.t.* **·spersed, ·spers·ing** **1.** To scatter among other things. **2.** To diversify or adorn with other things; interlard. [< L < *inter-* among + *spargere* to scatter] **—in′ter·spers′ed·ly** *adv.* **—in′ter·sper′sion** (-spûr′zhən) *n.*

in·ter·state (in′tər·stāt) *adj.* Between, among, or involving different States of the U.S., or their citizens.

in·ter·stel·lar (in′tər·stel′ər) *adj.* Among the stars.

in·ter·stice (in·tûr′stis) *n. pl.* **·sti·ces** (-stə·sēz) A narrow opening or crack. [< F < L *intersistere* to stand between] **—in′ter·sti′tial** (-stish′əl) *adj.* **—in′ter·sti′tial·ly** *adv.*

in·ter·twine (in′tər·twīn′) *v.t. & v.i.* **·twined, ·twin·ing** To unite by twisting together or interlacing; intertwist. **—in′·ter·twine′ment** *n.* **—in′ter·twin′ing·ly** *adv.*

in·ter·ur·ban (in′tər·ûr′bən) *adj.* Between or among cities. **—n.** An interurban railroad, electric trolley line, etc.

in·ter·val (in′tər·vəl) *n.* **1.** The time coming between two events, points in time, etc. **2.** A space between two objects or distance between two points. **3.** A break in the continuity or course of something. **4.** *Brit.* An intermission, as in a play or concert. **5.** *Music* The difference in pitch between two tones. [< OF < L *inter-* between + *vallum* rampart]

in·ter·vene (in′tər·vēn′) *v.i.* **·vened, ·ven·ing** **1.** To interfere or take a decisive role, esp. to correct or settle something.

2. To occur so as to modify an action, expectation, etc. **3.** To be located between. **4.** To take place between other events or times: Many years *intervened*. [< L < *inter-* between + *venire* to come] — **in'ter·ven'er** *n.*

in·ter·ven·tion (in'tər·ven'shən) *n.* **1.** The act of intervening. **2.** Interference with the acts of others. — **in'ter·ven'tion·ist** *adj. & n.*

in·ter·view (in'tər·vyōo) *n.* **1.** A conversation conducted, as by a reporter, with a person from whom information is sought; also, the record of such a conversation. **2.** A meeting with a person applying for a job. — *v.t.* To have an interview with. [< MF < L *inter-* between + *videre* to see] — **in'ter·view'er** *n.*

in·ter·weave (in'tər·wēv') *v.t. & v.i.* **·wove** or **·weaved, ·wo·ven, ·weav·ing** To weave together; blend.

in·tes·tate (in·tes'tāt, -tit) *adj.* **1.** Not having made a will or a valid will before death. **2.** Not legally disposed of by will. — *n.* One who dies intestate. [< L < *in-* not + *testari* to make a will] — **in·tes'ta·cy** (-tə·sē) *n.*

in·tes·ti·nal (in·tes'tə·nəl) *adj.* Of, found in, or affecting the intestine. — **in·tes'ti·nal·ly** *adv.*

in·tes·tine (in·tes'tin) *n. Anat.* Often *pl.* The section of the alimentary canal extending from the pylorus to the anus, consisting of the **small intestine,** including the duodenum, jejunum, and ileum; and the **large intestine,** including the cecum and vermiform appendix, the colon, and the rectum. — *adj.* Domestic; civil. [< L *intestinus* internal]

in·ti·ma·cy (in'tə·mə·sē) *n. pl.* **·cies** **1.** The state of being intimate. **2.** An instance of this. **3.** *Usu. pl.* Sexual relations, esp. when illicit.

in·ti·mate[1] (in'tə·mit) *adj.* **1.** Characterized by pronounced closeness of friendship or association. **2.** Deeply personal; private: *intimate* thoughts. **3.** Having illicit sexual relations: with *with*: a euphemism. **4.** Resulting from close study. — *n.* A close or confidential friend. [< F < L *intimus,* superl. of *intus* within] — **in'ti·mate·ly** *adv.* — **in'ti·mate·ness** *n.*

in·ti·mate[2] (in'tə·māt) *v.t.* **·mat·ed, ·mat·ing** To make known without direct statement; hint. [< L *intimus,* superl. of *intus* within]

in·ti·ma·tion (in'tə·mā'shən) *n.* **1.** Information given indirectly; a hint. **2.** A declaration or notification. [< F]

in·tim·i·date (in·tim'ə·dāt) *v.t.* **·dat·ed, ·dat·ing 1.** To make timid; scare. **2.** To discourage from acting by threats or violence: to *intimidate* a witness. [< Med.L < L *in-* very + *timidus* afraid] — **in·tim'i·da'tion** *n.* — **in·tim'i·da'tor** *n.*

in·to (in'tōo) *prep.* **1.** To or toward the inside of from outside: to go *into* the forest. **2.** To a time in the midst of: on *into* the night. **3.** To the form or condition of: to change water *into* steam. **4.** Dividing: Two *into* six is three. [OE]

in·tol·er·a·ble (in·tol'ər·ə·bəl) *adj.* Not tolerable; that cannot be borne or endured; insufferable. — **in·tol'er·a·bil'i·ty, in·tol'er·a·ble·ness** *n.* — **in·tol'er·a·bly** *adv.*

in·tol·er·ance (in·tol'ər·əns) *n.* **1.** The state of being intolerant. **2.** Incapacity or unwillingness to tolerate.

in·tol·er·ant (in·tol'ər·ənt) *adj.* **1.** Not tolerant, esp. of beliefs, racial or social types, etc., different from one's own; bigoted. **2.** Unable or unwilling to bear or endure. — *n.* One who is intolerant. — **in·tol'er·ant·ly** *adv.*

in·tomb (in·tōom'), **in·tomb·ment** (in·tōom'mənt), etc. See ENTOMB.

in·to·na·tion (in'tō·nā'shən) *n.* **1.** Way of speaking or language or utterance; esp., the meaning and melody given to speech by changing levels of pitch. **2.** The act of intoning. **3.** *Music* **a** The production of tones of accurate pitch. **b** Pitch or the accuracy of pitch.

in·tone (in·tōn') *v.* **·toned, ·ton·ing** *v.t.* **1.** To utter or recite in a musical monotone; chant. **2.** To give particular tones or intonation to. **3.** To sing the opening notes of (a plainsong, psalm, etc.). — *v.i.* **4.** To speak or sing in a monotone. **5.** To emit a slow, protracted sound. [< MF < Med.L *intonare* to intone, thunder] — **in·ton'er** *n.*

in to·to (in tō'tō) *Latin* In the whole; altogether; entirely.

in·tox·i·cant (in·tok'sə·kənt) *n.* That which intoxicates. — *adj.* Intoxicating.

in·tox·i·cate (in·tok'sə·kāt) *v.* **·cat·ed, ·cat·ing** *v.t.* **1.** To make drunk. **2.** To elate or excite to a degree of frenzy. **3.** *Med.* To poison. — *v.i.* **4.** To possess intoxicating properties. [< Med.L < L *toxicum* poison] — **in·tox'i·ca'tion** *n.* — **in·tox'i·ca'tive** *adj.* — **in·tox'i·ca'tor** *n.*

intra- *prefix* Situated or occurring within; inside of: intra-

abdominal; intracollegiate; intra-urban. [< L *intra-* *intra* within]

in·trac·ta·ble (in·trak'tə·bəl) *adj.* **1.** Not tractable; unruly. **2.** Difficult to manipulate, treat, or work. — **in·trac'ta·bil'i·ty, in·trac'ta·ble·ness** *n.* — **in·trac'ta·bly** *adv.*

in·tra·dos (in·trā'dos) *n.* The interior curved surface of an arch or vault. [< F < L *intra-* within + *dorsum* back]

in·tra·mu·ral (in'trə·myōo'rəl) *adj.* **1.** Taking place within a school, college, etc.: *intramural* football. **2.** Situated or occurring within the walls or limits of a city, building, organization, etc. — **in'tra·mu'ral·ly** *adv.*

in·tra·mus·cu·lar (in'trə·mus'kyə·lər) *adj.* Situated in or affecting the inside of a muscle. — **in'tra·mus'cu·lar·ly** *adv.*

in·tran·si·gent (in·tran'sə·jənt) *adj.* Refusing to compromise or come to terms, esp. in politics; unbending. — *n.* One who is intransigent: also **in·tran'si·gent·ist.** [< F < Sp. < L *in-* not + *transigere* to agree] — **in·tran'si·gence, in·tran'si·gen·cy** *n.* — **in·tran'si·gent·ly** *adv.*

in·tran·si·tive (in·tran'sə·tiv) *Gram. adj.* Of or pertaining to intransitive verbs. — *n.* An intransitive verb. — **in·tran'si·tive·ly** *adv.*

intransitive verb *Gram.* A verb that has or needs no complement to complete its meaning.

in·tra·state (in'trə·stāt') *adj.* Confined within or pertaining to a single state, esp. of the U.S.

in·tra·ve·nous (in'trə·vē'nəs) *adj.* Situated in or affecting the inside of a vein: an *intravenous* injection.

in·treat (in·trēt') See ENTREAT.

in·trep·id (in·trep'id) *adj.* Unshaken by fear; bold. [< L < *in-* not + *trepidus* agitated] — **in·tre·pid·i·ty** (in'trə·pid'ə·tē) *n.* — **in·trep'id·ly** *adv.*

in·tri·ca·cy (in'tri·kə·sē) *n. pl.* **·cies** **1.** The state or quality of being intricate. **2.** That which is intricate.

in·tri·cate (in'tri·kit) *adj.* **1.** Perplexingly entangled, complicated, or involved. **2.** Difficult to follow or understand; puzzling. [< L < *in-* in + *tricae* difficulties] — **in'tri·cate·ly** *adv.* — **in'tri·cate·ness** *n.*

in·trigue (in·trēg'; *for n., also* in'trēg) *v.* **·trigued, ·tri·guing** *v.t.* **1.** To arouse the interest or curiosity of; fascinate; beguile. — *v.i.* **2.** To use secret or underhand means; plot; conspire. **3.** To carry on a secret or illicit love affair. — *n.* **1.** A plotting or scheming by secret or underhand means. **2.** A plot or scheme. **3.** A secret or illicit love affair. **4.** The quality or power of arousing curiosity or interest. [< F < Ital. < L *intricare* to entangle] — **in·tri'guer** *n.*

in·trin·sic (in·trin'sik) *adj.* Belonging to or arising from the true or fundamental nature of a thing; essential; inherent. Also **in·trin'si·cal.** [< OF < Med.L < L *intrinsecus* internally] — **in·trin'si·cal·ly** *adv.* — **in·trin'si·cal·ness** *n.*

intro- *prefix* In; within: *introvert.* [< L < *intro* inwardly]

in·tro·duce (in'trə·dōos', -dyōos') *v.t.* **·duced, ·duc·ing 1.** To make (a person or persons) acquainted face to face, usu. in a formal manner: often with *to.* **2.** To bring into use or notice first; launch: to *introduce* a new technique. **3.** To broach or propose: to *introduce* an idea. **4.** To bring in as something added; establish as a new element. **5.** To present (a person, product, etc.) to a specific group or the general public. **6.** To bring (a person or persons) to first knowledge of something: with *to:* to *introduce* a class to algebra. **7.** To put in; insert. **8.** To bring forward for official notice or action. **9.** To begin; open. [< L < *intro-* within + *ducere* to lead] — **in'tro·duc'er** *n.* — **in'tro·duc'i·ble** *adj.*

in·tro·duc·tion (in'trə·duk'shən) *n.* **1.** The act of introducing. **2.** First knowledge or acquaintance; initiation. **3.** The presentation of a person to another, to a group, etc.; also, a means of acquainting persons, as a letter, etc. **4.** Something that leads up to what follows, as the first part of a book, etc. **5.** An elementary treatise in any branch of study. **6.** Something introduced.

in·tro·duc·to·ry (in'trə·duk'tər·ē) *adj.* Serving as an introduction; preliminary. Also **in'tro·duc'tive.** — **in'tro·duc'to·ri·ly** *adv.*

in·tro·it (in·trō'it) *n. Eccl.* **1.** In the Roman Catholic Church, the opening act of worship in the Mass, consisting usu. of a part of a psalm followed by the Gloria Patri. **2.** In the Anglican Church, a hymn sung at the beginning of public worship. [< F < L < *intro-* in + *ire* to go] — **in·tro'i·tal** (-təl) *adj.*

in·tro·spect (in'trə·spekt') *v.i.* To practice introspection or self-examination. [< L *intro-* within + *specere* to look]

in·tro·spec·tion (in'trə·spek'shən) *n.* The observation and analysis of one's own mental processes and emotional states. — **in'tro·spec'tive** *adj.* — **in'tro·spec'tive·ly** *adv.*

in·tro·ver·sion (in'trə·vûr'zhən, -shən) *n.* **1.** The act of introverting, or the state of being introverted. **2.** *Psychol.* The turning of one's interest inward upon the self rather than toward external objects. — **in·tro·ver'sive** (-vûr'siv) *adj.*

in·tro·vert (in'trə·vûrt) *n.* **1.** *Psychol.* A person whose in-

INTESTINES
a Duodenum. b Small intestine. c Large intestine. d Appendix. e Jejunum. f Ileum. g Cecum. h Rectum. A Ascending colon. B Transverse colon. C Descending colon.

terest is directed primarily toward the self. **2.** One who is sober, reserved, and withdrawn. — *v.t.* **1.** To turn inward; cause to bend in an inward direction. **2.** To turn (the mind or thoughts) toward the self. — *adj.* Characterized by or tending to introversion. [< INTRO- + L *vertere* to turn]

in·trude (in·trōōd/) *v.* **·trud·ed, ·trud·ing** *v.t.* **1.** To thrust or force in. **2.** *Geol.* To cause to enter by intrusion. — *v.i.* **3.** To come in without leave or invitation: often with *upon*. [< L < *in-* in + *trudere* to thrust] — **in·trud/er** *n.*

in·tru·sion (in·trōō/zhən) *n.* **1.** The act or condition of intruding; encroachment. **2.** That which intrudes. **3.** *Geol.* **a** The movement of molten rock into an earlier solid rock formation. **b** An intrusive rock.

in·tru·sive (in·trōō/siv) *adj.* **1.** Coming or thrusting in without warrant; obtrusive. **2.** Prone to intrude. **3.** *Geol.* Formed by intrusion. **4.** *Phonet.* Denoting speech sounds that result from the adjustment of the vocal organs to the sounds preceding and following and have no etymological basis, as the (d) in *spindle* (Old English *spinel*). [See INTRUDE.] — **in·tru/sive·ly** *adv.* — **in·tru/sive·ness** *n.*

in·trust (in·trust/) See ENTRUST.

in·tu·it (in·tyōō/it, -tōō/-) *v.t. & v.i.* **·tu·it·ed, ·tu·it·ing** To know or discover by intuition.

in·tu·i·tion (in/tōō·ish/ən, -tyōō-) *n.* **1.** A direct knowledge or awareness of something without conscious attention or reasoning. **2.** Anything perceived or learned without conscious attention, reasoning, concentration, etc. **3.** The ability or quality of perceiving without conscious attention or reasoning. [< Med.L < *in-* on + *tueri* to look] — **in·tu·i/tion·al** *adj.* — **in·tu/i·tion·al·ly** *adv.*

in·tu·i·tive (in·tōō/ə·tiv, -tyōō/-) *adj.* **1.** Perceived or learned by intuition; proceeding from intuition. **2.** Characterized by, or knowing through intuition. — **in·tu/i·tive·ly** *adv.* — **in·tu/i·tive·ness** *n.*

in·turn (in/turn/) *n.* A turning inward, as of the toes.

in·twine (in·twīn/) See ENTWINE.

in·un·dant (in·un/dənt) *adj.* Inundating; overflowing.

in·un·date (in/un·dāt) *v.t.* **·dat·ed, ·dat·ing** **1.** To cover by overflowing; flood. **2.** To overwhelm with abundance or excess. [< L < *in-* in, on + *undare* to overflow] — **in/un·da/tion** *n.* — **in/un·da/tor** *n.* — **in·un·da·to·ry** (in·un/də·tôr/ē, -tō/rē) *adj.*

in·ure (in·yōōr/) *v.* **·ured, ·ur·ing** *v.t.* **1.** To cause to accept or tolerate by use or exercise; accustom; habituate. — *v.i.* **2.** *Rare* To have or take effect. [< IN-² + obs. *ure* work < OF < L *opera* work] — **in·ure/ment** *n.*

in va·cu·o (in vak/yōō·ō) *Latin* In a vacuum.

in·vade (in·vād/) *v.* **·vad·ed, ·vad·ing** *v.t.* **1.** To enter by force with the intent of conquering or plundering. **2.** To rush or swarm into as if to occupy or overrun. **3.** To trespass upon; intrude upon: to *invade* privacy. **4.** To penetrate and spread through injuriously. — *v.i.* **5.** To make an invasion. [< L < *in-* in + *vadere* to go] — **in·vad/er** *n.*

in·vag·i·nate (in·vaj/ə·nāt) *v.* **·nat·ed, ·nat·ing** *v.t.* **1.** To put into or as into a sheath; ensheathe. **2.** To infold so as to form a depression or pouch. — *v.i.* **3.** To undergo invagination. [< L *in-* in + *vagina* sheath + -ATE²] — **in·vag/i·na·ble** (-nə·bəl) *adj.* — **in·vag/i·na/tion** *n.*

in·va·lid¹ (in/və·lid) *n.* A sickly or bedridden person; one disabled by injury or chronic disease. — *adj.* **1.** Enfeebled by ill health. **2.** Of or pertaining to disabled persons. — *v.t.* **1.** To cause to become an invalid; disable. **2.** *Chiefly Brit.* To release or classify (a soldier, sailor, etc.) as unfit for duty because of ill health. — *v.i.* **3.** To become an invalid. [< F < L *invalidus* not strong] — **in/va·lid·ism** *n.*

in·val·id² (in·val/id) *adj.* Not valid; having no force, weight, or cogency; null; void. [< L *invalidus*] — **in·val/id·ly** *adv.*

in·val·i·date (in·val/ə·dāt) *v.t.* **·dat·ed, ·dat·ing** To weaken or destroy the validity of; render invalid; annul. — **in·val/i·da/tion** *n.* — **in·val/i·da/tor** *n.*

in·va·lid·i·ty (in/və·lid/ə·tē) *n.* Lack of validity.

in·val·u·a·ble (in·val/yōō·ə·bəl, -yōō·bəl) *adj.* Having a value beyond estimation; priceless. — **in·val/u·a·bly** *adv.*

in·var·i·a·ble (in·vâr/ē·ə·bəl) *adj.* Not variable; not subject to alteration; unchangeable; constant. — **in·var/i·a·bil/i·ty, in·var/i·a·ble·ness** *n.* — **in·var/i·a·bly** *adv.*

in·var·i·ant (in·vâr/ē·ənt) *adj.* Not subject to change or variation; constant. — *n. Math.* A quantity that remains unchanged; constant. — **in·var/i·ance, in·var/i·an·cy** *n.*

in·va·sion (in·vā/zhən) *n.* **1.** The act of invading with hostile armed forces; a military inroad. **2.** Any attack or onset of something injurious or disagreeable, as a disease. **3.** Encroachment by intrusion or trespass. **4.** Entrance with intent to overrun or occupy. — **in·va/sive** *adj.*

in·vec·tive (in·vek/tiv) *n.* Violent accusation or denunciation; abuse. — *adj.* Using or characterized by vituperation or abuse. [< OF < LL < L *invectus*, pp. of *invehere* to carry into] — **in·vec/tive·ly** *adv.* — **in·vec/tive·ness** *n.*

in·veigh (in·vā/) *v.i.* To utter vehement censure or invective: with *against*. [< L < *in-* into + *vehere* to carry] — **in·veigh/er** *n.*

in·vei·gle (in·vē/gəl, -vā-) *v.t.* **·gled, ·gling** To entice or induce by guile or flattery; draw; cajole: often with *into*. [< F *aveugle* blind, ult. < L *ab-* without + *oculus* eye] — **in·vei/gle·ment** *n.* — **in·vei/gler** *n.*

in·vent (in·vent/) *v.t.* **1.** To devise or create by original effort; esp., to conceive or make originally (some mechanical, electrical, or other device). **2.** To make up, as something untrue or contrary to fact: to *invent* an excuse. [< L < *in-* on + *venire* to come] — **in·vent/i·ble** *adj.*

in·ven·tion (in·ven/shən) *n.* **1.** The act or process of inventing. **2.** A device or useful contrivance conceived or made by original effort. **3.** The skill or ingenuity needed for inventing or contriving; inventive powers. **4.** A mental fabrication or concoction. — **in·ven/tion·al** *adj.*

in·ven·tive (in·ven/tiv) *adj.* **1.** Skillful at invention or contrivance; ingenious. **2.** Characterized by or created by invention. **3.** Pertaining to invention. — **in·ven/tive·ly** *adv.* — **in·ven/tive·ness** *n.*

in·ven·tor (in·ven/tər) *n.* One who invents; esp., one who has originated some method, process, etc. Also **in·vent/er.**

in·ven·to·ry (in/vən·tôr/ē, -tō/rē) *n. pl.* **·ries 1.** A list of articles, with the description and quantity of each. **2.** A list of all finished goods in stock, goods in the process of manufacture, and the raw materials used, made annually by a business concern. **3.** The process of making such a list. **4.** The value of the goods or stock of a business. — *v.t.* **·ried, ·ry·ing 1.** To make an inventory of. **2.** To insert in an inventory. [< Med.L < L *inventorium*] — **in/ven·to/ri·al** (-tôr/ē·əl, -tō/rē) *adj.* — **in/ven·to/ri·al·ly** *adv.*

in·ver·ness (in/vər·nes/) *n. Often cap.* **1.** A type of overcoat having a detachable cape. **2.** The cape itself: also called **Inverness cape.** [after *Inverness*, Scotland]

in·verse (in·vûrs/, in/vûrs) *adj.* **1.** Reversed or opposite in order, effect, etc. **2.** Turned upside down; inverted. — *n.* That which is in direct contrast or opposition; the reverse; opposite. — **in·verse/ly** *adv.*

in·ver·sion (in·vûr/zhən, -shən) *n.* **1.** The act of inverting, or the state of being inverted. **2.** That which is inverted. **3.** In grammar and rhetoric, a reversing of the usual word order in a phrase, clause, or sentence. — **in·ver/sive** *adj.*

in·vert (*v.* in·vûrt/; *adj. & n.* in/vûrt) *v.t.* **1.** To turn upside down; turn completely over. **2.** To reverse the order, effect, or operation of. **3.** To alter by inversion, as in chemistry, music, etc. — *v.i.* **4.** To undergo inversion. — *adj. Chem.* Inverted. — *n.* **1.** One who or that which is inverted. **2.** *Psychiatry* A homosexual. [< L < *in-* in + *vertere* to turn] — **in·ver/ter** *n.* — **in·vert/i·ble** *adj.*

in·ver·te·brate (in·vûr/tə·brit, -brāt) *adj.* **1.** *Zool.* Not vertebrate; lacking a backbone or spinal column. **2.** Lacking firmness or character; irresolute. Also **in·ver/te·bral** (-brəl). — *n.* **1.** An invertebrate animal. **2.** One who lacks firmness of character.

in·vest (in·vest/) *v.t.* **1.** To commit or use (money, capital, etc.) for the purchase of property, securities, a business, etc., with the expectation of profit. **2.** To spend or use (money, time, effort, etc.) for: often with *in*. **3.** To place in office formally; install. **4.** To give power, authority, or rank to. **5.** To cover or surround as if with a garment; shroud. **6.** To provide or endow with qualities or traits: to *invest* a hero with glory. **7.** *Mil.* To surround or hem in; besiege. — *v.i.* **8.** To make an investment or investments. [< L < *in-* on + *vestire* to clothe] — **in·ves/tor** *n.*

in·ves·ti·gate (in·ves/tə·gāt) *v.* **·gat·ed, ·gat·ing** *v.t.* **1.** To search or inquire into; make a formal or official examination of. — *v.i.* **2.** To make an investigation. [< L < *in-* in + *vestigare* to trace] — **in·ves/ti·ga·ble** (-gə·bəl) *adj.* — **in·ves/ti·ga·tive** *adj.* — **in·ves/ti·ga·to·ry** (-gə·tôr/ē, -tō/rē) *adj.*

in·ves·ti·ga·tion (in·ves/tə·gā/shən) *n.* **1.** A formal or official examination or study, as by the police or a governmental body. **2.** The act of investigating. [< F]

in·ves·ti·ga·tor (in·ves/tə·gā/tər) *n.* **1.** A detective, esp. a private detective. **2.** One who investigates. — **in·ves/ti·ga·to/ri·al** (-tôr/ē·əl, -tō/rē·əl) *adj.*

in·ves·ti·tive (in·ves/tə·tiv) *adj.* **1.** Of or pertaining to investiture. **2.** Having the function of investing.

in·ves·ti·ture (in·ves/tə·chər) *n.* **1.** The act or ceremony of investing with an office, authority, or right. **2.** An investing or clothing, as with a quality, garment, etc.

in·vest·ment (in·vest/mənt) *n.* **1.** The investing of money or capital to gain interest or income. **2.** Money or capital so invested. **3.** The form of property in which one invests. **4.** The act of investing, or the state of being invested. **5.** Investiture. **6.** *Biol.* An outer covering of an animal, plant, organ, or part. **7.** *Mil.* The surrounding of a fort or town to create a state of siege; blockade.

in·vet·er·ate (in·vet/ər·it) *adj.* **1.** Firmly established by long continuance; deep-rooted. **2.** Confirmed or hardened in a particular character, habit, or opinion: an *inveterate* bigot. [< L < *in-* very + *vetus* old] — **in·vet/er·a·cy** *n.* — **in·vet/er·ate·ly** *adv.* — **in·vet/er·ate·ness** *n.*

in·vid·i·ous (in·vid/ē·əs) *adj.* **1.** Exciting or creating ill will or dislike; offensive: *invidious* remarks. **2.** Provoking anger or resentment by unjust discrimination. [< L < *invidia* envy.] **— in·vid/i·ous·ly** *adv.* **— in·vid/i·ous·ness** *n.*

in·vig·or·ate (in·vig/ər·āt) *v.t.* **·at·ed, ·at·ing** To give vigor and energy to; animate. [< L *in-* in + *vigor* vigor + -ATE²] **— in·vig/or·at/ing·ly** *adv.* **— in·vig/or·a/tion** *n.* **— in·vig/or·a/tive** *adj.* **— in·vig/or·a/tive·ly** *adv.* **— in·vig/or·a/tor** *n.*

in·vin·ci·ble (in·vin/sə·bəl) *adj.* Not to be overcome; unconquerable. [< F < L *invincibilis*] **— in·vin/ci·bil/i·ty, in·vin/ci·ble·ness** *n.* **— in·vin/ci·bly** *adv.*

in·vi·o·la·ble (in·vī/ə·lə·bəl) *adj.* **1.** Not to be profaned, defiled, etc.; sacrosanct. **2.** Not to be violated or broken. **— in·vi/o·la·bil/i·ty, in·vi/o·la·ble·ness** *n.* **— in·vi/o·la·bly** *adv.*

in·vi·o·late (in·vī/ə·lit) *adj.* **1.** Not violated; not profaned or broken; intact. **2.** Inviolable. **— in·vi/o·la·cy** *n.* **— in·vi/o·late·ly** *adv.* **— in·vi/o·late·ness** *n.*

in·vis·i·ble (in·viz/ə·bəl) *adj.* **1.** Not visible; not capable of being seen. **2.** Not in sight; concealed. **3.** Not publicly or openly acknowledged. **4.** *Econ.* Not appearing in regular processes or financial statements: *invisible* assets. **—** *n.* One who or that which is invisible. [< OF] **— in·vis/i·bil/i·ty, in·vis/i·ble·ness** *n.* **— in·vis/i·bly** *adv.*

in·vi·ta·tion (in/və·tā/shən) *n.* **1.** The act of inviting. **2.** The means or words by which one invites or is invited: a written *invitation.* **3.** The act of alluring or inducing; enticement. **— in/vi·ta/tion·al** *adj.*

in·vite (*v.* in·vīt/; *n.* in/vīt) *v.* **·vit·ed, ·vit·ing** *v.t.* **1.** To ask (someone) courteously to be present in some place, to attend some event, or to perform some action. **2.** To make formal or polite request for: to *invite* suggestions. **3.** To present opportunity or inducement for; attract: his opinions *invite* criticism. **4.** To tempt; entice. **—** *v.i.* **5.** To give invitation; entice. **—** *n. Slang* An invitation. [< F < L *invitare* to entertain] **— in·vit/er** *n.*

in·vit·ing (in·vī/ting) *adj.* That invites or allures; attractive. **— in·vit/ing·ly** *adv.* **— in·vit/ing·ness** *n.*

in·vo·ca·tion (in/və·kā/shən, -vō-) *n.* **1.** The act of invoking or appealing to a deity, or other agent for help, inspiration, witness, etc. **2.** A prayer, as at the opening of a ceremony. **3.** An appeal for assistance to the Muses or some divine being at the beginning of an epic or other poem. **4.** The act of conjuring an evil spirit. **— in·voc·a·tive** (in·vok/ə·tiv), **in·voc·a·to·ry** (in·vok/ə·tôr/ē, -tō/rē) *adj.*

in·voice (in/vois) *n.* **1.** A descriptive list of merchandise sent or services rendered to a purchaser, including quantities, prices, shipping and other costs, etc. **2.** The merchandise or services so itemized. **—** *v.t.* **·voiced, ·voic·ing** To make an invoice of; list on an invoice. [< F *envoyer* to send.]

in·voke (in·vōk/) *v.t.* **·voked, ·vok·ing** **1.** To call upon for aid, protection, witness, etc. **2.** To declare relevant and operative, as a law, power, right, etc.: to *invoke* the Fifth Amendment. **3.** To appeal to for confirmation; quote as an authority. **4.** To summon or conjure by incantation. **5.** To call or petition for: to *invoke* a blessing. [< F < L < *in-* on + *vocare* to call] **— in·vok/er** *n.*

in·vo·lu·cre (in/və·lōō/kər) *n. Bot.* A ring of bracts at the base of a compound flower. [< F < L < *involvere* to roll up] **— in/vo·lu/cral** (-krəl) *adj.*

in·vol·un·tar·y (in/vol/ən·ter/ē) *adj.* **1.** Done or occurring without one's consent or choice; unintentional. **2.** *Physiol.* Functioning without conscious control: *involuntary* muscles. **— in·vol/un·tar/i·ly** *adv.* **— in·vol/un·tar/i·ness** *n.*

in·vo·lute (in/və·lōōt) *adj.* **1.** Having complications and intricacies; involved. **2.** *Bot.* Having the edges rolled inward, as a leaf. **3.** *Zool.* Having the whorls nearly or entirely concealing the axis, as a shell. Also **in/vo·lut/ed.** [< L *involutus,* pp. of *involvere* to involve]

in·vo·lu·tion (in/və·lōō/shən) **1.** A complicating or intertwining; entanglement. **2.** Something involved or complicated. **3.** *Biol.* Arrest and reversal of development; degeneration. **4.** In rhetoric, complicated or cumbrous arrangement of words, clauses, or phrases. **— in/vo·lu/tion·al** *adj.*

in·volve (in·volv/) *v.t.* **·volved, ·volv·ing** **1.** To include as a relevant or necessary aspect. **2.** To have effect on; affect by drawing in or spreading. **3.** To implicate; associate significantly: usu. with *in* or *with:* He is *involved* in the scandal. **4.** To absorb or engross: usu. with *in.* **5.** To make intricate or tangled. **6.** To envelop: to *involve* an issue in obscurity. [< L < *in-* in + *volvere* to roll] **— in·volve/ment** *n.*

in·volved (in·volvd/) *adj.* Complicated; intricate. **— in·volv/ed·ness** (in·vol/vid·nis) *n.*

in·vul·ner·a·ble (in·vul/nər·ə·bəl) *adj.* **1.** Not capable of being wounded or physically injured. **2.** Not to be overcome or damaged by attack; unconquerable. **— in·vul/ner·a·bil/i·ty, in·vul/ner·a·ble·ness** *n.* **— in·vul/ner·a·bly** *adv.*

in·ward (in/wərd) *adv.* **1.** Toward the inside, center, or interior. **2.** In or into the mind or thoughts. Also *inwards.* **—** *adj.* **1.** Situated within, esp. with reference to the body; in-

ternal. **2.** Pertaining to the mind or spirit. **3.** Proceeding toward the inside: an *inward* thrust. **4.** Inland. **5.** Inherent; intrinsic. **—** *n.* The inner part. [OE *inweard*]

in·ward·ly (in/wərd·lē) *adv.* **1.** Within the mind or heart; secretly: *inwardly* anxious. **2.** On the inside; within. **3.** Toward the center or interior. **4.** Essentially; intrinsically.

in·ward·ness (in/wərd·nis) *n.* **1.** The state of being inward; existence within. **2.** Inner quality or meaning; essence. **3.** Intensity of feeling. **4.** Unworldliness.

in·wards (in/wərdz; *for n., also* in/ərdz) *adv.* Inward. **—** *n.pl.* The entrails.

in·weave (in·wēv/) *v.t.* **·wove** or **·weaved, ·wo·ven** or *less frequently* **·wove, ·weav·ing** To weave in or together.

in·wrap (in·rap/) See ENWRAP.

in·wrought (in·rôt/) *adj.* **1.** Worked into a fabric, metal, etc., as a pattern. **2.** Decorated with such a pattern or design. **3.** Closely combined with something; blended in.

i·o·dide (ī/ə·dīd) *n. Chem.* A compound of iodine and one other element. Also **i·o·did** (-did).

i·o·dine (ī/ə·dīn, -din; *in technical usage* ī/ə·dēn) *n.* **1.** A grayish black non-metallic element (symbol I), yielding, when heated, corrosive fumes of a rich violet color, used in medicine as an antiseptic and also in photography and organic synthesis. See ELEMENT. **2.** *Informal* A solution of iodine used as an antiseptic. Also **i·o·din** (-din). [< F < Gk. *iōdēs* violetlike (< *ion* a violet + *eidos* form) + -INE²]

i·o·dize (ī/ə·dīz) *v.t.* **·dized, ·diz·ing** To treat with, combine with, or expose to the vapor of iodine. **— i/o·diz/er** *n.*

i·o·do·form (ī·ō/də·fôrm) *n. Chem.* A light yellow crystalline compound, CHI₃, used in medicine as an antiseptic.

i·on (ī/ən, ī/on) *n. Physics* An electrically charged atom, radical, or molecule, resulting from the action of an electrolyte, electric fields, high temperatures, various forms of radiation, etc., in adding or removing electrons. [< Gk. *ion,* neut. of *iōn,* ppr. of *ienai* to go] **— i·on/ic** *adj.*

-ion *suffix of nouns* **1.** Action, state, quality, or process of: *communion.* **2.** State or result of being: *union.* Also *-ation, -tion.* [< F < L *-io, -ionis*]

ion exchange *Chem.* A process whereby ions may be reversibly interchanged at the boundary of a liquid and solid in contact, the composition of the solid not being altered.

I·o·ni·a (ī·ō/nē·ə) The ancient coastal region of western Asia Minor, colonized by the Greeks in the 11th century B.C. **— I·o/ni·an** *adj. & n.*

I·on·ic (ī·on/ik) *adj.* **1.** Ionian. **2.** *Archit.* Of or pertaining to an order of Greek architecture characterized by a capital having typical scroll-like ornaments. **—** *n.* A dialect of ancient Greek. [< L < Gk. *Iōnikos*]

i·o·ni·um (ī·ō/nē·əm) *n.* A radioactive isotope of thorium, of mass 230 and a half life of about 80,000 years. [< ION + (URAN)IUM; from its ionizing action]

i·on·ize (ī/ən·īz) *v.t. & v.i.* **·ized, ·iz·ing** To convert or become converted, totally or in part, into ions. **— i/on·i·za/tion** *n.* **— i/on·iz/er** *n.*

i·on·o·sphere (ī·on/ə·sfir) *n.* A region of the earth's atmosphere above the mesosphere, consisting of several layers subject to ionization, with seasonal variations. **— i·on/o·spher/ic** (-sfir/ik, -sfer/-) *adj.*

i·o·ta (ī·ō/tə) *n.* **1.** The ninth letter in the Greek alphabet (I, ι), corresponding to English *i.* See ALPHABET. **2.** A very small or insignificant amount. [< L < Gk. *iōta.*]

IOU A written acknowledgment of indebtedness having on it these letters (meaning *I owe you*). Also **I.O.U.**

-ious *suffix of adjectives* Characterized by; full of: occurring esp. in adjectives formed from nouns ending in *-ion: suspicious, cautious.* [< L *-iosus* full of]

ip·e·cac (ip/ə·kak) *n.* **1.** Either of two plants of the madder family, yielding a medicinal alkaloid. **2.** The dried root of either of these plants. **3.** An extract of this root, used as an emetic or cathartic. Also **ip·e·cac·u·an·ha** (ip/ə·kak/yōō·a/nə). [< Pg. < Tupi < *ipe* little + *kaa* tree, herb]

Iph·i·ge·ni·a (if/ə·jə·nī/ə) In Greek legend, a daughter of Agamemnon and Clytemnestra who was offered as a sacrifice to Artemis so that the Greek fleet might sail on to Troy.

ip·se dix·it (ip/sē dik/sit) *Latin* **1.** Literally, he himself said (it). **2.** An improved or dogmatic assertion.

ip·so fac·to (ip/sō fak/tō) *Latin* By the fact itself; by that very fact or act: outlawed *ipso facto.*

ir- Assimilated var. of IN-¹ and IN-².

I·ra·ni·an (ī·rā/nē·ən) *adj.* Of or pertaining to Iran, its people, or their language. **—** *n.* **1.** A native or inhabitant of Iran; a Persian. **2.** A branch of the Indo-Iranian subfamily of Indo-European languages, including Modern Persian, Kurdish, and Pashto, and such ancient languages as Old Persian and Scythian. **3.** Modern Persian.

I·ra·qi (ē·rä/kē) *adj.* Of or pertaining to Iraq, its people, or their language. **—** *n.* **1.** A native or inhabitant of Iraq. **2.** The dialect of Arabic spoken in Iraq.

---

i·ras·ci·ble (i·ras/ə·bəl, ī·ras/-) *adj.* **1.** Easily provoked to anger; quick-tempered. **2.** Resulting from or characterized by anger or irritability. [< OF < LL *irasci* to be angry] — **i·ras/ci·bil/i·ty, i·ras/ci·ble·ness** *n.* — **i·ras/ci·bly** *adv.*

i·rate (ī/rāt, ī·rāt/) *adj.* Angry; enraged. [< L *iratus,* pp. of *irasci* to be angry] — **i/rate·ly** *adv.*

IRBM The intermediate range ballistic missile, having a range between 200 and 1500 miles.

ire (īr) *n.* Wrath; anger. [< OF < L *ira* anger]

ire·ful (īr/fəl) *adj.* Full of ire; wrathful; angry. — **ire/ful·ly** *adv.* — **ire/ful·ness** *n.*

ir·i·des·cent (ir/ə·des/ənt) *adj.* Displaying the colors of the rainbow in shifting hues and patterns, as soap bubbles, mother-of-pearl, etc. [< Gk. *iris, iridos* rainbow] — **ir/i·des/cence** *adj.* — **ir/i·des/cent·ly** *adv.*

i·rid·i·um (i·rid/ē·əm, ī·rid/-) *n.* A hard, brittle, silver-gray metallic element (symbol Ir) of the platinum group, used in certain alloys for making penpoints, jewelry, etc. See ELEMENT. [< NL < L < Gk. *iris* rainbow + -IUM]

irido- *combining form* The iris of the eye. Also, before vowels, **irid-.** [< Gk. *iris, iridos* iris]

ir·i·dos·mine (ir/ə·doz/min, -dos/-, ī/rə-) *n.* Osmiridium. Also **ir·i·dos/mi·um** (-mē·əm). [< IRID(IUM) + OSMIUM]

i·ris (ī/ris) *n.* *pl.* **i·ris·es** or **ir·i·des** (ir/ə·dēz, ī/rə-) **1.** *Anat.* The colored, circular, contractile membrane between the cornea and the lens of the eye, having the pupil as its central aperture. For illus. see EYE. **2.** *Bot.* A plant with sword-shaped leaves and large handsome flowers, as the crocus, gladiolus, etc. [< L < Gk. *iris*]

I·ris (ī/ris) In Greek mythology, the goddess of the rainbow and a messenger of the gods.

I·rish (ī/rish) *adj.* Of or pertaining to Ireland, its people, or their language. — *n.* **1.** The people of Ireland or of Irish ancestry: preceded by *the.* **2.** The ancient or modern language of Ireland, belonging to the Goidelic branch of the Celtic languages: also called *Irish Gaelic:* sometimes called *Erse.* **3.** The dialect of English spoken in Ireland: also called *Irish English.* [ME *Irisc* < OE *Ir-* + *-isc*]

Irish English Irish (def. 3).

Irish Gaelic Irish (def. 2).

I·rish·man (ī/rish·mən) *n.* *pl.* **·men** (-mən) A man of Irish birth or ancestry.

Irish moss Carrageen, a seaweed.

Irish potato The common or white potato.

Irish setter A reddish brown variety of setter.

Irish terrier A small terrier having a wiry, reddish coat.

Irish wolfhound A large, powerful hunting dog of an ancient breed, characterized by a hard, rough coat.

irk (ûrk) *v.t.* To annoy or weary; vex. [ME *irken*]

irk·some (ûrk/səm) *adj.* Troublesome; tiresome; tedious. — **irk/some·ly** *adv.* — **irk/some·ness** *n.*

i·ron (ī/ərn) *n.* **1.** A tough, abundant, malleable, easily oxidized and strongly magnetic metallic element (symbol Fe): also called *Ferrum.* See ELEMENT. **2.** That which is firm, harsh, unyielding, or indestructible. **3.** An implement or tool made of iron. **4.** A metal implement or appliance having a smooth, flat undersurface and a handle, heated either by direct contact with fire or by electric current, and used to press or smooth cloth, etc. **5.** *pl.* Chains used to confine a prisoner; shackles. **6.** A golf club having a metal head with an angled face. **7.** *Slang* A pistol or similar firearm: also called *shooting iron.* **8.** *Med.* A preparation containing iron. — **to have irons in the fire** To be engaged in various enterprises. — **to strike while the iron is hot** To act at the right moment. — *adj.* **1.** Made of or consisting of iron. **2.** Resembling iron. **3.** Inexorable; unyielding; firm. **4.** Grim; pitiless. — *v.t.* **1.** To smooth or press, as with a heated flatiron. **2.** To add or apply iron to. **3.** To put in chains; shackle. — *v.i.* To press clothes, etc., with an iron. — **to iron out** To remove, as difficulties. [OE *īrenisen, īsern*]

Iron Age The most recent and advanced of three early stages of human progress, following the Stone Age and the Bronze Age.

i·ron·bound (ī/ərn·bound/) *adj.* **1.** Bound with iron. **2.** Surrounded with rocks, as a seacoast. **3.** Unyielding.

i·ron·clad (ī/ərn·klad/) *adj.* **1.** Covered by or in armor. **2.** Strict; unbreakable, as a rule, etc. — *n.* Formerly, a warship sheathed with armor.

iron curtain An impenetrable barrier of censorship and secrecy imposed by the Soviet Union between its sphere of influence and the rest of the world.

i·ron·er (ī/ərn·ər) *n.* One who or that which irons.

i·ron·hand·ed (ī/ərn·han/did) *adj.* Exerting severe discipline or rigorous control; despotic.

i·ron·ic (ī·ron/ik) *adj.* **1.** Of the nature of or characterized by irony. **2.** Given to the use of irony. Also **i·ron/i·cal.** — **i·ron/i·cal·ly** *adv.* — **i·ron/i·cal·ness** *n.*

i·ron·ing board (ī/ərn·ing) A board or folding table, usu. padded, on which articles of clothing, etc., are ironed.

iron lung A cabinetlike enclosure in which the respiration of a patient is artificially maintained.

i·ron·mon·ger (ī/ərn·mung/gər, -mong/-) *n.* *Brit.* One who sells iron articles; a hardware dealer. — **i/ron·mon/ger·y** *n.*

iron pyrites Pyrite.

I·ron·sides (ī/ərn·sīdz/) Nickname of Oliver Cromwell. — *n.pl.* Any of Cromwell's soldiers.

i·ron·stone (ī/ərn·stōn/) *n.* Glazed, usu. white pottery.

i·ron·ware (ī/ərn·wâr/) *n.* Articles made of iron; hardware.

i·ron·weed (ī/ərn·wēd/) *n.* An herb or shrub having mostly purple or reddish flowers.

i·ron·wood (ī/ərn·wŏŏd/) *n.* Any of various trees having unusually hard wood; also, the wood.

i·ron·work (ī/ərn·wûrk/) *n.* **1.** Parts or objects made of iron, as parts of a building. **2.** The act of working in iron. — **i/ron·work/er** *n.*

i·ron·works (ī/ərn·wûrks/) *n.pl.* (*often construed as sing.*) An establishment where iron or ironwork is made.

i·ro·ny (ī/rə·nē) *n.* *pl.* **·nies** **1.** A sarcastic or humorous manner of discourse in which what is said is meant to express its opposite, as when "That's very good" means "That's very bad". **2.** A result, ending, etc., the reverse of what was expected. **3.** A situation, event, pairing, etc., in which main elements are rationally or emotionally incompatible because of contrast, conflict, or surprise. **4.** The use of irony in literature, art, etc. **5.** The feigning of ignorance as a tehnique in argument; Socratic irony. — **Syn.** See SARCASM. [< L < Gk. *eirōn* dissembler]

Ir·o·quoi·an (ir/ə·kwoi/ən) *n.* **1.** A family of North American Indian languages, including Cayuga, Cherokee, Conestoga, Erie, Mohawk, Oneida, Seneca and other languages. **2.** A member of a tribe speaking these languages. — *adj.* Of the Iroquois Indians or their languages.

Ir·o·quois (ir/ə·kwoi, -kwoiz) *n.* *pl.* **·quois** **1.** A member of any of the North American Indian tribes known as the Five Nations; also, these tribes collectively. See FIVE NATIONS. **2.** A member of a tribe speaking an Iroquoian language. — *adj.* Of or pertaining to the Iroquois. [< F < Algonquian *Irinakoiw,* lit., real adders]

ir·ra·di·ant (i·rā/dē·ənt) *adj.* Sending forth light; shining. — **ir·ra/di·ance, ir·ra/di·an·cy** *n.*

ir·ra·di·ate (v. i·rā/dē·āt; *adj.* i·rā/dē·it, -āt) *v.* **·at·ed, ·at·ing** *v.t.* **1.** To light up; illuminate. **2.** To make clear or understandable. **3.** To send forth in or as in rays of light. **4.** To subject to X-rays, ultraviolet light, or similar rays. **5.** To expose to radiant energy. — *v.i.* **6.** To be radiant; shine. — *adj.* Made bright; illuminated. [< L in- thoroughly + *radiare* to shine] — **ir·ra/di·a/tion** *n.* — **ir·ra/di·a/tive** *adj.*

ir·ra·tion·al (i·rash/ən·əl) *adj.* **1.** Incapable of exercising the power of reason. **2.** Contrary to reason; absurd. **3.** *Math.* Denoting a number that cannot be expressed as an integer or a quotient of integers. [< L *irrationalis*] — **ir·ra/tion·al·ism** *n.* — **ir·ra/tion·al·ly** *adv.* — **ir·ra/tion·al·ness** *n.*

ir·ra·tion·al·i·ty (i·rash/ən·al/ə·tē) *n.* *pl.* **·ties** **1.** The state of being irrational. **2.** That which is irrational.

ir·re·claim·a·ble (ir/i·klā/mə·bəl) *adj.* Incapable of being reclaimed. — **ir·re·claim/a·bil/i·ty, ir/re·claim/a·ble·ness** *n.* — **ir/re·claim/a·bly** *adv.*

ir·re·con·cil·a·ble (i·rek/ən·sī/lə·bəl, i·rek/ən·sī/lə·bəl) *adj.* Not able or willing to be reconciled or brought into accord. — *n.* **1.** One who refuses to yield or compromise. **2.** *pl.* Incompatible ideas. — **ir·rec/on·cil/a·bil/i·ty, ir·rec/on·cil/a·ble·ness** *n.* — **ir·rec/on·cil/a·bly** *adv.*

ir·re·cov·er·a·ble (ir/i·kuv/ər·ə·bəl) *adj.* **1.** Incapable of being recovered. **2.** Incapable of being remedied. — **ir/re·cov/er·a·ble·ness** *n.* — **ir/re·cov/er·a·bly** *adv.*

ir·re·deem·a·ble (ir/i·dē/mə·bəl) *adj.* **1.** Incapable of being recovered, bought back, or paid off. **2.** Not to be converted into coin: said of some types of paper money. **3.** Beyond redemption or change; incorrigible. — **ir/re·deem/a·bly** *adv.*

ir·re·den·tist (ir/i·den/tist) *n.* *Usu. cap.* A member of a party formed in Italy about 1878, that had as its aim the acquisition of certain regions subject to other governments but having an Italian-speaking population. — *adj.* Of or pertaining to the irredentists or their policies. [< Ital. < L *in-* not + *redemptus* redeemed] — **ir/re·den/tism** (-tiz·əm) *n.*

ir·re·duc·i·ble (ir/i·dōō/sə·bəl, -dyōō/-) *adj.* **1.** Incapable of being decreased or diminished. **2.** Incapable of being converted to a simpler or more basic form. — **ir/re·duc/i·bil/i·ty** *n.* — **ir/re·duc/i·bly** *adv.*

ir·ref·ra·ga·ble (i·ref/rə·gə·bəl) *adj.* That cannot be refuted or disproved. [< LL < L in- not + *refragari* to oppose] — **ir·ref/ra·ga·bil/i·ty** *n.*

ir·ref·u·ta·ble (i·ref/yə·tə·bəl, ir/i·fyōō/tə·bəl) *adj.* Incapable of being disproved. — **ir·ref/u·ta·bil/i·ty** (i·ref/yə·tə·bil/ə·tē, ir/i·fyōō/-) *n.* — **ir·ref/u·ta·bly** (i·ref/yə·tə·blē, ir/i·fyōō/-) *adv.*

ir·re·gard·less (ir/i·gärd/lis) *adv.* Regardless: a nonstandard or humorous usage.

ir·reg·u·lar (i·reg/yə·lər) *adj.* 1. Lacking symmetry or uniformity. 2. Occurring at unequal intervals: an *irregular* pulse. 3. Not according to established rules or procedure. 4. Not conforming to accepted standards of conduct. 5. *Gram.* Not conforming to the usual pattern of inflection or conjugation. 6. *Mil.* Of troops, not belonging to a regularly organized military force. — *n.* One who or that which is irregular. [< OF < Med.L *irregularis*] — **ir·reg/u·lar·ly** *adv.*

ir·reg·u·lar·i·ty (i·reg/yə·lar/ə·tē) *n. pl.* **·ties** 1. The state or quality of being irregular. 2. That which is irregular.

ir·rel·a·tive (i·rel/ə·tiv) *adj.* Irrelevant. — **ir·rel/a·tive·ly** *adv.* — **ir·rel/a·tive·ness** *n.*

ir·rel·e·vant (i·rel/ə·vənt) *adj.* Not relevant; not pertinent; inapplicable. — **ir·rel/e·vance, ir·rel/e·van·cy** *n.* — **ir·rel/e·vant·ly** *adv.*

ir·re·lig·ion (ir/i·lij/ən) *n.* 1. Lack of religious faith. 2. Indifference or hostility toward religion. — **ir/re·lig/ion·ist** *n.*

ir·re·lig·ious (ir/i·lij/əs) *adj.* 1. Lacking in religious faith or piety. 2. Profane. — **ir/re·lig/ious·ly** *adv.*

ir·re·me·di·a·ble (ir/i·mē/dē·ə·bəl) *adj.* Incapable of being remedied; incurable; irreparable. [< L *irremediabilis*] — **ir/re·me/di·a·ble·ness** *n.* — **ir/re·me/di·a·bly** *adv.*

ir·re·mis·si·ble (ir/i·mis/ə·bəl) *adj.* Not remissible; unpardonable, as a sin. — **ir/re·mis/si·bil/i·ty, ir/re·mis/si·ble·ness** *n.* — **ir/re·mis/si·bly** *adv.*

ir·re·mov·a·ble (ir/i·mōō/və·bəl) *adj.* Not removable.

ir·rep·a·ra·ble (i·rep/ər·ə·bəl) *adj.* Incapable of being repaired, rectified, remedied, or made good. — **ir·rep/a·ra·bil/i·ty, ir·rep/a·ra·ble·ness** *n.* — **ir·rep/a·ra·bly** *adv.*

ir·re·place·a·ble (ir/i·plā/sə·bəl) *adj.* Not replaceable.

ir·re·pres·si·ble (ir/i·pres/ə·bəl) *adj.* Not repressible; incapable of being controlled or restrained. — **ir/re·pres/si·bil/i·ty, ir/re·pres/si·ble·ness** *n.* — **ir/re·pres/si·bly** *adv.*

ir·re·proach·a·ble (ir/i·prō/chə·bəl) *adj.* Not meriting reproach; blameless. [< F *irréprochable*] — **ir/re·proach/a·ble·ness** *n.* — **ir/re·proach/a·bly** *adv.*

ir·re·sis·ti·ble (ir/i·zis/tə·bəl) *adj.* 1. Not resistible. 2. Completely fascinating or enchanting. — **ir/re·sis/ti·bil/i·ty, ir/re·sis/ti·ble·ness** *n.* — **ir/re·sis/ti·bly** *adv.*

ir·res·o·lute (i·rez/ə·lōōt) *adj.* Not resolute or resolved; lacking firmness of purpose; wavering; hesitating. — **ir·res/o·lute/ly** *adv.* — **ir·res/o·lute/ness, ir·res/o·lu/tion** *n.*

ir·re·spec·tive (ir/i·spek/tiv) *adj.* Existing without relationship to something else: now chiefly in the phrase **irrespective of**, regardless of. — **ir/re·spec/tive·ly** *adv.*

ir·re·spon·si·ble (ir/i·spon/sə·bəl) *adj.* 1. Lacking in responsibility; unreliable. 2. Free from or incapable of responsibility. — *n.* One who is irresponsible. — **ir/re·spon/si·bil/i·ty, ir/re·spon/si·ble·ness** *n.* — **ir/re·spon/si·bly** *adv.*

ir·re·spon·sive (ir/i·spon/siv) *adj.* Not responsive. — **ir/re·spon/sive·ness** *n.*

ir·re·trace·a·ble (ir/i·trā/sə·bəl) *adj.* Incapable of being retraced, as a path, footsteps, etc.

ir·re·triev·a·ble (ir/i·trē/və·bəl) *adj.* Not retrievable; irrecoverable; irreparable. — **ir/re·triev/a·bil/i·ty, ir/re·triev/a·ble·ness** *n.* — **ir/re·triev/a·bly** *adv.*

ir·rev·er·ence (i·rev/ər·əns) *n.* 1. Lack of awe, veneration, or respect. 2. Behavior or utterance indicative of this.

ir·rev·er·ent (i·rev/ər·ənt) *adj.* Characterized by or showing irreverence. — **ir·rev/er·ent·ly** *adv.*

ir·re·vers·i·ble (ir/i·vûr/sə·bəl) *adj.* 1. Incapable of being turned in the opposite direction. 2. Incapable of being annulled, repealed, or undone. — **ir/re·vers/i·bil/i·ty, ir/re·vers/i·ble·ness** *n.* — **ir/re·vers/i·bly** *adv.*

ir·rev·o·ca·ble (i·rev/ə·kə·bəl) *adj.* 1. Incapable of being revoked. 2. Incapable of being brought back. — **ir·rev/o·ca·bil/i·ty, ir·rev/o·ca·ble·ness** *n.* — **ir·rev/o·ca·bly** *adv.*

ir·ri·ga·ble (ir/ə·gə·bəl) *adj.* Capable of being irrigated.

ir·ri·gate (ir/ə·gāt) *v.t.* **·gat·ed, ·gat·ing** 1. To supply (land) with water, as by means of ditches. 2. To revitalize or refresh by or as if by watering. 3. *Med.* To moisten or wash out with water. [< L < *in-* to + *rigare* to water] — **ir/ri·ga/tion** *n.* — **ir/ri·ga/tion·al** *adj.* — **ir/ri·ga/tor** *n.*

ir·ri·ta·bil·i·ty (ir/ə·tə·bil/ə·tē) *n. pl.* **·ties** The state or quality of being irritable.

ir·ri·ta·ble (ir/ə·tə·bəl) *adj.* 1. Easily annoyed or angered. 2. *Biol.* Responding to stimuli. 3. *Pathol.* Influenced abnormally by the action of stimulants. — **ir/ri·ta·ble·ness** *n.* — **ir/ri·ta·bly** *adv.*

ir·ri·tant (ir/ə·tənt) *n.* That which irritates or causes irritation. — *adj.* Causing irritation. — **ir/ri·tan·cy** *n.*

ir·ri·tate (ir/ə·tāt) *v.t.* **·tat·ed, ·tat·ing** 1. To excite annoyance, impatience, or ill temper in; vex. 2. To make sore or inflamed. 3. *Biol.* To stimulate (a cell, tissue, or organ) to a characteristic function or action. [< L *irritare* to irritate] — **ir/ri·ta/tive** *adj.* — **ir/ri·ta/tor** *n.*

ir·ri·tat·ing (ir/ə·tā/ting) *adj.* Causing irritation. — **ir/ri·tat/ing·ly** *adv.*

ir·ri·ta·tion (ir/ə·tā/shən) *n.* 1. The act of irritating, or the state of being irritated; annoyance. 2. *Pathol.* A condition of abnormal excitability or sensitivity in an organ or part.

ir·rup·tion (i·rup/shən) *n.* 1. A breaking or rushing in. 2. A violent, sudden invasion. [< L < *in-* in + *rumpere* to break] — **ir·rup/tive** *adj.*

is (iz) Present indicative, third person singular of BE. [OE]

is- Var. of ISO-.

I·saac (i/zək) A Hebrew patriarch, son of Abraham and Sarah. *Gen.* xxi 3. [< Hebrew *ṣaḥaq* to laugh]

i·sa·go·ge (i/sə·gō/jē) *n.* An introduction, as to a field of study. [< L < Gk. *eisagōgē* < *eisagein* to introduce < *eis-* into + *agein* to lead] — **i/sa·gog/ic** (-goj/ik) *adj.*

I·sa·iah (ī·zā/ə, ī·zī/ə) Eighth-century B.C. Hebrew prophet. — *n.* A book of the Old Testament attributed to him. Also, in the Douai Bible, **I·sai/as** (-əs). [< Hebrew *yesha'yāhu* Salvation of God]

Is·car·i·ot (is·kar/ē·ət) See JUDAS ISCARIOT.

is·che·mi·a (is·kē/mē·ə) *n. Pathol.* A localized anemia, due to a contracted blood vessel. Also **is·chae/mi·a**. [< NL < Gk. *ischein* to hold + *haima* blood] — **is·che/mic** *adj.*

is·chi·at·ic (is/kē·at/ik) *adj.* Of or pertaining to the ischium. Also **is/chi·ad/ic** (-ad/ik), **is·chi·al** (is/kē·əl).

is·chi·um (is/kē·əm) *n. pl.* **·chi·a** (-kē·ə) *Anat.* The lowest of the three sections composing the hipbone. For illus. see PELVIS. [< L < Gk. *ischion* hip, hip joint]

-ise Var. of -IZE.

I·seult (i·sōōlt/) In medieval romance Iseult the Beautiful of Ireland, married to King Mark and beloved of Tristan. See TRISTAN. Also called *Isolde, Isolt, Yseult.*

-ish¹ *suffix of adjectives* 1. Of or belonging to (a specified national group): *Danish.* 2. Of the nature of; like: *boyish.* 3. Having the bad qualities of: *selfish.* 4. Tending toward; inclined to: *bookish.* 5. Somewhat: *tallish.* 6. *Informal* Approximately: *fortyish.* [OE *-isc*, adjectival suffix]

-ish² *suffix of verbs* Appearing chiefly in verbs of French origin: *brandish, establish.* [< OF *-iss-*, stem ending of *-ir* verbs]

Ish·ma·el (ish/mē·əl) In the Bible, the son of Abraham and Hagar, banished with his mother. *Gen.* xxi 9–21. — *n.* An outcast. [< Hebrew *Yishmā'ēl* God heareth]

Ish·ma·el·ite (ish/mē·əl·īt/) *n.* 1. A descendant of Ishmael. 2. A wanderer. — **Ish/ma·el·it/ish** (-ī/tish) *adj.*

i·sin·glass (ī/zing·glas/, -gläs/, ī/zən-) *n.* 1. A preparation of nearly pure gelatin made from the swim bladders of certain fishes. 2. Mica, chiefly in the form of thin sheets. [Prob. < MDu. *huysenblas* sturgeon bladder]

I·sis (ī/sis) In Egyptian mythology, the goddess of fertility.

Is·lam (is·läm/, is/ləm, iz/-) *n.* 1. The religion of the Muslims, that maintains that there is but one God, Allah, and that Mohammed is his prophet: also called *Mohammedanism, Muslimism.* Also **Is·lam·ism** (is/ləm·iz/əm, iz/ləm-). 2. Muslims collectively. 3. The areas of the world where Islam is the main religion. [< Arabic *islām* submission]

Is·lam·ic (is·lam/ik, -läm/-, iz-) *adj.* Muslim. Also **Is/lam·it/ic** (-it/ik).

Is·lam·ite (is/ləm·īt, iz/-) *n.* A Muslim.

Is·lam·ize (is/ləm·īz, iz/-) *v.t. & v.i.* **·ized, ·i·zing** To convert or adapt to Islam.

is·land (ī/lənd) *n.* 1. A tract of land entirely surrounded by water. The major continental land masses are not usually considered islands. 2. Something resembling an island and set apart from its surroundings. 3. *Anat.* Any of various isolated cells of the body differentiated from those of the surrounding tissues. — *v.t.* To cause to become or resemble an island; isolate. [OE < *īg, īeg* island + *land*]

is·land·er (ī/lən·dər) *n.* A native or inhabitant of an island.

isle (īl) *n.* An island, esp. one of comparatively small size: used in place names, as the British *Isles,* or poetically. — *v.* **isled, isl·ing** *v.t.* 1. To island. — *v.i.* 2. To live on an isle or island. [< OF < L *insula*]

is·let (ī/lit) *n.* A small island. [< OF *islette*, dim. of *isle*]

ism (iz/əm) *n.* A distinctive theory, doctrine, or system: usually used disparagingly. [< -ISM]

-ism *suffix of nouns* 1. The act, process, or result of: *ostracism.* 2. The condition of being: *skepticism.* 3. The characteristic action or behavior of: *heroism.* 4. The beliefs, teachings, or system of: *Calvinism.* 5. Devotion to; adherence to the teachings of: *nationalism.* 6. A characteristic or peculiarity of: said especially of a language or idiom: *Americanism.* 7. *Med.* An abnormal condition resulting from an excess of: *alcoholism.* [< L *-ismus* < Gk. *-ismos*]

is·n't (iz/ənt) Is not.

iso- *combining form* 1. Equal; the same; identical. 2. *Chem.* Isomeric with, or an isomer of. Also, before vowels, **is-**. [< Gk. *isos* equal]

i·so·bar (ī/sə·bär) *n.* 1. *Meteorol.* A line drawn on a weather

---

map connecting all points having the same barometric pressure for a given time or period. **2.** *Physics* Any of two or more atoms having the same mass number but different atomic numbers. [< Gk. *isos* equal + *baros* weight] — **i·so·bar·ic** (ī'sə-bar'ik) *adj.*

i·so·cline (ī'sə-klīn) *n. Geol.* An anticline or syncline in which the strata are so closely folded that they have the same dip. [< ISO- + Gk. *klinein* to bend] —**i'so·cli'nal,** **i'so·clin'ic** (-klin'ik) *adj.*

i·so·gon·ic (ī'sə-gon'ik) *adj.* **1.** Having equal angles. **2.** Denoting a line on the earth's surface such that all points on it have equal magnetic declination. Also **i·sog·o·nal** (ī.sog'ə-nəl). — *n.* An isogonic line. [< Gk. *isogōnios* equiangular]

i·so·gram (ī'sə-gram) *n.* A line on a map, chart, diagram, etc., such that all points on it have equal value with respect to a given geographical feature, physical condition, etc.

i·so·late (ī'sə-lāt, is'ə-) *v.t.* **·lat·ed, ·lat·ing** **1.** To set apart, as from a mass, group, or situation; cause to be alone. **2.** *Chem.* To obtain (an element or substance) in a free or uncombined state. [< Ital. *isolare* to isolate] —**i'so·la·ble** *adj.* —**i'so·la'tor** *n.*

i·so·la·tion (ī'sə-lā'shən, is'ə-) *n.* **1.** The act of isolating. **2.** The state of being isolated; aloneness; solitude.

i·so·la·tion·ism (ī'sə-lā'shən·iz'əm, is'ə-) *n.* A national policy advocating freedom from foreign political and economic alliances. —**i'so·la'tion·ist** *adj. & n.*

I·solde (i·sōld', *Ger.* i·zōl'də) See ISEULT.

i·sol·o·gous (ī·sol'ə·gəs) *adj. Chem.* Having similar molecular structure but different atoms of the same valence.

i·so·mer (ī'sə·mər) *n.* **1.** *Chem.* One of two or more compounds identical in composition, but having different structural arrangements and different properties. **2.** *Physics* One of two or more nuclides having the same mass and atomic number but differing in energy characteristics. [< Gk. < *isos* equal + *meros* part] —**i·so·mer'ic** (-mer'ik) *adj.*

i·som·er·ism (ī·som'ə·riz'əm) *n. Chem.* The condition of being isomeric.

i·som·er·ous (ī·som'ər·əs) *adj.* **1.** Having an equal number of parts, organs, markings, etc. **2.** *Bot.* Equal in number, as the members of successive whorls of flowers.

i·so·met·ric (ī'sə·met'rik) *adj.* **1.** Pertaining to or characterized by equality in dimensions or measurements. **2.** Based upon contraction of muscles against resistance without shortening muscle fibers: *isometric exercises.* —**i'so·met'ri·cal·ly** *adv.*

i·so·mor·phic (ī'sə·môr'fik) *adj.* Having similar form or appearance but of different ancestry, genetic constitution, or chemical composition.

i·so·mor·phism (ī'sə·môr'fiz·əm) *n.* A similarity in form shown by substances of different composition, or by organisms belonging to different groups. —**i'so·morph** *n.*

i·so·oc·tane (ī'sō·ok'tān) *n. Chem.* Trimethylpentane.

i·so·prene (ī'sə·prēn) *n. Chem.* A volatile liquid hydrocarbon, C_5H_8, of the terpene group, obtained when crude rubber is subjected to pyrolysis. [Appar. an arbitrary coinage]

i·sos·ce·les (ī·sos'ə·lēz) *adj. Geom.* Of a triangle, having two sides of equal length. [< LL < Gk. *isos* equal + *skelos* leg]

i·sos·ta·sy (ī·sos'tə·sē) *n.* **1.** *Geol.* The equilibrium that the earth's crust tends to assume as a result of the action of terrestrial gravitation upon rock masses. **2.** Equilibrium resulting from equal pressure on all sides. [< ISO- + Gk. *stasis* standing] —**i·so·stat·ic** (ī'sə·stat'ik) *adj.*

i·so·therm (ī'sə·thûrm) *n. Meteorol.* A line drawn on a weather map connecting all points having the same mean temperature. [< ISO- + Gk. *thermē* heat] —**i'so·ther'mal** *adj. & n.*

i·so·ton·ic (ī'sə·ton'ik) *adj. Physiol.* Having the same osmotic pressure on opposite sides of a membrane: said of solutions, esp. blood or plasma. [< Gk. < *isos* equal + *tonos* accent]

i·so·tope (ī'sə·tōp) *n. Physics* Any of two or more forms of an element having the same atomic number and similar chemical properties but differing in mass number and radioactive behavior. [< ISO- + Gk. *topos* place] —**i·so·top·ic** (ī'sə·top'ik) *adj.* —**i·sot·o·py** (ī·sot'ə·pē) *n.*

i·so·trop·ic (ī'sə·trop'ik, -trō'pik) *adj. Physics* Exhibiting the same physical properties in every direction. Also **i·sot·ro·pous** (ī·sot'rə·pəs).

Is·ra·el (iz'rē·əl) The patriarch Jacob. *Gen.* xxxii 28. — *n.* The Jewish people, regarded as descended from Jacob. [< Hebrew *Yisrā'ēl* God persevereth]

Is·rae·li (iz·rā'lē) *adj.* Of modern Israel, its people, or their culture. — *n. pl.* **·lis** A native or inhabitant of Israel.

Is·ra·el·ite (iz'rē·əl·īt') *n.* Any of the people of Israel or their descendants; a Hebrew; a Jew. — *adj.* Of or pertaining to the Hebrews; Jewish: also **Is'ra·el·it'ish** (-ī'tish), **Is'ra·el·it'ic** (-it'ik).

Is·sei (ēs·sā') *n. pl.* **·sei** or **·seis** A Japanese who emigrated to the U.S. after 1907, and was not legally eligible to become an American citizen. [< Japanese *is* first + *sei* generation]

is·su·ance (ish'ōō·əns, -yōō-) *n.* The act or procedure of issuing; promulgation. —**is'su·ant** *adj.*

is·sue (ish'ōō, -yōō) *n.* **1.** The act of giving out or publishing, esp. from an official source. **2.** An item or set of items, as stamps, magazines, etc., published at a single time. **3.** A result; consequence; outcome. **4.** A matter of importance to be resolved. **5.** An outflow; discharge. **6.** A point of egress; outlet; exit. **7.** Offspring; progeny. **8.** Profits; proceeds, as from property. **9.** *Med.* A discharge, as of blood or pus. —**at issue** In question; in controversy. —**to join issue** To enter into a controversy. —**to take issue** To disagree. — *v.* **sued, ·su·ing** *v.i.* **1.** To come forth; flow out; emerge. **2.** To be derived or descended; originate. **3.** To come as a consequence; result. **4.** To terminate: often followed by *in.* **5.** To be circulated or published; appear. **6.** To be produced as profit. — *v.t.* **7.** To publish; announce. **8.** To give out; distribute, as supplies. [< OF < L < *ex-out of* + *ire* to go] —**is'su·a·ble** *adj.* —**is'su·er** *n.*

-ist *suffix of nouns* **1.** One who or that which does or has to do with: *catechist.* **2.** One whose profession is: *pharmacist.* **3.** A student or devotee of: *genealogist.* **4.** One who advocates or adheres to: *socialist.* [< F < L < Gk. *-istēs*]

isth·mus (is'məs, isth'-) *n. pl.* **·mus·es** or **·mi** (-mī) A narrow piece of land extending into a body of water and connecting two larger land masses. [< L < Gk. *isthmos* narrow passage] —**isth'mi·an** *adj. & n.*

-istic *suffix of adjectives* Having the qualities of: formed from nouns ending in *-ist* or *-ism: communistic.*

is·tle (is'lē, ist'lē) *n.* A fiber derived from an agave plant, used for carpets, etc.

it (it) *pron., possessive* **its***; pl. nominative* **they,** *possessive* **their** or **theirs,** *objective* **them** The nominative and objective singular neuter pronoun of the third person, used: **1.** As a substitute for a specific noun or name when referring to things or places or to infants or animals of unspecified sex. **2.** To represent some implied idea, condition, action, or situation: How was *it*? **3.** As the subject or predicate nominative of a verb whose logical subject is anticipated: Who is *it*? **4.** As the subject of an impersonal verb: *It* rained yesterday. **5.** As the indefinite subject of a verb introducing a clause or a phrase: *It* seems that he knew. **6.** As the indefinite object after certain verbs in idiomatic expressions: to brazen *it* out. — *n.* In certain children's games, the player required to perform some specified act. [OE *hit*]

I.T.A. Initial Teaching Alphabet.

I·tal·ian (i·tal'yən) *adj.* Of Italy, its people, or their language. — *n.* **1.** A native or naturalized inhabitant of Italy. **2.** The Romance language of Italy.

i·tal·ic (i·tal'ik) *n. Usu. pl.* A style of type in which the letters slant, often used to denote emphasis: *These words are printed in italics.* — *adj.* Designating or printed in italics.

I·tal·ic (i·tal'ik) *adj.* Relating to any of the peoples of ancient Italy. — *n.* A subfamily of the Indo-European languages, comprising three branches, and including Latin and the Romance languages.

i·tal·i·cize (i·tal'ə·sīz) *v.* **·cized, ·ciz·ing** *v.t.* **1.** To print in italics. **2.** To underscore to indicate italics. — *v.i.* **3.** To use or indicate the use of italics. —**i·tal'i·ci·za'tion** *n.*

itch (ich) *v.i.* **1.** To experience or produce an irritation that causes a desire to scratch or rub the affected area. **2.** To have a restless or unsatisfied desire to do something; hanker. — *n.* **1.** An itching sensation or irritation. **2.** Any of various usu. contagious skin diseases accompanied by itching. **3.** A restless desire or yearning. [ME < OE *giccan*]

itch·y (ich'ē) *adj.* **itch·i·er, itch·i·est** Having or producing an itching sensation. —**itch'i·ness** *n.*

-ite[1] *suffix of nouns* **1.** A native or inhabitant of: *suburbanite.* **2.** A follower of or sympathizer with: *Pre-Raphaelite.* **3.** A descendant of: *Israelite.* **4.** Resembling or related to: *dynamite.* **5.** *Mineral.* A rock or mineral: *graphite.* **6.** *Paleontol.* A fossil: *trilobite.* **7.** *Zool.* A part of the body or of an organ: *dendrite.* [< F < L. Gk. *-itēs*]

-ite[2] *suffix Chem.* A salt or ester of an acid having a name that ends in *-ous: sulfite.* [< F *-ite*]

-ite[3] *suffix* Derived from the past participial form of certain Latin verbs and occurring in: **1.** Adjectives: *infinite, polite.* **2.** Verbs: *unite.* **3.** Nouns: *appetite.* [< L *-itus*]

i·tem (ī'təm) *n.* **1.** A single unit or article included in a category, series, or enumeration. **2.** An entry in an account. **3.** A brief article of news, etc., as in a newspaper. — *v.t.* To record or take note of as an item. — *adv.* Likewise; also: used to introduce an entry in a list or series. [< L, thus]

i·tem·ize (ī'təm·īz) *v.t.* **·ized, ·iz·ing** To set down or specify by items. —**i'tem·i·za'tion** *n.* —**i'tem·iz'er** *n.*

it·er·ate (it'ə·rāt) *v.t.* **·at·ed, ·at·ing** To state or utter again or repeatedly. [< L *iterum* again] —**it'er·a'tion** *n.* —**it'er·a·tive** *adj.*

i·tin·er·an·cy (ī·tin'ər·ən·sē, i·tin'-) *n.* The act or state of being itinerant. Also **i·tin'er·a·cy** (-ə·sē).

ISOSCELES
TRIANGLE
$AB = CB$

i·tin·er·ant (ī·tin′ər·ənt, i·tin′-) *adj.* **1.** Going from place to place; wandering. **2.** Traveling to a series of places in order to fulfill official duties. — *n.* One who travels from place to place. [< LL *itineris* journey, route] — **i·tin′er·ant·ly** *adv.*
i·tin·er·ar·y (ī·tin′ə·rer′ē, i·tin′-) *n. pl.* **·ar·ies 1.** A route followed in traveling. **2.** A plan for or graphic representation of a journey. **3.** A detailed account or record of a journey. **4.** A guidebook for travelers. — *adj.* Pertaining to travel or routes of travel. [< LL *iter, itineris* journey, route]
-ition *suffix of nouns* **1.** Condition or quality: *ambition.* **2.** Act or process, or the result of an act or process: *audition.* [< L *-itio, -onis*]
-itious *suffix of adjectives* Characterized by; having the quality of: *ambitious.* [< L *-icius, -itius*]
-itis *suffix Pathol.* Inflammation of: *peritonitis.* [< Gk.]
it'll (it′l) **1.** It will. **2.** It shall.
-itol *suffix Chem.* Denoting a class of alcohols containing two or more hydroxyl radicals.
its (its) *pronominal adjective* The possessive case of the pronoun *it,* used attributively: *its* leaves. [< IT + 's, possessive case ending; written *it's* until the 19th century]
it's (its) **1.** It is. **2.** It has.
it·self (it·self′) *pron.* A form of the third person singular neuter pronoun, used: **a** As a reflexive or as object of a preposition in a reflexive sense: The motor started by *itself.* **b** As an intensifier or to give emphasis: simplicity *itself.* **c** As a designation for a normal or usual state: The house isn't *itself* with the children gone.
-ity *suffix of nouns* State or quality [< F < L *-itas*]
-ium *suffix Chem.* Denoting certain elements or compounds: *titanium.* [< L]
I've (īv) I have.
-ive *suffix of adjectives* **1.** Having a tendency or predisposition to: *disruptive.* **2.** Having the nature, character, or quality of: *massive.* Also *-ative.* [< F < L *-ivus*]
i·vied (ī′vēd) *adj.* Covered or overgrown with ivy.
i·vo·ry (ī′vər·ē) *n. pl.* **·ries 1.** A hard, white, smooth-textured dentine, the chief substance of the tusks of elephants, walruses, etc. **2.** Any substance resembling ivory. **3.** The creamy white color of ivory. **4.** *Usu. pl.* Articles made of ivory. **5.** Any form of dentine. **6.** A tusk, esp. of an elephant. **7.** *pl. Slang* **a** The teeth. **b** The keys of a piano. **c** Dice. — *adj.* **1.** Made of or resembling ivory. **2.** Of the color ivory. [< OF < L *ebur, -oris* ivory]
ivory tower A condition or attitude of withdrawal from the world and reality.
i·vy (ī′vē) *n. pl.* **i·vies** A climbing plant, having glossy, evergreen leaves: also **English ivy.** [OE *īfig*]
Ivy League An association of colleges in the NE U.S. (Brown, Columbia, Cornell, Dartmouth, Harvard, Princeton, the University of Pennsylvania, and Yale).
Iy·yar (ē·yär′, ē′yär) *n.* The eighth month of the Hebrew year. Also **I·yar′.** See (Hebrew) CALENDAR.
-ization *suffix* Used to form nouns from verbs in *-ize,* and denoting a condition, act, process, or result: *civilization.*
-ize *suffix of verbs* **1.** To cause to become or resemble: *Christianize.* **2.** To subject to the action of: *oxidize.* **3.** To change into: *mineralize.* **4.** To act in the manner of: *sympathize.* Also *-ise.* [< F < LL < Gk. *-izein*]
◆ The spelling of this suffix varies in British and American usage; *-ize* is the preferred spelling in the United States, while *-ise* is preferred in England. However, certain words, as *advise,* are always spelled with *-ise,* whereas others, as *baptize,* are always spelled with *-ize.*
iz·zard (iz′ərd) *n. Archaic* The letter Z. — **from A to iz·zard** From beginning to end. [< earlier *ezed,* var. of ZED]

J

j, J (jā) *n. pl.* **j's** or **js, J's** or **Js, jays** (jāz) **1.** The tenth letter of the English alphabet. **2.** The sound represented by the letter *j.*
jab (jab) *v.t. & v.i.* **jabbed, jab·bing 1.** To poke or thrust sharply. **2.** To punch or strike with short blows. — *n.* **1.** A sharp thrust. **2.** A rapid punch.
jab·ber (jab′ər) *v.t. & v.i.* To speak rapidly or without making sense. — *n.* Rapid or unintelligible talk; chatter. — **jab′ber·er** *n.*
ja·bot (zhā·bō′, *Fr.* zhà·bō′) *n. pl.* **·bots** (-bōz′, *Fr.* -bō′) A ruffle or similar decoration falling from the neckline or at the front of a blouse, shirt, or bodice. [< F, lit., gizzard]
ja·cinth (jā′sinth, jas′inth) *n.* Hyacinth. [< OF < L *hyacinthus*]
jack (jak) *n.* **1.** *Sometimes cap.* A man or boy; fellow; esp.: **a** A manual laborer: usu. in combination: *jack-of-all-trades; lumberjack.* **b** A sailor. **2.** Any of various devices that perform an operation formerly done by a man or boy: often used in combinations: *bootjack.* **3.** Any of various devices used for raising heavy weights through short distances, usu. by means of a lever. **4.** In names or designations of animals: **a** A male: sometimes used in combination: *jackass.* **b** Any of various kinds of animals, birds, or fish: often in combination: *jackdaw; jack rabbit.* **5.** A playing card showing the picture of a young man; the knave. **6.** A flag, flown at the bow of a ship as a signal or as an indication of nationality when in port. **7.** *U.S. Slang* Money. **8.** A jackstone. **9.** *Electr.* A metallic connecting device with spring clips to which the wires of a circuit may be attached. — *v.t.* **1.** To raise or lift with or as with a jack: usu. with *up.* **2.** *Informal* To increase, as a price or charge: with *up.* [after *Jack,* a nickname for John]
jack·al (jak′əl, -ôl) *n.* **1.** Any of various African or Asian doglike carnivorous mammals. **2.** One who does menial work to serve another. [< Turkish < Persian *shaghal*]
jack·a·napes (jak′ə·nāps) *n.* An impertinent fellow; an upstart. [< *Jack Napes,* nickname of William de la Pole, 15th c. Duke of Suffolk]
jack·ass (jak′as′) *n.* **1.** A male ass. **2.** A stupid person.
jack·boot (jak′bōōt′) *n.* A heavy topboot reaching above the knee.

jack·daw (jak′dô′) *n.* A glossy, black, crowlike bird of Europe, sometimes tamed as a pet.
jack·et (jak′it) *n.* **1.** A short coat, usu. not extending below the hips. **2.** An outer covering or case, as the removable paper cover for a bound book, the skin of a cooked potato, etc. — *v.t.* To cover or surround with or as with a jacket. [< OF *jaque* short jacket]
Jack Frost A personification of frost or winter weather.
jack-in-the-box (jak′in·thə·boks′) *n.* A toy consisting of a box containing a grotesque figure that springs up when the lid is unfastened: also **jack′-in-a-box′.**
jack-in-the-pul·pit (jak′in·thə·pōōl′pit) *n.* A common American herb of the arum family, growing from a turnip-shaped bulb.
jack·knife (jak′nīf′) *n. pl.* **·knives** (-nīvz′) **1.** A large pocketknife. **2.** A dive in which the body is doubled forward with the knees unbent and the hands touching the ankles, and then straightened before entering the water. — *v.t. & v.i.* **·knifed, ·knif·ing** To double up in the manner of a jackknife.
jack-of-all-trades (jak′əv·ôl′trādz′) *n.* One who is able to do many kinds of work.
jack-o'-lan·tern (jak′ə·lan′tərn) *n.* **1.** A lantern made of a pumpkin hollowed and carved into a grotesque face. **2.** A will-o'-the-wisp.
jack·pot (jak′pot′) *n.* **1.** In poker, a pot that accumulates until a player is dealt a pair of jacks or better with which he may open the betting. **2.** Any pot, pool, or prize in which the amount won is cumulative. — **to hit the jackpot** *U.S. Informal* **1.** To win the biggest possible prize. **2.** To achieve a major success.
jack rabbit A large American hare with long hind legs and long ears.
jacks (jaks) *n.pl.* (construed as sing.) The game of jackstones.
jack·stone (jak′stōn′) *n.* **1.** A stone or knobbed metal piece used in a children's game in which the pieces are tossed and picked up in a variety of ways: also called *jack.* **2.** *pl.* (construed as sing.) The game itself. [Var. of earlier *checkstone*]
jack·straw (jak′strô′) *n.* **1.** One of a set of thin strips of

JACK-IN-THE-PULPIT
a Flower.
b Fruit.

wood, bone, etc., used in a game in which the players attempt to pick up each strip without moving any of the others. **2.** *pl.* (*construed as sing.*) The game itself.

Ja·cob (jā′kəb) The second son of Isaac and father of the founders of the twelve Hebrew tribes. Also *Israel*. [< Hebrew *Ya'aqob* he grasps the heel. Cf. *Gen.* xxv 26.]

Jac·o·be·an (jak′ə·bē′ən) *adj.* Of or pertaining to James I of England or the period in which he reigned. — *n.* A notable person of the Jacobean era. [< LL < *Jacobus* James]

Jac·o·bin (jak′ə·bin) *n.* During the French Revolution, a member of a French political society that inaugurated the Reign of Terror. [< OF *Jacobin* of St. James; with ref. to the church of St. James, in Paris, where the society first met]

Jac·o·bite (jak′ə·bīt) *n.* An adherent of James II of England after his abdication in 1688. — *adj.* Of the Jacobites: also **Jac·o·bit·ic** (jak′ə·bit′ik) or **·i·cal**. [< L *Jacobus* James]

Jacob's ladder 1. A ladder from earth to heaven that Jacob saw in a dream. *Gen.* xxviii 12. **2.** *Naut.* A rope ladder, often with wooden rungs.

jade¹ (jād) *n.* **1.** A hard, translucent mineral, usu. green, used as a gemstone. **2.** A green color characteristic of jade. [< F < Sp. (*piedra de*) *ijada* (stone of) the side; because supposed to cure pain in the side]

jade² (jād) *n.* **1.** An old, worthless, or unmanageable hussy. **2.** A disreputable, ill-tempered, or perverse woman; hussy. — *v.t. & v.i.* **jad·ed, jad·ing** To weary or become weary through hard work or overuse; tire. [Origin uncertain]

jad·ed (jā′did) *adj.* **1.** Worn-out; exhausted. **2.** Dulled, as from overindulgence. — **jad′ed·ly** *adv.* — **jad′ed·ness** *n.*

jae·ger (yā′gər, jā′-) *n.* Any of a group of sea birds that pursue and harass gulls and terns until they drop or disgorge their prey. Also **jä′ger**. [< G, hunter]

jag¹ (jag) *n.* A sharp, projecting point; notch; tooth. — *v.t.* **1.** To cut notches or jags in. **2.** To cut unevenly or with slashing strokes. Also **jagg**. [ME *jagge*]

jag² (jag) *n. Slang* **1.** A period of unrestrained activity: a crying *jag*. **2.** A drunken spree.

jag·ged (jag′id) *adj.* Having jags or notches; serrate. — Syn. See ROUGH. — **jag′ged·ly** *adv.* — **jag′ged·ness** *n.*

jag·uar (jag′wär, jag′yōō·är) *n.* A large, spotted feline of Central and South America. [< Pg. < Tupi *jaguara*]

jai a·lai (hī ə·lī′) A game popular in Latin America, similar to handball but played with a long, curved, wicker basket strapped to the arm. [< Sp. < Basque, jolly festival]

jail (jāl) *n.* **1.** A place of confinement for those guilty of minor offenses or those awaiting trial. **2.** Loosely, any prison. — *v.t.* To put or hold in jail; imprison. Also, *Brit.*, **gaol**. [< OF *jaiole*, ult. < L *cavea* cave]

jail·bird (jāl′bûrd′) *n. Informal* A prisoner or ex-prisoner.

jail·er (jā′lər) *n.* The officer in charge of a jail: also, *Brit.*, **gaoler**. Also **jail′or**.

Jain·ism (jī′niz·əm) *n.* A religion of India, founded about 500 B.C., having elements of Brahmanism and Buddhism.

jal·ap (jal′əp) *n.* **1.** The dried root of any of several Mexican plants used as a purgative. **2.** Any allied plant yielding a similar drug. [< Sp. (*purga de*) *Jalapa* (medicine from) Jalapa] — **ja·lap·ic** (jə·lap′ik) *adj.*

ja·lop·y (jə·lop′ē) *n. pl.* **·lop·ies** *U.S. Informal* A decrepit automobile. [Origin uncertain]

ja·lou·sie (jal′ōō·sē, zhal′ōō·zē′) *n.* A window blind or shutter of overlapping horizontal slats or strips that may be tilted to keep out sun and rain while admitting air and some light. [< F, lit., jealousy]

jam¹ (jam) *v.* **jammed, jam·ming** *v.t.* **1.** To force or ram into or against something. **2.** To pack and block up by crowding. **3.** To cause (a machine, door, etc.) to become wedged or stuck. **4.** To interfere electronically with (a radio broadcast, etc.). **5.** To bruise or crush. — *v.i.* **6.** To become wedged; stick fast. **7.** To cease operation, as a machine, gun, etc., because parts have stuck or wedged together. **8.** To take part in a jam session. — *n.* **1.** A crowding together, as of people, cars, etc. **2.** The act of jamming. **3.** *Informal* An embarrassing or dangerous predicament. [Akin to CHAMP¹]

jam² (jam) *n.* A pulpy, sweet conserve of whole fruit boiled with sugar. [? < JAM¹, v.]

Ja·mai·can (jə·mā′kən) *adj.* Of or pertaining to Jamaica and its people. — *n.* A native or inhabitant of Jamaica.

jamb (jam) *n.* A side post or side of a doorway, window, etc. [< OF < LL *gamba* hoof, leg]

jam·bo·ree (jam′bə·rē′) *n.* **1.** *Informal* A boisterous frolic. **2.** A large, esp. international, assembly of Boy Scouts.

James (jāmz) One of the brothers of Jesus: called **Saint James**. — *n.* A book of the New Testament consisting of the epistle attributed to him.

jam session An informal gathering of jazz musicians performing improvisations on various themes.

jan·gle (jang′gəl) *v.* **·gled, ·gling** *v.i.* **1.** To make harsh, unmusical sounds. **2.** To wrangle; bicker. — *v.t.* **3.** To cause to sound discordantly. — *n.* **1.** A discordant sound. **2.** A quarrel; wrangling. [< OF *jangler*] — **jan′gler** *n.*

jan·i·tor (jan′i·tər) *n.* **1.** One who is employed to care for a building, etc. **2.** A doorkeeper; porter. [< L *janua* door] — **jan·i·to′ri·al** *adj.* — **jan′i·tress** *n.fem.*

jan·i·zar·y (jan′ə·zer′ē) *n. pl.* **·zar·ies** *Often cap.* **1.** A soldier in the Turkish sultan's army before 1826. **2.** Any Turkish soldier. Also **jan′i·sar·y, jan′is·sar·y** (-ser′ē). [< F < Turkish *yeničheri* new army]

Jan·u·ar·y (jan′yōō·er′ē) *n. pl.* **·ar·ies** or **·ar·ys** The first month of the year, containing 31 days. [< L *Januarius* < *Janus* Janus]

Ja·nus (jā′nəs) In Roman mythology, the god of portals and of beginnings and endings, usu. depicted as having two faces looking in opposite directions.

Ja·nus-faced (jā′nəs·fāst′) *adj.* Two-faced; deceitful.

Jap (jap) *adj. & n. Slang* Japanese: an offensive term.

ja·pan (jə·pan′) *n.* **1.** Any of various glossy black lacquers or varnishes, used for coating objects. **2.** A glossy, black, vitreous enamel baked onto machine parts, etc. **3.** Ornamental objects decorated or lacquered in the Japanese manner. — *adj.* Pertaining to, enameled with, or lacquered with japan. — *v.t.* **·panned, ·pan·ning** To enamel or lacquer with or as with japan. [< JAPAN]

Jap·a·nese (jap′ə·nēz′, -nēs′) *adj.* Of or pertaining to Japan, its people, or their language. — *n. pl.* **·nese 1.** A native of Japan, or a person of Japanese ancestry. **2.** The language of Japan.

Japanese beetle A destructive beetle introduced to the U.S. from Japan. The adults eat the leaves and fruits of various plants, and the larvae feed on grass roots.

jape (jāp) *Archaic v.* **japed, jap·ing** *v.i.* **1.** To joke; make jests. — *v.t.* **2.** To mock; jibe at. — *n.* A jest; jibe. [ME *jappen*] — **jap′er** *n.* — **jap′er·y** *n.*

Ja·pheth (jā′fith) Third and youngest son of Noah. *Gen.* v 32. Also **Ja′phet** (-fit). [< Hebrew *Yepheth*, lit., extension]

ja·pon·i·ca (jə·pon′i·kə) *n.* **1.** An Asian shrub with red flowers. **2.** The camellia. [< NL, Japanese]

jar¹ (jär) *n.* **1.** A wide-mouthed vessel of glass or earthenware, usu. deep and cylindrical. **2.** The quantity a jar contains: also **jar′ful** (-fŏŏl′). [< F < Arabic *jarrah*]

jar² (jär) *v.* **jarred, jar·ring** *v.t.* **1.** To strike against or bump so as to cause shaking, movement, etc.; jolt. **2.** To affect (one's nerves, feelings, etc.) unpleasantly or painfully. — *v.i.* **3.** To have an unpleasant or painful effect: with *on* or *upon*. **4.** To disagree or conflict; clash. **5.** To bump or jolt: with *against*. **6.** To make or have a disagreeable sound. — *n.* **1.** A shaking, shock, or jolt. **2.** A disagreeable sound or jumble of sounds; discord. **3.** A painful or irritating shock to the feelings. [Imit.]

jar·di·nière (jär′də·nir′, *Fr.* zhår·dē·nyâr′) *n.* An ornamental pot or stand for flowers or plants. [< F, fem. of *jardinier* gardener]

jar·gon (jär′gən) *n.* **1.** Confused, unintelligible speech; gibberish. **2.** A language, dialect, or form of speech regarded as meaningless or confusing. **3.** The technical or specialized vocabulary or phraseology used among themselves by the members of a particular profession, sect, or similarly restricted group: legal *jargon*. **4.** A mixture of two or more dissimilar languages, often serving as a lingua franca; pidgin. — *v.i.* To speak in jargon. [< OF, a chattering]

jar·gon·ize (jär′gən·īz) *v.* **·ized, ·iz·ing** *v.t.* **1.** To translate into jargon. — *v.i.* **2.** To express oneself in jargon.

jas·mine (jas′min, jaz′-) *n.* **1.** An ornamental plant of the olive family, with fragrant, generally white flowers. **2.** Any of various other similar plants. Also called *jessamine*. [< F < Persian *yāsmīn*]

Ja·son (jā′sən) In Greek legend, a prince who led the Argonauts in search of the Golden Fleece, and who married Medea. [< Gk., healer]

jas·per (jas′pər) *n.* **1.** An opaque, usu. red, brown, or yellow variety of quartz, admitting of a high polish: also **jas′per·ite**. **2.** In the Bible, one of the twelve stones in the breastplate of the high priest. *Ex.* xxviii 20. [< MF < L *jaspis* < Gk. < Semitic] — **jas′per·e·an** (-pid′ē·ən), **jas·pid′e·ous** (-pid′ē·əs) *adj.*

jaun·dice (jôn′dis, jän′-) *n.* **1.** *Pathol.* A diseased condition of the liver due to the presence of bile pigments in the blood and characterized by yellowness of the skin and eyeballs. **2.** A state of mind, feeling, perception, etc., that distorts the judgment. — *v.t.* **diced, dic·ing 1.** To affect with jaundice. **2.** To alter or influence (the mind, feelings, etc.) so as to affect the judgment. [< OF *jaune* < L *galbus* yellow]

jaunt (jônt, jänt) *n.* A short journey, esp. for pleasure. — *v.i.* To make such a journey. [Origin unknown]

jaunt·y (jôn′tē, jän′-) *adj.* **jaunt·i·er, jaunt·i·est 1.** Having a lively and self-confident air or manner; cheerfully brisk. **2.** Trim; dashing; a *jaunty* hat. [< F *gentil* genteel] — **jaunt′i·ly** *adv.* — **jaunt′i·ness** *n.*

ja·va (jav′ə, jä′və) *n. Sometimes cap. U.S. Slang* Coffee.

Ja·va (jav′ə, jä′və) *n.* A type of coffee. [after *Java*]

Java man Pithecanthropus.

Jav·a·nese (jav′ə·nēz′, -nēs′) *adj.* Of or pertaining to Java, its language, or its people. — *n. pl.* **·nese 1.** A native or naturalized inhabitant of Java. **2.** The Indonesian language of central Java, closely related to Malay.

jave·lin (jav′lin, jav′ə·lin) *n.* **1.** A light spear thrown as a weapon. **2.** A long spear with a wooden shaft, thrown for distance in an athletic contest. [< F, prob. < Celtic]

jaw (jô) *n.* **1.** *Anat.* **a** Either of the two bony structures forming the framework of the mouth and holding the teeth, consisting of the **upper jaw** or maxilla, and the **lower jaw** or mandible. **b** *pl.* The mouth and its associated parts. **2.** One of a pair of gripping parts capable of opening and closing, as of a tool. **3.** Anything suggesting the action of the jaws: the *jaws* of death. **4.** *pl.* The narrow entrance of a gorge, canyon, etc. **5.** *Informal* A talk; chat. **6.** *Informal* Impudent talk. — *v.i.* **1.** *Informal* To talk; jabber. — *v.t.* **2.** *Informal* To scold or abuse. [ME < F *joue* cheek]

jaw·bone (jô′bōn′) *n.* One of the bones of the jaw, esp. that of the lower jaw.

jaw·break·er (jô′brā′kər) *n.* **1.** *U.S. Informal* A type of very hard candy. **2.** A machine that crushes ore: also **jaw′crush′er** (-krush′ər). **3.** *Informal* A word hard to pronounce.

jay (jā) *n.* Any of various corvine birds, usu. of brilliant coloring, as the blue jay. [< OF < Med.L *gaius*]

jay·hawk·er (jā′hô′kər) *n.* **1.** A guerrilla raider of the Civil War period in Kansas; also, any freebooting guerrilla. **2.** *Usu. cap.* A Kansan. [Origin uncertain]

jay·walk (jā′wôk′) *v.i. Informal* To cross a street recklessly, violating traffic regulations or signals. — **jay′walk′er** *n.*

jazz (jaz) *n.* **1.** A kind of music, chiefly extemporaneous but sometimes arranged, characterized by melodic, harmonic, and rhythmic variation, syncopation, flatted thirds and sevenths, and a melody played against various chord patterns. **2.** Loosely, any contemporary popular dance music. **3.** *U.S. Slang* Lying and exaggerated talk; also, idle and foolish talk. **4.** *U.S. Slang* Liveliness and animation. — *adj.* Of or pertaining to jazz. — *v.t.* **1.** *U.S. Slang* To quicken the tempo of; speed up. **2.** To play or arrange (music) as jazz. — **to jazz up** *U.S. Slang* To make more exciting. [< Creole *jass* coition; from its origin in the brothels of New Orleans] — **jazz′y** *adj.* — **jazz′i·ly** *adv.*

jeal·ous (jel′əs) *adj.* **1.** Fearful or suspicious of being displaced by a rival in affection or favors. **2.** Vindictive toward another because of supposed or actual rivalry. **3.** Vigilant in guarding: to be *jealous* of a privilege. **4.** Resulting or arising from jealousy: *jealous* fears. **5.** Demanding exclusive worship and love: a *jealous* God. [< OF < Med.L LL < Gk. *zēlos* zeal] — **jeal′ous·ly** *adv.* — **jeal′ous·ness** *n.*

jeal·ous·y (jel′əs·ē) *n. pl.* **·ou·sies 1.** The state or quality of being jealous. **2.** The fact of being jealous.

jean (jēn, jān) *n.* **1.** A sturdy, twilled cotton cloth used in workclothes. **2.** *pl.* Trousers or overalls made of this material. [after F *Gênes* Genoa, where it was made]

jee (jē) See GEE.

jeep (jēp) *n.* A small, military and civilian motorcar equipped with four-wheel drive. [< G(ENERAL) P(URPOSE) (VEHICLE)]

jeer (jir) *v.i.* **1.** To speak or shout in a derisive, mocking manner; scoff. — *v.t.* **2.** To treat with derision or mockery; scoff at. — *n.* A derisive and flouting word or remark. [Origin unknown] — **jeer′er** *n.* — **jeer′ing·ly** *adv.*

Jef·fer·so·ni·an (jef′ər·sō′nē·ən) *adj.* Of, pertaining to, or characteristic of Thomas Jefferson or his political ideas and beliefs. — *n.* An adherent of Jefferson or his school of thought. — **Jef′fer·so′ni·an·ism** *n.*

Je·hosh·a·phat (ji·hosh′ə·fat, -hos′/-) Ninth-century B.C. king of Judah, I *Kings* xxii 41.

Je·ho·vah (ji·hō′və) In the Old Testament, God; the Lord. See YAHWEH. [< Hebrew *JHVH* Yahweh, either Creator or Eternal] **Je·ho′vi·an, Je·ho′vic** *adj.*

Jehovah's Witnesses A Christian sect opposed to war and the authority of the government in matters of conscience.

je·june (jə·jōōn′) *adj.* **1.** Lacking in substance or nourishment; barren. **2.** Lacking interest; insipid; dry. [< L *jejunus* hungry] — **je·june′ly** *adv.* — **je·june′ness** *n.*

je·ju·num (jə·jōō′nəm) *n. pl.* **·na** (-nə) *Anat.* That portion of the small intestine that extends from the duodenum to the ileum. [< NL < L *jejunus* hungry]

jell (jel) *v.t. & v.i. U.S. Informal* **1.** To jelly; congeal. **2.** To assume or cause to assume definite form. [< JELLY]

jel·lied (jel′ēd) *adj.* **1.** Made gelatinous, as by chilling: *jellied* consommé. **2.** Covered with or prepared in jelly.

jel·li·fy (jel′ə·fī) *v.t. & v.i.* **·fied, ·fy·ing** To make into or become a jelly. — **jel′li·fi·ca′tion** *n.*

Jel·lo (jel′ō) *n.* A fruit-flavored gelatin dessert. [< *Jell-O*, a trade name]

jel·ly (jel′ē) *n. pl.* **·lies 1.** Any food preparation made with gelatin or pectin, and having a consistency such that it quivers when shaken; esp., such a food made of boiled and sweet-

ened fruit juice and used as a spread or filler. **2.** Any gelatinous substance. — *v.* **·lied, ·ly·ing** *v.t.* **1.** To make into a jelly. **2.** To cover or fill with jelly. — *v.i.* **3.** To become jelly. [< OF < L *gelata*, pp. of *gelare* to freeze]

jel·ly·bean (jel′ē·bēn′) *n. U.S.* A bean-shaped candy having a hard, colored coating over a gelatinous center.

jel·ly·fish (jel′ē·fish′) *n. pl.* **·fish** or **·fish·es 1.** Any of a number of marine animals of jellylike substance, often having umbrella-shaped bodies with trailing tentacles. **2.** *Informal* One lacking determination or stamina; weakling.

je ne sais quoi (zhən se kwä′) *French* An indefinable something; literally, I know not what.

jen·net (jen′it) *n.* A breed of small Spanish horses. Also spelled *genet.* [< OF < Sp. *jinete* a light horseman.

jen·ny (jen′ē) *n. pl.* **·nies 1.** A spinning jenny. **2.** The female of some birds and animals: *jenny* wren; *jenny* ass. [after *Jenny*, a personal name]

jeop·ard·ize (jep′ər·dīz) *v.t.* **·ized, ·iz·ing** To put in jeopardy; expose to loss or injury; imperil. Also **jeop′ard.**

jeop·ar·dy (jep′ər·dē) *n.* **1.** Danger of death, loss, or injury; peril. **2.** *Law* The peril in which a defendant is put when placed on trial for a crime. [< OF < L *jocus partitus* divided play]

jer·bo·a (jər·bō′ə) *n.* Any of various nocturnal rodents of Asia and North Africa, with very long hind legs adapted for leaping. [< NL < Arabic *yarbu*′]

jer·e·mi·ad (jer′ə·mī′ad) *n.* A lament or tale of woe; complaint. [< F *Jérémie* Jeremiah]

Jer·e·mi·ah (jer′ə·mī′ə) Seventh-century B.C. Hebrew prophet. — *n.* The Old Testament book containing his prophecies. Also, in the Douai Bible, **Jer′e·mi′as** (-əs). [< Hebrew *Yirmĕyāhū*, lit., God looseneth (from the womb)]

jerk¹ (jûrk) *v.t.* **1.** To give a sharp, sudden pull or twist to. **2.** To throw, move, or thrust with a sharp, suddenly arrested motion. **3.** To utter in a gasping or broken manner: with *out.* — *v.i.* **4.** To give a jerk or jerks. **5.** To move with sharp, sudden motions; twitch. — *n.* **1.** A sudden sharp pull, twist, or thrust. **2.** *Physiol.* An involuntary contraction of a muscle caused by reflex action. **3.** *Slang* A stupid man. [? Var. of archaic *yerk*] — **jerk′y** *adv.* — **jerk′i·ly** *adv.* — **jerk′i·ness** *n.*

jerk² (jûrk) *v.t.* To cure (meat) by cutting into strips and drying. — *n.* Jerked meat, esp. beef. [< Sp. *charqui* < Quechua *echarqui* dried beef]

jer·kin (jûr′kin) *n.* **1.** A close-fitting jacket or vest, usu. sleeveless. **2.** Formerly, such a garment, often of leather, worn in the 16th and 17th centuries. [Origin unknown]

jerk·wa·ter (jûrk′wô′tər, -wot′ər) *U.S. Informal adj.* **1.** Not on the main line: a *jerkwater* town. **2.** Insignificant; small. — *n.* A train serving a branch line.

jer·ry·build (jer′ē·bild′) *v.t.* **·built, ·build·ing** To build flimsily and with inferior materials. [Origin unknown]

jer·sey (jûr′zē) *n. pl.* **·seys 1.** A ribbed elastic fabric of wool, cotton, etc., used for clothing. Also **jersey cloth. 2.** A close-fitting knit upper garment.

Jer·sey (jûr′zē) *n. pl.* **·seys** One of a breed of small cattle, usu. fawn-colored, originating in the island of Jersey and noted for milk rich in butterfat.

jes·sa·mine (jes′ə·min) *n.* Jasmine, a plant.

jest (jest) *n.* **1.** Something said or done to provoke laughter; joke. **2.** Playfulness; fun: to speak in *jest.* **3.** An object of laughter; laughingstock. — *v.i.* **1.** To make amusing remarks; tell jokes; quip. **2.** To speak or act in a playful way; trifle. [< OF < L *gesta* deeds]

jest·er (jes′tər) *n.* One who jests; esp., a court fool.

jest·ing (jes′ting) *n.* The action of one who jokes. — *adj.* Of the nature of a jest; prone to jest. — **jest′ing·ly** *adv.*

Jes·u·it (jezh′ōō·it, jez′yōō-) *n.* **1.** A member of the Society of Jesus, a religious order founded in 1534 by Ignatius Loyola to combat the Reformation and propagate the faith among the heathen. **2.** A crafty or scheming person; an equivocator: a derogatory term. [< NL < L *Jesus* Jesus] — **Jes′u·it′ic** or **·i·cal** *adj.* — **Jes′u·it′i·cal·ly** *adv.*

Jes·u·it·ize (jezh′ōō·it·īz′, jez′yōō-) *v.t. & v.i.* **·ized, ·iz·ing** To be or make Jesuitic.

Je·sus (jē′zəs) Founder of Christianity, 6? B.C.–29? A.D., son of Mary; regarded in the Christian faith as Christ, the Messiah. Also **Jesus Christ, Jesus of Nazareth.**

jet¹ (jet) *n.* **1.** A hard black lignite, taking a high polish, used for jewelry, buttons, etc. **2.** A deep, glossy black. — *adj.* **1.** Made of or resembling jet. **2.** Black as jet; **jetblack.** [< OF < L < Gk. *gagatēs*, after *Gagai*, a Lycian town where it was mined]

jet² (jet) *n.* **1.** A sudden spurt or gush of liquid or gas emitted from a narrow orifice. **2.** Liquid or gas that spurts from an orifice. **3.** A spout or nozzle. **4.** A jet-propelled aircraft. — *v.t.* **jet·ted, jet·ting** To spurt forth or emit in a stream. [< F, ult. < L *jactare*, freq. of *jacere* to throw]

Jet, meaning operating by, of, or relating to jet propulsion, may appear as a combining form or as the first element in two-word phrases; as in:

jet aircraft	jet bomber	jet pilot
jet airplane	jet fighter	jet plane
jet aviation	jetliner	jet-propelled

jet-black (jet′black′) *adj. & n.* Deep black, like jet.

jet engine A reaction and heat engine that takes in outside air to oxidize fuel that it converts into the energy of a powerful jet of heated gas expelled to the rear under high pressure.

jet lag A disruption of the body's accustomed rhythms of sleep, hunger, etc., owing to the change of time zones when traveling long distances by jet aircraft.

jet propulsion 1. Propulsion by means of a jet of gas or other fluid. 2. *Aeron.* Propulsion by means of jet engines.

jet·sam (jet′səm) *n.* 1. Goods thrown into the sea to lighten an imperiled vessel. 2. Such goods washed ashore. [Earlier *jetson,* short for JETTISON]

jet stream 1. The strong flow of gas or other fluid expelled from a jet engine, rocket motor, and the like. 2. *Meteorol.* A high-velocity wind circulating, usu. from west to east, near the base of the stratosphere.

jet·ti·son (jet′ə-sən) *v.t.* 1. To throw overboard (goods or cargo). 2. To discard (something that hampers). — *n.* 1. The act of jettisoning. 2. Jetsam. [< AF < L < *jactare* to throw]

jet·ty (jet′ē) *n. pl.* ·ties 1. A structure of piling, rocks, etc., extending out into a body of water to protect a harbor, etc. 2. A wharf or pier. [< OF *jeter* to throw]

Jew (jōō) *n.* 1. A member or descendant of the Hebrew people. 2. Any person professing Judaism. 3. Originally, a member of the tribe or the kingdom of Judah. — *adj.* Jewish: an offensive usage. [< OF < L < Gk. < Hebrew *y'hudi* descendant of Judah] — **Jew′ess** *n.fem.*

jew·el (jōō′əl) *n.* 1. A precious stone; gem. 2. An article for personal adornment, esp. one made of cut gems and precious metal. 3. A person or thing of rare excellence or value. 4. A bit of gem, crystal, glass, etc., used to form a durable bearing, as in a watch. — *v.t.* **jew·eled** or ·**elled,** **jew·el·ing** or ·**el·ling** To adorn with jewels; set jewels in. [< OF ult. < L *jocus* a joke, sport]

jew·el·er (jōō′əl·ər) *n.* A dealer in or maker of jewelry. Also **jew′el·ler.**

jew·el·ry (jōō′əl·rē) *n.* Jewels, collectively. Also *Brit.* **jew′el·ler·y.**

jew·el·weed (jōō′əl·wēd′) *n.* A species of touch-me-not having deep yellow flowers.

Jew·ish (jōō′ish) *adj.* Of or pertaining to Jews, their customs, religion, etc. — **Jew′ish·ness** *n.*

Jewish holidays See HANUKKAH, PASSOVER, ROSH HA-SHANA, SUKKOTH, and YOM KIPPUR.

Jew·ry (jōō′rē) *n.* The Jewish people.

jew's-harp (jōōz′härp′) *n.* A small, lyre-shaped musical instrument held between the teeth and played by plucking a flexible steel tongue with the finger. Also **jews′-harp.**

Jez·e·bel (jez′ə·bəl) The wife of Ahab, notorious for her evil actions. I *Kings* xvi 31. — *n.* A bold, vicious woman.

jib¹ (jib) *n.* 1. *Naut.* A triangular sail, set on a stay and extending from the foretopmast head to the jib boom or the bowsprit. For illus. see SCHOONER. 2. The boom of a crane or derrick. — *v.t. & v.i.* **jibbed, jib·bing** *Naut.* To jibe. [? Short for GIBBET]

jib² (jib) *v.i.* **jibbed, jib·bing** 1. To move restively sidewise or backward, as a horse. 2. To balk. — *n.* A horse that jibs: also **jib′ber.** [Cf. OF *giber* kick]

jib boom *Naut.* A spar forming a continuation of the bowsprit and holding a jib.

jibe¹ (jib) *v.* **jibed, jib·ing** *v.i.* 1. *Naut.* To swing from one side of a vessel to the other: said of a fore-and-aft sail or its boom. 2. To change course so that the sails shift in this manner. — *v.t.* 3. To cause to swing from one side of a vessel to the other. Also spelled *gibe, jib.* [< Du. *gijben*]

jibe² (jib) See GIBE¹.

jibe³ (jib) *v.i.* **jibed, jib·ing** *U.S. Informal* To agree; be in accordance. [Origin uncertain]

jif·fy (jif′ē) *n. pl.* ·**fies** *Informal* An instant; moment. Also **jiff.** [Origin unknown]

jig (jig) *n.* 1. A fast, lively dance; also, the music for such a dance. 2. *Mech.* A device for holding the material being worked or for guiding a tool. 3. In fishing, any of various combinations of hooks, spoons, etc., that are agitated in the water to attract and catch fish. 4. *Mining* A wire sieve or other device for separating or cleaning coal by jolting and shaking in water. — **the jig is up** *Slang* All hope of success is gone. — *v.* **jigged, jig·ging** *v.i.* 1. To dance or play a jig. 2. To move jerkily, esp. up and down; bob. 3. To use or operate a jig in working. 4. To fish with a jig. — *v.t.* 5. To jerk up and down or to and fro; jiggle. 6. To hold, form, process, etc., with a jig. 7. To catch (fish) with a jig. [Cf. OF *gigue* a fiddle]

jig·ger (jig′ər) *n.* 1. One who or that which jigs. 2. A

small glass or cup for measuring liquor, holding about one and one half ounces; also, the amount of liquor so measured. 3. A jig used in catching fish. 4. *Mech.* A jig. 5. Any of various types of jolting mechanisms, as an apparatus for separating ores, a potter's wheel, etc. 6. *Naut.* **a** A small sail set in the stern of a sailing craft, as a yawl. **b** A light tackle used on board ship. **c** A jigger mast. 7. *Informal* Any small device or thing one is unable to name definitely.

jigger mast *Naut.* The aftermost mast of a four- or five-masted vessel.

jig·gle (jig′əl) *v.t. & v.i.* ·**gled, ·gling** To move unsteadily up and down or backwards and forwards with slight, quick jerks. — *n.* A jerky, unsteady movement. [Freq. of JIG, v.]

jig·saw (jig′sô′) *n.* A saw having a slim blade set vertically in a frame and operated with a reciprocating motion, used for cutting curved or irregular lines.

jigsaw puzzle A puzzle consisting of a picture mounted on wood or cardboard and then cut or stamped into irregular interlocking pieces for reassembly.

jilt (jilt) *v.t.* To cast off or discard (a previously favored lover or sweetheart). — *n.* A woman or girl who discards a lover. [Cf. dial. E (Scottish) *jillet* giddy girl] — **jilt′er** *n.*

jim-crow (jim′krō′) *U.S. Slang adj.* Serving to segregate Negroes: *jim-crow* laws. — *v.t.* To subject (Negroes) to segregation or discrimination. Also **Jim′-Crow′.**

Jim Crow *U.S. Slang* 1. A Negro: an offensive term. 2. The segregation of Negroes. — **Jim-Crow′ism** *n.*

jim·my (jim′ē) *n. pl.* ·**mies** A burglar's crowbar. — *v.t.* ·**mied, ·my·ing** To break or pry open with or as with a jimmy. [after *Jimmy,* dim. of *James,* a personal name]

jim·son·weed (jim′sən·wēd′) *n.* A tall, coarse, evil-smelling, poisonous annual weed of the nightshade family, yielding atropine and scopolamine: also called *stramonium.* Also **Jimson weed.** [Alter. of *Jamestown weed* Jamestown, Va.]

jin·gle (jin′gəl) *v.* ·**gled, ·gling** *v.i.* 1. To make light ringing or tinkling sounds. 2. To have an intrusive rhyme or rhythm: said of writing or music, often in deprecation. — *v.t.* 3. To cause to make ringing or tinkling sounds. — *n.* 1. A tinkling, clinking, or rapidly ringing sound. 2. A catchy short song or poem, esp. one used for advertising. 3. Rapid repetition in rhyme, rhythm, alliteration, etc. [Imit.] — **jin′gly** *adj.*

jin·go (jing′gō) *n. pl.* ·**goes** One who boasts of his patriotism and favors an aggressive foreign policy. — *adj.* Of, pertaining to, or characteristic of the jingoes. [Originally a magician's nonsense word] — **jin′go·ish** *adj.* — **jin′go·ism** *n.* — **jin′go·ist** *n.* — **jin·go·is′tic** *adj.*

jin·ni (jin′ē, jin·ē′) *n. pl.* **jinn** (jin) In Moslem mythology, one of the supernatural beings able to assume human or animal form and often at the service of men: sometimes spelled *djinni, genie.* Also **jin·nee′.** [< Arabic *jinni*]

jin·rik·sha (jin-rik′shə, -shô) *n.* A small oriental two-wheeled carriage drawn by one or two men: also called *rickshaw, ricksha.* Also **jin·rick′sha, jin·rik′i·sha.** [< Japanese *jin* man + *riki* power + *sha* carriage]

jinx (jingks) *Slang n.* A person or thing supposed to bring bad luck. — *v.t.* To bring bad luck to. [< earlier *jynx* < Gk. *iynx* the wryneck (a bird anciently used in witchcraft)]

jit·ney (jit′nē) *n. U.S.* 1. A motor vehicle that carries passengers for a small fare. 2. *Obs. Slang* A small coin.

jit·ter (jit′ər) *v.i. U.S. Slang* To be nervous. — **the jitters** *Slang* Intense nervousness. — **jit′ter·y** *adj.*

jit·ter·bug (jit′ər·bug′) *U.S. Slang n.* One who dances rapidly and spasmodically to jazz. — *v.i.* ·**bugged, ·bugging** To dance to jazz in a fast, violent way.

jiu·jit·su (jōō·jit′sōō), **jiu·jut·su** (jōō·jit′sōō, -jōōt′sōō) See JUJITSU.

jive (jīv) *n. Slang* 1. The jargon of jazz music and musicians. 2. Jazz music. [Origin unknown]

job (job) *n.* 1. Anything that is to be done, esp. a definite single piece of work done for a set fee; also, the thing worked on. 2. A position or situation of employment. 3. Something done ostensibly for the public good, but actually for private profit. 4. *Informal* An affair; circumstance. 5. *Slang* A robbery or other criminal act. — **odd job** A piece of occasional or miscellaneous work. — **on the job** *Informal* 1. During working hours. 2. Attending strictly to the matter at hand. — **to lie** (or **lay**) **down on the job** *Informal* To evade work or responsibility. — *v.* **jobbed, job·bing** *v.i.* 1. To work by the job or piece. 2. To be a jobber or middleman. 3. To use a position of public trust for private advantage. — *v.t.* 4. To buy in bulk and resell in lots to dealers. 5. To sublet (work) among separate contractors. [Origin uncertain] — **job′less** *adj.* — **job′less·ness** *n.*

Job (jōb) In the Bible, the chief character in the Book of Job, who, despite great suffering and adversity, kept his faith in God. — *n.* The book itself.

job·ber (job′ər) *n.* 1. One who buys goods in bulk from the manufacturer or importer and sells to the retailer; wholesaler. 2. One who works by the job, or on small jobs; pieceworker.

job·ber·y (job′ər·ē) *n.* *pl.* **·ber·ies** Corrupt use of a public office or trust for private or partisan gain.

job·hold·er (job′hōl′dər) *n.* One who has a steady job.

job lot 1. A collection of miscellaneous goods sold to a retailer. 2. Any collection of things inferior in quality.

Jo·cas·ta (jō·kas′tə) In Greek legend, the queen who unwittingly marries her own son Oedipus.

jock·ey (jok′ē) *n.* *pl.* **·eys** One employed to ride horses in races. — *v.t.* & *v.i.* 1. To maneuver for an advantageous position. 2. To ride (a horse) in a race. 3. To cheat; trick. [Dim. of JOCK] — **jock′ey·ing** *n.* — **jock′ey·ism** *n.*

jo·cose (jō·kōs′) *adj.* Humorous; playful; joking. [< L *jocus* joke] — **jo·cose′ly** *adv.* — **jo·cose′ness, jo′cos·i·ty** (-kos′ə·tē) *n.*

joc·u·lar (jok′yə·lər) *adj.* Given to joking; also, like a joke. Also **joc′u·la·to·ry** (-tôr′ē, -tō′rē). [< L *jocus* joke] — **joc′u·lar′i·ty** (-lar′ə·tē) *n.* — **joc′u·lar·ly** *adv.*

jo·cund (jok′ənd, jō′kənd) *adj.* Cheerful; gay; jovial. [< OF < LL *juvare* to delight] — **jo·cun·di·ty** (jō·kun′də·tē) *n.* — **joc′und·ly** *adv.* — **joc′und·ness** *n.*

jodh·purs (jod′pərz) *n.pl.* Wide riding breeches, close-fitting from knee to ankle. [after *Jodhpur*, India]

Jo·el (jō′əl) A Hebrew prophet. — *n.* A book of the Old Testament by this prophet. [< Hebrew, the Lord is God]

jog (jog) *v.* **jogged, jog·ging** *v.i.* 1. To proceed slowly or monotonously: with *on* or *along.* — *v.t.* 2. To push or touch lightly; esp. to nudge (someone). 3. To stimulate: to *jog* the memory. — *n.* 1. The act of jogging. 2. A nudge. 3. A slow, jolting motion or pace. 4. *U.S.* An angle or projection in a surface, as in a wall; jag. 5. *U.S.* A sudden temporary turning or veering in a road, course, etc. [Prob. imit. Akin to SHOG.] — **jog′ger** *n.*

jog·gle (jog′əl) *v.* **·gled, ·gling** *v.t.* 1. To shake slightly; jog. 2. To fasten or join together by a joggle or joggles. — *v.i.* 3. To move with an irregular or jolting motion; shake. — *n.* 1. The act of joggling. 2. A projection formed on a piece, as of stone, timber, etc., that serves to fit it firmly to an adjoining piece having a corresponding notch. 3. A dowel. [Freq. of JOG, v.]

jog trot 1. A slow, easy trot, as of a horse. 2. A slow, humdrum habit of living or doing the daily tasks.

john (jon) *n.* *Slang* A toilet.

John (jon) *n.* One of the twelve apostles, son of Zebedee and brother of James: called **Saint John the Evangelist, Saint John the Divine.** — *n.* 1. The fourth Gospel of the New Testament, attributed to him. 2. One of the three New Testament epistles that bear his name.

John Bull 1. The English people. 2. A typical Englishman. Also **Johnny Bull.** [after a character in a satire (1712) by Dr. John Arbuthnot] — **John·Bul·lism** (jon′bool′iz·əm).

John Doe (dō) A name to designate a fictitious or real personage in any legal transaction or proceeding.

John Han·cock (han′kok) *U.S. Informal* A person's autograph. [after *John Hancock*]

john·ny·cake (jon′ē·kāk′) *n.* *U.S.* A flat cake of cornmeal, baked on a griddle. [? < obs. *jonikin*, a type of bread]

john·ny-jump-up (jon′ē-jump′up′) *n.* 1. Any of various American spring violets. 2. The wild pansy.

John·son·ese (jon′sən·ēz′, -ēs′) *n.* A ponderous and elaborate literary style similar to that of Samuel Johnson.

John·so·ni·an (jon·sō′nē·ən) *adj.* Pertaining to or resembling Samuel Johnson or his work. — *n.* An admirer of Dr. Johnson, esp. a student of his life and work.

John the Baptist, 6? B.C.–A.D. 30?, forerunner and baptizer of Jesus; beheaded by Herod Antipas.

joie de vi·vre (zhwà də vēv′r′) *French* Joy of living.

join (join) *v.t.* 1. To become a member of, as a club, party, staff, etc. 2. To come to as a companion or participant. 3. To unite in act or purpose. 4. To come to a junction with. 5. To connect. 6. To unite in marriage. 7. To take a place with, in, or among. 8. *Informal* To adjoin. — *v.i.* 9. To enter into association or agreement: often with *with.* 10. To take part: usually with *in.* 11. To come together; connect; unite. — **to join battle** To engage in a battle or conflict. — **to join up** *Informal* To enlist. — *n.* A joint or seam. [< OF < L *jungere* to join]

join·der (join′dər) *n.* 1. The act of joining. 2. *Law* a A joining of causes of action or defense. b A joining of parties in an action. c The acceptance of an issue tendered.

join·er (joi′nər) *n.* 1. One who or that which joins. 2. *U.S. Informal* One who joins many clubs, lodges, etc.

join·er·y (joi′nər·ē) *n.* 1. The art or skill of a joiner. 2. The articles constructed by a joiner.

joint (joint) *n.* 1. A place or point at which two or more parts of the same thing are joined together. 2. *Anat.* A place of union between two separate bones, usu. permitting movement; articulation. 3. *Bot.* The portion of the stem of a plant from which branches grow; a node. 4. A large cut of meat from a shoulder or leg containing the bone, used for roasting. 5. *Slang* a A place of low repute, as for drinking, gambling, etc. b Any place of dwelling or gathering. — **out of joint** 1. Dislocated. 2. Disordered; disorganized. — *adj.* 1. Belonging to or used by two or more: *joint* bank account. 2. Sharing with another: *joint* owner. 3. Produced by combined action: a *joint* literary effort. — *v.t.* 1. To fasten by means of a joint or joints. 2. To form or shape with a joint or joints, as a board. 3. To cut at the joints, as meat. [< OF < L *jungere* to join]

joint account A bank account in the name of two or more persons, each of whom may deposit and withdraw funds.

Joint Chiefs of Staff *U.S.* A body within the Department of Defense, consisting of a military chairman, the Chief of Staff of the Army, the Chief of Naval Operations, and the Chief of Staff of the Air Force.

joint·ed (join′tid) *adj.* 1. Having a joint or joints. 2. Having a (specified kind of) joint: *short-jointed.*

joint·ly (joint′lē) *adv.* In a joint manner; unitedly.

joint resolution *U.S.* A resolution passed by both houses of Congress, becoming a law if signed by the President.

joint-stock company (joint′stok′) An unincorporated business association of many persons, each of whom owns shares of stock which he may sell or transfer at will.

join·ture (join′chər) *n.* *Law* A settlement of property made to a woman by her husband after his death; also, the property. — *v.t.* **·tured, ·tur·ing** To settle a jointure on. [< F < L *jungere* to join]

joist (joist) *n.* Any of the parallel beams placed horizontally from wall to wall, to which the boards of a floor or the laths of a ceiling are fastened. — *v.t.* To furnish with joists. [< OF < L *jacere* to lie]

joke (jōk) *n.* 1. Something said or done to amuse; esp., a funny story. 2. Something said or done in fun rather than in earnest. 3. One who or that which excites mirth. 4. A trifling matter. — *v.* **joked, jok·ing** *v.i.* 1. To tell or make jokes; jest. 2. To say something in fun and not in earnest. [< L *jocus*] — **jok′ing·ly** *adv.*

jok·er (jō′kər) *n.* 1. One who jokes. 2. In a deck of cards, an extra card used in certain games. 3. *U.S.* An unobtrusive clause in a legislative bill, etc., that undermines or nullifies its original purpose. 4. Any hidden difficulty.

jol·li·fy (jol′ə·fī) *v.t.* & *v.i.* **·fied, ·fy·ing** *Informal* To be or cause to be merry or jolly. — **jol′li·fi·ca′tion** *n.*

jol·li·ty (jol′ə·tē) *n.* *pl.* **·ties** 1. The state or quality of being jolly; gaiety. 2. *Brit.* A festive occasion or gathering.

jol·ly (jol′ē) *adj.* **·li·er, ·li·est** 1. Full of good humor and high spirits. 2. Festive; merry. 3. *Brit. Informal* Extraordinary: a *jolly* bore. — *v.t.* **·lied, ·ly·ing** *Informal* 1. To attempt to put or keep in good humor: often with *along* or *up.* 2. To make fun of. — *n.* *pl.* **·lies** 1. *Brit. Informal* A merry or festive gathering. 2. *Brit. Slang* A sailor. — *adv. Brit. Informal* Extremely; very: *jolly* ugly. [< OF *joli*] — **jol′li·ly** *adv.* — **jol′li·ness** *n.*

jolly boat A small boat belonging to a ship. [< Dan. *jolle* yawl + BOAT]

Jolly Roger The pirate flag bearing the skull and crossbones.

jolt (jōlt) *v.t.* 1. To strike or knock against; jar; jostle. 2. To shake up or about with a blow or bump. — *v.i.* 3. To move with a series of irregular bumps or jars, as over a rough road. — *n.* 1. A sudden bump or jar as from a blow. 2. An unexpected surprise or emotional shock. [ME *jot* bump and *joll* bump] — **jolt′er** *n.* — **jolt′y** *adj.*

Jo·nah (jō′nə) Eighth- or ninth-century B.C. Hebrew prophet, who, cast overboard during a storm, was swallowed by a great fish and then cast up on the shore alive three days later. — *n.* 1. A book of the Old Testament containing his story: also, in the Douai Bible, **Jo′nas** (-nəs). 2. Any person bringing bad luck. [< Hebrew *Yōnāh*, lit., dove]

jon·gleur (jong′glər, *Fr.* zhôn·glœr′) *n.* A wandering minstrel of medieval England and France. [< OF < L *joculator.* See JUGGLER.]

jon·quil (jon′kwil, jong′-) *n.* 1. A species of narcissus related to the daffodil, having fragrant, white or yellow flowers. 2. The flower. [< F < L *juncus* a rush]

Jordan almond A large Spanish almond, frequently sugar-coated as a confection. [ME *jardyne almaunde*]

Jo·seph (jō′zəf) In the Old Testament, a son of Jacob and Rachel, sold into slavery in Egypt by his brothers. *Gen.* xxx 24. [< Hebrew *Yōsēph*, lit., He will add]

Joseph Husband of Mary, the mother of Jesus. *Matt.* i 18.

Joseph of Ar·i·ma·the·a (ar′ə·mə·thē′ə) A wealthy disciple of Christ who provided a tomb for his burial. *Matt.* xxvii 57–60.

josh (josh) *U.S. Slang* *v.t.* & *v.i.* To make good-humored fun of (someone); tease; banter. — *n.* A good-natured joke. [Blend of JOKE and BOSH] — **josh′er** *n.*

Josh·u·a (josh′ōō·ə) Israelite leader and successor of Moses. — *n.* The book of the Old Testament bearing his name. [< Hebrew *Yehōshua'* God is salvation]

joss (jos) *n.* A Chinese god. [Pidgin English < Pg. *deos* God]

joss house A Chinese temple or place for religious images.

joss paper Paper burnt by the Chinese at funerals, etc.

joss stick A stick of perfumed paste burnt by the Chinese.

jos·tle (jos′əl) *v.t. & v.i.* ·**tled**, ·**tling** To push or crowd roughly so as to shake up; elbow; shove. — *n.* A shoving or colliding against; jostling. [Freq. of JOUST] — **jos′tler** *n.*

jot (jot) *v.t.* **jot·ted**, **jot·ting** To make a hasty and brief note of: usually with *down.* — *n.* The least bit; iota. [< IOTA]

jot·ting (jot′ing) *n.* That which is jotted down; short note.

joule (joul, jōōl) *n. Physics* A unit of work equal to 10,000,-000 ergs or 0.737324 foot-pounds. [after J. P. *Joule*, 1818–1889, English physicist]

jounce (jouns) *v.t. & v.i.* **jounced**, **jounc·ing** To bounce; jolt. — *n.* A shake; a bump. [Origin unknown]

jour·nal (jûr′nəl) *n.* **1.** A diary or record of daily occurrences; esp. a ship's log. **2.** A newspaper, esp. one published daily. **3.** Any periodical or magazine. **4.** An official record of the daily proceedings of a legislature. **5.** In bookkeeping: **a** A daybook. **b** In double entry, a book in which daily transactions are entered to facilitate later posting in the ledger. **6.** *Mech.* The part of a shaft or axle that rotates in or against a bearing. [< OF < L *diurnalis* daily]

journal box *Mech.* The box or bearing for a journal.

jour·nal·ese (jûr′nəl·ēz′, -ēs′) *n.* The style of writing supposedly characteristic of newspapers, magazines, etc.: a derogatory term.

jour·nal·ism (jûr′nəl·iz′əm) *n.* The occupation, practice, and academic field concerned with writing, editing, and publishing newspapers and other periodicals.

jour·nal·ist (jûr′nəl·ist) *n.* One whose occupation is writing, editing, and publishing newspapers, etc. — **jour·nal·is·tic** (jûr′nəl·is′tik) *adj.* — **jour′nal·is′ti·cal·ly** *adv.*

jour·nal·ize (jûr′nəl·īz) *v.t.* ·**ized**, ·**iz·ing** *v.t.* **1.** To enter in a journal or diary. — *v.i.* **2.** To keep a journal or diary.

jour·ney (jûr′nē) *n.* **1.** Travel from one place to another. **2.** The distance traveled. — *v.i.* To make a trip; travel. [< OF *journee* a day's travel] — **jour′ney·er** *n.*

jour·ney·man (jûr′nē·mən) *n.* *pl.* ·**men** (-mən) A worker who has completed his apprenticeship in a skilled trade.

joust (just, joust, jōōst) *n.* **1.** A formal combat between two mounted knights armed with lances; tilt. **2.** *pl.* Tournament. — *v.i.* To engage in a joust. Also spelled *just.* [< OF < LL *juxtare* to approach] — **joust′er** *n.*

Jove (jōv) Jupiter. — **by Jove!** A mild oath expressing surprise, emphasis, etc. — **Jo′vi·an** *adj.*

jo·vi·al (jō′vē·əl) *adj.* Good-natured; convivial; jolly. [< F < LL *Jovialis* born under the influence of Jupiter] — **jo′vi·al·ly** *adv.* — **jo′vi·al·ness** *n.*

jo·vi·al·i·ty (jō′vē·al′ə·tē) *n.* The quality or state of being jovial; conviviality; merriment. Also **jo·vi·al·ty** (jō′vē·əl·tē).

jowl¹ (joul, jōl) *n.* The fleshy part under the lower jaw, esp. when fat; double chin. [ME *cholle* < OE *ceolu* throat]

jowl² (joul, jōl) *n.* **1.** The jaw, esp. the lower jaw. **2.** The cheek. [ME *chavel* < OE *ceafl*]

joy (joi) *n.* **1.** A strong feeling of happiness; gladness; delight. **2.** A state of contentment or satisfaction. **3.** Anything that causes delight or gladness. — *v.i.* To be glad; rejoice. [< OF < L *gaudere* to rejoice]

joy·ful (joi′fəl) *adj.* **1.** Full of joy. **2.** Showing or causing joy. — **joy′ful·ly** *adv.* — **joy′ful·ness** *n.*

joy·less (joi′lis) *adj.* Completely lacking in joy; causing no joy; dreary; sad. — **joy′less·ly** *adv.* — **joy′less·ness** *n.*

joy·ous (joi′əs) *adj.* Joyful. — **joy′ous·ly** *adv.* — **joy′ous·ness** *n.*

joy ride *Informal* **1.** A ride taken for pleasure. **2.** A reckless ride in a stolen vehicle. — **joy rider** — **joy riding**

joy stick *Informal* The control stick of an airplane.

ju·bi·lant (jōō′bə·lənt) *adj.* Exultingly joyful or triumphant. [< L *jubilare* to exult] — **ju′bi·lance**, **ju′bi·lan·cy** *n.* — **ju′bi·lant·ly** *adv.*

ju·bi·late (jōō′bə·lāt) *v.t. & v.i.* ·**lat·ed**, ·**lat·ing** To rejoice.

ju·bi·la·tion (jōō′bə·lā′shən) *n.* Rejoicing; exultation.

ju·bi·lee (jōō′bə·lē) *n.* **1.** In Jewish history, a celebration (*Lev.* xxv 8–17) observed every fiftieth year, at which time slaves were freed, alienated lands returned, and the fields left uncultivated. **2.** In the Roman Catholic Church, a year of special indulgence occurring usu. every twenty-fifth year. **3.** A special anniversary of an event. **4.** Any time of rejoicing. Also **ju′bi·le.** [< OF < LL < Gk. < Hebrew *yōbēl* ram's horn, trumpet]

Judaeo- See JUDEO-.

Judah (jōō′də) In the Old Testament, a son of Jacob and Leah. *Gen.* xxix 35. — *n.* The tribe of Israel descended from him. [< Hebrew *Yehūdhāh* praised]

Ju·da·ic (jōō·dā′ik) *adj.* Of or pertaining to the Jews. Also **Ju·da′i·cal.** [< L *Judaicus*] — **Ju·da′i·cal·ly** *adv.*

Ju·da·ism (jōō′dē·iz′əm) *n.* **1.** The religious beliefs or

practices of the Jews. **2.** The observance of Jewish rites or practices. See CONSERVATIVE JUDAISM, ORTHODOX JUDAISM, REFORM JUDAISM. — **Ju′da·ist** *n.* — **Ju′da·is′tic** *adj.*

Ju·da·ize (jōō′dē·īz) *v.* ·**ized**, ·**iz·ing** *v.t.* **1.** To bring into conformity with Judaism. — *v.i.* **2.** To accept Judaism.

Ju·das (jōō′dəs) **1.** The disciple of Jesus who betrayed him with a kiss: also **Judas Is·car·i·ot** (is·kar′ē·ət). **2.** Jude. — *n.* One who betrays another under the guise of friendship.

Judas tree A tree with reddish purple flowers. [from a tradition that Judas hanged himself upon a tree of this kind]

Jude (jōōd) **1.** One of the twelve apostles: called *Judas* (not Iscariot). *Luke* vi 16, *Acts* i 13, *John* xiv 22. **2.** The author of a book of the New Testament, possibly the brother of James and Jesus: called *Judas.* *Matt.* xiii 55, *Mark* vi 3. — *n.* A book of the New Testament by this author.

Ju·de·a (jōō·dē′ə) The southern part of ancient Palestine under Persian, Greek, and Roman dominion: also **Ju·dae′a.** — **Ju·de′an**, **Ju·dae′an** *n. & adj.*

Judeo- *combining form* Jewish. Also spelled *Judaeo-.* [< L *Judaeus*]

judge (juj) *n.* **1.** A public officer invested with the power to administer justice by hearing cases in a court of law. **2.** One appointed to make decisions. **3.** One considered competent to make critical evaluations: a *judge* of music. **4.** In Jewish history, one of the rulers of Israel before the kings. — *v.* **judged**, **judg·ing** *v.t.* **1.** To hear and decide the merits of (a case) or the guilt of (a person). **2.** To decide authoritatively, as a contest. **3.** To hold as judgment or opinion. **4.** To form an opinion or judgment concerning. **5.** To govern: said of the ancient Hebrew judges. — *v.i.* **6.** To act as a judge. **7.** To make a judgment or decision. [< OF < L *judex*, *-icis* < *ius* right + *dicere* to speak]

judge advocate *Mil.* **1.** A commissioned officer in the U.S. Army belonging to the Judge Advocate General's Corps. **2.** The legal staff officer for a commander.

Judge Advocate General A major general in the U.S. Army or the U.S. Air Force, serving as head of the Judge Advocate General's Department and supervising military justice and other legal matters.

Judg·es (juj′iz) *n.pl.* (*construed as sing.*) A book of the Old Testament, containing a history of the Jewish people.

judg·ment (juj′mənt) *n.* **1.** The act of judging. **2.** The decision or opinion reached through judging. **3.** The ability to judge wisely. **4.** *Law* **a** The sentence or decision. **b** A debt resulting from such a decision. **c** The record of such a decision. **5.** A disaster or misfortune regarded as inflicted by God. **judge′ment.**

Judgment Day *Theol.* The day or time of the Last Judgment: also *Day of Judgment.*

ju·di·ca·tor (jōō′də·kā·tər) *n.* One who acts as judge.

ju·di·ca·to·ry (jōō′də·kə·tôr′ē, -tō′rē) *adj.* Pertaining to the administration of justice. — *n.* *pl.* ·**ries** **1.** Any tribunal. **2.** The judicial process.

ju·di·ca·ture (jōō′də·kə·chŏŏr) *n.* **1.** The action or function of administering justice, as in courts of law. **2.** The right, power, or authority of administering justice; jurisdiction. **3.** A court of law; also, judges collectively.

ju·di·cial (jōō·dish′əl) *adj.* **1.** Of or pertaining to the administering of justice, to courts of law or to judges. **2.** Decreed or enforced by a court of law. **3.** Of or befitting a judge. **4.** Inclined to make judgments; discriminating; critical. [< L *judex*, *-icis* judge] — **ju·di′cial·ly** *adv.*

ju·di·ci·ar·y (jōō·dish′ē·er′ē, -dish′ə·rē) *adj.* Of or pertaining to courts, judges, or judgments. — *n.* *pl.* ·**ar·ies** **1.** The department of government that administers the law. **2.** The system of courts set up to carry out this function. **3.** The judges collectively.

ju·di·cious (jōō·dish′əs) *adj.* Having, showing, or exercising good judgment; prudent. [< F < L *judicium* judgment] — **ju·di′cious·ly** *adv.* — **ju·di′cious·ness** *n.*

Ju·dith (jōō′dith) **1.** A book in the Old Testament Apocrypha and the Douai Bible. **2.** A Jewish woman, heroine of this book, who rescued her countrymen by slaying the Assyrian general, Holofernes. [< Hebrew *Yehūdhīth*]

ju·do (jōō′dō) *n.* A system of physical conditioning devised in Japan in 1882, based on jujitsu. [< Japanese *ju* gentle, pliant + *do* way of life]

jug¹ (jug) *n.* **1.** A pitcher or similar vessel for holding liquids. **2.** *Slang* A prison or jail. — *v.t.* **jugged**, **jug·ging** **1.** To put into a jug. **2.** *Slang* To imprison; jail. [after *Jug*, a nickname for *Joan*]

jug² (jug) *n.* The sound of a nightingale's note. — *v.i.* **jugged**, **jug·ging** To make the sound of the nightingale.

ju·gate (jōō′git, -gāt) *adj.* **1.** *Biol.* Occurring in pairs. **2.** *Bot.* Having paired leaflets. [< L *jugare* to bind together]

jug·ger·naut (jug′ər·nôt) *n.* Any slow and irresistible destructive force.

Jug·ger·naut (jug′ər·nôt) The eighth avatar of Vishnu whose idol at Puri, India, is annually drawn on a heavy car under the wheels of which devotees are said to have thrown themselves. [< Skt. *jagannātha* lord of the universe]

jug·gle (jug′əl) v. **·gled**, **·gling** v.t. **1.** To keep (two or more balls or other objects) continuously moving from the hand into the air. **2.** To manipulate dishonestly. — v.i. **3.** To perform as a juggler. **4.** To practice deception or fraud. — n. **1.** An act of juggling. **2.** A trick or deception. [< OF < L *joculari* to jest] — **jug′gler** n.

jug·gler·y (jug′lər-ē) n. pl. **·gler·ies 1.** The juggler's art; legerdemain. **2.** Deception; fraud.

jug·u·lar (jug′yə-lər, jōō′gyə-) adj. Anat. Of or pertaining to the throat or the jugular vein. — n. Anat. A jugular vein. [< NL < L *jugulum* collar bone]

jugular vein Anat. One of the large veins on either side of the neck that returns blood from the brain, face, and neck.

juice (jōōs) n. **1.** The liquid part of a vegetable, fruit, or animal. **2.** Usually pl. The fluids of the body. **3.** U.S. Slang Electricity. **4.** U.S. Slang Gasoline. **5.** U.S. Slang Vital force; strength. [< OF *jus* < L]

juic·er (jōō′sər) n. A device for extracting juice.

juic·y (jōō′sē) adj. **juic·i·er**, **juic·i·est 1.** Abounding with juice; moist. **2.** Full of interest; colorful; spicy. — **juic′i·ly** adv. — **juic′i·ness** n.

ju·jit·su (jōō-jit′sōō) n. A Japanese system of hand-to-hand fighting in which surprise and a knowledge of anatomy and leverage are used: also spelled *jiujitsu*, *jiujutsu*. Also **ju·jut·su** (jōō-jit′sōō, -jōōt′sōō). Compare JUDO. [< Japanese *ju* pliant + *jutsu* art]

ju·jube (jōō′jōōb; for def. 1, also jōō′jōō-bē) n. **1.** A gelatinous candy lozenge. **2.** An Old World tree or shrub of the buckthorn family. [< F or < Med.L *jujuba*]

juke box (jōōk) A large automatic phonograph, usu. coin-operated and permitting selection of the records to be played.

juke joint U.S. Slang A roadhouse or barroom for drinking and dancing. [< Gullah *jook* disorderly, wicked]

ju·lep (jōō′lip) n. **1.** A mint julep. **2.** A sweetened, syrupy drink. [< OF < Persian < *gul* rose + *āb* water]

Jul·ian (jōōl′yən) adj. Of, pertaining to, or named after Julius Caesar.

ju·li·enne (jōō′lē·en′, Fr. zhü·lyen′) n. A clear meat soup containing vegetables chopped or cut into thin strips. — adj. Cut into thin strips: *julienne* potatoes. [< F]

Ju·li·et (jōō′lē·et, jōōl′yit) The heroine of Shakespeare's *Romeo and Juliet*.

Ju·ly (jōō·lī′, jōō-) pl. **·lys** The seventh month of the calendar year, having 31 days. [< AF < L (*mensis*) *Julius* (month) of Julius Caesar]

jum·ble (jum′bəl) v. **·bled**, **·bling** v.t. **1.** To mix in a confused mass; put or throw together without order. **2.** To mix up in the mind; muddle. — v.i. **3.** To meet or unite confusedly. — n. **1.** A confused mixture or collection; hodgepodge: also **jum′ble·ment**. **2.** A thin sweet cake. **3.** Any of various hairless bees. [Imit.]

jum·bo (jum′bō) n. pl. **·bos** A very large person, animal, or thing. — adj. Very large. [after *Jumbo*, an unusually large elephant exhibited by P. T. Barnum < ? W African]

jump (jump) v.i. **1.** To spring from the ground, floor, etc., by using the foot and leg muscles; leap; bound. **2.** To move or be moved jerkily; bob; bounce. **3.** To rise abruptly: Prices *jumped*. **4.** To pass suddenly, as if by leaping: to *jump* to a conclusion. **5.** To start in astonishment. **6.** To spring down from or out of a window, ladder, airplane, etc. **7.** In checkers, to capture a piece by passing another over it to a vacant square beyond. **8.** In bridge, to bid so as to exceed the preceding bid by more than the minimum. — v.t. **9.** To leap over or across. **10.** To cause to leap over or across: to *jump* a horse. **11.** To increase (prices, demands, etc.). **12.** To pass over; skip; omit. **13.** In bridge, to cause (a bid) to exceed the preceding bid by more than the minimum. **14.** U.S. To leave or quit abruptly: to *jump* town. **15.** Informal To get onto; board: to *jump* a train. **16.** Informal To attack suddenly or by surprise. — **to jump a claim** To take possession of another's mining or land claim by force and fraud. — **to jump at** To accept hastily. — **to jump bail** U.S. To forfeit one's bail bond by failing to appear when legally summoned. — **to jump off** Mil. To begin an attack. — **to jump on** (or **all over**) Informal To assail with abuse; scold. — **to jump ship** Naut. To end one's service in a ship's crew by desertion. — **to jump the gun** Slang **1.** To begin before the starting signal is given. **2.** To start prematurely. — **to jump the track** Of a train, etc., to leave the rails. — n. **1.** The act of jumping; a leap; spring; bound. **2.** An abrupt movement upward or outward; a jerk. **3.** A sudden rise or transition. **4.** The length or height of a leap. **5.** Something that is jumped over or across, as a hurdle, obstacle, or fence. **6.** A leap by parachute from an airplane. **7.** In sports, a competition in jumping: broad *jump*. — **on the jump** Informal Working or moving about at top speed; very busy. — **to get** (or **have**) **the jump on** U.S. Slang To get or have a head start

on or an advantage over. — adj. **1.** Mil. Of or pertaining to paratroops. **2.** U.S. Slang Of popular music, having a fast, excited tempo. [Cf. Scand. *gumpa* to jump]

jump·er¹ (jum′pər) n. **1.** One who or that which jumps. **2.** A piece of mechanism having a jumping motion. **3.** Electr. A short wire used to bypass or join parts of a circuit.

jum·per² (jum′pər) n. **1.** A sleeveless dress, usu. worn over a blouse or sweater. **2.** A loose jacket or smock worn over other clothes. [Prob. alter. of OF *juppe* jacket]

jump·ing bean (jump′ing) The seed of certain Mexican shrubs of the spurge family, that jumps about owing to the movements of a small larva inside.

jumping jack A toy figure of a man, whose jointed limbs are moved by strings.

jump·y (jum′pē) adj. **jump·i·er**, **jump·i·est 1.** Subject to sudden changes; fluctuating. **2.** Given to startled movements; nervous; apprehensive. — **jump′i·ness** n.

jun·co (jung′kō) n. pl. **·cos** Any of various small birds of North America, commonly seen in flocks during winter: also called *snowbird*. [< Sp. < L *juncus* rush]

junc·tion (jungk′shən) n. **1.** The act of joining, or the state of being joined. **2.** The place where lines or routes, as roads, railways, streams, etc., come together or cross.

junc·ture (jungk′chər) n. **1.** The act of joining, or the state of being joined; junction. **2.** A point or line of junction; a joint or seam. **3.** A point in time. **4.** A crisis; emergency. [< L *junctura* < *jungere* to join]

June (jōōn) The sixth month of the calendar year, having 30 days. [OE < L, or ME < OF *Juin* < L (*mensis*) *Junius* (month) of the Junii, a Roman family]

June bug A large, brightly colored beetle that flies in June. Also **June beetle**.

jun·gle (jung′gəl) n. **1.** A dense tropical thicket of high grass, reeds, vines, brush, or trees, usu. inhabited by wild animals. **2.** Any similar tangled growth. **3.** U.S. Slang A camp for hoboes. [< Hind. *jangal* forest] — **jun′gly** adj.

jun·ior (jōōn′yər) adj. **1.** Younger in years or lower in rank. **2.** Denoting the younger of two. **3.** Belonging to youth or earlier life. **4.** Later in effect or tenure. **5.** Pertaining to the third year of a high-school or collegiate course of four years. — n. **1.** The younger of two. **2.** One later or lower in service or standing. **3.** A student in the third or junior year. Abbr. *jr.*, *Jr.* [< L *junior*, compar. of *juvenis* young]

junior college A school giving college courses up to and including the sophomore year.

junior high school A school intermediate between grammar school and high school, in the U.S. typically comprising grades 7 and 8, and sometimes grade 9.

Junior League A local branch of the Association of the Junior Leagues of America, Inc., composed of young society women engaged in volunteer welfare work.

ju·ni·per (jōō′nə·pər) n. **1.** An evergreen pinaceous shrub of Europe and America. **2.** The dark blue berry of this shrub, used in making gin and as a diuretic. [< L *juniperus*]

junk¹ (jungk) n. **1.** Castoff material, as scrap iron, old bottles, or paper. **2.** Informal Worthless matter; rubbish; trash. **3.** Slang Narcotics; dope. **4.** Naut. Old cable or cordage used for making gaskets, oakum, etc. — v.t. Informal To discard as trash; scrap. [ME *jonke*]

junk² (jungk) n. A large Chinese vessel with high poop, prominent stem, and battened lugsails. [< Sp. and Pg. *junco* < Malay *djong* ship]

Jun·ker (yōōng′kər) n. One of the landed aristocracy of Prussia. [< G *jung* young + *herr* master] — **Jun′ker·dom** n. — **Jun′ker·ism** n.

jun·ket (jung′kit) n. **1.** A feast, banquet, picnic, or pleasure trip. **2.** U.S. A trip taken by a public official with all expenses paid from public funds. **3.** A delicacy made of curds or of sweetened milk and rennet. — v.i. **1.** To have a feast; banquet. **2.** U.S. To go on a trip, esp. at public expense. — v.t. **3.** To entertain by feasting; regale. [< It. < L *juncus* rush] — **jun′ket·er** n.

CHINESE JUNK

junk·ie (jung′kē) n. Slang A dope addict. Also **junk′y**.

junk·man (jungk′man′) n. pl. **·men** (-men′) One who purchases, collects, and sells junk. Also **junk′deal′er** (-dē′lər).

Ju·no (jōō′nō) In Roman mythology, the wife of Jupiter, queen of the gods and goddess of marriage: identified with the Greek *Hera*. — n. A woman of queenly beauty.

Ju·no·esque (jōō′nō·esk′) adj. Stately and beautiful.

jun·ta (jun′tə, Sp. hōōn′tä) n. **1.** A Central or South American legislative council. **2.** A body of men engaged in secret, usu. political intrigue: also **jun′to** (-tō). [< Sp. < L *jungere* to join]

Ju·pi·ter (jōō′pə·tər) In Roman mythology, the god ruling over all other gods and all men: identified with the Greek *Zeus*: also called *Jove*. — *n.* The largest planet of the solar system, fifth in order from the sun. See PLANET.

Ju·ras·sic (joo·ras′ik) *Geol. adj.* Of or pertaining to a period of the Mesozoic era succeeding the Triassic and followed by the Cretaceous. See chart for GEOLOGY. — *n.* The Jurassic period or rock system. [< F *jurassique*, after *Jura*]

ju·rid·i·cal (joo·rid′i·kəl) *adj.* Pertaining to the law and to the administration of justice. Also **ju·rid′ic.** [< L *juris* law + *dicere* to say, speak] — **ju·rid′i·cal·ly** *adv.*

ju·ris·dic·tion (joor′is·dik′shən) *n.* **1.** Lawful right to exercise authority, whether executive, legislative, or judicial. **2.** Those things over which such authority may be exercised. **3.** Power in general; authority. [< L *juris* law + *dicere* to say, speak] — **ju′ris·dic′tion·al** *adj.*

ju·ris·pru·dence (joor′is·prood′ns) *n.* **1.** The philosophy or science of law. **2.** A system of laws. [< L *juris* law + *prudentia* knowledge] — **ju′ris·pru·den′tial** (-proo·den′shəl) *adj.*

ju·ris·pru·dent (joor′is·prood′nt) *adj.* Skilled in the law. — *n.* One skilled in the law.

ju·rist (joor′ist) *n.* One versed in the law.

ju·ris·tic (joo·ris′tik) *adj.* Of or pertaining to a jurist or the profession of law. Also **ju·ris′ti·cal.** — **ju·ris′ti·cal·ly** *adv.*

ju·ror (joor′ər) *n.* **1.** One who serves on a jury. **2.** One who takes an oath. [< AF < L *jurare* to swear]

ju·ry[1] (joor′ē) *n., pl.* **·ries** A body of legally qualified persons summoned to serve on a judicial tribunal and give a verdict according to the evidence. See GRAND JURY, PETIT JURY. **2.** A committee of award in a competition. [< AF < L *jurare* to swear]

ju·ry[2] (joor′ē) *adj. Naut.* Rigged up temporarily: a *jury* mast. [Prob. < OF *ajurie* aid < L *adjutare* to help]

ju·ry·man (joor′ē·mən) *n., pl.* **·men** (-mən) A juror.

just[1] (just) *adj.* **1.** Fair and impartial in acting or judging. **2.** Upright; honest. **3.** Legally valid; legitimate. **4.** Merited; deserved. **5.** True; correct; accurate. **6.** Fitting; proper. **7.** *Archaic* Righteous in the sight of God. — *adv.* **1.** To the exact point; precisely: *just* right. **2.** Exactly now: He is *just* leaving. **3.** A moment ago: He *just* left. **4.** By very little; barely: It *just* missed. **5.** Only; merely: *just* a layman. **6.** *Informal* Simply; really; very: It's *just* lovely. [< OF < L *jus* law] — **just′ly** *adv.* — **just′ness** *n.*

just[2] (just) See JOUST.

jus·tice (jus′tis) *n.* **1.** The quality of being just. **2.** The rendering of what is due or merited; also, that which is due or merited. **3.** Conformity to the law. **4.** The administration of law. **5.** A judge. **6.** *Theol.* An attribute of God, and of his laws and judgments. **7.** The abstract principle by which right and wrong are defined. — **Department of Justice** An executive department of the U.S. government, headed by the Attorney General, that represents the government in legal matters, enforces antitrust laws, civil rights laws, etc., and supervises internal security and immigration. — **to bring to justice** To arrest and try (a wrongdoer). — **to do justice to** To show appreciation of. [See JUST[1].]

justice of the peace A local magistrate of limited jurisdiction with authority to fine and imprison in minor cases, commit to a higher court, perform marriages, etc.

jus·ti·fi·a·ble (jus′tə·fī′ə·bəl) *adj.* Capable of being justified; defensible. — **jus′ti·fi·a·bil′i·ty, jus′ti·fi′a·ble·ness** *n.* — **jus′ti·fi′a·bly** *adv.*

jus·ti·fi·ca·tion (jus′tə·fə·kā′shən) *n.* **1.** The act of justifying, or the state of being justified. **2.** The ground of justifying, or that which justifies. — **jus′ti·fi·ca′tive** *adj.*

jus·ti·fi·er (jus′tə·fī′ər) *n.* One who justifies.

jus·ti·fy (jus′tə·fī) *v.* **·fied, ·fy·ing** *v.t.* **1.** To show to be just, right, or reasonable; vindicate. **2.** To declare guiltless; absolve. **3.** To provide adequate grounds for; warrant. **4.** *Printing* To adjust (lines) to the proper length by spacing. — *v.i.* **5.** *Printing* To be properly spaced; fit. [< OF < LL < L *justus* just + *facere* to make]

jus·tle (jus′əl) See JOSTLE.

jut (jut) *v.i.* **jut·ted, jut·ting** To extend beyond the main portion; protrude; project: often with *out*. — *n.* Anything that juts; a projection. [Var. of JET[2].]

jute (joot) *n.* **1.** A tall annual Asian herb of the linden family. **2.** The tough fiber obtained from the inner bark of this plant, used for bags, cordage, etc. [< Bengali < Skt. *jūta* braid of hair]

Jute (joot) *n.* A member of a Germanic tribe, some of whom invaded Britain in the fifth century. [< LL *Jutae* the Jutes] — **Jut·ish** (joo′tish) *adj.*

ju·ve·nes·cent (joo′və·nes′ənt) *adj.* **1.** Becoming young; growing young again. **2.** Making young; rejuvenating. [< L *juvenescere* to grow younger] — **ju′ve·nes′cence** *n.*

ju·ve·nile (joo′və·nəl, -nīl) *adj.* **1.** Young; youthful; also, immature. **2.** Designed for young persons: *juvenile* books. — *n.* **1.** A young person. **2.** An actor of youthful roles. **3.** A book for young persons. [< L *juvenis* young person] — **ju′ve·nile·ly** *adv.* — **ju′ve·nile·ness, ju′ve·nil′i·ty** *n.*

juvenile court A court that has jurisdiction in cases involving dependent, neglected, and delinquent children.

juvenile delinquent One who is guilty of antisocial behavior or of violations of the law, but is too young to be punished as an adult criminal. — **juvenile delinquency**

ju·ve·nil·i·a (joo′və·nil′ē·ə, -nil′yə) *n.pl.* Works produced in youth, esp. writings or paintings.

juxta- *prefix* Near; next to. [< L *juxta* near]

jux·ta·pose (juks′tə·pōz′) *v.t.* **·posed, ·pos·ing** To place together; put side by side. [< F < L *juxta* near + *poser* to put down] — **jux·ta·po·si·tion** (juks′tə·pə·zish′ən) *n.*

K

k, K (kā) *n., pl.* **k's** or **ks, K's** or **Ks, kays** (kāz) **1.** The eleventh letter of the English alphabet. **2.** The sound represented by the letter. It normally has no phonetic value when initial before *n*, as in *knee, knight, know*, etc. — *symbol Chem.* Potassium (K for *kalium*).

Ka·a·ba (kä′ə·bə, kä′bə) *n.* The Moslem shrine at Mecca enclosing a sacred black stone, supposedly given to Abraham by the angel Gabriel, toward which worshipers face when praying: also spelled *Caaba*. [< Arabic *ka'b* cube]

kab·a·la (kab′ə·lə, kə·bä′lə), **kab·ba·la** See CABALA.

ka·bu·ki (kä·boo′kē) *n.* A form of Japanese play on popular or comic themes, employing elaborate costume, stylized gesture, music, and dancing. [< Japanese]

Kad·dish (kä′dish) *n.* In Judaism, a prayer recited by mourners and part of the daily service. [< Aramaic, holy]

kaf·fee·klatsch (kôf′ē·kläch′, *Ger.* käf′ā·kläch′) *n.* Sometimes *cap.* An informal conversational gathering where coffee is drunk. [< G < *kaffee* coffee + *klatsch* chitchat]

kaf·fir (kaf′ər) *n.* A variety of sorghum grown in dry regions as a grain and forage plant. Also **kaffir corn.** [after *Kaffir*]

Kaf·fir (kaf′ər) *n.* **1.** A member of a powerful group of South African Bantu tribes. **2.** Xhosa, the language of these tribes. Also **Kaf′ir.** [< Arabic *kāfir* unbeliever]

kaf·tan (kaf′tən, käf·tän′) See CAFTAN.

kai·ak (kī′ak) See KAYAK.

kai·ser (kī′zər) *n.* Emperor. [< G < L *Caesar* Caesar]

Kai·ser (kī′zər) Title of the emperors of the Holy Roman Empire, 962–1806; the Austrian emperors, 1804–1918; and the German emperors, 1871–1918.

kale (kāl) *n.* **1.** A variety of headless cabbage. **2.** *U.S. Slang* Money. [Var. of COLE]

ka·lei·do·scope (kə·lī′də·skōp) *n.* **1.** A tube-shaped optical toy that shows constantly changing symmetrical patterns as loose bits of colored glass are moved about under a set of mirrors. **2.** A swiftly changing scene, pattern, etc. [< Gk. *kalos* beautiful + *eidos* form + -SCOPE]

ka·lei·do·scop·ic (kə·lī′də·skop′ik) *adj.* **1.** Of or pertaining to a kaleidoscope. **2.** Rapidly changing and intricate. Also **ka·lei′do·scop′i·cal.** — **ka·lei′do·scop′i·cal·ly** *adv.*

kal·ends (kal′əndz) See CALENDS.

ka·lif (kā′lif, kal′if), **ka·liph** See CALIPH.

Kal·muck (kal′muk) *n.* **1.** A member of one of the Buddhistic Mongol tribes inhabiting a region extending from western China to the Volga river. **2.** The Mongolian language of these tribes. Also **Kal′muk, Kal·myk** (kal′mik).

kal·so·mine (kal′sə·mīn) See CALCIMINE.

kan·ga·roo (kang′gə·roo′) *n., pl.* **·roos** A herbivorous marsupial of Australia and Tasmania, having short, weak forelimbs, stout tails, and powerful hind limbs adapted for leaping. [< Australian]

kangaroo court *U.S.* An unauthorized court in which the law is disregarded or willfully misinterpreted.

kangaroo rat A pouched rodent of the SW U.S. and Mexico having elongated hind limbs and tail.

Kant·i·an (kan′tē-ən) *adj.* Of or pertaining to Kant or his philosophy. — *n.* A follower of Kantianism.

Kant·i·an·ism (kan′tē-ən-iz′əm) *n.* The philosophy of Immanuel Kant, stating that man experiences the material world through sense perception, but its reality is determined by mental forms and categories. Also **Kant′ism.**

ka·o·lin (kā′ō-lin) *n.* A claylike hydrous aluminum silicate used in making porcelain. Also **ka′o·line** (-lin). [< F < Chinese *Kao-ling* mountain where first mined]

ka·pok (kā′pok) *n.* A cottony or silky fiber covering the seeds of the kapok tree, used for mattresses, life preservers, insulation material, etc. [< Malay *kāpoq*]

kapok tree A tropical tree having seeds covered with silky fiber. Also called *silk-cotton tree.*

kap·pa (kap′ə) *n.* The tenth letter in the Greek alphabet (K, κ), corresponding to the English *k.* See ALPHABET.

ka·put (kä-pŏŏt′) *adj. Slang* Ruined; done for. [< G]

kar·a·kul (kar′ə-kəl) *n.* 1. A breed of sheep raised in the Soviet Union, Iran, Iraq, etc. 2. The black or gray, loosely curled fur made from the pelt of the karakul lamb. Also spelled *caracul.* [after *Kara Kul,* a lake in Bukhara]

kar·at (kar′ət) *n.* 1. The twenty-fourth part by weight of gold in an article: 18-*karat* gold has ¹⁸⁄₂₄ or ¾ gold by weight. 2. Loosely, a carat. [Var. of CARAT]

ka·ra·te (kä-rä′tä, -tē) *n.* An Oriental method of hand-to-hand combat utilizing a variety of sudden, forceful blows, as with the side of the hand or the fingertips. [< Japanese]

kar·ma (kär′mə) *n.* 1. *Hinduism & Buddhism* The spiritual force generated by one's actions, which determines one's reincarnated situation. 2. Loosely, fate. 3. Vibration (def. 3).

kar·roo (kə-rōō′, ka-) *n. pl.* **·roos** A dry plateau or tableland of South Africa. Also **ka·roo′.** [< Hottentot]

karyo- *combining form Biol.* Nucleus: also spelled *caryo-.* Also, before vowels, **kary-.** [< Gk. *karyon* nut]

kar·y·o·tin (kar′ē-ō′tin) *n. Biol.* Chromatin.

Kas·bah (käz′bä) See CASBAH.

Kash·mi·ri (kash-mir′ē) *n.* The Indic language of the Kashmirians.

Kash·mi·ri·an (kash-mir′ē-ən) *adj.* Of or pertaining to Kashmir or its people. — *n.* A native of Kashmir.

kata See CATA-.

ka·ty·did (kā′tē-did) *n.* A green, arboreal insect allied to the grasshoppers and crickets. [Imit., from sound produced by the males]

kau·ri (kou′rē) *n.* 1. A large timber tree of New Zealand. 2. Its wood. 3. Kauri gum. Also **kau′ry.** [< Maori]

kauri gum A resinous exudation of the kauri tree, used in varnishes, for linoleum, etc. Also **kauri copal, kauri resin.**

kay·ak (kī′ak) *n. U.S. & Canadian* The hunting canoe of arctic America, made of seal skins stretched over a frame, with a hole amidships where the user sits. [< Eskimo]

kay·o (kā′ō) *Slang v.t.* **kay·oed, kay·o·ing** In boxing, to knock out. — *n.* In boxing, a knockout. Also **K.O., KO, k.o.** [< k(nock) o(ut)]

kedge (kej) *Naut. n.* A light anchor used in warping, freeing a vessel from shoals, etc.: also **kedge anchor.** — *v.* **kedged, kedg·ing** *v.i.* 1. To move a vessel by hauling up to a kedge that has been dropped at a distance. 2. Of a vessel, to be moved in this way. — *v.t.* 3. To move (a vessel) in this way. [Origin uncertain]

keel (kēl) *n.* 1. *Naut.* The main structural member of a vessel, running fore and aft along the bottom, to which all the crosswise members are solidly fixed; the backbone of a ship. 2. A ship. 3. Any part or object resembling a keel in shape or function. 4. *Aeron.* **a** A vertical fin extending longitudinally at the bottom of an airship. **b** The center bottom of an airplane fuselage. 5. *Biol.* A longitudinal ridge or process, as of the breastbone of a fowl. — **on an even keel** In equilibrium; steady. — *v.t. & v.i.* To turn over with the keel uppermost; capsize. — **to keel over** 1. To turn bottom up; capsize. 2. To fall over or be felled, as from an injury. [< ON *kjölr* or OHG *kiol*]

keel·haul (kēl′hôl′) *v.t.* 1. *Naut.* To haul (a man) under the keel of a ship as punishment. 2. To reprove severely; castigate. Also **keel·hale** (kēl′hāl′). [< Du. *kielhalen*]

keel·son (kēl′sən) *n. Naut.* A beam running above the keel of a ship: also spelled *kelson.* [Akin to KEEL]

keen¹ (kēn) *adj.* 1. Able to cut or penetrate readily; very sharp. 2. Having mental acuteness, refined perception, etc. 3. Manifesting intense absorption or eagerness: a *keen* interest. 4. Of senses or sense organs, having great acuity and sensitivity. 5. Having a piercing, intense quality or impact. 6. Eager; enthusiastic: with *about, for, on,* or an infinitive. 7. *U.S. Slang* Fine; excellent. [ME < OE *cēne*] — **keen′ly** *adv.* — **keen′ness** *n.*

keen² (kēn) *n.* A wailing lamentation for the dead. — *v.i.* To wail loudly over the dead. [< Irish *caoinim* I wail] — **keen′er** *n.*

keep (kēp) *v.* **kept, keep·ing** *v.t.* 1. To retain possession or control of; avoid releasing or giving away: to *keep* one's earnings; to *keep* a secret. 2. To hold or continue to hold in some specified state, relation, place, etc.: *Keep* your hands off; *Keep* the car in repair. 3. To store, hold, or confine in a regular place. 4. To maintain: to *keep* the peace. 5. To be faithful to or abide by (a promise, vow, etc.). 6. To do the required work of; manage: to *keep* house. 7. To defend from harm. 8. To care for; tend: to *keep* the flocks. 9. To detain. 10. To prevent: with *from.* 11. To observe, as with rites or ceremony: to *keep* the Sabbath. 12. To be the support of; maintain in food, clothing, etc. 13. To write down and preserve in good order: to *keep* a diary. 14. To stay in or on: *Keep* your seat. 15. To have regularly for sale. 16. To maintain for use or employ for service: to *keep* a butler. 17. To preserve in good condition, as foods. — *v.i.* 18. To persist in; continue: often with *on:* to *keep* on working. 19. To remain; stay: *Keep* away; *Keep* indoors. 20. To stay in good condition. 21. To remain good for a later time: The news will *keep.* — **to keep back** 1. To restrain. 2. To withhold. — **to keep in with** *Informal* To remain in the good graces of. — **to keep to oneself** 1. To remain solitary. 2. To avoid revealing. — **to keep track of** (or **tabs on**) To continue to be informed about. — **to keep up** 1. To hold the pace. 2. To maintain in good condition. 3. To cause to continue: *Keep up* the good work. 4. To cause to stay awake or out of bed. — **to keep up with** To stay abreast of (someone or something). — *n.* 1. Means of subsistence: to earn one's *keep.* 2. Guard or custody: They are in my *keep.* 3. The donjon or strongest building of a castle; also, a castle or fortress. — **for keeps** 1. Very seriously; not for mere amusement. 2. Permanently. [OE *cēpan* to observe]

keep·er (kē′pər) *n.* 1. One who keeps or guards; as: **a** A guardian or protector. **b** The overseer of a prison. **c** The caretaker of a wild animal. 2. One in charge of (a specified place, thing, etc.): used in combination: *gatekeeper.*

keep·ing (kē′ping) *n.* 1. The act of one who keeps. 2. Custody, charge, or possession. 3. Maintenance; support. — **in keeping (with)** In right relation or proportion (to).

keep·sake (kēp′sāk′) *n.* Anything kept, or given to be kept, for the sake of the giver; a memento.

keg (keg) *n.* A small, strong barrel, usu. holding 5 to 10 gallons. [ME *cag,* prob. < ON *kaggi*]

keg·ler (keg′lər) *n. Informal* A bowler. [< G *kegel* ninepin]

kelp (kelp) *n.* 1. Any of various large, coarse, brown algae; esp., the **giant kelp,** found mainly on the Pacific coast. 2. The ashes of such algae, a source of iodine. [ME *culp*]

kel·pie (kel′pē) *n. Scot.* A water sprite in the form of a horse, supposed to be an omen of drowning. Also **kel′py.**

kel·son (kel′sən) See KEELSON.

Kelt (kelt), **Kelt·ic** (kel′tik). See CELT, CELTIC.

Kelvin scale (kel′vin) *Physics* The absolute scale of temperature, in which zero is equal to −273° Celsius or −459.4° Fahrenheit. [after William Thompson, 1824–1907, Lord *Kelvin,* English physicist]

ken (ken) *v.* **kenned** or **kent, ken·ning** *v.t.* 1. *Scot.* To know. 2. *Archaic* To see. — *v.i.* 3. *Scot. & Brit. Dial.* To have knowledge or understanding. — *n.* Range of sight or knowledge. [OE *cennan,* infl. by ON *kenna*]

ken·nel (ken′əl) *n.* 1. A house for a dog or for a pack of hounds. 2. *Often pl.* An establishment where dogs are bred for sale, boarded, trained, etc. 3. A pack of hounds. 4. The hole or lair of a fox or like beast. 5. A vile lodging. — *v.* **ken·neled** or **·nelled, ken·nel·ing** or **·nel·ling** — *v.t.* 1. To keep or confine in or as in a kennel. — *v.i.* 2. To lodge or take shelter in a kennel. [< MF < L *canis* dog]

Ken·nel·ly-Heav·i·side layer (ken′əl-ē-hev′ē-sīd) The Heaviside layer.

ken·o·tron (ken′ō-tron) *n. Electronics* A two-electrode electron tube used as a rectifier. [< Gk. *kenōsis* an emptying + (ELEC)TRON]

kept (kept) Past tense and past participle of KEEP.

ker·a·tin (ker′ə-tin) *n. Biochem.* An albuminous compound that forms the essential ingredient of horny tissue, as of horns, claws, and nails. — **ke·rat·i·nous** (kə-rat′ə-nəs) *adj.* [< Gk. *keras, -atos* horn + -IN]

ker·a·ti·tis (ker′ə-tī′tis) *n. Pathol.* Inflammation of the cornea.

kerb (kûrb) *n. Brit.* Curb (def. 2).

ker·chief (kûr′chif) *n.* A square of fabric used to cover the head or neck, or as a handkerchief. [ME < OF < *covrir* to cover + *chef* head]

ker·mes (kûr′mēz) *n.* The dried bodies of the females of a scale insect, used as a red dyestuff. [< Arabic *qirmiz*]

ker·mis (kûr′mis) *n.* 1. In Flanders, etc., a periodical outdoor festival. **2.** An indoor or outdoor festival imitative of this. [< Du < *kerk* church + *miss* mass]

kern (kûrn) *Printing n.* The part of the face of a type that projects beyond the shaft or shank. — *v.t.* To form (type) with a kern. [< F < L *cardo, -inis* hinge]

ker·nel (kûr′nəl) *n.* **1.** The entire contents of a seed or grain within its coating. **2.** The edible part of a nut. **3.** The central part of anything; nucleus; gist. — *v.i.* **ker·neled** or **·nelled, ker·nel·ing** or **·nel·ling** To envelop as a kernel. [OE *cyrnel*, dim. of *corn* seed]

ker·o·sene (ker′ə·sēn, ker′ə·sēn′) *n.* A mixture of hydrocarbons distilled from crude petroleum and used for burning in lamps, stoves, and some engines: also called *coal oil.* Also **ker·o·sine** (ker′ə·sēn, ker′ə·sēn′). [< Gk. *kēros* wax + -ENE]

ker·sey (kûr′zē) *n.* A coarse, ribbed, closely napped woolen cloth. [after *Kersey*, village in Suffolk, England]

kes·trel (kes′trəl) *n.* A European falcon resembling the American sparrow hawk. [ME < OF *cresserelle*]

ketch (kech) *n.* A fore-and-aft rigged, two-masted vessel similar to a yawl but having the mizzen or jiggermast forward of the rudder post. [ME *cache*, prob. < CATCH, v., because used as a pursuit vessel]

ketch·up (kech′əp) *n.* A spicy sauce or condiment for meat, fish, etc., of which the base is tomatoes, or sometimes mushrooms or walnuts: also spelled *catchup, catsup.* [< Malay *kēchap*, ? ult. < Chinese *ke-tsiap* brine of pickled fish]

ke·tone (kē′tōn) *n. Chem.* One of a class of organic compounds in which the carbonyl radical unites with two hydrocarbon radicals. The simplest member is acetone. [< G, var. of F *acétone* acetone] — **ke·ton·ic** (ki·ton′ik) *adj.*

ket·tle (ket′l) *n.* **1.** A metallic vessel for boiling or stewing. **2.** A teakettle. **3.** A kettle-shaped cavity, as in rock or glacial drift: also **kettle hole. 4.** A kettledrum. — **kettle of fish** A trying or difficult situation. [OE < L *catillus*, dim. of *catinus* a deep vessel]

ket·tle·drum (ket′l·drum′) *n.* A large drum having a brass hemispherical shell and a parchment head that can be tuned through a small range of definite pitches; timpano.

Kew·pie (kyōō′pē) *n.* A chubby, cherubic doll, made of plastic, etc.: a trade name. Also **kew′pie doll.**

key¹ (kē) *n. pl.* **keys 1.** An instrument for moving the bolt or tumblers of a lock in order to lock or unlock. **2.** An instrument for holding and turning a screw, nut, valve, or the like, as for winding a clock. **3.** Anything serving to disclose, open, or solve something. **4.** Something that opens or prepares a way: the *key* to the situation. **5.** A gloss, table, or group of notes interpreting certain symbols, ciphers, problems, etc. **6.** Any one of the finger levers in typewriters, computers, etc. **7.** *Telecom.* A circuit breaker or opener operated by the fingers, as in a telegraph or radiotelegraph sending apparatus. **8.** *Music* **a** In musical instruments, a lever to be pressed by the finger or thumb. **b** A system of tones in which a piece of music is written or performed, where all the tones bear a definite relationship to some specific tone (the keynote or tonic): the *key* of C. **9.** The tone or pitch of the voice. **10.** Level of intensity of expression, feeling, or artistic execution: He writes in a high *key.* **11.** *Mech.* **a** A wedge, cotter, bolt, or pin used to secure various parts. **b** One of various instruments for fixing a collar to a shaft. **12.** *Archit.* A keystone. **13.** *Bot.* A key fruit. — *v.t.* **keyed, key·ing 1.** To fasten with or as with a key. **2.** To wedge tightly or support firmly with a key, wedge, etc. **3.** To complete (an arch) by adding the keystone. **4.** To provide with a key or keys. **5.** To provide with a cross-reference or a system of cross-references. **6.** To provide with a solution. **7.** *Music* To regulate the pitch or tone of. — to **key up** To cause excitement, expectancy, etc., in. — *adj.* Of chief and decisive importance: a *key* figure. [OE *cæg*]

key² (kē) *n. pl.* **keys** A low island, esp. one of coral, along a coast; cay. [< Sp. < Taino, islet]

key·board (kē′bôrd′, -bōrd′) *n.* A row or rows of keys as in a piano or typewriter.

key·hole (kē′hōl′) *n.* A hole for a key, as in a door or lock.

key·note (kē′nōt′) *n.* **1.** The basic idea or principle of a philosophy, political platform, literary work, etc. **2.** *Music* The tonic of a key, from which it is named: also **key tone.** — *v.t.* **·not·ed, ·not·ing** To sound the keynote of.

keynote address *U.S.* An opening address, esp. at a political convention, presenting the basic issues and partisan principles. Also **keynote speech.**

key plug The part of a cylinder lock that receives the key. For illus. see LOCK.

key signature *Music* The sharps or flats following the clef sign at the beginning of each staff, placed so as to apply to specific tones whenever they occur.

key·stone (kē′stōn′) *n.* **1.** *Archit.* The uppermost and last-set stone of an arch, that completes it and locks its members together. **2.** The fundamental element, as of a science.

Keystone State Nickname of Pennsylvania.

khak·i (kak′ē, kä′kē; *in Canada, often* kär′kē) *n. pl.* **khak·is 1.** A color ranging from light sand to medium brown. **2.**

A stout cotton cloth of this color used for uniforms. **3.** *pl.* A uniform made of khaki. — *adj.* Of the color khaki. [< Hind. < Persian *khāk* dust]

kha·lif (kā′lif, kal′if) See CALIPH.

khan (kän, kan) *n.* **1.** The title of the imperial successors to the Mongol conqueror Genghis Khan. **2.** A title for rulers, officials, or dignitaries in Central Asia, Iran, etc. [< Turkic *khān* lord, prince] — **khan′ate** (-āt) *n.*

kib·butz (ki·bŏŏts′) *n. pl.* **·but·zim** (-bŏŏt·sēm′) A cooperative or collective farm in Israel. [< Hebrew, gathering]

kib·itz (kib′its) *v.i. Informal* To act as a kibitzer. [Back formation < KIBITZER]

kib·itz·er (kib′it·sər) *n. Informal* One who meddles in the affairs of others; esp., a spectator who gives gratuitous advice to card players. [< Yiddish < G *kiebitzen* to look on]

kick (kik) *v.i.* **1.** To strike out with the foot or feet, as in swimming, propelling a ball, etc. **2.** To strike out habitually with the foot, hooves, etc. **3.** Of firearms, to recoil. **4.** In football, to punt, try for an extra point or field goal by kicking, etc. **5.** *U.S. Informal* To object or complain. — *v.t.* **6.** To strike with the foot. **7.** To drive or impel by striking with the foot. **8.** In football, to score (an extra point or a field goal) by kicking the ball. **9.** Of firearms, to strike in recoiling. — to **kick around** *U.S. Informal* **1.** To abuse; neglect. **2.** To roam from place to place. **3.** To give thought to; discuss. — to **kick back 1.** To recoil violently or unexpectedly, as a gun. **2.** *U.S. Slang* To pay back (part of a salary, fee, etc.) to someone in a position to grant favors, usu. as a bribe. — to **kick in** *U.S. Informal* To contribute or participate by contributing. — to **kick off 1.** In football, to put the ball in play by kicking it toward the opposing team. **2.** *U.S. Slang* To die. — to **kick out** *U.S. Informal* To exclude or eject violently or suddenly, as with a kick. — to **kick the bucket** *Slang* To die. — to **kick up** *U.S. Slang* To make or stir up (trouble, confusion, etc.). — *n.* **1.** A blow or thrust with the foot. **2.** *U.S. Informal* An objection or complaint. **3.** *U.S. Slang* Power to stimulate, excite, or intoxicate: whisky with a *kick.* **4.** *U.S. Slang* A pleasant and exciting sensation; thrill. **5.** *U.S. Slang* Energy; pep. **6.** The recoil of a firearm. **7.** In football, a kicking of the ball; esp., a punt. [ME *kike*] — **kick′er** *n.*

kick·back (kik′bak′) *n.* **1.** *Informal* A strong reaction; recoil; repercussion. **2.** *U.S. Slang* A paying back of part of a salary, fee, etc., also, the money so paid.

kick·off (kik′ôf′, -of′) *n.* **1.** In football, the kick with which play is begun. **2.** Any beginning: the *kickoff* of a political campaign.

kid (kid) *n.* **1.** A young goat. **2.** Leather made from the skin of a kid. **3.** *pl.* Gloves or shoes made of kidskin. **4.** The meat of a young goat. **5.** *Informal* A child; youngster. — *adj. Informal* Younger: my *kid* brother. — *v.i. & v.t.* **kid·ded, kid·ding 1.** *Slang* To make fun of (someone); to tease. **2.** *Slang* To deceive or try to deceive (someone); fool. **3.** Of a goat, to give birth. [ME < ON *kith*] — **kid′der** *n.*

kid·dy (kid′ē) *n. pl.* **·dies** *Slang* A small child. Also **kid′die.**

kid glove A glove made of kidskin or similar material. — to **handle with kid gloves** To treat tactfully or gingerly.

kid·nap (kid′nap) *v.t.* **kid·naped** or **·napped, kid·nap·ing** or **·nap·ping 1.** To seize and carry off (someone) by force or fraud, usu. so as to demand a ransom. **2.** To steal (a child). [< KID (def. 5) + *nap*, dial. var. of NAB] — **kid′nap·er** or **kid′nap·per** *n.*

kid·ney (kid′nē) *n. pl.* **·neys 1.** *Anat.* Either of two glandular organs situated at the back of the abdominal cavity close to the spinal column in vertebrates, serving to separate waste products from the blood and to excrete them as urine. ◆ Collateral adjective: *renal.* **2.** The meat of the kidney of certain animals, used as food. **3.** Temperament, nature, or type: a man of my own *kidney.* [Origin unknown]

kidney bean 1. A kidney-shaped bean. **2.** The bean of the scarlet runner.

kidney stone *Pathol.* A hard mineral concretion formed in the kidney; renal calculus.

kid·skin (kid′skin′) *n.* Leather tanned from the skin of a young goat, used for gloves, shoes, etc.

HUMAN KIDNEY
a Pyramid.
b Papillae.
c Cortex. *d* Ureter. *e* Pelvis.

kill¹ (kil) *v.t.* **1.** To cause the death of. **2.** To slaughter for food; butcher. **3.** To bring to an end; destroy. **4.** *U.S. Slang* To make a strong emotional impression upon, as of amusement. **5.** To destroy the active qualities of; neutralize. **6.** To cancel by contrast, as a color. **7.** In printing, to delete. **8.** To turn off or stop (a motor, live circuit, etc.). **9.** To pass (time) aimlessly. **10.** To veto or quash (legislation). — *v.i.* **11.** To cause death. **12.** To murder; slay. **13.** To undergo death; die. — *n.* **1.** The act of killing, esp. in hunting. **2.** An animal or animals killed as prey. [ME *cullen, killen*]

—Syn. (verb) **1.** *Kill* is the general term applicable to all organisms, and frequently extended to inanimate things: frost *killed* the buds, to *kill* a story. *Murder*, *assassinate*, and *execute* are said only of persons. *Murder* refers to a deliberate, often premeditated, killing; *assassinate* is often applied to political killings. *Execute* refers to the carrying qut of a legal sentence of death.

kill² (kil) *n.* A creek, stream, or channel: an element in geographical names: *Schuylkill.* [< Du. < MDu. *kille*]

kill·deer (kil′dir) *n. pl.* **·deers** or **·deer** A North American wading bird of the plover family, having a loud cry. Also **kill′dee** (-dē). [Imit., from its cry]

kill·er (kil′ər) *n.* One who or that which kills.

killer whale A voracious whale related to the dolphins.

kill·ing (kil′ing) *n.* **1.** The act of one who or that which kills. **— to make a killing** To get or win a large amount of money. *—adj.* **1.** Used to kill. **2.** Likely to kill. **3.** Resulting in death; fatal.

kill-joy (kil′joi′) *n.* One who spoils pleasure for others.

kiln (kil, kiln) *n.* An oven or furnace for baking, burning, or drying bricks, pottery, etc. [OE < L *culina* kitchen]

kil·o (kil′ō, kē′lō) *n. pl.* **kil·os 1.** A kilogram. **2.** A kilometer.

kilo- *prefix* In the metric system, a thousand times (a specified unit): *kilogram.* [< F < Gk. *chilioi* a thousand]

kil·o·cy·cle (kil′ə·sī′kəl) *n.* **1.** *Telecom.* A unit of electromagnetic wave frequency of 1,000 cycles per second. **2.** One thousand cycles. Abbr. *kc, kc.*

kil·o·gram (kil′ə·gram) *n.* In the metric system, a thousand grams. Also **kil′o·gramme.** [< F *kilogramme*] Abbr. *k., K., kg, kg., kilo.* See table inside back cover.

kil·o·gram-me·ter (kil′ə·gram-mē′tər) *n.* A unit of work, the equivalent of the force expended in raising a mass of one kilogram one meter against gravity, about 7.2 foot-pounds.

kil·o·li·ter (kil′ə·lē′tər) *n.* In the metric system, a thousand liters. Abbr. *kl, kl.* See table inside back cover.

kil·o·me·ter (kil′ə·mē′tər, ki·lom′ə·tər) *n.* In the metric system, a thousand meters. Abbr. *km, km., kilo.* See table inside back cover. **— kil′o·met·ric** or **·ri·cal** *adj.*

kil·o·ton (kil′ə·tun′) *n.* **1.** A weight of 1,000 tons. **2.** A unit equivalent to the explosive power of 1,000 tons of TNT.

kil·o·watt (kil′ə·wät) *n. Electr.* A unit of power equal to 1,000 watts. Abbr. *kw, kw.*

kil·o·watt-hour (kil′ə·wät-our′) *n.* The work done or the energy resulting from one kilowatt acting for one hour, equal to approximately 1.34 horsepower-hours.

kilt (kilt) *n.* A short pleated skirt worn by Scottish Highland men and Irishmen. *—v.t.* To make broad, vertical pleats in; pleat. [ME; prob. < Scand.] **— kilt′ing** *n.*

kil·ter (kil′tər) *n. Informal* Proper or working order: now only in the phrase **out of kilter,** out or order. [Origin uncertain]

ki·mo·no (kə·mō′nə, ki·mō′nō) *n. pl.* **·nos 1.** A loose robe fastened with a wide sash, worn in Japan as an outer garment. **2.** A woman's negligee. [< Japanese]

kin (kin) *n.* **1.** One's relatives by blood, collectively; one's family. **— next of kin** In law, one's nearest relative or relatives. *—adj.* **1.** Related by blood. **2.** Similar; kindred; alike. [OE *cyn*]

-kin *suffix* Little; small: *lambkin.* [< MDu. *-kijn, -ken*]

kind¹ (kīnd) *adj.* **1.** Gentle and considerate; goodhearted. **2.** Proceeding from goodheartedness. [OE *gecynde*]

kind² (kīnd) *n.* **1.** A class or grouping; type. **2.** The distinguishing character of something: They differ in *kind.* **— in kind 1.** With a thing of the same sort: to return an insult *in kind.* **2.** In produce instead of money: to pay taxes *in kind.* **— kind of** *Informal* In a way; somewhat. **— of a kind** Inferior in quality. [OE *gecynd*]

kin·der·gar·ten (kin′dər·gär′tən) *n.* A school or class for young children, usu. from the ages of four to six. [< G]

kind·heart·ed (kīnd′här′tid) *adj.* Having or showing a kind nature. **— kind′heart′ed·ly** *adv.* **— kind′heart′ed·ness** *n.*

kin·dle (kin′dəl) *v.* **·dled, ·dling** *v.t.* **1.** To cause to burn; ignite. **2.** To excite, as the feelings. **3.** To make bright or glowing as if with flame. *—v.i.* **4.** To take fire. **5.** To become excited or inflamed. **6.** To become bright or glowing. [ME < ON *kynda*] **— kin·dler** *n.*

kin·dling (kind′ling) *n.* **1.** Sticks, wood chips, etc., with which a fire is started. **2.** The act of one who kindles.

kind·ly (kīnd′lē) *adj.* **·li·er, ·li·est 1.** Having or showing kindness; sympathetic. **2.** Having a favorable effect. *—adv.* **1.** In a kind manner; good-naturedly. **2.** Enthusiastically; heartily. **— to take kindly to 1.** To accept with liking. **2.** To be naturally attracted to. **— kind′li·ness** *n.*

kind·ness (kīnd′nis) *n.* **1.** The quality of being kind. **2.** A kind act or service; a favor. **3.** A kindly feeling.

kin·dred (kin′drid) *adj.* **1.** Related by blood; akin. **2.**

Having a like nature; similar. *— n.* One's relatives by blood. [ME < OE *cynn* kin + *rǣden* condition]

kine (kīn) *n. Archaic* Cattle: plural of COW¹.

kin·e·mat·ics (kin′ə·mat′iks) *n.pl. (construed as sing.)* The branch of physics treating of motion without reference to particular forces or bodies. [< Gk. < *kineein* to move] **— kin′e·mat′ic** or **·i·cal** *adj.* **— kin′e·mat′i·cal·ly** *adv.*

kin·e·mat·o·graph (kin′ə·mat′ə·graf, -gräf) See CINEMATOGRAPH.

kin·e·scope (kin′ə·skōp) *n.* **1.** The cathode-ray tube of a television set, which reproduces by the action of an electron beam upon a fluorescent screen, the image impinging upon a similar tube in the television camera: also called *picture tube.* **2.** A filmed record of a television program: also **kin·e** (kin′ē).

kinesi- *combining form* A movement. [< Gk. *kinēsis* motion]

-kinesis *combining form* A movement; motion. [< Gk. *kinēsis* motion]

kin·es·the·si·a (kin′is·thē′zhə, -zhē·ə) *n. Physiol.* The perception of muscular movement, tension, etc., derived from the functioning of afferent nerves connected with muscle tissue, skin, joints, and tendons. Also **kin·es·the′sis** (-thē′sis). [< NL < Gk. *kineein* to move + *aisthēsis* perception] **— kin′es·thet′ic** (-thet′ik) *adj.*

ki·net·ic (ki·net′ik) *adj.* **1.** Of or pertaining to motion. **2.** Producing or caused by motion: *kinetic* energy. [< Gk. < *kineein* to move]

ki·net·ics (ki·net′iks) *n.pl. (construed as sing.)* The branch of physics dealing with the effect of forces in the production or modification of motion in bodies.

kin·folk (kin′fōk′) *n.pl. Informal* Kinsfolk. Also **kin′folks′.**

king (king) *n.* **1.** The sovereign male ruler of a kingdom; monarch. ◆ Collateral adjective: *regal.* **2.** One who is preeminent: a cattle *king.* **3.** A playing card bearing the likeness of a king. **4.** In chess, the principal piece, for whose defense all the moves of the other pieces are made. **5.** In checkers, a piece that, having reached the opponent's last rank of squares, is then crowned and may move in any direction. Abbr. *k., K.* [OE *cyng, cyning*]

King Arthur See ARTHUR.

king·bird (king′bûrd′) *n.* Any of various North American flycatchers.

king·bolt (king′bōlt′) *n.* A vertical central bolt usu. attaching the body of a wagon or similar vehicle to the fore axle, and serving as a pivot in turning: also called *kingpin.*

king crab 1. The horseshoe crab. **2.** Any of a genus of usu. large crablike crustaceans common in the north Pacific, with a small, triangular body and very long legs.

king·dom (king′dəm) *n.* **1.** The territory, people, state, or realm ruled by a king or a queen; monarchy. **2.** Any place or area thought of as a sovereign domain. **3.** Any of the three primary divisions of natural objects known as the *animal, vegetable,* and *mineral kingdoms.* **4.** The spiritual dominion of God. [OE *cyningdom*]

king·fish (king′fish′) *n. pl.* **·fish** or **·fish·es** Any of various American food fishes.

king·fish·er (king′fish/ər) *n.* Any of several nonpasserine birds of world-wide distribution, that feed on fish.

King James Bible An English translation of the Bible from Hebrew and Greek, proposed by James I and completed in 1611. Also **Authorized Version.** Complete revisions were published in England in 1885 (**Revised Version**) and in the U.S. in 1901 (**American Standard Version**) and in 1952 (**Revised Standard Version**).

king·let (king′lit) *n.* **1.** A young or insignificant king. **2.** Any of several small birds, resembling the warblers.

king·ly (king′lē) *adj.* **·li·er, ·li·est** Of or worthy of a king; regal. *—adv.* In a kingly way. **— king′li·ness** *n.*

king·pin (king′pin′) *n.* **1.** In bowling or tenpins, the foremost pin of a set arranged in order for playing. **2.** In ninepins, the center pin. **3.** A kingbolt. **4.** *Informal* The person of central importance in a group, etc.

king post In carpentry, a single vertical strut supporting the apex of a triangular truss and resting on a crossbeam. For illustration see ROOF. Also **king·post** (king′pōst′).

Kings (kingz) *n.pl. (construed as sing.)* **1.** Either of two books, I Kings, and II Kings, of the Old Testament, recounting the histories of the Hebrew kings after David. **2.** In the Douai version of the Old Testament, a group of four books, comprising I Samuel, II Samuel, I Kings, and II Kings.

king's English Standard English considered as set by official authority: also called *queen's English.*

king·ship (king′ship) *n.* **1.** The state, power, office, or dignity of a king. **2.** The monarchical type of government. **3.** As a title, the person of a king: his royal *kingship.*

king-size (king′sīz′) *adj. Informal* Greater in length or size than is usual. Also **king′sized′.**

king snake A large, harmless snake of the southern U.S. that feeds on rats and mice.

kink (kingk) *n.* 1. An abrupt bend, curl, loop, or tangle in a line, wire, hair, etc. 2. A mental quirk. 3. A sharp, painful muscular spasm; crick. — *v.i.* & *v.t.* To form or cause to form a kink or kinks. [< Du., twist, curl]

kink·a·jou (king′kə-jōō) *n.* An arboreal, carnivorous mammal of Central and South America, having large eyes, soft woolly fur, and a long tail. [< F *quincajou* < Tupi]

kink·y (kingk′ē) *adj.* **kink·i·er, kink·i·est** Kinked; frizzy. — **kink′i·ness** *n.*

kins·folk (kinz′fōk′) *n.pl.* One's relatives or family; kin: also, *Informal,* kinfolk.

kin·ship (kin′ship) *n.* Relationship, esp. by blood. — **Syn.** See RELATIONSHIP.

kins·man (kinz′mən) *n.* *pl.* **·men** (-mən) A male blood relation. — **kins′wom′an** (-wōōm′ən) *n.fem.*

ki·osk (kē·osk′, kē′osk, ki′-) *n.* 1. In Turkey, a lightly constructed, open summerhouse or pavilion. 2. A similar structure, used as a booth, newsstand, etc. [< F < Turkish < Persian *kūshk* palace]

kip[1] (kip) *n.* 1. The untanned skin of a calf, a lamb, or an adult of any small breed of cattle. 2. A collection of such skins. Also **kip′skin′** (-skin′). [ME < Du.]

kip[2] (kip) *n.* *pl.* **kip** The monetary unit of Laos: in 1960 worth about one U.S. cent.

kip·per (kip′ər) *n.* 1. A salmon or herring cured by kippering. 2. The male salmon during the spawning season. — *v.t.* To cure (fish) by splitting, salting, and drying or smoking. [? OE *cypera* spawning salmon]

kirk (kûrk) *n.* *Scot & Brit. Dial.* A church.

kir·mess (kûr′mis) See KERMESS.

kir·tle (kûr′tl) *n.* *Archaic* 1. A woman's skirt. 2. A man's outer garment. [OE < L *curtus* short] — **kir′tled** *adj.*

Kis·lew (kis·lef′, kis′lef) *n.* The third month of the Hebrew year. Also **Kish′lev, Kis′lev.** See (Hebrew) CALENDAR.

kis·met (kiz′met, kis′-) *n.* Appointed lot; fate. [< Turkish < Arabic *qasama* to divide]

kiss (kis) *v.t.* & *v.i.* 1. To touch or caress with the lips as a sign of greeting, love, etc. 2. To meet or touch lightly. — *n.* 1. A touch or caress with the lips. 2. A light meeting or touching. 3. A small candy. [OE *cyssan*]

kiss·er (kis′ər) *n.* 1. One who kisses. 2. *Slang* The mouth or the face.

kit (kit) *n.* 1. A collection of articles, tools, etc., for a special purpose. 2. A set of parts, etc., from which something is to be made. 3. One's effects or outfit, esp. for traveling. 4. A box, bag, knapsack, etc. 5. *Informal* A collection of persons or things. [ME < MDu. *kitte* jug, vessel]

kitch·en (kich′ən) *n.* 1. A room set apart and equipped for cooking food. 2. A culinary department; cuisine. [OE < L *coquere* to cook]

kitch·en·ette (kich′ən·et′) *n.* A small, compactly arranged kitchen. Also **kitch′en·et′.**

kitchen police *Mil.* Enlisted men detailed to perform routine kitchen chores; also, such duty.

kitch·en·ware (kich′ən·wâr′) *n.* Kitchen utensils.

kite (kīt) *n.* 1. A lightweight structure of wood and paper, flown in the wind at the end of a long string. 2. A predatory bird of the hawk family (*Falconidae*) with long, pointed wings. 3. *Naut.* One of several light sails to use in a light wind. 4. In commerce, any negotiable paper not representing a genuine transaction, employed to obtain money, sustain credit, etc. — *v.* **kit·ed, kit·ing** *v.i.* 1. To soar or fly like a kite. 2. To obtain money, etc., by the use of kites. — *v.t.* 3. In commerce, to issue, as a kite. [OE *cȳta*]

kith (kith) *n.* *Archaic* One's friends, acquaintances, or associates: now only in **kith and kin.** [OE *cūth* known]

kitsch (kich) *n.* Art or literary works, etc., having broad popular appeal and little esthetic merit. [< G]

kit·ten (kit′ən) *n.* A young cat. [ME < OF *chaton* kitten]

kit·ten·ish (kit′ən·ish) *adj.* Playfully coy. — **kit′ten·ish·ly** *adv.* — **kit′ten·ish·ness** *n.*

kit·ti·wake (kit′ē·wāk) *n.* A gull of northern seas, having a rudimentary hind toe. [Imit.]

kit·ty[1] (kit′ē) *n.* *pl.* **·ties** 1. Money pooled, as by card players, for any specific purpose. 2. In card games, a hand or part of a hand left over after a deal. [Origin uncertain]

kit·ty[2] (kit′ē) *n.* *pl.* **·ties** A kitten or cat.

kit·ty-cor·nered (kit′ē·kôr′nərd) *adj.* Cater-cornered.

Ki·wa·nis (kə·wä′nis, -wô′-) An international chain of men's clubs to promote higher business standards and to provide service to the community. [< N. Am. Ind. *keewanis* to make oneself known] — **Ki·wa′ni·an** *adj.* & *n.*

ki·wi (kē′wē) *n.* A flightless bird of New Zealand, the apteryx. [< Maori]

Klan (klan) The Ku Klux Klan. — **Klans′man** *n.*

klep·to·ma·ni·a (klep′tə·mā′nē·ə) *n.* An obsessive impulse to steal. [< Gk. *kleptēs* thief + -MANIA] — **klep′to·ma′ni·ac** (-mā′nē·ak) *n.*

klieg light (klēg) A powerful arc floodlight, used in making motion pictures. [after the *Kliegl* brothers, lighting pioneers born in Germany]

knack (nak) *n.* 1. The ability to do something readily and well. 2. Cleverness; adroitness. [ME *knak, knekke*]

knap·sack (nap′sak′) *n.* A case or bag worn strapped across the shoulders, for carrying equipment or supplies; rucksack. [< Du < *knappen* to bite, eat + *zak* sack]

knave (nāv) *n.* 1. A dishonest person; rogue. 2. A playing card, the jack. [OE *cnafa* youth] — **knav′ish** *adj.*

knav·er·y (nā′vər·ē) *n.* *pl.* **·er·ies** 1. Deceitfulness; trickery; rascality. 2. An act of trickery or deceit.

knead (nēd) *v.t.* 1. To mix and work (dough, clay, etc.) into a uniform mass, usu. by pressing and pulling with the hands. 2. To work upon by squeezes of the hands; massage. 3. To make by kneading. [OE *cnedan*] — **knead′er** *n.*

knee (nē) *n.* 1. *Anat.* The joint of the human leg that articulates the femur with the tibia and fibula and includes the patella. 2. *Zool.* A part homologous to the human knee, as the stifle joint in horses, dogs, etc. 3. Something like a bent knee, as a bent piece of metal or wood used in construction, etc. 4. The part of a garment covering the knee. — *v.t.* To touch or strike with the knee. [OE *cnēow*]

knee·cap (nē′kap′) *n.* The patella. Also **knee′pan′.**

knee-deep (nē′dēp′) *adj.* Rising or sunk to the knee.

knee·hole (nē′hōl′) *n.* A space for the knees, as in a desk.

kneel (nēl) *v.i.* **knelt** or **kneeled, kneel·ing** To fall or rest on the bent knee or knees. [OE *cnēowlian*] — **kneel′er** *n.*

knell (nel) *n.* 1. The tolling of a bell, esp. one announcing a death. 2. Any sad or doleful sound. — *v.i.* 1. To sound a knell. 2. To toll mournfully. — *v.t.* 3. To proclaim by or as by a knell. [OE *cnyllan* to knock]

knelt (nelt) Past tense and past participle of KNEEL.

knew (nōō, nyōō) Past tense of KNOW.

Knick·er·bock·er (nik′ər·bok′ər) *n.* 1. A descendant of one of the early Dutch settlers in New York State. 2. A New Yorker. [after Diedrich *Knickerbocker,* fictitious Dutch author of Washington Irving's *History of New York*]

knick·er·bock·ers (nik′ər·bok′erz) *n.pl.* Wide short breeches gathered below the knee: also **knick·ers** (nik′ərz).

knick-knack (nik′nak) *n.* A trifling article; trinket; trifle: also spelled *nicknack.* [Reduplication of KNACK]

knife (nīf) *n.* *pl.* **knives** (nīvz) 1. An instrument for cutting, piercing, or spreading, with one or more sharp-edged, often pointed, blades, commonly set in a handle. 2. A blade forming a part of an implement or machine. 3. A weapon, such as a dagger. — *v.t.* **knifed, knif·ing** 1. To stab or cut with a knife. 2. *U.S. Slang* To discredit or betray behind one's back. [OE *cnīf*]

knight (nīt) *n.* 1. In medieval times: **a** A feudal tenant serving his superior as a mounted soldier. **b** A gentleman, usu. of the nobility, trained for mounted combat and raised to the order of chivalry. 2. In Great Britain, the holder of a nonhereditary dignity below the rank of baronet, conferred by the sovereign as a reward for personal merit or for service to the country. The holder is entitled to use *Sir* before his given name. 3. In chess, a piece bearing a horse's head. — *v.t.* To make (a man) a knight. [OE *cniht* boy, military attendant] — **knight′ly** *adv.*

knight errant *pl.* **knights errant** A wandering knight who went forth to redress wrongs or seek adventures.

knight-er·rant·ry (nīt′er′ən·trē) *n.* *pl.* **·ries** 1. The customs and practices of the knights errant; chivalry. 2. Quixotic behavior or action.

knight·hood (nīt′hōōd) *n.* 1. The character, rank, or vocation of a knight. 2. Knights collectively.

Knights of Columbus A fraternal society of American Roman Catholic men, founded 1882.

Knight Templar *pl.* **Knights Templars** *for def. 1,* **Knights Templar** *for def. 2.* 1. A member of a military and religious order founded in 1119 by the Crusaders for the protection of pilgrims. 2. A Freemason of an order claiming descent from the medieval order of Knights Templars.

knish (kə·nish′) *n.* A small square or round of dough filled with potatoes, meat, etc., and baked or fried. [< Yiddish]

knit (nit) *v.* **knit** or **knit·ted, knit·ting** *v.t.* 1. To form (a fabric or garment) by interlocking loops of a single yarn or thread by means of needles. 2. To fasten or unite closely and firmly. 3. To draw (the brows) together into wrinkles. — *v.i.* 4. To make a fabric by interlocking loops of yarn or thread. 5. To grow together, as broken bones. 6. To come together in wrinkles; contract. — *n.* The fabric made by knitting. [OE *cnyttan*] — **knit′ter** *n.*

knit·ting (nit′ing) *n.* 1. The act of one who or that which knits. 2. The fabric produced by knitting.

knitting needle A slender, pointed rod, used in knitting.

knives (nīvz) Plural of KNIFE.

knob (nob) *n.* 1. A rounded protuberance, bunch, or lump. 2. A rounded handle, as of a door. 3. A rounded mountain; knoll. [ME < MLG *knobbe*]

knob·by (nob′ē) *adj.* **·bi·er, ·bi·est** 1. Full of knobs. 2. Resembling a knob.

knock (nok) *v.t.* **1.** To deal a blow to; hit. **2.** To strike together. **3.** To drive or move by hitting. **4.** To make by striking or pounding: to *knock* a hole in the wall. **5.** To strike or push so as to make fall: with *down, over, off,* etc. **6.** *U.S. Slang* To find fault with; disparage. — *v.i.* **7.** To strike a blow or blows; rap: to *knock* at a door. **8.** To come into collision; bump. **9.** To make a pounding or clanking noise, as an engine. — **to knock around** (or **about**) **1.** *Informal* To wander from place to place. **2.** To treat roughly; abuse. — **to knock down 1.** To take apart for shipping or storing. **2.** At auctions, to sell to the highest bidder. — **to knock off 1.** *Informal* To stop or leave off (work, talking, etc.). **2.** To deduct. **3.** *Informal* To do or make quickly or easily. **4.** *U.S. Slang* To kill; also, to overwhelm or defeat. — **to knock (oneself) out** *U.S. Slang* **1.** To make a great effort; work very hard. **2.** To become exhausted. — **to knock out 1.** In boxing, to defeat (an opponent) by knocking to the canvas for a count of ten. **2.** To make unconscious. **3.** *U.S. Slang* To tire greatly. — **to knock together** To build or make roughly or hurriedly. — *n.* **1.** A sharp blow; rap. **2.** A noise made by an engine in faulty condition. **3.** A misfortune, setback, or reversal. **4.** *U.S. Slang* Hostile criticism; disparagement. [OE *cnocian*]

knock·a·bout (nok′ə·bout′) *n. Naut.* A small sailboat rigged like a sloop. — *adj.* **1.** Marked by roughness. **2.** Suitable for rough or casual occasions.

knock·down (nok′doun′) *adj.* **1.** Powerful enough to upset or overthrow. **2.** Made so as to be easily taken apart or put together: a *knockdown* chair. — *n.* **1.** A felling or upsetting, esp. by a blow. **2.** An article made for easy assembly.

knock·er (nok′ər) *n.* **1.** One who or that which knocks. **2.** A hinged metal hammer fastened to a door for knocking.

knock-knee (nok′nē′) *n.* **1.** An inward curvature of the legs that causes the knees to knock or rub together in walking. **2.** *pl.* Legs so curved.

knock-kneed (nok′nēd′) *adj.* Having knock-knees.

knock·out (nok′out′) *adj.* Forcible enough and so placed as to render unconscious. — *n.* **1.** A knocking unconscious or a knocking out of action. **2.** In boxing, a flooring of one fighter for a count of ten; a kayo. **3.** *Slang* A remarkably impressive person or thing.

knoll (nōl) *n.* A small round hill; a mound. [OE *cnoll* hill]

knot (not) *n.* **1.** An intertwining of rope, string, etc., one free end being passed through a loop and drawn tight; also, the lump thus made. **2.** An ornamental bow of silk, lace, braid, etc. **3.** A hard, gnarled portion of the trunk of a tree, or the round mark on sawed lumber left by this. **4.** A cluster or group of persons or things. **5.** A bond or union. **6.** An enlargement in a muscle, of a gland, etc. resembling a knot. **7.** Something not easily solved; problem. **8.** *Naut.* **a** A speed of a nautical mile in an hour, equivalent to 1.1516 statute miles per hour. **b** A nautical mile. — *v.* **knot·ted, knot·ting** *v.t.* **1.** To tie in a knot. **2.** To secure or fasten by a knot. **3.** To form knobs, bosses, etc., in. — *v.i.* **4.** To form a knot or knots. **5.** To become knotted or tangled. [OE *cnotta*]

KNOTS

a Square or reef. *b* Granny. *c* Overhand. *d* Figure-eight. *e* Slipknot. *f* Double bowknot. *g* Boat. *h* Surgeon's.

knot·grass (not′gras′, -gräs′) *n.* A widely distributed herb with jointed stems.

knot·hole (not′hōl′) *n.* A hole in a plank or board left by the falling out of a knot.

knot·ty (not′ē) *adj.* **·ti·er, ·ti·est 1.** Full of or tied in knots. **2.** Difficult or intricate; puzzling. — **knot′ti·ness** *n.*

knout (nout) *n.* A whip or scourge formerly used for flogging in Russia. — *v.t.* To flog with the knout. [< Russian < ON *knūtr*, knot < *knūta* knot]

know (nō) *v.* **knew, known, know·ing** *v.t.* **1.** To be cognizant of; have a concept of in the mind. **2.** To be certain of; apprehend as true. **3.** To be acquainted or familiar with. **4.** To be sure about the identity of; recognize. **5.** To have a practical grasp of through instruction, study, etc.: to *know* French. **6.** To be able: with *how:* to *know* how to swim. **7.** To distinguish between: to *know* good from bad. **8.** To have memorized: The actor *knows* his lines. **9.** To have experienced: We *know* poverty. — *v.i.* **10.** To have awareness; apprehend. **11.** To have understanding or certainty; be sure. — **to know better** To be aware of something truer or more correct than what one says or does. — *n. Informal* The fact of knowing: now only in the phrase **to be in the know,** to have inside or secret information. [OE *cnāwan*] — **know′a·ble** *adj.* — **know′er** *n.*

know-how (nō′hou′) *n. Informal* Mastery of a complicated operation or procedure; technical skill.

know·ing (nō′ing) *adj.* **1.** Perceptive; astute; also, hinting at having sly or secret knowledge concerning something. **2.** Conscious; intentional. **3.** Having knowledge or information. — **know′ing·ly** *adv.* — **know′ing·ness** *n.*

knowl·edge (nol′ij) *n.* **1.** A result or product of knowing; information or understanding acquired through experience; practical ability, or skill. **2.** Deep and extensive learning; erudition. **3.** The cumulative culture of the human race. **4.** A sure conviction; certainty. **5.** The act, process, or state of knowing; cognition. **6.** Any object of knowing or mental apprehension; that which is or may be known. **7.** Specific information; notice. **8.** *Archaic* Sexual intercourse: often preceded by *carnal.* [ME < OE *cnāwlǣc* acknowledgement] — **Syn. 5.** Cognition, apprehension, comprehension.

knowl·edge·a·ble (nol′ij·ə·bəl) *adj.* Having knowledge; well-informed; intelligent.

known (nōn) Past participle of KNOW. — *adj.* Recognized by all as the truth; understood; axiomatic: *known* facts.

know-noth·ing (nō′nuth′ing) *n.* An ignoramus.

knuck·le (nuk′əl) *n.* **1.** One of the joints of the fingers, or the region about it; esp., one of the joints connecting the fingers to the hand. **2.** The protuberance formed by one of these joints when the finger is bent. **3.** The carpal joint of the pig, calf, etc., the flesh of which is used as food. **4.** *pl.* Brass knuckles. — *v.* **knuck·led, knuck·ling** *v.t.* **1.** To rub, press, or hit with the knuckles. — *v.i.* **2.** To hold the knuckles on the ground in shooting a marble. — **to knuckle down** To apply oneself seriously and assiduously. — **to knuckle under** To yield; submit; give in. [ME *knokel*]

knuck·le·bone (nuk′əl·bōn′) *n.* **1.** In man, one of the bones forming a knuckle. **2.** In certain animals, as sheep, a leg bone with a knob at the end; also, this knob.

knuck·le·dus·ters (nuk′əl·dus′tərz) *n.pl.* Brass knuckles.

knurl (nûrl) *n.* **1.** A protuberance; lump. **2.** One of a series of small ridges on the edge of a metal object, as a coin, thumbscrew, etc. — *v.t.* To ridge or mill, as the edge of a coin. [? Dim. of KNUR] — **knurl′y** *adj.*

KO or **K.O.** or **k.o.** Knockout (boxing).

ko·a·la (kō·ä′lə) An arboreal marsupial having gray, woolly fur and no tail, and feeding on the leaves of the eucalyptus. [< native Australian name]

Ko·dak (kō′dak) *n.* A small portable camera carrying a roll of sensitized film: a trade name. Also **ko′dak.**

Ko·di·ak bear (kō′dē·ak) A very large brown bear found on Kodiak Island and adjacent islands off the Alaskan coast.

Koh·i·noor (kō′i·nŏŏr′) *n.* A famous Indian diamond weighing when cut about 106 carats, a British crown jewel since 1849. Also **Koh′i·nor′, Koh′i·nur′.** [< Persian *kōhinūr,* lit., mountain of light]

KOALAS
(28 to 32 inches long)

kohl·ra·bi (kōl′rä·bē, kōl·rä′-) *n. pl.* **·bies** A variety of cabbage with an edible turnip-shaped stem. [< L *caulis* cabbage + *rapa* turnip]

ko·la (kō′lə), **kola nut tree** See COLA.

kola nut See COLA NUT.

ko·lin·sky (kə·lin′skē, kō-) *n. pl.* **·skies 1.** Any of several minks of Asia and Russia. **2.** Their fur, often dyed to resemble sable. [< Russian *kolinski* of Kola]

kol·khoz (kol·khôz′) *n.* A collective farm in the Soviet Union. Also **kol·hoz′, kol·khos′.** [< Russian *kol(lektivnoe) collective* + *khoz(yaĭstvo)* farm, household]

kook (kŏŏk) *n. Slang* An unconventional, eccentric, or unbalanced person. [< CUCKOO] — **kook′y** *adj.*

ko·peck (kō′pek) *n.* A Russian bronze coin, the hundredth part of a ruble: also spelled *copeck.* Also **ko′pek.** Abbr. *k., K., kop.* [< Russian *kopye* lance]

Ko·ran (kō·rän′, -ran′) *n.* The sacred book of the Moslems, recording in Arabic the revelations of Allah (God) to Mohammed: also *Alcoran, Alkoran.* [< Arabic *Qur'ān,* lit., recitation < *qar'ā* to read]

Ko·re·an (kō·rē′ən, kō-) *adj.* Of or pertaining to Korea, its inhabitants, or their language. — *n.* **1.** A native of Korea, or a person of Korean ancestry. **2.** The language of Korea.

Korean War See table for WAR.

ko·ru·na (kō′rŏŏ·nä) *n. pl.* **ko·ru·ny** (kō′rŏŏ·nē) or **ko·run** (kō′rŏŏn) The monetary unit of Czechoslovakia. [< Czechoslovakian < L *corona* crown]

ko·sher (kō′shər) *adj.* **1.** Permitted by or conforming to Jewish (ceremonial) law: most often said of food. **2.** *Slang* Legitimate; proper. — *n.* Kosher food. — *v.t.* To make kosher. [< Hebrew *kāshēr* fit, proper]

kou·miss (kōō′mis), **kou·mys** See KUMISS.

kow·tow (kou′tou, kō′-) *v.i.* **1.** To behave in an obsequious, servile manner. **2.** To strike the forehead on the ground as a sign of reverence, etc. — *n.* The act of kowtowing. [< Chinese *k'o-t'ou*, lit., to knock the head] — **kow′tow′er** *n.*

kraal (kräl) *n.* **1.** In South Africa, a village or group of native huts, usu. surrounded by a stockade. **2.** A fenced enclosure for cattle or sheep, esp. in South or central Africa. [< Afrikaans < Pg. *curral* pen for cattle]

krait (krīt) *n.* Any of several venomous snakes of Asia, esp. India. [< Hind. *karait*]

K ration A highly condensed, packaged emergency ration provided for soldiers of the U.S. Army in World War II.

Krem·lin (krem′lin) **1.** The walled citadel of Moscow containing the government offices of the Soviet Union. **2.** The government of the Soviet Union. [< Russian *kreml′* citadel]

krill (kril) *n.* Tiny marine crustaceans, the main food of certain whales. [< Norw. *kril* very young fish]

kris (krēs) *n.* A Malay dagger or short sword with a wavy-edged blade: also spelled *crease, creese.* [< Malay]

Krish·na (krish′nə) A widely worshiped Hindu god, the eighth avatar of Vishnu. — **Krish′na·ism** *n.*

Kriss Krin·gle (kris kring′gəl) St. Nicholas; Santa Claus. [< G *Christkindl,* dim. of *Christkind* Christ child]

kró·na¹ (krō′nə) *n. pl.* **·nur** (-nər) The monetary unit of Iceland: also called *crown.* [< Icel.]

kro·na² (krō′nə, *Sw.* krōō′nə) *n. pl.* **·nor** (-nôr) The monetary unit of Sweden; also, a Swedish silver coin of this value. Also called *crown.* [< Sw.]

kro·ne (krō′ne) *n. pl.* **·ner** (-ner) **1.** The monetary unit of Denmark. **2.** The monetary unit of Norway. **3.** A Danish or Norwegian silver coin of this denomination. [< Dan.]

kryp·ton (krip′ton) *n.* A colorless, gaseous element (symbol Kr), present in minute amounts in the atmosphere, used in electric lamps. [< Gk. *kryptos* hidden]

ku·chen (kōō′kən) *n.* A yeast-dough coffee cake usu. containing fruits and nuts, and covered with sugar. [< G]

ku·dos (kyōō′dos, kōō-) *n.* Glory; credit; praise: used only in the singular. [< Gk. *kydos* glory]

Ku Klux Klan (kōō′ kluks′ klan′, kyōō′) **1.** A secret society formed in the South after the Civil War to prevent Negro equality. **2.** An anti-Negro, anti-Catholic, and anti-Jewish secret society founded in Georgia in 1915 and most active during the 1920's. — **Ku′ Klux′ Klan′ner**

ku·lak (kōō·läk′) *n.* In Russia, a wealthy peasant who employed labor, and opposed the Soviet collectivization of farms. [< Russian, lit., fist, tight-fisted man]

ku·miss (kōō′mis) *n.* Fermented mare's or camel's milk, used as a drink by nomads of central Asia. [< Russ. < Tatar]

küm·mel (kim′əl, *Ger.* kü′məl) *n.* A liqueur flavored with aniseed, cumin, or caraway. [< G, caraway seed]

kum·quat (kum′kwot) *n.* **1.** A small, round orange fruit with a sour pulp and edible rind, used in making preserves or confections. **2.** The tree bearing this fruit. [Cantonese alter. of Pekinese *chin-chü,* lit., golden orange]

Kuo·min·tang (kwō′min′tang′) *n.* The nationalist party of China. [< Chinese *kuo* nationalist + *min* people's + *tang* party]

Kurd (kûrd, kōōrd) *n.* One of a people living in Turkey, Iran, Iraq, Syria, and the Caucasus. — **Kurd′ish** *adj.*

kvass (kväs, kvas) *n.* A Russian fermented drink resembling sour beer, made from rye, barley, etc. [< Russian *kvas*]

L

l, L (el) *n. pl.* **l's** or **ls, L's** or **Ls, ells** (elz) **1.** The twelfth letter of the English alphabet. **2.** The sound represented by the letter *l.* **3.** Anything shaped like the letter L. — *symbol* The Roman numeral 50.

la¹ (lä) *n. Music* The sixth syllable used in solmization; the sixth degree of a major scale; also, the tone A.

la² (lä, lô) *interj.* An exclamation expressing surprise, emphasis, etc.: also spelled *law.* [OE *lā*]

lab (lab) *n. U.S. Informal* Laboratory.

la·bel (lā′bəl) *n.* **1.** A slip of paper, printed legend, etc., on a container or article showing its nature, producer, destination, etc. **2.** A term or phrase used to classify or describe persons, schools of thought, etc. — *v.t.* **la·beled** or **·belled, la·bel·ing** or **·bel·ling 1.** To mark with a label. **2.** To classify. [< OF, ribbon] — **la′bel·er** or **la′bel·ler** *n.*

la·bi·a (lā′bē-ə) Plural of LABIUM.

la·bi·al (lā′bē-əl) *adj.* **1.** Of or pertaining to a labium or the lips. **2.** *Phonet.* Articulated or modified by the lips, as are (p), (b), (m), (w), or the rounded vowels (ō) and (ōō). — *n.* A labial sound. [< Med.L < L *labium* lip]

la·bi·ate (lā′bē-āt, -it) *adj.* Having lips or liplike parts. Also **la′bi·at′ed.** [< NL < L *labium* lip]

la·bile (lā′bil) *adj.* Liable to lapse or change; unstable. [< L < *labi* to slip, fall] — **la·bil′i·ty** *n.*

labio- *combining form* Related to, or formed by the lips and (another organ): *labiodental.* [< L *labium* lip]

la·bi·o·den·tal (lā′bē·ō·den′təl) *Phonet. adj.* Formed with the lower lip and the upper front teeth, as (f) and (v) in English. — *n.* A sound so formed.

la·bi·um (lā′bē-əm) *n. pl.* **·bi·a** (-bē-ə) *Anat.* **1.** A lip or liplike part. **2.** One of the four folds of the vulva, comprising the two outer folds of skin (**labia majora**) and the two inner folds of mucous membrane (**labia minora**). [< L, lip]

la·bor (lā′bər) *n.* **1.** Physical or manual work done for hire in economic production. **2.** Arduous physical or mental exertion; toil. **3.** The working class collectively, esp. as organized into labor unions. **4.** A piece of work; task. **5.** *Med.* The pain and stress of childbirth; esp., the uterine contractions prior to giving birth. — **Department of Labor** An executive department of the U.S. government (established 1913), headed by the Secretary of Labor, that carries out policies regarding wages, unemployment, etc. — *v.i.* **1.** To work hard physically or mentally. **2.** To progress with great effort or painful exertion. **3.** To suffer the pangs of childbirth. **4.** To be oppressed or hampered. — *v.t.* **5.** To work out laboriously; overwork: to *labor* an argument. Also *Brit.* **la′bour.** [< OF < L *labor* toil, distress]

lab·o·ra·to·ry (lab′rə·tôr′ē, -tō′rē; *Brit.* lə·bor′ə·trē) *n. pl.* **·ries 1.** A building or room equipped for conducting scientific experiments, analyses, etc. **2.** A department, as in a factory, for research, testing, etc. Also, *Informal,* **lab.** [< Med.L < L *labor* toil]

Labor Day In most States of the United States and in Canada, a legal holiday, usu. the first Monday in September.

la·bored (lā′bərd) *adj.* **1.** Performed laboriously; difficult: *labored* breathing. **2.** Overelaborate: *labored* prose.

la·bor·er (lā′bər·ər) *n.* One who performs physical or manual labor, esp. unskilled labor.

la·bo·ri·ous (lə·bôr′ē·əs, -bō′rē-) *adj.* **1.** Requiring much labor; toilsome. **2.** Diligent; industrious. — **la·bo′ri·ous·ly** *adv.* — **la·bo′ri·ous·ness** *n.* [< OF < L *labor* labor, toil]

la·bor·ite (lā′bər·īt) *n.* One who supports labor interests, esp. in politics. Also *Brit.* **la′bour·ite.**

la·bor·sav·ing (lā′bər·sā′ving) *adv.* Doing away with, or diminishing the need for, manual work: *laborsaving* devices.

labor union An association of workers organized to improve and advance mutual interests: also called *trade union.*

La·bour·ite (lā′bər·īt) *n.* A member of a Labour party in Great Britain or in one of the Commonwealth nations.

Labour Party 1. In Great Britain, a political party drawing its chief support from labor and trade unions and committed to socialist reforms. **2.** A similar party in other members of the British Commonwealth of Nations.

la·bur·num (lə·bûr′nəm) *n.* Any of a group of leguminous Old World trees yielding a poisonous alkaloid, with pendulous yellow flowers and hard, dark wood. [< NL < L]

lab·y·rinth (lab′ə·rinth) *n.* **1.** A system of winding, intricate passages or paths designed to confuse whoever tries to go through and find the exit; maze. **2.** Anything resembling a labyrinth, as a confusing network of streets. **3.** Any intricate or perplexing set of difficulties. **4.** *Anat.* The winding passages of the inner ear.

Lab·y·rinth (lab′ə·rinth) In Greek mythology, the maze used to confine the Minotaur, constructed by Daedalus for Minos of Crete. [< L < Gk.]

lab·y·rin·thine (lab′ə·rin′thin, -thēn) *adj.* Of, pertaining to, or like a labyrinth. Also **lab′y·rin′thi·an, lab′y·rin′thic.**

lac (lak) *n.* A resinous deposit left on certain trees by the lac insect and used in making varnishes, paints, etc. [< Hind. < Prakrit < Skt. *lākshā*]

lace (lās) *n.* **1.** A cord or string passed through eyelets or over hooks for fastening together the edges of a shoe, garment, etc. **2.** A delicate openwork fabric or network, made by hand or on a machine, of linen, silk, cotton, etc. **3.** A silver or gold braid used to decorate uniforms, hats, etc. — *v.* **laced, lac·ing** *v.t.* **1.** To fasten or draw together by tying the lace or laces of. **2.** To pass (a cord or string) through eyelets or over hooks as a lace. **3.** To trim with or as with lace. **4.** To compress the waist of (a person) by tightening laces of a corset. **5.** To intertwine or interlace. **6.** To streak with lines or colors. — *v.i.* **7.** To be fastened by means of laces. — **to lace into** *Informal* **1.** To strike or attack. **2.** To scold; berate. [< OF < L *laqueus* noose, trap]

lac·er·ate (las′ər·āt) *v.t.* **·at·ed, ·at·ing 1.** To tear raggedly; esp., to wound the flesh by tearing. **2.** To injure: to *lacerate* one's feelings. — *adj.* **1.** Jagged; torn. **2.** Harrowed; distressed. **3.** *Biol.* Having the edges jagged or irregularly cleft. [< L *lacer* mangled] — **lac′er·a·ble** *adj.*

lac·er·a·tion (las′ər·ā′shən) *n.* **1.** The act of lacerating. **2.** The wound or jagged tear resulting from lacerating.

lace·wing (lās′wing′) *n.* An insect with four lacy wings.

lace·work (lās′wûrk′) *n.* **1.** Lace. **2.** Any decorative openwork resembling lace.

lach·es (lach′iz) *n. Law* Unreasonable delay in asserting a right, so that the court is warranted in refusing relief. [< AF, OF < L *laxus* lax]

Lach·e·sis (lak′ə·sis) One of the three Fates.

lach·ry·mal (lak′rə·məl) *adj.* Of, pertaining to, or producing tears. — *n. pl.* The organs secreting tears: also **lach·rymal glands.** [< Med.L < L *lacrima* tear]

lach·ry·ma·to·ry (lak′rə·mə·tôr′ē, -tō′rē) *n. pl.* **·ries** A small bottle found in ancient tombs, formerly supposed to have held the tears of mourners. — *adj.* Of or producing tears. [< Med.L < L *lacrima* tear]

lach·ry·mose (lak′rə·mōs) *adj.* **1.** Tearful. **2.** Provoking tears; sad. — **lach′ry·mose′ly** *adv.*

lac·ing (lā′sing) *n.* **1.** The act of one who or that which laces. **2.** A cord or string for holding together opposite parts of a shoe, etc.; lace. **3.** A fastening made with lacing. **4.** *Informal* A thrashing; beating. **5.** An ornamental braid.

lac insect Any of a family of insects, esp. an Indian species, the females of which exude lac.

lack (lak) *n.* **1.** Deficiency or complete absence of something. **2.** That which is absent or deficient; need. — *v.t.* **1.** To be without. **2.** To be short by. — *v.i.* **3.** To be wanting or deficient. [ME, prob. < MLG *lak* deficiency]

lack·a·dai·si·cal (lak′ə·dā′zi·kəl) *adj.* Affectedly pensive or melancholy; listless. — **lack′a·dai′si·cal·ly** *adv.*

lack·ey (lak′ē) *n. pl.* **·eys 1.** A male servant of low status, usu. in livery; footman. **2.** Any servile follower. — *v.t. & v.i.* To attend or act as a lackey. [< OF < Sp. *lacayo*]

lack·lus·ter (lak′lus′tər) *adj.* **1.** Lacking sheen and brightness; dull. **2.** Lacking spirit; mediocre: a *lackluster* performance. — *n.* A lack of brightness. Also **lack′lus′tre.**

la·con·ic (lə·kon′ik) *adj.* Brief and concise in expression. Also **la·con′i·cal.** [< L < Gk. *Lakōn* a Spartan; with ref. to the terseness of Spartan speech] — **la·con′i·cal·ly** *adv.*

lac·quer (lak′ər) *n.* **1.** A transparent varnish made from various resins, dissolved in volatile solvent. **2.** A resinous varnish obtained from the lacquer tree of China and Japan, and used to impart a high polish to wood. **3.** Decorative woodwork or articles of wood painted with this lacquer: also **lac′quer·work′** (-wûrk′). — *v.t.* To coat with or as with lacquer. [< MF *lacre* a kind of sealing wax < Pg. *lacca* gum lac] — **lac′quer·er** *n.*

la·crosse (lə·krôs′, -kros′) *n. U.S. & Canadian* A ball game of American Indian origin, played with long, racketlike implements by two teams of ten men each, the object being to advance the ball into the opponents' goal. [< dial. F (Canadian) *la crosse,* lit., the crozier, hooked stick]

lact- Var. of LACTO-.

lac·tate (lak′tāt) *v.i.* **·tat·ed, ·tat·ing 1.** To form or secrete milk. **2.** To suckle young. — *n.* A salt or ester of lactic acid. [< L *lactare* to suckle]

lac·ta·tion (lak·tā′shən) *n.* **1.** The mammalian formation or secretion of milk. **2.** The period during which milk is produced. **3.** The act of suckling young.

lac·te·al (lak′tē·əl) *adj.* **1.** Of, pertaining to, or resembling milk; milky. **2.** Carrying chyle. Also **lac′te·an, lac′te·ous.** — *n. Anat.* Any of the lymphatic vessels that carry chyle from the small intestine to the blood. [< L *lac, lactis* milk]

lac·tic (lak′tik) *adj.* Of, pertaining to, or derived from milk.

lactic acid *Chem.* A limpid, syrupy acid, $C_3H_6O_3$, with a bitter taste, present in sour milk.

lacto- *combining form* Milk. Also, before vowels, *lact-.* [< L *lac, lactis* milk]

lac·tose (lak′tōs) *n. Biochem.* A white, odorless, crystalline sugar, $C_{12}H_{22}O_{11}$, present in milk.

la·cu·na (lə·kyōō′nə) *n. pl.* **·nas** or **·nae** (-nē) **1.** A space from which something is missing or has been omitted, esp. in a manuscript; hiatus. **2.** *Anat.* Any of the minute cavities in bone containing bone cells. Also **la·cune′** (-kyōōn′).

[< L *lacus* basin, pond] — **la·cu′nal, la·cu′nar, lac·u·nar·y** (lak′yōō·ner′ē) *adj.*

lac·y (lā′sē) *adj.* **lac·i·er, lac·i·est** Made of or resembling lace. — **lac′i·ly** *adv.* — **lac′i·ness** *n.*

lad (lad) *n.* **1.** A boy or youth; stripling. **2.** Familiarly, any male. [< ME *ladde,* ? ult. < ON]

lad·der (lad′ər) *n.* A device of wood, metal, rope, etc., for climbing and descending, usu. consisting of two parallel side pieces connected by a series of rungs, or rounds, placed at regular intervals to serve as footholds. [OE *hlǽd(d)er*]

lad·die (lad′ē) *n.* A lad.

lade (lād) *v.* **lad·ed, lad·ed** or **lad·en, lad·ing** *v.t.* **1.** To load with a cargo or burden; also, to load as a cargo. **2.** To dip or lift (a liquid) in or out, as with a ladle. — *v.i.* **3.** To receive cargo. **4.** To dip or lift a liquid. [OE *hladan* to load]

lad·en[1] (lād′n) Alternative past participle of LADE. — *adj.* **1.** Burdened; oppressed. **2.** Weighed down; loaded.

lad·en[2] (lād′n) *v.t. & v.i.* **lad·ened, lad·en·ing** To lade.

lad·ing (lā′ding) *n.* **1.** The act of one who or that which lades. **2.** A load or cargo.

la·dle (lād′l) *n.* A cup-shaped vessel with a long handle, for dipping or conveying liquids. — *v.t.* **·dled, ·dling** To dip up or carry in a ladle. [OE *hladan* to lade] — **la′dler** *n.*

la·dy (lā′dē) *n. pl.* **·dies 1.** A woman showing refinement, gentility, and tact. **2.** A woman of superior position in society. **3.** A term of reference or address for any woman. **4.** A wife. — *adj.* Of or pertaining to a lady. [OE *hlǣfdige,* lit., bread-kneader < *hlāf* bread, loaf + *-dige,* a stem akin to *dah* dough]

La·dy (lā′dē) **1.** In Great Britain a title given to women of various ranks. **2.** The Virgin Mary: usu. with *Our.*

la·dy·bird (lā′dē·bûrd′) *n.* Any of a family of brightly colored beetles, usu. red spotted with black, that feeds on aphids and other insects. Also **lady beetle, la′dy·bug′.**

Lady Day 1. March 25, the church festival of the Annunciation. **2.** Formerly, a day honoring the Virgin Mary.

la·dy·fin·ger (lā′dē·fing′gər) *n.* A small sponge cake of about the size and shape of a finger. Also **la′dys·fin′ger** (lā′dēz-).

lady in waiting *pl.* **ladies in waiting** A lady appointed to attend upon a queen or princess.

la·dy·kill·er (lā′dē·kil′ər) *n. Slang* A man supposed to be unusually fascinating to women. — **la′dy-kill′ing** *adj. & n.*

la·dy·like (lā′dē·līk′) *adj.* **1.** Like or suitable to a lady; gentle; delicate. **2.** Effeminate.

la·dy·love (lā′dē·luv′) *n.* A woman beloved; sweetheart.

la·dy·ship (lā′dē·ship) *n.* The rank or condition of a lady: used as a title, with *Her* or *Your.*

lady's man A man attentive to and fond of the company of women. Also **ladies' man.**

lady's-slipper (lā′dēz·slip′ər) *n.* An orchid having a flower that suggests a slipper in shape. Also **la′dy·slip′per** (lā′dē-).

la·e·trile (lā′ə·tril) *n.* A drug derived from apricot pits, sometimes used in treating cancer. [<LAE(VO-) + (MANDEL-ONI)TRILE]

laevo- See LEVO-.

lag (lag) *v.i.* **lagged, lag·ging 1.** To move slowly; stay or fall behind; straggle: sometimes followed by *behind.* **2.** In marbles, to throw one's taw as near as possible to a line on the ground to decide the order of play. — *n.* **1.** The condition or act of retardation or falling behind. **2.** The amount or period of retardation. **3.** In marbles, an act of lagging. [? < Scand.] — **lag′ger** *n.*

lag·an (lag′ən) *n.* In maritime law, goods cast from a vessel in peril, but to which a buoy or float is attached as evidence of ownership: also called *ligan.* [< AF < Gmc.]

la·ger (lä′gər) *n.* A beer stored for sedimentation before use. Also **lager beer.** [< G < *lager* storehouse + *bier* beer]

lag·gard (lag′ərd) *n.* One who lags; straggler. — *adj.* Falling behind; loitering; slow. — **lag′gard·ly** *adv.*

la·gniappe (lan·yap′, lan′yap) *n.* **1.** *Southern U.S.* A small present given to the purchaser of an article by a merchant or storekeeper. **2.** *Informal* Anything given beyond strict obligation; an extra. Also **la·gnappe′.** [< dial. F (Creole) < F *la* the + Sp. *ñapa* lagniappe < Quechua *yapa*]

la·goon (lə·gōōn′) *n.* A body of shallow water, as a bay, inlet, pond, or lake, usu. connecting with a river, larger lake, or the sea; esp., the water within a coral atoll. Also **la·gune′.** [< F < Ital. < L *lacuna* pool]

la·ic (lā′ik) *adj.* Lay[2]. — *n.* A layman. [< LL < Gk. *laikos* < *laos* the people] — **la′i·cal·ly** *adv.*

la·i·cize (lā′ə·sīz) *v.t.* **·cized, ·ciz·ing** To remove from ecclesiastical control; secularize. — **la·i·ci·za′tion** *n.*

laid (lād) Past tense and past participle of LAY[1].

laid·back (lād′bak′) *Slang adj.* Relaxed.

lain (lān) Past participle of LIE[1].

lair (lâr) *n.* A resting place or den, esp. that of a wild animal. — *v.i.* **1.** To live or rest in a lair. — *v.t.* **2.** To place in a lair. **3.** To serve as a lair for. [OE *leger* bed]

laird (lârd) *n. Scot.* The proprietor of a landed estate. [Northern ME *laverd, lard*] — **laird′ly** *adj.* — **laird′ship** *n.*

lais·sez faire (les′ā·fâr′) **1.** In economics, the theory that the state should exercise as little control as possible in trade and industrial affairs. **2.** Noninterference or indifference. Also **lais′ser faire′**. [< F, lit., let do < *laisser* to let + *faire* to do, make]

la·i·ty (lā′ə·tē) *n. pl.* **·ties 1.** The people collectively; laymen: distinguished from *clergy.* **2.** All of those outside a specific profession or occupation.

La·i·us (lā′yəs) In Greek legend, a king of Thebes, husband of Jocasta, who was unwittingly killed by his son Oedipus.

lake¹ (lāk) *n.* **1.** A sizable inland body of either salt or fresh water. **2.** A large pool of any liquid: a *lake* of pitch. [Fusion of OE *lacu* stream, pool and OF *lac* basin, lake]

lake² (lāk) *n.* **1.** A deep red pigment made by combining cochineal with a metallic oxide. **2.** The color of this pigment. **3.** Any metallic compound yielding pigments by the interaction of mordant and dye. [Var. of LAC]

lake dwelling A habitation built on piles over the surface of a lake, esp. in prehistoric times. — **lake dweller**

lake herring A whitefish of the Great Lakes.

lake trout A salmonoid fish of the Great Lakes region of North America, somewhat resembling the brook trout.

la·la·pa·loo·za (lol′ə·pə·lōō′zə) See LOLLAPALOOZA. Also **lal/la·pa·loo′za.**

lam (lam) *Slang v.* **lammed, lam·ming** *v.i.* **1.** To run away, esp. to avoid arrest; flee. — *v.t.* **2.** To beat; thrash. — *n.* Sudden flight or escape. — **on the lam** In flight; fleeing. [? < ON *lemja* to thrash]

la·ma (lä′mə) *n.* A priest or monk of Lamaism. See DALAI LAMA. [< Tibetan *blama*]

La·ma·ism (lä′mə·iz′əm) *n.* The form of Buddhism practiced in Tibet and Mongolia, characterized by a complex hierarchy and Shamanistic beliefs and practices. — **La′ma·ist** *n.* — **La′ma·is′tic** *adj.*

La·marck·ism (lə·märk′iz·əm) *n. Biol.* The theory of organic evolution holding that species have developed through the inheritance of acquired characteristics. [after Chevalier de *Lamarck,* 1744–1829, French naturalist]

la·ma·ser·y (lä′mə·ser′ē) *n. pl.* **·ser·ies** A Lamaist monastery. [< F]

lamb (lam) *n.* **1.** A young sheep. **2.** The meat of a lamb used as food. **3.** Lambskin. **4.** Any gentle or innocent person, esp. a child. **5.** A gullible person. — **the Lamb** Christ. — *v.i.* To give birth: said of a ewe. [OE]

lam·baste (lam·bāst′) *v.t.* **·bast·ed, ·bast·ing** *Slang* **1.** To beat or thrash. **2.** To scold; castigate. — **lam·bast′ing** *n.*

lamb·da (lam′də) *n.* The eleventh letter in the Greek alphabet (Λ, λ), corresponding to the English *l*. See ALPHABET. [< Gk. < Phoenician *lamed*]

lam·bent (lam′bənt) *adj.* **1.** Playing over a surface with a soft, undulatory movement; flickering; licking: a *lambent* flame. **2.** Softly radiant. **3.** Lightly and playfully brilliant: *lambent* wit. [< L *lambens, -entis,* ppr. of *lambere* to lick] — **lam′ben·cy** *n.* — **lam′bent·ly** *adv.*

lamb·kin (lam′kin) *n.* **1.** A little lamb. **2.** A small child: a term of affection. Also **lamb′ie.** [Dim. of LAMB]

Lamb of God Christ, as the Paschal Lamb. *John* i 29.

lam·bre·quin (lam′bər·kin, -brə-) *n.* **1.** *U.S.* A draped strip of cloth, leather, etc., hanging from the casing above a window or doorway, and covering the upper half of the opening. **2.** In medieval times, a covering of heavy fabric for a helmet. [< F < Du. *lamperkin,* dim. of *lamper* veil]

lamb·skin (lam′skin) *n.* **1.** The dressed hide and wool of a lamb. **2.** Dressed leather made from a lamb's hide.

lame (lām) *adj.* **lam·er, lam·est 1.** Crippled or disabled, esp. in the legs or feet. **2.** Sore; painful: a *lame* back. **3.** Weak; ineffective: a *lame* effort. — *v.t.* **lamed, lam·ing** To make lame. [OE *lama*] — **lame′ly** *adv.* — **lame′ness** *n.*

la·mé (la·mā′) *n.* A fabric woven of flat gold or silver thread, sometimes mixed with silk or other fiber. [< F]

lame duck *Informal* **1.** *U.S.* An officeholder whose term continues for a time after his defeat for reelection. **2.** On the stock exchange, one who cannot fulfill his contracts. **3.** An ineffectual or disabled person.

la·mel·la (lə·mel′ə) *n. pl.* **·mel·lae** (-mel′ē) A thin plate, scale, or layer, as in bone or the gills of bivalves. [< NL < L, dim. of *lamina* plate, leaf] — **lam·el·lar** (lə·mel′ər, lam′ə·lər), **lam′el·late** *adj.*

la·mel·li·branch (lə·mel′i·brangk) *n. Zool.* One of a class of bivalve mollusks including clams, mussels, and oysters. [< NL < L *lamella* plate + Gk. *branchia* gills] — **lam·el′li·bran′chi·ate** (-brank′kē·āt, -it) *adj. & n.*

la·ment (lə·ment′) *v.t.* To feel remorse or regret over. — *v.i.* To feel or express sorrow, grief, or regret. — *n.* **1.** An expression of grief; lamentation. **2.** An elegiac melody or writing. [< L *lamentum* wailing, weeping] — **la·ment′er** *n.*

lam·en·ta·ble (lam′ən·tə·bəl, lə·ment′ə-) *adj.* **1.** That warrants lamenting; deplorable: a *lamentable* failure. **2.** *Archaic* Expressing grief; mournful. — **lam′en·ta·bly** *adv.*

lam·en·ta·tion (lam′ən·tā′shən) *n.* **1.** The act of lamenting or bewailing. **2.** A lament; wail; moan.

Lam·en·ta·tions (lam′ən·tā′shənz) *n.pl.* (*construed as sing.*) A lyrical poetic book of the Old Testament, attributed to Jeremiah the prophet.

lam·en·ted (lə·men′təd) *adj.* Mourned for; grieved over: usu. said of one who has died.

lam·i·na (lam′ə·nə) *n. pl.* **·nae** (-nē) or **·nas 1.** A thin scale or sheet. **2.** A layer or coat lying over another, as in bone, minerals, armor, etc. **3.** *Bot.* The blade or flat expanded portion of a leaf, or the blade of a petal. [< L]

lam·i·nate (lam′ə·nāt) *v.* **·nat·ed, ·nat·ing** *v.t.* **1.** To beat, roll, or press (metal) into thin sheets. **2.** To separate or cut into thin sheets. **3.** To make of layers united by the action of heat and pressure. **4.** To cover with thin sheets or laminae. — *v.i.* **5.** To separate into sheets. — *adj.* Laminated. [< NL < L *lamina* leaf] — **lam·i·na′tion** *n.*

lam·i·nat·ed (lam′ə·nā′təd) *adj.* Made up of or arranged in thin sheets; laminate.

lam·i·nose (lam′ə·nōs) *adj.* Laminate.

lamp (lamp) *n.* **1.** A device for holding one or more electric light bulbs and directing their light; also, an electric light bulb. **2.** Any of various devices for producing light by combustion, incandescence, electric arc, or fluorescence. **3.** A vessel in which oil or alcohol is burned through a wick to produce light or heat. **4.** Any of several devices for producing therapeutic heat or rays: sun *lamp*. [< OF < L < Gk. *lampein* to shine]

lamp·black (lamp′blak′) *n.* A black pigment consisting of fine carbon deposited from the smoke of burning oil or gas.

lamp·light (lamp′līt′) *n.* Light from lamps; artificial light.

lamp·light·er (lamp′lī′tər) *n.* **1.** One whose work is lighting lamps, esp. street lamps. **2.** Anything by which a lamp is lighted, as a torch, electric device, etc.

lam·poon (lam·pōōn′) *n.* A scurrilous, but often humorous, attack in prose or verse directed against a person. — *v.t.* To satirize in a lampoon. [< MF *lampons* let's drink (a song refrain)] — **lam·poon′er, lam·poon′ist** *n.* — **lam·poon′er·y** *n.*

lamp·post (lamp′pōst′) *n.* A post supporting a lamp.

lam·prey (lam′prē) *n. pl.* **·preys** An eellike, carnivorous, aquatic animal having a circular suctorial mouth with sharp rasping teeth on its inner surface. Also **lam·per eel** (lam′pər). [< OF < Med.L *lampreda lampetra*]

Lan·cas·ter (lang′kəs·tər), **House of** A royal house of England, reigning from 1399 to 1461. — **Lan·cas′tri·an** *adj. & n.*

lance (lans, läns) *n.* **1.** A spearlike weapon used by mounted soldiers or knights. **2.** One who is armed with a lance; lancer. **3.** Any of various long, slender weapons resembling a lance, as a whaler's spear, etc. **4.** A lancet. — *v.t.* **lanced, lanc·ing 1.** To pierce with a lance. **2.** To cut or open with a lancet. [ME < OF < L *lancea* light spear]

lance corporal 1. *Mil.* In the U.S. Marine Corps, an enlisted man. See table at GRADE. **2.** *Brit. Mil.* A private acting as a corporal, usu. without increased pay.

lance·let (lans′lit, läns′-) *n.* A small, fishlike animal having primitive vertebrate characteristics, and living in the sand: also called *amphioxus.* [Dim. of LANCE]

Lan·ce·lot of the Lake (lan′sə·lot, län′-) In Arthurian romance, the bravest and ablest of the knights of the Round Table. Also **Lancelot du Lac** (dü läk). [< F, servant]

lan·ce·o·late (lan′sē·ə·lit, -lāt) *adj.* **1.** Shaped like the head of a lance. **2.** *Bot.* Narrowing to a point; tapering, as certain leaves. [< LL < *lanceola* small lance]

lanc·er (lan′sər, län′-) *n.* A cavalryman armed with a lance.

lance sergeant *Brit. Mil.* A corporal acting temporarily as a sergeant without additional pay.

lan·cet (lan′sit, län′-) *n.* A small, two-edged, usu. pointed surgical knife, used to open abscesses, boils, etc. [< F *lancette,* dim. of *lance* < OF < L *lancea* light spear]

lancet arch *Archit.* A narrow, acutely pointed arch.

lancet window A narrow, acutely pointed window.

lance·wood (lans′wŏŏd′, läns′-) *n.* **1.** A tough, elastic wood used for carriage shafts, fishing rods, billiard cues, etc. **2.** Any of various tropical American trees yielding this wood.

land (land) *n.* **1.** The solid, exposed surface of the earth as distinguished from the waters of the seas. **2.** A country or region, esp. considered as a place of human habitation. **3.** The people of such a country or region. **4.** Ground considered with reference to its uses, location, character, etc.: pasture *land.* **5.** *Law* **a** Any tract of ground whatever that may be owned as goods together with all its appurtenances, as water, forests, buildings, etc. **b** A share or interest in such land. **6.** Rural places as distinguished from cities or towns. **7.** *Econ.* Natural resources as used in production. — *v.t.* **1.** To transfer from a vessel to the shore; put ashore. **2.** To bring (something in flight) down to rest. **3.** To bring to some point, condition, or state: His words *landed* him in trouble. **4.** To pull (a fish) out of the water; catch. **5.** *Informal* To obtain; win: to *land* a job. **6.** *Informal* To deliver (a blow) —*v.i.* **7.** To go or come ashore from a ship or boat. **8.** To touch at a port; come to land. **9.** To descend and come to rest after a flight or jump. **10.** To come to some place or state; end up: to *land* in jail. [OE]

-land *combining form* **1.** A region of a certain kind: *woodland*. **2.** The country of: *Scotland*. [< LAND]

lan·dau (lan′dô, -dou) *n.* **1.** A former type of closed sedan having a back seat with a collapsible top. **2.** A four-wheeled carriage with a collapsible top. [after *Landau*, a Bavarian city where it was first made]

land bank *U.S.* A bank making mortgage loans on land or other real property.

land·ed (lan′did) *adj.* **1.** Having an estate in land: *landed* gentry. **2.** Consisting in land: *landed* property.

-land·er *combining form* From or of a land. [< LAND]

land·fall (land′fôl′) *n.* A sighting of or coming to land; also, the land so sighted or reached.

land grant Government land granted to a railroad, educational institution, etc.

land-grant (land′grant) *adj.* Denoting a State college or university that received grants of land from the Federal government under the Morrill Act of 1862.

land·grave (land′grāv′) *n.* **1.** In medieval and Renaissance Germany, a count having jurisdiction over a specified territory. **2.** Later, the title of any of various German princes. [< MHG < *lant, land* land + *grave, graf* count]

land·hold·er (land′hōl′dər) *n.* An owner or occupant of land.

land·ing (lan′ding) *n.* **1.** The act of going or placing ashore from any kind of craft or vessel. **2.** The place where a craft or vessel lands; wharf; pier. **3.** The act of descending and settling on the ground after a flight, leap, etc. **4.** *Archit.* The platform or floor at the top of a flight of stairs, between flights of stairs, or interrupting a flight of stairs.

landing field A tract of ground selected or prepared for the landing and takeoff of aircraft.

land·la·dy (land′lā′dē) *n. pl.* ·**dies** **1.** A woman who owns and rents out real estate. **2.** The wife of a landlord. **3.** A woman who keeps an inn.

länd·ler (lent′lər) *n.* **1.** A slow Austrian country dance. **2.** Music for or in the manner of this dance, in triple meter. [< G < dial. G *Landl* upper Austria]

land·less (land′lis) *adj.* Owning no land.

land·locked (land′lokt′) *adj.* **1.** Surrounded by land; having no seacoast. **2.** Living in landlocked water: said esp. of a normally anadromous fish: *landlocked* salmon.

land·lord (land′lôrd′) *n.* **1.** A man who owns and rents out real estate. **2.** An innkeeper. **3.** *Brit.* The lord of a manor. [OE < *land* land + *hlaford* lord]

land·lub·ber (land′lub′ər) *n.* An awkward or inexperienced person on board a ship.

land·mark (land′märk′) *n.* **1.** A fixed object serving as a boundary mark to a tract of land, as a guide to travelers, etc. **2.** A prominent object in the landscape. **3.** A distinguishing fact, event, etc. [OE *land* land + *mearc* boundary]

land mine *Mil.* An explosive bomb placed in the ground.

land office A government office for the transaction of business pertaining to the public lands.

land-of·fice business (land′ô′fis, -of′is) *U.S. Informal* Business conducted at a rapid pace.

Land of Enchantment Nickname of New Mexico.

Land of Opportunity Nickname of Arkansas.

Land of Promise See PROMISED LAND.

Land of the Midnight Sun Norway.

Land of the Rising Sun Japan.

land·own·er (land′ō′nər) *n.* One who owns real estate. — **land′own′er·ship** *n.* — **land′own·ing** *n. & adj.*

land·scape (land′skāp) *n.* **1.** A stretch of inland natural scenery as seen from a single point. **2.** A picture representing such scenery. **3.** The branch of painting, photography, etc., that deals with inland natural scenery. — *v.* ·**scaped**, ·**scap·ing** *v.t.* **1.** To improve or change the features or appearance of a park, garden, etc. — *v.i.* **2.** To be a landscape gardener. [< Du. < *land* land + *-schap* -ship]

landscape architect One whose profession is to plan the decorative arrangement of outdoor features.

landscape gardener One who plans and carries out the arrangement of plants, trees, etc. — **landscape gardening**

land·scap·ist (land′skā′pist) *n.* A painter of landscapes.

land·slide (land′slīd′) *n.* **1.** The slipping down of a mass of soil, rock, and debris on a mountain side or other steep slope. **2.** The mass of soil, rock, etc., slipping down. Also *Chiefly Brit.*, **land′slip′** (-slip′). **3.** An overwhelming plurality of votes for one political party or candidate in an election.

lands·man (landz′mən) *n. pl.* ·**men** (-mən) One who lives and works on land: distinguished from *seaman*.

land·ward (land′wərd) *adj. & adv.* Being, facing, or going toward the land. Also **land′wards** (-wərdz).

lane (lān) *n.* **1.** A narrow rural path or way, confined between fences, walls, hedges, or similar boundaries; also, a narrow city street. **2.** Any narrow way, passage, or similar course. **3.** A prescribed route for transoceanic shipping or for aircraft. **4.** A marked division of a highway or road for traffic moving in the same direction. **5.** In sports, any of a set of parallel courses for contestants in races. [OE *lanu*]

Lang·er·hans (läng′ər·häns), **islands of** See ISLANDS OF LANGERHANS.

lang·lauf (läng′louf) *n.* A cross-country ski run. [< G < *lang* long + *lauf* course] — **lang′läu′fer** (-loi·fər) *n.*

lang·syne (lang′sīn′, -zīn′) *adv. Scot.* Long since; long ago.

lan·guage (lang′gwij) *n.* **1.** The expression and communication of emotions or ideas between human beings by means of speech and hearing. **2.** Transmission of emotions or ideas between any living creatures by any means. **3.** The words used in communication among members of a single nation or group at a given period. **4.** The impulses, capacities, and powers that induce and make possible the creation and use of language. **5.** The vocabulary used in a specific business, science, etc. **6.** One's characteristic manner of expression or use of speech. [< OF < L *lingua* tongue, language]

language arts Reading, spelling, literature, and composition, considered as basic language skills.

lan·guid (lang′gwid) *adj.* **1.** Indisposed toward physical exertion; affected by weakness or fatigue. **2.** Feeling little interest in or inclination toward anything; listless. **3.** Lacking in activity or quickness of movement. [< L *languere* to languish] — **lan′guid·ly** *adv.* — **lan′guid·ness** *n.*

lan·guish (lang′gwish) *v.i.* **1.** To become weak or feeble; fail in health or vitality; grow listless. **2.** To droop gradually from restless longing; pine. **3.** To pass through a period of external discomfort and mental anguish: to *languish* in prison. **4.** To adopt a look of sentimental longing or melancholy. [< OF < L *languescere*, inceptive of *languere* to be weary, languish] — **lan′guish·er** *n.* — **lan′guish·ment** *n.*

lan·guish·ing (lang′gwish·ing) *adj.* **1.** Lacking alertness or force. **2.** Sentimentally pensive or melancholy. **3.** Becoming weak or listless. — **lan′guish·ing·ly** *adv.*

lan·guor (lang′gər) *n.* **1.** Lassitude of body; weakness; fatigue. **2.** A lack of energy or enthusiasm. **3.** A mood of tenderness or sentimental dreaminess. **4.** The absence of activity; stagnation. **5.** Oppressiveness; stillness.

lan·guor·ous (lang′gər·əs) *adj.* **1.** Languid. **2.** Producing languor. — **lan′guor·ous·ly** *adv.* — **lan′guor·ous·ness** *n.*

lan·gur (lung·gŏŏr′) *n.* A slender, long-tailed Asian monkey. [< Hind. < Skt. *lāṅgūlin*, lit., having a tail]

lan·iard (lan′yərd) See LANYARD.

lank (langk) *adj.* **1.** Lean; shrunken. **2.** Long, flat, and straight; not curly: *lank* hair. [OE *hlanc* flexible] — **lank′·ly** *adv.* — **lank′ness** *n.*

lank·y (lang′kē) *adj.* **lank·i·er**, **lank·i·est** Ungracefully tall and thin; loose-jointed. — **lank′i·ly** *adv.* — **lank′i·ness** *n.*

lan·o·lin (lan′ə·lin) *n.* A fatty substance obtained from the wool of sheep and used in ointments, cosmetics, soaps, etc.; also called *wool fat*. Also **lan′o·line** (-lin, -lēn). [< L *lan(a)* wool + *ol(eum)* oil + -IN]

lan·tern (lan′tərn) *n.* **1.** A protective, usu. portable, case with transparent or translucent sides for enclosing a light. **2.** *Archit.* An open structure built on top of a building to admit light and air. **3.** A lighthouse, esp. the top that protects the light. **4.** *Archaic* A slide projector. [< F < L < Gk. *lampein* to shine]

lantern jaws Long, sunken jaws that make the face appear thin. — **lan·tern-jawed** (lan′tərn·jôd′) *adj.*

lan·tha·nide series (lan′thə·nīd) *Physics* The rare-earth elements beginning with lanthanum (according to some authorities, with cerium) and ending with lutetium. [< LANTHAN(UM) + -ide, var. of -ID²]

lan·tha·num (lan′thə·nəm) *n.* A dark lead gray metallic element (symbol La) chemically related to aluminum. See ELEMENT. [< NL < Gk. *lanthanein* to lie concealed]

lan·yard (lan′yərd) *n.* **1.** *Naut.* A small, usu. four-stranded hemp rope used on a ship for fastening riggings, etc. **2.** A cord used in firing certain types of cannon. **3.** A cord worn around the neck, used by sailors for attaching a knife. Also spelled *laniard*. [Alter. of obs. *lanyer* < OF *lasniere* thong]

La·o (lä′ō) *n. pl.* **La·o** **1.** A Buddhistic people living in Laos and parts of Thailand. **2.** Their Thai language.

La·oc·o·on (lā·ok′ə·won, -ō·won) In Greek legend, a Trojan priest who warned against the wooden horse and was destroyed with his two sons by two serpents.

La·o·tian (lou′shən, lā·ō′shən, lä·ō′shən) *adj.* Of or pertaining to Laos. — *n.* A native or inhabitant of Laos.

lap¹ (lap) *n.* **1.** The chairlike place formed by the lower torso and thighs of a person seated; also, the clothing that covers this part. **2.** The front part of a skirt when lifted up. **3.** A place of nurture or fostering: fortune's *lap*. **4.** Control, care, or custody: in the *lap* of the gods. — **to throw into someone's lap** To give over the responsibility or control of something to someone else. [OE *læppa*]

lap² (lap) *n.* **1.** The state of overlapping. **2.** A rotating disk used for grinding and polishing gems, etc. **3.** One circuit of a race course. **4.** The part of one thing that lies over another. — *v.t.* **1.** To fold or wrap about something. **2.** To lay (one thing) partly over or beyond another. **3.** To extend over or beyond; overlap. **4.** To grind or polish with a lap. **5.** To surround with love, etc.: now only in the passive: to be *lapped* in maternal tenderness. — *v.i.* **6.** To be folded. **7.** To overlap. **8.** To project beyond or into something else. [ME *lappen* to fold]

lap³ (lap) *v.t. & v.i.* **lapped, lap·ping 1.** To drink (a liquid) by taking it up with the tongue, as an animal does. **2.** To wash against (the shore, etc.) with a sound resembling that of lapping. — *n.* **1.** The act of one who or that which laps. **2.** The sound of lapping. — **to lap up 1.** To drink by lapping. **2.** *Informal* To eat or drink gluttonously. **3.** To listen to eagerly. [OE *lapian* to lap] — **lap'per** *n.*

lap dog A dog small enough to be held on the lap.

la·pel (lə·pel') *n.* The front of a coat, jacket, etc., that is folded back to form an extension of the collar. [< LAP¹]

lap·ful (lap'fŏŏl') *n.* As much as the lap can hold.

lap·i·dar·y (lap'ə·der'ē) *n. pl.* **·dar·ies** One whose work is to cut, engrave, or polish precious stones. — *adj.* Pertaining to the art of cutting or engraving precious stones. [< L *lapidarius* of stone]

lap·in (lap'in, *Fr.* là·pàn') *n.* **1.** A rabbit. **2.** Rabbit fur, usu. dyed to resemble more expensive furs. [< F]

lap·is laz·u·li (lap'is laz'yŏŏ·lī) **1.** A bluish violet variety of lazurite valued as a gemstone. **2.** The color of lapis lazuli. Also **lap'is.** [< NL < L *lapis* stone + Med.L *lazulus* azure]

lap joint A joint in which a layer of material laps over another, as in shingling. — **lap-joint·ed** (lap'join'tid) *adj.*

Lapp (lap) *n.* **1.** A member of a formerly nomadic Mongoloid people of Lapland, now settled largely in Sweden and Norway. Also **Lap·land·er** (lap'lan·dər). **2.** The Finno-Ugric language of the Lapps: also **Lap'pish.** [< Sw.]

lap·pet (lap'it) *n.* **1.** A flap or fold on a headdress or garment. **2.** A loose or pendent flap of flesh, as the lobe of the ear, the wattle of a bird, etc. [Dim. of LAP¹]

lapse (laps) *n.* **1.** A gradual passing away, as of time. **2.** A pronounced fall into ruin, decay, or disuse. **3.** A slip or mistake, usually trivial. **4.** A fault or negligence: a *lapse* of justice. **5.** *Law* A forfeiture brought about by the failure to perform some necessary act. — *v.i.* **lapsed, laps·ing 1.** To sink slowly; slip: to *lapse* into a coma. **2.** To fall into ruin or a state of neglect. **3.** To deviate from one's principles or beliefs. **4.** To become void, usually by failure to meet obligations. **5.** *Law* To pass or be forfeited to another because of negligence, failure, or death of the holder. **6.** To pass away, as time. [< L *labi* to glide, slip] — **laps'a·ble, laps'i·ble** *adj.* — **laps'er** *n.*

lap·wing (lap'wing') *n.* A ploverlike bird of the Old World, noted for its flopping flight and shrill cry. [OE *hleapan* to leap + *wince*, prob. < *wancol* unsteady]

lar·board (lär'bərd, -bôrd', -bōrd') *Naut. adj.* Being on or toward the left side of the ship as one faces the bow. — *n.* The left-hand side of a ship: now replaced by *port.* [ME *laddebord*, lit., prob., lading side]

lar·ce·ny (lär'sə·nē) *n. pl.* **·nies** *Law* The unlawful removal of the personal goods of another with intent to defraud the owner; theft. The distinction between **grand larceny** and **petty** (or **petit**) **larceny** is based on the value of the stolen property. — **Syn.** See THEFT. [< OF < L *latrocinari* to rob] — **lar'ce·ner, lar'cen·ist** *n.* — **lar'ce·nous** *adj.* — **lar'ce·nous·ly** *adv.*

larch (lärch) *n.* Any of several coniferous, deciduous trees of the pine family; also, the wood. [< G < L *larix, laricis*]

lard (lärd) *n.* The semisolid fat of a hog after rendering. — *v.t.* **1.** To cover or smear with lard. **2.** To prepare (lean meat or poultry) by inserting strips of fat before cooking. **3.** To intersperse (speech or writing) with embellishments, quotations, etc. [< OF, < L *lardum* lard] — **lard'y** *adj.*

lar·der (lär'dər) *n.* **1.** A room or cupboard where articles of food are stored. **2.** The provisions of a household. [< AF < Med.L *lardum* lard]

lar·es (lâr'ēz, lā'rēz) *n.pl. of lar* (lär) In ancient Rome, tutelary dieties, esp. those presiding over the household. **lares and pe·na·tes** (pə·nā'tēz) **1.** The household gods. **2.** The cherished belongings of one's household.

large (lärj) *adj.* **larg·er, larg·est 1.** Having considerable size, quantity, capacity, extent, etc.; big. **2.** Bigger than another. **3.** Sympathetic and broad in scope: to take a *large* view. — *adv.* In a size greater than usual: Print *large.* — **at large 1.** Free; at liberty: The maniac is *at large.* **2.** In general: the people *at large.* **3.** Elected from the whole State. **4.** Exhaustively; fully. [< OF < L *larga*, fem. of *largus* abundant] — **large'ness** *n.*

large-heart·ed (lärj'här'tid) *adj.* Generous; openhanded. — **large'heart'ed·ness** *n.*

large·ly (lärj'lē) *adv.* **1.** To a great extent; mainly; chiefly. **2.** On a big scale; extensively; abundantly.

large-scale (lärj'skāl') *adj.* **1.** Of large size or scope. **2.** Made according to a large scale: said of maps.

lar·gess (lär·jes', lär'jis, -jes) *n.* Liberal giving; also, something liberally given. Also **lar'gesse.** [< F *largesse*]

lar·ghet·to (lär·get'ō) *Music adj.* Moderately slow. — *adv.* In a moderately slow tempo. — *n. pl.* **·tos** A moderately slow movement. [< Ital., dim. of *largo.* See LARGO.]

lar·go (lär'gō) *Music adj.* Slow; broad. — *adv.* In a slow tempo. — *n. pl.* **·gos** A slow movement or passage. [< Ital., slow, large]

lar·i·at (lar'ē·ət) *n.* **1.** A rope for tethering animals. **2.** A lasso. — *v.t.* To fasten or catch with a lariat. [< Sp. *la reata* < *la* the + *reata* rope]

lark¹ (lärk) *n.* **1.** Any of numerous small singing birds, as the skylark. **2.** Any similar bird, as the meadowlark. [ME < OE *lāferce, læwerce*]

lark² (lärk) *n. Informal* A hilarious time. — *v.t.* **1.** To jump (a fence) on horseback. — *v.i.* **2.** To play pranks. [Origin uncertain] — **lark'er** *n.* — **lark'some** *adj.*

lark·spur (lärk'spûr') *n.* Any of several showy herbs of the crowfoot family with clusters of white, pink, blue, or red flowers.

lar·ri·gan (lar'ə·gən) *n. Canadian* A high moccasin, worn by lumbermen, trappers, etc. [Origin unknown]

lar·rup (lar'əp) *Informal v.t.* To beat; thrash. — *n.* A blow. [< dial. E, ? < Du. *larpen* to thrash]

lar·va (lär'və) *n. pl.* **·vae** (-vē) **1.** *Entomol.* The first stage of an insect after leaving the egg, as the maggot. **2.** *Zool.* The immature form of any animal that must undergo metamorphosis. [< L, ghost, mask] — **lar'val** *adj.*

la·ryn·ge·al (lə·rin'jē·əl, -jəl) *adj.* Of, pertaining to, or near the larynx. Also **la·ryn·gal** (lə·ring'gəl). [< NL < Gk. *larynx, laryngos* larynx]

lar·yn·gi·tis (lar'ən·jī'tis) *n. Pathol.* Inflammation of the larynx. — **lar'yn·git'ic** (-jit'ik) *adj.*

laryngo- *combining form* The larynx; pertaining to the larynx. Also, before vowels, **laryng-.** [< Gk. *larynx, laryngos* larynx]

la·ryn·go·scope (lə·ring'gə·skōp) *n.* An instrument for examining the larynx. — **la·ryn'go·scop'ic** (-skop'ik) *adj.* — **lar'yn·gos'co·py** (-gos'kə·pē) *n.*

lar·ynx (lar'ingks) *n. pl.* **la·ryn·ges** (lə·rin'jēz) or **lar·ynx·es** *Anat.* An organ of the respiratory tract situated at the upper part of the trachea, and consisting of a cartilaginous box containing the valvelike vocal cords. See illus. at LUNG. [< NL < Gk. *larynx* larynx]

la·sa·gna (lə·zän'yə) *n.* Broad, flat noodles, often served baked in a meat and tomato sauce. Also **la·sa'gne.** [< Ital.]

las·civ·i·ous (lə·siv'ē·əs) *adj.* Having, manifesting, or arousing sensual desires; lustful. [< LL < L *lascivus* lustful] — **las·civ'i·ous·ly** *adv.* — **las·civ'i·ous·ness** *n.*

la·ser (lā'zər) *n. Physics* A maser that can generate or amplify light waves: also called *optical maser.* [< l(ight) a(mplification by) s(timulated) e(mission of) r(adiation)]

lash¹ (lash) *n.* **1.** A whip or scourge. **2.** A single whip stroke. **3.** Anything that wounds the feelings. **4.** An eyelash. — *v.t.* **1.** To strike, punish, or command with or as with a whip; flog. **2.** To switch spasmodically: The lion *lashes* his tail. **3.** To beat or dash against violently. **4.** To assail sharply in speech or writing. **5.** To incite. — *v.i.* **6.** To deliver a whip stroke or strokes. **7.** To switch or wriggle rapidly. — **to lash out 1.** To hit out suddenly and violently. **2.** To break into angry verbal abuse. [< Prob. fusion of MLG *lasch* flap and OF *laz* cord] — **lash'er** *n.*

lash² (lash) *v.t.* To bind or tie with rope or cord. [< OF < L *laqueus* noose] — **lash'er** *n.*

lash·ing¹ (lash'ing) *n.* **1.** The act of one who or that which lashes. **2.** A flogging; whipping. **3.** A berating; scolding.

lash·ing² (lash'ing) *n.* The act of lashing with a rope, etc.; also, the rope.

lass (las) *n.* **1.** A young woman; girl. **2.** A sweetheart. **3.** *Scot.* A servant girl; maid. [< Scand.]

las·sie (las'ē) *n.* A little girl; lass. [Dim. of LASS]

las·si·tude (las'ə·tōōd, -tyōōd) *n.* A state of weariness or fatigue; languor. [< F < L *lassus* faint]

las·so (las'ō) *n. pl.* **·sos** or **·soes** A long rope with a running noose, used for catching horses, etc. — *v.t.* To catch with a lasso. [< Sp. < L *laqueus* snare] — **las'so·er** *n.*

last¹ (last, läst) *adj.* **1.** Coming after all others; final in order, sequence, or time: the *last* page. **2.** Being the only one remaining: his *last* dime. **3.** Most recent: *last* year. **4.** Least probable or suitable: the *last* man for the job. **5.** Newest; most fashionable. **6.** Conclusive; final: the *last* word. **7.** *Rare* Least: the *last* of nations. **8.** *Rare* Ultimate; utmost: to the *last* degree. — *adv.* **1.** After all others in time or order. **2.** At a time next preceding the present: He was *last* seen going west. **3.** In conclusion; finally. — *n.*

1. The end; final part or portion. **2.** The final appearance, experience, or mention: We'll never hear the *last* of this. **— at last** At length; finally. [OE *latost*, superl. of *læt* slow]

last² (last, läst) *v.i.* **1.** To remain in existence; continue to be; endure. **2.** To continue unimpaired or unaltered. **3.** To hold out: Will our supplies *last*? [OE *læstan*, to follow a track, continue, accomplish] **— last′er** *n.*

last³ (last, läst) *n.* A shaped form, usu. of wood, on which to make a shoe or boot. **—** *v.t.* To fit to or form on a last. **— to stick to one's last** To attend to one's own business. [OE *læste*, *læst* footstep, track] **— last′er** *n.*

Las·tex (las′teks) *n.* Rubber manufactured in fine strands and wound with rayon, cotton, silk, or wool: a trade name. Also **las′tex.** [< (E)LAS(TIC) + TEX(TILE)]

last·ing (las′ting, läs′-) *adj.* Continuing; durable; permanent. **—** *n.* Endurance; continuance. [< LAST²] **— last′ing·ly** *adv.* **— last′ing·ness** *n.*

Last Judgment *Theol.* **a** The final trial and sentencing by God of all mankind. **b** The time of this.

last·ly (last′lē, läst′-) *adv.* In the last place; in conclusion.

last rites *Eccl.* Sacraments administered to persons in peril of death.

Last Supper The last meal of Jesus Christ and his disciples before the Crucifixion: also called *Lord's Supper.*

last word **1.** The final and most authoritative utterance. **2.** *Informal* The most fashionable thing.

latch (lach) *n.* **1.** A fastening for a door or gate, usu. a movable bar that falls or slides into a notch. **2.** Any similar fastening. **— Syn.** See LOCK¹. **—** *v.t. & v.i.* To fasten by means of a latch; close. **— to latch on to** *U.S. Slang* To obtain, esp. something desirable. [OE *læccean* to seize]

latch·key (lach′kē′) *n.* A key for releasing a latch.

latch·string (lach′string′) *n.* A string on the outside of a door, used for lifting the latch.

late (lāt) *adj.* **lat·er** or **lat·ter, lat·est** or **last** **1.** Appearing or coming after the expected time; tardy. **2.** Occurring at an unusually advanced time: a *late* hour. **3.** Beginning at or continuing to an advanced hour. **4.** Recent or comparatively recent: the *late* war. **5.** Deceased: the *late* king. **—** *adv.* **1.** After the expected time; tardily. **2.** At or until an advanced time of the day, month, year, etc. **3.** *Archaic* Recently. **— of late** Recently. [OE *læt*] **— late′ness** *n.*

la·teen (la·tēn′) *adj. Naut.* Designating a rig common in the Mediterranean, having a triangular sail (**lateen sail**) suspended from a long yard set obliquely to the mast. [< F (*voile*) *latine* Latin (sail)]

la·tent (lā′tənt) *adj.* Not visible or apparent, but capable of developing or being expressed; dormant. [< L *latere* to be hidden] **— la′ten·cy** *n.* **— la′tent·ly** *adv.*

lat·er (lā′tər) *adv.* At a subsequent time; after some time.

lat·er·al (lat′ər·əl) *adj.* Pertaining to the side or sides; situated at, occurring, or coming from the side. **—** *n.* **1.** Something occurring at or on the side. **2.** In football, a lateral pass. [< L *latus, lateris* side] **— lat′er·al·ly** *adv.*

lateral pass In football, a pass that travels across the field or toward the passer's goal line, rather than forward.

Lat·er·an (lat′ər·ən) **1.** The basilica of St. John Lateran, the cathedral church of the pope as bishop of Rome. **2.** The adjoining palace. [< name of a Roman family]

la·tes·cent (lə·tes′ənt) *adj.* Becoming obscure, latent, or hidden. [< L *latere* to be hidden] **— la·tes′cence** *n.*

la·tex (lā′teks) *n. pl.* **lat·i·ces** (lat′ə·sēz) or **la·tex·es** The sticky emulsion secreted by certain plants, as the rubber tree, milkweed, etc., that coagulates on exposure to air and is the basis of natural rubber. [< L, liquid]

lath (lath, läth) *n.* **1.** Any of a number of thin strips of wood, etc., nailed to studs or joists to support a coat of plaster, or on rafters to support shingles or slates. **2.** Other similar materials used to support plaster, tiles, etc. **3.** Laths collectively: also **lath′work′** (-wûrk′). **—** *v.t.* To cover or line with laths. [Prob. fusion of OE *laett* and OE *laethth* (assumed)] **— lath′er** *n.*

lathe (lā̆th) *n.* A machine that holds and spins pieces of wood, metal, plastic, etc., so that they are cut and shaped when the operator holds cutting tools against them. **—** *v.t.* To form on a lathe. [< MDu. *lade*]

lath·er (lath′ər) *n.* **1.** The suds or foam formed by soap or detergents and water. **2.** The foam of profuse sweating, as of a horse. **— in a lather** *U.S. Slang* In a state of intense excitement or agitation. **—** *v.t.* **1.** To cover with lather. **2.** *Informal* To flog; thrash. **—** *v.i.* **3.** To form lather. **4.** To become covered with lather, as a horse. [OE *lēathor* washing soda, soap] **— lath′er·er** *n.* **— lath′er·y** *adj.*

lath·ing (lath′ing, läth′-) *n.* **1.** The act or process of covering with laths. **2.** Laths collectively.

lat·i·ces (lat′ə·sēz) Plural of LATEX.

Lat·in (lat′n) *adj.* **1.** Pertaining to ancient Latium, its inhabitants, culture, or language. **2.** Pertaining to or denot-

ing the peoples or countries of France, Italy, and Spain. **3.** Of or belonging to the Western or Roman Catholic Church. **—** *n.* **1.** The Indo-European, Italic language of ancient Latium and Rome, extensively used in western Europe until modern times as the language of learning, and still the official language of the Roman Catholic Church. **2.** A member of one of the modern Latin peoples. **3.** A member of the Western or Roman Catholic Church. **4.** One of the people of ancient Latium. **— Old Latin** The language before the first century B.C., as preserved in inscriptions and the comedies of Plautus. **— Classical Latin** The literary and rhetorical language of the period 80 B.C. to A.D. 200. **— Late Latin** The language from 200–600. **— Low Latin** The language of any period after the classical, such as Medieval Latin. **— Medieval Latin** The language used by the writers of the Middle Ages, from 600–1500: also called *Middle Latin.* **— New** (or **Neo-**) **Latin** A form of the language based on Latin and Greek elements, now used chiefly for scientific and taxonomic terms. **— Vulgar Latin** The popular speech of the Romans from about A.D. 200 through the medieval period. [< L *Latinus* Latin]

Latin America The countries of the western hemisphere south of the Rio Grande, in which the official languages are derived from Latin. See SPANISH AMERICA. **— Lat·in-A·mer·i·can** (lat′n·ə·mer′ə·kən) *adj.* **— Latin American**

Lat·in·ate (lat′ən·āt) *adj.* Of, like, or from Latin.

Latin Church The Roman Catholic Church.

Latin cross A cross in which the upright is longer than the beam that crosses it near the top.

Lat·in·ism (lat′ən·iz′əm) *n.* An idiom in another language taken from or imitating Latin.

Lat·in·ist (lat′ən·ist) *n.* One versed or learned in Latin.

Lat·in·ize (lat′ən·īz) *v.* **·ized, ·iz·ing** *v.t.* **1.** To translate into Latin. **2.** To make Latin in customs, thought, etc. **—** *v.i.* **3.** To use Latin words, forms, etc. **— Lat′in·i·za′· tion** *n.* **— Lat′in·iz′er** *n.*

Latin Quarter A section of Paris on the south bank of the Seine, known for its many artists and students.

lat·i·tude (lat′ə·tōōd, -tyōōd) *n.* **1.** *Geog.* Angular distance on the earth's surface northward or southward of the equator, measured in degrees along a meridian. **2.** *Often pl.* A region or place considered with reference to its distance from the equator. **3.** Freedom from narrow restrictions. **4.** *Astron.* The angular distance of a heavenly body from the ecliptic (**celestial latitude**). [< L *latitudo* breadth]

lat·i·tu·di·nal (lat′ə·tōō′də·nəl, -tyōō′-) *adj.* Of or pertaining to latitude. **— lat′i·tu′di·nal·ly** *adv.*

lat·i·tu·di·nar·i·an (lat′ə·tōō′də·nâr′ē·ən, -tyōō′-) *adj.* Characterized by or tolerant of liberal or unorthodox attitudes, beliefs, etc., esp. in matters of religion. **—** *n.* One who is latitudinarian. **— lat′i·tu′di·nar′i·an·ism** *n.*

La·ti·um (lā′shē·əm) An ancient country in central Italy.

la·trine (lə·trēn′) *n.* A public toilet, as in a camp, barracks, etc. [< F < L *latrina* bath, privy]

-latry *combining form* Worship of; excessive devotion to. [< Gk. *latreia* worship]

lat·ter (lat′ər) *adj.* **1.** Being the second of two persons or things referred to: often preceded by *the:* The *latter* statement is truer than the former. **2.** Later or nearer to the end: His *latter* years were happy. [OE *lætra*, compar. of *læt* late]

lat·ter-day (lat′ər-dā′) *adj.* Modern: a *latter-day* martyr.

Latter-day Saint A Mormon.

lat·ter·ly (lat′ər-lē) *adv.* **1.** Recently; lately. **2.** At a later time; toward the end.

lat·tice (lat′is) *n.* **1.** A structure consisting of strips of metal, wood, etc., crossed or interlaced to form regularly spaced openings. **2.** A window, screen, gate, etc., made from or consisting of such a structure. **—** *v.t.* **·ticed, ·tic·ing** **1.** To furnish or enclose with a lattice. **2.** To form into or arrange like a lattice. [< OF *latte* lath]

lat·tice·work (lat′is·wûrk′) *n.* Openwork made from or resembling a lattice. Also **lat′· tic·ing.**

LATTICE

Lat·vi·an (lat′vē·ən) *adj.* Of or pertaining to Latvia, its people, or their language; Lettish. **—** *n.* **1.** A native or inhabitant of Latvia; a Lett. **2.** The Lettish language.

laud (lôd) *v.t.* To praise highly; extol. **— Syn.** See PRAISE. **—** *n. pl. Eccl.* The prescribed prayers immediately following matins, the two offices together constituting the first of the seven canonical hours. [< OF < L *laus, laudis* praise]

laud·a·ble (lô′də·bəl) *adj.* Deserving approbation. **— laud′a·bil′i·ty, laud′a·ble·ness** *n.* **— laud′a·bly** *adv.*

lau·da·num (lô′də·nəm) *n.* **1.** Tincture of opium. **2.** Formerly, any opium preparation. [< NL < L *ladanum*]

laud·a·tion (lô·dā′shən) *n.* The act of lauding; praise.

laud·a·to·ry (lô′də·tôr′ē, -tō′rē) *adj.* Expressing or containing praise; complimentary. Also **laud′a·tive.**

laugh (laf, läf) *v.i.* **1.** To produce the characteristic physical manifestations expressive of merriment, elation, etc. **2.** To express or experience amusement, satisfaction, etc. —*v.t.* **3.** To express or utter with laughter. **4.** To induce, persuade, or bring about by or as by laughing: I *laughed* myself sick. —**to laugh at 1.** To express amusement at. **2.** To ridicule; mock. **3.** To make light of. —**to laugh away** To dispel or minimize with laughter. —**to laugh off** To rid one's self of or dismiss laughingly. —**to laugh up (or in) one's sleeve** To be covertly amused or exultant. —*n.* **1.** An act or sound of laughing. **2.** *Informal* A cause for or provocation to laughter. —**to have the last laugh** To triumph or succeed after seeming at a disadvantage. [OE *hliehhan, hlæhhan*] —**laugh'er** *n.*

laugh·a·ble (laf'ə·bəl, läf'-) *adj.* Provoking laughter; amusing. —**laugh'a·ble·ness** *n.* —**laugh'a·bly** *adv.*

laugh·ing (laf'ing, läf'-) *adj.* **1.** Like or expressing laughter. **2.** Causing laughter. —*n.* Laughter. —**laugh'ing·ly** *adv.*

laughing gas Nitrous oxide.

laugh·ing·stock (laf'ing·stok', läf'-) *n.* One who or that which provokes ridicule; a butt.

laugh·ter (laf'tər, läf'-) *n.* **1.** The sound, expression, or action of laughing. **2.** A cause of laughing.

Laun·ce·lot (lôn'sə·lot, län'-) See LANCELOT.

launch[1] (lônch, länch) *v.t.* **1.** To move or push (a vessel, etc.) into the water, esp. for the first time. **2.** To set in flight or motion, as a rocket, missile, etc. **3.** To start (a person, etc.) on a career or course of action. **4.** To initiate; open: to *launch* a campaign. **5.** To hurl; fling. —*v.i.* **6.** To make a beginning; start: usu. with *out* or *forth.* **7.** To begin (an action, speech, etc.) vehemently or impetuously: usu. with *into.* —*n.* The action of launching a vessel, missile, etc. [< AF *lancher* to launch] —**launch'er** *n.*

launch[2] (lônch, länch) *n.* **1.** An open or half-decked motor boat. **2.** Formerly, the largest of the boats carried by a ship. [< Sp. < Malay *lanca* three-masted boat]

launching pad *Aerospace* The platform from which a rocket or guided missile is fired. Also **launch pad.**

laun·der (lôn'dər, län'-) *v.t.* **1.** To wash (clothing, linens, etc.). **2.** To wash and prepare for use by or as by ironing. —*v.i.* **3.** To do the work of washing and ironing. **4.** To undergo washing: Nylon *launders* easily. [< OF < LL *lavare* to wash] —**laun'der·er** *n.*

laun·dress (lôn'dris, län'-) *n.* A woman paid or employed to do laundry; washerwoman.

laun·dro·mat (lôn'drə·mat, län'-) *n.* *U.S.* A place where laundry is washed and dried in coin-operated automatic machines. [< *Laundromat,* a trade name]

laun·dry (lôn'drē, län'-) *n.* *pl.* **·dries 1.** A room, commercial establishment, etc., where laundering is done. **2.** Articles to be laundered. **3.** The work of laundering.

laun·dry·man (lôn'drē·mən, län'-) *n.* *pl.* **·men** (-mən) **1.** A man who works in or manages a commercial laundry. **2.** A man who calls for and delivers laundry.

laun·dry·wom·an (lôn'drē·wŏom'ən, län'-) *n.* *pl.* **·wom·en** (-wim'ən) A laundress.

lau·re·ate (lô'rē·it; *v.* -āt) *adj.* **1.** Singled out for special honor. **2.** Crowned or decked with laurel as a mark of honor. —*n.* **1.** A person honored with a prize or award. **2.** A poet laureate (which see). —*v.t.* **·at·ed, ·at·ing 1.** To crown with or as with laurel. **2.** To confer the title of poet laureate upon. [< L *laureatus* crowned with laurel]

lau·rel (lôr'əl, lor'-) *n.* **1.** An evergreen tree or shrub typifying a family that includes cinnamon, sassafras, etc. **2.** Any of various similar trees and shrubs. **3.** *Often pl.* A crown or wreath of laurel leaves, considered as a symbol of honor, achievement, etc. **4.** *pl.* Honor or distinction gained by outstanding achievement. —**to look to one's laurels** To be on guard against losing a position of eminence, honor, etc. —**to rest on one's laurels** To be content with what one has already achieved. —*v.t.* **lau·reled** or **·relled, lau·rel·ing** or **·rel·ling 1.** To honor by or as by crowning with laurel. **2.** To adorn with laurel. [< OF < L *laurus*]

la·va (lä'və, lav'ə) *n.* **1.** Molten rock that issues from an active volcano or through a fissure in the earth's crust. **2.** Rock formed by the solidifying of this substance. [< Ital., orig., a stream formed by rain < *lavare* to wash]

lav·a·liere (lav'ə·lir') *n.* An ornamental pendant worn on a thin chain around the neck. Also **lav'a·lier'**, *French* **la·val·lière** (là·và·lyâr'). [< F *la vallière* a type of necktie, ? after Louise de *La Vallière*, 1644–1710, mistress of Louis XIV]

lav·a·to·ry (lav'ə·tôr'ē, -tō'rē) *n.* *pl.* **·ries 1.** A room equipped with washing and usu. toilet facilities. **2.** A basin, sink, etc., used for washing. [< LL < L *lavare* to wash]

lav·en·der (lav'ən·dər) *n.* **1.** An Old World plant of the mint family, having spikes of fragrant, pale violet flowers; esp., the **true lavender,** of which the dried flowers and aromatic oil (**oil of lavender**) are much used in perfumery. **2.** The dried flowers and foliage of this plant, used to scent linen, clothing, etc. **3.** A pale, reddish violet color. —*adj.*

Pale reddish violet. —*v.t.* To perfume with lavender. [< AF < Med.L, ? < L *lividus* blue]

la·ver (lā'vər) *n.* In the ancient Jewish Temple, a large ceremonial vessel for washing. [< OF < LL *lavatorium*]

lav·ish (lav'ish) *adj.* **1.** Generous and unrestrained in giving, spending, etc.; prodigal. **2.** Provided or expended in great abundance. —*v.t.* To give or bestow generously. [< OF *lavasse, lavacho* downpour of rain] —**lav'ish·er** *n.* —**lav'ish·ly** *adv.* —**lav'ish·ness** *n.*

law (lô) *n.* **1.** A rule of conduct, recognized by custom or decreed by formal enactment, considered as binding on the members of a community, nation, etc. **2.** A system or body of such rules. **3.** The condition of society when such rules are observed: to establish *law* and order. **4.** The body of authoritatively established rules relating to a specified subject or activity: criminal *law.* **5.** Remedial justice as administered by legal authorities: to resort to the *law.* **6.** The branch of knowledge concerned with jurisprudence. **7.** The vocation of an attorney, etc.; the legal profession. **8.** The rules and principles of common law and statute law, as distinguished from equity. **9.** An authoritative rule or command: His will is *law.* **10.** *Often cap.* Divine will, command, or precept; also, a body of rules having such divine origin. **11.** Any generally accepted rule, procedure, or principle governing a specified area of conduct, body of knowledge, etc. **12.** In science and philosophy, a formal statement of the manner or order in which a set of natural phenomena occur under certain conditions. **13.** *Math.* A rule or formula governing a function or operation. —**the law. 1.** The legal authorities; the police. **2.** *Informal* A policeman. —**the Law 1.** The Mosaic Law. **2.** The Torah. —**to go to law** To engage in litigation. —**to lay down the law** To utter one's wishes, instructions, etc., in an authoritative manner. [OE < ON *lag* something laid or fixed, in pl., law]

law·a·bid·ing (lô'ə·bī'ding) *adj.* Obedient to the law.

law·break·er (lô'brā'kər) *n.* One who violates the law. —**law'break'ing** *n.* & *adj.*

law·ful (lô'fəl) *adj.* **1.** Permitted by law. **2.** Recognized by the law: *lawful* debts. **3.** Valid, authentic, etc., according to law: *lawful* marriage. —**law'ful·ly** *adv.* —**law'ful·ness** *n.*

law·giv·er (lô'giv'ər) *n.* One who originates or institutes a law or system of laws. —**law'giv'ing** *n.* & *adj.*

law·less (lô'lis) *adj.* **1.** Not controlled by law, authority, discipline, etc. **2.** Contrary to law. —**law'less·ly** *adv.* —**law'less·ness** *n.*

law·mak·er (lô'mā'kər) *n.* One who enacts or helps to enact laws; a legislator. —**law'mak'ing** *n.* & *adj.*

lawn[1] (lôn) *n.* A stretch of grassy land; esp., an area of closely mown grass near a house, in a park, etc. [Obs. *laund* < OF *launde* heath] —**lawn'y** *adj.*

lawn[2] (lôn) *n.* A fine, thin linen or cotton fabric. [after *Laon,* France, where it was formerly made] —**lawn'y** *adj.*

lawn mower A machine operated by a motor or propelled by hand, used to cut the grass of lawns.

Law of Moses The Mosaic Law.

law·ren·ci·um (lô·ren'sē·əm) *n.* A very short-lived radioactive element (symbol Lw), originally produced by bombarding californium with the nuclei of a boron isotope. See ELEMENT. [after E. O. *Lawrence,* 1901–58, U.S. physicist]

law·suit (lô'sōōt') *n.* A case, action, or proceeding brought to a court of law for settlement.

law·yer (lô'yər) *n.* A member of any branch of the legal profession; esp., one who advises and acts for clients or pleads in court.

lax (laks) *adj.* **1.** Lacking strictness or disciplinary control. **2.** Lacking precision; vague. **3.** Lacking firmness or rigidity. [< L *laxus* loose] —**lax'ly** *adv.* —**lax'ness** *n.*

lax·a·tive (lak'sə·tiv) *n.* A medicine taken to produce evacuation of the bowels. —*adj.* **1.** Loosening or producing evacuation of the bowels. **2.** Characterized by or having loose bowel movements. [< F, fem. of *laxatif*]

lax·i·ty (lak'sə·tē) *n.* The state or quality of being lax.

lay[1] (lā) *v.* **laid, lay·ing 1.** To cause to lie; deposit; esp., to place in a horizontal, reclining, or low position. **2.** To put or place; esp., to cause to be in a specified place or condition. **3.** To construct or establish as a basis or support: to *lay* the groundwork. **4.** To place or arrange in proper position: to *lay* bricks. **5.** To produce internally and deposit (an egg or eggs). **6.** To think out; devise: to *lay* plans. **7.** To attribute or ascribe: to *lay* the blame. **8.** To impose as a penalty, obligation, etc.: to *lay* a fine. **9.** To set forth; present: to *lay* one's claim before a court. **10.** To cause to fall; knock down. **11.** To cause to settle, subside, or lie level: to *lay* the dust. **12.** To render ineffective; quell, as a rumor. **13.** To bury, as in a grave; inter. **14.** To apply in or as in a layer; spread, as paint. **15.** To set or prepare (a trap, etc.). **16.** To prepare (a table, etc.) for use by setting out the necessary equipment. **17.** To set or locate (a scene, action, etc.). **18.** To strike or inflict blows with. **19.** To offer or stake as a bet. **20.** To twist strands so as to produce (rope, cable, etc.). — *v.i.* **21.** To produce and deposit eggs. **22.** To make a bet or bets. **23.** *Naut.* To move to a specified place or position: to *lay* aloft. — **to lay away 1.** To store up; save. **2.** To bury in or as in a grave. — **to lay down 1.** To place or put aside, in a low position. etc. **2.** To give up; sacrifice: to *lay down* one's life. **3.** To state authoritatively or dogmatically: to *lay down* the rules. **4.** To bet. — **to lay for** *U.S. Informal* To await an opportunity to attack or harm (someone). — **to lay in** To procure and store. — **to lay into** To attack vigorously. — **to lay it on** *Informal* To be extravagant, lavish, or exorbitant, esp. in praise or flattery. — **to lay low 1.** To strike down; prostrate. **2.** *U.S. Slang* To go into hiding. — **to lay off 1.** To mark out; plan. **2.** *U.S.* To dismiss from a job, usu. temporarily. **3.** *U.S. Informal* To stop working; take a rest. **4.** *U.S. Slang* To stop or cease. — **to lay out 1.** To arrange or display for use, inspection, etc. **2.** To arrange according to a plan; map. **3.** To spend or supply (a sum of money). **4.** To prepare (a corpse) for burial. **5.** *Informal* To strike down; prostrate. — **to lay over 1.** To overlay. **2.** *U.S. Informal* To stop for a time in the course of a journey. — **to lay to 1.** To work vigorously at. **2.** *Naut.* To maintain a vessel facing into the wind in a stationary or nearly stationary position. — **to lay up 1.** To make a store of. **2.** To incapacitate or confine, as by illness, injury, etc. — *n.* The manner in which something lies or is placed. [OE pt. of *licyan* to lie, recline]

◆ **lay, lie** Formal writing demands a distinction between these two words. *Lay* takes an object: We *lay* the papers on his desk every morning. *Lie*, meaning recline or be situated, does not take an object: The papers *lie* on the desk. The past tenses of these verbs are particularly liable to misuse and should be handled carefully: We *laid* the papers on his desk, and they *lay* there until he arrived.

lay² (lā) *adj.* **1.** Of or belonging to the laity; secular. **2.** Not belonging to or endorsed by a learned profession: a *lay* opinion. [< OF < Med.L < Gk. *laos* the people]

lay³ (lā) Past tense of LIE¹.

lay⁴ (lā) *n.* **1.** A song, ballad, or narrative poem. **2.** A melody. [< OF *lai*]

lay·er (lā′ər) *n.* **1.** A single thickness, coating, covering, etc. **2.** One who or that which lays; esp., a hen considered as an egg producer. **3.** A shoot or twig constituting part of a growing plant, of which a part is placed in the ground for rooting. — *v.t. & v.i.* **1.** To form a layer or layers. **2.** To propagate (a plant) by means of a layer or layers.

layer cake A cake, usu. frosted, made in layers having a sweetened filling between them.

lay·ette (lā·et′) *n.* The supply of clothing, bedding, etc., provided for a newborn infant. [< F, dim. of *laie* packing box, drawer < Flemish < MDu. *lade* chest, trunk]

lay·man (lā′mən) *n. pl.* **·men** (mən) **1.** One without training or skill in a profession or branch of knowledge. **2.** A man belonging to the laity, as distinguished from the clergy.

lay·off (lā′ôf′, -of′) *n. U.S.* **1.** The temporary dismissal of employees. **2.** A period of enforced unemployment.

lay·out (lā′out′) *n.* **1.** A planned arrangement, as: **a** The relative positions of streets, rooms, etc. **b** Written matter, illustrations, etc., arranged for printing. **2.** That which is laid out or provided, as equipment.

lay·o·ver (lā′ō′vər) *n.* A break in a journey; a stopover.

la·zar (lā′zər, laz′ər) *n. Archaic* A beggar or pauper afflicted with a loathsome disease; esp., a leper. [< Med.L *lazarus*, after *Lazarus* (Luke xvi 20)]

laz·a·ret·to (laz′ə·ret′ō) *n. pl.* **·tos 1.** A hospital for the treatment of contagious diseases, as leprosy. Also **lazar house. 2.** A ship or building used as a place of quarantine. **3.** *Naut.* A storage space between decks in the stern of a vessel: also **laz·a·ret′**, **laz·a·rette′** (-ret′). [< Ital. dial. (Venetian) *lazareto*, *nazareto* (Santa Madonna di) *Nazaret*, Venetian church formerly used as a hospital]

Laz·a·rus (laz′ə·rəs) In the New Testament: **a** A brother of Martha and Mary, raised from the dead by Christ. *John* xi 1. **b** A sick beggar in the parable of the rich and the poor man. *Luke* xvi 20.

laze (lāz) *v.* **lazed**, **laz·ing** *v.i.* **1.** To be lazy; loaf; idle. — *v.t.* **2.** To pass (time) in idleness. [< LAZY]

laz·u·rite (laz′yŏō·rīt) *n.* A deep blue silicate of sodium and aluminum containing sulfur, the principal constituent of lapis lazuli. [< Med.L *lazur* azure]

la·zy (lā′zē) *adj.* **·zi·er**, **·zi·est 1.** Unwilling to work or engage in energetic activity; slothful. **2.** Moving or acting slowly or heavily. **3.** Characterized by idleness or languor. [Prob. < MLG *lusich* loose, feeble] — **la′zi·ly** *adv.* — **la′zi·ness** *n.*

la·zy·bones (lā′zē·bōnz′) *n. pl.* **·bones** *Informal* A lazy person.

Lazy Susan A revolving tray, often divided into compartments, used to hold condiments, etc. Also **lazy Susan.**

lea (lē) *n. Chiefly Poetic* A grassy field or tract; meadow. [OE *lēah*, orig., open ground in a wood]

leach (lēch) *v.t.* **1.** To cause (a liquid) to percolate or filter through something. **2.** To subject to the filtering action of a liquid. **3.** To remove or dissolve by or as by filtering. — *v.i.* **4.** To be removed or dissolved by percolation or filtration. — *n.* **1.** The process of leaching. **2.** A solution obtained from leaching. [OE *leccan* to wet, irrigate] — **leach′er** *n.*

lead¹ (lēd) *v.* **led**, **lead·ing** *v.t.* **1.** To go with or ahead of so as to show the way; guide. **2.** To cause to progress by or as by pulling or holding: to *lead* a child by the hand. **3.** To serve as or indicate a route for: The path *led* him to the hut. **4.** To control the actions or affairs of; direct. **5.** To influence the ideas, conduct, or actions of. **6.** To be first among. **7.** To be the principal participant in: to *lead* a discussion. **8.** To conduct the performance of (musicians or music). **9.** To experience or live; also, to cause to experience or go through: to *lead* a merry life; They *led* him a wild chase. **10.** To direct or effect the course of (water, conduits, cable, etc.). **11.** In card games, to begin a round by playing (a specified card). — *v.i.* **12.** To act as guide; conduct. **13.** To be led; yield readily to being pulled or guided. **14.** To afford a way or passage: The road *leads* through a swamp. **15.** To be conducive; tend: followed by *to*: Delinquency *leads* to crime. **16.** To have control or command. **17.** To be first or in advance. **18.** In card games, to make the first play. — **to lead off 1.** To make a start; begin. **2.** In baseball, to be the first batter in a line-up or inning. — **to lead on 1.** To entice or tempt, esp. to wrongdoing. **2.** To go first or in advance. — *n.* **1.** Position in advance or at the head. **2.** The distance or interval by which someone or something leads. **3.** Position of primary importance, responsibility, etc. **4.** Guidance; leadership; example: Follow his *lead*. **5.** Indication; clue: Give me a *lead*. **6.** In dramatic presentations: **a** A starring role. **b** A performer having such a role. **7.** In journalism, the introductory portion or paragraph of a news story. **8.** In card games: **a** The right or obligation to play first in a game or round. **b** The card, suit, etc., thus played. **9.** In baseball, a position taken by a runner part of the way between the base he has attained and the next base. **10.** *Electr.* A short wire or conductor, used as a connection to a source of current. **11.** A cord, leash etc., for leading an animal. [OE *lǣden* to cause to go]

lead² (led) *n.* **1.** A soft, heavy, malleable, dull gray metallic element (symbol Pb), occurring most commonly in the sulfide mineral galena. See ELEMENT. **2.** Any of various objects made of lead or similar metal; esp., a weight suspended from a line, used in sounding, etc. **3.** Graphite, esp. in the form of thin rods, used as the writing material in pencils. **4.** Bullets, shot, etc. **5.** White lead. **6.** *Printing* A thin strip of type metal used to provide space between printed lines. — *v.t.* **1.** To cover, weight, fasten, treat, or fill with lead. **2.** *Printing* To separate or space (lines of type) with leads. [OE *lēad*]

lead·en (led′n) *adj.* **1.** Dull gray, as lead. **2.** Made of lead. **3.** Weighty; inert: a *leaden* mass. **4.** Heavy or labored in movement, etc., sluggish. **5.** Oppressive; gloomy. — **lead′-en·ly** *adv.* — **lead′en·ness** *n.*

lead·er (lē′dər) *n.* **1.** One who or that which goes ahead or in advance. **2.** One who acts as a guiding force, commander, etc. **3.** An article of merchandise offered at a special low price to attract customers. **4.** A pipe for draining a liquid, as rainwater. **5.** In fishing, a length of gut, etc., used for attaching a hook or lure to the line. **6.** *pl. Printing* Dots or hyphens in a horizontal row, serving to guide the eye across a page, column, etc.

lead·er·ship (lē′dər·ship′) *n.* **1.** The office, position, or capacity of a leader; guidance. **2.** Ability to lead, exert authority, etc. **3.** A group of leaders.

lead-in (lēd′in′) *n. Telecom.* A wire connecting a radio receiving set with its antenna.

lead·ing¹ (lē′ding) *adj.* **1.** Having the capacity or effect of controlling, influencing, guiding, etc. **2.** Most important; chief. **3.** Situated or going at the head; first. — *n.* The act of one who or that which leads; guidance.

lead·ing² (led′ing) *n.* **1.** The act or process of filling, covering, or separating with lead. **2.** A border of lead. **3.** *Printing* Spacing between lines.

leading question (lē′ding) A question having the intention or effect of eliciting the reply desired by the questioner.

lead·off (lēd′ôf′, -of′) *n.* **1.** A beginning action, move, etc., as the opening play in a competitive game. **2.** A player or participant who begins the action in a game or competition.

lead pencil (led) A pencil having a thin stick of graphite as its writing material.

lead poisoning (led) *Pathol.* Poisoning caused by the absorption of lead by the tissues.

leaf (lēf) *n. pl.* **leaves** (lēvz) **1.** One of the outgrowths from the stem of a plant, commonly flat, thin, and green in color, and functioning as the principal area of photosynthesis. **2.** Foliage collectively; leafage. **3.** Loosely, a petal. **4.** A product, as tobacco, tea, etc., in the form of gathered leaves. **5.** One of the sheets of paper in a book, etc., each side being a single page. **6.** A flat piece, hinged or otherwise movable, constituting part of a table, gate, etc. **7.** Metal in a very thin sheet or plate: gold *leaf.* — **to turn over a new leaf** To begin anew, esp. with the intention of improving one's ways. — *v.i.* To put forth or produce leaves. [OE *lēaf*]

leaf·age (lē′fij) *n.* Leaves collectively; foliage.

leaf·less (lēf′lis) *adj.* Having or bearing no leaves. — **leaf′·less·ness** *n.*

leaf·let (lēf′lit) *n.* **1.** One of the divisions of a compound leaf. **2.** A small printed sheet or circular, often folded. **3.** A little leaf or leaflike part.

leaf·stalk (lēf′stôk) *n.* A petiole (def. 1).

leaf·y (lē′fē) *adj.* **leaf·i·er, leaf·i·est 1.** Bearing, covered with, or characterized by a profusion of leaves. **2.** Consisting of or resembling leaves. — **leaf′i·ness** *n.*

league[1] (lēg) *n.* A measure of distance varying from about 2.42 to 4.6 statute miles, but usu. reckoned as approximately 3 miles. [< OF < LL *leuga, leuca* Gaulish mile]

league[2] (lēg) *n.* **1.** An association or confederation of persons, organizations, or states. **2.** A compact or covenant binding such a union. **3.** An association of athletic teams. — **in league** In close alliance. — *v.t. & v.i.* **leagued, lea·guing** To unite in a league. [< OF < Ital. *legare* to bind]

League of Nations An international organization established in 1920, primarily for the preservation of world peace, and formally dissolved in 1946.

Le·ah (lē′ə) In the Old Testament, Rachel's elder sister, who became the first wife of Jacob. *Gen.* xxix 16.

leak (lēk) *n.* **1.** An opening, as a crack, permitting an undesirable escape or entrance of fluid, light, etc. **2.** Any condition or agency by which something is let through or escapes: *a leak* in the security system. **3.** An act or instance of leaking; leakage. — *v.i.* **1.** To let a fluid, etc., pass or escape through a hole, crack, or similar opening. **2.** To pass, flow, or escape through a hole, crack, etc. **3.** To be divulged despite secrecy: The plans *leaked* out. — *v.t.* **4.** To let (a liquid, etc.) escape. **5.** To disclose (information, etc.) without authorization. [< ON *leka* to drip]

leak·age (lē′kij) *n.* **1.** The act or circumstance of leaking. **2.** That which escapes or passes through by leaking.

leak·y (lē′kē) *adj.* **leak·i·er, leak·i·est** Having a leak; permitting leakage. — **leak′i·ness** *n.*

lean[1] (lēn) *v.* **leaned** or **leant** (lent), **lean·ing** *v.i.* **1.** To rest or incline for support: usu. with *against* or *on.* **2.** To bend or slant from an erect position. **3.** To have a tendency, preference, etc.: to *lean* toward conservatism. **4.** To depend for support, etc.; rely. — *v.t.* **5.** To cause to incline. **6.** To place or rest (something) so as to be supported by something else: usu. with *against, on,* or *upon.* — *n.* The act or condition of leaning; slant. [OE *hleonian, hlinian*]

lean[2] (lēn) *adj.* **1.** Not fat or plump; thin; spare. **2.** Not containing fat: *lean* meat. **3.** Not rich, plentiful, or satisfying; meager. — *n.* Meat or flesh having little or no fat. [OE *hlǣne* thin] — **lean′ly** *adv.* — **lean′ness** *n.*

Le·an·der (lē·an′dər) In Greek legend, the lover of Hero.

lean·ing (lē′ning) *n.* **1.** An inclination; tendency; predisposition. **2.** The act of one who or that which leans.

lean-to (lēn′tōō′) *n. pl.* **-tos** (-tōōz′) **1.** A crude hut of branches, etc., sloping to the ground from a raised support. **2.** A shed or extension of a building having a sloping roof and supported by an adjoining wall or structure.

leap (lēp) *v.* **leaped** or **leapt** (lept), **leap·ing** *v.i.* **1.** To rise or project oneself by a sudden thrust from the ground; jump; spring. **2.** To move, react, etc., suddenly or impulsively. **3.** To make an abrupt transition: to *leap* to a conclusion. — *v.t.* **4.** To traverse by a jump. **5.** To cause to jump. — *n.* **1.** The act of leaping. **2.** The space traversed by leaping. **3.** A place from which a leap may be made. **4.** An abrupt transition. [OE *hlēapan*] — **leap′er** *n.*

leap·frog (lēp′frog′, -frôg′) *n.* A game in which each player puts his hands on the back of another, who is bending over, and leaps over him in a straddling position.

leap year A year of 366 days, in which a 29th day is added to February. Every year divisible by 4 (as 1964) is a leap year, except those completing a century, which must be divisible by 400 (as 2000).

Lear (lir) Hero of Shakespeare's tragedy *King Lear.*

learn (lûrn) *v.* **learned** or **learnt, learn·ing** *v.t.* **1.** To acquire knowledge of or skill in by study, practice, etc. **2.** To find out; become aware of. **3.** To commit to memory; memorize. **4.** To acquire by experience or example. — *v.i.* **5.** To gain knowledge or acquire skill. **6.** To become informed; know: with *of* or *about.* [OE *leornian*] — **learn′er** *n.*

learn·ed (lûr′nid) *adj.* **1.** Having profound or extensive knowledge. **2.** Characterized by or devoted to scholarship.

learn·ing (lûr′ning) *n.* **1.** Knowledge obtained by study; erudition. **2.** The act of acquiring knowledge or skill.

lease (lēs) *n.* **1.** A contract for the temporary occupation or use of premises, property, etc., in exchange for payment of rent. **2.** The period of such occupation or use. — *v.t.* **1.** To grant use of under a lease. **2.** To hold under a lease. [< AF, OF < L *laxus* loose] — **leas′a·ble** *adj.*

leash (lēsh) *n.* **1.** A thong, cord, etc., by which a dog or other animal is led or restrained. **2.** Restraint; control. — *v.t.* To hold or secure by a leash. [< OF < L *laxus* loose]

least (lēst) Alternative superlative of LITTLE. — *adj.* Smallest in degree, value, size, etc.; most insignificant; slightest. — *n.* That which is smallest, slightest, or most insignificant. — **at least 1.** By the lowest possible estimate. **2.** At any rate. — **in the least** In the slightest degree; at all. — *adv.* In the lowest or smallest degree. [OE *lǣssa* less]

least·wise (lēst′wīz′) *adv. Informal* At least; at any rate. Also *Dial.* **least′ways′** (-wāz′).

leath·er (leth′ər) *n.* **1.** Animal skin, usu. with the hair removed, prepared for use by tanning. **2.** An article made of leather. — *v.t.* To cover or equip with leather. [OE *lether*]

leath·ern (leth′ərn) *adj. Archaic* **1.** Made of leather. **2.** Resembling leather; leathery. [OE *lether* leather]

leath·er·neck (leth′ər·nek′) *n. U.S. Slang* A marine.

leath·er·y (leth′ər·ē) *adj.* Resembling leather in texture or appearance; tough. — **leath′er·i·ness** *n.*

leave[1] (lēv) *v.* **left, leav·ing** *v.t.* **1.** To go or depart from. **2.** To allow to remain behind or in a specified place, condition, etc. **3.** To have or cause as an aftermath: Oil *leaves* stains. **4.** To cause to be made available in one's absence: *Leave* your name at the desk. **5.** To commit for action, etc.; entrust: *Leave* it to me. **6.** To terminate one's connection or association with. **7.** To abandon; forsake. **8.** To have remaining after one's death. **9.** To transmit as a legacy; bequeath. **10.** To have as a remainder as the result of an arithmetic operation. — *v.i.* **11.** To go away; set out. — **to leave alone 1.** To refrain from interfering with, etc. **2.** To allow to remain solitary. — **to leave off** To stop; cease. — **to leave out 1.** To omit. **2.** To exclude. [OE *lǣfan,* lit., to let remain] — **leav′er** *n.*

◆ **leave, let** *Leave* means to depart or to permit to remain (*He left the room; He left the book on the table*), as distinguished from *let,* which means simply to permit (*Let him stay*). *Let* can be followed by the infinitive without to; *leave* cannot. *Leave it to him to decide* and *Let him decide* are standard, but *Leave him decide* is nonstandard.

leave[2] (lēv) *n.* **1.** Permission to do something. **2.** Permission to be absent; esp., **a** Official permission to be absent from duty. **b** The period covered by such permission: also **leave of absence. 3.** Formal farewell: usu. in the phrase **to take (one's) leave.** — **on leave** Absent from work or duty with permission. [OE *lēaf* permission]

leave[3] (lēv) *v.i.* **leaved, leav·ing** To put forth leaves; leaf.

leaved (lēvd) *adj.* **1.** Having a leaf or leaves. **2.** Having or characterized by (a specified kind or number of) leaves.

leav·en (lev′ən) *n.* **1.** An agent of fermentation, as yeast, added to dough or batter to produce a light texture. **2.** A portion of fermented dough used for this purpose. **3.** Any pervasive influence that produces a significant change. Also **leav′en·ing.** — *v.t.* **1.** To cause fermentation in. **2.** To affect in character; temper. [< OF < L *levare* to raise]

leaves (lēvz) Plural of LEAF.

leave-tak·ing (lēv′tā′king) *n.* An act of departure.

leav·ings (lē′vingz) *n.pl.* Unused portion; remnants.

Leb·a·nese (leb′ə·nēz′, -nēs) *adj.* Of or pertaining to Lebanon or its people. — *n.* A native or citizen of Lebanon.

Le·bens·raum (lā′bəns·roum′) *n. German* Territory claimed by a nation as necessary for its economic independence or growth; literally, space for living.

lech·er (lech′ər) *n.* A lewd and prurient man. [< OF < OHG *leccôn* to lick]

lech·er·ous (lech′ər·əs) *adj.* Given to lewdness or inciting to lust. — **lech′er·ous·ly** *adv.* — **lech′er·ous·ness** *n.*

lech·er·y (lech′ər·ē) *n. pl.* **·ries** Unconstrained sexual indulgence.

lec·tern (lek′tərn) *n.* **1.** A stand on which a speaker, instructor, etc., may place books or papers. **2.** In some churches, a reading desk from which certain parts of the service are read. [< OF < LL < L *legere* to read]

lec·ture (lek′chər) *n.* **1.** A discourse on a specific subject, delivered to an audience for instruction or information. **2.** A formal reproof or lengthy reprimand. — *v.* **·tured, ·tur·ing** *v.i.* **1.** To deliver a lecture or lectures. — *v.t.* **2.** To deliver a lecture to. **3.** To rebuke sternly or at length. [< L *legere* to read] — **lec′tur·er** *n.*

led (led) Past tense and past participle of LEAD[1].

Le·da (lē′də) In Greek mythology, the mother of Clytemnestra, Castor, Pollux, and Helen, of which the latter three were fathered by Zeus in the form of a swan.

ledge (lej) *n.* **1.** A narrow, shelflike projection along the side of a rocky formation. **2.** A shelf or sill projecting from or forming the top of a wall, etc. **3.** An underwater or coastal ridge. **4.** *Mining* A metal-bearing rock stratum; vein. [ME *legge*] — **ledg'y** *adj.*

ledg·er (lej'ər) *n.* An account book in which all final entries of business transactions are recorded. [ME *legger*]

ledger line *Music* A short line added above or below the staff: also spelled *leger line.*

lee (lē) *n.* **1.** Shelter or protection, esp. from the wind. **2.** *Chiefly Naut.* **a** The side sheltered from the wind. **b** The direction opposite that from which the wind is blowing. — *adj. Chiefly Naut.* Pertaining to or being on the lee: opposed to *weather.* [OE *hlēo* shelter]

leech¹ (lēch) *n.* **1.** Any of a class of carnivorous or bloodsucking, chiefly aquatic annelid worms; esp. the **medicinal leech,** formerly used for bloodletting. **2.** One who clings to another for gain; a parasite. **3.** *Archaic* A physician. — *v.t. Archaic* To treat with leeches. [OE *lēce,* orig., physician]

leech² (lēch) *n. Naut.* **1.** Either of the side edges of a square sail. **2.** The after edge of a fore-and-aft sail. [ME *leche*]

leek (lēk) *n.* **1.** A culinary herb of the lily family, closely allied to the onion but having a narrow bulb and broader, dark green leaves: the national emblem of Wales. **2.** Any of various related plants. [OE *lēac*]

leer (lir) *n.* A sly look or sidewise glance expressing salacious desire, malicious intent, knowing complicity, etc. — *v.i.* To look with a leer. [OE *hlēor* cheek, face]

leer·y (lir'ē) *adj. Informal* **1.** Suspicious; wary. **2.** Sly.

lees (lēz) *n.pl.* Sediment, esp. in wine or liquor; dregs. [Pl. of obs. *lee* < OF *lie*]

lee·ward (lē'wərd, *Naut.* lōō'ərd) *adj.* **1.** Of or pertaining to the direction toward which the wind is blowing. **2.** Being on or toward the side sheltered from the wind. — *n.* The side or direction toward which the wind is blowing. — *adv.* Toward the lee. Opposed to *windward.*

lee·way (lē'wā') *n.* **1.** Additional space, time, range, etc., providing greater freedom of action. **2.** *Naut.* The lateral drift of a vessel or an aircraft in motion.

left¹ (left) Past tense and past participle of LEAVE¹.

left² (left) *adj.* **1.** Pertaining to, designating, or being on the side of the body that is toward the north when one faces east, and usu. having the weaker and less dominant hand, etc. **2.** Pertaining to or situated on the corresponding side of anything. **3.** Nearest to or tending in the direction of the left side. **4.** Worn on a left hand, foot, etc. **5.** *Sometimes cap.* Designating a person, party, faction, etc., having liberal, democratic, socialistic, or laborite views and policies. — *n.* **1.** Any part, area, etc., on or toward the left side. **2.** *Often cap.* A group, party, etc., whose views and policies are left (*adj.* def. 5); esp., in Europe, such parties whose members sit to the presiding officer's left in a deliberative assembly. **3.** In boxing: **a** A blow with the left hand. **b** The left hand. — *adv.* On, to, or toward the left. [ME (Kentish) var. of presumed OE *lyft* weak]

left face In military drill, a 90-degree pivot to the left, using the ball of the right foot and the heel of the left.

left-hand (left'hand') *adj.* **1.** Of, for, pertaining to, or situated on the left side or the left hand. **2.** Turning, opening, or swinging to the left.

left-hand·ed (left'han'did) *adj.* **1.** Using the left hand habitually and more easily than the right. **2.** Done with the left hand. **3.** Adapted or intended for use by the left hand. **4.** Turning or moving from right to left, or counterclockwise. **5.** Ironical or insincere in intent or effect: a *left-handed* compliment. **6.** Clumsy. — *adv.* With the left hand. — **left'-hand'ed·ly** *adv.* — **left'-hand'ed·ness** *n.*

left·ist (lef'tist) *n.* One whose views and policies are left (*adj.* def. 5). — *adj.* Left (*adj.* def. 5). — **left'ism** *n.*

left·o·ver (left'ō'vər) *n. Usu. pl.* An unused part or remnant, esp. of prepared food. — *adj.* Left as a remnant.

left wing *Sometimes cap.* A party, group, faction, etc., having leftist policies. **2.** The wing, part, etc., on the left side. — **left-wing** (left'wing') *adj.* — **left'-wing'er** *n.*

leg (leg) *n.* **1.** One of the limbs or appendages serving as a means of support and locomotion in animals and man. **2.** *Anat.* **a** A lower limb of the human body, extending from the hip to the ankle. **b** The part of the lower limb between the knee and the ankle. **3.** A support resembling a leg in shape, position, or function. **4.** The portion of an article of clothing, as hose, trousers, etc., that covers a leg. **5.** A division or section of a course or journey. **6.** One of the divisions of an angled or forked object, as a pair of compasses. **7.** *Geom.* Either of the sides of a triangle adjacent to the base or the hypotenuse. **8.** *Naut.* The distance traveled by a vessel in a single direction while tacking. — **on one's last legs** On the verge of collapse or death. — **to have not a leg to stand on** To have no sound or logical basis, as for argument, justifica-

tion, etc. — **to pull one's leg** *Informal* To make fun of; fool. — **to shake a leg** *Slang* **1.** To hurry. **2.** To dance. — *v.i.* **legged, leg·ging** *Informal* To walk or run: usu. followed by *it.* [< ON *leggr*]

leg·a·cy (leg'ə·sē) *n. pl.* **·cies** **1.** Personal property, money, etc., bequeathed by will; a bequest. **2.** Anything received from or passed on by an ancestor, predecessor, or earlier era. [< OF < Med.L *legatia* the district of a legate]

le·gal (lē'gəl) *adj.* **1.** Of, pertaining to, or concerned with law: *legal* documents. **2.** Established or authorized by law. **3.** Conforming with or permitted by law. **4.** According to, determined by, or coming under the jurisdiction of statute law, rather than equity. **5.** Characteristic of or appropriate to those who practice law. — **Syn.** See LAWFUL. [< OF < L *lex, legis* law] — **le'gal·ly** *adv.*

legal age Age (*n.* def. 3).

legal holiday *U.S.* A day on which banks are closed and official business is suspended or limited by law.

le·gal·ism (lē'gəl·iz'əm) *n.* Strict conformity to law; esp., the stressing of the letter and forms of the law rather than the spirit of justice. — **le'gal·ist** *n.* — **le·gal·is'tic** *adj.*

le·gal·i·ty (li·gal'ə·tē) *n. pl.* **·ties** **1.** The condition or quality of being legal; lawfulness. **2.** Adherence to law.

le·gal·ize (lē'gəl·īz) *v.t.* **·ized, ·iz·ing** To make legal. Also *Brit.* **le'gal·ise.** — **le·gal·i·za'tion** (-ə-zā'shən, -ī-zā'-) *n.*

legal medicine Medical jurisprudence.

legal tender Coin or other money that may be legally offered in payment of a debt, and that a creditor must accept.

leg·ate (leg'it) *n.* **1.** An ecclesiastic appointed as an official representative of the Pope. **2.** An official envoy, usu. acting as a diplomatic representative of a government. — **Syn.** See AMBASSADOR. [< OF < L *legare* to send as a deputy] — **leg·a·tine** (leg'ə·tin, -tīn) *adj.* — **leg'ate·ship** *n.*

leg·a·tee (leg'ə·tē') *n.* One to whom a legacy is bequeathed.

le·ga·tion (li·gā'shən) *n.* **1.** The official residence or business premises of a diplomatic minister or envoy of lower rank than an ambassador. **2.** The official staff of a foreign envoy or diplomatic mission. **3.** The position or rank of a legate.

le·ga·to (li·gä'tō) *Music adj.* Smooth and flowing, with unbroken transition between successive notes. — *adv.* In a legato manner. — *n. pl.* **·tos** A smooth, connected style, performance, or passage. [< Ital., lit., bound]

leg·a·tor (li·gā'tər, leg'ə·tôr') *n.* One who makes a will.

leg·end (lej'ənd) *n.* **1.** An unauthenticated story from earlier times, preserved by tradition and popularly thought to be historical. **2.** A body of such stories, as those connected with a people or culture. **3.** An inscription or motto, as on a coin, banner, etc. **4.** A caption or explanatory description accompanying an illustration, chart, etc. [< OF < Med.L < L *legere* to read]

leg·en·dar·y (lej'ən·der'ē) *adj.* **1.** Of, presented in, or of the nature of a legend. **2.** Famous; celebrated.

leg·end·ry (lej'ən·drē) *n.* Legends collectively; legend.

le·ger line (lej'ər) See LEDGER LINE.

leg·er·de·main (lej'ər·də·mān') *n.* **1.** Sleight of hand. **2.** Any artful trickery or deception. [ME < MF *léger de main,* lit., light of hand] — **leg'er·de·main'ist** *n.*

le·ges (lē'jēz) Plural of LEX.

leg·ged (leg'id, legd) *adj.* Having or characterized by (a specified kind or number of) legs: *bow-legged; two-legged.*

leg·ging (leg'ing) *n.* A gaiter or similar covering for the leg, usu. extending from the knee to the instep.

leg·gy (leg'ē) *adj.* **·gi·er, ·gi·est** **1.** Having disproportionately long legs. **2.** *Informal* Having or displaying attractive, shapely legs. — **leg'gi·ness** *n.*

leg·horn (leg'hôrn, -ərn) *n.* **1.** Finely plaited wheat straw. **2.** A hat made from this straw. **3.** *Usu. cap.* One of a breed of small, hardy domestic fowl. [after *Leghorn*]

leg·i·ble (lej'ə·bəl) *adj.* **1.** Capable of being read or deciphered; easy to read. **2.** Readily perceived or discovered from apparent signs or evidence. [< LL < L *legere* to read] — **leg'i·bil'i·ty, leg'i·ble·ness** *n.* — **leg'i·bly** *adv.*

le·gion (lē'jən) *n.* **1.** In ancient Rome, a major military unit consisting primarily of infantry troops with an auxiliary force of cavalry, altogether comprising between 4,200 and 6,000 men. **2.** *Usu. pl.* Any large military force; army. **3.** A great number; multitude. ◆ Sometimes used predicatively with the adjectival sense *innumerable,* as in Their members are *legion.* **4.** *Usu. cap.* Any of various military or honorary organizations, usu. national in character. [< OF < L *legere* to choose, levy troops]

le·gion·ar·y (lē'jən·er'ē) *adj.* Of, or pertaining to a legion. — *n. pl.* **·ar·ies** A soldier or member of a legion.

le·gion·naire (lē'jən·âr') *n. Often cap.* A member of a legion (def. 4). [< F *légionnaire*]

Legion of Merit *U.S.* A military decoration awarded for exceptionally meritorious conduct in the performance of outstanding services. See DECORATION.

leg·is·late (lej′is·lāt) v. **·lat·ed, ·lat·ing** v.i. **1.** To make a law or laws. — v.t. **2.** To cause to be in a specified state by legislation: often with *into* or *out of.* [Back formation < LEGISLATOR]

leg·is·la·tion (lej′is·lā′shən) n. **1.** The act or procedures of enacting laws. **2.** An officially enacted law or laws.

leg·is·la·tive (lej′is·lā′tiv) adj. **1.** Of, pertaining to, or involved in legislation. **2.** Having the power to legislate: the *legislative* branch of the government: distinguished from *executive, judicial.* **3.** Of or pertaining to a legislature. **4.** Enacted by or resulting from legislation. — n. The legislative branch of a government. — **leg′is·la′tive·ly** adv.

leg·is·la·tor (lej′is·lā′tər) n. **1.** One active in the formation and enactment of laws; a lawmaker. **2.** A member of a legislature. [< L lex, legis law + lator bearer, proposer] — **leg′is·la′tress** (-tris), **leg′is·la′trix** (-triks) n. fem.

leg·is·la·ture (lej′is·lā′chər) n. A body of persons officially constituted and empowered to make and enact the laws of a nation or state; esp., in the U.S., the lawmaking body of a State, Territory, etc., as distinguished from Congress.

le·git (lə·jit′) Slang n. Legitimate drama, theatrical productions, etc. — adj. Legitimate.

le·git·i·ma·cy (lə·jit′ə·mə·sē) n. The state or condition of being legitimate.

le·git·i·mate (adj. lə·jit′ə·mit; v. lə·jit′ə·māt) adj. **1.** In accordance with law; lawful. **2.** Based on or resulting from orderly, rational deduction or inference. **3.** Authentic; valid. **4.** Born in wedlock. **5.** According to or based on strict hereditary right. **6.** In the theater, denoting drama performed by living actors before an audience as distinguished from motion pictures, television, etc. — v.t. **·mat·ed, ·mat·ing 1.** To make or establish as legitimate. **2.** To show reason or authorization for. [< Med.L < L legitimus lawful < lex, legis law] — **le·git′i·mate·ly** adv. — **le·git′i·mate·ness** n. — **le·git′i·ma′tion** (-mā′shən) n.

le·git·i·mist (lə·jit′ə·mist) n. An advocate of rule or authority based on hereditary right; esp., of claims to a monarchy. — **le·git′i·mism** n. — **le·git′i·mis′tic** adj.

le·git·i·mize (lə·jit′ə·mīz) v.t. **·mized, ·miz·ing** To legitimate. Also **le·git′i·ma·tize** (-mə·tīz). — **le·git′i·mi·za′tion** n.

leg-of-mut·ton (leg′ə·mut′n) adj. Having the characteristically triangular or tapering shape of a haunch of mutton.

leg-of-mutton sleeve A sleeve puffed on the upper arm and fitting closely on the forearm: also called *gigot.*

leg·ume (leg′yōōm, lə·gyōōm′) n. **1.** The fruit or seed of any leguminous plant, esp. when used as food or fodder. **2.** Any leguminous plant. **3.** Bot. The characteristic, sutured seed vessel of such a plant; a pod. [< F < L legumen, lit., something gathered < legere to gather]

le·gu·mi·nous (lə·gyōō′mə·nəs) adj. Of or belonging to a large family of plants including peas, beans, etc.

leg·work (leg′wûrk′) n. Informal Chores, errands, etc., accomplished by or as by going about on foot.

lei (lā, lā′ē) n. pl. **leis** A festival garland of blossoms, feathers, etc., as worn in Hawaii. [< Hawaiian]

lei·sure (lē′zhər, lezh′ər) n. **1.** Freedom from the demands of work or duty. **2.** Time available for recreation or relaxation. — **at leisure 1.** Free from pressing necessity or obligation; having time to spare. **2.** Unoccupied; not employed. **3.** When one has time or opportunity: also **at one's leisure.** — adj. **1.** Not spent in work or necessary activity: *leisure* time. **2.** Having considerable leisure: the *leisure* classes. [< OF < L licere to be permitted]

lei·sure·ly (lē′zhər·lē, lezh′ər-) adj. Free from exertion or pressure; relaxed and unhurried. Also **lei′sured** (-zhərd). — adv. In a leisurely manner. — **lei′sure·li·ness** n.

leit·mo·tif (līt′mō·tēf′) n. Music A theme used for a certain person, event, or idea throughout an opera, etc. Also **leit′mo·tiv′** (-tēf′). [< G < leiten to lead + motiv motive]

LEM (lem) Lunar excursion module (which see).

lem·ming (lem′ing) n. Any of several small arctic rodents, having a short tail and furry feet; esp., a European species, noted for recurrent mass migrations often terminated by drowning in the ocean. [< Norw.]

LEMMING
(To 6 inches long)

lem·on (lem′ən) n. **1.** The oval, citrus fruit of an evergreen tree, having juicy, acid pulp and a yellow rind yielding an essential oil (**lemon oil**) used as a flavoring and perfuming agent. **2.** The tree. **3.** A bright, clear yellow. **4.** Slang Something or someone disappointing or unattractive. — adj. Bright, clear yellow. [< OF < Sp. < Arabic < Persian limūn]

lem·on·ade (lem′ən·ād′) n. A drink made of lemon juice, water, and sugar.

le·mur (lē′mər) n. Any of various small, arboreal, mostly nocturnal mammals related to the monkeys; esp., one having a foxlike face and soft fur, found chiefly in Madagascar. [< NL < L lemures ghosts]

Len·a·pe (len′ə·pē) n. The generic name of the Delawares, an Algonquian people; also, their language: also called Leni-

Lenape, Lenni-Lenape. [Short for Algonquian (Lenape) Leni-lenape, lit., real man < leni real + lenape man]

lend (lend) v. lent, lend·ing v.t. **1.** To grant the use or possession of with the understanding that the thing or its equivalent will be returned. **2.** To grant the use of (money) at a stipulated rate of interest. **3.** To impart, as an abstract quality. **4.** To make available, as for aid or support. **5.** To adapt or suit (itself or oneself) to a specific purpose. — v.i. **6.** To make a loan or loans. [OE lǣn a loan] — **lend′er** n.

lending library A circulating library.

length (lengkth, length) n. **1.** Linear extent from end to end; usu., the longest dimension of a thing, as distinguished from its width and thickness. **2.** Extent from beginning to end, as of a period of time, series, book, word, etc. **3.** The state or quality of being long or prolonged, either in time or space. **4.** Duration or continuance, esp. in respect to time. **5.** The measurement along, extent of, or distance equivalent to something specified: arm's *length.* **6.** A piece or standard unit of something, measured longitudinally. **7.** Often pl. The limit of one's efforts, ability, etc.: to go to great *lengths.* **8.** In racing, the extent from front to back of a competing horse, boat, etc., used as a unit of estimating position. — **at length 1.** Finally. **2.** In full. [OE lengthu < lang long]

length·en (lengk′thən, leng′-) v.t. & v.i. To make or become longer.

length·wise (lengkth′wīz′, length′-) adv. In the direction or dimension of length; longitudinally. Also **length′ways′** (-wāz′). — adj. According to length; longitudinal.

length·y (lengk′thē, leng′-) adj. **length·i·er, length·i·est** Unusually or unduly long. — **length′i·ly** adv. — **length′i·ness** n.

le·ni·en·cy (lē′nē·ən·sē, lēn′yən·sē) n. The state or quality of being lenient. — **le′ni·ence.** — Syn. See MERCY.

le·ni·ent (lē′nē·ənt, lēn′yənt) adj. Gentle or merciful in disposition, effect, etc.; mild. [< L leniens, -entis, ppr. of lenire to soothe] — **le′ni·ent·ly** adv.

Len·i-Len·a·pe (len′ē·len′ə·pē) n. Lenape. Also **Len′ni-Len′a·pe.**

Len·in·ism (len′in·iz′əm) A modification of Marxism constituting the doctrine and practice of the Bolsheviks and the Communist Party in the Soviet Union under Lenin. — **Len′in·ist, Len′in·ite** n. & adj.

len·i·tive (len′ə·tiv) adj. Having the power or tendency to allay pain or distress; soothing. — n. That which soothes or mitigates. [< Med.L < L lenitus, pp. of lenire to soothe]

len·i·ty (len′ə·tē) n. The state or quality of being lenient. [< OF < L lenitas, -tatis softness]

lens (lenz) n. **1.** Optics A piece of glass or other transparent substance, bounded by two curved surfaces or by one curved and one plane surface, by which rays of light are made to converge or diverge. See illus. for FOCUS. **2.** Two or more such pieces in combination. **3.** Any device that concentrates or disperses radiation, etc., other than light by action similar to that of an optical lens. **4.** Anat. A transparent, biconvex body situated behind the iris of the eye and serving to focus an image on the retina. For illus. see EYE. [< L lens, lentis lentil; so called from the form]

lent (lent) Past tense and past participle of LEND.

Lent (lent) n. Eccl. The period of forty days, excluding Sundays, from Ash Wednesday to Easter, observed annually as a season of fasting, penitence, and self-denial. [Short for Lenten < OE lencten, lengten the spring]

Len·ten (len′tən) adj. Of, pertaining to, suitable for, or characteristic of Lent. Also **len′ten.**

len·til (len′təl) n. **1.** A leguminous plant, having broad pods containing flattish, edible seeds. **2.** The seed of this plant. [< F < L lenticula, dim. of lens, lentis lentil]

len·to (len′tō) Music adj. Slow. — adv. Slowly: a direction to the performer. — n. pl. **·tos** A slow movement or passage. [< Ital. < L lentus]

l'en·voi (len′voi, Fr. län·vwä′) See ENVOY². Also **l'en′voy.**

Le·o (lē′ō) n. A constellation, the Lion; also, the fifth sign of the zodiac. See ZODIAC. [< NL < L]

Le·o Mi·nor (lē′ō mī′nər) A constellation, the Lesser Lion.

Le·o·nid (lē′ə·nid) n. pl. **Le·o·nids** or **Le·o·ni·des** (lē·on′ə·dēz) Astron. One of the meteors of a meteor shower having its radiant point in the constellation Leo, and appearing annually about November 14.

le·o·nine (lē′ə·nīn, -nin) adj. Pertaining to, resembling, or characteristic of a lion. [< L leo, leonis lion]

leop·ard (lep′ərd) n. **1.** A large member of the cat family, native to Asia and Africa, having a tawny coat with dark brown or black spots grouped in rounded clusters: also called *panther.* **2.** Any of various similar felines, as the cheetah, jaguar, or snow leopard. **3.** The fur of a leopard. [< OF < LL < Gk. < leōn lion + pardos panther]

le·o·tard (lē′ə·tärd) n. Often pl. A close-fitting, stretchable garment worn by dancers, acrobats, etc. [after Jules Léotard, 19th c. French aerialist]

lep·er (lep′ər) n. One afflicted with leprosy. [< obs. leper leprosy < OF < L < Gk., orig. fem. of lepros scaly]

lep·i·dop·ter·ous (lep′ə·dop′tər·əs) adj. Belonging or pertaining to an order of insects comprising the butterflies and moths, characterized by four wings covered with minute scales. [< NL < Gk. *lepis, -idos* scale + *pteron* wing] Also **lep·i·dop'ter·al.** — **lep·i·dop'ter·an** *n. & adj.*

lep·o·rine (lep'ə·rīn, -rin) *adj.* Pertaining to or characteristic of hares. [< L *lepus, leporis* hare]

lep·re·chaun (lep'rə·kôn) *n.* In Irish folklore, a tiny elfin cobbler supposed to own hidden treasure. [< Irish < OIrish < *lu* little + *corpān,* dim. of *corp* body < L *corpus, -oris*]

lep·ro·sy (lep'rə·sē) *n. Pathol.* A chronic, communicable disease caused by a microorganism and characterized by nodular skin lesions, nerve paralysis, and physical mutilation: also called *Hansen's disease.* [See LEPER.]

lep·rous (lep'rəs) *adj.* 1. Affected with leprosy. 2. Of or resembling leprosy. — **lep'rous·ly** *adv.*

-lepsy *combining form* Seizure; attack: *catalepsy.* Also **-lep·sia.** [< Gk. *lepsis* seizure]

lep·ton (lep'ton) *n. pl.* **·tons** *Physics* An atomic particle of very small mass, as the electron, positron, or neutrino. [< Gk., neut. of *leptos* fine]

les·bi·an (lez'bē·ən) *Sometimes cap. n.* A homosexual woman. — *adj.* Pertaining to or characteristic of homosexual women. [< LESBIAN] — **les'bi·an·ism** *n.*

Les·bi·an (lez'bē·ən) *n.* 1. A native or inhabitant of Lesbos. 2. Sappho or one of her followers, alleged to have been homosexuals. — *adj.* 1. Of or pertaining to Lesbos or its inhabitants. 2. Of or pertaining to Sappho or her poetry. [< L < Gk. *Lesbos* Lesbos, the home of Sappho]

lèse ma·jes·ty (lēz' maj'is·tē) An offense against sovereign authority or a sovereign; treason. Also *Fr.* **lèse-ma·jes·té** (lez'mȧ·zhes·tā'). [< F < L *laesa,* fem. of *laesus,* pp. of *laedere* to injure + *majestas* majesty]

le·sion (lē'zhən) *n.* 1. *Pathol.* Any abnormal or harmful change in the structure of an organ or tissue. 2. An injury; damage. [< F < L *laesus,* pp. of *laedere* to injure]

less (les) Alternative comparative of LITTLE. — *adj.* 1. Not as great in quantity or degree; not as much. 2. Inferior in degree; smaller; lower: with *than.* — *adv.* To a smaller degree or extent; not as: followed by an adjective or adverb. — *n.* A smaller amount or part. — *prep.* With the subtraction of; minus. [OE *lǣs*]

-less *suffix of adjectives* 1. Devoid of; without: *blameless, harmless.* 2. Deprived of; lacking: *motherless, stemless.* 3. Not able to (do something): *restless;* not susceptible of (some action): *countless.* [OE *leas* free from]

les·see (les·ē') *n.* One to whom a lease is granted. [< AF *lessee,* OF *lesse,* pp. of *lesser, laissier* to let, leave]

less·en (les'ən) *v.t.* 1. To decrease. 2. To make little of; disparage. — *v.i.* 3. To become less. — **Syn.** See DECREASE.

less·er (les'ər) *adj.* Not as large or important; minor.

Lesser Bear The constellation Ursa Minor.

lesser panda The panda (def. 1).

les·son (les'ən) *n.* 1. An instance or experience from which useful knowledge may be gained. 2. A division or portion of a course of study. 3. An assignment to be studied or learned, as by a student. 4. A reprimand; reproof. 5. A portion of the Bible read or designated to be read at a religious service. — *v.t. Rare* 1. To give a lesson or lessons to; instruct. 2. To admonish; rebuke. [< OF < L *lectio, -ionis* a reading]

les·sor (les'ôr, les·ôr') *n.* One who grants a lease; a landlord letting property under a lease. [See LESSEE]

lest (lest) *conj.* 1. In order to prevent the chance that (something might happen); for fear that. 2. That: after expressions denoting anxiety: We worried *lest* the money should not last. [OE *(thȳ) lǣs the* (by the) less that]

let¹ (let) *v.* **let, let·ting** *v.t.* 1. To allow; permit. 2. To permit to pass, come, go, etc.: followed by a preposition: *Let* him by. 3. To cause; make: with *know* or *hear: Let* me know when you arrive. 4. To grant or assign, as a contract for work to be performed. 5. An auxiliary verb, usu. in the imperative, signifying: **a** An exhortation or command: *Let's* go! **b** Acquiescence; inability to prevent the inevitable: *Let* it rain. **c** An assumption or suggestion: *Let* x equal the sum of two numbers. 6. *Chiefly Brit.* To rent (a house, room, etc.) to a tenant. 7. To cause to flow, as blood. — *v.i.* 8. *Chiefly Brit.* To be rented: rooms to let. — **let alone** *Informal* And surely not; not to say: He can't even float, *let alone* swim. — **to let down** 1. To cause to fall or descend; loosen, as hair. 2. To disappoint. — **to let in** To insert into the substance, material, or body of something. — **to let loose** To set free; release. — **to let off** 1. To emit; release, as from pressure or tension. 2. To discharge, dismiss, or excuse, as from work or obligation. 3. To allow to escape a punishment or penalty. — **to let on** *Informal* 1. To make it known; reveal. 2. To pretend. — **to let out** 1. To give vent to; emit. 2. To release or unfasten in order to make a garment, etc., wider or longer. — **to let up** 1. To grow less;

abate. 2. To reduce tension. — **to let up on** *Informal* To cease to subject to force or severe treatment. ◆ See note under LEAVE¹. [OE *lǣtan*]

let² (let) *n.* In tennis or similar games, a service, point, etc., that must be repeated because of some interruption or hindrance of playing conditions. — *v.t.* let or **let·ted, let·ting** *Archaic* To hinder; impede. [OE *lettan,* lit., to make late]

-let *suffix of nouns* 1. Small; little: *booklet.* 2. A band or ornament for (a specified part of the body): *anklet.* [< OF *-let, -lette* < *-el* + *-et,* dim. suffixes]

let·down (let'doun) *n.* 1. A decrease; slackening, as of speed, force, or energy. 2. *Informal* Disappointment.

le·thal (lē'thəl) *adj.* 1. Causing death; deadly; fatal. 2. Pertaining to or characteristic of death. [< L *lethum, letum* death] — **le·thal·i·ty** (lē·thal'ə·tē) *n.*

le·thar·gic (li·thär'jik) *adj.* 1. Affected with or characterized by lethargy; drowsy; apathetic. 2. Pertaining to or causing lethargy. Also **le·thar'gi·cal.** — **le·thar'gi·cal·ly** *adv.*

leth·ar·gize (leth'ər·jīz) *v.t.* **·gized, ·giz·ing** To make lethargic.

leth·ar·gy (leth'ər·jē) *n. pl.* **·gies** 1. A state of indifference; apathy. 2. *Pathol.* Excessive drowsiness or abnormally deep sleep. [< OF < LL < Gk. *lēthargos* forgetful]

Le·the (lē'thē) *n.* 1. In Greek mythology, a river in Hades, a drink from which produced oblivion. 2. Oblivion. [< Gk. *lēthē* oblivion] — **Le·the·an** (lē·thē'ən) *adj.*

Lett (let) *n.* 1. A Latvian. 2. The Latvian language.

let·ter (let'ər) *n.* 1. A standardized sign or character used in writing or printing to represent a speech sound. 2. A written or printed message directed to a specified person or group of persons. 3. An official document granting certain rights or privileges to a specified person: a *letter* of credit. 4. Literal meaning: the *letter* of the law. 5. *pl.* Literature in general; literary profession: a man of *letters.* 6. *U.S.* An emblem in the form of the initial letter of a college, school, etc., conferred as an award for outstanding performance in athletics. — **to the letter** In accordance with the exact words or literal meaning. — *v.t.* 1. To inscribe letters on; mark with letters. 2. To print or inscribe by means of letters. — *v.i.* 3. To form letters, as by hand. [< OF < L *littera* letter of the alphabet, in pl., epistle] — **let'ter·er** *n.*

let·tered (let'ərd) *adj.* 1. Versed in letters; learned; literary; educated. 2. Inscribed or marked with letters.

let·ter·head (let'ər·hed') *n.* A printed heading, as a name and address, on a sheet of writing paper; also, a sheet of paper bearing such a heading.

let·ter·ing (let'ər·ing) *n.* 1. The act or art of forming letters; process of marking or stamping with letters. 2. Letters collectively, esp. a single example.

letter of credit A letter issued by a bank and authorizing the bearer to draw a specified amount of money from other banks, etc.

let·ter-per·fect (let'ər·pûr'fikt) *adj.* 1. Perfect in memorization, as an actor. 2. Correct in all details, as a piece of writing. — *adv.* Perfectly: said of memorizing or writing.

let·ter·press (let'ər·pres') *n. Printing* 1. Any printed matter, as distinguished from illustrations, etc. 2. Printing produced from type or similar raised surfaces.

letters patent *Law* The instrument granting a patent.

Let·tish (let'ish) *adj. & n.* Latvian.

let·tuce (let'is) *n.* A cultivated herb having crisp, edible leaves; also, the leaves. [< OF < L *lac, lactis* milk]

let·up (let'up') *n. Informal* 1. A lessening or relaxation, as of force or intensity; lull. 2. A respite; pause; interlude.

leuco- *combining form* White; lacking color: also, before vowels, **leuc-.** Also **leuko-, leuk-.** [< Gk. *leukos* white]

leu·co·cyte (lōō'kə·sīt) *n. Physiol.* A white or colorless blood corpuscle, constituting an important agent in protection against infectious diseases. Also spelled *leukocyte.*

leu·co·cyt·ic (lōō'kə·sit'ik) *adj.* 1. Of or pertaining to leucocytes. 2. Characterized by an excess of leucocytes.

leuk- Var. of LEUCO-.

leu·ke·mi·a (lōō·kē'mē·ə) *n. Pathol.* A generally fatal disease of the blood and bloodmaking tissues, characterized by a marked increase in the number of leucocytes, accompanied by anemia, exhaustion, etc. Also **leu·kae'mi·a.** [< LEUK- + Gk. *haima* blood]

leuko- See LEUCO-.

leu·ko·cyte (lōō'kə·sīt) See LEUCOCYTE.

le·vant (lə·vant') *n.* A kind of morocco leather having an irregularly grained surface. Also **Levant morocco.**

Levant (lə·vant') *n.* The regions bordering the eastern Mediterranean, between western Greece and western Egypt: usu. preceded by *the.* [< F < L *levare* to raise] — **Le·van·tine** (lə·van'tin, lev'ən·tīn, -tēn) *adj. & n.*

le·va·tor (lə·vā'tər) *n. pl.* **lev·a·to·res** (lev'ə·tôr'ēz, -tō'rēz) or **le·va·tors** *Anat.* A muscle that raises an organ or part. [< LL < L *levare* to raise]

lev·ee[1] (lev′ē) _n. U.S._ **1.** An embankment along the shore of a river, built for protection against floods. **2.** A landing place; wharf. [< F _lever_ to raise < L _levare_]

lev·ee[2] (lev′ē, lə·vē′) _n._ A reception or formal gathering of visitors, usu. held early in the day by a person of rank or distinction. [< F _levé_ an arising]

lev·el (lev′əl) _n._ **1.** Relative place, degree, or stage: a high _level_ of development. **2.** Position in the vertical dimension: the _level_ of the lower branches. **3.** A horizontal line or surface: sea _level_. **4.** A flat expanse, as of land. **5.** Any of various devices used to find the conformity of a line or surface with the horizontal plane. — **on the level** _Informal_ Without deception; fair and square. — **to find one's (or its) level** To come to the appropriate place on a vertical scale of distances, values, etc. — _adj._ **1.** Having a surface with no irregularities in height; even; flat. **2.** Conforming to a horizontal plane. **3.** Being in the same plane with or at the same height as something else. **4.** Measured so as to have a surface even with the edge of the container. **5.** Equal to something or someone else, as in importance, development, etc. **6.** Even, as in quality or tone. — **a level head** A calm and sensible mind. — **one's level best** _Informal_ The best one can possibly do. — _v._ **lev·eled** or **·elled, lev·el·ing** or **·el·ling** _v.t._ **1.** To give an even or horizontal surface to. **2.** To destroy by or as by smashing to the ground. **3.** To knock down. **4.** To bring to a common state or condition. **5.** To aim or point as a weapon. **6.** To aim or direct (something) with force of emphasis: to _level_ an accusation. — _v.i._ **7.** To bring persons or things to a common state or condition. **8.** To take measurements with a level. **9.** To aim a weapon at a target. **10.** _U.S. Slang_ To be honest. — _adv._ In an even line or plane. [< OF < L _libra_ a balance] — **lev′el·er** or **·el·ler** _n._ — **lev′el·ly** _adv._ — **lev′el·ness** _n._

level crossing A grade crossing.

lev·el·head·ed (lev′əl·hed′id) _adj._ Characterized by common sense and cool judgment. — **lev′el·head′ed·ness** _n._

level of usage _Ling._ A distinguishable variety of vocabulary, grammar, pronunciation, etc., considered appropriate for a class within the speech community.

lev·er (lev′ər, lē′vər) _n._ **1.** _Mech._ A device consisting of a rigid structure, often a straight bar, pivoting on a fixed support (the fulcrum), and serving to impart pressure or motion from a force or effort applied at one point to a resisting force at another point. **2.** Any of various tools, devices or parts operating on the above principle, as a crowbar. **3.** Any means of exerting effective power. — _v.t. & v.i._ To move or pry with or as with a lever. [< OF < L _levare_ to raise]

lev·er·age (lev′ər·ij, lē′vər-) _n._ **1.** The use of a lever. **2.** The mechanical advantage gained by use of a lever.

lev·er·et (lev′ər·it) _n._ A young hare less than a year old. [< AF, OF _levre_ hare]

Le·vi (lē′vī) In the Old Testament, a son of Jacob and Leah. _Gen._ xxix 34. — _n._ The tribe of Israel descended from him.

le·vi·a·than (lə·vī′ə·thən) _n._ **1.** A gigantic water beast mentioned in the Bible. **2.** Any enormous creature or thing.

Le·vis (lē′vīz) _n.pl._ Close-fitting, heavy denim trousers having rivets to reinforce points of greatest strain: a registered trade mark. [after _Levi_ Strauss, U.S. manufacturer]

lev·i·tate (lev′ə·tāt) _v._ **·tat·ed, ·tat·ing** _v.i._ **1.** To rise and float in the air, as through buoyancy or supposed supernatural power. — _v.t._ **2.** To cause to rise and float in the air. [< L _levis_ light, on analogy with _gravitate_] — **lev′i·ta·tor** _n._

lev·i·ta·tion (lev′ə·tā′shən) _n._ **1.** The act of levitating, or the state of being levitated. **2.** The illusion of suspending a heavy object or the human body in the air without support.

Le·vite (lē′vīt) _n._ In Jewish history, one of the tribe of Levi, from whom were chosen those who assisted the priests.

Le·vit·i·cal (lə·vit′i·kəl) _adj._ **1.** Of or pertaining to the Levites. **2.** Of or pertaining to the book of Leviticus.

Le·vit·i·cus (lə·vit′i·kəs) The third book of the Old Testament, consisting chiefly of a compilation of ceremonial laws.

lev·i·ty (lev′ə·tē) _n. pl._ **·ties 1.** Lack of seriousness; inappropriate gaiety; frivolity. **2.** Fickleness; inconstancy. **3.** Lightness. [< L _levis_ light]

levo- _combining form_ Turned or turning to the left: used in chemistry and physics. Also spelled _laevo-_. [< L _laevus_ left]

le·vo·ro·ta·to·ry (lē′vō·rō′tə·tôr′ē, -tō′rē) _adj._ _Optics_ Causing the plane of polarization of light to rotate to the left, or counterclockwise: said of certain crystals: opposed to _dextrorotatory_.

lev·u·lose (lev′yə·lōs) _n. Biochem._ Fructose. [< L _laevus_ left + -UL(E) + -OSE[2]]

lev·y (lev′ē) _v._ **lev·ied, lev·y·ing** _v.t._ **1.** To impose and collect by authority or force, as a tax, fine, etc. **2.** To enlist or

call up (troops, etc.) for military service. **3.** To prepare for, begin, or wage (war). — _v.i._ **4.** To make a levy. **5.** _Law_ To seize property by judicial writ in order to fulfill a judgment: usu. with _on_. — _n. pl._ **lev·ies 1.** The act of levying. **2.** That which is levied, as money or troops. [< OF < L _levare_ to raise] — **lev′i·er** _n._

lewd (lood) _adj._ **1.** Characterized by or inciting to lust or debauchery. **2.** Obscene; ribald; bawdy. [OE _lǣwede_ lay[2], unlearned] — **lewd′ly** _adv._ — **lewd′ness** _n._

lew·is·ite (loo′is·īt) _n. Chem._ An oily liquid, $C_2H_2Cl_3As$, used in chemical warfare as a blistering agent. [after W. L. _Lewis_, 1878–1943, U.S. chemist]

lex (leks) _n. pl._ **le·ges** (lē′jēz) _Latin Law._

lex·i·cog·ra·pher (lek′sə·kog′rə·fər) _n._ One who works at writing or compiling a dictionary.

lex·i·cog·ra·phy (lek′sə·kog′rə·fē) _n._ The practice or profession of compiling dictionaries. [< NL < Gk. < _lexikon_ lexicon + _graphein_ to write] — **lex′i·co·graph′ic** (-kō·graf′ik) or **·i·cal** _adj._ — **lex′i·co·graph′i·cal·ly** _adv._

lex·i·con (lek′sə·kon) _n._ **1.** A dictionary; esp., a dictionary of Latin, Greek, or Hebrew. **2.** A vocabulary or list of words relating to a particular subject, occupation, or activity. [< Gk. _lexikos_ pertaining to words]

Leyden jar _Electr._ A device for accumulating a charge of static electricity, consisting principally of a glass jar coated with tinfoil inside and out. [after _Leyden_, earlier name of Leiden, where it was invented]

li·a·bil·i·ty (lī′ə·bil′ə·tē) _n. pl._ **·ties 1.** The state or condition of being liable. **2.** That for which one is liable, as a financial obligation or debt. **3.** _pl._ In accounting, the entries on a balance sheet showing the debts or obligations of a business: opposed to _assets_. **4.** Any obstacle or hindrance.

li·a·ble (lī′ə·bəl) _adj._ **1.** Justly or legally responsible, as for damages; answerable. **2.** Subject or susceptible, as to injury, illness, etc. **3.** Officially obligated to be available. **4.** _U.S. Informal_ Likely. [< F < L _ligare_ to bind]

li·ai·son (lē′ā·zon′, lē·ā′zon, lē′ə·zon; _Fr._ lē·e·zôń′) _n._ **1.** A means or agency for maintaining or furthering communication or unity, as between parts of an armed force or department of a government. **2.** An illicit love affair. **3.** In spoken French and in many other languages, the carrying over of a final consonant to the initial vowel of a succeeding word, as in _il est arrivé_ (ē le tả·rē·vā′). [< F < L _ligare_ to bind]

li·ar (lī′ər) _n._ One who lies or utters falsehoods. [OE _lēogere_]

li·ba·tion (lī·bā′shən) _n._ **1.** A liquid ceremonially poured out, as in honor of a deity; also, the act of pouring such liquid. **2.** Humorously, a drink. [< F < L _libare_ to pour out (as an offering)]

li·bel (lī′bəl) _n._ **1.** _Law_ **a** A written statement or graphic representation, esp. in published form, that damages a person's reputation. **b** The act or crime of publishing such a statement. **2.** Any defamatory or grossly unflattering statement. — _v.t._ **·beled** or **·belled, ·bel·ing** or **·bel·ling 1.** To publish or perpetrate a libel against. **2.** To defame or discredit, as by false or malicious statements. [< OF < L _libellus_, dim. of _liber_ book] — **li′bel·er, li′bel·ler** _n._

li·bel·ous (lī′bəl·əs) _adj._ Constituting, containing, or like a libel. Also, _esp. Brit._, **li′bel·lous**. — **li′bel·ous·ly** _adv._

lib·er·al (lib′ər·əl, lib′rəl) _adj._ **1.** Characterized by or inclining toward opinions or policies favoring progress or reform, as in politics or religion. **2.** Not intolerant or prejudiced; broad-minded. **3.** Characterized by generosity or lavishness in giving. **4.** Given or yielded freely or in large quantity; ample. **5.** Not literal or strict: a _liberal_ interpretation of the law. **6.** Suitable for persons of broad cultural interests: _liberal_ arts. — _n._ One having liberal opinions or convictions, esp. in politics or religion. [< OF < L _liberalis_ pertaining to a freeman] — **lib′er·al·ly** _adv._

Lib·er·al (lib′ər·əl, lib′rəl) _adj._ Designating or belonging to one of various political parties, as the Liberal Party of Canada or Great Britain. — _n._ A member of such a party.

liberal arts A group of subjects or college courses including literature, languages, history, etc., distinguished from scientific, technical, or purely practical subjects.

lib·er·al·ism (lib′ər·əl·iz′əm) _n._ **1.** Liberal beliefs or policies, esp. in regard to politics, social changes, religion, etc. **2.** _Sometimes cap._ The policies of the Liberal Party.

lib·er·al·i·ty (lib′ə·ral′ə·tē) _n. pl._ **·ties 1.** The quality of being liberal in giving; generosity. **2.** Broad-mindedness.

lib·er·al·ize (lib′ər·əl·īz′) _v.t. & v.i._ **·ized, ·iz·ing** To make or become liberal. — **lib′er·al·i·za′tion** (lib′ər·əl·ə·zā′shən, -ī·zā′-, lib′rəl-) _n._ — **lib′er·al·iz′er** _n._

Liberal Party 1. One of the principal political parties of Canada. **2.** In Great Britain, a Whiggish political party formed in the 1830's and the major opponent of the Conservative Party until after World War I.

lib·er·ate (lib′ə·rāt) _v.t._ **·at·ed, ·at·ing 1.** To set free, as from bondage or confinement. **2.** To release from chemical combination, as a gas. **3.** _Informal_ To free from oppression or from conventions considered oppressive. [< L _liberatus_, pp. of _liberare_ to free] — **lib′er·a′tion** _n._

lib·er·a·tor (lib′ər·ā′tər) *n.* One who liberates; esp., one who emancipates a nation, people, etc.

lib·er·tine (lib′ər·tēn) *n.* One completely lacking in moral restraint; a profligate. — *adj.* Characteristic of a libertine. [< L *libertus* freedman] — **lib′er·tin·ism** *n.*

lib·er·ty (lib′ər·tē) *n. pl.* **·ties 1.** Freedom from oppression, tyranny, or the domination of a government not freely chosen. **2.** The state of being free, as from confinement or slavery. **3.** Freedom of thought or action, or exemption from forms of compulsion or indignity, regarded as a human right. **4.** An overly free, familiar, or disrespectful act or manner. **5.** Permission to be present in and make free use of a specified place: followed by *of.* **6.** In the U.S. Navy and other maritime services, official permission to be absent from one's ship or place of duty, usu. for less than 48 hours. — **at liberty 1.** Free; authorized or permitted (to do something). **2.** Not engaged in an activity or occupation; unemployed. **3.** Able to move about freely. [< F < L < *liber* free]

Liberty Bell The bell in Independence Hall, Philadelphia, rung July 4, 1776, to celebrate the adoption of the Declaration of Independence, and cracked in 1835.

Liberty Ship A type of U.S. cargo ship built in large numbers during World War II.

li·bid·i·nous (li·bid′ə·nəs) *adj.* Characterized by or inclining toward excesses of sexual desire; lustful. — **li·bid′i·nous·ly** *adv.* — **li·bid′i·nous·ness** *n.*

li·bi·do (li·bē′dō, -bī-′) *n.* **1.** Sexual desire or impulse. **2.** *Psychoanal.* The instinctual craving or drive behind all human activities. [< L, lust] — **li·bid′i·nal** (-bid′ə·nal) *adj.*

Li·bra (lī′brə, lē′-) *n.* A constellation, the Balance or Scales; also, the seventh sign of the zodiac. See ZODIAC. [< L]

li·brar·i·an (lī·brâr′ē·ən) *n.* **1.** One who has charge of a library. **2.** A person qualified by training for library service.

li·brar·y (lī′brer·ē, -brə·rē) *n. pl.* **·brar·ies 1.** A collection of books, pamphlets, etc.; esp., such a collection arranged to facilitate reference. **2.** A building, room, etc., housing such a collection. **3.** A commercial establishment that rents books. [< OF < L *liber, libri* book]

Library of Congress The national library of the U.S. in Washington, D.C., established in 1800.

li·brate (lī′brāt) *v.i.* **·brat·ed, ·brat·ing 1.** To move back and forth; oscillate. **2.** To be poised; hover. [< L < *libra* balance] — **li·bra′tion** *n.* — **lī′bra·to·ry** *adj.*

li·bret·tist (li·bret′ist) *n.* The writer of a libretto.

li·bret·to (li·bret′ō) *n. pl.* **·tos** or **·ti** (-tē) **1.** The verbal text of an opera or other large-scale vocal work. **2.** A book containing such a text. [< Ital., little book, dim. of *libro*]

Lib·y·an (lib′ē·ən) *adj.* Of or pertaining to Libya, its inhabitants, or their language. — *n.* **1.** A native or inhabitant of Libya. **2.** The Hamitic language of ancient Libya.

lice (līs) Plural of LOUSE.

li·cense (lī′sens) *n.* **1.** An official document giving permission to engage in a specified activity, perform a specified act, etc. **2.** Unrestrained liberty of action. **3.** Abuse of freedom or privilege; laxity. **4.** Deviation from or relaxation of established rules or standards, esp. for artistic effect: poetic *license.* — *v.t.* **·censed, ·cens·ing** To grant a license to or for; authorize. Also, *esp. Brit.*, **li′cence.** [< OF < L *licens, -entis,* ppr. of *licere* to be permitted] — **li′cens·a·ble** *adj.* — **li′cen·ser** or **li′cen·cer** or *Law* **li′cen·sor** *n.*

li·cen·see (lī′sən·sē′) *n.* One to whom a license has been granted. Also **li′cen·cee′.**

li·cen·ti·ate (lī·sen′shē·it, -āt) *n.* **1.** A person licensed to practice a certain profession: a *licentiate* in dental surgery. **2.** In some Continental universities, a person holding a degree intermediate between bachelor and doctor.

li·cen·tious (lī·sen′shəs) *adj.* Lacking in moral restraint; lewd. [< F < L *licentiosus*] — **li·cen′tious·ly** *adv.* — **li·cen′tious·ness** *n.*

li·chee (lē′chē) *n.* **1.** The edible fruit of a tree native to China, having a hard seed and sweet pulp enclosed within a thin, brittle shell: also **lichee nut. 2.** The tree itself. [< Chinese *li-chih*]

li·chen (lī′kən) *n.* Any of various flowerless plants composed of fungi and algae, commonly growing in flat patches on rocks, trees, etc. [< L < Gk., prob. < *leichein* to lick] — **li′chen·ous, li′chen·ose** (-ōs) *adj.*

lic·it (lis′it) *adj.* Lawful. [< F ult. < L *licere* to be allowed] — **lic′it·ly** *adv.* — **lic′it·ness** *n.*

lick (lik) *v.t.* **1.** To pass the tongue over the surface of. **2.** To remove or consume by taking with the tongue: often followed by *up, off,* etc. **3.** To move or pass lightly over or about: The flames *licked* the coals. **4.** *Informal* To defeat. **5.** *Informal* To thrash; beat. — *v.i.* **6.** To move quickly or lightly; flicker. — **to lick into shape** To put in proper form or condition. — **to lick one's chops** To show pleased anticipation. — *n.* **1.** A stroke of the tongue in licking. **2.** A small amount. **3.** *U.S.* A salt lick. **4.** *Informal* A blow; whack. **5.** *Often pl. Informal* An opportunity to do something; a turn. **6.** *Informal* A stroke; spell, as of work. — **a lick and a promise** *Informal* Hasty washing or cleaning. [OE *liccian*]

lick·e·ty-split (lik′ə·tē·split′) *adv. U.S. Informal* At full speed.

lick·ing (lik′ing) *n.* **1.** The act of one who or that which licks. **2.** *Informal* A whipping; beating.

lic·o·rice (lik′ə·ris, -rish) *n.* **1.** A perennial leguminous herb of Europe. **2.** The dried root of this plant, or an extract made from it, used in medicine and confections. **3.** A confection flavored with this extract. Also, *esp. Brit., liquorice.* [< AF, OF < LL < Gk. < *glykys* sweet + *rhiza* root]

lic·tor (lik′tər) *n.* In ancient Rome, one of the officers or guards who attended the chief magistrates, and who bore the fasces as a symbol of office. [< L, prob. < *ligare* to tie]

lid (lid) *n.* **1.** A hinged or removable cover placed at the top of a receptacle or over an opening. **2.** An eyelid. **3.** *Bot.* A top, as of a pyxis, separating at a transverse dividing line; an operculum. [OE *hlid*] — **lid′ded** *adj.* — **lid′less** *adj.*

lie¹ (lī) *v.i.* **lay, lain, ly·ing 1.** To be in a recumbent or prostrate position. **2.** To place oneself in a recumbent position; rest at full length: often with *down.* **3.** To be placed upon or rest against a surface, esp. in a horizontal position. **4.** To be buried, as in a grave or tomb. **5.** To be or remain in a specified condition or state: to *lie* dormant. **6.** To exist; be inherent: often followed by *in* or *within.* **7.** To occupy a location; be situated. **8.** To continue or extend: The future *lies* before us. ◆ See note under LAY¹. — **to lie in wait (for)** To wait in concealment so as to attack by surprise. — **to lie low** *Informal* To remain in concealment; conceal one's intentions. — **to lie with** To rest with; be up to: The choice *lies with* him. — *n.* **1.** The position, manner, or situation in which something lies; aspect. **2.** The resting place or haunt of an animal, bird, or fish. [OE *licgan*]

lie² (lī) *n.* **1.** An untrue statement made with the intent of deceiving; a falsehood. **2.** That which creates or is intended to produce a false impression. — **to give the lie (to) 1.** To accuse (someone) of lying. **2.** To expose as false. — **white lie** A false statement made with the intent of being polite or kind. — *v.* **lied, ly·ing** *v.i.* **1.** To make an untrue statement or statements, esp. with intent to deceive. **2.** To give an erroneous or misleading impression: Figures don't *lie.* — *v.t.* **3.** To put or promote (oneself or someone) into a specified situation by telling lies. [OE *lyge*]

— **Syn.** (noun) **1.** A *lie* is a statement, known to be untrue, and made with the intent to deceive. *Falsehood* leaves open the question of intent to deceive, and *untruth* often implies error rather than malice; both *falsehood* and *untruth* are also used euphemistically for *lie. Fib* and *story* are almost exclusively used of *falsehoods* told by young children, and both are generally regarded as trivial.

lied (lēd, *Ger.* lēt) *n. pl.* **lied·er** (lē′dər) A German song; esp., a ballad or lyric poem set to music. [< G]

Lie·der·kranz (lē′dər·kränts) *n.* A soft cheese similar to but milder than Limburger: a trade name. Also **lie′der·kranz.** [< G, lit., garland of songs]

lie detector A polygraph (def. 3) used to establish the truth or falsity of an accused person's statements.

lief (lēf) *adv.* Willingly; readily: used chiefly in the phrase **would as lief.** — *adj. Archaic* **1.** Dear; beloved. **2.** Willing; inclined. [OE *lēof* dear]

liege (lēj) *n.* **1.** A lord or sovereign to whom allegiance or feudal service is due. **2.** A vassal or subject owing allegiance to a lord or sovereign. — *adj.* **1.** Entitled to feudal allegiance, as of a vassal: now used chiefly in the phrase **liege lord. 2.** Bound in vassalage or owing allegiance to a lord or sovereign. [< OF < Med.L < *laeticus* free < OHG *ledig*]

lien (lēn, lē′ən) *n.* A legal right to claim or dispose of property in payment of or as security for a debt or charge. [< L *ligare* to tie]

lieu (lōō) *n.* Place; stead: now only in the phrase **in lieu of.** [ME *live* < OF < L *locus* place]

lieu·ten·an·cy (lōō·ten′ən·sē, *Brit.* lef·ten′ən·sē, or *Brit. Naval* lə·ten′-) *n.* The office, rank, or authority of a lieutenant.

lieu·ten·ant (lōō·ten′ənt, *Brit.* lef·ten′ənt, or *Brit. Naval* lə·ten′-) *n.* **1.** *Mil.* A commissioned officer holding either of two ranks, **first** or **second lieutenant,** the former ranking next below a captain. See tables at GRADE. **2.** *Naval* a *U.S.* A commissioned officer holding either of two ranks, **lieutenant** or **lieutenant (junior grade),** the former ranking next below a lieutenant commander and the latter next above an ensign. **b** *Brit. & Canadian* A commissioned officer ranking next below a lieutenant-commander. See tables at GRADE. **3.** One deputized to perform the duties of a superior. [< F < *lieu* place + *tenant,* ppr. of *tenir* to hold]

lieutenant colonel *Mil.* An officer ranking next above a major. Also *Brit. & Canadian* **lieu·ten·ant-col·o·nel** (lef·ten′ənt·ker′nəl). See tables at GRADE.

lieutenant commander *Naval* An officer ranking next above a lieutenant and next below a commander. Also *Brit. & Canadian* **lieu·ten·ant-com·man·der** (lə·ten′ənt·kə·man′dər). See tables at GRADE.

lieutenant general *Mil.* An officer ranking next above a major general. Also *Brit. & Canadian* **lieu·ten·ant-gen·er·al** (lef·ten′ənt·gen′ər·əl). See tables at GRADE.

lieutenant governor   1. *U.S.* An elected official who performs the duties of the governor of a State during his absence or disability or who replaces him in case of death or resignation. 2. In the British Empire, a deputy governor of a territory under the jurisdiction of a governor general.

life (līf)   *n.*   *pl.* **lives** (līvz)   1. The form of existence that distinguishes animals and plants from inorganic substances and dead organisms, characterized by metabolism, growth, reproduction, irritability, etc.   2. The characteristic state of an organism that has not died.   3. Existence regarded as a desirable condition: *life*, liberty, and the pursuit of happiness.   4. A spiritual state regarded as a continuation or perfection of animate existence after death: eternal *life*.   5. Living organisms collectively.   6. A living being; person: to save a *life*.   7. The period of an individual's existence between birth and death; also, a specified portion of this period.   8. A biography.   9. The period during which something continues to be effective, useful, etc.: the *life* of an engine.   10. Human affairs or relationships: daily *life*.   11. Manner of existence; characteristic activities, as of a specified group, locality, etc.: city *life*.   12. Energetic force; animation: full of *life*.   13. A source of liveliness; animating spirit: the *life* of the party.   14. A living model; also, a representation of such a model.   **— for dear life** With urgent effort, speed, etc.   **— for life** For the remainder of one's existence.   **— for the life of me** (**him**, etc.) Under any circumstances; at all: usu. with the negative.   **— to bring to life**   1. To make vital; animate.   2. To recall vividly to the mind or senses.   **— to come to life**   1. To regain consciousness.   2. To become animated.   3. To seem to be real or alive.   **— to take life** To kill.   [OE *līf*]

life belt   A life preserver in the form of a belt.

life·blood (līf′blud′)   *n.*   1. The blood necessary to life.   2. Anything indispensable to existence; vital force.

life·boat (līf′bōt′)   *n.*   A boat constructed and equipped for saving lives at sea in the event of shipwreck, storm, etc.; esp., such a boat carried on board a larger vessel.

life buoy   A life preserver, often in the form of a ring.

life expectancy   The probable length of life of an individual, esp. as predicted statistically.

life·guard (līf′gärd′)   *n. U.S.* An expert swimmer employed at a beach, etc., to protect the safety of bathers.

life insurance   Insurance on the life of an individual, providing payment to the beneficiary or beneficiaries upon the death of the insured or to the insured upon reaching a certain age. Also *Brit.* **life assurance.**

life jacket   A life preserver in the form of a jacket or vest.

life·less (līf′lis)   *adj.*   1. Not possessing the characteristics of living organisms.   2. Deprived of life; dead.   3. Not inhabited by or incapable of sustaining living organisms: a *lifeless* desert.   4. Lacking animation or vitality.   5. Exhibiting no signs of life.   **— life′less·ly** *adv.*   **— life′less·ness** *n.*

life·like (līf′līk′)   *adj.*   1. Resembling actual life.   2. Accurately representing a person or thing.   **— life′like′ness** *n.*

life line   1. A rope affording support to those in precarious situations.   2. Any route used for transporting vital supplies.

life·long (līf′lông′, -long′)   *adj.*   Lasting through life.

life net   A strong net designed to rescue those who jump or fall from great heights, used by firemen, etc.

life preserver   A buoyant device, either inflatable or filled with cork, kapok, etc., and made as a belt, jacket, or ring, used to keep afloat those in danger of drowning.

lif·er (lī′fər)   *n. Slang* One sentenced to prison for life.

life raft   A raftlike structure used as a rescue craft; esp., an inflatable rubber boat equipped with oars.

LIFE PRESERVERS
A Solid block cork.
B Cork ring buoy.
C Collar-type jacket.

life·sav·er (līf′sā′vər)   *n.*   1. One who saves another's life.   2. A person trained to rescue those in danger of drowning.   3. *Informal* One who or that which provides aid, relief, etc., in time of need.   **— life′sav′ing** *n. & adj.*

life-size (līf′sīz′)   *adj.*   Having the same size as the thing or person portrayed. Also **life′-sized′.**

life span   The extreme length of life regarded as biologically possible in an organism or the group to which it belongs.

life·time (līf′tīm′)   *n.*   The period of animate existence; also, the period of effective functioning: the *lifetime* of the car.

life·work (līf′wûrk′)   *n.*   The work of a productive lifetime.

lift (lift)   *v.t.*   1. To take hold of and raise to a higher place or position; hoist.   2. To move, direct, or cause to rise to a higher position or level.   3. To hold up.   4. To bring to a higher or more desirable degree or condition; exalt.   5. To emit in loud or clearly audible tones, as the voice: to *lift* a cry.   6. To subject (the face) to surgery in order to remove signs of age.   7. *Informal* To take surreptitiously; steal; also, to plagiarize.   **— v.i.**   8. To exert effort in attempting to raise something.   9. To yield to upward pressure; rise.   10. To become dispersed or move away by or as by rising: the fog *lifted*.   **— n.**   1. The act of lifting or raising.   2. The power or ability to lift or impart upward motion.   3. The height, distance, or degree to which something rises or is raised.   4. Assistance given by or as by raising.   5. A ride given to a traveler by or in the direction of his destination.   6. A feeling of exaltation, exhilaration, or well-being.   7. Elevated or erect position, bearing, etc.: the *lift* of her chin.   8. A machine or device used in lifting or hoisting.   9. An amount lifted or capable of being lifted.   10. *Brit.* An elevator.   11. Any of the layers of leather, etc., constituting the heel of a shoe.   12. *Aeron.* The component of aerodynamic forces acting on an aircraft, exerted perpendicular to the relative wind and generally opposing the pull of gravity.   [ME < ON *lypta* to raise in the air.]   **— lift′er** *n.*

lift-off (lift′ôf′, -of′)   *n. Aerospace* The vertical ascent of a rocket or spacecraft from its launching pad.

lig·a·ment (lig′ə·mənt)   *n.*   1. *Anat.* A band of firm, fibrous tissue forming a connection between bones, or supporting an organ.   2. A bond or connecting tie.   [< L *ligare* to bind]   **— lig′a·men′tal, lig′a·men′ta·ry, lig′a·men′tous** *adj.*

li·gan (lī′gən)   *n.* Lagan.

li·gate (lī′gāt)   *v.t.* **·gat·ed, ·gat·ing** To bind or constrict with a ligature.   [< L *ligatus*, pp. of *ligare*, to bind, tie]

lig·a·ture (lig′ə·chŏŏr, -chər)   *n.*   1. The act of tying up or constricting by binding. Also **li·ga·tion** (lī·gā′shən).   2. A band, strip, etc., used to tie, bind, or constrict.   3. In printing, a character consisting of two or more connected letters, as æ, fi, ffi.   4. *Music* A slur indicating a group of notes sung or played as a connected phrase; also, the group of notes thus indicated.   **— v.t.** To ligate.

light[1] (līt)   *n.*   1. *Physics* **a** The form of radiant energy that stimulates the organs of sight, having for normal human vision wavelengths ranging from about 3900 to 7700 angstroms and traveling at a speed of about 186,300 miles a second. **b** A closely related form of radiant energy not stimulating human vision; ultraviolet or infrared light.   2. The condition or medium that makes vision possible; illumination.   3. The sensation produced by stimulation of the organs of vision and visual centers of the brain.   4. Any source of brightness, as a lamp, the sun, etc.   5. An emission of brightness, esp. from a particular source or direction.   6. The daily illumination shed on the earth by the sun; daylight; also the period of daylight.   7. Mental or spiritual understanding or insight.   8. The state of being unhidden and observable: to come to *light*.   9. Way of being regarded; aspect: to see things in a new *light*.   10. *pl.* Ability and understanding: to live according to one's own *lights*.   11. A lively or intense expression on the face, esp. in the eyes.   12. An instance of kindling; ignition.   13. An opening admitting illumination, as a window.   14. In graphic arts: **a** The representation of light or atmosphere. **b** A part of a picture showing an illuminated area.   15. A person of authority or eminence; luminary: a lesser *light*.   **— in the light of** In view of; considering.   **— to see the light**   1. To come into being.   2. To be presented to public notice.   3. To become enlightened.   **— to strike a light** To ignite something, as a match, by friction.   **— adj.**   1. Full of light; bright.   2. Diluted or combined with white, as a color; pale.   **— v.** **light·ed** or **lit, light·ing**   *v.t.*   1. To ignite; kindle.   2. To illuminate or cause to illuminate.   3. To make bright, cheerful, animated, etc.   4. To guide or conduct with light.   **— v.i.**   5. To become ignited.   6. To become luminous, radiant, or bright: often with *up*.   [OE *lēoht*]

light[2] (līt)   *adj.*   1. Having little weight; not heavy.   2. Having little weight in proportion to bulk or size; low in specific gravity.   3. Having less than standard or correct weight.   4. Not burdensome or oppressive.   5. Not difficult or arduous.   6. Having comparatively little effect; not intense, severe, etc.   7. Not great in degree or concentration; thin: a *light* fog.   8. Exerting little force or pressure; gentle: a *light* tap.   9. Characterized by buoyancy or ease in motion.   10. Moving or working swiftly and skillfully; deft.   11. Not clumsy, coarse, or massive in form or appearance; delicate.   12. Intended or enjoyed as entertainment; not lofty or heroic: *light* verse.   13. Slight in importance or consequence.   14. Frivolous; trivial.   15. Easily distracted or diverted; flighty.   16. Morally unrestrained; wanton.   17. Slightly faint or delirious; giddy.   18. Easily eaten or digested.   19. Comparatively low in alcoholic content: *light* wines.   20. Well-leavened; spongy or airy in texture: *light* biscuits.   21. Crumbly in texture; porous: *light* soil.   22. Relatively swift and maneuverable: a *light* cruiser.   23. *Mil.* **a** Designating the less massive types of weapons or equipment. **b** Formerly, designating troops or units with relatively less massive equipment: *light* cavalry.   24. *Meteorol.* Designating a breeze moving at 4 to 7 miles per hour. **25.** In phonetics, prosody, etc., designating an unaccented or unstressed syllable or vowel. **— to make light of** To treat or consider as trifling. *— v.i.* **light·ed** or **lit, light·ing 1.** To descend and settle down after flight, as a bird. **2.** To happen or come, as by chance: with *on* or *upon.* **3.** To get down, as from a horse or carriage. **4.** To fall; strike, as a blow. **— to light into** *U.S. Informal* To attack; assail. **— to light out** *U.S. Informal* To depart in haste. *— adv.* **1.** Lightly. **2.** Without encumbrance or excess equipment. [OE *lēoht, liht*]

light·en[1] (līt′n) *v.t.* **1.** To make light or bright; illuminate. *— v.i.* **2.** To become light; grow brighter. **3.** To glow with light; gleam. **4.** To emit or display lightning.

light·en[2] (līt′n) *v.t.* **1.** To reduce the weight or load of; make less heavy. **2.** To make less oppressive, troublesome, etc.; diminish the severity of. **3.** To relieve, as of distress, uneasiness, etc. *— v.i.* **4.** To become less heavy.

light·er[1] (līt′ər) *n.* One who or that which lights; esp., a device used to light cigarettes, cigars, etc.

light·er[2] (līt′ər) *Naut. n.* A bargelike vessel used in loading or unloading ships, or in transporting loads for short distances. *— v.t. & v.i.* To transport (goods) by lighter. [< Du. *lichten* to make light, unload]

light·er·age (lī′tər·ij) *n.* **1.** The removal or conveying of cargo by lighter. **2.** A price charged for this service.

light·er-than-air (lī′tər·thən·âr′) *adj. Aeron.* Designating aircraft, as balloons, dirigibles, etc., that depend for flight on a specific gravity less than that of air.

light·face (līt′fās′) *n. Printing* Type having characters formed of light, thin lines.

light-fin·gered (līt′fing′gərd) *adj.* Expert at picking pockets, etc. **— light′-fin′gered·ness** *n.*

light-foot·ed (līt′fŏŏt′id) *adj.* **1.** Stepping with buoyancy and grace. **2.** Running lightly and swiftly. Also *Poetic* **light′foot′. — light′-foot′ed·ly** *adv.* **— light′-foot′ed·ness** *n.*

light-head·ed (līt′hed′id) *adj.* **1.** Frivolous; giddy. **2.** Dizzy. **— light′-head′ed·ly** *adv.* **— light′-head′ed·ness** *n.*

light-heart·ed (līt′här′tid) *adj.* Free from care; blithe; gay. **— light′heart′ed·ly** *adv.* **— light′heart′ed·ness** *n.*

light·house (līt′hous′) *n.* A tower or similar structure equipped with a powerful beacon, erected at or near a dangerous place to serve as a warning or guide for ships.

light·ing (līt′ing) *n.* **1.** The providing of light or the state of being lighted. **2.** A system or apparatus supplying illumination, as in a public building, theater, etc. **3.** The arrangement or effect of lighted areas in a painting, etc.

light·ly (līt′lē) *adv.* **1.** With little weight or pressure; gently. **2.** To a slight degree; moderately. **3.** With a swift, buoyant step or motion. **4.** In a carefree manner or spirit. **5.** With insufficient seriousness or concern; frivolously; irresponsibly: often with the negative. **6.** With little esteem or appreciation; slightingly. **7.** *Archaic* Easily.

light-mind·ed (līt′mīn′did) *adj.* Thoughtless; frivolous. **— light′-mind′ed·ly** *adv.* **— light′-mind′ed·ness** *n.*

light·ness[1] (līt′nis) *n.* **1.** The state or quality of being illuminated or bright. **2.** Paleness of color.

light·ness[2] (līt′nis) *n.* **1.** The quality of having relatively little weight, force, etc. **2.** Buoyancy or ease of motion. **3.** Freedom from sorrow or care. **4.** Lack of seriousness.

light·ning (līt′ning) *n.* **1.** A sudden flash of light caused by the discharge of atmospheric electricity between electrified regions of cloud, or between a cloud and the earth. **2.** The discharge itself. [ME *lighten* to flash]

lightning bug *U.S.* A firefly.

lightning rod A pointed metal rod that protects buildings from lightning by grounding it harmlessly through a cable.

light opera Operetta.

light quantum *Physics* A photon.

lights (līts) *n.pl.* The lungs, esp. of animals used as food. [ME *lihtes*; so called from their light weight]

light·ship (līt′ship′) *n.* A vessel equipped with warning lights, signals, etc., and moored in dangerous waters as a guide to ships.

light·some (līt′səm) *adj.* **1.** Untroubled by care; cheerful; gay. **2.** Buoyant, airy, or graceful. **3.** Frivolous; flighty. **— light′some·ly** *adv.* **— light′some·ness** *n.*

light·weight (līt′wāt′) *n.* **1.** A person or animal of much less than average weight. **2.** A boxer or wrestler weighing between 127 and 135 pounds. **3.** *U.S. Informal* An unimportant, incompetent, or inadequate person. *— adj.* Of less than average or required weight.

light-year (līt′yir′) *n. Astron.* A unit of interstellar space measurement equal to the distance traversed by light in one year, approximately six trillion miles.

lig·ne·ous (lig′nē·əs) *adj.* Having the composition, texture, or appearance of wood. [< L < *lignum* wood]

ligni- *combining form* Wood. Also, before vowels, **lign-.** Also **ligno-.** [< L *lignum* wood]

lig·nite (lig′nīt) *n.* A compact, carbonized, brownish vegetable substance often retaining a woodlike structure, forming a fuel intermediate between peat and bituminous coal. [< F] **— lig·nit′ic** (-nit′ik) *adj.*

lig·num vi·tae (lig′nəm vī′tē) **1.** A tree of tropical America, having hard, greenish brown wood. **2.** The wood of this tree. **3.** Any of various related or similar trees. [< NL < L, wood of life]

lik·a·ble (lī′kə·bəl) *adj.* Of a nature to be liked; attractive; pleasing. Also **like′a·ble. — lik′a·ble·ness** *n.*

like[1] (līk) *v.* **liked, lik·ing** *v.t.* **1.** To take pleasure in; enjoy. **2.** To feel affectionately toward; be fond of. **3.** To desire; prefer: I *like* that one. *— v.i.* **4.** To feel disposed; choose: Do as you *like.* *— n. Usu. pl.* Preference; inclination: chiefly in the phrase **likes and dislikes.** [OE *lician*]

like[2] (līk) *prep.* **1.** Having a close resemblance to; similar to. **2.** With the characteristics or qualities of: to smell *like* a rose. **3.** Characteristic or typical of: How *like* him to behave that way! **4.** Indicative of; likely to result in: It looks *like* rain. **5.** As though having the need for: with *feel*: to feel *like* resting. **6.** Such as: cities *like* London, Rome, New York. **7.** In the manner of: He used the board like a hammer. **— like anything** (or **blazes, mad, hell,** etc.) *Informal* With great intensity, force, effort, etc. *— adj.* **1.** Having the same or similar characteristics; related. **2.** Equal or nearly equal; equivalent. **3.** Similar to what is portrayed or represented, as a portrait. **— like . . . , like . . .** As (the one is), so (is the other): *Like* father, *like* son. *— adv.* **1.** *Dial.* or *Informal* Probably: *Like* enough he'll go. **2.** *Dial.* or *Illit.* To a certain degree; somewhat: I'm hungry *like.* **3.** *U.S. Slang* or *Illit.* A meaningless interpolation, as before adjectives, etc.: It's *like* cool. *— n.* **1.** Anything similar or in the same category: preceded by *the*: physics, chemistry, and the *like.* **2.** One of equal value, standing, etc.: We will not see his *like* again. *— conj.* **1.** *Informal* or *Illit.* As; in the manner that: It turned out *like* you said. **2.** *Informal* As if: It looks *like* it's going to rain. [OE *gelic*]

-like *suffix of adjectives* **1.** Resembling or similar to: *wavelike.* **2.** Having the characteristics of: *childlike.* [< LIKE[2]] ◆ Compounds in *-like* are usu. solid, but are hyphenated when three *l's* occur together, as in *shell-like.*

like·li·hood (līk′lē·hŏŏd) *n.* **1.** The state or quality of being probable; probability. **2.** Something probable.

like·ly (līk′lē) *adj.* **·li·er, ·li·est 1.** Having or showing an apparent tendency or possibility: He is *likely* to go. **2.** Seemingly about to happen; imminent; probable: His promotion is *likely.* **3.** Apparently true; plausible; believable. **4.** Suitable; appropriate: a *likely* spot. **5.** Capable; promising: a *likely* lad. *— adv.* Probably.

like-mind·ed (līk′mīn′did) *adj.* Having similar opinions, purposes, tastes, etc.

lik·en (lī′kən) *v.t.* To represent as similar; compare.

like·ness (līk′nis) *n.* **1.** The state or quality of being like; resemblance. **2.** A pictorial representation; portrait; image. **3.** Imitative form; guise: to take on the *likeness* of someone.

like·wise (līk′wīz′) *adv.* **1.** Moreover; also; too. **2.** In like manner; similarly.

lik·ing (lī′king) *n.* **1.** Feeling of attraction or affection; fondness. **2.** Preference; taste.

li·lac (lī′lak, -lək, -lok) *n.* **1.** A flowering shrub of the olive family, having fragrant purplish or white flowers. **2.** A light pinkish purple color. *— adj.* Having a purplish color. [< F < Sp. < Arabic < Persian *lilak* bluish]

lil·i·a·ceous (lil′ē·ā′shəs) *adj.* Belonging to or characteristic of the lily family. [< LL < L *lilium* lily]

Lil·li·put (lil′i·put, -pət) In Swift's *Gulliver's Travels* (1726), a country inhabited by a race of tiny people. **— Lil/li·pu′tian** *adj., n.*

lilt (lilt) *n.* **1.** A lively quality of speech, voice, song, etc., with pronounced variations of pitch. **2.** A light, buoyant motion or manner. *— v.i. & v.t.* To speak, sing, move, etc., in a cheerful rhythmic manner. [ME *lulte*]

lil·y (lil′ē) *n. pl.* **·ies 1.** Any of numerous wild or cultivated plants, having bulbous rootstocks and showy, usu. funnel-shaped flowers. **2.** Any of various other plants resembling a lily, as the calla or the water lily. *— adj.* Resembling a lily in whiteness, delicacy, beauty, etc. [OE < L *lilium*]

lil·y-liv·ered (lil′ē·liv′ərd) *adj.* Cowardly; fainthearted.

lil·y-of-the-val·ley (lil′ē·əv·thə·val′ē) *n. pl.* **lil·ies-of-the-valley** A perennial herb having small, fragrant white flowers. Also **lily of the valley.**

lily pad One of the large, floating leaves of the water lily.

li·ma bean (lī′mə) **1.** A species of the common bean, having large, flat, edible seeds. **2.** The seed of this plant, eaten as a vegetable. Also **Lima bean.** [after *Lima*, Peru]

limb[1] (lim) *n.* **1.** A part of the animal or human body attached to but distinct from the torso, as an arm, leg, or wing. **2.** One of the major divisions of a tree trunk; a large branch.

3. An extended or branching part, division, etc. **4.** A person or thing regarded as a part of a larger body, group, etc. **— out on a limb** *U.S. Informal* In a risky, vulnerable, or questionable position. [OE *lim*] **— limb′less** *adj.*

limb² (lim) *n. Astron.* The edge of the disk of the sun, moon, or other heavenly body. [< F < L *limbus* edge, border]

limbed (limd) *adj.* **1.** Having limbs. **2.** Having or characterized by a (specified kind of) limb or (a specified number of) limbs: used in combination: *strong-limbed; four-limbed.*

lim·ber¹ (lim′bər) *adj.* **1.** Pliant; flexible. **2.** Able to bend or move easily; lithe. **— v.t.** **1.** To make pliant. **— v.i.** **2.** To exercise so as to become limber: with *up.* [Origin uncertain] **— lim′ber·ly** *adv.* **— lim′ber·ness** *n.*

lim·ber² (lim′bər) *n. Mil.* A two-wheeled, detachable vehicle at the forepart of a gun carriage. **— v.t. & v.i.** To attach a limber to (a gun). [Origin uncertain]

lim·bo¹ (lim′bō) *n. pl.* **·bos** **1.** *Theol.* A region on the edge of hell for the souls of the righteous who died before the coming of Christ, and those of infants who die before baptism. **2.** A place or condition for the relegation of unwanted or forgotten persons, things, etc. [< L *limbus* border]

lim·bo² (lim′bō) *n. pl.* **·bos** A dance popular in the West Indies, in which dancers pass under a bar placed at successively lower levels. [Origin uncertain]

Lim·burg·er cheese (lim′bûr′gər) A soft, white cheese having a strong odor and flavor. Also **Lim′burg cheese, Lim′burg·er.** Also **lim′burg·er.** [after *Limburg*, Belgium]

lime¹ (līm) *n.* A white, earthy substance, calcium oxide, CaO, prepared by calcining limestone or other forms of calcium carbonate, and used in mortars and cements. When dry it is called **quicklime** or **unslaked lime**, becoming **slaked lime** upon the addition of water. **— v.t.** **limed, lim·ing** To treat, mix, or spread with lime. [OE *līm*]

lime² (līm) *n.* **1.** A small, green, lemonlike citrus fruit whose juice is used for flavoring, in beverages, etc. **2.** The tropical tree yielding this fruit. [< F < Sp. *lima* < Arabic *līmah*]

lime³ (līm) *n.* The European linden tree. [OE *lind* linden]

lime·kiln (līm′kil′, -kiln′) *n.* A kiln in which limestone, seashells, etc., are burned to produce lime.

lime·light (līm′līt′) *n.* **1.** Public attention or notice. **2.** A bright light used to illuminate a performer, stage area, etc., and originally produced by heating lime to incandescence.

lim·er·ick (lim′rik, -ə-rik) *n.* A humorous verse of five anapestic lines. Also **Lim′er·ick.** [? from the line "Will you come up to *Limerick*,"]

lime·stone (līm′stōn′) *n.* A sedimentary rock composed wholly or in part of calcium carbonate.

lime·wa·ter (līm′wô′tər, -wot′ər) *n.* An aqueous solution of calcium hydroxide, used in medicine.

lim·ey (lī′mē) *n. pl.* **lim·eys** *U.S. Slang* **1.** A British sailor. **2.** Any Englishman. [from the former British maritime practice of drinking *lime* juice to prevent scurvy]

lim·it (lim′it) *n.* **1.** The furthest or utmost extent, range, degree, etc., beyond which an activity, power, or function cannot or may not proceed: one's *limit* of endurance. **2.** *Usu. pl.* The boundaries or extent of a specified area. **3.** An amount or quantity established as the greatest permissible: Four fish are the *limit.* **4.** *Math.* A definite quantity or value that a series is conceived or proved to approach but never reach. **— off limits** Forbidden to military personnel except on official business. **— the limit** *Informal* **1.** One who or that which tries one's patience, credulity, etc., to the utmost. **2.** To the utmost extent: usu. with *go.* **— v.t.** To set a bound or bounds to; confine; restrict. [< L *limes, limites*] **— lim′it·a·ble** *adj.* **— lim·i·ta·tive** (lim′ə-tā′tiv) *adj.* **— lim′it·er** *n.*

lim·i·ta·tion (lim′ə-tā′shən) *n.* **1.** That which limits; restriction; shortcoming. **2.** The act of limiting, or the state of being limited. **3.** *Law* **a** A restrictive condition. **b** A legally fixed period within which certain acts must be performed. [< L *limitatio, -onis*]

lim·it·ed (lim′it·id) *adj.* **1.** Confined within or defined by a limit or limits; restricted. **2.** Falling short of fullness or impressiveness: a *limited* success. **3.** Having powers restricted by constitutional law or authority, as a government. **4.** Of a train, bus, etc., making few stops. **5.** *Chiefly Brit. & Canadian* Restricted in liability to the amount invested by shareholders in its stock: a *limited* company. **— n.** A limited train, bus, etc. **— lim′it·ed·ly** *adv.* **— lim′it·ed·ness** *n.*

lim·it·ing (lim′it·ing) *adj. Gram.* Denoting adjectives that indicate the number or quantity of nouns rather than describe them, as *these* words, *seven* swans.

lim·it·less (lim′it·lis) *adj.* Having no limit; boundless.

limn (lim) *v.t.* To draw or paint; also, to describe in words. [ME < OF < L *illuminare*] **— lim·ner** (lim′nər) *n.*

Li·moges (lē·mōzh′, *Fr.* lē·môzh′) *n.* A type of fine porcelain manufactured at Limoges, France. Also **Limoges ware.**

lim·ou·sine (lim′ə·zēn′, lim′ə·zēn) *n.* **1.** A large automobile, originally having a closed compartment for passengers and an open driver's seat under a projecting roof. **2.** Any large, luxurious automobile. [< F]

limp¹ (limp) *v.i.* **1.** To walk with a halting or irregular step, as with an injured leg or foot. **2.** To progress in an irregular or labored manner. **— n.** The manner of walking of one who is lame. [OE *lemphealt* lame] **— limp′er** *n.*

limp² (limp) *adj.* **1.** Lacking stiffness or firmness; flabby. **2.** Lacking force or vigor; weak. [Origin uncertain] **— limp′ly** *adv.* **— limp′ness** *n.*

lim·pet (lim′pit) *n.* Any of various small marine animals having conical shells and noted for their ability to cling to rocks. [OE < LL *lampreda* limpet, lamprey]

lim·pid (lim′pid) *adj.* **1.** Characterized by crystalline clearness; transparent. **2.** Characterized by clarity, lucidity, or purity, as of style. **— Syn.** See CLEAR. [< L *limpidus* clear] **— lim·pid′i·ty, lim′pid·ness** *n.* **— lim′pid·ly** *adv.*

lim·y (lī′mē) *adj.* **lim·i·er, lim·i·est** Containing or resembling lime.

lin·age (lī′nij) *n.* **1.** The number of lines in a piece of written or printed matter. **2.** Alignment. Also *lineage.*

linch·pin (linch′pin′) *n.* A pin placed through the end of an axle in order to keep a wheel from sliding off. [OE *lynis*]

lin·den (lin′dən) *n.* Any of various shade trees having soft, white wood, heart-shaped leaves, and fragrant, cream-colored flowers: also called *basswood.* [OE *lind* linden]

line¹ (līn) *n.* **1.** A slender, continuous mark or indentation, as that drawn by a pen, pencil, or pointed tool. **2.** Any narrow band or strip resembling such a mark. **3.** A wrinkle or crease in the skin. **4.** Contour or profile, as of the edge of an area. **5.** A division or boundary between adjoining areas; border. **6.** A demarcation or limit separating contrasting concepts, kinds of behavior, etc. **7.** A row of persons or things. **8.** A chronological succession of persons: the royal *line.* **9.** A row of written or printed words. **10.** A short letter; note. **11.** A single row of words forming a verse, as of a stanza. **12.** Course of movement or progress; route: *line* of march. **13.** Course of action, thought, or performance: a *line* of thought. **14.** *Often pl.* General plan or concept, as of form, content, etc.: a work on heroic *lines.* **15.** Alignment; agreement; accord: to bring into *line.* **16.** Scope or field of activity, ability, etc.: that work is not in my *line.* **17.** Kind of work; occupation. **18.** Merchandise of a particular sort. **19.** *pl.* The words of an actor's or performer's part. **20.** *pl. Brit.* A certificate of marriage. **21.** *pl.* Lot in life; luck: hard *lines.* **23.** *U.S. Slang* A glib manner of speech intended to ingratiate or persuade. **24.** A pipe, conduit, or system of channels to convey liquids, gas, electricity, etc. **25.** In telephonic communication, etc.: **a** A wire or cable carrying power signals. **b** A system of such connections. **c** A connection or channel of communication: to keep a *line* open. **26.** Any system of public transportation over an established route or routes. **27.** The roadbed, track, or system of tracks of a railroad. **28.** A rope, string, cord, or the like, as used in fishing, measuring, etc. **29.** *Math.* The theoretical trace or course of a moving point, conceived of as having length, but no other dimension. **30.** In the arts: **a** The representation of form by the use of strokes, rather than by shading or coloring. **b** The distinctive form or contours of any artistic creation. **31.** *Mil.* **a** A trench or rampart. **b** A system of fortifications presenting an extended front. **c** *Often pl.* The disposition of troops: the front *lines.* **d** The combatant forces, as distinguished from the supporting services and the staff. **32.** In the naval services, those officers in charge of combat operations. **33.** In bridge, a horizontal division of the score, separating points counting toward game, written below it, and bonus points, written above it. **— in line** **1.** So as to form a line or row. **2.** In accordance with accepted standards or limitations. **— in line for** Next in order for. **— on a line** At the same level; evenly aligned. **— on the line** Paid directly and promptly. **— out of line** **1.** Not in conformity with accepted standards or practices. **2.** Insubordinate; unruly. **— to get a line on** *U.S. Informal* To acquire information about. **— to hold the line** **1.** To maintain a defense or opposition. **2.** To wait while maintaining an open telephone connection. **3.** In football, to prevent the opposing team from gaining ground. **— v. lined, lining** *v.t.* **1.** To mark with lines. **2.** To place in a line. **3.** To form a row or line along; border. **4.** To indicate by or as by lines; sketch. **5.** In baseball, to bat (a ball, hit, etc.) in an approximately horizontal trajectory. **— v.i.** **6.** To form a line; assume positions in a line: usually with *up.* **— to line out** In baseball, to be retired by hitting a line drive that is caught. **— to line up** **1.** To form a line. **2.** To bring into alignment. **3.** To take a stand, as in support of something. **4.** To gather; marshal. **5.** To compare. [OE *līne* cord]

line² (līn) *v.t.* **lined, lin·ing** **1.** To put a covering or facing on the inner surface of. **2.** To constitute a covering or surface for: Tapestries *lined* the room. **3.** To fill or stuff, as with money, food, etc. [OE *līn* flax]

lin·e·age¹ (lin′ē·ij) *n.* **1.** Line of descent from a progenitor. **2.** Ancestry; family; stock. [< OF < L *linea* line]

line·age² (lī′nij) See LINAGE.

lin·e·al (lin′ē·əl) *adj.* **1.** Being or occurring in the direct line of descent. **2.** Pertaining to or based upon direct descent. **3.** Consisting of lines; linear. — **lin′e·al·ly** *adv.*

lin·e·a·ment (lin′ē·ə·mənt) *n.* **1.** A facial contour or feature. **2.** A distinguishing characteristic.

lin·e·ar (lin′ē·ər) *adj.* **1.** Of or pertaining to a line or lines. **2.** Involving or pertaining to length. **3.** Composed of lines. **4.** Resembling a line. — **lin′e·ar·ly** *adv.*

Linear A, Linear B See under MINOAN.

linear measure 1. Measurement by length. **2.** A unit or system of units for measuring length. See table inside back cover.

line drive In baseball, a batted ball that travels in an approximately horizontal trajectory: also called *liner.*

line·man (līn′mən) *n. pl.* **·men** (-mən) **1.** A man who installs or repairs telephone or electric power lines: also *linesman.* **2.** A man who inspects a railroad track. **3.** In football, a center, guard, tackle, or end. **4.** In surveying, a man who holds the line, tape, or chain.

lin·en (lin′ən) *n.* **1.** A fabric woven from the fibers of flax. **2.** Articles or garments made of linen, or now often of cotton: bed *linen.* — *adj.* **1.** Made of the textile fiber of flax. **2.** Made of linen. [OE *linen* made of flax]

line of force *Physics* A hypothetical line in a field of force, coinciding at every point with the direction of the field.

lin·er¹ (lī′nər) *n.* **1.** A ship or airplane operated by a transportation line. **2.** In baseball, a line drive. **3.** One who or that which marks or produces lines.

lin·er² (lī′nər) *n.* **1.** One who makes or fits linings. **2.** Something used as a lining.

lines·man (līnz′mən) *n. pl.* **·men** (-mən) **1.** In certain games, as tennis, an official making decisions on play at the lines of the court. **2.** In football, the official marking the distances gained or lost in each play. **3.** A lineman (def. 1).

line-up (līn′up′) *n.* **1.** An arrangement of persons or things in a line. **2.** In sports: **a** The formation of players drawn up for action. **b** The players. **c** A list of the team members playing at the start of a game. **3.** In police work, a row of possible criminal suspects. Also **line′up′.**

lin·ey (lī′nē) See LINY.

ling (ling) *n. pl.* **ling** or **lings** A codlike food fish of the North Atlantic. [? < Du. *leng*]

-ling¹ *suffix of nouns* **1.** Little; young: *duckling.* **2.** Minor; petty: often used contemptuously: *princeling.* **3.** A person or thing related to or characterized by: *worldling.* [OE]

-ling² *suffix* Forming adverbs and adjectives: **1.** (from nouns) Toward: *sideling.* **2.** (from adjectives) Being; becoming: *darkling.* Also **-lings.** [OE *-ling, -linga*]

lin·ger (ling′gər) *v.i.* **1.** To stay on as if reluctant to leave. **2.** To proceed in a slow manner; dawdle. **3.** To continue to live or exist; endure. **4.** To pause or dwell with interest, pleasure, etc.: usually with *over.* — *v.t.* **5.** To spend or waste (time, one's life, etc.) idly or wearisomely: with *away* or *out.* [Northern ME *lenger* to delay] — **lin′ger·er** *n.*

lin·ge·rie (län′zhə·rē, län′zhə·rā′, *Fr.* laṅ·zhrē′) *n.* Women's light undergarments, nightgowns, etc. [< F]

lin·ger·ing (ling′gər·ing) *adj.* **1.** Protracted; drawn out. **2.** Long-lasting; enduring. **3.** Slow. — **ling′er·ing·ly** *adv.*

lin·go (ling′gō) *n. pl.* **·goes 1.** Language: used contemptuously or humorously of a tongue one does not understand. **2.** The specialized vocabulary and idiom of a profession, class, etc.: medical *lingo.* [< Pg. < L *lingua* tongue]

lin·gua fran·ca (ling′gwə fraṅ′kə) **1.** Any jargon or pidgin used as a commercial or trade language, as pidgin English. **2.** A mixture of French, Spanish, Italian, Greek, and Arabic, spoken in Mediterranean ports. [< Ital., lit., language of the Franks]

lin·gual (ling′gwəl) *adj.* Of or pertaining to the tongue or a tonguelike part. [< Med.L < L *lingua* tongue]

lin·gui·form (ling′gwi·fôrm) *adj.* Tongue-shaped.

lin·guist (ling′gwist) *n.* **1.** One who is fluent in several languages. **2.** A student of or specialist in linguistics.

lin·guis·tic (ling·gwis′tik) *adj.* Of or pertaining to language or linguistics. Also **lin·guis′ti·cal.** — **lin·guis′ti·cal·ly** *adv.*

lin·guis·tics (ling·gwis′tiks) *n.pl.* (*construed as sing.*) The scientific study of language.

linguistic stock A family of languages, including a parent language together with all the languages derived from it.

lin·i·ment (lin′ə·mənt) *n.* A liquid rubbed on the skin to relieve pain and stiffness. [< L *linire* to anoint]

lin·ing (lī′ning) *n.* An inner surface or facing inserted in a garment, container, etc., as for protection, reinforcement, etc.; also, the material used.

link (lingk) *n.* **1.** One of the loops, rings, or interlocking parts constituting a chain. **2.** A single element in a series, sequence, or set: a weak *link* in his argument. **3.** That which joins or connects separate parts, concepts, etc. **4.** A single sausage. **5.** In surveying, etc., the hundredth part of a chain, equal to 7.92 inches. — *v.t. & v.i.* To join or connect

by or as by links; interlock; couple; unite. — **Syn.** See UNITE. [ME *linke* < Scand.]

link·age (ling′kij) *n.* **1.** The act of linking, or the state of being linked. **2.** A system of links.

link·ing verb (ling′king) *Gram.* A verb that merely connects the subject and predicate of a sentence without asserting action, esp. the verbs *be, appear, become, feel, look, seem, smell, sound,* and *taste:* also called *copula.*

links (lingks) *n.pl.* A golf course. [OE *hlinc* slope]

Lin·ne·an (li·nē′ən) *adj.* Pertaining to Linnaeus or his system of classifying plants and animals. Also **Lin·nae′an.**

lin·net (lin′it) *n.* A common songbird of Europe. [< OF < L *linum* flax; from its feeding on flax seeds]

li·no·le·um (li·nō′lē·əm) *n.* A material used as a floor covering, etc., made from oxidized linseed oil and cork pressed upon canvas or burlap. [< L *linum* flax + *oleum* oil]

Li·no·type (lī′nə·tīp) *n.* A typesetting machine operated by a keyboard, and casting a complete line of type on a single metal piece: a trade name. Also **li′no·type.**

li·no·typ·er (lī′nə·tīp′ər) *n.* One who operates a Linotype. Also **li′no·typ·ist.**

lin·seed (lin′sēd′) *n.* Flaxseed. [OE *linsǣd*]

linseed oil A yellowish oil made from flaxseed and used as a drying agent in the preparation of oil paints, linoleum, etc.

lin·sey-wool·sey (lin′zē·wŏŏl′zē) *n. pl.* **-wool·seys** A coarse cloth woven of linen and wool or cotton and wool threads. [ME *lin* linen + *saye* cloth + WOOL]

lint (lint) *n.* **1.** Bits of thread, fluff, etc. **2.** A downy substance used as a surgical dressing. **3.** *U.S.* The fibers of seeds of unginned cotton. [ME *linnet* lint] — **lin′ty** *adj.*

lin·tel (lin′təl) *n.* A horizontal part above the opening of a door or window, supporting the structure above it. [< OF < LL *lintellus, limitellus,* dim. of *limes, limites* limit]

lint·ers (lin′tərz) *n.pl. U.S.* The short fibers adhering to cotton seeds after ginning.

lin·y (lī′nē) *adj.* **lin·i·er, lin·i·est 1.** Resembling a line; narrow. **2.** Marked with lines or streaks. Also *liney.*

li·on (lī′ən) *n.* **1.** A large, tawny or brownish gray carnivorous mammal of the cat family, native to Africa and SW Asia, the adult male having a shaggy mane. ◆ Collateral adjective: *leonine.* **2.** Any of various animals related or similar to the lion, as the mountain lion. **3.** One of noble courage, great strength, etc. **4.** A celebrity. — **the lion's share** The largest portion; an unduly large part. [< F < L *leo* < Gk. *león*] — **li′on·ess** (-is) *n.fem.*

Li·on (lī′ən) *n.* The constellation and sign of the zodiac Leo.

li·on·heart·ed (lī′ən·härt′id) *adj.* Admirably brave.

li·on·ize (lī′ə·nīz) *v.t.* **·ized, ·iz·ing** To treat or regard as a celebrity. — **li′on·i·za′tion** *n.* — **li′on·iz′er** *n.*

lip (lip) *n.* **1.** One of the two folds of flesh that bound the mouth and serve as organs of speech. ◆ Collateral adjective: *labial.* **2.** A marginal part or structure resembling this. **3.** The rim or edge of any opening or cavity. **4.** The flared edge of a pitcher, bell, etc. **5.** *Slang* Brash and impudent talk; sass. **6.** *Music* The shaping and control of the mouth in playing a wind instrument. **7.** *Anat.* A labium. **8.** *Bot.* Either of the two divisions, upper or lower, of a corolla or calyx. — **to button one's lip** *Slang* To stop talking; shut up. — **to hang on (someone's) lips** To listen to with rapt attention. — **to keep a stiff upper lip** To maintain one's fortitude. — **to smack one's lips** To express anticipatory or remembered gusto; gloat. — *v.t.* **lipped, lip·ping 1.** To touch with the lips; apply the lips to. **2.** *Music* In playing a wind instrument, to produce the correct pitch of (a tone) by adjusting the position of the lips. — *adj.* **1.** Of, pertaining to, or applied to the lips. **2.** Made or formed by the lips or a lip; labial. **3.** Insincere; hypocritical. [OE *lippa*]

lip·oid (lip′oid) *adj.* Resembling fat. — *n. Biochem.* A fatlike substance. [< Gk. *lipos* fat]

lipped (lipt) *adj.* Having a lip or lips.

lip·py (lip′ē) *adj.* **·pi·er, ·pi·est** *Slang* Sassy.

lip-read (lip′rēd′) *v.t. & v.i.* **-read** (red), **-read·ing** (rēd′ing) To interpret (speech) by watching the movements of lips.

lip reading The interpretation of speech by watching the movement of the lips, as by the deaf. — **lip reader**

lip·stick (lip′stik′) *n.* A pastelike cosmetic, usu. in the form of a small cylinder, used to color the lips.

liq·ue·fac·tion (lik′wə·fak′shən) *n.* The process of liquefying, or the state of being liquid.

liq·ue·fi·er (lik′wə·fī′ər) *n.* **1.** One who or that which liquefies. **2.** An apparatus in which ⊙ gas is liquefied.

liq·ue·fy (lik′wə·fī) *v.t. & v.i.* **·fied, ·fy·ing** To convert into or become liquid. [< L *liquere* to be liquid + *facere* to make] — **liq′ue·fi′a·ble** *adj.*

li·ques·cent (li·kwes′ənt) *adj.* Becoming or likely to become liquid; melting. [< L *liquere* to become liquid] — **li·ques′cence, li·ques′cen·cy** *n.*

li·queur (li·kûr′) *n.* An alcoholic beverage usu. made by adding sugar syrup and flavoring to brandy: also called *cordial*. [< F < OF *licur*]

liq·uid (lik′wid) *adj.* 1. Capable of flowing or of being poured. 2. Clear and flowing, as sounds. 3. Clear and bright; limpid. 4. Free and facile, as movement; fluent. 5. Consisting of or readily converted into cash. 6. *Physics* Not gaseous or solid. 7. *Phonet.* Of consonants, produced without friction; vowellike, as (l) and (r). — *n.* 1. A substance in that state in which the molecules move freely among themselves but remain in one mass; a fluid that is not a gas. 2. *Phonet.* The sound (l) or (r), or sometimes other sonorants. [< F < L *liquere* to be liquid] — **li·quid·i·ty** (li·kwid′ə·tē), **liq′uid·ness** *n.* — **liq′uid·ly** *adv.*

liquid air An extremely cold, liquid mixture of nitrogen and oxygen, used chiefly as a refrigerant.

liq·ui·date (lik′wə·dāt) *v.* **·dat·ed**, **·dat·ing** *v.t.* 1. To pay off or settle, as an obligation or debt. 2. To wind up the affairs of (a business firm, etc.) by using the assets to settle debts or obligations. 3. To convert into cash, as securities. 4. To do away with. 5. *Slang* To kill or murder. — *v.i.* 6. To settle one's debts. [< Med.L *liquidare* to make liquid]

liq·ui·da·tion (lik′wə·dā′shən) *n.* The act or procedure of liquidating, or the state of being liquidated. — **to go into liquidation** Of a business firm, to cease transacting business and to settle debts or discharge obligations.

liquid measure A unit or system of units for measuring liquids. See table inside back cover.

liquid oxygen Oxygen liquefied by a reduction of temperature and an increase of pressure, used extensively to oxidize other components of rocket fuels: also called *lox*.

liq·uor (lik′ər) *n.* 1. Any alcoholic beverage; esp., distilled spirits, as whisky, brandy, etc. 2. A liquid such as broth, juice, etc. — *v.t.* 1. *Slang* To ply with alcoholic drink: usu. with *up*. — *v.i.* 2. To drink liquor, esp. in large amounts: usu. with *up*. [< OF < L *liquor*]

liq·uo·rice (lik′ə·ris, -rish) See LICORICE.

li·ra (lir′ə, *Ital.* lē′rä) *n. pl.* **li·re** (lir′ə, *Ital.* lē′rā) or **li·ras** (lir′əz) The monetary unit of Italy equivalent to 100 centesimi: in 1960 worth about ⅒ of a U.S. cent; also a coin of this value. [< Ital. < L *libra* pound]

lisle (lil) *n.* 1. A fine twisted cotton thread used in knitting hosiery, etc. Also **lisle thread.** 2. A fabric, usu. knitted, made from such thread. [after *Lisle*, now Lille, France]

lisp (lisp) *n.* 1. A speech defect or affectation in which the sibilants (s) and (z) are articulated like (th) in *thank* and (**t**h) in *this*. 2. The act or habit of speaking with a lisp. 3. A sound resembling a lisp. — *v.t. & v.i.* 1. To pronounce with a lisp. 2. To speak in a childlike manner. [OE *āwlyspian*]

lis·some (lis′əm) *adj.* 1. Flexible; pliant. 2. Agile; lithe. Also **lis′som.** — **lis′some·ly** *adv.* — **lis′some·ness** *n.*

list[1] (list) *n.* 1. An itemized series of names, words, etc., usu. recorded in a set order. 2. A classification of persons or things belonging in the same category: usu. with *on*. — *v.t.* 1. To place on or in a list. 2. To include in a register, catalogue, etc. [< OF < OHG *lista*] — **list′a·ble** *adj.*

list[2] (list) *n.* 1. A strip, edging, or selvage, as of cloth. 2. Fabric consisting of or woven like a selvage. — *v.t.* To edge with list. [OE *līste*]

list[3] (list) *v.t. & v.i. Naut.* Of a vessel, to lean or tilt to one side. — *n.* A leaning or inclination to one side.

list[4] (list) *Poetic v.t.* 1. To listen to; hear. — *v.i.* 2. To listen. [OE *hlyst* hearing]

lis·ten (lis′ən) *v.i.* 1. To make conscious use of the sense of hearing; be attentive in order to hear. 2. To pay attention; give heed. 3. To be influenced or persuaded. — **to listen in** 1. To participate in hearing (a broadcast, etc.). 2. To eavesdrop. [OE *hlysnan*] — **lis′ten·er** *n.*

list·er (lis′tər) *n. U.S.* A plow with a double moldboard that produces a ridged furrow.

list·ing (lis′ting) *n.* 1. The act of one who or that which lists. 2. An entry in a list. 3. A list.

list·less (list′lis) *adj.* Languidly indifferent; apathetic; lackadaisical. — **list′less·ly** *adv.* — **list′less·ness** *n.*

list price The retail price of merchandise, from which a discount is sometimes made.

lists (lists) *n.pl.* 1. The barriers enclosing the jousting field of a medieval tournament. 2. The field thus enclosed. 3. Any arena or scene of conflict. — **to enter the lists** To engage in a contest or controversy. [OE *līste* border]

lit (lit) Alternative past tense and past participle of LIGHT[1] and LIGHT[2].

lit·a·ny (lit′ə·nē) *n. pl.* **·nies** *Eccl.* A liturgical form of prayer consisting of a series of supplications said by the clergy, to which the congregation repeat a fixed response. [OE < LL < Gk. *litaneuein* to pray]

-lite *combining form Mineral.* Stone; stonelike. [< F < Gk. *lithos* stone]

li·ter (lē′tər) *n.* In the metric system, a measure of capacity equal to the volume of one kilogram of water at 4° C. and normal atmospheric pressure, or to 1.0567 liquid quarts. Also, *esp. Brit., litre.* See table inside back cover.

lit·er·a·cy (lit′ər·ə·sē) *n.* The state of being literate.

lit·er·al (lit′ər·əl) *adj.* 1. Restricted to the exact, stated meaning; not figurative: the *literal* sense of the Scriptures. 2. Following the exact words and order of an original: a *literal* translation. 3. Tending to recognize or accept stated meanings only; matter-of-fact. 4. Free from figurative language, etc., as a literary style; factual. [< OF < LL < *littera* letter] — **lit·er·al·i·ty** (lit′ər·al′ə·tē), **lit′er·al·ness** *n.*

lit·er·al·ly (lit′ər·ə·lē) *adv.* 1. In a literal manner; in the strictest sense. 2. Actually; really. 3. In effect; virtually.

lit·er·ar·y (lit′ə·rer′ē) *adj.* 1. Of, pertaining to, or treating of literature. 2. Characteristic of or appropriate to literature. 3. Versed in or devoted to literature. 4. Professionally engaged in the field of literature. [< L *litterarius*]

lit·er·ate (lit′ər·it) *adj.* 1. Able to read and write. 2. Educated; cultured. 3. Literary. — *n.* 1. One able to read and write. 2. An educated person. [< L *littera* letter]

lit·er·a·ti (lit′ə·rä′tē, -rä′tī) *n.pl.* 1. Men of letters; scholars. 2. Literate or educated persons collectively. [< L]

lit·er·a·tim (lit′ə·rä′tim, -rä′-) *adv.* Letter for letter; literally. [< L]

lit·er·a·ture (lit′ər·ə·chŏŏr, -chər, lit′rə·chər) *n.* 1. Written works collectively, esp. those of enduring importance, exhibiting creative imagination and artistic skill. 2. Poetry, fiction, essays, etc., as distinguished from factual writing. 3. The writings of a particular period, language, etc.: Elizabethan *literature*. 4. The writings pertaining to a particular subject. 5. The occupation of a professional writer. 6. *Informal* Any printed matter used or distributed for advertising. [< L *littera* letter]

lith- Var. of LITHO-.

-lith *combining form* Stone; rock. [< Gk. *lithos* stone]

lith·arge (lith′ärj, li·thärj′) *n.* A yellowish monoxide of lead, PbO, made by heating lead in air, and used in glassmaking, as a pigment, etc. [< F *litarge* < L *lithargyrus* < Gk. *lithargyros* silver scum < *lithos* stone + *argyros* silver]

lithe (līth) *adj.* Bending easily or gracefully; supple; pliant; limber. [OE, soft] — **lithe′ly** *adv.* — **lithe′ness** *n.*

lithe·some (līth′səm) *adj.* Lithe.

lith·i·a (lith′ē·ə) *n.* Lithium oxide, Li_2O, a white, caustic compound. [< NL < Gk. *lithos* stone]

-lithic *combining form* Pertaining to a (specified) anthropological stage in the use of stone implements: *Neolithic*.

lith·i·um (lith′ē·əm) *n.* A soft, silver-white element (symbol Li), the lightest of the metals, found only in combination. See ELEMENT. [< NL < Gk. *lithos* stone]

litho- *combining form* Stone. Also, before vowels, **lith-**. [< Gk. *lithos* stone]

lith·o·graph (lith′ə·graf, -gräf) *n.* A print produced by the process of lithography. — *v.t.* To produce or reproduce by lithography. — **li·thog·ra·pher** (li·thog′rə·fər) *n.* — **lith′o·graph′ic** or **·i·cal** *adj.* — **lith′o·graph′i·cal·ly** *adv.*

li·thog·ra·phy (li·thog′rə·fē) *n.* The art or process of producing printed matter from a flat stone or zinc or aluminum plate on which a drawing or design has been made in a greasy or water-repellent material.

lith·o·sphere (lith′ə·sfir) *n.* The solid crust of the earth, as distinguished from the atmosphere and the hydrosphere.

Lith·u·a·ni·an (lith′ōō·ā′nē·ən) *adj.* Of or pertaining to Lithuania, its people, or their language. — *n.* 1. A native or inhabitant of Lithuania. 2. The Balto-Slavic language of the Lithuanians.

lit·i·ga·ble (lit′ə·gə·bəl) *adj.* Subject to legal dispute.

lit·i·gant (lit′ə·gənt) *n.* A participant in a lawsuit. — *adj.* Engaged in litigation. [< F < L < *litigare* to litigate]

lit·i·gate (lit′ə·gāt) *v.* **·gat·ed**, **·gat·ing** *v.t.* 1. To bring (a dispute, claim, etc.) before a court of law for decision; contest at law. — *v.i.* 2. To engage in a lawsuit. [< L < *lis*, *litis* lawsuit + *agere* to do, act] — **lit′i·ga′tor** *n.*

lit·i·ga·tion (lit′ə·gā′shən) *n.* 1. The act or process of engaging in legal action. 2. A judicial contest; lawsuit.

li·ti·gious (li·tij′əs) *adj.* 1. Inclined to litigation; quarrelsome. 2. Subject to litigation. 3. Of or pertaining to litigation. — **li·ti·gious·ly** *adv.* — **li·ti′gious·ness** *n.*

lit·mus (lit′məs) *n.* A blue dyestuff made from certain lichens. It is turned red by acids and remains blue when treated with an alkali. [< AF < ON < *litr* color + *mosi* moss]

litmus paper Paper dyed with litmus, used to test acidity.

li·tre (lē′tər) See LITER.

lit·ter (lit′ər) *n.* 1. Waste materials, scraps, or objects carelessly strewn about. 2. Untidy or chaotic condition; mess. 3. The young brought forth at one birth by any mammal normally having several offspring at one time. 4. A stretcher for carrying sick or wounded persons. 5. A couch carried between shafts by men or beasts of burden. 6. Straw, hay, etc., spread in animal pens, or over plants as protection. — *v.t.* 1. To make untidy or unsightly by carelessly discarding trash, etc. 2. To drop or scatter carelessly. 3. To provide with litter, as for bedding. 4. To give birth to (pups, kittens, etc.) — *v.i.* 5. To give birth to a litter of young. 6. To drop or scatter refuse. [< OF < Med.L < L *lectus* bed]

lit·ter·bug (lit′ər·bug′) *n. U.S. Slang* One who litters public places, roads, etc., with trash.

lit·tle (lit′l) *adj.* **lit·tler** or (for defs. 2 and 3) **less, lit·tlest** or (for defs. 2 and 3) **least 1.** Small, or smaller compared to others, in physical size: a *little* house. **2.** Not long; short; brief: a *little* time; a *little* distance away. **3.** Small or relatively small in quantity or degree: *little* wealth; *little* probability. **4.** Having small force or effectiveness; weak: a *little* effort. **5.** Not having great influence, power, or significance; minor; trivial. **6.** Narrow or limited in viewpoint; petty: *little* minds. — *adv.* **less, least 1.** Only slightly; not much: He sleeps *little*. **2.** Not at all: used before a verb: She *little* suspects. — *n.* **1.** A small amount: Give me a *little*. **2.** An insignificant amount: *Little* can be done about it. **3.** A short while or distance. — **little by little** By small degrees; gradually. — **to make little of** To treat or regard as inconsequential. [OE < *lȳt* small] — **lit′tle·ness** *n.*

little theater An amateur or community theater group.

lit·to·ral (lit′ər·əl) *adj.* Of a shore or coastal region. — *n.* A shore and its adjacent areas. [< L *lit(t)us, -oris* seashore]

li·tur·gi·cal (li·tûr′ji·kəl) *adj.* Of or associated with public worship, ritual, etc. Also **li·tur′gic.** — **li·tur′gi·cal·ly** *adv.*

lit·ur·gy (lit′ər·jē) *n. pl.* **·gies 1.** In various religions, the prescribed form for public worship; religious ritual. **2.** The rite of the Eucharist. [< Med.L < Gk. *leitourgia* public duty, ult. < *laos* people + *ergon* work]

liv·a·ble (liv′ə·bəl) *adj.* **1.** Suitable or agreeable for living in. **2.** Worth living; tolerable. **3.** Agreeable, as for companionship. Also **live′a·ble.**

live[1] (liv) *v.* **lived, liv·ing** *v.i.* **1.** To function as an animate organism; be alive. **2.** To remain alive: as long as you *live*. **3.** To remain or persist, as in the mind. **4.** To remain valid or operative; endure. **5.** To have as one's home; reside: with *in* or *at*. **6.** To use as one's sole or customary nourishment: with *on*: to *live* on air. **7.** To maintain or support oneself: with *on* or *by*: to *live* on one's income. **8.** To pass life in a specified manner: to *live* in peace. **9.** To regulate one's life, as in accordance with principles, etc.: to *live* by a strict code. **10.** To enjoy a varied or satisfying life. — *v.t.* **11.** To spend or pass (life, time, etc.). **12.** To put into practice: to *live* one's religion. — **to live down** To live or behave so as to expiate the memory of (an error, crime, etc.). — **to live in** To reside, as a domestic servant, at one's place of employment. — **to live through** To survive or withstand (an experience). — **to live up to 1.** To satisfy (an ideal, expectations, etc.). **2.** To fulfill (a bargain, obligation, etc.). [OE *libban, lifian*]
— **Syn. 5.** Dwell, reside, abide.

live[2] (līv) *adj.* **1.** Functioning as an animate organism; alive. **2.** Pertaining to, characteristic of, or abounding in life. **3.** Of present interest and importance: a *live* issue. **4.** Forceful and energetic; dynamic. **5.** Burning or glowing: a *live* coal. **6.** Vivid or brilliant, as color. **7.** Charged with electricity: a *live* wire. **8.** Capable of being detonated, as a bomb. **9.** In television, radio, etc., consisting of or performed by persons present at the time of transmission. **10.** In mechanical use, having motion or the power to impart motion or force. **11.** In printing, publishing, etc., ready or retained for use: *live* copy. **12.** In sports, being in play, as a ball.

live·bear·er (līv′bâr′ər) *n.* An ovoviviparous fish, as a guppy. — **live′bear′ing** *adj.*

lived (līvd) *adj.* Having a (specified kind of) life or life span: used in combination: *long-lived*.

live·li·hood (līv′lē·hŏŏd) *n.* Means of supporting or maintaining one's existence. [ME < OE < *līf* life + *lād* way]

live·long (liv′lông′, -long′) *adj.* Long or seemingly long in passing; entire: the *livelong* day. [ME *lefe longe*, lit., lief long; *lief*, here orig. intens., was later confused with *live*]

live·ly (līv′lē) *adj.* **·li·er, ·li·est 1.** Full of vigor or motion; energetic. **2.** Arousing activity or excitement: a *lively* tune. **3.** Vivid; keen: a *lively* imagination. **4.** Striking and forceful to the mind: a *lively* impression. **5.** Filled with activity: a *lively* day. **6.** Invigorating; brisk: a *lively* breeze. **7.** Bouncing readily, as a ball; resilient. — *adv.* In a lively manner; briskly: now usu. in the expression to **step lively,** to hurry up. [OE *līflīce*] — **live′li·ly** *adv.* — **live′li·ness** *n.*

li·ven (lī′vən) *v.t. & v.i.* To make or become lively or cheerful: often with *up.* — **liv′en·er** *n.*

live oak Any of several evergreen trees having hard, wood.

liv·er[1] (liv′ər) *n.* **1.** *Anat.* The largest glandular organ of vertebrates, secreting bile and active in metabolism, in man situated just under the diaphragm and on the right side. ◆ Collateral adjective: *hepatic.* **2.** A similar digestive gland in invertebrates. **3.** Food consisting of or prepared from the liver of certain animals. [OE *lifer*]

liv·er[2] (liv′ər) *n.* **1.** One who lives in a specified manner: a luxurious *liver.* **2.** A dweller.

liv·er·ied (liv′ər·ēd) *adj.* Dressed in livery, as a servant.

liv·er·ish (liv′ər·ish) *adj. Informal* Feeling or exhibiting supposed symptoms of disordered liver; bilious; irritable.

liv·er·wort (liv′ər·wûrt′) *n.* **1.** Any mosslike cryptogam forming mats in damp, shady places. **2.** A hepatica.

liv·er·wurst (liv′ər·wûrst′) *n.* A sausage made of or containing ground liver. [< G *leberwurst*]

liv·er·y (liv′ər·ē) *n. pl.* **·er·ies 1.** The distinctive clothing or uniform worn by male household servants. **2.** The distinguishing dress of an organization or group. **3.** Characteristic garb or outward appearance. **4.** The stabling and care of horses for pay. **5.** *U.S.* A livery stable. [< OF *livree* gift of clothes by a master to a servant < L *liber* free]

liv·er·y·man (liv′ər·ē·mən) *n. pl.* **·men** (-mən) A man who keeps or works in a livery stable.

livery stable A stable where horses and vehicles are cared for or kept for hire.

lives (līvz) Plural of LIFE.

live·stock (līv′stok′) *n.* Domestic farm animals, as cattle, horses, and sheep, esp. when raised for profit.

live wire 1. A wire carrying an electric current or potential. **2.** *Informal* An energetic, enterprising person; a go-getter.

liv·id (liv′id) *adj.* **1.** Having the skin abnormally discolored, as: **a** Flushed, purplish, etc., as from intense emotion. **b** Black-and-blue, as from contusion. **2.** Having a leaden pallor; bluish gray. **3.** *Informal* Furious; enraged. [< F < L *livere* to be livid] — **liv′id·ly** *adv.* — **liv′id·ness, li·vid·i·ty** (li·vid′ə·tē) *n.*

liv·ing (liv′ing) *adj.* **1.** Alive; animate; not dead. **2.** Of or characteristic of everyday life: *living* conditions. **3.** Used or intended for maintaining existence: a *living* wage. **4.** Having contemporary value, force, or application: *living* languages. **5.** Of or pertaining to those who are alive. **6.** Lifelike; real: the *living* image of his father. — *n.* **1.** The state of one who or that which lives. **2.** Those that are alive: preceded by *the.* **3.** Manner or conduct of life: virtuous *living.* **4.** Means of supporting existence; livelihood.

living death A prolonged painful existence.

living room A room designed and furnished for the general use, social activities, etc., of a household; sitting room.

liz·ard (liz′ərd) *n.* **1.** Any of various reptiles typically having elongate, scaly bodies, long tails, and four legs, as the chameleon, iguana, skink, etc. **2.** Loosely, any similar reptile or amphibian. **3.** Leather made from the skin of a lizard. [< OF < L *lacerta*]

-'ll Contracted form of SHALL or WILL (*v.*) or of TILL (*prep.*).

lla·ma (lä′mə) *n.* A camellike, humpless ruminant of South America, having thick, woolly hair, and frequently used as a beast of burden. [< Sp. < Quechua]

lla·no (lä′nō, *Sp.* lyä′nō) *n. pl.* **·nos** (-nōz, *Sp.* -nōs) A flat, treeless plain, as those of the SW U.S. and northern Latin America. [< Sp., plain, flat < L *planus*]

lo (lō) *interj.* See! observe!: *Lo* and behold! [OE *lā*]

loach (lōch) *n.* Any of various fresh-water fishes related to the carp and minnow. [< F *loche*]

LLAMA
(3½ to 4 feet high at shoulder)

load (lōd) *n.* **1.** The weight or quantity placed upon and sustained by a vehicle, bearer, surface, etc. **2.** A quantity borne or conveyed: often used in combination: *carload.* **3.** Something borne with difficulty; cause of physical or mental strain; burden. **4.** The charge or ammunition for a firearm. **5.** The hours or amount of work required of an employee. **6.** *pl. Informal* An ample amount; lots: *loads* of time. **7.** *Electr.* The power delivered by a generating system. **8.** *Mech.* The resistance overcome by a motor or engine in driving machinery. — **to get a load of** *U.S. Slang* To listen to or look at. — *v.t.* **1.** To place a large quantity, burden, cargo, etc., upon. **2.** To place or take (cargo, people, etc.) as on a conveyance. **3.** To burden, encumber, or oppress: often with *down.* **4.** To provide abundantly; heap: He was *loaded* with honors. **5.** To charge (a firearm, etc.) with explosive or ammunition. **6.** To put film or a photographic plate into (a camera). **7.** To tamper with, esp. by adding weight to: to *load* dice. **8.** To make prejudicial: to *load* the evidence. — *v.i.* **9.** To put on or receive a load or cargo. **10.** To charge a firearm, cartridge, etc., with ammunition. [OE *lād* way, journey] — **load′er** *n.*

load·star (lōd′stär′), **load·stone** (lōd′stōn′) See LODESTAR, LODESTONE.

loaf[1] (lōf) *v.i.* **1.** To loiter lazily or aimlessly. **2.** To shirk or dawdle over one's work. — *v.t.* **3.** To spend (time) idly: with *away.* [Back formation < LOAFER]

loaf[2] (lōf) *n. pl.* **loaves** (lōvz) **1.** A rounded or elongated mass of bread baked in a single piece. **2.** Any shaped mass of food, as of cake, chopped meat, etc. [OE *hlāf* bread]

loaf·er (lō'fər) *n.* **1.** One who loafs; an idler or slacker. **2.** A casual shoe resembling a moccasin.

loam (lōm) *n.* **1.** Loose-textured soil consisting of a mixture of sand and clay containing organic matter. **2.** A moistened mixture of clay, sand, and straw, used in plastering. — *v.t.* To coat or fill with loam. [OE *lām*] — **loam'y** *adj.*

loan (lōn) *n.* **1.** Something lent; esp., a sum of money lent at interest. **2.** The act of lending: the *loan* of a knife. — *v.t. & v.i.* To lend. [ME < ON *lān*]

loan shark *U.S. Informal* One who lends money at an excessively high or illegal rate of interest.

loan-word (lōn'wûrd') *n.* A word adopted from another language and partly or completely naturalized, as the English word *chauffeur*, taken from the French. Also **loan word, loan'word'.** [< G *lehnwort*]

loath (lōth) *adj.* Strongly disinclined; reluctant; unwilling: often followed by *to*. Also spelled *loth.* [OE *lāth* hateful]

loathe (lōth) *v.t.* **loathed, loath·ing** To feel great hatred or disgust for; abhor; detest. — **Syn.** See HATE. [OE *lāthian* to be hateful] — **loath'er** *n.*

loath·ing (lō'thing) *n.* Extreme dislike; abhorrence. — **loath'ing·ly** *adv.*

loath·some (lōth'səm) *adj.* Causing revulsion or disgust; repulsive. — **loath'some·ly** *adv.* — **loath'some·ness** *n.*

loaves (lōvz) Plural of LOAF.

lob (lob) *v.* **lobbed, lob·bing** *v.t.* **1.** To pitch, or strike (a ball, etc.) in a high, arching curve. — *v.i.* **2.** To move clumsily or heavily. **3.** To lob a ball. — *n.* In tennis, a stroke that sends the ball high into the air. [ME]

lo·bar (lō'bər, -bär) *adj.* **1.** Of or pertaining to a lobe. **2.** Affecting one or more lobes of the lungs. [< NL *lobaris*]

lo·bate (lō'bāt) *adj.* **1.** Having or consisting of lobes. **2.** Resembling a lobe. Also **lo'bat·ed.** [< NL *lobatus*]

lo·ba·tion (lō-bā'shən) *n.* **1.** The condition of having or forming lobes. **2.** A lobe or lobelike part.

lob·by (lob'ē) *n.* *pl.* **·bies 1.** An entrance hall, vestibule, or public lounge in an apartment house, hotel, theater, etc. **2.** *U.S.* A group representing persons or organizations with a common interest, who attempt to influence the votes of legislators. — *v.* **·bied, ·by·ing** *U.S. v.i.* **1.** To attempt to influence legislators in favor of some interest. — *v.t.* **2.** To attempt to influence (legislators, etc.). **3.** To exert influence for the passage of: often with *through.* [< Med.L *lobia*]

lob·by·ism (lob'ē·iz'əm) *n.* *U.S.* The practice of lobbying. — **lob'by·ist** *n.*

lobe (lōb) *n.* **1.** A rounded division, protuberance, or part, as of a leaf. **2.** The soft lower part of the human ear. **3.** *Anat.* Any of several well-defined, often symmetrical portions of an organ or part of the body, as of the brain, lungs, liver, etc. [< F < L < Gk. *lobos*] — **lobed** *adj.*

lo·be·li·a (lō·bē'lē·ə, -bēl'yə) *n.* Any of a genus of herbaceous plants having flowers usu. borne in racemes. [< NL, after Matthias de *Lobel,* 1538–1616, Flemish botanist]

lob·lol·ly (lob'lol'ē) *n.* *pl.* **·lies 1.** *U.S.* A pine of the southern U.S., having scaly bark and wood valuable as lumber. **2.** The wood of this tree. Also **loblolly pine.** [< dial. E *lob* bubble + *lolly* broth]

lo·bo (lō'bō) *n.* *pl.* **·bos** The timber wolf of the western U.S. [< Sp., wolf < L *lupus*]

lo·bot·o·my (lō·bot'ə·mē) *n.* *pl.* **·mies** *Surg.* The operation of cutting into or across a lobe of the brain, esp. in order to modify or eliminate some function associated with a mental disorder. [< Gk. *lobos* lobe + -TOMY]

lob·ster (lob'stər) *n.* **1.** Any of various ten-legged marine crustaceans having the first pair of legs modified as claws, and compound eyes on flexible stalks. **2.** Any of various similar crustaceans. **3.** The flesh of any of these crustaceans eaten as food. [OE < L *locusta* lobster, locust]

lob·ule (lob'yōōl) *n.* **1.** A small lobe. **2.** A subdivision of a lobe. [< NL < *lobus* lobe] — **lob'u·lar, lob'u·lose** *adj.*

lo·cal (lō'kəl) *adj.* **1.** Pertaining to, characteristic of, or confined to a relatively small area. **2.** Restricted, as by environmental influences, etc. **3.** Of or pertaining to a particular place or position in space: *local* time. **4.** Stopping at all stations along its run, as a train. **5.** *Med.* Relating to or affecting a specific part of the body. — *n.* **1.** A branch or chapter of an organization, as a trade union. **2.** A bus, train, etc., that stops at all stations. **3.** A news item of local interest. [< F < L < *locus* place] — **lo'cal·ly** *adv.*

local color The characteristic appearance, mannerisms, etc., of a place or period, esp. as presented in literature.

lo·cale (lō·kal') *n.* **1.** A place or locality, esp. with reference to some event or circumstance. **2.** The setting of a literary, dramatic, or artistic work; scene. [< F]

lo·cal·ism (lō'kəl·iz'əm) *n.* **1.** A local custom or idiom. **2.** A word, meaning of a word, pronunciation, etc., peculiar to a locality. **3.** Narrowness; provincialism.

lo·cal·i·ty (lō·kal'ə·tē) *n.* *pl.* **·ties 1.** A place, region, etc. **2.** Position, esp. in relation to surroundings, etc. **3.** The state of being local. [< F < LL *localitas*]

lo·cal·ize (lō'kəl·īz) *v.t.* **·ized, ·iz·ing 1.** To make local; con-

fine or assign to a specific area. **2.** To determine the place of origin of. — **lo'cal·iz'a·ble** *adj.* — **lo'cal·i·za'tion** *n.*

local option The right of a county or town, etc., to restrict or prohibit certain activities, as the sale of liquor.

lo·cate (lō'kāt, lō·kāt') *v.* **·cat·ed, ·cat·ing** *v.t.* **1.** To discover the position of; find. **2.** To establish or place at a particular site: The store is *located* on the corner. **3.** To place hypothetically as to setting, a relative position, etc. **4.** *U.S.* To survey and fix the site or boundaries of (property, a mining claim, etc.). — *v.i.* **5.** *U.S. Informal* To settle. [< L < *locus* place] — **lo'cat'a·ble** *adj.* — **lo'ca·ter** *n.*

lo·ca·tion (lō·kā'shən) *n.* **1.** The act of locating, or the state of being located. **2.** A site or situation, esp. considered in regard to its surroundings. **3.** Exact position or place occupied. **4.** A motion picture or television locale away from the studio on location. **5.** *U.S.* A tract of land having established boundaries. [< L *locatio*]

loc·a·tive (lok'ə·tiv) *adj.* *Gram.* In certain inflected languages, as Latin, Greek, and Sanskrit, designating a noun case denoting place where or at which. — *n. Gram.* **1.** The locative case. **2.** A word in this case. [< L *locatus*]

loch (lokh, lok) *n. Scot.* **1.** A lake. **2.** An arm of the sea.

lo·ci (lō'sī) Plural of LOCUS.

lock¹ (lok) *n.* **1.** A mechanical fastening device having a bolt or combination of bolts secured or released by a key, dial, etc., and used to prevent unauthorized entry, access, or operation. **2.** Any part or device that fastens, secures, or holds something firmly in place. **3.** A section of a canal, etc., enclosed by gates, within which the water depth may be varied to raise or lower boats from level to level. **4.** The mechanism that explodes the charge of a gun. **5.** An interlocking, fastening, or jamming together of parts. **6.** A wrestling grip or hold. — **lock, stock, and barrel** Altogether; completely. — *v.t.* **1.** To fasten, or secure by means of a lock. **2.** To keep, confine, etc., in or as in a locked enclosure: with *in, up,* or *away.* **3.** To fit together securely; interlock. **4.** To clasp or grip in or as in a firm hold. **5.** To make immovable by or as by jamming or fastening together. **6.** To move (a vessel) through a waterway by means of locks. — *v.i.* **7.** To become locked. **8.** To become firmly joined or interlocked. — **to lock out 1.** To prevent (employees) from working by closing a factory, shop, etc. **2.** To keep out by locking. [OE *loc* fastening, enclosure] — **lock'a·ble** *adj.*

LOCK

Insertion of key raises tumblers (*a*), thus releasing key plug (*b*) and permitting key to turn.

lock² (lok) *n.* **1.** Strands of hair forming a curl. **2.** *pl.* The hair of the head. **3.** A tuft of wool, etc. [OE *locc*]

lock·er (lok'ər) *n.* **1.** A closet, cabinet, storage space, etc., fastened with a lock; as: **a** One of a series of metal cabinets as in a school or gymnasium, in which clothes, equipment etc., are kept. **b** A cabinet in which frozen foods are kept **2.** A chest, etc., as on a ship, in which equipment or personal belongings are kept. **3.** One who or that which locks.

locker room A room having lockers for clothing, etc.

lock·et (lok'it) *n.* A small ornamental case for enclosing a picture or keepsake, usu. worn on a chain, ribbon, etc. around the neck. [< OF < *loc* latch + Gmc.]

lock·jaw (lok'jô') *n. Pathol.* A form of tetanus causing rigid closure of the jaws: also called *trismus.*

lock·out (lok'out') *n.* The closing of a place of business by an employer in order to make employees agree to terms.

lock·smith (lok'smith') *n.* A maker or repairer of locks.

lock step A marching style in which each marcher follows as closely as possible the one in front of him.

lock·up (lok'up') *n.* A jail or prison cell.

lo·co (lō'kō) *adj. U.S. Informal* Crazy; insane. — *n. pl.* **·cos** Locoweed. — *v.t.* **·coed, ·co·ing 1.** To poison with locoweed. **2.** *U.S. Slang* To make insane. [< Sp., insane]

lo·co·mo·tion (lō'kə·mō'shən) *n.* The act or power of moving from one place to another. [< L *loco* from a place + *motio, -onis* movement]

lo·co·mo·tive (lō'kə·mō'tiv) *n.* An engine that moves by its own power, used to pull passenger or freight trains on a railroad. — *adj.* **1.** Of, pertaining to, or used in locomotion. **2.** Moving or able to move from one place to another. **3.** Capable of moving by its own power, as an engine.

lo·co·weed (lō'kō·wēd') *n.* Any of several leguminous plants of the SW U.S., often poisonous to livestock.

lo·cus (lō'kəs) *n. pl.* **·ci** (-sī) **1.** A place; locality; area. **2.** *Math.* **a** A surface or curve regarded as traced by a line or point moving under specified conditions. **b** Any figure made up wholly of points or lines that satisfy given conditions.

lo·cust¹ (lō'kəst) *n.* **1.** Any of a family of widely distributed winged insects resembling grasshoppers but having short antennae, including those of migratory habits that destroy vegetation. **2.** A cicada. [< OF < L *locusta*]

lo·cust² (lō'kəst) *n.* A leguminous tree of North America, having compound leaves and clusters of fragrant white flowers. **2.** The wood of this tree. **3.** Any of various similar trees, as the acacia and honey locust. [< L *locusta*]

lo·cu·tion (lō·kyōō'shən) *n.* **1.** A verbal expression or phrase. **2.** Manner of speech or expression; phraseology. [< L *locutio, -onis* a speaking < *loqui* to speak]

lode (lōd) *n. Mining* **1.** A deposit of metallic ore filling a fissure or series of fissures in native rock. **2.** Any deposit of ore located between definite boundaries of associated rock. Also called *vein.* [OE *lād* way, journey]

lode·star (lōd'stär') *n.* **1.** A star used as a guide in navigation or travel; esp., the polestar. **2.** A guiding principle, etc. Also spelled *loadstar.* [ME *lode* course + STAR]

lode·stone (lōd'stōn') *n.* **1.** A variety of magnetite exhibiting magnetism. **2.** Something that attracts by or as by magnetism. [ME *lode* course + STONE]

lodge (loj) *n.* **1.** A local branch of a secret or fraternal society; also, the meeting place of such a society. **2.** A small hut, cabin, etc., esp. one used as a base for outdoor activity. **3.** A small house on the grounds of an estate, etc., usu. serving as quarters for an employee. **4.** A North American Indian tepee or wigwam, etc.; also, a group living in such a dwelling. **5.** The characteristic den of certain animals, as beavers. — *v.* **lodged, lodg·ing** *v.t.* **1.** To furnish with temporary quarters; house. **2.** To rent a room or rooms to. **3.** To serve as a shelter or dwelling for. **4.** To place or implant firmly, as by thrusting or inserting. **5.** To deposit for safekeeping or storage. **6.** To submit or enter (a complaint, etc.) formally. **7.** To confer or invest (power, etc.): usu. with *in* or *with*. — *v.i.* **8.** To take temporary quarters. **9.** To live in a rented room or rooms. **10.** To become fixed or embedded. [< OF < Med.L < OHG *loub* foliage]

lodg·er (loj'ər) *n.* **1.** One who lives in a rented room or rooms in another's residence. **2.** Something fixed in place.

lodg·ing (loj'ing) *n.* **1.** A temporary dwelling place. **2.** *pl.* Living quarters consisting of a rented room or rooms in another's house. **3.** Accommodation for living and sleeping.

lodg·ment (loj'mənt) *n.* The act of lodging, or the state of being lodged. Also **lodge'ment.**

loess (lō'is, lœs) *n. Geol.* A pale, yellowish silt or clay forming finely powdered, usu. wind-borne deposits. [< G *lösen* to pour, dissolve] — **loes'si·al** *adj.*

loft (lôft, loft) *n.* **1.** A floored space directly under a roof; attic. **2.** *U.S.* A large, open workroom or storeroom on an upper story of a commercial building. **3.** A hayloft. **4.** An upper section or gallery, as in a church: the choir *loft.* **5.** In golf: **a** The slope of the club face away from the vertical line of the shaft, intended to make a struck ball rise sharply in the air. **b** A stroke that causes the ball to rise sharply when struck. **c** The upward travel of a struck ball. — *v.t.* **1.** In sports, to strike (a ball) so that it travels in a high arc. **2.** To keep or store in a loft. — *v.i.* **3.** In golf, to drive a ball so that it rises in a high arc. [Late OE < ON, air, sky]

loft·y (lôf'tē, lof'-) *adj.* **loft·i·er, loft·i·est** **1.** Having great or imposing height. **2.** Elevated in character, quality, style, etc.; noble. **3.** Exalted in rank or position; eminent. **4.** Arrogant; haughty. — **loft'i·ly** *adv.* — **loft'i·ness** *n.*

log[1] (log, lôg) *n.* **1.** A full length or cut section of a felled tree trunk, limb, etc., stripped of branches. **2.** Something or someone inert, stupefied, etc. **3.** *Naut.* **a** A record of the daily progress of a vessel and of the events of a voyage. **b** Any of various devices for measuring the speed and mileage of a vessel. **4.** A record of operation or progress, as of an aircraft in flight. — *v.* **logged, log·ging** *v.t.* **1.** To cut down the trees of (a forest, etc.) for timber. **2.** To convert (timber) into logs. *Naut. & Aeron.* **a** To enter in a logbook. **b** To travel (a specified distance, etc.). **c** To travel at (a specified speed). — *v.i.* **4.** To engage in the operation of cutting and transporting timber. [ME *logge*]

log[2] (log, lôg) A logarithm.

log- Var. of LOGO-.

-log (log) Var. of -LOGUE.

lo·gan·ber·ry (lō'gən·ber'ē) *n. pl.* **·ries** **1.** A hybrid plant, obtained by crossing the red raspberry with the blackberry. **2.** The edible fruit of this plant. [after J. H. *Logan*, 1841–1928, U.S. horticulturist]

log·a·rithm (log'ə·rith'əm, lôg'-) *n. Math.* The power to which a fixed number, called the base, must be raised in order to produce a given number, the antilogarithm. [< NL < Gk. *logos* word, ratio + *arithmos* number] — **log'a·rith'mic** or **·mi·cal** *adj.* — **log'a·rith'mi·cal·ly** *adv.*

log·book (log'book', lôg'-) *n.* The book in which the official record of a ship, aircraft, etc., is entered. Also **log book.**

log chip *Naut.* A quadrant-shaped board weighted on the curved edge and suspended in the water from a moving vessel in order to measure its speed.

loge (lōzh) *n.* A box in a theater. [< F < OF]

log·ger (log'ər, lôg'-) *n.* **1.** A person engaged in logging; lumberjack. **2.** A machine for hauling and loading logs.

log·ger·head (log'ər·hed, lôg'-) *n.* A large marine turtle of tropical Atlantic waters. Also **loggerhead turtle.** — **at loggerheads** Engaged in a quarrel; unable to agree. [< dial. E *logger* log tied to a horse's leg + HEAD]

log·gi·a (loj'ē·ə, lō'jə; *Ital.* lôd'jä) *n.* A roofed gallery or portico that is open and supported by columns on one or more sides. [< Ital. < OF *loge*]

log·ging (log'ing, lôg'-) *n.* The occupation of felling timber and transporting logs to a mill or market.

log·ic (loj'ik) *n.* **1.** The science concerned with the principles of valid reasoning and correct inference, either deductive or inductive. **2.** Method of reasoning, inference, etc.; esp., correct or sound reasoning. **3.** Effective force, influence, etc. **4.** The apparently inevitable chain of events involved in an outcome, etc. **5.** A system of or treatise on logic. [< F < L < Gk. < *logos* word, speech, thought]

log·i·cal (loj'i·kəl) *adj.* **1.** Relating to or of the nature of logic. **2.** Conforming to the laws of logic. **3.** Capable of or characterized by clear reasoning. — **log'i·cal'i·ty** (-kal'ə·tē), **log'i·cal·ness** *n.* — **log'i·cal·ly** *adv.*

-logical *combining form* Of or related to a (specified) science or study: *biological, geological.* Also **-logic.**

lo·gi·cian (lō·jish'ən) *n.* One versed in logic.

lo·gis·tics (lō·jis'tiks) *n.pl.* (construed as *sing.*) The branch of military science dealing with supplying, equipping, and moving troops. [< F *loger* to quarter] — **lo·gis'tic** *adj.*

logo- *combining form* Word; speech. Also, before vowels, *log-.* [< Gk. *logos* word, speech]

Log·os (log'os, lôg'-, lō'gos) *n. Theol.* In the Christian religion, God, the second person of the Trinity, incarnate as Jesus Christ. *John* i 1–14.

log·roll (log'rōl', lôg'-) *U.S. v.t.* To obtain passage of (a bill) by logrolling. — *v.i.* To engage in logrolling. Also **log'-roll'.** [Back formation < LOGROLLING]

log·roll·ing (log'rō'ling, lôg'-) *n. U.S.* **1.** The trading of votes and influence between politicians; also, any such trading of help or approval for one's own benefit. **2.** Birling. Also **log'-roll'ing.** — **log'roll'er** *n.*

-logue *combining form* Discourse; recitation: *monologue, prologue.* Also **-log.** [< OF < L < Gk. *logos* word, speech]

log·wood (log'wood', lôg'-) *n.* **1.** The reddish wood of a Central American tree, used as a dyestuff. **2.** The tree itself.

lo·gy (lō'gē) *adj.* **·gi·er, ·gi·est** *U.S. Informal* Dull; heavy; lethargic. [Prob. < Du. *log* dull, heavy]

-logy *combining form* **1.** The science or study of. **2.** Speech; discourse. [< Gk. *logos* word, study]

Lo·hen·grin (lō'ən·grin) In medieval German legend, a knight of the Holy Grail and son of Parsifal.

loin (loin) *n. Usu. pl.* **1.** The part of the back and flanks between the lower ribs and the hipbone. ◆ Collateral adjective: *lumbar.* **2.** *pl. Chiefly Poetic* The lower back, thighs, and groin regarded as a zone to be clothed. **3.** The forepart of the hindquarters of beef, lamb, veal, etc., with the flank removed. — **to gird (up) one's loins** To prepare for action. [< OF *loigne, logne* < L *lumbus*]

loin·cloth (loin'klôth', -kloth') *n.* A garment consisting of a piece or strip of cloth worn about the loins and hips.

loi·ter (loi'tər) *v.i.* **1.** To linger idly or aimlessly; loaf. **2.** To dawdle. — *v.t.* **3.** To pass (time) idly: with *away.* [ME *lotere*] — **loi'ter·er** *n.*

Lo·ki (lō'kē) In Norse mythology, a god who created disorder and mischief. [< ON]

loll (lol) *v.i.* **1.** To lie or lean in a relaxed or languid manner; lounge. **2.** To hang loosely; droop. — *v.t.* **3.** To permit to droop or hang, as the tongue. — *n.* The act of lolling. [Cf. ME *lull*, MDu. *lollen* to sleep] — **loll'er** *n.*

lol·la·pa·loo·za (lol'ə·pə·loo'zə) *n. U.S. Slang* Something extraordinary. Also **lol·la·pa·loo'sa.** [Origin unknown]

Lol·lard (lol'ərd) *n.* A follower of John Wycliffe, 14th-century English religious reformer. Also **Lol'ler.** [< MDu. *lollaerd* mumbler (of prayers)]

lol·li·pop (lol'ē·pop') *n.* A lump or piece of candy on the end of a stick: also called *sucker.* Also **lol'ly·pop.** [Prob. < dial. E *lolly* tongue + POP[1]]

Lom·bard (lom'bard, -bärd, lum'-) *n.* **1.** One of a Germanic tribe that established a kingdom in northern Italy in the sixth century. **2.** A native or inhabitant of Lombardy. — **Lom·bar'dic** *adj.*

London broil Broiled flank steak sliced thin.

lone (lōn) *adj.* **1.** Being without companions; solitary. **2.** Isolated. **3.** Unfrequented; deserted. [< ALONE]

lone·ly (lōn'lē) *adj.* **·li·er, ·li·est** **1.** Unfrequented by human beings; deserted; desolate. **2.** Sad from lack of companionship or sympathy; lonesome. **3.** Characterized by or inducing loneliness. — **lone'li·ly** *adv.* — **lone'li·ness** *n.*

lone·some (lōn′səm) *adj.* **1.** Depressed or uneasy because of being alone; lonely; forlorn. **2.** Inducing a feeling of loneliness. **3.** Unfrequented; secluded: a *lonesome* retreat. — **lone′some·ly** *adv.* — **lone·some·ness** *n.*

Lone Star State Nickname of Texas.

lone wolf *U.S. Informal* One who prefers to work, live, etc., by himself: also **lon·er** (lō′nər).

long¹ (lông, long) *adj.* **1.** Characterized by extent or measurement relatively great in proportion to breadth or width; not short. **2.** Having relatively great duration in time; prolonged. **3.** Having relatively great extension from beginning to end: a *long* tunnel. **4.** Being of a specified measurement in extent or duration: ten miles *long*; three hours *long.* **5.** Having more than the standard or usual quantity, extent, or duration: a *long* ton, a *long* play. **6.** Consisting of many items or entries, as a list. **7.** Slow; tedious. **8.** Extending far into time or space; having considerable range. **9.** Well supplied: *long* on excuses. **10.** In gambling: **a** Denoting odds indicating little likelihood of winning. **b** Denoting a bet, chance, guess, etc., characterized by such odds. **11.** In finance, holding considerable amounts of a stock, commodity, etc., in anticipation of a rise in its price. **12.** *Phonet.* Denoting the vowel sounds of *Dane, dean, dine, dome, dune* as contrasted with those of *Dan, den, din, don, duck.* **13.** In prosody, stressed, as in English verse. — **in the long run** As the ultimate result of inevitable consequences; eventually. — *adv.* **1.** For or during an extensive period of time: Will he stay *long?* **2.** For a time or period (to be specified): How *long* will he stay? **3.** For the whole extent or duration (of a specified period): It rained all day *long.* **4.** At a considerably distant time: *long* after midnight. — **as** (or **so**) **long as 1.** For or during the time that. **2.** Inasmuch as; since. — *n.* **1.** Something relatively long. **2.** A long syllable or sound, as in phonetics, prosody, etc. — **before long** Soon. — **the long and the short** The entire sum and substance; the whole. [OE *long, lang*]

long² (lông, long) *v.i.* To have a strong or eager desire; wish earnestly; yearn. [OE *langian* to grow long]

long·boat (lông′bōt′, long′-) *n. Naut.* The largest boat carried by a sailing vessel.

long·bow (lông′bō′, long′-) *n.* A large bow drawn by hand and projecting long, feathered arrows.

long·cloth (lông′klôth′, long′klôth′) *n.* A fine, soft, cotton cloth used for making children's garments.

long·dis·tance (lông′dis′təns, long′-) *adj.* Connecting or covering relatively long distances or places. — *adv.* **1.** By long-distance telephone. **2.** At a distance.

long distance The telephone exchange, operator, or service that handles calls outside the immediate locality.

long division Arithmetical division, usu. with large numbers in which all the steps of the process are shown.

long·drawn (lông′drôn′, long′-) *adj.* Prolonged; protracted. Also **long′-drawn′-out′** (-out′).

lon·gev·i·ty (lon·jev′ə·tē) *n.* **1.** Great age or length of life. **2.** The tendency to live long. [< L < *longus* long + *aevum* age] — **lon·ge·vous** (lon·jē′vəs) *adj.*

long·hair (lông′hâr′, long′-) *U.S. Slang adj.* **1.** Of or pertaining to intellectuals or their tastes. **2.** Of or pertaining to serious rather than popular music. — *n.* **1.** A longhair person; intellectual. **2.** Longhair music. Also **long′-hair′.**

long·hand (lông′hand′, long′-) *n.* Ordinary handwriting with the words spelled in full.

long·head·ed (lông′hed′id, long′-) *adj.* **1.** Dolichocephalic. **2.** Characterized by shrewdness, foresight, etc. Also **long′head′ed.** — **long′head′ed·ly** *adv.* — **long′head′ed·ness** *n.*

long·horn (lông′hôrn′, long′-) *n.* One of a breed of domestic cattle with long horns. Also **Texas longhorn.**

long house Among North American Indians, esp. the Iroquois, a council house or community dwelling.

longi- *combining form* Long. [< L *longus* long]

long·ing (lông′ing, long′-) *n.* A strong, earnest, persistent craving; desire. — *adj.* Having or showing such a craving. — **Syn.** See APPETITE. — **long′ing·ly** *adv.*

lon·gi·tude (lon′jə·tōōd, -tyōōd, long′gə-) *n.* **1.** *Geog.* Distance east or west on the earth's surface, usu. measured by the angle that the meridian through a particular place makes with the prime meridian that runs through Greenwich, England. Longitude may be expressed either in hours and minutes (**longitude in time**) or in degrees (**longitude in arc**). **2.** *Astron.* The angular distance eastward from the vernal equinox to the intersection with the ecliptic of the perpendicular from a heavenly body (**celestial longitude**). [< F < L *longus* long]

lon·gi·tu·di·nal (lon′jə·tōō′də·nal, -tyōō′-, long′gə-) *adj.* **1.** Of or pertaining to longitude or length. **2.** Running lengthwise. — **lon′gi·tu′di·nal·ly** *adv.*

long-lived (lông′līvd′, -livd′, long′-) *adj.* Having a long life or period of existence. — **long′-lived′ness** *n.*

long measure Linear measure.

long-play·ing (lông′plā′ing, long′-) *adj.* LP.

long-range (lông′rānj′, long′-) *adj.* **1.** Designed to shoot

or move over distances. **2.** Taking account of, or extending over, a long span of future time: *long-range* plans.

long·shore·man (lông′shôr′mən, -shōr′-, long′-) *n. pl.* **·men** (-mən) A man employed on the waterfront to load and unload vessels; stevedore. [< *alongshore* + MAN]

long shot *Informal* **1.** In betting, a race horse or other gambling choice, backed at great odds and having little chance of winning. **2.** Any similar venture, scheme, etc. — **not by a long shot** *Informal* Decidedly not; not at all.

long-sight·ed (lông′sī′tid, long′-) *adj.* **1.** Far-sighted. **2.** Characterized by or having foresight; sagacious. — **long′sight′ed·ly** *adv.* — **long′-sight′ed·ness** *n.*

long-stand·ing (lông′stan′ding, long′-) *adj.* Having existed over a long period: a *long-standing* debt.

long-sta·ple (lông′stā′pəl, long′-) *adj.* Having a long fiber: said of fabrics, esp. cotton.

long-suf·fer·ing (lông′suf′ər·ing, long′-) *adj.* Patiently enduring injuries, misfortune, etc., for a long time. — *n.* Patient endurance of injuries, etc.: also **long′-suf′fer·ance.**

long-term (lông′tûrm′, long′-) *adj.* Involving or extending over a relatively long period of time: a *long-term* contract.

long-time (lông′tīm′, long′-) *adj.* Being such for a considerable period of time: a *long-time* friend.

long-wind·ed (lông′win′did, long′-) *adj.* **1.** Continuing for a long time in speaking or writing: a *long-winded* lecturer. **2.** Capable of vigorous activity without becoming short of breath. — **long′-wind′ed·ly** *adv.* — **long′-wind′ed·ness** *n.*

long·wise (lông′wīz′, long′-) *adv.* Lengthwise. Also **long′ways′** (-wāz′).

loo (lōō) *n. pl.* **loos** A game of cards in which each player deposits a forfeit in a pool. [< F *lanturelu*]

look (lŏŏk) *v.i.* **1.** To use one's sense of sight. **2.** To turn the eyes in a specified direction. **3.** To gaze so as to convey a specific feeling or meaning. **4.** To use one's eyes in order to examine, repair, etc.: Let's *look* at the engine. **5.** To consider: *Look* at his fine record. **6.** To seem: He *looks* reliable. **7.** To face in a specified direction. **8.** To expect: with an infinitive: I *look* to hear from you soon. — *v.t.* **9.** To express or influence by a glance or gaze: to *look* one's anger. — **it looks like 1.** It promises or suggests the coming of. **2.** *Informal* It seems as if: *It looks like* I'll have to move. — **to look after 1.** To take care of. **2.** To watch or follow with the eye. — **to look alive** *Informal* To be alert or attentive. — **to look back** To reflect on the past; recall. — **to look down on** (or **upon**) To regard with condescension or contempt. Also **to look down one's nose on** (or **upon**). — **to look for 1.** To search for. **2.** To anticipate; expect. — **to look forward to** To anticipate. — **to look in** (or **in on**) To make a short visit to. — **to look into 1.** To examine closely. **2.** To make inquiries about. — **to look on. 1.** To be a spectator. **2.** To consider; regard. — **to look oneself** To appear to be in a normal, usual, or healthy condition, etc. — **to look out for 1.** To protect: to *look out for* one's own interests. **2.** To be watchful; be on guard. — **to look over** To examine; scrutinize. — **to look the other way** To ignore or avoid an unpleasant or unfavorable situation, sight, etc. — **to look to 1.** To attend to. **2.** To turn to, as for help, advice, etc. **3.** To anticipate; expect. — **to look up 1.** *U.S.* To search for and find, as in a file, book, etc. **2.** *Informal* To discover the whereabouts of. **3.** *Informal* To improve; become better. — **to look up and down 1.** To inspect critically or appraisingly. **2.** To search everywhere. — **to look up to** To have respect for. — *n.* **1.** The act of looking. **2.** A search, examination, etc., by or as by means of one's eyes. **3.** Aspect or expression: a saintly *look.* **4.** *Often pl. Informal* General appearance: I like the *looks* of this place. **5.** *pl. Informal* Personal appearance: the *looks* of a model. — *interj.* **1.** See! **2.** Listen! [OE *lōcian*]

look·er (lŏŏk′ər) *n.* **1.** One who looks or watches. **2.** *U.S. Slang* A handsome or good-looking person.

look·er-on (lŏŏk′ər·on′, -ôn′) *n. pl.* **look·ers-on** A spectator; onlooker.

look·ing glass (lŏŏk′ing) A glass mirror.

look·out (lŏŏk′out′) *n.* **1.** The act of watching for someone or something. **2.** A place where such a watch is kept. **3.** The person or persons watching. **4.** *Naut.* A crow's-nest. **5.** *Informal* Concern; worry: It's your *lookout.*

look-see (lŏŏk′sē′) *n. Slang* A brief inspection or survey.

loom¹ (lōōm) *v.i.* **1.** To appear or come into view indistinctly, as through a mist. **2.** To appear to the mind as large or threatening. [Origin uncertain]

loom² (lōōm) *n.* Any of various machines on which thread or yarn is woven into fabric. [OE *gelōma* tool]

loon¹ (lōōn) *n.* Any of various diving, fish-eating waterfowl, having a weird, laughing cry. [Ult. < ON *lomr*]

loon² (lōōn) *n.* **1.** A stupid or crazy person. **2.** A worthless person; idler. [Cf. Du. *loen* stupid fellow]

loon·y (lōō′nē) *Informal adj.* **loon·i·er, loon·i·est 1.** Lunatic or demented. **2.** Foolish; erratic; silly. — *n. pl.* **·ies** A demented or insane person. [< LUNATIC]

loop (lōōp) *n.* **1.** A folding or doubling over of one end of a piece of thread, rope, wire, etc., so as to form an oval opening. **2.** A ring or bent piece of metal, wood, thread, etc., serving as a fastener, staple, or the like. **3.** Something having or suggesting the shape of a loop. **4.** *Electr.* A complete magnetic or electrical circuit. **5.** *Aeron.* A complete circular turn made by an aircraft flying in a vertical plane. —*v.t.* **1.** To form a loop in or of. **2.** To fasten, connect, or encircle by means of a loop. **3.** *Aeron.* To fly (an aircraft) in a loop or loops. —*v.i.* **4.** To make a loop or loops. **5.** To move forward by forming loops. —**to loop the loop** To make a vertical circular turn in the air, esp. in an aircraft. [ME *loupe*] —**loop′y** *adj.*

loop·hole (lōōp′hōl′) *n.* **1.** A narrow slit in a wall, esp. one in a fortification. **2.** An opportunity for escaping or evading something. —*v.t.* **·holed, ·hol·ing** To furnish with loopholes.

loose (lōōs) *adj.* **loos·er, loos·est 1.** Not fastened or confined; unattached. **2.** Not taut; slack: a *loose* rein. **3.** Freed from bonds or restraint. **4.** Not firmly fitted or embedded. **5.** Not closely fitted, as clothing. **6.** Not bound or fastened together. **7.** Not compact, firm, or dense: *loose* soil. **8.** Not packaged: *loose* butter. **9.** Not constricted; open: said of lax bowels or a cough. **10.** Not properly controlled: a *loose* tongue. **11.** Dissolute; unchaste. **12.** Lacking in exactness or precision: a *loose* translation. **13.** *Informal* Not set aside for a specific use: *loose* funds. —**on the loose 1.** Not confined; at large. **2.** *Informal* Behaving in a free, uninhibited, and usu. dissolute manner. —*adv.* **1.** In a loose manner; loosely. **2.** So as to be or become loose: to break *loose.* —**to cut loose** *Informal* To behave in a free, uninhibited manner. —*v.* **loosed, loos·ing** *v.t.* **1.** To set free, as from bondage, penalty, etc. **2.** To untie or undo. **3.** To loosen. **4.** To make less strict; relax. **5.** To let fly; shoot, as an arrow. —*v.i.* **6.** To become loose. **7.** To loose something. [< ON *lauss*] —**loose′ly** *adv.* —**loose′ness** *n.*

loose end Something left undecided or undone, as a task, decision, etc. —**at loose ends 1.** In an unsettled state. **2.** Without a job.

loose-joint·ed (lōōs′join′tid) *adj.* **1.** Having joints not tightly articulated. **2.** Limber or flexible in movement.

loose-leaf (lōōs′lēf′) *adj.* Designed for or having pages that are easily inserted or removed: a *loose-leaf* notebook.

loos·en (lōō′sən) *v.t.* **1.** To untie or undo, as bonds. **2.** To set free; release. **3.** To make less tight, firm, or compact. —*v.i.* **4.** To become loose or looser. —**to loosen up** *Informal* **1.** To relax. **2.** To talk with ease; talk freely. **3.** To give more generously, as money. —**loos′en·er** *n.*

loose-strife (lōōs′strīf′) *n.* **1.** Any of various plants of the primrose family. **2.** Any of several related plants. [< LOOSE + STRIFE; direct trans. of L *lysimachia*]

loot (lōōt) *n.* **1.** Goods taken as booty by a victorious army from a sacked city, enemy forces, etc. **2.** Anything unlawfully taken. **3.** *U.S. Slang* Money. —*v.t.* **1.** To plunder; pillage. —*v.i.* **2.** To engage in plundering. [< Hind. *lūt* < Skt. *lunt*] —**loot′er** *n.*

lop¹ (lop) *v.t.* **lopped, lop·ping 1.** To cut or trim the branches, twigs, etc., from. **2.** To cut off, as branches, twigs, etc. —*n.* A part lopped off. [Origin unknown]

lop² (lop) *v.* **lopped, lop·ping** *v.i.* **1.** To droop or hang down loosely. **2.** To move about in an awkward manner. —*v.t.* **3.** To permit to droop or hang down loosely. —*adj.* Pendulous; drooping. [Origin unknown]

lope (lōp) *v.t. & v.i.* **loped, lop·ing** To run or cause to run with a steady, swinging stride or gallop. —*n.* A slow, easy stride or gallop. [< ON *hlaupa* to leap, run]

lop-eared (lop′ird′) *adj.* Having drooping ears.

lop·py (lop′ē) *adj.* **·pi·er, ·pi·est** Pendulous; limp.

lop-sid·ed (lop′sī′did) *adj.* Heavier, larger, or sagging on one side. —**lop′sid′ed·ly** *adv.* —**lop′sid′ed·ness** *n.*

lo·qua·cious (lō-kwā′shəs) *adj.* Characterized by continuous talking. [< L *loqui* to speak] —**lo·qua′cious·ly** *adv.* —**lo·qua′cious·ness** *n.*

lo·quac·i·ty (lō-kwas′ə-tē) *n. pl.* **·ties** Talkativeness.

lo·ran (lôr′an, lō′ran) *n.* A system in which the position of a ship or aircraft is determined by comparing the time intervals between radio signals from a network of synchronized ground stations. [< LO(NG) RA(NGE) N(AVIGATION)]

lord (lôrd) *n.* **1.** One possessing great power and authority. **2.** In Great Britain: **a** Any one of the noblemen or peers (**lords temporal**) having the title of marquis, earl, viscount, or baron and having seats in the House of Lords. **b** Any of the higher churchmen (**lords spiritual**) who are members of the House of Lords. **3.** In feudal law, the owner of a manor. —*v.t.* To invest with the title of lord. —**to lord it** (**over**) To act in a domineering or arrogant manner (toward). [OE *hláford, hláfweard,* lit., bread keeper]

Lord (lôrd) **1.** God: preceded by *the* except in direct address. **2.** Jesus Christ: also *Our Lord.* **3.** In Great Britain, a title of honor or nobility.

lord·ly (lôrd′lē) *adj.* **·li·er, ·li·est 1.** Befitting the rank and position of a lord. **2.** Noble; dignified. **3.** Arrogant; haughty. —*adv.* In a lordly manner. —**lord′li·ness** *n.*

lor·do·sis (lôr-dō′sis) *n. Pathol.* Inward curvature of the spine resulting in a hollow back. [< NL < Gk. *lordos* bent backward] —**lor·dot′ic** (-dot′ik) *adj.*

Lord's Day Sunday; the Sabbath.

lord·ship (lôrd′ship) *n.* **1.** The dominion, power, or authority of a lord. **2.** Sovereignty in general; supremacy. **3.** *Often cap.* In Great Britain, the title by which noblemen (excluding dukes), bishops, and judges are addressed or spoken of: preceded by *Your* or *His.* [OE *hláfordscipe.* See LORD.]

Lord's Prayer The prayer beginning *Our Father,* taught by Christ to his disciples. *Matt.* vi 9–13.

Lord's Supper, the 1. The Last Supper. **2.** The Eucharist; Holy Communion.

lore (lôr, lōr) *n.* **1.** The body of traditional, popular, often anecdotal knowledge about a particular subject: the *lore* of the woods. **2.** Learning or erudition. [OE *lār*]

Lo·re·lei (lôr′ə-lī, *Ger.* lō′rə-lī) In German romantic literature, a siren on a rock in the Rhine who lured boatmen to shipwreck by her singing. [< G]

lor·gnette (lôr-nyet′) *n.* **1.** A pair of eyeglasses with an ornamental handle. **2.** An opera glass with a long handle. [< F < *lorgner* to spy, peer]

lo·ris (lôr′is, lō′ris) *n. pl.* **·ris** or **·ris·es** A small, arboreal and nocturnal Asian lemur. [< F < Du. *loeres* booby]

lorn (lôrn) *adj. Archaic & Poetic* Abandoned; lonely; wretched; forlorn. [OE *loren,* pp. of *lēosan* to lose]

lor·ry (lôr′ē, lor′ē) *n. pl.* **·ries 1.** A low, four-wheeled wagon without sides. **2.** A motor truck. [Prob. dial. E *lurry* to pull]

lo·ry (lō′rē, lôr′ē) *n. pl.* **·ries** Any of a number of small parrots of Australia and the neighboring islands. [< Malay *lūri*]

lose (lōōz) *v.* **lost, los·ing** *v.t.* **1.** To be unable to find; mislay. **2.** To fail to keep, control, or maintain: to *lose* one's footing. **3.** To be deprived of; suffer the loss of: to *lose* a leg. **4.** To fail to win. **5.** To fail to take advantage of; miss. **6.** To fail to see or hear. **7.** To fail to keep in sight, memory, etc. **8.** To occupy or absorb wholly; engross: usually in the passive. **9.** To cease to have: to *lose* one's courage. **10.** To squander; waste. **11.** To cause (someone or something) to be or become lost. **12.** To disappear: used reflexively: The river *loses* itself in the swamp. **13.** To outdistance or elude. **14.** To cause the loss of: His rashness *lost* him the election. **15.** To bring to destruction or death; ruin: usu. in the passive. —*v.i.* **16.** To suffer loss. **17.** To be defeated, as in battle or a contest. —**to lose oneself 1.** To lose one's way. **2.** To disappear or hide. **3.** To become engrossed or absorbed. —**to lose out** *Informal* To fail or be defeated. —**to lose out on** *Informal* To fail to secure; miss. [From OE *losian* to be lost and *lēosan* to lose] —**los′er** *n.*

los·ing (lōō′zing) *n.* **1.** The act of one who or that which loses. **2.** *pl.* Money lost, esp. in gambling. —*adj.* **1.** Incurring loss: a *losing* business. **2.** Not winning.

loss (lôs, los) *n.* **1.** The act of losing or the state of being lost. **2.** One who or that which is lost. **3.** The harm, inconvenience, deprivation, etc., caused by losing something or someone. **4.** *pl. Mil.* **a** Casualties. **b** The number of casualties. **5.** In insurance: **a** Death, injury, property damage, etc., sustained by an insured. **b** The sum payable by the insurer on that account. —**at a loss** Perplexed. [ME]

loss leader An article that a retail store sells below or near cost to promote sales of other merchandise.

lost (lôst, lost) *adj.* **1.** Not to be found or recovered. **2.** No longer possessed, seen, or known: *lost* friends. **3.** Not won, gained, or secured. **4.** Having gone astray. **5.** Bewildered; perplexed. **6.** Helpless. **7.** Not used or taken advantage of; wasted. **8.** Destroyed; ruined. **9.** No longer known or practiced: a *lost* art. —**to be lost in** To be absorbed or engrossed in. —**to be lost to 1.** To no longer belong to. **2.** To be impervious or insensible to. **3.** To be no longer available to. —**to be lost upon** (or **on**) To have no effect upon.

lot (lot) *n.* **1.** That which is used in determining something by chance, as objects drawn at random from a container. **2.** The process of deciding something by this method. **3.** The decisions arrived at by such means. **4.** The share or portion that comes to one as a result of drawing lots. **5.** One's portion in life as ascribed to chance, fate, custom, etc. **6.** A number of things or persons considered as a single group. **7.** A job lot. **8.** A plot or quantity of land: a parking *lot.* **9.** *Informal* A (specified) type of person: He's a bad *lot.* **10.** In motion pictures, a studio and the adjacent area. **11.** *Often pl. Informal* A great deal: a *lot* of money; *lots* of trouble. —**Syn.** See DESTINY. —**a lot** (or **lots**) *Informal* Very much: He is a *lot* better; *lots* better. —**the lot** The whole of a certain number or quantity: He bought the *lot.* —**to cast** (or

draw) lots To come to a decision or solution by the use of lots. **— to cast (or throw) in one's lot with** To join with and share the fortunes of. **—** v. **lot·ted, lot·ting** v.t. **1.** To apportion by lots; allot. **2.** To draw lots for. **3.** To divide, as land, into lots. **—** v.i. **4.** To cast lots. [OE *hlot*]

Lot (lot) In the Old Testament, a nephew of Abraham, whose wife was turned into a pillar of salt when she looked back upon the destruction of Sodom. *Gen.* xi 27, xix.

loth (lōth) See LOATH.

lo·tion (lō′shən) n. A liquid preparation used for external cleansing of the skin, eyes, etc. [< L < *lavare* to wash]

lot·ter·y (lot′ər·ē) n. pl. **·ter·ies** A method of distributing prizes in which numbered tickets are sold, the winning tickets being selected by lot. [< Ital. *lotto* lottery, lot]

lot·to (lot′ō) n. A game of chance played by drawing numbers from a container and covering with counters the corresponding numbers on cards, the winner being the first to cover a row of numbers. [< Ital.]

lo·tus (lō′təs) n. **1.** Any of various tropical water lilies noted for their large floating leaves and showy flowers; esp., the **white lotus** and the **blue lotus** of Egypt and the **sacred lotus** of India. **2.** A representation of any of these plants in art, architecture, sculpture, etc. **3.** Any of a genus of herbs of the bean family. Also **lo·tos.** [< L < Gk. *lōtos*]

lo·tus-eat·er (lō′təs·ē′tər) n. **1.** In the *Odyssey,* one of a people who lived a life of indolence induced by eating the fruit of the lotus tree. **2.** Anyone considered to be living an indolent, irresponsible existence.

lotus tree Any of a genus of Old World trees of the buckthorn family.

LOTUS
a Bud and leaf.
b Flower and leaf. c Stylized lotus in Egyptian architecture.

loud (loud) adj. **1.** Having great volume or intensity of sound: *loud* thunder. **2.** Making or uttering a great noise or sound: a *loud* trumpet. **3.** Emphatic or urgent; insistent: *loud* demands. **4.** *Informal* Crude; vulgar, as manners, persons, etc. **5.** *Informal* Excessively showy: a *loud* shirt. **—** adv. In a loud manner. [OE *hlūd*] **— loud′ly** adv. **— loud′ness** n.

loud·mouthed (loud′mouthd′, -mouth′) adj. Having a loud voice; offensively clamorous or talkative.

loud·speak·er (loud′spē′kər) n. Any of various devices for converting an electric current into sound, as in a public-address system, radio, etc.: also called *speaker.*

lou·is d'or (loo′ē dôr′) pl. **lou·is d'or 1.** A former French gold coin worth twenty francs. **2.** An old French coin, fluctuating in value, first minted in 1640. Also **lou′is.**

lounge (lounj) v. **lounged, loung·ing** v.i. **1.** To recline, walk, etc., in a relaxed, lazy manner. **2.** To pass time in doing nothing. **—** v.t. **3.** To spend or pass in idleness, as time. **—** n. **1.** A couch or sofa, esp. one with little or no back and a headrest at one end. **2.** A room in a hotel, club, train, etc., suitable for lounging and often having facilities for drinking. **3.** A lounging pace or gait. **4.** The act of lounging; also, a period of lounging. [Origin unknown] **— loung′er** n.

loupe (loop) n. A small magnifying glass, esp. one adapted as an eyepiece for jewelers or watchmakers. [< F]

louse (lous) n. pl. **lice** (līs) **1.** A small, flat-bodied, wingless insect living as an external parasite on man and some animals. **2.** Any of various other parasitic insects. **3.** *Slang* A contemptible person. **—** v.t. & v.i. **loused, lous·ing** *Slang* To ruin; bungle: with *up.* [OE *lūs*]

lous·y (lou′zē) adj. **lous·i·er, lous·i·est 1.** Infested with lice. **2.** *Slang* Contemptible; mean. **3.** *Slang* Worthless; inferior. **4.** *Slang* Having plenty (of): with *with: lousy* with money.

lout (lout) n. An awkward fellow; clown; boor. [? < ON *lutr* bent, stooped] **— lout′ish** adj.

lou·ver (loo′vər) n. **1.** A window or opening, as in a gable, provided with louver boards; also, a louver board. **2.** One of several narrow openings serving as an outlet for heated air. [OF *lover*]

louver board One of a series of horizontal, overlapping slats in a window or opening, sloped downward to shed rain while admitting light and air. Also **louver board·ing.**

Lou·vre (loo′vr′) A royal palace in Paris, begun in 1554 and made into an art museum in the late 18th century.

LOUVER
a Construction.
b Set in gable.

lov·a·ble (luv′ə·bəl) adj. Worthy of love; amiable; also, evoking love. Also **love′a·ble. — lov′a·bil·i·ty, lov′a·ble·ness** n. **— lov′a·bly** adv.

love (luv) n. **1.** A deep devotion or affection for another person or persons: *love* for one's children. **2.** A strong sexual passion for another person. **3.** Sexual passion in general or the gratification of it. **4.** One who is beloved. **5.** A very great interest in, or enjoyment of, something; also, the thing so enjoyed. **6.** In tennis, a score of nothing. **— in love**

Experiencing love for someone or something. **— to fall in love** To conceive a love for someone or something. **— to make love** To kiss, embrace, etc., as lovers. **—** v. **loved, lov·ing** v.t. **1.** To feel love or affection for. **2.** To take pleasure or delight in: to *love* good food. **3.** To show love for by kissing or caressing. **—** v.i. **4.** To be in love. [OE *lufu*]

Love (luv) A personification of love; Cupid or Eros.

love apple A former name for the tomato.

love·bird (luv′bûrd′) n. One of several small parrots often kept as cage birds: so called from the affection they show.

love knot A knot tied in pledge of love and constancy; also, a representation of it, as in jewelry.

love·less (luv′lis) adj. **1.** Having no love. **2.** Receiving no love. **— love′less·ly** adv. **— love′less·ness** n.

love-lies-bleed·ing (luv′līz′blē′ding) n. A species of amaranth having crimson flowers.

love·lorn (luv′lôrn) adj. Pining for one's lover.

love·ly (luv′lē) adj. **·li·er, ·li·est 1.** Possessing qualities that inspire admiration or love. **2.** Beautiful: a *lovely* rose. **3.** *Informal* Delightful; pleasing. **— love′li·ness** n.

love potion A magic draft or drink designed to arouse love toward a certain person in the one who drinks.

lov·er (luv′ər) n. **1.** One who loves: a *lover* of humanity. **2.** One in love with or making love to a person of the opposite sex: in the singular now used only of the man. **3.** One who especially enjoys diversion, pursuit, etc.: a *lover* of golf. **— lov′er·ly** adj. & adv.

love seat A double chair or small sofa for two persons.

love·sick (luv′sik′) adj. **1.** Languishing with love. **2.** Indicating such a state: a *lovesick* serenade. **— love′sick′ness** n.

lov·ing (luv′ing) adj. **1.** Affectionate; devoted; kind. **2.** Indicative of love. **— lov′ing·ly** adv. **— lov′ing·ness** n.

loving cup A wine cup, usu. with two or more handles, formerly passed around a circle of friends at a banquet.

lov·ing-kind·ness (luv′ing·kīnd′nis) n. Kindness that comes from or indicates personal affection or regard.

low¹ (lō) adj. **1.** Having relatively little upward extension; not high or tall. **2.** Located or placed below the normal or usual level: a *low* marsh. **3.** Near the horizon: a *low* moon. **4.** Pertaining to latitudes nearest the equator. **5.** Relatively small in depth, height, amount, degree, etc. **6.** Of or producing sounds of relatively long wavelengths: a *low* pitch. **7.** Not loud; faint: a *low* rustle. **8.** Extending far downward; deep: a *low* bow. **9.** Exposing part of the wearer's shoulders, back, or chest: a *low* blouse. **10.** Melancholy or sad; depressed: *low* spirits. **11.** Lacking vigor; feeble. **12.** Not adequately provided with; short of: to be *low* on groceries. **13.** *Informal* Having little or no ready cash. **14.** Inexpensive: a *low* price. **15.** Poor, unfavorable, or disparaging: to have a *low* estimate of one's abilities. **16.** Humble or inferior, as in origin, rank, position, etc. **17.** Inferior in quality: a *low* grade of tobacco. **18.** Lacking in refinement; vulgar: *low* companions. **19.** Morally base or mean. **20.** Relatively recent, as a date. **21.** Relatively simple in structure, function, or organization: a *low* form of animal life. **22.** In the Anglican Church, of or pertaining to the Low Church. **23.** *Mech.* Denoting a gear arrangement, as in transmissions, yielding a slow or the slowest output speed. **24.** *Phonet.* Of vowel sounds, produced with the tongue depressed and flat, as (ä) in *large:* opposed to *high.* **—** adv. **1.** In or to a low level, position, degree, etc. **2.** In a low manner. **3.** Softly; quietly. **4.** With a low pitch. **5.** At a low price; cheaply. **6.** In or to a humble, poor, or degraded condition. **—** n. **1.** A low level, position, degree, etc. **2.** *Meteorol.* An area of low barometric pressure. **3.** *Mech.* An arrangement of gears that yields a slow or the slowest output speed. [Early ME *lah* < ON *lagr*] **— low′ness** n.

low² (lō) v.i. **1.** To make the hollow, bellowing sound of cattle; moo. **—** v.t. **2.** To utter by lowing. **—** n. The vocal sound made by cattle: also **low′ing.** [OE *hlōwan*]

low·born (lō′bôrn′) adj. Of humble birth.

low·boy (lō′boi) n. A short-legged chest of drawers of about table height, similar to the lower part of a highboy.

low·bred (lō′bred′) adj. **1.** Of humble or inferior origin or birth. **2.** Vulgar; coarse.

low·brow (lō′brou′) n. *Informal* A person of uncultivated or vulgar tastes. **—** adj. Of or suitable for such a person: also **low′browed′. — low′brow′ism** n.

Low-Church (lō′chûrch′) adj. Of or belonging to a group **(Low Church)** in the Anglican Church that stresses evangelical doctrine and is, in general, opposed to extreme ritualism. **— Low′-Church′man** (-mən) n.

low comedy Comedy that is characterized by slapstick and lively physical action rather than by witty dialogue.

low·down (lō′doun′) n. *Slang* The truth.

low-down² (lō′doun′) adj. *Informal* **1.** Unethical or mean. **2.** In jazz, slow, sad, or sensuous, as the blues.

low·er (lou′ər) v.i. **1.** To look sullen; scowl. **2.** To appear dark and threatening, as the weather. **—** n. **1.** A sullen look; a scowl. **2.** A dark, threatening look, as of the weather. [Cf. G *lauern* to lurk]

low·er² (lō′ər) Comparative of LOW. — *adj.* **1.** Inferior in rank, value, etc. **2.** Situated below something else. **3.** *Often cap. Geol.* Older; designating strata normally beneath the newer (and upper) rock formations. — *n.* That which is beneath something else; esp., a lower berth. — *v.t.* **1.** To bring to a lower position or level; let down, as a window. **2.** To reduce in degree, quality, amount, etc.: to *lower* prices. **3.** To undermine or weaken. **4.** To bring down in estimation, rank, etc. **5.** To change (a sound) to a lower pitch or volume. — *v.i.* **6.** To become less; decrease; sink.

low·er-case (lō′ər·kās′) *Printing adj.* Of, in, or indicating small letters, as distinguished from capitals. — *v.t.* -cased, -cas·ing To set as or change to lower-case letters.

lower case *Printing* **1.** In type cases, the lower tray, containing the small letters of the alphabet. See CASE². **2.** The small letters of the alphabet.

lower class The socially or economically inferior group in society. — **low·er-class** (lō′ər·klas′, -kläs′) *adj.*

low·er-class·man (lō′ər·klas′mən, -kläs′-) *n. pl.* ·men (-mən) A student in either of the first two years of a four-year course; a freshman or sophomore.

Lower House The larger and more widely representative branch of a bicameral legislative body, as the House of Representatives in the U.S. Also **Lower Chamber.**

low·er·most (lō′ər·mōst′) *adj.* Lowest.

Lower Paleolithic See under PALEOLITHIC.

lower world 1. The abode of the dead; hell; Hades; Sheol. Also **lower regions. 2.** The earth.

low frequency *Telecom.* Radio waves having a frequency of from 30 to 300 kilocycles.

Low German See under GERMAN.

low·land (lō′lənd, -land′) *n. Usu. pl.* Land lying lower than the adjacent country. — *adj.* Of, pertaining to, or characteristic of a low or level country.

Low·land (lō′lənd, -land′) *n.* The speech or dialect of the Scottish Lowlands. — *adj.* Pertaining or belonging to the Scottish Lowlands.

Low Latin See under LATIN.

low·ly (lō′lē) *adj.* ·li·er, ·li·est **1.** Humble or low in rank, origin, nature, etc. **2.** Full of humility; meek. **3.** Situated or lying low. — *adv.* **1.** In a low condition, manner, position, etc. **2.** Modestly; humbly. — **low′li·ness** *n.*

Low Mass A form of Mass celebrated without music and by one priest usu. assisted by a server or altar boy.

low-mind·ed (lō′mīn′did) *adj.* Having low, vulgar, or mean thoughts, sentiments, or motives. — **low′-mind′ed·ly** *adv.* — **low′-mind′ed·ness** *n.*

low-necked (lō′nekt′) *adj.* Having a low neckline.

low-pitched (lō′picht′) *adj.* **1.** Low in tone or range of tone. **2.** Having little slope, as a roof. **3.** *Music* Built for a pitch lower than standard pitch: said of instruments.

low-pres·sure (lō′presh′ər) *adj.* **1.** Having or operating under a low degree of pressure. **2.** *Meteorol.* Designating atmospheric pressure below that normal at sea level.

low relief Bas-relief.

low-spir·it·ed (lō′spir′it·id) *adj.* Despondent; melancholy. — **low′-spir′it·ed·ly** *adv.* — **low′-spir′it·ed·ness** *n.*

low tide 1. The ebb tide at its lowest stage. **2.** The time this lowest stage occurs. **3.** The lowest point or level reached.

low water A very low level of water in a stream, etc.

lox¹ (loks) *n.* A salty, smoked salmon, often eaten with cream cheese, bagels, etc. [< Yiddish < G *lachs* salmon]

lox² (loks) *n.* Liquid oxygen.

loy·al (loi′əl) *adj.* **1.** Bearing true allegiance to a constituted authority, as to one's sovereign, government, etc. **2.** Constant and faithful in any relation or obligation implying trust, confidence, etc. **3.** Indicating or professing loyalty. [< OF < L *legalis*] — **loy′al·ism** *n.* — **loy′al·ly** *adv.*

loy·al·ist (loi′əl·ist) *n.* One who supports and defends his government, esp. in times of crisis or war.

Loy·al·ist (loi′əl·ist) *n.* **1.** In the American Revolution, a colonist who remained loyal to the British crown. **2.** In the Spanish Civil War, one who supported the government of the Republic against the uprising of Franco.

loy·al·ty (loi′əl·tē) *n. pl.* ·ties The state, quality, or fact of being loyal; fidelity; allegiance.

loz·enge (loz′inj) *n.* **1.** A small sweetened tablet or candy, now usu. medicated. **2.** *Math.* A diamond-shaped figure. [< OF < L *lapis*, -*idis* stone]

LP (el′pē′) *adj.* Designating a phonograph record pressed with microgrooves and played at a speed of 33⅓ revolutions per minute: also *long-playing.* — *n.* An LP record: a trade mark. [< l(ong)-p(laying)]

LSD (el′es′dē′) *n.* A drug that produces states similar to those of schizophrenia, used in medicine and illicitly as a hallucinogen. See LYSERGIC ACID. Also **LSD-25.** [< l(y)s-(ergic acid) d(iethylamide)]

lu·au (loo′ou′) *n.* A Hawaiian feast with entertainment.

lub·ber (lub′ər) *n.* **1.** An awkward, ungainly fellow. **2.** A landlubber. [Origin uncertain] — **lub′ber·ly** *adj. & adv.*

lu·bri·cant (loo′brə·kənt) *n.* A substance, as oil, grease, graphite, etc., used to coat moving parts in order to reduce friction and wear. — *adj.* Lubricating.

lu·bri·cate (loo′brə·kāt) *v.t.* ·cat·ed, ·cat·ing **1.** To apply a lubricant to. **2.** To make slippery or smooth. [< L < *lubricus* slippery] — **lu′bri·ca′tion** *n.* — **lu′bri·ca′tive** *adj.* — **lu′bri·ca′tor** *n.*

lu·bric·i·ty (loo·bris′ə·tē) *n. pl.* ·ties **1.** Lewdness; lasciviousness. **2.** Shiftiness; elusiveness. **3.** Slipperiness. [< F < L < *lubricus* slippery]

lu·cent (loo′sənt) *adj.* **1.** Showing or giving off radiance. **2.** Transparent or semitransparent. [< L *lucens*, -*entis*, ppr. of *lucere* to shine] — **lu′cen·cy** *n.* — **lu′cent·ly** *adv.*

lu·cerne (loo·sûrn′) *Brit.* Alfalfa. [< F]

lu·ces (loo′sēz) Plural of LUX.

lu·cid (loo′sid) *adj.* **1.** Easily understood; clear: a *lucid* explanation. **2.** Mentally sound, clear, or rational: a *lucid* interval. **3.** Shining; bright. [< L *lucere* to shine] — **lu·cid·i·ty** (loo·sid′ə·tē), **lu′cid·ness** *n.* — **lu′cid·ly** *adv.*

Lu·ci·fer (loo′sə·fər) *n.* **1.** The archangel who led the revolt of the angels and fell from Heaven: identified with *Satan.* **2.** The planet Venus when it appears as the morning star. [< L, light-bearer < *lux, lucis* light + *ferre* to bear]

Lu·cite (loo′sīt) *n.* A transparent acrylic resin, easily machined into various shapes.

luck (luk) *n.* **1.** That which happens by chance; fortune; lot. **2.** Good fortune; success. **3.** Any object regarded as bringing good fortune. — **to be down on one's luck** To suffer failure, poverty, etc. — **to be in luck** To meet with success or good fortune. — **to be out of luck** To be unlucky. — **to try one's luck** To attempt to do something without any certainty of success. [Prob. < MDu. *luk, geluk*]

luck·less (luk′lis) *adj.* Having bad luck; unlucky. — **luck′less·ly** *adv.* — **luck′less·ness** *n.*

luck·y (luk′ē) *adj.* **luck·i·er, luck·i·est 1.** Accompanied by or having good fortune. **2.** Bringing or resulting in good fortune. **3.** Believed to bring good fortune. — **luck′i·ly** *adv.* — **luck′i·ness** *n.*

lu·cra·tive (loo′krə·tiv) *adj.* Producing or yielding gain, profit, or wealth; profitable. [< L < *lucratus*, pp. of *lucrari* to gain] — **lu′cra·tive·ly** *adv.* — **lu′cra·tive·ness** *n.*

lu·cre (loo′kər) *n.* Money or riches: now chiefly in the humorous phrase: **filthy lucre.** [< F < L *lucrum* gain]

lu·cu·brate (loo′kyoo·brāt) *v.i.* ·brat·ed, ·brat·ing **1.** To study or write laboriously, esp. at night. **2.** To write in a learned manner. [< L *lucubrare* to work by candlelight]

lu·cu·bra·tion (loo′kyoo·brā′shən) *n.* **1.** Earnest and labored study. **2.** The product of such study, esp. a pedantic literary composition. **3.** *pl.* Any literary effort. — **lu′cu·bra′tor** *n.* — **lu′cu·bra·to′ry** (-brə·tôr′ē, -tō′rē) *adj.*

lu·di·crous (loo′də·krəs) *adj.* Exciting laughter or ridicule; ridiculous; absurd. [< L < *ludere* to play] — **lu′di·crous·ly** *adv.* — **lu′di·crous·ness** *n.*

luff (luf) *Naut. n.* **1.** The sailing of a ship close to the wind. **2.** The rounded and fullest part of a vessel's bow. **3.** The foremost edge of a fore-and-aft sail. — *v.i.* **1.** To bring the head of a vessel nearer the wind. **2.** To bring the head of a vessel into the wind, with the sails shaking. Also *loof.* [ME *lof, loven*]

Luft·waf·fe (looft′väf′ə) *n. German* The German air force during World War II.

lug¹ (lug) *n.* **1.** An earlike projection for holding or supporting something. **2.** *Mech.* A nut, closed at one end. **3.** *Slang* A fellow, esp. a clumsy one. [Origin uncertain]

lug² (lug) *v.* **lugged, lug·ging** *v.t.* **1.** To carry or pull with effort. — *v.i.* **2.** To pull or drag with effort; tug. — *n.* **1.** The act or exertion of lugging; also, that which is lugged. **2.** *Naut.* A lugsail. [Prob. Scand.]

lug³ (lug) *n.* A lugworm. [Origin uncertain]

lug·gage (lug′ij) *n.* Suitcases, trunks, etc., used for traveling; baggage. [< LUG²]

lug·ger (lug′ər) *n. Naut.* A one-, two-, or three-masted vessel having lugsails only. [< LUG(SAIL) + -ER²]

lug·sail (lug′səl, -sāl′) *n. Naut.* A four-cornered sail having no boom and bent to a yard that hangs obliquely on the mast: also called *lug.*

lu·gu·bri·ous (loo·goo′brē·əs, -gyoo′-) *adj.* Very sad, or mournful, esp. in a ludicrous manner. [< L < *lugere* to mourn] — **lu·gu′bri·ous·ly** *adv.* — **lu·gu′bri·ous·ness** *n.*

lug·worm (lug′wûrm′) *n.* An annelid worm with two rows of tufted gills on the back, living in the sand of seashores.

Luke (look) Physician and companion of St. Paul; traditionally thought to be the author of the third Gospel: called **Saint Luke.** — *n.* The third Gospel of the New Testament.

luke·warm (look′wôrm′) *adj.* **1.** Moderately warm; tepid. **2.** Lacking in ardor, enthusiasm, or conviction; indifferent:

a *lukewarm* greeting. [Prob. OE *hlēow* warm.] —**luke′·warm·ly** *adv.* —**luke′warm′ness** *n.*

lull (lul) *v.t.* **1.** To quiet or put to sleep by soothing sounds or motions. **2.** To calm or allay, esp. by deception: to *lull* someone's suspicions. —*v.i.* **3.** To become calm or quiet. —*n.* A brief period of calm, quiet, or diminished activity. [< ME *lullen*]

lull·a·by (lul′ə·bī) *n. pl.* **·bies 1.** A song to lull a child to sleep; a cradlesong. **2.** A piece of instrumental music in the manner of a lullaby. —*v.t.* **·bied, ·by·ing** *Rare* To soothe with a lullaby.

lum·ba·go (lum·bā′gō) *n.* Pain in the lumbar region of the back; backache, esp. in the small of the back.

lum·bar (lum′bər, -bär) *adj.* Pertaining to or situated near the loins. —*n.* A lumbar vertebra, nerve, artery, etc. [< NL < L *lumbus* loin]

lum·ber[1] (lum′bər) *n.* **1.** *U.S. & Canadian* Timber sawed into boards, planks, etc., of specified lengths. **2.** *Chiefly Brit.* Household articles no longer used and usu. stored away. —*adj.* Made of, pertaining to, or dealing in lumber. —*v.t.* **1.** *U.S. & Canadian* To cut down (timber); also, to cut down the timber of (an area). **2.** *Chiefly Brit.* To fill or obstruct with useless articles. —*v.i.* **3.** *U.S. & Canadian* To cut down or saw timber for marketing. [Var. of *Lombard* in obs. sense of "money-lender, pawnshop," hence, stored articles] —**lum′ber·er** *n.* —**lum′ber·ing** *n.*

lum·ber[2] (lum′bər) *v.i.* **1.** To move or proceed in a heavy or awkward manner. **2.** To move with a rumbling noise. —*n.* A rumbling noise. [ME *lomeren*] —**lum′ber·ing** *adj.* —**lum′ber·ing·ly** *adv.*

lum·ber·jack (lum′bər·jak) *n. U.S. & Canadian* A person who fells or transports timber; a logger. [< LUMBER[1] + *jack* man, boy]

lum·ber·man (lum′bər·mən) *n. pl.* **·men** (mən) *U.S. & Canadian* **1.** A lumberjack. **2.** One who is engaged in the business of lumbering.

lum·ber·yard (lum′bər·yärd) *n. U.S. & Canadian* A yard for the storage or sale of lumber.

lu·men (lōō′mən) *n. pl.* **·mens** or **·mi·na** (-mə·nə) *Physics* A unit for measuring the flow of light, equal to the flow of one international candle. [< L, light]

lu·mi·nar·y (lōō′mə·ner′ē) *n. pl.* **·nar·ies 1.** Any body that gives light, esp. the sun or the moon. **2.** One who has achieved great eminence. [< OF < LL < *lumen* light]

lu·mi·nesce (lōō′mə·nes′) *v.i.* **·nesced, ·nesc·ing** To be or become luminescent.

lu·mi·nes·cence (lōō′mə·nes′əns) *n.* An emission of light, such as fluorescence and phosphorescence, not directly attributable to the heat that produces incandescence. [< L *lumen* light + -ESCENT] —**lu′mi·nes′cent** *adj.*

lumini- *combining form* Light; luminescence. Also **lumin-** (before vowels), **lumino-**. [< L *lumen, luminis* light]

lu·mi·nif·er·ous (lōō′mə·nif′ər·əs) *adj.* Producing light.

lu·mi·nous (lōō′mə·nəs) *adj.* **1.** Full of light. **2.** Giving off light; shining. **3.** Easily understood; clear. **4.** Brilliantly intelligent. [< L *lumen* light] —**lu′mi·nous·ly** *adv.* —**lu′mi·nous·ness, lu′mi·nos′i·ty** *n.*

lum·mox (lum′əks) *n. U.S. Informal* An oaf.

lump[1] (lump) *n.* **1.** A shapeless mass, esp. a small mass. **2.** A swelling. **3.** A mass of things thrown together; aggregate. **4.** A heavy, ungainly, and usu. stupid person. —**a lump in one's throat** A feeling of tightness in the throat, as from emotion. —**in a** (or **the**) **lump** All together. —*adj.* Formed in a lump or lumps: *lump* sugar. —*v.t.* **1.** To put together in one mass, group, etc. **2.** To consider or treat as one mass, group, etc. **3.** To make lumps in or on. —*v.i.* **4.** To become lumpy. [< ME]

lump[2] (lump) *v.t. Informal* To put up with; endure: You can like it or *lump* it.

lump·ish (lum′pish) *adj.* **1.** Like a lump. **2.** Stupid; clumsy. —**lump′ish·ly** *adv.* —**lump′ish·ness** *n.*

lump sum A full or single sum of money paid at one time.

lump·y (lum′pē) *adj.* **lump·i·er, lump·i·est 1.** Full of lumps. **2.** Covered with lumps. **3.** Lumpish. **4.** Running in rough waves. —**lump′i·ly** *adv.* —**lump′i·ness** *n.*

Lu·na (lōō′nə) In Roman mythology, the goddess of the moon: identified with the Greek *Selene.* [< L]

lu·na·cy (lōō′nə·sē) *n. pl.* **·cies 1.** Irresponsible or senseless conduct. **2.** *Law* Insanity.

Luna moth A large North American moth having light green wings with long tails and lunate spots.

lu·nar (lōō′nər) *adj.* **1.** Of the moon. **2.** Round or crescentshaped like the moon. **3.** Measured by the revolutions of the moon: a *lunar* month. [< L < *luna* moon]

lunar excursion module *Aerospace* The vehicle that transports astronauts from the orbiting command module to the moon's surface and back.

lunar month See under MONTH.

lunar year A period of twelve lunar months, one month being added at intervals to make the mean length of the astronomical year, as in the Hebrew calendar.

lu·nate (lōō′nāt) *adj.* Crescent-shaped. Also **lu′nat·ed.**

lu·na·tic (lōō′nə·tik) *adj.* **1.** Insane. **2.** Wildly foolish or irrational. **3.** Of or for the insane. Also **lu·nat·i·cal** (lōō·nat′i·kəl). —*n.* An insane person. [< LL < L *luna* moon]

lunatic fringe Those followers or devotees of a movement, idea, etc., who are extreme or fanatical in their enthusiasm.

lunch (lunch) *n.* **1.** A light meal, esp. the noonday meal. **2.** Food for a lunch. —*v.i.* To eat lunch. —**lunch′er** *n.*

lunch·eon (lun′chən) *n.* A noonday meal, esp. a formal one.

lunch·eon·ette (lun′chən·et′) *n.* A restaurant where light lunches and other meals may be obtained.

lunch·room (lunch′rōōm′, -rŏŏm′) *n.* A restaurant serving light lunches; luncheonette. Also **lunch room.**

lung (lung) *n. Anat.* **1.** Either of two saclike organs of respiration in the thorax of man and other airbreathing vertebrates. ◆ Collateral adjective: *pulmonary.* ◆ An analogous organ in certain invertebrates. [OE *lungen*]

LUNGS

a Epiglottis. *b* Larynx. *c* Trachea. *d* Right lung. *e* Left lung. *f, i* Upper lobes. *g* Middle lobe. *h, j* Lower lobes. *k, l* Bronchi.

lunge (lunj) *n.* **1.** A sudden pass or thrust, as with a sword, etc. **2.** A quick movement or plunge forward. —*v.* **lunged, lung·ing** —*v.i.* **1.** To make a lunge; thrust. **2.** To move with a lunge. —*v.t.* **3.** To cause to lunge. [< F < L *ad* to + *longus* long]

lung·wort (lung′wûrt′) *n.* Any of various plants of the borage family, esp., a European herb having white blotches on its leaves.

luni- *combining form* Of or pertaining to the moon; lunar. [< L *luna* moon]

lu·pine[1] (lōō′pīn) *adj.* **1.** Of, like, or related to a wolf or wolves. **2.** Fierce; ravenous. [< L < *lupus* wolf]

lu·pine[2] (lōō′pin) *n.* **1.** Any of various plants of the pea family, bearing mostly blue, white, or purple flowers, as the white lupine of Europe, whose seeds are edible. **2.** The seeds of the white lupine. [< F < L *lupinus* wolflike]

lu·pus (lōō′pəs) *n. Pathol.* Any of various forms of a tuberculous disease of the skin, characterized by brownish nodules or scaly red patches. [< L, wolf]

lurch[1] (lûrch) *v.i.* **1.** To roll suddenly to one side. **2.** To stagger. —*n.* **1.** A sudden swaying. **2.** A reeling.

lurch[2] (lûrch) *n.* **1.** An embarrassing or difficult position; predicament: now only in the phrase **to leave** (**someone**) **in the lurch. 2.** In cribbage, the state of a player who has made 30 points or less while his opponent has won with 61. [< F *lourche* deceived < Gmc.]

lure (lŏŏr, lyŏŏr) *n.* **1.** Anything that attracts or entices. **2.** In angling, an artificial bait. **3.** In falconry, a device consisting of a bunch of feathers and a bait, fastened to a long cord and used to recall a hawk. —*v.t.* **lured, lur·ing 1.** To attract or entice; allure. **2.** To recall (a hawk) with a lure. [< OF < MHG *luoder* to bait] —**lur′er** *n.*

lu·rid (lŏŏr′id, lyŏŏr-) *adj.* **1.** Shocking or sensational. **2.** Pale and sickly in color. **3.** Lighted up with a yellowish red glare or glow esp. in smoke or darkness. [< L *luridus* sallow] —**lu′rid·ly** *adv.* —**lu′rid·ness** *n.*

lurk (lûrk) *v.i.* **1.** To lie hidden, as in ambush. **2.** To exist unnoticed or unsuspected. **3.** To move secretly or furtively; slink. [ME *lurken*] —**lurk′ing·ly** *adv.*

lus·cious (lush′əs) *adj.* **1.** Very pleasurable to the sense of taste or smell. **2.** Pleasing to any sense. **3.** Excessively sweet; cloying. —**lus′cious·ly** *adv.* —**lus′cious·ness** *n.*

lush[1] (lush) *adj.* **1.** Abounding in vigorous growth: a *lush* countryside. **2.** Delicious and succulent. **3.** Elaborate in effects, etc. [< OF < L *laxus* loose] —**lush′ness** *n.*

lush[2] (lush) *Slang n.* A heavy drinker; drunkard.

lust (lust) *n.* **1.** Sexual appetite. **2.** Excessive sexual appetite, esp. that seeking immediate or ruthless satisfaction. **3.** An overwhelming desire: a *lust* for power. —*v.i.* To have passionate or inordinate desire, esp. sexual desire: often with *after* or *for.* [OE, pleasure]

lus·ter (lus′tər) *n.* **1.** Sheen; gloss. **2.** Brilliance of light; radiance. **3.** Splendor, glory, or distinction. **4.** A source or center of light, esp. a chandelier. **5.** Any of various substances used to give a polish to a surface. **6.** In ceramics, a glossy, metallic, and often iridescent finish given to the surface of an object. **7.** A fabric of mixed wool and cotton and having a glossy finish. **8.** *Mineral.* The surface appearance of a mineral as determined by the intensity or quality of the light it reflects. —*v. lus·tered* and *Brit. ·tred, lus·ter·ing* or *Brit. ·tring v.t.* **1.** To give a luster or gloss to. —*v.i.* **2.** To be or become lustrous. Also *Brit.* **lus′tre.** [< F < Ital. < L < *lustrum* purification]

lus·ter·ware (lus′tər·wâr′) *n.* Pottery having a lustrous and often iridescent sheen.

lust·ful (lust′fəl) *adj.* Characterized or driven by lust. — **lust′ful·ly** *adv.* — **lust′ful·ness** *n.*

lus·trate (lus′trāt) *v.t.* **·trat·ed, ·trat·ing** To purify by an offering or ceremony. [< L *lustrum* purification] — **lus·tra′tion** *n.* — **lus·tra·tive** (lus′trə·tiv) *adj.*

lus·trous (lus′trəs) *adj.* **1.** Having a luster; glossy. **2.** Brilliant; shining. — **lus′trous·ly** *adv.* — **lus′trous·ness** *n.*

lus·trum (lus′trəm) *n.* **1.** A period of five years. **2.** In ancient Rome, the solemn ceremony of purification of the entire people made every five years.

lust·y (lus′tē) *adj.* **lust·i·er, lust·i·est 1.** Full of vigor; robust. **2.** Powerful. — **lust′i·ly** *adv.* — **lust′i·ness** *n.*

lu·ta·nist (lōō′tə·nist, lyōō′-) *n.* One who plays the lute. Also **lu′te·nist.**

lute[1] (lōōt, lyōōt) *n.* An old musical instrument having strings that are plucked by the fingers, a large body shaped like half of a pear, and a long, fretted neck usu. bent at a sharp angle just below the peg box. [< OF < Pg. < Arabic *al'ūd* the piece of wood]

lute[2] (lōōt, lyōōt) *n.* A composition of finely powdered clay, used as a sealing agent for joints of pipes, etc. Also **lut′ing.** — *v.t.* **lut·ed, lut·ing** To seal with lute. [< OF < L *lutum* mud]

lu·te·ous (lōō′tē·əs) *adj.* Light or moderate greenish yellow in color. [< L *luteus* < *lutum* weed used by dyers]

LUTE

lu·te·ti·um (lōō·tē′shē·əm, -tē′shəm) *n.* A metallic element (symbol Lu) of the lanthanide series, isolated from ytterbium. Also **lu·te′ci·um.** See ELEMENT.

Lu·ther·an (lōō′thər·ən) *adj.* Of or pertaining to Martin Luther, his doctrines, or to the Lutheran Church. — *n.* A member of the Lutheran Church. — **Lu′ther·an·ism** *n.*

lu·tist (lōō′tist) *n.* One who makes or plays lutes.

lux (luks) *n.* *pl.* **lux·es** or **lu·ces** (lōō′sēz) *Physics* The unit of illumination in the metric system, equivalent to .0929 foot-candle, or 1 lumen per square meter. [< L, light]

lux·u·ri·ance (lug·zhoor′ē·əns, luk·shoor′-) *n.* The state or quality of being luxuriant. Also **lux·u′ri·an·cy.**

lux·u·ri·ant (lug·zhoor′ē·ənt, luk·shoor′-) *adj.* **1.** Growing lushly and profusely, as vegetation. **2.** Abundant, exuberant, or ornate, as in design, etc. — **lux·u′ri·ant·ly** *adv.*

lux·u·ri·ate (lug·zhoor′ē·āt, luk·shoor′-) *v.i.* **·at·ed, ·at·ing 1.** To take great pleasure; indulge oneself fully: with *in.* **2.** To live sumptuously. **3.** To grow profusely. [See LUXURY.] — **lux·u′ri·a′tion** *n.*

lux·u·ri·ous (lug·zhoor′ē·əs, luk·shoor′-) *adj.* **1.** Characterized by or conducive to luxury or extreme comfort; opulent; sumptuous. **2.** Indulging in or given to luxury. — **lux·u′ri·ous·ly** *adv.* — **lux·u′ri·ous·ness** *n.*

lux·u·ry (luk′shər·ē, *occasionally* lug′zhər·ē) *n.* *pl.* **·ries 1.** Anything, usu. expensive or rare, that ministers to comfort or pleasure but is not a necessity to life, health, etc. **2.** Free indulgence in that which is expensive, rare, or extremely gratifying. [< OF < L *luxus* extravagance]

-ly[1] *suffix of adjectives* **1.** Like; characteristic of; pertaining to: *manly, godly.* **2.** Occurring every (specified interval): *weekly, daily.* Compare -LIKE. [OE *-līc*]

-ly[2] *suffix of adverbs* **1.** In a (specified) manner: used to form adverbs from adjectives, or (rarely) from nouns: *brightly, busily.* **2.** At every (specified interval): *hourly, yearly.* [OE *-līce* < *-līc* -ly*[1]*]

ly·cée (lē·sā′) *n.* *French* In France, a secondary school financed by the government. [See LYCEUM.]

ly·ce·um (lī·sē′əm, lī′-) *n.* *pl.* **·ce·ums** or **·ce·a** (-sē′ə) **1.** *U.S.* An organization providing popular instruction by lectures, concerts, etc.; also, its building. **2.** A lycée.

Ly·ce·um (lī·sē′əm, lī′-) *n.* A grove near Athens in which Aristotle taught. [< L < Gk. *lykeios,* epithet of Apollo]

lyd·dite (lid′īt) *n.* A high explosive, composed chiefly of picric acid, used in shells. [after *Lydd,* a town in England]

Lyd·i·a (lid′ē·ə) An ancient country in western Asia Minor, famous for its wealth and luxury. — **Lyd′i·an** *adj.* & *n.*

lye (lī) *n.* **1.** A solution leached from ashes, or derived from a substance containing alkali, used in making soap. **2.** Any solution obtained by leaching. [OE *lēah*]

ly·ing[1] (lī′ing) *n.* The act of telling lies; untruthfulness. — *adj.* Deceitful or false; untrue: a *lying* tongue.

ly·ing[2] (lī′ing) Present participle of LIE[1].

ly·ing-in (lī′ing·in′) *n.* The confinement of women during childbirth. — *adj.* Of or pertaining to childbirth.

lymph (limf) *n.* *Physiol.* A yellowish alkaline fluid derived from the body tissues, consisting of lymphcytes and a plasma similar to that of blood. [< L *limpa* water]

lym·phat·ic (lim·fat′ik) *adj.* **1.** Containing, conveying, or pertaining to lymph. **2.** Caused by or affecting the lymph nodes. **3.** Sluggish; indifferent. — *n.* A vessel that conveys lymph into the veins.

lymphato- *combining form* Lymphatic. Also, before vowels, **lymphat-.**

lymph node *Anat.* Any of numerous glandlike bodies found in the course of the lymphatic vessels and producing lymphocytes and monocytes. Also **lymph gland.**

lympho- *combining form* Lymph; of the lymph or the lymphatics. Also, before vowels, **lymph-.** [See LYMPH]

lym·pho·cyte (lim′fə·sīt) *n.* *Physiol.* A variety of nucleated, colorless leucocyte formed in the tissue of the lymph nodes and resembling white blood corpuscles. Also **lymph cell.**

lym·phoid (lim′foid) *adj.* Of, pertaining to, or resembling lymph or the tissues of a lymph node.

lynch (linch) *v.t.* To kill (a person accused of a crime) by mob action, as by hanging, without due process of law. [< LYNCH LAW] — **lynch′er** *n.* — **lynch′ing** *n.*

lynch law The practice of administering punishment by lynching. [? after Charles *Lynch,* 1736–96, or William *Lynch,* 1742–1820, Virginia magistrates]

lynx (lingks) *n.* *pl.* **lynx·es** or **lynx** A wildcat of Europe and North America having a short tail, tufted ears, and relatively long limbs. Also called *bobcat.* [< L < Gk. *lynx*]

lynx-eyed (lingks′īd′) *adj.* Having sharp sight.

ly·on·naise (lī′ə·nāz′, Fr. lē·ô·nez′) *adj.* Made with finely sliced onions; esp. designating a method of preparing potatoes with fried onions. [< F, fem. of *lyonnais* of Lyon]

ly·o·phil·ic (lī′ə·fil′ik) *adj.* *Chem.* Designating a colloidal system in which the solid particles attract and hold molecules of the dispersion medium. [< LYO- + Gk. *philos* loving]

ly·o·pho·bic (lī′ə·fō′bik) *adj.* *Chem.* Designating a colloidal system in which the solid particles are easily precipitated out of the dispersion medium. [< LYO- + Gk. *phobos* fear]

Ly·ra (lī′rə) *n.* A constellation, the Harp or the Lyre, containing the star Vega. [< L < Gk.]

ly·rate (lī′rāt) *adj.* Shaped like a lyre. Also **ly′rat·ed.** [< NL *lyratus*] — **ly′rate·ly** *adv.*

lyre (līr) *n.* An ancient harplike stringed instrument, used by the Greeks to accompany poetry and song. [< OF < L *lyra* < Gk.]

Lyre (līr) *n.* The constellation Lyra.

lyre·bird (līr′bûrd′) *n.* Either of two species of Australian birds, the male of which spreads its tail feathers into the shape of a lyre.

lyr·ic (lir′ik) *adj.* **1.** Of poetry, expressing the poet's personal or inner feelings; also, pertaining to the method, personality, etc., of a writer of such verse. **2.** Meant to be sung. **3.** *Music* Having a singing voice of a light, flexible quality: a *lyric* soprano. **4.** Pertaining to a lyre. Also **lyr′i·cal.** — *n.* **1.** *Usu. pl.* The words of a song. **2.** A lyric poem. [< L < Gk. *lyra* a lyre] — **lyr′i·cal·ly** *adv.*

lyr·i·cism (lir′ə·siz′əm) *n.* The quality of emotional self-expression in the arts.

lyr·i·cist (lir′ə·sist) *n.* **1.** One who writes the words of a song or the lyrics for a musical play. **2.** A lyric poet.

ly·ri·form (lī′rə·fôrm) *adj.* Shaped like a lyre.

lyse (līs) *v.t.* & *v.i.* **lysed, lys·ing** To undergo or cause to undergo lysis. [< Gk. *lysis* loosening]

ly·ser·gic acid (li·sûr′jik) *n.* *Biochem.* A crystalline alkaloid derived from ergot and forming the base of **lysergic acid di·eth·yl·am·ide-25** (d′eth·əl·am′īd), or LSD. [< LYS- + *erg(ot)* + -IC]

lysi- *combining form* A loosening; dissolving: *lysergic acid, lysine.* Also, before vowels, **lys-.** [< Gk. *lysis* a loosening]

ly·sine (lī′sēn, -sin) *n.* *Biochem.* An amino acid $C_6H_{14}O_2N_2$, necessary to animal growth, produced by the hydrolysis of various proteins. Also **ly′sin.** [< LYS- + -INE[2]]

ly·sis (lī′sis) *n.* **1.** *Med.* The gradual disappearing of the symptoms of a disease. **2.** *Biochem.* The process of disintegration or destruction of cells, bacteria, etc. [< NL < Gk., < *lyein* to loosen]

-lysis *combining form* A loosing, dissolving, etc.: *hydrolysis, paralysis.* [< Gk., *loosening*]

Ly·sol (lī′sôl, -sōl, -sol) *n.* Proprietary name for a liquid disinfectant containing soap and cresol. Also **ly′sol.**

-lyte *combining form* A substance decomposed by a (specified) process: *electrolyte.* [< Gk. *lytos* loosened, dissolved]

ly·tic (lit′ik) *adj.* Of, relating to, or effecting lysis, esp., of cells. [See -LYTIC.]

-lytic *combining form* Loosing; used in adjectives corresponding to nouns in *-lysis: hydrolytic, paralytic.* [< Gk. *lytikos* loosing < *lysis* a loosening]

-lyze *suffix of verbs* To perform, cause, or undergo: formed from nouns in *-lysis: electrolyze, paralyze.* Also *esp. Brit.* **-lyse.** [< -LYSIS]

M

m, M (em) *n.* *pl.* **m's** or **ms, M's** or **Ms** or **ems** (emz) **1.** The thirteenth letter of the English alphabet. **2.** The sound represented by the letter *m*, usually a bilabial nasal. — *symbol* **1.** The Roman numeral 1,000. **2.** *Printing* An em.

M-1 rifle *U.S. Mil.* A semiautomatic .30 caliber rifle adopted by the U.S. Army in World War II: also *Garand rifle.*

ma (mä, mô) *n. Informal & Dial.* Mama.

ma'am (mam, mäm, *unstressed* məm) *n.* **1.** A term of respectful address used to women; madam. **2.** *Brit.* A term of respectful address used to the queen or to a royal princess.

Mac- *prefix* In Scottish and Irish names, son of: *MacDougal,* son of Dougal: abbr. *Mc, Mᶜ,* or *M'.* See also Mc-. Compare Fitz-, O'. [< Scottish Gaelic and Irish, son]

ma·ca·bre (mə·kä'brə, -bər) *adj.* Suggesting death and decay; gruesome; ghastly. Also **ma·ca'ber.** [< F < OF (*danse*) *macabre* (dance) of death]

mac·ad·am (mə·kad'əm) *n.* A macadamized pavement. [after John L. *McAdam,* 1756–1836, Scottish engineer]

mac·ad·am·ize (mə·kad'ə·mīz) *v.t.* **·ized, ·iz·ing** To pave by spreading and compacting small stones, often with tar or asphalt. — **mac·ad'am·i·za'tion** *n.* — **mac·ad'am·iz'er** *n.*

mac·a·ro·ni (mak'ə·rō'nē) *n.* **1.** A dried paste of wheat flour made into short tubes and prepared as a food by boiling. **2.** An 18th-century English dandy. Also **mac'ca·ro'ni.** [< Ital. *maccaroni* pl. of *macherone* groats]

mac·a·roon (mak'ə·roōn') *n.* A small cooky made of ground almonds or coconut, egg, and sugar. [< MF *macaron*]

ma·caw (mə·kô') *n.* Any of various large tropical American parrots with a long tail, harsh voice, and brilliant plumage. [< Pg. *macao,* prob. < Tupi]

Mac·beth (mək·beth'), died 1057?; king of Scotland 1040–1057?; hero of Shakespeare's *Macbeth.*

Mac·ca·bees (mak'ə·bēz) The family of Jewish patriots who led a revolt against Syrian religious oppression. — *n.pl.* Four books in the Old Testament Apocrypha treating of oppression against the Jews from 222 to 135 B.C. [< LL < Gk. < Aramaic *maggābā* a hammer] — **Mac'ca·be'an** *adj.*

mace¹ (mās) *n.* **1.** A heavy medieval war club, usu. with a spiked metal head for use against armor. **2.** A club-shaped staff symbolic of office or authority. [< OF *masse, mace*]

mace² (mās) *n.* An aromatic spice ground from the covering between the husk and the seed of the nutmeg. [< OF < L < Gk. *maker* a spicy bark from India]

Mace (mās) *n.* A chemical solution similar to tear gas that temporarily blinds or incapacitates one when sprayed in the face, used as a weapon. — *v.t.* **Maced, Mac·ing** To spray with Mace. [< Chemical *Mace,* a trade name]

Mac·e·do·ni·a (mas'ə·dō'nē·ə) The ancient kingdom of **Mac·e·don** (mas'ə·don) that became a leading world power under Alexander the Great. — **Mac·e·do'ni·an** *adj. & n.*

mac·er·ate (mas'ə·rāt) *v.* **·at·ed, ·at·ing** *v.t.* **1.** To reduce (a solid substance) to a soft mass by soaking in liquid. **2.** To break down the structure of (food) in digestion. **3.** To cause to grow thin; emaciate. — *v.i.* **4.** To become macerated. [< L < *macerare* to make soft, knead] — **mac'er·a'ter** or **mac·er·a'tor** *n.* — **mac·er·a'tion** *n.*

mach (mäk) *n. Often cap.* A mach number.

ma·chet·e (mə·shet'ē, mə·shet'; *Sp.* mä·chā'tā) *n.* A heavy knife or cutlass used as an implement and a weapon in tropical America. [< Sp., dim. of *macho* an ax, hammer]

Mach·i·a·vel·li·an (mak'ē·ə·vel'ē·ən) *adj.* Pertaining to, resembling, or based upon the amoral principles for getting and keeping political power prescribed in Niccolò Machiavelli's *The Prince.* — *n.* A follower of Machiavelli's principles. Also **Mach'i·a·vel'i·an.** — **Mach'i·a·vel'li·an·ism, Mach'i·a·vel'lism** *n.* — **Mach'i·a·vel'list** *adj. & n.*

ma·chic·o·late (mə·chik'ə·lāt) *v.t.* **·lat·ed, ·lat·ing** *Archit.* To furnish with machicolations. [< Med.L < OF *macher* to crush + *couler* to flow]

ma·chic·o·la·tion (mə·chik'ə·lā'shən) *n. Archit.* An opening between the corbels of a projecting parapet, through which missiles or boiling liquids may be dropped.

mach·i·nate (mak'ə·nāt) *v.t. & v.i.* **·nat·ed, ·nat·ing** To scheme or contrive. [< L *machinari* to contrive] — **mach'·i·na'tor** *n.*

mach·i·na·tion (mak'ə·nā'shən) *n. Usu. pl.* A concealed working and scheming for some devious purpose.

ma·chine (mə·shēn') *n.* **1.** Any combination of interrelated parts for using or applying energy to do work. **2.** The party organization of a city, county, or state: a derogatory term. **3.** The organization and operating principles of a complex structure: the human *machine.* **4.** An automobile. **5.** A person who behaves with machinelike precision, regularity, etc. **6.** In the ancient theater, a windlass used for the spectacular entrance and exit of gods, etc. — *adj.* **1.** Of or pertaining to a machine or machines. **2.** Produced by machine. **3.** Characterized by the use of machines: *machine* age. — *v.t.* **·chined, ·chin·ing** To shape, mill, make, etc., by machine. [< F < L < Gk. *mēchos* a contrivance] — **ma·chin'a·ble, ma·chin'al** *adj.* — **ma·chin'a·bil'i·ty** *n.*

ma·chine-gun (mə·shēn'gun') *v.t.* **·gunned, ·gun·ning** To fire at or shoot with a machine gun.

machine gun A rapid-firing automatic gun, usually mounted, that fires small-arms ammunition. — **machine gunner.**

ma·chin·er·y (mə·shē'nər·ē, -shēn'rē) *n.* **1.** A collection of machines or machine parts. **2.** The mechanism or operating parts and principles of a complex structure: the *machinery* of the law. **3.** In literary works, plot devices.

machine shop A shop where metal and other materials are cut, shaped, milled, finished, etc., with machine tools.

machine tool A power-driven tool, partly or wholly automatic in action, for cutting, shaping, boring, milling, etc.

ma·chin·ist (mə·shē'nist) *n.* **1.** One who is skilled in the operation or repair of machines or machine tools. **2.** In the U.S. Navy and Coast Guard, a warrant officer who is assistant to the engineer officer.

ma·chis·mo (mä·chēz'mō, -chiz'-, -kēz'-) *n.* An exaggerated sense of masculinity. [< Sp. *macho* male]

mach number A number representing the ratio between the speed of an object moving through a fluid medium, as air, and the speed of sound in the same medium. Also **Mach number.** [after Ernst *Mach,* 1838–1916, Austrian physicist]

ma·cho (mä'chō) *adj.* Exaggeratedly masculine. [< Sp. *macho* male]

ma·chree (mə·krē') *n.* My heart; my love: an Anglo-Irish term of endearment. [< Irish < *mo* my + *croidhe* heart]

-machy *combining form* A fight between, or by means of. [< Gk. *-machia* < *machē* a battle]

mac·in·tosh (mak'ən·tosh) See MACKINTOSH.

mack·er·el (mak'ər·əl) *n.* **1.** A food fish of the Atlantic, steel blue with blackish bars above, and silvery beneath. **2.** Any of various fishes resembling it. [< OF *makerel*]

mackerel sky Cirrocumulus.

mack·i·naw (mak'ə·nô) A Mackinaw blanket, boat, or coat. [< dial. F (Canadian) *Mackinac* Mackinac Island]

Mackinaw blanket A thick, heavy blanket formerly used by Indians and traders of the western United States.

Mackinaw coat A thick, short, double-breasted woolen coat, commonly with a plaid pattern.

mack·in·tosh (mak'ən·tosh) *n. Chiefly Brit.* **1.** A waterproof overgarment or cloak; raincoat. **2.** Thin, rubber-coated cloth. Also *macintosh.* [after Charles *Macintosh,* 1766–1843, Scottish chemist, inventor of the cloth]

macro- *combining form* **1.** *Pathol.* Enlarged or overdeveloped. **2.** Large or long in size or duration: *macrocosm.* Also, before vowels, **macr-.** [< Gk. *makros* large]

mac·ro·ceph·a·ly (mak'rō·sef'ə·lē) *n.* Abnormal largeness of the head. [< MACRO- + Gk. *kephalē* head] — **mac'ro·ce·phal'ic** (-sə·fal'ik) *adj. & n.* — **mac'ro·ceph'a·lous** (-ləs) *adj.*

mac·ro·cosm (mak'rə·koz'əm) *n.* The whole universe, esp. when regarded in contrast to man. [< OF < Med.L < Gk. *makros* long, great + *kosmos* world] — **mac'ro·cos'mic** *adj.*

ma·cron (mā'kron, -kron) *n.* A straight line (—) over a vowel letter to show that it represents a long sound, as *ā* in *made.* [< Gk. *makron,* neut. of *makros* long]

mac·u·la (mak'yə·lə) *n. pl.* **·lae** (-lē) A spot, as on the skin, the sun, etc. [< L, a spot]

mad (mad) *adj.* **mad·der, mad·dest** **1.** Suffering from or manifesting severe mental disorder; insane; psychotic. **2.** *Chiefly U.S. Informal* Feeling or showing anger; angry. **3.** Wildly foolish; rash: a *mad* project. **4.** Subject to an overpowering emotion: *mad* with grief. **5.** Turbulent and confused: a *mad* jumble. **6.** Of animals, suffering from hydrophobia; rabid. **7.** *Informal* Showing a passionate infatuation with or desire for: with *about, for,* or *over.* **8.** *Informal* Flamboyant; daring. **— like mad** *Informal* As if insane; frantically. **— mad as a hatter** (or **March hare**) Totally insane; crazy. **— mad money** *Slang* Money to be used by a girl to pay her way home from a date in case she quarrels with her escort. **—** *n. U.S. Informal* A fit of temper: now only in the phrase **to have a mad on,** to be angry. **—** *v.t. & v.i.* **mad·ded, mad·ding** *Rare* To make or become mad. [OE *gemād* insane] **— mad′ly** *adv.* **— mad′ness** *n.*

mad·am (mad′əm) *n. pl.* **mes·dames** (mā·däm′, *Fr.* mā·däm′) *for def.1*; **mad·ams** *for def.2.* **1.** My lady; mistress: a title of courtesy. See MA′AM. **2.** A woman who manages a brothel. [< OF *ma dame* < *ma* my + *dame* lady]

mad·ame (mad′əm, *Fr.* mà·däm′) *n. pl.* **mes·dames** (mā·däm′, *Fr.* mā·däm′) The French title of courtesy for a married woman, equivalent to the English *Mrs.* Abbr. *Mme., Mme, Mdme.* [< F < OF *ma dame*]

mad·cap (mad′kap′) *adj.* Wild; rattlebrained. **—** *n.* One who acts wildly or rashly.

mad·den (mad′n) *v.t. & v.i.* To make or become mad or insane; inflame; infuriate. **— mad′den·ing·ly** *adv.*

mad·der[1] (mad′ər) Comparative of MAD.

mad·der[2] (mad′ər) *n.* **1.** Any of various perennial herbs, esp. an Old World species, the root of which yields a brilliant red extract. **2.** The red coloring matter. **3.** A brilliant red. **—** *v.t.* To dye with madder. [OE *mædere, mæddre*]

mad·ding (mad′ing) *adj.* Being or growing mad; delirious; raging. **— mad′ding·ly** *adv.*

made (mād) Past tense and past participle of MAKE. **—** *adj.* **1.** Produced by fabrication, invention, or skill; not occurring naturally. **2.** Assured of success or fortune. **— to have it made** *U.S. Slang* To be sure of success.

Ma·dei·ra (mə·dir′ə, *Pg.* mä·thā′rä) *n.* A fortified dessert wine made in the Madeira islands.

mad·e·moi·selle (mad′ə·mə·zel′, *Fr.* màd·mwà·zel′) *n. pl.* **mad·e·moi·selles,** *Fr.* **mes·de·moi·selles** (mād·mwà·zel′) **1.** The French title of courtesy for unmarried women, equivalent to the English *Miss.* **2.** A French nurse. [< F < *ma* my + *demoiselle* (< OF *dameisele* gentlewoman)]

made-to-order (mād′tōō·ôr′dər) *adj.* **1.** Made according to specific instructions. **2.** Perfectly adapted or useful.

made-up (mād′up′) *adj.* **1.** Devised by fabrication or invention; fictitious. **2.** Adorned or altered by cosmetics. **3.** Complete; finished: a *made-up* sample. **4.** Compensated for or provided: said of work, money, etc.

mad·house (mad′hous′) *n.* **1.** A hospital for the mentally ill; insane asylum. **2.** A place of confusion or uproar; bedlam.

mad·man (mad′man′) *n. pl.* **·men** (-men′) A maniac.

Ma·don·na (mə·don′ə) *n.* **1.** The Virgin Mary. **2.** A painting or statue of the Virgin Mary. [< Ital. < *ma* my + *donna* lady]

ma·dras (mə·dras′, -dräs′, mad′rəs) *n.* **1.** A cotton cloth with thick strands at intervals, giving either a striped, corded, or checked effect. **2.** A silk cloth, usually striped. [after *Madras,* India, because originally made there]

mad·re·pore (mad′rə·pôr, -pōr) *n. Zool.* Any of various stony corals that form reefs in tropical seas. [< NL < Ital. *madrepora,* lit., mother stone] **— mad′re·por′al** (-pôr′əl, -pō′rəl), **mad′re·po′ric** (-pôr′ik, -por′ik) *adj.*

mad·ri·gal (mad′rə·gəl) *n.* **1.** *Music* An unaccompanied part song, often in counterpoint, usu. for four to six voices, popular during the 16th and 17th centuries. **2.** A short lyric poem. **3.** Any song, esp. a part song. [< Ital. < LL *matricale* original, chief] **— mad′ri·gal·ist** *n.*

mad·wom·an (mad′wŏŏm′ən) *n. pl.* **·wom·en** (-wim′in) An insane woman; lunatic.

Mae·ce·nas (mi·sē′nəs) *n.* A patron, esp. of the arts. [after *Maecenas,* died 8 B.C., Roman patron of Horace and Vergil]

mael·strom (māl′strəm) *n.* **1.** Any dangerous and irresistible force, or a place where it prevails. **2.** A whirlpool. [< Du. < *malen* to whirl around + *stroom* stream]

Mael·strom (māl′strəm) A famous whirlpool in the Arctic Ocean off the NW coast of Norway.

mae·nad (mē′nad) *n.* **1.** A female votary or priestess of Dionysius, a bacchante. **2.** Any woman beside herself with frenzy. Also spelled *menad.* [< L < Gk. < *mainesthai* to rave] **— mae·nad′ic** *adj.* **— mae·nad′i·cal·ly** *adv.*

ma·es·to·so (mä′es·tō′sō) *Music adj.* Majestic; stately. **—** *adv.* In a stately manner. [< Ital., majestic]

ma·es·tro (mä′es·trō, mīs′trō) *n. pl.* **·tros** A master in any art, esp., an eminent conductor, composer, or performer of music. [< Ital., master]

Ma·fi·a (mä′fē·ä, maf′ē·ə) *n.* A secret criminal organization of Sicilians and Italians believed to exist in many countries, including the U.S. Also **Maf′fi·a.** [< Ital.]

mag·a·zine (mag′ə·zēn′, mag′ə·zēn) *n.* **1.** A periodical publication, usu. with a paper cover, containing articles, stories, etc., by various writers. **2.** A warehouse or depot, esp. for military supplies. **3.** A building or storeroom for explosives and ammunition. **4.** A receptacle or part of a gun holding ammunition ready for chambering. **5.** A supply chamber in a battery, camera, etc. [< MF < OF < Arabic *makhāzin* storehouses]

mag·da·len (mag′də·lin) *n.* A reformed prostitute. Also **mag·da·lene** (-lēn). [after Mary *Magdalene*]

Mag·da·le·ni·an (mag′də·lē′nē·ən) *adj. Anthropol.* Of or pertaining to the most advanced culture stage of the Paleolithic period in Europe. [< F, after *La Madeleine* in west central France, where artifacts were found]

Mag·el·lan·ic cloud (maj′ə·lan′ik) *Astron.* Either of two aggregations of star clusters and nebulae near the south celestial pole.

ma·gen·ta (mə·jen′tə) *n.* **1.** Fuchsin, a dye. **2.** The purplish red color produced by fuchsin. [after *Magenta,* Italy]

mag·got (mag′ət) *n.* The legless larva of an insect, as the housefly, esp. one found in decaying matter. [Prob. alter. of ME < ON *mathkr* worm] **— mag′got·y** *adj.*

Ma·gi (mā′jī) *n. pl.* of **Ma·gus** (mā′gəs) **1.** The three "wise men from the east" who came to Bethlehem to pay homage to the infant Jesus. *Matt.* ii 1–12. **2.** The priestly caste of the Medes and Persians: also **ma′gi.** [< L < Gk. < Persian *magu* priest, magician] **— Ma·gi·an** (mā′jē·ən) *adj. & n.*

mag·ic (maj′ik) *n.* **1.** Seeming control over or foresight of natural events, forces, etc., through supernatural agencies. **2.** An overpowering influence: the *magic* of his voice. **3.** Sleight of hand; legerdemain. **—** *adj.* **1.** Of or used in magic. **2.** Producing the effects of magic. **3.** Mysteriously impressive; beautiful. [< OF < LL *magica* (*ars*) magic (art) < Gk. < *magikos* of the Magi]

mag·i·cal (maj′i·kəl) *adj.* Of, pertaining to, or produced by or as by magic. **— mag′i·cal·ly** *adv.*

ma·gi·cian (mə·jish′ən) *n.* One who performs magic; esp., an entertainer who uses illusion and legerdemain.

magic lantern *Archaic* A slide projector.

mag·is·te·ri·al (maj′is·tir′ē·əl) *adj.* **1.** Of or like a master. **2.** Dictatorial; domineering. **3.** Of or pertaining to a magistrate. **— mag′is·te′ri·al·ly** *adv.*

mag·is·tra·cy (maj′is·trə·sē) *n. pl.* **·cies 1.** The office, function, or term of a magistrate. **2.** Magistrates collectively. **3.** The district under a magistrate's jurisdiction.

mag·is·trate (maj′is·trāt, -trit) *n.* **1.** A public official with the power to enforce the law. **2.** A minor judicial officer, as a justice of the peace. [< L < *magister* master]

mag·ma (mag′mə) *n. pl.* **·ma·ta** (-mə·tə) *Geol.* The molten, plastic mass of rock material from which igneous rocks are formed. [< L < Gk. < *massein* to knead]

Mag·na Car·ta (mag′nə kär′tə) **1.** The Great Charter of English liberties, delivered June 19, 1215, by King John on the demand of the English barons. **2.** Any document that secures liberty and rights. Also **Mag′na Char′ta.** [< Med.L, lit., Great Charter]

mag·na·nim·i·ty (mag′nə·nim′ə·tē) *n. pl.* **·ties 1.** The quality of being magnanimous. **2.** A magnanimous act.

mag·nan·i·mous (mag·nan′ə·məs) *adj.* **1.** Manifesting generosity in forgiving insults or injuries. **2.** Characterized by magnanimity. [< L < *magnus* great + *animus* mind, soul] **— mag·nan′i·mous·ly** *adv.* **— mag·nan′i·mous·ness** *n.*

mag·nate (mag′nāt) *n.* One notable or powerful, esp. in industry: a railroad *magnate.* [< LL *magnus* great]

mag·ne·sia (mag·nē′zhə, -shə, -zē·ə) *n. Chem.* Magnesium oxide, MgO, a light, white powder used in medicine as an antacid and laxative, and in the manufacture of firebrick. [< Med.L < Gk. *Magnēsia* (*lithos*) (stone) of Magnesia]

mag·ne·si·um (mag·nē′zē·əm, -zhē-, -shē-) *n.* A light, silver-white, malleable and ductile metallic element (symbol Mg), that burns with a very hot, bright flame and is used in lightweight alloys. See ELEMENT. [< NL < *magnesia*]

mag·net (mag′nit) *n.* **1.** A body that has a magnetic field and therefore attracts iron and other magnetic material. **2.** A lodestone. **3.** One who or that which exercises a strong attraction. [< OF < L < Gk. *Magnēs* (*lithos*) Magnesian (stone), i.e., a magnet]

mag·net·ic (mag·net′ik) *adj.* **1.** Pertaining to magnetism or a magnet. **2.** Capable of setting up a magnetic field. **3.** Capable of being attracted by a magnet or a lodestone. **4.** Possessing personal magnetism. Also **mag·net′i·cal.** **— mag·net′i·cal·ly** *adv.*

magnetic field That region in the neighborhood of a magnet or current-carrying body in which magnetic forces are observable.

magnetic needle A freely movable magnetized needle that tends to point to the magnetic poles of the earth.

magnetic north The direction, usu. differing from true north, toward which the needle of a compass points.

magnetic pickup A phonograph pickup that employs a

magnet and coils to transform vibrations into electrical impulses.

magnetic pole 1. Either of the poles of a magnet. 2. Either of two points (**north magnetic pole** and **south magnetic pole**) on the surface of the earth where the lines of magnetic force converge and are vertical. These poles attract the compass needle, slowly change position, and do not coincide with the geographical poles.

magnetic tape *Electronics* A thin ribbon coated with magnetic particles that form patterns corresponding to the electromagnetic impulses generated by a tape recorder.

mag·net·ism (mag′nə·tiz′əm) *n.* 1. The specific properties of a magnet. 2. The science that treats of the laws and conditions of magnetic phenomena. Also **mag·net·ics** (mag·net′iks). 3. The amount of magnetic moment in a magnetized body. 4. A personal quality that attracts.

mag·net·ite (mag′nə·tīt) *n.* A massive black iron oxide, Fe₃O₄, that is strongly magnetic and is called *lodestone* when it has polarity. — **mag·net·it′ic** (-tit′ik) *adj.*

mag·net·ize (mag′nə·tīz) *v.t.* **·ized, ·iz·ing** 1. To communicate magnetic properties to. 2. To attract by personal influence. — **mag′net·i·za′tion** *n.* — **mag′net·iz′er** *n.*

mag·ne·to (mag·nē′tō) *n.* *pl.* **·tos** Any of various devices in which the rotation of a coil of wire between the poles of a permanent magnet induces an electric current in the coil; esp., such a device used to produce the ignition spark in some internal-combustion engines. Also **mag·ne·to·dy·na·mo** (mag·nē′tō·dī′nə·mō), **mag·ne·to·gen·er·a·tor** (mag·nē′tō·jen′ə·rā′tər). [Short for *magnetoelectric machine*]

magneto- *combining form* Magnetic; magnetism.

mag·ne·to·e·lec·tric·i·ty (mag·nē′tō·i·lek·tris′ə·tē) *n.* 1. Electricity generated by the inductive action of a magnet. 2. The science that treats of such electricity. — **mag·ne·to·e·lec′tric, mag′ne·to·e·lec′tri·cal** *adj.*

mag·ne·to·hy·dro·dy·nam·ics (mag·nē′tō·hī′drō·dī·nam′iks) *n.pl.* (*construed as sing.*) The branch of physics that treats of the interaction of electromagnetic, thermal, and hydrodynamic forces. — **mag·ne′to·hy′dro·dy·nam′ic** *adj.*

mag·ne·tom·e·ter (mag′nə·tom′ə·tər) *n.* An instrument for measuring the intensity and direction of magnetic forces.

mag·ne·to·sphere (mag·nē′tə·sfir, -net′ə-) *n.* *Physics* A region of the upper atmosphere forming a continuous band of ionized particles trapped by the earth's magnetic field.

magni- *combining form* Great; large; long. [< L *magnus* great]

mag·nif·ic (mag·nif′ik) *adj. Archaic* 1. Magnificent; sumptuous. 2. Pompous. Also **mag·nif′i·cal.** [< F < L < *magnus* great + *facere* to make] — **mag·nif′i·cal·ly** *adv.*

Mag·nif·i·cat (mag·nif′ə·kat) *n.* 1. The canticle of the Virgin Mary. *Luke* i 46–55. 2. A musical setting for this. [< L, it magnifies]

mag·ni·fi·ca·tion (mag′nə·fə·kā′shən) *n.* 1. The act, process, or degree of magnifying. 2. The state of being magnified. 3. The magnifying power of a lens or other optical device. 4. A magnified representation of an object, as in a drawing, photograph, etc. [< L < *magnificus* great]

mag·nif·i·cence (mag·nif′ə·səns) *n.* The state or quality of being magnificent; splendor; impressiveness.

mag·nif·i·cent (mag·nif′ə·sənt) *adj.* 1. Presenting an extraordinarily imposing appearance; splendid; beautiful. 2. Exceptionally pleasing; superb. 3. Exalted or sublime in expression or concept. — **mag·nif′i·cent·ly** *adv.*

mag·nif·i·co (mag·nif′ə·kō) *n.* *pl.* **·coes** Any lordly personage. [< Ital.]

mag·ni·fy (mag′nə·fī) *v.* **·fied, ·fy·ing** *v.t.* 1. To increase the perceived size of, as by a lens. 2. To increase the size of; enlarge. 3. To cause to seem greater or more important; exaggerate. 4. *Archaic* To extol; exalt. — *v.i.* 5. To increase or have the power to increase the apparent size of an object, as a lens. [< OF < L < *magnificus* great] — **mag′ni·fi′a·ble** *adj.* — **mag′ni·fi′er** *n.*

mag·nil·o·quent (mag·nil′ə·kwənt) *adj.* Speaking or spoken in a grandiose style; grandiloquent. [< L *magnus* great + *loquens, -entis,* ppr. of *loqui* to speak] — **mag·nil′o·quence** *n.* — **mag·nil′o·quent·ly** *adv.*

mag·ni·tude (mag′nə·tōōd, -tyōōd) *n.* 1. Size or extent. 2. Greatness or importance: the *magnitude* of the achievement. 3. *Astron.* The relative brightness of a star, ranging from one for the brightest to six for those just visible to the naked eye. [< L *magnus* large]

mag·no·li·a (mag·nō′lē·ə, -nōl′yə) *n.* 1. An ornamental flowering shrub or tree with large fragrant flowers. 2. The fragrant white flower of the **evergreen magnolia,** the State flower of Louisiana and Mississippi. [< NL, genus name, after Pierre *Magnol,* 1638–1715, French botanist]

Magnolia State Nickname of Mississippi.

mag·num (mag′nəm) *n.* A wine bottle holding about two quarts; also, the quantity such a bottle will hold. [< L, neut. of *magnus* great]

magnum o·pus (ō′pəs) A great work; masterpiece; esp., the greatest single work of a writer, artist, etc. [< L]

mag·pie (mag′pī) *n.* 1. Any of various large, noisy corvine birds having a long tapering tail and black and white plumage: sometimes called *pie.* 2. A chatterbox. [< *Mag,* diminutive of MARGARET + PIE²]

mag·uey (mag′wā, *Sp.* mä·gā′ē) *n.* 1. Any of the agaves of Mexico with fleshy leaves, esp. the species yielding pulque, and the century plant. 2. The tough fibers taken from these plants and used in rope, etc. [< Sp., prob. < Taino]

Ma·gus (mā′gəs) Singular of MAGI.

Mag·yar (mag′yär, mäg′-; *Hungarian* mud′yär) *n.* 1. A member of the dominant group of the population of Hungary. 2. Hungarian, a Finno-Ugric language. — *adj.* Of or pertaining to the Magyars or their language.

ma·ha·ra·ja (mä′hə·rä′jə, *Hind.* mə·hä′rä′jə) *n.* A title of certain princes of India, particularly one ruling an Indian state. Also **ma′ha·ra′jah.** [< Hind. < Skt. < *maha* great + *rājā* king]

ma·ha·ra·ni (mä′hə·rä′nē, *Hind.* mə·hä′rä′nē) *n.* 1. The wife of a maharaja. 2. A sovereign princess of India. Also **ma′ha·ra′nee.** [< Hind. < *maha* great + *rāni* queen]

ma·hat·ma (mə·hat′mə, -hät′-) *n.* In theosophy and some Asian religions, one of a group of holy men possessed of special occult knowledge: often a title of respect. [< Skt. < *maha* great + *ātman* soul] — **ma·hat′ma·ism** *n.*

Ma·hi·can (mə·hē′kən) *n.* One of a tribe of North American Indians of Algonquian stock formerly occupying the territory from the Hudson River to Lake Champlain: also called *Mohican.* [< Algonquian, lit., wolf]

mah·jong (mä′zhong′, -zhông′) *n.* A game of Chinese origin, usu. played with 144 pieces or tiles. Also **mah′-jong′, mah′jongg′.** [< dial. Chinese < Chinese *ma ch'iao* house sparrow; from the design on one of the tiles]

ma·hog·a·ny (mə·hog′ə·nē) *n.* *pl.* **·nies** 1. Any of various tropical trees yielding fine-grained reddish hardwood much used for furniture and cabinet work. 2. The wood itself. 3. Any of various trees yielding a similar wood. 4. Any of the various shades of brownish red of the finished wood. — *adj.* Having a mahogany color. [< obs. Sp. *mahogani*]

Ma·hom·et (mə·hom′it) Mohammed.

Ma·hom·e·tan (mə·hom′ə·tən) *adj. & n.* Mohammedan.

ma·hout (mə·hout′) *n.* In India and the East Indies, the keeper and driver of an elephant. [< Hind. < Skt. *mahā-mātra,* lit., great in measure]

Mah·rat·i (mə·rät′ē) See MARATHI.

Mah·rat·ta (mə·rät′ə) *n.* One of a Hindu people of SW and central India: also *Maratha.* [< Hind. < Marathi < Skt. *Mahārāstra,* lit., great country]

Mai·a (mā′yə, mī′ə) In Greek mythology, the eldest of the Pleiades, mother by Zeus of Hermes.

maid (mād) *n.* 1. A young unmarried woman or girl; maiden. 2. A female servant. [Short for MAIDEN]

maid·en (mād′n) *n.* 1. An unmarried woman, esp. if young. 2. A virgin. — *adj.* 1. Of, pertaining to, or befitting a maiden. 2. Unmarried: said of women. 3. Of or pertaining to the first use, trial, or experience: *maiden* effort. 4. Untried. [OE *mægden,* prob. dim. of *mægeth* virgin]

maid·en·hair (mād′n·hâr′) *n.* A very delicate and graceful fern with an erect black stem, common in damp, rocky woods. Also **maidenhair fern.**

maid·en·head (mād′n·hed′) *n.* The hymen.

maid·en·hood (mād′n·hŏŏd) *n.* The state or time of being a maiden.

maid·en·ly (mād′n·lē) *adj.* Of, pertaining to, or befitting a maiden or young girl. — **maid′en·li·ness** *n.*

maiden name A woman's surname before marriage.

maid of honor 1. The chief unmarried attendant of a bride at a wedding. 2. An unmarried woman, usu. of noble birth, attendant upon an empress, queen, or princess.

maid·ser·vant (mād′sûr′vənt) *n.* A female servant.

mail¹ (māl) *n.* 1. Letters, printed matter, parcels, etc., sent or received through a governmental postal system. 2. The postal system itself. 3. Postal matter collected or delivered at a specified time: the morning *mail.* 4. A conveyance, as a train, plane, etc., for carrying postal matter. — *adj.* Pertaining to or used for the handling or conveyance of mail. — *v.t.* *U.S.* To send by mail, as letters; post. [< OF < OHG *malha* wallet] — **mail′a·ble** *adj.* — **mail′er** *n.*

mail² (māl) *n.* 1. Flexible armor made of interlinked rings or overlapping scales. 2. Loosely, any defensive armor. 3. A defensive covering, as a turtle's shell. — *v.t.* To cover with or as with mail. [< OF < L *macula* spot, mesh of a net]

mail·bag (māl′bag′) *n.* A bag in which mail is carried or shipped. Also **mail′pouch′** (-pouch′).

mail·box (māl′boks′) *n.* *U.S.* 1. A box in which letters, etc., are deposited for collection: also called *post box.* 2. A box into which private mail is delivered. Also **mail box.**

mail·man (māl′man′, -mən) *n.* *pl.* **·men** (-men′, -mən) One who carries and delivers letters: also called *postman.*

mail order An order for merchandise to be sent by mail.

mail-or·der house (māl′ôr′dər) A business enterprise that sells its merchandise wholly or in part by mail order.

maim (mām) *v.t.* **1.** To deprive of the use of a bodily part; mutilate; disable. **2.** To render imperfect; make defective. [< OF *mahaignier, mayner*] — **maim′er** *n.*

main¹ (mān) *adj.* **1.** First or chief in size, importance, etc.; leading: *main* event. **2.** Fully exerted; sheer: by *main* force. **3.** Of or pertaining to a broad expanse of land, sea, etc. — *n.* **1.** A principal conduit or pipe in a system conveying gas, water, etc. **2.** Utmost effort; force: now chiefly in the phrase **with might and main. 3.** The chief or most important point or part. **4.** *Naut.* The mainmast. — **in** (or **for**) **the main** For the most part; chiefly. [OE *mægen*]

main² (mān) *n.* In cockfighting, a match of several battles.

main clause *Gram.* An independent clause. See under CLAUSE.

main deck *Naut.* The chief deck of a vessel.

main·land (mān′land, -lənd) *n.* The main part of a continent, as distinguished from an island or peninsula.

main line The principal line of a railroad or highway.

main·ly (mān′lē) *adv.* Chiefly; principally.

main·mast (mān′məst, -mast′, -mäst′) *n. Naut.* **1.** The second mast from the bow in a schooner, brig, etc. **2.** The mast nearer the bow in a two-masted vessel.

main·sail (mān′səl, -sāl′) *Naut.* **1.** A sail bent to the main yard of a square-rigged vessel: also **main course. 2.** The principal sail on a mainmast.

main·sheet (mān′shēt′) *n. Naut.* The sheet by which the mainsail is trimmed and set.

main·spring (mān′spring′) *n.* **1.** The principal spring of a mechanism, as of a watch. **2.** The principal or most compelling cause or agency.

main·stay (mān′stā′) *n.* **1.** *Naut.* The rope from the mainmast head forward, used to steady the mast in that direction. **2.** A chief support: the *mainstay* of my old age.

main·stream (mān′strēm′) *n.* The main or middle course.

Main Street 1. The principal business street of a town. **2.** The typical manners, customs, etc., of a small town.

main·tain (mān·tān′) *v.t.* **1.** To carry on or continue; keep in existence. **2.** To preserve or keep. **3.** To keep in proper condition. **4.** To supply with a livelihood; support. **5.** To claim to be true; uphold. **6.** To hold or defend (a position, place, etc.) against attack. [< OF < L < *manu*, albative of *manus* hand + *tenere* to hold]

main·te·nance (mān′tə·nəns) *n.* **1.** The act of maintaining, or the state of being maintained. **2.** Means of support or subsistence; livelihood. **3.** The work of keeping roads, machines, buildings, etc., in good condition.

main·top (mān′top′) *n. Naut.* A platform at the head of the lower section of the mainmast.

main·top·mast (mān′top′məst) *n. Naut.* **1.** On a square-rigged vessel, the section of the mast above the maintopgallantmast. **2.** On a fore-and-aft-rigged ship, the section of the mast next above the mainmast.

main·top·sail (mān′top′səl) *n. Naut.* The sail set on the maintopmast.

main yard *Naut.* The lower yard on the mainmast.

maître d'hô·tel (me′tr′ dō·tel′) **1.** A headwaiter or steward. Also *U.S. Informal* **mai·tre d′** (mā′trə dē′). **2.** The proprietor or manager of a hotel. **3.** Having a sauce of melted butter, parsley, and lemon juice or vinegar. [< F]

maize (māz) *n.* **1.** Corn (def. 1). **2.** The deep shade of yellow of ripe corn. [< Sp. < Taino *mahiz*]

ma·jes·tic (mə·jes′tik) *adj.* Having or exhibiting majesty; stately; royal. Also **ma·jes′ti·cal.** — **ma·jes′ti·cal·ly** *adv.*

maj·es·ty (maj′is·tē) *n. pl.* **·ties 1.** Exalted dignity; stateliness; grandeur. **2.** Sovereign authority: the *majesty* of the law. [< OF < L *majestas, -tatis*]

Maj·es·ty (maj′is·tē) *n. pl.* **·ties** A title or form of address for a sovereign: preceded by *His, Her, Your,* etc. Abbr. *M.*

ma·jol·i·ca (mə·jol′i·kə, -yol′-) *n.* A kind of glazed and colorfully decorated Italian pottery. [< Ital., prob. < *Majorca*, where formerly made]

ma·jor (mā′jər) *adj.* **1.** Greater in quantity, number, or extent. **2.** Having primary or greater importance, excellence, rank, etc.: a *major* writer. **3.** Of, relating to, or making up a majority. **4.** *Music* **a** Denoting the larger of two similarly named intervals: *major* third. **b** Denoting a triad in which the third above the fundamental is major. **c** Denoting a type of diatonic scale, or a key based on this scale. Compare MINOR. **5.** *Logic* Having a greater degree of generality: *major* premise. **6.** *U.S.* In education, pertaining to the principal area of specialized study of a degree candidate in a college or university. **7.** Having attained the age of one's majority. — *n.* **1.** *Mil.* An officer ranking next above a captain. See tables at GRADE. **2.** *Music* A major interval, triad, or scale. **3.** *U.S.* The principal area of specialized study of a degree candidate in a college or university. **4.** One who has reached his majority or full legal age. **5.** One of superior status within a given group. **6.** *pl.*

U.S. The major leagues. — *v.i. U.S.* In education, to study as a major: with *in.* [< L, compar. of *magnus* great]

ma·jor-do·mo (mā′jər-dō′mō) *n. pl.* **·mos** The chief steward or butler, esp. of a royal or noble household. [< Sp. < Med.L < *major* an elder + *domus* house]

ma·jor·ette (mā′jər·et′) *n. U.S. Informal* A girl who marches and twirls a baton with a band, as in a parade.

major general *Mil.* An officer ranking next above a brigadier or brigadier general. Also *Brit. & Canadian* **ma·jor gen·er·al** (mā′jər·jen′ər·əl). See tables at GRADE.

ma·jor·i·ty (mə·jôr′ə·tē, -jor′-) *n. pl.* **·ties 1.** More than half of a given number or group; the greater part. **2.** The number of jurors, voters, etc., in accord who compose more than half of the total group. **3.** The number of votes cast for a particular candidate, bill, etc., over and above the total number of remaining votes. Distinguished from *plurality.* **4.** The party or group having the most power. **5.** The age when full civil and personal rights may be legally exercised. **6.** The rank, commission, or office of a major. [< MF < L *majoritas, -tatis*]

major key A key based on a major scale. See SCALE².

major league In baseball, either of the two main groups of professional teams in the U.S., the **National League** or the **American League.**

major mode An arrangement of tones found in or characteristic of a major key or scale. See SCALE².

major premise *Logic* The more general premise in a syllogism. See SYLLOGISM.

major scale See under SCALE².

major suit In bridge, either spades or hearts.

major term *Logic* The predicate of both the major premise and the conclusion of a syllogism. See SYLLOGISM.

ma·jus·cule (mə·jus′kyōōl) *adj.* **1.** Large, as either capital or uncial letters. **2.** Written in such letters. — *n.* A majuscule letter. [< F < L *majuscula* (*littera*), fem. of *majusculus,* dim. of *major* major] — **ma·jus′cu·lar** *adj.*

make (māk) *v.* **made, mak·ing** *v.t.* **1.** To bring about the existence of by shaping or combining of materials; produce; construct; fashion. **2.** To cause: Don't *make* trouble. **3.** To bring to some state: The wind *makes* him cold. **4.** To put into a specified rank or position: They *made* him president. **5.** To form or create in the mind, as a plan, conclusion, or judgment. **6.** To compose (a poem). **7.** To entertain mentally, as doubts, scruples, etc.: *Make* no mistake about it. **8.** To understand the meaning or significance; interpret: with *of.* **9.** To utter or express, as an announcement. **10.** To represent as being or appearing: That hat *makes* you look old. **11.** To put forward or proffer: to *make* friendly overtures. **12.** To engage in: to *make* war. **13.** To earn or acquire: to *make* a fortune. **14.** To act in such a way as to win or gain. **15.** To amount to; add up to. **16.** To bring the total to. **17.** To draw up, enact, or frame, as laws, treaties, etc. **18.** To effect or form, as an agreement or arrangement. **19.** To estimate to be; reckon. **20.** To prepare or arrange for use: to *make* a bed. **21.** To induce or force; compel. **22.** To be the essential element or determinant of: Nourishing food *makes* strong bodies. **23.** To afford or provide: Venison *makes* good eating. **24.** To become through development: He will *make* a good soldier. **25.** To cause the success of: His last book *made* him. **26.** To perform (a specific physical movement). **27.** To cover (distance) by traveling. **28.** To travel at the rate of. **29.** To arrive at; reach: to *make* Boston. **30.** To arrive in time for. **31.** In games and sports, to achieve as a score. **32.** *Electr.* To complete (a circuit). **33.** *U.S. Informal* To win a place or position, as on a team; also, to achieve the rank or status of: to *make* colonel. — *v.i.* **34.** To cause something to assume a specified condition: to *make* sure. **35.** To act or behave in a certain manner: to *make* merry. **36.** To start, or appear to start, to do something: They *made* to go. **37.** To be made: It *makes* easily. — **to make after** To pursue; follow. — **to make away with 1.** To carry off; steal. **2.** To kill. **3.** To get rid of; destroy. — **to make believe** To pretend; feign. — **to make do** To get along with what is available, esp. with an inferior substitute. — **to make for 1.** To go toward, esp. rapidly. **2.** To rush at in order to attack. — **to make it** *Informal* To succeed in doing something. — **to make off** To leave suddenly; run away. — **to make off with** To steal. — **to make or break** To bring about the success or failure of. — **to make out 1.** To see; discern. **2.** To comprehend. **3.** To establish by evidence. **4.** To fill out or draw up, as a document, bank check, etc. **5.** To succeed. **6.** To do well enough; get by. — **to make over 1.** To renovate; refashion. **2.** To transfer title or possession of. — **to make up 1.** To compose; compound, as a prescription. **2.** To be the parts of; constitute. **3.** To settle differences and become friendly again. **4.** To devise; fabricate. **5.** To supply what is lacking in. **6.** To compensate; atone. **7.** To settle; decide: to *make up* one's mind. **8.** *Printing* To arrange lines of type, illustrations, etc., for (a book, etc.). **9.** To put cosmetics on (the face). **10.** In education: **a** To repeat (an examination or course one has failed). **b** To take (an examination one has missed). — *n.* **1.** Style or type: a good *make* of car. **2.** The manner in which something is made. **3.** The quantity produced. **4.** The act of making. **5.** The closing of an electric circuit. — **on the make** *Informal* **1.** Greedy for profit or advancement. **2.** Eager for amorous conquest. [OE *macian*]

make-be-lieve (māk′bi-lēv′) *n.* **1.** Pretense; sham. **2.** One who pretends or feigns. — *adj.* Pretended; unreal.

mak-er (mā′kər) *n.* **1.** One who or that which makes. **2.** *Law* One who signs a promissory note.

Ma-ker (mā′kər) *n.* God, the creator.

make-shift (māk′shift′) *n.* A temporary means devised for an emergency; stopgap. — *adj.* Having the nature of or used as a temporary substitute: also **make′shift′y.**

make-up (māk′up′) *n.* **1.** The arrangement or combination of parts or qualities of which anything is composed. **2.** The cosmetics, etc., used by an actor in a specific role; also, the art of applying or assuming them. **3.** Cosmetics used by women. **4.** Physical or mental constitution. **5.** *Printing* The arranging of composed type and cuts into pages, columns, or forms. Also **make′up′.**

mak-ing (mā′king) *n.* **1.** The act of one who or that which makes, fashions, or constructs. **2.** That which contributes to improvement or success: Discipline is the *making* of a soldier. **3.** *Usu. pl.* The materials or qualities from which something can be made. **4.** A quantity made at one time; batch. **5.** *pl.* Paper and tobacco for cigarettes. — **in the making** In the process of being made.

mal- *prefix* **1.** Bad; ill; wrong: maladjustment. **2.** Defective; imperfect: malformation. [< F < L *malus* bad]

Ma-lac-ca (mə-lak′ə) *n.* The stem of a rattan palm, used for walking sticks, umbrella handles, etc. Also **Malacca cane.** [after *Malacca*, Malaya]

Mal-a-chi (mal′ə-kī) Fifth-century B.C. Hebrew prophet. — *n.* A book of the Old Testament containing his prophecies. Also, in the Douai Bible, **Ma-la-chi-as** (mal-ə-kī′əs).

mal-a-chite (mal′ə-kīt) *n.* A green basic copper carbonate, $Cu_2CO_3 (OH)_2$, a common ore of copper. [< OF, ult. < L < Gk. *malachē* mallow; so called because of its color]

mal-ad-just-ed (mal′ə-jus′tid) *adj.* **1.** Poorly adjusted. **2.** *Psychol.* Poorly adapted to one's environment through conflict between personal desires and external circumstances.

mal-ad-just-ment (mal′ə-just′mənt) *n.* Poor adjustment.

mal-a-droit (mal′ə-droit′) *adj.* Lacking skill; clumsy; blundering. [< F < *mal-* mal- + *adroit* clever] — **mal′a-droit′ly** *adv.* — **mal′a-droit′ness** *n.*

mal-a-dy (mal′ə-dē) *n.* *pl.* **-dies 1.** A disease, esp. when chronic or deep-seated. **2.** Any disordered or disturbed condition. [< OF < LL < L *male* ill + *habere* to have]

Mal-a-ga (mal′ə-gə) A rich, sweet white wine made in Málaga, Spain. **2.** A white, sweet grape of the muscat variety, grown in Spain and California.

mal-aise (mal-āz′, *Fr.* mȧ-lez′) *n.* A feeling of vague discomfort or lassitude, sometimes indicating the beginning of an illness. [< F < *mal* ill + *aise* ease]

ma-la-mute (mä′lə-myōōt, mal′ə-) *n.* *U.S. & Canadian* A large Alaskan sled dog with a thick, long coat: also spelled *malemute, malemiut.* [Orig. name of an Innuit tribe, alter. of Eskimo *Mahlemut < Mahle*, the tribe's name + *mut* village]

Mal-a-prop (mal′ə-prop), **Mrs.** A character in Sheridan's play *The Rivals* (1775), who uses words in an absurdly inappropriate manner. [< MALAPROPOS]

mal-a-prop-ism (mal′ə-prop-iz′əm) *n.* **1.** The absurd misuse of words. **2.** An instance of this.

mal-ap-ro-pos (mal′ap-rə-pō′) *adj.* Not appropriate. — *adv.* Inappropriately. [< F *mal à propos* not to the point]

ma-lar-i-a (mə-lâr′ē-ə) *n.* *Pathol.* Any of several forms of a disease caused by certain parasitic protozoans introduced into the blood by the bite of the infected female anopheles mosquito and characterized by periodic attacks of chills, fever, and profuse sweating. **2.** Foul or noxious vapors; miasma. [< Ital. *mal′ aria, mala aria,* lit., bad air] — **ma-lar′i-al, ma-lar′i-ous** *adj.*

ma-lar-key (mə-lär′kē) *n.* *U.S. Slang* Insincere or senseless talk; bunk. Also **ma-lar′ky.** [Origin unknown]

Ma-lay (mā′lā, mə-lā′) *n.* **1.** A member of a people dominant in Malaysia; a Malayan. **2.** The language spoken on the Malay Peninsula and now adopted as the official language of Indonesia. **3.** A variety of domestic fowl. —*adj.* Of or pertaining to the Malays; Malayan.

Mal-a-ya-lam (mal′ə-yä′ləm) *n.* The Dravidian language of the Malabar coast, India, related to Tamil.

Ma-lay-an (mə-lā′ən) *adj.* **1.** Malay. **2.** Indonesian. — *n.* **1.** A Malay (def. 1). **2.** An Indonesian. **3.** The Indonesian subfamily of Austronesian languages.

Ma-lay-o-Pol-y-ne-sian (mə-lā′ō-pol′ə-nē′zhən, -shən) *adj. & n.* Austronesian.

mal-con-tent (mal′kən-tent) *adj.* Discontented or dissatisfied, esp. with a government or economic system. — *n.* One who is malcontent.

mal de mer (mȧl′ də mâr′) *French* Seasickness.

male (māl) *adj.* **1.** Of or belonging to the sex that begets young or produces sperm. **2.** Of, characteristic of, or suitable for members of this sex; masculine. **3.** Made up of men or boys. **4.** *Bot.* **a** Designating a plant having stamens but no pistil. **b** Adapted to fertilize, but not to produce fruit, as stamens **5.** *Mech.* Denoting a part, as in some electric plugs, etc., designed to be inserted into a correlated slot or bore known as *female.* — *n.* **1.** A male person or animal. **2.** *Bot.* A plant with only staminate flowers. [< OF < L *masculus*] — **male′ness** *n.*

mal-e-dic-tion (mal′ə-dik′shən) *n.* **1.** The pronouncing of a curse against someone. **2.** Slander; calumny. [< L < *male* ill + *dicere* to speak] — **mal′e-dic′to-ry** (-tər-ē) *adj.*

mal-e-fac-tor (mal′ə-fak′tər) *n.* **1.** One who commits a crime; criminal. **2.** An evildoer. [< L < *male* ill + *facere* to do] — **mal′e-fac′tion** *n.* — **mal′e-fac′tress** (-tris) *n.fem.*

ma-lef-i-cent (mə-lef′ə-sənt) *adj.* Causing or doing evil or mischief; harmful: opposed to *beneficent.*

ma-le-mute (mä′lə-myōōt, mal′ə-) See MALAMUTE. Also **ma-le-miut.**

ma-lev-o-lent (mə-lev′ə-lənt) *adj.* Wishing evil toward others; malicious. [< OF < L < *male* ill + *volens, -entis,* ppr. of *velle* to wish] — **ma-lev′o-lence** *n.* — **ma-lev′o-lent-ly** *adv.*

mal-fea-sance (mal-fē′zəns) *n.* *Law* The performance of some act that is wrongful or that one has specifically contracted not to perform: said usu. of official misconduct. [< AF < OF < L *malus* bad + *facere* to do] — **mal-fea′-sant** *adj. & n.*

mal-for-ma-tion (mal′fôr-mā′shən) *n.* Defective structure, esp. in an organism.

mal-formed (mal-fôrmd′) *adj.* Badly formed; deformed.

mal-func-tion (mal-fungk′shən) *n.* **1.** Failure to function. **2.** Defective functioning. — *v.i.* **1.** To fail to function. **2.** To function improperly.

mal-ic (mal′ik, mā′lik) *adj.* Of, pertaining to, or made from apples. [< F < L *malum* apple]

mal-ice (mal′is) *n.* **1.** An intention or desire to injure another; specific ill will; spite. **2.** *Law* A willfully formed design to do another an injury: also, **malice aforethought, malice prepense.** [< OF < L *malus* evil]

ma-li-cious (mə-lish′əs) *adj.* **1.** Revealing or characterized by malice; spiteful. **2.** *Law* Resulting from or prompted by malice. — **ma-li′cious-ly** *adv.* — **ma-li′cious-ness** *n.*

ma-lign (mə-līn′) *v.t.* To speak slander of; defame. — *adj.* **1.** Having an evil disposition toward others; malevolent. **2.** Tending to injure; pernicious. [< OF < LL < L *malignus* ill-disposed] — **ma-lign′ly** *adv.* — **ma-lign′er** *n.*

ma-lig-nan-cy (mə-lig′nən-sē) *n. pl.* **-cies 1.** The state of being malignant. **2.** A malignant tumor. Also **ma-lig′nance.**

ma-lig-nant (mə-lig′nənt) *adj.* **1.** *Pathol.* **a** Of tumors, rapidly growing and liable to metastasize: opposed to *benign.* **b** Becoming progressively worse; virulent. **2.** Tending to do great harm. **3.** Having an evil disposition toward others; malign. — *n.* A malcontent. [< LL < L *malignus* ill-disposed] — **ma-lig′nant-ly** *adv.*

ma-lig-ni-ty (mə-lig′nə-tē) *n. pl.* **-ties 1.** The state or character of being malign; intense ill will. **2.** A harmful tendency; virulence. **3.** *Often pl.* Something evil.

ma-lines (mə-lēn′, *Fr.* mȧ-lēn′) *n.* A gauzelike veiling for trimming hats, etc.: also **ma-line′.** [< F, after *Malines* Mechlin]

ma-lin-ger (mə-ling′gər) *v.i.* To pretend sickness so as to avoid work or duty. [< F *malingre* sickly, ? < *mal* ill + OF *heingre* lean] — **ma-lin′ger-er** *n.*

mall¹ (môl, mal) See MAUL.

mall² (môl, mal, mel) *n.* **1.** A promenade or walk, usu. public and often shaded. **2.** *U.S. & Canadian* A street of shops closed off to vehicles and enhanced with trees, benches, etc. [Short for *Pall-Mall,* a street in London]

mal-lard (mal′ərd) *n. pl.* **-lards** or **-lard 1.** A common wild duck, the ancestor of the domestic breeds, having brownish plumage, and, in the male, a bright green head. **2.** The male or drake of this duck. [< OF < *masle* male]

mal-le-a-ble (mal′ē-ə-bəl) *adj.* **1.** Capable of being hammered or rolled out without breaking: said esp. of metals. **2.** Capable of being shaped or molded; flexible; pliable. [< OF < L *malleare* to hammer] — **mal′le-a-bil′i-ty, mal′le-a-ble-ness** *n.* — **mal′le-a-bly** *adv.*

mal-let (mal′it) *n.* **1.** A hammer having a head of wood, rubber, etc. **2.** A long-handled wooden hammer used in the game of croquet. **3.** A wooden-headed flexible stick used in the game of polo. [< OF < L *malleus* hammer]

mal-le-us (mal′ē-əs) *n. pl.* **-le-i** (-lē-ī) *Anat.* The club-shaped bone of the middle ear, articulating with the incus: also called *hammer.* For illus. see EAR. [< L, hammer]

mal-low (mal′ō) *n.* **1.** Any of various herbs having roundish leaves, pale pink flowers, and disklike fruit. **2.** Any similar plant, as the hibiscus. [OE < L *malva*]

malm·sey (mäm′zē) *n. pl.* **·seys** A rich, sweet wine made in the Canary Islands, Madeira, etc.; also, the grape used for this wine. [< Med.L < Gk. *Monembasia* Monemvasia, Greece, a town formerly exporting wine]

mal·nu·tri·tion (mal′nŏŏ·trish′ən, -nyŏŏ-) *n.* Faulty or inadequate nutrition; undernourishment.

mal·o·dor·ous (mal·ō′dər·əs) *adj.* Having a disagreeable smell. — **mal·o′dor·ous·ly** *adv.* — **mal·o′dor·ous·ness** *n.*

mal·prac·tice (mal·prak′tis) *n.* **1.** In medicine or surgery, the improper, injurious, or negligent treatment of a patient. **2.** Improper or immoral conduct in a professional or public position. — **mal·prac·ti·tion·er** (mal′prak·tish′ən·ər) *n.*

malt (môlt) *n.* **1.** Grain, usu. barley, germinated by soaking and then kiln-dried. **2.** Liquor made with malt, as beer, ale, etc. — *v.t.* **1.** To cause (grain) to become malt. **2.** To treat or combine with malt or malt extract. — *v.i.* **3.** To become malt. **4.** To change grain into malt. [OE *mealt*] — **malt·y** (môl′tē) *adj.*

malt·ed milk (môl′tid) **1.** A beverage made of milk, a powder of malted cereals and dried milk, and usu. ice cream: also **malt·ed.** **2.** The powder used in this beverage.

Mal·tese (môl·tēz′, -tēs′) *adj.* Of or pertaining to Malta, its inhabitants, or their language. — *n. pl.* **·tese 1.** A native or inhabitant of Malta. **2.** The language of Malta. **3.** A Maltese cat or dog.

Maltese cat A cat with long, silky, bluish gray hair.

Maltese cross An eight-pointed cross formed by four arrowheads joining at their points.

malt extract Wort (def. 2).

Mal·thu·si·an (mal·thŏŏ′zē·ən, môl′-, -zhən) *adj.* Of or pertaining to the theory of T. R. Malthus that population tends to outrun its means of support, and will be checked by disaster unless restricted by sexual restraint. — *n.* A believer in the theories of Malthus. — **Mal·thu′si·an·ism** *n.*

malt·ose (môl′tōs) *n. Biochem.* A white, crystalline sugar, $C_{12}H_{22}O_{11}H_2O$, formed by the action of diastase on starch. Also **malt sugar.**

mal·treat (mal·trēt′) *v.t.* To treat badly, roughly or unkindly; abuse. [< F *maltraiter*] — **mal·treat′ment** *n.*

malt·ster (môlt′stər) *n.* A maker of or dealer in malt.

ma·ma (mä′mə, mə·mä′) *n.* Mother: used familiarly. [Repetition of infantile syllable *ma*]

mam·bo (mäm′bō) *n. pl.* **·bos** A dance resembling the rumba; also the syncopated four-beat music for this dance. — *v.i.* To dance the mambo. [< Haitian Creole]

mam·ma (mam′ə) *n. pl.* **·mae** (-mē) In mammals, the organ that secretes milk; a breast; udder. [< L, breast]

mam·mal (mam′əl) *n.* Any of a class of vertebrates whose females have mammae to nourish their young, including man, all warm-blooded quadrupeds, seals, etc. [< NL < LL < L *mamma* breast] — **mam·ma·li·an** (ma·mā′lē·ən, -māl′yən) *adj. & n.*

mam·ma·ry (mam′ər·ē) *adj.* Of, pertaining to, or of the nature of a mamma or breast, or the mammae.

mam·mon (mam′ən) *n.* **1.** Riches regarded as an evil influence and ignoble goal. **2.** Worldliness; avarice. [< LL < Gk. < Aramaic *māmōnā* riches] — **mam′mon·ish** *adj.*

Mam·mon (mam′ən) The personification of riches, avarice, and worldly gain.

mam·moth (mam′əth) *n. Paleontol.* A large, once very abundant, now extinct elephant having a thick hairy coat and long curved tusks. — *adj.* Huge; gigantic. [< Russian *mammot, mamant*]

mam·my (mam′ē) *n. pl.* **·mies 1.** Mother: used familiarly. **2.** *Southern U.S.* A Negro nurse or foster mother of white children. Also spelled *mammie*. [Dim. of MAMA]

WOOLLY MAMMOTH
(9 to 12 feet high at shoulder)

man (man) *n. pl.* **men** (men) **1.** An adult male human being. **2.** Human beings collectively; the human race; mankind. **3.** A person or individual. **4.** One having pronounced masculine traits and virtues; a genuine male. **5.** An adult male subordinate or employee; as: **a** A worker in a factory, office, etc. **b** A servant, esp. a valet. **6.** A husband. **7.** A piece or counter used in certain games, as chess, checkers, etc. — **as one man** Unanimously. — **to a man** Unanimously. — **to be one's own man** To be independent. — *interj. Slang* An exclamation of surprise, pleasure, etc. — *adj.* Male. — *v.t.* **manned, man·ning 1.** To supply with men, as for work, defense, etc.: to *man* the fort. **2.** To take stations on, at, or in for work, defense, etc.: *Man* the pumps! [OE *monn, mann*]

man·a·cle (man′ə·kəl) *n.* **1.** *Usually pl.* A device for re-

straining the hands; shackle; handcuff. **2.** Anything that constrains. — *v.t.* **·cled, ·cling 1.** To put manacles on. **2.** To constrain or hamper. [< OF < L < *manus* hand]

man·age (man′ij) *v. ·aged, ·ag·ing v.t.* **1.** To direct or control the affairs or interests of: to *manage* a hotel. **2.** To arrange; contrive: usu. with an infinitive as object: He *managed* to stay. **3.** To control or guide the operation or performance of. **4.** To cause to do one's bidding: to *manage* a crowd. **5.** To handle or wield; use, as a weapon, etc. — *v.i.* **6.** To direct or control business, affairs, etc. **7.** To be able to continue or thrive. [< Ital. < L *manus* hand]

man·age·a·ble (man′ij·ə·bəl) *adj.* Capable of being managed. — **man′age·a·bil′i·ty, man′age·a·ble·ness** *n.* — **man′age·a·bly** *adv.*

man·aged currency (man′ijd) A monetary system in which the amount in circulation is regulated in an attempt to control prices, credit, etc.

man·age·ment (man′ij·mənt) *n.* **1.** The act, art, or practice of managing. **2.** The person or persons who manage a business, etc.. **3.** Managers collectively, esp. in their relations with labor unions. **4.** The skillful use of means.

man·ag·er (man′ij·ər) *n.* **1.** One who manages; esp., one who directs an enterprise, business, etc. **2.** One skilled in managing, esp. business affairs. — **man′ag·er·ship** *n.*

man·a·ge·ri·al (man′ə·jir′ē·əl) *adj.* Of or pertaining to a manager or management. — **man′a·ge′ri·al·ly** *adv.*

ma·ña·na (mä·nyä′nä) *n. & adv. Spanish* Tomorrow; some other time.

Ma·nas·seh (mə·nas′ə) In the Old Testament, a son of Joseph. *Gen.* xli 51. — *n.* The tribe of Israel descended from Manasseh. Also **Ma·nas·ses** (mə·nas′is).

man-at-arms (man′ət·ärmz′) *n. pl.* **men-at-arms** (men′-) A soldier; esp., an armed medieval mounted soldier.

man·a·tee (man′ə·tē′) *n.* A sluggish aquatic mammal of the coastal waters of Florida, the Gulf of Mexico, and the West Indies: also called *sea cow*. [< Sp. < Carib *manattoui*]

Man·chu (man·chŏŏ′, man′chŏŏ) *n.* **1.** One of a Mongoloid people that conquered China in 1643 and established the dynasty overthrown in 1912. **2.** The language of this people. — *adj.* Of or pertaining to Manchuria, its people, or its language. Also **Man·choo′.** [< Manchu, lit., pure]

-mancy *combining form* Divining or foretelling by means of: *necromancy*. [< OF < LL < Gk. *manteia* power of divination]

man·da·mus (man·dā′məs) *n. Law* A writ issued by a higher court to subordinate courts, corporations, etc., commanding them to do something. [< L, we command]

man·da·rin (man′də·rin) *n.* **1.** A member of any of the nine grades of well-educated officials of the Chinese Empire. **2.** A powerful person; esp., an intellectual arbiter. **3.** A tangerine: also **mandarin orange. 4.** An orange or reddish yellow dye. [< Pg. < Malay < Skt. *mantra* counsel]

Man·da·rin (man′də·rin) *n.* The Chinese language of north and west China, including the Peking dialect upon which the official language of the country is based.

man·da·tar·y (man′də·ter′ē) *n. pl.* **·tar·ies** One having or receiving a mandate.

man·date (man′dāt; *for n., also* -dit) *n.* **1.** In politics, an instruction from an electorate to its representative, expressed by the result of an election. **2.** Formerly, a charge to a nation from the League of Nations authorizing the administration of a territory, colony, etc.; also, the territory given in charge. **3.** An authoritative command; order. **4.** *Law* A judicial command issued by a higher court or official to a lower one. — *v.t.* **·dat·ed, ·dat·ing** To assign (a territory, etc.) to a specific nation under a mandate. [< L < *manus* hand + *dare* to give] — **man·da′tor** (-dā′tər) *n.*

man·da·to·ry (man′də·tôr′ē, -tō′rē) *adj.* **1.** Required by or as if by mandate or command; obligatory. **2.** Of or pertaining to a mandate. **3.** Holding a mandate. — *n. pl.* **·ries** A mandatary. — **man′da·to′ri·ly** *adv.*

man·di·ble (man′də·bəl) *n. Biol.* **1.** The lower jaw bone. **2.** Either part of the beak of a bird **3.** Either the upper or outer pair of jaws in an insect or other arthropod. [< L *mandere* to chew] — **man·dib·u·lar** (man·dib′yə·lər) *adj.*

man·do·lin (man′də·lin, man′də·lin′) *n.* A musical instrument with a fretted neck, a pear-shaped body, and eight metal strings. [< F < Ital. < L < Gk. *pandoura* lute]

man·drake (man′drāk) *n.* **1.** A short-stemmed Old World plant of the nightshade family with narcotic properties and fleshy forked roots sometimes resembling the human form. **2.** The May apple. Also **man·drag·o·ra** (man·drag′ə·rə). [< OE < LL < L < Gk. *mandragoras*]

man·drel (man′drəl) *n. Mech.* **1.** A shaft or spindle on which material may be fixed for working on a machine. **2.** A metal bar used as a core about which wire, glass, metal, etc., may be bent, forged, or shaped. Also **man′dril.** [Prob. alter. of F *mandrin* lathe]

man·drill (man′dril) *n.* A large, ferocious West African baboon.

mane (mān) *n.* The long hair growing on and about the neck of some animals, as the horse, lion, etc. [OE *manu*] — **maned** *adj.*

man-eat·er (man′ē′tər) *n.* 1. A cannibal. 2. An animal, as a tiger, shark, etc., that devours or is said to devour human flesh. — **man′-eat′ing** *adj.*

ma·nège (ma·nezh′) *n.* 1. The art of training and riding horses; also, a school for horsemanship. 2. The movements of a trained horse. Also **man·ege′**. [< F < Ital. *maneggiare* to handle, train horses]

MANDRILL (About 2½ feet high at shoulder; 3 to 4 feet long)

ma·nes (mā′nāz) *n.pl. Often cap.* In ancient Roman religion, the spirits of the dead, esp. of ancestors. [< L]

ma·neu·ver (mə·nōō′vər, -nyōō′-) *n.* 1. *Mil.* **a** A planned movement or shift, as of troops, warships, etc. **b** *pl.* Large-scale tactical exercises simulating war. 2. Any skillful move or stroke. — *v.t.* 1. To manage or conduct skillfully. 2. To put (troops, vessels, etc.) through a maneuver or maneuvers. — *v.i.* 3. To perform a maneuver or maneuvers. 4. To use artful moves or strokes. Also, *esp. Brit.*, **manoeuver**, **manoeuvre**. [< F < OF < LL < L *manu operari* to work with the hand] — **ma·neu′ver·a·bil′i·ty** or **·vra·bil′i·ty** *n.* — **ma·neu′ver·a·ble** or **·vra·ble** *adj.* — **ma·neu′ver·er** *n.*

man Friday A person devoted or subservient to another, like Robinson Crusoe's servant of that name; a factotum.

man·ful (man′fəl) *adj.* Having a manly spirit; sturdy. — **man′ful·ly** *adv.* — **man′ful·ness** *n.*

man·ga·nese (mang′gə·nēs, -nēz) *n. Chem.* A hard, brittle, grayish white metallic element (symbol Mn), oxidizing readily and forming an important component of certain alloys. See ELEMENT. [< F < Ital., alter. of Med.L *magnesia*]

mange (mānj) *n. Vet.* An itching skin disease of dogs and other domestic animals, caused by parasitic mites. [< OF *manjue* an itch, eating]

man·ger (mān′jər) *n.* A trough or box for feeding horses or cattle. [< OF < L *manducare* to chew]

man·gle[1] (mang′gəl) *v.t.* **·gled**, **·gling** 1. To disfigure or mutilate by cutting, bruising, crushing, etc. 2. To mar or ruin; spoil. [< AF, appar. freq. of OF *mahaignier*] — **man′gler** *n.*

man·gle[2] (mang′gəl) *n.* A machine for smoothing and pressing fabrics by passing them between rollers. — *v.t.* **·gled**, **·gling** To smooth with a mangle. [< Du. < MDu. < Ital. < LL < Gk. *manganon* a pulley, a war machine]

man·go (mang′gō) *n. pl.* **·goes** or **·gos** 1. An edible tropical fruit having a slightly acid taste. 2. The tree producing this fruit. [< Pg. < Malay < Tamil < *mān* mango tree + *kāy* a fruit]

man·grove (mang′gōv, man′-) *n.* A tropical evergreen shrub or tree, sometimes having aerial roots, growing in marshy and coastal areas. [< Sp. *mangle* < Taino]

man·gy (mān′jē) *adj.* **·gi·er**, **·gi·est** 1. Affected with or resembling mange. 2. Squalid; shabby. — **man′gi·ly** *adv.* — **man′gi·ness** *n.*

man·han·dle (man′han′dəl) *v.t.* **·dled**, **·dling** 1. To handle with rough force. 2. To handle by manpower alone.

Man·hat·tan District (Man·hat′an, man′-) In World War II, the project that developed the atomic bomb.

man·hole (man′hōl′) *n.* A usu. circular and covered opening by which a man may enter a sewer, boiler, etc.

man·hood (man′hŏŏd) *n.* 1. The state of being an adult male human being. 2. The masculine qualities collectively. 3. Men collectively. 4. The state of being human.

man-hour (man′our′) *n.* The amount of work a man can do in an hour.

ma·ni·a (mā′nē·ə, mān′yə) *n.* 1. An extraordinary enthusiasm, craving, etc. 2. *Psychiatry* An exaggerated sense of well-being with excessive but disordered mental and physical activity, often alternating with melancholia, as in manic-depressive psychosis. [< L < Gk., madness]

-mania *combining form* An exaggerated or irrational craving for or infatuation with. [< Gk. *mania* madness]

In the following list each entry denotes a mania for what is indicated:

acromania high places	**hodomania** travel
agoramania open places	**hylomania** woods
ailuromania cats	**hypnomania** sleep
anthomania flowers	**ichthyomania** fish
chionomania snow	**necromania** death or the dead
choreomania dancing	**noctimania** night
chrematomania money	**ophidiomania** reptiles
cynomania dogs	**ornithomania** birds
entomomania insects	**pedomania** children
gymnomania nakedness	**phonomania** noise
gynemania women	**thalassomania** ocean or sea
heliomania exposure to sun	**xenomania** strangers
hippomania horses	**zoomania** animals

ma·ni·ac (mā′nē·ak) *n.* A violently insane person; madman. — *adj.* Insane; mad. — **ma·ni·a·cal** (mə·nī′ə·kəl) *adj.* — **ma·ni′a·cal·ly** *adv.*

-maniac *combining form* Used to form nouns and adjectives from nouns ending in *-mania*: *kleptomaniac.*

man·ic (man′ik, mā′nik) *adj.* 1. Extraordinarily animated or excited. 2. *Psychiatry* Of or affected by mania.

man·ic-de·pres·sive (man′ik·di·pres′iv) *adj. Psychiatry* Denoting or characteristic of a mental disorder in which periods of depression alternate with periods of excitement. — *n.* One who suffers from this disorder.

man·i·cure (man′i·kyŏŏr) *n.* The care of the hands and fingernails. — *v.t. & v.i.* **·cured**, **·cur·ing** To treat (the nails, etc.). [< L *manus* hand + *cura* care]

man·i·cur·ist (man′ə·kyŏŏr′ist) *n.* One whose work is to care for the hands and fingernails.

man·i·fest (man′ə·fest) *adj.* Plainly apparent; obvious. — *v.t.* 1. To reveal; show; display. 2. To prove; be evidence of. 3. To record in a manifest. — *n.* In transportation, an itemized account or list, as of passengers, cargo, etc. [< L *manifestus* evident, lit., struck by the hand] — **man′i·fes·ta·ble** *adj.* — **man′i·fest′ly** *adv.* — **Syn.** (adj.) patent, visible, palpable, plain, evident.

man·i·fes·ta·tion (man′ə·fes·tā′shən) *n.* 1. The act of manifesting, or the state of being manifested. 2. A sign; indication.

man·i·fes·to (man′ə·fes′tō) *n. pl.* **·toes** or **·tos** A public and formal declaration or explanation of principles, intentions, etc., usually by a political faction or similar group.

man·i·fold (man′ə·fōld) *adj.* 1. Having many and varied forms, types, instances, etc.: *manifold* sorrows. 2. Having an assortment of features, etc. — **Syn.** See COMPLEX. — *n.* 1. *Mech.* A pipe or chest having several or many openings, as for exhaust gas. 2. A copy made by manifolding. 3. Something that is manifold. — *v.t.* 1. To make more than one copy of. 2. To multiply. — *adv.* By many or by much: to increase *manifold*. [OE *manigfeald* varied, numerous] — **man′i·fold·ly** *adv.* — **man′i·fold·ness** *n.*

man·i·kin (man′ə·kin) *n.* 1. A little man; dwarf. 2. See MANNEQUIN. [< Du. *manneken*, dim. of *man* man]

ma·nil·a (mə·nil′ə) *n. Often cap.* The fiber of the abaca, a banana plant, used for making rope, etc. Also **ma·nil′a hemp**.

Manila paper A heavy, light brown paper, originally made of Manila hemp, now made of various fibers.

Manila rope Rope made of Manila hemp.

man in the street The common or ordinary person.

man·i·oc (man′ē·ok, mā′nē-) *n.* Cassava (def. 1). [< F < Tupi *mandioca* manioc root]

ma·nip·u·late (mə·nip′yə·lāt) *v.* **·lat·ed**, **·lat·ing** *v.t.* 1. To manage (persons, figures, stocks, etc.) shrewdly and deviously for one's own profit. 2. To control, move, treat, etc., with or as with the hands; esp., to handle skillfully. — *v.i.* 3. To perform manipulation. [Back formation < MANIPULATION] — **ma·nip′u·la·ble** *adj.* — **ma·nip′u·la·tive**, **ma·nip′u·la·to′ry** *adj.* — **ma·nip′u·la′tor** *n.*

ma·nip·u·la·tion (mə·nip′yə·lā′shən) *n.* 1. The act of manipulating, or the state of being manipulated. 2. *Surg.* A manual procedure, esp. in orthopedics or obstetrics. [< F, ult. < L *manus* hand + *plere* to fill]

man·kind (man′kīnd′; *for def. 1, also* man′kīnd′) 1. The whole human species. 2. Men collectively, as distinguished from women.

man·ly (man′lē) *adj.* **·li·er**, **·li·est** 1. Pertaining to or appropriate for a man; virile: *manly* charm. 2. Having the qualities and virtues of a man, as courage, determination, strength, etc. — **the manly art** Boxing. — *adv. Archaic* Manfully. — **man′li·ly** *adv.* — **man′li·ness** *n.*

man·na (man′ə) *n.* 1. The food miraculously given to the Israelites in the wilderness as they fled from Egypt (*Ex.* xvi 14–36); also, any nourishment, help, etc., received as by divine bounty. 2. A sweetish substance obtained from various plants, esp. from the flowering ash, and used as a mild laxative. [< LL < Gk. < Aramaic < Hebrew *mān* What is it?]

man·ne·quin (man′ə·kin) *n.* 1. A full-sized model of a human figure used for cutting, fitting, or displaying garments. 2. A woman who models clothing; model. Also spelled *manikin*. [< F < Du. *manneken*. See MANIKIN.]

man·ner (man′ər) *n.* 1. A way of doing or a way in which something happens or is done. 2. A style of speech and action: a grave *manner*. 3. *pl.* Social conduct; etiquette; esp., polite and civil social behavior: to learn *manners* from Emily Post. 4. *pl.* The modes of social behavior prevailing in a group, nation, period, etc. 5. Typical or customary practice; esp., a characteristic style in literature, music, art, etc. — **in a manner of speaking** Approximately; more or less. — **to the manner born** Familiar or fitted from or as from birth. [< AF, OF, ult. < L *manuarius* of the hand]

man·nered (man′ərd) *adj.* 1. Having (a specific kind of) manner or manners: used in combination: *mild-mannered*. 2. Having mannerisms in writing, speaking, etc.

man·ner·ism (man′ər·iz′əm) *n.* 1. Marked use of a distinctive style, as in writing. **2.** A distinctive trait; idiosyncrasy. **— man′ner·ist** *n.* **— man′ner·is′tic** or **·ti·cal** *adj.*

man·ner·ly (man′ər·lē) *adj.* Well-behaved; polite. **—** *adv.* With good manners; politely. **— man′ner·li·ness** *n.*

man·ni·kin (man′ə·kin) See MANIKIN.

man·nish (man′ish) *adj.* Resembling a man; masculine; said of women. **— man′nish·ly** *adv.* **— man′nish·ness** *n.*

ma·noeu·ver (mə·nōō′vər, -nyōō′-), **ma·noeu·vre** See MANEUVER.

man of the world A worldly-wise and sophisticated man.

man-of-war (man′əv·wôr′, -ə·wôr′) *n. pl.* **men-of-war** (men′-) *Chiefly Archaic* An armed ship; warship.

man-of-war bird A frigate bird (which see). Also **man-of-war hawk.**

ma·nom·e·ter (mə·nom′ə·tər) *n.* Any of various instruments used to measure pressure, as of gases, liquids, vapors, etc. [< F < Gk. *manos* thin, rare + *-mètre* -meter] **— man·o·met·ric** (man′ə·met′rik) or **·ric·al** *adj.*

man on horseback A military leader whose popularity is a threat to the civil government.

man·or (man′ər) *n.* **1.** In England: **a** Formerly, a feudal domain. **b** A landed estate. **2.** A manor house. **3.** A mansion. **4.** In colonial America, a landed estate with hereditary feudal rights. [< OF < L *manere* to dwell] **— ma·no·ri·al** (mə·nôr′ē·əl, -nō′rē-) *adj.*

manor house The residence of the lord of a manor.

man·pow·er (man′pou′ər) *n.* **1.** The force of human physical strength. **2.** The number of men whose strength and skill are available to a nation, army, project, etc.; personnel.

man·qué (män·kā′) *adj. French* Lacking fulfillment; in wish but not in fact: a writer *manqué.*

man·sard (man′särd) *n. Archit.* A curb roof having the lower slope almost vertical and the upper almost horizontal, with the same profile on all four sides of the building. [after F. *Mansard,* 1598–1666, French architect who revived it]

manse (mans) *n.* **1.** A clergyman's house. **2.** *Archaic* A manor house. [< Med.L *mansa,* pp. of L *manere* to dwell]

man·ser·vant (man′sûr′vənt) *n.* An adult male servant.

man·sion (man′shən) *n.* A large and impressive house, typically that of a wealthy person or family. [< OF < L *mansio, -onis* a dwelling]

man·slaugh·ter (man′slô′tər) *n.* **1.** *Law* The unlawful killing of a human being without malice. **2.** Slaying of men.

man·ta (man′tə) *n.* **1.** Any of several very large rays common in tropical American waters: also called *devilfish.* Also **manta ray. 2.** A woman's shawl made of a coarse fabric. [< Sp., blanket < LL *mantum* cloak]

MANTA
(To 20 feet long)

man·teau (man′tō, *Fr.* män·tō′) *n. pl.* **·teaus** (-tōz) or **·teaux** (*Fr.* -tō′) A cloak or mantle. [< F. See MANTLE.]

man·tel (man′təl) *n.* **1.** The shelf above a fireplace. **2.** A facing of wood, brick, stone, etc., around a fireplace: also called *chimney piece.* Also **man′tel·piece′** (-pēs′). [< F *manteau* mantelpiece]

-mantic *combining form* Used to form adjectives from nouns ending in *-mancy.* [< Gk. *mantikos* prophetic]

man·til·la (man·til′ə) *n.* A light scarf often of black lace worn over the head and shoulders of women in Spain and Spanish America. [< Sp. dim. of *manta.* See MANTLE.]

man·tis (man′tis) *n. pl.* **·tis·es** or **·tes** (-tēz) A carnivorous, long-bodied insect with large eyes and swiveling head, that stands with its forelegs folded as if in prayer: also called *praying mantis.* [< NL < Gk., a prophet]

man·tle (man′təl) *n.* **1.** A loose and usu. sleeveless garment worn over other garments. **2.** Anything that clothes, envelops, or conceals. **3.** *Zool.* The variously modified flap or folds of the membranous covering of a mollusk. **4.** A mantel. **5.** A gas mantle. **—** *v.* **·tled, ·tling** *v.t.* **1.** To cover with or as with a mantle; conceal. **—** *v.i.* **2.** To overspread or cover the surface of something. **3.** To be or become covered or suffused, as a blush, etc. [OE < OF < L *mantellum*]

man·tu·a (man′chōō·ə, -tōō·ə) *n.* A woman's loose gown, about 1700. [Alter. of F *manteau*; infl. in form by *Mantua*]

man·u·al (man′yōō·əl) *adj.* Involving, used, or operated by the hands. **—** *n.* **1.** A small book of instructions. **2.** An organ keyboard. **3.** A prescribed drill in manipulating a rifle, flag, etc. [< OF < L *manus* hand] **— man′u·al·ly** *adv.*

manual alphabet A series of manual signs or gestures used by the deaf and deaf-mutes as a substitute for vocal speech: sometimes called *deaf-and-dumb alphabet.*

manual training In U.S. schools, practical training in carpentry, woodworking, etc.

man·u·fac·ture (man′yə·fak′chər) *v.* **·tured, ·tur·ing** *v.t.* **1.** To make or process a product, esp. on a large scale and with machinery. **2.** To fabricate or invent (a lie, alibi, etc.). **3.** To produce (poetry, art, etc.) mechanically. **—**

v.i. **4.** To make or process something. **—** *n.* **1.** The act or process of manufacturing. **2.** Something that is manufactured. [< MF < L *manus* hand + *factura* a making] **— man′u·fac′tur·a·ble** *adj.* **— man′u·fac′tur·er** *n.*

man·u·mit (man′yə·mit′) *v.t.* **·mit·ted, ·mit·ting** To free from bondage, as a slave. [< L *manumittere,* lit., to send forth from one's hand] **— man′u·mis′sion** (-mish′ən) *n.*

ma·nure (mə·nōōr′, -nyōōr′) *n.* Dung, compost, etc., used to fertilize soil. **—** *v.t.* **·nured, ·nur·ing** To apply manure or other fertilizer to, as soil. [< AF *maynoverer* to work with the hands] **— ma·nur′er** *n.*

man·u·script (man′yə·skript) *n.* **1.** A usu. typewritten copy of a book, article, document, etc., prepared or submitted for publication. **2.** Something written by hand. **—** *adj.* Written by hand. [< Med.L < LL < L *manus* hand + *scriptus,* pp. of *scribere* to write]

Manx (mangks) *adj.* Of or pertaining to the Isle of Man, its people, or their language. **—** *n.* **1.** The people of the Isle of Man. **2.** The Gaelic language of the Manx, nearly extinct. [< Scand. ult. < Celtic *Man* Isle of Man]

Manx cat A type of domestic cat having no tail.

Manx·man (mangks′mən) *n. pl.* **·men** (-mən) A native of the Isle of Man.

man·y (men′ē) *adj.* **more, most** Adding up to a large number; numerous. **—** *n.* **1.** A large number. **2.** The masses: with *the.* **— a great many** Many: with plural verb. **— many a** (or **an** or **another**) Many: with singular noun. **—** *pron.* A large number of persons or things. [OE *manig*]

Mao·ism (mou′iz′əm) *n.* The communist doctrines or practices of Mao Tse-tung. **— Mao′ist** *n., adj.*

Ma·o·ri (mä′ō·rē, mou′rē) *n.* **1.** One of an aboriginal, light brown people of New Zealand, chiefly Polynesian mixed with Melanesian. **2.** The Polynesian language of these people. **—** *adj.* Of or pertaining to the Maoris or their language.

map (map) *n.* **1.** A representation on a plane surface of any region, as of the earth's surface; a chart. **2.** Anything resembling a map. **3.** *Slang* The face. **— off the map** Out of existence. **—** *v.t.* **mapped, map·ping 1.** To make a map of. **2.** To plan in detail: often with *out.* [< OF < Med.L *mappa (mundi)* map (of the world)]

ma·ple (mā′pəl) *n.* **1.** Any of numerous deciduous trees of the north temperate zone, with opposite leaves and a fruit of two joined samaras, as the sugar maple, etc. **2.** The wood of these trees. **3.** The amber-yellow color of the finished wood. **4.** The flavor of the sap of the sugar maple. [OE *mapul (trēow)* maple (tree)]

maple sugar Sugar made from the sap of the sugar maple.

maple syrup The refined sap of the sugar maple.

ma·quis (mä·kē′) *n.* A zone of shrubby, mostly evergreen plants in the Mediterranean region, known as cover for game, bandits, etc. [< F < Ital. *macchia* thicket]

Ma·quis (mä·kē′) *n. pl.* **·quis 1.** The French resistance movement against the Germans during World War II. **2.** A member of this group. [< MAQUIS]

mar (mär) *v.t.* **marred, mar·ring 1.** To do harm to; damage. **2.** To injure so as to deface. **—** *n.* A disfiguring mark; blemish. [OE *mierran* to hinder] **— mar′rer** *n.*

mar·a·bou (mar′ə·bōō) *n.* **1.** A stork of Africa, whose soft, white, lower tail and wing feathers are used in millinery. **2.** A plume from the marabou. **3.** The adjutant (def. 2). Also **mar′a·bout** (-bōōt). [< F *marabou, marabout* hermit]

ma·ra·ca (mə·rä′kə, *Pg.* mä·rä·kä′) *n.* A percussion instrument made of a gourd or gourd-shaped rattle with beans or beads inside it. [< Pg *maracá,* ? < Tupi]

mar·a·schi·no (mar′ə·skē′nō) *n.* A cordial distilled from the fermented juice of a small wild cherry and flavored with the cracked pits. [< Ital. < *marasca.* See MARASCA.]

maraschino cherries Cherries preserved in a syrup usu. flavored with imitation maraschino.

mar·a·thon (mar′ə·thon) *n.* **1.** A footrace of 26 miles, 385 yards: so called from a messenger's run from Marathon to Athens to announce the Athenian victory over the Persians, 490 B.C. **2.** Any endurance contest.

Mar·a·thon (mar′ə·thon) A plain in Attica, Greece, scene of decisive victory of the Athenians over the Persians, 490 B.C.

ma·raud (mə·rôd′) *v.i.* **1.** To rove in search of plunder. **—** *v.t.* **2.** To invade for plunder. **—** *n.* A foray. [< F < *maraud* rogue] **— ma·raud′er** *n.*

mar·ble (mär′bəl) *n.* **1.** A compact, granular, partly crystallized limestone occurring in many colors, used for building, sculpture, etc. **2.** A piece, block, statue, etc., of this stone. **3.** A small ball of this stone, or of glass, porcelain, etc. **4.** *pl.* A boys' game played with balls of glass, etc. **—** *v.* **·bled, ·bling** *v.t.* **1.** To color or vein in imitation of marble, as book edges. **—** *v.i.* **2.** To be flecked with fat: said of meat. **—** *adj.* **1.** Made of or consisting of marble. **2.** Resembling marble as to chilliness, lack of feeling, etc. [< OF < L < Gk. *marmaros,* lit., sparkling stone] **— mar′bly** *adj.*

marble cake A cake made of light and dark batter mixed to give a marblelike appearance.

mar·ble·ize (mär′bəl·īz) v.t. & v.i. ·ized, ·iz·ing U.S. To marble.

mar·ca·site (mär′kə·sīt) n. 1. A pale, bronze-yellow, iron disulfide, FeS₂: also called white iron pyrites. 2. An ornament made of crystallized marcasite or of polished steel. [< Med.L marcasita]

mar·cel (mär·sel′) v.t. ·celled, ·cel·ling To dress (the hair) in even, continuous waves by means of special irons. [after M. Marcel, 19th c. French hairdresser] —**mar·cel′ler** n.

march¹ (märch) v.i. 1. To walk or proceed with measured, regular steps, as a soldier or body of troops. 2. To walk in a solemn or dignified manner. 3. To advance steadily. — v.t. 4. To cause to march. — n. 1. The act of marching. 2. A regular, measured step, as of a body of troops. 3. The distance passed over in marching: a full day's march. 4. Onward progress: the march of events. 5. A musical composition for marching. [< MF marcher to walk, orig., to trample] —**mar′cher** n.

march² (märch) n. A region or district lying along a boundary line; frontier. Also **march′land′** (-land′). [< OF < OHG marka mark]

March (märch) The third month of the year, containing 31 days. [< AF, OF < L Martius (mensis) (month) of Mars < Mars Roman god of war]

mar·che·se (mär·kā′zā) n. pl. ·che·si (-kā′zē) Italian A marquis. —**mar·che′sa** (-zä) n.fem.

Mar·ches·van (mär·khesh′vən) Heshwan. See (Hebrew) CALENDAR.

mar·chion·ess (mär′shən·is) n. 1. The wife or widow of a marquis. 2. A woman having in her own right the rank corresponding to that of a marquis. [< Med.L marchionissa < marchio, -onis captain of the marches]

march·pane (märch′pān) n. Marzipan. [< MF < Ital. marzapane. See MARZIPAN.]

Mar·di gras (mär′dē grä′) Shrove Tuesday, the last day before Lent, often a carnival. [< F, lit., fat Tuesday]

mare¹ (mâr) n. The female of the horse and other equine animals. [OE miere, fem. of mearh horse]

ma·re² (mär′ē) n. pl. ma·ri·a (mär′ē·ə) Any of a number of dark, seemingly flat areas of the moon's surface. [< L, sea; because of their resemblance to seas]

mare's nest 1. A discovery that proves worthless or false. 2. Loosely, a cluttered and confusing mess.

mare's-tail (mârz′tāl′) n. Meteorol. Long, fibrous, cirrus clouds, supposed to indicate rain.

mar·ga·rine (mär′jə·rin, -rēn, -gə-) n. 1. A substitute for butter, made from vegetable oils and milk. 2. Oleomargarine. Also **mar·ga·rin** (mär′jə·rin, -gə-). [< F]

mar·gin (mär′jin) n. 1. The part of a page around the body of printed or written text. 2. A bounding line or surface; border. 3. An extra amount of something, as space, time, money, etc. 4. A limiting or end point; limit. 5. In commerce, the difference between the cost and selling price of a commodity. 6. In the stock market, security deposited with a broker to protect him against loss in trading. — v.t. 1. To furnish with a margin. 2. To enter, place, or specify on the margin of a page, as a note. 3. In the stock market, to deposit a margin upon. [< L margo]

mar·gi·nal (mär′jə·nəl) adj. 1. Pertaining to or constituting a margin. 2. Situated or written at or on a margin. Also Archaic **mar′gent** (-jənt). 3. Having relatively low quality or value; meager. 4. Econ. Barely profitable. [< F] —**mar·gin·al′i·ty** n. **mar·gin·al·ly** adv.

mar·gi·na·li·a (mär′jə·nā′lē·ə, -nāl′yə) n.pl. Marginal notes.

marginal land Econ. Land so poor as to remain unused until the lack of more desirable land forces its development.

mar·grave (mär′grāv) n. 1. Formerly, the lord or governor of a German mark, march, or border. 2. A hereditary title of certain princes of the Holy Roman Empire. [< MDu. marke march + graf count]

mar·gra·vi·ate (mär·grā′vē·it) n. The territory of a margrave. Also **mar·gra·vate** (mär′grə·vāt).

mar·gue·rite (mär′gə·rēt′) n. Any of several flowers, esp. the oxeye daisy. [< F pearl, daisy]

Mar·i·an (mâr′ē·ən) n. A worshiper or devotee of the Virgin Mary. — adj. Of or pertaining to the Virgin Mary.

mar·i·gold (mar′ə·gōld) n. 1. Any of several plants of the composite family with golden-yellow flowers. 2. Any plant resembling these. [< Virgin Mary + GOLD]

mar·i·jua·na (mar′ə·wä′nə, Sp. mä′rē·hwä′nä) n. 1. Hemp (def. 1). 2. The dried leaves and flower tops of this plant, capable of producing disorienting or hallucinogenic effects when smoked in cigarettes or ingested. Also **ma′ri·hua′na**. [< Am. Sp. marihuana, mariguana]

ma·rim·ba (mə·rim′bə) n. A form of xylophone having a resonator beneath each tuned bar. [< Bantu marimba, malimba, pl. of limba, kind of musical instrument]

ma·ri·na (mə·rē′nə) n. U.S. A docking area or basin for small vessels. [< Ital., seacoast < L marinus. See MARINE.]

mar·i·nade (mar′ə·nād′) n. 1. A brine pickle sometimes flavored with wine, oil, spices, etc., in which meat or fish are soaked before cooking. 2. Pickled meat or fish. — v.t. ·nad·ed, ·nad·ing To marinate. [< F < Sp. marinar to pickle in brine]

mar·i·nate (mar′ə·nāt) v.t. ·nat·ed, ·nat·ing 1. To soak (food) in marinade. 2. To allow, as salad, to soak in French dressing before serving. [< Ital. marinare]

ma·rine (mə·rēn′) adj. 1. Of, pertaining to, existing in, or formed by the sea. 2. Pertaining to the navigation or handling of ships on the sea; nautical. 3. Relating to the navy; naval. 4. Used or intended for use at sea or in navigation. 5. Serving aboard ship. — n. 1. A soldier trained for service at sea and on land; a member of the Marine Corps: also **Ma·rine′**. 2. Shipping vessels, shipping, or the navy collectively. 3. A seascape. 4. The department of naval affairs in some countries. [< OF < L mare, maris sea] —**Syn.** (adj.) Maritime, nautical, naval.

Marine Corps A branch of the U.S. Navy, made up of combat troops, air forces, etc., under their own officers: officially, the United States Marine Corps.

mar·i·ner (mar′ə·nər) n. One who navigates or assists in navigating a ship; sailor; seaman. [< OF marinier]

mar·i·o·nette (mar′ē·ə·net′) n. A small jointed human or animal figure of wood, cloth, etc., used in shows and animated by manipulating strings: also called puppet. [< F marionnette, dim. of Marion, dim. of Marie]

Mar·i·po·sa lily (mar′ə·pō·sə, -zə) Any of various liliaceous Mexican and Californian plants. Also **Mariposa tulip**.

mar·i·tal (mar′ə·təl) adj. Of or pertaining to marriage. [< L maritus husband, orig., married] —**mar′i·tal·ly** adv.

mar·i·time (mar′ə·tīm) adj. 1. Situated on or near the sea. 2. Of or pertaining to the sea, its navigation, commerce, etc. —**Syn.** See MARINE. [< MF < L mare, maris sea]

Maritime Provinces New Brunswick, Nova Scotia, and Prince Edward Island on the Atlantic coast of Canada.

Mar·i·tim·er (mar′ə·tī′mər) n. A resident or native of the Maritime Provinces.

mar·jo·ram (mär′jər·əm) n. Any of several perennial herbs of the mint family, one of which, **sweet marjoram**, is used in cookery. [< OF majorane, ult. origin uncertain]

mark¹ (märk) n. 1. A visible trace, impression, or figure on something, as a line, scratch, spot, or dot. 2. An identifying symbol, seal, inscription, or label; trademark. 3. A cross or other sign made by one who cannot write. 4. A letter, number, or symbol used to indicate achievement, quality, defect, etc., as of a student's work. 5. A symbol, written or printed. 6. An object, point, sign, etc., serving to indicate, guide, or direct. 7. That which indicates the presence of a thing, quality, process, etc.: a mark of distinction. 8. A visible indication of some quality, trait, position, etc.: the mark of an outcast. 9. That which is aimed at, or toward which effort is directed. 10. A standard or criterion of quality, performance, etc. 11. Informal A person easily duped or victimized: a mark for every schemer. 12. In track sports, the starting line of the contest. 13. Naut. A knot, twist, rag, etc., on a lead line at intervals to indicate fathoms of depth. 14. Notice; attention; heed: worthy of mark. — **beside the mark** 1. Missing the point aimed at. 2. Irrelevant. — **hit the mark** 1. To be accurate. 2. To achieve one's goal. — **to leave** (or **make**) **a mark** To leave or make an impression; influence. — **to make one's mark** To succeed. — **of mark** Having, or worthy of distinction, renown, etc. — **up to the mark** Up to standard; in good health or condition, etc. — **wide of the mark** 1. Striking far from the point aimed at. 2. Irrelevant. — v.t. 1. To make a mark or marks on. 2. To trace the boundaries of; set limits to: often with out. 3. To indicate or show by a mark or sign. 4. To characterize; distinguish: a year marked by great events. 5. To designate, appoint, or select, as if by marking: to be marked for death. 6. To pay attention to; notice; heed. 7. To make known or clear; manifest; display. 8. To apply or attach a price tag, identification label, etc., to an article. 9. To evaluate by giving marks to. 10. To keep (record or score) in various games. 11. To produce by drawing, writing, etc. — v.i. 12. To take notice; pay attention; consider. 13. To make a mark or marks. 14. To keep score in games. — **to mark down** 1. To note down by writing. 2. To put a lower price on, as for sale. — **to mark time** 1. To keep time by moving the feet but not advancing. 2. To pause in action or progress temporarily. — **to mark up** 1. To make marks on; scar. 2. To increase the price of. [ME < OE meare, orig., boundary] —**mark′er** n.

mark² (märk) n. The former standard monetary unit and silver coin of Germany, equivalent to 100 pfennigs, superseded after World War II by the deutschemark in West Germany and a deutschemark of different value in East Germany. [OE marc a unit of weight]

Mark (märk) The evangelist who wrote the second of the gospel narratives in the New Testament: called **Saint Mark**. — n. The second Gospel of the New Testament.

marked (märkt) *adj.* **1.** Clearly evident; noticeable. **2.** Having a mark or marks. **— a marked man** One singled out for vengeance, punishment, etc. **— mark·ed·ly** (mär′ked·lē) *adv.* **— mark′ed·ness** *n.*

mar·ket (mär′kit) *n.* **1.** Trade and commerce in a specific service or commodity: the boat *market*; also, trade and commerce generally: with *the.* **2.** A region where one can buy or sell; also, a category of persons, institutions, etc., considered as buyers: the college *market.* **3.** The state of trade: a brisk *market.* **4.** A place where something is offered for sale. **5.** A public gathering, often weekly, for buying and selling. **6.** Market value (which see). **— in the market** Seeking to buy. **— on the market** Up for sale. **—** *v.t.* **1.** To sell. **—** *v.i.* **2.** To deal in a market. **3.** To buy household provisions. [ME < AF < L < *merx, mercis* merchandise]

mar·ket·a·ble (mär′kit·ə·bəl) *adj.* Suitable for sale; in demand. **— mar′ket·a·bil′i·ty** *n.*

mar·ket·place (mär′kit·plās′) *n.* **1.** A market (def. 4). **2.** The imagined place where ideas, opinions, works, etc., are tested and traded. Also **market place.**

market value The amount that can be obtained for goods on the open market. Also **market price.**

mark·ing (mär′king) *n.* **1.** A mark or an arrangement of marks. **2.** *Often pl.* The color pattern on a bird, animal, etc. **3.** The act of making a mark.

mark·ka (märk′kä) *n.* The standard monetary unit of Finland, equivalent to 100 pennia. [< Finnish < Sw. *mark*]

marks·man (märks′mən) *n. pl.* **·men** (-mən) **1.** One skilled in hitting the mark, as with a rifle or other weapon. **2.** *Mil.* In the U.S. Army, the lowest of three grades for skill in the use of small arms. **— marks′man·ship** *n.* **— marks′wom′an** (-woom′ən) *n.fem.*

mark·up (märk′up′) *n.* **1.** A raising of price. **2.** The amount of price increase.

marl (märl) *n.* **1.** An earthy deposit containing lime, clay, and sand, used as fertilizer. **2.** A soft, crumbly soil. **3.** *Poetic* Earth. **—** *v.t.* To spread with marl. [< OF < LL < L *marga* marl] **— marl′y, mar·la′ceous** (-lā′shəs) *adj.*

mar·lin (mär′lin) *n.* Any of various deep-sea game fishes; esp., the **blue marlin** of the Atlantic, and the **striped marlin** of the Pacific. [< MARLINE(SPIKE); because of its shape]

mar·line (mär′lin) *n. Naut.* A small rope of two strands loosely twisted together, used for winding ropes, cables, etc. [< Du. *marren* to tie + *lijn* a line]

mar·line·spike (mär′lin·spīk′) *n. Naut.* A sharp-pointed iron pin used in splicing ropes. Also **mar′lin·spike′, mar′· ling·spike′** (-ling-).

mar·ma·lade (mär′mə·lād) *n.* A preserve made by boiling with sugar the pulp and rind of fruits, usu. citrus fruits, to the consistency of jam. [< MF < Pg *marmelada*]

mar·mo·re·al (mär·môr′ē·əl, -mō′rē-) *adj.* Pertaining to, made of, or resembling marble. Also **mar·mo′re·an** (-môr′ē-, -mō′rē-). [< L *marmoreus* < *marmor.* See MARBLE.]

mar·mo·set (mär′mə·zet) *n.* Any of various small Central and South American monkeys with soft, woolly hair and a long hairy tail. [< OF *marmouset* grotesque figure]

mar·mot (mär′mət) *n.* Any of various rodents, as the woodchuck or ground hog. [Fusion of OF *marmotte* monkey and Romansch *murmont* marmot]

ma·roon[1] (mə·rōōn′) *v.t.* **1.** To put ashore and abandon on a desolate island or coast. **2.** To abandon; leave helpless. **—** *n.* One of a class of Negroes, chiefly fugitive slaves or their descendants, living wild in the mountains of some West Indies islands and of Guiana. [< Am. Sp. *cimarron* wild]

ma·roon[2] (mə·rōōn′) *n.* A dull, dark red color. **—** *adj.* Having a dull, dark red color. [< F *marron* chestnut]

mar·quee (mär·kē′) *n.* **1.** A canopy used as a shelter over the sidewalk in front of a theater, hotel, etc. **2.** A large field tent, as one used at outdoor parties. [< *marquise* canopy]

mar·quess (mär′kwis) See MARQUIS.

mar·que·try (mär′kə·trē) *n.* Inlaid work of wood often interspersed with stones, ivory, etc., esp. as used in furniture. Also **mar′que·te·rie.** [< MF < *marqueter* to variegate]

mar·quis (mär′kwis, *Fr.* mår·kē′) *n.* The title of a nobleman next in rank below a duke. Also, *Brit.,* **marquess.** [< OF < Med.L *markensis* commander of the marches]

Mar·quis (mär′kwis) *n.* An important variety of wheat, first developed in Canada.

mar·quis·ate (mär′kwiz·it) *n.* The rank of a marquis.

mar·quise (mär·kēz′) *n.* **1.** The wife or widow of a French marquis. **2.** An ornamental hood over a door; a marquee.

mar·qui·sette (mär′ki·zet′, -kwi-) *n.* A lightweight, open-mesh fabric of cotton, silk, rayon, or nylon, or a combination of these, used for curtains and women's and children's garments. [< F, dim. of *marquise* a marquise]

mar·riage (mar′ij) *n.* **1.** The state of being married; a legal contract, entered into by a man and a woman, to live together as husband and wife; wedlock. **◆** Collateral adjec-

tives: *hymeneal, marital.* **2.** The act of marrying; also, the accompanying rites or festivities; wedding; nuptials. **3.** Any close union. [< OF < L *maritare* to marry]

mar·riage·a·ble (mar′ij-ə·bəl) *adj.* Fitted or suitable for marriage. **— mar′riage·a·bil′i·ty, mar′riage·a·ble·ness** *n.*

mar·ried (mar′ēd) *adj.* **1.** United in matrimony; having a spouse. **2.** Of or pertaining to marriage or to persons united in marriage. **3.** Closely related or joined.

mar·ron (mar′ən, *Fr.* må·rôñ′) *n. Often pl.* A large variety of chestnut, esp. when preserved in syrup, etc. [< F]

mar·row (mar′ō) *n.* **1.** A soft, vascular tissue found in the central cavities of bones. **2.** The essence of anything; pith. **3.** Vitality. [OE *mearg*] **— mar′row·y** *adj.*

mar·row·bone (mar′ō·bōn′) *n.* **1.** A bone containing edible marrow. **2.** *pl.* One's knees: used humorously.

mar·row·fat (mar′ō·fat′) *n.* A variety of green pea, having a large, succulent seed. Also **marrow pea.**

mar·ry (mar′ē) *v.* **·ried, ·ry·ing** *v.t.* **1.** To accept as husband or wife; take in marriage. **2.** To join as husband and wife in marriage. **3.** To give in marriage. **4.** To unite closely. **—** *v.i.* **5.** To take a husband or wife. **6.** To join or unite closely. [< OF < L < *maritus* husband, married]

Mars (märz) In Roman mythology, the god of war: identified with the Greek *Ares.* **—** *n.* The seventh largest planet of the solar system and fourth from the sun. See PLANET.

Mar·sa·la (mär·sä′lä) *n.* A dark-colored, sweet, heavy wine, originally made in Marsala, Sicily.

Mar·seil·laise (mär′sə·lāz′, *Fr.* mår·se·yez′) The national anthem of France, written in 1792 by Rouget de Lisle.

mar·seille (mär·sāl′) *n.* A thick cotton fabric. Also **mar·seilles** (-sālz′). [after *Marseille,* France]

marsh (märsh) *n.* A tract of low, wet land; swamp. [OE *mersc, merisc*]

mar·shal (mär′shəl) *n.* **1.** In various foreign countries, a military officer of high rank, usu. just below the commander in chief: a field *marshal.* **2.** *U.S.* a An officer of the Federal courts, assigned to a judicial district and having duties similar to those of a sheriff. b In some cities, the chief of the police or fire department. **3.** An officer authorized to organize or regulate processions, ceremonies, etc. **4.** A title of certain royal court or household officials, often in charge of matters of protocol. **—** *v.t.* **mar·shaled** or **·shalled, mar·shal·ing** or **·shal·ling 1.** To arrange or dispose in order, as facts. **2.** To array or draw up, as troops for battle. **3.** To lead; usher. [< OF < Med.L < OHG < *marah* horse + *scalh* servant] **— mar′shal·cy, mar′shal·ship** *n.* **— mar′· shal·er, mar′shal·ler** *n.*

Marshal of the Royal Canadian Air Force In the Royal Canadian Air Force, a commissioned officer of the highest rank. See table at GRADE.

marsh gas Methane.

marsh hawk A marsh-dwelling American hawk having gray or brown plumage, a white rump, and rounded wings.

marsh·mal·low (märsh′mel′ō, -mal′ō) *n.* **1.** A confection made of starch, sugar, corn syrup, and gelatin, and coated with powdered sugar. **2.** A sweetmeat formerly made from the root of the marsh mallow.

marsh mallow A plant of the mallow family growing in marshy places.

marsh marigold A showy swamp plant of the crowfoot family, having yellow flowers: also called *cowslip.*

marsh·y (mär′shē) *adj.* **marsh·i·er, marsh·i·est 1.** Of, pertaining to, or containing a marsh. **2.** Swampy; boggy. **3.** Growing or produced in a marsh. **— marsh′i·ness** *n.*

mar·su·pi·al (mär·sōō′pē·əl) *n.* Any member of an order of mammals, as the kangaroos, opossums, wombats, etc., whose females carry their undeveloped young in a marsupium. **—** *adj.* Having a marsupium or pouch. **— mar·su′pi·a′li·an** (-ā′lē·ən), **mar·su′pi·an** *adj. & n.*

mar·su·pi·um (mär·sōō′pē·əm) *n. pl.* **·pi·a** (-pē·ə) A pouchlike receptacle on the abdomen of female marsupials, containing the teats and used for carrying the young. [< L < Gk. *marsypion,* dim. of *marsipos* bag]

mart (märt) *n.* A market. [< MDu. < L *mercatus*]

mar·ten (mär′ten) *n.* **1.** A weasellike carnivorous mammal having arboreal habits, as the **pine marten** of eastern North America. **2.** The valuable, dark brown fur of a marten. [< OF *martrine* of the marten < WGmc.]

Mar·tha (mär′thə) A sister of Lazarus and Mary, who served Jesus at Bethany. *Luke* x 38–41.

mar·tial (mär′shəl) *adj.* **1.** Of, pertaining to, or concerned with war or the military life. **2.** Suggestive of or suitable for war or military operations. **3.** Of or characteristic of a warrior. [< OF < L *martialis* pertaining to Mars] **— mar′· tial·ism** *n.* **— mar′tial·ist** *n.* **— mar′tial·ly** *adv.*

martial law Temporary jurisdiction or rule by military forces over the citizens of an area where civil law and order no longer function or exist.

Mar·tian (mär′shən) *adj.* *Astron.* Of or pertaining to the planet Mars. — *n.* One of the supposed inhabitants of Mars. [< L *Martius*]

mar·tin (mär′tən) *n.* **1.** Any of certain birds of the swallow family, having a tail that is less forked than that of the common swallow; esp., the **house martin** of Europe, and the **purple martin** of North America. **2.** Any of various similar birds. [< F]

mar·ti·net (mär′tə·net′) *n.* **1.** A strict military disciplinarian. **2.** One who demands rigid adherence to rules, etc. [after General Jean *Martinet*, 17th c. French drillmaster]

mar·tin·gale (mär′tən·gāl) *n.* A forked strap that prevents a horse from rearing its head, connecting the head gear with the bellyband. Also **mar′tin·gal** (-gal). [< F Provençal *martengalo*, appar. fem. of *martengo* an inhabitant of Martigues, miserly person < Sp. *almartaga* < Arabic]

mar·ti·ni (mär·tē′nē) *n.* *pl.* **·nis** A cocktail made of gin and dry vermouth, usu. served with an olive or lemon peel. [after *Martini* and *Rossi*, a company making vermouth]

mar·tyr (mär′tər) *n.* **1.** One who submits to death rather than renounce his religion. **2.** One who dies, suffers, or sacrifices everything for a principle, cause, etc. **3.** One who suffers much, as from ill health or misfortune. — *v.t.* **1.** To make a martyr of. **2.** To torture or persecute. [OE < LL < Gk. *martyr*, Aeolic form of *martyrs*, *martyros* witness] — **mar′tyr·dom** (-dəm) *n.*

mar·tyr·ize (mär′tər·īz) *v.* **·ized**, **·iz·ing** *v.t.* **1.** To make a martyr of. — *v.i.* **2.** To become a martyr. — **mar′tyr·i·za′tion** *n.*

mar·vel (mär′vəl) *v.* **mar·veled** or **·velled**, **mar·vel·ing** or **·vel·ling** *v.i.* **1.** To be filled with wonder, surprise, etc. — *v.t.* **2.** To wonder at or about: with a clause as object. — *n.* That which excites wonder; a prodigy. [< OF < L *mirabilia* neut. pl. of *mirabilis* wonderful]

mar·vel·ous (mär′vəl·əs) *adj.* **1.** Causing astonishment and wonder; amazing; extraordinary. **2.** Miraculous; incredible. **3.** *Informal* Very good; excellent; admirable. Also **mar′vel·lous.** — **mar′vel·ous·ly** *adv.* — **mar′vel·ous·ness** *n.*

Marx·ism (märk′siz·əm) *n.* The body of socialist doctrines formulated by Karl Marx and Friedrich Engels, the basic tenets of which are dialectical materialism, the theory of class struggle, and the labor theory of value. — **Marx′ist, Marx·ian** (märk′sē·ən) *n. & adj.*

Marx·ism-Len·in·ism (märk′siz·əm·len′in·iz·əm) *n.* The modification of Marxist philosophy or doctrines attributed to Lenin. — **Marx′ist-Len′in·ist** *n., adj.*

Mar·y (mâr′ē) The mother of Jesus: also *Virgin Mary.*

Mary The sister of Lazarus and Martha. *Luke* x 39–42.

Mary Mag·da·lene (mag′də·lēn, mag′də·lē′nē) A woman from Magdala out of whom Jesus cast seven devils, often identified with the penitent sinner whom Jesus forgave.

mar·zi·pan (märt′sə·pan, mär′zə-) *n.* A confection of grated almonds, sugar, and white of eggs, usu. made into a paste and molded into various shapes: also called *marchpane*. [< G < Ital. < Med.L *matapanus* a Venetian coin]

-mas *combining form* Mass; a (specified) festival or its celebration: *Christmas.* [< MASS²]

mas·car·a (mas·kar′ə) *n.* A cosmetic preparation used·to darken or tint the eyelashes and eyebrows. [< Sp. *mascara* mask < Arabic *maskharah* buffoon]

mas·cot (mas′kot, -kət) *n.* A person, animal, or object thought to bring good luck by its presence. [< F < Provençal *mascot*, dim. of *masco* sorcerer, lit., mask]

mas·cu·line (mas′kyə·lin) *adj.* **1.** Of or pertaining to the male sex; male. **2.** Of, pertaining to, typical of, or appropriate for men or boys: *masculine* sports. **3.** Mannish: said of a female. **4.** *Gram.* Applicable to males only or to persons or things classified, as in declension, as male. — *n. Gram.* **1.** The masculine gender. **2.** A word or form belonging to the masculine gender. [< OF < L < *masculus* male] — **mas′cu·line·ly** *adv.* — **mas′cu·lin′i·ty, mas′cu·line·ness** *n.*

masculine rhyme Rhyme in which the primary stress and the rhyme fall upon the final or only syllable, as in *breaks, takes* and *alert, convert.*

ma·ser (mā′zər) *n. Physics* Any of various devices that generate or amplify electromagnetic waves of precise frequency without loss of frequency and phase, by using the excess energy of an atomic or molecular system. [< *m(icrowave)* a(*mplification by*) s(*timulated*) e(*mission of*) r(*adiation*)]

mash (mash) *n.* **1.** A soft, pulpy mixture or mass. **2.** A mixture of meal, bran, etc., and water, fed warm to horses and cattle. **3.** Crushed or ground grain or malt, steeped in hot water to produce wort for making beer. — *v.t.* **1.** To crush into a mash or pulp. **2.** To steep (malt, grain meal, etc.) in hot water to produce wort. [OE *max-, mäsc* (*wyrt*) mash (wort), infused malt]

mash·er (mash′ər) *n.* **1.** One who or that which mashes. **2.** *Slang* A man who flirts or attempts familiarities, usu. with women unknown to him.

mash·ie (mash′ē) *n.* In golf, a five iron. Also **mash′·y** [? Alter. of F *massue* club < Celtic]

mask (mask, mäsk) *n.* **1.** A covering used to conceal all or part of the face; esp.: **a** A covering, often grotesque or comic, worn at a masquerade, at Halloween, etc. **b** A large, headlike covering for an actor's face, used to represent a specific character or trait, as in Greek and Roman drama. **c** A covering made of heavy wire or other material, worn to protect the face from a fencing foil, baseball, glass, etc. **d** A gas mask. **2.** A cast of a face, usu. made of plaster. **3.** That which hides or conceals something from the sight or mind: under the *mask* of piety. **4.** One who wears a mask. **5.** A masquerade. **6.** See MASQUE. **7.** *Mil.* A screen or cover for concealing any military installation or operation. — *v.t.* **1.** To cover (the face, head, etc.) with a mask. **2.** To disguise. — *v.i.* **3.** To put on a mask; assume a disguise. [< F < Ital. < Arabic *maskharah* buffoon] — **masked** *adj.* — **mas′ker** *n.*

MASKS
a Greek tragedy. *b* Greek comedy. *c* Tibetan ceremonial. *d* Ancient Shinto. *e* Domino.

mask·ing tape (mas′king, mäs′-) An adhesive tape to cover those parts of a surface not to be painted, sprayed, etc.

mas·o·chism (mas′ə·kiz′əm) *n.* **1.** *Psychol.* A condition in which sexual gratification depends largely on undergoing physical pain or humiliation. **2.** A tendency to derive pleasure from one's own suffering. [after Leopold von Sacher-*Masoch*, 1835–95, Austrian novelist, who described this condition] — **mas′o·chist** *n.* — **mas′o·chis′tic** *adj.* — **mas′o·chis′ti·cal·ly** (-kə·lē, -klē) *adv.*

ma·son (mā′sən) *n.* **1.** One skilled in building with stone, brick, concrete, etc. **2.** A stonecutter. — *v.t.* To build of or strengthen with brick, stone, etc. [< OF < Med.L *matio, macio, -onis*, prob. < Gmc.]

Ma·son (mā′sən) *n.* Freemason. — **Ma′son·ry** *n.*

ma·son·ic (mə·son′ik) *adj.* **1.** *Usu. cap.* Of, pertaining to, or like Freemasons or Freemasonry. **2.** Of or pertaining to masons or masonry.

Ma·son·ite (mā′sən·īt) *n.* A tough fiberboard made from wood fibers, used as a building and construction material: a trade name. Also **ma′son·ite.**

Ma·son jar (mā′sən) A glass jar having a tightly fitting screw top, used for canning and preserving. [after John L. *Mason*, 19th c. American inventor]

ma·son·ry (mā′sən·rē) *n. pl. ·ries* **1.** The art or work of a mason. **2.** That which is built by masons.

masque (mask, mäsk) *n.* **1.** An elaborately staged dramatic performance, popular during the 16th and 17th centuries in England; also, something written for this. **2.** A masquerade. [See MASK.]

mas·quer·ade (mas′kə·rād′, mäs′-) *n.* **1.** A social gathering in which the guests are masked and dressed in fancy costumes. **2.** The costumes worn at such a gathering. **3.** A false show, disguise, or pretense. Also called *mask, masque.* — *v.i.* **·ad·ed, ·ad·ing** **1.** To take part in a masquerade. **2.** To wear a mask or disguise. **3.** To disguise one's true character; assume a false appearance. [Alter. of F *mascarade* < Sp. < *máscara* mask] — **mas′quer·ad′er** *n.*

mass (mas, mäs) *n.* **1.** A body of matter having no definite shape but relatively large in size. **2.** An assemblage of individual parts or objects that collectively make up a single body. **3.** A great amount or number of anything. **4.** The principal or greater part of anything; majority. **5.** The volume or magnitude of a solid body; bulk; size. **6.** In painting, the solid, unified portions of color or light in a composition. **7.** *Physics* The measure of the inertia of a body, expressed as the quotient of the weight of the body divided by the acceleration due to gravity. — **the masses** The great body or majority of ordinary people. — *adj.* **1.** Attended by, designed for, characteristic of, or affecting a large mass of people. **2.** Done in a large-scale manner; produced in large amounts. **3.** Total; all-over: the *mass* effect. — *v.t. & v.i.* To form into a mass; assemble. [< OF < L *massa*, prob. < Gk. *maza* barley cake]

Mass (mas, mäs) *n. Eccl.* **1.** In the Roman Catholic and some Anglican churches, the eucharistic liturgy, consisting of various prayers and ritual ceremonies and regarded as a commemoration or repetition of Christ's sacrifice on the Cross. **2.** A celebration of this liturgy. **3.** A musical setting for some of the fixed portions of this liturgy. [OE < LL < L *missa*, pp. fem. of *mittere* to send, dismiss < *ite, missa est* go, you are dismissed; said by the priest]

Mas·sa·chu·set (mas′ə·chōō′sit) *n.* **1.** One of a large tribe of North American Indians of Algonquian stock, formerly inhabiting the region around Massachusetts Bay. **2.** Their language. Also **Mas′sa·chu′sett.** [< Algonquian (Massachuset) < *mass* big + *wadchu* hill + *es*, dim. + *et* at the]

mas·sa·cre (mas′ə-kər) *n.* **1.** A savage and indiscriminate killing of human beings, as in warfare, acts of persecution, revenge, etc. **2.** *U.S. Informal* A crushing defeat, as in sports. — *v.t.* **·cred** (-kərd), **·cring 1.** To kill indiscriminately or in great numbers. **2.** *U.S. Informal* To defeat severely, as in sports. [< MF < OF, ? < *mache-col* butcher < *macher* to smash + *col* neck] — **mas′sa·crer** *n.*
— **Syn.** (noun) A *massacre* is the killing of those who are defenseless or unresisting, as in barbarous warfare. *Slaughter* may be used in the same sense, but frequently is applied to any great loss of life in battle, riot, etc. In a more restricted sense, *slaughter* is used of the killing of animals for food. *Carnage* retains much of its original sense of the heaped up bodies of the slain, and refers to the result rather than to the process of a *massacre* or *slaughter*.
mas·sage (mə-säzh′) *n.* A manual or mechanical manipulation of parts of the body, as by rubbing, kneading, slapping or the like, used to promote circulation, relax muscles, etc. — *v.t.* **·saged, ·sag·ing** To treat by massage. [< F < L, ? < Gk. *massein* to knead] — **mas·sag′er, mas·sag′ist** *n.* — **mas·sa·geuse** (mas′ə-zhœz′) *n.fem.*
mas·seur (ma·sûr′, *Fr.* må·sœr′) *n.* A man who practices or gives massage. [< F] — **mas·seuse** (ma·sooz′, -soos′; *Fr.* må·sœz′) *n.fem.*
mas·sive (mas′iv) *adj.* **1.** Forming or constituting a large mass; having great bulk and weight; ponderous. **2.** Relatively large or heavy: a *massive* head. **3.** Imposing or impressive in scale, scope, degree, etc. **4.** *Mineral.* Lacking definite or externally observable crystalline form. **5.** *Geol.* Homogeneous, as certain rock formations. **6.** *Pathol.* Extending over or affecting a large area: a *massive* swelling. [< F *massif*] — **mas′sive·ly** *adv.* — **mas′sive·ness** *n.*
mass media The various means of disseminating information to a wide public audience, as newspapers, radio, etc.
mass meeting A large public gathering for the discussion or promotion of some topic or cause, usu. political.
mass number *Physics* The total number of nucleons of an atom; the integer nearest the observed mass of an isotope.
mass production The manufacture or production, usu. by machinery, of goods or articles in great numbers or quantities. — **mass-pro·duced** (mas′prə-doost′, -dyoost′) *adj.*
mass ratio *Aerospace* The ratio of the mass of a rocket at the time of liftoff to its mass after the fuel has been used up.
mass spectrograph *Physics* An instrument for determining the relative masses of electrically charged particles by passing a stream of them through a magnetic field and noting the variable deflections from a straight path.
mast¹ (mast, mäst) *n.* **1.** *Naut.* A pole or spar set upright in a sailing vessel to sustain the yards, sails, etc. **2.** Any large, upright pole, as of a derrick, crane, etc. — **before the mast** Serving as a common sailor. — *v.t.* To furnish with a mast or masts. [OE *mæst*]
mast² (mast, mäst) *n.* The fruit of the oak, beech, etc., when used as food for swine. [OE *mæst* mast, fodder]
mast- Var. of MASTO-.
mas·ta·ba (mas′tə-bə) *n.* In ancient Egypt, an oblong building with sloping sides and a flat top, covering the mouth of a burial pit and used as a chapel and place of offering. Also **mas′ta·bah.** [< Arabic *mastabah* bench]
mas·tec·to·my (mas·tek′tə-mē) *n. pl.* **·mies** The surgical removal of a breast. [< Gk. *mastos* breast + -ECTOMY]
mas·ter (mas′tər, mäs′-) *n.* **1.** One who has control, direction, or authority over someone or something, as over a household, an animal, etc. **2.** One exceptionally gifted or skilled in an art, science, etc.: a *master* of oratory. **3.** A craftsman or worker whose skill or experience qualifies him to practice his craft on his own and to train apprentices. **4.** One who has the ability to control or dispose of something to good advantage. **5.** A teacher or leader in philosophy, religion, etc., who has followers or disciples. **6.** *Chiefly Brit.* A male teacher. **7.** One who has received a Master of Arts degree. **8.** One who has charge of or presides over a place, institution, ceremony, etc.: a *master* of ceremonies. **9.** Something considered as having the power to control or influence: Never let fear be your *master*. **10.** Something, as a matrix, stencil, etc., from which copies or impressions are made. **11.** *Usu. cap.* A youth or boy; also, a title prefixed to a boy's name. **12.** *Usu. cap.* A title of respect or of address, now generally replaced by *Mister*. **13.** In the Scottish peerage, the title of the eldest son or heir apparent of a viscount or baron. **14.** A victor or conqueror. **15.** *Law* An officer of the court who assists the judge. — *v.t.* **1.** To bring under control; defeat. **2.** To become expert in: to *master* Greek. **3.** To control or govern as a master. — *adj.* **1.** Of, pertaining to, or characteristic of a master. **2.** Having or exercising control. **3.** Principal; main: the *master* plan. **4.** Designating a device or mechanism that controls, operates, or acts as a pattern or norm for something else: a *master* switch. [OE < L *magnus* great] — **mas′ter·dom** *n.* — **mas′ter·hood** *n.*

master builder 1. An architect. **2.** One who supervises building construction.
mas·ter·ful (mas′tər-fəl, mäs′-) *adj.* **1.** Vigorously bold or authoritative in conduct, decision, manner, etc. **2.** Domineering; imperious. **3.** Having or displaying the skill of a master. — **mas′ter·ful·ly** *adv.* — **mas′ter·ful·ness** *n.*
master key A key that will unlock two or more locks, each of which has its own key that fits no other lock.
mas·ter·ly (mas′tər-lē, mäs′-) *adj.* Characteristic of or befitting a master: a *masterly* performance. — *adv.* In a masterly manner. — **mas′ter·li·ness** *n.*
master mechanic An able, experienced mechanic.
mas·ter·mind (mas′tər-mīnd′, mäs′-) *n.* A person of great executive ability; esp., one who plans and directs at the highest levels of policy and strategy. — *v.t.* To plan and direct (a project, etc.) at the highest strategic level.
Master of Arts 1. A degree given by a college or university to a person who has completed a prescribed course of graduate study of at least one year in the humanities, social sciences, etc. **2.** A person who has received this degree.
master of ceremonies 1. A person presiding over an entertainment or dinner and introducing the performers or speakers. **2.** A person who supervises the ceremonies at a public or formal function. Also called *emcee*.
Master of Science 1. A degree given by a college or university to a person who has completed a prescribed course of graduate study of at least one year in science. **2.** A person who has received this degree.
mas·ter·piece (mas′tər-pēs′, mäs′-) *n.* **1.** Something of notable excellence; an unusually brilliant achievement. **2.** Something considered the greatest achievement of its creator. Also **mas′ter·work′.** [Trans. of G *meisterstück*]
mas·ter·ship (mas′tər-ship, mäs′-) *n.* **1.** The state of being a master or ruler. **2.** The status or function of a master. **3.** The skill, experience, or authority of a master.
mas·ter·stroke (mas′tər-strōk′, mäs′-) *n.* A masterly or decisive action or achievement.
mas·ter·y (mas′tər-ē, mäs′-) *n. pl.* **·ter·ies 1.** Superior knowledge or skill. **2.** Victory or superiority, as in a contest. **3.** The act of mastering a craft, technique, etc.
mast·head (mast′hed′, mäst′-) *n.* **1.** *Naut.* The top of a mast. **2.** The part of a periodical that gives the names of the editors, staff, and owners. — *v.t.* To display at the masthead.
mas·tic (mas′tik) *n.* **1.** A small Mediterranean evergreen tree of the cashew family. **2.** The resin obtained from this tree, used in varnishes and as a flavoring agent. [< F < LL < Gk. *mastichē*]
mas·ti·cate (mas′tə-kāt) *v.t.* **·cat·ed, ·cat·ing 1.** To chew. **2.** To reduce, as rubber, to a pulp by crushing or kneading. [< LL < Gk. *mastichaein* to gnash the teeth] — **mas′ti·ca′·tion** *n.* — **mas′ti·ca′tor** *n.*
mas·ti·ca·to·ry (mas′tə-kə-tôr′ē, -tō′rē) *adj.* **1.** Of or pertaining to mastication. **2.** Adapted for chewing. — *n. pl.* **·ries** A substance chewed to increase salivation.
mas·tiff (mas′tif, mäs′-) *n.* A breed of large hunting dogs, having a thickset, heavy body, drooping ears, and pendulous lips. [< OF < L < pp. of *mansuescere* to tame]
mas·ti·tis (mas·tī′tis) *n. Pathol.* Inflammation of the breast.
masto- *combining form Med.* The breast or the mammary glands. Also, before vowels, **mast-.** [< Gk. *mastos* breast]
mas·to·don (mas′tə-don) *n. Paleontol.* Any of various large, extinct mammals resembling the elephant. [< NL < MAST- + Gk. *odous, odontos* tooth]
mas·toid (mas′toid) *adj.* **1.** *Anat.* Designating a nipple-shaped process of the temporal bone located behind the ear. **2.** Having the shape of a breast or nipple. — *n.* The mastoid process. [< Gk. < *mastos* breast + *eidos* form]
mas·toid·i·tis (mas′toid-ī′tis) *n. Pathol.* Inflammation of the mastoid process.
mas·tur·bate (mas′tər-bāt) *v.i.* **·bat·ed, ·bat·ing** To perform masturbation. [< L *masturbatus*, pp. of *masturbari*]
mas·tur·ba·tion (mas′tər-bā′shən) *n.* Stimulation of the sexual organs, usu. by oneself: also called *onanism*. — **mas′·tur·ba′tor** *n.*
ma·su·ri·um (mə-soor′ē-əm) *n.* A supposed metallic element whose place in the periodic table is now occupied by technetium. [after *Masuria*, where first found]
mat¹ (mat) *n.* **1.** A flat piece of material made of fiber, rushes, rubber, etc., and used primarily to cover floors; also, a smaller piece of this material, used to sit or lie on. **2.** A thickly padded piece of material placed on the floor for protection in various gymnastic sports. **3.** A small, flat piece of material, as lace, straw, or plastic, used as a table protection, ornament, etc. **4.** Any dense, twisted, or tangled mass, as of hair. — *v.* **mat·ted, mat·ting** *v.t.* **1.** To cover with or as with a mat or mats. **2.** To knot or entangle into a mat. — *v.i.* **3.** To become entangled together. [OE < LL *matta*]

mat² (mat) *n.* **1.** A border of cardboard or other material, serving as the frame or part of the frame of a picture. **2.** *Printing* A matrix. **3.** A lusterless, dull, or roughened surface, as on metal or glass. — *v.t.* **mat·ted, mat·ting 1.** To produce a dull surface on, as on metal or glass. **2.** To furnish (a picture) with a mat. — *adj.* Having a lusterless surface. [OF, defeated]

mat·a·dor (mat′ə-dôr) *n.* In bullfighting, the man who kills the bull after completing various maneuvers with a cape in order to tire the animal. [< Sp. < *matar* to slay]

match¹ (mach) *n.* **1.** One who or that which is similar to another in some quality or characteristic. **2.** One who or that which is exactly equal to another. **3.** One who or that which is able to cope with or oppose another as an equal. **4.** Either of two things that harmonize or correspond with each other. **5.** A suitable or fit pair. **6.** A game or contest. **7.** A marriage or mating; also, an agreement to marry or mate. **8.** A possible partner in marriage. — *v.t.* **1.** To be similar to or in accord with in quality, degree, etc. **2.** To make, provide, or select as equals or as suitable for one another: to *match* pearls. **3.** To cause to correspond; adapt: *Match* your expenses to your income. **4.** To compare so as to decide superiority; test. **5.** To set (equal opponents) in opposition. **6.** To equal; oppose successfully. **7.** To flip (a coin or coins) so as to compare or bet on the faces that land upright; also, to flip coins in this manner with (another person). **8.** To place together as mates; marry. — *v.i.* **9.** To be equal or similar. **10.** To be married; mate. [OE *gemæcca* companion] — **match′a·ble** *adj.* — **match′er** *n.*

match² (mach) *n.* **1.** A splinter of soft wood or a piece of waxed thread or cardboard tipped with a combustible composition that ignites by friction. **2.** A wick or cord formerly used for firing cannon. [< OF *mesche* wick]

match·box (mach′boks′) *n.* A small box for matches.

match·less (mach′lis) *adj.* Having no match or equal; peerless. — **match′less·ly** *adv.* — **match′less·ness** *n.*

match·lock (mach′lok′) *n.* **1.** An old type of musket fired by igniting the powder with a slow-burning wick or match. **2.** The gunlock on such a musket.

match·mak·er¹ (mach′mā′kər) *n.* **1.** One who tries to bring about a marriage between other persons. **2.** One who arranges an athletic match. — **match′mak′ing** *adj. & n.*

match·mak·er² (mach′mā′kər) *n.* One who makes matches for lighting. — **match′mak′ing** *adj. & n.*

match play In golf, a form of competitive play in which the score is computed by totaling the number of holes won or lost by each side. Compare MEDAL PLAY.

mate¹ (māt) *n.* **1.** Something matched, paired, or joined with another. **2.** A husband or wife. **3.** The male or female of two animals paired for propagation. **4.** A companion; comrade. **5.** An officer of a merchant vessel, ranking next below the captain. **6.** *Naval* A petty officer. — *v.* **mat·ed, mat·ing** *v.t.* **1.** To join together; pair. **2.** To join in marriage. **3.** To unite for breeding, as animals. — *v.i.* **4.** To marry. **5.** To pair. **6.** To consort; associate. [< MLG < *ge-* together + *mat* meat, food]

mate² (māt) *v.t.* **mat·ed, mat·ing** In chess, to checkmate. — *n.* A checkmate. — *interj.* Checkmate.

ma·te³ (mä′tā, mat′ā) *n.* **1.** An infusion of the leaves of a Brazilian holly, much used as a beverage in South America. **2.** The plant itself. [< Sp. < Quechua *mati* calabash]

ma·ter (mā′tər, mä′-) *n. Brit. Informal* Mother. [< L]

ma·te·ri·al (mə-tir′ē-əl) *n.* **1.** That of which anything is or may be composed or constructed. **2.** Anything that may be used in creating, working up, or developing something. **3.** *pl.* The tools, instruments, etc., for doing something. **4.** Cloth or fabric. — *adj.* **1.** Of, pertaining to, or composed of matter; physical. **2.** Of, related to, or affecting the body or sensual appetites: *material* well-being. **3.** Concerned with or devoted to things primarily physical rather than spiritual or intellectual. **4.** Substantial; important. **5.** Relevant; pertinent: with *to.* [< LL < L *materia* matter, stuff]

ma·te·ri·al·ism (mə-tir′ē-əl-iz′əm) *n.* **1.** *Philos.* The doctrine that everything in the universe is reducible to matter and can be explained in terms of physical laws. **2.** Undue regard for the material rather than the spiritual or intellectual aspects of life. — **ma·te′ri·al·ist** *n.* — **ma·te′ri·al·is′tic** *adj.* — **ma·te′ri·al·is′ti·cal·ly** *adv.*

ma·te·ri·al·ize (mə-tir′ē-əl-īz′) *v.* **·ized, ·iz·ing** *v.t.* **1.** To give material or actual form to. **2.** In spiritualism, to cause (a spirit, etc.) to appear in visible form. **3.** To make materialistic. — *v.i.* **4.** To assume material or visible form; appear. **5.** To take form or shape; be realized. — **ma·te′ri·al·i·za′tion** *n.* — **ma·te′ri·al·iz′er** *n.*

ma·te·ri·al·ly (mə-tir′ē-əl-ē) *adv.* **1.** In an important manner or to a considerable degree. **2.** Physically. **3.** In respect to matter as distinguished from form.

ma·te·ri·a med·i·ca (mə-tir′ē-ə med′i-kə) *Med.* **1.** Substances, as drugs, etc., employed as remedial agents. **2.** The branch of medicine that treats of these substances. [< Med.L < *materia* matter + *medica*, fem. of *medicus* medical]

ma·te·ri·el (mə-tir′ē-el′) *n.* **1.** The equipment and supplies of a military force. **2.** The equipment of any organization. Also *Fr.* **ma·té·riel** (mȧ-tā-ryel′). [< F, material]

ma·ter·nal (mə-tûr′nəl) *adj.* **1.** Pertaining to a mother; motherly. **2.** Inherited from one's mother. **3.** Coming through the relationship of a mother. [< F < L < *mater* mother] — **ma·ter′nal·ly** *adv.*

ma·ter·ni·ty (mə-tûr′nə-tē) *n. pl.* **·ties 1.** The state of being a mother. **2.** The qualities of a mother. — *adj.* **1.** Fashioned for pregnant women: *maternity* clothes. **2.** Designed to accommodate women and babies during and after childbirth: a *maternity* ward. [< F < L *maternitas*]

math (math) *n. U.S. Informal* Mathematics.

math·e·mat·i·cal (math′ə-mat′i-kəl) *adj.* **1.** Of, pertaining to, or like mathematics. **2.** Used in mathematics. **3.** Rigidly exact or precise. Also **math′e·mat′ic.** [< L < Gk. < *manthanein* to learn] — **math′e·mat′i·cal·ly** *adv.*

math·e·ma·ti·cian (math′ə-mə-tish′ən) *n.* One who specializes or is expert in mathematics.

math·e·mat·ics (math′ə-mat′iks) *n.pl.* (construed as sing.) The study of quantity, form, arrangement, and magnitude; esp., the methods and processes for disclosing the properties and relations of quantities and magnitudes.

mat·in (mat′in) *n.* **1.** *pl. Eccl.* **a** The prescribed prayers that, with lauds, constitute the first of the seven canonical hours. **b** In the Anglican Church, the order for public worship in the morning. **2.** *Poetic* Any morning song. — *adj.* Of matins or the morning: also **mat′in·al.** Also spelled *mattin.* [< OF < L *matutinus* (tempus) (time) of the morning]

mat·i·nee (mat′ə-nā′) *n.* A performance or entertainment, as a play, concert, etc., held in the daytime, usu. in the afternoon. Also **mat′i·née.** [< F *matin* morning]

mat·ing (mā′ting) *n.* The act of pairing or matching.

matri- *combining form* Mother. [< L *mater* mother]

ma·tri·arch (mā′trē-ärk) *n.* A woman holding the position corresponding to that of a patriarch in her family or tribe. — **ma′tri·ar′chal, ma′tri·ar′chic** *adj.*

ma·tri·ar·chy (mā′trē-är′kē) *n. pl.* **·chies** A social organization having the mother as the head of the family, in which descent is traced through the mother.

mat·ri·cide (mat′rə-sīd) *n.* **1.** The killing of one's mother. **2.** One who kills his mother. [< L < *mater* mother + *caedere* to kill] — **mat′ri·ci′dal** *adj.*

ma·tric·u·late (mə-trik′yə-lāt) *v.t. & v.i.* **·lat·ed, ·lat·ing** To register or enroll in a college or university as a candidate for a degree. — *n.* One who is so enrolled. [< Med.L < *matriculare* to enroll < *matrix* womb] — **ma·tric′u·lant** *n.* — **ma·tric′u·la′tion** *n.* — **ma·tric′u·la′tor** *n.*

mat·ri·mo·ny (mat′rə-mō′nē) *n. pl.* **·nies 1.** The state or condition of being married. **2.** The act, ceremony, or sacrament of marriage. [< L < *mater* mother] — **mat′ri·mo′ni·al** *adj.* — **mat′ri·mo′ni·al·ly** *adv.*

ma·trix (mā′triks) *n. pl.* **ma·trix·es** or **ma·tri·ces** (mā′trə-sēz, mat′rə-) **1.** That in which anything originates, develops, takes shape, or is contained. **2.** The womb. **3.** A mold in or from which anything is cast or shaped. **4.** *Printing* **a** A mold in which the face of a type is cast. **b** In stereotyping, a papier-mâché or other impression of a form from which a plate for printing may be made. [< L, womb]

ma·tron (mā′trən) *n.* **1.** A married woman or widow who is usu. a mother. **2.** A female attendant or guard, as in a woman's prison, rest room, etc. **3.** A female superintendent of an institution, etc. [< OF < L *mater* mother] — **ma′tron·li·ness** *n.* — **ma′tron·ly** *adj. & adv.*

matron of honor A married woman acting as chief attendant to a bride at a wedding.

mat·ted (mat′id) *adj.* **1.** Covered with or made from mats or matting. **2.** Tangled or twisted in a mass. **3.** Covered with a dense or twisted growth.

mat·ter (mat′ər) *n.* **1.** That which makes up the substance of anything; constituent material. **2.** That which is material and physical, occupies space, and is perceived by the senses. **3.** A specific kind of substance: organic *matter.* **4.** A subject, event, or situation that is an object of discussion, concern, etc.: a *matter* of faith. **5.** Cause, occasion, or reason: usu. with *of* or *for:* a *matter* of great concern. **6.** Importance; consequence: It's of no *matter* what happens. **7.** Something of importance or consequence. **8.** A usu. unpleasant condition or circumstance: with *the:* What's the *matter* with you? **9.** The content or meaning of a book, etc., as distinguished from the style or form. **10.** An indefinite amount, quantity, etc.: a *matter* of a few dollars. **11.** Pus. **12.** That which is written, printed, etc.: *matter* for reading. **13.** Anything sent by mail: third-class *matter.* **14.** *Printing* **a** Type set up or composed. **b** Material to be set up; copy. — *v.i.* **1.** To be of concern; signify: It *matters* little. **2.** To form or discharge pus. [< OF < L *materia* stuff]

mat·ter-of-course (mat′ər-əv-kôrs′, -kōrs′) *adj.* **1.** To be expected. **2.** Accepting things as a matter of course.

matter of course Something expected to follow as a natural or logical result.

MATHEMATICAL SYMBOLS

$+$	Plus; positive; sign of addition	Σ	Summation of
$-$	Minus; negative; sign of subtraction	$\overset{n}{\underset{1}{\Sigma}}$	Summation of n terms, one for each positive integer from 1 to n
$\pm$	Plus or minus	Π	Product of
$\mp$	Minus or plus	$\overset{n}{\underset{1}{\Pi}}$	Product of n terms, one for each positive integer from 1 to n
$\times, \cdot$	Multiplied by		
$\div, :$	Divided by	$\int$	Integral of
$=, ::$	Equals	$\int_b^a$	Definite integral between limits a and b
$\cong$	Approximately equal; congruent	$\doteq, \rightarrow$	Approaches as a limit
$>$	Greater than	$f(x), F(x), \phi(x)$	Function of x
$<$	Less than	Δ	Increment of, as Δy
$/$	Is not; does not: drawn through another symbol, as $a \neq b$, a is not equal to b	d	Differential, as dx
$\geqq$	Greater than or equal to	$\dfrac{dy}{dx}, f'(x)$	Derivative of $y = f(x)$ with respect to x
$\leqq$	Less than or equal to		
$\sim$	Similar to; equivalent	δ	Variation, as δy
$\therefore$	Therefore	π	Pi; the ratio of the circumference and a diameter of the same circle; 3.14159...
$\because$	Since; because		
$\equiv$	Identical; identically equal to	$n!, \lfloor n$	n factorial; factorial n
$\propto$	Directly proportional to; varies directly as	$( ), [ ], \{ \}$	Indicate that the enclosed symbols are to be treated as a single number
∞	Infinity	$\overline{}$	Indicates that the symbols below it are to be treated as a single number, as $\overline{PQ}^2$. See VINCULUM.
i	Square root of minus one		
a_1, a_2, etc.	Particular values of a (a variable)	$\angle$	Angle
a^n	a multiplied by itself n times	$\parallel$	Parallel to
$\frac{a}{b}$	a divided by b	$\perp$	Perpendicular to; perpendicular
$\sqrt{a}$	Square root of a. See RADICAL SIGN.	$\triangle$	Triangle
$\sqrt[n]{a}$	nth root of a	$\llcorner$	Right angle
		$'$	Minutes of arc; prime
e, ϵ	Base of natural system of logarithms; 2.718...	$''$	Seconds of arc; double prime

mat·ter-of-fact (mat′ər·əv·fakt′) *adj.* Closely adhering to facts; not fanciful; unimaginative; practical.
Mat·thew (math′yōō) One of the twelve apostles and author of the first Gospel: called **Saint Matthew.** — *n.* The first Gospel of the New Testament.
mat·tin (mat′in) See MATIN.
mat·ting[1] (mat′ing) *n.* **1.** A woven fabric of fiber, straw, or other material, used as a floor covering, for packing, etc. **2.** The act of making mats. **3.** Mats collectively.
mat·ting[2] (mat′ing) *n.* **1.** A mat for framing a picture. **2.** A dull, lusterless surface, as on metal or glass.
mat·tock (mat′ək) *n.* Either of two tools resembling a pickax, having a blade on one end and a pick on the other, or a blade on each end. [OE *mattuc*]
mat·tress (mat′rəs) *n.* A large pad made of a strong fabric and filled with a resilient material, as cotton, rubber, hair, feathers, etc., used on or as a bed. [< OF < Ital. < Arabic *matrah* place where something is thrown]

MATTOCK

mat·u·rate (mach′ōō·rāt, mat′yōō-) *v.i.* **·rat·ed, ·rat·ing** **1.** To form pus; suppurate. **2.** To ripen or mature. [< L *maturus* ripe, fully developed] — **mat′u·ra′tion** *n.* — **mat′u·ra′tive** *adj.*
ma·ture (mə·tyŏŏr′, -tōōr′, -chŏŏr′) *adj.* **1.** Completely developed; fully ripe, as plants, fruit, animals, etc. **2.** Highly developed in intellect, outlook, etc.: a *mature* thinker. **3.** Thoroughly developed, perfected, etc.: a *mature* scheme. **4.** Due and payable: a *mature* bond. — *v.* **·tured, ·tur·ing** *v.t.* **1.** To cause to ripen; bring to full development. **2.** To perfect; complete. — *v.i.* **3.** To come to full development. **4.** To become due, as a note. [< L *maturus* ripe, of full age] — **ma·ture′ly** *adv.* — **ma·ture′ness** *n.*
ma·tur·i·ty (mə·tyŏŏr′ə·tē, -tōōr′-, -chŏŏr′-) *n.* **1.** The state of being mature. **2.** Full physical development. **3.** The time at which a note, etc., becomes due.
ma·tu·ti·nal (mə·tōō′tə·nəl, -tyŏŏr′-, mach·ə·tī′nəl) *adj.* Of, pertaining to, or taking place in the morning; early. [< L *matutinus* early in the morning] — **ma·tu′ti·nal·ly** *adv.*
mat·zo (mät′sə) *n.* *pl.* **·zos** or **·zot** (-sōt) or **·zoth** (-sōth, -sōt) A large, flat piece of unleavened bread, traditionally eaten during Passover. Also **mat′za, mat′zah, mat′zoh.** [< Hebrew *matstāh* unleavened bread]
maud·lin (môd′lin) *adj.* **1.** Excessively and tearfully emotional or sentimental. **2.** Overly sentimental or emotional from too much liquor. — **Syn.** See SENTIMENTAL. [< OF *Madeleine* (Mary) Magdalen, often depicted weeping]
maul (môl) *n.* A heavy mallet for driving wedges, piles, etc. — *v.t.* **1.** To beat and bruise. **2.** To handle roughly; manhandle; abuse. Also spelled *mall*. [< OF *mail* < L *malleus* hammer] — **maul′er** *n.*
Mau Mau (mou′ mou′) *pl.* **Mau Mau** or **Mau Maus** A member of a secret society of Kikuyu tribesmen in Kenya organized against European colonists. [< native name]
maun·der (môn′dər) *v.i.* **1.** To talk in a wandering or incoherent manner; drivel. **2.** To move dreamily or idly. [? Freq. of obs. *maund* to beg] — **maun′der·er** *n.*
Maun·dy Thursday (môn′dē) The day before Good Friday, commemorating the Last Supper of Christ. [< OF < L *mandatum* command]
Mau·ser (mou′zər) *n.* A magazine rifle having great range and velocity; also, a type of automatic pistol: a trade name. [after P. S. *Mauser*, 1838–1914, German inventor]
mau·so·le·um (mô′sə·lē′əm) *n.* *pl.* **·le·ums** or **·le·a** (-lē′ə) A large, stately tomb. [< L < Gk. *Mausōleion*, tomb of King Mausolus at Halicarnassus] — **mau′so·le′an** *adj.*
mauve (mōv) *n.* Any of various purplish rose shades. [< F, mallow]
mav·er·ick (mav′ər·ik) *n.* **1.** *U.S.* An unbranded or orphaned animal, as a calf, traditionally belonging to the first person to claim or brand it. **2.** *U.S. Informal* One who is unorthodox in his ideas, attitudes, etc. [after Samuel A. *Maverick*, 1803–70, Texas lawyer who did not brand his cattle]
ma·vour·neen (mə·vŏŏr′nēn, -vôr′-) *n.* My darling. Also **ma·vour′nin.** [< Irish *mo muirnin*]
maw (mô) *n.* **1.** The jaws, mouth, or gullet of a voracious mammal or fish. **2.** The craw of a bird. **3.** The stomach. [OE *maga* stomach]
mawk·ish (mô′kish) *adj.* **1.** Characterized by false or feeble sentimentality. **2.** Sickening or insipid. [< ON *mathkr* maggot] — **mawk′ish·ly** *adv.* — **mawk′ish·ness** *n.*

max·il·la (mak·sil'ə) *n. pl.* **max·il·lae** (mak·sil'ē) **1.** In vertebrates, the upper jaw or jawbone. **2.** *Zool.* In insects, crustaceans, etc., either of two pairs of jawlike appendages behind the mandibles. [< L *mala* jaw]

max·il·lar·y (mak'sə·ler'ē, mak·sil'ər·ē) *adj.* Of, pertaining to, or situated near the upper jaw or a maxilla. — *n. pl.* **·lar·ies** The upper jaw or a maxilla.

max·im (mak'sim) *n.* A brief statement of a general principle, truth, or rule of conduct. [< F < L *maxima* (*sententia, propositio*) greatest (authority, premise)]

max·i·mal (mak'sə·məl) *adj.* Of or being a maximum; greatest or highest possible. — **max'i·mal·ly** *adv.*

max·i·mize (mak'sə·mīz) *v.t.* **·mized, ·miz·ing** To make as great as possible; increase or intensify to the maximum.

max·i·mum (mak'sə·məm) *n. pl.* **·mums** or **·ma** (-mə) **1.** The greatest possible quantity, amount, or degree. **2.** The greatest quantity, degree, etc., reached or recorded. — *adj.* **1.** Consisting of the greatest amount or degree possible, permissible, attainable, etc. **2.** Of or pertaining to a maximum or maximums. [< L *magnus* great]

may¹ (mā) *v.* Present: *sing.* **may, may** (*Archaic* **may·est** or **mayst**), **may,** *pl.* **may**; past: **might** A defective verb now used only in the present and past tenses as an auxiliary followed by the infinitive without *to*, or elliptically with the infinitive understood, to express: **1.** Permission or allowance: *May* I go? **2.** Desire, prayer, or wish: *May* your tribe increase! **3.** Contingency, especially in clauses of result, concession, purpose, etc.: He died that we *might* live. **4.** Possibility: You *may* be right. **5.** *Law* Obligation or duty: the equivalent of *must* or *shall*. [OE *mæg*]

may² (mā) *n. Brit.* A species of hawthorn having white, rose, or crimson flowers. [< MAY, when it blooms]

May (mā) *n.* **1.** The fifth month of the year, containing 31 days. **2.** The prime of life; youth. **3.** May Day festivities. [< OF < L (*mensis*) *Maius* (month of) May]

Ma·ya¹ (mä'yə) *n.* In Hindu philosophy, illusion, often personified as a maiden: also **ma'ya.** [< Skt. *māyā* illusion]

Ma·ya² (mä'yə) *n.* **1.** One of a tribe of Central American Indians, having an early advanced civilization and still living in Yucatán, northern Guatemala, and British Honduras. **2.** The language of the Mayas. — *adj.* Of the Mayas, their culture, or their language. — **Ma'yan** *adj. & n.*

May apple A North American herb whose roots yield a purgative; also, its edible fruit. Also called *mandrake.*

may·be (mā'bē) *adv.* Perhaps; possibly. [< (*it*) *may be*]

May Day The first day of May, traditionally celebrated as a spring festival and, in recent times, celebrated in some countries by demonstrations commemorating labor.

may·est (mā'ist) May: archaic or poetic second person singular, present tense of MAY: used with *thou*. Also **mayst.**

may·flow·er (mā'flou'ər) *n.* Any of various plants that blossom in the spring; esp., in the U.S., the trailing arbutus, and in Great Britain, the hawthorn.

Mayflower The ship on which the Pilgrims came to America in 1620.

May fly Any of a large group of insects, having transparent forewings, a relatively long nymphal life, and a short-lived adult stage: also *dayfly, ephemerid.* Also **may'fly** *n.*

may·hem (mā'hem) *n.* **1.** *Law* The offense of injuring a person's body so as to render him less able to defend himself. **2.** Any situation characterized by violence, confusion, noise, etc. [< OF *mehaing, mahaym*]

may·on·naise (mā'ə·nāz', mā'-) *n.* **1.** A dressing, as for salads, made by beating together raw egg yolk, butter or olive oil, lemon juice or vinegar, and condiments. **2.** A dish, as of meat or fish, mixed with this dressing. [< F]

may·or (mā'ər, mâr) *n.* The chief magistrate of a city, borough, or municipal corporation. [< F < L *major* greater] — **may'or·al** *adj.*

may·or·al·ty (mā'ər·əl·tē, mâr'əl-) *n. pl.* **·ties** The office or term of service of a mayor. [< OF *mairalté*]

May·pole (mā'pōl') *n.* A decorated pole around which dancing takes place on May Day. Also **may'pole'.**

May·time (mā'tīm') *n.* The month of May. Also **May'tide'** (-tīd').

may tree *Brit.* The hawthorn.

maze (māz) *n.* **1.** An intricate network of paths or passages; a labyrinth. **2.** A state of bewilderment, uncertainty, or perplexity. [< AMAZE] — **ma'zy** *adj.* — **maz'i·ly** *adv*

ma·zur·ka (mə·zûr'kə, -zŏŏr'-) *n.* **1.** A lively Polish dance in 3/4 time. **2.** The music for such a dance. Also **ma·zour'ka.** [< Polish, woman from Mazovia, a province]

maz·zard cherry (maz'ərd) The sweet cherry, esp. the fruit of a wild sweet cherry. [Earlier *mazer* maple wood]

Mc— See also MAC—.

Mc·Car·thy·ism (mə·kär'thē·iz'əm) *n.* The practice of making public accusations of disloyalty or corruption, usu. with little evidence, ostensibly to expose pro-Communist activity. [after Joseph *McCarthy*, 1909–57, U.S. Senator]

Mc·Coy (mə·koi'), **the** (**real**) *U.S. Slang* The authentic person or thing.

Mc·In·tosh (mak'ən·tosh) *n. U.S. & Canadian* A red, early autumn, eating apple. Also **McIntosh red.** [after John *McIntosh* of Ontario, who discovered it about 1796]

M-Day (em'dā') *n. Mil.* Mobilization day, the day the Department of Defense orders mobilization for war.

me (mē) *pron.* The objective case of the pronoun *I*. [OE *mē*, dat. sing.]

◆ **It's me,** etc. Anyone who answers the question "Who's there?" by saying "It's me" is using acceptable informal idiom. Here *It is I* would seem stilted, although at the formal level of writing it is expected: They have warned me that *it is I*, and not he, who will have to bear the burden.

mead¹ (mēd) *n.* ʀAn alcoholic beverage of fermented honey and water to which yeast and spices are added. [OE *medu*]

mead² (mēd) *n. Poetic* A meadow. [OE *mǣd*]

mead·ow (med'ō) *n.* **1.** A tract of grassland, usu. used for grazing or for growing hay. **2.** A low or level piece of land, as near a river, used for growing grass or hay. [OE *mǣdwe,* oblique case of *mǣd*] — **mead'ow·y** *adj.*

mead·ow·lark (med'ō·lärk') *n.* Any of various songbirds of North America, marked with black on a yellow breast.

mea·ger (mē'gər) *adj.* **1.** Deficient in quantity or quality; scanty; inadequate. **2.** Lacking in fertility, strength, or richness: *meager* soil. **3.** Thin; emaciated. Also *Brit.* **mea'gre.** [< OF < L *macer* lean] — **mea'ger·ly** *adv.*

meal¹ (mēl) *n.* **1.** The edible seeds of any grain, coarsely ground and unbolted. **2.** Any powdery material. [OE *melu*]

meal² (mēl) *n.* **1.** The food served or eaten regularly at certain times during the day. **2.** The time or occasion of taking such food. [OE *mǣl* measure, time, meal]

meal·ie (mē'lē) *n.* In Africa: **a** An ear of corn (def. 1). **b** *pl.* Corn. [< Afrikaans *milje* < Pg. *milho* millet]

meal ticket **1.** A ticket or card bought for a specified price and redeemable at a restaurant for food. **2.** *U.S. Slang* One who or that which provides a livelihood for another.

meal·time (mēl'tīm') *n.* The habitual time for a meal.

meal·y (mē'lē) *adj.* **meal·i·er, meal·i·est** **1.** Resembling meal; dry; powdery; soft. **2.** Containing meal. **3.** Sprinkled or covered with or as with meal. **4.** Anemic or pale in color, etc. **5.** Mealy-mouthed. — **meal'i·ness** *n.*

meal·y-mouthed (mē'lē-moutht', -mouthd') *adj.* Unwilling to express facts or opinions plainly and frankly.

mean¹ (mēn) *v.* **meant** (ment), **mean·ing** *v.t.* **1.** To have in mind as a purpose or intent. **2.** To intend or design for some purpose, destination, etc.: Was that remark *meant* for me? **3.** To intend to express or convey: That's not what I *meant.* **4.** To have as the particular sense or significance. — *v.i.* **5.** To have disposition or intention: He *means* well. **6.** To be of specified importance or influence: Her work *means* everything to her. [OE *mǣnan* to tell]

mean² (mēn) *adj.* **1.** Poor or inferior in grade or quality. **2.** Having little worth or consequence. **3.** Ignoble in mind or character. **4.** Miserly; stingy. **5.** Poor in appearance; shabby. **6.** Humble in birth, rank, or station. **7.** *Informal* Disagreeable; nasty; vicious. **8.** *Informal* Ashamed; humiliated. **9.** *U.S. Informal* Ill; out of sorts: to feel *mean.* **10.** *U.S. Informal* Difficult; troublesome. **11.** *U.S. Slang* Excellent; expert. [OE (*ge*) *mǣne* ordinary]

mean³ (mēn) *n.* **1.** *pl.* The medium, method, or instrument by which some end is or may be accomplished. **2.** *pl.* Money; wealth. **3.** The middle point or state between two extremes. **4.** Avoidance of excess; moderation. **5.** *Math.* **a** A number or quantity contained within the range of a set of numbers or quantities and representative of each of the set; an average. **b** Arithmetic mean (which see). **c** Geometric mean (which see). **d** The second or third term in a proportion containing four terms. — **by all means** Without hesitation; certainly. — **by any means** In any manner possible; at all; somehow. — **by means of** With the help of; through using. — **by no** (or **no manner of**) **means** Most certainly not; on no account whatever. — *adj.* **1.** Intermediate or average in size, degree, quality, etc.; medium. **2.** Halfway between extremes; average. [< OF < L *medius* middle]

me·an·der (mē·an'dər) *v.i.* **1.** To wind and turn in a course. **2.** To wander aimlessly. — *n.* **1.** *Often pl.* A tortuous or winding course. **2.** Aimless wandering. [< L < Gk. *Maiandros,* the river Meander] — **me·an'der·er** *n.*

mean·ing (mē'ning) *n.* **1.** That which is intended or meant; aim; purpose; end. **2.** That which is signified; sense; import. **3.** Interpretation or significance. — *adj.* **1.** Having purpose or intention: usu. in combination: *well-meaning.* **2.** Significant; expressive. — **mean'ing·ly** *adv.*

mean·ing·ful (mē'ning·fəl) *adj.* Full of meaning. — **mean'ing·ful·ness** *n.* — **mean'ing·ful·ly** *adv.*

mean·ing·less (mē'ning·lis) *adj.* Having no meaning, significance, or importance. — **mean'ing·less·ly** *adv.* — **mean'ing·less·ness** *n.*

mean·ly (mēn'lē) *adv.* In a mean, poor, or ignoble manner.

mean·ness (mēn'nis) *n.* **1.** The state or quality of being mean. **2.** A mean act.

meant (ment) Past tense and past participle of MEAN[1].

mean·time (mēn′tīm′) *n.* Intervening time. —*adv.* **1.** In or during the intervening time. **2.** At the same time.

mean·while (mēn′hwīl′) *n. & adv.* Meantime.

mea·sles (mē′zəlz) *n.pl. (construed as sing. or pl.)* **1.** An acute, highly contagious virus disease affecting children and sometimes adults, characterized by an extensive eruption of small red spots: also called *rubeola.* **2.** Any similar disease, as German measles. [ME *maseles,* pl. of *masel* blister]

mea·sly (mēz′lē) *adj.* **·sli·er, ·sli·est 1.** Affected with measles. **2.** *Slang* Contemptibly stingy, scanty, or petty.

meas·ur·a·ble (mezh′ər·ə·bəl) *adj.* **1.** Capable of being measured or compared. **2.** Notable; significant. —**meas′ur·a·bil′i·ty, meas′ur·a·ble·ness** *n.* —**meas′ur·a·bly** *adv.*

meas·ure (mezh′ər) *n.* **1.** The extent, range, dimensions, capacity, etc., of anything. **2.** A standard or unit of measurement, as a yard. **3.** Any standard of criticism or judgment. **4.** A system of measurements: liquid *measure.* **5.** An instrument for taking measurements. **6.** The act of measuring. **7.** A specific quantity: a full *measure.* **8.** A fixed or suitable limit or bound: talkative beyond all *measure.* **9.** A certain amount, extent, or degree of anything: a *measure* of freedom. **10.** *Often pl.* A specific action, step, or procedure. **11.** A legislative bill. **12.** Rhythmic movement or beat. **13.** *Music* **a** A group of beats marked off by regularly recurring primary accents. **b** The portion of music contained between two bar lines; bar. **14.** In prosody: **a** Meter (def. 1). **b** A metrical foot. —**for good measure** As something additional or extra. —**in a measure** To some degree or extent. —**to take one's measure** To estimate or form an opinion of one's character, skill, etc. —*v.* **·ured, ·ur·ing** *v.t.* **1.** To take or ascertain the dimensions, quantity, capacity, etc., of. **2.** To set apart, mark off, allot, etc., by or as by measuring: often with *off* or *out.* **3.** To estimate; judge; weigh. **4.** To serve as the measure of. **5.** To bring into competition or comparison. **6.** To travel over. **7.** To adjust; regulate: *Measure* your actions to your aspirations. —*v.i.* **8.** To make or take measurements. **9.** To yield a specified measurement. **10.** To admit measurement. —**to measure one's length** To fall or lie prostrate at full length. —**to measure up to** To fulfill, or meet, as expectations. [< F < L *mensura* < *metiri* to measure] —**meas′ur·er** *n.*

meas·ured (mezh′ərd) *adj.* **1.** Determined by some standard. **2.** Slow and stately; rhythmical. **3.** Carefully considered or weighed; deliberate. **4.** Moderate. **5.** Metrical. —**meas′ured·ly** *adv.* —**meas′ured·ness** *n.*

meas·ure·less (mezh′ər·lis) *adj.* Incapable of being measured; very great; immense. —**Syn.** See INFINITE.

meas·ure·ment (mezh′ər·mənt) *n.* **1.** The act or process of measuring anything. **2.** The amount, capacity, or extent determined by measuring. **3.** A system of measures.

measuring worm The larva of a geometrid moth, that advances its body by a succession of loops: also *inchworm.*

meat (mēt) *n.* **1.** The flesh of animals used as food, esp. the flesh of mammals as opposed to fish or fowl. **2.** The edible part of anything. **3.** Anything eaten for nourishment, as in **meat and drink. 4.** The essence, gist, or main idea of something. **5.** *Informal* Anything one particularly enjoys or does with ease. [OE *mete*] —**meat′less** *adj.*

meat packing *U.S.* The commercial slaughtering of meat-producing animals and the processing, packaging, and distribution of meat and meat products. —**meat packer**

me·a·tus (mē·ā′təs) *n. pl.* **·tus** or **·tus·es** *Anat.* A passage, duct, or canal: the auditory *meatus.* [< L, passage]

meat·y (mē′tē) *adj.* **meat·i·er, meat·i·est 1.** Of, pertaining to, or like meat. **2.** Full of meat. **3.** Full of substance; significant. —**meat′i·ness** *n.*

mec·ca (mek′ə) *n.* **1.** A place or attraction visited by many people. **2.** The goal of one's aspirations. [after *Mecca*]

me·chan·ic (mə·kan′ik) *n.* One skilled in the making, operation, or repair of tools or machinery. —*adj.* **1.** Involving or pertaining to manual labor or skill. **2.** Mechanical. [< L < Gk. *mēchanē* machine]

me·chan·i·cal (mə·kan′i·kəl) *adj.* **1.** Of, involving, or having to do with the construction, operation, design, etc., of machinery or tools. **2.** Operated or produced by a machine. **3.** Of, pertaining to, or in accordance with the science of mechanics. **4.** Made or performed without spontaneity or by force of habit; automatic; lifeless. —**me·chan′i·cal·ly** *adv.* —**me·chan′i·cal·ness** *n.*

mechanical drawing A drawing done with the aid of compasses, squares, etc.

me·chan·ics (mə·kan′iks) *n.pl. (construed as sing. in defs. 1 and 2)* **1.** The branch of physics that treats of motion and of the action of forces on material bodies. **2.** The body of knowledge dealing with the design, operation, and maintenance of machinery. **3.** The technical aspects of anything.

mech·a·nism (mek′ə·niz′əm) *n.* **1.** The parts or arrange-

ment of parts of a machine. **2.** Something similar to a machine. **3.** The process or technique by which something works. **4.** A theory that all natural phenomena can be explained by the laws of chemistry and physics.

mech·a·nist (mek′ə·nist) *n.* **1.** A mechanic. **2.** A believer in mechanism (def. 4). —*adj.* Mechanistic.

mech·a·nis·tic (mek′ə·nis′tik) *adj.* **1.** Of, pertaining to, or of the nature of mechanics. **2.** Pertaining to or based on mechanism (def. 4). —**mech′a·nis′ti·cal·ly** *adv.*

mech·a·nize (mek′ə·nīz) *v.t.* **·nized, ·niz·ing 1.** To make mechanical. **2.** To convert (an industry, etc.) to machine production. **3.** *Mil.* To equip with tanks, trucks, etc. —**mech′a·ni·za′tion** *n.*

med·al (med′l) *n.* A small piece of metal, bearing an image, inscription, etc., and often given as an award for some outstanding act or service. —*v.t.* **med·aled** or **med·al·ing** or **·al·ling** To confer a medal upon. [< F < Ital. < L *metallum* mine]

med·al·ist (med′l·ist) *n.* **1.** A collector or maker of medals. **2.** The recipient of a medal awarded for services or merit. **3.** In golf, the winner at medal play.

me·dal·lion (mə·dal′yən) *n.* **1.** A large medal. **2.** An ornamental subject usu. set in a circular or oval frame, and used as a decorative element. [< F *médaillon*]

Medal of Honor The highest U.S. military decoration, awarded to one who risked his life beyond the call of duty. Also called *Congressional Medal of Honor.* See DECORATION.

medal play In golf, a form of competitive play in which the score is computed by counting the strokes of each competitor in a round of play. Compare MATCH PLAY.

med·dle (med′l) *v.i.* **·dled, ·dling 1.** To participate or interfere officiously: often with *in* or *with.* **2.** To tamper. [< OF *medler* < L *miscere* to mix] —**med′dler** *n.*

med·dle·some (med′l·səm) *adj.* Inclined to meddle. —**med′dle·some·ly** *adv.* —**med′dle·some·ness** *n.*

Me·de·a (mə·dē′ə) In Greek legend, a sorceress of Colchis who helped Jason obtain the Golden Fleece.

me·di·a (mē′dē·ə) Alternative plural of MEDIUM.

me·di·ae·val (mē′dē·ē′vəl, med′ē-), **me·di·ae·val·ism,** etc. See MEDIEVAL, etc.

me·di·al (mē′dē·əl) *adj.* **1.** Of, pertaining to, or situated in the middle. **2.** Of or pertaining to a mathematical average; mean. [< LL < L *medius* middle] —**me′di·al·ly** *adv.*

me·di·an (mē′dē·ən) *adj.* **1.** Pertaining to or situated in the middle; medial. **2.** *Stat.* Designating the middle point in a series of values: 8 is the *median* of 2, 5, 8, 10, 13. —*n.* A median point, line, or number. [< L < *medius* middle] —**me′di·an·ly** *adv.*

me·di·ate (*v.* mē′dē·āt; *adj.* -it) *v.* **·at·ed, ·at·ing** *v.t.* **1.** To settle or reconcile (differences) by intervening as a peacemaker. **2.** To serve as the medium for effecting (a result) or conveying (an object, etc.). —*v.i.* **3.** To act between disputing parties to bring about a settlement, etc. **4.** To be in an intermediate position. —*adj.* **1.** Acting as an intervening agency. **2.** Occurring or effected as a result of indirect or median agency. [< LL < *mediare* to stand between] —**me′di·ate·ly** *adv.* —**me′di·a·tive** *adj.*

me·di·a·tion (mē′dē·ā′shən) *n.* The act of mediating; intercession; interposition. —**me′di·a·tor** *n.*

me·di·a·to·ry (mē′dē·ə·tôr′ē, -tō′rē) *adj.* **1.** Of or pertaining to mediation. **2.** Serving to mediate. Also **me′di·a·to′ri·al** (-tôr′ē·əl, -tō′rē·əl). —**me′di·a·to′ri·al·ly** *adv.*

med·ic[1] (med′ik) *n.* Any of several cloverlike plants, esp. alfalfa. [< L < Gk. *Mēdikē* (*poa*) Median (grass)]

med·ic[2] (med′ik) *n. Informal* **1.** A physician or intern. **2.** A medical student. **3.** A corpsman.

med·i·ca·ble (med′ə·kə·bəl) *adj.* Capable of being relieved by medical treatment; curable.

Medicaid (med′i·kād) *n.* A governmental health insurance program for people with low incomes.

med·i·cal (med′i·kəl) *adj.* **1.** Of or pertaining to medicine. **2.** Having curative properties.

medical jurisprudence The application of medical principles in law: also called *forensic medicine, legal medicine.*

med·i·ca·ment (med′ə·kə·mənt, mə·dik′ə-) *n.* Any substance for the cure of disease or the alleviation of pain.

Medicare (med′i·kâr) *n.* A governmental health insurance program, esp. for the aged.

med·i·cate (med′ə·kāt) *v.t.* **·cat·ed, ·cat·ing 1.** To treat medicinally. **2.** To tincture or impregnate with medicine. [< L < *medicare* to heal] —**med′i·ca′tion** *n.* —**med′i·ca′tive** *adj.*

me·dic·i·nal (mə·dis′ə·nəl) *adj.* Pertaining to or having the properties of medicine; healing, curative, or alleviating.

med·i·cine (med′ə·sən, *Brit.* med′sən) *n.* **1.** Any substance used in the treatment of disease or in the relief of pain. **2.** The science of the preservation and restoration of health and of treating disease, esp., as distinguished from surgery. **3.**

The profession of medicine. **4.** Among American Indians, any magic spell or power. **— to take one's medicine** To endure punishment, etc. [< OF < L *medicus* physician]

medicine ball A large, heavy, leather-covered ball, thrown and caught for physical exercise.

medicine man Among North American Indians, one professing supernatural powers of healing, etc.; magician.

med·i·co (med′ə-kō) *n. pl.* **·cos** *Informal* A physician or a medical student. [< Ital. or Sp., physician]

medico- *combining form* Pertaining to medical science and: *medico-legal.* Also, before vowels, **medic-.** [< L *medicus* physician]

me·di·e·val (mē′dē-ē′vəl, med′ē-) *adj.* Of, like, or characteristic of the Middle Ages: also spelled *mediaeval.* [< L *medius* middle + *aevum* age] **— me′di·e′val·ly** *adv.*

me·di·e·val·ism (mē′dē-ē′vəl-iz′əm, med′ē-) *n.* **1.** The spirit, beliefs, customs, and practices of the Middle Ages. **2.** Devotion to the Middle Ages. **3.** Any custom, idea, etc., surviving from the Middle Ages. Also spelled *mediaevalism.*

me·di·e·val·ist (mē′dē-ē′vəl·ist, med′ē-) *n.* **1.** A scholar or specialist in medieval history, literature, or art. **2.** One devoted to the Middle Ages. Also spelled *mediaevalist.*

medio- *combining form* Middle. Also, before vowels, **medi-.** [< L *medius* middle]

me·di·o·cre (mē′dē·ō′kər, mē′dē·ō′kər) *adj.* Of only average quality; ordinary. [< F < L < *medius* middle]

me·di·oc·ri·ty (mē′dē-ok′rə-tē) *n. pl.* **·ties 1.** The condition or quality of being mediocre. **2.** Mediocre ability or performance. **3.** A mediocre person.

med·i·tate (med′ə-tāt) *v.* **·tat·ed, ·tat·ing** *v.i.* **1.** To engage in continuous and contemplative thought; muse; cogitate. **— *v.t.* 2.** To think about doing; plan. [< L < *meditari* to muse, ponder] **— med′i·tat′er, med′i·ta′tor** *n.* **— med′i·ta′tive** *adj.* **— med′i·ta′tive·ly** *adv.*

med·i·ta·tion (med′ə·tā′shən) *n.* The act of meditating; reflection upon a subject; contemplation.

med·i·ter·ra·ne·an (med′ə·tə·rā′nē·ən) *adj.* Enclosed nearly or wholly by land. [< L *medius* middle + *terra* earth]

Med·i·ter·ra·ne·an (med′ə·tə·rā′nē·ən) *adj.* Of or pertaining to the Mediterranean Sea or its shores. **— *n.* 1.** The Mediterranean Sea. **2.** One who lives in a Mediterranean country, or belongs to the Mediterranean race.

Mediterranean fever Undulant fever.

me·di·um (mē′dē-əm) *n. pl.* **·di·ums** (always for def. 5) or **·di·a** (-dē·ə) **1.** An intermediate degree or condition; mean. **2.** The surrounding or enveloping element; environment. **3.** An intervening substance in which something may act or an effect be produced. **4.** A means or agency; instrument: an advertising *medium.* **5.** One through whom the spirits of the dead are believed to communicate with the material world. **6.** An area or form of artistic expression, or the materials used. **7.** In painting, a liquid with which pigments are mixed to make them fluid enough to be applied. **8.** *Biol.* A culture medium. **— *adj.* Intermediate in quantity, quality, size, etc. [< L, orig. neut. sing. of *medius* middle]

medium frequency *Telecom.* Radio waves ranging in frequency from 300 to 3000 kilocycles.

med·lar (med′lər) *n.* **1.** A small, European tree of the rose family. **2.** The fruit of this tree, eaten when it begins to decay. [< OF *mesle* fruit of the medlar]

med·ley (med′lē) *n.* **1.** A mingled and confused mass of elements; jumble. **2.** A musical composition made up of different airs or parts of songs. **— *adj.* Made up of heterogeneous parts; jumbled; mixed. [< OF *medlee,* orig. fem. pp. of *medler* to meddle]

Mé·doc (mā-dôk′) *n.* A red wine made in Médoc, France.

me·dul·la (mə-dul′ə) *n. pl.* **·lae** (-lē) **1.** *Anat.* The soft inner portion of an organ or part, such as the kidney. **b** The marrow of bones. **c** The medulla oblongata. **2.** *Bot.* Pith (def. 1). [< L, marrow, pith] **— med·ul·lar·y** (med′ə-ler·ē, mi-dul′ər·ē), **me·dul′lar** *adj.*

medulla ob·lon·ga·ta (ob′lông-gä′tə) *Anat.* The hindmost and lowest part of the brain, narrowing down into the spinal cord, and controlling breathing, circulation, etc.

me·du·sa (mə-doō′sə, -zə, -dyoō′-) *n. pl.* **·sas** or **·sae** (-sē, -zē) A jellyfish. [< L] **— me·du′san, me·du′soid** *adj. & n.*

Me·du·sa (mə-doō′sə, -zə, -dyoō′-) In Greek mythology, one of the Gorgons, killed by Perseus.

meek (mēk) *adj.* **1.** Having a patient, gentle disposition. **2.** Lacking spirit or backbone; submissive. [ME < ON *miukr* gentle, soft] **— meek′ly** *adv.* **— meek·ness** *n.*

meer·schaum (mir′shəm, -shôm, -shoum) *n.* **1.** A light, heat-resisting magnesium silicate, used for tobacco pipes, etc. **2.** A tobacco pipe made from this. [< G < *meer* sea + *schaum* foam]

meet¹ (mēt) *v.* **met, meet·ing** *v.t.* **1.** To come upon; encounter. **2.** To be at, or go to the place of arrival of: to *meet* him at the station. **3.** To make the acquaintance of. **4.** To come into the company of or in association with, as for a conference. **5.** To come into contact or conjunction with. **6.** To keep an appointment with. **7.** To come into the ob-

servation, perception, or recognition of (the eye, ear, etc.). **8.** To experience; undergo: to *meet* adversity. **9.** To oppose in battle. **10.** To answer (a blow, move, etc.) by another in return. **11.** To deal or cope with; handle. **12.** To comply or act in accordance with: to *meet* the requirements for a diploma. **13.** To pay (a bill, debt, etc.). **14.** To fulfill (an obligation, need, etc.). **— *v.i.* 15.** To come together; come face to face. **16.** To come together in conjunction, or union. **17.** To assemble. **18.** To make acquaintance or be introduced. **19.** To come together in conflict or opposition; contend. **— to meet with 1.** To come upon; encounter. **2.** To deal or confer with. **3.** To experience. **— *n.* An** assembling for a sport or an athletic contest; also, the persons so assembled, or the place of assembly. [OE *mētan*]

meet² (mēt) *adj.* Suitable; proper. [OE *gemǣte*] **— meet′ly** *adv.*

meet·ing (mē′ting) *n.* **1.** A coming together. **2.** An assembly or gathering of persons; also, the persons present. **3.** A joining or conjunction of things. **4.** An assembly of Quakers for religious services; also, their meeting house.

meeting house 1. A house used for public meetings. **2.** A place of worship used by the Quakers.

mega- *combining form* **1.** Great; large: *megaphone.* **2.** In the metric system, a million times (a specified unit): *megacycle.* Also, before vowels, **meg-.** [< Gk. *megas* large]

meg·a·cy·cle (meg′ə-sī′kəl) *n.* **1.** *Telecom.* A unit of electromagnetic wave frequency of 1,000,000 cycles per second. **2.** One million cycles.

megalo- *combining form* Big; indicating excessive or abnormal size. Also, before vowels, **megal-.** [< Gk. *megas, megalou* big]

meg·a·lo·ceph·a·ly (meg′ə-lō-sef′ə-lē) *n.* Unusual largeness of the head. Also **meg′a·lo·ce·pha′li·a** (-sə-fā′lē·ə). [< MEGALO- + Gk. *kephalē* head] **— meg′a·lo·ce·phal′ic** (-sə-fal′ik), **meg′a·lo·ceph′a·lous** *adj.*

meg·a·lo·ma·ni·a (meg′ə-lō-mā′nē·ə, -mān′yə) *n.* **1.** *Psychiatry* A mental disorder in which the subject thinks himself great or exalted. **2.** A tendency to magnify and exaggerate. **— meg′a·lo·ma′ni·ac** *adj. & n.*

meg·a·phone (meg′ə-fōn) *n.* A funnel-shaped device for amplifying or directing sound. **— *v.t. & v.i.* ·phoned, ·phon·ing** To speak through or as through a megaphone.

meg·a·ton (meg′ə-tun′) *n.* **1.** One million tons. **2.** A unit equal to the explosive power of one million tons of TNT.

me·grim (mē′grim) *n.* **1.** *pl.* Depression of spirits; dullness. **2.** Migraine. [< F < L < Gk. *hēmi* half + *krania* skull]

mei·o·sis (mī-ō′sis) *n. Biol.* The cell divisions leading to the formation of gametes in which the number of chromosomes is reduced by half. [< Gk. *meiōn* less] **— mei·ot′ic** (-ot′ik) *adj.*

Meis·ter·sing·er (mīs′tər-sing′ər, *Ger.* mīs′tər-zing′ər) *n. pl.* **·sing·er** *German* Any of the poets and musicians, mainly artisans and tradesmen, active in the principal cities of Germany between the 14th and 16th centuries.

mel·a·mine (mel′ə-mēn, -min) *n. Chem.* A crystalline nitrogen compound, $C_3N_2(NH_2)_3$, that reacts with formaldehyde to produce a high-grade thermosetting resin. [< *melam)*, a chemical compound + AMINE]

melan- Var. of MELANO-.

mel·an·cho·li·a (mel′ən-kō′lē·ə) *n. Psychiatry* Great depression of spirits and excessive brooding without apparent or sufficient cause. [< L] **— mel′an·cho′li·ac** *adj. & n.*

mel·an·chol·y (mel′ən-kol′ē) *adj.* **1.** Excessively gloomy; sad. **2.** Suggesting or promoting sadness: a *melancholy* day. **3.** Somberly thoughtful; pensive. **— *n. pl.* ·chol·ies 1.** Low spirits; depression. **2.** Pensive or sober reflection. [< F < L < Gk. < *melas, -anos* black + *cholē* bile] **— mel′an·chol′ic** *adj.* **— mel′an·chol′i·cal·ly** *adv.*

Mel·a·ne·sian (mel′ə-nē′zhən, -shən) *adj.* Of or pertaining to Melanesia, its native inhabitants, or their languages. **— *n.* 1.** A member of any of the dark-skinned, kinky-haired peoples of Melanesia. **2.** Any of the languages of the Austronesian group spoken in Melanesia.

me·lange (mā-länzh′) *n. French* A mixture or medley.

mel·a·nin (mel′ə-nin) *n. Biochem.* A brownish black pigment contained in animal tissues, as the skin and hair.

melano- *combining form* Black; dark-colored. Also, before vowels, **melan-.** [< Gk. *melas, melanos* black]

Mel·ba toast (mel′bə) Thinly sliced bread toasted until brown and crisp.

meld (meld) *v.t. & v.i.* In pinochle and other card games, to announce or declare (a combination of cards) for inclusion in one's total score. **— *n.* A group of cards to be declared, or the act of declaring them. [< G *melden* to announce]

me·lee (mā′lā, mā·lā′) *n.* A confused, general hand-to-hand fight; affray. Also *Fr.* **me·lée** (me·lā′). [< F < OF *meslee,* var. of *medlee* medley]

mel·io·rate (mēl′yə·rāt) *v.t. & v.i.* **·rat·ed, ·rat·ing** To improve, as in quality or condition; ameliorate. [< LL < *melior* better] **— mel′io·ra·ble** *adj.* **— mel′io·ra′tion** *n.* **— mel′io·ra′tive** *adj.* **— mel′io·ra′tor** *n.*

mel·lif·er·ous (mə·lif′ər·əs) *adj.* Producing or bearing honey. Also **mel·lif′ic**. [< L < *mel* honey + *ferre* to bear]

mel·lif·lu·ent (mə·lif′lōō·ənt) *adj.* Mellifluous. **— mel·lif′lu·ence** *n.* **— mel·lif′lu·ent·ly** *adv.*

mel·lif·lu·ous (mə·lif′lōō·əs) *adj.* Sweetly or smoothly flowing: *mellifluous* speech. [< L < *mel* honey + *fluere* to flow] **— mel·lif′lu·ous·ly** *adv.* **— mel·lif′lu·ous·ness** *n.*

mel·low (mel′ō) *adj.* 1. Soft, sweet, and full-flavored by reason of ripeness, as fruit. 2. Well-matured, as wines. 3. Rich and soft in quality, as colors or sounds. 4. Made gentle and sympathetic by maturity or experience. 5. Made jovial or genial by liquor. 6. Soft and friable, as soil. **—** *v.t. & v.i.* To make or become mellow; soften. [ME, ? < OE *melu* meal] **— mel′low·ly** *adv.* **— mel′low·ness** *n.*

me·lo·de·on (mə·lō′dē·ən) *n.* A small reed organ or harmonium. [A pseudo-Greek formation < MELODY]

me·lod·ic (mə·lod′ik) *adj.* 1. Pertaining to or containing melody. 2. Melodious. **— me·lod′i·cal·ly** *adv.*

me·lo·di·ous (mə·lō′dē·əs) *adj.* 1. Producing or characterized by melody; tuneful. 2. Pleasant to hear. **— me·lo′di·ous·ly** *adv.* **— me·lo′di·ous·ness** *n.*

mel·o·dra·ma (mel′ə·drä′mə, -dram′ə) *n.* 1. A play or drama in which the emotions displayed are violent or extravagantly sentimental, and the plot is made up of sensational incidents. 2. Formerly, a romantic drama with sensational incidents, usu. including music and songs. 3. Sensational and highly emotional behavior or language. [< F < Gk. *melos* song + *drama* drama] **— mel′o·dram′a·tist** *n.*

mel·o·dra·mat·ic (mel′ə·drə·mat′ik) *adj.* Of, pertaining to, or like melodrama; sensational; exaggerated. **— mel′o·dra·mat′i·cal·ly** *adv.*

mel·o·dra·mat·ics (mel′ə·drə·mat′iks) *n.pl.* Melodramatic behavior.

mel·o·dy (mel′ə·dē) *n.* *pl.* **·dies** 1. Pleasing sounds, or an agreeable succession of such sounds. 2. *Music* **a** An organized succession of tones, usu. in the same voice or instrument. **b** The leading part in a homophonic composition; the air. [< OF < LL < Gk. < *melos* song + *aoidos* singer]

mel·on (mel′ən) *n.* 1. The large fruit of any of various plants of the gourd family, as the muskmelon and the watermelon. 2. Any of these plants. [< F < LL *melo, melonis*]

Mel·pom·e·ne (mel·pom′ə·nē) In Greek mythology, the Muse of tragedy.

melt (melt) *v.t. & v.i.* **melt·ed, melt·ed** (*Archaic* **mol·ten** (mōl′tən), **melt·ing** 1. To reduce or change from a solid to a liquid state by heat. 2. To dissolve, as in water. 3. To disappear or cause to disappear; dissipate: often with *away*. 4. To blend by imperceptible degrees: often with *into*. 5. To make or become softened in feeling or attitude. **—** *n.* 1. Something melted. 2. A single operation of fusing. 3. The amount of a single fusing. [OE *meltan, mieltan*] **— melt′a·ble** *adj.* **— melt′a·bil′i·ty** *n.* **— melt′er** *n.*

melt·down (melt′doun) *n.* The melting of the rods containing uranium fuel in the core of a nuclear reactor, or the melting of the fuel itself, resulting in a massive release of radiation.

melting point The temperature at which a specified solid substance melts or fuses.

melting pot 1. A vessel in which a substance is melted. 2. A country, city, or region in which immigrants of various racial and cultural backgrounds are assimilated.

mel·ton (mel′tən) *n.* A heavy woolen cloth with a short nap, used for overcoats. [after *Melton* Mowbray, England]

mem·ber (mem′bər) *n.* 1. One who belongs to a society, club, party, etc. 2. *Usu. cap.* One who belongs to a legislative body. 3. A part of a whole, as: **a** *Biol.* A part or organ of an animal body, esp. a limb. **b** *Math.* Either side of an algebraic equation. [< OF < L *membrum* limb]

mem·ber·ship (mem′bər·ship) *n.* 1. The state or fact of being a member. 2. The members of an organization, etc., collectively; also, the total number of members.

mem·brane (mem′brān) *n.* A thin, pliable, sheetlike layer of animal or vegetable tissue serving to cover or line an organ or part, separate adjoining cavities, or connect adjoining structures. [< L *membrana*, lit., limb coating]

mem·bra·nous (mem′brə·nəs) *adj.* 1. Of, pertaining to, or like a membrane. 2. Marked by the formation of a membrane. Also **mem·bra·na·ceous** (mem′brə·nā′shəs).

me·men·to (mə·men′tō) *n.* *pl.* **·tos** or **·toes** Anything that serves as a hint or reminder of the past; souvenir. [< L, remember, imperative of *meminisse* to remember]

memento mo·ri (mōr′ī) *Latin* An emblem or reminder of death, as a skull, etc.: literally, remember that you must die.

mem·o (mem′ō) *n.* *pl.* **mem·os** *Informal* A memorandum.

mem·oir (mem′wär) *n.* 1. *pl.* Personal reminiscences or records; esp., a narrative of events based on the writer's personal observations and experiences. 2. A biography. 3. *pl.* An account of the proceedings of a learned society. 4. A

monograph. [< F < L *memoria* memory]

mem·o·ra·bil·i·a (mem′ə·rə·bil′ē·ə) *n.pl.* Things or events worthy of remembrance and record. [< L]

mem·o·ra·ble (mem′ər·ə·bəl) *adj.* Worthy to be remembered; noteworthy. **— mem′o·ra·bil′i·ty, mem′o·ra·ble·ness** *n.* **— mem′o·ra·bly** *adv.*

mem·o·ran·dum (mem′ə·ran′dəm) *n.* pl. **·dums** or **·da** (-də) 1. A brief note of a thing or things to be remembered. 2. A record of transactions, etc., esp. for future use. 3. An informal letter, usu. sent between departments in an office. 4. *Law* A brief written outline of the terms of a transaction or contract. 5. In business, a statement of goods sent from a consignor to a consignee. [< L, a thing to be remembered]

me·mo·ri·al (mə·môr′ē·əl, -mō′rē-) *adj.* 1. Serving to keep in memory a deceased person or an event; commemorative. 2. Of or pertaining to memory. **—** *n.* 1. Something serving to keep in remembrance a person, event, etc. 2. A written summary or presentation of facts addressed to a legislative body, official, etc., as the grounds for or in the form of a petition. [< OF < L *memoria*]

Memorial Day *U.S.* A day set apart to honor the dead of any American war. Also called *Decoration Day.*

me·mo·ri·al·ize (mə·môr′ē·əl·īz′, -mō′rē-) *v.t.* **·ized, ·iz·ing** 1. To commemorate. 2. To present a memorial to; petition. Also *Brit.* **me·mo′ri·al·ise′**. **— me·mo′ri·al·i·za′tion** *n.*

mem·o·rize (mem′ə·rīz) *v.t.* **·rized, ·riz·ing** To commit to memory. **— mem′o·ri·za′tion** *n.* **— mem′o·riz′er** *n.*

mem·o·ry (mem′ər·ē) *n.* *pl.* **·ries** 1. The mental function or capacity of recalling or recognizing previously learned behavior or past experience. 2. The total of what is remembered. 3. One who or that which is remembered. 4. The period of time covered by the faculty of remembrance. 5. The state of being remembered. 6. Remembrance or commemoration. [< OF < L *memor* mindful]

mem·sah·ib (mem′sä·ib) *n.* *Anglo-Indian* A European lady: a name given by native servants. [< MA'AM + Hind. *sāhib* master < Arabic]

men (men) Plural of MAN.

men·ace (men′is) *v.* **·aced, ·ac·ing** *v.t.* 1. To threaten with evil or harm. **—** *v.i.* 2. To make threats; appear threatening. **—** *n.* 1. A threat. 2. *Informal* A troublesome person; pest. [< OF < L < *minax, -acis* threatening] **— men′ac·er** *n.* **— men′ac·ing·ly** *adv.*

mé·nage (mā·näzh′, *Fr.* mā·nazh′) *n.* A household. Also **me·nage′**. [< L *mansio, -onis* house]

me·nag·er·ie (mə·naj′ər·ē) *n.* A collection of wild animals kept for exhibition. [< F]

mend (mend) *v.t.* 1. To make sound or serviceable again by repairing. 2. To correct errors or faults in; improve. *Mend* your ways. 3. To correct (some defect). **—** *v.i.* 4. To become better, as in health. 5. To improve: said of conditions. **—** *n.* 1. A repairing. 2. A mended place, as on a garment. **— on the mend** Recovering health. [Var. of AMEND] **— mend′a·ble** *adj.* **— mend′er** *n.*

men·da·cious (men·dā′shəs) *adj.* 1. Lying; deceitful. 2. Untrue; false. [< L *mendax, -acis* lying] **— men·da′cious·ly** *adv.* **— men·da′cious·ness** *n.*

men·dac·i·ty (men·das′ə·tē) *n.* *pl.* **·ties** 1. The quality of being mendacious. 2. A lie; untruth.

men·de·le·vi·um (men′də·lē′vē·əm) *n.* A short-lived radioactive element (symbol Md). See ELEMENT. [after Dmitri Ivanovich *Mendeleyev*]

Mendel's laws *Genetics* Principles formulated by Gregor Mendel, stating that alternative unit characters of hybrids segregate from one another in transmission to offspring and that different pairs of such characters segregate independently of each other. **— Men·de·li·an** (men·dē′lē·ən) *adj.*

men·di·cant (men′də·kənt) *adj.* 1. Begging; depending on alms for a living. 2. Pertaining to or like a beggar. **—** *n.* 1. A beggar. 2. A begging friar. [< L < *mendicus* needy] **— men′di·can·cy, men·dic′i·ty** (men·dis′ə·tē) *n.*

Men·e·la·us (men′ə·lā′əs) In Greek legend, a king of Sparta and the husband of Helen of Troy.

men·ha·den (men·hād′n) *n.* A fish of North Atlantic and West Indian waters, used as a source of oil, as fertilizer, and as bait. [Alter. of Algonquian *munnawhat* fertilizer]

me·ni·al (mē′nē·əl, mēn′yəl) *adj.* 1. Pertaining to or appropriate to servants. 2. Servile; abject. **—** *n.* 1. A domestic servant. 2. One who has a servile nature. [< AF < OF < LL *mansio* house] **— me′ni·al·ly** *adv.*

me·nin·ges (mə·nin′jēz) *n.* *pl.* of **me·ninx** (mē′ningks) *Anat.* The three membranes enveloping the brain and spinal cord. [< NL < Gk. *mēninx, mēningos* membrane] **— me·nin′ge·al** *adj.*

men·in·gi·tis (men′ən·jī′tis) *n.* *Pathol.* Inflammation of the meninges, esp. through infection. **— men′in·git′ic** (-jit′ik) *adj.*

me·nis·cus (mə·nis'kəs) *n. pl.* **·nis·cus·es** or **·nis·ci** (-nis'ī) **1.** A crescent or crescent-shaped body. **2.** *Optics* A lens concave on one side and convex on the other. **3.** *Physics* The curved upper surface of a liquid column. [< L < Gk. *mēniskos* crescent, dim. of *mēnē* moon]

Men·non·ite (men'ən·īt) *n.* A member of a Protestant Christian sect founded in the 16th century, opposing the taking of oaths, the holding of public office, and military service. [after *Menno* Simons, 1492–1559, a leader of the sect]

Me·nom·i·nee (mə·nom'ə·nē) *n. pl.* **·nee 1.** One of an Algonquian tribe of North American Indians, inhabiting central Wisconsin. **2.** The Algonquian language of this tribe. Also **Me·nom·i·ni** (-nē).

men·o·pause (men'ə·pôz) *n. Physiol.* The final cessation of menstruation, occurring normally between the ages of 45 and 50. [< Gk. *mēn* month + *pauein* to cause to cease]

Me·no·rah (mə·nôr'ə, -nō'rə) *n.* In the Jewish religion, a candelabrum having nine candles lighted in increasing numbers during Hannukah. [< Hebrew, candlestick]

men·ses (men'sēz) *n.pl. Physiol.* Menstruation. [< L, pl. of *mensis* month]

Men·she·vik (men'shə·vik) *n. pl.* **·vi·ki** (-vē'kē) or **·viks** A member of the conservative element in the Russian Social Democratic Party. Compare BOLSHEVIK. Also **Men'she·vist.** [< Russian *menshe* minority] — **Men'she·vism** *n.*

men·stru·al (men'strōō·əl) *adj.* **1.** *Physiol.* Of or pertaining to menstruation. Also **men'stru·ous. 2.** Monthly. [< L < *menstruus* monthly]

men·stru·ate (men'strōō·āt) *v.i.* **·at·ed, ·at·ing** To undergo menstruation.

men·stru·a·tion (men'strōō·ā'shən) *n. Physiol.* **1.** The periodical flow of bloody fluid from the uterus, occurring normally about every 28 days: also called *menses.* **2.** An occurrence of this flow: also called *period.*

men·stru·um (men'strōō·əm) *n. pl.* **·stru·ums** or **·stru·a** (-strōō·ə) The medium in which a substance is dissolved.

men·su·ra·ble (men'shər·ə·bəl) *adj.* That can be measured. [< LL < *mensurare* to measure] — **men'su·ra·bil'i·ty** *n.*

men·su·ral (men'shər·əl) *adj.* Pertaining to measure.

men·su·ra·tion (men'shə·rā'shən) *n.* **1.** The art, act, or process of measuring. **2.** The branch of mathematics having to do with determining length, area, and volume.

-ment *suffix of nouns* **1.** The product or result of: *achievement.* **2.** The instrument or means of: *atonement.* **3.** The process or action of: *government.* **4.** The quality, condition, or state of being: *astonishment.* [< F < L *-mentum*]

men·tal (men'təl) *adj.* **1.** Of or pertaining to the mind or intellect. **2.** Effected by or taking place in the mind, esp. without the aid of written symbols: *mental calculations.* **3.** Affected by mental illness: a *mental* patient. **4.** For the care of the mentally ill: *mental* hospital. [< F < LL < L *mens, mentis* mind] — **men'tal·ly** *adv.*

mental age See under AGE.

mental deficiency *Psychol.* A condition characterized by subnormal intelligence to the extent that the individual is handicapped from participating fully in ordinary life.

mental healing The alleged curing of any disorder, ailment, or disease by mental concentration and suggestion.

mental hygiene The scientific study and application of methods to preserve and promote mental health.

men·tal·i·ty (men·tal'ə·tē) *n. pl.* **·ties 1.** The mental faculties or powers; mental activity. **2.** Intellectual capacity or power: an average *mentality.* **3.** Cast or habit of mind.

men·thol (men'thôl, -thol, -thol) *n. Chem.* A white, waxy, crystalline alcohol, $C_{10}H_{19}OH$, obtained from and having the odor of oil of peppermint, used as a flavoring agent, in perfumery, and in medicine. [< G < L *mentha* mint + -OL]

men·tho·lat·ed (men'thə·lā'tid) *adj.* Treated with, containing, or impregnated with menthol.

men·tion (men'shən) *v.t.* To refer to incidentally, briefly, or in passing. — *n.* **1.** The act of one who mentions. **2.** Slight reference; casual allusion. [< OF < L *mens, mentis* mind] — **men'tion·a·ble** *adj.* — **men'tion·er** *n.*

men·tor (men'tər, -tôr) *n.* A wise and trusted teacher or guide. [< MENTOR] — **men·to'ri·al** (-tôr'ē·əl, -tō'rē-) *adj.*

Men·tor (men'tər, -tôr) In the *Odyssey,* the sage guardian appointed by Odysseus for Telemachus.

men·u (men'yōō, mān'-; *Fr.* mə·nü') *n.* A bill of fare; also, the dishes included in it. [< F < L *minutus* small, detailed]

me·ow (mē·ou', myou) *n.* The crying sound made by a cat. — *v.t.* To make the sound of a cat. [Imit.]

Meph·is·toph·e·les (mef'is·tof'ə·lēz) **1.** In medieval legend, a devil to whom Faust sold his soul for wisdom and power. **2.** A leading character in Marlowe's *Dr. Faustus,* Goethe's *Faust,* etc. — *n.* A diabolical or crafty person. Also **Me·phis·to** (mə·fis'tō). — **Me·phis·to·phe·le·an** (mə·fis'tə·fē'lē·ən), **Me·phis·to·phe·li·an** *adj.*

me·phit·ic (mə·fit'ik) *adj.* **1.** Poisonous; foul. **2.** Offensive to the sense of smell. Also **me·phit'i·cal.**

me·pro·ba·mate (mə·prō'bə·māt, me·prō'bə·māt') *n. Chem.* A white, nearly odorless, bitter powder, $C_9H_{18}N_2O_4$, used in medicine as a tranquilizer. [< ME(THYL) + PRO(PANEDIOL) + (DI-) + (CAR)BAMATE]

mer·can·tile (mûr'kən·til, -tīl) *adj.* **1.** Of, pertaining to, or characteristic of merchants or commerce. **2.** Of or pertaining to the mercantile system. [< F < Ital. < L *mercans, -antis,* pp. of *mercari* to traffic]

mercantile system The theory in political economy that the wealth of a country consists in its quantity of gold and silver, and that the importation of precious metals, and the exportation of goods should be encouraged by the state. Also called **mer·can·til·ism** (mûr'kən·til·iz'əm).

Mer·ca·tor projection (mər·kā'tər) A map projection in which the earth is shown as projected on a cylinder, the meridians and parallels forming a rectangular grid, with areas and distances being less truly represented the farther they are from the equator. [after Gerardus *Mercator,* 1512–94, Flemish cartographer]

MERCATOR PROJECTION

mer·ce·nar·y (mûr'sə·ner'ē) *adj.* **1.** Influenced by a desire for gain or reward. **2.** Serving for pay: now said only of soldiers hired by a foreign state. — *n. pl.* **·nar·ies** A hireling; esp., a hired soldier in foreign service. [< L *merces* reward, hire] — **mer'ce·nar'i·ly** *adv.* — **mer'ce·nar'i·ness** *n.*

mer·cer·ize (mûr'sə·rīz) *v.t.* **·ized, ·iz·ing** To treat (cotton fabrics) with caustic soda so as to increase strength, impart a gloss, and render more receptive to dyes. [after John *Mercer,* 1791–1866, English inventor. — **mer'cer·i·za'tion** *n.*

mer·chan·dise (mûr'chən·dīz, -dīs) *n.* Anything bought and sold for profit; goods; wares. — *v.t. & v.i.* **·dised, ·dis·ing 1.** To buy and sell; trade. **2.** To promote the sale of (goods) through advertising, etc. Also **mer'chan·dize.** [See MERCHANT.] — **mer'chan·dis'er** *n.*

mer·chant (mûr'chənt) *n.* **1.** One who buys and sells commodities for profit. **2.** A storekeeper. — *adj.* **1.** Of or pertaining to merchants or trade. **2.** Of or pertaining to the merchant marine. [< OF < L *mercari* to traffic, buy]

mer·chant·a·ble (mûr'chən·tə·bəl) *adj.* Marketable.

mer·chant·man (mûr'chənt·mən) *n. pl.* **·men** (-mən) A trading or merchant vessel.

merchant marine 1. All the merchant or trading vessels of a nation, collectively. **2.** The officers and men employed on these vessels.

mer·ci (mer·sē') *interj. French* Thank you.

Mer·ci·a (mûr'shē·ə, -shə) An ancient Anglo-Saxon kingdom of central England. — **Mer'ci·an** *adj. & n.*

mer·ci·ful (mûr'sə·fəl) *adj.* **1.** Full of or exercising mercy; compassionate. **2.** Characterized by or indicating mercy: a *merciful* death. — **mer'ci·ful·ly** *adv.* — **mer'ci·ful·ness** *n.*

mer·ci·less (mûr'sə·lis) *adj.* Having or showing no mercy; pitiless. — **mer'ci·less·ly** *adv.* — **mer'ci·less·ness** *n.*

mer·cu·ri·al (mər·kyŏor'ē·əl) *adj.* **1.** Lively; volatile; clever: a *mercurial* wit. **2.** Of, pertaining to, containing, or caused by the action of mercury, or quicksilver. **3.** *Often cap.* Of or pertaining to the god Mercury or the planet Mercury. — *n. Med.* A preparation containing mercury. — **mer·cu'ri·al·ly** *adv.* — **mer·cu'ri·al·ness** *n.*

mer·cu·ri·al·ism (mər·kyŏor'ē·əl·iz'əm) *n. Pathol.* Poisoning produced by excessive amounts of mercury.

mer·cu·ri·al·ize (mər·kyŏor'ē·əl·īz') *v.t.* **·ized, ·iz·ing 1.** To make mercurial. **2.** To treat with mercury. — **mer·cu'ri·al·i·za'tion** *n.*

mer·cu·ric (mər·kyŏor'ik) *adj. Chem.* Of, pertaining to, or containing mercury in its highest valence.

mercuric chloride *Chem.* A white, crystalline, very poisonous compound, $HgCl_2$, used in industry, the arts, and as a strong disinfectant: also called *bichloride of mercury, corrosive sublimate.* Also **mercury chloride.**

mercuric sulfide Cinnabar.

mer·cu·rous (mər·kyŏor'əs) *adj. Chem.* Of, pertaining to, or containing mercury in its lowest valence.

mer·cu·ry (mûr'kyə·rē) *n. pl.* **·ries 1.** A heavy, silver-white metallic element (symbol Hg), liquid at ordinary temperatures: also called *hydrargyrum, quicksilver.* See ELEMENT. **2.** The quicksilver in a thermometer or barometer, as indicating temperature, etc. **3.** A messenger.

Mer·cu·ry (mûr'kyə·rē) **1.** In Roman mythology, the messenger of the gods, god of commerce, eloquence, and skill, and patron of travelers, merchants, and thieves: identified with the Greek *Hermes.* — *n.* The smallest planet of the solar system, and that nearest the sun. See PLANET.

mer·cy (mûr'sē) *n. pl.* **·cies 1.** Kind or compassionate treatment of an offender, adversary, prisoner, etc., in one's power. **2.** A disposition to be kind, forgiving, or helpful. **3.** The power to show mercy or compassion. **4.** A thing to be thankful for. — **at the mercy of** Wholly in the power of. [< OF < L *merces, mercedis* payment, reward; — **Syn. 1.** *Mercy* comes from compassion, kindness, or other ennobling sentiment. *Clemency* is a colder word, chiefly applied to moderation in the exercise of legal power to punish. *Leniency* denotes easygoing forbearance, sometimes with a suggestion of undue laxity or indulgence.

mercy killing Euthanasia.

mere (mir) *adj.* Being nothing more or less than: a *mere* trifle. [< L *merus* unmixed, bare]

-mere *combining form Zool.* A part or division. [< Gk. *meros* part]

mere·ly (mir'lē) *adv.* Nothing more than; solely; only.

mer·e·tri·cious (mer'ə-trish'əs) *adj.* Artificially and vulgarly attractive. [< L *merere* to earn, gain] — **mer'e·tri'cious·ly** *adv.* — **mer'e·tri'cious·ness** *n.*

mer·gan·ser (mər-gan'sər) *n.* Any of several fish-eating, diving ducks having the head usu. crested. [< NL < L *mergere* to plunge + *anser* goose]

merge (mûrj) *v.t. & v.i.* **merged, merg·ing** To combine or be combined so as to lose separate identity; blend. [< L *mergere* to dip, immerse] — **mer'gence** *n.*

merg·er (mûr'jər) *n.* **1.** The combining of two or more commercial interests into one. **2.** The act of merging.

me·rid·i·an (mə-rid'ē-ən) *n.* **1.** *Geog.* **a** A great circle drawn from any point on the earth's surface and passing through both poles. **b** Half of a circle so drawn between the poles. **2.** *Astron.* An imaginary great circle of the celestial sphere passing through its poles and the zenith of an observer at any point. **3.** The highest or culminating point; zenith. — *adj.* **1.** Of or pertaining to a meridian. **2.** Of or pertaining to midday. [< OF < L *medius* middle + *dies* day]

me·ringue (mə-rang') *n.* **1.** The stiffly beaten white of eggs blended with sugar and usu. baked, used as a topping for pastry or pies. **2.** A small cake or tart shell made of this. [< F < G *meringe*, lit., cake of Mehringen (in Germany)]

me·ri·no (mə-rē'nō) *n. pl.* **·nos 1.** A breed of sheep having fine, closely set, silky wool and heavy curled horns in the male; also, the wool of this sheep. **2.** A fine fabric originally made of merino wool. **3.** A type of fine yarn used for knitted underwear, hosiery, etc. — *adj.* Made of merino wool, yarn or cloth. [< Sp., roving from pasture to pasture, shepherd]

mer·it (mer'it) *n.* **1.** Worth or excellence; high quality. **2.** That which deserves esteem, praise, or reward. **3.** *Sometimes pl.* The quality or fact of being entitled to reward, praise, etc. **4.** *pl.* The actual rights or wrongs of a matter, esp. a legal matter. — *v.t.* To earn as a reward or punishment; deserve. [< OF < L *merere* to deserve] — **mer'it·ed** *adj.*

mer·i·to·ri·ous (mer'ə-tôr'ē·əs, -tō'rē-) *adj.* Deserving of reward or praise. — **mer'i·to'ri·ous·ly** *adv.* — **mer'i·to'ri·ous·ness** *n.*

merit system A system adopted in the U.S. Civil Service whereby appointments and promotions are made on the basis of merit, ascertained through qualifying examinations.

merle (mûrl) *n.* The European blackbird. Also **merl.** [< F < L *merula* blackbird]

Mer·lin (mûr'lin) In the Arthurian cycle and other medieval legends, a magician and prophet. [< Med.L < Welsh *Myrrdin*, lit., sea fortress]

mer·maid (mûr'mād') *n.* A legendary marine creature having the head and upper body of a woman and the tail of a fish. Also **mer'maid'en** (-mād'n). [OE *mere* sea, lake + MAID]

mero- *combining form* Part; partial. Also, before vowels, **mer-.** [< Gk. *meros* part, division]

-merous *suffix Zool.* Having a (specified number or kind of) parts. [< Gk. *meros* part, division]

Mer·o·vin·gi·an (mer'ə·vin'jē·ən, -jən) *adj.* Of or pertaining to the first Frankish dynasty founded about A.D. 500 and lasting until 751. — *n.* A member of the Merovingian dynasty. Also **Mer'o·win'gi·an.** [< L *Merovingi*, descendants of Maroveus, a legendary Frankish king]

mer·ri·ment (mer'i·mənt) *n.* Laughter; fun.

mer·ry (mer'ē) *adj.* **·ri·er, ·ri·est 1.** Full of mirth and laughter; joyous; gay. **2.** Characterized by or conducive to mirth, cheerfulness, etc. [OE *myrige* pleasant] — **mer'ri·ly** *adv.* — **mer'ri·ness** *n.*

mer·ry-an·drew (mer'ē·an'drōō) *n.* A clown or buffoon.

mer·ry-go-round (mer'ē·gō·round') *n.* **1.** A revolving platform fitted with wooden horses, seats, etc., on which people, esp. children, ride for amusement; carousel. **2.** A whirl, as of business or pleasure. Also, *Brit.*, **roundabout.**

mer·ry·mak·ing (mer'ē·mā'king) *n.* The act of having fun and making merry. — *adj.* Festive. — **mer'ry·mak'er** *n.*

mes- Var. of MESO-.

me·sa (mā'sə, *Sp.* mā'sä) *n.* A high, flat tableland descending sharply to the surrounding plain, common in the SW U.S. [< Sp. < L *mensa* table]

mé·sal·li·ance (mā·zal'ē·əns, *Fr.* mā·zȧ·lyäns') *n.* A marriage with one of inferior position; misalliance. [< F]

mes·cal (mes·kal') *n.* **1.** A spineless cactus, native to the SW U.S. and northern Mexico, whose dried tops, **mescal buttons,** are chewed by the Indians for their narcotic effect: also called *peyote.* **2.** An intoxicating liquor distilled from certain species of agave. [< Sp. < Nahuatl *mexicalli*]

mes·dames (mā·däm', *Fr.* mā·dàm') Plural of MADAME.

mes·de·moi·selles (mād·mwȧ·zel') *French* Plural of MADEMOISELLE.

me·seems (mē·sēmz') *v. impersonal Archaic* It seems to me.

mes·en·ceph·a·lon (mes'en·sef'ə·lon') *n. Anat.* One of the three principal divisions of the central nervous system of the embryo: also called *midbrain.* [< NL < MES- + ENCEPHALON] — **mes·en·ce·phal·ic** (mes·en'sə·fal'ik) *adj.*

mes·en·ter·y (mes'ən·ter'ē) *n. pl.* **·ter·ies** *Anat.* A membranous fold that invests an intestine and connects it with the posterior abdominal wall. Also **mes'en·te'ri·um** (-tir'ē·əm). [< Med.L < Gk. < *mesos* middle + *enteron* intestine] — **mes'en·ter'ic** *adj.*

mesh (mesh) *n.* **1.** One of the open spaces between the cords of a net or the wires of a screen. **2.** *pl.* The cords or wires bounding such a space or spaces. **3.** A net or network. **4.** *Usu. pl.* Anything that entangles or involves; a snare. **5.** *Mech.* The engagement of gear teeth. — *v.t. & v.i.* **1.** To make or become entangled, as in a net. **2.** To make or become engaged, as gear teeth. [< MDu. *maesche* mesh]

mesh·work (mesh'wûrk') *n.* Meshes; network.

mes·mer·ism (mes'mə·riz'əm, mez'-) *n.* Loosely, hypnotism: also called *animal magnetism.* [after Franz Anton Mesmer, 1733–1815, German physician] — **mes·mer·ic** (mes·mer'ik, mez-) *adj.* — **mes'mer·ist** *n.*

mes·mer·ize (mes'mə·rīz, mez'-) *v.t.* **·ized, ·iz·ing** To hypnotize. Also *Brit.* **mes'mer·ise.** — **mes'mer·i·za'tion** *n.*

meso- *combining form* **1.** Situated in the middle. **2.** Intermediate in size or degree. Also, before vowels, **mes-.** [< Gk. *mesos* middle]

mes·o·blast (mes'ə·blast, mē'sə-) *n. Biol.* The mesoderm in its early stages. [< MESO- + Gk. *blastos* sprout] — **mes'o·blas'tic** *adj.*

mes·o·carp (mes'ə·kärp, mē'sə-) *n. Bot.* The middle layer of a pericarp, as the fleshy part of certain fruits.

mes·o·derm (mes'ə·dûrm, mē'sə-) *n.* The middle of the three primary germ layers in the embryo of animals, developing into the skeletal and muscular systems.

Mes·o·lith·ic (mes'ə·lith'ik, mē'sə-) *adj. Anthropol.* Pertaining to or designating the period of human culture followed by the Neolithic and characterized by an economy transitional between food gathering and a settled agriculture.

mes·o·mor·phic (mes'ə·môr'fik, mē'sə-) *adj.* Designating a human body type characterized by a sturdy body structure. — **mes'o·morph** *n.* — **mes'o·mor'phy** *n.*

mes·on (mē'son, mes'on) *n. Physics* Any of a group of unstable nucleons having a mass intermediate between that of the electron and the proton. [< Gk. *mesos* middle]

mes·o·tho·ri·um (mes'ə·thôr'ē·əm, -thō'rē-; mē'sə-) *n.* Either of two isotopes resulting from the radioactive disintegration of thorium, intermediate between thorium and radiothorium.

Mes·o·zo·ic (mes'ə·zō'ik, mē'sə-) *Geol. adj.* Pertaining to the era between the Paleozoic and the Cenozoic. — *n.* This era, including the Triassic, Jurassic, and Cretaceous periods.

mes·quite (mes·kēt', mes'kēt) *n.* A spiny, leguminous shrub or small tree, found in SW U.S. and extending southward to Peru, that yields sweet pods used for cattle fodder: also called *honey mesquite.* Also spelled *mezquit, mesquit.* Also **mes·quit** (mes·kēt', mes'kēt). [< Sp. < Nahuatl *mizquitl*]

mess (mes) *n.* **1.** A state of disorder; esp., a condition of dirty or untidy confusion. **2.** A confusing, difficult, or embarrassing situation or condition; muddle. **3.** An unpleasant or confused mixture or collection; hodgepodge. **4.** A quantity of food sufficient for a meal or dish. **5.** A portion of soft, partly liquid food. **6.** A disagreeable or sloppy preparation of food. **7.** A number of persons who regularly take their meals together, as in the military; also, a meal taken by them. — *v.i.* **1.** To busy oneself; dabble: often with *around* or *about.* **2.** To make a mess; bungle: often with *up.* **3.** To interfere; meddle: often with *around.* **4.** To eat with as a member of a mess. — *v.t.* **5.** To make a mess of; botch: often with *up.* **6.** To make dirty: often with *up.* **7.** To provide meals for. [< OF < L *missus* course at a meal]

mes·sage (mes'ij) *n.* **1.** A communication sent by any of various means. **2.** An official or formal communication, as from a chief executive to a legislative body. **3.** A communication embodying important principles or counsel. [< OF < Med.L < *mittere* to send]

mes·sa·line (mes/ə·lēn/, mes/ə·lēn) *n.* A lightweight, lustrous, twilled silk fabric.

mes·sen·ger (mes/ən·jər) *n.* 1. One sent with a message or on an errand; esp., one whose work is running errands. 2. A bearer of official dispatches; courier. 3. *Archaic* A harbinger. [ME < OF *messagier*. The *n* is nonhistoric.]

mess hall A place where a group of persons regularly take their meals, as in the army, navy, etc.

Mes·si·ah (mə·sī/ə) *n.* 1. In Judaism, a deliverer of Israel promised by God and expected by the Jews. 2. In Christianity, Jesus regarded as this deliverer. 3. Any expected liberator of a country, people, etc. Also **Mes·si/as.** [< LL < Gk. < Aramaic *mĕshīhā*, Hebrew *māshīah* anointed] — **Mes·si·an·ship** *n.* — **Mes·si·an·ic** (mes/ē·an/ik) *adj.*

mes·sieurs (mes/ərz, *Fr.* mā·syœ/) *n.pl.* of *Fr.* **mon·sieur** (mə·syœ/) Sirs; gentlemen: in English in the contracted form *Messrs.*, used as plural of *Mr.*

mess jacket A man's tailored jacket, usu. white and terminating at the waistline, worn on semiformal occasions.

mess kit A small, compact unit containing cooking and eating utensils, used by soldiers in the field and campers.

mess sergeant A noncommissioned officer who plans meals, issues rations, and superintends the company mess.

mes·sy (mes/ē) *adj.* Being in or causing a condition of dirt or confusion; untidy. — **mess/i·ly** *adv.* — **mess/i·ness** *n.*

mes·ti·zo (mes·tē/zō) *n. pl.* **·zos** or **·zoes** Any one of mixed blood; in Mexico and the western U.S., a person of Spanish and Indian blood: also called *Ladino.* Also **mes·te/so, mes·ti/no** (-nō). [< Sp. < LL < L *mixtus*, pp. of *miscere* to mix] — **mes·ti/za** (-zə) *n.fem.*

met (met) Past tense and past participle of MEET[1].

met- Var. of META-.

meta- *prefix* 1. Changed in place or form; reversed; altered. 2. *Anat. & Zool.* Behind; after; on the farther side of; later: often equivalent to *post-* or *dorso-.* 3. With; alongside. 4. Beyond; over; transcending: *metaphysics, metapsychology.* 5. *Chem.* a A modification of. b A derivative of. Also, before vowels and *h,* **met-.** [< Gk. < *meta* after, beside, with]

met·a·bol·ic (met/ə·bol/ik) *adj. Biol. & Physiol.* Of, pertaining to, or having the nature of metabolism.

me·tab·o·lism (mə·tab/ə·liz/əm) *n. Biol. & Physiol.* The aggregate of all chemical processes constantly taking place in a living organism, including those that use energy to convert nutritive materials into protoplasm (anabolism) and those that release energy for vital processes in breaking down protoplasm into simpler substances (catabolism). [< Gk. < *meta-* beyond + *ballein* to throw]

me·tab·o·lize (mə·tab/ə·līz) *v.t. & v.i.* **·lized, ·liz·ing** To subject to or change by metabolism.

met·a·car·pus (met/ə·kär/pəs) *n. Anat.* The part of the forelimb between the carpus or wrist and the phalanges or bones of the finger. [< NL < Gk. < *meta-* beyond + *karpos* wrist] — **met·a·car/pal** *adj. & n.*

met·a·gal·ax·y (met/ə·gal/ək·sē) *n. pl.* **·ax·ies** *Astron.* The entire material universe, regarded esp. as a system including all the galaxies.

met·al (met/l) *n.* 1. Any of a class of elements characterized by a distinctive luster, malleability, ductility, thermal and electrical conductivity, and capable of forming positive ions. 2. A composition of such metallic elements; alloy. 3. Molten glass. 4. The constituent material of anything. — **white metal** Any one of the various white alloys, as pewter, Babbitt metal, etc., used for ornaments, castings, etc. — *v.t.* **met·aled** or **·alled, met·al·ing** or **·al·ling** To furnish or cover with metal. [< OF < L < Gk. *metallon*]

me·tal·lic (mə·tal/ik) *adj.* 1. Of, pertaining to, or consisting of metal. 2. Resembling or having the nature of metal: a *metallic* sound. 3. Yielding or containing metal.

met·al·lif·er·ous (met/ə·lif/ər·əs) *adj.* Yielding or containing metal.

met·al·lur·gy (met/ə·lûr/jē) *n.* 1. The art or science of extracting a metal or metals from ores. 2. The art or science of working with metals and alloys for the purpose of their development, improvement, etc. [< NL < Gk. < *metallon* mine + *-ergos* working] — **met·al·lur/gic** or **·gi·cal** *adj.* — **met·al·lur/gi·cal·ly** *adv.* — **met·al·lur/gist** *n.*

met·al·work (met/l·wûrk/) *n.* 1. Articles made of metal. 2. The art of making such things. — **met·al·work/er** *n.* — **met/al·work/ing** *n.*

met·a·mor·phic (met/ə·môr/fik) *adj.* 1. Of or pertaining to metamorphosis. 2. *Geol.* Of, pertaining to, or exhibiting metamorphism. Also **met·a·mor/phous.**

met·a·mor·phism (met/ə·môr/fiz·əm) *n.* 1. *Geol.* The changes in the composition and texture of rocks caused by force, heat, pressure, moisture, etc. 2. Metamorphosis.

met·a·mor·phose (met/ə·môr/fōz) *v.t.* **·phosed, ·phos·ing** 1. To change the form of. — *v.i.* 2. To undergo metamorphosis. Also **met·a·mor/phize.** [< MF *métamorphoser*]

met·a·mor·pho·sis (met/ə·môr/fə·sis) *n. pl.* **·pho·ses** (-fə-

sēz) 1. Change from one form, shape, or substance into another by any means. 2. Complete transformation of character, purpose, circumstances, etc. 3. One who or that which is metamorphosed. 4. *Biol.* Any marked change in the form and structure of an animal in its development from embryo to adult, as from tadpole to frog. [< L < Gk. < *meta-* beyond + *morphē* form]

met·a·phor (met/ə·fôr, -fər) *n.* A figure of speech in which one object is likened to another by speaking of it as if it were that other, as *He was a lion in battle*: distinguished from *simile.* — Syn. See SIMILE. — **mixed metaphor** A figurative expression in which two or more incongruous metaphors are used, as *He kept a tight rein on his boiling passions.* [< F < L < Gk. < *meta-* beyond, over + *pherein* to carry] — **met·a·phor/ic** (-fôr/ik, -for/ik) or **·i·cal** *adj.* — **met·a·phor/i·cal·ly** *adv.*

met·a·phys·i·cal (met/ə·fiz/i·kəl) *adj.* 1. Of, pertaining to, or of the nature of metaphysics. 2. Highly abstruse; abstract. 3. Of or designating certain English poets of the 17th century whose poetry is characterized by complex, intellectual imagery and paradox. [See METAPHYSICS.] — **met·a·phys/i·cal·ly** *adv.*

met·a·phys·ics (met/ə·fiz/iks) *n.pl.* (construed as sing.) 1. The branch of philosophy that investigates principles of reality transcending those of any particular science, traditionally including cosmology and ontology. 2. All speculative philosophy. [< Med.L < Med.Gk. < *ta meta ta physika* the (works) after the *Physics* of Aristotle]

me·tas·ta·sis (mə·tas/tə·sis) *n. pl.* **·ses** (-sēz) *Pathol.* 1. The transfer of a disease from one part of the body to another, as in certain types of cancer. 2. A site to which such a transfer has been made. [< L < Gk. < *meta-* after + *histanai* to place] — **met·a·stat/ic** (-stat/ik) *adj.* — **met·a·stat/i·cal·ly** *adv.*

me·tas·ta·size (mə·tas/tə·sīz) *v.i.* **·sized, ·siz·ing** *Pathol.* To shift or spread from one part of the body to another, as a malignant growth.

met·a·tar·sus (met/ə·tär/səs) *n. pl.* **·si** (-sī) *Anat.* 1. In man, the part of the foot situated between the tarsus and the bones of the toes. 2. An analogous part in the hind or pelvic limb of animals or birds. — **met·a·tar/sal** *adj. & n.*

me·tath·e·sis (mə·tath/ə·sis) *n. pl.* **·ses** (-sēz) The transposition of letters, syllables, or sounds in a word: Old English *bridd* became *bird* by *metathesis.* [< LL < Gk. < *meta-* over + *tithenai* to place] — **met·a·thet·ic** (met/ə·thet/ik) or **·i·cal** *adj.*

met·a·zo·an (met/ə·zō/ən) *n. Zool.* Any of a primary division of animals, whose bodies are made up of many cells. Also **met/a·zo/on.** — *adj.* Of the metazoans: also **met/a·zo/ic.** [< META- + Gk. *zōion* animal]

mete[1] (mēt) *v.t.* **met·ed, met·ing** To allot or distribute by or as by measure: usu. followed by *out.* [OE *metan* to measure]

mete[2] (mēt) *n.* A boundary line; limit: now chiefly in the phrase **metes and bounds.** [< OF < L *meta* goal, boundary]

me·tem·psy·cho·sis (mə·temp/sə·kō/sis, met/əm·sī-) *n.* Transmigration of souls. [< LL < Gk. < *meta-* over + *empsychoein* to animate]

met·en·ceph·a·lon (met/en·sef/ə·lon) *n. pl.* **·la** (-lə) *Anat.* That part of the brain comprising the cerebellum and the pons Varolii: also called *afterbrain.* — **met/en·ce·phal/ic** (-sə·fal/ik) *adj.*

me·te·or (mē/tē·ər, -ôr) *n.* 1. *Astron.* A meteoroid that on entering the earth's atmosphere at great speed is heated to luminosity and is visible as a streak of light: also called *shooting star.* 2. Loosely, a meteorite or meteoroid. [< Med.L < Gk. < *meta-* beyond + *eōra* suspension]

me·te·or·ic (mē/tē·ôr/ik, -or/ik) *adj.* 1. Of, pertaining to, or consisting of meteors. 2. Resembling a meteor; brilliant, rapid, and dazzling: a *meteoric* career. 3. Of or pertaining to atmospheric phenomena. — **me/te·or/i·cal·ly** *adv.*

me·te·or·ite (mē/tē·ə·rīt/) *n.* A portion of a meteor that has not been completely destroyed by combustion and has fallen to earth. — **me/te·or·it/ic** (-ə·rit/ik) *adj.*

me·te·or·oid (mē/tē·ə·roid/) *n. Astron.* One of the pieces of matter moving through outer space, that upon entering the earth's atmosphere form meteors.

me·te·or·ol·o·gy (mē/tē·ə·rol/ə·jē) *n.* 1. The science that treats of atmospheric phenomena, esp. those that relate to weather. 2. The weather conditions of any particular place. [< Gk. < *meteōros* high in the air + *logos* discourse] — **me/te·or/o·log/ic** (-ôr·ə·loj/ik) or **·i·cal** *adj.* — **me/te·or/o·log/i·cal·ly** *adv.* — **me/te·or·ol/o·gist** *n.*

meteor shower *Astron.* Any of various displays of meteors that recur at definite intervals and appear to radiate from a single point or region.

me·ter[1] (mē/tər) *n.* An instrument or device used to measure and indicate quantity or variation in amount, as of a liquid or gas, electric current, light, etc.; also, a similar device for measuring speed, time, distance, etc. — *v.t.* To measure or test by means of a meter. [< METE[1]]

me·ter[2] (mē/tər) *n.* 1. A measured verbal rhythm constituting one of the chief characteristics of verse, and, in prosody, forming definite groups (feet) of accented and unaccented syllables, usu. of a specified number for each line. **2.** *Music* The combining of rhythmic pulses into successive groups having like arrangement and duration. Also, *esp. Brit.*, *metre*. [OE < L < Gk. *metron* a measure]

me·ter[3] (mē′tər) *n.* The basic unit of length in the metric system, equivalent to 39.37 inches. Also *metre*. See table inside back cover. [< F *mètre* < Gk. *metron*]

-meter *combining form* **1.** A device for measuring (a specified quality, thing, etc.). **2.** Division into (a specified number of) prosodic feet: *pentameter*. **3.** A (specified kind of) unit in the metric system: *kilometer*: also, *esp. Brit.*, *-metre*.

me·ter-kil·o·gram-sec·ond (mē′tər·kil′ə·gram′sek′ənd) *adj.* See MKS.

meth- *combining form Chem.* Used to indicate the presence of a methyl group in a compound. Also, before consonants, *metho-*. [< METHYL]

meth·ane (meth′ān) *n. Chem.* A colorless, odorless, flammable gas, CH_4, the first member of the methane series, the chief constituent of firedamp and marsh gas, and commercially obtained from natural gas.

methane series *Chem.* A group of saturated hydrocarbons having the general formula C_nH_{2n+2}: also called *paraffin series*.

meth·a·nol (meth′ə·nōl, -nol) *n. Chem.* A colorless, flammable, highly toxic alcohol, CH_3OH, obtained by the destructive distillation of wood, and widely used in industry and the arts: also called *methyl alcohol*, *wood alcohol*.

me·thinks (mē·thingks′) *v. impersonal,* **me·thought** *Archaic & Poetic* It seems to me. [OE *thyncan* to seem]

metho- Var. of METH-.

meth·od (meth′əd) *n.* **1.** A way, means, or manner of proceeding; esp., a regular, systematic, or orderly way of doing anything. **2.** System, order, or regularity in action or thought. **3.** The techniques used in a particular field of knowledge, thought, practice, etc.: the scientific *method*. **4.** Systematic and orderly arrangement, as of ideas, facts, topics, etc. — **the method** A system or style of acting in which the actor makes a strong emotional identification with the role portrayed. [F < L < Gk. < *meta-* after + *hodos* way] — **meth′od·ism** *n.* — **meth′od·ist** *n.*

me·thod·i·cal (mə·thod′i·kəl) *adj.* **1.** Arranged in or performed in systematic order. **2.** Characterized by orderly or systematic habits, behavior, etc.: a *methodical* man. Also **me·thod′ic.** — **me·thod′i·cal·ly** *adv.* — **me·thod′i·cal·ness** *n.*

Meth·od·ist (meth′əd·ist) *n.* A member of any of the Protestant denominations having their origin in a religious movement begun in England in the first half of the 18th century by John and Charles Wesley and their followers. — *adj.* Pertaining to or characteristic of Methodism or Methodists. — **Meth′od·ism** *n.* — **Meth′od·is′tic** or **-ti·cal** *adj.*

meth·od·ize (meth′ə·dīz) *v.t.* **ized, ·iz·ing** To reduce to or arrange in accordance with a method. — **meth′od·i·za′tion** *n.*

meth·od·ol·o·gy (meth′ə·dol′ə·jē) *n. pl.* **·gies** **1.** The principles, practices, etc., of orderly thought or procedure applied to a particular branch of learning. **2.** The branch of logic dealing with such procedures. [< Gk. *methodos* method + -LOGY] — **meth·od·o·log·i·cal** (meth′əd·ə·loj′i·kəl) *adj.* — **meth′od·o·log′i·cal·ly** *adv.*

me·thought (mē·thôt′) Past tense of METHINKS.

Me·thu·se·lah (mə·thōō′zə·lə) In the Old Testament, a Hebrew patriarch reputed to have lived 969 years. *Gen.* v 27. — *n.* A very old man.

meth·yl (meth′əl) *n. Chem.* A univalent organic radical, CH_3, existing chiefly in combination, as in methanol, etc. [< METHYLENE] — **me·thyl·ic** (mə·thil′ik) *adj.*

methyl alcohol (meth′əl) *Chem.* Methanol.

meth·yl·ate (meth′əl·āt) *Chem. n.* A compound derived from methanol by replacing the hydroxyl group with a metal. — *v.t.* **·at·ed, ·at·ing 1.** To mix with methanol. **2.** To combine with the methyl radical. — **meth′yl·a′tion** *n.*

methylated spirit Denatured alcohol prepared by the admixture of methanol. Also **methylated spirits.**

me·tic·u·lous (mə·tik′yə·ləs) *adj.* Extremely or overly precise about details, esp. in minor or trivial matters. [< F < L *meticulosus* fearful] — **me·tic′u·los′i·ty** (-los′ə·tē), **me·tic′u·lous·ness** *n.* — **me·tic′u·lous·ly** *adv.* — **Syn.** Scrupulous, punctilious, fastidious.

mé·tier (mā·tyā′) *n.* **1.** One's occupation, trade, or profession. **2.** Work or activity for which one is esp. well suited. [< OF < L *ministerium* service, employment]

met·o·nym·i·cal (met′ə·nim′i·kəl) *adj.* **1.** Pertaining to or characterized by metonymy. **2.** Used in metonymy. Also **met′o·nym′ic.** — **met′o·nym′i·cal·ly** *adv.*

me·ton·y·my (mə·ton′ə·mē) *n.* A figure of speech that consists in substituting an associated term for the name itself, as in "the *crown* decrees" for "the *ruler* decrees." [< L

< Gk. < *meta-* altered + *onyma* name]

metr- Var. of METRO-.

Met·ra·zol (met′rə·zōl, -zol) *n.* Proprietary name of a synthetic drug, $C_6H_{10}N_4$, used in medicine as a heart stimulant and in the shock treatment of certain mental disorders. Also **met′ra·zol.**

me·tre[1] (mē′tər) See METER[2].

me·tre[2] (mē′tər) See METER[3].

-metre See -METER (def. 3).

met·ric (met′rik) *adj.* Of, pertaining to, or using the meter as a unit of measurement. [< F *métrique*]

met·ri·cal (met′ri·kəl) *adj.* **1.** Of, pertaining to, or characterized by meter; rhythmic. **2.** Composed in or constituting a unit of poetic meter. **3.** Of, pertaining to, or involving measurement. Also **met′ric.** — **met′ri·cal·ly** *adv.*

metric hundredweight A unit of weight equal to 50 kilograms.

met·ri·cize (met′rə·sīz) *v.t.* **·cized, ·ciz·ing** To convert to the metric system. — **met·ri·ca·tion** (met′ri·kā′shən) *n.*

met·rics (met′riks) *n.pl.* (construed as sing.) **1.** The art or branch of learning concerned with meter in prosody. **2.** The science or theory of measurement.

metric system A decimal system of weights and measures having as fundamental units the gram, the meter, and the liter. See table inside back cover.

metric ton A unit of weight equal to 1,000 kilograms, or 2,204.62 pounds avoirdupois.

met·rist (met′rist) *n.* One who is skillful in using poetic meter. Also **met′ri·cist** (-rə·sist). [< Med.L *metrista*]

met·ro (met′rō) *n. Often cap. Informal* An underground railroad; subway; esp., the subway system of Paris. Also **mé·tro** (mā·trō′). [< F *métro* < (*chemin de fer*) *métro-* (*politain*) metro(politan railroad)]

metro-[1] *combining form* The uterus; pertaining to the uterus. Also, before vowels, *metr-.* [< Gk. *metra* uterus]

metro-[2] *combining form* Measure. Also, before vowels, *metr-.* [< Gk. *metron* a measure]

met·ro·nome (met′rə·nōm) *n.* An instrument for indicating exact tempo in music, usu. producing audible clicks controlled by a reversed pendulum whose motion is regulated by a sliding weight. [< METRO-[2] + Gk. *nomos* law] — **met′ro·nom′ic** (-nom′ik) *adj.*

me·tro·nym·ic (mē′trə·nim′ik, met′rə-) *adj.* Derived from the name of one's mother or a female ancestor. — *n.* A metronymic name or designation. [< Gk. < *mētēr* mother + *onyma* name]

METRONOME

me·trop·o·lis (mə·trop′ə·lis) *n. pl.* **·lis·es 1.** The capital or the largest or most important city of a country, state, or area. **2.** An urban center of activity, culture, trade, etc. **3.** The see or city over which a metropolitan has authority. [< Gk. < *mētēr* mother + *polis* city]

met·ro·pol·i·tan (met′rə·pol′ə·tən) *adj.* **1.** Constituting a major urban center and its environs: the *metropolitan* area. **2.** Pertaining to or designating a bishop having authority over a metropolis (def. 3). — *n.* **1.** In various churches, an archbishop having authority over the bishops within his jurisdiction. **2.** One who lives in or has the viewpoint, etc., of one living in a metropolis.

-metry *combining form* The process, science, or art of measuring: *geometry*. [< Gk. *metria* < *metron* a measure]

met·tle (met′l) *n.* **1.** Character or temperament. **2.** Courage; pluck. — **on one's mettle** Aroused to one's best efforts. [Var. of METAL]

met·tle·some (met′l·səm) *adj.* Full of spirit; courageous; valiant. Also **met·tled** (met′ald).

mew[1] (myōō) *n.* **1.** A cage in which molting hawks are kept. **2.** *pl.* Stables built around a court or alley: so called from the royal stables in London. **3.** *pl.* (construed as sing.) Chiefly *Brit.* A narrow street or alley, often with dwellings converted from stables. — *v.t.* To confine in or as in a cage; often with up. [< OF *muer* to change, molt < L *mutare*]

mew[2] (myōō) *v.i.* To utter the high-pitched cry of a cat. — *n.* The high-pitched, plaintive cry of a cat. [Imit.]

mew[3] (myōō) *n.* A gull; esp. the common gull of Europe: also called *sea mew*. [OE *mæw*]

mewl (myōōl) *v.i.* To whimper or cry feebly, as an infant. — *n.* A whimper or feeble cry. [Freq. of MEW[2]]

Mex·i·can (mek′sə·kən) *n.* **1.** A native or inhabitant of Mexico. **2.** A language indigenous to Mexico, as Nahuatl. — *adj.* Of Mexico, its inhabitants, or their language.

Mexican hairless One of a breed of small dogs, hairless except for a tuft on the head and the end of the tail.

Mexican War See table for WAR.

mez·cal (mez·kal′) See MESCAL.

mez·quit (mez·kēt′, mez′kēt), **mez·quite** See MESQUITE.

mez·za·nine (mez′ə·nēn, -nin) *n.* **1.** An intermediate story, usu. not of full width, between two main floors. **2.** In a theater, the first balcony, or the front rows of the balcony. [< F < Ital. *mezzanino* < L *medianus*]

mez·zo (met′sō, med′zō, mez′ō) *adj.* Half; medium; moderate: often used in combination: *mezzo-soprano.* — *adv.* *Music* Moderately: *mezzo forte.* — *n.* *pl.* ·zos A mezzo-soprano. [< Ital., < L *medius* middle]

mez·zo-so·pran·o (met′sō·sə·pran′ō, -prä′nō, med′zō-, mez′ō-) *n.* *pl.* ·pran·os or ·pra·ni (-nē) **1.** A female voice intermediate between a soprano and a contralto. **2.** A person having such a voice. — *adj.* Of or pertaining to such a voice. [< Ital.]

mez·zo·tint (met′sō·tint′, med′zō-, mez′ō-) *n.* **1.** A method of engraving in which the roughened surface of a copper or steel plate is scraped or burnished to produce effects of light and shade. **2.** A print produced from such a plate. — *v.t.* To engrave by or represent in mezzotint. [< Ital. < *mezzo* middle + *tinto* painted] — **mez′zo·tint′er** *n.*

mi (mē) *n.* *Music* The third syllable used in solmization; the third tone of a major scale; also, the tone E.

Mi·am·i (mī·am′ē, -am′ə) *n.* *pl.* **Mi·ami** or **Mi·am·is** A member of an Algonquian tribe of North American Indians formerly inhabiting a region in Wisconsin, Indiana, and Ohio. [< N.Am.Ind.]

mi·aou, mi·aow (mē·ou′) See MEOW.

mi·as·ma (mī·az′mə, mē-) *n.* *pl.* ·mas or ·ma·ta (-mə·tə) **1.** Noxious or unwholesome influence, etc. **2.** The poisonous effluvium once supposed to rise from swamps, etc. Also **mi′asm** (-az·əm). [< NL < Gk. < *miainein* to stain, defile] — **mi·as′mal, mi·as·mat·ic** (mī′əz·mat′ik), **mi·as′mic** *adj.*

mib (mib) *n.* *U.S. Dial.* **1.** A marble. **2.** *pl.* The game of marbles. [? Alter. of MARBLE]

mi·ca (mī′kə) *n.* Any of a class of silicate minerals, cleaving into tough, often transparent and flexible laminae: sometimes called *isinglass.* [< L, crumb] — **mi·ca·ceous** (mī·kā′shəs) *adj.*

Mi·cah (mī′kə) Eighth-century B.C. Hebrew prophet. — *n.* A book of the Old Testament bearing his name. Also, in the Douai Bible, **Mi·che·as** (mī·kē′əs).

mice (mīs) Plural of MOUSE.

Mi·chael (mī′kəl) One of the archangels, represented as a militant protector and defender of the faithful: sometimes called *the Archangel. Dan.* x 10–12, *Rev.* xii 7–9.

Mich·ael·mas (mik′əl·məs) *n.* September 29, the church festival of the archangel Michael, in Great Britain serving as the fall quarter day. Also **Michaelmas Day.**

mick·ey (mik′ē) *n.* *pl.* ·eys *U.S. Slang* A Mickey Finn.

Mick·ey Finn (mik′ē fin′) *U.S. Slang* An alcoholic drink secretly drugged so as to render the drinker unconscious. Also **mick′ey finn.** [Origin unknown]

Mic·mac (mik′mak) *n.* *pl.* ·mac or ·macs A member of an Algonquian tribe living in Nova Scotia, New Brunswick, and Newfoundland. [< N.Am.Ind., lit., allies]

mi·cra (mī′krə) Plural of MICRON.

micro- *combining form* **1.** Very small; minute. **2.** Enlarging or magnifying size or volume: *microscope.* **3.** *Pathol.* Abnormally small or underdeveloped. **4.** Of a science, depending on, using, or requiring a microscope: *microbiology.* **5.** In the metric system and in technical usage, one millionth of (a specified unit): *microwatt.* Sometimes, before vowels, **micr-.** [< Gk. *mikros* small]

mi·crobe (mī′krōb) *n.* A microscopic organism; esp., one of the bacteria that cause disease. [< F < Gk. *mikros* small + *bios* life] — **mi·cro′bi·al, mi·cro′bi·an, mi·cro′bic** *adj.*

— Syn. *Microbe* was originally a general term, applied at first to protozoa, and then to *bacteria*; *germ* originally denoted a reproductive cell. Both words are now popularly used to refer to disease-producing *bacteria. Microorganism* developed as a general term for protozoa, bacteria, and *viruses. Bacteria* are unicellular organisms, distinguished from protozoa because they possess both plant and animal characteristics. *Bacillus* properly denotes one class only of *bacteria*. A *virus* is a complex protein molecule capable of invading the cells and there reproducing itself.

mi·cro·bi·ol·o·gy (mī′krō·bī·ol′ə·jē) *n.* The branch of biology concerned with the study of microorganisms. — **mi′cro·bi·o·log′i·cal** (-bī′ə·loj′i·kəl) *adj.* — **mi′cro·bi·ol′o·gist** *n.*

mi·cro·ceph·a·ly (mī′krō·sef′ə·lē) *n.* Abnormal smallness of the head and cranial capacity. [< MICRO- + Gk. *kephalē* head] — **mi′cro·ce·phal′ic** (-sə·fal′ik) *adj. & n.* — **mi′cro·ceph′a·lous** *adj.*

mi·cro·chem·is·try (mī′krō·kem′is·trē) *n.* A branch of chemistry dealing with minute quantities.

mi·cro·coc·cus (mī′krə·kok′əs) *n. pl.* ·coc·ci (-kok′sī) Any member of a group of spherical bacteria that occur in irregular masses and are often pathogenic. [< NL]

mi·cro·cop·y (mī′krə·kop′ē) *n. pl.* ·cop·ies A reduced photographic copy of a letter, manuscript, etc. — *v.t. & v.i.* ·cop·ied, ·cop·y·ing To reproduce in the form of microcopy.

mi·cro·cosm (mī′krə·koz′əm) *n.* **1.** A little world; the universe in miniature. **2.** Man regraded as epitomizing the universe. Also **mi′cro·cos′mos** (-koz′məs). [< LL < Gk. *mikros cosmos*, lit., little world] — **mi′cro·cos′mic** *adj.*

mi·cro·fiche (mī′krə·fēsh′) *n.* A piece of film suitable for a card file, containing images of 24, 48, 96, or more pages of microcopy. Also *fiche.* [< MICRO- + F *fiche* tag, slide]

mi·cro·film (mī′krə·film) *n.* A photographic reproduction on film of a printed page, document, or other object, highly reduced for ease in transmission and storage, and capable of reenlargement. — *v.t. & v.i.* To reproduce on microfilm.

mi·cro·gram (mī′krə·gram) *n.* In the metric system, one millionth of a gram. Also **mi′cro·gramme.**

mi·cro·groove (mī′krə·grōōv) *n.* An extremely fine groove cut in the surface of a long-playing phonograph record.

mi·crom·e·ter (mī·krom′ə·tər) *n.* **1.** An instrument used for measuring very small distances or dimensions, as in conjunction with a microscope or telescope. **2.** A micrometer caliper.

micrometer caliper A caliper or gauge having a micrometer screw, used for precise measurements.

micrometer screw A screw with a very finely cut thread and a graduated head, used in micrometers, etc.

mi·crom·e·try (mī·krom′ə·trē) *n.* Measurement by means of a micrometer. — **mi·cro·met·ric** (mī′krō·met′rik) or **·ri·cal** *adj.* — **mi′cro·met′ri·cal·ly** *adv.*

MICROMETER
a Frame. *b* Anvil.
c Movable spindle.
d Sleeve. *e* Thimble.

mi·cro·mil·li·me·ter (mī′krō·mil′ə·mē′tər) *n.* A millimicron. Also **mi′cro·mil′li·me·tre.**

mi·cron (mī′kron) *n. pl.* ·cra (-krə) A unit of measurement equal to one thousandth of a millimeter. [< NL < Gk. *mikron*, neut. of *mikros* small]

Mi·cro·ne·sian (mī′krə·nē′zhən, -shən) *adj.* Of or pertaining to Micronesia, its people, or their languages. — *n.* **1.** A native of Micronesia. **2.** Any of the Austronesian languages spoken in Micronesia.

mi·cro·or·gan·ism (mī′krō·ôr′gən·iz′əm) *n.* Any microscopic or ultramicroscopic organism, as a bacterium or protozoan. Also **mi′cro·or′gan·ism.** — Syn. See MICROBE.

mi·cro·phone (mī′krə·fōn) *n.* A device for converting sound waves into electric currents, forming the principal element of a telephone transmitter or of any sound-reproducing system, as in broadcasting. — **mi′cro·phon′ic** (-fon′ik) *adj.*

mi·cro·pho·to·graph (mī′krō·fō′tə·graf, -gräf) *n.* **1.** A very small or microscopic photograph, as on microfilm. **2.** Loosely, a photomicrograph. — **mi′cro·pho′to·graph′ic** *adj.* — **mi′cro·pho·tog′ra·phy** (-fə·tog′rə·fē) *n.*

mi·cro·print (mī′krə·print) *n.* A microphotograph reproduced in a print that may be examined or read by means of a magnifying glass. — *v.t. & v.i.* To represent or reproduce by means of a microprint.

mi·cro·scope (mī′krə·skōp) *n.* An optical instrument used for magnifying objects too small to be seen or clearly observed by ordinary vision. [< NL *microscopium*]

mi·cro·scop·ic (mī′krə·skop′ik) *adj.* **1.** So minute as to be visible only under a microscope. **2.** Exceedingly small. **3.** Of, pertaining to, or of the nature of a microscope or microscopy. **4.** Performed with or depending on use of a microscope. **5.** Characterized by or done with minute observation. Also **mi′cro·scop′i·cal.** — **mi′cro·scop′i·cal·ly** *adv.*

mi·cros·co·py (mī·kros′kə·pē, mī′krə·skō′pē) *n.* **1.** The process or technique of using the microscope. **2.** Investigation by means of the microscope. — **mi·cros·co·pist** (mī·kros′kə·pist, mī′krə·skō′pist) *n.*

mi·cro·tome (mī′krə·tōm) *n.* An instrument for cutting thin slices of organic tissue, etc., for microscopic study.

mi·cro·wave (mī′krə·wāv) *n.* An electromagnetic wave having a frequency between about 1,000 and 30,000 megacycles. Compare RADIO WAVE.

mic·tu·rate (mik′chə·rāt) *v.i.* ·rat·ed, ·rat·ing To urinate. [< L *micturire* to desire to urinate] — **mic′tu·ri′tion** (-rish′ən) *n.*

mid¹ (mid) *adj.* Being approximately in the middle; central. [OE *midd-*]

mid² (mid) *prep. Chiefly Poetic* Amid; among. Also **'mid.**

mid- *combining form* **1.** Middle point or part of, as in: **midafternoon, mid-century. 2.** Being in the middle or center, as in: **midpoint; mid-position 3.** With adjectives, of or pertaining to the middle part of that which is modified or implied, as in: **mid-Asian, midmonthly.**

mid·air (mid′âr′) *n.* A point or region seemingly in the middle or midst of the air. Also **mid′-air′.**

Mi·das (mī′dəs) In Greek legend, a king of Phrygia who had the power of turning whatever he touched into gold.

mid·brain (mid′brān′) *n. Anat.* The mesencephalon.

mid·day (mid′dā′) *n.* The middle of the day; noon. — *adj.* Of, pertaining to, or occurring in the middle of the day.

mid·den (mid′n) *n. Brit. Dial.* A dunghill or heap of refuse. [ME *midding* < Scand.]

mid·dle (mid'l) *adj.* **1.** Equally distant from the extremes, periphery, etc.; central. **2.** Intermediate in position, status, etc. **3.** Intervening between the earlier part and the latter part of a sequence, period of time, etc. **4.** Moderate, as in size or effect. **5.** *Usu. cap.* Designating a language in a stage between an earlier and a recent form: *Middle* English. — *n.* **1.** The area or point equally distant from the extremes, etc. **2.** The intermediate section of anything. **3.** The middle part of the body; the waist. — *v.t.* **dled, ·dling** To place in the middle. [OE *middel*]

middle age The time of life between youth and old age, usu. thought of as the years between 40 and 60. — **mid·dle-aged'** (mid'l·ājd') *adj.*

Middle Ages The period in European history between classical antiquity and the Renaissance, usu. regarded as extending from the downfall of Rome, in 476, to about 1450.

Middle Atlantic States New York, New Jersey, and Pennsylvania.

middle C *Music* The note written on the first ledger line above the bass staff and the first ledger line below the treble staff; also, the corresponding tone.

middle class The part of a society occupying a social or economic position between the laboring class and the very wealthy or the nobility. — **mid·dle-class** *adj.*

middle ear *Anat.* The portion of the ear between the tympanic membrane and the opening of the Eustachian tube; also, the membrane itself: also called *tympanum.*

Middle East 1. The region including Egypt and the countries of SW Asia west of Pakistan and India. **2.** *Brit.* This region with the exception of Turkey and including India, Pakistan, Burma, Tibet, Libya, Ethiopia, and Somaliland.

Middle Latin Medieval Latin. See under LATIN.

mid·dle·man (mid'l·man') *n.* *pl.* **·men** (-men') **1.** One who acts as an agent; go-between. **2.** One who buys in bulk from producers and sells to retailers or consumers.

mid·dle·most (mid'l·mōst') *adj.* Situated exactly or most nearly in the middle: also *midmost.*

middle of the road A moderate position or course.

mid·dle-of-the-road·er (mid'l·əv·thə·rō'dər) *n.* One who endorses a moderate course, esp. in politics.

mid·dle·weight (mid'l·wāt') *n.* **1.** A person or animal of average weight. **2.** A boxer or wrestler weighing between 147 and 160 pounds.

mid·dling (mid'ling) *adj.* **1.** Of middle size, quality, or condition; mediocre. **2.** *Informal* In fair health. — *adv. Informal* Fairly; moderately. — *n.* **1.** *pl.* Any of various commodities regarded as intermediate in quality, size, etc. **2.** *pl.* The coarser part of ground grain. — **mid'dling** *adv.*

mid·dy (mid'ē) *n.* *pl.* **·dies** *Informal* **1.** A midshipman. **2.** A middy blouse (which see).

middy blouse A loosely fitting blouse with a sailor collar.

midge (mij) *n.* **1.** A gnat or small fly; esp. any of various small, dipterous insects. **2.** An extremely small person or creature. [OE *mycge*]

mid·get (mij'it) *n.* **1.** A person of abnormally small size but of normal physical proportions. **2.** Anything very small of its kind. — *adj.* Very small; diminutive.

Mid·i·an·ite (mid'ē·ən·īt') *n.* One of an ancient nomadic tribe of Arabia. *Gen.* xxv 2. [< *Midian* a son of Abraham]

mid·i·ron (mid'ī'ərn) *n.* In golf, a five iron.

mid·land (mid'lənd) *n.* The central or interior part of a country or region. — *adj.* Of, pertaining to, or situated in an inland or interior region.

Mid·land (mid'lənd) *n.* The dialects of Middle English spoken in London and the Midlands; esp., **East Midland,** the direct predecessor of Modern English.

mid·most (mid'mōst') *adj.* Middlemost. — *adv.* In the midst or middle. [OE *mydmest*]

mid·night (mid'nīt') *n.* The middle of the night; twelve o'clock at night. — *adj.* **1.** Of or occurring at midnight. **2.** Resembling midnight; very dark. — **to burn the midnight oil** To work or study late into the night.

midnight sun The sun visible at midnight during summer at latitudes greater than 70° north or south of the equator.

mid·rib (mid'rib') *n. Bot.* The central vein of a leaf.

mid·riff (mid'rif) *n.* The part of the body between the chest and the abdomen, in the region of the diaphragm; also, the diaphragm itself. [OE *midd* mid + *hrif* belly]

mid·ship (mid'ship') *adj. Naut.* Of, pertaining to, or situated in the middle of a ship.

mid·ship·man (mid'ship'mən) *n.* *pl.* **·men** (-mən) **1.** In the U.S. Navy, a student training to be commissioned as an officer, esp. at the U.S. Naval Academy at Annapolis. **2.** In the Commonwealth navies, an officer ranking between a naval cadet and the lowest commissioned officer. See table at GRADE. [< *amidshipman*; so called from being amidships when on duty]

mid·ships (mid'ships') *Naut. adv.* Amidships.

midst (midst) *n.* **1.** The condition of being surrounded, as by people or things, engaged, as in an activity, or beset, as by troubles: used chiefly in the phrase **in the midst of.** **2.** The central part; middle. — **in our (your, their) midst** Among us (you, them). — *prep.* Amid. [ME *middest*]

mid·sum·mer (mid'sum'ər) *n.* The middle of summer.

mid·term (mid'tûrm') *n.* **1.** The middle of a term. **2.** *U.S.* An examination given in the middle of a school term.

mid-Vic·to·ri·an (mid'vik·tôr'ē·ən, -tō'rē-) *adj.* **1.** Of or pertaining to the middle period of Queen Victoria's reign, about 1850–80. **2.** Characteristic of the popular moral attitudes, culture, etc., of this period; prudishly old-fashioned. — *n.* **1.** One who lived during this period. **2.** One having mid-Victorian tastes, standards, or ideas.

mid·way (mid'wā') *n.* [*for adj. and adv.* mid'wā') *adv.* In the middle of the way or distance. — *adj.* Being in the middle of the way or distance. — *n. U.S.* At a fair, exposition, etc., the area or mall where amusements, side shows, or exhibitions are situated. [OE *midweg*]

mid·week (mid'wēk') *n.* The middle of the week.

mid·wife (mid'wīf') *n.* *pl.* **·wives** (-wīvz') A woman who assists women in childbirth. [OE *mid* with + *wīf* woman]

mid·wife·ry (mid'wī'fər·ē, -wīf'rē) *n.* The skill or practice of assisting women in childbirth; obstetrics.

mid·win·ter (mid'win'tər) *n.* The middle of winter.

mid·year (mid'yir') *n.* **1.** The middle of the year. **2.** *U.S.* An examination given in the middle of a school year.

mien (mēn) *n.* Manner, bearing, expression, etc. [? Aphetic form of DEMEAN]

miff (mif) *Informal v.t.* **1.** To cause to be offended or annoyed. — *v.i.* **2.** To take offense. — *n.* **1.** An ill-tempered mood; huff. **2.** A minor quarrel; tiff.

mig (mig) *n. U.S. Dial.* **1.** A marble. **2.** *pl.* The game of marbles. Also **mig·gle** (mig'əl).

might[1] (mīt) Past tense of MAY[1].

might[2] (mīt) *n.* **1.** Power to dominate; force; strength. **2.** Physical strength. — **with (all one's) might and main** With all one's strength or ability. [OE *miht*]

might·y (mī'tē) *adj.* **might·i·er, might·i·est 1.** Possessed of might; powerful. **2.** Of great size, importance, etc. — *adv. Informal* Very; exceedingly. — **might'i·ly** (mī'tə·lē) *adv.* — **might'i·ness** *n.*

mi·gnon·ette (min'yən·et') *n.* A plant having racemes of fragrant, yellowish green flowers. Also called *reseda.* [< F]

mi·graine (mī'grān) *n.* A type of severe, recurrent headache, usu. in one side of the head: also called *hemicrania.* [< F < LL < Gk. < *hēmi* half + *kranion* skull]

mi·grant (mī'grənt) *adj.* Migratory. — *n.* One who or that which migrates, as a bird or animal, an itinerant worker, etc. [< L *migrare* to roam, wander]

mi·grate (mī'grāt) *v.i.* **·grat·ed, ·grat·ing 1.** To move from one country, region, etc., to settle in another. **2.** To move seasonally from one region or climate to another, as birds or fish. [< L *migrare*] — **mi'gra·tor** *n.*

— **Syn. 1.** One may *migrate* to or from a place, whether permanently or transiently. *Emigrate* and *immigrate* imply a more or less permanent change. They are both applied to the same action performed by the same person, but *emigrate* refers to the place of departure and *immigrate* to the new home.

mi·gra·tion (mī·grā'shən) *n.* **1.** An act or instance of migrating. **2.** Those participating in a single instance of migrating. **3.** *Chem.* **a** The shifting of one or more atoms from one position to another. **b** The movement of ions under the influence of electromotive force toward one or the other electrode. [< L *migratio*] — **mi·gra'tion·al** *adj.*

mi·gra·to·ry (mī'grə·tôr'ē, -tō'rē) *adj.* **1.** Characterized by migration. **2.** Pertaining to or characteristic of migration or those that migrate. **3.** Roving; nomadic.

mi·ka·do (mi·kä'dō) *n.* *pl.* **·dos** The emperor of Japan. [< Japanese *mi* august + *kado* door]

mike (mīk) *n. Informal* A microphone.

mil (mil) *n.* **1.** A unit of length or diameter, equal to one thousandth of an inch. See table inside back cover. **2.** *Mil.* **a** A unit of angular measure equal to 1/6400 of a circle, or about 0.0560 degree. **b** A unit of angular measure equal to 0.001 radian. [< L *mille* thousand]

mi·la·dy (mi·lā'dē) *n.* *pl.* **·dies 1.** An English noblewoman or gentlewoman: a Continental term. **2.** A fashionable woman. Also **mi·la'di.** [< F < E *my lady*]

mil·age (mī'lij) See MILEAGE.

Mil·an·ese (mil'ən·ēz', -ēs') *adj.* Of or pertaining to Milan or its people. — *n.* *pl.* **·ese** A native or inhabitant of Milan.

milch (milch) *adj.* Giving milk, as a cow. [OE *-milc*]

mild (mīld) *adj.* **1.** Kind or amiable in disposition or manners. **2.** Gentle or moderate: *mild* words; *mild* weather. **3.** Not intense or strong: a *mild* flavor. [OE *milde*] — **mild'ly** *adv.* — **mild'ness** *n.*

mil·dew (mil'doo, -dyoo) *n.* **1.** A disease of plants usu.

caused by a parasitic fungus that deposits a whitish or discolored coating. **2.** Any of the fungi causing such a disease. —*v.t. & v.i.* To affect or be affected with mildew. [OE *meledēaw* honeydew] —**mil′dew·y** *adj.*

mile (mīl) *n.* **1.** A measure of distance used in the U.S. and other English-speaking countries, equal to 5,280 feet, 1,760 yards, or 1,609.35 meters: also called *statute mile.* See table inside back cover. **2.** Any considerable distance or amount. —**geographical, nautical, or air mile** One sixtieth of a degree of the earth's equator, or 6,080.2 feet. —**international nautical mile** A unit of distance by sea equal to 1,852 meters or 6,076.103 feet. [OE < LL < L *mille (passuum)* thousand (paces)]

mile·age (mī′lij) *n.* **1.** Total length or distance expressed in miles. **2.** Number of miles traveled by an automobile, etc., as estimated for each gallon of fuel used. **3.** Period of usefulness, estimated by miles used or traveled. **4.** U.S.A traveling allowance estimated at a fixed amount per mile. Also spelled *milage.*

mile·post (mīl′pōst′) *n.* A post or similar marker indicating distance in miles, as along a highway.

mil·er (mī′lər) *n.* A runner, racehorse, etc., trained to compete in mile races.

mile·stone (mīl′stōn′) *n.* **1.** A post or stone set up to indicate mileage from a given point. **2.** An important event or turning point.

mi·lieu (mē·lyœ′) *n.* Environment; surroundings. [< F < OF *mi* middle + *lieu* place]

mil·i·tant (mil′ə·tənt) *adj.* **1.** Combative or warlike; aggressive. **2.** Positive and forceful in action; resolute. **3.** Engaged in conflict; fighting. —*n.* One who is militant. [< L *militare* to be a soldier] —**mil′i·tan·cy** *n.* —**mil′i·tant·ly** *adv.*

mil·i·ta·rism (mil′ə·tə·riz′əm) *n.* **1.** The ideals characteristic of a military class; emphasis on martial qualities. **2.** A national policy that promotes a powerful military position. —**mil′i·ta·rist** *n.* —**mil′i·ta·ris′tic** *adj.*

mil·i·ta·rize (mil′ə·tə·rīz) *v.t.* **·rized, ·riz·ing 1.** To convert to a military system or adapt for military purposes. **2.** To prepare for warfare. —**mil′i·ta·ri·za′tion** *n.*

mil·i·tar·y (mil′ə·ter′ē) *adj.* **1.** Of or pertaining to the armed forces. **2.** Of or characteristic of warfare. **3.** Characteristic of or befitting a soldier or soldiers. —*n.* Soldiers collectively; armed forces: preceded by *the.* [< F < L < *miles, militis* soldier] —**mil′i·tar′i·ly** *adv.*

military police Soldiers who perform police duty.

mil·i·tate (mil′ə·tāt) *v.i.* **·tat·ed, ·tat·ing** To have influence or effect: with *against,* or, more rarely, *for:* The evidence *militated* against him. [< L *miles, militis* soldier]

mi·li·tia (mə·lish′ə) *n.* A body of citizens enrolled and drilled in military organizations other than the regular military forces, and called out only in emergencies. [< L, military service]

mi·li·tia·men (mə·lish′ə·mən) *n. pl.* **·men** (mən) A member of the militia.

milk (milk) *n.* **1.** The opaque, whitish liquid secreted by the mammary glands of female mammals for the nourishment of their young; esp., cow's milk. **2.** Any of various liquids resembling this, as the sap of certain plants, or the liquid contained in a coconut. —*v.t.* **1.** To draw or express milk from the mammary glands of. **2.** To draw off or drain by or as by milking. **3.** To draw or extract something from: to *milk* someone of information. **4.** To exploit; take advantage of: to *milk* a client. —*v.i.* **5.** To milk (a cow, cows, etc.). **6.** To yield milk. [OE *meolc, milc*]

milk leg A painful swelling of the leg in women shortly after childbirth, resulting from phlebitis of the femoral vein.

milk·maid (milk′mād′) *n.* A woman or girl who milks cows or works in a dairy.

milk·man (milk′man′) *n. pl.* **·men** (-men′) A man who sells or delivers milk.

milk of magnesia A white, aqueous suspension of magnesium hydroxide, $Mg(OH)_2$, used as a laxative and antacid.

milk shake A drink made of chilled, flavored milk, and sometimes ice cream, shaken, beaten, or whipped.

milk snake A nonpoisonous snake of eastern North America, feeding on rodents, frogs, etc.

milk·sop (milk′sop′) *n.* A weak, timorous fellow; sissy.

milk sugar Lactose.

milk·toast (milk′tōst′) *n.* **1.** A dish of buttered toast served in hot milk. **2.** See MILQUETOAST.

milk tooth A temporary tooth of a young mammal.

milk·weed (milk′wēd′) *n.* Any of various herbs, shrubs, and vines having milky juice.

milk·y (mil′kē) *adj.* **milk·i·er, milk·i·est 1.** Resembling or suggestive of milk. **2.** Containing or yielding milk or a milklike substance. **3.** Very mild or bland. —**milk′i·ly** *adv.* —**milk′i·ness** *n.*

Milky Way A luminous band visible across the night sky, composed of distant stars and nebulae not separately distinguishable to the naked eye: also called the *Galaxy.*

mill¹ (mil) *n.* **1.** A machine or mechanical device by means of which a solid or coarse substance is ground, crushed, or reduced to a pulp. **2.** A device, machine, building, or establishment in which grain is ground. **3.** Any of various machines that process materials used in combination: *sawmill; windmill.* **4.** A manufacturing or industrial establishment; factory. **5.** A steel roller for impressing a design on a printing plate, etc. **6.** A trying experience; ordeal: used chiefly in the phrase **through the mill.** —*v.t.* **1.** To grind, roll, shape, polish, etc., in or with a mill. **2.** To raise, indent, or ridge the edge of (a coin, etc.). **3.** To cause to move in a circle, as cattle. —*v.i.* **4.** To move with a circular or surging motion, as cattle. [OE < LL < L *mola* millstone]

mill² (mil) *n.* A monetary denomination of the U.S., one tenth of a cent. [< L *mille* thousand]

mill·dam (mil′dam′) *n.* A dam constructed across a watercourse to raise its level sufficiently to turn a mill wheel.

mil·len·ni·um (mi·len′ē·əm) *n. pl.* **·ni·a** (-nē·ə) or **·ni·ums** **1.** A period of a thousand years. **2.** The thousand years during which Christ is to rule the world. *Rev.* xx 1–5. **3.** Any period of happiness, prosperity, etc. [< NL < *mille* thousand + *annus* year] —**mil·len′ni·al** *adj.*

mil·le·ped (mil′ə·ped), **mil·le·pede** (mil′ə·pēd) See MILLIPEDE.

mil·le·pore (mil′ə·pôr, -pōr) *n. Zool.* Any of a group of corals that form large branching structures containing numerous tiny surface cavities.

mill·er (mil′ər) *n.* **1.** One who operates or tends a mill. **2.** A milling machine. **3.** Any of various moths having pale, dusty wings.

mil·let (mil′it) *n.* **1.** A grass cultivated in the U.S. for forage, and in many parts of the Old World for its small, edible seeds. **2.** Any of various similar grasses. **3.** The seed of these grasses. [< F, dim. of *mil* < L *milium*]

milli- *combining form* In the metric system and in technical use, one thousandth of a (specified unit), as in the following: **milliampere, millivolt.** [< L *mille* thousand]

mil·liard (mil′yərd) *n. Brit.* A thousand millions: called a *billion* in the U.S. [< F < Provençal *milhar* thousand]

mil·li·gram (mil′ə·gram) *n.* A unit of weight in the metric system, equal to one thousandth of a gram. Also **mil′li·gramme.** See table inside back cover.

mil·li·li·ter (mil′ə·lē′tər) *n.* A unit of capacity in the metric system, equal to one thousandth of a liter. Also **mil′li·li·tre.** See table inside back cover.

mil·li·me·ter (mil′ə·mē′tər) *n.* A unit of length in the metric system, equal to one thousandth of a meter. Also **mil′li·me′tre.** See table inside back cover.

mil·li·mi·cron (mil′ə·mī′kron) *n.* A unit of length equal to one thousandth of a micron: also called *micromillimeter.*

mil·li·ner (mil′ə·nər) *n.* One who makes or sells women's hats. [< *Milaner* an inhabitant of Milan, Italy]

mil·li·ner·y (mil′ə·ner′ē, -nər·ē) *n.* **1.** The articles made or sold by milliners. **2.** The business of a milliner.

mil·lion (mil′yən) *n.* **1.** A thousand thousands, written as 1,000,000: a cardinal number. **2.** A million units of money, as of dollars: He is worth a *million.* **3.** An indefinitely great number. —*adj.* **1.** Being a million in number. **2.** Very many. [< OF < Ital. *millione* (now *milione*), aug. of *mille* thousand] —**mil′lionth** *n. & adj.*

mil·lion·aire (mil′yən·âr′) *n.* One whose wealth is valued at a million or more, as of dollars, pounds, etc. Also **mil′·lion·naire′.** [< F *millionnaire*] —**mil′lion·air′ess** *n.fem.*

mil·li·pede (mil′ə·pēd) *n.* Any of various wormlike animals having a rounded body divided into numerous segments, nearly all of which bear two pairs of appendages: also called *wireworm:* also spelled *milliped, millepede.* Also **mil′li·ped** (-ped). [< L *mille* thousand + *pes, pedis* foot]

mill·pond (mil′pond′) *n.* A body of water dammed up to supply power for running a mill.

mill·race (mil′rās′) *n.* **1.** The current of water that operates a mill wheel. **2.** The channel in which it runs.

mil·li·rem (mil′ə·rem) *n.* One thousandth of a rem; the term used in measuring the absorption of radiation by humans.

mill·stone (mil′stōn′) *n.* **1.** One of a pair of thick, heavy, stone disks used for grinding grain, etc. **2.** That which crushes or bears down. **3.** A heavy or burdensome weight.

mill·stream (mil′strēm′) *n.* **1.** A stream whose current is used to operate a mill. **2.** The water in a millrace.

mill wheel A water wheel that drives a mill.

mill·wright (mil′rīt′) *n.* One who plans, builds, or repairs mills or mill machinery.

mi·lord (mi·lôrd′) *n.* An English nobleman or gentleman: a Continental term. [< F < E *my lord*]

milque·toast (milk′tōst′) *n.* A timid, meek, or very apologetic person: also spelled *milktoast.* [after Caspar *Milquetoast,* a creation by H. T. Webster, U.S. cartoonist]

milt (milt) *n.* **1.** Fish sperm. **2.** The reproductive organs of a male fish when filled with seminal fluid. —*v.t.* To impregnate (fish roe) with milt. [OE *milte*]

Mil·ton·ic (mil·ton′ik) *adj.* Of or like the poet Milton or his works; sublime. Also **Mil·to′ni·an** (-tō′nē·ən).

Mil·town (mil′toun) *n.* Proprietary name for a brand of meprobamate used in pill form as a tranquilizer.

mime (mīm) *n.* **1.** An actor, comedian, etc., who specializes in pantomime. **2.** In ancient Rome or Greece, a type of dramatic farce in which actual persons or events were ludicrously represented. **3.** An actor in such performances. — *v.* **mimed, mim·ing** — *v.i.* **1.** To play a part with gestures and, usu., without words. — *v.t.* **2.** To portray by pantomime. [< L < Gk. *mimos*] — **mim′er** *n.*

mim·e·o·graph (mim′ē·ə·graf′, -gräf′) *n.* **1.** A duplicating device that reproduces copies of written matter etc., by means of a stencil wrapped around a drum: also **Mim′e·o·graph′. 2.** A copy so made. — *v.t. & v.i.* To reproduce by mimeograph. [< *Mimeograph*, a trade name]

mi·met·ic (mi·met′ik, mī-) *adj.* **1.** Tending to imitate or mimic; imitative. **2.** Pertaining to or like mimicry. **3.** Make-believe. [< Gk. < *mimēsis* imitation] — **mi·met′i·cal·ly** *adv.*

mim·ic (mim′ik) *v.t.* **·icked, ·ick·ing 1.** To imitate the speech or actions of. **2.** To copy closely; ape. **3.** To have or assume the color, shape, etc., of. — *n.* **1.** One who mimics or imitates. **2.** A copy; imitation. — *adj.* **1.** Of the nature of mimicry; imitative; mimetic. **2.** Make-believe; simulated; mock. [< L < Gk. < *mimos* mime] — **mim′i·cal** *adj.* — **mim′ick·er** *n.*

mim·ic·ry (mim′ik·rē) *n. pl.* **·ries 1.** The act, practice, or art of mimicking or imitating. **2.** *Biol.* A resemblance of an organism to another or to its environment, for purposes of concealment, etc.

mi·mo·sa (mi·mō′sə, -zə) *n.* Any of a group of leguminous tropical herbs, shrubs, or trees with feathery foliage, and small, often yellow, flowers. [< NL < L *mimus* mime]

min·a·ret (min′ə·ret′) *n.* A high, slender tower attached to a Moslem mosque and surrounded by balconies, from which a muezzin calls the summons to prayer. [< Sp. < Turkish < Arabic *manārah* lamp, lighthouse]

min·a·to·ry (min′ə·tôr′ē, -tō′rē) *adj.* Conveying or expressing a threat. Also **min′a·to′ri·al.** [< OF < LL < *minari* to threaten] — **min′a·to′ri·al·ly, min′a·to′ri·ly** *adv.*

mince (mins) *v.* **minced, minc·ing** *v.t.* **1.** To cut or chop into small bits, as food. **2.** To subdivide minutely. **3.** To moderate the force or strength of (language, ideas, etc.): He didn't *mince* words with her. **4.** To say or express with affected primness or elegance. — *v.i.* **5.** To walk with short steps or affected daintiness. **6.** To speak or behave with affected primness. — *n. Chiefly Brit.* Any finely chopped food, as mincemeat. [< OF < L *minuere* to lessen, make smaller] — **minc′er** *n.*

mince·meat (mins′mēt′) *n.* A mixture of chopped apples, raisins, spices, etc., used as a pie filling. — **to make mincemeat of** To cut up, destroy, or annihilate utterly.

mince pie A pie filled with mincemeat.

minc·ing (min′sing) *adj.* Affectedly precise, refined, or dainty, as in manner, gait, etc. — **minc′ing·ly** *adv.*

mind (mīnd) *n.* **1.** The aggregate of processes originating in or associated with the brain, involving conscious and subconscious thought, interpretation of perceptions, insight, imagination, etc. **2.** Memory: within the *mind* of man. **3.** Opinion; sentiment: to change one's *mind.* **4.** Desire; inclination: to have a *mind* to leave. **5.** Way or state of thinking or feeling: a logical *mind.* **6.** Intellectual power or capacity: He has the *mind* for such work. **7.** A highly intelligent individual. **8.** Sound mental condition; sanity. **9.** Attention: to keep one's *mind* on a subject. — **Syn.** See INTELLECT. — **a piece of one's mind 1.** One's bluntly or candidly expressed opinion. **2.** A severe scolding. — **on one's mind** In one's thoughts, esp. so as to cause concern or worry. — **out of one's mind 1.** Insane; mad. **2.** Distracted; frantic. — **to bear (or keep) in mind** To focus one's thoughts or attention on; remember. — **to be of one mind** To be in accord; agree. — **to have a good (or great) mind** To feel strongly disposed (to do something). — **to have in mind** To be thinking about. — **to make up one's mind** To decide; be determined. — *v.t.* **1.** To pay attention to. **2.** To be careful concerning: *Mind* your step. **3.** To obey: *Mind* your leaders. **4.** To look after; tend. **5.** To object to: Do you *mind* the noise? **6.** *Dial.* To notice; perceive. **7.** *Dial.* To remember. — *v.i.* **8.** To pay attention; heed: *Mind* you now, not a word. **9.** To be obedient. **10.** To be concerned; care; object: I don't *mind.* **11.** To be careful. [OE *gemynd*] — **mind′er** *n.*

mind·ed (mīn′did) *adj.* **1.** Having or characterized by a (specified kind of) mind: used in combination: *evil-minded.* **2.** Having an inclination; disposed: often with *to.*

mind·ful (mīnd′fəl) *adj.* Keeping in mind; heeding; aware. — **mind′ful·ly** *adv.* — **mind′ful·ness** *n.*

mind·less (mīnd′lis) *adj.* **1.** Devoid of intelligence; senseless. **2.** Not giving heed or attention; careless. — **mind′less·ly** *adv.* — **mind′less·ness** *n.*

mind-set (mīnd′set′) *n.* Prevailing attitudes or opinions of an individual or of a region or country.

mine¹ (mīn) *n.* **1.** An excavation in the earth dug to obtain coal, precious stones, etc. **2.** The site of such an excavation, together with its buildings, equipment, etc. **3.** Any deposit of ore, coal, etc. **4.** Any source or abundant store of something: a *mine* of talent. **5.** *Mil.* **a** An encased explosive charge placed in the earth or water and designed to be actuated by contact, a time fuse, or remote control. **b** Formerly, an underground tunnel dug beneath an enemy's fortifications. — *v.* **mined, min·ing** *v.t.* **1.** To dig (coal, ores, etc.) from the earth. **2.** To dig into (the earth, etc.) for coal, ores, etc. **3.** To make by digging, as a tunnel. **4.** To obtain useful material or information from. **5.** To undermine by slow or secret means. **6.** To place an explosive mine in or under. — *v.i.* **7.** To dig in a mine for coal, ores, etc. **8.** To make a tunnel, etc., by digging. **9.** To place explosive mines. [< OF < Celtic. Cf. Irish *mein* vein of metal]

mine² (mīn) *pron.* **1.** The possessive case of the pronoun *I,* used predicatively: That book is *mine.* **2.** The one or ones belonging or relating to me: His work is better than *mine.* — **of mine** Belonging or relating to me; my. — *pronominal adj. Archaic* My: *mine* eyes. [OE *mīn*]

mine detector An electromagnetic device used to locate the position of explosive mines. — **mine detection**

mine·field (mīn′fēld′) *n.* An area on land or in water in which explosive mines have been systematically placed.

mine·lay·er (mīn′lā′ər) *n.* A vessel provided with special equipment for laying explosive mines.

min·er (mīn′ər) *n.* One who works in a mine.

min·er·al (min′ər·əl) *n.* **1.** A naturally ocurring inorganic substance having a characteristic set of physical properties, a definite range of chemical composition, and a molecular structure usu. expressed in crystalline form. **2.** Inorganic material, esp. as distinguished from animal or vegetable matter. — *adj.* Of, like, or containing a mineral or minerals. [< OF < Med.L < *mineralis* of a mine]

min·er·al·ize (min′ər·əl·īz′) *v.t.* **·ized, ·iz·ing 1.** To convert (a metal) to a mineral. **2.** To convert to a mineral substance; petrify. **3.** To impregnate with minerals. — **min′er·al·iz′er** *n.* — **min′er·al·i·za′tion** *n.*

min·er·al·o·gy (min′ə·ral′ə·jē, -rol′-) *n. pl.* **·gies 1.** The science of minerals, embracing their origin, structure, characteristics, properties, and classification. **2.** A treatise on minerals. — **min′er·a·log′i·cal** (-ər·ə·loj′i·kəl) *adj.* — **min′er·a·log′i·cal·ly** *adv.* — **min′er·al·o·gist** *n.*

mineral oil Any of various oils, esp. petroleum, derived from minerals and used as a fuel, in medicine, etc.

mineral spring A spring containing natural mineral water.

mineral water Any water naturally containing or artificially impregnated with mineral salts or gases.

mineral wool A fibrous, woollike material, used as packing and as insulation: also called *rock wool, slag wool.*

Mi·ner·va (mi·nûr′və) In Roman mythology, the goddess of wisdom and invention: identified with the Greek *Athena.*

min·e·stro·ne (min′ə·strō′nē, *Ital.* mē′nä·strō′nä) *n. Italian* A thick vegetable soup having a meat stock.

mine·sweep·er (mīn′swē′pər) *n.* A ship equipped to detect, destroy, and remove marine mines.

Ming (ming) *n.* In Chinese history, the last ruling dynasty (1368–1644) of truly Chinese origin, noted for its scholarly and artistic achievements, esp. for its porcelains.

min·gle (ming′gəl) *v.* **·gled, ·gling** *v.t.* **1.** To mix or unite together; blend. **2.** To make by combining. — *v.i.* **3.** To be or become mixed, united, or closely joined. **4.** To enter into company. [OE *mengan*] — **min′gler** *n.*

mini- *combining form* Small; tiny: *miniskirt.* [< L *minimus* least, smallest]

min·i·a·ture (min′ē·ə·chər, min′ə·chər) *n.* **1.** A portrayal or representation of anything on a small scale. **2.** Reduced dimensions, form, or extent. **3.** In art: **a** A painting done on a very small scale. **b** The art of executing such paintings. — *adj.* On a very small or reduced scale. [< F < Ital. < L *miniatus* painted red; later infl. by L *minuere* to lessen]

min·i·a·tur·ize (min′ē·ə·chər·īz′, min′ə·chər·īz′) *v.t.* **·ized, ·iz·ing** To reduce the size of. — **min′i·a·tur·i·za′tion** *n.*

min·im (min′im) *n.* **1.** A small liquid measure, ⅟₆₀ of a fluid dram, or about one drop. See table inside back cover. **2.** *Music Chiefly Brit.* A half note. **3.** One who or that which is very small or insignificant. **4.** A small particle; jot. — *adj.* Extremely small. [< L *minimus* least, smallest]

min·i·mal (min′ə·məl) *adj.* Of a minimum amount, degree, etc.; least possible; smallest. — **min′i·mal·ly** *adv.*

min·i·mize (min′ə·mīz) *v.t.* **·mized, ·miz·ing 1.** To reduce to the smallest amount or degree. **2.** To regard or represent as of the least possible importance, size, etc. Also *Brit.* **min′-i·mise.** — **min′i·mi·za′tion** *n.* — **min′i·miz′er** *n.*

min·i·mum (min′ə·məm) *n.* *pl.* **·mums** or **·ma** (-mə) **1.** The least possible quantity, amount, or degree. **2.** The lowest quantity, degree, number, etc., reached or recorded. — *adj.* **1.** Consisting of or showing the least amount or degree possible, permissible, attainable, etc. **2.** Of or pertaining to a minimum or minimums. [< L, neut. of *minimus*]

minimum wage The smallest wage, fixed by law or by agreement, an employer may offer an employee.

min·ing (mī′ning) *n.* The act, process, or business of extracting coal, ores, etc., from mines.

min·ion (min′yən) *n.* **1.** A servile favorite or follower. **2.** *Printing* A size of type, 7-point. [< F *mignon* darling]

min·i·skirt (min′i·skûrt) *n.* A very short skirt.

min·is·ter (min′is·tər) *n.* **1.** One who is authorized to administer the sacraments, preach, etc., in a church; clergyman; pastor. **2.** One appointed to head an administrative department of a government. **3.** One authorized to represent his government to another government in diplomatic matters and ranking next below an ambassador. **4.** One who or that which acts as the agent of another person or thing: a *minister* of good. — **Syn.** See AMBASSADOR. — *v.i.* **1.** To provide for the wants or needs of someone. **2.** To be helpful or useful. — *v.t.* **3.** To administer or apply (a sacrament, medicine, etc.). [< OF < L *minister* attendant]

min·is·te·ri·al (min′is·tir′ē·əl) *adj.* **1.** Of, or pertaining to a minister or to the ministry. **2.** Administrative; executive. **3.** Contributive; instrumental. — **min′is·te′ri·al·ly** *adv.*

min·is·trant (min′is·trənt) *adj.* Ministering — *n.* One who ministers. [< L < *ministrare* to serve]

min·is·tra·tion (min′is·trā′shən) *n.* **1.** The act of serving. **2.** *Often pl.* Help or aid. — **min′is·tra′tive** *adj.*

min·is·try (min′is·trē) *n.* *pl.* **·tries** **1.** The profession, duties, length of service, etc., of a minister of religion. **2.** The clergy. **3.** *Govt.* **a** An executive or administrative department presided over by a minister; also, its building. **b** A body of ministers collectively. **c** The duties of a minister; also, his term of office. **4.** The act of ministering.

min·i·track (min′i·trak′) *n.* *Aerospace* An electronic system for tracking earth satellites by the radio signals received from the satellite. Also **Min′i·track′.**

min·i·um (min′ē·əm) *n.* A vivid, opaque, red lead oxide Pb₃O₄, used chiefly as a pigment: also called *red lead.* [< L]

min·i·ver (min′ə·vər) *n.* **1.** A white or gray and white fur, used in the Middle Ages as trimming, etc. **2.** Any white fur, as ermine. [< OF *menu vair,* lit., little spotted (fur)]

mink (mingk) *n.* **1.** A semiaquatic, slender-bodied carnivorous mammal, resembling a weasel. **2.** The valuable, soft, brown fur of this mammal. [< Scand. Cf. Sw. *menk.*]

min·ne·sing·er (min′ə·sing′ər) *n.* A lyric poet and singer of medieval Germany. [< G < *minne* love + *singer* singer]

min·now (min′ō) *n.* *pl.* **min·nows** (*Rare* **min·now**) **1.** A small European cyprinoid fish of the carp family. **2.** Any of various related fishes. **3.** Any small fish. [ME *menawe*]

Mi·no·an (mi·nō′ən) *adj.* **1.** Of or pertaining to an advanced Bronze Age civilization that flourished in Crete from about 3000 to 1100 B.C. **2.** Designating two varieties of linear script, **Linear A,** deciphered in 1957, and **Linear B,** deciphered in 1952 and found to be an Achaean dialect of Greek.

mi·nor (mī′nər) *adj.* **1.** Less in quantity, number, or extent. **2.** Of secondary or lesser importance: a *minor* poet. **3.** Under legal age. **4.** *Music* **a** Denoting an interval smaller by a half step than the corresponding major interval. **b** Denoting a triad in which the third above the fundamental is minor. **c** Denoting a type of diatonic scale, or a key based on this scale. **5.** Sad or plaintive; mournful: said of a sound or voice. **6.** *U.S.* In education, of or pertaining to an area of specialized study usu. requiring fewer class hours than a major field of study. **7.** Of or constituting a minority — *n.* **1.** One who is below full legal age. **2.** *U.S.* In education, a minor subject or area of study. **3.** *Music* A minor chord, interval, scale, key, etc. — *v.i.* *U.S.* In education, to study as a minor subject: with *in*: to *minor* in philosophy. [< L]

mi·nor·i·ty (mə·nôr′ə·tē, -nor′-, mī-) *n.* *pl.* **·ties** **1.** The smaller in number of two parts or parties: opposed to *majority.* **2.** A racial, religious, political, or national group smaller than and usu. different in some ways from the larger group of which it is a part. **3.** The state or period of being under legal age. [< F *minorité* or L *minoritas*]

minor league *U.S.* Any professional sports league not having the standing of a major league. — **mi·nor-league** (mī′nər·lēg′) *adj.*

minor suit In bridge, diamonds or clubs.

Mi·nos (mī′nəs, -nos) In Greek mythology: **a** A king of Crete who became a judge of the lower world after his death. **b** His grandson. [< Gk. *Mīnōs*]

Min·o·taur (min′ə·tôr) In Greek mythology, a monster with the body of a man and the head of a bull, confined in the Labyrinth until it was killed by Theseus. [< L < Gk. *Minōtauros*]

min·ster (min′stər) *n.* *Chiefly Brit.* **1.** A monastery church. **2.** A cathedral or large church. [OE *mynster*]

min·strel (min′strəl) *n.* **1.** In the Middle Ages, a wandering musician who made his living by singing and reciting poetry. **2.** A performer in a minstrel show. **3.** *Poetic* A poet, musician, etc. [< OF < LL *ministerialis* servant, jester]

minstrel show A comic variety show of songs, dances, jokes, etc., given by a company of performers in blackface.

min·strel·sy (min′strəl·sē) *n.* *pl.* **·sies** **1.** The art or occupation of a minstrel. **2.** Ballads or lyrics collectively, esp. those sung by minstrels. **3.** A troupe of minstrels.

mint¹ (mint) *n.* **1.** A place where the coin of a country is lawfully manufactured. **2.** An abundant supply, esp. of money. **3.** A source of manufacture or inspiration. — *v.t.* **1.** To make (money) by stamping; to coin. **2.** To invent or fabricate (a word, etc.). — *adj.* In original condition; unused. [OE < L < *Moneta* epithet of Juno, whose temple at Rome was used as a mint] — **mint′er** *n.*

mint² (mint) *n.* **1.** Any of several aromatic herbs; esp. spearmint and peppermint, used as a flavoring, garnish, etc. **2.** A mint-flavored candy. [OE < L < Gk. *mintha*]

mint·age (min′tij) *n.* **1.** The act or process of minting. **2.** The money manufactured by a mint. **3.** The fee paid for coining. **4.** The authorized impression stamped upon a coin.

mint julep A drink made of bourbon mixed with crushed ice and sugar and flavored with sprigs of fresh mint.

min·u·end (min′yōō·end) *n.* *Math.* The number from which another is to be subtracted. [< L *minuere* to lessen]

min·u·et (min′yōō·et′) *n.* **1.** A stately dance for couples, introduced in France in the 17th century. **2.** Music for or in the manner of this dance, in moderate triple meter. [< F < L *minutus*]

mi·nus (mī′nəs) *prep.* **1.** Lessened or reduced by; less. **2.** *Informal* Lacking; deprived of. — *adj.* **1.** Of or denoting subtraction. **2.** Negative: a *minus* value. **3.** Less in quality or value than: a C *minus.* **4.** *Informal* Non-existent; lacking: His chances were *minus.* — *n.* **1.** The minus sign (−). **2.** A minus quantity. **3.** A deficit or loss. [< L, neut. of *minor*]

mi·nus·cule (mi·nus′kyōōl, min′ə·skyōōl) *n.* Any small or lower-case letter. — *adj.* **1.** Of, pertaining to, like, or composed of minuscules. **2.** Very small; miniature. [< L *minusculus,* dim. of *minor* less]

minus sign A sign (−) denoting subtraction or a negative quantity.

min·ute¹ (min′it) *n.* **1.** The 60th part of an hour; 60 seconds. **2.** Any very brief period of time; moment. **3.** A specific instant of time. **4.** A unit of angular measure equal to the 60th part of a degree, indicated by the sign (′) and called **a minute of arc.** **5.** A memorandum. **6.** *pl.* An official record of the business discussed and transacted at a meeting, conference, etc. — **up to the minute** In accord with the latest fashion, equipment, etc. — *v.t.* **·ut·ed, ·ut·ing** **1.** To make a minute or brief note of; record. **2.** To time to the minute. [< F < Med.L < L *minutus* small]

mi·nute² (mī·nōōt′, -nyōōt′, mi-) *adj.* **1.** Exceedingly small; tiny. **2.** Having little importance or value. **3.** Demonstrating or characterized by careful, precise attention to small details. [< L *minutus* small] — **mi·nute′ness** *n.*

min·ute·hand (min′it) The hand that indicates the minute on a clock or similar timepiece.

min·ute·ly¹ (min′it·lē) *adj. & adv.* At intervals of a minute.

mi·nute·ly² (mī·nōōt′lē, -nyōōt′-, mi-) *adv.* In a minute manner or degree; with great detail, precision, or exactness.

min·ute·man (min′it·man′) *n.* *pl.* **·men** (-men′) In the American Revolution, one of the armed citizens who volunteered to be ready for combat at a minute's notice.

minute steak (min′it) A small, thin cut of steak that can be cooked quickly.

mi·nu·ti·ae (mi·nōō′shi·ē, -nyōō′-) *n.* *pl.* of **mi·nu·ti·a** (-shē-ə, -shə) Small or unimportant details; trifles. [< L]

minx (mingks) *n.* **1.** A saucy, bold, or flirtatious girl. **2.** *Archaic* A wanton woman. [Prob. < LG *minsk* impudent woman. Akin to G *mensch* person.]

Mi·o·cene (mī′ə·sēn) *adj.* Pertaining to or designating the fourth geological epoch of the Tertiary period. See chart for GEOLOGY. — *n.* The Miocene epoch or series. [< Gk. *meiōn* less + *kainos* recent]

mir·a·cle (mir′ə·kəl) *n.* **1.** An event that appears to be neither a part nor result of any known natural law or agency and is therefore often attributed to a supernatural source. **2.** Any wonderful or amazing thing, fact, or event. **3.** One who or that which is of surpassing merit or excellence. **4.** A miracle play. [< F < L < *mirari* to wonder]

miracle play A medieval play dealing with the lives of saints and with their miracles. Compare MYSTERY PLAY.

mi·rac·u·lous (mi·rak′yə·ləs) *adj.* **1.** Wonderful and amazing. **2.** Apparently caused by the direct intervention of a supernatural power. **3.** Having the power to work miracles. — **Syn.** See SUPERNATURAL. — **mi·rac′u·lous·ly** *adv.* **mi·rac′u·lous·ness** *n.*

mi·rage (mi·räzh′) *n.* **1.** An optical illusion, as of a sheet of water, upside-down ship, etc., that sometimes appears in a desert or in the air, and is caused by reflection from layers of atmosphere having different densities. **2.** Anything that appears to be real but is not. [< F < L *mirari* to wonder at]

mire (mīr) *n.* **1.** An area of wet, yielding earth; swampy ground. **2.** Deep mud or slush. — *v.* **mired, mir·ing** *v.t.* **1.** To cause to sink or become stuck in mire. **2.** To smear or soil with mud; defile. **3.** To entangle or entrap. — *v.i.* **4.** To sink in mire; bog down. [< ON *mȳrr* swampy ground] — **mir′y** *adj.* — **mir′i·ness** *n.*

Mir·i·am (mir′ē·əm) Sister of Moses and Aaron. *Ex.* xv 20.

mirk (mûrk), **mirk·i·ly** (mûrk′i·lē), etc. See MURK, etc.

mir·ror (mir′ər) *n.* **1.** Any smooth reflecting surface, as of glass backed with a coating of silver, aluminum, etc. **2.** Whatever reflects or depicts truly. — *v.t.* To reflect or show an image of, as in a mirror. [< OF < LL < L *mirari* to wonder at, admire]

mirth (mûrth) *n.* Spirited gaiety; social merriment. [OE *myrig* pleasant, merry]

mirth·ful (mûrth′fəl) *adj.* Full of or characterized by mirth; merry. — **mirth′ful·ly** *adv.* — **mirth′ful·ness** *n.*

MIRV (mûrv) Multiple Independently-targeted Reentry Vehicle.

mis-[1] *prefix* Bad; amiss; badly; wrongly; unfavorably: used in combination, as in *miscalculate, miscolor, miscopy,* etc. [OE *mis-* wrong; infl. in meaning by ME *mes-* mis-[2]]

mis-[2] *prefix* Bad; amiss; not: found with negative or depreciatory force in words borrowed from Old French: *misadventure, miscreant.* [< OF *mes-* < L *minus* less]

mis-[3] Var. of MISO-.

mis·ad·ven·ture (mis′əd·ven′chər) *n.* A disastrous event.

mis·al·li·ance (mis′ə·lī′əns) *n.* An undesirable alliance or marriage. [< F *mésalliance*]

mis·al·ly (mis′ə·lī′) *v.t.* **·lied, ·ly·ing** To ally badly.

mis·an·thrope (mis′ən·thrōp, miz′-) *n.* One who hates or distrusts his fellow men. Also **mis·an·thro·pist** (mis·an′thrə·pist). [< Gk. < *misein* to hate + *anthrōpos* man]

mis·an·throp·ic (mis′ən·throp′ik) *adj.* Of, pertaining to, or like a misanthrope. Also **mis·an·throp′i·cal.** — **mis′an·throp′i·cal·ly** *adv.*

mis·an·thro·py (mis·an′thrə·pē) *n.* Hatred of mankind.

mis·ap·ply (mis′ə·plī′) *v.t.* **·plied, ·ply·ing** To use or apply incorrectly or wrongfully. — **mis′ap·pli·ca′tion** *n.*

mis·ap·pre·hend (mis′ap·ri·hend′) *v.t.* To apprehend or interpret wrongly. — **mis′ap·pre·hen′sion** *n.*

mis·ap·pro·pri·ate (mis′ə·prō′prē·āt) *v.t.* **·at·ed, ·at·ing** To use or take improperly or dishonestly; misapply. — **mis′ap·pro′pri·a′tion** *n.*

mis·be·come (mis′bi·kum′) *v.t.* **·came, ·come, ·com·ing** To be unbecoming or not appropriate to.

mis·be·have (mis′bi·hāv′) *v.i. & v.t.* **·haved, ·hav·ing** To behave badly. — **mis′be·hav′ior** *n.*

mis·be·lief (mis′bi·lēf′) *n.* False belief or opinion.

mis·be·lieve (mis′bi·lēv′) *v.* **·lieved, ·liev·ing** *v.i.* To hold a false, unorthodox, or heretical belief. — **mis′be·liev′er** *n.*

mis·cal·cu·late (mis·kal′kyə·lāt) *v.t. & v.i.* **·lat·ed, ·lat·ing** To calculate wrongly. — **mis′cal·cu·la′tion** *n.*

mis·call (mis·kôl′) *v.t.* To call by a wrong name.

mis·car·riage (mis·kar′ij) *n.* **1.** A premature delivery of a nonviable fetus. **2.** Failure to bring about a proper conclusion. **3.** Failure to reach an intended destination.

mis·car·ry (mis·kar′ē) *v.i.* **·ried, ·ry·ing** **1.** To fail; go wrong. **2.** To bring forth a fetus prematurely. **3.** To fail to reach an intended destination, as freight, mail, etc.

mis·cast (mis·kast′, -käst′) *v.t.* **·cast, ·cast·ing** To cast (a play, role, or an actor) inappropriately.

mis·ce·ge·na·tion (mis′i·jə·nā′shən) *n.* Interbreeding of ethnic stocks or races. [< L *miscere* to mix + *genus* race] — **mis′ce·ge·net′ic** (-jə·net′ik) *adj.*

mis·cel·la·ne·ous (mis′ə·lā′nē·əs) *adj.* **1.** Composed of various and diverse things or elements; mixed. **2.** Possessing diverse qualities or capabilities. [< L *miscellus* mixed] — **mis′cel·la′ne·ous·ly** *adv.* — **mis′cel·la′ne·ous·ness** *n.*

mis·cel·la·ny (mis′ə·lā′nē) *n. pl.* **·nies** A miscellaneous collection, esp. of literary works.

mis·chance (mis·chans′, -chäns′) *n.* Bad luck; also, an instance of bad luck; mishap.

mis·chief (mis′chif) *n.* **1.** Action, often playful, that causes some irritation, harm, or trouble. **2.** The disposition to annoy, tease, or disturb. **3.** Harm or injury: High winds can cause great *mischief.* **4.** A cause or source of damage, evil, etc. [< OF < *meschever* to come to grief]

mis·chief-mak·er (mis′chif·mā′kər) *n.* One who causes mischief. — **mis′chief-mak′ing** *adj. & n.*

mis·chie·vous (mis′chi·vəs) *adj.* **1.** Inclined to or full of mischief. **2.** Troubling or annoying. **3.** Having a playful, teasing nature or quality. **4.** Causing harm or injury. — **mis′chie·vous·ly** *adv.* — **mis′chie·vous·ness** *n.*

mis·ci·ble (mis′i·bəl) *adj.* Capable of being mixed. [< L *miscere* to mix] — **mis′ci·bil′i·ty** *n.*

mis·con·ceive (mis′kən·sēv′) *v.t. & v.i.* **·ceived, ·ceiv·ing** To conceive wrongly; misunderstand. — **mis′con·ceiv′er** *n.* — **mis′con·cep′tion** *n.*

mis·con·duct (*n.* mis·kon′dukt; *v.* mis′kən·dukt′) *n.* **1.** Improper or immoral behavior. **2.** Unlawful conduct. — *v.t.* **1.** To behave (oneself) improperly. **2.** To mismanage.

mis·con·strue (mis′kən·strōō′) *v.t.* **·strued, ·stru·ing** **1.** To interpret wrongly; misunderstand. **2.** *Gram.* To construe incorrectly. — **mis′con·struc′tion** *n.*

mis·count (mis·kount′) *v.t. & v.i.* To count incorrectly; miscalculate. — *n.* An incorrect count or reckoning.

mis·cre·ant (mis′krē·ənt) *n.* An unscrupulous wretch; evildoer. — *adj.* Villainous; vile. [< OF < *mes-* mis-[2] + *croire* to believe]

mis·cue (mis·kyōō′) *n.* **1.** In billiards, a stroke spoiled by a slipping of the cue. **2.** *Informal* An error; slip-up. — *v.i.* **·cued, ·cu·ing** **1.** To make a miscue. **2.** In the theater, etc., to miss one's cue or to answer another's cue.

mis·date (mis·dāt′) *v.t.* **·dat·ed, ·dat·ing** To date incorrectly; assign a wrong date to. — *n.* An incorrect date.

mis·deal (mis·dēl′) *v.t. & v.i.* **dealt** (-delt′)**, deal·ing** In card games, to deal incorrectly or improperly. — *n.* An incorrect deal. — **mis·deal′er** *n.*

mis·deed (mis·dēd′) *n.* An evil or immoral act.

mis·de·mean·or (mis′di·mē′nər) *n. Law* Any offense less serious than a felony, or for which the punishment is less severe.

mis·di·rect (mis′di·rekt′, -dī·rekt′) *v.t.* To direct or guide wrongly, as a letter, person, etc. — **mis′di·rec′tion** *n.*

mis·do (mis·dōō′) *v.t. & v.i.* **·did, ·done, ·do·ing** To do wrongly. [OE *misdōn*] — **mis·do′er** *n.* — **mis·do′ing** *n.*

mis·em·ploy (mis′im·ploi′) *v.t.* To put to a wrong or improper use. — **mis′em·ploy′ment** *n.*

mi·ser (mī′zər) *n.* One who saves or hoards avariciously, often sacrificing his own comfort. [< L, wretched]

mis·er·a·ble (miz′ər·ə·bəl, miz′rə-) *adj.* **1.** Being in a state of misery, poverty, or wretched unhappiness. **2.** *Informal* In poor health; not well. **3.** Causing misery or extreme discomfort: a *miserable* headache. **4.** Proceeding from or exhibiting misery: a *miserable* life. **5.** Of inferior quality; worthless. **6.** Paltry or meager; skimpy. **7.** Deserving of pity: a *miserable* creature. **8.** Disreputable; shameful: a *miserable* scoundrel. [< OF < L < *miserari* to pity] — **mis′er·a·ble·ness** *n.* — **mis′er·a·bly** *adv.*

Mis·e·re·re (miz′ə·râr′ē, -rir′ē) *n.* **1.** The 51st Psalm (in the Vulgate and Douai versions, the 50th): from the opening word of the Latin version. **2.** A musical setting of this psalm. [< L, imperative of *miserri* to have mercy]

mis·er·i·cor·di·a (miz′ə·ri·kôr′dē·ə) *n. Latin* Pity; mercy.

mi·ser·ly (mī′zər·lē) *adj.* Of, like, or characteristic of a miser; grasping; avaricious. — **mi′ser·li·ness** *n.*

mis·er·y (miz′ər·ē) *n. pl.* **·er·ies** **1.** A condition of great wretchedness or suffering, as caused by poverty, pain, etc. **2.** Intense mental or emotional anguish; extreme unhappiness. **3.** A cause or source of suffering or unhappiness. — *Syn.* See SUFFERING. [< OF < L < *miser* wretched]

mis·fea·sance (mis·fē′zəns) *n. Law* The performance of a lawful act in an unlawful or culpable manner. [< OF < *mes-* mis- + *faire* to do] — **mis·fea′sor** *n.*

mis·fire (*v.* mis·fīr′; *n.* mis′fīr) *v.i.* **·fired, ·fir·ing** **1.** To fail to fire, ignite, or explode at the desired time, as a firearm, internal-combustion engine, etc. **2.** To fail in achieving the proper or desired effect. — *n.* An instance of misfiring.

mis·fit (mis·fit′; *for n. def. 2,* mis′fit′) *v.t. & v.i.* **·fit·ted, ·fit·ting** To fail to fit or make fit. — *n.* **1.** Something that fits badly. **2.** One who is not well adjusted to his environment. **3.** The act or condition of fitting badly.

mis·for·tune (mis·fôr′chən) *n.* **1.** Adverse or ill fortune; bad luck; adversity. **2.** A calamity; mishap.

mis·giv·ing (mis·giv′ing) *n.* A feeling of doubt, distrust, or apprehension.

mis·gov·ern (mis·guv′ərn) *v.t.* To govern badly; administer improperly. — **mis·gov′ern·ment** *n.*

mis·guide (mis·gīd′) *v.t.* **·guid·ed, ·guid·ing** To guide wrongly; mislead. — **mis·guid′ance** *n.* — **mis·guid′er** *n.*

mis·guid·ed (mis·gī′did) *adj.* Guided or led wrongly in thought or action. — **mis·guid′ed·ly** *adv.*

mis·han·dle (mis·han′dəl) *v.t.* **·dled, ·dling** To handle, treat, or manage badly; abuse.

mis·hap (mis′hap, mis·hap′) *n.* An unfortunate accident.

mish·mash (mish′mash′, -mosh′) *n.* A confused mixture or collection of things; hodgepodge. Also **mish′-mash.**

mis·in·form (mis′in·fôrm′) *v.t.* To give false or erroneous information to. — **mis′in·form′ant, mis′in·form′er** *n.* — **mis′in·for·ma′tion** *n.*

mis·in·ter·pret (mis′in·tûr′prit) *v.t.* To interpret or understand incorrectly. —**mis·in·ter·pre·ta·tion** *n.* —**mis·in·ter·pret·er** *n.*

mis·judge (mis·juj′) *v.t. & v.i.* **·judged, ·judg·ing** To judge wrongly or unfairly. —**mis·judg′ment** or *Brit.* **mis·judge′·ment** *n.*

mis·lay (mis·lā′) *v.t.* **·laid, ·lay·ing** 1. To put or lay in a place not remembered; misplace. 2. To place or put down incorrectly: He *mislaid* the carpet. —**mis·lay′er** *n.*

mis·lead (mis·lēd′) *v.t.* **led** (-led′), **·lead·ing** 1. To guide or lead in the wrong direction. 2. To lead into error, as of judgment or conduct. —**mis·lead′er** *n.* —**mis·lead′ing** *adj.* —**mis·lead′ing·ly** *adv.*

mis·man·age (mis·man′ij) *v.t. & v.i.* **·aged, ·ag·ing** To manage badly or improperly. —**mis·man′age·ment** *n.* —**mis·man′ag·er** *n.*

mis·match (mis·mach′) *v.t.* To match badly or inappropriately, as in marriage. —*n.* A bad or incongruous match.

mis·mate (mis·māt′) *v.t. & v.i.* **·mat·ed, ·mat·ing** To mate unsuitably.

mis·name (mis·nām′) *v.t.* **·named, ·nam·ing** To call by a wrong name.

mis·no·mer (mis·nō′mər) *n.* 1. A name wrongly applied to someone or something. 2. The act of misnaming, esp. in a legal document. [< AF < OF < *mes-* wrongly + *nomer* < L *nominare* to name]

miso- *combining form* Hating; hatred. Also, before vowels, *mis-.* [< Gk. *misein* to hate]

mis·og·a·my (mis·og′ə·mē) *n.* Hatred of marriage. —**mis·og′a·mist** *n.*

mis·og·y·ny (mis·oj′ə·nē) *n.* Hatred of women [< Gk. < *misein* to hate + *gynē* woman] —**mis·og′y·nist** *n.* —**mis·og′y·nous** *adj.*

mis·place (mis·plās′) *v.t.* **·placed, ·plac·ing** 1. To put in a wrong place. 2. To put (confidence, faith, trust, etc.) in an unworthy or unsuitable person, thing, or idea. 3. To mislay (def. 1). —**mis·place′ment** *n.*

mis·play (mis·plā′; *for n., also* mis′plā) *v.t. & v.i.* In games, to play badly or incorrectly. —*n.* A bad play or move.

mis·print (mis·print′; *for n., also* mis′print′) *v.t.* To print incorrectly. —*n.* An error in printing.

mis·pri·sion (mis·prizh′ən) *n. Law* 1. Concealment of a crime, esp. of treason or felony. 2. Misconduct of a public official. 3. A mistake; often, a clerical error. [< OF < *mes- mis-* + *prendre* to take]

mis·prize (mis·prīz′) *v.t.* **·prized, ·priz·ing** To fail to appreciate the worth of; undervalue; despise.

mis·pro·nounce (mis′prə·nouns′) *v.t. & v.i.* **·nounced, ·nounc·ing** To pronounce incorrectly or in an unorthodox manner. —**mis·pro·nun·ci·a·tion** (mis′prə·nun′sē·ā′shən) *n.*

mis·quote (mis·kwōt′) *v.t. & v.i.* **·quot·ed, ·quot·ing** To quote incorrectly. —**mis·quo·ta·tion** (mis′kwō·tā′shən) *n.*

mis·read (mis·rēd′) *v.t.* **read** (-red′), **·read·ing** (-rē′ding) To read incorrectly or with the wrong sense; misinterpret.

mis·rep·re·sent (mis′rep·ri·zent′) *v.t.* 1. To give an incorrect or false representation of. 2. To represent inadequately or poorly. —**mis·rep·re·sen·ta·tion** *n.* —**mis·rep·re·sen′ta·tive** *adj. & n.* —**mis·rep·re·sent′er** *n.*

mis·rule (mis·rōōl′) *v.t.* **·ruled, ·rul·ing** To rule unwisely or unjustly; misgovern. —*n.* 1. Bad or unjust rule or government. 2. Disorder or confusion, as from lawlessness.

miss¹ (mis) *v.t.* 1. To fail to hit, reach, or land upon (a specified object). 2. To fail to meet or catch, as a train. 3. To fail to obtain, accomplish, or achieve: to *miss* the presidency by a few votes. 4. To fail to see, hear, perceive, etc. 5. To fail to attend, keep, perform, etc. 6. To overlook or fail to take advantage of. 7. To discover the absence of, usu. belatedly: to *miss* one's wallet. 8. To feel the loss or absence of. 9. To escape; avoid. —*v.i.* 10. To fail to hit; strike wide of the mark. 11. To be unsuccessful; fail. —*n.* A failure to hit, find, succeed, etc. [OE *missan*]

miss² (mis) *n.* 1. *Often cap.* A title used in speaking to an unmarried woman or girl: used without name. 2. A young girl: chiefly informal or trade usage. [Contr. of MISTRESS]

Miss (mis) *n.* A title of address used before the name of a girl or unmarried woman. ◆ In referring to two or more unmarried women bearing the same name, either *the Misses Brown* or *the Miss Browns* is acceptable.

mis·sal (mis′əl) *n.* 1. A book containing all the prayers, responses, etc., for celebrating Mass throughout the year. 2. Loosely, any prayer book. [< Med.L *missale*, neut. of *missalis* (*liber*) mass (book)]

mis·shape (mis·shāp′) *v.t.* **·shaped, ·shaped** or **·shap·en, ·shap·ing** To shape badly; deform. —**mis·shaped** *adj.*

mis·sile (mis′əl, *Brit.* mis′īl) *n.* 1. An object, esp. a weapon, intended to be thrown or discharged, as a bullet, arrow, etc. 2. A guided missile. —*adj.* 1. Such as may be thrown or discharged. 2. Used or adapted for throwing or discharging missiles. [< L < *missus*, pp. of *mittere* to send]

mis·sil·ry (mis′əl·rē) *n.* The science and art of designing, building, and operating missiles, esp. rockets and guided missiles. Also **mis′sile·ry.**

miss·ing (mis′ing) *adj.* 1. Not present; absent; lacking. 2. *Mil.* Absent: said of one whose whereabouts or fate in battle has not been determined: also **missing in action.**

missing link 1. A hypothetical animal intermediate in development between man and the anthropoid apes. 2. Something needed to complete a chain or series.

mis·sion (mish′ən) *n.* 1. Any body of persons sent some place in order to perform or accomplish a specific work or service; esp., such a body sent to a foreign country to conduct business, negotiations, etc., on behalf of its own country. 2. The specific task or responsibility that a person or body of persons is assigned to do or fulfill. 3. A body of missionaries sent by a religious organization to a foreign country or region to convert, aid, or instruct the inhabitants. 4. *pl.* The organized work of such missionaries. 5. The place or establishment where missionaries carry on their work and often live; also, the entire district or locality that they serve. 6. A special program or series of religious services or exercises for stimulating piety or converting unbelievers. 7. *U.S.* The permanent foreign office of an ambassador or envoy; embassy. 8. The particular work or goal that one is or feels destined to do or accomplish; a calling. 9. *Mil.* A definite task or field of operation assigned to an individual or unit of the armed forces. 10. A flight operation of a single aircraft or formation, esp. in wartime. —*adj.* Pertaining or belonging to a mission. —*v.t.* 1. To send on a mission. 2. To establish a mission in or among. [< L < *missus*, pp. of *mittere* to send] —**mis′sion·er** *n.*

mis·sion·ar·y (mish′ən·er′ē) *n. pl.* **·ar·ies** 1. A person sent to propagate religion or to do educational or charitable work in some foreign country or region. 2. One who advocates or spreads any new system or doctrine. —*adj.* Of, pertaining to, or characteristic of missionaries.

mis·sis (mis′əz) *n. Informal & Dial.* 1. A wife: often with *the.* 2. The female head of a household: with *the.* Also **mis′·sus.** [Alter. of MISTRESS]

Mis·sis·sip·pi·an (mis′ə·sip′ē·ən) *adj.* 1. Of or pertaining to the Mississippi River or to the State. 2. *Geol.* Relating to the earliest of the two geological periods or systems in the American Carboniferous division of the Paleozoic era. See chart for GEOLOGY. —*n.* 1. One born or residing in Mississippi. 2. The Lower Carboniferous geological formation.

mis·sive (mis′iv) *n.* A letter, esp. one of an official nature. —*adj.* Sent or designed to be sent. [< Med.L < L *missus*, pp. of *mittere* to send]

Mis·sou·ri (mi·zŏŏr′ē, -zŏŏr′ə) *n. pl.* **·ri** One of a tribe of North American Indians of the Siouan family, formerly inhabiting northern Missouri.

mis·speak (mis·spēk′) *v.t. & v.i.* **·spoke, ·speak·ing** To speak or pronounce incorrectly.

mis·spell (mis·spel′) *v.t. & v.i.* **·spelled** or **·spelt, ·spell·ing** To spell incorrectly.

mis·spell·ing (mis·spel′ing) *n.* An incorrect spelling.

mis·spend (mis·spend′) *v.t.* **·spent, ·spend·ing** To spend wrongfully or wastefully.

mis·state (mis·stāt′) *v.t.* **·stat·ed, ·stat·ing** To state wrongly or falsely. —**mis·state′ment** *n.*

mis·step (mis′step′) *n.* 1. A false step; a stumble. 2. An error or blunder, as in conduct.

mist (mist) *n.* 1. An aggregation of fine drops of water suspended in the atmosphere at or near the earth's surface. 2. *Meteorol.* A very thin fog with a horizontal visibility arbitrarily set at not more than two kilometers. 3. Watery vapor condensed on and blurring a surface. 4. Any cloud of particles forming a haze, as of dust, smoke, etc. 5. A film or haze before the eyes that blurs one's vision. 6. Anything that clouds or obscures one's memory, perceptions, etc. —*v.i.* 1. To be or become dim or misty; blur. 2. To rain in very fine drops. —*v.t.* 3. To make dim or misty. [OE]

mis·tak·a·ble (mis·tāk′ə·bəl) *adj.* Capable of being mistaken or misunderstood. —**mis·tak′a·bly** *adv.*

mis·take (mis·tāk′) *n.* An error or fault in action, judgment, perception, understanding, etc. —*v.* **took, ·tak·en, ·tak·ing** *v.t.* 1. To understand wrongly; acquire a wrong conception of. 2. To take (a person or thing) to be another. —*v.i.* 3. To make a mistake. [< ON *mistaka*]

mis·tak·en (mis·tā′kən) *adj.* 1. Based on or arising from error, as of judgment, understanding, perception, etc. 2. Wrong in opinion, action, etc. —**mis·tak′en·ly** *adv.*

mis·ter (mis′tər) *n. Informal* Sir: used without the name. [Var. of MASTER]

Mis·ter (mis′tər) *n.* 1. Master: a title of address prefixed to the name and to some official titles of a man: commonly written *Mr.* 2. The official term of address for certain military and naval persons.

mis·time (mis·tīm′) *v.t.* **·timed, ·tim·ing** 1. To time wrongly or inappropriately. 2. To misjudge the time of.

mis·tle·toe (mis′əl·tō) *n.* 1. A European parasitic shrub, found growing on various deciduous trees and having yellowish green leaves, inconspicuous flowers, and glutinous white berries, used as a Christmas decoration. 2. A related American plant used as a Christmas decoration and the State flower of Oklahoma. [OE *misteltān* mistletoe twig]

mis·took (mis·tŏŏk′) Past tense of MISTAKE.

mis·tral (mis′trəl, *Fr.* mēs·tràl′) *n.* A cold, dry, violent northerly wind blowing down the Rhône Valley through Southern France and adjacent areas. [< F < Provençal, lit., master wind < L < *magister* master]

mis·trans·late (mis′trans·lāt′, -tranz-, mis·trans′lāt, -tranz′-) *v.t.* ·lat·ed, ·lat·ing To translate incorrectly. — **mis′trans·la′tion** *n.*

mis·treat (mis·trēt′) *v.t.* To treat badly or improperly. — **mis·treat′ment** *n.*

mis·tress (mis′tris) *n.* **1.** A woman in a position of authority or control; as: **a** The head of a household, institution, or estate. **b** The head of a staff of servants. **c** The owner of an animal or slave. **2.** A woman who unlawfully cohabits with a man, usu. over an extended period of time. **3.** A woman having supreme control over anything. **4.** *Often cap.* Anything considered feminine that has actual or potential power over something else. **5.** A woman who has mastered a skill, craft, or branch of learning. **6.** *Chiefly Brit.* A female schoolteacher. [< OF *maistresse*, fem. of *maistre* master]

Mis·tress (mis′tris) *n.* Formerly, a title of address applied to women, now supplanted by *Mrs.* and *Miss.*

mis·tri·al (mis·trī′əl) *n. Law* **1.** A trial made void because of some legal errors or defects. **2.** A trial terminated by the jury's inability to agree on a verdict.

mis·trust (mis·trust′) *v.t.* **1.** To regard (someone or something) with suspicion or doubt; be skeptical of. — *v.i.* **2.** To be wary or suspicious. — *n.* Lack of trust or confidence. — **mis·trust′er** *n.* — **mis·trust′ing·ly** *adv.*

mis·trust·ful (mis·trust′fəl) *adj.* Full of mistrust; suspicious. — **mis·trust′ful·ly** *adv.* — **mis·trust′ful·ness** *n.*

mist·y (mis′tē) *adj.* **mist·i·er, mist·i·est** **1.** Consisting of, characterized by, or like mist. **2.** Dimmed or obscured. **3.** Lacking clarity; vague. — **mist′i·ly** *adv.* — **mist′i·ness** *n.*

mis·un·der·stand (mis′un·dər·stand′, mis·un′-) *v.t. & v.i.* ·stood, ·stand·ing To understand wrongly; misinterpret.

mis·un·der·stand·ing (mis′un·dər·stan′ding, mis·un′-) *n.* **1.** A failure to understand the meaning, motive, etc., of someone or something. **2.** A disagreement or quarrel.

mis·un·der·stood (mis′un·dər·stŏŏd′, mis·un′-) *adj.* **1.** Wrongly understood. **2.** Not valued or appreciated.

mis·us·age (mis·yōŏs′ij, -zij) *n.* **1.** Incorrect or improper use, as of words. **2.** Ill-treatment.

mis·use (*n.* mis·yōŏs′; *v.* mis·yōŏz′) *n.* Erroneous or improper use; misapplication. — *v.t.* ·used, ·us·ing **1.** To use or apply wrongly or improperly. **2.** To treat badly; abuse; maltreat. — **mis·us′er** *n.*

mis·val·ue (mis·val′yōŏ) *v.t.* ·ued, ·u·ing To value wrongly.

mite[1] (mīt) *n.* Any of various small arachnids, many of which are parasitic on men, animals, and plants, and feed upon stored grain. [OE *mīte*] — **mit′y** *adj.*

mite[2] (mīt) *n.* **1.** A very small particle, object, or creature. **2.** Any very small coin or sum of money. [< Du. *mijt*]

mi·ter (mī′tər) *n.* **1.** A tall ornamental headdress, rising in peaks at the front and back, worn by popes, bishops, and abbots. **2.** The office or dignity of a bishop. **3.** In carpentry: **a** A miter joint. **b** The beveled edges that come together to form a miter joint. — *v.t.* **1.** To confer a miter upon; raise to the rank of bishop. **2.** To make or join with a miter joint. Also, *Brit.,* **mitre.** [< OF < L *mitra* < Gk., belt, turban] — **mi′ter·er** *n.*

mi·tered (mī′tərd) *adj.* **1.** Shaped like an ecclesiastical miter. **2.** Wearing or permitted to wear a miter.

miter joint A joint made of two pieces of material whose joined ends have been beveled at equal angles, as at the corner of a picture frame.

mit·i·gate (mit′ə·gāt) *v.t. & v.i.* ·gat·ed, ·gat·ing To make or become milder or less severe. [< L *mitis* mild + *agere* to do, drive] — **mit′i·ga·ble** *adj.* — **mit′i·ga′tion** *n.* — **mit′i·ga′tor** *n.*

mit·i·ga·tive (mit′ə·gā′tiv) *adj.* Tending to mitigate. — *n.* Something that mitigates pain, discomfort, etc. Also **mit′i·gant** (-gənt), **mit′i·ga·to′ry** (-gə·tôr′ē, -tō′rē).

mi·to·chon·dri·a (mī′tə·kon′drē·ə) *n.pl. Biol.* Small granular bodies found in the cytoplasm of a cell, believed to function in certain phases of metabolism. For illus. see CELL. [< NL < Gk. *mitos* thread + *chondros* cartilage, granule]

mi·to·sis (mī·tō′sis) *n. Biol.* The series of changes in cell division by which the chromatin is modified into two sets of chromosomes, one set going to each pole before the cell divides into two mature daughter cells. [< NL < Gk. *mitos* thread + -OSIS] — **mi·tot·ic** (mī·tot′ik) *adj.* — **mi·tot′i·cal·ly** *adv.*

mi·tral (mī′trəl) *adj.* **1.** Pertaining to or resembling a miter. **2.** Of or pertaining to a mitral valve.

mitral valve *Anat.* A membranous valve between the left

atrium and the left ventrical of the heart, that prevents the blood from flowing back into the atrium.

mi·tre (mī′tər), **mi·tred** (mī′tərd), etc. See MITER, etc.

mitt (mit) *n.* **1.** In baseball, a covering somewhat like a mitten, to protect the hand catching the ball. **2.** A woman's glove, sometimes extending to or above the elbow but without fully covering the fingers. **3.** A mitten (def. 1). **4.** *Slang Usu. pl.* A hand. **5.** *Slang* A boxing glove.

mit·ten (mit′n) *n.* A covering for the hand, encasing the four fingers together and the thumb separately. [< F *mitaine*]

mix (miks) *v.* **mixed** or **mixt, mix·ing** *v.t.* **1.** To combine or put together in one mass or compound so as to render the constituent parts wholly or partially indistinguishable from one another. **2.** To make by combining ingredients: to *mix* cake batter. **3.** To put or add, as an ingredient: to *mix* two eggs into the batter. **4.** To combine or join: to *mix* age with wisdom. **5.** To bring into contact with; cause to mingle. **6.** To crossbreed. — *v.i.* **7.** To become mixed or have the capacity to become mixed; mingle. **8.** To associate; get along: He does not *mix* well with others. **9.** To take part; become involved. **10.** To crossbreed. — **to mix up 1.** To mix or blend together. **2.** To confuse. **3.** To mistake for another or others: He *mixed up* the meanings of those two words. **4.** To implicate or involve. — *n.* **1.** The act or product of mixing. **2.** A mixture of ingredients, often prepared and sold commercially: a cake *mix.* **3.** A beverage, as water, soda, ginger ale, etc., used in making cocktails and other mixed drinks. **4.** Confusion or bewilderment; a mess. **5.** *Telecom.* The correct blending of the outputs of two or more microphones. [Back formation < MIXED] — **mix′a·ble** or **mix′i·ble** *adj.*

mixed (mikst) *adj.* **1.** Mingled or blended together in a single mass or compound. **2.** Composed of different, dissimilar, or incongruous elements, qualities, classes, races, etc.: *mixed* motives. **3.** Made up of or involving persons of both sexes. **4.** Mentally confused: followed by *up.* Also **mixt.** [< F < L *mixtus,* pp. of *miscere* to mix]

mixed marriage Marriage between persons of different religions or races.

mixed metaphor See under METAPHOR.

mixed number A number, as 3½, 5¾, that is the sum of an integer and a fraction.

mix·er (mik′sər) *n.* **1.** One who or that which mixes. **2.** *Informal* A person with ability to mix socially or get along well in various groups. **3.** *Informal* A dance or gathering for the purpose of getting acquainted. **4.** A mix (def. 3).

mix·ture (miks′chər) *n.* **1.** Something formed by or resulting from mixing. **2.** Anything composed of unlike or various elements; as: **a** A cloth made of several types or colors of yarn. **b** A blend of different kinds or qualities of tea, tobacco, etc. **3.** *Chem.* A commingling of two or more substances in varying proportions, in which the components retain their individual chemical properties: distinguished from *compound.* **4.** The act of mixing, or the state of being mixed. [< F < L *miscere* to mix]

mix-up (miks′up′) *n.* **1.** A state of confusion; also, an instance of this. **2.** *Informal* A fight.

miz·zen (miz′ən) *Naut. n.* **1.** A triangular sail set on the mizzenmast. **2.** A mizzenmast. — *adj.* Of or pertaining to the mizzen or mizzenmast. Also **miz′en.** [< F < Ital. *mezzana,* fem. of *mezzano* middle, ? < L *medianus*]

miz·zen·mast (miz′ən·məst′, -mast′, -mäst′) *n. Naut.* **1.** In a ship with three masts, the mast nearest the stern. **2.** In a ship having more than three masts, the third mast from the forward end of the ship. **3.** In a ketch or yawl, the shorter of the two masts. Also **miz′en·mast′.**

mks The meter-kilogram-second system of measurement in which the unit of length is the meter, the unit of mass is the kilogram, and the unit of time is one second. Also **m.k.s., MKS, M.K.S.**

mne·mon·ic (nē·mon′ik, ni-) *adj.* **1.** Aiding or designed to aid the memory. **2.** Of or relating to mnemonics or memory. Also **mne·mon′i·cal.** — *n.* **1.** A device to assist memory. **2.** Mnemonics. [< Gk. < *mnasthai* to remember]

mne·mon·ics (nē·mon′iks, ni-) *n.pl.* (*construed as sing.*) A system of principles and formulas designed to assist or improve the memory. Also **mne·mo·tech·nics** (nē′mō·tek′niks).

mo·a (mō′ə) *n.* Any of a family of extinct, flightless birds of New Zealand, resembling the ostrich and having very powerful legs. [< Maori]

Mo·ab (mō′ab) An ancient country east of the Dead Sea. — **Mo′ab·ite** *adj. & n.*

moan (mōn) *n.* **1.** A low, sustained, mournful sound, as from grief or pain. **2.** Any similar sound. — *v.i.* **1.** To utter moans. **2.** To make a low, mournful sound, as wind. **3.** To complain or lament. — *v.t.* **4.** To lament; bewail. **5.** To utter with moans. [Cf. OE *mǣnan* to lament, moan]

moat (mōt) *n.* A deep, wide, and usu. water-filled trench around a castle, fortress, or town, designed to discourage attempts at invasion. —*v.t.* To surround with or as with a moat. [< OF *mote* embankment]

mob (mob) *n.* **1.** A disorderly or lawless crowd or throng; a rabble. **2.** Any large assemblage, group, or class of individuals or things: the ruling *mob.* **3.** The lower class or classes of people; the masses. **4.** *Informal* A gang of thieves, hoodlums, etc. —*v.t.* **mobbed, mob·bing 1.** To attack in a mob. **2.** To crowd around and jostle or molest, as from adulation or curiosity. **3.** To attend or crowd into (a hall, theater, etc.). [< L *mob(ile vulgus)* movable crowd] — **mob'ber** *n.* — **mob'bish** *adj.* — **mob'bish·ly** *adv.*

mo·bile (*adj.* mō'bəl, -bēl; *n.* mō'bēl; *Brit.* mō'bil) *adj.* **1.** Characterized by freedom of movement. **2.** Flowing freely: a *mobile* liquid. **3.** Capable of changing or responding easily or quickly, as to emotions, etc. **4.** Moving easily from one thing to another; versatile: a *mobile* mind. **5.** Capable of being easily and quickly moved. **6.** Capable of moving with relative ease from one social group or status to another. **7.** Of, pertaining to, or like a mobile. —*n.* A form of freely moving sculpture consisting of parts that are suspended from rods, wires, etc. [< F < L *mobilis* movable] — **mo·bil'i·ty** *n.*

mo·bi·lize (mō'bə·līz) *v.* **·lized, ·liz·ing** *v.t.* **1.** To make ready for war, as an army, industry, men, etc. **2.** To assemble for use; organize. **3.** To put into activity, circulation, or use: to *mobilize* one's talents. —*v.i.* **4.** To undergo mobilization. Also *Brit.* **mo'bi·lise.** [< F *mobiliser*] — **mo'bi·li·za'tion** (-lə·zā'shən, -lī·zā'-) *n.*

mob·ster (mob'stər) *n. Slang* A gangster.

moc·ca·sin (mok'ə·sin) *n.* **1.** A heelless foot covering, made of buckskin or of any soft leather and formerly worn by North American Indians. **2.** A shoe or slipper resembling a moccasin. **3.** The water moccasin. [< Algonquian *mohkisson*]

moccasin flower Any of certain lady's-slippers.

mo·cha (mō'kə) *n.* **1.** A choice, pungent coffee, originally brought from Mocha, Arabia. **2.** A flavoring made of an infusion of coffee or of coffee and chocolate. **3.** A fine sheepskin leather used for making gloves.

mock (mok) *v.t.* **1.** To treat or address scornfully or derisively. **2.** To mimic, as in sport, derision, or contempt. **3.** To deceive or disappoint; delude. **4.** To defy; make futile or meaningless. **5.** *Poetic* To imitate; counterfeit. —*v.i.* **6.** To express or show ridicule or contempt; scoff. —*adj.* Merely imitating or resembling the reality; sham. —*n.* **1.** An act of mocking or derision; a jeer. **2.** One who or that which is mocked. **3.** An imitation or counterfeit. [< OF *mocquer*] — **mock'er** *n.* — **mock'ing·ly** *adv.*

mock·er·y (mok'ər·ē) *n. pl.* **·er·ies 1.** Derision; ridicule. **2.** A contemptuous or derisive speech or action. **3.** An object of derision or ridicule. **4.** A deceitful, impudent, or contemptible imitation: His trial was a *mockery.* **5.** Something ludicrously futile, inadequate, or unsuitable.

mock-he·ro·ic (mok'hi·rō'ik) *adj.* Imitating or satirizing the heroic manner, style, attitude, or character. Also **mock'-he·ro'i·cal.**

mock·ing·bird (mok'ing·bûrd') *n.* **1.** A bird common in the southern U.S., noted for its ability to imitate the calls of other birds. **2.** Any of various birds of the same family.

mock turtle soup A soup prepared from calf's head or other meat and seasoned to taste like green turtle soup.

mock-up (mok'up') *n.* A model, usu. full-scale, of a proposed structure, machine, apparatus, etc.

mo·dal (mōd'l) *adj.* **1.** Of or pertaining to mode or a mode. **2.** *Gram.* **a** Of or pertaining to mood. **b** Conveying a meaning similar to those meanings conveyed by a mood. **3.** *Music* Of or pertaining to the modes. **4.** *Stat.* Typical. — **mo·dal'i·ty** (-dal'ə·tē) *n.* — **mo'dal·ly** *adv.*

mode (mōd) *n.* **1.** Manner or form of being, doing, etc.; way. **2.** Prevailing or current style or fashion, as in dress. **3.** *Gram.* Mood. **4.** *Music* Any of the arrangements of tones achieved by starting at various points in a given scale and proceeding through one octave; esp. the modes of the diatonic scale, as major mode, minor mode, etc. **5.** *Philos.* The manner or form in which a basic substance is manifested. **6.** *Stat.* The value, magnitude, or score that occurs the greatest number of times in a given series of observations: also called *norm.* [< L *modus* measure, manner]

mod·el (mod'l) *n.* **1.** An object, usu. in miniature and often built according to scale, that represents something to be made or something already existing. **2.** A pattern, example, or standard that is or may be used for imitation or comparison. **3.** A representation in clay, plaster, etc., of something later to be reproduced in more permanent material. **4.** One who or that which serves as a figure or pattern for an artist, sculptor, etc. **5.** One who is employed to display or advertise merchandise; esp. one who displays articles of clothing by wearing them. **6.** A representative style, plan, or design. **7.** In merchandise, a particular style or design. —*v.* **mod·eled** or **·elled, mod·el·ing** or **·el·ling** *v.t.* **1.** To plan or fashion after a model or pattern. **2.** To make a model of. **3.** To shape or fashion. **4.** To display by wearing. —*v.i.* **5.** To make a model or models. **6.** To pose or serve as a model (defs. 4 & 5). —*adj.* **1.** Serving or used as a model. **2.** Worthy or suitable to be used as a model. [< F < Ital. < L *modus* measure, manner] — **mod'el·er** or **mod'el·ler** *n.*

mod·el·ing (mod'ling, -əl·ing) *n.* **1.** The act or art of making a model, esp. a sculptor's clay or wax model. **2.** In painting, drawing, etc., the representation of depth or three-dimensional solidity. **3.** The surfaces or planes of a solid form or shape. **4.** The act or occupation of being a model (defs. 4 & 5). Also **mod'el·ling.**

mod·er·ate (*adj.* & *n.* mod'ər·it; *v.* mod'ə·rāt) *adj.* **1.** Keeping or kept within reasonable limits; temperate. **2.** Holding or characterized by ideas or convictions that are not extreme or radical. **3.** Of medium or average quality, quantity, scope, extent, etc. **4.** *Meteorol.* Designating a breeze (No. 4) or a gale (No. 7) on the Beaufort scale. —*n.* One having moderate views or practices, esp. in politics or religion. —*v.* **·at·ed, ·at·ing** *v.t.* **1.** To reduce the violence, severity, etc., of. **2.** To preside over. —*v.i.* **3.** To become less intense or violent. **4.** To act as a moderator. [< L *moderare* to regulate] — **mod'er·ate·ly** *adv.* — **mod'er·ate·ness** *n.*

mod·er·a·tion (mod'ə·rā'shən) *n.* **1.** The state or quality of being moderate. **2.** The act of moderating. —**in moderation** Within reasonable limits; temperately.

mod·e·ra·to (mod'ə·rä'tō) *Music adj.* Moderate. —*adv.* In moderate time; moderately. —*n. pl.* **·tos** A moderate passage or movement. Abbr. *mod.* [< Ital.]

mod·er·a·tor (mod'ə·rā'tər) *n.* **1.** One who or that which moderates. **2.** One who presides over a meeting, forum, or debate. **3.** The arbitrator of a dispute. **4.** *Physics* A substance, as graphite or beryllium, used to slow down neutrons in an atomic-energy reactor. — **mod'er·a'tor·ship** *n.*

mod·ern (mod'ərn) *adj.* **1.** Of or pertaining to the present or recent time. **2.** Characteristic of or serving to express the current times; up-to-date. **3.** *Usu. cap.* Of, pertaining to, or characteristic of the most recent period in the development of a language: *Modern* French. —*n.* **1.** One who lives in modern times. **2.** One who has opinions, habits, prejudices, etc., characteristic of modern times. **3.** *Printing* A style of type face characterized by heavy stems and extremely thin serifs. [< LL *modernus* recent] — **mod'ern·ly** *adv.*

mod·ern·ism (mod'ərn·iz'əm) *n.* **1.** The character or quality of thought, action, etc., that is peculiar to modern times. **2.** Something characteristic of modern times, as an act, practice, idiom, attitude, etc. **3.** *Often cap.* In religion, a movement to reinterpret the Bible and church teachings to make them consistent with modern science and philosophy.

mod·ern·ist (mod'ərn·ist) *n.* **1.** One who is sympathetic with or has a preference for modern things, practices, ideas, etc. **2.** *Often cap.* An advocate of religious modernism. — **mod'ern·is'tic** *adj.*

mo·der·ni·ty (mo·dûr'nə·tē) *n. pl.* **·ties 1.** The condition or quality of being modern. **2.** Something modern.

mod·ern·ize (mod'ərn·īz) *v.* **·ized, ·iz·ing** *v.t.* **1.** To make modern in method, style, character, etc.; bring up to date. —*v.i.* **2.** To accept or adopt modern ways, ideas, idioms, etc. — **mod'ern·i·za'tion** *n.* — **mod'ern·iz'er** *n.*

mod·est (mod'ist) *adj.* **1.** Having or displaying a moderate or unexaggerated regard for oneself or one's abilities, accomplishments, etc.; humble. **2.** Not showy, gaudy, or ostentatious. **3.** Not excessive or extreme; moderate. **4.** Reserved in speech, manner, dress, etc. [< L *modestus* moderate] — **mod'est·ly** *adv.*

mod·es·ty (mod'is·tē) *n. pl.* **·ties 1.** Freedom from vanity or excessive pride. **2.** Freedom from showiness or ostentation. **3.** Propriety in speech, dress, etc. **4.** Moderation.

mod·i·cum (mod'i·kəm) *n. pl.* **·cums** or **·ca** (-kə) A moderate or small amount. [< L < *modus* measure]

mod·i·fi·ca·tion (mod'ə·fə·kā'shən) *n.* **1.** The act of modifying, or the state of being modified. **2.** That which results from modifying. **3.** A small adjustment, alteration, or qualification. **4.** *Biol.* A noninheritable change in an organism, resulting from its own activity or its environment.

mod·i·fi·er (mod'ə·fī'ər) *n.* **1.** One who or that which modifies. **2.** *Gram.* A word, phrase, or clause that restricts or qualifies the meaning of another word or group of words.

mod·i·fy (mod'ə·fī) *v.* **·fied, ·fy·ing** *v.t.* **1.** To make somewhat different in form, character, etc. **2.** To revise by making less extreme, severe, or uncompromising. **3.** *Gram.* To qualify the meaning of; limit. —*v.i.* **4.** To be or become modified. [< F < L *modus* measure + *facere* to make] — **mod'i·fi'a·ble** *adj.*

mod·ish (mō'dish) *adj.* Conforming to the current mode or fashion; stylish. — **mod'ish·ly** *adv.* — **mod'ish·ness** *n.*

mo·diste (mō·dēst') *n.* A woman who deals in fashionable women's clothing, esp. hats or dresses. [< F]

mod·u·lar (moj'ōō·lər) *adj.* **1.** Of, like, or pertaining to a module or modulus. **2.** Composed of modules: *modular* homes.

mod·u·late (moj'oo-lāt) v. ·lat·ed, ·lat·ing v.t. 1. To vary the tone, inflection, pitch, or volume of. 2. To regulate or adjust; modify. 3. To sing or intone, as a prayer. 4. *Telecom.* To alter some characteristic of (a radio carrier wave). — v.i. 5. *Music* To change from one key to another. 6. *Telecom.* To alter some characteristic of a carrier wave. [< L *modulatus*, pp. of *modulari* to regulate] — **mod'u·la'tor** n. — **mod'u·la·to'ry** (-lə-tôr'ē, -tō'rē) adj.

mod·u·la·tion (moj'oo-lā'shən) n. 1. The act of modulating, or the state of being modulated. 2. *Music* A change from one key to another. 3. A melodious or rhythmical inflection of the voice. 4. A melodious use of language, as in prose or poetry. 5. *Telecom.* a The process whereby some characteristic of one carrier wave is varied in accordance with another wave. b The result of this process.

mod·ule (moj'ool) n. 1. A standard or unit of measurement. 2. *Archit.* A unit of measure used to determine the proportion among parts of a classical order. 3. A standard structural component repeatedly used, as in a building, computer, etc. 4. A self-contained component or subassembly: a housing *module.* [< L *modulus*, dim. of *modus* measure]

mo·dus op·er·an·di (mō'dəs op'ə·ran'dī) *Latin* A manner of operating or proceeding.

modus vi·ven·di (mō'dəs vi·ven'dī) *Latin* 1. A manner of living. 2. A temporary agreement in a dispute.

Mo·gul (mō'gul, mō·gul') n. 1. One of the conquerors of India, who in 1526 founded a Moslem empire. 2. Any of their descendants. 3. A member of the Mongoloid race. — adj. Of or pertaining to the Moguls or their empire. Also spelled *Mughal, Mughul:* also **Mo·ghal', Mo·ghul'.** [< Persian *mugal* Mongol]

mo·hair (mō'hâr) n. 1. The hair of the Angora goat. 2. A glossy, wiry fabric made of mohair and cotton in a plain or twill weave. 3. A fabric having a mohair pile, used for upholstery. [Earlier *mocayare* < Arabic *mukhayyar*]

Mo·ham·me·dan (mō·ham'ə·dən) adj. Of or pertaining to Mohammed or to his religion and institutions. — n. A follower of Mohammed or a believer in Islam; a Muslim. Also *Mahometan, Muhammadan, Muhammedan.*

Mohammedan calendar See under CALENDAR.

Mo·ham·me·dan·ism (mō·ham'ə·dən·iz'əm) n. Islam.

Mo·ha·ve (mō·hä'vē) n. One of a tribe of North American Indians of Yuman stock, formerly living along the Colorado River: also spelled *Mojave.*

Mo·hawk (mō'hôk) n. 1. One of a tribe of North American Indians of Iroquoian stock, one of the original Five Nations, formerly ranging from the Mohawk River to the St. Lawrence. 2. The language of this tribe. [< N.Am.Ind.]

Mo·he·gan (mō·hē'gən) n. 1. One of a tribe of North American Indians of Algonquian stock, formerly living along the Thames River in Connecticut. 2. Loosely, Mahican. [< Algonquian *maingan* wolf]

Mo·hi·can (mō·hē'kən) n. A Mahican.

Mo·hole (mō'hōl') n. A hole drilled or to be drilled through the ocean floor to the level of the Mohorovicic discontinuity.

Mo·hor·o·vic·ic discontinuity (mə·hôr'ə·vis'ik, -vich'ik) n. *Geol.* A rock layer forming a boundary zone beneath the earth's crust at depths of from about 6 to 25 miles and believed to explain certain changes in the character and velocity of seismic waves. Also **Mo·ho** (mō'hō). [after Andrija *Mohorovičić,* Yugoslavian geologist]

Mohs scale (mōz) *Mineral.* A qualitative scale in which the hardness of a mineral is determined by its ability to scratch, or be scratched by, any one of 15 minerals arranged in order of increasing hardness from talc to diamond. [after Friedrich *Mohs,* 1773–1839, German mineralogist]

moi·e·ty (moi'ə·tē) n. pl. ·ties 1. A half. 2. Any portion, part, or share. 3. *Anthropol.* Either of two basic groups that together constitute a tribe. [< F < L *medius* half]

moil (moil) v.i. 1. To work hard; toil. 2. To move about ceaselessly. — v.t. 3. To make wet. — n. 1. Toil; drudgery. 2. Confusion; uproar. [< OF *moillier, muiller* to wet < L *mollis* soft] — **moil'er** n. — **moil'ing·ly** adv.

moi·ré (mwä·rā') adj. Having a wavelike or watered appearance, as certain fabrics. — n. 1. A ribbed fabric, usu. silk or rayon, having a wavy or watered pattern: also *moire* (mwär, môr). 2. A wavy pattern produced on fabrics by engraved cylinders. [< F < *moire* watered silk]

moist (moist) adj. 1. Slightly wet or damp. 2. Saturated with or characterized by moisture or liquid. 3. Tearful or tearfully sentimental. [< OF, a fusion of L *musteus* dew + *mucidus* moldy] — **moist'ly** adv. — **moist'ness** n.

mois·ten (mois'ən) v.t. & v.i. To make or become moist. — **mois'ten·er** n.

mois·ture (mois'chər) n. 1. Water or other liquid diffused as a vapor in the air or as a liquid through or on the surface of objects. 2. Dampness. [< OF *moisteur*]

Mo·ja·ve (mō·hä'vē) See MOHAVE.

mo·lar (mō'lər) n. A grinding tooth, of which there are 12 in man, situated behind the canine and incisor teeth and having a broad, flattened crown. For illus. see TOOTH. — adj. 1. Grinding or adapted for grinding. 2. Pertaining to a molar. [< L < *mola* mill]

mo·las·ses (mə·las'iz) n. pl. **mo·las·ses** Any of various thick, dark-colored syrups obtained from sugar, sorghum, etc., during the refining process: also, *Brit., treacle.* [< Pg. < L *mellaceus* honeylike]

mold¹ (mōld) n. 1. A form or matrix that gives a particular shape to anything in a fluid or plastic condition. 2. A frame or model on or around which something is shaped or made: a basket *mold.* 3. That which is shaped or made in or on a mold. 4. The shape or pattern rendered by a mold. 5. General shape, form, or pattern. 6. Distinctive nature, character, or type. 7. *Archit.* A molding or set of moldings. — v.t. 1. To work into a particular shape or form. 2. To shape or form in or as in a mold. 3. To influence, determine, or direct: to *mold* public sentiment. 4. To follow the contours of; cling to. — v.i. 5. To assume or come to fit a particular shape or pattern. Also, *Brit., mould.* [< OF < L < *modus* measure, limit] — **mold'a·ble** adj. — **mold'er** n.

mold² (mōld) n. 1. Any of a variety of fungous growths commonly found on the surfaces of decaying food or in warm, moist places, and usu. having a woolly or furry texture. 2. A fungus producing one of these growths. — v.i. To become moldy. Also *Brit., mould.* [< obs. *mouled,* pp. of *moulen* to grow moldy]

mold³ (mōld) n. Soft, loose earth that is esp. suitable for plants because it is rich in decaying organic matter. — v.t. To cover with mold. Also, *Brit., mould.* [OE *molde* earth]

mold·board (mōld'bôrd', -bōrd') n. The curved metal plate of a plow that digs into and turns over the soil.

mold·er (mōl'dər) v.i. 1. To decay gradually and turn to dust; crumble. 2. To atrophy from lack of use. — v.t. 3. To cause to crumble. 4. To waste or squander. Also, *Brit., moulder.* [Freq. of obs. *mold* to crumble]

mold·ing (mōl'ding) n. 1. The act or process of one who or that which molds. 2. That which is molded. 3. *Archit.* a A cornice or other depressed or projecting member, used to decorate the surface or angle of a building, room, etc. b The decoratively molded surface of a cornice, jamb, etc. 4. A strip of decoratively shaped wood or other material, used to decorate or finish walls, doors, etc. Also, *Brit., moulding.*

mold·y (mōl'dē) adj. mold·i·er, mold·i·est 1. Covered with or containing mold. 2. Musty, as from age, lack of use, etc. Also, *Brit., mouldy.* — **mold'i·ness** n.

mole¹ (mōl) n. A small, permanent spot on the human skin, slightly protuberant and often dark and hairy. [OE *māl*]

mole² (mōl) n. Any of a number of small insectivorous mammals that live mainly underground and have soft fur, small eyes, and broad forefeet adapted for digging and burrowing: also called *taupe.* [ME *molle*]

COMMON MOLE
(6 to 8 inches long; tail 1 inch)

mole³ (mōl) n. 1. A massive, usu. stone barricade in the sea, built to enclose an anchorage or harbor for which it acts as a breakwater or pier. 2. An anchorage or harbor so enclosed. [< F < L < Gk. *mylē* millstone]

mole⁴ (mōl) *Chem.* The gram molecule: also spelled *mol.*

mo·lec·u·lar (mə·lek'yə·lər) adj. Pertaining to, consisting of, or caused by molecules. [< NL *molecularis*]

molecular weight *Chem.* The sum of the atomic weights of all the atoms in a molecule.

mol·e·cule (mol'ə·kyool) n. 1. *Chem.* One or more atoms constituting the smallest part of an element or compound that can exist separately without losing its chemical properties. 2. Any very small particle. [< F < NL *molecula,* dim. of L *moles* mass]

mole·hill (mōl'hil') n. 1. A small heap or mound of earth raised by a burrowing mole. 2. Something trivial or inconsequential: to make a mountain out of a *molehill.*

mole·skin (mōl'skin') n. 1. The dark gray pelt of a mole, very soft and fragile and used as a fur. 2. A heavy, twilled cotton fabric with a thick, soft nap on one side. 3. *Usu. pl.* Items of clothing, esp. trousers, made of this fabric.

mo·lest (mə·lest') v.t. 1. To disturb or annoy by unwarranted, excessive, or malicious interference. 2. To interfere with improperly or illicitly, esp. with a sexual motive. [< OF < L *molestus* troublesome] — **mo·les·ta·tion** (mō'les·tā'shən, mol'es-) n. — **mo·lest'er** n.

moll (mol) n. *Slang* 1. The girl friend of a gangster. 2. A prostitute. [< *Moll,* dim. of *Mary*]

mol·lie (mol'ē) n. Any of a variety of tropical fishes often raised in aquariums. Also **mol'ly.**

mol·li·fy (mol'ə·fī) v.t. ·fied, ·fy·ing 1. To make less angry, violent, or agitated; soothe. 2. To reduce the harshness, severity, or intensity of. [< F < LL < L *mollis* soft + *facere* to make] — **mol′li·fi′a·ble** *adj.* — **mol′li·fi·ca′tion** *n.* — **mol′li·fi′er** *n.* — **mol′li·fy·ing·ly** *adv.*

mol·lus·coid (mə·lus′koid) *adj.* Of or like a mollusk. Also **mol·lus·coi·dal** (mol′əs·koid′l).

mol·lusk (mol′əsk) *n. Zool.* A large group of unsegmented, soft-bodied invertebrates, usu. protected by a calcareous shell of one or more pieces, and including snails, mussels, oysters, clams, octopi, whelks, etc. Also **mol′lusc.** [< F < L *molluscus (nux)* soft, thin-shelled (nut)] — **mol·lus·can** (mə·lus′kən) *adj. & n.* — **mol′lus′cous** *adj.*

mol·ly·cod·dle (mol′ē·kod′l) *n.* Any overprotected or pampered person; also, an effeminate man or boy. — *v.t.* **·dled, ·dling** To pamper; coddle. [< *Molly* a personal name + CODDLE] — **mol′ly·cod′dler** *n.*

Mo·loch (mō′lok) In the Bible, a god of the Ammonites and Phoenicians to whom parents offered their children to be burnt in sacrifice. — *n.* Anything exacting merciless sacrifices. [< LL < Gk. < Hebrew *Mōlekh* a king]

molt (mōlt) *v.t. & v.i.* To cast off or shed (feathers, horns, skin, etc.) in preparation for periodic replacement by new growth. — *n.* 1. The act or process of molting. 2. That which is molted. Also, *Brit., moult.* [ME < OE < L *mutare* to change] — **molt′er** *n.*

mol·ten (mōl′tən) Archaic past participle of MELT. — *adj.* 1. Made fluid by heat; melted: *molten* metal. 2. Made by melting and casting in a mold: *molten* images.

mol·to (mōl′tō) *adv. Music* Much; very. [< Ital. < L *multum* much]

mo·lyb·de·nite (mə·lib′də·nīt) *n.* A soft, lead-gray molybdenum disulfide, MoS_2, the chief ore of molybdenum.

mo·lyb·de·num (mə·lib′də·nəm, mol′ib·dē′nəm) *n.* A hard, heavy, silver-white, metallic element (symbol Mo) of the chromium group, occurring only in combination, used to harden steel. See ELEMENT. [< NL < L < Gk. < *molybdos* lead]

mom (mom) *n.* Mother: used familiarly. [< MAMA]

mo·ment (mō′mənt) *n.* 1. A very short or relatively short period of time. 2. A particular point in time, usu. the present time. 3. A particular period or stage in a series of events: a great *moment* in history. 4. Importance; consequence: matters of great *moment.* 5. A brief period of excellence, distinction, enjoyment, etc. 6. *Mech.* **a** The tendency to produce motion, esp. rotatory motion. **b** A measure of such a tendency. [< F < L *momentum* movement]

mo·men·tar·i·ly (mō′mən·ter′ə·lē, mō′mən·ter′ə·lē) *adv.* 1. For a moment: *momentarily* at a loss. 2. In a moment; at any moment. 3. From moment to moment; progressively.

mo·men·tar·y (mō′mən·ter′ē) *adj.* 1. Lasting no more than a moment; fleeting. 2. Occurring or operating at every moment. — **mo′men·tar′i·ness** *n.*

mo·ment·ly (mō′mənt·lē) *adv.* 1. From moment to moment; at any instant. 2. For a moment.

mo·men·tous (mō·men′təs) *adj.* Of great importance or consequence. — **mo·men′tous·ly** *adv.* — **mo·men′tous·ness** *n.*

mo·men·tum (mō·men′təm) *n. pl.* **·ta** (-tə) or **·tums** 1. *Physics* The quantity of motion in a body as measured by the product of its mass and velocity. 2. Impetus, as of a body in motion.

mon- *combining form* Var. of MONO-.

mon·ad (mon′ad, mō′nad) *n.* 1. An indestructible unit; a simple and indivisible substance. 2. *Biol.* A minute, simple, single-celled organism. 3. *Chem.* An atom, radical, or element with a valence of one. — *adj.* Of, pertaining to, or consisting of a monad: also **mo·nad·ic** (mə·nad′ik) or **i·cal.** [< LL < Gk. < *monas* unit]

mon·arch (mon′ərk) *n.* 1. A hereditary constitutional ruler, as a king, queen, etc. 2. Formerly, a sole ruler of a state. 3. One who or that which surpasses others of the same kind. 4. *Entomol.* A large, orange and brown butterfly whose larvae feed on milkweed. [< LL < Gk. < *monos* alone + *archein* to rule] — **mo·nar·chal** (mə·när′kəl) *adj.* — **mo·nar′chal·ly** *adv.*

mo·nar·chi·cal (mə·när′ki·kəl) *adj.* 1. Of, pertaining to, or characteristic of a monarchy or monarch. 2. Governed by or favoring a monarch or monarchy. Also **mo·nar′chi·al, mo·nar′chic.** — **mo·nar′chi·cal·ly** *adv.*

mon·arch·ism (mon′ərk·iz′əm) *n.* 1. The principles or system of a monarchy. 2. The advocacy of a monarchy. — **mon′arch·ist** *n.* — **mon′arch·is′tic** *adj.*

mon·ar·chy (mon′ər·kē) *n. pl.* **·chies** 1. Government by a monarch; sovereign control. 2. A government or territory ruled by a monarch. — **absolute monarchy** A government in which the will of the monarch is positive law; a despotism. — **constitutional** or **limited monarchy** A monarchy in which the power and prerogative of the sovereign are limited by constitutional provisions.

mon·as·ter·y (mon′əs·ter′ē) *n. pl.* **·ter·ies** 1. A dwelling place occupied by monks living under religious vows and in seclusion. 2. The monks living in such a place. [< LL < LGk. < Gk. < *monazein* to live alone]

mo·nas·tic (mə·nas′tik) *adj.* 1. Of, pertaining to, or characteristic of monasteries or their inhabitants; ascetic. 2. Characteristic of a life of religious seclusion. Also **mon·as·te·ri·al** (mon′əs·tir′ē·əl), **mo·nas′ti·cal.** — *n.* A monk or other religious recluse. [< F < LL < Gk. *monastikos*] — **mon·as′ti·cal·ly** *adv.*

mo·nas·ti·cism (mə·nas′tə·siz′əm) *n.* The monastic life or system.

mon·a·tom·ic (mon′ə·tom′ik) *adj. Chem.* Consisting of a single atom, as the molecules of certain elements.

mon·au·ral (män·ôr′əl, mŏn′-) *adj.* 1. Pertaining to or characterized by the perception of sound by one ear only. 2. *Electronics* Designating a system of sound reproduction in which the sound is perceived as coming from one direction only.

mon·ax·i·al (mon·ak′sē·əl) *adj.* Having but one axis.

mon·a·zite (mon′ə·zīt) *n.* A resinous, brownish red or brown phosphate of the lanthanide metals, chiefly cerium, lanthanum, and didymium, an important source of thorium. [< G < Gk. *monazein* to live alone]

Mon·day (mun′dē, -dā) *n.* The second day of the week. [OE *mōn(an)dæg* day of the moon]

mo·ne·cious (mə·nē′shəs, mō-) See MONOECIOUS.

Mo·nel metal (mō·nel′) A corrosion-resistant nickel alloy containing copper, iron, and manganese, used for industrial equipment machine parts, etc.: a trade name. [after Ambrose *Monel*, d. 1921, U.S. manufacturer]

mon·e·tar·y (mon′ə·ter′ē, mun′-) *adj.* 1. Of or pertaining to currency or coinage. 2. Pertaining to or concerned with money. [< L *monetarius* of a mint] — **mon′e·tar′i·ly** *adv.*

mon·ey (mun′ē) *n. pl.* **mon·eys** or **mon·ies** 1. Officially issued coins and paper currency that serve as a medium of exchange and a measure of value and may be used as payment for goods and services and for settlement of debts. ◆ Collateral adjective: *pecuniary.* 2. Any substance or object used similarly, as checks, wampum, etc. 3. Property of any type having monetary value. 4. Money of account. 5. A system of coinage. 6. *pl.* Sums of money. 7. Pecuniary profits. — **to put money on** To place a bet on. [< OF < L *moneta* mint]

mon·ey·bag (mun′ē·bag) *n.* 1. A bag for holding money. 2. *pl. Slang* A wealthy person; also, wealth.

money belt A belt with pouches for carrying money.

mon·ey·chang·er (mun′ē·chān′jər) *n.* 1. One whose business it is to change money at a prescribed rate. 2. A device for holding and dispensing coins.

mon·eyed (mun′ēd) *adj.* 1. Possessed of money; wealthy. 2. Consisting of, arising from, or representing money or wealth: *moneyed* interests. Also spelled *monied.*

mon·ey·lend·er (mun′ē·len′dər) *n.* One whose business is the lending of money at interest.

mon·ey·mak·ing (mun′ē·mā′king) *adj.* Likely to bring in money; profitable. — *n.* The acquisition of money or wealth. — **mon′ey·mak′er** *n.*

money of account A monetary denomination used in keeping accounts, usu. not represented by a coin, as the U.S. mill.

money order An order for the payment of a specified sum of money; esp., such an order issued at one post office or telegraph office and payable at another.

mon·ger (mung′gər, mong′-) *n.* 1. *Brit.* A dealer or trader: chiefly in combination: *fishmonger.* 2. One who engages in discreditable matters: chiefly in compounds: a *scandalmonger.* [OE < L *mango* dealer]

Mon·gol (mong′gəl, -gol, -gŏl) *n.* 1. A member of any of the native tribes of Mongolia; esp., one inhabiting eastern Mongolia or a Kalmuck. 2. Any of the Mongolian languages. 3. A member of the Mongoloid ethnic division. — *adj.* Mongolian (def. 1). [< Mongolian *mong* brave]

Mon·go·li·an (mong·gō′lē·ən, -gōl′yən, mon-) *adj.* 1. Of or pertaining to Mongolia, its people, or their languages. 2. Exhibiting Mongolism. — *n.* 1. A native of Mongolia. 2. A subfamily of the Altaic languages, including the languages of the Mongols. 3. A person afflicted with Mongolism.

Mon·gol·ism (mong′gəl·iz′əm) *n.* A form of congenital mental deficiency characterized by a broad flat face and skull, obliquely set, narrow eyes, etc.

Mon·go·loid (mong′gə·loid) *adj.* 1. *Anthropol.* Of, pertaining to, or belonging to a major ethnic division of the human species, characterized by yellowish skin, slanting eyes, straight head hair, high cheek bones, etc. 2. Resembling, related to, or characteristic of Mongols or Mongolians. 3. Characterized by Mongolism. — *n.* A Mongoloid person.

mon·goose (mong′gōōs, mung′-) *n. pl.* **·goos·es** A small, ferretlike, carnivorous mammal that destroys rats and can kill venomous snakes without injury to itself. [< Marathi *mangus*]

MONGOOSE
(To 18 inches long; tail 18 inches)

mon·grel (mung′grəl, mong′-) *n.* 1. The progeny produced by crossing different breeds or varieties of plants or animals; esp. a dog of mixed breed. 2. Any incongruous mixture. —

adj. Of mixed breed, origin, nature, etc.: often a contemptuous term: a *mongrel* language. [ME < obs. *mong* mixture + *-rel,* dim. suffix]

'mongst (mungst) *prep. Poetic* Amongst.

mon·ied (mun′ēd) See MONEYED.

mon·i·ker (mon′ə·kər) *n. Informal* A name, signature, or nickname. Also **mon′ick·er.** [Prob. blend of MONOGRAM and MARKER]

mon·ism (mon′iz·əm, mō′niz·əm) *n. Philos.* The doctrine that there is but one principle of being or ultimate substance, as mind or matter. [< NL < Gk. *monos* single] — **mon′ist** *n.* — **mo·nis′tic** or **·ti·cal** *adj.*

mo·ni·tion (mō·nish′ən) *n.* 1. A warning or admonition, as of impending danger. 2. An official, legal, or formal notice. [< OF < L *monitus,* pp. of *monere* to warn]

mon·i·tor (mon′ə·tər) *n.* 1. In some schools, a student selected to perform certain duties in class, as helping to keep records, maintain order, etc. 2. One who advises or cautions, esp. in matters of conduct. 3. Something that warns or reminds. 4. Formerly, an ironclad warship having a low, flat deck and low freeboard, and fitted with one or more revolving turrets carrying heavy guns. 5. *Zool.* Any of several large, carnivorous lizards of Africa, Asia, and Australia. 6. *Telecom.* A receiver, loudspeaker, or other apparatus used to check radio or television broadcasts for quality of transmission, frequency, compliance with laws, material transmitted, etc. — *v.t. & v.i.* 1. *Telecom.* To listen to or watch (a broadcast) with a monitor. 2. To act or supervise as a monitor (def. 1). [< L *monere* to warn] — **mon′i·to′ri·al** (-tôr′ē·əl, -tō′rē-) *adj.* — **mon′i·tor·ship′** *n.*

mon·i·to·ry (mon′ə·tôr′ē, -tō′rē) *adj.* Conveying a warning; admonitory. — *n.* A monitory letter. [< L *monitor*]

monk (mungk) *n.* 1. One who has taken the religious vows of poverty, chastity, and obedience, usu. a member of a monastic order. 2. Formerly, a religious hermit. [OE < LL < LGk. *monos* alone]

mon·key (mung′kē) *n.* 1. Any of the primates, excluding the anthropoid apes, having elongate limbs, hands and feet adapted for grasping, and a highly developed nervous system; esp., the marmosets, baboons, macaques, etc. 2. One who acts in a way suggestive of a monkey, as a mischievous child. — *v.i. Informal* To play or trifle; meddle; fool: often with *with* or *around.* [? < MLG *Moneke,* name of the son of Martin the Ape in *Reynard the Fox*]

monkey business *Slang* Foolish tricks; deceitful or mischievous behavior.

mon·key·shine (mung′kē·shīn′) *n. Usu. pl. Slang* A mischievous or playful trick, prank, or joke.

monkey wrench A wrench having an adjustable jaw for grasping nuts, bolts, etc., of various sizes. — **to throw a monkey wrench into** *U.S. Informal* To disrupt.

monk's cloth (mungks) A sturdy cotton fabric with a basket weave used for drapes, curtains, etc.

monks·hood (mungks′hŏŏd′) *n.* A plant having the upper sepal arched like a hood; esp., a poisonous variety: also called *aconite.*

mono- *combining form* 1. Single; one: *monologue.* 2. *Chem.* Denoting the presence in a compound of a single atom, or an equivalent of the element or radical to the name of which it is prefixed. Also, before vowels, **mon-.** [< Gk. *monos* single]

mon·o·ba·sic (mon′ə·bā′sik) *adj. Chem.* Possessing but a single hydrogen atom replaceable by a metal or positive radical: applied to acids.

mon·o·chrome (mon′ə·krōm) *n.* A painting or drawing in a single color or in various shades of the same color. [< L < Gk. *monos* single + *chrōma* color] — **mon′o·chro·mat′ic,** **mon′o·chrom′ic** or **i·cal** *adj.* — **mon′o·chro′mist** *n.*

mon·o·cle (mon′ə·kəl) *n.* An eyeglass for one eye. [< F < LL < Gk. *monos* single + L *oculus* eye] — **mon′o·cled** *adj.*

mon·o·cli·nal (mon′ə·klī′nəl) *Geol. adj.* Having an inclination in only one direction, or composed of rock strata so inclined. — *n.* A monocline. — **mon′o·cli′nal·ly** *adv.*

mon·o·cline (mon′ə·klīn) *n. Geol.* A monoclinal rock structure. [< MONO- + Gk. *klinein* to incline]

mon·o·cli·nous (mon′ə·klī′nəs) *adj. Bot.* Containing both stamens and pistils in the same flower; hermaphrodite. [< MONO- + Gk. *klīne* bed, couch]

mon·o·cot·y·le·don (mon′ə·kot′ə·lēd′n) *n. Bot.* Any seed plant bearing one cotyledon in the embryo. Also **mon′o·cot′.** [< NL] — **mon′o·cot′y·le′do·nous** *adj.*

mon·o·dy (mon′ə·dē) *n. pl.* **·dies** 1. A poem in which the poet laments the death of another. 2. An ode performed by one voice; esp., a lyric ode in a Greek tragedy; dirge. 3. *Music* A composition in which there is only one vocal part; also, the style of such a composition. [< LL < Gk. *monos* alone + *aeidein* to sing] — **mo·nod′ic** (mə·nod′ik) or **·i·cal** *adj.* — **mo·nod′i·cal·ly** *adv.* — **mon′o·dist** *n.*

mo·noe·cious (mə·nē′shəs) *adj.* 1. *Biol.* Hermaphroditic. 2. *Bot.* Monoclinous. Also *monecious, monoicous.* Also **mo·ne′cian.** [< MON- + Gk. *oikos* house]

mo·nog·a·my (mə·nog′ə·mē) *n.* The condition or practice of having only one wife or husband at a time. [< F < LL < Gk. *monos* single + *gamos* marriage] — **mon·o·gam·ic** (mon′ə·gam′ik) *adj.* — **mo·nog′a·mist** *n.* — **mo·nog′a·mous** *adj.*

mon·o·gram (mon′ə·gram) *n.* Two or more letters intertwined into one; esp., the initials of one's name. — *v.t.* **mon·o·gramed** or **·grammed, mon·o·gram·ing** or **·gram·ming** To mark with a monogram. [< LL < Gk. *monos* single + *grammē* letter] — **mon′o·gram·mat′ic** (-grə·mat′ik) *adj.*

mon·o·graph (mon′ə·graf, -gräf) *n.* A book, pamphlet, or treatise on one subject or on a single aspect of a subject. — **mo·nog′ra·pher** (mə·nog′rə·fər) *n.* — **mon′o·graph′ic** *adj.*

mon·o·lith (mon′ə·lith) *n.* A single block of stone, usu. very large, used in architecture and sculpture. [< LL < Gk. < *mono-* + *lithos* stone]

mon·o·lith·ic (mon′ə·lith′ik) *adj.* 1. Of or resembling a monolith. 2. Having a massive, uniform structure that does not permit individual variations: a *monolithic* state.

mon·o·logue (mon′ə·lôg, -log) *n.* 1. A lengthy speech by one person, esp. one that interferes with conversation. 2. A play or dramatic composition for one actor only. 3. A soliloquy. 4. A poem, etc., written as a soliloquy. Also **mon′o·log.** [< F < Gk. < *monos* alone + *-logos* speech] — **mo·nol·o·gist** (mə·nol′ə·jist) *n.*

mon·o·ma·ni·a (mon′ə·mā′nē·ə, -mān′yə) *n.* 1. A mental disorder in which a person, otherwise rational, is obsessed with one idea or subject. 2. An exaggerated fondness or irrational enthusiasm for something; craze. [< NL] — **mon′o·ma′ni·ac** *n.* — **mon′o·ma·ni′a·cal** (-mə·nī′ə·kəl) *adj.*

mon·o·mer (mon′ə·mər) *n. Chem.* The structural unit of a polymer. [< MONO- + Gk. *mēros* part]

mon·o·met·al·ism (mon′ō·met′əl·iz′əm) *n.* The theory or system of a single metallic standard in coinage. Also **mon′o·met′al·ism.** — **mon′o·me·tal′lic** (-mə·tal′ik) *adj.*

mo·no·mi·al (mō·nō′mē·əl) *adj.* Consisting of a single word or term. — *n.* A monomial term or expression.

mon·o·nu·cle·ar (mon′ə·nōō′klē·ər, -nyōō′-) *adj.* Having only one nucleus, as certain cells of the body.

mon·o·nu·cle·o·sis (mon′ō·nōō′klē·ō′sis, -nyōō′-) *n. Pathol.* 1. The presence in the blood of an abnormal number of mononuclear leucocytes. 2. Infectious mononucleosis.

mon·o·plane (mon′ə·plān) *n. Aeron.* An airplane with only one wing or pair of wings.

mo·nop·o·lize (mə·nop′ə·līz) *v.t.* **·lized, ·liz·ing** 1. To obtain a monopoly of. 2. To assume exclusive possession or control of. — **mo·nop′o·li·za′tion** *n.* — **mo·nop′o·liz′er** *n.*

mo·nop·o·ly (mə·nop′ə·lē) *n. pl.* **·lies** 1. The exclusive control of a commodity, service, or means of production in a particular market, with the resulting power to fix prices. 2. *Law* An exclusive privilege, granted by a government, of buying, selling, making, or using anything. 3. A company having a monopoly. 4. The commodity, service, etc., controlled under a monopoly. 5. Exclusive possession or control of anything. [< L < Gk. < *monos* alone + *pōlein* to sell] — **mo·nop′o·lism** *n.* — **mo·nop′o·list** *n. & adj.* — **mo·nop′o·lis′tic** *adj.*

mon·o·pro·pel·lant (mon′ō·prə·pel′ənt) *n. Aerospace* A liquid rocket propellant consisting of fuel and oxidizer mixed and ready for simultaneous ignition.

mon·o·rail (mon′ō·rāl′) *n.* 1. A single rail serving as a track for cars either suspended from it or balanced upon it. 2. A railway using such a track.

mon·o·sac·cha·ride (mon′ə·sak′ə·rīd, -rid) *n. Biochem.* Any of a class of simple sugars that cannot be decomposed by hydrolysis, as glucose and fructose.

mon·o·syl·la·bic (mon′ə·si·lab′ik) *adj.* 1. Having only one syllable. 2. Using or speaking in monosyllables. 3. Composed of monosyllables. — **mon′o·syl·lab′i·cal·ly** *adv.*

mon·o·syl·la·ble (mon′ə·sil′ə·bəl) *n.* A word of one syllable, as *no.*

mon·o·the·ism (mon′ə·thē·iz′əm) *n.* The doctrine or belief that there is but one God. [< MONO- + Gk. *theos* god] — **mon′o·the·ist** *n.* — **mon′o·the·is′tic** or **·ti·cal** *adj.* — **mon′o·the·is′ti·cal·ly** *adv.*

mon·o·tone (mon′ə·tōn) *n.* 1. The utterance of a succession of words, etc., in a single tone. 2. Sameness in expression, style, color, etc. 3. A single musical tone unvaried in pitch. [< LGk. < Gk. *mōnos* single + *tōnos* tone]

mo·not·o·nous (mə·not′ə·nəs) *adj.* 1. Unvaried in tone. 2. Tiresome by reason of monotony. [< LGk. *monotonos*] — **mo·not′o·nous·ly** *adv.* — **mo·not′o·nous·ness** *n.*

mo·not·o·ny (mə·not′ə·nē) *n.* 1. Tiresome uniformity; irksome sameness. 2. Lack of variety in cadence, pitch, or inflection. [< LGk. < Gk. *monos* single + *tonos* tone]

mon·o·treme (mon′ə·trēm) *n.* A member of the lowest order of mammals, including the egg-laying platypuses and the echidnas, that have a single opening for the excretory and reproductive functions. [< MONO- + Gk. *trēma* hole] — **mon′o·trem′a·tous** (-trem′ə·təs) *adj.*

mon·o·type (mon′ə·tīp′) *n. Printing* A print from a metal plate on which a design, painting, etc., has been made.

Mon·o·type (mon′ə·tīp) *n. Printing* A machine that casts and sets type in single characters or units: a trade name.

mon·o·typ·ic (mon′ə·tip′ik) *adj. Biol.* 1. Having only one type: a *monotypic* genus. 2. Being a monotype.

mon·o·va·lent (mon′ə·vā′lənt) *adj. Chem.* Univalent. — **mon′o·va′lence, mon′o·va′len·cy** *n.* [< MONO- + L *valere* to be strong]

mon·ox·ide (mon·ok′sīd, mə·nok′-) *n. Chem.* An oxide containing a single atom of oxygen in each molecule.

Monroe Doctrine The doctrine, essentially formulated by President Monroe, that any attempt by European powers to interfere in the affairs of the American countries or to acquire territory on the American continents would be regarded by the U.S. as an unfriendly act.

mons (monz) *n. pl.* **mon·tes** (mon′tēz) *Anat.* The rounded fatty swelling over the pubic symphysis, covered with hair in the adult; the **mons pu·bis** (pyōō′bis) of the male, or the **mons ven·er·is** (ven′ər·is) of the female. [< L, hill]

Mon·sei·gneur (mon·sēn′yər; *Fr.* môn̂·se·nyœr′) *n. pl.* **Mes·sei·gneurs** (me·se·nyœr′) 1. My lord: a French title given to the higher nobility, bishops, etc. 2. One having this title. [< F *mon* my + *seigneur* lord < L *senior* older]

mon·sieur (mə·syûr′; *Fr.* mə·syœ′) *n. pl.* **mes·sieurs** (mes′ərz, *Fr.* me·syœ′) The French title of courtesy for men, equivalent to *Mr.* and *sir.* [< F *mon* + *sieur*, short for *seigneur* lord]

Mon·si·gnor (mon·sēn′yər, *Ital.* môn′sēn·nyōr′) *n. pl.* **·gnors** or *Ital.* **·gno·ri** (-nyō′rē) 1. In the Roman Catholic Church, a title of honor of certain prelates. 2. One having this title. [< Ital. < F *monseigneur*]

mon·soon (mon·sōōn′) *n. Meteorol.* 1. A seasonal wind that blows along the Asian coast of the Pacific and from the Indian Ocean, in winter from the northeast, in summer from the southwest. 2. The summer monsoon, characterized by heavy rains. [< MDu. < Pg. < Arabic *mausim* season]

mon·ster (mon′stər) *n.* 1. One who or that which is abnormal, unnatural, or hideous in form. 2. An animal or plant that is malformed; monstrosity. 3. One who or that which inspires hate or horror because of cruelty, wickedness, etc. 4. A huge person or thing. 5. A fabulous creature, as a centaur, dragon, etc. — *adj.* Enormous; huge. [< OF < L *monstrum* divine warning < *monere* to warn]

mon·strance (mon′strəns) *n.* In Roman Catholic ritual, a vessel in which the consecrated Host is exposed for adoration. [< OF < Med.L < L *monstrare* to show]

mon·stros·i·ty (mon·stros′ə·tē) *n. pl.* **·ties** 1. One who or that which is monstrous; also, a monster. 2. The condition or character of being monstrous. [< L *monstrositas*]

mon·strous (mon′strəs) *adj.* 1. Deviating greatly from the natural in form, structure, or character. 2. Enormous; huge. 3. Hideous; horrible; atrocious. 4. Strikingly wrong; ridiculous; absurd. 5. Having the appearance or nature of a fabulous monster. [< OF < LL < L *monstrum*] — **mon′strous·ly** *adv.* — **mon′strous·ness** *n.*

mon·tage (mon·täzh′) *n.* 1. A picture made by superimposing or arranging a number of different pictorial elements; also, the art or process of making such a picture. 2. In motion pictures or television, a rapid sequence of images used to illustrate a group of associated ideas. 3. Similar techniques in radio and writing. [< F < *monter* to mount]

mon·te (mon′tē) *n.* A Spanish or Spanish-American gambling game of cards. Also **monte bank.** [< Sp., lit., mountain < L; in ref. to the pile of unplayed cards]

month (munth) *n.* 1. One of the twelve parts (**calendar month**) into which the calendar year is divided. 2. A period of thirty days or four weeks. 3. The twelfth part (**solar month**) of the solar year. 4. The period (**lunar month**), equivalent to 29.53 days, during which the moon makes a complete revolution. ◆ Collateral adjective *men·sal.* [OE *mōnath*]

month·ly (munth′lē) *adj.* 1. Happening, done, appearing, etc., every month. 2. Of or pertaining to a month. 3. Pertaining to the menses. 4. Continuing or lasting for a month. — *adv.* Once a month. — *n. pl.* **·lies** 1. A periodical published once a month. 2. *pl.* Menstruation.

mon·u·ment (mon′yə·mənt) *n.* 1. A statue, pillar, plaque, etc., erected to perpetuate the memory of a person, event, or historical period. 2. A tombstone. 3. Any conspicuous or fine structure surviving from the past. 4. A work of art, scholarship, etc., regarded as having enduring value. 5. A stone boundary marker. [< L *monere* to remind]

mon·u·men·tal (mon′yə·men′təl) *adj.* 1. Of, pertaining to, or serving as a monument. 2. Like a monument; enduring; imposing; massive. 3. Having great significance: a

monumental study. 4. *Informal* Very large; huge. [< L *monumentalis*] — **mon′u·men′tal·ly** *adv.*

-mony *suffix of nouns* The condition, state, or thing resulting from: *parsimony.* [< L *-monia*]

moo (mōō) *v.i.* To make the deep, moaning sound of a cow; to low. — *n. pl.* **moos** The sound made by a cow. [Imit.]

mooch (mōōch) *Slang v.t.* 1. To obtain without paying; beg; cadge. 2. To steal. — *v.i.* 3. To loiter. 4. To skulk; sneak. [< OF *muchier* to hide, skulk] — **mooch′er** *n.*

mood[1] (mōōd) *n.* 1. A specific state of mind or feeling, esp. a temporary one. 2. *pl.* Fits of sullen or morose behavior. — **in the mood** Disposed; inclined. [OE *mōd* mind]

mood[2] (mōōd) *n. Gram.* The set of distinctive forms of a verb showing the attitude and understanding of the speaker regarding the action or condition expressed: also *mode.* See IMPERATIVE, INDICATIVE, SUBJUNCTIVE. [Var. of MODE]

mood·y (mōō′dē) *adj.* **mood·i·er, mood·i·est** 1. Given to sudden moods of moroseness. 2. Expressive of such moods. [OE *mōd* courage] — **mood′i·ly** *adv.* — **mood′i·ness** *n.*

moon (mōōn) *n.* 1. A celestial body revolving around the earth from west to east in a lunar month of 29.53 days, and accompanying the earth in its yearly revolution about the sun. 2. This celestial body at a specific time of the month: new *moon;* full *moon.* 3. Any satellite revolving about a planet. 4. A month; esp., a lunar month. 5. Something resembling a full moon or crescent. 6. Moonlight. — *v.i.* 1. *Informal* To stare or wander about abstractedly. — *v.t.* 2. To pass (time) in such a way. [OE *mōna*]

moon·beam (mōōn′bēm′) *n.* A ray of moonlight.

moon·calf (mōōn′kaf′, -käf′) *n.* An imbecile; idiot.

moon·light (mōōn′līt′) *n.* The light of the moon. — *adj.* Pertaining to, illuminated by, or performed by moonlight: a *moonlight* excursion. — **moon′lit′** (-lit′) *adj.*

moon·light·ing (mōōn′līt′ing) *n. Slang* The act of one who holds a job in addition to the regular day's work. — **moon′light′er** *n.*

moon·shine (mōōn′shīn′) *n.* 1. Moonlight. 2. Nonsense. 3. *Informal* Smuggled or illicitly distilled whisky, etc.

moon·shin·er (mōōn′shī′nər) *n. U.S. Informal* One who conducts an illegal trade by night, esp. distilling.

moon·stone (mōōn′stōn′) *n.* A pearly, opalescent variety of orthoclase and albite, valued as a gemstone.

moon·struck (mōōn′struk′) *adj.* Lunatic; deranged. Also **moon′strick′en** (-strik′ən).

moon·y (mōō′nē) *adj.* **moon·i·er, moon·i·est** *Informal* Absent-minded; dreamy.

moor[1] (mōōr) *n. Brit.* A tract of wasteland sometimes covered with heath, often elevated, marshy, and abounding in peat; a heath. [OE *mōr*]

moor[2] (mōōr) *v.t.* 1. To secure (a ship, etc.) in place by means of cables attached to shore, anchors, etc. 2. To secure; fix. — *v.i.* 3. To secure a ship, etc., in position. 4. To be secured by chains or cables. [ME < MDu. *māren* to fasten] — **moor′age** (-ij) *n.*

Moor (mōōr) *n.* 1. A Moslem of mixed Berber and Arab ancestry, esp. one of the Saracen invaders of Spain in the 8th century. 2. A native of Morocco. [< OF < L < Gk. *Mauros*, lit., dark] — **Moor′ish** *adj.*

moor cock The male of the red grouse.

moor·fowl (mōōr′foul′) *n.* The red grouse.

moor hen *n.* The female of the red grouse.

moor·ing (mōōr′ing) *n.* 1. *Chiefly pl.* A mooring place. 2. *Chiefly pl.* That which secures an object, as a cable.

moose (mōōs) *n. pl.* **moose** 1. A large, heavily built mammal of the deer family, found in northern U.S. and Canada, the male of which bears huge palmate antlers. 2. The elk (def. 1). [< Algonquian *moosu* he strips off; because it eats the bark of trees]

moot (mōōt) *adj.* Open to discussion: debatable: a *moot* point. — *v.t.* 1. To bring up for discussion or debate. 2. To argue (a case) in a moot court. — *n.* 1. Discussion or argument. 2. In early English history, a meeting of freemen to discuss local affairs. [OE *mōt* assembly, court] — **moot′er** *n.*

moot court A court for the trial of hypothetical legal cases by law students.

mop[1] (mop) *n.* 1. A device for cleaning floors, consisting of a bunch of heavy cotton yarn attached to a handle. 2. Any loosely tangled bunch, esp. of hair. — *v.t.* **mopped, mop·ping** To rub or wipe with or as with a mop. — **to mop up** *Informal* To finish. [ME *mappe*]

mop[2] (mop) *n.* A wry mouth. — *v.i.* To make a wry face.

mope (mōp) *v.* **moped, mop·ing** *v.i.* To be gloomy, listless, or dispirited. — *n.* 1. One who mopes. 2. *pl.* Dejection; depression. — **mop′er** *n.* — **mop′ish** *adj.* — **mop′ish·ly** *adv.* — **mop′ish·ness** *n.*

mo·ped (mō′ped) *n.* A motorized bicycle. [< MO(TOR) + PED(AL)] — **mo′ped·al·ing, mo′ped·ing** *n.* — **mo·ped′al·ist** *n.*

MOOSE
(To 7 feet high at shoulder)

mop·pet (mop′it) *n. Informal* A child. [Dim. of MOP¹]

mo·raine (mə·rān′, mō-) *n. Geol.* Debris in various topographic forms that has been carried by a glacier, either along its course, at its edges, or at its lower terminus. [< F dial. *morēna*] **— mo·rain′al, mo·rain′ic** *adj.*

mor·al (môr′əl, mor′-) *adj.* **1.** Of or related to conduct or character from the point of view of right and wrong: *moral* goodness. **2.** Of good character; right or proper in behavior. **3.** Sexually virtuous. **4.** Teaching standards of right and wrong. **5.** Capable of distinguishing between right and wrong: Man is a *moral* agent. **6.** Concerned with the establishment and application of principles of right and wrong: *moral* theology. **7.** Arising from a sense of duty and right conduct: a *moral* obligation. **8.** Acting not by physical force but by appeal to character, etc.: *moral* support. **9.** Based on probability rather than on objective evidence: *moral* certainty. *— n.* **1.** The lesson or teaching contained in or implied by a fable, poem, etc. **2.** *pl.* Conduct or behavior with regard to right and wrong, esp. in sexual matters. **3.** A maxim. [< OF < L *mos* custom; in the pl., *mores* manners, morals] **— mor′al·ly** *adv.*
— Syn. (adj.) **2.** ethical, conscientious, scrupulous, upright, just, honest. **— Ant.** See synonyms for IMMORAL.

mo·rale (mə·ral′, -räl′, mō-) *n.* State of mind with reference to confidence, courage, hope, zeal, etc. [< F]

mor·al·ist (môr′əl·ist, mor′-) *n.* **1.** A teacher of morals. **2.** One who practices morality. **— mor′al·is′tic** *adj.*

mo·ral·i·ty (mə·ral′ə·tē, mô-) *n. pl.* **·ties 1.** The quality of being morally right; virtue. **2.** Conformity to standards of right conduct. **3.** Virtuous conduct, often sexual virtue. **4.** A system of the principles of right and wrong conduct; ethics. **5.** A lesson in morals. **6.** A morality play.

morality play A form of allegorical drama of the 15th and 16th centuries in which the characters were personified virtues, vices, mental attributes, etc.

mor·al·ize (môr′əl·īz, mor′-) *v.* **·ized, ·iz·ing** *v.i.* **1.** To make moral reflections; talk about morality. *— v.t.* **2.** To explain in a moral sense; derive a moral from. **3.** To improve the morals of. [< MF *moralizer*] **— mor′al·i·za′tion** *n.* **— mor′al·iz′er** *n.*

mo·rass (mə·ras′, mô-, mō-) *n.* **1.** A tract of low-lying, soft, wet ground; marsh; bog. **2.** Anything that impedes, perplexes, or traps. [< Du. < OF *maresc* < Gmc.]

mor·a·to·ri·um (môr′ə·tôr′ē·əm, -tō′rē, mor′-) *n. pl.* **·ri·a** (-rē·ə) or **·ri·ums 1.** A legal authorization to a debtor to suspend payments for a given period. **2.** The period during which such suspension is in effect. **3.** Any authorized suspension or deferment of action. [< NL < LL < L *morari* to delay]

mor·a·to·ry (môr′ə·tôr′ē, -tō′rē, mor′-) *adj.* Pertaining to or intended to delay; especially, designating legislation authorizing a moratorium. [< LL < L *morari* to delay]

Mo·ra·vi·an (mô·rā′vē·ən, mō-) *adj.* Pertaining to Moravia, the Moravians, or the Moravian Church. *— n.* **1.** A native of Moravia. **2.** A member of the Moravian Church.

mo·ray (môr′ā, mō·rā′) *n.* A brightly colored, voracious eel inhabiting tropical and subtropical waters. Also **mo′ray eel.** [Origin uncertain]

mor·bid (môr′bid) *adj.* **1.** Taking or showing an excessive interest in matters of a gruesome or unwholesome nature. **2.** Grisly; gruesome: a *morbid* fantasy. **3.** Pertaining to, arising from, or affected by disease. [< L < *morbus* disease] **— mor′bid·ly** *adv.* **— mor·bid′i·ty, mor′bid·ness** *n.*

mor·dant (môr′dənt) *adj.* **1.** Biting; cutting; sarcastic: a *mordant* wit. **2.** Acting to fix colors in dyeing. *— n.* **1.** A substance that, by combining with a dyestuff, serves to produce a fixed color in a textile, leather, etc. **2.** In etching, a corrosive used to bite into the lines traced on a metal plate. *— v.t.* To treat or imbue with a mordant. [< F, ppr. of OF *modre* to bite] **— mor′dan·cy** *n.*

Mor·de·cai (môr′də·kī, -kā·ī) In the Old Testament, Esther's cousin, instrumental in saving the Jews. *Esth.* ii 5.

mor·dent (môr′dənt) *n. Music* A trill-like melodic ornamentation; also, the symbol that indicates this. [< G < Ital. < *mordere* to bite]

more (môr, mōr) *adj. superlative* **most 1.** Greater in amount, extent, degree, or number: comparative of *much* and *many.* **2.** Additional: *More* coffee, please. *— n.* **1.** A greater or additional quantity, amount, etc. **2.** That which exceeds or excels something else. *— adv.* **1.** In or to a greater extent or degree: used to form the comparative of many adjectives and adverbs of two or more syllables: *more* beautiful. **2.** In addition; further. **— more or less 1.** In some undetermined degree. **2.** Approximately. [OE *māra*]

more·o·ver (môr·ō′vər, mōr-) *adv.* Beyond what has been said; further; besides; likewise; in addition.

mo·res (môr′āz, mō′räz, môr′ēz, mō′rēz) *n.pl. Sociol.* **1.** The established, traditional customs regarded by a social group as essential to its preservation. **2.** The accepted conventions of a group. [< L, pl. of *mos, moris* custom]

mor·ga·nat·ic (môr′gə·nat′ik) *adj.* Of or designating a form of legitimate marriage between a member of certain royal families of Europe and a person of inferior rank, in which the titles and estates are not shared by the inferior partner or their children. [< NL < LL < OHG *morgangeba* morning gift] **— mor′ga·nat′i·cal·ly** *adv.*

morgue (môrg) *n.* **1.** A place where the bodies of unknown dead persons and of those killed in accidents are kept for identification. **2.** In a newspaper editorial office, the department in charge of filed items and biographical material used for obituary notices, etc. [< F]

mor·i·bund (môr′ə·bund, -bənd, mor′-) *adj.* **1.** At the point of death; dying. **2.** Approaching extinction. [< L < *mori* to die] **— mor′i·bun′di·ty** *n.* **— mor′i·bund·ly** *adv.*

mo·ri·on (môr′ē·on, mō′rē-) *n.* An open, crested, visorless helmet, worn in the 16th and 17th centuries. [< MF < Sp. < *morra* crown of the head]

Mo·ris·co (mə·ris′kō) *adj.* Moorish. *— n. pl.* **·cos** or **·coes** A Moor, especially one of Spain. [< Sp. < *moro* Moor]

Mor·mon (môr′mən) *n.* **1.** A member of the Mormon Church; a Latter-day Saint. **2.** In Mormon belief, a prophet of the fourth century who wrote, on golden tablets, a history of the early American people. *— adj.* Of or pertaining to the Mormons or their religion. **— Mor′mon·ism** *n.*

Mormon Church The Church of Jesus Christ of Latter-day Saints, founded by Joseph Smith in 1830.

Mormon State Nickname of Utah.

morn (môrn) *n. Poetic* The morning. [OE *morne*]

morn·ing (môr′ning) *n.* **1.** The early part of the day; the time from midnight to noon, or from sunrise to noon. **2.** The early part or stage of anything. *— adj.* Pertaining to or occurring in the morning. ♦ Collateral adjective: *matutinal.* [ME *morwen* + *-ing* by analogy with evening]

morn·ing-glo·ry (môr′ning·glôr′ē, -glō′rē) *n.* Any of various twining plants with colored, funnel-shaped flowers.

morning star A planet, esp. Venus, when rising in the east shortly before the sun.

Mo·ro (môr′ō, mō′rō) *n. pl.* **·ros 1.** A member of any of the various Moslem Malay tribes of the southern Philippines. **2.** The language of the Moros. *— adj.* Of or pertaining to the Moros or their language. [< Sp., Moor]

mo·roc·co (mə·rok′ō) *n.* **1.** A fine flexible leather, made originally in Morocco from goatskin tanned with sumac. **2.** Any soft, grained leather. Also **morocco leather.**

Mo·roc·can (mə·rok′ən) A native or inhabitant of Morocco. *— adj.* Of or pertaining to Morocco.

mo·ron (môr′on, mō′ron) *n.* **1.** A person exhibiting the mildest degree of mental deficiency, permitting adequacy in simple activities. **2.** Loosely, a very stupid person. **— Syn.** See IDIOT. [< Gk. < *mōros* stupid] **— mo·ron·ic** (mô·ron′ik, mō-) *adj.* **— mo·ron′i·cal·ly** *adv.*

mo·rose (mə·rōs′) *adj.* Ill-humored; sullen; gloomy, as a person, mood, etc. [< L < *mos, moris* manner, mood] **— mo·rose′ly** *adv.* **— mo·rose·ness** *n.*
— Syn. glum, dour, crabbed. **— Ant.** cheerful, genial.

-morph *combining form* Having the form or shape of: *allomorph.* [< Gk. *morphē* form]

mor·pheme (môr′fēm) *n. Ling.* The smallest meaningful unit of a language or dialect, whether a word, base, or affix. See ALLOMORPH. [< F < Gk. *morphē* form]

Mor·pheus (môr′fē·əs, -fyōōs) In Greek mythology, the god of dreams. [< L < Gk. *morphē* form; from the shapes he calls up in dreams] **— Mor′phe·an** *adj.*

-morphic *combining form* Having the form or shape of: *anthropomorphic.* [< Gk.*morphē* form]

mor·phine (môr′fēn) *n. Chem.* A bitter, white crystalline compound, $C_{17}H_{19}NO_3$, the principal alkaloid of opium, used as an analgesic and narcotic. Also **mor′phin** (-fin). [< F < L *Morpheus* god of dreams]

morpho- *combining form* Form; shape. Also, before vowels, **morph-.** [< Gk. *morphē* form]

mor·phol·o·gy (môr·fol′ə·jē) *n. pl.* **·gies 1.** *Biol.* The study of the form and structure of plants and animals considered apart from function. **2.** *Ling.* **a** The arrangement and interrelationship of morphemes in words. **b** The branch of linguistics dealing with this. **— mor·pho·log·ic** (môr′fə·loj′ik) or **·i·cal** *adj.* **— mor·phol′o·gist** *n.*

-morphous *combining form* Having a (specified) form: often equivalent to *-morphic: anthropomorphous.*

mor·ris (môr′is, mor′-) *n.* An old English dance, performed especially on May Day. [Earlier *morys, morish* Moorish]

Morris chair A large armchair with an adjustable back. [after William *Morris,* who invented it]

mor·ro (môr′ō, mor′ō; Sp. môr′rō) *n. pl.* **mor·ros** (môr′ōz, mor′-; Sp. môr′rōs) A round hill or promontory. [< Sp.]

mor·row (môr′ō, mor′ō) *n. Archaic & Poetic* **1.** The next succeeding day. **2.** A time immediately following a specified event. **3.** Formerly, morning. [See MORNING]

Morse code A system of telegraphic signals invented by S.F.B. Morse, composed of dots and dashes or short and long flashes representing the letters of the alphabet, numerals, etc., and used in transmitting messages.

mor·sel (môr′səl) *n.* **1.** A small fragment or bite of food. **2.** A tempting dish; tidbit. **3.** A small piece or bit of something. *— v.t.* **mor·seled** or **·selled, mor·sel·ing** or **·sel·ling** To divide into small pieces. [< OF, dim. of *mors* bite]

mor·tal (môr′təl) *adj.* **1.** Subject to death. **2.** Of or pertaining to humanity as subject to death. **3.** Of or relating to this life or world. **4.** Causing or liable to cause death. **5.** Relating to or accompanying death. **6.** Grievous; dire: *mortal* terror. **7.** Likely to remain so until death; implacable: a *mortal* enemy. **8.** *Theol.* Incurring spiritual death unless repented of and forgiven: distinguished from *venial*: *mortal* sin. **9.** *Informal* Possible; conceivable: There's no *mortal* reason for his action. *— n.* One who is mortal; a human being. *— adv. Informal* Very; exceedingly. [< OF < L *mors, mortis* death]

mor·tal·i·ty (môr·tal′ə·tē) *n. pl.* **·ties** **1.** The condition of being mortal or subject to death. **2.** Loss of life on a large scale, as caused by war, disease, etc. **3.** The frequency of death; death rate. **4.** Humanity; mankind.

mor·tal·ly (môr′təl·ē) *adv.* **1.** Fatally. **2.** After the manner of a mortal. **3.** Extremely: *mortally* offended.

mor·tar[1] (môr′tər) *n.* A bowl-shaped vessel in which substances are crushed with a pestle. For illustration see PESTLE. [OE < L *mortarium* mixing trough]

mor·tar[2] (môr′tər) *n.* A building material consisting of a mixture of lime, cement, etc., with sand and water, used in bricklaying, plastering walls, etc. [< OF < L *mortarium* trough, mixture of sand and lime]

mor·tar[3] (môr′tər) *n. Mil.* A smooth-bored or rifled muzzleloading weapon, firing a relatively heavy shell, having a shorter range and higher trajectory than a howitzer. [< F *mortier*]

mor·tar·board (môr′tər·bôrd′, -bōrd′) *n.* **1.** A square board with a handle, on which a mason holds mortar. **2.** A type of academic cap topped by a stiff, flat, four-cornered piece, worn at graduations.

mort·gage (môr′gij) *n. Law* **1.** A transfer of property pledged as security for the repayment of a loan. **2.** The contract specifying such a pledge. *— v.t.* **·gaged, ·gag·ing** **1.** To make over or pledge (property) by mortgage. **2.** To pledge; stake. [< OF, dead pledge]

mort·ga·gee (môr′gi·jē′) *n.* The holder of a mortgage.

mort·ga·gor (môr′gi·jər) *n.* One who mortgages his property to another as security for a loan. Also **mort′gag·er.**

mor·tice (môr′tis) *n.* A mortise. *— v.t.* **·ticed, ·tic·ing** To mortise.

mor·ti·cian (môr·tish′ən) *n. U.S.* A funeral director; undertaker. [< L *mors, mortis* death + -ICIAN]

mor·ti·fi·ca·tion (môr′tə·fə·kā′shən) *n.* **1.** A feeling of loss of self-esteem; humiliation; shame. **2.** That which causes such humiliation. **3.** The ascetic practice of subduing the appetites and strengthening the will by fasting, etc. **4.** *Pathol.* The death of a part by gangrene or necrosis.

mor·ti·fy (môr′tə·fī) *v.* **·fied, ·fy·ing** *v.t.* **1.** To humiliate. **2.** To discipline or punish (the body, appetites, etc.) by fasting or other ascetic practices. **3.** *Pathol.* To cause mortification in (part of an animal body). *— v.i.* **4.** To practice ascetic self-discipline. **5.** *Pathol.* To undergo mortification. [< OF < LL < L *mors, mortis* death + *facere* to make] *—* **mor′ti·fi′er** *n. —* **mor′ti·fy′ing·ly** *adv.*

mor·tise (môr′tis) *n.* A space hollowed out in a piece of timber, stone, etc., and shaped to fit a tenon to which it is to be joined. *— v.t.* **·tised, ·tis·ing** **1.** To cut or make a mortise in. **2.** To join by a tenon and mortise. Also spelled *mortice.* [< F < Arabic *murtazz* joined, fixed in]

mort·main (môrt′mān) *n. Law* The holding of lands and buildings in perpetual ownership. [< OF < Med.L *mortua manus* dead hand]

mor·tu·ar·y (môr′chōō·er′ē) *n. pl.* **·ar·ies** A place for the temporary reception of the dead before burial. *— adj.* **1.** Of the burial of the dead. **2.** Relating to death. [< MF < L *mortuarius* of the dead]

mo·sa·ic (mō·zā′ik) *n.* **1.** Inlaid work composed of bits of stone, glass, etc., forming a pattern or picture; also, the process of making this. **2.** A design, arrangement, etc., resembling such work. *— adj.* Of, pertaining to, or resembling mosaic. *— v.t.* **·icked, ·ick·ing** **1.** To make by or as if by combining in a mosaic. **2.** To decorate with mosaic. [< OF < Med.L < Gk. *mouseios* of the Muses, artistic] *—* **mo·sa·i·cist** (mō·zā′ə·sist) *n.*

Mo·sa·ic (mō·zā′ik) *adj.* Of or pertaining to Moses or the laws attributed to him. Also **Mo·sa′i·cal.**

Mosaic Law The code of civil and religious laws contained

in the Pentateuch and traditionally attributed to Moses: also called *Law of Moses, the Law.*

Mo·selle (mō·zel′) *n.* A light, dry wine made in the valley of the Moselle, chiefly in Luxembourg.

Mo·ses (mō′zis, -ziz) In the Old Testament, the leader who led the Israelites out of Egypt to the Promised Land and received the Ten Commandments from God. [< Hebrew *Mōsheh,* ? < Egyptian *mesu* son]

mo·sey (mō′zē) *v.i. U.S. Slang* **1.** To saunter, or stroll; shuffle along. **2.** To go away; move off. [Origin unknown]

Mos·lem (moz′lem) *n.* A believer in Islam; Mohammedan. *— adj.* Of or pertaining to Islam or the Muslims. Also *Muslim, Muslem.* [< Arabic *muslim* one who submits]

Mos·lem·ism (moz′lem·iz′əm) *n.* Islam.

mosque (mosk) *n.* A Moslem temple of worship. [< F < Ital. < Arabic *masjid* < *sajada* to worship, pray]

mos·qui·to (məs·kē′tō) *n. pl.* **·toes** or **·tos** Any of various winged insects, having in the female a long proboscis capable of puncturing the skin of man and animals for extracting blood, certain species of which transmit malaria, yellow fever, etc. [< Sp., dim. of *mosca* fly] *—* **mos·qui′tal** *adj.*

mosquito boat A patrol torpedo boat.

mosquito net A fine net or gauze (**mosquito netting**) placed over windows, beds, etc., to keep out mosquitoes.

moss (môs, mos) *n.* **1.** A delicate plant having a stem and distinct leaves, and growing in tufts or clusters on the ground, decaying wood, rocks, etc. **2.** A clump or tuft of such plants. **3.** Any of several similar plants, as certain lichens. **4.** *Chiefly Scot.* A peat bog. [OE *mos* marsh] *—* **moss′y** *adj. —* **moss′i·ness** *n.*

moss agate A variety of agate containing mineral oxides and showing patterns arranged in mosslike forms.

moss·back (môs′bak′, mos′-) *n.* **1.** An old fish or turtle on whose back is a growth of algae or the like. **2.** *U.S. Slang* A very conservative or old-fashioned person; fogy.

Möss·bau·er effect (mœs′bou′ər) The absorption of gamma rays emitted from a radioactive isotope by nuclei of the same isotope, both of which are anchored in crystals; used in the determination of wavelengths, and in testing various concepts of relativity and quantum theory. [after Rudolf L. *Mössbauer,* born 1929, U.S. physicist born in Germany.]

moss rose A cultivated variety of the rose with a mossy calyx and stem.

most (mōst) *adj.* **1.** Consisting of the greatest number: superlative of *many.* **2.** Consisting of the greatest amount or degree: superlative of *much.* **3.** In the greatest number of instances: *Most* people are honest. *—* **for the most part** Generally; mostly. *— n.* **1.** (*construed as pl.*) The greatest number; the largest part. **2.** (*construed as pl.*) The greatest number of persons: too difficult for *most.* **3.** The greatest amount, quantity or degree; utmost. *—* **at (the) most** Not more than; at the extreme point or limit. *—* **to make the most of 1.** To use to the fullest advantage. **2.** To exaggerate the importance of. *— adv.* **1.** In or to the greatest or highest degree, quantity, extent, etc.: used with adjectives and adverbs to form the superlative degree. **2.** Very. **3.** *Informal* Almost; nearly. [OE *mǣst, māst*]

-most *suffix* Most: added to adjectives and adverbs to form superlatives: *innermost; outmost.*

most·ly (mōst′lē) *adv.* For the most part; principally.

mot (mō) *n.* A witty or pithy saying: bon *mot.* [< F, word]

mote (mōt) *n.* A minute particle or speck, esp., of dust. [OE *mot* dust]

mo·tel (mō·tel′) *n. U.S.* A roadside hotel for motorists, often comprising private cabins that open on parking facilities: also called *motor court.*

mo·tet (mō·tet′) *n. Music* A polyphonic vocal composition of a sacred nature, usu. unaccompanied. [< OF]

moth (môth, moth) *n. pl.* **moths** (môthz, môths, mothz, moths) Any of a large group of insects, usu. nocturnal, distinguished from the butterflies by having smaller wings, stouter bodies, and duller coloring. [OE *moththe*]

moth·ball (môth′bôl′, moth′-) *Mil. & Nav. adj.* Designating ships or military equipment laid up in reserve and covered with protective materials. *— v.t.* To put in storage.

moth ball A small ball of camphor or naphthalene used to repel moths from clothing, etc., during storage.

moth-eat·en (môth′ēt′n, moth′-) *adj.* **1.** Eaten or damaged by moths. **2.** Worn out. **3.** Old-fashioned.

moth·er[1] (muth′ər) *n.* **1.** A female who has borne offspring. **2.** A female who adopts a child, or who otherwise holds a maternal relationship toward another. **3.** The characteristics regarded as belonging to a mother. **4.** Anything that creates, nurtures, or protects something else. **5.** *Usu. cap.* A title given to certain nuns. *— adj.* **1.** Native: *mother* tongue. **2.** Relating to or characteristic of a mother: *mother* love. **3.** Holding a maternal relation: the *mother* church. *— v.t.* **1.** To bring forth as a mother; produce; create. **2.** To care for or protect as a mother. **3.** To admit or claim parentage, authorship, etc., of. [OE *mōder*]

MORTISE
(a) AND
TENON (b)

moth·er² (muth/ər) *n.* A slimy film composed of bacteria and yeast cells, active in the production of vinegar.

Mother Goose **1.** The imaginary narrator of a volume of folk tales, compiled in French by Charles Perrault in 1697. **2.** The imaginary writer of a collection of nursery rhymes of English folk origin, first published in London about 1790.

moth·er·hood (muth/ər·hŏŏd) *n.* **1.** The state of being a mother. **2.** The spirit or qualities of a mother. **3.** Mothers collectively.

Mother Hub·bard (hub/ərd) A woman's loose, flowing gown, unconfined at the waist: also **mother hubbard**.

mother-in-law (muth/ər·in·lô/) *n. pl.* **moth·ers-in-law** The mother of one's spouse.

moth·er·land (muth/ər·land/) *n.* **1.** The land of one's birth; native land. **2.** The land of one's ancestors.

mother lode In mining, any principal or very rich vein.

moth·er·ly (muth/ər·lē) *adj.* Resembling, characteristic of, or like a mother. — *adv.* In the manner of a mother. — **moth/er·li·ness** *n.*

moth·er-of-pearl (muth/ər·əv·pûrl/) *n.* The pearly, iridescent internal layer of certain shells, as those of the pearl oyster and abalone, used in ornamental work, for buttons, etc.: also called *nacre.* — *adj.* Of mother-of-pearl.

Moth·er's Day (muth/ərz) *U.S.* A memorial day in honor of mothers, observed annually on the second Sunday in May.

mother's helper *U.S.* A girl or woman hired to help a mother care for her children and do light housekeeping chores.

mother tongue **1.** One's native language. **2.** A parent language.

mother wit Inherent or native intelligence; common sense.

moth·y (môth/ē, moth/ē) *adj.* **moth·i·er, moth·i·est 1.** Moth-eaten. **2.** Full of moths.

mo·tif (mō·tēf/) *n.* **1.** The underlying theme or main element in a literary or artistic work. **2.** In decoration, a distinct element of design. **3.** *Music* The shortest intelligible melodic or rhythmic fragment of a theme. Also *motive.* [< F]

mo·tile (mō/til, -təl) *adj. Zool.* Having the power of motion, as certain minute organisms. [< L *motus*, pp. of *movere* to move] — **mo·til/i·ty** *n.*

mo·tion (mō/shən) *n.* **1.** The act or process of changing position; movement: also, an instance of this. **2.** Change of place or position in the body or any of its parts. **3.** A formal proposal or suggestion in an assembly or meeting: to second the *motion.* **4.** An impulse; inclination. — **in motion** Moving; in operation. — *v.i.* **1.** To make a gesture of direction or intent, as with the hand. — *v.t.* **2.** To direct or guide by a gesture. [< OF < L *movere* to move]

motion picture **1.** A sequence of pictures of moving objects photographed on a strip of film, that, when projected on a screen, gives the optical illusion of continuous movement. **2.** A specific drama, story, etc., made by means of such photographs: also called *cinema, film, movie, moving picture, photoplay, picture, screen play.*

motion sickness Nausea, dizziness, etc., caused by the effects of motion, as in travel on land, water, and in the air.

mo·ti·vate (mō/tə·vāt) *v.t.* **·vat·ed, ·vat·ing** To provide with a motive. [< F *motiver*] — **mo/ti·va/tion** *n.* — **mo/·ti·va/tion·al** *adj.*

mo·tive (mō/tiv) *n.* **1.** A conscious or unconscious need, drive, etc., that incites a person to some action or behavior; incentive; goal. **2.** A motif. — **Syn.** See REASON. — *adj.* **1.** Causing or having the power to cause motion. **2.** Relating to or acting as a motive. — *v.t.* To motivate. [< OF < Med.L *movere* to move]

mot·ley (mot/lē) *adj.* **1.** Made up of diverse elements; heterogeneous. **2.** Variegated in color. **3.** Clothed in vari-colored garments. — *n.* **1.** A heterogeneous mixture or collection. **2.** A woolen cloth of mixed colors worn between the 14th and 17th centuries. **3.** A garment of various colors such as formerly worn by court jesters. [ME *motteley*]

mo·tor (mō/tər) *n.* **1.** An engine; esp., an internal-combustion engine propelling an automobile, motor boat, etc. **2.** Something that imparts or produces motion. **3.** *Chiefly Brit.* An automotive vehicle. — *adj.* **1.** Causing, producing, or imparting motion. **2.** Equipped with or driven by a motor. **3.** Of, pertaining to, or for automotive vehicles. **4.** *Psychol.* Transmitting impulses from nerve centers to the muscles. **5.** *Psychol.* Relating to or involving the movements of muscles. — *v.i.* To travel or ride in an automobile. [< L < *motus*, pp. of *movere* to move]

mo·tor·bike (mō/tər·bīk/) *n. Informal* **1.** A bicycle driven by a small motor. **2.** A motorcycle.

mo·tor·boat (mō/tər·bōt/) *n.* A boat propelled by a motor: also called *power boat.*

mo·tor·bus (mō/tər·bus/) *n.* A passenger bus powered by a motor. Also **motor bus, motor coach.**

mo·tor·cade (mō/tər·kād) *n.* A procession of automobiles.

mo·tor·car (mō/tər·kär/) *n.* An automobile.

motor court A motel.

mo·tor·cy·cle (mō/tər·sī/kəl) *n.* A two-wheeled vehicle, larger and heavier than a bicycle, propelled by an internal-combustion engine. — *v.i.* **·cled, ·cling** To travel or ride on a motorcycle. — **mo/tor·cy/clist** *n.*

mo·tor·ist (mō/tər·ist) *n.* One who drives or travels by automobile.

mo·tor·ize (mō/tər·īz) *v.t.* **·ized, ·iz·ing 1.** To equip with a motor. **2.** To equip with motor-propelled vehicles in place of horses or horse-drawn vehicles. — **mo/tor·i·za/tion** *n.*

mo·tor·man (mō/tər·mən) *n. pl.* **·men** (-mən) **1.** One who operates an electric street car or electric railway locomotive. **2.** One who operates a motor.

motor scooter A two-wheeled vehicle similar to a child's scooter, having a driver's seat and powered by an internal-combustion engine.

mot·tle (mot/l) *v.t.* **·tled, ·tling** To mark with spots or streaks of different colors or shades; blotch. — *n.* **1.** A spotted, blotched, or variegated appearance, as of skin or marble. **2.** A spot, blotch, etc. [back formation < MOTLEY]

mot·tled (mot/ld) *adj.* Marked with spots of different color or shade; blotched; spotted.

mot·to (mot/ō) *n. pl.* **·toes** or **·tos 1.** A word or phrase expressing a rule of conduct, principle, etc.; a maxim. **2.** An appropriate or indicative phrase inscribed on something, prefixed to a literary work, etc. [< Ital. < F *mot* word]

mouch (mōōch) See MOOCH.

mou·choir (mōō·shwär/) *n. French* A pocket handkerchief.

moue (mōō) *n.* A pouting grimace, as of disdain. [< F]

mou·jik (mōō·zhēk/) See MUZHIK.

mould (mōld), etc. See MOLD, etc.

moult (mōlt) See MOLT, etc.

mound (mound) *n.* **1.** A heap or pile of earth, debris, etc., either natural or artificial. **2.** A small natural elevation; a hillock. **3.** In baseball, the slightly raised ground from which the pitcher pitches. — *v.t.* **1.** To fortify or enclose with a mound. **2.** To heap up in a mound. [Origin unknown]

Mound Builder One of the prehistoric Indians who built the burial mounds and fortifications found in the Mississippi basin and adjoining regions.

mount¹ (mount) *v.t.* **1.** To ascend or climb (a slope, stairs, etc.). **2.** To get up on; climb upon. **3.** To put or set on horseback. **4.** To furnish with a horse. **5.** To set or place in an elevated position: to *mount* a picture on a wall. **6.** To set, fix, or secure in or on a support, frame, etc., as for exhibition or use: to *mount* a drawing; to *mount* a specimen on a microscope slide. **7.** To furnish with scenery, costumes, etc.: to *mount* a play. **8.** *Mil.* **a** To set or raise into position, as a gun. **b** To carry or be equipped with. **c** To stand or post (guard). **d** To prepare and begin: to *mount* an offensive. — *v.i.* **9.** To rise or ascend; go or come up. **10.** To increase in amount, number, or degree. **11.** To get up on something, as on a horse. — *n.* **1.** Anything on or in which an object is placed for use, preparation, display, etc., as a setting for a jewel, etc. **2.** A horse or other animal used for riding. **3.** The act or style of mounting. **4.** The act of riding a horse. [< OF < L *mons, montis* mountain] — **mount/a·ble** *adj.* — **mount/er** *n.*

mount² (mount) *n.* A mountain or hill: used poetically or as part of a proper name. [OE < L *mons, montis* mountain]

moun·tain (moun/tən) *n.* **1.** A natural elevation of the earth's surface, typically having steep sides and a narrow summit, and rising higher than a hill. **2.** Any large heap or pile: a *mountain* of paper. **3.** Anything of great size: a *mountain* of a man. — *adj.* **1.** Of, pertaining to, or like a mountain. **2.** Living, growing, or situated in or on mountains. [< OF < L *mons, montis* mountain]

mountain ash A small tree of the rose family, having white flowers and orange-red berries. **2.** Any of various related trees.

mountain cat **1.** The puma. **2.** The lynx.

moun·tain·eer (moun/tən·ir/) *n.* **1.** An inhabitant of a mountainous district. **2.** One who climbs mountains. — *v.i.* To climb mountains.

mountain goat The Rocky Mountain goat.

mountain laurel A low-growing evergreen shrub of the eastern U.S., having white or pink flowers: the State flower of Connecticut and Pennsylvania.

mountain lion The puma.

moun·tain·ous (moun/tən·əs) *adj.* **1.** Full of mountains. **2.** Huge; gigantic. — **moun/tain·ous·ly** *adv.*

moun·te·bank (moun/tə·bangk) *n.* **1.** One who sells quack medicines at fairs after drawing a crowd with jokes, tricks, etc. **2.** Any charlatan. [< Ital. < *montare* to mount + *in* upon + *banco* bench]

mount·ed (moun/tid) *adj.* **1.** Riding or seated on a horse.

2. Serving on or equipped with horses for transportation: *mounted* police. **3.** Set into position or fitted for use.

Moun·ty (moun′tē) *n. pl.* **·ties** *Informal* A member of the Royal Canadian Mounted Police. Also **Mount′ie.**

mourn (môrn, mōrn) *v.i.* **1.** To feel or express grief or sorrow, esp. for the dead; grieve. — *v.t.* **2.** To lament or sorrow for (someone dead). **3.** To grieve over or bemoan (misfortune, failure, etc.). [OE *murnan*] — **mourn′er** *n.*

mourners' bench *U.S.* At revival meetings, a bench near the preacher, reserved for penitents.

mourn·ful (môrn′fəl, mōrn′-) *adj.* **1.** Indicating, expressing, or exciting grief. **2.** Doleful; melancholy; sad. — **mourn′ful·ly** *adv.* — **mourn′ful·ness** *n.*

mourn·ing (môr′ning, mōr′-) *n.* **1.** The act of one who expresses grief or sorrow, esp. for the dead. **2.** The manifestations of grief, as the wearing of black dress, etc. **3.** The period during which one mourns. — *adj.* Of or expressive of mourning. — **mourn′ing·ly** *adv.*

mourning dove A dove common in North America, having a mournful cry: also called *turtledove.*

mouse (*n.* mous; *v.* mouz) *n. pl.* **mice** (mīs) **1.** One of various small rodents frequenting human habitations throughout the world. ◆ Collateral adjective: *murine.* **2.** Any of various similar animals. **3.** *U.S. Informal* A timid person. **4.** *Slang* A black eye. — *v.i.* **moused, mous·ing 1.** To hunt or catch mice. **2.** To hunt for something cautiously and softly; prowl. [OE *mūs*]

mous·er (mou′zər) *n.* Any animal that catches mice.

mouse·trap (mous′trap′) *n.* A trap for catching mice.

mousse (mōōs) *n.* Any of various light, frozen desserts made with whipped cream, egg white, etc., and sugar and flavoring. [< F < L *mulsus* sweetened with honey]

mous·tache (məs·tash′, mus′tash) See MUSTACHE.

Mous·te·ri·an (mōō·stir′ē·ən) *adj. Anthropol.* Pertaining to or describing a culture stage of the Paleolithic, represented in western Europe by artifacts of stone and generally found associated with Neanderthal men. [< F < *Le Moustier,* a village in France where such remains were found]

mous·y (mou′sē, -zē) *adj.* **mous·i·er, mous·i·est 1.** Of or resembling a mouse. **2.** Characterized by timidity, shyness, drabness, etc. **3.** Infested with mice. Also **mous′ey.**

mouth (*n.* mouth; *v.* mouth) *n. pl.* **mouths** (mouthz) **1.** The opening at which food is taken into the body; also, the cavity between the lips and throat containing the lingual and masticating structures. ◆ Collateral adjective: *oral.* **2.** One who needs food: so many *mouths* to feed. **3.** The organ or instrument of speech: to shut one's *mouth.* **4.** Something resembling a mouth; as: **a** The part of a stream where its waters are discharged into another body of water. **b** The entrance or opening of a cave, mine, etc. **c** The opening of a container: the *mouth* of a jar. — **down in** (or **at**) **the mouth** *Informal* Disconsolate; dejected. — **to have a big mouth** *Informal* **1.** To speak loudly or rudely. **2.** To talk too much. — *v.t.* **1.** To speak in a forced or affected manner. **2.** To seize or take into the mouth. **3.** To caress or rub with the mouth. **4.** To form (words, etc.) silently with the lips and tongue. — *v.i.* **5.** To speak in an affected manner. [OE *mūth*] — **mouth′er** (mou′thər) *n.*

mouthed (mouthd, moutht) *adj.* **1.** Having a mouth or mouths. **2.** Having a (specified kind of) mouth or (a specified number of) mouths: used in combination: *evil-mouthed.*

mouth·ful (mouth′fōōl′) *n. pl.* **·fuls** (-fōōlz) **1.** As much as can be held in the mouth. **2.** As much as is usu. taken or put in the mouth at one time. **3.** A small quantity. **4.** *Slang* An important or perceptive remark: chiefly in the phrase **to say a mouthful.**

mouth organ 1. A harmonica. **2.** A set of panpipes.

mouth·piece (mouth′pēs′) *n.* **1.** That part of a musical instrument, telephone, etc., that is used in or near the mouth. **2.** One who acts as spokesman for an individual, group, belief, etc. **3.** *Slang* A criminal lawyer. **4.** A rubber guard placed in the mouth of a boxer.

mouth·wash (mouth′wosh′, -wôsh′) *n.* An antiseptic and scented solution used for cleansing the mouth.

mouth·y (mou′thē, -thē) *adj.* **mouth·i·er, mouth·i·est** Garrulous; bombastic. — **mouth′i·ly** *adv.* — **mouth′i·ness** *n.*

mou·ton (mōō′ton) *n.* Sheepskin processed to simulate beaver or seal, used for women's coats, etc. [< F, sheep]

mov·a·ble (mōō′və·bəl) *adj.* **1.** Capable of being moved. **2.** *Eccl.* Varying in date from year to year: *movable* feast. **3.** *Law* Pertaining to personal property as distinguished from real property. — *n.* **1.** *Usu. pl.* Anything that can be

HUMAN MOUTH

a Hard palate. *b* Pharynx. *c* Soft palate. *d* Uvula. *e* Tonsil. *f* Epiglottis. *g* Esophagus. *h* Trachea. *i* Tongue. *j* Hyoid bone. *k* Larynx.

moved; esp., an article of furniture. **2.** *pl. Law* Personal property. Also **move′a·ble.** — **mov′a·bil·i·ty, mov′a·ble·ness** *n.* — **mov′a·bly** *adv.*

move (mōōv) *v.* **moved, mov·ing** *v.i.* **1.** To change place or position; go to or from a place. **2.** To change one's residence. **3.** To make progress; advance. **4.** To live or carry on one's life: to *move* in cultivated circles. **5.** To operate, work, revolve, etc., as a machine. **6.** To take or begin to take action; act. **7.** To be disposed of by sale. **8.** To make an application or proposal: to *move* for adjournment. **9.** To evacuate: said of the bowels. **10.** In checkers, chess, etc., to transfer a piece from one position to another. **11.** *Informal* To go fast. — *v.t.* **12.** To change the place or position of, as by carrying, pushing, pulling, etc. **13.** To set or keep in motion. **14.** To dislodge or force from a set position: to *move* him from his purpose. **15.** To cause, influence, or impel to some action: to *move* her to agree. **16.** To affect or arouse the emotions, sympathies, etc., of; touch. **17.** To propose for action, deliberation, etc. **18.** To cause (the bowels) to evacuate. **19.** In checkers, chess, etc., to transfer (a piece). — *n.* **1.** An act of moving; movement. **2.** An action for some purpose or design; step; maneuver. **3.** A change in residence. **4.** In checkers, chess, etc., the transfer of a piece. [< AF, OF < L *movere* to set in motion]

move·ment (mōōv′mənt) *n.* **1.** The act of moving; any change of place or position. **2.** A specific instance or manner of moving: a dance *movement.* **3.** A series of actions, plans, etc., tending toward some end: the temperance *movement.* **4.** An inclination or tendency. **5.** *Mech.* A particular arrangement of related moving parts. **6.** *Music* **a** One of the sections of a work, as of a symphony, string quartet, etc. **b** Tempo. **c** Rhythm. **7.** In prosody, rhythm or meter; cadence. **8.** An emptying of the bowels. **9.** *Mil.* A maneuver. [< OF < L *movere* to set in motion]

mov·er (mōō′vər) *n.* One who or that which moves; esp., one whose business is moving household goods.

mov·ie (mōō′vē) *Informal n.* **1.** A motion picture. **2.** A motion-picture theater. **3.** *pl.* The motion-picture industry. [Contr. of MOVING PICTURE]

mov·ing (mōō′ving) *adj.* **1.** Going or capable of going from place to place, position to position, etc. **2.** Causing or producing motion or change. **3.** That actuates, impels, or influences. **4.** Affecting, arousing, or touching the feelings or passions. **5.** Exciting or stirring up controversy, debate, etc. — **mov′ing·ly** *adv.* — **mov′ing·ness** *n.*

moving picture A motion picture.

moving staircase An escalator.

mow¹ (mō) *v.* **mowed, mowed** or **mown, mow·ing** *v.t.* **1.** To cut down (grain, grass, etc.) with a scythe or machine. **2.** To cut the grain or grass of (a field, lawn, etc.). **3.** *Informal* To cut down or kill rapidly or indiscriminately: with *down.* — *v.i.* **4.** To cut down grass or grain. [OE *māwan*] — **mow′er** *n.*

mow² (mou) *n.* Hay or grain stored in a barn; also, the place of storage. — *v.t.* To store in a mow. [OE *mūga*]

mowing machine A farm machine with cutting blades used for mowing hay, etc.

mox·ie (mok′sē) *n. Slang* Native shrewdness or common sense.

moz·za·rel·la (môd′dzä·rel′lä) *n.* A soft Italian curd cheese that is very stringy when cooked. [< Ital.]

Mrs. (mis′iz) *n.* A title prefixed to the name of a married woman: a contracted form of *Mistress.*

mu (myōō, mōō) *n.* **1.** The twelfth letter in the Greek alphabet (M, μ), corresponding to the English *m.* See ALPHABET. **2.** The micron (symbol μ).

much (much) *adj.* **more, most** Great in quantity, amount, extent, etc.: *much* noise. — *n.* **1.** A considerable quantity or amount; a great deal. **2.** A remarkable or important thing: It isn't *much.* — **to make much of 1.** To treat as very important. **2.** To treat (someone) with great courtesy, regard, etc. — *adv.* **1.** Greatly: *much* obliged. **2.** For the most part; almost. [ME < OE *mycel*] — **much′ness** *n.*

mu·ci·lage (myōō′sə·lij) *n.* **1.** An aqueous solution of vegetable gum or the like, used as an adhesive. **2.** Any of various gummy or gelatinous substances found in some plants. [< F < LL *mucilago* musty juice]

mu·ci·lag·i·nous (myōō′si·laj′ə·nəs) *adj.* **1.** Of, pertaining to, or producing mucilage. **2.** Resembling or characteristic of mucilage; slimy and viscid. — **mu·ci·lag′i·nous·ness** *n.*

muck (muk) *n.* **1.** Any wet and clinging material that soils; esp., viscid mud. **2.** Moist dung mixed with decomposed vegetable matter, used as a soil fertilizer; manure. **3.** A dark brown to black soil consisting largely of decomposing peat and other vegetable materials. **4.** A confusing or uncertain state or condition; mess. — *v.t.* **1.** To fertilize with manure. **2.** *Informal* To make dirty; pollute. **3.** To remove manure, dirt, rocks, etc., from. [ME *muk*] — **muck′y** *adj.*

muck·rake (muk′rāk′) *v.i.* **·raked, ·rak·ing** To search for or expose real or alleged corruption on the part of political officials, businessmen, etc. [Back formation < *muckrakes,* slang term in late 19th c. U.S. politics] **—muck′rak′er** n. **—muck′rak′ing** n.

mu·cous (myōō′kəs) adj. 1. Secreting mucus. 2. Pertaining to, consisting of, or resembling mucus. Also **mu′cose** (-kōs). **—mu·cos′i·ty** (-kos/ə·tē) n.

mucous membrane Anat. A membrane secreting or producing mucus, that lines passages communicating with the exterior, as the alimentary and respiratory passages, etc.

mu·cus (myōō′kəs) n. Biol. A viscid substance secreted by the mucous membranes. [< L]

mud (mud) n. 1. Soft and sticky wet earth. 2. Informal The most degrading place or situation: to drag one into the mud. **—clear as mud** Absolutely incomprehensible. — v.t. mud·ded, mud·ding To soil or cover with or as with mud. [ME < MLG mudde or MDu. modde]

mud·der (mud′ər) n. A race horse that runs well on a muddy track.

mud·dle (mud′l) v. ·dled, ·dling v.t. 1. To mix in a confused or disordered way; jumble. 2. To confuse or confound (the mind, speech, etc.). 3. To mess up or mismanage; bungle. 4. To make muddy or turbid. — v.i. 5. To act or think in a confused or ineffective manner. **—to muddle through** Chiefly Brit. To achieve one's object despite confusion or mistakes. — n. 1. A state or condition of confusion, disorder, or uncertainty. 2. A state of mental or intellectual disorder. [< MUD + freq. suffix -le]

mud·dle·head·ed (mud′l·hed′id) adj. Mentally confused; addlebrained; stupid. **—mud′dle·head′ed·ness** n.

mud·dler (mud′lər) n. 1. A stick for stirring liquids, esp. drinks. 2. One who muddles.

mud·dy (mud′ē) adj. ·di·er, ·di·est 1. Covered, spattered, or filled with mud. 2. Not clear, bright, or distinct, as color, liquid, etc. 3. Confused or obscure in thought, expression, meaning, etc. — v.t. & v.i. ·died, ·dy·ing To become or cause to become muddy. **—mud′di·ly** adv. **—mud′di·ness** n.

mud eel An eel-shaped amphibian, with no hind legs, that inhabits swamps of the southern U.S.: also called siren.

mud·fish (mud′fish′) n. pl. ·fish or ·fish·es Any of various fishes that inhabit mud or muddy waters.

mud flat A low-lying strip of muddy ground, esp. one between high and low tide.

mud puppy A tailed amphibian found in streams and lakes of North America.

mud·sling·er (mud′sling′ər) n. One who casts malicious slurs, esp. at a political opponent. **—mud′sling′ing** n.

mud·suck·er (mud′suk′ər) n. A fish of California, commonly used as bait.

mud turtle Any of various turtles inhabiting muddy waters in North and Central America.

mu·ez·zin (myōō·ez′in) n. In Islam, a crier who calls the faithful to prayer, as from a minaret of a mosque. Also **mu·ed′din** (-ed′in). [< Arabic mu′adhdhin < adhana to call]

muff[1] (muf) v.t. & v.i. To perform (some act) clumsily; esp., to fail to catch (a ball). — n. An awkward action. [< MUFF[2]; prob. to handle as if wearing a muff]

muff[2] (muf) n. 1. A pillowlike or tubular case of fur or cloth, open at the ends, into which the hands are put for warmth. 2. A tuft of feathers on the head or legs of certain birds. [< Du. < F moufle mitten]

muf·fin (muf′in) n. A small, cup-shaped portion of light bread, usu. eaten hot with butter. [Origin uncertain]

muf·fle (muf′əl) v.t. ·fled, ·fling 1. To wrap up in a blanket, scarf, etc., as for warmth or concealment: often with up. 2. To deaden the sound of by or as by wrapping. 3. To deaden (a sound). 4. To prevent (someone) from seeing, hearing, etc., by wrapping the head. — n. 1. Something used for muffling. 2. A chamber in a kiln or furnace that protects its contents from flame, gases, etc. [< F < moufle mitten]

muf·fler (muf′lər) n. 1. A device to reduce noise, as from the exhaust of an engine. 2. A heavy scarf worn about the neck for warmth. 3. Anything that muffles. [< MUFFLE]

muf·ti[1] (muf′tē) n. In Islam, an expounder of religious law. [< Arabic, active participle of aftā to expound the law]

muf·ti[2] (muf′tē) n. Civilian dress; plain clothes, esp. when worn by one who normally wears a uniform. [< MUFTI[1]]

mug[1] (mug) n. 1. A large drinking cup. 2. As much as will fill a mug. [Origin unknown]

mug[2] (mug) Slang n. 1. The face, esp. the mouth and chin. 2. U.S. A photograph of the face. Also **mug shot**. 3. U.S. A man; guy. 4. U.S. A criminal. — v. mugged, mug·ging v.t. 1. U.S. To photograph (someone's face), esp. for police files. 2. To assault viciously and rob. — v.i. 3. To make funny faces; overact to win an audience. Also **mugg**. [< MUG[1]] **—mug′ger** n.

mug·gy (mug′ē) adj. ·gi·er, ·gi·est Warm, humid, and close; sultry. [< dial. E mug drizzle] **—mug′gi·ness** n.

Mu·ghal (mōō′gəl) n. & adj. Mogul. Also **Mu′ghul**.

mug·wump (mug′wump′) n. U.S. 1. Usu. cap. A Republican who bolted the party in the presidential election of 1884. 2. Anyone who is independent, esp. in politics. [< Algonquian mugquomp great man, chief] **—mug′wump′er·y, mug′wump′ism** n.

Mu·ham·ma·dan (mōō·ham′ə·dən) adj. & n. Mohammedan. Also **Mu·ham′me·dan**.

mu·jik (mōō·zhēk′, mōō′zhik) See MUZHIK.

mu·lat·to (mə·lat′ō, myōō-, -lä′tō) n. pl. ·toes 1. A person having one white and one Negro parent. 2. Anyone having mixed white and Negro ancestry. — adj. Having the light brown color of a mulatto. [< Sp. < L mulus mule]

mul·ber·ry (mul′ber′ē, mul′bər·ē) n. pl. ·ries 1. Any of various trees whose leaves are valued for silkworm culture. 2. The berrylike fruit of any of these trees. 3. A purplish red color. [ME mulberie, var. of murberie, < OF < L morum mulberry + OE berie berry]

mulch (mulch) n. Any loose material, as straw, leaves, peat moss, etc., placed about the stalks of plants to protect their roots from drying, freezing, etc. — v.t. To cover with mulch. [ME molsh soft, OE milisc]

mulct (mulkt) v.t. 1. To defraud or cheat (someone). 2. To punish with a fine. — n. A fine or similar penalty. [< L mulcta, multa fine]

mule[1] (myōōl) n. 1. A hybrid between the ass and horse; esp., a hybrid between a jackass and mare. 2. Biol. Any hybrid or cross, esp. one that is sterile: said usu. of the hybrid between the canary and a related bird. 3. U.S. Informal A stubborn person. 4. A textile machine that spins fibers into yarn and winds it on spindles: also called spinning mule: also **mule′jen′ny**. [< OF < L mulus]

mule[2] (myōōl) n. A backless lounging slipper. [< F < L mulleus reddish (shoe)]

mule skinner U.S. Informal One who drives mules.

mu·le·teer (myōō′lə·tir′) n. A mule driver. [< F < MF mulet, dim. of OF mul mule] **—mu′le·tress** (-tris) n.fem.

mule train A train of mules carrying packs; also, a train of freight wagons drawn by mules.

mul·ish (myōō′lish) adj. Resembling a mule; stubborn. **—mul′ish·ly** adv. **—mul′ish·ness** n.

mull[1] (mul) v.t. To heat and spice, as wine or cider. [Origin uncertain]

mull[2] (mul) v.t. To ponder: usu. with over. [ME mullen to pulverize]

mul·lah (mul′ə, mōōl′ə) n. A Moslem religious leader or teacher, or any man of learned reputation: a title of respect. Also **mul′la**. [< Turkish, Persian, and Hind. < Arabic mawlā master, sir]

mul·lein (mul′ən) n. Any of various herbs of the figwort family; esp., the **great mullein** and the **moth mullein**. Also **mul′len**. [< AF moleine, prob. < OF mol soft < L mollis]

mul·let (mul′it) n. pl. ·lets or ·let Any of various marine and fresh-water fish, as the **striped mullet** of the Atlantic and Pacific. [< OF < L mullus red mullet]

mul·li·gan stew (mul′i·gən) U.S. Slang A stew, originally made by tramps, composed of odds and ends of meat, vegetables, etc. Also **mul′li·gan**. [? from personal name]

mul·li·ga·taw·ny (mul′i·gə·tô′nē) n. A strongly flavored soup of the East Indies, made of meat and curry. [< Tamil milagutannir pepper water]

mul·lion (mul′yən) n. Archit. A vertical dividing piece in an opening, esp. in a window. — v.t. To furnish with or divide by means of mullions. [? Var. of monial < OF < L medianus medial]

mul·lock (mul′ək) n. Waste rock or earth left from mining. [ME mull dust + -OCK] **—mul′lock·y** adj.

multi- combining form 1. Much; many; consisting of many; as in:

multiangular	multihued	multipurpose
multiblade	multimillion	multisection
multicellular	multimolecular	multistoried
multicolor	multipartisan	multisyllable
multidirectional	multipersonal	multivoiced
multifaced	multipointed	multivolumed

2. Having more than two (or more than one); as in:

multicuspid	multielectrode	multinucleate
multicylinder	multimammate	multispeed

3. Many times over: multimillionaire. 4. Med. Affecting many: multiglandular. Also, before vowels, sometimes **mult-**. [< L multus much]

mul·ti·col·ored (mul′ti·kul′ərd) adj. Having many colors.

mul·ti·far·i·ous (mul′ti·fâr′ē·əs) adj. Having great diversity or variety. [< LL multifarius] **—mul′ti·far′i·ous·ly** adv. **—mul′ti·far′i·ous·ness** n.

mul·ti·fold (mul′tə·fōld) adj. Many times doubled.

mul·ti·form (mul′tə·fôrm) adj. Having many forms or appearances. **—mul′ti·for′mi·ty** n.

mul·ti·lat·er·al (mul′ti·lat′ər·əl) adj. 1. Having many

sides. 2. *Govt.* Involving more than two nations: also *multi-partite*. — **mul·ti·lat·er·al·ly** *adv.*

mul·ti·lin·gual (mul′ti-ling′gwəl) *n. & adj.* Polyglot.

mul·ti·mil·lion·aire (mul′ti-mil′yən-âr′) *n.* One having a fortune of many millions; a very rich person.

mul·ti·no·mi·al (mul′ti-nō′mē-əl) *adj.* Polynomial.

mul·tip·a·ra (mul-tip′ə-rə) *n. pl.* **·rae** (-rē) A woman who has borne more than one child, or who is bearing her second. [< NL < MULTI- + L *parere* to give birth]

mul·tip·a·rous (mul-tip′ə-rəs) *adj.* 1. Giving birth to many at one time. 2. Of or relating to a multipara.

mul·ti·par·tite (mul′ti-pär′tīt) *adj.* 1. Divided into many parts. 2. *Govt.* Multilateral (def. 2).

mul·ti·ple (mul′tə-pəl) *adj.* 1. Having, consisting of, or relating to more than one part, aspect, individual, etc.; manifold. 2. Happening more than once; repeated: *multiple* echoes. 3. *Electr.* Denoting a circuit having two or more conductors arranged in parallel. — *n. Math.* Any of the products of a given number and some other number: 8 and 12 are *multiples* of 4. [< F]

mul·ti·ple-choice (mul′tə-pəl-chois′) *adj.* Giving several answers from which the correct one is to be selected.

multiple sclerosis *Pathol.* Sclerosis occurring in various areas of the brain or spinal cord or both, and characterized by tremors, failure of coordination, etc.

mul·ti·plex (mul′tə-pleks) *adj.* 1. Multiple; manifold. 2. *Telecom.* Designating a system for the simultaneous transmission of two or more signals over the same wire or radio frequency channel. [< L *multus* much + *plicare* to fold]

mul·ti·pli·cand (mul′tə-plə-kand′) *n. Math.* A number multiplied, or to be multiplied, by another. [< L *multiplicandus* to be multiplied]

mul·ti·pli·ca·tion (mul′tə-plə-kā′shən) *n.* 1. The act of multiplying, or the state of being multiplied. 2. *Math.* The process of finding the sum of a number repeated a given number of times.

multiplication sign The symbol (×) placed between two numbers or quantities to denote a multiplication of the first by the second, as $4 \times 2 = 8$.

mul·ti·plic·i·ty (mul′tə-plis′ə-tē) *n. pl.* **·ties** 1. The condition or quality of being manifold or various. 2. A large number. [< OF < LL < L *multiplicare* to multiply]

mul·ti·pli·er (mul′tə-plī′ər) *n.* 1. One who or that which multiplies or causes multiplication. 2. *Math.* The number by which a quantity is multiplied.

mul·ti·ply[1] (mul′tə-plī) *v.* **·plied**, **·ply·ing** *v.t.* 1. To increase the quantity, amount, or degree of. 2. *Math.* To determine the product of by multiplication. — *v.i.* 3. To become more in number, amount, or degree; increase. 4. *Math.* To determine the product by multiplication. 5. To grow in number by procreation; propagate. [< OF < L *multus* much + *plicare* to fold] — **mul·ti·pli·a·ble** *adj.*

mul·ti·ply[2] (mul′tə-plē) *adv.* So as to be multiple; in many ways.

mul·ti·pro·pel·lant (mul′ti-prə-pel′ənt) *Aerospace n.* A rocket propellant consisting of two or more chemicals separately fed into the combustion chamber.

mul·ti·stage (mul′ti-stāj) *adj.* 1. Having or characterized by a number of definite stages in the completion of a process or action. 2. *Aerospace* Having several sections, as in a rocket, each of which fulfills a given task before burnout.

mul·ti·tude (mul′tə-tōōd, -tyōōd) *n.* 1. A great number. 2. A large gathering of people. 3. The quality of being many or numerous. — **the multitude** The common people. [< OF < L *multus* many]

mul·ti·tu·di·nous (mul′tə-tōō′də-nəs, -tyōō′-) *adj.* 1. Existing in great numbers; numerous; myriad. 2. Consisting of or exhibiting many parts, features, etc. — **mul·ti·tu′di·nous·ly** *adv.* — **mul·ti·tu′di·nous·ness** *n.*

mul·ti·va·lent (mul′ti-vā′lənt) *adj. Chem.* Having three or more valences: also *polyvalent.* — **mul′ti·va′lence** *n.*

mum[1] (mum) *adj.* Silent; saying nothing. — *interj.* Hush! — **mum's the word** Keep silent; be secretive. [Imit.]

mum[2] (mum) *v.i.* **mummed**, **mum·ming** To play or act in a mask or disguise. Also **mumm.** [Prob. < MUM[1]]

mum[3] (mum) *n. Informal* A chrysanthemum.

mum·ble (mum′bəl) *v.t. & v.i.* **·bled**, **·bling** To speak low and indistinctly; mutter. — *n.* A low, indistinct speech or sound; mutter. [ME *momelen*] — **mum′bler** *n.*

mum·ble·ty-peg (mum′bəl-tē-peg′) *n.* A game played by manipulating a jackknife in various ways so as to stick it into the ground. Also **mum′ble-peg′, mum·ble-the-peg** (mum′bəl-thə-peg′).

mum·bo jum·bo (mum′bō jum′bō) 1. Meaningless, complicated, or obscure ritual, observance, incantation, etc. 2. *Usu. cap.* In certain African tribes, a village god or idol who opposes evil and terrifies the women into subjection. [< Mandingo *mama dyambo* a tutelary god]

mum·mer (mum′ər) *n.* 1. One who acts or makes sport in a mask or disguise. 2. An actor.

mum·mer·y (mum′ər-ē) *n. pl.* **·mer·ies** 1. A performance by mummers. 2. A pretentious or hypocritical ritual. [< MF *mommerie* dumb show]

mum·mi·fy (mum′ə-fī) *v.* **·fied**, **·fy·ing** *v.t.* 1. To make a mummy of; preserve by embalming, drying, etc. 2. To make dry and lifeless, as an idea, institution, etc. — *v.i.* 3. To dry up; shrivel. — **mum′mi·fi·ca′tion** *n.*

mum·my (mum′ē) *n. pl.* **·mies** 1. A human or animal body embalmed in the ancient Egyptian manner. 2. Any corpse that has been well preserved, as by cold, special preparation, etc. 3. One who is lifeless, withered, or torpid. — *v.t. & v.i.* **·mied**, **·my·ing** To mummify. [< F < Med.L < Arabic < Persian *mum* wax] — **mum′mi·form** *adj.*

mumps (mumps) *n.pl.* (*construed as sing.*) *Pathol.* A contagious virus disease usu. occurring in childhood, characterized by fever and swelling of the parotid and other facial glands, and occasionally of the testicles. [Pl. of obs. *mump* grimace]

munch (munch) *v.t. & v.i.* To chew steadily with a crunching noise. [ME, < MF *manger*] — **munch′er** *n.*

mun·dane (mun′dān, mun-dān′) *adj.* 1. Pertaining to or characterized by that which is practical, routine, or ordinary: *mundane* concerns. 2. Of or relating to the world or earth; earthly. [< F < L *mundus* world] — **mun·dane′ly** *adv.* — **mun·dane′ness** *n.*

Munich Pact A pact, signed in 1938 by Nazi Germany, Great Britain, France, and Italy, in which the Sudetenland was ceded to Germany. Also **Munich Agreement.**

mu·nic·i·pal (myōō-nis′ə-pəl) *adj.* 1. Of or pertaining to a town or city or its local government. 2. Having local self-government. [< L *municeps, -cipis* free citizen < *munia* duties + *capere* to take] — **mu·nic′i·pal·ly** *adv.*

municipal borough See under BOROUGH.

mu·nic·i·pal·i·ty (myōō-nis′ə-pal′ə-tē) *n. pl.* **·ties** An incorporated borough, town, or city.

mu·nic·i·pal·ize (myōō-nis′ə-pal·īz′) *v.t.* **·ized**, **·iz·ing** 1. To place within municipal authority or transfer to municipal ownership. 2. To make a municipality of. — **mu·nic′i·pal·i·za′tion** *n.*

mu·nif·i·cent (myōō-nif′ə-sənt) *adj.* Extraordinarily generous or bountiful; liberal. [< L < *munus* gift + *facere* to make] — **mu·nif′i·cence** *n.* — **mu·nif′i·cent·ly** *adv.*

mu·ni·tion (myōō-nish′ən) *n. Usu. pl.* Ammunition and all other necessary war materiel. — *v.t.* To furnish with munitions. [< F < L *munire* to fortify]

mu·ral (myōōr′əl) *n.* A painting or decoration applied to a wall or ceiling. — *adj.* 1. Placed or executed on a wall: a *mural* painting. 2. Of, pertaining to, or resembling a wall. [< F < L < *murus* wall] — **mu′ral·ist** *n.*

mur·der (mûr′dər) *n.* 1. The unlawful, malicious, and intentional killing of one human being by another. 2. *U.S. Informal* Something exceedingly difficult, painful, or hazardous. — **to get away with murder** *U.S. Slang* To avoid or elude punishment or responsibility. — *v.t.* 1. To kill (a human being) unlawfully and with deliberate malice. 2. To kill or slaughter in a brutal manner, as in war. 3. To spoil or mar by a bad performance, improper pronunciation, etc. — *v.i.* 4. To commit murder. — **Syn.** See KILL. [< OE *morthor*] — **mur′der·er** *n.* — **mur′der·ess** *n. fem.*

mur·der·ous (mûr′dər-əs) *adj.* 1. Of, pertaining to, or involving murder. 2. Capable of or given to murder. 3. Having the characteristics of or resembling murder; brutal; deadly. 4. Extremely difficult or dangerous. — **mur′der·ous·ly** *adv.* — **mur′der·ous·ness** *n.*

mu·ri·at·ic acid (myōōr′ē-at′ik) *n.* Hydrochloric acid, esp. an impure grade used commercially. [< L *muriaticus* pickled < *muria* brine]

mu·rine (myōōr′īn, -in) *adj.* Of or pertaining to a family or a subfamily of rodents that includes the true mice and rats. — *n.* A murine rodent. [< L *mus, muris* mouse]

murk (mûrk) *n.* Darkness; gloom. Also spelled **mirk.** [OE *mirce*]

murk·y (mûr′kē) *adj.* **murk·i·er**, **murk·i·est** 1. Dark, gloomy, or obscure: the *murky* depths. 2. Hazy, thick, or misty, as atmosphere, color, etc. 3. Not clear or distinct to the mind; confused; abstruse. Also **mirky.** — **murk′i·ly** *adv.* — **murk′i·ness** *n.*

mur·mur (mûr′mər) *n.* 1. A low, indistinct, continuously repeated sound, as of many voices. 2. An indistinct or mumbled complaint; grumbling. 3. *Med.* A soft, low sound heard on auscultation of certain organs; esp., an abnormal, rasping sound produced within the heart. — *v.i.* 1. To make a low, indistinct sound. 2. To complain in low, muttered tones; grumble. — *v.t.* 3. To mutter. [< OF < L *murmur*, ? ult. imit.] — **mur′mur·er** *n.* — **mur′mur·ing·ly** *adv.*

mur·mur·ous (mûr′mər-əs) *adj.* Characterized by, filled with, or making murmurs. — **mur′mur·ous·ly** *adv.* — **mur′mur·ous·ness** *n.*

mur·rain (mûr′in) *n.* Any of various contagious diseases affecting cattle. [< OF < L *mori* to die]

mur·rey (mûr′ē) *adj.* Of a purplish red color. — *n.* A dark purplish red. [< OF < L *morum* mulberry]

Mus·ca (mus′kə) *n.* A constellation, the Fly. [< NL]

mus·ca·dine (mus′kə·din, -dīn) *n.* A North American grape having a thick skin and a strong flavor. [Prob. < Provençal < LL *muscus* musk]

mus·cat (mus′kat, -kət) *n.* 1. Any of several varieties of musk-flavored Old World grapes. 2. A sweet wine made from such cultivated grapes. Also called *muscatel.* [< F < Provençal, smelling like musk < LL *muscus* musk]

mus·ca·tel (mus′kə·tel′) *n.* 1. A rich, sweet wine, made from the muscat grape. 2. The muscat grape. Also **mus′·ca·del′** (-del′).

mus·cle (mus′əl) *n.* 1. *Anat.* A contractile tissue composed of bundles of elongated fibers that function to produce bodily movements. 2. An organ or structure consisting of such tissue. 3. Muscular strength; brawn. —*v.i.* ·cled, ·cling *U.S. Slang* To force one's way by or as by sheer brawn: often with *in.* [< F < L *musculus*, lit., little mouse, dim. of *mus*] —**mus′cled** *adj.*

mus·cle-bound (mus′əl·bound′) *adj.* Having enlarged and inelastic muscles, as from excessive exercise.

Mus·co·vite (mus′kə·vīt) *n.* An inhabitant of Muscovy or of Moscow. —*adj.* 1. Of or pertaining to Muscovy.

Mus·co·vy (mus′kə·vē) Ancient Russia.

Muscovy duck A large greenish black duck of Central and South America. [Alter. of MUSK DUCK]

mus·cu·lar (mus′kyə·lər) *adj.* 1. Pertaining to or composed of muscle. 2. Having strong muscles; brawny. —**mus′cu·lar′i·ty** (-lar′ə·tē) *n.* —**mus′cu·lar·ly** *adv.*

muscular dystrophy *Pathol.* One of various diseases characterized by a progressive degeneration of muscle tissue.

mus·cu·la·ture (mus′kyə·lə·chŏŏr) *n.* 1. The disposition or arrangement of muscles in a part or organ. 2. The muscle system as a whole. Also **mus′cu·la′tion.** [< F]

muse¹ (myōōz) *n.* A spirit or power regarded as inspiring artists, poets, etc. [< MUSE]

muse² (myōōz) *v.t. & v.i.* mused, mus·ing To consider thoughtfully or at length; ponder; meditate. [< OF *muser* to reflect] —**muse′ful** *adj.* —**muse′ful·ly** *adv.*

Muse (myōōz) *n.* In Greek mythology, any of the nine goddesses who preside over the arts and sciences. [< F < L < Gk. *Mousa* a Muse, eloquence, music]

mu·se·um (myōō·zē′əm) *n.* A place or building for preserving and exhibiting works of art, scientific objects, curiosities, etc. [< L < Gk. *mouseion* shrine of the Muses]

mush¹ (mush) *n.* 1. *U.S.* A thick porridge made with corn meal boiled in water or milk. 2. Anything soft and pulpy. 3. *Informal* Maudlin sentimentality. [Var. of MASH]

mush² (mush) *Chiefly Canadian v.i.* In arctic regions, to travel over snow with a dog sled. —*interj.* Get along!: a command to a dog team. [Prob. < F (Canadian) *marche,* the cry of voyageurs and trappers to their dogs]

mush·mel·on (mush′mel′ən) *n. U.S. Dial.* A muskmelon.

mush·room (mush′rōōm, -rŏŏm) *n.* 1. Any of various fleshy, rapidly growing, umbrella-shaped fungi, esp., the common edible **field mushroom** and certain poisonous varieties loosely called toadstools. 2. Anything resembling a mushroom in shape or rapid growth. —*v.i.* To grow or spread rapidly or in a mushroomlike shape. [ME *muscheron*]

mush·y (mush′ē) *adj.* mush·i·er, mush·i·est 1. Soft; pulpy. 2. *Informal* Mawkishly sentimental. —**mush′i·ly** *adv.* —**mush′i·ness** *n.*

mu·sic (myōō′zik) *n.* 1. The art of producing significant arrangements of sounds, usu. with reference to rhythm, pitch, and tone color. 2. A musical composition or body of compositions; also, a musical score. 3. A succession or combination of musical sounds, esp. if pleasing to the ear. —**program music** Music intended to be heard with reference to a story, idea, situation, event, etc. —**to face the music** To accept the consequences of one's acts. [< OF < L < Gk. *mousikē* (*technē*), lit., the art of the Muse]

mu·si·cal (myōō′zi·kəl) *adj.* 1. Of, pertaining to, or capable of creating music. 2. Having the nature or characteristics of music; melodious; harmonious. 3. Fond of or versed in music. 4. Set to music. —*n.* A musical comedy. —**mu′si·cal·ly** *adv.* —**mu′si·cal′i·ty, mu′si·cal·ness** *n.*

musical comedy A show with music, songs, dances, jokes, colorful staging, etc., often based on a tenuous plot.

mu·si·cale (myōō′zə·kal′) *n.* A private concert or recital, as in a home. [< F (*soirée*) *musicale*]

musical saw A handsaw that is played with a violin bow and produces musical tones by being bent or flexed.

music box A mechanism that plays tunes, usu. by means of pins that strike the tuned teeth of a comblike metal plate.

music hall 1. A public building for musical performances. 2. *Brit.* A vaudeville theatre.

mu·si·cian (myōō·zish′ən) *n.* 1. A professional performer or composer of music. 2. One skilled in performing or composing music. —**mu·si′cian·ly** *adj.* —**mu·si′cian·ship** *n.*

mu·si·col·o·gy (myōō′zə·kol′ə·jē) *n. pl.* **·gies** The scientific and historical study of the forms, theory, methods, etc., of music. —**mu′si·col′o·gist** *n.*

music stand A rack to hold music for a performer.

musk (musk) *n.* 1. A soft, powdery secretion with a penetrating odor, obtained from the sac (**musk bag**) of the male musk deer, and used in making perfumes and in medicine. 2. Any similar substance, either natural or synthetic. 3. The odor of musk. [< OF < LL < LGk. *moskos*]

musk deer A small, hornless deer of Asia, of which the male has a musk-secreting gland.

mus·kel·lunge (mus′kə·lunj) *n. pl.* **·lunge** or **·lung·es** A large North American pike, valued as a game fish. Also **mus′kal·lunge, mus′kie** (-kē). [< Algonquian < *mas* great + *kinong* pike]

mus·ket (mus′kit) *n.* An archaic smoothbore, usually muzzleloading, firearm designed to be fired from the shoulder. [< MF < Ital. *moschetto* crossbow, dart]

mus·ket·eer (mus′kə·tir′) *n.* Formerly, a soldier armed with a musket. [< F *mousquetaire*]

mus·ket·ry (mus′kit·rē) *n.* 1. Muskets collectively. 2. The technique of firing small arms.

Mus·kho·ge·an (mus·kŏ′gē·ən, mus′kŏ·gē′ən) *n.* One of the principal North American Indian linguistic stocks formerly inhabiting the SE U.S. Also **Mus·ko′gi·an.**

musk·mel·on (musk′mel′ən) *n.* Any of several varieties of juicy, edible fruits of the gourd family, as the cantaloupe; also, the plant.

musk ox A shaggy, hollow-horned ruminant of arctic America and Greenland, emitting a strong odor of musk.

musk·rat (musk′rat) *n. pl.* **·rats** or **·rat** 1. An aquatic rodent of North America, having dark, glossy brown fur and a musky odor: also called *water rat.* 2. The valuable fur of this rodent. [< Algonquian *musquash*]

musk·y (mus′kē) *adj.* musk·i·er, musk·i·est Resembling musk in odor or taste. —**musk′i·ly** *adv.* —**musk′i·ness** *n.*

MUSKRAT (About 12 inches long; tail 10 inches)

Mus·lim (muz′lim, mŏŏz′-, mŏŏs′-) *n. pl.* **·lims** or **·lim** A believer in Islam; Mohammedan. —*adj.* Of or pertaining to Islam. Also called *Moslem:* also **Mus′lem.** [< Arabic, one who submits < *aslama* to surrender (to God)]

Mus·lim·ism (muz′ləm·iz′əm, mŏŏz′-, mŏŏs′-) *n.* Islam.

mus·lin (muz′lin) *n.* Any of several plain-weave cotton fabrics of varying fineness. [< F < Ital. < *Mussolo* Mosul, city in Iraq, where it was made]

muss (mus) *U.S. Informal n.* 1. A state of disorder or untidiness; mess. 2. A commotion or tumult. —*v.t.* To make messy or untidy; rumple: often with *up.* [Alter. of MESS]

mus·sel (mus′əl) *n.* 1. A bivalve marine mollusk, esp. the edible **blue mussel.** 2. Any of several fresh-water mollusks. [OE < L *musculus,* dim. of *mus* mouse]

Mus·sel·man (mus′əl·mən) *n. pl.* **·mans** (-mənz) or **·men** (-mən) A Muslim. [< Persian and Turkish *musulmān*]

muss·y (mus′ē) *adj. U.S. Informal* muss·i·er, muss·i·est Rumpled; messy. —**muss′i·ly** *adv.* —**muss′i·ness** *n.*

must¹ (must) *v. Present 3rd person sing.* must A defective verb now used only as an auxiliary followed by the infinitive without *to,* or elliptically with the infinitive understood, to express: **a** Compulsion: *Must* you go? **b** Requirement: You *must* be healthy to be accepted. **c** Probability or supposition: You *must* be tired. **d** Conviction or certainty: War *must* follow. ◆ A past conditional is formed by placing the following verb in the perfect infinitive: *He must have gone.* —*n. Informal* Anything that is required or vital: Safety is a *must.* —*adj. Informal* Important and essential: a *must* book. [OE *mōtan* to be able, to be obliged to]

must² (must) *n.* Mustiness; mold. [< MUSTY]

must³ (must) *n.* The expressed unfermented juice of the grape or other fruit. [OE < L *mustum* (*vinum*) new (wine)]

mus·tache (məs·tash′, mus′tash) *n.* 1. The growth of hair on the upper lip. 2. The hair or bristles growing near the mouth of an animal. Also **mus·ta·chio** (məs·tä′shō). Also, *Chiefly Brit.,* **moustache.** [< F < Ital. *mostaccio* face] —**mus·tached** (məs·tasht′) *adj.*

mus·tang (mus′tang) *n.* A wild horse of the American plains. [< Sp. *mesteño* belonging to a cattlemen's association]

mus·tard (mus′tərd) *n.* 1. A pungent condiment prepared as a paste or powder from the seed of the mustard plant. 2. Any of several plants of a large family that includes broccoli, cabbage, cress, etc. 3. The yellowish or brownish color of ground mustard. [< MF *mustarde*]

mustard gas *Chem.* An oily amber liquid, $C_4H_8Cl_2S$, having an odor of mustard or garlic, and used in warfare because of its powerful blistering effect.

mustard plaster A mixture of powdered black mustard and a suitable adhesive, used as a counterirritant.

mus·ter (mus′tər) *v.t.* **1.** To summon or assemble (troops, etc.), for service, review, roll call, etc. **2.** To collect, gather, or summon: often with *up.* —*v.i.* **3.** To gather or assemble, as troops for service, review, etc. **— to muster in** (or **out**) To enlist in (or leave) military service. —*n.* **1.** An assembling or gathering, as of troops. **2.** An assemblage or collection, as of troops. **3.** An official list of officers and men in a military unit or ship's crew: also **muster roll**. [< OF < L *monstrare* to show]

must·y (mus′tē) *adj.* **must·i·er, must·i·est 1.** Having a moldy odor or flavor, as a close room. **2.** Dull or stale with age. **3.** Without vigor; lifeless. [? Alter. of obs. *moisty* < MOIST] **— must′i·ly** *adv.* **— must′i·ness** *n.*

mu·ta·ble (myōō′tə·bəl) *adj.* **1.** Capable of or subject to change. **2.** Liable to frequent change. [< L < *mutare* to change] **— mu·ta·ble·ness, mu·ta·bil·i·ty** *n.* **— mu·ta·bly** *adv.*

mu·ta·gen·ic (myōō′tə·jen′ik) *adj. Genetics* Having the power to produce mutations in plant or animal organisms, as X-rays, certain chemicals, etc. [< L *mutare* to change]

mu·tant (myōō′tənt) *n.* A plant or animal organism differing from its parents in one or more characteristics that are inheritable; mutation; sport. —*adj.* Pertaining to, resulting from, or undergoing mutation. [< L *mutare* To change]

mu·tate (myōō′tāt) *v.t. & v.i.* **·tat·ed, ·tat·ing** To undergo or subject to change or mutation. [< L < *mutare* to change] **— mu′ta·tive** (-tə·tiv) *adj.*

mu·ta·tion (myōō·tā′shən) *n.* **1.** The act or process of changing; alteration. **2.** A change or modification in form, structure, function, etc. **3.** *Biol.* **a** A sudden, transmissible variation in a plant or animal. **b** An individual, species, etc., resulting from such a variation. [< OF < L < *mutare* to change] **— mu·ta′tion·al** *adj.*

mute (myōōt) *adj.* **1.** Not producing speech or sound; silent. **2.** Lacking the power of speech; dumb. **3.** Expressed or conveyed without speech; unspoken: a *mute* appeal. **4.** *Law* Deliberately refusing to plead on arraignment. **5.** *Phonet.* Not pronounced; silent, as the *e* in *gone.* —*n.* **1.** One who is unable to speak; esp. a deaf-mute. **2.** *Law* One who refuses to plead on arraignment. **3.** *Phonet.* **a** A silent letter. **b** A plosive. **4.** *Music* A device used to muffle the tone of an instrument. —*v.t.* **mut·ed, mut·ing 1.** To muffle or deaden the sound of (a musical instrument, etc.). **2.** In art, to soften (a color, a shade, etc.). [< L *mutus* dumb] **— mute′ly** *adv.* **— mute′ness** *n.*

mu·ti·late (myōō′tə·lāt) *v.t.* **·lat·ed, ·lat·ing 1.** To deprive (a person, animal, etc.) of a limb or essential part; maim. **2.** To damage or make imperfect: to *mutilate* a speech. [< L *mutilare* to maim] **— mu′ti·la·tion** *n.* **— mu′ti·la·tive** *adj.* **— mu′ti·la·tor** *n.*

mu·ti·neer (myōō′tə·nir′) *n.* One guilty of mutiny.

mu·ti·nous (myōō′tə·nəs) *adj.* **1.** Disposed to mutiny; seditious. **2.** Characterized by, expressing, or constituting mutiny. **— mu′ti·nous·ly** *adv.* **— mu′ti·nous·ness** *n.*

mu·ti·ny (myōō′tə·nē) *n. pl.* **·nies** Rebellion against constituted authority; insubordination; esp., a revolt of soldiers or sailors against their commanders. —*v.i.* **·nied, ·ny·ing** To take part in a mutiny. [< MF *mutin* rebellious < OF < Med.L < L *movere* to move]

mutt (mut) *n. Slang* **1.** A cur; mongrel dog. **2.** A stupid person; blockhead. Also **mut.** [< MUTT(ONHEAD)]

mut·ter (mut′ər) *v.i.* **1.** To speak in a low, indistinct tone, as in complaining. **2.** To complain; grumble. **3.** To make a low, rumbling sound. —*v.t.* **4.** To say in a low, indistinct tone. —*n.* A low, indistinct utterance or tone. [ME *muteren*] **— mut′ter·er** *n.* **— mut′ter·ing·ly** *adv.*

mut·ton (mut′n) *n.* The flesh of sheep used as food; esp. the flesh of mature sheep as distinguished from lambs. [< OF *molton* sheep] **— mut′ton·y** *adv.*

mutton chop A piece of mutton from the rib for broiling or frying.

mut·ton·chops (mut′n·chops′) *n.pl.* Side whiskers narrow at the temples and broad at the lower cheeks.

mut·ton·head (mut′n·hed′) *n. Slang* A stupid, dense person. **— mut′ton·head′ed** (-hed′id) *adj.*

mu·tu·al (myōō′chŏo·əl) *adj.* **1.** Felt, expressed, or performed for or toward each other; reciprocal: *mutual* dislike. **2.** Having the same attitude toward or relationship with each other or others: *mutual* friends. **3.** Possessed in common. [< OF < L *mutuus* borrowed, exchanged, reciprocal] **— mu′tu·al·ly** *adv.* **— mu′tu·al·i·ty** *n.*

muu-muu (mōō′mōō′) *n.* A loose, flowing gown for women, gathered from the neckline. [< Hawaiian]

mu·zhik (mōō·zhēk′) *n.* A Russian peasant in Czarist times. Also **mu·zjik.** [< Russian]

muz·zle (muz′əl) *n.* **1.** The projecting part of an animal's head, including the jaws, mouth, and snout. **2.** A guard or covering for the snout. **3.** The front end of the barrel of a firearm. —*v.t.* **·zled, ·zling 1.** To put a muzzle on (an animal, etc.). **2.** To restrain from speaking, expressing opinions, etc.; gag. [< OF < Med.L *musus* snout]

muz·zle-load·er (muz′əl·lō′dər) *n.* A gun loaded through the muzzle. **— muz′zle-load′ing** *adj.*

MVD The Ministry of Internal Affairs of the Soviet Union; the secret police. Also **M.V.D.**

my (mī) *pronominal adj.* The possessive case of the pronoun *I,* used attributively: also used in certain forms of address: *my* lord; *my* good man. —*interj.* An exclamation of surprise, dismay, etc.: Oh, *my!* [OE *mīn*]

my- Var. of MYO-.

my·as·the·ni·a (mī′əs·thē′nē·ə) *n. Pathol.* Muscular debility, often accompanied by progressive exhaustion.

my·ce·li·um (mī·sē′lē·əm) *n. pl.* **·li·a** (-lē·ə) *Bot.* The thallus or vegetative portion of a fungus, consisting of hyphae. Also **my′cele** (-sēl). [< NL < Gk. *mykēs* fungus] **— my·ce′li·al, my·ce′li·an** *adj.* **— my·ce′li·oid, my·ce·loid** (mī′sə·loid) *adj.*

My·ce·nae (mī·sē′nē) An ancient city in the NE Peloponnesus, Greece; first excavated 1876–77. **— My′ce·nae′an** *adj. & n.*

-mycete *combining form Bot.* A member of a class of fungi, corresponding in use to class names in *-mycetes.*

-mycetes *combining form Bot.* Used to form class names of fungi. [< Gk. *mykētes,* pl. of *mykēs* fungus]

myco- *combining form* Fungus. Also, before vowels, **myc-.** [< Gk. *mykēs* fungus]

my·col·o·gy (mī·kol′ə·jē) *n. pl.* **·gies** The branch of botany dealing with fungi. **— my·co·log·ic** (mī′kə·loj′ik) or **·i·cal** *adj.* **— my·col′o·gist** *n.*

my·co·sis (mī·kō′sis) *n. Pathol.* **1.** A fungous growth within the body. **2.** A disease caused by such a growth, as ringworm. **— my·cot′ic** (-kot′ik) *adj.*

my·e·len·ceph·a·lon (mī′ə·len·sef′ə·lon) *n. Anat.* The posterior part of the rhombencephalon or that portion of the medulla oblongata lying behind the pons Varolii and cerebellum.

my·e·li·tis (mī′ə·lī′tis) *n. Pathol.* **1.** Inflammation of the spinal cord. **2.** Inflammation of the bone marrow.

myelo- *combining form Anat.* The spinal cord or bone marrow. Also, before vowels, **myel-.** [< Gk. *myelos* marrow]

my·na (mī′nə) *n.* One of the various starlinglike Oriental birds, some of which are taught to speak words: sometimes spelled *mina.* Also **my′nah.** [< Hind. *mainā*]

myn·heer (mīn·hâr′, -hir′) *n.* **1.** *Cap.* The Dutch equivalent of *Mr.* **2.** A title of courtesy, equivalent to *sir.* [< Du. < *mijn* my + *heer* lord, master]

myo- *combining form* Muscle. Also, before vowels, **my-.** [< Gk. *mys, myos* muscle]

my·o·car·di·al (mī′ō·kär′dē·əl) *adj. Anat.* Of or pertaining to the heart muscle. [< MYO- + Gk. *kardia* heart]

my·o·car·di·um (mī′ō·kär′dē·əm) *n. Anat.* The muscular tissue of the heart. [< MYO- + Gk. *kardia* heart]

my·o·pi·a (mī·ō′pē·ə) *n.* **1.** *Pathol.* A visual defect in which objects are seen clearly only when close to the eye; nearsightedness. **2.** Lack of insight or discernment; obtuseness. Also **my·o·py** (mī′ə·pē). [< NL] **— my·op′ic** (-op′ik) *adj.*

my·o·sis (mī·ō′sis) See MIOSIS.

myria- *combining form* **1.** Very many; of great number. **2.** In the metric system, ten thousand. Also, before vowels, **myri-.** [< Gk. *myrios* numberless]

myr·i·ad (mir′ē·əd) *adj.* Countless; innumerable. —*n.* **1.** A vast indefinite number. **2.** A vast number of persons or things. **3.** Ten thousand. [< Gk. *myrios* numberless]

myr·i·a·pod (mir′ē·ə·pod) *n. Zool.* One of a group of arthropods whose bodies are made up of a certain number of segments, each of which bears one or two pairs of jointed appendages, including the centipedes. **— myr·i·ap·o·dan** (mir′ē·ap′ə·dən) *adj. & n.* **— myr′i·ap′o·dous** *adj.*

myr·mi·don (mûr′mə·don, -dən) *n.* A faithful, unquestioning follower. [< MYRMIDON]

Myr·mi·don (mûr′mə·don, -dən) *n.* In Greek legend, one of a warlike people of Thessaly, followers of Achilles in the Trojan War. [< L < Gk., pl. *Myrmidones*]

myrrh (mûr) *n.* **1.** An aromatic gum resin that exudes from certain small trees of Arabia and eastern Africa, used as incense, perfume, and in medicine. **2.** The shrub or tree. [OE < L < Gk. *myrra* < Hebrew *mōr, mar* bitter]

myr·tle (mûr′təl) *n.* Any of a group o? shrubs with evergreen leaves, white or rose-colored flowers, and black berries. **2.** One of various other plants, as the periwinkle. [< F < Med.L *myrtillus* myrtle]

my·self (mī·self′) *pron.* A form of the first person singular pronoun, used: **1.** As a reflexive or as the object of a preposition in a reflexive sense: I saw *myself* in the mirror. **2.** As an emphatic or intensive form of *I*: I *myself* invented the yo-yo. **3.** Informally as part of a direct compound object of a verb, or as an emphatic form of *me:* He asked John and *myself* to come along; They saw *myself* on television. **4.** As a designation of a normal, proper, or usual state: Once out of uniform, I was *myself* again in no time. [OE *mē* + *sylf*]

mys·te·ri·ous (mis·tir'ē·əs) *adj.* **1.** Implying or characterized by mystery. **2.** Unexplained; puzzling. — **mys·te'ri·ous·ly** *adv.* — **mys·te'ri·ous·ness** *n.*
— **Syn.** A *mysterious* occurrence contains something unknown, but not necessarily unknowable, while something *obscure* is hidden but may be brought to light. *Inscrutable* refers to that which is quite beyond the power of perception; *abstruse,* to that which is difficult to understand because of its complexity or profundity. *Esoteric* suggests something that is understood only by a small and select group possessing special knowledge. *Occult* marks those things considered to belong to a realm beyond human experience.

mys·ter·y (mis'tər·ē) *n. pl.* **·ter·ies** **1.** Something that is not or cannot be known, understood, or explained. **2.** Any action, affair, or thing that arouses curiosity or suspense because it is not fully revealed. **3.** A story, play, movie, etc., narrating or dramatizing such an affair. **4.** Obscurity or darkness: shrouded in *mystery.* **5.** Baffling character or property, as of a glance, gesture, etc. **6.** *Theol.* A truth that can be known only through divine revelation. **7.** *Eccl.* **a** A sacrament, esp. the Eucharist. **b** *pl.* The Eucharistic elements. **c** Any of fifteen events in the life of Christ. **8.** *Usu. pl.* In ancient times, one of certain religious cults. **9.** *Often pl.* A secret rite, doctrine, or practice. [< L < Gk. *mysterion* secret rite]

mystery play A medieval dramatic representation dealing with Scriptural events or characters and typically presented by a craft guild on a holiday. Compare MIRACLE PLAY.

mys·tic (mis'tik) *adj.* **1.** Of the nature of or pertaining to mysteries. **2.** Of or designating an occult or esoteric rite, practice, belief, religion, etc. **3.** Of or pertaining to mystics or mysticism. **4.** Baffling or enigmatic. — *n.* One who believes in mysticism, or professes to have had mystical experiences. [< L *mysticus* pertaining to secret rites]

mys·ti·cal (mis'ti·kəl) *adj.* **1.** Of the nature of a direct, intuitive, or subjective perception beyond the ordinary range of human experience, esp. one of a religious character.

2. Having a spiritual character or reality beyond human reason. **3.** Mystic (defs. 1, 2, & 3). — **mys'ti·cal·i·ty** (-kal'ə·tē), **mys'ti·cal·ness** *n.* — **mys'ti·cal·ly** *adv.*

mys·ti·cism (mis'tə·siz'əm) *n.* **1.** The doctrine or belief that through contemplation and love man can achieve a direct and immediate consciousness of God or of divine truth, etc., without the use of reason or of any of the ordinary senses. **2.** Any mystical theory. **3.** Vague thinking.

mys·ti·fy (mis'tə·fī) *v.t.* **·fied, ·fy·ing** **1.** To confuse or perplex, esp. deliberately. **2.** To make obscure or mysterious. [< F *mystique* mystic] — **mys'ti·fi·ca'tion** *n.* — **mys'ti·fi'er** *n.* — **mys'ti·fy'ing·ly** *adv.*

mys·tique (mis·tēk') *n.* A body of attitudes, opinions, or ideas that become associated with a person, thing, institution, etc., and give it a superhuman or mythical status: the *mystique* of bullfighting. [< F]

myth (mith) *n.* **1.** A traditional story, usu. focusing on the deeds of gods or heroes, often in explanation of some natural phenomenon, as the origin of the sun, etc. **2.** A theme, motif, character type, etc., in modern literature. **3.** Myths collectively. **4.** An imaginary or fictitious person, thing, event, or story. **5.** A false opinion, belief, or ideal. [< LL *mythos* < Gk., word, speech, story]

myth·i·cal (mith'i·kəl) *adj.* **1.** Pertaining to or like a myth; **2.** Derived from or contained in a myth. **3.** Imaginary. fictitious. Also **myth'ic.** — **myth'i·cal·ly** *adv.*

mytho- *combining form* Myth. Also, before vowels, **myth-.** [< Gk. *mythos* story]

myth·o·log·i·cal (mith'ə·loj'i·kəl) *adj.* **1.** Of, pertaining to, or described in mythology. **2.** Imaginary. Also **myth'o·log'ic.** — **myth'o·log'i·cal·ly** *adv.*

my·thol·o·gy (mi·thol'ə·jē) *n. pl.* **·gies** **1.** The collective myths and legends of a particular people, person, institution, etc. **2.** The scientific collection and study of myths. **3.** A volume of myths. [< F < LL < Gk. < *mythos* story + *logos* < *legein* to speak, tell] — **my·thol'o·gist** *n.*

N

n, N (en) *n. pl.* **n's** or **ns, N's** or **Ns, ens** (enz) **1.** The fourteenth letter of the English alphabet. **2.** The sound represented by the letter *n,* a voiced, alveolar nasal. — *symbol* **1.** *Printing* An en. **2.** *Chem.* Nitrogen (symbol N). **3.** *Math.* An indefinite number.

nab (nab) *v.t.* **nabbed, nab·bing** *Informal* **1.** To catch or arrest, as a fugitive or criminal. **2.** To take or seize suddenly; snatch. [Prob. of Scand. origin]

na·bob (nā'bob) *n.* **1.** A European who has become rich in India. **2.** Any very rich or powerful man. [< Hind. *nawwāb* < Arabic *nuwwab,* pl. of *nā'ib* viceroy]

na·celle (nə·sel') *n. Aeron.* A separate enclosure on an aircraft, esp. one for an engine. [< F, small boat]

na·cre (nā'kər) *n.* Mother-of-pearl. [< F < Ital. *naccara* < Arabic *naqqāra* drum]

na·cre·ous (nā'krē·əs) *adj.* **1.** Containing, resembling, or producing nacre. **2.** Iridescent; pearly.

Na-Dene (nə·dēn') *n.* A group of related North American Indian languages. Also **Na-Dé·né'** (-dā·nā').

na·dir (nā'dər, -dir) *n.* **1.** The point of the celestial sphere directly beneath the position of an observer, and opposite to the zenith. **2.** The lowest possible point: opposed to *zenith.* [< MF < Arabic *nazīr* (*as-samt*) opposite (the zenith)]

nae (nā) *adj. & adv. Scot.* No; not.

nag[1] (nag) *v.* **nagged, nag·ging** *v.t.* **1.** To bother or annoy by repeatedly urging, scolding, carping, etc. — *v.i.* **2.** To urge, scold, carp, etc., continually. — *n.* One who nags. [< Scand.] — **nag'ger** *n.* — **nag'ging·ly** *adv.*

nag[2] (nag) *n.* **1.** A pony or small horse used for riding. **2.** An old, broken-down, or worthless horse. [ME *nagge*]

Na·hua·tl (nä'wät·l) *n.* **1.** The Uto-Aztecan language of the Aztecs and certain other Indian peoples. **2.** The peoples whose native language is Nahuatl. — *adj.* Of or pertaining to Nahuatl or the people who speak it.

Na·hua·tlan (nä'wät·lən) *n.* **1.** A branch of the Uto-Aztecan linguistic family of North and Central American Indians, including the Aztec dialects. **2.** Nahuatl. — *adj.* Of or pertaining to Nahuatl or Nahuatlan.

Na·hum (nā'əm, -hum) Seventh-century B.C. Hebrew prophet. — *n.* A book of the Old Testament containing his prophecies. [< Hebrew, comfort]

nai·ad (nā'ad, nī'-) *n. pl.* **·ads** or **·a·des** (-ə·dēz) **1.** In classical mythology, one of the water nymphs believed to dwell in and preside over fountains, springs, rivers, lakes, and wells. **2.** *Entomol.* The aquatic nymphal stage in the life cycle of certain insects. [< L < Gk. *Naias, -ados.*]

na·if (nä·ēf') *adj. French* Masculine form of NAIVE. Also **na·if'.**

nail (nāl) *n.* **1.** A slender piece of metal, usu. pointed at one end and broadened at the other, used for driving into or through wood, etc., so as to hold or fasten one piece to another or to project as a peg. **2.** Something resembling a nail in shape or function. **3.** A thin, horny plate growing on one side of the ends of the fingers and toes of men and other primates. **4.** An animal part corresponding to the nail of a primate, as a claw, talon, or hoof. — **hard as nails 1.** In good physical condition; rugged. **2.** Not to be moved by sentiment, pity, etc. — **to hit the nail on the head** To do or say something exactly to the point. — *v.t.* **1.** To fasten or fix in place with a nail or nails. **2.** To close up or shut in by means of nails: often with *up.* **3.** To secure or make certain through quick or decisive action: often with *down.* **4.** To fix firmly or immovably: Terror *nailed* him to the spot. **5.** *Slang* To catch or arrest; intercept. **6.** *Slang* To expose, as a lie or liar. [OE *nægl,* orig., fingernail.]

nail file A small, fine file for shaping the fingernails.

nail·fold (nāl'fōld') *n. Anat.* The cuticle (def. 3).

nail polish A clear or colored lacquer or other substance applied to the nails to give a glossy finish. Also **nail enamel.**

nail·set (nāl'set') *n.* A punch for driving the head of a nail below or even with a surface. Also **nail set.**

nain·sook (nān'sŏŏk, nan'-) *n.* A soft, lightweight cotton fabric. [< Hind. *nainsukh,* lit., pleasure of the eye]

na·ive (nä·ēv') *adj.* **1.** Having an unaffected or simple nature that lacks worldly experience; artless. **2.** Lacking or revealing the lack of deliberate or careful analysis; uncritical: a *naive* idea. **3.** Uninstructed: a *naive* observer. Also **na·ive′**. [< F, fem. of *naïf* < L *nativus* natural, inborn] — **na·ive·ly** *adv.* — **na·ive·ness** *n.*

na·ive·té (nä·ēv·tā′, nä·ēv′tā) *n.* **1.** The state or quality of being naive. **2.** An incident, remark, etc., of a naive character. Also **na·ive·té′**, **na·ive·ty** (nä·ēv′tē). [< F]

na·ked (nā′kid) *adj.* **1.** Having no clothes on; nude. **2.** Having no covering, or lacking the usual covering; exposed. **3.** Bare or stripped, as of vegetation, furnishings, ornaments, etc. **4.** Without addition, adornment, or qualification; stark: the *naked* truth. **5.** Unaided by an optical instrument: the *naked* eye. **6.** Open or exposed to view: a *naked* sword. **7.** Without defense or protection; vulnerable. **8.** Being without means of sustenance; destitute. **9.** *Bot.* **a** Not enclosed in an ovary or case: said of seeds. **b** Without protective scales: said of buds. **c** Without a perianth: said of flowers. **d** Without leaves: said of stalks. **e** Having no hairs; smooth: said of leaves. **10.** *Zool.* Lacking fur, hair, feathers, etc. [OE *nacod*] — **na′ked·ly** *adv.* — **na′ked·ness** *n.*

nam·by-pam·by (nam′bē-pam′bē) *adj.* **1.** Full of or exhibiting weak sentimentality; insipid. **2.** Timid and irresolute. — *n. pl.* **·bies** One who is namby-pamby. [< The title of a satiric poem by Henry Carey, died 1743.]

name (nām) *n.* **1.** A word or group of words by which a person, thing, animal, class, or concept is distinctively known or referred to; esp., the proper appellation of a person or family. **2.** A usu. derogatory word or phrase evaluating character or quality: to call someone *names.* **3.** Popular or general reputation. **4.** A famous or important person, organization, or thing: a big *name* in industry. **5.** Mere semblance or outward form: a wife in *name* only. **6.** Fame or distinction. — **by the name of** Named. — **in the name of** **1.** For the sake of. **2.** By the authority of. — **to make a name for oneself** To achieve distinction or fame. — **to one's name** Of one's own: He hasn't a friend *to his name.* — *v.* **named, nam·ing** *v.t.* **1.** To give a name to; call. **2.** To mention or refer to by name; cite. **3.** To identify. **4.** To fix or determine: to *name* the day. **.5.** To nominate; appoint. — *adj.* **1.** Having or known by a name. **2.** *U.S. Informal* Famous. [OE *nama*] — **nam′er** *n.*

name day The feast day of the saint for whom one is named.

name·less (nām′lis) *adj.* **1.** Undistinguished or obscure: a *nameless* multitude. **2.** That cannot be named; indescribable: *nameless* terror. **3.** Not fit to be spoken of; unmentionable: *nameless* atrocities. **4.** Unmentioned by name. **5.** Having no name; esp., having no legal name; illegitimate. — **name′less·ly** *adv.* — **name′less·ness** *n.*

name·ly (nām′lē) *adv.* That is to say; to wit.

name·sake (nām′sāk′) *n.* One who is named after or has the same name as another.

nan·keen (nan·kēn′) *n.* **1.** A buff-colored Chinese cotton fabric. **2.** *pl.* Clothes made of nankeen. Also **nan·kin′** (-kēn′). [after *Nanking*, where originally made]

nan·ny (nan′ē) *n. pl.* **·nies** **1.** *Informal* A female goat: also **nanny goat.** **2.** *Brit.* A child's nurse. [after *Nanny*, a personal name, dim. of *Ann*]

nano- *combining form* **1.** Exceedingly small. **2.** In the metric system and in technical usage, one billionth of (a specified unit). Also, before vowels, **nan-.** [< Gk. *nānos* dwarf]

Nantes, Edict of (nants, *Fr.* nänt) An order granting political equality to the Huguenots, issued by Henry IV of France in 1598 and revoked by Louis XIV in 1685.

Na·o·mi (nā·ō′mē, nā′ə·mē, -mī) In the Bible, the mother-in-law of Ruth. *Ruth* i 2. [< Hebrew, my delight]

nap¹ (nap) *n.* A short sleep; doze. — *v.i.* **napped, nap·ping** **1.** To take a nap; doze. **2.** To be unprepared or off one's guard. [OE *hnappian* to doze]

nap² (nap) *n.* **1.** The short fibers forming a downy or fuzzy surface on flannel and certain other fabrics. **2.** A covering resembling this, as upon some plants. — *v.t.* **napped, nap·ping** To raise a nap on. [< MDu. *noppe*]

na·palm (nā′päm) *n.* A jellylike mixture that is combined with gasoline to form an incendiary fuel, as in bombs, flame throwers, etc. [< *na*(*phthenic*) and *palm*(*itic*) *acids*, chemical compounds used in its manufacture]

nape (nāp) *n.* The back of the neck. [Origin uncertain]

na·per·y (nā′pər·ē) *n. pl.* **·per·ies** Household linen, esp. napkins, tablecloths, etc. [See NAPKIN.]

Naph·ta·li (naf′tə·lī, -lē) In the Old Testament, a son of Jacob and Bilhah, Rachel's maid. *Gen.* xxx 7–8. — *n.* **1.** A tribe of Israel. **2.** The land occupied by the tribe of Naphtali. [< Hebrew, my wrestling]

naph·tha (naf′thə, nap′-) *n.* **1.** A volatile, colorless petroleum distillate intermediate between gasoline and benzene, used as a solvent, cleaning fluid, fuel, etc. **2.** Any similar substance obtained from another source, as from coal tar. **3.** Petroleum. [< L < Gk., prob. < Persian *naft* petroleum]

naph·tha·lene (naf′thə·lēn, nap′-) *n. Chem.* A colorless, odorous coal-tar compound, $C_{10}H_8$, used in the making of dyes, moth balls, etc. Also **naph′tha·line** (-lin, -lēn).

naph·thol (naf′thōl, -thol, nap′-) *n. Chem.* Either of two compounds, $C_{10}H_7OH$, derived from naphthalene and used in making dyes. Also **naph·tol** (naf′tol, -tōl, nap′-).

nap·kin (nap′kin) *n.* **1.** A small, usu. square cloth or paper, used at meals for wiping the hands and mouth or protecting the clothes. **2.** A small piece of toweling. **3.** *Chiefly Brit.* A diaper. [ME *napekyn,* < L *mappa* a cloth]

na·po·le·on (nə·pō′lē·ən, *Fr.* nà·pô·lā·ôn′) *n.* **1.** A rich pastry composed of layers of puff paste filled with cream, custard, etc. **2.** A former French gold coin. **3.** A card game. [after *Napoleon* Bonaparte]

Na·po·le·on·ic (nə·pō′lē·on′ik) *adj.* Characteristic of, pertaining to, or suggesting Napoleon Bonaparte.

Napoleonic Wars See table for WAR.

nappe (nap) *n.* **1.** The sheet of water overlying the top of a weir. **2.** *Geom.* In a cone, one of the two conical surfaces divided by the vertex. [< F, sheet]

nap·per¹ (nap′ər) *n.* One who takes naps.

nap·per² (nap′ər) *n.* One who or that which raises a nap.

nap·py¹ (nap′ē) *adj.* **·pi·er, ·pi·est** **1.** Having or coated with nap. **2.** Having a coarse or kinky quality, as hair.

nap·py² (nap′ē) *n. pl.* **·pies** *Brit. Informal* A baby's diaper. Also **nap′pie.** [< NAPKIN]

nar·cis·sism (när′sis·iz·əm, när·sis′iz·əm) *n.* **1.** Excessive admiration for or fascination with oneself. **2.** *Psychoanal.* The infantile stage of development in which the self is the object of one's erotic interest. Also **nar·cism** (när′siz·əm). [< NARCISSUS] — **nar′cis·sist** *n.* — **nar·cis·sis′tic** *adj.*

nar·cis·sus (när·sis′əs) *n. pl.* **·cis·sus·es** or **·cis·si** (-sis′ī) Any of various bulbous flowering plants of the amaryllis family, including the daffodil and jonquil.

Nar·cis·sus (när·sis′əs) In Greek mythology, a youth who fell in love with his own image in water and pined away for it until he died and changed into the narcissus.

narco- *combining form* Torpor; insensibility. Also, before vowels, **narc-.** [< Gk. *narkē* numbness]

nar·co·sis (när·kō′sis) *n.* Deep stupor produced by a drug.

nar·co·syn·the·sis (när′kō·sin′thə·sis) *n. Psychiatry* Therapy using narcotics to enable the patient to recall and relive painful experiences and minimize their hidden effects.

nar·cot·ic (när·kot′ik) *n.* **1.** A drug, as opium or morphine, that relieves pain and induces sleep, but may be habit-forming. **2.** One who is addicted to the use of narcotics. **3.** Anything that deadens or soothes. — *adj.* **1.** Capable of producing narcosis or stupor. **2.** Pertaining to, like, or induced by a narcotic or narcotics. **3.** Of, relating to, or for narcotic addicts or their treatment. [< L < Gk. < *narkē* torpor] — **nar·cot′i·cal·ly** *adv.*

nar·co·tism (när′kə·tiz′əm) *n.* **1.** Addiction to narcotics. **2.** Narcosis.

nar·co·tize (när′kə·tīz) *v.t.* **·tized, ·tiz·ing** To bring under the influence of a narcotic; stupefy. — **nar′co·ti·za′tion** *n.*

nard (närd) *n.* **1.** Spikenard. **2.** Any of several aromatic plants or roots formerly used in medicine. [< OF < L < Gk. *nardos,* prob. < Semitic]

nar·es (nâr′ēz) *n. pl. of* **nar·is** (nâr′is) *Anat.* Openings into the nasal cavities; esp., the nostrils. [< L, nostrils] — **nar·i·al** (nâr′ē·əl), **nar·ine** (nâr′in, -īn) *adj.*

nar·ghi·le (när′gə·lē) *n.* A hookah. Also **nar′gi·le, nar′gi·leh.** [< F < Persian < *nārgil* coconut]

Nar·ra·gan·set (nar′ə·gan′sit) *n. pl.* **·set** or **·sets** **1.** One of a tribe of North American Indians of Algonquian stock, formerly inhabiting Rhode Island. **2.** The language of this tribe. Also **Nar′ra·gan′sett.**

nar·rate (na·rāt′, nar′āt) *v.* **·rat·ed, ·rat·ing** *v.t.* **1.** To tell or relate, as a story. **2.** To speak in accompaniment and explanation of (a motion picture, television program, etc.). — *v.i.* **3.** To tell a story, etc. [< L *narratus,* pp. of *narrare* to relate] — **nar·ra·tor** or **nar·rat·er** (na·rāt′ər, nar′ā·tər) *n.*

nar·ra·tion (na·rā′shən) *n.* **1.** The act of narrating. **2.** A narrative. **3.** An account that narrates, as in fiction, etc.

nar·ra·tive (nar′ə·tiv) *n.* **1.** Something narrated, as an account, story, or tale. **2.** The act, art, or process of narrating. — *adj.* Of the nature of, pertaining to, or dealing with narration: a *narrative* poem. — **nar′ra·tive·ly** *adv.*

nar·row (nar′ō) *adj.* **1.** Having little width, esp. in comparison with length; not broad. **2.** Limited or small, as in extent or scope: *narrow* ambition. **3.** Narrow-minded. **4.** Nearly unsuccessful or disastrous: a *narrow* escape. **5.** Exhibiting or characterized by small means or resources. **6.** Minute or detailed; painstaking: *narrow* search. — *v.t. & v.i.* To make or become narrow or narrower, as in width or scope. — *n. Usu. pl.* A narrow passage; esp., the narrowest part of a strait, isthmus, etc. **2.** A narrow or contracted part, as of a street or valley. [OE *nearu*] — **nar′row·ness** *n.*

nar·row-gauge (nar′ō·gāj′) *adj.* Designed for or having a width of railroad track less than 56½ inches. Also **nar′row-gage′, nar′row-gaged′, nar′row-gauged′.**

narrow gauge A narrow-gauge railway, locomotive, or car. Also **narrow gage.**

nar·row·ly (nar′ō·lē) *adv.* 1. Barely; hardly. 2. So as to be narrow. 3. In a narrow manner.

nar·row-mind·ed (nar′ō·mīn′did) *adj.* Having or characterized by narrow views or sentiments; illiberal; bigoted. — **nar′row-mind′ed·ly** *adv.* — **nar′row-mind′ed·ness** *n.*

nar·whal (när′wəl -hwəl) *n.* A large, arctic cetacean having in the male a long, straight, spiral tusk, and valued for its oil and ivory. Also **nar′wal, nar·whale** (när′wāl′, -hwāl′). [< Dan. or Sw. *narhval*]

na·sal (nā′zəl) *adj.* 1. Of or pertaining to the nose. 2. *Phonet.* Produced with the voice passing partially or wholly through the nose, as (m), (n), and (ng), and the French nasal vowels. 3. Characterized by or suggestive of a sound so produced. —*n.* 1. *Phonet.* A nasal sound. 2. *Anat.* A part of the nose, as a bone. [< NL < L *nasus* nose] — **na·sal·i·ty** (nā·zal′ə·tē) *n.* — **na′sal·ly** *adv.*

na·sal·ize (nā′zəl·īz) *v.* **·ized, ·iz·ing** *v.t.* 1. To give a nasal sound to. —*v.i.* 2. To produce nasal sounds instead of oral ones. — **na′sal·i·za′tion** *n.*

nas·cent (nā′sənt, nas′ənt) *adj.* 1. Beginning to exist or develop; newly conceived. 2. *Chem.* Of, pertaining to, or being in the nascent state. [< L *nascens, -centis,* ppr. of *nasci* to be born] — **nas′cence, nas′cen·cy** *n.*

nascent state *Chem.* The uncombined condition of an atom in its most active state at the moment of its liberation from a compound. Also **nascent condition.**

naso- *combining form* 1. Nose. 2. Nasal and. [< L *nasus* nose]

na·stur·tium (nə·stûr′shəm) *n.* 1. Any of various garden plants with funnel-shaped flowers, commonly yellow, orange, or red. 2. A rich yellow or reddish orange color. [< L, cress < *nasus* nose + *tortus,* pp. of *torquere* to twist]

nas·ty (nas′tē) *adj.* **·ti·er, ·ti·est** 1. Offensive to the sense of taste or smell; disgusting. 2. Indecent; obscene: *nasty* language. 3. Disagreeable; unpleasant: *nasty* weather. 4. Mean, spiteful, or ill-natured: a *nasty* remark. 5. Serious or painful: a *nasty* cut. [< Du. *nestig* or Sw. *naskug* filthy] — **nas′ti·ly** *adv.* — **nas′ti·ness** *n.*

-nasty *combining form Biol.* An automatic response to a (specified) stimulus, or in a (specified) direction or character. [< Gk. *nastos* close-pressed]

na·tal (nāt′l) *adj.* 1. Of or pertaining to one's birth. 2. *Poetic* Native: said of a place. [< L *nasci* to be born]

na·ta·to·ry (nā′tə·tôr′ē, -tō′rē) *adj.* Of, pertaining to, or adapted for swimming. Also **na′ta·to′ri·al.**

Natch·ez (nach′iz) *n. pl.* **Natch·ez** One of a tribe of North American Indians of Muskhogean stock, formerly inhabiting the lower Mississippi valley.

Na·than (nā′thən) In the Bible, a prophet who denounced David for the death of Uriah. II *Sam.* xii 1. [< Hebrew *nāthān* he gave]

Na·than·a·el (nə·than′ē·əl, -than′yəl) A disciple of Jesus. *John* xxi 1. [< Hebrew, gift of God]

na·tion (nā′shən) *n.* 1. A body of persons associated with a particular territory, usu. organized under a government, and possessing a distinctive cultural and social way of life. 2. A body of persons having a common origin and language. 3. A tribe or federation, esp. of American Indians. [< F < L *nasci* to be born]

—**Syn.** 1. A *nation* is primarily the people under one government; a *state* is an independent *nation.* The words are often interchanged, but *nation* stresses ethnic unity, while *state* stresses political autonomy. We may speak of the many *nations* that made up the ancient Roman *state. Country* is primarily geographical, a region of the earth distinct from others by its topographical features or political character; Montenegro is a *country,* but no longer a *state.*

na·tion·al (nash′ən·əl, nash′nəl) *adj.* 1. Of, belonging to, or representative of a nation as a whole. 2. Characteristic of or peculiar to a particular nation. —*n.* A subject or citizen of a nation. [< F] — **na′tion·al·ly** *adv.*

national bank 1. *U.S.* A commercial bank organized by federal statute and chartered by the national government. 2. A bank associated with the national finances.

National Guard An organized militia force of a State, a Territory, or the District of Columbia, maintained in part by the U.S. government and subject to federal service in national emergencies.

na·tion·al·ism (nash′ən·əl·is′əm, nash′nəl-) *n.* 1. Devotion, often chauvinistic, to one's own nation. 2. The belief or doctrine that among nations the common welfare is best served by independent rather than collective or cooperative action. 3. A desire or movement for national independence. — **na′tion·al·ist** *adj. & n.* — **na′tion·al·is′tic** *adj.* — **na′·tion·al·is′ti·cal·ly** *adv.*

na·tion·al·i·ty (nash′ən·al′ə·tē) *n. pl.* **·ties** 1. A body of people having the same traditions, language, or ethnic origin, and potentially or actually constituting a nation. 2.

The state or fact of being related to a particular nation, as by birth or citizenship. 3. National character or quality. 4. The fact or quality of existing as a nation.

na·tion·al·ize (nash′ən·əl·īz′, nash′nəl-) *v.t.* **·ized, ·iz·ing** 1. To place (the industries, resources, etc., of a nation) under the control or ownership of the state. 2. To make national, as in character or scope. 3. To accept as a national; naturalize. Also *Brit.* **na′tion·al·ise′.** — **na′tion·al·i·za′tion** *n.* — **na′tion·al·iz′er** *n.*

National League See under MAJOR LEAGUE.

National Socialism See under NAZI.

Nation of Islam See under BLACK MUSLIM.

na·tion-wide (nā′shən·wīd′) *adj.* Extending throughout the nation.

na·tive (nā′tiv) *adj.* 1. Born in a particular place or region: a *native* New Yorker. 2. Linked to one by birth or by conditions existing at the time and place of one's birth: *native* language. 3. Produced, originated, or grown in a particular region or country; indigenous. 4. Of, pertaining to, or characteristic of any particular area or its inhabitants. 5. Natural rather than acquired; inborn: *native* shrewdness. 6. Of, pertaining to, or characteristic of the original inhabitants, chiefly nonwhites, of areas recently discovered or settled by foreigners: *native* ritual. 7. Occurring in nature in a pure state: *native* copper. —*n.* 1. A permanent or lifelong resident of a country or region. 2. One who was born in a specified country or place. 3. An original inhabitant of a country or region; aborigine. 4. An animal, plant, or mineral found only in a specified country or place. [< F < L < *nasci* to be born.] — **na′tive·ly** *adv.* — **na′tive·ness** *n.* —**Syn.** (adj.) 1, 3. indigenous, endemic.

na·tive-born (nā′tiv-bôrn′) *adj.* Born in the region or country specified.

na·tiv·i·ty (nā·tiv′ə·tē, nə-) *n. pl.* **·ties** 1. Birth, esp. with regard to the time, place, or circumstances surrounding it. 2. In astrology, a horoscope taken at the time of one's birth. [< OF < L *nativitas*]

Na·tiv·i·ty (nā·tiv′ə·tē, nə-) *n. pl.* **·ties** 1. The birth of Christ: with *the.* 2. A representation in a painting, drama, etc., of the birth of Christ. 3. Christmas Day.

NATO (nā′tō) North Atlantic Treaty Organization.

na·tri·um (nā′trē·əm) *n.* Sodium. [< NL < F, ult. < Gk. *nitron* niter]

nat·ty (nat′ē) *adj.* **·ti·er, ·ti·est** Neat and smart, as in dress or appearance: a *natty* vest. [? Akin to NEAT¹] — **nat′ti·ly** *adv.* — **nat′ti·ness** *n.*

nat·u·ral (nach′ər·əl, nach′rəl) *adj.* 1. Produced by or existing in nature; not artificial. 2. Of, pertaining to, or involving nature or the study of nature. 3. Derived from or defined by nature: *natural* day. 4. Belonging to or existing in one's nature; innate: *natural* talent. 5. Being so because of one's inherent ability, disposition, etc.: a *natural* athlete. 6. Conforming to nature or to its usual or expected course: death from *natural* causes. 7. Closely resembling nature; lifelike: a *natural* pose. 8. Untouched by man or by the influences of civilization; wild. 9. Free from affectation or awkwardness: *natural* manner. 10. Derived from or consistent with the nature or essence of a thing; expected: *natural* conclusion. 11. *Music* a Not sharped or flatted. b Denoting a scale or mode that is unaltered by accidentals. 12. Physical or actual, as distinguished from spiritual, etc.: *natural* man. 13. Determined by innate moral conviction: *natural* rights. 14. Related by blood rather than through adoption: *natural* mother. 15. Founded upon reason rather than faith: *natural* religion. 16. Born out of wedlock. —*n.* 1. *Music* a A note that is affected by neither a sharp nor a flat. b A character (♮) that cancels a sharp or flat at a specific line or space on the staff. 2. In keyboard musical instruments, a white key. 3. *U.S. Informal* One who or that which is naturally gifted, esp., well suited to some purpose, or obviously destined for success. [< F < L< *natura* nature, character] — **nat′u·ral·ness** *n.*

natural gas A gas consisting chiefly of methane, generated naturally in underground oil deposits and used as a fuel.

natural history The observation and study of the phenomena of the material universe, esp. the biological and earth sciences.

nat·u·ral·ism (nach′ər·əl·iz′əm, nach′rəl-) *n.* 1. Close adherence to nature or human life in literature, painting, etc. 2. *Philos.* The doctrine that all phenomena are derived from natural causes and can be explained by scientific laws. 3. Action or thought derived exclusively from natural desires and instincts.

nat·u·ral·ist (nach′ər·əl·ist, nach′rəl-) *n.* 1. One who is versed in natural history, as a zoologist or botanist. 2. An adherent of the doctrine of naturalism.

nat·u·ral·is·tic (nach′ər·əl·is′tik, nach′rəl-) *adj.* 1. Of, according to, or characteristic of naturalism. 2. In accordance with or closely resembling nature. **3.** Of or pertaining to naturalists or natural history.

nat·u·ral·ize (nach′ər·əl·īz′, nach′rəl-) *v.* **·ized, ·iz·ing** *v.t.* **1.** To confer the rights and privileges of citizenship upon, as an alien. **2.** To adopt (a foreign word, custom, etc.) into the common use of a country or area. **3.** To adapt (a foreign plant, animal, etc.) to the environment of a country or area. **4.** To explain by natural laws: to *naturalize* a miracle. **5.** To make natural or lifelike. — *v.i.* **6.** To become as if native; adapt. **7.** To observe or study nature. Also *Brit.* **nat′·u·ral·ise′.** — **nat′u·ral·i·za′tion** *n.*

nat·u·ral·ly (nach′ər·əl·ē, nach′rəl-ē) *adv.* **1.** In a natural, normal, or expected manner. **2.** By inherent nature. **3.** Of course; certainly.

natural number *Math.* A positive integer, as 1, 2, 3, etc.

natural philosophy **1.** The study of nature in general. **2.** The physical sciences collectively.

natural resource *Usu. pl.* **1.** A source of wealth provided by nature, as forests, minerals, and water supply. **2.** Any natural ability or talent.

natural science **1.** The sciences collectively that deal with the physical universe. **2.** Any one of these sciences, as biology, chemistry, or physics.

natural selection *Biol.* The process whereby individual variations advantageous to an organism in a certain environment tend to become perpetuated in later generations; survival of the fittest forms.

na·ture (nā′chər) *n.* **1.** The essential character of something: the *nature* of democracy. **2.** *Sometimes cap.* The overall pattern or system of natural objects, existences, forces, events, etc.; also, the principle or power that appears to guide it: laws of *nature.* **3.** The entire material universe and its phenomena. **4.** The basic character or disposition of a person or animal. **5.** *Sometimes cap.* A force, drive, or tendency that influences or determines the behavior or condition of a person or thing; instinct. **6.** Sort; kind; variety: nothing of that *nature.* **7.** A wild, naked, or uncivilized condition. **8.** That which is within the accepted or legal limits of morality: an act against *nature.* **9.** Natural aspect or appearance, as of a person or scene. — **by nature** By birth or disposition. [< OF < L *nasci* to be born]

-natured *combining form* Possessing a (specified) nature, disposition, or temperament: *good-natured.*

naught (nôt) *n.* **1.** Nothing. **2.** A cipher; zero; the character *0.* Also spelled **nought.** [OE < *nā* not + *wiht* thing]

naugh·ty (nô′tē) *adj.* **·ti·er, ·ti·est** **1.** Mischievous; disobedient; bad. **2.** Indecent or improper: a *naughty* word. — **naugh′ti·ly** *adv.* — **naugh′ti·ness** *n.*

nau·se·a (nô′zē·ə, -zhə, -sē·ə, -shə) *n.* **1.** A sick feeling in the stomach accompanied by an impulse to vomit; queasiness. **2.** Strong disgust or loathing. [< L < Gk. *nausia, nautia* seasickness]

nau·se·ate (nô′zē·āt, -sē-, -zhē-, -shē-) *v.t. & v.i.* **·at·ed, ·at·ing** To affect with or feel nausea or disgust.

nau·seous (nô′shəs, -zhē·əs, -zē·əs, -sē·əs) *adj.* **1.** Affected with nausea; queasy; sick. **2.** Nauseating; disgusting. — **nau′seous·ly** *adv.* — **nau′seous·ness** *n.*

nau·ti·cal (nô′ti·kəl) *adj.* Pertaining to or involving ships, seamen, or navigation. — **Syn.** See MARINE. [< L < Gk. < *naus* ship] — **nau′ti·cal·ly** *adv.*

nau·ti·lus (nô′tə·ləs) *n.* *pl.* **·lus·es** or **·li** (-lī) **1.** Any of a group of mollusks with a spiral shell whose chambers are lined with mother-of-pearl; esp., the **chambered** or **pearly nautilus. 2.** The paper nautilus. [< L < Gk. *nautilos sailor*]

Nav·a·ho (nav′ə·hō) *n.* *pl.* **hos** or **·hoes** or **·ho** One of a tribe of North American Indians now living on reservations in Arizona, New Mexico, and Utah. Also **Nav′a·jo.**

CHAMBERED NAUTILUS
(Cross-section; diameter to 10 inches)

na·val (nā′vəl) *adj.* **1.** Of, involving, or having a navy: a *naval* power. **2.** Of or pertaining to ships: a *naval* convoy. — **Syn.** See MARINE. [< L < *navis* ship]

nave[1] (nāv) *n.* *Archit.* The main body of a church, situated between the side aisles. [< L *navis* ship]

nave[2] (nāv) *n.* The hub of a wheel. [OE *nafu*]

na·vel (nā′vəl) *n.* **1.** The depression on the abdomen where the umbilical cord was attached; umbilicus. **2.** A central part or point. [OE < *nafu* nave[2]]

navel orange An orange, usu. seedless, having a navellike depression that contains a small, secondary fruit.

nav·i·cert (nav′ə·sûrt) *n.* *Brit.* A safe-conduct authorizing a vessel of a friendly or neutral nation to pass through a naval blockade.

nav·i·ga·ble (nav′ə·gə·bəl) *adj.* Capable of being navigated; as: **a** Broad or deep enough to admit of passage: said of a body of water. **b** Capable of being steered. — **nav′i·ga·bil′i·ty, nav′i·ga·ble·ness** *n.* — **nav′i·ga·bly** *adv.*

nav·i·gate (nav′ə·gāt) *v.* **·gat·ed, ·gat·ing** *v.t.* **1.** To travel or move across, over, on, or through, as by ship or aircraft. **2.** To plot the course of (a ship, aircraft, etc.). **3.** To manage or direct the course of; guide: to *navigate* a missile. — *v.i.* **4.** To guide or steer a ship, aircraft, etc. **5.** To compute and plot the course, position, etc., as of a ship or aircraft. **6.** To travel by ship. [< L < *navis* boat + *agere* to direct]

nav·i·ga·tion (nav′ə·gā′shən) *n.* **1.** The act or practice of navigating. **2.** The art or science of charting the course of ships, aircraft, etc. — **nav′i·ga′tion·al** *adj.*

navigation light *Aeron.* One of the colored lights on an aircraft, indicating its size, position, and course at night: also called *running light.*

nav·i·ga·tor (nav′ə·gā′tər) *n.* **1.** One who navigates. **2.** One who is trained in or practices navigation. [< L]

nav·vy (nav′ē) *n. pl.* **·vies** *Brit.* A laborer, esp. in construction work on railways, roads, etc. [< NAVIGATOR]

na·vy (nā′vē) *n. pl.* **·vies 1.** *Often cap.* The entire military sea force of a country, including vessels, servicemen, yards, etc.; also, the agency of government charged with its supervision. **2.** The warships of a nation, taken collectively. **3.** Navy blue. [< OF < L *navis* ship]

navy bean A small, dried, white bean related to the common kidney bean. [from its use in the U.S. Navy]

navy blue A very dark blue: also *navy.*

Navy Cross A decoration in the form of a bronze cross, awarded by the U.S. Navy for extraordinary heroism in action against the enemy. See DECORATION.

navy yard A government-owned dockyard for the building, repairing, docking, and equipping of warships.

nay (nā) *adv.* **1.** *Archaic* No. **2.** Not exactly that, but rather: She is a pretty, *nay*, a beautiful woman. — *n.* **1.** A negative vote or voter: opposed to *yea.* **2.** A denial or refusal. [ME < ON < *ne* not + *ei* ever]

Naz·a·rene (naz′ə·rēn) *n.* **1.** A native or inhabitant of Nazareth. **2.** A Christian. **3.** One of a sect of early Christians of Jewish origin who continued to observe much of the Jewish ritual. — **the Nazarene** Jesus Christ. — *adj.* Of Nazareth or the Nazarenes. Also **Naz′a·re′an** (-rē′ən).

Naz·a·rite (naz′ə·rīt) *n.* An ancient Hebrew who took vows of abstinence. *Num.* vi. Also **Naz′i·rite.** [< Hebrew < *nāzar* to abstain]

na·zi (nä′tsē, nat′sē, na′zē) *Often cap. n. pl.* **·zis** One who advocates or practices Nazism. — *adj.* Of the nature of, pertaining to, or involving Nazism. [< NAZI]

Na·zi (nä′tsē, nat′sē, na′zē) *n. pl.* **·zis** A member of the National Socialist German Workers' Party, founded in 1919, whose fascistic program (called **National Socialism**) was dominant in Germany from 1933 to 1945 under the dictatorship of Hitler. — *adj.* **1.** Of or pertaining to the Nazis or their party. **2.** Caused or committed by Nazis: *Nazi* atrocities. [< G, short for *nationalsozialist* National Socialist] — **Na′zism** or **Na′zi·ism** *n.*

Ne·an·der·thal (nē·an′dər·täl, -thôl, -thol; *Ger.* nä·än′dər·täl) *adj.* Of or characteristic of Neanderthal man.

Neanderthal man *Anthropol.* An extinct species of man that typifies the paleolithic cavedwellers preceding modern man. [< G *Neanderthal,* Neander valley, Germany, where the first bones of this species were found]

neap (nēp) *adj.* Designating or pertaining to a neap tide. — *n.* A neap tide. [OE *nēp-* in *nēpflod* low tide]

Ne·a·pol·i·tan (nē′ə·pol′ə·tən) *adj.* Of, relating to, or characteristic of Naples. — *n.* A native or resident of Naples.

neap tide The tide occurring shortly after the first and third quarters of the moon, when the rise and fall are minimal: also called *neap.*

near (nir) *adv.* **1.** At, to, or within a little distance; not remote in place, time, or degree. **2.** Nearly; almost: a team of *near* championship caliber. **3.** In a close relation; intimately. **4.** Stingily or frugally. — *adj.* **1.** Not distant in place, time, or degree. **2.** Closely approximating; almost achieved: a *near* success. **3.** Narrow; close: a *near* escape. **4.** Closely related, as by blood: someone *near* and dear. **5.** Closely touching one's interests or affections; intimate. **6.** That saves distance or time; short; direct. **7.** Stingy; miserly. **8.** On the left: used in riding or driving: the *near* ox: opposed to *off.* — *prep.* Close by or to. — *v.t. & v.i.* To come or draw near (to); approach. [OE *nēar,* compar. of *nēah* nigh] — **near′ness** *n.*

near·by (nir′bī′) *adj. & adv.* Close by; near; adjacent.

Near East The countries lying east of the Mediterranean, mostly in SW Asia, including Turkey, Syria, Lebanon, Israel, Jordan, Saudi Arabia, etc., and sometimes the Balkans and Egypt.

near·ly (nir′lē) *adv.* **1.** Almost; practically. **2.** Closely, as in distance, relation, degree, similarity, etc.

near·sight·ed (nir′sī′tid) *adj.* Able to see distinctly at short distances only; myopic. — **near′sight′ed·ly** *adv.* — **near′sight′ed·ness** *n.*

neat (nēt) *adj.* **1.** Characterized by or in a state of orderliness, tidiness, and cleanliness. **2.** Free from sloppiness, vagueness, or embellishment; precise. **3.** Ingeniously done or said; clever: a *neat* trick. **4.** Free from admixture; undiluted, as liquor. **5.** Remaining after all deductions; net. [< OF < L *nitidus* shining] **—neat′ly** *adv.* **—neat′ness** *n.*

'neath (nēth) *prep. Dial.* or *Poetic* Beneath. Also **neath.**

neat's-foot oil (nēts′foŏt′) A pale yellow oil obtained by boiling the shinbones and feet of cattle, used as a lubricant and softening agent for leather.

Neb·u·chad·nez·zar (neb′yoŏ-kəd-nez′ər), died 562 B.C., king of Babylonia 605–562 B.C.; conquered Jerusalem. II *Kings* xxiv and xxv. Also **Neb′u·chad·rez′zar** (-rez′ər).

neb·u·la (neb′yə-lə) *n. pl.* **·lae** (-lē) or **·las** *Astron.* Any interstellar mass of cloudlike appearance and vast extent, often luminous, and composed of gaseous matter. [< L, vapor, mist] **—neb′u·lar** *adj.*

nebular hypothesis *Astron.* The hypothesis that the solar system was formed from the consolidation of great masses of matter thrown off by a rotating nebula.

neb·u·lose (neb′yə-lōs) *adj.* Nebulous.

neb·u·los·i·ty (neb′yə-los′ə-tē) *n. pl.* **·ties** **1.** The state or quality of being nebulous. **2.** A nebula.

neb·u·lous (neb′yə-ləs) *adj.* **1.** Vague or confused; hazy. **2.** Cloudlike; misty. **3.** Of, pertaining to, or like a nebula. **—neb′u·lous·ly** *adv.* **—neb′u·lous·ness** *n.*

nec·es·sar·i·ly (nes′ə-ser′ə-lē) *adv.* **1.** As a necessary consequence. **2.** Of necessity; unavoidably.

nec·es·sar·y (nes′ə-ser′ē) *adj.* **1.** Absolutely needed to accomplish a certain result; essential. **2.** Being of such a nature that it must exist or occur; inevitable: a *necessary* belief. **3.** Caused by or acting under obligation or compulsion; required. **4.** That cannot be logically denied. **—** *n. pl.* **·sar·ies** Often *pl.* That which is indispensable; an essential requisite: the *necessaries* of life. [< OF < L *necessitas*]

ne·ces·si·tate (nə-ses′ə-tāt) *v.t.* **·tat·ed, ·tat·ing** **1.** To make necessary. **2.** To compel or oblige: No man is *necessitated* to lie. **—ne·ces′si·ta′tion** *n.* **—ne·ces′si·ta′tive** *adj.*

ne·ces·si·tous (nə-ses′ə-təs) *adj.* **1.** Extremely needy; destitute; poverty-stricken. **2.** Urgent; compelling. **—ne·ces′si·tous·ly** *adv.* **—ne·ces′si·tous·ness** *n.*

ne·ces·si·ty (nə-ses′ə-tē) *n. pl.* **·ties** **1.** Often *pl.* That which is indispensable or requisite, esp. toward the attainment of some end. **2.** The quality, condition, or fact of being necessary. **3.** The conditions that make compulsory a particular course of action: to resign out of *necessity.* **4.** Urgent or desperate need, as because of poverty or accident; also, a time of such need. **5.** That which is unavoidable because it is part of an invariable process, as in nature, logic, etc.; also, the process itself. **—of necessity** By necessity; inevitably. [< OF < L *necessitas*]

neck (nek) *n.* **1.** *Anat.* **a** The part of an animal that connects the head with the trunk. **b** Any similarly constricted part of an organ, bone, etc.: the *neck* of the uterus. ◆ Collateral adjective. *cervical.* **2.** The narrowed part of an object, esp. if near one end: the *neck* of a bottle. **3.** Something likened to a neck; as: **a** A narrow passage of water between two larger bodies of water. **b** A narrow strip of land, as a peninsula, isthmus, or cape. **4.** The part of a garment close to or covering the neck. **5.** The part of a violin, guitar, etc., that carries the fingerboard and tuning pegs. **6.** *Archit.* The upper part of the shaft of a column, just below the capital. **—neck and neck** Abreast of one another, as horses in a race. **—neck of the woods** *U.S. Informal* A neighborhood or region. **—to save one's (own) neck** To extricate oneself from difficult or dangerous circumstances, often without concern for others. **—** *v.i.* **1.** *U.S. Slang* To kiss and caress in lovemaking. **—** *v.t.* **2.** *U.S. Slang* To make love to (someone) in such a manner. [OE *hnecca*]

neck·band (nek′band′) *n.* **1.** The part of a garment that fits around the neck. **2.** A band around the neck.

necked (nekt) *adj.* **1.** Having a neck or necks. **2.** Having or characterized by (a specified kind of) neck or (a specified number of) necks: used in combination: *long-necked.*

neck·er·chief (nek′ər-chif) *n.* A kerchief for the neck.

neck·ing (nek′ing) *n. U.S. Slang* Kissing and caressing in lovemaking.

neck·lace (nek′lis) *n.* An ornament worn around the neck and usu. consisting of a string of beads, shells gems, etc.

neck·line (nek′līn′) *n.* The line or contour formed by the fit of a garment around the neck.

neck·piece (nek′pēs′) *n.* An article of clothing, usu. of fur, worn around the neck like a scarf.

neck·tie (nek′tī′) *n.* **1.** A strip of material worn knotted around the neck or collar and hanging down the front of a shirt. **2.** Any bow or tie worn under the chin.

neck·wear (nek′wâr′) *n.* Articles worn around the neck, as ties, collars, mufflers, etc.

necro- *combining form* Corpse; the dead; death. Also, before vowels, **necr-.** [< Gk. *nekros* corpse]

ne·crol·o·gy (ne-krol′ə-jē) *n. pl.* **·gies** **1.** A list of persons who have died in a certain place or time. **2.** An obituary notice. **—nec·ro·log·ic** (nek′rə-loj′ik) or **·i·cal** *adj.* **—nec′·ro·log′i·cal·ly** *adv.* **—ne·crol′o·gist** *n.*

nec·ro·man·cy (nek′rə-man′sē) *n.* **1.** The art of divining the future through alleged communication with the dead. **2.** Black magic; sorcery. [ME < OF < L < Gk. *<nekros* corpse + *manteia* divination] **—nec′ro·man′cer** *n.* **—nec′ro·man′tic** *adj.*

nec·ro·phil·i·a (nek′rō-fil′ē-ə) *n.* An abnormal attraction, esp. of an erotic nature, to corpses. **—nec·ro·phile** (nek′rə-fīl, -fil) *n.* **—nec′ro·phil′ic** *adj.*

ne·crop·o·lis (ne-krop′ə-lis) *n.* A cemetery. [< Gk. < *nekros* corpse + *polis* city]

ne·cro·sis (ne-krō′sis) *n.* **1.** *Pathol.* The death of tissue in a living animal, resulting from infection or burns; gangrene. **2.** *Bot.* A decay and death of plant tissue. [< Gk. *nekrōsis* death] **—ne·crot′ic** (-krot′ik) *adj.*

nec·tar (nek′tər) *n.* **1.** In Greek mythology, the drink of the gods. **2.** Any delicious drink. **3.** *Bot.* The saccharine secretion of plants, collected by bees to make honey. [< L < Gk. *nektar*] **—nec·tar·e·an** (nek-târ′ē-ən), **nec·tar·e·ous** (nek-târ′ē-əs), **nec·tar·ous** (nek′tər-əs) *adj.*

nec·tar·ine (nek′tə-rēn′, nek′tə-rēn) *n.* A variety of peach having a smooth, waxy skin and a firm pulp.

nec·ta·ry (nek′tər-ē) *n. pl.* **·ries** *Bot.* A gland that secretes nectar.

née (nā) *adj.* Born with the name of: used chiefly to note the maiden name of a married woman: Mrs. Mary Lincoln, *née* Todd. Also **nee.** [< F, pp. fem. of *naître* to be born]

need (nēd) *v.t.* **1.** To have an urgent or essential use for (something lacking); want; require. **—** *v.i.* **2.** To be in want. **3.** To be obliged or compelled; have to: He *need* not go. **—** *n.* **1.** The fact, quality, or condition of lacking or feeling the lack of something necessary or desirable. **2.** A desire or longing: the *need* for revenge. **3.** Obligation; necessity: no *need* to be afraid. **4.** A condition of want, danger, or helplessness. **5.** Something wanted or required: modest *needs.* **6.** Poverty; hardship. **— Syn.** See POVERTY. [OE *nīed, nēd*] **—need′er** *n.*

need·ful (nēd′fəl) *adj.* **1.** Needed; requisite; necessary. **2.** *Archaic* Needy. **—need′ful·ly** *adv.* **—need′ful·ness** *n.*

need·i·ness (nē′dē-nis, -di·nis) *n.* The state of being needy; poverty; want.

nee·dle (nēd′l) *n.* **1.** A small, slender, pointed instrument, usu. of steel, with an eye at one end to carry thread through fabric in sewing. **2.** A hypodermic needle. **3.** A pointer or index, as in a gauge or compass. **4.** A small, pointed instrument of steel, diamond, etc., that traverses the grooves of a phonograph record and transmits sound vibrations: sometimes called *stylus.* **5.** A slender, pointed rod of steel, bone, etc., used in knitting; also, a similar, hooked rod used in crocheting. **6.** A needleshaped leaf, as that of a pine tree. **7.** Any object suggesting a needle in shape. **8.** A fine-pointed instrument used in etching. **9.** *Mech.* A needle valve (which see). **—on the needle** *U.S. Slang* Addicted to narcotics. **—** *v.* **·dled, ·dling** *v.t.* **1.** To sew or pierce with a needle. **2.** *Informal* To tease or heckle repeatedly. **3.** *U.S. Informal* To increase the alcoholic content of: to *needle* the beer. **—** *v.i.* **4.** To sew or work with a needle. **5.** To crystallize in the form of needles. [OE *nǣdle*]

nee·dle·point (nēd′l·point′) *n.* **1.** Embroidery on canvas, as in a tapestry; also, a single stitch. **2.** Lace made with a sewing needle on a paper pattern: also called *point lace.*

need·less (nēd′lis) *adj.* Not needed or necessary; useless. **—need′less·ly** *adv.* **—need′less·ness** *n.*

needle valve *Mech.* A valve having a needlelike plug capable of closely regulating the flow of a liquid or gas.

nee·dle·wom·an (nēd′l·woŏm′ən) *n. pl.* **·wom·en** (-wim′in) A seamstress.

nee·dle·work (nēd′l·wûrk′) *n.* Work done with a needle.

need·n't (nēd′nt) Need not.

needs (nēdz) *adv. Archaic* Of necessity: often with *must*: He *needs* must go. [OE *nīedes*]

need·y (nē′dē) *adj.* **need·i·er, need·i·est** Being in need, want, or poverty; necessitous.

ne'er (nâr) *adv. Poetic* Never.

ne'er-do-well (nâr′doō-wel′) *n.* A worthless, unreliable person. **—** *adj.* Shiftless; good-for-nothing.

ne·far·i·ous (ni-fâr′ē-əs) *adj.* Extremely wicked; vile. [< L < *ne-* not + *fas* divine law] **—ne·far′i·ous·ly** *adv.* **—ne·far′i·ous·ness** *n.*

ne·gate (ni-gāt′, nē′gāt) *v.t.* **·gat·ed, ·gat·ing** **1.** To render ineffective or void; nullify. **2.** To deny; contradict; rule out. [< L *negatus*, pp. of *negare* to deny]

ne·ga·tion (ni-gā′shən) *n.* **1.** The absence or opposite of something: Sleep is the *negation* of consciousness. **2.** The act of denying or contradicting. **3.** That which is negative.

neg·a·tive (neg′ə·tiv) *adj.* **1.** Expressing, containing, or characterized by negation, denial, or refusal. **2.** Marked by the absence of positive or affirmative qualities: a *negative* attitude. **3.** *Math.* Less than zero; to be subtracted; minus. **4.** *Electr.* Having the kind of electricity exhibited by a resinous object when rubbed with wool. **5.** *Med.* Not indicating the presence of a particular disease, organism, etc.: a *negative* blood test. **6.** *Photog.* Having the lights and darks reversed. — *n.* **1.** *Photog.* An image showing the lights and darks reversed; also, the film or plate on which it appears. **2.** An expression of denial or refusal. **3.** The side of a question that denies or contradicts what the other side affirms, as in a debate. **4.** *Math.* A negative symbol or quantity. **5.** *Electr.* A negative pole, plate, terminal, etc. **6.** *Gram.* A negative particle, as *not*. — *adv.* No; not so: a military usage. — **double negative** *Gram.* The use of two negatives in the same statement, as in "I didn't see nobody." ◆ This usage is now considered nonstandard. Such statements as "I am not unhappy," however, are standard English and have the effect of weak affirmatives. — **in the negative 1.** By or with an expression of refusal; no. **2.** On the negative or opposing side. — *v.t.* **·tived**, **·tiv·ing 1.** reject; veto. **2.** To deny; contradict. **3.** To prove to be false. **4.** To make ineffective. [< F < L *negare* to deny] — **neg′a·tive·ly** *adv.* — **neg′a·tive·ness**, **neg′a·tiv′i·ty** *n.*

neg·a·tiv·ism (neg′ə·tiv·iz′əm) *n.* **1.** An attitude characterized by the questioning of traditional beliefs; skepticism. **2.** A tendency to deny, contradict, etc. **3.** *Psychol.* An attitude characterized by resistance to suggestion. — **neg′a·tiv·ist** *n. & adj.* — **neg′a·tiv·is′tic** *adj.*

neg·lect (ni·glekt′) *v.t.* **1.** To fail to heed or take note of; disregard. **2.** To fail to give proper attention to: to *neglect* one's business. **3.** To fail to do or perform; leave undone. — *n.* **1.** Habitual want of attention or care; negligence. **2.** The act of neglecting, or the state of being neglected. **3.** An instance of neglect. [< L < *nec-* not + *legere* to gather] — **neg·lect′er** or **neg·lec′tor** *n.*

neg·lect·ful (ni·glekt′fəl) *adj.* Exhibiting or indicating neglect. — **neg·lect′ful·ly** *adv.* — **neg·lect′ful·ness** *n.*

neg·li·gee (neg′li·zhā′, neg′li·zhā) *n.* **1.** A loose, flowing, usu. decorative dressing gown worn by women. **2.** Any informal attire. Also **neg′li·gée′**, *French* **né·gli·gé** (nā·glē·zhā′). [< F *négligé*, pp. of *négliger* to neglect]

neg·li·gence (neg′lə·jəns) *n.* **1.** The state, quality, or fact of being negligent. **2.** A negligent act or omission. [< OF]

neg·li·gent (neg′lə·jənt) *adj.* **1.** Habitually neglecting to do what ought to be done; neglectful. **2.** Free-and-easy; informal; nonchalant. — **neg′li·gent·ly** *adv.*

neg·li·gi·ble (neg′lə·jə·bəl) *adj.* Not worth considering, as because of trifling size, amount, or extent. — **neg′li·gi·bil′i·ty**, **neg′li·gi·ble·ness** *n.* — **neg′li·gi·bly** *adv.*

ne·go·ti·a·ble (ni·gō′shē·ə·bəl, -shə·bəl) *adj.* **1.** Capable of being negotiated. **2.** Open to negotiation. **3.** That can be legally transferred to another party. — **ne·go′ti·a·bil′i·ty** *n.*

ne·go·ti·ate (ni·gō′shē·āt) *v.* **·at·ed**, **·at·ing** *v.i.* **1.** To confer with another party with the aim of reaching an agreement. — *v.t.* **2.** To arrange or conclude by negotiation. **3.** To transfer (a note, bond, etc.) to another for a value received; sell. **4.** To manage to execute, traverse, or cope with (something difficult): to *negotiate* a steep hill. [< L *negotiari* to do business] — **ne·go′ti·a′tor** *n.*

ne·go·ti·a·tion (ni·gō′shē·ā′shən) *n.* **1.** The act or process of negotiating. **2.** A conference or discussion designed to produce an agreement.

Ne·gri·to (ni·grē′tō) *n. pl.* **·tos** or **·toes** *Anthropol.* One of the Pygmy peoples of the Malay Peninsula, the Philippine Islands, central Africa, and southeast Asia. [< Sp., dim. of *negro* black]

ne·gri·tude (nē′grə·tood′, -tyood′) *n.* *Often cap.* **1.** Awareness of and pride in one's black African heritage. **2.** The fact of being a Negro; Negroness. Also *French* **né·gri·tude** (nā′grə·tüd′). [< F < L *niger* black]

Ne·gro (nē′grō) *n. pl.* **·groes 1.** A member of the Negroid ethnic division of mankind. **2.** One who is of Negroid stock or has Negro ancestors. — *adj.* **1.** Of, pertaining to, or having the characteristics of a Negro or Negroes. **2.** Of Negroid ethnic stock. Also **ne′gro**. [< Sp. < L *niger* black]

Ne·groid (nē′groid) *adj.* **1.** *Anthropol.* Of, pertaining to, or belonging to a major ethnic division of the human species characterized by skin color ranging from dark brown to almost black. **2.** Resembling, related to, or characteristic of Negroes. — *n.* A Negroid person.

Ne·gro·ness (nē′grō·nis) *n.* The fact of being a Negro.

Ne·he·mi·ah (nē′hə·mī′ə) Fifth-century B.C. Hebrew statesman and historian. — *n.* A book of the Old Testament: also, in the Douai Bible, II *Esdras*. [< Hebrew *Nehemyāh* Jehovah comforts]

neigh (nā) *v.i.* To utter the cry of a horse; whinny. — *n.* The cry of a horse. [OE *hnǣgan*; imit.]

neigh·bor (nā′bər) *n.* **1.** One who lives near another. **2.** One who or that which is near another. **3.** *Chiefly Dial.*

Friend; mister: a term of address. — *adj.* Living nearby. — *v.t. & v.i.* To live or be near to or next to; adjoin. Also *Brit.* **neigh′bour**. [OE < *nēah* near + *gebur* dweller]

neigh·bor·hood (nā′bər·hood) *n.* **1.** A comparatively small region possessing some specific quality or character. **2.** The people who live in such a region. **3.** Any region or area; vicinity. Also *Brit.* **neigh′bour·hood**. — **in the neighborhood of 1.** Near. **2.** *Informal* Approximately.

neigh·bor·ing (nā′bər·ing) *adj.* Situated or living nearby.

neigh·bor·ly (nā′bər·lē) *adj.* Like a good neighbor; kind, sociable, etc. — **neigh′bor·li·ness** *n.*

nei·ther (nē′thər, nī′-) *adj.* Not the one nor the other; not either. — *pron.* Not the one nor the other: *Neither* of the hats is becoming. — *conj.* **1.** Not either; not: used with the correlative *nor* to list alternatives and to signify their negation: He *neither* reads nor writes. **2.** Nor yet: He cannot write: *neither* can he read. ◆ See usage note under EITHER. [ME *naither*, *neyther* < OE *nāhwaether*]

nemato- *combining form* Thread; filament: also, before vowels, **nemat-**. Also **nema-**. [< Gk. *nēma*, *-matos* thread]

nem·a·tode (nem′ə·tōd) *Zool. adj.* Of or belonging to a phylum or class of roundworms, as the hookworm. — *n.* A nematode worm. [< NL *Nematoda*]

nem·e·sis (nem′ə·sis) *n. pl.* **·ses** (-sēz) **1.** An unusually tenacious opponent or antagonist. **2.** An instrument of vengeance. [< Gk., retributive justice]

Nem·e·sis (nem′ə·sis) In Greek mythology, the goddess of retributive justice or vengeance. [< NEMESIS]

neo- *combining form* New; recent; a modern or modified form of. Also, before vowels, usu. **ne-**. [< Gk. < *neos* new]

ne·o·clas·sic (nē′ō·klas′ik) *adj.* Of, pertaining to, or denoting a revival of classical style in literature, art, music, etc. Also **ne′o·clas′si·cal**. — **ne′o·clas′si·cism** *n.* — **ne′o·clas′si·cist** *n.*

ne·o·dym·i·um (nē′ō·dim′ē·əm) *n.* A metallic element (symbol Nd) forming rose-colored salts, found in combination with cerium, etc. See ELEMENT. [< NEO- + (DI)DYMIUM]

Ne·o·lith·ic (nē′ə·lith′ik) *adj.* *Anthropol.* Of or pertaining to the period of human culture following the Mesolithic, characterized by polished stone implements and a settled agriculture. [< Gk. *neos* new + *lithos* stone]

ne·ol·o·gism (nē·ol′ə·jiz′əm) *n.* **1.** A new word or phrase. **2.** The use of new words or of new meanings for old words. Also **ne·ol′o·gy**. [< F *néologisme*] — **ne·ol′o·gist** *n.* — **ne·ol′o·gis′tic** or **·ti·cal** *adj.*

ne·o·my·cin (nē′ə·mī′sin) *n.* An antibiotic related to streptomycin, used in the treatment of certain infections.

ne·on (nē′on) *n.* A gaseous element (symbol Ne) occurring in the atmosphere in very small amounts. See ELEMENT. — *adj.* **1.** Of or pertaining to neon. **2.** Composed of or employing neon. [< NL < Gk., neut. of *neos* new]

ne·o·phyte (nē′ə·fīt) *n.* **1.** A recent convert, esp. in the early Christian Church. **2.** Any beginner. [< LL < Gk. *neophytos* newly planted] — **ne′o·phyt′ic** (-fit′ik) *adj.*

ne·o·plasm (nē′ə·plaz′əm) *n.* *Pathol.* Any abnormal growth of tissue in the body; a tumor. — **ne′o·plas′tic** *adj.*

ne·o·prene (nē′ə·prēn) *n.* *Chem.* Any of various types of synthetic rubber. [< NEO- + (CHLORO)PRENE]

Nep·a·lese (nep′ə·lēz′, -lēs′) *adj.* Of Nepal, its people, or their culture. — *n.* A native or inhabitant of Nepal.

ne·pen·the (ni·pen′thē) *n.* **1.** A drug or potion supposed by the ancient Greeks to banish pain and sorrow. **2.** Anything causing oblivion. [< L < Gk. < *nē-* not + *penthos* sorrow]

neph·ew (nef′yoo, *esp. Brit.* nev′yoo) *n.* The son of a brother or brother-in-law or of a sister or sister-in-law. [< OF < L *nepos* grandson, nephew.]

nepho- *combining form* Cloud. Also, before vowels, **neph-**. [< Gk. *nephos* cloud]

neph·rite (nef′rīt) *n.* A very hard, compact, white to dark-green mineral formerly worn as a remedy for diseases of the kidney. [< G *nephrit* < Gk. *nephros* kidney]

ne·phrit·ic (ni·frit′ik) *adj.* **1.** Of or pertaining to the kidney or kidneys; renal: also **neph′ric**. **2.** Of, pertaining to, or suffering from nephritis. Also **ne·phrit′i·cal**. — *n.* Any medicine applicable to disease of the kidney.

ne·phri·tis (ni·frī′tis) *n.* *Pathol.* Inflammation of the kidneys. [< LL < Gk. *nephros* kidney]

nephro- *combining form* A kidney. Also, before vowels, **nephr-**. [< Gk. *nephros* kidney]

ne·phro·sis (ni·frō′sis) *n.* *Pathol.* Disease of the kidney.

ne plus ul·tra (nē plus ul′trə) *Latin* The extreme or utmost point; perfection; literally, nothing more beyond.

nep·o·tism (nep′ə·tiz′əm) *n.* Favoritism; esp. governmental patronage to relatives. [< F < L *nepos*, *-potis* grandson, nephew] — **ne·pot·ic** (ni·pot′ik) *adj.* — **nep′o·tist** *n.*

Nep·tune (nep′toon, -tyoon) In Roman mythology, the god of the sea: identified with the Greek *Poseidon*. — *n.* The fourth largest planet and eighth in order from the sun. See PLANET. [< L *Neptunus*] — **Nep·tu′ni·an** *adj.*

nep·tu·ni·um (nep·too′nē·əm, -tyoo′-) *n.* A radioactive element (symbol Np), artificially produced from a uranium isotope by neutron bombardment and decaying to plutonium by emission of a beta particle. See ELEMENT.

Ne·re·id (nir′ē·id) *pl.* **Ne·re·i·des** (ni·rē′ə·dēz) or **Ne·re·ids** In Greek mythology, one of the fifty daughters of Nereus.

Ne·reus (nir′ōōs, -ē·əs) In Greek mythology, a sea god, father of the Nereides.

nerve (nûrv) *n.* **1.** *Physiol.* Any of the cordlike bundles of fibers that convey impulses of sensation, etc., between the brain or spinal cord and other parts or organs. **2.** Courage or boldness; daring. **3.** *Informal* Arrogant assurance; brashness. **4.** *Usu. pl.* Unsteadiness of mind and muscle; nervousness: a case of *nerves.* **5.** Muscle; sinew: now only in the phrase **to strain every nerve.** — **to get on one's nerves** *Informal* To irritate; exasperate; upset. — *v.t.* **nerved, nerv·ing** To provide with nerve or nerves. — **to nerve oneself** To summon up one's courage. [< L *nervus* sinew]

nerve cell *Physiol.* A neuron.

nerve center **1.** *Physiol.* An aggregation of neurons having a specific function, as hearing, sight, etc. **2.** The focus of command and communication; headquarters.

nerve impulse *Physiol.* A wave of electrical disturbance along a nerve fiber and continuing until it has been discharged into the appropriate sensory or motor channels.

nerve·less (nûrv′lis) *adj.* **1.** Lacking force; feeble. **2.** Completely controlled and calm in crises; cool. **3.** *Anat.* Having no nerves. — **nerve′less·ly** *adv.* — **nerve′less·ness** *n.*

nerve-rack·ing (nûrv′rak′ing) *adj.* Extremely irritating; harrowing. Also **nerve′-wrack′ing.**

ner·vous (nûr′vəs) *adj.* **1.** Characterized by or exhibiting restlessness, anxiety, tension, etc.; high-strung; excitable. **2.** Neural. **3.** Caused by or acting on the nerves or nervous system. — **ner′vous·ly** *adv.* — **ner·vos′i·ty** (-vos′ə·tē), **ner′vous·ness** *n.* — **Syn. 1.** uneasy, fidgety, jittery, skittish.

nervous breakdown Popularly, any severe mental or emotional disturbance, usu. requiring hospitalization.

nervous system *Physiol.* A system in animals that coordinates, controls, and regulates various organic activities by means of the reception and transmission of stimuli.

ner·vure (nûr′vyŏŏr) *n.* *Biol.* A vein, as on a leaf or an insect's wing. Also **ner′vule** (-vyŏōl). [< F < L *nervus* sinew] — **ner·vu·ra·tion** (nûr′vyə·rā′shən) *n.*

nerv·y (nûr′vē) *adj.* **nerv·i·er, nerv·i·est** **1.** *U.S. Informal* Brazen; impudent; brash. **2.** *Brit. Informal* Nervous; jumpy. **3.** Having or requiring courage.

nes·cience (nesh′əns, -ē·əns) *n.* Lack or absence of knowledge; ignorance. [< L < *ne-* not + < *scire* to know] — **nes′cient** *adj. & n.* — **nes′cient·ist** *n.*

-ness *suffix of nouns* **1.** State or quality of being: *darkness.* **2.** An example of this state or quality: to do someone a *kindness.* [OE *-nes(s), -nis(s)*]

nest (nest) *n.* **1.** The habitation prepared or the place selected by a bird for the hatching of its eggs and the rearing of its young. **2.** A place used by fishes, insects, turtles, etc., for laying eggs. **3.** The group of animals, birds, etc., occupying such a place. **4.** A cozy or snug place. **5.** A haunt or den; also, those occupying such a place: a *nest* of thieves. **6.** A series or set of similar things designed to fit into one another, as bowls, boxes, etc. — *v.t.* **1.** To place in or as in a nest. **2.** To pack or place one inside another. — *v.i.* **3.** To build or occupy a nest. **4.** To hunt for nests. [OE]

n'est-ce pas (nes pä′) *French* Isn't that so?

nest egg **1.** A sum of money set aside for emergencies, etc. **2.** An artificial egg put in a nest to induce a hen to lay eggs.

nes·tle (nes′əl) *v.* **tled, ·tling** *v.i.* **1.** To lie or press closely and snugly; cuddle; snuggle. **2.** To lie or be embedded, or half-hidden. — *v.t.* **3.** To place or press snugly or lovingly. **4.** To place, or shelter in or as in a nest. [OE *nestlian* to nest] — **nes′tler** *n.*

nest·ling (nest′ling, nes′-) *n.* **1.** A bird too young to leave the nest. **2.** A young child. — *adj.* Recently hatched.

Nes·tor (nes′tər) In Greek legend, the oldest and wisest Greek chief in the Trojan War. — *n.* Any wise old man.

net¹ (net) *n.* **1.** A fabric of thread, cord, rope, etc., woven or knotted to form an open pattern or meshwork and used to catch fish, birds, etc. ♦ Collateral adjective: *reticular.* **2.** Anything that traps or entangles; a snare. **3.** A piece of fine lace. **4.** Any of various devices constructed with meshes: cargo *net;* tennis *net.* **5.** Something resembling a net. — *v.t.* **net·ted, net·ting** **1.** To catch in or as in a net; ensnare. **2.** To make into a net. **3.** To cover, enclose, or shelter with a net. **4.** In tennis, etc., to hit (the ball) into the net. [OE]

net² (net) *adj.* **1.** Obtained after deducting all expenses, losses, taxes, etc.: distinguished from *gross*: *net* proceeds. **2.** Free from anything extraneous; fundamental; basic: *net* results. — *n.* A net profit, amount, weight, etc. — *v.t.* **net·ted, net·ting** To earn or yield as clear profit. [< F]

neth·er (neth′ər) *adj.* Situated beneath or below. [OE *nither* < Gmc.]

neth·er·most (neth′ər·mōst′) *adj.* Lowest.

nether world **1.** The world of the dead. **2.** The world of punishment after death; hell.

net·ting (net′ing) *n.* **1.** A net; network. **2.** The act or operation of making net. **3.** The right of using fishing nets.

net·tle (net′l) *n.* **1.** An herb having minute stinging hairs. **2.** Any of various plants having some real or fancied resemblance to this herb. — *v.t.* **·tled, ·tling** **1.** To annoy or irritate; provoke. **2.** To sting like nettle. [OE *netle* < Gmc.]

nettle rash Urticaria. Also **nettle fever.**

net ton A short ton. See under TON¹.

net·work (net′wûrk′) *n.* **1.** A system of interlacing lines, tracks, or channels. **2.** An openwork fabric; netting. **3.** *Telecom.* A chain of broadcasting stations. **4.** Any interconnected system: an espionage *network.*

Neuf·châ·tel (nœ′shə·tel′, *Fr.* nœ·shà·tel′) *n.* A soft, white cheese produced in Neufchâtel, a town in northern France.

neu·ral (nŏŏr′əl, nyŏŏr′-) *adj.* Of or pertaining to the nerves or nervous system. [< Gk. *neuron* cord, sinew]

neu·ral·gi·a (nŏŏ·ral′jē·ə, -jə, nyŏŏ-) *n.* *Pathol.* Acute pain along the course of a nerve. — **neu·ral′gic** *adj.*

neu·ras·the·ni·a (nŏŏr′əs·thē′nē·ə, -then′yə, nyŏŏr′-) *n.* A condition marked by general debility, depression, and bodily disturbances, formerly believed to be due to weakness or exhaustion of the nervous system. [< NL < Gk. *neuron* cord, sinew + *astheneia* weakness] — **neu·ras·then′ic** (-then′ik) *adj. & n.*

neu·ri·tis (nŏŏ·rī′tis, nyŏŏ-) *n.* *Pathol.* Inflammation of a nerve. — **neu·rit′ic** (-rit′ik) *adj.*

neuro- *combining form* Nerve. Also **neur-** (before vowels), **neuri-.** [< Gk. *neuron* sinew]

neu·rol·o·gy (nŏŏ·rol′ə·jē, nyŏŏ-) *n.* The branch of medicine that deals with the nervous system and its disorders. [< NL *neurologia*] — **neu·ro·log·i·cal** (nŏŏr′ə·loj′i·kəl, nyŏŏr′-) *adj.* — **neu·rol′o·gist** *n.*

neu·ron (nŏŏr′on, nyŏŏr′-) *n.* *Physiol.* The fundamental cellular unit of the nervous system, consisting of a nucleus with all its processes and extensions: also called *nerve cell.* Also **neu′rone** (-ōn). [< NL < Gk. *neuron* sinew] — **neu·ron·ic** (nŏŏ·ron′ik, nyŏŏ-) *adj.*

neu·rop·ter·an (nŏŏ·rop′tər·ən, nyŏŏ-) *n.* A neuropterous insect. Also **neu·rop′ter, neu·rop′ter·on** (-on). — *adj.* Neuropterous. Also **neu·rop′ter·oid.**

neu·rop·ter·ous (nŏŏ·rop′tər·əs, nyŏŏ-) *adj.* Of or pertaining to an order of insects having two pairs of membranous net-veined wings and chewing mouth parts. Also **neu·rop′ter·al.** [< NL *Neuroptera*]

neu·ro·sis (nŏŏ·rō′sis, nyŏŏ-) *n.* *pl.* **·ses** (-sēz) *Psychiatry* Any of various emotional disturbances, less severe than the psychoses, and usu. involving anxiety, depression, and unresolved psychic conflicts: also called *psychoneurosis.* [< NL]

neu·rot·ic (nŏŏ·rot′ik, nyŏŏ-) *adj.* **1.** Pertaining to or suffering from neurosis. **2.** Neural. — *n.* A neurotic person.

neu·ter (nŏŏ′tər, nyŏŏ′-) *adj.* **1.** *Gram.* Neither masculine nor feminine in gender. **2.** *Biol.* Having nonfunctioning or imperfectly developed sex organs, as a worker bee. — *n.* **1.** *Biol.* A neuter plant or animal. **2.** A castrated animal. **3.** *Gram.* **a** The neuter gender. **b** A word in this gender. [ult. < L < *ne-* not + *uter* either]

neu·tral (nŏŏ′trəl, nyŏŏ′-) *adj.* **1.** Not taking the part of either side in a dispute or war. **2.** Of or belonging to neither side in a dispute, war, etc.: *neutral* territory. **3.** Neither one thing nor the other; indefinite; middling. **4.** Having no decided hue or color; grayish. **5.** *Biol.* Neuter; esp., without stamens or pistils. **6.** *Chem.* Neither acid nor alkaline: a *neutral* solution. **7.** *Electr.* Neither positive nor negative. **8.** *Phonet.* Produced with the tongue in a relaxed, midcentral position, as the *a* in *about.* — *n.* **1.** One who or that which is neutral. **2.** *Mech.* The state in which transmission gears are disengaged: a car in *neutral.* [< L < *neuter* neither] — **neu′tral·ly** *adv.*

neu·tral·ism (nŏŏ′trəl·iz′əm, nyŏŏ′-) *n.* In foreign affairs, the policy of not associating or aligning a nation with any side of a power conflict. — **neu′tral·ist** *adj. & n.*

neu·tral·i·ty (nŏŏ·tral′ə·tē, nyŏŏ-) *n.* *pl.* **·ties** Neutral condition, status, attitude, policy, etc., as of a nation during a war. [< F < Med.L *neutralitas*]

neu·tral·ize (nŏŏ′trəl·īz, nyŏŏ′-) *v.t.* **·ized, ·iz·ing** **1.** To counteract or destroy the force, influence, effect, etc., of. **2.** To declare (a nation, area, etc.) neutral during a war. **3.** *Chem.* To make neutral or inert. **4.** *Electr.* To render electrically neutral by combining equal negative and positive units. [< F *neutraliser*] — **neu′tral·i·za′tion** (-ə·zā′shən, -ī·zā′-) *n.* — **neu′tral·iz′er** *n.*

neu·tri·no (nŏŏ·trē′nō, nyŏŏ-) *n.* *pl.* **·nos** *Physics* An atomic particle associated with the radioactive emission of beta rays, carrying no electric charge and having a mass approaching zero. [< Ital., little neutron]

neu·tron (nōō′tron, nyōō′-) *n. Physics* An electrically neutral particle of the atomic nucleus having a mass approximately equal to that of the proton.

neutron star *Astron.* A hypothetical star of great density that is a source of strong X-rays and believed to be a collapsed large star.

nev·er (nev′ər) *adv.* **1.** Not at any time; not ever: also used in combination to form adjectives: *never-ending.* **2.** Not at all; positively not: *Never* fear. [OE *nǣfre*]

nev·er·more (nev′ər·môr′, -mōr′) *adv.* Never again.

nev·er·the·less (nev′ər·thə·les′) *adv.* Nonetheless; however; yet. — Syn. See BUT[1].

ne·vus (nē′vəs) *n. pl.* **·vi** (-vī) A birthmark or congenital mole. [< L *naevus* blemish] — **ne′void** *adj.*

new (nōō, nyōō) *adj.* **new·er, new·est** **1.** Having recently been made, used, developed, etc. **2.** Having never existed, occurred, etc., before. **3.** Recently discovered, observed, etc.: a *new* river. **4.** Different from that which is older or previous: a *new* dispensation. **5.** Unfamiliar; strange. **6.** Not accustomed or experienced: *new* at the job. **7.** Having recently come into a certain place, condition, relationship, etc.: a *new* member. **8.** Built, made, etc., in place of something older: a *new* post office. **9.** Fresh; unspoiled. **10.** Repeated; renewed: a *new* plea. **11.** Additional; increased: a *new* supply. **12.** Rejuvenated; refreshed: a *new* man. **13.** Modern; current; fashionable. **14.** *Usu. cap.* Designating the most recent form or period: said of languages. — *adv.* Newly; freshly; recently. — *n.* That which is new. [OE *nīwe* < Gmc.] — **new′ish** *adj.* — **new′ness** *n.*

new·born (nōō′bôrn′, nyōō′-) *adj.* **1.** Just lately born. **2.** Reborn. — *n.* A newborn infant or animal.

New·burg (nōō′bûrg, nyōō′-) See À LA NEWBURG.

new·com·er (nōō′kum′ər, nyōō′-) *n.* One who has recently arrived.

New Deal The political, economic, and social policies of the administration under Franklin D. Roosevelt.

new·el (nōō′əl, nyōō′-) *n. Archit.* **1.** The post that terminates the handrail of a staircase. **2.** The central pillar or upright of a spiral staircase. Also **newel post.** [< OF < LL < L *nux* nut]

New England The NE section of the United States, including Maine, New Hampshire, Vermont, Massachusetts, Rhode Island, and Connecticut. — **New Englander**

new·fan·gled (nōō′fang′gəld, nyōō′-) *adj.* Lately come into fashion; novel: a derogatory term. [ME < *newe* new + *fangel* contrivance, prob. < *fōn* to seize, grasp]

New·found·land (nōō′fənd·lənd, nyōō′-) *n.* A large dog of a breed originating in Newfoundland, having a broad head, square muzzle, and thick, abundant, usu. black coat.

New·gate (nōō′git, -gāt, nyōō′-) Formerly, a London prison.

New Jerusalem The city of God; heaven. *Rev.* xxi 2.

New Latin See under LATIN.

new·ly (nōō′lē, nyōō′-) *adv.* **1.** Very recently; lately. **2.** Once more; anew; afresh. **3.** In a new or different way.

new·ly·wed (nōō′lē·wed′, nyōō′-) *n.* A person recently married.

new moon **1.** The phase of the moon when it is directly between the earth and the sun, its disk then being invisible; also, the first visible crescent of the disk. **2.** The period when the moon is new.

new·mown (nōō′mōn′, nyōō′-) *adj.* Recently mown, as hay.

New Neth·er·land (neth′ər·lənd) The Dutch colony in North America, 1613–1664, near the mouth of the Hudson River; capital, New Amsterdam.

new penny A penny (def. 3).

news (nōōz, nyōōz) *n.pl.* (*construed as sing.*) **1.** Information of a recent event, development, etc., esp. as reported in a newspaper, on the radio, etc. **2.** Any new or unfamiliar information. [< NEW]

news·boy (nōōz′boi′, nyōōz′-) *n.* A boy who sells or delivers newspapers.

news·cast (nōōz′kast′, -käst′, nyōōz′-) *n.* A radio or television broadcast of news. — **news′cast′er** *n.*

news·let·ter (nōōz′let′ər, nyōōz′-) *n.* A brief, specialized, periodical news report or set of reports sent by mail.

news·mag·a·zine (nōōz′mag′ə·zēn, -mag′ə·zēn′, nyōōz′-) *n.* A periodical, especially a weekly, that summarizes the news.

news·man (nōōz′man′, -mən, nyōōz′-) *n. pl.* **·men** (-men′, -mən) **1.** A news reporter. **2.** A newsdealer.

news·pa·per (nōōz′pā′pər, nyōōz′-) *n.* **1.** A printed publication usu. issued daily or weekly, containing news, editorials, advertisements, etc. **2.** Newsprint.

news·print (nōōz′print′, -nyōōz′-) *n.* The thin, unsized paper on which the ordinary newspaper is printed.

news·reel (nōōz′rēl′, nyōōz′-) *n.* A short motion picture showing current events.

news·stand (nōōz′stand′, nyōōz′-) *n. U.S.* A stand or stall at which newspapers and periodicals are offered for sale.

New Style See (Gregorian) CALENDAR.

news·worth·y (nōōz′wûr′thē, nyōōz′-) *adj.* Having sufficient importance to be reported in a newspaper or newscast.

news·y (nōō′zē, nyōō′-) *Informal adj.* **news·i·er, news·i·est** Full of news. — *n. pl.* **news·ies** *U.S.* A newsboy.

newt (nōōt, nyōōt) *n.* Any of various semiaquatic salamanders. [Earlier *ewt;* in ME *an ewt* was taken as *a newt*]

New Testament That portion of the Bible containing the life and teachings of Christ and his followers.

New World The Western Hemisphere.

New Year The first day of the year; in the Gregorian calendar, January 1. Also **New Year's Day** (yirz).

New Year's Eve The night of December 31.

New York·er (yôr′kər) An inhabitant of New York; esp., a native or resident of New York City.

New Zea·land·er (zē′lən·dər) **1.** A resident of New Zealand. **2.** Formerly, a Maori.

next (nekst) *adj.* **1.** Coming directly after in time, order, position, etc. **2.** Nearest or closest in space. **3.** Adjacent or adjoining: in the *next* room. — *adv.* **1.** Immediately afterward. **2.** On the first succeeding occasion: when *next* we meet. — *prep.* Nearest to: *next* his heart. — **next door** **1.** The adjacent house, building, apartment, etc. **2.** In, at, or to the adjacent house, etc. — **next to** Almost; nearly: *next to* impossible. [OE *niehst,* superl. of *neah* near]

next of kin The person most closely related to one.

nex·us (nek′səs) *n. pl.* **·us·es** or **·us** **1.** A bond or tie between the several members of a group or series; link. **2.** A connected series. [< L, pp. of *nectere* to tie]

ni·a·cin (nī′ə·sin) *n.* Nicotinic acid.

nib (nib) *n.* **1.** The point of a pen. **2.** The projecting, pointed part of anything; tip. — *v.t.* **nibbed, nib·bing** To furnish with a nib. [Var. of NEB < OE *nebb* beak]

nib·ble (nib′əl) *v.* **·bled, ·bling** *v.t.* **1.** To eat with small, quick, gentle bites: to *nibble* grass. **2.** To take little, soft bites of: to *nibble* an ear. — *v.i.* **3.** To eat or bite, esp. with small, gentle bites: often with *at.* — *n.* **1.** A little bit or morsel. **2.** The act of one who or that which nibbles. [< Gmc] — **nib′bler** *n.*

Ni·be·lung (nē′bə·lŏŏng) *n. pl.* **·lungs** or **·lung·en** (-lŏŏng′ən) In Teutonic mythology, one of a dwarf people who held a magic ring and a hoard of gold, taken from them by Siegfried.

Ni·be·lung·en·lied (nē′bə·lŏŏng′ən·lēt′) The lay of the Nibelungs, a Middle High German epic poem written by an unknown author during the early 13th century.

nib·lick (nib′lik) *n.* In golf, a nine iron. [? < Du. < *kneppel* club]

Nic·a·ra·guan (nik′ə·rä′gwən) *adj.* Of or pertaining to Nicaragua. — *n.* A native of Nicaragua.

nice (nīs) *adj.* **nic·er, nic·est** **1.** Agreeable; pleasing; respectable; suitable. **2.** Friendly; kind. **3.** Characterized by, revealing, or demanding discrimination, delicacy, or subtlety: a *nice* distinction. **4.** Precise, accurate, or minute, as an instrument. — **nice and** Gratifyingly; properly: *nice and* dry. [< OF, innocent, foolish < L *nescius* ignorant] — **nice′ly** *adv.* — **nice′ness** *n.*

Ni·cene Creed (nī′sēn, nī·sēn′) *Eccl.* **1.** A Christian confession of faith, adopted by the first Council of Nicaea, A.D. 325. **2.** Any of several other creeds later adopted by Christian churches. [after *Nicaea,* an ancient town in Asia Minor]

ni·ce·ty (nī′sə·tē) *n. pl.* **·ties** **1.** *Usu. pl.* A minute or subtle point; detail, or distinction. **2.** *Usu. pl.* A delicacy or refinement: *niceties* of living. **3.** The quality of requiring careful and delicate treatment. **4.** Precision or accuracy; exactness. **5.** The quality of being nice. — **to a nicety** Exactly.

niche (nich) *n.* **1.** A recessed space or hollow, usu. in a wall, for a statue or the like. **2.** Any position specially adapted to its occupant: to find one's *niche.* — *v.t.* **niched, nich·ing** To put in a niche. [Prob. < F, ult. < L *nidus* nest]

NICHE

Nich·o·las, (nik′ə·ləs, -lus) **Saint** See SANTA CLAUS.

nick (nik) *n.* A slight cut, chip, or indentation on a surface or edge. — **in the nick of time** At the exact or crucial moment. — *v.t.* To make a nick in or on.

nick·el (nik′əl) *n.* **1.** A hard, ductile, malleable, silver-white metallic element (symbol Ni) having a wide variety of uses. See ELEMENT. **2.** A five-cent coin of the U.S., made of an alloy of nickel and copper. — *v.t.* **·eled** or **·elled, ·el·ing** or **·el·ling** To plate with nickel. [< Sw. < G < (*kupfer*)*nickel,* lit., copper demon; because its ore looks like copper]

nick·el·o·de·on (nik′əl·ō′dē·ən) *n. U.S.* **1.** Formerly, a motion-picture theater charging an admission fee of five cents. **2.** Formerly, a jukebox or other automatic music machine. [< NICKEL (def. 2) + *odeon* < F *odéon* theater]

nick·el-plate (nik′əl·plāt′) *v.t.* **-plat·ed, -plat·ing** To cover with nickel by electroplating.

nickel plate A thin layer of nickel deposited on the surface of objects by electroplating.

nickel silver   German silver.

nick·er (nik′ər) *n.* **1.** A neigh. **2.** A neighing laugh. — *v.i.* **1.** To neigh. **2.** To snicker. [Imit.]

nick·nack (nik′nak′)   See KNICKKNACK.

nick·name (nik′nām′) *n.* **1.** A familiar form of a proper name, as *Tom* for *Thomas.* **2.** A descriptive name given instead of or in addition to the actual name of a person, place, or thing, as *Honest Abe.* — *v.t.* ·**named**, ·**nam·ing 1.** To give a nickname to or call by a nickname. **2.** To misname. [ME *ekename* surname, *an ekename* becoming a *nickname*]

nic·o·tine (nik′ə-tēn, -tin) *n.* An acrid, poisonous, oily alkaloid, $C_{11}H_{14}N_2$, contained in the leaves of tobacco. Also **nic′o·tin.** [< F, after Jean *Nicot,* 1530–1600, French courtier, who introduced tobacco into France from Portugal] — **nic·o·tin·ic** (nik′ə-tin′ik) *adj.*

nicotinic acid   *Biochem.* A colorless, water-soluble compound, $C_6H_5NO_2$, prepared by the oxidation of nicotine and forming part of the vitamin B complex, used to prevent pellagra: also called *niacin.*

nic·ti·tate (nik′tə-tāt) *v.i.* ·**tat·ed**, ·**tat·ing** To wink. Also **nic′tate.** [< Med.L, freq. of L *nictare* to wink] — **nic′ti·ta′tion** *n.*

nictitating membrane   A transparent third eyelid at the inner corner of the eye in various birds, reptiles, etc.

niece (nēs) *n.* The daughter of a brother or sister. [< OF, ult. < L *neptis* niece, granddaughter]

Nie·tzsche·an (nē′chi·ən) *adj.* Of or relating to Friedrich Nietzsche, or to his philosophy. — **Nie′tzsche·an·ism, Nie′.tzsche·ism** *n.*

nif·ty (nif′tē) *adj.* ·**ti·er**, ·**ti·est** *Slang* Stylish; pleasing.

nig·gard (nig′ərd) *n.* A stingy person. — *adj.* Niggardly. [? < AF, < ON *hnøggr*]

nig·gard·ly (nig′ərd·lē) *adj.* **1.** Stingy; parsimonious. **2.** Meanly insufficient; scanty. — *adv.* In the manner of a niggard. — **nig′gard·li·ness** *n.*

nig·ger (nig′ər) *n.* A Negro or member of any dark-skinned people: a vulgar and offensive term. [See NEGRO.]

nig·gle (nig′əl) *v.i.* ·**gled**, ·**gling** To occupy oneself with trifles; behave trivially. [Cf. dial. Norw. *nigla*]

nig·gling (nig′ling) *adj.* **1.** Fussy; overprecise. **2.** Mean; petty. **3.** Annoying; nagging. — *n.* Overelaborate or overprecise work or behavior. — **nig′gling·ly** *adv.*

nigh (nī) *Chiefly Archaic & Dial. adj.* **nigh·er**, **nigh·est** or **next 1.** Close; near. **2.** Convenient; direct. — *adv.* **1.** Near in time or place. **2.** Almost: often with *on* or *onto:* *nigh* on a year. — *prep.* Near. — *v.t. & v.i.* To draw near; approach. [OE *nēah, nēh*] — **nigh′ness** *n.*

night (nīt) *n.* **1.** The period from sunset to sunrise, esp. the part that is dark. ◆ Collateral adjective: *nocturnal.* **2.** The period of evening and darkness before midnight of a given day. **3.** Darkness; the dark. **4.** A condition of ignorance, gloom, painful confusion, etc. [OE *niht, neaht*]

night blindness   Vision that is abnormally poor in dim light but normal in daylight.

night-bloom·ing ce·re·us (nīt′blōō′ming sir′ē·əs)   A tall tropical cactus having large white flowers that open at night.

night·cap (nīt′kap′) *n.* **1.** A cap to be worn in bed. **2.** *Informal* A drink of liquor taken just before going to bed.

night·clothes (nīt′klōz′, -klōthz′) *n.pl.* Clothes to be worn in bed.

night club   A restaurant open until late at night, providing entertainment, food, and drink.

night crawler   Any large earthworm that emerges at night.

night·fall (nīt′fôl′) *n.* The close of day.

night·gown (nīt′goun′) *n.* A loose gown worn in bed by women and children. Also **night′dress′** (-dres′).

night·hawk (nīt′hôk′) *n.* **1.** Any of various birds related to the whippoorwill. **2.** The nightjar.

night·in·gale (nīt′ən-gāl, nī′ting-) *n.* A small, Old World migratory bird allied to the thrushes and noted for the melodious song of the male. [OE < *niht* night + *galan* to sing]

night·jar (nīt′jär′) *n.* Any of various goatsuckers of Europe: also called *nighthawk.*

night letter   A telegram sent at night, at reduced rates.

night·light (nīt′līt′) *n.* A usu. dim light kept on at night.

night·long (nīt′lông′, -long′) *adj.* Lasting through the night. — *adv.* Through the whole night.

night·ly (nīt′lē) *adj.* **1.** Of, pertaining to, or occurring each night. **2.** Pertaining to or occurring at night. — *adv.* **1.** By night. **2.** Each night: to take place *nightly.*

night·mare (nīt′mâr) *n.* **1.** A horrible and frightening dream. **2.** Any experience or condition resembling a nightmare. [< NIGHT + MARE²] — **night′mar·ish** *adj.*

night owl   One who stays up late.

nights (nīts) *adv. Informal* At night. [OE *nihtes*]

night school   A school that holds classes during the evening, esp. for those who cannot attend day school.

night·shade (nīt′shād′) *n.* **1.** Any of various flowering plants typical of a family that includes tobacco, pepper, jimsonweed, the potato, and the tomato. **2.** Belladonna.

night·shirt (nīt′shûrt′) *n.* A long, loose garment worn in bed, usu. by men or boys.

night·spot (nīt′spot′) *U.S. Informal* A night club.

night·stick (nīt′stik′) *n. U.S.* A long, heavy club carried by policemen.

night table   A bedside table or stand.

night·time (nīt′tīm′) *n.* The time from sunset to sunrise, or from dark to dawn.

night-walk·er (nīt′wô′kər) *n.* A night crawler.

night watch 1. A watch or guard kept at night. **2.** A night watchman. **3.** A period of watch or guard.

night·wear (nīt′wâr′) *n.* Nightclothes.

night·y (nī′tē) *n. pl.* **night·ies** *U.S. Informal* A nightgown.

nigri- *combining form* Black. Also, before vowels, **nigr-.** [< L *niger, nigris* black]

ni·hil·ism (nī′əl·iz′əm, nī′hil-) *n.* **1.** *Philos.* **a** A doctrine that denies existence. **b** A doctrine that denies any basis for knowledge or truth. **c** Total denial of all traditional principles, values, and institutions. **2.** In politics: **a** A doctrine advocating the destruction of all political, economic, and social institutions. **b** *Usu. cap.* A revolutionary movement in Russia in the 19th century advocating violence and terror. **3.** Any revolutionary movement advocating terror and violence. — **ni′hil·ist** *n.* — **ni′hil·is′tic** *adj.*

Ni·ke (nī′kē)   In Greek mythology, the winged goddess of victory: identified with the Roman *Victoria.* — *n.* An antiaircraft guided missile. [< Gk. *Nikē* victory]

nil (nil) *n.* Nothing. [< L, contr. of *nihil* nothing]

Nile green   Any of several light green tints.

nil·gai (nil′gī) *n.* A large, short-maned antelope of India. Also **nil′gau** (-gô), **nil′ghai, nil′ghau** (-gô). [< Hind. < *nīl* blue + *gāi* cow]

nim·ble (nim′bəl) *adj.* ·**bler**, ·**blest 1.** Light and quick in movement; lively. **2.** Characterized by a quick and ready intellect. [OE *numel* quick at grasping] — **nim′ble·ness** *n.* — **nim′bly** *adv.*

nim·bo·stra·tus (nim′bō·strā′təs, -strat′əs) *n. Meteorol.* A low, formless, dark gray cloud layer, precipitating continuous rain or snow.

nim·bus (nim′bəs) *n. pl.* ·**bus·es** or ·**bi** (-bī) **1.** A luminous emanation believed to envelop a deity or holy person. **2.** Any atmosphere or aura, as of fame, glamor, etc. **3.** Formerly, a nimbostratus. [< L, cloud]

Nim·rod (nim′rod)   Grandson of Ham, described as a mighty hunter. *Gen.* x 8. — *n.* A hunter. Also **nim′rod.**

Ni·ña (nē′nə, *Sp.* nē′nyä) *n.* One of the three ships of Columbus on his first voyage to America.

nin·com·poop (nin′kəm·pōōp) *n.* An idiot; fool. [Origin unknown]

nine (nīn) *n.* **1.** The sum of eight and one: a cardinal number. **2.** Any symbol of this number, as 9, ix, IX. **3.** Anything consisting of or representing nine units, as a baseball team, etc. — **the Nine** The Muses. — *adj.* Being one more than eight. [OE *nigon*] — **ninth** *adj. & n.*

nine iron   In golf, an iron with an extremely slanted face, used for lofting the ball: also called *niblick.*

nine·pence (nīn′pəns) *n. Brit.* **1.** The sum of nine pennies. **2.** A coin of this value, no longer minted.

nine·pins (nīn′pinz′) *n.pl.* (construed as *sing.*) A bowling game similar to tenpins, using nine large wooden pins.

nine·teen (nīn′tēn′) *n.* **1.** The sum of eighteen and one: a cardinal number. **2.** Any symbol of this number, as 19, xix, XIX. **3.** Anything consisting of or representing nineteen units. — *adj.* Being one more than eighteen. [OE *nigontiene*] — **nine′teenth′** *adj. & n.*

nine·ty (nīn′tē) *n. pl.* ·**ties 1.** The sum of eighty and ten: a cardinal number. **2.** Any symbol of this number, as 90, xc, XC. **3.** Anything consisting of or representing ninety units, as an organization, game token, etc. — *adj.* Being ten more than eighty. [OE *nigontig*] — **nine′ti·eth** *adj. & n.*

Nin·e·veh (nin′ə·və)   An ancient city on the Tigris, capital of Assyria. — **nin′e·vite** (-vīt) *n.*

Ni·o·be (nī′ə·bē)   In Greek mythology, the mother whose children were killed by Apollo and Artemis after she had vaunted their superiority. She was turned by Zeus into a stone from which tears continued to flow.

ni·o·bi·um (nī·ō′bē·əm) *n.* A rare, steel gray, metallic element (symbol Nb), valuable as an alloy metal: formerly called *columbium.* See ELEMENT. [< NIOBE]

nip¹ (nip) *v.* **nipped**, **nip·ping** *v.t.* **1.** To pinch or compress between two surfaces; bite. **2.** To sever or remove by pinching, biting, or clipping: usually with *off.* **3.** To check, arrest, or destroy the growth or development of. **4.** To affect painfully or injuriously, as by cold. **5.** *Slang* To steal; pilfer. **6.** *Slang* To catch; take. — *v.i.* **7.** *Brit. Informal* To move nimbly or rapidly: with *off*, *away*, etc. — *n.* **1.** The act of one who or that which nips. **2.** That which is nipped off. **3.** Any small portion: a *nip* of tea. **4.** A sharp, stinging quality. **5.** Severe cold or frost. **6.** A cutting remark. **7.** A sharp, pungent flavor. — **nip and tuck** *U.S.* Very close or even; precariously uncertain. [Cf. Du. *nijpen* to pinch]

nip² (nip) *n.* A small quantity of liquor. — *v.t.* & *v.i.* To sip (liquor). [? < earlier *nipperkin* a small liquid measure]

nip·per (nip'ər) *n.* **1.** One who or that which nips. **2.** *pl.* Any of various implements used for nipping, as pliers, pincers, etc. **3.** The large claw of a crab or lobster. **4.** *pl. Slang* Handcuffs. **5.** *Brit. Informal* A small boy; lad.

nip·ple (nip'əl) *n.* **1.** The protuberance on the breasts of higher mammals, esp. that of the female; teat. **2.** The rubber teatlike mouthpiece of a nursing bottle. **3.** Something resembling a nipple, as a short pipe coupling with threaded ends. [Earlier *nible*, ? dim. of NIB]

nip·py (nip'ē) *adj.* **·pi·er**, **·pi·est** **1.** Biting or sharp, as cold weather. **2.** *Brit. Informal* Active; alert. — **nip'pi·ly** *adv.* — **nip'pi·ness** *n.*

nir·va·na (nir·vä'nə, nər·van'ə) *n.* **1.** In Buddhism, the state of absolute felicity attained through the annihilation of the self. **2.** Freedom from care and pain; bliss. [< Skt. *nirvāna* extinction]

Ni·san (nē·sän', nis'ən) *n.* The seventh month of the Hebrew year. Also **Nis'san**. See (Hebrew) CALENDAR.

Ni·sei (nē·sā') *n. pl.* **·sei** or **·seis** A native American of immigrant Japanese parentage.

ni·si (nī'sī) *conj. Law* Unless: used after the word *order*, *rule*, *decree*, etc., signifying that it shall become effective at a certain time, unless modified or avoided. [< L]

Nis·sen hut (nis'ən, nēs'-) A prefabricated sheet steel building resembling a long half-cylinder lying flat on the ground. [after P. N. *Nissen*, 1871–1930, who invented it]

nit (nit) *n.* **1.** The egg of a louse or other parasitic insect. **2.** An immature louse. [OE *hnitu*] — **nit'ty** *adj.*

ni·ter (nī'tər) *n.* **1.** Potassium or sodium nitrate; saltpeter. **2.** *Obs.* Natron. Also **ni'tre**. [< OF < L < Gk. *nitron*]

ni·ton (nī'ton) *n.* Radon. [< L *nit)ere* to shine) + -ON]

nit-pick (nit'pik') *Informal v.t.* **1.** To fuss over or find fault with. — *v.i.* **2.** To engage in nit-picking. Also **nit'-pick**. [Back formation < NIT-PICKING] — **nit'-pick'er** *n.*

nit-pick·ing (nit'pik'ing) *n. Informal* A fussing over trivial details, often with the aim of finding fault.

ni·trate (nī'trāt) *Chem. n.* **1.** A salt or ester of nitric acid. **2.** Niter. — *v.t.* **·trat·ed**, **·trat·ing** To treat or combine with nitric acid or a compound. [See NITER.]

ni·tric (nī'trik) *adj. Chem.* **1.** Of, pertaining to, or obtained from nitrogen. **2.** Containing nitrogen in the higher valence.

nitric acid *Chem.* A colorless, highly corrosive liquid, HNO_3, having strong oxidizing properties.

ni·tride (nī'trīd, -trid) *n. Chem.* A compound of nitrogen with some more electropositive element. Also **ni'trid** (-trid).

ni·tri·fy (nī'trə·fī) *v.t.* **·fied**, **·fy·ing** *Chem.* **1.** To treat or combine with nitrogen. **2.** To convert, as ammonium salts in the soil, into nitrates or nitrites by oxidation. **3.** To treat or impregnate (soil, etc.) with nitrates. [< F *nitrifier*] — **ni'tri·fi'a·ble** *adj.* — **ni'tri·fi·ca'tion** *n.*

ni·trite (nī'trīt) *n. Chem.* A salt of nitrous acid.

nitro- *combining form Chem.* Containing the univalent radical NO_2. Also, before vowels, **nitr-**. Also **nitri-**. [< L *nitrum* < Gk. *nitron*]

ni·tro·ben·zene (nī'trō·ben'zēn, -ben·zēn') *n. Chem.* A yellow, oily compound, $C_6H_5NO_2$, formed by the nitration of benzene and used in the making of aniline.

ni·tro·gen (nī'trə·jən) *n.* An odorless, colorless, gaseous element (symbol N) forming about four-fifths of the atmosphere by volume and playing a decisive role in the formation of compounds essential to life. See ELEMENT. [< F *nitrogène* < *nitro-* NITRO- + *-gène* -GEN]

nitrogen fixation **1.** The conversion of atmospheric nitrogen into nitrates by soil bacteria. **2.** The production of nitrogen compounds, as for fertilizers and explosives, by processes utilizing free nitrogen. — **ni'tro·gen-fix'ing** *adj.*

ni·trog·en·ize (nī·troj'ən·īz, nī'trə·jən·īz') *v.t.* **·ized**, **·iz·ing** To treat or combine with nitrogen.

ni·trog·e·nous (nī·troj'ə·nəs) *adj.* Pertaining to or containing nitrogen. Also **ni·tro·ge·ne·ous** (nī'trō·jē'nē·əs).

ni·tro·glyc·er·in (nī'trō·glis'ər·in) *n. Chem.* A colorless to pale yellow, oily liquid, $C_3H_5(ONO_2)_3$, made by nitrating glycerol, used as an explosive and propellant, etc. Also **ni'tro**, **ni'tro·glyc'er·ine**. [< NITRO- + GLYCERIN]

nitro group *Chem.* The univalent NO_2 radical.

ni·trous (nī'trəs) *adj. Chem.* Of, pertaining to, or derived from nitrogen: esp. applied to those compounds containing less oxygen than the nitric compounds.

nitrous oxide A gas, N_2O, used as an anesthetic in dental surgery, etc., and sometimes having an exhilarating effect when inhaled: also called *laughing gas*.

nit·ty-grit·ty (nit'ē-grit'ē) *U.S. Slang n.* The basic questions or details; essence. — *adj.* Down-to-earth; basic.

nit·wit (nit'wit') *n.* A silly or stupid person.

ni·val (nī'vəl) *adj.* Of or pertaining to the snow; also, growing under the snow. [< L *nivalis* < *nix, nivis* snow]

nix¹ (niks) *n.* In Germanic mythology, a water sprite.

nix² (niks) *Slang n.* **1.** Nothing. **2.** No. — *adv.* No. — *interj.* Stop! Watch out! — *v.t.* To forbid or disagree with: He *nixed* our suggestions. [< G *nichts* nothing]

no¹ (nō) *adv.* **1.** Nay; not so. **2.** Not at all; not in any wise: *no* better than the other. **3.** Not: used to express an alternative after *or*: whether or no. — *n. pl.* **noes** **1.** A negative reply; a denial. **2.** A negative vote or voter: The *noes* have it. [OE *nā* < *ne* not + *ā* ever]

no² (nō) *adj.* Not any; not one. [OE < *ne* not + *ān* one]

no³ (nō) *n. pl.* **no** *Sometimes cap.* The classical drama of Japan, traditionally tragic or noble in theme, having music and dancing: also spelled *noh*. Also **nō**. Compare KABUKI.

No·ah (nō'ə) In the Old Testament, a patriarch who built an ark that saved him, his family, and every kind of animal from the Flood. [Gen. v-ix. < Hebrew]

nob¹ (nob) *n.* **1.** *Slang* The head. **2.** In cribbage, the jack of trumps. [Var. of KNOB]

nob² (nob) *n. Slang* One who is rich, influential, etc.

No·bel Prizes (nō·bel') Any of five prizes founded by the will of Alfred Nobel and awarded annually in the fields of physics, chemistry, medicine, literature, and the furtherance of world peace.

no·be·li·um (nō·bē'lē·əm) *n.* An unstable radioactive element (symbol No) originally produced by the bombardment of curium by an isotope of carbon. See ELEMENT. [after A. B. *Nobel*]

no·bil·i·ty (nō·bil'ə·tē) *n. pl.* **·ties** **1.** A class in society composed of persons having hereditary title, rank, and privileges. **2.** In Great Britain, the peerage. **3.** The state or quality of being noble.

no·ble (nō'bəl) *adj.* **·bler**, **·blest** **1.** Having excellence or dignity; eminent; illustrious; worthy. **2.** Characterized by or displaying superior moral qualities. **3.** Magnificent and imposing in appearance; grand; stately. **4.** Of or pertaining to the nobility; aristocratic. **5.** Chemically inert. — *n.* **1.** A nobleman. **2.** In Great Britain, a peer. [< MF < L *nobilis* noble, well-known] — **no'ble·ness** *n.* — **no'bly** *adv.*

no·ble·man (nō'bəl·mən) *n. pl.* **·men** (-mən) A man of noble rank; in England, a peer.

no·blesse o·blige (nō·bles' ō·blēzh') *French* Those of high birth, wealth, or social position must behave generously or nobly toward others; literally, nobility obligates.

no·ble·wom·an (nō'bəl·wŏŏm'ən) *n. pl.* **·wom·en** (-wim'in) **1.** A woman of noble rank. **2.** In England, a peeress.

no·bod·y (nō'bod'ē, -bəd·ē) *pron.* Not anybody. — *n. pl.* **·bod·ies** A person of no importance or influence.

nock (nok) *n.* **1.** The notch for the bowstring on the butt end of an arrow. **2.** The notch on the horn of a bow for securing the bowstring. [ME *nocke*]

nocti- *combining form* By or at night. Also, before vowels, **noct-**. [< L *nox, noctis* night]

noc·tu·id (nok'chŏŏ·id) *n.* Any of a large family of medium-sized moths, esp. those whose larvae are destructive. — *adj.* Of this family of moths. [< NL < L *noctua* night owl]

noc·tur·nal (nok·tûr'nəl) *adj.* **1.** Of, pertaining to, or occurring at night. **2.** *Biol.* Active, blooming, etc., by night. [< LL < L *nocturnus* nightly] — **noc·tur'nal·ly** *adv.*

noc·turne (nok'tûrn) *n.* **1.** In painting, a night scene. **2.** *Music* A composition of a pensive or romantic nature.

nod (nod) *v.* **nod·ded**, **nod·ding** *v.i.* **1.** To lower the head forward briefly, as in agreement, assent, invitation, etc. **2.** To let the head fall forward slightly and involuntarily, as when drowsy. **3.** To be inattentive or careless. **4.** To sway or bend the top or upper part, as trees. — *v.t.* **5.** To lower (the head) by nodding. **6.** To express or signify (assent, agreement, etc.) by nodding the head. — *n.* The act of one who or that which nods. — **to give** (or **get**) **the nod** *U.S. Slang* To give (or receive) the sign to go ahead, assent, approval, etc. [ME *nodden*] — **nod'der** *n.*

nod·dle (nod'l) *Informal n.* The head; noodle. — *v.t.* & *v.i.* **·dled**, **·dling** To nod frequently. [Freq. of NOD]

nod·dy (nod'ē) *n. pl.* **·dies** **1.** A dunce; a fool. **2.** One of several terns of the Atlantic coast. [? < NOD]

node (nōd) *n.* **1.** A knot, knob, or swelling; protuberance. **2.** *Bot.* A joint or knob of a stem. **3.** *Math.* A point at which a curve crosses itself. **4.** *Astron.* Either of two points at which the orbit of a heavenly body intersects the ecliptic. **5.** *Physics* A point, line, or surface in a standing wave system at which some component wave has virtually zero amplitude. **6.** *Anat.* A swelling. [< L *nodus* knot] — **nod·al** (nōd'l) *adj.* — **nod'al·ly** *adv.*

nod·ule (noj'ŏŏl, nod'yŏŏl) *n.* **1.** A little knot or node. **2.** *Bot.* A tubercle. [< L < *nodus* knot] — **nod·u·lar** (noj'ŏŏ·lər), **nod'u·lose** (-lōs), **nod'u·lous** (-ləs) *adj.*

no·ël (nō·el') *n.* A Christmas carol. Also **no·el'**.

No·ël (nō·el') *n.* Christmas. Also **No·el'**. [< F < LL (*dies*) *natalis* birthday]

no-fault (nō′fôlt′) *adj.* Describing a form of motor vehicle insurance that insures the policyholder against his own loss rather than against loss to others he may have caused.

nog (nog) *n.* 1. Eggnog (which see). 2. *Brit. Dial.* A strong ale. Also **nogg.** [Origin unknown]

nog·gin (nog′in) *n.* 1. *Informal* A person's head. 2. A small mug or cup. 3. A measure of liquor equal to about one fourth of a pint or a gill. [Origin unknown]

noh (nō) See NŌ³.

no·how (nō′hou′) *adv. Dial.* In no way; not by any means.

noise (noiz) *n.* 1. Loud, confused, or disturbing sound of any kind. 2. In communication theory, any random disturbance that causes a received signal to differ from what was transmitted. —*v.* **noised, nois·ing** *Rare v.t.* 1. To spread, report, or rumor: often with *about* or *abroad.* —*v.i.* 2. To be noisy; make a noise. [< OF, ? < L *nausea*] —**Syn.** 1. din, clamor, uproar, hubbub, racket, clatter, blare. See SOUND¹.

noise·less (noiz′lis) *adj.* Causing or making little or no noise; quiet; silent. —**noise′less·ly** *adv.* —**noise′less·ness** *n.*

noise·mak·er (noiz′mā′kər) *n.* A horn, bell, etc., for making noise at celebrations. —**noise′mak′ing** *n. & adj.*

noi·some (noi′səm) *adj.* 1. Offensive or disgusting, esp. in smell; stinking. 2. Injurious; noxious. [ME < *noy* annoyance + OE *-sum* like, resembling] —**noi′some·ly** *adv.* —**noi′some·ness** *n.*

nois·y (noi′zē) *adj.* **nois·i·er, nois·i·est** 1. Making a loud noise. 2. Characterized by or full of noise. —**nois′i·ly** *adv.* —**nois′i·ness** *n.*

no·li-me-tan·ge·re (nō′li-mē-tan′jə-rē) *n.* A warning against touching or meddling. [< L, touch me not]

nol·le pros·e·qui (nol′ē pros′ə-kwī) *Law* An entry in a civil or criminal case, to signify that the plaintiff or prosecutor will not press it. [< L, to be unwilling to prosecute]

no·lo con·ten·de·re (nō′lō kən·ten′də·rē) *Law* A plea by a defendant in a criminal action that has the same legal effect as an admission of guilt but does not debar him from denying the truth of the charges in any other proceedings. [< L, I am unwilling to contend]

nol-pros (nol′pros′) *v.t.* **-prossed, -pros·sing** *Law* To subject to a nolle prosequi. [Short for NOLLE PROSEQUI]

no·mad (nō′mad, nom′ad) *n.* 1. One of a group of people that habitually shifts its abode to find food, avoid drought, etc. 2. One who constantly moves about, usu. without purpose; a wanderer. —*adj.* Nomadic. [< L < Gk. *nomas* < *nemein* to graze] —**no′mad·ism** *n.*

no·mad·ic (nō-mad′ik) *adj.* Of, pertaining to, or like nomads. Also **no·mad′i·cal.** —**no·mad′i·cal·ly** *adv.*

no man's land 1. A tract of waste or unowned land. 2. In war, the land between opposing armies. 3. An area of human activity characterized by ambiguity or peril.

nom de guerre (nôn də gâr′) *French* A pseudonym; literally, a war name.

nom de plume (nom′ də ploom′, *Fr.* nôn də plüm′) A pen name; a writer's assumed name. —**Syn.** See PSEUDONYM. [< F *nom* name + *de* of + *plume* pen]

no·men·cla·ture (nō′mən-klā′chər, nō-men′klə-) *n.* 1. The system of names used to describe the various elements of a science, art, etc.; terminology. 2. The specific names for the parts or stages of a device, process, etc.

nom·i·nal (nom′ə-nəl) *adj.* 1. Existing in name only; not actual. 2. Slight or inconsiderable; trifling. 3. Of or like a name. 4. *Gram.* Of, pertaining to, or like a noun. [< L < *nomen* name]

nom·i·nal·ism (nom′ə-nəl-iz′əm) *n. Philos.* The doctrine that universals (abstract concepts) exist only as names and without a basis in reality: opposed to *realism.* [< F *nominalisme*] —**nom′i·nal·ist** *adj. & n.*

nom·i·nal·ly (nom′ə-nəl-ē) *adv.* In name only; not actually.

nom·i·nate (nom′ə-nāt) *v.t.* **-nat·ed, -nat·ing** 1. To name or propose as a candidate for elective office. 2. To appoint to some office or duty. —*adj.* Having a particular or special name. [< L *nominare* to name] —**nom′i·na′tion** *n.* —**nom′i·na′tor** *n.*

nom·i·na·tive (nom′ə-nə-tiv, nom′ə-nā′-) *adj.* 1. *Gram.* Designating the case of the subject of a finite verb, or of a word agreeing with or in apposition to the subject. 2. Appointed by nomination; nominated. —*n. Gram.* 1. The nominative case. 2. A word in this case.

nom·i·nee (nom′ə-nē′) *n.* One who receives a nomination.

-nomy *combining form* The science or systematic study of: *astronomy, economy.* [< Gk. *nomos* law]

non- *prefix* Not. [< F < L *non* not]

◆ *Non-* is the Latin negative adverb adopted as an English prefix. It denotes in general simple negation or absence of, as in *nonheroic,* not heroic, *nonattendance,* lack of attendance. Numerous words beginning with *non-* are self-explaining, as in the list beginning below.

nonabsolute	nonassertive	noncereal	noncompression	nonconventional	nonderivable
nonabsorbent	nonassignable	noncerebral	noncompulsion	nonconvergent	nonderivative
nonabstainer	nonassimilation	nonceremonial	nonconcealment	nonconversant	nonderogatory
nonaccent	nonathletic	noncertified	nonconcentration	nonconversion	nondespotic
nonacceptance	nonatmospheric	nonchargeable	nonconception	nonconvertible	nondestructive
nonaccomplishment	nonattached	nonchemical	nonconcurrence	nonconviction	nondetachable
nonacid	nonattendance	non-Chinese	noncondensation	nonconvivial	nondetonating
nonacquaintance	nonattention	non-Christian	nonconditioned	noncoordinating	nondevelopment
nonacquiescence	nonattributive	nonchurch	nonconducive	noncorrective	nondevotional
nonaction	nonaugmentative	noncitizen	nonconducting	noncorresponding	nondialectical
nonactive	nonauthoritative	noncivilized	nonconferrable	noncorroborative	nondictatorial
nonadherence	nonautomatic	nonclassifiable	nonconfidential	noncorrosive	nondifferentiation
nonadjacent	nonautomotive	nonclerical	nonconflicting	noncosmic	nondiffusing
nonadministrative	nonbacterial	nonclinical	nonconforming	noncreative	nondiplomatic
nonadmission	non-Baptist	nonclotting	noncongealing	noncreditor	nondirectional
nonadult	nonbasic	noncoagulating	noncongenital	noncriminal	nondirigible
nonadvantageous	nonbeliever	noncoalescing	noncongestion	noncritical	nondisappearing
nonadverbial	nonbelieving	noncoercive	non-Congressional	noncrucial	nondischarging
nonaffiliated	nonbelligerent	noncognition	nonconnective	noncrystalline	nondisciplinary
non-African	nonbenevolent	noncognitive	nonconnivance	noncrystallized	nondiscontinuance
nonaggression	non-Biblical	noncoherent	nonconnotative	nonculpable	nondiscountable
nonagreement	nonblending	noncohesive	nonconnubial	noncultivated	nondiscovery
nonagricultural	nonblooming	noncoincident	nonconscious	noncultivation	nondiscrimination
nonalcoholic	non-Bolshevik	noncollaborative	nonconsecutive	noncumulative	nondiscriminatory
nonalgebraic	non-Bolshevist	noncollapsible	nonconsent	noncurrency	nondisfranchised
nonaligned	nonbreakable	noncollectable	nonconsenting	nondamageable	nondisinterested
nonallergic	non-British	noncollegiate	nonconsequence	nondecaying	nondispersion
nonalphabetic	non-Buddhist	noncolonial	nonconservative	nondeceptive	nondisposal
nonamateur	nonbudding	noncombat	nonconsideration	nondefensive	nondisqualifying
nonamendable	nonbureaucratic	noncombining	nonconspiring	nondeferential	nondissenting
non-American	nonburnable	noncombustible	nonconstitutional	nondeferrable	nondistinctive
non-Anglican	nonbusiness	noncombustion	nonconstructive	nondefilement	nondistribution
nonantagonistic	noncaffeine	noncommendable	nonconsular	nondefining	nondistributive
nonapologetic	noncaking	noncommercial	nonconsultative	nondegeneration	nondivergence
nonapostolic	non-Calvinist	noncommunicable	nonconsumption	nondelineation	nondivergent
nonappearance	noncanonical	noncommunicating	noncontagious	nondelirious	nondivisible
nonappearing	noncapitalistic	noncommunist	noncontemporary	nondelivery	nondivision
nonapprehensive	noncarnivorous	non-Communist	noncontiguous	nondemand	nondoctrinal
nonaquatic	noncategorical	noncompensating	noncontinental	nondemocratic	nondocumentary
non-Arab	non-Catholic	noncompensation	noncontinuous	nondepartmental	nondogmatic
non-Arabic	non-Caucasian	noncompetent	noncontradiction	nondeparture	nondomesticated
nonaristocratic	noncelestial	noncompeting	noncontradictory	nondependence	nondramatic
nonarithmetical	noncellular	noncompetitive	noncontributing	nondepletion	nondrying
nonarrival	non-Celtic	noncomplaisant	noncontributory	nondeportation	nonearning
non-Aryan	noncensored	noncompletion	noncontrolled	nondepositor	nonecclesiastical
non-Asiatic	noncentral	noncontroversial	noncontroversial	nondepreciating	noneconomic

non·age (non′ij, nō′nij) *n.* **1.** The period of legal minority. **2.** A period of immaturity. [< OF < *non* not + *age* age]

non·a·ge·nar·i·an (non′ə-jə-nâr′ē-ən, nō′nə-) *n.* A person between 90 and 100 years of age. —*adj.* **1.** Being ninety years old, or between 90 and 100. **2.** Of or pertaining to a nonagenarian. [< L *nonagenarius* of ninety]

non·a·gon (non′ə-gon) *n. Geom.* A polygon having nine sides and nine angles. [< L *nonus* ninth + Gk. *gōnia* angle]

nonce (nons) *n.* Present time or occasion: now chiefly in the phrase **for the nonce.** [ME *for then ones* for the one (occasion), misread as *for the nones*]

nonce word A word coined for a single occasion.

non·cha·lant (non′shə-lənt, non′shə-länt′) *adj.* Marked by or exhibiting a lack of interest or excitement; casually indifferent. [< F < L *non* not + *calere* to be warm, to be desirous] —**non′cha·lance** *n.* —**non′cha·lant·ly** *adv.*

non·com (non′kom′) *U.S. Informal n.* A noncommissioned officer. —*adj.* Noncommissioned.

non·com·bat·ant (non′kəm-bat′ənt, non′kom′bə-tənt, -kum′-) *n.* **1.** One whose duties as a member of a military force do not entail fighting, as a chaplain or medical officer. **2.** A civilian in wartime.

non·com·mis·sioned (non′kə-mish′ənd) *adj.* Not holding a commission: said of certain grades of the armed forces.

noncommissioned officer *Mil.* An enlisted man appointed to a noncommissioned grade, as from corporal to sergeant major in the U.S. Army. See table for GRADE.

non·com·mit·tal (non′kə-mit′l) *adj.* Not involving or revealing a commitment to any particular attitude, opinion, etc. —**non′com·mit′tal·ly** *adv.*

non·com·pli·ance (non′kəm-plī′əns) *n.* Failure or neglect to comply. —**non′com·pli′ant** *adj. & n.*

non com·pos men·tis (non kom′pəs men′tis) *Law* Not of sound mind; mentally unbalanced: often **non compos.** [< L]

non·con·duc·tor (non′kən-duk′tər) *n.* A substance that offers resistance to the passage of some form of energy, as of heat or electricity. —**non′con·duct′ing** *adj.*

non·con·form·ist (non′kən-fôr′mist) *n.* **1.** One who does not conform to an approved manner of behaving or thinking. **2.** *Often cap.* An English Protestant who refuses to conform to the Church of England. —**non′con·form′ing** *adj.* —**non′con·for′mi·ty** *n.*

non·co·op·er·a·tion (non′kō-op′ə-rā′shən) *n.* Failure to cooperate; esp.: resistance to a government through civil disobedience, including the refusal to pay taxes. —**non′co·op′er·a′tion·ist** *n.* —**non′co·op′er·a·tive** (-kō-op′rə-tiv, -kō-op′ə-rā′tiv) *adj.* —**non′co·op′er·a·tor** *n.*

non·de·script (non′di-skript) *adj.* Not distinctive enough to be described; lacking individual character. —*n.* A nondescript person or thing: often used disparagingly. [< NON- + L *descriptus,* pp. of *describere* to describe]

none (nun) *pron.* (construed as *sing.* or *pl.*) **1.** Not one; no one. **2.** No or not one (specified person or thing); not any (of a class of things). **3.** No part or portion; not any: It is *none* of my business. —*adv.* By no means; not at all: He is *none* too bright. [OE < *ne* not + *an* one]

non·ef·fec·tive (non′i-fek′tiv) *adj.* **1.** Not effective. **2.** Unfit or unavailable for active service or duty, as in the army or navy. —*n.* A noneffective soldier, sailor, etc.

non·en·ti·ty (non-en′tə-tē) *n. pl.* **·ties 1.** One who or that which is of little or no account; a nothing. **2.** That which does not exist, or exists solely in the imagination. **3.** The negation of being; nonexistence.

nones (nōnz) *n.pl.* **1.** In the ancient Roman calendar, the ninth day before the ides. **2.** *Often cap. Eccl.* Prescribed prayers constituting the fifth of the seven canonical hours. [< OF < L *nonae,* fem. pl. of *nonus* ninth]

none·such (nun′such′) *n.* **1.** One who or that which has no equal; nonpareil. **2.** A variety of apple. Also **nonsuch.**

none·the·less (nun′thə-les′) *adv.* In spite of everything; nevertheless. Also **none the less.**

non·fea·sance (non-fē′zəns) *n. Law* The nonperformance of some act that one is legally bound to perform. —**non·fea′sor** *n.*

non·fer·rous (non-fer′əs) *adj.* Not containing iron; esp., pertaining to metals other than iron, as copper, tin, platinum, etc.

non·fic·tion (non′fik′shən) *n.* Prose literature other than fiction, as historical works, biographies, etc. —**non′fic′tion·al** *adj.* —**non′fic′tion·al·ly** *adv.*

non·flam·ma·ble (non′flam′ə-bəl) *adj.* Not flammable.

no·nil·lion (nō-nil′yən) *n.* **1.** *U.S.* A thousand octillions, written as 1 followed by thirty zeros: a cardinal number. **2.** *Brit.* A million octillions (def. 2), written as 1 followed by fifty-four zeros: a cardinal number. —*adj.* Being a nonillion in number. [< MF < L *nonus* ninth + F (m)*illion* million] —**no·nil′lionth** (-yənth) *adj. & n.*

non·in·ter·ven·tion (non′in-tər-ven′shən) *n.* **1.** The refusal or failure to intervene; esp., the policy or practice of a nation of not intervening in the affairs of other nations. **2.** An instance of this. —**non′in·ter·ven′tion·ist** *adj. & n.*

non·join·der (non-join′dər) *n. Law* An omission to join an action or suit, as by a person who should be a party to it.

non·ju·ror (non-jŏŏr′ər) *n.* One who refuses to take an oath, as of allegiance, supremacy, or abjuration. [< NON- + JUROR, in obs. sense "one who takes an oath"]

non·met·al (non-met′l) *n. Chem.* Any element, as nitrogen, carbon, or sulfur, that has acid rather than basic properties.

non·mor·al (non-môr′əl, -mor′-) *adj.* Having no relation to morals; neither moral nor immoral. —**non′mo·ral′i·ty** *n.*

non·ob·jec·tive (non′əb-jek′tiv) *adj.* Not objective; esp., denoting a style of nonrepresentational art.

non·pa·reil (non′pə-rel′) *adj.* Having no equal; unrivaled. —*n.* **1.** One who or that which has no equal; a paragon. **2.** Any of various brilliantly colored finches of the southern U.S. **3.** *Printing* A size of type, 6 points, between agate and minion. [< MF < *non* not + OF *pareil* equal]

non·par·ti·san (non-pär′tə-zən) *adj.* Not partisan; esp., not controlled by, associated with, or in support of the interests of any one political party. Also **non·par′ti·zan.**

non·plus (non-plus′, non′plus) *v.t.* **·plused** or **·plussed, ·plus·ing** or **·plus·sing** To cause to be at a loss; baffle; perplex. —*n.* A mental standstill; bewilderment, esp. as causing speechlessness or indecision. [< L *non plus* no further]

non·pro·duc·tive (non′prə-duk′tiv) *adj.* **1.** Not productive; esp., pertaining to that part of the labor force that does not directly contribute to the production of goods, as office workers, salesmen, etc. **2.** Unproductive. —**non′pro·duc′·tive·ly** *adv.* —**non′pro·duc′tive·ness** *n.*

---

nonedible	nonesthetic	nonextensile	nonforfeiture	nonhumorous	noninheritable
noneditorial	noneternity	nonextension	nonformal	nonidentical	noninjurious
noneducable	nonethereal	nonextinct	nonfortuitous	nonidentity	noninjury
noneducational	nonethical	nonextinction	nonfraudulent	nonidiomatic	noninstruction
noneffervescent	nonethnological	nonextortion	nonfreezing	nonidolatrous	noninstrumental
nonefficacious	non-Euclidean	nonextradition	non-French	nonignitable	noninsurance
nonefficiency	noneugenic	nonextraneous	nonfulfillment	nonimaginary	nonintellectual
nonefficient	non-European	nonfactual	nonfunctional	nonimitative	nonintelligent
nonelastic	nonevanescent	nonfading	nonfundamental	nonimmunity	noninterchangeable
nonelective	nonevangelical	nonfanatical	nongaseous	nonimpairment	noninterference
nonelectric	nonevasion	nonfanciful	nongelatinous	nonimperative	nonintermittent
nonelementary	nonevolutionary	non-Fascist	nongenealogical	nonimperial	noninternational
nonelimination	nonexcessive	nonfastidious	nongenerative	nonimportant	noninterrupted
nonemotional	nonexchangeable	nonfatal	nongenetic	nonimportation	nonintersecting
nonemphatic	nonexciting	nonfatalistic	non-Gentile	nonimpregnated	nonintestinal
nonempirical	nonexclusive	nonfederal	non-German	nonimprovement	nonintrospective
nonenforcement	nonexcusable	nonfederated	nongovernmental	nonincandescent	nonintuitive
non-English	nonexecution	nonfermented	nongranular	noninclusive	noninverted
nonentailed	nonexemplary	nonfertility	non-Greek	nonincrease	nonionized
nonenteric	nonexempt	nonfestive	nongregarious	nonindependent	non-Irish
nonentry	nonexercise	nonfeudal	nonhabitable	nonindictable	nonirrigation
nonephemeral	nonexistence	nonfigurative	nonhabitual	nonindictment	nonirritant
nonepicurean	nonexisting	nonfilamentous	nonharmonious	nonindividual	non-Islamic
nonequal	nonexpansive	nonfinancial	nonhazardous	nonindividualistic	nonisolation
nonequation	nonexpendable	nonfinite	nonheathen	non-Indo-European	non-Israelite
nonequatorial	nonexperienced	nonfireproof	non-Hellenic	nonindustrial	non-Italian
nonequilateral	nonexperimental	nonfiscal	nonhereditary	noninfallible	non-Japanese
nonequilibrium	nonexpert	nonfissionable	nonheretic	noninfection	non-Jew
nonequivalent	nonexploitation	nonflowering	nonheritable	noninfinite	non-Jewish
nonequivocating	nonexplosive	nonflowing	nonheroic	noninflammatory	nonjudicial
nonerasure	nonexportable	nonfluctuating	nonhistoric	noninflected	nonjuristic
nonerotic	nonexportation	nonflying	nonhomogeneous	noninflectional	nonlaminated
nonerudite	nonextant	nonfocal	nonhostile	noninflectional	non-Latin
nonessential	nonextended	nonforfeitable	nonhuman	noninformative	

non·prof·it (non-prof′it) *adj.* Not organized or maintained for the making of a profit: *nonprofit* charities.

non·pros (non-pros′) *v.t.* **·prossed**, **·pros·sing** *Law* To enter judgment against (a plaintiff who fails to prosecute). [Short for NON PROSEQUITUR]

non pro·se·qui·tur (non prō-sek′wi·tər) *Law* A judgment entered against a plaintiff who fails to prosecute an action. [< L, lit., he does not prosecute]

non·rep·re·sen·ta·tion·al (non′rep′ri·zen·tā′shən·əl) *adj.* Not representational; esp., denoting a style of art that does not seek to represent objects as they appear in nature.

non·res·i·dent (non-rez′ə·dənt) *adj.* Not resident; esp., not residing permanently in the locality where one works, owns property, attends school, etc. — *n.* One who is non-resident. — **non·res′i·dence**, **non·res′i·den·cy** *n.*

non·re·sis·tant (non′ri·zis′tənt) *adj.* 1. Not resistant; esp., incapable of resistance, as to infection. 2. Of, pertaining to, or characteristic of a nonresistant. — *n.* One who is passive in the face of violence. — **non′re·sis′tance** *n.*

non·re·stric·tive (non′ri·strik′tiv) *adj.* 1. Not restrictive. 2. *Gram.* Denoting a word or word group, esp. an adjective clause, that describes its antecedent, but may be omitted without loss of essential meaning, as *which is for sale* in *Our house, which is for sale, needs repairs.*

non·sec·tar·i·an (non′sek·târ′ē·ən) *adj.* Not restricted to or associated with any one religion, sect, or faction.

non·sense (non′sens, -səns) *n.* 1. That which is without sense, or without good sense; esp., words or actions that are meaningless or absurd. 2. Things of no importance or use; trifles. 3. Foolish or frivolous conduct. — **non·sen′si·cal** *adj.* — **non·sen′si·cal·ly** *adv.* — **non·sen′si·cal·ness** *n.*

non se·qui·tur (non sek′wə·tər) 1. *Logic* An inference that does not follow from the premises. 2. Any comment not relevant to what has preceded it. [< L, it does not follow]

non·skid (non′skid′) *adj.* Having a surface that resists skidding.

non·stan·dard (non′stan′dərd) *adj.* 1. Varying or deviating from the standard. 2. *Ling.* Designating those usages or varieties of a language that differ from the standard.

nonstandard English *Ling.* Those usages in English that differ from standard English: also *substandard English.*

non·stop (non′stop′) *adj.* Making, having made, or scheduled to make no stops: a *nonstop* flight; *nonstop* train.

non·such (nun′such′) See NONESUCH.

non·suit (non′sōōt′) *Law v.t.* To order the dismissal of the suit of. — *n.* 1. The abandonment of a suit. 2. A judgment dismissing a suit, when the plaintiff either abandons it or fails to establish a cause of action.

non·sup·port (non′sə·pôrt′, -pōrt′) *n.* Failure to provide for the support of a legal dependent.

non trop·po (non trŏp′ō) *Music* Not too much. [< Ital.]

non·un·ion (non-yōōn′yən) *adj.* 1. Not belonging to or associated with a trade union. 2. Not recognizing or contracting with any trade union; also, not employing the members of any union: *nonunion* shop. 3. Not produced or maintained by union labor.

non·un·ion·ism (non-yōōn′yən·iz′əm) *n.* Opposition to trade unions. — **non·un′ion·ist** *n.*

non·white (non′hwīt′) *n.* One who is not a member of the Caucasoid ethnic division of mankind. — *adj.* 1. Of or pertaining to nonwhites. 2. Not white.

noo·dle[1] (nōōd′l) *n.* 1. A simpleton. Also **noo′dle·head′** (-hed′). 2. *Informal* The head. [? < NOD]

noo·dle[2] (nōōd′l) *n.* A thin strip of dried dough, usu. containing egg, used in soup, etc. [< G *nudel*]

nook (nŏŏk) *n.* 1. An interior corner or angle, as in a room. 2. Any narrow or retired place, as a recess. [ME *nok* corner]

noon (nōōn) *n.* 1. The middle of the day; twelve o'clock in the daytime. 2. The highest or culminating point; zenith: the *noon* of life. — *adj.* Of, pertaining to, or occurring at or about noon. [OE < L *nona* (*hora*) ninth (hour)]

noon·day (nōōn′dā′) *n.* Noon. — *adj.* Of or at noon.

no one Not any person; nobody.

noon·time (nōōn′tīm′) *n.* 1. Midday. 2. The culminating point or period. Also *Archaic* **noon′tide′**. [OE *nōntīd*]

noose (nōōs) *n.* 1. A loop furnished with a running knot, as in a hangman's halter or a snare. 2. Anything that entraps, restrains, or binds. — *v.t.* **noosed**, **noos·ing** 1. To capture or secure with a noose. 2. To make a noose in or with. [< Provençal < L *nodus* knot]

Noot·ka fir (nōōt′kə) The Douglas fir.

no-par (nō′pär′) *adj.* Having no par or face value, as certain stock.

nope (nōp) *adv. Chiefly U.S. Slang* No.

nor (nôr) *conj.* And not; likewise not. ◆ *Nor* is used chiefly as a correlative of a preceding negative, as *neither*, *not*, or *never*: He is neither tall *nor* short; He has not come, *nor* will he. *Nor* is also used to introduce a clause following an affirmative clause: He hates me, *nor* does he hide it. [Contr. of ME *nother* neither]

Nor·dic (nôr′dik) *adj. Anthropol.* Pertaining or belonging to the tall, long-headed, blond-haired subdivision of the Caucasian ethnic stock, distributed mainly in NW Europe. — *n.* A Nordic person. [< NL *nordicus*]

nor′·east·er (nôr·ēs′tər), etc. See NORTHEASTER, etc.

Nor·folk jacket (nôr′fək) A loose-fitting men's jacket with a belt and two box pleats at the back and front.

no·ri·a (nō′rē·ə) *n.* An undershot water wheel having buckets on its rim to raise water, used in Spain and the Orient: also called *Persian wheel.* [< Sp. < Arabic *nā'ūrah*]

NORIA

norm (nôrm) *n.* 1. A pattern, model, or standard regarded as typical of a specified group. 2. *Psychol.* The standard of performance in a given function or test, usu. the average achievement based on the group concerned. 3. *Stat.* The mode. [< L *norma* rule]

nor·mal (nôr′məl) *adj.* 1. Conforming to or consisting of a pattern, process, or standard regarded as usual or typical; natural. 2. *Psychol.* a Well adjusted; without

nonlegal	nonmedical	nonnuclear	nonparental	nonplausible	nonproportional
nonlethal	nonmember	nonnucleated	nonparishioner	nonplutocratic	nonproprietary
nonlicensed	nonmercantile	nonnutrient	nonparliamentary	nonpoetic	nonprotection
nonlicentiate	nonmetaphysical	nonnutritious	nonparochial	nonpoisonous	nonprotective
nonlimiting	nonmeteoric	nonnutritive	nonparticipation	nonpolarizable	non-Protestant
nonliquefying	non-Methodist	nonobedient	nonpartisanship	non-Polish	non-Prussian
nonliquidation	nonmetrical	nonobligatory	nonpaternal	nonpolitical	nonpsychic
nonliterary	nonmetropolitan	nonobservable	nonpathogenic	nonporous	nonpublication
nonliturgical	nonmigratory	nonobservance	nonpaying	non-Portuguese	nonpulmonary
nonliving	nonmilitant	nonobservant	nonpayment	nonpredatory	nonpuncturable
nonlocal	nonmilitary	nonobstructive	nonpenalized	nonpredicative	nonpunishment
nonloving	nonmimetic	nonoccupational	nonperceptual	nonpredictable	nonpurulent
nonluminescent	nonmineral	nonoccurrence	nonperforated	nonpreferential	nonracial
nonluminosity	nonministerial	nonodorous	nonperforating	nonprehensile	nonradical
nonlustrous	nonmiraculous	nonoffensive	nonperformance	nonprejudicial	nonratable
non-Lutheran	nonmischievous	nonofficial	nonperiodical	nonprepositional	nonrated
nonmagnetic	nonmobile	nonoperating	nonperishable	non-Presbyterian	nonrational
non-Magyar	non-Mohammedan	nonoperative	nonpermanent	nonprescriptive	nonreactive
non-Malay	non-Mongolian	nonoptional	nonpermeability	nonpreservative	nonreality
nonmalignant	non-Moslem	nonorganic	nonpermeable	nonpresidential	nonreasonable
nonmalleable	nonmunicipal	non-Oriental	nonpermissible	nonpressure	nonreceptive
nonmarital	nonmuscular	nonorthodox	nonperpendicular	nonprevalent	nonreciprocal
nonmaritime	nonmystical	nonowner	nonperpetual	nonpriestly	nonrecognition
nonmarriageable	nonmythical	nonoxidizing	nonpersecution	nonproducer	nonrecourse
nonmarrying	nonnatural	nonoxygenated	nonperseverance	nonprofessional	nonrecoverable
nonmartial	nonnautical	nonpacific	nonpersistence	nonprofessorial	nonrectangular
nonmaterial	nonnaval	nonpagan	nonpersistent	nonproficiency	nonrecurrent
nonmaterialistic	nonnavigable	nonpalatal	nonphilanthropic	nonprofiteering	nonrecurring
nonmateriality	nonnecessity	nonpalatalization	nonphilosophical	nonprogressive	nonredeemable
nonmaternal	nonnegotiation	nonpapist	nonphysical	nonprohibitive	nonrefillable
nonmathematical	non-Negro	nonpar	nonphysiological	nonprolific	nonrefueling
nonmatrimonial	nonneutral	nonparallel	nonpigmented	nonpromiscuous	nonregenerating
nonmechanical	non-Norman	nonparalytic	nonplanetary	nonprophetic	nonregenerative
nonmechanistic	non-Norse	nonparasitic	nonplastic	nonpropitiation	nonregent

marked or persistent mental aberrations. **b** Of average skill, intelligence, etc. **3.** *Chem.* **a** Denoting a solution containing one gram equivalent weight of solute per liter: used as a unit, as *two normal, three normal,* etc. **b** Denoting a hydrocarbon having a straight, unbranched chain of carbon atoms: *normal* butane. **4.** *Math.* Perpendicular. — *n.* **1.** *Math.* A perpendicular; esp., a perpendicular to a tangent line or plane at the point of tangency. **2.** The common or natural condition, form, degree, etc. **3.** The usual or accepted rule or process. [< L < *norma* rule] — **nor'mal·cy, nor·mal·i·ty** (nôr·mǎl'ə·tē), **nor'mal·ness** *n.*

normal curve *Stat.* A bell-shaped curve representing the distribution of a series of values of a variable.

normal distribution *Stat.* A frequency distribution represented by a normal curve.

nor·mal·ize (nôr'məl·īz) *v.t.* **·ized, ·iz·ing** To bring into accord with a norm or standard form; make normal. — **nor'·mal·i·za'tion** *n.* — **nor'mal·iz'er** *n.*

nor·mal·ly (nôr'mə·lē) *adv.* **1.** As a rule; usually: The mail *normally* comes before noon. **2.** In a normal manner.

normal school A school that prepares secondary-school graduates to become teachers.

Nor·man (nôr'mən) *n.* **1.** One of the Scandinavian people who conquered Normandy in the tenth century. **2.** One of the people of mixed Scandinavian and French descent who conquered England in 1066. **3.** A resident of Normandy. **4.** Norman French. — *adj.* Of or pertaining to Normandy or the Normans. [< OF *Normans* Northmen]

Norman Conquest The subjugation of England by William the Conqueror in 1066. See table for WAR.

Norman French **1.** The dialect of French spoken by the Normans in the Middle Ages. **2.** The legal parlance of England from the Norman Conquest to the 17th century. **3.** The dialect of French spoken in Normandy. Also *Norman.*

nor·ma·tive (nôr'mə·tiv) *adj.* **1.** Of, pertaining to, or based upon a norm, esp. one regarded as a standard or rule of usage. **2.** Implying, supporting, or establishing a norm.

Norse (nôrs) *adj.* **1.** Scandinavian. **2.** Of or pertaining to Norway, Iceland, and the Faroe Islands; West Scandinavian. — *n.* **1.** The Scandinavians or West Scandinavians collectively: used with *the.* **2.** The Scandinavian or North Germanic group of the Germanic languages; esp., Norwegian. **3.** The West Scandinavian languages. — **Old Norse 1.** The ancestor of the North Germanic languages, best represented by Old Icelandic: also called *Old Scandinavian.* **2.** Old Icelandic: see under ICELANDIC. [< Du. < MDu. *nordsch, nortsch* northern]

Norse·man (nôrs'mən) *n.* *pl.* **·men** (-mən) A Scandinavian of Viking times.

north (nôrth) *n.* **1.** The direction along a meridian that falls to the left of an observer on earth facing the sun at sunrise. **2.** One of the four cardinal points of the compass, directly opposite *south* and 90° counterclockwise from *east.* See COMPASS CARD. **3.** Any direction near this point. **4.** *Sometimes cap.* Any region north of a specified point. — **the North** In the U.S.: **a** The population or territory of the northern or northeastern States; esp., the region north of Maryland, the Ohio River, and Missouri. **b** The Free States op-

posed to the Confederacy (*the South*) in the Civil War. — *adj.* **1.** To, toward, facing, or in the north. **2.** Coming from the north. — *adv.* In or toward the north. [OE]

North American Indian An Indian of any of the tribes formerly inhabiting North America north of Mexico, now the United States and Canada. Abbr. *N.Am.Ind.*

North Atlantic Drift The terminal current of the Gulf Stream system, flowing from near Newfoundland northeast to Western Europe. Also **North Atlantic Current.**

North Atlantic Treaty Organization A military and naval alliance of Belgium, Canada, Denmark, France, Greece, Iceland, Italy, Luxemburg, the Netherlands, Norway, Portugal, Turkey, the United Kingdom, the U.S., and West Germany, organized under the **North Atlantic Treaty** of Washington, Apr. 4, 1919. Abbr. *NATO*

north·bound (nôrth'bound') *adj.* Going northward. Also **north'-bound'.**

north·east (nôrth'ēst', *Naut.* nôr·ēst') *n.* **1.** The direction midway between north and east. **2.** A point on the mariner's compass, four points or 45° clockwise from due north. See COMPASS CARD. **3.** Any region lying in or toward this point. — *adj.* **1.** To, toward, facing, or in the northeast. **2.** Coming from the northeast. — *adv.* In or toward the northeast. — **north'east'ern** *adj.*

north·east·er (nôrth'ēs'tər, *Naut.* nôr·ēs'tər) *n.* **1.** A gale or storm from the northeast. **2.** A sailor's hat with a sloping brim worn in stormy weather. Also spelled *nor'easter.*

north·east·er·ly (nôrth'ēs'tər·lē, *Naut.* nôr·ēs'tər·lē) *adj.* **1.** In, of, or toward the northeast. **2.** From the northeast, as a wind. — *adv.* Toward or from the northeast. — *n.* A wind or storm from the northeast. Also spelled *nor'easterly.*

north·east·ward (nôrth'ēst'wərd, *Naut.* nôr·ēst'wərd) *adv.* Toward the northeast. Also **north'east'wards** (-wərdz). — *adj.* To, toward, facing, or in the northeast. — *n.* Northeast.

north·east·ward·ly (nôrth'ēst'wərd·lē, *Naut.* nôr·ēst'wərd·lē) *adj. & adv.* Toward or from the northeast.

north·er (nôr'thər) *n.* **1.** A gale or storm from the north. **2.** *U.S.* A violent, cold north wind blowing over the plains of the SW States.

north·er·ly (nôr'thər·lē) *adj.* **1.** In, of, toward, or pertaining to the north. **2.** From the north, as a wind. — *adv.* Toward or from the north. — *n.* A wind or storm from the north. — **north'er·li·ness** *n.*

north·ern (nôr'thərn) *adj.* **1.** To, toward, or in the north. **2.** Native to or inhabiting the north: a *northern* species. **3.** *Sometimes cap.* Of, pertaining to, or characteristic of the north or the North. **4.** From the north, as a wind.

north·ern·er (nôr'thər·nər) *n.* **1.** One who is native to or lives in the north. **2.** *Usu. cap.* One who lives in or comes from the North.

northern lights The aurora borealis.

north·ern·most (nôr'thərn·mōst') *adj.* Farthest north.

Northern Spy A large, yellowish red variety of apple.

north·land (nôrth'lond) *n.* A land or region in the north. [OE] — **north'land·er** *n.*

North·man (nôrth'mən) *n.* *pl.* **·men** (-mən) A Scandinavian; esp., a Scandinavian of the Viking period. [OE]

North Star Polaris.

nonregimented	nonrevertible	non-Semitic	nonspeculative	nonsymptomatic	nonunited
nonregistered	nonrevival	nonsensitive	nonspherical	nonsynchronous	nonuniversal
nonreigning	nonrevolving	nonsensitized	nonspiritual	nonsyntactical	nonuser
nonrelative	nonrhetorical	nonsensual	nonspontaneous	nonsynthesized	nonuterine
nonrelevant	nonrhymed	nonsensuous	nonstainable	nonsystematic	nonutilitarian
nonreligious	nonrhythmic	nonsentient	nonstandardized	nontarnishable	nonutilization
nonremunerative	nonritual	nonseparable	nonstarter	nontaxable	nonvalidity
nonrenewable	nonrival	nonservile	nonstarting	nonteachable	nonvascular
nonpayable	non-Roman	nonsexual	nonstatic	nontechnical	nonvegetative
nonrepentant	nonromantic	non-Shakespearean	nonstationary	nontemporal	nonvenereal
nonrepetition	nonrotating	nonsharing	nonstatistical	nontemporizing	nonvenomous
nonrepetitive	nonroyal	nonshattering	nonstatutory	nonterminating	nonvenous
nonreprehensible	nonruminant	nonshatterproof	nonstimulating	nonterrestrial	nonverbal
nonrepresentative	nonrural	nonshrinkable	non-Stoic	nonterritorial	nonvesicular
nonreproductive	non-Russian	nonsignificant	nonstrategic	nontextual	nonviable
nonresemblance	nonrusting	nonsilver	nonstretchable	nontheatrical	nonvibratory
nonresidential	nonsacramental	nonsimplification	nonstriker	nontheological	nonviolation
nonresidual	nonsacred	nonsinkable	nonstriking	nontherapeutic	nonviolence
nonresinous	nonsacrificial	non-Slavic	nonstructural	nonthinking	nonvirulent
nonresisting	nonsalable	nonslipping	nonsubmissive	nontitular	nonviscous
nonresistive	nonsalaried	nonsmoker	nonsubscriber	nontoxic	nonvisiting
nonresolvable	nonsaturated	nonsmoking	nonsubstantial	nontraditional	nonvisual
nonresonant	non-Scandinavian	nonsocial	nonsuccessful	nontransferable	nonvitreous
nonrestraint	nonscheduled	nonsocialist	nonsuccessive	nontransitional	nonvocal
nonrestricted	nonscholastic	nonsocialistic	nonsulfurous	nontransparent	nonvocational
nonretention	nonscientific	nonsolid	nonsupporter	nontransposing	nonvolatile
nonretinal	nonscoring	nonsolvent	nonsupporting	nontributary	nonvolcanic
nonretiring	nonseasonal	nonsovereign	nonsustaining	nontropical	nonvolition
nonretraceable	nonsecretarial	nonsparing	non-Swedish	nontruth	nonvoluntary
nonretractile	nonsecretive	nonsparkling	nonsyllabic	nontuberculous	nonvortical
nonretrenchment	nonsecular	non-Spartan	nonsymbolic	nontypical	nonvoter
nonretroactive	nonsedentary	nonspecialized	nonsymmetrical	nontypographical	nonvoting
nonreturnable	nonseditious	nonspecific	nonsympathetic	nontyrannical	nonvulcanizable
nonrevealing	nonsegmented	nonspectacular	nonsympathizer	nonulcerous	nonworking
nonreversible	nonselective	nonspectral	nonsymphonic	non-Unitarian	nonyielding

North·um·bri·a (nôr·thum′brē·ə) An ancient Anglo-Saxon kingdom, extending from the Humber to the Firth of Forth.

North·um·bri·an (nôr·thum′brē·ən) *adj.* 1. Of or pertaining to Northumbria or to its inhabitants. 2. Of or pertaining to the Old English dialect used in Northumbria. — *n.* 1. A native or inhabitant of Northumbria. 2. The Old English Northumbrian dialect.

north·ward (nôrth′wərd, *Naut.* nôr′thərd) *adv.* Toward the north. Also **north·wards** (-wərdz). — *adj.* To, toward, facing, or in the north. — *n.* A northward direction or point; also, a northern part or region.

north·ward·ly (nôrth′wərd·lē, *Naut.* nôr′thərd·lē) *adj. & adv.* 1. Toward the north. 2. Coming from the north.

north·west (nôrth′west′, *Naut.* nôr·west′) *n.* 1. The direction midway between north and west. 2. A point on the mariner's compass, four points or 45° counterclockwise from due north. See COMPASS CARD. 3. Any region, lying in or toward this point. — *adj.* 1. To, facing, or in the northwest. 2. Coming from the northwest. — *adv.* In or toward the northwest. — **north·west′ern** *adj.*

north·west·er (nôrth′wes′tər, *Naut.* nôr·wes′tər) *n.* A gale or storm from the northwest: also spelled *nor'wester.*

north·west·er·ly (nôrth′wes′tər·lē, *Naut.* nôr·wes′tər·lē) *adj.* 1. In, of, or toward the northwest. 2. From the northwest, as a wind. — *adv.* Toward or from the northwest.

north·west·ward (nôrth′west′wərd, *Naut.* nôr·west′wərd) *adv.* Toward the northwest. Also **north·west′wards.** — *adj.* To, toward, or in the northwest. — *n.* Northwest.

north·west·ward·ly (nôrth′west′wərd·lē, *Naut.* nôr·west′·wərd·lē) *adj. & adv.* Toward or from the northwest.

Nor·way maple (nôr′wā) A tall European maple.

Nor·we·gian (nôr·wē′jən) *adj.* Of or pertaining to Norway, its people, or their language. — *n.* 1. A native or inhabitant of Norway. 2. The North Germanic language of Norway. [< Med.L < *nor*(thr) north + *vegr* way]

nor′·west·er (nôr·wes′tər), etc. See NORTHWESTER, etc.

nose (nōz) *n.* 1. The part of the face or forward end of an animal that contains the nostrils and the organ of smell, and that in man encloses cavities used in the respiratory process. ◆ Collateral adjectives: *nasal, rhinal.* 2. The sense of smell or the power of smelling; scent. 3. The ability to perceive or discover by or as if by the sense of smell: a *nose* for scandal. 4. Something resembling a nose, as a spout or nozzle. 5. *Aeron.* The forward part of an aircraft. 6. The prow of a ship. 7. *Informal* The nose (def. 1), considered as its owner's agent for prying or interfering: Keep your *nose* out of this. — **by a nose** *Slang* By a narrow margin. — **on the nose** *Slang* 1. Designating a racing bet on a horse, etc., to win. 2. Exactly; precisely. — **to pay through the nose** *Slang* To pay an excessively high price. — *v.* **nosed, nos·ing** *v.t.* 1. To nuzzle. 2. To make (one's way) carefully with the front end foremost. 3. To perceive or discover by or as if by smell; scent. — *v.i.* 4. To pry or interfere; snoop: with *around* or *about.* 5. To move forward, esp. carefully. 6. To smell; sniff. — **to nose out** To defeat by a narrow margin. [OE *nosu*]

nose·band (nōz′band′) *n.* The part of a bridle that passes over the nose of a horse: also called *nosepiece.*

nose·bleed (nōz′blēd′) *n.* Bleeding from the nose.

nose cone *Aerospace* The cone-shaped forward section of a rocket or missile, separable from the main body and carrying the payload, and able to withstand great heat.

nose-dive (nōz′dīv′) *v.i.* **-dived, -div·ing** To take a nose dive; plunge downward.

nose dive 1. A steep, downward plunge of an aircraft, nose end foremost. 2. Any steep, sudden drop.

nose·gay (nōz′gā′) *n.* A small bunch of flowers; bouquet. [< NOSE + GAY, in obs. sense "a pretty thing"]

nose·piece (nōz′pēs′) *n.* 1. Any piece or part, as of a helmet, that covers or protects the nose. 2. A noseband.

nos·ey (nō′zē) See NOSY.

nos·tal·gi·a (nos·tal′jə, -jē·ə) *n.* 1. A longing for familiar or beloved circumstances that are now remote or irrecoverable. 2. Any longing for something far away or long ago. 3. Severe homesickness. [< NL < Gk. *nostos* return home + *algos* pain] — **nos·tal′gic** *adj.*

nos·tril (nos′trəl) *n.* One of the external openings of the nose. [OE < *nos*(u) nose + *thyrel* hole]

nos·trum (nos′trəm) *n.* 1. A medicine of one's own preparation; also, a quack medicine. 2. A favorite remedy or plan. 3. A cure-all. [< L *noster* our own]

nos·y (nō′zē) *adj.* **nos·i·er, nos·i·est** *Informal* Prying; snooping; inquisitive: also spelled *nosey.*

not (not) *adv.* In no way, or to no extent or degree: used to note the absence, reverse, or opposite of something or to express negation, prohibition, or refusal. [OE < *ne* not + *ā* ever + *wiht* thing however small]

not- Var. of NOTO-.

no·ta·ble (nō′tə·bəl) *adj.* Worthy of note; remarkable; distinguished. — *n.* One who is distinguished, famous, etc. [< OF < L *nota* mark] — **no′ta·bil′i·ty** *n.* — **no′ta·ble·ness** *n.* — **no′ta·bly** *adv.*

no·ta·rize (nō′tə·rīz) *v.t.* **-rized, ·riz·ing** To attest to or authenticate as a notary public. — **no′ta·ri·za′tion** *n.*

no·ta·ry public (nō′tə·rē) *pl.* **no·ta·ries public** One who is legally authorized to administer oaths, certify contracts, etc. Also **notary.** — **no·tar′i·al** (-târ′ē·əl) *adj.*

no·ta·tion (nō·tā′shən) *n.* 1. A system of signs, figures, or abbreviations used for convenience in recording a quantity, relation, process, etc.: musical *notation*; algebraic *notation.* 2. The act or process of using notation. 3. A note or comment. [< L *notare* to note] — **no·ta′tion·al** *adj.*

notch (noch) *n.* 1. A V-shaped cut in a surface. 2. A nick cut into a stick, etc., as for keeping count. 3. A narrow passage between mountains; a defile. 4. *Informal* A degree; level: He is a *notch* above the others. — *v.t.* 1. To make a notch or notches in. 2. To record by or as if by notches; score. [Prob. ME < OF *oschier* to notch]

note (nōt) *n.* 1. *Often pl.* A brief record or summary of facts set down for future study or reference: to take *notes.* 2. A brief account or jotting to aid the memory. 3. *Music* **a** A symbol representing a tone or sound of a given duration and pitch. **b** A tone or sound of a definite pitch. **c** A key of the keyboard. 4. Any more or less musical sound, as the call of a bird. 5. Any distinctive vocal sound, as the cry of an animal. 6. A distinctive mark: a *note* of sadness; a *note* of spring in the air. 7. A piece of paper currency issued by a government or authorized bank and negotiable as money: a bank *note.* 8. A promissory note (which see). 9. A formal, written communication of an official or diplomatic nature. 10. A brief letter, esp. of an informal character. 11. *pl.* A record of impressions, observations, reflections, etc. 12. A marginal comment amending, criticizing, or explaining a passage in a book, etc.; annotation. 13. Distinction; importance; reputation: a gentleman of *note.* 14. Notice; attention: worthy of *note.* 15. *Archaic* or *Poetic* A melody or song. — *v.t.* **not·ed, not·ing** 1. To become aware of; observe. 2. To pay attention to; heed carefully: to *note* well. 3. To make special mention of. 4. To set down for remembering; make a note of. 5. To point out or indicate. [< OF < L *nota*] — **not′er** *n.*

note·book (nōt′bŏŏk′) *n.* 1. A book with blank pages on which notes may be entered. 2. A book in which notes of hand are registered; bill book.

not·ed (nō′tid) *adj.* 1. Well known by reputation; famous. 2. Taken note of. — **not′ed·ly** *adv.* — **not′ed·ness** *n.*

note paper Paper for writing notes or letters.

note·wor·thy (nōt′wûr′thē) *adj.* Remarkable; significant. — **note′wor′thi·ly** *adv.* — **note′wor′thi·ness** *n.*

noth·ing (nuth′ing) *n.* 1. Not anything; naught. 2. No part or element: He knew *nothing* of it. 3. One who or that which is of little or no importance. 4. Insignificance or unimportance: to rise from *nothing.* 5. Zero. 6. A state of nonexistence; also, that which is nonexistent. — **for nothing** 1. Without charge; free. 2. To no avail. 3. Without cause. — *adv.* In no degree; not at all: now only in the expression **nothing like.** [ME < OE *nān* thing]

noth·ing·ness (nuth′ing·nis) *n.* 1. The condition, quality, or fact of being nothing; nonexistence. 2. Utter worthlessness or insignificance. 3. That which is petty, trivial, or nonexistent. 4. Unconsciousness.

no·tice (nō′tis) *v.t.* **·ticed, ·tic·ing** 1. To pay attention to or become aware of. 2. To refer to or comment on. 3. To treat courteously or with favor. — *n.* 1. The act of noticing or observing. 2. Announcement; information; warning. 3. A formal announcement: to give *notice.* 4. A written or printed communication publicly displayed. 5. A short advertisement or review. 6. Respectful treatment; civility. [< OF < L *notitia* fame, renown]

no·tice·a·ble (nō′tis·ə·bəl) *adj.* 1. That can be noticed; perceptible. 2. Worthy of notice. — **no′tice·a·bly** *adv.*

no·ti·fi·ca·tion (nō′tə·fə·kā′shən) *n.* 1. The act of notifying. 2. Notice given. 3. A sign, advertisement, etc., by which notice is conveyed.

no·ti·fy (nō′tə·fī) *v.t.* **·fied, ·fy·ing** 1. To give notice to; inform. 2. *Chiefly Brit.* To make known. [< OF < L *notus* known + *facere* to make] — **no′ti·fi′er** *n.*

no·tion (nō′shən) *n.* 1. A general idea or impression; a vague conception. 2. An opinion, belief, or idea. 3. Intention; inclination. 4. *pl. U.S.* Small miscellaneous articles for sale. — Syn. See IDEA. See NOTIFY.

no·tion·al (nō′shən·əl) *adj.* 1. Pertaining to, expressing, or consisting of notions or concepts. 2. Existing in imagination only. — **no′tion·al·ly** *adv.*

noto- *combining form* Back. Also, before vowels, **not-.** [< Gk. *nōton* back]

no·to·chord (nō′tə·kôrd) *n. Biol.* In invertebrate embryos, a flexible rod of cells along the median line on the dorsal side, a precursor of the spinal column.

no·to·ri·e·ty (nō′tə·rī′ə·tē) *n. pl.* **·ties** 1. The state or character of being notorious. 2. One who or that which is notorious.

no·to·ri·ous (nō·tôr′ē·əs, -tō′rē-) *adj.* 1. Widely known and generally disapproved of or deplored. 2. Generally known; acknowledged. [< Med.L < *noscere* to know] — **no·to′ri·ous·ly** *adv.*

no-trump (nō′trump′) *n.* 1. In bridge, a bid calling for play without a trump suit. 2. Play without a trump suit. — *adj.* Of or denoting a bid or play of no-trump.

not·with·stand·ing (not′with·stan′ding, -with-) *prep.* In spite of: He left *notwithstanding* your orders. — *adv.* All the same; nevertheless: Though closely guarded, he escaped *notwithstanding.* — *conj.* In spite of the fact that; although. — **notwithstanding that** Although.

nou·gat (nōō′gət, *Fr.* nōō·gä′) *n.* A confection made with chopped almonds, pistachios, etc., mixed in a honey or sugar paste. [< F < Provençal]

nought (nôt) See NAUGHT.

noun (noun) *n. Gram.* 1. A word used as the name of a thing, quality, or action. 2. Anything that can be used either as subject, object, or appositive, as a noun clause. — *adj.* Of or pertaining to a noun or nouns: also **noun′al.** [< AF, OF < L *nomen* name] — **noun′al·ly** *adv.*

noun clause *Gram.* A dependent clause that functions as a noun in a sentence, as *Whoever finds my wallet* in *Whoever finds my wallet will be rewarded.*

nour·ish (nûr′ish) *v.t.* 1. To furnish food or other material to sustain the life and promote the growth of (a living plant or animal). 2. To support; maintain; foster. [< OF < L *nutrire* to nourish] — **nour′ish·a·ble** *adj.* — **nour′ish·er** *n.* — **nour′ish·ing·ly** *adv.*

nour·ish·ment (nûr′ish·mənt) *n.* 1. That which nourishes; nutriment. 2. The act of nourishing, or the state of being nourished.

nou·veau riche (nōō′vō′ rēsh′) *French pl.* **nou·veaux riches** (nōō′vō′ rēsh′) One who has recently become rich.

no·va (nō′və) *n. pl.* **·vae** (-vē) or **·vas** *Astron.* A star that suddenly flares up and fades away after a period of a few months or years. [< L, fem. of *novus* new]

nov·el (nov′əl) *adj.* New, strange, or unusual. — *n.* A fictional prose narrative of considerable length, usu. having an overall pattern or plot. [< F < Ital. < L *novus* new]

nov·el·ette (nov′əl·et′) *n.* A short novel: also *novella.*

nov·el·ist (nov′əl·ist) *n.* A writer of novels.

nov·el·is·tic (nov′əl·is′tik) *adj.* Of, pertaining to, characteristic of, or found in novels. — **nov′el·is′ti·cal·ly** *adv.*

nov·el·ize (nov′əl·īz) *v.t.* **·ized, ·iz·ing** To put into the form of a novel. — **nov′el·i·za′tion** *n.*

no·vel·la (nō·vel′ə, *Ital.* nō·vel′lä) *n. pl.* **·vel·las,** *Ital.* **·vel·le** (-vel′lā) 1. A short tale or narrative, usu. with a moral. 2. A novelette. [< Ital. See NOVEL.]

nov·el·ty (nov′əl·tē) *n. pl.* **·ties** 1. Something novel or unusual. 2. The quality of being novel or new. 3. *Usu. pl.* A small manufactured article.

No·vem·ber (nō·vem′bər) *n.* The eleventh month of the year, containing 30 days. [< L, ninth month (of the old Roman calendar) < *novem* nine]

no·ve·na (nō·vē′nə) *n.* In the Roman Catholic Church, devotions made on nine successive days, for some special religious purpose. [< Med.L < L *novem* nine]

nov·ice (nov′is) *n.* 1. A beginner in any occupation; an inexperienced person. 2. *Eccl.* One who enters a religious order or community on probation. [< F < L *novicius* new] — **Syn.** 1. *Novice* is a general term, often used as the official designation for those who have yet to demonstrate proficiency in a game or sport. *Beginner* is a homelier synonym for *novice,* sometimes implying depreciation; even more depreciatory is *tyro.*

no·vi·ti·ate (nō·vish′ē·it, -āt) *n.* 1. The state or period of being a novice. 2. *Eccl.* **a** The period of probation of a novice in a religious order or community. **b** The quarters occupied by such novices. 3. A novice (defs. 1 and 2). Also **no·vi′ci·ate.** [< F *novicat* or Med.L *novitiatus*]

No·vo·cain (nō′və·kān) *n.* Proprietary name for a brand of procaine used as a local anesthetic, less toxic than cocaine. Also **no′vo·cain, no′vo·caine, No′vo·caine.**

now (nou) *adv.* 1. At once. 2. At or during the present time. 3. Nowadays. 4. In the immediate past: He said so just *now.* 5. In the immediate future: He is going just *now.* 6. In such circumstances: *Now* we can be sure of getting home. 7. At this point in the proceedings, narrative, etc.: The war was *now* virtually over. — *conj.* Seeing that; since: *Now* that you've come, stay a while. — *n.* The present time, moment, or occasion. — **now and then** From time to time; occasionally: also **now and again.** [OE *nū*]

now·a·days (nou′ə·dāz′) *adv.* In the present time or age.

no·way (nō′wā′) *adv.* 1. In no way, manner, or degree. 2. *U.S. Dial.* By any means. Also **no′ways′** (-wāz′).

no·where (nō′hwâr′) *adv.* In no place; not anywhere. — *n.* No place. Also *U.S. Dial.* **no′wheres′** (-hwârz′).

no·wise (nō′wīz′) *adv.* In no manner or degree.

nox·ious (nok′shəs) *adj.* Causing or tending to cause injury to health or morals; hurtful. — **Syn.** See PERNICIOUS. [< L < *noxa* harm] — **nox′ious·ly** *adv.* — **nox′ious·ness** *n.*

noz·zle (noz′əl) *n.* A projecting spout or pipe serving as an outlet, as of a teapot, hose, or rifle. [Dim. of NOSE]

nth (enth) *adj.* 1. *Math.* Representing an ordinal equivalent to *n.* 2. Infinitely or indefinitely large (or small); most extreme: to the *nth* degree.

nu (nōō, nyōō) *n.* The thirteenth letter in the Greek alphabet (N, ν), corresponding to English *n.* See ALPHABET.

nu·ance (nōō·äns′, nōō′äns, nyōō′-; *Fr.* nü·äns′) *n.* A fine or subtle variation, as in color, tone, or meaning; gradation. [< F < OF *nuer* to shade < *nue* cloud]

nub (nub) *n.* 1. A knob or protuberance. 2. A small piece, as of coal. 3. *U.S. Informal* Core; gist. [Var. of KNOB]

nub·bin (nub′in) *n. U.S.* 1. An imperfectly developed fruit or ear of corn. 2. Anything small or stunted. [< NUB]

nub·ble (nub′əl) *n.* A small protuberance or lump; nub. [Dim. of NUB] — **nub′bly** *adj.*

Nu·bi·an (nōō′bē·ən, nyōō′-) *adj.* Of Nubia, its people, or their language. — *n.* 1. A native of Nubia; esp., a member of any of the tribes formerly ruling the territory between Egypt and Abyssinia. 2. The language of the Nubians.

nu·bile (nōō′bil, nyōō′-) *adj.* Ready or suitable for marriage: said of young women. [< L < *nubere* to wed] — **nu·bil′i·ty** *n.*

nu·cle·ar (nōō′klē·ər, nyōō′-) *adj.* 1. Of, pertaining to, or resembling a nucleus or nuclei. Also **nu′cle·al** (-klē·əl). 2. Of or using atomic energy: *nuclear* reactor. [< F *nucléaire*]

nuclear family A family consisting of parents and child or children considered as a discrete group.

nuclear fission *Physics* Fission.

nuclear fusion *Physics* Fusion.

nuclear physics The branch of physics that investigates the structure and properties of the atomic nucleus.

nuclear reaction *Physics* A change in the properties of one or more atomic nuclei, esp. as a result of a collision between two nuclei.

nu·cle·ase (nōō′klē·ās, nyōō′-) *n. Biochem.* An enzyme that hydrolyzes nucleic acids.

nu·cle·ate (nōō′klē·āt, nyōō′-) *adj.* Having a nucleus. — *v.t. & v.i.* **·at·ed, ·at·ing** To form or gather into a nucleus. [< L *nucleare* to form a kernel] — **nu′cle·a′tion** *n.*

nu·cle·ic acid (nōō·klē′ik, nyōō-) *Biochem.* Any of a group of complex noncrystalline acids derived from nucleoproteins and containing carbohydrates combined with phosphoric acids and bases derived from purine or pyrimidine.

nu·cle·in (nōō′klē·in, nyōō′-) *n. Biochem.* A colorless, amorphous protein containing nucleic acid, found as a normal constituent of cell nuclei.

nucleo- *combining form* Nucleus. [< L *nucleus* kernel]

nu·cle·o·late (nōō′klē·ə·lāt, nyōō′-) *adj.* Having a nucleolus or nucleoli. Also **nu′cle·o·lat′ed.**

nu·cle·o·lus (nōō·klē′ə·ləs, nyōō′-) *n. pl.* **·li** (-lī) *Biol.* A rounded body sometimes found within the nucleus of a cell. Also **nu′cle·ole** (-ōl). For illus. see CELL. [< L, dim. of NUCLEUS] — **nu·cle′o·lar** *adj.*

nu·cle·on (nōō′klē·on, nyōō′-) *n. Physics* Any of the particles composing the nucleus of an atom, as the proton, neutron, neutrino, etc.

nu·cle·on·ics (nōō′klē·on′iks, nyōō′-) *n.pl.* (*usually construed as sing.*) The practical applications of nuclear physics in any field of science, engineering, or technology. — **nu′cle·on′ic** *adj.*

nu·cle·o·plasm (nōō′klē·ə·plaz′əm, nyōō′-) *n. Biol.* The protoplasm of a cell nucleus. — **nu′cle·o·plas′mic** *adj.*

nu·cle·o·pro·te·in (nōō′klē·ə·prō′tē·in, -tēn, nyōō′-) *n. Biochem.* Any of a class of substances found in the nuclei of plant and animal cells, containing one or more protein molecules combined with nucleic acid.

nu·cle·us (nōō′klē·əs, nyōō′-) *n. pl.* **·cle·i** (-klē·ī) 1. A central point or part around which other things are gathered; core. 2. A center of growth or development. 3. *Biol.* A complex spherical body surrounded by a thin membrane and embedded in the protoplasm of most plant and animal cells, containing chromatin and essential to the processes of heredity and to other vital activities of the cell. For illus. see CELL. 4. *Astron.* The brightest portion in the head of a comet or in the center of a nebula. 5. *Physics* The central core of an atom, containing nucleons that provide its effective mass and carrying a positive electric charge balanced by the negative charge of the surrounding electrons. 6. *Chem.* A group or ring of atoms so related structurally that their fundamental arrangement remains intact through a series of chemical changes. [Contr. of L *nuculeus,* dim. of *nux, nucis* nut]

nu·clide (nōō′klīd, nyōō′-) *n. Physics* A specific, relatively stable atom as defined by the composition and properties of its nucleus.

nude (nōōd, nyōōd) *adj.* Without clothing or covering; naked. — *n.* **1.** A nude figure, esp. in painting, sculpture, etc. **2.** The state of being nude. [< L *nudus* naked, bare] — **nude**/**ly** *adv.* — **nude**/**ness** *n.*

nudge (nuj) *v.t.* **nudged, nudg·ing** To touch or push gently, as with the elbow, in order to attract attention, etc. — *n.* A gentle push, as with the elbow. [? < Scand.]

nudi– *combining form* Without covering; naked; bare. [< L *nudus* naked]

nud·ism (nōō/diz·əm, nyōō/-) *n.* The doctrine or practice of living in the state of nudity.

nud·ist (nōō/dist, nyōō/-) *n.* One who believes in or practices nudism. — *adj.* Of or pertaining to nudism.

nu·di·ty (nōō/də·tē, nyōō/-) *n. pl.* **·ties 1.** The state or fact of being nude. **2.** A naked part; anything uncovered.

nud·nik (nōōd/nik) *n. U.S. Slang* A pestiferous or annoying person. Also **nud/nick.** [< Yiddish]

nug·get (nug/it) *n.* A lump; esp., a lump of gold found in its native state. [? Dim. of dial. E *nug* lump]

nui·sance (nōō/səns, nyōō/-) *n.* Anything that annoys, bothers, or irritates. [< F < *nuire* to harm]

nuisance tax A tax on various consumer goods and services, etc., regarded as more of a bother than a burden.

null (nul) *adj.* **1.** Of no legal force or effect; void; invalid. **2.** Nonexistent; negative. **3.** Of no avail; useless. — **null and void** Without legal force or effect. [< L < *ne* not + *ullus* any]

nul·li·fi·ca·tion (nul/ə·fə·kā/shən) *n.* **1.** The act of nullifying, or the state of being nullified. **2.** In U.S. history, the refusal of a State to obey an act of Congress, or the doctrine that such refusal is legal.

nul·li·fy (nul/ə·fī) *v.t.* **·fied, ·fy·ing 1.** To make useless or ineffective; undo. **2.** To deprive of legal force or effect. — **Syn.** See ANNUL. [< LL < *nullus* none + *facere* to make] — **nul/li·fi/er** *n.*

nul·li·ty (nul/ə·tē) *n. pl.* **·ties 1.** The state of being null. **2.** That which is null.

numb (num) *adj.* **1.** Having no sensation; without feeling. **2.** Unable to move. — *v.t.* To make numb. [ME < OE < *niman* to take] — **numb/ly** *adv.* — **numb/ness** *n.*

num·ber (num/bər) *n.* **1.** A specific quantity or place in a sequence, usu. designated by one of a series of symbols or words called *numerals.* **2.** A symbol or word used to designate number; a numeral. **3.** *Often pl.* A sizable collection or grouping: *numbers* of people. **4.** An indefinite quantity or collection: a *number* of facts. **5.** A specific sum or total count. **6.** *pl.* A large group; multitude. **7.** One of a series of things to which numbers are assigned: the March *number* of a magazine. **8.** A part of a program of music or entertainment. **9.** Quantity, as composed of units. **10.** A particular group, esp. of a privileged character. **11.** *Gram.* The representation in a language, by inflection or otherwise, of singleness or plurality. English has the singular and the plural number. **12.** *pl.* In poetry, metrical feet or rhythm; also, verse or verses. **13.** *Informal* An item or article, as of merchandise. Symbol #. — **any number of** A good many; rather a lot. — **beyond** (or **without**) **number** Too numerous to be counted. — **to get** (or **have**) **one's number** *Informal* To have insight into a person's motives, character, etc. — *v.t.* **1.** To determine the total number of; reckon. **2.** To assign a number to. **3.** To include as one of a collection or group. **4.** To amount to; total. **5.** To set or limit the number of. **6.** To be (a number of years, etc.) old or older. — *v.i.* **7.** To make a count; total. **8.** To be included, as in a particular group. **9.** To count off or call out numbers. [< OF < L *numerus*] — **num/ber·er** *n.*

num·ber·less (num/bər·lis) *adj.* **1.** Very numerous; countless. **2.** Having no number.

Num·bers (num/bərz) *n.pl.* (construed as sing.) The fourth book of the Old Testament.

num·bles (num/bəlz) *n.pl. Archaic* The entrails of an animal, as a deer. [< OF, ult. < LL *lumbellus*, dim. of L *lumbus* loin]

numb·skull (num/skul/) See NUMSKULL.

nu·mer·a·ble (nōō/mər·ə·bəl, nyōō/-) *adj.* That can be numbered. [< L *numerare* to count]

nu·mer·al (nōō/mər·əl, nyōō/-) *n.* A symbol, letter, or word that is used alone or in combination with others to express a number. — *adj.* **1.** Used in expressing or representing a number. **2.** Of or pertaining to number. [< LL < *numerus* number] — **nu/mer·al·ly** *adv.*

nu·mer·ate (nōō/mə·rāt, nyōō/-) *v.t.* **·at·ed, ·at·ing 1.** To enumerate; count. **2.** To read, as a numerical expression. [< L *numerare* to number]

nu·mer·a·tion (nōō/mə·rā/shən, nyōō/-) *n.* **1.** The act, process, or system of reading or naming numbers. **2.** An instance or example of this.

nu·mer·a·tor (nōō/mə·rā/tər, nyōō/-) *n. Math.* The term

of a fraction indicating how many of the parts of a unit are to be taken. In a common fraction it appears above or to the left of the line. **2.** One who or that which numbers.

nu·mer·i·cal (nōō·mer/i·kəl, nyōō-) *adj.* **1.** Of or denoting number. **2.** Numerable. **3.** Represented by or consisting of numbers or figures rather than letters. [< NL < L *numerus* number] — **nu·mer/i·cal·ly** *adv.*

nu·mer·ous (nōō/mər·əs, nyōō/-) *adj.* Consisting of a great number of units; being many. — **nu/mer·ous·ly** *adv.* — **nu/mer·os/i·ty** (nōō/mə·ros/ə·tē, nyōō/-), **nu/mer·ous·ness** *n.*

Nu·mid·i·a (nōō·mid/ē·ə, nyōō-) An ancient kingdom and Roman province in northern Africa. — **Nu·mid/i·an** *adj. & n.*

nu·mis·mat·ics (nōō/miz·mat/iks, -mis-, nyōō/-) *n.pl.* (construed as sing.) The study of coins, medals, and related objects, as paper money. [< F < L *numisma* coin < Gk. < *nomos* law] — **nu/mis·mat/ic** *adj.* — **nu·mis/ma·tist** *n.*

num·skull (num/skul/) *n.* A blockhead; dunce: also spelled *numbskull.*

nun (nun) *n.* A woman belonging to a religious order and living in a convent under vows of poverty, chastity, and obedience. [OE < LL *nonna* child's nurse, fem. of *nonnus*, orig., old man] — **nun/nish** *adj.*

nun·ci·o (nun/shē·ō, -sē·ō, nōōn/-) *n. pl.* **·ci·os** A permanent diplomatic envoy of the Pope to a foreign government. — **Syn.** See AMBASSADOR. [< Ital. < L *nuntius* messenger]

nun·ner·y (nun/ər·ē) *n. pl.* **·ner·ies** A convent for nuns.

nun's veiling (nunz) A soft, thin fabric, usu. of worsted, used for veiling and as a dress material.

nup·tial (nup/shəl) *adj.* Of or pertaining to marriage or the marriage ceremony. — *n. Usu. pl.* A marriage or wedding. [< L *nubere* to marry] — **nup/tial·ly** *adv.*

nurse (nûrs) *n.* **1.** A person who cares for the sick, injured, or infirm; esp., one who is trained to do such work. **2.** One who is a graduate of a school of nursing. **3.** A nursemaid. **4.** One who or that which fosters, nourishes, protects, or promotes. — *v.* **nursed, nurs·ing** *v.t.* **1.** To take care of (the sick, injured, or infirm). **2.** To feed (an infant) at the breast; suckle. **3.** To promote the growth and development of; foster; cherish. **4.** To feed and care for, as a child. **5.** To take steps to cure. **6.** To use or operate carefully: to *nurse* a weak wrist. **7.** To preserve or prolong deliberately. **8.** To fondle. **9.** To suckle at the breast of. — *v.i.* **10.** To act or serve as a nurse. **11.** To take nourishment from the breast. **12.** To suckle an infant. [Earlier *nurice* < OF < LL < L *nutrix* nursing mother] — **nurs/er** *n.*

nurse·maid (nûrs/mād/) *n.* A woman employed to care for children. Also **nurs·er·y·maid** (nûr/sər·ē·mād/, nûrs/rē-).

nurs·er·y (nûr/sər·ē, nûrs/rē) *n. pl.* **·er·ies 1.** A place where trees, shrubs, etc., are raised, as for sale. **2.** A room or area set apart for the use of children. **3.** A nursery school. **4.** Anything that fosters, breeds, or develops.

nurs·er·y·man (nûr/sər·ē·mən, nûrs/rē-) *n. pl.* **·men** (-mən) One who raises or cultivates plants in a nursery.

nursery rhyme A simple story, riddle, proverb, etc., presented in rhymed verse or jingle for children.

nursery school A place where children of preschool age regularly meet for training and supervised play.

nursing home A residence for persons who are unable to care for themselves, as the aged or the infirm.

nurs·ling (nûrs/ling) *n.* **1.** An infant or animal in the stage of being nursed. **2.** Anything that is carefully tended or supervised. Also **nurse/ling.**

nur·ture (nûr/chər) *n.* **1.** That which nourishes; food; sustenance. **2.** Training; breeding; education. — *v.t.* **·tured, ·tur·ing 1.** To feed or support; nourish; rear. **2.** To bring up or train; educate. [< OF < LL < L *nutrire* to nourish]

nut (nut) *n.* **1.** A dry fruit consisting of a kernel or seed enclosed in a woody shell, as a walnut, pecan, acorn, etc. **2.** The kernel of such fruit, esp. when edible. **3.** A small block of metal having an internal screw thread so that it may be fitted upon a bolt, screw, or the like. **4.** A person or matter difficult to deal with; a problem. **5.** *U.S. Slang* A crazy, irresponsible, or eccentric person. **6.** *Slang* The head. **7.** *Usu. pl. Slang* A testicle. — *v.i.* **nut·ted, nut·ting** To gather nuts. [OE *hnutu*] — **nut/ter** *n.*

nut·brown (nut/broun/) *adj.* Of a dark shade of brown suggesting the color of certain nuts, as the walnut.

nut·crack·er (nut/krak/ər) *n.* **1.** *Sometimes pl.* A device for cracking the hard shells of nuts. **2.** Any of certain crow-like birds, as the common nutcracker of Europe.

nut·gall (nut/gôl/) *n.* A nut-shaped gall, as on an oak tree.

nut·hatch (nut/hach/) *n.* A small, short-tailed bird related to the titmouse and feeding on nuts.

nut·meg (nut/meg) *n.* **1.** The aromatic kernel of the fruit of various tropical trees, esp. of the nutmeg tree of the Molucca Islands. **2.** The tree itself. [ME < OF < *nois* nut + *mugue* musk]

Nutmeg State Nickname of Connecticut.

nut·pick (nut′pik′) *n.* A small, sharp-pointed instrument for picking out the kernels of nuts.

nu·tri·a (nōō′trē·ə, nyōō′-) *n.* The soft brown fur of the coypu, often dyed to resemble beaver. [< Sp., otter]

nu·tri·ent (nōō′trē·ənt, nyōō′-) *adj.* 1. Giving nourishment; nutritious. 2. Conveying nutriment. — *n.* Something that nourishes; food. [< L < *nutrire* to nourish]

nu·tri·ment (nōō′trə·mənt, nyōō′-) *n.* 1. That which nourishes; food. 2. Anything that promotes development. [< L < *nutrire* to nourish] — **nu′tri·men′tal** *adj.*

nu·tri·tion (nōō·trish′ən, nyōō-) *n.* 1. The act or process of nourishing; esp., the processes by which food is converted into tissue in living organisms. 2. That which nourishes. [< L < *nutrire* to nourish] — **nu·tri′tion·al** *adj.* — **nu·tri′tion·al·ly** *adv.* — **nu·tri′tion·ist** *n.*

nu·tri·tious (nōō·trish′əs, nyōō-) *adj.* Promoting growth and repairing the waste of living organisms; nourishing. — **nu·tri′tious·ly** *adv.* — **nu·tri′tious·ness** *n.*

nu·tri·tive (nōō′trə·tiv, nyōō′-) *adj.* 1. Having nutritious properties. 2. Of or relating to nutrition. — **nu′tri·tive·ly** *adv.* — **nu′tri·tive·ness** *n.*

nuts (nuts) *Chiefly U.S. Slang adj.* 1. Crazy; demented; eccentric. 2. Extremely enthusiastic or in love: with *about.* — *interj.* An exclamation of contempt, disappointment, etc. [< pl. of NUT]

nut·shell (nut′shel′) *n.* The shell of a nut. — **in a nutshell** In brief and concise statement or form.

nut·ty (nut′ē) *adj.* **·ti·er, ·ti·est** 1. Abounding in or producing nuts. 2. Having the flavor of nuts. 3. *Chiefly U.S. Slang* Crazy; nuts. — **nut′ti·ly** *adv.* — **nut′ti·ness** *n.*

nux vom·i·ca (nuks′ vom′i·kə) 1. The silky disklike seed of an Indian tree containing strychnine and other poisons. 2. The tree itself. [< L *nux* nut + *vomere* to vomit]

nuz·zle (nuz′əl) *v.* **·zled, ·zling** *v.i.* 1. To rub, press, or dig with or as with the nose. 2. To nestle or snuggle; lie close. — *v.t.* 3. To push or rub the nose, etc., into or against. 4. To root up with the nose or snout. [Freq. of NOSE, v.]

nycto- *combining form* Night; nocturnal. Also, before vowels, **nyct-**. Also **nycti-**. [< Gk. *nyx, nyktos* night]

ny·lon (nī′lon) *n.* 1. A synthetic material yielding fibers and bristles of great toughness, strength, and elasticity; esp., cloth made from these fibers. 2. *pl. Informal* Stockings made of nylon. [< *Nylon*, a trade name]

nymph (nimf) *n.* 1. In Greek and Roman mythology, any of a class of minor female divinities dwelling in groves, forests, fountains, etc. 2. *Chiefly Poetic.* A young woman or girl. 3. *Entomol.* The young of an insect undergoing incomplete metamorphosis, at which stage the wing pads are first evident: also **nym·pha** (nim′fə). [< OF < L < Gk. *nymphē* nymph, bride] — **nymph′al, nym·phe·an** (nim·fē′·ən) *adj.*

nympho- *combining form* Nymph; bride. Also, before vowels, **nymph-**. [< Gk. *nymphē* bride, nymph]

nym·pho·ma·ni·a (nim′fə·mā′nē·ə, -mān′yə) *n. Psychiatry* An extreme and ungovernable sexual desire in women. — **nym′pho·ma′ni·ac** *adj. & n.*

Nyx (niks) In Greek mythology, the goddess of night.

O

o, O (ō) *n. pl.* **o's** or **os, O's** or **Os, oes** (ōz) 1. The fifteenth letter of the English alphabet. 2. Any sound represented by the letter *o.* 3. Anything shaped like an *O.* — *symbol* 1. *Math.* Zero or nought. 2. *Chem.* Oxygen.

o' (ō, ə) *prep.* Of: one o'clock, man-o'-war, jack-o'-lantern.

o- Var. of OB-.

O (ō) *interj.* 1. An exclamation used in direct address, as in prayer or invocation: *O Lord!* 2. An exclamation of surprise, disappointment, fear, longing, etc.: *O dear!* — *n. pl.* **O's** An exclamation or lamentation.

O' (ō) A descendant of: *O'Conor*: a patronymic prefix commonly used in Irish surnames, equivalent to the English and Scandinavian suffixes *-son, -sen.* Compare FITZ-, MAC-.

oaf (ōf) *n. pl.* **oafs** or *Rare* **oaves** (ōvz) A stupid, bungling person. [Earlier *auf* < ON *ālfr* elf] — **oaf′ish** *adj.* — **oaf′ish·ly** *adv.* — **oaf′ish·ness** *n.*

oak (ōk) *n.* 1. An acorn-bearing tree or shrub of the beech family, valued for the hardness, strength, and durability of its timber. ◆ Collateral adjective: *quercine.* 2. The wood of the oak. 3. Any of various plants resembling the oak. [OE *āc*] — **oak′en** *adj.*

oak apple A rounded gall produced on an oak by an insect. Also **oak gall.**

oak leaf cluster A bronze decoration given to holders of certain U.S. military medals in recognition of further merit.

oak·um (ō′kəm) *n.* Hemp fiber obtained by untwisting and picking out the fibers of old rope, used for caulking seams, etc. [OE *ācumba* < ā- out + *cemban* to comb]

oar (ôr, ōr) *n.* 1. A wooden implement for propelling or steering a boat, consisting of a long shaft with a blade at one end. 2. A person using an oar. 3. An oarlike part or appendage, as in certain worms. — *v.t.* 1. To propel with or as with oars; row. 2. To make (one's way) or traverse (water) with or as with oars. — *v.i.* 3. To proceed by or as by rowing; row. [OE *ār*]

oared (ôrd, ōrd) *adj.* Having or equipped with oars.

oar·lock (ôr′lok′, ōr′-) *n.* A device on the side of a boat for keeping an oar in place. Also, *Brit.,* **rowlock.**

oars·man (ôrz′mən, ōrz′-) *n. pl.* **·men** (-mən) One who rows.

o·a·sis (ō·ā′sis, ō′ə·sis) *n. pl.* **·ses** (-sēz) An area in a desert made fertile by groundwater or by irrigation. [< L < Gk.]

oat (ōt) *n.* 1. *Usu. pl.* A cereal grass widely cultivated for its edible grain. 2. *Usu. pl.* The grain itself. 3. Any similar grass, as the wild oat. 4. A musical pipe made from the stem of an oat. — **to feel one's oats** *Informal* 1. To be exuberant or high-spirited. 2. To feel bold or self-assured. — **to sow one's wild oats** *Informal* To experience the adventures and follies characteristic of youth. [OE *āte*] — **oat′en** *adj.*

oat·cake (ōt′kāk′) *n.* A thin, hard cake of oatmeal.

oath (ōth) *n. pl.* **oaths** (ōths, ō*th*s) 1. A formal declaration in support of a pledge or promise, usu. based on an appeal to God or some other higher institution or figure; also, the form of the declaration. 2. The careless or profane use of the name of God or other sacred person or thing. 3. A profane or vulgar utterance. [OE *āth*]

oat·meal (ōt′mēl′) *n.* A cereal food made from the cooked meal of oats; also, the meal itself. Also **oat meal.**

ob- *prefix* 1. Toward; to; facing: *obvert.* 2. Against; in opposition to: *object, obstruct.* 3. Over; upon: *obliterate.* 4. Completely: *obdurate.* 5. Inversely: prefixed to adjectives in scientific terms. Also: o- before *m*, as in *omit*; oc- before *c*, as in *occur*; of- before *f*, as in *offend*; op- before *p*, as in *oppress.* [< L *ob* toward, for, against]

O·ba·di·ah (ō′bə·dī′ə) Sixth-century B.C. minor Hebrew prophet. — *n.* A book of the Old Testament containing his prophecies.

ob·bli·ga·to (ob′lə·gä′tō, *Ital.* ōb′blē·gä′tō) *Music adj.* Denoting a part or accompaniment essential to the performance of a composition. — *n.* An obbligato part. Also spelled *obligato.* [< Ital. < L *obligare.* See OBLIGE.]

ob·du·rate (ob′dyə·rit, -rāt) *adj.* 1. Unmoved by or hardened against human feelings or moral influence; hardhearted. 2. Difficult to manage or manage; intractable. [< L < ob- against + *durare* to harden] — **ob′du·rate·ly** *adv.* — **ob′du·ra·cy** (-rə·sē) — **ob′du·rate·ness** *n.*

o·be·di·ence (ō·bē′dē·əns, ə·bē′-) *n.* The act of obeying, or the condition of being obedient; submission; compliance.

o·be·di·ent (ō·bē′dē·ənt, ə·bē′-) *adj.* 1. Complying with or conforming to a command, restraint, etc.; dutiful. 2. Deferring habitually to laws, superiors, etc.; docile; compliant. [See OBEY.] — **o·be′di·ent·ly** *adv.*

o·bei·sance (ō·bā′səns, ō·bē′-) *n.* Courtesy, reverence, or homage; also, an act or gesture expressing this: chiefly in phrases **to do (make, or pay) obeisance.** [< OF < *obeisant,* ppr. of *obeir* to obey] — **o·bei′sant** *adj.*

ob·e·lisk (ob′ə·lisk) *n.* 1. A square shaft of stone with a pyramidal top, usu. tapering, and often used as a monument in ancient Egypt. 2. *Printing* The dagger sign (†), used as a mark of reference: also **ob·e·lus** (ob′ə·ləs). [< L < Gk. *obelos* a spit, hence pointed pillar] — **ob′e·lis′cal, ob′e·lis′koid** (-koid) *adj.*

O·ber·on (ō′bə·ron) In medieval legend and folklore, the king of the fairies, husband of Titania.

o·bese (ō·bēs′) *adj.* Very fat or corpulent. [< L *obesus* fat] — **o·bese′ly** *adv.*

o·bes·i·ty (ō·bē′sə·tē, ō·bes′ə-) *n.* The condition of being obese; corpulence. Also **o·bese′ness** *n.*

o·bey (ō·bā′, ə·bā′) *v.t.* **1.** To comply with or carry out the command, request, etc., of. **2.** To comply with or execute (a command, request, etc.). **3.** To be guided, controlled, or actuated by. — *v.i.* **4.** To be obedient; comply. [< OF < L *oboedire* to give ear, obey] — **o·bey′er** *n.*

ob·fus·cate (ob·fus′kāt, ob′fəs-) *v.t.* **·cat·ed, ·cat·ing 1.** To confuse or perplex; bewilder. **2.** To darken or obscure. [< L *obfuscare* to darken, obscure] — **ob′fus·ca′tion** *n.*

o·bi (ō′bē) *n.* A broad sash tied with a stylized bow or loop in the back, worn by Japanese women. [< Japanese *ōbi*]

o·bit (ō′bit) *n. Informal* An obituary.

ob·i·ter dic·tum (ob′ə·tər dik′təm) *Latin pl.* **ob·i·ter dic·ta** (dik′tə) **1.** *Law* A judicial opinion that is not binding. **2.** Any incidental remark.

o·bit·u·ar·y (ō·bich′ōō·er′ē) *n. pl.* **·ar·ies** A published notice of a person's death, usu. including a biographical sketch. — *adj.* Of or recording a death. [< Med.L < L *obitus* a going down, death]

ob·ject (əb·jekt′) *v.i.* **1.** To offer an argument in opposition or disagreement. **2.** To feel or state disapproval. — *v.t.* **3.** To offer in opposition or criticism. [< L < *ob-* towards, against + *jacere* to throw] — **ob·jec′tor** *n.*

ob·ject² (ob′jikt, -jekt) *n.* **1.** Anything that is or may be apprehended by the senses. **2.** The purpose or end of an action. **3.** One who or that which is the focus or center of thought, action, etc. **4.** *Gram.* **a** A substantive that receives or is affected by the action of the verb, called the **direct object** when it receives the direct action, as *pie* in *She gave him the pie*, and the **indirect object** when it receives the secondary action, as *him* in the same sentence. **b** A substantive following a preposition, as *mountain* in the phrase *on the mountain.* — **Syn.** See PURPOSE. [< Med.L *objectum* something thrown in the way]

object glass *Optics* An objective (*n.* def. 3).

ob·jec·ti·fy (əb·jek′tə·fī) *v.t.* **·fied, ·fy·ing** To make objective. — **ob·jec′ti·fi·ca′tion** *n.*

ob·jec·tion (əb·jek′shən) *n.* **1.** A statement or feeling of disagreement, opposition, etc. **2.** The cause or reason for disagreement, etc. **3.** The act of objecting.

ob·jec·tion·a·ble (əb·jek′shən·ə·bəl) *adj.* Deserving of disapproval; offensive. — **ob·jec′tion·a·bil′i·ty** *n.* — **ob·jec′tion·a·bly** *adv.*

ob·jec·tive (əb·jek′tiv) *adj.* **1.** Free from personal feelings, opinions, prejudice, etc.; unbiased. **2.** Pertaining to what is external to or independent of the mind; real: opposed to *subjective.* **3.** Treating of or stressing external or actual phenomena, as distinct from inner or imaginary feelings and thoughts. **4.** *Gram.* Denoting the case of the object of a transitive verb or preposition; accusative. **5.** Pertaining to a goal or end. — *n.* **1.** That which is striven for or aimed at; a goal; end. **2.** *Gram.* **a** The objective or accusative case. **b** A word in this case. **3.** *Optics* A lens or lenses, as in a telescope, that is nearest to the object being viewed: also called *object glass.* — **ob·jec′tive·ly** *adv.*

ob·jec·tiv·i·ty (ob′jek·tiv′ə·tē) *n.* **1.** The state or quality of being objective. **2.** Material reality. Also **ob·jec′tive·ness.**

object lesson An example of a principle or moral in a concrete form or striking instance.

ob·jet d'art (ôb·zhe′ där′) *French pl.* **ob·jets d'art** (ôb·zhe′) Any work of artistic value.

ob·jur·gate (ob′jər·gāt, əb·jûr′-) *v.t.* **·gat·ed, ·gat·ing** To rebuke severely; scold sharply. [< L < *ob-* against + *jurgare* to scold] — **ob′jur·ga′tion** *n.* — **ob′jur·ga′tor** *n.* — **ob·jur·ga·to·ri·ly** (ob·jûr′gə·tôr′ə·lē, -tō′rə·lē) *adv.* — **ob·jur·ga·to′ry** (-tôr′ē, -tō′rē) *adj.*

ob·late¹ (ob′lāt, ob·lāt′) *adj.* Flattened at the poles. [< NL < L *ob-* towards + (*pro*)*latus* lengthened out] — **ob′late·ly** (ob′lāt·lē, ob·lāt′-) *adv.*

ob·late² (ob′lāt, ob·lāt′) *adj.* Consecrated or devoted to a religious life. — *n.* A person so devoted, as in a monastery. [< Med.L *oblatus* < L, pp. of *offerre* to present]

ob·la·tion (ob·lā′shən) *n.* **1.** The act of offering religious worship, sacrifice, etc., esp. in the Eucharist. **2.** That which is offered, esp. the elements of the Eucharist. **3.** Any solemn offering. [See OBLATE².] — **ob·la′tion·al** *adj.* — **ob·la·to·ry** (ob′lə·tôr′ē, -tō′rē) *adj.*

ob·li·gate (ob′lə·gāt; for *adj.*, *also* -git) *v.t.* **·gat·ed, ·gat·ing** To bind or compel, as by contract, conscience, promise, etc. — *adj.* Bound or restricted. — **ob′li·ga·tor** *n.*

ob·li·ga·tion (ob′lə·gā′shən) *n.* **1.** The act of obligating, or the state of being obligated. **2.** The duty, promise, contract, etc., by which one is bound. **3.** Any duty or requirement. **4.** The constraining or binding power of a law, promise, conscience, etc. **5.** What one owes in return for a service, favor, etc.; also, the service or favor itself. [< OF < LL < L *obligare.* See OBLIGE.]

ob·li·ga·tive (ob′lə·gā′tiv) *adj.* Implying or expressing obligation.

ob·li·ga·to (ob′lə·gä′tō, *Ital.* ōb′blē·gä′tō) See OBBLIGATO.

ob·lig·a·to·ry (ə·blig′ə·tôr′ē, -tō′rē, ob′lə·gə-) *adj.* Of the nature of or constituting a duty or obligation; imperative.

o·blige (ə·blīj′) *v.t.* **o·bliged, o·blig·ing 1.** To place (one) under obligation, as for a service, favor, etc.: with *to.* **2.** To compel, bind, or constrain, as by command, promise, etc. **3.** To do a favor or service for. [< OF < L *obligare,* orig., to tie around] — **o·blig′er** *n.*

o·blig·ing (ə·blī′jing) *adj.* Disposed to do favors; accommodating; kind. — **o·blig′ing·ly** *adv.* — **o·blig′ing·ness** *n.*

ob·lique (ə·blēk′, *in military usage* ·ə·blīk′) *adj.* **1.** Deviating from the perpendicular or horizontal; slanting. **2.** Not direct or straightforward in meaning, expression, etc.: *oblique* praise. **3.** Indirectly aimed at or attained. **4.** *Geom.* Having an acute or obtuse angle. **5.** Not in the direct line of descent; collateral. — *n.* **1.** An oblique thing, as a line. **2.** *Naut.* The act of veering less than ninety degrees. — *v.i.* **·liqued, ·li·quing** To deviate from the perpendicular or horizontal; slant. [< L *obleiquus*] — **ob·lique′ly** *adv.* — **ob·liq·ui·ty** (ə·blik′wə·tē), **ob·lique′ness** *n.*

oblique angle *Geom.* An angle not a right angle; an acute or obtuse angle.

ob·lit·er·ate (ə·blit′ə·rāt) *v.t.* **·at·ed, ·at·ing 1.** To destroy utterly. **2.** To blot or wipe out, as writing. [< L < *obliterare* to efface] — **ob·lit·er·a′tion** *n.* — **ob·lit′er·a′tive** *adj.* — **ob·lit′er·a′tor** *n.*

ob·liv·i·on (ə·bliv′ē·ən) *n.* **1.** The state or fact of being completely forgotten. **2.** The state or fact of forgetting completely. [< OF < L < *oblivisci* to forget]

ob·liv·i·ous (ə·bliv′ē·əs) *adj.* **1.** Not conscious or aware; unmindful: with *of* or *to.* **2.** Forgetful or given to forgetfulness. [< L *obliviosus*] — **ob·liv′i·ous·ly** *adv.* — **ob·liv′i·ous·ness** *n.*

ob·long (ob′lông, -long) *adj.* Longer in one dimension than in another: said usually of rectangles. — *n.* An oblong figure, object, etc. [< L *oblongus* somewhat long]

ob·lo·quy (ob′lə·kwē) *n. pl.* **·quies 1.** Abusive and defamatory language, esp. by a large group of people; vilification. **2.** Disgrace resulting from such abuse. [< LL < *ob-* against + *loqui* to speak]

ob·nox·ious (əb·nok′shəs) *adj.* Highly disagreeable; objectionable; offensive. [< L < *ob-* towards + *nozius* harmful] — **ob·nox′ious·ly** *adv.* — **ob·nox′ious·ness** *n.*

o·boe (ō′bō, ō′boi) *n.* A double-reed woodwind instrument with a conical bore, having a high, penetrating tone. [< Ital. < F *hautbois.* See HAUTBOY.] — **o′bo·ist** *n.*

ob·scene (əb·sēn′, ob-) *adj.* **1.** Offensive or abhorrent to prevailing concepts of morality or decency; indecent; lewd. **2.** Disgusting; loathsome; foul. [< MF < L *obscenus* ill-omened, filthy] — **ob·scene′ly** *adv.* — **ob·scene′ness** *n.*

ob·scen·i·ty (əb·sen′ə·tē, -sē′nə-, ob-) *n. pl.* **·ties 1.** The quality or state of being obscene. **2.** Something obscene.

ob·scur·ant (əb·skyŏŏr′ənt) *n.* One who or that which obscures, esp. by opposing or hindering educational progress, free thought, etc. — *adj.* **1.** Causing obscurity. **2.** Of an obscurant. [< L *obscurare* to darken]

ob·scur·ant·ism (əb·skyŏŏr′ən·tiz′əm) *n.* **1.** The act or principles of an obscurant. **2.** Opposition to learning and inquiry. — **ob·scur′ant·ist** *n. & adj.*

ob·scure (əb·skyŏŏr′) *adj.* **·scur·er, ·scur·est 1.** Not clear or plain to the mind; hard to understand. **2.** Not clear or distinct to the senses, difficult to discern. **3.** Not readily discovered; hidden; remote. **4.** Without distinction or fame; inconspicuous. **5.** Having little or no light, dark. — *v.t.* **·scured, ·scur·ing 1.** To render obscure, vague, indefinite, etc. **2.** To cover or darken so as to make dim, indistinct, etc. [< OF < L *obscurus* covered over] — **ob·scure′ly** *adv.* — **ob·scure′ness** *n.*

ob·scu·ri·ty (əb·skyŏŏr′ə·tē) *n. pl.* **·ties 1.** The state or quality of being obscure. **2.** An obscure person or thing.

ob·se·quies (ob′sə·kwēz) *n.pl.* Funeral rites. [< OF *obseques* < Med.L *obsequiae,* pl. funeral rites]

ob·se·qui·ous (əb·sē′kwē·əs) *adj.* Excessively obedient or submissive; sycophantic; servile. [< L < *obsequi* to comply with] — **ob·se′qui·ous·ly** *adv.* — **ob·se′qui·ous·ness** *n.*

ob·serv·a·ble (əb·zûr′və·bəl) *adj.* **1.** Capable of being observed; noticeable. **2.** Worthy of notice or mention; noteworthy. **3.** That may or must be observed, as a holiday. — **ob·serv′a·bly** *adv.* — **ob·serv′a·ble·ness** *n.*

ob·ser·vance (əb·zûr′vəns) *n.* **1.** The act of observing a command, law, etc. **2.** The act of celebrating a holiday, ceremony, etc. **3.** A customary rite, ceremony, etc. **4.** Observation; notice; attention. **5.** *Eccl.* The rule or constitution of a religious order.

ob·ser·vant (əb·zûr′vənt) *adj.* **1.** Attentive or quick in observing; heedful; alert. **2.** Strict or careful in obeying or keeping a custom, law, ceremony, etc.: often with *of: observant* of ritual. — **ob·ser′vant·ly** *adv.*

ob·ser·va·tion (ob′zər·vā′shən) *n.* **1.** The act of observing, or the fact of being observed; also, that which is observed. **2.** Close examination for the purpose of scientific study. **3.** An opinion or judgment. **— to take (or work out) an observation** *Naut.* To calculate the latitude and longitude from the altitude and position of the sun or other celestial body. **— ob′ser·va′tion·al** *adj.* **— ob′ser·va′tion·al·ly** *adv.*

ob·ser·va·to·ry (əb·zûr′və·tôr′ē, -tō′rē) *n. pl.* **·ries 1.** A building or station for the systematic observation of natural phenomena; esp., one for astronomical observation. **2.** A place affording a panoramic view.

ob·serve (əb·zûrv′) *v.* **·served, ·serv·ing** *v.t.* **1.** To see or notice; perceive. **2.** To watch attentively. **3.** To make careful observation of, esp. for scientific purposes. **4.** To say or comment; remark. **5.** To follow or comply with (a law, custom, etc.); abide by. **6.** To celebrate as a holiday. **— v.i. 7.** To make a remark; comment: often with *on* or *upon.* **8.** To take notice. **9.** To look on or attend without taking part, as at a meeting. [< OF < L *observare* to watch] **— ob·serv′er** *n.* **— ob·serv′ing·ly** *adv.*

ob·sess (əb·ses′) *v.t.* To occupy or trouble the mind of to an excessive degree; preoccupy; harass; haunt. [< L *obsidere* to occupy, beseige] **— ob·ses′sive** *adj.* **— ob·ses′sor** *n.*

ob·ses·sion (əb·sesh′ən) *n.* **1.** That which obsesses, as a persistent idea or feeling. **2.** *Psychiatry* An unwanted or compulsive idea or emotion persistently coming to awareness. **3.** The act of obsessing, or the state of being obsessed.

ob·sid·i·an (əb·sid′ē·ən, ob-) *n.* A glassy volcanic rock, usu. black. [< L *obsidianus*]

ob·so·les·cent (ob′sə·les′ənt) *adj.* Growing obsolete. **— ob′so·les′cence** *n.* **— ob′so·les′cent·ly** *adv.*

ob·so·lete (ob′sə·lēt, ob′sə·lēt′) *adj.* **1.** Gone out of fashion; out-of-date. **2.** No longer used or practiced. **3.** *Biol.* Imperfectly developed; atrophied or vestigial. [< L *obsolescere* to wear out] **— ob′so·lete′ly** *adv.* **— ob′so·lete′ness** *n.* **— ob′so·let′ism** *n.*

— Syn. 1. An *obsolete* word is no longer used either in speech or writing, usually because it has been supplanted by a different word. *Archaic* words were current at some time in the past, and appear in the works of Shakespeare, the Bible, etc., but unlike obsolete words they are still used for effect because they have an unmistakable flavor of their period or milieu. *Rare* words may be *archaic* or current, but are little used.

ob·sta·cle (ob′stə·kəl) *n.* That which stands in the way; a hindrance or obstruction. [< OF < L *ob-* before, against + *stare* to stand]

ob·stet·ric (əb·stet′rik) *adj.* Of or pertaining to obstetrics or childbirth. Also **ob·stet′ri·cal.** [< L *obstetrix, -icis* midwife, lit., one who stands by] **— ob·stet′ri·cal·ly** *adv.*

ob·ste·tri·cian (ob′stə·trish′ən) *n.* A medical and surgical specialist in obstetrics.

ob·stet·rics (əb·stet′riks) *n.pl.* (*construed as sing.*) The branch of medicine dealing with pregnancy and childbirth.

ob·sti·na·cy (ob′stə·nə·sē) *n. pl.* **·cies 1.** The state or quality of being obstinate. **2.** An obstinate act, feeling, etc.

ob·sti·nate (ob′stə·nit) *adj.* **1.** Unreasonably fixed in one's purpose or opinion; unyielding; stubborn. **2.** Difficult to overcome or cure: an *obstinate* habit. [< L *obstinare* to persist] **— ob′sti·nate·ly** *adv.* **— ob′sti·nate·ness** *n.*

ob·strep·er·ous (əb·strep′ər·əs) *adj.* Unruly, noisy, or boisterous, esp. in resistance to control, advice, etc. [< L *ob-* towards + *strepere* to make noise] **— ob·strep′er·ous·ly** *adv.* **— ob·strep′er·ous·ness** *n.*

ob·struct (əb·strukt′) *v.t.* **1.** To stop or impede movement through (a way or passage) by obstacles or impediments; barricade. **2.** To block or retard the progress or way of; impede. **3.** To come or be in front of so as to prevent a clear view. [< L *ob-* before + *struere* to pile, build] **— ob·struct′er** *or* **ob·struc′tor** *n.* **— ob·struc′tive** *adj.* **— ob·struc′tive·ly** *adv.* **— ob·struc′tive·ness** *n.*

ob·struc·tion (əb·struk′shən) *n.* **1.** That which obstructs. **2.** The act of obstructing, or the state of being obstructed.

ob·struc·tion·ist (əb·struk′shən·ist) *n.* One who makes a practice of obstructing, esp. in politics, one who obstructs debate, legislation, etc. **— ob·struc′tion·ism** *n.*

ob·tain (əb·tān′) *v.t.* **1.** To gain possession of, esp. by effort; acquire; get. **— v.i. 2.** To be prevalent or in effect. **— Syn.** See GET. [< OF < L *ob-* towards + *tenere* to hold] **— ob·tain′a·ble** *adj.* **— ob·tain′er** *n.* **— ob·tain′ment** *n.*

ob·trude (əb·trōōd′) *v.* **·trud·ed, ·trud·ing** *v.t.* **1.** To thrust or force (oneself, an opinion, etc.) upon another without request or warrant. **2.** To push forward or out; eject. **— v.i. 3.** To intrude oneself. [< L *ob-* towards + *trudere* to thrust] **— ob·trud′er** *n.* **— ob·tru′sion** *n.*

ob·tru·sive (əb·trōō′siv) *adj.* Tending to obtrude. **— ob·tru′sive·ly** *adv.* **— ob·tru′sive·ness** *n.*

ob·tuse (əb·tōōs′, -tyōōs′) *adj.* **1.** Lacking acuteness of intellect or feeling; insensible. **2.** Not clear or distinct to the senses; dull, as a sound or pain. **3.** *Bot.* Blunt or rounded at the extremity, as a leaf or petal. [< L *obtusus* blunt, dulled] **— ob·tuse′ly** *adv.* **— ob·tuse′ness** *n.*

obtuse angle *Geom.* An angle greater than a right angle and less than a straight angle.

ob·verse (ob′vûrs; *for adj., also* ob·vûrs′) *adj.* **1.** Turned toward or facing one. **2.** Narrower at the base than at the apex: an *obverse* leaf. **3.** Constituting a counterpart. **— n. 1.** The front or principal side of anything; esp., the side of a coin bearing the main design or device: distinguished from *reverse.* **2.** A counterpart. [< L < *ob-* towards + *vertere* to turn] **— ob·verse′ly** *adv.*

ob·vi·ate (ob′vē·āt) *v.t.* **·at·ed, ·at·ing** To prevent or counter (an objection, difficulty, etc.) by effective measures; provide for. [< L *obviatus,* pp. of *obviare* to meet, withstand] **— Syn.** preclude, forestall, avert.

ob·vi·ous (ob′vē·əs) *adj.* **1.** Immediately evident; palpably true; manifest. **2.** Behaving without equivocation or subtlety. [< L < *ob-* before + *via* way] **— ob′vi·ous·ly** *adv.* **— ob′vi·ous·ness** *n.*

oc- Assimilated var. of OB-.

oc·a·ri·na (ok′ə·rē′nə) *n.* A small musical instrument in the shape of a sweet potato, with a mouthpiece and finger holes, and yielding soft, sonorous notes. [< Ital., dim. of *oca* goose < L *auca*; so called with ref. to its shape]

oc·ca·sion (ə·kā′zhən) *n.* **1.** The particular time of an event or occurrence; also, the event or occurrence itself. **2.** An important or extraordinary event. **3.** A favorable time or condition; opportunity. **4.** The immediate cause or grounds for some action or state: to give one *occasion* to complain. **5.** A need or requirement. **— on occasion** On suitable opportunity; now and then. **— to take the (this,** etc.) *occasion* To avail oneself of the (this, etc.) opportunity. **— v.t.** To cause or bring about, esp. in an accidental or incidental manner. [< L *ob-* towards + *cadere* to fall]

oc·ca·sion·al (ə·kā′zhən·əl) *adj.* **1.** Occurring, appearing, etc., irregularly or now and then. **2.** Made, intended, or suitable for a particular occasion: *occasional* verse. **3.** Pertaining to or designating a small chair, table, etc., that is not part of a set. **— oc·ca′sion·al·ly** *adv.*

oc·ci·dent (ok′sə·dənt) *n.* The west: opposed to *orient.* [< OF < L *occidens, -entis* region where the sun sets.]

Oc·ci·dent (ok′sə·dənt) **1.** The countries west of Asia; esp., Europe. **2.** The western hemisphere.

oc·ci·den·tal (ok′sə·den′təl) *adj.* Of or belonging to the west, or to the countries constituting the Occident: distinguished from *oriental.* **— n.** One born or living in a western country. Also **Oc′ci·den′tal.**

oc·cip·i·tal (ok·sip′ə·təl) *adj.* Pertaining to the occiput. **— n.** The occipital bone.

occipital bone *Anat.* The hindmost bone of the skull, between the parietal and temporal bones.

oc·ci·put (ok′sə·put, -pət) *n. pl.* **oc·cip·i·ta** (ok·sip′ə·tə) *Anat.* The lower back part of the skull. [< L, back of the head < *ob-* against + *caput* head]

oc·clude (ə·klōōd′) *v.* **·clud·ed, ·clud·ing** *v.t.* **1.** To shut up or close, as pores or openings. **2.** To shut in, out, or off. **3.** *Chem.* To take up, either on the surface or internally, but without change of properties. **4.** *Meteorol.* To displace, as a mass of warm air by an advancing front of cold air. **— v.i. 5.** *Dent.* To meet so that the corresponding cusps fit closely together: said of the teeth of the upper and lower jaws. [< L < *ob-* against + *claudere* to close] **— oc·clu′dent** *adj.* **— oc·clu·sion** (ə·klōō′zhən) *n.*

oc·clu·sive (ə·klōō′siv) *adj.* **1.** Characterized by or bringing about occlusion or closure. **2.** *Phonet.* Pertaining to a stop. **— n.** *Phonet.* A stop.

oc·cult (ə·kult′, ok′ult) *adj.* **1.** Of or pertaining to various magical arts and practices, as astrology, alchemy, etc. **2.** Beyond human understanding; mysterious. **3.** Not divulged or disclosed; secret. **— Syn.** See MYSTERIOUS. **— n.** Occult arts or practices: usu. with *the.* **— v.t.** To hide or conceal from view. **— v.i.** To become hidden or concealed from view. [< L *occultus,* pp. of *occulere* to cover over, hide] **— oc·cult′ism** *n.* **— oc·cult′ist** *n.* **— oc·cult′ly** *adv.*

oc·cul·ta·tion (ok′ul·tā′shən) *n.* *Astron.* Concealment of one celestial body by another interposed in the line of vision.

oc·cu·pan·cy (ok′yə·pən·sē) *n. pl.* **·cies 1.** The act of occupying, or the state of being occupied. **2.** *Law* The act of taking possession of something previously unowned. **3.** The condition of being an occupant or tenant. **4.** The time during which something is occupied.

oc·cu·pant (ok′yə·pənt) *n.* **1.** One who occupies a place, position, etc. **2.** A tenant. [See OCCUPY.]

oc·cu·pa·tion (ok′yə·pā′shən) *n.* **1.** One's regular, principal, or immediate business or job. **2.** The act of occupying, or the state of being occupied. **3.** The taking and holding of land by a military force: the *occupation* of Germany.

— Syn. 1. *Occupation* and *vocation* are general terms, meaning little more than line of work. A *profession* requires special knowledge and training: Law and medicine are *professions.* A *business* is usually industrial, commercial, or mercantile, but may also be general: the clothing *business,* the *business* of government. A *trade* requires manual skill, as does a *craft,* but the latter suggests a greater degree of skill and even artistic creation: the bricklayer's *trade*, the jeweler's *craft*.

oc·cu·pa·tion·al (ok'yə·pā'shən·əl) *adj.* Of, pertaining to, or caused by an occupation. **— oc'cu·pa'tion·al·ly** *adv.*

occupational therapy *Med.* The treatment of nervous, mental, or physical disabilities by means of work designed to promote recovery or readjustment.

oc·cu·py (ok'yə·pī) *v.t.* **·pied, ·py·ing** 1. To take and hold possession of, as by conquest. 2. To fill or take up (space or time). 3. To inhabit; dwell in. 4. To hold; fill, as an office or position. 5. To busy or engage; employ. [< OF < L < *ob-* against + *capere* to take] **— oc'cu·pi'er** *n.*

oc·cur (ə·kûr') *v.i.* **·curred, ·cur·ring** 1. To happen or take place; come about. 2. To be found or met with; appear. 3. To suggest itself; come to mind. [< L < *ob-* towards, against + *currere* to run]

oc·cur·rence (ə·kûr'əns) *n.* 1. The act or fact of occurring. 2. That which occurs; an event. **— oc·cur'rent** *adj.*

o·cean (ō'shən) *n.* 1. The great body of salt water that covers about 70 percent of the earth's surface. 2. *Often cap.* Any one of the divisions of this body of water, usu. reckoned as five, the Atlantic, Pacific, Indian, Arctic, and Antarctic. 3. A very large expanse or quantity. [< OF < L < Gk. *ōkeanos*]

ocean current Any of a large number of riverlike masses of water flowing in all oceans, each having a characteristic direction, length, depth, speed, and temperature.

o·ce·an·ic (ō'shē·an'ik) *adj.* 1. Of, relating to, or living in the ocean; pelagic. 2. Resembling an ocean; vast.

O·ce·an·ic (ō'shē·an'ik) *n.* A subfamily of the Austronesian family of languages, including the Melanesian languages of the Solomon Islands, Fiji, New Caledonia, the New Hebrides, etc., and the Micronesian group of languages.

o·ce·an·og·ra·phy (ō'shē·ən·og'rə·fē, ō'shən·og'-) *n.* The branch of physical geography that treats of oceanic life and phenomena. **— o'ce·an·og'ra·pher** *n.* **— o'ce·an·o·graph'ic** (-ə·graf'ik) or **·i·cal** *adj.* **— o'ce·an·o·graph'i·cal·ly** *adv.*

oc·el·lat·ed (os'ə·lā'tid, ō·sel'ā·tid) *adj.* 1. Having an ocellus or ocelli. 2. Resembling an ocellus. 3. Spotted. Also **oc·el·late** (os'ə·lāt, ō·sel'āt). [< L *ocellatus* small-eyed]

o·cel·lus (ō·sel'əs) *n.* *pl.* **·li** (-lī) 1. *Biol.* A minute simple eye, as of many invertebrates. 2. An eyelike spot, as in the tail of a peacock. [< L, dim. of *oculus* eye] **— o·cel'lar** *adj.*

o·ce·lot (ō'sə·lət, -lot, os'ə-) *n.* A large cat of Central and South America, having a spotted yellowish or reddish gray coat. [< F, short for Nahuatl *tlaocelotl* < *tlalli* field + *ocelotl* jaguar]

o·cher (ō'kər) *n.* 1. A naturally occurring iron oxide mixed with various earthy materials and varying from light yellow to deep orange or red, largely used as a pigment. 2. A dark yellow color derived from or resembling ocher. Also *Brit.* **o'chre.** [< OF < L < Gk. *ōchra* yellow ocher < *ōchros* pale yellow] **— o'cher·ous, o·chre·ous** (ō'krē·əs), **o'cher·y, o·chry** (ō'krē) *adj.*

-ock *suffix of nouns* Small: *hillock.* [OE *-oc, -uc*]

o'clock (ə·klok') Of or according to the clock: six *o'clock*.

oct-, octa- See OCTO-.

oc·ta·gon (ok'tə·gon) *n.* *Geom.* A polygon having eight sides and eight angles. [< L < Gk. < *oktō* eight + *gōnia* angle] **— oc·tag·o·nal** (ok·tag'ə·nəl) *adj.* **— oc·tag'o·nal·ly** *adv.*

oc·ta·he·dron (ok'tə·hē'drən) *n.* *pl.* **·dra** (-drə) *Geom.* A polyhedron bounded by eight plane faces. [< Gk. < *oktō* eight + *hedra* seat] **— oc'ta·he'dral** *adj.*

oc·tane (ok'tān) *n.* *Chem.* One of a group of saturated hydrocarbons that have the formula C_8H_{18}.

octane number A measure of the antiknock properties of gasoline, expressed as the percentage, by volume, of isooctane that must be blended with normal heptane until the mixture has the same knock rating as the gasoline under test.

oc·tant (ok'tənt) *n.* An eighth part of a circle; an arc subtending an angle of 45 degrees. [< LL *octans, -antis* an eighth part < L *octo* eight] **— oc·tant'al** (-tan'təl) *adj.*

oc·tave (ok'tiv, -tāv) *n.* 1. *Music* a The interval between a tone and another having twice as many or half as many vibrations per second. b A tone at this interval above or below any other, considered in relation to that other. c Two tones at this interval, sounded together; also, the resulting consonance. d An organ stop giving tones an octave above those normally corresponding to the keys played. 2. *Eccl.* The eighth day from a feast day, beginning with the feast day as one; also, the lengthening of a festival so as to include a period of eight days. 3. Any group or series of eight. 4. In prosody, an octet. **— adj.** 1. Composed of eight. 2. *Music* Producing tones an octave higher. [< L *octavus* eighth < *octo* eight] **— oc·ta·val** (ok·tā'vəl, ok'tə-) *adj.*

oc·ta·vo (ok·tā'vō, -tä'-) *n.* *pl.* **·vos** 1. The page size (6 x 9½ inches except where otherwise specified) of a book made

up of printer's sheets folded into eight leaves. 2. A book consisting of pages of this size. **— adj.** In octavo. Also *eightvo.* Also written 8vo or 8°. [< L *in octavo* in an eighth]

oc·tet (ok·tet') *n.* 1. A musical composition for eight singers or instrumentalists. 2. A group of eight singers or instrumentalists. 3. Any group of eight. Also **oc·tette'.** [< Ital. < L *octo* eight]

oc·til·lion (ok·til'yən) *n.* 1. *U.S.* A thousand septillions, written as 1 followed by 27 zeros: a cardinal number. 2. *Brit.* A million septillions (def. 2), written as 1 followed by 48 zeros: a cardinal number **— adj.** Being an octillion in number. [< MF < *octo* eight + F (*m*)*illion*]

octo- *combining form* Eight: also, before vowels, *oct-.* Also *octa-.* [< L *octo* and Gk. *oktō* eight]

Oc·to·ber (ok·tō'bər) The tenth month of the year, containing 31 days. [< L, eighth month of early Roman calendar < *octo* eight]

October Revolution See RUSSIAN REVOLUTION under REVOLUTION.

oc·to·dec·i·mo (ok'tə·des'ə·mō) *n.* *pl.* **·mos** 1. The page size (approximately 4 x 6½ inches) of a book made up of printer's sheets folded into 18 leaves. 2. A book consisting of pages of this size. **— adj.** In octodecimo; consisting of pages of this size. Also *eighteenmo.* Also written 18mo or 18°. [< L *in octodecimo* in an eighteenth]

oc·to·ge·nar·i·an (ok'tə·jə·nâr'ē·ən) *adj.* Being eighty or from eighty to ninety years of age. **— n.** One between eighty and ninety years of age. Also **oc·tog·e·nar·y** (ok·toj'ə·ner'ē) *adj. & n.* [< L *octoginta* eighty]

oc·to·pod (ok'tə·pod) *n.* *Zool.* Any of a group of eight-armed cephalopods, as the octopus.

oc·to·pus (ok'tə·pəs) *n.* *pl.* **·pus·es** or **·pi** (-pī) or **oc·top·o·des** (ok·top'ə·dēz) 1. An eight-armed marine mollusk having a large oval head and rows of suckers along the arms; a devilfish. 2. Any organized power regarded as far-reaching and potentially destructive; esp., a powerful business organization. [< NL < Gk. < *oktō* eight + *pous* foot]

oc·to·roon (ok'tə·rōōn') *n.* A person who is one-eighth Negro. [< L *octo* eight + (QUAD)ROON]

oc·u·lar (ok'yə·lər) *adj.* Of, like, or related to the eye or sight. **— n.** The lenses forming the eyepiece of an optical instrument. [< L < *oculus* eye] **— oc'u·lar·ly** *adv.*

oc·u·list (ok'yə·list) *n.* A physician skilled in treating diseases of the eye; ophthalmologist. [< MF < L *oculus* eye]

o·da·lisque (ō'də·lisk) *n.* A female slave or concubine in an Oriental harem. Also **o'da·lisk.** [< F < Turkish *ōdaliq* chambermaid]

odd (od) *adj.* 1. Strange or unusual in appearance, behavior, etc.; peculiar; queer. 2. Not part of what is regular, usual, required, etc.: an *odd* job. 3. Constituting a member of an incomplete pair, set, etc.: an *odd* slipper. 4. Leaving a remainder when divided by two; not even: Five is an *odd* number; also, characterized by such a number. 5. Additional to a specified round number: seventy *odd* dollars. [< ON *oddi* point, hence, third point of a triangle, hence, odd number] **— odd'ly** *adv.* **— odd'ness** *n.*

odd·i·ty (od'ə·tē) *n.* *pl.* **·ties** 1. One who or that which is odd. 2. An odd or peculiar quality or trait; an eccentricity. 3. The state of being odd; singularity; strangeness.

odd·ment (od'mənt) *n.* *Usu. pl.* A fragment, scrap, or leftover; odds and ends.

odds (odz) *n.pl.* (*sometimes construed as sing.*) 1. An equalizing allowance or advantage given to a weaker opponent. 2. The proportion by which one bet differs from that of another. 3. The ratio between the probability for and the probability against something being true or happening. 4. A difference to the advantage of one side. **— at odds** At variance; disagreeing. [< plural of ODD]

odds and ends Miscellaneous things; fragments; scraps.

ode (ōd) *n.* A lyric poem often in the form of an elaborate address and usually characterized by loftiness of tone, feeling, and style. [< MF < LL < Gk. *ōidē* song]

-ode¹ *combining form* Way; path: *anode, cathode.* [< Gk. *hodos* way]

-ode² *suffix* Like; resembling; having the nature of. [< Gk. *-ōdēs* < *eidos* form]

O·din (ō'din) In Norse mythology, the supreme deity, god of war, art, culture, and the dead.

o·di·ous (ō'dē·əs) *adj.* Exciting hate, repugnance, or disgust; offensive; abhorrent. [< OF < L < *odium* hatred] **— o'di·ous·ly** *adv.* **— o'di·ous·ness** *n.*

o·di·um (ō'dē·əm) *n.* 1. The state of being odious. 2. Extreme dislike or aversion; hatred. 3. The reproach, disgrace, or stigma associated with something hateful; opprobrium. [< L, hatred]

o·dom·e·ter (ō·dom'ə·tər) *n.* A device for measuring distance traveled by a vehicle. [< Gk. < *hodos* way, road + *metron* a measure] **— o·dom'e·try** *n.*

-odont *combining form* Toothed. [< Gk. *odous, odontos* tooth]

odonto- *combining form* Tooth; of the teeth. Also, before vowels, **odont-**. [< Gk. *odous, odontos* tooth]

o·don·tol·o·gy (ō'don·tol'ə·jē) *n.* The body of scientific knowledge that relates to the structure, health, and growth of the teeth. **—o·don·to·log·i·cal** (ō·don'tə·loj'i·kəl) *adj.* **—o·don·to·log'i·cal·ly** *adv.* **—o'don·tol'o·gist** *n.*

o·dor (ō'dər) *n.* **1.** That quality of a substance that renders it perceptible to the sense of smell; smell; scent. **2.** Regard or estimation. **3.** A perfume; incense. **—Syn.** See SMELL. Also *Brit.* **o'dour.** [< OF < L] **—o'dored** *adj.*

o·dor·if·er·ous (ō'də·rif'ər·əs) *adj.* Having or giving off an odor, especially a pleasant odor. [< L < *odor* odor + *ferre* to bear] **—o'dor·if'er·ous·ly** *adv.* **—o'dor·if'er·ous·ness** *n.*

o·dor·less (ō'dər·lis) *adj.* Having no odor. **—o'dor·less·ly** *adv.* **—o'dor·less·ness** *n.*

o·dor·ous (ō'dər·əs) *adj.* Having an odor, esp. a fragrant odor. **—o'dor·ous·ly** *adv.* **—o'dor·ous·ness** *n.*

-odynia *combining form Med.* Pain; chronic pain in a (specified) part of the body. [< Gk. *odynē* pain]

O·dys·seus (ō·dis'yōōs, -ē·əs) In Greek legend, king of Ithaca, one of the Greek leaders in the Trojan War and hero of the *Odyssey:* Latin *Ulysses.*

Od·ys·sey (od'ə·sē) An ancient Greek epic poem attributed to Homer, describing the wanderings of Odysseus during the ten years after the fall of Troy. **—n.** A long, wandering journey: often **od'ys·sey. —Od'ys·sey'an** *adj.*

oe- See also words beginning with E-.

oe·de·ma (i·dē'mə) See EDEMA.

Oed·i·pus (ed'ə·pəs, ē'də-) In Greek legend, the son of Laius and Jocasta, rulers of Thebes, who unwittingly killed his father and married his mother.

Oedipus complex *Psychoanal.* A strong, typically unconscious attachment of a child to the parent of the opposite sex, esp. of a son to his mother, with antagonism toward the other parent. **—Oed·i·pal** (ed'ə·pəl, ē'də-) *adj.*

o'er (ôr, ōr) *prep. & adv. Poetic* Over.

oe·soph·a·gus (i·sof'ə·gəs) See ESOPHAGUS.

oes·tro·gen (es'trə·jən, ēs'-) See ESTROGEN.

oes·trous (es'trəs, ēs'-) See ESTROUS.

of (uv, ov; *unstressed* əv) *prep.* **1.** Coming from: Anne of Cleves; an actor of noble birth. **2.** Included among: Is he of your party? **3.** Located at: the Leaning Tower of Pisa. **4.** Away or at a distance from: within six miles of home. **5.** Named; specified as: the city of Newark; a fall of ten feet. **6.** Characterized by: a man of strength. **7.** With reference to; as to: quick of wit. **8.** About; concerning: Good is said of him. **9.** Because of: dying of pneumonia. **10.** Possessing: a man of means. **11.** Belonging to: the lid of a box. **12.** Pertaining to: the majesty of the law. **13.** Composed of: a ship of steel. **14.** Containing: a glass of water. **15.** From the number or class of: six of the seven conspirators. **16.** So as to be without: relieved of anxiety. **17.** Produced by: the plays of Shakespeare. **18.** Directed toward: exerted upon: a love of opera. **19.** During, on, or at a specified time or occasion: of recent years. **20.** Set aside for or devoted to: a program of music. **21.** *U.S.* Before; until: used in telling time: ten minutes of ten. **22.** *Archaic* By: loved of all men. [OE, away from, off]

of- Assimilated var. of OB-.

of course 1. In the usual order of procedure; naturally; as expected. **2.** Doubtless; certainly.

off (ôf, of) *adj.* **1.** Farther or more distant; remote: an *off* chance. **2.** In a (specified) circumstance or situation: to be well *off.* **3.** Not in accordance with the facts; wrong: Your reckoning is *off.* **4.** Not up to standard: an *off* season for roses. **5.** No longer considered active or effective: The deal is *off.* **6.** Away from work; not on duty: *off* hours. **7.** In riding or driving, on the right: opposed to *near:* Pass on the *off* side. **8.** *Naut.* Seaward. **—adv. 1.** To a distance; so as to be away: My horse ran *off.* **2.** To or at a (specified) future time: to put it *off* for a week. **3.** To or at a (specified) distance: to stand five feet *off.* **4.** So as to be no longer in place, connection, etc.: Take *off* your hat. **5.** So as to be no longer functioning, continuing, or in operation: to break *off* talks. **6.** So as to be away from one's work, duties, etc.: to take the day *off.* **7.** So as to be completed, exhausted, etc.: to kill *off* one's enemies. **8.** So as to deviate from or be below what is regarded as standard: His game dropped *off.* **9.** *Naut.* Away from land, a ship, the wind, etc. **— off and on** Now and then; intermittently. **— to be off 1.** To leave; depart. **2.** *Informal* To be insane. **—prep. 1.** So as to be separated, detached, distant, or removed from (a position, source, etc.): twenty miles *off* course. **2.** Not engaged in or occupied with; relieved from: *off* duty. **3.** Extending away or out from; no longer on: *off* Broadway. **4.** So as to deviate from or be below (what is regarded as standard): to be *off* one's game. **5.** On or from (the material or substance of): living *off* nuts and berries. **6.** *Informal* No longer using, engaging in, or advocating: to be *off* drinking. **7.** *Naut.*

Opposite to and seaward of: the battle *off* the eastern cape. **— off of** *Informal* Off; from: He fell *off* of the horse. **—n.** The state or condition of being off. [ME]

of·fal (ô'fəl) *n.* **1.** The waste parts of a butchered animal. **2.** Rubbish or refuse of any kind. [ME *ofall* < OFF + FALL]

off·beat (ôf'bēt', of'-) *n. Music* Any secondary or weak beat in a measure. **—adj.** *U.S. Slang* Out of the ordinary; strange; unconventional; unusual.

off-Broad·way (ôf'brôd'wā) *adj.* **1.** Not situated in the Broadway entertainment district: an *off-Broadway* theater. **2.** Designating a play that is regarded as experimental, noncommercial, etc. **— n.** Any area in New York City in which off-Broadway plays are produced.

off·cast (ôf'kast', -käst', of'-) *adj.* Rejected; castoff. **— n.** Anything thrown away or rejected.

off chance A bare possibility.

off-col·or (ôf'kul'ər, of'-) *adj.* **1.** Unsatisfactory in color, as a gem. **2.** Indelicate or indecent; risqué.

of·fence (ə·fens') See OFFENSE.

of·fend (ə·fend') *v.t.* **1.** To give displeasure or offense to. **2.** To be disagreeable to (the sense of smell, sight, etc.). **— v.i. 3.** To give displeasure or offense; be offensive. [< L < *ob-* against + *fendere* to hit] **—of·fend'er** *n.* **—Syn. 1.** Insult, affront, exasperate, outrage.

of·fense (ə·fens'; *for defs. 4 & 5, also* ô'fens, of'ens) *n.* **1.** Any violation of a rule, duty, propriety, etc.; esp., a breach of law. **2.** The act of offending or causing displeasure. **3.** That which offends: an *offense* to the ear. **4.** The act of attacking or assaulting; attack. **5.** In football, hockey, etc., the team possessing the ball or puck. **— to give offense** To offend or cause anger, resentment, etc. **— to take offense** To be offended; feel angry, hurt, etc. Also *esp. Brit.,* **offence.**

of·fen·sive (ə·fen'siv) *adj.* **1.** Unpleasant or disagreeable; obnoxious; disgusting. **2.** Causing anger, resentment, etc.; insulting. **3.** Of, pertaining to, or characterized by attack: distinguished from *defensive.* **— n.** The movement, attitude, or position of offense or attack. **—of·fen'sive·ly** *adv.* **—of·fen'sive·ness** *n.*

of·fer (ô'fər, of'ər) *v.t.* **1.** To present for acceptance or rejection. **2.** To suggest for consideration or action; propose. **3.** To make an offering of: often with *up.* **4.** To show readiness to do or attempt; propose or threaten: to *offer* battle. **5.** To attempt to do or inflict; also, to do or inflict. **6.** To suggest as payment; bid. **7.** To present for sale. **— v.i. 8.** To present itself; appear. **9.** To make an offering in worship or sacrifice. **— n.** **1.** The act of offering. **2.** That which is offered, as a bid, suggestion, etc. [OE *offrian* < L < *ob-* before + *ferre* to bring] **—of'fer·er** or **of'fer·or** *n.*

of·fer·ing (ô'fər·ing, of'ər-) *n.* **1.** The act of making an offer. **2.** That which is offered, as a sacrifice or contribution.

of·fer·to·ry (ô'fər·tôr'ē, -tō'rē, of'ər-) *n. pl.* **·ries** *Eccl.* **1.** *Usu. cap.* A section of the eucharistic liturgy during which the bread and wine to be consecrated are offered, and the alms of the congregation are collected. **2.** Any collection taken during a religious service. **3.** An antiphon, hymn, or anthem sung during this service. **4.** A prayer of oblation said by the celebrant over the bread and wine to be consecrated. [< Med.L *offertorium* < LL, place of offerings]

off·hand (ôf'hand', of'-) *adv.* Without preparation; unceremoniously; extempore. Also **off'hand'ed·ly.** **— adj. 1.** Done, said, or made offhand. **2.** Casual; informal; curt. Also **off'hand'ed.**

of·fice (ô'fis, of'is) *n.* **1.** A place in which the business of an individual, corporation, government bureau, etc., is carried out; also, the staff and administrative officials working in such a place. **2.** *Usu. cap. U.S.* An executive branch of the federal government ranking below the departments. **3.** Any post or position held by a person; especially, a position of authority or trust in the government, a corporation, etc. **4.** The duty, charge, or trust of a person. **5.** Any act done or intended to be done for another; a service; favor: through his kind *offices.* **6.** *Eccl.* A prescribed religious or devotional service, as: **a** The canonical hours. **b** The Morning or Evening Prayer. **7.** Any ceremony or rite, esp., a rite for the dead. [< OF < L *officium* service]

of·fice·hold·er (ô'fis·hōl'dər, of'-) *n.* One who holds an office under a government.

of·fi·cer (ô'fə·sər, of'ə-) *n.* **1.** In the armed forces, one appointed to a certain rank and authority; esp., one holding a commission. **2.** One elected or appointed to a position of authority or trust in a corporation, government, institution, etc. **3.** On a merchant or passenger ship, the captain or any of the mates. **4.** One who enforces the law, as a policeman. **— v.t. 1.** To furnish with officers. **2.** To command; direct; manage.

officer of the day At a military installation, the officer who on a given day is responsible for the performance of the guard, maintenance of order or security, etc.

of·fi·cial (ə·fish'əl, ō-) *adj.* **1.** Of or relating to an office or position of authority. **2.** Supported by or derived from authority. **3.** Authorized to carry out some special duty.

4. Formal: *official* banquets. — *n.* One who holds an office or position; esp., one who is authorized to act for a corporation, government agency, etc., in a subordinate capacity. — **of·fi′cial·ly** *adv.*

of·fi·cial·dom (ə-fish′əl-dəm, ō-) *n.* **1.** Officials collectively or as a class. **2.** Rigid adherence to official forms, routines, etc.: also **of·fi′cial·ism.**

of·fi·ci·ate (ə-fish′ē-āt, ō-) *v.i.* **·at·ed, ·at·ing** **1.** To act or serve as a priest or minister. **2.** To perform the duties or functions of any office or position. — **of·fi′ci·a′tion** *n.* — **of·fi′ci·a′tor** *n.*

of·fic·i·nal (ə-fis′ə-nəl) *adj.* Prepared and kept in stock by a pharmacy. — *n.* Any drug or medicine kept ready for sale. [< Med.L < L *officina* workshop]

of·fi·cious (ə-fish′əs, ō-) *adj.* Unduly forward in offering one's services or advice; obtrusive; meddling. [< L *officiosus* obliging < *officium* service] — **of·fi′cious·ly** *adv.* — **of·fi′cious·ness** *n.*

off·ing (ô′fing, of′ing) *n.* **1.** That part of the visible sea offshore but beyond anchorage. **2.** A position some distance offshore. — **in the offing 1.** In sight and not very distant. **2.** Ready or soon to happen, arrive, etc.

off·ish (ô′fish, of′ish) *adj.* Inclined to be distant in manner; aloof. — **off′ish·ly** *adv.* — **off′ish·ness** *n.*

off·scour·ing (ôf′skour′ing, of′-) *n.* **1.** *Usu. pl.* Trash; garbage. **2.** A social outcast; wretch.

off·set (*n.* ôf′set′, of′-; *v.* ôf′set′, of′-) *n.* **1.** That which balances or compensates for something else. **2.** That which derives, develops, or springs from something else; offshoot. **3.** *Archit.* A ledge formed along a wall by a reduction in thickness above; setoff. **4.** *Printing* **a** Offset printing. **b** An impression made by offset printing. **5.** A bend or curve made in a pipe, rod, etc., to allow it to pass an obstacle. — *v.* **·set, ·set·ting** *v.t.* **1.** To balance or compensate for. **2.** *Printing* **a** To reproduce by offset printing. **b** To transfer (an impression) by offset printing. **3.** *Archit.* To make an offset in. — *v.i.* **4.** To branch off or project as an offset.

offset printing A method of printing in which the inked impression from a lithographic plate is transferred to a rubber-coated cylinder, and then onto the paper.

off·shoot (ôf′shoot′, of′-) *n.* **1.** *Bot.* A lateral shoot or branch from the main stem of a plant. **2.** Anything that derives or branches off from a principal source, stock, etc.

off·shore (ôf′shôr′, -shōr′, of′-) *adj.* **1.** Moving or directed away from the shore. **2.** Situated or occurring at some distance from the shore. — *adv.* From or away from the shore.

off·side (ôf′sīd′, of′-) *adj.* In football, in front of the ball before it is put into play: said of a player, team, or play. Also **off side.**

off·spring (ôf′spring′, of′-) *n.* *pl.* **·spring** or **·springs** **1.** The progeny or issue of a person, animal, or plant; descendant. **2.** Any result or product: the *offspring* of his mind.

off·stage (ôf′stāj, of′-) *n.* The area behind or to the side of a stage, out of the view of the audience. — *adj.* In or from this area: *off-stage* dialogue. — *adv.* To this area.

off·white (ôf′hwīt′, of′-) *n.* Oyster white.

oft (ôft, oft) *adv.* Often: archaic or poetic except in certain combinations, as **oft-repeated, oft-recurring,** etc. [OE]

oft·en (ôf′ən, of′-) *adv.* Frequently or repeatedly. [Var. of ME *ofte,* OE *oft*]

oft·en·times (ôf′ən-tīmz′, of′-) *adv. Archaic* Frequently; often. Also **oft·times** (ôf′tīmz′, of′-).

o·gee (ō′jē, ō-jē′) *n. Archit.* **1.** Any S-shaped curve used in a construction. **2.** An arch having two S-shaped curves meeting at the apex: also **ogee arch.** [OF *ogive*]

o·give (ō′jīv, ō-jīv′) *n. Archit.* **1.** A diagonal rib of a vaulted arch or bay. **2.** A pointed arch. [< OF *ogive*]

o·gle (ō′gəl, og′əl) *v.* **o·gled, o·gling** *v.t.* **1.** To look at with admiring or impertinent glances. **2.** To stare at; eye. — *v.i.* **3.** To look or stare in an admiring or impertinent manner. — *n.* An amorous or coquettish look. [< LG *oegeln,* freq. of *oegen* to look at < *oege* eye] — **o′gler** *n.*

o·gre (ō′gər) *n.* **1.** In fairy tales, a man-eating giant or monster. **2.** One who is brutal, hideous, or feared. [< F] — **o·gre·ish** (ō′gər-ish), **o·grish** (ō′grish) *adj.* — **o′gress** (-grəs) *n.fem.*

oh (ō) *interj.* An exclamation expressing surprise, sudden emotion, etc. — *n.* The interjection *oh.*

ohm (ōm) *n.* The unit of electrical resistance, equal to the resistance of a conductor carrying a current of one ampere at a potential difference of one volt between the terminals.

ohm·age (ō′mij) *n.* Electrical resistance of a conductor, expressed in ohms.

ohm·me·ter (ōm′mē′tər) *n.* A galvanometer for measuring the resistance of a conductor in ohms.

o·ho (ō-hō′) *interj.* An exclamation expressing astonishment, exultation, etc.

-oid *suffix* Like; resembling; having the form of: *ovoid, hydroid.* [< NL *-oides* < Gk. *-oeidēs* < *eidos* form]

oil (oil) *n.* **1.** A greasy or unctuous, sometimes combustible liquid of vegetable, animal, or mineral origin, soluble in alcohol and ether, but not in water, variously used as food, for lubricating, illuminating, and fuel, and in the manufacture of soap, candles, cosmetics, perfumery, etc. **2.** Petroleum. **3.** An oil color; also, an oil painting. **4.** Anything of an oily consistency. — *v.t.* **1.** To smear, lubricate, or supply with oil. **2.** To bribe; flatter. — *adj.* **1.** Of or resembling oil. **2.** Using, obtained from, or yielding oil. [< OF < L *prob.* < Gk. *elaion* olive oil]

oil burner A heating unit that operates on oil fuel.

oil cake The mass of compressed seeds of cotton, flax, etc., or coconut pulp from which oil has been expressed, used as food (**oil meal**) for livestock, etc.

oil·cloth (oil′klôth′, -kloth′) *n.* A fabric waterproofed with oils and pigments, used as a covering for tables, etc.

oil color A color or paint made of pigment ground in linseed or other oil, used chiefly by artists.

oil of vitriol Sulfuric acid.

oil painting 1. A painting done in pigments mixed in oil. **2.** The art of painting in oils.

oil·paper (oil′pā′pər) *n.* Paper treated with oil for transparency and resistance against moisture and dryness.

oil·skin (oil′skin′) *n.* Cloth made waterproof with oil, or a garment of such material.

oil slick A smooth area on water caused by a film of oil.

oil·stone (oil′stōn) *n.* A whetstone moistened with oil.

oil well A well that is dug or drilled to obtain petroleum.

oil·y (oi′lē) *adj.* **oil·i·er, oil·i·est** **1.** Of, pertaining to, or containing oil. **2.** Coated, smeared, or soaked with oil; greasy. **3.** Smooth or suave in behavior, speech, etc.; unctuous. — **oil′i·ly** *adv.* — **oil′i·ness** *n.*

oint·ment (oint′mənt) *n.* A fatty or unctuous preparation applied to the skin as a medicine or cosmetic; unguent. [< OF *oignement,* ult. < L *unguentum < ungere* to anoint]

O·jib·wa (ō-jib′wä, -wə) *n. pl.* **·wa** or **·was** **1.** One of a tribe of North American Indians formerly inhabiting the regions around Lake Superior. **2.** Their Algonquian language. Also called *Chippewa:* also **O·jib′way.**

OK (*interj., adj., adv. & n.* ō′kā′; *v.* ō-kā′) *interj., adj., & adv.* All correct; all right: used to express approval, agreement, etc. — *v.t.* To approve, endorse, or agree to; especially, to sign with an *OK.* — *n.* Approval; agreement; endorsement. Also **O.K., o′kay′, o′keh′.** [? < *o(ll) k(orrect),* humorous misspelling of "all correct," reinforced by *O(ld) K(inderhook)* in the name of a political club (1840) supporting Martin Van Buren of Kinderhook, N.Y.]

o·ka·pi (ō-kä′pē) *n.* An African ruminant related to the giraffe, but with a smaller body and a shorter neck. [< native African name]

O·kie (ō′kē) *n. U.S. Slang* A migrant farmworker, originally one from Oklahoma.

o·kra (ō′krə) *n.* **1.** A tall annual herb of the mallow family. **2.** Its green mucilaginous pods, used in soups and stews, or as a vegetable. **3.** Gumbo. [< West African]

-ol[1] *suffix Chem.* Denoting an alcohol or phenol: *methanol, glycerol.* [< (ALCOH)OL]

-ol[2] *suffix Chem.* Var. of -OLE[1], as in *benzol.*

old (ōld) *adj.* **old·er** or **eld·er, old·est** or **eld·est** **1.** Living, existing, made, known, etc., for a relatively long time. **2.** Exhibiting the characteristics of advanced life. **3.** Having a specified age or duration: a child two months *old.* **4.** Worn with age or repeated use; shabby. **5.** Familiar through long acquaintance or use: an *old* friend. **6.** Skilled through long experience: an *old* hand at politics. **7.** Belonging to or associated with a relatively remote period in history; ancient. **8.** *Usu. cap.* Denoting the earlier or earliest of two or more things, periods, developments, etc.; *Old* English; the *Old* Testament. **9.** *Informal* Good; cherished; dear: a general term of affection or endearment: *old* buddy of mine. **10.** *Informal* Plentiful; great; wonderful: used to express intense pleasure, excess, etc.: a grand *old* time. **11.** *Geog.* In a late stage of a cycle of development: said of topographic features, streams, etc. — *n.* Past time: days of *old.* [OE *ald*] — **old′ness** *n.*
— **Syn.** (adj.) **1.** *Old* and *aged* mean having lived a long time, but *old* more often suggests feebleness or senility than *aged.* An *elderly* man has passed middle age, but is generally regarded as younger than an *old* man, both in years and in vigor.

Old Bailey The central criminal court of London.

old country The native country of an immigrant, esp. a European country.

old·en (ōl′dən) *adj. Archaic & Poetic* Old; ancient.

Old English *Printing* Black letter.

old·fan·gled (ōld′fang′gəld) *adj.* Having a fondness for what is old-fashioned. [On analogy with NEWFANGLED]

old·fash·ioned (ōld'fash'ənd) *adj.* Of, pertaining to, characteristic of, or favoring former times, old customs, etc.

old fashioned A cocktail of whisky, sugar, fruit, etc.

old fo·gy (fō'gē) One who is extremely conservative or old-fashioned. Also **old fo'gey.** — **old'-fo'gy·ish** *adj.*

Old French See under FRENCH.

Old Glory The flag of the United States.

old guard The conservative element in a community, political party, etc.

old hat *U.S. Slang* Out of style; old-fashioned; obsolete.

Old Hickory Nickname of Andrew Jackson.

Old High German See under GERMAN.

Old Icelandic See under ICELANDIC.

old·ish (ōl'dish) *adj.* Somewhat old.

old lady *Slang* 1. One's mother. 2. One's wife.

old-line (ōld'līn') *adj.* 1. Traditional or conservative in action or thought. 2. Long-established; traditional.

Old Line State Nickname of Maryland.

old maid 1. A spinster. 2. *Informal* One who is prim, prudish, fastidious, etc.

old man *Slang* 1. One's father. 2. One's husband. 3. Any man in a position of authority, as an employer.

old master Any of the famous painters who lived between the 13th and 16th centuries, esp. in Italy and the Low Countries; also, any of their paintings.

Old Nick The devil.

Old Prussian See under PRUSSIAN.

old rose Any of various shades of grayish or purplish red.

old·ster (ōld'stər) *n. Informal* An old or elderly person.

Old Stone Age The Paleolithic period of human culture.

old-style (ōld'stīl') *adj.* Of a former or old-fashioned style.

old style *Printing* A style of type having the stems and the serifs of nearly the same thickness.

Old Style See (Gregorian) CALENDAR.

Old Testament The first of the two main divisions of the Bible, divided into the Pentateuch, the Prophets, and the Hagiographa.

old-time (ōld'tīm') *adj.* 1. Of or characteristic of a former time. 2. Of long standing; long-established.

old-tim·er (ōld'tī'mər) *n. Informal* 1. One who has been a member, resident, etc., for a long time. 2. An old-fashioned person.

Ol·du·vai Gorge (ōl'doo-vī', ōl'doo-vī') A gorge about 100 mi. SE of Lake Victoria in Tanzania; site of fossils of extinct mammals believed to be forerunners of early man.

old-wom·an·ish (ōld'woom'ən·ish) *adj.* Characteristic of or suitable for an old woman; fussy.

old-world (ōld'wûrld') *adj.* 1. Of or pertaining to the Old World or Eastern Hemisphere. 2. Ancient; antique.

Old World The Eastern Hemisphere, including Europe, Asia and Africa; esp., Europe.

-ole[1] *suffix Chem.* Denoting a closed-chain compound having a five-membered ring. Also spelled **-ol.** [< L *oleum* oil]

-ole[2] *suffix* Small; little: *nucleole.* [< L *-olus,* dim. suffix]

o·le·a·ceous (ō'lē·ā'shəs) *adj. Bot.* Pertaining or belonging to the olive family of plants and including the lilac, jasmine, and ash. [< NL *oleaceae* < L *olea* olive tree]

o·le·ag·i·nous (ō'lē·aj'ə·nəs) *adj.* Of or pertaining to oil; oily. [< F < L *olea* olive tree] — **o·le·ag'i·nous·ly** *adv.*

o·le·an·der (ō'lē·an'dər) *n.* An Old World, evergreen shrub, having leaves that yield a poisonous glycoside and clusters of fragrant rose or white flowers. [< Med.L]

o·le·ate (ō'lē·āt) *n. Chem.* A salt or ester of oleic acid.

o·le·ic (ō·lē'ik, ō'lē-) *adj.* Of, pertaining to, or derived from oil. [< L *oleum* oil + -IC]

oleic acid *Chem.* An oily compound, C₁₇H₃₃COOH, contained as an ester in most mixed oils and fats.

o·le·o (ō'lē·ō) Short for OLEOMARGARINE.

oleo- *combining form* Oil; of oil. [< L *oleum* oil]

o·le·o·mar·ga·rine (ō'lē·ō·mär'jə·rin, -rēn) *n.* A substitute for butter made usu. from vegetable oils: also called *margarine.* Also **o·le·o·mar'ga·rin.**

o·le·o·res·in (ō'lē·ō·rez'in) *n.* 1. A naturally occurring compound of an essential oil and a resin. 2. A pharmaceutical preparation consisting of a resin and sometimes other active matter in solution with a fixed or volatile oil.

ol·fac·tion (ol·fak'shən) *n.* The act, sense, or process of smelling odors. [< L *olfactus.* See OLFACTORY.]

ol·fac·to·ry (ol·fak'tər·ē, -trē) *adj.* Of or pertaining to the sense of smell. — *n. pl.* **·ries** *Usu. pl.* The organ of smell. [< L < *olere* to have a smell + *facere* to make]

ol·i·garch (ol'ə·gärk) *n.* A ruler in an oligarchy.

ol·i·gar·chy (ol'ə·gär'kē) *n. pl.* **·chies** 1. A form of government in which power is restricted to a few; also, a state so governed. 2. The ruling oligarchs. [< Gk. < *oligos* few + *archein* to rule] — **ol'i·gar·chic, ol'i·gar'chal, ol'i·gar·chi·cal** *adj.*

Ol·i·go·cene (ol'ə·gō·sēn') *Geol. adj.* Pertaining to the third oldest of the epochs or series comprised in the Tertiary system. — *n.* This epoch, with its included rock series. [< OLIGO- + Gk. *kainos* new, recent]

o·li·o (ō'lē·ō) *n. pl.* **o·li·os** A miscellaneous collection, as of musical pieces or numbers. [< Sp. *olla* pot, stew]

ol·ive (ol'iv) *n.* 1. A small, oily fruit native to Southern Europe and the Middle East. 2. The evergreen tree yielding this fruit, having leathery leaves and hard yellow wood. 3. The dull, yellowish green color of the unripe olive: also **olive green.** — *adj.* 1. Pertaining to or characteristic of the olive. 2. Having a dull, yellowish green color. 3. Tinged with this color: an *olive* complexion. [< L *oliva*]

olive branch 1. A branch of the olive tree as an emblem of peace. 2. Any peace offering.

olive drab 1. Any of several shades of greenish brown. 2. A woolen material of this color, formerly used by the armed services of the U.S. for uniforms. 3. *Often pl.* A uniform or a pair of trousers made of this cloth.

olive oil Oil pressed from olives, used in cooking, etc.

Olives, Mount of A hill just east of Jerusalem: *Matt.* xvi 1. Also **Ol·i·vet** (ol'ə·vet, -vit).

ol·i·vine (ol'ə·vēn, -vin) *n.* A vitreous, often transparent, magnesium-iron silicate, often used as a gemstone.

ol·la (ol'ə, *Sp.* ō'lyä, ō'yä) *n.* 1. A wide-mouthed pot or jar, usu. of earthenware. 2. A highly seasoned stew. [< Sp. < L *olla* pot]

ol·o·gy (ol'ə·jē) *n. pl.* **·gies** *Informal* A science or branch of learning: a humorous term. [< -LOGY] — **ol'o·gist** *n.*

O·lym·pi·a (ō·lim'pē·ə) An ancient city in the western Peloponnesus, Greece; scene of the Olympic games.

O·lym·pi·ad (ō·lim'pē·ad) *n.* 1. The interval of four years between two successive celebrations of the Olympic games. 2. The modern Olympic games.

O·lym·pi·an (ō·lim'pē·ən) *adj.* 1. Of or pertaining to the great gods of Olympus, or to Mount Olympus. 2. Godlike. 3. Of or pertaining to Olympia or the Olympic games. Also **O·lym·pic** (ō·lim'pik, ə-). — *n.* 1. One of the twelve higher gods who dwelt on Mount Olympus. 2. A contestant in the Olympic games. 3. A native of Olympia.

Olympic games 1. In ancient Greece, athletic games, races, and contests in poetry held every four years at the plain of Olympia in Elis in honor of Zeus. 2. A modern international revival of the ancient athletic games, held every four years at some city chosen for the event. Also **Olympian games, O·lym'pics.**

-oma *suffix Med.* Tumor: *carcinoma.* [< Gk. *-ōma*]

o·ma·sum (ō·mā'səm) *n. pl.* **·sa** (-sə) The third stomach of a ruminant. [< L]

om·buds·man (om·budz'mən) *n. pl.* **·men** (-mən) A government official appointed to receive and report grievances against the government. [< Sw.]

-ome *combining form Bot.* Group; mass. [< Gk. *-ōma*]

o·me·ga (ō·mē'gə, ō·meg'ə, ō'meg·ə) *n.* 1. The twenty-fourth and last letter in the Greek alphabet (Ω, ω), corresponding to English long *o.* See ALPHABET. ♦ In the etymologies in this dictionary, omega is transliterated as ō. 2. The end; the last. [< Gk. ō *mega* great o]

om·e·let (om'lit, om'ə·lit) *n.* A dish of eggs beaten together with milk and cooked in a frying pan, often with other ingredients. Also *Brit.* **om'e·lette.** [< F *omelette*]

o·men (ō'mən) *n.* A phenomenon or incident regarded as a prophetic sign. — *v.t.* To foretell as or by an omen. [< L] — **Syn.** (noun) portent, foretoken, augury, presage.

om·i·cron (om'ə·kron, ō'mə-) *n.* The fifteenth letter of the Greek alphabet (Ο, ο), corresponding to English short *o.* Also **om'i·kron.** See ALPHABET. [< Gk. *o mikron* little o]

om·i·nous (om'ə·nəs) *adj.* 1. Of the nature of or fore-shadowed by an omen or by a presentiment of evil; threatening. 2. Serving as an omen; prognostic. [< L < *omen* omen] — **om'i·nous·ly** *adv.* — **om'i·nous·ness** *n.*

o·mis·si·ble (ō·mis'ə·bəl) *adj.* Capable of being omitted.

o·mis·sion (ō·mish'ən) *n.* 1. The act of omitting, or the state of being omitted. 2. Anything omitted or neglected.

o·mis·sive (ō·mis'iv) *adj.* Failing to do or include. — **o·mis'sive·ly** *adv.*

o·mit (ō·mit') *v.t.* **o·mit·ted, o·mit·ting** 1. To leave out; fail to include. 2. To fail to do, make, etc.; neglect. [< L *omittere* to let go < *ob-* to, towards + *mittere* to send]

omni- *combining form* All; totally: *omnipotent.* [< L *omnis* all]

om·ni·a vin·cit a·mor (om'nē·ə vin'sit ä'môr) *Latin* Love conquers all things.

om·ni·bus (om'nə·bəs, -bus) *n.* 1. A bus. 2. A printed anthology: a Conrad *omnibus.* — *adj.* Covering a full collection of objects or cases. [< F < L, for all]

om·nif·er·ous (om·nif'ər·əs) *adj.* Producing all kinds. [< L *omnifer* < *omnis* all + *ferre* to bear]

om·nip·o·tence (om·nip'ə·təns) *n.* 1. Unlimited and universal power, esp. as a divine attribute. 2. *Usu. cap.* God. 3. Unlimited power. Also **om·nip'o·ten·cy.**

om·nip·o·tent (om·nip'ə·tənt) *adj.* Almighty; not limited in authority or power. — **the Omnipotent** God. [< OF < L < *omnis* all + *potens, -entis* able, powerful] — **om·nip'o·tent·ly** *adv.*

om·ni·pres·ence (om/nə-prez/əns) *n.* The quality of being everywhere present at the same time. [< Med.L < L *omnis* all + *praesens, -entis* present] — **om/ni·pres/ent** *adj.*

om·ni·range (om/nə-rānj/) *n. Aeron.* A network of very-high-frequency radio signals emitted simultaneously in all directions from a transmitting station, enabling aircraft pilots to plot their bearings from the station.

om·nis·cience (om-nish/əns) *n.* **1.** Infinite knowledge. **2.** *Usu. cap.* God. **3.** Extensive knowledge. Also **om·nis/-cien·cy.**

om·nis·cient (om-nish/ənt) *adj.* Knowing all things; all-knowing. — **the Omniscient** God. [< NL < L *omnis* all + *sciens, -entis,* ppr. of *scire* to know] — **om·nis/cient·ly** *adv.*

om·ni·um-gath·er·um (om/nē-əm-gath/ər-əm) *n.* A miscellaneous collection: a humorous pseudo-Latin term.

om·niv·o·rous (om-niv/ər-əs) *adj.* **1.** Eating both animal and vegetable food. **2.** Eating food of all kinds indiscriminately. **3.** That assimilates everything: an *omnivorous* taste for literature. [< L *omnis* all + *vorare* to devour] — **om·niv/o·rous·ly** *adv.* — **om·niv/o·rous·ness** *n.*

on (on, ôn) *prep.* **1.** Above and supported by. **2.** In contact with any surface or outer part of: a blow *on* the head. **3.** Attached to or suspended from: *on* a string. **4.** Directed or moving along the course of. **5.** Near; adjacent to. **6.** Within the duration of. **7.** At the occasion of; because of: *On* seeing her, I left. **8.** At the moment or point of: *on* the hour. **9.** In a state or condition of: *on* fire; *on* record. **10.** By means of: *on* wheels. **11.** Using as a means of sustenance, activity, etc.: living *on* fruit. **12.** In addition to: thousands *on* thousands. **13.** Sustained or confirmed by: *on* good authority. **14.** With reference to: to bet *on* a horse. **15.** Concerning; about: a work *on* economics. **16.** Engaged in; occupied with: *on* a journey; *on* duty. **17.** As a consequence or result of: making a profit *on* tips. **18.** In accordance with or relation to; in terms of. **19.** Directed, tending, or moving toward or against: making war *on* the enemy. **20.** Following after: disease on the heels of famine. **21.** *Informal* With, as about one's person: Do you have five dollars *on* you? **22.** *Informal* At the expense of: The joke is *on* them; drinks *on* the house. **23.** *Informal* So as to annoy or make difficulty for: The car stalled *on* me. — **Syn.** See AT. ♦ See note under UPON. — **to have something on** *U.S. Informal* To have knowledge, possess evidence, etc., against. — *adv.* **1.** In or into a position or condition of contact, adherence, covering, etc.: He put his hat *on.* **2.** In the direction of an activity, performance, etc.: He looked *on* while they played. **3.** In advance; ahead, in space or time: later *on.* **4.** In continuous course or succession: The music went *on.* **5.** In or into operation, performance, or existence. — **and so on** And like what has gone before; et cetera. — **on and on** Without interruption; continuously. — **to be on to** *Informal* To be aware of, informed about, or alert to. — *adj.* **1.** Being in operation, progress, or application. **2.** Near; located nearer. [OE *on, an*]

-on *suffix* **1.** *Physics* Atomic or charged particle: *meson.* **2.** *Chem.* Inert gas; neon. [< Gk., neuter *-on*]

o·nan·ism (ō/nən-iz/əm) *n.* **1.** Withdrawal before orgasm; incomplete coitus. **2.** Masturbation. [after *Onan.* Cf. *Gen.* xxxviii 9.] — **o/nan·ist** *n.* — **o/nan·is/tic** *adj.*

once (wuns) *adv.* **1.** One time; without repetition. **2.** At or during some past time. **3.** At any time; ever. — **once (and) for all** Finally. — **once in a while** Occasionally. — *adj.* Former; formerly existing; quondam. — *conj.* As soon as; whenever. — *n.* One time. — **all at once 1.** All at the same time. **2.** All of a sudden. — **at once 1.** Simultaneously. **2.** Immediately. [ME < OE *ānes,* genitive of *ān* one]

once-o·ver (wuns/ō/vər) *n. Slang* **1.** A quick glance or survey. **2.** A quick putting of things in order.

on·com·ing (on/kum/ing, ôn/-) *adj.* Approaching. — *n.* An approach.

one (wun) *adj.* **1.** Being a single individual, object, or unit. **2.** Being or designating an unspecified or not precisely identified individual, thing, or time. **3.** Designating a person, thing, or group as contrasted with another or others. **4.** Single in kind; the same; closely united or alike. — *n.* **1.** A single unit, the first and lowest integer in the numerical series, preceding two: a cardinal number. **2.** Any symbol of this number, as 1, i, I. **3.** A single person or thing. — *pron.* **1.** Someone or something; anyone or anything. **2.** An individual or thing among persons or things already mentioned. — **all one 1.** Of equal consequence. **2.** Unimportant; of no significance. — **at one** In harmony or accord. — **one another** Each other. — **one by one** Singly and in succession. [OE *ān*]

♦ Expressions like *one of those who* may be followed by a plural or a singular verb, either *one* or *those* being regarded as the antecedent of *who* according to the sense or emphasis of the idea expressed. One may say *He is one of those who never*

break rules or *He is one of those who is always sure of what he is doing.*

One must work at one's own pace and *One must work at his own pace* are both correct, but the latter form is more common in the U.S.

-one *suffix Chem.* Denoting an organic compound of the ketone group: *acetone.* [< Gk. *-ōnē,* fem. patronymic]

one-horse (wun/hôrs/) *adj.* **1.** Drawn or adapted to be worked by one horse. **2.** *Informal* Of inferior resources or capacity; small; unimportant: a *one-horse* town.

O·nei·da (ō-nī/də) *n.* A member of a tribe of North American Indians of Iroquoian stock.

one·ness (wun/nis) *n.* **1.** Singleness; unity; sameness. **2.** Agreement; concord. **3.** Quality of being unique.

on·er·ous (on/ər-əs) *adj.* **1.** Burdensome or oppressive. **2.** *Law* Legally subject to an obligation. [< OF < L < *onus* burden] — **on/er·ous·ly** *adv.* — **on/er·ous·ness** *n.*

one·self (wun/self/, wunz/-) *pron.* A form of the indefinite pronoun *one,* used as a reflexive or as object of a preposition. Also **one's self.**

one-sid·ed (wun/sī/did) *adj.* **1.** Having, involving, or on one side. **2.** Biased; unfair. **3.** Having unequal or unbalanced sides. — **one/-sid/ed·ly** *adv.* — **one/-sid/ed·ness** *n.*

on-the-job (on-thə-job/, ôn-) *adj.* Pertaining to skills acquired while actually doing the job: *on-the-job* training.

one-time (wun/tīm/) *adj.* Former: a *one-time* winner.

one-track (wun/trak/) *adj.* **1.** Having or consisting of a single track. **2.** *Informal* Limited to a single idea or pursuit: a *one-track* mind.

one-way (wun/wā/) *adj.* Moving, or permitting movement, in one direction only: *one-way* traffic.

on·ion (un/yən) *n.* **1.** The edible, succulent bulb of an herb of the lily family, having a pungent odor and taste. **2.** Any of various allied plants. [< OF < L *unio* pearl, onion]

on·ion·skin (un/yən-skin/) *n.* A thin, translucent paper.

on·look·er (on/lŏŏk/ər, ôn/-) *n.* One who looks on; a spectator. — **on/look/ing** *adj.*

on·ly (ōn/lē) *adv.* **1.** In one manner or for one purpose alone. **2.** Solely; exclusively. **3.** Merely; just. — *adj.* **1.** Alone in its class; sole; single. **2.** Standing alone by reason of superior excellence. — *conj.* Except that; but. [OE *ānlīc*]

on·o·mat·o·poe·ia (on/ə-mat/ə-pē/ə, ō-nom/ə-tə-) *n.* **1.** The formation of words in imitation of natural sounds, as *crack, splash,* or *bow-wow.* **2.** An imitative word. **3.** The use of such words. Also **on/o·mat/o·po·e/sis** (-pō-ē/sis), **on/-o·mat/o·py** (-mat/ə-pē). [< L < Gk. < *onoma* name + *poieein* to make] — **on/o·mat/o·poe/ic** or **·i·cal, on/o·mat/o·po·et/ic** (-pō-et/ik) *adj.* — **on/o·mat/o·po·et/i·cal·ly** *adv.*

On·on·da·ga (on/ən-dô/gə, -dä/-) *n. pl.* **·ga** or **·gas 1.** A tribe of North American Indians of Iroquoian stock formerly living in New York and Ontario. **2.** A member of this tribe.

on·rush (on/rush/, ôn/-) *n.* An onward rush or flow.

on·set (on/set/, ôn/-) *n.* **1.** An attack; assault. **2.** An initial stage, as of illness. **3.** A setting about; outset; start.

on·shore (on/shôr/, -shōr/, ôn/-) *adv. & adj.* To, toward, or on the shore.

on·slaught (on/slôt/, ôn/-) *n.* A violent, often hostile assault. [< Du. *annslag,* or < ON + ME *slaught* slaughter]

on·to (on/tōō, ôn/-) *prep.* **1.** Upon the top of; to and upon. **2.** *Informal* Aware of: I'm *onto* your tricks. Also **on to.**

onto- *combining form* Being; existence: *ontogeny.* Also, before vowels, **ont-.** [< Gk. *ōn, ontos,* ppr. of *einai* to be]

on·tog·e·ny (on-toj/ə-nē) *n. pl.* **·nies** *Biol.* The history of the development of the individual organism. Also **on·to·gen·e·sis** (on/tō-jen/ə-sis). — **on·to·ge·net·ic** (on/tō-jə-net/ik), **on/to·gen/ic** *adj.* — **on/tog·e·nist** *n.*

on·tol·o·gy (on-tol/ə-jē) *n. pl.* **·gies** The branch of metaphysics dealing with the philosophical theory of reality. — **on/to·log/i·cal** *adj.* — **on·tol/o·gist** *n.*

o·nus (ō/nəs) *n.* A burden or responsibility. [< L]

on·ward (on/wərd, ôn/-) *adv.* In the direction of progress; forward in space or time; ahead. Also **on/wards.** — *adj.* Moving or tending to be forward or ahead. [ME]

on·yx (on/iks) *n.* A variety of chalcedony having layers of different colors, used as a semiprecious gemstone. [< L < Gk., nail, onyx]

oo- *combining form* **1.** Egg; pertaining to eggs: *oology.* **2.** *Biol.* An ovum: *oogenesis.* [< Gk. *ōon* egg]

oo·dles (ōōd/lz) *n.pl. Informal* A great deal; many. [< dial. E *oodle,* var. of HUDDLE, n.]

o·o·lite (ō/ə-līt) *n.* A granular variety of limestone made up of round grains resembling the roe of a fish. [< F < Gk. *ōon* egg + *lithos* stone] — **o/o·lit/ic** (-lit/ik) *adj.*

o·ol·o·gy (ō-ol/ə-jē) *n.* The branch of ornithology that deals with the study of eggs. — **o·o·log/ic** (ō/ə-loj/ik) or **·i·cal** *adj.* — **o·ol/o·gist** *n.*

oo·long (ōō/lông) *n.* A dark tea that is partly fermented before being dried. [< Chinese *wu-lung* black dragon]

oo·mi·ak (oō′mē·ak) See UMIAK.

oophoro- *combining form* Ovary; ovarian. Also, before vowels, **oophor-**. [< Gk. *ōophoros* egg-bearing]

ooze¹ (ōōz) *v.* **oozed, ooz·ing** *v.i.* **1.** To flow or leak out slowly or gradually. **2.** To exude moisture. **3.** To escape or disappear little by little. —*v.t.* **4.** To give off or exude in or as in droplets or a trickle. —*n.* **1.** A slow, gradual leak. **2.** That which oozes. [ME < OE *wāse* slimy mud]

ooze² (ōōz) *n.* **1.** Slimy mud or moist, spongy soil. **2.** A deposit of calcareous matter found on the ocean bottom and largely made up of the remains of foraminifers. **3.** Muddy or marshy ground; bog; fen. [OE *wāse* slimy mud]

oo·zy¹ (ōō′zē) *adj.* **·zi·er, ·zi·est** Slowly leaking.

oo·zy² (ōō′zē) *adj.* **·zi·er, ·zi·est** Of or resembling mud or ooze; slimy. —**oo′zi·ly** *adv.* —**oo′zi·ness** *n.*

op- Assimilated var. of OB-.

o·pac·i·ty (ō·pas′ə·tē) *n.* *pl.* **·ties 1.** The state or quality of being opaque. **2.** That which is opaque.

o·pal (ō′pəl) *n.* An amorphous, variously colored hydrous silica, including some iridescent varieties esteemed as gemstones. [< L < Gk. < Skt. *upala* precious stone]

o·pal·esce (ō′pəl·es′) *v.i.* **·esced, ·esc·ing** To exhibit opalescence.

o·pal·es·cence (ō′pəl·es′əns) *n.* An iridescent play of brilliant or milky colors, as in an opal. —**o′pal·es′cent** *adj.*

o·pal·ine (ō′pəl·ēn, -in) *adj.* Resembling or characteristic of an opal; opalescent. —*n.* A milky variety of glass.

o·paque (ō·pāk′) *adj.* **1.** Impervious to light; not translucent or transparent. **2.** Impervious to reason; unintelligent. **3.** Impervious to radiant heat, electric radiation, etc. **4.** Having no luster; dull. **5.** Unintelligible; obscure. —*n.* **1.** That which is opaque. **2.** A pigment used to darken or eliminate portions of a print, photographic negative, etc. [ME *opake* < L *opacus* dark] —**o·paque′ly** *adv.* —**o·paque′ness** *n.*

op art (op) A style of art of the 1960's characterized by complex geometric patterns. [< *op*(*tical*) *art*]

o·pen (ō′pən) *adj.* **1.** Affording approach, view, passage, or access. **2.** Public; accessible to all. **3.** Not secret or hidden: *open* hostility. **4.** Expanded; unfolded: an *open* flower. **5.** Not enclosed or covered: an *open* car. **6.** Ready for business, appointment, etc. **7.** Not settled or decided; pending: an *open* question. **8.** Available: The job is still *open.* **9.** Unbiased; receptive: often with *to:* an *open* mind; *open* to conviction. **10.** Generous; liberal: an *open* hand. **11.** *Phonet.* **a** Produced with a wide opening above the tongue; low: said of vowels, as the *a* in *father* and *calm:* opposed to *close.* **b** Ending in a vowel or diphthong: said of a syllable. **12.** Not deceptive: an *open* face. **13.** Eager or willing to receive: with *open* arms. **14.** In hunting or fishing, without prohibition: *open* season. **15.** Liable to attack, robbery, temptation, etc. **16.** Having openings, holes, or perforations, as needlework. **17.** *Music* **a** Not stopped by the finger, as a string. **b** Not produced by the stopping of a string or hole, or the use of a valve or slide; not fingered, as the tone of an instrument. **c** Not stopped by the hand or by a mute, as a brass instrument or its tone. **18.** Unrestricted by union regulations in employment: an *open* shop. **19.** *U.S. Informal* Permitting illicit activities, as gambling and prostitution: an *open* town. **20.** Out of doors. **21.** Not to be defended in war: *open* city. **22.** Not restricted by rigid classes, control, etc.: an *open* society. **23.** *U.S.* Of or designating a policy of admitting students for matriculation to a college or university without regard to their academic preparedness: *open* admissions. **24.** In the elementary grades, of or characterized by an educational environment designed to encourage self-motivated learning: *open* classrooms. —*v.t.* **1.** To set open or ajar, as a door; unclose; unfasten. **2.** To make passable; free from obstacles. **3.** To make or force (a hole, passage, etc.). **4.** To remove the covering, lid, etc., of. **5.** To expand, as for viewing; unroll; unfold, as a map. **6.** To make an opening or openings into: to *open* an abscess. **7.** To make or declare ready for commerce, use, etc.: to *open* a store. **8.** To make or declare public or free of access, as a park. **9.** To make less compact; expand: to *open* ranks. **10.** To make more receptive to ideas or sentiments; enlighten: to *open* the mind. **11.** To bare the secrets of; divulge; reveal: to *open* one's heart. **12.** To begin, as negotiations. **13.** *Law* To undo or recall (a judgment or order) so as to permit its validity to be questioned. —*v.i.* **14.** To become open. **15.** To come apart or break open; rupture. **16.** To come into view; spread out; unroll. **17.** To afford access or view: The door *opened* on a courtyard. **18.** To become receptive or enlightened. **19.** To begin: The season *opened* with a ball. **20.** In the theater, to begin a season or tour. —*n.* Any wide space not enclosed, obstructed, or covered, as by woods, rocks, etc.: usu. with the definite article: in the open. [OE] —**o′pen·er** *n.* —**o′pen·ly** *adv.* —**o′pen·ness** *n.*

o·pen-air (ō′pən·âr′) *adj.* Occurring, done, etc., out of doors: an *open-air* concert.

o·pen-and-shut (ō′pən·ən·shut′) *adj. Informal* Obvious; easily determined.

open door 1. The policy or practice of giving to all nations the same commercial privileges in a region or area open for trade or exploitation. **2.** Admission to all without charge. **o·pen-door** (ō′pən·dôr′, -dōr′) *adj.* Of or characterized by the commercial policies or practices of the open door.

o·pen-eyed (ō′pən·id′) *adj.* **1.** Having the eyes open; aware; watchful. **2.** Amazed: in *open-eyed* wonder.

o·pen-faced (ō′pən·fāst′) *adj.* **1.** Having an honest face. **2.** Having a face or side uncovered.

o·pen-hand·ed (ō′pən·han′did) *adj.* Giving freely; liberal.

o·pen-heart·ed (ō′pən·här′tid) *adj.* Disclosing the thoughts and intentions plainly; frank; candid.

o·pen-hearth (ō′pən·härth′) *adj. Metall.* Designating a steel-making process in which the material is melted in a shallow furnace open at each end to admit fuel and air.

open house 1. A house or a social event in which hospitality is extended to all who wish to come. **2.** An occasion when a school, factory, institution, etc., is open to visitors.

o·pen·ing (ō′pən·ing) *n.* **1.** The act of becoming open or of causing to be open. **2.** A vacant or unobstructed space, as a hole, passage, or gap. **3.** An aperture in a wall, esp. one for the admission of light or air. **4.** The first part or stage, as of a period, act, or process. **5.** A first time for or the beginning of something: the play's *opening.* **6.** In chess, checkers, etc., a specific series of opening moves. **7.** An opportunity for action, esp. in business.

open market A market accessible to all buyers and sellers.

o·pen-mind·ed (ō′pən·min′did) *adj.* Free from prejudiced conclusions; amenable to reason; receptive. —**o′pen-mind′ed·ly** *adv.* **o′pen-mind′ed·ness** *n.*

o·pen-mouthed (ō′pən·mouthd′, -moutht′) *adj.* **1.** Having the mouth open; gaping, as in wonder or surprise. **2.** Noisy; clamorous. **3.** Greedy; voracious.

open sesame An unfailing means or formula for opening secret doors and gaining entrance: an allusion to the tale of *Ali Baba and the Forty Thieves* in the *Arabian Nights.*

open shop 1. An establishment employing both union and nonunion labor. **2.** An establishment whose policy is to hire only nonunion labor.

o·pen·work (ō′pən·wûrk′) *n.* Any product of art or handicraft containing numerous small openings.

op·er·a (op′ər·ə, op′rə) Plural of OPUS. —*n.* **1.** A form of drama in which music is a dominant factor, made up of arias, recitatives, choruses, etc., with orchestral accompaniment, scenery, acting, and sometimes dance. **2.** An opera house. [< Ital. < L, service, work < *opus* work] —**op·er·at·ic** (op′ə·rat′ik) *adj.* —**op′er·at′i·cal·ly** *adv.*

op·er·a·ble (op′ər·ə·bəl) *adj.* **1.** Capable of treatment by surgical operation. **2.** Practicable. —**op′er·a·bil′i·ty** *n.*

o·pé·ra bouffe (ō·pā·rä bōōf′) *French* A farcical comic opera. Also *Ital.* **o·pe·ra buf·fa** (ō′pä·rä bōōf′fä).

opera glass Small binoculars suitable for use at the theater. Also **opera glasses.**

opera hat A man's top hat, having a collapsible crown.

opera house A theater adapted for performance of operas.

op·er·ate (op′ə·rāt) *v.* **·at·ed, ·at·ing** *v.i.* **1.** To act or function; work. **2.** To bring about the proper or intended effect. **3.** *Surg.* To perform an operation. **4.** To carry on a military or naval operation: usu. with *against.* —*v.t.* **5.** To control the working of, as a machine. **6.** To manage or conduct the affairs of. **7.** To bring about or cause; effect. [< L *operari* to work] —**op′er·at′a·ble** *adj.*

op·er·a·tion (op′ə·rā′shən) *n.* **1.** The act or process of operating. **2.** A method of operating; mode of action. **3.** An act or transaction, esp. in the stock market. **4.** A course or series of acts to effect a certain purpose; process. **5.** The state of being in action: to be in *operation.* **6.** *Surg.* Any manipulation upon or within the body, performed with or without instruments, to restore disunited or deficient parts, to remove diseased or injured parts, etc. **7.** *Math.* **a** The act of making a change in the value or form of a quantity. **b** The change itself as indicated by symbols or rules. **8.** A military or naval campaign.

op·er·a·tion·al (op′ə·rā′shən·əl) *adj.* **1.** Pertaining to an operation. **2.** Checked and serviced for ready operation.

operations research The application of scientific methods and skills to insure maximum efficiency in industry and government. Also called **operational research.**

op·er·a·tive (op′ər·ə·tiv, -ə·rā′tiv) *adj.* **1.** Exerting force or influence. **2.** Moving or working efficiently; effective. **3.** Being in operation or in force. **4.** Connected with surgical operations. **5.** Concerned with practical work, mechanical or manual. —*n.* **1.** A skilled worker, as in a mill or factory. **2.** *Informal* A detective. —**op′er·a·tive·ly** *adv.*

op·er·a·tor (op′ə·rā′tər) *n.* **1.** One who operates a machine or mechanism. **2.** One who runs a commercial or industrial establishment. **3.** A broker. **4.** *Math.* A symbol that briefly indicates a mathematical process. **5.** *Slang* One who craftily obtains things with little or no cost to himself.

op·er·cu·late (ō-pûr′kyŏŏ-lit, -lāt) *adj.* Having an operculum. Also **o·per′cu·lat·ed.**

o·per·cu·lum (ō-pûr′kyŏŏ-ləm) *n. pl.* **·la** (-lə) *Biol.* A lidlike part or organ in certain plants, esp. one serving to close an aperture or provide protection. Also **o·per·cele** (ō-pûr′sĕl), **o·per′cule** (-kyōōl). [< L, a covering, lid < *operire* to cover] — **o·per′cu·lar** *adj.*

o·pe·re ci·ta·to (op′ə-rē sī-tā′tō) *Latin* In the work cited, or quoted. Abbr. *o.c., op. cit.*

op·e·ret·ta (op′ə-ret′ə) *n.* A type of short, humorous opera with dialogue: also called *light opera.* [< Ital., dim. of *opera*]

o·phid·i·an (ō-fid′ē-ən) *n.* One of a group of limbless reptiles with jaws connected by elastic ligaments; a serpent or snake. — *adj.* Snakelike. [< NL < Gk. *ophis* serpent]

oph·thal·mi·a (of-thal′mē-ə) *n. Pathol.* Inflammation of the eye, its membranes, or its lids. Also **oph·thal′my** (-mē). [< LL < Gk. < *ophthalmos* eye]

oph·thal·mic (of-thal′mik) *adj.* Of or pertaining to the eye.

oph·thal·mi·tis (of′thal-mī′tis) *n. Pathol.* Inflammation of the eye, including the outer and internal structures.

ophthalmo- *combining form* Eye; pertaining to the eyes. [< Gk. *ophthalmos* eye]

oph·thal·mol·o·gy (of′thal-mol′ə-jē) *n.* The science dealing with the structure, functions, and diseases of the eye. — **oph·thal′mo·log′ic** (-mə-loj′ik) or **·i·cal** *adj.* — **oph·thal·mol′o·gist** *n.*

oph·thal·mo·scope (of-thal′mə-skōp) *n.* An optical instrument for illuminating and viewing the center of the eye. — **oph·thal′mo·scop′ic** (-skop′ik) or **·i·cal** *adj.* — **oph·thal·mos′co·py** (of′thal-mos′kə-pē) *n.*

-opia *combining form Med.* A (specified) defect of the eye, or condition of sight: *myopia.* Also spelled **-opy.** [< Gk. *-ōpia* < *ōps, ōpos* the eye]

o·pi·ate (*n. & adj.* ō′pē·it, -āt; *v.* ō′pē-āt) *n.* **1.** Medicine containing opium or one of its derivatives. **2.** Something inducing relaxation or sleep. — *adj.* **1.** Consisting of opium. **2.** Tending to induce sleep. — *v.t.* **·at·ed, ·at·ing** **1.** To treat with opium or an opiate. **2.** To deaden; dull.

o·pine (ō-pīn′) *v.t. & v.i.* **o·pined, o·pin·ing** To hold or express as an opinion; think; conjecture: now usu. humorous. [< MF < L *opinari* to think, suppose]

o·pin·ion (ə-pin′yən, ō-) *n.* **1.** A conclusion or judgment held with confidence, but falling short of positive knowledge. **2.** An expert judgment given more or less formally. **3.** An evaluation. **4.** A prevailing sentiment: public *opinion.* **5.** *Law* The formal announcement of the conclusions of a court. [< OF < L < *opinari* to think]

o·pin·ion·at·ed (ə-pin′yən-ā′tid, ō-) *adj.* Obstinately attached to one's own opinion. — **o·pin′ion·at′ed·ness** *n.*

o·pin·ion·a·tive (ə-pin′yən-ā′tiv, ō-) *adj.* **1.** Opinionated. **2.** Of the nature of opinion. — **o·pin′ion·a·tive·ly** *adv.* **o·pin′ion·a·tive·ness** *n.*

o·pi·um (ō′pē-əm) *n.* A narcotic drug obtained from the unripe capsules of the **opium poppy,** containing a mixture of alkaloids, including morphine. [< L < Gk. *opion* opium, dim. of *opos* vegetable juice]

o·pos·sum (ə-pos′əm, pos′əm) *n.* An American marsupial of largely arboreal and nocturnal habits, having a prehensile tail and toes adapted for grasping. [< Algonquian]

op·po·nent (ə-pō′nənt) *n.* One who opposes another, as in battle; antagonist. — **Syn.** See ENEMY. — *adj.* **1.** Acting against something or someone; opposing. **2.** *Anat.* Bringing one part, as of a muscle, into opposition to another. **3.** Standing in front; opposite. [< L < *ob-* against + *ponere* to place] — **op·po′nen·cy** *n.*

op·por·tune (op′ər-tōōn′, -tyōōn′) *adj.* **1.** Meeting some need; esp. right or fit. **2.** Occurring at the right moment; timely. [< MF < L *opportunus* favorable, lit., (a wind) blowing towards port] — **op′por·tune′ly** *adv.* — **op′por·tune′ness** *n.*

op·por·tu·nist (op′ər-tōō′nist, -tyōō′-) *n.* One who uses every opportunity to contribute to the achievement of some end, and who is relatively uninfluenced by moral principles or sentiment. — **op′por·tu·nis′tic** *adj.* — **op′por·tu′nism** *n.*

op·por·tu·ni·ty (op′ər-tōō′nə-tē, -tyōō′-) *n. pl.* **·ties** A fit or convenient time; favorable occasion or circumstance.

op·pos·a·ble (ə-pō′zə-bəl) *adj.* **1.** Capable of being placed opposite something else: said esp. of the thumb. **2.** That can be opposed. — **op·pos′a·bil′i·ty** *n.*

op·pose (ə-pōz′) *v.* **·posed, ·pos·ing** *v.t.* **1.** To act or be in opposition to; resist; combat. **2.** To set in opposition or contrast: to *oppose* love to hatred. **3.** To place before or in front. — *v.i.* **4.** To act or be in opposition. [< OF < L < *ob-* against + *ponere* to place] — **op·pos′er** *n.*
— **Syn. 1.** Combat, fight, resist, withstand, dispute, contradict, contravene.

op·po·site (op′ə-zit) *adj.* **1.** Situated or placed on the other side, or on each side, of an intervening space or thing. **2.**

Facing or moving the other way: *opposite* directions. **3.** Contrary in tendency or character: *opposite* opinions. **4.** *Bot.* **a** Arranged in pairs, as leaves on a stem. **b** Having one part or organ immediately before or vertically over another, as a stamen before a petal. — *n.* Something or someone that is opposite, opposed, or contrary. — *adv.* In an opposite or complementary direction or position. — *prep.* **1.** Across from; facing. **2.** Complementary to, as in theatrical roles: He played *opposite* her. [< OF < L *oppositus.* See OPPOSE.] — **op′po·site·ly** *adv.* — **op′po·site·ness** *n.*

op·po·si·tion (op′ə-zish′ən) *n.* **1.** The act of opposing or resisting. **2.** The state of being opposite or opposed; antithesis. **3.** A position confronting another or a placing in contrast. **4.** That which is or furnishes an obstacle to some result: The stream flows without *opposition.* **5.** *Often cap.* The political party opposed to the party or administration in power. — **op′po·si′tion·al** *adj.* — **op·po·si′tion·ist** *n.* — **op′po·si′tion·less** *adj.*

op·pos·i·tive (ə-poz′ə-tiv) *adj.* Placed or capable of being placed in contrast. — **op·pos′i·tive·ly** *adv.*

op·press (ə-pres′) *v.t.* **1.** To burden or keep down by harsh and unjust use of force or authority. **2.** To lie heavy upon physically or mentally. [< OF < Med.L *oppressare,* ult. < L *ob-* against + *premere* to press] — **op·pres′sor** *n.*

op·pres·sion (ə-presh′ən) *n.* **1.** The act of oppressing, or the state of being oppressed. **2.** A sense of weight or constriction; mental depression. **3.** That which oppresses.

op·pres·sive (ə-pres′iv) *adj.* **1.** Burdensome; tyrannical; harsh; cruel. **2.** Producing a state of oppression. — **op·pres′sive·ly** *adv.* — **op·pres′sive·ness** *n.*

op·pro·bri·ous (ə-prō′brē-əs) *adj.* **1.** Contemptuously abusive; imputing disgrace. **2.** Shameful; disgraceful. — **op·pro′bri·ous·ly** *adv.* — **op·pro′bri·ous·ness** *n.*

op·pro·bri·um (ə-prō′brē-əm) *n.* **1.** The state of being scornfully reproached; ignominy. **2.** Reproach mingled with disdain. **3.** A cause of disgrace or reproach. [< L < *ob-* against + *probum* disgrace]
— **Syn. 1.** odium, obloquy, infamy, disgrace.

op·pugn (ə-pyōōn′) *v.t.* To assail or oppose with argument; call in question; controvert. [< L < *ob-* against + *pugnare* to fight] — **op·pugn′er** *n.*

-opsia *combining form Med.* A (specified) type or condition of sight. Also **-opsy.** [< NL < Gk. *opsis* aspect, sight]

opt (opt) *v.i.* To choose; decide. [< F < L *optare*]

op·ta·tive (op′tə-tiv) *adj.* **1.** Expressing desire or choice. **2.** *Gram.* Denoting the mood that expresses wish or desire. — *n. Gram.* **1.** The optative mood. **2.** A word or construction in this mood. [< F < LL < L *optare* to wish] — **op′ta·tive·ly** *adv.*

op·tic (op′tik) *adj.* Pertaining to the eye or vision. — *n. Informal* The eye. [< MF < Med.L < Gk. *optikos* < stem *op-* as in *opsomai* I shall see]

op·ti·cal (op′ti-kəl) *adj.* **1.** Pertaining to optics. **2.** Of or pertaining to eyesight. **3.** Designed to assist or improve vision. — **op′ti·cal·ly** *adv.*

optical fiber Any of various fibers of glass or other clear plastic through which light may be conducted along any desired path and in compact bundles will transmit images of high fidelity and resolution.

optical maser *Physics* A laser.

op·ti·cian (op-tish′ən) *n.* One who makes or deals in optical goods.

optic nerve *Anat.* The special nerve of vision, connecting the retina with the cerebral centers. For illus. see EYE.

op·tics (op′tiks) *n.pl.* (*construed as sing.*) The science that treats of the phenomena of light, vision, and sight.

op·ti·mal (op′tə-məl) *adj.* Most favorable; best.

op·ti·mism (op′tə-miz′əm) *n.* **1.** A disposition to look on the bright side of things. **2.** The doctrine that everything is ordered for the best. **3.** The doctrine that the universe is constantly tending toward a better state. [< F < L *optimus* best] — **op′ti·mist** *n.* — **op′ti·mis′tic** or **·ti·cal** *adj.* — **op′ti·mis′ti·cal·ly** *adv.*

op·ti·mum (op′tə-məm) *n. pl.* **·ma** (-mə) or **·mums** The condition or degree producing the best result. — *adj.* Producing or conducive to the best results. [< L, neut. of *optimus* best]

op·tion (op′shən) *n.* **1.** The right, power, or liberty of choosing; discretion. **2.** The act of opting or choosing. **3.** The purchased privilege of either buying or selling something at a specified price within a specified time. **4.** A thing that is or can be chosen. [< MF < L < *optare* to choose]

op·tion·al (op′shən-əl) *adj.* Left to one's preference; not required; elective. — **op′tion·al·ly** *adv.*

op·tom·e·try (op-tom′ə-trē) *n.* The profession or occupation of measuring vision and prescribing corrective lenses to compensate for visual defects. — **op·tom′e·trist** *n.*

op·u·lence (op′yə-ləns) *n.* **1.** Wealth; affluence. **2.** Lux-

uriance; abundance. Also **op′u·len·cy** (-lən·sē).
— **Syn. 1.** riches, fortune, means, prosperity.
op·u·lent (op′yə·lənt) *adj.* **1.** Possessing great wealth; rich; affluent. **2.** Plentiful; abundant; profuse. [< L *opulentus* < *ops, opis* power, wealth] — **op′u·lent·ly** *adv.*
o·pus (ō′pəs) *n., pl.* **op·er·a** (op′ər·ə, op′rə) A literary or musical work or composition. Abbr. *op.* [< L, work]
-opy See -OPIA.
or (ôr, *unstressed* ər) *conj.* **1.** Introducing an alternative: stop *or* go. **2.** Offering a choice of a series: Will you take milk *or* coffee *or* chocolate? **3.** Introducing an equivalent: the culinary art *or* art of cookery. **4.** Indicating uncertainty: He lives in Chicago *or* thereabouts. **5.** Introducing the second alternative of a choice limited to two: with *either or whether*: It must be either black *or* white; I don't care whether he goes *or* not. **6.** *Poetic* Either; whether: *or* in the heart *or* in the head. [ME contraction of *other, auther* either, OE *æther*; infl. in meaning by OE *oththe* or]
-or¹ *suffix of nouns* The person or thing performing the action expressed in the root verb: *competitor.* ◆ See note under -ER¹. [< AF -*our*, OF -*or* < L -*or*, -*ator*]
-or² *suffix of nouns* Quality, state, or condition: *favor.* [< OF < L]
or·a·cle (ôr′ə·kəl, or′-) *n.* **1.** The seat of worship of some ancient divinity, as of Apollo at Delphi, where prophecies were given out by the priests in answer to inquiries. **2.** A prophecy thus given. **3.** The deity whose prophecies were given. **4.** A person of unquestioned wisdom or knowledge, or something regarded as of infallible authority. **5.** A wise saying. [< OF < L *oraculum* < *orare* to speak, pray]
o·rac·u·lar (ō·rak′yə·lər, ō-) *adj.* **1.** Of or pertaining to an oracle. **2.** Obscure; enigmatical. **3.** Prophetic; farseeing. — **o·rac′u·lar′i·ty** *n.* — **o·rac′u·lar·ly** *adv.*
o·ral (ôr′əl, ō′rəl) *adj.* **1.** Uttered through the mouth; spoken. **2.** Of or pertaining to the mouth; also, situated at or near the mouth. **3.** Of, pertaining to, or using speech. **4.** Taken or administered by mouth. — **Syn.** See VERBAL. — *n. Usu. pl.* An academic examination in which the student speaks his answers aloud. [< L *os, oris* mouth] — **o′ral·ly** *adv.*
o·rang (ō·rang′) *n.* An orang-utan.
or·ange (ôr′inj, or′-) *n.* **1.** A round, juicy fruit of a low, much-branched, evergreen tree with a reddish yellow rind enclosing membranous divisions and a refreshing, sweetish or subacid pulp. **2.** Any of the trees yielding this fruit. **3.** Any of many related species. **4.** A reddish yellow color; also, a pigment of this color. — *adj.* **1.** Reddish yellow. **2.** Of an orange. [< OF < Provençal < Sp. < Arabic < Persian *nārang*]
or·ange·ade (ôr′inj·ād′, or′-) *n.* A beverage made of orange juice, sugar, and water. [< F]
orange blossom The white, fragrant blossom of the orange tree, often worn by brides: State flower of Florida.
Or·ange·man (ôr′inj·mən, or′-) *n., pl.* **·men** (-mən) A member of a secret society founded in northern Ireland in 1795 for upholding Protestant ascendancy and succession in England. [named in honor of William III, king of England and Prince of Orange]
orange pekoe A black tea from India, Ceylon, and Java.
or·ange·wood (ôr′inj·wŏŏd′, or′-) *n.* The fine-grained, yellowish wood of the orange tree, used in lathe work.
o·rang-u·tan (ō·rang′ə·tan, -ōō·tan) *n., pl.* **·tans** or **·tan** A large, anthropoid ape of Borneo and Sumatra, having brownish red hair and extremely long arms: also called *orang, ourang.* Also **o·rang′-ou·tang** (-ə·tang), **o·rang′-ou·tang** (-ə·tang). [< Malay < *oran* man + *utan* forest]
o·rate (ô·rāt′, ō-rāt′, ō′rāt, ō·rāt′) *v.i.* **o·rat·ed, o·rat·ing** To talk oratorically or pompously; speechify. [See ORATION.]
o·ra·tion (ô·rā′shən, ō-rā′-) *n.* An elaborate public speech, esp. one given at a formal occasion. [< L < *orare* to speak]
or·a·tor (ôr′ə·tər, or′-) *n.* **1.** One who delivers an oration; an eloquent public speaker. **2.** *Law* The complainant in a chancery proceeding. — **or′a·tor·ship′** *n.*
or·a·to·ri·o (ôr′ə·tôr′ē·ō, -tō′rē·ō, or′-) *n., pl.* **·os** A large musical composition for solo voices, chorus, and orchestra, usu. dramatizing a sacred story, but without scenery or acting. [< Ital. < LL. See ORATORY².]
or·a·to·ry¹ (ôr′ə·tôr′ē, -tō′rē, or′-) *n.* **1.** The art of public speaking; eloquence. **2.** Eloquent language. [< L *oratoria* (*ars*) the oratorical (art)] — **or′a·tor′i·cal** (-tôr′i·kəl, -tor′-) *adj.* — **or′a·tor′i·cal·ly** *adv.*
or·a·to·ry² (ôr′ə·tôr′ē, -tō′rē, or′-) *n., pl.* **·ries** A place for prayer; private chapel. [< LL *oratorium* (*templum*) (temple) for prayer < *orare* to pray]
orb (ôrb) *n.* **1.** A rounded mass; a sphere or globe. **2.** A circle or orbit; anything circular. **3.** A sphere topped by a cross, used as a symbol of royal power. **4.** *Poetic* The eye. — *v.t.* **1.** To shape into a sphere or circle. **2.** *Poetic* To enclose; encircle. [< L *orbis* circle]
or·bic·u·lar (ôr·bik′yə·lər) *adj.* **1.** Having the form of an orb or orbit. **2.** Well-rounded. **3.** *Bot.* Circular, as a leaf.

[< F, or < L < *orbiculus*, dim. of *orbis* circle] — **or·bic′u·lar′i·ty** (-lar′ə·tē) *n.* — **or·bic′u·lar·ly** *adv.*
or·bic·u·late (ôr·bik′yə·lit, -lāt) *adj.* Having a rounded form; orbicular. Also **or·bic′u·lat′ed.** — **or·bic′u·late·ly** *adv.*
or·bit (ôr′bit) *n.* **1.** The path in space along which a heavenly body or artificial satellite moves about its center of attraction. **2.** A range of influence or action: the *orbit* of imperialism. — *v.t.* **1.** To cause to move in an orbit, as an artificial satellite. **2.** To revolve around (the earth, etc.), as a satellite. — *v.i.* **3.** To move in or as in an orbit. [< L *orbita* track of a wheel < *orbis* wheel, circle] — **or′bi·tal** *adj.*
or·chard (ôr′chərd) *n.* A plantation of trees grown for their products, as fruit, nuts, oils, etc.; also, the enclosure or ground containing them. [OE < *ort-geard* garden]
or·ches·tra (ôr′kis·trə) *n.* **1.** A comparatively large group of musicians playing together; esp., a symphony orchestra; also, the instruments they play. **2.** *U.S.* In theaters, the place immediately before the stage, occupied by the musicians: also **orchestra pit. 3.** The main floor of a theater. [< L < Gk. *orchēstra* dancing space] — **or·ches·tral** (ôr·kes′·trəl) *adj.* — **or·ches′tral·ly** *adv.*
or·ches·trate (ôr′kis·trāt) *v.t. & v.i.* **·trat·ed, ·trat·ing** To compose or arrange (music) for an orchestra. — **or′ches·tra′tion** *n.*
or·chid (ôr′kid) *n.* **1.** Any of a family of herbs of temperate regions, having bulbous roots and often very showy flowers. **2.** Any of various delicate, rosy purple colors. [< NL < L *orchis* orchid < Gk., orig., a testicle; so called because of the shape of its rootstocks]
orchio- *combining form* Testicle; pertaining to the testicles. Also, before vowels, **orchi-.** [< Gk. *orchis* testicle]
or·chis (ôr′kis) *n.* Any of various plants having dense spikes of small flowers. [< L, orchid]
or·dain (ôr·dān′) *v.t.* **1.** To order or decree; enact. **2.** To predestine; destine: said of God, fate, etc. **3.** To invest with ministerial or priestly functions. [< OF < L *ordinare* to set in order] — **or·dain′er** *n.*
or·deal (ôr·dēl′, -dē′əl, ôr′dēl) *n.* **1.** A severe test of character or endurance. **2.** A former method of judicial trial in which the accused was subjected to painful physical tests that were supposed to do him no harm if he were innocent. [OE *ordāl, ordēl* judgment < *or-* out + *dæl* a deal]
or·der (ôr′dər) *n.* **1.** A condition in which there is a methodical, proper, or harmonious arrangement of things. **2.** The disposition or arrangement of things. **3.** Established method, procedure, or condition. **4.** A proper or working condition. **5.** A command, direction, or regulation. **6.** *Law* Any direction of a court, entered in the record but not included in the final judgment. **7.** A commission or instruction to supply, purchase, or sell something; also, that which is supplied or purchased. **8.** A body of persons united by some common bond: the *Order* of Odd Fellows. **9.** A monastic or religious body. **10.** A group of persons upon whom an honor has been conferred, entitling them to wear specific insignia; also, the insignia so worn. **11.** *Eccl.* **a** *Usu. pl.* Any of the various grades or degrees of the Christian ministry. **b** The rite or sacrament of ordination. **c** A liturgical form for a service or the performance of a rite. **12.** *Archit.* **a** A style of classical architecture, as Doric, Ionic, or Corinthian, etc. represented by the general character of its columns. **b** A column with its entablature. **13.** *Biol.* A taxonomic category ranking next below the class, and above the family. — **in order 1.** In accordance with rule or proper procedure. **2.** Neat; tidy. — **in order that** So that; to the end that. — **in order to** For the purpose of. — **in short order** Quickly; without delay. — **on order** Ordered but not yet delivered. — **on the order of** Similar to. — **out of order 1.** Not in working condition. **2.** Not in proper arrangement or sequence. **3.** Not according to rule. **4.** Not suitable or appropriate. — **to order** According to the buyer's specifications. — *v.t.* **1.** To give a command or direction to. **2.** To command to go, come, etc. **3.** To give an order that (something) be done. **4.** To give an order for. **5.** To put in orderly or systematic arrangement. **6.** To ordain. — *v.i.* **7.** To give an order or orders. — **to order arms** *Mil.* To bring a rifle against the right side, with the butt on the ground. [< OF < L *ordo, -inis* row, series, order] — **or′der·er** *n.*
or·der·ly (ôr′dər·lē) *adj.* **1.** Having regard for arrangement, method, or system. **2.** Peaceful. **3.** Characterized by neatness and order. **4.** Pertaining to orders. — *n., pl.* **·lies 1.** A hospital attendant. **2.** A soldier detailed to carry orders. — *adv.* Methodically; regularly. — **or′der·li·ness** *n.*
or·di·nal¹ (ôr′də·nəl) *adj.* **1.** Denoting position in an order or succession. **2.** Pertaining to an order, as of plants, animals, etc. [< LL < L *ordo, -inis* order]
or·di·nal² (ôr′də·nəl) *n. Eccl.* A book of rites for certain church services. [< Med.L < LL < L *ordo, -inis* order]
ordinal number *Math.* A number that shows the order of a unit in a given series, as first, second, third, etc.: distinguished from *cardinal number.*
or·di·nance (ôr′də·nəns) *n.* **1.** An order, decree, or law of

a municipal body. **2.** A religious rite or ceremony. [< OF < Med.L < L < *ordinare* to set in order]

or·di·nar·i·ly (ôr′də·ner′ə·lē, ôr′də·nâr′ə·lē) *adv.* **1.** In ordinary cases; usually. **2.** In the usual manner. **3.** To the usual extent; normally.

or·di·nar·y (ôr′də·ner′ē) *adj.* **1.** Of common or everyday occurrence; customary; usual. **2.** According to an established order; normal. **3.** Common in rank or degree; average; commonplace. — *n. pl.* **·nar·ies 1.** That which is usual or common. **2.** *Brit.* **a** A meal provided regularly at a fixed price. **b** An eating house where such meals are served. **3.** *Law* One who exercises jurisdiction in his own right, and not by delegation. **4.** *Eccl.* **a** A rule or book prescribing the form for saying Mass. **b** The practically unchangeable part of the Mass: with *the*: distinguished from the *proper.* — **in ordinary 1.** In actual and constant service. **2.** *Naut.* Out of commission; laid up: said of a ship. — **out of the ordinary** Not common or usual; extraordinary. [< OF < L *ordinarius* regular, usual] — **or′di·nar′i·ness** *n.*

or·di·nate (ôr′də·nit) *adj.* Characterized by order; regular. — *n. Math.* **1.** The distance of any point from the X-axis, measured on a line parallel to the Y-axis in a coordinate system. **2.** The line or number indicating such distance.

or·di·na·tion (ôr′də·nā′shən) *n.* **1.** *Eccl.* The rite of consecration to the ministry. **2.** The state of being ordained, regulated, or settled.

ord·nance (ôrd′nəns) *n.* **1.** Military weapons, ammunition, and associated equipment and materiel. **2.** Cannon or artillery. [Contr. of ORDINANCE]

Or·do·vi·cian (ôr′də·vish′ən) *adj. Geol.* Of or designating a period of the Paleozoic era, following the Cambrian and preceding the Silurian. — *n.* An epoch of the Paleozoic era. See chart for GEOLOGY. [< L *Ordovices* the Ordovices, an ancient Celtic tribe]

or·dure (ôr′jər, -dyŏor) *n.* Excrement; feces. [< OF < *ord* foul, nasty < L *horridus* bristling]

ore (ôr, ōr) *n.* **1.** A natural substance, as a mineral or rock, containing a valuable metal. **2.** A natural substance containing a nonmetallic mineral: sulfur *ore.* [OE *ār, ǣr* brass, copper; infl. in meaning by OE *ōra* unwrought metal]

ö·re (œ′rə) *n. pl.* **ö·re** A coin or monetary unit equivalent to one hundredth of a krone in Denmark and Norway, and of a krona in Sweden. [< Norw., Dan., and Sw.]

o·reg·a·no (ō·reg′ə·nō) *n.* A perennial herb of the mint family, having aromatic leaves used as a seasoning. [< Sp. < L *origanum* wild marjoram]

Oregon grape An evergreen shrub having dark blue berry clusters resembling grapes: the State flower of Oregon.

O·res·tes (ō·res′tēz, ō-) In Greek legend, the son of Agamemnon and Clytemnestra who, together with his sister Electra, avenged his father's murder by killing his mother and her lover. [< L < Gk.]

or·fray (ôr′frā) See ORPHREY.

or·gan (ôr′gən) *n.* **1.** A musical instrument consisting of a collection of pipes and reeds made to sound by means of compressed air controlled by one or more keyboards and by various knobs used to vary registration: often called *pipe organ.* **2.** Any musical instrument resembling this, either in sound or in some aspect of its mechanism. **3.** Any part of a plant or animal, as a stamen, the heart, etc., performing some definite function. **4.** An instrument or agency of communication; esp., a newspaper or periodical published in the interest of a political party, religious denomination, etc. [< OE *organa*, or < OF < L < Gk. *organon* instrument]

or·gan·dy (ôr′gən·dē) *n. pl.* **·dies** A thin, crisp, transparent, cotton muslin, used for dresses, collars, cuffs, etc. Also **or′gan·die.** [< F *organdi*; ult. origin uncertain]

organ grinder A street musician playing a hand organ.

or·gan·ic (ôr·gan′ik) *adj.* **1.** Of, pertaining to, or of the nature of animals and plants. **2.** Affecting or altering the structure of an organ or part: *organic* disease: distinguished from *functional.* **3.** Serving the purpose of an organ. **4.** *Chem.* Of or pertaining to compounds containing carbon. **5.** Inherent in or pertaining to the fundamental structure of something; constitutional. **6.** Of or characterized by systematic coordination of parts; organized; systematized. **7.** *Law* Designating the system of laws or principles forming the foundation of a government. Also **or·gan′i·cal.** [< L < Gk. < *organon* instrument] — **or·gan′i·cal·ly** *adv.*

organic chemistry The branch of chemistry that relates to the structure, formation, and properties of compounds containing carbon.

organic disease *Pathol.* A disease that affects or alters the structure of some particular organ or part.

or·gan·ism (ôr′gən·iz′əm) *n.* **1.** An animal or plant considered as a totality of interdependent parts functioning to maintain vital activities. **2.** Anything that is analogous in structure and function to a living thing: the social *organism.*

or·gan·ist (ôr′gən·ist) *n.* One who plays the organ.

or·gan·i·za·tion (ôr′gən·ə·zā′shən, -ī·zā′-) *n.* **1.** The act of organizing, or the state of being organized; also, that which is organized. **2.** A number of individuals systematically united for some end or work. **3.** The officials who control a political party. Also *Brit.* **or′gan·i·sa′tion.**

or·gan·ize (ôr′gən·īz) *v.* **·ized, ·iz·ing** *v.t.* **1.** To bring together or form as a whole or combination, as for a common objective. **2.** To arrange systematically; order. **3.** To furnish with organic structure. **4.** To enlist (workers) in a trade union. **5.** To unionize the workers of (a factory, etc.). — *v.i.* **6.** To form or join an organization. Also *Brit.* **or′gan·ise.** — **or′gan·iz′a·ble** *adj.* — **or′gan·iz′er** *n.*

organo- *combining form* **1.** *Biol.* Related to an organ or to the organs of the body. **2.** *Chem.* Organic. [< Gk. *organon* instrument, organ]

or·ga·no·me·tal·lic (ôr′gə·nō·mə·tal′ik) *adj. Chem.* Designating or pertaining to a compound of metal and carbon.

organ pipe One of the tubes of a pipe organ in which a column of air is made to vibrate so as to produce a tone.

or·gasm (ôr′gaz·əm) *n. Physiol.* The acme of excitement at the culmination of a sexual act. [< NL < Gk. *orgaein* to swell] — **or·gas·mic** (ôr·gaz′mik) *adj.*

or·gi·as·tic (ôr′jē·as′tik) *adj.* **1.** Pertaining to or resembling an orgy. **2.** Marked by orgies.

or·gy (ôr′jē) *n. pl.* **·gies 1.** Wild or wanton revelry. **2.** Any immoderate or excessive indulgence. **3.** *pl.* The secret rites in honor of certain Greek and Roman deities, marked by frenzied songs and dances. [Earlier *orgies*, pl. < MF < L *orgia* < Gk., secret rites]

o·ri·el (ôr′ē·əl, ō′rē-) *n. Archit.* A bay window, esp. one built out from a wall and resting on a bracket or similar support. [< OF *oriol* porch, gallery, ? < Med.L *oriolum*]

o·ri·ent (*n. & adj.* ôr′ē·ənt, ō′rē-, -ent; *v.* ôr′ē·ent, ō′rē-) *n.* **1.** The east: opposed to *occident.* **2.** The eastern sky; also, sunrise. — *v.t.* **1.** To cause to face or turn to the east. **2.** To place or adjust, as a map, in exact relation to the points of the compass. **3.** To adjust in relation to something else. Also **orientate.** — *adj.* **1.** Resembling sunrise; bright. **2.** Ascending; rising. [< OF < L (*sol*) *oriens, -entis* rising (sun), east, ppr. of *oriri* to rise]

O·ri·ent (ôr′ē·ənt, ō′rē-, -ent) **1.** The countries east of Europe; esp., eastern Asia. **2.** The eastern hemisphere.

o·ri·en·tal (ôr′ē·en′təl, ō′rē-) *adj.* **1.** Of or pertaining to the East, or to the countries constituting the Orient: distinguished from *occidental.* **2.** Very bright, clear, and pure: said of gems. **3.** Denoting a variety of precious corundum, esp. sapphire: an *oriental* topaz. — **o·ri·en·tal·ly** *adv.*

O·ri·en·tal (ôr′ē·en′təl, ō′rē-) *adj.* Of or pertaining to the Orient; Eastern. — *n.* An inhabitant of Asia; an Asian.

O·ri·en·tal·ism (ôr′ē·en′təl·iz′əm, ō′rē-) *n.* **1.** An Oriental quality, mannerism, characteristic, etc. **2.** Knowledge of or proficiency in Oriental languages, literature, etc. Also **o′ri·en′tal·ist.** — **O′ri·en′tal·ist** *n.*

Oriental rug 1. A rug or carpet hand-woven in one piece in the Orient. **2.** Any rug having a design or texture resembling those made in the Orient.

o·ri·en·tate (ôr′ē·en·tāt′, ō′rē-) *v.* **·tat·ed, ·tat·ing** *v.t.* **1.** To orient. — *v.i.* **2.** To face or turn eastward or in some specified direction. **3.** To become adjusted or oriented.

o·ri·en·ta·tion (ôr′ē·en·tā′shən, ō′rē-) *n.* **1.** The act of orienting, or the state of being oriented. **2.** The determination or adjustment of one's position with reference to circumstances, ideals, etc.

o·ri·en·ted (ôr′ē·en·tid, ō′rē-, -ən·tid) *adj.* **1.** Directed toward; interested in: *oriented* to the arts. **2.** Directed or centered: used in combination: *child-oriented.*

or·i·fice (ôr′ə·fis, or′-) *n.* An opening into a cavity; aperture. [< MF < LL < L *os, oris* mouth + *facere* to make]

or·i·flamme (ôr′ə·flam) *n.* **1.** The red banner of the abbey of St. Denis, used as a battle standard by the kings of France until the 15th century. **2.** Any flag or standard. [< F < OF < *orie* golden (< L *aureus*) + *flambe* banner]

or·i·ga·mi (ôr′i·gä′mē) *n.* The ancient Japanese art of folding single sheets of paper into realistic animal forms, usu. without the aid of scissors or paste. [< Japanese]

or·i·gin (ôr′ə·jin, or′-) *n.* **1.** The beginning of the existence of anything. **2.** A primary source; cause. **3.** Parentage; ancestry. **4.** *Math.* **a** The point at which the axes of a Cartesian coordinate system intersect. **b** The point in a polar coordinate system where the radius vector equals zero. [< OF < L *origo, -inis* source, beginning]

o·rig·i·nal (ə·rij′ə·nəl) *adj.* **1.** Of or belonging to the beginning, origin, or first stage of existence of a thing. **2.** Produced by one's own mind and thought; not copied or imitative. **3.** Able to produce works requiring thought without copying or imitating others; creative; inventive. — *n.* **1.** The first form of anything. **2.** An original work, as a painting, sculpture, etc., as distinct from a reproduction or copy. 3. A person or thing represented in a painting, biography, etc. 4. A person of unique character or genius. 5. An eccentric. — **Syn.** See NEW.

o·rig·i·nal·i·ty (ə·rij/ə·nal/ə·tē) n. pl. **·ties** 1. The power of originating; inventiveness. 2. The quality of being original or novel. 3. Something original.

o·rig·i·nal·ly (ə·rij/ə·nəl·ē) adv. 1. At the beginning. 2. In a new and striking manner.

original sin Theol. The corruption and depravity held to be inherent in all mankind as a consequence of Adam's first sinful disobedience.

o·rig·i·nate (ə·rij/ə·nāt) v. **·nat·ed, ·nat·ing** v.t. 1. To bring into existence; create; initiate. — v.i. 2. To come into existence; have origin; arise. — **o·rig/i·na/tion** n. — **o·rig/i·na/tive** adj. — **o·rig/i·na/tive·ly** adv. — **o·rig/i·na/tor** n. — **Syn.** 1. institute, propagate, produce.

o·ri·ole (ôr/ē·ōl, ō/rē-) n. 1. Any of a family of black and yellow birds of the Old World, related to the crows. 2. Any of various black and yellow American songbirds that build hanging nests; esp., the Baltimore oriole and the orchard oriole. [< OF < Med.L < L aureolus, dim. of aureus golden]

O·ri·on (ō·rī/ən) In Greek and Roman mythology, a giant hunter who pursued the Pleiades and was killed by Diana. — n. A constellation. [< L < Gk.]

or·i·son (ôr/i·zən, or/-) n. Usu. pl. A devotional prayer. [< OF < LL oratio, -onis prayer]

Or·lon (ôr/lon) n. A synthetic fiber woven from an acrylic resin, having high resistance to heat, light, and chemicals, widely used as a textile material: a trade name. Also **or/lon.**

or·mo·lu (ôr/mə·lōō) n. Any of various alloys of copper, tin, and zinc that resemble gold in appearance, used in furniture decorations, jewelry, etc. [< F < or gold + moulu, pp. of moudre to grind]

or·na·ment (n. ôr/nə·mənt; v. ôr/nə·ment) n. 1. Something that adorns or beautifies; a decoration. 2. Ornaments, collectively. 3. A person regarded as a source of honor or credit. 4. The act of adorning, or the state of being adorned; ornamentation. 5. Music A tone or group of tones used to embellish a melody without materially affecting its harmonic content. — v.t. 1. To furnish with ornaments; decorate. 2. To be an ornament to. [< OF < L < ornare to adorn] — **or/na·ment/er** (-ment/ər) n.

or·na·men·tal (ôr/nə·men/təl) adj. Of the nature of or serving as an ornament. — n. An ornamental object; esp., a plant used as decoration. — **or/na·men/tal·ly** adv.

or·na·men·ta·tion (ôr/nə·men·tā/shən) n. 1. The act or result of ornamenting. 2. The state of being ornamented. 3. That which ornaments; also, ornaments, collectively.

or·nate (ôr·nāt/) adj. 1. Elaborately or excessively ornamented; overdecorative. 2. Florid or showy, as a style of writing. [< L ornatus, pp. of ornare to adorn] — **or·nate/ly** adv. — **or·nate/ness** n.

or·ner·y (ôr/nər·ē, ôrn/rē) adj. Dial. 1. U.S. Disposed to be contrary or stubborn. 2. U.S. Mean; ugly; low; snide: an ornery trick. 3. Ordinary; common. [Alter. of ORDINARY] — **or/ner·i·ness** n.

ornitho- combining form Bird; of or relating to birds. Also, before vowels, **ornith-.** [< Gk. ornis, onithos bird]

or·ni·thol·o·gy (ôr/nə·thol/ə·jē) n. The branch of zoology that treats of birds. [< NL < Gk. ornithologos treating of birds] — **or/ni·tho·log/ic** (-thə·loj/ik) or **·i·cal** adj. — **or/ni·tho·log/i·cal·ly** adv. — **or/ni·thol/o·gist** n.

oro-¹ combining form Mouth; oral: oropharynx. [< L os, oris mouth]

oro-² combining form Geol. Mountain; of mountains. [< Gk. oros mountain]

o·ro·tund (ôr/ə·tund, ō/rə-) adj. 1. Full, clear, rounded, and resonant: said of the voice. 2. Pompous; inflated, as a manner of speech. [< L os, oris mouth + rotundus round] — **o·ro·tun·di·ty** (ôr/ə·tun/də·tē) n.

or·phan (ôr/fən) n. 1. A child whose parents are dead; also, less commonly, a child with one surviving parent. 2. A cast-off or waif. — adj. 1. That is an orphan. 2. Of or for orphans. — v.t. To make an orphan of. [< L < Gk. orphanos orphaned] — **or/phan·hood** (-hŏŏd) n.

or·phan·age (ôr/fən·ij) n. 1. An institution for the care of orphans or other abandoned children. 2. The condition of being an orphan; also, orphans collectively.

Or·phe·us (ôr/fē·əs) In Greek mythology, the son of a Muse, whose singing to the lyre could charm beasts and even rocks and trees. When his wife Eurydice died he was permitted to lead her back from Hades provided he did not turn to look at her until they had arrived in the upper world, but he did look back and she was lost. — **Or/phe·an** adj.

or·phic (ôr/fik) adj. Sometimes cap. Of a mystical nature; oracular. Also **or/phi·cal.** — **or/phi·cal·ly** adv.

Or·phic (ôr/fik) adj. 1. Of, pertaining to, or associated with Orpheus. 2. Having the quality of the music of Orpheus; enchanting. Also **Or/phi·cal.** [< L < Gk. < Orpheus]

or·pine (ôr/pin) n. Any of a large, widely distributed family of plants including the sedums and houseleeks as the **common** or **garden orpine,** having succulent stems and leaves and clusters of whitish flowers. Also **or/pin.**

Or·ping·ton (ôr/ping·tən) n. Any of a variety of large domestic fowls having single combs and unfeathered legs. [after Orpington, a village in Kent, England]

or·ris (ôr/is, or/-) n. Any of the several species of iris having a scented root; esp. one whose dried rootstock is used in medicine, as a perfume, etc. Also **or/rice.** [Prob. alter. of Ital. ireos < L iris iris]

ort (ôrt) n. Usu. pl. Archaic or Dial. A worthless scrap or leaving, as of food. [ME; ult. origin uncertain]

or·thi·con (ôr/thə·kon) n. A sensitive television camera tube using low-velocity electrons in scanning: also called image orthicon. Also **or·thi·con·o·scope** (ôr/thi·kon/ə·skōp).

ortho- combining form 1. Straight; upright; in line: orthodontics. 2. At right angles; perpendicular: orthorhombic. 3. Correct; proper; right: orthography. 4. Med. The correction of irregularities or deformities of: orthopedics. 5. Chem. **a** Designating that one of a series of acids that is most fully hydrated: orthophosphoric acid: distinguished from meta-. **b** Noting a benzene derivative in which the substituted atoms or radicals occupy adjoining positions. Also, before vowels, **orth-.** [< Gk. orthos straight]

or·tho·clase (ôr/thō·klās, -klāz) n. A brittle, vitreous, potassium-aluminum silicate of the feldspar group, a constituent of many igneous rocks: also called potash feldspar. [< ORTHO- + Gk. klasis fracture]

or·tho·don·tics (ôr/thə·don/tiks) n. The branch of dentistry concerned with the prevention and correction of irregularities of the teeth. Also **or/tho·don/tia** (-don/sha, -shē·ə). [< NL < Gk. orthos right, straight + odous, odontos tooth] — **or/tho·don/tic** adj. — **or/tho·don/tist** n.

or·tho·dox (ôr/thə·doks) adj. 1. Holding the commonly accepted or established faith, esp. in religion; correct or sound in doctrine. 2. Conforming to the Christian faith as represented in the early ecumenical creeds. 3. Adhering to traditional practice or belief. [< LL < Gk. < orthos right + doxa opinion] — **or/tho·dox/ly** adv.

Or·tho·dox (ôr/thə·doks) adj. 1. Of, belonging to, or characteristic of the Eastern Orthodox Church. 2. Designating any of the bodies in this Church.

Orthodox Church The Eastern Orthodox Church.

Orthodox Judaism The branch of Judaism that accepts the Mosaic Laws and their authoritative rabbinical interpretations in the Talmud and elsewhere as binding for today.

or·tho·dox·y (ôr/thə·dok/sē) n. pl. **·dox·ies** 1. Orthodox belief or practice; also, an instance of it. 2. The quality or condition of being orthodox. — **or/tho·dox/i·cal** adj.

or·thog·ra·phy (ôr·thog/rə·fē) n. pl. **·phies** 1. A mode or system of spelling, esp. of spelling correctly. 2. The study dealing with letters and spelling. [< OF < L < Gk. < orthographos] — **or·thog/ra·pher, or·thog/ra·phist** n. — **or·tho·graph·ic** (ôr/thə·graf/ik), **or/tho·graph/i·cal** adj. — **or/tho·graph/i·cal·ly** adv.

or·tho·pe·dics (ôr/thə·pē/diks) n.pl. (construed as sing.) The branch of surgery concerned with the correction of deformities of the skeletal system. Also **or/tho·pae/dics, or·tho·pe·dy** (ôr/thə·pē/dē). [< F < Gk. orthos right + paideia rearing of children] — **or/tho·pe/dic** adj. — **or/tho·pe/dist** n.

or·thop·ter·on (ôr·thop/tə·ron) n. An orthopterous insect.

or·thop·ter·ous (ôr·thop/tər·əs) adj. Designating any of an order of insects with membranous hind wings and leathery, usually straight, fore wings, including locusts, crickets, grasshoppers, etc. [< NL < Gk. orthos straight + pteron wing] — **or·thop/ter·an** adj. & n.

or·to·lan (ôr/tə·lən) n. A bunting of Europe, having an olive-green head and a yellow throat. [< F < Provençal < Ital. < L hortulus, dim. of hortus garden]

-ory¹ suffix of nouns A place or instrument for (performing the action of the main element): dormitory, lavatory. [< OF -oir, -oire. See -ORY².]

-ory² suffix of adjectives Related to; like; resembling: amatory, laudatory. [< F -oir, -oire, or < L -orius, -oria, -orium]

o·ryx (ôr/iks, or/-, ō/riks) n. pl. **o·ryx·es** or **o·ryx** Any of several long-horned antelopes, as the **Arabian oryx** and the gemsbok. [< NL < L < Gk.]

os¹ (os) n. pl. **o·ra** (ôr/ə, ō/rə) Anat. A mouth or opening. [< L]

os² (os) n. pl. **os·sa** (os/ə) Anat. A bone. [< L]

O·sage (ō/sāj) n. 1. One of a tribe of North American Indians of Siouan stock now living in Oklahoma. 2. The language of this tribe. [< Siouan Wazhazhe war people]

Osage orange 1. A showy tree of the mulberry family, native to Arkansas and adjacent regions, widely used as a hedge. 2. Its orangelike fruit.

Os·car (os/kər) n. One of the gold statuettes awarded annually in the U.S. for outstanding achevements in motion pictures. [Origin uncertain]

os·cil·late (os/ə·lāt) v.i. **·lat·ed, ·lat·ing** 1. To swing back and forth, as a pendulum. **2.** To fluctuate; waver. [< L *oscillare* to swing] — **os·cil·la′tor** *n.*

os·cil·lat·ing universe *Astron.* A hypothetical model of the universe, according to which the matter in the universe alternately expands and contracts. Compare BIG-BANG THEORY, STEADY-STATE THEORY.

os·cil·la·tion (os′ə·lā′shən) *n.* **1.** The act or state of oscillating. **2.** A single swing of an oscillating body. **3.** *Physics* A periodic fluctuation between extreme values of a quantity or force. — **os′cil·la·to·ry** (-lə·tôr′ē, -tō′rē) *adj.*

os·cil·lo·graph (ə·sil′ə·graf, -gräf) *n.* A device for recording and measuring any oscillating system convertible into wave forms, as sound, light, heartbeats, etc.

os·cil·lo·scope (ə·sil′ə·skōp) *n.* Any of various electronic instruments for projecting the forms of electromagnetic waves on the fluorescent screen of a cathode-ray tube.

os·cine (os′in, -īn) *adj.* Of or belonging to a suborder of birds, including those having the most highly developed vocal ability, as thrushes, sparrows, etc. Also **os′ci·nine.** — *n.* An oscine bird. [< NL < L *oscen, oscinis* singing bird]

Os·co-Um·bri·an (os′kō·um′brē·ən) *n.* A branch of the Italic subfamily of Indo-European languages.

os·cu·late (os′kyə·lāt) *v.t. & v.i.* **·lat·ed, ·lat·ing** **1.** To kiss: used humorously. **2.** To come into close contact or union. **3.** *Biol.* To have (characteristics) in common. [< L *osculari* to kiss]

os·cu·la·tion (os′kyə·lā′shən) *n.* The act of kissing; also, a kiss. — **os′cu·la·to·ry** (-lə·tôr′ē, -tō′rē) *adj.*

-ose¹ *suffix of adjectives* **1.** Full of or abounding in (the main element): *verbose.* **2.** Like; resembling (the main element): *grandiose.* Compare -OUS. [< L *-osus*]

-ose² *suffix Chem.* Indicating a sugar or other carbohydrate: *lactose, fructose.* [< (GLUC)OSE]

O·see (ō′zē, ō′sē) The Douai Bible name for HOSEA.

o·sier (ō′zhər) *n.* Any of various willows producing long, flexible shoots used in wickerwork. [< OF]

O·si·ris (ō·sī′ris) In Egyptian mythology, the god of the underworld and lord of the dead, husband of his sister Isis.

-osis *suffix of nouns* **1.** The condition, process, or state of: *metamorphosis.* **2.** *Med.* **a** A diseased or abnormal condition of: *neurosis.* **b** A formation of: *sclerosis.* [< L < Gk. *-ōsis;* or directly < Gk.]

-osity *suffix of nouns* Forming nouns corresponding to adjectives in *-ose: verbosity.* [< L *-ositas*]

Os·man·li (oz·man′lē, os-) *n. pl.* **·lis** **1.** An Ottoman Turk. **2.** The language of the Ottoman Turks; Turkish. — *adj.* Ottoman. [< Turkish *Osman* Osman < Arabic *'Othmān*]

os·mi·rid·i·um (os′mə·rid′ē·əm, oz′-) *n.* A mixture of iridium and osmium that occurs naturally, used in pen points: also called *iridosmine, iridosmium.* [< OSM(IUM) + IRIDIUM]

os·mi·um (oz′mē·əm, os′-) *n.* A hard, brittle, extremely heavy, white, metallic element (symbol Os) of the platinum group. See ELEMENT. [< Gk. *osmē* odor]

os·mose (oz′mōs, os′-) *v.t. & v.i.* **·mosed, mos·ing** To subject to or undergo osmosis.

os·mo·sis (oz·mō′sis, os-) *n. Chem.* **1.** The diffusion of a fluid through a semipermeable membrane, resulting in equalization of the pressures on each side. **2.** The tendency of a fluid to act in such a manner. Also **os′mose.** [< Gk. *ōsmos* < *ōthein* to impel] — **os·mot·ic** (oz·mot′ik, os-) *adj.*

os·prey (os′prē) *n.* An American hawk, brown above and white below, that preys upon fish: also called *fish hawk.* [ME < L < *os, ossis* bone + *frangere* to break]

ossi- *combining form* Bone: *ossify.* [< L *os, ossis* bone]

Os·sian (osh′ən, os′ē·ən) A legendary Irish hero and bard of the third century. — **Os·si·an·ic** (os′ē·an′ik) *adj.*

os·sif·er·ous (o·sif′ər·əs) *adj.* Yielding or containing bones. [< L *os, ossi(s)* + -FEROUS]

os·si·fy (os′ə·fī) *v.t. & v.i.* **·fied, ·fy·ing** **1.** To convert or be converted into bone. **2.** To make or become rigid or inflexible in habits, beliefs, etc.; harden. [< L *os, ossis* + *facere* to make] — **os·sif·ic** (o·sif′ik) *adj.* — **os′si·fi·ca′tion** *n.*

os·te·al (os′tē·əl) *adj.* Of, pertaining to, or like bone; bony. [< Gk. *osteon* bone]

os·ten·si·ble (os·ten′sə·bəl) *adj.* Offered as real or genuine; apparent. [< L *ostendere* to show] — **os·ten′si·bly** *adv.*

os·ten·sive (os·ten′siv) *adj.* Manifest; apparent; ostensible. — **os·ten′sive·ly** *adv.*

os·ten·ta·tion (os′tən·tā′shən) *n.* **1.** The act of displaying vainly or pretentiously in order to excite admiration, awe, etc. **2.** Excessive or uncalled-for exhibition; showiness. [< OF < L < *ostendere* to show]

os·ten·ta·tious (os′tən·tā′shəs) *adj.* **1.** Intended to attract notice; showy. **2.** Marked by ostentation. — **os′ten·ta′tious·ly** *adv.* — **os′ten·ta′tious·ness** *n.*

osteo- *combining form* Bone; pertaining to bone or bones. Also, before vowels, **oste-.** [< Gk. *osteon* bone]

os·te·ol·o·gy (os′tē·ol′ə·jē) *n.* The study of the skeleton and

of the structure of bones. — **os′te·o·log′i·cal** (-ə·loj′i·kəl) *adj.* — **os′te·ol′o·gist** *n.*

os·te·o·ma (os′tē·ō′mə) *n. pl.* **·o·mas** or **·o·ma·ta** (-ō′mə·tə) *Pathol.* A tumor of bony tissue. [< OSTE(O)- + -OMA]

os·te·o·my·e·li·tis (os′tē·ō·mī′ə·lī′tis) *n. Pathol.* Suppurative inflammation of the bone, sometimes involving the marrow. [< OSTEO- + MYEL(O)- + -ITIS]

os·te·op·a·thy (os′tē·op′ə·thē) *n.* A system of healing based on the theory that most diseases are the result of structural abnormalities of the body and may be cured by manipulation of the affected parts. — **os′te·o·path′, os·te·op·a·thist** (os′·te·op′ə·thist) *n.* — **os·te·o·path·ic** (os′tē·ə·path′ik) *adj.*

Os·ti·a (os′tē·ə, *Ital.* ō′styä) An ancient port city of Rome.

ost·ler (os′lər) See HOSTLER.

os·tra·cism (os′trə·siz′əm) *n.* **1.** In ancient Greece, temporary banishment by popular vote. **2.** The act of ostracizing or the state of being ostracized.

os·tra·cize (os′trə·sīz) *v.t.* **·cized, ·ciz·ing** **1.** To shut out or exclude, as from society or from a particular group; banish. **2.** To exile by ostracism. Also *Brit.* **os′tra·cise.** [< Gk. *ostrakizein* < *ostrakon* potsherd, shell, voting tablet]

os·trich (ôs′trich, os′-) *n. pl.* **·trich·es** or **·trich** **1.** A large, two-toed, flightless bird of Africa and Arabia, the largest of existing birds, having long, powerful legs and a plumage highly valued for ornamental purposes. **2.** A rhea. [< OF < LL < L *avis* bird + LL *struthio* ostrich]

Os·tro·goth (os′trə·goth) *n.* A member of the eastern branch of the Goths, who established a kingdom in Italy from 493 to 555. [< LL *Ostrogothi*] — **Os′tro·goth′ic** *adj.*

Os·ty·ak (os′tē·ak) *n.* **1.** One of a Finno-Ugric people inhabiting western Siberia and the Ural Mountains. **2.** The Ugric language of these people. Also **Os′ti·ak.**

Os·we·go tea (os·wē′gō) A species of mint with bright red flowers, found in the eastern U.S. [after *Oswego,* city in New York State]

ot- Var. of OTO-.

O·thel·lo (ō·thel′ō, ə-) In Shakespeare's play of this name, the hero, a Moor of Venice, whose jealousy, inspired by Iago, provokes him to kill his innocent wife Desdemona.

oth·er (uth′ər) *adj.* **1.** Different from the one or ones specified or implied. **2.** Noting the remaining one of two persons or things: the *other* eye. **3.** Additional; more: Have you no *other* children? **4.** Alternate; second: every *other* day. **5.** Different: The truth is *other* than what you suppose. **6.** Former: in *other* times. — *pron.* **1.** Another or different person or thing. **2.** The other person or thing: this hand, not the *other.* — *adv.* Differently; otherwise: with *than.* [OE *ōther*] — **oth′er·ness** *n.*

oth·er·wise (uth′ər·wīz′) *adv.* **1.** In a different manner; by other means. **2.** In other circumstances or conditions. **3.** In all other respects: an *otherwise* sensible person. — *adj.* **1.** Other than supposed; different: The facts are *otherwise.* **2.** Other: He could not be *otherwise* than proud.

other world A world peopled by the dead.

oth·er·world·ly (uth′ər·wurld′lē) *adj.* Concerned with matters of the spirit or intellect, esp. to the neglect of material things. — **oth′er·world′li·ness** *n.*

Oth·man (oth′mən, *Arabic* ōōth·män′) Ottoman.

-otic *suffix of adjectives* **1.** *Med.* Of, related to, or affected by: corresponding to nouns in *-osis: sclerotic.* **2.** Causing or producing: *narcotic.* [< Gk. *-ōtikos,* suffix of adjectives]

o·ti·ose (ō′shē·ōs, -tē-) *adj.* **1.** Being at rest; indolent; lazy. **2.** Having no use or effect; futile. [< L *otiosus* idle] — **o′ti·ose′ly** *adv.* — **o′ti·os′i·ty** (-os′ə·tē) *n.*

o·ti·tis (ō·tī′tis) *n. Pathol.* Inflammation of the ear. [< OT(O)- + -ITIS]

oto- *combining form* Ear; pertaining to the ear: *otology.* Also, before vowels, **ot-.** [< Gk. *ous, ōtos* ear]

o·tol·o·gy (ō·tol′ə·jē) *n.* The science of the ear and its diseases. — **o·to·log·i·cal** (ō′tə·loj′i·kəl) *adj.* — **o·tol′o·gist** *n.*

ot·ta·va (ōt·tä′vä) *n. Ital.* An octave.

ottava ri·ma (rē′mä) In prosody, a stanza form of Italian origin consisting of eight lines in iambic pentameter and rhyming in the pattern *abababcc.* [< Ital., octave rhyme]

Ot·ta·wa (ot′ə·wə) *n.* One of a tribe of North American Indians of Algonquian stock, originally inhabiting the region around Georgian Bay, Lake Huron and Ontario. [< dial. F *otauan;* ult. < Algonquian. Akin to Cree *atāweu* a trader.]

ot·ter (ot′ər) *n.* **1.** Any of various web-footed mammals of aquatic habits, related to the weasel and having a long, flattened tail. **2.** Its valuable, dark brown fur. [OE *otor*]

ot·to·man (ot′ə·mən) *n.* **1.** An upholstered, armless seat or sofa, usu. without a back. **2.** A cushioned footrest. [< F *ottomane,* orig. fem. of *ottoman* Ottoman]

OSTRICH

(To about 8 feet high)

Ot·to·man (ot′ə·mən) *n. pl.* **·mans** A Turk: also *Othman.* — *adj.* Of or pertaining to the Turks. [< F < Ital. *Ottomano* < Med.L *Ottomanus* < Arabic *'Othmāni* of Osman]

Ottoman Empire A former empire (1300–1919) of the Turks in Asia Minor, NE Africa, and SE Europe; capital, Constantinople: also *Turkish Empire.*

ouch (ouch) *interj.* An exclamation of sudden pain.

ought[1] (ôt) *v. Present 3rd person sing.* **ought** An auxiliary followed by the infinitive with *to* expressed or understood, meaning: **1.** To have a moral duty: A person *ought* to keep his promises. **2.** To be advisable: You *ought* to be careful. **3.** To be expected as something probable, natural, or logical: The engine *ought* to run. ◆ A past is formed by placing the following verb in the perfect infinitive, as in *He ought to have been there.* [OE past tense of *āgan* to owe]

ought[2] (ôt) See AUGHT[1].

ought[3] (ôt) See AUGHT[2].

oui (wē) *adv. French* Yes.

Oui·ja (wē′jə) *n.* A device consisting of a large board inscribed with the alphabet and other characters and over which moves a small rectangular board resting on three legs, the pointer of which is thought to spell out mediumistic communications: a trade name. Also **oui′ja.**

ounce (ouns) *n.* **1.** A unit of weight; one sixteenth of a pound avoirdupois, or 28.349 grams; one twelfth of a pound troy, or 31.1 grams. See table inside back cover. **2.** A fluid ounce. **3.** A small quantity. [< OF < L *uncia* twelfth part (of a pound or foot)]

our (our) *pronominal adj.* The possessive case of the pronoun *we,* used attributively: *our* child. [OE *ūre,* gen. of *wē*]

ours (ourz) *pron.* **1.** The possessive case of the pronoun *we,* used predicatively: That dog is *ours.* **2.** The one or ones belonging or relating to us: their country and *ours.* — **of ours** Belonging or relating to us: a double possessive.

our·self (our·self′) *pron.* Myself or ourselves, considered collectively: used in formal or regal contexts.

our·selves (our·selvz′) *pron.pl.* A form of the first person plural pronoun, used: **1.** As a reflexive: We helped *ourselves.* **2.** As an emphatic or intensive form of *we:* We *ourselves* want to know. **3.** As a designation of a normal, proper, or usual state: We weren't *ourselves* then.

-ous *suffix of adjectives* **1.** Full of, having, given to, like: *joyous, glorious.* **2.** *Chem.* Having a lower valence than that indicated by *-ic:* said of elements in compounds: *nitrous* oxide. [< OF < L *-osus*]

ou·sel (oo′zəl) See OUZEL.

oust (oust) *v.t.* To force out or remove, as from a place or position. [< AF < LL < *ob-* against + *stare* to stand]

oust·er (ous′tər) *n.* **1.** The act or condition of ousting. **2.** One who ousts. **3.** *Law* The act of putting one out of possession or occupancy of real property to which he is legally entitled; wrongful dispossession.

out (out) *adv.* **1.** Away from the inside or center: to branch *out.* **2.** In or into the open air: to go *out.* **3.** Away from a specified or usual place, as from one's home or place of business: *out* to lunch. **4.** From a receptacle or source: to pour *out* wine. **5.** From among others: to pick *out.* **6.** So as to remove, deplete, or exhaust: to sweep *out;* to dry *out.* **7.** Thoroughly: tired *out.* **8.** Into extinction or inactivity: The flame went *out;* The excitement died *out.* **9.** To a conclusion; to the end: Hear me *out.* **10.** Into being or activity, or into a state manifest to the senses: An epidemic broke *out;* The sun came *out.* **11.** Into or within the realm of public knowledge: The secret leaked *out.* **12.** In or into circulation: to bring *out* a new edition. **13.** Aloud and boldly: to speak *out.* **14.** So as to be extended or projecting: to lean *out.* **15.** Into the care or control of another or others: to deal *out* cards. **16.** From a state of composure to a state of tension, irritation, etc.: to be put *out* over trifles. **17.** In or into a condition of being out-of-date or retired from use: Latin went *out* as a spoken language. **18.** In baseball, etc., so as to be or count as an out. **19.** *Informal* Into unconsciousness: to pass *out.* — **out and away** By far; incomparably. — **out of 1.** From the inside of; from among. **2.** Beyond the limits, scope, or usual position of: *out of* sight; *out of* joint. **3.** From (a material, etc.): made *out of* tin. **4.** Inspired or caused by: *out of* pity. **5.** Without (any): *out of* breath. — **out to** With the intention of. — *adj.* **1.** External; exterior. **2.** Irregular: an *out* size. **3.** Not in effective working order: The bridge is *out.* **4.** At a financial loss: *out* five dollars. **5.** Not to be considered: That method is altogether *out.* **6.** Exposed, as by tears in the clothing: *out* at the seams. **7.** In error; mistaken: *out* in one's reckoning. **8.** Not in office or in power. **9.** No longer skillful, as at a game. **10.** Distant; outlying. ◆ *Out* may also be used in many of its adverbial senses as a predicate adjective with a form of the verb *to be,* as in the following examples: *He is out to lunch* (adv., def. 3); *The fire is out* (adv., def. 8); *The stars are out* (adv. def. 10). — *prep.* From within; forth from: *out* the door. — *n.* **1.** One who or that which is out. **2.** A way of dodging responsibility or involvement: to look for an *out.* **3.** In baseball, etc., the retirement of a batter or base runner; also, a player so retired. **4.** In tennis, etc., a return that falls outside the court. — **on the outs** (or **at outs**) Involved in a disagreement; at odds. — *v.i.* **1.** To come out; be revealed: Murder will *out.* **2.** To go out or outside. — *v.t.* **3.** To put (someone or something) out. — *interj.* Get out! Away! [OE *ūt*]

out- *combining form* **1.** Living or situated outside; away from the center; detached: *outlying, outpatient.* **2.** Going forth; outward: *outbound, outstretch.* **3.** Denoting the time, place, or result of the action expressed by the root verb: *outcome, outcry.* **4.** To a greater extent; more; better.
Out is widely used to form compounds, as in the list below.

out-and-out (out′ənd·out′) *adj.* Unqualified; outright.

out·bid (out·bid′) *v.t.* **·bid,** **·bid·den** or **·bid,** **·bid·ding** To bid more than; offer a higher bid than: also *overbid.*

out·board (out′bôrd′, -bōrd′) *adj. & adv. Naut.* **1.** Outside the hull. **2.** Away from the center line of a vessel.

outboard motor A portable gasoline or electric motor for temporary attachment to the stern of a small boat.

out·bound (out′bound′) *adj.* Outward bound.

out·break (out′brāk′) *n.* A sudden bursting forth, as of an emotion or a disease; an eruption.

out·build·ing (out′bil′ding) *n.* A building separate from and subordinate to a main building, as a woodshed or barn: also *outhouse.*

out·burst (out′bûrst′) *n.* A bursting out; esp., a sudden and violent display, as of anger.

out·cast (out′kast′, -käst′) *n.* **1.** One who is cast out or excluded. **2.** A homeless person or vagabond. **3.** Anything cast out, as refuse. — *adj.* Rejected; discarded; forlorn.

outact	outbuild	outfeel	outkeep	outpromise	outsit	outthreaten
outadd	outbully	outfight	outkiss	outpush	outskirmish	outthrob
outambush	outburn	outfigure	outlaugh	outquestion	outslander	outtower
outanswer	outcaper	outfind	outleap	outquibble	outsleep	outtrade
outargue	outcatch	outfire	outlearn	outquote	outsmile	outtravel
outask	outcavil	outflatter	outlie	outrace	outsmoke	outtrick
outbabble	outcharm	outfool	outlighten	outraise	outsnore	outtrot
outbake	outchatter	outfrown	outlinger	outrank	outsparkle	outtrump
outbalance	outcheat	outgabble	outlisten	outrave	outspell	outvalue
outbanter	outchide	outgain	outlove	outread	outsprint	outvaunt
outbargain	outclimb	outgallop	outmanage	outreason	outstare	outvoice
outbark	outcompete	outgamble	outmaneuver	outredden	outstart	outvote
outbawl	outcook	outgather	outmarch	outring	outstate	outwait
outbeam	outcrawl	outgive	outmatch	outrival	outstay	outwalk
outbeg	outcrow	outglare	outmove	outrear	outsteer	outwallop
outbeggar	outcurse	outglitter	outpaint	outrock	outstrain	outwar
outbellow	outdance	outglow	outpass	outroll	outstride	outwarble
outblaze	outdare	outgnaw	outperform	outrun	outstrive	outwaste
outbleat	outdazzle	outgrin	outpity	outsail	outstudy	outwatch
outbless	outdodge	outguess	outplan	outsatisfy	outstunt	outweary
outbloom	outdream	outguide	outplod	outsavor	outsuffer	outweep
outblossom	outdress	outhasten	outpoison	outscold	outsulk	outwhirl
outbluff	outdrink	outhear	outpopulate	outscorn	outswagger	outwile
outblunder	outdrive	outhit	outpractice	outscream	outswear	outwill
outblush	outdrop	outhowl	outpraise	outsee	outswim	outwish
outbluster	outeat	outhumor	outpray	outserve	outswindle	outwrangle
outboast	outecho	outinvent	outpreach	outshame	outtalk	outwrestle
outbox	outfable	outjinx	outpreen	outshout	outtask	outwriggle
outbrag	outfast	outjockey	outpress	outshriek	outthank	outyell
outbrazen	outfawn	outjourney	outprice	outsin	outthieve	outyelp
outbribe	outfeast	outjump	outproduce	outsing	outthink	outyield

out·class (out·klas´, -kläs´)   *v.t.*   To surpass decisively.

out·come (out´kum´)   *n.*   Consequence or result.

out·crop (*n.* out´krop´; *v.* out·krop´)   *Geol.*   *n.*   **1.** The exposure at or above the surface of the ground of any rock stratum, vein, etc.   **2.** The rock so exposed.   —*v.i.*   **·cropped, ·crop·ping**   To crop out above the ground, as rocks.

out·cry (*n.* out´krī´; *v.* out·krī´)   *n.*   *pl.*   **·cries**   **1.** A loud cry or clamor.   **2.** A vehement outburst of alarm, indignation, etc.   —*v.t.*   **·cried, ·cry·ing**   To surpass in noise or crying.

out·date (out·dāt´)   *v.t.*   **·dat·ed, ·dat·ing**   To make obsolete or out-of-date.

out·dat·ed (out·dā´tid)   *adj.*   Out-of-date; old-fashioned.

out·dis·tance (out·dis´təns)   *v.t.*   **·tanced, ·tanc·ing**   **1.** To outrun, as in a race; outstrip.   **2.** To surpass completely.

out·do (out·dōo´)   *v.t.*   **·did, ·done, ·do·ing**   To exceed in performance; surpass.   —**out·do´er** *n.*

out·done (out·dun´)   *adj.*   *U.S. Dial.*   Provoked; exasperated.

out·door (out´dôr´, -dōr´)   *adj.*   **1.** Being or done in the open air.   **2.** Intended for the outdoors. Also *out-of-door*.

out·doors (out·dôrz´, -dōrz´)   *adv.*   Outside of the house; in the open air.   —*n.*   The world beyond the house; the open air. Also *out-of-doors*.

out·er (ou´tər)   *adj.*   **1.** Being on the exterior side.   **2.** Farther from a center or from something regarded as the inside.

out·er·most (ou´tər·mōst)   *adj.*   Most remote from the inside or inner part; farthest out.

outer space   The space beyond the extreme limits of the earth's atmosphere; interplanetary and interstellar space.

out·face (out·fās´)   *v.t.*   **·faced, ·fac·ing**   **1.** To face or stare down.   **2.** To defy or confront fearlessly or impudently.

out·field (out´fēld´)   *n.*   In baseball: **a** The space beyond the infield. **b** The outfielders collectively.

out·field·er (out´fēl´dər)   *n.*   In baseball, any of three players whose positions are in the outfield.

out·fit (out´fit´)   *n.*   **1.** The tools or equipment needed for any particular purpose, as a trade, etc.   **2.** *U.S. Informal* A group of persons regarded as a unit; esp., a military unit.   **3.** *U.S. Informal* A set of clothing.   —*v.t. & v.i.*   **·fit·ted, ·fit·ting** To provide with or acquire an outfit.   —**out´fit´ter** *n.*

out·flank (out·flangk´)   *v.t.*   To get around and in back of the flank of (an opposing force or army); flank.

out·flow (out´flō´)   *n.*   **1.** That which flows out.   **2.** The act or process of flowing out.

out·fox (out·foks´)   *v.t.*   *U.S. Informal* To outwit.

out·go (*v.* out·gō´; *n.* out´gō´)   *v.t.*   **·went, ·gone, ·go·ing**   To go farther than; exceed.   —*n.*   *pl.*   **·goes**   **1.** That which goes out; outlay.   **2.** The act of going out.   —**out´go´er** *n.*

out·go·ing (out´gō´ing)   *adj.*   **1.** Going out; leaving.   **2.** Friendly; expansive.   —*n.*   The act of going out.

out·group (out´grōop´)   *n.*   *Sociol.*   Those not in an in-group.

out·grow (out·grō´)   *v.t.*   **·grew, ·grown, ·grow·ing**   **1.** To grow too large for.   **2.** To lose or get rid of in the course of time or growth: to *outgrow* a habit.   **3.** To surpass in growth.

out·growth (out´grōth´)   *n.*   **1.** That which grows out of something else; an excrescence.   **2.** A natural result or development.   **3.** The process of growing out.

out·house (out´hous´)   *n.*   **1.** An outdoor privy or toilet.   **2.** An outbuilding.

out·ing (ou´ting)   *n.*   **1.** A short pleasure trip; an excursion.   **2.** The act of going out; an airing.

out·land·er (out´lan´dər)   *n.*   **1.** A foreigner.   **2.** A stranger.

out·land·ish (out·lan´dish)   *adj.*   **1.** Strange or unfamiliar, as in appearance or manners.   **2.** *Informal* Freakish; crazy.   **3.** Far-off; remote.   [OE *ūtland*]   —**out·land´ish·ly** *adv.*   —**out·land´ish·ness** *n.*

out·last (out·last´, -läst´)   *v.t.*   To last longer than.

out·law (out´lô´)   *n.*   **1.** One who habitually breaks or defies the law; a criminal.   **2.** A person deprived of the protection or benefit of the law.   —*v.t.*   **1.** To prohibit; ban.   **2.** To deprive of legal force or protection, as a contract.   **3.** To declare an outlaw.   [OE < ON *ūtlagi*]   —**out·law´ry** *n.*

out·lay (*n.* out´lā´; *v.* out·lā´)   *n.*   **1.** The act of disbursing or spending.   **2.** The amount spent; expenditure.   —*v.t.*   **·laid, ·lay·ing** To expend (money, etc.).

out·let (out´let)   *n.*   **1.** A passage or vent for escape or discharge.   **2.** A channel of expression or escape: an *outlet* for creative energy.   **3.** In commerce, a market for any commodity; also, a store handling the goods of a particular manufacturer.   **4.** *Electr.* The point in a wiring system at which the current is taken to supply electrical apparatuses.

out·line (out´līn´)   *n.*   **1.** *Sometimes pl.* A preliminary sketch showing the principal features of a thing; general plan.   **2.** A systematic statement of the structure or content of an essay, etc.   **3.** The bordering line that serves to define a figure.   **4.** A sketch made only of such lines.   —*v.t.*   **·lined, ·lin·ing**   **1.** To make or give an outline of.   **2.** To draw the outline of.

out·live (out·liv´)   *v.t.*   **·lived, ·liv·ing**   **1.** To live longer than (another).   **2.** To live through; survive.

out·look (out´lŏok´)   *n.*   **1.** A point of view.   **2.** The prospect of a thing.   **3.** A place where something is viewed.   **4.** The expanse in view.   **5.** The act of looking out. .

out·man (out·man´)   *v.t.*   **·manned, ·man·ning**   **1.** To surpass in number of men.   **2.** To excel in manliness.

out·mod·ed (out·mō´did)   *adj.*   Out of fashion.

out·most (out´mōst´)   *adj.*   Farthest out; outermost.

out-of-date (out´əv·dāt´)   *adj.*   Old-fashioned; archaic.

out-of-door (out´əv·dôr´, -dōr´)   *adj.*   Outdoor.

out-of-doors (out´əv·dôrz´, -dōrz´)   *adv. & n.*   Outdoors.

out-of-the-way (out´əv·thə·wā´)   *adj.*   **1.** Remote; difficult to reach; secluded.   **2.** Out of the common range; odd.

out·pa·tient (out´pā´shənt)   *n.*   A patient treated at but not formally admitted to a hospital, dispensary, etc.

out·play (out·plā´)   *v.t.*   To play better than; defeat.

out·point (out·point´)   *v.t.*   **1.** To score more points than.   **2.** *Naut.* To sail closer to the wind than.

out·post (out´pōst´)   *n.*   **1.** A detachment of troops stationed at a distance from the main body as a guard against surprise attack.   **2.** The station occupied by such troops.   **3.** Any outlying settlement, as at a frontier.

out·pour (*v.* out·pôr´, -pōr´; *n.* out´pôr´, -pōr´)   *v.t. & v.i.*   To pour out.   —*n.*   A free outflow.   —**out´pour´er** *n.*

out·put (out´pŏot´)   *n.*   **1.** The amount of anything produced in a given time, as by a mine, factory, mill, etc.   **2.** The effective work done by a machine.   **3.** *Electr.* The electrical energy delivered by a generator, circuit, amplifier, etc.

out·rage (*n.* out´rāj´; *v.* out·rāj´)   *n.*   **1.** An act of shocking violence or cruelty.   **2.** A gross violation of morality or decency.   **3.** A profound insult or injury.   —*v.t.*   **·raged, ·rag·ing**   **1.** To commit an outrage upon.   **2.** To subject to an outrage.   **3.** To rape.   [ME < OF ult. < L *ultra* beyond]   —**Syn.** (noun) **1.** crime, atrocity. —(verb) See OFFEND.

out·ra·geous (out·rā´jəs)   *adj.*   **1.** Of the nature of an outrage; awful; atrocious.   **2.** Heedless of authority or decency.   —**out·ra´geous·ly** *adv.*   —**out·ra´geous·ness** *n.*

ou·tré (ōō·trā´)   *adj.*   *French*   Strikingly odd; exaggerated.

out·reach (*v.* out·rēch´; *n.* out´rēch´)   *v.t.*   **1.** To reach or go beyond; surpass.   **2.** To extend (something).   —*v.i.*   **3.** To reach out.   —*n.*   The act or extent of reaching out.

out·ride (out·rīd´)   *v.t.*   **·rode, ·rid·den, ·rid·ing**   To ride faster, farther, or better than.

out·rid·er (out´rī´dər)   *n.*   A mounted attendant who rides in advance or to one side of a carriage.

out·rig·ger (out´rig´ər)   *n.*   **1.** A part built or arranged to project beyond a natural outline, as of a vessel or machine.   **2.** A projecting contrivance terminating in a boatlike float, braced to the side of a canoe to prevent capsizing.   **3.** A bracket projecting from the side of a narrow rowboat, and provided with a rowlock for an oar; also, a boat so equipped.

out·right (*adj.* out´rīt´; *adv.* out´rīt´)   *adj.*   **1.** Free from reserve or restraint; downright.   **2.** Complete; entire.   **3.** Going straight on.   —*adv.*   **1.** Without reservation or limitation; openly.   **2.** Entirely; utterly.   **3.** Without delay.

out·sell (out·sel´)   *v.t.*   **·sold, ·sell·ing**   **1.** To sell more readily or for a higher price than.   **2.** To sell more goods than.

out·set (out´set´)   *n.*   A setting out; beginning.

out·shine (out·shīn´)   *v.*   **·shone, ·shin·ing** *v.t.*   **1.** To shine brighter than.   **2.** To surpass.   —*v.i.*   **3.** To shine forth.

out·side (*n., adj., & adv.* out´sīd´; *prep.* out·sīd´)   *n.*   **1.** The outer or exterior surface or side.   **2.** The space beyond a bounding line or surface.   **3.** The part that is seen; outward appearance.   **4.** Something empty of significance or substance; mere outward display.   —**at the outside** *Informal* At the farthest, longest, or most.   —*adj.*   **1.** Pertaining to, located on, or restricted to the outside.   **2.** Originating, caused by, or situated beyond designated limits or boundaries.   **3.** Reaching the limit; extreme: an *outside* estimate.   **4.** Slight; slim: an *outside* possibility.   —*adv.*   **1.** On or to the outside; externally.   **2.** Beyond the outside limits of.   **3.** In the open air; outdoors.   —*prep.*   **1.** On or to the exterior of.   **2.** Beyond the limits of.   —**outside of 1.** *U.S. Informal* Except: No one came *outside* of me.   **2.** Outside.

out·sid·er (out´sī´dər)   *n.*   One who is outside or excluded.   —**Syn.** stranger, alien, foreigner.

out·size (out´sīz´)   *n.*   An irregular size, as of clothing; esp., an uncommonly large size.   —*adj.*   Being of an outsize: also **out´sized´**.

out·skirts (out´skûrts´)   *n.pl.*   A place remote from the main or central area; an outlying district.

out·smart (out·smärt´)   *v.t.*   *Informal*   To outwit; fool.

out·spo·ken (out·spō´kən)   *adj.*   **1.** Bold or free in speech; frank.   **2.** Spoken boldly or frankly.   —**out´spo´ken·ly** *adv.*   —**out´spo´ken·ness** *n.*

out·spread (*v.* out·spred´; *n.* out´spred´)   *v.t. & v.i.*   **spread, spread·ing** To spread out; extend.   —*n.*   The act of spreading out.

out·stand·ing (out·stan´ding)   *adj.*   **1.** Prominent; excellent. **2.** Still standing or unsettled, as a debt. **3.** Projecting; abutting.

out·stretch (out-strech′) *v.t.* **1.** To stretch out; expand; extend. **2.** To extend beyond.

out·strip (out-strip′) *v.t.* **·stripped**, **·strip·ping 1.** To leave behind; outrun. **2.** To excel; surpass.

out·ward (out′wərd) *adj.* **1.** Of or pertaining to the outside; external. **2.** Relating to the physical as distinguished from the mental or spiritual aspect. **3.** Readily apparent, esp. to sight: no *outward* sign of trouble. **4.** Superficially evident: *outward* display of wealth. **5.** Not inherent; extrinsic: *outward* grace. — *adv.* **1.** In an outward direction. **2.** In an outward manner. **3.** Away from a place regarded as central, as home. [OE *ūtweard*] — **out′ward·ness** *n.*

out·ward·ly (out′wərd-lē) *adv.* **1.** On or toward the outside. **2.** In outward form or aspect; seemingly.

out·wards (out′wərdz) *adv.* Outward.

out·wear (out-wâr′) *v.t.* **·wore**, **·worn**, **·wear·ing 1.** To wear or stand use longer than; outlast. **2.** To wear out.

out·weigh (out-wā′) *v.t.* **1.** To weigh more than. **2.** To exceed in importance, value, etc.

out·wit (out-wit′) *v.t.* **·wit·ted**, **·wit·ting** To trick or baffle by superior ingenuity or cunning.

out·work[1] (out-wûrk′) *v.t.* **·worked** or **·wrought**, **·work·ing** To work faster or better than.

out·work[2] (out′wûrk′) *n. Mil.* Any outer defense, as beyond the ditch of a fort.

out·worn (out-wôrn′) Past participle of OUTWEAR.

ou·zel (ōō′zəl) *n.* **1.** One of various European thrushes, as the blackbird. **2.** The water ouzel. Also spelled *ousel.* [OE *ōsle*]

o·va (ō′və) Plural of OVUM.

o·val (ō′vəl) *adj.* **1.** Having the shape of an egg. **2.** Resembling an ellipse. — *n.* An oval shape or figure. [< MF < L *ovum* egg] — **o′val·ly** *adv.* — **o′val·ness** *n.*

o·va·ry (ō′və-rē) *n. pl.* **·ries 1.** *Zool.* The genital gland of female animals in which the ova are produced. **2.** *Bot.* In plants, that organ in which the ovules are contained. For illus. see FLOWER. [< NL < L *ovum* egg] — **o·var′i·an, o·var′i·al** *adj.*

o·vate (ō′vāt) *adj. Bot.* Egg-shaped: said of leaves. [< L *ovum*] — **o′vate·ly** *adv.*

o·va·tion (ō·vā′shən) *n.* A spontaneous acclamation of popularity; enthusiastic applause. [< L *ovare* to rejoice, exult] — **o·va′tion·al** *adj.*

ov·en (uv′ən) *n.* An enclosed chamber in which substances are heated in order to cook or dry them. [OE *ofen*]

ov·en·bird (uv′ən·bûrd′) *n.* A North American warbler with an olive-colored back and a golden crown, having a grassy nest suggesting an oven.

o·ver (ō′vər) *prep.* **1.** In or to a place or position above; higher than. **2.** So as to pass or extend across: walking *over* the bridge. **3.** On the other side of: lying *over* the ocean. **4.** Upon the surface or exterior of. **5.** Here and there upon or within; throughout all parts of: traveling *over* land and sea. **6.** At or up to a level higher than: The mud is *over* my boots. **7.** So as to close or cover: Put the lid *over* the jar. **8.** During: a diary kept *over* several years. **9.** Up to the end of and beyond: Stay *over* Christmas. **10.** More than; in excess of, as in amount, extent, etc.: *over* a million dollars. **11.** In preference to: chosen *over* all other candidates. **12.** In a position to guide or control: They want a strong man *over* them. **13.** Upon, as an effect: his influence *over* her. **14.** With regard to: time wasted *over* trifles. — **over all** From one end or aspect to the other. — **over and above** In addition to; besides. — *adv.* **1.** Above; overhead. **2.** To another or opposite side, or to a specified place; across: to leap *over* a puddle; to bring *over* a friend. **3.** At or on the other side; at a distance in a specified direction or place: *over* in France. **4.** From one side, opinion, or attitude to another. **5.** From one person, condition, or custody to another. **6.** So as to close, cover, or be covered: The pond froze *over.* **7.** From beginning to end: I'll think the matter *over.* **8.** So as to bring the underside upward: to turn *over* the boat. **9.** From an upright position: to topple *over.* **10.** Once more; again. **11.** So as to constitute a surplus; to have some left *over.* **12.** Beyond or until a stated time: Stay *over* until tomorrow. — **over again** Once more; anew. — **over against** Opposite to; as contrasted with. — **over and over** Time and again; repeatedly. — *adj.* **1.** Finished; done; past. **2.** On the other side; having got across. **3.** Outer; superior; upper. **4.** In excess or addition; extra. — *n.* **1.** Something remaining or in addition. **2.** *Mil.* A shot hitting or exploding beyond the target. [OE *ofer*]

over- *combining form* **1.** Above; superior: *overlord.* **2.** Passing above; going beyond the top or limit of: *overflow.* **3.** Moving or causing to move downward, as from above: *overturn.* **4.** Excessively; excessive; too much: *overcharge.* *Over-* is widely used to form compounds, as in the list beginning below.

overability	overblithe	overcloseness	overcunningly	overearnest	overfeatured
overable	overboastful	overcold	overcured	overearnestly	overfed
overabound	overbold	overcolor	overcurious	overeasily	overfeed
overabstemious	overboldly	overcommend	overcuriousness	overeasy	overfeminine
overabundance	overbookish	overcompetitive	overdaintiness	overeducate	overfierce
overabundant	overboorish	overcomplacency	overdainty	overelaborate	overfill
overabundantly	overborrow	overcomplacent	overdance	overelaboration	overflatten
overaccentuate	overbounteous	overcomplete	overdare	overelate	overflourish
overaccumulation	overbravely	overcomplex	overdaring	overelegant	overfluent
overactive	overbred	overcompliant	overdazzle	overembellish	overfond
overactivity	overbreed	overconcentration	overdear	overemotional	overfondle
overadvance	overbright	overconcern	overdeck	overemphasis	overfondly
overagitate	overbrilliant	overcondense	overdecorate	overemphasize	overfondness
overagitation	overbroaden	overconfidence	overdecorative	overemphatic	overfoolish
overambition	overbroil	overconfident	overdeepen	overempty	overforce
overambitious	overbrown	overconfidently	overdeeply	overenjoy	overforged
overambitiously	overbrush	overconscientious	overdeliberate	overenrich	overforward
overanalyze	overbrutal	overconscious	overdeliberation	overenter	overforwardness
overanxiety	overbulky	overconsciousness	overdelicate	overenthusiastic	overfoul
overanxious	overburdensome	overconservatism	overdelicately	overesteem	overfrail
overanxiously	overbusily	overconservative	overdelighted	overexcelling	overfrank
overapprehension	overbusy	overconsiderate	overdemand	overexcitable	overfraught
overapprehensive	overbuy	overconsideration	overdemocratic	overexcite	overfree
overapprehensively	overcapability	overconsume	overdepress	overexcitement	overfreedom
overapt	overcapable	overconsumption	overdepressive	overexercise	overfreely
overargue	overcapacity	overcontented	overdesirous	overexert	overfreight
overassert	overcaptious	overcontribute	overdestructive	overexertion	overfrequency
overassertion	overcaptiousness	overcook	overdestructiveness	overexpand	overfrequent
overassertive	overcareful	overcool	overdevoted	overexpansion	overfrighten
overassess	overcareless	overcoolly	overdevotion	overexpect	overfruitful
overassessment	overcaring	overcopious	overdiffuse	overexpectant	overfull
overassumption	overcarry	overcorrect	overdignified	overexpenditure	overfulness
overattached	overcasual	overcorrupt	overdiligence	overexpress	overfunctioning
overattention	overcaution	overcostly	overdiligent	overexuberant	overfurnish
overattentive	overcautious	overcount	overdilute	overfacile	overgamble
overattentively	overcautiously	overcourteous	overdiscipline	overfaithful	overgarrison
overattentiveness	overcautiousness	overcovetous	overdiscourage	overfamiliar	overgeneralize
overbake	overcentralization	overcoy	overdistant	overfamiliarly	overgenerous
overballast	overcharitable	overcram	overdiversification	overfanciful	overgenial
overbanked	overcheap	overcredit	overdiversify	overfast	overgentle
overbarren	overcherish	overcredulity	overdogmatic	overfastidious	overgifted
overbarrier	overchildish	overcredulous	overdominate	overfastidiousness	overgird
overbashful	overchill	overcritical	overdoubt	overfasting	overglad
overbashfully	overcivil	overcriticize	overdramatic	overfat	overgloomy
overbelief	overcivility	overcrowd	overdredge	overfatigue	overglorious
overbet	overcivilized	overcull	overdrink	overfatten	overgoad
overbig	overclean	overcultivate	overdry	overfavor	overgodly
overbitter	overclever	overcultivation	overeager	overfear	overgorge
overblame	overclose	overcunning	overeagerness	overfearful	overgracious

o·ver·act (ō′vər·akt′) *v.t. & v.i.* To act with exaggeration.

o·ver·age[1] (ō′vər·ij) *n.* In commerce, an amount of money or goods in excess of that which is listed as being on hand.

o·ver·age[2] (ō′vər·āj) *adj.* 1. Over the usual or specified age. 2. Too old to be of use: *overage guns.*

o·ver·all (ō′vər·ôl′) *adj.* 1. From one end to the other. 2. Including or covering everything.

o·ver·alls (ō′vər·ôlz′) *n.pl.* Loose, coarse trousers, often with suspenders and a piece extending over the breast, worn over the clothing as protection against soiling and wear.

o·ver·arm (ō′vər·ärm′) *adj.* Done with the arm above the level of the shoulder, as a swimming stroke.

o·ver·awe (ō′vər·ô′) *v.t.* **awed, aw·ing** To subdue or restrain by awe.

o·ver·bal·ance (ō′vər·bal′əns) *v.* **anced, anc·ing** *v.t.* 1. To exceed in weight, importance, etc. 2. To cause to lose balance. — *v.i.* 3. To lose one's balance. — *n.* Excess of weight or value.

o·ver·bear (ō′vər·bâr′) *v.* **bore, borne, bear·ing** *v.t.* 1. To crush or bear down by physical weight or force. 2. To prevail over; domineer. — *v.i.* 3. To be too fruitful.

o·ver·bear·ing (ō′vər·bâr′ing) *adj.* 1. Arrogant; domineering. 2. Overwhelming. — **o·ver·bear′ing·ly** *adv.*

o·ver·bid (ō′vər·bid′) *v.t. & v.i.* **bid, bid·den** or **bid, bid·ding** 1. To bid more than the value of (something). 2. To outbid (someone).

o·ver·blown (ō′vər·blōn′) *adj.* 1. Blown up or swollen, as with conceit or pretentiousness; inflated; bombastic. 2. Past full bloom, as a flower.

o·ver·board (ō′vər·bôrd′, -bōrd′) *adv.* Over the side of or out of a boat or ship. — **to go overboard** *U.S. Informal* To be extremely enthusiastic about someone or something.

o·ver·bur·den (ō′vər·bûr′dən) *v.t.* To load with too much weight, care, etc. — *n.* That which overburdens.

o·ver·cap·i·tal·ize (ō′vər·kap′i·təl·īz′) *v.t.* **ized, iz·ing** 1. To invest capital in to an extent not warranted by actual prospects. 2. To affix an unjustifiable or unlawful value to the nominal capital of (a corporation). 3. To estimate the value of (a property, company, etc.) too highly. — **o′ver·cap′i·tal·i·za′tion** *n.*

o·ver·cast (ō′vər·kast′, -käst′; *for v. defs. 1, 2, & 4, also* ō′vər·kast′, -käst′) *adj.* 1. Covered or obscured, as with clouds. 2. Gloomy; melancholy. 3. Sewn with long wrapping stitches to prevent raveling. — *n.* 1. A covering or mantle, as of clouds. 2. *Meteorol.* A cloud or clouds covering more than nine-tenths of the sky. — *v.* **cast, cast·ing** *v.t.* 1. To make

overcast. 2. To cast beyond. 3. To sew with an overcast stitch. — *v.i.* 4. To become overcast.

o·ver·charge (*v.* ō′vər·chärj′; *n.* ō′vər·chärj′) *v.t.* **charged, charg·ing** 1. To charge (someone) too high a price. 2. To overburden. 3. To overdo. — *n.* An excessive charge.

o·ver·cloud (ō′vər·kloud′) *v.t.* 1. To cover with clouds; darken. 2. To make gloomy. — *v.i.* 3. To become cloudy.

o·ver·coat (ō′vər·kōt′) *n.* An outdoor coat worn over a suit, etc., esp. in cold weather.

o·ver·come (ō′vər·kum′) *v.t.* **came, come, com·ing** 1. To get the better of in any conflict or struggle; defeat; conquer. 2. To prevail over or surmount, as difficulties, obstacles, etc. 3. To render (someone) helpless, as by emotion, sickness, etc. — *v.i.* 4. To gain mastery; win. [OE *ofercuman*]

o·ver·com·pen·sa·tion (ō′vər·kom′pən·sā′shən) *n. Psychol.* Excessive or abnormal reaction, esp. to compensate for the fact or feeling of inferiority.

o·ver·de·vel·op (ō′vər·di·vel′əp) *v.t.* 1. To develop excessively. 2. *Photog.* To develop (a plate or film) to too great a degree. — **o′ver·de·vel′op·ment** *n.*

o·ver·do (ō′vər·dōō′) *v.* **did, done, do·ing** *v.t.* 1. To do excessively; exaggerate. 2. To overtax the strength of; exhaust. 3. To cook too much, as meat. [OE *oferdōn*]

o·ver·dose (*v.* ō′vər·dōs′; *n.* ō′vər·dōs′) *v.t.* **dosed, dos·ing** To dose to excess. — *n.* An excessive dose.

o·ver·draft (ō′vər·draft′, -dräft′) *n.* 1. The act of overdrawing an account, as at a bank. 2. The amount by which an account is overdrawn. Also **o′ver·draught′.**

o·ver·draw (ō′vər·drô′) *v.t.* **drew, drawn, draw·ing** 1. To draw against (an account) beyond one's credit. 2. To draw or strain excessively, as a bow. 3. To exaggerate.

o·ver·drive (*v.* ō′vər·drīv′; *n.* ō′vər·drīv′) *v.t.* **drove, driv·en, driv·ing** To drive too hard or too far. — *n. Mech.* A gearing device that turns a drive shaft at a speed greater than that of the engine, thus decreasing power output.

o·ver·due (ō′vər·dōō′, -dyōō′) *adj.* 1. Remaining unpaid after becoming due. 2. Past due: an *overdue* plane or train.

o·ver·eat (ō′vər·ēt′) *v.i.* **ate** (-āt′, *Brit.* -et′) or *Archaic* **eat** (-et′, -ēt′), **eat·en, eat·ing** To eat to excess.

o·ver·es·ti·mate (*v.* ō′vər·es′tə·māt; *n.* ō′vər·es′tə·mit) *v.t.* **mat·ed, mat·ing** To value or estimate too highly. — *n.* An estimate that is too high. — **o′ver·es′ti·ma′tion** *n.*

o·ver·ex·pose (ō′vər·ik·spōz′) *v.t.* **posed, pos·ing** 1. To expose excessively. 2. *Photog.* To expose (a film or plate) too long. — **o′ver·ex·po′sure** (-spō′zhər) *n.*

o·ver·flow (*v.* ō′vər·flō′) *v.* **flowed, flown,**

overgraciously	overidealistic	overlate	overmerry	overparticular	overprovident
overgrasping	overidle	overlaudatory	overmighty	overpassionate	overprovision
overgrateful	overillustrate	overlaunch	overmild	overpassionately	overprovocation
overgratify	overimaginative	overlavish	overminutely	overpatient	overprovoke
overgraze	overimitate	overlawful	overminuteness	overpatriotic	overpublic
overgreasy	overimitative	overlax	overmix	overpensive	overpublicity
overgreat	overimpress	overlaxness	overmodest	overpeople	overpunish
overgreatness	overimpressible	overlearnedness	overmodestly	overpessimistic	overpunishment
overgreediness	overinclination	overlet	overmodesty	overpicture	overquantity
overgreedy	overinclined	overlewd	overmoist	overpiteous	overquick
overgrieve	overindividualistic	overliberal	overmoisten	overplain	overquiet
overgross	overindulge	overliberality	overmoisture	overplausible	overquietness
overhandle	overindulgence	overliberally	overmortgage	overplease	overrank
overhappy	overindulgent	overlighted	overmournful	overplentiful	overrapturous
overharass	overindustrialize	overlinger	overmultiply	overplenty	overrash
overhard	overinflate	overliterary	overnarrow	overplump	overrational
overharden	overinflation	overliveliness	overnear	overply	overrationalize
overhardy	overinfluence	overlively	overneat	overpolemical	overreadily
overharsh	overinfluential	overload	overneglect	overpolish	overreadiness
overhaste	overinsistence	overlofty	overnegligence	overponderous	overready
overhastily	overinsistent	overlogical	overnegligent	overpopular	overrealism
overhastiness	overinsolent	overlong	overnervous	overpopulate	overrealistic
overhasty	overinstruct	overloud	overnervousness	overpopulated	overrefine
overhate	overinsure	overlove	overnew	overpopulation	overrefined
overhaughty	overintellectual	overloyal	overnice	overpopulous	overrefinement
overheap	overintense	overluscious	overnimble	overpositive	overreflection
overheartily	overinterest	overlustiness	overnotable	overpotent	overreflective
overhearty	overinventoried	overlusty	overnourish	overpowerful	overregulation
overheavy	overinvest	overluxuriant	overnumerous	overpraise	overrelax
overhelpful	overirrigate	overluxurious	overobedient	overprecise	overreliant
overhigh	overirrigation	overmagnify	overobese	overpreciseness	overreligious
overhold	overjealous	overmany	overoblige	overpreoccupation	overrepresent
overholy	overjocular	overmarch	overobsequious	overpress	overreserved
overhomely	overjoyful	overmasterful	overobsequiousness	overpresumptuous	overresolute
overhonest	overjoyous	overmasterfulness	overoffensive	overproductive	overrestrain
overhonor	overjudicious	overmature	overofficious	overproficient	overretention
overhope	overjust	overmeanness	overofficiousness	overprolific	overreward
overhot	overkeen	overmeasure	overoften	overprominent	overrich
overhotly	overkind	overmeddle	overoptimistic	overprompt	override
overhuman	overknowing	overmeek	overornamented	overpromptness	overrighteous
overhumanize	overlabor	overmellow	overpainful	overprosperous	overrighteousness
overhurriedly	overlactation	overmelt	overpamper	overprotract	overrigid
overhysterical	overlade	overmerciful	overpartial	overproud	overrigorous
overidealism	overlarge	overmerrily	overpartiality	overprovide	overripe

·flow·ing *v.i.* **1.** To flow or run over the brim or bank, as water, rivers, etc. **2.** To be filled beyond capacity; superabound. — *v.t.* **3.** To flow over the brim or bank of. **4.** To flow or spread over; cover; flood. **5.** To cause to overflow. — *n.* **1.** The act or process of overflowing. **2.** That which flows over. **3.** The amount by which a capacity is exceeded; surplus. **4.** An outlet for liquid. [OE *oferflōwan*]

o·ver·grow (ō′vər-grō′) *v.* **grew, ·grown, ·grow·ing** *v.t.* **1.** To grow over; cover with growth. **2.** To grow too big for; outgrow. — *v.i.* **3.** To increase excessively; grow too large.

o·ver·hand (ō′vər-hand′) *adj.* **1.** In baseball, etc., executed with the hand above the level of the elbow or the shoulder. Also **o′ver·hand′ed** (-han/did). **2.** In sewing, made by carrying the thread over both edges, as a seam. — *adv.* In an overhand manner. — *n.* **1.** An overhand stroke or delivery, as in tennis. **2.** A kind of knot. For illus. see KNOT[1].

o·ver·hang (ō′vər-hang′) *v.* **·hung** (-hung′), **·hang·ing** *v.t.* **1.** To hang or project over (something); jut over. **2.** To threaten; menace. **3.** To adorn with hangings. — *v.i.* **4.** To hang or jut over something. — *n.* An overhanging portion of a structure; also, the amount of such projection.

o·ver·haul (*v.* ō′vər-hôl′; *n.* ō′vər-hôl′) *v.t.* **1.** To examine carefully for needed repairs. **2.** To make all needed repairs in; renovate. **3.** To catch up with; gain on. — *n.* A thorough inspection and repair. Also **o′ver·haul′ing.**

o·ver·head (*adj.* & *n.* ō′vər-hed′; *adv.* ō′vər-hed′) *adj.* **1.** Situated or working above the level of one's head: an *overhead* light. **2.** Of or relating to the overhead of a business. — *n.* The operating expenses of a business, as rent, light, heat, taxes, etc. — *adv.* Over or above the head.

o·ver·hear (ō′vər-hir′) *v.t.* **heard** (-hûrd′), **·hear·ing** To hear (something said or someone speaking) without the knowledge or intention of the speaker. — **o′ver·hear′er** *n.*

o·ver·joy (ō′vər-joi′) *v.t.* To delight or please greatly.

o·ver·kill (ō′vər-kil′) *n.* The military capacity for destruction far beyond the resources and population of an enemy.

o·ver·land (ō′vər-land′) *adj.* Proceeding over or accomplished by land. — *adv.* Across, over, or via land.

o·ver·lap (*v.* ō′vər-lap′; *n.* ō′vər-lap′) *v.t.* & *v.i.* **lapped, ·lap·ping 1.** To lie or extend partly over or upon (another or each other); lap over. **2.** To cover and project beyond (something). — *n.* **1.** The state or extent of overlapping. **2.** The part that overlaps.

o·ver·lay (*v.* ō′vər-lā′; *n.* ō′vər-lā′) *v.t.* **laid, ·lay·ing 1.** To spread something over, as with a decorative pattern or layer. **2.** To lay or place over or upon something else. **3.** To overburden. — *n.* **1.** *Printing* A piece of paper placed on the tympan of a press to make the impression heavier or to compensate for a depression. **2.** Anything that covers or partly covers something. **3.** An ornamental layer, as veneer, applied to wood, etc. **4.** A transparent sheet laid over a map to add or emphasize certain features.

o·ver·leaf (ō′vər-lēf′) *adv.* On the other side of a page.

o·ver·leap (ō′vər-lēp′) *v.t.* **leaped** or **leapt, ·leap·ing 1.** To leap over or across. **2.** To omit; overlook. **3.** To leap farther than; outleap. — **to overleap oneself** To miss one's purpose by going too far. [OE *oferhlēapan*]

o·ver·lie (ō′vər-lī′) *v.t.* **·lay** (-lā′), **·lain** (-lān′), **·ly·ing 1.** To lie over or upon. **2.** To suffocate by lying upon.

o·ver·load (*v.* ō′vər-lōd′; *n.* ō′vər-lōd′) *v.t.* To load excessively; overburden. — *n.* **1.** An excessive burden. **2.** *Electr.* An amperage in excess of that which can be safely carried.

o·ver·look (*v.* ō·vər-look′; *n.* ō′vər-look′) *v.t.* **1.** To fail to see or notice; miss. **2.** To disregard purposely or indulgently; ignore. **3.** To look over or see from a higher place. **4.** To afford a view of: The castle *overlooks* the harbor. **5.** To supervise; oversee. **6.** To examine or inspect. — *n.* **1.** The act of looking over, as from a height; an inspection; survey. **2.** An elevated place affording a view.

o·ver·lord (ō′vər-lôrd′) *n.* **1.** A superior lord or chief. **2.** One who holds supremacy over others. — **o′ver·lord/ship** *n.*

o·ver·ly (ō′vər-lē) *adv.* *Chiefly U.S.* To an excessive degree; too much; too.

o·ver·man (ō′vər-man′) *v.t.* **·manned, ·man·ning** To provide with more men than necessary.

o·ver·mas·ter (ō′vər-mas′tər, -mäs′-) *v.t.* To overcome; overpower. — **o′ver·mas′ter·ing** *n.* & *adj.*

o·ver·match (*v.* ō′vər-mach′; *n.* ō′vər-mach′) *v.t.* To be more than a match for; surpass. — *n.* One who or that which is superior in strength, skill, etc.

o·ver·much (ō′vər-much′) *adj.* Excessive; too much. — *adv.* In too great a degree. — *n.* An excess; too much.

o·ver·night (*adj.* & *adv.* ō′vər-nīt′) *adj.* **1.** Done during the previous evening; lasting all night. **2.** Away from home for one night: *overnight* trip. **3.** Used for nighttime travel or for short visits: an *overnight* bag. — *adv.* **1.** During or through the night. **2.** On the previous evening.

o·ver·pass (*n.* ō′vər-pas′, -päs′; *v.* ō′vər-pas′, -päs′) *n.* An elevated section of highway crossing other lines of travel. — *v.t.* **1.** To pass over, across, or through; cross. **2.** To surpass. **3.** To overlook. **4.** To transgress.

o·ver·play (ō′vər-plā′) *v.t.* **1.** To play or act (a part or role) to excess. **2.** To rely too much on the strength or value of. **3.** In golf, to send (the ball) beyond the putting green.

o·ver·pow·er (ō′vər-pou′ər) *v.t.* **1.** To gain supremacy over; subdue. **2.** To render wholly helpless or ineffective; overcome. **3.** To supply with more power than necessary.

o·ver·pow·er·ing (ō′vər-pou′ər·ing) *adj.* **1.** That overpowers. **2.** Intense. — **o′ver·pow′er·ing·ly** *adv.*

o·ver·print (*v.* ō′vər-print′; *n.* ō′vər-print′) *v.t.* To print additional material of another color on (sheets already printed). — *n.* Any word, symbol, etc., printed on a postage stamp, changing its value or use.

o·ver·pro·duce (ō′vər-prə-dōōs′, -dyōōs′) *v.t.* **·duced, ·duc·ing** To produce too much of or so as to exceed demand.

o·ver·pro·duc·tion (ō′vər-prə-duk′shən) *n.* Production in excess of demand, or of the possibility of profitable sale.

o·ver·rate (ō′vər-rāt′) *v.t.* **·rat·ed, ·rat·ing** To rate or value too highly; credit with undue merit; overestimate.

o·ver·reach (ō′vər-rēch′) *v.t.* **1.** To reach over or beyond. **2.** To spread over; cover. **3.** To defeat (oneself), as by attempting something beyond one's capability. **4.** To miss by stretching or reaching too far. **5.** To outwit; cheat. — *v.i.* **6.** To reach too far. **7.** To cheat. — **o′ver·reach′er** *n.*

o·ver·ride (ō′vər-rīd′) *v.t.* **·rode** (-rōd′), **·rid·den** (-rid′ən), **·rid·ing 1.** To disregard summarily, as if trampling down; supersede. **2.** To ride (a horse, etc.) to exhaustion. **3.** To ride over. **4.** To trample down; suppress.

o·ver·rule (ō′vər-rōōl′) *v.t.* **·ruled, ·rul·ing 1.** To decide against or nullify; set aside; invalidate. **2.** To disallow the arguments of (someone). **3.** To have control over; rule. **4.** To prevail over.

o·ver·run (*v.* ō′vər-run′; *n.* ō′vər-run′) *v.* **·ran** (-ran′), **·run, ·run·ning** *v.t.* **1.** To spread or swarm over, as vermin or in-

overripen	overservile	oversophistication	overstress	overtax	overurge
overroast	oversettled	oversorrow	overstretch	overtaxation	overuse
overrough	oversevere	overspacious	overstrict	overteach	overvaluable
overrude	overseverely	oversparing	overstrident	overtechnical	overvaluation
oversad	overseverity	oversparingly	overstriving	overtedious	overvariety
oversale	oversexual	overspecialization	overstrong	overtenacious	overvehement
oversalt	oversharp	overspecialize	overstudious	overtender	overventilate
oversalty	overshort	overspecific	overstudiousness	overtenderness	overventuresome
oversanguine	overshorten	overspeculate	overstudy	overtense	overventurous
oversaturate	overshrink	overspeculation	oversublime	overtension	overvigorous
oversaturation	oversick	overspeculative	oversubscribe	overthick	overviolent
oversaucy	oversilent	overspeed	oversubscription	overthin	overvote
oversave	oversimple	overspeedily	oversubtle	overthoughtful	overwarm
overscare	oversimplicity	overspent	oversubtlety	overthrifty	overwarmed
overscented	oversimplification	overspin	oversufficient	overthrong	overwary
overscrub	oversimplify	oversqueamish	oversup	overthrust	overweak
overscrupulosity	overskeptical	oversqueamishness	oversuperstitious	overtight	overwealthy
overscrupulous	overslander	overstale	oversupination	overtimid	overwet
overscrupulousness	overslight	overstaring	oversure	overtimorous	overwide
overseason	overslow	overstately	oversusceptible	overtinseled	overwilling
overseasoned	oversmall	oversteadfast	oversuspicious	overtire	overwily
oversecure	oversmooth	oversteadfastness	oversuspiciously	overtoil	overwise
overseed	oversoak	oversteady	oversweet	overtorture	overwoody
oversensible	oversoft	overstiff	oversystematic	overtrain	overworry
oversensitive	oversoftness	overstimulate	oversystematize	overtrim	overworship
oversensual	oversolemn	overstimulation	overtalkative	overtrust	overyoung
oversensuality	oversolicitous	overstir	overtalkativeness	overtrustful	overyouthful
oversententious	oversoon	overstore	overtame	overtruthful	overzeal
oversentimental	oversoothing	overstout	overtart	overunionized	overzealous
overserious	oversophisticated	overstrain	overtask	overurbanization	overzealously

vaders. **2.** To overflow. **3.** To spread rapidly across or throughout, as a fashion or fad. **4.** To run beyond; pass the limit of. **5.** *Printing* To shift or rearrange (words, lines of type, etc.) from one line, page, or column to another. — *v.i.* **6.** To run over; overflow. **7.** To pass the usual or desired limit. — *n.* An instance of overrunning; also, the amount of overrunning.

o·ver·score (ō′vər·skôr′, -skōr′) *v.t.* **·scored, ·scor·ing** To draw a line or lines over a word, letter, etc.

o·ver·seas (ō′vər·sēz′) *adv.* Beyond the sea; abroad. — *adj.* Situated, coming from, or for use beyond the sea; foreign: also **o′ver·sea′**.

o·ver·see (ō′vər·sē′) *v.t.* **·saw, ·seen, ·see·ing 1.** To direct; superintend. **2.** To survey; watch. [OE *ofersēon*]

o·ver·se·er (ō′vər·sē′ər, -sir′) *n.* A person who oversees; esp., one who superintends laborers at their work.

o·ver·sell (ō′vər·sel′) *v.t.* **·sold** (-sōld′), **·sell·ing 1.** To sell to excess. **2.** To sell more of (a stock, etc.) than one can provide.

o·ver·set (*v.* ō′vər·set′; *n.* ō′vər·set′) *v.* **·set, ·set·ting** *v.t.* **1.** To disconcert. **2.** *Printing* To set too much (type or copy). — *v.i.* **3.** To overturn; fall over. — *n.* **1.** A turning over; upset. **2.** *Printing* Excess of composed type.

o·ver·shad·ow (ō′vər·shad′ō) *v.t.* **1.** To render unimportant or insignificant by comparison; loom above; dominate. **2.** To throw a shadow over; obscure.

o·ver·shoe (ō′vər·shōō′) *n.* A shoe worn over another for protection against water, mud, cold, etc.; a galosh.

o·ver·shoot (ō′vər·shōōt′) *v.* **·shot, ·shoot·ing 1.** To shoot or go over or beyond (the mark, target, etc.). **2.** To go beyond; exceed, as a limit. **3.** To drive or force (something) beyond the proper limit. — *v.i.* **4.** To shoot or go over or beyond the mark. **5.** To go too far.

o·ver·shot (ō′vər·shot′) *adj.* **1.** Surpassed in any way. **2.** Projecting, as the upper jaw beyond the lower jaw. **3.** Driven by water flowing over from above: an *overshot* wheel.

o·ver·sight (ō′vər·sīt′) *n.* **1.** An inadvertent mistake or omission. **2.** Watchful supervision; superintendence.

o·ver·size (ō′vər·sīz′) *adj.* Of a larger size than necessary or normal: also **over·sized′**. — *n.* A large size.

o·ver·sleep (ō′vər·slēp′) *v.* **·slept, ·sleep·ing** *v.i.* To sleep too long.

o·ver·spread (ō′vər·spred′) *v.t.* **·spread, ·spread·ing** To spread or extend over; cover completely.

o·ver·state (ō′vər·stāt′) *v.t.* **·stat·ed, ·stat·ing** To state in too strong terms; exaggerate. — **o′ver·state′ment** *n.*

o·ver·stay (ō′vər·stā′) *v.t.* To stay beyond the limits or duration of.

o·ver·step (ō′vər·step′) *v.t.* **·stepped, ·step·ping** To step over or go beyond; exceed, as a limit or restriction.

o·ver·stock (*v.* ō′vər·stok′, *n.* ō′vər·stok′) *v.t.* To stock to excess. — *n.* An excessive supply.

o·ver·strung (ō′vər·strung′) *adj.* Too tense or sensitive.

o·ver·stuff (ō′vər·stuf′) *v.t.* **1.** To stuff to excess. **2.** To cover completely with deep upholstery: said of furniture.

o·ver·sup·ply (*n.* ō′vər·sə·plī′; *v.* ō′vər·sə·plī′) *n.* *pl.* **·plies** An excessive supply. — *v.t.* **·plied, ·ply·ing** To supply in excess.

o·vert (ō′vûrt, ō·vûrt′) *adj.* **1.** Open to view; observable. **2.** *Law* Done with criminal intent. [< OF, pp. of *ovrir* to open] — **o·vert′ly** (ō′vûrt·lē, ō·vûrt′lē) *adv.* — **Syn. 1.** evident, plain, open. See MANIFEST. — **Ant.** covert, hidden, secret.

o·ver·take (ō′vər·tāk′) *v.t.* **took** (-tōōk′), **·tak·en, ·tak·ing 1.** To catch up with. **2.** To come upon suddenly.

o·ver-the-count·er (ō′vər·thə·koun′tər) *adj.* Not sold on the floor of a stock exchange: said of stocks, bonds, etc.

o·ver·throw (*v.* ō′vər·thrō′; *n.* ō′vər·thrō′) *v.t.* **·threw** (-thrōō′), **·thrown, ·throw·ing 1.** To bring down or remove from power by force; defeat; ruin. **2.** To throw over or down; upset. — *n.* **1.** The act of overthrowing; destruction; demolition. **2.** In baseball, a throwing of the ball over and beyond the player or base aimed at.

o·ver·time (*n., adj., & adv.* ō′vər·tīm′; *v.* ō′vər·tīm′) *n.* Time used in working beyond the specified hours. — *adj.* During or for extra working time: *overtime* pay. — *adv.* Beyond the stipulated time. — *v.t.* **timed, ·tim·ing** *Photog.* To expose too long, as a plate or film.

o·ver·tone (ō′vər·tōn′) *n.* **1.** *Music* An upper partial tone: so called because it is heard with and above the fundamental tone produced by a musical instrument. **2.** Connotations, implications, etc., of language, thoughts, etc.

o·ver·top (ō′vər·top′) *v.t.* **topped, ·top·ping 1.** To rise above the top of; tower over. **2.** To surpass; excel.

o·ver·ture (ō′vər·chər) *n.* **1.** *Music* **a** An instrumental prelude to an opera or other large work. **b** Any of various orchestral pieces, often having programmatic content. **2.** An act or proposal intended to initiate a relationship, negotiations,

etc. — *v.t.* **·tured, ·tur·ing 1.** To offer as an overture or proposal. **2.** To introduce with or as an overture. [See OVERT.]

o·ver·turn (*v.* ō′vər·tûrn′; *n.* ō′vər·tûrn′) *v.t.* **1.** To turn or throw over; capsize; upset. **2.** To overthrow; defeat; ruin. — *v.i.* **3.** To turn over; capsize; upset. — *n.* **1.** The act of overturning, or the state of being overturned. **2.** A subversion or destruction. **3.** Turnover (def. 6).

o·ver·view (ō′vər·vyōō′) *n.* A broad survey or review of a subject, activity, etc.

o·ver·ween·ing (ō′vər·wē′ning) *adj.* **1.** Presumptiously proud or conceited. **2.** Excessive; exaggerated. [OE *oferwēnan* to become insolent] — **o′ver·ween′ing·ly** *adv.*

o·ver·weigh (ō′vər·wā′) *v.t.* **1.** To outweigh; overbalance. **2.** To overburden; oppress.

o·ver·weight (*n.* ō′vər·wāt′; *adj. & v.* ō′vər·wāt′) *n.* **1.** Excess weight, as beyond the legal or customary amount. **2.** Greater importance; preponderance. — *adj.* Being more than the usual or permitted weight. — *v.t.* To overburden.

o·ver·whelm (ō′vər·hwelm′) *v.t.* **1.** To bury or submerge completely, as with a wave or flood. **2.** To overcome or defeat; crush. [ME *oferwhelmen* to turn upside down] — **Syn. 1.** inundate, bury. **2.** rout, vanquish.

o·ver·whelm·ing (ō′vər·hwel′ming) *adj.* Crushing by reason of force, weight, or numbers; irresistible. — **o′ver·whelm′ing·ly** *adv.*

o·ver·work (*v.* ō′vər·wûrk′; *n.* ō′vər·wûrk′) *v.* **·worked** (*Archaic* **·wrought**), **·work·ing** *v.t.* **1.** To cause to work too hard. **2.** To work on or elaborate excessively: to *overwork* an argument. — *v.i.* **3.** To work too hard; do too much work. — *n.* Excessive work. [OE *oferwiercan*]

o·ver·write (ō′vər·rīt′) *v.t. & v.i.* **·wrote** (-rōt′), **·writ·ten** (-rit′ən), **·writ·ing 1.** To write in too elaborate or labored a style. **2.** To write too much about (a subject) or at too great length. **3.** To write over other writing.

o·ver·wrought (ō′vər·rôt′) *adj.* **1.** Worked up or excited excessively; overstrained. **2.** Worked all over, as with embroidery. **3.** Worked too hard. **4.** Too elaborate.

ovi- *combining form* Egg; of or pertaining to eggs: *oviparous*. Also **ovo-**. [< L *ovum* egg]

o·vi·duct (ō′vi·dukt) *n.* *Anat.* A Fallopian tube.

o·vi·form (ō′vi·fôrm) *adj.* Shaped like an egg or ovum.

o·vip·a·ra (ō·vip′ər·ə) *n.pl.* Animals that lay eggs. [< NL < L < *ovum* egg + *parus < parere* to bring forth]

o·vip·a·rous (ō·vip′ər·əs) *adj.* *Zool.* Producing eggs or ova that mature and are hatched outside the body, as birds, most fishes, and reptiles. — **o·vip′a·rous·ly** *adv.* — **o·vip′·a·rous·ness** *n.*

o·vi·pos·i·tor (ō′vi·poz′ə·tər) *n.* *Entomol.* The tubular organ at the extremity of the abdomen in many insects by which the eggs are deposited. [< OVI- + L *ponere* to place]

o·void (ō′void) *adj.* Egg-shaped: also **o·voi′dal**. — *n.* An egg-shaped body.

o·vo·vi·vip·a·rous (ō′vō·vī·vip′ər·əs) *adj.* *Zool.* Producing eggs that are hatched within the parent's body, but without formation of a placenta, as some reptiles and fishes. — **o′vo·vi·vip′a·rous·ly** *adv.* — **o′vo·vi·vip′a·rous·ness** *n.*

o·vu·late (ō′vyə·lāt) *v.i.* **·lat·ed, ·lat·ing** To produce ova; discharge ova from an ovary. [See OVULE.]

o·vu·la·tion (ō′vyə·lā′shən) *n.* *Biol.* **1.** The formation and discharge of ova. **2.** The period when this occurs.

o·vule (ō′vyōōl) *n.* **1.** *Bot.* The body within the ovary that upon fertilization becomes the seed. For illus. see FLOWER. **2.** *Zool.* An immature ovum. [< F < NL *ovulum*, dim. of L *ovum* egg] — **o·vu·lar, o·vu·lar·y** (ō′vyə·lər′ē) *adj.*

o·vum (ō′vəm) *n.* *pl.* **o·va** (ō′və) *Biol.* The female reproductive cell of animals, produced in the ovary.

owe (ō) *v.* **owed** (*Obs.* **ought**), **ow·ing** *v.t.* **1.** To be indebted to the amount of. **2.** To be obligated to render or offer: to *owe* an apology. **3.** To have or possess by virtue of some condition or cause: with *to*: He *owes* his success to his own efforts. **4.** To cherish (a certain feeling) toward another. — *v.i.* **5.** To be in debt. [OE *āgan* to own]

ow·ing (ō′ing) *adj.* Due; yet to be paid. — **owing to** Attributable to; on account of; in consequence of.

owl (oul) *n.* **1.** A predatory nocturnal bird, having large eyes and head, short, sharply hooked bill, long powerful claws, and a circular facial disk of radiating feathers. **2.** A person with nocturnal habits. [OE *ūle*]

owl·et (ou′lit) *n.* A small or young owl.

owl·ish (ou′lish) *adj.* **1.** Like an owl. **2.** *Brit. Dial.* Stupid. — **owl′ish·ly** *adv.* — **owl′ish·ness** *n.*

own (ōn) *adj.* **1.** Belonging or relating to oneself: following the possessive (usu. a possessive pronoun) as an intensive or to indicate the exclusion of others: my *own* horse; his *own* idea. **2.** Being of the nearest degree: *own* cousin. — **to come into one's own 1.** To obtain possession of one's property. **2.** To receive one's reward. — **to hold one's own 1.** To maintain one's place or position. **2.** To keep up with one's work, or remain undefeated. **— on one's own** Entirely dependent on one's self for support or success. **—** *v.t.* 1. To have or hold as one's own; possess. 2. To admit or acknowledge. **—** *v.i.* 3. To confess: with *to.* **— to own up** *Informal* To confess forthrightly and fully. **— Syn.** See CONFESS. [OE *āgan* to possess, have] **— own'a·ble** *adj.*

own·er (ō′nər) *n.* One who has the legal title or right to or has possession of a thing. **— own'er·less** *adj.*

own·er·ship (ō′nər·ship) *n.* The state of being an owner.

ox (oks) *n. pl.* **ox·en** (ok′sən) 1. An adult castrated male of the genus *Bos,* used for draft and food. 2. Any bovine quadruped, as a buffalo, bison, or yak. [OE *oxa*]

ox·al·ic acid (ok·sal′ik) *Chem.* A white, crystalline, poisonous compound, $C_2H_2O_4 \cdot 2H_2O$, found in plant tissues and made artificially, used in bleaching, dyeing, etc.

ox·blood (oks′blud′) *n.* A deep red color.

ox·bow (oks′bō′) *n.* 1. A bent piece of wood in an ox yoke, that forms a collar for the ox. 2. A bend in a river shaped like this.

ox·eye (oks′ī′) *n.* 1. Any of several plants of the composite family having large yellow heads. 2. The oxeye daisy. 3. Any of various shore birds, as the sandpiper. 4. An oval dormer window.

ox·eyed (oks′īd) *adj.* Having large, calm eyes, as an ox.

ox·ford (oks′fərd) *n. U.S.* 1. A low shoe laced at the instep. Also **oxford shoe.** 2. A cotton cloth of basket weave, used for men's shirts. Also **Oxford.** [after *Oxford*]

oxford gray 1. A very dark gray. 2. A woolen fabric of this color.

ox·heart (oks′härt′) *n.* A variety of sweet cherry.

ox·i·da·tion (ok′sə·dā′shən) *n. Chem.* 1. The process or state of undergoing combination with oxygen. 2. The process by which atoms lose or are deprived of valence electrons, or begin sharing them with a more electronegative element.

ox·ide (ok′sīd, -sid) *n. Chem.* Any binary compound of oxygen with another element: iron *oxide.* Also **ox'id** (-sid). [< F < *ox(ygène)* oxygen + *(ac)ide* acid]

ox·i·dize (ok′sə·dīz) *v.* **·dized, ·diz·ing** *Chem. v.t.* 1. To convert (an element) into its oxide; combine with oxygen. 2. To increase the valence of an atom or group of atoms by the loss of electrons. **—** *v.i.* 3. To become oxidized. Also **ox·i·date** (ok′sə·dāt). Also *Brit.* **ox'i·dise.** — **ox'i·diz'a·ble** *adj.*

ox·lip (oks′lip′) *n.* A species of primrose, closely resembling the cowslip: also called *five-fingers.* [OE < *oxa, oxan* ox + *slyppe* slime]

Ox·o·ni·an (ok·sō′nē·ən) *adj.* Of or pertaining to Oxford, England, or to its university. **—** *n.* A student or graduate of Oxford University. [< LL *Oxonia* Oxford]

ox·tail (oks′tāl′) *n.* The tail of an ox, esp. when skinned for use in soup.

oxy-¹ *combining form* 1. Sharp; pointed; keen. 2. Acid: *oxygen.* [< Gk. *oxys* sharp, acid]

oxy-² *combining form Chem.* 1. Oxygen; of or containing oxygen, or one of its compounds. 2. An oxidation product. 3. Containing the hydroxyl group. [< OXYGEN]

ox·y·acet·y·lene (ok′sē·ə·set′ə·lēn) *adj.* Designating or pertaining to a mixture of acetylene and oxygen, used to obtain high temperatures, as in welding.

ox·y·gen (ok′sə·jin) *n.* A colorless, tasteless, odorless gaseous element (symbol O), occurring free in the atmosphere, of which it forms about one-fifth by volume. It is an abundant and active element, combining with hydrogen to form water, supporting combustion, and essential in the respiration of plants and animals. See ELEMENT. [< F < *oxy-* oxy-¹ + *-gène* -gen]

ox·y·gen·ate (ok′sə·jən·āt′) *v.t.* **·at·ed, ·at·ing** To treat, combine, or impregnate with oxygen. **— ox'y·gen·a'tion** *n.*

ox·y·gen·ize (ok′sə·jən·īz′) *v.t.* **·ized, ·iz·ing** To oxidize.

oxygen mask A device worn over the nose and mouth by means of which the user can inhale oxygen as an aid to breathing.

oxygen tent A tentlike canopy placed over a patient's head and shoulders, within which pure oxygen may be circulated for the purpose of facilitating respiration.

ox·y·hy·dro·gen (ok′si·hī′drə·jən) *n.* A mixture of oxygen and hydrogen.

ox·y·mo·ron (ok′si·môr′on, -mō′ron) *n. pl.* **·mo·ra** (-môr′ə, -mō′rə) A figure of speech in which contradictory terms are brought together, as in the phrase, "*O heavy lightness, serious vanity!*" [< Gk. < *oxys* sharp + *moros* foolish]

o·yez (ō′yes, ō′yez) *interj.* Hear! hear ye! an introductory word to call attention to a proclamation, as by a court crier: usu. repeated three times. Also **o'yes.** [< OF *oyez,* imperative of *oir,* ult. < L *audire* to hear]

oys·ter (ois′tər) *n.* 1. A bivalve mollusk, found in salt and brackish water and moored by the shell to stones, other shells, etc.; esp., a common edible species of Europe and America. 2. An analogous bivalve, as the **pearl oyster.** 3. Some delicacy; tidbit; prize. **—** *v.i.* To gather or farm oysters. [< OF < L < Gk. *ostreon*]

oyster bed A place where oysters breed or are grown.

oyster crab A smooth-bodied crab living nonparasitically in the mantle of the oyster.

oyster cracker A small biscuit or hard, salted cracker.

oyster plant Salsify.

oyster white Any of several very light gray tints.

O·zark State (ō′zärk) Nickname of Missouri.

o·zo·ce·rite (ō·zō′kə·rīt, -sə-, ō′zō·sir′īt) *n.* A waxy, translucent mixture of natural hydrocarbons, used in candles, etc. Also **o·zo'ke·rite.** [< G < Gk. *ozein* to smell + *keros* wax]

o·zone (ō′zōn) *n.* 1. An unstable allotropic form of oxygen, O_3, with a pungent odor like that of chlorine, formed variously, as by the passage of electricity through the air. It is a powerful oxidizing agent, and is used for bleaching oils, waxes, ivory, flour, and starch, and for sterilizing drinking water. 2. *Informal* Fresh air. [< F < Gk. *ozein* to smell] **— o·zon·ic** (ō·zon′ik, ō·zō′nik), **o·zo·nous** (ō′zə·nəs) *adj.*

o·zon·ize (ō′zō·nīz) *v.t.* **·nized, ·niz·ing** 1. To treat or charge with ozone. 2. To convert (oxygen) into ozone. **— o'zo·ni·za'tion** *n.* **— o'zo·niz'er** *n.*

o·zon·o·sphere (ō·zon′ə·sfir) *n. Meteorol.* A narrow layer in the stratosphere, containing a high concentration of ozone. Also **ozone layer.** **— o·zon'o·spher'ic** or **·i·cal** *adj.*

P

p, P (pē) *n. pl.* **p's** or **ps, P's** or **Ps, pees** (pēz) 1. The sixteenth letter of the English alphabet. 2. The sound represented by the letter *p,* the voiceless bilabial stop. **— symbol** 1. *Chem.* Phosphorus (symbol P). 2. *Genetics* The parental generation: followed by a subscript numeral, as P_1, P_2, to indicate the first, second, etc., parental generation. **— to mind one's P's and Q's** To be careful of one's behavior.

pa (pä) *n. Informal* Papa.

paba or **PABA** *Biochem.* Para-aminobenzoic acid.

pab·u·lum (pab′yə·ləm) *n.* Any substance giving nourishment; aliment. [< L *pabulum* fodder] **— pab'u·lar** *adj.*

pace (pās) *n.* 1. A step in walking; also, the distance covered in one such movement. 2. A conventional measure of length approximating the average length of stride in walking: usu. 3 feet, but sometimes making 5 paces to the rod. The U.S. Army **regulation pace** is 30 inches, quick time; 36 inches, double time. 3. The manner or speed of movement in going on the legs; carriage and action, esp. of a horse. 4. Rate of speed, as in movement, work, etc. 5. A gait of a horse, etc., in which both feet on the same side are lifted and moved forward at once. **— to put (one) through his paces** To test the abilities, speed, etc., of. **—** *v.* **paced, pac·ing** *v.t.* 1. To walk back and forth across. 2. To measure by paces. 3. To set or make the pace for. 4. To train to a certain gait or pace. **—** *v.i.* 5. To walk with slow or regular steps. 6. To move at a pace (def. 5). [< F < L *passus,* pp. of *pandere* to stretch.] **— pac'er** *n.*

paced (pāst) *adj.* 1. Having a particular pace: used in compounds: *slow-paced.* 2. Measured in paces or by pacing. 3. Done after or with the help of a pacemaker.

pace·mak·er (pās′mā′kər) *n.* 1. One who makes or sets the pace for another in a race. 2. *Anat.* A mass of tissue in the right atrium of the heart that normally regulates the heartbeat. **— pace'mak'ing** *n. & adj.*

pa·cha (pə·shä′, pash′ə), **pa·cha·lic** (pə·shä′lik) See PASHA, PASHALIK.

pach·ou·li (pach′ōō·lē, pə·chōō′lē) See PATCHOULI.

pachy- *combining form* Thick; massive. [< Gk. *pachys* thick]

pach·y·derm (pak′ə·dûrm) *n.* 1. Any of certain thick-skinned, nonruminant hoofed animals, esp. an elephant, hippopotamus, or rhinoceros. 2. A thick-skinned, insensitive

person. [< F < Gk. < *pachys* thick + *derma* skin] — **pach'y·der'ma·tous** (-dûr'mə-təs), **pach'y·der'mous** *adj.*
pa·cif·ic (pə-sif'ik) *adj.* **1.** Tending or leading to peace or conciliation. **2.** Peaceful. Also **pa·cif'i·cal.** [< MF < L < *pax, pacis* peace + *facere* to make] — **pa·cif'i·cal·ly** *adv.*
Pa·cif·ic (pə-sif'ik) *adj.* Pertaining to the Pacific Ocean.
pa·cif·i·cate (pə-sif'ə-kāt) *v.t.* **·cat·ed, ·cat·ing** To pacify; calm. — **pac·i·fi·ca·tion** (pas'ə-fə-kā'shən) *n.* — **pa·cif'i·ca'tor** *n.* — **pa·cif'i·ca·to'ry** (-kə-tôr'ē, -tō'rē) *adj.*
pac·i·fi·er (pas'ə-fī'ər) *n.* **1.** One who or that which pacifies. **2.** A rubber nipple or ring, for babies to suck or bite on.
pac·i·fist (pas'ə-fist) *n.* One who opposes war or military preparedness, and proposes that all disputes be settled by arbitration. — **pac'i·fism** *n.* — **pac'i·fis'tic** *adj.*
pac·i·fy (pas'ə-fī) *v.t.* **·fied, ·fy·ing 1.** To bring peace to (an area). **2.** To allay the anger or agitation of; quiet; soothe. [< F < L < *pax, pacis* peace + *facere* to make]
pack¹ (pak) *n.* **1.** A bundle or large package, esp. one to be carried on the back of a man or animal. **2.** A collection of anything; heap. **3.** A full set of like or associated things usu. handled collectively, as cards. **4.** A group of dogs or wolves that hunt together. **5.** Any gang or band, esp. a criminal gang. **6.** An ice pack. **7.** A cosmetic paste for the face. **8.** A wrapping of sheets or blankets used in certain water-cure treatments; also, the sheets or blankets used. **9.** A parachute, fully assembled and folded for use. **10.** The quantity of something, as foods, put in containers for preservation at one time or in one season. — **Syn.** See FLOCK. — *v.t.* **1.** To make a pack or bundle of. **2.** To place compactly in a trunk, box, etc., for storing or carrying. **3.** To fill compactly, as for storing or carrying. **4.** To put up for preservation or sale. **5.** To compress tightly; crowd together. **6.** To fill completely or to overflowing; cram. **7.** To cover, fill, or surround so as to prevent leakage, damage, etc.: to *pack* a piston rod. **8.** To load with a pack; burden. **9.** To carry or transport on the back or on pack animals. **10.** To carry or wear habitually: to *pack* a gun. **11.** To send or dispatch summarily: with *off* or *away.* **12.** To treat with a pack (def. 7). **13.** *Slang* To be able to inflict: He *packs* a wallop. — *v.i.* **14.** To place one's clothes and belongings in trunks, boxes, etc., for storing or carrying. **15.** To be capable of being stowed or packed. **16.** To crowd together. **17.** To settle in a hard, firm mass **18.** To leave in haste: often with *off* or *away.* — **to send packing** To send away or dismiss summarily. [ME *pakke*, appar. < LG *pak*] — **pack'er** *n.*
pack² (pak) *v.t.* To arrange, select, or manipulate to one's own advantage: to *pack* a jury. [? < PACK¹]
pack·age (pak'ij) *n.* **1.** Something packed, wrapped up, or bound together, as for transportation. **2.** A box, case, or other receptacle used for packing. **3.** The act of packing. **4.** A combination of items considered as a unit. — *v.t.* **·aged, ·ag·ing** To arrange or tie into a package.
package store *U.S.* A store that sells liquor by the bottle.
pack animal An animal used to carry packs or burdens.
pack·et (pak'it) *n.* **1.** A small package; parcel. **2.** A steamship for conveying mails, passengers, and freight at stated times: also **packet boat.** — *v.t.* To make into a packet or parcel. [< AF *pacquet*, dim. of ME *pakke*]
pack·ing (pak'ing) *n.* **1.** The act or operation of one who or that which packs. **2.** The canning or putting up of meat, fish, fruit, etc. **3.** Any material used in packing, closing a joint, stopping a wound, etc.
packing box 1. A stout box in which goods are packed. Also **packing case. 2.** *Mech.* A stuffing box.
packing plant *U.S.* A factory where meats and meat products are processed and packed. Also *U.S.* **packing house.**
pack rat A North American rat that carries off and hides small articles in its nest.
pack·sad·dle (pak'sad'l) *n.* A saddle for a pack animal, to which the packs are fastened so as to balance evenly.
pack·thread (pak'thred') *n.* Strong thread used for wrapping.
pact (pakt) *n.* An agreement; compact. [< OF < L *pactum* agreement]
pad¹ (pad) *n.* **1.** A cushion; also, any stuffed, cushionlike thing serving to protect from jarring, friction, etc. **2.** A number of sheets of paper gummed together at one edge; a tablet. **3.** A large floating leaf of an aquatic plant: a lily *pad.* **4.** A soft cushionlike enlargement of skin on the undersurface of the toes of many animals. **5.** The foot of a fox, otter, etc. **6.** The footprint of an animal. **7.** A launching pad. — *v.t.* **pad·ded, pad·ding 1.** To stuff, line, or protect with pads or padding. **2.** To lengthen (speech or writing) by inserting unnecessary matter. **3.** To add to (an expense account, voting register, etc.) for fraudulent purposes. [Origin unknown]
pad² (pad) *v.i.* **pad·ded, pad·ding 1.** To travel by walking. **2.** To move with soft, almost noiseless footsteps. — *n.* A dull, padded sound, as of a footstep. [Akin to PAD³]

pad³ (pad) *n.* **1.** An easy-paced road horse. **2.** A highwayman. [< LG *pad* path]
pad·ding (pad'ing) *n.* **1.** The act of one who or that which pads. **2.** Material with which to pad. **3.** Extraneous matter used in writing, etc., merely to fill space.
pad·dle (pad'l) *n.* **1.** A broad-bladed implement resembling a short oar, used without a rowlock in propelling a canoe or small boat. **2.** The distance covered during one trip in a canoe over a given time. **3.** A flat board for inflicting bodily punishment. **4.** A small, rounded, flat piece of wood with a handle, used in table tennis. **5.** The act of paddling. — *v.* **·dled, ·dling** *v.i.* **1.** To move a canoe, etc., on or through water by means of a paddle. **2.** To row gently or lightly. **3.** To swim with short, downward strokes, as ducks do. **4.** To play in water with the hands or feet; wade. — *v.t.* **5.** To propel by means of a paddle or paddles. **6.** To convey by paddling. **7.** To beat with a paddle; spank. **8.** To stir. — **to paddle one's own canoe** To be independent. [ME, ? var. of *patel* < L *patella* shallow pan] — **pad'dler** *n.*
paddle board One of the broad, paddlelike boards set on the circumference of a paddle wheel or water wheel.
pad·dle·fish (pad'l-fish') *n.* *pl.* **·fish** or **·fish·es** A large fish having a scaleless body and paddle-shaped snout, found in the Mississippi Valley streams.
paddle wheel A wheel having projecting floats or boards for propelling a vessel.
pad·dling (pad'ling) *n.* **1.** The act of propelling with a paddle. **2.** A beating or spanking.
pad·dock (pad'ək) *n.* **1.** A pasture, lot, or enclosure for exercising horses, adjoining a stable. **2.** A grassed enclosure at a racecourse where horses are walked and saddled. — *v.t.* To confine in a paddock, as horses. [Alter. of dial. E *parrock*, OE *pearruc* enclosure]
pad·dy¹ (pad'ē) *n.* *pl.* **·dies** The ruddy duck. [after *Paddy*, a proper name]
pad·dy² (pad'ē) *n.* *pl.* **·dies** Rice in the husk, whether gathered or growing. [< Malay *pādĭ*]
paddy wagon *U.S. Slang* A patrol wagon.
pa·di·shah (pä'di-shä) *n.* Lord protector; chief ruler: a title of the shah of Iran. Also **pad·shah** (päd'shä). [< Persian < *pati* master + *shāh* king]
pad·lock (pad'lok') *n.* A detachable lock, having a pivoted hasp to be passed through a staple or ring and then locked. — *v.t.* To fasten with or as with a padlock. [ME]
pa·dre (pä'drā) *n.* **1.** Father: a title used in Italy, Spain, and Spanish America in addressing or speaking of priests. **2.** An army or navy chaplain. [< L *pater, patris* father]
pae·an (pē'ən) *n.* A song of joy or exultation. Also spelled *pean.* [< L < Gk. *paian* hymn addressed to Apollo]
paed-, paedo- See PEDO-.
paed·e·rast (ped'ər·ast), etc. See PEDERAST, etc.
pa·gan (pā'gən) *n.* **1.** One who is neither a Christian, a Jew, nor a Moslem; a heathen. **2.** In early Christian use, an idol worshiper. **3.** An irreligious person. — *adj.* **1.** Of, pertaining to, or like pagans; heathenish. [< LL < L, orig., villager < *pagus* the country] — **pa'gan·dom** *n.* — **pa'gan·ish** *adj.* — **pa'gan·ism** *n.*
pa·gan·ize (pā'gən·īz) *v.t. & v.i.* **ized, ·iz·ing** To make or become pagan.
page¹ (pāj) *n.* **1.** A male attendant; esp., in chivalry, a lad or young man in training for knighthood, or a youth attending a royal or princely personage. **2.** In Congress or other legislatures, a boy who attends upon legislators when in session. **3.** A boy employed in a hotel, club, etc., to perform light duties. — *v.t.* **paged, pag·ing 1.** To seek or summon (a person) by calling his name. **2.** To wait on as a page. [< OF < Ital. < Gk. < *pais, paidos* boy]
page² (pāj) *n.* **1.** One side of a leaf of a book, letter, etc. **2.** The printing or the type used on one side. **3.** Any event or events worthy of being noted or recorded: a sad *page* in history. **4.** *Usu. pl.* Any source or record of knowledge. — *v.* **paged, pag·ing** *v.t.* **1.** To mark the pages of with numbers. — *v.i.* **2.** To turn pages: usu. with *through.* [< F < L *pagina* written page < *pangere* to fasten]
pag·eant (paj'ənt) *n.* **1.** A community outdoor celebration presenting scenes from local history and tradition. **2.** An exhibition or spectacular parade devised for a public celebration. **3.** A theatrical spectacle. **4.** Unsubstantial display. [< Med.L *pagina* scaffold of a stage]
pag·eant·ry (paj'ən·trē) *n.* *pl.* **·ries 1.** Pageants collectively. **2.** Ceremonial splendor or display. **3.** Empty or showy display.
pag·i·nate (paj'ə·nāt) *v.t.* **nat·ed, ·nat·ing** To number the pages of (a book) consecutively. [< L *pagina* page + -ATE¹]
pag·i·na·tion (paj'ə·nā'shən) *n.* **1.** The numbering of the pages, as of a book. **2.** The system of figures and marks used in paging.
pa·go·da (pə-gō'də) *n.* In the Far East, a sacred tower or

temple, usu. pyramidal. Also **pag·od** (pag/əd, pə·god/).
[< Pg. < Tamil < Skt. *bhagavati* belonging to a deity]
paid (pād) Past tense and past participle of PAY.
pail (pāl) *n.* **1.** A cylindrical vessel for carrying liquids, etc.,
properly having a handle; bucket. **2.** The amount carried
in this vessel. [OE *paegel* wine measure] —**pail/ful/** *n.*
pail·lasse (pal·yas/, pal/yas) *n.* A mattress of straw, ex-
celsior, etc.: also spelled *palliasse*. [< MF < L *palea* chaff]
pain (pān) *n.* **1.** The unpleasant sensation or feeling resulting from or accompanying some injury, overstrain, or obstruction of the physical powers. **2.** Any distressing or afflicting emotion. **3.** *pl.* Care, effort, etc. expended on anything: with much *pains*. **4.** *pl.* The pangs of childbirth.
—**on** (or **upon** or **under**) **pain of** With the penalty of (some
specified punishment). —**to take pains** To be careful; to
make an effort. —*v.t.* **1.** To cause pain to; hurt. —*v.i.*
2. To cause pain. [< OF < L < Gk. *poinē* fine, penalty]
pained (pānd) *adj.* **1.** Hurt physically or mentally; distressed. **2.** Showing pain: a *pained* expression.
pain·ful (pān/fəl) *adj.* **1.** Giving pain; distressing. **2.** Requiring labor or care; arduous. **3.** Affected with pain: said
of the body. —**pain/ful·ly** *adv.* —**pain/ful·ness** *n.*
pain·less (pān/lis) *adj.* Free from pain; causing no pain.
—**pain/less·ly** *adv.* —**pain/less·ness** *n.*
pains·tak·ing (pānz/tā/king, pān/stā/-) *adj.* Careful; assiduous. —*n.* Careful effort. —**pains/tak/ing·ly** *adv.*
paint (pānt) *n.* **1.** A color or pigment, either dry or mixed
with oil, water, etc. **2.** A cosmetic, as rouge. **3.** Grease
paint. **4.** A film, layer, or coat of pigment applied to the
surface of an object; also, the dry coating of such a pigment:
cracked *paint*. —*v.t.* **1.** In art: **a** To make a representation
of in paints or colors. **b** To make, as a picture, by applying
paints or colors. **2.** To describe vividly, as in words. **3.** To
cover, coat, or decorate with paint. **4.** To apply cosmetics
to. **5.** To apply (medicine, etc.) with or as with a swab. —
v.i. **6.** To practice the art of painting; paint pictures. **7.**
To apply cosmetics to the face, etc. [< OF < L *pingere* to
paint] —**paint·y** (pān/tē) *adj.*
paint·brush (pānt/brush/) *n.* A brush for applying paint.
paint·ed (pān/tid) *adj.* **1.** Coated with paint. **2.** Depicted
in colors. **3.** Having no reality, truth, or value; artificial.
painted bunting A brilliantly colored finch widely distributed in the southern U.S. Also **painted finch.**
paint·er[1] (pān/tər) *n.* **1.** One who covers surfaces with a
coat of paint. **2.** An artist who paints in oils, etc.
paint·er[2] (pān/tər) *n. Naut.* A rope with which to fasten a
boat by its bow. [Prob. < OF < L *pendere* to suspend]
paint·er[3] (pān/tər) *n. U.S. Dial.* The puma, or cougar.
[Var. of PANTHER]
paint·ing (pān/ting) *n.* **1.** The act of laying on paints with
a brush. **2.** The art of creating meaningful effects on a surface by the use of pigments. **3.** A picture.
pair (pâr) *v.t.* **1.** To bring together or arrange in a pair or
pairs; match; couple; mate. —*v.i.* **2.** To come together as
a couple or pair. **3.** To marry or mate. —**to pair off 1.**
To separate into couples. **2.** To arrange by pairs. —*n.* **1.**
Two persons or things of a kind, that are joined, related, or
associated; a couple; brace. **2.** A single thing having two
correspondent parts dependent on each other: a *pair* of scissors. **3.** A married couple; also, two animals mated. **4.** In
legislative bodies, two opposed members who agree to abstain from voting, and so offset each other. **5.** A set of similar things making a whole: a *pair* of pajamas. **6.** In some
games of cards, two cards of the same denomination: a *pair*
of queens. ◆ Current usage calls for *pair* in the plural after
a numeral of two or more, as, four *pairs* of shoes, though informally the singular is often used, as, four *pair* of shoes.
[< F < L neut. plural of *par* equal]
Pais·ley (pāz/lē) *adj.* Made of or resembling a
patterned woolen fabric originally made in Paisley, Scotland. —*n.* **1.** Paisley fabric. **2.** A
Paisley shawl.
pa·ja·mas (pə·jä/məz, -jam/əz) *n. pl.* of **pa·ja-**
ma (-mə) **1.** A garment consisting of loose
trousers of silk, cotton, etc., and an accompanying jacket or blouse, used for sleeping. **2.**
In the Orient, similar trousers worn by both
men and women Also, *Brit.*, *pyjamas.* [< Hind. < Persian
pāi leg + *jāmāh* garment]
pal (pal) *Informal n.* A friend or chum. —*v.i.* **palled, pal·**
ling To associate as pals. [< Romany ult. < Skt. *bharatr*
brother]
pal·ace (pal/is) *n.* **1.** A royal residence, or the official residence of some high dignitary, as of a bishop. **2.** Any splendid residence or stately building. [< OF < L *Palatium*
Palatine Hill at Rome, on which stood the palace of Caesar
Augustus]
pal·a·din (pal/ə·din) *n.* **1.** Any of the twelve peers of
Charlemagne. **2.** A paragon of knighthood. [< F < Ital.
< L *palatium*. See PALACE.]
palae- Var. of PALEO-.

PAISLEY
DESIGN

palaeo- See PALEO-.
pal·an·quin (pal/ən·kēn/) *n.* A type of covered litter used
as a means of conveyance in the Orient, borne by poles on
the shoulders of two or more men. Also **pal·an·keen/.** [<
Pg. < Javanese < Skt. *palyanka*]
pal·at·a·ble (pal/ət·ə·bəl) *adj.* **1.** Agreeable to the taste or
palate; savory. **2.** Acceptable. —**pal/at·a·bil/i·ty, pal/at·**
a·ble·ness *n.* —**pal/at·a·bly** *adv.*
pal·a·tal (pal/ə·təl) *adj.* **1.** Pertaining to the palate. **2.**
Phonet. **a** Produced by placing the front (not the tip) of the
tongue near or against the hard palate, as *y* in English *yoke.*
b Produced with the blade of the tongue near the hard palate, as *ch* in *child, j* in *joy.* —*n. Anat.* **1.** A bone of the
palate. **2.** *Phonet.* **a** A palatal consonant. **b** A front vowel.
[< F < L *palatum* palate]
pal·a·tal·ize (pal/ə·təl·īz) *v.t. & v.i.* **·ized, ·iz·ing** *Phonet.*
To change a nonpalatal sound to a palatal by assimilation,
as (-yōōr) to (-shər) in *censure.* —**pal/a·tal·i·za/tion** *n.*
pal·ate (pal/it) *n.* **1.** *Anat.* The roof of the mouth, consisting of the anterior **hard palate,** having a bony skeleton, and
the posterior **soft palate,** that is composed of muscular tissue. For illus. see MOUTH, THROAT. **2.** The sense of taste.
[< L *palatum.*]
pa·la·tial (pə·lā/shəl) *adj.* Of, like, or befitting a palace;
magnificent. —**pa·la/tial·ly** *adv.*
pa·lat·i·nate (pə·lat/ə·nāt, -nit) *n.* A political division ruled
over by a prince possessing certain prerogatives of royalty
within his own domain.
pal·a·tine[1] (pal/ə·tīn, -tin) *adj.* Of or pertaining to the palate. —*n. Anat.* Either of the two bones forming the hard
palate. [< F < L *palatum* palate]
pal·a·tine[2] (pal/ə·tīn, -tin) *adj.* **1.** Of or pertaining to a
royal palace or its officials. **2.** Possessing royal prerogatives:
a count *palatine.* —*n.* **1.** A lord exercising sovereign power
over a province. **2.** A vassal exercising royal privileges over
his territory. **3.** The ruler of a palatinate or county palatine. [< F < L < *palatium* palace]
pa·la·ver (pə·lav/ər) *n.* **1.** Empty talk, esp. that intended
to flatter or deceive. **2.** A public discussion or conference.
3. Originally, a parley with native or aboriginal inhabitants,
as by explorers. —*v.t.* **1.** To flatter; cajole. —*v.i.* **2.** To
talk idly and at length. [< Pg. < LL *parabola* story, word]
—**pa·lav/er·er** *n.*
pale[1] (pāl) *n.* **1.** A pointed stick or stake. **2.** A fence enclosing a piece of ground. **3.** Any boundary or limit. **4.**
That which is enclosed within bounds. —*v.t.* **paled, pal·ing**
To enclose with pales; fence in. [< OF < L *palus* stake]
pale[2] (pāl) *adj.* **1.** Of a whitish or ashen appearance. **2.**
Of a very light shade of any color; lacking in brightness or
intensity of color. **3.** Feeble or weak. —*v.t. & v.i.* **paled,**
pal·ing To make or turn pale; blanch. [< OF < L < *pal-*
lere to be pale] —**pale/ly** *adv.* —**pale/ness** *n.*
pale·face (pāl/fās/) *n.* A white person: a term allegedly
originated by North American Indians.
paleo- *combining form* **1.** Ancient; old. **2.** Primitive. Also,
before vowels, **pale-.** Also *palae-, palaeo-.* [< Gk. *palaios*
old, ancient]
Pa·le·o·cene (pā/lē·ə·sēn/) *Geol. adj.* Of or pertaining to
the oldest epoch of the Tertiary period, preceding the Eo-
cene. —*n.* This epoch. See chart for GEOLOGY.
pa·le·og·ra·phy (pā/lē·og/rə·fē) *n.* **1.** An ancient mode of
writing; ancient writings collectively. **2.** The science of
describing or deciphering ancient writings. —**pa/le·og/ra·**
pher *n.* —**pa/le·o·graph/ic** (-ə·graf/ik) or **·i·cal** *adj.*
Pa·le·o·lith·ic (pā/lē·ō·lith/ik) *adj. Anthropol.* Designating, pertaining to, or associated with a period of human culture preceding the Mesolithic and characterized by chipped
or flaked stone implements, cave paintings, etc.
pa·le·ol·o·gy (pā/lē·ol/ə·jē) *n.* The study of antiquity or
antiquities; archeology. —**pa/le·o·log/i·cal** (-ə·loj/i·kəl) *adj.*
—**pa/le·ol/o·gist** *n.*
pa·le·on·tol·o·gy (pā/lē·on·tol/ə·jē) *n. pl.* **·gies 1.** The science that treats of ancient forms of life or of fossil organisms.
2. A work dealing with this subject. [< PALEO- + Gk. *ōn,*
ontos being, ppr. of *einai* to be + -LOGY] —**pa/le·on/to·log/**
ic (-on/tə·loj/ik) or **·i·cal** *adj.* —**pa/le·on·tol/o·gist** *n.*
Pa·le·o·zo·ic (pā/lē·ō·zō/ik) *adj. Geol.* Of or pertaining to
the era following the Pre-Cambrian and preceding the Mesozoic. —*n.* The Paleozoic era, with its life forms and rock
systems. See chart for GEOLOGY. [< PALEO- + Gk. *zōē* life]
Pal·es·tine (pal/is·tīn) In Biblical times, a territory on the
eastern coast of the Mediterranean, the country of the Jews:
Old Testament *Canaan:* also *Holy Land.* —**Pal/es·tin/i·an**
(-tin/ē·ən) *adj. & n.*
pa·les·tra (pə·les/trə) *n. pl.* **·trae** (-trē) In ancient Greece,
a school or practice place for athletics. [< L < Gk. < *pa-*
laiein to wrestle] —**pa·les/tral, pa·les/tri·an** *adj.*
pal·ette (pal/it) *n.* **1.** A thin board or tablet with a hole for
the thumb, upon which artists lay and mix their colors **2.**
The range of colors characteristic of a particular artist,
painting, etc. Also spelled *pallet.* [< L < F < L *pala* spade]

Pa·li (pä′lē) *n.* The sacred language of the early Buddhist writings, still surviving in the religious literature of Burma and Thailand. [< Skt. *pāli* (*bhasa*) canonical (language)]

pal·imp·sest (pal′imp·sest) *n.* A parchment, manuscript, etc., written upon two or three times, the earlier writing having been wholly or partially erased to make room for the next. [< L < Gk. < *palin* again + *psaein* to rub]

pal·in·drome (pal′in·drōm) *n.* A word, sentence, verse, etc., that is the same read forward or backward, as "Madam, I'm Adam." [< Gk. < *palin* again + *dromos* run]

pal·ing (pā′ling) *n.* **1.** One of a series of upright pales forming a fence. **2.** Pales or pickets collectively. **3.** A fence or enclosure made of pales or pickets. **4.** The act of erecting a fence with pales.

pal·i·sade (pal′ə·sād′) *n.* **1.** A barrier or fortification made of strong timbers set in the ground. **2.** One of the stakes forming such a barrier. **3.** *pl.* An extended cliff or rocky precipice. — *v.t.* **·sad·ed, ·sad·ing** To enclose or fortify with a palisade. [< MF < Provençal < L *palus* stake]

pal·ish (pāl′ish) *adj.* Somewhat pale.

pall[1] (pôl) *n.* **1.** A covering, usu. of black cloth, thrown over a coffin or over a tomb. **2.** A dark, heavy covering, cloud, etc. **3.** A gloomy or oppressive atmosphere, effect, etc. **4.** *Eccl.* **a** A chalice cover, consisting of a square piece of cardboard faced on both sides with lawn or linen. **b** An altar cloth. — *v.t.* To cover with or as with a pall. [OE < L *pallium* cloak]

pall[2] (pôl) *v.i.* **1.** To become insipid or uninteresting. **2.** To have a dulling or displeasing effect: followed by *on*. — *v.t.* **3.** To satiate; cloy. [Appar. aphetic var. of APPALL]

Pal·la·di·an (pə·lā′dē·ən) *adj.* **1.** Pertaining to or characteristic of the goddess Pallas. **2.** Characterized by wisdom or learning. [< L < Gk. *Palladios* of Pallas]

pal·la·di·um[1] (pə·lā′dē·əm) *n.* *pl.* **·di·a** (-dē·ə) Any object considered essential to the safety of a community or organization; a safeguard. [< PALLADIUM]

pal·la·di·um[2] (pə·lā′dē·əm) *n.* A rare, silver-white, malleable and ductile metallic element (symbol Pd) occurring in combination with platinum, iridium, and rhodium. See ELEMENT. [< NL, after the asteroid *Pallas*]

Pal·la·di·um (pə·lā′dē·əm) *n.* In Greek and Roman legend, a statue of Pallas Athena, esp. one in Troy, on the preservation of which the safety of the city depended.

Pal·las (pal′əs) In Greek mythology, a name of Athena, the goddess of wisdom: often **Pallas Athena.** — *n.* The second largest asteroid. [< Gk., prob. orig. maiden]

pall·bear·er (pôl′bâr′ər) *n.* One who forms part of an escort for a coffin at a funeral.

pal·let[1] (pal′it) *n.* **1.** *Mech.* **a** A click or pawl used to regulate the motion of a ratchet wheel, etc., as by converting reciprocating into rotary motion, or the reverse. **b** The lip or point of a pawl. **2.** A paddle for mixing and shaping clay for crucibles, etc. **3.** A tool used in gilding the backs of books or for taking up gold leaf. **4.** A painter's palette. [< F < L *pala* spade]

pal·let[2] (pal′it) *n.* **1.** A small, mean bed or mattress, usu. of straw. **2.** A blanket laid on the floor for a bed. [< OF < L *palea* chaff, straw]

pal·liasse (pal·yas′, pal′yas) See PAILLASSE.

pal·li·ate (pal′ē·āt) *v.t.* **·at·ed, ·at·ing** **1.** To cause (a crime, fault, etc.) to appear less serious or offensive. **2.** To relieve the symptoms or effects of (a disease, etc.) without curing. [< L *palliatus*, pp. of *palliare* to cloak] — **pal′li·a′tion** *n.* — **pal′li·a′tive** *adj. & n.* — **pal′li·a′tor** *n.*

pal·lid (pal′id) *adj.* Of a pale or wan appearance; weak or lacking in color. [< L < *pallere* to be pale] — **pal′lid·ly** *adv.* — **pal′lid·ness** *n.*

pal·lor (pal′ər) *n.* The state of being pale or pallid; paleness. [< L < *pallere* to be pale]

palm[1] (päm) *n.* **1.** The inner surface of the hand between the wrist and the base of the fingers. **2.** A linear measure equal to the approximate breadth (3 or 4 inches) or length (about 8½ inches) of the hand. **3.** That which covers the palm, as part of a glove. **4.** The flattened terminal portion of the antler of a moose, etc. **5.** The flat, expanding end of any armlike projection, as the blade of an oar. — *v.t.* **1.** To hide (cards, dice, etc.) in or about the hand, as in sleight of hand. **2.** To handle or touch with the palm. — **to palm off** To pass off or impose fraudulently. [< F < OF < L *palma*]

palm[2] (päm) *n.* **1.** Any of a large and varied group of tropical evergreen trees or shrubs usu. having an unbranched trunk topped by a crown of large palmate or pinnate leaves. **2.** A leaf or branch of the palm, used as a symbol of victory or joy. **3.** Triumph; victory. [OE < L *palma* palm tree]

pal·ma·ceous (pal·mā′shəs, pä·mā′-) *adj.* Belonging to or characteristic of the group of plants comprising the palms.

pal·mar (pal′mər, pä′mər) *adj.* Of, pertaining to, or similar to the palm of the hand.

pal·mate (pal′māt, pä′māt) *adj.* **1.** Resembling an open hand. **2.** Broad and flat, with fingerlike projections, as the antlers of the moose, or some corals. **3.** *Bot.* Having lobes that diverge from the apex of the petiole: a *palmate* leaf. **4.** *Zool.* Webbed, as a bird's foot. Also **pal′mat·ed.** [< L *palmatus*, pp. of *palmare* to mark with the palm of the hand] — **pal′mate·ly** *adv.* — **pal·ma′tion** *n.*

palm·er (pä′mər) *n.* In the Middle Ages, one who had visited Palestine and brought back a palm branch as a token of the pilgrimage.

pal·met·to (pal·met′ō) *n.* *pl.* **·tos** or **·toes** Any of various palms having fanlike foliage. [< Sp. *palmito*, dim. of *palma* palm tree < L]

Palmetto State Nickname of South Carolina.

palmi- *combining form* Palm. [< L *palma* palm]

palm·ist (pä′mist) *n.* One who practices palmistry.

palm·is·try (pä′mis·trē) *n.* The art or practice of supposedly discovering a person's past or future from the lines and marks in the palm of the hand. [ME < *palme* palm + *-estrie*, prob. < OF *maistrie* mastery]

palm oil A yellowish, butterlike oil obtained from the fruit of several varieties of palm, and used in the manufacture of soap, candles, etc.

palm sugar Sugar made from palm sap.

Palm Sunday The Sunday before Easter, being the last Sunday in Lent and the first day in Holy Week. [Named for Christ's triumphal entry into Jerusalem, when palm branches were strewn before him]

palm·y (pä′mē) *adj.* **palm·i·er, palm·i·est** **1.** Marked by prosperity; flourishing. **2.** Abounding in palms.

pal·my·ra (pal·mī′rə) *n.* An East Indian palm having large fan-shaped leaves. [< Pg. *palmeira* palm tree]

pal·o·mi·no (pal′ə·mē′nō) *n.* *pl.* **·nos** A light tan or golden brown horse with a cream-colored mane and tail. [< Am. Sp., orig., dove-colored horse < Sp. < L *palumbus* ringdove]

pa·loo·ka (pə·lōō′kə) *n.* *U.S. Slang* **1.** An inferior or bungling pugilist. **2.** A lout; lummox. [Coined by Jack Conway, U.S. journalist, d. 1928; ult. origin uncertain]

palp (palp) *n.* A palpus. [< F < L *palpus* feeler]

pal·pa·ble (pal′pə·bəl) *adj.* **1.** Capable of being touched or felt. **2.** Readily perceived; obvious. **3.** Perceptible by touching. [< LL < L *palpare* to touch] — **pal·pa·bil′i·ty, pal′pa·ble·ness** *n.* — **pal′pa·bly** *adv.*

pal·pate (pal′pāt) *v.t.* **·pat·ed, ·pat·ing** To feel or examine by touch, esp. for medical diagnosis. — *adj.* Having a palpus or palpi. [< L *palpare* to touch] — **pal·pa′tion** *n.*

pal·pi·tate (pal′pə·tāt) *v.i.* **·tat·ed, ·tat·ing** **1.** To quiver; tremble. **2.** To beat more rapidly than normal; flutter: said esp. of the heart. [< L *palpitatus*, pp. of *palpitare* to tremble, freq. of *palpare* to touch] — **pal′pi·ta′tion** *n.*

pal·pus (pal′pəs) *n.* *pl.* **·pi** (-pī) *Zool.* A feeler; esp., one of the jointed sense organs attached to the mouth parts of arthropods: also called *palp*. [< NL < L *palpus* feeler]

pal·sied (pôl′zēd) *adj.* Affected with palsy; trembling.

pal·sy (pôl′zē) *n.* *pl.* **·sies** **1.** Paralysis. **2.** Any impairment or loss of ability to control movement. — *v.t.* **·sied, ·sy·ing** **1.** To paralyze. **2.** To cause to tremble or become helpless, as from fear or rage. [< OF < L *paralysis*]

pal·ter (pôl′tər) *v.i.* **1.** To speak or act insincerely; equivocate; lie. **2.** To be fickle or capricious; trifle. **3.** To haggle or quibble. [Origin unknown] — **pal′ter·er** *n.*

pal·try (pôl′trē) *adj.* **·tri·er, ·tri·est** **1.** Having little or no worth or value; trifling; trivial. **2.** Contemptible; petty. [< LG < *palte* rag.] — **pal′tri·ly** *adv.* — **pal′tri·ness** *n.*

pa·lu·dal (pə·lōōd′l) *adj.* Pertaining to a marsh; swampy. [< L *palus, paludis* marsh]

pam·pas (pam′pəz, *Sp.* päm′päs) *n.pl.* The great treeless plains south of the Amazon river, extending from the Atlantic to the Andes. [< Sp. < Quechua *pampa* plain]

pam·pe·an (pam′pē·an, pam·pē′ən) *adj.* Of or pertaining to the pampas or to their native inhabitants. — *n.* An Indian of the pampas.

pam·per (pam′pər) *v.t.* To treat very indulgently; gratify the whims or wishes of; coddle. [Appar. < LG < *pampen* to live luxuriously] — **pam′per·er** *n.*

pam·phlet (pam′flit) *n.* **1.** A printed work stitched or pasted, but not permanently bound. **2.** A brief treatise or essay, often on a subject of current interest, printed and published without a binding. [< OF *pamphilet*, dim. of *Pamphilus*, title of a 12th c. Latin love poem]

pam·phlet·eer (pam′flə·tir′) *n.* One who writes pamphlets: sometimes a term of contempt. — *v.i.* To write and issue pamphlets.

pan[1] (pan) *n.* **1.** A wide, shallow vessel, usu. of metal, used for holding liquids or in cooking. **2.** Any similar receptacle or vessel, as one used for boiling and evaporating. **3.** A circular iron dish with sloping sides, in which gold is separated. **4.** The powder cavity of a flintlock. **5.** The skull; brainpan.

6. Hardpan. **7.** Either of the two receptacles on a pair of scales or a balance. — *v.* **panned, pan·ning** *v.t.* **1.** To separate (gold) by washing gold-bearing earth in a pan. **2.** To wash (earth, gravel, etc.) for this purpose. **3.** To cook and serve in a pan. **4.** *Informal* To criticize severely. — *v.i.* **5.** To search for gold by washing earth, gravel, etc., in a pan. **6.** To yield gold, as earth. — **to pan out** *U.S. Informal* To succeed. [OE < Gmc. < LL < L < Gk. *patanē*]

pan² (pan) *v.t.* **panned, pan·ning** To move (a motion-picture or television camera) so as to photograph an entire scene, following a particular character, etc. [< PANORAMA]

pan- *combining form* **1.** All; every; the whole: *panchromatic.* **2.** Comprising, including, or applying to all: usually capitalized when preceding proper nouns or adjectives, as in: **Pan-African, Pan-Asia, Pan-Arab.** [< Gk., neut. of *pas* all]

Pan (pan) In Greek mythology, a god identified with the Roman *Faunus.*

pan·a·ce·a (pan′ə·sē′ə) *n.* A remedy for all diseases or ills; a cure-all. [< L < Gk. < *pan*, neut. of *pas* all + *akos* cure] — **pan′a·ce′an** *adj.*

Panama hat A hat woven from the leaves of a palmlike tree of Central and South America.

Pan·a·ma·ni·an (pan′ə·mā′nē·ən, -mä′-) *adj.* Of or pertaining to the Isthmus of Panama or its inhabitants. — *n.* A native or naturalized inhabitant of Panama. Also **Pan·a·man** (pan′ə·män′).

Pan-A·mer·i·can (pan′ə·mer′ə·kən) *adj.* Including or pertaining to the whole of America, both North and South, or to all Americans. Also **Pan American.**

Pan-A·mer·i·can·ism (pan′ə·mer′ə·kən·iz′əm) *n.* The advocacy of a closer political and economic cooperation among the republics of the western hemisphere.

Pan American Union A bureau established in Washington, D.C., in 1890, by the 21 American republics to promote mutual peace.

pan·a·tel·a (pan′ə·tel′ə) See PANETELA.

pan-broil (pan′broil′) *v.t. & v.i.* To cook in a heavy frying pan placed over direct heat, using little or no fat.

pan·cake (pan′kāk′) *n.* **1.** A thin, flat cake made from batter fried in a pan or baked on a griddle. **2.** A cosmetic resembling face powder: also **pancake make-up. 3.** *Aeron.* An abrupt landing in which an airplane is leveled off and stalled well above the surface so that it drops flat. — *v.i.* **·caked, ·cak·ing** *Aeron.* To make a pancake landing.

pan·chro·mat·ic (pan′krō·mat′ik) *adj. Photog.* Sensitive to light of all colors of the spectrum, as film or a plate. — **pan·chro′ma·tism** (-krō′mə·tiz′əm) *n.*

pan·cre·as (pan′krē·əs, pang′-) *n. Anat.* A large gland situated behind the lower part of the stomach, secreting digestive enzymes into the duodenum and producing insulin in the islands of Langerhans. [< NL < Gk. < *pan-* all + *kreas* flesh] — **pan′cre·at′ic** (-at′ik) *adj.*

pan·da (pan′də) *n. pl.* **·das** or **·da 1.** A small, raccoonlike carnivore of the southeastern Himalayas, with long reddish brown fur and ringed tail: also called *bearcat.* **2.** A large, bearlike mammal of Tibet and China, with black-and-white coat and rings around the eyes: also called *giant panda.* [Prob. < Nepalese]

Pan·de·an (pan·dē′ən) *adj.* Of or pertaining to the god Pan.

pan·dem·ic (pan·dem′ik) *adj.* **1.** *Med.* Widely epidemic. **2.** Universal; general. — *n.* A pandemic disease. [< < *pan-* all + *dēmos* people]

pan·de·mo·ni·um (pan′də·mō′nē·əm) *n.* **1.** The abode of all demons. **2.** Loosely, hell. **3.** A place marked by disorder and uproar. **4.** Riotous uproar. Also **pan′dae·mo′ni·um.** [< NL < Gk. < *pan-* all + *daimōn* demon]

pan·der (pan′dər) *n.* **1.** A go-between in sexual intrigues; pimp. **2.** One who ministers to the passions or base desires of others. Also **pan′der·er.** — *v.i.* **1.** To act as a pander. — *v.t.* **2.** To act as a pander for. [< L < Gk. *Pandaros;* or < *Pandare,* character in Chaucer's Troilus and Criseyde]

Pan·do·ra (pan·dôr′ə, -dō′rə) In Greek mythology, the first mortal woman, who brought with her a box (**Pandora's box**) containing all human ills which, when she opened the lid, escaped into the world. [< Gk., all-gifted]

pan·dow·dy (pan·dou′dē) *n. pl.* **·dies** *U.S.* A deep-dish pie or pudding make of baked sliced apples and having only a top crust. Also **apple pandowdy.** [Origin unknown]

pane (pān) *n.* **1.** One of the sections of a window, door, etc., filled with a sheet of glass. **2.** A sheet of glass for such a section. **3.** One of the flat surfaces on an object having several sides, as a nut, bolthead, or cut diamond. **4.** A panel in a door, ceiling, etc. [< OF < L *pannus* piece of cloth]

pan·e·gyr·ic (pan′ə·jir′ik) *n.* **1.** A formal public eulogy, either written or spoken. **2.** Elaborate praise; laudation. [< MF < L < Gk. < *pan-* all + *agyris* assembly] — **pan′·e·gyr′i·cal** *adj.* **pan′e·gyr′i·cal·ly** *adv.*

pan·e·gyr·ist (pan′ə·jir′ist) *n.* One who panegyrizes.

pan·e·gy·rize (pan′ə·jə·rīz′) *v.* **·rized, ·riz·ing** *v.t.* **1.** To deliver or write a panegyric upon; eulogize. — *v.i.* **2.** To make panegyrics.

pan·el (pan′əl) *n.* **1.** A rectangular or square piece forming part of a wainscot, ceiling, door, etc., usu. raised above or sunk below the general level, surrounded by a molding, etc. **2.** A window pane. **3.** One or more pieces of the same or different fabric inserted lengthwise in a woman's skirt. **4.** A tablet of wood used as the surface for an oil painting; also, the picture painted on such a tablet. **5.** A picture very long for its width. **6.** *Law* **a** The official list of persons summoned for jury duty. **b** The body of persons composing a jury **7.** A small group of persons selected to hold a discussion, judge a contest, etc. **8.** An instrument panel. — *v.t.* **pan·eled** or **·elled, pan·el·ing** or **·el·ling 1.** To fit, furnish, or adorn with panels. **2.** To divide into panels. [< OF < Med.L < L *pannus* piece of cloth]

panel discussion A discussion before an audience of a specific topic by a group of selected speakers.

pan·el·ing (pan′əl·ing) *n.* **1.** Wood or other materials used in making panels. **2.** Panels collectively. Also **pan′el·ling.**

pan·el·ist (pan′əl·ist) *n.* A person serving on a panel.

pan·e·tel·a (pan′ə·tel′ə) *n.* A long, slender cigar: also spelled *panatela.* Also **pan′e·tel′la.** [< Sp.]

pan fish Any little fish that can be fried whole.

pang (pang) *n.* **1.** A sudden sharp pain. **2.** A spasm of mental anguish. [Origin unknown]

pan·go·lin (pang·gō′lin) *n.* A heavily armored, typically long-tailed toothless mammal of Asia and Africa: also called *scaly anteater.* [< Malay *peng-gōling* roller, in ref. to its power of rolling itself up]

pan·han·dle¹ (pan′han′dəl) *v.i.* **·dled, ·dling** *U.S. Informal* To beg, esp. on the street. [PAN-HAN-DLER]

pan·han·dle² (pan′han′dəl) *n.* **1.** The handle of a pan. **2.** *Usu. cap. U.S.* A narrow strip of land shaped like the handle of a pan, as in Texas or West Virginia.

pan·han·dler (pan′han′dlər) *n. U.S. Informal* A beggar. [< PAN¹ (used to receive alms) + HANDLE, v.]

Pan-Hel·len·ic (pan′he·len′ik) *adj.* **1.** Of or pertaining to all Greeks. **2.** Of college fraternities or sororities.

pan·ic (pan′ik) *n.* **1.** A sudden, unreasonable, overpowering fear, esp. when affecting a large number simultaneously. **2.** An instance of such fear. — *adj.* **1.** Of the nature of or resulting from panic. **2.** *Usu. cap.* Of or pertaining to the Greek god Pan. — *v.t. & v.i.* **·icked, ·ick·ing** To affect or become affected with panic. [< MF < Gk. *panikos* of or for the god Pan, who was believed to cause sudden or groundless fear] — **pan′ick·y** *adj.*

pan·i·cle (pan′i·kəl) *n. Bot.* A loose compound flower cluster, produced by irregular branching. [< L *panicula,* dim. of *panus* swelling]

pan·ic-strick·en (pan′ik·strik′ən) *adj.* Overcome by panic. Also **pan′ic-struck′** (-struk′).

pa·nic·u·late (pə·nik′yə·lāt, -lit) *adj. Bot.* Arranged in panicles. Also **pa·nic′u·lat′ed.** — **pa·nic′u·late·ly** *adv.*

pan·jan·drum (pan·jan′drəm) *n.* A mock title for an official of exaggerated importance or great pretensions. [Coined by Samuel Foote, 1720–1777, English dramatist and actor]

pan·nier (pan′yər) *n.* **1.** One of a pair of baskets adapted to be slung on both sides of a beast of burden. **2.** A basket for carrying a load on the back. **3.** A light framework for extending a woman's dress at the hips; also, a skirt or overskirt so extended. [< MF < L *panarium* bread basket]

pa·no·cha (pə·nō′chə) *n.* A coarse Mexican sugar. Also **pa·no′che.** [< Am. Sp., dim. of Sp. *pan*]

pan·o·ply (pan′ə·plē) *n. pl.* **·plies 1.** The complete equipment of a warrior. **2.** Any complete covering that protects or arrays. [< Gk. *panoplia* full armor] — **pan′o·plied** *adj.*

pan·o·ram·a (pan′ə·ram′ə, -rä′mə) *n.* **1.** A series of pictures representing a continuous scene, arranged to unroll and pass before the spectator. **2.** A complete view in every direction; also, a complete or comprehensive view of a subject or of passing events. [< PAN- + Gk. *horama* sight] — **pan′o·ram′ic** *adj.* — **pan′o·ram′i·cal·ly** *adv.*

pan·pipe (pan′pīp′) *n. Sometimes cap. Often pl.* An instrument consisting of a graduated series of short flutes, originally reeds, bound together in proper order to produce a scale.

Pan-Slav·ism (pan′slô′viz·əm) *n.* The idea of uniting all Slavic peoples, esp. under the hegemony of Russia. — **Pan′-Slav′ic** *adj.* — **Pan′-slav′ist** *n.*

pan·sy (pan′zē) *n. pl.* **·sies 1.** A garden violet having blossoms of a variety of colors. **2.** *U.S. Slang* An effeminate or homosexual man. [< MF *pensée* thought]

pant (pant) *v.i.* **1.** To breathe rapidly or spasmodically; gasp for breath. **2.** To emit smoke, steam, etc., in loud puffs. **3.** To gasp with desire; yearn: with *for* or *after.* **4.** To beat or pulsate rapidly. — *v.t.* **5.** To breathe out or utter gaspingly. — *n.* **1.** The act of panting. **2.** A gasp. **3.** A throb, as of the heart. **4.** A puff, as from an engine. [Appar. < OF, ult. < L *phantasiare* to have a nightmare]

pant- Var. of PANTO-.

pan·ta·lets (pan'tə-lets') *n.pl.* 1. Formerly, long ruffled or embroidered drawers extending below the hem of the skirt. 2. Separate frilled leg coverings to be attached to drawers. Also **pan'ta·lettes'.** [Dim. of PANTALOON]

pan·ta·loon (pan'tə-lōōn') *n. pl.* Formerly, a tight-fitting garment for the hips and legs; trousers. [< MF < Ital. *pantalone* clown < *Pantaleone*, popular Venetian saint]

Pan·ta·loon (pan'tə-lōōn') In early Italian comedy, a skinny, foolish old man wearing pantaloons.

pan·the·ism (pan'thē-iz'əm) *n.* 1. The doctrine that the whole universe is God, or that every part of the universe is a manifestation of God. 2. Worship of all the gods. [<PAN- + Gk. *theos* god] — **pan'the·ist** *n.* — **pan'the·is'tic** *adj.*

pan·the·on (pan'thē-on) *n.* 1. All the gods of a people collectively. 2. A temple commemorating the great of a nation. [< L < Gk. < *pan-* all + *theios* of or sacred to a god]

Pan·the·on (pan'thē·on) A circular domed temple at Rome, dedicated to all the gods, built 27 B.C., rebuilt A.D. 120–124.

pan·ther (pan'thər) *n.* 1. A leopard, esp. the black variety of Asia. 2. The puma or cougar. 3. The jaguar. [< OF < L Gk. *panthēr*] — **pan'ther·ess** *n.fem.*

pant·ies (pan'tēz) *n.pl.* A woman's or child's underpants.

panto- *combining form* All; every. Also, before vowels, *pant-.* [< Gk. *pantos*, genitive of *pas* all]

pan·to·graph (pan'tə-graf, -gräf) *n.* An instrument used for copying drawings, maps, etc., to any scale. — **pant'o·graph'ic** or **·i·cal** *adj.* — **pan·tog'ra·phy** (pan·tog'rə-fē) *n.*

pan·to·mime (pan'tə-mīm) *n.* 1. Any play in which the actors express their meaning by action without dialogue. 2. Gestures without speech. 3. In ancient Roman drama, a part of a play in which the actor used only gestures to the accompaniment of the chorus. — *v.t. & v.i.* **·mimed, ·mim·ing** To act or express in pantomime. [< F < L < Gk. < *panto(s)* of all + *mimos* imitator] — **pan'to·mi'mist** *n.*

pan·try (pan'trē) *n. pl.* **·tries** A room or closet for provisions, dishes, table linen, etc. [ME < OF < L *panis* bread]

pants (pants) *n.pl.* *Chiefly U.S.* 1. Trousers. 2. Drawers; underpants. [Short for PANTALOONS]

pant·suit (pant'sōōt') *n.* A woman's two-piece garment consisting of a jacket and pants. Also **pants suit.**

pan·ty·waist (pan'tē-wāst') *n.* 1. A child's waist on which to fasten short pants. 2. *Slang* An effeminate young man.

pan·zer (pan'zər, *Ger.* pän'tsər) *adj.* Armored. [< G, armor plating < MHG < OF < Ital. *panzia* belly]

pap¹ (pap) *n.* *Archaic* A teat; nipple. [ME *pappe*]

pap² (pap) *n.* 1. Any soft food for babies. 2. *Slang* The fees and privileges of public office. [Prob. akin to L *pappa*]

pa·pa (pä'pə, pə-pä') *n.* Father: used familiarly. [< F < L < Gk. *papas*, child's word for father]

pa·pa·cy (pā'pə-sē) *n. pl.* **·cies** 1. The dignity, office, or jurisdiction of the pope. 2. The succession of popes. 3. The period during which a pope is in office. [< Med.L < Gk. *papas* father]

Pa·pa·cy (pā'pə-sē) *n.* The Roman Catholic system of church government.

pa·pal (pā'pəl) *adj.* 1. Of, pertaining to, or ordered by the pope. 2. Of or pertaining to the papacy. 3. Of or pertaining to the Roman Catholic Church.

Papal cross A cross having three crossbars or transoms, the top one the shortest and the bottom one the longest.

pa·paw (pə-pô', pô'pô) *n.* 1. The fleshy, edible fruit of a North American shrub or small tree. 2. The tree bearing this fruit. Also spelled *pawpaw.* [< PAPAYA]

pa·pa·ya (pä-pä'yä, pə-pä'yə) *n.* 1. The yellow, melonlike fruit of a tropical American evergreen tree, valued for its flavor and nutritious qualities. 2. The tree bearing this fruit. [< Sp. and Pg.; ult of Carib origin]

pa·per (pā'pər) *n.* 1. A substance made from pulp obtained from rags, wood, bark, etc., usu. formed into thin sheets for writing, printing, wrapping, etc. 2. A sheet of this material. 3. Something similar in appearance to paper, as papier-mâché. 4. Wallpaper. 5. A small paper wrapper or card holding a limited number or amount: a *paper* of pins. 6. A printed or written document. 7. A newspaper. 8. A written discourse or treatise. 9. In schools and colleges, a piece of written work, as an assignment, a report, etc. 10. *pl.* A collection of letters, diaries, and other writings, especially by one person. 11. *pl.* Personal documents or identification; credentials. 12. *pl.* A ship's papers. 13. In business, written or printed pledges to pay, that are negotiable. 14. *Slang* Free passes to a theater, etc.; also, an audience so admitted. 15. *pl. U.S.* Documents leading to naturalization: see FIRST PAPERS, SECOND PAPERS. — **on paper** 1. In written or printed form. 2. In theory, as distinguished from fact. — *v.t.* 1. To cover with wallpaper. 2. To fold or enclose in paper. 3. To supply with paper. 4. *Slang* To issue free tickets of admission to (a place of amusement). — *adj.* 1. Made of paper. 2. Existing only in writing. [< OF < L *papyrus*] — **pa'per·y** *adj.*

pa·per·back (pā'pər-bak') *adj.* Of books, having a flexible paper cover or binding. — *n.* A book so bound.

pa·per·hang·er (pā'pər-hang'ər) *n.* One whose business is to cover walls, etc., with paper. — **pa'per·hang'ing** *n.*

pa·per·knife (pā'pər-nīf') *n. pl.* **·knives** (-nīvz') A dull blade for opening letters, leaves of books, etc.

paper money Currency consisting of paper imprinted with certain fixed values issued by a government or by authorized banks for circulation as a substitute for metallic money.

paper nautilus One of various eight-armed marine mollusks having delicate shells.

pa·per·weight (pā'pər-wāt') *n.* A small, heavy object, often ornamental, placed on loose papers to secure them.

pap·er·work (pā'pər-wûrk') *n.* Work involving the preparation or handling of reports, letters, forms, etc.

pa·pier-mâ·ché (pā'pər-mə-shā', *Fr.* pà·pyā'mä·shā') *n.* A material consisting of paper pulp mixed with size, paste, oil, resin, etc., that can be molded into various shapes when wet and that becomes hard when dry. [< F *papier* paper + *mâché*, pp. of *mâcher* to chew]

pa·pil·la (pə-pil'ə) *n. pl.* **·pil·lae** (-pil-ē) 1. *Anat.* **a** The nipple. **b** Any small nipplelike process of connective tissue, as on the tongue or at the root of a hair. 2. *Bot.* A small nipple-shaped projection. [< L] — **pap·il·la·ry** (pap'ə-ler'ē) *adj.*

pap·il·lo·ma (pap'ə-lō'mə) *n. pl.* **·ma·ta** (-mə-tə) *Pathol.* An abnormality of the skin or mucous membrane consisting of tumorous outgrowths, as corns, warts, etc. [< PAPILLA]

pap·il·lose (pap'ə-lōs) *adj.* Having many papillae. — **pap·il·los'i·ty** (-los'ə-tē) *n.*

pa·pist (pā'pist) *n.* An adherent of the papacy; a Roman Catholic: usu. a disparaging term. [See PAPACY.] — **pa·pis·ti·cal** (pə-pis'ti-kəl), **pa·pis·tic** *adj.* — **pa'pis·try** *n.*

pa·poose (pa-pōōs') *n.* A North American Indian infant or small child. Also **pap·poose'.** [< Algonquian *papoos*]

pap·pus (pap'əs) *n. pl.* **pap·pi** (pap'ī) *Bot.* A downy tuft of hairs, as in thistles, or on certain fruits. [< NL < Gk. *pappos* grandfather] — **pap'pose** (-ōs), **pap'pous** (-əs) *adj.*

pap·py (pap'ē) *n. pl.* **·pies** Papa; father. [Dim. of PAPA¹]

pa·pri·ka (pa-prē'kə, pap'rə-kə) *n.* A condiment made from the ripe fruit of a mild variety of red pepper. Also **pa·pri'ca.** [< Magyar, red pepper]

Pap smear A method of early detection of cervical cancer. Also **Pap test.** [after George *Papanicolaou*, 1883–1962, U.S. scientist]

Pap·u·an (pä'pōō-ən, pap'ōō·ən) *adj.* Of or pertaining to the Island of Papua or to the Papuan peoples. — *n.* A member of any of the dark peoples inhabiting Melanesia.

pap·u·la (pap'yə-lə) *n. pl.* **·lae** (-lē) *Pathol.* A pimple. Also **pap'ule** (-yōōl). [< L, pimple] — **pap'u·lan** *adj.*

pa·py·rus (pə-pī'rəs) *n. pl.* **·ri** (-rī) 1. A tall rushlike aquatic plant of the sedge family, formerly common in Egypt. 2. A type of writing paper made by the ancient Egyptians from this plant. 3. A manuscript written on this material. [< L < Gk. *papyros*]

par (pär) *n.* 1. An accepted standard or level used for comparison: usu. preceded by *on* or *upon:* His work is on a *par* with that of the other students. 2. The normal average in amount, quality, or degree: His health is up to *par.* 3. In commerce, the state of equality between the nominal, or face, value and the market value of shares of stock, bonds, bills of exchange, etc: also *parity.* 4. In golf, the number of strokes allotted to a hole or round when played perfectly. — *adj.* 1. Normal; average. 2. In commerce, having the face value normal. [< L, equal]

para-¹ *prefix* 1. Beside; nearby; along with: *paradigm.* 2. Beyond; aside from; amiss: *paradox.* 3. *Chem.* A modification of or a compound similar to (not necessarily isomeric or polymeric): *paramorphine.* 4. *Med.* **a** A functionally disordered or diseased condition: *paraplegia.* **b** Similar to but not identical with a true condition or form: *paratyphoid.* Also, before vowels and *h,* usu. **par-.** [< Gk. *para* beside]

para-² *combining form* Shelter or protection against: *parasol.* [< Ital *para,* imperative of *parare* to defend]

par·a-a·mi·no·ben·zo·ic acid (par'ə-ə-mē'nō-ben-zō'ik, -am'ə-nō-) *Biochem.* A colorless crystalline compound, $C_7H_7NO_2$, forming part of the vitamin B complex, present in yeast and also made synthetically.

par·a·ble (par'ə-bəl) *n.* A short narrative making a moral or religious point by comparison with natural or homely things. [< OF < LL < Gk. *parabolē* a placing side by side]

pa·rab·o·la (pə-rab'ə-lə) *n. Math.* The curve formed by the edges of a plane when cutting through a right circular cone at an angle parallel to one of its sides. [< L < Gk. *parabolē* a placing side by side]

par·a·bol·ic (par'ə-bol'ik) *adj.* 1. Pertaining to or having the nature of a parable. **2.** Pertaining to or like a parabola. Also **par'a·bol'i·cal.** — **par'a·bol'i·cal·ly** *adv.*

pa·rab·o·lize (pə·rab'ə·līz) *v.t.* **·lized, ·liz·ing 1.** To relate in parable form. **2.** *Math.* To give the form of a parabola to.

par·a·chute (par'ə·shoot) *n.* A large, umbrella-shaped apparatus for retarding the speed of a body descending through the air, esp. from an airplane. — *v,* **·chut·ed, ·chut·ing** *v.t.* **1.** To land (troops, materiel, etc.) by means of parachutes. — *v.i.* **2.** To descend by parachute. [< F < PARA² + *chute* fall] — **par'a·chut'ist** *n.*

par·a·clete (par'ə·klēt) *n.* One called to the aid of another. — **the Paraclete** The Holy Spirit as a helper or comforter. [< OF < LL < LGk. *paraklētos* comforter, advocate]

pa·rade (pə·rād') *n.* **1.** A procession or march for ceremony or display. **2.** A marshaling and maneuvering of troops for display or inspection. **3.** A ground where military reviews are held. **4.** A promenade or public walk; also, the persons promenading. **5.** Pompous show, ostentation. — **on parade** On display. — *v.* **·rad·ed, ·rad·ing** *v.t.* **1.** To walk or march through or about. **2.** To display ostentatiously; flaunt. **3.** To cause to assemble for military parade. — *v.i.* **4.** To march formally. **5.** To walk in public for the purpose of showing oneself. **6.** To assemble in military order for inspection or review. [< MF < Sp. *parada* stopping place, exercise ground] — **pa·rad'er** *n.*

par·a·digm (par'ə·dim, -dīm) *n.* *Gram.* **1.** A list or table of all the inflected forms of a word or class of words, as of a particular declension, conjugation, etc. **2.** Any pattern or example. [< LL < Gk. *paradeigma* pattern] — **par'a·dig·mat'ic** (-dig·mat'ik) *adj.*

par·a·dise (par'ə·dīs) *n.* **1.** Heaven. **2.** A place or state of great beauty or delight. [< F < LL < Gk. *paradeisos* park] — **par'a·di·sa'ic** (-di·sā'ik) or **·i·cal,** **par'a·dis'i·ac** (-dis'ē·ak) or **par·a·di·si·a·cal** (par'ə·di·sī'ə·kəl) *adj.*

Par·a·dise (par'ə·dīs) Eden or heaven.

par·a·dox (par'ə·doks) *n.* **1.** A statement seemingly absurd or contradictory, yet in fact true. **2.** A statement essentially self-contradictory, false, or absurd. **3.** One whose character or behavior is inconsistent or contradictory. [< F < L < Gk. *paradoxos* incredible] — **par'a·dox'i·cal** *adj.* — **par'a·dox'i·cal'i·ty** (-kal'ə·tē), **par'a·dox'i·cal·ness** *n.* — **par'a·dox'i·cal·ly** *adv.*

par·af·fin (par'ə·fin) *n.* *Chem.* **1.** A waxy mixture of hydrocarbons, distilled from petroleum and widely used for candles, as a preservative, etc. **2.** Any hydrocarbon of the methane series. — *v.t.* To treat or impregnate with paraffin. Also **par'af·fine** (-fin, -fēn). [< G < L *par(um)* too little + *affin(is)* related to; so named because it has little affinity for other substances]

paraffin series *Chem.* The methane series.

paraffin wax Paraffin in its solid state.

par·a·gon (par'ə·gon) *n.* A model or pattern of excellence, esp. of a specific excellence: *a paragon of manhood.* [< OF < Ital. *paragone* touchstone, prob. < Gk. *parakonan* to sharpen one thing against another]

par·a·graph (par'ə·graf, -gräf) *n.* **1.** A distinct part or section of a written discourse, begun on a new and usu. indented line and generally containing a unified statement of a particular point. **2.** A short article, item, or comment, as in a newspaper. **3.** A mark (¶) used to indicate where a paragraph is to be begun. — *v.t.* **1.** To arrange in or into paragraphs. **2.** To comment on or express in a paragraph. [< OF < LL < Gk. < *para* beside + *graphein* to write] — **par'a·graph'er** *n.* — **par'a·graph'ic, par'a·graph'i·cal** *adj.*

par·a·keet (par'ə·kēt) *n.* Any of certain small parrots, with long, wedge-shaped tails: also spelled *paraquet, paroquet, parrakeet, parroket, parroquet.* [< OF < Ital. *parrochetto*]

Par·a·li·pom·e·non (par'ə·li·pom'ə·non) *n.pl.* The Douai Bible name for CHRONICLES.

par·al·lax (par'ə·laks) *n.* The apparent displacement of an object, esp. of a star or other heavenly body, when it is viewed successively from two points not in the same line of sight. [< F < Gk. *parallassein* to deviate]

par·al·lel (par'ə·lel) *adj.* **1.** Being a uniform distance away or apart throughout a certain area or extent. **2.** *Geom.* Not meeting, however far extended: said of straight lines and of planes. **3.** Having a close resemblance. **4.** *Music* **a** Denoting consecutive identical or similar intervals in the same two voices. **b** Denoting consecutive identical chords. **5.** *Electr.* Connected between like terminals, as a group of cells, condensers, etc. — *n.* **1.** An object or surface equidistant from another. **2.** *Geom.* A parallel line or plane. **3.** Essential likeness. **4.** A counterpart; match. **5.** Comparison: to draw a *parallel* between two things. **6.** *Geog.* Any of the circles imagined as drawn upon the earth's surface at right angles to its axis, every point on which marks a given latitude north or south of the equator. **7.** *Electr.* Connection between like terminals: usu. in the phrase **in parallel:** also called *multiple.* — *v.t.* **·leled** or **·lelled, ·lel·ing** or **·lel·ling 1.** To place in parallel; make parallel. **2.** To be, go, or extend parallel to. **3.** To furnish with a parallel

or equal; find a parallel to. **4.** To be a parallel to; correspond to. **5.** To compare; liken. [< MF < L < Gk. < *para* beside + *allēlos* one another]

parallel bars Two horizontal crossbars, parallel to each other and supported by upright posts, used for gymnastics.

par·al·lel·e·pi·ped (par'ə·lel'ə·pī'pid, -pip'id) *n.* A prism with six faces, each of which is a parallelogram. Also **par·al·lel'o·pi'ped, par·al·lel'e·pip'e·don, par·al·lel'o·pip'e·don** (-pip'ə·don, -pī'pə-). [< Gk. < *parallēlos* parallel + *epipe·don* a plane surface]

par·al·lel·ism (par'ə·lel·iz'əm) *n.* **1.** The state or quality of being parallel. **2.** Likeness; similarity. **3.** A comparison.

par·al·lel·o·gram (par'ə·lel'ə·gram) *n.* **1.** *Geom.* A foursided plane figure whose opposite sides are parallel and equal. **2.** Any area or object having such form. [< MF < L < Gk. < *parallēlos* parallel + *grammē* line]

pa·ral·y·sis (pə·ral'ə·sis) *n. pl.* **·ses** (-sēz) **1.** *Pathol.* Partial or complete loss of motor function, esp., voluntary motion, resulting from injury to the nervous system or to a muscular mechanism. **2.** Cessation or crippling of normal activities. [< L < Gk. < *paralyein* to disable] — **par·a·lyt·ic** (par'ə·lit'ik) *adj. & n.*

par·a·lyze (par'ə·līz) *v.t.* **·lyzed, ·lyz·ing 1.** To bring about paralysis in; make paralytic. **2.** To render powerless, ineffective, or inactive. [< F *paralyser,* back formation < *paralysie* palsy] — **par'a·lyz'er** *n.* — **par·a·ly·za'tion** *n.*

par·a·me·ci·um (par'ə·mē'shē·əm, -sē·əm) *n. pl.* **·ci·a** (shē·ə, -sē·ə) Any of various species of ciliate protozoa having a flattened, elongate body, and feeding by a primitive oral groove. [< NL < Gk. *paramēkēs* oblong, oval]

par·a·med·ic (par'ə·med'ik) *n.* One trained to assist a physician. — **par'a·med'i·cal** *adj.*

pa·ram·e·ter (pə·ram'ə·tər) *n.* **1.** *Math.* A constant whose values determine the operation or characteristics of a system. **2.** A fixed limit or guideline. [< NL < Gk. *para* beside + *metron* measure]

par·a·mil·i·tar·y (par'ə·mil'ə·ter'ē) *adj.* Having a military structure although not officially military; capable of becoming, replacing, or supplementing a military force: said of certain political movements, etc. [< PARA-¹ + MILITARY]

par·a·mount (par'ə·mount) *adj.* **1.** Superior to all others; chief in importance. **2.** Having the highest authority or rank. — *n.* A supreme lord; highest ruler. [< AF < OF *par* by + *à mont* up, above] — **par'a·mount·ly** *adv.*

par·a·mour (par'ə·moor) *n.* A lover, esp. one who unlawfully takes the place of a spouse. [< OF *par amour* with love]

par·a·noi·a (par'ə·noi'ə) *n.* *Psychiatry* A form of mental disorder characterized by delusions of persecution or of grandeur. [< NL < Gk., < *para* beside + *noos, nous* mind]

par·a·noi·ac (par'ə·noi'ak) *adj.* Relating to or affected by paranoia. — *n.* One affected by paranoia.

par·a·noid (par'ə·noid) *adj.* Resembling or suggestive of paranoia. — *n.* One affected by paranoia.

par·a·pet (par'ə·pit, -pet) *n.* A low wall about the edge of a roof, terrace, bridge, etc. [< MF, or < Ital. *parapetlu*] — **par'a·pet·ed** *adj.*

par·a·pher·na·li·a (par'ə·fər·nā'lē·ə, -nāl'yə, -fə-) *n.pl.* **1.** Personal effects. **2.** A group of articles, esp. as used in some activity; equipment; gear. [< Med.L *paraphernalia* (bona) a wife's own (goods)]

par·a·phrase (par'ə·frāz) *n.* A restatement of the meaning of a passage, work, etc., as for clarity. — *v.t. & v.i.* **·phrased, ·phras·ing** To express in or make a paraphrase. [< MF < L < Gk. < *para* beside + *phrazein* to tell] — **par'a·phras'er, par'a·phrast** (-frast) *n.* — **par'a·phras'tic** or **·ti·cal** *adj.* — **par'a·phras'ti·cal·ly** *adv.*

par·a·ple·gi·a (par'ə·plē'jē·ə) *n.* *Pathol.* Paralysis of the lower half of the body, due to disease or injury of the spinal cord. Also **par'a·ple'gy** (-plē'jē). [< NL < Gk. < *para* beside + *plēssein* to strike] — **par·a·ple'gic** *adj. & n.*

par·a·pro·fes·sion·al (par'ə·prə·fesh'ə·nəl) *n.* One who assists professionals, as teachers, by performing tasks not requiring professional skills.

par·a·psy·chol·o·gy (par'ə·sī·kol'ə·jē) *n.* The study of extrasensory perception and related psychic phenomena.

pa·ra·quet (par'ə·kēt) See PARAKEET.

par·a·site (par'ə·sīt) *n.* **1.** *Biol.* An animal or plant that lives in or on another organism, the host, and from whom it obtains nourishment. **2.** One who lives at another's expense without making proper return. [< L < Gk. *parasitos,* lit., one who eats at another's table] — **par'a·sit'ic, par·a·sit'i·cal** *adj.* — **par'a·sit'i·cal·ly** *adv.*

par·a·sit·ism (par'ə·sī'tiz·əm) *n.* The condition of being a parasite; parasitic mode of existence.

par·a·sol (par'ə·sôl, -sol) *n.* A small, light umbrella carried by women, used as protection against the sun. [< MF < Ital. < *para-* para-² + *sole* sun]

par·a·sym·pa·thet·ic (par'ə·sim'pə·thet'ik) *adj. Anat.* Denoting a part of the nervous system having among its functions the constriction of the pupil, the slowing of the heart, and the dilation of the blood vessels.

par·a·thy·roid (par'ə-thī'roid) *adj. Anat.* 1. Lying near the thyroid gland. 2. Of or pertaining to any of the several, usu. four, small glands found near the thyroid gland and serving to control the amount of calcium in the blood. — *n.* One of the parathyroid glands.

par·a·troops (par'ə-trōōps) *n.pl.* Troops trained and equipped to drop behind enemy lines by parachute. — **par'a·troop·er** *n.*

par·a·ty·phoid (par'ə-tī'foid) *Pathol. adj.* Of or pertaining to paratyphoid fever. — *n.* Paratyphoid fever.

paratyphoid fever *Pathol.* An infectious disease having symptoms resembling those of typhoid fever, but caused by a different bacterium.

par a·vi·on (par'ä-vyôn') *French* By airmail.

par·boil (par'boil') *v.t.* 1. To boil partially. 2. To make uncomfortable with heat. [< OF < LL *perbullire* to boil thoroughly]

par·buck·le (par'buk'əl) *n.* A sling for vertically raising a heavy object by passing a doubled rope around it, the free ends being pulled through the loop. — *v.t.* **·led, ·ling** To hoist or lower by means of a parbuckle. [Earlier *parbunkle*; origin uncertain]

par·cel (par'səl) *n.* 1. Something that is wrapped up; package. 2. A quantity of some commodity put up for sale; lot. 3. An indefinite number of persons or things. 4. A distinct portion of land. — *v.t.* **par·celed** or **·celled, par·cel·ing** or **·cel·ling** 1. To divide or distribute in parts or shares: usu. with *out.* 2. To make up a parcel or parcels. — *adj. & adv.* Part; partly. [< F < L *pars, partis* part]

parcel post A postal service for the conveying and delivering of parcels not exceeding a specified weight and size.

parch (parch) *v.t.* 1. To make extremely dry. 2. To make very thirsty. 3. To dry (corn, peas, etc.) by exposing to great heat. 4. To dry up or shrivel by exposing to cold. — *v.i.* 5. To become dry. 6. To become dry with thirst. [ME *parchen*; ult. origin uncertain]

par·chee·si (par-chē'zē) *n.* A board game derived from pachisi. Also **par·che'si, par·chi'si.**

parch·ment (parch'mənt) *n.* 1. The skin of sheep, goats, and other animals prepared and polished with pumice stone, used as a material for writing or painting upon. 2. A writing on this material. 3. Any of several types of paper made in imitation of parchment. [< OF < L *pergamenus* of Pergamum, the city where it was first used]

pard¹ (pard) *n. Archaic* A leopard or panther. [< OF < L < Gk. *pardos*]

pard² (pard) *n. Slang* A partner. [Short for PARDNER]

pard·ner (pard'nər) *n. U.S. Dial* Chum; friend. [Alter. of PARTNER]

par·don (par'dən) *v.t.* 1. To remit the penalty of (an offense, insult, etc.). 2. To forgive (a person) for an offense. 3. To grant courteous allowance for or to. — *n.* 1. The act of pardoning; forgiveness. 2. An official warrant declaring such a remission. 3. In the Roman Catholic Church, an indulgence. [< OF < LL < *per-* through + *donare* to give] — **par'don·a·ble** *adj.* — **par'don·a·bly** *adv.*

par·don·er (par'dən·ər) *n.* 1. One who pardons. 2. In the Middle Ages, a layman who sold ecclesiastical indulgences.

pare (pâr) *v.t.* **pared, par·ing** 1. To cut off the covering layer or part of. 2. To cut off or trim away (a covering layer or part): often with *off* or *away* 3. To diminish gradually. [< OF *parer* to prepare, trim] — **par'er** *n.*

par·e·gor·ic (par'ə·gôr'ik, -gor'ik) *n. Med.* A camphorated tincture of opium, used primarily to treat diarrhea. [< LL < Gk. < *parēgoros* soothing]

pa·ren·chy·ma (pə·reng'ki·mə) *n.* 1. *Biol.* The essential functioning cellular substance of an animal organ, as distinguished from connective tissue. 2. *Bot.* The soft cell tissue of higher plants, as found in stem pith or fruit pulp. Also **pa·ren·chyme** (-kim) [< NL < Gk. < *para* beside + *enchyma* infusion] — **par·en·chym·a·tous** (par'eng·kim'ə·tes) *adj.*

par·ent (pâr'ənt) *n.* 1. A father or mother. 2. One exercising the functions of a father or mother. 3. A progenitor; forefather. 4. Any organism that generates another. 5. Source; cause. [< OF < L *parere* to beget] — **pa·ren·tal** (pa·ren'tal) *adj.* — **pa·ren'tal·ly** *adv.* — **par'ent·hood** *n.*

par·ent·age (pâr'ən·tij) *n.* 1. Descent or derivation from parents; lineage; origin. 2. Derivation from a source or origin. 3. Parenthood. [< OF]

pa·ren·the·sis (pə·ren'thə·sis) *n. pl.* **·ses** (-sēz) 1. Either or both of the upright curved lines ( ) used to enclose an interjected, explanatory, or qualifying remark, mathematical quantities, etc. 2. *Gram.* A word, phrase, or clause inserted in a sentence that is grammatically complete without it, set off usu. by commas, dashes, or upright curved lines. 3. An intervening episode or incident. [< Med. L < Gk. < *para* beside + *en* in + *tithenai* to place]

pa·ren·the·size (pə·ren'thə·sīz) *v.t.* **·sized, ·siz·ing** 1. To insert as a parenthetical statement. 2. To insert parentheses in. 3. To place within parentheses (def. 1).

par·en·thet·i·cal (par'ən·thet'i·kəl) *adj.* 1. Thrown in; episodic. 2. Abounding in or like parentheses; also, given to using parentheses. — **par'en·thet'i·cal·ly** *adv.*

pa·re·sis (pə·rē'sis, par'ə·sis) *n. Pathol.* 1. Partial paralysis affecting muscular motion but not sensation. 2. General paresis. [< NL < Gk., a letting go] — **pa·ret·ic** (pə·ret'ik, -rē'tik) *adj.* — **pa·ret'i·cal·ly** *adv.*

par ex·cel·lence (par ek'sə·läns, *Fr.* par ek·se·läns') Beyond comparison; preeminently. [< F, lit., by excellence]

par·fait (par·fā') *n.* A frozen dessert or confection made with eggs, sugar, whipped cream, and fruit or other flavoring. [< F, perfect]

par·he·li·on (par·hē'lē·ən) *n. pl.* **·li·a** (-lē·ə) *Meteorol.* One of two bright images sometimes appearing on a solar halo. Also **par·he'li·um** (-əm). [< L < Gk. < *para* beside + *hēlios* sun] — **par·he'lic, par·he·li·a·cal** (par'hi·lī'ə·kəl) *adj.*

pari- *combining form* Equal. [< L *par, paris* equal]

pa·ri·ah (pə·rī'ə, par'ē·ə) *n.* 1. A member of an extensive low caste of southern India and Burma. 2. A social outcast. [< Tamil *paraiyon*, lit., (hereditary) drummer]

pa·ri·e·tal (pə·rī'ə·tal) *adj.* 1. *Anat.* a Of, pertaining to, or forming the walls of a cavity or hollow organ. b Of or pertaining to the parietal bones. 2. *Bot.* Attached to the wall of the ovary. 3. *U.S.* Pertaining to residence or authority within the walls of a college. — *n.* A parietal bone. [< MF < L *paries* wall]

parietal bone *Anat.* Either of two bones that form a part of the top and sides of the cranium.

pa·ri·mu·tu·el (par'i·myōō'chōō·əl) *n.* 1. A system of betting at races in which those who have bet on the winners share in the total amount wagered. Also **par'i·mu'tu·el.** 2. A pari-mutuel machine. [< F, stake or mutual wager]

pari-mutuel machine A machine for recording pari-mutuel bets: also called *totalizator, totalizer.*

par·ing (pâr'ing) *n.* 1. The act of one who pares. 2. *Often pl.* The part pared off.

Par·is (par'is) In Greek mythology, a son of Priam whose abduction of Helen caused the Trojan War.

Paris green A poisonous compound prepared from copper acetate and arsenic trioxide, used chiefly as an insecticide.

par·ish (par'ish) *n.* 1. *Eccl.* In the Anglican, Roman Catholic, and some other churches, a district with its own church. 2. *U.S.* All those who worship at the same church. 3. *Brit.* A political subdivision of a county. 4. In Louisiana, a civil district corresponding to a county. 5. The people of a parish. ◆ Collateral adjective: *parochial.* [< OF < LL < Gk. *paroikia*, orig., neighborhood, later diocese]

pa·rish·ion·er (pə·rish'ən·ər) *n.* A member of a parish.

Pa·ri·sian (pə·rizh'ən, -riz'ē·ən) *adj.* Of or pertaining to the city of Paris. — *n.* A native or resident of Paris.

par·i·ty (par'ə·tē) *n. pl.* **·ties** 1. Equality, as of condition, rank, value, etc.; also, a like state or degree. 2. The equivalence in legal weight and quality of the legal tender of one class of money to another. 3. Par (def. 3). 4. Equality between the currency or prices of commodities of two countries or cities. 5. Perfect analogy; close resemblance. 6. *U.S.* A level for farm prices that gives to the farmer the same purchasing power that he averaged during each year of a chosen base period. [< MF < *paritas* equality]

park (park) *n.* 1. A tract of land for public use in or near a city. 2. An open square in a city. 3. A national park (which see). 4. An amusement park (which see). 5. A large tract of land surrounding a country estate. 6. *Mil.* An open area where guns, trucks, etc., are assembled for servicing and storage. 7. In English law, a tract of land held through royal grant or by prescription. — *v.t.* 1. To place or leave (an automobile, etc.) standing for a time, as on a street. 2. *U.S. Slang* To place; set. 3. To assemble or mass together: to *park* artillery. 4. To enclose in or as in a park. — *v.i.* 5. To park an automobile, etc. [< OF *parc* game preserve]

par·ka (par'kə) *n. U.S. & Canadian* 1. A hooded outer garment of undressed skins worn by Eskimos. 2. A similar garment worn for skiing and other winter sports. [< Aleut]

Par·kin·son's disease *Pathol.* A form of paralysis characterized by muscular rigidity, tremor, and weakness. Also **Park'in·son·ism.** [after James *Parkinson*, 1755–1824, English physician]

park·land (park'land') *n. Often pl.* 1. Land used or designated as a park. 2. Grassland with trees.

park·way (park'wā') *n.* A wide thoroughfare adorned with spaces planted with turf and trees.

par·lance (par'ləns) *n.* Manner of speech; language: legal *parlance.* [< OF < *parler* to speak]

par·lay (par·lā', par'lē) *v.t. & v.i.* To place (an original bet and its winnings) on a later race, contest, etc. — *n.* Such a bet. [< F < Ital *paroli* grand cast at dice]

par·ley (pär′lē) *n.* A conference, as with an enemy; a discussion of terms. — *v.i.* To hold a conference, esp. with an enemy. [< F *parlée*, fem. pp. of *parler* to speak]

par·lia·ment (pär′lə·mənt) *n.* 1. An assembly for consultation and deliberation. 2. A national legislature, esp. when composed of various estates. [< OF *parlement* speaking < *parler* to speak]

Par·lia·ment (pär′lə·mənt) *n.* 1. The supreme legislature of Great Britain and Northern Ireland, composed of the House of Lords and the House of Commons. 2. The legislature in any of Great Britain's colonies or dominions.

par·lia·men·tar·i·an (pär′lə·men·târ′ē·ən) *n.* One versed in parliamentary procedure or debate.

par·lia·men·ta·ry (pär′lə·men′tər·ē) *adj.* 1. Of, pertaining to, or enacted by a parliament. 2. According to the rules of a parliament: *parliamentary* procedure. 3. Of a government, having a parliament.

parliamentary procedure The rules by which meetings of deliberative assemblies, societies, boards, clubs, etc., are formally conducted. Also **parliamentary law.**

par·lor (pär′lər) *n.* 1. A room for reception of callers or entertainment of guests. 2. A room in an inn, hotel, etc., for private conversation, appointments, etc. Also *Brit.* **par′lour.** [< AF < Med.L < ML *parabolare* to speak]

parlor car A railway car fitted with luxurious chairs, and run as a day coach: also called *chair car.*

par·lous (pär′ləs) *Archaic adj.* 1. Dangerous or exciting. 2. Shrewd. — *adv.* Exceedingly. [Var. of PERILOUS]

Par·me·san cheese (pär′mə·zan) A hard, dry Italian cheese made from skim milk, grated and used to flavor spaghetti, soups, etc. [after *Parma*, a city in Italy]

Par·nas·sus (pär·nas′əs), **Mount** 1. A mountain in central Greece, anciently regarded as sacred to Apollo and the Muses. 2. The domain of poetry or of literature. 3. A collection of poems or other literary works. — **Par·nas′si·an** (pär·nas′ē·ən) *adj.*

pa·ro·chi·al (pə·rō′kē·əl) *adj.* 1. Pertaining to, supported by, or confined to a parish. 2. Narrow; provincial; restricted in scope. [See PARISH.] — **pa·ro′chi·al·ism** *n.* **pa·ro′chi·al·ly** *adv.*

parochial school A school, usu. elementary, supported and directed by the parish of a church.

par·o·dy (par′ə·dē) *n. pl.* **·dies** 1. A humorous or burlesque imitation of a literary or musical work or style. 2. An incompetent attempt to imitate another's work or style. — *v.t.* **·died, ·dy·ing** To make a parody of. [Ult. < Gk. *parōidia* burlesque poem or song] — **pa·rod·ic** (pə·rod′ik) or **·i·cal** *adj.* — **par′o·dist** *n.*

pa·rol (pə·rōl′) *n.* A word: now only in phrase **by parol,** by word of mouth. [< OF *parole* word]

pa·role (pə·rōl′) *n.* 1. The conditional release of a prisoner before his sentence has expired. 2. The duration of such conditional freedom. 3. *Mil.* A pledge of honor by a prisoner of war that he will not seek to escape or will not serve against his captors until exchanged. — **on parole** Freed from prison under conditions of parole. — *v.t.* **·roled, ·rol·ing** To release (a prisoner) on parole. [< F *parole* (d'honneur) word (of honor)]

pa·rol·ee (pə·rō′lē) *n.* One released from prison on parole.

pa·ro·quet (par′ə·ket) See PARAKEET.

pa·rot·id (pə·rot′id) *Anat. adj.* 1. Situated near the ear. 2. Designating one of the paired salivary glands in front of and below the ear. — *n.* A parotid gland. [< F < L < Gk. *parōtis,* < *para-* beside + *ous, ōtos* ear]

par·ox·ysm (par′ək·siz′əm) *n.* 1. A sudden and violent outburst, as of emotion or action: a *paroxysm* of tears. 2. *Pathol.* A sudden intensification of the symptoms of a disease, usu. occurring at intervals. [< MF < Med.L < Gk. < *para-* beside + *oxynein* to goad < *oxys* sharp] — **par·ox·ys′mal** (-siz′məl) *adj.* — **par·ox·ys′mal·ly** *adv.*

par·quet (pär·kā′, -ket′) *n.* 1. Flooring of parquetry. 2. The main floor of a theater, esp. the section from the orchestra pit to the parquet circle: also called *orchestra.* — *v.t.* **·quet·ed** (-kād′, -ket′id), **·quet·ing** (-kā′ing, -ket′ing) To make (a floor, etc.) of parquetry. [< F < OF *parchet* small compartment, dim. of *parc*]

parquet circle The section of theater seats at the rear of the parquet and under the balcony.

par·quet·ry (pär′kit·rē) *n. pl.* **·ries** Inlaid mosaic of wood, used esp. for floors.

parr (pär) *n.* 1. A young salmon before its first migration seaward. 2. The young of some other fishes, as the cod or pollack. [? < dial. E (Scottish)]

PARQUETRY

par·ra·keet (par′ə·kēt) See PARAKEET.

par·ri·cide (par′ə·sīd) *n.* 1. The killing of a parent. 2. One who has killed a parent. [< F < L *paricida* killer of a relative] — **par′ri·ci′dal** *adj.* — **par′ri·ci′dal·ly** *adv.*

par·ro·ket (par′ə·ket) See PARAKEET.

par·ro·quet (par′ə·ket) See PARAKEET.

par·rot (par′ət) *n.* 1. Any of certain birds native in warm regions, having a hooked bill, and often brilliant plumage, including the macaws, parakeets, etc., some of which imitate human speech and laughter. 2. One who repeats without understanding. — *v.t.* To repeat or imitate by rote. [ME, var. of *Perrot* < F < LL *Petrus*] — **par′rot·er** *n.*

parrot fish Any of many small fishes inhabiting warm seas and having vivid coloring and beaklike jaws.

par·ry (par′ē) *v.* **·ried, ·ry·ing** *v.t.* 1. To ward off (a thrust, blow, etc.) in fencing. 2. To avoid or evade. — *v.i.* 3. To ward off a thrust or blow. — *n. pl.* **·ries** 1. A defensive movement, as in fencing. 2. An evasion or diversion in a contest of wits. [< Ital. *parare* to ward off]

parse (pärs) *v.t.* **parsed, pars·ing** 1. To analyze (a sentence) grammatically by giving the form, function, and syntactical relation of each of its words. 2. To describe and analyze (a word) grammatically. [< L *pars, partis* part]

par·sec (pär′sek) *n. Astron.* A unit of length used in expressing stellar distances, corresponding to an annual parallax of one second of arc, or 3.26 light-years.

Par·see (pär′sē, pär·sē′) *n.* A member of a religious sect practicing a form of Zoroastrianism, descendants of Persians who fled to India in the eighth century to escape Moslem persecution. Also **Par′si.** [< Persian *Pārsī* a Persian] — **Par′see·ism, Par′si·ism, Par′sism** *n.*

Par·si·fal (pär′si·fäl, -fəl) A knight in Wagner's opera (1882) of this name.

par·si·mo·ni·ous (pär′sə·mō′nē·əs) *adj.* Characterized by or showing parsimony; penurious; niggardly. — **par′si·mo′ni·ous·ly** *adv.* — **par′si·mo′ni·ous·ness** *n.*

par·si·mo·ny (pär′sə·mō′nē) *n. pl.* **·nies** Undue sparingness in the expenditure of money; stinginess. [< L *parsus,* pp. of *parcere* to spare]

pars·ley (pärs′lē) *n.* A cultivated herb, having aromatic leaves, widely used to garnish and flavor foods. [< OF < LL < L < Gk. < *petra* rock + *selinon* parsley]

pars·nip (pärs′nip) *n.* A European herb of the parsley family, with a large, sweetish, edible root. [ME < OF *pasnaie* + OE *nǣp* turnip]

par·son (pär′sən) *n.* 1. A clergyman; minister. 2. In the Anglican Church, a clergyman having full charge of a parish; a rector. [< OF < Med.L *persona* rector] — **par·son·i·cal** (pär·son′i·kəl), **par·son′ic** *adj.*

par·son·age (pär′sən·ij) *n.* 1. A clergyman's dwelling; esp., a free official residence provided by the church. 2. In English ecclesiastical law, the benefice of a parson.

part (pärt) *n.* 1. A portion of a whole; segment. 2. *Math.* One of a specified number of equal divisions; an aliquot division. 3. A distinct piece or portion of a machine that fulfills a specific function in the working of the whole. 4. Something less than the whole. 5. An organ, member, or other portion of an animal or plant body. 6. *Usu. pl.* A region; territory: in foreign *parts.* 7. One's proper share, as of obligation or performance: to do one's *part.* 8. Individual concern or participation in something. 9. The role or lines assigned to an actor in a play. 10. *Usu. pl.* An endowment of mind or character: a man of *parts.* 11. *Music* **a** The melody intended for a single voice or instrument in a concerted piece: sometimes called *voice.* **b** The written or printed copy for the performer's use. 12. Division, section, or installment of a literary work. 13. The dividing line on the scalp made by combing sections of the hair in opposite directions. — **for one's part** As far as one is concerned. — **for the most part** To the greatest extent; in general. — **in good part** With good grace; good-naturedly. — **in part** Partly. — **part and parcel** An essential part: an emphatic phrase. — **to take part** To participate; share or cooperate: usu. with *in.* — **to take someone's part** To support someone in a contest or disagreement. — *v.t.* 1. To divide or break (something) into parts. 2. To sever or discontinue (a relationship or connection). 3. To separate by being or coming between; keep or move apart. 4. To comb (the hair) so as to leave a dividing line on the sides or elsewhere on the scalp. 5. To separate (mingled substances) chemically or mechanically. — *v.i.* 6. To become divided or broken into parts. 7. To go away from each other; cease associating. 8. To depart. — **to part from** To separate from; leave. — **to part with** 1. To give up; relinquish. 2. To part from. — *adv.* To some extent; partly. [< OF and OE < L *pars, partis*]

par·take (pär·tāk′) *v.* **·took, ·tak·en, ·tak·ing** *v.i.* 1. To take part or have a share: with *in.* 2. To receive or take a portion or share: with *of.* 3. To have something of the quality or character: with *of.* — *v.t.* 4. To take or have a part in; share. [Back formation < *partaker* < L < *pars, partis* part + *capere* to take] — **par·tak′er** *n.*

part·ed (pär′tid) *adj.* **1.** Situated or placed apart; separated. **2.** *Bot.* Cut almost but not quite to the base, as certain leaves. **3.** Divided into parts.

par·terre (pär·târ′) ` *n.* **1.** A flower garden having beds arranged in a pattern. **2.** The part of a theater on the main floor under the balcony and behind the parquet. [< MF < L *per* through, all over + *terra* land]

par·the·no·gen·e·sis (pär′thə·nō·jen′ə·sis) *n. Biol.* Reproduction by means of unfertilized eggs, seeds, or spores, as in many rotifers, insects, and algae. Also **par′the·nog′e·ny** (-noj′ə·nē). [< Gk. *parthenos* virgin + GENESIS] — **par′· the·no·ge·net′ic** (-jə·net′ik), **par′the·no·gen′ic** *adj.*

Par·the·non (pär′thə·non) The temple of Athena on the Acropolis at Athens, dedicated in 438 B.C., regarded as one of the finest examples of Doric architecture.

Par·thi·a (pär′thē·ə) An ancient kingdom occupying what is now NE Iran.

Par·thi·an (pär′thē·ən) *n.* An inhabitant of Parthia. — *adj.* Of or pertaining to Parthia or the Parthians. — **Parthian shot** Any aggressive remark or action made in leaving or fleeing, after the manner of Parthian cavalry who shot at their enemies while retreating.

par·tial (pär′shəl) *adj.* **1.** Pertaining to, constituting, or involving a part only. **2.** Favoring one side; biased. **3.** Having a special liking: usu. with *to.* — *n.* In acoustics, a partial tone. [< OF < LL < L *pars, partis* part] — **par′· tial·ly** *adv.*

partial eclipse *Astron.* An eclipse in which only part of the disk of a celestial body is obscured from view.

par·ti·al·i·ty (pär′shē·al′ə·tē) *n. pl.* **·ties 1.** The state of being partial. **2.** Unfairness; bias. **3.** A particular fondness; predilection. Also **par′tial·ness** (-shəl·nis).

partial tone Any of the simple or pure tones that, taken collectively, constitute a complex tone

par·tic·i·pant (pär·tis′ə·pənt) *adj.* Sharing; taking part in. — *n.* One who participates; a sharer.

par·tic·i·pate (pär·tis′ə·pāt) *v.* **·pat·ed, ·pat·ing** *v.i.* To take part or have a share in common with others: with *in.* [< L < *pars, partis* part + *capere* to take] — **par·tic′i· pa′tion, par·tic′i·pa′tor** *n.*

par·tic·i·pa·to·ry (pär·tis′·ə·pə·tôr′ē, -tō′rē) *adj.* Based on or involving active participation, as in a political system.

par·ti·cip·i·al (pär′tə·sip′ē·əl) *Gram. adj.* **1.** Having the nature, form, or use of a participle. **2.** Characterized by, consisting of, or based on a participle. — *n.* A participle.

par·ti·ci·ple (pär′tə·sip′əl) *n. Gram.* A verbal adjective, often retaining some of the attributes of a verb, such as tense and the power of taking an object, but often also having the adjectival function of qualifying nouns. The **present participle** ends in *-ing* and the **past participle** commonly in *-d, -ed, -en, -n,* or *-t.* — **dangling participle** A participle that modifies the wrong substantive, as in *"Opening the door, the room looked large."* [< OF, var. of *participe* < L *participium* a sharing, partaking]

par·ti·cle (pär′ti·kəl) *n.* **1.** A minute part, piece, or portion, as of matter. **2.** A very small amount or slight degree. **3.** *Physics* One of the elementary components of an atom, as an electron, proton, neutron, meson, etc. **4.** *Gram.* **a** A short, uninflected part of speech, as an article, preposition, interjection, or conjunction. **b** A prefix or suffix. **5.** A small section or clause, as of a document. [< L *particula,* dim. of *pars, partis* part]

par·ti-col·ored (pär′tē·kul′ərd) *adj.* **1.** Differently colored in different parts. **2.** Diversified. Also spelled *party-colored.* [< F *partir,* to divide + COLORED]

par·tic·u·lar (pər·tik′yə·lər) *adj.* **1.** Peculiar or pertaining to a specified person, thing, time, or place; specific. **2.** Referring to one as distinguished from others. **3.** Especially noteworthy: of *particular* importance. **4.** Comprising all details or circumstances: a *particular* description. **5.** Requiring or giving minute attention to details; fastidious: *particular* in dress. **6.** *Logic* Including some, not all, of a class: opposed to *universal.* — *n.* **1.** *Usu. pl.* An item; detail. **2.** An individual instance; a single or separate case. **3.** *Logic* A particular proposition. — **in particular** Particularly. [< OF < LL *particularis* concerning a part]

par·tic·u·lar·i·ty (pər·tik′yə·lar′ə·tē) *n. pl.* **·ties 1.** The state or quality of being particular, as: **a** Exactitude in description. **b** Strict or careful attention to details; fastidiousness. **2.** That which is particular, as: **a** A circumstance or detail. **b** A special characteristic; peculiarity.

par·tic·u·lar·ize (pər·tik′yə·lə·rīz′) *v.* **·ized, ·iz·ing** *v.t.* **1.** To speak of or treat individually or in detail. — *v.i.* **2.** To give particular details; be specific. — **par·tic′u·lar·i·za′· tion** *n.* — **par·tic′u·lar·iz′er** *n.*

par·tic·u·lar·ly (pər·tik′yə·lər·lē) *adv.* **1.** With specific reference; distinctly. **2.** In an unusually great degree. **3.** Part by part; in detail. **4.** Severally; personally.

par·tic·u·late (pər·tik′yə·lāt) *adj.* Consisting of minute, separate particles.

part·ing (pär′ting) *adj.* **1.** Given or done at parting: a *parting* glance. **2.** Of or pertaining to a parting or a going away. **3.** Departing; declining. **4.** Separating; dividing. — *n.* **1.** The act of separating, or the state of being separated. **2.** A leave-taking; esp., a final separation. **3.** A place, line, or surface of separation. **4.** That which serves to part or separate objects.

parting shot Any retort or aggressive action made as one is leaving or fleeing. [< PARTHIAN SHOT by folk etymology]

par·ti·san (pär′tə·zən) *n.* **1.** One who supports or upholds a party, cause, etc.; esp., an overly zealous adherent or devotee. **2.** *Mil.* A member of a body of detached or irregular troops; a guerrilla. — *adj.* **1.** Of, relating to, or characteristic of a partisan. **2.** Advocated by or composed of members of one party. **3.** *Mil.* Of or carried on by partisans. Also **par′ti·zan.** — **Syn.** See ADHERENT. [< F < Ital. < L *pars, partis* part] — **par′ti·san·ship** *n.*

par·tite (pär′tīt) *adj.* Divided into or composed of parts: used in combination: *bipartite, tripartite.* [< L *partitus,* pp. of *partire* to divide]

par·ti·tion (pär·tish′ən) *n.* **1.** The act of dividing, separating, distributing; also, the state of being divided, etc. **2.** Something that divides or separates, as a light interior wall dividing a room, an enclosure, a septum in a plant or animal structure, etc. **3.** One of the parts, sections, compartments, etc., into which a thing is divided. — *v.t.* **1.** To divide into parts, sections, segments, etc. **2.** To separate by a partition: often with *off.* [< OF < L *partire* to divide] — **par·ti′tion·er** *n.* — **par·ti′tion·ment** *n.*

par·ti·tive (pär′tə·tiv) *adj.* **1.** Separating into integral parts or distinct divisions. **2.** *Gram.* Denoting a part as distinct from the whole. Example: *Of them* is the *partitive* genitive in the sentence "Many of them were there." — *n. Gram.* A partitive word or case. [< F *partitif* or L < *partitus,* pp. of *partire* to divide] — **par′ti·tive·ly** *adv.*

part·ly (pärt′lē) *adv.* In some part; partially.

part·ner (pärt′nər) *n.* One who is united or associated with another or others in some action, enterprise, etc.; as: **a** *Law* A member of a partnership. **b** A husband or wife; spouse. **c** One of a couple who dance together. **d** One of two or more players on the same side in a game. **e** A colleague or associate in some undertaking; a sharer. — *v.t. Rare* **1.** To make a partner. **2.** To be the partner of. [ME < fusion of *parcener* and *part*]

part·ner·ship (pärt′nər·ship) *n.* **1.** The state or relationship of being a partner; association. **2.** *Law* **a** A contractual relationship in which two or more persons combine capital, labor, etc., to carry on a business. **b** The contract that creates such a relationship. **c** The persons associated.

part of speech *Gram.* One of the eight traditional classes of words in English, noun, pronoun, verb, adverb, adjective, conjunction, preposition, and interjection.

par·took (pär·took′) Past tense of PARTAKE.

par·tridge (pär′trij) *n.* **1.** Any of certain small, plump game birds of the Old World. **2.** Any of various similar birds, as the ruffed grouse or the bobwhite. [< OF < L < Gk. *perdix, -ikos* partridge]

part song A song of three or more parts; esp., a secular choral piece without accompaniment.

part-time (pärt′tīm′) *adj.* For, during, or by part of the time: a *part-time* student.

par·tu·ri·ent (pär·tyōŏr′ē·ənt, -tōŏr′-) *adj.* **1.** Bringing forth or about to bring forth young. **2.** Of or pertaining to parturition. **3.** Producing or about to produce an idea, discovery, etc. [< L *parturiens, -entis,* ppr. of *parturire* to be in labor] — **par·tu′ri·en·cy** *n.*

par·tu·ri·tion (pär′tyōŏ·rish′ən, -chōŏ-) *n.* The act of bringing forth young; delivery; childbirth.

par·ty (pär′tē) *n. pl.* **·ties 1.** A social gathering for pleasure or entertainment. **2.** A group of persons associated or gathered together for some common purpose; as: **a** A group united in promoting or maintaining a cause, policy, system, etc.; esp., a political group organized to gain control of a government through the election of its candidates to public office. **b** A small body of persons selected for some special mission or assignment: a demolition *party.* **c** A group formed for a sport or other diversion. **3.** *Law* Either of the persons or groups involved in legal proceedings. **4.** One who takes part or participates in an action, plan, etc.: a *party* to his crime. **5.** *Informal* A person. — *adj.* Of or pertaining to a party or parties. [< OF *partir* to divide]

par·ty-col·ored (pär′tē·kul′ərd) See PARTI-COLORED.

party line **1.** A telephone line or circuit serving two or more subscribers. Also **party wire.** **2.** A boundary line between the properties of two or more owners. **3.** The essential beliefs or policies of a political party.

party politics Policies and acts aimed at furthering the interests of one political party.

party whip A whip (def. 4).

par value The nominal or stated value of stock; face value: distinguished from *market value.*

par·ve·nu (pär′və-nōō, -nyōō) n. One who has risen above his class through the sudden attainment of wealth or position; an upstart. —adj. 1. Being a parvenu. 2. Characteristic of or resembling a parvenu. [< F, orig., pp. of *parvenir* to arrive < L *pervenire*]

pas (pä) n. A dance step. [< F < L *passus* step]

pas·chal (pas′kəl) adj. Pertaining to the Jewish Passover or to Easter: *paschal* sacrifice. [< OF < LL < Gk. < Hebrew *pesakh* a passing over]

paschal flower The pasqueflower.

Paschal Lamb 1. Jesus Christ. 2. Any symbolic representation of Christ.

pas de deux (pä də dœ′) *French* A dance or ballet figure for two persons.

pa·sha (pə-shä′, pash′ə, pä′shə) n. Formerly, a Turkish honorary title placed after the name of generals, governors of provinces, etc.: also *pacha.* [< Turkish *bāsh* head]

pa·sha·lik (pə-shä′lik) n. The province or jurisdiction of a pasha: also spelled *pachalic.* Also **pa·sha·lic.** [< Turkish]

Pash·to (push′tō) n. The Iranian language dominant in Afghanistan: also called *Afghan:* also *Pushtu.*

pasque·flow·er (pask′flou′ər) n. Any of several plants of the crowfoot family, having white, red, or purple flowers blooming about Easter, the State flower of South Dakota: also called *paschal flower.* Also **pasch′flow′er.**

pas·quin·ade (pas′kwin-ād′) n. An abusive or coarse personal satire posted in a public place. —v.t. **·ad·ed, ·ad·ing** To attack or ridicule in pasquinades; lampoon. [< Ital. < *Pasquino*, orig., a disinterred statue at Rome on which satirical verses were pasted] —**pas′quin·ad′er** n.

pass (pas, päs) v. **passed** (*Rare*, past), **passed** or **past, pass·ing** v.t. 1. To go by or move past. 2. To succeed in meeting the requirements of (a test, trial, etc.). 3. To go beyond or surpass. 4. To spend (a specified period of time). 5. To cause or allow to move, go past, proceed, advance, etc.: to *pass* him through the ranks. 6. To approve or sanction; enact: to *pass* a bill. 7. To be approved or sanctioned by: The bill *passed* the senate. 8. To cause or allow to get through (a test, trial, etc.). 9. To convey or transfer from one to another; transmit: to *pass* a bad check. 10. In football, hockey, etc., to transfer (the ball, etc.) to another player on the same team. 11. In baseball, to walk (a batter). 12. To utter or pronounce, esp. judicially: to *pass* sentence. 13. To discharge or excrete (waste); void. 14. To omit paying (a dividend). 15. *Law* To transfer ownership or title of to another; make over. 16. *Rare* To permit to go unnoticed or unmentioned. 17. *Rare* To pledge or promise. —v.i. 18. To go or move; proceed; advance. 19. To go by or move past. 20. To obtain or force a way: to *pass* through a crowd. 21. To lead or extend; run: The river *passes* under a bridge. 22. To go by or elapse: The years *passed* slowly. 23. To come to an end; terminate. 24. To die. 25. To go about or circulate; be current. 26. To change or move from one condition, place, form, etc., to another: to *pass* from hot to cold. 27. To be mutually exchanged or transacted: Whispers *passed* between them. 28. To take place; occur: It came to *pass.* 29. To be allowed or permitted without challenge, censure, etc. 30. To undergo a test, etc., successfully. 31. To be approved, sanctioned, ratified, etc. 32. To be excreted or voided. 33. *Law* To give or pronounce sentence, judgment, etc.: with *on* or *upon.* 34. In football, hockey, etc., to transfer the ball, etc., to another player on the same team. 35. In fencing, to make a pass or thrust; lunge. 36. In card games, to decline to make a play, bid, etc. —**to pass away** 1. To come to an end. 2. To die. 3. To allow (time) to elapse. —**to pass for** To be accepted or regarded as, usu. erroneously. —**to pass off** 1. To come to an end; disappear. 2. To give out or circulate as genuine; palm off. 3. To be emitted, as vapor. —**to pass out** 1. To distribute or circulate. 2. *Informal* To faint. —**to pass over** To fail to notice or consider, as an applicant. —**to pass up** *U.S. Informal* 1. To reject or fail to take advantage of, as an offer or opportunity. 2. To pass over. —n. 1. A way or opening through which one can pass; esp., a narrow passage between the peaks of a mountain range. 2. A permit, order, or license giving the bearer authority to enter, move about, depart, etc., without the usual restrictions; as: **a** *Mil.* A written form granting permission to the holder to be absent from duty; also, the permission itself or the period of absence covered by it. **b** A ticket allowing one to enter a theater, movie, train, etc., free of charge. 3. The passing of an examination or course. 4. In magic, hypnotism, etc.: **a** A movement of the hand, a wand, etc., over a person or thing. **b** The manipulation of objects by sleight of hand. 5. A state of affairs; situation: to bring events to a critical *pass.* 6. In fencing, a thrust or lunge. 7. In cards, a refusal to bid or raise a bid. 8. In baseball, a walk. —**to bring to pass** To cause to be fulfilled or accomplished. —**to come to pass** To happen. —**to make a pass** 1. To attempt to hit. 2. *Slang* To invite intimacies; proposition. [< OF < L *passus* step]

pass·a·ble (pas′ə-bəl, päs′-) adj. 1. Capable of being passed, penetrated, crossed, etc.: *passable* rivers. 2. Fairly good or acceptable; tolerable. 3. Fit for general circulation, as money. —**pass′a·ble·ness** n. —**pass′a·bly** adv.

pas·sage (pas′ij) n. 1. A portion of a writing, speech, or musical composition, usu. of small or moderate length. 2. *Music* A short section of a composition designed primarily to display the performer's skill, as a run or flourish. 3. A way, channel, duct, etc., by which a person or thing may pass. 4. A hall, corridor, etc., between apartments in a building. 5. The act of passing, changing, etc.; esp., the transition from one state or period to another: the *passage* from winter to summer. 6. A journey, esp. by sea: a stormy *passage*; also, the right or privilege of making a journey: to secure *passage.* 7. The right, power, or freedom to pass. 8. The passing or enactment of a legislative measure. 9. An evacuation of the bowels. —v.i. **·saged, ·sag·ing** *Rare* 1. To make a journey. 2. To fight or quarrel. [< OF]

pas·sage·way (pas′ij-wā′) n. A way affording passage, esp. a hall or corridor.

pass·book (pas′bŏŏk′, päs′-) n. A bankbook.

pas·sé (pa-sā′, pas′ā; Fr. pȧ-sā′) adj. 1. Past the prime; faded. 2. Out-of-date; old-fashioned. [< F, orig., pp. of *passer* to pass] —**pas·sée′** adj. fem.

passed ball (past, päst) In baseball, a misplay charged to the catcher for allowing a runner to advance by failing to catch a pitch that passes reasonably close to him.

pas·sen·ger (pas′ən·jər) n. One who travels in a conveyance. [< MF *passager* < *passage* passage]

passe par·tout (pas pär-tōō′, Fr. päs pär-tōō′) In picture framing: **a** A light frame consisting of a glass, the picture, and a pasteboard back put together with strips of tape pasted around the edges. **b** The tape. [< MF < *passer* to pass + *partout* everywhere]

pas·ser·by (pas′ər-bī′, päs′-) n. pl. **pas·sers·by** One who passes by, usu. casually.

pas·ser·ine (pas′ər-ēn, -in) adj. 1. Of or pertaining to an order of birds including all singing birds, and more than half of the living birds of various sizes. 2. Resembling or characteristic of a sparrow. —n. A passerine bird. [< L *passer* sparrow + -INE[1]]

pas·sim (pas′im) adv. *Latin* Here and there; in various passages: a reference note in books.

pass·ing (pas′ing, päs′-) adj. 1. Going by or away. 2. Transitory; fleeting. 3. Happening or occurring; current. 4. Done, said, etc., in a cursory or casual manner. 5. Fulfilling all requirements: a *passing* grade. —Syn. See TRANSIENT. —n. 1. The act of one who or that which passes. 2. A means or place of passing, as a ford. —**in passing** Incidentally. —adv. *Archaic* In a surpassing degree or manner.

pas·sion (pash′ən) n. 1. Any intense, extreme, or overpowering emotion or feeling. 2. Ardent affection or love. 3. Intense sexual desire or lust. 4. Overwhelming anger or rage. 5. An outburst of strong feeling, esp. of violence or anger. 6. A strong desire or affection for some object, cause, etc. 7. The object of such a desire or affection. [< OF < L < *passus* pp. of *pati* to suffer] —**pas′sion·less** adj.

Pas·sion (pash′ən) n. 1. The sufferings of Christ, esp. after the Last Supper and on the Cross. 2. The part of the Gospels that relates the sufferings and death of Christ. 3. A representation of Christ's sufferings in art, music, etc.

pas·sion·ate (pash′ən-it) adj. 1. Capable of or inclined to strong passion; excitable. 2. Easily moved to anger; quick-tempered. 3. Expressing, displaying, or characterized by passion or strong emotion; ardent. 4. Strong or vehement, as a feeling or emotion. —Syn. See ARDENT. —**pas′sion·ate·ly** adv. —**pas′sion·ate·ness** n.

pas·sion·flow·er (pash′ən-flou′ər) n. Any of various vines or shrubs having showy flowers and sometimes edible berries: so called from the fancied resemblance of certain parts to the wounds, crown of thorns, etc., of Christ. [Trans. of Med.L *flos passionis*]

passion fruit The berries of the passion flower.

Passion play A religious drama representing the Passion of Christ.

pas·sive (pas′iv) adj. 1. Not acting, working, or operating; inactive; inert. 2. Acted upon, affected, or influenced by something external. 3. Receiving or receptive to an external force, etc. 4. Submitting or yielding without resistance or opposition; submissive. 5. *Gram.* Designating a voice of the verb that indicates that the subject is receiving the action, as *was killed* is in the passive voice in *Caesar was killed by Brutus:* distinguished from *active.* —n. *Gram.* 1. The passive voice. 2. A verb or construction in this voice. [< L *passus* pp. of *pati* to suffer] —**pas′sive·ly** adv. —**pas′sive·ness** n.

passive resistance A method of opposing some authority or law by nonviolent acts, as voluntary fasting, etc.

pas·siv·i·ty (pa·siv'ə·tē) *n.* The state of being passive.

pass·key (pas'kē', päs'-) *n.* A master key.

Pass·o·ver (pas'ō'vər, päs'-) *n.* A Jewish feast commemorating the night when God, smiting the first-born of the Egyptians, "passed over" the houses of the children of Israel.

pass·port (pas'pôrt', -pōrt', päs'-) *n.* 1. An official warrant certifying the citizenship of the bearer and affording protection to him when traveling abroad. 2. A permit to travel or convey goods through a foreign country. 3. Anything that enables one to gain entrance, acceptance, etc. [< MF < *passer* to pass + *port* harbor]

pass·word (pas'wûrd', päs'-) *n.* 1. A secret word or phrase enabling the speaker to pass a guard or sentry. 2. Anything that gains entrance or access for one.

past (past, päst) *adj.* 1. Ended or finished; done with. 2. Having existed in or belonging to a former time: *past* civilizations. 3. Just passed or gone by: the *past* few days. Having formerly served in a public office, committee, etc.: a *past* governor. — *n.* 1. Past or antecedent time, conditions, or events: usu. with *the.* 2. Something, as a former life or career, that is kept secret. 3. *Gram.* **a** A verb tense denoting any action or condition that occurred at a former time. **b** A verb or construction in this tense. — *adv.* In such a manner as to go by: to run *past.* — *prep.* 1. Beyond in time; after. 2. Beyond in place or position; farther than. 3. Beyond the reach, power, or influence of: *past* hope. 4. Beyond in amount or degree. [Orig. pp. of PASS]

pas·ta (päs'tə) *n.* A noodlelike paste or dough, as spaghetti, macaroni, etc. [< Ital. < LL, dough, paste]

paste (pāst) *n.* 1. A mixture, usu. of flour and water, used as an adhesive for paper, etc. 2. Any of various soft, moist, smooth preparations used as foods, in cooking, etc.; as: **a** Dough used in making pastry. **b** A soft, creamy mass made from fish, fruit, etc. 3. A vitreous composition used in making imitation gems; also, a gem made of this composition. — *v.t.* **past·ed, past·ing** 1. To stick or fasten with or as with paste. 2. To cover by applying pasted material. [< OF < LL < Gk. *pastē* barley porridge] — **past'er** *n.*

paste·board (pāst'bôrd', -bōrd') *n.* 1. Paper pulp compressed, or paper pasted together and rolled into a stiff sheet. 2. A board on which dough for pastry is rolled. 3. *Informal* A visiting card; also, a playing card. — *adj.* Flimsy.

pas·tel (pas·tel', pas'tel) *n.* 1. A picture drawn with colored crayons. 2. The art of drawing such pictures. 3. A dried paste made of pipe clay, pigment, and gum water, used for crayons; also, a hard crayon made of this paste: also called *pastille.* 4. A delicate, soft, or slightly grayish tint. — *adj.* 1. Of or pertaining to a pastel. 2. Having a delicate, soft, or slightly grayish tint. [See PASTE.] — **pas'tel·ist** or **pas'tel·list** *n.*

pas·tern (pas'tərn) *n.* 1. The part of a horse's foot that is between the fetlock and the hoof. 2. A hobble for a horse's foot. [< OF < *pasture* tether for a grazing animal]

pas·teur·i·za·tion (pas'tər·ə·zā'shən, -chər-) *n.* A process of arresting or preventing fermentation in liquids, as beer, milk, wine, etc., by heating so as to destroy the vitality of the ferment. Also *Brit.* **pas'teur·i·sa'tion.**

pas·teur·ize (pas'tə·rīz, -chə·rīz) *v.t.* **·ized, ·iz·ing** To treat by pasteurization. Also *Brit.* **pas'teur·ise.**

pas·tic·cio (päs·tē'chō) *n.* *pl.* **·ci** (-chē) A work of art, music, or literature made up of fragments from various sources. [< Ital., paste]

pas·tiche (pas·tēsh', päs-) *n.* A pasticcio, esp. one imitating or satirizing the style of other artists. [< F]

pas·tille (pas·tēl', -til') *n.* 1. A compound of aromatic substances with niter for fumigating. 2. A troche; lozenge. 3. A flavored confection. 4. Pastel (def. 3). Also **pas·til** (pas'til). [< MF < L *pastillus* little loaf, lozenge]

pas·time (pas'tīm', päs'-) *n.* Something that serves to make time pass agreeably. [Trans. of F *passe-temps*]

past master 1. One who has held the office of master in certain social or benevolent organizations. 2. One who has thorough experience in something; an expert; adept.

pas·tor (pas'tər, päs'-) *n.* A Christian clergyman who has a church or congregation under his charge. [< AF, OF < L *pastor, -oris* shepherd, lit., feeder] — **pas'tor·ship** *n.*

pas·tor·al (pas'tər·əl, päs'-) *adj.* 1. Of or pertaining to shepherds, rustics, or rural life. 2. Having the characteristics usu. associated with rural life, as innocence, simplicity, etc. 3. Dealing with or portraying rural life. 4. Pertaining to a clergyman or to his duties. — *n.* 1. A literary work, esp. a poem, dealing with rural life, scenes, etc. 2. A picture illustrating rural scenes. 3. *Eccl.* A letter from a pastor or bishop to his diocese. [< L *pastor* shepherd] — **pas'tor·al·ism** *n.* — **pas'tor·al·ist** *n.* — **pas'tor·al·ly** *adv.*

pas·tor·ate (pas'tər·it, päs'-) *n.* 1. The office or jurisdiction of a pastor. 2. The duration of a pastoral charge. 3. Pastors collectively.

past participle See under PARTICIPLE.

past perfect *Gram.* The verb tense indicating an action completed prior to the occurrence of some other past action or specified past time, as *had finished* is the past perfect in *He had finished before the bell rang.* Also called *pluperfect.*

pas·tra·mi (pə·strä'mē) *n.* Heavily seasoned, smoked beef, usu. cut from the shoulder. [< Yiddish < Rumanian]

pas·try (pās'trē) *n.* *pl.* **·tries** Articles of food that are sweet, baked, and are usu. made with a crust of shortened dough, as pies, tarts, etc.; also, any sweet baked foods.

pas·tur·age (pas'chər·ij, päs'-) *n.* 1. Grass and herbage for cattle. 2. Ground used or suitable for grazing.

pas·ture (pas'chər, päs'-) *n.* 1. Ground for the grazing of domestic animals. 2. Grass or herbage that grazing domestic animals eat. — *v.t.* **·tured, ·tur·ing** 1. To put in a pasture to graze. 2. To graze on (grass, etc.). 3. To provide pasturage for (cattle, etc): said of land. [< OF < LL < L < *pascere* to feed] — **pas'tur·a·ble** *adj.*

past·y¹ (pās'tē) *adj.* **past·i·er, past·i·est** Like paste. — **past'i·ness** *n.*

past·y² (pās'tē, *Brit.* pas'tē, päs'tē, -) *n.* *pl.* **pas·ties** A pie; esp., a meat pie. [< OF < LL *pasta* paste]

pat (pat) *v.* **pat·ted, pat·ting** *v.t.* 1. To touch or tap lightly with something flat, esp. with the hand in caressing, etc. 2. To shape or mold by a pat or pats. — *v.i.* 3. To run or walk with light steps. — *n.* 1. A light, caressing stroke; a gentle tap. 2. The sound of patting or pattering. 3. A small, molded mass, as of butter. — *adj.* 1. Exactly suitable; apt. 2. Needing no change: a *pat* hand in a card game. 3. Glib; facile. — *adv. Informal* 1. Firm; steadfast: to stand *pat.* 2. Aptly. [ME *patte*] — **pat'ness** *n.* — **pat'ter** *n.*

patch (pach) *n.* 1. A small piece of material used to repair a garment, etc. 2. A piece of courtplaster or the like, applied to the skin to hide a blemish or to set off the complexion. 3. A small piece of ground; also, the plants growing on it: a *patch* of corn. 4. A piece of material worn over an injured eye. 5. Any small part of a surface not sharing the general character of the whole. 6. A shred or scrap. — *v.t.* 1. To put a patch or patches on. 2. To repair or put together, esp. hurriedly or crudely: often with *up* or *together.* 3. To make of patches, as a quilt. [ME *pacche*] — **patch'a·ble** *adj.* — **patch'er** *n.*

patch·ou·li (pach'oo·lē, pə·choo'lē) *n.* 1. An East Indian herb of the mint family. 2. A perfume obtained from it. Also spelled *pachouli.* Also **patch'ou·ly.** [< F < Tamil < *paccu* green + *ilai* leaf]

patch pocket A pocket sewn to the outside of a garment.

patch·work (pach'wûrk') *n.* 1. A fabric made of patches of cloth, as for quilts, etc. 2. Work made up of heterogeneous materials; work done hastily or carelessly; a jumble.

patch·y (pach'ē) *adj.* **patch·i·er, patch·i·est** 1. Made up of or abounding in patches. 2. Careless; jumbled. 3. Peevish; irritable. — **patch'i·ly** *adv.* — **patch'i·ness** *n.*

pate (pāt) *n.* The head or top of the head; also, the brains or intellect: usu. humorous or derogatory. [ME]

pâ·té de foie gras (pä·tā' də fwà grä') *French* A paste of fat goose liver.

pa·tel·la (pə·tel'ə) *n.* *pl.* **·tel·lae** (-tel'ē) *Anat.* The flat, movable, oval bone in front of the knee joint; kneecap. For illus. see SKELETON. [< L, dim. of *patina* pan, bowl] — **pa·tel'lar** *adj.* — **pa·tel·late** (pə·tel'āt, -it) *adj.*

pat·en (pat'n) *n.* 1. A plate; esp., a plate for the eucharistic bread: also called *patina*: also spelled *patin, patine.* 2. A thin, metallic plate or disk. [< OF < L *patina* pan]

pa·ten·cy (pāt'n·sē) *n.* 1. The condition of being patent or evident. 2. *Chiefly Med.* The state of being open, spread, enlarged, or without obstruction.

pat·ent (pat'nt, *Brit.* pāt'nt; *for adj. defs.* 1, 4, & 5, *usu.* pāt'nt) *n.* 1. A government protection to an inventor, securing to him for a specific time the exclusive right of manufacturing, exploiting, using, and selling an invention; also, the right granted. 2. Any official document securing a right. 3. That which is protected by a patent or its distinctive marks or features. — *v.t.* To obtain a patent on (an invention). — *adj.* 1. Manifest or apparent to everybody. 2. Protected or conferred by letters patent. 3. Open for general inspection or use: letters *patent.* 4. Expanded; spreading widely, as leaves from the stem of a plant. 5. *Chiefly Med.* Open; unobstructed, as an intestine. [< F < L < *patere* to lie open] — **pat'ent·a·bil·i·ty** *n.* — **pat'ent·a·ble** *adj.*

pat·en·tee (pat'n·tē') *n.* One who holds a patent.

patent leather Leather with a glossy, varnishlike finish.

pat·ent·ly (pāt'nt·lē, pat'nt-) *adv.* Manifestly; clearly.

patent medicine A medicine manufactured and sold under patent and usu. of secret composition.

pat·en·tor (pat'n·tər) *n.* One who grants a patent.

pa·ter (pā′tər) *n. Brit. Informal* Father. [< L]
pa·ter·fa·mil·i·as (pā′tər·fə·mĭl′ē·əs) *n.* The father of a family. [< L < *pater* father + *familia* family]
pa·ter·nal (pə·tûr′nəl) *adj.* 1. Of, pertaining to, or characteristic of a father; fatherly. 2. Derived from, related through, or connected with one's father. [< LL < L < *pater* father] — **pa·ter′nal·ly** *adv.*
pa·ter·nal·ism (pə·tûr′nəl·ĭz′əm) *n.* The care or control of a country, community, group of employees, etc., in a manner suggestive of a father looking after his children. — **pa·ter′·nal·is·tic** *adj.* — **pa·ter′nal·is′ti·cal·ly** *adv.*
pa·ter·ni·ty (pə·tûr′nə·tē) *n.* 1. The condition of being a father. 2. Parentage on the male side. 3. Origin in general.
pa·ter·nos·ter (pā′tər·nŏs′tər) *n.* 1. The Lord's Prayer. *Matt.* vi 9–13. Also **Pa′ter Nos′ter.** 2. A large bead of the rosary, indicating that a paternoster is to be recited. [< L *pater noster* our father]
path (path, päth) *n. pl.* **paths** (pathz, päthz, paths, päths) 1. A walk or way used by man or animals on foot. 2. A track or course. 3. A course of life or action. [OE *pæth*]
Pa·than (pə·tän′, pət·hän′) *n.* An Afghan; esp., one of a people of Afghanistan of Indo-Iranian stock and Moslem religion. [< Hind. < Afghan *Pĕstūn* an Afghan]
pa·thet·ic (pə·thĕt′ĭk) *adj.* Of the nature of, expressing, or arousing sadness, pity, tenderness, etc. Also **pa·thet′i·cal.** [< LL < Gk. < *pathos* suffering] — **pa·thet′i·cal·ly** *adv.* — **pa·thet′i·cal·ness** *n.*
pathetic fallacy The ascribing of human emotions and characteristics to nature or things of nature, as *a sad day.*
path·find·er (path′fīn′dər, päth′-) *n.* One skilled in leading or finding a way, esp. in unknown regions.
-pathia See **-PATHY.**
path·less (path′lis, päth′-) *adj.* Trackless; untrodden.
patho- *combining form* Suffering; disease. Also, before vowels, **path-.** [< Gk. *pathos* suffering]
path·o·gen (path′ə·jən) *n.* Any disease-producing bacterium or microorganism. Also **path′o·gene** (-jēn).
path·o·gen·e·sis (path′ə·jen′ə·sis) *n. Med.* The production or development of any diseased condition. Also **pa·thog·e·ny** (pə·thŏj′ə·nē).
path·o·gen·ic (path′ə·jen′ĭk) *adj. Med.* Productive of or pertaining to the production of disease. Also **path′o·ge·net′·ic** (-jə·nĕt′ĭk).
path·o·log·i·cal (path′ə·lŏj′i·kəl) *adj.* 1. Of pathology. 2. Related to, involving, concerned with, or caused by disease. Also **path′o·log′ic.** — **path′o·log′i·cal·ly** *adv.*
pa·thol·o·gist (pə·thŏl′ə·jist) *n.* One skilled in pathology.
pa·thol·o·gy (pə·thŏl′ə·jē) *n. pl.* **·gies** 1. The branch of medical science that treats of the origin, nature, causes, and development of disease. 2. The sum of the conditions, processes, and effects in the course of a disease.
pa·thos (pā′thŏs) *n.* The quality, esp. in literature or art, that arouses feelings of pity, sorrow, compassion, etc. — **Syn.** See FEELING. [< Gk. < *pathein* to suffer]
path·way (path′wā′, päth′-) *n.* A path; footway.
-pathy *combining form* 1. Suffering; affection. 2. *Med.* Disease, or the treatment of disease: *psychopathy.* Also spelled *-pathia.* [< Gk. *pathos* suffering]
pa·tience (pā′shəns) *n.* 1. The state, quality, or fact of being patient; also, the ability to be patient. 2. *Chiefly Brit.* Solitaire (def. 2). [< OF < L *pati* to suffer]
pa·tient (pā′shənt) *adj.* 1. Possessing or demonstrating quiet, uncomplaining endurance under distress or annoyance. 2. Tolerant, tender, and forbearing. 3. Capable of tranquilly awaiting results. 4. Persevering; diligent. — *n.* A person undergoing treatment for disease or injury. [< OF < L < *pati* to suffer] — **pa′tient·ly** *adv.*
pat·in (pat′n) See PATEN (def. 1).
pat·i·na¹ (pat′ə·nə, pə·tē′nə) *n. pl.* **·nae** (-nē) 1. An earthen ware or metal bowl or basin used as a domestic utensil by the Romans. 2. A paten (def. 1). [< L < Gk. *patanē*]
pat·i·na² (pat′ə·nə, pə·tē′nə) *n.* 1. A green rust that covers ancient bronzes, copper coins, medals, etc. 2. Any surface of antique appearance. Also called *patine.* [< F, prob. < L *patina* plate]
pat·ine (pə·tēn′ *for def.1,* pat′n *for def. 2*) *n.* 1. Patina². 2. See PATEN (def. 1).
pa·ti·o (pā′tē·ō, pat′ē·ō; *Sp.* pä′tyō) *n. pl.* **·ti·os** 1. The open inner court of a Spanish or Spanish-American dwelling. 2. *U.S.* A paved area adjoining a house, used for parties, barbecues, etc. [< Sp., ? < L *patere* to lie open]
pat·ois (pat′wä, *Fr.* pä·twä′) *n. pl.* **pat·ois** (pat′wäz, *Fr.* pä·twä′) A type of local dialect, esp. one that is rustic or illiterate. [< F; origin uncertain]
patri- *combining form* Father: *patricide.* [< L *pater, -tris* father]
pa·tri·arch (pā′trē·ärk) *n.* 1. The leader of a family or tribe who rules by paternal right. 2. One of the fathers of the Hebrew race, Abraham, Isaac, or Jacob. 3. One of the twelve sons of Jacob considered as the progenitors of the tribes of Israel. 4. A venerable man; esp., the founder of a

religion, order, etc. 5. *Eccl.* **a** In the primitive Christian church, any of the bishops of Antioch, Alexandria, Rome, Constantinople, or Jerusalem. **b** In the Greek Orthodox Church, any of the bishops of Constantinople, Alexandria, Antioch, or Jerusalem. [< OF < L < Gk. < *patria* family, clan + *archein* to rule]
pa·tri·ar·chal (pā′trē·är′kəl) *adj.* 1. Of, pertaining to, or governed by a patriarch. 2. Of the nature of a patriarchy. 3. Having the nature or character of a patriarch. — **pa′tri·ar′chal·ly** *adv.*
pa·tri·ar·chate (pā′trē·är′kit) *n.* 1. The office, dominion, or residence of a patriarch. 2. A patriarchal system of government.
pa·tri·ar·chy (pā′trē·är′kē) *n. pl.* **·chies** 1. A system of government in which the father or the male heir of his choice rules. 2. Government by men.
pa·tri·cian (pə·trish′ən) *adj.* 1. Of or pertaining to the aristocracy. 2. Noble or aristocratic. — *n.* 1. An aristocrat; esp., in ancient Rome, a member of the hereditary aristocracy. 2. Any one of the upper classes. 3. An honorary title bestowed by the later Roman emperors. [< OF < L *pater, -tris* senator, lit., father] — **pa·tri′cian·ly** *adv.*
pat·ri·cide (pat′rə·sīd) *n.* 1. The killing of one's father. 2. One who has killed his father. [< LL *patricidium*] — **pat′·ri·ci′dal** *adj.*
pat·ri·lin·e·al (pat′rə·lin′ē·əl) *adj.* Derived from or descending through the male line.
pat·ri·mo·ny (pat′rə·mō′nē) *n. pl.* **·nies** 1. An inheritance from a father or an ancestor; also, anything inherited. 2. An endowment, as of a church. [< OF < L < *pater, -tris* father] — **pat′ri·mo′ni·al** *adj.* — **pat′ri·mo′ni·al·ly** *adv.*
pa·tri·ot (pā′trē·ət, -ŏt) *n.* One who loves his country and zealously guards its welfare; esp., a defender of popular liberty. [< F < LL < Gk. *patris* fatherland] — **pa′tri·ot′ic** *adj.* — **pa′tri·ot′i·cal·ly** *adv.*
pa·tri·ot·ism (pā′trē·ə·tiz′əm) *n.* Devotion to one's country.
pa·tris·tic (pə·tris′tik) *adj.* Of or pertaining to the fathers of the Christian church or to their writings. Also **pa·tris′ti·cal.** — **pa·tris′ti·cal·ly** *adv.*
pa·trol (pə·trōl′) *v.t. & v.i.* **·trolled, ·trol·ling** To walk or go through or around (an area, town, etc.) for the purpose of guarding or inspecting. — *n.* 1. One or more soldiers, policemen, etc., patrolling a district. 2. A reconnaissance or combat group sent out from the main body in air, ground, or naval warfare. 3. The act of patrolling. 4. A division of a troop of Boy Scouts. [< MF < *patrouiller,* var. of *patouiller,* orig., to paddle in mud] — **pa·trol′ler** *n.*
patrol car A squad car.
pa·trol·man (pə·trōl′mən) *n. pl.* **·men** (-mən) 1. One who patrols. 2. *U.S.* A policeman assigned to a beat.
patrol torpedo boat A small, highly maneuverable vessel, armed with torpedoes for action against enemy shipping: also called *PT boat.*
patrol wagon *U.S.* A police wagon for conveying prisoners.
pa·tron (pā′trən) *n.* 1. One who protects, fosters, or supports some person, thing, or enterprise. 2. A regular customer. 3. A patron saint. [< OF < L *patronus* protector] — **pa′tron·al** *adj.* — **pa′tron·ess** *n.fem.*
pa·tron·age (pā′trən·ij, pat′rən-) *n.* 1. The protection, support, or position of a patron. 2. In the public service, the power or right to distribute offices, esp. political offices; also, the offices so distributed. 3. The financial support given by customers to a commercial establishment. 4. An overly condescending manner.
pa·tron·ize (pā′trən·īz, pat′rən-) *v.t.* **·ized, ·iz·ing** 1. To act as a patron toward; give support to. 2. To treat in a condescending manner. 3. To trade with as a regular customer; frequent. — **pa′tron·iz′er** *n.* — **pa′tron·iz′ing·ly** *adv.*
patron saint A saint regarded as the special protector of a country, city, person, cause, etc.
pat·ro·nym·ic (pat′rə·nim′ik) *adj.* Pertaining to or derived from the name of one's father or paternal ancestor. — *n.* 1. A family name. 2. A name formed by adding a prefix or suffix to a proper name, as *Johnson,* son of John. [< L < Gk. < *patēr* father + *onoma* name] — **pat′ro·nym′i·cal·ly** *adv.*
pa·troon (pə·trōōn′) *n.* Formerly, under the old Dutch law, a holder of entailed estates, having some manorial rights. [< Du. < F < L *patronus* protector]
pat·ter¹ (pat′ər) *v.i.* 1. To make a succession of light, sharp sounds. 2. To move with light, quick steps. — *v.t.* 3. To cause to patter. — *n.* The act or sound of pattering. [Freq. of PAT¹]
pat·ter² (pat′ər) *v.t. & v.i.* To speak or say glibly or rapidly; mumble mechanically or indistinctly. — *n.* 1. Glib and rapid talk, as used by comedians, etc. 2. Patois or dialect. 3. Any professional jargon. 4. Rapid speech set to music. [Short for PATERNOSTER] — **pat′ter·er** *n.*
pat·tern (pat′ərn) *n.* 1. An original or model proposed for or worthy of imitation. 2. Anything shaped or designed to serve as a model or guide in making something else. 3. Any

decorative design or figure; also, such design worked on something. **4.** Arrangement of natural or accidental markings: the *pattern* of a butterfly's wings. **5.** The stylistic composition or design of a work of art. **6.** A complex of integrated parts functioning as a whole: the behavior *pattern* of a five-year-old. **7.** A representative example, sample, or instance. — *v.t.* **1.** To make after a model or pattern: with *on, upon,* or *after.* **2.** To decorate or furnish with a pattern. [< F *patron* patron]

pat·ty (pat′ē) *n.* *pl.* **·ties 1.** A small, flat piece of chopped meat, fish, etc. **2.** A small pie. [Alter. of F *pâté*]

patty shell A small puff-paste shell in which creamed meat, fish, vegetables, or fruit are served.

pau·ci·ty (pô′sə·tē) *n.* **1.** Smallness of number or quantity. **2.** Scarcity; insufficiency. [< OF or < L *paucus* few]

Paul (pôl), died 67? A.D., one of the apostles; the chief early Christian missionary to the Gentiles; author of several New Testament epistles: original name *Saul.* Also **Saint Paul, Paul the Apostle, Saul of Tarsus.** — **Paul′ine** *adj.*

Paul Bunyan The famous hero lumberjack of American folklore, of superhuman size and strength.

paunch (pônch) *n.* **1.** The abdomen or the belly, esp. if protruding. **2.** A rumen (def. 1). [< OF < L *pantex, -ticis* belly] — **paunch′y** *adj.* — **paunch′i·ness** *n.*

pau·per (pô′pər) *n.* **1.** One who receives, or is entitled to receive, public charity. **2.** Any very poor person. [< Med.L < *pauper* poor] — **pau′per·ism** *n.*

pau·per·ize (pô′pər·īz) *v.t.* **·ized, ·iz·ing** To make a pauper of.

pause (pôz) *v.i.* **paused, paus·ing 1.** To cease action or utterance temporarily; hesitate. **2.** To dwell or linger: with *on* or *upon.* — *n.* **1.** A temporary ceasing of action; rest. **2.** A holding back because of doubt or irresolution; hesitation. **3.** A momentary cessation in speaking or music for the sake of meaning or expression; also, a sign indicating such cessation. **4.** *Music* A hold. **5.** In prosody, a calculated interval of silence in a meter, or the place at which the voice naturally pauses in reading a verse: see CAESURA. [< OF < L < Gk. < *pauein* to stop] — **paus′er** *n.*

pav·an (pə·van′, -vän′) *n.* A slow, stately dance of the 16th and 17th centuries. Also **pav·ane** (pə·van′, -vän′; *Fr.* pà·vàn′). [< MF < Sp. ? < L *pavo, -onis* peacock]

pave (pāv) *v.t.* **paved, pav·ing** To cover or surface with asphalt, gravel, concrete, etc., as a road. — **to pave the way (for)** To make preparation (for); lead up to. [< OF < L *pavire* to ram down] — **pav′er** *n.*

pave·ment (pāv′mənt) *n.* **1.** A hard, solid, surface covering for a road or footway. **2.** A paved road or footway. **3.** The material with which a surface is paved.

pa·vil·ion (pə·vil′yən) *n.* **1.** A movable or open structure, as a large tent or summerhouse. **2.** A related or connected part of a principal building, as for hospital patients. **3.** A canopy. — *v.t.* **1.** To provide with a pavilion. **2.** To shelter by a pavilion. [< OF < L *papilio, -onis* butterfly, tent]

pav·ing (pā′ving) *n.* **1.** The laying of a pavement. **2.** A pavement; also, the material used for pavement.

Pa·vo (pā′vō) A constellation, the Peacock. [< L]

pav·o·nine (pav′ə·nīn, -nin) *adj.* **1.** Resembling or characteristic of the peacock. **2.** Iridescent like the tail of a peacock. [< L *pavo, -onis* peacock]

paw (pô) *n.* **1.** The foot of an animal having nails or claws. **2.** *Informal* A human hand. — *v.t. & v.i.* **1.** To strike or scrape with the feet or paws: to *paw* the air. **2.** *Informal* To handle or caress rudely or clumsily; maul. [< OF *powe,* prob. of Gmc. origin] — **paw′er** *n.*

pawl (pôl) *n.* *Mech.* A hinged or pivoted member shaped to engage with ratchet teeth, either to drive a ratchet wheel or to stop its reverse motion. [Origin uncertain]

pawn[1] (pôn) *n.* **1.** A chessman of lowest rank, that moves on file but captures diagonally. **2.** Any insignificant person used at another's will. [< AF, OF *peon* foot soldier]

pawn[2] (pôn) *n.* **1.** Something pledged as security for a loan. **2.** The condition of being held as a pledge for money loaned. **3.** The act of pawning. — *v.t.* **1.** To give as security for a loan. **2.** To risk. [< OF *pan,* var. of early Frisian *pand* pledge] — **pawn′a·ble** *adj.* — **pawn′er, pawn′or** *n.*

pawn·brok·er (pôn′brō′kər) *n.* One engaged in the business of lending money at interest on pledged personal property.

Paw·nee (pô·nē′) *n.* *pl.* **·nees** or **·nee** A member of one of four tribes of North American Indians formerly inhabiting the region between the Arkansas River and the Platte River, Nebraska, now living in Oklahoma.

pawn·shop (pôn′shop′) *n.* The shop of a pawnbroker.

pawn ticket A receipt for goods pawned.

paw·paw (pô′pô) See PAPAW.

pay[1] (pā) *v.* **paid** or (*Obs.* except for def. 2 of *to pay out*) **payed, pay·ing** *v.t.* **1.** To give (someone) what is due for a debt, purchase, etc.; remunerate. **2.** To give (money, etc.)

for a purchase, service rendered, etc. **3.** To provide or hand over the amount of, as a debt, bill, etc. **4.** To yield as return or recompense. **5.** To afford profit or benefit to. **6.** To defray, as expenses. **7.** To requite, as for an insult. **8.** To render or give, as a compliment, attention, etc. **9.** To make, as a call or visit. — *v.i.* **10.** To make recompense or payment. **11.** To be worthwhile: It *pays* to be honest — **to pay back** To repay. — **to pay off 1.** To pay the entire amount of (a debt, mortgage, etc.). **2.** To pay the wages of and discharge. **3.** To gain revenge upon or for. **4.** *U.S. Informal* To afford full return. **5.** *Naut.* To turn or cause to turn to leeward. **6.** *U.S. Slang* To bribe. — **to pay out 1.** To disburse or expend. **2.** *Naut.* To let out by slackening, as a rope or cable. — **to pay up** To make full payment (of). — *n.* **1.** That which is given as a recompense; wages. **2.** The act of paying, or the state of being paid. **3.** Paid employment. **4.** Requital; reward; also, retribution. — *adj.* **1.** Of or pertaining to payments, persons who pay, or services paid for: *pay* day. **2.** Constructed so as to require payment on use. **3.** Yielding enough metal to be worth mining: *pay* dirt. [< OF < L *pacare* to appease] — **pay′er** *n.*
— **Syn.** (verb) **1.** compensate, indemnify. **2.** spend, expend, disburse. **3.** settle, liquidate.

pay[2] (pā) *v.t.* **paid** or **payed, pay·ing** To coat with a waterproof substance, as pitch. [< AF < L < *pix, picis* pitch]

pay·a·ble (pā′ə·bəl) *adj.* **1.** Due and unpaid. **2.** That can or will be paid. **3.** Likely to be profitable. — **pay′a·bly** *adv.*

pay·day (pā′dā′) *n.* The day on which wages are distributed.

pay dirt 1. Soil containing enough metal, esp. gold, to be profitable to mine. **2.** Anything profitable.

pay·ee (pā·ē′) *n.* A person to whom money has been or is to be paid.

pay·load (pā′lōd′) *n.* **1.** That part of a cargo producing revenue. **2.** The warhead of a guided missile. **3.** The persons, instruments, etc., carried in a spacecraft that are directly related to the objective of the flight.

pay·mas·ter (pā′mas′tər, -mäs′-) *n.* One who has charge of paying employees. — **pay′mis′tress** (-mis′tris) *n.fem.*

pay·ment (pā′mənt) *n.* **1.** The act of paying, or that which is paid. **2.** Recompense. **3.** Punishment.

pay·off (pā′ôf′, -of′) *n.* **1.** *Informal* Any settlement, reward, or punishment. **2.** *Informal* The climax or outcome of an incident or narrative. **3.** *U.S. Slang* A bribe.

pay·roll (pā′rōl′) *n.* A list of those entitled to receive pay, with the amounts due them; also, the total sum of money needed to make the payments. Also **pay roll.**

pays (pās) See PAIS.

pea (pē) *n.* *pl.* **peas** or **pease 1.** A climbing annual leguminous herb having pinnate leaves and round, green, usu. edible seeds. **2.** The seed of any one of various related plants. [< PEASE, incorrectly taken as a plural]

peace (pēs) *n.* **1.** A state of mental or physical quiet or tranquillity; calm. **2.** The absence or cessation of war. **3.** Public order and tranquillity. **4.** A state of reconciliation after strife or enmity. **5.** Freedom from mental agitation or anxiety. — **at peace 1.** In a quiet state; tranquil. **2.** In a state or condition of order and harmony. — **to hold** (or **keep**) **one's peace** To be silent. — *v.i.* *Obs. except as an imperative* To be or become quiet. [< OF < L *pax, pacis*]

Peace Corps A U.S. government organization, established in 1961, that trains and sends volunteers to live in and aid underdeveloped countries by teaching, farming, building, etc.

peace·a·ble (pē′sə·bəl) *adj.* **1.** Inclined to peace. **2.** Peaceful; tranquil. — **peace′a·ble·ness** *n.* — **peace′a·bly** *adv.*

peace·ful (pēs′fəl) *adj.* **1.** Not in a state of war, riot, or commotion; undisturbed. **2.** Averse to strife. **3.** Inclined to or characteristic of peace. — **peace′ful·ly** *adv.* — **peace′ful·ness** *n.*

peace·mak·er (pēs′mā′kər) *n.* One who effects a reconciliation between unfriendly parties.

peace·nik (pēs′nik) *n.* *Informal* One who demonstrates against war or a particular war: a derogatory term. [< PEACE + Yiddish *-nik* (< Russ.), suffix meaning "a person"]

peace pipe The calumet.

peace·time (pēs′tīm′) *n.* A time of peace. — *adj.* Of, characterized by, or used in such a time.

peach[1] (pēch) *n.* **1.** The edible fruit of a tree of the rose family, wildly cultivated in many varieties. **2.** The tree itself. **3.** The yellowish pink color characteristic of the fruit. **4.** *Slang* Any particularly beautiful, pleasing, or excellent person or thing. [< OF < LL < L < Gk. *Persikon (melon)* Persian (fruit)]

peach[2] (pēch) *v.i.* *Slang* To inform against an accomplice; turn informer. [Aphetic var. of obs. *appeach* to accuse]

peach·y (pē′chē) *adj.* **peach·i·er, peach·i·est 1.** Resembling a peach, esp. in color or downiness. **2.** *Slang* Delightfully pleasant, beautiful, etc. — **peach′i·ness** *n.*

pea·coat (pē′kōt′) *n.* A pea jacket. Also **pea coat.**

pea·cock (pē′kok′) *n.* The male of a gallinaceous crested bird having erectile, brilliantly iridescent tail coverts enormously elongated and marked with eyelike spots, and the neck and breast of a greenish blue. ◆ Collateral adjective: *pavonine.* — *v.i.* To strut vainly; make a display. [OE *pēa, pāwa* peacock (< L *pavo*) + COCK[1]]

peacock blue A vivid greenish blue.

pea·fowl (pē′foul′) *n.* A peacock or peahen.

pea green A light yellowish green.

pea·hen (pē′hen′) *n.* A female peafowl.

pea jacket A short coat of thick woolen cloth, worn by seamen. Also called *peacoat.* [< Du. *pij* coat of coarse wool + JACKET]

MALE PEACOCK
(Body to 36 inches long; tail coverts to 6 feet)

peak (pēk) *n.* 1. A projecting point or edge; an end terminating in a point. 2. A conspicuous or precipitous mountain; also, the summit of such a mountain. 3. A point formed by the growth or cut of hair. 4. The maximum development, strength, value, etc., of something. 5. *Naut.* **a** The after upper corner of a fore-and-aft sail. **b** The upper end of a gaff. **c** The sharply narrowed part of a vessel at the bow or stern. — *v.t.* 1. *Naut.* To raise to or almost to a vertical position, as a gaff or yard. 2. To make into a peak or point. — *v.i.* 3. To assume the form of a peak. [Var. of PIKE[4]]

peak·ed (pē′kid, pēkt) *adj.* Having a thin or sickly appearance. [Origin uncertain]

peal (pēl) *n.* 1. A prolonged, sonorous sound, as of a bell or thunder. 2. A set of large bells. 3. A change rung on a set of bells. — *v.t. & v.i.* To sound with a peal or peals. [ME *pele,* aphetic var. of *apele* < OF *apeler* to appeal]

pe·an (pē′ən) See PAEAN.

pea·nut (pē′nut′) *n.* 1. The nutlike seed or seed pod of an annual herbaceous vine ripening underground from the flowers that bury themselves after fertilization. 2. The plant bearing this nut.

peanut brittle A hard candy containing roasted peanuts.

peanut butter A spread resembling butter in consistency, made from ground, roasted peanuts.

pear (pâr) *n.* 1. The juicy, edible, fleshy fruit of a tree of the rose family. 2. The tree bearing this fruit. [OE < W Gmc. < LL < L *pira,* pl. of *pirum* pear]

pearl[1] (pûrl) *n.* 1. A smooth, rounded, variously tinted nacreous concretion formed as a deposit around a foreign body in the shells of various mollusks, and largely used as a gem. 2. Something like or likened to such a jewel in form, luster, value, etc. 3. Nacre or mother-of-pearl. 4. A very pale bluish gray: also **pearl blue, pearl gray.** 5. *Printing* A size of type smaller than agate, 5 points. — *adj.* 1. Pertaining to, consisting of, set with, or made of pearl or mother-of-pearl. 2. Shaped like a pearl. — *v.i.* 1. To seek or fish for pearls. 2. To form beads like pearls. — *v.t.* 3. To adorn or set with or as with pearls. 4. To color or shape like pearls. 5. To make into small round grains, as barley. [< OF < Med.L *perna* pearl < L, mussel] — **pearl′ly** *adj.*

pearl[2] (pûrl) See PURL[2].

pearl·ash (purl′ash) *n.* Commercial potassium carbonate.

peas·ant (pez′ənt) *n.* 1. In Europe, a farmer, farm laborer, or rustic workman. 2. A boorish, uncouth, or simple-minded person. [< AF < OF *pais* country < LL < *pagus* district]

peas·ant·ry (pez′ən·trē) *n.* 1. The peasant class; a body of peasants. 2. Rusticity.

pease (pēz) Alternate plural of PEA: now used only in the collective sense. [OE < LL < L, pl. of *pisum* < Gk. < *pisos,* pulse, pease]

pease·cod (pēz′kod) *n.* A pea pod. Also **peas′cod.**

pea·soup·er (pē′soop′ər) *n.* 1. *Canadian* A French Canadian. 2. *Brit.* A thick fog.

peat (pēt) *n.* 1. A substance consisting of partially carbonized vegetable material, found usu. in bogs. 2. A block of this substance, pressed and dried for fuel: also called *turf.* [ME < Med.L *peta* piece of peat] — **peat′y** *adj.*

peat bog A marsh with an accumulation of peat.

peat moss 1. A moss of which peat is largely composed. 2. *Brit.* A peat bog.

pea·vey (pē′vē) *n. pl.* **·vies** An iron-pointed lever fitted with a movable hook and used for handling logs. Also **pea′vy.** [after Joseph *Peavey,* its inventor]

peb·ble (peb′əl) *n.* 1. A small, rounded fragment of rock, shaped by the action of water, ice, etc. 2. Quartz crystal; also, a lens made of it. 3. Leather that has been pebbled. — *v.t.* **·bled, ·bling** 1. To impart a rough grain to (leather). 2. To cover or pelt with pebbles. [Back formation of OE *papol(stān)* pebble(stone)]

peb·bly (peb′lē, peb′əl·ē) *adj.* **·bli·er, ·bli·est** 1. Covered with or full of pebbles. 2. Having a texture resembling pebbles.

pe·can (pi·kan′, -kän′, pē′kan) *n.* 1. A large hickory of the central and southern U.S., with edible, oval, thin-shelled nuts. 2. The nut of this tree. [Earlier *paccan* < Algonquian (Cree) *pacan*]

pec·ca·dil·lo (pek′ə·dil′ō) *n. pl.* **·los** or **·loes** A slight or trifling sin. [< Sp., dim. of *pecado* sin < L < *peccare* to sin]

pec·cant (pek′ənt) *adj.* 1. Guilty of sin; sinful. 2. Corrupt and offensive. — **pec′can·cy** *n.* — **pec′cant·ly** *adv.*

pec·ca·ry (pek′ər·ē) *n. pl.* **·ries** A hoglike animal of Central and South America. [< Sp. < Carib *pakira*]

pec·ca·vi (pe·kä′vī, -kä′vē) *n. pl.* **·vis** *Latin* A confession of guilt; literally, I have sinned.

peck[1] (pek) *v.t.* 1. To strike with the beak, as a bird does, or with something pointed. 2. To make by striking thus: to *peck* a hole in a wall. 3. To pick up, as food, with the beak. — *v.i.* 4. To make strokes with the beak or with something pointed. 5. To eat in small amounts or without appetite: with *at.* — *n.* 1. A quick, sharp blow, as with a beak. 2. A mark or hole made by such a blow. 3. *Informal* A quick kiss. [ME. Var. of PICK.] — **peck′er** *n.*

peck[2] (pek) *n.* 1. A measure of capacity: the fourth of a bushel. See table inside back cover. 2. A vessel for measuring a peck. 3. *Slang* A great quantity. [< OF *pek*]

pec·tin (pek′tin) *n. Biochem.* Any of a class of carbohydrates contained in the cell walls of various fruits as apples, lemons, etc., used as the basis of fruit jellies.

pec·to·ral (pek′tər·əl) *adj.* 1. Of or pertaining to the breast or chest. 2. Of or for diseases of the lungs or chest. — *n.* 1. A pectoral organ, fin, or muscle. 2. Any medicine for ailments of the chest. [< L < *pectus, -oris* breast]

pectoral fin *Zool.* One of the anterior paired fins of fishes, homologous with the anterior limb of higher vertebrates.

pec·u·late (pek′yə·lāt) *v.t. & v.i.* **·lat·ed, ·lat·ing** To steal or appropriate wrongfully (funds, esp. public funds entrusted to one's care); embezzle. [< L *peculatus,* pp. of *peculari* to embezzle] — **pec′u·la′tion** *n.* — **pec′u·la′tor** *n.*

pe·cu·li·ar (pi·kyōōl′yər) *adj.* 1. Having a character exclusively its own; specific. 2. Singular; strange. 3. Select or special; separate. 4. Belonging particularly or exclusively to one. — *n.* A person or thing that is peculiar; formerly, any private possession. [< MF *peculier* or < L < *peculium* private property] — **pe·cu′liar·ly** *adv.*

pe·cu·li·ar·i·ty (pi·kyōō′lē·ar′ə·tē, -kyōōl′yar′-) *n. pl.* **·ties** 1. A characteristic. 2. The quality of being peculiar. — **Syn.** See CHARACTERISTIC.

pe·cu·ni·ar·y (pi·kyōō′nē·er′ē) *adj.* 1. Consisting of or relating to money. 2. Having a monetary penalty; entailing a fine. [< L < *pecunia* money < *pecus* cattle]

ped-[1] Var. of PEDI-[1].

ped-[2] Var. of PEDO-.

-ped Var. of -PEDE.

ped·a·gog·ic (ped′ə·goj′ik, -gō′jik) *adj.* 1. Of or pertaining to the science or art of teaching. 2. Of or belonging to a pedagogue; affected with a conceit of learning. Also **ped′a·gog′i·cal.** — **ped′a·gog′i·cal·ly** *adv.*

ped·a·gog·ism (ped′ə·gog′iz·əm, -gōg′-) *n.* The nature, character, or business of a teacher. Also **ped′a·gogu·ism.**

ped·a·gogue (ped′ə·gog, -gôg) *n.* 1. A schoolmaster; educator. 2. A pedantic, narrow-minded teacher. Also **ped′a·gog.** [< OF < L < Gk. < *pais, paidos* child + *agōgos* leader]

ped·a·go·gy (ped′ə·gō′jē, -goj′ē) *n.* 1. The science or profession of teaching. 2. The theory of how to teach.

ped·al (ped′l) *adj.* 1. Of or pertaining to a foot, feet, or a footlike part. 2. Of or pertaining to a pedal. — *n. Mech.* A lever operated by the foot and having various functions: a bicycle *pedal;* a piano *pedal.* — *v.t. & v.i.* **ped·aled** or **·alled, ped·al·ing** or **·al·ling** To move or operate by working pedals. [< L < *pes, pedis* foot]

ped·al-push·ers (ped′l-pŏŏsh′ərz) *n.pl.* Slacks that come to just below the knees, worn by women and girls.

ped·ant (ped′ənt) *n.* One who makes needless display of his learning, or who insists upon the importance of trifling points of scholarship. [< MF < Ital. *pedante,* prob. < Med.L *paedagogans, -antis,* ppr. of *paedagogare* to teach] — **pe·dan·tic** (pi·dan′tik) *adj.* — **pe·dan′ti·cal·ly** *adv.*

ped·ant·ry (ped′ən·trē) *n. pl.* **·ries** 1. Ostentatious display of knowledge. 2. Slavish adherence to forms or rules.

ped·ate (ped′āt) *adj.* 1. Resembling or having the functions of a foot; also, having feet. 2. *Bot.* Divided or parted as a fan, the lateral divisions being subdivided: said esp. of leaves. [< L *pedatus* having feet] — **ped′ate·ly** *adv.*

ped·dle (ped′l) *v.* **·dled, ·dling** *v.i.* 1. To travel about selling small wares. 2. To piddle. — *v.t.* 3. To carry about and sell in small quantities. 4. To sell or dispense in small quantities. [Appar. back formation < ME *pedlere* peddler]

ped·dler (ped′lər) *n.* One who peddles; a hawker. [ME < *ped* basket] — **ped′dler·y** *n.*

-pede *combining form* Footed: *centipede.* Also spelled *-ped,* as in *quadruped.* [< L *pes, pedis* foot]

ped·er·ast (ped′ə·rast, pē′də-) *n.* One addicted to pederasty: also spelled *paederast.*

ped·er·as·ty (ped′ə·ras′tē, pē′də-) *n.* Sex relations between men, esp. between men and boys. [< NL < Gk. < *pais, paidos* boy + *erastēs* lover] — **ped′er·as′tic** *adj.*

ped·es·tal (ped′is·təl) *n.* 1. A base or support for a column, statue, or vase. 2. Any foundation or support. — **to put on a pedestal** To hold in high estimation; to put in the position of an idol or hero. — *v.t.* **·taled** or **·tailed**, **·tal·ing** or **·tal·ling** To place on a pedestal. [< MF < Ital. < *piè, piede* foot + *di* of + *stallo* stall, standing place]

pe·des·tri·an (pə·des′trē·ən) *adj.* 1. Moving on foot; walking. 2. Pertaining to common people; plebeian. 3. Commonplace, prosaic, or dull, as prose. — *n.* One who journeys or moves from place to place on foot; a walker. [< L *pedester, -tris* on foot] — **pe·des′tri·an·ism** *n.*

pedi-¹ *combining form* Foot; related to the foot or feet. Also, before vowels, **ped-**. [< L *pes, pedis* foot]

pedi-² Var. of PEDO-.

pe·di·a·tri·cian (pē′dē·ə·trish′ən, ped′ē-) *n.* A physician specializing in pediatrics. Also **pe·di·a·trist** (pē′dē·at′rist).

pe·di·at·rics (pē′dē·at′riks, ped′ē-) *n.pl.* (*construed as sing.*) That branch of medicine dealing with the diseases and hygienic care of children: also spelled *paediatrics*. [< Gk. *pais, paidos* child + -IATRICS] — **pe′di·at′ric** *adj.*

ped·i·cab (ped′i·kab) *n.* A three-wheeled vehicle operated by pedaling and used for public hire, esp. in Asia.

ped·i·cel (ped′ə·səl) *n.* 1. A stalk or supporting part. 2. *Bot.* The stalk supporting a single flower in an inflorescence composed of flowers arranged upon a common peduncle. 3. *Zool.* A footlike sucker or part. [< NL *pedicellus*, dim. of L *pediculus*, dim. of *pes, pedis* foot]

ped·i·cel·late (ped′ə·sə·lit, -lāt′) *adj.* On or having a pedicel.

ped·i·cle (ped′i·kəl) *n.* A pedicel.

pe·dic·u·lo·sis (pə·dik′yə·lō′sis) *n. Pathol.* The condition of being infested with lice; lousiness. [< L *pediculus* little louse + -OSIS] — **pe·dic′u·lous** *adj.*

ped·i·cure (ped′i·kyŏŏr) *n.* 1. Chiropody. 2. A chiropodist; podiatrist. 3. The cosmetic treatment of the feet and toenails. [< F < L *pes, pedis* foot + *curare* to care for]

ped·i·gree (ped′ə·grē) *n.* 1. A line of ancestors; lineage. 2. A list or table of descent and relationship, esp. of an animal of pure breed. [< MF *pié de grue* a crane's foot; from a three line mark denoting succession in pedigrees] — **ped′i·greed** *adj.*

ped·i·ment (ped′ə·mənt) *n. Archit.* 1. A broad triangular part above a portico or door. 2. Any similar piece surmounting a door, screen, bookcase, etc. [Earlier *periment*, prob. alter. of PYRAMID; infl. in form by L *pes, pedis* foot] — **ped′i·men′tal** (-men′təl) *adj.*

PEDIMENT
(Supreme Court Building, Washington, D.C.)

pedo- *combining form* Child; children; offspring: also, before vowels, **ped-**, as in *pedagogy*. Also spelled **paedo-**. [< Gk. *pais, paidos* child]

pe·dom·e·ter (pi·dom′ə·tər) *n.* An instrument that records the number of steps taken by the person who carries it. [< F < L *pes, pedis* foot + Gk. *metron* measure]

pe·dun·cle (pi·dung′kəl) *n.* 1. *Bot.* The general stalk or support of an inflorescence. 2. *Zool.* A stalk or stalklike part. [< NL *pedunculus* footstalk, dim. of *pes, pedis* foot] — **pe·dun′cu·lar** (-kyə·lər) *adj.* — **pe·dun′cu·late** (-kyə·lit, -lāt), **pe·dun′cu·lat′ed** *adj.*

peek (pēk) *v.i.* To look furtively, slyly, or quickly; peep. — *n.* A peep, glance. [ME *piken*; origin uncertain]

peek·a·boo (pē′kə·bōō′) *n.* A children's game in which one hides one's face and calls out "peekaboo!"

peel¹ (pēl) *n.* The natural coating of certain kinds of fruit, as oranges and lemons; skin; rind. — *v.t.* 1. To strip off the bark, skin, etc., of. 2. To strip off; remove. — *v.i.* 3. To lose bark, skin, etc. 4. To come off: said of bark, skin, etc. 5. *Slang* To undress. — **to keep one's eye peeled** *Informal* To keep watch; be alert. — **to peel off** *Aeron.* To veer off from a flight formation so as to dive or prepare for a landing. [ME < L *pilare* to deprive of hair] — **peel′er** *n.*

peel² (pēl) *n.* A long-handled implement used in moving bread, etc., about an oven. [< OF < L *pala* shovel]

peel·ing (pē′ling) *n.* Something peeled off, as rind, skin, etc.

peen (pēn) *n.* The end of a hammer head opposite the flat, striking face, usu. shaped like a wedge. — *v.t.* To beat, bend, or shape with the peen. [< ON]

peep¹ (pēp) *v.i.* 1. To utter the small, sharp cry of a young bird or chick; chirp; cheep. 2. To speak in a weak, small voice. — *n.* 1. The cry of a chick or small bird, or of a young frog; chirp. 2. A small sandpiper. [ME *pepen*; imit.]

peep² (pēp) *v.i.* 1. To look through a small hole, from concealment, etc.; peek. 2. To look furtively or quickly; peek. 3. To begin to appear; be just visible. — *n.* 1. A furtive look; a glimpse or glance. 2. A peephole. 3. The earliest appearance: the *peep* of day. [Prob. alter. of PEEK]

peep·er¹ (pē′pər) *n.* An animal that peeps, as a chick or any of several tree frogs.

peep·er² (pē′pər) *n.* 1. One who peeps or peeks; a spying person. 2. *Slang* An eye.

peep·hole (pēp′hōl′) *n.* An aperture, as a hole or crack, through which one may peep; also, a small window in a door.

peep·ing Tom (pē′ping tom′) An overly inquisitive or prying person; esp., one who peeps in at windows.

Peeping Tom of Coventry In British legend, a curious tailor who peeped at Lady Godiva and was struck blind.

peep·show (pēp′shō′) *n.* An exhibition of pictures, etc., viewed through a small orifice fitted with a magnifying lens.

peer¹ (pir) *v.i.* 1. To look narrowly or searchingly, as in an effort to see clearly. 2. To come partially into view. 3. *Poetic* To appear. [Origin uncertain]

peer² (pir) *n.* 1. An equal, as in natural gifts or in social rank. 2. An equal before the law. 3. A noble, esp. a British duke, marquis, earl, viscount, or baron; also, a prelate in the House of Lords. [< OF < L *par* equal]

peer·age (pir′ij) *n.* 1. The office or rank of a peer or nobleman. 2. Peers collectively. 3. A book containing a genealogical list of the nobility.

peer·ess (pir′is) *n.* A woman who holds a title of nobility, either in her own right or by marriage with a peer.

peer·less (pir′lis) *adj.* Of unequaled excellence. — **peer′less·ly** *adv.* — **peer′less·ness** *n.*

peer of the realm One of the lords of Parliament.

peeve (pēv) *v.t.* **peeved, peev·ing** *Informal* To make peevish. — *n. Informal* A complaint, annoyance, or grievance. [Back formation < PEEVISH]

pee·vish (pē′vish) *adj.* 1. Irritable or querulous; cross. 2. Showing discontent and vexation. [ME *pevische*; origin uncertain] — **pee′vish·ly** *adv.* — **pee′vish·ness** *n.*

pee·wee (pē′wē) *n.* 1. See PEWEE. 2. *Informal* Anything or anyone small or diminutive. — *adj.* Tiny. [Imit.]

peg (peg) *n.* 1. A pin, usu. of wood or metal, used to fasten articles together, to stop a hole, etc. 2. A projecting pin upon which something may be hung; or which may serve to keep a score, etc. 3. In a stringed musical instrument, a pin for holding fast the end of a string and adjusting its tension. 4. A reason or excuse. 5. A degree or step, as in rank or estimation. 6. *Brit.* A drink of brandy or whisky and soda. 7. *Informal* A leg, often of wood. 8. *Informal* A throw, as in baseball. — **to take (one) down a peg** To lower the self-esteem of (a person). — *v.* **pegged, peg·ging** *v.t.* 1. To drive or force a peg into; fasten with pegs. 2. To mark with pegs. 3. To strike or pierce with a peg or sharp instrument. 4. *Informal* To throw. — *v.i.* 5. To work or strive hard and perseveringly: usu. with *away*. 6. In croquet, to hit a peg. 7. To mark the score with pegs. — *adj.* Peg-top. [ME < MDu. *pegge*]

Peg·a·sus (peg′ə·səs) In Greek mythology, a winged horse, symbol of poetic inspiration. — *n.* A constellation, the Winged Horse. [< L < Gk. *Pēgasos*]

peg·board (peg′bôrd) *n.* 1. Any perforated board into which pegs may be inserted for holding things, keeping score, etc. 2. *Brit.* A game in which a player arranges pegs in certain patterns on a perforated board: also called *solitaire*.

peg leg *Informal* 1. An artificial leg of rodlike or tapering shape. 2. A person with such a leg.

peg-top (peg′top′) *adj.* Wide at the hip and narrow at the ankle: said of trousers: also **peg**. Also **pegged**.

peg top A child's wooden spinning top, pear-shaped and having a sharp metal peg.

pei·gnoir (pān·wär′, pān′wär) *n.* A loose dressing gown or negligee worn by women. [< F < *peigner* to comb]

pe·jo·ra·tion (pē′jə·rā′shən, pej′ə-) *n.* The condition of becoming worse; deterioration.

pe·jo·ra·tive (pē′jə·rā′tiv, pej′ə-, pi·jôr′ə·tiv, -jor′-) *adj.* Having or giving a derogatory or disparaging meaning or sense: a *pejorative* statement. — *n.* A pejorative word. [< LL *pejorare* to make worse] — **pe′jo·ra′tive·ly** *adv.*

Pe·king·ese (pē′kə·nēz′ for def. 1; pē′king·ēz′ for defs. 2, 3) *n. pl.* **·ese** 1. A variety of a pug dog, having long, silky hair, snub nose, and short legs. 2. A native or inhabitant of Peking. 3. The dialect spoken in Peking. — *adj.* Of or pertaining to Peking. Also **Pe·kin·ese** (pē′kə·nēz′).

Pe·king man (pē′king′) *Paleontol.* An extinct manlike primate whose fossil remains were found near Peking, China.

pe·koe (pē′kō, *Brit.* pek′ō) *n.* A superior black tea of India, Ceylon, and Java, made from the downy tips of the young buds of the tea plant. [< dial. Chinese *pek* white + *ho* hair]

pe·lag·ic (pə·laj′ik) *adj.* Of, pertaining to, or inhabiting the sea or ocean far from land. [< L < Gk. < *pelagos* the sea]

pel·ar·go·ni·um (pel′är·gō′nē·əm) *n.* Any of a number of strong-scented, ornamental herbs or shrubs generally known as *geraniums*, having handsome, variously colored flowers. [< NL < Gk. *pelargos* stork]

pelf (pelf) *n.* Money; wealth, esp. if dishonestly acquired. [< OF *pelfre* booty; ult. origin uncertain]

pel·i·can (pel′i·kən) *n.* A large, gregarious, web-footed bird of warm regions, having a pouch on the lower jaw for the temporary storage of fish. [OE < LL < Gk. *pelekan*]

Pelican State Nickname of Louisiana.

pe·lisse (pə·lēs′) *n.* A long outer garment or cloak, originally made of fur or lined with fur. [< F < Med.L < L (*vestis*) *pellicia* (a garment) of skins or fur]

pel·la·gra (pə·la′grə, -lag′rə) *n. Pathol.* A disease characterized by gastric disturbance, skin eruptions, etc., caused by a deficiency of nicotinic acid. [< NL, prob. < Ital. *pelle agra* rough skin] **— pel·la′grous** *adj.*

pel·let (pel′it) *n.* 1. A small round ball, as of wax, paper, etc. 2. A small bullet. 3. A very small pill. 4. A stone. 5. A cannonball. **—** *v.t.* 1. To make into pellets. 2. To strike or hit with pellets. [< OF < Med.L < L *pila* ball]

pell-mell (pel′mel′) *adv.* 1. In a confused or disordered way or manner. 2. With a headlong rush; in wild haste. **—** *adj.* Devoid of order or method; confused. **—** *n.* A jumble; disorder. Also **pell′mell′**. [< F *pêlemêle* < OF *pesle-mesle*]

pel·lu·cid (pə·loō′sid) *adj.* 1. Permitting to a certain extent the passage of light. 2. Transparently clear and simple: a *pellucid* style. [< L < *per-* through + *lucere* to shine] **— pel·lu′cid·ly** *adv.* **— pel·lu′cid·ness, pel·lu·cid′i·ty** (pel′oō·sid′ə·tē) *n.*

Pel·o·pon·ne·sian (pel′ə·pə·nē′zhən, -shən) *adj.* Of or pertaining to the Peloponnesus. **—** *n.* A native or inhabitant of the Peloponnesus.

Peloponnesian War See table for WAR.

pe·lo·ta (pe·lō′tə) *n.* A game popular among Basques, Spaniards, and Spanish Americans. It is played in a walled court with a hard rubber ball and a curved, wicker racquet. [< Sp., lit., a ball, aug. of *pella* < L *pila*]

pelt[1] (pelt) *n.* 1. The skin of an animal, usu. with the fur left on. 2. A garment made of skin. 3. The human skin: a humorous term. [< OF < L *pellis* skin]

pelt[2] (pelt) *v.t.* 1. To strike repeatedly with or as with blows. 2. To throw or hurl (missiles). 3. To assail with words. **—** *v.i.* 4. To beat or descend with violence. 5. To move rapidly; hurry. **—** *n.* 1. A blow. 2. A swift pace. [ME *pelten*, ? var. of *pulten* to thrust] **— pelt′er** *n.*

pel·tate (pel′tāt) *adj. Bot.* Attached at or near the center of the lower surface, as a leaf. Also **pel′tat·ed**. [< L *peltatus* armed with a shield] **— pel′tate·ly** *adv.*

pel·try (pel′trē) *n. pl.* **·ries** 1. Pelts collectively. 2. A pelt. 3. A place for keeping or storing pelts.

pelvi- *combining form* Pelvis. [< L *pelvis* basin]

pel·vic (pel′vik) *adj.* Of, pertaining to, or near the pelvis.

pelvic arch *Anat.* In vertebrates, that part of the skeleton to which the hind limbs (in man, the lower limbs) are attached. Also **pelvic girdle**.

pel·vis (pel′vis) *n. pl.* **·ves** (-vēz) 1. *Anat.* a The part of the skeleton that forms a bony girdle joining the lower or hind limbs to the body, composed, in man, of the two innominate bones and the sacrum. b The hollow interior portion of the kidney, into which the urine is discharged. For illus. see KIDNEY. 2. A basinlike structure. [< L, basin]

pem·mi·can (pem′ə·kən) *n. U.S. & Canadian* 1. Lean meat, usu. venison, cut into strips, dried, pounded into paste with fat and a few berries, and pressed into cakes. 2. A similar concentrated and nutritious food made from beef and dried fruits, used by Arctic explorers, etc. Also **pem′i·can**. [< Algonquian (Cree) *pimekan* < *pime* fat]

pen[1] (pen) *n.* 1. An instrument for writing with fluid ink, usu. a metal point split in the middle and fitted to a holder. 2. A ball-point pen. 3. The quality of one's penmanship. 4. The profession of writing. 5. The style of writing. 6. A writer. **—** *v.t.* **penned, pen·ning** To write with a pen. [< OF < LL < L, wing, feather] **— pen′ner** *n.*

pen[2] (pen) *n.* 1. A small enclosure, as for pigs; also, the animals contained in a pen. 2. Any small place of confinement. 3. *Slang* A penitentiary. **—** *v.t.* **penned** or **pent, pen·ning** To enclose in or as in a pen; confine. [OE *penn*]

HUMAN PELVIS
a Crest of ilium. *b* Ilium. *c* Coccyx. *d* Acetabulum. *e* Ischium. *f* Pubic symphysis. *g* Head of femur. *h* Sacrum. *i* Lumbar vertebrae.

pe·nal (pē′nəl) *adj.* 1. Of or pertaining to punishment. 2. Liable, or rendering liable, to punishment. 3. Enacting or prescribing punishment: a *penal* code. 4. Relating to the means, or place of punishment. [< OF < L *poena* penalty]

pe·nal·ize (pē′nəl·īz, pen′əl-) *v.t.* **·ized, ·iz·ing** 1. To subject to a penalty, as for a violation. 2. To declare, as an action, subject to a penalty. Also *Brit.* **pe′nal·ise**. **— pe′nal·i·za′tion** *n.*

pen·al·ty (pen′əl·tē) *n. pl.* **·ties** 1. The legal punishment for having violated a law. 2. A sum of money to be forfeited as punishment for illegal acts; fine. 3. The disadvantage, loss, or suffering incurred by some act, error, state of being, etc.: the *penalty* of sin. 4. In sports and games, any handicap imposed for a violation of rules.

pen·ance (pen′əns) *n.* 1. *Eccl.* A sacramental rite involving contrition, confession of sins to a priest, the acceptance of penalties, and absolution; also, the penalty imposed. 2. Any penalty, mortification, or act of piety voluntarily undertaken as an atonement for sin. **— to do penance** To perform an act or acts of penance. **—** *v.t.* **·anced, ·anc·ing** To impose a penance upon. [< OF < L *paenitere* to repent]

pence (pens) *Brit.* The plural of PENNY: used mostly in combination: *twopence*.

pen·chant (pen′chənt, *Fr.* päṅ·shäṅ′) *n.* A strong liking or inclination for something. [< F *pencher* to incline]

pen·cil (pen′səl) *n.* 1. A writing, drawing, or marking implement consisting of a stick or thin strip of graphite, colored chalk, slate, etc., encased in wood or inserted in a mechanically operated holder. 2. A pencillike instrument for applying cosmetics. 3. A small stick of some substance: a styptic *pencil*. 4. A set of rays, as of light, diverging from or converging upon a given point. 5. In drawing or painting, the artist's skill or style. **—** *v.t.* **pen·ciled** or **·cilled, pen·cil·ing** or **·cil·ling** 1. To mark, write, draw, or color with or as with a pencil. 2. To use a pencil on. [< OF < L *penicillum* paintbrush] **— pen′cil·er** or **pen′cil·ler** *n.*

pend (pend) *v.i.* 1. To await adjustment or settlement. 2. *Dial.* To hang; depend. [< MF < L *pendere* to hang]

pen·dant (pen′dənt) *n.* 1. Anything that hangs from something else, either for ornament or for use. 2. Something hanging from a chandelier, ceiling, lamp, etc., by which a light is turned on and off. 3. *Archit.* An ornament hanging from a ceiling, roof, etc. Also spelled *pendent*. **—** *adj.* See PENDENT. [See PEND.]

pen·dent (pen′dənt) *adj.* 1. Hanging downward; suspended. 2. Projecting; overhanging. 3. Undetermined; pending. Also spelled *pendant*. **—** *n.* See PENDANT. [Var. of PENDANT] **— pen′dent·ly** *adv.*

pend·ing (pen′ding) *adj.* 1. Remaining unfinished or undecided. 2. Imminent; impending. **—** *prep.* 1. During the process or continuance of. 2. While awaiting; until.

pen·drag·on (pen·drag′ən) *n.* In ancient Britain, a supreme ruler or chief. [< Welsh, a chief leader in war]

pen·du·lous (pen′joō·ləs) *adj.* 1. Hanging, esp. so as to swing. 2. Undecided; wavering. [< L *pendere* to hang] **— pen′du·lous·ly** *adv.* **— pen′du·lous·ness** *n.*

pen·du·lum (pen′joō·ləm, -də-) *n.* 1. A suspended body free to oscillate between two extremes. 2. Such a device serving to regulate the movement of a clock. 3. Something that changes often. [See PENDULOUS.]

Pe·nel·o·pe (pə·nel′ə·pē) In the *Odyssey*, the faithful wife of Odysseus, who, during his absence kept her many suitors in check under pretext of having to weave a shroud.

pen·e·tra·ble (pen′ə·trə·bəl) *adj.* That can be penetrated. **— pen′e·tra·bil′i·ty** *n.* **— pen′e·tra·bly** *adv.*

pen·e·trate (pen′ə·trāt) *v.* **·trat·ed, ·trat·ing** *v.t.* 1. To force a way into or through; pierce; enter. 2. To spread or diffuse itself throughout. 3. To perceive the meaning of; understand. 4. To affect or move profoundly. **—** *v.i.* 5. To enter or pass through something. 6. To have an effect on the mind or emotions. [< L *penetrare* to put within] **— pen′e·tra·ble** (-trə·bəl) *adj.* **— pen′e·tra·bil′i·ty** *n.*

pen·e·trat·ing (pen′ə·trā′ting) *adj.* 1. Tending or having power to penetrate. 2. Acute; discerning: a *penetrating* mind. Also **pen′e·tra·tive**. **— pen′e·trat′ing·ly** *adv.* **— pen′e·trat′ing·ness** *n.*

pen·e·tra·tion (pen′ə·trā′shən) *n.* 1. The act or power of penetrating physically. 2. Ability to penetrate mentally; acuteness; discernment. 3. The depth to which a bullet sinks in a target.

pen·guin (pen′gwin, peng′-) *n.* A web-footed, flightless, aquatic bird of the southern hemisphere, with flipperlike wings and short legs. [< Welsh *pen* head + *gwyn* white]

pen·hold·er (pen′hōl′dər) *n.* 1. A handle with a device for inserting a metallic pen. 2. A rack for pens.

pen·i·cil·lin (pen′ə·sil′in) *n.* A powerful antibiotic found in a mold fungus, used to treat bacterial infections.

pen·i·cil·li·um (pen′ə·sil′ē·əm) *n. pl.* **·cil·li·a** (-ē·ə) Any of various fungi growing on decaying fruits, ripening cheese, etc.; one of which is the principal source of penicillin. [< NL < L *penicillus* paintbrush]

pe·nin·su·la (pə-nin′sə-lə, -syə-) *n.* A piece of land almost surrounded by water, and connected with the mainland by an isthmus. [< L < *paene* almost + *insula* island] — **pe·nin′su·lar** *adj.*

Peninsula State A nickname for FLORIDA.

pe·nis (pē′nis) *n. pl.* **·nis·es** or **·nes** (-nēz) The copulatory organ of male animals. [< L, orig., *tail*] — **pe′ni·al** (-nē-əl), **pe′nile** (-nil, -nīl) *adj.*

pen·i·tence (pen′ə-təns) *n.* The state of being penitent; contrition. [< OF < L < *paenitere* to repent]

pen·i·tent (pen′ə-tənt) *adj.* Affected by a sense of one's own guilt, and resolved on amendment. — *n.* 1. One who is penitent. 2. One who confesses his sins to a priest and submits to the penance prescribed. — **pen′i·tent·ly** *adv.*

pen·i·ten·tial (pen′ə-ten′shəl) *adj.* Of or expressing penitence or penance. — *n.* A penitent. — **pen′i·ten′tial·ly** *adv.*

pen·i·ten·tia·ry (pen′ə-ten′shər-ē) *n. pl.* **·ries** A prison, esp. one operated by a state or federal government for those convicted of serious crimes. — *adj.* 1. Of or pertaining to penance. 2. Relating to or used for the punishment of criminals. 3. Rendering the offender liable to imprisonment. [See PENITENCE.]

pen·knife (pen′nīf′) *n. pl.* **·knives** (-nīvz′) A small pocket knife.

pen·man (pen′mən) *n. pl.* **·men** (-mən) 1. A person considered with regard to his handwriting. 2. An author.

pen·man·ship (pen′mən-ship) *n.* 1. The art of writing. 2. The style or quality of handwriting.

pen name An author's assumed name; pseudonym; nom de plume. — **Syn.** See PSEUDONYM.

pen·nant (pen′ənt) *n.* 1. A long, narrow flag, usu. triangular, used as a school emblem, etc. 2. A similar flag awarded to sports winners. [< PENNON]

pen·nate (pen′āt) *adj.* Having wings or feathers. Also **pen′nat·ed.** [< L *pennatus* winged < *penna* feather] **-pennate** *combining form* Having wings or feathers.

pen·ni (pen′ē) *n. pl.* **pen·nis** or **pen·ni·a** (pen′ē-ə) A Finnish coin and monetary unit, the hundredth part of a markka. [< Finnish < G *pfennig* penny]

pen·ni·less (pen′i-lis) *adj.* Poverty-stricken.

pen·non (pen′ən) *n.* 1. A small, pointed flag, borne by medieval knights on their lances. 2. Any banner or flag. 3. A wing. [< OF *penon* streamer < L *penna* feather]

Pennsylvania Dutch 1. Descendants of immigrants from SW Germany and from Switzerland, who settled in Pennsylvania in the 17th and 18th centuries. 2. The language spoken by these people, a High German dialect with an admixture of English. [< early and dial. E *Dutch* (< G *Deutsch*) German] — **Penn′syl·va′ni·a-Dutch** *adj.*

Penn·syl·va·ni·an (pen′səl-vā′nē-ən, -vān′yən) *adj.* 1. Of or relating to the State of Pennsylvania. 2. *Geol.* Belonging to or denoting a Paleozoic period following the Mississippian and preceding the Permian periods. See table for GEOLOGY. — *n.* 1. A native or inhabitant of Pennsylvania. 2. *Geol.* The Pennsylvanian period or rock system.

pen·ny (pen′ē) *n. pl.* **pen·nies** or *Brit.* **pence** (pens) 1. In the U.S. and Canada, a cent. 2. A coin of Great Britain, Ireland, and various Commonwealth Nations, equivalent to ½ shilling. 3. In the United Kingdom, a coin equal in value to ⅟₁₀₀ pound: also *new penny.* 4. Money in general. — **a pretty penny** *Informal* A large or relatively large amount of money. [OE *penning, penig, pending*]
-penny *combining form* Costing (a specified number of) pennies: formerly designating the cost of nails per hundred, but now denoting their length, beginning at 1 inch for two-penny nails. [< PENNY]

penny ante 1. A poker game in which the ante is limited to one cent. 2. *Informal* Any piddling transaction.

penny pincher A parsimonious person. — **pen·ny-pinch·ing** (pen′ē-pinch′ing) *adj. & n.*

pen·ny·roy·al (pen′ē-roi′əl) *n.* A low, erect, strong-scented herb of North America yielding oil of pennyroyal, used in medicine. [Alter. of earlier *pulyole ryale*]

pen·ny·weight (pen′ē-wāt′) *n.* In troy weight, the twentieth part of an ounce, 24 grains, or 1.56 grams. See table inside back cover.

pen·ny-wise (pen′ē-wīz′) *adj.* Unduly economical in small matters. — **penny-wise and pound-foolish** Economical in small matters, but wasteful in large ones.

pen·ny·worth (pen′ē-wûrth′) *n.* 1. As much as can be bought for a penny. 2. A bargain. 3. A small amount.

Pe·nob·scot (pə-nob′skot) *n.* One of a tribe of North American Indians of the Algonquian confederacy of 1749.

pe·nol·o·gy (pē-nol′ə-jē) *n. pl.* **·gies** The science that treats of crime and of the management of prisons and reformatories. [< L *poena* penalty + -LOGY] — **pe·no·log·i·cal** (pē′nə-loj′i-kəl) *adj.* — **pe·nol′o·gist** *n.*

pen·sile (pen′sil) *adj.* 1. Hanging loosely. 2. Constructing pensile nests: said of birds. [< L < *pendere* to hang] — **pen′sile·ness, pen·sil′i·ty** *n.*

pen·sion¹ (pen′shən) *n.* 1. A periodic allowance to an individual or to his family, given when certain conditions, as age, length of service, etc., have been fulfilled. 2. A grant or allowance paid to someone of recognized ability in the arts or sciences. — *v.t.* 1. To grant a pension to. 2. To dismiss with a pension: with *off.* [< OF < L *pensio, -onis* payment] — **pen′sion·a·ble** *adj.*

pen·sion² (pen′shən, *Fr.* pän-syôn′) *n. French* A boarding house; also, a boarding school. [< OF, payment, rent]

pen·sion·ar·y (pen′shən-er′ē) *adj.* 1. Living by means of a pension. 2. Consisting of or like a pension. — *n. pl.* **·ar·ies** 1. A pensioner. 2. A hireling.

pen·sion·er (pen′shən-ər) *n.* 1. One who receives a pension or is dependent on the bounty of another. 2. At Cambridge University, a student who pays his own expenses. 3. A boarder, as in a convent or school.

pen·sive (pen′siv) *adj.* 1. Engaged in or addicted to serious, quiet reflection. 2. Expressive of, suggesting, or causing a melancholy thoughtfulness. [< OF < L *pensare* to think] — **pen′sive·ly** *adv.* — **pen′sive·ness** *n.*

pen·stock (pen′stok′) *n.* 1. A trough or conduit for carrying water to a water wheel. 2. A sluice or floodgate controlling the discharge of water, as from a pond.

pent (pent) Past participle of PEN². — *adj.* Penned up or in; closely confined.

penta- *combining form* Five: *pentagon.* Also, before vowels, **pent-.** [< Gk. *pente* five]

pen·ta·gon (pen′tə-gon) *n. Geom.* A polygon having five sides and five angles. [< L < Gk. < *pente* five + *gōnia* angle] — **pen·tag·o·nal** (pen-tag′ə-nəl) *adj.* — **pen·tag′o·nal·ly** *adv.*

Pentagon, the 1. A five-sided building in Arlington, Virginia, housing the U.S. Department of Defense and other offices. 2. The military leadership of the U.S.

pen·ta·he·dron (pen′tə-hē′drən) *n. pl.* **·dra** (-drə) *Geom.* A polyhedron bounded by five plane faces. — **pen′ta·he′dral** *adj.*

pen·tam·e·ter (pen-tam′ə-tər) *n.* 1. A line of verse consisting of five metrical feet. 2. Verse comprised of pentameters. — *adj.* Having five metrical feet. [< L < Gk. < *pente* five + *metron* a measure]

pen·tane (pen′tān) *n. Chem.* Any one of three isomeric, volatile, liquid hydrocarbons of the methane series, C_5H_{12}, two of which are contained in petroleum.

Pen·ta·teuch (pen′tə-tōōk, -tyōōk) *n.* The first five books of the Old Testament collectively, consisting of Genesis, Exodus, Leviticus, Numbers, and Deuteronomy. [< LL < Gk. < *pente* five + *teuchos* book] — **Pen′ta·teuch′al** *adj.*

pen·tath·lon (pen-tath′lən) *n.* An athletic contest consisting of five separate events, in all of which each contestant must participate. [< Gk. < *pente* five + *athlos* contest]

pen·ta·va·lent (pen′tə-vā′lənt, pen-tav′ə-) *adj. Chem.* Having a valence of five. [< PENTA- + L *valere* to have power or value]

Pen·te·cost (pen′tə-kôst, -kost) *n.* 1. A Christian festival, the seventh Sunday after Easter, commemorating the descent of the Holy Ghost upon the apostles (*Acts* ii): also called *Whitsunday.* 2. A Jewish festival, fifty days after the first day of Passover: also called *Shabuoth.* [< LL < Gk. *pentēkostē* (*hēmera*) the fiftieth (day)]

pen·te·cos·tal (pen′tə-kôs′təl, -kos′-) *adj. Often cap.* Of, pertaining to, or occurring at Pentecost.

pent·house (pent′hous′) *n.* An apartment or other structure on the roof of a building. [< OF, ? < LL *appendicium* appendage]

Pen·to·thal Sodium (pen′tə-thôl) A proprietary name for a brand of thiopental sodium.

pent-up (pent′up′) *adj.* Repressed: *pent-up* emotions.

pe·nuch·le (pē′nuk-əl), **pe·nuck·le** See PINOCHLE.

pe·nult (pē′nult, pi-nult′) *n.* The syllable next to the last in a word. Also **pe·nul·ti·ma** (pi-nul′tə-mə). [Short for *penultima* < L *paene* almost + *ultimus* last]

pe·nul·ti·mate (pi-nul′tə-mit) *adj.* 1. Next to the last. 2. Of or belonging to the next to the last syllable. — *n.* A penultimate part. [< L *paene* almost + ULTIMATE]

pe·num·bra (pi-num′brə) *n. pl.* **·brae** (-brē) or **·bras** 1. A partial shadow, as in an eclipse, within which the rays of light from an illuminating body are partly but not wholly intercepted. 2. The dark fringe around the central part of a sunspot. [< NL < L *paene* almost + *umbra* shadow] — **pe·num′bral, pe·num′brous** (-brəs) *adj.*

pe·nu·ri·ous (pə-nŏŏr′ē-əs, -nyŏŏr′-) *adj.* 1. Excessively sparing in the use of money; stingy. 2. Extremely poor; needy. 3. Affording or yielding little; scanty. [< MF < Med.L < L *penuria* want, poverty] — **pe·nu′ri·ous·ly** *adv.* — **pe·nu′ri·ous·ness** *n.*

---

pen·u·ry (pen′yə·rē) *n.* Extreme poverty or want. [< OF < L *penuria* want]

pe·on (pē′ən) *n.* **1.** In Latin America, a laborer; servant. **2.** Formerly, a debtor kept in servitude until he had worked out of his debt. [< Sp. < LL *pedo, -onis* foot soldier < L *pes, pedis* foot]

pe·on·age (pē′ən·ij) *n.* **1.** The condition of being a peon. **2.** The system by which debtors are held in servitude until they have worked out their debt. Also **pe′on·ism** (-iz′əm).

pe·o·ny (pē′ə·nē) *n.* *pl.* **·nies 1.** A plant of the crowfoot family, having large crimson, rose, or white flowers. **2.** The flower. [OE < L < Gk. *Paion* Paeon, the Healer]

peo·ple (pē′pəl) *n.* *pl.* **peo·ple;** *for defs. 1 & 2, also* **peo·ples 1.** The entire body of human beings living in the same country, under the same government, and speaking the same language: the *people* of England. **2.** A body of human beings having the same history, culture, and traditions, and usu. speaking the same language: the Polish *people*. **3.** In a state or nation, the body of persons invested with political rights. **4.** A group of persons having the same interests, profession, condition of life, etc.: poor *people*. **5.** Persons considered collectively: *people* say. **6.** Ordinary persons; the populace: usu. with *the*. **7.** One's family or relatives. **8.** Human beings as distinguished from animals. **9.** Animals collectively: the ant *people*. — *v.t.* **·pled, ·pling** To fill with inhabitants; populate. [< OF < L *populus* populace] — **peo′pler** *n.*
— **Syn.** A group having a common descent, language, culture, habitat, or government may be called a *people*. *Folk* is a homelier word for *people*, nearly as broad, and usu. stressing common traditions, customs, or behavior. A *nation* is a political entity, comprising the *people* (or *peoples*) under one government.

pep (pep) *n.* *Informal* Energy and high spirits; vigorous activity. — *v.t.* **pepped, pep·ping** To fill or inspire with energy or pep: usu. with *up*. [Short for PEPPER]

pep·lum (pep′ləm) *n.* *pl.* **·lums** or **·la** (-lə) A short overskirt, ruffle, or flounce attached to a blouse or coat at the waist. [< L < Gk. *peplos* a woman's shawl]

pep·per (pep′ər) *n.* **1.** A pungent, aromatic condiment consisting of the dried immature berries of a plant. When ground entire it is **black pepper,** but when the outer coating of the seeds is removed, the product is **white pepper. 2.** Any plant of the pepper family. **3.** Red pepper. **4.** Green pepper. — *v.t.* **1.** To sprinkle or season with pepper. **2.** To sprinkle freely. **3.** To shower, as with missiles; spatter; pelt. **4.** To make (speech or writing) vivid or pungent, as with humor, sarcasm, etc. — *v.i.* **5.** To discharge missiles at something. [OE, ult. < L < Gk. *peperi*]

pep·per-and-salt (pep′ər·ən·sôlt′) *adj.* Having or consisting of a mixture of white and black, so as to present a grayish appearance. — *n.* A pepper-and-salt cloth.

pep·per·box (pep′ər·boks′) *n.* **1.** A container for sprinkling pepper. **2.** A quick-tempered person.

pep·per·corn (pep′ər·kôrn′) *n.* **1.** A berry of the pepper plant. **2.** Anything trifling or insignificant.

pep·per·grass (pep′ər·gras′, -gräs′) *n.* A plant of the mustard family, having a pungent flavor, and used as a salad vegetable. Also **pep′per·wort** (-wûrt).

pepper mill A hand mill, often designed for table use, in which peppercorns are ground.

pep·per·mint (pep′ər·mint′) *n.* **1.** A pungent, aromatic herb used in medicine and confectionery. **2.** An oil made from this herb. **3.** A confection flavored with peppermint.

pepper pot 1. A pepperbox. **2.** A stew of meat or fish with vegetables, flavored with pepper, etc.

pepper tree A tree of Central and South America whose seeds are used as a spice.

pep·per·y (pep′ər·ē) *adj.* **1.** Pertaining to or like pepper; pungent. **2.** Quick-tempered; hasty. **3.** Spicy and vivid, as speech or writing. — **pep′per·i·ness** *n.*

pep pill *Slang* Any of various pills or tablets acting to stimulate the central nervous system.

pep·py (pep′ē) *adj.* **·pi·er, ·pi·est** *Informal* Full of energy; lively. — **pep′pi·ness** *n.*

pep·sin (pep′sin) *n.* **1.** *Biochem.* An enzyme secreted by the gastric juices that promotes the digestion of proteins. **2.** A medicinal preparation obtained from the stomachs of various animals, as the pig and the calf, used to aid digestion. Also **pep′sine** (-sin). [< G < Gk. *pepsis* digestion]

pep talk *Informal* A brief, vigorous talk meant to inspire confidence or enthusiasm.

pep·tic (pep′tik) *adj.* **1.** Of, pertaining to, or promotive of digestion. **2.** Of, pertaining to, or caused by pepsin. **3.** Able to digest. — *n.* An agent that promotes digestion. [< Gk. *pepsis* digestion]

pep·tone (pep′tōn) *n.* *Biochem.* Any of the soluble compounds into which proteins are converted when acted upon by pepsin, by acids and alkalis, by putrefaction, etc. [< G < Gk. *peptos* digested] — **pep·ton·ic** (pep·ton′ik) *adj.*

Pe·quot (pē′kwot) *n.* One of a tribe of Algonquian Indians, formerly inhabiting southern New England.

per (pûr) *prep.* **1.** By; by means of; through: used in commercial and business English: *per* bearer. **2.** To or for each: ten cents *per* yard. **3.** By the; every: esp. in Latin phrases: *per diem.* [< L, through, by]

per- *prefix* **1.** Through; throughout: *pervade, perennial.* **2.** Thoroughly: *perturb.* **3.** Away: *pervert.* **4.** Very: *perfervid.* **5.** *Chem.* Indicating an excess amount of a specified element in a compound: hydrogen peroxide. [< L *per* through]

per·ad·ven·ture (pûr′əd·ven′chər) *adv. Archaic* Perchance; perhaps. [< OF *par aventure* by chance]

per·am·bu·late (pə·ram′byə·lāt) *v.* **·lat·ed, ·lat·ing** *v.t.* **1.** To walk through or over. **2.** To walk through or around so as to inspect, etc. — *v.i.* **3.** To stroll. [< L *per* through + *ambulare* to walk] — **per·am·bu·la·tion** (pə·ram′byə·lā′shən) *n.* — **per·am′bu·la·to·ry** (-tôr′ē, -tō′rē) *adj.*

per·am·bu·la·tor (pə·ram′byə·lā′tər) *n.* **1.** One who perambulates. **2.** *Chiefly Brit.* A baby carriage.

per an·num (pûr an′əm) *Latin* By the year.

per·cale (pər·kāl′, -kal′) *n.* A closely woven cotton fabric without gloss. [< F, prob. < Persian *pergālah*]

per cap·i·ta (pûr kap′ə·tə) *Latin* For each person; literally, by heads.

per·ceive (pər·sēv′) *v.t. & v.i.* **·ceived, ·ceiv·ing 1.** To become aware of (something) through the senses; see, hear, feel, taste, or smell. **2.** To come to understand; apprehend with the mind. [< OF < L < *per-* thoroughly + *capere* to take] — **per·ceiv′a·ble** *adj.* — **per·ceiv′a·bly** *adv.*
— **Syn. 1.** sense. Compare SEE, DISCERN. **2.** comprehend.

per·cent (pər·sent′) *n.* **1.** Number of parts in or to every hundred, often specified: fifty *percent* of the people. **2.** Amount or quantity commensurate with the number of units in proportion to one hundred: ten *percent* of fifty is five: symbol, %. **3.** *pl.* Securities bearing a certain percentage of interest. Also **per cent., per cent** [Short for L *per centum* by the hundred]

per·cent·age (pər·sen′tij) *n.* **1.** Rate per hundred, or proportion in a hundred parts. **2.** A proportion or part considered in its quantitative relation to the whole. **3.** In commerce, the allowance, commission, duty, or interest on a hundred. **4.** *Informal* Advantage; profit.

per·cen·tile (pər·sen′tīl, -til) *n. Stat.* Any of 100 points spaced at equal intervals within the range of a plotted variable, each point denoting that percentage of the total cases lying below it in the series. — *adj.* Of a percentile.

per·cept (pûr′sept) *n. Psychol.* **1.** Something perceived. **2.** Immediate knowledge derived from perceiving. [< L *percipere* to perceive]

per·cep·ti·ble (pər·sep′tə·bəl) *adj.* That can be perceived; appreciable. — **per·cep′ti·bil′i·ty** *n.* — **per·cep′ti·bly** *adv.*

per·cep·tion (pər·sep′shən) *n.* **1.** The act or process of perceiving. **2.** The result or effect of perceiving. **3.** Any insight, knowledge, etc., arrived at by or as by perceiving. **4.** The capacity for perceiving. — **per·cep′tion·al** *adj.* — **per·cep′tu·al** (-chōō·əl) *adj.*

per·cep·tive (pər·sep′tiv) *adj.* **1.** Having the power of perception. **2.** Having a quick capacity for perceiving. **3.** Of or pertaining to perception. — **per·cep′tive·ly** *adv.* — **per·cep·tiv·i·ty** (pûr′sep·tiv′ə·tē), **per·cep′tive·ness** *n.*

perch¹ (pûrch) *n.* **1.** A horizontal staff or pole used as a roost for poultry. **2.** Any place on which birds alight or rest. **3.** Any place for sitting or standing, esp. if elevated. **4.** A rod (def. 9). — *v.i.* **1.** To alight or sit on or as on a perch; roost. — *v.t.* **2.** To set on or as on a perch. [< OF < L *pertica* pole] — **perch·er** (pûr′chər) *n.*

perch² (pûrch) *n.* *pl.* **perch** or **perches 1.** A small, spiny-finned fresh-water food fish. **2.** Any of various other re-related fishes. [< OF < L < Gk. *perkē*]

per·chance (pər·chans′, -chäns′) *adv.* Possibly; perhaps. [< OF *par chance* by chance]

Per·che·ron (pûr′chə·ron, -shə-) *n.* A breed of large draft horses. [after *Perche*, a region of nothern France]

per·cip·i·ent (pər·sip′ē·ənt) *adj.* **1.** Having the power of perception. **2.** Perceiving rapidly or keenly. — *n.* One who or that which perceives. [< L < *per-* thoroughly + *capere* to take] — **per·cip′i·ence** or **·en·cy** *n.*

per·coid (pûr′koid) *adj.* Of or pertaining to an order of spiny-finned fishes, including the fresh-water perches; perch-like. — *n.* A percoid fish. Also **per·coi·de·an** (pər·koi′dē·ən). [< L *perca* perch² + -OID]

per·co·late (pûr′kə·lāt; *for n., also* pur′kə·lət) *v.t. & v.i.* **·lat·ed, ·lat·ing** Of a liquid, to pass or cause to pass through fine interstices; filter. — *n.* That which has percolated. [< L < *per-* through + *colare* to strain] — **per′co·la′tion** *n.*

per·co·la·tor (pûr′kə·lā′tər) *n.* A type of coffeepot in which boiling water rises to the top in a tube and then filters down through finely ground coffee to a container below.

per·cus·sion (pər·kush′ən) *n.* **1.** The sharp striking of one body against another. **2.** The shock, vibration, or sound produced by a striking of one body against another. **3.** *Med.* A light, quick tapping of the finger tips upon the back, chest, or abdomen, for determining by resonance the condition of the organ beneath. **4.** The act of striking the percussion cap in a firearm. **5.** *Music* Percussion instruments. —*adj.* Of, pertaining to, or operating by percussion. [< L < *per-* through + *quatere* to shake]

percussion cap A small cap of thin metal, containing mercury fulminate or some other detonator, formerly used in ammunition to explode the propelling charge.

percussion instruments Musical instruments whose tone is produced by striking, as the timpani, cymbals, piano, etc.

per·di·em (per dē′əm, dī′əm) **1.** By the day. **2.** An allowance for expenses each day. [< L]

per·di·tion (pər·dish′ən) *n.* **1.** Eternal damnation; the utter loss of a soul. **2.** The place of eternal damnation; hell. [< OF < L < *per-* through, away + *dare* to give]

père (pâr) *n.* French Father: often used after a surname to distinguish father from son: Dumas *père*.

per·e·gri·nate (per′ə·gri·nāt′) *v.* **·nat·ed, ·nat·ing** *v.i.* **1.** To travel from place to place. —*v.t.* **2.** To travel through or along. [< L *peregrinari* to travel abroad] —**per′e·gri·na′tion** *n.* —**per′e·gri·na′tor** *n.*

per·e·grine (per′ə·grin) *adj.* **1.** Coming from foreign regions. **2.** Wandering. —*n.* The peregrine falcon. [< L < *peregre* abroad < *per-* through + *ager* land]

peregrine falcon 1. A falcon generally blackish blue above and white or gray below, formerly much used in falconry. **2.** An American subspecies of this falcon.

per·emp·to·ry (pə·remp′tər·ē, per′əmp·tôr′ē, -tō′rē) *adj.* **1.** Not admitting of appeal; decisive; absolute. **2.** Positive in opinion, etc.; imperious. **3.** Intolerant of opposition; dictatorial. **4.** *Law* Precluding or putting an end to debate or discussion; final. [< L < *per-* entirely + *emere* to take] —**per·emp′to·ri·ly** *adv.* —**per·emp′to·ri·ness** *n.*

per·en·ni·al (pə·ren′ē·əl) *adj.* **1.** Continuing or enduring through the year or through many years. **2.** Perpetual; everlasting; unceasing. **3.** *Bot.* Lasting more than two years. —*n.* A plant that grows for three or more years, usu. blossoming and fructifying annually. [< L < *per-* through + *annus* year] —**per·en′ni·al·ly** *adv.*

per·fect (*adj. & n.* pûr′fikt; *v.* pər·fekt′) *adj.* **1.** Having all the elements or qualities requisite to its nature or kind; complete. **2.** Without defect; flawless: *perfect* weather. **3.** Thoroughly and completely skilled or informed: a *perfect* violinist. **4.** Accurately corresponding to a type or original; exact: a *perfect* replica. **5.** Thorough; utter: He made a *perfect* nuisance of himself. **6.** Completely effective: a *perfect* answer. **7.** *Informal* Very great: a *perfect* horror of spiders. **8.** *Gram.* Denoting the tense of a verb expressing action completed in the past. Grammarians note in English a present perfect, past perfect (or pluperfect), and a future perfect tense. **9.** *Music* a Denoting the three intervals whose accuracy of intonation the human ear can recognize within precise limits, the **perfect octave**, the **perfect fifth**, and the **perfect fourth.** **b** Complete: a *perfect* cadence. —*n. Gram.* The perfect tense; also, a verb in this tense. —*v.t.* **1.** To bring to perfection; complete. **2.** To make thoroughly skilled or accomplished: to *perfect* oneself in an art. [< OF < L < *per-*thoroughly + *facere* to do, make] —**per·fect′er** *n.* —**per′fect·ly** *adv.* —**per′fect·ness** *n.*

per·fect·i·ble (pər·fek′tə·bəl) *adj.* Capable of being made perfect or of arriving at perfection. —**per·fect′i·bil′i·ty** *n.*

per·fec·tion (pər·fek′shən) *n.* **1.** The state or quality of being perfect. **2.** The embodiment of something that is perfect: As a hostess, she is *perfection*. **3.** Any quality, characteristic, or trait considered to be perfect. **4.** The highest degree of something. **5.** The act or process of perfecting.

per·fec·tion·ist (pər·fek′shən·ist) *n.* One who demands of himself or of others an exceedingly high degree of excellence.

per·fec·tive (pər·fek′tiv) *adj.* Tending to make perfect. —**per·fec′tive·ly** *adv.* —**per·fec′tive·ness** *n.*

per·fec·to (pər·fek′tō) *n. pl.* **·tos** A cigar of medium size, shaped to taper at either end. [< Sp., perfect]

perfect participle Past participle.

perfect pitch Absolute pitch.

per·fer·vid (pər·fûr′vid) *adj.* Excessively fervid; ardent; zealous. [< NL < L *per-* thoroughly + *fervidus* burning]

per·fid·i·ous (pər·fid′ē·əs) *adj.* Marked by or guilty of perfidy; treacherous. [< L *perfidia*] —**per·fid′i·ous·ly** *adv.* —**per·fid′i·ous·ness** *n.*

per·fi·dy (pûr′fə·dē) *n. pl.* **·dies** The act of violating faith, trust, or allegiance; treachery. [< MF < L < *per* through, under pretext of + *fides* faith]

per·fo·li·ate (pər·fō′lē·it, āt) *adj. Bot.* Growing so that the stem seems to pass through it, as a leaf. [< NL < L *per-* through + *folium* leaf] —**per·fo′li·a′tion** *n.*

per·fo·rate (*v.* pûr′fə·rāt; *adj.* pûr′fə·rit) *v.t.* **·rat·ed, ·rat·ing 1.** To make a hole or holes through, by or as by stamping or drilling. **2.** To pierce with holes in rows or patterns. —*adj.* Perforated. [< L < *per-* through + *forare* to bore]

—**per′fo·ra·ble** *adj.* —**per′fo·ra′tive, per′fo·ra·to′ry** (-rə·tôr′ē, -tō′rē) *adj.* —**per′fo·ra′tor** *n.*

per·fo·rat·ed (pûr′fə·rā′tid) *adj.* Pierced with a hole or holes; esp., pierced with lines of holes, as sheets of stamps.

per·fo·ra·tion (pûr′fə·rā′shən) *n.* **1.** The act of perforating, or the state of being perforated. **2.** A hole or series of holes drilled in or stamped through something.

per·force (pər·fôrs′, -fōrs′) *adv.* By or of necessity; necessarily. [< OF < *par* by (< L *per-*) + *force* force]

per·form (pər·fôrm′) *v.t.* **1.** To carry out in action; execute; do. **2.** To fulfil; discharge, as a duty or command. **3.** To act (a part) or give a performance of (a play, piece of music, etc.). —*v.i.* **4.** To carry through to completion an action, undertaking, etc. **5.** To give an exhibition or performance. [< OF < *par-* thoroughly (< L *per-*) + *fournir* to accomplish] —**per·form′a·ble** *adj.*

per·form·ance (pər·fôr′məns) *n.* **1.** An entertainment of some kind before an audience or spectators. **2.** A public presentation: The music had its first *performance* here. **3.** The act or manner of performing a play, part, piece of music, etc. **4.** Manner of operating or functioning: The car's *performance* improved. **5.** Any act, deed, or accomplishment.

per·form·er (pər·fôr′mər) *n.* One who performs; esp., an actor, musician, etc.

per·fume (pər·fyōōm′; *for n., usu.* pûr′fyōōm) *n.* **1.** A fragrant substance, usu. a volatile liquid, prepared to emit a pleasant odor; scent. **2.** A pleasant odor, as from flowers; fragrance. —**Syn.** See SMELL. —*v.t.* **·fumed, ·fum·ing** To fill or scent with a fragrant odor. [< MF < Ital. < *per-* through (< L) + *fumare* to smoke < LL *fumus* smoke]

per·fum·er (pər·fyōō′mər) *n.* **1.** One who makes or deals in perfumes. **2.** One who or that which perfumes.

per·fum·er·y (pər·fyōō′mər·ē) *n. pl.* **·er·ies 1.** The art or business of preparing perfumes. **2.** Perfumes in general, or a specific perfume. **3.** A place where perfumes are made.

per·func·to·ry (pər·fungk′tər·ē) *adj.* **1.** Done mechanically; careless; cursory. **2.** Having no zest or enthusiasm; dull. [< LL < L < *per-* through + *fungi* to perform] —**per·func′to·ri·ly** *adv.* —**per·func′to·ri·ness** *n.*

per·fuse (pər·fyōōz′) *v.t.* **·fused, ·fus·ing 1.** To permeate, suffuse, or sprinkle with a liquid, color, etc. **2.** To spread (a liquid, etc.) over or through something; diffuse. [< L < *per-* throughout + *fundere* to pour] —**per·fu′sion** (-fyōō′zhən) *n.* —**per·fu′sive** (-fyōō′siv) *adj.*

per·go·la (pûr′gə·lə) *n.* An arbor or covered walk made of trelliswork covered with vegetation or flowers. [< Ital., arbor < L *pergula* projecting roof, arbor]

per·haps (pər·haps′) *adv.* Maybe; possibly. [< PER + *happes*, pl. of *hap* chance]

peri- *prefix* **1.** Around; encircling: *periphery.* **2.** Situated near; adjoining: *perihelion.* [< Gk. *peri* around]

per·i·anth (per′ē·anth) *n. Bot.* The envelope of a flower, esp. one in which the calyx and corolla are so alike as to be indistinguishable. [< F < NL < Gk. *peri-* around + *anthos* flower]

per·i·car·di·al (per′ə·kär′dē·əl) *adj.* Of or pertaining to the pericardium. Also **per′i·car′di·ac** (-ak), **per′i·car′di·an.**

per·i·car·di·tis (per′ə·kär·dī′tis) *n. Pathol.* Inflammation of the pericardium.

per·i·car·di·um (per′ə·kär′dē·əm) *n. pl.* **·di·a** (-dē·ə) *Anat.* A membranous bag that surrounds and protects the heart. [< NL < Gk. < *peri-* around + *kardia* heart]

per·i·carp (per′ə·kärp) *n. Bot.* The wall of a ripened ovary or fruit, usu. in three layers, the epicarp, mesocarp, and endocarp: also called *seedcase, seed vessel.* [< NL < Gk. < *peri-* around + *karpos* fruit] —**per′i·car′pi·al** *adj.*

Per·i·cle·an (per′ə·klē′ən) *adj.* Pertaining to, characteristic of, or named after Pericles, or the period of his supremacy, when Greek art, drama, and statesmanship are considered to have been at their height.

per·i·cra·ni·um (per′ə·krā′nē·əm) *n. pl.* **·ni·a** (-nē·ə) *Anat.* The periosteum of the external surface of the cranium. [< NL < Gk. < *peri-* around + *kranion* skull] —**per′i·cra′ni·al** *adj.*

per·i·gee (per′ə·jē) *n. Astron.* The point in the orbit of the moon or of an artificial satellite at which it is nearest the earth: opposed to *apogee.* [< MF < Med.L < Gk. < *peri-*, near + *gē* earth] —**per′i·ge′al, per′i·ge′an** *adj.*

per·i·gon (per′ə·gon) *n. Geom.* An angle equal to two straight angles or 360 degrees.

per·i·he·li·on (per′ə·hē′lē·ən) *n. pl.* **·li·a** (-lē·ə) *Astron.* The point in the orbit of a planet or comet where it is nearest the sun: opposed to *aphelion.* [< NL < Gk. *peri-* around, near + *helios* sun]

per·il (per′əl) *n.* **1.** Exposure to the chance of injury; danger; risk. —*v.t.* **·iled** or **·illed, ·il·ing** or **·il·ling** To expose to danger; imperil. [< OF < L *periculum* trial, danger]

per·i·lous (per′əl·əs) *adj.* Involving, or attended with peril;

hazardous; risky. — **per'il·ous·ly** *adv.* — **per'il·ous·ness** *n.*

per·i·lune (per'ə-lōōn') *n.* That point in the lunar orbit of an artificial satellite or other celestial body which is nearest to the moon. [< PERI- + Fr. *lune* moon]

pe·rim·e·ter (pə-rim'ə-tər) *n.* **1.** The boundary line of any figure of two dimensions. **2.** The sum of the sides of a plane figure. [< L < Gk. < *peri-* around + *metron* measure] — **per·i·met·ric** (per'ə-met'rik) or **·ri·cal** *adj.*

per·i·ne·um (per'ə-nē'əm) *n. pl.* **·ne·a** (-nē'ə) *Anat.* **1.** The region of the body between the genital organs and the rectum. **2.** The entire region comprising the anus and the internal genitals. Also **per·i·nae'um.** [< LL < Gk. < *peri-* around + *inein* to empty out] — **per'i·ne'al** *adj.*

pe·ri·od (pir'ē-əd) *n.* **1.** A portion of time marked or defined by certain conditions, events, etc.: a *period* of rest. **2.** A portion or lapse of time, as in a process or development, a stage. **3.** A portion of time into which something is divided: Our new school day has seven *periods*. **4.** *Astron.* The time it takes a planet or satellite to revolve once about its primary. **5.** *Geol.* One of the divisions of geologic time. **6.** *Physics* The time that elapses between any two successive similar phases of an oscillation or other regularly repeated cyclical motion. **7.** A dot (.) placed on the line, used as a mark of punctuation after every complete declarative sentence, after most abbreviations, etc. **8.** The pause at the end of a sentence. **9.** *Pathol.* A stage distinguished in the course of a disease. **10.** Menstruation. **11.** The completion of something. [< OF < L < Gk. < *peri-* around + *hodos* way]

pe·ri·od·ic (pir'ē-od'ik) *adj.* **1.** Of, pertaining to, or like a period. **2.** Recurring at regular intervals. **3.** Intermittent. **4.** Of or expressed in periodic sentences. **5.** *Physics* Recurring after a definite interval. — **pe'ri·od'i·cal·ly** *adv.*

pe·ri·od·i·cal (pir'ē-od'i-kəl) *adj.* **1.** Of or pertaining to publications that appear at fixed intervals of more than one day; also, published at regular intervals. **2.** Periodic. — *n.* A periodical publication.

pe·ri·o·dic·i·ty (pir'ē-ə-dis'ə-tē) *n.* The quality of being periodic or of recurring at definite intervals of time.

periodic law *Chem.* The statement that the physical and chemical properties of the elements are related to their atomic numbers, and that they recur periodically when the elements are arranged in the order of these numbers.

periodic sentence A sentence so constructed as to suspend completion of both sense and structure until the close.

periodic table *Chem.* A table in which the elements are arranged in groups as determined by the periodic law.

per·i·os·te·um (per'ē-os'tē-əm) *n. Anat.* A tough, fibrous vascular membrane that surrounds and nourishes the bones. [< NL < LL < Gk. < *peri-* around + *osteon* bone] — **per'i·os'te·al, peri·os'te·ous** *adj.*

per·i·pa·tet·ic (per'i-pə-tet'ik) *adj.* Walking about from place to place. — *n.* One given to walking about. [< MF < L < Gk. < *peri-* around + *pateein* to walk]

Per·i·pa·tet·ic (per'i-pə-tet'ik) *adj.* Of or pertaining to the philosophy of Aristotle, who lectured to his disciples while walking. — *n.* A disciple of Aristotle.

pe·riph·er·al (pə-rif'ər-əl) *adj.* **1.** Of or consisting of a periphery. **2.** Capable of perceiving images laterally that are not directly in one's line of sight: *peripheral* vision. **3.** Not central; marginal: of *peripheral* importance. **4.** *Anat.* Outer; external. — **pe·riph'er·al·ly** *adv.*

pe·riph·er·y (pə-rif'ər-ē) *n. pl.* **·er·ies** **1.** The outer part surface, or boundary of something. **2.** A surrounding region, area, or country. [< OF < LL < Gk. < *peri-* around + *pherein* to carry]

pe·riph·ra·sis (pə-rif'rə-sis) *n. pl.* **·ses** (-sēz) A roundabout method or instance of expressing something; circumlocution. [< L < Gk. < *peri-* around + *phrazein* to declare]

per·i·phras·tic (per'ə-fras'tik) *adj.* **1.** Of the nature of or involving periphrasis; circumlocutory. **2.** *Gram.* Denoting a construction in which a phrase is substituted for an inflected form, as, *the hat of John* for *John's hat.* Also **per'i·phras'ti·cal.** — **per'i·phras'ti·cal·ly** *adv.*

per·i·scope (per'ə-skōp) *n.* An instrument consisting of prisms or mirrors so arranged as to reflect light rays down a vertical tube, used to guide submarines, etc. [< Gk. *peri-* around + *skopeein* to look] — **per·i·scop·ic** (per'ə-skop'ik) or **i·cal** *adj.*

per·ish (per'ish) *v.i.* **1.** To suffer a violent or untimely death. **2.** To pass from existence. [< OF < L < *per-* away + *ire* to go]

per·ish·a·ble (per'ish-ə-bəl) *adj.* **1.** Liable to perish. **2.** Liable to speedy decay, as fruit in transportation. — *n. Usu. pl.* Something liable to decay, as food. — **per'ish·a·ble·ness, per'ish·a·bil'i·ty** *n.* — **per'ish·a·bly** *adv.*

PERISCOPE

per·i·stal·sis (per'ə-stôl'sis, -stal'-) *n. pl.* **·ses** (-sēz) *Physiol.* A contractile muscular movement of any hollow organ, as of the alimentary canal, whereby the contents are gradually propelled toward the point of expulsion.

[< NL < Gk. < *peri-* around + *stellein* to place] — **per'i·stal'tic** *adj.*

per·i·style (per'ə-stīl) *n. Archit.* **1.** A system of columns about a building or an internal court. **2.** An area or space so enclosed. [< MF < L < Gk. < *peri-* around + *stylos* pillar] — **per'i·sty·lar** *adj.*

per·i·to·ne·um (per'ə-tə-nē'əm) *n. pl.* **·ne·a** (-nē'ə) *Anat.* A serous membrane that lines the abdominal cavity and is a more or less complete covering for the viscera. Also **per·i·to·nae'um.** [< LL < Gk. < *peri-* around + *teinein* to stretch] — **per'i·to·ne'al** or **·nae'al** *adj.*

per·i·to·ni·tis (per'ə-tə-nī'tis) *n. Pathol.* Inflammation of the peritoneum.

per·i·wig (per'ə-wig) *n.* A peruke or wig. [Earlier *perwyke*, alt. of *perruck* < MF *perruque*]

per·i·win·kle[1] (per'ə-wing'kəl) *n.* Any of several small marine snails, some of which are edible. [OE *pinewincle*, ? < L *pina* mussel + OE *wincle* a shellfish]

per·i·win·kle[2] (per'ə-wing'kəl) *n.* A plant having shining, evergreen leaves and blue or sometimes white flowers: also called *myrtle.* [OE < L *pervinca*]

per·jure (pûr'jər) *v.t.* **·jured, ·jur·ing** **1.** To make (oneself) guilty of perjury. **2.** To find guilty of or involved in perjury. [< OF < L < *per-* thoroughly + *jurare* to swear] — **per'jur·er** *n.*

per·jured (pûr'jərd) *adj.* Guilty of or constituting perjury.

per·ju·ry (pûr'jə-rē) *n. pl.* **·ries** *Law* The wilful giving of false testimony or the withholding of material facts or evidence while under oath in a judicial proceeding.

perk[1] (pûrk) *v.i.* **1.** To recover one's spirits or vigor: with *up.* **2.** To carry oneself or lift one's head jauntily. — *v.t.* **3.** To raise quickly or smartly, as the ears: often with *up.* **4.** To make (oneself) trim and smart in appearance: often with *up* or *out.* — *adj.* Perky. [ME *perken;* ? var. of PERCH[1]]

perk[2] (pûrk) *v.i. Informal* To percolate.

perk·y (pûr'kē) *adj.* **perk·i·er, perk·i·est** **1.** Jaunty; sprightly; pert. **2.** Spirited and self-assured. Also **perk.** — **perk'i·ly** *adv.* — **perk'i·ness** *n.*

per·ma·frost (pûr'mə-frôst, -frost) *n.* The part of the earth's surface in arctic regions that is permanently frozen.

per·ma·nence (pûr'mə-nəns) *n.* The state or quality of being permanent.

per·ma·nen·cy (pûr'mə-nən-sē) *n. pl.* **·cies** **1.** Permanence. **2.** Something permanent.

per·ma·nent (pûr'mə-nənt) *adj.* Continuing in the same state or without essential change; enduring; durable; fixed. — *n.* A permanent wave. [< OF < L < *per-* through + *manere* to remain] — **per'ma·nent·ly** *adv.*

Permanent Court of International Justice An international tribunal established under the Covenant of the League of Nations (1921) and superseded in 1945 by the International Court of Justice: also called *World Court.*

permanent wave An artificial wave mechanically or chemically set in the hair and lasting several months.

per·man·ga·nate (pər-mang'gə-nāt) *n. Chem.* A dark purple salt of permanganic acid.

per·man·gan·ic acid (pûr'man-gan'ik) *Chem.* An acid, $HMnO_4$, that is a powerful oxidizer in aqueous solutions.

per·me·a·bil·i·ty (pûr'mē-ə-bil'ə-tē) *n.* The quality or condition of being permeable, as by liquids, gases, etc.

per·me·a·ble (pûr'mē-ə-bəl) *adj.* Allowing passage, esp. of fluids. — **per'me·a·bly** *adv.*

per·me·ance (pûr'mē-əns) *n.* **1.** The act of permeating. **2.** *Electr.* The ability to be traversed by magnetic lines of force.

per·me·ate (pûr'mē-āt) *v.* **·at·ed, ·at·ing** *v.t.* **1.** To spread thoroughly through; pervade. **2.** To pass through the pores or interstices of. — *v.i.* **3.** To spread itself. [< L < *per-* through + *meare* to pass] — **per'me·ant** *adj.* — **per'me·a'tion** *n.* — **per'me·a'tive** *adj.*

Per·mi·an (pûr'mē-ən) *Geol. adj.* Of or pertaining to the latest period of the Paleozoic era. — *n.* The Permian rock system or period. See table for GEOLOGY. [after *Perm,* former E. Russian province]

per·mis·si·ble (pər-mis'ə-bəl) *adj.* That can be permitted; allowable. — **per·mis'si·bil'i·ty** *n.* — **per·mis'si·bly** *adv.*

per·mis·sion (pər-mish'ən) *n.* **1.** The act of permitting or allowing. **2.** Formal authorization or consent.

per·mis·sive (pər-mis'iv) *adj.* **1.** Permitting; granting permission. **2.** Permitted; optional. **3.** Not strict in discipline. — **per·mis'sive·ly** *adv.* — **per·mis'sive·ness** *n.*

per·mit (*v.* pər-mit'; *n.* pûr'mit) *v.* **·mit·ted, ·mit·ting** *v.t.* **1.** To allow the doing of; consent to. **2.** To give (someone) leave or consent; authorize. **3.** To afford opportunity for. — *v.i.* **4.** To afford possibility or opportunity. **5.** To allow. — *n.* **1.** Permission to do something. **2.** An official document or certificate authorizing performance of a specified activity; license. [< L < *per-* through + *mittere* to send, let go] — **per·mit'ter** *n.*

per·mut·a·ble (pər-myōō'tə-bəl) *adj.* Capable of being changed or of undergoing change or interchange.

per·mu·ta·tion (pûr′myŏŏ·tā′shən)   n.   **1.** The act of re-arranging; transformation. **2.** *Math.* Change in the order of sequence of elements or objects in a series; esp., the making of all possible changes of sequence, as *abc, acb, bac,* etc.

per·mute (pər·myōōt′)   v.t.   **·mut·ed, ·mut·ing** To subject to permutation, esp., to change the order of. [< OF < L < *per-* thoroughly + *mutare* to change]

per·ni·cious (pər·nish′əs)   adj.   **1.** Having the power of destroying or injuring; very injurious; deadly. **2.** Malicious; wicked. [< MF < L < *per-* thoroughly + *nex, necis* death] **—per·ni′cious·ly** adv. **—per·ni′cious·ness** n. **—Syn. 1.** Noxious, baneful, deleterious, detrimental.

pernicious anemia   *Pathol.*   Severe anemia characterized by inadequate development of red blood corpuscles and progressive disturbances in the muscular, nervous, and gastrointestinal systems.

per·nick·e·ty (pər·nik′ə·tē)   adj.   Persnickety.

per·o·rate (per′ə·rāt)   v.i.   **·rat·ed, ·rat·ing 1.** To speak at length; harangue. **2.** To sum up or conclude a speech.

per·o·ra·tion (per′ə·rā′shən)   n.   The concluding portion of an oration or the summing up of an argument. [< L < *per-* through + *orare* to speak]

per·ox·ide (pə·rok′sīd)   n.   *Chem.* **1.** An oxide having the highest proportion of oxygen for a given series. **2.** Hydrogen peroxide. Also **per·ox′id** (-sid). **—v.t. ·id·ed, ·id·ing** To bleach, as hair, with peroxide.

per·pen·dic·u·lar (pûr′pən·dik′yə·lər)   adj.   **1.** Being at right angles to the plane of the horizon; upright or vertical. **2.** *Math.* Meeting a given line or plane at right angles **—** n. **1.** A perpendicular line or plane. **2.** A plumb rule. **3.** A line at right angles to another line or to a plane. [< OF < L *perpendiculum* plumb line] **—per′pen·dic′u·lar′i·ty** (-lar′ə·tē) n. **—per′pen·dic′u·lar·ly** adv.

per·pe·trate (pûr′pə·trāt)   v.t.   **·trat·ed, ·trat·ing** To do, perform, or commit (a crime, etc.). [< L < *per-* thoroughly + *patrare* to accomplish] **—per′pe·tra′tion** n. **—per′pe·tra′tor** n.

per·pet·u·al (pər·pech′ŏŏ·əl)   adj.   **1.** Continuing or lasting forever or for an unlimited time. **2.** Incessant. [< OF < L < *per-* through + *petere* to seek] **—per·pet′u·al·ly** adv. **—Syn. (adj.) 1.** eternal, endless, interminable.

perpetual motion   Continuous motion of a mechanism, conceived of as a capacity of doing work indefinitely by the energy supplied through its own operation.

per·pet·u·ate (pər·pech′ŏŏ·āt)   v.t.   **·at·ed, ·at·ing 1.** To make perpetual or enduring. **2.** To cause to remain known, current, etc.: to *perpetuate* a myth. [< L *perpetuare* to perpetuate] **—per·pet′u·a′tion** n. **—per·pet′u·a′tor** n.

per·pe·tu·i·ty (pûr′pə·tōō′ə·tē, -tyōō′-)   n., pl. **·ties 1.** The quality or state of being perpetual. **2.** Something perpetual, as a perpetual annuity. **3.** Unending or unlimited time. [See PERPETUAL.]

per·plex (pər·pleks′)   v.t.   **1.** To cause to hesitate or become confused, as from doubt, difficulties encountered, etc.; puzzle. **2.** To make complicated, intricate, or confusing. **—Syn. 1.** bewilder, mystify, confound. Compare BAFFLE.

per·plexed (pər·plekst′)   adj.   **1.** Confused; puzzled; bewildered. **2.** Of a complicated character; involved. [Appar. alter. of obs. *perplex*, adj., intricate < L *perplexus* involved] **—per·plex′ed·ly** (-plek′sid·lē) adv.

per·plex·ing (pər·plek′sing)   adj.   Confusing; puzzling. **—per·plex′ing·ly** adv.

per·plex·i·ty (pər·plek′sə·tē)   n., pl. **·ties 1.** The state, quality, or condition of being perplexed; doubt; confusion; bewilderment. **2.** That which perplexes. **3.** The quality or condition of being intricate or complicated.

per·qui·site (pûr′kwə·zit)   n.   **1.** Any incidental profit, payment, etc., beyond what is earned as salary or wages. **2.** Any privilege or benefit owed or claimed as one's due. [< L *perquisitum* a thing diligently sought]

perse (pûrs)   adj.   Dark grayish blue. **—** n. A dark grayish blue. [< OF *pers* < LL *persus* < *Persicus* Persian]

per se (pûr sē′, sā′)   *Latin*   By itself; intrinsically.

per·se·cute (pûr′sə·kyōōt)   v.t.   **·cut·ed, ·cut·ing 1.** To annoy or harass persistently. **2.** To maltreat or oppress because of race, religion, or beliefs. [< F < L *persecutus,* pp. of *persequi* to pursue] **—per′se·cu′tion** n. **—per′se·cu′tive** adj. **—per′se·cu′tor** n.

Per·seph·o·ne (pər·sef′ə·nē)   In Greek mythology, the daughter of Zeus and Demeter, abducted to the underworld by Pluto, but allowed to return to the earth for part of each year: identified with the Roman *Proserpine.*

Per·seus (pûr′syōōs, -sē·əs)   In Greek mythology, the son of Zeus and Danae, slayer of Medusa and rescuer of Andromeda. **—** n. A northern constellation. See CONSTELLATION.

per·se·ver·ance (pûr′sə·vir′əns)   n.   **1.** The act or habit of persevering. **2.** *Theol.* In Calvinism, the continuance in grace and certain salvation of those chosen by God.

per·se·vere (pûr′sə·vir′)   v.i.   **·vered, ·ver·ing** To persist in any purpose or enterprise; strive in spite of difficulties, etc. [< OF < L < *per-* thoroughly + *severus* strict] **—per′se·ver′ing** adj. **—per′se·ver′ing·ly** adv.

Per·sian (pûr′zhən, -shən)   adj.   Of or pertaining to Persia (now Iran), or its people, language, or culture. **—** n. **1.** A native or inhabitant of Persia or Iran. **2.** The Iranian language of the Persians. [< OF < L *Persia* Persia]

Persian Empire   An empire of SW Asia, extending from the Indus to the Mediterranean, destroyed by Alexander the Great (331 B.C.).

Persian lamb   **1.** The lamb of the karakul sheep. **2.** Its black, gray, or brown curled fur.

Persian wheel   A noria.

per·si·flage (pûr′sə·fläzh)   n.   A light, flippant style of conversation or writing. [< F < *persifler* to banter]

per·sim·mon (pər·sim′ən)   n.   **1.** Any of several trees having reddish orange fruit with an astringent taste when not ripe. **2.** The fruit of these trees. [< Algonquian]

per·sist (pər·sist′, -zist′)   v.i.   **1.** To continue firmly in some course, state, etc., esp. despite opposition or difficulties. **2.** To be insistent, as in repeating or continuing an action. **3.** To continue to exist; endure. [< L < *per-* thoroughly + *sistere* causative of *stare* to stand]

per·sis·tence (pər·sis′təns, -zis′-)   n.   **1.** The act, condition, or quality of persisting. **2.** Perseverance. **3.** The continuance of an effect longer than the cause that first produced it. Also **per·sis′ten·cy.**

per·sis·tent (pər·sis′tənt, -zis′-)   adj.   **1.** Persevering or stubborn in a course or resolve. **2.** Enduring; permanent. **3.** Constantly repeated. **—per·sis′tent·ly** adv.

per·snick·e·ty (pər·snik′ə·tē)   adj.   *Informal* **1.** Unduly fastidious; fussy. **2.** Demanding minute care or pains. Also *pernickety.* [< dial. E] **—per·snick′e·ti·ness** n.

per·son (pûr′sən)   n.   **1.** Any human being considered as a distinct entity or personality; an individual. **2.** The body of a human being. **3.** One's characteristic appearance or physical condition. **4.** *Law* Any human being, corporation, or body politic having legal rights and duties. **5.** *Theol.* One of the three individualities in the Trinity **6.** *Gram.* **a** A modification of the pronoun and verb that distinguishes the speaker (**first person**), the person or thing spoken to (**second person**), and the person or thing spoken of (**third person**). **b** Any of the forms or inflections indicating this, as *I* or *we, you, he, she, it.* **—in person 1.** Physically present. **2.** Acting for oneself. [< F < L *persona* actor's mask, character]

per·so·na (pər·sō′nə)   n., pl. **·nae** (-nē)   *Usu. pl.* A character in a drama, novel, etc. [L, person]

per·son·a·ble (pûr′sən·ə·bəl)   adj.   Attractive or pleasing in personal appearance. **—per′son·a·bly** adv.

per·son·age (pûr′sən·ij)   n.   **1.** A man or woman of importance or rank. **2.** A person; individual. **3.** A character in fiction, drama, history, etc.

per·so·na gra·ta (pər·sō′nə grä′tə, grā′tə)   *Latin* An acceptable or welcome person.

per·son·al (pûr′sən·əl)   adj.   **1.** Pertaining to or concerning a particular person; not general or public. **2.** Relating to, having the qualities of, or constituting a person or persons. **3.** Done in person: a *personal* service. **4.** Of or pertaining to the body or appearance: *personal* beauty. **5.** Directly referring to an individual, esp. in a critical or disparaging manner: *personal* remarks. **6.** *Law* Pertaining to property regarded as movable or temporary: distinguished from *real.* **7.** *Gram.* Denoting or indicating person: *personal* pronouns. **—** n. **1.** *Law* A movable or temporary article or property; chattel. **2.** A paragraph or advertisement of personal reference or application. [< OF < LL < L *persona* a person]

per·son·al·i·ty (pûr′sən·al′ə·tē)   n., pl. **·ties 1.** Distinctive qualities or characteristics of a person. **2.** A person of outstanding or distinctive qualities. **3.** That which constitutes a person; personal existence. **4.** *Often pl.* A remark or reference, often disparaging, of a personal nature.

per·son·al·ize (pûr′sən·əl·īz′)   v.t.   **·ized, ·iz·ing 1.** To make personal. **2.** To personify. **3.** To mark with one's name, initials, etc., as stationery or handkerchiefs.

per·son·al·ly (pûr′sən·əl·ē)   adv.   **1.** In person; not through an agent. **2.** As regards one's own opinions, tastes, etc. **3.** With regard to a person as an individual. **4.** As though intended for or directed toward oneself.

personal pronoun   *Gram.*   A pronoun that varies in form according to person, gender, case, and number, as *we, their, him.*

per·son·al·ty (pûr′sən·əl·tē)   n., pl. **·ties** *Law* Personal property.

per·so·na non gra·ta (pər·sō′nə non grä′tə, grā′tə)   *Latin* A person who is not welcome or acceptable.

per·son·ate (pûr′sən·āt)   v.t.   **·at·ed, ·at·ing 1.** To act the part of, as a character in a play. **2.** *Law* To impersonate with intent to deceive. [See PERSON.] **—per·son·a·tion** *n.* **—per·son·a·tive** *adj.* **—per·son·a·tor** *n.*

per·son·i·fi·ca·tion (pər·son′ə·fə·kā′shən) *n.* **1.** The figurative endowment of inanimate objects or qualities with personality or human attributes. **2.** Exemplification of a quality or attribute in one's person; embodiment: She was the *personification* of joy. **3.** Impersonation.

per·son·i·fy (pər·son′ə·fī) *v.t.* **·fied**, **·fy·ing 1.** To think of or represent as having life or human qualities. **2.** To represent (an abstraction or inanimate object) as a person. **3.** To be the embodiment of; typify. [< F < L *persona* mask, person + *facere* to make] **—per·son′i·fi′er** *n.*

per·son·nel (pûr′sə·nel′) *n.* The persons employed in a business, in military service, etc. [See PERSONAL.]

per·spec·tive (pər·spek′tiv) *n.* **1.** The art or theory of representing solid objects on a flat surface in such a way as to convey the impression of depth and distance. **2.** The effect of distance upon the appearance of objects. **3.** The relative importance of facts or matters from any special point of view. **4.** Judgment of facts, circumstances, etc., with regard to their importance. **5.** A distant view, vista, or prospect. **—adj.** Pertaining to, characterized by, or represented in perspective. [< Med.L < LL < L < *per-* through + *specere* to look] **—per·spec′tive·ly** *adv.*

per·spi·ca·cious (pûr′spə·kā′shəs) *adj.* **1.** Keenly discerning or understanding. **2.** *Archaic* Sharp-sighted. [< L *perspicax, -acis* sharp-sighted] **—per′spi·ca′cious·ly** *adv.* **—per′spi·ca′cious·ness** *n.*

per·spi·cac·i·ty (pûr′spə·kas′ə·tē) *n.* Keenness in mental penetration or discernment.

per·spi·cu·i·ty (pûr′spə·kyōō′ə·tē) *n.* **1.** Clearness of expression or style; lucidity. **2.** Perspicacity.

per·spic·u·ous (pər·spik′yōō·əs) *adj.* Having the quality of perspicuity; clear; lucid. **—per·spic′u·ous·ly** *adv.* **—per·spic′u·ous·ness** *n.*

per·spi·ra·tion (pûr′spə·rā′shən) *n.* **1.** The act or process of perspiring. **2.** The fluid excreted; sweat. **3.** Arduous physical effort. **—per·spir·a·to·ry** (pər·spī′rə·tôr′ē) *adj.*

per·spire (pər·spīr′) *v.* **·spired**, **·spir·ing** *v.i.* **1.** To give off a saline fluid through the pores of the skin; sweat. **—v.t.** **2.** To give off through pores; exude. [< MF < L < *per-* through + *spirare* to breathe]

per·suade (pər·swād′) *v.t.* **·suad·ed**, **·suad·ing 1.** To induce (someone) to do something. **2.** To induce to a belief; convince. [< MF < L < *per-* thoroughly + *suadere* to advise] **—per·suad′a·ble** *adj.* **—per·suad′er** *n.*

per·sua·sion (pər·swā′zhən) *n.* **1.** The act of persuading or of using persuasive methods. **2.** Ability to persuade. **3.** The state of being persuaded; settled opinion; conviction. **4.** An accepted creed or belief. **5.** A religious sect. **6.** Party; group; faction.

per·sua·sive (pər·swā′siv) *adj.* Having power or tendency to persuade. **—n.** That which persuades or tends to persuade. **—per·sua′sive·ly** *adv.* **—per·sua′sive·ness** *n.*

pert (pûrt) *adj.* **1.** Impertinent; saucy. **2.** *Dial.* Handsome and lively. [Aphetic var. of ME *apert* < OF, open, impudent] **—pert′ly** *adv.* **—pert′ness** *n.*

per·tain (pər·tān′) *v.i.* **1.** To have reference; relate. **2.** To belong as an adjunct, function, quality, etc. **3.** To be fitting or appropriate. **—pertaining to** Having to do with; belonging or relating to. [< OF < L < *per-* through + *tenere* to hold]

per·ti·na·cious (pûr′tə·nā′shəs) *adj.* **1.** Tenacious of purpose; adhering fixedly to a pursuit or opinion. **2.** Stubbornly or doggedly persistent. [< L < *per-* thoroughly, very + *tenax, -acis* tenacious] **—per′ti·na′cious·ly** *adv.*

per·ti·nac·i·ty (pûr′tə·nas′ə·tē) *n.* *pl.* **·ties 1.** Tenacity of purpose; unyielding adherence. **2.** Obstinacy.

per·ti·nent (pûr′tə·nənt) *adj.* Related to or properly bearing upon the matter in hand; relevant. [See PERTAIN.] **—per′ti·nence, per′ti·nen·cy** *n.* **—per′ti·nent·ly** *adv.*

per·turb (pər·tûrb′) *v.t.* **1.** To disquiet or disturb greatly; alarm; agitate. **2.** To throw into disorder; cause confusion in. [< OF < L < *per-* thoroughly + *turbare* to disturb] **—per·turb′a·ble** *adj.* **—per′tur·ba′tion** *n.*

pe·ruke (pə·rōōk′) *n.* A wig; esp. one worn by men in the 17th and 18th centuries: also *periwig*. [< MF *perruque* < Ital. *perrucca*]

pe·rus·al (pə·rōō′zəl) *n.* The act or procedure of reading or examining carefully; a thorough reading or scrutiny.

pe·ruse (pə·rōōz′) *v.t.* **·rused**, **·rus·ing 1.** To read carefully or attentively. **2.** To read. **3.** To examine; scrutinize. [< PER- + USE, v.] **—pe·rus′a·ble** *adj.* **—pe·rus′er** *n.*

Pe·ru·vi·an (pə·rōō′vē·ən) *adj.* Of or pertaining to Peru or its inhabitants, etc. **—n.** A native or inhabitant of Peru. **Peruvian bark** Cinchona.

per·vade (pər·vād′) *v.t.* **·vad·ed**, **·vad·ing** To spread through every part of; be diffused throughout; permeate. [< L < *per-* through + *vadere* to go] **—per·va′sion** (-zhən) *n.*

per·va·sive (pər·vā′siv) *adj.* Thoroughly penetrating or permeating. **—per·va′sive·ly** *adv.* **—per·va′sive·ness** *n.*

per·verse (pər·vûrs′) *adj.* **1.** Willfully deviating from acceptable or conventional behavior, opinion, etc. **2.** Refractory; capricious. **3.** Petulant; cranky. **4.** Morally wrong or erring; wicked; perverted. [See PERVERT.] **—per·verse′ly** *adv.* **—per·verse′ness** *n.*

per·ver·sion (pər·vûr′zhən, -shən) *n.* **1.** The act of perverting, or the state of being perverted. **2.** A perverted form, act, use, etc. **3.** Deviation from the normal in sexual desires or activities.

per·ver·si·ty (pər·vûr′sə·tē) *n.* *pl.* **·ties 1.** The state or quality of being perverse. **2.** An instance of perverseness.

per·vert (*v.* pər·vûrt′; *n.* pûr′vərt) *v.t.* **1.** To turn to an improper use or purpose; misapply. **2.** To distort the meaning or intent of; misconstrue. **3.** To turn from approved opinions or conduct; lead astray. **4.** To deprave; debase; corrupt. **—n.** One characterized by or practicing sexual perversion. [< F < L < *per-* away + *vertere* to turn] **—per·vert′er** *n.* **—per·vert′i·ble** *adj.*

per·vert·ed (pər·vûr′tid) *adj.* **1.** Deviating widely from what is right or acceptable; distorted. **2.** Characterized by viciousness, sexual perversion, etc. **—per·vert′ed·ly** *adv.*

per·vi·ous (pûr′vē·əs) *adj.* **1.** Capable of being penetrated. **2.** Open to reason, suggestions, etc. [< L *pervius* having a way through] **—per′vi·ous·ly** *adv.* **—per′vi·ous·ness** *n.*

pe·se·ta (pə·sā′tə, *Sp.* pā·sā′tä) *n.* The standard monetary unit of Spain, equivalent to 100 centimos: in 1960 worth about 2 U.S. cents; also, a silver coin of this value. [< Sp., dim. of *pesa* weight]

pes·ky (pes′kē) *adj.* **·ki·er**, **·ki·est** *U.S. Informal* Annoying; troublesome. [Prob. < PEST + -Y²] **—pes′ki·ly** *adv.*

pe·so (pā′sō) *n.* *pl.* **·sos 1.** The standard monetary unit of various Spanish-speaking countries, as Argentina, Mexico, or the Philippines, equivalent to 100 centavos. **2.** A coin or note of this denomination. [< Sp., orig., a weight < L *pensum*, orig. pp. neut. of *pendere* to weigh]

pes·sa·ry (pes′ə·rē) *n.* *pl.* **·ries** *Med.* **1.** A device worn internally to remedy a uterine displacement. **2.** A contraceptive device worn over or in the uterine cervix. [< Med.L < L < Gk. *pessos* oval stone]

pes·si·mism (pes′ə·miz′əm) *n.* **1.** A disposition to take a gloomy or cynical view of affairs: opposed to *optimism.* **2.** The doctrine that the world and life are essentially evil. [< L *pessimus* worst + -ISM] **—pes′si·mist** *n.* **—pes′si·mis′tic** or **·ti·cal** *adj.* **—pes′si·mis′ti·cal·ly** *adv.*

pest (pest) *n.* **1.** An annoying person or thing. **2.** A destructive or injurious insect, plant, etc. **3.** A virulent epidemic, esp. of plague. [< MF < L *pestis* plague]

pes·ter (pes′tər) *v.t.* To harass with petty and persistent annoyances; bother; plague. [< OF < *em-* in + LL *pastorium* foot shackles] **—pes′ter·er** *n.*

pest·hole (pest′hōl′) *n.* A squalid or insanitary place in which disease is likely to occur and spread.

pes·ti·cide (pes′tə·sīd) *n.* A chemical or other substance used to destroy plant and animal pests. **—pes′ti·ci′dal** *adj.*

pes·tif·er·ous (pes·tif′ər·əs) *adj.* **1.** *Informal* Annoying; bothersome. **2.** Carrying or spreading infectious disease. **3.** Having an evil or harmful influence. [< L < *pestis* plague + *ferre* to bear] **—pes·tif′er·ous·ly** *adv.* **—pes·tif′er·ous·ness** *n.*

pes·ti·lence (pes′tə·ləns) *n.* **1.** Any widespread, often fatal infectious or contagious disease, as cholera or the bubonic plague. **2.** A noxious or malign doctrine, influence, etc. **—pes′ti·len′tial** (-len′shəl) *adj.*

pes·ti·lent (pes′tə·lənt) *adj.* **1.** Tending to produce infectious or epidemic disease. **2.** Having a malign influence or effect. **3.** Making trouble; vexatious. [< OF < L < *pestis* plague] **—pes′ti·lent·ly** *adv.*

pes·tle (pes′əl) *n.* **1.** An implement used for crushing, pulverizing, or mixing substances in or as in a mortar. **2.** A vertical moving bar employed in pounding, as in a stamp mill, etc. **—** *v.t. & v.i.* **·tled**, **·tling** To pound, grind, or mix with or as with a pestle. [< OF < L < *pistus*, pp. of *pinsere* to pound]

PESTLE (a) IN MORTAR (b)

pet¹ (pet) *n.* **1.** A tame animal treated lovingly or kept as a companion or playmate. **2.** Any loved and cherished creature or thing. **3.** A favorite: teacher's *pet.* **—adj. 1.** Tamed or kept as a pet. **2.** Regarded as a favorite; cherished. **—v.** **pet·ted**, **pet·ting** **—v.t. 1.** To stroke or caress. **2.** To treat indulgently; coddle. **—v.i. 3.** *U.S. Slang* To make love by kissing and caressing. [< dial. E (Scottish), ? < F *petit* little one]

pet² (pet) *n.* A fit of pique or ill temper. [Origin unknown]

pet·al (pet′l) *n. Bot.* One of the divisions or leaflike parts of a corolla. For illus. see FLOWER. [< NL < Gk. *petalon* leaf] **—pet′aled** or **pet′alled** *adj.*

-petal *combining form* Seeking: *centripetal.* [< L *petere* to seek]

pet·a·lif·er·ous (pet′ə·lif′ər·əs) *adj.* Bearing petals.

pe·tard (pi·tärd′) *n.* **1.** An explosive device formerly used to break through walls, gates, etc. **2.** A small firecracker exploding with a loud report. [< MF < OF < L *peditum*, orig. pp. neut. of *pedere* to break wind]

pet·cock (pet′cock′) *n. Mech.* A small valve or faucet, used for draining, releasing pressure, etc. Also **pet cock.** [? < obs. *pet* a fart + COCK¹]

pe·ter (pē′tər) *v.i. Informal* To diminish gradually and then cease or disappear: followed by *out.* [Orig. U.S. mining slang, ? < F *péter* (*dans la main*) to come to nothing]

Pe·ter (pē′tər) One of the twelve apostles, reputed author of two New Testament epistles: called **Saint Peter.** Also **Simon Peter.** — *n.* Either of the two books of the New Testament that bear his name. [< LL < Gk. *petros* stone]

Peter Pan The hero of J. M. Barrie's play (1904) of the same name, a little boy who remained perpetually a child.

Peter Pan collar A flat collar with rounded ends, used on girls' and women's blouses, dresses, etc.

pet·i·o·late (pet′ē·ə·lāt) *adj.* Having a petiole. Also **pet′i·o·lat′ed.**

pet·i·ole (pet′ē·ōl) *n.* **1.** *Bot.* The stem or slender stalk of a leaf; a leafstalk. **2.** *Anat.* A peduncle. [< L *petiolus*, orig. dim. of *pes, pedis* foot] — **pet′i·o·lar** *adj.*

pet·it (pet′ē) *adj. Law* Small; lesser; minor: *petit* jury: also spelled *petty.* [< OF, small]

pe·tite (pə·tēt′) *adj. fem.* Diminutive; little. [< F]

pet·it four (pet′ē fôr′, fōr′; *Fr.* pə·tē′fōōr′) *pl.* **pet·its fours** or **pet·it fours** (pet′ē fôrz′, fōrz′; *Fr.* pə·tē′fōōr′) A little, decoratively iced cake. [< F, lit., little oven]

pe·ti·tion (pə·tish′ən) *n.* **1.** A formal request or prayer. **2.** A formal request addressed to a person or group in authority and asking for some benefit, the redress of a grievance, etc. **3.** *Law* A formal application in writing made to a court, requesting judicial action concerning some matter therein set forth. **4.** Something formally requested or entreated. — *v.t.* **1.** To make a petition to. **2.** To ask for. — *v.i.* **3.** To make a petition. [< OF < L < *petere* to seek] — **pe·ti′tion·ar′y** *adj.* — **pe·ti′tion·er** *n.*

petit jury The jury that sits at a trial in civil and criminal cases: also called *trial jury:* also spelled *petty jury.*

petit larceny See under LARCENY.

pe·tit mal (pə·tē′ mäl′) *Pathol.* A mild form of epilepsy characterized by a momentary loss of consciousness: distinguished from *grand mal.* [< F, lit., little sickness]

pet·it point (pet′ē) **1.** A fine tapestry stitch used in decorative needlework: also called *tent stitch.* **2.** Needlework done in this stitch.

Pe·trar·chan sonnet (pə·trär′kən) A sonnet having the rhyme scheme *abbaabba* in the octave, and having in the sestet a set of two or three different, variously combined rhymes, as *cdcdcd*, or *cdecde*, etc.

pet·rel (pet′rəl) *n.* Any of various small sea birds as the storm petrel. [? < LL *Petrellus*, dim. of *Peter*, after St. Peter, in an allusion to his walking on the water. *Matt.* xiv 29]

pet·ri·fac·tion (pet′rə·fak′shən) *n.* **1.** The act or process of petrifying, or the state of being petrified. **2.** Anything petrified. Also **pet′ri·fi·ca′tion** (-fə·kā′shən). [< PETRIFY.] — **pet′ri·fac′tive** *adj.*

pet·ri·fy (pet′rə·fī) *v.* **·fied, ·fy·ing** *v.t.* **1.** To convert (organic material) into a substance of stony character. **2.** To make fixed and unyielding. **3.** To daze or paralyze with fear, surprise, etc. — *v.i.* **4.** To become stone or like stone. [< MF < L *petra* a rock + *facere* to make]

petro- *combining form* Rock; stone. Also, before vowels, **petr-.** [< F < L < Gk. *petra* rock and *petros* stone]

pet·ro·chem·is·try (pet′rō·kem′is·trē) *n.* The chemistry of petroleum and its derivatives, esp. the natural and synthetic hydrocarbons. — **pet′ro·chem′i·cal** *adj. & n.*

pe·trog·ra·phy (pə·trog′rə·fē) *n.* The systematic description and classification of rocks. — **pe·trog′ra·pher** *n.* — **pet·ro·graph·ic** (pet′rə·graf′ik) or **·i·cal** *adj.* — **pet′ro·graph′i·cal·ly** *adv.*

pet·rol (pet′rəl) *n. Brit.* Gasoline.

pet·ro·la·tum (pet′rə·lā′təm) *n.* A greasy, semisolid substance obtained from petroleum, used as a stabilizer for certain explosives and in ointments. Also **petroleum jelly.**

pe·tro·le·um (pə·trō′lē·əm) *n.* An oily, liquid mixture of numerous hydrocarbons, found in subterranean deposits, used in its natural state for heat and light, and as the source of gasoline, benzine, kerosene, paraffin, etc.: also called *naphtha, rock oil.* [< Med.L < L *petra* rock (< Gk.) + *oleum* oil]

petroleum ether *Chem.* A distillate of petroleum used as a solvent of fats, waxes, etc.

pe·trol·ic (pə·trol′ik) *adj.* Of or pertaining to petroleum.

pe·trol·o·gy (pə·trol′ə·jē) *n.* The science of the origin, structure, constitution, and characteristics of rocks. — **pet·ro·log·ic** (pet′rə·loj′ik) or **·i·cal** *adj.* — **pet′ro·log′i·cal·ly** *adv.* — **pe·trol′o·gist** *n.*

pet·ti·coat (pet′ē·kōt) *n.* **1.** A skirt or skirtlike garment hanging from the waist; esp., a woman's underskirt. **2.**

Something resembling a petticoat. **3.** A woman: a humorous or disparaging term. **4.** An electric insulator shaped like an inverted cup, for use on high-tension wires. — *adj.* Of or influenced by women: *petticoat* politics.

pet·ti·fog (pet′i·fog, -fôg) *v.i.* **·fogged, ·fog·ging 1.** To be unduly concerned over trivial matters; fuss. **2.** To be a pettifogger. [Appar. back formation < PETTIFOGGER]

pet·ti·fog·ger (pet′i·fog′ər, -fôg′ər) *n.* **1.** An inferior lawyer, esp. one dealing with insignificant cases, or resorting to tricks. **2.** One who quibbles or fusses over trivialities. [Earlier *petty fogger* < PETTY + obs. *fogger* a trickster for gain] — **pet′ti·fog′ger·y** *n.*

pet·tish (pet′ish) *adj.* Capriciously ill-tempered; petulant; peevish. [Prob. < PET² + -ISH] — **pet′tish·ly** *adv.*

pet·ty (pet′ē) *adj.* **·ti·er, ·ti·est 1.** Having little worth or importance; trifling; insignificant. **2.** Having little scope or generosity; narrow-minded. **3.** Mean; spiteful. **4.** Having a comparatively low rank or position; minor. **5.** *Law* Petit. [< F *petit* small] — **pet′ti·ly** *adv.* — **pet′ti·ness** *n.*

petty cash A supply of money kept for minor expenses, as in a business office.

petty jury See PETIT JURY.

petty larceny See under LARCENY.

petty officer *Naval* Any of a class of noncommissioned officers. See table at GRADE.

pet·u·lant (pech′ōō·lənt) *adj.* Displaying or characterized by capricious fretfulness; peevish. [< OF < L *petulans, -antis* forward, ult. < *petere* to rush at] — **pet′u·lant·ly** *adv.* — **pet′u·lance, pet′u·lan·cy** *n.*

pe·tu·ni·a (pə·tōō′nē·ə, -tyōō′-) *n.* Any of various tropical American plants cultivated widely for their funnel-shaped, variously colored flowers. [< NL < F *petun* tobacco]

pew¹ (pyōō) *n.* **1.** A bench for seating people in church, frequently with a kneeling rack attached. **2.** Formerly, a boxlike enclosure with seats on three sides, occupied by a family attending church. [ME < OF < LL *podia*, pl. of *podium* height, balcony < Gk. *podion* base]

pew² (pyōō) *interj.* An expression of disgust or displeasure, as at a bad odor. [Origin unknown]

pe·wee (pē′wē) *n.* Any of various small, greenish gray flycatchers: also spelled *peewee.* [Imit.]

pe·wit (pē′wit, pyōō′it) *n.* Any of various birds having a high or shrill cry. [Imit.]

pew·ter (pyōō′tər) *n.* **1.** An alloy, usu. of tin and lead, formerly much used for tableware. **2.** Pewter articles collectively. **3.** The characteristic dull gray of pewter. — *adj.* **1.** Made of pewter. **2.** Dull gray. [< OF *peutre, pialtre*]

pe·yo·te (pā·ō′tē, *Sp.* pā·yō′tā) *n.* Mescal. Also **pe·yo′tl** (-yōt′l). [< Am. Sp. < Nahuatl *peyotl*, lit., caterpillar]

pfen·nig (pfen′ikh) *n. pl.* **·nigs** or **pfen·ni·ge** (pfen′i·gə) A small bronze coin of Germany, equivalent to one hundredth of a deutschemark. [< G, penny]

Phae·dra (fē′drə) In Greek mythology, the wife of Theseus, who fell in love with her stepson and killed herself because he spurned her. Also **Phæ′dra.**

Pha·e·thon (fā′ə·thon) In Greek mythology, the son of Helios, who borrowed his father's chariot of the sun, and would have set heaven and earth on fire by his careless driving if Zeus had not slain him with a thunderbolt.

pha·e·ton (fā′ə·tən, *esp. Brit.* fā′tən) *n.* **1.** A light, fourwheeled carriage, open at the sides, and sometimes having a top. **2.** An open automobile having front and back seats. [< F, ult. < Gk. *Phaethōn* Phaethon]

-phage *combining form* One who or that which eats or consumes: *bacteriophage.* [< Gk. *phagein* to eat]

phago- *combining form* Eating. Also, before vowels, **phag-.** [< Gk. *phagein* to eat]

phag·o·cyte (fag′ə·sīt) *n. Physiol.* A leucocyte that ingests and destroys harmful bacteria, etc., in the blood and tissues of the body. — **phag′o·cyt′ic** (-sit′ik) or **·i·cal** *adj.*

-phagous *combining form* Consuming; tending to eat. [< Gk. *phagein* to eat]

-phagy *combining form* The consumption or eating of. Also **-phagia.** [< Gk. *phagein* to eat]

phal·ange (fal′ənj, fə·lanj′) *n. Anat.* A phalanx.

pha·lan·ge·al (fə·lan′jē·əl) *adj.* Of, pertaining to, or resembling the phalanges of the fingers and toes. Also **pha·lan′gal** (-gəl), **pha·lan′ge·an.**

pha·lan·ger (fə·lan′jər) *n.* Any one of a family of small marsupials of Australia and New Guinea, having long, often prehensile tails. [< NL < *phalanges*, pl. of *phalanx* phalanx]

pha·lanx (fā′langks, *esp. Brit.* fal′angks) *n. pl.* **pha·lan·ges** (fə·lan′jēz) or **pha·lanx·es 1.** In ancient Greece, a marching order of heavy infantry, with close ranks and files, joined shields, and spears overlapping. **2.** Any massed or compact body or corps. **3.** *Anat.* One of the bones articulating with the joints of the fingers or toes: also called *phalange.* [< L < Gk. *phalanx, phalangos* line of battle]

PRONUNCIATION KEY: add, āce, cāre, pälm; end, ēven; it, īce; odd, ōpen, ôrder; tŏŏk, pōōl; up, bûrn; ə = a in *above*, e in *sicken*, i in *flexible*, o in *melon*, u in *focus*; yōō = u in *fuse*; oil; pout; check; go; ring; thin; this; zh, vision. For ā, œ, ü, kh, ṅ, see inside front cover.

phal·a·rope (fal′ə·rōp) *n.* Any of several swimming birds resembling the sandpiper, but having lobate toes. [< F < NL < Gk. *phalaris* coot + *pous* foot]

phal·lism (fal′iz·əm) *n.* Worship of the generative power in nature as symbolized by the phallus. Also **phal′li·cism.** — **phal′li·cist, phal′list** *n.*

phal·lus (fal′əs) *n.* *pl.* **·li** (-ī) **1.** A representation of the male generative organ, often used as a symbol of the generative power of nature. **2.** *Anat.* The penis or the clitoris. [< L < Gk. *phallos* penis] — **phal′lic** *adj.*

-phane *combining form* Something resembling or similar to (a specified substance or material): *cellophane.* [< Gk. *-phanēs* < *phainein* to show]

phan·tasm (fan′taz·əm) *n.* **1.** An imaginary appearance; phantom. **2.** A mental image; fancy. [< Gk. *phantasma*]

phan·tas·ma·go·ri·a (fan·taz′mə·gôr′ē·ə, -gō′rē·ə) *n.* **1.** A changing, incoherent series of apparitions or phantasms, as in a dream. **2.** An exhibition of pictures projected on a screen and made to increase or diminish in size rapidly while continuously in focus; also, any exhibition of optical effects. **3.** An apparition. Also **phan·tas′ma·go·ry.** [< Gk. *phantasma* apparition + (prob.) *agora* crowd] — **phan·tas′ma·go′ri·al, phan·tas′ma·gor′ic** (-gôr′ik, -gor′ik) or **·i·cal** *adj.*

phan·tas·mal (fan·taz′məl) *adj.* Of or like a phantasm; unreal or illusive; spectral. Also **phan·tas′mic.**

phan·ta·sy (fan′tə·sē, -zē) See FANTASY.

phan·tom (fan′təm) *n.* **1.** Something that exists only in appearance. **2.** An apparition; specter. **3.** The visible representative of an abstract state or incorporeal person. — *adj.* Illusive; ghostlike. Also spelled *fantom.* [< OF < L < Gk. *phantasma* apparition < *phainein* to show]

-phany *combining form* Appearance; manifestation: *epiphany.* [< Gk. < *phainein* to appear]

Phar·aoh (fâr′ō, fā′rō) *n.* Any one of the monarchs of ancient Egypt. [< LL < Gk. < Hebrew < Egyptian *pr-ʿōh* the great house] — **Phar′a·on′ic** (-ē·on′ik) or **·i·cal** *adj.*

phar·i·sa·ic (far′ə·sā′ik) *adj.* **1.** Of or pertaining to the Pharisees. **2.** Observing the form, but neglecting the spirit, of religion; self-righteous. Also **phar′i·sa′i·cal** — **phar′i·sa′i·cal·ly** *adv.* — **phar′i·sa′i·cal·ness** *n.*

phar·i·sa·ism (far′ə·sā·iz′əm) *n.* **1.** *Often cap.* The principles of the Pharisees. **2.** Formality, self-righteousness, or hypocrisy. Also **phar′i·see·ism** (-sē·iz′əm).

Phar·i·see (far′ə·sē) *n.* **1.** A member of an ancient Jewish sect that accepted the Mosaic law and the oral traditions associated with it, and emphasized strict observance of ritual. **2.** A formal, sanctimonious, hypocritical person: also **phar′i·see.** [OE *fariseus,* infl. by OF *pharise,* both < L < Gk. < Aramaic *perishayā,* pl. of *perish*]

phar·ma·ceu·ti·cal (fär′mə·sōō′ti·kəl) *adj.* Pertaining to, using, or relating to pharmacy or the pharmacopoeia: also **phar·ma·cal** (fär′mə·kəl). Also **phar′ma·ceu′tic.** — *n.* A pharmaceutical product. [< L < Gk. < *pharmakon* drug] — **phar′ma·ceu′ti·cal·ly** *adv.* — **phar′ma·ceu′tist** *n.*

phar·ma·ceu·tics (fär′mə·sōō′tiks) *n.pl.* (construed as sing.) Pharmacy (def. 1).

phar·ma·cist (fär′mə·sist) *n.* A qualified druggist.

pharmaco- *combining form* A drug; of or pertaining to drugs. Also, before vowels, **pharmac-.** [< Gk. *pharmakon* drug]

phar·ma·col·o·gy (fär′mə·kol′ə·jē) *n.* The science of the nature, preparation, administration, and effects of drugs. — **phar′ma·co·log′ic** (-kə·loj′ik) or **·i·cal** *adj.* — **phar′ma·co·log′i·cal·ly** *adv.* — **phar′ma·col′o·gist** *n.*

phar·ma·co·poe·ia (fär′mə·kə·pē′ə) *n.* **1.** A book, usu. published by an authority, containing standard formulas and methods for the preparation of medicines, drugs, and other remedial substances. **2.** A collection of drugs. [< NL < Gk. < *pharmakon* drug + *poieein* to make] — **phar′ma·co·poe′ial** *adj.* — **phar′ma·co·poe′ist** *n.*

phar·ma·cy (fär′mə·sē) *n.* *pl.* **·cies 1.** The art or business of compounding and identifying drugs, and of compounding and dispensing medicines: also called *pharmaceutics.* **2.** A drugstore. [< OF < LL < Gk. < *pharmakon* drug]

pha·ryn·ge·al (fə·rin′jē·əl, far′in·jē′əl) *adj.* Of or pertaining to the pharynx. Also **pha·ryn′gal** (-gəl).

phar·yn·gi·tis (far′in·jī′tis) *n.* *Pathol.* Inflammation of the pharynx, as in diphtheria and sore throat.

pharyngo- *combining form* The throat; related to the throat. Also, before vowels, **pharyng-.** [< Gk. *pharynx* throat]

phar·ynx (far′ingks) *n.* *pl.* **pha·ryn·ges** (fə·rin′jēz) or **phar·ynx·es** *Anat.* The part of the alimentary canal between the palate and the esophagus, serving as a passage for air and food. For illus. see MOUTH, THROAT. [< NL < Gk. *pharynx, -yngos* throat]

phase (fāz) *n.* **1.** The view that anything presents to the eye; any one of varying distinctive manifestations of an object. **2.** *Astron.* One of the appearances or forms presented periodically by the moon and planets. **3.** *Physics* **a** Any particular stage in the complete cycle of a periodic system. **b** The fraction of a cycle through which a wave has passed at any instant. **4.** *Chem.* Any homogeneous part of a material system separated from other parts by physical boundaries, as ice in water. **5.** *Biol.* Any characteristic or decisive stage in the growth, development, or life pattern of an organism. Also **pha·sis** (fā′sis). — **in phase** Reaching corresponding phases simultaneously, as two waves. — **to phase out** (or **in**) *U.S.* To plan and execute the orderly and gradual completion or initiation of an enterprise. [< NL < Gk. *phainein* to show] — **pha·sic** (fā′zik) *adj.* — **Syn.** (noun) **1.** Aspect, side, facet.

-phasia *combining form* *Med.* Defect or malfunction of speech: *dysphasia.* Also **-phasy.** [< Gk. < *phanai* to speak]

pheas·ant (fez′ənt) *n.* **1.** A long-tailed, gallinaceous bird, originally of Asia, noted for the gorgeous plumage of the male; esp. the **ring-necked pheasant,** widely bred in the U.S. **2.** One of various other birds, as the ruffed grouse. [< AF < L < Gk. *Phasianos* (*ornis*) the Phasian (bird) < *Phasis* the Phasis, a river in the Georgian S.S.R.]

Phe·be (fē′bē) See PHOEBE.

phen- Var. of PHENO-.

phe·nac·e·tin (fə·nas′ə·tin) *n.* *Chem.* A white, crystalline, coal-tar compound, $C_{10}H_{13}NO_2$, used in medicine as an antipyretic. Also **phe·nac′e·tine.**

phe·nix (fē′niks) See PHOENIX.

pheno- *combining form* *Chem.* Related to benzene; a derivative of benzene. Also, before vowels, **phen-.** [< Gk. *phaino-* shining < *phainein* to show]

phe·no·bar·bi·tal (fē′nō·bär′bə·tal, -tôl) *n.* *Chem.* A white, odorless, slightly bitter, crystalline powder, $C_{12}H_{12}O_3N_2$, used as a sedative. Also **phe′no·bar′bi·tone** (-tōn).

phe·nol (fē′nol, -nol) *n.* *Chem.* A white, crystalline, caustic compound, C_6H_5OH, derived from coal tar and used as a disinfectant: also called *carbolic acid.* [< Gk. *phaino-* shining < *phainein* to show + -OL¹]

phe·nol·phthal·ein (fē′nol·thal′ēn, fē′nolf·thal′ē·in) *n.* *Chem.* A yellowish white derivative of phenol, $C_{20}H_{14}O_4$, used as a laxative, an indicator in acid-base titrations, etc.

phe·nom·e·na (fi·nom′ə·nə) Plural of PHENOMENON.

phe·nom·e·nal (fi·nom′ə·nəl) *adj.* **1.** Pertaining to phenomena. **2.** Extraordinary or marvelous. **3.** *Philos.* Perceptible through the senses. — **phe·nom′e·nal·ly** *adv.*

phe·nom·e·nal·ism (fi·nom′ə·nəl·iz′əm) *n.* *Philos.* The doctrine that denies either our knowledge or the existence of a reality beyond phenomena. — **phe·nom′e·nal·ist** *n.* — **phe·nom′e·nal·is′tic** *adj.* — **phe·nom′e·nal·is′ti·cal·ly** *adv.*

phe·nom·e·non (fi·nom′ə·non) *n.* *pl.* **phe·nom·e·na** (-nə); *for defs.* **2** & **3, often phe·nom·e·nons 1.** Something visible or directly observable, as an appearance, action, change, etc. **2.** Any unusual occurrence; marvel. **3.** *Informal* A person having some remarkable talent, power, or ability; prodigy. **4.** *Med.* Any notable characteristic or disease. [< LL < Gk. < *phainein* to show]

phe·no·type (fē′nə·tīp) *n.* *Biol.* The aggregate of genetic characteristics visibly manifested by an organism. [< F < Gk. *phainein* to show + -TYPE] — **phe′no·typ′ic** (-tip′ik) or **·i·cal** *adj.* — **phe′no·typ′i·cal·ly** *adv.*

phen·yl (fen′əl, fē′nəl) *n.* *Chem.* The univalent radical C_6H_5, the basis of numerous aromatic compounds.

phew (fyōō, fōō) *interj.* An exclamation of disgust or surprise.

phi (fī, fē) *n.* The twenty-first letter in the Greek alphabet (Φ, φ): corresponding to English *ph* and *f.* See ALPHABET.

phi·al (fī′əl) See VIAL.

Phi Be·ta Kap·pa (fī bā′tə kap′ə, bē′tə) An American honorary society founded in 1776, having its membership based on conditions of high academic standing.

phil- Var. of PHILO-.

phi·lan·der (fi·lan′dər) *v.i.* To make love without serious intentions: said of a man. — *n.* A male flirt: also **phi·lan′der·er.** [< Gk. *philandros,* orig., loving men < *phileein* to love + *anēr, andros* man]

phi·lan·thro·py (fi·lan′thrə·pē) *n.* *pl.* **·pies 1.** The effort to promote the happiness or social elevation of mankind, as by making donations, etc. **2.** Love or benevolence toward mankind in general. [< LL < Gk. < *phileein* to love + *anthropos* man] — **phil′an·throp·ic** (fil′ən·throp′ik) or **·i·cal** *adj.* — **phil′an·throp′i·cal·ly** *adv.* — **phi·lan′thro·pist** *n.*

phi·lat·e·ly (fi·lat′ə·lē) *n.* The study and collection of postage stamps, stamped envelopes, etc.; stamp collecting. [< F < Gk. *philos* loving + *ateleia* exemption from tax as indicated by a stamp] — **phil·a·tel·ic** (fil′ə·tel′ik) or **·i·cal** *adj.* — **phil′a·tel′i·cal·ly** *adv.* — **phi·lat′e·list** (-lat′ə·list) *n.*

-phile *combining form* One who supports or is fond of; one devoted to: *bibliophile.* Also **-phil.** [< Gk. *-philos* loving]

Phi·le·mon (fi·lē′mən) A Greek of Colossae, converted to Christianity by Saint Paul. — *n.* A book of the New Testament consisting of an epistle addressed by Saint Paul to him.

phil·har·mon·ic (fil′här·mon′ik, -ər·mon′-) *adj. Sometimes cap.* Fond of music: often used in the names of musical societies. [< F < Ital. < Gk. *philos* loving + *harmonia* music]

-philia *combining form* 1. A tendency toward: *hemophilia.* 2. An excessive affection or fondness for: *necrophilia.* Also spelled *-phily.* [< Gk. *-philia* < *phileein* to love]

Phil·ip (fil′ip) One of the twelve apostles: called **Saint Philip.**

Phi·lip·pi (fi·lip′ī) An ancient town in northern Macedonia, Greece; scene of the defeat of Brutus and Cassius by Octavian and Antony, 42 B.C., and of Saint Paul's first preaching in Europe. *Acts* xvi 12. — **Phi·lip′pi·an** *adj. & n.*

Phi·lip·pi·ans (fi·lip′ē·ənz) *n.pl.* (construed as sing.) A book of the New Testament consisting of an epistle of Saint Paul addressed to Christians at Philippi.

phi·lip·pic (fi·lip′ik) *n.* An impassioned speech characterized by invective. — **the Philippics** A series of twelve speeches in which Demosthenes denounced Philip of Macedon. [< L < Gk. *Philippikos* pertaining to Philip]

Phi·lis·ti·a (fi·lis′tē·ə) An ancient region on the Mediterranean, SW Palestine. *Ps.* lx 8.

Phi·lis·tine (fi·lis′tin, -tēn, -tīn, fil′əs-) *n.* One of a warlike race of ancient Philistia. I *Sam.* xvii 23. [< F < LL < Gk. < Hebrew *p'lishtīm*]

Phi·lis·tine (fi·lis′tin, -tēn, -tīn, fil′əs-) *n.* An ignorant, narrow-minded person, devoid of culture and indifferent to art. [< G student slang *Philister* one of the ancient Philistines] — **Phi·lis′tin·ism** *n.*

philo- *combining form* Loving; fond of. Also, before vowels, *phil-.* [< Gk. *philos* loving < *phileein* to love]

phil·o·den·dron (fil′ə·den′drən) *n.* Any of various climbing plants of the arum family, having glossy, evergreen leaves and cultivated as an ornamental house plant. [< NL < Gk., neut. of *philodendros* fond of trees.]

phi·log·y·ny (fi·loj′ə·nē) *n.* Fondness for or devotion to women. [< Gk. < *philos* loving + *gynē* woman] — **phi·log′y·nist** *n.* — **phi·log′y·nous** *adj.*

phi·lol·o·gy (fi·lol′ə·jē) *n.* 1. The study of written records, chiefly literary works, to set up accurate texts and determine their meaning. 2. Linguistics, esp. comparative and historical. [< F < L < Gk. *philologos* fond of argument or words.] — **phi·lo·log·ic** (fil′ə·loj′ik) or **·i·cal** *adj.* — **phil′·o·log′i·cal·ly** *adv.* — **phi·lol′o·gist, phi·lol′o·ger** *n.*

phil·o·mel (fil′ə·mel) *n. Poetic* The nightingale. Also **phil′o·me′la** (-mē′lə). [< F < L < Gk. ? < *philos* loving + *melos* song]

phi·los·o·pher (fi·los′ə·fər) *n.* 1. A student of or specialist in philosophy. 2. One who lives, makes judgments, etc., according to a philosophy. 3. One who is calm and patient under all circumstances. [< OF < L < Gk. *philosophos* lover of wisdom]

philosopher's stone An imaginary stone or substance capable of transmuting the baser metals into gold.

phil·o·soph·i·cal (fil′ə·sof′i·kəl) *adj.* 1. Of or founded on the principles of philosophy. 2. Proper to or characteristic of a philosopher. 3. Self-restrained; rational; thoughtful. Also **phil′o·soph′ic.** — **phil′o·soph′i·cal·ly** *adv.* — **phil′o·soph′i·cal·ness** *n.*

phi·los·o·phize (fi·los′ə·fīz) *v.i.* **·phized, ·phiz·ing** To speculate like a philosopher; moralize. — **phi·los′o·phiz′er** *n.*

phi·los·o·phy (fi·los′ə·fē) *n. pl.* **·phies** 1. The inquiry into the most comprehensive principles of reality in general, or of some sector of it, as human knowledge or human values. 2. The love of wisdom, and the search for it. 3. A philosophical system; also, a treatise on such a system. 4. The general laws that furnish the rational explanation of anything: the *philosophy* of banking. 5. Practical wisdom; fortitude. [< OF < L < Gk. *philosophos* lover of wisdom]

-philous *combining form* Loving; fond of. [< Gk. *-philos*]

phil·ter (fil′tər) *n.* 1. A charmed draft supposed to have power to excite sexual love. 2. Any magic potion. — *v.t.* To charm with a philter. Also **phil′tre.** [< MF < L < Gk. < *phileein* to love]

-phily Var. of -PHILIA.

phle·bi·tis (fli·bī′tis) *n. Pathol.* Inflammation of the inner membrane of a vein. [< Gk. *phleps, phlebos* blood vessel + -ITIS] — **phle·bit′ic** (-bit′ik) *adj.*

phlebo- *combining form* Venous. Also, before vowels, **phleb-.** [< Gk. *phleps, phlebos* blood vessel]

phle·bot·o·mize (fli·bot′ə·mīz) *v.t.* **·mized, ·miz·ing** To treat by phlebotomy.

phle·bot·o·my (fli·bot′ə·mē) *n. Surg.* The practice of opening a vein for letting blood as a remedial measure; bloodletting. [< OF < L < Gk. *phleps, phlebos* blood vessel + *temnein* to cut] — **phleb·o·tom·ic** (fleb′ə·tom′ik) or **·i·cal** *adj.* — **phle·bot′o·mist** *n.*

phlegm (flem) *n.* 1. *Physiol.* A viscid, stringy mucus secreted in the air passages, esp. when produced as a discharge through the mouth. 2. Cold, undemonstrative temper. 3. One of the four natural humors in ancient physiology. [< MF < LL < Gk., flame, phlegm < *phlegein* to burn]

phleg·mat·ic (fleg·mat′ik) *adj.* Not easily moved or excited. Also **phleg·mat′i·cal.** — **phleg·mat′i·cal·ly** *adv.*

phlo·em (flō′əm) *n. Bot.* The complex tissue serving for the conduction of the sap in plants. [< G < Gk. *phloos* bark]

phlo·gis·ton (flō·jis′tən) *n.* The hypothetical substance formerly assumed to be a necessary constituent of all combustible bodies, and to be given up by them in burning. [< NL < Gk., < *phlogizein* to set on fire]

phlox (floks) *n.* Any of various herbs with opposite leaves and clusters of variously colored flowers. [< NL < L < Gk., wallflower, lit., flame]

-phobe *combining form* One who fears or has an aversion to. [< LL < Gk. *phobeesthai* to fear]

pho·bi·a (fō′bē·ə) *n.* 1. A compulsive and persistent fear of any specified type of object, stimulus, or situation. 2. Any strong aversion or dislike. [< L < Gk. < *phobos* fear] — **pho′bic** (-bik) *adj.*

-phobia *combining form* An exaggerated and persistent dread of or aversion to. [< Gk. *phobos* fear]

In the following list each entry denotes a phobia for what is indicated:

acrophobia high places	**hemophobia** blood
agoraphobia open spaces	**musophobia** mice
ailurophobia cats	**necrophobia** dead bodies
androphobia men	**nyctophobia** night, darkness
astraphobia thunderstorms	**ophidiophobia** reptiles
autophobia self, being alone	**phonophobia** noise
bathophobia depths	**pyrophobia** fire
cynophobia dogs	**taphephobia** being buried alive
demophobia crowds	**thanatophobia** death
gynophobia women	**zoophobia** animals

phoe·be (fē′bē) *n.* An American bird, a flycatcher, having grayish brown plumage and a slightly crested head. [Imit. of its cry; infl. in form by PHOEBE.]

Phoe·be (fē′bē) In Greek mythology, Artemis as goddess of the moon. — *n. Poetic* The moon. Also spelled *Phebe.* [< L < Gk., bright]

Phoe·bus (fē′bəs) In Greek mythology, Apollo as god of the sun. Also **Phoebus Apollo.** — *n. Poetic* The sun.

Phoe·ni·cian (fə·nē′shən, -nish′ən) *adj.* Of ancient Phoenicia, its people, or its language. — *n.* 1. One of the people of ancient Phoenicia or any of its colonies. 2. The Northwest Semitic language of these people.

phoe·nix (fē′niks) *n.* In Egyptian mythology, a bird of great beauty, said to live for 500 or 600 years and then consume itself by fire, rising from its ashes to live through another cycle, often used as a symbol of immortality. Also spelled *phenix.* [OE < Med.L < L < Gk. *phoinix* phoenix, Phoenician, purple red, crimson]

phon- Var. of PHONO-.

pho·nate (fō′nāt) *v.i.* **·nat·ed, ·nat·ing** To make speech sounds. [< Gk. *phōnē* voice] — **pho·na′tion** *n.*

phone¹ (fōn) *Informal n.* A telephone. — *v.t. & v.i.* **phoned, phon·ing** To telephone. [Short for TELEPHONE]

phone² (fōn) *n. Phonet.* A sound used in human speech. [< Gk. *phōnē* a sound, voice]

-phone *combining form* Voice; sound: *microphone.* [< Gk. *phōnē* voice]

pho·neme (fō′nēm) *n. Ling.* A class of phonetically similar phones that alternate with each other according to phonetic environment and that function to distinguish utterances from one another, as /t/ and /p/ in the words *tin* and *pin.* See ALLOPHONE. [< F < Gk. *phōnēma* utterance]

pho·ne·mic (fə·nē′mik, fō-) *adj.* 1. Of or referring to phonemes. 2. Involving distinctive speech sounds: a *phonemic* difference. — **pho·ne′mi·cal·ly** *adv.*

pho·ne·mics (fə·nē′miks, fō-) *n.pl.* (construed as sing.) 1. A phonemic system. 2. The study of phonemic systems.

pho·net·ic (fə·net′ik, fō-) *adj.* 1. Of or pertaining to phonetics, or to speech sounds and their production. 2. Representing the sounds of speech. Also **pho·net′i·cal.** [< NL < Gk. *phōnē* sound] — **pho·net′i·cal·ly** *adv.*

pho·ne·ti·cian (fō′nə·tish′ən) *n.* A specialist in phonetics. Also **pho·net·i·cist** (fə·net′ə·sist), **pho′ne·tist.**

pho·net·ics (fə·net′iks, fō-) *n.pl.* (construed as sing.) 1. The branch of linguistics dealing with the analysis, description, and classification of the sounds of speech. 2. The system of sounds of a language: the *phonetics* of American English. 3. Loosely, phonetic transcription.

pho·ney (fō′nē) See PHONY.

-phonia See -PHONY.

phon·ic (fon′ik, fō′nik) *adj.* Pertaining to or of the nature of sound, esp. speech sounds.

phon·ics (fon′iks, fō′niks) *n.pl.* (construed as sing.) 1. The phonetic rudiments used in teaching reading and pronunciation. 2. The science of sound; acoustics.

phono- *combining form* Sound; speech; voice. Also, before vowels, **phon-.** [< Gk. *phōnē* voice]

pho·no·gram (fō'nə·gram) *n.* A character symbolizing a speech sound, word, etc. — **pho'no·gram'ic** or **·gram'mic** *adj.* — **pho'no·gram'i·cal·ly** or **·gram'mi·cal·ly** *adv.*

pho·no·graph (fō'nə·graf, -gräf) *n.* A record player.

pho·no·graph·ic (fō'nə·graf'ik) *adj.* 1. Pertaining to or produced by a phonograph. 2. Pertaining to or written in phonography. — **pho'no·graph'i·cal·ly** *adv.*

phonograph record A grooved disk that reproduces sounds on a record player.

pho·nog·ra·phy (fō·nog'rə·fē, fə-) *n.* 1. The art or science of representing words according to a system of sound elements; esp. a style of shorthand. 2. The art of representing speech sounds by marks or letters.

pho·nol·o·gy (fō·nol'ə·jē) *n.* 1. Phonemics. 2. Phonemics and phonetics taken together. 3. The history of the sound changes that have taken place in a language, or the study thereof. — **pho·no·log·ic** (fō'nə·loj'ik) or **·i·cal** *adj.* — **pho'·no·log'i·cal·ly** *adv.* — **pho·nol'o·gist** *n.*

pho·ny (fō'nē) *U.S. Slang* *adj.* **·ni·er, ·ni·est** Fake; false; spurious; counterfeit. — *n.* *pl.* **·nies** 1. Something fake or not genuine. 2. One who tries to be something he is not. Also spelled *phoney.* [? < British slang *fawney man* peddler of imitation jewelry, ult. < Irish *fainne* ring]

-phony *combining form* A (specified) type of sound or sounds: *cacophony.* [< Gk. *phōnē* sound, voice]

-phore *combining form* A bearer or producer of: *semaphore.* [< NL < Gk. < *pherein* to bear]

-phorous *combining form* Bearing or producing: found in adjectives corresponding to nouns in *-phore.*

phos·gene (fos'jēn) *n.* *Chem.* A colorless, highly toxic gas, $COCl_2$, having a suffocating odor, used in organic chemistry and in warfare. [< Gk. *phōs* light + *-gene* -GEN]

phosph- Var. of PHOSPHO-.

phos·phate (fos'fāt) *n.* 1. *Chem.* A salt or ester of phosphoric acid. 2. *Agric.* Any fertilizer valued for its phosphoric acid. 3. A beverage of carbonated water, containing small amounts of phosphoric acid. [< F]

phos·phat·ic (fos·fat'ik) *adj.* 1. Relating to the phosphates. 2. Containing some phosphate.

phos·phide (fos'fīd, -fid) *n.* *Chem.* A compound of phosphorus with a metal, as **calcium phosphide,** Ca_3P_2.

phos·phite (fos'fīt) *n.* A salt of phosphorous acid.

phospho- *combining form* Phosphorus; of or containing phosphorus, or any of its compounds.

phos·phor (fos'fər) *n.* Any of a class of substances that will emit light under the action of certain chemicals or radiations. [< L < Gk. *phōs* light + *pherein* to bear]

Phos·phor (fos'fər) *n.* *Poetic* The morning star, esp. Venus. [< L *Phosphorus* morning star < Gk. *Phosphoros*]

phos·pho·rate (fos'fə·rāt') *v.t.* **·rat·ed, ·rat·ing** To combine with phosphorus.

phos·phor·esce (fos'fə·res') *v.i.* **·esced, ·esc·ing** To glow with a faint light unaccompanied by perceptible heat.

phos·phor·es·cence (fos'fə·res'əns) *n.* 1. The emission of light without sensible heat; also, the light so emitted. 2. The property of continuing to shine in the dark after exposure to light, shown by many mineral substances.

phos·phor·es·cent (fos'fə·res'ənt) *adj.* Exhibiting phosphorescence.

phos·phor·et·ed (fos'fə·ret'id) *adj.* *Chem.* Combined with phosphorus. Also **phos'phor·et'ted.**

phos·phor·ic (fos·fôr'ik, -for'-) *adj.* *Chem.* Pertaining to or derived from phosphorus, esp. in its highest valence.

phosphoric acid *Chem.* One of three acids of phosphorus, esp. *orthophosphoric acid* (H_3PO_4), used as a reagent.

phos·pho·rous (fos'fər·əs, fos·fôr'əs, -fō'rəs) *adj.* *Chem.* Of, pertaining to, resembling, containing, or derived from phosphorus, esp. in its lower valence.

phosphorous acid *Chem.* A crystalline acid, H_3PO_3, with a garlic taste, obtained by the oxidation of phosphorus.

phos·pho·rus (fos'fər·əs) *n.* A soft, nonmetallic element (symbol P), found only in combination; white or yellow phosphorus is luminous in the dark, highly flammable, and poisonous; red phosphorus does not glow, is less flammable, and nonpoisonous. See ELEMENT. [< NL < L *Phosphorus* morning star < Gk. *phōs* light + *pherein* to bear]

pho·tic (fō'tik) *adj.* 1. Of or relating to light or to the production of light. 2. Designating those underwater regions penetrated by sunlight: the *photic* zone.

pho·to (fō'tō) *n.* *pl.* **·tos** *Informal* A photograph.

photo- *combining form* 1. Light; of, pertaining to, or produced by light. 2. Photograph; photographic: *photoengrave.* [< Gk. *phōs* light]

pho·to·cell (fō'tō·sel') *n.* A photoelectric cell.

pho·to·chem·is·try (fō'tō·kem'is·trē) *n.* The branch of chemistry dealing with chemical reactions produced or influenced by light. — **pho'to·chem'i·cal** *adj.*

pho·to·cop·y (fō'tō·kop'ē) *n.* *pl.* **·cop·ies** A photographic reproduction of printed or other graphic material. — *v.* **·cop·ied, ·cop·y·ing** *v.t.* 1. To make a photocopy of. — *v.i.* 2. To make a photocopy. — **pho'to·cop'i·er** *n.*

pho·to·e·lec·tric (fō'tō·i·lek'trik) *adj.* Of or pertaining to the electrical or electronic effects due to the action of light. Also **pho'to·e·lec'tri·cal.**

photoelectric cell An electron tube, one of whose electrodes is sensitive to variations in the intensity of light, incorporated in electrical circuits as a controlling, testing, and counting device: also *electric eye, photocell, phototube.*

pho·to·e·lec·tron (fō'tō·i·lek'tron) *n.* An electron emitted from a metal surface when exposed to suitable radiation.

pho·to·en·grave (fō'tō·in·grāv') *v.t.* **·graved, ·grav·ing** To reproduce by photoengraving. — **pho'to·en·grav'er** *n.*

pho·to·en·grav·ing (fō'tō·in·grā'ving) *n.* 1. The act or process of producing by the aid of photography a relief block or plate for printing. 2. A plate or picture so produced.

photo finish 1. A race so closely contested that only a photograph of the finish can determine the winner. 2. *Informal* Any race or competition decided by a slim margin.

pho·to·flash bulb (fō'tō·flash') *Photog.* A flash bulb.

pho·to·flood lamp (fō'tō·flud') *Photog.* An electric lamp operating at excess voltage to give high illumination.

pho·to·gen·ic (fō'tō·jen'ik) *adj.* 1. Being a good subject for a photograph, esp. for esthetic reasons. 2. *Biol.* Producing phosphorescence. — **pho'to·gen'i·cal·ly** *adv.*

pho·to·gram·me·try (fō'tō·gram'ə·trē) *n.* The art and technique of making surveys or maps by photographs.

pho·to·graph (fō'tə·graf, -gräf) *n.* A picture taken by photography. — *v.t.* 1. To take a photograph of. — *v.i.* 2. To practice photography. 3. To be depicted in photographs: He *photographs* beautifully. — **pho·tog·ra·pher** (fə·tog'rə·fər) *n.*

pho·to·graph·ic (fō'tə·graf'ik) *adj.* 1. Pertaining to, used in, or produced by photography. 2. Of or like a photograph. Also **pho'to·graph'i·cal.** — **pho'to·graph'i·cal·ly** *adv.*

pho·tog·ra·phy (fə·tog'rə·fē) *n.* 1. The process of forming and fixing an image of an object or objects by the chemical action of light and other forms of radiant energy on photosensitive surfaces. 2. The art or business of producing and printing photographs.

pho·to·gra·vure (fō'tō·grə·vyŏŏr', -grāv'yər) *n.* 1. The process of making an intaglio plate from a photograph for use in printing. 2. A picture so produced. [< F]

pho·to·lith·o·graph (fō'tō·lith'ə·graf, -gräf) *v.t.* To reproduce by photolithography. — *n.* A picture produced by photolithography.

pho·to·li·thog·ra·phy (fō'tō·li·thog'rə·fē) *n.* The art or operation of producing on stone, largely by photographic means, a printing surface from which impressions may be taken by a lithographic process. — **pho'to·lith'o·graph'ic** (-lith'ə·graf'ik) *adj.*

pho·tol·y·sis (fō·tol'ə·sis) *n.* Chemical or biological decomposition due to the action of light. [< NL < Gk. *phōs* light + *lyein* to loosen] — **pho·to·lyt·ic** (fō'tə·lit'ik) *adj.*

pho·to·map (fō'tō·map') *n.* A map composed of one or more aerial photographs.

pho·tom·e·ter (fō·tom'ə·tər) *n.* Any instrument for measuring or comparing the intensity of light.

pho·tom·e·try (fō·tom'ə·trē) *n.* 1. The measurement of the intensity of light, esp. with a photometer. 2. The branch of optics that treats of such measurement. — **pho·to·met·ric** (fō'tə·met'rik) or **·ri·cal** *adj.* — **pho·tom'e·trist** n.

pho·to·mi·cro·graph (fō'tō·mī'krə·graf, -gräf) *n.* A photograph taken through a microscope; a microphotograph. — **pho·to·mi·crog·ra·phy** (fō'tō·mī·krog'rə·fē) *n.*

pho·to·mon·tage (fō'tō·mon·täzh', -môn-) *n.* Montage produced by photography.

pho·to·mu·ral (fō'tō·myŏŏr'əl) *n.* A photograph enlarged to a considerable size, used for wall decoration.

pho·ton (fō'ton) *n.* *Physics* A quantum of radiant energy moving with the velocity of light and an energy proportional to its frequency: also called *light quantum.* — **pho·ton'ic** *adj.*

pho·to·nu·cle·ar (fō'tō·nōō'klē·ər, -nyōō'-) *adj.* *Physics* Of, pertaining to, or designating a reaction initiated in an atomic nucleus by a photon.

pho·to·off·set (fō'tō·ôf'set, -of'-) *n.* Offset printing from a metal surface on which the text or design has been imprinted by photography.

pho·to·play (fō'tō·plā') *n.* A play arranged for or presented in a motion-picture performance.

pho·to·sen·si·tive (fō'tō·sen'sə·tiv) *adj.* Sensitive to light. — **pho'to·sen'si·tiv'i·ty** *n.*

pho·to·sphere (fō'tə·sfir) *n.* *Astron.* The visible shining surface of the sun. — **pho'to·spher'ic** (-sfir'ik, -sfer'-) *adj.*

pho·to·stat (fō'tə·stat) *v.t. & v.i.* **·stat·ed** or **·stat·ted, ·stat·ing** or **·stat·ting** To make a reproduction (of) with a Photostat. — *n.* The reproduction so produced. — **pho'to·stat'·ic** *adj.* — **pho'to·stat'i·cal·ly** *adv.*

Pho·to·stat (fō'tə·stat) *n.* A camera designed to reproduce facsimiles of documents, drawings, etc., directly as positives: a trade name. Also **pho'to·stat.**

pho·to·syn·the·sis (fō'tō·sin'thə·sis) *n.* *Biochem.* The process by which plants form carbohydrates from carbon dioxide, inorganic salts, and water through the agency of sunlight acting upon chlorophyll. — **pho′to·syn·thet·ic** (-sin·thet′ik) *adj.*

pho·to·tel·e·graph (fō′tō·tel′ə·graf, -gräf) *v.t. & v.i.* To transmit by phototelegraphy. — *n.* Something so transmitted.

pho·to·te·leg·ra·phy (fō′tō·tə·leg′rə·fē) *n.* The electrical or telegraphic transmission of messages, photographs, etc., by facsimile; telephotography. — **pho′to·tel′e·graph′ic** (-tel′ə·graf′ik) *adj.*

pho·to·trop·ic (fō′tə·trop′ik) *adj. Biol.* Turning in a particular direction under the influence of light. — **pho′to·trop′i·cal·ly** *adv.*

pho·tot·ro·pism (fō·tot′rə·piz′əm) *n. Biol.* Phototropic growth or response.

pho·to·tube (fō′tō·tōōb′, -tyōōb′) *n.* A photoelectric cell.

pho·to·type (fō′tə·tīp′) *n.* **1.** A relief plate made for printing by photography. **2.** The process by which it is produced: also **pho·to·typ·y** (fō′tō·tī′pē). **3.** A picture printed from such a plate. — **pho′to·typ′ic** (-tip′ik) *adj.*

phrase (frāz) *n.* **1.** *Gram.* A group of two or more associated words, not containing a subject and predicate: distinguished from *clause*. **2.** A word or group of words spoken in one breath. **3.** A concise, catchy expression. **4.** *Music* A short division of time comprising several statements of one or more motifs. — *v.t. & v.i.* **·phrased, ·phras·ing 1.** To express in words or phrases. **2.** To divide (a sentence, etc.) into phrases when speaking. **3.** *Music* To divide (a melody) into phrases. [< LL < Gk. *phrazein* to point out] — **phras·al** (frā′zəl) *adj.* — **phras′ing** *n.*

phra·se·ol·o·gy (frā′zē·ol′ə·jē) *n. pl.* **·gies 1.** The choice and arrangement of words and phrases in expressing ideas. **2.** A compilation or handbook of phrases. [< NL < Gk. *phrasis* speech + *logos* word] — **phra′se·o·log′i·cal** (-ə·loj′i·kəl) *adj.* — **phra′se·ol′o·gist** (-jist) *n.*

phren·ic (fren′ik) *adj.* **1.** Of or pertaining to the mind. **2.** *Anat.* Of or pertaining to the diaphragm: the *phrenic* nerve. [< NL < Gk. *phrēn, phrenos* diaphragm, mind]

phreno- *combining form* **1.** Mind; brain. **2.** Diaphragm; of or related to the diaphragm. Also, before vowels, **phren-**. [< Gk. *phrēn, phrenos* the diaphragm (thought to be the seat of intellect)]

phre·nol·o·gy (fri·nol′ə·jē) *n.* The doctrine that the conformation of the human skull allegedly indicates the degree of development of various mental faculties and characteristics. [< Gk. *phrēn, phrenos* mind + -LOGY] — **phren·o·log·ic** (fren′ə·loj′ik) or **·i·cal** *adj.* — **phre·nol′o·gist** *n.*

Phryg·i·a (frij′ē·ə) An ancient country in west central Asia Minor. — **Phryg′i·an** *n. & adj.*

phthal·e·in (thal′ē·in, -ēn, fthal′-) *n. Chem.* Any of a series of compounds formed by combining a phenol with phthalic acid or its anhydride, and yielding dyes in some derivatives. Also **phthal′e·ine.** [< PHTHAL(IC) + -ein, var. of -IN]

phthal·ic acid (thal′ik, fthal′-) *Chem.* One of three aromatic crystalline compounds, $C_8H_6O_4$, derived variously.

phthi·sis (thī′sis, fthī′-) *n. Pathol.* Tuberculosis of the lungs. Also **phthis′ic.** [< L < Gk., a wasting away < *phthinein* to decay] — **phthis′i·cal, phthis·ick·y** (fiz′ik·ē) *adj.*

-phyceae *combining form Bot.* Seaweed: used in the names of various classes of algae. [< Gk. *phykos* seaweed]

phyco- *combining form* Seaweed; of or related to seaweed. [< Gk. *phykos* seaweed]

phy·la (fī′lə) Plural of PHYLUM.

phy·lac·ter·y (fi·lak′tər·ē) *n. pl.* **·ter·ies 1.** In traditional Judaism, one of two small leather cases containing a strip or strips of parchment inscribed with Scriptural passages, and bound on the forehead or around the left arm during morning prayer. [< LL < Gk. *phylaktērion* safeguard]

phyllo- *combining form* Leaf; pertaining to a leaf. Also, before vowels, **phyll-.** [< Gk. *phyllon* leaf]

phyl·lo·tax·is (fil′ə·tak′sis) *n. Bot.* **1.** The arrangement of leaves upon a stem. **2.** The laws of this arrangement. Also **phyl′lo·tax′y.** [< NL < Gk. *phyllon* leaf + *taxis* arrangement] — **phyl′lo·tac′tic** (-tak′tik) *adj.*

-phyllous *combining form* Having (a specified kind or number of) leaves. [< Gk. *phyllon* leaf]

phylo- *combining form* Tribe; race; species. Also, before vowels, **phyl-.** [< Gk. *phylē, phylon* tribe]

phy·log·e·ny (fī·loj′ə·nē) *n. pl.* **·nies 1.** *Biol.* The history of the evolution of a species or group: distinguished from *ontogeny*. **2.** Tribal or racial history. Also **phy·lo·gen·e·sis** (fī′lə·jen′ə·sis). [< Gk. *phylon* race + -*geneia* birth, origin] — **phy·lo·ge·net·ic** (-jə·net′ik) or **phy′lo·ge·net′i·cal·ly** *adv.* — **phy′lo·gen′ic** *adj.*

phy·lum (fī′ləm) *n. pl.* **·la** (-lə) *Biol.* A great division of animals or plants of which the members are believed to have a common evolutionary ancestor. [< NL < Gk. *phylon* race]

-phyre *combining form Geol.* A porphyritic rock. [See PORPHYRY.]

physi- Var. of PHYSIO-.

phys·ic (fiz′ik) *n.* A cathartic; a purge. — *v.t.* **·icked, ·ick·ing 1.** To treat with medicine, esp. with a cathartic. **2.** To cure or relieve. [< L < Gk. *physikē* (*epistēmē*) (the knowledge) of nature]

phys·i·cal (fiz′i·kəl) *adj.* **1.** Of or relating to the human body, as distinguished from the mind or spirit. **2.** Of the nature of or pertaining to matter or material things. **3.** Of or relating to the material universe or to the sciences that treat of it. **4.** Of or pertaining to physics: a *physical* law. **5.** Apparent to the senses; external: *physical* changes. [See PHYSIC.] — **phys′i·cal·ly** *adv.*

physical chemistry The branch of chemistry that deals with the physical properties of substances, esp. with reference to the laws governing their quantitative energy transformations and chemical interactions.

physical education Athletic training and development of the human body; also, education in hygiene.

physical geography Geography dealing with the natural features of the earth, as vegetation, land forms, drainage, ocean currents, climate, etc.: also called *physiography*.

physical science Any of the sciences that treat of inanimate matter or energy, as physics, astronomy, chemistry, geology, etc.

physical therapy The treatment of disability, injury, and disease by external physical means, as by electricity, heat, light, massage, exercise, etc.: also called *physiotherapy*.

phy·si·cian (fi·zish′ən) *n.* **1.** One who is legally authorized to practice medicine; a doctor. **2.** A doctor engaged in general practice. **3.** Any healer. [See PHYSIC.]

phys·i·cist (fiz′ə·sist) *n.* A specialist in physics.

physico- *combining form* Physics. [< Gk. *physikos* < *physis* nature. See PHYSIC.]

phys·i·co·chem·i·cal (fiz′i·kō·kem′i·kəl) *adj.* **1.** Of or pertaining to the physical and chemical properties of matter. **2.** Pertaining to physical chemistry.

phys·ics (fiz′iks) *n.pl.* (construed as sing.) The science that treats of motion, matter, and energy, and of their interactions.

physio- *combining form* Nature; related to natural functions or phenomena. Also, before vowels, *physi-*. [< Gk. *physis* nature. See PHYSIC.]

phys·i·og·no·my (fiz′ē·og′nə·mē, *esp. Brit.* fiz′ē·on′ə·mē) *n. pl.* **·mies 1.** The face or features considered as revealing character or disposition. **2.** The outward look of a thing. **3.** The practice of discerning character in the features of the face or form of the body. [< OF < Med.L *phisnomia* < Gk. *physiognōmonia* the judging of a man's nature (by his features)] — **phys′i·og·nom′ic,** *esp. Brit.* **-ə·nom′ik)** or **·i·cal** *adj.* — **phys′i·og·nom′i·cal·ly** *adv.* — **phys′i·og′no·mist** *n.*

phys·i·og·ra·phy (fiz′ē·og′rə·fē) *n.* **1.** A description of nature. **2.** Physical geography. — **phys′i·og′ra·pher** *n.* — **phys′i·o·graph′ic** (-ə·graf′ik) or **·i·cal** *adj.* — **phys′i·o·graph′i·cal·ly** *adv.*

phys·i·ol·o·gy (fiz′ē·ol′ə·jē) *n. pl.* **·gies 1.** The science that treats of the processes and mechanisms by which living animals and plants function under varied conditions. **2.** The aggregate of vital processes: the *physiology* of the frog. [< F < L < Gk. < *physiologos* speaker on nature] — **phys′i·o·log′i·cal, phys′i·o·log′ic** *adj.* — **phys′i·o·log′i·cal·ly** *adv.* — **phys′i·ol′o·gist** *n.*

phys·i·o·ther·a·py (fiz′ē·ō·ther′ə·pē) *n.* Physical therapy.

phy·sique (fi·zēk′) *n.* The structure, strength, or appearance of the body. [< F, orig. adj., physical]

-phyte *combining form* A (specified) kind of plant; a plant having a (specified) habitat. [< Gk. *phyton* plant]

phyto- *combining form* Plant; of or related to vegetation. Also, before vowels, *phyt-*. [< Gk. *phyton* plant]

pi¹ (pī) *n.* **1.** The sixteenth letter in the Greek alphabet (Π, π): corresponding to English *p*. See ALPHABET. **2.** *Math.* **a** This letter used to designate the ratio of the circumference of a circle to its diameter. **b** The ratio itself (3.14159 . . .). [def. 2 < Gk. *p(eriphereia)* periphery]

pi² (pī) *n.* **1.** *Printing* Type that has been thrown into disorder. **2.** Any jumble or disorder. — *v.t.* **pied, pie·ing** To jumble or disorder, as type. Also spelled *pie*. [Var. of PIE¹]

pi·a ma·ter (pī′ə mā′tər) *Anat.* The delicate inner membrane that envelops the brain and spinal cord. [< Med.L, tender mother]

pi·a·nis·si·mo (pē′ə·nis′i·mō, *Ital.* pyä·nēs′sē·mo) *Music adj. & adv.* Very soft or very softly: a direction to the performer. — *n. pl.* **·mos** A passage so played. [< Ital. < L *planissimus,* superl. of *planus* soft]

pi·an·ist (pē·an′ist, pē′ə·nist) *n.* One who plays the piano; esp., an expert or professional performer on the piano. [< F *pianiste* and < Ital. *pianista*]

pi·an·o¹ (pē·an′ō) *n. pl.* **·os** A musical instrument having felt-covered hammers operated from a manual keyboard that strike upon steel wires to produce musical tones; a pianoforte. [< Ital., short for *pianoforte*. See PIANOFORTE.]

pi·a·no² (pē·ä′nō, *Ital.* pyä′nō) *Music adj. & adv.* Soft or softly: a direction to the performer. — *n. pl.* **·os** A passage so played. [< Ital. < L *planus* flat, soft]

pi·an·o·for·te (pē·an′ə·fôr′tā, -fôr′-, -fôrt′, -fôrt′) *n.* A piano. [< Ital. < *piano e forte* soft and loud]

pi·as·ter (pē·as′tər) *n.* **1.** A monetary unit of various countries, as Egypt, Libya, Sudan, and Syria: the hundredth part of a pound. **2.** A Turkish coin and monetary unit: also called *kurus*. **3.** The Spanish peso or dollar. Also **pi·as′tre**. [< F < Ital. *piastra*, lit., plate of metal]

pi·az·za (pē·az′ə, *Ital.* pyät′tsä) *n.* **1.** An open area or public square in a city or town, esp. in Italy. **2.** A covered outer walk or gallery. **3.** *Chiefly U.S.* A veranda or porch. [< Ital., square, market place]

pi·broch (pē′brokh) *n.* A martial air played on the bagpipe. [< Gaelic *piobaireachd* art of playing the bagpipe]

pi·ca (pī′kə) *n.* **1.** A size of type; 12-point; about ⅙ inch; also, a standard unit of measurement for thickness and length of leads, borders, etc. **2.** A size of typewriter type equivalent to 12-point, with 10 characters to the inch. [< Med.L, a book of church rules]

pic·a·dor (pīk′ə·dôr, *Sp.* pē′kä·thôr′) *n.* In bullfighting, a horseman who seeks to weaken the bull by pricking him with a lance. [< Sp., lit., pricker < *picar* to prick]

pic·a·resque (pik′ə·resk′) *adj.* **1.** Of or involving rogues or vagabonds. **2.** Denoting a form of fiction involving rogues and vagabonds. [< Sp. *picaresco* roguish]

pic·a·roon (pik′ə·rōōn′) *n.* **1.** One who lives by cheating or robbery; a pirate, rogue, or adventurer. **2.** A pirate vessel. [< Sp. *picarón*, aug. of *picaro* rogue]

pic·a·yune (pik′i·yōōn′) *adj. U.S.* **1.** Of small value; paltry; contemptible. **2.** Petty; niggling; mean. Also **pic′a·yun′ish**. — *n.* **1.** *U.S.* A coin of little value. **2.** *U.S.* Anything of trifling value. [< F *picaillon* farthing]

pic·ca·lil·li (pik′ə·lil′ē) *n.* A relish of chopped vegetables.

pic·co·lo (pik′ə·lō) *n. pl.* **·los** A small flute pitched an octave higher than the ordinary flute. [< Ital., small]

pick¹ (pik) *v.t.* **1.** To choose; select, as from a group or number. **2.** To detach or pluck, as with the fingers. **3.** To clear (a field, tree, etc.) in such a manner. **4.** To clear of or harvest; gather. **5.** To prepare by removing the feathers, hulls, leaves, etc. **6.** To remove extraneous matter from (the teeth, etc.), as with the fingers or with a pointed instrument. **7.** To touch, irritate, or remove (something) with a fingernail, etc. **8.** To nibble at or peck. **9.** To eat in a dainty or overfastidious manner. **10.** To break up, penetrate, or indent with or as with a pointed instrument. **11.** To form in this manner: to *pick* a hole. **12.** To pull apart, as rags. **13.** To seek or point out critically: to *pick* flaws. **14.** To remove the contents of by stealth: to *pick* a pocket. **15.** To open (a lock) by means other than the key. **16.** To provoke: to *pick* a fight. — *v.i.* **17.** To work with a pick. **18.** To pluck or remove fruit, flowers, etc.; harvest. **19.** To eat daintily or without appetite; nibble. **20.** To select carefully. **21.** To steal. — **to pick apart** (or **to pieces**) **1.** To pull apart. **2.** To destroy by shrewd or critical analysis. — **to pick at 1.** To touch or toy with. **2.** To eat without appetite. **3.** *U.S. Informal* To nag at. — **to pick off 1.** To remove by picking. **2.** To hit, as with a bullet. **3.** In baseball, to catch (a base runner) off base. — **to pick on 1.** To determine on; choose. **2.** *Informal* To tease or annoy. — **to pick one's way** (or **steps**) To advance by careful selection of one's course. — **to pick out 1.** To choose or select. **2.** To distinguish (something) from its surroundings. **3.** To produce the notes of (a tune, etc.) singly or slowly, as by ear. — **to pick over** To examine carefully or one by one. — **to pick up 1.** To take up, as with the hand. **2.** To take up or receive into a group, vehicle, etc. **3.** To acquire casually or by chance. **4.** To gain speed; accelerate. **5.** To be able to perceive or receive, as a radio station. **6.** To break (ground, etc.) with a pick. **7.** *U.S.* To make (a room, etc.) tidy. **8.** *Informal* To recover spirits, health, etc.; improve. **9.** *Informal* To make the acquaintance of (a stranger, esp. of the opposite sex) under casual circumstances. — *n.* **1.** Right of selection; choice. **2.** That which is selected, esp. the choicest part. **3.** The quantity of certain crops that are picked by hand. **4.** The act of picking. [ME *piken, pikken* < OE *pīcan, pīcian*] — **pick′er** *n.*

pick² (pik) *n.* **1.** A double-headed, pointed metal tool mounted on a wooden handle, used for breaking ground, etc. **2.** Any of various implements used for picking. **3.** A plectrum. [Appar. var. of PIKE¹]

pick·a·back (pik′ə·bak′) *adv.* Piggyback. [Earlier *pick-back, pickpack*]

pick·a·nin·ny (pik′ə·nin′ē) *n. pl.* **·nies** A Negro child: a condescending or offensive term. Also **pic′ca·nin′ny**. [Dim. of Sp. *pequeño* little, small]

pick·ax (pik′aks′) *n.* A pick or mattock with one end of the head edged like a chisel and the other pointed; also, a pick with both ends pointed. Also **pick′axe′**.

picked (pikt) *adj.* **1.** Carefully selected. **2.** Cleaned by picking out refuse, stalks, etc.

picked-o·ver (pikt′ō′vər) *adj.* Handled; left after the best have been removed.

pick·er·el (pik′ər·əl, -rel) *n.* Any of various North American fresh-water fishes of the pike family, esp. the small species having a narrow snout and sharp teeth. [Dim. of PIKE¹]

pick·er·el·weed (pik′ər·əl·wēd′) *n.* Any of various perennial plants found in the shallows of North American lakes.

pick·et (pik′it) *n.* **1.** A pointed stick or post, used as a fence paling, tent peg, etc.; a stake. **2.** A person stationed at the outside of a place affected by a strike, for the purpose of publicizing alleged grievances, etc. **3.** A person engaged in publicly protesting a proposed law, policy, etc. **4.** *Mil.* A soldier or detachment of soldiers posted to guard a camp, army, etc. — *v.t.* **1.** To be a picket or station pickets outside of. **2.** To fence or fortify with pickets. **3.** To tie to a picket, as a horse. **4.** *Mil.* **a** To guard by means of a picket. **b** To post as a picket. — *v.i.* **5.** To act as a picket (defs. 2 & 3). [< F *piquet* pointed stake]

pick·et·er (pik′it·ər) *n.* A picket (defs. 2 & 3).

picket fence A fence made of upright pickets.

picket line A line of people picketing a business, etc.

pick·ing (pik′ing) *n.* **1.** The act of picking; also, that which is or may be picked. **2.** *pl.* That which is left: scanty *pickings*. **3.** *Usu. pl.* That which is taken by questionable means; spoils.

pick·le (pik′əl) *n.* **1.** A cucumber that has been preserved and flavored in a liquid solution, usu. of brine or vinegar. **2.** Any article of food so preserved or flavored. **3.** A liquid preservative, as brine or vinegar, sometimes spiced, for meat, fish, etc. **4.** Diluted acid used in cleaning metal castings, etc. **5.** *Informal* An embarrassing condition or position. — *v.t.* **·led, ·ling 1.** To preserve or flavor in pickle. **2.** *Metall.* To treat with a pickle. [Appar. < MDu. *pekel, peeckel*]

pick·led (pik′əld) *adj.* **1.** Preserved in pickle. **2.** Of wood work, etc., having a bleached finish. **3.** *Slang* Drunk.

pick·lock (pik′lok′) *n.* **1.** A special implement for opening a lock. **2.** One who picks locks, esp. illegally.

pick-me-up (pik′mē′up′) *n. Informal* A drink, esp. an alcoholic drink, taken to renew one's energy or spirits.

pick·pock·et (pik′pok′it) *n.* One who steals from pockets.

pick·up (pik′up′) *n.* **1.** Acceleration, as in the speed of an automobile, engine, etc. **2.** *Electronics* A crystal, ceramic, or magnetic device that converts the oscillations of a needle in a record groove into electrical impulses. **3.** The tone arm of a record player. **4.** A small, usu. open truck for light loads. **5.** *Telecom.* **a** In radio, the location of microphones in relation to program elements. **b** The place where a broadcast originates. **c** In television, the scanning of an image by the electron beam. **d** The scanning apparatus. **6.** In baseball, the act of fielding a ball that has touched the ground. **7.** *Informal* A period of renewed or increased activity: a *pickup* in business. **8.** *Informal* Something that stimulates or renews in spirit. **9.** *Slang* A stranger with whom a casual acquaintance is made.

pic·nic (pik′nik) *n.* **1.** An outdoor social outing for which food is usu. provided by the people participating. **2.** *Slang* An easy or pleasant time or experience. — *v.i.* **·nicked, ·nick·ing** To have or attend a picnic. [< F *pique-nique*, prob. reduplication of *piquer* to pick, peck] — **pic′nick·er** *n.*

pico- *combining form* One trillionth (10⁻¹²) of a specified quantity or dimension. [< NL < Sp., small quantity]

pi·cot (pē′kō) *n.* A small thread loop on ornamental edging, ribbon, etc. — *v.t. &v.i.* **·coted** (-kōd) **·cot·ing** (-kō·ing) To sew with this edging. [< F, dim. of OF *pic* point]

pic·ric acid (pik′rik) *Chem.* A yellow, crystalline, bitter compound, $C_6H_2(NO_2)_3OH$, used in dyeing and in certain explosives.

picro- *combining form* Bitter. Also, before vowels, **picr-**. [< Gk. *pikros* bitter]

Pict (pikt) *n.* One of an ancient people of uncertain origin who inhabited Britain and the Scottish Highlands.

Pict·ish (pik′tish) *n.* The language of the Picts, of undetermined relationship. — *adj.* Of or pertaining to the Picts.

pic·to·graph (pik′tə·graf, -gräf) *n.* **1.** A picture representing an idea, as a hieroglyph. **2.** A record of such pictures. [< L *pictus* painted + -GRAPH] — **pic′to·graph′ic** *adj.* — **pic·to·graph′i·cal·ly** *adv.* — **pic·tog·ra·phy** (pik·tog′rə·fē) *n.*

pic·to·ri·al (pik·tôr′ē·əl, -tō′rē-) *adj.* **1.** Pertaining to, composed of, or concerned with pictures. **2.** Graphic; vivid **3.** Containing or illustrated by pictures. — *n.* A periodical that devotes considerable space to pictures [< LL < L *pictus*, pp. of *pingere* to paint] — **pic·to′ri·al·ly** *adv.*

pic·ture (pik′chər) *n.* **1.** A visual representation of an object or scene upon a flat surface, as a painting, drawing, engraving, or photograph. **2.** A vivid or graphic verbal description. **3.** A mental image or impression of the nature of a situation, event, etc. **4.** An overall situation, esp. as perceived from a particular vantage point. **5.** One who or that which resembles or embodies another person or thing: She is the *picture* of despair. **6.** A motion picture. **7.** Something attractive or pleasant: pretty as a *picture*. — *v.t.* **·tured, ·tur·ing 1.** To form a mental image of. **2.** To describe graphically; depict verbally. **3.** To make a picture of. [< L *pictus*, pp. of *pingere* to paint]

picture gallery A room or hall for exhibiting pictures.

picture hat A woman's hat having a very wide brim and often trimmed with plumes.

pic·tur·esque (pik'chə·resk') *adj.* **1.** Having a striking, irregular beauty, quaintness, or charm. **2.** Abounding in striking or original expression or imagery; richly graphic. **3.** Like or suitable for a picture; having pictorial quality. — **pic'tur·esque'ly** *adv.* — **pic'tur·esque'ness** *n.*

picture tube Kinescope.

picture window A large window consisting of a single pane of glass, designed to frame a view of the outside.

picture writing 1. The use of pictures or pictorial symbols in writing. **2.** A writing so made.

pid·dle (pid'l) *v.* **·dled, ·dling** *v.t.* **1.** To trifle; dawdle: usually with *away.* — *v.i.* **2.** To trifle; dawdle. **3.** To urinate. [Origin uncertain]

pid·dling (pid'ling) *adj.* Unimportant; trivial; trifling.

pidg·in (pij'in) *n.* A mixed language combining the vocabulary and grammar of dissimilar languages. [< Chinese pronun. of *business*]

Pidgin English A jargon composed of English and elements of local non-English dialects, used as the language of commerce in areas of China, Melanesia, Northern Australia, and West Africa. Also called **Pidgin.**

pie[1] (pī) *n.* **1.** A baked food consisting of one or two layers or crusts of pastry with a filling of fruit, custard, meat, etc. **2.** A layer cake filled with cream, jam, etc. **3.** See PI[2]. **4.** *Slang* Anything very good or very easy. **5.** *Slang* Political graft. [? < PIE[2]; with ref. to the variety of objects collected by magpies]

pie[2] (pī) *n.* A magpie. [< OF < L *pica* magpie]

pie·bald (pī'bôld') *adj.* Having spots, esp. of white and black. — *n.* A spotted or mottled animal, esp. a horse. [< PIE[2] + BALD; because like a magpie's plumage]

piece (pēs) *n.* **1.** A portion or quantity existing as an individual entity or mass: a *piece* of paper. **2.** A small portion considered as forming or having formed a distinct part of a whole. **3.** A coin: a fifty-cent *piece.* **4.** An instance; example: a *piece* of luck. **5.** One of a class or group: a *piece* of furniture. **6.** A work of esthetic interest, as a literary or musical composition, a play, etc. **7.** Point of view; opinion: to speak one's *piece.* **8.** One of the disks or counters used in checkers, backgammon, etc. **9.** A quantity or length, as of wallpaper, in which an article is manufactured or sold. **10.** *Dial.* A short time, space, or distance: to walk a *piece.* **11.** *Dial.* A snack between regular meals. **12.** *Archaic or Dial.* A person; individual. — **a piece of one's mind** *Informal* Criticism or censure frankly expressed. — **of a (or one) piece 1.** Of the same kind, sort, or class. **2.** Of the same piece; undivided. — **to go to pieces 1.** To fall apart. **2.** *Informal* To lose moral or emotional self-control. — **to have a piece of** *U.S. Slang* To have a financial interest in. — *v.t.* **pieced, piec·ing 1.** To add or attach a piece or pieces to, as for enlargement. **2.** To unite or reunite the pieces of, as in mending. **3.** To unite (parts) into a whole. [< OF < Med.L *pecia*; ult. origin uncertain] — **piec'er** *n.*

pièce de ré·sis·tance (pyes də rā·zē·stäns') *French* **1.** A principal or most important item. **2.** The chief dish of a dinner.

piece goods Fabrics made in standard lengths.

piece·meal (pēs'mēl') *adv.* **1.** Piece by piece; gradually. **2.** In pieces. — *adj.* Made up of pieces. [ME < *pece* piece + -*mele* a part]

piece·work (pēs'wûrk') *n.* Work done or paid for by the piece or quantity. — **piece'work'er** *n.*

pie chart *Stat.* A graph in the form of a circle divided into sectors.

pied (pīd) *adj.* Spotted; piebald; mottled. [< PIE[2]]

pied-à-terre (pyā·dà·târ') *n. French* A temporary or secondary lodging; literally, foot on the ground.

pied·mont (pēd'mont) *adj. Geog.* At the foot of a mountain. [< L < pes, *pedis* foot + *mons, montis* mountain]

pie plant *U.S. Dial.* The common variety of rhubarb.

pier (pir) *n.* **1.** A structure extending over the water, secured by piles and serving as a landing place for vessels; wharf. **2.** A plain, detached mass of masonry, usu. serving as a support: the *pier* of a bridge. **3.** An upright projecting portion of a wall; a buttress. **4.** A solid portion of a wall between window openings, etc. [< OF *per* < Med.L *pera*]

pierce (pirs) *v.* **pierced, pierc·ing** *v.t.* **1.** To pass into or

through, with or as if with a pointed instrument; puncture; stab. **2.** To force a way into or through: to *pierce* the wilderness. **3.** To make an opening or hole in, into, or through. **4.** To make or cut (an opening or hole) in or through something. **5.** To cut through as if stabbing; cleave. **6.** To affect sharply or deeply, as with emotion, pain, etc. **7.** To solve; understand: to *pierce* a mystery. — *v.i.* **8.** To enter; penetrate. [< OF *percer*] — **pierc'er** *n.* — **pierc'ing·ly** *adv.* — **pierc'ing·ness** *n.*

pier glass A large, high mirror intended to fill the space, or pier, between two windows.

Pi·e·ri·a (pī·ir'ē·ə) A coastal region of ancient Macedon, at the base of Mount Olympus, legendary birthplace of the nine Muses. — **Pi·e'ri·an** *adj.*

Pier·rot (pye·rō') Formerly, a stock character in French pantomimes, wearing white pantaloons and a loose white jacket with big buttons. [< F, dim. of *Pierre* Peter]

Pie·tà (pyā·tä') *n.* In painting, sculpture, etc., a representation of Mary mourning over the body of Christ in her arms. [< Ital., lit., pity]

pi·e·tism (pī'ə·tiz'əm) *n.* **1.** Piety or godliness; devotion. **2.** Affected or exaggerated piety. [< G *pietismus*] — **pi'e·tist** *n.* — **pi'e·tis'tic** or **·ti·cal** *adj.* — **pi·e·tis'ti·cal·ly** *adv.*

pi·e·ty (pī'ə·tē) *n. pl.* **·ties 1.** Reverence toward God or the gods. **2.** Honor and obedience due to parents, etc. **3.** A pious act, wish, etc. **4.** The state or quality of being pious. [< OF < L < *pius* dutiful]

piezo- *combining form* Pressure; related to or produced by pressure. [< Gk. *piezien* to press]

pi·e·zo·e·lec·tric·i·ty (pī·ē'zō·i·lek'tris'ə·tē, -ē'lik-) *n.* Electricity or electric phenomena resulting from pressure upon certain bodies, esp. crystals. — **pi·e'zo·e·lec'tric** or **·tri·cal** *adj.* — **pi·e'zo·e·lec'tri·cal·ly** *adv.*

pif·fle (pif'əl) *Informal v.i.* **·fled, ·fling** To talk nonsensically; babble. — *n.* Nonsense; babble. [? Blend of PIDDLE and TRIFLE]

pig (pig) *n.* **1.** A cloven-hoofed mammal having a long, mobile snout; esp., a small, young one: also called *hog, swine.* ◆ Collateral adjective: *porcine.* **2.** The flesh of a pig; pork. **3.** An oblong mass of metal, esp. iron or lead, just run from the smelter and cast in a rough mold; also, the mold. **4.** Pig iron or iron pigs in general. **5.** *Informal* A person who is filthy, gluttonous, or coarse. **6.** *Informal* A railroad locomotive. — *v.i.* **pigged, pig·ging 1.** To bring forth pigs. **2.** To act or live like pigs: with *it.* [ME *pigge*; ult. origin uncertain]

pig·eon (pij'ən) *n.* **1.** A bird having short legs, a small head and a sturdy body; esp., the domestic pigeon or rock dove. **2.** *Slang* One who is easily swindled. [< OF < LL *pipio, -onis* young chirping bird]

pigeon breast *Pathol.* A deformity in which the chest is narrow and pointed. — **pig'eon-breast'ed** *adj.*

pigeon hawk A small American falcon.

pig·eon·heart·ed (pij'ən·här'tid) *adj.* Timid; fearful.

pig·eon·hole (pij'ən·hōl') *n.* **1.** A hole for pigeons to nest in. **2.** A small compartment, as in a desk, for filing papers. — *v.t.* **·holed, ·hol·ing 1.** To place in a pigeonhole; file. **2.** To file away and ignore. **3.** To place in categories.

pig·eon-toed (pij'ən·tōd') *adj.* Having the toes or feet turned inward.

pig·ger·y (pig'ər·ē) *n. pl.* **·ger·ies** A place for keeping or raising pigs.

pig·gish (pig'ish) *adj.* Like a pig; greedy; dirty; selfish. — **pig'gish·ly** *adv.* — **pig'gish·ness** *n.*

pig·gy (pig'ē) *n. pl.* **·gies** A little pig. Also **pig'gie.**

pig·gy·back (pig'ē·bak') *adv.* **1.** On the back or shoulders: to ride *piggyback:* also *pickaback.* **2.** On a railway flat car: to ship trailers *piggyback.* — **pig'gy·back'ing** *n.*

piggy bank A coin bank in the shape of a pig.

pig·head·ed (pig'hed'id) *adj.* Stupidly obstinate. — **pig'head'ed·ly** *adv.* — **pig'head'ed·ness** *n.*

pig iron Crude iron poured from a blast furnace into variously shaped molds or pigs of sand or the like.

pig latin A jargon in which the initial sound of a word is usu. transposed to the end and to which -*ay* (ā) is added, as in *Illkay the umbay* for *Kill the bum.* Also **pig Latin.**

pig·ment (pig'mənt) *n.* **1.** Any of a class of finely powdered, insoluble coloring matters suitable for making paints, enamels, etc. **2.** Any substance that imparts color to animal or vegetable tissues, as melanin and chlorophyll. [< L *pingere* to paint] — **pig'men·tar·y** (-ter'ē) *adj.*

pig·men·ta·tion (pig'mən·tā'shən) *n.* **1.** Coloration resulting from pigment. **2.** *Biol.* Deposition of pigment by cells.

pig·ment·ed (pig'mən·tid) *adj.* Having pigmentation.

pig·my (pig'mē) See PYGMY.

Pig·my (pig'mē) See PYGMY.

pig·nut (pig'nut') *n.* **1.** The fruit of a species of hickory common in the U.S. **2.** The tree.

pig·pen (pig'pen') *n.* A pen or sty where pigs are kept.

pig·skin (pig'skin') *n.* 1. The skin of a pig. 2. Something made of this skin, as a saddle. 3. *U.S. Informal* A football.

pig·sty (pig'stī') *n.* *pl.* **·sties** A sty or pen for pigs.

pig·tail (pig'tāl') *n.* 1. A braid or plait of hair extending down from the back of the head. 2. A twist of tobacco.

pike[1] (pīk) *n.* A long pole having a metal spearhead. — *v.t.* **piked, pik·ing** To run through or kill with a pike. [< MF *pique*]

pike[2] (pīk) *n.* 1. A widely-distributed, voracious fresh-water food fish having a slender body and a long snout. 2. Any of several other fishes resembling the pike. [< PIKE[5] with ref. to its pointed snout]

pike[3] (pīk) *n.* 1. A turnpike. 2. The fee for using a turn-pike road. — *v.i.* **piked, pik·ing** *Slang* To go in haste: usu. with *along*. [Short for TURNPIKE]

pike[4] (pīk) *n.* *Brit. Dial.* A mountain peak or pointed hill.

pike[5] (pīk) *n.* A spike or sharp point, as the end of a spear.

piked (pīkt, pī'kid) *adj.* Having a pike; pointed. [< PIKE[5]]

pik·er (pī'kər) *n.* *U.S. Slang* 1. One who bets or speculates in a small, niggardly way. 2. One who acts in a petty or niggling way. [Origin uncertain]

pike·staff (pīk'staf', -stäf') The wooden handle of a pike. [< PIKE[5] + STAFF[1]]

pi·laf (pi·läf') *n.* An Oriental dish of rice, raisins, spice, and a meat or fowl sauce. Also **pi·laff**, **pi·lau** (pi·lou', -lô'), **pi·law** (-lô'). [< Persian and Turkish *pilāw*]

pi·lar (pī'lər) *adj.* Of, pertaining to, or covered with hair. [< NL < L *pilus* hair]

pi·las·ter (pi·las'tər) *n.* *Archit.* A rectangular column, with capital and base, engaged in a wall. [< MF < Ital. < L *pila* column]

pil·chard (pil'chərd) *n.* A small, herringlike food fish, the sardine of Mediterranean and European Atlantic waters. [Earlier *pilcher*; origin uncertain]

pile[1] (pīl) *n.* 1. A quantity of anything gathered or thrown together in one place; a heap. 2. A funeral pyre. 3. A massive building or group of buildings. 4. *Informal* A large accumulation, quantity, or number of something. 5. *Physics* A reactor. 6. *Slang* A large amount of money. — *v.* **piled, pil·ing** *v.t.* 1. To make a heap or pile of: often with *up.* 2. To cover or burden with a pile or piles: to *pile* a plate with food. — *v.i.* 3. To form a heap or pile. 4. To proceed or go in a confused mass: with *in, on, off, out,* etc. — **to pile up** To accumulate. [< OF < L *pila* pillar, pier]

PILASTER

pile[2] (pīl) *n.* 1. A heavy timber forced into the earth to form a foundation for a building, pier, etc.: also called *spile.* 2. Any similar supporting structure, as of steel or concrete. — *v.t.* **piled, pil·ing** 1. To drive piles into. 2. To furnish or strengthen with piles. [OE *pil* dart, pointed stake]

pile[3] (pīl) *n.* 1. The cut or uncut loops that form the surface of certain fabrics, as velvets, plushes, and corduroys. 2. The surface so formed. 3. Hair collectively; fur; wool. 4. Soft, fine hair; down. [< L *pilus* hair] — **piled** *adj.*

pi·le·at·ed (pī'lē·ā'tid, pil'ē-) *adj.* 1. *Bot.* Provided with a pileus or cap. 2. *Ornithol.* Having the feathers of the pileum elongated or conspicuous; crested. Also **pi'le·ate.** [< L *pileatus* capped]

pile driver A machine for driving piles.

pi·le·ous (pī'lē·əs) *adj.* Pilose.

piles (pīlz) *n.pl.* Hemorrhoids. [< LL *pila* ball]

pi·le·um (pī'lē·əm, pil'ē-) *n.* *pl.* **·le·a** (-lē·ə) *Ornithol.* The top of the head of a bird, from the base of the bill to the nape and above the eyes. [< L, var. of *pileus* felt cap]

pi·le·us (pī'lē·əs, pil'ē-) *n.* *pl.* **·le·i** (-lē·ī) *Bot.* The umbrella-shaped portion of a mushroom. [< L, felt cap]

pil·fer (pil'fər) *v.t. & v.i.* To steal in small quantities. [< OF *pelfrer* to rob] — **pil'fer·age** (-fər·ij) *n.* — **pil'fer·er** *n.*

pil·grim (pil'grim) *n.* 1. One who journeys to some sacred place from religious motives. 2. Any wanderer or wayfarer. [ME < OF < L < *per-* through + *ager, agri* land]

Pil·grim (pil'grim) *n.* One of the English Puritans who founded Plymouth Colony in 1620.

pil·grim·age (pil'grə·mij) *n.* 1. A journey made to a shrine or sacred place. 2. Any long or arduous journey.

Pilgrim Fathers The founders of Plymouth Colony, Massachusetts, in 1620.

Pilgrim's Progress A religious allegory by John Bunyan.

pil·ing (pī'ling) *n.* 1. Piles collectively. 2. A structure formed of piles. 3. The act or process of driving piles.

pill (pil) *n.* 1. A pellet or globule containing medicine, convenient for swallowing whole. 2. A disagreeable necessity. 3. *Slang* A person difficult to bear with; a bore. 4. *Slang* A ball or disk, as a baseball or golfball. — **the pill** or **the Pill** Any of various oral contraceptive drugs in tablet form, taken by women. — *v.t.* 1. To form into pills. 2. To dose with pills. [< L *pila* ball]

pil·lage (pil'ij) *n.* 1. The act of taking money or property by open violence; looting. 2. Spoil; booty. — *v.* **·laged, ·lag·ing** *v.t.* 1. To plunder. 2. To take as loot. — *v.i.* 3. To take plunder. [< OF < *piller* to plunder] — **pil'lag·er** *n.*

pil·lar (pil'ər) *n.* 1. A vertical, freestanding support, usu. slender in relation to its height; column; shaft. 2. A structure of similar form used as a decoration or monument. 3. Anything resembling a pillar in form or function. 4. One who strongly supports a work or cause. — **from pillar to post** From one predicament to another. — *v.t.* To support or adorn with pillars. [< OF < LL < L *pila* pillar]

pill·box (pil'boks') *n.* 1. A small box for pills. 2. A small, round, concrete emplacement for a machine gun, antitank gun, etc. 3. A small, round hat with a flat top.

pil·lion (pil'yən) *n.* A pad or seat behind the saddle of a horse or motorcycle for a second rider. [Appar. < Scottish Gaelic *pillean,* dim. of *pell* cushion]

pil·lo·ry (pil'ə·rē) *n.* *pl.* **·ries** A framework in which an offender was fastened by the neck and wrists and exposed to public scorn. — *v.t.* **·ried, ·ry·ing** 1. To set in the pillory. 2. To hold up to public scorn or ridicule. [< OF *pellori*]

pil·low (pil'ō) *n.* 1. A case, usu. of cloth, filled with a soft or yielding material, as feathers or foam rubber, used to cushion the head, as during sleep. 2. A small, usu. decorative cushion. 3. Any body rest. 4. Anything resembling a pillow. — *v.t.* 1. To rest on or as on a pillow. 2. To act as a pillow for. — *v.i.* 3. To recline on or as on a pillow. [ME < OE < L *pulvinus* cushion] — **pil'low·y** *adj.*

pil·low·case (pil'ō·kās') *n.* A covering drawn over a pillow. Also **pillow slip.**

pi·lose (pī'lōs) *adj.* Hairy; also *pileous, pilous.* [< L *pilus* hair] — **pi·los·i·ty** (pī·los'ə·tē) *n.*

pi·lot (pī'lət) *n.* 1. One who operates or guides an aircraft or spacecraft during flight. 2. One who is trained and licensed to conduct ships in and out of port or through certain waters difficult to navigate. 3. The helmsman of a ship. 4. Any guide. 5. *Mech.* A part that steadies or guides the action of a tool or other part. 6. A pilot light (which see). — *v.t.* 1. To act as the pilot of; steer. 2. To guide or conduct, as through difficult circumstances. 3. To serve as a pilot on, over, or in. — *adj.* 1. Serving as a guide or control. 2. Serving as a trial situation. 3. Of or pertaining to a pilot or pilots. [< MF *pillotte, pilot* < Ital. *pilota*]

pi·lot·age (pī'lət·ij) *n.* 1. The act of piloting a vessel or aircraft. 2. The fee for such service.

pilot balloon A small balloon sent aloft to show the direction and velocity of the wind.

pilot fish An oceanic fish often seen in warm latitudes in company with sharks.

pi·lot·house (pī'lət·hous') *n.* An enclosed structure, usu. in the forward part of a ship, containing the steering wheel and compass: also called *wheelhouse.*

pilot lamp A small electric light that shows whether a given circuit, motor, etc., is functioning: also called *pilot light.*

pilot light 1. A minute jet of gas kept burning for igniting an ordinary burner as soon as the gas is turned on: also **pilot burner.** 2. A pilot lamp (which see).

pilot officer In the Royal, Royal Canadian, and other Commonwealth air forces, a commissioned officer ranking next below a flight officer. See table at GRADE.

pi·lous (pī'ləs) *adj.* Pilose.

pil·sner (pil'znər) *n.* *Often cap.* Beer of a kind originally brewed in Pilsen, Czechoslovakia. Also **pil'sen·er** (-zə·nər).

Pilt·down man (pilt'doun) A spurious type of early man postulated from skull fragments planted by a hoaxer near Piltdown, England.

Pi·ma (pē'mə) *n.* *pl.* **Pi·mas** or **Pi·ma** 1. One of a tribe of North American Indians of southern Arizona and Northern Mexico. 2. The Uto-Aztecan language of this tribe.

Pi·man (pē'mən) *n.* A branch of the Uto-Aztecan stock of North American Indians. — *adj.* Of or pertaining to this linguistic branch.

pi·men·to (pi·men'tō) *n.* *pl.* **·tos** 1. The dried, unripe, aromatic berries of a West Indian tree of the myrtle family. 2. Pimento. [< Sp. < Med.L *pigmentum* spiced drink, spice]

pimento cheese A cheese with pimentos added.

pi·mien·to (pi·myen'tō) *n.* *pl.* **·tos** A sweet pepper or its ripe fruit, used as a relish and as a stuffing in olives: also called *pimento.* [< Sp. < *pimienta* pepper]

pimp (pimp) *n.* A pander; esp., one who solicits for a prostitute in exchange for part of her earnings. — *v.i.* To act as a pimp. [? < F < MF < L *pipire* to murmur seductively]

pim·per·nel (pim'pər·nel) *n.* A plant of the primrose family, usu. with red flowers, as the common **scarlet pimpernel.** [< OF < Med.L < LL, ? < L *piper* pepper]

pim·ple (pim'pəl) *n.* A small swelling or elevation of the skin, with an inflamed base. [ME < OE *piplian* to break out in pimples] — **pim'pled, pim'ply** *adj.*

pin (pin) *n.* 1. A short, stiff piece of wire with a sharp point and a round, usu. flattened head, used for fastening together parts of clothing, sheets of paper, etc. **2.** An ornament mounted on a pin or having a pin with a clasp. **3.** Anything resembling a pin in form or use, as a hairpin or clothespin. **4.** A peg or bar, as of metal or wood, used in fastening or supporting, as the bolt of a door, a linchpin, etc. **5.** A rolling pin. **6.** Something of no importance; a trifle. **7.** In bowling and other ball-throwing games, one of the rounded wooden clubs, that are set up as the target. **8.** In golf, a pole with a small flag attached to mark the position of a hole. **9.** *pl. Informal* The legs. **10.** *Music* A peg. **11.** *Naut.* **a** A belaying pin. **b** A thole. — **on pins and needles** Uneasy or anxious; nervous. — *v.t.* **pinned, pin·ning 1.** To fasten with or as with a pin or pins. **2.** To seize and hold firmly; make unable to move. **3.** To transfix with a pin, spear, etc. **4.** To force (someone) to make up his mind, follow a definite course of action, etc.: usu. with *down.* **5.** *U.S. Slang* In colleges and universities, to give one's fraternity pin to (a girl) as an expression of the intention to become engaged. **6.** *U.S. Slang* To hold responsible for (a wrongdoing, etc.); accuse of: with *on.* [OE *pinn* peg] — **pin′ner** *n.*

pi·na·ceous (pī-nā′shəs) *adj. Bot.* Pertaining or belonging to the pine family of widely distributed coniferous trees and shrubs having needlelike leaves and bearing hard, woody cones. [< NL < L *pinus* pine]

pin·a·fore (pin′ə-fôr, -fōr) *n.* A sleeveless apronlike garment. esp. one for protecting a child's dress.

pin·ball (pin′bôl′) *n.* A game in which a ball is propelled by a spring to the top of an inclined board, and in its descent touches any of various numbered pins, holes, etc., the contacts so made determining the player's score.

pince-nez (pans′nā′, pins′-, *Fr.* paṅs-nā′) *n. pl.* **pince-nez** Eyeglasses held upon the nose by a spring. [< F, lit., pinch-nose < *pincer* to pinch + *nez* nose]

pin·cer·like (pin′sər·līk′) *adj.* Resembling the action or form of one or both jaws of pincers: a *pincerlike* movement.

pin·cers (pin′sərz) *n.pl.* (*sometimes construed as sing.*) **1.** An instrument having two handles and a pair of jaws working on a pivot, used for holding objects. **2.** *Zool.* A pincerlike organ, as the claw of a lobster. Also **pinch·ers** (pin′chərz). [ME *pinsours*, appar. < AF *pincer* to pinch]

pinch (pinch) *v.t.* **1.** To squeeze between two hard edges or surfaces, as a finger and thumb, etc. **2.** To bend or compress painfully. **3.** To affect with pain or distress: The cold *pinched* his fingers. **4.** To contract or make thin, as from cold or hunger. **5.** To reduce in means; distress, as for lack of money. **6.** *Slang* To capture or arrest. **7.** *Slang* To steal. — *v.i.* **8.** To squeeze; hurt. **9.** To be careful with money; be stingy. — **to pinch pennies** To be economical or stingy — *n.* **1.** The act of pinching, or the state of being pinched. **2.** So much of a substance as can be taken between the finger and thumb; a small amount. **3.** An emergency. **4.** *Slang* A theft. **5.** *Slang* An arrest or raid. [< AF *pincher*, OF *pincier*] — **pinch′er** *n.*

pinch·beck (pinch′bek) *n.* **1.** An alloy of copper, zinc, and tin, forming a cheap imitation of gold. **2.** Anything spurious or pretentious. — *adj.* **1.** Made of pinchbeck. **2.** Cheap; spurious. [after Christopher *Pinchbeck,* 1670?–1732, English inventor]

pinch-hit (pinch′hit′) *v.i.* **-hit, -hit·ting 1.** In baseball, to go to bat in place of a regular player. **2.** *U.S. Informal* To substitute for another in an emergency. — **pinch hitter**

pin·cush·ion (pin′kŏsh′ən) *n.* A small cushion into which pins are stuck when they are not in use.

pine¹ (pīn) *n.* **1.** Any of various cone-bearing trees having needle-shaped evergreen leaves growing in clusters, and including many important timber trees. **2.** Loosely, any tree of the pine family. **3.** The wood of any pine tree. [Fusion of OE *pīn* and OF *pin,* both < L *pinus* pine tree]

pine² (pīn) *v.* **pined, pin·ing** *v.i.* **1.** To grow thin or weak with longing, grief, etc. **2.** To have great longing; usu. with *for.* [OE *pīn* torment, ult. < L *poena* punishment]

pin·e·al (pin′ē-əl) *adj.* **1.** Shaped like a pine cone. **2.** Pertaining to the pineal body. [< F < L *pinea* pine cone]

pineal body *Anat.* A small, reddish gray, vascular, conical body of rudimentary glandular structure found in the brain and having no known function. Also **pineal gland.**

pine·ap·ple (pīn′ap′əl) *n.* **1.** A tropical American plant having spiny, recurved leaves and a cone-shaped fruit tipped with a rosette of spiked leaves. **2.** Its edible fruit. **3.** *Slang* A hand grenade.

pine cone The cone-shaped fruit of the pine tree.

pine needle The needle-shaped leaf of a pine tree.

pine tar A dark, viscous tar obtained by the destructive distillation of the wood of pine trees, used to treat skin ailments.

PINEAPPLE

Pine-Tree (pīn′trē′) **State** Nickname of Maine.

pine·y (pī′nē) See PINY.

pin·feath·er (pin′feth′ər) *n. Ornithol.* A rudimentary feather, esp. one just beginning to grow through the skin.

pin·fold (pin′fōld′) *n.* A pound for stray animals, esp. for cattle. — *v.t.* To shut in a pinfold. [OE *pundfald*]

ping (ping) *n.* A brief, sharp, high-pitched sound. — *v.i.* To make this sound. [Imit.]

ping-pong (ping′pong′, -pông′) *n.* The game of table tennis. [< *Ping Pong,* a trade name]

pin·head (pin′hed′) *n.* **1.** The head of a pin. **2.** Any small or insignificant object. **3.** A small minnow. **4.** A microcephalic. **5.** *Slang* A brainless or stupid person.

pin·hole (pin′hōl′) *n.* A minute puncture made by or as by a pin.

pin·ion¹ (pin′yən) *n.* **1.** The wing of a bird. **2.** A feather; quill. **3.** The outer segment of a bird's wing, bearing the flight feathers. **4.** The anterior border of the wing of an insect. — *v.t.* **1.** To cut off one pinion or bind the wings of (a bird) so as to prevent flight. **2.** To cut or bind (the wings) of a bird. **3.** To bind or hold the arms of (someone). **4.** To shackle; confine. [< OF < L *pinna,* *penna* feather]

pin·ion² (pin′yən) *n. Mech.* A toothed wheel driving or driven by a larger cogwheel. For illus. see DIFFERENTIAL GEAR. [< F < OF < L *pinna,* orig., pinnacle]

pink¹ (pingk) *n.* **1.** A pale hue of crimson. **2.** Any of several garden plants with narrow, grasslike leaves and fragrant flowers. **3.** The flower of any of these plants, as the carnation. **4.** The highest or best condition, degree, or example. **5.** *Informal* A person who holds somewhat radical economic or political views: a contemptuous term. — **in the pink (of condition)** *Informal* In excellent health. — *adj.* **1.** Being pink in color. **2.** *Informal* Moderately radical. [Origin uncertain] — **pink′ish** *adj.*

pink² (pingk) *v.t.* **1.** To prick or stab with a pointed weapon. **2.** To decorate, as cloth or leather, with a pattern of holes. **3.** To cut or finish the edges of (cloth) with a notched pattern, as to prevent raveling or for decoration. **4.** *Brit.* To adorn; deck. [ME *pynken*]

pink·eye (pingk′ī′) *n.* **1.** *Pathol.* An acute, contagious conjunctivitis marked by redness of the eyeball. **2.** *Vet.* A febrile, contagious keratitis of sheep.

pink·ie (pingk′ē) *n. U.S. Informal* The little or fifth finger. Also **pink′y.** [Prob. < obs. *pink* small]

pink·ing shears (pingk′ing) Shears with serrated blades for scalloping the edges of fabrics.

pink rhododendron A tall rhododendron having rosy purple flowers: State flower of Washington.

pin money 1. An allowance of money for minor incidental expenses. **2.** An allowance made by a husband to his wife for her personal expenses.

pin·na (pin′ə) *n. pl.* **pin·nae** (pin′ē) **1.** *Bot.* A single leaflet of a pinnate leaf. **2.** *Anat.* The auricle of the ear. **3.** *Zool.* A feather, wing, fin, or the like. [< NL < L *pinna,* *penna* feather] — **pin′nal** *adj.*

pin·nace (pin′is) *n. Naut.* **1.** Any ship's boat. **2.** Formerly, a small vessel used as a tender, scout, etc. [< OF < Ital. *pinaccia,* prob. < L *pinus* pine]

pin·na·cle (pin′ə·kəl) *n.* **1.** A small turret or tall ornament, as on a parapet. **2.** Anything resembling a pinnacle, as a mountain peak. **3.** The highest point or place; apex; summit. — *v.t.* **·cled, ·cling 1.** To place on or as on a pinnacle. **2.** To furnish with a pinnacle; crown. [< OF < LL *pinnaculum,* dim. of L *pinna* wing, pinnacle]

pin·nate (pin′āt, -it) *adj.* **1.** Like a feather. **2.** *Bot.* Having the shape or arrangement of a feather: said of compound leaves or leaflets arranged on each side of a common axis. Also **pin′nat·ed.** [< L < *pinna* feather, wing] — **pin′nate·ly** *adv.* — **pin·na′tion** *n.*

pinnati- *combining form* **1.** *Bot.* Feathered; resembling a feather. **2.** *Zool.* Pinni-. [< L *pinna* feather]

pinni- *combining form Zool.* Web; fin: *pinniped.* Also **pinnati.** [< L *pinna* feather]

pi·noch·le (pē′nuk·əl, -nok-) *n.* A card game for two, three, or four persons, played with a double deck of 48 cards with no card below a nine: also spelled *penuchle,* *penuckle.* Also **pi′noc·le.** [Origin uncertain]

pi·ñon (pin′yən; *Sp.* pē·nyōn′) *n.* **1.** Any of various pine trees of the southwestern U.S., having edible seeds: also spelled *pinyon.* **2.** A seed from such a tree. [< Sp. < L *pinea* pine cone]

pin·point (pin′point′) *n.* **1.** The point of a pin. **2.** Something extremely small. — *v.t.* To locate or define precisely.

pin·scher (pin′shər) *n.* A Doberman pinscher. [< G, terrier]

pint (pint) *n.* **1.** A dry and liquid measure of capacity equal to half a quart. See table inside back cover. **2.** A container having such a capacity. [< OF *pinte*]

Pin·ta (pin′tə, *Sp.* pēn′tä) *n.* One of the three ships of Columbus on his initial voyage to America.

pin·tail (pin′tāl′) *n.* **1.** A duck of the northern hemisphere, the male of which has a long, sharp tail. **2.** A sharp-tailed grouse of North America.

pin·tle (pin′təl) *n.* A pin upon which anything pivots, as a rudder, hinge, etc. [OE *pintel* penis]

pin·to (pin′tō) *adj. SW U.S.* Piebald; pied, as an animal. — *n. pl.* **·tos 1.** *SW U.S.* A pied animal: said esp. of a horse or pony. **2.** A kind of spotted bean of the southwestern U.S.: also **pinto bean.** [< Am. Sp. < Sp., lit., painted, ult. < L *pingere* to paint]

pin·up (pin′up′) *n. Slang* **1.** A picture of a sexually attractive young woman hung on a wall. **2.** A young woman who is the subject of such a picture. — *adj.* **1.** Capable of being affixed to a wall, etc.: a *pinup* lamp. **2.** *U.S. Slang* Having the qualities of or suitable for a pinup: a *pinup* girl.

pin·wheel (pin′hwēl′) *n.* **1.** A firework that revolves when ignited, forming a wheel of fire. **2.** A child's toy resembling a windmill, revolving on a pin attached to a stick.

pin·worm (pin′wûrm′) *n.* A nematode worm parasitic in the lower intestines and rectum of man, esp. of children.

pin·y (pī′nē) *adj.* **pin·i·er, pin·i·est** Pertaining to, suggestive of, or covered with pines: also spelled *piney.*

pin·yon (pin′yən) See PIÑON (def. 1).

pi·o·neer (pī′ə·nir′) *n.* **1.** One of the first explorers, settlers, or colonists of a new country or region. **2.** One of the first investigators or developers in a new field of research, enterprise, etc. **3.** *Mil.* An engineer who goes before the main body, building roads, bridges, etc. — *v.t.* **1.** To prepare (a way, etc.). **2.** To prepare the way for. **3.** To be a pioneer of. — *v.i.* **4.** To act as a pioneer. [< OF *peonier* foot soldier < ML < L *pes, pedis* foot]

pi·ous (pī′əs) *adj.* **1.** Actuated by reverence for a Supreme Being; religious; godly. **2.** Marked by a reverential spirit. **3.** Practiced in the name of religion. [< L *pius* dutiful, respectful] — **pi′ous·ly** *adv.* — **pi′ous·ness** *n.*

pip¹ (pip) *n.* The seed of an apple, orange, etc. [Short for PIPPIN]

pip² (pip) *n.* **1.** A spot, as on a playing card, domino, or die. **2.** A sharp audible or visible signal produced mechanically or electronically, as in radar. [< earlier *peep*; origin unknown]

pip³ (pip) *v.* **pipped, pip·ping** *v.t.* **1.** To break through (the shell), as a chick in the egg. — *v.i.* **2.** To peep; chirp. [Prob. var. of PEEP¹]

pip⁴ (pip) *n.* **1.** *Vet.* A contagious disease of fowls marked by mucus in the throat or by a scale on the tongue. **2.** *Slang* A mild human ailment: used humorously. [< MDu. < LL < L *pituita* mucus, the pip]

pipe (pīp) *n.* **1.** An apparatus, usu. a small bowl with a hollow stem, for smoking tobacco, opium, etc. **2.** Enough tobacco to fill the bowl of a pipe. **3.** A long conducting passage of wood, metal, tiling, etc., for conveying a fluid. **4.** A single tube or long, hollow case. **5.** Any hollow or tubular part in an animal or plant body. **6.** *Music* **a** A tubular flute or woodwind instrument. **b** An organ pipe. **c** *pl.* The bagpipe. **7.** The voice; also, a bird's note or call. **8.** A large cask for wine; also, a liquid measure of half a tun. **9.** A boatswain's whistle. — *v.* **piped, pip·ing** *v.i.* **1.** To play on a pipe. **2.** To make a shrill sound. **3.** *Naut.* To signal the crew by means of a boatswain's pipe. — *v.t.* **4.** To convey by or as by means of pipes. **5.** To provide with pipes. **6.** To play, as a tune, on a pipe. **7.** To utter shrilly or in a high key. **8.** *Naut.* To call to order by means of a boatswain's pipe. **9.** To lead, entice, or bring by piping. **10.** To trim, as a dress, with piping. — **to pipe down** *Slang* To become silent; stop talking or making noise. — **to pipe up 1.** To start playing or singing. **2.** To speak out, esp. in a shrill voice. [OE, ult. < L *pipare* to cheep]

pipe-clay (pīp′klā′) *v.t.* To whiten with pipe clay.

pipe clay A white clay used for pottery, for making tobacco pipes, and for whitening military accouterments.

pipe dream A groundless hope or wish; a daydream.

pipe·fit·ting (pīp′fit′ing) *n.* **1.** A piece of pipe used to connect two or more pipes together. **2.** The work of joining pipes together. — **pipe′fit′ter** *n.*

pipe·line (pīp′līn′) *n.* **1.** A line of pipe, as for the transmission of water, oil, etc. **2.** A channel for the transmission of information, usu. private or secret. — *v.t.* **·lined, ·lin·ing 1.** To convey by pipeline. **2.** To furnish with a pipeline.

pipe organ An organ having pipes, as distinguished from an electric organ, etc.

pip·er (pī′pər) *n.* **1.** One who plays upon a pipe, esp. a bagpipe. **2.** One who installs pipes.

pipe stem 1. The stem of a tobacco pipe. **2.** Anything resembling this. Also **pipe-stem** (pīp′stem′).

pi·pette (pī·pet′, pi-) *n.* A small tube, often graduated, for removing or transferring measured quantities of a liquid. Also **pi·pet′.** [< F, dim. of *pipe* pipe]

pip·ing (pī′ping) *adj.* **1.** Playing on the pipe. **2.** Hissing or sizzling: *piping* hot. **3.** Having a shrill sound. **4.** Char-

acterized by peaceful rather than martial music. — *n.* **1.** The act of one who pipes. **2.** Music of or suggesting that of pipes; a wailing or whistling sound. **3.** A system of pipes, as for drainage. **4.** A narrow strip of cloth folded on the bias, used for trimming dresses, etc.

pip·it (pip′it) *n.* One of various larklike singing birds widely distributed in North America. [Prob. imit. of its call]

pip·kin (pip′kin) *n.* A small earthenware jar. [? Dim. of PIPE]

pip·pin (pip′in) *n.* **1.** An apple of many varieties. **2.** A seed; pip. [< OF *pepin* seed of a fruit]

pip·sis·se·wa (pip·sis′ə·wə) *n.* An evergreen of the heath family, with white or pink flowers and thick leaves, used in medicine as an astringent and diuretic. [< Algonquian]

pip-squeak (pip′skwēk′) *n.* **1.** A petty and contemptible person or thing. **2.** A small, insignificant person.

pip·y (pī′pē) *adj.* **pip·i·er, pip·i·est 1.** Pipelike; tubular; containing pipes. **2.** Piping; thin and shrill.

pi·quant (pē′kənt, -känt, -kwənt, pē·känt′) *adj.* **1.** Having an agreeably pungent or tart taste. **2.** Tart; racy. **3.** Lively and interesting. — **Syn.** See RACY. [< F, orig. ppr. of *piquer* to sting]

pique (pēk) *n.* A feeling of irritation or resentment. — *v.t.* **piqued, pi·quing 1.** To excite resentment in. **2.** To stimulate or arouse; provoke. **3.** To pride (oneself): with *on* or *upon.* [< MF < *piquer* to sting, prick] — **Syn.** (noun) displeasure, offense, umbrage, huff.

pi·qué (pē·kā′) *n.* A fabric of cotton, rayon, or silk, with raised cord or welts running lengthwise in the fabric. [< F, lit., quilted, orig. pp. of *piquer* to prick, backstitch]

pi·ra·cy (pī′rə·sē) *n. pl.* **·cies 1.** Robbery on the high seas. **2.** The unauthorized publication, reproduction, or use of another's invention, idea, or literary creation.

pi·ra·nha (pi·rä′nyə) *n.* A small fish of tropical South America with massive jaws and sharp teeth, known to attack man and larger animals. [< Pg. (Brazilian) < Tupi, toothed fish]

pi·rate (pī′rit) *n.* **1.** A rover and robber on the high seas. **2.** A vessel engaged in piracy. **3.** A person who appropriates without right the work of another. — *v.t. & v.i.* **·rat·ed, ·rat·ing 1.** To practice or commit piracy (upon). **2.** To plagiarize. [< L < Gk. *peiran* to attempt] — **pi·rat·ic** (pī·rat′ik) or **·i·cal** *adj.* — **pi·rat′i·cal·ly** *adv.*

pir·ou·ette (pir′ōō·et′) *n.* A rapid whirling upon the toes in dancing. — *v.i.* **·et·ted, ·et·ting** To make a pirouette. [< F spinning top, origin uncertain]

pis·ca·to·ri·al (pis′kə·tôr′ē·əl, -tō′rē-) *adj.* **1.** Pertaining to fishes or fishing. **2.** Engaged in fishing. Also **pis′ca·to·ry.** [< L < *piscator* fisherman] — **pis·ca·to·ri·al·ly** *adv.*

Pis·ces (pis′ēz, pī′sēz) *n.pl.* A constellation, the Fish or Fishes; also, the twelfth sign of the zodiac. See ZODIAC. [< L, pl. of *piscis* a fish]

Pis·cis Aus·tri·nus (pis′is ô·strī′nəs) A constellation containing the star Fomalhaut. [< L]

pisci- *combining form* Fish; of or related to fish. Also, before vowels, **pisc-.** [< L *piscis* fish]

pis·ci·cul·ture (pis′i·kul′chər) *n.* The hatching and rearing of fish. — **pis′ci·cul′tur·al** *adj.* — **pis′ci·cul′tur·ist** *n.*

pis·cine (pis′īn, -ēn, -in) *adj.* Of, pertaining to, or resembling a fish or fishes [< L *piscis* a fish + -INE¹]

pis·civ·o·rous (pi·siv′ər·əs) *adj.* Feeding on fish.

pis·mire (pis′mīr) *n. Archaic & Dial.* An ant. Also **piss·ant** (pis′ant). [ME < *pisse* urine + *mire* an ant]

pis·ta·chi·o (pis·tä′shē·ō, -tash′ē·ō) *n. pl.* **·chi·os 1.** A small tree of western Asia and the Levant. **2.** Its edible nut. **3.** The flavor produced by the pistachio nut. **4.** A delicate shade of green, the color of the pistachio nut. Also **pis·tache′** (-täsh′). [< Ital. < L < Gk. < *pistakē* a pistachio tree, prob. < OPersian *pistah* a pistachio nut]

pis·til (pis′til) *n. Bot.* The seed-bearing organ of flowering plants, composed of the ovary, with its contained ovules, and the stigma, usu. with a style. For illus. see FLOWER. [< F < L *pistillum* pestle]

pis·til·late (pis′tə·lit, -lāt) *adj. Bot.* **1.** Having a pistil. **2.** Having pistils and no stamens. Also **pis′til·lar·y** (-ler′ē).

pis·tol (pis′təl) *n.* A small firearm having a stock to fit the hand, and a short barrel, and fired from one hand. — *v.t.* **pis·toled** or **·tolled, pis·tol·ing** or **·tol·ling** To shoot with a pistol. [< MF < MHG < Czechoslovakian *pišt'al*]

pis·tole (pis·tōl′) *n.* A former European gold coin of varying value. [< F, short for MF *pistolet* pistol]

pis·ton (pis′tən) *n.* **1.** *Mech.* A rigid disk fitted to slide in a cylinder, and connected with a rod for receiving the pressure of or exerting pressure upon a fluid in the cylinder. **2.** A valve in a wind instrument for altering the pitch of tones. [< F < Ital. < LL *pistare*, freq. of L *pinsere* to pound]

piston ring *Mech.* An adjustable metal ring fitted into a groove around the piston and designed to prevent leakage between the piston and the cylinder wall.

pit¹ (pit) *n.* **1.** A natural or artificial cavity in the ground, esp. when relatively wide and deep. **2.** A pitfall for snaring animals; snare. **3.** An abyss so deep that one cannot return from it, as the grave. **4.** Great distress or trouble. **5.** The main floor of the auditorium of a theater, esp. the rear part; also, the audience occupying this area. **6.** An enclosed space in which fighting cocks, etc., are pitted against each other. **7.** Any natural cavity or depression in the body: the *pit* of the stomach. **8.** Any slight depression or excavation, as a pockmark. **9.** That part of the floor of an exchange where a special line of trading is done: the wheat *pit*. **10.** A mining excavation, or the shaft of a mine. — *v.* **pit·ted, pit·ting** *v.t.* **1.** To mark with dents, pits, or hollows. **2.** To put, bury, or store in a pit. **3.** To match as antagonists; set in opposition. — *v.i.* **4.** To become marked with pits. [OE < L *puteus* a well]

pit² (pit) *n.* The kernel of certain fruits, as the plum. — *v.t.* **pit·ted, pit·ting** To remove pits from, as fruits. [< Du. < MDu. *pitte* kernel, pith]

pit·a·pat (pit′ə·pat′) *v.i.* **·pat·ted, ·pat·ting** To move or sound with light, quick steps or pulsations. — *n.* A tapping or succession of taps, steps, or similar sounds. — *adv.* With a pitapat; flutteringly. Also *pitty-pat*. [Imit.]

pitch¹ (pich) *n.* **1.** A thick, viscous, dark substance obtained by boiling down tar from the residues of distilled turpentine, etc., used in coating seams. **2.** Any of a class of residues obtained from the refining of fats, oils, and greases. **3.** The resinous sap of pines. **4.** Bitumen or asphalt, esp. when unrefined. — *v.t.* To smear, cover, or treat with or as with pitch. [OE < L *pix, picis* pitch]

pitch² (pich) *v.t.* **1.** To throw or hurl; fling. **2.** To erect or set up (a tent, camp, etc.). **3.** To set the level, angle, degree, etc., of. **4.** To put in a definite place or position. **5.** To set in order; arrange: now chiefly in the phrase **pitched battle.** **6.** In baseball, to deliver (the ball) to the batter. **7.** To set or be set in a pitch or key. — *v.i.* **8.** To fall or plunge forward or headlong. **9.** To lurch; stagger. **10.** To rise and fall alternately at the bow and stern, as a ship. **11.** To incline downward; slope. **12.** To encamp; settle. **13.** In baseball, to deliver the ball to the batter; act as pitcher. — **to pitch in** *Informal* **1.** To work together; cooperate. **2.** To start vigorously. — **to pitch into** To attack; assail. — *n.* **1.** Point or degree of elevation or depression. **2.** The extreme top or bottom point. **3.** The degree of descent of a declivity; also, a descent, slope, or inclination to the horizon. **4.** In building, the inclination of a roof. **5.** *Aeron.* The movement of an aircraft about its lateral axis. **6.** *Mech.* **a** The amount of advance of a screw thread in a single turn. **b** The distance between two corresponding points on the teeth of a gearwheel. **7.** *Physics* The dominant frequency of a sound wave perceived by the ear, ranging from a low tone of about 20 cycles per second to a maximum high approaching 30,000 cycles. **8.** *Music* **a** The sensory impression of the acuteness or gravity of a tone or sound. **b** The exact vibration frequency of a tone expressed in cycles per second. **9.** The act of pitching; a throw. **10.** In baseball: **a** The delivery of the ball by the pitcher. **b** The place of pitching. **c** The distance pitched. **11.** The act of dipping or plunging downward, as a ship. **12.** *U.S. Slang* A practiced talk or appeal intended to influence or persuade. [ME *picchen*]

pitch-black (pich′blak′) *adj.* Intensely black, as pitch.

pitch·blende (pich′blend′) *n.* A black or brown variety of a mineral occurring in the massive form and resembling pitch in luster, the chief source of uranium and radium. [< G < *pech* pitch¹ + *blende* blende]

pitch-dark (pich′därk′) *adj.* Very dark; as black as pitch.

pitch·er¹ (pich′ər) *n.* One who pitches; esp., in baseball, the player who delivers the ball to the batter. [< PITCH²]

pitch·er² (pich′ər) *n.* **1.** *Chiefly U.S.* A container with a spout and a handle, used for holding liquids to be poured out. **2.** A form of leaf suggestive of a pitcher. [< OF < LL < Gk. *bikos* wine jar]

pitcher plant Any of several carnivorous plants having tubular leaves arranged in the form of pitchers that function as insect traps.

pitch·fork (pich′fôrk′) *n.* A large fork with which to handle hay, straw, etc. — *v.t.* To lift and throw with or as with a pitchfork.

pitch·man (pich′mən) *n.* *pl.* **·men** (-mən) *Slang* One who sells small articles from a temporary stand, as at a fair, etc.; a sidewalk vender.

pitch pine Any of several American pines that yield pitch or turpentine.

pitch pipe *Music* A small pipe that sounds a particular tone when blown, used to adjust the pitch of a voice or instrument; also, a group of such pipes combined in a unit.

PITCHER PLANT
(About 2 feet tall)

pitch·y (pich′ē) *adj.* **pitch·i·er, pitch·i·est** **1.** Resembling pitch; intensely dark; pitchlike. **2.** Full of or daubed with pitch. — **pitch′i·ly** *adv.* — **pitch′i·ness** *n.*

pit·e·ous (pit′ē·əs) *adj.* Exciting pity, sorrow, or sympathy. [See PITY] — **pit′e·ous·ly** *adv.* — **pit′e·ous·ness** *n.*

pit·fall (pit′fôl′) *n.* **1.** A hidden danger or unexpected difficulty. **2.** A pit for entrapping wild beasts or men. [ME < PIT¹ + *falle, fal* < OE *fealle* a trap]

pith (pith) *n.* **1.** *Bot.* The cylinder of soft, spongy tissue in the center of the stems and branches of certain plants. **2.** *Ornithol.* The spongy substance of the interior of the shaft of a feather. **3.** The marrow of bones or of the spinal cord. **4.** Concentrated force; vigor. **5.** The essential part; gist. — *v.t.* **1.** To destroy the central nervous system or spinal cord of (a frog, etc.) by passing a wire through the vertebral column. **2.** To remove the pith from. **3.** To kill (cattle) by severing the spinal cord. [OE *pitha*]

Pith·e·can·thro·pus (pith′ə·kan′thrə·pəs, -kan·thrō′pəs) *n.* *adj.* **·pi** (-pī) *n. Paleontol.* An extinct manlike primate represented by skeletal remains discovered in central Java: also called *Java man.* [< NL < Gk. *pithēkos* ape + *anthropos* man] — **pith′e·can′thro·pine** (-pēn, -pin) *adj.*

pith helmet A topi.

pith·less (pith′lis) *adj.* Having no pith; lacking force.

pith·y (pith′ē) *adj.* **pith·i·er, pith·i·est** **1.** Consisting of pith; like pith. **2.** Forceful; effective: a *pithy* remark. — **Syn.** See TERSE. — **pith′i·ly** *adv.* — **pith′i·ness** *n.*

pit·i·a·ble (pit′ē·ə·bəl) *adj.* **1.** Arousing or meriting pity or compassion. **2.** Insignificant; contemptible. — **pit′i·a·ble·ness** *n.* — **pit′i·a·bly** *adv.*

pit·i·ful (pit′i·fəl) *adj.* **1.** Calling forth pity or compassion; wretched. **2.** Evoking a feeling of contempt. — **pit′i·ful·ly** *adv.* — **pit′i·ful·ness** *n.*

pit·i·less (pit′i·lis) *adj.* Having no pity; ruthless. — **pit′i·less·ly** *adv.* — **pit′i·less·ness** *n.*

pit·man (pit′mən) *n.* *pl.* **·men** (-mən) *for def 1,* **·mans** (-mənz) *for def. 2* **1.** One who works in a pit, as in a mine. **2.** *Mech.* A connecting rod.

pit·tance (pit′əns) *n.* A small allowance of money. [< OF *pitance*, monk's food allotment, pity]

pit·ter-pat·ter (pit′ər·pat′ər) *n.* A rapid series of light sounds or taps. [Varied reduplication of PATTER¹]

pit·ty-pat (pit′ē·pat′) See PITAPAT.

pi·tu·i·tar·y (pi·too′ə·ter′ē, -tyoo′-) *adj. Physiol.* **1.** Secreting mucus. **2.** *Anat.* Of the pituitary gland. — *n.* *pl.* **·tar·ies** **1.** *Anat.* The pituitary gland. **2.** *Med.* Any of various preparations made from extracts of the pituitary gland. [< L < *pituita* mucus]

pituitary gland *Anat.* A small, rounded body at the base of the brain that secretes hormones affecting growth, metabolism, and other functions of the body. Also **pituitary body.**

pit viper Any of various venomous snakes, as the rattlesnake, bushmaster, copperhead, etc., characterized by a small depression between the nostril and the eye.

pit·y (pit′ē) *n.* *pl.* **pit·ies** **1.** Grief or pain awakened by the misfortunes of others; compassion. **2.** That which arouses compassion; misfortune. — *v.t. & v.i.* **pit·ied, pit·y·ing** To feel pity (for). [< OF < L *pietas, -tatis* dutiful conduct] — **pit′i·er** *n.* — **pit′y·ing·ly** *adv.*

— **Syn.** (noun) **1.** Both *pity* and *compassion* are keen regret or sorrow, but *compassion* more strongly suggests the inclination to give aid or support, or to show mercy. *Sympathy* is a sharing of the feelings of another; it becomes akin to *pity* when those feelings are sorrow, chagrin, disappointment, etc.

più (pyoo) *adv. Music* More: a direction. [< Ital. < L *plus*]

piv·ot (piv′ət) *n.* **1.** *Mech.* Something upon which a related part turns, oscillates, or rotates, as a pin or short cylindrical bearing fixed on only one end, for carrying or rotating a swinging part. **2.** A person or thing upon which an important matter hinges or turns. — *v.t.* **1.** To place on, attach by, or provide with a pivot or pivots. — *v.i.* **2.** To turn on a pivot; swing. [< F, origin unknown] — **piv′ot·al** *adj.* — **piv′ot·al·ly** *adv.*

pix·i·lat·ed (pik′sə·lā′tid) *adj.* **1.** Affected by the pixies; mentally unbalanced; fey. **2.** *Slang* Drunk. [Prob. alter. of dial. E (Cornish) *pixy-led* bewitched]

pix·y (pik′sē) *n.* *pl.* **pix·ies** A fairy or elf. Also **pix′ie.** [< dial. E *pixey, pisky;* origin uncertain]

piz·za (pēt′sə, *Ital.* pēt′sä) *n.* An Italian food comprising a doughy crust overlaid with a mixture of cheese, tomatoes, spices, etc., and baked. [< Ital.]

piz·ze·ri·a (pēt′sə·rē′ə) *n.* A place where pizzas are prepared, sold, and eaten. [< Ital. < *pizza* pizza]

piz·zi·ca·to (pit′sə·kä′tō, *Ital.* pēt′tse·kä′tō) *Music adj.* Plucked with the fingers. — *adv.* In a pizzicato manner. — *n.* *pl.* **·ti** (-tē) A tone or passage played in a pizzicato manner. [< Ital., pp. of *pizzicare* to pluck, pinch]

pla·ca·ble (plā′kə·bəl, plak′ə-) *adj.* Appeasable; yielding; forgiving. [< OF < L < *placare* to appease] — **pla′·ca·bil′i·ty, pla′ca·ble·ness** *n.* — **pla′ca·bly** *adv.*

plac·ard (plak′ärd; *for v., also* plə·kärd′) *n.* **1.** A paper publicly displayed, as a poster. **2.** A tag or plate bearing the owner's name. — *v.t.* **1.** To announce by means of placards. **2.** To post placards on or in. [< F *plaquer* to veneer, plate]

pla·cate (plā′kāt, plak′āt, plak′ət) *v.t.* **·cat·ed, ·cat·ing** To appease the anger of; pacify. [< L < *placare* to appease] — **pla′cat·er** *n.* — **pla·ca′tion** *n.*

pla·ca·to·ry (plā′kə·tôr′ē, -tō′rē, plak′ə-) *adj.* Tending or intended to placate. Also **pla′ca·tive.**

place (plās) *n.* **1.** A particular point or portion of space, esp. that part occupied by or belonging to a thing under consideration; a definite locality or location. **2.** An occupied situation or building; space regarded as abode or quarters. **3.** An open space or square in a city; also, a court or street. **4.** Position in a sequence or series. **5.** Station in life; rank. **6.** An office, appointment, or employment; position. **7.** Room for occupation. **8.** Room; way: One thing gives *place* to another. **9.** A particular passage or page in a book, etc. **10.** The second position among the first three finishers in a race, as in a horse race. **11.** *Math.* The position of a figure in relation to the other figures of a given arithmetical series or group. — **in place 1.** In a natural or suitable position. **2.** In its original site. — **in place of** Instead of. — **out of place** Removed from or not situated in the natural or appropriate place, order, or relation. — **to take place** To happen; occur. — *v.* **placed, plac·ing** *v.t.* **1.** To put in a particular place or position. **2.** To put or arrange in a particular relation or sequence. **3.** To find a place, situation, home, etc., for. **4.** To appoint to a post or office. **5.** To identify; classify. **6.** To arrange for the satisfaction, handling, or disposition of. **7.** To bestow or entrust. — *v.i.* **8.** In racing: **a** To finish second: distinguished from *show, win.* **b** To finish among the first three finishers. [< OF, ult. < L < Gk. < *platys* wide]

pla·ce·bo (plə·sē′bō) *n.* *pl.* **·bos** or **·boes 1.** *Med.* Any harmless substance given to humor a patient or as a test in controlled experiments. **2.** Anything said in order to flatter. [< L < *placere* to please]

place kick In football, a kick for a goal in which the ball is placed on the ground for kicking.

place mat A mat on which a table setting is placed.

place·ment (plās′mənt) *n.* **1.** The act of placing, or the state of being placed. **2.** Relative position; arrangement. **3.** The business of placing persons in jobs. **4.** In football, the setting of the ball for a place kick; also, the kick itself.

pla·cen·ta (plə·sen′tə) *n.* *pl.* **·tas** or **·tae** (-tē) **1.** *Anat.* In higher mammals, the vascular, spongy organ of interlocking fetal and uterine structures by which the fetus is nourished in the uterus. **2.** *Bot.* The part of the ovary that supports the ovules. [< L, cake < Gk. < *plax, plakos* flat object] — **pla·cen′tal, plac·en·tar·y** (plas′ən·ter′ē, plə·sen′tər·ē) *adj.*

pla·cen·tate (plə·sen′tāt) *adj.* Having a placenta.

plac·er¹ (plā′sər) *n.* One who or that which places.

plac·er² (plas′ər) *n.* *Mining* **1.** An alluvial or glacial deposit of sand, gravel, etc., containing gold in particles large enough to be obtained by washing. **2.** Any place where deposits are washed for valuable minerals. [Var. of Sp. *placel* sandbank < *plaza* place]

plac·id (plas′id) *adj.* Having a smooth surface or nature; unruffled; calm. [< L < *placere* to please] — **pla·cid·i·ty** (plə·sid′ə·tē), **plac′id·ness** *n.* — **plac′id·ly** *adv.*

plack·et (plak′it) *n.* The opening in the upper part of a dress, blouse, or skirt to make it easy to put on and take off. Also **placket hole.** [Origin unknown]

pla·gia·rism (plā′jə·riz′əm, -jē·ə-) *n.* **1.** The act of plagiarizing. **2.** Something plagiarized. — **pla′gia·rist** *n.* — **pla′gia·ris′tic** *adj.*

pla·gia·rize (plā′jə·rīz, -jē·ə-) *v.* **·rized, ·riz·ing** *v.t.* **1.** To appropriate and pass off as one's own (the writings, ideas, etc., of another). **2.** To appropriate and use passages, ideas, etc., from. — *v.i.* **3.** To commit plagiarism. — **pla′gia·riz′er** *n.*

pla·gia·ry (plā′jər·ē, -jē·ər·ē) *n.* *pl.* **·ries 1.** The act or result of plagiarism. **2.** One who plagiarizes; a plagiarist. [< L *plagium* kidnapping < Gk. *plagios* treacherous]

plagio- *combining form* Oblique; slanting. Also, before vowels, **plagi-.** [< Gk. *plagios* oblique]

pla·gi·o·clase (plā′jē·ə·klās′) *n.* Feldspar consisting chiefly of the silicates of sodium, calcium, and aluminum, and crystallizing in the triclinic system. [< PLAGIO- + Gk. *klasis* cleavage] — **pla′gi·o·clas′tic** (-klas′tik) *adj.*

plague (plāg) *n.* **1.** Anything troublesome or harassing; affliction; calamity. **2.** *Pathol.* Any of various forms of a virulent, febrile, highly contagious, and often pandemic disease, esp. the bubonic plague. **3.** The Black Death. **4.** *Informal* Nuisance; bother. — *v.t.* **plagued, pla·guing 1.** To vex; annoy. **2.** To afflict with plague or disaster. [< OF < LL < L *plaga*, prob. < Gk. *plēssein* to strike]

pla·guy (plā′gē) *Informal adj.* Troublesome. — *adv.* Vexatiously; intolerably: also **pla′gui·ly.** Also **pla′guey.**

plaice (plās) *n.* **1.** A flounder of European waters. **2.** Any of various American flatfishes. [< OF < LL *platessa* flatfish, ult. < Gk. *platys* broad]

plaid (plad) *adj.* Having a tartan pattern; checkered. — *n.* An oblong woolen scarf of tartan or checkered pattern, worn in the Scottish Highlands as a cloak over one shoulder; also, any fabric of this pattern. [< Scottish Gaelic *plaide* blanket] — **plaid′ed** *adj.*

plain (plān) *adj.* **1.** Flat; smooth. **2.** Presenting few difficulties; easy. **3.** Clear; understandable. **4.** Straightforward; guileless. **5.** Lowly in condition or station. **6.** Unadorned; without ornamentation. **7.** Not figured, twilled, or variegated: *plain* cloth. **8.** Homely. **9.** Not rich; simple: *plain* food. — *n.* An expanse of level land; a prairie. [< OF < L *planus* flat] — **plain′ly** *adv.* — **plain′ness** *n.*

plain-clothes man (plān′klōz′, -klōthz′) A member of a police force not in uniform; esp., a detective.

plains·man (plānz′mən) *n.* *pl.* **·men** (-mən) A dweller on the plains.

plain·song (plān′sông, -song) *n.* The old ecclesiastical chant, having simple melody, not governed by strict rules of meter but by accentuation of the words. Also **plain·chant** (plān′chant, -chänt). [Trans. of Med.L *cantus planus*]

plain-spo·ken (plān′spō′kən) *adj.* Candid; frank.

plaint (plānt) *n.* **1.** A lamentation. **2.** A complaint. [< OF < L *planger* to lament]

plain·tiff (plān′tif) *n.* *Law* The party that begins an action at law; the complaining party in an action: opposed to *defendant.* [< OF < L *plangere* to lament]

plain·tive (plān′tiv) *adj.* Expressing a subdued sadness; mournful. [< OF, fem. of *plaintif*] — **plain′tive·ly** *adv.* — **plain′tive·ness** *n.*

plait (plāt, plat) *v.t.* **1.** To braid (hair, etc.). **2.** To pleat. — *n.* **1.** A braid, esp. of hair. **2.** A pleat. [< OF < L *plicare* to fold]

plan (plan) *n.* **1.** A scheme, method, or design for the attainment of some object. **2.** A drawing showing the proportion and relation of parts, as of a building. **3.** Any sketch; draft. **4.** A mode of action. — *v.* **planned, plan·ning** *v.t.* **1.** To form a scheme or method for doing, achieving, etc. **2.** To make a plan of, as a building; design. **3.** To have as an intention or purpose. — *v.i.* **4.** To make plans. [< MF < OF < L *planus* flat] — **plan′ner** *n.*

pla·nar·i·an (plə·nâr′ē·ən) *n.* *Zool.* Any of an order of chiefly aquatic flatworms having elongate flattened bodies, and the power of regenerating themselves when cut apart. [< NL < L *planus* flat]

plane¹ (plān) *n.* **1.** *Geom.* A surface such that a straight line joining any two of its points lies wholly within the surface. **2.** Any flat surface. **3.** A grade of development; level: a *plane* of thought. **4.** *Aeron.* A supporting surface of an airplane. **5.** An airplane. — *adj.* **1.** Lying in a plane. **2.** Level; flat. **3.** Dealing only with flat surfaces: *plane* geometry. [< L *planus* flat] — **pla′nar** (plā′nər) *adj.*

plane² (plān) *n.* A tool used for smoothing boards or other surfaces of wood. — *v.* **planed, plan·ing** *v.t.* **1.** To make smooth or even with a plane. **2.** To remove with a plane. — *v.i.* **3.** To use a plane. **4.** To do the work of a plane. [< F < L < OF < L *planare* to level] — **plan·er** (plā′nər) *n.*

plane³ (plān) *v.i.* **planed, plan·ing 1.** To rise partly out of the water, as a power boat when driven at high speed. **2.** To glide; soar. [< F < OF < L *planus* flat]

plan·et (plan′it) *n.* **1.** *Astron.* One of the celestial bodies revolving around the sun and shining only by reflected light. Those within the Earth's orbit, Mercury and Venus, are called **inferior planets.** Those beyond it, the **superior planets,** are Mars, Jupiter, Saturn, Uranus, Neptune, and Pluto. Between Mars and Jupiter are the asteroids or **minor planets. 2.** In ancient astronomy, one of the seven heavenly bodies (the Sun, Moon, Mercury, Venus, Mars, Jupiter, and Saturn) having a motion relative to the fixed stars. **3.** In astrology, a planet considered as an influence on human beings. [< OF < LL < Gk. < *planaesthai* to wander]

plan·e·tar·i·um (plan′ə·târ′ē·əm) *n.* *pl.* **·i·ums** or **·i·a** (-ē·ə) **1.** An apparatus for exhibiting the features of the heavens as they exist at any time and for any place on earth, consisting of an array of suitably mounted stereopticons installed in a room having a circular dome. **2.** A room or building having such an apparatus. **3.** An apparatus or model representing the planetary system.

plan·e·tar·y (plan′ə·ter′ē) *adj.* **1.** Of or pertaining to a planet or the planets. **2.** Mundane; terrestrial. **3.** Wandering; erratic. **4.** *Mech.* Pertaining to or denoting a type of gearing in which one or more small wheels mesh with the toothed circumference of a larger wheel, around which they revolve, at the same time rotating axially.

plan·e·tes·i·mal (plan′ə·tes′ə·məl) *Astron. adj.* Of or pertaining to very small, solid, planetary bodies. — *n.* Any of such bodies.

TABLE OF PLANETS

Name	MERCURY	VENUS	EARTH	MARS	JUPITER	SATURN	URANUS	NEPTUNE	PLUTO
Symbol	☿	♀	⊕	♂	♃	♄	♅	♆	♇
Distance from sun, millions of miles	36	67	93	142	483	886	1780	2790	3670
Mean diameter, miles	3000	7600	7918	4200	87,000	72,000	29,600	27,700	4000
Period of sidereal revolution	88 days	225 days	365.25 days	687 days	12 years	29.5 years	84 years	165 years	248 years
Period of rotation	88 days	20–30 days?	23 hr., 56 min.	24 hr., 37 min.	9 hr., 50 min.	10 hr., 14 min.	10 hr., 45 min.	15 hr., 48 min.	?
No. of satellites	0	0	1	2	12	9	5	2	0
Mass, Earth considered as 1.	0.0543	0.8148	1.0000	0.1069	318.35	95.3	14.58	17.26	0.1?
Escape velocity, miles per second	2	6.3	6.95	3.1	37	22	13	15	?
Mean density, water = 1	5.3	4.95	5.52	3.95	1.33	0.69	1.56	2.27	5?
Surface gravity, Earth = 1	0.38	0.87	1.00	0.39	2.65	1.17	1.05	1.23	0.5?
Mean orbital velocity, miles per second	29.76	21.78	18.52	15.00	8.12	6.00	4.23	3.37	2.95

planetesimal hypothesis *Astron.* The hypothesis that the solar system developed from large masses of planetesimals that coalesced to form planets and satellites.

plan·et·fall (plan′it·fôl′) *n.* The descent of a rocket or artificial satellite to the surface of a planet.

plan·e·toid (plan′ə·toid) *n. Astron.* An asteroid. **— plan′·e·toi′dal** *adj.*

plane tree Any of various large deciduous trees characterized by broad, lobed leaves and spreading growth. [< OF < L < Gk. *platys* broad]

plan·et·struck (plan′it·struk′) *adj.* Affected by the influence of planets. Also **plan′et·strick′en** (-strik′ən).

planet wheel One of the smaller wheels in an epicyclic train.

plan·gent (plan′jənt) *adj.* Dashing noisily; resounding, as the sound of bells. [< L *plangens, -entis,* ppr. of *plangere* to lament, strike] **— plan·gen·cy** *n.* **— plan′gent·ly** *adv.*

plan·gor·ous (plang′gər·əs) *adj.* Wailing; lamenting. [< L *plangor* lamentation < *plangere.* See PLANGENT.]

pla·ni·form (plā′nə·fôrm, plan′ə-) *adj.* Having the surfaces nearly flat.

pla·nim·e·ter (plə·nim′ə·tər) *n.* An instrument for measuring the area of any plane surface, however irregular, by moving a pointer around its boundary and reading the indications of a scale. [< F *planimètre* — **pla·ni·met·ric** (plā′nə·met′rik, plan′ə-) or **·ri·cal** *adj.* **— pla·nim′e·try** *n.*

plan·i·sphere (plan′ə·sfir) *n.* A plane projection of the sphere; especially, a polar projection of the heavens on a chart, showing the stars visible at a given time. [< OF < Med.L *planisphaerium* < L *planus* flat + *sphaera* sphere] **— plan′i·spher′ic** (-sfir′ik, -sfer′-) *adj.*

plan·ish (plan′ish) *v.t.* To condense, smooth, toughen, or polish, as metal, by hammering, rolling, etc. [< MF < L *planus* flat]

plank (plangk) *n.* 1. A broad piece of sawed timber, thicker than a board. 2. A support. 3. One of the principles of a political platform. **— to walk the plank** To walk off a plank projecting from the side of a ship, a method once used by pirates for executing prisoners. **— v.t.** 1. To cover, furnish, or lay with planks. 2. To broil or bake and serve on a plank, as fish. 3. *Informal* To put down forcibly. 4. *Informal* To pay: with *out, down,* etc. [< OF < LL *planca*]

plank·ing (plangk′ing) *n.* 1. The act of laying planks. 2. Anything made of planks. 3. Planks collectively.

plank·ton (plangk′tən) *n. Biol.* The marine animal and plant organisms that drift or float with currents, waves, etc., unable to influence their own course and ranging in size from microorganisms to jellyfish. [< G < Gk. *plazesthai* to wander] **— plank·ton′ic** *adj.*

plano-¹ *combining form* Roaming; wandering. Also, before vowels, **plan-**. [< Gk. *planos* wandering]

plano-² *combining form* Flat; level; plane: *plano-concave, planometer.* Also, before vowels, **plan-**. Also **plani-**. [< L *planus* flat]

pla·no·con·cave (plā′nō·kon′kāv) *adj.* Plane on one side and concave on the other.

pla·no·con·vex (plā′nō·kon′veks) *adj.* Plane on one side and convex on the other.

pla·nom·e·ter (plə·nom′ə·tər) *n.* A device for gauging a plane surface, especially as used in metalworking. [< PLANO-² + -METER] **— pla·nom′e·try** *n.*

plant (plant, plänt) *n.* 1. A living organism belonging to the vegetable kingdom, as distinguished from the animal kingdom, having typically rigid cell walls and characterized by growth chiefly from the synthesis of simple, usually inorganic food materials from soil, water, and air. 2. One of the smaller forms of vegetable life, as distinct from shrubs and trees. 3. A set of machines, tools, apparatus, etc., necessary to conduct a manufacturing enterprise or other business: a chemical *plant.* 4. The buildings, grounds, and permanent appliances needed for any institution, as a post office, college, etc. 5. A slip or cutting from a tree or bush; sapling. 6. A person placed in a theater audience to encourage applause, speak lines, or contribute to the action of a play. 7. An apparently trivial passage early in a story or play that later becomes important in shaping the outcome of the action. 8. *Slang* A trick; dodge; swindle. **— v.t.** 1. To set in the ground for growing. 2. To furnish with plants or seed: to *plant* a field. 3. To set or place firmly; put in position. 4. To found; establish. 5. To introduce into the mind; implant, as an idea or principle. 6. To introduce into a country, as a breed of animal. 7. To deposit (fish or spawn) in a body of water. 8. To stock, as a river. 9. To bed (oysters). 10. *Slang* To deliver, as a blow. 11. *Slang* To place or station for purposes of deception, observation, etc.: to *plant* evidence. 12. *Slang* To hide; bury: Where did you *plant* the loot? [OE *plante* < L *planta* a sprout, cutting; ult. origin uncertain]

Plan·tag·e·net (plan·taj′i·net) *n.* A patronymic of the Angevin dynasty of English sovereigns from Henry II (1154) to the accession of the House of Tudor (1485). [< Med.L *planta genista* sprig of broom; with ref. to the habit of Geoffrey of Anjou, founder of the line, of wearing one]

plan·tain¹ (plan′tin) *n.* An annual or perennial herb (genus *Plantago*) widely distributed in temperate regions; especially, the **common** or **greater plantain** (*P. major*) with large, ovate, ribbed leaves. [< OF < L *plantago, -ginis* < *planta* sole of the foot; with ref. to the shape of the leaves]

plan·tain² (plan′tin) *n.* 1. A tropical, perennial herb (*Musa paradisiaca*), sometimes growing to 30 feet. 2. The long, bananalike fruit of this plant, edible when cooked. [< Sp. *plátano*; infl. in form by PLANTAIN¹]

plan·tar (plan′tər) *adj.* Pertaining to the sole of the foot. [< L *planta* sole of the foot]

plan·ta·tion (plan-tā′shən) *n.* **1.** Any place that is planted. **2.** A farm or estate of many acres, planted in cotton, tobacco, etc., worked by resident laborers. **3.** A colony. **4.** A grove cultivated for its wood. [< L < *plantare* to plant]

plant·er (plan′tər) *n.* **1.** One who plants. **2.** An early settler or colonizer. **3.** An owner of a plantation. **4.** An agricultural implement for dropping seed in soil. **5.** A decorative container in which shrubs and flowers are planted, especially outdoors. **6.** *Canadian* In Newfoundland, a trader who hires and provisions fishermen in return for a share of the catch.

plan·ti·grade (plan′tə-grād) *Zool. adj.* Walking on the whole sole of the foot: distinguished from *digitigrade*. [< F < L *planta* sole of the foot + *gradi* to walk]

plant louse 1. An aphid. **2.** Any of a family of leaping insects that infest plants and suck their juices.

plaque (plak) *n.* **1.** A plate, disk, or slab of metal, porcelain, ivory, etc., artistically ornamented, as for wall decoration. **2.** A small disk or brooch worn as a badge of membership, etc. [< F < MDu. *placke* flat disk, tablet]

plash¹ (plash) *n.* A slight splash. — *v.t. & v.i.* To splash lightly, as water. [Prob. imit.] — **plash′y** *adj.*

plash² (plash) *n.* A small pool. [OE *plæsc* pool]

-plasia *combining form* Growth; development; formative action. Also **-plasis.** [< Gk. *plassein* to mold, form]

-plasm *combining form Biol.* The viscous material of an animal or vegetable cell: *protoplasm*. [< LL < Gk. *plassein* to mold, form]

plas·ma (plaz′mə) *n.* **1.** The liquid portion of nutritive animal fluids, as blood, lymph, or intercellular fluid. **2.** The clear, fluid portion of blood, freed from blood cells and used for transfusions. **3.** The viscous material of a cell; protoplasm. **4.** *Physics* **a** The region in a gas-discharge tube in which there are approximately equal numbers of positive ions and electrons. **b** Any gas composed of such particles. Also **plasm** (plaz′əm). [< LL < Gk. *plassein* to mold, form] — **plas·mat·ic** (plaz-mat′ik), **plas′mic** *adj.*

plasma engine A reaction engine producing a small but sustained thrust by emission of a plasma jet.

plasma jet *Physics* A beam of plasma ejected from a specially constructed generator that forms a brilliantly luminous jet of extremely high energy and temperature.

plasmo- *combining form* Plasma; of or pertaining to plasma. Also, before vowels, **plasm-.** [See -PLASM]

plas·mo·di·um (plaz-mō′dē-əm) *n.* *pl.* **·di·a** (-dē-ə) **1.** A mass of protoplasm resulting from the fusion of ameboid organisms, typical of the slime molds. **2.** Any of a genus of parasitic protozoans that include the causative agents of malaria. [< NL < PLASM(O)- + Gk. *eidos* form]

-plast *combining form* An organized living particle or cell. [< Gk. < *plassein* to form]

plas·ter (plas′tər, pläs′-) *n.* **1.** A composition of lime, sand, and water, sometimes mixed with hair, for coating walls and partitions. **2.** Plaster of Paris. **3.** A viscid substance spread on linen, silk, etc., and applied to some part of the body, used for healing. — *v.t.* **1.** To cover or overlay with or as with plaster. **2.** To apply a plaster to, as a part of the body. **3.** To apply like plaster or a plaster: to *plaster* posters on a fence. **4.** To cause to adhere or lay flat like plaster. [OE reinforced by OF *plastre* < LL < L < Gk. *emplassain* < en upon, into + *plassein* to mold] — **plas′ter·er** *n.* — **plas′ter·ing** *n.* — **plas′ter·y** *adj.*

plas·ter·board (plas′tər-bôrd′, pläs′-, -bōrd′) *n.* A wallboard made of gypsum or plaster and fibrous paper.

plaster cast 1. A cast or model of a person or object made by molding plaster of Paris. **2.** *Surg.* A cast.

plaster of Paris Calcined gypsum, setting readily when mixed with water, useful in making molds, casts, bandages, etc. [With ref. to use of gypsum from Paris]

plas·tic (plas′tik) *adj.* **1.** Giving form or fashion to matter. **2.** Capable of being molded; pliable. **3.** Pertaining to modeling or molding. **4.** *Surg.* Efficacious in recreating or remodeling injured or destroyed parts: *plastic* surgery. — *n.* **1.** Any substance or material that may be molded. **2.** *Chem.* One of a large class of synthetic organic compounds capable of being molded, extruded, cast, or otherwise fabricated into various shapes, or of being drawn into filaments for textiles. [< L < Gk. *plastikos* moldable] — **plas′ti·cal·ly** *adv.*

-plastic *combining form* Growing; developing; forming. [< Gk. *plastikos* plastic, moldable]

plas·tic·i·ty (plas-tis′ə-tē) *n.* **1.** The quality or state of being plastic. **2.** Capacity for being shaped or molded.

plas·ti·ciz·er (plas′tə-sī′zər) *n.* That which functions to make a substance plastic, preserve softness, etc.

plastic surgery Surgery that deals with the restoration or healing of lost, wounded, or deformed parts of the body.

plas·tid (plas′tid) *n.* *Biol.* **1.** A small, specialized mass in the cytoplasm of a cell. For illus. see CELL. **2.** An elementary organism, as a cell. [< G < Gk. < *plassein* to mold]

plas·tron (plas′trən) *n.* **1.** A leather shield worn on the breast by fencers. **2.** *Zool.* The ventral part of the shell of a turtle or tortoise: also **plas/trum.** [< F, < Ital. < *piastra* sheet of metal] — **plas/tral** (-trəl) *adj.*

-plasty *combining form Surg.* An operation involving: **a** A (specified) part of the body: *osteoplasty*. **b** Tissue from a (specified) source: *zooplasty*. **c** A (specified) process or formation: *neoplasty*. [< Gk. *-plastia* formation]

-plasy See -PLASIA.

plat (plat) *v.t.* **plat·ted, plat·ting** To plait or braid. — *n.* A plait; braid. [Var. of PLAIT]

plat- Var. of PLATY-.

plate (plāt) *n.* **1.** A flat, extended, rigid body of metal or any material of slight but even thickness. **2.** A shallow vessel made of crockery, wood, glass, etc., in which food is served or from which it is eaten at table. **3.** Household articles, as trays, carving sets, etc., that are plated with a precious metal. **4.** A portion of food served at table; plateful. **5.** A piece of flat metal bearing a design or inscription or intended for reproduction, as in a bookplate. **6.** Metal in sheets. **7.** An impression from an engraving, woodcut, etc., as reproduced in a book. **8.** An electrotype or stereotype. **9.** A horizontal timber laid on a wall to receive a framework. **10.** *Dent.* A piece of metal, vulcanite, or plastic fitted to the mouth and holding one or more artificial teeth. **11.** A thin part of the brisket of beef. **12.** *Photog.* A sensitized sheet of glass, metal, or the like, for taking photographs. **13.** In baseball, the home base. **14.** *Biol.* A platelike part or structure; a lamina. **15.** A dish used in taking up collections, as in churches; also, a collection. **16.** *Electronics* The principal anode in an electron tube. — *v.t.* **plat·ed, plat·ing 1.** To coat with a thin layer of gold, silver, etc. **2.** To cover or sheathe with metal plates for protection. **3.** In papermaking, to give a high gloss to (paper) by pressure between metal plates. **4.** *Printing* To make an electrotype or stereotype from. [< OF < LL *plattus* flat] — **plat′er** *n.*

pla·teau (pla-tō′, *esp. Brit.* plat′ō) *n.* *pl.* **·teaus** or **·teaux** (-tōz′) **1.** An extensive stretch of elevated and comparatively level land; mesa. **2.** A stage or period of leveling off in the development of something or in the process of learning. [< F < OF *plat* flat]

plat·ed (plā′tid) *adj.* **1.** Coated with a layer of gold, silver, etc.: often used in combination: *gold-plated*. **2.** Provided with plates, as of metal.

plate·ful (plāt′fŏŏl′) *n.* *pl.* **·fuls** The quantity that fills a plate.

plate glass Glass in clear, thick sheets, suitable for mirrors, display windows, etc.

plate·let (plāt′lit) *n.* **1.** A small, platelike object. **2.** *Physiol.* A blood platelet. [Dim. of PLATE]

plat·en (plat′n) *n.* *Mech.* **1.** The part of a printing press, typewriter, or the like, on which the paper is supported to receive the impression. **2.** In a machine tool, the adjustable table that carries the work. [See PLATE]

plat·form (plat′fôrm) *n.* **1.** Any floor or flat surface raised above the adjacent level, as a stage for public speaking or a raised walk upon which railroad passengers alight. **2.** A projecting stage at the end of a car or similar vehicle. **3.** A formal scheme of principles put forth by a religious, political, or other body; also, the document stating the principles of a political party. [< MF < *plate* flat + *forme* form]

plat·ing (plā′ting) *n.* **1.** A layer or coating of metal. **2.** A sheathing of metal plates, as armor. **3.** The act or process of sheathing or coating something with plates or metal.

pla·tin·ic (plə-tin′ik) *adj.* *Chem.* Of, pertaining to, or containing platinum, esp. in its higher valence.

plat·i·nize (plat′ə-nīz) *v.t.* **·nized, ·niz·ing** To coat or combine with platinum, esp. by electroplating.

platino- *combining form* Platinum; of or containing platinum. Also, before vowels, **platin-.** [< PLATINUM]

plat·i·nous (plat′ə-nəs) *adj.* *Chem.* Of, pertaining to, or containing platinum, esp. in its lower valence.

plat·i·num (plat′ə-nəm) *n.* **1.** A heavy, steel-gray, malleable and ductile metallic element (symbol Pt) that is very infusible, resistant to most acids, and that has a high electrical resistance. It is widely used as a catalyst, in industry and the arts, and in jewelry. See ELEMENT. **2.** A color resembling that of platinum. [< NL < Sp. *plata* silver]

platinum blond 1. A very light, almost white blond. **2.** One having platinum blond hair.

plat·i·tude (plat′ə-tōōd, -tyōōd) *n.* **1.** A flat, dull, or commonplace statement; an obvious truism. **2.** Dullness; triteness. [< F *plat* flat] — **plat·i·tu′di·nous** *adj.*

plat·i·tu·di·nize (plat′ə-tōō′də-nīz, -tyōō′-) *v.i.* **·nized, ·niz·ing** To utter platitudes.

pla·ton·ic (plə-ton′ik) *adj.* *Often cap.* Purely spiritual, or devoid of sensual feeling. — **pla·ton′i·cal·ly** *adv.*

Pla·ton·ic (plə-ton′ik) *adj.* Of, pertaining to, or characteristic of Plato or of Platonism; academic; theoretical. Also **Pla·ton′i·cal.** — **Pla·ton′i·cal·ly** *adv.*

Pla·to·nism (plā′tə-niz′əm) *n.* The philosophy of Plato;

esp., the doctrine that objects are merely copies or images of eternal ideas and that these ideas are the ultimate realities. — **Pla·to·nist** n.

pla·toon (plə·tōōn′) n. **1.** A subdivision of a company, troop, or other military unit, commanded by a lieutenant. **2.** A company of people; esp., in football, a defensive or offensive unit. — v.t. In football, to use as or in a platoon. [< F peloton ball, group of men]

platoon sergeant In the U.S. Army, the senior noncommissioned officer in a platoon. See table for GRADE.

Platt·deutsch (plät′doich′) n. The low German vernacular of the north of Germany. [< G]

plat·ter (plat′ər) n. **1.** Chiefly U.S. An oblong shallow dish on which meat or fish is served. **2.** Informal A phonograph record. [< AF plat dish]

platy- combining form Flat. Also, before vowels, plat-. [< Gk. platys flat]

plat·y·pus (plat′ə·pəs) n. A burrowing, egg-laying, aquatic monotreme of Australia, having a ducklike bill: also called duckbill. [< NL < Gk. < platus flat + pous foot]

plau·dit (plô′dit) n. An expression of applause; praise bestowed. [< L plaudite, pl. imperative of plaudere to applaud]

plau·si·ble (plô′zə·bəl) adj. **1.** Seeming to be likely or probable, but open to doubt. **2.** Apparently trustworthy or believable. [< L plausibilis deserving applause] — **plau′si·bil′i·ty, plau′si·ble·ness** n. — **plau′si·bly** adv.

PLATYPUS
(To 2 feet long; tail about 5¼ inches)

play (plā) v.i. **1.** To engage in sport or diversion; amuse oneself. **2.** To take part in a game of skill or chance. **3.** To act in a way that is not to be taken seriously. **4.** To act or behave in a specified manner: to play false. **5.** To make love sportively. **6.** To make love sportively. **7.** To move quickly or irregularly as if frolicking: lights playing along a wall. **8.** To discharge or be discharged freely or continuously: a fountain playing in the square. **9.** To perform on a musical instrument. **10.** To give forth musical sounds. **11.** To be performed or exhibited. **12.** To act on or as on a stage; perform. **13.** To move freely or loosely, esp. within limits, as part of a mechanism. — v.t. **14.** To engage in (a game etc.). **15.** To imitate in play: to play cowboys and Indians. **16.** To perform sportively or wantonly: to play a trick. **17.** To oppose in a game or contest. **18.** To move or employ (a piece, card, etc.) in a game. **19.** To employ (someone) in a game as a player. **20.** To cause: to play havoc. **21.** To perform upon (a musical instrument). **22.** To perform or produce, as a piece of music, a play, etc. **23.** To act the part of on or as on the stage: to play the fool. **24.** To perform or act in: to play Chicago. **25.** To cause to move quickly or irregularly. **26.** To put into or maintain in action. **27.** In angling, to let (a hooked fish) tire itself by maintaining pressure on the line. **28.** To bet or bet on. — **to play at 1.** To take part in. **2.** To pretend to be doing; do half-heartedly. — **to play down** To minimize. — **to play into the hands of** To act to the advantage of (a rival or opponent). — **to play off 1.** To oppose against one another. **2.** To decide (a tie) by playing one more game. — **to play on 1.** To take unscrupulous advantage of (another's hopes, emotions, etc.) for one's own advantage. **2.** To continue. — **to play out 1.** To come to an end; be exhausted. **2.** To continue to the end. — **to play the game** To behave in a fair manner. — **to play up** Informal To emphasize. — **to play up to** Informal To try to win the favor of by flattery, etc. — n. **1.** A dramatic composition; drama. **2.** The performance of such a composition. **3.** Exercise or action for recreation or diversion. **4.** A maneuver or turn in a game. **5.** Manner of playing: rough play. **6.** In sports, a state of being actively and legitimately in use or motion: in play. **7.** The act of playing a game, esp. gambling. **8.** Fun; joking: to say something in play. **9.** The active operation of something: the play of one's mind. **10.** Action or operation that is light, free, and unencumbered. **11.** Light, quick, fitful movement. **12.** Manner of acting toward or dealing with others: fair play. — **to make a play for** Informal **1.** To attempt to gain something, as a favor, votes, etc. **2.** To attempt to seduce. [OE plegan] — **play′a·ble** adj.

play·back (plā′bak′) n. **1.** The act of reproducing a sound recording, as from a record or tape. **2.** A method or machine for reproducing sound recordings.

play·bill (plā′bil′) n. **1.** A bill or poster advertising a play. **2.** A program of a play.

play·boy (plā′boi′) n. Informal One who constantly seeks pleasure at nightclubs, social gatherings, etc.

play-by-play (plā′bī-plā′) adj. Dealing with each play or event as it happens: a play-by-play report.

play·er (plā′ər) n. **1.** One who takes part or specializes in a game: a tennis player. **2.** An actor. **3.** A performer on a musical instrument. **4.** A gambler. **5.** An automatic device for playing a musical instrument.

player piano A piano having a mechanical device by which it may be played automatically.

play·fel·low (plā′fel′ō) n. An associate in play; playmate.

play·ful (plā′fəl) adj. **1.** Lightly humorous; joking: a playful remark. **2.** Full of high spirits and play; frolicsome: a playful puppy. — **play′ful·ly** adv. — **play′ful·ness** n.

play·go·er (plā′gō′ər) n. One who goes often to the theater.

play·ground (plā′ground′) n. An area, usu. adjoining a school, used for playing games and for recreation.

play·house (plā′hous′) n. **1.** A theater. **2.** A small house for children to play in. **3.** A toy house.

playing card One of a pack of cards used in playing various games, the pack usu. consisting of four suits (spades, hearts, diamonds, clubs) of 13 cards each.

play·let (plā′lit′) n. A short play.

play·mate (plā′māt′) n. A companion in sports or in play.

play·off (plā′ôf′, -of′) n. In sports: **a** A decisive game or contest to break a tie. **b** A series of games to decide a championship, award, etc.

play·pen (plā′pen′) n. A small, usu. collapsible enclosure in which a baby or small child is left to amuse himself.

play·thing (plā′thing′) n. A thing to play with; a toy.

play upon words Words used with double meaning; a pun.

play·wright (plā′rīt′) n. A writer of plays.

pla·za (plä′zə, plaz′ə) n. An open square or market place in a town or city. [< Sp. < L platea wide street]

plea (plē) n. **1.** An appeal or entreaty. **2.** An excuse, pretext, or justification: the tyrant's plea. **3.** Law An allegation made by either party in a cause: a pleading. **b** A statement made by or for the defendant concerning the charge or indictment against him. [< OF < L placitum opinion, orig. pp. of placere to please]

plead (plēd) v. **plead·ed** or **pled** (pled), **plead·ing** v.i. **1.** To make earnest entreaty; beg. **2.** Law To advocate a case in court. **b** To file a pleading. — v.t. **3.** To allege as an excuse or defense. **4.** Law To discuss or maintain (a case) by argument. [See PLEA.] — **plead′a·ble** adj. — **plead′er** n.

plead·ing (plē′ding) n. **1.** The act of making a plea. **2.** Law **a** The art, science, or system of preparing the formal written statements of the parties to an action. **b** Usu. pl. Any one of such statements. — **plead′ing·ly** adv.

pleas·ant (plez′ənt) adj. **1.** Giving or promoting pleasure; pleasing. **2.** Agreeable in manner, act, appearance, etc. **3.** Merry; gay. [< OF < L placere to please] — **pleas′ant·ly** adv. — **pleas′ant·ness** n.

pleas·ant·ry (plez′ən·trē) n. pl. **·tries 1.** A playful, amusing, or good-natured remark, jest, or trick. **2.** The quality or spirit of pleasant conversation or companionship.

please (plēz) v. **pleased, pleas·ing** v.t. **1.** To give pleasure to; be agreeable to. **2.** To be the wish or will of. **3.** To be so kind as to; be willing to: usu. in the imperative: Please pass the bread. — v.i. **4.** To give satisfaction or pleasure. **5.** To have the will or preference; wish: Go when you please. [< OF < L placere to please]
— Syn. **1.** cheer, gladden, delight, rejoice, exhilarate.

pleas·ing (plē′zing) adj. Affording pleasure or satisfaction; gratifying. — **pleas′ing·ly** adv. — **pleas′ing·ness** n.

pleas·ur·a·ble (plezh′ər·ə·bəl) adj. Gratifying; pleasant; satisfying. — **pleas′ur·a·ble·ness** n. — **pleas′ur·a·bly** adv.

pleas·ure (plezh′ər) n. **1.** An agreeable sensation or emotion; enjoyment. **2.** Something that gives a feeling of enjoyment, delight, or satisfaction. **3.** Amusement or diversion: a search for pleasure. **4.** Sensual gratification. **5.** One's preference; choice. [See PLEASE.]

pleat (plēt) n. A fold of cloth doubled on itself and pressed or sewn in place. — v.t. To make a pleat or pleats in. Also plait. [Var. of PLAIT] — **pleat′er** n.

plebe (plēb) n. U.S. A member of the freshman class in the U.S. Military Academy at West Point or the U.S. Naval Academy at Annapolis. [Short for PLEBEIAN]

ple·be·ian (pli·bē′ən) adj. **1.** Of or pertaining to the common people, esp. those of ancient Rome. **2.** Common or vulgar. — n. **1.** One of the common people, esp. of ancient Rome. **2.** Anyone who is coarse or vulgar. [< L < plebs the common people] — **ple·be′ian·ism** n.

pleb·i·scite (pleb′ə·sīt, -sit) n. An expression of the popular will by means of a vote by the whole people, as to change a constitution. [< F < L < plebs common people + scitum decree] — **ple·bis·ci·tar·y** (plə·bis′ə·ter′ē) adj.

plec·trum (plek′trəm) n. pl. **·trums** or **·tra** (-trə) A small implement with which the player on a lyre, guitar, etc., picks or strikes the strings: also called pick. Also **plec′tron** (-tron). [< L < Gk. < plessein to strike]

pled (pled) Alternate past tense and past participle of PLEAD.

pledge (plej) v.t. **pledged, pledg·ing 1.** To give or deposit as security for a loan, etc. **2.** To bind by or as by a pledge.

3. To promise solemnly, as assistance. 4. To offer (one's word, life, etc.) as a guaranty or forfeit. 5. To drink a toast to. 6. To promise to join (a fraternity). 7. To accept (someone) as a pledge (def. 6). — *n.* 1. A promise or agreement to perform or fulfill some act, contract, or duty. 2. A formal promise to do or not to do something. 3. The drinking of a toast to one's health, etc. 4. Something given as security for a debt or obligation. 5. The state of being given or held as security: to put property in *pledge.* 6. One who has promised to join a fraternity but who has not yet been formally inducted. [< OF < Med.L *plebium,* prob. < Gmc.] — **pledg′er** *n.*

pledg·ee (plej·ē′) *n.* 1. One to whom something is pledged. 2. One with whom a pledge is deposited.

pledg·or (plej′ər) *n. Law* A pledger. Also **pledge′or.**

-plegia *combining form Pathol.* A (specified) kind of paralysis, or paralytic condition: *hemiplegia.* Also **-plegy.** [< Gk. < *plēgē* stroke]

Plei·a·des (plē′ə·dēz, plī′-) *n.pl.* 1. In Greek mythology, the seven daughters of Atlas, who were set by Zeus among the stars. 2. *Astron.* A loose cluster of many hundred stars in the constellation Taurus, six of which are visible to ordinary sight.

Plei·o·cene (plī′ə·sēn) See PLIOCENE.

Pleis·to·cene (plīs′tə·sēn) *Geol. adj.* Of or pertaining to the earlier of the two epochs of the Quaternary, characterized by the glacial epoch of northern Asia, Europe, and North America. — *n.* The rock series of this epoch. See chart for GEOLOGY. [< Gk. *pleistos* most + *kainos* recent]

ple·na·ry (plē′nə·rē, plen′ə-) *adj.* 1. Full in all respects or requisites; complete. 2. Fully or completely attended, as an assembly. [< LL < L *plenus* full] — **ple′na·ri·ly** *adv.* — **ple′na·ri·ness** *n.*

plenary indulgence In the Roman Catholic Church, the remission of all temporal penalties incurred by sin.

plen·i·po·ten·ti·ar·y (plen′i·pə·ten′shē·er′ē, -shə·rē) *adj.* Possessing or conferring full powers. — *n. pl.* **·ar·ies** A person fully empowered to represent a government, as an ambassador, minister, or envoy. [< Med.L < LL < L *plenus* full + *potens* powerful < *potere* to be able]

plen·i·tude (plen′ə·tood, -tyood) *n.* The state of being full, complete, or abounding.

plen·te·ous (plen′tē·əs) *adj.* 1. Characterized by plenty; amply sufficient. 2. Yielding an abundance. — **plen′te·ous·ly** *adv.* — **plen′te·ous·ness** *n.*

plen·ti·ful (plen′ti·fəl) *adj.* 1. Existing in great quantity; abundant. 2. Yielding or containing plenty; affording ample supply. — **plen′ti·ful·ly** *adv.* — **plen′ti·ful·ness** *n.*

— **Syn.** 1. *Plentiful* suggests comparison with a need or demand, and can be applied to almost anything concrete: wheat is *plentiful* this year, aspirants for movie jobs are always *plentiful. Abundant* suggests, in the concrete, the works of nature rather than of man: *abundant* foliage. *Ample* means both just enough and more than enough, and so tends to imply an amount between enough and *plentiful.* — **Ant.** scanty, scarce.

plen·ty (plen′tē) *n.* 1. The state of being sufficient and in abundance. 2. As much as can be required; an abundance or sufficiency: I have *plenty.* — *adj.* Existing in abundance; plentiful. — *adv. Informal* In a sufficient degree: The house is *plenty* large enough. [< OF < L *plenus* full]

ple·o·nasm (plē′ə·naz′əm) *n.* 1. The use of needless words; redundancy; also, an instance of it. 2. A redundant word or phrase. 3. Superabundance. [< L < Gk. < *pleōn* more] — **ple·o·nas′tic** (-nas′tik) *adj.* — **ple·o·nas′ti·cal·ly** *adv.*

pleth·o·ra (pleth′ər·ə) *n.* 1. A state of excessive fullness; superfluity. 2. *Med.* Superabundance of blood in the whole system or in an organ or part. [< LL < Gk. < *plēthein* to be full] — **ple·thor′ic** *adj.* — **ple·thor′i·cal·ly** *adv.*

pleu·ra (ploor′ə) *n. pl.* **pleu·rae** (ploor′ē) *Anat.* The serous membrane that envelops the lungs and is folded back upon the walls of the thorax and upon the diaphragm. [< Gk. *pleura* side] — **pleu′ral** *adj.*

pleu·ri·sy (ploor′ə·sē) *n. Pathol.* Inflammation of the pleura, commonly attended with fever, pain in the chest, difficult breathing, exudation, etc. [< OF < LL < L < Gk. *pleura* side] — **pleu·rit·ic** (ploo·rit′ik) *adj.*

pleuro- *combining form* 1. Of or pertaining to the side. 2. *Med.* Of, related to, or affecting the pleura. Also, before vowels, **pleur-.** [< Gk. *pleura* side]

Plex·i·glas (plek′si·glas′, -gläs′) *n.* A lightweight thermoplastic acrylic resin, very weather-resistant and highly transparent: a trade name. Also **plex′i·glas, plex′i·glass.**

plex·us (plek′səs) *n. pl.* **plex·us·es** or **plex·us** 1. A network or complicated interlacing of parts. 2. *Anat.* A network of cordlike structures, as blood vessels or nerves. [< L, pp. of *plectere* to intertwine]

pli·a·ble (plī′ə·bəl) *adj.* 1. Easily bent or twisted; flexible. 2. Easily persuaded or controlled; tractable. — **pli′a·bil′i·ty, pli′a·ble·ness** *n.* — **pli′a·bly** *adv.*

pli·an·cy (plī′ən·sē) *n.* The state or quality of being pliant.

pli·ant (plī′ənt) *adj.* 1. Capable of being bent or twisted

with ease. 2. Easily yielding to influence; compliant. [< OF, ppr. of *plier* < L *plicare* to fold] — **pli′ant·ly** *adv.*

pli·cate (plī′kāt) *adj.* Folded or pleated, as a fan. Also **pli·cat·ed.** — **pli′cate·ness** *n.* — **pli′cate·ly** *adv.* — **pli·ca′tion, plic·a·ture** (plik′ə·choor) *n.*

pli·er (plī′ər) *n.* 1. *pl.* Small pincers for bending, holding, or cutting: also **pair of pliers.** 2. One who or that which plies.

plight¹ (plīt) *n.* A condition, state, or circumstance, usu. of a dangerous or complicated nature. [< AF *plit* fold, condition < OF *pleit*]

plight² (plīt) *v.t.* 1. To pledge (one's word, faith, etc.). 2. To promise, as in marriage; betroth. — **to plight one's troth** 1. To pledge one's solemn word. 2. To promise oneself in marriage. [OE *plihtan* to expose to danger] — **plight′er** *n.*

Plim·soll mark (plim′sol, -səl) A mark painted on the outside of the hull of a British vessel to show how deeply she may be loaded. Also **Plimsoll line.** [after Samuel *Plimsoll,* 1824–98, English statesman]

plinth (plinth) *n. Archit.* 1. The slab, block, or stone, usu. square, on which a column, pedestal, or statue rests. 2. A thin course, as of slabs, usu. projecting beneath a wall: also **plinth course.** [< L < Gk. *plinthos* brick]

Pli·o·cene (plī′ə·sēn) *Geol. adj.* Of or pertaining to the latest epoch of the Tertiary, and succeeded by the Pleistocene. — *n.* The Pliocene epoch or rock series. Also spelled *Pleiocene.* See chart for GEOLOGY. [< Gk. *pleiōn* more + *kainos* new] — **Pli′o·cen′ic** (-sen′ik) *adj.*

plod (plod) *v.* **plod·ded, plod·ding** *v.i.* 1. To walk heavily or laboriously. 2. To work in a steady, laborious manner. — *v.t.* 3. To walk along heavily or laboriously. — *n.* 1. The act or duration of plodding. 2. The sound of a heavy step, as of a horse. [Imit.] — **plod′der** *n.* — **plod′ding·ly** *adv.*

-ploid *combining form Biol.* In cytology and genetics, having a (specified) number of chromosomes: *polyploid.* Corresponding nouns end in **-ploidy.** [< Gk. *-ploos* fold + -OID]

plop (plop) *v.t. & v.i.* **plopped, plop·ping** To drop with a sound like that of something striking the water without making a splash. — *n.* The act or sound of plopping. — *adv.* Suddenly with a plopping sound. [Imit.]

plo·sion (plō′zhən) *n. Phonet.* The sudden release of breath after closure of the oral passage in the articulation of a stop consonant, as after the *p* in *pat.* [< EXPLOSION]

plo·sive (plō′siv) *Phonet. adj.* Designating a sound produced by plosion. — *n.* A consonant so produced; a·stop.

plot (plot) *n.* 1. A piece or patch of ground, usu. used for some special purpose. 2. A chart or diagram, as of a building, for showing certain data; also, a surveyor's map. 3. A secret plan to accomplish some questionable purpose; conspiracy. 4. The scheme or pattern of the events, incidents, or situations of a story, play, etc. — *v.* **plot·ted, plot·ting** *v.t.* 1. To make a map, chart, or plan of, as of a ship's course, a building, etc. 2. To plan for secretly. 3. To arrange the plot of (a novel, etc.). 4. *Math.* **a** To represent graphically the position of (a measured value) by a point located with reference to its coordinates on graph paper. **b** To draw (a curve) through a series of such points. — *v.i.* 5. To form a plot; scheme. [OE] — **plot′ter** *n.*

plov·er (pluv′ər, plō′vər) *n.* 1. Any of various shore birds, having long, pointed wings and a short tail. 2. Any of certain related shore birds, as the **upland plover.** [< OF *plovier,* ult. < L *pluvia* rain]

plow (plou) *n.* 1. An implement for cutting, turning over, stirring, or breaking up the soil, usu. drawn by horses or oxen, or by mechanical power. 2. Any implement that operates like a plow: often in combination: a *snowplow.* — *v.t.* 1. To turn up the surface of (land) with a plow. 2. To make or form (a furrow, one's way, etc.) by or as by means of a plow. 3. To furrow or score the surface of: Shot *plowed* the field. 4. To dig out or remove with a plow: with *up* or *out.* 5. To move or cut through (water). — *v.i.* 6. To turn up soil with a plow. 7. To undergo plowing in a specified way, as land. 8. To move or proceed as a plow does: usu. with *through* or *into.* 9. To advance laboriously; plod. — **to plow into** *Informal* 1. To hit hard. 2. To undertake vigorously to accomplish, finish, or solve (a meal, problem, etc.). Also, *esp. Brit.,* **plough.** [OE *plōh,* prob. < ON *plōgr*] — **plow′a·ble** *adj.* — **plow′er** *n.*

plow·boy (plou′boi′) *n.* 1. A boy who drives or guides a team in plowing. 2. A country boy. Also **plough′boy′.**

plow·man (plou′mən) *n. pl.* **·men** (-mən) 1. One who plows. 2. A farmer; rustic. Also **plough′man.**

plow·share (plou′shâr′) *n.* The blade of a plow. Also **plough′share′.**

ploy (ploi) *n.* A maneuver or stratagem, as in a game or conversation. [< EMPLOY]

pluck (pluk) *v.t.* 1. To pull out or off; pick. 2. To pull with force; snatch or drag: with *off, away,* etc. 3. To pull out the feathers, hair, etc., of. 4. To give a twitch or pull to, as a sleeve. 5. To cause the strings of (a musical instrument) to sound by quickly pulling or picking them. 6. *Slang* To rob; swindle. — *v.i.* 7. To give a sudden pull;

tug: with *at.* — **to pluck up** To rouse or summon (one's courage). — *n.* **1.** Confidence and spirit in the face of difficulty or danger. **2.** A sudden pull; twitch. — **pluck′er** *n.* [OE *pluccian* to pick out, ? ult. < LL *pilus* hair′]

pluck·y (pluk′ē) *adj.* **pluck·i·er, pluck·i·est** Brave and spirited; courageous. — **pluck′i·y** *adv.* — **pluck′i·ness** *n.*

plug (plug) *n.* **1.** Anything, as a piece of wood or a cork, used to stop a hole. **2.** *Electr.* A usu. two-pronged device attached to the end of a wire or cable and inserted in a socket or jack to make a connection. **3.** A spark plug. **4.** A fireplug. **5.** A flat cake of pressed or twisted tobacco. **6.** A piece of tobacco for chewing. **7.** *Informal* Anything useless or defective. **8.** *Informal* An old, worn-out horse. **9.** *Slang* A favorable word, recommendation, or piece of publicity for someone or something. **10.** *Geol.* A core of hard, igneous rock that has filled the neck of a volcano. — *v.* **plugged, plug·ging** *v.t.* **1.** To stop or close, as a hole, by inserting a plug; often with *up.* **2.** To insert as a plug. **3.** *Slang* To shoot a bullet into. **4.** *Slang* To hit or punch. **5.** *Slang* To advertise frequently or insistently. — *v.i.* **6.** *Informal* To work doggedly. **7.** *Slang* To hit or shoot. **8.** *Slang* To favor or work for a cause, person, etc.: usu. with *for.* — **to plug in** To insert the plug of (a lamp, etc.) in an electrical outlet. [< MDu. *plugge*] — **plug′ger** *n.*

plug-ug·ly (plug′ug′lē) *n. pl.* **-lies** *U.S. Slang* A gangster, ruffian, or rowdy.

plum[1] (plum) *n.* **1.** The edible fruit of any of various trees of the rose family. **2.** The tree itself. **3.** The plumlike fruit of any of various other trees; also, a tree bearing such fruit. **4.** A raisin, esp. as used in cooking. **5.** Any of various shades of dark, reddish purple. **6.** The best or most choice part of anything. **7.** Something desirable, as a post or appointment. **8.** A sugarplum. [OE *plūme* < LL < L *prunum* < Gk. *prounon*]

plum[2] (plum) See PLUMB (*adj.* def. 2 and *adv.* def. 2).

plum·age (ploo′mij) *n.* **1.** The feathers of a bird; esp., a bird's entire covering of feathers. **2.** Gaudy costume or adornment. [< F < *plume* plume]

plumb (plum) *n.* A lead weight (*plumb bob*) on the end of a line (*plumb line*) used to find the exact perpendicular, to sound the depth of water, etc. — **off** (or **out of**) **plumb** Not exactly vertical; not in alignment. — *adj.* **1.** Conforming to a true vertical or perpendicular. **2.** *Informal* Sheer; absolute; complete: also spelled *plum.* — *adv.* **1.** In a line perpendicular to the plane of the horizon; vertically. **2.** *Informal* Utterly; completely; entirely: also spelled *plum.* — *v.t.* **1.** To test the perpendicularity of with a plumb. **2.** To make vertical; straighten: usu. with *up.* **3.** To test the depth of; sound. **4.** To reach the lowest level or extent of: to *plumb* the depths of despair. [< F < L *plumbum* lead]

plumb- Var. of PLUMBO-.

plumb bob The weight used at the end of a plumb line.

plumb·er (plum′ər) *n.* One whose occupation is the installing or repairing of plumbing.

plumb·er's friend (plum′ərz) A plunger (def. 3).

plumb·ing (plum′ing) *n.* **1.** The art or trade of putting into buildings the tanks, pipes, etc., for water, gas, sewage, etc. **2.** The pipe system of a building. **3.** The act of sounding for depth, etc., with a plumb line.

plumb line 1. A cord by which a weight is suspended to test the perpendicularity or depth of something. **2.** Such a cord.

plumbo- *combining form* Lead; of or containing lead. Also, before vowels, *plumb-*. [< L *plumbum* lead]

plume (ploom) *n.* **1.** A feather, esp. when long and ornamental. **2.** A large feather or tuft of feathers used as an ornament. **3.** *Biol.* A featherlike form or part. **4.** Plumage. **5.** Anything resembling a plume. **6.** A decoration of honor or achievement. — *v.t.* **plumed, plum·ing 1.** To adorn, dress, or furnish with or as with plumes. **2.** To smooth (itself or its feathers); preen. **3.** To congratulate or pride (oneself): with *on* or *upon.* [< F < L *pluma*]

plum·met (plum′it) *n.* **1.** A plumb bob. **2.** Something that oppresses or weighs down. — *v.i.* To drop straight down; plunge. [< OF *plom* < L *plumbum* lead]

plu·mose (ploo′mōs) *adj.* **1.** Bearing feathers or plumes. **2.** Plumelike; feathery. [< L *pluma* feather] — **plu′mose·ly** *adv.* — **plu·mos·i·ty** (ploo·mos′ə·tē) *n.*

plump[1] (plump) *adj.* **1.** Somewhat fat; chubby. **2.** Well filled or rounded out. — *v.t. & v.i.* To make or become plump: often with *up* or *out.* [< MDu., var. of *plomp* blunt] — **plump′ly** *adv.* — **plump′ness** *n.*

plump[2] (plump) *v.i.* **1.** To fall suddenly or heavily; drop with full impact. **2.** To give one's complete support: with

for. **3.** To come or go abruptly or in a hurry: with *in* or *out.* — *v.t.* **4.** To drop or throw down heavily or all at once. **5.** To utter bluntly or abruptly: often with *out.* — *n.* **1.** The act of plumbing or falling. **2.** The sound made by this. — *adj.* Containing no reservation or qualification; blunt; downright. — *adv.* **1.** With a sudden impact or fall. **2.** Straightforwardly; bluntly. **3.** Straight down. [< MDu. *plompen*; ult. imit.] — **plump′er** *n.* — **plump′ly** *adv.*

plum·y (ploo′mē) *adj.* **plum·i·er, plum·i·est 1.** Made of, covered, or adorned with feathers. **2.** Like a plume or feather.

plun·der (plun′dər) *v.t.* **1.** To rob of goods or property by open violence, as in war; pillage. **2.** To despoil by robbery or fraud. **3.** To take as plunder. — *v.i.* **4.** To take plunder. — *n.* **1.** That which is taken by plundering; booty. **2.** The act of plundering or robbing. [< G < MHG *plundern*, orig., to remove household goods] — **plun′der·er** *n.*

plunge (plunj) *v.* **plunged, plung·ing** *v.t.* **1.** To thrust or force suddenly into a fluid, penetrable substance, hole, etc. **2.** To force into some condition or state: to *plunge* a nation into debt. — *v.i.* **3.** To dive, jump, or fall into a fluid, chasm, etc. **4.** To move suddenly or with a rush. **5.** To move violently forward and downward, as a horse or ship. **6.** To descend abruptly or steeply, as a road or cliff. **7.** *Informal* To gamble or speculate heavily. — *n.* **1.** The act of plunging; a leap; dive. **2.** A sudden and violent motion, as of a breaking wave. **3.** A place for diving or swimming. **4.** A swim. **5.** A heavy or extravagant bet, expenditure, or speculation. [< OF *plongier*, ult. < L *plumbum* lead]

plung·er (plun′jər) *n.* **1.** One who or that which plunges. **2.** *Informal* One who gambles recklessly. **3.** A cuplike device made of rubber and attached to a stick, used to clean out clogged drains, etc.: also called *plumber's friend.* **4.** *Mech.* Any appliance having a plunging motion, as a piston.

plunk (plungk) *Informal v.t.* **1.** To pluck, as a banjo or its strings; strum. **2.** To place or throw heavily and suddenly: with *down.* — *v.i.* **3.** To emit a twanging sound. **4.** To fall heavily. — *n.* A heavy blow, or its sound. — *adv.* Directly; exactly: *plunk* in the middle. [Imit.]

plu·per·fect (ploo·pûr′fikt) *n. Gram.* The past perfect. [< L *plus quam perfectus*, lit., more than completed]

plu·ral (ploor′əl) *adj.* **1.** Containing, consisting of, or designating more than one. **2.** *Gram.* Of or designating a linguistic form that denotes more than one (in languages that have dual number, as Sanskrit and Greek, more than two): distinguished from *dual, singular.* — *n. Gram.* The plural number or a word in this number. [< OF < L < *plus, pluris* more] — **plu′ral·ly** *adv.*

♦ English nouns regularly form their plurals by adding *s* to the singular. However, nouns that end in *y* preceded either by a consonant or by *qu* form their plurals by changing the *y* to *i* and adding *es*, as, body, *bodies*, city, *cities*, colloquy, *colloquies*; if the *y* is preceded by a vowel (other than *u*), the plural is formed by adding *s*, as, day, *days*, monkey, *monkeys.* Nouns ending in *ss, sh, ch, s, x,* and *zz* usually form their plurals by adding *es*, as, brass, *brasses*, crash, *crashes*, crutch, *crutches*, gas, *gases*, box, *boxes*, buzz, *buzzes.* Many nouns ending in *f* change the *f* to *v* and add *es*, as, wolf, *wolves*, half, *halves.* Nouns ending in *o* form their plurals by adding either *s* or *es*, and the preferable form will be found at the word entry. Some nouns of Old English origin have an irregular plural in *en*, as, child, *children*, and some form the plural by a vowel change, as mouse, *mice*; goose, *geese*; man, *men.* A few nouns retain the singular form unchanged in the plural, as, *deer, hose, moose, series.* Some such nouns, especially the names of animals, have also an alternative plural regularly formed, as fish, *fish* or *fishes. Fish* is the usual collective plural; *fishes* is used to indicate more than one genus, variety, species, etc. Many words of foreign derivation retain the plural forms peculiar to the languages from which they are derived, as, addendum, *addenda*; crisis, *crises*; datum, *data.* Many nouns of this class have also a plural of the regular English form, as, appendix, *appendixes* or *appendices*; beau, *beaus* or *beaux*; cherub, *cherubs* or *cherubim*; focus, *focuses* or *foci.* Compounds commonly form the plural regularly by adding *s* or to the complete word, as, armful, *armfuls*; football, *footballs.* If the last element of the compound forms its plural irregularly, the same form usually appears in the plural of the compound, as, footman, *footmen.* Some nouns that end in *-man*, but are not compounds, form the plural regularly by adding *s*, as, Mussulman, *Mussulmans.* Hyphenated compounds in which the principal word forms the first element change that element to form the plural, as, father-in-law, *fathers-in-law.*

plu·ral·ism (ploor′əl·iz′əm) *n.* **1.** The condition of being plural. **2.** A social condition in which disparate religious, ethnic, and racial groups are part of a common community. **3.** *Eccl.* The holding at the same time of more than one office. **4.** *Philos.* The doctrine that there are several ulti-

PLUMB BOB
a Plumb line.
b Plumb bob.
c Wall.

mate substances. Compare DUALISM, MONISM. — **plu′ral‑ist** *n*. — **plu′ral‑is′tic** *adj*.

plu‑ral‑i‑ty (ploo‑ral′ə‑tē) *n*. *pl*. **‑ties** 1. In U.S. politics: **a** The number of votes cast for a candidate over and above the number cast for his nearest opponent. **b** In a contest having more than two candidates, the greatest number of votes cast for any one candidate but not more than half the total number of votes cast. Distinguished from *majority*. 2. The larger or greater portion of anything. 3. The state or condition of being plural or numerous.

plu‑ral‑ize (ploor′əl‑īz) *v.t.* **‑ized, ‑iz‑ing** 1. To make plural. 2. To express in the plural. — **plu′ral‑i‑za′tion** *n*.

pluri‑ *combining form* More; many; several. [< L *plus, pluris* more]

plus (plus) *prep*. 1. Added to: Three *plus* two equals five. 2. Increased by: salary *plus* commission. — *adj*. 1. Of, pertaining to, or involving addition. 2. Extra; supplemental. 3. Denoting a value higher than ordinary in a specified grade: B *plus*. 4. Positive: a *plus* quantity. 5. *Informal* More of something than can be stated or described: He has personality *plus*. 6. *Electr*. Positive. — *n*. *pl*. **plus‑es** 1. The plus sign. 2. An addition or an extra quantity. 3. A positive quantity. — *adv*. *Electr*. Positively. [< L, more]

plus fours Knickerbockers cut very full and bagging below the knees. [Orig. tailor's cant; because they were four inches longer than ordinary knickerbockers]

plush (plush) *n*. A pile fabric of silk, rayon, mohair, etc., having a deeper pile than velvet. — *adj*. 1. Of plush. 2. *Slang* Luxurious. [< MF < OF < Ital. < L *pilus* hair]

plush‑y (plush′ē) *adj*. **plush‑i‑er, plush‑i‑est** Of or resembling plush. — **plush′i‑ly** *adv*.

plus sign A sign (+) denoting addition or a positive quantity.

Plu‑to (ploo′tō) In Greek and Roman mythology, the god of the dead. — *n*. A planet of the solar system, ninth in order from the sun. See PLANET. [< L < Gk. *Ploutōn*]

plu‑toc‑ra‑cy (ploo‑tok′rə‑sē) *n*. *pl*. **‑cies** 1. Government by the wealthy. 2. A wealthy class that controls the government. [< Gk. *ploutos* wealth + *kratein* to rule]

plu‑to‑crat (ploo′tə‑krat) *n*. 1. A member of a plutocracy. 2. *Informal* Any wealthy person. — **plu′to‑crat′ic, plu′to‑crat′i‑cal** *adj*. — **plu′to‑crat′i‑cal‑ly** *adv*.

plu‑ton‑ic (ploo‑ton′ik) *adj*. *Geol*. Deeply subterranean in original position: said of igneous rocks. [< L *Pluto, ‑onis*]

plu‑to‑ni‑um (ploo‑tō′nē‑əm) *n*. A radioactive element (symbol Pu), formed in the bombardment of neptunium by deuterons. See ELEMENT. [< NL < *Pluto* (the planet)]

Plu‑tus (ploo′təs) In Greek mythology, the god of riches, blinded by Zeus. [< L < Gk. *Ploutos < ploutos* wealth]

plu‑vi‑al (ploo′vē‑əl) *adj*. 1. Of or pertaining to rain. 2. Caused by the action of rain. [< L *pluvia* rain]

pluvio‑ *combining form* Rain; pertaining to rain. Also before vowels, **pluvi‑**. [< L *pluvia* rain]

ply¹ (plī) *v.t.* **plied, ply‑ing** To bend; mold; shape. — *n*. *pl*. **plies** 1. A layer, fold, or thickness, as of cloth, etc. 2. A strand of rope, yarn, thread, etc.; used in combination to mean (a certain) number of folds, twists, or strands: three‑*ply* yarn. 3. A bent; inclination. [< F < L *plicare* to fold]

ply² (plī) *v.t.* **plied, ply‑ing** *v.t.* 1. To use in working, fighting, etc.; wield; employ. 2. To work at; be engaged in. 3. To supply with or offer repeatedly: to *ply* a person with drink. 4. To address (a person) repeatedly with questions, requests, etc. 5. To strike or assail persistently: He *plied* the donkey with a whip. 6. To traverse regularly: ferryboats that *ply* the river. — *v.i.* 7. To make regular trips; sail: usu. with *between*. 8. To work steadily. 9. To proceed; steer. 10. *Naut*. To beat; tack. [< APPLY]

Plymouth Rock One of a breed of domestic fowls. [after *Plymouth Rock*]

ply‑wood (plī′wood′) *n*. A structural material consisting of sheets or layers of wood glued together, the grains of adjoining layers usu. being at right angles to each other.

pneu‑mat‑ic (noo‑mat′ik, nyoo‑) *adj*. 1. Pertaining to pneumatics. 2. Operated by compressed air. 3. Pertaining to or containing air or gas. 4. Spiritual. 5. Containing air, as cavities in the bones of certain birds. Also **pneu‑mat′i‑cal**. — *n*. A tire inflated with compressed air. [< L < Gk. < *pneuma* breath, wind] — **pneu‑mat′i‑cal‑ly** *adv*.

pneu‑mat‑ics (noo‑mat′iks, nyoo‑) *n.pl*. (*construed as sing*.) The branch of physics that treats of the mechanical properties of air and other gases.

pneumato‑ *combining form* 1. Air. 2. Breath; breathing. 3. Spirit; spirits. Also, before vowels, **pneumat‑**. [< Gk. *pneuma, pneumatos* air, spirit, breath < *pneein* to blow]

pneu‑ma‑tol‑o‑gy (noo′mə‑tol′ə‑jē, nyoo‑) *n*. *pl*. **‑gies** The doctrine or study of the nature and operation of spirit and spiritual beings. — **pneu′ma‑to‑log′ic** (‑tə‑loj′ik) or **‑i‑cal** *adj*. — **pneu′ma‑tol′o‑gist** *n*.

pneumo‑ *combining form* Lung; related to the lungs; respiratory. Also **pneum‑** (before vowels), **pneumono‑**. [< Gk. *pneumōn, pneumonos* a lung]

pneu‑mo‑coc‑cus (noo′mə‑kok′əs, nyoo′‑) *n*. *pl*. **‑coc‑ci** (‑kok′sī) Any of a group of bacteria that inhabit the respiratory tract, some of which cause lobar pneumonia. — **pneu′‑mo‑coc′cal, pneu′mo‑coc′cic** (‑kok′sik) *adj*.

pneu‑mo‑ni‑a (noo‑mōn′yə, nyoo‑) *n*. *Pathol*. Inflammation of the lungs, a disease of bacterial or viral origin occurring in many forms, as **bronchial pneumonia** or **lobar pneumonia**. [< NL < Gk. < *pneumōn* lung]

pneu‑mon‑ic (noo‑mon′ik, nyoo‑) *adj*. 1. Of, pertaining to, or affected with pneumonia. 2. Pulmonary. [< NL *pneumonicus* < Gk. *pneumonikos < pneumōn* lung]

poach¹ (pōch) *v.t.* To cook (eggs, fish, etc.) in boiling water, milk, or other liquid. [< OF *poche* pocket, pouch; because the egg white forms a pouch around the yolk]

poach² (pōch) *v.i.* 1. To trespass on another's property, etc., esp. for the purpose of taking game or fish. 2. To take game or fish unlawfully. — *v.t.* 3. To trespass on, as for taking game or fish. 4. To take (game or fish) unlawfully. [< OF *pocher* to thrust, encroach upon] — **poach′er** *n*.

pock (pok) *n*. 1. A pustule in an eruptive disease, as in smallpox. 2. A pockmark. [OE *pocc*]

pock‑et (pok′it) *n*. 1. A small pouch inserted in a garment, for carrying money, etc. 2. A small bag or pouch. 3. Any opening, receptacle, or container. 4. Money, means, or financial interests. 5. *Mining* **a** A cavity containing ore. **b** An accumulation of ore. 6. One of the pouches in a billiard or pool table. 7. An air pocket (which see). 8. A region or area, usu. small and differentiated in some way from the surrounding area. — **in one's pocket** 1. On terms of close intimacy. 2. Under one's influence or control. — *adj*. 1. Diminutive, as if pocketable. 2. Pertaining to, for, or carried in a pocket: *pocket* lining. — *v.t.* 1. To put into or confine in a pocket. 2. To appropriate as one's own, esp. dishonestly. 3. To enclose as if in a pocket. 4. To conceal or suppress: *Pocket* your pride. 5. To retain without signing. 6. In billiards, etc., to drive (a ball) into a pocket. [< AF *pokete*, dim. of OF *poque, poche* pouch] — **pock′et‑a‑ble** *adj*.

pocket billiards Pool² (def. 5).

pock‑et‑book (pok′it‑book′) *n*. 1. A wallet. 2. A woman's purse or handbag. 3. A book, usu. paperbound and smaller than standard size: also **pocket book**. 4. Money or financial resources.

pock‑et‑ful (pok′it‑fool′) *n*. *pl*. **‑fuls** As much as a pocket will hold.

pock‑et‑knife (pok′it‑nīf′) *n*. *pl*. **‑knives** (‑nīvz′) A knife having one or more blades that fold into the handle.

pocket money Money for small expenses.

pocket veto *U.S.* An act whereby the President, on being presented a bill by Congress for his signature of approval, retains ("pockets") it unsigned until the session has adjourned, thus causing it to fail without a direct veto.

pock‑mark (pok′märk′) *n*. A pit or scar left on the skin by smallpox or a similar disease. — **pock′‑marked′** *adj*.

pock‑y (pok′ē) *adj*. **pock‑i‑er, pock‑i‑est** 1. Pertaining to, resembling, or affected with smallpox. 2. Marked by pocks.

po‑co (pō′kō) *adv*. *Music* Slightly; a little. [< Ital.]

pod¹ (pod) *n*. 1. A seed vessel or capsule, esp. of a leguminous plant. 2. *Aeron*. A separate enclosure on an aircraft, esp. one beneath the wing for a jet engine. — *v.i.* **pod‑ded, pod‑ding** To produce pods. [Origin unknown]

pod² (pod) *n*. A flock or collection of animals, esp. of seals, whales, or walruses. [Origin unknown]

‑pod *combining form* 1. One who or that which has (a specified number or kind of) feet: *arthropod*. 2. A (specified kind of) foot. Also **‑pode**. [< Gk. *pous, podos* foot]

‑poda *combining form* *Zool*. Plural of ‑POD: used in names of phyla, orders, classes, etc.: *Arthropoda*.

podg‑y (poj′ē) *adj*. **podg‑i‑er, podg‑i‑est** Pudgy. [< dial. *podge* to walk slowly and heavily] — **podg′i‑ness** *n*.

po‑di‑a‑try (pə‑dī′ə‑trē, pō‑) *n*. *Chiropody*. [< Gk. *pous, podos* foot + ‑IATRY] — **po‑di′a‑trist** *n*.

po‑di‑um (pō′dē‑əm) *n*. *pl*. **‑di‑ums** or **‑di‑a** (‑dē‑ə) 1. A small platform or dais for the conductor of an orchestra, a speaker, etc. 2. *Zool*. A foot, or any footlike structure. [< L < Gk. *podion*, dim. of *pous, podos* foot]

‑podium *combining form* A footlike part. [< NL < Gk. *podion*, dim. of *pous, podos* a foot]

‑podous *combining form* ‑footed: used in adjectives corresponding to nouns in ‑pod and ‑poda: *arthropodous*.

Po‑dunk (pō′dungk) *n*. Any small town regarded as dull and nonprogressive. [? after *Podunk*, Massachusetts]

po‑em (pō′əm) *n*. 1. A composition in verse, characterized by the imaginative treatment of experience and a condensed use of language. 2. Any composition in verse. 3. Any composition or work of art characterized by intensity and beauty. [< F < L < Gk. *poieein* to make]

po‑e‑sy (pō′ə‑sē, ‑zē) *n*. *pl*. **‑sies** 1. *Poetic* Poetry taken collectively. 2. *Poetic* The art of writing poetry.

po‑et (pō′it) *n*. 1. One who writes poems. 2. One esp. endowed with imagination and the creative faculty or power of artistic expression. — **po′et‑ess** *n.fem*.

po·et·as·ter (pō'it·as'tər) *n.* An inferior poet. [< NL]

po·et·ic (pō·et'ik) *adj.* **1.** Of or pertaining to a poet or poetry. **2.** Having the nature or quality of or expressed in poetry: a *poetic* theme. **3.** Having or showing the sensibility, feelings, faculty, etc., of a poet. Also **po·et'i·cal.**

poetic justice The ideal distribution of rewards to the good and punishment to the evil as often represented in literature.

poetic license The departure from fact or rigid rule for the sake of an artistic effect.

po·et·ics (pō·et'iks) *n.pl.* (*usu. construed as sing.*) **1.** The nature, principles, and forms of poetry or, by extension, of any art. **2.** A treatise on poetry.

po·et·ize (pō'it·īz) *v.t. & v.i.* **·ized, ·iz·ing** To write or express in poetry. — **po'et·iz'er** *n.*

poet laureate *pl.* **poets laureate 1.** In Great Britain, the official poet of the realm, a member of the royal household charged with writing verses for particular occasions. **2.** A poet acclaimed as the most eminent in a locality.

po·et·ry (pō'it·rē) *n.* **1.** The art or craft of writing poems. **2.** Poems collectively. **3.** The quality, effect, or spirit of a poem or of anything poetic. **4.** Something that is poetic.

po·go stick (pō'gō) A stiltlike toy, with a spring at the base and fitted with two projections for the feet, on which a person may stand and propel himself in a series of hops.

po·grom (pō'grəm, pō·grom') *n.* An organized and often officially instigated local massacre, esp. one directed against the Jews. [< Russian, destruction]

po·gy (pō'gē, pog'ē) *n.* *pl.* **·gies** or **·gy** The menhaden, a fish. [< Algonquian *pauhagen*]

poi (poi, pō'ē) *n.* A native Hawaiian food made from the root of the taro that is first cooked, ground to a paste, then fermented. [< Hawaiian]

-poietic *combining form* Making; producing; creating. [< Gk. *poiētikos* forming < *poieein* to make]

poign·ant (poin'yənt, poi'nənt) *adj.* **1.** Painful and afflicting to the feelings: *poignant* grief. **2.** Piercing, sharp, and cutting: *poignant* sarcasm. **3.** Penetrating and apt: *poignant* observations. [< OF, ppr. of *poindre* to prick] — **poign'an·cy** *n.* — **poign'ant·ly** *adv.*

poi·lu (pwȧ·lü') *French adj.* Hairy. — *n.* A French soldier, esp. of World War I.

poin·ci·a·na (poin'sē·a'nə, -än'ə) *n.* **1.** A tropical tree or shrub of the bean family. **2.** A similar tree, the **royal poinciana,** having bright orange and scarlet flowers. [< N L, after M. de *Poinci,* a 17th c. governor of the West Indies]

poin·set·ti·a (poin·set'ē·ə) *n.* Any of various American plants of the spurge family, having large, showy red bracts. [after J. R. *Poinsett,* 1779–1851, U.S. statesman]

point (point) *n.* **1.** The sharp, tapering end of a thing. **2.** Something sharp or tapering, as a needle or dagger. **3.** In printing or writing, a dot, mark, etc. **4.** Any mark of punctuation, esp. a period. **5.** That which is conceived to have position, but not parts, dimension, or extent, as the extremity of a line. **6.** A spot, place, or locality. **7.** A tapering tract of land extending into water. **8.** A fixed place from which position and distance are reckoned. **9.** A particular degree, state, or limit reached or determined: the boiling *point.* **10.** One of the 32 equal divisions that indicate direction on a mariner's compass card, each division equal to an angular distance of 11° 15', reckoning from north at 0°. For illustration see COMPASS CARD. **11.** A particular moment of time: on the *point* of starting; at the *point* of death. **12.** The important or main purpose or aim: the whole *point* of the inquiry. **13.** Advantage: What's the *point* of telling her? **14.** The main idea; gist: the *point* of the joke. **15.** An important, striking, or effective fact, idea, etc.: She has some good *points* in her argument. **16.** A tip, idea, or suggestion. **17.** Any single item or particular; detail. **18.** A prominent or distinguishing feature, attribute, or peculiarity. **19.** *pl.* The extremities of an animal, as a horse. **20.** A spike or prong on the antler of a deer. **21.** A unit, as in measuring, evaluating, rating, scoring, etc.: A touchdown equals six *points.* **22.** In schools and colleges, a unit of credit equal to a certain number of hours of academic work. **23.** *Printing* A unit of type size, about ½₂ of an inch. **24.** In commerce, one dollar, used in quoting prices of stocks, etc.: Wheat fell four *points.* **25.** The attitude of a pointer or setter when it finds game: The dog came to a *point.* **26.** *Electr.* **a** A contact or conducting part for making or breaking a circuit, as in a distributor, relay, etc. **b** *Brit.* An outlet or socket. **27.** *Brit.* In railroads, a movable rail that tapers to a point, as in a switch. **28.** *Mil.* The individual or group that goes ahead of an advance guard. **29.** The act of pointing. **30.** *Electr.* Any of a set of contacts determining the direction of current flow in a circuit. — **at** (or **on, upon**) **the point of** On the verge of. — **beside the point** Irrelevant. — **in point** Pertinent. — **in point of** In the matter of; as regards. — **to make a point of** To treat as vital or essential. — **to see the point**

To understand the purpose of a course of action; get the important meaning of a story, joke, etc. — **to stretch a point** To make an exception. — **to the point** Relevant; apt. — *v.t.* **1.** To direct or aim, as a finger or weapon. **2.** To indicate; direct attention to: often with *out:* to *point* the way; to *point* out errors. **3.** *Chiefly U.S.* To give force or point to, as a meaning or remark: often with *up.* **4.** To shape or sharpen to a point. **5.** To punctuate, as writing. **6.** To mark or separate with points, as decimal fractions: with *off.* **7.** In hunting, to indicate the presence or location of (game) by standing rigid and directing the muzzle toward it: said of dogs **8.** In masonry, to fill and finish the joints of (brickwork) with mortar. — *v.i.* **9.** To call attention or indicate direction by or as by extending the finger: usually with *at* or *to.* **10.** To direct the mind: Everything *points* to your being wrong. **11.** To be directed; have a specified direction; tend; face: with *to* or *toward.* **12.** To point game: said of hunting dogs. **13.** *Med.* To come to a head, as an abscess. **14.** *Naut.* To sail close to the wind. [< OF *point* dot and *pointe* sharp tip]

point·blank (point'blangk') *adj.* **1.** Aimed directly at the mark; in gunnery, fired horizontally. **2.** Close enough to aim directly at the mark: *pointblank* range. **3.** Direct; plain: a *pointblank* question. — *n.* A shot with direct aim. — *adv.* **1.** In a straight line; from close range. **2.** Directly; without circumlocution. [? < F *de pointe en blanc* from a point into the white (of a target)]

point·ed (poin'tid) *adj.* **1.** Having a point. **2.** Sharply precise and cutting, as an epigram. **3.** Made clearly evident; emphasized. **4.** Directed or aimed, as at a particular person. — **point'ed·ly** *adv.* — **point'ed·ness** *n.*

point·er (poin'tər) *n.* **1.** One who or that which points. **2.** A hand, index finger, or other indicator, as on a clock or scale. **3.** A long tapering rod used in classrooms to point out things. **4.** One of a breed of smooth-haired dogs trained to scent and point out game. **5.** *Informal* A hint; tip.

pointes (points) *n.pl.* In ballet, dancing on tiptoe. [< F]

poin·til·lism (pwan'tə·liz'əm) *n.* In painting, a method of producing effects of light by placing small spots of varying hues close together on a surface. [< F < *pointiller* to mark with dots] — **point'til·list** *n.*

point lace Needlepoint (def. 2).

point·less (point'lis) *adj.* **1.** Having no point; blunt. **2.** Having no relevance or meaning. **3.** Having no force; ineffective. **4.** Having no points scored. — **point'less·ly** *adv.* — **point'less·ness** *n.*

point of honor Something that vitally affects one's honor.

point of no return That stage or position in any enterprise, course, action, etc., beyond which there can be no return to the starting point; a state of total commitment.

point of order A question as to whether or not the correct parliamentary procedure is being observed.

point of view 1. The place or position from which one views an object, situation etc. **2.** An attitude or viewpoint.

poise (poiz) *v.* **poised, pois·ing** *v.t.* **1.** To bring into or hold in balance; maintain in equilibrium. **2.** To hold; support, as in readiness. — *v.i.* **3.** To be balanced or suspended; hover. — *n.* **1.** The state or quality of being balanced; equilibrium. **2.** Repose and dignity of manner; self-possession. **3.** Physical ease or balance. **4.** Any condition of hovering or suspended motion. **5.** Indecision; suspense. [< OF < L *pendere* to weigh, suspend]

poi·son (poi'zən) *n.* **1.** Any substance that, either taken internally by or coming into contact with an organism, acts chemically upon the tissues in such a way as to harm or destroy. **2.** Anything that tends to harm, destroy, or corrupt. — *v.t.* **1.** To administer poison to; kill or injure with poison. **2.** To put poison into or on. **3.** To corrupt; pervert: to *poison* one's mind. — *adj.* Poisonous. [< OF < L *potio, -onis* drink, esp. a poisonous one] — **poi'son·er** *n.*

poison dogwood Poison sumac. Also **poison elder.**

poison ivy A climbing shrub related to sumac, having glossy, variously notched, trifoliate leaves, greenish flowers, whitish berries, and blistering poison.

poison oak 1. Any of various shrubs related to poison ivy or poison sumac. **2.** A species of poison ivy common in the western U.S.

poi·son·ous (poi'zən·əs) *adj.* **1.** Containing or being a poison. **2.** Having the effect of a poison; toxic. — **poi'son·ous·ly** *adv.* — **poi'son·ous·ness** *n.*

poison sumac A shrub or small tree growing in swamps in

POISON IVY (*a*) AND POISON SUMAC (*b*)

the U.S. and Canada, having smooth, entire leaflets, panicles of greenish yellow berries, and a strong poison.

poke[1] (pōk) v. **poked, pok·ing** v.t. 1. To push or prod, as with the elbow; jab. 2. To make by or as by thrusting. 3. To thrust or push in, out, through, from, etc.: to poke one's head from a window. 4. To stir (a fire, etc.) by prodding: often with up. — v.i. 5. To make thrusts, as with a stick: often with at. 6. To intrude or meddle. 7. To go or look curiously; pry. 8. To appear or show. 9. To proceed slowly; dawdle; putter: often with along. — **to poke one's nose into** To meddle in. — **to poke fun at** To ridicule, esp. slyly. — n. 1. A push; prod. 2. One who moves sluggishly; a dawdler. 3. Informal A punch. [< MLG poken]

poke[2] (pōk) n. A pocket or small bag. [< OF < Gmc.]

poke[3] (pōk) n. A large bonnet with projecting front or brim. Also **poke bonnet**. [Prob. < POKE[1]]

poke·ber·ry (pōk′ber′ē) n. pl. **·ries** 1. A berry of the pokeweed. 2. The pokeweed plant.

pok·er[1] (pō′kər) n. 1. One who or that which pokes. 2. A metal rod for poking a fire.

po·ker[2] (pō′kər) n. Any of several games of cards in which the players bet on the value of the cards dealt to them, the winner being he whose hand contains the cards of highest value. [Cf. G pochspiel, lit., boast game < pochen to boast]

poker face Informal A face that reveals nothing: so called from the inscrutable faces of skillful poker players.

poke·weed (pōk′wēd′) n. A stout perennial North American herb, having purple berries, edible shoots, and a medicinal root: also called pokeberry. Also **poke′root′** (-rōōt′, -rŏŏt′). [< Algonquian (Virginian) pakon weed used for staining < pak blood]

pok·y (pō′kē) adj. **pok·i·er, pok·i·est** Informal 1. Lacking briskness; dull; slow. 2. Shabby or dowdy, as dress. 3. Cramped; stuffy. Also **poke′y**.

Poland China An American mixed breed of large pigs.

po·lar (pō′lər) adj. 1. Of the poles of a sphere, magnet, etc. 2. Of, from, or near the North or South Pole. 3. Directly opposite in character, etc. 4. Chem. Exhibiting ionization. [< Med.L < L < Gk. polos pivot, pole]

polar bear A large, white bear of arctic regions.

Po·lar·is (pō·lar′is, -lâr′-) n. One of the 20 brightest stars, 2.12 magnitude; Alpha in the constellation Ursa Minor: also called Cynosure, polestar, North Star. [< L]

po·lar·i·scope (pō·lar′ə·skōp) n. An optical instrument for exhibiting or measuring the polarization of light, or for examining substances in polarized light.

po·lar·i·ty (pō·lar′ə·tē, -lâr′-) n. pl. **·ties** 1. The quality or condition of having poles. 2. Physics The possession by a body of two poles, the properties at one pole being of opposite or contrasting nature to the properties at the other pole, as in a magnet. 3. The quality or condition of being attracted to one pole and repelled from the other. 4. The possession of two contrary qualities, tendencies, etc.

po·lar·i·za·tion (pō′lər·ə·zā′shən, -ī·zā′-) n. 1. The possession or bestowal of polarity. 2. Physics A condition of electromagnetic waves, most noticeable in light, in which one component of its oscillation is limited to a certain plane, as by transmission through variously oriented crystals or other suitable media. 3. Electr. A change in the potential of a cell due to the accumulation of liberated gases.

po·lar·ize (pō′lə·rīz) v. **·ized, ·iz·ing** v.t. 1. To develop polarization in; give polarity to. — v.i. 2. To acquire polarity. — **po′lar·iz′a·ble** adj. — **po′lar·iz′er** n.

Po·lar·oid (pō′lə·roid) n. A plastic capable of polarizing the light passing through: a trade name. Also **po′lar·oid**.

Polar Regions The areas within the Arctic and Antarctic circles.

pole[1] (pōl) n. 1. Either of the two extremities of the axis of a sphere or any spheroidal body. 2. One of the two points where the earth's axis of rotation meets the surface, called the North Pole and the South Pole. 3. Physics One of the two points at which opposite qualities or forces are concentrated, as in a magnet. 4. Either of two diametrically opposite forces, tendencies, etc. — **to be poles apart** (or **asunder**) To differ greatly. [< OF < L < Gk. polos pivot, pole]

pole[2] (pōl) n. 1. A long, comparatively slender piece of wood or metal. 2. A unit of linear measure, usu. equal to 16.5 feet. 3. A unit of square measure equal to a square rod or 30.25 square yards. — v.t. & v.i. **poled, pol·ing** To propel or push (a boat, raft, etc.) with a pole. [OE < L palus stake]

Pole (pōl) n. A native or inhabitant of Poland.

pole·ax (pōl′aks′) n. An ax, or a combined ax and pick, set on a long pole; a battle-ax. — v.t. To strike or fell with a poleax. Also **pole′axe′**. [ME pol poll + AX]

pole·cat (pōl′kat′) n. 1. A European carnivore allied to the weasel, noted for its offensive odor. 2. U.S. A skunk. [< F poule pullet + CAT; from its predacity]

po·lem·ic (pō·lem′ik) adj. Of or pertaining to controversy; disputatious. Also **po·lem′i·cal**. — n. 1. An argument or controversy. 2. One who engages in argument or controversy. [< Gk. < polemos war]

po·lem·ics (pō·lem′iks) n.pl. (construed as sing.) The art or practice of disputation, esp., theological disputation. — **po·lem′i·cist** (-ə·sist) n.

pole·star (pōl′stär′) n. Polaris.

pole-vault (pōl′vōlt′) v.i. To perform a pole vault. — **pole′-vault′er** n.

pole vault An athletic event in which a vault or jump over a high, horizontal bar is made with the help of a long pole.

po·lice (pə·lēs′) n. 1. An official civil force or department organized to maintain order, prevent and detect crime, and enforce law. 2. (construed as pl.) The members of such a force. 3. In a community, the maintenance of order, law, health, safety, etc. 4. In the U.S. Army: **a** The cleaning or keeping clean of a camp or garrison. **b** A group of soldiers assigned to some specific duty or duties: kitchen police. — v.t. **·liced, ·lic·ing** 1. To protect, regulate, or maintain order in (a city, etc.) with or as with police. 2. U.S. To make clean or orderly, as a military camp. [< MF < LL < Gk. < politēs citizen < polis city]

police dog A German shepherd dog.

po·lice·man (pə·lēs′mən) n. pl. **·men** (-mən) A member of a police force.

police state A country whose citizens are rigidly supervised by a national police, often working secretly.

po·lice·wom·an (pə·lēs′wŏŏm′ən) n. pl. **·wom·en** (-wim′-in) A woman member of a police force.

pol·i·clin·ic (pol′i·klin′ik) n. The department of a hospital in which outpatients are treated. Compare POLYCLINIC. [< G < Gk. polis city + klinik clinic]

pol·i·cy[1] (pol′ə·sē) n. pl. **·cies** 1. Any plan of action, esp. in governmental or business administration: a nation's foreign policy. 2. Prudence, wisdom, or shrewdness, as in conduct or the management of one's affairs; also, any act or plan based on such principles: It was his policy always to be silent. [< OF < LL < Gk. politeia polity]

pol·i·cy[2] (pol′ə·sē) n. pl. **·cies** A written contract of insurance. [< MF < Ital. < Med.L < Gk. apodeiknynai to show forth] — **pol′i·cy·hol′der** n.

po·li·o (pō′lē·ō) n. Informal Poliomyelitis.

polio- combining form Med. Of or pertaining to the gray matter of the brain or the spinal cord. [< Gk. polios gray]

po·li·o·my·e·li·tis (pol′ē·ō·mī′ə·lī′tis, pō′lē-) n. Pathol. An acute, infectious virus disease, occurring esp. in children, and characterized by inflammation of the gray matter of the spinal cord, followed by paralysis and atrophy of various muscle groups: also called infantile paralysis. [< NL < Gk. polios gray + myelos marrow + -ITIS]

pol·ish (pol′ish) n. 1. Smoothness or glossiness of surface. 2. A substance used to produce a smooth or glossy surface. 3. Refinement or elegance. 4. The process of polishing. — v.t. 1. To make smooth or lustrous, as by rubbing. 2. To complete; perfect. 3. To free from crudity, etc. — v.i. 4. To take a gloss. 5. To become elegant or refined. — **to polish off** 1. To do or finish completely. 2. To dispose of. — **to polish up** To improve. [< OF < L polire to smooth] — **pol′ished** adj. — **pol′ish·er** n.

Po·lish (pō′lish) adj. Of or pertaining to Poland, its inhabitants, or their language. — n. The West Slavic language of the Poles.

Po·lit·bu·ro (pol′it·byŏŏr′ō) n. The leading committee of the Communist party in the Soviet Union, replaced in 1952 by the Presidium. [< Russian polit(icheskoe) buro]

po·lite (pə·līt′) adj. **·lit·er, ·lit·est** 1. Courteous; mannerly. 2. Refined; cultured; polished: polite society. [< L polire to polish] — **po·lite′ly** adv. — **po·lite′ness** n.

— **Syn. 1.** Polite implies punctilious observance of the forms of speech and action customary among well-bred persons. Civil is weaker, implying little more than the avoidance of rudeness: To be courteous is to be polite while having also a warmer regard for the feelings and dignity of others. — **Ant.** impolite, rude, boorish.

po·li·tesse (pō·lē·tes′) n. French Politeness; civility.

pol·i·tic (pol′ə·tik) adj. 1. Skillful, ingenious, or shrewd. 2. Crafty; sly; cunning. 3. Wise, prudent, or expedient: a politic move. 4. Political: see BODY POLITIC. [< OF < L < Gk. politēs citizen < polis city] — **pol′i·tic·ly** adv.

— **Syn. 1.** diplomatic, discreet. **2.** wily. **3.** See EXPEDIENT.

po·lit·i·cal (pə·lit′i·kəl) adj. 1. Of or concerned with government. 2. Of, relating to, or involved in politics. 3. Characteristic of or similar to politics or politicians. 4. Having an organized system of government. [< L < Gk. politēs citizen] — **po·lit′i·cal·ly** adv.

political economist A person skilled in political economy.

political economy Economics.

political science The science of the form, principles, and conduct of civil government.

pol·i·ti·cian (pol′ə·tish′ən) n. 1. One who is engaged in politics, esp. professionally. 2. One who engages in politics for personal or partisan aims. 3. One who is skilled in the science of government or politics; a statesman.

po·lit·i·co (pə·lit′i·kō) n. pl. **·cos** A politician. [< Sp. < L politicus]

pol·i·tics (pol′ə·tiks) *n.pl.* (*Usu.* construed as *sing.*) **1.** The science or art of government. **2.** The affairs or activities of those engaged in controlling or seeking to control a government; also, the profession or area of activity of such persons. **3.** The principles, aims, or policies of a government. **4.** The acts or practices of those who seek any position of power or advantage. **5.** Political opinions. [< OF < L < Gk. *politēs* citizen]

pol·i·ty (pol′ə·tē) *n.* *pl.* **·ties 1.** The form or method of government of a nation, state, church, etc. **2.** Any community living under some definite form of government. [< MF < L < Gk. *politeia* polity]

pol·ka (pōl′kə, pō′-) *n.* **1.** A lively round dance consisting of three quick steps and a hop. **2.** Music for this dance, in duple meter. — *v.i.* **·kaed, ·ka·ing** To dance the polka. [< F < Czech *pulka* half step < *Polak* a Pole]

polka dot 1. One of a series of round dots decorating a textile fabric. **2.** A pattern or fabric made up of such dots.

poll (pōl) *n.* **1.** The voting at an election. **2.** The total number of votes cast or registered. **3.** *pl.* The place where votes are cast and counted. **4.** A survey of public opinion on a given subject, usu. obtained from a sample group. **5.** A list of persons. **6.** The head, esp. the top or back of the head where hair grows. — *v.t.* **1.** To receive (a specified number of votes). **2.** To enroll, as for taxation or voting; register. **3.** To cast (a vote) at the polls. **4.** To canvass in a poll (def. 4). **5.** To cut off or trim, as hair, horns, etc. **6.** To cut off or trim the hair, horns, top, etc, of: to *poll* cattle. — *v.i.* **7.** To vote at the polls; cast one's vote. [< MDu. *polle* top of the head] — **poll′er** *n.*

pol·lack (pol′ək) *n.* A food fish of the North Atlantic: also spelled *pollock.* [< Scot. *podlok*]

pol·len (pol′ən) *n.* The male or fertilizing element in a seed plant, consisting of fine yellowish powder formed within the anther of the stamen. [< L, fine flour]

pollen count A measure of the relative concentration of pollen grains in the atmosphere at a given locality and date, usually expressed as the number of grains per cubic yard.

pol·li·nate (pol′ə·nāt) *v.t.* **·nat·ed, ·nat·ing** *Bot.* To supply or convey pollen to. Also **pol′len·ate.** — **pol′li·na′tion** *n.*

pol·li·wog (pol′ē·wog) *n.* A tadpole. Also **pol′ly·wog.** [ME *polwygle*]

poll·ster (pōl′stər) *n.* One who takes polls. Also **poll′ist.**

poll tax A tax on a person, as distinguished from that on property, esp. as a prerequisite for voting.

pol·lute (pə·lōōt′) *v.t.* **·lut·ed, ·lut·ing** To make unclean or impure; dirty; corrupt; profane. [< L < *polluere* to defile] — **pol·lut′er** *n.* — **pol·lu′tion** *n.*

Pol·lux (pol′əks) In Greek mythology, the twin brother of Castor. See CASTOR AND POLLUX. — *n.* One of the 20 brightest stars, 1.21 magnitude; Beta in the constellation Gemini.

Pol·ly·an·na (pol′ē·an′ə) *n.* One who persistently finds good in everything. [after stories by Eleanor H. Porter, 1868–1920]

po·lo (pō′lō) *n.* **1.** A hockeylike game played on horseback, usu. with a light wooden ball and long-handled mallets. **2.** A similar game played on ice, roller skates, in the water, etc. [Prob. < Tibetan *pulu* ball] — **po′lo·ist** *n.*

po·lo·naise (pol′ə·nāz′, pō′lə-) *n.* **1.** A stately, marchlike Polish dance. **2.** Music for this dance, in triple meter. [< F (*danse*) *polonaise* Polish (dance)]

po·lo·ni·um (pə·lō′nē·əm) *n.* A radioactive element (symbol Po) produced by the disintegration of various uranium minerals, discovered in 1898 by Pierre and Marie Sklodowska Curie. See ELEMENT. [< NL < Med.L *Polonia* Poland]

pol·ter·geist (pōl′tər·gīst) *n.* A ghost or spirit reputed to make much noise. [< G, lit., noisy ghost]

pol·troon (pol·trōōn′) *n.* A mean-spirited coward; craven; dastard. — *adj.* Cowardly; contemptible. [< F < Ital. *poltrone* coward < *poltro* colt] — **pol·troon′er·y** *n.*

poly- *combining form* **1.** Many; several; much: *polygamy.* **2.** Excessive; abnormal. [< Gk. *polys* much, many]

pol·y·an·dry (pol′ē·an′drē) *n.* The condition of having more than one husband at the same time. [< Gk. < *poly-* many + *anēr, andros* man, husband] — **pol′y·an′drous** *adj.*

pol·y·cen·trism (pol′ē·sen′triz·əm) *n.* The existence of several centers of power in the Communist world, as Peking and Belgrade, where Moscow had formerly been the single undisputed center. — **pol′y·cen′trist** *n. & adj.*

pol·y·clin·ic (pol′ē·klin′ik) *n.* A hospital or clinic in which all forms of diseases are treated. Compare POLICLINIC.

po·lyg·a·mous (pə·lig′ə·məs) *adj.* **1.** Of, pertaining to, practicing, or characterized by polygamy. **2.** *Bot.* Bearing unisexual and bisexual or hermaphrodite flowers on the same plant. — **po·lyg′a·mous·ly** *adv.*

po·lyg·a·my (pə·lig′ə·mē) *n.* The condition or practice of having more than one wife or husband at the same time.

2. *Zool.* The state of having more than one mate at the same time. [< F < LL < Gk. < *poly-* many + *gamos* marriage] — **po·lyg′a·mist** *n.*

pol·y·glot (pol′i·glot) *adj.* Expressed in several tongues or speaking several languages; multilingual. — *n.* **1.** A polyglot book or person. **2.** A mixture of several languages. [< Gk. < *poly-* many + *glōtta* tongue] — **pol′y·glot′ism** *n.*

pol·y·gon (pol′i·gon) *n.* *Geom.* A closed, usu. plane, figure bounded by straight lines or arcs, esp. by more than four. [< L < Gk. < *poly-* many + *gōnia* angle] — **po·lyg·o·nal** (pə·lig′ə·nəl), **po·lyg′o·nous** *adj.* — **po·lyg′o·nal·ly** *adv.*

pol·y·graph (pol′i·graf, -gräf) *n.* **1.** A device for multiplying or reproducing a drawing or writing. **2.** A versatile or prolific author. **3.** An electrical device for simultaneously recording variations in the heartbeat, blood pressure, muscle reflexes, and respiratory movements, sometimes used as a lie detector. [< Gk. *polygraphos* writing much] — **pol′y·graph′ic** or **·i·cal** *adj.* — **po·lyg·ra·phy** (pə·lig′rə·fē) *n.*

po·lyg·y·ny (pə·lij′ə·nē) *n.* The condition of having more than one wife at the same time. [< POLY- + Gk. *gynē* woman] — **po·lyg′y·nous** (pə·lij′ə·nəs) *adj.*

pol·y·he·dron (pol′i·hē′drən) *n.* *pl.* **·dra** (-drə) or **·drons** *Geom.* A solid bounded by plane faces, esp. by more than four. [< NL < Gk. < *poly-* many + *hedra* base, side] — **pol′y·he′dral** *adj.*

Pol·y·hym·ni·a (pol′i·him′nē·ə) The Muse of sacred song. Also **Po·lym·ni·a** (pə·lim′nē·ə).

pol·y·mer (pol′i·mər) *n.* *Chem.* Any of two or more compounds formed by polymerization. [< Gk. *polymerēs* manifold < *poly-* many + *meros* part]

pol·y·mer·ic (pol′i·mer′ik) *adj. Chem.* Having the same chemical composition but different molecular weights and different properties, as acetylene and benzene.

po·lym·er·ism (pə·lim′ə·riz′əm, pol′i·mə-) *n. Chem.* The condition of being polymeric.

po·lym·er·i·za·tion (pə·lim′ər·ə·zā′shən, pol′i·mər·ə-) *n. Chem.* The process of changing the molecular arrangement of a compound so as to form new compounds having the same percentage composition as the original, but of greater molecular weight and different properties.

po·lym·er·ize (pə·lim′ə·rīz, pol′i·mə·rīz′) *v.t. & v.i.* **·ized, ·iz·ing** To subject to or undergo polymerization. Also *Brit.* **po·lym′er·ise.**

pol·y·morph (pol′i·môrf) *n.* A substance or organism that exhibits polymorphism. [< Gk. < *poly-* many + *morphē* form]

pol·y·morph·ism (pol′i·môr′fiz·əm) *n.* The property of having, assuming, or passing through several forms or characters. — **pol′y·mor′phic, pol′y·mor′phous** *adj.*

Pol·y·ne·sian (pol′i·nē′zhən, -shən) *n.* **1.** One of the native brown-skinned people of Polynesia. **2.** A subfamily of the Austronesian family of languages spoken by these people. — *adj.* Of or pertaining to Polynesia, its people, or their languages.

pol·y·no·mi·al (pol′i·nō′mē·əl) *adj.* Of, pertaining to, or consisting of many names or terms. — *n.* **1.** *Math.* An expression, as in algebra, containing two or more terms. **2.** *Biol.* A scientific name consisting of more than two terms. [< POLY- + *-nomial*, as in BINOMIAL]

pol·yp (pol′ip) *n.* **1.** *Pathol.* **a** A smooth growth of hypertrophied mucus found in mucous membrane, as in the nasal passages. **b** A tumor. **2.** *Zool.* **a** A single individual forming part of a colonial marine animal, esp. a hydrozoan. **b** A hydra. [< MF < L < Gk. < *poly-* many + *pou-* foot] — **pol′y·pous** *adj.*

pol·y·pet·al·ous (pol′i·pet′əl·əs) *adj. Bot.* Having the petals free and distinct. [< NL *polypetalus* < Gk. *poly-* many + *petalon* leaf]

pol·y·phase (pol′i·fāz) *adj. Electr.* Having or producing several phases, as an alternating current.

pol·y·phon·ic (pol′i·fon′ik) *adj.* **1.** Consisting of many sounds or voices. **2.** *Music* Designating or involving the simultaneous combination of two or more independent melodic parts. Also **po·lyph·o·nous** (pə·lif′ə·nəs). [< Gk. < *poly-* many + *phōnē* voice]

po·lyph·o·ny (pə·lif′ə·nē, pol′i·fō′nē) *n.* *pl.* **·nies 1.** Multiplicity of sounds, as in an echo. **2.** The representation by one written character or sign of more than one sound. **3.** Polyphonic music.

pol·y·ploid (pol′i·ploid′) *adj. Genetics* Having more than twice the normal number of chromosomes. — *n.* An organism with more than two chromosome sets.

pol·y·pod (pol′i·pod) *adj.* **1.** Having many feet. **2.** *Zool.* Pertaining to many-footed organisms. — *n.* A myriapod. [< POLY- + -POD]

pol·y·pus (pol′i·pəs) *n.* *pl.* **·pi** (-pī) *Pathol.* A polyp.

pol·y·syl·lab·ic (pol′i·si·lab′ik) *adj.* **1.** Having or pertaining to several syllables, esp. to more than three. **2.** Characterized by words of more than three syllables. Also **pol′y·syl′lab′i·cal.** [< MF < Med.L < Gk. < *poly-* many + *syllabē* syllable]

pol·y·syl·la·ble (pol′i·sil′ə·bəl) *n.* A polysyllabic word. — **pol′y·syl′la·bism** or **·syl·lab′i·cism** (pol′i·sil·ə·siz′əm) *n.*

pol·y·tech·nic (pol′i·tek′nik) *adj.* Embracing many arts: also **pol′y·tech′ni·cal.** — *n.* A school of applied science and the industrial arts. [< F < Gk. < *poly-* many + *technē* craft, art]

pol·y·the·ism (pol′i·thē·iz′əm) *n.* The belief in and worship of more gods than one. [< F < Gk. < *poly-* many + *theos* god] — **pol′y·the·ist** *n.* — **pol′y·the·is′tic** or **·is′ti·cal** *adj.*

pol·y·va·lent (pol′i·vā′lənt) *adj.* 1. *Bacteriol.* Designating a type of vaccine containing antibodies derived from two or more different strains of microorganisms. 2. *Chem.* Multivalent. — **pol′y·va′lence** *n.*

pom·ace (pum′is) *n.* 1. The pulpy substance of apples or similar fruit after grinding. 2. The pulpy substance of anything ground. [< Med.L *pomacium* cider < L *pomum* apple]

po·ma·ceous (pō·mā′shəs) *adj.* 1. Relating to or made of apples. 2. Of or pertaining to a pome.

po·made (pō·mād′, -mäd′) *n.* A perfumed dressing for the hair or scalp. — *v.t.* **·mad·ed, ·mad·ing** To anoint with pomade. [< MF < Ital. < L *pomum* apple]

pome (pōm) *n. Bot.* A fleshy fruit with a core, as an apple, quince, pear, or the like. [< OF, apple < L *pomum*]

pome·gran·ate (pom′gran·it, pum′-, pəm·gran′it) *n.* 1. The fruit of a tropical Asian and African tree about the size of an orange and having many seeds. 2. The tree itself. [< OF *pome* apple + *grenate* < L *granatum* seeded]

Pom·e·ra·ni·an (pom′ə·rā′nē·ən) *adj.* Relating to Pomerania or its inhabitants. — *n.* 1. A native or inhabitant of Pomerania. 2. One of a breed of small dog with pointed ears, a bushy tail, and long, straight, silky coat.

pom·mel (pum′əl, pom′-) *n.* 1. A knob, as on the hilt of a sword, bayonet, etc. 2. A knob at the front and on the top of a saddle. — *v.t.* **pom·meled** or **·melled, pom·mel·ing** or **·mel·ling** To beat with or as with the fists or a pommel. Also spelled *pummel.* [< OF *pomel* rounded knob]

po·mol·o·gy (pō·mol′ə·jē) *n.* The science that deals with fruits and fruit culture. [< NL < L *pomum* an apple, fruit + -LOGY] — **po·mo·log·i·cal** (pō′mə·loj′i·kəl) *adj.* — **po′·mo·log′i·cal·ly** *adv.* — **po·mol′o·gist** *n.*

pomp (pomp) *n.* 1. Magnificent or stately display; splendor. 2. Ostentatious display; vain show. [< OF < L < Gk. *pompē* a sending, procession]

pom·pa·dour (pom′pə·dôr, -dŏŏr, -dŏr) *n.* A style of arranging hair by puffing it over the forehead. [after the Marquise de *Pompadour,* 1721–64]

pom·pa·no (pom′pə·nō) *n. pl.* **·nos** Any of various spiny-finned food fishes of warm seas. [< Sp. *pámpano*]

pom·pon (pom′pon, *Fr.* pôṅ·pôṅ′) *n.* 1. A tuft or ball, as of wool, ribbon, etc., worn on hats, on costumes, etc. 2. A small, compact variety of chrysanthemum or dahlia. [< F]

pom·pos·i·ty (pom·pos′ə·tē) *n. pl.* **·ties** The state or quality of being pompous in manner or speech.

pom·pous (pom′pəs) *adj.* 1. Marked by exaggerated dignity or self-importance. 2. Bombastic and florid, as speech. 3. Full of pomp. [See POMP.] — **pom′pous·ness** *n.* — **pom′·pous·ly** *adv.*

pon·cho (pon′chō) *n. pl.* **·chos** 1. A South American cloak like a blanket with a hole in the middle for the head. 2. A similar waterproofed garment, used as a raincoat. [< Sp.]

pond (pond) *n.* A body of still water, smaller than a lake. [ME *ponde,* var. of POUND²]

pon·der (pon′dər) *v.t.* 1. To weigh in the mind; consider carefully. — *v.i.* 1. To meditate; reflect. [< OF < L *ponderare* to weigh] — **pon′der·er** *n.*

pon·der·a·ble (pon′dər·ə·bəl) *adj.* Capable of being weighed; having appreciable weight. — **pon′der·a·bil′i·ty** *n.*

pon·der·ous (pon′dər·əs) *adj.* 1. Having great weight; also, huge; bulky. 2. Heavy to the extent of dullness; lumbering. [< F < L < *pondus, ponderis* weight] — **pon′der·os′i·ty** (-də·ros′ə·tē), **pon′der·ous·ness** *n.* — **pon′der·ous·ly** *adv.*

pond lily Any of various plants of the water-lily family.

pond scum Any of a group of free-floating, fresh-water green algae that form a scum on ponds.

pond·weed (pond′wēd′) *n.* Any of various perennial aquatic plants that grow in ponds and streams.

pone (pōn) *n. Southern U.S.* Corn pone.

pon·gee (pon·jē′) *n.* A thin, natural, unbleached silk with a rough weave, originally made in China from wild silkworms. [? < Chinese *pen chi* home loom]

pon·iard (pon′yərd) *n.* A dagger. — *v.t.* To stab with a poniard. [< MF < OF *poing* fist < L *pugnus*]

pons (ponz) *n. pl.* **pon·tes** (pon′tēz) 1. A bridge: used in Latin phrases. 2. The pons Varolii. [< L]

pons Va·ro·li·i (ponz və·rō′lē·ī) *Anat.* A broad band of nerve fibers that connect the cerebrum, cerebellum, and medulla oblongata. [< NL, bridge of Varoli; after Costanzo *Varoli,* 1543?–75, Italian anatomist]

pon·ti·fex (pon′tə·feks) *n. pl.* **pon·tif·i·ces** (pon·tif′ə·sēz) In ancient Rome, a priest belonging to the Pontifical College. [< L *pons, pontis* bridge + *facere* to make]

pon·tiff (pon′tif) *n.* 1. In the Roman Catholic Church: **a** The Pope. **b** Any bishop. 2. In ancient Rome, a pontifex. [< MF *pontife* < L *pontifex* pontifex] — **pon·tif′ic** *adj.*

pon·tif·i·cal (pon·tif′i·kəl) *adj.* 1. Of, pertaining to, or suitable for a pope or bishop. 2. Haughty; pompous; dogmatic. — **pon·tif′i·cal·ly** *adv.*

Pontifical College In ancient Rome, the highest priestly group that had supreme jurisdiction in religious matters.

pon·tif·i·cate (*n.* pon·tif′ə·kit, -kāt′; *v.* -kāt′) *v.i.* **·cat·ed, ·cat·ing** 1. To act or speak pompously or dogmatically. 2. To perform the office of a pontiff. — *n.* The office or term of a pontiff.

pon·toon (pon·tōōn′) *n.* 1. *Mil.* A flat-bottomed boat, air-tight metal cylinder, or the like, used in the construction of temporary floating bridges over rivers. 2. A pontoon bridge. 3. Either of the floats on the landing gear of a seaplane. [< MF < L *pons, pontis* bridge]

pontoon bridge A bridge supported on pontoons.

po·ny (pō′nē) *n. pl.* **·nies** 1. A breed of very small horse, esp. one not over 14 hands high. 2. Any small horse. 3. *U.S. Slang* A translation used to prepare foreign language lessons: also called *trot.* 4. Anything that is small for its kind. 5. *Informal* A very small glass for liquor or its contents. — *v.t.* & *v.i.* **·nied, ·ny·ing** *U.S. Slang* 1. To translate lessons with the aid of a pony. 2. To pay (money) that is due: with *up.* [< dial. E (Scottish) *powney*]

pony express A former postal system by which mail was relayed by riders mounted on swift ponies.

po·ny·tail (pō′nē·tāl′) *n.* 1. A style of arranging long hair by gathering it tightly at the back of the head and letting it hang down like a pony's tail. 2. Hair so worn.

pooch (pōōch) *n. Slang* A dog; esp., a small mongrel. [? < dial. E and obs. *pooch,* var. of POUCH]

poo·dle (pōōd′l) *n.* One of a breed of dogs of high intelligence, with long, curly, usu. white or black hair. [< G *pudel* < *pudeln* to splash in water]

pooh (pōō) *interj.* An exclamation of contempt, disdain, etc.

Pooh-Bah (pōō′bä′) *n. Informal* A pompous official. [after a character in Gilbert and Sullivan's *The Mikado*]

pooh-pooh (pōō′pōō′) *v.t.* To reject or speak of disdainfully. [Reduplication of POOH] — **pooh′-pooh′er** *n.*

pool¹ (pōōl) *n.* 1. A small body of fresh water, as a spring. 2. A deep place in a stream. 3. Any small, isolated body of liquid: a *pool* of blood. 4. A swimming pool. [OE *pōl*]

pool² (pōōl) *n.* 1. In certain gambling games, a collective stake. 2. In business, a combination whereby companies agree to fix prices in order to overcome competition. 3. In finance, any combination formed for a speculative operation, as in stocks. 4. Any combining of efforts or resources: a typists' *pool.* 5. Any of various games played on a six-pocket billiard table: also *pocket billiards.* See BILLIARDS. — *v.t.* 1. To combine in a mutual fund or pool. — *v.i.* 2. To form a pool. [< F < L *pulla* stake]

pool·room (pōōl′rōōm′, -rŏŏm′) *n.* A commercial establishment or room equipped for the playing of pool, billiards, etc.

pool table A six-pocket billiard table for playing pool.

poop¹ (pōōp) *Naut. n.* 1. The after part or stern of a ship. 2. A short deck built over the main deck at the stern of a ship: also **poop deck.** — *v.t.* 1. To break over the stern or poop of: said of a wave. 2. To take (a wave) over the stern. [< OF < OProvencal < L *puppis*]

poop² (pōōp) *U.S. Slang v.t.* To tire: usu. in the passive: He was *pooped* by the long climb. [Origin unknown]

poor (pōŏr) *adj.* 1. Lacking means of comfortable subsistence; needy. 2. Characterized by poverty: a *poor* neighborhood. 3. Lacking in abundance; scanty; meager: a *poor* crop. 4. Lacking in fertility; sterile: *poor* soil. 5. Inferior in workmanship or quality. 6. Feeble; frail: *poor* health. 7. Thin from bad feeding; lean, as cattle. 8. Contemptible; mean. 9. Lacking proper ability; unsatisfactory. 10. Deserving of pity. [< OF < L *pauper* poor] — **poor′ly** *adv.* & *adj.* — **poor′ness** *n.*

poor·house (pŏŏr′hous′) *n.* A public establishment maintained as a dwelling for paupers.

poor-spir·it·ed (pŏŏr′spir′it·ed) *adj.* Having little spirit or courage. — Syn. See COWARDLY. — **poor′-spir′it·ed·ness** *n.*

poor white In the southern U.S., a member of a class of poverty-stricken white farmers or laborers: an offensive term. Also **poor white trash.**

pop¹ (pop) *v.* **popped, pop·ping** *v.i.* 1. To make a sharp, explosive sound. 2. To burst open or explode with such a sound. 3. To move or go suddenly or quickly: with *in, out,* etc. 4. To bulge: His eyes *popped.* — *v.t.* 5. To cause to burst or explode, as kernels of corn. 6. To thrust or put suddenly: with *in, out,* etc. 7. To fire (a gun, etc.). 8. To shoot. 9. *Slang* To take (habit-forming or harmful drugs) by mouth or injection: to *pop* pills. — **to pop the question** *Informal* To make a proposal of marriage. — *n.* 1. A sharp, explosive noise. **2.** A shot with a firearm. **3.** Soda (def. 2). **4.** A shot, as in basketball. — *adv.* **1.** Like, or with the sound of a pop. **2.** Suddenly. [Imit.]

pop² (pop) *n. Slang* **1.** Papa. **2.** A familiar term of address for an old man. [Short for *poppa*, var. of PAPA]

pop³ (pop) *n.* A concert of popular or light classical music. — *adj.* Featuring popular or light classical music: a *pop* concert; a *pop* orchestra. Also **pops**. [Short for POPULAR]

pop art *Sometimes cap.* A style of art of the 1960's influenced by popular commercial art.

pop·corn (pop'kôrn') *n.* A variety of maize, the kernels of which explode when heated, forming large white balls; also, the corn after popping, eaten as a confection.

pope (pōp) *n. Often cap.* In the Roman Catholic Church, the bishop of Rome and the head of the Church. [OE < LL < LGk. < Gk. *pappas* father] — **pope'dom** *n.*

pop·er·y (pō'pər·ē) *n.* The practices, doctrines, etc., of the Roman Catholic Church: an offensive term.

pop-eyed (pop'īd') *adj.* **1.** Having bulging or protruding eyes. **2.** Filled with astonishment; amazed.

pop·gun (pop'gun') *n.* A child's toy gun that expels a pellet with a popping sound by compressed air.

pop·in·jay (pop'in·jā) *n.* A pretentious, conceited person. [< OF *papegai* < Sp. < Arabic *babaghā*]

pop·ish (pō'pish) *adj.* Pertaining to popes or popery: an offensive term. — **pop'ish·ly** *adv.* — **pop'ish·ness** *n.*

pop·lar (pop'lər) *n.* **1.** Any of a genus of dioecious trees and bushes of the willow family. **2.** The wood of any of these trees. [< OF < L *populus*]

pop·lin (pop'lin) *n.* A durable silk, cotton, or rayon fabric with a ribbed surface, used for dresses, etc. [< F < Ital. *papalina* papal; because made in Avignon, a papal residence]

pop·o·ver (pop'ō'vər) *n.* A very light egg muffin.

pop·per (pop'ər) *n.* **1.** One who or that which pops. **2.** A container or device for popping corn.

pop·pet valve (pop'it) *Mech.* A valve that rises and falls perpendicularly, used in gasoline engines.

pop·py (pop'ē) *n.* *pl.* **·pies** **1.** Any of various plants having lobed or toothed leaves and showy red, violet, orange, or white flowers, as the opium poppy. **2.** A medicinal extract, as opium, from such a plant. **3.** The bright scarlet color of certain poppy blossoms: also **poppy red**. [OE < L *papaver*]

pop·py·cock (pop'ē·kok) *n. Informal* Pretentious talk; humbug; nonsense. [< Dial. Du. *pappekak*, lit., soft dung]

poppy seed The small, black seed of the poppy plant used to flavor and top rolls, bread, etc.

pop·u·lace (pop'yə·lis) *n.* The common people; the masses. [< MF < Ital. < L *populus* people]

pop·u·lar (pop'yə·lər) *adj.* **1.** Approved of, admired, or liked by most people: *popular* music. **2.** Having many friends. **3.** Of, pertaining to, or engaged in by the people at large: *popular* government. **4.** Suited to the intelligence of ordinary people. **5.** Prevalent among the people in general. **6.** Suited to the means of the people: *popular* prices [< L *popularis* of the people] — **pop'u·lar·ly** *adv.*

popular front A coalition of leftist, labor, and liberal parties formed to combat fascism and promote reform.

pop·u·lar·i·ty (pop'yə·lar'ə·tē) *n.* The state of being popular.

pop·u·lar·ize (pop'yə·lə·rīz) *v.t.* **·ized, ·iz·ing** To make popular. Also *Brit.* **pop'u·lar·ise'.** — **pop'u·lar·i·za'tion** *n.* — **pop'u·lar·iz'er** *n.*

pop·u·late (pop'yə·lāt) *v.t.* **·lat·ed, ·lat·ing** **1.** To furnish with inhabitants, as by colonization; people. **2.** To inhabit. [< Med.L < L *populus* the people]

pop·u·la·tion (pop'yə·lā'shən) *n.* **1.** The total number of persons living in a country, city, or other specified area. **2.** The total number of persons of a particular group, class, race, etc., residing in a place. **3.** The act or process of populating or furnishing with inhabitants. **4.** *Stat.* A group of items or individuals. [< LL < L *populus* the people]

Pop·u·list (pop'yə·list) *n.* A member of the Populist or People's Party, formed in the U.S. in 1891 and advocating public control of railways, an income tax, and limitation of ownership of land. — *adj.* Of or pertaining to Populists or to their party. — **Pop'u·lism** *n.*

pop·u·lous (pop'yə·ləs) *adj.* Containing many inhabitants; thickly settled. — **pop'u·lous·ly** *adv.* — **pop'u·lous·ness** *n.*

porce·lain (pôrs'lin, pôrs'-, pôr'sə-, pôr'-) *n.* **1.** A white, hard, translucent ceramic ware, usu. glazed; chinaware. **2.** An object made of this material. [< MF < Ital. *porcellana* shell < L *porcella*, dim. fem. of *porcus* pig] — **por·ce·la·ne·ous** (pôr'sə·lā'nē·əs, pôr'-) or **por'cel·la'ne·ous** *adj.*

porch (pôrch, pōrch) *n.* **1.** A covered structure or recessed space at the entrance to a building; a stoop. **2.** *U.S.* A veranda. **3.** A covered walk or portico. [< OF < L *porticus* colonnade < *porta* gate]

por·cine (pôr'sīn, -sin) *adj.* Of, pertaining to, or characteristic of swine. [< F, fem. of *porcin* < L *porcus* pig]

por·cu·pine (pôr'kyə·pīn) *n.* Any of various large, clumsy rodents covered with erectile spines or quills used for defense: also, *U.S.* hedgehog. [< OF < OProvençal < It. < L *porcus* pig + *spina* thorn]

pore¹ (pôr, pōr) *v.i.* **pored, por·ing** **1.** To gaze steadily or intently. **2.** To study or read with care and application: with *over*: to *pore* over one's accounts. **3.** To meditate; ponder: with *on*, *over*, or *upon*. [ME *pouren*]

pore² (pôr, pōr) *n.* **1.** A minute orifice or opening, as in the skin or a leaf, serving as an outlet for perspiration or as a means of absorption. **2.** Any similar opening, as in rock. [< OF < L < Gk. *poros* pore, passage]

por·gy (pôr'gē) *n.* *pl.* **·gies** or **·gy** **1.** Any of various saltwater food fishes, esp. the **red porgy** of Mediterranean and European waters. **2.** Any of various related fishes, as the scup. [Origin uncertain]

pork (pôrk, pōrk) *n.* **1.** The flesh of swine used as food. **2.** *U.S. Slang* Government money, favors, etc., obtained through political patronage. [< OF < L *porcus* pig]

pork barrel *U.S. Slang* A Federal appropriation for some local enterprise that will favorably impress a representative's constituents.

pork·er (pôr'kər, pōr'-) *n.* A pig or hog, esp. one fattened for slaughter.

pork·pie (pôrk'pī, pōrk'-) *n.* **1.** A pie filled with chopped pork and having a thick crust. **2.** A man's hat with a low, flat crown. Also **pork pie**.

pork·y (pôr'kē, pōr'-) *adj.* **pork·i·er, pork·i·est** **1.** Of or like pork. **2.** Obese; fat, as from overeating.

porn (pôrn) *Slang adj.* Pornographic. — *n.* Pornography. Also **por·no** (pôr'nō).

por·nog·ra·phy (pôr·nog'rə·fē) *n.* *pl.* **·phies** Obscene literature or art. [< Gk. < *pornē* prostitute + *graphein* to write] — **por·nog'ra·pher** *n.* — **por·no·graph·ic** (pôr'nə·graf'ik) *adj.*

po·ros·i·ty (pô·ros'ə·tē, pō-) *n.* *pl.* **·ties** **1.** The property of being porous; porousness. **2.** A porous part or structure.

po·rous (pôr'əs, pō'rəs) *adj.* **1.** Having pores. **2.** Permeable by fluids or light. — **po'rous·ly** *adv.* — **po'rous·ness** *n.*

por·phy·ry (pôr'fə·rē) *n.* *pl.* **·ries** An igneous rock that has a groundmass enclosing crystals of feldspar or quartz. [< OF < Med.L < Gk. *porphyros* purple]

por·poise (pôr'pəs) *n.* *pl.* **·es** or **·poise** **1.** A dolphinlike animal with a blunt, rounded snout; esp., the **harbor porpoise** of the North Atlantic and Pacific, blackish above and white below. **2.** Loosely, any small cetacean, as the common dolphin. [< OF < L *porcus pisces*, lit., hog fish]

PORPOISE (def. 1) (To 6 feet long)

por·ridge (pôr'ij, por-) *n.* **1.** *Chiefly Brit.* A soft food made by boiling oatmeal or other meal in water or milk until thickened. **2.** Originally, pottage. [Alter. of POTTAGE]

por·rin·ger (pôr'in·jər, por'-) *n.* A small, relatively shallow bowl for porridge or soup; esp., such a bowl used by small children. [Earlier *pottanger* < MF *potager* soup bowl]

port¹ (pôrt, pōrt) *n.* **1.** A city or place of customary entry and exit of ships, esp. for commerce. **2.** A harbor or haven. **3.** *Law* A port of entry. [OE < L *portus* harbor]

port² (pôrt, pōrt) *Naut. n.* The left side of a vessel as one faces the front or bow: formerly called *larboard*: opposed to *starboard*. — *v.t. & v.i.* To put or turn to the port or larboard side. — *adj.* Left: *port* side. [Prob. < PORT¹]

port³ (pôrt, pōrt) *n.* **1.** *Naut.* **a** A porthole. **b** A covering for a porthole. **2.** *Mech.* An orifice for the passage of air, gas, etc.: a steam *port*. [Prob. < OF < L *porta* gate, door]

port⁴ (pôrt, pōrt) *n.* A variety of sweet wine, usu. dark red. [Short for *Oporto* wine, after *Oporto*, Portugal]

port⁵ (pôrt, pōrt) *v.t. Mil.* To carry (a rifle, saber, etc.) diagonally across the body and sloping to the left shoulder. — *n.* **1.** *Mil.* The position of a rifle or other weapon when ported. **2.** The way in which one bears or carries himself. [< MF < L *portare* to carry]

port·a·ble (pôr'tə·bəl, pōr'-) *adj.* That can be readily carried or moved. — *n.* Something portable, as a typewriter or radio. [< MF < LL < L *portare* to carry] — **port·a·bil'i·ty, port'a·ble·ness** *n.* — **port'a·bly** *adv.*

port·age (pôr'tij, pōr'-) *n.* *U.S. & Canadian* **1.** The act of transporting (canoes, boats, and goods) from one navigable water to another; also, that which is transported. **2.** The route over which and the place where such transportation is made. **3.** The charge for transportation.

por·tal (pôr'təl, pōr'-) *n.* **1.** *Often pl.* An entrance, door, or gate, esp. one that is grand and imposing. **2.** The portal vein. — *adj.* Pertaining to the portal vein. [< MF < Med.L, ult. < L *porta* gate]

port authority Any official body having charge of the coordination of all rail and water traffic of a port.

port·cul·lis (pôrt·kul'is, pōrt-) *n.* A grating made of strong bars of wood or iron that can be let down suddenly to close the gateway of a fortified place. [< OF < *porte* gate + fem. of *coleis,* pp. of *couler* to slide]

Porte (pôrt, pōrt) *n.* The former Ottoman Turkish government: with *the.* [< F (*la Sublime*) *Porte* (the High) Gate, trans. of Turkish *Babi Ali*]

porte-co·chère (pôrt'kō·shâr', pōrt'-; Fr. pôrt·kô·shâr') *n.* 1. A large covered gateway for vehicles, leading into a courtyard. 2. A porch over a driveway at the entrance of a building for sheltering persons entering or leaving vehicles. [< F < *porte* gate + *cochère,* fem. adj. < *coche* coach]

por·tend (pôr·tend', pōr-) *v.t.* To warn of as an omen; forebode. [< L < *pro-* forth + *tendere* to stretch]

por·tent (pôr'tent, pōr'-) *n.* 1. An indication or sign of what is to happen, esp. of something momentous or calamitous. 2. Ominous significance. 3. A prodigy; marvel.

por·ten·tous (pôr·ten'təs, pōr-) *adj.* 1. Having the nature of a portent; foreboding. 2. Causing astonishment or awe; extraordinary. — **por·ten'tous·ly** *adv.* — **por·ten'tous·ness** *n.*

por·ter¹ (pôr'tər, pōr'-) *n.* 1. One who carries travelers' luggage, etc., for hire, as at a railroad station. 2. *U.S.* An attendant in a Pullman car. [< OF < LL *portator* to carry]

por·ter² (pôr'tər, pōr'-) *n.* A keeper of a door or gate; janitor. [< OF < LL < L *porta* gate, door]

por·ter³ (pôr'tər, pōr'-) *n.* A dark brown, heavy, English liquor resembling ale, formerly drunk chiefly by porters.

por·ter·house (pôr'tər·hous', pōr'-) *n.* 1. A place where porter, ale, etc., are retailed. 2. A restaurant; chophouse. 3. A choice cut of beefsteak including a part of the tenderloin, usu. next to the sirloin: also **porterhouse steak.**

port·fo·li·o (pôrt·fō'lē·ō, pōrt-) *n.* *pl.* **·li·os** 1. A portable case for holding drawings, papers, etc. 2. Such a case for carrying documents of a department of state. 3. The office of a minister of state or a cabinet member. 4. An itemized list of investments, securities, etc., of a bank or investor. [< Ital. < L *portare* to carry + *folium* leaf, sheet of paper]

port·hole (pôrt·hōl', pōrt'-) *n.* 1. A small opening in a ship's side for admitting light and air, for shooting a weapon through, or for loading cargo. 2. A loophole in the wall of a fort for shooting through; embrasure. 3. An opening into a furnace, engine, or the like, shaped like a porthole.

por·ti·co (pôr'ti·kō, pōr'-) *n.* *pl.* **·coes** or **·cos** An open space or ambulatory with roof upheld by columns; a porch. [< Ital. < L *porticus* < *porta* door] — **por'ti·coed** *adj.*

por·tière (pôr·tyâr', pōr-; Fr. pôr·tyâr') *n.* A curtain for a doorway, used instead of a door. Also **por·tiere'.** [< F]

por·tion (pôr'shən, pōr'-) *n.* 1. A part of a whole, whether separated from it or not. 2. An allotment or share. 3. The quantity of food usu. served to one person. 4. The part of an estate coming to an heir or next of kin. 5. A dowry (def. 1). — *v.t.* 1. To divide into shares for distribution; parcel: usu. with *out.* 2. To give a dowry or inheritance to. 3. To assign; allot. [< OF < L *portio, -onis*] — **por'tion·a·ble** *adj.* — **por'tion·less** *adj.*

— Syn. (noun) 1. *Portion, fraction,* and *section* denote a part of a whole. A *portion* was originally an alloted share, and so suggests a measured quantity: to devote a *portion* of one's time to study. A *fraction,* originally a very small part, now denotes a part taken away: the first *fraction* in the distillation of petroleum. Unlike the other synonyms, *fraction* has little or no suggestion of measurement. A *section* is the part lying between two cuts; hence, any clearly demarcated part: a *section* of a book.

por·tion·er (pôr'shən·ər, pōr'-) *n.* One who divides in shares or holds a share or shares.

port·ly (pôrt'lē, pōrt'-) *adj.* **·li·er, ·li·est** 1. Somewhat corpulent; stout. 2. Having a stately appearance and carriage; impressive. [< PORT⁵ + -LY] — **port'li·ness** *n.*

port·man·teau (pôrt·man'tō, pōrt-) *n.* *pl.* **·teaus** or **·teaux** (-tōz) *Chiefly Brit.* A large, leather suitcase hinged at the back to form two distinct compartments. [< MF < *porter* to carry + *manteau* coat < L *mantellum*]

port of call A port where vessels put in for supplies, repairs, discharge or taking on of cargo, etc.

port of entry *Law* A place, whether on the coast or inland, designated as a point at which persons or merchandise may enter or pass out of a country: also called *port.*

por·trait (pôr'trit, pōr'-, -trāt) *n.* 1. A likeness of a person, esp. of the face, produced, usu. from life, by an artist or photographer. 2. A vivid word description, esp. of a person. [See PORTRAY] — **por'trait·ist** *n.*

por·trai·ture (pôr'tri·chər, pōr'-) *n.* 1. The art or practice of making portraits. 2. A portrait. 3. Portraits collectively.

por·tray (pôr·trā', pōr-) *v.t.* 1. To represent by drawing, painting, etc. 2. To describe or depict in words. 3. To represent, as in a play; act. [< OF < Med.L < L < *pro-* forward + *trahere* to draw] — **por·tray'a·ble** *adj.* — **por·tray'al** *n.* — **por·tray'er** *n.*

por·tress (pôr'tris, pōr'-) *n.* A woman porter or doorkeeper. Also **por·ter·ess** (pôr'tris, -tər·is, pōr'-).

Por·tu·guese (pôr'chə·gēz', -gēs', pōr'-) *adj.* Pertaining to Portugal, its inhabitants, or their language. — *n.* 1. A native or inhabitant of Portugal. 2. The people of Portugal. 3. The Romance language of Portugal and Brazil.

Portuguese man-of-war Any of several large marine organisms, having long, stinging tentacles hanging down from a bladderlike float.

pose¹ (pōz) *n.* 1. The position of the whole or part of the body, esp. such a position assumed for or represented by an artist or photographer. 2. A mental attitude adopted for effect. — *v.* **posed, pos·ing** *v.i.* 1. To assume or hold an attitude or position, as for a portrait. 2. To affect mental attitudes. 3. To represent oneself: to *pose* as an expert. — *v.t.* 4. To cause to assume an attitude or position, as an artist's model. 5. To state or propound; put forward as a question, etc. [< OF, fusion of LL *pausare* to place < L, to pause and *pos-,* stem of L *ponere* to put]

pose² (pōz) *v.t.* **posed, pos·ing** To puzzle or confuse by asking a difficult question. [< obs. *appose,* var. of OPPOSE]

Po·sei·don (pō·sī'dən) In Greek mythology, brother of Zeus, god of the sea and of horses: identified with the Roman *Neptune.* — **Po'sei·do·ni·an** (-dō'nē·ən) *adj.*

pos·er¹ (pō'zər) *n.* One who poses. [< POSE¹, v.]

pos·er² (pō'zər) *n.* A question that baffles. [< POSE²]

po·seur (pō·zœr') *n.* One who affects a particular attitude to make an impression on others. [< F < *poser* to pose]

pos·it (poz'it) *v.t.* 1. To put in position; place. 2. To lay down or assume as a fact or basis of argument; postulate. [< L *positus,* pp. of *ponere* to place]

po·si·tion (pə·zish'ən) *n.* 1. The manner in which a thing is placed. 2. Disposition of the body or parts of the body. 3. The locality or place occupied by a person or thing. 4. *Med.* The placement or arrangement of the body of a patient in order to facilitate therapeutic, surgical, or obstetrical procedures. 5. The proper or appropriate place: in *position.* 6. State or situation in relation to other conditions: to be in a false *position.* 7. An attitude or point of view; stand. 8. Relative social standing; status; also, high social standing. 9. Employment; job. 10. In sports, the assignment of an area covered by a particular player. — **to be in a position** To have the means or opportunity to. — *v.t.* To place in a particular or appropriate position. [< OF < L < *ponere* to place] — **po·si'tion·al** *adj.*

— Syn. (noun) 1. See PLACE. 9. office, post, situation.

pos·i·tive (poz'ə·tiv) *adj.* 1. That is or may be directly affirmed; actual. 2. Expressing, containing, or characterized by affirmation: a *positive* attitude. 3. Inherent in a thing by and of itself, regardless of its relations to other things. 4. Openly and plainly expressed: a *positive* denial. 5. Imperative. 6. Not admitting of doubt or denial. 7. Noting one of two opposite directions, qualities, properties, etc., which is taken as primary, or as indicating increase or progression. 8. *Math.* Greater than zero; plus: said of quantities and usu. denoted by the sign (+). 9. *Med.* Denoting the presence of a specific condition or organism: a *positive* Wasserman reaction. 10. *Photog.* Having the lights and darks in their original relation, as in a print made from a negative. 11. *Biol.* Noting the response of an organism toward a stimulus: a *positive* tropism. 12. *Electr.* Having the kind of electricity exhibited by a glass object when rubbed with silk; characterized by a deficiency of electrons on a charged body. 13. *Chem.* Basic. 14. *Gram.* Denoting the simple, uncompared degree of the adjective or adverb. 15. *Stat.* Designating a correlation in which the values of two variables tend to increase or decrease together: also *direct.* — *n.* 1. That which is positive or capable of being directly or certainly affirmed. 2. *Math.* A positive symbol or quantity. 3. *Electr.* A positive pole, terminal, etc. 4. *Photog.* A positive picture or print. 5. *Gram.* The positive degree of an adjective or adverb; also, a word in this degree. [< OF, fem. of *positif* < L < *ponere* to place] — **pos'i·tive·ly** *adv.* — **pos'i·tive·ness** *n.*

pos·i·tiv·ism (poz'ə·tiv·iz'əm) *n.* 1. A way of thinking that regards nothing as ascertained or ascertainable beyond the facts of physical science or of sense. 2. *Philos.* A system of philosophy elaborated by Auguste Comte, holding that man can have no knowledge of anything but actual phenomena and facts and their interrelations. 3. Certitude, or the claim of certitude, in knowledge. — **pos'i·tiv·ist** *n.* — **pos'i·tiv·is·tic** *adj.*

pos·i·tron (poz'ə·tron) *n.* *Physics* The positive counterpart of an electron.

pos·se (pos'ē) *n.* 1. A posse comitatus. 2. A force of men; squad. [< Med.L, armed force < L, to be able]

pos·se com·i·ta·tus (pos'ē kom/ə·tā'təs) The body of men that a sheriff or other peace officer calls or may call to his assistance in the discharge of his official duty, as to quell a riot. [< Med.L < *posse* power + *comitatus* county]

pos·sess (pə·zes') *v.t.* 1. To have as property; own. 2. To have as a quality, attribute, etc. 3. To enter and exert control over; dominate: often used passively: The idea *possessed* him. 4. To maintain control over (oneself, one's mind, etc.). **5.** To put in possession, as of property, news, etc.: with *of*. **6.** To have knowledge of; gain mastery of, as a language. **7.** To imbue or impress, as with wonder or an idea: with *with*. **8.** To have sexual intercourse with. [< F < L < *potis* master + *sedere* to sit (as)]

pos·sessed (pə·zest′) *adj.* **1.** Having; owning: *possessed* of a ready tongue. **2.** Calm; cool: to be *possessed* in time of danger. **3.** Controlled by or as if by evil spirits; beyond self-control; frenzied.

pos·ses·sion (pə·zesh′ən) *n.* **1.** The act or fact of possessing. **2.** The state of being possessed. **3.** That which is possessed or owned. **4.** *pl.* Property; wealth. **5.** The state of being possessed by, or as by, evil spirits. **6.** Self-possession.

pos·ses·sive (pə·zes′iv) *adj.* **1.** Of or pertaining to possession or ownership. **2.** Having a strong desire for complete emotional domination of another person. **3.** *Gram.* Designating a case of the noun or pronoun that denotes possession, origin, or the like. In English, this is formed in nouns by adding 's to the singular and to irregular plurals: *John's* book; *men's* souls; and a simple apostrophe to the regular plural and sometimes to singulars and proper names ending in a sibilant: *boys'* shoes; *James'* (or *James's*) brother. Pronouns in the possessive case have special forms, as *my, mine, his, her, hers, its, our, ours, your, yours, their, theirs, whose.* — *n. Gram.* **1.** The possessive case. **2.** A possessive form or construction. — **pos·ses′sive·ness** *n.*

pos·set (pos′it) *n.* A drink of hot milk curdled with wine or ale, sweetened and spiced. [< ME *poshote, possot*]

pos·si·bil·i·ty (pos′ə·bil′ə·tē) *n. pl.* **·ties 1.** The fact or state of being possible. **2.** That which is possible.

pos·si·ble (pos′ə·bəl) *adj.* **1.** Capable of happening or proving true: not contrary to fact, natural laws, or experience. **2.** Capable of being done or of coming about; feasible. **3.** That may or may not happen. [< OF < L < *posse* to be able + *esse* to be] — **pos′si·bly** *adv.*

pos·sum (pos′əm) *n. Informal* An oppossum. — **to play possum** To feign death, illness, etc. [< OPOSSUM.]

post¹ (pōst) *n.* An upright piece of timber or other material; as: **a** A support for a sign. **b** A bearing or framing member in a building. **c** An indicator of the starting or finishing point of a racecourse, etc. — *v.t.* **1.** To put up (a poster, etc.) in some public place. **2.** To fasten posters upon. **3.** To announce by or as by a poster: to *post a reward.* **4.** To publish the name of on a list. [OE < L *postis* door post]

post² (pōst) *n.* **1.** A position or employment, esp. a public office. **2.** *Mil.* **a** A place occupied by a detachment of troops. **b** The buildings and grounds of such a place. **3.** An assigned beat, position, or station, as of a sentry, policeman, etc. **4.** A trading post or settlement. **5.** *U.S.* A local unit of a veterans' organization. — *v.t.* To assign to a particular post; station, as a sentry. [< MF < Ital. < LL *postum,* contr. of L *positum.* pp. neut. of *ponere* to place]

post³ (pōst) *n.* **1.** *Chiefly Brit.* A single delivery of mail to a home, office, etc.; also, the mail itself. **2.** *Chiefly Brit.* An established, usu. government, system, for transporting the mails; also, a local post office. **3.** *Brit.* A mailbox. **4.** A rider or courier who carries mail over a fixed route. **5.** Any of the stations furnishing relays of men and horses on such a route. — *v.t.* **1.** *Chiefly Brit.* To place in a mailbox or post office; mail. **2.** To inform. **3.** In bookkeeping: **a** To transfer (items or accounts) to the ledger. **b** To make the proper entries in (a ledger). — *v.i.* **4.** To travel with post horses. **5.** To travel with speed; hasten. — *adv.* **1.** By post horses. **2.** Speedily; rapidly. [< MF < Ital. *posta,* orig., a station < LL, contr. of L *posita,* pp. fem. of *ponere* to place]

post- *prefix* **1.** After in time or order; following: *postdate, postwar.* **2.** Chiefly in scientific terms, after in position; behind. [< L *post* behind, after]

post·age (pōs′tij) *n.* **1.** The charge levied on mail matter. **2.** The act of going by post.

postage stamp A small, printed label issued and sold by a government to be affixed to letters, parcels, etc., in payment of postage.

pos·tal (pōs′təl) *adj.* Pertaining to the mails or to mail service. — *n.* A postal card.

postal card A card, issued officially, for carrying a written or printed message through the mails.

post-bel·lum (pōst′bel′əm) *adj.* Occurring after a war, esp. after the Civil War. [< L < *post* after + *bellum* war]

post·box (pōst′boks′) *n.* A mailbox (def. 1).

post card 1. A postal card. **2.** An unofficial card of any regulation size, usu. having a picture on one side, transmissible through the mails on prepayment of postage.

post chaise A closed carriage used for traveling and drawn by post horses.

post·date (pōst′dāt′) *v.t.* **·dat·ed, ·dat·ing 1.** To assign or fix a date later than the actual date to (a check, document, etc.). **2.** To follow in time.

post·er (pōs′tər) *n.* **1.** A placard or bill used for advertising, public information, etc., to be posted on a wall or other surface. **2.** A billposter. [< POST¹]

pos·te·ri·or (pos·tir′ē·ər) *adj.* **1.** Situated behind or toward the hinder part. **2.** Coming after another in a series. **3.** Subsequent in time; later. **4.** *Anat.* **a** In animals, pertaining to the tail end of the body. **b** In man, pertaining to the back side of the body. — *n. Sometimes pl.* The buttocks. [< L, comp. of *posterus* coming after < *post* after, behind] — **pos·te′ri·or′i·ty** (-ôr′ə·tē, -or′ə-) *n.* — **pos·te′ri·or·ly** *adv.*

pos·ter·i·ty (pos·ter′ə·tē) *n.* **1.** Future generations taken collectively. **2.** All of one's descendants. [< OF < L < *posterus* coming after]

pos·tern (pōs′tərn, pos′-) *n.* A small back gate or door, esp. in a fortification or castle. — *adj.* Situated at the back or side. [< OF < L < *posterus* back door, gate]

post exchange *Mil.* An establishment for the sale of merchandise and services to military personnel. Abbr. *PX*

post·grad·u·ate (pōst′graj′ōō·it, -āt) *adj.* Of or pertaining to studies pursued after the taking of an advanced degree. — *n.* One who pursues such studies.

post·haste (pōst′hāst′) *Archaic n.* Great haste or speed, like that of the post. — *adv.* With utmost speed.

post horse A horse kept at a post house.

post house A house where post horses were kept for relay; also, formerly, a post office.

post·hu·mous (pos′chōō·məs) *adj.* **1.** Denoting a child born after the father's death. **2.** Published after the author's death, as a book. **3.** Arising or continuing after one's death. [< LL < L *postumus* latest, last] — **post′hu·mous·ly** *adj.*

pos·til·lon (pōs·til′yən, pos-) *n.* One who guides a team drawing a carriage or other heavy vehicle by riding the near horse when one pair is used or the near horse of the leaders when two or more pairs are used. Also **pos·til′lion.** [< MF < Ital. < *posta* post, station]

post·im·pres·sion·ism (pōst′im·presh′ən·iz′əm) *n.* The theories and practice of a group of expressionist painters of the late 19th century, who rejected the objective naturalism of the Impressionists and emphasized the subjective point of view of the artist. — **post′im·pres′sion·ist** *n. & adj.* — **post′im·pres′sion·is′tic** *adj.*

post·lude (pōst′lōōd) *n. Music* **1.** An organ voluntary concluding a church service. **2.** Loosely, a coda.

post·man (pōst′mən) *n. pl.* **·men** (-mən) A mailman.

post·mark (pōst′märk′) *n.* Any official mark stamped on mail to cancel stamps and to give the date and place of sending or receiving. — *v.t.* To stamp with a postmark.

post·mas·ter (pōst′mas′tər, -mäs′-) *n.* **1.** An official having charge of a post office. **2.** One who provides horses for posting. — **post′mis′tress** (-mis′tris) *n.fem.*

postmaster general *pl.* **postmasters general** The executive head of the postal service of a government.

post·me·rid·i·an (pōst′mə·rid′ē·ən) *adj.* Pertaining to or occurring in the afternoon. Also **post′me·rid′i·o·nal.** [< L < *post* after + *meridies* noon]

post me·rid·i·em (pōst mə·rid′ē·əm) After midday. Abbr. *p.m., P.M.* [< L]

post·mortem (pōst·môr′təm) *adj.* **1.** Happening or performed after death. **2.** Of or pertaining to a post-mortem examination. — *n.* **1.** A post-mortem examination. **2.** *Informal* An analysis or discussion of an accomplished fact. [< L *post mortem* after death]

post-mortem examination *Med.* A thorough examination of a human body after death: also called *autopsy.*

post·na·tal (pōst·nāt′l) *adj.* Occurring after birth.

post office 1. The branch of the civil service of a government charged with carrying and delivering the mails. **2.** Any local office that receives, sorts, and delivers mail, sells stamps, etc. **3.** Any town or place having a post office.

post·op·er·a·tive (pōst·op′ər·ə·tiv, -ə·rā′-) *adj. Surg.* Occurring or done after a surgical operation: *postoperative* care.

post·paid (pōst′pād′) *adj.* Having postage prepaid.

post·par·tum (pōst′pär′təm) *adj. Med.* After childbirth. [< POST- + L *partus* childbirth < *parere* to bear]

post·pone (pōst·pōn′) *v.t.* **·poned, ·pon·ing 1.** To put off to a future time; defer; delay. **2.** To subordinate. [< L < *post-* after + *ponere* to put] — **post·pon′a·ble** *adj.* — **post·pone′ment** *n.* — **post·pon′er** *n.*
— **Syn. 1.** Delay, defer, procrastinate, adjourn, stay.

post·pran·di·al (pōst·pran′dē·əl) *adj.* After-dinner. [< POST- + L *prandium* lunch + -AL¹]

post road A road built for the transportation of mail, formerly having post houses at specified distances.

post·script (pōst′skript′) *n.* **1.** A sentence or paragraph added to a letter after the writer's signature. **2.** A supplemental addition to a written or printed document. Abbr. *p.s., P.S.* [< L *postscriptum,* pp. of *postscribere* to write after]

pos·tu·lant (pos′chə·lənt) *n.* **1.** One who presents a request. **2.** *Eccl.* An applicant for admission into a religious order. [< L < *postulare*, freq. of *poscere* to ask] — **pos′·tu·lant·ship** *n.*

pos·tu·late (*v.* pos′chə·lāt; *n.* pos′chə·lit) *v.t.* **·lat·ed, ·lat·ing** **1.** To claim, demand, or require. **2.** To set forth as self-evident. **3.** To assume the truth or reality of. — *n.* **1.** A self-evident truth. **2.** A prerequisite. **3.** A fundamental principle. — **pos′tu·la′tion** *n.* — **pos′tu·la′tor** *n.*

pos·ture (pos′chər) *n.* **1.** The position or carriage of the body or parts of the body. **2.** Such a position assumed during posing for an artist, etc. **3.** The visible disposition of the various parts of a material thing. **4.** A mental attitude; frame of mind. **5.** A situation or condition, esp. if a consequence of policy: national defense posture. — *v.t.* **1.** To place (a person) in a specific position or pose. — *v.i.* **2.** To assume or adopt a bodily pose or a character not natural to one. [< F < L *positura* position] — **pos′tur·al** *adj.* — **pos′tur·er, pos′tur·ist** *n.*

pos·tur·ize (pos′chə·rīz) *v.t. & v.i.* **·ized, ·iz·ing** To posture; pose.

post·war (pōst′wôr′) *adj.* After a war.

po·sy (pō′zē) *n. pl.* **·sies** A single flower or a bouquet. [Contr. of POESY]

pot (pot) *n.* **1.** A round, fairly deep vessel of metal, earthenware, or glass, generally having a handle, used for cooking and other domestic purposes. **2.** Such a vessel and its contents. **3.** The amount a pot will hold. **4.** A large drinking cup, as a tankard; also, drink or liquor. **5.** In cardplaying, the amount of stakes wagered or played for, esp. in poker. **6.** *Informal* A large sum of money. **7.** In fishing, a basketlike trap for catching lobsters, eels, etc. — **to go to pot** To deteriorate. — *v.* **pot·ted, pot·ting** *v.t.* **1.** To put into a pot or pots: to *pot* plants. **2.** To preserve (meat, etc.) in pots or jars. **3.** To cook in a pot. **4.** To shoot (game) for food rather than for sport. **5.** To shoot or kill with a pot shot. **6.** *Informal* To secure, capture, or win; bag. — *v.i.* **7.** To take a pot shot; shoot. [OE *pott*]

po·ta·ble (pō′tə·bəl) *adj.* Suitable for drinking: said of water. — *n. Often pl.* Something drinkable; a drink. [< MF < LL < *potare* to drink]

po·tage (pō·täzh′) *n.* French Any thick soup.

pot·ash (pot′ash′) *n.* **1.** Potassium hydroxide. **2.** Crude potassium carbonate. **3.** The oxide of potassium, K_2O. [< Du. *potasch*]

po·tas·si·um (pə·tas′ē·əm) *n.* A bluish white, highly reactive, metallic element (symbol K), never found free in nature, but yielding many compounds of great practical value in industry, medicine, etc.: also called *kalium*. See ELEMENT. [< NL < *potass* potash] — **po·tas′sic** *adj.*

potassium bitartrate *Chem.* A white crystalline compound, $HKC_4H_4O_6$, having an acid taste; an ingredient of baking powder: also called *cream of tartar.*

potassium bromide *Chem.* A crystalline compound, KBr, used in photography, and in medicine as a sedative.

potassium carbonate *Chem.* A white, strongly alkaline compound, K_2CO_3, used in making soap and glass.

potassium cyanide *Chem.* An intensely poisonous compound, KCN, used in photography, and as a reagent.

potassium hydroxide *Chem.* A whitish deliquescent solid, KOH, yielding a strong caustic solution: used in salt-making, electroplating, as a chemical reagent, etc. Also called *caustic potash, potash.*

potassium nitrate *Chem.* A crystalline white salt, KNO_3, used in gunpowder, fertilizers, and in medicine. Also called *niter, saltpeter.*

potassium permanganate *Chem.* A purple red crystalline salt, $KMnO_4$, used as an oxidizing agent in antiseptics and deodorizing substances.

potassium sulfate *Chem.* A salt, K_2SO_4, used in the manufacture of glass and alum, and in the crude state as a component of fertilizer.

po·ta·tion (pō·tā′shən) *n.* **1.** The act of drinking; also, a drink, esp. of an alcoholic beverage. **2.** A drinking bout. [< OF < L < *potare* to drink]

po·ta·to (pə·tā′tō) *n. pl.* **·toes** **1.** One of the edible tubers of a plant of the nightshade family: also called *Irish potato, white potato.* **2.** The plant. **3.** The sweet potato. [< Sp. *patata* < Arawakan (Taino) *batata*]

potato beetle A beetle having long black stripes on the wing covers, that feeds on the leaves of the potato, tomato, and similar plants. Also **potato bug.**

potato chip *U.S.* A very thin slice of potato fried crisp and salted.

pot·bel·ly (pot′bel′ē) *n. pl.* **·lies** **1.** A protuberant belly. **2.** An upright wood- or coal-burning stove with bulging sides: also **potbellied stove.** — **pot′bel′lied** *adj.*

pot·boil·er (pot′boi′lər) *n. Informal* A literary or artistic work produced simply to obtain the means of subsistence.

po·tent (pōt′nt) *adj.* **1.** Physically powerful. **2.** Having great authority. **3.** Exerting great influence on mind or morals; very convincing: a *potent* argument. **4.** Of a drug, liquor, etc., strong in its physical and chemical effects. **5.** Sexually competent: said of the male. [< L < *potis* able + *esse* to be] — **po′ten·cy, po′tence** *n.* — **po′tent·ly** *adv.* — **po′tent·ness** *n.*

po·ten·tate (pōt′n·tāt) *n.* One having great power or sway; a sovereign. [< LL *potentatus*]

po·ten·tial (pə·ten′chəl) *adj.* **1.** Possible but not actual. **2.** Having capacity for existence, but not yet existing; latent. **3.** *Gram.* Indicating possibility, power, or liberty, as a verb phrase including *may, can, must,* etc. — *n.* **1.** A possible development; potentiality. **2.** *Electr.* The charge on a body as referred to another body or to a given standard, as the earth, considered as having zero potential. [< LL *potentialis*] — **po·ten′tial·ly** *adv.*

po·ten·ti·al·i·ty (pə·ten·chē·al′ə·tē) *n. pl.* **·ties** **1.** Inherent capacity for development or accomplishment. **2.** That which is potential ro capable of being realized.

poth·er (poth′ər) *n.* Excitement mingled with confusion; bustle; fuss. — *v.t. & v.i.* To worry; bother.

pot·herb (pot′ûrb′, -hûrb′) *n.* Any plant or herb, esp. greens, when cooked or used to flavor boiled foods.

pot·hole (pot′hōl′) *n.* A deep hole, as in a road.

pot·hook (pot′hook′) *n.* **1.** A curved or hooked piece of iron for lifting or hanging pots. **2.** A curved mark or elementary stroke used in teaching penmanship.

pot·house (pot′hous′) *Brit. n.* An alehouse; saloon.

po·tion (pō′shən) *n.* A draft, as a large dose of liquid medicine: often used of a magic or poisonous draft. [< OF < L < *potare* to drink]

pot·luck (pot′luk′) *n.* Whatever food may have been prepared for the family: usu. in the phrase **to take potluck.**

pot·pie (pot′pī′) *n.* **1.** A meat pie baked in a deep dish. **2.** Meat stewed with dumplings.

pot·pour·ri (pot·poor′ē, *Fr.* pô·pōō·rē′) *n.* **1.** A mixture of dried flower petals kept in a jar and used to perfume a room. **2.** A musical medley or literary miscellany. **3.** Any incongruous mixture. [< F, lit., rotten pot]

pot roast Meat braised and cooked in a covered pot.

pot·sherd (pot′shûrd) *n.* A bit of broken earthenware.

pot shot **1.** A shot fired to kill, without regard to the rules of sports. **2.** A shot fired, as from ambush, at a person or animal within easy range. **3.** A random shot.

pot·stone (pot′stōn′) *n.* A variety of steatite or soapstone.

pot·tage (pot′ij) *n.* A thick broth or stew of vegetables with or without meat. [< OF *pot pot*]

pot·ted (pot′id) *adj.* **1.** Placed or kept in a pot. **2.** Cooked or preserved in a pot. **3.** *Slang* Drunk.

pot·ter¹ (pot′ər) *v.t. & v.i. Chiefly Brit.* To putter. [Freq. of dial, *pote*] — **pot′ter·er** *n.*

pot·ter² (pot′ər) *n.* One who makes earthenware or porcelain vessels.

potter's field A piece of ground appropriated as a burial ground for the destitute and the unknown. *Matt.* xxvii 7.

potter's wheel A horizontal rotating disk used by potters for holding and manipulating prepared clay.

pot·ter·y (pot′ər·ē) *n. pl.* **·ter·ies** **1.** Ware molded from clay and hardened by intense heat. **2.** The art of making earthenware or porcelain. **3.** A place where pottery is made. [< OF < Med.L *pot pot*]

POTTER'S WHEEL
a Molding clay. *b* Rotating wheel. *c* Shaft. *d* Treadle.

pot·tle (pot′l) *n.* **1.** A drinking vessel, pot, or tankard holding about half a gallon. **2.** An old liquid measure of half a gallon. **3.** Liquor. [< OF *pot* pot)

pot·ty¹ (pot′ē) *adj. Brit. Informal* **1.** Insignificant. **2.** Slightly drunk; also, a little silly.

pot·ty² (pot′ē) *n. pl.* **·ties** A receptacle that fits under a child's toilet seat; also, the toilet seat.

pouch (pouch) *n.* **1.** A small bag, sack, or other container, used for carrying money, pipe tobacco, ammunition, etc. **2.** *Zool.* **a** A saclike part for temporarily containing food, as in gophers and pelicans. **b** A marsupium. **3.** *Bot.* Any baglike cavity, as the pod of the mustard plant. **4.** A mailbag. — *v.t.* **1.** To put in a pouch. **2.** To fashion in pouchlike form. — *v.i.* **3.** To form a pouchlike cavity. [< OF *poche*] — **pouch′y** *adj.*

poul·tice (pōl′tis) *n.* A moist, mealy mass of flour, mustard, etc., applied hot to a sore part of the body. — *v.t.* **·ticed, ·tic·ing** To cover with a poultice. [< L *puls* porridge]

poul·try (pōl′trē) *n.* Domestic fowls, generally or collectively, as hens, ducks, etc. [< OF *poule* hen]

pounce¹ (pouns) *v.i.* **pounced, pounc·ing** To swoop or spring in or as in seizing prey: with *on, upon,* or *at.* — *n.* **1.** A talon or claw of a bird of prey. **2.** The act of pouncing.

pounce² (pouns) *n.* **1.** A powder, as of cuttlebone, formerly used to absorb excess of ink, as on a manuscript.

2. A finely pulverized substance used in transferring designs. — *v.t.* To sprinkle, smooth, or rub with pounce. [< F < L *pumex* pumice]

pound¹ (pound) *n.* **1.** A unit of weight varying in different countries and at different periods. **2.** In Great Britain and the U.S., either of two legally fixed units, the avoirdupois pound and the troy pound. See table inside back cover. **3.** The standard monetary unit of the United Kingdom, equivalent to 20 shillings: in 1960 worth about $2.81: also **pound sterling.** Symbol £. **4.** A similar monetary unit of Ireland and several members of the Commonwealth of Nations. **5.** A standard monetary unit of various other countries; esp. Egypt, Israel, and Turkey. [OE < L *pondus* weight]

pound² (pound) *n.* **1.** A place, enclosed by authority, in which stray animals or distrained possessions are left until claimed or redeemed. **2.** A place of confinement for law-breakers. **3.** A trap for wild animals. **4.** An area or place in which to catch or stow fish. — *v.t.* To confine in a pound; impound. [OE *pund-*]

pound³ (pound) *v.t.* **1.** To strike heavily and repeatedly; beat. **2.** To reduce to a pulp or powder by beating. — *v.i.* **3.** To strike heavy, repeated blows: with *on, at,* etc. **4.** To move or proceed heavily. **5.** To throb heavily or resoundingly. — *n.* **1.** A heavy blow. **2.** The act of pounding. [OE *pūnian* to bruise] — **pound′er** *n.*

pound·age (poun′dij) *n.* A rate on the pound sterling.

pound·al (poun′dəl) *n. Physics* A unit of force that, acting on a mass of one pound, imparts to it a velocity of one foot per second.

pound·cake (pound′kāk′) *n.* A rich cake having ingredients equal in weight, as a pound each of flour, butter, and sugar, with eggs added.

pound·er (poun′dər) *n.* **1.** Anything weighing a pound. **2.** One who or that which weighs, has, etc., a given number of pounds: used in combination: an eight-*pounder.*

pound-fool·ish (pound′fōō′lish) *adj.* Extravagant with large sums, but watching small sums closely.

pour (pôr, pōr) *v.t.* **1.** To cause to flow in a continuous stream, as water, sand, etc. **2.** To send forth, emit, or utter profusely or continuously — *v.i.* **3.** To flow in a continuous stream; gush. **4.** To rain heavily. **5.** To move in great numbers; swarm. — *n.* A pouring, flow, or downfall. [ME *pouren*] — **pour′er** *n.* — **pour′ing·ly** *adv.*

pour·boire (pōōr·bwär′) *n. French* A gratuitous gift of money, as a tip. [< F, lit., in order to drink]

pout¹ (pout) *v.i.* **1.** To thrust out the lips, esp. in ill humor. **2.** To be sullen; sulk. **3.** To swell out; protrude. — *v.t.* **4.** To thrust out (the lips, etc.). **5.** To utter with a pout. — *n.* **1.** A pushing out of the lips as in pouting. **2.** A fit of ill humor. [ME *pouten*]

pout² (pout) *n.* Any of various fresh-water catfishes. [OE (*æle*) *pūte* eelpout]

pout·er (pou′tər) *n.* **1.** One who pouts. **2.** A breed of pigeon having the habit of puffing out the crop.

pov·er·ty (pov′ər·tē) *n.* **1.** The condition or quality of being poor. **2.** Scantiness of supply: a *poverty* of imagination. **3.** Absence or scarcity of necessary qualities, elements, etc.: *poverty* of soil. [< OF < L < *pauper* poor] — **Syn. 1.** Privation, indigence, penury.

pov·er·ty-strick·en (pov′ər·tē·strik′ən) *adj.* Suffering from poverty; destitute.

pow·der (pou′dər) *n.* **1.** A finely ground or pulverized mass of loose particles formed from a solid substance in the dry state. **2.** Any of various substances prepared in this form, as a cosmetic, medicine, or explosive. — *v.t.* **1.** To reduce to powder; pulverize. **2.** To sprinkle or cover with or as with powder. — *v.i.* **3.** To be reduced to powder. **4.** To use powder as a cosmetic. [< OF < L *pulvis* dust] — **pow′der·er** *n.*

powder blue A soft medium blue.

powder horn The hollow horn of an ox or cow, formerly fitted with a cover and used for holding gunpowder.

powder puff A soft pad used to apply powder to the skin.

pow·der·y (pou′dər·ē) *adj.* **1.** Consisting of or like fine powder or dust. **2.** Covered with or as with powder; mealy; dusty. **3.** Capable of being easily powdered; friable.

pow·er (pou′ər) *n.* **1.** Ability to act; capability. **2.** Potential capacity. **3.** Strength or force actually put forth. **4.** The right, ability, or capacity to exercise control; legal authority. **5.** Any agent that exercises power, as in control or dominion; an important and influential sovereign nation. **6.** Great or telling force or effect. **7.** Often *pl.* A mental or physical faculty. **8.** Any form of energy available for doing work; esp., electrical energy. **9.** *Physics* The time rate at which energy is transferred, or converted into work. **10.** *Math.* **a** The product of a number multiplied by itself a given number of times: The third *power* of 2 is 8.

b An exponent. **11.** *Optics* Magnifying capacity, as of a lens. — *v.t.* To provide with means of propulsion. [< OF < LL < L *posse* to be able]

power boat A motorboat.

pow·er·ful (pou′ər·fəl) *adj.* **1.** Possessing great force or energy; strong. **2.** Exercising great authority, or manifesting high qualities. **3.** Having great effect on the mind. — *adv. Dial. & Informal* Very. — **pow′er·ful·ly** *adv.*

pow·er·house (pou′ər·hous′) *n. Electr.* A station where electricity is generated.

pow·er·less (pou′ər·lis) *adj.* **1.** Destitute of power; unable to accomplish an effect; impotent. **2.** Without authority. — **pow′er·less·ly** *adv.* — **pow′er·less·ness** *n.*

power of attorney *Law* **1.** The authority or power to act conferred upon an agent. **2.** The instrument or document by which that power or authority is conferred.

power politics The use or threatened use of superior force to exact international concessions.

pow·wow (pou′wou′) *U.S. n.* **1.** *Informal* Any meeting or conference. **2.** A North American Indian ceremony to cure the sick or effect success in war, etc. **3.** A conference with or of American Indians. — *v.i.* To hold a powwow. [< Algonquian (Massachusetts) *pauwaw,* lit., he dreams]

pox (poks) *n.* **1.** Any disease characterized by purulent eruptions: *chickenpox.* **2.** Syphilis. [Var. of *pocks,* pl. of POCK]

prac·ti·ca·ble (prak′ti·kə·bəl) *adj.* **1.** That can be put into practice; feasible. **2.** That can be used; usable. [< F < Med.L < LL < Gk. *prassein* to do] — **prac′ti·ca·bil′i·ty, prac′ti·ca·ble·ness** *n.* — **prac′ti·ca·bly** *adv.*

prac·ti·cal (prak′ti·kəl) *adj.* **1.** Pertaining to or governed by actual use and experience or action, as contrasted with speculation. **2.** Trained by or derived from practice or experience. **3.** Applicable to use. **4.** Manifested in practice. **5.** Being such to all intents and purposes; virtual. — **Syn.** See PRACTICABLE. [< MF < LL < Gk. *prassein* to do] — **prac′ti·cal′i·ty** (-kal′ə·tē), **prac′ti·cal·ness** *n.*

practical joke A trick having a victim or victims.

prac·ti·cal·ly (prak′tik·lē) *adv.* **1.** In a practical manner. **2.** To all intents and purposes; in fact or effect; virtually.

practical nurse One who has some training and practice in nursing but who is not a registered nurse.

prac·tice (prak′tis) *v.* **·ticed, ·tic·ing** *v.t.* **1.** To make use of habitually or often: to *practice* economy. **2.** To apply in action; make a practice of. **3.** To work at a profession. **4.** To do or perform repeatedly in order to acquire skill or training; rehearse. **5.** To instruct, as pupils, by repeated exercise or lessons. — *v.i.* **6.** To repeat or rehearse something in order to acquire skill or proficiency. **7.** To work at a profession. — *n.* **1.** Any customary action or proceeding; habit. **2.** An established custom or usage. **3.** The act of doing or performing: distinguished from *theory.* **4.** The regular prosecution of a profession. **5.** Frequent and repeated exercise in any matter. **6.** *pl.* Stratagems or schemes for bad purposes; tricks. **7.** The rules by which legal proceedings are governed. Also **prac′tise.** [< MF < Med.L < LL < Gk. *praktikos* < *prassein* to do] — **prac′tic·er** *n.* — **Syn.** (noun) **5.** *Practice* is the putting into action of what one has learned in theory, to gain skill and facility. *Exercise* is primarily physical action to acquire and maintain strength. *Drill* is systematic and rigorous *practice* under an instructor.

prac·ticed (prak′tist) *adj.* **1.** Expert by practice; experienced. **2.** Acquired by practice. Also **prac′tised.**

prac·ti·tion·er (prak·tish′ən·ər) *n.* One who practices an art or profession.

prae- See PRE-.

prae·fect (prē′fekt) See PREFECT.

prae·no·men (prē·nō′mən) *n. pl.* **·nom·i·na** (-nom′ə·nə) The first name of an ancient Roman; also, any given name: also spelled *prenomen.* [< L]

praeter- See PRETER-.

prae·tor (prē′tər) *n.* A city magistrate of ancient Rome; also spelled *pretor.* [< L < *praeire* to go before] — **prae·to·ri·al** (pri·tôr′ē·əl, -tō′rē-) *adj.* — **prae′tor·ship** *n.*

prae·to·ri·an (pri·tôr′ē·ən, -tō′rē-) *adj.* Of a praetor; praetorial. — *n.* A praetor or ex-praetor. Also spelled *pretorian.*

Prae·to·ri·an (pri·tôr′ē·ən, -tō′rē-) *adj.* Denoting the Praetorian Guard. — *n.* A soldier of the Praetorian Guard. Also spelled *Pretorian.*

Praetorian Guard **1.** The bodyguard of the Roman emperors. **2.** A member of this bodyguard.

prag·mat·ic (prag·mat′ik) *adj.* **1.** Pertaining to the study of events with emphasis on cause and effect. **2.** *Philos.* Pertaining to pragmatism. **3.** Pragmatical. [< L < Gk. < *pragma, pragmatos* thing done < *prassein* to do]

prag·mat·i·cal (prag·mat′i·kəl) *adj.* Relating to everyday business; practical; commonplace.

prag·mat·i·cal·ly (prag·mat/i·kəl·ē) *adv.* In a pragmatic or pragmatical manner. —**prag·mat/i·cal·ness** *n.*

prag·ma·tism (prag/mə·tiz/əm) *n.* **1.** *Philos.* The doctrine that ideas have value only in terms of their practical consequences, and that results are the sole test of the validity or truth of one's beliefs. **2.** The quality or condition of being pragmatic. —**prag/ma·tist** *n.*

prai·rie (prâr/ē) *n.* *U.S. & Canadian* A tract of grassland; esp., the broad, grassy plain of central North America. [< F < L *pratum* meadow]

prairie chicken Either of two gallinaceous game birds inhabiting the plains of western North America. Also **prairie hen.**

prairie dog A burrowing rodent of the plains of North America. Also **prairie squirrel.**

prairie schooner *U.S.* A covered wagon used for travel by pioneers.

Prairie State Nickname of ILLINOIS.

prairie wolf A coyote.

praise (prāz) *n.* **1.** An expression of approval or commendation. **2.** The glorifying and honoring of a god, ruler, hero, etc. —*v.t.* **praised, prais·ing 1.** To express approval and commendation of; applaud. **2.** To express adoration of; glorify, esp. in song. [< OF < LL *pretiare* to prize] —**prais/er** *n.*

—**Syn.** (verb) **1.** *Praise* is a weak word, and may refer to the mere speaking of compliments. To *laud* is to *praise* highly. *Extol* stresses the intention to elevate or magnify a person or thing by praise. *Applaud* and *acclaim* point to a public show of approval, as by clapping the hands or shouting. —**Ant.** blame, decry.

praise·wor·thy (prāz/wûr/thē) *adj.* Worthy of praise. —**praise/wor/thi·ly** *adv.,* —**praise/wor·thi·ness** *n.*

Pra·krit (prä/krit) *n.* Any of several vernacular languages of ancient India. [< Skt. *prakrtā* natural]

pra·line (prä/lēn, prā/-) *n.* A confection made of pecans or other nuts browned in boiling sugar. [< F, after Marshal Duplessis-*Praslin*, 1598–1675, whose cook invented it]

pram (pram) *n. Chiefly Brit. Informal* A baby carriage. [Short for PERAMBULATOR]

prance (prans, präns) *v.* **pranced, pranc·ing** *v.i.* **1.** To move proudly with high steps, as a spirited horse; spring from the hind legs; also, to ride a horse moving thus. **2.** To move in an arrogant or elated manner; swagger. **3.** To gambol; caper. —*v.t.* **4.** To cause to prance. —*n.* The act of prancing; a high step; caper. [ME *prauncen*] —**pranc/er** *n.*

pran·di·al (pran/dē·əl) *adj.* Of or pertaining to a meal, esp. dinner. [< L *prandium* breakfast or lunch]

prank[1] (prangk) *v.t.* **1.** To decorate gaudily. —*v.i.* **2.** To make an ostentatious show. [Prob. < MLG *prank* pomp]

prank[2] (prangk) *n.* A mischievous or frolicsome act; a trick. —*v.i.* To play pranks or tricks. [Origin uncertain; ? < PRANK[1]] —**prank/ish** *adj.*

pra·se·o·dym·i·um (prā/zē·ō·dim/ē·əm, prā/sē-) *n.* A yellowish white metallic element (symbol Pr) of the lanthanide series, having olive-green salts. See ELEMENT. [< NL < Gk. *prasios* light green + (DI)DYMIUM]

prate (prāt) *v.* **prat·ed, prat·ing** *v.i.* **1.** To talk idly and at length; chatter. —*v.t.* **2.** To utter idly or emptily. —*n.* Idle talk; prattle. [< MDu.-MLG *praten*] —**prat/er** *n.* —**prat/ing·ly** *adv.*

prat·fall (prat/fôl/) *n.* *U.S. Slang* A fall on the buttocks.

prat·tle (prat/l) *v.* **·tled, ·tling** *v.i.* **1.** To talk foolishly or like a child. —*v.t.* **2.** To utter in a foolish or childish way. —*n.* **1.** Childish speech. **2.** Idle or foolish talk. [See PRATE.] —**prat/tler** *n.*

prawn (prôn) *n.* Any of various shrimplike crustaceans of tropical and temperate waters, used as food. —*v.i.* To fish for prawns. [ME *prane, prayne*]

pray (prā) *v.i.* **1.** To address prayers to a deity, idol, etc. **2.** To make earnest request or entreaty; beg. —*v.t.* **3.** To say prayers to. **4.** To ask (someone) earnestly; entreat. **5.** To ask for by prayers or entreaty. [< OF < LL < L *prex, precis* request, prayer] —**pray/er** *n.*

prayer (prâr) *n.* **1.** A devout request or petition to a deity. **2.** The act of praying, esp. to God. **3.** A set form of words used for a devout request, petition, etc. **4.** Spiritual and wordless communion with God. **5.** *Often pl.* A religious service. **6.** Something prayed for. **7.** Any earnest request.

prayer book 1. A book of prayers for divine service. **2.** *Usu. cap.* The Book of Common Prayer.

prayer·ful (prâr/fəl) *adj.* Inclined or given to prayer; devotional. —**prayer/ful·ly** *adv.* —**prayer/ful·ness** *n.*

prayer wheel A wheel, cylinder, or vertical drum containing written prayers, used by the Buddhists of Tibet.

praying mantis The mantis (which see).

pre- *prefix* **1.** Before in time or order; prior to; preceding; as in: *prearrange, pre-Roman.* **2.** Before in position; anterior: chiefly in scientific terms; as in: *preabdomen, preanal.* **3.** Preliminary to; preparing for; as in: *precollege.* Also *prae-.* [< L *prae* before]

preach (prēch) *v.t.* **1.** To advocate or recommend urgently. **2.** To proclaim or expound upon: to *preach* the gospel. **3.** To deliver (a sermon, etc.). —*v.i.* **4.** To deliver a sermon. **5.** To give advice, esp. in an officious or moralizing manner. [< OF < L *praedicare* to proclaim]

preach·er (prē/chər) *n.* **1.** *Informal* A clergyman, esp. a Protestant minister. **2.** One who preaches.

preach·i·fy (prē/chə·fī) *v.i.* **·fied, ·fy·ing** *Informal* To preach or discourse tediously. —**preach/i·fi·ca/tion** *n.*

preach·ment (prēch/mənt) *n.* A sermon or moral lecture, esp. a tedious one.

preach·y (prē/chē) *adj.* **preach·i·er, preach·i·est** Given to preaching; santimonious.

pre·am·ble (prē/am·bəl) *n.* **1.** An introductory statement or preface, esp. to a formal document. **2.** An introductory act, event, fact, etc. [< OF < Med.L < L *prae-* before + *ambulare* to walk] —**pre·am/bu·lar/y** (-byə·ler/ē) *adj.*

pre·am·pli·fi·er (prē·am/plə·fī/ər) *n.* In a sound reproduction system, an auxiliary amplifier used to reinforce very weak signals before sending them into the main amplifier. Also **pre·amp** (prē/amp).

preb·end (preb/ənd) *n.* **1.** A stipend allotted from the revenues of a cathedral or conventual church to a clergyman. **2.** The land or tithe yielding the stipend. **3.** A prebendary. [< MF < Med.L < L *praebere* to supply] —**preb/en·dal** *adj.*

preb·en·dar·y (preb/ən·der/ē) *n.* *pl.* **·dar·ies** A canon or clergyman who holds a prebend. Also called *prebend.*

Pre-Cam·bri·an (prē·kam/brē·ən) *adj. Geol.* Of or pertaining to all geological time and rock formations preceding the Cambrian. See table for GEOLOGY. —*n.* Pre-Cambrian era or rocks.

pre·can·cel (prē·kan/səl) *v.t.* **·celed** or **·celled, ·cel·ing** or **·cel·ling** To cancel (stamps) before use on mail. —*n.* A precanceled stamp.

pre·car·i·ous (pri·kâr/ē·əs) *adj.* **1.** Subject to continued risk; uncertain. **2.** Subject or exposed to danger; hazardous. —**Syn.** See RISKY. **3.** Without foundation or basis. [< L *precarius* obtained by prayer]

pre·cau·tion (pri·kô/shən) *n.* **1.** A step or preparation taken to avoid a possible danger, evil, etc. **2.** Caution observed in preparation for a possible emergency. [< F < LL < L < *prae-* before + *cavere* to take care] —**pre·cau/tion·ar/y** *adj.*

pre·cau·tious (pri·kô/shəs) *adj.* Exercising precaution. —**pre·cau/tious·ly** *adv.* —**pre·cau/tious·ness** *n.*

pre·cede (pri·sēd/) *v.* **·ced·ed, ·ced·ing** *v.t.* **1.** To go or be before in order, place, rank, time, etc. **2.** To preface; introduce. —*v.i.* **3.** To go or be before; take precedence. [< F < L < *prae-* before + *cedere* to go]

pre·ce·dence (pri·sēd/əns, pres/ə·dəns) *n* **1.** The act, right, or state of preceding in place, time, or rank. **2.** The ceremonial order observed by persons of different ranks on formal occasions. Also **pre·ce·den·cy** (pri·sēd/ən·sē, pres/ə·dən·sē).

prec·e·dent (*n.* pres/ə·dənt; *adj.* pri·sēd/nt) *n.* An act or instance capable of being used as a guide or standard in evaluating future actions. —*adj.* Former; preceding. —**prec/e·den/tial** *adj.*

pre·ced·ing (pri·sē/ding) *adj.* Going before, as in time, place, or rank; earlier; foregoing. —**the preceding** That which precedes or has been mentioned before.

pre·cen·tor (pri·sen/tər) *n.* One who leads the singing of a church choir or congregation. [< LL < L < *prae-* before + *canere* to sing] —**pre·cen·to·ri·al** (prē/sen·tôr/ē·əl, -tō/rē-) *adj* —**pre·cen/tor·ship** *n.*

pre·cept (prē/sept) *n.* **1.** A rule prescribing a particular kind of conduct or action. **2.** A proverbial standard or guide to morals; a maxim. [< L *praecipere* to prescribe]

pre·cep·tive (pri·sep/tiv) *adj.* **1.** Consisting of or expressing a precept or precepts. **2.** Pertaining to or of the nature of a precept.

pre·cep·tor (pri·sep/tər) *n.* A teacher; instructor. [< L *praeceptor*] —**pre·cep·to·ri·al** (prē/sep·tôr/ē·əl, -tō/rē-) *adj.* —**pre·cep/tress** (-tris) *n.fem.*

pre·ces·sion (pri·sesh/ən) *n.* The act of preceding. —**pre·ces/sion·al** *adj.*

pre·cinct (prē/singkt) *n.* **1.** *U.S.* An election district of a town, township, county, etc. **2.** *U.S.* **a** A subdivision of a city or town under the jurisdiction of a police unit. **b** The police station for such an area. **3.** A place marked off by fixed limits; also, the boundary of such a place. **4.** *pl.* Neighborhood; environs. **5.** A limited area of thought, action, etc. [< Med.L < L *praecingere* < *prae-* before + *cingere* to encircle]

pre·ci·os·i·ty (presh/ē·os/ə·tē) *n. pl.* **·ties** Extreme fastidiousness or affected refinement, as in speech, style, etc.

pre·cious (presh/əs) *adj.* **1.** Highly priced or prized; valuable. **2.** Greatly esteemed: truth is *precious.* **3.** Beloved; cherished. **4.** Affectedly delicate or sensitive, as a style of writing. **5.** *Informal* Flagrant; surpassing: a *pre-*

cious scoundrel. — *n.* Precious one; sweetheart. — *adv.* Extremely; very. [< OF < L < *pretium* price] — **pre′·cious·ly** *adv.* — **pre′·cious·ness** *n.*

precious stone A valuable, rare gem, as the diamond, ruby, sapphire, or emerald.

prec·i·pice (pres′i·pis) *n.* 1. A high vertical or overhanging face of rock; the brink of a cliff. 2. A perilous situation. [< F < L < *prae-* before + *caput* head]

pre·cip·i·ta·ble (pri·sip′ə·tə·bəl) *adj. Chem.* Capable of being precipitated: a *precipitable* salt.

pre·cip·i·tant (pri·sip′ə·tənt) *adj.* 1. Rushing or falling quickly or heedlessly. 2. Rash; overhasty; impulsive. 3· Very sudden; abrupt. — *n. Chem.* Any substance that, when added to a solution, results in the formation of a precipitate. — **pre·cip′i·tance, pre·cip′i·tan·cy** *n.* — **pre·cip′i·tant·ly** *adv.*

pre·cip·i·tate (pri·sip′ə·tāt; *for adj. & n.,* also pri·sip′ə·tit) *v.* ·tat·ed, ·tat·ing *v.t.* 1. To hasten the occurrence of. 2. To hurl from or as from a height; throw headlong. 3. *Meteorol.* To cause (vapor, etc.) to condense and fall as dew, rain, etc. 4. *Chem.* To separate (a substance) in solid form, as from a solution. — *v.i.* 5. *Meteorol.* To fall as condensed vapor, etc. 6. *Chem.* To separate and settle, as a substance held in solution. 7. To fall headlong. — *adj.* 1. Moving speedily or hurriedly; rushing headlong. 2. Lacking due deliberation; hasty; rash. 3. Sudden and brief, as a disease. — *n. Chem.* A deposit of solid matter formed by precipitation. [< L < *praeceps.* See PRECIPICE.] — **pre·cip′i·tate·ly** *adv.* — **pre·cip′i·tate·ness** *n.* — **pre·cip′i·ta′tive** *adj.* — **pre·cip′i·ta′tor** *n.*

pre·cip·i·ta·tion (pri·sip′ə·tā′shən) *n.* 1. *Meteorol.* **a** The depositing of moisture from the atmosphere upon the surface of the earth. **b** The amount of rain, snow, etc., deposited. 2. *Chem.* The process of separating any of the constituents of a solution. 3. The act of precipitating, or the state of being precipitated. 4. Rash haste or hurry.

pre·cip·i·tous (pri·sip′ə·təs) *adj.* 1. Consisting of or like a precipice; very steep. 2. Having many precipices. 3. Hasty. — **pre·cip′i·tous·ly** *adv.* — **pre·cip′i·tous·ness** *n.*

pré·cis (prā′sē, prā·sē′) *n. pl.* **pré·cis** (prā′sēz, prā·sēz′) A concise summary of a book, article, or document; abstract. — **Syn.** See ABRIDGMENT. [< F]

pre·cise (pri·sīs′) *adj.* 1. Sharply and clearly determined or defined. 2. No more and no less than; exact in amount. 3. Noting or confined to a certain thing; particular. 4. Exact or distinct in sound, statement, etc. 5. Scrupulously observant of rule. [< F < L < *prae-* before + *caedere* to cut] — **pre·cise′ly** *adv.* — **pre·cise′ness** *n.*

pre·ci·sion (pri·sizh′ən) *n.* The state or quality of being precise; accuracy; definition. — *adj.* 1. Designed for extremely accurate measurement: *precision* instruments. 2. Characterized by precision. — **pre·ci′sion·ist** *n.*

pre·clude (pri·klo͞od′) *v.t.* ·clud·ed, ·clud·ing 1. To make impossible or ineffectual by prior action. 2. To shut out; exclude. — **Syn.** See PREVENT. [< L < *prae-* before + *claudere* to shut] — **pre·clu′sion** (-klo͞o′zhən) *n.* — **pre·clu′sive** (-klo͞o′siv) *adj.* — **pre·clu′sive·ly** *adv.*

pre·co·cious (pri·kō′shəs) *adj.* 1. Unusually developed or advanced for one's age. 2. Pertaining to or showing premature development. [< L < *prae-* beforehand, early + *coquere* to cook] — **pre·co′cious·ly** *adv.* — **pre·co′cious·ness, pre·coc′i·ty** (-kos′ə·tē) *n.*

pre·con·ceive (prē′kən·sēv′) *v.t.* ·ceived, ·ceiv·ing To conceive in advance; form an idea or opinion of beforehand.

pre·con·cep·tion (prē′kən·sep′shən) *n.* 1. An idea or opinion formed or conceived in advance. 2. A prejudice or misconception; bias. — **pre′con·cep′tion·al** *adj.*

pre·con·di·tion (prē′kən·dish′ən) *n.* A condition that must be met before a certain result is attained; prerequisite.

pre·cur·sor (pri·kûr′sər) *n.* One who or that which precedes and suggests the course of future events. [< L < *prae-* before + *currere* to run]

pre·cur·so·ry (pri·kûr′sər·ē) *adj.* Going before as a precursor or harbinger; preliminary. Also **pre·cur′sive** (-kûr′siv).

pre·da·cious (pri·dā′shəs) *adj.* Living by preying upon others, as a beast or bird; raptorial: also **predatory.** Also **pre·da′ceous.** [< L *praeda* prey] — **pre·da′cious·ness, pre·dac′i·ty** (-das′ə·tē) *n.*

pre·date (prē′dāt′) *v.t.* ·dat·ed, ·dat·ing 1. To date before the actual time. 2. To precede in time.

pred·a·tor (pred′i·tər) *n.* A predatory person or animal.

pred·a·to·ry (pred′ə·tôr′ē, -tō′rē) *adj.* 1. Of, relating to, or characterized by plundering. 2. Accustomed to or living by pillaging. 3. Predacious. [< L *praeda* prey] — **pred′a·to′ri·ly** *adv.* — **pred′a·to′ri·ness** *n.*

pre·de·cease (prē′di·sēs′) *v.t.* ·ceased, ·ceas·ing To die before: She *predeceased* her husband by five years.

pred·e·ces·sor (pred′ə·ses′ər) *n.* 1. One who goes or has gone before another in point of time. 2. A thing succeeded

by something else. 3. An ancestor. [< OF < LL < *prae-* before + *decessor* withdrawer]

pre·des·ti·nate (prē·des′tə·nāt) *v.t.* ·nat·ed, ·nat·ing 1. *Theol.* To foreordain by divine decree or purpose. 2. To predestine. [< L < *prae-* before + *destinare* to determine]

pre·des·ti·na·tion (prē·des′tə·nā′shən) *n.* 1. The act of predestinating, or the state of being predestined; destiny; fate. 2. *Theol.* The foreordination of all things by God, including the salvation or damnation of men.

pre·des·tine (prē·des′tin) *v.t.* ·tined, ·tin·ing To destine or decree beforehand; foreordain; predestinate.

pre·de·ter·mine (prē′di·tûr′min) *v.t.* ·mined, ·min·ing 1. To determine beforehand; foreordain. 2. To urge to accept (a point of view, etc.) beforehand; influence. — **pre′de·ter′mi·nate** (-mə·nit, -nāt) *adj.* — **pre′de·ter′mi·na′tion** *n.*

pred·i·ca·ble (pred′i·kə·bəl) *adj.* Capable of being predicated or affirmed. — *n.* 1. Anything predicable. — **pred′·i·ca·bil′i·ty, pred′i·ca·ble·ness** *n.*

pre·dic·a·ment (pri·dik′ə·mənt) *n.* 1. A trying or embarrassing situation; plight. 2. A specific state, position, or situation. [< LL < *praedicare* to proclaim. See PREACH.]

pred·i·cate (*v.* pred′i·kāt; *n. & adj.* pred′i·kit) *v.* ·cat·ed, ·cat·ing *v.t.* 1. *U.S.* To found or base (an argument, proposition, etc.): with *on* or *upon.* 2. To affirm as a quality or attribute of something. 3. To imply or connote. 4. To declare; proclaim. 5. *Logic* To state or affirm concerning the subject of a proposition. — *v.i.* 6. To make a statement or affirmation. — *n.* 1. *Gram.* The verb in a sentence or clause together with its complements and modifiers. 2. *Logic* In a proposition, that which is stated about a subject. — *adj.* 1. That predicates. 2. *Gram.* Belonging to, relating to, or of the nature of a predicate. [< L < *praedicare* to proclaim] — **pred′i·ca′tive** *adj.* — **pred′i·ca′tive·ly** *adv.*

predicate adjective *Gram.* An adjective that describes the subject of a linking verb, as *sad* in *He is sad.*

predicate noun *Gram.* A noun that designates or identifies the subject of a linking verb, as *king* in *He was king.*

pred·i·ca·tion (pred′i·kā′shən) *n.* 1. The act of predicating. 2. Something predicated. — **pred′i·ca′tion·al** *adj.*

pre·dict (pri·dikt′) *v.t.* 1. To make known beforehand; prophesy. 2. To assert on the basis of data, theory, or experience but in advance of proof. — *v.i.* 3. To make a prediction. [< L < *prae-* before + *dicere* to say] — **pre·dict′a·ble** *adj.* — **pre·dict′a·bly** *adv.* — **pre·dic′tor** *n.*

pre·dic·tion (pri·dik′shən) *n.* 1. The act of predicting. 2. Something predicted. — **pre·dic′tive** *adj.* — **pre·dic′tive·ly** *adv.*

pre·di·gest (prē′di·jest′, -dī-) *v.t.* To treat (food) by a process of partial digestion before introduction into the stomach.

pre·di·lec·tion (prē′də·lek′shən, pred′ə-) *n.* A preference or bias in favor of something; a partiality: with *for.* [< F < Med.L < L *prae-* before + *diligere* to love, choose]

pre·dis·pose (prē′dis·pōz′) *v.t.* ·posed, ·pos·ing 1. To give a tendency or inclination to; make susceptible: Exhaustion *predisposes* one to sickness. 2. To dispose of beforehand.

pre·dom·i·nant (pri·dom′ə·nənt) *adj.* Superior in power, influence, effectiveness, number, or degree; prevailing over others. — **pre·dom′i·nance, pre·dom′i·nan·cy** *n.* — **pre·dom′i·nant·ly** *adv.*

pre·dom·i·nate (pri·dom′ə·nāt) *v.i.* ·nat·ed, ·nat·ing 1. To have governing influence or control; be in control: often with *over.* 2. To be superior to all others. 3. To prevail. — **pre·dom′i·nat′ing·ly** *adv.* — **pre·dom′i·na′tion** *n.*

pre·em·i·nent (prē·em′ə·nənt) *adj.* Supremely eminent; distinguished above all others; outstanding; conspicuous. [< L < *prae-* before + *eminere* to stand out] — **pre·em′i·nent·ly** *adv.* — **pre·em′i·nence** *n.*

pre·empt (prē·empt′) *v.t.* 1. To acquire or appropriate beforehand. 2. To occupy (public land) so as to acquire by preemption. — *v.i.* 3. In bridge, to make a preemptive bid. — **pre·emp′tor** *n.* — **pre·emp′to·ry** (-tər·ē) *adj.*

pre·emp·tion (prē·emp′shən) *n.* 1. The right to purchase something before others; also, the act of so purchasing. 2. Public land obtained by exercising this right. [< Med.L < L *prae-* before + *emptus,* pp. of *emere* to buy]

pre·emp·tive (prē·emp′tiv) *adj.* 1. Pertaining to or capable of preemption. 2. In bridge, designating a bid that is unnecessarily high, intended to discourage subsequent bidding.

preen (prēn) *v.t.* 1. To trim and dress (feathers, etc.) with the beak, as a bird. 2. To dress or adorn (oneself) carefully. 3. To pride or congratulate (oneself): with *on.* — *v.i.* 4. To primp; prink. [ME *proyne, preyn, prene*]

pre·ex·ist (prē′ig·zist′) *v.t. & v.i.* To exist before. — **pre′ex·is′tence** *n.* — **pre′ex·is′tent** *adj.*

pre·fab (prē′fab′) *n.* A prefabricated structure or part.

pre·fab·ri·cate (prē·fab′rə·kāt) *v.t.* ·cat·ed, ·cat·ing 1. To build beforehand. 2. To manufacture in standard sections that can be rapidly assembled. — **pre·fab′ri·ca′tion** *n.*

pref·ace (pref′is) *n.* **1.** A statement or brief essay, included in the front matter of a book, etc., and dealing primarily with the purpose and scope of the work. **2.** Any introductory speech, writing, etc. — *v.t.* **·aced, ·ac·ing 1.** To introduce or furnish with a preface. **2.** To serve as a preface for. [< OF < L < *prae-* before + *fari* to speak]

pref·a·to·ry (pref′ə·tôr′ē, -tō′rē) *adj.* Of the nature of a preface; introductory. Also **pref′a·to′ri·al.** — **pref′a·to′ri·ly** *adv.*

pre·fect (prē′fekt) *n.* **1.** In ancient Rome, any of various civil and military officials. **2.** Any magistrate, chief official, etc.; esp., in France: **a** The chief administrator of a department. **b** The head of the Paris police. **3.** The dean of certain private or religious schools. Also spelled *praefect.* [< OF < L *praeficere* to set over]

pre·fec·ture (prē′fek·chər) *n.* The office, jurisdiction, or province of a prefect. — **pre·fec′tur·al** *adj.*

pre·fer (pri·fûr′) *v.t.* **·ferred, ·fer·ring 1.** To hold in higher regard or esteem; value more. **2.** To choose (something or someone) over another or others; like better. **3.** To give priority to, as certain securities over others. — **Syn.** See CHOOSE. [< F < L < *prae-* before + *ferre* to carry] — **pre·fer′rer** *n.*

pref·er·a·ble (pref′ər·ə·bəl) *adj.* That is preferred; more desirable; worthy of choice. — **pref′er·a·ble·ness, pref′er·a·bil′i·ty** *n.* — **pref′er·a·bly** *adv.*

pref·er·ence (pref′ər·əns) *n.* **1.** The choosing of one person or thing over another or others; also, the privilege of so choosing. **2.** One who or that which is preferred. **3.** The granting of special advantage to one over others, as to one country or group of countries. **4.** The act of preferring, or the state of being preferred.

pref·er·en·tial (pref′ə·ren′shəl) *adj.* **1.** Showing or arising from preference or partiality. **2.** Giving preference, as in tariffs. — **pref′er·en′tial·ism** *n.* — **pref′er·en′tial·ly** *adv.*

preferential shop A shop that gives preferential treatment to union members when hiring, laying off, promoting, etc.

pre·fer·ment (pri·fûr′mənt) *n.* **1.** The act of promoting to higher office; advancement. **2.** A position, rank, or office of social prestige or profit. **3.** The act of preferring.

preferred stock Stock on which dividends must be paid before dividends can be paid on common stocks, usu. also receiving preference in the distribution of assets on liquidation. Also *Brit.* **preference shares.**

pre·fig·u·ra·tion (prē·fig′yə·rā′shən) *n.* **1.** The act of prefiguring. **2.** That which prefigures; a prototype. — **pre·fig·ur·a·tive** (prē·fig′yər·ə·tiv) *adj.* — **pre·fig′ur·a·tive·ly** *adv.* — **pre·fig′ur·a·tive·ness** *n.*

pre·fig·ure (prē·fig′yər) *v.t.* **·ured, ·ur·ing 1.** To serve as an indication or suggestion of; foreshadow. **2.** To imagine or picture to oneself beforehand. [< LL < L *prae-* before + *figurare* to form]

pre·fix (*n.* prē′fiks; *v.* prē·fiks′) *n.* **1.** *Gram.* A bound form affixed to the beginning of a base, stem, or root, altering or modifying its meaning, as *re-* in *renew.* Compare COMBINING FORM, SUFFIX. **2.** Something placed before, as a title before a name. — *v.t.* To put or attach before or at the beginning; add as a prefix. [< OF < L < *prae-* before + *figere* to fasten, fix] — **pre′fix·al** *adj.* — **pre′fix·al·ly** *adv.* — **pre·fix·ion** (prē·fik′shən) *n.*

preg·na·ble (preg′nə·bəl) *adj.* **1.** Capable of being captured, as a fort. **2.** Open to attack; vulnerable; assailable. [< OF < L *prehendere* to seize] — **preg′na·bil′i·ty** *n.*

preg·nan·cy (preg′nən·sē) *n. pl.* **·cies** The state or quality of being pregnant.

preg·nant (preg′nənt) *adj.* **1.** Carrying a growing fetus in the uterus. **2.** Having considerable weight or significance; full of meaning. **3.** Teeming with ideas. **4.** Bearing issue or results; fruitful; prolific. [< L < *prae-* before + *gnasci* to be born] — **preg′nant·ly** *adv.*

pre·hen·si·ble (pri·hen′sə·bəl) *adj.* Capable of being grasped.

pre·hen·sile (pri·hen′sil) *adj.* Adapted for grasping or holding, as the tail of a monkey. [See PREHENSION.] — **pre·hen·sil·i·ty** (prē′hen·sil′ə·tē) *n.*

pre·hen·sion (pri·hen′shən) *n.* The act of grasping, physically or mentally. [< L *prehendere* to seize]

pre·his·tor·ic (prē′his·tôr′ik, -tor′-) *adj.* Of or belonging to the period before written history. Also **pre′his·tor′i·cal.** — **pre′his·tor′i·cal·ly** *adv.*

pre·his·to·ry (prē·his′tə·rē) *n. pl.* **·ries** The history of mankind in the period preceding written records.

pre·judge (prē·juj′) *v.t.* **·judged, ·judg·ing** To judge beforehand or without proper inquiry. [< F < Med.L < *prae-* before + *judicare* to judge] — **pre·judg′er** *n.* — **pre·judg′ment** or **pre·judge′ment** *n.*

prej·u·dice (prej′ōō·dis) *n.* **1.** A judgment or opinion formed before the facts are known; esp., an unfavorable, irrational opinion. **2.** The act or state of holding preconceived, irrational opinions. **3.** Hatred of or dislike for a particular group, race, religion, etc. **4.** Injury or damage to a person arising from a hasty and unfair judgment by others. — **in (or to) the prejudice of** To the injury or detriment of. — *v.t.* **·diced, ·dic·ing 1.** To cause to have a prejudice; bias; influence. **2.** To damage or impair by some act, judgment, etc. [< OF < L < *prae-* before + *judicium* judgment] — **Syn.** (noun) *Prejudice, bias,* and *partiality* are compared as they denote an attitude of mind that interferes with fair judgment. Only *prejudice* is necessarily a term of opprobrium; literally, it signifies prejudgment without adequate hearing or consideration, but it is chiefly used to refer to a strong emotional *bias.* A *bias* is an imbalance of mind, an inclination in some direction that prevents a fair weighing of issues. *Partiality* is an inclination to favor one person or view unfairly. A *bias* may be for or against someone or something, but *partiality* always implies favor.

prej·u·di·cial (prej′ōō·dish′əl) *adj.* Tending to prejudice or injure; detrimental. — **prej′u·di′cial·ly** *adv.*

prel·a·cy (prel′ə·sē) *n. pl.* **·cies 1.** The system of church government by prelates: sometimes used disparagingly. **2.** The dignity or function of a prelate; also, prelates collectively: also **prel·a·ture** (prel′ə·chər).

prel·ate (prel′it) *n.* An ecclesiastic of high rank, as a bishop, archbishop, etc. [< OF *prelat* < L *praelatus* set over] — **prel′ate·ship** *n.* — **pre·lat·ic** (pri·lat′ik) or **·i·cal** *adj.*

pre·lim·i·nar·y (pri·lim′ə·ner′ē) *adj.* Before or introductory to the main event, proceeding, or business; prefatory; preparatory. — *n. pl.* **·nar·ies 1.** A preparatory step or act. **2.** A preliminary examination. **3.** In sports, a minor, introductory event, as a boxing match. [< F *pré-* pre- + *liminaire* prefactory] — **pre·lim′i·nar′i·ly** *adv.*

pre·lit·er·ate (prē·lit′ər·it) *adj.* Of a culture, lacking or predating the existence of written language or records.

prel·ude (prel′yōōd, prē′lōōd) *n.* **1.** *Music* **a** An instrumental composition of moderate length, in a free style. **b** An opening section or movement of a musical composition. **2.** Any introductory or opening performance or event. — *v.* **·ud·ed, ·ud·ing** *v.t.* **1.** To introduce with a prelude. **2.** To serve as a prelude to. — *v.i.* **3.** To serve as a prelude. **4.** To provide or play a prelude. [< Med.L < L < *prae-* before + *ludere* to play] — **pre·lud·er** (pri·lōō′dər, prel′yə·dər) *n.* — **pre·lu·di·al** (pri·lōō′dē·əl) *adj.*

pre·ma·ture (prē′mə·chŏŏr′, -tŏŏr′, -tyŏŏr′; *Brit.* prem′ə·tyŏŏr′) *adj.* Existing, happening, or developed before the natural or proper period; untimely. [< L < *prae-* before + *maturus* ripe] — **pre′ma·ture′ly** *adv.* — **pre′ma·ture′ness, pre′ma·tu′ri·ty** *n.*

pre·med·i·cal (prē·med′i·kəl) *adj.* Preparatory to or preparing for the study of medicine. Also *Informal* **pre·med′.**

pre·med·i·tate (prē·med′ə·tāt) *v.t. & v.i.* **·tat·ed, ·tat·ing** To plan or consider beforehand. [< L < *prae-* before + *meditari* to muse, ponder] — **pre·med′i·tat′ed·ly** *adv.* — **pre·med′i·ta′tive** *adj.* — **pre·med′i·ta′tor** *n.*

pre·med·i·ta·tion (prē·med′ə·tā′shən) *n.* **1.** The act of premeditating. **2.** *Law* The deliberation and planning of a crime before its commission, showing intent to commit it.

pre·mi·er (prē′mē·ər, *esp. Brit.* prem′yər; *for n.,* also pri·mir′) *adj.* **1.** First in rank or position; principal. **2.** First in order of occurrence; senior. — *n.* **1.** Prime minister. **2.** In Canada, the head of a Provincial cabinet. [< F < L *primus* first] — **pre′mi·er·ship′** *n.*

pre·mière (pri·mir′, *Fr.* prə·myâr′) *n.* The first performance of a play, movie, etc. [< F, fem. of *premier* first]

pre·mil·len·ni·al (prē′mi·len′ē·əl) *adj.* Pertaining to or occurring before the millennium.

prem·ise (prem′is; *for v.,* also pri·mīz′) *n.* **1.** A proposition that serves as a ground for argument or for a conclusion. **2.** *pl.* A definite portion of real estate; land with its appurtenances; also, a building or part of a building. **3.** In a syllogism, either of the two propositions that combine to form a conclusion. **4.** *pl. Law* That part in a deed that sets forth the date, names of parties, the land or thing conveyed or granted, etc. Also **prem′iss.** — *v.* **·mised, ·mis·ing** *v.t.* **1.** To state beforehand, as by way of introduction or explanation. **2.** To state or assume a premise or basis of argument. — *v.i.* **3.** To make a premise. [< MF < Med.L < L < *prae-* before + *mittere* to send]

pre·mi·um (prē′mē·əm) *n.* **1.** An object or service offered free as an inducement to buy, rent, or contract for another object or service. **2.** The amount paid or payable for insurance, usu. in periodical installments. **3.** An extra amount or bonus paid in addition to a fixed price, wage, etc. **4.** A price paid for a loan, usu. in addition to interest. **5.** The rate or price at which stocks, shares, or money are valued in excess of their nominal or par value: bank shares at a *premium* of five percent. **6.** High regard or value. **7.** A reward or prize awarded in a competition. — **at a premium 1.** Valuable and in demand. **2.** Above par. [< L ult. < *prae-* before + *emere* to take]

pre·mo·lar (prē·mō′lər) *Anat. n.* One of the teeth situated in front of the molars and behind the canines: also called *bicuspid.* — *adj.* Situated in front of the molar teeth.

pre·mo·ni·tion (prē′mə·nish′ən, prem′ə-) *n.* **1.** A presentiment of the future not based on information received; an instinctive foreboding. **2.** An actual warning of something yet to occur. [< LL < *prae-* before + *monere* to advise] — **pre·mon·i·to·ry** (pri·mon/ə·tôr/ē, -tō/rē) *adj.* — **pre·mon/i·to/ri·ly** *adv.*

pre·na·tal (prē·nāt/l) *adj.* Prior to birth: *prenatal* care. — **pre·na/tal·ly** *adv.*

pre·no·men (prē·nō/mən) See PRAENOMEN.

pre·oc·cu·pied (prē·ok/yə·pīd) *adj.* **1.** Engrossed in thought or in some action. **2.** Previously occupied.

pre·oc·cu·py (prē·ok/yə·pī) *v.t.* **·pied, ·py·ing 1.** To engage fully; engross the mind. **2.** To occupy or take possession of first. [< L *praeoccupare* to seize beforehand] — **pre·oc/u·pan·cy** (-pən·sē), **pre·oc/cu·pa/tion** *n.*

pre·or·dain (prē/ôr·dān/) *v.t.* To ordain beforehand; foreordain. — **pre·or·di·na·tion** (prē/ôr·də·nā/shən) *n.*

prep (prep) *adj. Informal* Preparatory: a *prep* school.

pre·pack·age (prē·pak/ij) *v.t.* **·aged, ·ag·ing** To package (meats, etc.) before offering them for sale.

prep·a·ra·tion (prep/ə·rā/shən) *n.* **1.** The act or process of preparing. **2.** An act or proceeding undertaken in advance of some event; provision. **3.** The fact or state of being prepared. **4.** Something made or prepared, as a medicine.

pre·par·a·to·ry (pri·par/ə·tôr/ē, -tō/rē) *adj.* **1.** Serving as preparation. **2.** Occupied in preparation: a *preparatory* scholar. — *adv.* As a preparation: *Preparatory* to writing, I will consider this: also **pre·par/a·to/ri·ly.**

preparatory school A private school that prepares students for college admission.

pre·pare (pri·pâr/) *v.* **·pared, ·par·ing** *v.t.* **1.** To make ready, fit, or qualified; put in readiness. **2.** To provide with what is needed; equip: to *prepare* an expedition. **3.** To bring to a state of completeness: to *prepare* a meal. — *v.i.* **4.** To make preparations; get ready. [< F < L < *prae-* before + *parare* to produce] — **pre·par/ed·ly** (pri·pâr/id·lē) *adv.* — **pre·par/er** *n.*

pre·par·ed·ness (pri·pâr/id·nis, -pârd/-) *n.* Readiness; esp., a condition of military readiness for war.

pre·pay (prē·pā/) *v.t.* **·paid, ·pay·ing** To pay or pay for in advance. — **pre·pay/ment** *n.*

pre·pense (pri·pens/) *adj.* Considered beforehand; premeditated: chiefly in the phrase **malice prepense.** [< OF < L *pro-* ahead + *pensare* to think] — **pre·pense/ly** *adv.*

pre·pon·der·ant (pri·pon/dər·ənt) *adj.* Having superior force, weight, importance, quantity, etc.. — **pre·pon/der·ance, pre·pon/der·an·cy** *n.* — **pre·pon/der·ant·ly** *adv.*

pre·pon·der·ate (pri·pon/də·rāt) *v.i.* **·at·ed, ·at·ing 1.** To be of greater weight. **2.** To incline downward or descend, as the scale of a balance. **3.** To be of greater power, importance, quantity, etc.; predominate; prevail. [< L < *prae-* before + *ponderare* to weigh] — **pre·pon/der·a/tion** *n.*

prep·o·si·tion (prep/ə·zish/ən) *n. Gram.* **1.** In some languages, a word as *by, for, from,* functioning to indicate the relation of a substantive (the object of the preposition) to another substantive, verb, or adjective and usu. placed before its object. Together they constitute a prepositional phrase that serves as an adjectival or an adverbial modifier as: sitting *beside the fire;* a man *of honor.* **2.** Any word or construction that functions in a similar manner, as *in reference to* in *He telephoned in reference to your letter.*
◆ It was once maintained that a sentence should never end with a preposition, but natural English sentences often do. *What did you laugh at?* is good English. *At what did you laugh?* is awkward and unnatural. [< F < L < *prae-* before + *ponere* to place] — **prep/o·si/tion·al** *adj.* — **prep/o·si/tion·al·ly** *adv.*

pre·pos·sess (prē/pə·zes/) *v.t.* **1.** To preoccupy to the exclusion of other ideas, beliefs, etc.; prejudice; bias. **2.** To impress or influence beforehand or at once, esp. favorably. — **pre/pos·ses/sion** *n.*

pre·pos·sess·ing (prē/pə·zes/ing) *adj.* Inspiring a favorable opinion; pleasing. — **pre/pos·sess/ing·ly** *adv.*

pre·pos·ter·ous (pri·pos/tər·əs) *adj.* Contrary to nature, reason, or common sense; utterly absurd or impracticable. [< L *prae-* before + *posterus* last] — **pre·pos/ter·ous·ly** *adv.* — **pre·pos/ter·ous·ness** *n.*

pre·puce (prē/pyoōs) *n. Anat.* The fold of skin covering the glans of the penis or clitoris: also called *foreskin.* [< F < L *praeputium*] — **pre·pu·tial** (pri·pyoō/shəl) *adj.*

Pre-Raph·a·el·ite (prē·raf/ē·ə·līt, -rā/fē-) *n.* **1.** A follower of the **Pre-Raphaelite Brotherhood,** a society of artists formed in England, 1847–49, stressing characteristics supposedly typical of Italian art before the time of Raphael. **2.** Any modern artist with similar aims. — *adj.* Of or pertaining to the Pre-Raphaelites. — **Pre-Raph/a·el·it/ism** *n.*

pre·req·ui·site (prē·rek/wə·zit) *adj.* Required as an antecedent condition; necessary to something that follows. — *n.* Something prerequisite.

pre·rog·a·tive (pri·rog/ə·tiv) *n.* **1.** An exclusive and unquestionable right belonging to a person or body of persons; esp., a hereditary or official right. **2.** Any characteristic privilege peculiar to a person or class. **3.** Precedence; preeminence. — *adj.* Of, pertaining to, or possessing a prerogative. [< OF < L < *prae-* before + *rogare* to ask]

pres·age (*n.* pres/ij; *v.* pri·sāj/) *n.* **1.** An indication of something to come; omen. **2.** A presentiment; foreboding. **3.** Prophetic meaning or import. — *v.* **·saged, ·sag·ing** *v.t.* **1.** To give a presage or portent of; foreshadow. **2.** To have a presentiment of. **3.** To predict; foretell. — *v.i.* **4.** To make a prediction. [< MF < L < *prae-* before + *sagire* to perceive keenly] — **pres·sag/er** *n.*

pres·by·ter (prez/bə·tər, pres/-) *n. Eccl.* **1.** In the early Christian church, one of the elders of a church. **2.** In various hierarchical churches, a priest. **3.** In the Presbyterian Church: **a** An ordained clergyman: also called *teaching elder.* **b** A layman who is a member of the governing body of a congregation. [< LL < Gk. *presbyteros* elder, compar. of *presbys* old, important]

pres·by·te·ri·al (prez/bə·tir/ē·əl, pres/-) *adj.* Pertaining to a presbytery or a presbyter. Also **pres·byt/er·al.** — **pres/by·te/ri·al·ly** *adv.*

pres·by·te·ri·an (prez/bə·tir/ē·ən, pres/-) *adj.* Pertaining to or characterized by church government by presbyters. — **pres/by·te/ri·an·ism** *n.*

Pres·by·te·ri·an (prez/bə·tir/ē·ən, pres/-) *adj.* Pertaining to any of various Protestant churches that have church government by presbyters. — *n.* A member of a Presbyterian church. — **Pres/by·te/ri·an·ism** *n.*

pres·by·ter·y (prez/bə·ter/ē, pres/-) *n. pl.* **·ter·ies 1.** In the Presbyterian Church, a court composed of the ministers and one or two presbyters of each church in a district. **2.** Presbyters collectively. **3.** Government of a church by presbyters. **4.** That part of a church set apart for the clergy. [< OF < LL *presbyterium* assembly of elders]

pre·school (prē/skoōl/) *adj.* Of, intended for, or designating a child past infancy but under school age.

pre·sci·ence (prē/shē·əns, presh/ē-) *n.* Knowledge of events before they take place; foreknowledge. [< OF < L < *prae-* before + *scire* to know]

pre·sci·ent (prē/shē·ənt, presh/ē-) *adj.* Having prescience; farseeing. — **pre/sci·ent·ly** *adv.*

pre·scribe (pri·skrīb/) *v.* **·scribed, ·scrib·ing** *v.t.* **1.** To set down as a direction or rule to be followed; enjoin. **2.** *Med.* To order the use of (a medicine, treatment, etc.). — *v.i.* **3.** To lay down laws or rules; give directions. **4.** *Med.* To order a remedy; give prescriptions. [< L < *prae-* before + *scribere* to write] — **pre·scrib/er** *n.*

pre·script (prē/skript; *for adj., also* pri·skript/) *n.* Something prescribed; a rule or regulation, esp. a rule of conduct. — *adj.* Laid down, prescribed.

pre·scrip·tion (pri·skrip/shən) *n.* **1.** *Med.* **a** A physician's order for a medicine including directions for its use. **b** The remedy so prescribed. **2.** The act of prescribing. **3.** That which is prescribed; a prescript.

pre·scrip·tive (pri·skrip/tiv) *adj.* **1.** Making strict requirements or rules: *prescriptive* grammar. **2.** Sanctioned by custom or long use. — **pre·scrip/tive·ly** *adv.*

pres·ence (prez/əns) *n.* **1.** The state or fact of being present. **2.** The area immediately surrounding a person or thing; close proximity. **3.** The immediate vicinity of a person of superior rank, esp., a sovereign; also, the person or personality of a sovereign, ruler, etc. **4.** Personal appearance; bearing; esp., a pleasing or dignified bearing. **5.** An invisible spirit or influence felt to be near.

presence of mind Full command of one's faculties, esp. in an emergency; coolness, alertness, and readiness.

pres·ent¹ (prez/ənt) *adj.* **1.** Now going on; not past or future. **2.** Of or pertaining to time now occurring; current. **3.** Being in the place or company referred to or considered; being at hand. **4.** Being actually considered, written, discussed, etc.: the *present* issue. **5.** *Gram.* Denoting a tense or verb form that expresses a current or habitual action or state. — *n.* **1.** Present time; the time being; now. **2.** *Gram.* The present tense; also, a verb form denoting it. **3.** *pl. Law* Present writings: a term for the document in which the word occurs: Know all men by these *presents.* — **at present** Now. [< OF < L < *prae-* before + *esse* to be]

pre·sent² (*v.* pri·zent/; *n.* prez/ənt) *v.t.* **1.** To bring into the presence or acquaintance of another; introduce, esp. to one of higher rank. **2.** To exhibit to view or notice. **3.** To suggest to the mind: This *presents* a problem. **4.** To put forward for consideration or action; submit, as a petition. **5.** To make a gift or presentation of or to, usu. formally. **6.** To aim or level (a weapon, etc.). — **to present arms** *Mil.* To salute by holding a gun vertically in front of one's body with the muzzle up and the trigger facing forward. — *n.* Something presented or given; a gift. [< OF < L *praeesse* to be before] — **pre·sent′er** *n.*

pre·sent·a·ble (pri-zen′tə-bəl) *adj.* **1.** Fit to be presented; in suitable condition or attire for company. **2.** Capable of being offered, exhibited, or bestowed. — **pre·sent′a·bil′i·ty, pre·sent′a·ble·ness** *n.* — **pre·sent′a·bly** *adv.*

pres·en·ta·tion (prez′ən·tā′shən, prē′zən-) *n.* **1.** The act of presenting or proffering for acceptance, approval, etc., or the state of being presented. **2.** The formal offering of a complimentary gift. **3.** The act of introducing or bringing to notice, esp. to one of higher rank: *presentation* at court. **4.** An exhibition or representation, as of a play.

pres·ent-day (prez′ənt·dā′) *adj.* Modern; current.

pre·sen·ti·ment (pri·zen′tə·mənt) *n.* A prophetic sense of something to come; a foreboding. [< F < L < *prae-* before + *sentire* to perceive]

pres·ent·ly (prez′ənt·lē) *adv.* **1.** After a little time; shortly. **2.** At the present time; now.

pre·sent·ment (pri·zent′mənt) *n.* **1.** The act of presenting. **2.** Something represented or exhibited.

present participle See under PARTICIPLE.

present perfect *Gram.* The verb tense expressing an action completed by the present time, usu. constructed with a form of the verb *to have*, as *has finished* in *By now he has finished the task.*

present tense *Gram.* The verb tense marking present time, as in *I am here*, or *are going* in *You are going home.*

pre·ser·va·tive (pri·zûr′və·tiv) *adj.* Serving or tending to preserve. — *n.* A preservative agent; esp., a chemical substance added to food to retard spoilage.

pre·serve (pri·zûrv′) *v.* **·served, ·serv·ing** *v.t.* **1.** To keep in safety; guard: May the gods *preserve* you. **2.** To keep intact or unimpaired; maintain. **3.** To prepare (food) for future consumption, as by boiling with sugar or by salting. **4.** To keep from decomposition or change, as by chemical treatment. **5.** To keep for one's private hunting or fishing: to *preserve* foxes. — *v.i.* **6.** To make preserves, as of fruit. **7.** To maintain a game preserve. — *n.* **1.** *Usu. pl.* Fruit that has been cooked, usu. with sugar, to prevent its fermenting. **2.** Something that preserves or is preserved. **3.** An area set apart for the protection of wildlife, forests, etc.; also, such an area reserved for restricted or private hunting or fishing. [< OF < LL < L *prae-* before + *servare* to keep] — **pre·serv′a·bil·i·ty** *n.* — **pre·serv′a·ble** *adj.* — **pres·er·va′tion** (prez′ər·vā′shən) *n.* — **pre·serv′er** *n.*

pre·shrunk (prē′shrungk′) *adj.* Shrunk during manufacture to minimize later shrinkage during cleaning.

pre·side (pri·zīd′) *v.i.* **·sid·ed, ·sid·ing** **1.** To sit in authority, as over a meeting; act as chairman or president. **2.** To exercise direction or control. **3.** To occupy a featured place, as an instrumentalist on a program. [< F < L *prae-* before + *sedere* to sit] — **pre·sid′er** *n.*

pres·i·den·cy (prez′ə·dən·sē) *n.* *pl.* **·cies** **1.** The office, function, or term of office of a president. **2.** *Often cap.* The office of president of the U.S.

pres·i·dent (prez′ə·dənt) *n.* **1.** One who is chosen to preside over an organized body. **2.** *Often cap.* The chief executive of a republic. **3.** The chief executive officer of a government department, corporation, society, or similar body. **4.** The chief officer of a college or university. **5.** The chairman of a meeting conducted under parliamentary rules. [< OF < L *praesidens, -entis*, ppr. of *praesidere* to preside] — **pres·i·den·tial** (prez′ə·den′shəl) *adj.* — **pres′i·dent·ship′** *n.*

pre·sid·i·o (pri·sid′ē·ō) *n.* *pl.* **·sid·i·os** A garrisoned post; fortified settlement; fort. [< Am. Sp. < L *praesidium*]

pre·sid·i·um (pri·sid′ē·əm) *n.* An executive committee in the Soviet Union serving as the permanent organ of a larger governmental body.

Pre·sid·i·um (pri·sid′ē·əm) *n.* **1.** A governmental body of the Soviet Union that exercises the powers of the Supreme Soviet between plenary sessions. **2.** The supreme policy-making committee of the Communist party of the Soviet Union, headed by the party secretary. See POLITBURO.

pre·sig·ni·fy (prē·sig′nə·fī) *v.t.* **·fied, ·fy·ing** To signify or give token of in advance; presage; foreshadow.

press¹ (pres) *v.t.* **1.** To act upon by weight or pressure: to *press* a button. **2.** To compress so as to extract the juice: to *press* grapes. **3.** To extract by pressure, as juice. **4.** To exert pressure upon so as to smooth, shape, make compact, etc. **5.** To smooth or shape by heat and pressure, as clothes; iron. **6.** To embrace closely; hug. **7.** To force or impel. **8.** To distress or harass; place in difficulty. **9.** To urge persistently; entreat: They *pressed* me for an answer. **10.** To advocate persistently; emphasize. **11.** To put forward insistently: to *press* a claim. **12.** To urge onward; hasten. **13.** To proceed further in, as a lawsuit. **14.** To produce (a phonograph record) from a matrix. — *v.i.* **15.** To exert pressure; bear heavily. **16.** To advance forcibly or with speed. **17.** To press clothes, etc. **18.** To crowd; cram. **19.** To be urgent or importunate. — *n.* **1.** Newspapers or periodical literature collectively, or the persons concerned

THE PRESIDENTS OF THE UNITED STATES

Number—Name	Birthplace—Inaugurated: year		Age
1 George Washington	Westmoreland Co., Va.	1789	57
2 John Adams	Quincy, Mass.	1797	61
3 Thomas Jefferson	Shadwell, Va.	1801	57
4 James Madison	Port Conway, Va.	1809	57
5 James Monroe	Westmoreland Co., Va.	1817	58
6 John Quincy Adams	Quincy, Mass.	1825	57
7 Andrew Jackson	Union Co., N.C.	1829	61
8 Martin Van Buren	Kinderhook, N.Y.	1837	54
9 William H. Harrison	Berkeley, Va.	1841	68
10 John Tyler	Greenway, Va.	1841	51
11 James K. Polk	Little Sugar Creek, N.C.	1845	49
12 Zachary Taylor	Orange Co., Va.	1849	64
13 Millard Fillmore	Summerhill, N.Y.	1850	50
14 Franklin Pierce	Hillsboro, N.H.	1853	48
15 James Buchanan	Cove Gap, Pa.	1857	65
16 Abraham Lincoln	Hardin Co., Ky.	1861	52
17 Andrew Johnson	Raleigh, N.C.	1865	56
18 Ulysses S. Grant	Point Pleasant, O.	1869	46
19 Rutherford B. Hayes	Delaware, O.	1877	54
20 James A. Garfield	Cuyahoga Co., O.	1881	49
21 Chester A. Arthur	Fairfield, Vt.	1881	50
22 Grover Cleveland	Caldwell, N.J.	1885	47
23 Benjamin Harrison	North Bend, O.	1889	55
24 Grover Cleveland	Caldwell, N.J.	1893	55
25 William McKinley	Niles, O.	1897	54
26 Theodore Roosevelt	New York, N.Y.	1901	42
27 William H. Taft	Cincinnati, O.	1909	51
28 Woodrow Wilson	Staunton, Va.	1913	56
29 Warren G. Harding	Corsica, O.	1921	55
30 Calvin Coolidge	Plymouth, Vt.	1923	51
31 Herbert C. Hoover	West Branch, Ia.	1929	55
32 Franklin D. Roosevelt	Hyde Park, N.Y.	1933	51
33 Harry S Truman	Lamar, Mo.	1945	60
34 Dwight D. Eisenhower	Denison, Tex.	1953	62
35 John F. Kennedy	Brookline, Mass.	1961	43
36 Lyndon B. Johnson	Stonewall, Tex.	1963	55
37 Richard M. Nixon	Yorba Linda, Calif.	1969	57
38 Gerald R. Ford	Omaha, Neb.	1974	61
39 Carter, Jimmy [James Earl, Jr.]	Plains, Ga.	1977	53

with such publications, as editors, reporters, etc. **2.** Criticism, news, etc., in newspapers and periodicals. **3.** The place of business where printing is carried on. **4.** The art, process, or business of printing. **5.** A printing press. **6.** An apparatus by which pressure is applied, as for crushing grapes to make wine. **7.** The act of crowding together. **8.** Hurry or presures of affairs: the *press* of business. **9.** The proper creases and folds in a pressed garment. **10.** A movable upright closet. [< OF < L *pressare*, freq. of *premere* to press] — **press′er** *n.*

press² (pres) *v.t.* **1.** To force into military or naval service. **2.** To put to use in a manner not intended or desired. — *n.* A commission to impress men into the public service; also, the impressment of men. [< obs. *prest* enlistment for advance pay < OF < L < *prae-* before + *stare* to stand]

press agent A person employed to advance the interests of an actor, singer, etc., by means of publicity.

press conference An interview granted by a celebrity, official, etc., to a number of journalists at the same time.

press gang A detachment of men detailed to press men into naval or military service. Also **press·gang** (pres/gang/).

press·ing (pres/ing) *adj.* **1.** Demanding immediate attention; urgent. **2.** Importunate. — **press/ing·ly** *adv.*

press·man (pres/mən) *n. pl.* **·men** (-mən) **1.** A man in charge of a press, as a printing press. **2.** *Brit.* A journalist.

press of canvas *Naut.* The maximum spread of sail that can be carried with safety. Also **press of sail.**

press·or (pres/ər) *adj. Physiol.* Increasing the functional activities of an organ, as a nerve. [< PRESS¹]

press release A bulletin prepared by a public relations department, etc., announcing an event, decision, etc.

pres·sure (presh/ər) *n.* **1.** The act of pressing, or the state of being pressed. **2.** Any force that acts against an opposing force. **3.** An impelling or constraining moral force. **4.** Urgent demands on one's time or strength. **5.** The oppressive influence or depressing effect of something hard to bear; weight. **6.** *Physics* The force acting upon a surface per unit of area. — *v.t.* **·sured, ·sur·ing** *Informal* To compel, as by forceful persuasion. [< OF < L < *premere* to press]

pressure cabin *Aeron.* An enclosed compartment in an aircraft in which air is pressurized.

pressure cooker A strong, airtight pot for cooking food at high temperature under pressure: also called *autoclave.*

pressure group A group that seeks to influence legislators and public opinion in behalf of its own special interests.

pres·sur·ize (presh/ər·īz) *v.t.* **·ized, ·iz·ing 1.** To subject to high pressure. **2.** To establish (in an aircraft compartment, special suit, etc.) an air pressure higher than the low atmospheric pressure at high altitudes. — **pres/sur·i·za/tion** *n.*

press·work (pres/wûrk/) *n.* **1.** The operating or management of a printing press. **2.** The work done by it.

pres·ti·dig·i·ta·tion (pres/tə·dij/ə·tā/shən) *n.* The practice of sleight of hand; legerdemain. [< F < Ital. < LL *praestus* nimble + L *digitus* finger] — **pres/ti·dig/i·ta/tor** *n.*

pres·tige (pres·tēzh/, pres/tij, pres·tēj/) *n.* **1.** Authority or importance based on past achievements, reputation, power, etc. **2.** Importance, respect, etc., due to the appearance of wealth or power. [< F < L *praestigium* illusion < *prae-* before + *stringere* to bind]

pres·tig·ious (pres·tij/əs, -tē/jəs) *adj.* Having a famous reputation or name; honored or well-known; illustrious. — **pres·tig/ious·ly** *adv.* — **pres·tig/ious·ness** *n.*

pres·to (pres/tō) *adj. Music* Quick; faster than allegro. — *adv.* **1.** *Music* In a presto manner: a direction to the performer. **2.** At once; speedily. — *n. Music* A presto movement or passage. [< Ital. < L *praesto* at hand]

pre·sum·a·ble (pri·zōō/mə·bəl) *adj.* That may be assumed or presumed; reasonable. — **pre·sum/a·bly** *adv.*

pre·sume (pri·zōōm/) *v.* **·sumed, ·sum·ing** *v.t.* **1.** To take for granted; assume to be true until disproved. **2.** To take upon oneself without warrant or permission; venture: usu. with the infinitive. **3.** To indicate the probability of; seem to prove: A concealed weapon *presumes* the intent to commit a crime. — *v.i.* **4.** To act or proceed presumptuously or over-confidently. **5.** To make excessive demands: with *on* or *upon.* [< OF < L < *prae-* before + *sumere* to take] — **pre·sum·ed·ly** (pri·zōō/mid·lē) *adv.* — **pre·sum/er** *n.*

pre·sump·tion (pri·zump/shən) *n.* **1.** Offensively forward or arrogant conduct or speech; insolence. **2.** The act of presuming; also, something presumed. **3.** A ground or reason for presuming. **4.** That which may be logically assumed true until disproved. **5.** *Law* The inference of a fact from circumstances that usually or necessarily attend such a fact. — **Syn. 1.** arrogance, boldness, impudence, impertinence.

pre·sump·tive (pri·zump/tiv) *adj.* **1.** Creating or affording reasonable grounds for belief. **2.** Based upon presumption: an heir *presumptive.* — **pre·sump/tive·ly** *adv.*

pre·sump·tu·ous (pri·zump/chōō·əs) *adj.* Unduly confident or bold; audacious; arrogant. — **pre·sump/tu·ous·ly** *adv.* — **pre·sump/tu·ous·ness** *n.*

pre·sup·pose (prē/sə·pōz/) *v.t.* **·posed, ·pos·ing 1.** To assume to start with. **2.** To imply as a necessary antecedent condition. — **pre·sup·po·si·tion** (prē/sup·ə·zish/ən) *n.*

pre·tend (pri·tend/) *v.t.* **1.** To assume or display a false appearance of; feign. **2.** To claim or assert falsely. **3.** To feign in play; make believe. — *v.i.* **4.** To make believe, as in play or deception. **5.** To put forward a claim: with *to.* [< L < *prae-* before + *tendere* to spread out]

pre·tend·ed (pri·ten/did) *adj.* **1.** Alleged or asserted; professed. **2.** Deceptive; false. — **pre·tend/ed·ly** *adv.*

pre·tend·er (pri·ten/dər) *n.* **1.** One who advances a claim or title; a claimant to a throne. **2.** One who pretends.

pre·tense (pri·tens/, prē/tens) *n.* **1.** A pretended claim; pretext. **2.** A false assumption of a character or condition. **3.** The act or state of pretending. **4.** A right or title asserted. **5.** The condition of being a claimant. Also *Brit.* **pre·tence/.** [< AF < Med.L < L *praetendere* to pretend]

pre·ten·sion (pri·ten/shən) *n.* **1.** A claim put forward, as to an office, privilege, rank, etc. **2.** Affectation; display. **3.** A bold or presumptuous assertion.

pre·ten·tious (pri·ten/shəs) *adj.* **1.** Making an ambitious outward show; ostentatious. **2.** Making claims, esp. when exaggerated or false. [< F *prétentieux*] — **pre·ten/tious·ly** *adv.* — **pre·ten/tious·ness** *n.*

preter- *prefix* Beyond; past; more than: also spelled *praeter-.* [< L *praeter* beyond < *prae* before]

pret·er·it (pret/ər·it) *Gram. adj.* Signifying past time or completed past action. — *n.* The tense that expresses absolute past time; also, a verb in this tense. Also **pret/er·ite.** [< OF < L < *praeter-* beyond + *ire* to go]

pre·ter·i·tive (pri·ter/ə·tiv) *adj. Gram.* Used only in a past tense or past tenses: said of certain verbs.

pre·ter·mit (prē/tər·mit/) *v.t.* **·mit·ted, ·mit·ting** To fail or cease to do; neglect; omit. [< L < *praeter-* beyond + *mittere* to send] — **pre·ter·mis·sion** (-mish/ən) *n.*

pre·ter·nat·u·ral (prē/tər·nach/ər·əl) *adj.* **1.** Diverging from or exceeding the common order of nature, but not outside the natural order: distinguished from *supernatural.* **2.** Outside the natural order. — **Syn.** See SUPERNATURAL. — **pre/ter·nat/u·ral·ism** *n.* — **pre/ter·nat/u·ral·ly** *adv.*

pre·text (prē/tekst) *n.* **1.** A fictitious reason or motive advanced to conceal a real one. **2.** A specious excuse or explanation. [< F < L < *prae-* before + *texere* to weave]

pre·tor (prē/tər), **pre·to·ri·an** (pri·tôr/ē·ən, -tō/rē-), etc. See PRAETOR, etc.

pret·ti·fy (prit/i·fī) *v.t.* **·fied, ·fy·ing** To make pretty; embellish overmuch.

pret·ty (prit/ē) *adj.* **·ti·er, ·ti·est 1.** Characterized by delicacy, gracefulness, or proportion rather than by striking beauty. **2.** Pleasant; attractive: a *pretty* melody. **3.** Decent; good; sufficient: often used ironically: A *pretty* mess you've made of it! **4.** *Informal* Rather large in size or degree; considerable. **5.** Foppish. — *adv.* To a fair extent; rather: He looked *pretty* well. — **sitting pretty** *Informal* In good circumstances. — *n. pl.* **·ties** (-tēz) A pretty person or thing. [OE *prættig* sly, cunning] — **pret/ti·ly** *adv.* — **pret/ti·ness** *n.*

pret·zel (pret/səl) *n.* A glazed, salted biscuit, usu. baked in the form of a loose knot. [< G *brezel*]

pre·vail (pri·vāl/) *v.i.* **1.** To gain mastery; triumph: with *over* or *against.* **2.** To be effective or efficacious. **3.** To use persuasion or influence successfully: with *on, upon,* or *with.* **4.** To be or become a predominant feature or quality; be prevalent. **5.** To have general or widespread use or acceptance. [< OF or L < *prae-* before + *valere* to be strong]

pre·vail·ing (pri·vā/ling) *adj.* **1.** Current; prevalent. **2.** Having effective power or influence; efficacious. — **pre·vail/ing·ly** *adv.* — **pre·vail/ing·ness** *n.*

prev·a·lent (prev/ə·lent) *adj.* **1.** Of wide extent or frequent occurrence; common. **2.** Predominant; superior. **3.** Efficacious; effective. — **prev/a·lence** *n.* — **prev/a·lent·ly** *adv.*

pre·var·i·cate (pri·var/ə·kāt) *v.i.* **·cat·ed, ·cat·ing** To speak or act in a deceptive, ambiguous, or evasive manner; lie. [< L < *prae-* before + *varicare* to straddle] — **pre·var/i·ca/tion** *n.* — **pre·var/i·ca/tor** *n.*

pre·vent (pri·vent/) *v.t.* **1.** To keep from happening, as by previous measures or preparations; preclude; thwart. **2.** To keep from doing something; forestall; hinder. [< L < *prae-* before + *venire* to come] — **pre·vent/a·ble** or **pre·vent/i·ble** *adj.* — **pre·vent/a·bil/i·ty** or **pre·vent/i·bil/i·ty** *n.* — **pre·vent/er** *n.*

— **Syn. 1.** *Prevent* suggests forcible restraint and complete stoppage. The sense of anticipation, originally understood in *prevent,* is now to be found in *preclude* and *forestall.* An event is *precluded* by circumstances which make its occurrence impossible; to *forestall* is to make advance preparation to deal with, esp. to restrain. *Avert* suggests a warding off of something. — **Ant.** permit, facilitate.

pre·ven·tion (pri·ven/shən) *n.* **1.** The act of preventing. **2.** A hindrance; obstruction.

pre·ven·tive (pri·ven/tiv) *adj.* Intended or serving to ward off harm, disease, etc.: *preventive* medicine. — *n.* That which prevents or hinders. Also **pre·vent·a·tive** (pri·ven/tə·tiv). — **pre·ven/tive·ly** *adv.* — **pre·ven/tive·ness** *n.*

pre·view (prē/vyōō/) *n.* **1.** An advance showing of a motion picture, a fashion show, etc., to invited guests. **2.** Any advance display or viewing. — *v.t.* To view in advance. Also spelled *prevue.*

pre·vi·ous (prē′vē·əs) *adj.* **1.** Existing or taking place before something else in time or order; antecedent; prior to. **2.** *Informal* Acting or occurring too soon; premature. — **previous to** Antecedent to; before. [< L < *prae-* before + *via* way] — **pre′vi·ous·ly** *adv.* — **pre′vi·ous·ness** *n.*

pre·vise (prē·vīz′) *v.t.* ·vised, ·vis·ing **1.** To foresee. **2.** To notify beforehand. [< L < *prae-* before + *videre* to see]

pre·vi·sion (prē·vizh′ən) *n.* **1.** The act or power of foreseeing; prescience; foresight. **2.** An anticipatory vision.

pre·vue (prē′vyōō′) See PREVIEW.

pre·war (prē′wôr′) *adj.* Of or pertaining to a condition, arrangement, time, etc., before a war.

prex·y (prek′sē) *pl.* ·ies *n. Slang* A president; esp., a college president. Also **prex.**

prey (prā) *n.* **1.** Any animal seized by another for food. **2.** A victim of a harmful or hostile person or influence. — *v.i.* **1.** To seek or take prey for food. **2.** To make someone a victim, as by cheating. **3.** To exert a wearing or harmful influence. Usu. with *on* or *upon.* [< OF < L *praeda* booty] — **prey′er** *n.*

Pri·am (prī′əm) In Greek legend, the father of Hector and Paris, the last king of Troy who was killed at the end of the Trojan War.

price (prīs) *n.* **1.** The amount of money, goods, etc., for which something is bought or sold. **2.** The cost at which something is obtained. **3.** Value; worth. **4.** A bribe, or anything used for a bribe. **5.** A reward for the capture or death of someone. — **beyond price 1.** Invaluable; priceless. **2.** Not bribable. — **to price out of the market** To lose one's share of a market by overpricing. — **to set a price on one's head** To offer a reward for the capture of a person, dead or alive. — *v.t.* **priced, pric·ing 1.** To set a price on; establish a price for. **2.** *Informal* To ask the price of. [< OF < L *pretium*]

price cutting The act of reducing the price of an article below the price at which it is usually advertised or sold.

price fixing 1. The establishment and maintenance of a scale of prices by specified groups of producers or distributors. **2.** The establishing by law of maximum or minimum or fixed prices for certain goods and services. **3.** The fixing of the retail price of a product by a manufacturer or producer. — *adj.* Pertaining to price fixing.

price·less (prīs′lis) *adj.* **1.** Beyond price or valuation; invaluable. **2.** *Informal* Wonderfully amusing or absurd.

price list A catalogue of goods listing their prices.

price rigging The concealed illegal fixing of prices.

prick (prik) *v.t.* **1.** To pierce slightly, as with a sharp point; puncture. **2.** To affect with sharp mental pain; sting; spur. **3.** To outline or indicate by punctures. **4.** To transplant (young plants) preparatory to later planting. **5.** To trace (a ship's course, etc.) on a chart: with *off.* **6.** To urge on with or as with a spur; goad. — *v.i.* **7.** To have or cause a stinging or piercing sensation. — **to prick up one's** (or **its**) **ears 1.** To raise the ears erect. **2.** To listen attentively. — *n.* **1.** The act of pricking; also, the sensation of being pricked. **2.** A mental sting or spur. **3.** A slender, sharp-pointed thing, as a thorn or weapon. **4.** A puncture; dot. [OE *prica* point, dot] — **prick′er** *n.*

prick·le (prik′əl) *n.* **1.** A small, sharp point, as on the bark of a plant. **2.** A tingling or stinging sensation. — *v.* ·led, ·ling *v.t.* **1.** To prick; pierce. **2.** To cause a tingling or stinging sensation in. — *v.i.* **3.** To have a stinging sensation; tingle. [OE *pricel*]

prick·ly (prik′lē) *adj.* **1.** Furnished with prickles. **2.** Stinging, as if from a prick or sting: a *prickly* sensation.

prickly heat A rash characterized by redness, itching, and small eruptions: also called *heat rash.*

prickly pear 1. A flat-stemmed cactus bearing a pear-shaped and often prickly fruit. **2.** The fruit itself.

pride (prīd) *n.* **1.** An undue sense of one's own superiority; arrogance; conceit. **2.** A proper sense of personal dignity and worth. **3.** That of which one is justly proud. **4.** The most excellent part of anything: the nation's *pride.* **5.** The best time or the flowering of something: the *pride* of summer. **6.** A group or company: said of lions. — *v.t.* **prid·ed, prid·ing** To take pride in (oneself) for something: with *on* or *upon.* [OE *prūt* proud]

— **Syn.** (noun) **1.** *Pride* manifests itself in disdain or haughtiness toward others; *self-esteem,* in more deference to one's opinions than others grant. *Conceit* is an exaggerated opinion of one's ability or worth. *Vanity* is seen in an excessive desire for admiration, while *vainglory* points to undue boasting about one's accomplishments. **6.** See FLOCK. — **Ant.** humility, modesty.

pride·ful (prīd′fəl) *adj.* Full of pride; haughty; disdainful.

prie-dieu (prē·dyœ′) *n.* A small desk with a shelf for a book, at which to kneel at prayers. [< F, pray God]

pri·er (prī′ər) *n.* One who pries: also spelled *pryer.*

priest (prēst) *n.* **1.** One esp. consecrated to the service of a divinity, and serving as mediator between the divinity and

his worshipers. **2.** In the Anglican, Greek, and Roman Catholic churches, a clergyman in the second order of the ministry, ranking next below a bishop, and having authority to administer the sacraments. [OE < L *presbyter*]

priest·craft (prēst′kraft′, -kräft′) *n.* **1.** Priestly arts and wiles: a disparaging term. **2.** The knowledge of priests.

priest·ess (prēs′tis) *n.* A woman or girl who exercises priestly functions.

priest·hood (prēst′hŏŏd) *n.* **1.** The priestly office or character. **2.** Priests collectively. [OE *prēosthad*]

priest·ly (prēst′lē) *adj.* Of, pertaining to, or befitting a priest or the priesthood. — **priest′li·ness** *n.*

priest-rid·den (prēst′rid′n) *adj.* Completely under the influence or domination of priests.

prig (prig) *n.* A formal and narrow-minded person who assumes superior virtue and wisdom. [Origin uncertain]

prig·gish (prig′ish) *adj.* Like a prig; smug. — **prig′gish·ly** *adv.* — **prig′gish·ness** *n.*

prim (prim) *adj.* Minutely or affectedly precise and formal; stiffly proper and neat. — *v.t.* **primmed, prim·ming** To fix (the face, mouth, etc.) in a precise or prim expression. [Origin uncertain] — **prim′ly** *adv.* — **prim′ness** *n.*

pri·ma·cy (prī′mə·sē) *n.* *pl.* ·cies **1.** The state of being first, as in rank or excellence. **2.** The office or province of a primate; archbishopric: also **pri′mate·ship** (-mit-ship). **3.** In the Roman Catholic Church, the office of the Pope. [< OF < Med.L < LL *primas, primatis* one of the first]

pri·ma don·na (prē′mə don′ə) **1.** A leading female singer, as in an opera company. **2.** *Informal* A temperamental or vain person. [< Ital., lit., first lady]

pri·ma fa·ci·e (prī′mə fā′shi·ē, fā′shē) *Latin* At first view; so far as at first appears. — **pri′ma-fa′ci·e** *adj.*

prima-facie evidence Evidence that, if unexplained or uncontradicted, would establish the fact alleged.

pri·mal (prī′məl) *adj.* **1.** Being at the beginning or foundation; first; original. **2.** Most important; chief. [< Med.L < L *primus*]

pri·ma·ri·ly (prī·mâr′ə·lē, prī′mə·rə·lē) *adv.* In the first place; originally; essentially.

pri·ma·ry (prī′mer·ē, -mər·ē) *adj.* **1.** First in time or origin; primitive. **2.** First in a series or sequence. **3.** First in rank or importance; chief. **4.** Constituting the fundamental or original elements of which a whole is composed; basic; elemental. **5.** Of the first stage of development; elementary; lowest: *primary* school. **6.** *Electr.* Of, pertaining to, or noting an inducing current or its circuit: a *primary* coil. **7.** *Chem.* **a** Having some characteristic in the first degree, as an initial replacement of one atom or radical. **b** Having a carbon atom directly joined to only one other carbon atom in a molecule. — *n.* *pl.* ·ries **1.** That which is first in rank, dignity, or importance. **2.** *Usu. pl.* A direct primary election. **3.** One of the primary colors. **4.** A primary cell. **5.** *Ornithol.* One of the large flight feathers of the pinion of a bird's wings. **6.** *Astron.* A body, as a planet, as distinguished from another body that revolves around it, as a satellite. [< L *primus* first]

primary cell *Electr.* Any of several devices consisting of two electrodes immersed in an electrolyte and capable of generating a current by chemical action when the electrodes are in contact through a conducting wire. Also called *voltaic cell.*

primary colors Any of several sets of colors considered basic to all other colors, as red, green, and blue (**physiological, fundamental,** or **additive primaries**); red, yellow, green, blue, black, and white (**psychological** or **subtractive primaries**); and red, yellow, and blue (**painting primaries**).

primary election A direct primary election.

primary school A school for very young pupils, usu. the first four grades of elementary school.

pri·mate (prī′mit, -māt) *n.* **1.** The prelate highest in rank in a nation or province. **2.** Any of an order of mammals, including the tarsiers, lemurs, marmosets, monkeys, apes, and man. [< OF < LL < L *primus*] — **pri·ma·tial** (prī·mā′shəl) *adj.*

pri·ma·tol·o·gy (prī′mə·tol′ə·jē) *n.* The study of the origin, structure, evolution, and classification of primates. — **pri′ma·tol′o·gist** *n.*

prime¹ (prīm) *adj.* **1.** First in rank, dignity, or importance. **2.** First in value or quality; first-rate. **3.** First in time or order; original; primitive. **4.** *Math.* Divisible by no whole number except itself and unity. Two or more numbers are said to be *prime* to each other when they have no common factor except unity. **5.** Not derived; first. — *n.* **1.** The period of full vigor, beauty, and power succeeding youth and preceding age. **2.** The period of full perfection in anything. **3.** The beginning of anything; dawn; spring. **4.** The best of anything: a *prime* grade. **5.** *Math.* A prime number. **6.** A mark or accent (′) written above and to the right of a letter or figure; also, an inch, a minute, etc., as indicated by that sign. **7.** *Music* Unison. — *v.* **primed, prim·ing** *v.t.* **1.** To prepare; make ready. **2.** To put a primer into (a gun, etc.) preparatory to firing. **3.** To pour water into (a pump) so as to displace air and promote suction. 4. To cover (a surface) with sizing, a first coat of paint, etc. 5. To supply beforehand with facts, information, etc.; brief. — *v.i.* 6. To make something ready, as for firing, pumping, etc. [< OF < L *primus*] — **prime′ly** *adv.* — **prime′ness** *n.*

prime² (prīm) *n. Often cap. Eccl.* The second of the seven canonical hours. [OE < LL *prima (hora)* first (hour)]

prime meridian A meridian from which longitude is reckoned, now, generally, the one that passes through Greenwich, England.

prime minister The chief minister and head of a cabinet, and often the chief executive of a government.

prim·er¹ (prim′ər) *n.* 1. An elementary textbook; esp., a beginning reading book. 2. *Printing* Either of two sizes of type, **great primer** (18-point) and **long primer** (10-point). [< Med.L < L *primus*]

prim·er² (prī′mər) *n.* 1. Any device, as a cap, tube, etc., used to detonate the main charge of a gun, mine, etc. 2. One who or that which primes.

pri·me·val (prī·mē′vəl) *adj.* Belonging to the first ages; primitive. [< L *primus* first + *aevum* age] — **pri·me′val·ly** *adv.*

primi- *combining form* First. [< L *primus* first]

pri·mi·ge·ni·al (prī′mi·jē′nē·əl) *adj.* Being the first or first-born; primal; original. [< L *primus* + *genus* kind]

prim·ing (prī′ming) *n.* 1. That with which anything is primed. 2. A combustible composition used to ignite an explosive charge. 3. The first layer of paint laid on a surface.

prim·i·tive (prim′ə·tiv) *adj.* 1. Pertaining to the beginning or origin; earliest; primary; not derived. 2. Resembling the manners or style of early times; simple; crude. 3. *Anthropol.* Of or pertaining to the earliest anthropological forms or civilizations. 4. *Biol.* a Being or occurring at an early stage of development or growth; first-formed; rudimentary. b Not much changed by evolution: a *primitive* species. — *n.* 1. An artist, or a work of art, belonging to an early period; also, a work resembling such art, or an artist producing it. 2. One who or that which is primitive. [< F < L < *primus* first] — **prim′i·tive·ly** *adv.* — **prim′i·tive·ness, prim′i·tiv·i·ty** *n.*

prim·i·tiv·ism (prim′ə·tiv·iz′əm) *n.* Belief in or adherence to primitive forms and customs.

pri·mo·gen·i·tor (prī′mə·jen′ə·tər) *n.* An earliest ancestor; a forefather. [< Med.L < L *primo* first + *genitor* father]

pri·mo·gen·i·ture (prī′mə·jen′ə·chər) *n.* 1. The state of being the first-born child. 2. The exclusive right of the eldest son to inherit the property, title, etc., of a parent. [< Med.L < L *primo* first + *gignere* to beget]

pri·mor·di·al (prī·môr′dē·əl) *adj.* 1. First in time; original; elemental. 2. *Biol.* First in order or appearance in the growth or development of an organism. [< LL < L *primus* first + *ordiri* to begin a web] — **pri·mor′di·al·ly** *adv.*

primp (primp) *v.t. & v.i.* To prink; dress up, esp. with superfluous attention to detail.

prim·rose (prim′rōz) *n.* 1. An early-blossoming perennial herb with tufted basal leaves and variously colored flowers. 2. The evening primrose. 3. A pale yellow color. [ME < OF < Med.L < L *primus* first]

prince (prins) *n.* 1. A nonreigning male member of a royal family. 2. A male monarch or sovereign. 3. *Brit.* The son of a sovereign or of a son of the sovereign. 4. One of a high order of nobility. 5. The ruler of a small state. 6. One of the highest rank of any class: a merchant *prince*. [< OF < L < *primus* first + stem of *capere* to take]

Prince Al·bert (al′bûrt) A long, double-breasted frock coat.

prince consort The husband of a reigning female sovereign.

prince·ling (prins′ling) *n.* 1. A young prince. 2. A subordinate prince. Also **prince′let** (-lit).

prince·ly (prins′lē) *adj.* **li·er, ·li·est** 1. Liberal; generous. 2. Like or suitable for a prince. 3. Having the rank of a prince. — *adv.* In a princely manner. — **prince′li·ness** *n.*

Prince of Darkness Satan.

Prince of Peace Jesus Christ.

Prince of Wales The title conferred on the eldest son of the British sovereign, to make that son heir apparent.

prin·cess (prin′sis) *n.* 1. A nonreigning female member of a royal family. 2. The consort of a prince. 3. Formerly, a female sovereign. 4. *Brit.* A daughter of the sovereign or of a son of the sovereign. [< F *princesse*]

prin·cesse (prin·ses′, prin′sis) *adj.* Designating a woman's close-fitting garment hanging in an unbroken line from shoulder to flared hem. Also **prin′cess.** [< F, princess]

princess royal The eldest daughter of a sovereign.

prin·ci·pal (prin′sə·pəl) *adj.* First in rank, character, or importance. — *n.* 1. One who takes a leading part in some action. 2. *Law* a The actor in a crime, or one present aiding and abetting. b The employer of one who acts as an agent. c One primarily liable for whom another has become surety. d The capital or body of an estate. 3. One who is at the head

of some body or society. 4. The head teacher, master, or officer of a school. 5. Property or capital, as opposed to interest or income. 6. The chief truss or rafter of a roof. [< F < L *princepe* first, principal] — **prin·ci·pal·ly** *adv.* — **prin′ci·pal·ship** *n.*

principal axis *Optics* The imaginary line passing through the center of a lens or mirror at right angles to each surface.

principal clause *Gram.* An independent clause. See under CLAUSE.

prin·ci·pal·i·ty (prin′sə·pal′ə·tē) *n. pl. ·ties* 1. The territory of a reigning prince, or one that gives to a prince a title of courtesy. 2. The state, office, or jurisdiction of a prince.

principal parts The inflected forms of a verb from which all other inflected forms may be derived. In English, the principal parts of a verb are the infinitive (go, walk), the past tense (went, walked), and the past participle (gone, walked). In this dictionary, when appropriate, the past, past participle, and present participle are shown (gave, given, giving). When, however, the principal parts are entirely regular in formation, adding *-ed* and *-ing* directly to the infinitive without spelling modification, they are not shown. In cases where the past tense and past participle are identical, only the one is shown (behaved, behaving).

prin·ci·ple (prin′sə·pəl) *n.* 1. A general truth or law, basic to other truths. 2. A rule of personal conduct. 3. Moral standards collectively: a man of *principle*. 4. That which is inherent in anything, determining its nature. 5. A primary source or fundamental cause. 6. An established mode of action or operation in natural phenomena: the *principle* of relativity. 7. *Chem.* An essential constituent of a compound or substance. [< L *principium* a beginning]

prin·ci·pled (prin′sə·pəld) *adj.* Having or characterized by ethical principles: often in combination: high-principled.

prink (pringk) *v.t.* 1. To dress (oneself) for show. — *v.i.* 2. To dress oneself showily or fussily. — **prink′er** *n.*

print (print) *n.* 1. An impression with ink from type, plates, etc.; printed characters collectively; also, any printed matter. 2. Anything printed from an engraved plate or lithographic stone; a proof; also, a printed picture or design. 3. An impression or mark made upon a substance by pressure; imprint: the *print* of a shoe in the snow. 4. Any fabric stamped with a design. 5. Any tool or device bearing a pattern or design, or that upon which it is impressed. 6. *Photog.* A positive picture made from a negative. — **in print** Printed; also, for sale in printed form. — **out of print** No longer on sale, the edition being exhausted: said of books, etc. — *v.t.* 1. To mark, as with inked type, a stamp, die, etc. 2. To stamp or impress (a mark, seal, etc.) on or into a surface. 3. To fix as if by impressing: The scene is *printed* on my memory. 4. To produce (a book, newspaper, etc.) by the application of inked type, plates, etc., to paper or similar material. 5. To cause to be put in print; publish. 6. To write in letters similar to those used in print. 7. *Photog.* To produce (a positive picture) by transmitting light through a negative onto a sensitized surface. — *v.i.* 8. To be a printer. 9. To take or give an impression in printing. 10. To form letters similar to printed ones. [< OF < L *premere* to press] — **print′a·ble** *adj.* — **print′er** *n.*

printer's devil Devil (def. 7).

print·ing (prin′ting) *n.* 1. The making and issuing of printed matter. 2. The act of reproducing a design upon a surface. 3. That which is printed. 4. The number of copies of anything printed at one time. 5. Writing that resembles printed matter. 6. The act of one who or that which prints.

printing press A mechanism for printing from an inked surface, operating by pressure.

print·out (print′out′) *n.* Material printed automatically, as by a computer.

pri·or¹ (prī′ər) *adj.* Preceding in time, order, or importance. — **prior to** Before. [< L, earlier, superior]

pri·or² (prī′ər) *n.* A monastic officer next in rank below an abbot. [OE < L] — **pri′or·ate** (-it) *n.*

pri·or·ess (prī′ər·is) *n.* A woman holding a position corresponding to that of a prior; a nun next below an abbess.

pri·or·i·ty (prī·ôr′ə·tē, -or′-) *n. pl. ·ties* 1. Antecedence; precedence. 2. A first right established on emergency or need. 3. A certificate giving a first right to a manufacturer or contractor.

pri·or·y (prī′ər·ē) *n. pl. ·or·ies* A monastic house presided over by a prior or prioress. [< OF *priorie* < Med.L *prioria*]

prism (priz′əm) *n.* 1. *Geom.* A solid whose bases or ends are any similar equal and parallel plane figures, and whose lateral faces are parallelograms. 2. *Optics* A prism made of glass or other transparent substance and usually having triangular ends, used to produce a spectrum or to refract light beams. [< LL < Gk. < *prizein* to saw]

pris·mat·ic (priz·mat′ik) *adj.* 1. Refracted or formed by a prism. 2. Resembling the spectrum; exhibiting rainbow tints. **3.** Pertaining to or shaped like a prism. Also **pris-mat'i-cal.** — **pris-mat'i-cal-ly** adv.

pris-on (priz'ən) n. **1.** A public building for the safekeeping of persons in legal custody; a penitentiary. **2.** Any place of confinement. **3.** Imprisonment. — v.t. To imprison. [< OF < F < prehendere to seize]

pris-on-er (priz'ən-ər, priz'nər) n. **1.** One who is confined in a prison or whose liberty is forcibly restrained. **2.** A person confined for any reason. [< OF prisonier]

pris-sy (pris'ē) Informal adj. **·si-er, ·si-est** Effeminate; overprecise; prim. [Blend of PRIM or PRECISE + SISSY]

pris-tine (pris'tēn, -tin; Brit. pris'tīn) adj. **1.** Of or pertaining to the earliest state or time; primitive. **2.** Extremely pure; untouched; unspoiled. [< L pristinus primitive]

prith-ee (prith'ē) interj. Archaic I pray thee.

pri-va-cy (prī'və-sē) n. pl. **·cies 1.** The condition of being private; seclusion. **2.** The state of being secret; secrecy.

pri-vate (prī'vit) adj. **1.** Removed from public view; secluded. **2.** Not for public or common use. **3.** Having no official rank, character, office, etc.: a private citizen. **4.** Not generally known; secret. **5.** Not common or usual; special: a private interpretation. **6.** Individual; personal: one's private opinion. — n. **1.** Mil. An enlisted man ranking below a corporal. Abbr. Pvt. See table at GRADE. **2.** pl. The genitals. — **in private** In secret. [< L privatus apart from the state] — **pri'vate-ly** adv. — **pri'vate-ness** n.

private detective A detective employed by a private citizen, business enterprise, etc., rather than by a city or state.

private enterprise Free enterprise.

pri-va-teer (prī'və-tir') n. **1.** A vessel owned and commanded by private persons, but carrying on maritime war under letters of marque. **2.** The commander or one of the crew of a privateer: also **pri'va-teers'man** (-tirz'mən) — v.i. To cruise in or as a privateer. — **pri'va-teer'ing** n.

private eye Informal A private detective.

private first class A soldier ranking next above a private and below a corporal. Abbr. Pfc, Pfc. See table at GRADE.

private school U.S. A school maintained under private or corporate management, usu. for profit.

private secretary A secretary who works for one individual only and is usu. entrusted with confidential matters.

pri-va-tion (prī-vā'shən) n. The state of lacking something necessary or desirable; esp., want of the common comforts of life. [< L privare to set apart]

priv-a-tive (priv'ə-tiv) adj. **1.** Causing privation, want, or destitution; depriving. **2.** Gram. Altering a word so as to express a negative instead of a positive meaning: privative particles (such prefixes and suffixes as a-, an-, in-, -less). — n. Gram. A privative prefix or suffix. [< L privativus] — **priv'a-tive-ly** adv. — **priv'a-tive-ness** n.

priv-et (priv'it) n. An ornamental, bushy shrub of the olive family, with white flowers and black berries, used for hedges. [Earlier primet; origin unknown]

priv-i-lege (priv'ə-lij) n. **1.** A special or peculiar benefit, favor, or advantage. **2.** An exemption or immunity by virtue of one's office or station. **3.** A fundamental or basic civil, legal, or political right; the privilege of voting. — v.t. **·leged, ·leg-ing 1.** To grant a privilege to. **2.** To exempt or free: with from. [< OF < L privus one's own + lex law]

priv-i-leged (priv'ə-lijd) adj. Having or enjoying a privilege.

priv-y (priv'ē) adj. **1.** Participating with another or others in the knowledge of a secret transaction: with to: privy to the plot. **2.** Archaic Secret. — n. pl. **priv-ies 1.** Law One who is concerned with another in a matter affecting the interests of both. **2.** A small toilet or outhouse. [< F < L privatus. See PRIVATE.] — **priv'i-ly** adv.

privy council Any body of advisers or counselors, as appointed by a sovereign for his personal use.

Privy Council 1. In Great Britain, the sovereign's personal council whose duties have been largely assumed by the cabinet. **2.** In Canada, a body that advises the Governor General.

privy seal In Great Britain, the seal used by the sovereign on papers that later pass under the great seal or do not demand the great seal.

prix fixe (prē fēks') A meal served at a fixed price; table d'hôte. Compare À LA CARTE. [< F, fixed price]

prize[1] (prīz) n. **1.** That which is offered or won as a reward for superiority or success, as in a contest. **2.** Anything to be striven for. **3.** Anything offered or won, as in a lottery, etc. — adj. **1.** Offered or awarded as a prize: a prize medal. **2.** Having drawn a prize; entitled to a prize. **3.** Highly valued or esteemed. — v.t. **prized, priz-ing 1.** To value highly. **2.** To estimate the value of; appraise. [Var. of PRICE.]

prize[2] (prīz) n. In international law, property, as a vessel and cargo, captured by a belligerent at sea in conformity with the laws of war. — v.t. **prized, priz-ing 1.** To seize as a prize, as a ship. **2.** To raise or force with a lever; pry: also spelled prise. [< F prise something taken; booty]

prize court A court sitting for the adjudication of prizes taken at sea in wartime.

prize fight A fight between professional boxers for a prize, a certain sum of money, etc., generally limited to a specified number of rounds. — **prize fighter** — **prize fighting**

prize ring A roped enclosure within which boxers fight.

pro[1] (prō) n. pl. **pros 1.** An argument or vote in favor of something: in the phrase pros and cons. **2.** Usu. pl. One who votes for or favors a proposal. — adv. In behalf of; in favor of; for: to argue pro and con. [< L, for]

pro[2] (prō) n. pl. **pros** Informal **1.** A professional athlete. **2.** Any expert in any field.

pro-[1] prefix **1.** Forward; to or toward the front from a position behind; forth: produce, to lead forth; project, to throw forth. **2.** Forth from its place; away: profugate, to flee away. **3.** To the front of; forward and down: prolapse, to slip forward and down. **4.** Forward in time or direction: proceed, to go forward. **5.** In behalf of: prolocutor. **6.** In place of; substituted for: proconsul. **7.** In favor of: pro-Russian. [< L pro- < pro before, forward, for]

pro-[2] prefix **1.** Prior; occurring earlier in time: prognosis. **2.** Situated in front; forward; before: prognathous. [< Gk. pro- < pro before, in front]

pro-a (prō'ə) n. A swift Malaysian vessel, propelled by sails or oars. Also called prahu. [< Malay prāu]

prob-a-bil-i-ty (prob'ə-bil'ə-tē) n. pl. **·ties 1.** The state or quality of being probable; likelihood. **2.** A probable event, statement, condition, etc.

prob-a-ble (prob'ə-bəl) adj. **1.** Likely to be true or to happen, but leaving room for doubt. **2.** That renders something worthy of belief, but falls short of demonstration: probable evidence. — **Syn.** See APPARENT. [< OF < L probare to prove, test]

prob-a-bly (prob'ə-blē) adv. In all probability.

pro-bate (prō'bāt) adj. **1.** Of or pertaining to a probate court. **2.** Pertaining to making proof. — n. **1.** Formal, legal proof, as of a will. **2.** The right or jurisdiction of proving wills. — v.t. **·bat-ed, ·bat-ing** To obtain probate of, as a will. [< L < probare to prove]

probate court A court having jurisdiction of the proof of wills, of guardianships, and of the settlement of estates.

pro-ba-tion (prō-bā'shən) n. **1.** Law A method of allowing a person convicted of a minor offense to go at large but usu. under the supervision of a probation officer. **2.** A proceeding or period designed to test character, qualifications, etc., as of a new employee. **3.** The status or condition of one being tried out, or free under suspension of sentence: to be on probation. **4.** The act of proving; also, proof. — **pro-ba'tion-al, pro-ba'tion-ar'y** adj.

pro-ba-tion-er (prō-bā'shən-ər) n. One on probation.

probation officer A person delegated to supervise an offender on suspended sentence.

pro-ba-tive (prō'bə-tiv) adj. **1.** Serving to prove or test. **2.** Pertaining to probation; proving. Also **pro-ba-to-ry** (prō'bə-tôr'ē, -tō'rē)

probe (prōb) v. **probed, prob-ing** v.t. **1.** To explore with a probe. **2.** To investigate or examine thoroughly. — v.t. **3.** To penetrate; search. — n. **1.** Surg. An instrument for exploring cavities, wounds, etc. **2.** That which proves or tests. **3.** U.S. A searching investigation or inquiry, esp. into crime. [< LL proba proof] — **prob'er** n.

pro-bi-ty (prō'bə-tē, prob'ə-) n. Virtue or integrity tested and confirmed. [< F < L probus good, honest]

prob-lem (prob'ləm) n. **1.** A perplexing question or situation, esp. when difficult or uncertain of solution. **2.** Any puzzling or difficult circumstance or person. **3.** Math. A proposition in which some operation or construction is required, as to bisect an angle. — adj. **1.** Presenting and dealing with a problem. **2.** Being a problem. [< OF < L < Gk. < pro- forward + ballein to throw]

prob-lem-at-ic (prob'ləm-at'ik) adj. Constituting or involving a problem; questionable; contingent. Also **prob'lem-at'i-cal.** — **prob'lem-at'i-cal-ly** adv.

pro-bos-cis (prō-bos'is) n. pl. **·bos-cis-es** or **·bos-ci-des** (-bos'ə-dēz) **1.** Zool. **a** A long flexible snout, as of the tapir. **b** The trunk of an elephant. **2.** Entomol. Any of various tubular feeding structures of certain insects, as bees and mosquitoes. **3.** A human nose: a humorous term. [< L < Gk. < pro- before + boskein to feed]

pro-caine (prō-kān', prō'kān) n. A white crystalline compound, $C_{13}H_{20}O_2N_2$, used chiefly in its hydrochloride form as a local anesthetic. [< PRO-[1] + (CO)CAINE]

pro-ce-dure (prə-sē'jər) n. **1.** A manner of proceeding or acting in any course of action. **2.** The methods or forms of conducting a business, parliamentary affairs, etc. **3.** A course of action; a proceeding. — **pro-ce'du-ral** adj.

pro-ceed (prə-sēd') v.i. **1.** To go on or forward, esp. after a stop. **2.** To begin and carry on an action or process. **3.** To issue or come, as from some cause, source, or origin: with from. **4.** Law To institute and carry on legal proceedings. [< OF < L < pro- forward + cedere to go] — **pro-ceed'er** n.

pro-ceed-ing (prə-sē'ding) n. **1.** An act or course of action; also, a particular act or course of action. **2.** The act of one

who or that which proceeds. **3.** *pl.* The records or minutes of the meetings of a society, etc. **4.** *Law* Any action instituted in a court.
pro·ceeds (prō′sēdz) *n.pl.* The amount derived from the disposal of goods, work, or the use of capital; return; yield.
proc·ess (pros′es, *esp.* Brit. prō′ses) *n.* **1.** A course or method of operations in the production of something. **2.** A series of continuous actions that bring about a particular result, end, or condition: the *process* of growth. **3.** A forward movement; advance; course. **4.** *Law* A judicial writ or order. **b** A writ issued to bring a defendant into court. **c** The whole course of proceedings in a cause. **5.** *Biol.* An accessory outgrowth or prominence of an organism or any of its parts: vertebral *process*. — *adj.* **1.** Produced by a special method: *process* butter; *process* cheese. **2.** Pertaining to, for, or made by a mechanical or chemical photographic process: a *process* illustration. — *v.t.* **1.** To subject to a routine procedure: to *process* an application. **2.** To treat or prepare by a special method. **3.** *Law* **a** To issue or serve a process on. **b** To proceed against. [See PROCEED.] — **proc′es·sor** or **proc′ess·er** *n.*
pro·ces·sion (prə·sesh′ən, prō-) *n.* **1.** An array, as of persons or vehicles, arranged in succession and moving in a formal manner; a parade; also, any continuous course: the *procession* of the stars. **2.** The act of proceeding or issuing forth: the *procession* of the Holy Ghost from the Father. — *v.i.* To march in procession. [See PROCEED.]
pro·ces·sion·al (prə·sesh′ən·əl) *adj.* Of, pertaining to, or moving in a procession. — *n.* **1.** A hymn sung at the opening of a church service, during the entrance of the choir, etc. **2.** The music played or sung during a procession. — **pro·ces′sion·al·ly** *adv.*
pro·claim (prō·klām′) *v.t.* **1.** To announce or make known publicly or officially; declare. **2.** To make plain; manifest. **3.** To outlaw, prohibit, or restrict by proclamation. [< L < *pro-* before + *clamare* to call] — **pro·claim′er** *n.*
proc·la·ma·tion (prok′lə·mā′shən) *n.* **1.** The act of proclaiming. **2.** That which is proclaimed.
pro·cliv·i·ty (prō·kliv′ə·tē) *n.* *pl.* **·ties** Natural tendency: usu. with *to*. [< L < *pro-* before + *clivus* slope]
pro·con·sul (prō·kon′səl, prō′kon′-) *n.* **1.** In ancient Rome, an official who exercised authority over a province or an army. **2.** A governor of a dependency; a viceroy. [< L] — **pro·con′su·lar** (-sə·lər, -syə-) *adj.* — **pro·con′su·late** (-sə·lit, -syə-), **pro·con′sul·ship** *n.*
pro·cras·ti·nate (prō·kras′tə·nāt) *v.* **·nat·ed, ·nat·ing** *v.i.* **1.** To put off taking action until a future time; be dilatory. — *v.t.* **2.** To defer or postpone. [< L *procrastinare*] — **pro·cras′ti·na′tion** *n.* — **pro·cras′ti·na′tor** *n.*
pro·cre·ate (prō′krē·āt) *v.t.* **·at·ed, ·at·ing** **1.** To engender or beget (offspring). **2.** To originate; produce. [< L < *pro-* before + *creare* to create] — **pro′cre·ant** *adj.* — **pro′cre·a′tion** *n.* — **pro′cre·a′tor** *n.*
pro·cre·a·tive (prō′krē·ā′tiv) *adj.* **1.** Possessed of generative power; reproductive. **2.** Pertaining to procreation.
Pro·crus·te·an (prō·krus′tē·ən) *adj.* **1.** Pertaining to or characteristic of Procrustes. **2.** Ruthlessly or violently bringing about conformity.
Pro·crus·tes (prō·krus′tēz) In Greek mythology, a giant of Attica, who tied travelers to an iron bed and amputated or stretched their limbs until they fitted it.
procto- *combining form* *Med.* Related to or affecting the rectum. Also, before vowels, **proct-.** [< Gk. *proktos* anus]
proc·tol·o·gy (prok·tol′ə·jē) *n.* The branch of medicine that treats of the diseases of the rectum. — **proc·to·log·i·cal** (prok′tə·loj′i·kəl) *adj.* — **proc·tol′o·gist** *n.*
proc·tor (prok′tər) *n.* **1.** An agent acting for another; attorney; proxy. **2.** A university or college official charged with maintaining order, supervising examinations, etc. — *v.t. & v.i.* To supervise (an examination). [ME *proketour, procutour*] — **proc·to·ri·al** (prok·tôr′ē·əl, -tō′rē-) *adj.*
pro·cum·bent (prō·kum′bənt) *adj.* **1.** *Bot.* Lying on the ground; trailing, as certain vines and plants. **2.** Lying down or on the face; prone; prostrate. [< L < *pro-* forward + *cumbere* to lie down]
pro·cur·a·ble (prō·kyoor′ə·bəl) *adj.* That can be procured.
pro·cur·ance (prō·kyoor′əns) *n.* The process of procuring.
proc·u·ra·tor (prok′yə·rā′tər) *n.* **1.** A person authorized to act for and manage the affairs of another. **2.** In ancient Rome, one who had charge of the imperial revenues or, in a province, was an administrator. [See PROCURE.] — **proc′u·ra·to·ri·al** (-rə·tôr′ē·əl, -tō′rē-) *adj.* — **proc′u·ra·tor·ship** *n.*
pro·cure (prō·kyoor′) *v.* **·cured, ·cur·ing** *v.t.* **1.** To obtain by some effort or means; acquire. **2.** To bring about; cause. **3.** To obtain (women) for the gratification of the lust of others. — *v.i.* **4.** To be a procurer or procuress. — **Syn.** See GET. [< OF < L < *pro-* on behalf of + *curare* to attend to] — **pro·cure′ment** *n.*

pro·cur·er (prō·kyoor′ər) *n.* One who procures for another, as to gratify lust; a pimp. — **pro·cur′ess** *n.fem.*
Pro·cy·on (prō′sē·on) *n.* One of the 20 brightest stars, 2.12 magnitude; Alpha in the constellation Canis Minor: also called *Dog Star*. [< L < Gk. *Prokyōn*]
prod (prod) *v.t.* **prod·ded, prod·ding** **1.** To punch or poke with or as with a pointed instrument. **2.** To arouse mentally; urge; goad. — *n.* **1.** Any pointed instrument used for prodding; a goad. **2.** A thrust or punch; a poke. **3.** A reminder. [Origin unknown] — **prod′der** *n.*
prod·i·gal (prod′ə·gəl) *adj.* **1.** Addicted to wasteful expenditure, as of money, time, or strength; extravagant. **2.** Yielding in profusion; bountiful. **3.** Lavish; profuse. — *n.* One who is wasteful or profligate; a spendthrift. [< L *prodigus* wasteful] — **prod′i·gal·ly** *adv.*
prod·i·gal·i·ty (prod′ə·gal′ə·tē) *n.* *pl.* **·ties** **1.** Extravagance; wastefulness. **2.** Great abundance; lavishness. **3.** Extreme generosity; bounteousness.
pro·di·gious (prə·dij′əs) *adj.* **1.** Enormous or extraordinary in size, quantity, or degree; vast. **2.** Marvelous; amazing. [< L *prodigium* omen] — **pro·di′gious·ly** *adv.* — **pro·di′gious·ness** *n.*
prod·i·gy (prod′ə·jē) *n.* *pl.* **·gies** **1.** A person having remarkable qualities or powers: a violin *prodigy*. **2.** Something extraordinary. **3.** Something out of the ordinary course of nature; a monstrosity. [< L *prodigium*]
pro·duce (*v.* prə·d(y)ōōs′, -dyōōs′; *n.* prod′ōōs, -yōōs, prō′d(y)ōōs, -dyōōs) *v.* **·duced, ·duc·ing** *v.t.* **1.** To bring forth or bear; yield, as young or a natural product. **2.** To bring forth by mental effort; compose, write, etc. **3.** To bring about: His words *produced* a violent reaction. **4.** To bring to view; exhibit: to *produce* evidence. **5.** To manufacture; make. **6.** To bring to performance before the public, as a play. **7.** To extend or lengthen, as a line. **8.** *Econ.* To create (anything with exchangeable value). — *v.i.* **9.** To yield or generate an appropriate product or result. — *n.* That which is produced; a product; esp. farm products collectively. [< L < *pro-* forward + *ducere* to lead] — **pro·duc′i·ble** *adj.*
pro·duc·er (prə·d(y)ōō′sər, -dyōō′-) *n.* **1.** One who or that which produces, esp. one who makes things for sale and use. **2.** One who finances and generally controls the production of a play, concert, motion picture, etc.
prod·uct (prod′əkt, -ukt) *n.* **1.** Anything produced or obtained as a result of some operation or work, as by generation, growth, labor, study, or skill. **2.** A result. **3.** *Math.* The result obtained by multiplication.
pro·duc·tion (prə·duk′shən) *n.* **1.** The act or process of producing. **2.** That which is produced. **3.** Any tangible result of industrial, artistic, or literary effort.
pro·duc·tive (prə·duk′tiv) *adj.* **1.** Producing or tending to produce; fertile; creative, as of artistic things. **2.** Producing or tending to produce profits or increase in quantity, quality, or value. **3.** Causing; resulting in: with *of*. — **pro·duc′tive·ly** *adv.* — **pro·duc·tiv·i·ty** (prō′duk·tiv′ə·tē), **pro·duc′tive·ness** *n.*
pro·em (prō′əm) *n.* An introductory statement; preface. [< OF < L < Gk. *prooimion* overture] — **pro·e·mi·al** (prō·ē′mē·əl) *adj.*
prof·a·na·tion (prof′ə·nā′shən) *n.* **1.** The act of profaning; also, an instance of it. **2.** Abusive or improper treatment of anything.
pro·fane (prə·fān′, prō-) *v.t.* **·faned, ·fan·ing** **1.** To treat (something sacred) with irreverence or abuse; desecrate; pollute. **2.** To put to an unworthy or degrading use; debase. — *adj.* **1.** Manifesting irreverence or disrespect toward the Deity or sacred things. **2.** Not religious or concerned with religious things; secular. **3.** Vulgar; common; coarse. [< F < L < *profanus* before or outside the temple, hence, unsacred] — **pro·fan·a·to·ry** (prə·fan′ə·tôr′ē, -tō′rē) *adj.* — **pro·fane′ly** *adv.* — **pro·fan′er** *n.* — **pro·fane′ness** *n.*
pro·fan·i·ty (prə·fan′ə·tē) *n.* *pl.* **·ties** **1.** The state of being profane. **2.** Profane speech or action.
— **Syn.** **2.** *Profanity* may refer to irreverent use of a sacred name, as well as to the use of words considered lewd or coarse. *Blasphemy* is a much stronger word; *profanity* may be thoughtless or careless speech, but *blasphemy* denotes a degree of malicious insult to sacred things. *Cursing* and *swearing* are types of *profanity*; *cursing* involves the uttering of imprecations in the name of God, generally as an expression of rage or frustration, while *swearing* is the uttering of rash or empty oaths.
pro·fess (prə·fes′) *v.t.* **1.** To declare openly; avow; affirm. **2.** To assert, usu. insincerely: to *profess* remorse. **3.** To declare or affirm faith in. **4.** To have as one's profession: to *profess* the law. **5.** To receive into a religious order. — *v.i.* **6.** To make open declaration; avow. **7.** To take the vows of a religious order. [< L < *pro-* before < *fateri* to confess]
pro·fess·ed·ly (prə·fes′id·lē) *adv.* **1.** By open profession; avowedly. **2.** Pretendedly.

pro·fes·sion (prə-fesh′ən) *n.* **1.** An occupation that properly involves a liberal, scientific, or artistic education. **2.** The collective body of those following such occupations. **3.** The act of professing or declaring; declaration: *professions* of good will. **4.** That which is avowed or professed; a declaration. **5.** The act of binding oneself to a religious order; also, the condition of being so bound. — **Syn.** See OCCUPATION.

pro·fes·sion·al (prə-fesh′ən-əl) *adj.* **1.** Connected with, preparing for, engaged in, appropriate to, or conforming to a profession: *professional* courtesy. **2.** Of or pertaining to an occupation pursued for gain: a *professional* ball player. — *n.* **1.** One who pursues as a business some vocation or occupation. **2.** One who engages for money to compete in sports. **3.** One skilled in a profession, craft, or art. — **pro·fes′sion·al·ism** *n.* — **pro·fes′sion·al·ly** *adv.*

pro·fes·sor (prə-fes′ər) *n.* **1.** A teacher of the highest rank in a university or college, or in an institution where professional or technical studies are pursued. ◆ *Professor* may be abbreviated *Prof.* before the full name but is usu. written out before the surname, as *Professor Smith.* **2.** One who professes skill and offers instruction in some sport or art. — **pro·fes′sor·ship** *n.*

pro·fes·so·ri·al (prō′fə-sôr′ē-əl, -sō′rē-, prof′ə-) *adj.* Of, pertaining to, or characteristic of a professor; pedagogic; academic. — **pro′fes·so′ri·al·ly** *adv.*

prof·fer (prof′ər) *v.t.* To offer for acceptance. — *n.* The act of proffering, or that which is proffered. [< AF, OF < L *pro-* in behalf of + *offere* to offer] — **prof′fer·er** *n.*

pro·fi·cien·cy (prə-fish′ən-sē) *n.* *pl.* **·cies** A high state of attainment in some knowledge, art, or skill; expertness.

pro·fi·cient (prə-fish′ənt) *adj.* Thoroughly versed, as in an art or science. — *n.* An expert. [< L < *pro-* forward + *facere* to do] — **pro·fi′cient·ly** *adv.*

pro·file (prō′fīl, *esp. Brit.* prō′fēl) *n.* **1.** The outline of a human face or figure as seen from the side; also, a drawing of this outline. **2.** Any outline or contour. **3.** A short biographical sketch vividly presenting the most striking characteristics of a personality. **4.** *Archit.* The outline of a perpendicular section of a building, etc., or the contour of an architectural member. **5.** *Geol.* A vertical section of the earth's crust. — *v.t.* **·filed, ·fil·ing** **1.** To draw a profile of. **2.** To write or make a profile of. [< Ital. *profilare* to draw in outline < L *pro-* forward + *filum* thread, line]

prof·it (prof′it) *n.* **1.** Any advantage or gain; benefit. **2.** *Often pl.* Excess of returns over outlay or expenditure. **3.** The return from the employment of capital after deducting the amount paid for raw material and for wages, rent, interest, etc. **4.** That part of the amount received for goods which exceeds the sum originally paid for them with or without all secondary expenses involved. — **gross profit** The excess of receipts from sales over expenditures for production or purchase. — **net profit** The surplus remaining after all necessary deductions, as for interest, bad debts, etc. — *v.i.* **1.** To be of advantage or benefit. **2.** To derive gain or benefit. — *v.t.* **3.** To be of profit or advantage to. [< OF < L *profectus,* pp. of *proficere* to go forward] — **prof′it·less** *adj.*

prof·it·a·ble (prof′it·ə·bəl) *adj.* Bringing profit or gain; advantageous. — **prof′it·a·ble·ness** *n.* — **prof′it·a·bly** *adv.*

prof·i·teer (prof′ə·tir′) *v.i.* To seek or obtain excessive profits. — *n.* One who is given to making excessive profits, esp. to the detriment of others. — **prof′i·teer′ing** *n.*

profit sharing A system of remuneration by which workmen are given a share of the net profits of a business. — **prof·it·shar·ing** ((prof′it·shär′ing) *adj.*

prof·li·ga·cy (prof′lə·gə·sē) *n.* *pl.* **·cies** The state or quality of being profligate.

prof·li·gate (prof′lə·git, -gāt) *adj.* **1.** Lost or insensible to principle, virtue, or decency. **2.** Recklessly extravagant; in great profusion. — *n.* **1.** A depraved or dissolute person. **2.** A reckless spendthrift. [< L, pp. of *profligare* to destroy < *pro-* forward + *fligere* to dash] — **prof′li·gate·ly** *adv.* — **prof′li·gate·ness** (-git·nis, -gāt′nis) *n.*

prof·lu·ent (prof′lōō·ənt) *adj.* Flowing smoothly or plentifully. [< L < *pro-* before + *fluere* to flow] — **prof′lu·ence** *n.*

pro·found (prə·found′, prō-) *adj.* **1.** Intellectually deep or penetrating. **2.** Reaching to, arising from, or affecting the depth of one's nature: *profound* respect. **3.** Situated far below the surface; unfathomable. **4.** Deep. **5.** Thorough; exhaustive: *profound* changes. — *n.* **1.** A fathomless depth. **2.** The ocean; the deep. [< OF < L *pro-* very + *fundus* deep] — **pro·found′ly** *adv.* — **pro·found′ness** *n.*

pro·fun·di·ty (prə·fun′də·tē, prō-) *n.* *pl.* **·ties** **1.** The state or quality of being profound, in any sense. **2.** A deep place or thing. **3.** A profound or abstruse statement, theory, etc.

pro·fuse (prə·fyōōs′, prō-) *adj.* **1.** Giving or given forth lavishly; liberal; extravagant. **2.** Copious; overflowing; abundant: *profuse* vegetation. [< L < *pro-* forward + *fundere* to pour] — **pro·fuse′ly** *adv.* — **pro·fuse′ness** *n.*

pro·fu·sion (prə·fyōō′zhən, prō-) *n.* **1.** A lavish supply or condition: a *profusion* of ornaments. **2.** The act of pouring forth or supplying in great abundance; prodigality.

pro·gen·i·tor (prō-jen′ə·tər) *n.* A forefather or parent. [< F < L < *pro-* forth + *gignere* to beget]

prog·e·ny (proj′ə·nē) *n.* *pl.* **·nies** Offspring.

pro·ges·ter·one (prō·jes′tə·rōn) *n.* *Biochem.* A female hormone, isolated as a white, crystalline compound, $C_{21}H_{30}O_2$, and also made synthetically. It is active in preparing the uterus for the fertilized ovum. Also **pro·ges·tin** (prō·jes′tin).

prog·na·thous (prog′nə·thəs, prog·nā′thəs) *adj.* Having abnormally projecting jaws. Also **prog·nath·ic** (prog·nath′ik). — **prog·na·thism** (prog′nə·thiz′əm) *n.*

prog·no·sis (prog·nō′sis) *n.* *pl.* **·ses** (-sēz) **1.** *Med.* **a** A prediction or conclusion regarding the course of a disease and the probability of recovery. **b** Likelihood of recovery: The *prognosis* is excellent. **2.** Any prediction or forecast. [< NL < Gk. < *pro-* before + *gignōskein* to know]

prog·nos·tic (prog·nos′tik) *adj.* **1.** Of, pertaining to, or serving as a prognosis. **2.** Predicting or foretelling. — *n.* **1.** A sign of some future occurrence; an omen. **2.** *Med.* A symptom indicative of the course of a disease.

prog·nos·ti·cate (prog·nos′tə·kāt) *v.t.* **·cat·ed, ·cat·ing** **1.** To foretell (future events, etc.) by present indications. **2.** To indicate beforehand. — **prog·nos′ti·ca′tion** *n.* — **prog·nos′ti·ca′tor** *n.*

pro·gram (prō′gram, -grəm) *n.* **1.** A performance or show, esp. one given at a scheduled time on television or radio. **2.** A printed announcement or schedule of events, esp. one for a theatrical performance. **3.** Any prearranged, proposed, or desired plan or course of proceedings. **4.** *Electronics* A sequence of instructions set up on the control panels of an electronic computer as guides in the performance of a desired operation or group of operations. Also *Brit.* **pro′gramme.** — *v.t.* **·gramed** or **·grammed, ·gram·ing** or **·gram·ming** **1.** To arrange or include in a program. **2.** To make up a program for (a radio station, a computer, etc.). [< LL < Gk. < *pro-* before + *graphein* to write] — **pro·gram·mat·ic** (prō′grə·mat′ik) or **pro′gram·at′ic** *adj.*

pro·gram·mer (prō′gram·ər) *n.* One who makes up a computer program. Also **pro′gram·er.**

program music See under MUSIC.

prog·ress (*n.* prog′res, *esp. Brit.* prō′gres; *v.* prə·gres′) *n.* **1.** A moving forward in space; movement forward nearer a goal. **2.** Advancement toward maturity or completion; improvement. — *v.i.* **1.** To move forward or onward. **2.** To advance toward completion or fuller development. [< L < *pro-* forward + *gradi* to walk]

pro·gres·sion (prə·gresh′ən) *n.* **1.** The act of progressing; advancement. **2.** *Math.* A sequence of numbers or quantities, each of which is derived from the preceding by a constant relationship. **3.** *Music* **a** A movement from one tone or chord to another. **b** A succession of tones, chords, etc. **4.** Course or lapse of time; passage. — **pro·gres′sion·al** *adj.* — **pro·gres′sion·ism** *n.*

pro·gres·sive (prə·gres′iv) *adj.* **1.** Moving forward; advancing. **2.** Proceeding gradually or step by step. **3.** Aiming at or characterized by progress. **4.** Spreading from one part to others; increasing: said of a disease: *progressive* paralysis. **5.** Striving for or favoring progress or reform, esp. social, political, educational, or religious. **6.** Denoting or pertaining to a tax or taxes in which the tax rate increases as the amount taxed increases. **7.** *Gram.* Designating an aspect of the verb that expresses the action as being in progress at some time in the past, present, or future: formed with any tense of the auxiliary *be* and the present participle; as, He *is speaking;* he *had been speaking;* he *will be speaking.* — *n.* **1.** One who believes in progress or in progressive methods; esp., one who favors or promotes reforms or changes, as in politics or religion. **2.** *Gram.* A progressive verb form. [< OF *progressif*] — **pro·gres′sive·ly** *adv.* — **pro·gres′sive·ness** *n.* — **pro·gres′sive·ism** *n.* — **pro·gres′siv·ist** *n.*

Pro·gres·sive-Con·ser·va·tive Party (prə·gres′iv·kən·sûr′və·tiv) In Canada, one of the principal political parties, formerly called the Conservative Party.

Progressive Party **1.** A political party formed under the leadership of Theodore Roosevelt in 1912. **2.** A political party formed in 1924 under the leadership of Robert M. LaFollette. **3.** A political party formed in 1948, which nominated Henry A. Wallace for president.

pro·hib·it (prō·hib′it) *v.t.* **1.** To forbid, esp. by authority or law; interdict. **2.** To prevent or hinder. [< L < *pro-* before + *habere* to have] — **pro·hib′it·er** *n.*

pro·hi·bi·tion (prō′ə·bish′ən) *n.* **1.** The act of prohibiting, preventing, or stopping; also, a decree or order forbidding anything. **2.** The forbidding of the manufacture, transportation, and sale of alcoholic liquors as beverages.

pro·hi·bi·tion·ist (prō′ə·bish′ən·ist) *n.* One who favors legal prohibition of the manufacture and sale of alcoholic liquors.

pro·hib·i·tive (prō·hib′ə·tiv) *adj.* **1.** Prohibiting or tending to prohibit. **2.** Preventing the sale, purchase, etc., of something: *prohibitive* costs. Also **pro·hib′i·to·ry** (-tôr′ē, -tō′rē). — **pro·hib′i·tive·ly** *adv.*

proj·ect (n. proj′ekt; v. prə·jekt′) n. 1. Something proposed or mapped out in the mind, as a course of action; a plan. 2. In schools, a problem, task, or piece of work given to a student or group of students. 3. A housing project. —v.t. 1. To cause to extend forward or out. 2. To throw forth or forward, as missiles. 3. To visualize as an external reality. 4. To cause (an image, shadow, etc.) to fall on a surface. 5. To propose or plan. 6. Math. a To make a projection of (a solid, etc.) on a plane. b To reproduce (a figure) by drawing lines from a vertex through every point (of the figure) to the corresponding point of the reproduction. 7. To use or produce (one's voice, words, etc.) so as to be heard clearly and at a distance. —v.i. 8. To protrude. 9. Psychol. To attribute one's own ideas, impulses, etc., to others. 10. To speak or sing so as to be heard clearly and at a distance. [< L < pro- before + jacere to throw]

pro·jec·tile (prə·jek′təl, esp. Brit. -til) adj. 1. Projecting, or impelling forward. 2. Capable of being or intended to be projected or shot forth. 3. Protrusile. —n. 1. A body projected or thrown forth by force. 2. Mil. A missile for discharge from a gun or cannon. [< NL < L projectus thrown out]

pro·jec·tion (prə·jek′shən) n. 1. The act of projecting; a jutting, throwing, or shooting out or forth. 2. That which projects; a projecting part. 3. A scheme; project. 4. A system of lines drawn on a given fixed plane, as in a map, representing point for point a given terrestrial or celestial surface. 5. Psychol. a The unconscious process of attributing one's own feelings, attitudes, etc., to others. b An instance of this process. 6. Photog. a The process of exhibiting motion pictures or slides on a screen. b The picture so produced. —pro·jec′tive adj. —pro·jec′tive·ly adv.

pro·jec·tor (prə·jek′tər) n. 1. An apparatus for throwing illuminated images or motion pictures upon a screen. 2. A mirror or combination of lenses for projecting a beam of light. 3. One who devises projects; schemer; promoter.

pro·lapse (prō·laps′) Pathol. v.i. ·lapsed, ·laps·ing To fall out of place, as an organ or part. —n. The falling down of an organ or part, as the uterus, from its normal position. Also **pro·lap·sus** (prō·lap′səs). [< L < pro- forward + labi to glide, fall]

pro·late (prō′lāt) adj. 1. Extended lengthwise. 2. Lengthened toward the poles, as a spheroid. [< L < pro- forward + ferre to carry]

pro·le·gom·e·non (prō′lə·gom′ə·non) n. pl. ·na (-nə) Often pl. An introductory remark or remarks; a preface. [< Gk. < pro- before + legein to say] —pro′le·gom′e·nous adj.

pro·le·tar·i·an (prō′lə·târ′ē·ən) adj. Of or pertaining to the proletariat. —n. A member of the proletariat. [< L < proles offspring: so called because they served the Roman state only by having children] —pro′le·tar′i·an·ism n.

pro·le·tar·i·at (prō′lə·târ′ē·ət) n. 1. Wageworkers collectively; the working class: a term used esp. in Marxism. 2. In ancient Rome, the lowest class of the state.

pro·lif·er·ate (prō·lif′ə·rāt) v.t. & v.i. ·at·ed, ·at·ing To produce, reproduce, or grow, esp. with rapidity, as cells in tissue formation. —pro·lif′er·a′tion n. —pro·lif′er·a′tive adj.

pro·lif·er·ous (prō·lif′ər·əs) adj. 1. Producing offspring freely. 2. Bot. a Developing buds, branches, and flowers from unusual places. b Bearing progeny in the way of offshoots, buds, etc. [< Med.L < L proles, prolis offspring + ferre to bear]

pro·lif·ic (prō·lif′ik) adj. 1. Producing abundantly, as offspring or fruit; fertile. 2. Producing results abundantly: a prolific writer. [< F < Med.L < L proles, prolis offspring + stem of facere to make] —pro·lif′i·ca·cy (-i·kə·sē), pro·lif′ic·ness n. —pro·lif′i·cal·ly adv.

—Syn. 1. fruitful, fecund. 2. productive.

pro·lix (prō′liks, prō·liks′) adj. 1. Unduly long and verbose, as an address. 2. Indulging in long and wordy discourse. [< F < L < pro- before + stem of liquere to flow] —pro·lix·i·ty (prō·lik′sə·tē), pro·lix·ness n. —pro′lix·ly adv.

pro·logue (prō′lôg, -log) n. 1. A prefatory statement to a poem, discourse, or performance; esp., an introduction, often in verse, spoken or sung before a play or opera. 2. Any anticipatory act or event. —v.t. To introduce with a prologue or preface. Also **pro′log.** [< OF < L < Gk. < pro- before + logos discourse]

pro·logu·ize (prō′lôg·īz, -log-) v.i. ·ized, ·iz·ing To make or utter a prologue. Also **pro′log·ize.** —pro′logu·iz′er n.

pro·long (prə·lông′, -long′) v.t. To extend in time or space; continue; lengthen. Also **pro·lon′gate** (-lông·gāt, -long′-). [< OF < LL < L pro- forth + longus long] —pro′lon·ga′tion n. —pro·long′er n. —pro·long′ment n.

prom (prom) n. U.S. Informal A formal college or school dance or ball. [Short for promenade]

prom·e·nade (prom′ə·nād′, -näd′) n. 1. A walk for amusement or exercise, or as part of a formal or social entertain-ment. 2. A place for promenading. 3. A concert or ball opened with a formal march; also, the march. —v. ·nad·ed, ·nad·ing v.i. 1. To take a promenade. —v.t. 2. To take a promenade through or along. 3. To take or exhibit on or as on a promenade. [< MF < LL < pro- before + minare to drive (cattle)] —prom′e·nad′er n.

Pro·me·theus (prə·mē′thyōōs, -thē·əs) In Greek mythology, a Titan who stole fire from heaven for mankind and as a punishment was chained to a rock, where an eagle daily devoured his liver, which was made whole again at night. [< L < Gk. Promētheus] —Pro·me′the·an adj. & n.

pro·me·thi·um (prə·mē′thē·əm) n. A radioactive element (symbol Pm) separated from uranium fission products and belonging to the lanthanide series: formerly called illinium. See ELEMENT. [< NL < PROMETHEUS]

prom·i·nence (prom′ə·nəns) n. 1. The state of being prominent. 2. That which is prominent. 3. Astron. One of the great tongues of flame shooting out from the sun's surface, seen during total eclipses. Also **prom′i·nen·cy.**

prom·i·nent (prom′ə·nənt) adj. 1. Jutting out; projecting; protuberant. 2. Conspicuous in position, character, or importance. 3. Well-known; eminent. [< L < prominere to project] —prom′i·nent·ly adv.

pro·mis·cu·ous (prə·mis′kyōō·əs) adj. 1. Composed of individuals or things confusedly or indiscriminately mingled. 2. Indiscriminate, esp. in sexual relations. 3. Informal Lacking plan or purpose; casual; irregular. [< L < pro- thoroughly + stem of miscere to mix] —pro·mis·cu·i·ty (prō′mis·kyōō′ə·tē, prom′is-) n. —pro·mis′cu·ous·ly adv. —pro·mis′cu·ous·ness n.

prom·ise (prom′is) n. 1. An assurance given by one person to another that the former will or will not perform a specified act. 2. Reasonable ground for hope or expectation, esp. of future excellence or satisfaction. 3. Something promised. —v. ·ised, ·is·ing v.t. 1. To engage or pledge by a promise: used with the infinitive or a clause. 2. To make a promise of (something) to someone. 3. To give reason for expectation. 4. Informal To assure (someone). —v.i. 5. To make a promise. 6. To give reason for expectation. [< L < pro- forth + mittere to send] —prom′is·ee n. —prom′is·er n.

Promised Land 1. Canaan, promised to Abraham by God. Gen. xv 18. 2. Any longed-for place of happiness or improvement. 3. Heaven; paradise. Also Land of Promise.

prom·is·ing (prom′is·ing) adj. Giving promise of good results: a promising sign. —prom′is·ing·ly adv.

prom·is·so·ry (prom′ə·sôr′ē, -sō′rē) adj. 1. Containing or of the nature of a promise. 2. Indicating what is to be required after the signing of an insurance contract.

promissory note A written promise by one party to pay another party a certain sum of money at a specified time, or upon demand.

prom·on·to·ry (prom′ən·tôr′ē, -tō′rē) n. pl. ·ries 1. A high point of land extending into the sea; headland. 2. Anat. A rounded projection or part. [< Med.L < L, ? < prominere to project]

pro·mote (prə·mōt′) v.t. ·mot·ed, ·mot·ing 1. To contribute to the progress, development, or growth of; further; encourage. 2. To advance to a higher position, grade, or honor. 3. To work in behalf of; advocate actively. 4. In education, to advance (a pupil) to the next higher school grade. 5. To seek to make (a commercial product, business venture, etc.) popular or successful, as by securing capital or by advertising. [< L < pro- forward + movere to move] —pro·mot′er n. —pro·mo′tion n. —pro·mo′tion·al adj. —pro·mo′tive adj.

prompt (prompt) v.t. 1. To incite to action; instigate. 2. To suggest or inspire (an act, thought, etc.). 3. To remind of something forgotten or next in order; give a cue to. —v.i. 4. To give help or suggestions. —adj. 1. Acting or ready to act at the moment; punctual. 2. Done or rendered with readiness or alacrity; taking place at the appointed time. —n. 1. An act of prompting. 2. The information imparted by prompting. [< OF < L < pro- forth + emere to take] —prompt′ness n.

prompt·er (promp′tər) 1. In a theater, one who follows the lines and prompts the actors. 2. One who or that which prompts.

promp·ti·tude (promp′tə·tōōd, -tyōōd) n. The quality, habit, or fact of being prompt; promptness.

prompt·ly (prompt′lē) adv. In a prompt manner; at once.

pro·mul·gate (prō·mul′gāt, prom′əl·gāt) v.t. ·gat·ed, ·gat·ing To make known or announce officially and formally; put into effect by public proclamation, as a law or dogma. [< L < pro- forth + vulgus people] —pro′mul·ga′tion n. —pro·mul′ga·tor (prō·mul′gā·tər, prom′əl-) n.

prone (prōn) adj. 1. Lying flat, esp. with the face, front, or palm downward; prostrate. 2. Leaning forward or downward; also, moving or sloping sharply downward. 3. Mentally inclined or predisposed: with *to*. [< L *pronus* prostrate] **—prone′ly** *adv.* **—prone′ness** *n.*

prong (prông, prong) *n.* **1.** A pointed end of an instrument, as the tine of a fork. **2.** Any pointed, projecting part, as the end of an antler. **—v.t.** To prick or stab with or as with a prong. [Cf. LG *prange* pointed stick, Du. *prangen* to pinch]

prong·horn (prông′hôrn′, prong′-) *n. pl.* **·horns** or **·horn** A ruminant of western North America, resembling an antelope, with deciduous branched horns.

pro·nom·i·nal (prō·nom′ə·nəl) *adj.* Of, pertaining to, or of the nature of a pronoun. **—pro·nom′i·nal·ly** *adv.*

pronominal adjective The possessive case of a personal pronoun used attributively, as *my, your, his, her,* etc.

pro·noun (prō′noun) *n. Gram.* A word that may be used instead of a noun or noun phrase, as an adjective, or to introduce a question. [< OF < L < *pro-* in place of + *nomen* name, noun]

pro·nounce (prə·nouns′) *v.* **·nounced, ·nounc·ing** *v.t.* **1.** To utter or deliver officially or solemnly; proclaim: to *pronounce* judgment. **2.** To assert; declare, esp. as one's judgment. **3.** To enunciate or articulate (sounds). **4.** To utter the constituent sounds of (a word or phrase) in a particular sequence or with a particular accentual pattern. **5.** To utter (the sound of a letter). **—v.i. 6.** To make a judgment or pronouncement. **7.** To articulate words; speak. [< OF < LL < L < *pro-* forth + *nuntiare* to announce] **—pronounce′a·ble** *adj.* **—pro·nounc′er** *n.*

pro·nounced (prə·nounst′) *adj.* Of marked or clearly indicated character. **—pro·nounc·ed·ly** (prə·noun′sid·lē) *adv.*

pro·nounce·ment (prə·nouns′mənt) *n.* **1.** The act of pronouncing. **2.** A formal declaration or announcement.

pron·to (pron′tō) *adv. U.S. Informal* Quickly; promptly; instantly. [< Sp. < L *promptus* brought forth]

pro·nun·ci·a·men·to (prə·nun′sē·ə·men′tō, -shē·ə-) *n. pl.* **·tos** A public announcement; proclamation; manifesto. [< Sp. < L *pronuntiare* to pronounce]

pro·nun·ci·a·tion (prə·nun′sē·ā′shən) *n.* **1.** The act or manner of uttering words. **2.** Articulation.

proof (prōōf) *n.* **1.** The act or process of proving; esp., the establishment of a fact by evidence or a truth by other truths. **2.** A trial of strength, truth, excellence, etc. **3.** Evidence and argument sufficient to induce belief. **4.** *Law* Anything that serves to determine a verdict. **5.** The state or quality of having successfully undergone a test. **6.** Impenetrability; also, impenetrable armor. **7.** The standard of strength of alcoholic liquors. **8.** *Printing* A printed trial sheet showing the contents or condition of matter in type or of a plate, or the like. **9.** In engraving and etching, a trial impression taken from an engraved plate, stone, or block; also, a perfect impression from such a plate, etc., when finished. **10.** *Photog.* A trial print from a negative. **11.** *Math.* A process to check a computation by using its result; also, a demonstration. **12.** In philately, an experimental printing of a stamp. **—adj. 1.** Employed in or connected with proving or correcting. **2.** Capable of resisting successfully: with *against.* **3.** Of standard alcoholic strength, as liquors. [< OF < LL < *probare* to test]

-proof *combining form* **1.** Impervious to; able to withstand; not damaged by: *bombproof.* **2.** Protected against: *mothproof.* **3.** As strong as: *armorproof.* **4.** Resisting; showing no effects of: *panicproof.* Adjectives formed with *-proof* may also be used as verbs. [< PROOF, adj.]

proof·read (prōōf′rēd′) *v.t. & v.i.* **·read** (-red′), **·read·ing** (-rē′ding) To read and correct (printers' proofs). **—proof′·read′er** *n.* **—proof′read′ing** *n.*

proof spirit An alcoholic liquor that contains a standard amount of alcohol. In the U.S. 100 proof indicates a liquor half of whose volume is ethyl alcohol having a specific gravity of 0.7939 at 60° F.

prop¹ (prop) *n.* **1.** A rigid object, as a beam or pole, that bolsters or sustains an incumbent weight. **2.** One who gives support to an institution, organization, etc. **—v.t. propped, prop·ping 1.** To support or keep from falling with or as with a prop. **2.** To lean or place: usu. with *against.* **3.** To support; sustain. [< MDu. *proppe* a support]

prop² (prop) *n.* A property (def. 7.).

prop·a·ga·ble (prop′ə·gə·bəl) *adj.* That can be propagated.

prop·a·gan·da (prop′ə·gan′də) *n.* **1.** A systematic effort to persuade a body of people to support or adopt a particular opinion, attitude, or course of action. **2.** Any selection of facts, ideas, or allegations forming the basis of such an effort. **3.** An institution or scheme for propagating a doctrine or system. ◆ *Propaganda* is now often used in a disparaging sense, as of a body of distortions and half-truths calculated to bias one's judgment or opinions. [< PROPAGANDA.] **—prop′a·gan′dism** *n.* **—prop′a·gan′dist** *n. & adj.*

Prop·a·gan·da (prop′ə·gan′də) *n.* In the Roman Catholic Church, a society of cardinals charged with overseeing the foreign missions. [< NL (*congregatio de*) *propaganda* (*fide*) (the council for) propagating the faith)]

prop·a·gan·dize (prop′ə·gan′dīz) *v.* **·dized, ·diz·ing** *v.t.* **1.**

To spread by means of propaganda. **2.** To subject to propaganda. **—v.i. 3.** To carry on or spread propaganda.

prop·a·gate (prop′ə·gāt) *v.* **·gat·ed, ·gat·ing** *v.t.* **1.** To cause (animals, plants, etc.) to multiply by natural reproduction. **2.** To spread from person to person, as a doctrine or belief; disseminate. **3.** To transmit through a medium: to *propagate* heat. **4.** To reproduce (itself), as a species of plant or animal. **5.** To pass on (traits, qualities, etc.) to one's offspring. **—v.i. 6.** To have offspring; breed. [< L < *pro-* forth + *pag-* root of *pangere* to fasten] **—prop′a·ga′tion** *n.* **—prop′a·ga′tive** *adj.* **—prop′a·ga′tor** *n.*

pro·pane (prō′pān) *n. Chem.* A gaseous hydrocarbon of the methane series, C_3H_8, obtained from petroleum and sometimes used as a fuel gas.

pro pa·tri·a (prō pā′trē·ə) *Latin* For one's country.

pro·pel (prə·pel′) *v.t.* **·pelled, ·pel·ling** To cause to move forward or ahead; drive or urge forward. [< L < *pro-* forward + *pellere* to drive]

pro·pel·lant (prə·pel′ənt) *n.* **1.** One who or that which propels. **2.** *Mil.* An explosive that upon ignition propels a projectile from a gun. **3.** A solid or liquid fuel that serves to propel a rocket, guided missile, etc.: also spelled *propellent.*

pro·pel·lent (prə·pel′ənt) *adj.* Able to propel; propelling. **—n.** See PROPELLANT.

pro·pel·ler (prə·pel′ər) *n.* **1.** One who or that which propels. **2.** Any device for propelling a craft through water or air; esp., one having blades mounted at an angle on a power-driven shaft and producing a thrust by their rotary action on the medium.

pro·pe·no·ic acid (prō′pə·nō′ik) *Chem.* Acrylic acid.

pro·pen·si·ty (prə·pen′sə·tē) *n. pl.* **·ties** A natural disposition or tendency; bent. [< L < *pro-* forward + *pendere* to hang]

prop·er (prop′ər) *adj.* **1.** Specially suited or adapted for some end; appropriate. **2.** Conforming to a prevalent standard of conduct or manners; fitting. **3.** Understood in a strict or literal sense: usu. following the noun modified: part of the book *proper.* **4.** Naturally belonging to a particular person, thing, or class: Crying is *proper* to babies. **5.** Modest; decent. **6.** *Gram.* Designating a particular person, place, or the like: a *proper* name. **7.** *Brit. Informal* Thorough; unmitigated: a *proper* bore. **—n.** *Sometimes cap. Eccl.* The portion of the breviary, missal, or Mass containing the prayers and collects suitable to special occasions or feasts: with *the:* distinguished from *ordinary.* [< OF < L *propius* one's own] **—prop′er·ly** *adv.* **—prop′er·ness** *n.*

proper fraction *Math.* A fraction in which the numerator is less than the denominator.

proper noun *Gram.* A noun that names a particular person, place, or thing, and is always capitalized, as *Paul, Venice, U.S.S. Nautilus:* distinguished from *common noun.*

prop·er·tied (prop′ər·tēd) *adj.* Owning property.

prop·er·ty (prop′ər·tē) *n. pl.* **·ties 1.** Any object of value that a person may lawfully acquire and hold; that which may be owned, as stocks, land, etc. **2.** The legal right to the possession, use, enjoyment, and disposal of a thing. **3.** Holdings, land, etc., owned; wealth. **4.** A parcel of land. **5.** Any of the qualities or characteristics that together make up the nature or basic structure of a thing. **6.** A quality or feature that belongs distinctively to a particular object or class; a peculiarity. **7.** In the theater, any portable article used in a performance other than scenery and the costumes, as books, dishes, etc.: also called *prop.* [< OF < L *proprius* one's own.] **—prop′er·ty·less** *adj.*

—Syn. 3. chattels, goods, estate. **6.** See CHARACTERISTIC.

proph·e·cy (prof′ə·sē) *n. pl.* **·cies 1.** A prediction made under divine influence and direction. **2.** Any prediction. **3.** Discourse delivered by a prophet under divine inspiration. **4.** A book of prophecies. [< OF < LL < Gk. < *pro* before + *phanai* to speak]

proph·e·sy (prof′ə·sī) *v.* **·sied, ·sy·ing** *v.t.* **1.** To utter or foretell with or as with divine inspiration. **2.** To predict (a future event). **3.** To point out beforehand. **—v.i. 4.** To speak by divine influence, or as a medium between God and man. **5.** To foretell the future. **6.** To explain or teach religious subjects; preach. [See PROPHECY] **—proph′e·si′er** *n.*

—Syn. 1. *Prophesy* and *foretell* are often interchangeable, but in Scriptural sense *prophesy* refers to the uttering of religious truths under divine inspiration, and does not necessarily include the prediction of future events. *Foretell* always bears the latter sense.

proph·et (prof′it) *n.* **1.** One who delivers divine messages or interprets the divine will. **2.** One who foretells the future; esp., an inspired predictor. **3.** A religious leader. **4.** An interpreter or spokesman for any cause. **5.** A mantis. **—the Prophet** According to Islam, Mohammed. **—the Prophets** The second of the three ancient divisions of the Old Testament, containing all those books not found in the Pentateuch or the Hagiographa. [< OF < LL < Gk. < *pro-* before + *phanai* to speak] **—proph′et·ess** *n.fem.*

pro·phet·ic (prə·fet′ik) *adj.* **1.** Of or pertaining to a prophet or prophecy. **2.** Pertaining to or involving prediction or presentiment; predictive. Also **pro·phet/i·cal. — pro·phet/i·cal·ly** adv. **— pro·phet/i·cal·ness** n.

pro·phy·lac·tic (prō/fə·lak/tik, prof/ə-) adj. Tending to protect against or ward off something, esp. disease; preventive. **— n.** A prophylactic medicine or appliance. [< Gk. < pro- before + phylassein to guard]

pro·phy·lax·is (prō/fə·lak/sis, prof/ə-) n. Preventive treatment for disease. [< NL < Gk. pro- before + phylaxis guarding]

pro·pin·qui·ty (prō·ping/kwə·tē) n. **1.** Nearness in place or time. **2.** Kinship. **— Syn.** See APPROXIMATION. [< L prope near]

pro·pi·ti·ate (prō·pish/ē·āt) v.t. **·at·ed, ·at·ing** To cause to be favorably disposed; conciliate. [See PROPITIOUS.] **— pro·pi·ti·a·ble** (prō·pish/ē·ə·bəl) adj. **— pro·pi/ti·at·ing·ly** adv. **— pro·pi/ti·a·tion** n. **— pro·pi/ti·a·tive** adj. **— pro·pi/ti·a/tor** n.

pro·pi·ti·a·to·ry (prō·pish/ē·ə·tôr/ē, -tō/rē) adj. Pertaining to or causing propitiation.

pro·pi·tious (prō·pish/əs) adj. **1.** Attended by favorable circumstances; auspicious. **2.** Kindly disposed; gracious. [< OF < L propitius favorable, ? < pro- before + petere to seek] **— pro·pi/tious·ly** adv. **— pro·pi/tious·ness** n.

— Syn. Propitious may be applied to persons, while auspicious is not so used.

prop·jet (prop/jet/) n. Aeron. A turboprop.

pro·po·nent (prə·pō/nənt) n. **1.** One who makes a proposal or proposition. **2.** One who advocates or supports a cause or doctrine. [< L < pro- forth + ponere to put]

pro·por·tion (prə·pôr/shən, -pōr/-) n. **1.** Relative magnitude, number, or degree, as existing between parts, a part and a whole, etc. **2.** Fitness and harmony; symmetry. **3.** A proportionate or proper share. **4.** An equality or identity between ratios. **5.** Math. The relationship among four terms such that the product of the second and third terms is equal to the product of the first and fourth. **6.** pl. Size; dimensions. **— v.t. 1.** To adjust properly as to relative magnitude, amount, or degree. **2.** To form with a harmonious relation of parts. [< OF < L < pro- for + portio, -onis share] **— pro·por/tion·a·ble** adj. **— pro·por/tion·a·bly** adv. **— pro·por/tion·er** n. **— pro·por/tion·ment** n.

pro·por·tion·al (prə·pôr/shən·əl, -pōr/-) adj. **1.** Of or being in proportion. **2.** Math. **a** Constituting the terms of a proportion. **b** Varying so that corresponding values form a proportion. **— n.** Any quantity or number in proportion to another or others. **— pro·por/tion·al·ly** adv. **— pro·por/tion·al/i·ty** (-al/ə·tē) n.

pro·por·tion·ate (adj. prə·pôr/shən·it, -pōr/-; v. prə·pôr/shən·āt, -pōr/-) adj. Being in due proportion; proportional. **— v.t. ·at·ed, ·at·ing** To make proportionate. **— pro·por/tion·ate·ly** adv. **— pro·por/tion·ate·ness** n.

pro·po·sal (prə·pō/zəl) n. **1.** An offer proposing something to be accepted or adopted. **2.** An offer of marriage. **3.** Something proposed, as a scheme or plan.

pro·pose (prə·pōz/) v. **·posed, ·pos·ing** v.t. **1.** To put forward for acceptance or consideration. **2.** To nominate, as for appointment. **3.** To intend; aim. **4.** To suggest the drinking of (a toast or health). **— v.i. 5.** To form or announce a plan or design. **6.** To make an offer, as of marriage. [< OF < pro- forth (< L) + poser to put down, rest] **— pro·pos/er** n.

— Syn. 3. What we propose to do is subject to further consideration. What we purpose to do is settled; the word suggests that the mind has been made up.

prop·o·si·tion (prop/ə·zish/ən) n. **1.** A scheme or proposal offered for consideration or acceptance. **2.** U.S. Informal Any matter or person to be dealt with. **3.** A subject or statement presented for discussion. **4.** Logic A statement in which something (the subject) is affirmed or denied in terms of something else (the predicate). **5.** Math. A statement of a truth to be demonstrated (a theorem) or of an operation to be performed (a problem). [< OF < L < pro- forth + ponere to put] **— prop/o·si/tion·al** adj. **— prop/o·si/tion·al·ly** adv.

pro·pound (prə·pound/) v.t. To put forward for consideration, solution, etc.; submit. [Earlier propone < L proponere to set forth] **— pro·pound/er** n.

pro·pri·e·tar·y (prə·prī/ə·ter/ē) adj. **1.** Of or belonging to a proprietor. **2.** Subject to exclusive ownership. **3.** Designating an article, as a medicine, protected by copyright, patent, secrecy, etc. **— n.** pl. **·tar·ies 1.** A proprietor or proprietors collectively. **2.** Proprietorship; ownership. [< LL < L proprius one's own]

pro·pri·e·tor (prə·prī/ə·tər) n. A person having the exclusive title to anything. **— pro·pri/e·tor·ship/** n. **— pro·pri/e·tress** n.fem.

pro·pri·e·ty (prə·prī/ə·tē) n. pl. **·ties** The character or

quality of being proper; esp., accordance with recognized usage or principles. **— the proprieties** The standards of good society. [< OF propriete < L proprius one's own]

pro·pul·sion (prə·pul/shən) n. **1.** The act or operation of propelling. **2.** A propelling force. **— pro·pul/sive** (-siv) adj.

pro·pyl (prō/pil) n. Chem. The univalent radical, C_3H_7, derived from propane.

pro ra·ta (prō rā/tə, rat/ə, rä/tə) In proportion. [< L pro rata (parte) according to the calculated (share)]

pro·rate (prō·rāt/, prō/rāt/) v.t. & v.i. **·rat·ed, ·rat·ing** To distribute or divide proportionately. [< PRO RATA] **— pro·rat/a·ble** adj. **— pro·ra/tion** n.

pro·ro·ga·tion (prō/rə·gā/shən) n. **1.** The act of proroguing. **2.** The act of prolonging; also, continuance.

pro·rogue (prō·rōg/) v.t. **·rogued, ·ro·guing** To discontinue a session of (an assembly). [< MF < L < pro- forward + rogare to ask]

pro·sa·ic (prō·zā/ik) adj. **1.** Unimaginative; commonplace; dull. **2.** Of or like prose. Also **pro·sa/i·cal.** [< LL < L prosa prose] **— pro·sa/ic·ness** n.

pro·sce·ni·um (prō·sē/nē·əm) n. pl. **·ni·a** (-nē·ə) The part of a theater stage in front of the curtain, sometimes including the curtain and its arch. [< L < Gk. < pro- before + skēnē stage, tent]

pro·scribe (prō·skrīb/) v.t. **·scribed, ·scrib·ing 1.** To denounce or condemn; prohibit. **2.** To outlaw or banish. **3.** In ancient Rome, to publish the name of (one condemned or exiled). [< L proscribere to write publicly] **— pro·scrib/er** n. **— pro·scrip/tion** (-skrip/shən) n. **— pro·scrip/tive** adj.

prose (prōz) n. **1.** Speech or writing without metrical structure: distinguished from verse. **2.** Commonplace or tedious discourse. **— adj. 1.** Of or pertaining to prose. **2.** Tedious; tiresome. **— v.t. & v.i. prosed, pros·ing** To write or speak in prose. [< OF < L prosa (oratio) straightforward (discourse)]

pros·e·cute (pros/ə·kyōōt) v. **·cut·ed, ·cut·ing** v.t. **1.** To go on with so as to complete. **2.** To carry on or engage in, as a trade. **3.** Law **a** To bring suit against. **b** To seek to enforce, as a claim, by legal process. **— v.i. 4.** To begin and carry on a legal proceeding. **— Syn.** See PUSH. [< L < pro- forward + sequi to follow]

prosecuting attorney The attorney empowered to act in behalf of the state, county, or national government in prosecuting for penal offenses.

pros·e·cu·tion (pros/ə·kyōō/shən) n. **1.** The act or process of prosecuting. **2.** Law The instituting and carrying forward of a judicial or criminal proceeding. **3.** The party instituting and conducting it.

pros·e·cu·tor (pros/ə·kyōō/tər) n. **1.** One who prosecutes. **2.** Law **a** One who institutes and carries on a suit, esp. a criminal suit. **b** A prosecuting attorney.

pros·e·lyte (pros/ə·līt) n. One who has been brought over to any opinion, belief, sect, or party, esp. from one religious belief to another. **— v.t. & v.i. ·lyt·ed, ·lyt·ing** To proselytize. [< LL < Gk. proselytos, orig., a newcomer] **— pros·e·lyt/ism** (-lə·tiz/əm, -līt/iz·əm) n.

pros·e·lyt·ize (pros/ə·lit·īz/) v. **·ized, ·iz·ing** v.i. **1.** To make proselytes. **— v.t. 2.** To make a convert of. Also proselyte: also Brit. **pros/e·lyt·ise/.**

pros·en·ceph·a·lon (pros/en·sef/ə·lon) n. Anat. The anterior segment of the three divisions of the brain in embryos, developing into the cerebrum and the optic thalamus, with related structures: also called forebrain. [< NL < Gk. pros toward + encephalon brain] **— pros/en·ce·phal/ic** (-sə·fal/ik) adj.

Pros·er·pine (pros/ər·pīn, prō·sûr/pə·nē) In Roman mythology, the daughter of Ceres and wife of Pluto: identified with the Greek Persephone. Also **Pro·ser·pi·na** (prō·sûr/pə·nə).

pro·sit (prō/sit, Ger. prō/zit) interj. To your good health: used as a drinking toast, esp. by the Germans. Also **prost** (prōst). [< L, lit., may it benefit]

pro·slav·er·y (prō·slā/vər·ē, -slāv/rē) adj. In U.S. history, advocating Negro slavery.

pro·sod·ic (prō·sod/ik) adj. Of or pertaining to prosody. Also **pro·sod/i·cal.**

prosodic symbols In the scansion of verse, those signs used to indicate the various kinds of syllables, stresses, feet, etc.: these include the breve (˘), macron (—), acute (´), caesura (||), and vertical bar (|).

pros·o·dy (pros/ə·dē) n. The science of poetical forms, including quantity and accent of syllables, meter, versification, and metrical composition. [< L < Gk. prosōidia a song sung to music] **— pro·so·di·ac** (prō·sō/dē·ak), **pro·so·di·al** (prō·sō/dē·əl) adj. **— pros/o·dist** n.

pros·pect (pros/pekt) n. **1.** A future probability; esp., often in the plural, the chance for future success. **2.** An extended view. **3.** An exposure; outlook. **4.** A prospective buyer. **— v.t. & v.i.** To explore (a region) for gold, oil, etc. [< L < pro- forward + specere to look]

pro·spec·tive (prə·spek′tiv) *adj.* **1.** Anticipated. **2.** Looking toward the future. **— pro·spec′tive·ly** *adv.*

pros·pec·tor (pros′pek·tər) *n.* One who searches or examines a region for mineral deposits or precious stones.

pro·spec·tus (prə·spek′təs) *n. pl.* **·tus·es 1.** A paper containing information of a proposed undertaking. **2.** A summary; outline. [< L < *pro-* forward + *specere* to look]

pros·per (pros′pər) *v.i.* To be prosperous; thrive; flourish. [< OF < L *prosperus* favorable, prosperous]

pros·per·i·ty (pros·per′ə·tē) *n. pl.* **·ties** The state of being prosperous; material well-being.

pros·per·ous (pros′pər·əs) *adj.* **1.** Successful; flourishing. **2.** Auspicious. **3.** Favorable. [< MF < L *prosperus* favorable] **— pros′per·ous·ly** *adv.* **— pros′per·ous·ness** *n.*

pros·tate (pros′tāt) *Anat. adj.* Of or designating the prostate gland. **—** *n.* The prostate gland. [< NL < Gk. *prostatēs* stander before < *pro-* before + *histanai* to set]

prostate gland *Anat.* A partly muscular gland at the base of the bladder and surrounding the urethra in male mammals, providing some of the chemicals necessary to maintain the sperm for reproduction. **— pro·stat·ic** (prō·stat′ik) *adj.*

pros·the·sis (pros′thə·sis) *n. pl.* **·ses** (-sēz) **1.** *Surg.* The fitting of artificial parts to the body. **2.** A part so fitted, as an artificial limb, false tooth, etc. [< L < Gk. < *pros-* to + *tithenai* to put] **— pros·thet·ic** (pros·thet′ik) *adj.*

pros·thet·ics (pros·thet′iks) *n.pl.* (construed as sing.) The branch of surgery that specializes in artificial parts. **— pros·the·tist** (pros′thə·tist) *n.*

pros·tho·don·tics (pros′thə·don′tiks) *n.* The branch of dentistry concerned with the making of crowns, bridges, dentures, and artificial teeth; dental prosthetics. Also **pros′·tho·don′ti·a.** (-thə·don′shē·ə). [< NL < Gk. *prosthesis* addition + *odous* tooth] **— pros·tho·don·tist** (pros′thə·don′tist) *n.*

pros·ti·tute (pros′tə·tōot, -tyōot) *n.* **1.** A woman who offers her body for hire for purposes of sexual intercourse. **2.** One who sells his services for unworthy purposes. **—** *v.t.* **·tut·ed, ·tut·ing 1.** To apply (talent, etc.) to unworthy purposes. **2.** To offer (oneself or another) for lewd purposes, esp. for hire. [< L < *pro-* forward + *statuere* to place] **— pros′ti·tu′tion** *n.* **— pros′ti·tu′tor** *n.*

pros·trate (pros′trāt) *adj.* **1.** Lying prone, or with the face to the ground. **2.** Brought low in mind or spirit. **3.** Lying at the mercy of another. **4.** *Bot.* Trailing along the ground. **—** *v.t.* **·trat·ed, ·trat·ing 1.** To bow or cast (oneself) down, as in adoration or pleading. **2.** To throw flat; lay on the ground. **3.** To overcome; make helpless. [< L < *pro-* before + *sternere* to stretch out] **— pros·tra′tion** *n.*

pros·y (prō′zē) *adj.* **pros·i·er, pros·i·est 1.** Like prose; prosaic. **2.** Dull; tedious. **— pros′i·ly** *adv.* **— pros′i·ness** *n.*

prot- Var. of PROTO-.

pro·tac·tin·i·um (prō′tak·tin′ē·əm) *n.* A radioactive metallic element (symbol Pa) of the actinide series, intermediate between thorium and uranium: also called *protoactinium.* See ELEMENT.

pro·tag·o·nist (prō·tag′ə·nist) *n.* **1.** The actor who played the chief part in a Greek drama. **2.** Any leading character, contender, etc. [< Gk. < *prōtos* first + *agōnistēs* actor]

pro·te·an (prō′tē·ən, prō·tē′ən) *adj.* Readily assuming different forms or various aspects; changeable. [< PROTEUS]

pro·te·ase (prō′tē·ās) *n.* *Biochem.* An enzyme that digests proteins.

pro·tect (prə·tekt′) *v.t.* **1.** To shield or defend from attack, harm, or injury. **2.** *Econ.* To assist (domestic industry) by means of protective tariffs. **3.** In commerce, to provide funds to guarantee payment of (a draft, etc.). [< L < *pro-* before + *tegere* to cover] **— pro·tect′ing·ly** *adv.*

pro·tec·tion (prə·tek′shən) *n.* **1.** The act of protecting, or the state of being protected. **2.** One who or that which protects. **3.** *Econ.* A system aiming to protect the industries of a country by imposing duties. See PROTECTIVE TARIFF. **— pro·tec′tive** *adj.* **— pro·tec′tive·ly** *adv.*

pro·tec·tion·ism (prə·tek′shən·iz′əm) *n.* The economic doctrine or system of protection. **— pro·tec′tion·ist** *n.*

protective tariff A tariff that is intended to insure protection of domestic industries against foreign competition.

pro·tec·tor (prə·tek′tər) *n.* **1.** One who protects; a defender. **2.** In English history, one appointed as a regent of the kingdom during minority or incapacity of the sovereign. Also **pro·tect′er. — pro·tec′tress** *n.fem.*

Pro·tec·tor (prə·tek′tər) *n.* The title borne by Oliver Cromwell, 1653–58, and by Richard Cromwell, his son, 1658–59 during the Protectorate: in full, **Lord Protector.**

pro·tec·tor·ate (prə·tek′tər·it) *n.* **1.** A relation of protection and partial control by a strong nation over a weaker power. **2.** A country or region under the protection of another. **3.** The office, or period of office, of a protector of a kingdom. Also **pro·tec′tor·ship.**

Pro·tec·tor·ate (prə·tek′tər·it) *n.* The English government during the rule of the Cromwells, 1653–59.

pro·té·gé (prō′tə·zhā, *Fr.* prô·tā·zhā′) *n.* One specially cared

for by another who is older or more powerful. [< F < L *protegere* to protect] **— pro′té·gée** *n.fem.*

pro·te·in (prō′tē·in, -tēn) *n.* *Biochem.* Any of a class of highly complex nitrogenous compounds originally synthesized by plants, and forming an essential constituent in the processes of animal metabolism. Also **pro′te·id** (-id). [< G < Gk. *prōtos* first]

pro tem·po·re (prō tem′pə·rē) *Latin* For the time being.

Prot·er·o·zo·ic (prot′ər·ə·zō′ik) *Geol. adj.* Of or designating the geological era following the Archeozoic and succeeded by the Paleozoic. See chart for GEOLOGY. **—** *n.* The Proterozoic era. [< Gk. *proteros* former + ZOIC]

pro·test (*n.* prō′test; *v.* prə·test′) *n.* **1.** A solemn or formal objection or declaration. **2.** A public expression of dissent. **3.** A formal notarial certificate attesting the fact that a note or bill of exchange has been presented for acceptance or payment and that it has been refused. **4.** The act of protesting. **—** *adj.* Of or relating to public protest: *protest* demonstrations. **—** *v.t.* **1.** To assert earnestly or positively. **2.** *U.S.* To make a protest against; object to. **3.** To declare formally that payment of (a promissory note, etc.) has been duly submitted and refused. **—** *v.i.* **4.** To make solemn affirmation. **5.** To make a protest; object. [< OF < L < *pro-* forth + *testari* to testify] **— pro·test′er** *n.* **— pro·test′ing·ly** *adv.*

prot·es·tant (prot′is·tənt, prə·tes′-) *n.* One who makes a protest. [< MF < L < *protestari*]

Prot·es·tant (prot′is·tənt) *n.* A member of one of those bodies of Christians that adhere to Protestantism, as distinguished from Roman Catholicism. **—** *adj.* Pertaining to Protestants or Protestantism.

Protestant Episcopal Church A religious body in the United States that is descended from the Church of England: also called *Episcopal Church.*

Prot·es·tant·ism (prot′is·tənt·iz′əm) *n.* **1.** The principles and common system of doctrines of the Protestants. **2.** The ecclesiastical system founded upon this faith; also, Protestants, collectively. **3.** The state of being a Protestant.

prot·es·ta·tion (prot′is·tā′shən) *n.* **1.** The act of protesting; also, that which is protested. **2.** A formal declaration of dissent. **3.** Any solemn or urgent avowal.

Pro·te·us (prō′tē·əs, -tyōos) In Greek mythology, a sea god who had the power of assuming different forms.

pro·tist (prō′tist) *n.* *Biol.* Any member of a large division or kingdom of one-celled or noncellular plants and animals, including bacteria, flagellates, rhizopods, and ciliates. [< NL < Gk. *prōtos* first] **— pro·tis′tan** *adj. & n.* **— pro·tis′tic** *adj.*

pro·ti·um (prō′tē·əm) *n.* *Chem.* The hydrogen isotope of atomic mass 1 (symbol, H^1): sometimes so called in distinction from deuterium and tritium. [< NL < Gk. *prōtos* first]

proto- *combining form* **1.** First in rank or time; chief; typical. **2.** Primitive; original: *prototype.* Also, before vowels, **prot-.** [< Gk. *prōtos* first]

pro·to·ac·tin·i·um (prō′tō·ak·tin′ē·əm) *n.* Protactinium.

pro·to·col (prō′tə·kōl, -kol) *n.* **1.** The rules of diplomatic and state etiquette and ceremony. **2.** The preliminary draft of a diplomatic negotiation or of an official document, as a treaty. **—** *v.i.* **·coled** or **·colled, ·col·ing** or **·col·ling** To write or form protocols. [< OF < Med.L < LGk. *prōto·kollon* the first sheet glued to a papyrus roll enumerating the contents < *prōtos* first + *kolla* glue]

pro·ton (prō′ton) *n.* *Physics* One of the elementary particles in the nucleus of an atom, having a unitary positive charge and a mass of approximately 1.672×10^{-24} gram. [< NL < Gk. < *prōtos* first]

pro·to·plasm (prō′tə·plaz′əm) *n.* *Biol.* The physico-chemical basis of living matter, a viscid, grayish, translucent substance of complex composition than forms the essential part of plant and animal cells. [< G < Gk. *prōtos* first + *plasma* form] **— pro′to·plas′mic** *adj.*

pro·to·type (prō′tə·tīp) *n.* **1.** *Biol.* A primitive or ancestral organism; an archetype. **2.** An original model on which subsequent forms are to be based. [< F < NL < Gk. < *prōtos* first + *typos* form] **— pro′to·typ′al** (-tī′pəl), **pro′to·typ′ic** (-tip′ik), **pro′to·typ′i·cal** *adj.*

pro·to·zo·an (prō′tə·zō′ən) *n.* Any of a phylum of microscopic, single-celled organisms, largely aquatic and including many parasites. Also **pro′to·zo′on.** [< NL < Gk. *prōtos* first + *zōion* animal] **— pro′to·zo′an** *adj.* **— pro′to·zo′ic** *adj.*

pro·tract (prō·trakt′) *v.t.* **1.** To extend in time; prolong. **2.** In surveying, to draw or map by means of a scale and protractor; plot. **3.** *Anat.* To protrude or extend. [< L < *pro-* forward + *trahere* to draw] **— pro·trac′tion** *n.* **— pro·trac′tive** *adj.*

pro·trac·tile (prō·trak′til) *adj.* Capable of being protracted or protruded.

pro·trac·tor (prō·trak′tər) *n.* **1.** One who protracts. **2.** An instrument for measuring and laying off angles. **3.** *Anat.* A muscle that extends a limb or moves it forward.

pro·trude (prō·trōōd′) *v.t. & v.i.* **·trud·ed, ·trud·ing** To push or thrust out; project outward. [< L < *pro-* forward + *trudere* to thrust] — **pro·tru'sion** (-trōō'zhən) *n.*

pro·tru·sile (prō·trōō'sil) *adj.* Adapted to being thrust out, as the tongue of an anteater. Also **pro·tru'si·ble.**

pro·tru·sive (prō·trōō'siv) *adj.* **1.** Tending to protrude; protruding. **2.** Pushing or driving forward. — **pro·tru'·sive·ly** *adv.* — **pro·tru'sive·ness** *n.*

pro·tu·ber·ance (prō·tōō'bər·əns, -tyōō'-) *n.* **1.** Something that protrudes; a knob; prominence. **2.** The state of being protuberant. Also **pro·tu'ber·an·cy, pro·tu'ber·a'tion.**

pro·tu·ber·ant (prō·tōō'bər·ənt, -tyōō-) *adj.* Swelling out beyond the surrounding surface; bulging. [< LL < L *pro-* forth + *tuber* a swelling] — **pro·tu'ber·ant·ly** *adv.*

proud (proud) *adj.* **1.** Actuated by, possessing, or manifesting pride; arrogant; also, self-respecting. **2.** Sensible of honor and personal elation: generally followed by *of* or by a verb in the infinitive. **3.** High-mettled, as a horse. **4.** Proceeding from or inspired by pride. **5.** Being a cause of honorable pride, as a distinction. — **to do oneself proud** To do extremely well. [OE < OF, prob. ult. < L < *pro-* for + *esse* to be] — **proud'ly** *adv.*

proud flesh *Pathol.* A granulated growth resembling flesh in a wound or sore. [So called from its swelling up]

prove (prōōv) *v.* **proved, proved** or **prov·en, prov·ing** *v.t.* **1.** To show to be true or genuine, as by evidence or argument. **2.** To determine the quality or genuineness of; test: to *prove* a gun. **3.** To establish the authenticity or validity of, as a will. **4.** *Math.* To verify the accuracy of (a calculation, etc.). — *v.i.* **5.** To be shown to be by the result or outcome; turn out to be. [< OF < L < *probus* upright] — **prov'a·ble** *adj.* — **prov'er** *n.*

Pro·ven·cal (prō'vən·säl', *Fr.* prō·vän·sàl') *n.* **1.** A native or resident of Provence, France. **2.** The Roman language of Provence, used esp. in the 12th and 13th centuries in the lyric literature of the troubadours. — *adj.* Of or pertaining to Provence, its inhabitants, or their language.

prov·en·der (prov'ən·dər) *n.* **1.** Food for cattle; esp., dry food, as hay. **2.** *Rare* Provisions generally. — *v.t.* To provide with food, as cattle. [< OF < L *praebere* to supply]

prov·erb (prov'ûrb) *n.* **1.** A pithy saying, esp. one condensing the wisdom of experience; adage; saw; maxim. **2.** An enigmatic saying. **3.** A typical example; byword. [< OF < L < *pro-* before + *verbum* word]
  — **Syn.** A *proverb* is usually a homely illustration of a general truth, as: A rolling stone gathers no moss. An *adage* is a time-honored and generally accepted *proverb*, as: A man is known by the company he keeps. Any ancient and hackneyed *adage* is a *saw*, as: All that glitters is not gold.

pro·ver·bi·al (prə·vûr'bē·əl) *adj.* **1.** Pertaining to, or like a proverb. **2.** Well-known; notorious. — **pro·ver'bi·al·ly** *adv.*

Prov·erbs (prov'ûrbz) *n.pl.* (*construed as sing.*) An Old Testament book of moral teaching.

pro·vide (prə·vīd') *v.* **vid·ed, vid·ing** *v.t.* **1.** To supply or furnish. **2.** To afford; yield. **3.** To prepare, make ready, or procure beforehand. **4.** To set down as a condition; stipulate. — *v.i.* **5.** To take measures in advance: with *for* or *against*. **6.** To furnish means of subsistence: usu. with *for*. **7.** To make a stipulation. [< L < *pro-* before + *videre* to see] — **pro·vid'er** *n.*

pro·vid·ed (prə·vī'did) *conj.* On condition; if: He will get the loan *provided* he offers good security.

prov·i·dence (prov'ə·dəns) *n.* **1.** The care exercised by God over the universe. **2.** An event or circumstances ascribable to divine interposition. **3.** The exercise of foresight and care for the future. [< OF < L *providere* to foresee]

Prov·i·dence (prov'ə·dəns) God; the Deity.

prov·i·dent (prov'ə·dənt) *adj.* Anticipating and making ready for future wants. — **prov'i·dent·ly** *adv.*

prov·i·den·tial (prov'ə·den'shəl) *adj.* Resulting from or involving God's providence. — **prov'i·den'tial·ly** *adv.*

pro·vid·ing (prə·vī'ding) *conj.* On condition; provided.

prov·ince (prov'ins) *n.* **1.** A country incorporated with a kingdom or empire and subject to central administration. **2.** Any large administrative division of a country with a permanent local government. **3.** *pl.* Regions lying at a distance from the capital or most populous part of a country. **4.** A sphere of knowledge, activity, or endeavor. [< OF < L *provincia* province]

pro·vin·cial (prə·vin'shəl) *adj.* **1.** Of or pertaining to a province. **2.** Confined to a province; rustic; local. **3.** Narrow; uncultured; illiberal. — *n.* **1.** A native or inhabitant of a province. **2.** One who is provincial. — **pro·vin'ci·al'i·ty** (-shē·al'ə·tē) *n.* — **pro·vin'cial·ly** *adv.*

pro·vin·cial·ism (prə·vin'shəl·iz'əm) *n.* **1.** The quality of being provincial. **2.** A provincial custom, esp. of speech.

pro·vi·sion (prə·vizh'ən) *n.* **1.** The act of providing, or the state of being provided. **2.** Measures taken or means made ready in advance. **3.** *pl.* Food or a supply of food. **4.**

Something provided or prepared, as against future need. **5.** The part of an agreement, instrument, etc., referring to one specific thing; a stipulation. — *v.t.* To provide with food or provisions. [< OF < L < *pro-* before + *videre* to see] — **pro·vi'sion·er** *n.*

pro·vi·sion·al (prə·vizh'ən·əl) *adj.* Provided for a present service or temporary necessity; adopted tentatively. Also **pro·vi'sion·ar'y.** — **pro·vi'sion·al·ly** *adv.*

pro·vi·so (prə·vī'zō) *n.* *pl.* **·sos** or **·soes** A stipulation or clause, as in a contract or statute, limiting, modifying, or rendering conditional its operation. [< Med.L *proviso* it being provided < L *providere* to foresee]

pro·vi·so·ry (prə·vī'zər·ē) *adj.* **1.** Conditional. **2.** Provisional. — **pro·vi'so·ri·ly** *adv.*

prov·o·ca·tion (prov'ə·kā'shən) *n.* **1.** The act of provoking. **2.** An incitement to action; stimulus.

pro·voc·a·tive (prə·vok'ə·tiv) *adj.* Serving to provoke; stimulating. — *n.* That which provokes or tends to provoke. — **pro·voc'a·tive·ly** *adv.* — **pro·voc'a·tive·ness** *n.*

pro·voke (prə·vōk') *v.t.* **·voked, ·vok·ing 1.** To stir to anger or resentment; irritate; vex. **2.** To arouse or stimulate to some action. **3.** To stir up or bring about: to *provoke* a quarrel. **4.** To induce or cause; elicit: to *provoke* a smile. [< OF < L < *pro-* forth + *vocare* to call] — **pro·vok'ing·ly** *adv.* — **pro·vok'ing·ness** *n.*

prov·ost (prov'əst) *n.* **1.** A person having charge or authority over others. **2.** The chief magistrate of a Scottish city. **3.** In some English and American colleges, the head of the faculty. **4.** The head of a collegiate chapter or a cathedral; a dean. [< OE and OF, both < LL *propositus*, var. of L *praepositus* chief] — **prov'ost·ship** *n.*

pro·vost marshal (prō'vō) A military or naval officer exercising police functions: also called *provost.*

prow (prou) *n.* **1.** The fore part of the hull of a vessel; the bow. **2.** Any projection. [< MF < L < Gk. *prōira*]

prow·ess (prou'is) *n.* **1.** Strength, skill, and courage, esp. in battle. **2.** A daring and valiant deed. [< OF *prouesse*, *proece* < *prou* brave]

prowl (proul) *v.t. & v.i.* To roam about stealthily, as in search of prey or plunder. — *n.* The act of prowling. [ME *prollen* to search] — **prowl'er** *n.*

prowl car *U.S.* A police patrol car.

prox·i·mal (prok'sə·məl) *adj.* **1.** *Anat.* Relatively nearer the central portion of the body or point of origin. **2.** Proximate. — **prox'i·mal·ly** *adv.*

prox·i·mate (prok'sə·mit) *adj.* Being in immediate relation with something else; next: also *proximal.* [< LL < L *proximus*, superl. of *prope* near] — **prox'i·mate·ly** *adv.*

prox·im·i·ty (prok·sim'ə·tē) *n.* The state or fact of being near or next; nearness. [See PROXIMATE.]

proximity fuse A fuse in a projectile, usu. activated by an electronic device, that detonates by simple proximity to the target: also called *VT fuse.*

prox·i·mo (prok'sə·mō) *adv.* In or of the next or coming month. [See PROXIMATE.]

prox·y (prok'sē) *n.* *pl.* **prox·ies 1.** A person empowered by another to act for him. **2.** The office or right to so act, or the instrument conferring it. [ME *prokecie*]

prude (prōōd) *n.* A person who makes an affected display of modesty and propriety, esp. in matters relating to sex. [< F *preude* (*femme*) strong, hence, modest (woman)] — **prud'ish** *adj.* — **prud'ish·ly** *adv.* — **prud'ish·ness** *n.*

pru·dence (prōōd'ns) *n.* The quality or state of being prudent; sagacity; discretion.

pru·dent (prōōd'nt) *adj.* **1.** Cautious; worldly-wise. **2.** Exercising sound judgment. **3.** Not extravagant. **4.** Decorously discreet. [< OF < L *prudens, -entis* knowing, foreseeing] — **pru'dent·ly** *adv.*
  — **Syn. 1.** discreet, circumspect, wary. **3.** thrifty, economical, frugal. — **Ant.** imprudent, indiscreet, rash, reckless.

pru·den·tial (prōō·den'shəl) *adj.* **1.** Proceeding from or marked by prudence. **2.** Exercising prudence and wisdom. — **pru·den'tial·ly** *adv.*

prud·er·y (prōō'dər·ē) *n.* *pl.* **·er·ies 1.** Extreme priggishness; primness. **2.** Prudish action or language.

prune¹ (prōōn) *n.* The dried fruit of the plum. [< OF < LL < L *prunum*]

prune² (prōōn) *v.t. & v.i.* **pruned, prun·ing 1.** To trim or cut branches or parts (from) so as to improve growth, appearance, etc. **2.** To cut off (branches or parts). [< OF *proöignier, proignier,* ? < *provaignier* to cut] — **prun'er** *n.*

pru·ri·ent (prōōr'ē·ənt) *adj.* **1.** Having lustful cravings or desires. **2.** Lewd. [< L *pruriens, -entis,* ppr. of *prurire* to itch] — **pru'ri·ence, pru'ri·en·cy** *n.* — **pru'ri·ent·ly** *adv.*

pru·ri·tus (prōō·rī'təs) *n.* *Pathol.* Intense itching. [< L < *prurire* to itch] — **pru·rit·ic** (-rit'ik) *adj.*

Prus·sian (prush'ən) *adj.* **1.** Of or pertaining to Prussia, its inhabitants, or their language. **2.** Characteristic of the

Junkers of Prussia; militaristic; overbearing. — *n.* A native or inhabitant of Prussia.

Prussian blue 1. *Chem.* Any one of a group of cyanogen compounds containing chiefly ferric ferrocyanide, formerly much used in dyeing. 2. A deep blue pigment.

prus·sic acid (prus'ik) Hydrocyanic acid.

pry[1] (prī) *v.i.* **pried, pry·ing** To look or peer carefully, curiously, or slyly; snoop. — *n. pl.* **pries** 1. A sly and searching inspection. 2. One who pries; an inquisitive, prying person. [ME *prien*] — **pry'ing·ly** *adv.*

pry[2] (prī) *v.t.* **pried, pry·ing** *Chiefly U.S.* 1. To raise, move, or open by means of a lever; prize. 2. To obtain by effort. — *n.* A lever, as a bar, stick, or beam; also, leverage. [Back formation < *prize* lever]

pry·er (prī'ər) See PRIER.

psalm (säm) *n.* 1. *Often cap.* A sacred song or lyric contained in the Old Testament Book of Psalms. 2. Any sacred song. — *v.t.* To celebrate or praise in psalms. [OE < LL < Gk. *psalmos* song accompanied by a harp]

psalm·ist (sä'mist) *n.* A maker or composer of psalms. — **the Psalmist** King David, as the traditional author of many of the Scriptural psalms.

psalm·o·dy (sä'mə·dē, sal'-) *n. pl.* **·dies** 1. The use of psalms in divine worship. 2. A collection of psalms. [< OF < LL < Gk. < *psalmos* psalm + *aeidein* to sing]

Psalms (sämz) A lyrical book of the Old Testament, containing 150 hymns. Also **Book of Psalms.**

psal·ter (sôl'tər) *n.* The psalms appointed to be read or sung at any given service. [See PSALTERY.] — **psal·te·ri·an** (sôl·tir'ē·ən, sal-) *adj.*

Psal·ter (sôl'tər) *n.* The Book of Psalms, esp. for use in religious services. Also **Psal'ter·y.**

psal·ter·y (sôl'tər·ē) *n. pl.* **·ter·ies** An ancient stringed musical instrument played by plucking with a plectrum. [< OF < L < Gk. < *psallein* to pluck]

pseu·do (sōō'dō) *adj.* Pretended; sham.

pseudo- *combining form* 1. False; pretended: *pseudonym.* 2. Counterfeit; not genuine. 3. Closely resembling: *pseudopodium.* 4. Illusory; apparent. 5. Abnormal; erratic. Also, before vowels, **pseud-.** [< Gk. < *pseudēs* false]

pseu·do·nym (sōō'də·nim) *n.* A fictitious name; pen name. [< F < Gk. < *pseudēs* false + *onoma* name] — **pseu·don·y·mous** (sōō·don'ə·məs) *adj.* — **pseu·don'y·mous·ly** *adv.* — **pseu·don'y·mous·ness, pseu·do·nym'i·ty** *n.*

— **Syn.** *Pseudonym, alias, pen name,* and *nom de plume* denote an assumed name. Pseudonym is the general term, including all the others. An *alias* is a name taken to conceal one's true identity, most often for some wrongful purpose. *Pen name* and *nom de plume* refer to a fictitious name signed to a literary work by its author.

pseu·do·po·di·um (sōō'də·pō'dē·əm) *n. pl.* **·di·a** (-dē·ə) *Zool.* A temporary extension of the protoplasm of a cell or of a protozoan, used for taking in food, locomotion, etc. Also **pseu·do·pod** (-pod), **pseu·do·pode** (-pōd). [< NL]

pshaw (shô) *interj.* An exclamation of annoyance, disapproval, disgust, or impatience. — *v.t. & v.i.* To exclaim *pshaw* at (a person or thing).

psi (sī, psī, psē) *n.* The twenty-third letter in the Greek alphabet (Ψ, ψ): equivalent to English *ps*. See ALPHABET.

psit·ta·co·sis (sit'ə·kō'sis) *n.* An acute, infectious virus disease of parrots and related birds, transmissible to man and resembling influenza: also called *parrot fever.* [< NL < Gk. *psittakos* parrot + -OSIS]

pso·ri·a·sis (sə·rī'ə·sis) *n. Pathol.* A noncontagious, inflammatory skin disease, chronic or acute, characterized by reddish patches and white scales. [< NL < Gk. *psōra* an itch] — **pso·ri·at·ic** (sôr'ē·at'ik, sō'rē-) *adj.*

psych- Var. of PSYCHO-.

psy·che (sī'kē) *n.* 1. The human soul. 2. *Psychoanal.* The mind, often regarded as an entity functioning apart from or independently of the body. [< Gk. *psychē* soul]

Psy·che (sī'kē) In Greek and Roman mythology, a maiden who is united with Eros and is a personification of the soul.

psy·che·del·ic (sī'kə·del'ik) *adj.* Causing or having to do with an abnormal stimulation of consciousness or perception. [< Gk. *psychē* soul + *del(os)* manifest + -IC]

psy·chi·a·trist (sī·kī'ə·trist, si-) *n.* A physician specializing in the practice of psychiatry.

psy·chi·a·try (sī·kī'ə·trē, si-) *n.* The branch of medicine that deals with the diagnosis and treatment of mental disorders. — **psy·chi·at·ric** (sī'kē·at'rik) or **·ri·cal** *adj.*

psy·chic (sī'kik) *adj.* 1. Pertaining to the mind. 2. Pertaining to mental phenomena that appear to be independent of normal sensory stimuli, as clairvoyance, telepathy, and extrasensory perception. 3. Caused by, proceeding from, or attributed to a nonmaterial or occult agency. 4. Sensitive to mental or occult phenomena. Also **psy'chi·cal.** — *n.* One sensitive to extrasensory phenomena. [See PSYCHE.] — **psy'chi·cal·ly** *adv.*

psycho- *combining form* Mind; soul; spirit: *psychosomatic.* Also, before vowels, *psych-.* [< Gk. *psychē.* See PSYCHE.]

psy·cho·a·nal·y·sis (sī'kō·ə·nal'ə·sis) *n.* A system of psy-

chotherapy that seeks to alleviate neuroses and other mental disorders by the analysis of unconscious factors as revealed in dreams, free association, lapses of memory, etc. — **psy'·cho·an'a·lyt'ic** (-an'ə·lit'ik) or **·i·cal** *adj.* — **psy'cho·an'·a·lyt'i·cal·ly** *adv.*

psy·cho·an·a·lyst (sī'kō·an'ə·list) *n.* One who practices psychoanalysis.

psy·cho·an·a·lyze (sī'kō·an'ə·līz) *v.t.* **·lyzed, ·lyz·ing** To treat by psychoanalysis. Also *Brit.* **psy'cho·an'a·lyse.**

psy·cho·chem·i·cal (sī'kō·kem'i·kəl) *n. Chem.* A drug or compound that affects consciousness and behavior. — *adj.* Consisting or of the nature of a psychochemical.

psy·cho·gen·ic (sī'kō·jen'ik) *adj.* Having mental origin, or being affected by mental conflicts and states.

psy·cho·log·i·cal (sī'kə·loj'i·kəl) *adj.* 1. Of or pertaining to psychology. 2. Of or in the mind. Also **psy'cho·log'ic.** — **psy'cho·log'i·cal·ly** *adv.*

psy·chol·o·gist (sī·kol'ə·jist) *n.* A student of or a specialist in psychology.

psy·chol·o·gize (sī·kol'ə·jīz) *v.i.* **·gized, ·giz·ing** 1. To study psychology. 2. To theorize on psychology.

psy·chol·o·gy (sī·kol'ə·jē) *n. pl.* **·gies** 1. The science of the human mind in any of its aspects, operations, powers, or functions. 2. The systematic investigation of mental phenomena, especially those associated with consciousness, behavior, and the problems of adjustment to the environment. 3. The behavior patterns regarded as characteristic of an individual, type, group, etc. 4. A work on psychology.

psy·cho·mo·tor (sī'kō·mō'tər) *adj. Physiol.* Of or pertaining to muscular movements resulting from mental processes.

psy·cho·neu·ro·sis (sī'kō·nōō·rō'sis, -nyōō-) *n. pl.* **·ses** (-sēz) *Psychiatry* Neurosis. — **psy'cho·neu·rot'ic** (-rot'ik) *adj. & n.*

psy·cho·path (sī'kō·path) *n.* One who is mentally unstable, esp. in a criminal or antisocial manner.

psy·cho·path·ic (sī'kō·path'ik) *adj.* Of or characterized by psychopathy.

psy·cho·pa·thol·o·gy (sī'kō·pə·thol'ə·jē) *n.* The pathology of the mind. — **psy'cho·path'o·log'i·cal** (-path'ə·loj'i·kəl) *adj.* — **psy'cho·pa·thol'o·gist** *n.*

psy·chop·a·thy (sī·kop'ə·thē) *n.* Mental disorder.

psy·cho·phar·ma·col·o·gy (sī'kō·fär'mə·kol'ə·jē) *n.* The branch of pharmacology dealing with drugs that affect the mind. — **psy'cho·phar'ma·co·log'ic** (-kə·loj'ik) *adj.*

psy·cho·sis (sī·kō'sis) *n. pl.* **·ses** (-sēz) *Psychiatry* A severe mental disorder, often involving disorganization of the total personality, with or without organic disease. [< NL < Gk. *psychōsis* giving of life < *psychoein* to animate]

psy·cho·so·mat·ic (sī'kō·sō·mat'ik) *adj.* 1. Of or pertaining to the effect of emotional states upon the body, with special reference to certain disorders. 2. Designating a branch of medicine that treats such disorders with a psychological approach.

psy·cho·ther·a·py (sī'kō·ther'ə·pē) *n. pl.* **·pies** The treatment of nervous and mental disorders, by psychological methods, as hypnosis, re-education, psychoanalysis, etc. Also **psy'cho·ther'a·peu'tics** (-ther'ə·pyōō'tiks). — **psy'·cho·ther'a·peu'tic** *adj.* — **psy'cho·ther'a·pist** *n.*

psy·chot·ic (sī·kot'ik) *n.* One suffering from a psychosis. — *adj.* Of or characterized by a psychosis.

psy·chot·o·mi·met·ic (sī·kot'ō·mi·met'ik, -mī·met'ik) *adj.* Designating a group of drugs capable of inducing altered states of consciousness and having possible therapeutic value.

psychro- *combining form* Cold. [< Gk. *psychros* cold]

ptar·mi·gan (tär'mə·gən) *n. pl.* **·gans** or **·gan** A grouse of the northern hemisphere, having a white winter plumage, and feathered toes. [< Scottish Gaelic *tarmachan*]

PT boat A patrol torpedo boat.

ptero- *combining form* Wing; feather; winglike. Also, before vowels, **pter-.** [< Gk. *pteron* wing]

pter·o·dac·tyl (ter'ə·dak'til) *n. Paleontol.* Any of a genus of extinct flying reptiles of the Jurassic period. [< NL < Gk. *pteron* wing + *daktylos* finger]

-pterous *combining form* Having (a specified number or kind of) wings: *dipterous.* [< Gk. *pteron* wing]

Ptol·e·ma·ic (tol'ə·mā'ik) *adj.* Of or pertaining to Ptolemy, the astronomer, or to the dynasty of Egyptian kings that began with Ptolemy I. [< Gk. *Ptolemaïkos*]

Ptolemaic system The ancient astronomical system of Ptolemy. It assumed that the earth was the central body around which the sun, planets, and celestial bodies revolved.

Ptol·e·ma·ist (tol'ə·mā'ist) *n.* A believer in or adherent of the Ptolemaic system.

pto·maine (tō'mān, tō·mān') *n. Biochem.* Any of a class of basic nitrogenous compounds, some of which are poisonous, derived from decomposing animal or vegetable protein. Also **pto'main.** [< Ital. < Gk. *ptōma* corpse]

ptomaine poisoning An erroneous term for food poisoning.

pty·a·lin (tī'ə·lin) *n. Biochem.* An enzyme, contained in saliva, that converts starch into dextrin and maltose. [< Gk. *ptyalon* saliva < *ptuein* to spit + -IN]

pub (pub) *n. Brit. Informal* A public house; inn; tavern.

pu·ber·ty (pyōō'bər·tē) *n. pl. ·ties* The period during which an individual becomes physiologically capable of reproduction. [< L < *pubes, puberis* an adult]

pu·bes (pyōō'bēz) *n.* 1. *Anat.* The part of the lower abdomen covered with hair in the adult; the pubic region. 2. The hair that appears on the body at puberty; esp., the hair on the pubic region. [< L, pubic hair]

pu·bes·cent (pyōō·bes'ənt) *adj.* 1. Arriving or having arrived at puberty. 2. Having a growth of soft, fine hairs, as certain plants. [< MF < L *pubescens, -entis*, ppr. of *pubescere* to grow hair, attain puberty] — **pu·bes'cence** *n.*

pu·bic (pyōō'bik) *adj.* Of or pertaining to the region in the lower part of the abdomen: the *pubic* bones.

pu·bis (pyōō'bis) *n. pl. ·bes* (-bēz) *Anat.* Either of the two bones that join with a third to form an arch on either ventral side of the pelvis. [See PUBES.]

pub·lic (pub'lik) *adj.* 1. Of, pertaining to, or affecting the people at large or the community. 2. Maintained by or for the public: *public* parks. 3. Participated in by the people: a *public* demonstration. 4. For the use of the public: especially, for hire: a *public* cab, hall, etc. 5. Well-known; open; notorious: a *public* scandal. 6. Acting before or for the community: a *public* official. — *n.* 1. Those who may be grouped together for any given purpose. 2. An audience; esp., the admirers of an actor or other celebrity. — **the public** The people of a locality or nation. [< MF < L *publicus*] — **pub'lic·ly** *adv.* — **pub'lic·ness** *n.*

pub·lic-ad·dress system (pub'lik·ə·dres') An apparatus for the amplification of speech, music, etc., in public places.

pub·li·can (pub'lə·kən) *n.* 1. In England, the keeper of a public house. 2. In ancient Rome, a tax collector. [< OF < L < *publicum* public revenue, orig. neut. of *publicus*]

pub·li·ca·tion (pub'lə·kā'shən) *n.* 1. The act of publishing or offering to public notice. 2. Any printed work placed on sale or otherwise distributed or offered for distribution. 3. Notification to people at large orally or by writing or print; promulgation; proclamation. [See PUBLISH.]

public domain Lands owned by a state or national government; public lands. — **in the public domain** Available for unrestricted use: said of material on which copyright or patent right has expired.

public enemy 1. A person, esp. a criminal, regarded as a menace to the public. 2. An enemy state.

public house 1. An inn, tavern, or hotel. 2. In England, a place licensed to sell intoxicating liquors; a saloon.

pub·li·cist (pub'lə·sist) *n.* 1. A writer on international law or on topics of public interest. 2. A public-relations man or publicity agent.

pub·lic·i·ty (pub·lis'ə·tē) *n.* 1. Information or personal news intended to promote the interests of individuals, institutions, etc. 2. The state of being public, or the act of making or becoming public; exposure; notoriety. 3. The attention or interest of the public gained by any method.

pub·li·cize (pub'lə·sīz) *v.t. ·cized, ·ciz·ing* To advertise.

public library 1. A library maintained for the use of the public. 2. The building in which it is contained.

public opinion The prevailing ideas, beliefs, and aims of the people, collectively.

public relations The activities and techniques used by organizations and individuals to establish favorable attitudes and responses in their behalf on the part of the general public or of special groups; also, the occupation of establishing such attitude and responses.

public school 1. *U.S.* A school maintained by public funds for the free education of the children of the community, usu. covering elementary and secondary grades. 2. *Brit.* A private or endowed school not run for profit, esp. one preparing students for the universities, as Eton, Harrow, etc.

public servant A government official.

public utility A business organization or industry that supplies water, electricity, gas, etc., to the public, and is subject to particular governmental regulations.

public works Architectural or engineering works or improvements built with public money, as parks, roads, etc.

pub·lish (pub'lish) *v.t.* 1. To print and issue (a book, magazine, map, etc.) to the public. 2. To make known or announce publicly; promulgate; proclaim. [See PUBLIC.] — **pub'lish·a·ble** *adj.*

pub·lish·er (pub'lish·ər) *n.* One who publishes; esp., one whose business is publishing books, etc.

puce (pyōōs) *adj.* Of a dark brown or purplish brown. [< F, flea color, flea < L *pulex, -icis* flea]

puck¹ (puk) *n.* An evil sprite or hobgoblin. [OE *pūca*]

puck² (puk) *n.* The black, hard, rubber disk used in playing ice hockey. [? < dial. E, to strike]

Puck (puk) A mischievous elf or goblin in Shakespeare's *A Midsummer Night's Dream.* [< PUCK¹]

puck·a (puk'ə) See PUKKA.

puck·er (puk'ər) *v.t. & v.i.* To gather or draw up into small folds or wrinkles. — *n.* A wrinkle or group of wrinkles. [Appar. freq. of POKE²] — **puck'er·y** *adj.*

puck·ish (puk'ish) *adj.* Mischievous; impish.

pud·ding (pōōd'ing) *n.* 1. A sweetened and flavored dessert of soft food, usu. made of milk, flavoring, a thickening agent, etc. 2. A sausage of seasoned minced meat, blood, or the like, usu. boiled or broiled. [ME *poding*, orig., sausage, black pudding]

pud·dle (pud'l) *n.* 1. A small pool of water, esp. dirty water. 2. A small pool of any liquid. — *v.t.* **·dled, ·dling** 1. *Metall.* To convert (molten pig iron) into wrought iron by melting and stirring in the presence of oxidizing substances. 2. To mix (clay, etc.) with water so as to obtain a watertight paste. 3. To make muddy; stir up. [ME *podel*, dim. of OE *pudd* ditch] — **pud'dly** *adj.*

pud·dle·ball (pud'l·bôl') *n. Metall.* A ball of iron reduced to a pasty condition in the puddling furnace and ready for hammering or rolling.

pud·dler (pud'lər) *n.* 1. One who puddles. 2. A device for stirring fused metal.

pud·dling (pud'ling) *n. Metall.* The operation or business of making wrought iron from pig iron in a puddling furnace.

puddling furnace A reverberatory furnace for puddling pig iron: also called *hearth.*

pudg·y (puj'ē) *adj.* **pudg·i·er, pudg·i·est** Short and fat; dumpy; chubby: also *podgy.* [< Scot.]

pueb·lo (pweb'lō *for def. 1;* pwä'blō *for def. 2*) *n. pl. ·los* 1. A communal adobe or stone building or group of buildings of the Indians of the SW U.S. 2. A town or village of Indians or Spanish Americans, as in Mexico. [< Sp., village]

Pueb·lo (pweb'lō) *n.* A member of one of the Indian tribes of Mexico and the SW U.S., as a Zuni, Hopi, etc.

pu·er·ile (pyōō'ər·il, pyōō'rəl, -rīl, pwer'əl, -il) *adj.* 1. Pertaining to or characteristic of childhood; juvenile. 2. Immature; weak; silly: a *puerile* suggestion. [< L < *puer* boy, child] — **pu'er·ile·ly** *adv.* — **pu'er·ile·ness** *n.*

pu·er·il·i·ty (pyōō'ə·ril'ə·tē, pyōō·ril'-, pwer·il'-) *n. pl. ·ties* 1. Puerile state. 2. A childish act or expression.

pu·er·per·al (pyōō·ûr'pər·əl) *adj. Med.* Of or connected with childbirth. [< L < *puer* child + *parere* to bear]

puff (puf) *n.* 1. A breath emitted suddenly and with force; also, a sudden emission, as of air, smoke, or steam. 2. A light, air-filled piece of pastry. 3. A light ball, tuft, wad, or pad for dusting powder on the hair or skin. 4. A loose roll of hair in a coiffure, or a light cushion over which it is rolled. 5. A quilted bed coverlet; a comforter. 6. In dressmaking, a part of a fabric so gathered as to produce a loose, fluffy distention. 7. Excessive praise, as in a newspaper or advertisement. 8. A puffball. — *v.i.* 1. To blow in puffs, as the wind. 2. To breathe hard, as after violent exertion. 3. To emit smoke, steam, etc., in puffs. 4. To smoke a cigar, etc., with puffs. 5. To move, act, or exert oneself while emitting puffs: often with *away, up,* etc. 6. To swell, as with air or pride; dilate: often with *up* or *out.* — *v.t.* 7. To send forth or emit with short puffs or breaths. 8. To move, impel, or stir up with or in puffs. 9. To smoke, as a pipe or cigar, with puffs. 10. To swell or distend. 11. To praise excessively. 12. To arrange (hair, etc.) in a puff. [ME *puf*]

puff adder A large, sluggish, venomous African viper with a habit of violently puffing out its breath.

puff·ball (puf'bôl') *n.* Any of various globular fungi that puff out dustlike spores when broken open.

puff·er (puf'ər) *n.* One who or that which puffs.

puf·fin (puf'in) *n.* A sea bird allied to the auk and having a deep, compressed, highly colored bill. [ME *poffin*]

puff·y (puf'ē) *adj.* **puff·i·er, puff·i·est** 1. Swollen with or as with air, etc. 2. Inflated in manner; bombastic. 3. Blowing in puffs. — **puff'i·ly** *adv.* — **puff'i·ness** *n.*

pug¹ (pug) *n.* Clay worked with water, for molding pottery or bricks. — *v.t.* **pugged, pug·ging** 1. To knead or work (clay) with water, as in brickmaking. 2. To fill in with clay, etc. [Origin unknown]

pug² (pug) *n.* 1. A breed of dog characterized by a short square body, upturned nose, curled tail, and short smooth coat. 2. A pug nose. [Prob. alter. of PUCK]

pug³ (pug) *n. Anglo-Indian* An animal's footprint; trail. [< Hind. *pag* foot]

pug⁴ (pug) *n. Slang* A professional pugilist. [Short for PUGILIST]

pugh (pyōō, pōō) *interj.* An exclamation of disgust.

pu·gi·lism (pyōō'jə·liz'əm) *n.* The art or practice of boxing or fighting with the fists. [< L *pugil* boxer] — **pu'gi·list** *n.* — **pu'gi·lis·tic** *adj.*

pug·na·cious (pug·nā'shəs) *adj.* Disposed or inclined to fight; quarrelsome. [< L *pugnare* to fight] — **pug·na'·cious·ly** *adv.*

pug·nac·i·ty (pug·nas′ə·tē) *n.* *pl.* **·ties** The quality of being pugnacious; quarrelsome disposition; combativeness. Also **pug·na′cious·ness** (-nā′shəs·nis).

pug nose A short nose tilted upward at the end. [< PUG²] —**pug-nosed** (pug′nōzd′) *adj.*

puis·ne (pyōo′nē) *adj.* *Law* Junior as to rank; younger. [< OF < *puis* afterwards + *né* born]

pu·is·sant (pyōo′ə·sənt, pyōo·is′ənt, pwis′ənt) *adj.* Powerful; mighty. [< OF < L *posse* to be able] —**pu′is·sance** *n.* —**pu′is·sant·ly** *adv.*

puke (pyōōk) *v.t. & v.i.* **puked, puk·ing** To vomit or cause to vomit. —*n.* Vomit. [Origin unknown]

puk·ka (puk′ə) *adj.* *Anglo-Indian* 1. Made of good materials; substantial. 2. Genuine; superior. Also spelled *pucka.* [< Hind. *pakkā* substantial, cooked, ripe]

pul·chri·tude (pul′krə·tōōd, -tyōōd) *n.* Beauty; grace; physical charm. [< L *pulchritudo, -inis* < *pulcher* beautiful]

pul·chri·tu·di·nous (pul′krə·tōō′də·nəs, -tyōō′-) *adj.* Beautiful; lovely; esp., having physical beauty.

pule (pyōōl) *v.i.* **puled, pul·ing** To cry plaintively, as a child; whimper; whine. [Prob. imit.] —**pul′er** *n.*

Pul·itz·er Prize (pyōo′lit·sər, pool′it-) One of several annual awards for outstanding work in American journalism, letters, music, and art, established by Joseph Pulitzer, 1847–1911, U.S. journalist.

pull (pool) *v.t.* 1. To apply force so as to cause motion toward or in the direction of the source of force; drag; tug. 2. To draw or remove from a natural or fixed place. 3. To give a pull or tug to. 4. To pluck, as a fowl. 5. To rip; tear; rend. 6. To strain so as to cause injury. 7. In golf, etc., to strike (the ball) so that it curves obliquely from the direction in which the striker faces. 8. In baseball, to hit (the ball) to the field that the batter faces on completing his swing. 9. *Slang* To put into effect; carry out: often with *off.* 10. *Slang* To make a raid on; arrest. 11. *Slang* To draw out so as to use. 12. *Printing* To make or obtain by impression from type: to *pull* a proof. 13. In boxing, to deliver (a punch, etc.) with less than one's full strength. 14. In rowing: **a** To operate (an oar) by drawing toward one. **b** To propel or transport by rowing. **c** To be propelled by: The gig *pulls* four oars. —*v.i.* 15. To use force in hauling, dragging, moving, etc. 16. To move: with *out, in, away, ahead,* etc. 17. To drink or inhale deeply. 18. To propel a boat with oars; row. —**to pull for** 1. To strive in behalf of. 2. *Informal* To declare one's allegiance to. —**to pull oneself together** To regain one's composure. —**to pull out** To withdraw, as from established position. —**to pull through** To manage to succeed, recover, etc. —**to pull up** To come to a halt. —**to pull up with** To advance to a position even with. —*n.* 1. The act of pulling. 2. Something that is pulled, as the handle of a drawer. 3. An impression made by pulling the lever of a hand press. 4. A long swallow, or a deep puff. 5. Any steady, continuous effort. 6. *Slang* A means of influencing those in power; influence. 7. Attraction; appeal. 8. The amount of resistance met in drawing a bowstring, pulling a trigger or the like, usu. measured in pounds. [OE *pullian* to pluck] —**pull′er** *n.*

pull·back (pool′bak′) *n.* 1. A restraint or drawback. 2. A device for drawing or holding something back, as part of a dress, or a window.

pul·let (pool′it) *n.* A young hen, or one not fully grown. [< OF *polete, poulet,* dim. of *poule* hen]

pul·ley (pool′ē) *n.* *pl.* **·leys** 1. A wheel grooved to receive a rope, and usu. mounted in a block, used to increase the mechanical advantage of an applied force. 2. A block with its pulleys or tackle. 3. A wheel driving, carrying, or being driven by a belt. [< OF < Med.L *poleia,* prob. ult. < Gk. *polos* pivot, axis]

Pull·man (pool′mən) *n.* A sleeping car or chair car on a passenger train: a trade name. Also **Pullman car.** [after George M. *Pullman,* 1831–97, U.S. inventor]

pull·out (pool′out′) *n.* 1. A withdrawal, as of troops. 2. *Aeron.* The maneuver of an airplane in passing from a dive to horizontal flight.

pull·o·ver (pool′ō′vər) *adj.* Put on by being drawn over the head. —*n.* A garment so put on, as a sweater or shirt.

pulmo- *combining form* Lung. [< *pulmo, -onis* lung]

pul·mo·nar·y (pul′mə·ner′ē) *adj.* 1. Of, pertaining to, or affecting the lungs: also *pneumonic.* 2. Having lunglike organs. [< L *pulmo, -onis* lung]

pulmonary artery *Anat.* An artery that conveys venous blood from the right ventricle of the heart to the lungs.

pulmonary tuberculosis Tuberculosis.

pul·mon·ic (pul·mon′ik) *adj.* Pulmonary.

Pul·mo·tor (pul′mō′tər, pool′-) *n.* An apparatus for producing artificial respiration by forcing oxygen into the lungs: a trade name. Also **pul′mo·tor.** [< PUL(MO)- + MOTOR]

pulp (pulp) *n.* 1. A moist, soft, slightly cohering mass of matter, as the succulent part of fruit. 2. A mixture of wood fibers or rags reduced to a pulpy consistency and forming the substance of paper. 3. *Often pl.* A magazine printed on rough, unglazed paper, and usu. having contents of a cheap, sensational nature: distinguished from *slick.* 4. *Dent.* The soft tissue of vessels and nerves that fills the central cavity of a tooth. —*v.t.* 1. To reduce to pulp. 2. To remove the pulp or envelope from. —*v.i.* 3. To be or become of a pulpy consistency. [< MF < L *pulpa* flesh, pulp of fruit, pith] —**pulp′i·ness** *n.* —**pulp′y** *adj.*

pul·pit (pool′pit) *n.* 1. An elevated stand or desk for a preacher in a church. 2. The office or work of preaching. 3. The clergy as a class. [< L *pulpitum* scaffold, stage]

pulp·wood (pulp′wood′) *n.* The soft wood of certain trees, as the spruce, used in the manufacture of paper.

pul·que (pul′kē, pool′-; *Sp.* pool′kä) *n.* A fermented drink made from various species of agave, esp. from the juice of the maguey. [< Am. Sp.]

pul·sar (pul′sär) *n.* A rotating neutron star, a source of regularly pulsing radio waves. [< PULSE + QUASAR]

pul·sate (pul′sāt) *v.i.* **·sat·ed, ·sat·ing** 1. To move or throb with rhythmical impulses, as the pulse or heart. 2. To vibrate; quiver. [< L *pellere* (pp. *pulsus*) to beat] —**pul·sa′tion** *n.* —**pul′sa·tive** (-sə·tiv) *adj.* —**pul′sa·tor** *n.* —**pul·sa·to·ry** (pul′sə·tôr′e) *adj.*

pulse¹ (puls) *n.* 1. *Physiol.* The rhythmical beating of the arteries resulting from the successive contractions of the heart. 2. Any throbbing or pulsation. 3. *Telecom.* A brief surge of electrical or electromagnetic energy, usu. transmitted as a signal in communication. 4. An indication of general opinion or sentiment. —*v.i.* **pulsed, puls·ing** To pulsate; throb. [< OF < L *pulsus* (*venarum*) the beating (of the veins)] —**pulse′less** *adj.*

pulse² (puls) *n.* Leguminous plants collectively, as peas, beans, etc.; also, their edible seeds. [< OF < L *puls* pottage of meal or pulse]

pulse·jet (puls′jet′) *n.* *Aeron.* A jet engine having movable vanes that intermittently take in air to develop power in rapid bursts. Also **pul′so·jet′** (-sō·jet′).

pul·som·e·ter (pul·som′ə·tər) *n.* A device for pumping liquids by steam pressure, consisting of two pear-shaped chambers connected by valves: also called *vacuum pump.*

pul·ver·ize (pul′və·rīz) *v.* **·ized, ·iz·ing** *v.t.* 1. To reduce to powder or dust, as by crushing. 2. To demolish; annihilate. —*v.i.* 3. To become reduced to powder or dust. Also *Brit.* **pul′ver·ise.** [< MF < LL < L *pulvis, pulveris* powder, dust] —**pul′ver·iz′a·ble** *adj.* —**pul′ver·i·za′tion** *n.* —**pul′ver·iz′er** *n.*

pu·ma (pyōo′mə) *n.* A reddish carnivore of the cat family, ranging from Canada to Patagonia: also called *cougar, mountain cat, mountain lion.* [< Sp. < Peruvian]

pum·ice (pum′is) *n.* Spongy volcanic lava, used as an abrasive and polishing material, esp. when powdered. Also **pumice stone.** —*v.t.* **·iced, ·ic·ing** To smooth, polish, or clean with pumice. [< OF < L *pumex, pumicis*] —**pu·mi·ceous** (pyōo·mish′əs) *adj.*

pum·mel (pum′əl) *v.t.* **·meled** or **·melled, ·mel·ing** or **·mel·ling** To pommel. —*n.* A pommel.

pump¹ (pump) *n.* A mechanical device for raising, circulating, exhausting, or compressing a liquid or gas by drawing or pressing it through openings and pipes. —*v.t.* 1. To raise with a pump, as water or other liquid. 2. To remove the water, etc., from. 3. To inflate with air by means of a pump. 4. To propel, discharge, force, etc., from or as if from a pump. 5. To obtain information from persistently or subtly: to *pump* a witness. 6. To obtain (information) in such a manner. —*v.i.* 7. To work a pump; raise water or other liquid with a pump. 8. To move up and down like a pump handle. [< MDu. *pompe*] —**pump′er** *n.*

pump² (pump) *n.* A low-cut shoe without a fastening, having either a high or a low heel. [Origin uncertain]

pum·per·nick·el (pum′pər·nik′əl) *n.* A coarse, dark, sour bread made from unsifted rye. [< G]

pump·kin (pump′kin, pung′-) *n.* 1. A large, round, edible, yellow-orange fruit borne by a coarse trailing vine with heart-shaped leaves. 2. The vine. 3. Any of several related European plants. [< MF < L < Gk. *pepon* melon]

pun (pun) *n.* The humorous use of two words having the same or similar sounds but different meanings, or of two different, more or less incongruous meanings of the same word. —*v.i.* **punned, pun·ning** To make a pun. [Origin uncertain] —**pun′ning·ly** *adv.*

punch¹ (punch) *n.* 1. A tool for perforating or indenting, or for driving out or in an object inserted in a hole, as a bolt or pin. 2. A machine for impressing a design or stamping a die. —*v.t.* To perforate, shape, indent, etc., with a punch. [Prob. short for PUNCHEON¹]

punch² (punch) *v.t.* 1. To strike sharply, esp. with the fist. 2. To poke with a stick; prod. 3. To operate; work; use: to *punch* a time clock. 4. *U.S.* In the West, to drive (cattle). —*n.* 1. A swift blow with the fist; also, a thrust or nudge. 2. *Slang* Vitality; force: an editorial with *punch.* [Prob. var. of POUNCE²] —**punch′er** *n.*

punch³ (punch) *n.* A beverage having wine or spirits, milk, tea, or fruit juices as a basic ingredient, sweetened, sometimes spiced, and diluted with water. [? < Hind. < Skt. *panchan* five; from the five original ingredients]

Punch (punch) The quarrelsome, grotesque hero of a comic puppet show, **Punch and Judy**, who habitually fights with his wife, Judy. **— pleased as Punch** Extremely pleased; highly gratified. [Short for PUNCHINELLO]

punch card In data processing, a card marked by an arrangement of positions to record information indicated by the presence or absence of punched holes. Also **punched card**.

punch-drunk (punch′drungk′) *adj.* **1.** Groggy, slow in movement, speech, etc., from repeated blows to the head: said of prize fighters. **2.** Confused; dazed.

pun·cheon[1] (pun′chən) *n.* **1.** An upright supporting timber. **2.** A punch or perforating tool. **3.** A broad, heavy piece of roughly dressed timber. [< OF *poncon*, *poinchon* a punch]

pun·cheon[2] (pun′chən) *n.* **1.** A liquor cask of variable capacity, from 72 to 120 gallons. **2.** A liquor measure of varying amount. [< OF *ponçon*, *poinchon*]

Pun·chi·nel·lo (pun′chə·nel′ō) *n.* *pl.* **·los** or **·loes** A comic character; buffoon, esp. in an Italian puppet show. Also **pun′chi·nel′lo**. [< dial. Ital. (Neapolitan) *Polcenella*]

punch·ing bag (pun′ching) An inflated or stuffed ball, usu. suspended, that is punched with the fists for exercise.

punch press A machine equipped to cut or form metal.

punc·til·i·o (pungk·til′ē·ō) *n.* *pl.* **·til·i·os** **1.** A fine point of etiquette. **2.** Preciseness in the observance of etiquette or ceremony. [< Sp. < Ital. < L *punctum* point]

punc·til·i·ous (pungk·til′ē·əs) *adj.* **1.** Very careful in the observance of forms of etiquette, etc. **2.** Very precise. **— punc·til′i·ous·ly** *adv.* **— punc·til′i·ous·ness** *n.*

punc·tu·al (pungk′chōō·əl) *adj.* **1.** Acting or arriving promptly. **2.** Done or made precisely at an appointed time. **3.** Punctilious; exact. [< Med.L < L *punctus* pricking, point] **— punc′tu·al·ly** *adv.*

punc·tu·al·i·ty (pungk′chōō·al′ə·tē) *n.* *pl.* **·ties** The quality, characteristic, act, or habit of being punctual.

punc·tu·ate (pungk′chōō·āt) *v.* **·at·ed**, **·at·ing** *v.t.* **1.** To divide or mark with punctuation. **2.** To interrupt at intervals. **3.** To emphasize; stress. **—** *v.i.* **4.** To use punctuation. [< Med.L < L *punctus* point] **— punc′tu·a′tor** *n.*

punc·tu·a·tion (pungk′chōō·ā′shən) *n.* The use of points or marks in written or printed matter to indicate the separation of the words into sentences, clauses, and phrases, and to aid in the better comprehension of the meaning; also, the marks so used (**punctuation marks**). **— punc′tu·a′tive** *adj.* The chief punctuation marks are:

period	.	parentheses	( )
colon	:	brackets	[ ]
semicolon	;	dash (em-dash)	—
comma	,	(en-dash)	–
question mark	?	hyphen	-
(interrogation point)		quotation marks	" "
exclamation mark	!	virgule (virgil)	/

punc·ture (pungk′chər) *v.* **·tured**, **·tur·ing** *v.t.* **1.** To pierce with a sharp point. **2.** To make by pricking, as a hole. **3.** To cause to collapse: to *puncture* a tire. **—** *v.i.* **4.** To be pierced or punctured. **—** *n.* **1.** A small hole made by piercing with a sharp point. **2.** A minute depression; pit. **3.** The act of puncturing. [< L < *pungere* to prick]

pun·dit (pun′dit) *n.* **1.** In India, one versed in Sanskrit lore and in the science, laws, and religion of the Hindus. **2.** Any learned man. [< Hind. < Skt. *pandita*]

pun·gent (pun′jənt) *adj.* **1.** Sharp or acrid to taste or smell; keen; penetrating: a *pungent* odor. **2.** Affecting the mind or feelings so as to cause pain; poignant. **3.** Caustic; biting: *pungent* sarcasm. [< L < *pungere* to prick] **— pun′·gence** (-jəns), **pun′gen·cy** *n.* **— pun′gent·ly** *adv.*

Pu·nic (pyōō′nik) *adj.* **1.** Of or pertaining to ancient Carthage or the Carthaginians. **2.** Untrustworthy, as the Carthaginians. **—** *n.* The language of the Carthaginians. [< L < *Poenus* Carthaginian, Phoenician]

Punic Wars See table for WAR.

pun·ish (pun′ish) *v.t.* **1.** To subject (a person) to pain, confinement, or other penalty for a crime or fault. **2.** To impose a penalty on. **3.** To use roughly; injure. **4.** To deplete, as a stock of food. [< OF < L *punire* to punish] **— pun′ish·a·ble** *adj.* **— pun′ish·a·bil′i·ty** *n.* **— pun′ish·er** *n.*

pun·ish·ment (pun′ish·mənt) *n.* **1.** A penalty imposed, as for transgression of law. ◆ Collateral adjective: *penal.* **2.** Any ill suffered in consequence of wrongdoing. **3.** The act of punishing. **4.** *Informal* Rough handling, as in a prize fight.

pu·ni·tive (pyōō′nə·tiv) *adj.* **1.** Pertaining to or inflicting punishment: *punitive* measures. **2.** *Law* Of a character to punish or vindicate. Also **pu′ni·to·ry** (-tôr′ē, -tō′rē). **— pu′ni·tive·ly** *adv.* **— pu′ni·tive·ness** *n.*

Pun·ja·bi (pun·jä′bē) *n.* **1.** A native of the Punjab. **2.** The Sanskritic language of the Punjab: also spelled *Panjabi.*

punk[1] (pungk) *n.* **1.** Wood decayed through the action of a fungus, useful as tinder. **2.** An artificial preparation that will smolder without flame. [< Algonquian]

punk[2] (pungk) *U.S. Slang n.* **1.** Nonsense. **2.** A petty hoodlum. **3.** A young, inexperienced boy or man: a contemptuous term. **—** *adj.* **1.** Worthless. **2.** Unwell. [Origin uncertain]

pun·ka (pung′kə) *n.* A fan; esp., a rectangular strip of cloth, etc., swung from the ceiling and moved by a servant or by machinery. Also **pun′kah**. [< Hind. *pankhā* fan]

pun·ster (pun′stər) *n.* One who puns. Also **pun′ner**.

punt[1] (punt) *n.* A flat-bottomed, square-ended boat, often propelled by a pole, used in shallow waters. **—** *v.t.* **1.** To propel (a boat) by pushing with a pole against the bottom of a shallow stream, lake, etc. **2.** To convey in a punt. **—** *v.i.* **3.** To go or hunt in a punt. [OE < L *ponto*, *-onis* punt, pontoon] **— punt′er** *n.*

PUNT

punt[2] (punt) *v.i.* In certain card games, to gamble or bet, esp. against a bank. [< F < Sp. < L *punctum* point] **— punt′er** *n.*

punt[3] (punt) *n.* In football, a kick made by dropping the ball from the hands and kicking it before it strikes the ground. **—** *v.t. & v.i.* In football, to propel (the ball) with a punt. [? Var. of BUNT] **— punt′er** *n.*

pun·ty (pun′tē) *n.* *pl.* **·ties** An iron rod used in glassmaking to handle the hot glass. [< F *pontil*]

pu·ny (pyōō′nē) *adj.* **·ni·er**, **·ni·est** Of small and feeble development or importance; weak and insignificant. [See PUISNE.] **— pu′ni·ly** *adv.* **— pu′ni·ness** *n.*

pup (pup) *n.* **1.** A puppy (def. 1). **2.** The young of the seal, the shark, and certain other animals. **—** *v.i.* **pupped**, **pupping** To bring forth pups. [Short for PUPPY]

pu·pa (pyōō′pə) *n.* *pl.* **·pae** (-pē) *Entomol.* **1.** The quiescent stage in the development of an insect, following the larval and preceding the adult stage. **2.** An insect in such a stage. [< NL < L, girl, doll, puppet] **— pu′pal** *adj.*

pu·pil[1] (pyōō′pəl) *n.* A person of any age under the care of a teacher; learner. **— Syn.** See STUDENT. [< OF < L *pupillus*, dim. of *pupus* boy and *pupilla*, dim. of *pupa* girl]

pu·pil[2] (pyōō′pəl) *n.* *Anat.* The contractile opening in the iris of the eye, through which light reaches the retina. [< OF < L *pupilla* pupil of the eye]

pup·pet (pup′it) *n.* **1.** A small figure of a person, animal, etc., and animated by the hand. **2.** A marionette. **3.** One slavishly subject to the will of another; a tool. **—** *adj.* **1.** Of or pertaining to puppets. **2.** Not autonomous: a *puppet* state. [< OF < L *pupa* girl, doll, puppet]

pup·pet·eer (pup′i·tir′) *n.* One who manipulates puppets.

puppet show A drama with puppets for the actors.

pup·py (pup′ē) *n.* *pl.* **·pies** **1.** A young dog: also called *pup.* **2.** A pup (def. 2). [< OF < L *pupa* girl, doll] **— pup′py·ish** *adj.*

puppy love Sentimental, adolescent love or infatuation.

pup tent A shelter tent.

pur·blind (pûr′blīnd′) *adj.* **1.** Partly blind. **2.** Having little or no insight or understanding. [ME] **— pur′blind·ly** *adv.* **— pur′blind·ness** *n.*

pur·chase (pûr′chəs) *v.t.* **·chased**, **·chas·ing** **1.** To acquire by paying money or its equivalent; buy. **2.** To obtain by exertion, sacrifice, flattery, etc. **3.** To move, hoist, or hold by a mechanical purchase. **—** *n.* **1.** Something purchased. **2.** The act of purchasing. **3.** A device that holds or grips something so as to prevent slipping, etc. **4.** A device that gives a mechanical advantage, as a tackle or lever; also, leverage. **5.** Any means of increasing influence or advantage. **6.** Value; worth. [< OF *porchacier* to seek for] **— pur′chas·a·ble** *adj.* **— pur′chas·er** *n.*

pur·dah (pûr′də) *n.* *Anglo-Indian* **1.** A curtain or screen used to seclude women. **2.** The state or system of such seclusion. [< Urdu and Persian *pardah*]

pure (pyōōr) *adj.* **pur·er**, **pur·est** **1.** Free from anything that weakens, impairs, or pollutes. **2.** Free from adulteration; clear; clean. **3.** Genuine; stainless: *pure* food; *pure* motives. **4.** Free from moral defilement; innocent; chaste. **5.** Free from foreign or imported elements, as a language. **6.** Free of harsh qualities, as music; also, correct in form or style; finished. **7.** Abstract; nonobjective: *pure* form. **8.** *Phonet.* Having a single, unvarying tone or sound: said of vowels. **9.** Concerned with fundamental research, as distinguished from practical application; theoretical: said of sciences. **10.** *Genetics* Breeding true with respect to one or more characters; purebred. **11.** Nothing but; sheer: *pure* luck. [< OF < L *purus* clean, pure] **— pure′ness** *n.*

pure·bred (*adj.* pyōōr′bred′; *n.* pyōōr′bred′) *adj. Biol.* Bred from stock having had no admixture for many generations: said especially of livestock. **—** *n.* A purebred animal.

pu·rée (pyŏō·rā′, pyŏōr′ā; *Fr.* pü·rā′) *n.* A thick pulp, usu. of vegetables, boiled and strained. [< F < OF < L *purare* to purify]

pure·ly (pyŏōr′lē) *adv.* 1. So as to be free from admixture, taint, or any harmful substance. 2. Chastely; innocently. 3. Completely; totally. 4. Merely; simply.

pur·ga·tion (pûr·gā′shən) *n.* The act of purging; catharsis.

pur·ga·tive (pûr′gə·tiv) *adj.* Tending to purge; esp., precipitating a bowel movement. —*n.* A purgative agent.

pur·ga·to·ry (pûr′gə·tôr′ē, -tō′rē) *n. pl.* **·ries** 1. In Roman Catholic theology, a state or place where the souls of those who have died penitent are made fit for paradise by expiating venial sins and undergoing any punishment remaining for previously forgiven sins. 2. Any place or state of temporary banishment, suffering, or punishment. [See PURGE.] — **pur′ga·to′ri·al** *adj.*

purge (pûrj) *v.* **purged, purg·ing** *v.t.* 1. To cleanse of what is impure or extraneous; purify. 2. To remove (impurities, etc.) in cleansing: with *away, off,* or *out.* 3. To rid (a group, nation, etc.) of elements regarded as undesirable or inimical, esp. by killing. 4. To cleanse or rid of sin, fault, or defilement. 5. *Med.* **a** To cause evacuation of (the bowels, etc.). **b** To induce evacuation of the bowels of. — *v.i.* 6. To become clean or pure. 7. *Med.* To have or induce evacuation of the bowels, etc. — *n.* 1. The act or process of purging. 2. That which purges, esp. a cathartic. [< OF < L *purgare* to cleanse < *purus* pure] — **purg′er** *n.* — **purg′ing** *n.*

pu·ri·fy (pyŏōr′ə·fī) *v.* **·fied, ·fy·ing** *v.t.* 1. To make pure or clean. 2. To free from sin. 3. To free of foreign or debasing elements, as a language. — *v.i.* 4. To become pure or clean. [< OF < L < *purus* pure + *facere* to make] — **pu′ri·fi·ca′tion** *n.* — **pu·rif·i·ca·to·ry** (pyŏō·rif′ə·kə·tôr′ē, -tō′rē) *adj.* — **pu′ri·fi′er** *n.*

Pu·rim (pŏōr′im, pyŏōr′im; *Hebrew* pōō·rēm′) *n.* A Jewish festival commemorating the defeat of Haman's plot to massacre the Jews (*Esth.* ix 26), observed about the first of March. [< Hebrew *pūrim,* pl. of *pūr* lot]

pur·ist (pyŏōr′ist) *n.* 1. One who believes in or practices exact or meticulous usage, as of a language, style, etc. 2. One who practices or advocates an art form in which primary stress is placed on structural simplicity, as in works of a geometric nature. — **pur′ism** *n.* — **pu·ris′tic** *adj.*

pu·ri·tan (pyŏōr′ə·tən) *n.* *Sometimes cap.* One who is scrupulously strict or exacting in his religious or moral life: often used disparagingly. — *adj.* Puritanical. — **pu′ri·tan·ism** *n.*

Pu·ri·tan (pyŏōr′ə·tən) *n.* One of a group of English Protestants who in the 16th and 17th centuries advocated simpler forms of creed and ritual in the Church of England. — *adj.* Of or pertaining to the Puritans or to their beliefs or customs. [< LL < L *purus* pure] — **Pu′ri·tan·ism** *n.*

pu·ri·tan·i·cal (pyŏōr′ə·tan′i·kəl) *adj.* 1. Rigidly scrupulous or exacting in religious observance or morals; strict. 2. *Often cap.* Of or characteristic of the Puritans. Also **pu′ri·tan′ic.** — **pu′ri·tan′i·cal·ly** *adv.* — **pu′ri·tan′i·cal·ness** *n.*

pu·ri·ty (pyŏōr′ə·tē) *n.* 1. The quality or state of being pure. 2. Saturation: said of a color.

purl¹ (pûrl) *v.i.* 1. To whirl; turn. 2. To flow with a bubbling sound. 3. To move in eddies. — *n.* 1. A circling movement of water; an eddy. 2. A gentle, continued murmur, as of a rippling stream. [Cf. Norw. *purla* to gush out]

purl² (pûrl) *v.t.* 1. In knitting, to make (a stitch) backward. 2. To edge with lace, embroidery, etc. Also spelled *pearl.* — *v.i.* 3. To do edging with lace, etc.: also spelled *pearl.* — *n.* 1. An edge of lace, embroidery, etc. 2. In knitting, the inversion of the knit stitch, giving a horizontal rib effect. Also spelled *pearl.* 3. A spiral of gold or silver wire used in lacework. [Earlier *pyrle* < *pyrl* twist]

pur·lieu (pûr′lōō) *n.* 1. *pl.* The outlying districts or outskirts of any place. 2. A place in which one is free to come and go. 3. Formerly, ground unlawfully taken for a royal forest, but afterward disafforested and restored to its rightful owners. [< AF < OF < *puraler* to go through]

pur·lin (pûr′lin) *n.* A horizontal timber supporting rafters. Also **pur′line** (-lin). For illus. see ROOF. [ME *purlyn*]

pur·loin (pûr·loin′) *v.t. & v.i.* To steal; filch. [< OF *por-loignier* to remove, put far off] — **pur·loin′er** *n.*

pur·ple (pûr′pəl) *n.* 1. A color of mingled red and blue, between crimson and violet. 2. Cloth or a garment of this color, worn formerly by sovereigns. 3. Royal power or dignity: usu. in the phrase **born to the purple.** 4. The office of a cardinal, from the official red hat and robes. 5. The office of a bishop. — *v.t. & v.i.* **·pled, ·pling** To make or become purple. — *adj.* 1. Of the color of purple. 2. Imperial; regal. 3. Ornate; flowery: a *purple* passage of prose. [OE < OF < L *purpura,* orig., shellfish yielding Tyrian purple dye, or cloth dyed with it]

Purple Heart A decoration, the **Order of the Purple Heart,** awarded to members of the armed forces or to citizens of the U.S. honorably wounded in action. See DECORATION.

pur·plish (pûr′plish) *adj.* Somewhat purple.

pur·port (pûr′pôrt, -pōrt; *for v.,* also pər·pôrt′, -pōrt′) *v.t.* 1. To have or bear as its meaning; signify; imply. 2. To claim or profess (to be), esp. falsely. — *n.* 1. That which is conveyed or suggested to the mind as the meaning or intention; import. 2. The substance of a statement, etc., given in other than the exact words. [< AF or OF < L *pro-* forth + *portare* to carry] — **pur·port′ed·ly** *adv.*

pur·pose (pûr′pəs) *n.* 1. An idea or ideal kept before the mind as an end of effort or action; design; aim. 2. A particular thing to be effected or attained. 3. Practical advantage or result; use: words to little *purpose.* 4. Settled resolution; determination. 5. Purport; intent, as of spoken or written language. 6. A proposition; question at issue. — **on purpose** Intentionally. — *v.t. & v.i.* **·posed, ·pos·ing** To have the intention of doing or accomplishing (something); intend; aim. [< OF *pro-* forth + *poser* to put] — **pur′pose·ful** *adj.* — **pur′pose·ful·ly** *adv.* — **pur′pose·ful·ness** *n.* — **pur′pose·less** *adj.* — **pur′pose·less·ly** *adv.* — **Syn.** (noun) 1. Intent, intention, aim, goal, design, end.

pur·pose·ly (pûr′pəs·lē) *adv.* For a purpose; intentionally.

pur·po·sive (pûr′pə·siv) *adj.* 1. Pertaining to, having, or indicating purpose. 2. Functional; useful. — **pur′po·sive·ly** *adv.* — **pur′po·sive·ness** *n.*

purr (pûr) *n.* A murmuring sound, such as a cat makes when pleased. — *v.i.* 1. To make such a sound. — *v.t.* 2. To express by or as by purring. [Imit.]

purse (pûrs) *n.* 1. A small bag or pouch, esp. one for carrying money. 2. Available resources or means; treasury: the public *purse.* 3. A sum of money offered as a prize. — *v.t.* **pursed, purs·ing** To contract into wrinkles or folds: to *purse* the lips. [OE < LL < Gk. *byrsa* skin, hide]

purs·er (pûr′sər) *n.* 1. An officer having charge of the accounts, etc., of a vessel. 2. Formerly, a naval paymaster.

purs·lane (pûrs′lin, -lān) *n.* A common garden herb with reddish green stem and leaves and small yellow flowers, used as a salad: also called *pussley.* [< OF < L *porcilaca*]

pur·su·ance (pər·sōō′əns) *n.* The act of pursuing; a following up; prosecution: usu. in the phrase **in pursuance of.**

pur·su·ant (pər·sōō′ənt) *adj.* Done in accordance with or by reason of something; conformable. — *adv.* In accordance; conformably: usu. with *to:* also **pur·su′ant·ly.**

pur·sue (pər·sōō′) *v.* **·sued, ·su·ing** *v.t.* 1. To follow in an attempt to overtake or capture; chase. 2. To seek or attain. 3. To advance along the course of; keep to the direction or provisions of, as a path, plan, or system. 4. To apply one's energies to or have as one's profession or chief interest: to *pursue* one's studies. 5. To follow persistently; harass. — *v.i.* 6. To follow; chase. 7. To continue; persist. [< AF, OF < LL < L < *pro-* forth + *sequi* to follow] — **pur·su′a·ble** *adj.* — **pur·su′er** *n.*

pur·suit (pər·sōōt′) *n.* 1. The act of pursuing; a chase. 2. That which is followed as a continued employment, pastime, etc. — **Syn.** See OCCUPATION.

pursuit plane *Mil.* A fighter plane.

purs·y (pûr′sē) *adj.* **purs·i·er, purs·i·est** 1. Short-breathed; asthmatic. 2. Fat; hefty. [Earlier *pursive* < AF *pursif,* OF *polsif* < *polser* to pant, gasp] — **purs′i·ness** *n.*

pu·ru·lent (pyŏōr′ə·lənt, -yə-lənt) *adj.* Consisting of or secreting pus; suppurating. [< L < *pus, puris* pus] — **pu′ru·lence** or **·len·cy** *n.* — **pu′ru·lent·ly** *adv.*

pur·vey (pər·vā′) *v.t. & v.i.* To furnish (provisions, etc.). [< AF < L *providere*] — **pur·vey′or** *n.*

pur·vey·ance (pər·vā′əns) *n.* 1. The act of purveying. 2. That which is purveyed or supplied; provisions.

pur·view (pûr′vyōō) *n.* 1. Extent, sphere, or scope of anything, as of official authority. 2. Range of view, experience, or understanding; outlook. 3. *Law* The body or the scope or limit of a statute. [< AF *purveu* provided]

pus (pus) *n.* A yellowish secretion from inflamed tissues. [< L] — **pus·sy** (pus′ē) *adj.*

push (pŏōsh) *v.t.* 1. To exert force upon or against (an object) for the purpose of moving. 2. To force (one's way), as through a crowd, jungle, etc. 3. To press forward, prosecute, or develop with vigor and persistence. 4. To urge, advocate, or promote vigorously and persistently: to *push* a new product. 5. To bear hard upon; harass: I am *pushed* for time. — *v.i.* 6. To exert steady pressure against something so as to move it. 7. To move or advance vigorously or persistently. 8. To exert great effort. — *n.* 1. The act of pushing; a shove. 2. *Informal* An extremity; exigency: at a *push* for money. 3. Determined activity; energy. 4. Anything pushed to cause action. 5. An influential clique. [< OF < L *pusare* to beat]

push button A button or knob that on being pushed opens or closes a circuit in an electric system. — **push·but·ton** (pŏōsh′but′n) *adj.*

push·cart (pŏōsh′kärt′) *n.* A two- or four-wheeled cart pushed by hand, used by fruit venders, peddlers, etc.

push·er (pŏōsh′ər) *n.* 1. One who or that which pushes; esp., an active, energetic person. 2. *Aeron.* An airplane with the propeller in the rear of the wings. 3. *U.S. Slang* One who illegally sells narcotics to addicts.

push·ing (pŏŏsh′ing) *adj.* **1.** Possessing enterprise and energy. **2.** Aggressive; impertinent. — **push′ing·ly** *adv.*

push·o·ver (pŏŏsh′ō′vər) *n. Slang* **1.** One who is easily defeated, overcome, taken advantage of, etc.; an easy mark. **2.** Anything that can be done with little or no effort.

push·pin (pŏŏsh′pin′) *n.* A pin with a large head, inserted by thumb pressure and used for mounting papers, etc.

push-pull (pŏŏsh′pŏŏl′) *adj. Electronics* Designating a circuit or system that uses two similar components operating in opposite phase.

Push·tu (push′tōō) *n.* Pashto.

push·y (pŏŏsh′ē) *adj.* **·i·er, ·i·est** *Informal* Offensively aggressive; bossy. — **push′i·ly** *adv.* — **push′i·ness** *n.*

pu·sil·lan·i·mous (pyōō′sə·lan′ə·məs) *adj.* **1.** Lacking courage, or spirit; cowardly. **2.** Characterized by weakness of purpose or lack of courage. [< LL < L *pusillus* very little + *animus* soul] — **pu′sil·la·nim′i·ty** (-lə·nim′ə·tē) *n.* — **pu·sil·lan′i·mous·ly** *adv.* — **pu·sil·lan′i·mous·ness** *n.*

puss¹ (pŏŏs) *n. Informal* **1.** A cat. **2.** A child or young woman: a term of affection. [< LG *puus*, name for a cat]

puss² (pŏŏs) *n. Slang* The mouth; face. [< Irish *pus* mouth]

puss·ley (pus′lē) *n.* Purslane. [Alter. of PURSLANE]

pus·sy (pŏŏs′ē) *n. pl.* **·sies** *Informal* **1.** A cat. **2.** A fuzzy catkin, as of a willow, birch, etc. [Dim. of PUSS¹]

pus·sy·foot (pŏŏs′ē·fŏŏt′) *v.i.* **1.** To move softly and stealthily, as a cat does. **2.** To act or proceed without committing oneself or revealing one's intentions.

pus·sy willow (pŏŏs′ē) A small American willow with silky catkins in early spring.

pus·tu·late (pus′chŏŏ·lāt; *for adj.,* also pus′chŏŏ-lit) *v.t. & v.i.* **·lat·ed, ·lat·ing** To form into or become pustules. — *adj.* Covered with pustules. [< L *pustulatus,* pp. of *pustulare* to blister] — **pus′tu·la′tion** *n.*

pus·tule (pus′chŏŏl) *n.* **1.** *Pathol.* A small elevation of the skin with an inflamed base containing pus. **2.** Any elevation resembling a pimple or a blister. [< L *pustula*] — **pus′tu·lar, pus′tu·lous** *adj.*

PUSSY
WILLOW

put (pŏŏt) *v.* **put, put·ting** *v.t.* **1.** To bring into or set in a specified or implied place or position; lay. **2.** To bring into a specified state or relation: to *put* a prisoner to death. **3.** To bring to bear; apply: *Put* your back into it! **4.** To impose. **5.** To ascribe or attribute, as the wrong interpretation on a remark. **6.** To place according to one's estimation: I *put* the time at five o'clock. **7.** To throw with a pushing motion of the arm: to *put* the shot. **8.** To incite; prompt. **9.** To bring forward for debate, answer, consideration, etc. **10.** To subject. **11.** To express in words: That's *putting* it mildly. **12.** To bet: I'll *put* six dollars on that horse. — *v.i.* **13.** To go; proceed: to *put* to sea. — **to put about** *Naut.* To change to the opposite tack; change direction. — **to put aside (or away or by)** **1.** To place in reserve; save. **2.** To thrust aside; discard. — **to put down** **1.** To repress; crush. **2.** To degrade; demote. **3.** To write down; record. **4.** *Slang* To disparage. — **to put forth** **1** To extend, as the arm or hand. **2.** To grow, as shoots or buds. **3.** To exert. **4.** To set out; leave port. — **to put forward** To advance; urge, as a claim. — **to put in** **1.** *Naut.* To enter a harbor or place of shelter. **2.** To interpolate; interpose. **3.** *Informal* To devote; expend, as time. **4.** To advance (a claim, etc.). **5.** To submit, as an application. — **to put off** **1.** To delay; postpone. **2.** To discard. — **to put on** **1.** To don. **2.** To bring into action; turn on. **3.** To simulate; pretend. **4.** To give a representation of; stage. **5.** *Slang* To deceive; mock. — **to put out** **1.** To extinguish. **2.** To expel; eject. **3.** To disconcert; embarrass. **4.** To inconvenience. **5.** In baseball, to retire (a batter or base runner). — **to put over** **1.** To place in command or charge. **2.** *Informal* To accomplish successfully. — **to put one (or something) over on** *Informal* To deceive or dupe. — **to put through** **1.** To bring to successful completion. **2.** To cause to undergo. — **to put up** **1.** To erect; build. **2.** To preserve or can. **3.** To wager; bet. **4.** To provide (money, capital, etc.). **5.** To sheathe, as a weapon. — **to put upon** To take advantage of. — **to put up with** To endure. — *n.* The act of putting, as a throw. — *adj. Informal* Fixed; settled: My hat won't stay *put.* [Fusion of OE *pūtian* to instigate, *potian* to push, and *pȳtan* to put out]

pu·ta·tive (pyōō′tə·tiv) *adj.* Supposed; reputed. [< MF or LL < L, pp. of *putare* to think] — **pu′ta·tive·ly** *adv.*

put·off (pŏŏt′ôf′, -of′) *n.* An evasion; excuse.

put-on (pŏŏt′on′) *n. Slang* A hoax or deception.

put·out (pŏŏt′out′) *n.* In baseball, the act of causing an out, as of a batter or base runner.

pu·tre·fac·tion (pyōō′trə·fak′shən) *n.* **1.** The decomposition of organic matter. **2.** The state of being putrefied. **3.** Putrescent or putrefied matter.

pu·tre·fac·tive (pyōō′trə·fak′tiv) *adj.* **1.** Of or pertaining to putrefaction. **2.** Producing putrefaction.

pu·tre·fy (pyōō′trə·fī) *v.t. & v.i.* **·fied, ·fy·ing** **1.** To decay or cause to decay with a fetid odor; rot. **2.** To make or become gangrenous. — **Syn.** See DECAY. [< F < L < *putrere* to decay + *facere* to make] — **pu′tre·fi′er** *n.*

pu·tres·cent (pyōō·tres′ənt) *adj.* **1.** Becoming putrid; **2.** Pertaining to putrefaction. — **pu·tres′cence** *n.*

pu·trid (pyōō′trid) *adj.* **1.** Being in a state of putrefaction; rotten. **2.** Indicating or produced by putrefaction: a *putrid* smell. **3.** Rotten; corrupt. [< L *putrere* to decay] — **pu·trid′i·ty** *n.* — **pu′trid·ly** *adv.* — **pu′trid·ness** *n.*

Putsch (pŏŏch) *n.* An outbreak or rebellion; an attempted *coup d'état.* [< G < dial. G (Swiss), lit., push, blow]

putt (put) *n.* In golf, a light stroke made on a putting green to place the ball in or near the hole. — *v.t. & v.i.* To strike (the ball) with such a stroke. [Var. of PUT]

put·tee (put′ē, pu·tē′) *n.* A strip of cloth wound spirally about the leg from knee to ankle, used by soldiers, sportsmen, etc.; also, a leather gaiter strapped around the leg. Also **put′ty.** [< Hind. < Skt. *patta* strip of cloth]

put·ter¹ (put′ər) *n.* **1.** In golf, one who putts. **2.** An upright, stiff-shafted golf club used on the putting green.

put·ter² (put′ər) *v.i.* **1.** To act or work in a dawdling manner. — *v.t.* **2.** To waste (time, etc.) in dawdling or puttering. [Var. of POTTER²]

put·ting green (put′ing) In golf: **a** Green (*n.* def. 5). **b** A place set aside for putting practice.

put·ty (put′ē) *n.* **1.** Whiting mixed with linseed oil to the consistency of dough, used for filling holes or cracks in wood surfaces, securing panes of glass in the sash, etc. **2.** Any of various similar substances. — *v.t.* **·tied, ·ty·ing** To fill, stop, fasten, etc., with putty. [< OF *potée* calcined tin, lit., potful] — **put′ti·er** *n.*

putty knife A knife with a spatulalike blade, used in applying putty.

put-up (pŏŏt′up′) *adj. Informal* Prearranged or contrived in an artful manner: a *put-up* job.

puz·zle (puz′əl) *v.* **·zled, ·zling** *v.t.* **1.** To confuse or perplex. **2.** To solve by investigation and study, as something perplexing: with *out.* — *v.i.* **3.** To be perplexed or confused. — **to puzzle over** To attempt to understand or solve. — *n.* **1.** Something that puzzles; enigma. **2.** A toy, word game, etc., designed to test one's ingenuity or patience. **3.** The state of being puzzled; perplexity. [Origin unknown] — **puz′zler** *n.* — **puz′zle·ment** *n.*

— **Syn.** (verb) **1.** confound, bewilder, baffle, daze. — (noun) **1.** A *puzzle* is usually intricate but can be solved by ingenuity and patience; many *puzzles* are made for amusement. An *enigma* is something said or written whose meaning is hidden and can only be inferred from clues. A *conundrum* is a baffling question, the answer to which depends upon some trick of words. *Conundrums* are also *riddles,* but a *riddle* is usually less playful in character.

py- Var. of PYO-.

pyelo- *combining form* Pelvis. Also, before vowels, **pyel-.** [< Gk. *pyelos* pelvis, trough]

py·e·mi·a (pī·ē′mē·ə) *n. Pathol.* A type of blood poisoning characterized by many abscesses. [< NL < Gk. *pyon* pus + *haima* blood] — **py·e′mic** *adj.*

Pyg·ma·li·on (pig·māl′ē·ən, -māl′yən) In Greek mythology, a sculptor of Cyprus who fell in love with his statue, Galatea, which Aphrodite later brought to life.

pyg·my (pig′mē) *adj.* **1.** Diminutive; dwarfish. **2.** Trivial; unimportant. — *n. pl.* **·mies** A small person or thing regarded as insignificant. Also spelled *pigmy.* [< L < Gk. *pygmē* the length from elbow to knuckles]

Pyg·my (pig′mē) *n. pl.* **·mies** **1.** A member of a Negroid people of equatorial Africa, ranging in height from four to five feet. **2.** Any of the Negrito peoples of the Philippines, Andaman Islands, and Malaya.

py·ja·mas (pə·jä′məz, -jam′əz) See PAJAMAS.

py·lon (pī′lon) *n.* **1.** *Archit.* A monumental structure constituting an entrance to an Egyptian temple, consisting of a central gateway, flanked on each side by a truncated pyramidal tower. **2.** A stake marking the course in an airport or turning point in an air race. **3.** One of the steel towers supporting a high-tension electric power line. **4.** *Surg.* An artificial leg, esp. temporary. [< Gk. *pylōn* gateway]

py·lo·rus (pī·lôr′əs, -lō′rəs, pi-) *n. pl.* **·ri** (-rī) *Anat.* The opening between the stomach and the duodenum, surrounded by a sphincter. [< LL < Gk. < *pylē* gate + *ouros* watcher] — **py·lor′ic** (-lôr′ik, -lor′ik) *adj.*

pyo- *combining form* Pus; of or related to pus. Also, before vowels, **py-.** [< Gk. *pyon* pus]

py·or·rhe·a (pī′ə·rē′ə) *n. Pathol.* A continuous discharge of pus; esp., from the gums, with loosening of the teeth. [< NL < Gk. *pyon* pus + *rheein* to flow] — **py′or·rhe′al** *adj.*

pyr- Var. of PYRO-.

pyr·a·mid (pir′ə·mid) *n.* 1. *Archit.* A structure of masonry typically having a square base and triangular sides meeting in an apex, sometimes vast in size, as those used as tombs or temples in ancient Egypt. 2. Something pyramidal in form. 3. *Geom.* A solid consisting of a polygonal base and triangular sides, having a common vertex. 4. *Mineral.* A crystal form consisting of three or more similar planes having a common point of intersection. —*v.t. & v.i.* 1. To arrange or form in the shape of a pyramid. 2. To buy or sell (stock) with paper profits, and to continue so buying or selling. [ME *piramis* (pl. *pyramids*) and later borrowing of F *pyramide*, both < L < Gk. *pyramis, -idos*] — **py·ram·i·dal** (pi·ram′ə·dəl), **pyr′a·mid′ic** or **·i·cal** *adj.* — **py·ram′i·dal·ly** *adv.*

pyre (pīr) *n.* 1. A heap of combustibles arranged for burning a dead body. 2. Any pile or heap of combustible material. [< L *pyra* hearth, funeral pile < Gk. *pyr* fire]

py·reth·rum (pi·reth′rəm, -rē′thrəm) *n.* The powdered flowers of a chrysanthemum, used medically as an ointment, and as an insecticide. [< L, feverfew < Gk. *pyrethron*]

py·ret·ic (pi·ret′ik) *adj.* 1. Affected with or relating to fever. 2. Remedial in fevers. [< NL < Gk. *pyretos* fever]

Py·rex (pī′reks) *n.* A type of heat-resisting glass having a high silica content, with additions of soda, aluminum, and boron: a trade name. Also **py′rex.**

pyr·i·dox·ine (pir′ə·dok′sēn, -sin) *n. Biochem.* Vitamin B₆, a water-soluble compound, $C_8H_{10}NO_3$, occurring in cereal grains, vegetable oils, legumes, yeast, meats, and fish, and also made synthetically. [PYRID(INE) + OX(Y)-² + -INE²]

py·rite (pī′rīt) *n.* *pl.* **py·ri·tes** (pi·rī′tēz) A metallic, pale yellow iron disulfide, FeS₂, a source of sulfuric acid: also called *fool's gold, iron pyrites.* [< L < Gk. < *pyritēs* (*lithos*) fire (stone)] — **py·rit′ic** (-rit′ik) or **·i·cal** *adj.*

py·ri·tes (pi·rī′tēz) *n.pl.* Any of various metallic sulfides.

pyro- *combining form* Fire; heat. Also, before vowels, *pyr-.* [< Gk. *pyr, pyros* fire]

py·ro·e·lec·tric (pī′rō·i·lek′trik, pir′ō-) *adj.* Of, pertaining to, or manifesting pyroelectricity; developing poles when heated. — *n.* A pyroelectric substance.

py·ro·e·lec·tric·i·ty (pī′rō·i·lek′tris′ə·tē, -ē′lek-, pir′ō-) *n.* Electrification or electric polarity developed in certain minerals by a change in temperature.

py·ro·gen·ic (pī′rə·jen′ik, pir′ə-) *adj.* 1. Causing or produced by heat. 2. Caused by or inducing fever. Also **py·rog·e·nous** (pī·roj′ə·nəs, pi-).

py·rog·ra·phy (pī·rog′rə·fē, pi-) *n.* The art or process of producing a design, as on wood or leather, by a red-hot point or fine flame. — **py·ro·graph** (pī′rə·graf, -gräf, pir′ə-) *n.* — **py·rog′ra·pher** *n.* — **py′ro·graph′ic** *adj.*

py·rol·y·sis (pī·rol′ə·sis) *n.* *Chem.* Decomposition of organic compounds or other substances by the action of heat. [< NL < Gk. *pyr, pyros* fire + *lysis* loosing] — **py·ro·lit·ic** (pī′rə·lit′ik, pir′ə-) *adj.*

py·ro·mag·net·ic (pī′rō·mag·net′ik, pir′ō-) *adj.* Of, pertaining to, or produced by changes in magnetic properties caused by change of temperature.

py·ro·ma·ni·a (pī′rə·mā′nē·ə, -mān′yə, pir′ə-) *n.* A compulsion to set things on fire. — **py′ro·ma′ni·ac** (-ak) *adj. & n.* — **py·ro·ma·ni·a·cal** (pī′rō·mə·nī′ə·kəl, pir′ō-) *adj.*

py·rom·e·ter (pī·rom′ə·tər) *n.* An instrument for measuring high degrees of heat. — **py·ro·met·ric** (pī′rə·met′rik, pir′ə-) or **·ri·cal** *adj.* — **py·rom′e·try** *n.*

py·ro·tech·nic (pī′rə·tek′nik, pir′ə-) *adj.* Pertaining to fireworks or their manufacture. Also **py′ro·tech′ni·cal.**

py·ro·tech·nics (pī′rə·tek′niks, pir′ə-) *n.pl.* (construed as *sing. in defs.* 1, 4) 1. The art of making or using fireworks. Also **py·ro·tech·ny** (pī′rə·tek′nē, pir′ə-) 2. A display of fireworks. 3. An ostentatious display, as of oratory. 4. *Mil.* Rockets, flares, or the like, that produce flame or smoke for signaling, lighting, screening, etc. [< MF < Gk. *pyr, pyros* fire + *technē* art] — **py·ro·tech′nist** *n.*

py·ro·tox·in (pī′rə·tok′sin, pir′ə-) *n.* *Biochem.* Any of various toxins found in the body and inducing a rise of bodily temperature or symptoms of fever.

py·rox·y·lin (pī·rok′sə·lin) *n.* *Chem.* A cellulose nitrate mixture, less explosive than guncotton, and widely used in making Celluloid, collodion, lacquers, adhesives, etc. Also **py·rox′y·line** (-lēn, -lin). [< F < Gk. *pyr, pyros* fire + *xylon* wood + F *-in* -in]

Pyr·rhic victory (pir′ik) A victory gained at a ruinous loss, such as that of Pyrrhus over the Romans in 279 B.C. [after *Pyrrhus* king of Epirus]

Py·thag·o·re·an·ism (pi·thag′ə·rē′ən·iz′əm) *n.* The mystical philosophy taught by Pythagoras, including the idea that number is the essence of all things. — **Py·thag·o·re·an** (pi·thag′ə·rē′ən) *n. & adj.*

Pythagorean theorem *Geom.* The theorem that the sum of the squares of the legs of a right triangle is equal to the square of the hypotenuse.

PYTHAGOREAN THEOREM

Sum of squares ABDE and BCGF equals square ACHK
$(a^2 + b^2 = c^2)$

Pyth·i·an (pith′ē·ən) *adj.* 1. Relating to Delphi, to Apollo's temple there, its oracle, or its priestess. 2. Relating to the Pythian games. — *n.* 1. A native or inhabitant of Delphi. 2. The priestess of Apollo. 3. An epithet of the Delphic Apollo. [< L *Pythius* < Gk. *Pythios*]

Pythian games In ancient Greece, games held every four years at Delphi in honor of Apollo.

Pyth·i·as (pith′ē·əs) See DAMON AND PYTHIAS.

py·thon (pī′thon, -thən) *n.* 1. A large, nonvenomous serpent that crushes its prey. 2. Any nonvenomous constrictor. [< L < Gk. *Python*, a serpent slain by Apollo]

py·tho·ness (pī′thə·nis, pith′ə-) *n.* 1. The priestess of the Delphic oracle. 2. Any woman supposed to be possessed of the spirit of prophecy.

pyx (piks) *n.* *Eccl.* A vessel or casket, usu. of precious metal, in which the Host is preserved. [< L < Gk. *pyxos* box tree]

pyx·i·di·um (pik·sid′ē·əm) *n.* *pl.* **·i·a** (-ē·ə) *Bot.* A seed vessel with two parts, the upper separating as a lid.

pyx·is (pik′sis) *n.* *pl.* **pyx·i·des** (pik′sə·dēz) 1. A box or pyx; esp., an ancient form of ornamental jewel case or toilet box. 2. An emollient ointment. 3. *Bot.* A pyxidium. [< L]

Q

q, Q (kyōō) *n.* *pl.* **q's** or **qs, Q's** or **Qs, cues** (kyōōz) 1. The 17th letter of the English alphabet. 2. The sound represented by the letter *q.* In English *q* is always followed by *u* and represents (kw), as in *quack, quest, quote, equal,* etc. In some words borrowed from French, however, English follows the French pronunciation with (k) alone, as in *appliqué, conquer, coquette, pique.* Final *-que* always represents (k), as in *antique, oblique, physique, unique,* etc.

qua (kwā, kwä) *adv.* In the capacity of; by virtue of being; insofar as. [< L, ablative sing. fem. of *qui* who]

quack¹ (kwak) *v.i.* To utter a harsh, croaking cry, as a duck. — *n.* The sound made by a duck, or a similar croaking noise. [Imit.]

quack² (kwak) *n.* 1. A pretender to medical knowledge or skill. 2. One who falsely poses as an expert; a charlatan. — *adj.* Of or pertaining to quacks or quackery. — *v.i.* To play the quack. [Short for QUACKSALVER] — **quack′ish** *adj.* — **quack′ish·ly** *adv.*

quack·er·y (kwak′ər·ē) *n.* *pl.* **·er·ies** Ignorant or fraudulent practice. Also **quack′hood** (-hŏŏd), **quack′ism.**

quack·sal·ver (kwak′sal′vər) *n.* A medical quack. [< MDu. < *quacken* quack¹ + *salf* salve]

quad¹ (kwod) *n.* *Informal* A quadrangle, as of a college.

quad² (kwod) *n.* *Printing* A piece of type metal of less height than the letters, used for spacing: also called *quadrat.*

quad·ran·gle (kwod′rang·gəl) *n.* 1. *Geom.* A plane figure having four sides and four angles. 2. A court, either square or oblong; also, the building or buildings that surround such a court. [< OF < LL < L *quattuor* four + *angulus* angle] — **quad·ran′gu·lar** (-gyə·lər) *adj.*

quad·rant (kwod′rənt) *n.* 1. A quarter section of a circle, subtending an arc of 90°; also, the arc subtended. 2. An in-

strument having a graduated arc of 90°, with a movable radius for measuring angles on it, used in navigation, surveying, and astronomy for measuring altitudes. [< L *quattuor* four]
— **quad·ran·tal** (kwod·ran′təl) *adj.*

quad·ra·phon·ic (kwod′rə·fon′ik) *adj.* Designating a system of stereophonic sound that uses four loudspeakers.

quad·rat (kwod′rət) *n. Printing* A quad².

quad·rate (kwod′rāt; *for n., also* kwod′rit) *n.* **1.** In astrology, an aspect of two heavenly bodies in which they are distant from each other 90°. **2.** A cubical or square object. — *adj.* Square; four-sided. [< L *quadrare* to square]

quad·rat·ic (kwod·rat′ik) *adj.* **1.** Pertaining to or resembling a square. **2.** *Math.* Pertaining to or designating an equation, curve, surface, etc., of the second degree. — *n. Math.* A quadratic equation, curve, etc.

quad·rat·ics (kwod·rat′iks) *n.pl.* (*construed as sing.*) *Rare* The branch of algebra dealing with quadratic equations.

quad·ren·ni·al (kwod·ren′ē·əl) *adj.* **1.** Occurring once in four years. **2.** Lasting four years. — **quad·ren′ni·al·ly** *adv.*

quadri- *combining form* Four: *quadrilateral.* Also *quadru-*: also **quadr-** (before vowels). [< L *quattuor* four]

quad·ri·lat·er·al (kwod′rə·lat′ər·əl) *adj.* Formed or bounded by four lines; four-sided. — *n. Geom.* A figure bounded by four straight lines terminated at four angles. [< L *quattuor* + *latus* side]

qua·drille (kwə·dril′) *n.* **1.** A square dance for four couples, having five figures. **2.** Music for or in the manner of this dance. [< F < Sp. < L *quattuor* four]

quad·ril·lion (kwod·ril′yən) *n.* **1.** *U.S.* A thousand trillions, written as 1 followed by fifteen zeros: a cardinal number. **2.** *Brit.* A million trillions (def. 2), written as 1 followed by twenty-four zeros: a cardinal number. — *adj.* Being a quadrillion in number. [< MF < *quadri-* four + (*mi*)*llion* million] — **quad·ril′lionth** *adj. & n.*

quad·ri·no·mi·al (kwod′rə·nō′mē·əl) *n. Math.* An algebraic expression having four terms.

quad·ri·va·lent (kwod′rə·vā′lənt) *adj. Chem.* Having a valence of four, as carbon: also *tetratomic, tetravalent.* [< QUADRI- + L *valere* to be worth] — **quad′ri·va′lence,** **quad′ri·va′len·cy** *n.*

quad·roon (kwod·rōōn′) *n.* A person having one Negro grandparent. [< Sp. *cuarto* fourth]

quadru- Var. of QUADRI-.

quad·ru·ped (kwod′rōō·ped) *n.* An animal having four feet; esp., a four-footed mammal. — *adj.* Having four feet. [< L *quattuor* four + *pes* foot] — **quad·ru·pe·dal** (kwod·rōō′pə·dəl, kwod′rōō·ped′l) *adj.*

quad·ru·ple (kwod′rōō·pəl, kwod·rōō′pəl) *v.t. & v.i.* **·pled,** **·pling** To multiply by four; make or become four times larger. — *adj.* **1.** Consisting of four. **2.** Multiplied by four. — *n.* A sum four times as great as another. — *adv.* So as to make four times larger. [< OF < L *quadruplus*]

quad·ru·plet (kwod′rōō·plit, kwod·rōō′-) *n.* **1.** A compound or combination of four things or objects. **2.** One of four offspring born of the same mother at one birth.

quad·ru·pli·cate (kwod·rōō′plə·kāt; *for adj. & n., also* kwod·rōō′plə-kit) *adj.* Quadruple; fourfold. — *n.* One of four like things. [< L *quattuor* four + stem of *plicare* to fold] — **quad·ru′pli·cate·ly** *adv.* — **quad·ru′pli·ca′tion** *n.*

quaff (kwaf, kwof, kwôf) *v.t. & v.i.* To drink, esp. copiously or with relish. — *n.* A drink; swallow. — **quaff′er** *n.*

quag·gy (kwag′ē, kwog′ē) *adj.* **·gi·er,** **·gi·est** Yielding to or quaking under the foot, as soft, wet earth; boggy.

quag·mire (kwag′mīr′, kwog′-) *n.* **1.** Marshy ground that gives way under the foot. **2.** A difficult situation. [< obs. *quag* to shake + MIRE] — **quag′mired′, quag′mir′y** *adj.*

qua·hog (kwô′hôg, -hog, kwə·hôg′, -hog′) *n.* An edible American clam called *hard-shelled clam.* Also **qua′haug.** [< Algonquian (Narraganset) *poquauhock*]

quail¹ (kwāl) *n.* Any of various small American game birds related to the partridge, esp. the bobwhite. [< OF *quaille,* prob. of Gmc. origin]

quail² (kwāl) *v.i.* To shrink with fear; lose heart or courage. [ME *quailen*]

quaint (kwānt) *adj.* **1.** Combining an antique appearance with a pleasing oddity, fancifulness, or whimsicalness. **2.** Pleasingly odd or old-fashioned; fanciful. [< OF < L < *cognoscere* to ascertain] — **quaint′ly** *adv.* — **quaint′ness** *n.*

quake (kwāk) *v.i.* **quaked, quak·ing 1.** To shake, as with violent emotion or cold. **2.** To shake or tremble, as earth during an earthquake. — **Syn.** See SHAKE. — *n.* **1.** The act of quaking. **2.** An earthquake. [OE *cwacian* to shake]

Quak·er (kwā′kər) *n.* A member of the Society of Friends: originally a term of derision. [< QUAKE, v.; with ref. to their founder's admonition to tremble at the word of the Lord] — **Quak′er·ish** *adj.* — **Quak′er·ism** (kwā′kə·riz′əm) *n.* — **Quak′er·ly** *adj. & adv.*

qual·i·fi·ca·tion (kwol′ə·fə·kā′shən) *n.* **1.** The act of quali-

fying, or the state of being qualified. **2.** Any ability, training, etc., that fits a person for a specific office, role, position, etc. **3.** A restriction: to accept without *qualification.*

qual·i·fied (kwol′ə·fīd) *adj.* **1.** Competent or fit, as for public office. **2.** Restricted or modified. — **qual′i·fied′ly** *adv.*

qual·i·fy (kwol′ə·fī) *v.* **·fied, ·fy·ing** *v.t.* **1.** To make fit or capable, as for an office, occupation, or privilege. **2.** To make legally capable. **3.** To limit or restrict. **4.** To attribute a quality to; describe; characterize. **5.** To make less strong or extreme. **6.** To change the strength or flavor of. **7.** *Gram.* To modify. — *v.i.* **8.** To be or become qualified or fit; meet the requirements, as for entering a race. [< MF < Med.L < L *qualis* of such a kind + *facere* to make] — **qual′i·fi′a·ble** *adj.* — **qual′i·fi′er** *n.*

qual·i·ta·tive (kwol′ə·tā′tiv) *adj.* Of or pertaining to quality: distinguished from *quantitative.* [< LL < L *qualis* of such a kind] — **qual′i·ta′tive·ly** *adv.*

qualitative analysis *Chem.* The process of determining the kind and number of ingredients present in a substance.

qual·i·ty (kwol′ə·tē) *n.* *pl.* **·ties 1.** That which makes something such as it is; a distinguishing element or characteristic. **2.** The basic or essential character, nature, etc., of something. **3.** Excellence: *quality* rather than quantity. **4.** The degree of excellence. **5.** A moral or personality trait or characteristic. **6.** *Music* The timbre of a voice or musical instrument. **7.** *Archaic* High or superior social rank or birth; also, persons of superior rank collectively. — *adj.* Of superior quality. [< F < L *qualis* of such a kind]

qualm (kwäm, kwôm) *n.* **1.** A feeling of sickness. **2.** A twinge of conscience; moral scruple. **3.** A sensation of fear or misgiving. [? OE *cwealm* death] — **qualm′ish** *adj.* — **qualm′ish·ly** *adv.* — **qualm′ish·ness** *n.* — **qualm′y** *adj.*

quan·da·ry (kwon′dər·ē, -drē) *n.* *pl.* **·da·ries** A state of hesitation or perplexity; predicament.

quan·ta (kwon′tə) Plural of QUANTUM.

quan·ti·ta·tive (kwon′tə·tā′tiv) *adj.* **1.** Of or pertaining to quantity. **2.** Having to do with quantities only: distinguished from *qualitative.* — **quan′ti·ta′tive·ly** *adv.* — **quan′ti·ta′tive·ness** *n.*

quantitative analysis *Chem.* The process of finding the amount or percentage of each element or ingredient present in a material or compound.

quan·ti·ty (kwon′tə·tē) *n.* *pl.* **·ties 1.** A specified or indefinite number, amount, weight, etc. **2.** The property of a thing that admits of exact measurement. **3.** *Often pl.* A large amount: abundance: *quantities* of food. **4.** Measure; amount: *quantity* rather than quality. **5.** *Math.* An entity regarded as possessing a certain determinable magnitude, as length, size, volume, or number. **6.** The relative length of a speech sound, prosodic syllable, or musical tone. **7.** *Electr.* The amount of current. [< OF < L *quantus* how much]

quan·tize (kwon′tīz) *v.t.* **·tized, ·tiz·ing** *Physics* **1.** To restrict the possible values of (an observable quantity or magnitude). **2.** To express as multiples of a given quantity or quantum. — **quan′ti·za′tion** *n.*

quan·tum (kwon′təm) *n.* *pl.* **·ta** (-tə) *Physics* A fundamental unit of energy as provided for in the quantum theory. [< L, neuter of *quantus* how much]

quantum theory *Physics* The theory that energy is not a smoothly flowing continuum but is manifested by the emission from radiating bodies of discrete particles or *quanta,* the values of which are expressed as the product of Planck's constant multiplied by the frequency of the given radiation.

quar·an·tine (kwôr′ən·tēn, kwor′-) *n.* **1.** The enforced isolation for a fixed period of time of persons, ships, or goods arriving from places infected with or exposed to contagious disease. **2.** A place designated for the enforcement of such interdiction. **3.** The enforced isolation of any person or place infected with contagious disease. **4.** Any enforced isolation. **5.** A period of forty days. — *v.t.* **·tined, ·tin·ing** To subject to or retain in quarantine; isolate by or as by quarantine. [< Ital. < ult. < L *quadraginta* forty]

quark (kwärk, kwôrk) *n. Physics* A hypothetical elementary particle. [after "Three *quarks* for Muster Mark" in James Joyce's *Finnegans Wake*]

quar·rel (kwôr′əl, kwor′-) *n.* **1.** An unfriendly, angry, or violent dispute. **2.** A falling out; breach of amity. **3.** The cause for dispute. — *v.i.* **quar·reled** or **·relled, quar·rel·ing** or **·rel·ling 1.** To engage in a quarrel. **2.** To break off a mutual friendship. **3.** To find fault. [< F < L *queri* to complain] — **quar′rel·er** or **quar′rel·ler** *n.*

— **Syn.** (noun) **1.** Wrangle, bicker, squabble, altercation, scrap.

quar·rel·some (kwôr′əl·səm, kwor′-) *adj.* Inclined to quarrel. — **quar′rel·some·ly** *adv.* — **quar′rel·some·ness** *n.*

quar·ry¹ (kwôr′ē, kwor′ē) *n.* *pl.* **·ries 1.** A beast or bird hunted or killed, as in the chase. **2.** Anything hunted, slaughtered, or pursued. [< OF < L *corium* hide]

quar·ry² (kwôr′ē, kwor′ē) *n.* *pl.* **·ries** An excavation from

---

which stone is taken by cutting, blasting, or the like. — *v.t.* **·ried**, **·ry·ing 1.** To cut, dig, or take from or as from a quarry. **2.** To establish a quarry in. [< OF < L *quadrus* square] — **quar′ri·er** *n.*

quart (kwôrt) *n.* **1.** A measure of capacity, the fourth part of a gallon, or two pints. In the U.S., the dry quart is equal to 1.10 liters and the liquid quart is equal to 0.946 liter. See table inside back cover. **2.** A container having such a capacity. [< OF < L *quartus* fourth]

quar·ter (kwôr′tər) *n.* **1.** One of four equal parts into which anything is or may be divided. **2.** In the U.S. and Canada, a coin having the value of 25 cents. **3.** Fifteen minutes or the fourth of an hour; also, the moment such a period begins or ends. **4.** Three months or a fourth of a year. **5.** A term of school, usu. one fourth of a year. **6.** *Astron.* A fourth part of the moon's revolution about the earth. **7.** One of the four periods into which a game, as football, is divided. **8.** One of the four principal points of the compass. **9.** A particular district or locality, as of a city: the native *quarter*. **10.** A place or source from which something comes: on authority of the highest *quarter*. **11.** *Usu. pl.* Proper or assigned station, as of officers and crew on a warship. **12.** *pl.* A place of lodging or residence. **13.** Mercy shown to a vanquished enemy. **14.** Either of the four limbs of a quadruped, together with the adjacent parts. **15.** *Naut.* The upper part of a vessel's side, near the stern. **16.** *Heraldry* **a** Any of four equal divisions into which a shield is divided. **b** An ordinary occupying such a division. — **at close quarters** Close by; at close range. — *adj.* **1.** Being one of four equal parts. **2.** Having one fourth of a standard value. — *v.t.* **1.** To divide into four equal parts. **2.** To divide into a number of parts or pieces. **3.** To cut the body of (an executed person) into four parts. **4.** To range from one side to the other of (a field, etc.) while advancing. **5.** To furnish with quarters or shelter; lodge. **6.** *Heraldry* **a** To divide (a shield) into quarters. **b** To bear or arrange (different coats of arms) quarterly upon a shield. — *v.i.* **7.** To be stationed or lodged. **8.** To range from side to side of an area, as dogs in hunting. **9.** *Naut.* To blow on a ship's quarter: said of the wind. [< OF < L *quartus* fourth]

quar·ter·back (kwôr′tər·bak′) *n.* In American football, one of the backfield, who often calls the signals.

quarter day Any of the four days of the year when quarterly payments are due.

quar·ter-deck (kwôr′tər·dek′) *n. Naut.* The rear part of a ship's upper deck, reserved for officers.

quar·tered (kwôr′tərd) *adj.* **1.** Divided into four quarters. **2.** Lodged; stationed; also, having quarters. **3.** Quartersawed. **4.** *Heraldry* Divided into quarters.

quar·ter·ly (kwôr′tər·lē) *adj.* **1.** Containing or being a fourth part. **2.** Occurring at intervals of three months. — *n. pl.* **·lies** A publication issued once every three months. — *adv.* **1.** Once in a quarter of a year. **2.** In or by quarters.

quar·ter·mas·ter (kwôr′tər·mas′tər, -mäs′-) *n.* **1.** *Usu. cap. Mil.* An officer responsible for the supply of food, fuel, clothing, etc. **2.** On shipboard, a petty officer responsible for steering and related functions.

quar·tern (kwôr′tərn) *n.* A fourth part of certain measures or weights, as of a peck or pound. [< OF < L *quartus* fourth]

quarter note *Music* A note having one fourth the time value of a whole note: also called *crotchet*.

quar·ter·saw (kwôr′tər·sô′) *v.t.* **·sawed**, **·sawed** or **·sawn**, **·saw·ing** To saw (a log) lengthwise into quarters so that each face corresponds with one of the log's radii.

quarter section A tract of land half a mile square, containing one fourth of a square mile, or 160 acres.

quarter sessions A court held quarterly.

quar·ter·staff (kwôr′tər·staf′, -stäf′) *n. pl.* **·staves** (-stāvz′) A stout, iron-tipped staff about 6½ feet long, formerly used in England as a weapon; also, the use of the quarterstaff.

quarter tone *Music* Half of a semitone. Also **quar·ter·tone** (kwôr′tər·tōn′).

quar·tet (kwôr·tet′) *n.* **1.** A composition for four voices or instruments. **2.** The four persons who perform such compositions. **3.** Any group or set of four things of a kind. Also **quar·tette′**. [< F *quartette* < Ital.]

quar·to (kwôr′tō) *adj.* Having four leaves or eight pages to the sheet: a *quarto* book. — *n. pl.* **·tos** A book or pamphlet having pages the size of a fourth of a sheet: often written 4to or 4°. [< L (*in*) *quarto* fourth]

quartz (kwôrts) *n.* Silicon dioxide, SiO_2, a hard, vitreous mineral occurring in many varieties, sometimes massive, as jasper and chalcedony, or sometimes in colorless and transparent or diversely colored forms crystallizing in the hexagonal system. [< G *quarz*; ult. origin uncertain]

quartz crystal A thin section of pure quartz, accurately ground and polished for use in certain optical instruments and as a high-frequency oscillator in some electron tubes.

quartz lamp A mercury-vapor lamp that is enclosed in a quartz tube and transmits ultraviolet wavelengths.

qua·sar (kwā′zär) *n.* A galaxylike formation in remote space that emits radio waves and vast energy. [QUAS(I-STELL)AR(RADIO SOURCE)]

quash¹ (kwosh) *v.t. Law* To make void or set aside, as an indictment; annul. — **Syn.** See ANNUL. [< OF < L *quassare* to shatter; meaning infl. by SQUASH¹]

quash² (kwosh) *v.t.* To put down or suppress forcibly or summarily: to *quash* a rebellion. [< OF < L *quassare* to shatter]

quasi- *prefix* **1.** (With nouns) Resembling; not genuine, as in *quasi-adult*, *quasi-physics*. **2.** (With adjectives) Nearly; almost, as in *quasi-complex*, *quasi-official*. [< L, as if]

qua·si-ju·di·cial (kwä′sī-jōō-dish′əl, -zī-, kwä′sē-) *adj.* Exercising functions of a judicial nature as a guide for official action, as a committee investigating facts and drawing conclusions from them.

quas·si·a (kwosh′ē·ə, kwosh′ə) *n.* **1.** The wood of either of two tropical American trees yielding a variety of economic products. **2.** A bitter drug prepared from this wood, used in medicine as a tonic, etc. **3.** The tree itself. [< NL, after Graman *Quassi* who discovered its use in 1730]

qua·ter·na·ry (kwə·tûr′nə·rē) *adj.* **1.** Consisting of four. **2.** Fourth in order. — *n. pl.* **·ries 1.** The number four; a group of four things. **2.** *Math.* A quantic function having four variables. [< L *quaternarius* < *quaterni* by fours]

Qua·ter·na·ry (kwə·tûr′nə·rē) *adj. Geol.* Of, pertaining to, or designating a geological period and system of the Cenozoic era, following the Tertiary and still continuing. See chart for GEOLOGY. — *n.* The Quaternary system or period.

qua·ter·ni·on (kwə·tûr′nē·ən) *n.* A set, system, or file of four. [< LL < *quattuor* four < L *quattor*]

quat·rain (kwot′rān) *n.* A stanza or poem of four lines. [< F < *quatre* four]

quat·re·foil (kat′ər·foil′, kat′rə-) *n.* **1.** A leaf, etc., having four leaflets. **2.** *Archit.* An ornament with four foils or lobes. [< OF *quatre* four + *foil* leaf]

quat·tro·cen·to (kwat′rō·chen′tō) *n.* The 15th century as connected with the revival of art and literature, esp. in Italy. — *adj.* Of or pertaining to the quattrocento. [< Ital.]

QUATREFOILS

qua·ver (kwā′vər) *v.i.* **1.** To tremble or shake: said usu. of the voice. **2.** To produce trills or quavers in singing or in playing a musical instrument. — *v.t.* **3.** To utter or sing in a tremulous voice. — *n.* **1.** A quivering or tremulous motion. **2.** A shake or trill, as in singing. **3.** *Music Chiefly Brit.* An eighth note. [Freq. of obs. *quave*, ME *cwafian* to tremble] — **qua′ver·y** *adj.*

quay (kē) *n.* A wharf or artificial landing place where vessels may load or unload. [< OF *cai* hedge, wall]

quean (kwēn) *n.* A brazen or ill-behaved woman; harlot; prostitute. [OE *cwene* prostitute]

quea·sy (kwē′zē) *adj.* **quea·si·er**, **quea·si·est 1.** Sick at the stomach. **2.** Nauseating; also, caused by nausea. **3.** Easily nauseated. **4.** Fastidious; squeamish. **5.** Requiring to be carefully treated; delicate. **6.** Hazardous. [ME *coisy*; origin unknown] — **quea′si·ly** *adv.* — **quea′si·ness** *n.*

Quech·ua (kech′wä) *n.* **1.** One of a tribe of South American Indians. **2.** The language of the Quechuas: also called *Incan*. Also spelled *Kechua*. — **Quech′uan** (kech′wən) *adj. & n.*

queen (kwēn) *n.* **1.** The wife of a king. **2.** A female sovereign or monarch. **3.** A woman preeminent in a given sphere. **4.** In chess, the most powerful piece, capable of moving any number of squares in a straight or diagonal line. **5.** A playing card bearing a conventional picture of a queen. **6.** *Entomol.* The single fully developed female in a colony of social insects, as bees, ants, etc. — *v.t.* **1.** To make a queen of. **2.** In chess, to make a queen of (a pawn) by moving it to the eighth row. — *v.i.* **3.** To reign as or play the part of a queen. — **to queen it** To act in a domineering, queenly manner. [OE *cwēn* woman, queen]

Queen Anne's lace The wild carrot.

Queen Anne's War See WAR OF THE SPANISH SUCCESSION in table for WAR.

queen consort The wife of a reigning king, who does not share his sovereignty.

queen dowager The widow of a king.

queen·ly (kwēn′lē) *adj.* **queen·li·er**, **queen·li·est 1.** Of or like a queen. **2.** Fit for a queen. — *adv.* In the manner of a queen. — **queen′li·ness** *n.*

queen mother A queen dowager who is mother of a reigning sovereign.

queen's English King's English.

queer (kwir) *adj.* **1.** Unusual; singular; odd. **2.** Of questionable character. **3.** *Slang* Counterfeit. **4.** *Slang* Homosexual. — *n. Slang* **1.** Counterfeit money. **2.** *Slang* A homosexual person. — *v.t. U.S. Slang* To jeopardize or spoil. [Origin unknown] — **queer′ly** *adv.* — **queer′ness** *n.*

quell (kwel) *v.t.* **1.** To put down or suppress by force; extinguish. **2.** To quiet; allay, as pain. [OE *cwellan* to kill] — **Syn. 1.** subdue, crush. **2.** soothe, still.

quel·que chose (kel'kə shōz') *French* A trifle; something.

quench (kwench) *v.t.* **1.** To put out or extinguish, as a fire. **2.** To put an end to. **3.** To slake or satisfy (thirst). **4.** To suppress or repress, as emotions. **5.** To cool, as heated iron or steel, by thrusting into water or other liquid. [OE *cwincan* to grow less, disappear] — **quench'a·ble** *adj.* — **quench'er** *n.* — **quench'less** *adj.*

quer·u·lous (kwer'ə·ləs, -yə·ləs) *adj.* **1.** Disposed to complain or be fretful; captious. **2.** Indicating or expressing a complaining or whining disposition. [< LL < *queri* to complain] — **quer'u·lous·ly** *adv.* — **quer'u·lous·ness** *n.*

que·ry (kwir'ē) *v.* **·ried, ·ry·ing** *v.t.* **1.** To inquire into; ask about. **2.** To ask questions of; interrogate. **3.** To express doubt concerning the correctness or truth of. — *v.i.* **4.** To have or express doubt; question. — **Syn.** See ASK. — *n. pl.* **·ries 1.** An inquiry or question. **2.** A doubt; interrogation. [< L < *quaerere* to ask]

quest (kwest) *n.* **1.** The act of seeking or looking for something; a search. **2.** An adventure or expedition, as in medieval romance. **3.** The person or persons engaged in a quest. — *v.t. & v.i.* To go on a quest or to search for (something). [< OF < L < *quaerere* to ask, seek] — **quest'er** *n.*

ques·tion (kwes'chən) *n.* **1.** An interrogative sentence calling for an answer; an inquiry. **2.** A subject of inquiry or debate; a matter to be decided; problem. **3.** A subject of dispute; a controversy. **4.** A proposition under discussion in a deliberative assembly. **5.** Possibility of disagreement or dispute; doubt: no *question* about it. **6.** The act of asking or inquiring. — **beside the question** Irrelevant; not pertinent. — **beyond (all) question** Not open to dispute; settled. — **out of the question** Not to be thought of; impossible. — *v.t.* **1.** To put a question or questions to; interrogate. **2.** To be uncertain of; doubt. **3.** To make objection to; challenge; dispute. — *v.i.* **4.** To ask a question or questions. — **Syn.** See ASK. [< OF < L < *quaerere* to ask] — **ques'tion·er** *n.*

ques·tion·a·ble (kwes'chən·ə·bəl) *adj.* **1.** Characterized by doubtful integrity, honesty, respectability, etc. **2.** Liable to be called in question; debatable. **3.** Uncertain; difficult to decide. — **ques'tion·a·bil'i·ty, ques'tion·a·ble·ness** *n.* — **ques'tion·a·bly** *adv.*

question mark A mark of punctuation (?) indicating that the sentence it closes is a direct question: also called *interrogation point.*

ques·tion·naire (kwes'chə·nâr') *n.* A written or printed form comprising a series of questions submitted to a number of persons to obtain data for a survey or report. [< F]

quet·zal (ket·säl') *n. pl.* **·zal·es** (-sä'lās) **1.** A bird of long, brilliant plumage, the national symbol of Guatemala, regarded as a deity by the Mayas. **2.** The standard monetary unit of Guatemala: in 1962 worth about one U.S. dollar. Also **que·zal** (kā·säl'). [< Sp.]

queue (kyōō) *n.* **1.** A pigtail. **2.** A line of persons or vehicles. — *v.i.* **queued, queu·ing** *Brit.* To form a line: usu. with *up.* Also **cue.** [< MF < L *cauda* a tail]

quib·ble (kwib'əl) *n.* **1.** An evasion of a point or question. **2.** A trivial distinction or objection; cavil. — *v.i.* **·bled, ·bling** To evade the truth or the point in question, as by raising trivial objections. [< obs. *quib* < L *quibus,* ablative pl. of *qui* who, which] — **quib'bler** *n.*

quick (kwik) *adj.* **1.** Done or occurring in a short time; rapid; swift. **2.** Responding readily or eagerly to impressions or instruction: a *quick* mind. **3.** Alert; sensitive; perceptive: a *quick* ear. **4.** Easily aroused or excited; hasty: a *quick* temper. **5.** Nimble: *quick* fingers. **6.** Pregnant; with child. **7.** Refreshing; bracing. **8.** Burning briskly. — *n.* **1.** Those who are alive: chiefly in the phrase **the quick and the dead. 2.** The living flesh, esp. the tender flesh under a fingernail. **3.** The feelings: cut to the *quick.* **4.** A plant suitable for hedges. — *adv.* Quickly; rapidly. [OE *cwic* alive] — **quick'ness** *n.*

quick bread Any bread, biscuits, etc., whose leavening agent makes immediate baking possible.

quick·en (kwik'ən) *v.t.* **1.** To cause to move more rapidly; hasten or accelerate. **2.** To give or restore life to. **3.** To excite or arouse; stimulate: to *quicken* the appetite. — *v.i.* **4.** To move or act more quickly; become more rapid. **5.** To come or return to life; revive. **6.** To begin to manifest signs of life: said of the fetus. — **quick'en·er** *n.*

quick-freeze (kwik'frēz') *v.t.* **-froze, -fro·zen, -freez·ing** To subject (food) to rapid refrigeration for storing at or below freezing temperatures.

quick·ie (kwik'ē) *n. U.S. Slang* Anything done hastily, as by short cuts or makeshift methods.

quick·lime (kwik'līm') *n.* See under LIME[1].

quick·ly (kwik'lē) *adv.* In a quick manner; rapidly; soon.

quick march A march in quick time; quickstep.

quick·sand (kwik'sand') *n.* A bed of sand, often of considerable depth, so water-soaked as to engulf any object, person, or animal resting or moving upon it.

quick·set (kwik'set') *n.* **1.** A plant suitable for hedges, esp. hawthorn. **2.** A hedge made of it.

quick·sil·ver (kwik'sil'vər) *n.* **1.** Mercury in its liquid form. **2.** An amalgam of tin, used for the backs of mirrors. [OE *cwicseolfor.* Trans. of L *argentum vivum.*]

quick·step (kwik'step') *n.* A march or dance written in a rapid tempo; also, a quick march.

quick-tem·pered (kwik'tem'pərd) *adj.* Easily angered.

quick time A marching step of 120 paces a minute, each pace of 30 inches, used in military drills and ceremonies.

quick-wit·ted (kwik'wit'id) *adj.* Having a ready wit or quick discernment; keen; alert. — **quick'-wit'ted·ly** *adv.* — **quick'-wit'ted·ness** *n.*

quid[1] (kwid) *n.* **1.** A small portion of chewing tobacco. **2.** A cud, as of a cow. [OE *cwudu.* Var. of CUD.]

quid[2] (kwid) *n. pl.* **quid** *Brit. Slang* A pound sterling, or a sovereign. [? Suggested by L QUID PRO QUO]

quid·di·ty (kwid'ə·tē) *n. pl.* **·ties 1.** The essence of a thing. **2.** A quibble; cavil. [< LL < L *quid* which, what]

quid·nunc (kwid'nungk') *n.* One who seeks to know all that is going on; a busybody. [< L *quid nunc* what now]

quid pro quo (kwid' prō kwō') *Latin* **1.** Something for something; an equivalent in return. **2.** A substitution.

qui·es·cent (kwī·es'ənt) *adj.* **1.** Being in a state of repose or inaction; quiet; still. **2.** Resting free from anxiety, emotion, or agitation. [< L *quiescere* to be quiet] — **qui·es'cence** *n.* — **qui·es'cent·ly** *adv.*

qui·et (kwī'ət) *adj.* **1.** Making little or no noise. **2.** Having little or no motion; still; calm. **3.** Characterized by silence; also, retired or secluded: a *quiet* nook. **4.** Free from excessive activity, turmoil, or vexation: a *quiet* day at the office. **5.** Gentle; mild: a *quiet* temperament. **6.** Restful to the eye; reposeful: a *quiet* scene. **7.** Not showy or pretentious; modest: *quiet* decorations. **8.** Not loud or brash; reserved: a *quiet* sense of humor. **9.** In commerce, not busy or active. — **Syn.** See CALM. — *n.* **1.** The quality or condition of being quiet. **2.** Peace; tranquillity; calmness. — *v.t. & v.i.* To make or become quiet: often with *down.* — *adv.* In a quiet or peaceful manner. [< OF < L *quies, quietis* rest, repose] — **qui'et·ly** *adv.* — **qui'et·ness** *n.*

qui·et·ism (kwī'ə·tiz'əm) *n.* **1.** A form of religious mysticism in which the will and the intellect fix themselves in a passive contemplation of God. **2.** A state of quiet.

qui·et·ist (kwī'ə·tist) *n.* **1.** An advocate or practicer of quietism. **2.** One who seeks or enjoys quiet.

qui·e·tude (kwī'ə·tōōd, -tyōōd) *n.* A state or condition of calm or tranquillity; repose; rest.

qui·e·tus (kwī·ē'təs) *n.* **1.** A silencing or suppressing, as of a rumor. **2.** Anything that kills, as a blow. **3.** A final discharge, as of a debt. [< L *quietus est* he is quit]

quill (kwil) *n. Ornithol.* One of the large, strong flight feathers or tail feathers of a bird. **2.** Something made from a quill, as a pen or plectrum. **3.** *Zool.* One of the large, sharp spines of a porcupine or hedgehog. [ME *quil*]

quilt (kwilt) *n.* **1.** A bedcover made by stitching together firmly two layers of cloth or patchwork with some soft and warm substance (as wool or cotton) between them. **2.** Any bedcover, esp. if thick. **3.** A quilted skirt or other quilted article. — *v.t.* **1.** To stitch together (two pieces of material) with a soft substance between. **2.** To stitch in ornamental patterns or crossing lines. **3.** To pad or line with something soft. — *v.i.* **4.** To make a quilt or quilted work. [< OF < L *culcita* bed, cushion]

quilt·ing (kwil'ting) *n.* **1.** The act or process of making a quilt, or of stitching as in making a quilt. **2.** Material for quiltwork. **3.** A quilting bee or party.

quilting bee A social gathering of women for working on a quilt or quilts. Also **quilting frolic, quilting party.**

quince (kwins) *n.* **1.** The hard, acid, applelike fruit of a small tree of the rose family, used for preserves. **2.** The tree. [< MF < OF *cooin* < L < Gk. *kydōnion*]

qui·nine (kwī'nīn, *esp. Brit.* kwi·nēn') *n. Chem.* A white, amorphous or slightly crystalline, very bitter alkaloid, $C_{20}H_{24}N_2O_2$, contained in cinchona barks, the salts of which are used in medicine for their tonic and antipyretic qualities and in the treatment of malaria. Also **quin·in** (kwin'in). [< Sp. *quina* cinchona bark and its extract]

quinine water A carbonated beverage flavored with quinine: also called *tonic.*

quin·qua·ge·nar·i·an (kwin'kwə·jə·nâr'ē·ən) *adj.* Of or pertaining to the age of 50 years, or to the decade between 50 and 60 years of age. — *n.* One who is of this age.

Quin·qua·ges·i·ma Sunday (kwin'kwə·jes'ə·mə) The Sunday before Ash Wednesday: also called *Shrove Sunday.* [< L *quinquagesima* (*dies*) fiftieth (day)]

quinque- *combining form* Five: *quinquennial.* Also, before vowels, **quinqu-.** [< L *quinque* five]

quin·quen·ni·al (kwin·kwen'ē·əl) *adj.* Occurring every five years, or once in five years; also, lasting five years. — *n.* A quinquennial anniversary. [< L *quinque* five + *annus* year]

quin·sy (kwin'zē) *n. Pathol.* A suppurative inflammation of the tonsils. [< Med.L < Gk. *kynanchē* dog's collar]

quint (kwint) *n.* 1. A fifth. 2. A set of five. 3. *Informal* A quintuplet. [< L *quintus* fifth]

quin·tal (kwin'təl) *n.* 1. A measure of weight, a hundredweight. 2. In the metric system, 100 kilograms. [< MF < Med.L *quintale* < Arabic *quintar* < LL *centarium* one hundred pieces of gold]

quin·tes·sence (kwin·tes'əns) *n.* 1. An extract from anything, containing in concentrated form its most essential principle. 2. The purest and most essential part of anything. [< F < Med.L *quinta essentia* fifth essence] — **quin·tes·sen·tial** (kwin'tə·sen'shəl) *adj.*

quin·tet (kwin·tet') *n.* 1. A musical composition for five voices or instruments; also, the five persons performing it. 2. Any group of five persons or things. Also **quin·tette'.** [< F < Ital. *quintetto,* dim. of *quinto* fifth]

quin·til·lion (kwin·til'yən) *n.* 1. *U.S.* A thousand quadrillions, written as 1 followed by 18 zeros: a cardinal number. 2. *Brit.* A million quadrillions (def. 2), written as 1 followed by 30 zeros: a cardinal number. — *adj.* Being a quintillion in number. [< *quinti-* five + (*mi*)*llion*] — **quin·til'lionth** *adj. & n.*

quin·tu·ple (kwin'tōō·pəl, -tyōō-, kwin·tōō'pəl, -tyōō'-) *v.t. & v.i.* **·pled, ·pling** To multiply by five; make or become five times as much or as large. — *adj.* 1. Consisting of five things united or of five parts. 2. Multiplied by five. — *n.* A number or a sum five times as great as another. [< F < LL *quintuplex* fivefold]

quin·tu·plet ((kwin'tōō·plit, -tyōō-, kwin·tōō'plit, -tyōō'-, -tup'lit) *n.* 1. Five things of a kind used or occurring together. 2. One of five born of the same mother at one birth.

quin·tu·pli·cate (*adj.* kwin·tōō'plə·kit, -tyōō'-; *v.* kwin·tōō'plə·kāt, -tyōō'-) *adj.* 1. Fivefold. 2. Raised to the fifth power. — *v.t. & v.i.* **·cat·ed, ·cat·ing** To multiply by five; quintuple. — *n.* One of five identical things. — **in quintuplicate** So as to have five identical copies. — **quin·tu'pli·cate·ly** *adv.* — **quin·tu·pli·ca'tion** *n.*

quip (kwip) *n.* 1. A sarcastic or witty jest or retort. 2. A quibble. 3. An odd, fantastic action or object. — *v.i.* **quipped, quip·ping** To make a witty remark; jest. [Prob. < L *quippe* indeed] — **quip'pish** *adj.*

quip·ster (kwip'stər) *n.* One who makes quips.

quire (kwīr) *n.* 1. The twentieth part of a ream of paper; 24 (or 25) sheets. 2. A set of all the sheets necessary to make a book. — *v.t.* **quired, quir·ing** To fold or separate into quires. [< OF *quaer,* ult. < L *quaterni* a set of four]

Quir·i·nal (kwir'ə·nəl) *n.* 1. One of the Seven Hills of Rome, containing the **Quirinal palace,** after 1870 the official residence of the kings of Italy. 2. The monarchical or civil government of Italy: distinguished from the *Vatican.* — *adj.* Pertaining to or situated on the Quirinal.

quirk (kwûrk) *n.* 1. A personal peculiarity, mannerism, or caprice. 2. A quibble. 3. A sharp turn or twist. 4. A sudden curve or flourish, as in writing. 5. A bright retort; quip. [Origin uncertain] — **quirk'y** *adj.*

quirt (kwûrt) *n.* A short-handled riding whip with a braided lash. — *v.t.* To strike with a quirt. [< Am. Sp. *cuarta*]

quis·ling (kwiz'ling) *n.* One who betrays his country to the enemy and is then given political power by the conquerors. [after Vidkun *Quisling,* 1887–1945, Norwegian Nazi party leader and traitor] — **quis'ling·ism** *n.*

quit (kwit) *v.* **quit** or **quit·ted, quit·ting** *v.t.* 1. To cease or desist from; discontinue. 2. To give up; renounce. 3. To go away from; leave. 4. To let go of (something held). — *v.i.* 5. To stop; cease; discontinue. 6. To leave; depart. 7. *Informal* To resign from a position, etc. — *adj.* Released, relieved, or absolved from something; clear; free; rid. — *n.* The act of quitting. — **to be quits** To be even (with another). — **to cry quits** To declare (oneself) willing to stop competing. [< OF < Med.L < L *quietus* at rest]

quit·claim (kwit'klām') *n. Law* A full release and acquittance given by one to another in regard to a certain demand, suit, or right of action. Also **quit·claim'ance** (-əns). — *v.t.* To relinquish or give up claim or title to; release from a claim. [< MF *quite clamer* to declare quit or free]

quite (kwīt) *adv.* 1. To the fullest extent; totally: *quite dead.* 2. Really; truly. 3. *Informal* To a great or considerable extent; noticeably; very: *quite ill.* ◆ The phrase *quite a* is used in many idioms to indicate considerable but indefinite number, size, quantity, etc., as in *quite a lot* (a good deal), *quite a few* (many), *quite a while* (a long while). It is also used in informal expressions with the sense of "wonderful, great, etc.," as in *quite a guy.* [ME; var. of QUIT, adj.]

quit·rent (kwit'rent') *n.* A fixed rent formerly paid by a freeholder, whereby he was released from feudal services.

quit·tance (kwit'ns) *n.* 1. Discharge or release, as from a debt or obligation. 2. A document or receipt certifying this. 3. A recompense or repayment. [< OF < *quitter* to quit]

quit·ter (kwit'ər) *n.* One who quits needlessly; a shirker.

quiv·er¹ (kwiv'ər) *v.i.* To shake with a slight, tremulous motion; vibrate; tremble. — *n.* The act or fact of quivering; a trembling or shaking. [Var. of QUAVER]

quiv·er² (kwiv'ər) *n.* A portable case for arrows; also, its contents. [< AF *quiver,* OF *cuivre* < OHG *kochar*]

quix·ot·ic (kwik·sot'ik) *adj.* 1. Of, pertaining to, or like Don Quixote. 2. Ridiculously chivalrous or romantic; having high but impractical sentiments, aims, etc. — **quix·ot'i·cal·ly** *adv.* — **quix·ot·ism** (kwik'sə·tiz'əm) *n.*

quiz (kwiz) *n.* 1. The act of questioning; esp., an informal oral or written examination of a class or individual. 2. An eccentric person or thing. 3. A hoax; practical joke. — *v.t.* **quizzed, quiz·zing** 1. To examine by asking questions; question. 2. *Brit.* To make fun of; ridicule. — **Syn.** See ASK. [Origin unknown] — **quiz'zer** *n.*

quiz·zi·cal (kwiz'i·kəl) *adj.* 1. Given to chaffing or bantering. 2. Queer; odd. 3. Questioning; puzzled: a *quizzical* smile. — **quiz·zi·cal·ly** *adv.*

quoin (koin, kwoin) *n.* 1. An external angle or corner of a building. 2. A stone or stones forming such an angle. 3. A wedge or wedgelike piece, as one of the stones in an arch. 4. *Printing* A wedge or pair of wedges for locking type in a chase or galley. — *v.t.* To provide, secure, or support with a quoin or quoins. [Var. of COIN]

QUOINS

A Printer's: *a* Single quoin, *b* Pair ready for locking with key.
B Quoins of dressed stone.

quoit (kwoit, *esp. Brit.* koit) *n.* 1. A ring of metal, rope, etc., thrown in a game at a short stake, either encircling it or coming as close to it as possible. 2. *pl.* (*construed as sing.*) The game so played. — *v.t.* To pitch as a quoit. [< MF *coite,* ? flat stone < OF *cuille.* See QUILT.]

quon·dam (kwon'dəm) *adj.* Having been formerly; former. [< L]

Quon·set hut (kwon'sit) A prefabricated, metal structure the roof of which is half of a cylinder cut lengthwise and resting on the ground: a trade name. [after *Quonset,* Rhode Island, where first made]

quo·rum (kwôr'əm, kwō'rəm) *n.* The number of members of any deliberative or corporate body as is necessary for the legal transaction of business, commonly, a majority. [< L, genitive plural of *qui* who]

quo·ta (kwō'tə) *n.* A proportional part or share required from each person, group, state, etc., for making up a certain number or quantity. [< Med.L < L *quotus* how many]

quot·a·ble (kwō'tə·bəl) *adj.* Suitable for quotation. — **quot·a·bil'i·ty** *n.*

quo·ta·tion (kwō·tā'shən) *n.* 1. The act of quoting. 2. The words quoted or cited. 3. A price quoted or current, as of securities, etc.: the *quotations* for wheat. — **quo·ta'tion·al** *adj.* — **quo·ta'tion·al·ly** *adv.* — **quo·ta'tion·ist** *n.*

quotation mark Either of the marks placed at the beginning and end of a word or passage that is an exact quotation of the original. In English usage, one or two inverted commas (" ") mark the beginning of a quotation, and correspondingly, one or two apostrophes (' ") the close, the single marks being used to set off a quotation within a quotation.

quote (kwōt) *v.* **quot·ed, quot·ing** *v.t.* 1. To reproduce the words of. 2. To repeat or cite (a rule, author, etc.), as for authority or illustration. 3. In commerce: **a** To state (a price). **b** To give the current or market price of. 4. *Printing* To enclose within quotation marks. — *v.i.* 5. To make a quotation, as from a book. — *n.* 1. Loosely, a quotation. 2. A quotation mark. [< Med.L *quotare* to distinguish by number < L *quot* how many] — **quot'a·ble** *adj.* — **quot'er** *n.* — **quote'wor'thy** (-wûr'thē) *adj.* — **quot'ing·ly** *adv.*

quoth (kwōth) *v.t.* Said or spoke; uttered: the imperfect tense of the obsolete verb *queth,* used only in the first and third persons, the subject always following the verb: *quoth* he. [OE *cwæth,* pt. of *cwethan* to say]

quo·tid·i·an (kwō·tid'ē·ən) *adj.* Recurring or occurring every day. — *n.* A fever that returns every day. [< OF, or < L *quotidianus* daily]

quo·tient (kwō'shənt) *n. Math.* The result obtained by division; a number indicating how many times one quantity is contained in another. [< L *quotiens* how often]

quo war·ran·to (kwō wô·ran'tō, wo-) *Law* A proceeding, usu. criminal in form but in substance civil, by which a government or sovereign seeks to recover an office or franchise. [< L, by what warrant]

R

r, R (är) *n. pl.* **r's** or **rs, R's** or **Rs, ars** (ärz) **1.** The 18th letter of the English alphabet. **2.** The sound represented by the letter *r.* — *symbol* **1.** *Chem.* An alkyl group. **2.** *Math.* Ratio. **3.** *Electr.* Resistance. — **the three R's** Reading, writing, and arithmetic regarded as the essential elements of a primary education.

Ra (rä) The supreme Egyptian deity, the sun god, usu. represented as a hawk-headed man crowned with the solar disk and the sacred serpent: also *Re.*

rab·bet (rab′it) *n.* **1.** A recess or groove in or near the edge of one piece of wood, etc., cut so as to receive the edge of another piece. **2.** A joint so made. — *v.* **·bet·ed,** **·bet·ing** *v.t.* **1.** To cut a rabbet in. **2.** To unite in a rabbet. — *v.i.* **3.** To be jointed by a rabbet. [< OF < *rabattre* to beat down]

RABBET JOINTS

rab·bi (rab′ī) *n. pl.* **·bis** or **·bies** In Judaism: **a** The spiritual head of a Jewish community, authorized to perform religious duties. **b** Master; teacher: a title for one learned in the Law. Also **rab′bin** (-in). [< Hebrew *rabbī* my master]

rab·bin·ate (rab′in·āt) *n.* **1.** The office or term of office of a rabbi. **2.** Rabbis collectively.

Rab·bin·ic (rə·bin′ik) *n.* The Hebrew language as used in late ancient and early medieval periods.

rab·bin·i·cal (rə·bin′i·kəl) *adj.* Pertaining to the rabbis or to their opinions, languages, or writings. Also **rab·bin′ic.** — **rab·bin′i·cal·ly** *adv.*

rab·bit (rab′it) *n.* **1.** Any of a family of various small, long-eared mammals allied to but smaller than the hare, as the common American cottontail. **2.** The pelt of a rabbit or hare. **3.** Welsh rabbit. — *v.i.* To hunt rabbits. [Akin to Walloon *robett,* Flemish *robbe*] — **rab′bit·er** *n.*

rabbit fever Tularemia.

rabbit foot The left hind foot of a rabbit, carried as a good-luck charm. Also **rab·bit's foot.**

rabbit hutch A coop in which domestic rabbits are bred.

rabbit punch A short chopping blow at the base of the skull or back of the neck.

rab·ble (rab′əl) *n.* A disorderly crowd or mob. — **the rabble** The populace or lower classes: a contemptuous term. — *adj.* Of, suited to, or characteristic of a rabble; disorderly. — *v.t.* **·bled,** **·bling** To mob. [? < RABBLE³]

rab·ble-rous·er (rab′əl·rou′zər) *n.* One who tries to incite mobs by arousing prejudices and passions.

Rab·e·lai·si·an (rab′ə·lā′zē·ən, -zhən) *adj.* **1.** Of, pertaining to, or resembling Rabelais or his works. **2.** Bawdy and boisterous. — *n.* A student or imitator of Rabelais. — **Rab′e·lai′si·an·ism, Rab′e·la′ism** *n.*

rab·id (rab′id) *adj.* **1.** Affected with, arising from, or pertaining to rabies; mad. **2.** Unreasonably zealous; fanatical; violent. **3.** Furious; raging. Also **rab′ic.** [< L *rabere* to be mad] — **rab′id·ly** *adv.* — **rab′id·ness** *n.*

ra·bies (rā′bēz, -bi·ez) *n.* An acute, infectious, usu. fatal disease of certain animals, esp. of dogs, readily transmissible to man by the bite of an affected animal: also called *hydrophobia.* [< L, madness] — **ra′bi·et′ic** (-et′ik) *adj.*

rac·coon (ra·kōōn′) *n.* **1.** A North American nocturnal carnivore, grayish brown with a black cheek patch and a black-and-white-ringed bushy tail. **2.** The fur of this animal. Also spelled *racoon.* [Alter. of Algonquian *arakunem* hand-scratcher]

race¹ (rās) *n.* **1.** One of the major zoological subdivisions of mankind, regarded as having a common origin and exhibiting a relatively constant set of physical traits, such as pigmentation, hair form, and facial and bodily proportions. **2.** Any group of people or any grouping of peoples having, or assumed to have, common characteristics, habits, appearance, etc. **3.** A nation: the German *race.* **4.** A genealogical or family stock; clan: the *race* of MacGregor. **5.** Pedigree; lineage: a noble *race.* **6.** Any class of beings having characteristics uniting them, or differentiating them from others: the *race* of lawyers. **7.** *Biol.* A group of plants or animals having distinct characteristics that are passed on to offspring. [< MF < Ital. *razza;* origin uncertain]

race² (rās) *n.* **1.** A contest to determine the relative speed of the contestants. **2.** Any contest. **3.** Movement or progression, esp. when regular or swift. **4.** Duration of life; course; career. **5.** A swift current of water or its channel. **6.** A sluice or channel by which to conduct water to or from a water wheel or around a dam. **7.** Any groove along which some part of a machine slides or is guided. — *v.* **raced, racing** *v.i.* **1.** To take part in a contest of speed. **2.** To move at great or top speed. **3.** To move at an accelerated or too great speed: said of machinery. — *v.t.* **4.** To contend against in a race. **5.** To cause to race. [< ON *rās*]

race·course (rās′kôrs′, -kōrs′) *n.* A racetrack.

race·horse (rās′hôrs′) *n.* A horse bred and trained for contests of speed.

ra·ceme (rā·sēm′, rə-) *n.* **1.** *Bot.* An inflorescence in which the flowers are arranged singly at intervals on a common axis. **2.** *Chem.* A racemic compound. [< L *racemus* cluster]

ra·ce·mic (rā·sē′mik, -sem′ik, rə-) *adj.* **1.** *Bot.* Of, pertaining to, or contained in racemes. **2.** *Chem.* Indicating any compound that is optically inactive, but separable into two isomers, one dextrorotatory, the other levorotatory. Also **rac·e·moid** (ras′ə·moid).

rac·e·mose (ras′ə·mōs) *adj.* Like a raceme in form or nature. Also **rac′e·mous** (-məs). — **rac′e·mose·ly** *adv.*

rac·er (rā′sər) *n.* **1.** One who races. **2.** Anything designed or used for racing, as a car, yacht, etc. **3.** One of various colubrine snakes, as the blacksnake.

race riot A violent conflict between groups in the same community, based on differences of color or creed.

race suicide The slow reduction in numbers of a people through voluntary failure on the part of individuals to maintain the birth rate at or above the level of the death rate.

race·track (rās′trak′) *n.* A track or course over which a horse race, dog race, etc., is run: also called *racecourse.*

race·way (rās′wā′) *n.* **1.** A channel for conducting water. **2.** A tube for protecting wires, as in a subway. **3.** *U.S.* A racetrack for trotting horses.

Ra·chel (rā′chəl) The wife of Jacob; mother of Joseph and Benjamin. *Gen.* xxix 6. [< Hebrew, lit., ewe]

ra·chi·tis (rə·kī′tis) *n. Pathol.* Rickets. [< NL < Gk. < *rachis* spine] — **ra·chit′ic** (-kit′ik) *adj.*

ra·cial (rā′shəl) *adj.* Of, pertaining to, or characteristic of a race, races, or descent. — **ra′cial·ly** *adv.*

ra·cial·ism (rā′shəl·iz′əm) *n.* Racism. — **ra′cial·ist** *n.*

ra·cism (rā′siz·əm) *n.* **1.** An irrational belief in or advocacy of the superiority of a given group, people, or nation, usu. one's own, on the basis of racial differences having no scientific validity. **2.** Social action or government policy based upon such assumed differences. — **ra′cist** *n.*

rack¹ (rak) *n.* **1.** An open grating, framework, or the like, in or on which articles may be placed. **2.** A triangular frame for arranging the balls on a billiard table. **3.** A container or framework in an airplane for carrying bombs. **4.** *Mech.* A bar or the like having teeth that engage with those of a gearwheel, pinion, or worm gear. **5.** A machine for stretching or making tense; esp., an instrument of torture that stretches the limbs of victims. **6.** Torture or punishment as by the rack; also, intense mental or physical suffering. **7.** A wrenching or straining, as from a storm. — *v.t.* **1.** To place or arrange in or on a rack. **2.** To torture on the rack. **3.** To torment. **4.** To strain, as with the effort of thinking: to *rack* one's brains. **5.** To raise (rents) excessively. — **to rack up** *U.S. Informal* To achieve: to *rack up* a perfect score. [< MDu. < *recken* to stretch] — **rack′er** *n.*

rack² (rak) *n.* **1.** Thin, flying, or broken clouds. **2.** Any floating vapor. — *v.i.* To move rapidly; send, as clouds before the wind. Also spelled *wrack.* [< Scand.]

rack³ (rak) *n.* Destruction; wreck; demolition: now usu. in the phrase **rack and ruin.** — **to rack up** *U.S. Slang* To wreck. [Var. of WRACK²]

rack·et¹ (rak′it) *n.* **1.** A nearly elliptical hoop of bent wood, usu. strung with catgut or nylon, and having a handle, used in striking a tennis ball, etc. **2.** A large wooden sole or shoe to support the weight of a man or horse on swampy ground.

3. A snowshoe. 4. An organ stop. 5. *Often pl.* A game resembling court tennis, played in a court with four walls. Often *racquet*. [< MF < Arabic *rāha* palm of the hand]

rack·et² (rak/it) *n.* 1. A clattering, vociferous, or confused noise. 2. *Informal* A scheme for getting money or other benefits by fraud, intimidation, or other illegitimate means. 3. *Slang* Any business or occupation. 4. Social activity or excitement. — *v.i.* 1. To make a loud, clattering noise. 2. To indulge in noisy sport or diversion. [Prob. imit.]

rack·et·eer (rak/ə·tir/) *n.* 1. One engaged in a racket. 2. Formerly, a bootlegger or rumrunner. — **rack/et·eer/ing** *n.*

rack·et·y (rak/it·ē) *adj.* Making a racket; noisy.

rac·on·teur (rak/on·tûr/, *Fr.* ra·kôn·tœr/) *n.* A skilled storyteller.

ra·coon (ra·kōōn/) See RACCOON.

rac·quet (rak/it) See RACKET¹.

rac·y (rā/sē) *adj.* **rac·i·er, rac·i·est** 1. Having a spirited or pungent interest; spicy; piquant. 2. Having a characteristic flavor assumed to be indicative of origin, as wine; rich, fresh, or fragrant. 3. Suggestive; slightly immodest: a *racy* story. [< RACE] — **rac/i·ly** *adv.* — **rac/i·ness** *n.*

ra·dar (rā/där) *n. Telecom.* An electronic device that locates objects by beaming radio-frequency impulses that are reflected back from the object, and determines its distance by a measurement of the time elapsed between transmission and reception of the impulses. [< *ra(dio) d(etection) a(nd) r(anging)*]

radar beacon *Telecom.* The part of a radar that transmits radio-frequency waves. Also **ra·con** (rā/kon).

ra·dar·scope (rā/där·skōp) *n. Telecom.* The oscilloscope of a radar set.

rad·dle (rad/l) *v.t.* **·dled, ·dling** To intertwine or weave together. [< OF < MHG *reidel* stout stick]

ra·di·al (rā/dē·əl) *adj.* 1. Pertaining to, consisting of, or resembling a ray or radius. 2. Extending from a center like rays. 3. Of or pertaining to the radius or a radiating part. 4. *Anat.* Denoting the radius. 5. Developing uniformly on all sides. — *n.* A radiating part. — **ra/di·al·ly** *adv.*

radial engine A multicylinder internal-combustion engine having its cylinders arranged like the spokes in a wheel.

ra·di·an (rā/dē·ən) *n. Math.* 1. An arc equal in length to the radius of the circle of which it is a part. 2. The angle subtended by such an arc, equal to 57° 17′ 44.80625″ +.

ra·di·ance (rā/dē·əns) *n.* The quality or state of being radiant; brightness; effulgence. Also **ra/di·an·cy, ra/di·ant·ness.**

ra·di·ant (rā/dē·ənt) *adj.* 1. Emitting rays of light or heat. 2. Beaming with light or brightness, kindness, or love: a *radiant* smile. 3. Resembling rays. 4. Consisting of or transmitted by radiation: *radiant* heat. — *n.* 1. A straight line proceeding from and conceived as revolving around a given point. 2. *Astron.* That point in the heavens from which, during a meteoric shower, the meteors seem to shoot. 3. The luminous point from which light proceeds or is made to radiate. 4. That which radiates. [< L *radians, -antis,* ppr. of *radiare* to emit rays] — **ra/di·ant·ly** *adv.*

radiant energy *Physics* The energy associated with and transmitted in the form of waves, esp. those of electromagnetic frequencies, as heat, light, radio waves, X-rays, etc.

ra·di·ate (*v.* rā/dē·āt; *adj. & n.* rā/dē·it) *v.* **·at·ed, ·at·ing** *v.i.* 1. To emit rays or radiation; be radiant. 2. To issue forth in rays, as light from the sun. 3. To spread out from a center, as the spokes of a wheel. — *v.t.* 4. To send out or emit in rays. 5. To cause to spread as if from a center; diffuse. 6. To show as if shining with. — *adj.* Divided or separated into rays; having rays; radiating. — **ra/di·a/tive** *adj.*

ra·di·a·tion (rā/dē·ā/shən) *n.* 1. The act of radiating, or the state of being radiated. 2. *Physics* **a** The emission and propagation of radiant energy, esp. by radioactive substances capable of affecting living tissue. **b** The stages of emission, absorption, and transmission involved in this.

radiation sickness *Pathol.* A condition due to absorption of excess radiation and marked by fatigue, vomiting, internal hemorrhage, and progressive tissue breakdown.

ra·di·a·tor (rā/dē·ā/tər) *n.* 1. That which radiates. 2. A chamber, coil, or flat hollow vessel, through which is passed steam or hot water for warming a building or apartment. 3. In engines, a nest of tubes for cooling water flowing through them. 4. *Physics* Any source of radiant energy, whether in the form of particles or of electromagnetic waves. — **ra/di·a·to/ry** (-ə·tôr/ē, -tō/rē) *adj.*

rad·i·cal (rad/i·kəl) *adj.* 1. Of, proceeding from, or pertaining to the root or foundation; fundamental. 2. Thoroughgoing; extreme: *radical* measures. 3. *Math.* Pertaining to the root or roots of a number. 4. In etymology, belonging or referring to a root or a root syllable. 5. *Chem.* Pertaining to a radical. 6. Of or pertaining to political radicals. — *n.* 1. One who carries his theories or convictions to their furthest application. 2. In politics, one who advocates widespread governmental changes and reforms at the earliest opportunity. 3. The primitive or underived part of a word; a root. 4. *Math.* **a** A quantity that is the root of another

quantity. **b** The radical sign. 5. *Chem.* A group of atoms that acts as a unit in a compound and may pass unchanged through a series of reactions. [< LL *radicalis* having roots] — **rad/i·cal·ly** *adv.* — **rad/i·cal·ness** *n.*

rad·i·cal·ism (rad/i·kəl·iz/əm) *n.* 1. The state of being radical. 2. Advocacy of radical measures.

radical sign *Math.* The symbol √ placed before a quantity to indicate that a designated root is to be taken.

rad·i·cle (rad/i·kəl) *n.* 1. *Bot.* **a** The embryonic root below the cotyledon of a plant. **b** A small root or rootlet. 2. *Anat.* A rootlike part, as the initial fiber of a nerve. [< L *radicula,* dim. of *radix, -icis* root]

ra·di·i (rā/dē·ī) Plural of RADIUS.

ra·di·o (rā/dē·ō) *n. pl.* **·os** 1. The science and technique of communicating by means of radio waves that have been modulated to carry information either in the form of sound or of a code. 2. A radio program or broadcast. 3. A receiver, transmitter, or other radio apparatus. 4. A radio message or radiogram. 5. The radio business and industry. — *adj.* Of, pertaining to, designating, employing, or produced by radiant energy, esp. in the form of electromagnetic waves. — *v.t. & v.i.* **ra·di·oed, ra·di·o·ing** To transmit (a message, etc.) or communicate with (someone) by radio. Also, *Brit., wireless.* [< RADIO(TELEGRAPHY)]

radio- *combining form* 1. Radial. 2. Radio; produced or obtained by or related to radio. 3. Radioactive. 4. Radiation. [< L *radius* ray]

ra·di·o·ac·tive (rā/dē·ō·ak/tiv) *adj.* Pertaining to, exhibiting, caused by, or characteristic of radioactivity.

radioactive series *Physics* The sequence of disintegration products through which a radioactive element passes before reaching a stable form as an isotope of lead. The three principal series are those of uranium, thorium, and actinium.

ra·di·o·ac·tiv·i·ty (rā/dē·ō·ak·tiv/ə·tē) *n. Physics* The spontaneous nuclear disintegration of certain elements and isotopes, with the emission of nucleons or of electromagnetic radiation; also, a particular form of such disintegration.

radio astronomy The branch of astronomy and astrophysics that studies celestial objects by the analysis of radio waves intercepted by radio telescopes.

radio beacon A stationary radio transmitter that sends out characteristic signals for the guidance of ships and aircraft.

radio beam *Aeron.* A continuous radio signal along an airway to guide aircraft.

ra·di·o·bi·ol·o·gy (rā/dē·ō·bī·ol/ə·jē) *n.* The study of the effects of radiation upon living organisms.

ra·di·o·broad·cast (rā/dē·ō·brôd/kast/, -käst/) *v.t. & v.i.* **·cast** *or* **·cast·ed, ·cast·ing** To broadcast by radio. — *n.* A broadcast. — **ra/di·o·broad/cast/er** *n.*

ra·di·o·car·bon (rā/dē·ō·kär/bən) *n. Physics* The radioactive isotope of carbon of mass 14 with a half life of about 5570 years, much used in the dating of fossils, artifacts, and certain kinds of geological formations: also called *carbon 14.*

radio compass *Aeron.* A directional radio receiver that indicates the bearing of a radio transmitting station.

ra·di·o·dat·ing (rā/dē·ō·dā/ting) *n.* The technique of dating objects by measuring their radioactivity.

ra·di·o·el·e·ment (rā/dē·ō·el/ə·mənt) *n. Physics* Any isotope or element exhibiting radioactivity.

radio fix The position of an aircraft, ship, or radio transmitter, as determined by use of radio signals.

radio frequency Any wave frequency lying between about 10 kilocycles and 30,000 megacycles.

ra·di·o·gram (rā/dē·ō·gram/) *n.* 1. A message sent by radio. 2. A radiograph.

ra·di·o·graph (rā/dē·ō·graf/, -gräf/) *n.* A picture made by means of radioactivity; an X-ray photograph. — *v.t.* To make a radiograph of. — **ra/di·og/ra·pher** (-og/rə·fər) *n.* — **ra/di·o·graph/ic** *or* **·i·cal** *adj.* — **ra/di·og/ra·phy** *n.*

ra·di·o·i·so·tope (rā/dē·ō·ī/sə·tōp) *n. Physics* A radioactive isotope, usu. one produced artificially from a normally stable element, used in biological and physical research and in medicine for diagnostic and therapeutic purposes.

ra·di·ol·o·gy (rā/dē·ol/ə·jē) *n.* The branch of science that relates to radiant energy and its applications, especially in the diagnosis and treatment of disease. — **ra/di·o·log/i·cal** (rā/dē·ə·loj/i·kəl) *or* **ra/di·o·log/ic** *adj.* — **ra/di·ol/o·gist** *n.*

ra·di·om·e·ter (rā/dē·om/ə·tər) *n.* An instrument for detecting and measuring radiant energy by converting it into mechanical energy, as by the rotation of blackened vanes suspended in a vacuum and exposed to sunlight. — **ra/di·o·met/ric** (-ō·met/rik) *adj.* — **ra/di·om/e·try** *n.*

ra·di·o·phone (rā/dē·ō·fōn/) *n.* 1. Any device for the production or transmission of sound by radiant energy. 2. A radiotelephone. — **ra/di·o·phon/ic** (-fon/ik) *adj.* — **ra/di·oph/o·ny** (-of/ə·nē) *n.*

ra·di·o·pho·tog·ra·phy (rā/dē·ō·fə·tog/rə·fē) *n.* The transmission of a photograph by radio waves. — **ra/di·o·pho/to·graph** (-fō/tə·graf, -gräf) *n.*

radio pill *Med.* A tiny radio transmitter that can be introduced into the body to transmit physiological data.

ra·di·o·scope (rādē·ō·skōp′) n. An apparatus for detecting radioactivity or X-rays.

ra·di·os·co·py (rā′dē·os′kə·pē) n. Examination of opaque bodies with the aid of X-rays or some other form of radiant energy. — **ra′di·o·scop′ic** (-skop′ik) or -**i·cal** adj.

ra·di·o·sonde (rā′dē·ō·sond′) n. Meteorol. An airborne device, usu. attached to a balloon, that radios meteorological data to the ground. [< F < radio radio + sonde sounding]

radio spectrum The full range of frequencies pertaining to and associated with radiant energy; esp., the radio frequencies.

radio star Any of a large number of stars that may be identified and studied by means of the radio waves they emit.

radio station An installation of all the equipment needed for effective radio broadcasting, esp. when used for commercial or educational purposes and licensed to employ an assigned frequency and power.

ra·di·o·stron·tium (rā′dē·ō·stron′shəm, -tē·əm) n. Physics Strontium 90.

ra·di·o·tel·e·gram (rā′dē·ō·tel′ə·gram) n. A message sent by radiotelegraphy.

ra·di·o·te·leg·ra·phy (rā′dē·ō·tə·leg′rə·fē) n. Telegraphic communication using radio waves. — **ra′di·o·tel′e·graph′ic** (-tel′ə·graf′ik) adj. — **ra′di·o·tel′e·graph** (-graf, -gräf) n.

ra·di·o·tel·e·phone (rā′dē·ō·tel′ə·fōn) n. A telephone that operates by means of radio waves. — **ra′di·o·tel′e·phon′ic** (-tel′ə·fon′ik) adj. — **ra′di·o·te·leph′o·ny** (-tə·lef′ə·nē) n.

radio telescope Astron. A highly sensitive radio receiver, designed to receive radio waves from outer space.

ra·di·o·ther·a·py (rā′dē·ō·ther′ə·pē) n. Med. The treatment of disease by X-rays and other forms of radioactivity.

ra·di·o·ther·my (rā′dē·ō·thûr′mē) n. Med. Diathermy.

ra·di·o·tho·ri·um (rā′dē·ō·thôr′ē·əm, -thō′rē·əm) n. A radioactive isotope of thorium, with a half life of 1.9 years.

radio tube An electron tube.

radio wave Any electromagnetic wave having a radio frequency; a Hertzian wave.

rad·ish (rad′ish) n. 1. The pungent, edible root of a tall, branching herb of the mustard family. 2. The herb yielding this root. [OE rædic < L radix, radicis root]

ra·di·um (rā′dē·əm) n. A powerfully radioactive metallic element (symbol Ra), obtained principally as a disintegration product of uranium. It has a half life of about 1,600 years, emitting alpha and beta particles and gamma rays in a succession of stages beginning with radon and continuing to radium G, a stable isotope of lead. See ELEMENT. [< NL < L radius ray + -IUM]

radium therapy The treatment of diseases, esp. cancer, by means of radium.

ra·di·us (rā′dē·əs) n. pl. **·di·i** (-dē·ī) 1. A straight line from the center of a circle or sphere to the circumference or surface. 2. Anat. The thicker and shorter bone of the forearm, on the same side as the thumb. 3. Zool. A similar bone in the forelimb of other vertebrates. 4. Bot. A ray floret of a composite flower. 5. A ray or radiating part. 6. A circular area or boundary measured by the length of its radius. 7. Sphere, scope, or limit, as of activity. 8. A fixed limit of travel or operation under specified conditions: the cruising radius of a ship. [< L, orig. rod, hence spoke of a wheel]

radius vector n. pl. **radius vectors** or **ra·di·i vec·to·res** (rā′dē·ī vek·tôr′ēz, -tō′rēz) Math. The straight-line distance from a fixed origin to any point of a curve.

ra·dix (rā′diks) n. pl. **rad·i·ces** (rad′ə·sēz, rā′də-) or **ra·dix·es** 1. Math. A number or symbol used as the basis of a scale of enumeration. 2. Bot. The root of a plant. [< L, root]

ra·dome (rā′dōm) n. A protective housing for the antenna of a radar assembly. [< RA(DAR) + DOME]

ra·don (rā′don) n. A heavy, gaseous, radioactive element (symbol Rn), an emanation of radium with a half life of about 14 days: formerly called niton. See ELEMENT.

raff (raf) n. The rabble; riffraff. [< dial. raff to rake < OF rafler < rafle]

raf·fi·a (raf′ē·ə) n. 1. A cultivated palm of Madagascar, the leafstalks of which furnish fiber for making hats, mats, baskets, etc. 2. Its fiber. [< Malagasy]

raff·ish (raf′ish) adj. 1. Tawdry; gaudy; flashy. 2. Disreputable.

raf·fle (raf′əl) n. A form of lottery in which one buys a chance on an object. — v. **fled, fling** v.t. 1. To dispose of by a raffle: often with off. — v.i. 2. To take part in a raffle. [< OF rafle a game of dice < Du. rafelen] — **raf′fler** n.

raft¹ (raft, räft) n. 1. A float of logs, planks, etc., fastened together for transportation by water. 2. A life raft. — v.t.

1. To transport on a raft. 2. To form into a raft. — v.i. 3. To travel by, be employed on, or manage a raft. [< ON raptr rafter]

raft² (raft, räft) n. Informal A large number or indiscriminate collection of any kind. [< RAFF]

raft·er (raf′tər, räf′-) n. A beam giving form, slope, and support to a roof. For illus. see ROOF. [OE ræfter]

rafts·man (rafts′mən, räfts′-) n. pl. **·men** (-mən) One who manages or works on a raft.

rag¹ (rag) v.t. **ragged, rag·ging** Slang 1. To tease or annoy. 2. To scold. — n. Brit. A ragging. [Origin uncertain]

rag² (rag) n. 1. A torn or discarded piece of cloth. 2. A small cloth used for washing, cleaning, etc. 3. A fragment of anything. 4. pl. Cotton or linen textile remnants used in the making of rag paper. 5. pl. Tattered or shabby clothing. 6. Any clothing: a jocular usage. 7. Anything resembling a rag in appearance or worth: used humorously or in disparagement. — **glad rags** Slang One's best clothes. — **to chew the rag** Slang To talk or argue at great length. [OE < ON rögg tuft]

rag³ (rag) v.t. **ragged, rag·ging** To compose or play in ragtime. — n. Ragtime.

rag·a·muf·fin (rag′ə·muf′in) n. Anyone, esp. a child, wearing very ragged clothes. [after Ragamoffyn, demon in William Langland's Piers Plowman, 1393]

rage (rāj) n. 1. Violent anger; wrath; fury. 2. Any great violence or intensity, as of a fever or a storm. 3. Extreme eagerness or emotion; great enthusiasm. 4. Something popular or in demand; a fad. — v.i. **raged, rag·ing** 1. To speak, act, or move with unrestrained anger. 2. To act or proceed with great violence. 3. To spread or prevail uncontrolled, as an epidemic. [< OF < LL < L rabere to rage] — **rag′ing·ly** adv.

rag·ged (rag′id) adj. 1. Rent or worn into rags; frayed. 2. Wearing worn, frayed, or shabby garments. 3. Of rough or uneven character or aspect. 4. Naturally of a rough or shaggy appearance. — **rag′ged·ly** adv. — **rag′ged·ness** n.

ragged edge Informal The extreme or precarious edge; the verge; the ragged edge of starvation. — **on the ragged edge** Dangerously near to losing one's self-control, sanity, etc.

rag·lan (rag′lən) n. An overcoat or topcoat, the sleeves of which extend in one piece up to the collar. — adj. Denoting a garment with such sleeves. [after Lord Raglan, 1788–1855, English field marshal]

rag·man (rag′man′, -mən) n. pl. **·men** (-men′, -mən) One who buys and sells old rags and other waste; a ragpicker.

ra·gout (ra·gōō′) n. A highly seasoned dish of stewed meat and vegetables. — v.t. **ra·gouted** (-gōōd′), **ra·gout·ing** (-gōō′ing) To make into a ragout. [< F]

rag·pick·er (rag′pik′ər) n. One who picks up rags and other junk for a livelihood.

rag·time (rag′tīm′) n. 1. A kind of American dance music, developed from about 1890 to 1920, characterized by highly syncopated rhythm in fast time. 2. The rhythm of this music. Also called rag. [< ragged time]

rag·weed (rag′wēd′) n. A coarse, very common annual or perennial herb, the pollen of which induces hay fever.

rag·wort (rag′wûrt′) n. Any of several herbs of the composite family, with bright yellow flowers.

rah (rä) interj. Hurrah: a cheer used chiefly in college yells.

raid (rād) n. 1. A hostile or predatory incursion by a rapidly moving body of troops or an armed vessel; a foray. 2. An air raid. 3. Any sudden invasion, capture, or seizure. 4. An attempt by speculators to lower stock prices. — v.t. 1. To make a raid on. — v.i. 2. To participate in a raid. [< Scottish form of OE rād a riding] — **raid′er** n.

rail¹ (rāl) n. 1. A bar of wood, metal, etc., resting on supports, as in a fence, at the side of a stairway, or capping the bulwarks of a ship; a railing. 2. One of a series of parallel bars of iron or steel, resting upon crossties and forming a support and guide for wheels, as of a railroad. 3. A railroad considered as a means of transportation: to ship by rail. — v.t. To furnish or shut in with rails; fence. [< OF < L regula wooden ruler]

RAIL FENCE

rail² (rāl) n. Any of numerous marsh birds having very short wings, moderately long legs and toes, and a short turned-up tail. [< OF raale]

rail³ (rāl) v.i. 1. To use scornful, insolent, or abusive language; scold: with at or against. — v.t. 2. To drive or force by railing. [< MF < Provençal ralhar to jest at] — **rail′er** n.

rail·ing (rā′ling) n. 1. A series of rails; a balustrade. 2. Rails, or material from which rails are made.

rail·ler·y (rā′lər·ē) n. pl. **·ler·ies** Merry jesting or teasing; banter. [< F raillerie jesting]

rail·road (rāl′rōd′) n. 1. A graded road having metal rails

(Note: RADIO-SONDE. a Instrument box. — caption beside balloon illustration in first column)

supported by ties or sleepers, for the passage of trains or rolling stock drawn by locomotives. **2.** The system of tracks, stations, etc., used in transportation by rail. **3.** The corporation or persons owning or operating such a system. — *v.t.* **1.** To transport by railroad. **2.** *U.S. Informal* To rush or force with great speed or without deliberation: to *railroad* a bill through Congress. **3.** *U.S. Slang* To cause to be imprisoned on false charges or without fair trial. — *v.i.* **4.** To work on a railroad. — **rail'road'er** *n.* — **rail'road'ing** *n.*

rail-split-ter (rāl'split'ər) *n.* One who splits logs into fence rails.

rail-way (rāl'wā') *n.* **1.** *Chiefly Brit.* A railroad. **2.** Rails similar to those of a railroad, as for streetcars. **3.** A track or set of rails, as in a factory, for handling heavy articles, etc.

rai-ment (rā'mənt) *n.* *Archaic* Wearing apparel; clothing; garb. [Aphetic var. of *arrayment* < ARRAY + -MENT]

rain (rān) *n.* **1.** The condensed water vapor of the atmosphere falling in drops. ◆ Collateral adjective: *pluvial*. **2.** The fall of such drops. **3.** A fall or shower of anything in the manner of rain. **4.** A rainstorm; shower. **5.** *pl.* The rainy season, as in a tropical country. — *v.i.* **1.** To fall from the clouds in drops of water: usu. with *it* as the subject. **2.** To fall like rain, as tears. **3.** To send or pour down rain, as clouds. — *v.t.* **4.** To send down like rain; shower. — **to rain out** To cause (a game, outdoor event, etc.) to be canceled or postponed because of rain. [OE *regn*]

rain-bow (rān'bō') *n.* **1.** An arch of prismatic colors formed in the sky opposite the sun and caused by refraction, reflection, and dispersion of light in raindrops falling through the air. **2.** Any similar display of color. [OE *regnboga*]

rain check *U.S.* **1.** The stub of a ticket to an outdoor event, as a baseball game, entitling the holder to admission at a future date if for any reason the event is called off. **2.** A postponed invitation.

rain-coat (rān'kōt') *n.* A coat, often waterproof, intended to be worn in rainy weather. Also, *Brit.*, *waterproof.*

rain-fall (rān'fôl') *n.* **1.** A fall of rain. **2.** *Meteorol.* The amount of water, measured in inches, precipitated in a given region over a stated time, as rain, hail, snow, or the like.

rain gauge An instrument for measuring the amount of rainfall at a given place or time. Also **rain gage.**

rain-mak-er (rān'mā'kər) *n.* One reputedly able to cause rain; esp., among certain American Indians, one who uses incantations to produce rain. — **rain'mak'ing** *n.*

rain-out (rān'out') *n.* *Physics* Precipitation of radioactive water droplets following an underwater nuclear explosion.

rain-proof (rān'prōōf') *adj.* Shedding rain, as garments.

rain-storm (rān'stôrm') *n.* A storm accompanied by rain.

rain-wa-ter (rān'wô'tər, -wot'-) *n.* Water that falls or has fallen in the form of rain. Also **rain water.**

rain-y (rā'nē) *adj.* **rain-i-er, rain-i-est** Characterized by, abounding in, or bringing rain. — **rain'i-ness** *n.*

rainy day A time of need; hard times.

raise (rāz) *v.* **raised, rais-ing** *v.t.* **1.** To cause to move upward or to a higher level; elevate. **2.** To place erect; set up. **3.** To construct or build. **4.** To make greater in amount, size, or value: to *raise* prices. **5.** To advance or elevate in rank, estimation, etc. **6.** To increase the strength, intensity, or degree of. **7.** To breed; grow: to *raise* tomatoes. **8.** *U.S.* To rear (children, a family, etc.). **9.** To cause to be heard: to *raise* a hue and cry. **10.** To cause; occasion, as a smile or laugh. **11.** To stir to action or emotion. **12.** To waken; animate or reanimate. **13.** To gather together; obtain or collect, as an army, capital, etc. **14.** To bring up for consideration, as a question. **15.** To cause to swell or become lighter; leaven. **16.** To put an end to, as a siege. **17.** In poker, to bet more than. **18.** *Naut.* To cause to appear above the horizon, as land or a ship, by approaching nearer. — *v.i.* **19.** *Informal* To cough up phlegm. **20.** In poker, to make a raise. — **to raise the devil** (or **the dickens, hell, the roof, a rumpus,** etc.) *Informal* To make a great disturbance; stir up confusion. — *n.* **1.** The act of raising. **2.** An increase, as of wages or a bet. ◆ In British usage, a *rise* is an increase in wages. [< ON *risa* to rise] — **rais'er** *n.*

raised (rāzd) *adj.* **1.** Elevated in low relief. **2.** Made with yeast or leaven.

rai-sin (rā'zən) *n.* A grape of a special sort dried in the sun or in an oven. [< OF < L *racemus* bunch of grapes]

rai-son d'ê-tre (re-zôn' de'tr') *French* Reason or excuse for existing; literally, reason for being.

raj (räj) *n.* In India, sovereignty; rule. [< Hind. *rāj*]

ra-jah (rä'jə) *n.* A Hindu prince or chief of a tribal state in India; also, a Malay or Javanese ruler: often used as a courtesy title. Also **ra'ja.** [< Hind. < Skt. *rājan* king]

Raj-put (räj'pōōt) *n.* One of a powerful and warlike Hindu caste. Also **Raj'poot.** [< Hind. < Skt. < *rājan* king + *putra* son]

rake[1] (rāk) *n.* A toothed implement for drawing together loose material, loosening the surface of the soil, etc. — *v.* **raked, rak-ing** *v.t.* **1.** To scrape or gather together with or as with a rake. **2.** To smooth, clean, or prepare with a rake.

3. To gather by diligent effort; scrape together. **4.** To search or examine carefully. **5.** To direct heavy gunfire along the length of, as a ship or column of troops; enfilade. — *v.i.* **6.** To use a rake. **7.** To scrape or pass roughly or violently: with *across, over,* etc. **8.** To make a search. — **to rake in** *Informal* To earn or acquire (money, etc.) in large quantities. [OE *raca*] — **rak'er** *n.*

rake[2] (rāk) *v.* **raked, rak-ing** *v.i.* **1.** To lean from the perpendicular, as a ship's masts. — *v.t.* **2.** To cause to lean; incline. — *n.* Inclination from the perpendicular or horizontal, as of the edge of a cutting tool. [Origin uncertain]

rake[3] (rāk) *n.* A dissolute, lewd man; a roué. [Earlier *rake-hell* < ME *rakel* rash, wild]

rake-off (rāk'ôf', -of') *n.* *U.S. Slang* **1.** A share, as of profits; commission. **2.** A rebate, usu. illegitimate.

rak-ish[1] (rā'kish) *adj.* **1.** Dashing; jaunty; smart. **2.** *Naut.* Having the masts unusually inclined, so as to suggest speed. [< RAKE²] — **rak'ish-ly** *adv.* — **rak'ish-ness** *n.*

rak-ish[2] (rā'kish) *adj.* Characteristic of a rake; dissolute; profligate. — **rak'ish-ly** *adv.* — **rak'ish-ness** *n.*

râle (räl) *n.* *Pathol.* A sound additional to that of normal respiration, heard on auscultation of the chest and indicative of the presence, nature, or stage of a disease. [< F, rattle]

ral-len-tan-do (räl'ən-tän'dō, *Ital.* räl'len-tän'dō) *Music* *adj. & adv.* Gradually slower. [< Ital.]

ral-ly[1] (ral'ē) *n.* *pl.* **-lies** **1.** A meeting or assembly of persons for a common purpose. **2.** A rapid recovery of a normal condition as after exhaustion, depression, etc. **3.** A return, as of scattered troops, to order or action. **4.** In tennis, the interchange of several strokes before one side wins the point. **5.** A driving competition or procession over a fixed, often extensive course, as for sports cars, antique automobiles, etc. — *v.* **-lied, -ly-ing** *v.t.* **1.** To bring together and restore to effective discipline: to *rally* fleeing troops. **2.** To summon up or revive: to *rally* one's spirits. **3.** To bring together for common action. — *v.i.* **4.** To return to effective discipline or action: The enemy *rallied*. **5.** To unite for common action. **6.** To make a partial or complete return to a normal condition; improve. **7.** In tennis, to engage in a rally. [< F < *re-* again + *allier* to join] — **ral'li-er** *n.*

ral-ly[2] (ral'ē) *v.t. & v.i.* **-lied, -ly-ing** To mock or tease with raillery; banter. [< F *railler* to banter] — **ral'li-er** *n.*

ram (ram) *n.* **1.** A male sheep. **2.** A device for driving, forcing, or crushing by heavy blows or thrusts. **3.** A hydraulic ram. — *v.t.* **rammed, ram-ming** **1.** To strike with or as with a ram; dash against. **2.** To drive or force down or into something. **3.** To cram; stuff. [OE *ramm*] — **ram'-mer** *n.* — **ram'mish** *adj.*

ram-ble (ram'bəl) *v.i.* **-bled, -bling** **1.** To walk about freely and aimlessly; roam. **2.** To write or talk aimlessly or without sequence of ideas. **3.** To proceed with turns and twists; meander. — **Syn.** See WANDER. — *n.* **1.** The act of rambling; an aimless or leisurely stroll. **2.** A meandering path; maze. [? ME *romblen,* freq. of *romen* to roam]

ram-bler (ram'blər) *n.* **1.** One who or that which rambles. **2.** Any of several varieties of climbing roses, with clusters of deep red flowers.

ram-bunc-tious (ram-bungk'shəs) *adj.* *U.S. Informal* Boisterous; rough. [Prob. var. of *robustious* < ROBUST]

ram-e-kin (ram'ə-kin) *n.* **1.** A seasoned dish of bread crumbs with eggs and cheese, baked and served in a shallow dish. **2.** A dish, usu. with a handle, in which ramekins are baked. **3.** Any dish used both for baking and serving. Also **ram'e-quin.** [< F *ramequin* < Du.]

ram-ie (ram'ē) *n.* The fiber yielded by a shrubby Chinese and East Indian perennial of the nettle family, used for cordage and certain textiles. Also **ram'ee.** [< Malay *rami*]

ram-i-fi-ca-tion (ram'ə-fə-kā'shən) *n.* **1.** The act or process of ramifying. **2.** An offshoot or subdivision. **3.** A result, consequence, etc., stemming from a main source.

ram-i-form (ram'ə-fôrm) *adj.* **1.** Branch-shaped. **2.** Branched. [< L *ramus* branch + -FORM]

ram-i-fy (ram'ə-fī) *v.t. & v.i.* **-fied, -fy-ing** To divide or spread out into or as into branches; branch out. [< F < Med.L < L *ramus* branch + *facere* to make]

ram-jet (ram'jet') *n.* A type of jet engine that provides continuous jet propulsion.

ra-mose (rā'mōs, rə-mōs') *adj.* **1.** Branching. **2.** Consisting of or having branches. [< L *ramus* branch]

ra-mous (rā'məs) *adj.* **1.** Of or like branches. **2.** Ramose. [See RAMOSE]

ramp[1] (ramp) *n.* **1.** An inclined passageway or roadway, as between floors of a building. **2.** A movable stairway by which passengers enter or leave an airplane. [< F < OF *ramper* to climb]

ramp[2] (ramp) *v.i.* **1.** To rear up on the hind legs and stretch out the forelegs, as a horse. **2.** To act in a violent or threatening manner; rampage. — *n.* The act of ramping. [< OF *ramper* to climb]

ram-page (*n.* ram'pāj; *v.* ram-pāj') *n.* Boisterous agitation or excitement. — *v.i.* **-paged, -pag-ing** **1.** To rush or act violently. **2.** To storm; rage. [Orig. Scot., ? < RAMP²] — **ram·pag′er** *n.* — **ram·pa′geous** *adj.*

ram·pant (ram′pənt) *adj.* **1.** Exceeding all bounds; wild. **2.** Widespread or unchecked, as an erroneous belief. **3.** Standing on the hind legs; rearing: said of a quadruped. **4.** *Heraldry* Standing on the hind legs, with both forelegs elevated. [< OF, ppr. of *ramper.* See RAMP².] — **ram′pan·cy** *n.* — **ram′pant·ly** *adv.*

ram·part (ram′pärt, -pərt) *n.* **1.** The embankment surrounding a fort, on which the parapet is raised. **2.** A bulwark or defense. — *v.t.* To supply with or as with ramparts; fortify. [< F *remparer* to fortify]

ram·rod (ram′rod′) *n.* **1.** A rod used to drive home the charge of a muzzleloading gun or pistol. **2.** A similar rod used for cleaning the barrel of a rifle, etc.

ram·shack·le (ram′shak′əl) *adj.* Likely to go to pieces, as from age or neglect. [< *ransackle,* freq. of RANSACK]

ran (ran) Past tense of RUN.

ranch (ranch) *n.* **1.** An establishment for raising or grazing cattle, sheep, horses, etc., in large herds. **2.** The buildings, personnel, and lands connected with it. **3.** A large farm. — *v.i.* To manage or work on a ranch. [< Sp. *rancho* soldiers' mess] — **ranch′er, ranch′man** *n.*

ranch house 1. The main building of a ranch. **2.** *U.S.* A one-story house usu. having a low roof with a wide overhang.

ran·cid (ran′sid) *adj.* Having the unpleasant taste or smell of oily substances that have begun to spoil; rank; sour. [< L < *rancere* to be rank] — **ran·cid′i·ty, ran′cid·ness** *n.*

ran·cor (rang′kər) *n.* Bitter enmity; spitefulness. Also *Brit.* **ran′cour.** [< OF < LL < L *rancere* to be rank] — **ran′cor·ous** *adj.* — **ran′cor·ous·ly** *adv.* — **ran′cor·ous·ness** *n.*

rand (rand, ränd) *n.* The monetary unit of South Africa.

ran·dom (ran′dəm) *n.* Lack of definite aim or intention: now chiefly in the phrase **at random,** without definite purpose or aim; haphazardly. — *adj.* Done at random. [< OF *random* rapidity, impetuosity] — **ran′dom·ly** *adv.*

rang (rang) Past tense of RING².

range (rānj) *n.* **1.** The area over which anything moves, operates, or is distributed. **2.** *U.S.* An extensive tract of land over which cattle, sheep, etc., roam and graze. **3.** Extent or scope: the whole *range* of politics. **4.** The extent to which any power can be made effective: *range* of influence. **5.** The extent of variation of anything: the temperature *range.* **6.** A line, row, or series, as of mountains. **7.** The maximum distance that an aircraft, ship, vehicle, etc., can travel before its fuel is exhausted; also, the maximum distance at which a weapon, transmitter, etc., is effective. **8.** A place for shooting at a mark: a rifle *range.* **9.** A large cooking stove. — *adj.* Of or pertaining to a range. — *v.* **ranged, rang·ing** *v.t.* **1.** To arrange in definite order, as in rows. **2.** To assign to a class, division, or category. **3.** To move about or over (a region, etc.). **4.** To put (cattle) to graze on a range. **5.** To adjust or train, as a telescope or gun. — *v.i.* **6.** To move over an area in a thorough, systematic manner. **7.** To rove; roam. **8.** To extend or proceed: The shot *ranged* to the right. **9.** To exhibit variation within specified limits. **10.** To lie in the same direction, line, etc. [< OF < *ranc* row]

range finder An instrument for determining the distance of an object from a given point.

rang·er (rān′jər) *n.* **1.** One who or that which ranges; a rover. **2.** One of an armed band designed to protect large tracts of country. **3.** One of a herd of cattle that feeds on a range. **4.** *U.S.* A warden employed in patrolling forest tracts. — **rang′er·ship** *n.*

Rang·er (rān′jər) *n.* One of a select group of U.S. soldiers trained for raiding action on enemy territory.

rang·y (rān′jē) *adj.* **rang·i·er, rang·i·est 1.** Disposed to roam, or adapted for roving, as cattle. **2.** Having long, slender limbs, as a person. **3.** Affording wide range; roomy. **4.** Resembling a mountain range.

ra·ni (rä′nē) *n.* **1.** The wife of a raja or prince. **2.** A reigning Hindu queen or princess. Also spelled **ra′nee.** [< Hind. < Skt. *rājñī,* fem. of *rajan* king]

rank¹ (rangk) *n.* **1.** A series of objects ranged in a line or row; a range. **2.** Degree of official standing, esp. in the armed forces. See table for GRADE. **3.** A line of soldiers drawn up side by side in close order. **4.** *pl.* An army; also, the mass of soldiery. **5.** Relative position or status; degree; grade. **6.** High degree or position: a lady of *rank.* — **Syn.** See CLASS. — *v.t.* **1.** To arrange in a rank or ranks. **2.** To place in a class, order, etc. **3.** To outrank: Sergeants *rank* corporals. — *v.i.* **4.** To hold a specified place or rank. **5.** To have the highest rank or grade. [< OF *ranc*]

rank² (rangk) *adj.* **1.** Very vigorous and flourishing in growth, as vegetation. **2.** Strong and disagreeable to the taste or smell. **3.** Utter; complete: *rank* injustice. **4.** Producing a luxuriant growth; fertile. [OE *ranc* strong] — **rank′ly** *adv.* — **rank′ness** *n.*

rank and file 1. The common soldiers of an army, including all from the corporals downward. **2.** Those who form the bulk of any organization, as distinct from officers or leaders.

rank·ing (rangk′ing) *adj.* Superior in rank; taking precedence over others in the same category: a *ranking* senator.

ran·kle (rang′kəl) *v.* **·kled, ·kling** *v.i.* **1.** To cause continued resentment: The defeat *rankles* in his breast. **2.** To become irritated or inflamed; fester. — *v.t.* **3.** To irritate; embitter. [< OF *rancler* to fester]

ran·sack (ran′sak) *v.t.* **1.** To search through every part of. **2.** To search throughout for plunder; pillage. [< ON *rannsaka* to search a house] — **ran′sack·er** *n.*

ran·som (ran′səm) *v.t.* **1.** To secure the release of (a person, property, etc.) for a required price, as from captivity or detention. **2.** To set free on payment of ransom. — *n.* **1.** The payment for the release of a person or property detained. **2.** Release purchased. [< OF < L < *re-* back + *emere* to buy] — **ran′som·er** *n.*

rant (rant) *v.i.* **1.** To speak in loud, violent, or extravagant language; rave. — *v.t.* **2.** To utter in a ranting manner. — *n.* Bombastic talk. [< MDu. *ranten* rave] — **rant′er** *n.*

rap¹ (rap) *v.* **rapped, rap·ping** *v.t.* **1.** To strike sharply and quickly; hit. **2.** To utter in a sharp manner: with *out.* **3.** *Slang* To criticize severely. — *v.i.* **4.** To strike sharp, quick blows. **5.** *Slang* To have a frank discussion; talk. — *n.* **1.** A sharp blow. **2.** A sound caused by or as by knocking. **3.** *Slang* A charge of wrongdoing; blame. **4.** *Slang* A talk; discussion. [ME, prob. imit.] — **rap′per** *n.*

rap² (rap) *n.* The least bit: I don't care a *rap.* [< RAPT]

ra·pa·cious (rə-pā′shəs) *adj.* **1.** Given to plunder or rapine. **2.** Grasping; greedy. **3.** Subsisting on prey seized alive, as hawks, etc. [< L *rapere* to seize] — **ra·pa′cious·ly** *adv.* — **ra·pa′cious·ness** *n.* — **ra·pac′i·ty** (-pas′ə-tē) *n.*

rape¹ (rāp) *v.* **raped, rap·ing** *v.t.* **1.** To commit rape upon; ravish. **2.** *Archaic* To carry off by force. — *n.* **1.** The forcible and unlawful carnal knowledge of a woman against her will. **2.** *Archaic* A capturing or snatching away by force. [< AF < L *rapere* to seize] — **rap′ist** *n.*

rape² (rāp) *n.* A plant related to the cabbage, grown as a forage crop for sheep and hogs, and having seeds that yield rape oil. [< L *rapum* turnip]

rape oil An oil obtained from rapeseed, and used as a lubricant, etc.: also called *colza oil.*

rape·seed (rāp′sēd′) *n.* The seed of the rape.

Raph·a·el (raf′ē·əl, rā′fē-) One of the archangels.

rap·id (rap′id) *adj.* **1.** Having or moving with great speed; swift. **2.** Characterized by rapidity: a *rapid* style. **3.** Done or completed in a short time: *rapid* growth. — **Syn.** See SWIFT¹. — *n. Usu. pl.* A swift-running descent in a river. [< L *rapere* to seize, rush] — **ra·pid·i·ty** (rə-pid′ə-tē) *n.* — **rap′id·ly** *adv.* — **rap′id·ness** *n.*

rapid eye movement Rapid movement of the closed eyes during sleep, associated with dreaming and a characteristic pattern of electrical activity of the brain. Also *REM.*

rap·id-fire (rap′id·fīr′) *adj.* **1.** Firing or designed for firing shots in rapid succession. **2.** Characterized by speed.

ra·pi·er (rā′pē·ər, rāp′yər) *n.* **1.** A long, straight, two-edged sword with a large cup hilt, used for dueling, chiefly for thrusting. **2.** A shorter straight sword without cutting edge and therefore used for thrusting only. [< MF *rapière*]

rap·ine (rap′in) *n.* The taking of property by force, as in war; spoliation; pillage. [< OF < L *rapere* to seize]

rap·port (ra·pôr′, -pōr′) *n.* Harmony or sympathy of relation; agreement; accord. — **en rapport** (än rà·pôr′) *French* In close accord. [< F *rapporter* to bring back]

rap·proche·ment (rà·prôsh·män′) *n. French* A state of harmony or reconciliation; restoration of cordial relations.

rap·scal·lion (rap·skal′yən) *n.* A rogue; scamp; rascal. [< earlier *rascallion,* extension of RASCAL]

rapt (rapt) *adj.* **1.** Carried away with lofty emotion; enraptured; transported. **2.** Engrossed; intent; deeply engaged. [< L *rapere* to seize]

rap·to·ri·al (rap·tôr′ē·əl, -tō′rē-) *adj.* **1.** Seizing and devouring living prey; predatory. **2.** Having talons adapted for seizing prey: said esp. of hawks, vultures, eagles, and other carnivorous birds. [< L *rapere* to seize]

rap·ture (rap′chər) *n.* **1.** The state of being rapt or transported; ecstatic joy; ecstasy. **2.** *Often pl.* An act or expression of excessive delight. — *v.t.* **·tured, ·tur·ing** *Poetic* To enrapture. [< RAPT] — **rap′tur·ous** *adj.* — **rap′tur·ous·ly** *adv.* — **rap′tur·ous·ness** *n.*

rare¹ (râr) *adj.* **rar·er, rar·est 1.** Infrequent in occurrence, distribution, etc. **2.** Highly esteemed because of infrequency or uncommonness. **3.** Rarefied: now said chiefly of the atmosphere, etc. [< L *rarus* rare] — **rare′ness** *n.* — **Syn. 1.** scarce, unusual, exceptional. See OBSOLETE.

rare² (râr) *adj.* Not thoroughly cooked, as roasted or broiled meat retaining its redness and juices. [OE *hrēre*]

rare·bit (râr'bit) *n.* Welsh rabbit.

rare earth *Chem.* Any of the metallic oxides of the lanthanide series of elements.

rare-earth element (râr'ûrth') *Chem.* Any of a group of metallic elements constituting the lanthanide series. Also **rare-earth metals.**

rar·e·fy (râr'ə·fī) *v.* **·fied, ·fy·ing** *v.t.* 1. To make rare, thin, less solid, or less dense. 2. To refine or purify. — *v.i.* 3. To become rare, thin, or less solid. 4. To become pure. [< F < L *rarus* rare + *facere* to make] — **rar'e·fac'tion** (-fak'shən) *n.* — **rar'e·fac'tive** *adj.* — **rar'e·fi'a·ble** *adj.*

rare·ly (râr'lē) *adv.* 1. Not often; infrequently. 2. With unusual excellence or effect; finely 3. Exceptionally.

rar·ing (râr'ing) *adj. U.S. Informal* Extremely eager or enthusiastic. [< Pres. part. of *rare*, dial. of REAR²]

rar·i·ty (râr'ə·tē) *n.* *pl.* **·ties** 1. That which is exceptionally valued because of scarceness. 2. The state of being rare.

ras·cal (ras'kəl) *n.* An unprincipled fellow; rogue; knave: sometimes used playfully. — *adj. Obs.* Base; mean. [< OF, ult. < L *radere* to scratch] — **ras·cal'i·ty** (-kal'ə·tē) *n.* — **ras'cal·ly** *adj. & adv.*

rase (rāz) *v.t.* **rased, ras·ing** To raze.

rash¹ (rash) *adj.* 1. Acting without due caution or regard of consequences; reckless. 2. Exhibiting recklessness or precipitancy. [Prob. < MLG < OHG *rasc* lively] — **rash'ly** *adv.* — **rash'ness** *n.*

rash² (rash) *n.* A superficial eruption of the skin, often localized. [< OF, ult. < L *radere* to scratch]

rash·er (rash'ər) *n.* A thin slice of meat, esp. bacon.

rasp (rasp, räsp) *n.* 1. A file having coarse pyramidal projections for abrasion. 2. The act or sound of rasping. — *v.t.* 1. To scrape or rub with or as with a rasp. 2. To affect unpleasantly; irritate. 3. To utter in a rough voice. — *v.i.* 4. To grate; scrape. 5. To make a rough, harsh sound. [< OF *rasper* to scrape] — **rasp'er** *n.* — **ras'py** *adj.*

rasp·ber·ry (raz'ber'ē, -bər·ē, räz'-) *n.* *pl.* **·ries** 1. The round fruit of certain brambles of the rose family, composed of drupes clustered around a fleshy receptacle. 2. Any plant yielding this fruit. 3. *Slang* A Bronx cheer: also spelled *razzberry.* [< earlier *raspis* (berry)]

rat (rat) *n.* 1. A destructive and injurious rodent of worldwide distribution, larger and more aggressive than the mouse. 2. *Slang* A cowardly or selfish person who deserts or betrays his associates. 3. A pad over which a woman's hair is combed to give a coiffure body. — **to smell a rat** To suspect that something is wrong. — *v.i.* **rat·ted, rat·ting** 1. To hunt rats. 2. *Slang* To desert one's party, etc. — *Slang* To inform; betray: with *on.* [OE *ræt*]

rat·a·ble (rā'tə·bəl) *adj.* 1. *Brit.* Legally liable to taxation. 2. Estimated proportionally; pro rata: a *ratable* distribution. 3. That may be rated or valued. Also **rate'a·ble.** — **rat'a·bil'i·ty, rat'a·ble·ness** *n.* — **rat'a·bly** *adv.*

ra·tan (ra·tan') See RATTAN.

ratch·et (rach'it) *n.* 1. A mechanism consisting of a notched wheel, the teeth of which engage with a pawl, permitting motion of the wheel in one direction only. 2. The pawl or the wheel thus used. Also **ratchet wheel.** [< F *rochet* bobbin]

rate¹ (rāt) *n.* 1. The measure of a variable in relation to some fixed unit: a *rate* of 5 miles per hour. 2. Degree of value; price; also, the unit cost of a commodity or service. 3. Comparative rank or class. 4. *Brit.* A local tax on property. 5. Proportion, as of an incidence, to some fixed number of cases: the death *rate* per 100,000 adults. 6. A fixed allowance, amount, or ratio. — **at any rate** In any case; anyhow. — *v.* **rat·ed, rat·ing** *v.t.* 1. To estimate the value or worth of; appraise. 2. To place in a certain rank or grade. 3. To consider; regard. 4. To fix the rate for the transportation of (goods), as by rail. 5. *Informal* To deserve. — *v.i.* 6. To have rank, rating, or value. 7. *Informal* To stand in comparison with others. [< OF < L < *reri* to calculate] — **rat'er** *n.*

rate² (rāt) *v.t. & v.i.* **rat·ed, rat·ing** To reprove with vehemence; rail at.

rath·er (rath'ər, rä'thər) *adv.* 1. More willingly. 2. With more reason, justice, wisdom, etc. 3. More precisely, strictly, or accurately. 4. Somewhat; in a greater or less degree: *rather* cold. 5. On the contrary. 6. *Brit.* Yes indeed! ◆ Both *had rather* and *would rather* are acceptable forms. [OE *hrathor*, compar. of *hrathe* soon, quickly]

raths·kel·ler (rath'skel·ər, räts'kel·ər) *n.* A beer hall or similar restaurant, usu. located in a cellar. [< G *rat* council, town hall + *keller* cellar]

rat·i·fy (rat'ə·fī) *v.t.* **·fied, ·fy·ing** To give sanction to, esp. official sanction; confirm. [< OF < Med.L < L *ratus* fixed, calculated + *facere* to make] — **rat'i·fi·ca'tion** (-fə·kā'shən) *n.* — **rat'i·fi'er** *n.*

— **Syn.** The U.S. Senate *ratifies* a proposed treaty; Congress *confirms* Presidential appointments; notarization *validates* a bill of sale. These words are chiefly used of governmental process.

rat·i·né (rat·ə·nā') *n.* A heavy, loosely woven fabric with a nubby surface. [< F < *ratiner* to make nubby]

rat·ing (rā'ting) *n.* 1. Classification according to a standard; grade; rank; status. 2. An evaluation of the financial standing of a business firm or an individual. 3. Any specialist grade held by an enlisted man or officer: the *rating* of pilot in the Air Force.

ra·tio (rā'shō, -shē·ō) *n.* *pl.* **·tios** 1. Relation of degree, number, etc.; proportion; rate. 2. The relation of two quantities, esp. the quotient of the first divided by the second. A ratio of 3 to 5 is expressed as 3 : 5 or ⅗. [< L *reri* to think]

ra·ti·oc·i·nate (rash'ē·os'ə·nāt) *v.i.* **·nat·ed, ·nat·ing** To make a deduction from premises; reason. [< L *reri* to think] — **ra'ti·oc'i·na'tion** *n.* — **ra'ti·oc'i·na'tive** *adj.* — **ra'ti·oc'i·na'tor** *n.*

ra·tion (rash'ən, rā'shən) *n.* 1. A portion; share. 2. A fixed allowance or portion of food, etc., allotted in time of scarcity. 3. *Mil.* Food for one person for one day. — *v.t.* 1. To issue rations to, as an army. 2. To give out or allot in rations. 3. To restrict to limited rations. [< F < L *ratio, -onis*] — **ra'tion·ing** *n.*

ra·tion·al (rash'ən·əl) *adj.* 1. Possessing the faculty of reasoning. 2. Having full possession of one's mental faculties; sane. 3. Conformable to reason; judicious; sensible. 4. Attained by reasoning. 5. *Math.* Denoting an algebraic expression containing no variables within irreducible radicals. [See RATIO.] — **ra'tion·al'i·ty** (rash'ən·al'ə·tē) *n.* — **ra'tion·al·ly** *adv.* — **ra'tion·al·ness** *n.*

ra·tion·ale (rash'ən·al', -äl'ē, -āl'ē) *n.* 1. The rational or logical basis of something. 2. A rational explanation of principles.

ra·tion·al·ism (rash'ən·əl·iz'əm) *n.* 1. The formation of opinions by reason alone, independently of authority or of revelation. 2. *Philos.* The theory that truth and knowledge are attainable through reason rather than by empirical means. — **ra'tion·al·ist** *n.* — **ra'tion·al·is'tic** or **·ti·cal** *adj.* — **ra'tion·al·is'ti·cal·ly** *adv.*

ra·tion·al·ize (rash'ən·əl·īz') *v.* **·ized, ·iz·ing** *v.t.* 1. *Psychol.* To explain or base (one's behavior) on grounds ostensibly rational but not in accord with the actual or unconscious motives. 2. To explain or treat from a rationalistic point of view. 3. To make rational or reasonable. — *v.i.* 4. To think in a rational or rationalistic manner. Also *Brit.* **ra'tion·al·ise'.** — **ra'tion·al·i·za·tion** (rash'ən·əl·ə·zā'shən, -ī·zā'shən) *n.* — **ra'tion·al·iz'er** *n.*

rat·ite (rat'īt) *adj.* Designating a group of flightless birds including ostriches, cassowaries, kiwis, emus, etc. — *n.* A ratite bird. [< L *ratis* raft + -ITE²]

rat·line (rat'lin) *n. Naut.* 1. One of the small ropes fastened across the shrouds of a ship, used as a ladder for going aloft or descending. 2. The rope so used. Also **rat'lin** (-lin). [Origin unknown]

RA·TO (rā'tō) *n.* An airplane takeoff assisted by an auxiliary rocket motor or unit; also, the rocket motor or unit used. Also **ra'to.** [< *r(ocket)* + *a(ssisted)* + *t(ake)o(ff)*]

rat race *Slang* A frantic, usu. fruitless, struggle.

rats·bane (rats'bān') *n.* Rat poison.

rat's nest *Informal* A cluttered and messy place.

rat·tan (ra·tan') *n.* 1. The long, tough, flexible stem of various tropical palms, used in making wickerwork, light furniture, etc. 2. The palm itself. Also spelled *ratan.* [< Malay *rotan*]

rat·ter (rat'ər) *n.* 1. A dog or cat that catches rats. 2. *Slang* A deserter; traitor.

rat·tle (rat'l) *v.* **·tled, ·tling** *v.i.* 1. To make a series of sharp noises in rapid succession, as of hard objects striking one another. 2. To move or act with such noises; also, to make a gurgling sound in the throat. 3. To talk rapidly and foolishly; chatter. — *v.t.* 4. To cause to rattle: to *rattle* pennies in a tin cup. 5. To utter or perform rapidly or noisily. 6. *Informal* To confuse; disconcert; agitate. — *n.* 1. A series of short, sharp sounds in rapid succession. 2. A plaything, implement, etc., made to produce a rattling noise. 3. Any of the jointed horny rings in the tail of a rattlesnake. 4. Rapid and noisy talk; chatter. [Imit.]

rat·tle·brain (rat'l·brān') *n.* A talkative, flighty person; foolish chatterer. Also **rat'tle·head'** (-hed'), **rat'tle·pate'** (-pāt'). — **rat'tle·brained'** *adj.*

rat·tler (rat'lər) *n.* 1. One who or that which rattles. 2. A rattlesnake.

rat·tle·snake (rat'l·snāk') *n.* Any of several venomous American snakes with a tail ending in a series of horny, loosely connected, modified joints, that make a rattling noise when the tail is vibrated.

RATTLESNAKE
(To 8 feet long)

rat·tle·trap (rat'l·trap') *n.* Any rickety, clattering, or worn-out vehicle or article.

rat·trap (rat'trap') *n.* 1. A trap for catching rats. 2. Any hopeless or involved predicament.

rat·ty (rat'ē) *adj.* **·ti·er, ·ti·est** 1. Ratlike. 2. Abounding in rats. 3. *Slang* Disreputable; shabby.

rau·cous (rô′kəs) *adj.* **1.** Rough in sound; hoarse; harsh. **2.** Boisterous; unruly; disorderly. [< L *raucus*] **— rau′city** (-sə·tē), **rau′cous·ness** *n.* **— rau′cous·ly** *adv.*

rau·wol·fi·a (rou·wŏŏl′fē·ə) *n.* Any of a genus of tropical trees or shrubs, several of which contain alkaloids having valuable medicinal properties. [after Leonard *Rauwolf*, 17th c. German botanist]

rav·age (rav′ij) *v.* **·aged, ·ag·ing** *v.t.* **1.** To lay waste, as by pillaging or burning; despoil. **—** *v.i.* **2.** To wreak havoc; be destructive. **—** *n.* Violent and destructive action, or its result; ruin. [See RAVISH.] **— rav′ag·er** *n.*

rave (rāv) *v.* **raved, rav·ing** *v.i.* **1.** To speak wildly or incoherently. **2.** To speak with extravagant enthusiasm. **3.** To make a wild, roaring sound; rage. **—** *v.t.* **4.** To utter wildly or incoherently. **—** *n.* The act or state of raving; a frenzy. **—** *adj. Informal* Extravagantly enthusiastic: *rave* reviews. [< OF *raver* to wander, to be delirious]

rav·el (rav′əl) *v.* **rav·eled** or **·elled, rav·el·ing** or **·el·ling** *v.t.* **1.** To separate the threads or fibers of; unravel. **2.** To make clear or plain; explain: often with *out.* **—** *v.i.* **3.** To become separated, as threads or fibers; unravel; fray. **—** *n.* **1.** A broken or rejected thread. **2.** A raveling. [< MDu. *ravelen* to tangle] **— rav′el·er** or **rav′el·ler** *n.*

rav·el·ing (rav′əl·ing) *n.* A thread or threads raveled from a fabric. Also **rav′el·ling.**

ra·ven[1] (rā′vən) *n.* A large, omnivorous, widely distributed corvine bird, having lustrous black plumage. **—** *adj.* Black and shining, like a raven. [OE *hræfn*]

rav·en[2] (rav′ən) *v.t.* **1.** To devour hungrily or greedily. **2.** To take by force; ravage. **—** *v.i.* **3.** To search for prey or plunder. **4.** To eat voraciously. **—** *n.* The act of plundering; spoliation; pillage. [< OF *raviner* < L *rapina* < *rapere* to seize] **— rav′en·er** *n.*

Ra·ven (rā′vən) *n.* The constellation Corvus.

rav·en·ing (rav′ən·ing) *adj.* **1.** Seeking eagerly for prey; rapacious. **2.** Devouring; voracious. **3.** Mad.

rav·en·ous (rav′ən·əs) *adj.* **1.** Violently voracious or hungry. **2.** Extremely eager for gratification. [See RAVEN[2].] **— rav′en·ous·ly** *adv.* **— rav′en·ous·ness** *n.*

ra·vine (rə·vēn′) *n.* A deep gorge or gully, esp. one worn by a flow of water. [< F]

rav·ing (rā′ving) *adj.* **1.** Furious; delirious; frenzied. **2.** *Informal* Outstandingly attractive: a *raving* beauty. **—** *n.* A furious, incoherent, or irrational utterance.

ra·vi·o·li (rä·vyō′lē, rä′vē·ō′lē, rav′ē-) *n.pl.* Little envelopes of dough for encasing meat or cheese, boiled, and often served in a tomato sauce. [< Ital. pl. of *raviolo* little turnip]

rav·ish (rav′ish) *v.t.* **1.** To fill with strong emotion, esp. delight; enrapture. **2.** To commit a rape upon. **3.** *Archaic* To seize and carry off by force. [< OF < L *rapere* to seize] **— rav′ish·er** *n.* **— rav′ish·ment** *n.*

rav·ish·ing (rav′ish·ing) *adj.* Filling with delight; enchanting. **— rav′ish·ing·ly** *adv.*

raw (rô) *adj.* **1.** Not changed or prepared by cooking; uncooked. **2.** Having the skin irritated or abraded. **3.** Bleak; chilling: a *raw* wind. **4.** In a natural state; crude. **5.** Newly done; fresh: *raw* paint, *raw* work. **6.** Inexperienced; undisciplined. **7.** Obscene; coarse; off-color. **8.** Harshly unfair; ruthless. **—** *n.* A sore or abraded spot: with *the.* **— in the raw 1.** In a raw, unrefined, or untempered state. **2.** *U.S. Informal* Naked; nude. [OE *hrēaw.*] **— raw′ly** *adv.* **— raw′ness** *n.*

raw·boned (rô′bōnd′) *adj.* Bony; gaunt.

raw·hide (rô′hīd′) *n.* **1.** A hide dressed without tanning. **2.** A whip made of such hide.

ray[1] (rā) *n.* **1.** A narrow beam of light. **2.** Anything representing or suggesting this. **3.** A slight manifestation; glimmer; hint. **4.** *Geom.* One of several straight lines emerging from a point and unlimited in one direction. **5.** *Zool.* **a** One of the rods supporting the membrane of a fish's fin. **b** One of the radiating parts of a radiate animal, as a starfish. **6.** *Bot.* A ray flower. **7.** *Physics* **a** A line of propagation of any form of radiant energy. **b** A stream of particles spontaneously emitted by a radioactive substance. **—** *v.i.* **1.** To emit rays; shine. **2.** To issue forth as rays; radiate. **—** *v.t.* **3.** To send forth as rays. **4.** To mark with rays or radiating lines. **5.** To treat with X-rays, etc. [< OF < L *radius* rod]

ray[2] (rā) *n.* Any of various fishes having a flattened body with expanded pectoral fins and gill openings on the lower surface. [< OF < L *raia*]

ray flower *Bot.* Any of the flat marginal flowers surrounding the disk, as the daisy or sunflower. Also **ray floret.**

ray·on (rā′on) *n.* **1.** A synthetic fiber produced from cellulose, the material being forced through fine jets to produce threadlike filaments. **2.** A fabric made from such fibers. [Coined from RAY[1]; prob. infl. by F *rayon* ray]

raze (rāz) *v.t.* **razed, raz·ing** **1.** To demolish, as a building. **2.** *Rare* To scrape or shave off. Also spelled *rase.* **— Syn.** See DEMOLISH. [< OF < L *radere* to scrape]

ra·zor (rā′zər) *n.* A sharp cutting implement used for shaving off the beard or hair, etc. [< OF < LL *rasorium* scraper]

ra·zor·back (rā′zər·bak′) *n.* **1.** The rorqual, a whale. **2.** A lean, long-legged, half-wild hog, common in the southeastern U.S. **3.** A hill with a sharp, narrow ridge.

razor blade A thin, metal blade, having either one or two sharpened edges, inserted in a safety razor.

razz (saz) *Slang* *n.* A Bronx cheer. **—** *v.t.* To heckle; deride. [< RAZZBERRY]

razz·ber·ry (raz′ber′ē, -bər·ē, räz′-) *n.* *pl.* **·ries** *U.S. Slang* A Bronx cheer. [< RASPBERRY]

raz·zle-daz·zle (raz′əl·daz′əl) *n.* *U.S. Slang* Bewildering, exciting, or dazzling activity or performance. Also **razz·ma·tazz** (raz′mə·taz′). [Varied reduplication of DAZZLE]

re[1] (rā) *n.* *Music* The second of the syllables used in solmization; the second degree of a major scale; also, the tone D. [< L *re*(*sonare*). See GAMUT.]

re[2] (rē) *prep.* Concerning; about; in the matter of: used in business letters, law, etc. [< L, ablative of *res* thing]

re- *prefix* **1.** Back: *rebound, remit.* **2.** Again; anew; again and again. [< L *re-, red-* back, again]

◆ Sense 2 of *re-* is freely used in forming words, particularly verbs or words derived from verbs. Some words thus formed are hyphenated to prevent confusion with similarly spelled words, as *recoil,* to spring back, and *re-coil,* to coil again, but in current usage most other words using *re-* as a prefix are written solid. However, many writers still prefer to hyphenate some combinations of *re-* and a word beginning with a vowel, especially *e.*

A list of self-explanatory words containing the prefix *re-* (def. 2) appears below.

reabandon	reappointment	reblossom	recondense	rediscover	reengage
reabsorb	reapportion	reboil	reconduct	rediscovery	reengagement
reabsorption	reapportionment	reborn	reconfirm	redissolve	reengrave
reaccept	reargue	rebuild	reconquer	redistill	reenjoy
reaccommodate	reargument	rebuilt	reconquest	redistribute	reenjoyment
reaccompany	reascend	rebury	reconsecrate	redivide	reenkindle
reaccuse	reascension	recapitalize	reconsolidate	redivision	reenlist
reacquire	reascent	recarry	reconvene	redo	reenlistment
readapt	reassemble	recelebrate	recopy	redraw	reenslave
readdress	reassembly	rechallenge	recoronation	redrive	reenter
readjourn	reassert	rechange	recross	redry	reentrance
readjournment	reassertion	recharge	recrown	redye	reerect
readjust	reassign	recharter	recrystallization	reecho	reestablish
readjustment	reassimilate	recheck	recrystallize	reedit	reestablishment
readmission	reassimilation	rechoose	recultivate	reelect	reexamination
readmit	reassociate	rechristen	recultivation	reelection	reexamine
readopt	reassume	recircle	rededicate	reelevate	reexchange
readorn	reassumption	recirculate	rededication	reembark	reexhibit
readvance	reattach	reclasp	redefeat	reembody	reexpel
reaffirm	reattack	reclean	redefine	reembrace	reexperience
reaffirmation	reattain	reclothe	redemand	reemerge	reexport
realign	reattempt	recoin	redemonstrate	reemergence	reexpulsion
realignment	reavow	recoinage	redeny	reemigrate	reface
reannex	reawake	recolonize	redeposit	reenact	refashion
reannoint	reawaken	recolor	redescend	reenaction	refasten
reappear	rebaptism	recombine	redescent	reenactment	refertilize
reappearance	rebaptize	recombination	redescribe	reencourage	refire
reapply	rebind	recommence	redetermine	reencouragement	reflow
reappoint	rebloom	recommission	redigest	reendow	reflower

reach (rēch) *v.t.* **1.** To stretch out or forth, as the hand; extend. **2.** To present or hand over. **3.** To be able to touch or grasp: Can you *reach* the top shelf? **4.** To arrive at or come to by motion or progress. **5.** To achieve communication with; gain access to. **6.** To amount to; total. **7.** To strike or hit, as with a blow or missile. — *v.i.* **8.** To stretch the hand, foot, etc., out or forth. **9.** To attempt to touch or grasp something: He *reached* for his wallet. **10.** To have extent in space, time, etc.: The ladder *reached* to the ceiling. **11.** *Naut.* To sail on a tack with the wind on or forward of the beam. — *n.* **1.** The act or power of reaching. **2.** The distance one is able to reach, as with the hand, an instrument, or missile. **3.** Extent of thought, influence, etc.; scope; range. **4.** An unbroken stretch, as of a stream; a vista or expanse. **5.** *Naut.* The sailing, or the distance sailed, by a vessel on one tack. [OE *rǣcan*] — **reach′er** *n.*

re·act (rē·akt′) *v.i.* **1.** To act in response, as to a stimulus. **2.** To act in a manner contrary to some preceding act. **3.** *Physics* To exert an opposite and equal force on an acting or impinging body. **4.** *Chem.* To undergo a reaction.

re·act (rē·akt′) *v.t.* To act again.

re·ac·tance (rē·ak′təns) *n.* *Electr.* In a circuit, the opposition to an alternating current caused by inductance and capacitance.

re·ac·tion (rē·ak′shən) *n.* **1.** Responsive action, attitude, etc. **2.** Tendency toward a former state of things; esp., a trend toward an earlier social, political, or economic policy or condition. **3.** The action of a muscle, nerve, organ, etc., in response to a stimulus; reflex action. **4.** *Psychol.* A response to an experience, situation, influence, etc. **5.** *Physics* **a** The equal and opposite force exerted on an agent by the body acted upon. **b** A nuclear reaction. **6.** *Chem.* The reciprocal action of substances subjected to chemical change. **7.** *Med.* The effect upon an organism of any foreign substance introduced for therapeutic purposes, or for testing, immunizing, etc.

re·ac·tion·ar·y (rē·ak′shən·er′ē) *adj.* Pertaining to, favoring, or characterized by reaction (def. 2). — *n. pl.* **·ar·ies** One who favors political or social reaction; one hostile toward change or progress. Also **re·ac′tion·ist.**

re·ac·ti·vate (rē·ak′tə·vāt) *v.t.* **·vat·ed, ·vat·ing** To make active or effective again. — **re·ac′ti·va′tion** *n.*

re·ac·tive (rē·ak′tiv) *adj.* **1.** Reacting or tending to react. **2.** Resulting from reaction. **3.** Responsive to a stimulus.

re·ac·tiv·i·ty (rē·ak·tiv′ə·tē) *n.* **1.** The state or quality of being reactive. **2.** *Chem.* The relative tendency of an element to enter into chemical reactions.

re·ac·tor (rē·ak′tər) *n.* **1.** One who or that which reacts. **2.** *Electr.* A device for introducing reactance into a circuit, as for starting motors, controlling current, etc. **3.** *Physics* Any of various assemblies for the generation and control of atomic energy: formerly called *pile.*

read (*v. & n.* rēd; *adj.* red) *v.* **read** (red), **read·ing** (rē′ding) *v.t.* **1.** To apprehend the meaning of (a book, writing, etc.) by perceiving the form and relation of the printed or written characters. **2.** To utter aloud (something printed or written). **3.** To understand the significance, intent, etc., of as if by reading: to *read* the sky. **4.** To apprehend the meaning of something written in (a foreign language). **5.** To make a study of: to *read* law. **6.** To discover the true nature of (a person, character, etc.) by observation or scrutiny. **7.** To interpret (something read) in a specified manner. **8.** To take as the meaning of something read. **9.** To have as its wording: The passage *reads* "principal," not "principle." **10.** To indicate or register, as an instrument or device. **11.** To bring into a specified condition by reading: I *read* her to sleep. — *v.i.* **12.** To apprehend written or printed characters, as of words, music, etc. **13.** To utter aloud the words or contents of a book, etc. **14.** To gain information by reading: with *of* or *about*. **15.** To learn by means of books; study. **16.** To have a specified wording: How does the contract *read*? **17.** To admit of being read in a specified manner: The first verse *reads* well. **18.** To have the quality of a specified style or manner of writing: His work *reads* like poetry. **19.** To give a public reading or recital. — **to read between the lines** To perceive or infer what is not expressed or obvious. — **to read out 1.** To read aloud. **2.** To expel from a religious body, political party, etc., by proclamation or concerted action. — **to read up** (or **up on**) To learn by reading. — *adj.* Informed by books: well *read*. [OE *rǣdan* to read]

read·a·ble (rē′də·bəl) *adj.* **1.** Legible. **2.** Interesting or enjoyable to read. — **read′a·bil′i·ty, read′a·ble·ness** *n.* — **read′a·bly** *adv.*

read·er (rē′dər) *n.* **1.** One who reads. **2.** A professional reciter. **3.** One who reads and criticizes manuscripts offered to publishers. **4.** A textbook containing exercises in reading. **5.** *Eccl.* A church functionary authorized to read in church services.

read·ing (rē′ding) *n.* **1.** The act or practice of one who reads. **2.** A public or formal recital of something written. **3.** Literary research; study; scholarship. **4.** Matter that is read or is designed to be read. **5.** The indication of a meter, dial, graduated instrument, etc. **6.** The form in which any passage or word appears in any copy of a work. **7.** A specific interpretation. — *adj.* **1.** Pertaining to or suitable for reading. **2.** Of or pertaining to a reader or readers.

read·y (red′ē) *adj.* **read·i·er, read·i·est 1.** Prepared for use or action. **2.** Prepared in mind; willing. **3.** Likely or liable: with *to*: *ready* to sink. **4.** Quick to act, follow, occur, or appear; prompt. **5.** Immediately available or at hand; convenient; handy. **6.** Designating the standard position in which a rifle is held just before aiming. **7.** Quick to perceive or understand; alert; facile: a *ready* wit. — *n.* The position in which a rifle is held before aiming. — *v.t.* **read·ied, read·y·ing** To make ready; prepare. [ME < OE *rǣde, gerǣde* + *ig*, suffix of adverbs] — **read′i·ly** *adv.* — **read′i·ness** *n.*

read·y-made (red′ē·mād′) *adj.* **1.** Not made to order; prepared or kept on hand for general demand: said especially of clothing. **2.** Prepared beforehand; not impromptu.

read·y-mix (red′ē-miks) *adj.* *U.S.* Ready to use after adding liquid, etc.: *ready-mix* pancake flour.

ready money Money on hand; cash.

read·y-to-wear (red′ē-tə-wâr′) *adj.* Ready-made: said of clothing.

refold	reinaugurate	reinvite	renavigate	repurify	restrive
reforge	reincite	reinvolve	renominate	repursue	restudy
reformulate	reincorporate	rejudge	renomination	requicken	resubject
refortification	reincur	rekindle	renotify	reradiate	resubjection
refortify	reinduce	relabel	renumber	reread	resummon
reframe	reinfect	relace	reobtain	rerecord	resummons
refreeze	reinfection	relaunch	reobtainable	rerise	resupply
refuel	reinflame	relaunder	reoccupation	reroll	resurvey
refurnish	reinform	relearn	reoccupy	reroute	reteach
regather	reinfuse	relight	reoccur	resaddle	retell
regear	reinhabit	reline	reoccurrence	resail	retest
regerminate	reinoculate	reliquidate	reopen	resalute	retie
regermination	reinoculation	reliquidation	reoppose	reseal	retranslate
regild	reinscribe	relive	reordain	reseed	retraverse
reglaze	reinsert	reload	reordination	reseek	retrim
reglorify	reinsertion	reloan	repacify	resegregate	retype
reglue	reinspect	relocate	repack	reseize	reuse
regrade	reinspection	relocation	repaint	reseizure	reutilize
regraft	reinspire	remade	repaper	resell	reutter
regrant	reinstall	remake	repass	resend	revaluate
regroup	reinstruct	remanufacture	repave	resettle	revalue
rehandle	reintegrate	remarriage	repenalize	resettlement	revarnish
rehear	reintegration	remarry	replant	reshape	reverification
rehearing	reinter	rematch	replantation	resharpen	reverify
reheat	reinterment	remeasure	replay	reshuffle	revictual
reheel	reinterrogate	remelt	repledge	resift	revictualment
rehire	reintrench	remerge	replunge	resolder	revindicate
reignite	reintroduce	remigrate	repolish	resolidify	revindication
reimplant	reintroduction	remigration	repopulate	resow	revisit
reimpose	reinundate	remilitarization	repopulation	respread	revitalize
reimposition	reinvent	remilitarize	repour	restack	rewarm
reimpregnate	reinvest	remix	reprocess	restipulate	rewash
reimpress	reinvestigate	remodification	reproclaim	restipulation	reweigh
reimprint	reinvestigation	remodify	republication	restrengthen	rewin
reimprison	reinvigorate	remold	republish	restrike	rewind
reimprisonment	reinvigoration	rename	repurchase	restring	rework

re·a·gent (rē·ā′jənt) *n. Chem.* Any substance used to ascertain the nature or composition of another by means of their reciprocal chemical action. [< RE- + AGENT]

real[1] (rēl, rē′əl) *adj.* 1. Having existence or actuality as a thing or state; not imaginary: a *real* event. 2. Not artificial or counterfeit; genuine. 3. Representing the true or actual, as opposed to the apparent or ostensible: the *real* reason. 4. Unaffected; unpretentious: a *real* person. 5. *Philos.* Having actual existence. 6. *Law* Pertaining to property regarded as immovable or permanent, as land or tenements: distinguished from *personal.* — *adv. Informal* Very; extremely: to be *real* glad. [< OF < LL *realis* < L *res* thing] — **real′ness** *n.*

re·al[2] (rē′əl, *Sp.* rā·äl′) *n. pl.* **re·als** or **re·a·les** (rā·ä′lās) *for def. 1,* **reis** (rās) *for def. 2* 1. A former small silver coin of Spain and various Latin-American countries. 2. A former Portuguese and Brazilian coin. [< Sp., lit., royal]

real estate Land, including whatever is made part of or attached to it by man or nature, as trees, houses, etc. — **real-es·tate** (rēl′ə·stāt′, rē′əl-) *adj.*

re·al·ism (rē′əl·iz′əm) *n.* 1. The tendency to be concerned with and act in accordance with actual facts rather than ideals, feelings, etc. 2. In literature and art, the treatment of subject matter in conformance with nature or real life and without idealization: opposed to *idealism.* 3. *Philos.* **a** The doctrine that abstract concepts have objective existence and are more real than concrete objects: opposed to *nominalism.* **b** The doctrine that things have reality apart from the conscious perception of them. — **re·al·ist** *n.* — **re·al·is·tic** *adj.* — **re·al·is·ti·cal·ly** *adv.*

re·al·i·ty (rē·al′ə·tē) *n. pl.* **·ties** 1. The fact, state, or quality of being real or genuine. 2. That which is real; an actual thing, situation, or event. 3. The sum or totality of real things. 4. *Philos.* The absolute or ultimate, as contrasted with the apparent. [< Med.L < L *realis* real]

re·al·ize (rē′əl·īz, rē′līz) *v.* **·ized, ·iz·ing** *v.t.* 1. To understand or appreciate fully. 2. To make real or concrete. 3. To cause to appear real. 4. To obtain as a profit or return. 5. To obtain money in return for: He *realized* his holdings for a profit. — *v.i.* 6. To sell property for cash. Also *Brit.* **re′al·ise.** — **re·al·iz′a·ble** *adj.* — **re·al·i·za′tion** *n.*

re·al-life (rē′əl·līf′, rēl′-) *adj. U.S. Informal* Actual; true.

re·al·ly (rē′ə·lē, rē′lē) *adv.* 1. In reality; as a matter of fact; actually; indeed. 2. Honestly; truly: used for emphasis: *Really,* the situation is impossible.

re·al·ly (rē′ə·lī′) *v.t. & v.i.* **-al·lied, -al·ly·ing** To ally again.

realm (relm) *n.* 1. A kingdom or domain. 2. The scope or range of any power or influence: the *realm* of imagination. 3. A primary zoogeographical division of the globe: also called *region.* [< OF *realme*]

Re·al·tor (rē′əl·tər, -tôr) *n. U.S.* A realty broker who is a member of the National Association of Real Estate Boards: a trade name. Also **re′al·tor.** [< REALTY + -OR[1]]

re·al·ty (rē′əl·tē) *n. pl.* **·ties** *U.S. Law* Real estate or real property in any form. [< REAL[1] (def. 6) + -TY[1]]

real wages Wages evaluated in terms of purchasing power.

ream[1] (rēm) *n.* 1. A unit of quantity for sheets of paper consisting of twenty quires or 480 sheets (**short ream**), 500 sheets (**long ream**), or 516 sheets (**printer's** or **perfect ream**). 2. *pl. Informal* A prodigious amount of printed, written, or spoken material: *reams* of footnotes. [< OF < Sp. < Arabic *rizmah* bundle]

ream[2] (rēm) *v.t.* 1. To increase the size of (a hole). 2. To enlarge or taper (a hole) with a rotating cutter or reamer. 3. To get rid of (a defect) by reaming. [? OE *ryman* to enlarge]

ream·er (rē′mər) *n.* 1. One who or that which reams. 2. A finishing tool with a rotating cutting edge for reaming: sometimes called *rimmer.* 3. A device with a ridged cone for extracting juice from citrus fruits.

re·an·i·mate (rē·an′ə·māt) *v.t.* **·mat·ed, ·mat·ing** 1. To bring back to life; resuscitate. 2. To give renewed strength or vigor to; revive. — **re·an·i·ma′tion** *n.*

reap (rēp) *v.t.* 1. To harvest or gather (a crop) with a scythe, reaper, etc. 2. To cut the growth from or gather the fruit of, as a field. 3. To obtain as the result of action or effort; receive as a return or result. — *v.i.* 4. To harvest grain, etc. 5. To receive a return or result. [OE *rēopan, ripan*] — **reap′a·ble** *adj.*

reap·er (rē′pər) *n.* 1. One who reaps. 2. A reaping machine.

reaping machine (rē′ping) A machine for harvesting standing grain, often equipped with appliances for pressing, bundling, and binding the cut grain: also called *harvester.*

rear[1] (rir) *n.* 1. The back or hind part. 2. A place or position behind any person or thing. 3. The portion of a military force that is last or farthest from the front: opposed to *van.* — *adj.* Being in the rear. [Var. of ARREAR]

rear[2] (rir) *v.t.* 1. To place upright; raise. 2. To build; erect. 3. To care for and bring to maturity. 4. To breed or grow. — *v.i.* 5. To rise upon the hind legs, as a horse. 6. To rise high; tower, as a mountain. [OE *rēran,* causative of *rīsan* to rise] — **rear′er** *n.*

rear admiral *Naval* A commissioned officer ranking next below a vice admiral. Also *Brit. & Canadian* **rear-ad·mi·ral** (rir′ad′mər·əl). See tables at GRADE.

rear guard A body of troops to protect the rear of an army.

re·arm (rē·ärm′) *v.t. & v.i.* 1. To arm again. 2. To arm with more modern weapons. — **re·ar′ma·ment** *n.*

rear·most (rir′mōst′) *adj.* Coming or stationed last.

re·ar·range (rē′ə·rānj′) *v.t. & v.i.* **·ranged, ·rang·ing** To arrange again or in some new way. — **re′ar·range′ment** *n.*

rear·ward (rir′wərd) *adj.* Coming last or toward the rear; hindward. — *adv.* Toward or at the rear; backward: also **rear′wards.** — *n.* Hindward position; the rear; end.

rea·son (rē′zən) *n.* 1. A motive or cause for an action, belief, thought, etc. 2. An explanation for or defense of an action, belief, etc.; justification. 3. The faculty of thinking logically. 4. Good judgment; common sense. 5. A normal state of mind; sanity. — **by reason of** Because of. — **in reason** In accordance with reason or good sense. — **it stands to reason** It is logical or reasonable. — **with reason** Justifiably; properly. — *v.i.* 1. To think logically; obtain inferences or conclusions from known or presumed facts. 2. To talk or argue logically. — *v.t.* 3. To think out carefully and logically; analyze: with *out.* 4. To influence by means of reason; persuade or dissuade. 5. To argue; debate. [< OF *raison* < L < *reri* to think, reckon] — **rea′son·er** *n.* — **rea′son·less** *adj.*

— **Syn.** (noun) A *reason* seeks to explain or justify an action by citing facts, circumstances, inducement, and the like, together with the workings of the mind upon them. The *purpose* of an action is the effect that it is intended to produce; its *motive* is the inner impulse that sets it in motion and guides it. *Grounds* are the facts, data, etc., that the mind weighs in reaching a decision; and *argument* is the logical demonstration of how these facts and data determine the decision. 3. See INTELLECT.

rea·son·a·ble (rē′zən·ə·bəl) *adj.* 1. Conformable to reason; sensible. 2. Having the faculty of reason; rational. 3. Governed by reason. 4. Moderate, as in price; fair. — **rea′son·a·bil′i·ty, rea′son·a·ble·ness** *n.* — **rea′son·a·bly** *adv.*

rea·son·ing (rē′zən·ing) *n.* 1. The mental process of drawing conclusions from known or presumed facts. 2. The proofs, data, etc., employed in or resulting from this process.

re·as·sure (rē′ə·shŏŏr′) *v.t.* **·sured, ·sur·ing** 1. To restore to courage or confidence. 2. To assure again. 3. To reinsure. — **re′as·sur′ance** *n.* — **re′as·sur′ing·ly** *adv.*

re·bate (rē′bāt, ri·bāt′) *v.t.* **·bat·ed, ·bat·ing** 1. To allow as a deduction. 2. To make a deduction from. 3. *Obs.* To blunt, as an edge. — *n.* A deduction from a gross amount; discount: also **re·bate′ment.** [< OF *rabattre* to beat down < *re-* again + *abattre.* See ABATE.] — **re′bat·er** *n.*

re·bec (rē′bek) *n.* An early violinlike instrument. Also **re′beck.** [< F, alter. of OF *rebebe* < Arabic *rabāb*]

Re·bec·ca (ri·bek′ə) In the Bible, the wife of Isaac, and mother of Esau and Jacob. *Gen.* xxiv 15.

re·bel (*v.* ri·bel′; *n. & adj.* reb′əl) *v.i.* **·belled, ·bel·ling** 1. To rise in armed resistance against the established government or ruler of one's land. 2. To resist any authority or established usage. 3. To react with violent aversion: usu. with *at.* — *n.* One who rebels. — *adj.* Rebellious; refractory. [< OF < L < *re-* again + *bellare* to make war]

re·bel·lion (ri·bel′yən) *n.* 1. The act of rebelling. 2. Organized resistance to a lawful government or authority.

re·bel·lious (ri·bel′yəs) *adj.* 1. Being in a state of rebellion; insubordinate. 2. Of or pertaining to a rebel or rebellion. 3. Resisting control; refractory: *rebellious* curls. — **re·bel′lious·ly** *adv.* — **re·bel′lious·ness** *n.*

re·birth (rē·bûrth′, rē′bûrth′) *n.* 1. A new birth. 2. A revival or renaissance.

re·bound (ri·bound′; *for n.,* also rē′bound′) *v.i.* 1. To bound back; recoil. — *v.t.* 2. To cause to rebound. — *n.* 1. Recoil. 2. Something that rebounds or resounds. 3. *Informal* Reaction of feeling after a disappointment: to fall in love on the *rebound.* [< F < *re-* back + *bondir* to bound]

re·broad·cast (rē·brôd′kast′, -käst′) *v.t.* **·cast** or **·cast·ed, ·cast·ing** 1. To broadcast (the same program) more than once. 2. To broadcast (a program received from another station). — *n.* A program so transmitted.

re·buff (ri·buf′) *v.t.* 1. To reject or refuse abruptly or rudely. 2. To drive or beat back; repel. — *n.* 1. A sudden repulse; curt denial. 2. A sudden check; defeat. 3. A beating back. [< MF < Ital. *ribuffare* to reprimand]

re·buke (ri·byōōk′) *v.t.* **·buked, ·buk·ing** To reprove sharply; reprimand. — *n.* A strong expression of disapproval. [< AF < OF < *re-* back + *buchier* to beat] — **re·buk′a·ble** *adj.* — **re·buk′er** *n.*

re·bus (rē′bəs) *n. pl.* **·bus·es** A puzzle representing a word, phrase, sentence, etc., by letters, numerals, pictures, etc., whose names have the same sounds as the words represented. [< L, ablative pl. of *res* thing]

re·but (ri·but′) *v.t.* **·but·ted, ·but·ting** To refute by contrary evidence or proof, as in formal argument; disprove. — **Syn.** See REFUTE. [< OF < *re-* back + *bouter* to strike, push] — **re·but′ter** *n.*

re·but·tal (ri·but′l) *n.* The act of rebutting; refutation.

re·cal·ci·trant (ri·kal′sə·trənt) *adj.* Not complying; obstinate; rebellious; refractory. — *n.* One who is recalcitrant. [< L < *re-* back + *calcitrare* to kick < *calx* heel] — **re·cal′·ci·trance, re·cal′ci·tran·cy** *n.*

re·call (ri·kôl′; *for n., also* rē′kôl) *v.t.* **1.** To call back; order or summon to return. **2.** To summon back in awareness or attention. **3.** To recollect; remember. **4.** To take back; revoke. — *n.* **1.** A calling back or to mind. **2.** Revocation. **3.** A system whereby officials may be removed from office by popular vote.

re·cant (ri·kant′) *v.t.* **1.** To withdraw formally one's belief in (something previously believed or maintained). — *v.i.* **2.** To disavow an opinion or belief previously held. [< L < *re-* back + *cantare* to sing] — **re·can·ta·tion** (rē′kan·tā′·shən) *n.* — **re·cant′er** *n.*

re·cap (*v.* rē′kap′, rē·kap′; *n.* rē′kap′) *v.t.* **capped, ·cap·ping** To recondition (an automobile tire) by vulcanizing new rubber onto the surface that comes in contact with the road. — *n.* A tire that has been recapped.

re·ca·pit·u·late (rē′kə·pich′ŏŏ·lāt) *v.t. & v.i.* **·lat·ed, ·lat·ing 1.** To review briefly; sum up. **2.** *Zool.* To reproduce (typical ancestral forms) in the course of embryonic development. [< LL < *re-* again + *capitulare* to draw up in chapters] — **re·ca·pit′u·la·tion** *n.* — **re·ca·pit′u·la·tive** (-lā′tiv), **re·ca·pit′u·la·to·ry** (-lə·tôr′ē, -tō′rē) *adj.*

re·cap·ture (rē·kap′chər) *v.t.* **·tured, ·tur·ing 1.** To capture again; obtain by recapture. **2.** To recall; remember. — *n.* **1.** The act of retaking. **2.** Anything recaptured.

re·cast (*v.* rē′kast′, -käst′; *n.* rē′kast′, -käst′) *v.t.* **·cast, ·cast·ing 1.** To form anew; cast again. **2.** To fashion anew by changing style, arrangement, etc., as a discourse. **3.** To calculate anew. — *n.* Something that has been recast.

re·cede (ri·sēd′) *v.i.* **·ced·ed, ·ced·ing 1.** To move back, as flood waters. **2.** To withdraw, as from an agreement, etc. **3.** To slope backward: a *receding* forehead. **4.** To become more distant. [< L < *re-* back + *cedere* to go]

re·cede (rē·sēd′) *v.t.* **·ced·ed, -ced·ing** To cede back.

re·ceipt (ri·sēt′) *n.* **1.** The act or state of receiving anything. **2.** *Usu. pl.* That which is received: cash *receipts*. **3.** A written acknowledgment of the payment of money, of the delivery of goods, etc. **4.** A recipe. — *v.t.* **1.** To give a receipt for the payment of. **2.** To write acknowledgment of payment on, as a bill. [< OF < L < *re-* back + *capere* to take]

re·ceiv·a·ble (ri·sē′və·bəl) *adj.* **1.** Capable of being received; fit to be received, as legal tender. **2.** Maturing for payment: said of a bill. — *n., pl.* Outstanding accounts listed among the assets of a business.

re·ceive (ri·sēv′) *v.* **·ceived, ·ceiv·ing** *v.t.* **1.** To take into one's hand or possession (something given, delivered, etc.); acquire. **2.** To gain knowledge of: He *received* the news at breakfast. **3.** To take from another by hearing or listening: The king *received* his oath of fealty. **4.** To bear; support: These columns *receive* the weight of the building. **5.** To experience; meet with: to *receive* abuse. **6.** To undergo; suffer: He *received* a wound. **7.** To contain; hold. **8.** To allow entrance to; admit; greet. **9.** To accept as true, proven, etc. — *v.i.* **10.** To be a recipient. **11.** To welcome visitors or callers. **12.** *Telecom.* To convert radio waves into some useful form by means of a receiver. [< OF < L < *re-* back + *capere* to take]

— **Syn. 1.** *Receive* has no close synonym; he who *receives* takes what is given or what comes entirely passively. *Acquire* implies an active role, or some effort to obtain; the same is true of *get*, for the most part, but this word is broad enough to include some of the sense of *receive*.

re·ceiv·er (ri·sē′vər) *n.* **1.** One who receives; a recipient. **2.** An official assigned to receive money due. **3.** *Law* A person appointed by a court to take into his custody, control, and management the property or funds of another pending judicial action concerning them. **4.** Something that receives; a receptacle. **5.** *Telecom.* **a** An instrument serving to receive and reproduce signals transmitted from another part of a circuit: a telephone *receiver*. **b** Any of various electronic devices that convert radio waves into audio signals, video signals, etc., or into forms useful as a basis for observation, as in radio telescopes or radar: also **receiving set.**

re·ceiv·er·ship (ri·sē′vər·ship) *n.* **1.** The office and functions pertaining to a receiver under appointment of a court. **2.** The state of being in the hands of a receiver.

re·cent (rē′sənt) *adj.* Pertaining to, or formed, developed, or created in time not long past; modern. [< MF < L *recens*] — **re′cent·ly** *adv.* — **re′cen·cy, re′cent·ness** *n.*

Re·cent (rē′sənt) *adj. Geol.* Pertaining to or designating the present geological epoch, succeeding the Pleistocene. See chart for GEOLOGY.

re·cep·ta·cle (ri·sep′tə·kəl) *n.* **1.** Anything that serves to contain or hold something else. **2.** *Bot.* The base to which the parts of the flower, fruit, or seeds are fixed. For illus. see FLOWER. [< L < *re-* back + *capere* to take] — **re·cep·tac·u·lar** (rē′sep·tak′yə·lər) *adj.* — **Syn. 1.** container, repository.

re·cep·tion (ri·sep′shən) *n.* **1.** The act of receiving, or the state of being received. **2.** A formal social entertainment of guests: a wedding *reception*. **3.** The manner of receiving a person or persons: a warm *reception*. **4.** *Telecom.* The act or process of receiving, or the quality of reproduction achieved. [< OF < L < *re-* back + *capere* to take]

re·cep·tion·ist (ri·sep′shən·ist) *n.* One employed to receive callers at the entrance to an office.

re·cep·tive (ri·sep′tiv) *adj.* **1.** Able or inclined to receive, as truths or impressions. **2.** Able to take in or hold. — **re·cep′tive·ly** *adv.* — **re·cep·tiv·i·ty** (rē′sep·tiv′ə·tē), **re·cep′tive·ness** *n.*

re·cep·tor (ri·sep′tər) *n. Anat.* The terminal structure of a neuron, specialized to receive stimuli and transmit them to the spinal cord and brain. [< OF or L, receiver]

re·cess (*n.* ri·ses′, rē′ses; *for def. 2. usu.* rē′ses; *v.* ri·ses′) *n.* **1.** A depression or indentation in any otherwise continuous line or surface, esp. in a wall; niche. **2.** A time of cessation from employment or occupation: The school took a *recess.* **3.** *Usu. pl.* A secluded spot; withdrawn or inner place: the *recesses* of the mind. — *v.t.* **1.** To place in or as in a recess. **2.** To make a recess in. — *v.i.* **3.** To take a recess. [< L < *re-* back + *cedere* to go]

re·ces·sion (ri·sesh′ən) *n.* **1.** The act of receding; a withdrawal. **2.** The procession of the clergy, choir, etc., as they leave the chancel after a church service. **3.** An economic setback in commercial and industrial activity, esp. one occurring as a downward turn during a period of generally rising prosperity.

re·ces·sion (rē·sesh′ən) *n.* The act of ceding again; a giving back.

re·ces·sion·al (ri·sesh′ən·əl) *adj.* Of or pertaining to recession. — *n.* A hymn sung as the choir or clergy leave the chancel after service.

re·ces·sive (ri·ses′iv) *adj.* **1.** Having a tendency to recede or go back; receding. **2.** *Genetics* Designating one of a pair of hereditary characters that, appearing in a hybrid offspring, is masked by a contrasting character. — *n. Genetics* A recessive character. — **re·ces′sive·ly** *adv.*

re·cher·ché (rə·sher·shā′) *adj. French* **1.** Rare and exquisite; choice. **2.** Elegant and refined; also, overrefined.

rec·i·pe (res′ə·pē) *n.* **1.** A formula or list of ingredients of a mixture, giving proper directions for compounding, cooking, etc. **2.** A medical prescription: usu. abbreviated to ℞. **3.** A method prescribed for attaining a desired result. [< L < *re-* back + *capere* to take]

re·cip·i·ent (ri·sip′ē·ənt) *adj.* Receiving or ready to receive; receptive. — *n.* One who or that which receives. [< L < *re-* back + *capere* to take] — **re·cip′i·ence, re·cip′i·en·cy** *n.*

re·cip·ro·cal (ri·sip′rə·kəl) *adj.* **1.** Done or given by each of two to the other; mutual. **2.** Mutually interchangeable. **3.** Alternating; moving to and fro. **4.** Expressive of mutual relationship or action: used in connection with certain pronouns and verbs or their meaning. **5.** *Math.* Of or pertaining to various types of mutual relations between two quantities. — *n.* **1.** That which is reciprocal. **2.** *Math.* The quotient obtained by dividing unity by a number or expression, as ½ is the *reciprocal* of *x.* In a fraction, this reverses the numerator and denominator, as ⅔ is the *reciprocal* of ⅔. [< L *reciprocus*] — **re·cip′ro·cal·i·ty** (-kal′ə·tē), **re·cip′ro·cal·ness** *n.* — **re·cip′ro·cal·ly** *adv.*

reciprocal pronouns *Gram.* Pronouns or phrases denoting reciprocal action or relation, as *each other, one another.*

re·cip·ro·cate (ri·sip′rə·kāt) *v.* **·cat·ed, ·cat·ing** *v.t.* **1.** To cause to move backward and forward alternately. **2.** To give and receive mutually; interchange. **3.** To give, feel, do, etc., in return; requite, as an emotion. — *v.i.* **4.** To move backward and forward. **5.** To make a return in kind. **6.** To give and receive favors, gifts, etc., mutually. [< L < *reciprocus* reciprocal] — **re·cip′ro·ca′tion** *n.* — **re·cip′ro·ca′tive** *adj.* — **re·cip′ro·ca′tor** *n.* — **re·cip′ro·ca·to·ry** (-kə·tôr′ē, -tō′rē) *adj.*

rec·i·proc·i·ty (res′ə·pros′ə·tē) *n.* **1.** Reciprocal obligation, action, or relation. **2.** A trade relation between two countries by which each makes concessions favoring the importation of the other's products. [< F *réciprocité*]

re·cit·al (ri·sīt′l) *n.* **1.** A telling over in detail, or that which is thus told. **2.** A public delivery of something previously memorized. **3.** A musical program performed usu. by one person or several appearing as soloists.

rec·i·ta·tion (res′ə·tā′shən) *n.* **1.** The act of repeating from memory. **2.** The reciting of a lesson, or the meeting of a class for that purpose. **3.** That which is allotted for recital or actually recited. [< L < *re-* again + CITE]

rec·i·ta·tive (res/ə·tə·tēv/, rə·sit/ə·tiv) *n. Music* **1.** Language uttered in the phrasing of ordinary speech, but set to music. **2.** This style of singing, or a passage so rendered. Also *Italian* re·ci·ta·ti·vo (rä/chē·tä·tē/vō). [< Ital. *recitativo*]

re·cite (ri·sīt/) *v.* **·cit·ed, ·cit·ing** *v.t.* **1.** To declaim or say from memory, esp. formally, as a lesson in class. **2.** To tell in particular detail; relate. **3.** To enumerate. — *v.i.* **4.** To declaim or speak something from memory. **5.** To repeat or be examined in a lesson or part of a lesson in class. [< OF < L < *re-* again + CITE] — **re·cit/er** *n.*
—**Syn. 1.** repeat. **2.** recount, narrate, recapitulate.

reck (rek) *v.t. & v.i. Archaic* **1.** To have a care (for); heed; mind. **2.** To be of concern (to). [OE *reccan*]

reck·less (rek/lis) *adj.* **1.** Foolishly heedless of danger; rash. **2.** Proceeding from carelessness or rashness. [OE *reccelēas*] — **reck/less·ly** *adv.* — **reck/less·ness** *n.*

reck·on (rek/ən) *v.t.* **1.** To count; compute; calculate. **2.** To look upon as being; regard: They *reckon* him a fool. — *v.i.* **3.** To make computation; count up. **4.** To rely or depend: with *on* or *upon*: to *reckon* on help. — **to reckon with 1.** To settle accounts with. **2.** To take into consideration. [OE *recenian* to explain] — **reck/on·er** *n.*

reck·on·ing (rek/ən·ing) *n.* **1.** The act of counting; computation; a settlement of accounts. **2.** Account; score; bill, as at a hotel. **3.** *Naut.* Dead reckoning (which see).

re·claim (ri·klām/) *v.t.* **1.** To bring (swamp, desert, etc.) into a condition to support cultivation or life, as by draining or irrigating. **2.** To obtain (a substance) from used or waste products. **3.** To cause to return from wrong or sinful ways of life. — *n.* The act of reclaiming, or state of being reclaimed. [< OF < L < *re-* back + *clamare* to cry out] — **re·claim/a·ble** *adj.* — **re·claim/ant, re·claim/er** *n.*

re-claim (rē·klām/) *v.t.* To claim again.

rec·la·ma·tion (rek/lə·mā/shən) *n.* **1.** The act of reclaiming. **2.** Restoration, as to usefulness or a moral life.

re·cline (ri·klīn/) *v.* **·clined, ·clin·ing** *v.i. & v.t.* To assume or cause to assume a recumbent position; lie or lay down or back. [< L < *re-* back + *clinare* to lean] — **rec·li·na·tion** (rek/lə·nā/shən) *n.* — **re·clin/er** *n.*

rec·luse (ri·kloos/; *for n., also* rek/loos) *n.* **1.** One who lives in retirement or seclusion. **2.** A religious devotee who lives voluntarily shut up in a cell. — *adj.* Secluded or retired from the world. [< OF < L < *re-* back + *claudere* to shut] — **re·clu/sion** *n.* — **re·clu/sive** *adj.*

rec·og·ni·tion (rek/əg·nish/ən) *n.* **1.** The act of recognizing, or the state of being recognized. **2.** Acknowledgment of a fact or claim. **3.** Friendly notice; salutation; attention. **4.** Acknowledgment and acceptance on the part of one government of the independence of another. [< L < *re-* again + *cognoscere* to know] — **re·cog/ni·to·ry** (ri·kog/nə·tôr/ē, tō/rē) *or* **re·cog/ni·tive** *adj.*

re·cog·ni·zance (ri·kog/nə·zəns, -kon/ə-) *n. Law* **1.** An obligation of record, with condition to do some particular act, as to appear and answer. **2.** A sum of money deposited as surety for fulfillment of such act or obligation, and forfeited by its nonperformance. [< OF < L. See RECOGNITION] — **re·cog/ni·zant** *adj.*

rec·og·nize (rek/əg·nīz) *v.t.* **·nized, ·niz·ing 1.** To perceive as identical with someone or something previously known. **2.** To identify, as by previous experience: I *recognize* poor poetry when I see it. **3.** To perceive as true; realize: to *recognize* the facts in a case. **4.** To acknowledge the independence and validity of, as a newly constituted government. **5.** To indicate appreciation or approval of. **6.** To regard as valid or genuine: to *recognize* a claim. **7.** To give (someone) permission to speak, as in a legislative body. **8.** To admit the acquaintance of; greet. [Back formation < RECOGNIZANCE] — **rec·og·niz·a·ble** (rek/əg·nī/zə·bəl) *adj.* — **rec/og·niz/a·bly** *adv.* — **rec/og·niz/er** *n.*

re·coil (*v.* ri·koil/; *n.* rē/koil/) *v.i.* **1.** To start back, as in fear or loathing; shrink. **2.** To spring back, as from force of discharge or impact. **3.** To return to the source; react: with *on* or *upon*: Crime *recoils* upon its perpetrator. — *n.* A backward movement, as of a gun at the moment of firing; also, a shrinking. [< OF < *re-* backwards + *cul* backside < L *culus*] — **re·coil/er** *n.*

re-coil (rē·koil/) *v.t. & v.i.* To coil again.

rec·ol·lect (rek/ə·lekt/) *v.t.* **1.** To call back to the mind. — *v.i.* **2.** To have a recollection of something. [< L < *re-* again + COLLECT]

re-col·lect (rē/kə·lekt/) *v.t.* **1.** To collect again, as things scattered. **2.** To collect or compose (one's thoughts or nerves); compose or recover (oneself). — **re/-col·lec/tion** *n.*

rec·ol·lec·tion (rek/ə·lek/shən) *n.* **1.** The act or power of remembering. **2.** Something remembered. — **rec/ol·lec/tive** *adj.* — **rec/ol·lec/tive·ly** *adv.*

rec·om·mend (rek/ə·mend/) *v.t.* **1.** To commend with favorable representations. **2.** To make attractive or acceptable. **3.** To advise; urge. **4.** To give in charge; commend. [< Med.L < L *re-* again + COMMEND] — **rec/om·mend/er** *n.*

rec·om·men·da·tion (rek/ə·men·dā/shən) *n.* **1.** The act of recommending, or of being recommended. **2.** A letter recommending a person.

re·com·mit (rē/kə·mit/) *v.t.* **·mit·ted, ·mit·ting 1.** To commit again. **2.** To refer back to a committee, as a bill. — **re/com·mit/tal** *n.*

rec·om·pense (rek/əm·pens) *v.t.* **·pensed, ·pens·ing 1.** To give compensation to; pay or repay; reward. **2.** To compensate for, as a loss. — *n.* **1.** An equivalent for anything given or done; payment. **2.** Compensation or reward. [< OF < LL < L *re-* again + *compensare*. See COMPENSATE.]
—**Syn.** (verb) **1.** reimburse. **2.** indemnify.

rec·on·cil·a·ble (rek/ən·sī/lə·bəl) *adj.* Capable of being reconciled, adjusted, or harmonized. — **rec/on·cil/a·bil/i·ty, rec/on·cil/a·ble·ness** *n.* — **rec/on·cil/a·bly** *adv.*

rec·on·cile (rek/ən·sīl) *v.t.* **·ciled, ·cil·ing 1.** To bring back to friendship after estrangement. **2.** To settle or adjust, as a quarrel. **3.** To bring to acquiescence, content, or submission. **4.** To make or show to be consistent or congruous; harmonize: often with *to* or *with*: Can he *reconcile* his statement with his conduct? [< OF < L < *re-* again + *conciliare* to unite] — **rec/on·cile/ment** *n.* — **rec/on·cil/er** *n.* — **rec·on·cil·i·a·tion** (rek/ən·sil/ē·ā/shən) *n.*

rec·on·dite (rek/ən·dīt, ri·kon/dīt) *adj.* **1.** Remote from ordinary or easy perception; abstruse; secret. **2.** Dealing in abstruse matters. **3.** Hidden. [< L < *recondere* to hide] — **rec/on·dite/ly** *adv.* — **rec/on·dite/ness** *n.*

re·con·di·tion (rē/kən·dish/ən) *v.t.* To put into good or working condition, as by making repairs; overhaul.

re·con·nais·sance (ri·kon/ə·səns, -säns) *n.* **1.** A reconnoitering; a preliminary examination or survey, as of the territory and resources of a country. **2.** *Mil.* The act of obtaining information of military value, especially regarding the position, strength, and movement of enemy forces. Also **re·con/nois·sance.** [< F]

re·con·noi·ter (rē/kə·noi/tər, rek/ə-) *v.t.* To examine or survey, as for military, engineering, or geological purposes. — *v.i.* To make a reconnaissance. [< OF < L < *re-* again + *cognoscere* to know] — **re/con·noi/ter·er** *n.*

re·con·sid·er (rē/kən·sid/ər) *v.t. & v.i.* To consider again, esp. with a view to a reversal of previous action. — **re/con·sid/er·a/tion** *n.*

re·con·sti·tute (rē·kon/stə·tōōt, -tyōōt) *v.t.* **·tut·ed, ·tut·ing** To constitute again; make over. — **re·con/sti·tu/tion** *n.*

re·con·struct (rē/kən·strukt/) *v.t.* To build again; rebuild.

re·con·struc·tion (rē/kən·struk/shən) *n.* **1.** The act of reconstructing, or the state of being reconstructed. **2.** *Often cap.* The restoration of the seceded States as members of the Union under the **Reconstruction Acts** of March 2 and 23, 1867. — **re/con·struc/tive** *adj.*

Reconstruction period *U.S.* The period following the Civil War during which the seceded Southern States were reorganized in accordance with the Congressional program.

re·con·vert (rē/kən·vûrt/) *v.t.* **1.** To change back to a state or form previously possessed. **2.** To convert back to a previously held religious belief. — **re/con·ver/sion** *n.*

rec·ord (*n. & adj.* rek/ərd; *v.* ri·kôrd/) *n.* **1.** An account in written or other permanent form serving as a memorial or authentic evidence of a fact or event. **2.** Something on which such an account is made, as a document or monument. **3.** Information preserved and handed down: the heaviest rainfall on *record*. **4.** The known career or performance of a person, animal, organization, etc. **5.** The best listed achievement, as in a competitive sport. **6.** *Law* **a** A written account of an act, statement, or transaction made by an officer acting under authority of law, and intended as permanent evidence thereon. **b** An official written account of a judicial or legislative proceeding. **7.** A phonograph record. — **off the record 1.** Unofficial or unofficially. **2.** Not for quotation or publication, or not from a source to be identified. — *adj.* Surpassing any previously recorded achievement or performance of its kind. — *v.t.* **1.** To write down or otherwise inscribe, as for preserving a record. **2.** To indicate; register, esp. in permanent form, as a cardiograph does. **3.** To make a tape or phonograph record of. — *v.i.* **4.** To record something. [< OF < L *recordari* to remember]
—**Syn.** (noun) **1.** note, memorandum, register, roll, catalogue.

record changer A device on some record players that automatically feeds successive records onto the turntable.

re·cord·er (ri·kôr/dər) *n.* **1.** One who records. **2.** A magistrate having criminal jurisdiction in a city or borough. **3.** A registering apparatus. **4.** Any of a group of fipple flutes having eight finger holes, and various ranges. **5.** A tape or wire recorder. — **re·cord/er·ship** *n.*

re·cord·ing (ri·kôr′ding) *n.* **1.** *Telecom.* The process of registering a relatively permanent physical record of sounds or other communicable signals. **2.** A phonograph record.

record player A motor-driven turntable with a pickup attachment and auxiliary equipment for the playing of phonograph records: also called *gramophone, phonograph.*

re·count (ri·kount′) *v.t.* **1.** To relate the particulars of; narrate in detail. **2.** To enumerate; recite. [< OF *reconter* to relate]

re-count (rē·kount′; *for n., also* rē′kount′) *v.t.* To count again. — *n.* A repetition of a count; esp., a second count of votes cast. — **re·count′al** *n.*

re·coup (ri·kōōp′) *v.t.* **1.** To recover or obtain an equivalent for; make up, as a loss. **2.** To reimburse for a loss; indemnify. — *n.* The act or process of recouping. [< OF < *re-* back + *couper* to cut] — **re·coup′a·ble** *adj.* — **re·coup′ment** *n.*

re·course (rē′kôrs, -kōrs, ri·kôrs′, -kōrs′) *n.* **1.** Resort to or application for help or security. **2.** One who or that which is resorted to for help or supply. [< OF < L < *re-* back + *currere* to run]

re·cov·er (ri·kuv′ər) *v.t.* **1.** To regain after losing. **2.** To make up for; retrieve, as a loss. **3.** To restore (oneself) to natural balance, health, etc. **4.** To reclaim, as land. **5.** *Law* To gain or regain in legal proceedings. — *v.i.* **6.** To regain health, composure, etc. [< OF < L < *re-* back + *capere* to take] — **re·cov′er·a·ble** *adj.* — **re·cov′er·er** *n.*

re-cov·er (rē·kuv′ər) *v.t.* To cover again.

re·cov·er·y (ri·kuv′ər·ē) *n. pl.* **·er·ies** **1.** The act or process of recovering. **2.** Restoration from sickness or from any undesirable or abnormal condition. **3.** The retrieval of a flying object, as a balloon, space vehicle, meteorite, etc., after it has fallen to earth.

rec·re·ant (rek′rē·ənt) *adj.* **1.** Unfaithful to a cause or pledge; false. **2.** Craven; cowardly. — *n.* A cowardly or faithless person; also, a deserter. [< OF < Med.L < L *re-* back + *credere* to believe] — **rec′re·ance, rec′re·an·cy** *n.* — **rec′re·ant·ly** *adv.*

rec·re·ate (rek′rē·āt) *v.* **·at·ed, ·at·ing** *v.t.* **1.** To impart fresh vigor to; refresh. — *v.i.* **2.** To take recreation. [< L < *re-* again + *creare* to create] — **rec′re·a′tive** *adj.*

re-cre·ate (rē′krē·āt′) *v.t.* **·at·ed, ·at·ing** To create anew. — **re′-cre·a′tion** *n.*

rec·re·a·tion (rek′rē·ā′shən) *n.* **1.** Refreshment of body or mind; diversion; amusement. **2.** Any pleasurable exercise or occupation. — **rec′re·a′tion·al** *adj.*

rec·rim·i·nate (ri·krim′ə·nāt) *v.* **·nat·ed, ·nat·ing** *v.t.* **1.** To accuse in return. — *v.i.* **2.** To repel one accusation by making another in return. [< Med.L < L *re-* again + *criminare* to accuse of crime] — **re·crim′i·na′tive, re·crim′i·na·to·ry** (ri·krim′ə·nə·tôr′ē, -tō′rē) *adj.* — **re·crim′i·na′tor** *n.*

re·crim·i·na·tion (ri·krim′ə·nā′shən) *n.* **1.** The act of recriminating. **2.** A countercharge.

re·cru·desce (rē′krōō·des′) *v.i.* **·desced, ·desc·ing** To break out afresh. [< L < *re-* again + *crudescere* to become raw] — **re′cru·des′cence** *n.* — **re′cru·des′cent** *adj.*

re·cruit (ri·krōōt′) *v.t.* **1.** To enlist (men) for military or naval service. **2.** To muster; raise, as an army, by enlistment. **3.** To supply with recruits. **4.** To regain or revive (lost health, strength, etc.). — *v.i.* **5.** To enlist new men for military or naval service. **6.** To regain lost health or strength. **7.** To gain or raise new supplies of anything lost or needed. — *n.* A newly enlisted member of an organization, esp. of the armed forces. See tables at GRADE. [< F < OF < L < *re-* again + *crescere* to grow] — **re·cruit′er** *n.* — **re·cruit′ment** *n.*

rec·tal (rek′təl) *adj. Anat.* Of, for, or in the rectum.

rec·tan·gle (rek′tang′gəl) *n.* A parallelogram with all its angles right angles. [< F < LL < L *rectus* straight + *angulus* angle]

rec·tan·gu·lar (rek·tang′gyə·lər) *adj.* **1.** Having one or more right angles. **2.** Resembling a rectangle in shape. — **rec·tan′gu·lar′i·ty** (-lər′ə·tē) *n.* — **rec·tan′gu·lar·ly** *adv.*

recti- *combining form* Straight: *rectilinear.* Also, before vowels, **rect-.** [< L *rectus* straight < *regere* to guide]

rec·ti·fi·er (rek′tə·fī′ər) *n.* **1.** One who or that which rectifies. **2.** *Electr.* A device used to convert an alternating current into a direct current.

rec·ti·fy (rek′tə·fī) *v.t.* **·fied, ·fy·ing** **1.** To make right; correct; amend. **2.** *Chem.* To refine and purify, as a liquid, by repeated distillations. **3.** *Electr.* To change (an alternating current) into a direct current. **4.** To allow for errors or inaccuracies in, as a compass reading. [< MF < LL < L *rectus* straight] — **rec′ti·fi′a·ble** *adj.* — **rec′ti·fi·ca·tion** (rek′·tə·fə·kā′shən) *n.*

rec·ti·lin·e·ar (rek′tə·lin′ē·ər) *adj.* Pertaining to, consisting of, moving in, or bounded by a straight line or lines; straight. Also **rec′ti·lin′e·al** (-ē·əl). — **rec′ti·lin′e·ar·ly** *adv.*

rec·ti·tude (rek′tə·tōōd, -tyōōd) *n.* **1.** Uprightness in principles and conduct. **2.** Correctness, as of judgment. [< F < LL < L *rectus* straight]

rec·to (rek′tō) *n. pl.* **·toes** A right-hand page, as of a book: opposed to *verso.* [< L *recto (folio)* on the right (page)]

recto- *combining form Anat.* Rectal; pertaining to or located in the rectum. Also, before vowels **rect-.** [See RECTUM]

rec·tor (rek′tər) *n.* **1.** In the Church of England, a priest who has full charge of a parish, and receives the parochial tithes. **2.** In the Protestant Episcopal Church, a priest in charge of a parish. **3.** In the Roman Catholic Church: **a** A priest in charge of a congregation or church, esp. one not having parochial status. **b** The head of a seminary or religious house. **4.** In certain universities, colleges, and schools, the head or chief officer. [< L < *regere* to guide, rule] — **rec′tor·ate** (-it) *n.* — **rec·to·ri·al** (rek·tôr′ē·əl, -tō′rē) *adj.*

rec·to·ry (rek′tər·ē) *n. pl.* **·ries** **1.** A rector's dwelling. **2.** In England, a parish domain with its buildings, revenue, etc.

rec·tum (rek′təm) *n. pl.* **·ta** (-tə) *Anat.* The terminal portion of the large intestine, connecting the colon with the anus. [< NL *rectum (intestinum)* straight (intestine)]

re·cum·bent (ri·kum′bənt) *adj.* **1.** Lying down, wholly or partly. **2.** *Biol.* Tending to rest upon or extend from a surface, as certain plant or animal organs. [< L < *re-* back + -*cumbere* < *cubare* to lie down] — **re·cum′bence, re·cum′ben·cy** *n.* — **re·cum′bent·ly** *adv.*

re·cu·per·ate (ri·kōō′pə·rāt, -kyōō′-) *v.* **·at·ed, ·at·ing** *v.i.* **1.** To regain health or strength. **2.** To recover from loss, as of money. — *v.t.* **3.** To obtain again after loss; recover. **4.** To restore to vigor and health. — **Syn.** See RECOVER. [< L < *re-* back + *capere* to take] — **re·cu′per·a′tion** *n.* — **re·cu′per·a′tive, re·cu′per·a·to′ry** (-pər·ə·tôr′ē, -tō′rē) *adj.*

re·cur (ri·kûr′) *v.i.* **·curred, ·cur·ring** **1.** To happen again or repeatedly, esp. at regular intervals. **2.** To come back or return; esp., to return to the mind or in recollection. [< L < *re-* back + *currere* to run]

re·cur·rent (ri·kûr′ənt) *adj.* **1.** Happening or appearing again or repeatedly; recurring. **2.** *Anat.* Running back: said of arteries and nerves. — **re·cur′rence, re·cur′ren·cy** *n.* — **re·cur′rent·ly** *adv.*

re·cur·vate (ri·kûr′vit, -vāt) *adj.* Bent back. — **re·cur′va·ture** (-və·chər) *n.*

re·curve (ri·kûrv′) *v.t. & v.i.* **·curved, ·curv·ing** To curve or bend back or down. [< L < *re-* back + *curvus* curved] — **re·cur·va·tion** (rē′kûr·vā′shən) *n.*

re·cy·cle (rē·sī′kəl) *v.t.* **·cy·cled, ·cy·cling** To reclaim (waste materials, as newsprint) by using in the manufacture of new products. — **re·cy′cla·ble** *adj.*

red (red) *adj.* **red·der, red·dest** **1.** Being of or having a bright color resembling that of blood. **2.** Communistic. — *n.* **1.** One of the primary colors, occurring at the opposite end of the spectrum from violet; the color of blood. **2.** Any pigment or dye having or giving this color. **3.** An ultraradical in political views, esp. a communist. **4.** A red object considered with reference to its color. — **in the red** *Informal* Operating at a loss; owing money. — **to see red** *Informal* To be very angry. [OE *rēad*] — **red′dish** *adj.* — **red′ly** *adv.* — **red′ness** *n.*

Red (red) *n.* **1.** A member of the Communist party of Russia. **2.** A member of the Communist party of any country. **3.** Any person who supports or approves of the aims of the Communist party. **4.** An ultraradical; anarchist.

re·dact (ri·dakt′) *v.t.* **1.** To prepare, as for publication; edit; revise. **2.** To draw up or frame, as a message or edict. [< L < *re-* back + *agere* to drive] — **re·dac′tion** *n.* — **re·dac′tor** *n.*

red algae Any of a class of algae of a reddish color.

red·bait·ing (red′bā′ting) *n.* The practice of denouncing groups or individuals as communist or sympathetic to communism, often with little evidence. — **red′bait′er** *n.*

red·bird (red′bûrd′) *n.* **1.** The cardinal (def. 2). **2.** The scarlet tanager.

red-blood·ed (red′blud′id) *adj.* Having vitality and vigor.

red·breast (red′brest′) *n.* A bird having a red breast, as the American or European robin.

red·cap (red′kap′) *n. U.S.* A railroad porter.

red cedar **1.** An American juniper tree of the cypress family, having a fine-grained, durable wood of a bright or dark red color resembling cedar. **2.** The wood of this tree.

Red Chamber The chamber of the Canadian Senate at Ottawa.

Red China *Informal* The People's Republic of China.

red·coat (red′kōt′) *n.* A British soldier of the period when a red coat was part of the uniform, esp. during the American Revolution and the War of 1812.

Red Cross An international organization for the care of the sick and wounded in war, formed in accordance with the international convention signed at Geneva in 1864, the members wearing a red Geneva cross as a badge of neutrality. These societies are now national organizations, as the American Red Cross, and continue their activities in times of peace, as in fighting disease, etc.

red deer **1.** The common European and Asian stag. **2.** The white-tailed deer in its rufous summer coat.

red·den (red/n) *v.t.* **1.** To make red. — *v.i.* **2.** To grow red; flush; blush.

re·dec·o·rate (ri-dek/ə-rāt) *v.t. & v.i.* ·rat·ed, ·rat·ing To renovate or remodel, as an apartment. — **re/dec/o·ra/tion** *n.*

re·deem (ri-dēm/) *v.t.* **1.** To regain possession of by paying a price; esp., to recover, as mortgaged property. **2.** To pay off; receive back and satisfy, as a promissory note. **3.** To set free; ransom. **4.** *Theol.* To rescue from sin and its penalties. **5.** To fulfill, as an oath or promise. **6.** To compensate for: The play was *redeemed* by its acting. [< MF < L < back + *emere* to buy] — **re·deem/a·ble, re·demp/ti·ble** (-demp/tə·bəl) *adj.*

re·deem·er (ri-dē/mər) *n.* One who redeems. — **The Re·deemer** Jesus Christ.

re·deem·ing (ri-dē/ming) *adj.* Compensating for faults, lacks, poor quality, etc.: the *redeeming* feature.

re·de·liv·er (rē/di-liv/ər) *v.t.* **1.** To deliver again, as a message or a speech. **2.** To give back; return; restore. — **re/·de·liv/er·ance, re/de·liv/er·y** *n.*

re·demp·tion (ri-demp/shən) *n.* **1.** The act of redeeming, or the state of being redeemed. **2.** The recovery of what is mortgaged or pledged. **3.** The payment of a debt or obligation; esp., the paying of the value of its notes, warrants, etc., by a government. [< OF < L < *redimere* to redeem.]

re·demp·tive (ri-demp/tiv) *adj.* Serving to redeem, or connected with redemption. Also **re·demp/to·ry** (-tər-ē).

Red Ensign The Canadian flag, bearing both the Union Jack and the arms of Canada.

re·de·vel·op (rē/di-vel/əp) *v.t.* **1.** To develop again. **2.** *Photog.* To intensify with chemicals and put through a second developing process. — *v.i.* **3.** To develop again. Also **re/de·vel/ope.** — **re/de·vel/op·er** *n.* — **re/de·vel/op·ment** *n.*

red·eye (red/ī/) *n.* **1.** *U.S. Informal* The danger signal in a railroad semaphore system. **2.** *U.S. Slang* Inferior whisky.

red-hand·ed (red/han/did) *adj.* **1.** Having just committed any crime. **2.** Caught in the act of doing some particular thing. — **red/hand/ed·ly** *adv.* — **red/-hand/ed·ness** *n.*

red·head (red/hed/) *n.* **1.** A person with red hair. **2.** An American duck, sometimes mistaken for the canvasback.

red herring 1. Herring dried and smoked to a reddish color. **2.** A diverting of attention from the main subject by introducing some irrelevant topic.

red-hot (red/hot/) *adj.* **1.** Heated to redness. **2.** New, as if just from the fire: *red-hot* news. **3.** Heated; excited.

red·in·gote (red/ing-gōt) *n.* An outer coat with long full skirts. [< F *rédingote*, alter. of E *riding coat*]

re·din·te·grate (ri-din/tə-grāt) *v.t.* ·grat·ed, ·grat·ing To restore to a perfect state. — *adj.* Restored. [< L < *red-* again + *integrare* to make whole] — **re·din/te·gra/tion** *n.*

re·di·rect¹ (rē/di-rekt/) *v.t.* To direct again or anew: to *redirect* a letter. — **re/di·rec/tion** *n.*

re·di·rect² (rē/di-rekt/) *adj. Law* Designating the examination of a witness, after cross-examination, by the party who first examined him.

re·dis·trict (rē-dis/trikt) *v.t.* To district again; esp., to redraw the boundaries of the election districts of.

red lead (led) Minium.

red-let·ter day (red/let/ər) A memorable occasion: from the use on calendars of red letters to indicate holidays.

red light A red traffic or signal light meaning "stop."

red-light district (red/līt/) A part of a city or town in which brothels, often marked by a red light, are numerous.

red man An American Indian.

red·neck (red/nek/) *n.* In the rural South, a poor, uneducated white person: a disparaging term.

red oak Any of several oaks having a dense, cross-grained wood. **2.** The wood of any of these oaks.

red·o·lent (red/ə-lənt) *adj.* Full of or diffusing a pleasant fragrance. [< OF < L < *red-* thoroughly + *olere* to smell] — **red/o·lence, red/o·len·cy** *n.* — **red/o·lent·ly** *adv.*

re·dou·ble (rē-dub/əl) *v.t. & v.i.* ·led, ·ling **1.** To make or become double. **2.** To increase greatly. **3.** To echo or reecho. **4.** To fold or turn back. **5.** In bridge, to double (an opponent's double). — *n.* In bridge, the doubling of an opponent's double.

re·doubt (ri-dout/) *n.* **1.** An enclosed fortification, esp. a temporary one of any form. **2.** An earthwork or simple fortification placed within the main rampart line of a permanent fortification. [< F < Ital. < Med.L < L *reductus* secret place, pp. of *reducere* to reduce]

re·doubt·a·ble (ri-dou/tə-bəl) *adj.* **1.** Inspiring fear; formidable. **2.** Deserving respect or deference. Also **re·doubt/·ed** (-dou/tid). [< F, ult. < L *re-* thoroughly + *dubitare* to doubt] — **re·doubt/a·ble·ness** *n.* — **re·doubt/a·bly** *adv.*

re·dound (ri-dound/) *v.i.* **1.** To have an effect, as by reaction, to the credit, discredit, advantage, etc., of the original agent; accrue. — *n.* A return by way of consequence; requital. [< F < L < *red-* back + *undare* to surge]

red pepper A species of capsicum cultivated in many varieties and used as a condiment: also called *cayenne pepper*.

red·poll (red/pōl/) *n.* Any of various small finches of northern regions, having a reddish crown.

re·draft (*n.* rē/draft/, -dräft/; *v.* rē-draft/, -dräft/) *n.* **1.** A second draft or copy. **2.** A bill of exchange drawn by the holder of a protested bill on the drawer or endorsers for the reimbursement of the amount of the original bill with costs and charges. — *v.t. & v.i.* To make a redraft (of).

re·dress (ri-dres/; *for n.,* also rē/dres) *v.t.* **1.** To set right, as a wrong, by compensation or by punishment of the wrongdoer; make reparation for. **2.** To make reparation to; compensate. **3.** To remedy; correct. **4.** To adjust, as balances. — *n.* **1.** Satisfaction for wrong done; reparation; amends. **2.** A restoration; correction. [< F < *re-* again + *dresser* to arrange] — **re·dress/er** or **re·dres/sor** *n.*

re-dress (rē-dres/) *v.t. & v.i.* To dress again.

red salmon The sockeye.

red·skin (red/skin/) *n.* A North American Indian.

red snapper A reddish fish found in Atlantic waters and esteemed as a food fish.

red·start (red/stärt/) *n.* **1.** A small European singing bird allied to the warblers; having a black throat, white forehead, and rust-red breast, sides, and tail. **2.** A small fly-catching warbler of eastern North America, with bright orange-red patches against black and white.

red tape Rigid official procedure involving delay or inaction: from the tying of public documents with red tape.

red tide A reddish coloration of the sea due to the presence of great numbers of red protozoan flagellates.

re·duce (ri-dōōs/, -dūs/) *v.* ·duced, ·duc·ing *v.t.* **1.** To make less in size, amount, number, intensity, etc.; diminish. **2.** To bring to a lower condition; degrade. **3.** To bring to submission; conquer. **4.** To bring to a specified condition or state: with *to*: to *reduce* a person to desperation. **5.** To thin (paint, etc.) with oil or turpentine. **6.** *Math.* To change (an expression) to a more elementary form. **7.** *Surg.* To restore (displaced parts) to normal position. **8.** *Chem.* **a** To decrease the valence of (an atom or group of atoms) by adding electrons. **b** To remove oxygen from (a compound). **9.** *Metall.* To extract (a metal) from a combined state, as in an ore. — *v.i.* **10.** To become less in any way. **11.** To decrease one's weight, as by dieting. — **Syn.** See DECREASE. [< L < *re-* back + *ducere* to lead] — **re·duc/er** *n.* — **re·duc/i·bil/i·ty** *n.* — **re·duc/i·ble** *adj.* — **re·duc/i·bly** *adv.*

reducing agent *Chem.* A substance that effects reduction, while increasing its valence and becoming oxidized.

re·duc·ti·o ad ab·sur·dum (ri-duk/shē-ō ad ab-sûr/dəm) *Latin* Reduction to an absurdity; disposal of a proposition by showing that its logical conclusion is absurd.

re·duc·tion (ri-duk/shən) *n.* **1.** The act or process of reducing, or its results. **2.** *Chem.* **a** The process of depriving a compound of oxygen. **b** The process by which atoms gain valence electrons or cease to share them with a more electronegative element. — **re·duc/tion·al** *adj.* — **re·duc/tive** (-tiv) *adj.*

re·dun·dance (ri-dun/dəns) *n.* **1.** The condition or quality of being redundant. **2.** That which is redundant.

re·dun·dan·cy (ri-dun/dən-sē) *n. pl.* ·cies **1.** Redundance. **2.** In information theory, the extent to which a signal repeats the same message, reducing the probability of error and reducing the effective capacity of the channel.

re·dun·dant (ri-dun/dənt) *adj.* **1.** Being more than is required; constituting an excess. **2.** Unnecessarily verbose; tautological. [< L *redundans, -antis*, ppr. of *redundare* to overflow] — **re·dun/dant·ly** *adv.*

re·du·pli·cate (*v.* ri-dōō/plə-kāt, -dyōō/-; *adj.* ri-dōō/plə-kit, -dyōō/-) *v.* ·cat·ed, ·cat·ing *v.t.* **1.** To repeat again and again; redouble; iterate. **2.** *Ling.* To affix a reduplication to. — *v.i.* **3.** To undergo reduplication. — *adj.* **1.** Repeated again and again; duplicated. **2.** *Bot.* Valvate with the margins reflexed. [< L < *re-* again + *duplicare* to double] — **re·du/pli·ca/tive** *adj.*

re·du·pli·ca·tion (ri-dōō/plə-kā/shən, -dyōō/-) *n.* **1.** The act of reduplicating, or the state of being reduplicated; a redoubling. **2.** *Ling.* **a** The repetition of an initial element or elements in a word. **b** The doubling of all or part of a word, often with vowel or consonant change, as in *razzle-dazzle*.

red·wing (red/wing/) *n.* **1.** An American blackbird with bright scarlet patches on the wings of the male. Also **red/-winged/ blackbird.** **2.** An Old World red-winged thrush, with bright reddish orange on the sides and underwings.

red·wood (red/wŏŏd/) *n.* **1.** A sequoia. **2.** Its durable reddish wood. **3.** Any of various similar trees.

re·ech·o (ri-ek/ō) *v.t.* **1.** To echo back, as a sound. **2.** To echo again; repeat, as an opinion. — *v.i.* **3.** To echo again; reverberate. — *n.* That which is reechoed.

reed (rēd) *n.* **1.** The slender, frequently jointed stem of certain tall grasses growing in wet places, or the grasses themselves. **2.** A thin, elastic plate of reed, wood, or metal nearly closing an opening, as in a pipe, used in reed organs, oboes, clarinets, etc., to produce a musical tone. **3.** A musical pipe made of the hollow stem of a plant. **4.** *Archit.* A semicylindrical ornamental molding or bead. **5.** An arrow. **6.** The abomasum. — *v.t.* **1.** To fashion into or decorate with reeds. **2.** To thatch with reeds. [OE *hrēod*]

reed·ing (rē'ding) *n.* **1.** Beading or semicylindrical moldings collectively. **2.** Ornamentation by such moldings. **3.** A molding of this kind. **4.** The knurling on the edge of a coin, as distinguished from milling.

reed organ A keyboard musical instrument sounding by means of free reeds vibrated by air currents.

reed pipe An organ pipe that acts as a resonator for a tuned reed. Compare FLUE PIPE.

re·ed·u·cate (rē·ej'ŏō·kāt) *v.t.* **·cat·ed, ·cat·ing 1.** To educate again. **2.** To rehabilitate, as a criminal, by education.

reed·y (rē'dē) *adj.* **reed·i·er, reed·i·est 1.** Full of reeds. **2.** Like a reed. **3.** Having a thin, sharp tone, like a reed instrument. — **reed'i·ness** *n.*

reef¹ (rēf) *n.* **1.** A ridge of sand or rocks, or esp. of coral, at or near the surface of the water. **2.** A lode, vein, or ledge. Compare SHOAL¹. [< ON *rif*] — **reef'y** *adj.*

reef² (rēf) *Naut.* *n.* **1.** The part of a sail that is folded and secured or untied and let out in regulating its size on the mast. **2.** The tuck taken in a sail when reefed. — *v.t.* **1.** To reduce (a sail) by folding a part and fastening it to a yard or boom. **2.** To shorten or lower, as a topmast by taking part of it in. [< ON *rif* rib]

reef·er¹ (rē'fər) *n.* **1.** One who reefs. **2.** A close-fitting, often double-breasted coat or jacket of heavy material.

reef·er² (rē'fər) *n.* *U.S. Slang* A marihuana cigarette. [? from its resemblance to the reef of a sail]

reef knot A square knot.

reek (rēk) *v.i.* **1.** To give off smoke, vapor, etc. **2.** To give off a strong, offensive smell. **3.** To be pervaded with anything offensive. — *v.t.* **4.** To expose to smoke or its action. **5.** To give off or emit (fumes, an odor, etc.) [OE *rēocan* to smoke] — **reek'er** *n.* — **reek'y** *adv.*

reel¹ (rēl) *n.* **1.** A rotary device or frame for winding rope, film, or other flexible substance. **2.** Motion picture film wound on one reel, used as a unit of length. **3.** A wooden spool for wire, thread, etc. **4.** Material, as thread, paper, etc., wound on a reel. — *v.t.* **1.** To wind on a reel or bobbin, as a line. **2.** To pull by reeling a line: with *in*: to *reel* a fish in. **3.** To say, do, etc., easily and fluently: with *off*. [OE *hrēol*] — **reel'a·ble** *adj.* — **reel'er** *n.*

reel² (rēl) *v.i.* **1.** To stagger, sway, or lurch, as when giddy or drunk. **2.** To whirl round and round. **3.** To have a sensation of giddiness or whirling. **4.** To waver or fall back, as attacking troops. — *v.t.* **5.** To cause to reel. — *n.* A staggering motion; giddiness. [< REEL¹] — **reel'er** *n.*

reel³ (rēl) *n.* A lively dance, chiefly Scottish or Irish; also, the music for this dance. [? < REEL¹]

re·en·force (rē'en·fôrs', -fōrs'), **re·en·force·ment** (rē'en·fôrs'mənt, -fōrs'-), etc. See REINFORCE, etc.

re·en·try (rē·en'trē) *n.* *pl.* **·tries 1.** The act of entering again. **2.** In whist and bridge, an entry. **3.** *Aerospace* The return of a rocket or other object to the atmosphere of the earth after travel to very high altitudes.

re·e·val·u·ate (rē'i·val'yŏō·āt) *v.t.* **·at·ed, ·at·ing** To evaluate or consider anew. — **re·e·val'u·a·tion** *n.*

reeve¹ (rēv) *v.t.* **reeved** or **rove, reev·ing** *Naut.* **1.** To pass, as a rope or rod, through a hole, block, or aperture. **2.** To fasten in such manner. **3.** To pass a rope, etc., through (a block or pulley). [Origin uncertain]

reeve² (rēv) *n.* **1.** In Canada, the elected head of a rural municipal council. **2.** In medieval England: **a** A high administrative officer. **b** A bailiff; steward. [OE *gerēfa*]

reeve³ (rēv) *n.* The female of the ruff, a sandpiper.

re·fec·tion (ri·fek'shən) *n.* **1.** Refreshment with food and drink. **2.** A light meal. [< OF < L < *re-* again + *facere* to make]

re·fec·to·ry (ri·fek'tə·rē) *n.* *pl.* **·ries** A room or hall for eating, esp. in a religious house or college.

re·fer (ri·fûr') *v.* **·ferred, ·fer·ring** *v.t.* **1.** To direct or send for information, assistance, etc. **2.** To hand over or submit for consideration, settlement, etc. **3.** To assign or attribute to a source, cause, class, period, etc. — *v.i.* **4.** To make reference; allude. **5.** To turn, as for information, help, or authority. — **Syn.** See ATTRIBUTE. [< OF < L < *re-* back + *ferre* to carry] — **ref·er·a·ble** (ref'ər·ə·bəl), **re·fer'ra·ble** or **re·fer'ri·ble** *adj.* — **re·fer'ral** *n.* — **re·fer'rer** *n.*

ref·er·ee (ref'ə·rē') *n.* **1.** A person to whom something is referred, esp. for settlement or arbitration. **2.** In certain sports, as football, a supervisory official. — **Syn.** See JUDGE. — *v.t. & v.i.* **·reed, ·ree·ing** To judge as a referee.

ref·er·ence (ref'ər·əns, ref'rəns) *n.* **1.** The act of referring. **2.** An incidental allusion or direction of the attention: *reference* to a recent event. **3.** A note or other indication in a

book, referring to some other book or passage. Compare CROSS-REFERENCE. **4.** One who or that which is or may be referred to. **5.** The state of being referred or related: used in the phrases **with** (or **in**) **reference to. 6.** The person or persons to whom one seeking employment may refer for recommendation. — **ref'er·enc·er** *n.*

ref·er·en·dum (ref'ə·ren'dəm) *n.* *pl.* **·dums** or **·da** (-də) **1.** The submission of a proposed public measure or law that has been passed upon by a legislature or convention to a vote of the people for ratification or rejection. **2.** The vote in such a procedure. [< L, gerund of *referre* to refer]

ref·er·ent (ref'ər·ənt) *n.* The object, concept, etc., to which reference is made in a statement or its symbolic equivalent.

re·fill (*v.* rē·fil'; *n.* rē'fil') *v.t.* To fill again. — *n.* Any commodity packaged to fit and fill a container originally containing that commodity: a *refill* for a lipstick case.

re·fine (ri·fīn') *v.* **·fined, ·fin·ing** *v.t.* **1.** To make fine or pure; free from impurities or extraneous matter. **2.** To make polished or cultured. **3.** To improve or change by subtle or precise alterations. — *v.i.* **4.** To become fine or pure. **5.** To become more polished or cultured. **6.** To make fine distinctions. [< RE- + FINE¹, v.] — **re·fin'er** *n.*

re·fined (ri·fīnd') *adj.* **1.** Characterized by refinement; cultivated; polished. **2.** Free from impurity; purified. **3.** Exceedingly precise or exact; subtle.

re·fine·ment (ri·fīn'mənt) *n.* **1.** Fineness of thought, taste, language, etc.; freedom from coarseness or vulgarity; delicacy; culture. **2.** The act, effect, or process of refining. **3.** A nice distinction; subtlety. **4.** Fastidiousness.

— **Syn. 1.** *Refinement* implies not only the elimination of vulgarity and grossness but also the development of delicate perception and understanding. *Cultivation* is the self-discipline, study, and exercise that bring urbanity, learning, esthetic taste, etc. *Culture* primarily contrasts the enlightenment of the civilized man with that of a savage or a child; *breeding* suggests the training that manifests itself in good manners, tact, and consideration for others. — **Ant.** coarseness, grossness, vulgarity.

re·fin·er·y (ri·fī'nər·ē) *n.* *pl.* **·er·ies** A place where some crude material, as sugar or petroleum, is purified.

re·fit (rē·fit') *v.t. & v.i.* **·fit·ted, ·fit·ting** To make or be made fit or ready again, as by repairs, replacing equipment, etc. — *n.* The repair of damages or wear, esp. of a ship.

re·flect (ri·flekt') *v.t.* **1.** To turn or throw back, as waves of light, heat, or sound. **2.** To give back an image of; mirror. **3.** To cause as a result of one's actions, character, etc.; cast: He *reflects* credit on his teacher. **4.** To manifest as a result of influence, imitation, etc. — *v.i.* **5.** To send back rays, as of light or heat. **6.** To shine back. **7.** To give back an image; be mirrored. **8.** To think carefully; ponder. **9.** To bring blame, discredit, etc.: with *on* or *upon*. **10.** *Anat.* To fold back upon itself, as a membrane or tissue. [< OF < L < *re-* back + *flectere* to bend]

re·flec·tion (ri·flek'shən) *n.* **1.** The act of reflecting, or the state of being reflected. **2.** *Physics* The throwing off or back from a surface of impinging light, heat, sound, or any form of radiant energy. **3.** The result of reflecting; reflected rays or an image thrown by reflection. **4.** Meditation; careful consideration. **5.** An imputation of blame or censure. **6.** *Anat.* The folding of a part upon itself. Also **re·flex'ion.** — **re·flec'tion·al** or **re·flex'ion·al** *adj.*

— **Syn. 4.** rumination, reverie, thought. **5.** aspersion, animadversion.

re·flec·tive (ri·flek'tiv) *adj.* **1.** Given to reflection or thought; meditative. **2.** Of, pertaining to, or caused by reflection. **3.** Having the quality of throwing back light, heat, etc. — **re·flec'tive·ly** *adv.* — **re·flec'tive·ness** *n.* — **re'flec·tiv'i·ty** *n.*

re·flec·tor (ri·flek'tər) *n.* **1.** That which reflects. **2.** A polished surface for reflecting light, heat, sound, etc. **3.** A telescope that transmits an image from a reflecting surface to the eyepiece. **4.** *Physics* A substance placed around the core of a nuclear reactor for the purpose of maintaining the level of the chain reaction.

re·flex (*adj. & n.* rē'fleks; *v.* ri·fleks') *adj.* **1.** *Physiol.* Of, pertaining to, or produced by involuntary response to a stimulus. **2.** Turned, thrown, or directed backward or in the opposite direction. **3.** Bent back; reflexed. — *n.* **1.** *Physiol.* An involuntary movement or response to a stimulus, as in winking, sneezing, shivering, etc.: also **reflex action. 2.** Reflection, or an image produced by reflection, as from a mirror or like surface. **3.** Light reflected from an illuminated surface to a shady one. — *v.t.* To bend back; turn back or reflect. [See REFLECT.]

reflex angle *Geom.* An angle greater than 180 degrees.

reflex arc *Physiol.* The entire path of a nerve impulse from the receptors to the nerve center, and thence to the effectors.

re·flex·ive (ri·flek'siv) *adj.* **1.** *Gram.* **a** Of verbs, having an object that is identical with the subject, as "dresses" in "He dresses himself." **b** Of pronouns in the objective case, being identical with the subject, as "herself" in "She hurt herself." **2.** Of or pertaining to a reflex or reflection. — *n.* *Gram.* A reflexive verb or pronoun. — **re·flex'ive·ly** adv. — **re·flex'· ive·ness, re·flex·iv·i·ty** (rē'flek·siv'ə·tē) n.

ref·lu·ent (ref'lōō·ənt) adj. Flowing back; ebbing, as the tide. [< L < re- back + fluere to flow] — **ref'lu·ence** n.

re·flux (rē'fluks') n. A flowing back; ebb: the flux and reflux of fortune. [< L refluxus, pp. of refluere. See REFLUENT.]

re·for·est (rē·fôr'ist, -for'-) v.t. & v.i. To replant (an area) with trees. — **re·for·es·ta'tion** n.

re·form (ri·fôrm') v.t. 1. To make better by removing abuses, altering, etc. 2. To improve morally; persuade or educate to a better life. 3. To put an end to (an abuse, malpractice, etc.). — v.i. 4. To give up sin or error; become better. — n. 1. An act or result of reformation; change for the better, esp. in administration. 2. Improvement in one's personal life, esp. by abandonment of bad habits. [< OF < L < re- again + formare to form] — **re·form'a·tive** adj. — **re·form'er, re·form'ist** n.

re-form (rē'fôrm') v.t. & v.i. To form again. — **re'·for·ma'tion** n.

ref·or·ma·tion (ref'ər·mā'shən) n. The act of reforming, or the state of being reformed; esp., moral improvement.

Ref·or·ma·tion (ref'ər·mā'shən) n. The 16th-century religious revolution that aimed at reforming Catholicism and ended with the establishment of Protestantism.

re·for·ma·to·ry (ri·fôr'mə·tôr'ē, -tō'rē) n. pl. ·ries An institution for the reformation and instruction of juvenile offenders. Also **reform school**. — adj. Tending to reform.

re·formed (ri·fôrmd') adj. 1. Restored to a better state; corrected or amended. 2. Improved in conduct, habits, etc.

Reform Judaism The branch of Judaism that does not accept in entirety the Mosaic Laws, the Talmud, and rabbinical interpretations as binding in modern times.

re·fract (ri·frakt') v.t. 1. To deflect (a ray) by refraction. 2. Optics To determine the degree of refraction of (an eye or lens). [< L < refringere to turn aside]

re·frac·tion (ri·frak'shən) n. 1. Physics The change of direction of a ray, as of light or heat, in passage from one medium to another of different density. 2. Optics The refracting of light rays by the eye so as to form an image upon the retina. — **re·frac'tive** adj. — **re·frac'tive·ly** adv. — **re·frac'tive·ness, re·frac·tiv·i·ty** (rē'frak·tiv'ə·tē) n.

refractive index Optics The ratio of the velocity of a specific radiation in a vacuum to its velocity in a given medium.

re·frac·tor (ri·frak'tər) n. 1. That which refracts. 2. A refracting telescope. See under TELESCOPE.

LIGHT REFRACTION

re·frac·to·ry (ri·frak'tər·ē) adj. 1. Not amenable to control; unmanageable; obstinate. 2. Resisting heat or ordinary methods of reduction, as an ore. 3. Resisting treatment, as a disease. — n. pl. ·ries 1. One who or that which is refractory. 2. Any of various materials highly resistant to the action of great heat, as fire clay. [See REFRACT.] — **re·frac'to·ri·ly** adv. — **re·frac'to·ri·ness** n.

re·frain' (ri·frān') v.i. To keep oneself back; abstain from action. [< OF < L refrenare to curb] — **re·frain'er** n.

re·frain² (ri·frān') n. 1. A phrase or strain in a poem or song repeated at the end of each stanza. 2. Any saying repeated over and over. [< OF < L refringere to turn aside]

re·fran·gi·ble (ri·fran'jə·bəl) adj. Capable of being refracted, as light. [< RE- + L frangere to break + -IBLE] — **re·fran'gi·bil'i·ty, re·fran'gi·ble·ness** n.

re·fresh (ri·fresh') v.t. 1. To make fresh or vigorous again, as by food or rest; reinvigorate; revive. 2. To make fresh, clean, cool, etc. 3. To stimulate, as the memory. 4. To renew or replenish with or as with new supplies. — v.i. 5. To become fresh again; revive. 6. To take refreshment. [< OF < re- again + fres fresh]

re·fresh·er (ri·fresh'ər) adj. Reviewing material previously studied. — n. One who or that which refreshes.

re·fresh·ing (ri·fresh'ing) adj. 1. Serving to refresh. 2. Enjoyably novel or unusual. — **re·fresh'ing·ly** adv.

re·fresh·ment (ri·fresh'mənt) n. 1. The act of refreshing, or the state of being refreshed. 2. That which refreshes, as food or drink. 3. pl. Food, or food and drink.

re·frig·er·ant (ri·frij'ər·ənt) adj. 1. Cooling or freezing. 2. Allaying bodily heat or fever. — n. 1. Any medicine or material, as ice, that reduces abnormal heat of the body. 2. A substance used for obtaining and maintaining a low temperature, as frozen carbon dioxide or ammonia.

re·frig·er·ate (ri·frij'ə·rāt') v.t. ·at·ed, ·at·ing 1. To keep or make cold. 2. To freeze or chill (foodstuffs, etc.) for preservative purposes. [< L < re- thoroughly + frigerare to cool] — **re·frig'er·a'tion** n. — **re·frig'er·a·tive** adj. & n. — **re·frig'er·a·to·ry** (-tôr'ē, -tō'rē) adj.

re·frig·er·a·tor (ri·frij'ə·rā'tər) n. A box, cabinet, room,

railroad car, etc., equipped with a cooling apparatus for preserving perishable foods, etc.

reft (reft) Past tense and past participle of REAVE.

ref·uge (ref'yōōj) n. 1. Shelter or protection, as from danger or distress. 2. One who or that which shelters or protects. 3. A safe place; asylum. [< OF < L < re- back + fugere to flee]
— Syn. (noun) 3. sanctuary, retreat, haven.

ref·u·gee (ref'yōō·jē', ref'yōō·jē') n. One who flees from invasion, persecution, or political danger.

re·ful·gent (ri·ful'jənt) adj. Shining brilliantly; radiant. [< L < re- back + fulgere to shine] — **re·ful'gence, re·ful'·gen·cy** n. — **re·ful'gent·ly** adv.

re·fund' (v. ri·fund'; n. rē'fund) v.t. 1. To give or pay back (money, etc.). 2. To repay; reimburse. — v.i. 3. To make repayment. — n. A repayment; also, the amount repaid. [< OF < L < re- back + fundere to pour] — **re·fund'er** n.

re·fund² (rē·fund') v.t. To fund anew; replace (an old loan) by issuing new securities.

re·fur·bish (re·fûr'bish) v.t. To furbish again; renovate or freshen; polish up; brighten.

re·fus·al (ri·fyōō'zəl) n. 1. The act of refusing; declination. 2. The privilege of accepting or rejecting; option.

re·fuse' (ri·fyōōz') v. ·fused, ·fus·ing v.t. 1. To decline to do, permit, take, or yield. 2. Mil. To turn back (the wing of a line of troops), so that it stands at an angle with the main body. 3. To decline to jump over: said of a horse at a ditch, hedge, etc. — v.i. 4. To decline to do, permit, take, or yield something. [< OF < L refusus, pp. of refundere to refund]

re·fuse² (ref'yōōs) n. Anything worthless; rubbish. — adj. Rejected as worthless. [See REFUSE'.]

re·fute (ri·fyōōt') v.t. ·fut·ed, ·fut·ing 1. To prove the incorrectness or falsity of (a statement). 2. To prove (a person) to be in error; confute. [< L refutare to repulse] — **re·fut'·a·bil'i·ty** n. — **re·fut'a·ble** adj. — **re·fut'a·bly** adv. — **ref·u·ta·tion** (ref'yōō·tā'shən), **re·fut'al** n. — **re·fut'er** n.
— Syn. 1. Refute, disprove, rebut, and confute mean to show to be incorrect or fallacious. Refute emphasizes the fact of opposing a statement or argument; disprove emphasizes the result of such opposition. To rebut is to refute in formal debate, while to confute is to disprove, overthrow, or put to confusion; confute may include the use of ridicule, as well as of logical argument.

re·gain (ri·gān') v.t. 1. To get possession of again, as something lost; recover. 2. To reach again; get back to: He regained the street. [< MF regaigner] — **re·gain'er** n.

re·gal (rē'gəl) adj. 1. Of a king; royal. 2. Stately. [< OF < L regalis < rex, regis king] — **re'gal·ly** adv.

re·gale (ri·gāl') v. ·galed, ·gal·ing v.t. 1. To give unusual pleasure to; delight. 2. To entertain sumptuously; feast. — v.i. 3. To feast. [< F < ré- again + OF gale pleasure] — **re·gale'ment** n.

re·ga·li·a (ri·gā'lē·ə, -gāl'yə) n.pl. 1. The insignia and emblems of royalty, as the crown, scepter, etc. 2. The distinctive symbols, insignia, etc., of any society, order, or rank. 3. Fine clothes; fancy trappings. [See REGAL]

re·gard (ri·gärd') v.t. 1. To look at or observe closely or attentively. 2. To look on or think of in a certain or specified manner; consider: I regard him as a friend. 3. To take into account; consider. 4. To have relation or pertinence to; concern. — v.i. 5. To pay attention. 6. To gaze or look. — n. 1. Careful attention or notice; heed; consideration. 2. Esteem; respect. 3. Reference; relation: in regard to this matter. 4. A look or aspect. 5. Usu. pl. Good wishes; affection. [< OF < re- again + garder to guard, heed]

re·gard·ful (ri·gärd'fəl) adj. 1. Having or showing regard; heedful. 2. Respectful; deferential. — **re·gard'ful·ly** adv.

re·gard·ing (ri·gär'ding) prep. In reference to; concerning.

re·gard·less (ri·gärd'lis) adj. Having no regard or consideration; heedless; negligent: often with of. — adv. Informal In spite of everything. — **re·gard'less·ly** adv.

re·gat·ta (ri·gat'ə, -gä'tə) n. 1. A boat race, or a series of such races. 2. Originally, a gondola race. [< Ital.]

re·gen·cy (rē'jən·sē) n. pl. ·cies 1. The government or office of a regent or body of regents. 2. The period during which a regent governs. 3. A body of regents. 4. The district under the rule of a regent. Also **re'gent·ship**.

re·gen·er·ate (v. ri·jen'ə·rāt'; adj. ri·jen'ər·it) v. ·at·ed, ·at·ing v.t. 1. To cause complete moral and spiritual reformation or regeneration in. 2. To produce or form anew; recreate; reproduce. 3. To make use of (heat or other energy that might otherwise be wasted) by means of various devices. 4. Biol. To grow or form by regeneration. 5. Telecom. To return (part of the output of an amplifier) to the input in reinforcing phase to control gain, selectivity, etc. — v.i. 6. To form anew; be reproduced. 7. To become spiritually regenerate. 8. To effect regeneration. — adj. 1. Having new life; restored. 2. Spiritually renewed; regenerated.

[< L < *re-* again + *generare* to generate] **—re·gen'er·a·cy, re·gen'er·a'tion** *n.* **—re·gen·er·a·tive** (ri·jen'ə·rā'tiv, -ər·ə-tiv) *adj.* **—re·gen'er·a'tive·ly** *adv.* **—regen'er·a'tor** *n.*

re·gent(rē'jənt) *n.* **1.** One who rules in the name and place of a sovereign. **2.** A resident master who takes part in the government of a university or college. **3.** One of various educational officers, as of a state. **—** *adj.* **1.** Exercising authority in another's place. **2.** Governing; ruling. [< OF < L < *regere* to rule]

reg·i·cide (rej'ə·sīd) *n.* **1.** The killing of a king or sovereign. **2.** One who has killed a king or sovereign. [< L *rex, regis* king + -CIDE] **—reg'i·ci'dal** *adj.*

re·gime (ri·zhēm') *n.* **1.** System of government or administration. **2.** A social system. **3.** Regimen. Also **ré·gime** (rā·zhēm'). [< F < L < *regere* to rule, guide]

reg·i·men (rej'ə·mən) *n.* A systematized course of living, as to food, clothing, etc.: also *regime*. [< L *regere* to rule]

reg·i·ment (rej'ə·mənt) *n.* **1.** *Mil.* An administrative and tactical unit of infantry, artillery, etc., larger than a battalion and smaller than a division, usu. commanded by a colonel. **2.** Any large body of persons. **—** *v.t.* **1.** To form into a regiment or regiments; organize. **2.** To assign to a regiment. **3.** To form into well-defined units or groups; systematize. **4.** To make uniform. [< OF < LL < L *regere* to rule] **—reg'i·men'tal** *adj.* **—reg'i·men·ta'tion** *n.*

reg·i·men·tals (rej'ə·men'təlz) *n.pl.* **1.** A military uniform. **2.** The uniform worn by a regiment.

re·gion (rē'jən) *n.* **1.** An indefinite portion of territory or space, usu. of considerable extent. **2.** A particular area or place: the delta *region* of the Nile. **3.** General area; scope; province: in the *region* of literature. **4.** A portion of the body. **5.** A realm (def. 3). [< AF < L < *regere* to rule]

re·gion·al (rē'jən·əl) *adj.* **1.** Of or pertaining to a particular region; sectional; local: *regional* planning. **2.** Of or pertaining to an entire region or section. **—re'gion·al·ly** *adv.*

reg·is·ter (rej'is·tər) *n.* **1.** A formal or official record or account, as of names or transactions; also, a book containing such a record. **2.** An individual entry in a register. **3.** Any of various devices for counting or recording: a cash *register*. **4.** An official keeper of records; registrar. **5.** *Music* **a** A portion of the compass of a voice or instrument having tones of a relatively homogeneous timbre. **b** A full set of organ pipes or harpsichord strings controlled by a single stop. **6.** A device by which heated or cooled air is admitted to a room. **7.** *Printing* **a** Exact correspondence of the lines and margins on the opposite sides of a printed sheet. **b** Correct relation of the colors in color printing. **8.** The act of recording or registering; registry. **—** *v.t.* **1.** To enter in or as in a register; record officially or exactly. **2.** To indicate, as on a scale. **3.** To express; show: His face *registered* shock. **4.** To cause (mail) to be recorded, on payment of a fee, when deposited with the postal system, so as to insure delivery. **5.** *Printing* To effect the exact correspondence of; put in register. **—** *v.i.* **6.** To enter one's name in a register. **7.** To cause one's name to be included on a list of eligible voters by fulfilling certain requirements. **8.** *Informal* To have effect; make an impression. **9.** *Printing* To be in register. [< OF < Med.L < LL < L < *re-* back + *gerere* to carry] **—reg·is·tra·ble** (rej'is·trə·bəl) *adj.* **—reg'is·trant** *n.*

reg·is·tered (rej'is·tərd) *adj.* **1.** Recorded, as a birth, a voter, an animal's pedigree, etc. **2.** Having a required or official certificate, as a nurse.

registered nurse A graduate nurse licensed to practice by the appropriate State authority and entitled to add R.N. after her name.

reg·is·trar (rej'is·trär, rej'is·trär') *n.* An authorized keeper of a register or of records; esp., a college or university officer who records the enrollment of students, their grades, etc.

reg·is·tra·tion (rej'is·trā'shən) *n.* **1.** The act of entering in a registry; also, such an entry. **2.** The registering of voters; also, the number of voters registered. **3.** Enrollment in a school, college, or university. **4.** *Music* The combination of stops used in playing a composition on the organ.

reg·is·try (rej'is·trē) *n. pl.* **·tries 1.** The act of registering; registration. **2.** A register, or the place where it is kept.

reg·nant (reg'nənt) *adj.* **1.** Reigning in one's own right. **2.** Dominant. [< *regnum* reign] **—reg'nan·cy** *n.*

re·gorge (ri·gôrj') *v.t.* **gorged, ·gorg·ing** To vomit up; disgorge. [< F < *re-* again + *gorger* to gorge]

re·gress (*n.* rē'gres; *v.* ri·gres') *n.* **1.** Passage back; return. **2.** The power or right of passing back. **3.** Withdrawal; retrogression. **—** *v.i.* To go back; move backward; return. [< L < *re-* back + *gradi* to walk] **—re·gres'sor** *n.*

re·gres·sion (ri·gresh'ən) *n.* **1.** The act of regressing. **2.** *Psychoanal.* A retreat of the libido to earlier and less mature forms of behavior. **3.** *Stat.* The return to a mean or average value. **4.** *Med.* The subsidence of a disease.

re·gres·sive (ri·gres'iv) *adj.* **1.** Tending to regress. **2.** Of or marked by regression. **3.** Denoting or pertaining to a tax or taxes in which the tax rate decreases as the amount taxed increases. **—re·gres'sive·ly** *adv.*

re·gret (ri·gret') *v.t.* **gret·ted, ·gret·ting 1.** To look back upon with a feeling of distress or loss. **2.** To feel sorrow or grief concerning. **—** *n.* **1.** Distress of mind over loss or circumstances beyond one's control. **2.** Remorseful sorrow; compunction. **3.** *pl.* A polite refusal in response to an invitation. [< OF *regreter* < Gmc.] **—re·gret'ta·ble** *adj.* **—re·gret'ta·bly** *adv.* **—re·gret'ter** *n.*

re·gret·ful (ri·gret'fəl) *adj.* Feeling, expressive of, or full of regret. **—re·gret'ful·ly** *adv.* **—re·gret'ful·ness** *n.*

reg·u·lar (reg'yə·lər) *adj.* **1.** Made according to rule; symmetrical; normal. **2.** Acting according to rule; methodical; orderly: *regular* habits. **3.** Constituted, appointed, or conducted in the proper manner; duly authorized: a *regular* meeting. **4.** *Gram.* Undergoing the inflection that is normal or most common to the class of words to which it belongs: said esp. of weak verbs. **5.** *Bot.* Having all the parts or organs of the same kind uniform in structure or shape and size: said mainly of flowers. **6.** *Eccl.* Bound by a religious rule. **7.** *Mil.* Pertaining or belonging to the permanent military services. **8.** In politics, adhering loyally to a party organization or platform. **9.** *Geom.* Having equal sides and angles. **10.** *Math.* Controlled or governed by one law or operation throughout: a *regular* equation. **11.** *Informal* Thorough; unmitigated; absolute. **12.** *U.S.* Designating the component of the armed services that consists of persons in continuous service on active duty in both peace and war: the *regular* Army. **—** *n.* **1.** A regular soldier. **2.** *Informal* One regularly employed or engaged; also, a habitual customer. **3.** *Eccl.* A member of a religious or monastic order. **4.** A person loyal to a certain political party. [< OF < L < *regula* rule] **—reg'u·lar·ly** *adv.* **—reg'u·lar·ness** *n.*

reg·u·lar·i·ty (reg'yə·lar'ə·tē) *n. pl.* **·ties** The state, quality, or character of being regular; also, an instance of this.

reg·u·lar·ize (reg'yə·lə·rīz') *v.t.* **·ized, ·iz·ing** To make regular. Also *Brit.* **reg'u·lar·ise'.** **—reg'u·lar·i·za'tion** *n.*

reg·u·late (reg'yə·lāt) *v.t.* **·lat·ed, ·lat·ing 1.** To direct or control according to certain rules, principles, etc. **2.** To adjust according to a standard, degree, etc.: to *regulate* currency. **3.** To adjust to accurate operation. **4.** To put in order. [< LL < *regulare* to rule] **—reg'u·la·tive, reg'u·la·to'ry** *adj.*

reg·u·la·tion (reg'yə·lā'shən) *n.* **1.** The act of regulating, or the state of being regulated. **2.** A rule of conduct.

reg·u·la·tor (reg'yə·lā'tər) *n.* **1.** One who or that which regulates. **2.** A device for regulating the rate of a watch. **3.** *Mech.* A contrivance for regulating or equalizing motion or flow. **—reg'u·la'tor·ship** *n.*

Reg·u·lus (reg'yə·ləs) A white star, one of the 20 brightest, 1.34 magnitude; Alpha in the constellation Leo. [< L]

re·gur·gi·tate (ri·gûr'jə·tāt) *v.* **·tat·ed, ·tat·ing** *v.i.* **1.** To rush, pour, or surge back. **—** *v.t.* **2.** To cause to surge back, as partially digested food; vomit. [< Med.L < *re-* back + LL *gurgitare* to swallow, engulf] **—re·gur'gi·tant** *adj.* **—re·gur'gi·ta'tion** *n.*

re·ha·bil·i·tate (rē'hə·bil'ə·tāt) *v.t.* **·tat·ed, ·tat·ing 1.** To restore to a former state, capacity, privilege, rank, etc.; reinstate. **2.** To restore to a state of health, useful activity, etc., through training, therapy, guidance. [< Med.L < *re-* back + HABILITATE] **—re·ha·bil'i·ta'tion** *n.*

re·hash (*v.* rē·hash'; *n.* rē'hash') *v.t.* To work into a new form; go over again. **—** *n.* Something hashed over, or made or served up from something used before.

re·hear·ing (rē·hir'ing) *n.* A new hearing, as in court.

re·hears·al (ri·hûr'səl) *n.* **1.** A practice session or performance of a play, etc. **2.** The act of practicing or drilling for public performance. **3.** The act of telling over again.

re·hearse (ri·hûrs') *v.* **·hearsed, ·hears·ing** *v.t.* **1.** To perform privately in preparation for public performance, as a play or song. **2.** To instruct by rehearsal. **3.** To say over again; repeat aloud; recite. **4.** To give an account of; relate. **—** *v.i.* **5.** To rehearse a play, song, dance, etc. [< OF < *re-* again + *hercier* to harrow] **—re·hears'er** *n.*

Reich (rīkh) *n.* Germany or its government. **— First Reich** The Holy Roman Empire from its establishment in the ninth century to its collapse in 1806. **— Second Reich** Either of two German governments in the period 1871–1933. **— Third Reich** The Nazi state under Adolf Hitler, 1933–45. [< G, realm]

reichs·mark (rīkhs'märk') *n.* A former standard monetary unit of Germany, worth about 24 U.S. cents.

Reichs·tag (rīkhs'täkh') *n.* The former legislative assembly of Germany. [< G]

reign (rān) *n.* **1.** The possession or exercise of supreme power, esp. royal power; sovereignty. **2.** The time or duration of a sovereign's rule. **—** *v.i.* **1.** To hold and exercise sovereign power. **2.** To hold sway; prevail: Winter *reigns*. [< F < L *regnum* rule]

Reign of Terror The period of the French Revolution from May, 1793, to August, 1794, during which thousands were guillotined, including Louis XVI and Marie Antoinette.

re·im·burse (rē'im·bûrs') *v.t.* **·bursed, ·burs·ing 1.** To pay back (a person) an equivalent for what has been spent or lost; recompense; indemnify. **2.** To pay back; refund. [< RE- + obs. *imburse*] — **re·im·burs/a·ble** *adj.* — **re/im·burse/ment** *n.* — **re/im·burs/er** *n.*

re·im·port (*v.* rē/im·pôrt/, -pōrt/, rē·im/pôrt, -pōrt; *n.* rē·im/pôrt, -pōrt) *v.t.* To import (goods, etc., previously exported) again. — *n.* **1.** The act of importing again. **2.** That which is reimported. — **re/im·por·ta/tion** *n.*

rein (rān) *n.* **1.** *Usu. pl.* A strap attached to the bit to control a horse or other draft animal. **2.** Any means of restraint or control; a check. — *v.t.* **1.** To guide, check, or halt with or as with reins. **2.** To furnish with reins. — *v.i.* **3.** To check or halt a horse by means of reins: with *in* or *up*. [< AF < L *retinere* to retain]

re·in·car·nate (rē/in·kär/nāt) *v.t.* **·nat·ed, ·nat·ing** To cause to undergo reincarnation.

re·in·car·na·tion (rē/in·kär·nā/shən) *n.* **1.** A rebirth of the soul in successive bodies; also, the belief in such rebirth. **2.** In Vedic religions, the becoming of an avatar again.

rein·deer (rān/dir/) *n.* *pl.* **·deer** A deer of northern regions, having branched antlers in both sexes, long domesticated for its milk, hide, and flesh, and used as a pack animal. [< ON < *hreinn* reindeer + *dýr* deer]

re·in·force (rē/in·fôrs/, -fōrs/) *v.t.* **·forced, ·forc·ing 1.** To give new force or strength to. **2.** *Mil.* To strengthen with additional personnel or equipment. **3.** To add some strengthening part or material to. **4.** *Psychol.* To strengthen (a response) by the addition of another stimulus, as a reward. Also spelled *reenforce.* [< RE- + *inforce*, var. of ENFORCE]

reinforced concrete Concrete containing metal bars, rods, or netting disposed through the mass to increase its tensile strength and durability: also called *ferro-concrete.*

re·in·force·ment (rē/in·fôrs/mənt, -fōrs/-) *n.* **1.** The act of reinforcing. **2.** *Often pl. Mil.* A fresh body of troops or additional vessels. Also spelled *reenforcement.*

re·in·state (rē/in·stāt/) *v.t.* **·stat·ed, ·stat·ing** To restore to a former state, position, etc. — **re/in·state/ment** *n.*

re·in·sure (rē/in·shōōr/) *v.t.* **·sured, ·sur·ing 1.** To protect (the risk on a policy already issued) by obtaining insurance from a second insurer: said of a first insurer. **2.** To insure anew. — **re/in·sur/ance** *n.* — **re/in·sur/er** *n.*

re·is·sue (rē·ish/ōō) *n.* **1.** A second or subsequent issue, as of a publication changed in form or price. **2.** A second printing of postage stamps from the same plates. — *v.t.* **·sued, ·su·ing** To issue again.

re·it·er·ate (rē·it/ə·rāt) *v.t.* **·at·ed, ·at·ing** To say or do again and again. [< L *re-* again + ITERATE] — **re·it/er·a/tion** *n.* — **re·it/er·a/tive** *adj.* — **re·it/er·a/tive·ly** *adv.*

re·ject (*v.* ri·jekt/; *n.* rē/jekt) *v.t.* **1.** To refuse to accept, recognize, believe, etc. **2.** To refuse to grant; deny, as a petition. **3.** To refuse (a person) recognition, acceptance, etc. **4.** To expel, as from the mouth; vomit. **5.** To cast away as worthless; discard. — *n.* One who or that which has been rejected. [< L *re-* back + *jacere* to throw] — **re·ject/er** or **re·jec/tor** *n.* — **re·jec/tion** *n.*

re·joice (ri·jois/) *v.* **·joiced, ·joic·ing 1.** To feel joyful; be glad. — *v.t.* **2.** To fill with joy; gladden. [< OF < *re-* again + *esjoir* to be joyous] — **re·joic/er** *n.*

re·joic·ing (ri·joi/sing) *adj.* Pertaining to or characterized by joyfulness. — *n.* The feeling or expression of joy.

re·join[1] (ri·join/) *v.t.* **1.** To say in reply; answer. — *v.i.* **2.** To answer; respond. [< F < *re-* again + *joindre* to join]

re·join[2] (rē/join/) *v.t.* **1.** To come again into company with. **2.** To join together again; reunite. — *v.i.* **3.** To come together again. [< RE- + JOIN]

re·join·der (ri·join/dər) *n.* **1.** An answer to a reply; also, any reply or retort. **2.** *Law* The answer filed by a defendant to a plaintiff's replication.

re·ju·ve·nate (ri·jōō/və·nāt) *v.t.* **·nat·ed, ·nat·ing** To give new vigor or youthfulness to. Also **re·ju/ve·nize.** [< RE- + L *juvenis* young + -ATE[1]] — **re·ju/ve·na/tion** *n.*

re·lapse (ri·laps/; *for n., also* rē/laps) *v.i.* **lapsed, ·laps·ing 1.** To lapse back, as into a disease. **2.** To return to bad habits or ways; backslide. — *n.* The act or condition of relapsing. [< L < *re-* back + *labi* to slide] — **re·laps/er** *n.*

re·late (ri·lāt/) *v.* **·lat·ed, ·lat·ing** *v.t.* **1.** To tell the events or the particulars of; narrate. **2.** To bring into connection or relation. — *v.i.* **3.** To have relation: with *to.* **4.** To have reference: with *to.* [< F *relater*] — **re·lat/er, re·la/tor** *n.*
— **Syn. 1.** report, recount, recite, rehearse, state. **2.** connect, link, join, associate. **3.** pertain, apply.

re·lat·ed (ri·lā/tid) *adj.* **1.** Standing in relation; connected. **2.** Connected by blood or marriage; of common ancestry; akin. **3.** Narrated; told. — **re·lat/ed·ness** *n.*

re·la·tion (ri·lā/shən) *n.* **1.** The fact or condition of being related or connected in some way. **2.** Connection by blood or marriage; kinship. **3.** A person connected by blood or marriage; kinsman. **4.** Reference; regard; allusion: in *rela-*

tion to that matter. **5.** The position of one person with respect to another: the *relation* of ruler to subject. **6.** *pl.* Conditions or connections that bring an individual in touch with his fellows; also, any conditions or connections by which one country may come into contact with another politically and commercially. **7.** The act of narrating; also, that which is narrated. [< F < L. See REFER.] — **re·la/tion·al** *adj.*

re·la·tion·ship (ri·lā/shən·ship) *n.* The state of being related; connection.
— **Syn.** *Relationship, kinship, consanguinity,* and *affinity* are compared as they apply to persons of the same descent or family. *Relationship* is the most general term, embracing all the others and also the connection between things. *Kinship* is *relationship* by blood or marriage, and suggests mutual regard and affection. *Consanguinity* is *relationship* by blood only, and *affinity, relationship* by marriage only.

rel·a·tive (rel/ə·tiv) *adj.* **1.** Having connection; pertinent: an inquiry *relative* to one's health. **2.** Resulting from or depending upon relation; comparative: a *relative* truth. **3.** Intelligible only in relation to each other: the *relative* terms "father" and "son." **4.** Referring to, relating to, or qualifying an antecedent term: a *relative* pronoun. — *n.* **1.** One who is related; a kinsman. **2.** A relative word or term, esp. a relative pronoun. [< OF < Med.L < L *relatus*] — **rel/a·tive·ly** *adv.* — **rel/a·tive·ness** *n.*

relative clause *Gram.* An adjective clause.

relative pronoun *Gram.* A pronoun that relates to an antecedent and introduces a qualifying clause, as *who* in *We found a boatman who ferried us.*

rel·a·tiv·i·ty (rel/ə·tiv/ə·tē) *n.* **1.** The quality or condition of being relative. **2.** *Philos.* Existence only as an object of, or in relation to, a thinking mind. **3.** A condition of dependence or of close relation, as of the solar system on the sun. **4.** *Physics* The principle of the interdependence of matter, energy, space, and time, as mathematically formulated by Albert Einstein. The **special theory of relativity** states that the velocity of light is the maximum velocity possible in the universe, that it is constant and independent of the motion of its source, and that energy and mass are interconvertible in accordance with the equation *energy* = *mass* $\times$ *the square of the speed of light* or $E = mc^2$. The **general theory of relativity** extends these principles to the law of gravitation and the motions of the heavenly bodies.

re·lax (ri·laks/) *v.t.* **1.** To make lax or loose; make less tight or firm. **2.** To make less stringent or severe, as discipline. **3.** To abate; slacken, as efforts. **4.** To relieve from strain or effort. — *v.i.* **5.** To become lax or loose; loosen. **6.** To become less stringent or severe. **7.** To rest; repose. **8.** To become less formal; unbend. [< L < *re-* again + *laxare* to loosen] — **re·lax/a·ble** *adj.* — **re/lax·a/tion** *n.* — **re·lax/er** *n.*

re·lay (rē/lā, ri·lā/) *n.* **1.** A fresh set, as of men, horses, or dogs, to replace or relieve a tired set. **2.** A supply of anything kept in store for anticipated use or need. **3.** A relay race, or one of its laps or legs. **4.** *Electr.* A device that utilizes variations in the condition of a current in a circuit to effect the operation of similar devices in the same or another circuit. — *v.t.* **1.** To send onward by or as by relays. **2.** To provide with relays. **3.** *Electr.* To operate or retransmit by means of a relay. [< MF < L *relaxare* to loosen again]

re·lay (rē·lā/) *v.t.* **·laid, ·lay·ing** To lay again.

relay race A race between teams each member of which races a set part of the course and is relieved by a teammate.

re·lease (ri·lēs/) *v.t.* **·leased, ·leas·ing 1.** To set free; liberate. **2.** To deliver from worry, pain, obligation, etc. **3.** To free from something that holds, binds, etc. **4.** To permit the circulation, sale, performance, etc., of, as a motion picture, phonograph record, or news item. — *n.* **1.** The act of releasing or the state of being released. **2.** A discharge from responsibility or penalty, as from a debt. **3.** *Law* An instrument of conveyance by which one surrenders and relinquishes all claim to something; quitclaim. **4.** Anything formally released to the public, as news, a motion picture, etc. **5.** *Mech.* Any catch or device to hold and release a mechanism, weights, etc. [< OF < L *relaxare* to relax] — **re·leas/er** *n.*

re·lease (rē/lēs/) *v.t.* **·leased, ·leas·ing** To lease again.

released time *U.S.* A period during which school children are released from classes to receive religious instruction.

rel·e·gate (rel/ə·gāt) *v.t.* **·gat·ed, ·gat·ing 1.** To send off or consign, as to an obscure position or place. **2.** To assign, as to a particular class or sphere. **3.** To refer (a matter) to someone for decision **4.** To banish; exile. [< L < *re-* back + *legare* to send] — **rel/e·ga/tion** *n.*

re·lent (ri·lent/) *v.i.* To soften in temper; become more gentle or compassionate. [< L < *re-* again + *lentus* soft]

re·lent·less (ri·lent/lis) *adj.* **1.** Unremitting; continuous. **2.** Indifferent to the pain of others; pitiless. — **re·lent/less·ly** *adv.* — **re·lent/less·ness** *n.*

rel·e·vant (rel′ə·vənt) *adj.* Fitting or suiting given requirements; pertinent; applicable: usu. with *to*. [< Med.L ppr. of *relevare* to bear upon] — **rel′e·vance, rel′e·van·cy** *n.* — **rel′e·vant·ly** *adv.*

re·li·a·ble (ri·lī′ə·bəl) *adj.* That may be relied on; worthy of confidence; trustworthy. — **re·li′a·bil′i·ty, re·li′a·ble·ness** *n.* — **re·li′a·bly** *adv.*

re·li·ance (ri·lī′əns) *n.* 1. The act of relying, or the condition of being reliant. 2. Something relied upon.

re·li·ant (ri·lī′ənt) *adj.* Manifesting reliance, esp. upon oneself. — **re·li′ant·ly** *adv.*

rel·ic (rel′ik) *n.* 1. Some remaining portion or fragment of that which has vanished or been destroyed. 2. A keepsake or memento. 3. The body or part of the body of a saint, or any sacred memento. 4. Any outworn custom, institution, etc. [< OF < L *reliquiae* remains, leavings.]

re·lief (ri·lēf′) *n.* 1. The act of relieving, or the state of being relieved. 2. That which relieves. 3. Charitable aid, as food or money. 4. The release, as of a sentinel or guard, from his post or duty, and the substitution of some other person or persons; also, the person or persons so substituted. 5. In architecture and sculpture, the projection of a figure, ornament, etc., from a surface: also, any such figure. 6. In painting, the apparent projection of forms and masses. 7. *Geog.* **a** The elevations and unevenness of land surface. **b** The parts of a map that portray the configuration of the district represented; contour lines. [See RELIEVE.]

re·lieve (ri·lēv′) *v.t.* **·lieved, ·liev·ing** 1. To free wholly or partly from pain, embarrassment, etc. 2. To lessen or alleviate, as pain or anxiety. 3. To give aid or assistance to. 4. To free from obligation, injustice, etc. 5. To release from duty, as a sentinel, by providing or serving as a substitute. 6. To make less monotonous, harsh, or unpleasant; vary. 7. To bring into relief or prominence. 8. To rid (oneself) of urine or excrement. [< OF < L < *re-* again + *levare* to lift, raise] — **re·liev′a·ble** *adj.* — **re·liev′er** *n.*

re·lig·ion (ri·lij′ən) *n.* 1. The beliefs, attitudes, emotions, behavior, etc., constituting man's relationship with the powers and principles of the universe, esp. with a deity or deities. 2. An object of conscientious devotion or scrupulous care: His work is a *religion* to him. [< OF < L < *re-* back + *ligare* to bind]

re·lig·ious (ri·lij′əs) *adj.* 1. Feeling and manifesting religion; devout; pious 2. Of or pertaining to religion: a *religious* teacher. 3. Strict in performance; conscientious: a *religious* loyalty. 4. Belonging to the monastic life. — *n. pl.* **·ious** A person devoted to a life of piety; a monk or nun. [< OF < Med.L *religiosus*] — **re·lig′ious·ly** *adv.* — **re·lig′ious·ness** *n.*

re·lin·quish (ri·ling′kwish) *v.t.* 1. To give up; abandon. 2. To renounce: to *relinquish* a claim. 3. To let go (a hold, etc.). [< OF < L < *re-* back, from + *linquere* to leave] — **re·lin′quish·er** *n.* — **re·lin′quish·ment** *n.*

rel·i·quar·y (rel′ə·kwer′ē) *n. pl.* **·quar·ies** A repository for relics, as a casket, coffer, or shrine. [< F < L < *re-* back, from + *linquere* to leave]

rel·ish (rel′ish) *n.* 1. Appetite; appreciation; liking. 2. The flavor, esp. when agreeable, in food and drink. 3. The quality in anything that lends spice or zest: Danger gives *relish* to adventure. 4. Something taken with food to lend it flavor, as chopped pickles and spices. 5. A small but important characteristic; flavoring. — *v.t.* 1. To like the savor of; enjoy. 2. To give pleasant flavor to. — *v.i.* 3. To have an agreeable flavor; afford gratification. [ME < OF *relaissier* to leave behind] — **rel′ish·a·ble** *adj.*
— **Syn.** (noun) 1. gusto, zest.

re·luc·tance (ri·luk′təns) *n.* 1. The state of being reluctant. 2. *Electr.* Capacity for opposing magnetic induction. Also **re·luc′tan·cy.**
— **Syn.** 1. disinclination, unwillingness.

re·luc·tant (ri·luk′tənt) *adj.* 1. Marked by unwillingness or rendered unwillingly. 2. Disinclined to yield to some requirement. [< L < *re-* back + *luctari* to fight] — **re·luc′tant·ly** *adv.*
— **Syn.** 1. averse, hesitant, indisposed, loath.

rel·uc·tiv·i·ty (rel′ək·tiv′ə·tē) *n. pl.* **·ties** *Electr.* The specific electrical resistance to magnetization, of a given substance per unit of length or cross section.

re·ly (ri·lī′) *v.i.* **·lied, ·ly·ing** To place trust or confidence: with *on* or *upon*. [< OF < L < *re-* again + *ligare* to bind]

rem (rem) *n.* *Physics* The quantity of absorbed ionizing radiation that has the same biological effect as one roentgen of X-ray or gamma ray radiation. [< R(OENTGEN) + E(QUIVA-LENT) + M(AN)]

REM (rem) *n.* Rapid eye movement.

re·main (ri·mān′) *v.i.* 1. To stay or be left behind after the removal, departure, or destruction of other persons or things. 2. To continue in one place, condition, or character: He *remained* in office. 3. To be left as something to be done, dealt with, etc.: It *remains* to be proved. 4. To endure or last; abide. [< OF < L < *re-* back + *manere* to stay]

re·main·der (ri·mān′dər) *n.* 1. That which remains. 2. *Math.* The quantity left after subtraction or division. 3. A book disposed of by a publisher at a reduced price. — *adj.* Left over. — *v.t.* To sell (books) as remainders.

re·mains (ri·mānz′) *n.pl.* 1. That which is left after a part has been removed or destroyed. 2. The body of a deceased person. 3. Writings of an author published after his death. 4. Survivals of the past, as fossils, etc.

re·mand (ri·mand′, -mänd′) *v.t.* 1. To order or send back. 2. *Law* To recommit to custody, as an accused person after a preliminary examination. — *n.* 1. A remanding, or being remanded. 2. A remanded person. [< OF < LL < L *re-* back + *mandare* to order] — **re·mand′ment** *n.*

re·mark (ri·märk′) *n.* 1. An oral or written comment or saying; a casual observation. 2. The act of observing or noticing; observation; notice. — *v.t.* 1. To say or write by way of comment. 2. To take particular notice of. — *v.i.* 3. To make remarks: with *on* or *upon*. [< F < *re-* again + *marquer* to mark] — **re·mark′er** *n.*

re·mark·a·ble (ri·mär′kə·bəl) *adj.* 1. Worthy of notice. 2. Extraordinary; unusual; conspicuous; distinguished. — **re·mark′a·ble·ness** *n.* — **re·mark′a·bly** *adv.*

re·me·di·a·ble (ri·mē′dē·ə·bəl) *adj.* Capable of being cured or remedied. [< MF < L *remediabilis*] — **re·me′di·a·ble·ness** *n.* — **re·me′di·a·bly** *adv.*

re·me·di·al (ri·mē′dē·əl) *adj.* Of the nature of or adapted to be used as a remedy: *remedial* measures. [< L < *remediare* to remedy] — **re·me′di·al·ly** *adv.*

rem·e·dy (rem′ə·dē) *n. pl.* **·dies** 1. That which cures or affords relief to bodily disease or ailment; a medicine; also, remedial treatment. 2. A means of counteracting or removing an error, evil, etc. 3. *Law* A legal mode for enforcing a right or redressing or preventing a wrong. — *v.t.* **·died, ·dy·ing** 1. To cure or heal, as by medicinal treatment. 2. To make right; correct. 3. To overcome or remove (an evil, defect, etc.). [< AF < OF < L < *re-* again + *mederi* to heal]

re·mem·ber (ri·mem′bər) *v.t.* 1. To bring back or recall again to the mind or memory. 2. To keep in mind carefully, as for a purpose. 3. To bear in mind as worthy of a reward, gift, etc.: She *remembered* me in her will. 4. To reward; tip. — *v.i.* 5. To have or use one's memory. — **to remember (one)** to To inform a person of the regard of: *Remember* me *to* your wife. [< OF < LL < L *re-* again + *memorare* to bring to mind] — **re·mem′ber·er** *n.*

re·mem·brance (ri·mem′brəns) *n.* 1. The act or power of remembering, or the state of being remembered. 2. The period within which one can remember. 3. That which is remembered. 4. *Often pl.* A memento; keepsake. 5. Mindful regard. [< OF]

re·mind (ri·mīnd′) *v.t.* To bring to (someone's) mind; cause to remember. — **re·mind′er** *n.* — **re·mind′ful** *adj.*

rem·i·nisce (rem′ə·nis′) *v.i.* **·nisced, ·nisc·ing** *Chiefly U.S.* To recall incidents or events of the past; indulge in reminiscences. [Back formation < REMINISCENCE]

rem·i·nis·cence (rem′ə·nis′əns) *n.* 1. The recalling to mind of past incidents and events. 2. The narration of past experiences. 3. A feature, etc., serving as a reminder of something else. [< MF or LL < L < *re-* again + *memini* to remember] — **rem′i·nis′cent** *adj.* — **rem′i·nis′cent·ly** *adv.*

re·miss (ri·mis′) *adj.* Slack or careless in matters requiring attention; dilatory; negligent. [< L < *re-* back + *mittere* to send] — **re·miss′ness** *n.*

re·mis·si·ble (ri·mis′ə·bəl) *adj.* Capable of being remitted or pardoned, as sins. [< F *rémissible*] — **re·mis′si·bil′i·ty** *n.*

re·mis·sion (ri·mish′ən) *n.* 1. The act of remitting, or the state of being remitted. 2. Discharge from penalty; pardon; deliverance, as from a debt or obligation. 3. *Med.* Temporary abatement of a disease or pain. Also **re·mit·tal** (ri·mit′l). [See REMIT.]

re·mit (ri·mit′) *v.* **·mit·ted, ·mit·ting** *v.t.* 1. To send, as money in payment for goods; transmit. 2. To refrain from exacting or inflicting, as a penalty. 3. To pardon; forgive, as a sin or crime. 4. To abate; relax, as vigilance. 5. To refer or submit for judgment, settlement, etc., as to one in authority. 6. *Law* To refer (a legal proceeding) to a lower court for further consideration. 7. *Rare* To send back, as to prison. — *v.i.* 8. To send money, as in payment. 9. To diminish; abate. [< L < *re-* back + *mittere* to send] — **re·mit′ta·ble** *adj.* — **re·mit′ter** or **re·mit′tor** *n.*

re·mit·tance (ri·mit′əns) *n.* The act of sending money or credit; also, the money or credit so sent.

re·mit·tent (ri·mit′ənt) *adj.* Having temporary diminutions of energy or action, as a fever. — *n.* A remittent fever. — **re·mit′tence, re·mit′ten·cy** *n.* — **re·mit′tent·ly** *adv.*

rem·nant (rem′nənt) *n.* 1. That which remains of anything. 2. The piece of cloth, etc., left over after the last cutting. 3. Any small piece or quantity. — *adj.* Remaining. [< OF < L < *re-* back + *manere* to stay, remain]

re·mod·el (rē·mod′l) *v.t.* **·eled** or **·elled, ·el·ing** or **·el·ling** 1. To model again. 2. To make over or anew.

re·mon·e·tize (rī-mon'ə-tīz) *v.t.* **·tized, ·tiz·ing** To reinstate (esp. silver) as lawful money. — **re·mon'e·ti·za'tion** *n.*

re·mon·strance (ri-mon'strəns) *n.* **1.** The act of remonstrating; protest; expostulation. **2.** Expostulatory counsel.

re·mon·strant (ri-mon'strənt) *adj.* Having the character of a remonstrance; expostulatory. — *n.* One who presents or signs a remonstrance.

re·mon·strate (ri-mon'strāt) *v.* **·strat·ed, ·strat·ing** *v.t.* **1.** To say or plead in protest. — *v.i.* **2.** To urge strong reasons against any course or action; protest; object. [< Med.L < L < *re-* again + *monstrare* to show] — **re·mon·stra·tion** (rē'mon·strā'shən, rem'ən-) *n.* — **re·mon'stra·tive** (-strə·tiv) *adj.* — **re·mon'stra·tor** (-strā'tər) *n.*

re·morse (ri-môrs') *n.* The keen or hopeless anguish caused by a sense of guilt; distressing self-reproach. [< OF < LL < L < *re-* again + *mordere* to bite] — **re·morse'ful** *adj.* — **re·morse'ful·ly** *adv.* — **re·morse'ful·ness** *n.* — **re·morse'less** *adj.* — **re·morse'less·ly** *adv.* — **re·morse'less·ness** *n.*

re·mote (ri-mōt') *adj.* **·mot·er, ·mot·est** **1.** Located far from a specified place. **2.** Distant in time. **3.** Having slight relation or connection: a *remote* cousin. **4.** Not obvious; slight. **5.** Distant in manner; aloof. [< L < *re-* again + *movere* to move] — **re·mote'ly** *adv.* — **re·mote'ness** *n.*

remote control Control from a distance by electrical or radio circuits, as in the operation of a machine, aircraft, guided missile, etc.

re·mount (*v.* rē·mount'; *n.* rē'mount') *v.t. & v.i.* To mount again. — *n.* **1.** A new setting or framing. **2.** A fresh riding horse. [< OF < *re-* again (< L) + *monter* to climb]

re·mov·a·ble (ri·mōō'və·bəl) *adj.* Capable of being removed. — **re·mov'a·bil'i·ty, re·mov'a·ble·ness** *n.* — **re·mov'a·bly** *adv.*

re·mov·al (ri-mōō'vəl) *n.* **1.** The act of removing, or the state of being removed. **2.** Dismissal, as from office. **3.** Changing of place, as of residence or business.

re·move (ri·mōōv') *v.* **·moved, ·mov·ing** *v.t.* **1.** To take or move away, as from one place to another. **2.** To take off; doff, as a hat. **3.** To get rid of; do away with: to *remove* abuses. **4.** To kill. **5.** To displace or dismiss, as from office. **6.** To take out; extract: with *from.* — *v.i.* **7.** To change one's place of residence or business. **8.** *Poetic* To go away. — *n.* **1.** The act of removing, as one's business or belongings. **2.** The space moved over in changing an object from one position to another. **3.** A degree of difference; step: He is only one *remove* from a fool. [< OF < L < *re-* again + *movere* to move] — **re·mov'er** *n.*
— **Syn.** (verb) **1.** transfer, transplant, transpose. **3.** eliminate, obliterate, eradicate. **5.** depose, disestablish.

re·moved (ri·mōōvd') *adj.* Separated, as by intervening space, time, or relationship, or by difference in kind: a cousin twice *removed.* — **re·mov·ed·ness** (ri-mōō'vid·nis) *n.*

re·mu·ner·ate (ri·myōō'nə·rāt) *v.t.* **·at·ed, ·at·ing** To make just or adequate return to or for; pay or pay for. [< L < *re-* again + *munus* gift] — **re·mu'ner·a·bil'i·ty** *n.* — **re·mu'ner·a·ble** *adj.* — **re·mu'ner·a'tion** *n.* — **re·mu'ner·a'tive** (-nə·rā'tiv, -nər·ə·tiv) *adj.* — **re·mu'ner·a·tive·ly** *adv.*

Re·mus (rē'məs) In Roman mythology, the twin brother of Romulus. See ROMULUS.

ren- Var. of RENI-.

ren·ais·sance (ren'ə·säns', -zäns', ri·nā'səns; *Fr.* rə·ne·säns') *n.* A new birth; resurrection; renascence. [< F < L < *re-* again + *nasci* to be born]

Ren·ais·sance (ren'ə·säns', -zäns', ri·nā'səns; *Fr.* rə·ne·säns') *n.* **1.** The revival of letters and art in Europe, marking the transition from medieval to modern history. **2.** The period of this revival, roughly from the 14th through the 16th century. **3.** The style of art, literature, etc., that was developed in and characteristic of this period. Also *Renascence.* — *adj.* **1.** Of the Renaissance. **2.** Pertaining to a style of architecture developed in Italy in the 15th century, and based on the classic Roman style.

re·nal (rē'nəl) *adj.* Of, pertaining to, affecting, or near the kidneys. [< F < LL < L *renes* kidneys]

Ren·ard (ren'ərd) See REYNARD.

re·nas·cence (ri·nas'əns) *n.* A rebirth; revival. [< L < *re-* again + *nasci* to be born] — **re·nas'cent** *adj.*

Re·nas·cence (ri·nas'əns) *n.* The Renaissance.

rend (rend) *v.* **rent** or **rend·ed, rend·ing** *v.t.* **1.** To tear apart forcibly. **2.** To pull or remove forcibly: with *away,*

from, off, etc. **3.** To pass through (the air) violently and noisily. **4.** To distress (the heart, etc.). — *v.i.* **5.** To split; part. [OE *rendan* to tear] — **rend'er** *n.*

ren·der (ren'dər) *v.t.* **1.** To give, present, or submit for action, approval, payment, etc. **2.** To provide; give: to *render* aid to the poor. **3.** To give as due: to *render* obedience. **4.** To perform; do: to *render* great service. **5.** To give or state formally. **6.** To give by way of requital: to *render* double for one's sins. **7.** To represent or depict, as in music or painting. **8.** To cause to be: to *render* a ship seaworthy. **9.** To translate. **10.** To melt and clarify, as lard. **11.** To give back; return: often with *back.* **12.** To surrender; give up. [< F < LL < L < *re-* back + *dare* to give] — **ren'der·a·ble** *adj.* — **ren'der·er** *n.*

ren·dez·vous (rän'dā·vōō, -də-; *Fr.* rän·dā·vōō') *n. pl.* **·vous** (-vōōz, *Fr.* -vōō') **1.** An appointed place of meeting. **2.** A meeting or an appointment to meet. — *v.t. & v.i.* **·voused** (-vōōd), **·vous·ing** (-vōō'ing) To assemble or cause to assemble at a certain place or time. [< F < *se rendre* to betake oneself]

ren·di·tion (ren·dish'ən) *n.* **1.** The interpretation of a text; a translation. **2.** Artistic, dramatic, or musical interpretation; also, the performance or execution of a dramatic or musical composition. **3.** The act of rendering; also, that which is rendered. [< obs. F < *rendre* to render]

ren·e·gade (ren'ə·gād) *n.* **1.** One who forsakes his faith, etc. **2.** A traitor; deserter. Also **ren'e·ga'do** (-gā'dō). — *adj.* Of or characteristic of a renegade; traitorous. [< Sp. < Med.L < L *re-* again + *negare* to deny]

re·nege (ri·nig', -neg', -nēg') *v.i.* **·neged, ·neg·ing** **1.** In card games, to fail to follow suit when able and required by the rules to do so; revoke. **2.** *Informal* To fail to fulfill a promise. [See RENEGADE.] — **re·neg'er** *n.*

re·new (ri·nōō', -nyōō') *v.t.* **1.** To make new or as if new again; restore to a former or sound condition. **2.** To begin again; resume. **3.** To repeat: to *renew* an oath. **4.** To regain (vigor, strength, etc.). **5.** To cause to continue in effect; extend. **6.** To revive; reestablish. **7.** To replenish or replace, as provisions. — *v.i.* **8.** To become new again. **9.** To begin or commence again. [< RE- + NEW] — **re·new'a·ble** *adj.* — **re·new'ed·ly** *adv.*

reni- *combining form* Kidney; of or related to the kidneys. Also **ren-** (before vowels): also **reno-**. [< L *ren, renis* kidney]

ren·i·form (ren'ə·fôrm, rē'nə-) *adj.* Kidney-shaped.

ren·net (ren'it) *n.* **1.** The mucous membrane lining the fourth stomach of a suckling calf or sheep. **2.** *Biochem.* A substance that yields rennin, obtained from the stomach of such an animal. [ME *rennen* to cause to run]

ren·nin (ren'in) *n. Biochem.* A milk-curdling enzyme present in rennet. [< RENN(ET) + -IN]

re·nounce (ri·nouns') *v.* **·nounced, ·nounc·ing** *v.t.* **1.** To give up, resign, or formal statement. **2.** To disown; repudiate. [< F < L < *re-* back, against + *nuntiare* to report] — **re·nounce'ment** *n.* — **re·nounc'er** *n.*
— **Syn.** **1.** *Renounce* and *abjure* are often used in the general sense of put aside or abandon: to *renounce* one's citizenship, to *abjure* vice. *Forswear* has acquired an implication of perjury, esp. in the reflexive form: he *forswore* himself, that is, he swore falsely.

ren·o·vate (ren'ə·vāt) *v.t.* **·vat·ed, ·vat·ing** **1.** To make as good as new; repair. **2.** To renew; refresh. [< L < *re-* again + *novare* to make new] — **ren'o·va'tion** *n.* — **ren'o·va'tor** *n.*

re·nown (ri·noun') *n.* Exalted reputation; celebrity; fame. [< AF < OF < L *re-* again + *nominare* to name]

re·nowned (ri·nound') *adj.* Having renown; famous.

rent[1] (rent) *n.* **1.** Compensation made in any form by a tenant to a landlord or owner for the use of land, buildings, etc., esp., when paid in money at regular or specified intervals. **2.** Similar payment for the use of any property, movable or fixed. **3.** *Econ.* Income derived by the owner from the use or cultivation of his land or property. — **for rent** Available for use or occupancy by the paying of rent. — *v.t.* **1.** To obtain temporary possession and use of for a rent. **2.** To grant such temporary possession and use. — *v.i.* **3.** To be let for rent. [< OF < L *re-* back + *dare* to give] — **rent'a·ble** *adj.* — **rent'er** *n.*

rent[2] (rent) Alternative past tense and past participle of REND. — *n.* **1.** A hole or slit made by rending or tearing; rip; fissure. **2.** A violent separation; schism.

rent·al (ren'təl) *n.* **1.** The revenue from rented property **2.** A schedule of rents. — *adj.* Of or for rent. [< AF]

ren·tier (rän·tyā') *n. French* One who owns or derives a fixed income from invested capital or lands.

re·nun·ci·a·tion (ri·nun'sē·ā'shən, -shē-) *n.* **1.** The act of renouncing or disclaiming; repudiation. **2.** A declaration or statement in which something is renounced. [< L *renunciatio, -onis* proclamation] — **re·nun'ci·a'tive** *adj.* — **re·nun'ci·a·to·ry** (ri·nun'sē·ə·tôr'ē, -tō'rē, -shē-) *adj.*

RENAISSANCE ARCHITECTURE
(Church of the Redentore, Venice, 1578–80)

re·or·der (rē·ôr′dər) *v.t.* 1. To order (goods) again. 2. To put back into order. 3. To give a different order to; rearrange. — *n.* Goods ordered again.

re·or·gan·i·za·tion (rē′ôr·gən·ə·zā′shən, -ī·zā′-) *n.* 1. The act of reorganizing, or the condition of being reorganized. 2. The legal reconstruction of a corporation.

re·or·gan·ize (rē·ôr′gən·īz) *v.t. & v.i.* ·ized, ·iz·ing To organize anew. — **re·or′gan·iz′er** *n.*

rep¹ (rep) *n.* A silk, cotton, rayon, or wool fabric having a crosswise rib: also spelled *repp.* [< F *reps,* prob. < E *ribs*]

rep² (rep) *n. Slang* Reputation.

re·pair¹ (ri·pâr′) *v.t.* 1. To restore to sound or good condition after damage, decay, etc.; mend. 2. To make amends for (an injury); remedy. 3. To make up, as a loss; compensate for. — *n.* 1. The act or process of repairing. 2. Condition after use or after repairing: in good *repair.* [< OF < L < *re-* again + *parare* to prepare, make ready] — **re·pair′er** *n.*

re·pair² (ri·pâr′) *v.i.* To betake oneself; go: to *repair* to the garden. [< OF < LL < L *re-* again + *patria* native land]

re·pair·man (ri·pâr′man′, -mən) *n. pl.* ·men (-men′, -mən) A man whose work is to make repairs.

rep·a·ra·ble (rep′ər·ə·bəl) *adj.* Capable of being repaired. Also **re·pair·a·ble** (ri·pâr′ə·bəl). — **rep′a·ra·bil′i·ty** *n.* — **rep′a·ra·bly** *adv.*

rep·a·ra·tion (rep′ə·rā′shən) *n.* 1. The act of making amends; atonement. 2. That which is done by way of amends or satisfaction. 3. The act of repairing or the state of being repaired. 4. *pl.* Indemnities paid by defeated countries for acts of war. [< OF < LL < L. See REPAIR.¹] — **re·par·a·tive** (ri·par′ə·tiv) *adj.*

rep·ar·tee (rep′ər·tē′, -är·-, -tā′) *n.* 1. Conversation marked by quick and witty replies. 2. Skill or quickness in such conversation. 3. A witty or quick reply; a sharp rejoinder. [< OF < *repartir* to depart again, reply]

re·past (ri·past′, -päst′) *n.* 1. Food taken at a meal. 2. A meal. [< OF < Med.L < LL < L *re-* again + *pascere* to feed]

re·pa·tri·ate (*v.* rē·pā′trē·āt; *n.* rē·pā′trē·it) *v.t.* ·at·ed, ·at·ing To send back to one's own country or to the place of citizenship. — *n.* One who has been repatriated. [< LL < L *re-* again + *patria* native land] — **re·pa′tri·a′tion** *n.*

re·pay (ri·pā′) *v.* ·paid, ·pay·ing *v.t.* 1. To pay back; refund. 2. To pay back or refund something to. 3. To give a reward or inflict a penalty for; recompense or retaliate for. — *v.i.* 4. To make repayment or requital. [< OF *repaier*] — **re·pay′a·ble** *adj.* — **re·pay′ment** *n.*

re·peal (ri·pēl′) *v.t.* To rescind, as a law; revoke. — **Syn.** See ANNUL. — *n.* The act of repealing; revocation. [< OF < *re-* back, again + *apeler* to call, summon] — **re·peal′a·ble** *adj.* — **re·peal′er** *n.*

re·peat (ri·pēt′) *v.t.* 1. To say again; iterate. 2. To recite from memory. 3. To say (what another has just said) 4. To tell, as a secret, to another. 5. To do, make, or experience again. — *v.i.* 6. To say or do something again; esp., to vote more than once in an election. — *n.* 1. The act of repeating; a repetition. 2. *Music* A passage that is repeated; also, any notations indicating this. 3. Anything repeated. [< OF < L < *re-* again + *petere* to seek, demand]

re·peat·ed (ri·pē′tid) *adj.* Occurring or spoken again and again; reiterated. — **re·peat′ed·ly** *adv.*

re·peat·er (ri·pē′tər) *n.* 1. One who or that which repeats. 2. A repeating firearm. 3. *U.S.* One who votes, or attempts to vote, more than once at the same election. 4. One who has been repeatedly imprisoned.

re·peat·ing decimal (ri·pē′ting) A decimal in which a series of digits is repeated indefinitely, as 0.16353535. . . .

repeating firearm A gun, rifle, or pistol capable of shooting several bullets without reloading.

re·pel (ri·pel′) *v.* ·pelled, ·pel·ling *v.t.* 1. To force or drive back; repulse. 2. To reject; refuse, as a suggestion. 3. To cause to feel distaste or aversion. 4. To refuse to mix with or adhere to. 5. To push or keep away, esp. with invisible force. — *v.i.* 6. To act so as to drive something back or away. 7. To cause distaste or aversion. [< L < *re-* back + *pellere* to drive] — **re·pel′ler** *n.*

re·pel·lent (ri·pel′ənt) *adj.* 1. Serving, tending, or having power to repel. 2. Waterproof. 3. Repugnant; repulsive. — *n.* Something that repels, as a compound to repel insects. — **re·pel′lence, re·pel′len·cy** *n.*

re·pent (ri·pent′) *v.i.* 1. To feel remorse or regret, as for something one has done or failed to do; be contrite. 2. To change one's mind concerning past action: with *of:* He *repented* of his generosity. — *v.t.* 3. To feel remorse or regret for (an action, sin, etc.). 4. To change one's mind concerning (a past action). [< OF < L *re-* again + *poenitere* to cause to repent] — **re·pent′er** *n.*

re·pen·tance (ri·pen′təns) *n.* The act of repenting or the condition of being repentant.

re·pen·tant (ri·pen′tənt) *adj.* Showing, feeling, or characterized by repentance. [< OF] — **re·pen′tant·ly** *adv.*

re·peo·ple (rē·pē′pəl) *v.t.* ·pled, ·pling 1. To people anew. 2. To provide again with animals; restock.

re·per·cus·sion (rē′pər·kush′ən) *n.* 1. The act of driving back, or the state of being driven back; repulse. 2. Echo; reverberation. 3. A stroke or blow given in return; also, the recoil after impact. 4. The indirect result of something; aftereffect. [< L < *re-* again + *percutere* to strike] — **re′per·cus′sive** *adj.*

rep·er·toire (rep′ər·twär, -twôr) *n.* A list of songs, plays, operas, or the like, that a person or company is prepared to perform; also, such pieces collectively: also called *repertory.* [See REPERTORY.]

rep·er·to·ry (rep′ər·tôr′ē, -tō′rē) *n. pl.* ·ries 1. Repertoire. 2. A place where things are gathered together. 3. The things so gathered. [< LL *repertorium* inventory < L *repe-rire* to discover]

repertory company A theatrical group having a repertoire of productions, each typically running for a few weeks. Also **repertory theater.**

rep·e·ti·tion (rep′ə·tish′ən) *n.* 1. The act of repeating; the doing, making, or saying of something again. 2. Recital from memory. 3. That which is repeated; a copy. — **re·pet·i·tive** (ri·pet′ə·tiv) *adj.* — **re·pet′i·tive·ly** *adv.*

rep·e·ti·tious (rep′ə·tish′əs) *adj.* Characterized by or containing repetition, esp. useless or tedious repetition. — **rep′e·ti′tious·ly** *adv.* — **rep′e·ti′tious·ness** *n.*

re·phrase (rē·frāz′) *v.t.* ·phrased, ·phras·ing To phrase again; esp., to express in a new way.

re·pine (ri·pīn′) *v.i.* ·pined, ·pin·ing To be discontented or fretful; complain; murmur. [< RE- + PINE²] — **re·pin′er** *n.*

re·place (ri·plās′) *v.t.* ·placed, ·plac·ing 1. To put back in place. 2. To take or fill the place of; supersede. 3. To refund; repay. — **re·place′a·ble** *adj.* — **re·plac′er** *n.*

re·place·ment (ri·plās′mənt) *n.* 1. One who or that which takes the place of another person or thing. 2. The act of replacing or the state of being replaced.

re·plen·ish (ri·plen′ish) *v.t.* 1. To fill again, as something wholly or partially emptied. 2. To bring back to fullness or completeness, as supplies. [< OF < L *re-* again + *plenus* full] — **re·plen′ish·er** *n.* — **re·plen′ish·ment** *n.*

re·plete (ri·plēt′) *adj.* 1. Full or supplied to the uttermost. 2. Gorged with food or drink; sated. [< OF < L < *re-* again + *plere* to fill] — **re·ple′tion** *n.*

re·plev·in (ri·plev′in) *Law n.* 1. An action to regain possession of personal property unlawfully retained, on giving security to try the title and respond to the judgment; also, recovery of property by such action 2. The writ or process by which such proceedings are instituted. — *v.t.* To recover (goods) by a writ of replevin. Also **re·plev·y** (ri·plev′ē). [< AF < OF < *re-* back + *plevir* to pledge]

rep·li·ca (rep′lə·kə) *n.* Any close copy or reproduction, esp. of a work of art, etc. [< Ital. < L *replicare* to reply]

rep·li·ca·tion (rep′lə·kā′shən) *n.* 1. A reply. 2. *Law* A plaintiff's reply to a defendant's plea or answer. [< OF < L < *replicare* to answer to] — **rep′li·ca′tive** *adj.*

re·ply (ri·plī′) *v.* ·plied, ·ply·ing *v.i.* 1. To give an answer orally or in writing. 2. To respond by some act, gesture, etc. 3. To bounce back, as a sound; echo. 4. *Law* To file a pleading in answer to the statement of the defense. — *v.t.* 5. To say in answer: often with a clause as object. — *n. pl.* ·plies Something said, written, or done by way of answer. [< OF < L *replicare* to fold back, answer to] — **re·pli′er** *n.*

re·port (ri·pôrt′, -pōrt′) *v.t.* 1. To make or give an account of, often formally. 2. To relate, as information obtained by investigation. 3. To repeat to another, as an answer. 4. To complain about, esp. to a superior. 5. To state the result of consideration concerning: The committee *reported* the bill. — *v.i.* 6. To make a report. 7. To act as a reporter. 8. To present oneself, as for duty. — *n.* 1. That which is reported. 2. A statement or record of an investigation, transaction, etc. 3. Common talk; rumor. 4. Fame, reputation, or character. 5. An explosive sound. [< OF < L < *re-* back + *portare* to carry] — **re·port′a·ble** *adj.*

report card *U.S.* A periodic statement of a pupil's scholastic record, which is presented to the parents or guardian.

re·port·ed·ly (ri·pôr′tid·lē, -pōr′-) *adv.* According to report.

re·port·er (ri·pôr′tər, -pōr′-) *n.* 1. One who reports; esp., one who reports news for a newspaper, magazine, etc. 2. One who reports cases in court for official publication. — **rep·or·to·ri·al** (rep′ər·tôr′ē·əl, -tō′rē-) *adj.*

re·pose¹ (ri·pōz′) *n.* 1. The act of taking rest or the state of being at rest. 2. Calm; peace. 3. Ease of manner; graceful and dignified calmness. 4. That which conduces to rest or calm. — *v.* ·posed, ·pos·ing *v.t.* 1. To lay or place in a position of rest. — *v.i.* 2. To lie at rest. 3. To rely; depend: with *on, upon,* or *in.* [< F < LL < *re-* again + *pausare* to pause] — **re·pos′al** *n.* — **re·pose′ful** *adj.* — **re·pos′er** *n.*

re·pose² (ri·pōz′) *v.t.* ·posed, ·pos·ing To place, as confidence or hope: with *in.* [ME < L *reponere* to put back] — **re·pos′al** *n.*

re·pos·i·to·ry (ri·poz′ə·tôr′ē, -tō′rē) *n. pl.* **·ries** **1.** A place in which goods are or may be stored. **2.** A person to whom a secret is entrusted **3.** A burial vault. **4.** A receptacle for relics. [< L < *re-* back, again + *ponere* to place]

re·pos·sess (rē′pə·zes′) *v.t.* **1.** To have possession of again; regain possession of. **2.** To give back possession or ownership to. — **re′pos·ses′sion** (-zesh′ən) *n.*

re·pous·sé (rə·pōō·sā′) *adj.* **1.** Formed in relief, as a design in metal. **2.** Adorned with such designs. [< F]

repp (rep) *n.* Rep, the fabric.

rep·re·hend (rep′ri·hend′) *v.t.* To criticize sharply; find fault with; blame. [< L < *re-* back + *prehendere* to hold]

rep·re·hen·si·ble (rep′ri·hen′sə·bəl) *adj.* Deserving blame or censure. — **rep′re·hen′si·bil′i·ty**, **rep′re·hen′si·ble·ness** *n.* — **rep′re·hen′si·bly** *adv.*

rep·re·hen·sion (rep′ri·hen′shən) *n.* The act of reprehending; also, an expression of blame; a rebuke. — **rep′re·hen′sive** *adj.* — **rep′re·hen′sive·ly** *adv.*

rep·re·sent (rep′ri·zent′) *v.t.* **1.** To serve as the symbol, expression, or designation of; symbolize. **2.** To express or symbolize in this manner. **3.** To depict; portray, as in painting or sculpture. **4.** To produce on the stage, as an opera. **5.** To act the part of; impersonate. **6.** To serve as or be the delegate, agent, etc., of. **7.** To describe: They *represented* him as a genius. **8.** To set forth in words; state; explain. **9.** To bring before the mind; present clearly. **10.** To serve as an example, specimen, type, etc., of. [< OF < L < *re-* again + PRESENT²] — **rep′re·sent′a·ble** *adj.* — **rep′re·sent′a·bil′i·ty** *n.*

re-present (rē′pri·zent′) *v.t.* To present again. — **re′-pre′sen·ta′tion** *n.*

rep·re·sen·ta·tion (rep′ri·zen·tā′shən) *n.* **1.** The act of representing or the state of being represented. **2.** Anything that represents, as a picture, a statue, etc. **3.** A dramatic performance. **4.** The right of acting authoritatively for others, esp. in a legislative body. **5.** Representatives collectively. **6.** A setting forth by statement or account, esp. to object or propose.

rep·re·sen·ta·tion·al (rep′ri·zen·tā′shən·əl) *adj.* **1.** Serving to represent; esp., denoting a style of art that seeks to represent objects realistically. **2.** Of, pertaining to, or of the nature of representation.

rep·re·sen·ta·tive (rep′ri·zen′tə·tiv) *adj.* **1.** Typifying or typical of a group or class. **2.** Acting as a qualified agent. **3.** Made up of representatives. **4.** Based on or pertaining to the political principle of representation. **5.** Presenting, portraying, or representing, or capable of so doing — *n.* **1.** One who or that which is fit to stand as a type; a typical instance. **2.** One who is a qualified agent of any kind. **3.** A member of a legislative body, esp. a member of the lower house of Congress or of a State legislature. — **rep′re·sen′ta·tive·ly** *adv.* — **rep′re·sen′ta·tive·ness** *n.*

re·press (ri·pres′) *v.t.* **1.** To keep under restraint or control. **2.** To put down; quell, as a rebellion. **3.** *Psychoanal.* To effect the repression of, as fears, impulses, etc. [< L < *re-* back + PRESS] — **re·press′er** or **re·pres′sor** *n.* — **re·press′i·ble** *adj.*
— **Syn. 1.** check, curb, rein, restrain, subdue, suppress.

re-press (rē′pres′) *v.t. & v.i.* To press again.

re·pres·sion (ri·presh′ən) *n.* **1.** The act of repressing or the condition of being repressed. **2.** That which holds in check; a restraint. **3.** *Psychoanal.* The exclusion from consciousness of painful or unacceptable memories, etc.

re·pres·sive (ri·pres′iv) *adj.* **1.** Tending to repress. **2.** Capable of repressing. — **re·pres′sive·ly** *adv.* — **re·pres′sive·ness** *n.*

re·prieve (ri·prēv′) *v.t.* **·prieved**, **·priev·ing** **1.** To suspend temporarily the execution of a sentence upon. **2.** To relieve for a time from suffering, danger, or trouble. — *n.* **1.** The temporary suspension of a sentence, or the instrument ordering such a suspension. **2.** Temporary relief or cessation of pain or ill. **3.** The act of reprieving or the state of being reprieved. [< earlier *repry* < F *repris*, pp. of *reprendre* to take back] — **re·priev′a·ble** *adj.*

rep·ri·mand (rep′rə·mand, -mänd) *v.t.* To reprove sharply or formally. — *n.* Severe reproof or censure. [< F *réprimande* reproof]

re·print (n. rē′print′; v. rē·print′) *n.* An edition of a printed work that is a verbatim copy of the original. — *v.t.* To print a new edition or copy of. — **re·print′er** *n.*

re·pri·sal (ri·prī′zəl) *n.* **1.** The application of force short of war by one nation against another in retaliation for acts committed; also, an instance of such use of force. **2.** Any act of retaliation. [< OF *reprendre* < L < *re-* back + *prehendere* to hold]

re·prise (rə·prēz′, -prīz′) *n. Music* A repeated phrase; esp., the repetition of or return to the subject after an intermediate movement. [See REPRISAL.]

re·proach (ri·prōch′) *v.t.* **1.** To charge with or blame for something wrong; rebuke; censure. **2.** To bring discredit and disgrace upon; to disgrace. — *n.* **1.** The act of reproaching, or the words of one who reproaches; censure; reproof; rebuke. **2.** A cause of blame or disgrace. **3.** Disgrace; discredit. [< F *reprocher*; ult. origin uncertain.] — **re·proach′a·bly** *adj.* — **re·proach′a·ble·ness** *n.* — **re·proach′a·bly** *adv.* — **re·proach′er** *n.*

re·proach·ful (ri·prōch′fəl) *adj.* Containing or full of reproach; expressing reproach. — **re·proach′ful·ly** *adv.* — **re·proach′ful·ness** *n.*

rep·ro·bate (rep′rə·bāt) *adj.* **1.** Having lost all sense of duty; depraved. **2.** Abandoned to punishment; condemned. — *n.* A depraved or profligate person. — *v.t.* **·bat·ed**, **·bat·ing** To disapprove of heartily; condemn. [See REPROVE.] — **rep′ro·ba′tion** *n.* — **rep′ro·ba′tive** *adj.*

re·pro·duce (rē′prə·dōōs′, -dyōōs′) *v.* **·duced**, **·duc·ing** *v.t.* **1.** To make a copy, image, or reproduction of. **2.** *Biol.* **a** To give rise to (offspring) by sexual or asexual generation. **b** To replace (a lost part or organ) by regeneration. **3.** To produce again. **4.** To recall to the mind; visualize again. — *v.i.* **5.** To produce offspring. **6.** To undergo copying, reproduction, etc. — **re′pro·duc′er** *n.* — **re′pro·duc′i·ble** *adj.*

re·pro·duc·tion (rē′prə·duk′shən) *n.* **1.** The act or power of reproducing. **2.** *Biol.* The process by which an animal or plant gives rise to another of its kind **3.** That which is reproduced, as a revival of a play or a copy of a picture.

re·pro·duc·tive (rē′prə·duk′tiv) *adj.* Pertaining to, employed in, or tending to reproduction. — **re′pro·duc′tive·ly** *adv.* — **re′pro·duc′tive·ness** *n.*

re·proof (ri·prōōf′) *n.* **1.** The act of reproving. **2.** A rebuke; blame; censure. Also **re·prov·al** (ri·prōō′vəl).

re·prove (ri·prōōv′) *v.t.* **·proved**, **·prov·ing** **1.** To censure, as for a fault; rebuke. **2.** To express disapproval of (an act). [< OF < LL < *re-* again + *probare* to test] — **re·prov′a·ble** *adj.* — **re·prov′er** *n.* — **re·prov′ing·ly** *adv.*
— **Syn. 1.** chide, upbraid, reprimand.

re-prove (rē·prōōv′) *v.t.* **·proved**, **·prov·ing** To prove (a theory, assertion, etc.) anew.

rep·tile (rep′til, -tīl) *n.* **1.** Any of a class of cold-blooded, air-breathing vertebrates, including the snakes, crocodiles, lizards, and turtles. **2.** A groveling, abject person. — *adj.* **1.** Crawling on the belly. **2.** Groveling morally; sly and base; treacherous. **3.** Of or resembling a reptile [< LL < *reptus*, pp. of *repere* to creep]

rep·til·i·an (rep·til′ē·ən) *adj.* Of, pertaining to, or characteristic of a reptile or reptiles. — *n.* Any reptile.

re·pub·lic (ri·pub′lik) *n.* A state in which the sovereignty resides in the people and the legislative and administrative powers are lodged in officers elected by them; also, such a government. [< F < L *respublica* commonwealth]

re·pub·li·can (ri·pub′li·kən) *adj.* **1.** Of, like, or suitable for a republic. **2.** Supporting republican government. — *n.* One who advocates a republican form of government.

Re·pub·li·can (ri·pub′li·kən) *adj.* Pertaining to or belonging to the Republican Party of the U.S. — *n.* A member of the Republican Party.

Republican calendar See under CALENDAR.

re·pub·li·can·ism (ri·pub′li·kən·iz′əm) *n.* **1.** The theory or principles of republican government. **2.** Advocacy of or adherence to republican principles.

Re·pub·li·can·ism (ri·pub′li·kən·iz′əm) *n.* The policy and principles of the Republican Party of the U.S.

Republican Party One of the two major political parties of the United States, founded in 1854 in opposition to the extension of slavery.

re·pu·di·ate (ri·pyōō′dē·āt) *v.t.* **·at·ed**, **·at·ing** **1.** To refuse to accept as valid or binding; reject. **2.** To refuse to acknowledge or pay. **3.** To cast off; disown, as a son. [< L < *repudiare* to divorce] — **re·pu′di·a′tion** *n.* — **re·pu′di·a′tive** *adj.* — **re·pu′di·a′tor** *n.*

re·pug·nance (ri·pug′nəns) *n.* The state of feeling aversion and resistance; antipathy. Also **re·pug′nan·cy.**

re·pug·nant (ri·pug′nənt) *adj.* **1.** Offensive to taste or feeling; exciting aversion or repulsion **2.** Being inconsistent or opposed; antagonistic. **3.** Hostile; resisting. [< OF < L < *re-* back + *pugnare* to fight]

re·pulse (ri·puls′) *v.t.* **·pulsed**, **·puls·ing** **1.** To drive back; repel, as an attacking force. **2.** To repel by coldness, discourtesy, etc.; reject; rebuff. — *n.* **1.** The act of repulsing or the state of being repulsed. **2.** Rejection; refusal [< L *repulsus*, pp. of *repellere*. See REPEL.] — **re·puls′er** *n.*

re·pul·sion (ri·pul′shən) *n.* **1.** The act of repelling, or the state of being repelled. **2.** Aversion; repugnance **3.** *Physics* The mutual action of two bodies that tends to drive them apart.

re·pul·sive (ri·pul′siv) *adj.* **1.** Exciting feelings of dislike, disgust, or horror; grossly offensive. **2.** Such as to forbid approach or familiarity; forbidding. **3.** Acting by repulsion: *repulsive* forces. — re·pul'sive·ly *adv.* — re·pul'sive·ness *n.*

rep·u·ta·ble (rep'yə·tə·bəl) *adj.* **1.** Having a good reputation; estimable; honorable. **2.** Consistent with proper usage, as words — rep'u·ta·bil'i·ty *n.* — rep'u·ta·bly *adv.*

rep·u·ta·tion (rep'yə·tā'shən) *n.* **1.** The general estimation in which a person or thing is held by others. **2.** The state of being in high regard or esteem **3.** A particular credit or character ascribed to a person or thing: a *reputation* for honesty. [See REPUTE.]

re·pute (ri·pyōōt') *v.t.* ·put·ed, ·put·ing To regard or consider to be as specified; esteem: usu. in the passive: They are *reputed* to be an intelligent people. — *n.* **1.** Reputation (defs. 1 and 2). **2.** Public opinion; general report. [< OF < L *reputare* to reckon, be reputed]

re·put·ed (ri·pyōō'tid) *adj.* Generally thought or supposed: a *reputed* criminal. — re·put'ed·ly *adv.*

re·quest (ri·kwest') *v.t.* **1.** To express a desire for. **2.** To ask (a person) to do a favor, answer an inquiry, etc. — **Syn.** See ASK. — *n.* **1.** The act of requesting; petition. **2.** That which is requested. **3.** The state of being in demand: in *request.* — *adj.* Having been asked for: a *request* program. [See REQUIRE.]

re·qui·em (rē'kwē·əm, rek'wē-) *n.* **1.** Any musical composition, or service for the dead. **2.** *Often cap. Eccl.* In the Roman Catholic Church, a solemn mass sung for the dead: also **Requiem mass.** **3.** *Often cap.* A musical setting for such a mass. [< L *Requiem (aeternam dona eis, Domine)* rest (eternal give unto them, O Lord)]

req·ui·es·cat in pa·ce (rek'wē·es'kat in pä'sē) May he rest in peace Abbr. *R.I.P.* [< L]

re·quire (ri·kwīr') *v.* ·quired, ·quir·ing *v.t.* **1.** To have need of; find necessary. **2.** To demand authoritatively; insist upon. — *v.i.* **3.** To make demand or request. [< OF < L < *re-* again + *quaerere* to ask, seek] — re·quir'a·ble *adj.* — re·quir'er *n.* — re·quire'ment *n.*

req·ui·site (rek'wə·zit) *adj.* Required by the nature of things or by circumstances; indispensable. — *n.* That which cannot be dispensed with; a necessity. [See REQUEST.] — req'ui·site·ly *adv.* — req'ui·site·ness *n.*

req·ui·si·tion (rek'wə·zish'ən) *n.* **1.** A formal request, summons, or demand, as for supplies. **2.** A necessity or requirement. **3.** The state of being required. — *v.t.* To make a requisition for or upon; demand or take upon requisition. [See REQUIRE.]

re·quite (ri·kwīt') *v.t.* ·quit·ed, ·quit·ing **1.** To make equivalent return for, as kindness, service, or injury; make up for. **2.** To make return to; compensate or repay in kind. **3.** To give or do in return. [< RE- + *quite,* obs. var. of QUIT] — re·quit'al (ri·kwīt'l) *adj.* — re·quit'er *n.*

rere·dos (rir'dos) *Chiefly Brit.* *n.* **1.** An ornamental screen behind an altar. **2.** The back of an open fire hearth. [< AF < *rere* rear + *dos* back]

re·run (*n.* rē'run; *v.* rē·run') *n.* The presenting of a motion picture, play, etc., after its original run is over; also, the motion picture, play, etc., so presented. — *v.t.* ·ran, ·run·ning To run again or a second time.

re·sale (rē'sāl, rē·sāl') *n.* The act of selling again.

re·scind (ri·sind') *v.t.* To make void, as an act; abrogate; repeal. — **Syn.** See ANNUL. [< L < *re-* back + *scindere* to cut] — re·scind'a·ble *adj.* — re·scind'er *n.*

re·scis·sion (ri·sizh'ən) *n.* The act of rescinding or abrogating. — re·scis'si·ble (-sis'-) *adj.* — re·scis'so·ry *adj.*

re·script (rē'skript) *n.* **1.** A formal answer to questions of state, law, morality, etc., as given by a Roman emperor or a Pope. **2.** Any decree, edict or formal announcement. [< L < *re-* back + *scribere* to write]

res·cue (res'kyōō) *v.t.* ·cued, ·cu·ing **1.** To save or free from danger, captivity, evil, etc.; deliver. **2.** *Law* To remove forcibly from the custody of the law. — *n.* The act of rescuing; deliverance. [< OF *rescourre* < *re-* back + *escorre* to move, shake] — res'cu·a·ble *adj.* — res'cu·er *n.*

re·search (ri·sûrch', rē'sûrch) *n.* **1.** Diligent, protracted investigation; studious inquiry. **2.** A systematic investigation of some phenomenon — *v.i.* To undertake research. [< F < *re-* back + *chercher* to seek] — re·search'·er *n.*

re·seat (rē·sēt') *v.t.* **1.** To seat again. **2.** To put a new seat or seats in or on.

re·sect (ri·sekt') *v.t.* *Surg.* To cut or pare off. [< L < *re-* back + *secare* to cut] — re·sec'tion *n.*

re·sem·blance (ri·zem'bləns) *n.* **1.** The quality of similarity in nature, form, etc.; likeness. **2.** A semblance or likeness of a person or thing. — **Syn.** See ANALOGY.

re·sem·ble (ri·zem'bəl) *v.t.* ·bled, ·bling To be similar to in appearance, quality, or character. [< OF < *re-* again + *sembler* to seem] — re·sem'bler *n.*

re·sent (ri·zent') *v.t.* To feel or show resentment at; be indignant at. [< F < *re-* again + *sentir* to feel] — re·sent'ful *adj.* — re·sent'ful·ly *adv.* — re·sent'ful·ness *n.*

re·sent·ment (ri·zent'mənt) *n.* Anger and ill will in view of real or fancied wrong or injury.

re·ser·pine (ri·sûr'pēn, -pin, res'ər-) *n.* A drug originally prepared from alkaloids found in rauwolfia, used as a tranquilizer. [< NL *Rauwolfia serpentina,* genus name + -INE]

res·er·va·tion (rez'ər·vā'shən) *n.* **1.** The act of reserving. **2.** That which is reserved, kept back, or withheld. **3.** A qualification or condition, as to an opinion or commitment. **4.** An agreement by which a seat on a train, hotel room, etc., is reserved in advance. **5.** A tract of government land reserved for a special purpose, as for the use and occupancy of an Indian tribe, or for the preservation of forests, wildlife, etc. [< OF < LL *reservatio, -onis*]

re·serve (ri·zûrv') *v.t.* ·served, ·serv·ing **1.** To hold back or set aside for special or future use. **2.** To keep as one's own; retain. **3.** To arrange for ahead of time; have set aside for one's use. — *n.* **1.** Something stored up for future use or set apart for a particular purpose. **2.** A reservation of land. **3.** In banking, the amount of funds reserved in order to meet regular or emergent demands. **4.** The act of reserving. **5.** Silence or reticence as to one's feelings, opinions, or affairs. **6.** A fighting force held back from action to meet possible emergencies. **7.** A branch of the armed forces composed of persons trained for military service and subject to call in emergencies. — *adj.* Held in reserve; constituting a reserve. [< OF < L < *re-* back + *servare* to keep] — re·serv'a·ble *adj.* — re·serv'er *n.*

re·serve (rē·sûrv') *v.t. & v.i.* -served, -serv·ing To serve again.

re·served (ri·zûrvd') *adj.* **1.** Characterized by reserve of manner; distant; undemonstrative. **2.** Retained; kept back. — re·serv·ed·ly (-rizûr'vid·lē) *adv.* — re·serv·ed·ness *n.*

Reserve Officers' Training Corps In the U.S., a military corps to train students at colleges and universities to qualify as officers in a reserve. Abbr. *ROTC, R.O.T.C.*

re·serv·ist (ri·zûr'vist) *n.* A member of a military reserve.

res·er·voir (rez'ər·vwôr, -vwär, -vôr) *n.* **1.** A lake, either natural or artificial, for collecting and containing a supply of water, as for use in a city or for water power. **2.** An attachment to a stove, machine, or instrument, for containing a fluid to be used in its operation. **3.** An extra supply; a store of anything. [< F *réservoir*]

re·set (*v.* rē·set'; *n.* rē'set') *v.t.* ·set, ·set·ting To set again. — *n.* The act of resetting, or that which is reset.

re·ship (rē·ship') *v.* ·shipped, ·ship·ping *v.t.* **1.** To ship again. **2.** To transfer (oneself) to another vessel. — *v.i.* **3.** To go on a vessel again. **4.** To sign for another voyage as a crew member or a passenger. — re·ship'ment *n.*

re·side (ri·zīd') *v.i.* ·sid·ed, ·sid·ing **1.** To dwell for a considerable time; make one's home; live. **2.** To exist as an attribute or quality: with *in.* **3.** To be vested: with *in.* — **Syn.** See LIVE. [< F < L *residere* to abide]

res·i·dence (rez'ə·dəns) *n.* **1.** The place or the house where one resides. **2.** The act of residing. **3.** The fact of being officially present, esp. in the phrase **in residence.** **4.** The seat of power of government. **5.** The length of time one resides in a place. Also *residency.* [< OF < LL *residentia*]

res·i·den·cy (rez'ə·dən·sē) *n.* *pl.* ·cies **1.** Residence. **2.** An official abode of the representative of a government. **3.** *Med.* The period of clinical training served by a physician in his chosen specialty.

res·i·dent (rez'ə·dənt) *n.* **1.** One who resides or dwells in a place. **2.** A diplomatic representative residing at a foreign seat of government. **3.** *Med.* One serving a residency. — *adj.* **1.** Having a residence. **2.** Abiding in a place in connection with one's official work: a *resident* physician. **3.** Inherent: Pungency is *resident* in pepper. **4.** Not migratory: said of certain birds.

res·i·den·tial (rez'ə·den'shəl) *adj.* **1.** Of, pertaining to, or resulting from residence; having residence. **2.** Of, consisting of, or suitable for residences or living quarters.

re·sid·u·al (ri·zij'ōō·əl) *adj.* **1.** Pertaining to or having the nature of a residue or remainder. **2.** Left over as a residue. — *n.* Something left over.

re·sid·u·ar·y (ri·zij'ōō·er'ē) *adj.* Of or pertaining to a residuum or remainder; residual.

res·i·due (rez'ə·dōō, -dyōō) *n.* **1.** A remainder or surplus after a part has been separated or otherwise treated. **2.** *Chem.* Insoluble matter left after filtration or separation from a liquid. **3.** *Law* The portion of an estate that remains after all charges, debts, and particular bequests have been satisfied. Also re·sid·u·um (ri·zij'ōō·əm). [< OF < L < *re-* back + *sedere* to sit]

re·sign (ri·zīn') *v.t.* **1.** To give up, as a position, office, or trust. **2.** To relinquish (a privilege, claim, etc.). **3.** To give over (oneself, one's mind, etc.), as to fate or domination. — *v.i.* **4.** To resign a position, etc. [< OF < L < *re-* back + *signare* to seal] — re·sign'er *n.*

re·sign (rē·sīn') *v.t.* To sign again.

res·ig·na·tion (rez'ig·nā'shən) *n.* **1.** The act of resigning, as a position or office. **2.** A written statement declaring one's intention to resign. **3.** The quality of being submissive or acquiescent.

re·signed (ri·zīnd′) *adj.* Characterized by resignation; submissive. **— re·sign·ed·ly** (ri·zī′nid·lē) *adv.*
re·sil·ience (ri·zil′yəns) *n.* The quality or power of being resilient; elasticity; rebound. Also **re·sil′ien·cy.**
re·sil·ient (ri·zil′yənt) *adj.* **1.** Springing back to a former shape or position. **2.** Capable of recoiling from pressure or shock unchanged or undamaged; buoyant. [< MF < L *re*- back + *salire* to leap] **— re·sil′ient·ly** *adv.*
res·in (rez′in) *n.* **1.** An amorphous organic substance exuded from certain plants and trees, yellowish or dark in color. **2.** Any of a class of similar substances made by chemical synthesis, esp. those used in the making of plastics. **3.** Rosin (def. 1). **— v.t.** To apply resin to. [< OF < L < Gk. *rhētinē*] **— res·i·na·ceous** (rez′ə·nā′shəs) *adj.*
res·i·nous (rez′ə·nəs) *adj.* **1.** Like or containing resin. **2.** Obtained from resin. Also **res·in·y** (rez′ən·ē).
re·sist (ri·zist′) *v.t.* **1.** To strive against; act counter to. **2.** To be proof against; withstand. **— v.i.** **3.** To offer opposition. [< OF < L *resistere* to withstand] **— re·sist′er** *n.*
re·sis·tance (ri·zis′təns) *n.* **1.** The act of resisting. **2.** Any force tending to hinder motion. **3.** *Electr.* The opposition that a conductor offers to the passage of a current, resulting from the conversion of energy into heat, light, etc. **4.** *Psychoanal.* The action of the ego in preventing the return to consciousness of unpleasant incidents and experiences. **5.** The underground and guerrilla movement opposing an occupying power. **— re·sis′tant** *n.*
re·sist·i·ble (ri·zis′tə·bəl) *adj.* Capable of being resisted. **— re·sist′i·bil′i·ty** *n.* **— re·sist′i·bly** *adv.*
re·sis·tive (ri·zis′tiv) *adj.* Having or exercising the power of resistance. **— re·sis′tive·ly** *adv.*
re·sis·tiv·i·ty (rē′zis·tiv′ə·tē) *n.* **1.** The capacity to resist, or the degree of that capacity. **2.** *Electr.* Specific resistance to electric or magnetic force of a substance as tested in a cube measuring one centimeter.
re·sist·less (ri·zist′lis) *adj.* **1.** Incapable of resisting; irresistible. **2.** Offering no resistance; powerless. **— re·sist′less·ly** *adv.* **— re·sist′less·ness** *n.*
re·sis·tor (ri·zis′tər) *n.* *Electr.* A device, as a coil of wire, for introducing resistance into an electrical circuit.
res·na·tron (rez′nə·tron) *n.* *Electronics* A tetrode electron tube operating on the resonance principle and capable of generating large power at high frequency and maximum efficiency. [< RES(O)NA(TOR) + -TRON]
re·sole (rē·sōl′) *v.t.* **·soled, ·sol·ing** To sole (a shoe, etc.) again.
res·o·lute (rez′ə·lōōt) *adj.* **1.** Having a fixed purpose; determined. **2.** Bold; unflinching. [See RESOLVE.] **— res′o·lute·ly** *adv.* **— res′o·lute·ness** *n.*
res·o·lu·tion (rez′ə·lōō′shən) *n.* **1.** The act of resolving or of reducing to a simpler form. **2.** The state of being resolute; active fortitude. **3.** The making of a resolve; also, the purpose or course resolved upon. **4.** The separation of anything into component parts. **5.** A proposition offered to or adopted by an assembly. **6.** *Med.* The termination of an abnormal condition. **— res′o·lu′tion·er, res′o·lu′tion·ist** *n.*
re·solve (ri·zolv′) *v.* **·solved, ·solv·ing** *v.t.* **1.** To decide or determine (to do something). **2.** To cause to decide or determine. **3.** To separate or break down into constituent parts. **4.** To make clear; explain or solve, as a problem. **5.** To explain away; remove (doubts, etc.). **6.** To state or decide by vote, as in a legislative assembly. **7.** To transform; convert: He *resolves* his anger into pride. **8.** *Optics* To make distinguishable the structure or parts of, as in a microscope or telescope. **— v.i. 9.** To make up one's mind; arrive at a decision: with *on* or *upon*. **10.** To become separated into constituent parts. **— n. 1.** Fixity of purpose; resolution. **2.** A fixed determination; a resolution. **3.** The action of a deliberative body expressing formally its intention or purpose. [< L < *re*- again + *solvere* to loosen] **— re·solv′a·ble** *adj.* **— re·solv′a·bil′i·ty** *n.* **— re·solv′er** *n.*
re·solve (rē·solv′) *v.t.* **-solved, -solv·ing** To solve anew.
re·solved (ri·zolvd′) *adj.* Fixed or set in purpose; determined. **— re·solv·ed·ly** (ri·zol′vid·lē) *adv.*
res·o·nance (rez′ə·nəns) *n.* **1.** The state or quality of being resonant. **2.** *Physics* The property whereby any vibratory system responds with maximum amplitude to an applied force having a frequency equal or nearly equal to its own. **3.** *Electr.* The condition of an electric circuit in which maximum flow of current is obtained by impressing an electromotive force of given frequency.
res·o·nant (rez′ə·nənt) *adj.* **1.** Sending back or having the quality of sending back or prolonging sound. **2.** Resounding. **3.** Having resonance. [< L < *re*- again + *sonare* to sound] **— res′o·nant·ly** *adv.*
res·o·nate (rez′ə·nāt) *v.i.* **·nat·ed, ·nat·ing** **1.** To exhibit resonance. **2.** To manifest sympathetic vibration, as a resonator. [< L *resonatus*, pp. of *resonare*. See RESONANT.]

res·o·na·tor (rez′ə·nā′tər) *n.* **1.** That which resounds. **2.** Any device utilizing the effects of resonance, esp. in connection with sound or electromagnetic waves. [< NL]
re·sorb (ri·sôrb′) *v.t.* To absorb again. [< L < re- back + *sorbere* to suck up] **— re·sorp·tion** (ri·sôrp′shən) *n.*
re·sor·cin·ol (ri·zôr′sin·ōl, -ol) *n.* *Chem.* A colorless crystalline compound, $C_6H_6O_2$, used as an antiseptic and in the making of dyes. Also **re·sor′cin. — re·sor′cin·al** *adj.*
re·sort (ri·zôrt′) *v.i.* **1.** To go frequently or habitually; repair. **2.** To have recourse; apply or betake oneself for relief or aid: with *to*. **— n. 1.** A place frequented for recreation or rest: health *resort.* **2.** The use of something as a means; a recourse. **3.** The act of frequenting a place. [< OF < *re*- again + *sortir* to go out] **— re·sort′er** *n.*
re·sort (rē·sôrt′) *v.t. & v.i.* To sort anew or again.
re·sound (ri·zound′) *v.i.* **1.** To be filled with sound; echo; reverberate. **2.** To make a loud, prolonged, or echoing sound. **3.** To ring; echo: said of sounds. **— v.t. 4.** To give back (a sound, etc.); re-echo. **5.** *Poetic* To extol. [ME < OF < L *resonare* to echo]
re·sound (rē·sound′) *v.t. & v.i.* To sound again.
re·source (ri·sôrs′, -zors′, -sôrs′, rē′sôrs, -sōrs) *n.* **1.** That which is resorted to for aid or support; resort. **2.** *pl.* Available means or property; any natural advantages or products. **3.** Capacity for finding or adapting means; power of achievement. **4.** Fertility in expedients; skill or ingenuity in meeting any situation; resourcefulness. [< OF < *re*- again + *sourdre* < L *surgere* to rise]
re·source·ful (ri·sôrs′fəl, -sôrs′-, -zors′-) *adj.* **1.** Fertile in resources or expedients. **2.** Full of resources. **— re·source′ful·ly** *adv.* **— re·source′ful·ness** *n.*
re·spect (ri·spekt′) *v.t.* **1.** To have deferential regard for; esteem. **2.** To treat with propriety or consideration. **3.** To regard as inviolable; avoid intruding upon. **4.** To have relation or reference to; concern. **— n. 1.** Regard for and appreciation of worth; honor and esteem. **2.** Demeanor or deportment indicating deference; courteous regard. **3.** *pl.* Expressions of consideration or esteem; compliments: to pay one's *respects.* **4.** Conformity to duty or obligation: *respect* for the law. **5.** The condition of being honored or respected. **6.** A specific aspect: In what *respect* is he wanting? **7.** Reference or relation: usu. with *to*: with *respect* to profits. [< L < *re*- again + *specere* to look] **— re·spect′er** *n.*
re·spect·a·ble (ri·spek′tə·bəl) *adj.* **1.** Deserving of respect; being of good name or repute; also, respected. **2.** Being of moderate excellence; average. **3.** Considerable in number, size, quality, etc. **4.** Having a good appearance; presentable. **5.** Conventionally correct or socially acceptable in conduct. **— re·spect′a·bil′i·ty** *n.* **— re·spect′a·bly** *adv.*
re·spect·ful (ri·spekt′fəl) *adj.* Marked by or manifesting respect. **— re·spect′ful·ly** *adv.* **— re·spect′ful·ness** *n.*
re·spect·ing (ri·spek′ting) *prep.* In relation to; regarding.
re·spec·tive (ri·spek′tiv) *adj.* Pertaining or relating severally to each of those under consideration; particular.
re·spec·tive·ly (ri·spek′tiv·lē) *adv.* As singly or severally considered; singly in the order designated: The first three go to John, James, and William *respectively.*
re·spell (rē·spel′) *v.t.* To spell again, esp. in a system whereby pronunciation is indicated.
res·pi·ra·tion (res′pə·rā′shən) *n.* **1.** The act of inhaling and exhaling; breathing. **2.** The process by which a plant or animal takes in oxygen from the air and gives off carbon dioxide and other products of oxidation. [< MF < L < *re*- again + *spirare* to breathe]
res·pi·ra·tor (res′pə·rā′tər) *n.* **1.** A screen, as of fine gauze, worn over the mouth or nose, as a protection against dust, etc. **2.** A device worn over the nose and mouth for the inhalation of medicated vapors, or of oxygen for lung patients. **3.** An apparatus for artificial respiration.
res·pi·ra·to·ry (ri·spīr′ə·tôr′ē, -tō′rē, res′pər·ə-) *adj.* Of, pertaining to, used in, or caused by respiration.
res·pite (res′pit) *n.* **1.** Postponement; delay. **2.** Temporary intermission of labor or effort; an interval of rest. **3.** *Law* Temporary suspension of the execution of a sentence for a capital offense; reprieve. **— v.t. ·pit·ed, ·pit·ing 1.** To relieve by a pause or rest. **2.** To grant delay in the execution of (a penalty, sentence, etc.). **3.** To postpone. [< OF < L *respectus* regard, refuge]
re·splen·dent (ri·splen′dənt) *adj.* Shining with brilliant luster; vividly bright; splendid; gorgeous. [< L < *re*- back + *splendere* to shine] **— re·splen′dence, re·splen′den·cy** *n.* **— re·splen′dent·ly** *adv.*
re·spond (ri·spond′) *v.i.* **1.** To give an answer; reply. **2.** To act in reply or return; react. **3.** *Law* To be liable or answerable. **— v.t. 4.** To say in answer; reply. **— n. 1.** *Archit.* A pilaster or similar feature placed against a wall, to receive an arch. **2.** *Eccl.* A response (def. 2). [< OF < *re*- back + *spondere* to pledge] **— re·spon′der** *n.*

re·spon·dence (ri·spon′dəns) *n.* **1.** The character or condition of being respondent. **2.** The act of responding. Also **re·spon′den·cy.**

re·spon·dent (ri·spon′dənt) *adj.* **1.** Giving response, or given as a response; answering; responsive. **2.** *Law* Occupying the position of defendant. — *n.* **1.** One who responds or answers. **2.** *Law* A defendant.

re·sponse (ri·spons′) *n.* **1.** The act of responding, or that which is responded; reply; reaction. **2.** *Eccl.* **a** A portion of a liturgy or church service said or sung by the congregation or choir in reply to the officiating priest. **b** An anthem sung or said during or after a reading. Also called *respond.* **3.** *Biol.* The behavior of an organism resulting from a stimulus or influence; a reaction. **4.** In bridge, the play of a high or low card in following suit, as a signal to one's partner.

re·spon·si·bil·i·ty (ri·spon′sə·bil′ə·tē) *n. pl.* **·ties 1.** The state of being responsible or accountable. **2.** That for which one is answerable; a duty or trust. **3.** Ability to meet obligations or to act without superior authority or guidance. Also **re·spon′si·ble·ness.**

re·spon·si·ble (ri·spon′sə·bəl) *adj.* **1.** Answerable legally or morally for the discharge of a duty, trust, or debt. **2.** Having capacity to perceive the distinctions of right and wrong. **3.** Able to meet legitimate claims; having sufficient property or means for the payment of debts. **4.** Involving accountability or obligation. [See RESPOND.] — **re·spon′si·bly** *adv.*

re·spon·sive (ri·spon′siv) *adj.* **1.** Inclined or ready to respond; being or reacting in accord, sympathy, or harmony; responding. **2.** Constituting, or of the nature of, response or reply. **3.** Characterized by or containing responses. — **re·spon′sive·ly** *adv.* — **re·spon′sive·ness** *n.*

rest[1] (rest) *v.i.* **1.** To cease working, exerting oneself, etc., so as to refresh oneself. **2.** To cease from effort or activity for a time. **3.** To seek or obtain ease or refreshment by lying down, sleeping, etc. **4.** To sleep. **5.** To be at peace; be tranquil. **6.** To lie in death; be dead. **7.** To remain unchanged. **8.** To be supported; stand, lean, lie, or sit: with *against, on,* or *upon.* **9.** To be founded or based: with *on* or *upon.* **10.** To rely; depend: with *on* or *upon.* **11.** To be placed as a burden or responsibility: with *on* or *upon.* **12.** To be or lie in a specified place. **13.** To be directed; remain, as the gaze or eyes, on something. **14.** *Law* To cease presenting evidence in a case. **15.** *Agric.* To lie fallow. — *v.t.* **16.** To give rest to; refresh by rest. **17.** To put, lay, lean, etc., as for support or rest. **18.** To found; base. **19.** To direct (the gaze, eyes, etc.). **20.** *Law* To cease presenting evidence in (a case). — *n.* **1.** The act or state of resting; repose; quiet. **2.** Freedom from disturbance or disquiet; tranquillity. **3.** Sleep; also, death. **4.** That on which anything rests; a support. **5.** In billiards and pool, a support for a cue; a bridge. **6.** A place of repose or quiet; a stopping place; abode. **7.** *Music* A pause or interval of silence that corresponds to the time value of a note; also, the character indicating such a pause. **8.** In prosody, a pause in a verse; caesura. **9.** *Mil.* A command given troops, allowing them to relax. — **at rest 1.** In a state of repose, as in sleep or death. **2.** Not in motion; still. **3.** Free from anxiety or worry: to set one's mind *at rest.* [OE *restan*] — **rest′er** *n.*

rest[2] (rest) *n.* **1.** That which remains or is left over; a remainder. **2.** (*construed as pl.*) Those remaining or not enumerated; the others. — *v.i.* To be and remain; stay: *Rest content.* [< OF < L < *re-* back + *stare* to stand]

re·state (rē·stāt′) *v.t.* **·stat·ed, ·stat·ing** To state again or anew. — **re·state′ment** *n.*

res·tau·rant (res′tər·ənt, -tə·ränt) *n.* A place where refreshments or meals are provided; a public dining room. [< F, lit., restoring]

res·tau·ra·teur (res′tər·ə·tûr′, *Fr.* res·tō·rȧ·tœr′) *n.* The proprietor or keeper of a restaurant. [< F]

rest·ful (rest′fəl) *adj.* **1.** Full of or giving rest; affording freedom from disturbance, work, or trouble. **2.** Being at rest or in repose; quiet. — **rest′ful·ly** *adv.* — **rest′ful·ness** *n.*

rest·ing (res′ting) *adj.* **1.** In a state of rest; reposing; also, dead. **2.** *Bot.* Dormant: a *resting* spore.

res·ti·tu·tion (res′tə·tōō′shən, -tyōō′-) *n.* **1.** The act of restoring something that has been taken away or lost. **2.** The act of making good or rendering an equivalent for injury or loss. **3.** Restoration to, return to, or recovery of a former position or condition. **4.** *Physics* The tendency of elastic bodies to recover their shape after compression. [< OF < L < *re-* again + *statuere* to set up]

res·tive (res′tiv) *adj.* **1.** Impatient of control; unruly. **2.** Restless; fidgety. [< F < L *restare* to stand] — **res′tive·ly** *adv.* — **res′tive·ness** *n.*

rest·less (rest′lis) *adj.* **1.** Having no rest; never quiet. **2.** Unable or disinclined to rest. **3.** Constantly seeking change; discontented. **4.** Obtaining no rest or sleep; sleepless. — **rest′less·ly** *adv.* — **rest′less·ness** *n.*

re·stock (rē·stok′) *v.t.* To stock again or anew.

res·to·ra·tion (res′tə·rā′shən) *n.* **1.** The act of restoring a person or thing to a former place or condition. **2.** The state of being restored; renewal. **3.** The reconstruction or repair of something so as to restore it to its original or former state; also, an object that has been so restored. — **the Restoration** The return of Charles II to the English throne in 1660, after the overthrow of the Protectorate; also, the following period until 1685.

re·stor·a·tive (ri·stôr′ə·tiv, -stō′rə-) *adj.* **1.** Tending or able to restore. **2.** Pertaining to restoration. — *n.* That which restores; esp. something to restore consciousness.

re·store (ri·stôr′, -stōr′) *v.t.* **·stored, ·stor·ing 1.** To bring into existence or effect again. **2.** To bring back to a former or original condition, appearance, etc., as a painting. **3.** To put back in a former place or position; reinstate, as a deposed monarch. **4.** To bring back to health and vigor. **5.** To give back (something lost or taken away). [< OF < L < *re-* again + *-staurare* to make firm] — **re·stor′er** *n.*

re·store (rē·stôr′, -stōr′) *v.t.* **·stored, ·stor·ing** To store again or anew.

re·strain (ri·strān′) *v.t.* **1.** To hold back from acting, proceeding, or advancing; repress. **2.** To deprive of freedom or liberty, as by placing in a prison. **3.** To restrict or limit. [< OF < L < *re-* back + *stringere* to draw tight] — **re·strain′a·ble** *adj.* — **re·strain′ed·ly** *adv.* — **re·strain′er** *n.*

re·straint (ri·strānt′) *n.* **1.** The act of restraining. **2.** The state of being restrained; confinement. **3.** That which restrains; a restriction. **4.** Self-repression; constraint.

restraint of trade Interference with the free flow of goods or with fair competition, as by price fixing.

re·strict (ri·strikt′) *v.t.* To hold or keep within limits or bounds. [< L *restrictus,* pp. or *restringere* to restrain]

re·strict·ed (ri·strik′tid) *adj.* **1.** Limited; confined. **2.** Not available to the general public; limited to a specific group: *restricted* information. **3.** Excluding people of certain races, religions, or nationalities. — **re·strict′ed·ly** *adv.*

re·stric·tion (ri·strik′shən) *n.* **1.** The act of restricting, or the state of being restricted. **2.** That which restricts.

re·stric·tive (ri·strik′tiv) *adj.* **1.** Serving, tending, or operating to restrict. **2.** *Gram.* Denoting a word or word group, esp. an adjective clause, that limits the identity of its antecedent and is therefore essential to the meaning of the sentence, as *who votes for Jones* in *Any man who votes for Jones is a fool.* — **re·stric′tive·ly** *adv.*

rest room A toilet and washroom in a public building.

re·sult (ri·zult′) *n.* **1.** The outcome of an action, course, process, or agency; consequence; effect; conclusion. **2.** *Math.* A quantity or value ascertained by calculation. — *v.i.* **1.** To be a result or outcome; be a physical or logical consequent; follow: with *from.* **2.** To have an issue; terminate; end: with *in.* [< L < *re-* back + *salire* to leap]

re·sul·tant (ri·zul′tənt) *adj.* Arising or following as a result. — *n.* **1.** That which results; a consequence. **2.** *Physics* A force, velocity, or other quantity, resulting from and equivalent in effect to the action of two or more quantities of the same kind.

re·sume (ri·zōōm′) *v.* **·sumed, ·sum·ing** *v.t.* **1.** To take up again after cessation or interruption; begin again. **2.** To take or occupy again. **3.** To take for oneself again: to *resume* a title. — *v.i.* **4.** To continue after cessation or interruption. [< MF < L < *re-* again + *sumere* to take] — **re·sum′a·ble** *adj.* — **re·sum′er** *n.*

ré·su·mé (rez′ŏŏ·mā′, rez′ŏŏ·mā) *n.* A summary, as of one's employment record. [< F]

re·sump·tion (ri·zump′shən) *n.* The act of resuming.

re·sur·face (rē·sûr′fis) *v.t.* **·faced, ·fac·ing** To provide with a new surface.

re·surge (ri·sûrj′) *v.i.* **·surged, ·surg·ing 1.** To rise again; be resurrected. **2.** To surge or sweep back again, as the tide. [< L < *re-* again + *surgere* to rise]

re·sur·gent (ri·sûr′jənt) *adj.* **1.** Rising again. **2.** Surging back or again. — **re·sur′gence** *n.*

res·ur·rect (rez′ə·rekt′) *v.t.* **1.** To bring back to life; raise from the dead. **2.** To bring back into use or to notice. — *v.i.* **3.** To rise again from the dead. [Back formation < RESURRECTION]

res·ur·rec·tion (rez′ə·rek′shən) *n.* **1.** A rising again from the dead. **2.** The state of those who have risen from the dead. **3.** Any revival or renewal, as of a practice or custom, after disuse, decay, etc.; restoration. — **the Resurrection** *Theol.* **1.** The rising of Christ from the dead. **2.** The rising again of all the dead at the day of judgment. [See RESURGE.] — **res′ur·rec′tion·al** *adj.* — **res′ur·rec′tion·ar·y** *adj.*

re·sus·ci·tate (ri·sus′ə·tāt) *v.t. & v.i.* **·tat·ed, ·tat·ing** To bring or come back to life; revive from unconsciousness. [< L < *re-* again + *suscitare* to revive] — **re·sus′ci·ta′tion** *n.* — **re·sus′ci·ta′tive** *adj.* — **re·sus′ci·ta′tor** *n.*

ret (ret) *v.t.* **ret·ted, ret·ting** To steep or soak, as flax, to separate the fibers: also *rot.* [ME < MDu. *reten*]

re·tail (*n. & adj.* rē′tāl; *v.* ri·tāl′) *n.* The selling of goods in small quantities, esp. to the ultimate consumer: distinguished from *wholesale.* — *adj.* Pertaining to, involving, or engaged in the sale of goods at retail. — *v.t.* **1.** To sell at retail. **2.** To repeat, as gossip. — *v.i.* **3.** To be sold at retail. [< OF < *re-* back + *tailler* to cut] — **re'tail·er** *n.*

re·tain (ri·tān') *v.t.* **1.** To keep or continue to keep in one's possession; hold. **2.** To maintain in use, practice, etc. **3.** To keep in a fixed condition or place. **4.** To keep in mind; remember. **5.** To hire; also, to engage (an attorney or other representative) by paying a retainer. [< OF < L < *re-* back + *tenere* to hold] — **re·tain'a·ble** *adj.*

re·tain·er[1] (ri·tā'nər) *n.* **1.** A servant. **2.** One who retains or keeps. **3.** *Mech.* A device for holding the parts of ball or roller bearings in place.

re·tain·er[2] (ri·tā'nər) *n.* **1.** The fee paid, or the agreement made, to employ an attorney to serve in a suit; a retaining fee. **2.** A similar fee paid to anyone to retain his services. [< OF *retenir* to hold back, used as noun]

re·tain·ing wall (ri·tā'ning) A wall to prevent the material of an embankment or cut from sliding, as a revetment.

re·take (*v.* rē·tāk'; *n.* rē'tāk) *v.t.* **·took, ·tak·en, ·tak·ing 1.** To take back; receive again. **2.** To recapture. **3.** To photograph again. — *n.* A motion-picture or television scene, part of a musical or other recording, etc., done again.

re·tal·i·ate (ri·tal'ē·āt) *v.* **·at·ed, ·at·ing** *v.i.* **1.** To return like for like; esp., to repay evil with evil. — *v.t.* **2.** To repay (an injury, wrong, etc.) in kind; revenge. [< L < *re-* back + *talio* punishment in kind] — **re·tal'i·a·tive** *adj.* — **re·tal'i·a·to'ry** *adj.*

re·tal·i·a·tion (ri·tal·ē·ā'shən) *n.* The act of retaliating; reprisal; requital. — **Syn.** See REVENGE.

re·tard (ri·tärd') *v.t.* **1.** To cause to move or proceed slowly; hinder the advance or course of; delay. — *v.i.* **2.** To be delayed. — *n.* The act of retarding; delay. [< MF < L < *re-* back + *tardare* to make slow] — **re·tard'ant** *n.* & *adj.* — **re'tar·da'tion** *n.* — **re·tard'a·tive** *adj.* & *n.*

re·tard·ed (ri·tär'did) *adj. Psychol.* Slowed down or backward in mental development or school achievement.

re·tard·er (ri·tär'dər) *n.* **1.** One who or that which retards. **2.** *Chem.* A substance that slows a chemical reaction, usu. when added in small quantity: compare CATALYST.

retch (rech) *v.i.* To make an effort to vomit; strain; heave. [OE *hræcan* to clear one's throat]

re·ten·tion (ri·ten'shən) *n.* **1.** The act of retaining, or the state of being retained. **2.** The ability to remember. **3.** The capacity or ability to retain. **4.** *Med.* A retaining within the body of materials normally excreted, as urine.

re·ten·tive (ri·ten'tiv) *adj.* Having the power or tendency to retain. — **re·ten·tiv'i·ty** *n.* — **re·ten'tive·ness** *n.*

ret·i·cent (ret'ə·sənt) *adj.* Habitually silent or reserved in utterance. [< L < *re-* again + *tacere* to be silent] — **ret'i·cence, ret'i·cen·cy** *n.* — **ret'i·cent·ly** *adv.*

re·tic·u·lar (ri·tik'yə·lər) *adj.* Like a network; reticulate; intricate. Also **re·tic'u·lar'y.**

re·tic·u·late (ri·tik'yə·lāt; *for adj., also* ri·tik'yə·lit) *v.* **·lat·ed, ·lat·ing** *v.t.* **1.** To make a network of. **2.** To cover with or as with lines of network. — *v.i.* **3.** To form a network. — *adj.* **1.** Having the form or appearance of a network. **2.** *Bot.* Having lines or veins crossing: also **re·tic'u·lat'ed.** — **re·tic'u·la'tion** *n.*

ret·i·cule (ret'ə·kyōōl) *n.* A small bag formerly used by women for carrying personal articles, etc. [See RETICULUM.]

re·tic·u·lum (ri·tik'yə·ləm) *n.* *pl.* **·la** (-lə) **1.** A netlike structure; network. **2.** *Zool.* The second stomach of a ruminant. [< L, dim. of *rete* net]

ret·i·na (ret'ə·nə, ret'nə) *n.* *pl.* **·nas** or **·nae** (-nē) *Anat.* The inner membrane at the back of the eyeball, containing light-sensitive rods and cones that transmit the image to the optic nerve. For illus. see EYE. [< Med.L < L *rete* net] — **ret'i·nal** *adj.*

ret·i·ni·tis (ret'ə·nī'tis) *n.* *Pathol.* Inflammation of the retina.

ret·i·nue (ret'ə·nōō, -nyōō) *n.* The body of retainers attending a person of rank; cortège. [< F < *retenir* to retain]

re·tire (ri·tīr') *v.* **·tired, ·tir·ing** *v.i.* **1.** To go away or withdraw, as for privacy, shelter, or rest. **2.** To go to bed. **3.** To withdraw oneself from business, public life, or active service. **4.** To fall back; retreat, as troops under attack. **5.** To move back; recede or appear to recede. — *v.t.* **6.** To remove from active service. **7.** To pay off and withdraw from circulation: to *retire* bonds. **8.** To withdraw (troops, etc.) from action. **9.** In baseball, etc., to put out (a batter or side). [< MF < *re-* back + *tirer* to draw]

re·tired (ri·tīrd') *adj.* **1.** Withdrawn from public view; solitary; secluded: a *retired* life. **2.** Withdrawn from active service, business, office, etc. **3.** Due to or received by a person withdrawn from active service: *retired* pay.

re·tire·ment (ri·tīr'mənt) *n.* **1.** The act of retiring, or the state of being retired. **2.** A secluded place; a retreat.

re·tir·ing (ri·tīr'ing) *adj.* **1.** Shy; modest; reserved; unobtrusive. **2.** Pertaining to retirement: a *retiring* pension.

re·tort[1] (ri·tôrt') *v.t.* **1.** To direct (a word or deed) back upon the originator. **2.** To reply to, as an accusation or argument, by a similar accusation, etc. — *v.i.* **3.** To make answer, esp. sharply. — *n.* **1.** A keen rejoinder or retaliatory speech; caustic repartee. **2.** The act of retorting. [< L < *re-* back + *torquere* to twist] — **re·tort'er** *n.*

re·tort[2] (ri·tôrt') *n.* **1.** *Chem.* A vessel with a bent tube for the heating of substances, or for distillation. **2.** *Metall.* A vessel in which ore may be heated for the removal of its metal content. [< L *retortus* bent back.]

re·touch (rē·tuch'; *for n., also* rē'tuch) *v.t.* **1.** To add new touches to; modify; revise. **2.** *Photog.* To change or improve, as a print. — *n.* An additional touch, as to a picture, model, or other work of art. — **re·touch'er** *n.*

re·trace (ri·trās') *v.t.* **·traced, ·trac·ing 1.** To go back over; follow backward, as a path. **2.** To trace the whole story of, from the beginning. **3.** To go back over with the eyes or mind. [< F *retracer*] — **re·trace'a·ble** *adj.*

re·trace (rē·trās') *v.t.* **·traced, ·trac·ing** To trace again, as an engraving, drawing, or map.

re·tract (ri·trakt') *v.t.* & *v.i.* **1.** To take back (an assertion, admission, etc.); make a disavowal (of); recant. **2.** To draw back or in, as the claws of a cat. [< F < L < *re-* again + *tractare* to handle, freq. of *trahere* to draw] — **re·tract'a·ble** or **·i·ble** *adj.* — **re·trac·ta·tion** (rē'trak·tā'shən), **re·trac'·tion** *n.*

re·trac·tile (ri·trak'til) *adj. Zool.* Capable of being drawn back or in, as a cat's claws or the head of a tortoise. — **re·trac·til·i·ty** (rē'trak·til'ə·tē) *n.*

re·trac·tive (ri·trak'tiv) *adj.* Having the power or tendency to retract; retracting.

re·trac·tor (ri·trak'tər) *n.* **1.** One who or that which retracts. **2.** *Surg.* An instrument used to hold apart the edges of a wound, incision, etc.

re·tread (*n.* rē'tred; *v.* rē·tred') *n.* A pneumatic tire furnished with a new tread. — *v.t.* **·tread·ed, ·tread·ing** To fit or furnish (an automobile tire) with a new tread.

re·tread (rē·tred') *v.t.* **·trod, ·trod·den, ·tread·ing** To tread again.

re·treat (ri·trēt') *v.i.* **1.** To go back or backward; withdraw; retire. **2.** To curve or slope backward. — *v.t.* **3.** In chess, to move (a piece) back. — *n.* **1.** The act of retreating. **2.** The retirement of a military force from a position of danger or from an enemy; also, a signal for retreating, made by a trumpet or drum **3.** *Mil.* A signal, as by bugle, for the lowering of the flag at sunset. **4.** Retirement; seclusion; solitude. **5.** A place of retirement, quiet, or security; a refuge; haunt. **6.** Religious retirement; also, the time spent in religious retirement. — **to beat a retreat 1.** To give a signal for retreat, as by the beat of drums. **2.** To turn back; flee. [< OF < L < *re-* back + *trahere* to draw]

re·trench (ri·trench') *v.t.* **1.** To cut down or reduce; curtail (expenditures). **2.** To cut off or away; remove; omit. — *v.i.* **3.** To make retrenchments; economize. [< MF < *re-* back + *trencher* to cut]

re·trench·ment (ri·trench'mənt) *n.* **1.** The act of retrenching. **2.** Reduction, as of expenses, for the sake of economy. **3.** *Mil.* An interior fortification from which the enemy can be resisted should the outer line be taken.

re·tri·al (rē·trī'əl) *n.* A second or succeeding trial, as of a judicial case.

ret·ri·bu·tion (ret'rə·byōō'shən) *n.* **1.** The act of requiting; esp., impartial infliction of punishment. **2.** That which is done or given in requital, as a reward or punishment. [< OF < L < *re-* back + *tribuere* to divide, grant]

re·trib·u·tive (ri·trib'yə·tiv) *adj.* Tending to reward or punish. Also **re·trib'u·to'ry** (-tôr'ē, -tō'rē).

re·triev·al (ri·trē'vəl) *n.* **1.** The act or process of retrieving. **2.** Possibility of restoration or recovery.

re·trieve (ri·trēv') *v.* **·trieved, ·triev·ing** *v.t.* **1.** To get back; regain. **2.** To restore; revive, as flagging spirits. **3.** To make up for. **4.** To call to mind. **5.** To find and bring in (wounded or dead game): said of dogs. **6.** *Electronics* To obtain or extract (specific information) from the storage unit of an electronic computer. — *v.i.* **7.** To retrieve game. — *n.* The act of retrieving; recovery. [ME < OF < *re-* again + *trouver* to find] — **re·triev'a·bil'i·ty** *n.* — **re·triev'a·ble** *adj.* — **re·triev'a·bly** *adv.*

re·triev·er (ri·trē'vər) *n.* **1.** A sporting dog specifically trained to retrieve game. **2.** One who retrieves.

retro- *prefix* **1.** Back; backward. **2.** Behind. [< L *retro* back, backward]

RETORTS
a Retort with receiver. *b* Common retort.

---

ret·ro·ac·tive (ret'rō·ak'tiv, rē'trō-) *adj.* Taking effect at a (usu. specified) time prior to its enactment, ratification, etc., as a provision in a law or contract; applying retrospectively. — **ret'ro·ac'tive·ly** *adv.* — **ret'ro·ac·tiv'i·ty** *n.*

ret·ro·cede (ret'rō·sēd') *v.* **·ced·ed**, **·ced·ing** *v.t.* **1.** To cede or give back — *v.i.* **2.** To recede. [< L < *retro*- back + *cedere* to go] — **ret'ro·ces'sion** (-sesh'ən) *n.*

ret·ro·fire (ret'rə·fīr') *n. Aerospace* The operation or moment of firing a retrorocket.

ret·ro·flex (ret'rə·fleks) *adj.* Bent backward; reflexed: said esp. of the tongue. Also **ret·ro·flexed** (ret'rə·flexst). [< LL < L *retro*- back + *flectere* to bend]

ret·ro·grade (ret'rə·grād) *adj.* **1.** Going or tending backward; reversed. **2.** Declining to or toward a worse state or character. **3.** *Astron.* Apparently moving from east to west relative to the fixed stars. **4.** Reversed; inverted. — *v.* **·grad·ed**, **·grad·ing** *v.i.* **1.** To move or appear to move backward. **2.** To degenerate. **3.** *Astron.* To have a retrograde motion. — *v.t.* **4.** To cause to move backward; reverse. [< L < *retro*- backward + *gradi* to walk] — **ret'ro·gra·da'tion** (-grā·dā'shən) *n.*

ret·ro·gress (ret'rə·gres) *v.i.* To go back to an earlier or worse state. [< L < *retro*- backward + *gradi* to walk] — **Syn.** In strict usage, *retrogress* suggests a return to a former place or condition, while *degenerate* implies a passing into a worse condition.

ret·ro·gres·sion (ret'rə·gresh'ən) *n.* **1.** The act or process of retrogressing. **2.** *Biol.* Return to or toward an earlier form or structure. — **ret'ro·gres'sive** *adj.*

ret·ro·rock·et (ret'rō·rok'it) *n. Aerospace* An auxiliary rocket whose reverse thrust decelerates a rocket or spaceship.

re·trorse (ri·trôrs') *adj.* Turned or directed backward. [< L *retrorsus*, contr. of *retroversus* < *retro*- backward + *versus*, pp. of *vertere* to turn] — **re·trorse'ly** *adv.*

ret·ro·spect (ret'rə·spekt) *n.* A view or contemplation of something past. [< L < *retro*- back + *specere* to look] — **ret'ro·spec'tion** *n.*

ret·ro·spec·tive (ret'rə·spek'tiv) *adj.* **1.** Looking back on the past. **2.** Looking or facing backward. **3.** Applying retroactively, as legislation. **4.** Characterized by retrospection. — **ret'ro·spec'tive·ly** *adv.*

ret·rous·sé (ret'rōō·sā', *Fr.* rə·trōō·sā') *adj.* Turned up at the end: said of a nose. [< F, pp. of *retrousser* to turn up]

re·try (rē·trī') *v.t.* **·tried**, **·try·ing** To try again, as a judicial case.

re·turn (ri·tûrn') *v.i.* **1.** To come or go back, as to or toward a former place or condition. **2.** To come back or revert in thought or speech. **3.** To revert to a former owner. **4.** To answer; respond. — *v.t.* **5.** To bring, carry, send, or put back; replace. **6.** To give in return for something. **7.** To repay or requite, esp. with an equivalent: to *return* a compliment. **8.** To yield or produce, as a profit or interest. **9.** To send back; reflect, as light or sound. **10.** To render (a verdict, etc.). **11.** To submit, as a report or writ, to one in authority. **12.** To report or announce officially. **13.** In card games, to lead (a suit previously led by one's partner). — *n.* **1.** The act, process, state, or result of coming back or returning. **2.** That which is returned. **3.** That which accrues, as from investments, labor, or use; profit. **4.** A coming back, reappearance, or recurrence, as of a periodical event. **5.** A report, list, etc.; esp., a formal or official report. **6.** *pl.* A set of tabulated statistics: election *returns*. **7.** In card games, a lead in a suit formerly led, esp. by one's partner **8.** In tennis, etc., the act of returning a ball to one's opponent; also, the ball, etc., so returned. — *adj.* **1.** Of, pertaining to, or for a return: a *return* ticket. **2.** Given, taken, or done in return: a *return* visit. **3.** Occurring or presented a second time or again. **4.** Reversing direction; doubling back, as a U-shaped bend. [< OF < *re*- back + *torner* to turn] — **re·turn'a·ble** *adj.* — **re·turn'er** *n.*

re·turn (rē·tûrn') *v.t. & v.i.* To turn or fold back again.

return ticket A round-trip ticket.

Reu·ben (rōō'bin) In the Old Testament, the eldest son of Jacob and Leah. *Gen.* xxix 32. — *n.* The tribe of Israel descended from Reuben.

re·un·ion (rē·yōōn'yən) *n.* **1.** The act of reuniting. **2.** A gathering of persons who have been separated.

re·u·nite (rē'yōō·nīt') *v.t. & v.i.* **·nit·ed**, **·nit·ing** To unite, cohere, or combine again after separation. — **re'u·nit'er** *n.*

Reu·ters (roi'tərz) *n.* A British organization for collecting news and distributing it to member newspapers. Also **Reuter's News Agency.** [after Baron P. J. von *Reuter*, 1816–99, born in Germany]

rev (rev) *n.* A revolution, as of a motor. — *v.t. & v.i.* **revved**, **rev·ving** To alter the speed of (a motor): with *up*.

re·vamp (rē·vamp') *v.t.* **1.** To patch up; make over; renovate. **2.** To vamp (a boot or shoe) anew.

re·veal (ri·vēl') *v.t.* **1.** To make known; disclose; divulge. **2.** To make visible; expose to view; show. [< OF < L to unveil < *re*- back + *velum* veil] — **re·veal'a·ble** *adj.* — **re·veal'er** *n.* — **re·veal'ment** *n.*

rev·eil·le (rev'i·lē) *n.* **1.** A morning signal by drum or bugle, notifying soldiers or sailors to rise. **2.** The hour at which this signal is sounded. [< F, ult. < L < *re*- again + *vigilare* to keep watch]

rev·el (rev'əl) *v.i.* **rev·eled** or **·elled**, **rev·el·ing** or **·el·ling 1.** To take delight: with *in*: He *revels* in his freedom. **2.** To engage in boisterous festivities; make merry. — *n.* **1.** Merrymaking; carousing. **2.** *Often pl.* An occasion of boisterous festivity; a celebration. [< OF *reveler* to make an uproar < L *rebellare*] — **rev'el·er** or **rev'el·ler** *n.*

rev·e·la·tion (rev'ə·lā'shən) *n.* **1.** The act or process of revealing. **2.** That which is or has been revealed. **3.** *Theol.* **a** The act of revealing or communicating divine truth, esp. by divine agency. **b** That which has been so revealed, as concerning God in his relations to man.

Rev·e·la·tion (rev'ə·lā'shən) *n. Often pl.* The Apocalypse, or book of Revelation, the last book of the New Testament: in full, **The Revelation of Saint John the Divine.**

rev·el·ry (rev'əl·rē) *n. pl.* **·ries** Noisy or boisterous merriment.

re·venge (ri·venj') *v.* **·venged**, **·veng·ing** *v.t.* **1.** To inflict punishment, injury, or loss in return for. **2.** To take or seek vengeance in behalf of. — *n.* **1.** The act of revenging. **2.** A means of avenging oneself or others. **3.** A desire for vengeance. [< OF < *re*- again + *vengier* to take vengeance] — **re·veng'er** *n.* — **Syn.** (noun) *Revenge* stresses personal bitterness that seeks relief in harming or humiliating an enemy. *Vengeance*, originally the indignant vindication of justice, is now applied to any furious and thoroughgoing *revenge*. *Retaliation* suggests the repayment of an act by a like act.

re·venge·ful (ri·venj'fəl) *adj.* Disposed to or full of revenge; vindictive. — **re·venge'ful·ly** *adv.* + **re·venge'ful·ness** *n.*

rev·e·nue (rev'ə·nyōō, -nōō) *n.* **1.** Total current income of a government, except duties on imports: also called *internal revenue.* **2.** Income from any form of property. **3.** A source of income. [< F < L < *re*- back + *venire* to come]

re·ver·ber·ant (ri·vûr'bər·ənt) *adj.* Reverberating.

re·ver·ber·ate (ri·vûr'bə·rāt) *v.* **·at·ed**, **·at·ing** *v.i.* **1.** To resound or re-echo. **2.** To be reflected. **3.** To rebound or recoil. — *v.t.* **4.** To echo back (a sound); re-echo. **5.** To reflect. [< L < *re*- back + *verberare* to beat]

re·ver·ber·a·tion (ri·vûr'bə·rā'shən) *n.* **1.** The act or process of reverberating. **2.** That which is reverberated. **3.** The rebound or reflection of light, heat, or sound waves. — **re·ver'ber·a'tive** *adj.* — **re·ver'ber·a·to·ry** (-bər·ə·tôr'ē, -tō'rē) *adj.*

re·vere (ri·vir') *v.t.* **·vered**, **·ver·ing** To regard with reverence; venerate. — **Syn.** See VENERATE. [< L < *re*- again + *vereri* to fear] — **re·ver'er** *n.*

rev·er·ence (rev'ər·əns) *n.* **1** A feeling of profound respect often mingled with awe and affection; veneration. **2.** An act of respect; an obeisance. — *v.t.* **·enced**, **·enc·ing** To regard with reverence. — **Syn.** See VENERATE.

Rev·er·ence (rev'ər·əns) *n.* A title or form of address for clergymen: often preceded by *His, Your*, etc.

rev·er·end (rev'ər·ənd) *adj.* **1.** Worthy of reverence. **2.** *Often cap.* A title of respect often used with the name of a clergyman. — *n. Informal* A clergyman; minister. [See REVERE.]

rev·er·ent (rev'ər·ənt) *adj.* **1.** Feeling reverence. **2.** Expressing reverence. [See REVERE.] — **rev'er·ent·ly** *adv.*

rev·er·en·tial (rev'ə·ren'shəl) *adj.* Proceeding from or expressing reverence. — **rev'er·en'tial·ly** *adv.*

rev·er·ie (rev'ə·rē) *n. pl.* **·er·ies 1.** Abstracted musing; dreaming. **2.** A product of such musing. Also **rev'er·y.** [< F < MF *resver* to be delirious, dream]

re·vers (rə·vir', -vâr') *n. pl.* **vers** (-virz', -vârz') A part of a garment folded over to show the inside, as the lapel of a coat. Also **re·vere'.** [< OF. See REVERSE.]

re·ver·sal (ri·vûr'səl) *n.* The act of reversing, or the state of being reversed.

re·verse (ri·vûrs') *adj.* **1.** Having a contrary or opposite direction, character, order, etc.; turned backward. **2.** Causing backward motion: the *reverse* gear of an automobile. — *n.* **1.** That which is directly opposite or contrary. **2.** The back or secondary side of anything: distinguished from *obverse.* **3.** A change to an opposite position, direction, or state. **4.** A change for the worse; a check or partial defeat. **5.** *Mech.* A reversing gear or movement. — *v.* **·versed**, **·vers·ing** *v.t.* **1.** To turn upside down or inside out. **2.** To turn in an opposite direction. **3.** To change into something different or opposite. **4.** To set aside; annul: to *reverse* a decree. **5.** *Mech.* To cause to have an opposite motion or effect. — *v.i.* **6.** To move or turn in the opposite direction. **7.** To reverse its action, as an engine. [< OF < L < *re*- back + *vertere* to turn] — **re·verse'ly** *adv.* — **re·vers'er** *n.*

re·vers·i·ble (ri·vûr'sə·bəl) *adj.* **1.** Capable of being reversed in direction or position. **2.** Capable of going either forward or backward, as a chemical reaction or physiological process. **3.** Capable of being used or worn inside out or backward, as a coat. **4.** Having the finish on both sides, as a fabric. — *n.* A reversible coat. — **re·vers'i·bil'i·ty, re·vers'i·ble·ness** *n.* — **re·vers'i·bly** *adv.*

re·ver·sion (ri·vûr'zhən, -shən) *n.* **1.** A return to or toward some former state, condition, practice, or belief. **2.** The act of reversing, or the state of being reversed. **3.** *Biol.* **a** The reappearance in an individual of characteristics that had not been evident for two or more generations: also called *atavism*. **b** An example of such reappearance. **4.** *Law* **a** The return of an estate to the grantor or his heirs after the expiration of the grant. **b** The right of succession to an estate. [See REVERT.] — **re·ver'sion·al, re·ver'sion·ar'y** (-er'ē) *adj.*

re·vert (ri·vûrt') *v.i.* **1.** To go or turn back to a former place, condition, attitude, etc. **2.** *Biol.* To return to or show characteristics of an earlier type. **3.** *Law* To return to the former owner or his heirs. [< OF < LL < L < *re-* back + *vertere* to turn] — **re·vert'i·ble** *adj.* — **re·vert'ive** *adj.*

re·vet·ment (ri·vet'mənt) *n.* A facing or sheathing, as of masonry, for protecting earthworks, river banks, etc. [< F < OF < LL < L < *re-* again + *vestire* to clothe]

re·view¹ (ri·vyōō') *v.t.* **1.** To go over or examine again; look at or study again. **2.** To look back upon; think of retrospectively. **3.** To make an inspection of, esp. formally. **4.** To write or make a critical review of, as a new book. **5.** *Law* To reexamine (something done or adjudged by a lower court). — *v.i.* **6.** To write a review or reviews, as for a magazine. [< RE- + VIEW]

re·view² (ri·vyōō') *n.* **1.** A repeated or new view or study of something; a retrospective survey. **2.** A lesson studied or recited again. **3.** Critical study or examination. **4.** An article containing a critical discussion of some work. **5.** A periodical devoted to essays in criticism and on general subjects. **6.** A formal inspection, as of troops. **7.** *Law* A judicial revision by a superior court of the order or decree of a subordinate court. See REVUE. [< MF < L < *re-* again + *videre* to see]

re·view·al (ri·vyōō'əl) *n.* The act of reviewing; a review.

re·view·er (ri·vyōō'ər) *n.* One who reviews; esp., one who critically reviews new books, plays, movies, etc.

re·vile (ri·vīl') *v.* **·viled, ·vil·ing** *v.t.* **1.** To assail with abusive or contemptuous language; vilify; abuse. — *v.i.* **2.** To use abusive or contemptuous language. — **Syn.** See SCOLD. [< OF *reviler* to despise] — **re·vile'ment** *n.* — **re·vil'er** *n.* — **re·vil'ing·ly** *adv.*

re·vis·al (ri·vī'zəl) *n.* The act of revising; revision.

re·vise (ri·vīz') *v.t.* **·vised, ·vis·ing** **1.** To read or read over so as to correct errors, suggest or make changes, etc. **2.** To change; alter. — *n.* **1.** The act or result of revising; a revision. **2.** A corrected proof after revision. [< MF < L < *re-* again + *visere* to scrutinize] — **re·vis'er** or **re·vi'sor** *n.*

re·vi·sion (ri·vizh'ən) *n.* **1.** The act or process of revising. **2.** Something revised, as a new version of a book. — **re·vi'sion·al, re·vi'sion·ar'y** *adj.*

re·vi·so·ry (ri·vī'zər·ē) *adj.* Effecting, or capable of effecting, revision; revising: *revisory* powers.

re·vi·val (ri·vī'vəl) *n.* **1.** The act of reviving or, the state of being revived. **2.** A recovery, as from depression. **3.** A restoration, as after neglect or obscurity. **4.** A renewal of interest in religion. **5.** A series of evangelical meetings to reawaken faith.

re·vi·val·ist (ri·vī'vəl·ist) *n.* A preacher or leader in a religious revival movement.

re·vive (ri·vīv') *v.* **·vived, ·viv·ing** *v.t.* **1.** To bring back to life or to consciousness. **2.** To give new health, etc., to. **3.** To bring back into use. **4.** To make effective or operative again. **5.** To renew in the mind or memory. **6.** To produce again, as an old play. — *v.i.* **7.** To come back to life again. **8.** To assume new vigor, health, etc. **9.** To come back into use. **10.** To become effective or operative again. [< MF < L < *re-* again + *vivere* to live] — **re·viv'er** *n.*

re·viv·i·fy (ri·viv'ə·fī) *v.t.* **·fied, ·fy·ing** To give new life to; revive. [< L < *re-* again + *vivus* alive + *facere* to make] — **re·viv'i·fi·ca'tion** *n.*

rev·o·ca·ble (rev'ə·kə·bəl) *adj.* Capable of being revoked. Also **re·vok·a·ble** (ri·vō'kə·bəl). — **rev'o·ca·bil'i·ty** *n.* — **rev'o·ca·bly** *adv.*

rev·o·ca·tion (rev'ə·kā'shən) *n.* The act of revoking, or the state of being revoked; repeal; reversal; annulment.

re·voke (ri·vōk') *v.* **·voked, ·vok·ing** *v.t.* **1.** To annul or make void by recalling; cancel; rescind. — *v.i.* **2.** In card games, to fail to follow suit when possible and when required by the rules. — **Syn.** See ANNUL. — *n.* In card games, neglect to follow suit; a renege. [< OF < L < *re-* back + *vocare* to call] — **re·vok'er** *n.*

re·volt (ri·vōlt') *n.* **1.** An uprising against authority; rebellion. **2.** An act of protest, refusal, or disgust. **3.** The state of a person or persons who revolt: to be in *revolt*. —

v.i. **1.** To rise in rebellion against constituted authority; mutiny. **2.** To turn away in disgust: with *against, at,* or *from.* — *v.t.* **3.** To cause to feel disgust; repel. [< MF < Ital. < L < *re-* back + *volvere* to roll] — **re·volt'er** *n.*

re·volt·ing (ri·vōl'ting) *adj.* Abhorrent; loathsome; nauseating. — **re·volt'ing·ly** *adv.*

rev·o·lu·tion (rev'ə·lōō'shən) *n.* **1.** The act or state of revolving. **2.** A motion in a closed curve around a center, or a complete circuit made by a body in such a course. **3.** *Mech.* Rotation about an axis, as in a spiral, so as to come to a point corresponding to the starting point. **4.** *Astron.* The movement of a planet around the sun or of any celestial body around a center of attraction. **5.** A cycle of successive events or changes. **6.** The overthrow and replacement of a government or political system by those governed. **7.** A drastic change in a condition, method, idea, etc.: a *revolution* in industry. [< OF < LL < L < *re-* back + *volvere* to roll]
— **American Revolution** The war for independence carried on by the thirteen American colonies against Great Britain, 1775–83. Also *Revolutionary War.* See table for WAR.
— **Chinese Revolution** The events in China during the years 1911–12, inspired by Sun Yat-sen, that overthrew the Manchu Empire and established a republic.
— **English Revolution** The course of events in England in 1642–89 that brought about the execution of Charles I, the rise of the Commonwealth, the dethronement of James II, and the establishment of a constitutional government.
— **French Revolution** The revolution that began in France in 1789, overthrew the French monarchy, and culminated in the start of the Napoleonic era in 1799.
— **Russian Revolution** The conflict (1917–22), beginning in a Petrograd uprising on March 12, 1917, that resulted in a provisional moderate government and the abdication of Nicholas II. On November 6, the Bolsheviks under Lenin overthrew this government (the **October Revolution**), and in December, 1922, united the soviet states in the Union of Soviet Socialist Republics under Communist (Bolshevik) control.

rev·o·lu·tion·ar·y (rev'ə·lōō'shən·er'ē) *adj.* **1.** Pertaining to or of the nature of revolution, esp. political; causing or tending to produce revolution. **2.** Rotating; revolving.

Revolutionary calendar See (Republican) CALENDAR.

Revolutionary War The American Revolution. See under REVOLUTION.

rev·o·lu·tion·ize (rev'ə·lōō'shən·īz) *v.t.* **·ized, ·iz·ing** To effect a radical change in the character, operation, etc., of.

re·volve (ri·volv') *v.* **·volved, ·volv·ing** *v.i.* **1.** To move in an orbit about a center. **2.** To spin around on an axis; rotate. **3.** To recur periodically. — *v.t.* **4.** To cause to move in a circle or orbit. **5.** To cause to rotate. **6.** To turn over mentally; consider. [< L < *re-* back + *volvere* to roll] — **re·volv'a·ble** *adj.*

re·volv·er (ri·volv'ər) *n.* **1.** A type of pistol having a revolving cylinder in the breech chambered to hold several cartridges that may be fired in succession without reloading. **2.** One who or that which revolves.

revolving door A door rotating like a turnstile about a central post and consisting of three or four adjustable leaves so encased in a doorway as to exclude drafts of air.

re·vue (ri·vyōō') *n.* A musical show consisting of songs, dances, and skits that lampoon or burlesque contemporary people and events: also spelled *review*. [< F]

re·vul·sion (ri·vul'shən) *n.* **1.** A sudden change of or strong reaction in feeling. **2.** The drawing back from something; violent withdrawal or recoil. [< OF < L < *re-* back + *vellere* to pull] — **re·vul'sive** (-siv) *adj.*

re·ward (ri·wôrd') *n.* **1.** Something given or done in return; esp., a gift, prize, etc., for merit, service, or achievement. **2.** Money offered for information, for the return of lost goods, etc. **3.** Profit; return. — *v.t.* **1.** To give a reward to or for. **2.** To be a reward for. [< OF < *re-* back (< L) + *warder* to guard] — **re·ward'er** *n.*

re·wire (rē·wīr') *v.t.* **·wired, ·wir·ing** To wire again, as a house or a machine.

re·word (rē·wûrd') *v.t.* **1.** To say again in other words; express differently. **2.** To utter or say again in the same words.

re·write (*v.* rē·rīt'; *n.* rē'rīt') *v.t.* **·wrote, ·writ·ten, ·writ·ing** **1.** To write over again. **2.** In American journalism, to put into publishable form (a story submitted by a reporter). — *n.* A news item written in this manner.

rex (reks) *n. pl.* **re·ges** (rē'jēs) *Usu. cap. Latin* King.

Reyn·ard (ren'ərd, rā'nərd) *n.* The fox, esp. as the personification of cunning: also spelled *Renard*. [< MDu. < OHG, name of fox in medieval legend]

-rhage, -rhagia, -rhagy See -RRHAGIA.

-rhaphy See -RRHAPHY.

rhap·so·dize (rap'sə·dīz) *v.t. & v.i.* **·dized, ·diz·ing** To express or recite rhapsodically. — **rhap'so·dist** *n.*

---

rhap·so·dy (rap′sə·dē) *n.   pl. ·dies* 1. A series of disconnected and often extravagant sentences, extracts, or utterances, gathered or composed under excitement. 2. *Music* An instrumental composition of irregular form, often suggestive of improvisation. 3. A miscellaneous collection. [< Gk. < Gk. *rhaptein* to stitch together + *ōidē* song] —**rhap·sod·ic** (rap·sod′ik) *or* ·i·cal *adj.* —**rhap·sod′i·cal·ly** *adv.*

rhe·a (rē′ə) *n.* A flightless bird of the plains of South America, smaller than true ostriches, and having three toes: also called *ostrich.* [< NL < L < Gk.]

Rhe·a (rē′ə) In Greek mythology, the daughter of Uranus and Gaea and mother of Zeus.

-rhea See -RRHEA.

Rhen·ish (ren′ish) *adj.* Pertaining to the river Rhine, or to the adjacent lands. —*n.* Rhine wine. [< L *Rhenus* Rhine]

rhe·ni·um (rē′nē·əm) *n.* A heavy, lustrous, rare metallic element (symbol Re) of the manganese group. See ELEMENT. [< NL < L *Rhenus* Rhine]

rheo- *combining form* Current or flow, as of water or electricity. [< Gk. *rheos* a current]

rhe·o·stat (rē′ə·stat) *n.   Electr.* A variable resistor used to control current and voltage strength in a circuit. [< RHEO- + Gk. *statos* standing] —**rhe′o·stat′ic** *adj.*

rhe·sus (rē′səs) *n.* A monkey with a short tail, common throughout India and widely used in biological and medical research. [< NL < Gk. *Rhēsos* Rhesus]

Rhe·sus factor (rē′səs) Rh factor.

rhet·o·ric (ret′ə·rik) *n.* 1. The art of discourse, both written and spoken. 2. The power of pleasing or persuading. 3. Affected and exaggerated display in the use of language. 4. The art of prose as distinct from verse. [< MF < Gk. < *rhētōr* public speaker]

rhe·tor·i·cal (ri·tôr′i·kəl, -tor′-) *adj.* 1. Pertaining to rhetoric; oratorical. 2. Designed for showy oratorical effect. —**rhe·tor′i·cal·ly** *adv.* —**rhe·tor′i·cal·ness** *n.*

rhetorical question A question put only for oratorical or literary effect, the answer being implied in the question.

rhet·o·ri·cian (ret′ə·rish′ən) *n.* 1. A master of rhetoric. 2. One who writes or speaks eloquently. [< F *rhétoricien*]

rheum (rōōm) *n.   Pathol.* 1. A thin, watery discharge from the nose and eyes. 2. A cold. [< OF < L < Gk. *rheuma* stream < *rheein* to flow] —**rheum′y** *adj.*

rheu·mat·ic (rōō·mat′ik) *adj.* 1. Of or relating to rheumatism. 2. Affected with rheumatism. —*n.* One affected with rheumatism. [< OF < L < Gk. *rheuma* a stream]

rheumatic fever *Pathol.* An infectious disease chiefly affecting children, characterized by painful inflammation around the joints, typically intermittent fever, and inflammation of the pericardium and valves of the heart.

rheu·ma·tism (rōō′mə·tiz′əm) *n.   Pathol.* 1. A painful inflammation and stiffness of the muscles, joints, etc. 2. Rheumatoid arthritis. [< L < Gk. *rheumatismos* < *rheuma* a stream]

rheu·ma·toid (rōō′mə·toid) *adj.   Pathol.* 1. Resembling rheumatism. 2. Rheumatic. Also **rheu′ma·toi′dal** (-toid′l). —**rheu′ma·toi′dal·ly** *adv.*

rheumatoid arthritis *Pathol.* A persisting inflammatory disease of the joints, marked by atrophy, rarefaction of the bones, and deformities.

Rh factor *Biochem.* An agglutinogen present in the blood of most persons (who are said to be **Rh positive**) and that may cause hemolytic reactions under certain conditions, as during pregnancy or following transfusions with persons lacking this factor (who are said to be **Rh negative**): also called *Rhesus factor.*

rhin- Var. of RHINO-.

rhi·nal (rī′nəl) *adj.* Of or pertaining to the nose; nasal.

rhine·stone (rīn′stōn′) *n.* A refractive, colorless glass or paste, used as an imitation gemstone. [Trans. of F *caillou du Rhin*; so called because orig. made at Strasbourg]

Rhine wine 1. Wine made from grapes grown in the neighborhood of the Rhine: also called *Rhenish.* 2. Any of various white, dry, still wines.

rhi·ni·tis (rī·nī′tis) *n.   Pathol.* Inflammation of the mucous membranes of the nose.

rhi·no[1] (rī′nō) *n.   pl. ·nos* A rhinoceros.

rhi·no[2] (rī′nō) *n.   Slang* Money; cash. [Origin unknown]

rhino- *combining form* Nose; nasal. Also, before vowels, *rhin-.* [< Gk. *rhis, rhinos* nose]

rhi·noc·e·ros (rī·nos′ər·əs) *n.   pl. ·ros·es *or* ·ros* A large, herbivorous mammal of Africa and Asia, having one or two horns on the snout and a very thick hide. [< LL < Gk. < *rhis, rhinos* nose + *keras* horn]

rhizo- *combining form* Root; pertaining to a root or roots. Also, before vowels, **rhiz-.** [< Gk. *rhiza* root]

rhi·zoid (rī′zoid) *adj.* Rootlike. —*n.   Bot.* A hairlike, branching organ by which mosses and liverworts obtain nourishment and support. —**rhi·zoi′dal** (rī·zoid′l) *adj.*

rhi·zome (rī′zōm) *n.   Bot.* A subterranean rootlike stem, producing roots from its lower surface and leaves or shoots from its upper surface: also called *rootstalk, rootstock.* Also

rhi·zo·ma (rī·zō′mə). [< NL *rhizoma* < Gk. *rhizōma*, ult. < *rhiza* root] —**rhi·zom·a·tous** (rī·zom′ə·təs, -zō′mə-) *adj.*

rhi·zo·pod (rī′zə·pod) *n.* Any of a class or subclass of protozoans with rootlike pseudopodia. —**rhi·zop·o·dan** (rīzop′ə·dən) *adj. & n.* —**rhi·zop′o·dous** *adj.*

rho (rō) *n.* The seventeenth letter in the Greek alphabet (P, ρ), corresponding to the English *r* aspirated. See ALPHABET. [< Gk. *rhō*]

Rhode Island Red An American breed of domestic fowls, reddish and black in color, with yellow smooth legs.

Rhodes scholarships One of a number of scholarships at Oxford University, provided for in the will of Cecil Rhodes, for selected scholars (**Rhodes scholars**) from the U.S. and the British dominions and colonies.

Rho·di·an (rō′dē·ən) *adj.* Of or pertaining to the island of Rhodes. —*n.* A native of Rhodes.

rho·di·um (rō′dē·əm) *n.* A whitish gray, metallic element (symbol Rh) of the platinum group, whose salts are for the most part rose-colored, used in electroplating to prevent corrosion. See ELEMENT. [< NL < Gk. *rhodon* rose]

rho·do·den·dron (rō′də·den′drən) *n.* Any of a genus of evergreen shrubs or small trees of the heath family, with clusters of white, pink, or purple flowers: the State flower of West Virginia. [< L < Gk. < *rhodon* rose + *dendron* tree]

-rhoea See -RRHEA.

rhomb (rom, romb) *n.* A rhombus. [< F *rhombe*]

rhom·ben·ceph·a·lon (rom′ben·sef′ə·lon) *n.   Anat.* A segment of the embryonic brain that divides into the metencephalon and myelencephalon: also called *hindbrain.* [< NL]

rhom·bic (rom′bik) *adj.* Pertaining to or having the shape of a rhombus. Also **rhom′bi·cal.**

rhom·boid (rom′boid) *n.   Geom.* 1. A parallelogram having opposite sides and opposite angles equal but having no right angle. 2. A solid bounded by such parallelograms. —*adj.* 1. Having the character or shape of a rhomboid. 2. Having a shape approaching that of a rhombus. [< F *rhomboïde*] —**rhom·boi·dal** (rom·boid′l) *adj.*

rhom·bus (rom′bəs) *n.   pl. ·bus·es *or* ·bi** (-bī) *Geom.* An equilateral parallelogram having the angles usu., but not necessarily, oblique. [< L < Gk. *rhombos* spinning top]

rhu·barb (rōō′bärb) *n.* 1. A stout, coarse, perennial herb having large leaves and small clusters of flowers on tall stalks, esp. one whose acid leafstalks are used in cooking. 2. *U.S. Slang* A heated argument or quarrel. [< MF < LL < Gk. *rha rhubarb,* ? < *Rha* the Volga River + L *barbarus* foreign]

rhumb (rum, rumb) *n.   Naut.* 1. One of the 32 points of the mariners' compass, separated by arcs of 11° 15′. 2. One of these arcs or divisions. [< OF *rumb*]

rhum·ba (rum′bə) See RUMBA.

rhumb line A line or course along the surface of a sphere crossing successive meridians at the same angle.

rhyme (rīm) *n.* 1. A correspondence of sounds in two or more words, esp. at the ends of lines of poetry. 2. A verse whose lines have a correspondence of sounds in the end words. 3. Poetry; verse. —*v.* **rhymed, rhym·ing** *v.i.* 1. To make rhymes or verses. 2. To correspond in sound or in terminal sounds. —*v.t.* 3. To put or write in rhyme or verse. 4. To use as a rhyme. Also spelled *rime.* [< OF *rime* < L *rhythmus* rhythm] —**rhym′er** *n.*

rhyme·ster (rīm′stər) *n.* A writer of jingles: also spelled *rimester.*

rhythm (rith′əm) *n.* 1. The recurrence or repetition of stress, beat, sound, accent, motion, etc., usu. occurring in a regular or harmonious pattern or manner. 2. *Music* **a** The relative duration and accent of musical sounds. **b** Any specific arrangement of the accents or durations of musical sounds. 3. In poetry, the cadenced flow of sound as determined by the succession of long and short syllables (**classical rhythm**), or accented and unaccented syllables (**modern rhythm**). 4. In painting, sculpture, etc., a regular or harmonious recurrence of lines, forms, colors, etc. [< MF < L < Gk. *rhythmos* < *rheein* to flow]

rhyth·mi·cal (rith′mə·kəl) *adj.* Of or possessing rhythm. Also **rhyth·mic** (rith′mik). —**rhyth′mi·cal·ly** *adv.*

rhythm method Birth control by sexual abstinence during the woman's estimated monthly period of fertility.

ri·al (rī′al) *n.* A standard monetary unit and coin of Iran: in 1961 worth about 13 U.S. cents. [< OF *rial, real* royal]

ri·al·to (rē·al′tō) *n.   pl. ·tos* A market or place of exchange. [< RIALTO]

Ri·al·to (rē·al′tō, *Ital.* rē·äl′tō) In New York City, the theater district. [after *Rialto,* the ancient business quarter of Venice]

rib (rib) *n.* 1. *Anat.* One of the series of bony rods attached to the spine of most vertebrates, and nearly encircling the thoracic cavity. In man there are twelve ribs on each side, forming the walls of the thorax. For illus. see SKELETON. ◆ Collateral adjective: *costal.* 2. Something likened to a rib: the *rib* of an umbrella. 3. A curved side timber bending away from the keel in a boat or ship. 4. A raised wale or stripe in cloth or knit goods. **5.** *Bot.* A vein of a leaf, esp. a central one. **6.** A cut of meat including one or more ribs. — *v.t.* **ribbed, rib·bing 1.** To make with ridges: to *rib* a piece of knitting. **2.** To strengthen or protect by or enclose within ribs. **3.** *Slang* To make fun of; tease. [OE]

rib·ald (rib′əld) *adj.* Pertaining to or indulging in coarse language or vulgar jokes. — *n.* One who uses coarse or abusive language. [< OF *ribauld* < Gmc.]

rib·ald·ry (rib′əl·drē) *n. pl.* **·ries** Ribald language.

rib·and (rib′ənd) *n. Archaic* A decorative ribbon.

rib·bing (rib′ing) *n.* An arrangement or collection of ribs, as in ribbed cloth, etc.

rib·bon (rib′ən) *n.* **1.** A narrow strip of fine fabric, usu. silk or satin, having finished edges and made in a variety of weaves, used as trimming. **2.** Something shaped like or suggesting a ribbon, as a watch spring. **3.** *Often pl.* A narrow strip; a shred: torn to *ribbons.* **4.** An ink-bearing strip of cloth for giving the impression in a typewriter or similar device. **5.** A colored strip of cloth worn to signify membership in an order, the award of a prize, or as a military badge. — *v.t.* To ornament with ribbons; also, to form or tear into ribbons. [< MF *riban* < Gmc.]

ri·bo·fla·vin (rī′bō·flā′vin) *n. Biochem.* A member of the vitamin B complex, vitamin B₂, an orange-yellow, crystalline compound, $C_{17}H_{22}N_4O_6$, found in milk, leafy vegetables, eggs, and meats: also *vitamin G.* [< RIBO(SE) + FLAVIN]

ri·bo·nu·cle·ase (rī′bō·nōō′klē·ās, -nyōō′-, -āz) *n. Biochem.* A pancreatic enzyme, effective in splitting ribonucleic acid.

ri·bo·nu·cle·ic acid (rī′bō·nōō·klē′ik, -nyōō-) *Biochem.* A nucleic acid of high molecular weight found in the cytoplasm and nuclei of cells and associated with DNA in the synthesis of cell proteins. *Abbr. RNA*

ri·bose (rī′bōs) *n. Chem.* A sugar, $C_5H_{10}O_5$, derived from pentose and occurring in certain nucleic acids. [< G *ribon-säure*, arbitrary alteration of ARABINOSE + *-säure* acid]

ri·bo·some (rī′bə·sōm) *n. Biol.* One of a class of minute protein particles found in the cytoplasm of plant and animal cells, associated with ribonucleic acid in the transmission of genetic characteristics. — **ri·bo·so·mal** (rī′bə·sō′məl) *adj.*

-ric *combining form* Realm: bishopric. [OE *rīce*]

rice (rīs) *n.* **1.** The edible seeds of an annual cereal grass, rich in carbohydrates and forming a staple food throughout the world. **2.** The grass itself, cultivated in warm climates. [< OF < Ital. < L < Gk. *oryza*]

rice paper 1. Paper made from rice straw. **2.** A delicate vegetable paper made from the pith of a Chinese shrub, pared into thin rolls and flattened into sheets.

ric·er (rī′sər) *n.* A kitchen utensil consisting of a container perforated with small holes through which potatoes and other vegetables are pressed.

rich (rich) *adj.* **1.** Having large possessions, as of money, goods, or lands; wealthy; opulent. **2.** Composed of rare or precious materials; valuable; costly: *rich* fabrics. **3.** Luscious to the taste, often implying an excess of fats, flavoring, etc. **4.** Full, satisfying, and pleasing, as a tone, voice, color, etc. **5.** Luxuriant; abundant: *rich* hair; *rich* crops. **6.** Yielding abundant returns; fruitful. **7.** Abundantly supplied: often with *in* or *with.* **8.** Abounding in desirable qualities; of full strength, as blood. **9.** *Informal* Exceedingly humorous; amusing or ridiculous: a *rich* joke. **10.** Of a fuel-air mixture, containing a relatively high ratio of fuel to air. [Fusion of OE *rīce* powerful, rich and OF *riche* < Gmc.] — **rich′ly** *adv.* — **rich′ness** *n.*

rich·es (rich′iz) *n.pl.* **1.** Abundant possessions; wealth. **2.** Abundance of whatever is precious.

Rich·ter scale (rikh′tər) A scale for measuring the magnitude of earthquakes. [after C. F. *Richter*, born 1900, U.S. seismologist]

rick (rik) *n.* A stack, as of hay, having the top covered to protect the interior from rain. — *v.t.* To pile in ricks. [OE *hrēac*]

rick·ets (rik′its) *n. Pathol.* A disease of early childhood, chiefly due to a deficiency of calcium salts or vitamin D, characterized by softening of the bones and consequent deformity: also called *rachitis.* [? Alter. of Gk. *rachitis* inflammation of the spine]

rick·ett·si·a (rik·et′sē·ə) *n. pl.* **·si·ae** (-si·ē) Any of a genus of microorganisms typically parasitic in the bodies of certain ticks and lice, but transmissible to other animals and to man and the causative agent of typhus, Rocky Mountain spotted fever, etc. [after Howard T. *Ricketts*, 1871–1910, U.S. pathologist] — **rick·ett′si·al** *adj.*

rick·et·y (rik′it·ē) *adj.* **·et·i·er, ·et·i·est 1.** Ready to fall; tottering. **2.** Affected with or like rickets. **3.** Irregular, as motion. **4.** Feeble; infirm; unsteady. — **rick′et·i·ly** *adv.* — **rick′et·i·ness** *n.*

rick·ey (rik′ē) *n. pl.* **·eys** A cooling drink of which a liquor, as gin, lime juice, and carbonated water are the chief ingre-

dients. [Said to be after a Colonel *Rickey*]

rick·rack (rik′rak′) *n.* Flat braid in zigzag form, made of cotton, rayon, silk, or wool; also, the openwork trimming made with this braid. [Reduplication of RACK¹]

rick·shaw (rik′shô) *n.* A jinriksha. Also **rick′sha.**

ric·o·chet (rik′ə·shā′, -shet′) *v.i.* **·cheted** (-shād′) or **·chet·ted** (-shet′id), **·chet·ing** (-shā′ing) or **·chet·ting** (-shet′ing) To glance from a surface, as a stone thrown over the water; make a series of skips or bounds. — *n.* **1.** A bounding, as of a projectile over or off a surface. **2.** A projectile so bounding. [< F; origin uncertain]

rid (rid) *v.t.* **rid** or **rid·ded, rid·ding** To free, as from a burden or annoyance: usu. with *of.* — *adj.* Free; clear; quit: with *of:* We are well *rid* of him. [< ON *rythja* to clear land]

rid·dance (rid′ns) *n.* A ridding of something undesirable, or the state of being rid. — **good riddance** A welcome deliverance from something undesirable.

rid·den (rid′n) Past participle of RIDE.

rid·dle¹ (rid′l) *v.t.* **·dled, ·dling 1.** To perforate in numerous places, as with shot. **2.** To sift through a coarse sieve. **3.** To damage, injure; criticize, etc., as if by perforating. — *n.* A coarse sieve. [OE *hriddel* sieve] — **rid′dler** *n.*

rid·dle² (rid′l) *n.* **1.** A puzzling question stated as a problem to be solved by clever ingenuity; a conundrum. **2.** Any puzzling object or person. — *Syn.* See PUZZLE. — *v.* **·dled, ·dling** *v.t.* **1.** To solve; explain. — *v.i.* **2.** To utter or solve riddles. [OE *rædels* advice, interpretation]

ride (rīd) *v.* **rode** (*Archaic* **rid**), **rid·den** (*Archaic* **rid**), **rid·ing** *v.i.* **1.** To sit on and be borne along by a horse or other animal. **2.** To be borne along as if on horseback. **3.** To travel or be carried on or in a vehicle or other conveyance. **4.** To be supported in moving: The wheel *rides* on the shaft. **5.** To support and carry a rider in a specified manner: This car *rides* easily. **6.** To seem to float in space, as a star. **7.** *Naut.* To lie at anchor, as a ship. **8.** To work or move upward out of place: with *up.* **9.** *Slang* To continue unchanged: Let it *ride.* — *v.t.* **10.** To sit on and control the motion of (a horse, bicycle, etc.). **11.** To move or be borne or supported upon. **12.** To overlap or overlie. **13.** To travel or traverse (an area, etc.) on horseback, in an automobile, etc. **14.** To control imperiously or oppressively: usually in the past participle: a king-*ridden* people. **15.** To accomplish by riding: to *ride* a race. **16.** To cause to ride. **17.** *Naut.* To keep at anchor. **18.** *Informal* To tease or harass by ridicule or petty criticisms; tyrannize. — **to ride out** To survive; endure successfully. — *n.* **1.** An excursion by any means of conveyance, as on horseback, by car, etc. **2.** A road intended for riding. [OE *rīdan*] — **rid′a·ble** *adj.*

rid·er (rī′dər) *n.* **1.** One who or that which rides. **2.** One who breaks in horses. **3.** Any device that rides upon or weighs down something else. **4.** A separate piece of writing or print added to a document, record, or the like. **5.** An addition or proposed addition to a legislative bill.

ridge (rij) *n.* **1.** An elevation long in proportion to its width and height and generally having sloping sides. **2.** A long, relatively narrow elevation of land. **3.** That part of a roof where the rafters meet the ridgepole. **4.** Any raised strip, as on fabric, etc. **5.** The back or backbone of an animal, especially of a whale. — *v.* **ridged, ridg·ing** *v.t.* **1.** To mark with ridges. **2.** To form into ridges. — *v.i.* **3.** To form ridges. [OE *hrycg*] — **ridg′y** *adj.*

ridge·pole (rij′pōl′) *n.* A horizontal timber at the ridge of a roof. Also **ridge beam, ridge piece, ridge plate.** For illus. see ROOF.

rid·i·cule (rid′ə·kyōōl) *n.* **1.** Language or actions calculated to make a person or thing the object of contemptuous or humorous derision or mockery. **2.** An object of mocking merriment; butt. — *v.t.* **·culed, ·cul·ing** To make fun of; deride. [< OF < L *ridiculum* a joke] — **rid′i·cul′er** *n.*

ri·dic·u·lous (ri·dik′yə·ləs) *adj.* Exciting ridicule; absurd and unworthy of consideration. — **ri·dic′u·lous·ly** *adv.* — **ri·dic′u·lous·ness** *n.*

rid·ing¹ (rī′ding) *n.* The act of one who rides; a ride. — *adj.* **1.** Suitable for riding. **2.** For use while at anchor.

rid·ing² (rī′ding) *n.* **1.** One of the three administrative divisions into which Yorkshire, England, was formerly divided. **2.** In Canada, an administrative or electoral district. [OE *thrithing* < ON *thrithjungr* third part]

rife (rīf) *adj.* **1.** Great in number or quantity; plentiful; abundant. **2.** Prevalent; current. **3.** Containing in abundance: followed by *with.* [OE *rȳfe*]

riff (rif) *n.* In jazz music, a melodic phrase or motif, played repeatedly as background or used as the main theme. [? Back formation < RIFFLE, or ? < REFRAIN]

Riff (rif) *n.* One of a Berber tribe inhabiting the mountainous region of northern Morocco. — **Rif′fi·an** *adj. & n.*

rif·fle (rif′əl) *n.* **1.** *U.S.* A shoal or rocky obstruction lying beneath the surface of a river or other stream. **2.** A stretch

riff·raff (rif'raf') *n.* **1.** The populace; rabble. **2.** Miscellaneous rubbish. [ME *riff and raff* one and all < OF *rif et raf*]

ri·fle (rī'fəl) *n.* **1.** A firearm having a rifled or spirally grooved bore, fired from the shoulder. **2.** An artillery piece having a rifled bore. **3.** *pl.* A body of soldiers equipped with rifles. —*v.t.* **·fled, ·fling.** To cut a spirally grooved bore in (a firearm, etc.). [< *rifled gun* < OF *rifler* to file]

ri·fle² (rī'fəl) *v.t.* **·fled ·fling** **1.** To search through and rob, as a safe. **2.** To search and rob (a person). **3.** To seize and take away by force. [< OF *rifler* to plunder] — **ri'fler** *n.*

U.S. RIFLES
A Springfield, 1903. *B* Garand semi-automatic, World War II. *C* M-14 automatic, 1958.

ri·fle·man (rī'fəl·mən) *n. pl.* **·men** (-mən) One armed or skilled with the rifle.

rifle range An area used for shooting rifles at a target.

ri·fling (rī'fling) *n.* **1.** The operation of forming the grooves in a rifle. **2.** The grooves of a rifle collectively.

rift¹ (rift) *n.* **1.** An opening made by riving or splitting; a cleft; fissure. **2.** Any disagreement or lack of harmony, as between friends, nations, etc. —*v.t. & v.i.* To rive; burst open; split. [< Scand. Cf. Dan. *rift*, ON *rifa*.]

rift² (rift) *n.* A shallow place in a stream.

rig¹ (rig) *v.t.* **rigged, rig·ging** **1.** To fit out; equip. **2.** *Naut.* **a** To fit, as a ship, with rigging. **b** To fit (sails, stays, etc.) to masts, yards, etc. **3.** *Informal* To dress; clothe, esp. in finery. **4.** To make or construct hurriedly: often with *up*. —*n.* **1.** *Naut.* The arrangement of sails, rigging, spars, etc., on a vessel. **2.** *Informal* A style of dress; costume. **3.** *U.S. Informal* A horse or horses and vehicle. **4.** Any apparatus, gear, or tackle: an oil-well *rig*. **5.** Fishing tackle. [< Scand. Cf. Norwegian and Sw. *rigga*.]

rig² (rig) *v.t.* **rigged, rig·ging** To control fraudulently; manipulate: to *rig* an election. [Origin uncertain]

rig·a·doon (rig'ə·dōōn') *n.* **1.** A gay, quick dance for two, originating in Provence. **2.** Music for this dance. [< F]

Ri·gel (rī'jəl, -gəl) One of the 20 brightest stars, 0.34 magnitude; Beta in the constellation Orion. [< Arabic *rijl* foot]

rig·ger (rig'ər) *n.* **1.** One who rigs. **2.** One who fits the rigging of ships. **3.** A ship having a specified rig: used in combination: a *square-rigger*.

rig·ging (rig'ing) *n.* **1.** *Naut.* The entire cordage system of a vessel. **2.** Tackle used in logging. **3.** The act of one who or that which rigs.

right (rīt) *adj.* **1.** Done in accordance with or conformable to moral law or to some standard of rightness; equitable; just; righteous. **2.** Conformable to truth or fact. **3.** Conformable to a standard of propriety or to the conditions of the case; proper; fit; suitable. **4.** Most desirable or preferable; also, fortunate. **5.** Pertaining to, designating, or situated on the side of the body that is toward the south when one faces east. **6.** Holding one direction, as a line; straight; direct. **7.** Properly placed, disposed, or adjusted; well-regulated; orderly. **8.** Sound in mind or body; healthy; well. **9.** *Geom.* Formed with reference to a line or plane perpendicular to another line or plane: a *right* angle. **10.** Designed to be worn outward or when in use placed toward an observer: the *right* side of cloth. **11.** *Sometimes cap.* Designating a person, party, faction, etc., having absolutely or relatively conservative or reactionary views and policies. — **to rights** In a proper or orderly condition: to put a room *to rights.* —*adv.* **1.** In accordance with justice or moral principle. **2.** According to the fact or truth; correctly. **3.** In a straight line; directly. **4.** Very: used dialectally or in some titles: a *right* good time, *Right* Reverend. **5.** Suitably; properly. **6.** Precisely; just; also, immediately. **7.** Without delay or evasion. **8.** Toward the right. **9.** Completely or quite: The house burned *right* to the ground. —*n.* **1.** That which is right; moral rightness; also, justice. **2.** *Often pl.* A just and proper claim or title to anything. **3.** The right hand, side, or direction. **4.** Anything adapted for right-hand use or position. **5.** *Often cap.* A group, party, etc., whose views and policies are right (adj. def. 11) or, in Europe, whose members sit to the presiding officer's right in a deliberative assembly. **6.** In boxing, a blow delivered with the right hand. —*v.t.* **1.** To restore to an upright or normal position. **2.** To put in order; set right. **3.** To make

correct or in accord with facts. **4.** To make reparation for. **5.** To make reparation to (a person). —*v.i.* **6.** To regain an upright or normal position. [OE *riht*] — **right'er** *n.*

right·a·bout (rīt'ə·bout') *n.* **1.** The opposite direction. **2.** A turning in or to the opposite direction.

right angle *Geom.* An angle whose sides are perpendicular to each other; an angle of 90°.

right-an·gled (rīt'ang'gəld) *adj.* Forming or containing a right angle or angles: a *right-angled* triangle.

right·eous (rī'chəs) *adj.* **1.** Conforming to a standard of right and justice; virtuous. **2.** Morally right; equitable: a *righteous* act. [OE < *riht* right + *wīs* wise] — **right'eous·ly** *adv.* — **right'eous·ness** *n.*

right face In military drill, a 90-degree pivot to the right, using the ball of the left foot and the heel of the right.

right·ful (rīt'fəl) *adj.* **1.** Characterized by or conforming to a right or just claim: *rightful* heritage. **2.** Consonant with moral right or with justice and truth. **3.** Proper. **4.** Upright; just. [OE *rihtful*] — **right'ful·ly** *adv.* — **right'ful·ness** *n.*

right-hand (rīt'hand') *adj.* **1.** Of, for, pertaining to, or situated on the right side or right hand. **2.** Chiefly depended on: *right-hand* man. **3.** Toward the right.

right-hand·ed (rīt'han'did) *adj.* **1.** Using the right hand more easily than the left. **2.** Done with the right hand. **3.** Moving from left to right, as the hands of a clock. **4.** Adapted for use by the right hand. — **right'-hand'ed·ness** *n.*

right·ist (rī'tist) *n.* One whose views and policies are right (adj. def. 11). —*adj.* Right (adj. def. 11). — **right'ism** *n.*

right·ly (rīt'lē) *adv.* **1.** Correctly. **2.** Honestly; uprightly. **3.** Properly; aptly.

right-mind·ed (rīt'mīn'did) *adj.* Having right feelings or opinions. — **right'mind'ed·ly** *adv.* — **right'mind'ed·ness** *n.*

right·ness (rīt'nis) *n.* **1.** The quality or condition of being right. **2.** Rectitude. **3.** Correctness. **4.** Straightness.

right·o (rī'tō) *interj. Brit. Informal* Right: All right!

right of asylum In international law, the right to protection from arrest in a place recognized by law or custom.

right of search In international law, the right of a belligerent vessel in time of war to verify the nationality of a vessel and to ascertain, if neutral, whether it carries contraband goods. Also **right of visit and search.**

right of way **1.** *Law* The right of a person to pass over the land of another; also, the path or piece of land. **2.** The strip of land over which a railroad lays its tracks, on which a public highway is built, or above which a high-tension power line is built. **3.** The legal or customary precedence which allows one vehicle or vessel to cross in front of another. Also **right-of-way** (rīt'əv·wā).

right triangle A triangle containing one right angle.

right whale Any of several whales of polar seas, having a large head and elastic whalebone plates in its mouth.

right wing **1.** *Sometimes cap.* A party, group, faction, etc., having rightist policies. **2.** The wing, division, part, etc., on the right side. — **right-wing** (rīt'wing') *adj.* — **right'-wing'er** *n.*

rig·id (rij'id) *adj.* **1.** Resisting change of form; stiff. **2.** Rigorous; inflexible; severe. **3.** Not moving; fixed. **4.** Strict; exact, as reasoning. **5.** *Aeron.* Designating a dirigible whose cells are enclosed within a rigid framework. [< L *rigere* to be stiff] — **rig'id·ly** *adv.* — **ri·gid'i·ty, rig'id·ness** *n.*

Rig·il Cen·tau·rus (rij'il ken·tôr'əs) One of the 20 brightest stars, 0.6 magnitude; Beta in the constellation Centaurus.

rig·ma·role (rig'mə·rōl) *n.* Incoherent talk or writing; nonsense. Also **rig'a·ma·role** (-ə·mə-). [Alter. of *ragman roll* deed on parchment]

rig·or (rig'ər) *n.* **1.** The condition of being stiff or rigid. **2.** Stiffness of opinion or temper; harshness. **3.** Exactness without allowance or indulgence; inflexibility; strictness; severity. **4.** Inclemency, as of the weather; hardship. Also *Brit.* **rig'our.** [< OF < L < *rigere* to be stiff] — **rig'or·ist** *n.* — **rig'or·is'tic** *adj.*

rig·or mor·tis (rig'ər·môr'tis, rī'gər) The muscular rigidity that ensues shortly after death. [L, stiffness of death]

rig·or·ous (rig'ər·əs) *adj.* **1.** Marked by or acting with rigor; uncompromising; severe. **2.** Logically accurate; exact; strict. **3.** Inclement; severe: a *rigorous* climate. — **rig'or·ous·ly** *adv.* — **rig'or·ous·ness** *n.*

rile (rīl) *v.t.* **riled, ril·ing** *Informal or Dial* **1.** To vex; irritate. **2.** To make (a liquid) muddy. Also *roil*. [Var. of ROIL]

rill (ril) *n.* **1.** A small stream. **2.** A long, narrow valley on the face of the moon: also **rille.** [Prob. < LG *rille*]

rim (rim) *n.* **1.** The edge of an object, usu. of a circular object. **2.** The peripheral part of a wheel, connected to the hub by spokes. **3.** The frame of a pair of spectacles, surrounding the lenses. —*v.t.* **rimmed, rim·ming** **1.** To provide with a rim; border. **2.** In sports, to roll around the edge of (the basket, cup, etc.) without falling in. [OE *rima*]

rime¹ (rīm) See RHYME.

rime² (rīm) *n.* **1.** A milky white, granular deposit of ice formed on objects by fog or water vapor that has frozen. **2.** Frost. — *v.i.* & *v.t.* **rimed, rim·ing** To cover with or congeal into rime. [OE *hrīm* frost] — **rim′y** *adj.*

rim·er (rī′mər) See RHYMER.

rime·ster (rīm′stər) See RHYMESTER.

rim·mer (rim′ər) *n.* A reamer (def. 2).

rind (rīnd) *n.* The skin or outer coat that may be peeled or taken off, as of bacon, fruit, cheese, etc. [OE *rind* bark]

rin·der·pest (rin′dər·pest) *n. Vet.* An acute intestinal virus disease of cattle and sometimes of sheep. [< G]

ring¹ (ring) *n.* **1.** Any circular object, line, mark, etc. **2.** A circular band, usu. of precious metal, worn on a finger. **3.** Any metal or wooden band used for holding or carrying something. **4.** A group of persons or things in a circle; also, a circular movement. **5.** A group of persons, as in business or politics; a clique. **6.** One of a series of concentric layers of wood in the trunk of a tree, formed by annual growth. **7.** An area or arena, usu. square, as that in which boxers fight; prize fighting in general. **8.** Political competition or rivalry: He tossed his hat into the *ring.* **9.** *Chem.* An arrangement of atoms in a closed chain: the benzene *ring.* **10.** The space between two concentric circles. — **to run rings around** *Informal* To be superior to in some way. — *v.* **ringed, ring· ing** *v.t.* **1.** To surround with a ring; encircle. **2.** To form into a ring or rings. **3.** To provide or decorate with a ring or rings. **4.** To cut a ring of bark from (a branch or tree). **5.** To hem in (cattle, etc.) by riding in a circle around them. **6.** In certain games, to cast a ring over (a peg or pin). — *v.i.* **7.** To form a ring or rings. **8.** To move or fly in rings or spirals; circle. [OE *hring*]

ring² (ring) *v.* **rang** (*Archaic* or *Dial.* **rung**), **rung, ring·ing** *v.i.* **1.** To give forth a resonant, sonorous sound, as a bell when struck. **2.** To sound loudly or be filled with sound or resonance; reverberate; resound. **3.** To cause a bell or bells to sound. **4.** To have or suggest a sound expressive of a specified quality: His story *rings* true. **5.** To have a continued sensation of ringing or buzzing: My ears *ring.* — *v.t.* **6.** To cause (a bell, etc.) to ring. **7.** To produce, as a sound, by or as by ringing. **8.** To announce or proclaim by ringing: to *ring* the hour. **9.** To summon, escort, usher, etc., in this manner: with *in* or *out:* to *ring* out the old year. **10.** To call on the telephone: often with *up.* — *n.* **1.** The sound produced by a bell or other vibrating, sonorous body. **2.** The act of sounding a bell. **3.** A telephone call. **4.** Any reverberating sound, as of acclamation. **5.** Characteristic sound or impression: the *ring* of truth. **6.** A set, chime, or peal of bells. [OE *hringan;* imit.]

ring·bolt (ring′bolt′) *n.* A bolt having a ring through an eye in its head.

ring·dove (ring′duv′) *n.* One of several other pigeons having a black ring partially surrounding the neck.

ringed (ringd) *adj.* **1.** Having a wedding ring; lawfully married. **2.** Encircled by raised or depressed lines or bands. **3.** Marked by a ring or rings. **4.** Composed of rings.

rin·gent (rin′jənt) *adj. Biol.* Gaping, as a corolla in which the lips are widely separated. [< L < *ringi* to gape]

ring·er¹ (ring′ər) *n.* **1.** One who or that which rings (a bell or chime). **2.** *Slang* An athlete, horse, etc., illegally entered in a contest by concealing disqualifying facts, as age, professional status, etc. **3.** *Slang* A person who bears a marked resemblance to another: You are a *ringer* for Jones.

ring·er² (ring′ər) *n.* **1.** One who or that which rings. **2.** A quoit or horseshoe that falls around one of the posts.

ring·lead·er (ring′lē′dər) *n.* A leader or organizer of any undertaking, esp. of an unlawful one, as a riot.

ring·let (ring′lit) *n.* **1.** A long, spiral lock of hair; a curl. **2.** A small ring.

ring·mas·ter (ring′mas′tər, -mäs′-) *n.* One who has charge of a circus ring and of the performances in it.

ring·side (ring′sīd′) *n.* The space or seats immediately surrounding a ring, as at a prize fight.

ring·worm (ring′wûrm′) *n. Pathol.* Any of several contagious skin diseases, caused by certain fungi, and marked by the appearance of discolored, scaly patches on the skin.

rink (ringk) *n.* **1.** A smooth, artificial surface of ice, used for ice-skating or hockey. **2.** A smooth floor, used for roller-skating. **3.** A building containing a surface for ice-skating or roller-skating. [< Scot., course, race]

rinse (rins) *v.t.* **rinsed, rins·ing** **1.** To remove soap from by putting through clear water. **2.** To wash lightly, as by dipping in water or by running water over or into. **3.** To remove (dirt, etc.) by this process. — *n.* **1.** The act of rinsing, or the solution in which something is rinsed. **2.** A hair coloring agent. [< OF < L *recens* fresh] — **rins′er** *n.*

rins·ing (rin′sing) *n.* **1.** A rinse. **2.** The liquid in which anything is rinsed. **3.** That which is removed by rinsing.

ri·ot (rī′ət) *n.* **1.** A disturbance consisting of wild and tur-

bulent conduct of a large number of persons, as a mob. **2.** A brilliant or sometimes confusing display: a *riot* of color. **3.** Boisterous festivity; revelry. **4.** Loose or profligate living or activity. **5.** *U.S. Slang* An uproariously amusing person, thing, or performance. — **to run riot 1.** To act or move wildly and without restraint. **2.** To grow profusely or luxuriantly, as vines. — *v.i.* **1.** To take part in a riot or public disorder. **2.** To live a life of feasting, drinking, etc.; revel. — *v.t.* **3.** To spend (time, money, etc.) in riot or revelry. [< OF < *rioter* to quarrel] — **ri′ot·er** *n.*

riot act Any forceful or vigorous warning or reprimand. — **to read the riot act to** To reprimand bluntly and severely.

ri·ot·ous (rī′ət·əs) *adj.* **1.** Of, pertaining to, or like a riot. **2.** Engaged in a riot. **3.** Loud; uproarious. **4.** Profligate: *riotous* spending. — **ri′ot·ous·ly** *adv.* — **ri′ot·ous·ness** *n.*

riot squad A group of policemen specially trained, armed, and equipped to deal with riots.

rip¹ (rip) *v.* **ripped, rip·ping** *v.t.* **1.** To tear or cut apart roughly or violently; slash. **2.** To tear or cut from something else in a rough or violent manner: with *off, away, out,* etc. **3.** To saw or split (wood) in the direction of the grain. — *v.i.* **4.** To be torn or cut apart; split. **5.** *Informal* To utter with vehemence: with *out.* **6.** *Informal* To rush headlong. — **to rip off** *Slang* **1.** To steal or steal from. **2.** To swindle. — *n.* **1.** A place torn or ripped open; a tear. **2.** A ripsaw. [Cf. MLG *reppen,* MDu. *rippen*] — **rip′per** *n.*

rip² (rip) *n.* **1.** A ripple; a rapid in a river. **2.** A riptide. [? < RIP¹]

ri·par·i·an (ri·pâr′ē·ən, rī-) *adj.* Of or growing on a bank of a river or stream. [< L < *ripa* river bank]

rip·cord (rip′kôrd′) *n. Aeron.* The cord, together with the handle and fastening pins, that when pulled releases a parachute from its pack.

ripe (rīp) *adj.* **1.** Grown to maturity and fit for food, as fruit or grain. **2.** Brought by keeping and care to a condition for use, as wine or cheese. **3.** Fully developed; matured. **4.** Advanced in years. **5.** In full readiness to do or try; prepared; ready. **6.** Fit; opportune. **7.** Resembling ripe fruit; rosy; luscious. [OE *rīpe*] — **ripe′ly** *adv.* — **ripe′ness** *n.*

rip·en (rī′pən) *v.t.* & *v.i.* To make or become ripe; mature.

rip-off (rip′of′, -ôf′) *n.* **1.** An act of stealing or cheating. **2.** Anything dishonest, illegal, or exploitative.

ri·poste (ri·pōst′) *n.* **1.** A return thrust, as in fencing. **2.** A quick, clever reply; repartee. — *v.i.* **post·ed, ·post·ing** **1.** To make a riposte. **2.** To reply quickly. Also **ri·post′.** [< F < Ital. *risposta* reply]

rip·ping (rip′ing) *Brit. Slang adj.* Splendid; excellent. — *adv.* Very; extraordinarily: a *ripping* good time.

rip·ple (rip′əl) *v.* **·pled, ·pling** *v.i.* **1.** To become slightly agitated on the surface, as water blown on by a light breeze. **2.** To flow with small waves or undulations on the surface. **3.** To make a sound like water flowing in small waves. — *v.t.* **4.** To cause to form ripples. — *n.* **1.** One of the wavelets on the surface of water. **2.** Any sound like that made by rippling. **3.** Any appearance like a wavelet [? Fusion of RIFFLE + RIP²] — **rip′pler** *n.* — **rip′ply** *adj.*

rip·plet (rip′lit) *n.* A small ripple.

rip-roar·ing (rip′rôr′ing, -rōr′-) *adj. U.S. Slang* Good and lively; boisterous.

rip·saw (rip′sô′) *n.* A coarse-toothed saw used for cutting wood in the direction of the grain: also called *rip.*

rip·snort·er (rip′snôr′tər) *n. Archaic Slang* Any person or thing excessively noisy, violent, or striking.

rip·tide (rip′tīd′) *n.* Water agitated and made dangerous for swimmers by conflicting tides or currents.

rise (rīz) *v.* **rose, ris·en, ris·ing** *v.i.* **1.** To move upward; go from a lower to a higher position. **2.** To slope gradually upward. **3.** To have height or elevation: The city *rises* above the plain. **4.** To gain elevation in rank, status, fortune, or reputation. **5.** To swell up: Dough *rises.* **6.** To become greater in force, intensity, height, etc.; also, to become higher in pitch, as the voice. **7.** To become greater in amount, value, etc. **8.** To become erect after lying down, sitting, etc.; stand up. **9.** To get out of bed. **10.** To return to life. **11.** To revolt; rebel. **12.** To adjourn. **13.** To appear above the horizon: said of heavenly bodies. **14.** To come to the surface, as a fish after a lure. **15.** To have origin; begin. **16.** To become perceptible to the mind or senses. **17.** To occur; happen. **18.** To be able to cope with an emergency, danger, etc. — *v.t.* **19.** To cause to rise. — **to rise above** To prove superior to; show oneself indifferent to. — *n.* **1.** The act of rising; ascent. **2.** Degree of ascent; elevation; also, an ascending course. **3.** The act of beginning to be: the *rise* of a stream. **4.** An elevated place; a small hill. **5.** The act of appearing above the horizon. **6.** Increase or advance, as in price or value. **7.** Advance or elevation, as in rank, prosperity, or importance. **8.** The spring or height of an arch above the impost level. **9.** The height of a stair step.

10. Ascent in a musical scale; also, increase in volume of tone. **11.** The ascent of a fish to food or bait; also, the flying up of a game bird. **12.** *Informal* An emotional reaction; a response or retort. **13.** *Brit.* An increase in salary. [OE *rīsan*]

ris·en (riz′ən) Past participle of RISE.

ris·er (rī′zər) *n.* **1.** One who rises or gets up, as from bed: He is an early *riser*. **2.** The vertical part of a step or stair.

ris·i·bil·i·ty (riz′ə·bil′ə·tē) *n. pl.* **·ties 1.** A tendency to laughter. **2.** *pl.* Impulses to laughter: also **ris′i·bles** (-bəlz)

ris·i·ble (riz′ə·bəl) *adj.* **1.** Having the power of laughing. **2.** Of a nature to excite laughter. **3.** Pertaining to laughter. [< F < LL < L *ridere* to laugh] — **ris′i·bly** *adv.*

ris·ing (rī′zing) *adj.* **1.** Increasing in wealth, power, or distinction. **2.** Ascending; also, sloping upward: a *rising* hill. **3.** Advancing to adult years or to a state of vigor and activity; growing: the *rising* generation. — *n.* **1.** The act of one who or that which rises. **2.** That which rises above the surrounding surface. **3.** An insurrection or revolt. **4.** Yeast or leaven used to make dough rise.

risk (risk) *n.* **1.** A chance of encountering harm or loss; hazard; danger. **2.** In insurance: **a** The hazard or chance of loss. **b** The degree of exposure to loss. **c** An insurance applicant who is considered a hazard to the insurer. — *v.t.* **1.** To expose to a chance of injury or loss. **2.** To incur the risk of. [< F < Ital. *risco*] — **risk′er** *n.*

risk·y (ris′kē) *adj.* **risk·i·er, risk·i·est** Attended with risk; hazardous; dangerous.

ri·sot·to (rē·sôt′tō) *n.* Rice cooked in broth and served with meat, cheese, etc. [< Ital. < *riso* rice]

ris·qué (ris·kā′, *Fr.* rēs·kā′) *adj.* Bordering on or suggestive of impropriety; bold; daring; off-color: a *risqué* story or play. [< F, pp. of *risquer* to risk] — **Syn.** racy, ribald, suggestive.

ris·sole (ris′ōl, *Fr.* rē·sôl′) *n.* In cookery, a sausagelike roll consisting of minced meat or fish, enclosed in a thin puff paste and fried. [< F, ult. < LL *russeolus* reddish]

ri·tar·dan·do (rē′tär·dän′dō) *Music adj.* Slackening in tempo gradually; retarding. — *n. pl.* **·dos** A gradual slackening of tempo. [< Ital.]

rite (rīt) *n.* **1.** A solemn or religious ceremony performed in an established or prescribed manner, or the words or acts constituting or accompanying it. **2.** Any formal practice or custom. [< L *ritus*]

rit·u·al (rich′ōō·əl) *n.* **1.** A prescribed form or method for the performance of a religious or solemn ceremony; any body of rites or ceremonies. **2.** A book setting forth such a system of rites. — *adj.* Of, pertaining to, or practiced as a rite or rites. [< L < *ritus* rite] — **rit′u·al·ly** *adv.*

rit·u·al·ism (rich′ōō·əl·iz′əm) *n.* **1.** Insistence upon ritual; adherence to ritual. **2.** The study of religious ritual. **3.** A love of ritual. — **rit′u·al·ist** *n.* — **rit′u·al·is′tic** *adj.* — **rit′u·al·is′ti·cal·ly** *adv.*

ritz·y (rit′sē) *adj.* **ritz·i·er, ritz·i·est** *U.S. Slang* Smart; elegant; classy. [< the *Ritz*-Carlton Hotel, New York; after César *Ritz*, 1850–1918, who founded it]

ri·val (rī′vəl) *n.* **1.** One who strives to equal or excel another, or is in pursuit of the same object as another; a competitor. **2.** One equaling or nearly equaling another, in any respect. — *v.* **ri·valed** or **·valled, ri·val·ing** or **·val·ling** *v.t.* **1.** To strive to equal or excel; compete with. **2.** To be the equal of or a match for. — *adj.* Being a rival; competing. [< L *rivalis*, pl. *rivales* those living near the same stream]

ri·val·ry (rī′vəl·rē) *n. pl.* **·ries 1.** The act of rivaling. **2.** The state of being a rival or rivals; competition.

rive (rīv) *v.* **rived, rived** or **riv·en, riv·ing** *v.t.* **1.** To split asunder by force; cleave. **2.** To break (the heart, etc.). — *v.i.* **3.** To become split. [< ON *rifa*] — **riv·er** (rī′vər) *n.*

riv·er (riv′ər) *n.* **1.** A large, natural stream of water, usu. fed by converging tributaries along its course and discharging into a larger body of water, as the ocean, a lake, or another stream. ◆ Collateral adjective: *fluvial.* **2.** A large stream of any kind; copious flow — **to sell down the river** To betray the trust of; deceive. — **to send up the river** To send to the penitentiary. [< OF *rivière*]

river basin *Geog.* An extensive area of land drained by a river and its branches.

riv·er·ine (riv′ə·rīn, -ər·in) *adj.* Pertaining to or like a river; riparian.

riv·er·side (riv′ər·sīd′) *n.* The space alongside of or adjacent to a river.

riv·et (riv′it) *n.* A short, soft metal bolt, having a head on one end, used to join objects, as metal plates, by passing the shank through holes and forming a new head by flattening out the other end. — *v.t.* **1.** To fasten with or as with a rivet. **2.** To batter the headless end of (a bolt, etc.) so as to make fast. **3.** To fasten firmly. **4.** To engross or attract (the eyes, attention, etc.). [< OF, prob. < MDu. *wriven* to cause to turn] — **riv′et·er** *n.*

riv·u·let (riv′yə·lit) *n.* A small stream or brook; streamlet. [< Ital. < L *rivulus*, dim. of *rivus* stream]

roach[1] (rōch) *n.* **1.** A European fresh-water fish of the carp family, with a greenish back. **2.** Any of various related fishes. [< OF *roche*.]

roach[2] (rōch) *n.* A cockroach.

road (rōd) *n.* **1.** An open way for public passage, esp. from one city, town, or village to another; a highway. **2.** Any way of advancing or progressing: the *road* to fame. **3.** *Usu. pl.* A roadstead: Hampton *Roads.* **4.** *U.S.* A railroad. — **on the road 1.** On tour: said of circuses, theatrical companies, etc. **2.** Traveling, as a canvasser or salesman. **3.** Living the life of a tramp or hobo. [OE *rād* journey < *rīdan* to ride]

road·bed (rōd′bed′) *n.* **1.** The graded foundation of gravel, etc., on which the ties, rails, etc., of a railroad are laid. **2.** The graded foundation or surface of a road.

road·block (rōd′blok′) *n.* **1.** An obstruction in a road. **2.** Any arrangement of men and materials for blocking passage, as of enemy troops.

road·house (rōd′hous′) *n.* A restaurant, dance hall, etc., located at the side of the road in a rural area.

road metal Broken stone or the like, used for making or repairing roads.

road runner A long-tailed ground cuckoo inhabiting open regions of southwestern North America, and running with great swiftness.

road·side (rōd′sīd′) *n.* The area along the side of a road. — *adj.* Situated on the side of a road.

road·stead (rōd′sted) *n. Naut.* A place of anchorage offshore, but less sheltered than a harbor. [< ROAD + *stead*, a place]

road·ster (rōd′stər) *n.* A light, open automobile, usu. with a single seat for two people and a luggage compartment or rumble seat in the rear.

ROAD RUNNER
(Body to 24 inches; tail 12 inches)

road·way (rōd′wā′) *n.* A road, esp. that part over which vehicles pass.

roam (rōm) *v.i.* **1.** To move about purposelessly from place to place; rove. — *v.t.* **2.** To wander over; range. — *n.* The act of roaming. [ME *romen*] — **roam′er** *n.*

roan (rōn) *adj.* Of a horse, having a color consisting of bay, sorrel, or chestnut, thickly interspersed with gray or white. — *n.* **1.** A roan color. **2.** An animal of a roan color. [< MF < Sp. *roano*.]

roar (rôr, rōr) *v.i.* **1.** To utter a deep, prolonged cry, as of rage or distress. **2.** To make a loud noise or din, as the sea or a cannon. **3.** To laugh loudly. **4.** To move, proceed, or function with a roar, as an automobile. — *v.t.* **5.** To utter or express by roaring. — *n.* **1.** A full, deep, resonant cry, as of a beast, or of a human being in pain, grief, anger, etc. **2.** Any loud, prolonged sound, as of wind or waves. [OE *rārian*] — **roar′er** *n.*

roast (rōst) *v.t.* **1.** To cook (meat, etc.) by subjecting to the action of heat, as in an oven. **2.** To cook before an open fire, or by placing in hot ashes, embers, etc. **3.** To heat to an extreme degree. **4.** To dry and parch under the action of heat. **5.** *Metall.* To heat (ores) with access of air for the purpose of dehydration, purification, or oxidation. **6.** *Informal* To criticize or ridicule severely. — *v.i.* **7.** To roast food in an oven, etc. **8.** To be cooked or prepared by this method. **9.** To be uncomfortably hot. — *n.* **1.** Something roasted; esp., a piece of roasted meat. **2.** A piece of meat adapted or prepared for roasting. **3.** The act of roasting. — *adj.* Roasted. [< OF *rostir* < Gmc.]

roast·er (rōs′tər) *n.* **1.** One who or that which roasts. **2.** A pan or contrivance for roasting something. **3.** Something suitable for roasting, esp. a pig.

rob (rob) *v.* **robbed, rob·bing** *v.t.* **1.** To seize and carry off the property of by unlawful violence or threat of violence. **2.** To deprive of something belonging or due. **3.** To plunder; rifle, as a house. **4.** To steal. — *v.i.* **5.** To commit robbery. [< OF *robe* booty] — **rob′ber** (-ər) *n.*

robber baron *U.S.* One of the powerful and unscrupulous financial adventurers of the late 19th century.

rob·ber·y (rob′ər·ē) *n. pl.* **·ber·ies** The act of one who robs; the taking away of the property of another unlawfully, by force or fear. — **Syn.** See THEFT.

robe (rōb) *n.* **1.** A long, loose, flowing garment, worn over other dress; a gown. **2.** A bathrobe. **3.** *pl.* Such a garment worn as a badge of office or rank. **4.** Anything that covers in the manner of a robe. **5.** *U.S.* A blanket or covering, as for use in an automobile: lap *robe.* — *v.* **robed, rob·ing** *v.t.* **1.** To put a robe upon; dress. — *v.i.* **2.** To put on robes. [< OF, orig. booty < Gmc.]

rob·in (rob′in) *n.* **1.** A large North American thrush with black head and tail, grayish wings and sides, and reddish brown breast and underparts. **2.** A small European bird of the thrush family, with the cheeks, and breast yellowish red. Also **robin redbreast.** [< OF *Robin*, dim. of *Robert*]

Robin Hood A legendary medieval outlaw of England, famed for his chivalry and daring, who lived in Sherwood Forest and robbed from the rich to help the poor.

rob·in's-egg blue (rob'inz·eg') A light greenish blue.
Rob·in·son Cru·soe (rob'in·sən krōō'sō) The hero of Defoe's *Robinson Crusoe* (1719), a sailor shipwrecked on a tropical island.
ro·bot (rō'bət, rob'ət) *n.* **1.** A mechanical man constructed to perform work in the place of human beings. **2.** One who works mechanically; automaton. **3.** Any mechanism or device that operates automatically or is remotely controlled. [< Czechoslovakian *robota* forced labor]
robot bomb A high-explosive bomb provided with a jet engine or rocket permitting it to travel under its own power after being launched on the target, as the German V-1 of World War II: also called *buzz bomb.*
ro·bust (rō·bust', rō'bust) *adj.* **1.** Possessing or characterized by great strength or endurance; rugged. **2.** Requiring strength. **3.** Violent; rude. [< L < *robur* oak, hence strength] — **ro·bust'ly** *adv.* — **ro·bust'ness** *n.*
roc (rok) *n.* In Arabian and Persian legend, an enormous and powerful bird of prey. [< Arabic < Persian *rukh*]
Ro·chelle salt (rō·shel') A white crystalline tartrate of potassium and sodium, KNaC₄H₄O₆·4H₂O, used as a cathartic. [after La *Rochelle*]
rock¹ (rok) *n.* **1.** A large mass of stone or stony material. **2.** A fragment of rock small enough to be thrown; stone. **3.** *Geol.* The material forming the essential part of the earth's crust, classified principally according to mode of formation, as igneous or sedimentary. **4.** Something resembling or suggesting a rock, as a firm support, source of strength, etc. **5.** *U.S. Slang* A gemstone, esp. a large diamond. — **on the rocks** *U.S. Informal* **1.** Ruined; also, destitute or bankrupt. **2.** Served with ice cubes but without soda or water: said of whisky or other liquors. — *adj.* Made or composed of rock. [< OF *roque, roche*]
rock² (rok) *v.i.* **1.** To move backward and forward or from side to side; sway **2.** To sway, reel, or stagger, as from a blow; shake. — *v.t.* **3.** To move backward and forward or from side to side, esp. so as to soothe or put to sleep. **4.** To cause to sway or reel. — *n.* The act of rocking; a rocking motion. [OE *roccian*]
rock·a·by (rok'ə·bī) *interj.* Go to sleep: from a nursery song intended to lull a child to slumber. — *n.* A lullaby. Also **rock'a·bye, rock'-a-bye.**
rock-and-roll (rok'ən·rōl') *adj.* Denoting a form of popular music derived from hillbilly styles, characterized by repetitious melody and rhythm and exaggerated vocal mannerisms. — *n.* Rock-and-roll music. Also **rock 'n' roll.**
rock bottom The very bottom; the lowest possible level: Prices hit *rock bottom.* — **rock-bot·tom** (rok'bot'əm) *adj.*
rock-bound (rok'bound') *adj.* Encircled by or bordered with rocks.
rock candy Large crystals of sugar.
rock crystal Colorless transparent quartz.
rock dove The wild pigeon of Europe, the parent of domestic varieties.
rock·er (rok'ər) *n.* **1.** One who rocks, as a cradle or rocking chair. **2.** One of the curved pieces on which a rocking chair or a cradle rocks. **3.** A rocking chair. **4.** A rocking horse. — **off one's rocker** *Slang* Mentally unbalanced; nuts.
rock·et (rok'it) *n.* **1.** A firework, projectile, missile, or other device, usu. cylindrical in form, that is propelled by the reaction of escaping gases produced during flight. **2.** A type of vehicle operated by rocket propulsion and designed for space travel. — *v.i.* **1.** To move like a rocket. **2.** To fly straight up into the air, as a bird. — *v.t.* **3.** To propel by means of a rocket. [< Ital. *rocchetta,* dim. of *rocca* distaff < Gmc.]
rocket bomb A bomb delivered to its target by means of a rocket.
rock·et·eer (rok'ə·tir') *n.* One who designs or launches rockets; a student of rocket flight.
rocket engine A reaction engine fueled by a liquid or solid propellant containing its own oxidizing agent.
rocket gun Any gunlike device used for the discharge of rocket projectiles, as a bazooka.
rock·et·ry (rok'it·rē) *n.* The science, art, and technology of rocket flight, design, construction, etc.
rock·et·sonde (rok'it·sond') *n. Meteorol.* A radiosonde adapted for use on high-altitude rockets.
rock·fish (rok'fish') *n. pl.* **·fish** or **·fish·es** Any of several spiny finned fishes of the Pacific coast of North America.
rock garden A garden with flowers and plants growing in rocky ground or among rocks.
rocking chair A chair having the legs set on rockers.
rocking horse A toy horse mounted on rockers, large enough to be ridden by a child: also called *hobbyhorse.*
rock lobster The spiny lobster.
rock maple The sugar maple.
rock oil Petroleum.
rock·oon (rok·ōōn') *n.* A small rocket equipped with various meteorological recording devices and attached to a balloon, from which it is released at predetermined altitudes. [< ROCK(ET) + (BALL)OON]
rock-ribbed (rok'ribd') *adj.* **1.** Having rocky ridges. **2.** Unyielding; inflexible.
rock salt Halite.
rock-shaft (rok'shaft', -shäft') A shaft made to rock on its bearings; esp., such a shaft for operating a slide valve in an engine.
rock wool Mineral wool.
rock·y¹ (rok'ē) *adj.* **rock·i·er, rock·i·est** **1.** Consisting of, abounding in, or resembling rocks. **2.** Tough; unfeeling; hard. — **rock'i·ness** *n.*
rock·y² (rok'ē) *adj.* **rock·i·er, rock·i·est** **1.** Inclined to rock or shake; unsteady. **2.** *Informal* Dizzy or weak, as from dissipation. — **rock'i·ness** *n.*
Rocky Mountain goat A goatlike, shaggy white ruminant with short black horns, found in the mountains of NW North America: also called *mountain goat.*
Rocky Mountain sheep The bighorn.
Rocky Mountain spotted fever *Pathol.* An acute infectious disease caused by a microorganism transmitted by the bite of certain ticks, and marked by skin eruptions.
ro·co·co (rə·kō'kō, rō'kə·kō') *n.* **1.** A style of art that developed in France in the 18th century and spread throughout Europe; esp., architecture and ornament characterized by curvilinear designs, often imitating shells, foliage, and scrolls in asymmetrical arrangements. **2.** *Music* The elegant, formal style of European music from about 1726 to 1775, immediately following the baroque. **3.** Florid, fantastic, or odd style, as in literature. — *adj.* **1.** In the rococo style. **2.** Overelaborate; florid. [< F, alter. of *rocaille* shellwork]
rod (rod) *n.* **1.** A straight, slim piece of wood, metal, or other material. **2.** A shoot or cane of any woody plant. **3.** A switch or several switches together, used as an instrument of punishment. **4.** Discipline; correction: with *the.* **5.** A scepter or badge of office; a wand. **6.** Dominion; power. **7.** A bar, typically of metal, forming part of a machine: a connecting *rod.* **8.** A light pole used to suspend and manipulate a fishing line. **9.** A measure of length, equal to 5.5 yards; also, a square rod: sometimes called *perch, pole.* See table inside back cover. **10.** A measuring rule. **11.** One of the rodlike bodies of the retina sensitive to faint light. **12.** A rod-shaped bacterium. **13.** In Biblical usage, a line of family descent. **14.** A lightning rod. **15.** The drawbar of a freight train. **16.** *U.S. Slang* A pistol. [OE *rodd*]
rode (rōd) Past tense of RIDE.
ro·dent (rōd'nt) *n.* Any of a large cosmopolitan order of gnawing mammals, having in each jaw two (rarely four) incisors growing continually from persistent pulps, and no canine teeth, as a squirrel, beaver, or rat. — *adj.* **1.** Gnawing; corroding. **2.** Of or pertaining to a rodent or rodents. [< L *rodens, -entis,* ppr. of *rodere* to gnaw]
rodent ulcer *Pathol.* A malignant ulcer that progressively destroys soft tissues and bones, especially of the face.
ro·de·o (rō'dē·ō, rō·dā'ō) *n. pl.* **·os** **1.** The driving of cattle together to be branded, counted, inspected, etc.; a roundup. **2.** A public spectacle in which the more exciting features of a roundup are presented, as the riding of broncos, branding, lariat throwing, etc. **3.** An enclosure for cattle. [< Sp. *rodear* to go around < L *rota* wheel]
roe¹ (rō) *n.* **1.** The spawn or eggs of female fish. **2.** The milt of male fish. **3.** The eggs of crustaceans. [Var. of dial. *roan,* appar. < ON *hrogn* or MDu. *roch*]
roe² (rō) *n.* A small, graceful deer of Europe and western Asia. Also **roe deer.** [OE *rā*]
roe·buck (rō'buk') *n.* The male of the roe deer.
roent·gen (rent'gən, runt'-; *Ger.* rœnt'gən) *n.* A measure of the intensity of gamma or X-rays, being the quantity of radiation that will produce 1 electrostatic unit of electricity in 1 cubic centimeter of air at normal temperature and pressure: also spelled *röntgen.* [after Wilhelm Konrad *Roentgen*]
roent·gen·ize (rent'gən·īz, runt'-) *v.t.* **·ized, ·iz·ing** To subject to the action of X-rays. — **roent'gen·i·za'tion** *n.*
roentgeno- *combining form* X-rays; using, produced by, or producing X-rays. Also, before vowels, **roentgen-.** [< ROENTGEN]
roent·gen·o·gram (rent'gən·ə·gram', runt'-) *n.* An X-ray photograph. Also **roent'gen·o·graph'** (-graf', -gräf').
roent·gen·og·ra·phy (rent'gən·og'rə·fē, runt'-) *n. Med.* Photography means of X-rays; radiography. — **roent'gen·o·graph'ic** (-ə·graf'ik) *adj.* — **roent'gen·o·graph'i·cal·ly** *adv.*
Roentgen rays X-rays.
Ro·gal·lo wing (rō·gal'ō) *Aeron.* A kitelike triangular flexible wing that can be used on simple aircraft, as a kite, or type of parachute. [after F. M. *Rogallo,* U.S. engineer, the inventor]

---

ro·ga·tion (rō·gā′shən) *n. Often pl.* Litany; supplication, esp. as part of the rites of the Rogation Days. [< L < *rogatus,* pp. of *rogare* to ask]

Rogation Days *Eccl.* The three days immediately preceding Ascension Day, observed as days of special supplication.

rog·er (roj′ər) *interj.* 1. *Often cap.* Message received: used in radio communication. 2. *Informal* All right; O.K. [after *Roger,* personal name representing *r* in telecommunication]

rogue (rōg) *n.* 1. A dishonest and unprincipled person; rascal. 2. One who is innocently mischievous or playful. 3. *Biol.* A variation from a standard. 4. A fierce and dangerous animal, as an elephant, separated from the herd. 5. *Archaic* A vagrant. — *v.* **rogued, ro·guing** *v.t.* 1. To practice roguery upon; defraud. 2. *Bot.* To eliminate (inferior individuals) from a plot of plants undergoing selection. [Origin uncertain]

ro·guer·y (rō′gər·ē) *n. pl.* **·guer·ies** 1. Conduct characteristic of a rogue; trickery. 2. A roguish act.

rogues′ gallery A collection of photographs of criminals taken to aid the police in identification.

ro·guish (rō′gish) *adj.* 1. Playfully mischievous. 2. Knavish; dishonest. — **ro′guish·ly** *adv.* — **ro′guish·ness** *n.*

roil (roil) *v.t.* 1. To make muddy or turbid, as by stirring up sediment. 2. To vex; irritate; rile. [< F *rouiller, ruiler*] **roil·y** (roi′lē) *adj.* **roil·i·er, roil·i·est** Turbid; muddy.

roist·er (rois′tər) *v.i.* 1. To act in a blustery manner; swagger. 2. To engage in tumultuous merrymaking; revel. [< OF < L *rusticus* rustic] — **roist′er·er** *n.*

Ro·land (rō′lənd, Fr. rô·län′) Legendary nephew of Charlemagne and hero of the medieval French epic *Chanson de Roland,* in which he dies fighting the Saracens.

role (rōl) *n.* 1. A part or character taken by an actor. 2. Any assumed character or function. Also **rôle.** [< F *rôle*]

roll (rōl) *v.i.* 1. To move forward on a surface by turning round and round, as a ball or wheel. 2. To move or be moved on wheels or rollers. 3. To move or appear to move in undulations or swells, as waves. 4. To assume the shape of a ball or cylinder by turning over and over upon itself, as a ball of yarn. 5. To pass; elapse: with *on* or *by.* 6. Of sounds: **a** To make a deep, prolonged sound, as thunder. **b** To trill, as a bird. **c** To produce a roll, as on a drum. 7. To rotate wholly or partially: his eyes *rolled.* 8. To sway or move from side to side, as a ship. 9. To wander or travel about. 10. To walk with a swaying motion; also, to stagger. 11. To become spread or flat because of pressure applied by a roller, etc.: The metal *rolls* easily. 12. To perform a periodic revolution or cycle, as the seasons. 13. To move ahead; progress. — *v.t.* 14. To cause to move along a surface by turning round and round, as a ball, log, etc. 15. To move, push forward, etc. on wheels or rollers. 16. To wrap round and round upon itself or on an axis: often with *up.* 17. To cause to assume the shape of a ball or cylinder by means of rotation and pressure: to *roll* a cigarette. 18. To impel or cause to move onward with a steady, surging motion. 19. To spread or make flat by pressing with a roller or rollers, as dough. 20. To impart a swaying motion to. 21. To wrap or envelop in or as in a covering. 22. To rotate, as the eyes. 23. Of sounds: **a** To utter with a trilling sound: to *roll* one's r's. **b** To emit in a full and swelling manner. **c** To beat a roll upon (a drum, etc.). 24. To cast (dice) in the game of craps. 25. *Printing* To apply ink to (a form) by means of a roller or rollers. 26. *U.S. Slang* To rob (a drunk or a person who is asleep). — **to roll back** In commerce, to cause (prices, wages, etc.) to return to a previous, lower level, as by government direction. — **to roll in** *Informal* 1. To arrive, esp. in numbers; congregate. 2. To wallow; luxuriate: to *roll in* money. — **to roll up** *Informal* 1. To accumulate; amass, as profits. 2. To arrive, as an automobile. — *n.* 1. Anything rolled up in cylindrical form. 2. A register or list of names. 3. A roller; esp., a cylinder in fixed bearings used as a roller. 4. A strip of material, as of ribbon or carpeting, that is rolled upon itself or upon a core, often of an agreed length for use as a measure. 5. Any food rolled up in preparation for eating; also, a small, individually shaped portion of bread. 6. A rolling gait or movement, as of a ship. 7. Of sounds: **a** reverberation, as of thunder. **b** A rapid sustained series of short sounds: a drum *roll.* **c** A trill, as of a bird. 8. A swell or undulation of a surface, as of land or water. 9. *U.S. Slang* **a** A wad of paper money. **b** Money in general. 10. The act of rolling, or the state of being rolled. 11. *Aeron.* A complete rotation of an airplane about its longitudinal axis without change in the direction of flight. [< OF < L *rotula* < *rota* wheel]

roll·a·way (rōl′ə·wā′) *adj.* Mounted on rollers for easy movement into storage: a *rollaway* bed.

roll call 1. The act of calling a roll or list of the names of a number of persons, as soldiers, to determine which are present. 2. The time of or signal for calling the roll.

roll·er (rō′lər) *n.* 1. One who or that which rolls. 2. Any of various cylindrical devices that roll or rotate. 3. The wheel of a caster or roller skate. 4. A rod on which a win-

dow shade, towel, map, etc., is rolled. 5. A heavy cylinder for rolling, smoothing, or crushing something: a steam *roller.* 6. *Surg.* A long rolled bandage. 7. One of a series of long, swelling waves that break on a coast, esp. after a storm. 8. *Ornithol.* **a** Any of various European birds having gaudy colors and remarkable for their rolling and tumbling flight. **b** A canary having a trilling song.

roller bearing A bearing employing steel rollers to lessen friction between the parts of a mechanism.

roller coaster *U.S.* A railway with small, open cars run over a route of steep inclines and sharp turns, common at amusement parks.

roller skate A skate having wheels instead of a runner.

rol·lick (rol′ik) *v.i.* To move or behave in a careless, frolicsome manner. [? Blend of ROLL and FROLIC]

rol·lick·ing (rol′ik·ing) *adj.* 1. Acting in a carefree, swaggering manner. 2. Jovial; light-hearted; merry. Also **rol′·lick·some** (-səm), **rol′lick·y.**

roll·ing (rō′ling) *adj.* 1. Turning round and round, esp. so as to move forward on a surface. 2. Having a succession of sloping elevations and depressions: *rolling* hills. 3. Turning on or as if on wheels; rotating. 4. Turned back or down as if over a roll: a *rolling* collar. 5. Surging in puffs, billows, or waves, as smoke, water, etc. 6. Of sounds: **a** Trilled. **b** Resounding; reverberating. 7. Swaying from side to side. 8. Recurring; elapsing. — *n.* The act of one who or that which rolls or is rolled.

rolling hitch A knot having one or more intermediate turns between the first and last hitch. For illus. see HITCH.

rolling mill 1. An establishment in which metal is rolled into sheets, bars, etc. 2. A machine used to roll metal.

rolling pin A cylindrical device, usu. of wood and with a handle at each end, for rolling out dough, etc.

rolling stock The wheeled transportation equipment of a railroad, as locomotives and passenger cars.

roll-top (rōl′top′) *adj.* Designating a type of desk having a flexible, slatted cover that rolls back out of the way.

ro·ly-po·ly (rō′lē·pō′lē) *adj.* Short and fat; pudgy; dumpy. — *n. pl.* **-pol·ies** 1. A roly-poly person or thing. 2. *Chiefly Brit.* A pudding made of pastry dough spread with fruit, preserves, etc., rolled up and cooked. [Reduplication of ROLL]

Ro·ma·ic (rō·mā′ik) *adj.* Pertaining to or characteristic of the language or people of modern Greece. — *n.* Modern Greek, esp. the popular spoken form. [< LL < Gk. *Rhōmaikos* Roman]

ro·maine (rō·mān′) *n.* A variety of lettuce characterized by long, crisp leaves. [< F, fem. of *romain* Roman]

ro·man (rō′mən) *Sometimes cap. n.* A common style of type or lettering characterized by serifs, perpendicularity, and thicker vertical strokes than horizontal strokes: This line is set in roman. — *adj.* Pertaining to, designating, or printed in roman. Distinguished from *italic.* [< ROMAN]

Ro·man (rō′mən) *adj.* 1. Of, pertaining to, or characteristic of modern or ancient Rome or its people. 2. Of or belonging to the Roman Catholic Church. 3. Of, pertaining to, or characteristic of the language of ancient Rome; Latin. 4. Of or pertaining to the Holy Roman Empire. — *n.* 1. A native, resident, or citizen of ancient or modern Rome. 2. The language of ancient Rome; Latin. 3. *Informal* A Roman Catholic. [< OF < L *Roma* Rome]

Roman calendar See under CALENDAR.

Roman candle A firework consisting of a tube filled with a composition that discharges colored balls and sparks of fire.

Roman Catholic A member of the Roman Catholic Church. — **Roman Catholicism**

Roman Catholic Church The Christian church that recognizes the Pope as its supreme head: also called *Catholic Church, Church of Rome.*

ro·mance (rō·mans′; *for n., also* rō′mans) *n.* 1. A love affair. 2. A kind of love between the sexes, usu. youthful and nonmarital, characterized by high ideals of purity and devotion, strong ardor, etc. 3. Adventurous, heroic, or picturesque character or nature: the *romance* of faraway places. 4. A tendency toward the mysterious or adventurous. 5. A long narrative, sometimes in verse, presenting chivalrous ideals and usu. involving heroes in strange adventures and affairs of love. 6. Any long fictitious narrative embodying scenes and events filled with extravagant adventures. 7. An extravagant or fanciful falsehood. — *v.* **·manced, ·manc·ing** *v.i.* 1. To tell or write romances. 2. To think or act in a romantic manner. 3. *Informal* To make love. — *v.t.* 4. *Informal* To make love to; woo. [< OF *romans* story written in French < L < *Romanicus* Roman] — **ro·manc′er** *n.*

Ro·mance (rō·mans′, rō′mans) *adj.* Pertaining or belonging to one or more, or all, of the languages that have developed from Vulgar Latin and that exist now as French, Italian, Spanish, Portuguese, Catalan, Provençal, and Rumanian. — *n.* One or all collectively, of the Romance languages.

Roman Empire The empire of ancient Rome, established in 27 B.C. and continuing until A.D. 395.

Ro·man·esque (rō′mən·esk′) *adj.* Of, pertaining to, or designating a style of Western architecture that developed from Roman principles, prevailed from the 5th to the 12th century, and was characterized by round arches and general massiveness. — *n.* The Romanesque style of architecture.

Roman holiday 1. Enjoyment or profit derived from the suffering of others. 2. A day of gladiatorial and other contests in ancient Rome.

Ro·man·ic (rō·man′ik) *adj.* 1. Roman. 2. Romance.

Ro·man·ism (rō′mən·iz′əm) *n.* The dogmas, forms, etc., of the Roman Catholic Church: often used disparagingly. — **Ro′man·ist** *n.*

Ro·man·ize (rō′mən·īz) *v.t. & v.i.* **·ized, ·iz·ing** 1. To make or become Roman or Roman Catholic. 2. To write in the Roman style, language, etc. — **Ro′man·i·za′tion** *n.*

Roman nose A nose that is somewhat aquiline.

Roman numerals The letters used by the ancient Romans as symbols in arithmetical notation. The basic letters are I(1), V(5), X(10), L(50), C(100), D(500), and M(1000), and intermediate and higher numbers are formed as follows: Any symbol following another of equal or greater value adds to its value, as II = 2, XI = 11; any symbol preceding one of greater value subtracts from its value, as IV = 4, IX = 9, XC = 90. When a symbol stands between two of greater value, it is subtracted from the second and the remainder added to the first, as XIV = 14, LIX = 59.

Ro·ma·nov (rō′mə·nôf, *Russian* rô·mä′nôf) A Russian dynasty founded in 1613, and ended in 1918 with the execution of Nicholas II. Also **Ro′ma·noff.**

Ro·mans (rō′mənz) *n.pl.* (*construed as sing.*) One of the books of the New Testament, a letter from the apostle Paul to the Christians at Rome: in full **Epistle to the Romans.**

ro·man·tic (rō·man′tik) *adj.* 1. Of, characterized by, or of the nature of romance. 2. Characterized by or given to feelings or thoughts of love or romance. 3. Suitable for or conducive to love or amorousness. 4. Visionary; impractical. 5. Not based on fact; imaginary; fictitious. 6. Of or pertaining to romanticism in art, literature, and music. — *n.* One who is romantic. [< F *romant* romance, novel] — **ro·man′ti·cal·ly** *adv.*

ro·man·ti·cism (rō·man′tə·siz′əm) *n.* 1. *Usu. cap.* A movement in art, music, and literature originating in Europe in the late 18th century, characterized by a revolt against the neoclassic adherence to rules, forms, and traditions, an exalting of the feelings, and a marked preference for individualism, etc.: distinguished from *classicism.* Also **Romantic Movement.** 2. Romantic quality. — **ro·man′ti·cist** *n.*

ro·man·ti·cize (rō·man′tə·sīz) *v.* **·cized, ·ciz·ing** *v.t.* To regard or interpret in a romantic manner.

Rom·a·ny (rom′ə·nē, rō′mə-) *n. pl.* **·nies** 1. A Gypsy (def. 1). 2. The Indic language of the Gypsies: also called *Gypsy.* — *adj.* Of or pertaining to the Gypsies or their language. Also **Rom′ma·ny** (rom′ə·nē). [< Romany < *rom* man]

Rome (rōm) 1. Capital of the former Roman republic, the Roman Empire, and the States of the Church: Italian and Latin *Roma.* 2. The Roman Catholic Church.

Ro·me·o (rō′mē·ō) The hero of Shakespeare's *Romeo and Juliet.*

romp (romp) *v.i.* 1. To play boisterously. 2. To win easily. — *n.* 1. One who romps, esp. a girl. 2. Noisy, exciting frolic or play. 3. *Informal* An easy win. — **romp′ish** *adj.* — **romp′ish·ly** *adv.* — **romp′ish·ness** *n.*

romp·er (rom′pər) *n.* 1. One who romps. 2. *pl.* A garment combining a waist and bloomers, worn by young children.

Rom·u·lus (rom′yə·ləs) In Roman mythology, a son of Mars and founder of Rome, who with his twin brother Remus was reared by a she-wolf. Later Romulus slew his brother to become the first ruler of Rome.

ron·deau (ron′dō, ron·dō′) *n. pl.* **·deaux** (-dōz, -dōz′) A poem of thirteen (or sometimes ten) lines with only two rhymes, and in which the opening words are repeated in two places as an unrhymed refrain. [< F *rond* round]

ron·del (ron′dəl, -del) *n.* A verse form consisting of 13 or 14 lines, the first two lines being repeated, as a refrain, in the seventh and eighth lines, and again in the thirteenth and fourteenth. [< F *rond* round]

ron·do (ron′dō, ron·dō′) *n. Music* A composition or movement having a main theme and several contrasting episodes, the main theme being repeated after each subordinate theme. [< Ital. < F *rond* round]

ROMANESQUE ARCHITECTURE (Notre Dame de la Grande, Poitiers, France, 11th century)

rönt·gen (rent′gən, runt′-; *Ger.* rœnt′gən) See ROENTGEN.

rood (rōōd) *n.* 1. A cross or crucifix; esp., a large crucifix or representation of the Crucifixion over the altar screen of a church. 2. A land measure equivalent to one-fourth of an acre, or 40 square rods: also **square rood.** [OE *rōd* rod, measure of land, cross]

roof (rōōf, rŏŏf) *n.* 1. The exterior upper covering of a building. For other illustrations see GABLE ROOF, GAMBREL ROOF. 2. Any top covering, as of a car or oven. 3. The most elevated part of anything. — *v.t.* To cover with or as with a roof. [OE *hrōf*] — **roof′less** *adj.*

roof·er (rōō′fər, rŏŏf′ər) *n.* One who makes or repairs roofs.

roof garden 1. A garden on the roof of a building. 2. A space on a roof including a garden and used as a restaurant, etc.

ROOF, KINGPOST TYPE
a Common rafter. *b* Purlin. *c* Kingpost. *d* Ridge pole. *e* Principal rafter. *f* Strut. *g* Pole plate. *h* Tie beam.

roof·ing (rōō′fing, rŏŏf′ing) *n.* 1. The act of covering with a roof. 2. Material for roofs. 3. A roof; covering.

roof·tree (rōōf′trē′, rŏŏf′-) *n.* 1. The ridgepole of a roof; also, the roof itself. 2. A home or dwelling.

rook¹ (rŏŏk) *n.* 1. An Old World crow noted for its gregariousness. 2. A trickster or cheat; a sharper. — *v.t. & v.i.* To cheat; defraud. [OE *hrōc*]

rook² (rŏŏk) *n.* A castle-shaped chessman that can move any number of unoccupied squares parallel to the sides of the board: also called *castle.* [< OF *roc* ult. < Persian *rukh*]

rook·er·y (rŏŏk′ər·ē) *n. pl.* **·er·ies** 1. A colony or breeding place of rooks. 2. A breeding place of sea birds, seals, etc.

rook·ie (rŏŏk′ē) *n. Slang* 1. A raw recruit in the army, etc. 2. Any novice, as in baseball. [Prob. alter. of RECRUIT]

room (rōōm, rŏŏm) *n.* 1. An extent of space used for some implied or specified purpose. 2. A space for occupancy or use enclosed on all sides, as in a building. 3. *pl.* Lodgings. 4. Warrantable occasion; opportunity: *room* for doubt. — *v.i.* To occupy a room; lodge. [OE *rūm* space]

room·er (rōō′mər, rŏŏm′ər) *n.* A lodger; esp., one who rents a room and eats elsewhere.

room·ette (rōōm·et′, rŏŏm·et′) *n.* A small compartment in a railroad sleeping car furnished with a folding bed.

room·ful (rōōm′fŏŏl′, rŏŏm′-) *n. pl.* **·fuls** 1. As many or as much as a room will hold. 2. A number of persons present in a room.

room·ing house (rōō′ming, rŏŏm′ing) *U.S.* A house for roomers.

room·mate (rōōm′māt′, rŏŏm′-) *n. U.S.* One who shares lodgings with another or others.

room·y (rōō′mē, rŏŏm′ē) *adj.* **room·i·er, room·i·est** Having abundant room; spacious. — **room′i·ness** *n.*

roor·back (rŏŏr′bak) *n. U.S.* A slanderous report circulated for political purposes. [after *Roorback*, purported author of a (nonexistent) book of travel that was cited as authority for certain defamatory charges made against President Polk in the 1844 campaign]

roost (rōōst) *n.* 1. A perch upon which fowls rest at night; also, any place where birds resort to spend the night. 2. Any temporary resting place. — *v.i.* 1. To sit or perch upon a roost. 2. To come to rest; settle. [OE *hrōst*]

roost·er (rōōs′tər) *n.* The male of the chicken; cock.

root¹ (rōōt, rŏŏt) *n.* 1. The underground portion of a plant, that absorbs moisture, obtains or stores nourishment, and provides support. 2. Any underground growth, as a tuber or bulb. 3. That from which anything derives origin, growth, or support, or life and vigor: Money is the *root* of evil. 4. An ancestor. 5. A rootlike part of an organ or structure: the *root* of a tooth or nerve. 6. *Ling.* A base to which affixes and thematic vowels may be added to form words, as *know* in *unknown, knowable,* and *unknowingly.* See STEM. 7. *Math.* A quantity that, multiplied by itself a specified number of times, will give a given quantity: 3 is the square *root* of 9 and the cube *root* of 27. 8. *Music* The fundamental tone of a chord. — *v.i.* 1. To put forth roots and begin to grow. 2. To be or become firmly fixed. — *v.t.* 3. To fix by or as by roots. 4. To pull, dig, or tear up by or as by the roots: with *up* or *out.* [OE *rōt* < ON] — **root′less** *adj.* — **root′y** *adj.*

root² (rōōt, rŏŏt) *v.t.* 1. To dig with the snout, as swine. — *v.i.* 2. To turn up the earth with the snout. 3. To search; rummage. 4. To toil. [OE *wrōtan* to root up] — **root′er** *n.*

root³ (rōōt, rŏŏt) *v.i.* *U.S. Informal* To cheer for or encourage a contestant, team, etc., with *for.* [Prob. var. of ROUT²] **— root′er** *n.*

root beer A beverage made with yeast and root extracts.

root hair *Bot.* Hairlike outgrowths of plant roots, having an absorbent and protective function.

root·let (rōōt′lit, rŏŏt′-) *n.* A small root.

root·stalk (rōōt′stôk′, rŏŏt′-) *n. Bot.* A rhizome.

root·stock (rōōt′stok′, rŏŏt′-) *n.* 1. Original source; origin. 2. *Bot.* A rhizome.

rope (rōp) *n.* 1. A construction of twisted fibers, as of hemp, cotton, flax, etc., so intertwined in several strands as to form a thick cord. 2. A collection of things plaited or united in a line. 3. A slimy or glutinous filament or thread. 4. A cord or halter used in hanging. 5. Execution or death by hanging: to die by the *rope.* 6. (*U.S.* A lasso. **— to give (one) plenty of rope** To allow (a person) to pursue unchecked a course that will end in disaster. **— to know the ropes** *Informal* To be familiar with all the conditions in any sphere of activity. **— v. roped, rop·ing** *v.t.* 1. To tie or fasten with or as with rope. 2. To enclose or divide with a rope: usu. with *off.* 3. *U.S.* To catch with a lasso. **— v.i.** 4. To become drawn out or extended into a filament or thread. [OE *rāp*]

rope·danc·er (rōp′dan′sər, -dän′-) *n.* A tightrope walker.

rope·walk (rōp′wôk′) *n.* A long alley or building used for the spinning of rope yarn.

rope·walk·er (rōp′wô′kər) *n.* A tightrope walker.

rop·y (rō′pē) *adj.* **rop·i·er, rop·i·est** 1. That may be drawn into threads, as a glutinous substance; stringy. 2. Resembling ropes or cordage. **— rop′i·ly** *adv.* **— rop′i·ness** *n.*

Roque·fort cheese (rōk′fərt, *Fr.* rôk·fôr′) A strong cheese with a blue mold, made from ewe's and goat's milk in the town of Roquefort, France.

ror·qual (rôr′kwəl) *n.* A whalebone whale of the Atlantic and Pacific oceans: also called *finback, razorback.* [< F < Norw. *röyrkval*]

Ror·schach test (rôr′shäk, -shäkh, rōr′-) *Psychol.* A test in which personality characteristics are made capable of analysis by the subject's interpretation of a series of standard inkblot patterns. [after Hermann *Rorschach,* 1884–1922, Swiss psychiatrist]

ro·sa·ceous (rō·zā′shəs) *adj.* 1. *Bot.* Of, pertaining to, or designating the rose family of trees, shrubs, and herbs. 2. Resembling a rose. [< L *rosa* rose]

ro·sa·ry (rō′zə·rē) *n. pl.* **·ries** 1. *Eccl.* **a** A series of prayers. **b** A string of beads for keeping count of these prayers. 2. A garden or bed of roses. [< L *rosa* rose]

rose¹ (rōz) *n.* 1. Any of a large genus of hardy, erect or climbing shrubs, with rodlike, prickly stems: the national flower of England and the State flower of New York, North Dakota, and Iowa. 2. The flower of such a shrub, usu. having five sepals and exhibiting a wide range of colors, principally white, yellow, pink, or red. 3. Any of various other plants or flowers likened to the true rose. 4. A light pinkish red. 5. An ornamental knot; a rosette. 6. A form in which gems, esp. diamonds, are often cut; also, a diamond so cut. **— bed of roses** A peaceful or carefree time, place, or condition. **— v.t. rosed, ros·ing** To cause to blush; redden; flush. [OE < L *rosa,* prob. < Gk. *rhodea*]

rose² (rōz) Past tense of RISE.

ro·se·ate (rō′zē·it, -āt) *adj.* 1. Rosy; rose-colored. 2. Cheerful; optimistic. [< L *roseus*] **— ro′se·ate·ly** *adv.*

rose·bud (rōz′bud′) *n.* The bud of a rose.

rose·bush (rōz′bŏŏsh′) *n.* A rose-bearing shrub or vine.

rose campion An herbaceous plant, cultivated for its pink or crimson flowers.

rose chafer A hairy, fawn-colored beetle injurious to roses: also called *rose beetle.* Also **rose bug.**

rose-col·ored (rōz′kul′ərd) *adj.* Pink or crimson, as a rose. **— to see through rose-colored glasses** To see things in an unduly favorable light.

rose fever *Pathol.* A variety of hay fever, assumed to be caused by rose pollen. Also **rose cold.**

rose·mar·y (rōz′mâr′ē) *n. pl.* **·mar·ies** An evergreen, fragrant Old World shrub of the mint family, commonly with blue flowers, cultivated for use in making perfume and in cookery. [ME < L < *ros* dew + *marinus* of the sea]

rose of Sharon 1. A hardy shrub of the mallow family: also called *shrub althea.* 2. A species of St. Johnswort having large, yellow flowers.

rose quartz A semitransparent variety of quartz, pink or rose in color and often used for ornament and as a gemstone.

Ro·set·ta stone (rō·zet′ə) A tablet of basalt inscribed with two forms of Egyptian hieroglyphics and in Greek, found near Rosetta, Egypt, in 1799. It supplied the key to the ancient inscriptions of Egypt.

ro·sette (rō·zet′) *n.* 1. An ornament or badge having some resemblance to a rose; esp., an architectural ornament with parts circularly arranged. 2. A flowerlike cluster of leaves, organs, or markings, arranged in circles, as in certain plants. [< F, dim. of *rose*]

rose water A fragrant preparation made variously by the distillation of rose petals or rose oil with water, used as a toilet water and in cooking.

rose window A circular window filled with tracery, often radiating from the center like spokes.

rose·wood (rōz′wŏŏd′) *n.* 1. A hard, close-grained, dark-colored, fragrant wood yielded by certain tropical American trees. 2. Any of various other woods resembling true rosewood. 3. Any tree yielding such a wood.

Rosh Ha·sha·na (rosh hə·shä′nə, rōsh) The Jewish New Year, celebrated in September or early October. Also **Rosh Ha·sho′nah** (-shō′-). [< Hebrew *rōsh* head + *hash-shānāh* of the year]

ros·in (roz′in) *n.* 1. The hard, amber-colored resin forming the residue after the distillation of oil from crude turpentine: also called *resin.* 2. Resin (defs. 1 & 2). **— v.t.** To apply rosin to. [Alter. of RESIN] **— ros′in·y** *adj.*

ros·ter (ros′tər) *n.* 1. A list of officers and men enrolled for duty; also, a list of active military organizations. 2. Any list of names. [< Du. *rooster* list, lit. gridiron]

ros·trum (ros′trəm) *n. pl.* **·trums** or **·tra** (-trə) *for defs.1 & 3,* **·tra** *for def. 2* 1. A pulpit or platform. 2. In ancient Rome: **a** A beaklike part on the prow of a ship. **b** The orators' platform in the Roman forum, embellished with such parts. 3. *Biol.* A beaklike process or part. [< L *rostrum* beak] **— ros′tral, ros′trate** (-trāt) *adj.*

ros·y (rō′zē) *adj.* **ros·i·er, ros·i·est** 1. Like a rose; rose red; blushing. 2. Bright, pleasing, or flattering. 3. Made of or ornamented with roses. 4. Auguring success; optimistic. **— ros′i·ly** *adv.* **— ros′i·ness** *n.*

rot (rot) *v.* **rot·ted, rot·ting** *v.i.* 1. To undergo decomposition; decay. 2. To become morally rotten. **— v.t.** 3. To cause to decompose; decay. 4. To ret. **— Syn.** See DECAY. **— n.** 1. The process of rotting or the state of being rotten. 2. That which is rotten. 3. Any of various diseases involving decay in humans, plants, and animals, esp., sheep. 4. *Informal* Trashy and nonsensical opinions or expressions. **— interj.** Nonsense. [OE *rotian*]

Ro·tar·i·an (rō·târ′ē·ən) *n.* A member of a Rotary Club. **— adj.** Of or pertaining to Rotary Clubs or their members. **— Ro·tar′i·an·ism** *n.*

ro·ta·ry (rō′tər·ē) *adj.* 1. Turning or designed to turn around its axis, like a wheel. 2. Having some part that turns on its axis. 3. Characterized by movement around an axis; rotatory. **— n. pl. ·ries** A rotary device or part. [< LL < L *rota* wheel]

Rotary Club A club belonging to an international association of clubs, **Rotary International,** whose aim is to improve civic service.

rotary engine *Mech.* 1. An engine in which rotary motion is directly produced, as in a turbine. 2. In internal-combustion engines, a radial engine revolving about a fixed crankshaft.

rotary press A printing press using curved type plates that revolve against the paper.

ro·tate (rō′tāt) *v.t. & v.i.* **·tat·ed, ·tat·ing** 1. To turn or cause to turn on or as on its axis. 2. To alternate in a definite order or succession. [< L < *rotare* to turn < *rota* wheel] **— ro′tat·a·ble, ro·ta·tive** (rō′tə·tiv) *adj.* **— ro′ta·tor** *n.* **— Syn.** (verb) 1. spin, whirl, twirl, turn, gyrate. See REVOLVE.

ro·ta·tion (rō·tā′shən) *n.* 1. The act or state of rotating; rotary motion. 2. Change or alternation in a particular sequence; regular variation. [< L *rotatio, -onis*] **— ro·ta′tion·al** *adj.*

ro·ta·to·ry (rō′tə·tôr′ē, -tō′rē) *adj.* 1. Having, pertaining to, or producing rotation. 2. Following in succession. 3. Alternating or recurring.

rote (rōt) *n.* 1. Mechanical routine. 2. Repetition of words as a means of learning them, with slight attention to the sense. **— by rote** Mechanically, without intelligent attention: to learn *by rote.* [ME; origin uncertain]

ro·te·none (rō′tə·nōn) *n. Chem.* A crystalline compound, $C_{23}H_{22}O_6$, the effective principle in insecticides and fish poisons, obtained from the roots of various plants. [Origin unknown]

rot·gut (rot′gut′) *U.S.* An inferior raw whisky.

ro·ti·fer (rō′tə·fər) *n.* One of a division of microscopic organisms usu. found in stagnant fresh water, having rings of cilia that in motion resemble revolving wheels. [< NL < L *rota* wheel + *ferre* to bear] **— ro·tif·er·al** (rō·tif′ər·əl), ro·tif′er·ous *adj.*

ro·tis·se·rie (rō·tis′ər·ē) *n.* 1. A restaurant where patrons select uncooked food and have it roasted and served. 2. A shop where food is roasted and sold. 3. A rotating device for roasting meat, etc. [< F < *rôtir* to roast]

ro·to·gra·vure (rō′tə·grə·vyŏŏr′, -grāv′yər) *n.* 1. The process of printing photographs, letters, etc., from cylinders etched from photographic plates and run through a rotary press. 2. A picture printed by this process. 3. The section of a newspaper containing such pictures. [< L *rota* wheel + GRAVURE]

ro·tor (rō′tər) *n.* **1.** The rotating section of a motor, dynamo, turbine, or other power generator: distinguished from *stator.* **2.** *Aeron.* The horizontally rotating unit of a helicopter or autogiro, consisting of the airfoils and hub. [Contraction of ROTATOR]

rot·ten (rot′n) *adj.* **1.** Decomposed by natural process; putrid. **2.** Untrustworthy; treacherous. **3.** Corrupt; venal. **4.** Liable to break; unsound. **5.** *Informal* Worthless. [< ON *rotinn*] **— rot′ten·ly** *adv.* **— rot′ten·ness** *n.* **— Syn. 1.** decayed, putrefied, putrescent, carious, fetid. Compare DECAY. **— Ant.** fresh, sweet, sound, wholesome, healthy.

rot·ter (rot′ər) *n. Chiefly Brit. Slang* A worthless or objectionable person; scoundrel.

ro·tund (rō·tund′) *adj.* **1.** Rounded out; spherical; plump. **2.** Full-toned, as a voice or utterance; sonorous. [< L *tundus* round] **— ro·tun′di·ty** *n.* **— ro·tund′ly** *adv.* **— ro·tund′ness** *n.*

ro·tun·da (rō·tun′də) *n.* A circular building or an interior hall, surmounted with a dome. [< Ital. < L *rotundus.* See ROTUND.]

rou·ble (rōō′bəl) See RUBLE.

rou·é (rōō·ā′) *n.* A sensualist; debauchee. [< F < *rouer* to break on the wheel]

rouge (rōōzh) *n.* **1.** Any cosmetic used for coloring the cheeks or lips pink or red. **2.** A ferric oxide used in polishing metals and glass. **— v. rouged, roug·ing** *v.t.* **1.** To color with rouge. **— v.i. 2.** To apply rouge. [< F < L *rubeus* ruby]

rough (ruf) *adj.* **1.** Having an uneven surface; not smooth or polished. **2.** Coarse in texture; shabby. **3.** Disordered or ragged; shaggy. **4.** Having the surface broken; uneven. **5.** Characterized by rude or violent action. **6.** Boisterous or tempestuous; stormy. **7.** Characterized by harshness of spirit; brutal. **8.** Lacking the finish and polish bestowed by art or culture; crude. **9.** Done or made hastily and without attention to details, as a drawing. **10.** Harsh to the ear; grating; inharmonious. **— n. 1.** A low, rude, and violent fellow; a rowdy. **2.** A crude, incomplete, or unpolished object, material, or condition. **3.** Any part of a golf course on which tall grass, bushes, etc., grow. **— in the rough** In a crude or unpolished state. **— v.t. 1.** To make rough; roughen. **2.** To treat roughly. **3.** To make, cut, or sketch roughly: with *in* or *out.* **— v.i. 4.** To become rough. **5.** To behave roughly. **— to rough it** To live, camp, or travel under rough, hard, or impoverished conditions. **— adv.** In a rude manner; roughly. [OE *rūh*] **— rough′ly** *adv.* **— rough′ness** *n.*

rough·age (ruf′ij) *n.* **1.** Any coarse or tough substance. **2.** Food material containing a high percentage of indigestible constituents, as cellulose.

rough-and-read·y (ruf′ən·red′ē) *adj.* **1.** Characterized by or acting with rude but effective promptness. **2.** Unpolished but good enough.

rough-and-tum·ble (ruf′ən·tum′bəl) *adj.* **1.** Marked by the disregard of all rules, as a fight. **2.** Scrambling; disorderly. **— n.** A rough-and-tumble fight or scuffle.

rough·cast (ruf′kast′, -käst′) *v.t.* **·cast, ·cast·ing 1.** To shape or prepare in a preliminary or incomplete form. **2.** To coat, as a wall, with coarse plaster, and cover with thin mortar by dashing it on. **— n. 1.** Very coarse plaster for the outside of buildings. **2.** A form or model of something in its first rough stage. **— rough′cast′er** *n.*

rough·draw (ruf′drô′) *v.t.* **·drew, ·drawn, ·draw·ing** To sketch hastily or crudely.

rough·dry (ruf′drī′) *v.t.* **·dried, ·dry·ing** To dry without ironing, as washed clothes.

rough·en (ruf′ən) *v.t. & v.i.* To make or become rough.

rough·hew (ruf′hyōō′) *v.t.* **·hewed, ·hewed** or **·hewn, ·hew·ing 1.** To hew or shape roughly or irregularly. **2.** To make crudely; roughcast.

rough·house (ruf′hous′) *Slang n.* A noisy, boisterous, or violent game; rough play. **— v. ·housed, ·hous·ing** *v.i.* **1.** To make a disturbance; engage in horseplay or violence. **— v.t. 2.** To handle or treat roughly but without hostile intent.

rough·neck (ruf′nek′) *n. U.S. Slang* A rowdy.

rough·rid·er (ruf′rī′dər) *n. U.S.* One skilled in breaking broncos or performing dangerous feats in horsemanship.

Rough Riders The 1st U.S. Volunteer Cavalry in the Spanish-American War of 1898, mainly organized and subsequently commanded by Theodore Roosevelt.

rough·shod (ruf′shod′) *adj.* Shod with rough shoes to prevent slipping, as a horse. **— to ride roughshod (over)** To act overbearingly; domineer without compunction.

rou·lette (rōō·let′) *n.* **1.** A game played at a table divided into spaces numbered and colored red and black, and having a rotating disk (**roulette wheel**) on which a ball is rolled until it drops into one of 37 or 38 correspondingly marked spaces. **2.** An engraver's disk of tempered steel, as for trac-

ing points on a copperplate; also, a draftsman's wheel for making dotted lines. **— v.t. ·let·ted, ·let·ting** To perforate or mark with a roulette. [< F < *roue* wheel]

round (round) *adj.* **1.** Having a contour that is circular or approximately so; spherical, ring-shaped, or cylindrical. **2.** Having a curved contour or surface; not angular or flat; convex or concave. **3.** Liberal; ample; large. **4.** Easy and free, as in motion; brisk. **5.** Of full cadence; well-balanced; full-toned. **6.** Made without reserve; outspoken. **7.** Open; just. **8.** Formed or moving in rotation or a circle. **9.** Returning to the point of departure: a *round* trip. **10.** Of a number, increased or decreased by a relatively small amount for the sake of simplicity: 3,992 is 4,000 in *round* numbers. **11.** Semicircular: a *round* arch. **12.** *Phonet.* Labialized; rounded. **— n. 1.** Something round, as a globe, ring, or cylinder, a rung of a ladder, a portion of the thigh of a beef, etc. **2.** *Often pl.* A circular course or range; circuit; beat. **3.** A single revolution; also revolving motion. **4.** A series of recurrent movements; routine; order: the daily *round* of life. **5.** One of a series of concerted actions performed in succession: a *round* of applause. **6.** One of the divisions of a boxing match; a bout. **7.** In golf, a number of holes or an interval of play in a match. **8.** *Music* A short canon in the octave or unison, in which each voice enters in turn and returns to the beginning upon reaching the end. **9.** A firing by a company or squad in which each soldier fires once; volley. **10.** A single shot or complete unit of ammunition. **11.** The state of being carved out on all sides: sculpture in the *round.* **12.** The state or condition of being circular; roundness. **13.** A thick slice from a haunch. **— to go** (or **make**) **the rounds 1.** To take a usual walk or tour, as of inspection. **2.** To pass from person to person of a certain group. **— v.t. 1.** To make round. **2.** To bring to completion; perfect: usually with *off* or *out.* **3.** To free of angularity; fill out to fullness of form. **4.** *Phonet.* To utter (a vowel) with the lips in a rounded position; labialize. **5.** To travel or go around; make a circuit of. **— v.i. 6.** To become round. **7.** To come to completeness or perfection. **8.** To fill out; become plump. **9.** To make a circuit; travel a circular course. **10.** To turn around. **— to round off 1.** To make round or rounded. **2.** To make into a round number. **— to round up 1.** To collect (cattle, etc.) in a herd, as for driving to market. **2.** *Informal* To assemble. **— adv. 1.** On all sides; in such a manner as to encircle. **2.** With a circular or rotating motion. **3.** Through a circle or circuit, as from person to person or point to point: provisions enough to go *round.* **4.** In circumference: a log 3 feet *round.* **5.** From one view or position to another; to and fro. **6.** In the vicinity: to hang *round.* **— prep. 1.** Enclosing; encircling. **2.** On every side of, or from every side toward; surrounding. **3.** Toward every side from; about. [< OF < L *rotundus* round] **— round′ish** *adj.* **— round′ish·ness** *n.* **— round′ness** *n.*

round·a·bout (round′ə·bout′) *adj.* **1.** Circuitous; indirect. **2.** Encircling. **— n. 1.** An outer garment reaching to the waist; a jacket. **2.** *Brit.* A merry-go-round.

round·ed (roun′did) *adj.* **1.** Round or spherical. **2.** *Phonet.* Formed or uttered with the lips rounded; labialized.

roun·de·lay (roun′də·lā) *n.* **1.** A simple melody. **2.** A musical setting of a poem with a recurrent refrain. [< OF < *rond* round]

round·er (roun′dər) *n.* **1.** A tool for rounding. **2.** *U.S. Slang* A drunkard, drifter, or petty criminal. **3.** *pl.* (*construed as sing.*) An English game somewhat resembling baseball.

Round·head (round′hed′) *n.* A member of the parliamentary party in England in the civil war of 1642–49.

round·house (round′hous′) *n.* **1.** A cabin on the after part of the quarter-deck of a vessel. **2.** A round building with a turntable in the center for housing and switching locomotives. **3.** In pinochle, a meld of four kings and four queens.

round·ly (round′lē) *adv.* **1.** In a round manner or form; circularly; spherically. **2.** Severely; vigorously: to be *roundly* denounced. **3.** Frankly; bluntly. **4.** Thoroughly.

round number A number expressed to the nearest ten, hundred, thousand, etc. Also **round figure.**

round robin 1. A tournament, as in tennis or chess, in which each player meets every other player. **2.** A letter circulated among the members of a group. **3.** A number of signatures, as to a petition, written in a circle so as to avoid giving prominence to any one name.

round-shoul·dered (round′shōl′dərd) *adj.* Having the back rounded or the shoulders stooping.

round table 1. A meeting place for conference. **2.** Any discussion group. **— round-ta·ble** (round′tā′bəl) *adj.*

Round Table 1. The table around which King Arthur and his knights sat. **2.** King Arthur and his knights.

round-the-clock (round′thə·klok′) *adj.* Through all twenty-four hours of the day.

round trip A trip to a place and back again; a two-way trip. — **round′-trip′** *adj.*

round·up (round′up′) *n. U.S.* **1.** The bringing together of cattle scattered over a range, as for inspection or branding. **2.** The cowboys, horses, etc., employed in this work. **3.** *Informal* A bringing together of persons or things.

round·worm (round′wûrm′) *n.* A nematode worm, esp. one parasitic in the human intestines.

rouse (rouz) *v.* **roused, rous·ing** *v.t.* **1.** To cause to awaken from slumber, repose, unconsciousness, etc. **2.** To excite to vigorous thought or action; stir up. **3.** To startle or drive (game) from cover. — *v.i.* **4.** To awaken. **5.** To become active. **6.** To start from cover: said of game. — *n.* The act of rousing. [Orig. technical term in hawking and hunting] — **rous′er** *n.*

rous·ing (rou′zing) *adj.* **1.** Able to rouse or excite: a *rousing* speech. **2.** Lively; active; vigorous: a *rousing* trade. **3.** *Informal* Outrageous; astonishing: a *rousing* lie.

roust (roust) *v.t. & v.i. Informal* To arouse and drive (a person or thing); stir up: usu. with *out*. [< ROUSE]

roust·a·bout (roust′tə·bout′) *n.* **1.** A laborer on river craft or on the waterfront. **2.** One who is employed for casual work; esp., a transient laborer on a cattle ranch, etc. **3.** A laborer in a circus.

rout¹ (rout) *n.* **1.** A disorderly and overwhelming defeat or flight. **2.** A boisterous crowd. — *v.t.* To defeat disastrously; put to flight. [< OF < L *rumpere* to break]

rout² (rout) *v.i.* **1.** To root, as swine. **2.** To search; rummage. — *v.t.* **3.** To dig or turn up with the snout. **4.** To turn up as if with the snout; disclose to view: with *out*. **5.** To hollow, gouge, or scrape, as with a scoop. **6.** To drive or force out. [Var. of ROOT²]

route (root, rout) *n.* **1.** A course, road, or way taken in traveling from one point to another. **2.** The specific course over which mail is sent. **3.** The territory covered by a newsboy. — *v.t.* **rout·ed, rout·ing** To dispatch or send by a certain way, as passengers, goods, etc. [< OF < L *rupta* (*via*) broken (road), fem. of *ruptus*. See ROUT¹.]

rout·er (rou′tər) *n.* **1.** One who scoops or routs. **2.** A tool for routing. **3.** A plane devised for working a molding around a circular sash. [< ROUT²]

rou·tine (rō̄o·tēn′) *n.* **1.** A detailed method of procedure, regularly followed: an official *routine*. **2.** Habitual methods of action induced by circumstances. — *adj.* Customary; habitual. [< F < *route* way, road] — **rou·tine′ly** *adv.*

rou·tin·ism (rō̄o·tē′niz·əm) *n.* Adherence to routine or routine methods in general. — **rou·tin′ist** *n.*

rou·tin·ize (rō̄o·tē′nīz) *v.t.* **·ized, ·i·zing** To reduce or fit to a routine.

roux (rō̄o) *n. French* Butter and an equal portion of flour mixed and browned together, used for sauces, etc.

rove¹ (rōv) *v.* **roved, rov·ing** *v.i.* **1.** To wander from place to place; go or move without any definite destination. — *v.t.* **2.** To roam over, through, or about. — *n.* The act of roving; a ramble. [ME *roven*] — **rov′er** *n.*

rove² (rōv) Alternate past tense and past participle of REEVE¹.

row¹ (rō) *n.* **1.** An arrangement or series of persons or things in a continued line; a rank; file. **2.** A street lined with houses on both sides. **3.** A line of seats, as in a theater. — **a long row to hoe** A hard task or undertaking. — *v.t.* To arrange in a row: with *up*. [OE *rāw*, var. of *ræw* line]

row² (rō) *v.i.* **1.** To use oars, etc., in propelling a boat. — *v.t.* **2.** To propel across the surface of the water with oars, as a boat. **3.** To transport by rowing. **4.** To be propelled by (a specific number of oars): said of boats. **5.** To make use of (oars or rowers), esp. in a race. **6.** To row against in a race. — *n.* **1.** The act of rowing. **2.** A turn at the oars. **3.** A trip in a rowboat. [OE *rōwan*]

row³ (rou) *n.* **1.** A noisy disturbance or quarrel; a brawl. **2.** Any dispute or disturbance. — *v.t. & v.i.* To engage in a row or brawl. [Origin uncertain]

row·an (rō′ən, rou′-) *n.* A small tree native to Europe, having clusters of bright orange berries: also called *mountain ash*.

row·boat (rō′bōt′) *n. U.S.* A boat propelled by oars.

row·dy (rou′dē) *n. pl.* **·dies** One inclined to create disturbances; a rough, disorderly person. — *adj.* **·di·er, ·di·est** Rough and loud; disorderly. [Origin unknown] — **row′dy·ish** *adj.* — **row′dy·ism, row′di·ness** *n.*

row·el (rou′əl) *n.* A spiked or toothed wheel, as on a spur. — *v.t.* **row·eled** or **·elled, row·el·ing** or **·el·ling** To prick with a rowel; spur. [< OF *roele* < L *rota* wheel]

row·lock (rō′lok′) *n. Brit.* An oarlock.

roy·al (roi′əl) *adj.* **1.** Pertaining to a monarch; kingly. **2.** Under the patronage or authority of a king, or connected with a monarchical form of government: a *royal* governor. **3.** Like or befitting a king; regal. **4.** Of superior quality or size. **5.** *Informal* Extraordinarily good, large, impressive, etc. — *n.* **1.** A size of paper, 19 x 24 inches for writing, 20 x 25 inches for printing. **2.** *Naut.* A sail next above the topgallant. [< OF < L *rex* king] — **roy′al·ly** *adv.*

royal blue A brilliant blue, often with reddish overtones.

Royal Canadian Mounted Police The federal police force of Canada.

royal flush See under FLUSH³.

roy·al·ist (roi′əl·ist) *n.* A supporter of a royal dynasty. — *adj.* Of or pertaining to royalists: also **roy′al·is′tic**.

Roy·al·ist (roi′əl·ist) *n.* **1.** In English history, a Cavalier or adherent of King Charles I. **2.** In French history, a supporter of the Bourbon or Orléans claims to the throne since 1793. **3.** In the American Revolution, a supporter of the king; Loyalist; Tory.

roy·al·mast (roi′əl·mast′, -mäst′) *n. Naut.* The section of a mast next above the topgallant mast.

royal palm Any of various palms native in tropical America, noted for their height and striking appearance.

royal purple **1.** A very deep violet color verging toward blue. **2.** Originally, a rich crimson.

roy·al·ty (roi′əl·tē) *n. pl.* **·ties** **1.** The rank, birth, or lineage of a king or queen. **2.** A royal personage; also, royal persons collectively. **3.** A share of proceeds paid to a proprietor, author, or inventor. **4.** A tax paid to the crown on the produce of royal mines, or on gold and silver coinage. **5.** A royal possession or domain. [< OF *roialte*]

-rrhagia *combining form Pathol.* An abnormal or violent discharge or flow; an eruption: also *-rhage, -rhagia, -rhagy*. Also **-rrhage, -rrhagy.** Corresponding adjectives are formed with **-rrhagic.** [< Gk. < *rrhag-*, root of *rrhēgnynai* to burst]

-rrhaphy *combining form* A sewing together; a suture. [< F *-rrhaphie* < Gk. *rhaptein* to sew together]

-rrhea *combining form Pathol.* An abnormal or excessive flow or discharge: also spelled *-rhea, -rhoea*. Also **-rrhoea.** [< Gk. *-rrhoia* < *rheein* to flow]

rub (rub) *v.* **rubbed, rub·bing** *v.t.* **1.** To move or pass over the surface of with pressure and friction. **2.** To cause (something) to move or pass with friction; scrape; grate. **3.** To cause to become frayed, worn, or sore from friction. **4.** To clean, shine, burnish, etc., by means of pressure and friction. **5.** To apply or spread with pressure and friction. **6.** To remove or erase by friction: with *off* or *out*. — *v.i.* **7.** To move along a surface with friction; scrape. **8.** To exert pressure and friction. **9.** To become frayed, worn, or sore from friction; chafe. **10.** To undergo rubbing or removal by rubbing: with *off, out*, etc. — **to rub it in** *Slang* To harp on someone's errors, faults, etc. — **to rub out** *Slang* To kill. — **to rub the wrong way** *Slang* To irritate; annoy. — *n.* **1.** A rubbing: Give it a *rub*. **2.** A hindrance, doubt, etc.: There's the *rub*. **3.** Something that rubs or is rough to the feelings; a sarcasm. **4.** A roughness or unevenness of surface, quality, or character. [ME *rubben*, prob. < LG]

ru·ba·to (rō̄o·bä′tō) *Music adj.* Denoting the lengthening of one note at the expense of another. — *n. pl.* **·tos** A rubato modification. — *adv.* In a rubato manner. [< Ital., robbed]

rub·ber¹ (rub′ər) *n.* **1.** A resinous elastic material obtained by coagulating the milky latex of certain tropical plants, and also made synthetically: sometimes called *India rubber*. **2.** Anything used for rubbing, erasing, polishing, etc. **3.** An article made of rubber, as an elastic band or an overshoe. **4.** In baseball, the pitcher's plate. **5.** *Slang* A condom. **6.** One who or that which rubs. — *adj.* Made of rubber. [< RUB] — **rub′ber·y** *adj.*

rub·ber² (rub′ər) *n.* In bridge, whist, and other card games, a series of two or three games terminated when one side has won two games; also, the odd game that breaks a tie between the players. [Origin unknown]

rubber check *U.S. Slang* A worthless check.

rub·ber·ize (rub′ər·īz) *v.t.* **·ized, ·iz·ing** To coat, impregnate, or cover with a preparation of rubber.

rub·ber·neck (rub′ər·nek′) *U.S. Slang n.* One who cranes his neck in order to see something; a sightseer; tourist. — *v.i.* To stretch or crane one's neck; gape.

rubber plant **1.** Any of several plants yielding rubber. **2.** A house plant of the mulberry family, having large, glossy, leathery leaves.

rub·ber-stamp (rub′ər·stamp′) *v.t.* **1.** To endorse, initial, or approve with the mark made by a rubber stamping device. **2.** *Informal* To pass or approve as a matter of routine.

rub·bish (rub′ish) *n.* **1.** Waste refuse, or broken matter; trash. **2.** Nonsense; rot. [ME *rubbous*] — **rub′bish·y** *adj.*

rub·ble (rub′əl) *n. for def. 3, also* **rub′el** *n.* **1.** Rough, irregular pieces of broken stone. **2.** The debris to which buildings of brick, stone, etc., are reduced by violent actions, as by earthquakes or bombings. **3.** Rough pieces of stone for use in construction; also, masonry composed of such pieces. [Origin uncertain] — **rub′bly** *adj.*

rub·down (rub′doun′) *n.* A type of massage.

rube (rō̄ob) *n. Slang* A farmer; rustic. [Abbreviation of *Reuben*, a personal name]

ru·bel·la (rō̄o·bel′ə) *n. Pathol.* German measles. [< NL, neut. pl. of L *rubellus* reddish, dim. of *ruber* red]

ru·be·o·la (rōō·bē′ə·lə) *n. Pathol.* 1. Measles (def. 1). 2. German measles. [< NL, neut. pl. dim. of L *rubeus* red] — **ru·be′o·lar** *adj.*

Ru·bi·con (rōō′bi·kon) A river in north central Italy, forming the boundary separating Caesar's province of Gaul from Italy, and by crossing it he committed himself to war with Pompey. — **to cross the Rubicon** To be committed definitely to some course of action.

ru·bi·cund (rōō′bə·kənd) *adj.* Red, or inclined to redness; rosy. [< L *rubicundus* red] — **ru′bi·cun′di·ty** *n.*

ru·bid·i·um (rōō·bid′ē·əm) *n.* A soft, rare, silvery white, metallic element (symbol Rb) resembling potassium. See ELEMENT. [< NL < L *rubidus* red]

ru·ble (rōō′bəl) *n.* 1. A standard monetary unit of the U.S.S.R.: in 1960 worth about 25 U.S. cents: also spelled *rouble*. 2. Formerly, a Russian silver coin.

ru·bric (rōō′brik) *n.* 1. A part of an early manuscript or a book that appears in red, used to indicate initial letters, headings, etc. 2. *Eccl.* A direction or rule printed in a devotional or liturgical office. 3. A heading or title, as of a chapter, statute, etc. 4. Any direction or rule of conduct. — *adj.* 1. Red or reddish. 2. Written in red. [< F < L *rubrica* red earth] — **ru′bri·cal** *adj.* — **ru′bri·cal·ly** *adv.*

ru·bri·cate (rōō′brə·kāt) *v.t.* **·cat·ed, ·cat·ing** To mark or tint with red; illuminate with red, as a book. [< L *rubricare* to redden] — **ru′bri·ca′tion** *n.* — **ru′bri·ca′tor** *n.*

ru·by (rōō′bē) *n. pl.* **·bies** 1. A translucent, deep purplish red variety of corundum, highly valued as a gemstone: also called *Oriental ruby.* 2. A rich red color like that of a ruby. — *adj.* Pertaining to or like a ruby; being of a rich crimson. — *v.t.* **·bied, ·by·ing** To tint with the color of a ruby; redden. [< OF *rubi*, ult. < L *rubeus* red]

ruche (rōōsh) *n.* A quilted or ruffled strip of fine fabric, worn about the neck or wrists of a woman's costume. [< F, beehive, frill]

ruch·ing (rōō′shing) *n.* Material for ruches; also, ruches collectively.

ruck·sack (ruk′sak′, rŏŏk′-) *n.* A canvas knapsack. [< G < *rucken*, var. of *rücken* back + *sack* sack]

ruck·us (ruk′əs) *n. U.S. Slang* An uproar; commotion; rumpus. [Prob. blend of RUMPUS and RUCTION]

rud·der (rud′ər) *n.* 1. *Naut.* A broad, flat, movable device hinged vertically at the stern of a vessel to direct its course. 2. Anything that guides or directs a course. 3. *Aeron.* A hinged or pivoted surface, used to control the position of an aircraft about its vertical axis. [OE *rōthor* oar, scull]

rud·dy (rud′ē) *adj.* **·di·er, ·di·est** 1. Tinged with red. 2. Having a healthy glow; rosy: a *ruddy* complexion. 3. *Brit. Slang* Bloody: a euphemism. [OE *rudig*] — **rud′di·ly** *adv.* — **rud′di·ness** *n.*

ruddy duck A small North American duck having stiffened tail feathers and, in the adult male, a bright chestnut-colored body.

rude (rōōd) *adj.* **rud·er, rud·est** 1. Offensively blunt or uncivil; rough or abrupt; impudent. 2. Characterized by lack of polish or refinement; uncultivated; uncouth. 3. Unskillfully made or done; crude; rough. 4. Robust; strong. 5. Barbarous; savage. [< OF, or < L *rudis* rough] — **rude′ly** *adv.* — **rude′ness** *n.*

ru·di·ment (rōō′də·mənt) *n.* 1. A first principle, step, stage, or condition. 2. That which is as yet undeveloped or only partially developed. 3. *Biol.* An undeveloped or functionless organ or part. [< F < L *rudiment* first attempt]

ru·di·men·ta·ry (rōō′də·men′tər·ē) *adj.* 1. Pertaining to or of the nature of a rudiment or first principle; elementary. 2. Being or remaining in an imperfectly developed state; vestigial; abortive. Also **ru′di·men′tal.** — **ru′di·men′ta·ri·ly** *adv.* — **ru′di·men′ta·ri·ness** *n.*

rue¹ (rōō) *v.* **rued, ru·ing** *v.t.* 1. To feel sorrow or remorse for. — *v.i.* 2. To feel sorrow or remorse; be regretful. — Syn. See MOURN. — *n.* Sorrowful remembrance; regret. [OE *hrēowan* to be sorry] — **ru′er** *n.*

rue² (rōō) *n.* 1. A small, bushy herb with bitter, acrid leaves, formerly much used in medicine. 2. Any bitter draft. [< F < L *ruta* < Gk. *rhytē*]

rue·ful (rōō′fəl) *adj.* 1. Feeling or causing sorrow, regret, or pity; deplorable; sorrowful. 2. Expressing sorrow or pity. — **rue′ful·ly** *adv.* — **rue′ful·ness** *n.*

ruff¹ (ruf) *n.* 1. A pleated, round, heavily starched collar popular in the 16th century. 2. Ruffle¹ (defs. 1 and 2). 3. A natural collar of projecting feathers or hair around the neck of a bird or mammal. 4. An Old World sandpiper of which the male in the breeding season has an erectile frill of feathers about the neck. [Short for RUFFLE¹]

ruff² (ruf) *n.* The playing of a trump upon another suit when one has no cards of that suit. — *v.t. & v.i.* To trump when unable to follow suit. [< OF *roffle, rouffle, ronfle*]

ruffed (ruft) *adj.* Having a ruff, ruffle, or frill; ruffled.

ruffed grouse A North American grouse: called *partridge* in the northern and *pheasant* in the southern U.S.

ruf·fi·an (ruf′ē·ən, ruf′yən) *n.* A lawless, brutal fellow; a tough. — *adj.* Lawlessly or recklessly brutal or cruel. [< OF *ruffian*] — **ruf′fi·an·ism** *n.* — **ruf′fi·an·ly** *adj.*

ruf·fle¹ (ruf′əl) *n.* 1. A pleated strip or frill of fabric, lace, etc., used as trim or ornament. 2. Anything resembling such a strip. Also called *ruff.* 3. A temporary discomposure. 4. A slight disturbance, as a ripple. — *v.* **fled, ·fling** *v.t.* 1. To disturb or destroy the smoothness or regularity of. 2. To draw into folds or ruffles; gather. 3. To furnish with ruffles. 4. To erect (the feathers) in a ruff. 5. To disturb or irritate; upset. 6. To riffle (the pages of a book). 7. To shuffle (cards). — *v.i.* 8. To be or become rumpled or disordered. 9. To become disturbed or irritated. [< RUFFLE²]

ruf·fle² (ruf′əl) *n.* A low continuous beat of a drum, not as loud as a roll. — *v.t.* **fled, ·fling** To beat a ruffle upon, as a drum. [< earlier *ruff;* prob. imit.]

ru·fous (rōō′fəs) *adj.* Dull red. [< L *rufus* red]

rug (rug) *n.* 1. A heavy textile fabric, made in one piece, to cover a portion of a floor. 2. A covering made from the skins of animals. 3. *Chiefly Brit.* A heavy coverlet or lap robe. [< Scand. Cf. Norw. *rugga* coarse coverlet.]

rug·by football (rug′bē) 1. *Usu. cap. Brit.* A form of football in which the ball is propelled toward the opponents' goal by kicking or carrying. 2. *Canadian* Football (def. 3).

rug·ged (rug′id) *adj.* 1. Having a surface full of abrupt inequalities; broken into irregular points or crags; rough; uneven. 2. Shaggy; unkempt; ragged. 3. Rough in temper, character, or action. 4. Having strongly marked features; wrinkled. 5. Lacking culture or refinement; rude. 6. Rough to the ear; grating. 7. Robust; sturdy; hale. 8. Tempestuous; stormy. [< Scand.] — **rug′ged·ly** *adv.* — **rug′ged·ness** *n.*

ru·gose (rōō′gōs) *adj.* Full of wrinkles, as some leaves. Also **ru′gous** (-gəs). [< L < *ruga* wrinkle]

ru·in (rōō′in) *n.* 1. Total destruction of value or usefulness. 2. Loss of honor, position, wealth, etc.; degradation. 3. *Often pl.* That which remains of something demolished or decayed. 4. A condition of desolation or destruction. 5. That which causes destruction, downfall or injury. — *v.t.* 1. To bring to ruin; destroy. 2. To bring to bankruptcy or poverty. 3. To deprive of chastity; seduce. — *v.i.* 4. To fall into ruin. — Syn. See DEMOLISH. [< OF < L < *ruere* to fall] — **ru′in·a·ble** *adj.* — **ru′in·er** *n.*

ru·in·a·tion (rōō′in·ā′shən) *n.* 1. The act of ruining, or the state of being ruined. 2. Something that ruins.

ru·in·ous (rōō′in·əs) *adj.* 1. Causing or tending to ruin. 2. Falling to ruin; decayed. — **ru′in·ous·ly** *adv.* — **ru′in·ous·ness** *n.*

rule (rōōl) *n.* 1. Controlling power, or its possession and exercise; government; dominion; authority. 2. A method or principle of action: I make early rising my *rule.* 3. An authoritative direction or enactment respecting the doing or method of doing something: the *rules* of a game. 4. A regulation or body of directions laid down by or for a religious order. 5. A prescribed form, method, or set of instructions for solving a given class of mathematical problems. 6. An established usage or law, fixing the form or use of words or the construction of sentences. 7. Something belonging to the ordinary course of events or condition of things. 8. Regular or proper method; propriety, as of conduct; regularity. 9. *Law* A judicial decision on some motion or special application: a *rule* to show cause. 10. A straightedged instrument for use in measuring, or as a guide in drawing lines. 11. *Printing* A strip of type-high metal for handling type or for printing a rule or line. — **as a rule** Ordinarily; usually. — *v.* **ruled, rul·ing** *v.t.* 1. To have authority or control over; govern. 2. To influence greatly; dominate. 3. To decide or determine judicially or authoritatively. 4. To restrain; keep in check. 5. To mark with straight, parallel lines. 6. To make (a straight line) with or as with a ruler. — *v.i.* 7. To have authority or control; be in command. 8. To maintain a standard of rates. 9. To form and express a decision. [< OF < L *regula* ruler, rule] — **rul′a·ble** *adj.*

rule of thumb 1. Measurement by the thumb. 2. Roughly practical rather than scientifically accurate measure.

rul·er (rōō′lər) *n.* 1. One who rules or governs, as a sovereign. 2. A straight-edged instrument for use in measuring, or as a guide in drawing lines, usu. marked in inches.

rul·ing (rōō′ling) *adj.* Exercising dominion; controlling; predominant. — *n.* 1. The act of one who rules or governs. 2. A decision, as of a judge or presiding officer.

rum¹ (rum) *n.* 1. An alcoholic liquor distilled from fermented molasses or cane juice. 2. Any alcoholic liquor. [Origin uncertain; ? short for obs. *rumbullion* rum]

rum² (rum) *adj. Brit. Slang* Queer; strange; peculiar. [? < Romany *rom* man]

Ru·ma·ni·an (rōō·mā′nē·ən, -mān′yən) *adj.* Of Rumania, its people, or their language. —*n.* **1.** A native or inhabitant of Rumania. **2.** The Romance language of the Rumanians.

rum·ba (rum′bə, *Sp.* rōōm′bä) *n.* **1.** A dance having its origin among Cuban Negroes. **2.** A modern ballroom dance based on this; also, music for or in the manner of such a dance. Also spelled *rhumba.* [< Am.Sp.]

rum·ble (rum′bəl) *v.* ·**bled**, ·**bling** *v.i.* **1.** To make a low, heavy, rolling sound, as thunder. **2.** To move or proceed with such a sound. —*v.t.* **3.** To cause to make a low, heavy, rolling sound. **4.** To utter with such a sound. —*n.* **1.** A continuous low, heavy, rolling sound. **2.** A seat or baggage compartment in the rear of a carriage. **3.** A folding seat in the back of a coupé or roadster: in full **rumble seat. 4.** *U.S. Slang* A gang fight, usu. involving teenagers. [ME *romblen*] —**rum′bler** *n.* —**rum′bling·ly** *adv.* —**rum′bly** *adj.*

ru·men (rōō′men) *n.* *pl.* **ru·mi·na** (rōō′mə·nə) The first stomach or the cud of a ruminant. [< L *gullet*]

ru·mi·nant (rōō′mə·nənt) *n.* One of a division or suborder of even-toed, cud-chewing mammals, as the deer, sheep, cow, camel, etc., having a stomach with four cavities, the rumen, reticulum, omasum, and abomasum. —*adj.* **1.** Chewing the cud. **2.** Of or pertaining to a ruminant. **3.** Meditative or contemplative. [< L < *ruminare* to chew over]

ru·mi·nate (rōō′mə·nāt) *v.t. & v.i.* ·**nat·ed**, ·**nat·ing** **1.** To chew (food previously swallowed and regurgitated) over again; chew (the cud). **2.** To meditate or reflect (upon); ponder. [See RUMINANT.] —**ru′mi·nat′ing·ly** *adv.* —**ru′mi·na′tion** *n.* —**ru′mi·na·tive** *adj.* —**ru′mi·na·tive·ly** *adv.* —**ru′mi·na·tor** *n.*

rum·mage (rum′ij) *v.* ·**maged**, ·**mag·ing** *v.t.* **1.** To search through (a place, box, etc.) by turning over and disarranging the contents; ransack. **2.** To find or bring out by searching: with *out* or *up.* —*v.i.* **3.** To make a thorough search. —*n.* **1.** Any act of rummaging. **2.** An upheaval or stirring up; bustle. [< MF < *arrumer* to stow cargo] —**rum′mag·er** *n.*

rummage sale 1. A sale of second-hand objects to obtain money for some charitable purpose. **2.** A sale of unclaimed articles, or a sale for clearing out articles prior to restocking.

rum·my[1] (rum′ē) *n.* A card game in which each player draws a card and discards another card, the object being to combine or get rid of one's hand in sequences of three cards or more of the same suit. [? < Brit. slang *rummy, queer*]

rum·my[2] (rum′ē) *n.* *pl.* ·**mies** *Slang* A drunkard. —*adj.* ·**mi·er, ·mi·est** Of or resembling rum: a *rummy* flavor.

ru·mor (rōō′mər) *n.* **1.** An unverified or unfounded report, story, etc., circulating from person to person. **2.** Common gossip; hearsay. —*v.t.* To tell or spread as a rumor; noise about. Also *Brit.* **ru′mour.** [< OF < L]

rump (rump) *n.* **1.** The rounded or fleshy upper part of the hind quarters of an animal. **2.** The analogous region in man; the buttocks. **3.** A cut of beef between the loin and the round. **4.** A legislative group, representative body, etc., having only a remnant of its original membership, and therefore regarded as unauthoritative. **5.** A last, often undesirable remnant. [ME *rumpe* < Scand.]

rum·ple (rum′pəl) *v.t. & v.i.* ·**pled**, ·**pling** To form into creases or folds; wrinkle; ruffle. —*n.* **1.** An irregular fold; untidy wrinkling. **2.** The condition of being rumpled. [< MDu. *rumpelen*]

rum·pus (rum′pəs) *n.* *Informal* A row; wrangle; to-do. [Origin uncertain]

rumpus room A room for games, informal gatherings, etc.

rum·run·ner (rum′run′ər) *n.* A person or ship illicitly transporting alcoholic liquors across a border.

run (run) *v.* **ran** (*Archaic* or *Dial.* **run**), **run, run·ning** *v.i.* **1.** To move by rapid steps, faster than walking, in such a manner that both feet are off the ground for a portion of each step. **2.** To move rapidly; go swiftly. **3.** To flee; take flight. **4.** To make a brief or rapid journey. **5.** To make regular trips; ply. **6.** To be a candidate or contestant. **7.** To finish a race in a specified position. **8.** To move or pass easily: The rope *runs* through the block. **9.** To elapse: The hours *run* by. **10.** To proceed in direction or extent: This road *runs* north. **11.** To move in or as in a stream; flow. **12.** To become liquid and flow, as wax; also, to spread or mingle confusedly, as colors when wet. **13.** To move or pass into a specified condition: to *run* into trouble. **14.** To climb or grow in long shoots, as vines. **15.** To become torn by unraveling, as a knitted fabric. **16.** To suppurate. **17.** To leak. **18.** To continue or proceed: The conversation *ran* on and on. **19.** To be in operation; be operative; work: Will the engine *run*? **20.** To continue in existence or effect; extend in time: Genius *runs* in her family. **21.** To be reported or expressed: The story *runs* as follows. **22.** To migrate, as salmon from the sea. **23.** To occur or return, as to the mind. **24.** To incline; tend: Her taste *runs* to luxuries. **25.** To be performed or repeated in continuous succession, as a play. **26.** To make a rapid succession of demands for payment, as on a bank. **27.** To continue unexpired or unpaid, as a debt;

become payable. —*v.t.* **28.** To go along by running, as a route, course, or path. **29.** To make one's way over, through, or past: to *run* rapids. **30.** To perform or accomplish by or as by running: to *run* an errand. **31.** To compete against in or as in a race. **32.** To enter (a horse, etc.) for a race. **33.** To present and support as a candidate. **34.** To hunt or chase, as game. **35.** To bring to a specified condition by or as by running: to *run* oneself out of breath. **36.** To drive or force: with *out of, off, into, through*, etc. **37.** To cause (a vessel) to move rapidly or freely. **38.** To move (the eye, hand, etc.) quickly or lightly. **39.** To cause to move, slide, etc., as into a specified position. **40.** To cause to go or ply: to *run* a train. **41.** To transport or convey in a vessel or vehicle. **42.** To smuggle. **43.** To cause to flow. **44.** To give forth a flow of; emit: Her eyes *ran* tears. **45.** To mold, as from melted metal. **46.** To sew or stitch in a continuous line. **47.** To maintain or control the motion or operation of, as a machine. **48.** To direct or control; manage; oversee. **49.** To allow to continue or mount up, as a bill: often with *up.* **50.** To become liable to; incur: to *run* a risk. **51.** In games, to make (a number of points, strokes, etc.) successively. **52.** To publish in a magazine or newspaper: to *run* an ad. **53.** To mark, set down, or trace, as a boundary line. **54.** To suffer from (a fever, etc.). —**to run across** To meet by chance. —**to run down 1.** To pursue and overtake, as a fugitive. **2.** To strike down while moving. **3.** To speak of disparagingly; decry. —**to run in 1.** To insert; include. **2.** *Printing* To print without a paragraph or break. **3.** *Slang* To arrest and place in confinement. —**to run into 1.** To meet by chance. **2.** To collide with. —**to run off 1.** To produce on a typewriter, printing press, etc. **2.** To decide (a tied race, game, etc.) by the outcome of another, subsequent race, game, etc. **3.** To flee or escape; elope. —**to run out** To come to an end; be exhausted, as supplies. —**to run out of** To exhaust one's supply of. —**to run over 1.** To ride or drive over; run down. **2.** To overflow. **3.** To go over or examine hastily or quickly; rehearse. —**to run through 1.** To spend wastefully; squander. **2.** To stab or pierce. **3.** To run over (def. 3). —**to run up** To produce; make hurriedly, as on a sewing machine. —*n.* **1.** An act or instance of running or going rapidly. **2.** The movement or gait of running: to break into a *run.* **3.** A distance covered by running. **4.** A distance traveled between two points, as by a train or vessel. **5.** A rapid, brief journey. **6.** A course or route followed, as in reaching a destination. **7.** The privilege of free use or access: to have the *run* of the place. **8.** A series, succession, or sequence, as of playing cards in consecutive order. **9.** A continuous spell of a specified condition: a *run* of luck. **10.** A continuous period of consecutive performances, as of a theatrical production. **11.** A trend or tendency: the *run* of the market. **12.** A broadly inclusive category, type, or class: the general *run* of readers. **13.** A period of continuous operation, as of a machine or factory. **14.** The output during such a period. **15.** A continuous length or extent of something: a *run* of pipe. **16.** A lengthwise rip in knitted fabric. **17.** Characteristic direction, tendency, or linear form: the *run* of the grain in wood. **18.** Flowing movement, as of a stream. **19.** The period of such flow. **20.** A swift stream or current. **21.** Mass migration or movement of animals, esp. of fish to spawn. **22.** A trail, burrow, or terrain frequented by a specific kind of animal. **23.** An enclosure for animals or poultry. **24.** A steep course or runway, as for skiing or sledding. **25.** An unusually large number of demands for payment, as on a bank. **26.** Any great sustained demand, as for a commodity. **27.** *Music* A rapid succession of tones. **28.** In baseball, the scoring of a point by a player's making a complete circuit of the bases; also, a point so scored. **29.** In football, the ball carrier's attempt to run through or around the line of the opposing team. **30.** In cricket, the scoring of a point by both batsmen successfully reaching opposite popping creases after a hit. **31.** *Naut.* The after part of a ship's bottom. **32.** *Mining* A vein of ore or rock. **33.** An approach to a target made by a bombing plane: also *bomb run.* —**a run for one's money** A successful or satisfactory instance of activity, esp. in competition. —**in the long run** As the ultimate outcome of any train of circumstances. —*adj.* **1.** Made liquid; melted. **2.** Made by a process of melting and casting or molding: *run* metal; *run* butter. [OE *rinnan*]

run·a·bout (run′ə·bout′) *n.* **1.** A small, open automobile. **2.** A light, open wagon. **3.** A small motorboat.

run·a·round (run′ə·round′) *n.* **1.** *Slang* Artful deception; evasion. **2.** *Printing* Type set narrower than the body of the text, as around illustrations.

run·a·way (run′ə·wā′) *adj.* **1.** Escaping or escaped from restraint or control; fugitive. **2.** Brought about by running away: a *runaway* marriage. **3.** Easily won as a horse race. **4.** Of, pertaining to, or characterized by a rapid price rise. —*n.* **1.** One who or that which runs away; also, a horse whose driver has lost control. **2.** An act of running away. **3.** *Informal* An easily won victory, as in a race.

run·down (run′doun′)   n. A summary; resumé.

run·down (run′doun′)   adj. 1. Debilitated; physically weak; tired out. 2. Dilapidated; shabby. 3. Stopped because not wound: said of a timepiece.

rune (rōōn)   n. 1. Any of the characters in the runic alphabet. 2. A Finnish poem or one of its cantos. 3. pl. Old Norse lore expressed in or as in runes. 4. Any obscure or mystic song, poem, verse, or saying. [< OE and ON *rūn* mystery, secret conversation] — ru′nic adj.

RUNES
(Tomb inscription, Sweden, 11th century)

rung[1] (rung)   n. 1. A round crosspiece forming one of the steps of a ladder. 2. A crosspiece used in chairs to strengthen or support the legs or back. 3. The spoke of a wheel. [OE *hrung* staff, pole]

rung[2] (rung)   Past participle of RING[2].

runic alphabet   An old Germanic alphabet, probably originating in both the Latin and Greek, consisting originally of 24 characters, or runes.

run-in (n. run′in′; adj. run′in′)   n. 1. A quarrel; bicker. 2. *Printing* Inserted or added matter. — adj. *Printing* Inserted or added.

run·nel (run′əl)   n. A rivulet. [OE *rynel* < *rinnan* to run]

run·ner (run′ər)   n. 1. One who or that which runs, as one who runs a race. 2. One who operates or manages anything. 3. One who runs errands or goes about on any kind of business. 4. That part on which an object runs or slides: the *runner* of a skate. 5. *Mech.* A device to assist sliding motion. 6. Any of various fishes of warm and temperate seas. 7. *Bot.* **a** A slender, procumbent stem rooting at the end and nodes, as in the strawberry. **b** Any of various twining plants. 8. A smuggler. 9. A long, narrow rug or carpeting, used in hallways, etc. 10. A narrow strip of cloth, used on tables, dressers, etc.

run·ner-up (run′ər-up′)   n. A contestant or team finishing in second place.

run·ning (run′ing)   adj. 1. Moving or going rapidly. 2. Inclined or trained to run rather than to pace or trot: said of horses. 3. Creeping or clinging, as a plant. 4. Flowing: *running* water. 5. Slipping or untying easily: a *running* knot. 6. Moving or pulling easily and freely: a *running* rope. 7. Being or able to be in operation: a *running* engine. 8. Cursive: a *running* handwriting. 9. Liquid or fluid. 10. Discharging, as pus from a sore. 11. In a straight line: three feet *running*. 12. Current, as an account. 13. Continuous; repeated: a *running* design. 14. Kept up continuously. 15. Passing; cursory: a *running* glance. 16. Following one another without intermission; successive: He talked three hours *running*. 17. Accomplished or performed with a run. 18. Of or pertaining to a trip or run: the train's *running* time. — n. 1. The act of one who or that which runs. 2. That which runs or flows. 3. The amount or quantity that runs. 4. Ability or power to run. 5. Competition or race: He is out of the *running*.

running board   A footboard on the side of a locomotive, street car, automobile, etc.

running gear   *Mech.* The wheels and axles of any vehicle and their immediate attachments, as distinguished from the body that they support.

running knot   A knot made so as to slip along a noose and tighten when pulled upon: also called *slipknot*.

running light   *Aeron.* A navigation light.

running mate   The candidate for the lesser of two offices closely linked by constitutional provisions, as the vice-presidency with the presidency.

running title   *Printing* A title or headline repeated at the head of every page or every other page throughout a book or chapter. Also **running head**.

Run·ny·mede (run′i·mēd)   A meadow in Surrey, England, where King John is said to have signed the Magna Carta.

run·off (run′ôf′, -of′)   n. 1. The part of the rainfall that is not absorbed directly by the soil but is drained off in rills or streams. 2. A special contest held to break a tie.

run-of-the-mill (run′əv-thə-mil′)   adj. Not special in any way; average. Also **run-of-the-mine**.

run-on (run′on′, -ôn′)   n. *Printing* Appended matter.

runt (runt)   n. 1. An unusually small, weak, or stunted animal or plant. 2. A small person: often a contemptuous term. [< Scot. *runt* old cow]

runt·y (runt′ē)   adj. runt·i·er, runt·i·est Dwarfish; stunted. — runt′i·ness n.

run·way (run′wā′)   n. 1. A way or path over or through which something runs. 2. A pathway extending from a stage into the audience, used for certain types of theatrical entertainment. 3. The channel or bed of a stream. 4. In lumbering, a chute. 5. Any track specially laid for wheeled vehicles. 6. *Aeron.* An improved or unimproved roadlike surface, used for the takeoff and landing of aircraft.

ru·pee (rōō·pē′)   n. 1. The standard monetary unit of various countries; esp., the rupee of India and Pakistan, in 1960 worth about 21 U.S. cents. 2. A coin of this denomination. [< Hind. < Skt. *rūpya* coined silver]

rup·ture (rup′chər)   n. 1. The act of breaking apart, or the state of being broken apart. 2. *Pathol.* Hernia. 3. Breach of friendship or concord between individuals or nations. — v.t. & v.i. ·tured, ·tur·ing 1. To break apart; separate into parts. 2. To affect with or suffer a rupture. [< Med.L *ruptura* < *rumpere* to break] — rup′tur·a·ble adj.

ru·ral (rōōr′əl)   adj. 1. Of or pertaining to the country as distinguished from the city or the town; rustic. 2. Of or pertaining to farming or agriculture. [< MF < L < *rus, ruris* country] — ru′ral·ism n. — ru′ral·ist n. — ru′ral·ly adv.

— **Syn.** 1. Rustic, pastoral, bucolic. — **Ant.** urban.

rural free delivery   A government service of house-to-house free mail delivery in rural districts.

ru·ral·i·ty (rōō·ral′ə·tē)   n. pl. ·ties 1. The condition or quality of being rural. 2. A rural characteristic.

ru·ral·ize (rōōr′əl·īz)   v. ·ized, ·iz·ing v.t. 1. To make rural. — v.i. 2. To go into or live in the country; rusticate. — ru′ral·i·za′tion n.

ruse (rōōz)   n. An action intended to mislead or deceive; a stratagem; trick. [< MF *ruser* to turn aside.]

rush[1] (rush)   v.i. 1. To move or go swiftly or with violence. 2. To make an attack; charge: with *on* or *upon*. 3. To proceed recklessly or rashly; plunge: with *in* or *into*. 4. To come, surge, flow, etc., suddenly. — v.t. 5. To drive or push with haste or violence: hurry. 6. To do or perform hastily or hurriedly. 7. To make a sudden assault upon; also, to capture by such an assault. 8. *Slang* To seek the favor of with assiduous attentions. 9. In football, to move (the ball) toward the goal of the other team by a rush or rushes. 10. *U.S.* To consider for membership in a fraternity or sorority. — n. 1. The act of rushing; a sudden turbulent movement, drive, or onset. 2. A state of pressed or impatient activity; hurry. 3. A sudden surge, flow, or outpouring. 4. A sudden pressing demand. 5. A sudden or urgent press of traffic, business, etc. 6. A sudden flocking of people to a new region, esp. to an area rumored to be rich in a precious mineral: a gold *rush*. 7. *U.S.* A general contest or scrimmage between students, as between sophomores and freshmen. 8. In football, an attempt to take the ball through the opposing linemen and toward the goal. 9. pl. In motion pictures, the first film prints of a scene or series of scenes, before editing or selection. — adj. 1. Requiring urgency or haste: a *rush* order. 2. Characterized by much traffic, business, etc. 3. *U.S.* Denoting a time or function set aside for fraternity or sorority members to meet new students to consider them for membership: *rush* week. [< AF < OF *ruser, reuser* to push back < L *recusare* to refuse] — rush′er n.

rush[2] (rush)   n. 1. Any one of various grasslike, usu. aquatic herbs, growing in marshy ground and having pliant, cylindrical, leafless stems, often used for making mats, etc. 2. A thing of little or no value. 3. A rushlight. [OE *risc*]

rush hour   A time when traffic or business is at its height. — **rush-hour** (rush′our′) adj.

rush·light (rush′līt′)   n. A candle made by dipping a rush in tallow. Also **rush candle**.

rush·y (rush′ē)   adj. rush·i·er, rush·i·est 1. Abounding in, covered with, or made of rushes. 2. Like a rush.

rusk (rusk)   n. 1. A light, sweetened bread or biscuit. 2. Bread or cake that has been crisped and browned in an oven. [< Sp. *rosca*, twisted loaf of bread]

rus·set (rus′it)   n. 1. A reddish or yellowish brown. 2. Coarse homespun cloth or clothing of this color. 3. Russet leather. 4. A winter apple of greenish color, mottled with brown. — adj. 1. Of a reddish or yellowish brown color. 2. Made of russet cloth; also, coarse; homespun. 3. Finished, but not blacked: said of leather. [< OF < L *russus* red]

Rus·sian (rush′ən)   adj. Of or pertaining to Russia, its people, or their language. — n. 1. A native or citizen of the Soviet Union or the former Russian Empire; esp., a Great Russian, Ukrainian, or Byelorussian. 2. The East Slavic language of Russia, including Great Russian, Ukrainian, and Byelorussian.

Russian dressing   Mayonnaise dressing to which chili sauce, pimientos, chopped pickles, etc., have been added.

Rus·sian·ize (rush′ən·īz)   v.t. ·ized, ·iz·ing To make Russian in manner, character, etc.

Russian leather   A smooth, well-tanned, high-grade leather of calfskin or light cattle hide, dressed with birch oil.

Russian Orthodox Church An autonomous branch of the Eastern Orthodox Church in the Soviet Union, under the patriarch of Moscow.

Russian Revolution See under REVOLUTION.

Russian roulette A suicidal stunt in which one aims a revolver containing one cartridge at one's head and pulls the trigger, with one chance in six of being shot.

Russian wolfhound The borzoi.

Russo- *combining form* Russia; pertaining to the Russians.

Russo-Japanese War (rus/ō·jap/ə·nēz/, -nēs/) See table for WAR.

Rus·so·pho·bi·a (rus/ə·fō/bē·ə) *n.* Fear of the policy or influence of Russia. — **Rus/so·phobe** *n.*

rust (rust) *n.* **1.** The reddish or yellow coating formed on iron and steel by exposure to air and moisture, consisting of ferric hydroxide, $Fe(OH)_3$, and ferric oxide, Fe_2O_3. **2.** Any film formed on the surface of a metal by oxidation. **3.** A disease caused by a parasitic fungi living on the tissues of higher plants and characterized by the appearance of orange or reddish brown spots on the host plant. **4.** Any coating or accretion formed by a corrosive or degenerative process. **5.** A condition or tendency that destroys or weakens energy or active qualities: the *rust* of idleness. **6.** Any of several shades of reddish brown, somewhat like the color of rust, but containing more orange. — *v.t. & v.i.* **1.** To become or cause to become rusty. **2.** To contract or cause to contract rust. **3.** To become or cause to become weakened or impaired because of inactivity or disuse. **4.** To make or become rust-colored. [OE *rūst*]

rus·tic (rus/tik) *adj.* **1.** Typical of or appropriate to simple country life. **2.** Plain; simple; homely: *rustic* garments. **3.** Uncultured; rude; awkward. **4.** Unaffected; artless: *rustic* simplicity. **5.** Of or pertaining to any irregular style of work or decoration appropriate to the country; also, of or pertaining to work in natural, unpolished wood. — **Syn.** See RURAL. — *n.* **1.** One who lives in the country. A country person of simple manners or character; also, a coarse or clownish person. **3.** Rusticwork. **4.** Country dialect. [< L < *rus* country] — **rus/ti·cal·ly** *adv.*

rus·ti·cate (rus/tə·kāt) *v.* **·cat·ed, ·cat·ing** *v.i.* **1.** To go to the country. **2.** To stay or live in the country. — *v.t.* **3.** To send or banish to the country. **4.** To make rustic. **5.** To construct (masonry) with rusticwork. — **rus/ti·ca/tion** *n.* — **rus/ti·ca/tor** *n.*

rus·tic·i·ty (rus·tis/ə·tē) *n. pl.* **·ties** **1.** Rustic condition, character, or manners; simplicity; homeliness; awkwardness. **2.** A rustic trait or peculiarity.

rus·tic·work (rus/tik·wûrk/) *n.* **1.** Ashlar masonry having rough surfaces, and often deeply sunk grooves at the joints. **2.** Furniture, etc., made of the natural limbs and roots of trees. Also **rustic work.**

rus·tle¹ (rus/əl) *v.t. & v.i.* **·tled, ·tling** To fall, move, or cause to move with a quick succession of small, light, rubbing sounds, as dry leaves or sheets of paper. — *n.* A rustling sound. [ME *rustel*, alter. of OE *hrūxlian* to make a noise] — **rus/tler** *n.* — **rus/tling·ly** *adv.*

rus·tle² (rus/əl) *v.t. & v.i.* **·tled, ·tling** **1.** *Informal* To act with or obtain by energetic or vigorous action. **2.** *U.S. Informal* To steal (cattle, etc.). [Blend of RUSH and HUSTLE]

rus·tler (rus/lər) *n. U.S. Informal* **1.** A cattle or horse thief. **2.** A pushing, energetic person.

rust·y (rus/tē) *adj.* **rust·i·er, rust·i·est** **1.** Covered or affected with rust. **2.** Consisting of or produced by rust. **3.** Having the reddish or yellowish appearance of rust: said often of salted fish or meat that has become rancid. **4.** Impaired by inaction or want of exercise; also, stiff. **5.** Ineffective or weakened through neglect; also, having lost skill for want of practice. **6.** *Biol.* Appearing as if covered with rust; brownish red. — **rust/i·ly** *adv.* — **rust/i·ness** *n.*

rut¹ (rut) *n.* **1.** A sunken track worn by a wheel, as in a road; also, a groove forming a path for anything. **2.** A settled habit or course of procedure; routine. — *v.t.* **rut·ted, rut·ting** To wear or make a rut or ruts in. [Var. of ROUTE]

rut² (rut) *n.* **1.** The sexual excitement of various animals, esp. of deer and other ruminants; estrus. **2.** The period during which this excitement lasts. — *v.* **rut·ted, rut·ting** *v.i.* To be in rut. [< MF < L < *rugire* to roar]

ru·ta·ba·ga (rōō/tə·bā/gə) *n.* **1.** A cultivated plant allied to the turnip. **2.** Its edible root. [< dial. Sw. *rotabagge*]

ruth (rōōth) *n. Archaic* **1.** Compassion; pity. **2.** Grief; repentance; regret. [ME < OE *hrēow* sad]

Ruth (rōōth) A widow of Moab who left her own people and went with her mother-in-law Naomi to Bethlehem. — *n.* The book of the Old Testament in which this story is told.

Ru·the·ni·an (rōō·thē/nē·ən) *n.* **1.** One of a group of Ukrainians living in eastern Czechoslovakia and the Transcarpathian Oblast, formerly Ruthenia. **2.** The Ukrainian language. — *adj.* Of or pertaining to the Ruthenians or their language.

ru·the·ni·um (rōō·thē/nē·əm) *n.* A gray, brittle, rare metallic element (symbol Ru) of the platinum group. See ELEMENT. [< NL, after *Ruthenia*]

ruth·less (rōōth/lis) *adj.* Having no compassion; merciless. [< RUTH] — **ruth/less·ly** *adv.* — **ruth/less·ness** *n.*

rut·tish (rut/ish) *adj.* Disposed to rut; lustful; libidinous.

rut·ty (rut/ē) *adj.* **·ti·er, ·ti·est** Full of ruts. — **rut/ti·ness** *n.*

-ry Var. of -ERY.

rye (rī) *n.* **1.** The grain or seeds of a hardy cereal grass closely allied to wheat, used in the making of flour and whisky, and as a feed for livestock. **2.** The plant. **3.** Whisky distilled from rye or partly from rye. [OE *ryge*]

rye grass Darnel.

S

s, S (es) *n. pl.* **s's** or **ss, S's** or **Ss, ess·es** (es/iz) **1.** The 19th letter of the English alphabet. **2.** The sound represented by the letter *s*, usu. a voiceless sibilant, but often voiced between vowels, as in *easy*. — *symbol* **1.** Anything shaped like an S. **2.** *Chem.* Sulfur (symbol S).

s- *Chem.* Symmetrical.

-s¹ A variant of *-es¹*, inflectional ending of the plurals of nouns, attached to nouns not ending in a sibilant or an affricate: *books, words, cars.* It represents (s) after a voiceless consonant, and (z) after a voiced consonant or a vowel. Compare -ES¹.

-s² An inflectional ending used to form the third person singular present indicative of verbs not ending in a sibilant, affricate, or vowel: *reads, walks, sings.* Compare -ES².

-s *suffix* On; of a; at: often used in adverbs without appreciable force: *nights, Mondays, always, towards.* [OE *-es*, forming adverbial genitives]

-'s¹ An inflectional ending used to form the possessive of singular nouns and of plural nouns not ending in *-s*: a *man's* world, *women's* fashions. In plurals ending in *-s* (or *-es*) a simple apostrophe is used as a sign of the possessive: a *girls'* school, the *churches'* steeples.

-'s² Contraction of: **a** Is: *He's* here. **b** Has: *She's* left. **c** Us: *Let's* go.

Sa *Chem.* Samarium.

Sab·ba·tar·i·an (sab/ə·târ/ē·ən) *adj.* Pertaining to the Sabbath or its strict observance. — *n.* **1.** A Christian who observes Sunday strictly. **2.** A Christian who observes the seventh day as the Sabbath. — **Sab/ba·tar/i·an·ism** *n.*

Sab·bath (sab/əth) *n.* **1.** The seventh day of the week, appointed in the Decalogue as a day of rest to be observed by the Jews; now, Saturday. **2.** The first day of the week as observed by Christians; Sunday. **3.** The institution or observance of a day of rest; a time of rest, peace, or quiet. **4.** The sabbatical year of the Jews. *Lev.* xxv 4. [Fusion of OE *sabat* and OF *sabbat, sabat,* both < L *sabbatum* < Gk. < Hebrew *shābath* to rest] — **Sab·bat/ic** or **·i·cal** *adj.* — **Sab·bat/i·cal·ly** *adv.*

sab·bat·i·cal (sə·bat/i·kəl) *adj.* Of the nature of the Sabbath as a day of rest; offering rest at regular intervals. Also **sab·bat/ic.** — *n.* A sabbatical year. [See SABBATH]

sabbatical year **1.** In the ancient Jewish economy, every seventh year, in which the people were required to refrain from tillage. **2.** A year's vacation awarded to teachers in some American educational institutions every seven years.

sa·ber (sā/bər) *n.* **1.** A heavy one-edged cavalry sword, with a thick-backed blade, often curved. **2.** In fencing, a light swordlike instrument, used for both thrusting and slashing, hits being scored with the point or either edge. — *v.t.* To strike, wound, or kill with a saber. Also, *Brit., sabre.* [< F < G, prob. < Hung. *szabni* to cut]

Sa·bine (sā/bīn) *n.* One of an ancient central Italian people, conquered and absorbed by Rome in 290 B.C. — *adj.* Of or pertaining to the Sabines.

sa·ble (sā′bəl) *n.* **1.** A carnivore of northern Asia and Europe, related to the marten and prized for its valuable fur. **2.** The dressed fur of a sable, esp. of the Asian sable. **3.** *pl.* Garments made wholly or partly of this fur. **4.** The color black; also, mourning or a mourning garment. — *adj.* **1.** Black, esp. as the color of mourning. **2.** Made of or having the color of sable fur; dark brown. [< OF < Med.L *sabelum*]

sa·bot (sab′ō, *Fr.* sà·bō′) *n.* **1.** A wooden shoe. **2.** A shoe having a wooden sole but flexible shank. [< F < OF *savate*, ult. < Arabic *sabbat* sandal]

sab·o·tage (sab′ə·täzh, *Fr.* sà·bô·tàzh′) *n.* An act of malicious damage or destruction, as one intended to obstruct the production of war materiel by the enemy. — *v.* **·taged**, **·tag·ing** *v.i.* **1.** To engage in sabotage. — *v.t.* **2.** To damage or destroy by sabotage. [< F < *sabot* sabot; with ref. to damage done to machinery with sabots]

sab·o·teur (sab′ə·tûr′, *Fr.* sà·bô·tœr′) *n.* One who engages in sabotage. [< F]

sa·bra (sä′brə) *n.* A native Israeli. [< Hebrew, cactus]

sa·bre (sā′bər)   See SABER.

sac (sak) *n. Biol.* A membranous pouch or receptacle in an animal or plant, as for containing a liquid: the ink *sac* of a squid. [< F < L *saccus* sack[1]]

Sac (sak, sôk)   See SAUK.

sac·cha·ride (sak′ə·rīd, -rid) *n. Chem.* Any of a large group of carbohydrates containing sugar, usu. classified as *monosaccharide*, *disaccharide*, etc.

sac·cha·rin (sak′ər·in) *n. Chem.* A white crystalline coaltar compound, $C_7H_5O_3NS$, from 300 to 500 times sweeter than cane sugar, used as a noncaloric sweetening agent. [< L < Gk. ult. < Skt. *sharkarā* grit, sugar]

sac·cha·rine (sak′ər·in, -ə·rīn) *adj.* **1.** Of, pertaining to, or of the nature of sugar. **2.** Cloyingly sweet: a *saccharine* manner. — *n.* Saccharin. — **sac′cha·rine·ly** *adv.* — **sac′cha·rin·i·ty** *n.*

saccharo- *combining form* Sugar; of or pertaining to sugar. Also, before vowels, **sacchar-**. [See SACCHARIN]

sac·cha·rose (sak′ə·rōs) *n.* Sucrose.

sac·er·do·tal (sas′ər·dōt′l) *adj.* **1.** Pertaining to a priest or priesthood; priestly. **2.** Believing in the divine authority of the priesthood. [< MF < L *sacerdos*, *-dotis* priest] — **sac′er·do′tal·ly** *adv.*

sac·er·do·tal·ism (sas′ər·dōt′l·iz′əm) *n.* **1.** The character and methods of the priesthood; priestcraft. **2.** Zeal for priestly things.

sa·chem (sā′chəm) *n.* A North American Indian hereditary chief. [< Algonquian (Narraganset)]

sa·chet (sa·shā′, *esp. Brit.* sash′ā) *n.* A small ornamental bag for perfumed powder. [< MF, dim. of *sac* sack]

sack[1] (sak) *n.* **1.** A bag for holding bulky articles. **2.** A measure or weight of varying amount. **3.** A loose jacketlike garment, worn by women and babies: also **sacque**. **4.** *Slang* Dismissal: esp. in the phrases **to get the sack**, **to give (someone) the sack**. **5.** In baseball slang, a base. **6.** *U.S. Slang* A bed; mattress. — **to hit the sack** *U.S. Slang* To go to bed. — **to sack out** *U.S. Slang* To go to bed. — *v.t.* **1.** To put into a sack or sacks. **2.** To dismiss, as a servant. [OE < L < Gk. < Hebrew *saq* sack, sackcloth]

sack[2] (sak) *v.t.* To plunder or pillage (a town or city) after capturing. — *n.* **1.** The pillaging of a captured town or city. **2.** Loot or booty obtained by pillage. [< MF *sac* < Ital. *sacco*, orig., plunder < Med.L < L *saccus* sack[1]] — **sack′er** *n.*

sack[3] (sak) *n.* Light-colored Spanish dry wine; also, any strong white wine from southern Europe. [Earlier (*wyne*) *seck* < F (*vin*) *sec* dry (wine) < L *siccus* dry] •

sack·but (sak′but) *n.* **1.** An early instrument resembling the trombone. **2.** In the Bible, a stringed instrument. [< MF < OF *saquer* to draw + *bouter* to push]

sack·cloth (sak′klôth′, -kloth′) *n.* **1.** A coarse cloth used for making sacks. **2.** Coarse cloth or haircloth worn in penance. — **in sackcloth and ashes** **1.** In the Bible, wearing garments of sackcloth and sprinkling ashes on one's head as marks of penance or sorrow. **2.** In any state of sorrow, penance, or self-abasement.

sack coat A short, loose-fitting coat with no waist seam.

sack·ful (sak′fool′) *n. pl.* **·fuls** Enough to fill a sack.

sack·ing (sak′ing) *n.* A coarse cloth made of hemp or flax and used for sacks.

sack race A race run with the feet in a sack.

sa·cral[1] (sā′krəl) *adj.* Of, pertaining to, or situated near the sacrum. — *n.* A sacral vertebra or nerve.

sa·cral[2] (sā′krəl) *adj.* Pertaining to sacred rites. [< L *sacrum* rite < *sacer* sacred]

sac·ra·ment (sak′rə·mənt) *n.* **1.** *Eccl.* Any of certain rites ordained by Christ or by the church, as baptism, the Eu-

charist, confirmation, etc. **2.** *Often cap. Eccl.* **a** The Eucharist; the Lord's Supper. **b** The consecrated bread and wine of the Eucharist: often with *the*. **3.** Any sign or token of a solemn covenant or pledge. **4.** Anything considered to have a secret or mysterious meaning. [< OF < L *sacrare* to consecrate]

sac·ra·men·tal (sak′rə·men′təl) *n.* **1.** One of certain rites, such as the use of holy water, oil, or salt, employed as adjuncts to sacraments, or regarded as analogous to a sacrament. **2.** *pl.* The objects, words, or ceremonies used in administering a sacrament. — *adj.* **1.** Of or pertaining to a sacrament. **2.** Constituting or composing a sacrament. **3.** Having the influence or efficacy of a sacrament. **4.** Consecrated, as by sacred vows. — **sac′ra·men′tal·ism** *n.* — **sac′ra·men′tal·ist** *n.* — **sac′ra·men′tal·ly** *adv.*

sa·cred (sā′krid) *adj.* **1.** Set apart or dedicated to religious use; hallowed. **2.** Pertaining or related to deity, religion, or hallowed places or things. **3.** Consecrated or dedicated to a person or purpose. **4.** Entitled to reverence or respect; not to be profaned; inviolable. [< OF < L *sacrare* to treat as sacred] — **sa′cred·ly** *adv.* — **sa′cred·ness** *n.*

Sacred College The College of Cardinals.

sacred cow **1.** *U.S. Informal* Something or someone regarded as above criticism or reproach. **2.** A cow when considered sacred, as by the Hindus.

sac·ri·fice (sak′rə·fīs) *n.* **1.** The act of making an offering to a deity, in worship or atonement; also, that which is so offered. **2.** A giving up of some cherished or desired object, person, idea, etc., usu. for the sake of something else; also, that which is so given up. **3.** Loss incurred or suffered without return. **4.** A reduction of price that leaves little or no profit or involves loss. **5.** In baseball, a sacrifice hit. — *v.* **·ficed**, **·fic·ing** *v.t.* **1.** To make an offering or sacrifice of, as to a god or deity. **2.** To give up, yield, permit injury to, or relinquish (something valued) for the sake of something else, as a person, thing, or idea. **3.** To sell at a reduced price; part with at a loss. **4.** In baseball, to advance (one or more runners) by means of a sacrifice hit. — *v.i.* **5.** To make a sacrifice. **6.** To make a sacrifice hit. [< OF < L < *sacer* sacred + *facere* to perform, do] — **sac′ri·fic′er** *n.* — **sac′ri·fic′ing·ly** *adv.*

sacrifice fly In baseball, a fly ball hit with less than two out that enables a runner on third base to score after the catch.

sacrifice hit In baseball, a bunt made with less than two out that enables a runner or runners to advance a base while the batter is being retired. Also **sacrifice bunt**.

sac·ri·fi·cial (sak′rə·fish′əl) *adj.* Of, pertaining to, performing, or like a sacrifice. — **sac′ri·fi′cial·ly** *adv.*

sac·ri·lege (sak′rə·lij) *n.* The act of violating or profaning anything sacred, including sacramental vows. [< OF < L *sacer*, *sacris* sacred + *legere* to gather, steal] — **sac′ri·le′gist** (-lē′jist) *n.*

sac·ri·le·gious (sak′rə·lij′əs, -lē′jəs) *adj.* **1.** Having committed sacrilege; impious. **2.** Of, pertaining to, or like sacrilege. — **sac′ri·le·gious·ly** *adv.* — **sac′ri·le·gious·ness** *n.*

sac·ris·tan (sak′ris·tən) *n.* An officer having charge of the sacristy of a church. [< Med.L < L *sacer*, *sacris* sacred]

sac·ris·ty (sak′ris·tē) *n. pl.* **·ties** A room in a religious house for the sacred vessels and vestments; vestry.

sacro- *combining form Med.* Near, or related to the sacrum. [< L (*os*) *sacrum* the sacral (bone)]

sac·ro·il·i·ac (sak′rō·il′ē·ak) *adj. Anat.* Pertaining to the sacrum and the ilium and to the joints or ligaments connecting them. [< SACRO- + ILIAC]

sac·ro·sanct (sak′rō·sangkt) *adj.* Peculiarly and exceedingly sacred; inviolable: sometimes used ironically. [< L < *sacro*, ablative of *sacrum* rite + *sanctus*, pp. of *sancire* to make holy, inviolable] — **sac′ro·sanc′ti·ty** *n.*

sa·crum (sā′krəm) *n. pl.* **·cra** (-krə) *Anat.* A composite bone formed by the union of the five vertebrae between the lumbar and caudal regions, constituting the dorsal part of the pelvis. For illus. see PELVIS. [< NL < L (*os*) *sacrum* sacred (bone); from its use in sacrifices]

sad (sad) *adj.* **sad·der**, **sad·dest** **1.** Sorrowful or depressed in spirits. **2.** Causing sorrow or pity; unfortunate. **3.** *Informal* Pitifully inadequate; bad; contemptible. **4.** Dark-hued; somber. [OE *sæd*, orig., sated] — **sad′ly** *adv.* — **sad′ness** *n.*

sad·den (sad′n) *v.t. & v.i.* To make or become sad.

sad·dle (sad′l) *n.* **1.** A seat or pad for a rider, as on the back of a horse or on a bicycle. **2.** A padded cushion for a horse's back, used as part of a harness or to support a pack, etc. **3.** A part of an animal that is similar to a saddle in shape, position, etc.; esp., the lower part of the back of a fowl. **4.** The two hindquarters of a carcass, as of mutton, veal, or venison; also, the undivided loins of such a carcass. **5.** Something resembling a saddle in form or position, as a bearing for a car axle. — **in the saddle** In control. — *v.* **·dled**, **·dling** *v.t.*

1. To put a saddle on. 2. To load, as with a burden. 3. To place as a burden or responsibility: with *upon.* — *v.i.* 4. To get into a saddle. [OE *sadol*]

sad·dle-backed (sad/l·bakt) *adj.* 1. Concave, as a saddle, in the back or upper part. 2. Having a saddlelike mark, as some birds.

sad·dle-bag (sad/l·bag) *n.* One of a pair of pouches connected by a strap or band and slung over an animal's back or attached to a saddle.

sad·dle-cloth (sad/l·klôth', -kloth') *n.* A cloth placed under and attached to a saddle.

saddle horse A horse used with or trained for the saddle.

sad·dler (sad/lər) *n.* 1. A maker of saddles, harness, etc. 2. A saddle horse.

saddle roof A ridge roof having two gables.

sad·dler·y (sad/lər·ē) *n. pl.* **·dler·ies** 1. Saddles, harnesses, etc., collectively. 2. A shop where such articles are sold. 3. The craft or business of a saddler.

saddle shoe A white sport shoe having a dark band of leather across the instep.

saddle soap A softening and preserving soap for leather, containing pure white soap, as Castile, and neat's-foot oil.

Sad·du·cee (saj/ŏŏ·sē, sad/yŏŏ·sē) *n.* A member of an ancient Jewish sect that adhered to the written Mosaic law but repudiated oral tradition, rejecting the resurrection of the body, etc. Compare PHARISEE. [Appar. ult. after *Zadok,* a high priest (*Ezek.* xl 46)] — **Sad/du·ce'an, Sad/du·cae'an** *adj.* — **Sad/du·cee'ism** *n.*

sad·i·ron (sad/ī'ərn) *n.* An iron for pressing clothes.

sad·ism (sā/diz·əm, sad/iz·əm) *n.* 1. *Psychol.* A condition in which sexual gratification depends largely on the infliction of pain upon others. 2. A tendency to take delight in being cruel. Compare MASOCHISM. [after Comte Donatien de *Sade,* 1740–1814, who described such sexual aberrations in his writings] — **sa·dist** (sā/dist, sad/ist) *n. & adj.* — **sa·dis·tic** (sə·dis/tik, sā-) *adj.* — **sa·dis/ti·cal·ly** *adv.*

sad sack *U.S. Slang* A blundering, pitiable person.

sa·fa·ri (sə·fä/rē) *n. pl.* **·ris** An expedition or journey, often on foot, as for hunting. [< Swahili < Arabic *safara* to travel.]

safe (sāf) *adj.* **saf·er, saf·est** 1. Free or freed from danger or evil. 2. Having escaped injury or damage; unharmed. 3. Not involving risk or loss. 4. Conferring safety. 5. Prudent or trustworthy. 6. Not likely to cause or do harm or injury. 7. In baseball, having reached base without being retired. — *n.* 1. A strong metal receptacle for protecting valuables. 2. Any place of safe storage. [< OF < L *salvus* whole, healthy] — **safe/ly** *adv.* — **safe/ness** *n.*

safe·break·er (sāf/brā'kər) *n.* A safecracker.

safe-con·duct (sāf/kon'dukt) *n.* 1. An official document assuring protection on a journey or voyage, as in time of war; a passport. 2. The act of conducting in safety.

safe·crack·er (sāf/krak'ər) *n.* One who breaks into safes to rob them. — **safe/crack'ing** *n.*

safe-de·pos·it box (sāf/di·poz'it) A box or other fireproof receptacle for valuables, generally in a bank.

safe·guard (sāf/gärd') *n.* One who or that which guards or protects against accident or injury. — *v.t.* To defend; protect; guard.

safe·keep·ing (sāf/kē'ping) *n.* The act or state of keeping or being kept in safety; protection.

safe·ty (sāf/tē) *n. pl.* **·ties** 1. Freedom from danger or injury. 2. A device or catch designed as a safeguard, as in a firearm. 3. In football, the act or play of touching the ball to the ground behind the player's own goal line when the impetus that sent the ball over the goal line was given to it by one of his own side. Also **safe/ty-touch'down'** (-tuch'doun'). [< OF < Med.L < L *salvus* sound]

safety belt 1. A strap or strip of strong belting encircling the user and fastened to a fixed object, worn by linemen, window cleaners, etc., as a safeguard against falling. 2. A strap fixed to the seat of an aircraft or vehicle, by which the occupant is secured against sudden shocks or turning movements: also called *seat belt.*

safety glass Two sheets of glass having a film of transparent, adhesive plastic tightly pressed between them: also called *shatterproof glass.*

safety lamp A miner's lamp having the flame surrounded by fine wire gauze that prevents the ignition of explosive gases: also called *davy.*

safety match A match that will ignite only when struck upon a chemically prepared surface.

safety pin A pin whose point springs into place within a protecting sheath.

safety razor A razor provided with a guard or guards for the blade to prevent accidental gashing of the skin.

safety valve 1. *Mech.* A valve in a steam boiler, etc., for automatically relieving excessive pressure. 2. Any outlet for pent-up energy or emotion.

saf·fron (saf/rən) *n.* 1. An autumn-flowering species of crocus. 2. The dried orange-colored stigmas of this plant,

used for coloring confectionery, etc., and as a flavoring in cookery. 3. A deep yellow-orange: also **saffron yellow.** — *adj.* Yellow-orange. [< OF < Med.L < Arabic *za'farān*]

sag (sag) *v.* **sagged, sag·ging** *v.i.* 1. To bend or sink downward from weight or pressure, esp. in the middle. 2. To hang unevenly. 3. To lose firmness or determination; weaken, as from exhaustion, age, etc. 4. To decline, as in price or value. — *v.t.* 5. To cause to sag. — *n.* 1. A sagging. 2. A sagging or sunken place or part. [ME *saggen*]

sa·ga (sä/gə) *n.* 1. A medieval Scandinavian prose narrative dealing with legendary or historical exploits, usu. of a single hero or family. 2. A long story, sometimes poetic, often chronicling the history of a family. [< ON]

sa·ga·cious (sə·gā/shəs) *adj.* 1. Characterized by discernment, shrewdness, and wisdom. 2. Ready and apt to apprehend. [< L *sagax*] — **sa·ga/cious·ly** *adv.* — **sa·ga/cious·ness** *n.*

sa·gac·i·ty (sə·gas/ə·tē) *n.* The quality of being sagacious; discernment and judgment; shrewdness.

sag·a·more (sag/ə·môr, -mōr) *n.* A chief among the Algonquian Indians of North America, usu. inferior to sachem. [< Algonquian (Penobscot) *sagamo* he prevails]

sage[1] (sāj) *n.* A venerable man of recognized wisdom, experience, prudence, and foresight. — *adj.* **sag·er, sag·est** 1. Characterized by or proceeding from calm, far-seeing wisdom and prudence. 2. Profound; learned. — **Syn.** See WISE[1]. [< OF, ult. < LL *sapius* prudent, wise] — **sage/ly** *adv.* — **sage/ness** *n.*

sage[2] (sāj) *n.* 1. A plant of the mint family, having gray-green leaves used for flavoring meats. 2. The leaves of this plant. 3. The sagebrush. [< F < L *salvus* safe]

sage·brush (sāj/brush') *n.* An aromatic, bitter, typically perennial herb or small shrub, widely distributed on the alkali plains of the western U.S.

Sagebrush State Nickname of Nevada.

sage hen A large grouse of the western U.S.

sag·it·tal (saj/ə·təl) *adj.* 1. Of, pertaining to, or resembling an arrow or arrowhead. 2. *Anat.* Of or pertaining to the longitudinal plane dividing an animal into right and left halves. [< L *sagitta* arrow] — **sag/it·tal·ly** *adv.*

Sag·it·ta·ri·us (saj/ə·târ/ē·əs) *n.* A constellation, the Archer; also, the ninth sign of the zodiac. See ZODIAC. [< L *sagitta* arrow]

sag·it·tate (saj/ə·tāt) *adj. Bot.* Shaped like an arrowhead, as certain leaves. [< L *sagitta* arrow]

sa·go (sā/gō) *n. pl.* **·gos** 1. Any of several varieties of East Indian palm. 2. The pith of this palm, used as a thickening agent in puddings, etc. [< Malay *sāgū*]

sa·gua·ro (sə·gwä/rō, -wä/-) *n. pl.* **·ros** A large desert cactus with an erect, columnar trunk, strong spines, and flowering tops. Also **sa·hua/ro** (-wä/-). [< Sp. < Piman]

Sa·hib (sä/ib) *n.* Master; sir: used in India and Pakistan for people of rank and, esp. formerly, for Europeans. Also **Sa/heb.** [< Urdu < Arabic *sāhib* lord, companion]

said (sed) Past tense and past participle of SAY. — *adj. Law* Previously mentioned; aforesaid.

sail (sāl) *n. pl.* **sails;** *for def. 3, often* **sail** 1. *Naut.* A piece of canvas, or other strong material, attached to a vessel so that it may be spread to the wind and aid in the vessel's propulsion. 2. Sails collectively. 3. A sailing vessel or craft. 4. A trip or passage in any watercraft. 5. Anything resembling a sail in form or use, as the broad part of the arm of a windmill. — **to make sail** 1. To unfurl a sail or sails. 2. To set out on a voyage. — **to set sail** To begin a voyage; get under way. — **under sail** Sailing; with sails spread. — *v.i.* 1. To move across the surface of water by the action of wind or mechanical power. 2. To travel over water in a ship or boat. 3. To begin a voyage. 4. To manage a sailing craft. 5. To glide or float in the air. 6. To move along in a stately or dignified manner. 7. *Informal* To pass rapidly. 8. *Informal* To proceed boldly into action: with *in.* — *v.t.* 9. To move or travel across the surface of (a body of water) in a ship or boat. 10. To navigate (a ship, etc.). — **to sail into** 1. To begin with energy. 2. To attack violently. [OE *segl*] — **sail/a·ble** *adj.*

sail·boat (sāl/bōt') *n. U.S.* A small boat propelled by a sail or sails.

sail·cloth (sāl/klôth', -kloth') *n.* A very strong, firmly woven cotton canvas suitable for sails.

sail·er (sā/lər) *n.* A vessel that sails; a ship having a specified sailing power: a fast *sailer.*

sail·fish (sāl/fish') *n. pl.* **·fish** or **·fish·es** A marine fish allied to the spearfish, having a large or conspicuous dorsal fin likened to a sail.

sail·or (sā/lər) *n.* 1. A seaman; mariner. 2. A sailor hat.

sailor hat A low-crowned, flat-topped straw hat with a brim, worn by both sexes: also called *sailor.*

saint (sānt) *n.* 1. A holy or godly person. 2. In certain churches, such a person who has died and been canonized. 3. Any one of the blessed in heaven. 4. A very patient, unselfish person. — *v.t.* To canonize; venerate as a saint. —

adj. Holy; canonized. [< OF < L *sancire* to make sacred] — **saint′hood, saint′ship** *n.*

Saint For entries not found under *Saint*, see under **St.**

Saint (sānt) *n.* A member of one of the religious bodies known as **Saints**: Latter-day *Saint.*

Saint Bernard A working dog of great size and strength, characterized by a massive head, and a thick, white, red, or brindled coat, used to rescue travelers by the hospice at Great St. Bernard Pass in the Swiss Alps.

saint·ed (sān′tid) *adj.* 1. Canonized. 2. Of holy character; saintly.

saint·ly (sānt′lē) *adj.* ·li·er, ·li·est Like, concerned with, or suitable for a saint. — **saint′li·ness** *n.*

SAINT BERNARD
(About 27 inches high at shoulder)

Saint Patrick's Day March 17, a day traditionally celebrated by the Irish in honor of their patron saint.

Saint Valentine's Day February 14, the anniversary of the beheading of St. Valentine by the Romans, and also a day when valentines are exchanged.

saith (seth) *Archaic* Present indicative third person singular of SAY.

sake¹ (sāk) *n.* 1. Purpose of obtaining or accomplishing: to speak slowly for the *sake* of clarity. 2. Interest; account; advantage: for your own *sake.* [OE *sacu* lawsuit]
— **Syn.** 2. Something done for the *sake* of a person, or on his *behalf*, is intended to promote his welfare. But *sake* suggests the benevolence of a parent or friend, while *behalf* suggests a somewhat less personal relationship, as that of an attorney or patron.

sa·ke² (sä′kē) *n.* A fermented liquor made in Japan from rice. Also **sa′ki.** [< Japanese]

sal (sal) *n.* Salt. [< L]

sa·laam (sə-läm′) *n.* An oriental salutation or obeisance made with a low bow, the palm of the right hand being held to the forehead; also, a respectful or ceremonious verbal greeting. — *v.t. & v.i.* To greet with or make a salaam. [< Arabic *salām* peace, a salutation]

sal·a·ble (sā′lə-bəl) *adj.* Such as can be sold; marketable: also spelled **saleable.** — **sal′a·bil′i·ty, sal′a·ble·ness** *n.*

sa·la·cious (sə-lā′shəs) *adj.* 1. Lustful; lewd. 2. Obscene: a *salacious* joke. [< L *salax* inclined to leap] — **sa·la′cious·ly** *adv.* — **sa·la′cious·ness, sa·lac′i·ty** (-las′ə-tē) *n.*

sal·ad (sal′əd) *n.* Green herbs or vegetables, usu. uncooked and served with a dressing, sometimes mixed with chopped cold meat, fish, etc.; also, a similar dish made with fruit. [< OF < Provençal < L *sal* salt]

sal·a·man·der (sal′ə-man′dər) *n.* 1. Any of a variety of tailed, lizardlike amphibians having a smooth, moist skin and two pairs of limbs. 2. A mythical lizard or other creature fabled to live in fire. 3. Any person or thing that can stand great heat. 4. A large poker or other implement used around or in fire, or when red-hot. [< OF < L *salamandra* < Gk.] — **sal′a·man′drine** (-drin) *adj.*

sa·la·mi (sə-lä′mē) *n.* A salted, spiced sausage, originally Italian. [< Ital. < L *sal* salt]

sal ammoniac *Chem.* A white, crystalline, soluble compound, NH_4Cl, used in medicine and industry. [< L *sal Ammoniacum*, lit. salt of Ammon]

sal·a·ried (sal′ə-rēd, sal′rēd) *adj.* 1. In receipt of a salary. 2. Yielding a salary.

sal·a·ry (sal′ər-ē, sal′rē) *n. pl.* ·ries A periodic, fixed payment for services, esp. for official or professional services as distinguished from manual or menial labor. — *v.t.* ·ried, ·ry·ing To pay or allot a salary to. [< AF < L *salarium* money paid Roman soldiers for their salt]

sale (sāl) *n.* 1. The act of selling; the exchange or transfer of property of any kind for money or its equivalent. 2. An auction. 3. The selling of something at bargain prices. 4. Opportunity of selling; market. — **for sale** (or **on sale**) Offered or ready for sale. [OE *sala* < ON]

sale·a·ble (sā′lə-bəl) See SALABLE.

sal·e·ra·tus (sal′ə-rā′təs) *n.* Sodium bicarbonate, for use in cookery; baking soda. [< NL *sal aëratus* aerated salt]

sales·girl (sālz′gûrl′) *n. U.S.* A woman or girl hired to sell merchandise, especially in a store.

sales·la·dy (sālz′lā′dē) *n. pl.* ·dies *Informal* A woman or girl hired to sell merchandise, esp. in a store.

sales·man (sālz′mən) *n. pl.* ·men (-mən) A man hired to sell goods, stock, etc., in a store or by canvassing.

sales·man·ship (sālz′mən·ship) *n.* 1. The work or profession of a salesman. 2. Ability or skill in selling.

sales·peo·ple (sālz′pē′pəl) *n.pl.* Salespersons.

sales·per·son (sālz′pûr′sən) *n.* A person hired to sell merchandise, esp. in a store.

sales resistance The ability to resist any attempts to induce one to buy certain goods or services.

sales·room (sālz′rōōm′, -rŏŏm′) *n.* A room where merchandise is displayed for sale.

sales tax A tax on money received from sales of goods.

sales·wom·an (sālz′wŏŏm′ən) *n. pl.* ·wom·en (-wim′in) A woman or girl hired to sell merchandise, esp. in a store.

sal·ic (sal′ik) *adj. Geol.* Belonging to a group of igneous rocks composed chiefly of silica and alumina, as the feldspars, quartz, etc. [< S(ILICA) + AL(UMINUM) + -IC]

sal·i·cyl·ate (sal′ə-sil′āt, sə-lis′ə-lāt) *n. Chem.* A salt or ester of salicylic acid.

sal·i·cyl·ic acid (sal′ə-sil′ik) *Chem.* A white crystalline compound, $C_7H_6O_3$, occurring in many plants and also made synthetically, one acetyl form of which is widely known as aspirin. [< SALIC(IN) + -YL + -IC]

sa·li·ent (sā′lē-ənt) *adj.* 1. Standing out prominently; striking; conspicuous. 2. Protruding; projecting. 3. Leaping; springing. — *n.* The part of a fortification, etc., that most protrudes towards the enemy. [< L < *salire* to leap] — **sa′li·ence** *n.* — **sa′li·ent·ly** *adv.* — **sa′li·ent·ness** *n.*

sa·line (sā′līn) *adj.* 1. Of, constituting, or characteristic of salt. 2. Containing salt; salty. — *n.* 1. A metallic salt. 2. A salt solution used in the investigation of biological and physiological processes, and also in medicine. [< F < LL < L *sal, salis* salt] — **sa·lin·i·ty** (sə-lin′ə-tē) *n.*

Salisbury steak Hamburger (def. 2).

sa·li·va (sə-lī′və) *n. Physiol.* The slightly alkaline fluid secreted by the glands of the mouth, considered a promoter of digestion. [< L] — **sal·i·var·y** (sal′ə-ver′ē) *adj.*

sal·i·vate (sal′ə-vāt) *v.* ·vat·ed, ·vat·ing *v.i.* To secrete saliva. — *v.t.* To produce salivation in. [< L < *saliva* saliva] — **sal′i·va′tion** *n.*

sal·low (sal′ō) *adj.* Of an unhealthy yellowish color: said chiefly of the human skin. [OE *salu*] — **sal′low·ish** *adj.* — **sal′low·y** *adv.* — **sal′low·ness** *n.*

sal·ly (sal′ē) *v.i.* ·lied, ·ly·ing 1. To rush out suddenly. 2. To set out energetically. 3. To go out, as from a room or building. — *n. pl.* ·lies 1. A rushing forth, as of troops against besiegers; sortie. 2. Any sudden rushing forth. 3. A going forth, as on a walk. 4. A bantering remark or witticism. [< OF < L *salire* to leap]

sal·ma·gun·di (sal′mə·gun′dē) *n.* 1. A saladlike dish of chopped meat, anchovies, eggs, onions, oil, etc. 2. Any medley or mixture. Also **sal′ma·gun′dy.** [< F *salmigondis*]

salm·on (sam′ən) *n.* 1. Any of various food fishes inhabiting the North Atlantic coastal waters and ascending to adjacent rivers to spawn, having a brownish color above, silvery sides, black spots, and a delicate pink flesh. 2. Any of various other salmonoid fishes. 3. A reddish or pinkish orange color: also **salmon pink.** — *adj.* Having a salmon color. [< OF < L *salmo, -onis*, prob. akin to *salire* to leap] — **sal·mo·noid** (sal′mə·noid) *adj. & n.*

salmon trout 1. The European brown trout. 2. The lake trout. 3. The steelhead.

Sa·lo·me (sə-lō′mē) The daughter of Herodias, who asked Herod for the head of John the Baptist in return for her dancing. *Matt.* xiv 8.

sa·lon (sə-lon′, *Fr.* så·lôn′) *n.* 1. A room in which guests are received; a drawing room. 2. The periodic gathering of noted persons, under the auspices of some distinguished figure. 3. A hall or gallery used for exhibiting works of art. 4. An establishment devoted to some specific purpose: a beauty *salon.* [< F < Ital. < *sala* hall < Gmc.]

sa·loon (sə-lōōn′) *n.* 1. A place where alcoholic drinks are sold; a bar. 2. A large apartment or room for assemblies, public entertainment, exhibitions, etc. 3. The main cabin of a passenger ship. [< F *salon* salon]

sa·loon·keep·er (sə-lōōn′kē′pər) *n.* One who owns or manages a saloon (def. 1).

sal·si·fy (sal′sə-fē, -fī) *n. pl.* ·fies An Old World plant with a white, edible root and an oysterlike flavor: also called *oyster plant.* [< F < Ital. *sassefrica*]

sal soda Sodium carbonate.

salt (sôlt) *n.* 1. Sodium chloride, NaCl, a compound found in sea water and as a mineral, used as a seasoning and as a preservative. ◆ Collateral adjective: *saline.* 2. *Chem.* Any compound consisting of the cation of a base and the anion of an acid, combined in proportions that give a balance of electropositive and electronegative charges. 3. *pl.* A salt used as a laxative or cathartic; also, smelling salts. 4. Piquant humor; dry wit; repartee. 5. That which preserves or purifies. 6. *Informal* A sailor: an old *salt.* 7. A saltcellar. — **to take with a grain of salt** To have doubts about. — *adj.* 1. Flavored with salt; briny. 2. Cured or preserved with salt. 3. Containing, or growing or living in or near, salt water. — *v.t.* 1. To season with salt. 2. To preserve or cure with salt. 3. To furnish with salt: to *salt* cattle. 4. To add zest or piquancy to. 5. To add something to so as to increase the value fraudulently: to *salt* a mine with gold. — **to salt away**

1. To pack in salt for preserving. **2.** *Informal* To store up; save. [OE *sealt*] — **salt'ness** *n.*

salt·cel·lar (sôlt'sel'ər) *n.* A small receptacle for salt; a saltshaker. [ME < *salt* + F *salière* saltcellar]

salt·ed (sôl'tĭd) *adj.* **1.** Treated with salt; preserved. **2.** *Informal* Experienced or expert in some occupation.

sal·tine (sôl·tēn') *n.* A crisp, salty cracker.

salt lick A place to which animals go to lick salt from superficial deposits; a salt spring or dried salt pond.

salt·pe·ter (sôlt'pē'tər) *n.* Potassium nitrate. — **Chile saltpeter** Mineral sodium nitrate, found chiefly in Chile. [< OF < Med.L < L *sal* salt + *petra* a rock < Gk.]

salt·shak·er (sôlt'shā'kər) *n.* A container with small holes for sprinkling table salt.

salt·wa·ter (sôlt'wô'tər, -wot'ər) *adj.* Of, composed of, or living in salty water.

salt·works (sôlt'wûrks') *n. pl.* **·works** An establishment where salt is made on a commercial scale.

salt·wort (sôlt'wûrt') *n.* **1.** Any of various maritime plants of the goosefoot family. **2.** Any of various glassworts.

salt·y (sôl'tē) *adj.* **salt·i·er, salt·i·est 1.** Of, containing, or tasting like salt. **2.** Reminiscent of the sea; smelling of the sea. **3.** Piquant; sharp; pungent, as literature or speech. — **salt'i·ly** *adv.* — **salt'i·ness** *n.*

sa·lu·bri·ous (sə·lōō'brē·əs) *adj.* Conducive to health; healthful; wholesome. [< L < *salus* health] — **sa·lu'bri·ous·ly** *adv.* — **sa·lu'bri·ous·ness, sal·u'bri·ty** *n.*

sal·u·tar·y (sal'yə·ter'ē) *adj.* **1.** Calculated to bring about a sound condition by correcting evil or promoting good; beneficial. **2.** Salubrious. [< F < L *salus, salutis* health] — **sal'u·tar'i·ly** *adv.* — **sal'u·tar'i·ness** *n.*

sal·u·ta·tion (sal'yə·tā'shən, -yōō-) *n.* **1.** The act of saluting. **2.** Any form of greeting. **3.** The opening words of a letter, as *Dear Sir.* [< MF < L *salus, salutis* health]

sa·lu·ta·to·ri·an (sə·lōō'tə·tôr'ē·ən, -tō'rē-) *n. U.S.* In schools, the graduating student, usu. receiving second highest honors, who delivers the salutatory. [< SALUTATORY]

sa·lu·ta·to·ry (sə·lōō'tə·tôr'ē, -tō'rē) *n. pl.* **·ries** An opening oration, as at a school commencement. — *adj.* Of or consisting in greeting; esp., relating to a salutatory address. [< L < *salutare.* See SALUTE.]

sa·lute (sə·lōōt') *n.* **1.** A greeting by display of military or other official honors, as by presenting arms, firing cannon, etc. **2.** The act of or attitude assumed in giving a military salute. **3.** A gesture of greeting, compliment, etc. — *v.* **·lut·ed, ·lut·ing** *v.t.* **1.** To greet with a sign of welcome, respect, etc. **2.** To honor in some prescribed way, as by raising the hand to the cap. — *v.i.* **3.** To make a salute. [< F < L *salus, salutis* health] — **sa·lut'er** *n.*

sal·va·ble (sal'və·bəl) *adj.* Capable of being saved or salvaged. [< LL < L *salvus* safe] — **sal'va·bil'i·ty** *n.*

sal·vage (sal'vij) *v.t.* **·vaged, ·vag·ing** To save, as a ship or its cargo, from wreck, capture, etc. — *n.* **1.** The saving of a ship, cargo, etc., from loss. **2.** Any act of saving property. **3.** Compensation to persons who save a vessel, her cargo, or the lives of those belonging to her. **4.** That which is saved from a wrecked or abandoned vessel or from a fire. **5.** Anything saved from destruction. [< MF < Med.L < L *salvus* safe] — **sal'vage·a·ble** *adj.* — **sal'vag·er** *n.*

sal·va·tion (sal·vā'shən) *n.* **1.** The process or state of being saved. **2.** *Theol.* Deliverance from sin and penalty, realized in a future state. **3.** Any means of deliverance from danger, evil, or ruin. [< OF < LL < L *salvus* safe]

Salvation Army A religious and charitable organization on semimilitary lines, founded by William Booth in 1865.

salve¹ (sav, säv) *n.* **1.** A thick, adhesive ointment for local ailments. **2.** Anything that heals, soothes, or mollifies. **3.** Praise or flattery. — *v.t.* **salved, salv·ing 1.** To dress with ointment. **2.** To soothe; appease. [OE *sealf*]

salve² (salv) *v.t.* **salved, salv·ing** To save from loss; salvage. [< Med.L *salvare*]

sal·ve³ (sal'vē) *interj.* Hail. [< L < *salvere* to be well]

sal·ver (sal'vər) *n.* A tray, as of silver. [< OF < Sp. < *salvar* to taste]

sal·vi·a (sal'vē·ə) *n.* Any of a genus of ornamental plants of the mint family, as the sage. [< L. See SAGE².]

sal·vo (sal'vō) *n. pl.* **·vos** or **·voes 1.** A simultaneous discharge of artillery, or of two or more bombs. **2.** A salute given by firing all the guns. **3.** Any salute or simultaneous outburst: a *salvo* of applause. [< Ital. *salva* salute]

sal vo·lat·i·le (sal võ·lat'ə·lē) *n.* Ammonium carbonate; also, an aromatic solution of ammonium carbonate, used as smelling salts. [< NL, volatile salt < L]

sam·a·ra (sam'ər·ə, sə·mâr'ə) *n. Bot.* A one-seeded fruit, as of the elm, ash, or maple, provided with a membrane or wing. [< L, elm seed]

Sa·mar·i·a (sə·mâr'ē·ə) In the Bible, a city of Palestine, capital of the northern kingdom of Israel, or, later, a restricted portion of central Palestine west of the Jordan occupied by the Samaritans.

Sa·mar·i·tan (sə·mar'ə·tən) *n.* **1.** One of the people of Sa-

maria. **II** *Kings* xvii. **2.** Good Samaritan (which see). — *adj.* Of or pertaining to Samaria.

sa·mar·i·um (sə·mâr'ē·əm) *n.* A hard, brittle, yellowish gray, metallic element (symbol Sm) of the lanthanide series. See ELEMENT. [< NL < *samarskite*, an orthorhombic, vitreous, black mineral]

sam·ba (sam'bə, säm'bä) *n.* **1.** A popular dance of Brazilian origin. **2.** Music for this dance, in duple meter. — *v.i.* To dance the samba. [< Pg. < native African name]

Sam Browne belt (sam' broun') A military belt with a shoulder strap running diagonally across the chest. [after Sir *Samuel J. Browne*, 1824–1901, British general]

same (sām) *adj.* **1.** Having individual or specific identity or quality; identical; equal: with *the.* **2.** Similar in kind or quality. **3.** Similar in quantity or measure; equivalent. **4.** Aforesaid; identical: said of a person or thing just mentioned. — **all the same 1.** Nevertheless; yet. **2.** Equally acceptable or unacceptable. — **just the same 1.** Nevertheless; yet. **2.** Unchanged. — *pron.* The identical person, thing, etc. — *adv.* In like manner; equally: with *the.* [< ON *samr*]

same·ness (sām'nis) *n.* **1.** Lack of change or variety; monotony. **2.** Close similarity; likeness. **3.** Identity; unity.

Sam Hill (sam' hil') *U.S. Slang* Hell: a euphemism.

sam·i·sen (sam'i·sen) *n.* A Japanese guitarlike instrument with three strings, played with a plectrum. [< Japanese < Chinese *san hsien* three strings]

SAMISEN

sa·mite (sā'mīt, sam'it) *n.* A rich medieval fabric of silk, often interwoven with gold or silver. [< OF < Med.L < Gk. *hex* six + *mitos* thread]

Sa·mo·an (sə·mō'ən) *adj.* Of or pertaining to Samoa, to its aboriginal Polynesian inhabitants, or to their language. — *n.* **1.** A native of the Samoan islands. **2.** The Polynesian language of the Samoans.

sam·o·var (sam'ə·vär, sam'ə·vär') *n.* A metal urn for heating water, as for making tea. [< Russian, lit., self-boiler]

Sam·o·yed (sam'ə·yed') *n.* **1.** One of a Mongoloid people inhabiting the Arctic coasts of Siberia. **2.** A large dog having a thick white coat of long hair. — *adj.* Of the Samoyeds or their language; Samoyedic. Also **Sam'o·yede'** (-yed'). [< Russian, lit., self-eater]

Sam·o·yed·ic (sam'ə·yed'ik) *adj.* Of or pertaining to the Samoyeds or their language. — *n.* A subfamily of the Uralic languages, including the language of the Samoyeds.

samp (samp) *n.* Coarse Indian corn; also, a porridge made of it. [< Algonquian *nasaump* softened with water]

sam·pan (sam'pan) *n.* A small flat-bottomed boat or skiff used along rivers and coasts of China and Japan. [< Chinese *san* three + *pan* board, plank]

sam·ple (sam'pəl) *n.* A portion, part, or piece taken or shown as a representative of the whole. — *v.t.* **·pled, ·pling** To test or examine by means of a sample. [See EXAMPLE.]

sam·pler¹ (sam'plər) *n.* One who tests by sampling.

sam·pler² (sam'plər) *n.* A piece of needlework, originally designed to show a beginner's skill. [See EXAMPLE.]

sam·pling (sam'pling) *n.* **1.** A small part of something or a number of items from a group selected for examination or analysis in order to estimate the quality or nature of the whole. **2.** The act or process of making such a selection.

Sam·son (sam'sən) A Hebrew judge of great strength, betrayed to the Philistines by Delilah. *Judges* xii–xvi.

Sam·u·el (sam'yōō·əl) A Hebrew judge and prophet. — *n.* Either of two historical books, I and II Samuel, of the Old Testament.

sam·u·rai (sam'ŏŏ·rī) *n. pl.* **·rai** Under the Japanese feudal system, a member of the soldier class of the lower nobility; also, the class itself. [< Japanese]

san·a·tive (san'ə·tiv) *adj.* Healing; sanatory; health-giving. [< OF < Med.L < L *sanare* to heal]

san·a·to·ri·um (san'ə·tôr'ē·əm, -tō'rē-) *n. pl.* **·ri·ums** or **·ri·a** (-tôr'ē·ə, -tō'rē·ə) **1.** An institution for the treatment and care of invalids and convalescents. **2.** A health resort. Also *sanitarium.* [< NL < LL < L *sanare* to heal]

sanc·ti·fied (sangk'tə·fīd) *adj.* **1.** Made holy; freed from sin; consecrated. **2.** Sanctimonious; self-righteous.

sanc·ti·fy (sangk'tə·fī) *v.t.* **·fied, ·fy·ing 1.** To set apart as holy or for holy purposes; consecrate. **2.** To purify or make holy. **3.** To render sacred or inviolable, as a vow. [< OF < LL < L *sanctus* holy + *facere* to make] — **sanc'ti·fi·ca'tion** *n.* — **sanc'ti·fi'er** *n.*

sanc·ti·mo·ni·ous (sangk'tə·mō'nē·əs) *adj.* Making an ostentatious display or pretense of sanctity. — **sanc'ti·mo'ni·ous·ly** *adv.* — **sanc'ti·mo'ni·ous·ness** *n.*

sanc·ti·mo·ny (sangk'tə·mō'nē) *n.* Assumed or outward sanctity; a show of holiness or devoutness. [< OF < L *sanctimonia* holiness]

sanc·tion (sangk'shən) *v.t.* **1.** To approve authoritatively; confirm; ratify. **2.** To countenance; allow. — *n.* **1.** Final and authoritative confirmation or ratification. **2.** A formal decree. **3.** A provision for securing conformity to law, as by the enactment of rewards or penalties or both. **4.** *Usu. pl.* In international law, coercive measures adopted to force a nation that is violating international law to desist. **5.** In ethics, that which makes virtue morally obligatory. [< L < *sancire* to render sacred, inviolable]

sanc·ti·ty (sangk′tə·tē) *n. pl.* **·ties 1.** The state of being sanctified; holiness. **2.** Sacredness; solemnity.

sanc·tu·ar·y (sangk′chōō·er′ē) *n. pl.* **·ar·ies 1.** A holy or sacred place. **2.** The most sacred part of a place in a sacred structure. **3.** A place of refuge; asylum; also, immunity. [< OF < LL < L *sanctus* holy]

sanc·tum (sangk′təm) *n. pl.* **·tums** or **·ta** (-tə) **1.** A sacred place. **2.** A private room where one is not to be disturbed. [< L, neut. of *sanctus* holy]

sanc·tum sanc·to·rum (sangk′təm sangk·tôr′əm, -tō′rəm) **1.** The holy of holies. **2.** A place of great privacy: often used humorously.

Sanc·tus (sangk′təs) *n. Eccl.* **1.** An ascription of praise to God, occurring at the end of the Preface in many eucharistic liturgies. **2.** A musical setting for this. [< L *sanctus* holy]

sand (sand) *n.* **1.** A hard, granular rock material finer than gravel and coarser than dust. **2.** *pl.* Stretches of sandy beach, desert, etc. **3.** *pl.* Sandy grains in an hourglass. **4.** *pl.* Moments of time or life. **5.** A reddish yellow color. — *v.t.* **1.** To sprinkle or cover with sand. **2.** To smooth or abrade with sand or sandpaper. **3.** To mix sand with. **4.** To fill with sand. [OE] — **sand′er** *n.*

san·dal (san′dəl) *n.* **1.** A foot covering, consisting usu. of a sole only, held to the foot by thongs. **2.** A light slipper. **3.** An overshoe of rubber, cut very low. [< OF < Gk. *sandalon*] — **san′daled, san′dalled** *adj.*

san·dal·wood (san′dəl·wŏŏd′) *n.* **1.** The fine-grained, dense, fragrant wood of any of several East Indian trees. **2.** The similar wood of other trees, whose dark red wood is used as a dyestuff. [< Med.L < Skt. *çandana*]

sand·bag (sand′bag′) *n.* **1.** A bag filled with sand, used for building fortifications, for ballast, etc. **2.** A long, narrow bag filled with sand and used as a club or weapon. — *v.t.* **·bagged, ·bag·ging 1.** To fill or surround with sandbags. **2.** To strike with a sandbag. — **sand′bag′ger** *n.*

sand·bar (sand′bär′) *n.* A ridge of silt or sand in rivers, along beaches, etc., formed by the action of currents or tides.

sand·blast (sand′blast′, -bläst′) *n.* **1.** A fine jet of sand, propelled under pressure and used to clean, grind, or decorate hard surfaces. **2.** The apparatus used in applying this blast. — *v.t.* To clean or engrave by means of a sandblast.

sand·box (sand′boks′) *n.* **1.** A box on a locomotive or streetcar filled with sand to be poured on the rail treads to prevent slipping. **2.** A box of sand for children to play in.

sand·cast (sand′kast′, -käst′) *v.t.* **·cast, ·cast·ing** To make (a casting) by pouring metal into a mold of sand.

sand crack *Vet.* A crack running down from the coronet of a horse's hoof and apt to cause lameness if neglected.

sand flea Any of various fleas that live in sand, as the chigoe.

sand·hog (sand′hôg′, -hog′) *n.* One who works under air pressure, as in caisson sinking, tunnel building, etc.

sand·lot (sand′lot′) *adj.* Of or in a vacant lot in or near an urban area: *sand-lot* baseball.

sand·man (sand′man′) *n.* In nursery lore, a person supposed to make children sleepy by casting sand in their eyes.

sand painting A form of painting by the American Indians in which fine colored sand is trickled on a ground base.

sand·pa·per (sand′pā′pər) *n.* Heavy paper coated with sand for smoothing or polishing. — *v.t.* To rub or polish with sandpaper.

sand·pi·per (sand′pī′pər) *n.* Any of certain small wading birds related to the snipes and frequenting seashores. Also **sand′peep′** (-pēp′).

sand·stone (sand′stōn′) *n.* A rock consisting chiefly of quartz sand cemented with silica, feldspar, lime, or clay.

sand·storm (sand′stôrm′) *n.* A high wind by which sand or dust is carried along.

sand·wich (sand′wich, san′-) *n.* **1.** Two thin slices of bread, having between them meat, cheese, etc. **2.** Any combination of alternating dissimilar things pressed together. — *v.t.* **1.** To place between two layers or objects. **2.** To insert between dissimilar things. [after John Montagu, fourth Earl of *Sandwich*, 1718–92, who originated it in order to eat without leaving the gaming table]

sandwich man *n. pl.* **men** *Informal* A man carrying advertising boards (**sandwich boards**) slung in front and behind.

sand·y (san′dē) *adj.* **sand·i·er, sand·i·est 1.** Consisting of or characterized by sand; containing, covered with, or full of sand. **2.** Yellowish red: a *sandy* beard. — **sand′i·ness** *n.*

sane (sān) *adj.* **1.** Mentally sound; not deranged. **2.** Proceeding from a sound mind. [< L *sanus* whole, healthy] — **sane′ly** *adv.* — **sane′ness** *n.*

San·for·ize (san′fə·rīz) *v.t.* **·ized, ·iz·ing** To treat (cloth) so as to prevent shrinkage: a trade name. Also **san′for·ize.** [after *Sanford* L. Cluett, 1874–1968, U.S. inventor]

sang (sang) Past tense of SING.

sang-froid (sän·frwä′) *n.* Calmness amid trying circumstances; coolness; composure. [< F, lit., cold blood]

san·gri·a (säng·grē′ə) *n.* Red wine mixed with fruit and/or fruit juices. [< Sp. *sangría*, lit., bleeding]

sangui- *combining form* Blood. [< L *sanguis* blood]

san·gui·nar·y (sang′gwə·ner′ē) *adj.* **1.** Attended with bloodshed. **2.** Bloodthirsty. **3.** Consisting of blood. — **san′gui·nar′i·ly** *adv.* — **san′gui·nar′i·ness** *n.*

san·guine (sang′gwin) *adj.* **1.** Of cheerful, hopeful disposition. **2.** Ruddy; robust. **3.** Of, like, or full of blood. **4.** *Obs.* Bloodthirsty; sanguinary. [< OF < L *sanguis, -inis* blood] — **san′guine·ly** *adv.* — **san′guine·ness** *n.*

san·i·tar·i·um (san′ə·târ′ē·əm) *n. pl.* **·tar·i·ums** or **·tar·i·a** (-târ′ē·ə) A sanatorium. [< NL < L *sanitas* health]

san·i·tar·y (san′ə·ter′ē) *adj.* **1.** Relating to the preservation of health. **2.** Favorable to health; hygienic. [< F < L *sanitas* health] — **san′i·tar′i·ly** *adv.*

sanitary napkin An absorbent pad worn by women during menstruation.

san·i·ta·tion (san′ə·tā′shən) *n.* The use and practical application of sanitary measures; the removal or neutralization of elements injurious to health.

san·i·ta·tion·man (san′i·tā′shən·man′) *n. pl.* **·men** (-mən) A person, esp. a municipal employee, whose work is the collection of refuse and trash.

san·i·tize (san′ə·tīz) *v.t.* **·tized, ·tiz·ing 1.** To make sanitary. **2.** To make acceptable or unobjectionable.

san·i·ty (san′ə·tē) *n. pl.* **·ties 1.** The state of being sane; soundness of mind. **2.** Sane moderation or reasonableness.

San Jo·sé scale (san′ hō·zā′) A scale insect destructive to various fruit trees.

sank (sangk) Past tense of SINK.

sans (sanz, *Fr.* sän) *prep.* Without. [< OF *sanz*]

sans-cu·lotte (sanz′kyōō·lot′, *Fr.* sän·kü·lôt′) *n.* **1.** A revolutionary: originally a term of contempt applied by the aristocrats to the French revolutionists in 1789. **2.** Any revolutionary or radical. [< F, lit., without knee breeches] — **sans-cu·lot′tic** *adj.* — **sans′-cu·lot′tism** *n.*

San·sei (sän·sā′) *n. pl.* **·sei** or **·seis** An American citizen of Japanese descent whose grandparents settled in the U.S. [< Japanese, third generation]

san·se·vi·e·ri·a (san′sə·vi·ir′ē·ə) *n.* Any of several perennial herbs of the lily family, cultivated as an ornamental plant. [after the Prince of *Sanseviero*, 1710–71]

San·skrit (san′skrit) *n.* The ancient and classical language of the Hindus of India, belonging to the Indic branch of the Indo-Iranian subfamily of Indo-European languages. Also **San′scrit.** [< Skt. *samskrita* artificial, highly cultivated]

San·skrit·ic (san·skrit′ik) *adj.* **1.** Of, pertaining to, or written in Sanskrit. **2.** Designating a group of some 30 to 40 ancient and modern languages and dialects of India.

sans ser·if (sanz ser′if) *Printing* A type face without serifs: also called *gothic.*

San·ta Claus (san′tə klôz′) In nursery lore, a fat, jolly old man who brings presents at Christmas time. [< Du. *Sant Nikolaas* Saint Nicholas]

San·ta Ma·ri·a (san′tə mə·rē′ə) One of the three ships of Columbus on his maiden voyage to America.

sap¹ (sap) *n.* **1.** The juices of plants, that contain and transport the materials necessary to growth. **2.** Any vital fluid; vitality. **3.** *Slang* A foolish or gullible person. [OE *sæp*]

sap² (sap) *v.* **sapped, sap·ping** *v.t.* **1.** To weaken or destroy gradually and insidiously; enervate; exhaust. **2.** To approach or undermine (an enemy fortification) by digging a sap. — *v.i.* **3.** To dig a sap or saps. — *n.* A deep, narrow trench or tunnel dug so as to approach or undermine a fortification. [< MF < Ital. *zappa* spade, goat]

sap·head (sap′hed′) *n. Slang* A simpleton; sap. — **sap′head′ed** *adj.*

sa·pi·ent (sā′pē·ənt) *adj.* Wise; sagacious: often used ironically. [< OF < L < *sapere* to have good taste] — **sa′pi·ence, sa′pi·en·cy** *n.* — **sa′pi·ent·ly** *adv.*

sap·less (sap′lis) *adj.* **1.** Destitute of sap; withered. **2.** Wanting vitality, spirit, or vivacity; insipid; dull.

sap·ling (sap′ling) *n.* **1.** A young tree. **2.** A youth. [Dim. of SAP¹]

sap·o·dil·la (sap′ə·dil′ə) *n.* **1.** A large evergreen tree of the West Indies and tropical America. **2.** Its edible, apple-shaped fruit, a source of chicle: also **sapodilla plum.** Also **sa·po·ta** (sə·pō′tə), **sap′a·dil′lo, sap′o·dil′lo.** [< Sp. < Nahuatl *tzapotl*]

sap·o·na·ceous (sap/ə·nā/shəs) *adj.* Soapy.

sa·pon·i·fy (sə·pon/ə·fī) *v.t.* **·fied, ·fy·ing** *Chem.* To convert (a fat or oil) into soap by the action of an alkali. [< F < L *sapo, saponis* soap + *facere* to make] — **sa·pon/i·fi/a·ble** *adj.* — **sa·pon·i·fi·ca·tion** (sə·pon/ə·fə·kā/shən) *n.* — **sa·pon/i·fi/er** *n.*

sap·per (sap/ər) *n.* **1.** One who or that which saps. **2.** A soldier employed in making a sap². [< SAP² + -ER]

Sap·phic (saf/ik) *adj.* **1.** Pertaining to or in the manner of Sappho. **2.** In prosody, denoting a line of trochaic pentameter with a dactyl in the third foot, much used by Sappho. [after *Sappho*]

sap·phire (saf/īr) *n.* **1.** Any of the hard, translucent, colored varieties of corundum other than the red variety, that when cut are used as gems; esp., a deep blue corundum. **2.** Deep pure blue. [< OF < L < Gk. *sappheiros*]

sap·py (sap/ē) *adj.* **·pi·er, ·pi·est 1.** Full of sap; juicy. **2.** *Slang* Immature; silly. — **sap/pi·ly** *adv.* — **sap/pi·ness** *n.*

sapro- *combining form* **1.** Decomposition or putrefaction. **2.** Saprophytic. [< Gk. *sapros* rotten]

sap·ro·phyte (sap/rə·fīt) *n.* A vegetable organism that lives on dead or decaying organic matter, as certain funguses, various bacteria, etc. — **sap/ro·phyt/ic** (-fit/ik) *adj.*

sap·suck·er (sap/suk/ər) *n.* Any of various small black and white woodpeckers that damage orchard trees by exposing and drinking the sap.

sap·wood (sap/wŏŏd/) *n. Bot.* The new wood next to the bark of an exogenous tree.

sar·a·band (sar/ə·band) *n.* **1.** A slow, stately dance of the 17th and 18th centuries. **2.** Music for this dance, in triple meter. Also **sar/a·bande.** [< F < Sp. < Persian *sarband* a kind of dance and song]

Sar·a·cen (sar/ə·sən) *n.* **1.** Originally, a nomad Arab of the Syrian-Arabian desert. **2.** A Moslem, esp. during the Crusades. **3.** Any Arab. [< LL < LGk. *Sarakēnos*] — **Sar/a·cen/ic** (-sen/ik) or **·i·cal** *adj.*

Sar·ah (sâr/ə) The wife of Abraham. *Gen.* xvii 15.

sa·ran (sə·ran/) *n.* Any of a class of synthetic fibers and textile materials obtained by the polymerization of vinyl chloride. [Coined by Dow Chemical Co.]

sa·ra·pe (sə·räp/ē) See SERAPE.

Saratoga trunk A very large traveling trunk used formerly by ladies. [after *Saratoga* Springs]

sar·casm (sär/kaz·əm) *n.* **1.** An ironical or scornful utterance; contemptuous and taunting language. **2.** The use of biting gibes or cutting rebukes. [< LL < Gk. *sarkazein* to tear flesh, sneer < *sarx, sarkos* flesh]
— **Syn. 1.** *Sarcasm* may describe a man's weakness in subtly pejorative terms, or may show the vanity of his pretensions, or his absurdity. *Irony* is more limited, and is sometimes regarded as one of the methods of *sarcasm*; it consists of the assertion of the opposite of what is really meant.

sar·cas·tic (sär·kas/tik) *adj.* **1.** Characterized by or of the nature of sarcasm; taunting. **2.** Given to the use of sarcasm. Also **sar·cas/ti·cal.** — **sar·cas/ti·cal·ly** *adv.*

sarce·net (särs/nit) See SARSENET.

sarco- *combining form* Flesh; of or related to flesh. Also, before vowels, **sarc-.** [< Gk. *sarx, sarkos* flesh]

sar·co·carp (sär/kō·kärp) *n. Bot.* The succulent part of a stone fruit, as the fleshy edible part of a plum or peach.

sar·co·ma (sär·kō/mə) *n. pl.* **·ma·ta** (-mə·tə) *Pathol.* A tumor, often malignant, made up of cells resembling those of embryonic connective tissue. [< Gk. < *sarx, sarkos* flesh] — **sar·co/ma·toid, sar·co/ma·tous** (-kō/mə·təs, -kom/ə-) *adj.*

sar·coph·a·gus (sär·kof/ə·gəs) *n. pl.* **·gi** (-jī) **1.** A stone coffin or tomb. **2.** A large ornamental coffin of marble or stone placed in a crypt or exposed to view. **3.** A kind of limestone, used by the Greeks for coffins. [< L < Gk. < *sarx, sarkos* flesh + *phagein* to eat]

sar·cous (sär/kəs) *adj.* Of, pertaining to, or composed of flesh or muscle. [< Gk. *sarx, sarkos* flesh]

sard (särd) *n.* The deep brownish red variety of chalcedony, used as a gem. [< OF < L < Gk. *Sardeis* Sardis]

sar·dine (sär·dēn/) *n.* **1.** A small, herringlike fish commonly preserved in oil as a food delicacy, esp. the pilchard. **2.** Any of various related fishes similarly preserved. [< OF < L < Gk. *sardēnē, ?* < *Sardo* Sardinia]

Sar·dis (sär/dis) An ancient city of Asia Minor, capital of Lydia; destroyed by Tamerlane. Also **Sar/des.**

sar·don·ic (sär·don/ik) *adj.* Scornful or derisive; mocking; cynical. [< F < L < Gk. *sardanios* bitter, scornful] — **sar·don/i·cal·ly** *adv.* — **sar·don/i·cism** *n.*

sar·do·nyx (sär/də·niks) *n.* A variety of chalcedony in bands varying from light to reddish brown, with other colors. [< L < Gk., appar. < *sardios* sard + *onyx* onyx]

sar·gas·so (sär·gas/ō) *n.* An olive-brown seaweed having small air bladders on its stalks, native in tropical American waters: also called *gulfweed.* Also **sar·gas/sum.** [< Pg. < *sarga, ?* < L *salicastrum*]

sa·ri (sä/rē) *n. pl.* **·ris** A long piece of cotton or silk cloth, constituting the principal garment of Hindu women, worn round the waist, one end falling to the feet, and the other crossed over the bosom and shoulder, and sometimes over the head. Also **sa/ree.** [< Hind. *sarī* < Skt. *śāṭī*]

sa·rong (sə·rong/) *n.* **1.** A skirtlike garment of colored silk or cotton cloth worn by both sexes in the Malay Archipelago, etc. **2.** The material used for this garment. [< Malay *sārung,* prob. < Skt. *sāranga* variegated]

sar·sa·pa·ril·la (sas/pə·ril/ə, sär/sə·pə·ril/ə) *n.* **1.** The dried roots of certain tropical American climbing plants of the lily family. **2.** A medicinal preparation or a beverage made from such roots. [< Sp. < *zarza* bramble + *parilla,* dim. of *parra* vine]

sarse·net (särs/nit) *n.* A fine, thin silk, used for linings: also spelled *sarcenet.* [< AF, dim. of ME *sarzin* Saracen]

sar·to·ri·al (sär·tôr/ē·əl, -tō/rē-) *adj.* **1.** Pertaining to a tailor or his work. **2.** Pertaining to men's clothes. [< L *sartor* patcher, mender] — **sar·to/ri·al·ly** *adv.*

sash¹ (sash) *n.* An ornamental band or scarf, worn as a girdle, or around the waist or over the shoulder. [Orig. *shash* < Arabic *shāsh* muslin, turban]

sash² (sash) *n.* A frame, as of a window, in which glass is set. — *v.t.* To furnish with a sash. [Alter. of CHASSIS, taken as a pl.]

sa·shay (sa·shā/) *v.i. U.S. Informal* To move with a swinging or gliding motion. [Alter. of *chassé,* a dance motion]

sass (sas) *Informal n.* Impudence; back talk. — *v.t.* To talk to impudently or disrespectfully. [Dial. alter. of SAUCE]

sas·sa·fras (sas/ə·fras) *n.* **1.** An aromatic, deciduous tree of the laurel family. **2.** The root bark of this tree, used for flavoring, and yielding a volatile oil. [< Sp. *sasafrás,* prob. < N. Am. Ind. name]

sas·sy¹ (sas/ē) *adj.* **·si·er, ·si·est** *U.S. Dial.* Saucy; impertinent; cheeky.

sas·sy² (sas/ē) *n.* A West African tree having a bark that yields a poisonous alkaloid. Also **sas/sy·bark/** (-bärk/), **sas/sy·wood/** (-wŏŏd/). [< native W. African name]

sat (sat) Past tense of SIT.

Sa·tan (sā/tən) In the Bible, the great adversary of God and tempter of mankind; the Devil: identified with *Lucifer. Luke* iv 5–8; *Rev.* xii 7–9. Also **Sa/than** (sā/tən), **Sath·a·nas** (sath/ə·nəs). [< Hebrew *sātān* enemy]

sa·tan·ic (sā·tan/ik) *adj.* Devilish; infernal; wicked. Also **sa·tan/i·cal.** — **sa·tan/i·cal·ly** *adv.*

satch·el (sach/əl) *n.* A small handbag or suitcase. [< OF < L *sacellus,* dim. of *saccus* sack]

sate (sāt) *v.t.* **sat·ed, sat·ing** To satisfy the appetite of; satiate. [Appar. alter. of obs. *sade* to sate, OE *sadian;* refashioned after L *sat, satis* enough]

sa·teen (sa·tēn/) *n.* A cotton fabric woven so as to give it a satin surface. [Alter. of SATIN]

sat·el·lite (sat/ə·līt) *n.* **1.** *Astron.* A smaller body attending upon and revolving round a larger one; a moon. **2.** One who attends upon a person in power. **3.** Any obsequious attendant. **4.** A small nation that is politically, economically, or militarily dependent on a great power. **5.** A town or community whose activities are largely determined by those of a neighboring metropolis. **6.** Any manmade object launched from and revolving around the earth. [< F < L *satelles, satellitis* attendant, guard]

sa·ti·a·ble (sā/shē·ə·bəl, -shə·bəl) *adj.* Capable of being satiated. — **sa/ti·a·bil/i·ty,** **sa/ti·a·ble·ness** *n.* — **sa/ti·a·bly** *adv.*

sa·ti·ate (sā/shē·āt) *v.t.* **·at·ed, ·at·ing 1.** To satisfy the appetite or desire of; gratify. **2.** To fill or gratify beyond natural desire; glut. — **Syn.** See SATISFY. — *adj.* Filled to satiety; satiated. [< L < *satis* enough] — **sa/ti·a/tion** *n.*

sa·ti·e·ty (sə·tī/ə·tē) *n. pl.* **·ties** The state of being satiated.

sat·in (sat/ən) *n.* A silk, cotton, rayon, or acetate fabric of thick texture, with glossy face and dull back. — *adj.* Of or resembling satin; glossy; smooth. [< OF < Med.L *satinus, setinus,* ult. < *seta* silk] — **sat·in·y** *adj.*

sat·i·net (sat/ə·net/) *n.* **1.** A strong fabric with cotton warp and woolen filling. **2.** A thin satin. Also **sat/i·nette/.** [< F, dim. of *satin* satin]

sat·in·wood (sat/ən·wŏŏd/) *n.* **1.** The satinlike wood of an East Indian tree of the mahogany family. **2.** The tree.

sat·ire (sat/īr) *n.* **1.** The use of sarcasm, irony, or wit in exposing abuses or follies; ridicule. **2.** A written composition in which vice, folly, etc., is held up to ridicule. [< MF < L *satira, satura* satire, orig. medley < (*lanx*) *satura* fruit salad, lit., full (dish), fem. of *satur* full]
— **Syn. 1.** chaff, raillery, mockery, derision.

sa·tir·ic (sə·tir/ik) *adj.* Of, pertaining to, or resembling satire, esp. literary satire: *satiric* verse. Also *satirical.*

sa·tir·i·cal (sə·tir/i·kəl) *adj.* **1.** Given to or characterized by satire. **2.** Severely sarcastic; caustic: a *satirical* laugh. **3.** Satiric. — **sa·tir/i·cal·ly** *adv.* — **sa·tir/i·cal·ness** *n.*

sat·i·rist (sat/ə·rist) *n.* **1.** A writer of satire. **2.** A satirical person.

sat·i·rize (sat/ə·rīz) *v.t.* **·rized, ·riz·ing** To criticize by means of satire; subject to satire. — **sat/i·riz/er** *n.*

sat·is·fac·tion (sat/is·fak/shən) *n.* **1.** The act of satisfying or the state of being satisfied; gratification. **2.** The making of amends, reparation, or payment, as of a claim or obligation. **3.** That which satisfies; atonement; compensation.

sat·is·fac·to·ry (sat/is·fak/tər·ē) *adj.* **1.** Giving satisfaction; answering fully all desires, expectations, or requirements. **2.** Atoning; expiatory. — **Syn.** See ADEQUATE. — **sat/is·fac/to·ri·ly** *adv.* — **sat/is·fac/to·ri·ness** *n.*

sat·is·fy (sat/is·fī) *v.* **·fied, ·fy·ing** *v.t.* **1.** To supply fully with what is desired, expected, or needed; gratify. **2.** To free from doubt or anxiety; convince. **3.** To give what is due to. **4.** To pay or discharge (a debt, obligation, etc.). **5.** To answer sufficiently or convincingly, as a question or objection. **6.** To fulfill the conditions or requirements of, as an equation. **7.** To make reparation for; expiate. — *v.i.* **8.** To give satisfaction. [< OF < L < *satis* enough + *facere* to do] — **sat/is·fi/er** *n.* — **sat/is·fy/ing·ly** *adv.*
— **Syn. 1.** *Satisfy* suggests the giving of just enough, and no more, and a state of mind that is merely content. To *gratify* is to please, hence to give liberally, while *satiate* is now chiefly used to indicate an excess or oversupply.

sa·to·ri (sä·tôr/ē) *n.* The illumination of spirit sought by Zen Buddhists. [< Japanese]

sa·trap (sā/trap, sat/rap) *n.* **1.** A governor of a province in ancient Persia. **2.** A subordinate, often despotic, ruler or governor. [< L < Gk. < OPersian *shathrapavan*, lit., protector of a province]

sa·trap·y (sā/trə·pē, sat/rə·pē) *n. pl.* **·trap·ies** The territory or the jurisdiction of a satrap. Also **sa·trap·ate** (sā/trə·pit, sat/rə-).

sat·u·rate (sach/ə·rāt; *for adj., also* sach/ə·rit) *v.t.* **·rat·ed, ·rat·ing 1.** To soak or imbue thoroughly. **2.** To fill, impregnate, or charge (a substance or material) to its full capacity. — *adj.* **1.** Filled to repletion; saturated. **2.** Very intense; deep: said of colors. [< L *saturatus*, pp. of *saturare* to fill up] — **sat·u·ra·ble** (sach/ər·ə·bəl) *adj.* — **sat/u·ra/ter** *or* **·tor** *n.* — **sat/u·ra/tion** *n.*

sat·u·rat·ed (sach/ə·rā/tid) *adj.* **1.** Incapable of holding more of a substance or material; completely satisfied; replete: *saturated* vapor. **2.** *Chem.* Designating an organic compound, as paraffin or methane, having no free valences and without double or triple bonds. **3.** Designating a color or hue exhibiting high saturation.

Sat·ur·day (sat/ər·dē, -dā) *n.* The seventh or last day of the week. [OE *Sæterdæg, Sæternesdæg*]

Sat·urn (sat/ərn) In Roman mythology, the god of agriculture: identified with the Greek *Cronus.* — *n.* The second largest planet of the solar system and sixth in order from the sun. See PLANET. [< L *Saturnus*] — **Sa·tur·ni·an** (sə·tûr/nē·ən) *adj.*

sat·ur·na·li·a (sat/ər·nā/lē·ə) *n.pl.* (*Usu. construed as sing.*) Any season or period of general license or revelry.

Sat·ur·na·li·a (sat/ər·nā/lē·ə) *n.pl.* The feast of Saturn, held at Rome in mid-December, and marked by wild reveling and licentious abandon. — **Sat/ur·na/li·an** *adj.*

sat·ur·nine (sat/ər·nīn) *adj.* Having a grave, gloomy, or morose disposition or character. [< OF < Med.L *Saturnus* lead, Saturn]

sat·yr (sat/ər, sā/tər) *n.* **1.** In Greek mythology, a lecherous woodland diety in human form, having pointed ears, goat's legs, and budding horns. **2.** A very lascivious man. [< L < Gk. *satyros*] — **sa·tyr·ic** (sə·tir/ik) *or* **·i·cal** *adj.*

sat·y·ri·a·sis (sat/ə·rī/ə·sis) *n. Psychiatry* An excessive and uncontrollable sexual desire in men. [< NL < Gk. < *satyros* satyr]

sauce (sôs) *n.* **1.** An appetizing dressing or liquid relish for food. **2.** Any appetizing garnish of a meal. **3.** Formerly, any condiment, as salt or pepper. **4.** A dish of fruit pulp stewed and sweetened. **5.** *Informal* Pert or impudent language. — *v.t.* **sauced, sauc·ing 1.** To flavor with sauce; season. **2.** To give zest or piquancy to. **3.** *Informal* To flavor saucy to. [< OF < LL *salsa*, orig. fem. of L *salsus* salted]

sauce·pan (sôs/pan/) *n.* A metal or enamel pan with projecting handle, for cooking food.

sau·cer (sô/sər) *n.* **1.** A small dish for holding a cup. **2.** Any small, round, shallow vessel of similar shape. [< OF < *sauce* sauce]

sau·cy (sô/sē) *adj.* **·ci·er, ·ci·est 1.** Disrespectful to superiors; impudent. **2.** Piquant; sprightly; amusing. — **sau/ci·ly** *adv.* — **sau/ci·ness** *n.*

sau·er·bra·ten (sour/brät·n, *Ger.* zou/ər·brät·n/) *n.* Beef marinated in vinegar before being braised. [< G < *sauer* sour + *braten* to roast]

sau·er·kraut (sour/krout/) *n.* Shredded and salted cabbage fermented in its own juice: also called *kraut.* [< G < *sauer* sour + *kraut* cabbage]

Sauk (sôk) *n.* One of a tribe of North American Indians of Algonquian stock, formerly occupying Michigan, later Wis-consin and the Mississippi valley, now on reservations in Oklahoma, Iowa, and Kansas. Also spelled *Sac.*

Saul (sôl) **1.** The first king of Israel. *I Sam.* ix 2. **2.** The Hebrew name of the Apostle Paul (*Acts* xiii 9): also **Saul of Tarsus.**

sau·na (sou/nə) *n.* A room or house for taking steam baths by the Finnish method, in steam produced by throwing water on hot stones; also, such a steam bath. [< Finnish]

saun·ter (sôn/tər) *v.i.* To walk in a leisurely or lounging way; stroll. — *n.* **1.** A slow, aimless manner of walking. **2.** An idle stroll. [ME *santren* to muse, meditate]

sau·ri·an (sôr/ē·ən) *n.* One of a suborder of reptiles, including the lizards, geckos, and chameleons. — *adj.* Pertaining to saurians. [< NL < Gk. *sauros* lizard]

sauro- *combining form* Lizard. Also, before vowels, **saur-.** [< Gk. *sauros* lizard]

-saurus *combining form* Lizard: used to form genus names: *Brontosaurus.* [< Gk. *sauros* lizard]

sau·sage (sô/sij) *n.* **1.** Finely chopped and highly seasoned meat, commonly stuffed into the cleaned entrails of some animal or into artificial casings. **2.** *Aeron.* A type of barrage or observation balloon, shaped like a sausage. [< AF < LL *salsicia*, ult. < L *salsus* salted]

sau·té (sō·tā/, sô-) *adj.* Fried quickly with little grease. — *v.t.* **·téed, ·té·ing** To fry quickly in a little fat. [< F, pp. of *sauter* to leap < L *saltare*]

sau·terne (sō·tûrn/, sô-; *Fr.* sō·tern/) *n.* A sweet, white French wine. Also **sau·ternes/.** [after *Sauternes*, district in SW France]

sav·age (sav/ij) *adj.* **1.** Having a wild and untamed nature; not domesticated. **2.** Ferocious; fierce. **3.** Living in or belonging to a primitive condition of human life and society; uncivilized: *savage* tribes. **4.** Vicious; cruel; furious. **5.** Rude; uncultivated; rough. — *n.* **1.** A primitive or uncivilized human being. **2.** A brutal, fierce, and cruel person; a barbarian. — *v.t.* **·aged, ·ag·ing** To attack savagely, esp. with the teeth. [< OF < L *salvaticus, silvaticus < silva* a wood] — **sav/age·ly** *adv.* — **sav/age·ness** *n.*

sav·age·ry (sav/ij·rē) *n. pl.* **·ries 1.** The state of being savage. **2.** Cruelty in disposition or action; a cruel or savage act. **3.** Savages collectively: also **sav/age·dom** (-dəm). Also **sav/ag·ism.**

sa·van·na (sə·van/ə) *n.* **1.** A tract of level land covered with low vegetation. **2.** Any large area of tropical or subtropical grassland, covered in part with trees and spiny shrubs. Also **sa·van/nah.** [Earlier *zavana* < Sp. < Carib]

sa·vant (sə·vänt/, sav/ənt; *Fr.* sà·vän/) *n.* A man of exceptional learning. [< F < L *sapere* to be wise]

save¹ (sāv) *v.* **saved, sav·ing** *v.t.* **1.** To preserve or rescue from danger, harm, etc. **2.** To keep from being spent, expended, or lost. **3.** To set aside for future use; accumulate: often with *up.* **4.** To treat carefully so as to avoid fatigue, harm, etc.: to *save* one's eyes. **5.** To prevent by timely action: A stitch in time *saves* nine. **6.** *Theol.* To deliver from spiritual death or the consequences of sin. — *v.i.* **7.** To avoid waste; be economical. **8.** To preserve something from danger, harm, etc. **9.** To admit of preservation, as food. [< OF < LL < L *salvus* safe] — **sav/a·ble** *or* **save/a·ble** *adj.* — **sav/a·ble·ness** *n.* — **sav/er** *n.*

save² (sāv) *prep.* Except; but. — *conj.* **1.** Except; but: usu. with *that.* **2.** *Archaic* Unless. [< OF *sauf* being excepted, orig., safe < L *salvus*]

sav·ing (sā/ving) *adj.* **1.** That saves; preserving, as from destruction. **2.** Redeeming; delivering. **3.** Avoiding needless waste or expense; economical; frugal. **4.** Incurring no loss, if not gainful: a *saving* investment. **5.** Holding in reserve; making an exception; qualifying: a *saving* clause. — *n.* **1.** Preservation from loss or danger. **2.** Avoidance of waste; economy. **3.** The extent of something saved: a *saving* of 16 percent. **4.** *pl.* Sums of money not expended. **5.** That which is saved. — *prep.* **1.** With the exception of; save. **2.** With due respect for: *saving* your presence. — *conj.* Save; but. — **sav/ing·ly** *adv.* — **sav/ing·ness** *n.*

savings account An account drawing interest at a bank.

savings bank 1. A bank whose chief functions are receiving and investing savings and paying interest on deposits. **2.** A container with a slot for depositing coins.

sav·ior (sāv/yər) *n.* One who saves. Also *Brit.* **sav/iour.** [< OF < LL < L *salvare* to save]

Sav·iour (sāv/yər) *n.* A title sometimes applied directly to God, but chiefly to Jesus Christ, as the Redeemer: usu. with *the.* Also **Sav/ior.**

sa·voir-faire (sà·vwär·fâr/) *French* Ability to say and do the right thing; tact; literally, to know how to act.

sa·vor (sā/vər) *n.* **1.** The quality of a thing that affects the sense of taste or smell, or both; flavor; odor. **2.** Specific or characteristic quality or approach to a quality; flavor. **3.** Relish; zest: The conversation had *savor.* — *v.i.* **1.** To have a specified savor; taste or smell: with *of*. **2.** To have a specified quality or character: with *of*. — *v.t.* **3.** To give flavor to; season. **4.** To taste or enjoy with pleasure; relish. **5.** To have the savor or character of. Also *Brit.* **sa'vour.** [< OF < L < *sapere* to taste, know] — **sa'vor·er** *n.* — **sa'·vor·ous** *adj.*

sa·vor·less (sā'vər·lis) *adj.* Tasteless; insipid.

sa·vor·y[1] (sā'vər·ē) *adj.* **1.** Of an agreeable taste and odor; appetizing. **2.** Piquant to the taste. **3.** In good repute; respectable. — *n. Brit.* A small, hot serving of food eaten at the end or beginning of a dinner. Also *Brit.* **sa'vour·y.** [< OF *savouré*, pp. of *savourer* to taste] — **sa'vor·i·ly** *adv.* — **sa'vor·i·ness** *n.*

sa·vor·y[2] (sā'vər·ē) *n.* A hardy, annual, aromatic herb of the mint family, used for seasoning. Also **summer savory.** [OE < L *satureia*]

sa·voy (sə·voi') *n.* A variety of cabbage with wrinkled leaves. [< F (*chou de*) *Savoie* (cabbage of) Savoy]

Sa·voy·ard (sə·voi'ərd, *Fr.* sȧ·vwȧ·yȧr') *n.* **1.** An actor or actress in the Gilbert and Sullivan operas. **2.** An admirer of these operas. [after the *Savoy* Theater in London]

sav·vy (sav'ē) *Slang v.i.* **·vied, ·vy·ing** To understand; comprehend. — *n.* Understanding; good sense. [Alter. of Sp. *¿ Sabe* (*usted*)? Do (you) know? < L *sapere* to know]

saw[1] (sô) *n.* **1.** A cutting instrument with pointed teeth arranged continuously along the edge of the blade, used to cut or divide wood, bone, metal, etc. **2.** A machine for operating a saw or gang of saws. **3.** Any tool or instrument without teeth used like a saw. — *v.* **sawed, sawed** or **sawn, saw·ing** *v.t.* **1.** To cut or divide with a saw. **2.** To shape or fashion with a saw. **3.** To cut or slice (the air, etc.) as if using a saw. **4.** To cause to move with a to-and-fro motion like that of a saw. — *v.i.* **5.** To use a saw. **6.** To cut: said of a saw. **7.** To be cut with a saw: This wood *saws* easily. [OE *sagu*] — **saw'er** *n.*

saw[2] (sô) *n.* A proverbial or familiar saying; old maxim. — **Syn.** See PROVERB. [OE *sagu*]

saw[3] (sô) Past tense of SEE[1].

saw·bones (sô'bōnz') *n. Slang* A surgeon.

saw·buck (sô'buk') *n.* **1.** A sawhorse consisting of two X-shaped ends joined by a connecting bar or bars. **2.** *U.S. Slang* A ten-dollar bill: so called from the resemblance of X, Roman numeral ten, to the ends of a sawbuck. [Trans. of Du. *zaagbok*]

saw·dust (sô'dust') *n.* Small particles of wood produced by the action of sawing.

sawed-off (sôd'ôf', -of') *adj.* **1.** Having one end sawed off, as a shotgun. **2.** *U.S. Slang* Short; not of average height.

saw·fish (sô'fish') *n. pl.* **·fish** or **·fish·es** Any of various elongate, sharklike tropical fish with the snout prolonged into a flat blade with teeth on each edge.

saw·fly (sô'flī') *n. pl.* **·flies** Any of various winged insects having in the female a sawlike ovipositor for piercing plants, soft wood, etc.

saw·horse (sô'hôrs') *n.* A frame on which to rest wood, etc., for sawing, usu. consisting of a long wooden bar or plank supported by four extended legs.

saw log A log of suitable size for sawing.

saw·mill (sô'mil') *n.* **1.** An establishment for sawing logs with power-driven machinery. **2.** A large sawing machine.

sawn (sôn) Alternative past participle of SAW[1].

saw-toothed (sô'tōōtht') *adj.* Serrate; having teeth or toothlike processes similar to those of a saw.

saw·yer (sô'yər) *n.* **1.** One whose occupation is the sawing of wood, as in lumbering or in a sawmill. **2.** Any of various longicorn beetles having larvae that bore into wood, as the **pine sawyer.** [Alter. of SAWER]

sax (saks) *n. Informal* A saxophone.

sax·horn (saks'hôrn') *n.* Any of a family of valved brass instruments resembling the bugle, made in a wide series of ranges. [after the inventor, Antoine Joseph *Sax* (called Adolphe), 1814–94, Belgian instrument maker + HORN]

sax·i·frage (sak'sə·frij) *n.* Any of a large, widely distributed genus of herbaceous plants growing in rocky places, bearing small white, yellow, or purplish flowers. [< OF < L (*herba*) *saxifraga*, lit., stone-breaking (herb)]

Sax·on (sak'sən) *n.* **1.** A member of a Germanic tribal group formerly inhabiting what is now Schleswig-Holstein. **2.** A member of any of the offshoots of this group, as those who, with the Angles and Jutes, invaded England in the fifth and sixth centuries A.D. **3.** An Anglo-Saxon. **4.** An inhabitant of Saxony. **5.** The modern High German dialect of Saxony. — **Old Saxon** The dialect of Low German current in the valley of the lower Elbe in the early Middle Ages. — *adj.* **1.** Of or pertaining to the Saxons or to their language. **2.** Anglo-Saxon; English. **3.** Of or pertaining to Saxony, Germany. [< F < L *Saxo, Saxonis* < WGmc.]

sax·o·phone (sak'sə·fōn) *n.* Any of a family of metal wind instruments having a single reed and conical bore, made in a wide series of ranges. [after A. J. *Sax* (see SAXHORN) + -PHONE] — **sax'o·phon'ist** *n.*

say (sā) *v.* **said, say·ing** *v.t.* **1.** To pronounce or utter; speak. **2.** To declare or express in words; tell; state. **3.** To state positively or as an opinion: *Say* which you prefer. **4.** To recite: to *say* one's prayers. **5.** To report; allege. **6.** To assume; suppose. — *v.i.* **7.** To make a statement; speak. — **that is to say** In other words. — *adv.* **1.** Approximately; at a guess: He is worth, *say*, a million. **2.** For example: Choose a number, *say*, ten. — *n.* **1.** What one has said or has to say; word. **2.** Right or turn to speak or choose: to have one's *say*. **3.** Authority: to have the *say*. — *interj. U.S. Informal* A hail or an exclamation to command attention: also *Brit.* **I say.** [OE *secgan*] — **say'er** *n.*

say·ing (sā'ing) *n.* **1.** A maxim; adage. **2.** Something said.

says (sez) Third person singular, present indicative of SAY.

say-so (sā'sō') *n. Informal* **1.** An unsupported assertion or decision. **2.** Right or power to make decisions.

scab (skab) *n.* **1.** A crust formed on the surface of a wound or sore. **2.** *Vet.* Scabies. **3.** Any of certain plant diseases characterized by a roughened or warty appearance. **4.** *Slang* A mean, contemptible fellow. **5.** *Informal* A workman who will not join or act with a labor union; esp., a strikebreaker. — *v.i.* **scabbed, scab·bing** **1.** To form or become covered with a scab. **2.** *Informal* To take the job of a striker. [Fusion of ON *skabbr* (assumed) and OE *sceabb*]

scab·bard (skab'ərd) *n.* A sheath for a weapon, as for a bayonet or a sword. — *v.t.* To sheathe in or furnish with a scabbard. [< OF *escalberc*, prob. < OHG *scar* sword + *bergan* to hide, protect]

scab·by (skab'ē) *adj.* **·bi·er, ·bi·est** **1.** Having, consisting of, or resembling a scab or scabs. **2.** Having scabies. **3.** *Informal* Contemptible. — **scab'bi·ly** *adv.* — **scab'bi·ness** *n.*

sca·bies (skā'bi·ēz, -bēz) *n.* **1.** A skin disease caused by the itch mite; itch. **2.** *Vet.* A similar skin disease of sheep: also called *scab*. [< L, roughness, an itch < *scabere* to scratch, scrape.] — **sca·bi·et·ic** (skā'bē·et'ik) *adj.*

sca·bi·ous[1] (skā'bē·əs) *adj.* **1.** Pertaining to or resembling scabies. **2.** Having scabs.

sca·bi·ous[2] (skā'bē·əs) *n.* Any of a genus of herbs allied to the teasel, with heads of variously colored flowers. Also **sca·bi·o'sa** (-ō'sə). [< NL < Med.L (*herba*) *scabiosa*, fem. sing. of *scabiosus* scabious[1]]

sca·brous (skab'rəs, skā'brəs) *adj.* **1.** Roughened with minute points; scurfy. **2.** Off-color; risqué. **3.** Difficult to handle tactfully; knotty. [< LL < *scabere* to scratch] — **sca'·brous·ly** *adv.* — **sca'brous·ness** *n.*

scads (skadz) *n.pl. Informal* A large amount or quantity. [? Var. of dial E *scald* a large amount, great number]

scaf·fold (skaf'əld, -ōld) *n.* **1.** A temporary elevated structure for the support of workmen, materials, etc., as in building. **2.** Any raised wooden framework. **3.** A platform for the execution of criminals. — *v.t.* To furnish or support with a scaffold. [< OF (*e*)*schaffaut*]

scaf·fold·ing (skaf'əl·ding) *n.* A scaffold, or system of scaffolds, or the materials for constructing them. Also **scaf·fold·age** (skaf'əl·dij).

sca·lar (skā'lər) *Math. adj.* Definable by a number on a line or scale: said of a quantity having magnitude only, as a volume or mass: distinguished from *vector*. [< L < *scala* ladder]

scal·a·wag (skal'ə·wag) *n.* **1.** *Informal* A worthless fellow; scamp. **2.** *U.S.* During the Reconstruction period, a native Southern white Republican: a contemptuous term. Also called *scallywag*: also spelled *scallawag*. [Origin uncertain]

scald (skôld) *v.t.* **1.** To burn with or as with hot liquid or steam. **2.** To cleanse or treat with boiling water. **3.** To heat (a liquid) to a point just short of boiling. — *v.i.* **4.** To be or become scalded. — *n.* **1.** A burn or injury to the skin by a hot fluid. **2.** A destructive parasitic disease of plants. **3.** A discoloration of plant tissue due to improper conditions of growth, storage, etc. [< AF < LL < L < *ex-* very + *calidus* hot]

scale[1] (skāl) *n.* **1.** One of the thin, flat, horny, membranous or bony outgrowths of the skin of various animals, as most fishes, usu. overlapping and forming a nearly complete covering. **2.** Any similar thin, flat formation, piece, or part. **3.** A scab. **4.** A scale insect. **5.** *Bot.* A rudimentary or metamorphosed leaf, as of a pine cone. **6.** *Metall.* The coating of oxide that forms on heated iron, etc. **7.** An incrustation formed on the inside of boilers, etc. — *v.* **scaled, scal·ing** *v.t.* **1.** To strip or clear of scales. **2.** To form scales on. **3.** To take off in layers. — *v.i.* **4.** To come off in scales; peel. **5.** To shed scales. **6.** To become incrusted with scales. [< OF *escale* husk < Gmc.] — **scal'er** *n.*

scale[2] (skāl) *n.* **1.** Any instrument bearing accurately spaced lines or gradations for use in measurement. **2.** The series of marks so used. **3.** Any system of designating units of measurement: the Fahrenheit *scale*. **4.** A fixed proportion used in determining measurements or dimensions: a *scale* of one inch to the mile. **5.** Any progressive or graded classification: wage *scale*. **6.** Relative proportion, degree, scope, etc.: with *on*: to live on a grand *scale*. **7.** *Math.* A system of notation in which the successive places determine the value of the figures: the decimal *scale.* **8.** *Music* An arrangement of tones in ascending or descending order through the interval of an octave: a diatonic *scale.* **— major scale** *Music* A scale having semitones after the third and seventh steps, all the other intervals being whole tones. **— minor scale** A scale having semitones after the second and fifth steps (the natural form), or after the second, fifth, and seventh steps (the harmonic form), or after the second and seventh steps when ascending and the sixth and third when descending (the melodic form), all the other intervals being whole tones. **—** *v.* **scaled, scal·ing** *v.t.* **1.** To climb to the top of. **2.** To make according to a scale. **3.** To regulate or adjust according to a scale or ratio: with *up, down,* etc. **—** *v.i.* **4.** To climb; ascend. **5.** To rise in steps or stages. [< Ital. < *scala* to climb] **— scal′a·ble** *adj.* **— scal′er** *n.*

scale³ (skāl) *n.* **1.** Any weighing machine. **2.** A pan, scoop, platform, etc., that holds the object or material to be weighed in a weighing instrument or balance. **3.** *Usu. pl.* A balance (defs. 1 & 2). **— to turn the scales** To determine; decide. **—** *v.* **scaled, scal·ing** *v.t.* **1.** To weigh in scales. **2.** To amount to in weight. **—** *v.i.* **3.** To be weighed. [< ON *skāl* bowl, in pl., a weighing balance]

scale insect One of numerous small insects that feed on plants and as adults have a scalelike, protective shield.

sca·lene (skā′lēn, skā·lēn′) *adj. Geom.* Designating a triangle having no two sides equal. [< LL < Gk. *skalēnos* uneven]

Scales (skālz) *n.pl.* The constellation and sign of the zodiac Libra.

scal·la·wag (skal′ə·wag) See SCALAWAG.

scal·lion (skal′yən) *n.* **1.** A young, tender onion with a small white bulb. **2.** A shallot or leek. [< OF < L (*caepa*) *Ascalonia* (onion) of Ashkelon, a Palestinian seaport]

scal·lop (skal′əp, skol′-) *n.* **1.** A bivalve mollusk having a rounded, ridged shell whose valves are snapped together in swimming. **2.** The edible adductor muscle of certain species of this mollusk. **3.** The shell of a scallop; esp., one in which seafood is cooked or served. **4.** One of a series of semicircular curves along an edge, as for ornament. **—** *v.t.* **1.** To shape the edge of with scallops. **2.** To bake (food) in a casserole with a sauce, often topped with bread crumbs. Also spelled *escallop, scollop.* [< OF *escalope* < Gmc.] **— scal′lop·er** *n.*

SCALLOP SHELL

scal·ly·wag (skal′ē·wag) *n.* A scalawag.

scalp (skalp) *n.* **1.** The skin of the top and back of the human skull, usu. covered with hair. A portion of this, formerly cut or torn away as a war trophy among certain North American Indians. **—** *v.t.* **1.** To cut or tear the scalp from. **2.** *Informal* To buy and resell (tickets) at prices exceeding the established rate. **3.** *Informal* To buy and sell again quickly in order to make a small profit. **4.** *Informal* To defeat utterly. **—** *v.i.* **5.** *Informal* To scalp bonds, tickets, etc. [ME, prob. < Scand.] **— scalp′er** *n.*

scal·pel (skal′pəl) *n.* A small pointed knife with a very sharp, thin blade, used in dissections and in surgery. [< L *scalpere* to cut]

scal·y (skā′lē) *adj.* **scal·i·er, scal·i·est** Having, resembling, or incrusted with scales. **— scal′i·ness** *n.*

scaly anteater A pangolin.

scamp¹ (skamp) *n.* A confirmed rogue; good-for-nothing fellow; rascal. [< obs. verb *scamp* to roam, contr. of SCAMPER] **— scamp′ish** *adj.*

scamp² (skamp) *v.t.* To perform (work) carelessly or dishonestly. [Orig. dial. E] **— scamp′er** *n.*

scam·per (skam′pər) *v.i.* To run quickly or hastily. **—** *n.* A hurried run or departure. [< OF, ult. < L *ex* out from + *campus* plain, battlefield] **— scam′per·er** *n.*

scan (skan) *v.* **scanned, scan·ning** *v.t.* **1.** To examine in detail; scrutinize closely. **2.** To pass the eyes over quickly; glance at. **3.** To separate (verse) into metrical feet; ascertain or indicate the rhythm of. **4.** *Telecom.* To pass a beam of light or electrons rapidly over every point of (a surface, etc.) for television, sound, or other reproduction. **—** *v.i.* **5.** To scan verse. **6.** To conform to metrical rules: said of verse. [< LL < L *scandere* climb] **— scan′na·ble** *adj.* **— scan′ner** *n.*

scan·dal (skan′dəl) *n.* **1.** Heedless or malicious gossip. **2.** Disgrace or reproach caused by outrageous or improper conduct. **3.** A discreditable circumstance, event, or action. **4.** Censure or open disapproval. **5.** One whose conduct results in disgrace or censure. [< AF < L < Gk. *skandalon* snare]

scan·dal·ize (skan′dəl·īz) *v.t.* **·ized, ·iz·ing** To shock the moral feelings of, as by improper, frivolous, or offensive conduct; outrage. **— scan′dal·i·za′tion** *n.* **— scan′dal·iz′er** *n.*

scan·dal·mon·ger (skan′dəl·mung′gər, -mong′-) *n.* One who spreads or repeats scandal.

scan·dal·ous (skan′dəl·əs) *adj.* **1.** Causing or tending to cause scandal; disgraceful. **2.** Consisting of or spreading scandal. **— scan′dal·ous·ly** *adv.* **— scan′dal·ous·ness** *n.*

Scan·di·na·vi·an (skan′də·nā′vē·ən) *adj.* Of or pertaining to Scandinavia, its people, or their languages. **—** *n.* **1.** A native or inhabitant of Scandinavia. **2.** The North Germanic group of languages: see under GERMANIC. Also *Norse.* **— Old Scandinavian** Old Norse. See under NORSE.

scan·di·um (skan′dē·əm) *n.* A metallic element (symbol Sc) of the lanthanide series. See ELEMENT. [< NL < L *Scandia* Scandinavia]

scan·sion (skan′shən) *n.* The division or analysis of lines of verse according to a metrical pattern. Compare METER² (def. 1). [< F < LL < L *scandere* scan]

scant (skant) *adj.* **1.** Scarcely enough; meager in measure or quantity. **2.** Being just short of the measure specified: a *scant* half-hour; a *scant* five yards. **3.** Insufficiently supplied with: with *of:* We were *scant* of breath. **—** *v.t.* **1.** To restrict or limit in supply; stint. **2.** To treat briefly or inadequately. **—** *adv. Dial.* Scarcely; barely. [< ON *skammr* short] **— scant′ly** *adv.* **— scant′ness** *n.*

scant·ling (skant′ling) *n.* **1.** A piece of lumber of small or moderate cross section, used for studding, etc. **2.** Such lumber collectively. [< OF *eschantillon* cornerpiece]

scant·y (skan′tē) *adj.* **scant·i·er, scant·i·est 1.** Limited in extent. **2.** Restricted in quantity or amount; scarcely sufficient; meager. **— scant′i·ly** *adv.* **— scant′i·ness** *n.*

scape (skāp) *Archaic v.t. & v.i.* To escape. **—** *n.* An escape or means of escape. Also **'scape.**

scape·goat (skāp′gōt′) *n.* **1.** In the Bible, the goat upon whose head the high priest symbolically laid the sins of the people on the day of atonement, after which it was led away into the wilderness. *Lev.* xvi. **2.** An animal, person, or group that bears the blame or suffers for the errors or sins of others.

scape·grace (skāp′grās′) *n.* A mischievous or incorrigible person; rogue.

scapi- *combining form* A stalk, stem, or shaft. [< L *scapus* stalk]

scap·u·la (skap′yə·lə) *n. pl.* **·lae** (-lē) *Anat.* Either of a pair of large, flat, triangular bones in the back of the shoulder in man and having an analogous position in the skeleton of vertebrates: also called *shoulder blade.* [< LL < L *scapulae* shoulder blades]

scap·u·lar (skap′yə·lər) *n.* **1.** An outer garment consisting of two strips of cloth joined across the shoulders, worn by members of certain religious orders. **2.** A badge or sign of devotion worn about the neck by members of certain religious orders and groups. **3.** *pl. Ornithol.* The shoulder feathers of a bird. **—** *adj.* Of or pertaining to the scapula.

scap·u·lar·y (skap′yə·ler′ē) *n. pl.* **·ries** A scapular. **—** *adj.* Scapular.

scar (skär) *n.* **1.** The mark left on the skin after the healing of a wound or sore. **2.** Any mark, damage, or lasting effect resulting from past injury, stress, etc. **—** *v.t. & v.i.* **scarred, scar·ring** To mark or become marked with a scar. [< OF < L *eschara* scab < Gk.]

scar·ab (skar′əb) *n.* **1.** A large, black beetle held sacred by the ancient Egyptians. **2.** A gem or ornament representing this beetle. [< MF < L *scarabaeus*]

scar·a·bae·us (skar′ə·bē′əs) *n. pl.* **·bae·us·es** or **·bae·i** (-bē′ī) A scarab. [< L]

scar·a·mouch (skar′ə·mouch, -mōōsh) *n.* A swaggering rascal. [< *Scaramouch*]

Scar·a·mouch (skar′ə·mouch, -mōōsh) In old Italian comedy, a stock character represented as a boastful, cowardly buffoon. [< F < Ital. *Scaramuccia,* lit., skirmish]

scarce (skârs) *adj.* **scarc·er, scarc·est 1.** Rarely seen or found. **2.** Not plentiful; insufficient. **— to make oneself scarce** *Informal* To go away or stay away. [< OF, ult. < L < *ex-* out + *carpere* to pluck] **— scarce′ness** *n.*

scarce·ly (skârs′lē) *adv.* **1.** Only just; barely. **2.** Not quite; hardly.

scar·ci·ty (skâr′sə·tē) *n. pl.* **·ties 1.** Inadequate supply; insufficiency; dearth. **2.** Infrequency of occurrence; rarity.

scare (skâr) *v.* **scared, scar·ing** *v.t.* **1.** To strike with sudden fear; frighten. **2.** To drive or force by frightening: with *off* or *away.* **—** *v.i.* **3.** To become scared. **— to scare up** *Informal* To get together or produce hurriedly. **—** *n.* **1.** Sudden fright, esp. from slight cause. **2.** Panic. [< ON < *skiarr* shy] **— scar′er** *n.* **— scar′ing·ly** *adv.*

scare·crow (skâr′krō′) *n.* **1.** Any effigy set up to scare crows and other birds away from growing crops. **2.** Something frightening but not dangerous. **3.** A person of ragged or disreputable appearance.

scare·head (skâr′hed′) *n. Informal* An exceptionally large newspaper headline giving news of sensational interest.

scarf¹ (skärf) *n. pl.* **scarfs** or **scarves** (skärvz) **1.** A band or square of cloth worn about the head, neck, etc., for warmth or protection, or as a decorative accessory. **2.** A necktie, cravat, kerchief, etc. **3.** A runner for a bureau or dresser. **4.** An official sash denoting rank. — *v.t.* To cover or decorate with or as with a scarf. [< OF *escharpe*]

scarf² (skärf) *n. pl.* **scarfs 1.** In carpentry, a lapped joint made by notching two timbers at the ends and joining them so as to form one continuous piece. Also **scarf joint. 2.** The notched end of a timber so cut. — *v.t.* **1.** To unite with a scarf joint. **2.** To cut a scarf in. [? < ON *skarfr* notch in a timber]

SCARF JOINTS

scar·i·fy (skar′ə·fī) *v.t.* **·fied, ·fy·ing 1.** To scratch or make slight incisions in, as the skin in surgery. **2.** To criticize severely. **3.** To stir or break up the surface of, as soil. [< MF < LL < Gk. < *skariphos* stylus] — **scar′i·fi′er** *n.* — **scar′i·fi·ca′tion** *n.*

scar·la·ti·na (skär′lə·tē′nə) *n. Pathol.* **1.** Scarlet fever. **2.** A mild form of scarlet fever. [< Ital. See SCARLET.]

scar·let (skär′lit) *n.* **1.** A brilliant red, inclining to orange. **2.** Cloth or clothing of this color. — *adj.* **1.** Being scarlet in color. **2.** Unchaste; whorish. [< OF < Med.L, prob. < Arabic < Persian *saqalāt* a rich, scarlet cloth]

scarlet fever *Pathol.* An acute infectious bacterial disease characterized by a diffused scarlet rash.

scarlet runner A tall climbing bean of tropical America, having vividly red flowers and long seed pods.

scarlet tanager An American tanager, the male of which has brilliant red plumage with black wings and tail.

scarp (skärp) *n.* **1.** A steep slope. **2.** An embankment or wall at the outer part of a fortification. — *v.t.* To cut or form to a steep slope. [< AF < Ital. *scarpa*]

scarves (skärvz) Alternative plural of SCARF¹.

scar·y (skâr′ē) *adj.* **scar·i·er, scar·i·est** *Informal* **1.** Easily scared; timid. **2.** Causing fear or alarm; frightening.

scat (skat) *v.i.* **scat·ted, scat·ting** *Informal* To go away; depart: usu. in the imperative. [? < SCATTER]

scathe (skāth) *v.t.* **scathed, scath·ing 1.** To criticize severely. **2.** To injure severely; harm. — *n.* Severe injury; harm. [< ON < *skathi* to harm] — **scathe′ful** *adj.*

scathe·less (skāth′lis) *adj.* Free from harm.

scath·ing (skā′thing) *adj.* Mercilessly severe; blasting; withering: a *scathing* rebuke. — **scath′ing·ly** *adv.*

scato- *combining form* Dung; excrement. [< Gk. *skōr* dung]

scat·o·log·i·cal (skat′ə·loj′i·kəl) *adj.* Of or pertaining to scatology; obscene. Also **scat′o·log′ic.**

sca·tol·o·gy (skə·tol′ə·jē) *n.* The study of, or a preoccupation with, excrement. — **sca·tol′o·gist** *n.*

scat·ter (skat′ər) *v.t.* **1.** To throw about in various places; sprinkle. **2.** To separate and drive away in different directions; disperse. — *v.i.* **3.** To separate and go in different directions. [ME *scateren* to squander] — **scat′ter·er** *n.*

scat·ter·brain (skat′ər·brān′) *n.* A flighty or forgetful person. — **scat′ter·brained′** *adj.*

scatter rug A small rug used to cover only part of a floor.

scaup (skôp) *n.* A sea duck of northern regions, having the head and neck black in the male. [Var. of SCALP]

scav·enge (skav′inj) *v.* **·enged, ·eng·ing** *v.t.* **1.** To remove filth, rubbish, and refuse from, as streets. — *v.i.* **2.** To act as a scavenger. **3.** To search or rummage, as for food. [Back formation < SCAVENGER]

scav·en·ger (skav′in·jər) *n.* **1.** An animal that feeds on carrion, as the buzzard. **2.** One who searches refuse, garbage, etc., for usable material. **3.** A street cleaner. [ME < AF < Flemish *scauwen* to see]

sce·nar·i·o (si·nâr′ē·ō, -nä′rē·ō) *n. pl.* **·nar·i·os 1.** A summary or outline of the plot of a dramatic work. **2.** The written plot and arrangement of incidents of a motion picture. **3.** An outline or plan of a projected series of actions or events. [< Ital. < LL < L < Gk. *skēnē* tent, stage]

sce·nar·ist (si·nâr′ist, -nä′rist) *n.* One who writes scenarios.

scene (sēn) *n.* **1.** A locality as presented to view. **2.** The place in which the action of a drama is supposed to occur; setting. **3.** The place and surroundings of any event: the *scene* of the crime. **4.** A division of an act of a play; one comprehensive event in a play. **5.** Any incident or episode that may serve as the subject of a description. **6.** The painted canvas screens for the background for a play. **7.** Any striking display; esp., a display of excited feeling. **8.** *Slang* A place or realm of a currently popular activity: the pop music *scene*. — **behind the scenes 1.** Out of sight of a theater audience. **2.** Privately; in secret. [< OF < L < Gk. *skēnē* tent, stage]

scen·er·y (sē′nər·ē) *n. pl.* **·er·ies 1.** The appearance or visible aspects of a landscape, locality, etc. **2.** The settings, backdrops, etc., of a theatrical production.

sce·nic (sē′nik, sen′ik) *adj.* **1.** Of or pertaining to natural scenery; picturesque. **2.** Relating to stage scenery. Also **sce′ni·cal.** — **sce′ni·cal·ly** *adv.*

scent (sent) *n.* **1.** A distinctive odor. **2.** A residual odor by which an animal can be tracked. **3.** A trail, trace, or clue aiding pursuit or investigation. **4.** A perfume. **5.** The sense of smell. — **Syn.** See SMELL. — *v.t.* **1.** To perceive by the sense of smell. **2.** To form a suspicion of. **3.** To cause to be fragrant; perfume. — *v.i.* **4.** To hunt by the sense of smell: said of hounds. [< OF *sentir* to discern by the senses, feel] — **scent′less** *adj.*

scep·ter (sep′tər) *n.* **1.** A staff carried as the badge of command or sovereignty. **2.** Kingly office or power. — *v.t.* To confer the scepter on; invest with royal power. Also *esp. Brit.* **scep′tre** (-tər). [< OF < L < Gk. *skēptron* staff]

scep·tic (skep′tik), **scep·ti·cal**, etc. See SKEPTIC, etc.

sched·ule (skej′ool, -əl, -ōō·əl; *Brit.* shed′yool) *n.* **1.** A written or printed statement specifying the details of some matter. **2.** A list; catalogue. **3.** A timetable, as for a transportation service. **4.** A detailed and timed plan; program. — *v.t.* **·uled, ·ul·ing 1.** To place in or on a schedule. **2.** To make a schedule of. **3.** To appoint or plan for a specified time or date. [ME < OF < LL < L *scida, scheda* leaf of paper]

sche·ma (skē′mə) *n. pl.* **·ma·ta** (-mə·tə) **1.** A scheme or summary. **2.** A plan or diagram, of a process, organization, etc. [< Gk. See SCHEME.] — **sche·mat′ic** (skē·mat′ik) or **·i·cal** *adj.* — **sche·mat′i·cal·ly** *adv.*

sche·ma·tize (skē′mə·tīz) *v.t.* **·tized, ·tiz·ing** To form into or arrange according to a scheme or schema.

scheme (skēm) *n.* **1.** A plan of something to be done; a plot or device for the accomplishment of an object. **2.** A systematic arrangement, plan, or design. **3.** A secret or underhand plot or plan. **4.** An outline drawing or sketch; diagram. — *v.* **schemed, schem·ing** *v.t.* **1.** To make a scheme for; plan. **2.** To plan or plot in an underhand manner. — *v.i.* **3.** To make schemes; plan or plot. [< L < Gk. *schēma, -atos* a form, plan] — **schem′er** *n.*

scher·zan·do (sker·tsän′dō) *Music adv.* In a sportive or playful manner. — *adj.* Sportive; playful. [See SCHERZO.]

scher·zo (sker′tsō) *n. pl.* **·zos** or **·zi** (-tsē) *Music* A playful or satirical movement, often following a slow movement, as in a symphony or sonata. [< Ital., a jest < G *scherz*]

Schick test (shik) A test to determine the susceptibility of a person to diphtheria by the subcutaneous injection of a diluted diphtheria toxin. [after Dr. Béla *Schick*, born 1877]

schil·ling (shil′ing) *n.* **1.** The standard monetary unit of Austria: in 1960 worth about 4 U.S. cents; also, a coin of this value. **2.** Formerly, a minor coin of Germany. [< G]

schism (siz′əm) *n.* **1.** A division of a church or other organized body into factions. **2.** The offense of causing such division. **3.** Any group, esp., an ecclesiastical one, separated from a larger body. [< OF < LL < Gk. *schizein* to split] — **schis·mat′ic** (siz·mat′ik) *adj.*

schist (shist) *n. Geol.* Any rock that readily splits or cleaves into parallel layers: also spelled **shist.** [< F < L < Gk. < *schizein* to split] — **schist′ous, schist·ose** (shis′tōs) *adj.*

schizo- *combining form* Split; divided. Also, before vowels, **schiz-.** [< Gk. *schizein* to split]

schiz·o·carp (skiz′ə·kärp) *n. Bot.* A pericarp splitting at maturity into two or more one-seeded indehiscent portions. — **schiz′o·car′pous, schiz′o·car′pic** *adj.*

schiz·oid (skit′soid, skiz′oid) *Psychiatry n.* One who is abnormally shy and withdrawn. — *adj.* **1.** Of, pertaining to, or like a schizoid. **2.** Of or pertaining to schizophrenia.

schiz·o·phre·ni·a (skit′sō·frē′nē·ə, skiz′ō-) *n. Psychiatry* Any of a group of psychotic disorders characterized by delusions, withdrawal, conflicting emotions, and deterioration of the personality. [< NL < Gk. *schizein* to split + *phrēn* mind] — **schiz′o·phren′ic** (-fren′ik) *adj. & n.*

schle·miel (shlə·mēl′) *n. Slang* An inept, easily duped person; a bungler; dolt. Also **schle·mihl′.** [< Yiddish < Hebrew *Shelumiēl*, a personal name]

schlep (shlep) *Slang v.* **schlepped, schlep·ping** *v.t.* **1.** To drag awkwardly; lug. — *v.i.* **2.** To drag something awkwardly. **3.** To proceed wearily or heavily. — *n.* **1.** A difficult journey. **2.** A stupid, awkward person. Also **schlepp.** [< Yiddish *shleppen* to drag] — **schlep′per** *n.*

schlock (shlok) *Slang n.* Shoddy, inferior merchandise. — *adj.* Of inferior quality. [< Yiddish] — **schlock′y** *adj.*

schnapps (shnäps, shnaps) *n. pl.* **schnapps** Any strong liquor, esp. a type of gin. Also **schnaps.** [< G, < Du. *snaps* gulp, mouthful]

schnau·zer (shnou′zər) *n.* A terrier originally developed in Germany, having a wiry, black or pepper-and-salt coat. [< G *Schnauze* snout]

schol·ar (skol′ər) *n.* **1.** A person eminent for learning, esp. in the humanities. **2.** One who does authoritative research and writing in some special field. **3.** The holder of a scholarship. **4.** A pupil. [See SCHOOL¹.]

schol·ar·ly (skol′ər·lē) *adj.* **1.** Of or befitting a scholar: *scholarly* methods. **2.** Having the qualities of a scholar. — *adv.* After the manner of a scholar.

schol·ar·ship (skol′ər·ship) *n.* **1.** The mental attainments and qualities of a scholar; learning; erudition. **2.** Scholarly inquiry or research. **3.** Maintenance or a stipend awarded to a student; also, the position of such a student.

scho·las·tic (skŏ·las′tik, skə-) *adj.* **1.** Of, or characteristic of scholars, education, or schools. **2.** Of, or characteristic of the medieval schoolmen. **3.** Precise; pedantic. Also **scho·las′ti·cal.** — *n.* **1.** *Often cap.* An advocate of scholasticism. **2.** A pedant. [< L < Gk. < *scholazein* to be at leisure, devote leisure to study] — **scho·las′ti·cal·ly** *adv.*

scho·las·ti·cism (skŏ·las′tə·siz′əm, skə-) *n.* **1.** *Often cap.* The systematized Christian logic, philosophy, and theology of medieval scholars. **2.** Any system of teaching that insists on traditional doctrines, etc.

school[1] (skōōl) *n.* **1.** Any institution devoted primarily to imparting knowledge or to developing certain skills or talents; esp., an educational institution for children. **2.** A place where formal instruction is given; a schoolhouse or schoolroom. **3.** A session or course of study at an educational institution. **4.** The pupils in an educational institution. **5.** A subdivision of a university: the *school* of medicine, law, etc. **6.** A body of disciples of a teacher or system; also, the system, methods, or opinions characteristic of those thus associated: a painting of the Flemish *school*. **7.** A general style of life, manners, etc.: a gentleman of the old *school*. **8.** Any sphere or means of instruction: the *school* of hard knocks. — *v.t.* **1.** To instruct in or as in a school; train; educate. **2.** To subject to rule or discipline. — **Syn.** See TEACH. [OE < L < Gk. *scholē* leisure, school]

school[2] (skōōl) *n.* A large number of fish, whales, etc., swimming together; shoal. — *v.i.* To swim together in a school. [< Du., a crowd, school of fishes]

school board A board of education.

school·book (skōōl′bŏŏk′) *n.* A book for use in school.

school·boy (skōōl′boi′) *n.* A boy attending school.

school·girl (skōōl′gûrl′) *n.* A girl attending school.

school·house (skōōl′hous′) *n.* A building in which a school is conducted.

school·ing (skōōl′ing) *n.* **1.** Instruction given at school. **2.** The process of teaching or being taught in a school.

school·man (skōōl′mən) *n.* *pl.* **·men** (-mən) One of the theologians of the Middle Ages; a scholastic.

school·marm (skōōl′märm′) *n.* *Informal* A woman schoolteacher. Also **school′ma′am′** (-mäm′).

school·mas·ter (skōōl′mas′tər, -mäs′-) *n.* **1.** A man who teaches in or directs a school. **2.** Anything that instructs or disciplines: Necessity was his *schoolmaster*.

school·mate (skōōl′māt′) *n.* A fellow pupil.

school·mis·tress (skōōl′mis′tris) *n.* A woman who teaches school.

school·room (skōōl′rōōm′, -rŏŏm′) *n.* A room in which classes are held or instruction is given.

school·teach·er (skōōl′tē′chər) *n.* One who gives instruction in a school below the college level.

school year The part of the year during which a school or the schools of an educational system are in session.

schoon·er (skōō′nər) *n.* **1.** A fore-and-aft rigged vessel having two or more masts. **2.** A large beer glass. [New England < dial. *scoon* to skim on water]

schot·tische (shot′ish) *n.* **1.** A round dance similar to the polka, but slower. **2.** Music for this dance, in duple meter. [< G (*der*) *schottische* (*tanz*) (the) Scottish (dance)]

schwa (shwä, shvä) *n.* *Phonet.* A weak, neutral vowel sound occurring in most of the unstressed syllables in English speech, as the *a* in *alone*, the *e* in *happen*, or the *u* in *circus*: written ə. [< G < Hebrew *shewa*]

SCHOONER
a Jib topsail. *b* Flying jib. *c* Jib. *d* Foresail. *e* Fore club topsail. *f* Maintopmast staysail. *g* Main club topsail. *h* Mainsail.

sci·at·ic (sī·at′ik) *adj.* Pertaining to or affecting the hip or its nerves. — *n.* A sciatic nerve or part. [< MF < Med.L < Gk. < *ischion* hip, hip joint]

sci·at·i·ca (sī·at′i·kə) *n.* *Pathol.* **1.** Neuralgia affecting the sciatic nerve. **2.** Any painful affection of the hip or adjoining areas. [See SCIATIC.]

sci·ence (sī′əns) *n.* **1.** Any department of knowledge in which the results of investigation have been logically arranged and systematized. **2.** Knowledge of facts, phenomena, laws, and proximate causes, gained and verified by exact observation, organized experiment, and ordered thinking. **3.** An orderly presentation of facts, reasonings, doctrines, and beliefs concerning some subject or group of subjects. **4.** Systematic knowledge in general. **5.** Expertness or skill resulting from knowledge. [< OF < L < *scire* to know]

science fiction Fiction in which facts or theories of contemporary science are imaginatively employed.

sci·en·tif·ic (sī′ən·tif′ik) *adj.* **1.** Of, discovered by, derived from, or used in science. **2.** Agreeing with the rules, principles, or methods of science; accurate; systematic; exact. **3.** Versed in science or a science; eminently learned or skillful. Also **sci′en·tif′i·cal.** [< LL < *scientia* knowledge + *facere* to make] — **sci′en·tif′i·cal·ly** *adv.*

sci·en·tist (sī′ən·tist) *n.* One versed in science or devoted to scientific study or investigation.

scil·i·cet (sil′ə·set) *adv.* Namely; to wit; that is to say. [< L *scire licet* it is permitted to know]

scim·i·tar (sim′ə·tər) *n.* A curved Oriental sword or saber. Also **scim′e·tar, scim′i·ter.** [< MF < Ital. *scimitarra*]

scin·til·la (sin·til′ə) *n.* A spark; trace; iota: a *scintilla* of truth. [< L]

scin·til·late (sin′tə·lāt) *v.* **·lat·ed, ·lat·ing** *v.i.* **1.** To give off sparks. **2.** To sparkle; glitter. **3.** To twinkle, as a star. — *v.t.* **4.** To give off as a spark or sparks. [< L *scintilla* spark] — **scin′til·lant** *adj.* — **scin′til·lat′ing·ly** *adv.* — **scin′til·la′tion** *n.*

sci·o·lism (sī′ə·liz′əm) *n.* Superficial knowledge; charlatanism. [< L *scius* < *scire* to know] — **sci′o·lis′tic** *adj.*

sci·on (sī′ən) *n.* **1.** A twig or shoot cut from a plant or tree, esp. for grafting. **2.** A child or descendant. [< OF < L *secare* to cut]

scis·sile (sis′il) *adj.* Capable of being cut or split easily and evenly. [< L *scindere* to cut]

scis·sion (sizh′ən, sish′-) *n.* **1.** The act of cutting or splitting, or the state of being cut. **2.** Any division. [< OF < LL < *scissus*, pp. of *scindere* to cut]

scis·sor (siz′ər) *v.t. & v.i.* To cut with scissors.

scis·sors (siz′ərz) *n.pl.* (*construed as sing. in defs. 2 & 3*) **1.** A cutting implement with handles and a pair of blades pivoted face to face so that the opposed edges may be brought together on the object to be cut. Also **pair of scissors. 2.** In wrestling, a hold secured by clasping the legs about the body or head of the opponent. **3.** A gymnastic feat in which the movement of the legs suggests that of scissors. [< OF < LL *cisoria*, pl. of *cisorium* cutting instrument]

scissors kick In swimming, a kick performed usu. with the side stroke, in which both legs are thrust apart, the upper leg bent at the knee while the lower is kept straight, then brought sharply together.

scis·sor·tail (siz′ər·tāl′) *n.* A flycatcher of the SW U.S. and Mexico, having a scissorlike tail.

scis·sure (sizh′ər, sish′-) *n.* **1.** A lengthwise cut; fissure. **2.** Any division, rupture, or schism. [See SCISSION.]

scle·ra (sklir′ə) *n.* *Anat.* The hard, white, fibrous outer coat of the eyeball, continuous with the cornea. For illus. see EYE. [< NL < Gk. *sklēros* hard]

scle·ren·chy·ma (sklə·reng′kə·mə) *n.* *Bot.* A tough, thick-walled tissue that protects and supports plants. [< NL < Gk. *sklēros* hard + *enchyma* infusion]

sclero- *combining form* Hardness; hard. Also, before vowels, **scler-.** [< Gk. *sklēros* hard]

scle·rosed (sklə·rōst′) *adj.* Affected with sclerosis; grown abnormally hard.

scle·ro·sis (sklə·rō′sis) *n.* *pl.* **·ses** (-sēz) **1.** *Pathol.* The thickening and hardening of a tissue or part. **2.** *Bot.* The hardening of a plant cell wall by the formation of lignin in it. [< Med.L < Gk. *sklēros* hard] — **scle·ro′sal** *adj.*

scle·rot·ic (sklə·rot′ik) *adj.* **1.** Dense; hard, as the sclera. **2.** Of or pertaining to the sclera. **3.** *Pathol.* Pertaining to or affected with sclerosis.

scle·rous (sklir′əs) *adj.* Hard or indurated; bony.

scoff (skôf, skof) *v.i.* **1.** To speak with contempt or derision; jeer: often with *at.* — *v.t.* **2.** To deride; mock. — *n.* An expression or an object of contempt or derision. [ME *scof*, prob. < Scand.] — **scoff′er** *n.* — **scoff′ing·ly** *adv.*

scoff·law (skôf′lô′, skof′-) *n.* One who scoffs at or flouts the law; esp., a habitual violator of traffic laws, etc.

scold (skōld) *v.t.* **1.** To find fault with harshly. — *v.i.* **2.** To find fault harshly or continuously. — *n.* One who scolds, esp. a shrewish woman. [Appar. < ON *skáld* poet, satirist] — **scold′er** *n.* — **scold′ing·ly** *adv.*

scol·lop (skol′əp), etc. See SCALLOP, etc.

scom·broid (skom′broid) *adj.* Of or pertaining to a widely distributed family of fishes, including mackerels. — *n.* A scombroid fish. [< NL < L < Gk. *skombros* mackerel]

sconce[1] (skons) *n.* **1.** A small earthwork or fort. **2.** A protective shelter, covering, or screen. [< Du. *schanz* fortress, wicker basket; infl. in form by SCONCE[2]]

sconce[2] (skons) *n.* An ornamental wall bracket for holding a candle or other light. [< OF < Med.L *sconsa* < L *abscondere* to hide]

scone (skōn, skon) *n.* A round tea cake or biscuit usu. eaten with butter. [? < MDu. *schoonbrot* fine bread]

scoop (skōōp) *n.* **1.** A shovellike instrument or large shovel with high sides. **2.** A small shovellike implement or ladle used by grocers, druggists, etc. **3.** An implement for bailing, as water from a boat. **4.** A spoon-shaped instrument for using in a cavity: a surgeons' *scoop.* **5.** An implement for dispensing uniform, spherical portions of ice cream, etc.; also, a portion thus dispensed. **6.** An act of scooping; a scooping movement. **7.** *Informal* A large gain, esp. in speculation. **8.** A bowl-shaped cavity. **9.** *Slang* In journalism, a news story obtained and published ahead of rival papers. **10.** *Slang* Any item of recent news. — *v.t.* **1.** To take or dip out with or as with a scoop. **2.** To hollow out, as with a scoop; excavate. **3.** To empty with a scoop. **4.** *Informal* To heap up or gather in or as in scoopfuls. **5.** *Slang* In journalism, to obtain and publish a news story before (a rival). [Fusion of MDu. *schope* vessel for bailing out water, and *schoppe* shovel] — **scoop'er** *n.*

scoot (skōōt) *v.i. Informal* To go quickly; dart off. — *n.* The act of scooting; a hurried darting off. [Prob. < Scand.]

scoot·er (skōō'tər) *n.* **1.** A child's vehicle consisting of a footboard mounted between two tandem wheels and steered by means of a long handle attached to the front axle. **2.** A motor scooter (which see). **3.** A sailboat with runners that may be used in water and on ice.

scope (skōp) *n.* **1.** Room for the exercise of faculties or function; capacity for achievement or effectiveness. **2.** Range of view or activity; outlook: a mind of limited *scope.* **3.** The area or sphere in which any activity takes place: the *scope* of a scientific work. **4.** *Naut.* The length or sweep of a cable at which a ship rides at anchor. **5.** *Informal* Any of various optical or detecting instruments, as a telescope. [< Ital. < L < Gk. < *skopeein* to look at]

-scope *combining form* An instrument for viewing, observing, or indicating: *telescope.* [< Gk. *skopeein* to watch]

sco·pol·a·mine (skō·pol'ə·mēn, -min, skō'pə·lam'ēn, -in) *n. Chem.* An alkaloid, $C_{17}H_{12}O_4N$, extracted from certain plants, the salts of which are used in medicine as a hypnotic and sedative. [< G < NL, after G. A. *Scopoli*, 1723–88, Italian naturalist]

-scopy *combining form* Observation; viewing: *microscopy.* [< Gk. < *skopeein* to watch]

scor·bu·tic (skôr·byōō'tik) *adj.* Relating to, characteristic of, or affected with scurvy: also **scor·bu'ti·cal.** [< NL < Med.L *scorbutus* scurvy] — **scor·bu'ti·cal·ly** *adv.*

scorch (skôrch) *v.t.* **1.** To change the color, taste, etc., of by slight burning; char the surface of. **2.** To wither or shrivel by heat. **3.** To criticize severely. — *v.i.* **4.** To become scorched. **5.** *Informal* To go at high speed. — *n.* **1.** A superficial burn. **2.** A mark caused by heat, as a slight burn. [Prob. akin to ME *skorken* < ON *skorpna* to dry up, shrivel] — **scorch'ing** *adj.* — **scorch'ing·ly** *adv.*

scorched-earth policy (skôrcht'ûrth') The military policy of destroying all crops, industrial equipment, dwellings, etc., so as to leave nothing for the use of the enemy.

scorch·er (skôr'chər) *n.* **1.** One who or that which scorches. **2.** *Informal* An extremely hot day. **3.** *Informal* Severe or caustic criticism. **4.** *Informal* One who or that which moves at great speed.

score (skôr, skōr) *n.* **1.** The record of the winning points in a competition or game; also, the total of such points made by a player or a team. **2.** *Psychol.* A quantitative value assigned to an individual or group response to a test or series of tests. **3.** Grade or rating in a test or examination. **4.** Any record, esp. of indebtedness. **5.** A notch or groove cut in something for keeping a tally. **6.** Something charged or laid up against one: to settle old *scores.* **7.** A set of twenty. **8.** *pl.* An indefinitely large number. **9.** *Music* The complete notation for a composition, showing the various instrumental or vocal parts. — **to know the score** *Informal* To be aware of the real facts of a situation. — *v.* **scored, scor·ing** *v.t.* **1.** To mark with notches, cuts, or lines. **2.** To mark with cuts or lines for the purpose of keeping a tally or record. **3.** To obliterate or cross out by means of a line drawn through: with *out.* **4.** To make or gain, as points, runs, etc. **5.** To count for a score of, as in games. **6.** To rate or grade, as an examination paper. **7.** *Music* a To orchestrate. **b** To arrange or adapt for an instrument. **8.** *Informal* To criticize severely. **9.** In cooking, to make superficial cuts in (meat, etc.). — *v.i.* **10.** To make points, runs, etc., as in a game. **11.** To keep score. **12.** To make notches, cuts, etc. **13.** To win an advantage or success. [OE < ON *skor* notch, tally] — **scor'er** *n.*

sco·ri·a (skôr'ē·ə, skō'rē·ə) *n. pl.* **·ri·ae** (-ri·ē) **1.** Refuse or slag remaining after metal has been smelted. **2.** Loose, clinkerlike pieces of lava. [< L < Gk. *skōria* refuse] — **sco'ri·a·ceous** (-ā'shəs) *adj.*

sco·ri·fy (skôr'ə·fī, skō'rə-) *v.t.* **·fied, ·fy·ing** *Metall.* **1.** To separate, as gold or silver, from an ore by smelting with lead, borax, etc. **2.** To reduce to scoria or dross. — **sco'ri·fi·ca'·tion** *n.*

scorn (skôrn) *n.* **1.** A feeling of contempt or loathing, as for someone or something deemed inferior or unworthy of attention; disdain. **2.** Behavior characterized by such a feeling; derision. **3.** An expression of contempt or disdain. **4.** An object of contempt. — *v.t.* **1.** To hold in or treat with contempt; despise. **2.** To reject with scorn; disdain; spurn. [< OF < *escarnir* < Gmc.] — **scorn'er** *n.* — **scorn'ful** *adj.* — **scorn'ful·ly** *adv.* — **scorn'ful·ness** *n.*

Scor·pi·o (skôr'pē·ō) *n.* A constellation, the Scorpion, containing the bright star Antares; also, the eighth sign of the zodiac. Also **Scor'pi·us** (-əs). See ZODIAC. [< L]

scor·pi·on (skôr'pē·ən) *n.* **1.** One of an order of arachnids found chiefly in warmer regions, having an elongated, lobsterlike body and a segmented tail that bears a venomous sting. **2.** An instrument of chastisement; a whip or scourge. I *Kings* xii 11. [< OF < L < Gk. *skorpios*]

SCORPION
s Stinger.
(To 8 inches long)

scot (skot) *n.* An assessment or tax. [Fusion of ON *skot* and OF *escot*]

Scot (skot) *n.* **1.** A native of Scotland: also called *Scotsman.* **2.** Formerly, a Gaelic Highlander. **3.** One of a Gaelic people who migrated in the fifth century to northwestern Britain from Ireland. [OE *Scottas,* pl., the Irish < LL *Scotus Scoti*]

scotch (skoch) *v.t.* **1.** To cut; scratch. **2.** To wound so as to maim or cripple. **3.** To put down; crush or suppress. — *n.* **1.** A superficial cut; a scratch; notch. **2.** A line traced on the ground, as for hopscotch. [Origin uncertain]

Scotch (skoch) *n.* **1.** The people of Scotland collectively: with *the.* **2.** One or all of the dialects spoken by the people of Scotland. **3.** Scotch whisky. — *adj.* Of or pertaining to Scotland, its inhabitants, or their language; Scottish; Scots.

Scotch·man (skoch'mən) *n. pl.* **·men** (-mən) A Scot; Scotsman. ◆ These forms are preferred to *Scotchman.*

Scotch tape A rolled strip of transparent cellulose tape having an adhesive on one side: a trade name.

Scotch terrier A Scottish terrier.

Scotch whisky Whisky made in Scotland from malted barley and having rather a smoky flavor.

sco·ter (skō'tər) *n.* Any of several dark sea ducks. [< dial. E *scote* scoot]

scot-free (skot'frē') *adj.* **1.** Without injury or loss; unharmed; whole. **2.** Free from scot; untaxed.

Scotland Yard (skot'land) The headquarters of the London Metropolitan Police and of the London Criminal Investigation Department, since 1890 located at the **New Scotland Yard** on the Thames Embankment.

Scots (skots) *adj. Scottish.* — *n.* The Scottish dialect of English. [Earlier *Scottis,* var. of SCOTTISH]

Scots·man (skots'mən) *n. pl.* **·men** (-mən) A Scot.

Scot·ti·cism (skot'ə·siz'əm) *n.* A form of expression or an idiom peculiar to the Scottish people.

Scot·tish (skot'ish) *adj.* Pertaining to or characteristic of Scotland, its inhabitants, or their language: also *Scots.* — *n.* **1.** The dialect of English spoken in Scotland, esp. in the Lowlands; Scots. **2.** The people of Scotland collectively: with *the.* [OE *Scottisc*]

Scottish Gaelic The Goidelic language of the Scottish Highlands: also called *Erse.*

Scottish terrier A small, short-legged terrier originating in Scotland, having a large head and a wiry coat: also *Scotch terrier.* Also *Informal* **Scot·tie** (skot'ē), **Scot·ty.**

scoun·drel (skoun'drəl) *n.* A mean, unprincipled rascal; a rogue. — *adj.* Of or characteristic of a scoundrel. [? < AF, OF < L *ex-* off + *condere* to hide] — **scoun'drel·ly** *adj.*

scour[1] (skour) *v.t.* **1.** To clean or brighten by thorough washing and rubbing, as with sand or steel wool. **2.** To remove dirt, etc., from; clean: to *scour* wool. **3.** To remove by or as by rubbing away. **4.** To clear by means of a strong current of water; flush. **5.** To purge the bowels of. **6.** To clean (wheat) before milling. — *v.i.* **7.** To rub something vigorously so as to clean or brighten it. **8.** To become bright or clean by rubbing. — *n.* **1.** The act of scouring. **2.** A place scoured, as by running water. **3.** A cleanser used in cleaning wool. **4.** *Usu. pl.* A watery diarrhea in cattle. [Prob. < MDu. < OF *escurer,* ult. < L *ex-* out + *curare* to take care of] — **scour'er** *n.*

scour[2] (skour) *v.t.* **1.** To range over or through, as in making a search. **2.** To move or run swiftly over or along. — *v.i.* **3.** To range about, as in making a search. **4.** To move swiftly. [ME *scoure*] — **scour'er** *n.*

scourge (skûrj) *n.* **1.** A whip for inflicting suffering or punishment. **2.** Any instrumentality or means for causing suffering or death. **3.** Severe punishment. **4.** A cause of suffering or trouble. — *v.t.* **scourged, scourg·ing** **1.** To whip severely; flog. **2.** To punish severely; afflict. [< AF < LL *excoriare* to flay] — **scourg'er** *n.*

scour·ings (skour'ingz) *n.pl.* **1.** The residue after scouring grain. **2.** Dirt or other residue left after any scouring.

scout[1] (skout) *n.* **1.** One who or that which is engaged in scouting; esp., a person sent out to observe and get information, as of a war enemy, rival team in sports, etc. **2.** The act of scouting. **3.** *Slang* A fellow or friend. **4.** A Boy or Girl

Scout. — *v.t.* **1.** To observe or spy upon for the purpose of gaining information. — *v.i.* **2.** To go or act as a scout. — **to scout around** To go in search. [< OF < L *auscultare* to listen] — **scout'er** *n.*

scout² (skout) *v.t. & v.i.* To mock; jeer. [< Scand.]

scout car An armored motor car for reconnaissance work.

scout·ing (skout'ing) *n.* The activities of a scout, esp. of a Boy Scout or Girl Scout.

scout·mas·ter (skout'mas'tər, -mäs'-) *n.* The leader of a troop of Boy Scouts.

scow (skou) *n.* A large boat with a flat bottom and square ends, chiefly used for freight and usually towed. [< Du. *schouw* boat propelled by a pole < MDu. *schoude*]

scowl (skoul) *n.* **1.** A lowering of the brows, as in anger, disapproval, or sullenness. **2.** Gloomy aspect. — *v.i.* **1.** To lower and contract the brows in anger, sullenness, or disapproval. **2.** To look threatening; lower. — *v.t.* **3.** To affect or express by scowling. [ME *skoul*, prob. < Scand.] — **scowl'er** *n.* — **scowl'ing·ly** *adv.*

scrab·ble (skrab'əl) *v.* **·bled**, **·bling** *v.i.* **1.** To scratch, scrape, or paw, as with the hands. **2.** To make irregular or meaningless marks; scribble. **3.** To struggle or strive. — *v.t.* **4.** To make meaningless marks on; scribble on. **5.** To gather hurriedly; scrape together. — *n.* **1.** The act of scrabbling or scrambling. **2.** A scrawling character, mark, etc.; scribble. **3.** A sparse growth, as of underbrush. [< Du. *schrabbelen*, freq. of *schrabben* to scratch]

scrag (skrag) *v.t.* **scragged**, **scrag·ging** *Informal* To use roughly; wring the neck of; esp., to kill by hanging. — *n.* **1.** Something thin or lean, as a person. **2.** *Slang* The human neck. **3.** A lean or bony piece of meat. [? < Scand.]

scrag·gly (skrag'lē) *adj.* **·gli·er**, **·gli·est** Unkempt; shaggy.

scrag·gy (skrag'ē) *adj.* **·gi·er**, **·gi·est 1.** Rough. **2.** Lean; scrawny; bony. — **scrag'gi·ly** *adv.* — **scrag'gi·ness** *n.*

scram (skram) *v.i.* **scrammed**, **scram·ming** *U.S. Slang* To go away; leave quickly. [Prob. short for SCRAMBLE]

scram·ble (skram'bəl) *v.* **·bled**, **·bling** *v.i.* **1.** To move by clambering or crawling on hands and feet. **2.** To struggle with others in a disorderly manner; scuffle; also, to strive for something in such a manner. **3.** *Aeron.* To put interceptor aircraft into the air hurriedly to meet enemy aircraft. — *v.t.* **4.** To mix together haphazardly. **5.** To gather or collect hurriedly or confusedly. **6.** To fry (eggs) with the yolks and whites stirred together. **7.** *Telecom.* To alter or garble (a signal) so that a special receiving apparatus is needed to render it comprehensible. — *n.* **1.** The act of scrambling. **2.** A disorderly performance or struggle. **3.** A difficult climb or trek, as over rocks or rough terrain. [Prob. nasalized var. of SCRABBLE] — **scram'bler** *n.*

scrap¹ (skrap) *n.* **1.** A small piece cut or broken from something; fragment. **2.** A brief printed or written extract. **3.** *pl.* Pieces of crisp fat tissue after the oil has been expressed by cooking; also, any bits of food. **4.** Old or refuse metal. — *v.t.* **scrapped**, **scrap·ping 1.** To break up into scrap. **2.** To discard. — *adj.* Having the form of scraps; discarded after use. [< ON *skrapa* to scrape]

scrap² (skrap) *v.i.* **scrapped**, **scrap·ping** *Slang* To fight; quarrel. — *n.* A quarrel, fight, or disagreement. [< SCRAPE (n. def. 2)] — **scrap'per** *n.*

scrap·book (skrap'book') *n.* **1.** A blank book in which to paste pictures, clippings, etc. **2.** A personal notebook.

scrape (skrāp) *v.* **scraped**, **scrap·ing** *v.t.* **1.** To rub, as with something rough or sharp, so as to abrade or to remove an outer layer or adherent matter. **2.** To remove thus: with *off*, *away*, etc. **3.** To rub (a rough or sharp object) across a surface. **4.** To rub roughly across or against (a surface). **5.** To dig or form by scratching or scraping. **6.** To gather or accumulate with effort or difficulty: usu. with *up* or *together.* — *v.i.* **7.** To scrape something. **8.** To rub with a grating noise. **9.** To emit or produce a grating noise. **10.** To draw the foot backward along the ground in bowing. **11.** To manage or get along with difficulty. **12.** To be very or overly economical. — *n.* **1.** The act or effect of scraping; also, the noise made by scraping. **2.** A difficult situation; predicament. **3.** A scraping or drawing back of the foot in bowing. [Prob. fusion of OE *scrapian* and ON *skrapa* to scrape, erase] — **scrap'er** *n.*

scrap·ing (skrā'ping) *n.* **1.** The act of someone or something that scrapes. **2.** The sound so produced. **3.** *Often pl.* That which is scraped off or together.

scrap iron Old pieces of iron suitable for reworking.

scrap·ple (skrap'əl) *n.* A mixture of meal or flour boiled with scraps of pork, seasoned, and allowed to set, usu. cooked by frying. [Dim. of SCRAP¹]

scrap·py¹ (skrap'ē) *adj.* **·pi·er**, **·pi·est** Composed of scraps; fragmentary. — **scrap'pi·ly** *adv.* — **scrap'pi·ness** *n.*

scrap·py² (skrap'ē) *adj.* **·pi·er**, **·pi·est** Pugnacious; given to picking fights. — **scrap'pi·ly** *adv.* — **scrap'pi·ness** *n.*

scratch (skrach) *v.t.* **1.** To tear or mark the surface of with something sharp or rough. **2.** To scrape or dig with something sharp or rough, as the claws or nails. **3.** To scrape lightly with the nails, etc., as to relieve itching. **4.** To rub with a grating sound; scrape. **5.** To write or draw awkwardly or hurriedly. **6.** To erase or cancel by or as by scratches or marks. **7.** To erase or cancel the name of (a candidate) from a political ticket, while supporting the rest of the ticket; also, to bolt (a ticket or party) in this way. **8.** To withdraw (an entry) from a race, game, etc. — *v.i.* **9.** To use the nails or claws, as in fighting or digging. **10.** To scrape the skin, etc., lightly, as to relieve itching. **11.** To make a harsh, grating noise. **12.** To manage or get along with difficulty. **13.** To withdraw from a game, race, etc. **14.** In billiards and pool, to make a scratch. — *n.* **1.** A mark or incision made on a surface by scratching; also, a quick mark or scribble, as made by a pencil. **2.** A slight flesh wound or cut. **3.** A harsh, grating sound. **4.** The act of scratching. **5.** The line from which contestants start, as in racing. **6.** The contestant who competes against an allowance. **7.** In billiards, a chance shot; also, a fluke; in billiards and pool, a shot resulting in a penalty. — **from scratch** From the beginning; from nothing. — **up to scratch** *Informal* Meeting the standard or requirement in courage, stamina, or performance. — *adj.* **1.** Done by chance; haphazard. **2.** In sports, without handicap or allowance. **3.** Used for quick notes, a memorandum, etc.: a *scratch* pad. **4.** Chosen at random or by chance. [Prob. blend of ME *scratte* to scratch and *cracchen* to scratch] — **scratch'er** *n.*

scratch test *Med.* A test to determine the substances to which a person is allergic by rubbing allergens in small scratches made in his skin.

scratch·y (skrach'ē) *adj.* **scratch·i·er**, **scratch·i·est 1.** Characterized by or covered with scratches. **2.** Making a scratching noise. **3.** Straggling; shaggy; rough. **4.** That scratches or irritates. — **scratch'i·ly** *adv.* — **scratch'i·ness** *n.*

scrawl (skrôl) *v.t. & v.i.* To write hastily or illegibly. — *n.* Irregular or careless writing. [? < dial. E, var. of CRAWL]

scrawl·y (skrô'lē) *adj.* **scrawl·i·er**, **scrawl·i·est** Consisting of or characterized by ill-formed or irregular characters.

scraw·ny (skrô'nē) *adj.* **·ni·er**, **·ni·est** Skinny; thin. [< dial. E *scranny*, var. of SCRANNEL] — **scraw'ni·ness** *n.*

scream (skrēm) *v.i.* **1.** To utter a prolonged, piercing cry, as of pain, terror, or surprise. **2.** To make a prolonged, piercing sound. **3.** To laugh loudly or immoderately. **4.** To use heated, hysterical language. **5.** To have an odd or startling effect, as of screaming. — *v.t.* **6.** To utter with a scream. — *n.* **1.** A loud, shrill, prolonged cry or sound, generally denoting fear or pain. **2.** *U.S. Slang* A person or situation arousing great mirth. [ME *scraemen*]

scream·er (skrē'mər) *n.* **1.** One who or that which screams. **2.** Any of various birds of South America related to the ducks.

screech (skrēch) *n.* **1.** A shrill, harsh cry; shriek. **2.** *Canadian Slang* Cheap rum or wine. — *v.t.* **1.** To utter with or as with a screech. — *v.i.* **2.** To make a prolonged, harsh, piercing sound. [Var. of obs. *scritch*, prob. imit.] — **screech'er** *n.* — **screech'y** *adv.*

screech owl Any of various owls common from Canada to Brazil; esp. a small, gray species of the eastern U.S. **2.** The barn owl of England.

screed (skrēd) *n.* **1.** A prolonged tirade; harangue. **2.** A long piece of discursive prose. — *v.t.* To rend or tear into shreds. [Var. of SHRED]

screen (skrēn) *n.* **1.** That which separates or cuts off, shelters, or protects, as a light partition. **2.** A network, as of wire, forming a partition or panel in a window, door, etc., to exclude insects and admit air. **3.** A sieve or riddle for sifting. **4.** A smooth surface, on which motion pictures, etc., may be shown. **5.** A motion picture or motion pictures collectively. — *v.t.* **1.** To shield from observation or annoyance with or as with a screen. **2.** To cause to pass through a screen or sieve; sift. **3.** To show or exhibit on a screen, as a motion picture. **4.** To determine the competence or eligibility of (an individual) for a specified task. — *v.i.* **5.** To be shown or be suitable for showing on a motion-picture screen. [Prob. < OF *escren*, *escrin*, prob. < OHG *skirm*] — **screen'a·ble** *adj.* — **screen'er** *n.*

screen·ing (skrē'ning) *n.* **1.** The act or instance of exhibiting a motion picture. **2.** The work of one who screens. **3.** Mesh, as of wire, fabric, or plastic, suitable for window screens and the like. **4.** *pl.* The residue of anything passed through a sieve; siftings.

screen play A motion picture.

screw (skrōō) *n.* **1.** A device resembling a nail but having a slotted head and a tapering grooved spiral for driving into wood with a screwdriver. **2.** A similar device of cylindrical form, for insertion into a corresponding grooved part: also

male or **external** screw. **3.** A cylindrical socket with a spiral groove: also **female** or **internal** screw. **4.** Anything having the form of a screw. **5.** A screw propeller. **6.** A turn of or as of a screw. **7.** Pressure; force. **8.** *Brit. Slang* Salary; pay. **9.** *Slang* A prison guard. **10.** A haggler over prices. **— to have a screw loose** *Slang* To be mentally deranged, eccentric, etc. **— to put the screws on** (or **to**) *Slang* To exert pressure or force upon. **—** *v.t.* **1.** To tighten, fasten, attach, etc., by or as by a screw or screws. **2.** To turn or twist. **3.** To force as if by the pressure of a screw; urge: to *screw* one's courage to the sticking point. **4.** To twist out of shape; contort, as one's features. **5.** To practice oppression or extortion on. **6.** To obtain by extortion. **7.** *Slang* To have sexual intercourse with: a vulgar term. **8.** *Slang* To act maliciously toward; harm. **—** *v.i.* **1.** To turn or admit of being turned as a screw. **2.** To be attached or become detached by means of screws: with *on, off,* etc. **11.** *Slang* To have sexual intercourse: a vulgar term. **— to screw up** *Slang* To make a mess of; botch. [Appar. < OF *escroue* nut, female screw] **— screw′er** *n.*

screw·ball (skrōō′bôl′) *n. U.S. Slang* An unconventional or erratic person.

screw·driv·er (skrōō′drī′vər) *n.* **1.** A tool with a flattened metal end that fits into the slot of a screw in order to turn it. **2.** A cocktail consisting of vodka and orange juice.

screw propeller A mechanism consisting of a revolving shaft with radiating blades set at an angle to produce a spiral action, used in propelling ships, etc.

screw thread **1.** The projecting spiral ridge of uniform pitch on the outer or inner surface of a screw or nut. **2.** A complete revolution of any point on this ridge.

screw·y (skrōō′ē) *adj.* **screw·i·er, screw·i·est** *Slang* Extremely irrational; crazy.

scrib·ble (skrib′əl) *v.* **·bled, ·bling** *v.t.* **1.** To write hastily and carelessly. **2.** To cover with careless or illegible writing or marks. **—** *v.i.* **3.** To write in a careless or hasty manner. **4.** To make illegible or meaningless marks. **—** *n.* **1.** Hasty, careless writing. **2.** Any scrawl. [< Med.L *scribillare,* freq. of L *scribere* to write] **— scrib′bler** *n.*

scribe (skrīb) *n.* **1.** One who writes or copies manuscripts. **2.** A clerk, public writer, or amanuensis. **3.** An ancient Jewish teacher, interpreter, or writer of the Mosaic law. **—** *v.* **scribed, scrib·ing** *v.t.* **1.** To mark or scratch with a pointed instrument. **2.** To write, inscribe, or engrave. **—** *v.i.* **3.** *Rare* To write; work as a scribe. [< L < *scribere* to write] **— scrib′al** *adj.*

scrim (skrim) *n.* **1.** A lightweight, open-mesh, cotton fabric, usu. white or ecru, used for draperies, etc. **2.** In the theater, a similar fabric, often painted, used as a transparency, to support artificial foliage, etc. [Origin unknown]

scrim·mage (skrim′ij) *n.* **1.** A rough-and-tumble contest; fracas. **2.** In American football, a mass play from the line of scrimmage after the ball has been placed on the ground and snapped back, the play ending when the ball is dead. **3.** In Rugby football, a scrummage. **4.** In football, a practice session or unofficial game played by opposing teams. **line of scrimmage** In football, the hypothetic line on which the ball rests and along which the opposing linemen take position at the start of play. **—** *v.t. & v.i.* **·maged, ·mag·ing** To engage in a scrimmage. Also *scrummage.* [Alter. of *scrimish,* var. of SKIRMISH]

scrimp (skrimp) *v.i.* **1.** To be very or overly economical. **—** *v.t.* **2.** To be overly sparing with; skimp. **3.** To cut too small, narrow, etc. **—** *adj.* Scanty; scrimpy. [Prob. akin to OE *scrimman* to shrink, shrivel]

scrimp·y (skrim′pē) *adj.* **·i·er, ·i·est** **1.** Scanty; skimpy; short. **2.** Tending to scrimp; niggardly. **— scrimp′i·ness** *n.*

scrip[1] (skrip) *n.* **1.** A scrap of paper, esp. one containing writing. **2.** A writing; a certificate, schedule, or written list. **3.** A piece of paper money less than a dollar, formerly issued in the U.S. [< SCRIPT]

scrip[2] (skrip) *n.* A provisional document (or documents collectively) certifying that the holder is entitled to receive something else, as shares of stock or land. [Short for obs. *subscription receipt*]

script (skript) *n.* **1.** Writing of the ordinary cursive form. **2.** Type, or printed or engraved matter, in imitation of handwriting. **3.** *Law* A writing, esp. an original. **4.** A piece of writing; esp., a prepared copy of a play or dramatic role, for the use of actors. **5.** Alphabet; writing system: phonetic *script.* **—** *v.t. & v.i. U.S. Informal* To prepare a script for (a radio, television, or theatrical performance). [< OF < L *scribere* to write]

scrip·tur·al (skrip′chər·əl) *adj.* Relating to writing; written. **— scrip′tur·al·ly** *adv.* **— scrip′tur·al·ness** *n.*

Scrip·ture (skrip′chər) *n.* **1.** The books of the Old and New Testaments, including often the Apocrypha. **2.** A text or passage from the Bible. **— Scrip′tur·al** *adj.* **— Scrip′tur·al·ly** *adv.* **— Scrip′tur·al·ness** *n.*

script·writ·er (skript′rī′tər) *n.* A writer who prepares copy for the use of an actor or announcer.

scrive (skrīv) *v.t.* **scrived, scriv·ing** To engrave. [? < OF < L *scribere*]

scriv·en·er (skriv′ən·ər, skriv′nər) *n. Archaic* One who prepares deeds, contracts, and other writings; a clerk or scribe. [< obs. *scrivein* < OF < Ital. < L *scribere* to write]

scrod (skrod) *n.* A young codfish, esp. when split and prepared for broiling. [? < MDu. *schrode* piece cut off]

scrof·u·la (skrof′yə·lə) *n. Pathol.* A tuberculous condition of the lymphatic glands, characterized by enlargement, abscesses, and cheeselike degeneration: also called *struma.* [Orig. pl. < LL *scrofulae,* dim. pl. of *scrofa* breeding sow]

scrof·u·lous (skrof′yə·ləs) *adj.* **1.** Pertaining to, affected with, or of the nature of scrofula. **2.** Morally corrupt; degraded. **— scrof′u·lous·ly** *adv.* **— scrof′u·lous·ness** *n.*

scroll (skrōl) *n.* **1.** A roll of parchment, paper, or the like, esp. one containing or intended for writing; also, the writing on such a roll. **2.** Anything resembling or suggestive of a parchment roll; esp. a convoluted ornament or an ornamental space or tablet on sculptured work. [Earlier *scrowle,* alter. of obs. *scrow* < AF *escrowe*]

scroll saw A narrow-bladed hand or power saw for doing curved or irregular work.

scroll·work (skrōl′wûrk′) *n.* Ornamental work of scroll-like pattern.

Scrooge (skrōōj), **Ebenezer** In Dickens's *A Christmas Carol,* a miser whose hard nature is transformed on Christmas Eve.

scro·tum (skrō′təm) *n. pl.* **·ta** (-tə), **·tums** *Anat.* The pouch of skin that contains the testicles in most mammals. [< L] **— scro′tal** *adj.*

scrounge (skrounj) *v.t. & v.i.* **scrounged, scroung·ing** *Slang* **1.** To hunt about in order to take (something); pilfer. **2.** To mooch; sponge; beg. **—** *n.* One who scrounges: also **scroung′er.** [? < dial. E *scrunge* to steal]

scrub[1] (skrub) *v.* **scrubbed, scrub·bing** *v.t.* **1.** To rub vigorously in washing. **2.** To remove (dirt, etc.) by such action. **3.** *U.S. Slang* To cancel; call off. **—** *v.i.* **4.** To rub something vigorously, as in washing. **—** *n.* The act of scrubbing. [? < Scand. Cf. Dan. *skrubbe,* MDu. *shrubben.*] **— scrub′ber** *n.*

scrub[2] (skrub) *n.* **1.** A stunted tree; also, such trees collectively. **2.** A thicket or group of stunted trees or shrubs. **3.** A domestic animal of inferior breed. **4.** A poor, insignificant person. **5.** In sports, a player not on the varsity or regular team. **—** *adj.* **6.** Undersized or stunted-looking; inferior. [Dial. var. of SHRUB[1]]

scrub·by (skrub′ē) *adj.* **·bi·er, ·bi·est** **1.** Of stunted growth. **2.** Covered with or consisting of scrub or underbrush. **— scrub′bi·ness** *n.*

scrub·land (skrub′land′) *n.* Land covered with scrub.

scrub oak Any of various dwarf oaks of the United States.

scrub pine Any of several American pines having a tendency toward stunted or crowded growth.

scruff (skruf) *n.* The nape of the neck. [Earlier *scuff,* ? < ON *skopt* hair]

scrum·mage (skrum′ij) *v.t. & v.i.* **·maged, ·mag·ing** To scrimmage. **—** *n.* **1.** A scrimmage. **2.** In Rugby football, a formation around the ball, out of which the ball is kicked to begin play. [Var. of SCRIMMAGE] **— scrum′mag·er** *n.*

scrump·tious (skrump′shəs) *adj. Slang* Elegant or stylish; fine; delightful; splendid. [Prob. alter. of SUMPTUOUS]

scrunch (skrunch) *v.t. & v.i.* To crush; squeeze; crunch. **—** *n.* A crunch. [Imit. alter. of CRUNCH]

scru·ple (skrōō′pəl) *n.* **1.** Doubt or uncertainty regarding a question of moral right or duty. **2.** An apothecaries' weight of twenty grains, or 1.296 grams (symbol: ℈). See table inside back cover. **3.** A minute quantity. **—** *v.t. & v.i.* **·pled, ·pling** To have scruples (about). [< OF < L *scrupulus* small sharp stone]

scru·pu·lous (skrōō′pyə·ləs) *adj.* **1.** Cautious in action because of a wish to do right; nicely conscientious. **2.** Resulting from the exercise of scruples; exact; careful. **— Syn.** See METICULOUS. **— scru′pu·lous·ly** *adv.* **— scru′pu·los′i·ty** (-los′ə·tē), **scru′pu·lous·ness** *n.*

scru·ti·nize (skrōō′tə·nīz) *v.t.* **·nized, ·niz·ing** To observe carefully; examine in detail. Also *Brit.* **scru′ti·nise.** **— scru′ti·niz′er** *n.* **— scru′ti·niz′ing·ly** *adv.*

scru·ti·ny (skrōō′tə·nē) *n. pl.* **·nies** **1.** The act of scrutinizing; close examination or investigation. **2.** A searching look or glance. [< OF < LL < L *scrutari* to examine]

scu·ba (skōō′bə, skyōō′-) *n. Sometimes cap.* An underwater breathing apparatus needing no connection with the surface, worn by divers. Also called *Aqua-Lung, aqualung.* [< s(elf)-c(ontained) u(nderwater) b(reathing) a(pparatus)]

scud (skud) *v.i.* **scud·ded, scud·ding** **1.** To move, run, or fly swiftly. **2.** *Naut.* To run rapidly before the wind. **—** *n.* **1.** The act of scudding or moving swiftly. **2.** Light clouds driven rapidly before the wind. [Prob. < Scand.; ? infl. in meaning by *scut,* in earlier sense of "hare"]

scuff (skuf) *v.i.* **1.** To walk with a dragging movement of the feet; shuffle. **—** *v.t.* **2.** To scrape (the floor, ground, etc.) with the feet. **3.** To roughen or wear down the surface of by rubbing or scraping. — *n.* **1.** The act of scuffing; also, the noise or mark so made. **2.** A flat slipper having no covering for the heel. [Prob. < ON *skúfa* to shove]

scuf·fle (skuf′əl) *v.i.* **·fled, ·fling 1.** To struggle roughly or confusedly. **2.** To drag one's feet; shuffle. — *n.* A disorderly struggle. [Prob. freq. of SCUFF] — **scuf′fler** *n.*

scull (skul) *n.* **1.** A long oar worked from side to side over the stern of a boat. **2.** A light, short-handled oar, used in pairs by one person. **3.** A small boat for sculling. — *v.t. & v.i.* To propel (a boat) by a scull or sculls. [ME *sculle, skulle;* origin unknown] — **scull′er** *n.*

scul·ler·y (skul′ər·ē) *n.* *pl.* **·ler·ies** A room where kitchen utensils are kept and cleaned, vegetables washed, etc. [< OF *escuelerie* care of dishes]

scul·lion (skul′yən) *n.* *Archaic* **1.** A servant who washes and scours dishes, pots, and kettles. **2.** A base, contemptible person. [< OF *escouillon* mop < *escouve* broom]

scul·pin (skul′pin) *n.* *pl.* **·pins** or **·pin** One of several broad-mouthed fishes with a large, spiny head. [Prob. alter. of F *escorpene* < L *scorpaena* scorpionlike fish]

sculpt (skulpt) *v.t. & v.i.* *Informal* To sculpture.

sculp·tor (skulp′tər) *n.* One who creates sculpture by carving wood, modeling clay or plastics, working metal, or chiseling stone, etc. — **sculp′tress** (-tris) *n.fem.*

sculp·ture (skulp′chər) *n.* **1.** The art of fashioning figures of wood, clay, plastics, metal, or stone. **2.** Figures or groups carved, cut, hewn, cast, or modeled in such materials. **3.** Raised or incised lines or markings, as upon a shell. — *v.t.* **·tured, ·tur·ing 1.** To fashion, as statuary, by modeling, carving, casting, or welding. **2.** To represent or portray in sculpture. **3.** To embellish with sculpture. **4.** To change, as the face of a valley or canyon, by erosion and deposition. [< L *sculpere* to carve in stone] — **sculp′tur·al** *adj.*

sculp·tur·esque (skulp′chə·resk′) *adj.* Resembling sculpture; coldly, calmly, or grandly beautiful; statuesque.

scum (skum) *n.* **1.** Impure or extraneous matter that rises to the surface of boiling or fermenting liquids. **2.** Minute vegetation on stagnant water. **3.** Worthless element; refuse. **4.** A vile or worthless person or group of persons: often in the phrase **the scum of the earth.** — *v.* **scummed, scum·ming** *v.t.* **1.** To take scum from; skim. — *v.i.* **2.** To become covered with or form scum. [< MDu. *schuum*] — **scum′mer** *n.*

scum·my (skum′ē) *adj.* **·mi·er, ·mi·est 1.** Covered with, containing, or resembling scum. **2.** Vile; contemptible.

scup (skup) *n.* *pl.* **scup** or **scups** A food fish of the eastern coast of the U.S.: also called *porgy.* Also **scup·paug** (skup′ôg, skə·pôg′). [< Algonquian (Narraganset) *mishcup* thick-scaled]

scup·per (skup′ər) *n.* *Naut.* A hole or gutter along the side of a ship's deck, to let water run off. [? Short for *scupper hole* < OF *escope* bailing scoop]

scup·per·nong (skup′ər·nông, -nong) *n.* **1.** A variety of muscadine grape cultivated in the southern United States. **2.** A sweet, straw-colored wine made from this grape. [after the *Scuppernong* River in North Carolina]

scurf (skûrf) *n.* **1.** Loose outer skin thrown off in minute scales, as in dandruff. **2.** Any scaly matter. [OE] — **scurf′y** *adj.*

scur·ril·i·ty (skə·ril′ə·tē) *n.* *pl.* **·ties 1.** A scurrilous remark. **2.** The quality of being obscenely jocular.

scur·ri·lous (skûr′ə·ləs) *adj.* **1.** Grossly and offensively abusive. **2.** Expressed with or given to coarse jocularity. Also **scur·rile** (skûr′il), **scur′ril.** [< L *scurrilis* buffoonlike] — **scur′ri·lous·ly** *adv.* — **scur′ri·lous·ness** *n.*

scur·ry (skûr′ē) *v.i.* **·ried, ·ry·ing** To move or go hurriedly; scamper. — *n.* *pl.* **·ries** The act or sound of scurrying. [Short for HURRY-SCURRY]

scur·vy (skûr′vē) *adj.* **·vi·er, ·vi·est 1.** Meanly low or contemptible; base. **2.** *Obs.* Scurfy; scabby. — *n.* *Pathol.* A disease caused by lack of vitamin C in the diet, and characterized by swollen and bleeding gums, and great weakness. [< SCURF] — **scur′vi·ly** *adv.* — **scur′vi·ness** *n.*

scut (skut) *n.* A short tail, as of a rabbit or deer. [ME, tail, hare, prob. < Scand. Cf. Icelandic *skott* fox's tail.]

scu·tate (skyoo′tāt) *adj.* *Zool.* Covered with horny, shieldlike plates or large scales. **2.** *Bot.* Shaped like a shield. [< L *scutatus* provided with a shield < *scutum* shield]

scutch·eon (skuch′ən) *n.* An escutcheon.

scu·tel·late (skyoo′tel·it, skyoo′tə·lāt) *adj.* *Zool.* **1.** Platterlike; shield-shaped. **2.** Covered with scales; scutate. Also **scu′tel·lat·ed** (-tə·lā′tid). [< NL *scutellatus* < L *scutella* platter, dim. of *scutra* tray] — **scu′tel·la′tion** *n.*

scu·tel·lum (skyoo·tel′əm) *n.* *pl.* **·la** (-lə) *Biol.* A small, shieldlike organ or part, as on the leg of a bird. [< NL, dim. of L *scutum* shield] — **scu·tel′lar** *adj.*

scut·tle[1] (skut′l) *n.* **1.** A small opening or hatchway with a movable lid or cover, esp. on the deck of a ship. **2.** The lid closing such an opening. **3.** A sea cock in the bottom of a ship. — *v.t.* **·tled, ·tling** To sink (a ship) by making holes in the bottom or by opening the sea cocks. [< MF *escoutille* hatchway]

scut·tle[2] (skut′l) *n.* A metal vessel or hod for coal. [OE *scutel* dish, platter < L *scutella*]

scut·tle[3] (skut′l) *v.i.* **·tled, ·tling** To run in haste; scurry. — *n.* A hurried run or departure. [? Var. of *scuddle*]

scut·tle·butt (skut′l·but) *n.* **1.** A drinking fountain aboard ship. **2.** Formerly, a cask containing the day's drinking water. **3.** *U.S. Slang* Rumor; gossip. [Orig. *scuttled butt* a lidded cask for drinking water]

scu·tum (skyoo′təm) *n.* *pl.* **·ta** (-tə) **1.** *Zool.* A platelike piece or part, as on a turtle. **2.** In ancient Rome, the large oval or rectangular shield of the legionaries. [< L]

Scyl·la (sil′ə) In Greek mythology, a six-headed sea monster who dwelt in a cave on the Italian coast opposite the whirlpool Charybdis. — **between Scylla and Charybdis** Between two dangers, where one cannot be avoided without incurring equally great peril from the other.

scythe (sīth, *sometimes* sī) *n.* An implement used for mowing, reaping, etc., consisting of a long, curved blade fixed at an angle to a long bent handle. — *v.t.* **scythed, scyth·ing** To cut or mow with or as with a scythe. [OE *sīthe*]

Scyth·i·a (sith′ē·ə) An ancient region of southern Europe, generally considered as lying north of the Black Sea. — **Scyth′i·an** *adj. & n.*

sea (sē) *n.* **1.** The great body of salt water covering the larger portion of the earth's surface; the ocean. **2.** A large body of oceanic water partly enclosed by land. **3.** A large inland body of water, salt or fresh. **4.** The swell or surface of the ocean: a calm *sea.* **5.** Anything that suggests the sea, as something vast. **6.** The occupation of a seaman. — **at sea 1.** On the ocean. **2.** At a loss; bewildered. — **to follow the sea** To follow the occupation of a sailor. — **to go to sea 1.** To become a sailor. **2.** To take an ocean voyage. — **to put to sea** To start on a voyage, as a ship. [OE *sǣ*]

sea anchor A large canvas bag or sail dragged from the stern of a ship to reduce yawing, as in a gale.

sea anemone Any of various marine animals that attach themselves to rocks, etc., suggesting flowers by their coloring and outspread tentacles.

sea bass 1. Any of various large-mouthed food fishes of Atlantic waters; esp., the **black sea bass. 2.** Any of various similar or related fishes.

Sea·bee (sē′bē′) *n.* A member of the Construction Battalions of the U.S. Navy, organized to build base facilities, airfields, etc. [< C(*on*)struction) B(*attalion*)]

sea·board (sē′bôrd′, -bōrd′) *n.* The seashore or seacoast; also, the land or region bordering the sea. — *adj.* Bordering on the sea. [ME < SEA + *board* border, OE *bord*]

sea breeze A cool breeze blowing inland from the ocean.

sea calf The harbor seal.

sea captain The captain of a seagoing vessel.

sea·coast (sē′kōst′) *n.* The seashore; seaboard.

sea cock A cock or valve controlling connection with the water through a vessel's hull.

sea coconut The very large and heavy seed of a palm native to islands of the Indian Ocean.

sea cow 1. Any acquatic mammal, as the manatee or the dugong. **2.** The walrus.

sea cucumber Any of a group of marine animals shaped like a cucumber and having long branched tentacles.

sea dog 1. The harbor seal. **2.** The sea lion. **3.** An old or experienced sailor.

sea·drome (sē′drōm′) *n.* *Aeron.* A floating airport for aircraft making overseas flights. [< SEA + -DROME]

sea duck Any of various diving ducks, esp. the eider.

sea·far·er (sē′fâr′ər) *n.* A seaman; a mariner.

sea·far·ing (sē′fâr′ing) *adj.* **1.** Following the sea as a calling. **2.** Traveling by sea. — *n.* **1.** Travel by sea. **2.** The profession of a seaman.

sea·flow·er (sē′flou′ər) *n.* A sea anemone.

sea foam 1. Foam of the ocean. **2.** Meerschaum. **3.** A fluffy candy made of spun sugar.

sea·food (sē′food′) *n.* *U.S.* Edible marine fish or shellfish.

sea·fowl (sē′foul′) *n.* A sea bird, or sea birds collectively.

sea front Land or buildings that border on the sea.

sea·girt (sē′gûrt′) *adj.* Surrounded by waters of the sea.

sea·go·ing (sē′gō′ing) *adj.* **1.** Adapted for use on the ocean. **2.** Seafaring.

sea green A deep bluish green, like the color of sea water.

sea gull Any gull or large tern.

sea hog A porpoise.

SEA ANEMONE

(3 to 5 inches high) *a* Tentacles contracted. *b* Tentacles extended.

sea horse 1. A marine fish, having a prehensile tail and a head resembling that of a horse. 2. A walrus. 3. A fabulous animal, half horse and half fish, driven by Neptune. 4. A large, white-crested wave.

Sea Islands A chain of small islands off the coast of South Carolina, Georgia, and northern Florida.

sea king A viking pirate king of the Middle Ages.

seal¹ (sēl) n. 1. An instrument or device used for making an impression upon some plastic substance, as wax or a wafer; also, the impression made. 2. The wax, wafer, or similar token affixed to a document as a proof of authenticity; also, an impression, scroll, or mark on the paper. 3. A substance or device employed to secure a letter, door, etc., firmly or to prevent tampering. 4. Anything that confirms or ratifies; a pledge. 5. An ornamental stamp for packages, etc. — **under seal** Fastened or secured with an authoritative seal. — v.t. 1. To affix a seal to, as to prove authenticity or prevent tampering. 2. To stamp or impress a seal upon in order to attest to weight, quality, etc. 3. To fasten or close with or as with a seal. 4. To grant or assign under seal. 5. To establish or settle finally; determine. 6. In Mormon usage, to solemnize forever, as a marriage. 7. To secure, set, or fill up, as with plaster. 8. Mech. To supply with a device or trap for preventing a return flow of gas or air. [< OF < L sigillum small picture, seal] — **seal'a·ble** adj. — **seal'er** n.

seal² (sēl) n. 1. Any of a group of acquatic carnivorous mammals mostly of northern latitudes. 2. The fur of a fur seal; sealskin. 3. Leather made from the hide of a seal. 4. Any fur prepared so as to look like sealskin. — v.i. To hunt seals. [OE seolh]

sea legs Informal The ability to walk aboard ship, esp. in rough seas, without losing one's balance.

seal·er·y (sē'lər·ē) n. pl. ·er·ies 1. The occupation of hunting seals. 2. A place where seals are regularly hunted.

sea lettuce A green seaweed often used for food.

sea level 1. The assumed mean level of the ocean surface, esp. as used in determining elevation on maps, etc. 2. The actual mean level of the ocean surface.

sealing wax A mixture of shellac and resin with turpentine and pigment that is fluid when heated but becomes solid as it cools, used for sealing papers, packages, etc.

sea lion Any of various large, eared seals, esp., the **California sea lion**: also called sea dog.

seal ring A finger ring containing an engraved stone or signet: also called signet ring.

seal·skin (sēl'skin') n. 1. The under fur of the fur seal when prepared for use by removing the long hairs and dyeing dark brown or black. 2. A coat, etc., made of this fur. — adj. Made of this fur.

Sea·ly·ham terrier (sē'lē·ham, -əm) A breed of terrier first developed at Sealyham, Wales, having short legs and a wiry, usu. white coat.

seam (sēm) n. 1. A visible line of junction between parts, esp. the edges of two pieces of cloth sewn together. 2. A crack; fissure. 3. A ridge made in joining two pieces or left by a mold upon a casting. 4. A scar; also, a wrinkle. 5. A thin stratum of rock. — v.t. 1. To unite by means of a seam. 2. To mark with a cut, furrow, wrinkle, etc. 3. In knitting, to give the appearance of a seam to; purl. — v.i. 4. To crack open; become fissured. 5. In knitting, to form seams. [OE seam] — **seam'er** n.

sea·man (sē'mən) n. pl. ·men (-mən) 1. A sailor. 2. Naval An enlisted man of any of the lowest grades. See tables at GRADE. — **sea'man·like'** (-līk') adj. — **sea'man·ly** adj. & adv.

sea·man·ship (sē'mən·ship) n. The skill and ability of a seaman in the operation and handling of a boat or ship.

seam·less (sēm'lis) adj. Having no seam.

seam·stress (sēm'stris, Brit. sem'-) n. A woman skilled in needlework, esp. one whose occupation is sewing. Also sempstress. [< OE sēamestre seamster + -ESS]

seam·y (sē'mē) adj. seam·i·er, seam·i·est 1. Full of seams, as the wrong side of a garment. 2. Showing the worst aspect; distasteful: the seamy side. — **seam'i·ness** n.

sé·ance (sā'äns, Fr. sā·äns') n. 1. A session or sitting. 2. A meeting of persons seeking spiritualistic manifestations. [< F < OF seoir to sit < L sedere]

sea onion Squill¹.

sea otter A large, nearly extinct marine animal of the North Pacific coast, having a valuable dark brown fur.

sea·plane (sē'plān') n. An airplane equipped to land on or take off from the water.

sea·port (sē'pôrt', -pōrt') n. 1. A harbor or port on a coast accessible to seagoing ships. 2. A town located on such a harbor.

SEA HORSE
(2 to 12 inches long)

sea purse Zool. The horny capsule enclosing the eggs of certain sharks, skates, and rays.

sea·quake (sē'kwāk') n. A seismic disturbance of the ocean floor.

sear (sir) v.t. 1. To wither; dry up. 2. To burn the surface of; scorch. 3. To burn or cauterize, as with a hot iron; brand. 4. To make callous; harden. — v.i. 5. To cause dryness. — adj. Poetic Dried or blasted; withered. — n. A scar or brand. Also spelled sere. [OE sēarian to wither]

search (sûrch) n. 1. The act of seeking or looking diligently. 2. Investigation; inquiry. 3. A critical examination or scrutiny. 4. Law Right of search. — v.t. 1. To look through or explore thoroughly in order to find something. 2. To subject (a person) to an examination, as for concealed weapons, etc. 3. To examine with close attention; probe. 4. To penetrate or pierce. 5. To learn by investigation: with out. — v.i. 6. To make a search. [< OF < L circare to go round, explore] — **search'a·ble** adj. — **search'er** n.

search·ing (sûr'ching) adj. 1. Investigating minutely. 2. Keenly penetrating; observant: a searching gaze. — **search'ing·ly** adv. — **search'ing·ness** n.

search·light (sûrch'līt') n. 1. An apparatus containing a reflector and an intensely brilliant light that may be thrown in various directions for search or signaling. 2. The beam of light from this apparatus.

search warrant A warrant authorizing an officer to search a house or other specified place for things alleged to be unlawfully concealed there.

sea·scape (sē'skāp') n. 1. An ocean view. 2. A picture presenting a marine view. [< SEA + (LAND)SCAPE]

sea·shell (sē'shel') n. The shell of any marine mollusk.

sea·shore (sē'shôr', -shōr') n. 1. Land adjacent to or bordering on the ocean. 2. Law The ground between high- and low-water marks.

sea·sick (sē'sik') adj. Suffering from seasickness.

sea·sick·ness (sē'sik'nis) n. Nausea, dizziness, and prostration caused by the motion of a vessel at sea.

sea·side (sē'sīd') n. The seashore, esp. as a place of resort. — adj. Of or pertaining to the seashore.

sea·son (sē'zən) n. 1. A division of the year as determined by the earth's position with respect to the sun, and as marked by the temperature, moisture, vegetation, etc. 2. A period of time. 3. Any of the periods into which the Christian year is divided. 4. A period of special activity: the hunting season. 5. A fit or suitable time. 6. That which imparts relish; seasoning. — **in season** 1. In condition and obtainable for use. 2. In good or sufficient time; opportunely. 3. Legally permitted to be killed or taken, as game. 4. Ready to mate or breed: said of animals. — v.t. 1. To increase the flavor or zest of (food), as by adding spices, etc. 2. To add zest or piquancy to. 3. To render more suitable for use. 4. To make accustomed or inured; harden. 5. To mitigate or soften. — v.i. 6. To become seasoned. [< OF < LL satio, -onis sowing time < L, a sowing] — **sea'son·er** n.

sea·son·a·ble (sē'zən·ə·bəl) adj. 1. Being in keeping with the season. 2. Done at the proper time. — **sea'son·a·ble·ness** n. — **sea'son·a·bly** adv.

sea·son·al (sē'zən·əl) adj. Characteristic of, affected by, or occurring at a certain season. — **sea'son·al·ly** adv.

sea·son·ing (sē'zən·ing) n. 1. The act or process by which something, as lumber, is rendered fit for use. 2. Something added to food to give relish; esp., a condiment. 3. Something added to increase enjoyment, zest, etc.

season ticket A ticket or pass, usually at a reduced rate, entitling the holder to daily trips on a train for a certain period or to admission to a series of sporting events, etc.

seat (sēt) n. 1. That on which one sits, as a chair, bench, or stool. 2. The part of a thing upon which one rests in sitting, or upon which an object or another part rests. 3. The buttocks; also, the portion of a garment covering them. 4. The place where anything is situated, settled, or established. 5. A place of abode. 6. The privilege or right of membership in a legislative body, stock exchange, etc. 7. The manner of sitting, as on horseback. 8. A surface or part upon which the base of anything rests. — v.t. 1. To place on a seat or seats; cause to sit down. 2. To have seats for. 3. To put or repair a seat on or in. 4. To locate, settle, or center: usually in the passive. 5. To fix or set firmly or in place. [< ON sǣti. Akin to SIT.]

seat belt A safety belt.

seat·ing (sē'ting) n. 1. The act of providing with seats. 2. Fabric for upholstering seats. 3. The arrangement of seats, as in a room, auditorium, etc.

sea urchin A marine animal having a soft rounded body covered with a shell bearing numerous movable spines.

sea wall A wall or an embankment to prevent the encroachments of the sea, the erosion of the shore, etc.

sea·ward (sē'wərd) adj. 1. Going toward the sea. 2. Blowing, as wind, from the sea. — adv. In the direction of the sea: also **sea'wards** (-wərdz).

sea·way (sē'wā') *n.* **1.** A way or lane over the sea. **2.** An inland waterway that receives ocean shipping. **3.** The headway made by a ship. **4.** A rough sea: usu. in **in a seaway.**

sea·weed (sē'wēd') *n.* **1.** Any of a widely distributed class of plants growing in the sea, including the kelps, rockweeds, dulse, etc. **2.** Any marine plant.

sea·wor·thy (sē'wûr'thē) *adj.* In fit condition for a voyage: said of a vessel. **— sea'wor'thi·ness** *n.*

se·ba·ceous (si·bā'shəs) *adj. Physiol.* **1.** Of, pertaining to, or like fat. **2.** Designating any of the glands in the skin that secrete sebum. [< NL *sebaceus* < L *sebum* tallow]

sebi- *combining form* Fat; fatty matter: also, before vowels, **seb-.** Also **sebo-.** [< L *sebum* tallow]

se·bum (sē'bəm) *n. Physiol.* A fatty matter secreted by the sebaceous glands. [< L, tallow]

sec (sek) *adj. French* Dry: said of wines.

se·cant (sē'kənt, -kant) *adj.* Cutting, esp. into two parts; intersecting. **— n. 1.** *Geom.* **a** A straight line intersecting a given curve. **b** A line drawn from the center of a circle through one extremity of an arc to the tangent drawn from the other extremity of the same arc. **2.** *Trig.* A function of an acute angle, equal to the ratio of the hypotenuse to the side adjacent to the angle when the angle is included in a right triangle. [< L *secans, -antis*, ppr. of *secare* to cut]

se·cede (si·sēd') *v.i.* **·ced·ed, ·ced·ing** To withdraw formally from a union, fellowship, or association, esp. from a political or religious organization. [< L < *se-* apart + *cedere* to go] **— se·ced'er** *n.*

se·ces·sion (si·sesh'ən) *n.* **1.** The act of seceding, esp. from political or religious association. **2.** *Usually cap. U.S.* The withdrawal of the Southern States from the Union in 1860–61. **— se·ces'sion·al** *adj.* **— se·ces'sion·ist** *adj. & n.*

Seck·el (sek'əl, sik'əl) *n.* A variety of small, sweet pear. [after the Pennsylvania farmer who introduced it]

se·clude (si·klood') *v.t.* **·clud·ed, ·clud·ing 1.** To remove and keep apart from the company or society of others; isolate. **2.** To screen or shut off, as from view. [< L < *se-* apart + *claudere* to shut]

se·clud·ed (si·kloo'did) *adj.* **1.** Separated; withdrawn; living apart from others. **2.** Protected or screened. **— se·clud'ed·ly** *adv.* **— se·clud'ed·ness** *n.*

se·clu·sion (si·kloo'zhən) *n.* **1.** The act of secluding, or the state or condition of being secluded; solitude; retirement. **2.** A secluded place. **— se·clu'sive** *adj.* **— se·clu'sive·ly** *adv.* **— se·clu'sive·ness** *n.*

sec·ond[1] (sek'ənd) *n.* **1.** A unit of time, ⅟₆₀ of a minute. **2.** *Geom.* A unit of angular measure, ⅟₆₀ of a minute of arc. Symbol: ″. [< OF *seconde*]

sec·ond[2] (sek'ənd) *adj.* **1.** Next in order, authority, responsibility, etc., after the first: the ordinal of *two.* **2.** Ranking next to or below the first or best; secondary; subordinate. **3.** Identical in character with another or preceding one; another; other. **4.** *Music* Designating one of two parts for like instruments or voices, usu. the one lower in pitch or in some manner subordinate. **— n. 1.** The one next after the first in position, rank, importance, or quality. **2.** An attendant who supports or aids another, as in a duel. **3.** *pl.* Articles of merchandise of imperfect manufacture or of inferior quality. **4.** *Music* **a** The interval between any note and the next above or below in the diatonic scale. **b** A note separated by this interval from any other. **c** Two notes at this interval written or sounded together. **d** A second or subordinate part, instrument, or voice. **5.** In parliamentary law, an utterance whereby a motion is seconded: Do I hear a *second*? **— v.t. 1.** To act as a supporter or assistant of; promote; encourage. **2.** In deliberative bodies, to support formally, as a motion, resolution, etc. **— adv.** In the second order, place, or rank: also, in formal discourse, **sec'ond·ly.** [< OF < L *secundus* following]

sec·on·dar·y (sek'ən·der'ē) *adj.* **1.** Of second rank, grade, or influence; subordinate; auxiliary. **2.** Depending on what is primary or original: *secondary* sources. **3.** *Electr.* Of, pertaining to, or noting an induced current or its circuit, esp. in an induction coil. **— n.** *pl.* **·dar·ies 1.** One who acts in a secondary or subordinate capacity; an assistant. **2.** Anything of secondary size, position, or importance. **3.** *Ornithol.* One of the feathers that grow on the second joint or forearm of a bird's wing. **— sec'on·dar'i·ly** *adv.*

secondary accent See under ACCENT.

secondary cell *Electr.* A type of cell that can be recharged by the passage of direct current in reverse direction through the electrolyte: also called *storage cell.*

secondary education High school or preparatory school education between the elementary and college levels.

secondary school A high school or preparatory school intermediate between the elementary school and college.

second base In baseball, the base situated between first and third base.

second base·man (bās'mən) *n. pl.* **·men** (-mən) A baseball player stationed at or near second base.

sec·ond-best (sek'ənd·best') *adj.* Next to the best.

second childhood Senility; dotage.

sec·ond-class (sek'ənd·klas', -kläs') *adj.* **1.** Ranking next below the first or best; inferior; mediocre. **2.** Of or pertaining to travel accommodations ranking between first class and third class. **3.** Of or pertaining to a class of mail including all printed periodicals. **— adv.** By second-class ticket or by using second-class conveniences.

Second Coming The expected second coming of Christ.

second estate The nobility.

second fiddle Any secondary or inferior status, esp. in the phrase **to be** (or **play**) **second fiddle.**

sec·ond-guess (sek'ənd·ges') *v.t. & v.i.* To judge or conjecture about (something) after it has occurred.

sec·ond-hand (sek'ənd·hand') *adj.* **1.** Having been previously owned, worn, or used by another; not new. **2.** Received from another: *secondhand* information. **3.** Handling or dealing in merchandise that is not new.

second hand The hand that marks the seconds on a clock or a watch.

second lieutenant *Mil.* The lowest grade of commissioned officer, ranking below first lieutenant.

second nature A disposition or character that is acquired and not innate; deep-seated habits that have become fixed.

second papers A popular name for a certificate of naturalization.

sec·ond-rate (sek'ənd·rāt') *adj.* Second in quality, size, rank, importance, etc.; second-class. **— sec'ond-rat'er** *n.*

second sight The alleged power of seeing events occurring at distant places, in the future, etc.; clairvoyance.

sec·ond-sto·ry man (sek'ənd·stôr'ē, -stō'rē) *U.S. Slang* A burglar.

sec·ond-string (sek'ənd·string') *adj. U.S. Informal* In sports, ranking next to the regular or starting player or team.

Second World War See WORLD WAR II in table for WAR.

se·cre·cy (sē'krə·sē) *n. pl.* **·cies 1.** The condition or quality of being secret or hidden; concealment. **2.** The character of being secretive; secretiveness. **3.** Privacy; retirement; solitude. Also **se·cret·ness** (sē'krit·nis).

se·cret (sē'krit) *adj.* **1.** Kept separate or hidden from view or knowledge; concealed; hidden. **2.** Beyond normal comprehension; obscure; recondite. **3.** Known or revealed only to the initiated: *secret* rites. **4.** Affording privacy; secluded. **5.** Good at keeping secrets; close-mouthed. **6.** *U.S. Mil.* Denoting the second highest category of security classification. Compare TOP-SECRET. **— n. 1.** Something not to be told. **2.** A thing undiscovered or unknown. **3.** An underlying reason; that which, when known, explains; key. **4.** A secret contrivance. **5.** Secrecy. **— in secret** In privacy; in a hidden place. [< OF < L < *se-* apart + *cernere* to separate] **— se'cret·ly** *adv.*

sec·re·tar·i·at (sek'rə·târ'ē·it, -at) *n.* **1.** A secretary's position. **2.** The place where a secretary transacts his business. **3.** The executive department of an organization, esp. of the United Nations. **4.** The entire staff of secretaries in an office. Also **sec're·tar'i·ate.**

sec·re·tar·y (sek'rə·ter'ē) *n. pl.* **·tar·ies 1.** A person employed to deal with correspondence, keep records, and handle clerical business for an individual, business, committee, etc. **2.** An executive officer presiding over and managing a department of government. **3.** A writing desk with a bookcase or cabinet. [< Med.L < L *secretum* secret] **— sec're·tar'i·al** (-târ'ē·əl) *adj.*

secretary bird A South African bird that has long legs and a crest suggesting quill pens stuck behind the ear.

secretary general *pl.* **secretaries general** A chief secretary; an assistant to a governor general. **— sec're·tar'y-gen'er·al·cy** (-jen'ər·əl·sē) *n.*

se·crete (si·krēt') *v.t.* **·cret·ed, ·cret·ing 1.** To conceal; hide. **2.** *Physiol.* To produce (a secretion). [See SECRET.] **— se·cre'tor** *n.*

se·cre·tion (si·krē'shən) *n. Physiol.* **1.** The process, generally glandular, by which materials are separated from the blood and elaborated into new substances, as milk, etc. **2.** The substance secreted. [See SECRET.]

se·cre·tive (si·krē'tiv; *for def. 1, also* sē'krə·tiv) *adj.* **1.** Inclined to secrecy; reticent. **2.** *Physiol.* Producing or causing secretion. **— se·cre'tive·ly** *adv.* **— se·cre'tive·ness** *n.*

se·cre·to·ry (si·krē'tər·ē) *adj.* Of, or functioning as, a secretion. **— n.** *pl.* **·ries** A secreting organ or gland.

secret service 1. Investigation conducted secretly for a government. **2.** The secret or espionage work of various government agencies in time of war.

Secret Service A section of the Department of the Treasury concerned with the suppression of counterfeiting, the protection of the President of the United States, etc.

---

sect (sekt) *n.* **1.** A body of persons distinguished by peculiarities of faith and practice from other bodies adhering to the same general system, esp., the adherents of a particular religious creed. **2.** Any number of persons united in opinion, interest beliefs. [< OF < L < *sequi* to follow]

-sect *combining form* To cut; divide (in a specified manner): *vivisect, bisect.* [< L < *secare* to cut]

sec·tar·i·an (sek·târ′ē·ən) *adj.* **1.** Pertaining to or belonging to a particular sect. **2.** Adhering or confined to a specific group, party, etc.; partisan. — *n.* A member of a sect, esp. if bigoted. — **sec·tar′i·an·ism** *n.*

sec·ta·ry (sek′tər·ē) *n.* *pl.* **·ries 1.** A sectarian. **2.** A dissenter from an established church; a nonconformist. Also **sec′ta·rist.** [< MF or Med.L < L. See SECT.]

sec·tion (sek′shən) *n.* **1.** A separate part or division; as a portion of a book or a chapter. **2.** A distinct part of a country, community, etc. **3.** *U.S.* An area of land containing 640 acres, ⅟₃₆ of a township. **4.** Any of two or more trains, buses, airplanes, etc., represented by a single entry in a timetable or schedule. **5.** A portion of railroad track under the care of a particular set of men. **6.** In a sleeping car, a space containing two berths. **7.** A picture of a building, geological formation, etc., as if cut by an intersecting plane; also, the thing so viewed. **8.** The act of cutting; division by cutting. — **Syn.** See PORTION. — *v.t.* **1.** To cut or divide into sections. **2.** To shade (a drawing) so as to designate a section or sections. [< MF or L < *secare* to cut]

-section *combining form* The act or process of cutting or dividing: *vivisection.* [< L. See SECTION.]

sec·tion·al (sek′shən·al) *adj.* **1.** Pertaining to a section, as of a country; local: a *sectional* dialect. **2.** Dividing or alienating one section from another. **3.** Made up of sections. — *n.* *U.S.* A long sofa having several separate units. — **sec′tion·al·ly** *adv.*

sec·tion·al·ism (sek′shən·əl·iz′əm) *n.* Undue concern for a particular section of the country; intense consciousness of sectional differences. — **sec′tion·al·ist** *n.*

sec·tor (sek′tər) *n.* **1.** *Geom.* A part of a circle or ellipse bounded by two radii and the arc subtended by them. A part or portion: a wooded *sector* of land; the conservative *sector* of the population. **3.** *Mil.* A defined area for which a unit is responsible. — *v.t.* To divide into sectors. [< LL < L < *secare* to cut] — **sec·to·ri·al** (sek·tôr′ē·al) *adj.*

SECTOR (*abc*) OF A CIRCLE

sec·u·lar (sek′yə·lər) *adj.* **1.** Of this world or the present life; temporal; worldly: distinguished from *spiritual.* **2.** Not under the control of the church; civil. **3.** Not concerned with religion; not sacred. **4.** Not bound by monastic vows. — *n.* **1.** One in holy orders who is not bound by monastic vows. **2.** A layman. [< OF < LL < L *saeculum* generation, an age]

sec·u·lar·ism (sek′yə·lə·riz′əm) *n.* **1.** The belief that morality should be determined without reference to religious systems. **2.** The view that religion should not be introduced into public education or civil affairs. — **sec′u·lar·ist** *n.*

sec·u·lar·ize (sek′yə·lə·rīz′) *v.t.* **·ized, ·iz·ing 1.** To convert from sacred to secular uses. **2.** To make worldly. — **sec′u·lar·i·za′tion** *n.*

se·cure (si·kyŏŏr′) *adj.* **1.** Guarded against or not likely to be exposed to danger; safe. **2.** Free from fear, apprehension, etc. **3.** Fixed or holding firmly in place. **4.** So strong or well-made as to render loss, escape, or failure impossible. **5.** Assured; certain; guaranteed. — *v.* **·cured, ·cur·ing** *v.t.* **1.** To make secure; protect. **2.** To make firm or tight; fasten. **3.** To make certain; ensure. **4.** To obtain possession of; get. — *v.i.* **5.** To be or become secure; take precautions; visit *against,* etc. [< L < *se-* without + *cura* care] — **se·cur′a·ble** *adj.* — **se·cure′ly** *adv.* — **se·cure′ment** *n.* — **se·cure′ness** *n.* — **se·cur′er** *n.*

se·cu·ri·ty (si·kyŏŏr′ə·tē) *n.* *pl.* **·ties 1.** The state of being secure; freedom from danger, poverty, etc. **2.** One who or that which secures or guarantees. **3.** Something deposited or pledged as a guarantee for payment. **4.** *pl.* Stocks, bonds, notes, etc. **5.** Protection of secrecy, as in wartime.
— **Syn. 2, 3.** Both *security* and *surety* may mean property given as a guarantee or the person who gives it, but *security* is chiefly used in the first sense, and *surety* in the second. A *bond* is a written promise to pay compensation for loss, damage, etc.

Security Council A permanent organ of the United Nations charged with the maintenance of international peace.

security risk *U.S.* A person regarded as unfit for employment in government or in a job connected with national defense, as because of dubious associations.

se·dan (si·dan′) *n.* **1.** A closed automobile having two or four doors and a front and back seat. **2.** A sedan chair. [? Ital. *sedere* to sit < L]

sedan chair A portable, enclosed chair, usu., for one passenger, carried by means of poles at the front and back.

se·date (si·dāt′) *adj.* **1.** Characterized by habitual composure; unhurried; calm. **2.** Sober and decorous. [< L < *sedere* to sit] — **se·date′ly** *adv.* — **se·date′ness** *n.*

se·da·tion (si·dā′shən) *n.* *Med.* The act or process of reducing distress, irritation, excitement, etc., by administering sedatives.

sed·a·tive (sed′ə·tiv) *adj.* **1.** Having a soothing effect. **2.** *Med.* Allaying irritation; assuaging pain. — *n.* Any means, as a medicine, of soothing distress or allaying pain.

sed·en·tar·y (sed′ən·ter′ē) *adj.* **1.** Characterized by, requiring, or resulting from much sitting or a habitual sitting posture. **2.** Settled in one place, as certain tribes; sluggish; inactive. **3.** Accustomed to sitting. **4.** *Zool.* Remaining in one place; attached or fixed to an object. [< L *sedere* to sit] — **sed′en·tar′i·ly** *adv.* — **sed′en·tar′i·ness** *n.*

Se·der (sā′dər) *n.* *pl.* **Se·ders** or **Se·dar·im** (sə·där′im) In Judaism, the Passover feast commemorating the departure of the Israelites from Egypt. [< Hebrew *sedher* service]

sedge (sej) *n.* Any of various grasslike herbs widely distributed in marshy places. [OE *secg*] — **sedg′y** *adj.*

sed·i·ment (sed′ə·mənt) *n.* **1.** Matter that settles to the bottom of a liquid; settlings; dregs; lees. **2.** *Geol.* Fragmentary material deposited by water or air. — **Syn.** See WASTE. [< MF < L *sedere* to sit, settle] — **sed′i·men′ta·ry, sed′i·men′tal** *adj.*

se·di·tion (si·dish′ən) *n.* **1.** Language or conduct directed against public order and the safety of the state. **2.** The clandestine incitement of such disorder. **3.** Dissension; revolt. [< OF < L < *sed-* aside + *itio, -onis* a going] — **se·di′tion·ar·y, se·di′tion·ist** *adj.* & *n.*

se·di·tious (si·dish′əs) *adj.* **1.** Of, promoting, or having the character of sedition. **2.** Taking part in or guilty of sedition. [See SEDITION.] — **se·di′tious·ly** *adv.*

se·duce (si·dōōs′, -dyōōs′) *v.t.* **·duced, ·duc·ing 1.** To lead astray; entice into wrong, disloyalty, etc.; tempt. **2.** To induce to engage in illicit sexual intercourse, esp. for the first time. [< L < *se-* apart + *ducere* to lead] — **se·duc′er** *n.* — **se·duc′i·ble** or **se·duce′a·ble** *adj.*

se·duc·tion (si·duk′shən) *n.* **1.** The act of seducing. **2.** Something that seduces; an enticement. Also **se·duce·ment** (si·dōōs′mənt, -dyōōs′-). [See SEDUCE.]

se·duc·tive (si·duk′tiv) *adj.* Tending to seduce; enticing. — **se·duc′tive·ly** *adv.* — **se·duc′tive·ness** *n.*

se·du·li·ty (si·dōō′lə·tē, -dyōō′-) *n.* The state or character of being sedulous.

sed·u·lous (sej′ŏŏ·ləs) *adj.* Constant in application or attention; assiduous. [< L *sedulus* careful] — **sed′u·lous·ly** *adv.* — **sed′u·lous·ness** *n.*
— **Syn.** diligent, persevering. Compare BUSY.

se·dum (sē′dəm) *n.* Any of a large genus of chiefly perennial plants, having very thick leaves and usu. white, yellow, or pink flowers. [< L, houseleek]

see[1] (sē) *v.* **saw, seen, see·ing** *v.t.* **1.** To perceive with the eyes; gain knowledge or awareness of by means of one's vision. **2.** To perceive with the mind; understand. **3.** To find out or ascertain. **4.** To have experience or knowledge of. **5.** To encounter; chance to meet. **6.** To have a meeting or interview with; visit or receive as a guest, patient, etc. **7.** To attend as a spectator; view. **8.** To accompany; escort. **9.** To take care; be sure: *See* that you do it! **10.** In poker, to accept a bet by betting an equal sum. — *v.i.* **11.** To have or exercise the power of sight. **12.** To find out; inquire. **13.** To understand. **14.** To think; consider. — **to see about 1.** To inquire into the facts, causes, etc., of. **2.** To take care of; attend to. — **to see (someone) off** To accompany to a point of departure, as for a journey. — **to see (someone) through** To aid or protect, as throughout a period of difficulty or danger. — **to see through** To penetrate, as a disguise or deception. — **to see to** To be responsible for; give one's attention to. [OE *sēon*]

see[2] (sē) *n.* **1.** The local seat from which a bishop, archbishop, or pope exercises jurisdiction. **2.** Episcopal or papal jurisdiction, authority, rank, or office. — **Holy See** The Pope's jurisdiction or office. [< OF < L *sedes* seat]

seed (sēd) *n.* **1.** The ovule from which a plant may be reproduced; the fertilized ovule containing an embryo. **2.** That from which anything springs; source. **3.** Offspring; children. **4.** The male fertilizing element; semen; milt. **5.** Any small, usu. hard fruit; also, any part of a plant from which it may be propagated, as bulbs, tubers, etc. **6.** Seeds collectively. **7.** Ancestry; stock. — **to go to seed 1.** To develop and shed seed. **2.** To become shabby, useless, etc.; deteriorate. — *v.t.* **1.** To sow with seed. **2.** To sow (seed). **3.** To remove the seeds from. **4.** In sports, to arrange positions in a tournament, etc., so that the more skilled competitors meet only in the later events. **5.** To intersperse (clouds) with particles of silver iodide or other substances in order to produce rainfall. — *v.i.* **6.** To sow seed. **7.** To grow to maturity and produce or shed seed. [OE *sæd*] — **seed′er** *n.* — **seed′less** *adj.*

seed bud *Bot.* The germ within a seed; also, the ovule.

seed cake A sweet cake containing aromatic seeds.

seed·case (sēd′kās′) *n. Bot.* A pericarp.

seed leaf *Bot.* A cotyledon.

seed·ling (sēd′ling) *n.* **1.** *Bot.* A plant grown from seed, as distinguished from one propagated by grafting. **2.** A very small or young tree or plant.

seed oyster A young oyster, esp. one transplanted to another bed.

seed pearl A small pearl, used in jewelry, embroidery, etc.

seeds·man (sēdz′mən) *n. pl.* **·men** (-mən) **1.** A dealer in seeds. **2.** A sower. Also **seed′man.**

seed vessel *Bot.* A pericarp.

seed·y (sē′dē) *adj.* **seed·i·er, seed·i·est 1.** Full of seeds. **2.** Gone to seed. **3.** Poor; shabby. **4.** *Informal* Feeling or looking wretched. — **seed′i·ly** *adv.* — **seed′i·ness** *n.*

see·ing (sē′ing) *n.* The act of seeing; vision; sight. — *conj.* Taking into consideration; since; in view of the fact.

seek (sēk) *v.* **sought, seek·ing** *v.t.* **1.** To go in search of; look for. **2.** To strive for; try to get or obtain. **3.** To endeavor or try: He *seeks* to mislead me. **4.** To ask or inquire for; request. **5.** To go to; betake oneself to: to *seek* a warmer climate. — *v.i.* **6.** To make a search or inquiry. [OE *sēcan*] — **seek′er** *n.*

seem (sēm) *v.i.* **1.** To give the impression of being; appear. **2.** To appear to oneself: I *seem* to hear strange voices. **3.** To appear to exist. **4.** To be evident or apparent: It *seems* to be raining. [ME < ON *sœma* to conform to] — **seem′er** *n.*

seem·ing (sē′ming) *adj.* Having the appearance of reality; apparent but not necessarily actual. — *n.* Appearance; semblance; esp., false show. — **seem′ing·ly** *adv.* — **seem′ing·ness** *n.*

seem·ly (sēm′lē) *adj.* **·li·er, ·li·est** Befitting the proprieties; decorous. — *adv.* Becomingly; decently; appropriately. [< ON < *sœmr* fitting] — **seem′li·ness** *n.*

seen (sēn) Past participle of SEE.

seep (sēp) *v.i.* To soak through pores or small interstices; percolate; ooze. — *n.* A small spring or a place out of which water, oil, etc., oozes. [Alter. of OE *sypian* to soak]

seep·age (sē′pij) *n.* **1.** The act or process of seeping or oozing. **2.** The fluid or moisture that oozes.

seer (sē′ər for def. 1; also sir for defs. 2 and 3) *n.* **1.** One who sees. **2.** A prophet. **3.** One believed to have second sight. [< SEE[1] + -ER] — **seer′ess** *n. fem.*

seer·suck·er (sir′suk′ər) *n.* A thin fabric of cotton, rayon, nylon, etc., usu. striped in colors, with a crinkled surface. [< Hind. < Persian *shīr o shakkar*, lit., milk and sugar]

see·saw (sē′sô′) *n.* **1.** A balanced plank or board made to move alternately up and down by persons at opposite ends: also called *teeter.* **2.** The action or diversion of balancing on such a board. **3.** Any up-and-down or to-and-fro movement. — *v.t. & v.i.* **1.** To move or cause to move on or as if on a seesaw. **2.** To alternate; fluctuate. — *adj.* Moving to and fro; vacillating. [Reduplication of SAW[1]]

seethe (sēth) *v.* **seethed, seethed, seeth·ing** *v.i.* **1.** To boil. **2.** To foam or bubble as if boiling. **3.** To be agitated, as by rage. — *v.t.* **4.** To soak in liquid; steep. — *n.* The act or condition of seething; turmoil. [OE *sēothan*]

seg·ment (seg′mənt) *n.* **1.** A part cut off or divided from the other parts of anything; a section. **2.** *Geom.* **a** A part of a figure, esp., of a circle, cut off by a line or plane. **b** A finite part of a line. — *v.t. & v.i.* To divide into segments. [< L < *secare* to cut] — **seg·men·tar·y** (seg′mən·ter′ē) *adj.*

seg·men·tal (seg·men′təl) *adj.* **1.** Of a segment or segments. **2.** Divided into segments. — **seg·men′tal·ly** *adv.*

seg·men·ta·tion (seg′mən·tā′shən) *n.* **1.** The act of cutting or dividing into segments. **2.** The state of being so divided. **3.** *Biol.* The cleavage of a cell.

se·go (sē′gō) *n. pl.* **·gos 1.** A perennial herb of the lily family, having white flowers: the State flower of Utah. **2.** Its edible bulb. [< Shoshonean (Ute) *sīgo*]

seg·re·gate (seg′rə·gāt; *for adj. also* seg′rə·git) *v.* **·gat·ed, ·gat·ing** *v.t.* **1.** To place apart from others or the rest; isolate. **2.** To subject to segregation. — *v.i.* **3.** To separate from a mass and gather about nuclei or along lines of fracture, as in crystallization. **4.** To undergo segregation. — *adj.* Set apart from others. [< L < *se-* apart + *grex, gregis* flock] — **seg′re·ga′tive** *adj.* — **seg′re·ga′tor** *n.*

seg·re·ga·tion (seg′rə·gā′shən) *n.* **1.** The act or process of segregating. **2.** The practice of requiring separate facilities, as in housing, schools, and transportation, for use by whites and nonwhites, esp. Negroes. — **seg′re·ga′tion·ist** *n.*

Seid·litz powder (sed′lits) An aperient consisting of two separate parts, tartaric acid, and sodium bicarbonate mixed with Rochelle salt, dissolved separately and then combined. [after *Seidlitz*, a Czech village, site of a medicinal spring]

seign·ior (sēn′yər) *n.* **1.** A lord; noble. **2.** A title of respect equivalent to *Sir.* Also **sei·gneur** (sēn·yûr′). [< AF, OF < L *senior* older] — **sei·gnio·ri·al** (sēn·yôr′ē·əl, -yō′rē-) *adj.*

seign·ior·y (sēn′yər·ē) *n. pl.* **·ies 1.** The territory or juris-

diction of a seignior; a manor. **2.** Right belonging to feudal superiority. Also **sei′gneur·y.**

seine (sān) *n.* A long fishnet hanging vertically in the water and having floats at the top edge and weights at the bottom. — *v.t. & v.i.* **seined, sein·ing** To fish or catch with a seine. [OE < L < Gk. *sagēnē* fishnet]

seis·mic (sīz′mik, sīs′-) *adj.* Of, characteristic of, or produced by earthquakes. Also **seis′mal, seis′mi·cal, seis·mat·i·cal** (sīz·mat′ə·kəl, sīs-). [< Gk. < *seiein* to shake]

seismic sea wave A large and often destructive wave caused by a submarine earthquake; a tsunami.

seismo- *combining form* Earthquake. Also, before vowels, **seism-.** [< Gk. *seismos* earthquake]

seis·mo·gram (sīz′mə·gram, sīs′-) *n.* The record of an earthquake or earth tremor made by a seismograph.

seis·mo·graph (sīz′mə·graf, -gräf, sīs′-) *n.* An instrument for recording automatically the intensity, direction, and duration of an earthquake shock. — **seis′mo·graph′ic** *adj.* — **seis·mog·ra·pher** (sīz·mog′rə·fər, sīs-) *n.*

seis·mog·ra·phy (sīz·mog′rə·fē, sīs-) *n.* The study and recording of earthquake phenomena.

seis·mol·o·gy (sīz·mol′ə·jē, sīs-) *n.* The science of earthquake phenomena. — **seis·mo·log·ic** (sīz′mə·loj′ik, sīs′-) or **·i·cal** *adj.* — **seis′mo·log′i·cal·ly** *adv.* — **seis·mol′o·gist** *n.*

seize (sēz) *v.* **seized, seiz·ing** *v.t.* **1.** To take hold of suddenly and forcibly. **2.** To grasp mentally; comprehend. **3.** To take possession of by authority or right. **4.** To take possession of by force. **5.** To take prisoner; capture; arrest. **6.** To act upon with sudden and powerful effect: Terror *seized* the enemy. **7.** To take advantage of immediately, as an opportunity. **8.** *Law* To put into legal possession. **9.** *Naut.* To fasten or bind by turns of cord, etc. — *v.i.* **10.** To take a sudden or forcible hold. [< OF < Med.L (*ad propriam*) *sacire* to take (into one's own possession)] — **seiz′a·ble** *adj.* — **seiz′er** *n.*

sei·zure (sē′zhər) *n.* **1.** The act of seizing. **2.** A sudden or violent attack, as of epilepsy; fit; spell.

se·la·chi·an (si·lā′kē·ən) *adj.* Of or belonging to a group of fishes including the sharks, skates, and rays. — *n.* A selachian fish. [< NL < Gk. *selachos* shark]

se·lah (sē′lə) A word of unknown meaning occurring often at the end of a verse in the Psalms, usu. considered as a direction to readers or musicians. [< Hebrew *selāh*]

sel·dom (sel′dəm) *adv.* At widely separated intervals, as of time or space; infrequently. [OE *seldum*]

se·lect (si·lekt′) *v.t.* **1.** To take in preference to another or others. — *v.i.* **2.** To make a choice. — *adj.* **1.** Chosen in preference to others; choice. **2.** Exclusive. **3.** Very particular in selecting. [< L < *se-* apart + *legere* to choose] — **se·lect′ness** *n.* — **se·lec′tor** *n.*

se·lec·tee (si·lek′tē′) *n.* One selected; esp., one drafted for military or naval service.

se·lec·tion (si·lek′shən) *n.* **1.** Choice. **2.** Anything selected. **3.** A thing or collection of things chosen with care. **4.** *Biol.* The process by which certain organisms, or any of their characteristics, are favored in the struggle for survival.

se·lec·tive (si·lek′tiv) *adj.* **1.** Pertaining to selection; tending to select. **2.** Having or characterized by good selectivity.

selective service Compulsory military service according to specified conditions of age, fitness, etc.

se·lec·tiv·i·ty (si·lek′tiv′ə·tē) *n.* **1.** The state or quality of being selective. Also **se·lec′tive·ness. 2.** *Telecom.* That characteristic of a radio or television receiver, electrical circuit, etc., by which certain frequencies can be received to the exclusion of others.

se·lect·man (si·lekt′mən) *n. pl.* **·men** (-mən) In New England, one of a board of town officers, elected annually to exercise executive authority in local affairs.

Se·le·ne (si·lē′nē) In Greek mythology, goddess of the moon: identified with the Roman *Luna.* Also **Se·le′na** (-nə). [< Gk. *Selēnē*, lit., the moon]

sel·e·nite (sel′ə·nīt) *n.* A pearly, usu. transparent variety of gypsum. [< L < Gk. *selēnītēs* (*lithos*), lit., moonstone < *selēnē* the moon]

se·le·ni·um (si·lē′nē·əm) *n.* A gray, crystalline, nonmetallic element (symbol Se) of the sulfur group, varying greatly in electrical resistance under the influence of light. See ELEMENT. [< NL < Gk. *selēnē* the moon]

selenium cell A photoelectric cell in which plates of selenium respond to the action of light upon them.

seleno- *combining form* Moon; pertaining to the moon; lunar. Also, before vowels, **selen-.** [< Gk. *selēnē* the moon]

self (self) *n. pl.* **selves 1.** An individual known or considered as the subject of his own consciousness. **2.** Anything considered as having a distinct personality. **3.** Personal interest or advantage. **4.** Any thing, class, or attribute that, abstractly considered, maintains a distinct and characteristic individuality or identity. — *adj.* **1.** Being of the same color, substance, etc., throughout; uniform. **2.** Of a part, accessory, etc., made of the same material as that with which it is used. [OE]

◆ *Self* may appear as a combining form with various meanings as shown in the list below:

1. Of the self (the object of the root word); as in:

self-abandonment	self-disclosure	self-murderer
self-abasing	self-discovery	self-mutilation
self-abhorrence	self-disgrace	self-neglect
self-accusation	self-disparagement	self-neglectful
self-adaptive	self-display	self-nourishment
self-admiration	self-disposal	self-observation
self-admission	self-disquieting	self-offense
self-adornment	self-dissolution	self-opinion
self-adulation	self-doubt	self-painter
self-advancement	self-easing	self-paying
self-advertisement	self-enriching	self-perceiving
self-advertising	self-estimate	self-perceptive
self-affliction	self-evacuation	self-perfecting
self-analysis	self-exalting	self-perfection
self-annihilation	self-exculpation	self-perpetuating
self-applause	self-excuse	self-perpetuation
self-appreciation	self-expansion	self-persuasion
self-approbation	self-expatriation	self-pleasing
self-approval	self-exploiting	self-praise
self-asserting	self-exposure	self-praising
self-awareness	self-fearing	self-preparation
self-bedizenment	self-flatterer	self-presentation
self-betrayal	self-flattering	self-preserving
self-blame	self-flattery	self-projection
self-castigation	self-folding	self-protecting
self-chastisement	self-forgetful	self-protection
self-cognizance	self-formation	self-punishment
self-commendation	self-glorification	self-raising
self-committal	self-gratification	self-recollection
self-comparison	self-guidance	self-reconstruction
self-condemnation	self-harming	self-reduction
self-condemning	self-helpful	self-regulation
self-conditioning	self-humbling	self-representation
self-confinement	self-humiliation	self-repressing
self-confounding	self-hypnosis	self-repression
self-conquest	self-hypnotism	self-reproach
self-conservative	self-hypnotized	self-reproachful
self-conserving	self-idolatry	self-restriction
self-consideration	self-idolizing	self-revealing
self-consoling	self-ignorance	self-revelation
self-consuming	self-ignorant	self-ruin
self-contempt	self-imitation	self-satirist
self-contradicting	self-immolation	self-scrutinizing
self-conviction	self-immurement	self-scrutiny
self-correction	self-impairment	self-searching
self-corruption	self-indignation	self-slaughter
self-creation	self-indulging	self-soothing
self-criticism	self-inspection	self-study
self-cure	self-instruction	self-subjection
self-damnation	self-insurer	self-subordination
self-debasement	self-integration	self-suppression
self-deceit	self-intensifying	self-surrender
self-deceiving	self-interrogation	self-suspicious
self-dedication	self-introduction	self-taxation
self-defeating	self-judgment	self-teacher
self-deflation	self-justification	self-terminating
self-degradation	self-justifying	self-tolerant
self-deifying	self-laudatory	self-torment
self-dejection	self-limitation	self-torture
self-delusion	self-limiting	self-treatment
self-deprecating	self-loss	self-trust
self-depreciation	self-maceration	self-trusting
self-depreciative	self-maintenance	self-undoing
self-destroying	self-martyrdom	self-upbraiding
self-destruction	self-mastery	self-valuing
self-destructive	self-mistrust	self-vaunting
self-direction	self-mortification	self-vindication
self-disapproval	self-murder	self-worship

2. By oneself or itself; by one's own effort (the agent of the root word); as in self-employed.

self-abandoned	self-doomed	self-named
self-administered	self-elaborated	self-offered
self-approved	self-elected	self-ordained
self-authorized	self-explained	self-paid
self-balanced	self-exposed	self-pampered
self-beguiled	self-furnished	self-performed
self-betrayed	self-generated	self-perpetuated
self-blinded	self-honored	self-perplexed
self-caused	self-idolized	self-planted
self-chosen	self-illumined	self-posed
self-condemned	self-imposed	self-powered
self-conducted	self-incurred	self-proclaimed
self-constituted	self-initiated	self-professed
self-convicted	self-instructed	self-punished
self-corrupted	self-invited	self-renounced
self-declared	self-judged	self-repressed
self-defended	self-justified	self-restrained
self-deluded	self-kindled	self-revealed
self-deprived	self-limited	self-schooled
self-destroyed	self-maimed	self-sown
self-determined	self-matured	self-subdued
self-devised	self-misused	self-sustained
self-divided	self-mortified	self-tempted

3. To, toward, in, for, on, or with oneself; as in:

self-absorbed	self-desire	self-permission
self-aid	self-despair	self-pictured
self-aim	self-directed	self-pleased
self-amusement	self-direction	self-preference
self-application	self-disdain	self-prescribed
self-applied	self-disgust	self-pride
self-assumed	self-dislike	self-procured
self-assuming	self-dissatisfied	self-produced
self-benefit	self-elation	self-profit
self-care	self-enamored	self-purifying
self-comment	self-enclosed	self-reflection
self-communing	self-exultation	self-relation
self-compassion	self-focusing	self-relying
self-complacence	self-gain	self-repellent
self-complacency	self-helpfulness	self-repose
self-complacent	self-injurious	self-reproof
self-conflict	self-injury	self-repulsive
self-consistency	self-kindness	self-resentment
self-consistent	self-liking	self-resigned
self-content	self-loathing	self-respectful
self-contented	self-oblivious	self-rigorous
self-delight	self-occupied	self-sent
self-dependence	self-panegyrical	self-tenderness
self-dependent	self-penetration	self-vexation

4. From oneself or itself; from one's own nature or power; as in:

self-apparent	self-fruition	self-poise
self-arising	self-healing	self-poised
self-born	self-inclusive	self-refuting
self-coherence	self-initiative	self-renewing
self-complete	self-intelligible	self-resourceful
self-defining	self-issuing	self-resplendent
self-derived	self-luminous	self-restoring
self-desirable	self-manifestation	self-reward
self-developing	self-moving	self-rewarding
self-effort	self-operative	self-sprung
self-evolving	self-opinionated	self-stability
self-explaining	self-originating	self-stimulated
self-forbidden	self-perfect	self-warranting

5. Independent; as in:

self-agency	self-dominance	self-existence
self-authority	self-dominion	self-ownership
self-credit	self-entity	self-sovereignty

6. In technology, automatic or automatically; as in:

self-acting	self-cocking	self-moving
self-adapting	self-cooled	self-oiling
self-adjustable	self-defrosting	self-primer
self-adjusting	self-emptying	self-priming
self-aligning	self-feeder	self-recording
self-burning	self-feeding	self-registering
self-changing	self-filling	self-regulated
self-charging	self-inking	self-regulating
self-checking	self-lighting	self-righting
self-cleaning	self-locking	self-screwing
self-closing	self-lubricating	self-setting

self·a·base·ment (self'ə·bās'mənt) *n.* Abasement or degradation of oneself.

self·ab·ne·ga·tion (self'ab/ni·gā'shən) *n.* The complete putting aside of oneself and one's own claims for the sake of some other person or object; self-sacrifice.

self·ab·sorp·tion (self'ab·sôrp'shən, -zôrp'-) *n.* Absorption in or concentration on one's own affairs, work, interests, etc.

self·a·buse (self'ə·byōōs') *n.* **1.** The disparagement of one's own person or powers. **2.** Masturbation.

self·ad·dressed (self'ə·drest') *adj.* Addressed to oneself.

self·ap·point·ed (self'ə·poin'təd) *adj.* Appointed or designated by oneself rather than by others: a *self-appointed* boss.

self·as·ser·tion (self'ə·sûr'shən) *n.* The asserting or putting forward of oneself, one's opinions, claims, or rights. — **self'-as·ser'tive·ly** *adv.*

self·as·sured (self'ə·shoŏrd') *adj.* Confident in one's own abilities; self-reliant. — **self'-as·sur'ance** *n.*

self·cen·tered (self'sen'tərd) *adj.* Concerned chiefly with one's own affairs and interests, often with a lack of consideration for others. Also *Brit.* **self'-cen'tred.** — **self'-cen'tered·ness** *n.* — **self'-cen'tered·ly** *adv.*

self·col·ored (self'kul'ərd) *adj.* **1.** Having the natural color. **2.** Of but one color or tint.

self·com·mand (self'kə·mand', -mänd') *n.* The state of having all the faculties and powers fully at command.

self·con·ceit (self'kən·sēt') *n.* An unduly high opinion of oneself; vanity. — **self'-con·ceit'ed** *adj.*

self·con·fi·dence (self'kon'fə·dəns) *n.* Confidence in oneself or in one's own unaided powers, judgment, etc. — **self'-con'fi·dent** *adj.* — **self'-con'fi·dent·ly** *adv.*

self·con·scious (self'kon'shəs) *adj.* **1.** Unduly conscious that one is observed by others; ill at ease. **2.** Manifesting embarrassment. — **self'-con'scious·ly** *adv.* — **self'-con'·scious·ness** *n.*

self·con·tained (self'kən·tānd') *adj.* **1.** Keeping one's thoughts and feelings to oneself. **2.** Exercising self-control. **3.** Complete and independent; self-sustaining. **4.** Having all parts needed for working order, as a machine bearing its own motor.

self-con·tra·dic·tion (self′kon′trə·dik′shən) *n.* **1.** The act or state of contradicting oneself or itself. **2.** That which contradicts itself. **— self′-con′tra·dic′to·ry** *adj.*

self-con·trol (self′kən·trōl′) *n.* The act, power, or habit of having one's faculties or energies under control of the will.

self-de·fense (self′di·fens′) *n.* Defense of oneself, one's property, or one's reputation. **— self′-de·fen′sive** *adj.*

self-de·ni·al (self′di·nī′əl) *n.* The act or power of denying oneself gratification. **— self′-de·ny′ing** *adj.* **— self′-de·ny′ing·ly** *adv.*

self-de·ter·mi·na·tion (self′di·tûr′mə·nā′shən) *n.* **1.** The principle of free will; decision by oneself. **2.** Decision by the people of a country or section as to its future political status. **— self′-de·ter′min·ing** *adj.* & *n.*

self-de·vo·tion (self′di·vō′shən) *n.* Devotion of oneself, with one's claims, wishes, or interests, to the service of a person or a cause. **— self′-de·vo′tion·al** *adj.*

self-dis·ci·pline (self′dis′ə·plin) *n.* The discipline or training of oneself, often for improvement.

self-ed·u·cat·ed (self′ej′ŏŏ·kā′tid) *adj.* **1.** Educated through one's own efforts without the aid of instructors. **2.** Educated at one's own expense. **— self′-ed′u·ca′tion** *n.*

self-ef·face·ment (self′i·fās′mənt) *n.* The keeping of oneself in the background through modesty, timidity, etc.

self-es·teem (self′ə·stēm′) *n.* A good opinion of oneself; an overestimate of oneself. **— Syn.** See PRIDE.

self-ev·i·dent (self′ev′ə·dənt) *adj.* Carrying its evidence or proof in itself; requiring no proof of its truth. **— self′-ev′i·dence** *n.* **— self′-ev′i·dent·ly** *adv.*

self-ex·am·i·na·tion (self′ig·zam′ə·nā′shən) *n.* Examination of one's own motives, desires, habits, etc.

self-ex·ist·ence (self′ig·zis′təns) *n.* Inherent, underived, independent existence. **— self′-ex·ist′ent** *adj.*

self-ex·plan·a·to·ry (self′ik·splan′ə·tôr′ē, -tō′rē) *adj.* Easily comprehended without explanation; obvious.

self-ex·pres·sion (self′ik·spresh′ən) *n.* Expression of one's own temperament or emotions, as in art.

self-fer·til·i·za·tion (self′fûr′təl·ə·zā′shən, -ī·zā′shən) *n.* *Biol.* Fertilization of an ovum by sperm from the same animal or of a plant ovule by its own pollen.

self-gov·ern·ment (self′guv′ərn·mənt, -ər·mənt) *n.* **1.** Government of a country or region by its own people. **2.** The state of being so governed. **3.** *Archaic* Self-control. **— self′-gov′erned, self′-gov′ern·ing** *adj.*

self-heal (self′hēl′) *n.* Any of various weedy, perennial herbs with violet flowers, formerly reputed to cure disease.

self-help (self′help′) *n.* The act or condition of getting along by one's own efforts without the aid of others.

self-hood (self′hŏŏd) *n.* **1.** The state of being an individual; personality. **2.** Selfishness; self-centeredness.

self-im·por·tance (self′im·pôr′təns) *n.* Pompous self-conceit. **— self′-im·por′tant** *adj.*

self-im·prove·ment (self′im·prōōv′mənt) *n.* Improvement of one's abilities or condition through one's own efforts.

self-in·duced (self′in·dōōst′, -dyōōst′) *adj.* **1.** Induced by oneself or itself. **2.** *Electr.* Produced by self-induction.

self-in·duc·tion (self′in·duk′shən) *n.* *Electr.* Induction within the same circuit, causing it to resist any change in the amount of current flowing in it. **— self′-in·duc′tive** *adj.*

self-in·dul·gence (self′in·dul′jəns) *n.* The indulgence or gratification of one's own desires, weaknesses, etc. **— self′-in·dul′gent** *adj.* **— self′-in·dul′gent·ly** *adv.*

self-in·flict·ed (self′in·flik′tid) *adj.* Inflicted on oneself by oneself: a *self-inflicted* wound. **— self′-in·flic′tion** *n.*

self-in·ter·est (self′in′tər·ist, -in′trist) *n.* Personal interest or advantage, or the pursuit of it; selfishness. **— self′-in′ter·est·ed** *adj.*

self·ish (sel′fish) *adj.* **1.** Caring chiefly for oneself or one's own interests or comfort, esp. to the point of disregarding the welfare or wishes of others. **2.** Proceeding from or characterized by undue love of self. **— self′ish·ly** *adv.*

self·ish·ness (sel′fish·nis) *n.* The quality of being selfish.

self-knowl·edge (self′nol′ij) *n.* Knowledge of one's own character, motives, limitations, etc.

self·less (self′lis) *adj.* Regardless of self; unselfish. **— self′less·ly** *adv.* **— self′less·ness** *n.*

self-load·ing (self′lō′ding) *adj.* Of firearms, utilizing a portion of the force of the exploding gas or of recoil to extract and eject the empty case and chamber the next round.

self-love (self′luv′) *n.* The desire or tendency that leads one to seek his own well-being. **— self′-lov′ing** *adj.*

self-made (self′mād′) *adj.* **1.** Having attained honor, wealth, etc., by one's own efforts. **2.** Made by oneself.

self-pit·y (self′pit′ē) *n.* The act or state of pitying oneself. **— self′-pit′y·ing** *adj.* **— self′-pit′y·ing·ly** *adv.*

self-pol·li·na·tion (self′pol′ə·nā′shən) *n.* *Bot.* The transfer of pollen from stamens to pistils of the same flower. **— self′-pol′li·nat·ed** *adj.*

self-pos·ses·sion (self′pə·zesh′ən) *n.* **1.** The full possession or control of one's powers or faculties. **2.** Presence of mind; self-command. **— self′-pos·sessed′** *adj.*

self-pres·er·va·tion (self′prez′ər·vā′shən) *n.* **1.** The protection of oneself from destruction. **2.** The urge to protect oneself, regarded as an instinct.

self-pro·nounc·ing (self′prə·noun′sing) *adj.* Having marks of pronunciation and stress applied to a word without phonetic alteration of the spelling.

self-pro·pelled (self′prə·peld′) *adj.* **1.** Able to propel itself. **2.** Having the means of propulsion contained within itself, as an automobile.

self-re·gard (self′ri·gärd′) *n.* **1.** Regard or consideration for oneself or one's own interests. **2.** Estimation of self.

self-re·li·ance (self′ri·lī′əns) *n.* Reliance on one's own abilities, resources, or judgment. **— self′-re·li′ant** *adj.*

self-re·spect (self′ri·spekt′) *n.* Proper respect for oneself and one's own character. **— self′-re·spect′ing** *adj.*

self-re·straint (self′ri·strānt′) *n.* Restraint, as of the passions, by the force of one's own will; self-control.

self-right·eous (self′rī′chəs) *adj.* Righteous in one's own estimation; pharisaic. **— self′-right′eous·ly** *adv.* **— self′-right′eous·ness** *n.*

self-ris·ing (self′rī′zing) *adj.* **1.** That rises of itself. **2.** Having the leaven already added, as some flours.

self-sac·ri·fice (self′sak′rə·fīs) *n.* The sacrifice of one's self or one's personal welfare or wishes for the sake of duty or for the good of others. **— self′-sac′ri·fic′ing** *adj.*

self·same (self′sām′) *adj.* Exactly the same; identical. **— self′same′ness** *n.*

self-sat·is·fac·tion (self′sat′is·fak′shən) *n.* Satisfaction with one's own actions and characteristics; conceit; complacency. **— self′-sat′is·fied** *adj.* **— self′-sat′is·fy′ing** *adj.*

self-seek·ing (self′sē′king) *adj.* Exclusively seeking one's own interests or gain. **—** *n.* Actions, motives, etc., characteristic of a self-seeking person. **— self′-seek′er** *n.*

self-ser·vice (self′sûr′vis) *adj.* Designating a restaurant, store, etc., where patrons serve themselves.

self-ser·ving (self′sûr′ving) *adj.* Tending to advance one's own interests, often at the expense of others.

self-start·er (self′stär′tər) *n.* A starter (def. 3).

self-styled (self′stīld′) *adj.* Characterized (as such) by oneself: a *self-styled* gentleman.

self-suf·fi·cient (self′sə·fish′ənt) *adj.* **1.** Able to support or maintain oneself without aid or cooperation from others. **2.** Having overweening confidence in oneself. Also **self′-suf·fic′ing** (-sə·fī′sing). **— self′-suf·fi′cien·cy** *n.*

self-sup·port (self′sə·pôrt′, -pōrt′) *n.* The act or state of supporting oneself entirely by one's own efforts. **— self′-sup·port′ed, self′-sup·port′ing** *adj.*

self-sus·tain·ing (self′sə·stān′ing) *adj.* Sustaining oneself or itself without outside help; self-supporting.

self-taught (self′tôt′) *adj.* Taught by oneself or through one's own efforts, without the aid of formal instruction.

self-will (self′wil′) *n.* Strong or tenacious adherence to one's own will or wish, esp. with disregard of the wishes of others; obstinacy. **— self′-willed′** *adj.*

self-wind·ing (self′wīn′ding) *adj.* *Mech.* Having a device that automatically winds a clock or other mechanism.

sell (sel) *v.* **sold, sell·ing** *v.t.* **1.** To transfer (property) to another for money or for some other consideration. **2.** To deal in; offer for sale. **3.** To deliver, surrender, or betray for a price or reward: to *sell* one's honor. **4.** To promote the sale of: Good advertising *sells* many products. **5.** *Informal* To cause to accept or approve something: with *on*: They *sold* him on the scheme. **6.** *Informal* To cause the acceptance or approval of: He always sold himself well. **7.** *Slang* To deceive; cheat. **—** *v.i.* **8.** To transfer ownership for money, etc.; engage in selling. **9.** To be on sale; be sold. **10.** *Informal* To attract buyers: This item *sells* well. **11.** *Informal* To gain acceptance or approval: Will his plan *sell*? **— to sell off** To get rid of by selling. **— to sell out 1.** To sell all one's merchandise, possessions, etc. **2.** *Slang* To betray. **—** *n.* **1.** On the stock exchange, a stock that ought to be sold. **2.** *Slang* A trick; joke; swindle. [OE *sellan* to give]

sell·er (sel′ər) *n.* **1.** One who sells. **2.** Something with a measure of salability: This book is a good *seller.*

sell-out (sel′out′) *n.* **1.** An act of selling out. **2.** *Informal* A performance for which all seats have been sold. **3.** *Slang* A betrayal through a secret bargain or agreement.

Selt·zer (selt′sər) *n.* An effervescing mineral water. Also **Seltzer water.** [Alter. of G *Selterser,* from *Nieder Selters,* a village in SW Prussia, its place of origin]

sel·vage (sel′vij) *n.* The edge of a woven fabric so finished that it will not ravel. Also **sel′vedge.** [< SELF + EDGE, trans. of MDu. *selfegghe*]

selves (selvz) Plural of SELF.

se·man·tic (si·man′tik) *adj.* **1.** Of or pertaining to meaning. **2.** Of or relating to semantics. [< Gk. *sēmainein* to signify] — **se·man'ti·cal·ly** *adv.*

se·man·ti·cist (si·man'tə·sist) *n.* A specialist in semantics.

se·man·tics (si·man'tiks) *n.pl.* (*construed as sing.*) **1.** *Ling.* The study of the meanings of speech forms, esp. of the development and changes in meaning of words and word groups. **2.** *Logic* The relation between signs or symbols and what they signify or denote. **3.** Loosely, verbal trickery.

sem·a·phore (sem'ə·fôr, -fōr) *n.* An apparatus for making signals, as with movable arms, disks, flags, or lanterns. [< F < Gk. *sēma* a sign + -PHORE] — **sem'a·phor'ic** (-fôr'ik, -for'ik) or **·i·cal** *adj.*

sem·blance (sem'bləns) *n.* **1.** A mere show without reality; pretense. **2.** Outward appearance. **3.** A likeness or resemblance. [< OF < L *simulare, similare* to simulate]

se·men (sē'mən) *n.* The impregnating fluid of male animals that contains spermatozoa; seed. [< L < *serere* to sow]

se·mes·ter (si·mes'tər) *n.* **1.** A college half year. **2.** In U.S. colleges and universities, a period of instruction, usu. lasting 17 or 18 weeks. [< G < L (*cursus*) *semestris* (a period) of six months] — **se·mes'tral** *adj.*

sem·i (sem'ī) **1.** *U.S. Informal* A semitrailer. **2.** *Canadian Slang* An American.

semi- *prefix* **1.** Not fully; partially; partly: *semiautomatic, semicivilized.* **2.** Exactly half: *semicircle.* **3.** Occurring twice (in the periods specified): *semiweekly.* [< L]

◆ *Semi-* (def. 1) appears as a prefix in many words, as in the following words and in the list below. It is pronounced sem'ē, sem'ə, or sometimes sem'ī.

semiacquaintance	semidivine	semiovoid
semiadherent	semidomestic	semipagan
semiaffectionate	semidomesticated	semipanic
semiagricultural	semidry	semiparallel
semialcoholic	semi-Empire	semiparalysis
semiallegiance	semienclosed	semipastoral
semianarchist	semierect	semipeace
semiangular	semieremitical	semiperfect
semianimal	semiexposed	semiperishable
semianimated	semiextinction	semipermanent
semiarborescent	semifailure	semiperspicuous
semiarchitectural	semifatalistic	semipinnate
semiarid	semifeudalism	semiplastic
semiatheist	semifictional	semipolitical
semiattached	semifinished	semipolitician
semiautonomous	semifit	semiporous
semiautonomy	semifitting	semipublic
semibald	semifixed	semiradical
semibarbarian	semiflexed	semiraw
semibarbaric	semifluctuating	semireactionary
semibarbarism	semiforeign	semirebellion
semibarbarous	semifriable	semireligious
semibarren	semifrontier	semiresolute
semibleached	semifunctional	semirespectability
semiblind	semigala	semirespectable
semiblunt	semigenuflection	semiretirement
semiboiled	semi-Gothic	semiriddle
semibourgeois	semigranulate	semi-Romanesque
semichannel	semihard	semi-Romanized
semichaotic	semihigh	semiroyal
semichivalrous	semihistorical	semirustic
semi-Christian	semihobo	semisacred
semiclerical	semihostile	semisatiric
semiclosed	semihumanitarian	semisatirical
semiclosure	semihumorous	semiscientific
semicoagulated	semi-idle	semisecrecy
semicollapsible	semi-idleness	semisecret
semicolonial	semi-incandescent	semiserious
semicoma	semi-independence	semiseriousness
semicomplete	semi-independent	semisocial
semiconceal	semi-intoxicated	semisocialism
semiconfident	semi-intoxication	semisoft
semiconfinement	semi-invalid	semispontaneity
semiconformist	semileafless	semispontaneous
semiconnection	semilegendary	semistagnant
semiconservative	semiliberal	semistagnation
semiconversion	semilined	semistarvation
semicooperation	semiliterate	semistarved
semicooperative	semilucent	semisuccess
semicured	semimilitary	semisuccessful
semicylindrical	semimobile	semisuspension
semidangerous	semimodern	semisymmetric
semidarkness	semimonastic	semisymmetrical
semideaf	semimonopoly	semitailored
semidelirious	semimute	semitechnical
semidenatured	semimystical	semitrained
semidependent	seminecessary	semitruth
semidestructive	seminervous	semivirtue
semideveloped	semioblivious	semivital
semidiaphanous	semiobscurity	semivoluntary
semidigested	semiopened	semiwarfare
semidirect	semiorganized	semiwild

sem·i·an·nu·al (sem'ē·an'yoo·əl) *adj.* Issued or occurring twice a year; half-yearly. — *n.* A publication issued twice a year. — **sem'i·an·nu·al·ly** *adv.*

sem·i·au·to·mat·ic (sem'ē·ô'tə·mat'ik) *adj.* **1.** Partly au-

tomatic. **2.** Of firearms, self-loading but firing once at each pull on the trigger.

sem·i·breve (sem'ē·brēv', -brev') *n. Chiefly Brit. Music* A whole note.

sem·i·cir·cle (sem'ē·sûr'kəl) *n.* **1.** A half-circle; an arc or a segment of 180°. **2.** Anything formed or arranged in a half-circle. — **sem'i·cir'cu·lar** (-kyə·lər) *adj.*

semicircular canal *Anat.* One of the three tubular structures in the labyrinth of the ear, serving as the organ of equilibrium. For illus. see EAR.

sem·i·civ·i·lized (sem'ē·siv'ə·līzd) *adj.* Partly civilized.

sem·i·co·lon (sem'ē·kō'lən, sem'ə-) *n.* A mark (;) of punctuation, indicating a greater degree of separation than the comma.

sem·i·con·duc·tor (sem'ē·kən·duk'tər) *n. Physics* One of a class of substances whose electrical conductivity at ordinary temperatures is between that of a metal and an insulator, used in the manufacture of transistors.

sem·i·con·scious (sem'ē·kon'shəs) *adj.* Partly conscious.

sem·i·de·tached (sem'ē·di·tacht') *adj.* Joined to another on one side only; esp. designating a house having one wall in common with another house.

sem·i·fi·nal (sem'ē·fī'nəl) *n.* **1.** In sports, a competition that precedes the final event. **2.** One of two competitions in a tournament, the winners of each meeting in the final. — *adj.* Next before the final. — **sem'i·fi'nal·ist** *n.*

sem·i·flu·id (sem'ē·floo'id) *adj.* Fluid, but thick and viscous. Also **sem'i·flu·id'ic** (-floo·id'ik). — *n.* A thick, viscous fluid.

sem·i·month·ly (sem'ē·munth'lē) *adj.* Taking place twice a month. — *n. pl.* **·lies** A publication issued twice a month. — *adv.* At half-monthly intervals.

sem·i·nal (sem'ə·nəl) *adj.* **1.** Of, pertaining to, or containing seeds or semen. **2.** Having productive power; germinal. **3.** Not developed; rudimentary. Also *seminary.* [< OF < L < *semen, seminis* semen, seed] — **sem'i·nal·ly** *adv.*

sem·i·nar (sem'ə·när) *n.* **1.** A group of advanced students at a college or university, meeting regularly and informally with a professor for discussion of research problems. **2.** The course thus conducted or the room where it meets.

sem·i·nar·y (sem'ə·ner'ē) *n. pl.* **·nar·ies** **1.** A special school, as of theology. **2.** A school of higher education. **3.** The place where anything is nurtured. — *adj.* **1.** Seminal. **2.** Pertaining to a seminary. [< L *seminarium* seed plot]

sem·i·na·tion (sem'ə·nā'shən) *n.* **1.** The act of sowing or spreading; dispersion of seeds. **2.** Propagation; reproduction. [< L *seminare* to sow < *semen* seed]

sem·i·nif·er·ous (sem'ə·nif'ər·əs) *adj.* **1.** Carrying or producing semen. **2.** Bearing a seed or seeds.

Sem·i·nole (sem'ə·nōl) *n.* One of a Florida tribe of North American Indians of Muskhogean stock, an offshoot of the Creeks, now chiefly in Oklahoma. [< Muskhogean (Creek) *Simanóle*, lit., separatist, runaway]

sem·i·of·fi·cial (sem'ē·ə·fish'əl) *adj.* Having some official authority or sanction; official to a certain extent. — **sem'i·of·fi'cial·ly** *adv.*

sem·i·per·me·a·ble (sem'ē·pûr'mē·ə·bəl) *adj.* Partially permeable, as membranes that separate a solvent from the dissolved substance.

sem·i·pre·cious (sem'ē·presh'əs) *adj.* Of, pertaining to, or designating gemstones, as jade, garnet, opal, amethyst, etc., that are somewhat less rare or valuable than precious stones.

sem·i·pri·vate (sem'ē·prī'vit) *adj.* Partly but not wholly private, as a hospital room for two or several patients.

sem·i·pro·fes·sion·al (sem'ē·prə·fesh'ən·əl) *adj.* Engaged in a sport for profit, but not as a full-time occupation. — *n.* A semiprofessional athlete. Also *Informal* **sem'i·pro'** (-prō'). — **sem'i·pro·fes'sion·al·ly** *adv.*

sem·i·qua·ver (sem'ē·kwā'vər) *n. Chiefly Brit. Music* A sixteenth note.

sem·i·rig·id (sem'ē·rij'id) *adj. Aeron.* Partly rigid, as an airship in which an exterior stiffener supports the load. — *n.* A semirigid airship.

sem·i·skilled (sem'ē·skild') *adj.* Partly skilled.

sem·i·sol·id (sem'ē·sol'id) *adj.* Nearly solid; partly solid.

Sem·ite (sem'īt, sē'mīt) *n.* **1.** One of a people of Caucasian stock, now represented by the Jews and Arabs, but originally including the ancient Babylonians, Assyrians, Arameans, Phoenicians, etc. **2.** A person believed to be a descendant of Shem. Also *Shemite.* [< NL < Gk. < Hebrew *Shēm*]

Se·mit·ic (sə·mit'ik) *adj.* Of or pertaining to the Semites, or to any of their languages. — *n.* A subfamily of the Hamito-Semitic family of languages.

Sem·i·tism (sem'ə·tiz'əm) *n.* **1.** A Semitic word or idiom. **2.** Semitic practices, opinions, or customs. **3.** Any policy favoring or thought to favor the Jews.

sem·i·tone (sem'ē·tōn') *n. Music* The smallest interval of the chromatic scale; a minor second: also called *half step, half tone.* — **sem'i·ton'ic** (-ton'ik) *adj.*

sem·i·trail·er (sem'ē·trā'lər) *n.* A trailer having wheels only at the rear, the front end resting on the tractor.

sem·i·vow·el (sem′ē·vou′əl) *n. Phonet.* A vowellike sound used as a consonant, as (w), (y), and (r): also called *glide*.

sem·i·week·ly (sem′ē·wēk′lē) *adj.* Issued or occurring twice a week. — *n. pl.* **·lies** A publication issued twice a week. — *adv.* At half-weekly intervals.

sem·i·year·ly (sem′ē·yir′lē) *adj.* Issued or occurring twice a year. — *n. pl.* **·lies** A semiyearly occurrence. — *adv.* At half-yearly intervals.

sem·o·li·na (sem′ə·lē′nə) *n.* The gritty or grainlike portions of wheat retained in the bolting machine after the fine flour has been passed through. [< L *simila* fine flour]

sem·per fi·de·lis (sem′pər fi·dē′lis, fi·dā′lis) *Latin* Always faithful: motto of the U.S. Marine Corps.

sem·per pa·ra·tus (sem′pər pə·rā′təs) *Latin* Always prepared: motto of the U.S. Coast Guard.

sem·pi·ter·nal (sem′pə·tûr′nəl) *adj.* Eternal; everlasting. [< OF < L *sempiternus* everlasting] — **sem′pi·ter′ni·ty** *n.*

semp·stress (semp′stris, sem′-) *n.* A seamstress.

sen (sen) *n. pl.* **sen** (sen) **1.** A former monetary unit and coin of Japan, equal to one hundredth of a yen. **2.** A monetary unit and coin of Indonesia.

sen·ate (sen′it) *n.* **1.** The governing body of some universities and institutions of learning. **2.** A council or legislative body. [< OF < L *senatus*, lit., council of old men]

Sen·ate (sen′it) *n.* **1.** The upper branch of national or state legislative bodies of the U.S., Canada, France, and other governments. The **United States Senate** is composed of two Senators elected by popular vote from each State. **2.** In ancient Rome, the state council.

sen·a·tor (sen′ə·tər) *n. Often cap.* A member of a senate.

sen·a·to·ri·al (sen′ə·tôr′ē·əl, -tō′rē-) *adj.* Of, pertaining to, or befitting a senator or senate. — **sen′a·to′ri·al·ly** *adv.*

send (send) *v.* **sent, send·ing** *v.t.* **1.** To cause or direct (a person or persons) to go; dispatch. **2.** To cause to be taken or directed to another place; transmit; forward: sometimes with *off*. **3.** To cause to issue; emit or discharge, as heat, light, smoke, etc. **4.** To throw or drive by force; impel. **5.** To cause to come, happen, etc.; grant. **6.** To bring into a specified state or condition. **7.** *U.S. Slang* To make rapturous with joy. — *v.i.* **8.** To dispatch an agent, messenger, or message. — **to send** (someone) **about his** (or her) **business** To dismiss with reproach or warning. — **to send down** *Brit.* To expel from a university. — **to send flying 1.** To scatter or knock violently away. **2.** To cause to flee. — **to send for** To summon by a message or messenger. — **to send packing** To dismiss quickly and forcefully. — **to send up** *Informal* To sentence to prison. [OE *sendan*] — **send′er** *n.*

send·off (send′ôf′, -of′) *n.* **1.** The act of sending off; a start. **2.** A farewell dinner or other celebration or demonstration at parting. **3.** Encouragement, as in starting a career.

Sen·e·ca (sen′ə·kə) *n.* One of a tribe of Indians of Iroquoian stock formerly inhabiting western New York. [< Du. *Sennacaas* the Five Nations < Algonquian *A′sinnika*]

Sen·e·ga·lese (sen′gə·lēz′, -lēs) *adj.* Of or pertaining to Senegal. — *n.* A native or inhabitant of Senegal.

se·nes·cent (si·nes′ənt) *adj.* **1.** Growing old. **2.** Characteristic of old age. [< L *senescere* to grow old] — **se·nes′cence** *n.*

sen·e·schal (sen′ə·shəl) *n.* **1.** An official in the household of a medieval prince or noble, having charge of feasts, etc.; a steward or major-domo. **2.** *Brit.* A cathedral official. [< OF < Gmc. Cf. OHG *siniskalk* old servant.]

se·nile (sē′nīl, -nil, sen′īl) *adj.* **1.** Pertaining to, proceeding from, or characteristic of old age. **2.** Infirm; weak; doting. **3.** *Geog.* Almost worn away to base level. [< L *senilis* < *senex* old] — **se′nile·ly** *adv.* — **se·nil·i·ty** (si·nil′ə·tē) *n.*

sen·ior (sēn′yər) *adj.* **1.** Older in years or higher in rank. **2.** Denoting the older of two: opposed to *junior*. ◆ The form used to distinguish a father from a son of the same name is usu. written *Albert Jones, Sr.* or *Albert Jones, senior.* **3.** Belonging to maturity or later life. **4.** Pertaining to the last year of a high-school or collegiate course of four years. — *n.* **1.** The older of two. **2.** One longer in service or higher in standing. **3.** A student in the senior year of a high-school, college, or university. [< L, comparative of *senex* old]

senior citizen An elderly person, esp. one of or over the age of retirement.

senior high school A high school, in the U.S. typically comprising grades 10, 11, and 12.

sen·ior·i·ty (sēn·yôr′ə·tē, -yor′-) *n. pl.* **·ties 1.** The state of being senior; priority of age or rank. **2.** Precedence or priority due to length of service.

sen·na (sen′ə) *n.* **1.** The dried leaflets of any of several leguminous plants, used medicinally as purgatives. **2.** Any plant yielding senna. [< NL < Arabic *sanā*]

se·ñor (sā·nyôr′) *n. pl.* **·ño·res** (-nyō′rās) *Spanish* **1.** A gentleman. **2.** Sir; Mr.: used as a title of address.

se·ño·ra (sā·nyō′rä) *n. Spanish* **1.** A lady. **2.** Mrs.

se·ño·ri·ta (sā′nyō·rē′tä) *n. Spanish* **1.** A young, unmarried lady. **2.** Miss.

sen·sate (sen′sāt) *adj.* Perceived by the senses. Also **sen′sat·ed.** — *v.t.* **·sat·ed, ·sat·ing** To perceive by the senses. [< LL < L *sensus* sense]

sen·sa·tion (sen·sā′shən) *n.* **1.** The aspect of consciousness resulting from the stimulation of any of the sense organs, as hearing, taste, touch, smell, or sight. **2.** *Physiol.* The capacity to respond to such stimulation. **3.** That which produces great interest or excitement. **4.** An excited condition: to cause a *sensation.* [See SENSATE.]

sen·sa·tion·al (sen·sā′shən·əl) *adj.* **1.** Pertaining to emotional excitement. **2.** Of or pertaining to physical sensation. **3.** Causing excitement; startling; melodramatic. — **sen·sa′tion·al·ly** *adv.*

sen·sa·tion·al·ism (sen·sā′shən·əl·iz′əm) *n.* The use of sensational or melodramatic methods, words, etc. — **sen·sa′tion·al·ist** *n.* — **sen·sa′tion·al·is′tic** *adj.*

sense (sens) *n.* **1.** The faculty of sensation; sense perception. **2.** Any of certain agencies by or through which an individual receives impressions of the external world, as taste, touch, hearing, smell, or sight. **3.** *Physiol.* Any receptor, or group of receptors, specialized for the perception of external objects or internal bodily changes. **4.** Rational perception accompanied by feeling: a *sense* of wrong. **5.** *Often pl.* Normal power of mind or understanding; sound or natural judgment: She is coming to her *senses.* **6.** Signification; import; meaning. **7.** Opinion, view, or judgment of the majority. **8.** Sound reason or judgment; wisdom. **9.** Capacity to perceive or appreciate: a *sense* of color. — *v.t.* **sensed, sens·ing 1.** To become aware of through the senses. **2.** *Informal* To comprehend; understand. [< F < L *sensus* perception]

sense·less (sens′lis) *adj.* **1.** Devoid of sense; making no sense; irrational. **2.** Unconscious. **3.** Incapable of feeling or perception. — **sense′less·ly** *adv.* — **sense′less·ness** *n.*

sense organ A structure specialized to receive sense impressions, as the eye, nose, ear, etc.

sen·si·bil·i·ty (sen′sə·bil′ə·tē) *n. pl.* **·ties 1.** The capability of sensation; power to perceive or feel. **2.** The capacity of sensation and rational emotion, as distinguished from intellect and will. **3.** *Often pl.* Susceptibility or sensitiveness to outside influences or mental impressions. **4.** Appreciation accompanying mental apprehension; discerning judgment.

— **Syn. 1, 3.** *Sensibility* may be used of mere physical sensation, but more often denotes qualities of mind: *sensibility* to heat and cold, the *sensibility* of the artist to beauty. *Sensitivity* suggests great *sensibility*, and the readiness to be excited by small cause. *Susceptibility* is the capacity to receive, contain, or be influenced: *susceptibility* to colds. *Feeling* specifically refers to the tactile sense, but is also used in the sense of emotional response as a general, but less precise, substitute for the other words.

sen·si·ble (sen′sə·bəl) *adj.* **1.** Possessed of good practical judgment; exhibiting sound sense and understanding. **2.** Capable of physical sensation. **3.** Perceptible through the senses: *sensible* heat. **4.** Emotionally or mentally sensitive. **5.** Having a perception or cognition; fully aware; persuaded. **6.** Great enough to be perceived. [< OF < L < *sentire* to feel, perceive] — **sen′si·ble·ness** *n.* — **sen′si·bly** *adv.*

sen·si·tive (sen′sə·tiv) *adj.* **1.** Easily affected by outside operations or influences; excitable or impressionable; touchy. **2.** Reacting readily to external agents or forces: paper *sensitive* to light. **3.** Pertaining to or depending on the senses or sensation. **4.** Closing or moving when touched or irritated, as certain plants. **5.** Liable to fluctuation. **6.** Capable of indicating minute changes or differences; delicate. [See SENSIBLE.] — **sen′si·tive·ly** *adv.* — **sen′si·tive·ness** *n.*

sensitive plant 1. A shrubby tropical herb whose leaves close at a touch. **2.** Any of various similar or related plants.

sen·si·tiv·i·ty (sen′sə·tiv′ə·tē) *n. pl.* **·ties** The state or degree of being sensitive. — **Syn.** See SENSIBILITY.

sen·si·tize (sen′sə·tīz) *v.t.* **·tized, ·tiz·ing 1.** To render sensitive. **2.** *Photog.* To make sensitive to light, as a plate or film. — **sen′si·ti·za′tion** *n.* — **sen′si·tiz′er** *n.*

sen·sor (sen′sər) *n.* That which receives and responds to a stimulus or signal; esp., an instrument or device designed to detect and respond to some force, change, or radiation.

sen·so·ri·um (sen·sôr′ē·əm, -sō′rē-) *n. pl.* **·ri·a** (-rē·ə) **1.** *Anat.* The nervous system, including the cerebrum, as the collective organ of sensation. **2.** *Biol.* The entire sensory apparatus. [< LL < L *sensus* sense]

sen·so·ry (sen′sər·ē) *adj.* **1.** Of or pertaining to sensation. **2.** Conveying or producing sense impulses. **3.** Pertaining to the sensorium. Also **sen·so·ri·al** (sen·sôr′ē·əl, -sō′rē-).

sen·su·al (sen′shoo·əl) *adj.* **1.** Unduly indulging the appetites or sexual pleasure; lewd. **2.** Pertaining to the body or to the physical senses; carnal. **3.** Pertaining to sensualism. ◆ See note under SENSUOUS. [< MF < LL < L *sensus* sense] — **sen′su·al·ly** *adv.*

sen·su·al·ism (sen′shŏō-əl-iz′əm) n. 1. Sensuality. 2. A system of ethics predicating the pleasures of sense to be the highest good. — **sen′su·al·ist** n. — **sen′su·al·is′tic** adj.

sen·su·al·i·ty (sen′shŏō-al′ə-tē) n. pl. **·ties** 1. The state of being sensual, or sensual acts collectively. 2. Sensual indulgence. Also called sensualism: also **sen′su·al·ness**.

sen·su·al·ize (sen′shŏō-əl-īz′) v.t. **·ized, ·iz·ing** To make sensual. Also Brit. **sen′su·al·ise′**. — **sen′su·al·i·za′tion** n.

sen·su·ous (sen′shŏō-əs) adj. 1. Pertaining or appealing to or derived from the senses: used in a higher and purer signification than sensual. 2. Keenly appreciative of and aroused by beauty, refinement, or luxury. 3. Resembling imagery that appeals to the senses: a sensuous portrayal. — **sen′su·ous·ly** adv. — **sen′su·ous·ness** n.

◆ **sensuous, sensual** Sensuous refers not only to the physical senses but to any means of feeling, as intellectual or esthetic sensitivity, intuition, etc.: the sensuous pleasure of walking in the rain. Sensual is generally restricted to bodily sensations and to the satisfaction of physical appetites.

sent (sent) Past tense and past participle of SEND.

sen·tence (sen′təns) n. 1. Gram. A group of words containing a subject and a predicate, as declarative, interrogative, imperative, and exclamatory sentences, or a single word in the case of the simple imperative. — **simple sentence** A sentence consisting of a subject and a predicate without any subordinate clauses. — **compound sentence** A sentence consisting of two or more independent clauses, usu. connected by a semicolon or a coordinating conjunction or both. — **complex sentence** A sentence consisting of an independent clause and one or more subordinate clauses. 2. Law A penalty pronounced upon a person convicted. 3. A formal determination or opinion. — v.t. **·tenced, ·tenc·ing** To pass sentence upon. [< OF < L < sentire to feel, be of opinion] — **sen′tenc·er** n. — **sen·ten′tial** (sen·ten′shəl) adj.

sen·ten·tious (sen·ten′shəs) adj. 1. Abounding in or giving terse expression to thought; axiomatic. 2. Habitually using terse, laconic, or aphoristic language. 3. Pompously formal; moralizing. [< L sententia < sentire to feel, be of an opinion] — **sen·ten′tious·ly** adv. — **sen·ten·ti·os·i·ty** (sen·ten′shē·os′ə·tē), **sen·ten′tious·ness** n.

sen·ti·ent (sen′shē·ənt, ·shənt) adj. Possessing powers of sense or sense perception; having sensation or feeling. — n. 1. A sentient person or thing. 2. The mind. [< L sentiens, -entis, ppr. of sentire to feel] — **sen′ti·ence, sen′ti·en·cy** n. — **sen′ti·ent·ly** adv.

sen·ti·ment (sen′tə-mənt) n. 1. Noble, tender, or artistic feeling, or susceptibility to such feeling; sensibility. 2. A verbal expression of such feeling. 3. A mental attitude or response to a person, object, or idea, based on feeling instead of reason. 4. An exaggerated emotional reaction. 5. Often pl. An opinion or judgment. 6. An expressive thought or idea in appropriate language [< OF < Med.L < L sentire to feel]

sen·ti·men·tal (sen′tə-men′təl) adj. 1. Characterized by sentiment or emotion. 2. Experiencing, displaying, or given to sentiment, often in an extravagant or mawkish manner: a sentimental novel. — **sen·ti·men′tal·ly** adv.

sen·ti·men·tal·i·ty (sen′tə-men·tal′ə·tē) n. pl. **·ties** 1. The state or quality of being mawkishly sentimental. 2. Any expression of sentiment. Also **sen′ti·men′tal·ism** (-men′təl·iz′əm). — **sen′ti·men′tal·ist** n.

sen·ti·men·tal·ize (sen′tə-men′təl-īz′) v. **·ized, ·iz·ing** v.t. 1. To make sentimental. 2. To cherish sentimentally. — v.i. 3. To behave sentimentally. Also Brit. **sen′ti·men′tal·ise**.

sen·ti·nel (sen′tə-nəl) n. 1. A sentry. 2. Any watcher or guard. — v.t. **·neled** or **·nelled, ·nel·ing** or **·nel·ling** 1. To watch over as a sentinel. 2. To furnish with sentinels. 3. To station or appoint as a sentinel. [< OF < Ital. < LL sentinare to avoid danger]

sen·try (sen′trē) n. pl. **·tries** 1. A soldier placed on guard to see that only authorized persons pass his post and to warn of danger. 2. The watch or guard kept by a sentry. [? Short for obs. centrenel, var. of SENTINEL.]

se·pal (sē′pəl) n. Bot. One of the individual leaves of a calyx. [< F < NL < L sep(aratus) separate + (pet)alum petal]

sep·a·ra·ble (sep′ər-ə-bəl, sep′rə-) adj. Capable of being separated. — **sep′a·ra·bil′i·ty, sep′a·ra·ble·ness** n. — **sep′a·ra·bly** adv.

sep·a·rate (v. sep′ə-rāt; adj. sep′ər-it, sep′rit) v. **·rat·ed, ·rat·ing** v.t. 1. To set asunder; disunite or disjoin; sever. 2. To occupy a position between; serve to keep apart. 3. To divide into components, parts, etc. 4. To isolate or obtain from a compound, mixture, etc. 5. To consider separately; distinguish between. 6. Law To part by separation. — v.i. 7. To become divided or disconnected; draw apart. 8. To part company; withdraw from association or combination. — adj. 1. Existing or considered apart from others; individual. 2. Disunited from the body; disembodied. 3. Separated; disjoined. [< L < se- apart + parare to prepare] — **sep′a·rate·ly** adv. — **sep′a·rate·ness** n. — **sep′a·ra′-**

tive, sep·a·ra·to·ry (sep′ər-ə·tôr′ē, -tō′rē, sep′rə-). — **sep′a·ra′tor** n.

sep·a·ra·tion (sep′ə-rā′shən) n. 1. The act or process of separating; division. 2. The state of being disconnected or apart. 3. Something that separates. 4. Law Relinquishment of cohabitation between husband and wife by mutual consent: distinguished from divorce.

separation center A central army or navy point that handles the discharging and releasing of personnel.

sep·a·ra·tist (sep′ər-ə·tist, sep′rə-) n. One who advocates or upholds separation, esp. one who secedes. Also **sep′a·ra′tion·ist**. — **sep′a·ra·tism** n.

Se·phar·dim (si-fär′dim) n.pl. The Spanish and Portuguese Jews or their descendants. Also **Se·phar′a·dim** (-ə·dim). [< Hebrew sephārādhīm] — **Se·phar′dic** adj.

se·pi·a (sē′pē-ə) n. 1. A reddish brown pigment prepared from the inky secretion of the cuttlefish. 2. The color of this pigment. 3. A picture done in this pigment. — adj. Executed in or colored like sepia; dark brown with a tinge of red. [< L < Gk. sēpia cuttlefish]

se·poy (sē′poi) n. A native Indian soldier who was employed in the former British Indian Army. [< Pg. sipae < Urdu sipāhī soldier < Persian sipāh army]

sep·pu·ku (sep·pōō-kōō) n. Japanese Hara-kiri.

sep·sis (sep′sis) n. Pathol. Infection by pathogenic microorganisms. [< NL < Gk. < sēpein to make putrid]

sep·ta (sep′tə) Plural of SEPTUM.

Sep·tem·ber (sep-tem′bər) The ninth month of the year, containing 30 days; the seventh month in the old Roman calendar. [< L septem seven]

sep·te·nar·y (sep′tə-ner′ē) adj. Consisting of, pertaining to, or being seven. — n. pl. **·nar·ies** 1. The number seven. 2. Anything having a definite relation to the number seven. Also **sep′te·nar′i·us** (sep′tə-nâr′ē-əs). [< L < septem seven]

sep·ten·ni·al (sep-ten′ē-əl) adj. 1. Recurring every seven years. 2. Continuing or capable of lasting seven years. [< L < septem seven + annus year] — **sep·ten′ni·al·ly** adv.

sep·tet (sep·tet′) n. 1. A group of seven persons, things, etc. 2. Music A composition for seven singers or instrumentalists. Also **sep·tette′**. [< G < L septem seven]

septi-¹ combining form Seven. Also, before vowels, **sept-**. [< L septem seven]

septi-² combining form A partition; fence. Also, before vowels, **sept-**. Also **septo-**. [< L septum enclosure, wall]

sep·tic (sep′tik) adj. 1. Of, pertaining to, or caused by sepsis. 2. Producing sepsis; infective. Also **sep′ti·cal.** — n. Any agent producing sepsis. [< LL < Gk. sēpein to putrefy] — **sep·tic·i·ty** (sep·tis′ə·tē) n.

sep·ti·ce·mi·a (sep′tə-sē′mē-ə) n. Pathol. An infection of the blood by pathogenic microorganisms; blood poisoning. Also **sep′ti·cae′mi·a**. [< NL < Gk. sēptikos putrefactive + haima blood] — **sep′ti·ce′mic** (-sē′mik) adj.

septic tank A tank in which sewage is allowed to remain until purified by the action of anaerobic bacteria.

sep·til·lion (sep-til′yən) n. 1. U.S. A thousand sextillions, written as 1 followed by twenty-four zeros: a cardinal number. 2. Brit. A million sextillions (def. 2), written as 1 followed by forty-two zeros: a cardinal number. — adj. Being a septillion in number. [< MF < septi- seven + (mi)llion million] — **sep·til′lionth** adj. & n.

sep·tu·a·ge·nar·i·an (sep′chōō-ə·jə·nâr′ē-ən, sep′tōō-) n. A person 70 years old, or between 70 and 80. — adj. 1. Seventy years old, or between 70 and 80. 2. Of or pertaining to a septuagenarian. [< L septuaginta seventy]

sep·tu·ag·e·nar·y (sep′chōō-aj′ə·ner′ē, sep′tōō-) adj. & n. Septuagenarian.

Sep·tu·a·ges·i·ma (sep′chōō-ə·jes′ə·mə, sep′tōō-) n. The third Sunday before Lent. Also **Septuagesima Sunday**. [< L, seventieth]

Sep·tu·a·gint (sep′chōō-ə·jint′, sep′tōō-) n. An old Greek version of the Old Testament Scriptures. [< L septuaginta seventy]

sep·tum (sep′təm) n. pl. **·ta** (-tə) Biol. 1. A dividing wall between two cavities: the nasal septum. 2. A partition, as in coral or in a spore. [< L < sepire to enclose] — **sep′tal, sep′tate** adj.

sep·ul·cher (sep′əl-kər) n. 1. A burial place; tomb; vault. 2. A receptacle for relics, esp. in an altar slab. — v.t. **·chered** or **·chred, ·cher·ing** or **·chring** To place in a sepulcher; bury. Also Brit. **sep′ul·chre** (-kər). [< OF < L sepulcrum burial place, tomb]

se·pul·chral (si-pul′krəl) adj. 1. Pertaining to a sepulcher. 2. Suggestive of the grave; dismal. 3. Unnaturally low and hollow in tone, as a voice. — **se·pul′chral·ly** adv.

sep·ul·ture (sep′əl-chər) n. 1. The act of entombing; burial. 2. Archaic A sepulcher.

se·quel (sē′kwəl) n. 1. Something that follows and serves as a continuation; a development from what went before. 2. A narrative discourse that, though complete in itself, develops from a preceding one. 3. A consequence; upshot; result. [< OF < L sequela < sequi to follow]

se·quence (sē′kwəns) *n.* **1.** The process or fact of following in space, time, or thought; succession or order: also **se′quen·cy. 2.** Order of succession; arrangement. **3.** A number of things following one another, considered collectively; a series. **4.** An effect or consequence. **5.** In card games, a set of three or more cards next each other in value. **6.** A section of motion-picture film presenting a single episode, without time lapses or interruptions. **7.** *Math.* An ordered succession of quantities, as 2*x*, 4*x*², 8*x*³, 16*x*⁴. [< L < *sequi* to follow]

sequence of tenses See under TENSE².

se·quent (sē′kwənt) *n.* That which follows; a consequence; result. —*adj.* **1.** Following in the order of time; succeeding. **2.** Consequent; resultant. [See SEQUENCE.]

se·quen·tial (si·kwen′shəl) *adj.* **1.** Characterized by or forming a sequence, as of parts. **2.** Sequent. —**se·quen·ti·al·i·ty** (si·kwen′shē·al′ə·tē) *n.* —**se·quen′tial·ly** *adv.*

se·ques·ter (si·kwes′tər) *v.t.* **1.** To place apart; separate. **2.** To seclude; withdraw: often used reflexively. **3.** *Law* To take (property) into custody until a controversy, claim, etc., is settled or satisfied. **4.** In international law, to confiscate and control (enemy property) by preemption. **5.** *Chem.* To render inactive, as by the process of chelation. [< OF < L *sequestrare* to remove, lay aside < *sequester* trustee] —**se·ques′tra·ble** *adj.* —**se·ques′tered** *adj.*

se·ques·trate (si·kwes′trāt) *v.t.* **·trat·ed, ·trat·ing 1.** To seize, esp. for the use of the government; confiscate. **2.** To take possession of for a time, with a view to the just settlement of the claims of creditors. **3.** To seclude; sequester. —**se·ques·tra·tion** (sē′kwes·trā′shən, sek′wəs-) *n.* —**se·ques·tra·tor** (sē′kwes·trā′tər, si·kwes′trā·tər) *n.*

se·quin (sē′kwin) *n.* A small coinlike ornament sewn on clothing. [< F < Ital. < Arabic *sikka* coining-die]

se·quoi·a (si·kwoi′ə) *n.* **1.** A gigantic evergreen tree of the western U.S., with spreading, lanceolate leaves and small cones: also called *redwood*. **2.** A closely related tree of the Sierra Nevada mountains of California, sometimes reaching a height of 300 feet. [< NL, after *Sequoyah*, 1770?–1843, a half-breed Cherokee Indian who invented the Cherokee alphabet]

ser (sir) See SEER².

ser- Var. of SERO.

se·ra (sir′ə) Plural of SERUM.

se·ra·glio (si·ral′yō, -räl′-) *n.* **1.** The portion of a Moslem house reserved for the wives and concubines; a harem. **2.** Any residence of a sultan. Also **se·rail** (se·rāl′). [< Ital. *serraglio* enclosure, ult. < LL *serrare*, var. of L *serare* to lock up]

se·ra·pe (sə·räp′ē) *n.* A blanketlike outer garment worn in Latin America, esp. in Mexico: also *sarape, zarape.* [< Am. Sp.]

ser·aph (ser′əf) *n. pl.* **ser·aphs** or **ser·a·phim** (ser′ə·fim) A celestial being having three pairs of wings. *Isa.* vi 2. [Back formation < *Seraphim*, pl. < LL < Hebrew] —**se·raph·ic** (si·raf′ik), *also* **se·raph′i·cal** *adj.* —**se·raph′i·cal·ly** *adv.*

ser·a·phim (ser′ə·fim) *n.* **1.** Plural of SERAPH: also **se·a·phin** (-fin). **2.** *pl.* **·phims** A seraph: an erroneous usage.

Ser·bo-Cro·a·tian (sûr′bō-krō·ā′shən) *n.* **1.** The South Slavic language of Yugoslavia, including all the old languages and dialects. **2.** One whose native tongue is Serbo-Croatian. Also **Ser′bo-Cro′at** (-krō′at, -ət). —*adj.* Of the Serbo-Croatian language or those who speak it.

sere¹ (sir) See SEAR¹.

sere² (sir) *n. Ecol.* The series of changes found in a given plant formation from the initial to the ultimate stage. [Back formation < SERIES] —**ser′al** *adj.*

ser·e·nade (ser′ə·nād′) *n.* **1.** An evening song, usu. that of a lover beneath his sweetheart's window. **2.** Music performed in honor of some person in the open air at night. **3.** The music for such a song. **4.** *Music* A form of instrumental music similar to the suite, and usu. including a march and a minuet: also called *serenata.* —*v.t.* & *v.i.* **·nad·ed, ·nad·ing** To entertain with a serenade. [< F < Ital. < L *serenus* clear, serene] —**ser′e·nad′er** *n.*

ser·e·na·ta (ser′ə·nä′tə) *n. pl.* **·tas, ·te** (tā) *Music* **1.** A dramatic cantata on any imaginative or simple subject, often composed as a complimentary offering for a royal personage. **2.** A serenade. [< Ital. See SERENADE.]

ser·en·dip·i·ty (ser′ən·dip′ə·tē) *n.* The faculty of happening upon fortunate discoveries when not in search of them. [Coined by Horace Walpole (1754), in *The Three Princes of Serendip* (Ceylon)] —**ser′en·dip′i·tous** *adj.*

se·rene (si·rēn′) *adj.* **1.** Clear; calm: a *serene* sky. **2.** Marked by peaceful repose; tranquil; placid: a *serene* spirit. **3.** Of exalted rank: chiefly in the titles of certain European princes: His *Serene* Highness. —**Syn.** See CALM. [< L *serenus*] —**se·rene′ly** *adv.* —**se·rene′ness** *n.*

se·ren·i·ty (si·ren′ə·tē) *n. pl.* **·ties 1.** The state or quality of being serene; peacefulness; repose. **2.** Clearness; brightness. **3.** *Usu. Cap.* A title of honor given to certain members of royal families: preceded by *His, Your,* etc.

serf (sûrf) *n.* **1.** In feudal times, a person bound in servitude on an estate. **2.** Anyone in servile subjection. [< OF < L *servus* slave] —**serf′age, serf′dom, serf′hood** *n.*

serge (sûrj) *n.* **1.** A strong twilled fabric made of wool yarns and characterized by a diagonal rib on both sides of the cloth. **2.** A rayon lining fabric. [< OF < L *serica* (*lana*) (wool) of the Seres < *Seres* the Seres, an eastern Asian people]

ser·geant (sär′jənt) *n.* **1.** *Mil.* Any of several noncommissioned officer grades. See tables at GRADE. **2.** A police officer ranking next below a captain (sometimes lieutenant) in the U.S., and next below an inspector in England. **3.** A sergeant at arms. **4.** A constable or bailiff. Also, *esp. Brit.,* **ser·jeant.** [< OF < L *serviens, -entis,* ppr. of *servire* to serve] —**ser′gean·cy, ser′geant·cy, ser′geant·ship** *n.*

sergeant at arms 1. An executive officer in a legislative body who enforces order. **2.** The title of certain court or city officials who have ceremonial duties.

sergeant major A noncommissioned officer in the highest enlisted grade of the U.S. Army and Marine Corps. See table at GRADE.

Sergeant Major of the Army The highest enlisted rank in the U.S. Army. See table at GRADE.

se·ri·al (sir′ē·əl) *adj.* **1.** Of the nature of a series. **2.** Published in a series at regular intervals. **3.** Arranged in rows or ranks; successive: also **se·ri·ate** (sir′ē·it, -āt). —*n.* **1.** A novel or other story regularly presented in successive instalments, as in a magazine, on radio or television, or in motion pictures. **2.** *Brit.* A periodical. [< NL < L *series* row, order] —**se′ri·al·ly** *adv.*

se·ri·al·ize (sir′ē·əl·īz′) *v.t.* **·ized, ·iz·ing** To arrange or publish in serial form. —**se′ri·al·i·za′tion** *n.*

serial number A number assigned to a person, object, item of merchandise, etc., as a means of identification.

se·ri·a·tim (sir′ē·ā′tim, ser′ē-) *adv.* One after another; serially. [< Med.L < L *series,* on analogy with *gradatim*]

ser·i·cul·ture (sir′ə·kul′chər) *n.* The raising and care of silkworms for the production of raw silk. [Contr. of F *sériciculture* < L *sericum* silk + *cultura* a raising, culture] —**ser′i·cul′tur·al** *adj.* —**ser′i·cul′tur·ist** *n.*

se·ries (sir′ēz) *n. pl.* **se·ries 1.** An arrangement of one thing after another; a connected succession of persons, things, data, etc. on the basis of like relationships. **2.** *Math.* An ordered arrangement of terms the sum of which is indicated. **3.** *Electr.* **a** An arrangement of sources or utilizers of electricity in which the positive electrode of one is connected with the negative electrode of another. **b** The circuit so produced. [< L *serere* to join, weave together]

series winding *Electr.* The winding of a dynamo or an electric motor in such a way that the field circuit is connected in series with the armature circuit. —**se·ries-wound** (sir′ēz·wound′) *adj.*

ser·if (ser′if) *n. Printing* A light line or stroke crossing or projecting from the end of a main line or stroke in a letter: also spelled *ceriph.* [< Du. < L *scribere* to write]

se·ri·o·com·ic (sir′ē·ō·kom′ik) *adj.* Mingling the serious with the comic. Also **se′ri·o·com′i·cal.**

se·ri·ous (sir′ē·əs) *adj.* **1.** Grave and earnest in quality, feeling, or disposition; sober. **2.** Said, planned, or done with full practical intent; being or done in earnest. **3.** Of grave importance: a *serious* problem. **4.** Attended with considerable danger or loss: a *serious* accident. [< MF < LL < L *serius*] —**se′ri·ous·ly** *adv.* —**se′ri·ous·ness** *n.*

ser·jeant (sär′jənt) See SERGEANT.

ser·mon (sûr′mən) *n.* **1.** A discourse based on a passage or text of the Bible, delivered as part of a church service. **2.** Any discourse intended for the pulpit. **3.** Any speech of a serious or solemn kind, as a formal exhortation. [< AF, OF < L *sermo, -onis* talk] —**ser·mon·ic** (-mon′ik) or **·i·cal** *adj.*

ser·mon·ize (sûr′mən·īz) *v.t.* & *v.i.* **·ized, ·iz·ing 1.** To compose or deliver a sermon or sermons (to). **2.** To address at length in a moralizing manner. —**ser′mon·iz′er** *n.*

Sermon on the Mount The discourse of Jesus found recorded in *Matt.* v, vi, vii: properly distinguished from the **Sermon on the Plain,** *Luke* vi 20–49.

sero- *combining form* Connected with or related to serum. Also, before vowels, **ser-.** [< L *serum* whey]

se·rol·o·gy (si·rol′ə·jē) *n.* The science of serums and their actions. —**se·ro·log·i·cal** (sir′ə·loj′i·kəl) *adj.*

se·ro·to·nin (ser′ə·tō′nin) *n. Biochem.* A crystalline protein found in many body tissues but chiefly in the brain and blood, a powerful vasoconstrictor. [< SERO- + TON- + -IN]

ser·pent (sûr′pənt) *n.* **1.** A scaly, limbless reptile; a snake.

SEQUOIA

(To over 300 feet high)

2. Anything of serpentine form or appearance. **3.** An insinuating and treacherous person. **4.** Satan; the devil. [< OF < L < ppr. of *serpere* to creep]

ser·pen·tine (sûr'pən·tēn, -tīn) *adj.* **1.** Pertaining to or like a serpent; sinuous. **2.** Subtle; cunning. — *n.* A mottled green or yellow magnesium silicate, used as a source of asbestos, and as architecturally decorative stonework.

ser·rate (ser'āt, -it) *adj.* **1.** Toothed or notched like a saw. **2.** *Bot.* Having notched edges, as certain leaves. Also **ser'·rat·ed.** [< L *serratus*, ult. < *serra* saw]

ser·ra·tion (se·rā'shən) *n.* **1.** The state of being serrated. **2.** One of the projections of a serrate formation, or a series of such projections. Also **ser·ra·ture** (ser'ə·chər).

ser·ried (ser'ēd) *adj.* Compacted in rows or ranks, as soldiers in company formation. [Pp. of obs. *serry* to press close together in ranks < MF *serré*, pp. of *serrer* to tighten]

se·rum (sir'əm) *n.* *pl.* **se·rums** or **se·ra** (sir'ə) **1.** The clear, slightly yellow portion of an animal liquid after separation from its solid constituents, esp. that formed by the clotting of blood. **2.** Loosely, an antiserum. **3.** Serum of milk; whey. **4.** Any similar secretion. [< L, whey, watery fluid]

ser·val (sûr'vəl) *n.* An African wildcat, yellow with black spots and having a ringed tail and long legs. [< F < Pg. *lobo cerval* lynx < *lobo* wolf + *cerval* stag]

ser·vant (sûr'vənt) *n.* **1.** A person hired to assist in domestic matters, sometimes living within the employer's house; hired help. **2.** A person employed to work for another; an employee. **3.** A slave or bondman. **4.** A public servant.

serve (sûrv) *v.* **served, serv·ing** *v.t.* **1.** To work for, esp. as a servant; be in the service of. **2.** To be of service to; wait on. **3.** To promote the interests of; aid. **4.** To obey and give homage to: to *serve* God. **5.** To satisfy the requirements of. **6.** To perform the duties connected with, as a public office. **7.** To go through (a period of enlistment, etc.). **8.** To furnish or provide, as with a regular supply. **9.** To offer or bring food or drink to (a guest, etc.). **10.** To bring and place on the table or distribute among guests, as food or drink. **11.** To operate or handle: to *serve* a cannon. **12.** To copulate with: said of male animals. **13.** In tennis, etc., to put (the ball) in play by hitting it to one's opponent. **14.** *Law* **a** To deliver (a summons or writ) to a person. **b** To deliver a summons or writ to. **15.** *Naut.* To wrap (a rope, stay, etc.), as with marlin or spun yarn, so as to strengthen or protect. — *v.i.* **16.** To work as or perform the functions of a servant. **17.** To wait at table; distribute food or drink. **18.** To perform the duties of any employment, office, etc. **19.** To go through a term of service, as in the army or navy. **20.** To be suitable or usable, as for a purpose. **21.** In tennis, etc., to put the ball in play. — *n.* **1.** In tennis, etc., the delivering of the ball by striking it toward an opponent. **2.** The turn of the server. [< OF < L < *servus* slave]

serv·er (sûr'vər) *n.* **1.** One who serves. **2.** That which is used in serving, as a tray. **3.** The male of any domestic animal used for breeding. **4.** In games, the player who serves.

ser·vice (sûr'vis) *n.* **1.** Assistance or benefit afforded another. **2.** A useful result or product of labor that is not a tangible commodity. **3.** *pl.* Such products collectively, as distinguished from goods. **4.** The manner in which one is waited upon or served: the *service* in this restaurant is only fair. **5.** A system of labor and material aids for the public or a portion of it: telephone *service*. **6.** A division of public employment devoted to a particular function: the diplomatic *service*. **7.** Employment as a public servant in government. **8.** A public duty or function: jury *service*. **9.** Any branch of the armed forces. **10.** Military duty or assignment. **11.** Devotion to God, as demonstrated by obedience and good works. **12.** A formal and public exercise of worship. **13.** A ritual prescribed for a particular ministration or observance: a marriage *service*. **14.** The music for a liturgical office or rite. **15.** The state or position of a servant, esp. a domestic servant. **16.** A set of tableware for a specific purpose. **17.** Installation, maintenance, and repair of an article provided a buyer by a seller. **18.** *Law* The legal communication of a writ or process to a designated person. **19.** In tennis, etc., the act or manner of serving a ball. **20.** *Naut.* The protective cordage wrapped around a rope. **21.** In animal husbandry, the copulation or covering of a female. — *adj.* **1.** Pertaining to or for service. **2.** For the use of servants or tradespeople: a *service* entrance. **3.** Of, pertaining to, or belonging to a military service. — *v.t.* **·viced, ·vic·ing** **1.** To maintain or repair. **2.** To supply service to. [< OF < L < *servus* slave]

ser·vice·a·ble (sûr'vis·ə·bəl) *adj.* **1.** That can be made of service; beneficial; usable. **2.** Capable of rendering long service; durable. — **ser'vice·a·bil'i·ty, ser'vice·a·ble·ness** *n.* — **ser'vice·a·bly** *adv.*

ser·vice·ber·ry (sûr'vis·ber'ē) *n.* *pl.* **·ries** **1.** A small tree bearing racemes of white flowers and purple edible berries: also called *service tree, shadbush*. **2.** A berry from this tree.

service cap A military uniform cap with a visor.

ser·vice·man (sûr'vis·man') *n.* *pl.* **·men** (-men') **1.** A member of one of the armed forces. **2.** A man who performs services of maintenance, supply, repair, etc. Also **service man.** — **ser'vice·wom'an** (-wŏŏm'ən) *n.fem.*

service ribbon A distinctively colored ribbon worn on the U.S. service uniform to indicate the wearer's right to the corresponding campaign medal or decoration.

service station A place for supplying automobiles, trucks, etc., with gasoline, oil, water, etc.

service tree **1.** Either of two deciduous trees of Europe, having alternate pinnate leaves and panicled cream-colored flowers. **2.** The serviceberry.

ser·vi·ette (sûr'vē·et', -vyet') *n.* *Brit. & Canadian* A table napkin. [< MF, prob. < *servir* to serve]

ser·vile (sûr'vil, -vil) *adj.* **1.** Having the spirit of a slave; abject: a *servile* flatterer. **2.** Pertaining to or appropriate for slaves or servants. **3.** Being in a condition of servitude. **4.** Obedient; subject: with *to*. [< L < *servus* slave] — **ser'vile·ly** *adv.* — **ser'vile·ness, ser·vil'i·ty** (sûr·vil'ə·tē) *n.*

serv·ing (sûr'ving) *n.* A portion of food for one person. — *adj.* Used for serving food at table: a *serving* platter.

ser·vi·tor (sûr'və·tər) *n.* One who waits upon and serves another; an attendant; servant. — **ser'vi·tor·ship'** *n.*

ser·vi·tude (sûr'və·tood, -tyood) *n.* **1.** The condition of a slave; bondage. **2.** Enforced service as a punishment for crime: penal *servitude*. **3.** A state of subjection to a person or thing. **4.** The condition or duties of a servant; menial service. **5.** *Law* A right that one man may have to use the land of another for a special purpose.

ser·vo (sûr'vō) *n.* *pl.* **·vos** Any of various relay devices used in the automatic control of a complex machine, instrument, operation, or process. Also **ser'vo·mech'a·nism** (-mek'-ə·niz'əm). [< L *servus* slave]

servo- *combining form* In technical use, auxiliary. [< L *servus* slave]

ser·vo·mo·tor (sûr'vō·mō'tər) *n.* An electric motor connected with and supplying power for a servo.

ses·a·me (ses'ə·mē) *n.* **1.** An East Indian plant. **2.** The seeds of this plant, used as food and as a source of **sesame oil**, an emollient. [< F < L < Gk. *sēsamon, sēsamē*]

sesqui- *prefix* One and a half; one and a half times: *sesquicentennial*. [< L < *semis* half + *que* and]

ses·qui·cen·ten·ni·al (ses'kwi·sen·ten'ē·əl) *adj.* Of or pertaining to a century and a half. — *n.* A 150th anniversary, or its celebration.

ses·sile (ses'il) *adj.* **1.** *Bot.* Attached by its base, without a stalk, as a leaf. **2.** *Zool.* Firmly or permanently attached; fixed. [< L < *sessus*, pp. of *sedere* to sit] — **ses·sil'i·ty** *n.*

ses·sion (sesh'ən) *n.* **1.** The sitting together of a legislative assembly, court, etc., for the transaction of business. **2.** A single meeting or series of meetings of a group of persons, convened for a specific purpose or activity. **3.** A division of a school year; term. **4.** A part of a day during which classes meet in a school. [< F < L *sessio, -onis* < *sedere* to sit] — **ses'sion·al** *adj.* — **ses'sion·al·ly** *adv.*

ses·tet (ses·tet') *n.* **1.** The last six lines of a sonnet; also, any six-line stanza. **2.** *Music* See SEXTET (def. 1). [< Ital. < *sesto* sixth (< L *sextus*) + *-etto*, dim. suffix]

set[1] (set) *v.* **set, set·ting** *v.t.* **1.** To put in a certain place or position; place. **2.** To put into a fixed or immovable position or state: to *set* one's jaw. **3.** To bring to a specified state: to *set* a boat adrift. **4.** To restore to proper position for healing, as a broken bone. **5.** To place in readiness for operation or use: to *set* a trap. **6.** To adjust according to a standard: to *set* a clock. **7.** To adjust (an instrument, dial, etc.) to a particular calibration or position. **8.** To place knives, forks, etc., on (a table) in preparing for a meal. **9.** To bend the teeth of (a saw) to either side alternately. **10.** To appoint or establish: to *set* a time. **11.** To fix or establish a time for. **12.** To assign for performance, completion, etc.; allot: to *set* a task. **13.** To assign to some specific duty or function; station: to *set* a guard. **14.** To cause to sit. **15.** To present or perform so as to be copied or emulated: to *set* a bad example. **16.** To direct: He *set* his course for the Azores. **17.** To put in place so as to catch the wind: to *set* the jib. **18.** To place in a mounting or frame, as a gem. **19.** To stud or adorn with gems. **20.** To arrange (hair) in waves, curls, etc., while moist. **21.** To place (a hen) on eggs to hatch them. **22.** To place (eggs) under a fowl or in an incubator for hatching. **23.** To place (a price or value): with *by* or *on*. **24.** To point (game): said of hunting dogs. **25.** *Printing* **a** To arrange (type) for printing; compose. **b** To put into type, as a sentence, manuscript, etc. **26.** *Music* **a** To arrange (music) for words. **b** To write (words) to accompany music. **27.** To describe (a scene) as taking place: to *set* the scene in Monaco. **28.** In the theater, to arrange (a stage) so as to depict a scene. **29.** In some games, as bridge, to defeat. **30.** *Dial.* or *Illit.* To sit. — *v.i.* **31.** To go or pass below the horizon, as the sun. **32.** To wane; decline. **33.** To sit on eggs, as fowl. **34.** To become hard or firm; congeal. **35.** To begin a journey; start: with *forth, out, off*, etc. **36.** To have a specified direction; tend. **37.** To hang or fit, as clothes. **38.** To point game: said of hunting dogs. **39.** *Bot.* To begin development or growth, as a rudimentary fruit. **40.** *Dial.* or *Illit.* To sit. **— to set about** To start doing; begin. **— to set against 1.** To balance; compare. **2.** To make unfriendly to. **— to set aside 1.** To place apart or to one side. **2.** To reject; dismiss. **3.** To declare null and void. **— to set back** To reverse; hinder. **— to set down 1.** To place on a surface. **2.** To write or print; record. **3.** To judge or consider. **4.** To attribute; ascribe. **— to set forth** To state or declare; express. **— to set in 1.** To begin to occur: Rigor mortis *set in.* **2.** To blow or flow toward shore, as wind or tide. **— to set off 1.** To put apart by itself. **2.** To serve as a contrast or foil for. **3.** To cause to explode. **— to set on** To incite or instigate; urge. **— to set out 1.** To present to view; exhibit. **2.** To establish the limits or boundaries of, as a town. **3.** To plant. **4.** To start a journey, enterprise, etc. **— to set to 1.** To start; begin. **2.** To start fighting. **— to set up 1.** To place in an upright position. **2.** To raise. **3.** To place in power, authority, etc. **4.** To construct or build; assemble. **5.** To establish. **6.** To provide with the means to start a new business. **7.** To cause to be heard: to *set up* a cry. **8.** *Informal* **a** To pay for the drinks, etc., of; treat. **b** To pay for (drinks, etc.). *— adj.* **1.** Established by authority or agreement; appointed: a *set* time; a *set* method. **2.** Customary; conventional: a *set* phrase. **3.** Deliberately and systematically conceived; formal: a *set* speech. **4.** Fixed and motionless; rigid. **5.** Fixed in opinion or disposition. **6.** Formed; made: with a qualifying adverb: deep-*set* eyes. **7.** Ready; prepared: to get *set.* *— n.* **1.** The act or condition of setting. **2.** Permanent change of form, as by chemical action, cooling, pressure, etc. **3.** The arrangement, tilt, or hang of a garment, sail, etc. **4.** Carriage or bearing: the *set* of his shoulders. **5.** The sinking of a heavenly body below the horizon. **6.** The direction of a current or wind. **7.** A young plant for setting out; a cutting, slip, or seedling. **8.** A group of games constituting a division of a tennis match. [OE *settan* to cause to sit]

set² (set) *n.* **1.** A number of persons regarded as associated through status, common interests, etc. **2.** A social group having some exclusive character; clique: the fast *set.* **3.** A number of things belonging together and customarily used together: a *set* of dishes. **4.** A number of specific things so grouped as to form a whole: a *set* of lyrics. **5.** A group of volumes issued together and related by common authorship or subject. **6.** In motion pictures, television, etc., the complete assembly of properties, structures, etc., required in a scene. **7.** Radio or television receiving equipment assembled for use. **8.** *Math.* An array of objects, quantities, magnitudes, etc., arranged in some particular way: the *set* of integers. [< OF < L *secta* sect]

se·ta (sē′tə) *n. pl.* **·tae** (-tē) *Biol.* **1.** A bristle, or slender, bristlelike part or process of an organism. **2.** A slender spine or prickle. **3.** A coarse, rigid hair. [< L]

se·ta·ceous (si·tā′shəs) *adj.* **1.** Bristly; more or less covered with bristles. **2.** Of the nature or form of setae. Also **se′tal** (sēt′l). [< NL < L *seta* bristle]

set·back (set′bak′) *n.* **1.** An unexpected reverse or relapse. **2.** *Archit.* In tall buildings, the stepping of upper sections so that they progressively recede from the street line.

Seth (seth) The third son of Adam. *Gen.* v 3.

seti- *combining form* A bristle. Also, before vowels, **set-**. [< L *seta* bristle]

set·off (set′ôf′, -of′) *n.* **1.** That which offsets or counterbalances; a counterpoise. **2.** A counterclaim or the discharge of a debt by a counterclaim.

set·screw (set′skrōō′) *n.* A screw used as a clamp, esp. one used to screw through one part and slightly into another to bind the parts tightly.

set·tee (se·tē′) *n.* **1.** A long wooden seat with a high back. **2.** A sofa suitable for two or three people. [< SET¹ or SET- (TLE), n. + *-ee*, dim. suffix]

set·ter (set′ər) *n.* **1.** One who or that which sets. **2.** One of a breed of medium-sized, silky-coated, lithe hunting dogs trained to indicate the presence of game birds by standing rigid. See ENGLISH SETTER, GORDON SETTER, IRISH SETTER.

set·ting (set′ing) *n.* **1.** The act of anything that sets. **2.** An insertion. **3.** That in which something is set; a frame; environment. **4.** The act of indicating game like a setter. **5.** A number of eggs placed together for hatching. **6.** The music adapted to a song or poem. **7.** The scene or background of a play or narrative. **8.** The apparent sinking of the sun, etc., below the horizon. **9.** The tableware set out for one person.

set·tle (set′l) *v.* **·tled, ·tling** *v.t.* **1.** To put in order; set to rights. **2.** To put firmly in place: He *settled* himself on the couch. **3.** To free of agitation or disturbance; quiet: to *settle* one's nerves. **4.** To cause (sediment or dregs) to sink to the bottom. **5.** To cause to subside or come to rest; make

firm or compact: to *settle* dust or ashes. **6.** To make clear or transparent, as by causing sediment or dregs to sink. **7.** *Informal* To make quiet or orderly: One blow *settled* him. **8.** To decide or determine finally, as an argument or difference. **9.** To pay, as a debt; satisfy, as a claim. **10.** To establish residents or residence in (a country, town, etc.). **11.** To establish as residents. **12.** To establish in a permanent occupation, home, etc. **13.** To decide (a suit at law) by agreement between the litigants. **14.** *Law* To make over or assign (property) by legal act: with *on* or *upon. — v.i.* **15.** To come to rest, as after moving about or flying. **16.** To sink gradually; subside. **17.** To sink or come to rest, as dust or sediment. **18.** To become more firm or compact. **19.** To become clear or transparent, as by the sinking of sediment. **20.** To take up residence. **21.** To come to a decision; resolve: with *on, upon,* or *with.* **22.** To pay a bill, etc. **— to settle down 1.** To start living a regular, orderly life, esp. after a period of wandering or irresponsibility. **2.** To apply steady effort or attention. *— n.* **1.** A long seat or bench, generally of wood, with a high back, often with arms and sometimes having a chest from seat to floor. **2.** A wide step; platform. [OE *setl* seat, *setlan* to seat]

set·tle·ment (set′l·mənt) *n.* **1.** The act of settling, or the state of being settled; esp., an adjustment of affairs by public authority. **2.** The settling of a new region; colonization. **3.** An area of country newly occupied by those who intend to live and labor there; a colony. **4.** A collection of frontier dwellings forming a community. **5.** *Brit.* A regular or settled place of living. **6.** An accounting; adjustment; liquidation in regard to amounts. **7.** The conveyance of property in such form as to provide for some future object, esp. the support of members of the settler's family; also, the property so settled. **8.** A welfare institution established in a congested part of a city, that conducts educational and recreational activities for the community: also **settlement house.**

set·tler (set′lər) *n.* **1.** One who settles; esp., one who establishes himself in a colony or new country; a colonist. **2.** One who or that which settles or decides something.

set-to (set′tōō′) *n. pl.* **-tos** A bout at fighting, fencing, arguing, or any other mode of contest.

set-up (set′up′) *n.* **1.** *U.S. Informal* The overall scheme or pattern of organization or construction; circumstances. **2.** *U.S. Slang* A contest or match arranged to result in an easy victory. **3.** *U.S. Informal* Ice, soda water, etc., provided for use in alcoholic drinks. **4.** Physique; physical build; make-up. **5.** Carriage of the body; bearing.

sev·en (sev′ən) *n.* **1.** The sum of six and one: a cardinal number. **2.** Any symbol of this number, as 7, vii, VII. **3.** Anything consisting of or representing seven units. *— adj.* Being one more than six. [OE *seofon*]

seven deadly sins *Often cap.* Pride, lust, envy, anger, covetousness, gluttony, and sloth: also called *cardinal sins.*

seven seas All the oceans of the world, now considered to be the North and South Atlantic, the North and South Pacific, the Indian, the Arctic, and the Antarctic oceans.

sev·en·teen (sev′ən·tēn′) *n.* **1.** The sum of sixteen and one: a cardinal number. **2.** Any symbol of this number, as 17, xvii, XVII. **3.** Anything consisting of or representing seventeen units. *— adj.* Being one more than sixteen. [OE *seofontiene*] **— sev′en·teenth′** *adj. & n.*

sev·en·teen-year locust (sev′ən·tēn′yir′) A dark-bodied, wedge-shaped cicada native to the eastern U.S., having an underground nymphal stage of from 13 to 17 years.

sev·enth (sev′ənth) *adj.* **1.** Next after the sixth: the ordinal of *seven.* **2.** Being one of seven equal parts. *— n.* **1.** One of seven equal parts. **2.** That which follows the sixth. **3.** *Music* **a** The interval between any tone and the seventh tone above it in the diatonic scale. **b** A tone separated by this interval from any other, considered with reference to that other. *— adv.* In the seventh order, place, or rank: also, in formal discourse, **sev′enth·ly.** [ME < *seven* + -TH, replacing OE *seofotha*]

sev·enth-day (sev′ənth·dā′) *adj.* **1.** Pertaining to the seventh day of the week. **2.** *Often cap.* Advocating the observance of this day as the Sabbath: a *Seventh-Day* Adventist.

seventh day Saturday: a Quaker term.

Seventh-Day Adventist See under ADVENTIST.

seventh heaven 1. A condition of great happiness. **2.** The highest heaven according to various ancient systems of astronomy or in certain theologies.

sev·en·ty (sev′ən·tē) *n. pl.* **·ties 1.** The sum of sixty and ten: a cardinal number. **2.** Any symbol of this number, as 70, lxx, LXX. **3.** Anything consisting of or representing seventy units. *— adj.* Being ten more than sixty. [OE (*hund-*) *seofontig*] **— sev′en·ti·eth** *adj. & n.*

Seven Wonders of the World The seven works of man considered the most remarkable in the ancient world: the Egyptian pyramids, the hanging gardens of Babylon, the temple of Diana at Ephesus, the statue of Zeus at Olympia, the mausoleum of King Mausolos at Halicarnassus, the Colossus of Rhodes, and the lighthouse of Alexandria.

Seven Years' War See table for WAR.

sev·er (sev′ər) *v.t.* **1.** To put or keep apart; separate. **2.** To cut or break into two or more parts. **3.** To break off; dissolve, as a relationship or tie. — *v.i.* **4.** To come or break apart or into pieces. **5.** To go away or apart; separate. [< AF, OF < L *separare* to separate] — **sev′er·a·ble** *adj.*

sev·er·al (sev′ər·əl, sev′rəl) *adj.* **1.** More than two, yet not many. **2.** Considered individually; single; separate. **3.** Individually different; various or diverse. — *n.* Several persons or things. [< AF < Med.L < L *separ* separate]

sev·er·al·ly (sev′ər·əl·ē, sev′rəl·ē) *adv.* **1.** Individually; separately. **2.** Respectively.

sev·er·ance (sev′ər·əns, sev′rəns) *n.* **1.** The act of severing, or the condition of being severed. **2.** Separation; partition.

se·vere (si·vir′) *adj.* **·ver·er**, **·ver·est** **1.** Rigorous in the treatment of others; unsparing. **2.** Conforming to rigid rules; accurate. **3.** Serious and austere in disposition or manner. **4.** Causing extreme anguish: a *severe* pain. **5.** Causing extreme hardship; harsh: a *severe* snowstorm. [< MF < L *severus*] — **se·vere′ly** *adv.* — **se·vere′ness** *n.*

se·ver·i·ty (si·ver′ə·tē) *n. pl.* **·ties** **1.** The quality of being severe. **2.** Harshness or cruelty of disposition or treatment. **3.** Extreme strictness; rigor; exactness. **4.** Seriousness; austerity. **5.** Strict conformity to truth or law.

sew (sō) *v.* **sewed**, **sewed** or **sewn**, **sew·ing** *v.t.* **1.** To make, mend, or fasten with needle and thread. — *v.i.* **2.** To work with needle and thread. — **to sew up** *U.S. Informal* To conclude (a deal, etc.). [OE *sīwian*] — **sew′·er** *n.*

sew·age (sōō′ij) *n.* The waste matter from domestic, commercial, and industrial establishments carried off in sewers.

sew·er (sōō′ər) *n.* **1.** A conduit, usu. laid underground, to carry off drainage and excrement. ◆ Collateral adjective: *cloacal.* **2.** Any large public drain. [< OF, ult. < L *ex-* off + *aqua* water]

sew·er·age (sōō′ər·ij) *n.* **1.** A system of sewers. **2.** Systematic draining by sewers. **3.** Sewage.

sew·ing (sō′ing) *n.* **1.** The act or occupation of one who sews. **2.** That which is sewed.

sewing circle A group of women, meeting periodically to sew, usu. for some charitable purpose.

sewing machine A machine for stitching or sewing.

sewn (sōn) Alternative past participle of SEW.

sex (seks) *n.* **1.** Either of two divisions, male and female, by which organisms are distinguished with reference to the reproductive functions. **2.** The character of being male or female. **3.** The activity or phenomena of life concerned with sexual desire or reproduction. **4.** *Informal* Sexual gratification. [< OF < L, prob. orig. < *secare* to divide]

sex- *combining form* Six: also *sexi-*. [< L *sex* six]

sex·a·ge·nar·i·an (sek′sə·jə·nâr′ē·ən) *n.* A person between sixty and seventy years of age. — *adj.* Sixty years old, or between sixty and seventy. [< SEXAGENARY]

sex·ag·e·nar·y (seks·aj′ə·ner′ē) *adj.* Sexagenarian. — *n. pl.* **·nar·ies** A sexagenarian. [< L < *sexaginta* sixty]

sex appeal A physical quality that attracts sexual interest.

sex chromosome *Genetics* A chromosome whose presence in the reproductive cells of certain plants and animals is associated with the determination of the sex of offspring.

sex gland A gonad; either of the testes or ovaries.

sexi- Var. of SEX-.

sex·ism (seks′iz·əm) *n.* Sexual prejudice against women. [< SEX + -ISM, on analogy with *racism*] — **sex′ist** *n., adj.*

sex·less (seks′lis) *adj.* **1.** Having or appearing to have no sex; neuter. **2.** Provoking or showing little sexual desire. — **sex′less·ly** *adv.* — **sex′less·ness** *n.*

sex linkage *Biol.* That type of inheritance that is associated with the transmission of genes attached to the sex chromosomes. — **sex-linked** (seks′ lingkt′) *adj.*

sex·ol·o·gy (seks·ol′ə·jē) *n.* The study of human sexual behavior. — **sex·o·log·ic** (sek′sə·loj′ik) or **·i·cal** *adj.* — **sex·ol′o·gist** *n.*

sex·ploi·ta·tion (seks′ploi·tā′shən) *n.* The commercial exploitation of interest in sex, as by means of pornography. [Blend of SEX + EXPLOITATION]

sext (sekst) *n. Often cap. Eccl.* Prescribed prayers constituting the fourth of the seven canonical hours. [< LL < L *sexta* (*hora*) the sixth (hour)]

sex·tant (seks′tənt) *n.* **1.** An instrument for measuring angular distance between two objects, as a heavenly body and the horizon, used esp. in determining latitude at sea. **2.** An arc of 60 degrees, one-sixth of a circle. [< L *sextus* sixth]

sex·tet (seks·tet′) *n.* **1.** *Music* A group of six singers or players; also, a musical composition for six performers: also called *sestet.* **2.** Any collection of six persons or things. Also **sex·tette′**. [Alter. of SESTET; refashioned after L *sex* six]

sex·til·lion (seks·til′yən) *n.* **1.** *U.S.* A thousand quintillions, written as 1 followed by twenty-one zeros: a cardinal number. **2.** *Brit.* A million quintillions (def. 2), written as

1 followed by thirty-six zeros: a cardinal number. — *adj.* Being a sextillion in number. [< MF < *sexti-* six + (*mi*)*lion* million] — **sex·til′lionth** *adj. & n.*

sex·to·dec·i·mo (seks′tō·des′ə·mō) *n. pl.* **·mos** **1.** A page size made from a printer's sheet folded so as to have 16 leaves, usu. measuring 4½ x 6⅝ inches. **2.** A book or pamphlet having pages this size. — *adj.* Having or consisting of pages this size. Also *sixteenmo.* Also written **16mo., 16°** [< L < *sextus* sixth + *decimus* tenth]

sex·ton (seks′tən) *n.* A janitor of a church having charge also of ringing the bell, overseeing burials, etc. [< OF < Med.L *sacristanus*] — **sex′ton·ship** *n.*

sex·tu·ple (seks′tōō·pəl, -tyōō-, seks·tōō′-, -tyōō′-) *v.t.* **·pled**, **·pling** To multiply by six. — *adj.* **1.** Consisting of six or of six parts. **2.** Multiplied by six. **3.** *Music* Having six beats to the measure. — *n.* A number or sum six times as great as another. [< L *sex* six, formed on analogy with *quadruple*]

sex·tu·plet (seks′tōō·plit, -tyōō-, seks·tōō′-, -tyōō′-) *n.* **1.** A set of six similar things. **2.** One of six offspring produced at a single birth. [< SEXTUPLE on analogy with *triplet*]

sex·u·al (sek′shōō·əl) *adj.* **1.** Of, pertaining to, or characteristic of sex, the sexes, or the organs or functions of sex. **2.** Having sex. **3.** *Biol.* Designating a type of reproduction involving both sexes. [< LL < L *sexus* sex] — **sex′u·al′i·ty** (-al′ə·tē) *n.* — **sex′u·al·ly** *adv.*

sex·y (sek′sē) *adj.* **sex·i·er**, **sex·i·est** *Slang* **1.** Provocative of sexual desire. **2.** Concerned in large degree with sex.

sfor·zan·do (sfôr·tsän′dō) *Music adj.* Accented more forcibly than the rhythm requires. — *adv.* In a sforzando manner. Also **sfor·za′to** (-tsä′tō). [< Ital. *sforzare* to force]

shab·by (shab′ē) *adj.* **·bi·er**, **·bi·est** **1.** Threadbare; ragged. **2.** Wearing worn or seedy garments. **3.** Mean; paltry. [OE *sceabb* scab + -Y¹] — **shab′bi·ly** *adv.* — **shab′bi·ness** *n.*

Sha·bu·oth (shä·vōō′ōth, shə·vōō′əs) *n.pl.* The Jewish festival of Pentecost. [< Hebrew *shebuōth*, lit., weeks]

shack (shak) *n. U.S. & Canadian Informal* A rude cabin, as of logs. [? < dial. Sp. (Mexican) *jacal* wooden hut < Nahuatl *xacalli*]

shack·le (shak′əl) *n.* **1.** A ring, clasp, or braceletlike fastening for encircling and fettering a limb. **2.** Impediment or restraint. **3.** One of various forms of fastenings. — *v.t.* **·led**, **·ling** **1.** To restrain or confine with shackles. **2.** To keep or restrain from free action or speech. **3.** To connect or fasten with a shackle. [OE *sceacul*] — **shack′ler** *n.*

shack·o (shak′ō) See SHAKO.

shad (shad) *n. pl.* **shad** Any of several food fishes related to the herring. [OE *sceadd*]

shad·ber·ry (shad′ber′ē) *n. pl.* **·ries** The serviceberry.

shad·bush (shad′bōōsh′) *n.* **1.** The serviceberry (def. 1). **2.** Any of various other related plants. Also **shad′blow′** (-blō′). [< SHAD + BUSH; so called because it flowers when the shad appear in U.S. rivers]

shade (shād) *v.* **shad·ed**, **shad·ing** *v.t.* **1.** To screen from light by intercepting its rays. **2.** To make dim; darken. **3.** To screen or protect with or as with a shade. **4.** To cause to change by gradations. **5.** In graphic arts: **a** To represent (degrees of shade, colors, etc.) by gradations of light or dark lines or shading. **b** To represent varying shades, colors, etc., in (a picture, etc.) thus. **6.** To make slightly lower, as a price. — *v.i.* **7.** To change or vary by degrees. — *n.* **1.** Relative obscurity due to interception of the rays of light; darkness. **2.** The state of being outshone. **3.** A shady place; secluded retreat. **4.** *U.S.* A screen that shuts off light, heat, dust, etc. **5.** A gradation of color; also, slight degree; minute difference. **6.** A disembodied spirit; ghost. — **the shades** Hades. [OE *sceadu*] — **shade′less** *adj.*

shad·ing (shā′ding) *n.* **1.** Protection against light or heat. **2.** The lines, dots, etc., by which degrees of darkness, color, or depth are represented in a picture. **3.** A slight variation.

shad·ow (shad′ō) *n.* **1.** A comparative darkness within an illuminated area, esp. that caused by the interception of light by a body. **2.** The dark image thus produced on a surface and representing the approximate shape of the intercepting body. **3.** The shaded portion of a picture. **4.** A mirrored image. **5.** A delusive image or semblance. **6.** A phantom; ghost; shade. **7.** A faint representation or indication; a symbol. **8.** A remnant; vestige. **9.** An insignificant trace or portion. **10.** Gloom; a saddening influence. **11.** An inseparable companion. **12.** One who trails another, as a detective. — *v.t.* **1.** To cast a shadow upon. **2.** To darken; make gloomy. **3.** To represent or foreshow dimly: with *forth* or *out.* **4.** To follow closely or secretly. **5.** To shade in painting, etc. [OE *sceadu* shade] — **shad′ow·er** *n.*

shad·ow·box (shad′ō·boks′) *v.i.* To spar with an imaginary opponent as a form of exercise. — **shad′ow·box′ing** *n.*

shad·ow·y (shad′ō·ē) *adj.* **·ow·i·er**, **·ow·i·est** **1.** Full of or affording shadow. **2.** Vague; dim. **3.** Unsubstantial or illusory. — **shad′ow·i·ness** *n.*

shad·y (shā′dē) *adj.* **shad·i·er**, **shad·i·est** **1.** Full of shade; casting a shade. **2.** Shaded, sheltered, or hidden. **3.** *Informal* Questionable as to honesty or legality; dubious. —

on the shady side of Older than; past the age of. **— shad′i· ly** *adv.* **— shad′i·ness** *n.*

shaft¹ (shaft, shäft) *n.* **1.** The long narrow rod of an arrow, spear, etc. **2.** An arrow. **3.** Anything resembling a missile in appearance or effect: *shafts* of ridicule. **4.** A beam of light. **5.** A long handle, as of a hammer, etc. **6.** *Mech.* A long bar, esp. if rotating and transmitting motive power. **7.** *Archit.* **a** The portion of a column between capital and base. **b** A slender column. **8.** An obelisk or memorial column. **9.** The stem of a feather. **10.** One of two poles by which a horse is harnessed to a vehicle. [OE *sceat*]

shaft² (shaft, shäft) *n.* **1.** A narrow, vertical or inclined, excavation connected with a mine. **2.** The tunnel of a blast furnace. **3.** An opening through the floors of a building, as for an elevator. [< LG *schacht* rod, shaft]

shag (shag) *n.* **1.** A rough coat or mass, as of hair. **2.** A wild growth, as of weeds. **3.** A long nap on cloth. **4.** Cloth having a rough or long nap. **5.** A coarse, strong tobacco: also **shag tobacco.** **—** *v.* **shagged, shag·ging** *v.t.* To make shaggy; roughen. [OE *sceacga* rough hair, wool]

shag·bark (shag′bärk′) *n.* **1.** A rough-barked hickory yielding high-grade, light-colored nuts. **2.** Its tough, durable wood. Also called *shellbark.*

shag·gy (shag′ē) *adj.* **·gi·er, ·gi·est 1.** Having, consisting of, or resembling rough hair or wool; rugged; rough. **2.** Covered with any rough, tangled growth; fuzzy; scrubby. **3.** Unkempt. **— shag′gi·ly** *adv.* **— shag′gi·ness** *n.*

sha·green (shə·grēn′) *n.* **1.** The rough skin of various sharks and rays. **2.** A rough-grained leather, usu. dyed green. [< F < Turkish *sāghrī* horse's hide]

shah (shä) *n.* An eastern king or ruler, esp. of Iran. [< Persian *shāh*]

shake (shāk) *v.* **shook, shak·en, shak·ing** *v.t.* **1.** To cause to move to and fro or up and down with short, rapid movements. **2.** To affect in a specified manner by or as by vigorous action: with *off, out, from,* etc. **3.** To cause to tremble or quiver; vibrate. **4.** To cause to stagger or totter. **5.** To weaken or disturb: I could not *shake* his determination. **6.** To agitate or rouse: often with *up.* **7.** *Slang* To get rid of or away from. **8.** *Music* To trill. **—** *v.i.* **9.** To move to and fro or up and down in short, rapid movements. **10.** To be affected in a specified way by vigorous action: with *off, out, from,* etc. **11.** To tremble or quiver, as from cold or fear. **12.** To become unsteady; totter. **13.** *Music* To trill on a note, etc. **— to shake down 1.** To cause to fall by shaking; bring down. **2.** To cause to settle. **3.** *Slang* To extort money from. **— to shake hands** To clasp hands as a form of greeting, etc. **— to shake off** To rid oneself of by or as by shaking. **— to shake up 1.** To shake, mix, or stir. **2.** *U.S. Informal* To shock or jar mentally or physically. **—** *n.* **1.** A shaking; concussion; agitation; vibration; shock; jolt. **2.** The state of being shaken. **3.** *pl. Informal* The chill or ague of intermittent fever. **4.** A frost or wind crack in timber; also, a tight fissure in rock. **5.** An earthquake. **6.** *Slang* An instant. **7.** *Music* A trill. **— no great shakes** *Informal* Of no great importance; mediocre. [OE *scacan*] **— shak′a·ble, shake′a·ble** *adj.*

shake·down (shāk′doun′) *n.* **U.S. Slang** A swindle; extortion. **—** *adj.* *U.S. Informal* For the purpose of adjusting mechanical parts or habituating people: a *shakedown* cruise.

shak·er (shā′kər) *n.* **1.** One who or that which shakes. **2.** A container for shaking or pouring something: cocktail *shaker.*

Shak·er (shā′kər) *n.* One of a sect practicing celibacy and communal living: so called from their characteristic bodily movements during religious meetings. **— Shak′er·ism** *n.*

Shake·spear·e·an (shāk·spir′ē·ən) *adj.* Of, pertaining to, or characteristic of Shakespeare, his work, or his style. **—** *n.* A specialist on Shakespeare or his writings. Also **Shake·spear′i·an.** **— Shake·spear′e·an·ism** *n.*

Shakespearean sonnet A sonnet having the rhyme scheme *ababcdcdefefgg*: also called *Elizabethan sonnet, English sonnet.*

shake·up (shāk′up′) *n.* A radical change of personnel or organization, as in a business office, etc.

shak·o (shak′ō) *n.* *pl.* **·os** A kind of high, stiff military headdress, originally of fur, having a peak and an upright plume: also spelled *shacko.* [< F < Hungarian *csákó*]

shak·y (shā′kē) *adj.* **shak·i·er, shak·i·est 1.** Habitually shaking or tremulous; tottering; weak; unsound. **2.** Wavering; unreliable. **— shak′i·ly** *adv.* **— shak′i·ness** *n.*

shale (shāl) *n.* A fissile claylike rock resembling slate, with fragile, uneven laminae. **— shal′y** *adj.*

shall (shal) *v.* Present *3rd person sing.* **shall;** past **should** A defective verb having a past tense that is now used only as an auxiliary followed by the infinitive without *to,* or elliptically without the infinitive, to express: **1.** In the first person, simple futurity, with a matter-of-fact attitude toward the action or state projected: We *shall* take only the usual precautions. (But see usage note below.) **2.** In the second and third persons, futurity combined with a mood or feeling of: **a** Determination: They *shall* not pass. **b** Promise: You *shall* have whatever you need. **c** Threat: You *shall* pay for this. **d** Command: No one *shall* twice be put in jeopardy. **e** Inevitability: When earthly time *shall* end, will life survive? **3.** In all persons, indefinite future time in conditional statements: If and when you or we or the divers *shall* locate the treasure, it will (or, in legal use, the mandatory *shall*) be shared out according to the agreement. **4.** In all persons, futurity involving ideal certainty, in clauses following expressions of anxiety, demand, or desire: They are anxious that you or I or both of us *shall* go, rather than any outsider. [OE *sceal* I am obliged]

◆ **shall, will** The formal view on the use of *shall* and *will* is that to indicate simple futurity *shall* is used in the first person, *will* in the second and third; their roles are reversed to express determination, command, inevitability, etc., while in questions the choice depends on the form expected in the answer. These rules apply to American usage only at the most formal level.

shal·lop (shal′əp) *n.* An open boat propelled by oars or sails. [< F < Du. *sloep.* See SLOOP.]

shal·lot (shə·lot′) *n.* **1.** An onionlike vegetable allied to garlic but having milder bulbs that are used in seasoning and for pickles. **2.** A small onion. [< OF *eschalotte*]

shal·low (shal′ō) *adj.* **1.** Having the bottom not far below the surface; lacking depth. **2.** Lacking intellectual depth; not wise; superficial. **—** *n.* A shallow place in a body of water; shoal. **—** *v.t. & v.i.* To make or become shallow. [ME *schalowe*] **— shal′low·ly** *adv.* **— shal′low·ness** *n.*

shalt (shalt) Archaic or poetic second person singular, present tense of SHALL: used with *thou.*

sham (sham) *v.* **shammed, sham·ming** *v.t.* **1.** To assume or present the appearance of; counterfeit; feign. **2.** To represent oneself as; pretend to be. **—** *v.i.* **3.** To make false pretenses. **—** *adj.* False; counterfeit. **—** *n.* **1.** A pretense; imposture; deception. **2.** One who simulates a certain character; a pretender: also **sham′mer.** **3.** A deceptive imitation. [Prob. dial. var. of SHAME]

sha·man (shä′mən, shä′-, sham′ən) *n.* **1.** A priest of Shamanism; a magician. **2.** A North American Indian medicine man. **—** *adj.* Of a shaman: also **sha·man·ic** (shə·man′ik). [< Russian < Tungusic < Skt. *śamaṇa* ascetic]

Sha·man·ism (shä′mən·iz′əm, shä′-, sham′ən-) *n.* **1.** A religion of NE Asia and Europe holding that gods and spirits work only through the shamans. **2.** Any similar religion, as of certain Indians of the American Northwest. **— Sha′man·ist** *adj. & n.* **— Sha′man·is′tic** *adj.*

sham·ble (sham′bəl) *v.i.* **·bled, ·bling** To walk with shuffling or unsteady gait. **—** *n.* A shambling walk; shuffling gait. [Origin uncertain]

sham·bles (sham′bəlz) *n.pl.* (*usu.* construed *as sing.*) **1.** A place where butchers kill animals; slaughterhouse. **2.** Any place of carnage. **3.** A place marked by great destruction or disorder. [OE < L < *scamnum* bench, stool]

shame (shām) *n.* **1.** A painful sense of guilt or degradation caused by consciousness of guilt or of anything degrading, unworthy, or immodest. **2.** Susceptibility to such feelings. **3.** One who or that which brings reproach or disgrace. **4.** A state of regret, dishonor, or disgrace. **— to put to shame 1.** To disgrace; make ashamed. **2.** To surpass or eclipse. **—** *v.t.* **shamed, sham·ing 1.** To make ashamed; cause to feel shame. **2.** To bring shame upon; disgrace. **3.** To impel by a sense of shame: with *into* or *out of.* [OE *scamu*]

shame·faced (shām′fāst′) *adj.* Easily abashed; showing shame or bashfulness in one's face; modest; bashful. [< ME < OE *scamfæst* abashed] **— shame·fac·ed·ly** (shām′· fā′sid·lē, shām′fāst′lē) *adv.* **— shame′fac′ed·ness** *n.*

shame·ful (shām′fəl) *adj.* **1.** Deserving or bringing shame or disgrace; disgraceful; scandalous. **2.** Exciting shame; indecent. **— shame′ful·ly** *adv.* **— shame′ful·ness** *n.*

shame·less (shām′lis) *adj.* **1.** Impudent; brazen; immodest. **2.** Done without shame; indicating a want of pride or decency. **— shame′less·ly** *adv.* **— shame′less·ness** *n.*

sham·my (sham′ē), **sham·ois** (sham′ē) See CHAMOIS.

sham·poo (sham·pōō′) *n.* **1.** Any of various liquid preparations of soap, chemical solvents, etc., used to cleanse the hair and scalp. **2.** The act or process of shampooing. **—** *v.t.* To cleanse (the hair and scalp) with a shampoo. [< Hind. *chāmpnā* to press] **— sham·poo′er** *n.*

sham·rock (sham′rok) *n.* Any of several trifoliate plants, accepted as the national emblem of Ireland. [< Irish < *seamar* trefoil]

shang·hai (shang′hī, shang·hī′) *v.t.* **·haied, ·hai·ing 1.** To

SHAKO

drug or render unconscious and kidnap for service aboard a ship. **2.** To cause to do something by force or deception. [after *Shanghai*, China]

Shan·gri-la (shang'gri·lä') *n.* Any imaginary hidden utopia or paradise. [after the locale of *Lost Horizon*, a novel by James Hilton, 1900–54, English author]

shank (shangk) *n.* **1.** The part of the leg between the knee and the ankle. **2.** A cut of meat from the leg of an animal; the shin. **3.** Something resembling a leg. **4.** The part of a tool connecting the handle with the working part. **5.** The projecting piece or loop by which some forms of buttons are attached. **6.** The straight part of a hook. **7.** *Printing* The body of a type. **13.** The narrow part of a shoe sole. [OE *scanca*]

sha'nt (shant, shänt) Shall not. Also **shan't.**

shan·tey (shan'tē) See CHANTEY.

shan·tung (shan'tung, shan·tung') *n.* A fabric with a rough, nubby surface, originally made of wild silk, now often made of rayon combined with cotton. [after the Chinese town *Shantung*]

shan·ty¹ (shan'tē) *n.* *pl.* **·ties** A hastily built shack or cabin; a ramshackle or rickety dwelling. [< F (Canadian) *chantier* lumberer's shack]

shan·ty² (shan'tē) See CHANTEY.

shape (shāp) *n.* **1.** Outward form or construction; configuration; contour. **2.** A developed expression or definite formulation; embodiment; cast: to put an idea into *shape*. **3.** A phantom. **4.** The character or form in which a thing appears; guise; aspect. **5.** A pattern or mold; in millinery, a stiff frame. **6.** The lines of a person's body; figure. **7.** Manner of execution. **8.** Condition: Everything is in good *shape*. **— to take shape** To have or assume a definite form. *— v.* **shaped, shaped** (*Rare* **shap·en**), **shap·ing** *v.t.* **1.** To give shape to; mold. **2.** To adjust or adapt; modify. **3.** To devise; prepare. **4.** To give direction or character to. **5.** To put into or express in words. *— v.i.* **6.** To take shape; develop; form: often with *up* or *into*. **— to shape up** *Informal* **1.** To proceed satisfactorily or favorably. **2.** To develop proper form. [OE < *scieppan* to create] **— shap'er** *n.*

shaped (shāpt) *adj.* **1.** Formed. **2.** Resembling in shape: used in compounds: leaf-*shaped*.

shape·less (shāp'lis) *adj.* Having no definite shape; lacking symmetry. **— shape'less·ly** *adv.* **— shape'less·ness** *n.*

shape·ly (shāp'lē) *adj.* **·li·er, ·li·est** Having a pleasing shape; well-formed; graceful. **— shape'li·ness** *n.*

shard (shärd) *n.* **1.** A broken piece of a brittle substance, as of an earthen vessel; a potsherd; a fragment: also called *sherd*. **2.** A hard, thin shell, or a wing cover, of a beetle. [OE *sceard*. Related to SHEAR.]

share¹ (shâr) *n.* **1.** A portion; allotted or equitable part. **2.** One of the equal parts into which the capital stock of a company or corporation is divided. **3.** An equitable part of something enjoyed or suffered in common. **— to go shares** To partake equally, as in an enterprise. *— v.* **shared, shar·ing** *v.t.* **1.** To divide and give out in shares or portions; apportion. **2.** To enjoy or endure in common; participate in. *— v.i.* **3.** To have a part; participate: with *in*. [OE < *scieran* to shear] **— shar'er** *n.*

share² (shâr) *n.* A plowshare.

share-crop·per (shâr'krop'ər) *n.* A tenant farmer who pays a share of his crop as rent for his land.

share-hold·er (shâr'hōl'dər) *n.* An owner of a share or shares of a company's stock; a stockholder.

shark¹ (shärk) *n.* One of a group of fishes, mostly marine, of medium to large size, having dun-colored bodies covered with plate-like scales. Some species are dangerous to man. *— v.i.* To fish for sharks. [Origin uncertain]

shark² (shärk) *n.* A bold and dishonest person; a rapacious swindler. Also **shark'er.** *— v.i.* To live by trickery. [Prob. < G *schürke* scoundrel; infl. by SHARK¹]

shark·skin (shärk'skin') *n.* **1.** The skin of a shark. **2.** A fabric with a smooth, almost shiny surface, made of acetate rayon and used for sports clothes.

sharp (shärp) *adj.* **1.** Having a keen edge or an acute point; capable of cutting or piercing. **2.** Coming to an acute angle; not obtuse; abrupt: a *sharp* peak. **3.** Keen of perception or discernment; also, shrewd in bargaining; artful; overreaching. **4.** Ardent; eager; keen; impetuous or fiery; attentive. **5.** Affecting the mind or senses, as if by cutting or piercing; poignant; acrimonious. **6.** Shrill. **7.** Pinching; cutting, as cold. **8.** Having an acrid or pungent taste. **9.** Distinct, as an outline. **10.** *Music* A raised in pitch by a semitone. **b** Above the right, true pitch. **c** Having sharps in the key signature. **11.** Hard and rough; gritty. **12.** *Phonet.* Of consonants, voiceless: opposed to *flat*. *— adv.* **1.** In a sharp manner; sharply. **2.** Promptly; exactly: at 4 o'clock *sharp*. **3.** *Music* Above the proper pitch. *— n.* **1.** *Music* A sign (♯) placed before a note to indicate that the note is sharped; also, the note so altered. **2.** A cheat; a cardsharp. *— v.t. Music* To raise in pitch, as by a half step. [OE *scearp*] **— sharp'ly** *adv.* **— sharp'ness** *n.*

sharp·en (shär'pən) *v.t. & v.i.* To make or become sharp. **— sharp'en·er** *n.*

sharp·er (shär'pər) *n.* A swindler; cheat.

sharp-eyed (shärp'īd') *adj.* **1.** Having acute eyesight. **2.** Keenly observant; alert.

sharp·ie (shär'pē) *n.* A long, sharp, flat-bottomed sailboat having a centerboard and one or two masts, each having a triangular sail, originally used for fishing. [< SHARP]

sharp-shoot·er (shärp'shoō'tər) *n.* A skilled marksman, especially in the use of the rifle. **— sharp'shoot'ing** *n.*

sharp-tongued (shärp'tungd') *adj.* Bitter or caustic in speech.

sharp-wit·ted (shärp'wit'id) *adj.* Acute; intelligent. **— sharp'-wit'ted·ness** *n.*

shat·ter (shat'ər) *v.t.* **1.** To break into pieces suddenly, as by a blow. **2.** To break the health or tone of, as the body or mind; disorder; damage. *— v.i.* **3.** To break into pieces; burst. [ME *schateren*]

shave (shāv) *v.* **shaved, shaved** or **shav·en, shav·ing** *v.i.* **1.** To cut hair or beard close to the skin with a razor. *— v.t.* **2.** To remove hair or beard from (the face, head, etc.) with a razor. **3.** To cut (hair or beard) close to the skin with a razor: often with *off*. **4.** To trim closely: to *shave* a lawn. **5.** To cut thin slices from, as in preparing the surface; pare; plane. **6.** To cut into thin slices. **7.** To touch or scrape in passing; graze; come close to. *— n.* **1.** The act or operation of cutting off the beard with a razor. **2.** A knife or blade, mounted between two handles, as for shaving wood: also **draw shave, spoke shave.** **3.** A shaving; thin slice. **4.** *Informal* The act of barely grazing something; a narrow escape: a close *shave*. [OE *scafan* to shave]

shave·ling (shāv'ling) *n.* **1.** One who is shaven; opprobriously, a monk or priest. **2.** A youth.

shav·en (shā'vən) Alternative past participle of SHAVE. **—** *adj.* **1.** Shaved; also, tonsured. **2.** Trimmed closely.

Sha·vi·an (shā'vē·ən) *n.* An admirer of George Bernard Shaw, his books, or his theories. **—** *adj.* Of, pertaining to, or like George Bernard Shaw, or his style and methods.

shav·ing (shā'ving) *n.* **1.** The act of one who or that which shaves. **2.** A thin paring shaved from anything, as a board.

shawl (shôl) *n.* A wrap, as a square cloth, or large scarf, worn over the upper part of the body. [< Persian *shāl*]

Shaw·nee (shô·nē') *n.* One of a tribe of North American Indians of Algonquian stock, now living in Oklahoma. [< Algonquian (Shawnee) *Shawunogi* southerners]

she (shē) *pron., possessive* **her** or **hers,** *objective* **her;** *pl. nominative* **they,** *possessive* **their** or **theirs,** *objective* **them** **1.** The nominative singular pronoun of the third person, used of the female person or being previously mentioned or understood, or of things conventionally regarded as feminine, as ships, machines, etc. **2.** That woman or female; any woman: *She* who listens learns. *— n.* *pl.* **shes** A female person or being. [ME < OE *sēo, sīo,* fem. of *sē* the]

she- *combining form* Female; feminine: in hyphenated compounds: a *she*-lion; *she*-devil.

sheaf (shēf) *n.* *pl.* **sheaves** (shēvz) **1.** A quantity of the stalks of cut grain or the like, bound together. **2.** Any collection of things, as papers, tied together. **3.** A quiverful of arrows. *— v.t.* To bind in a sheaf. [OE *scēaf*]

shear (shir) *n.* **1.** A two-bladed cutting instrument; obsolete except in the plural. See SHEARS. **2.** *Physics* A deformation of a solid body, equivalent to a sliding over each other of adjacent laminar elements, with a progressive relative displacement; also **shearing stress.** **3.** The act or result of shearing. **4.** A plowshare. *— v.* **sheared, sheared** or **shorn, shear·ing** *v.t.* **1.** To cut the hair, fleece, etc., from. **2.** To remove by cutting or clipping: to *shear* wool. **3.** To deprive; strip, as of wealth. **4.** To cut or clip with or as with shears. *— v.i.* **5.** To use shears. **6.** To slide or break from a shear (def. 2). **7.** To proceed by or as by cutting away: with *through*. [OE < *scieran* to shear] **— shear'er** *n.*

shears (shirz) *n.pl.* **1.** Any large cutting or clipping instrument worked by the crossing of cutting edges. Also **pair of shears. 2.** The ways or guides, as of a lathe. [See SHEAR.]

shear·wa·ter (shir'wô'tər, -wot'ər) *n.* Any of various far-ranging sea birds related to the fulmars and petrels: so called because they skim close to the water.

sheath (shēth) *n.* *pl.* **sheaths** (shēthz, shēths) **1.** An envelope or case, as for a sword; scabbard. **2.** A covering in plants or animals resembling a sheath. **3.** A close-fitting dress having straight, unbroken lines. *— v.t.* To sheathe. [OE *scæth*] **— sheath'less** *adj.*

sheathe (shēth) *v.t.* **sheathed, sheath·ing** **1.** To put into a sheath. **2.** To encase or protect with a covering. **3.** To draw in, as claws. [< SHEATH]

sheath·ing (shē'thing) *n.* **1.** A protective covering, as of a ship's hull; that which sheathes; also, the material used. **2.** The act of one who sheathes. **3.** The covering or waterproof material on outside walls or roofs.

sheave¹ (shēv) *v.t.* **sheaved, sheav·ing** To gather into sheaves; collect. [< SHEAF]

sheave² (shēv) *n.* A grooved pulley wheel; also, a pulley wheel and its block. [ME *schive*]

sheaves (shēvz) Plural of SHEAF¹.

She·ba (shē′bə), **Queen of** A queen who visited Solomon to test his wisdom. I *Kings* x 1–3.

she·bang (shi·bang′) *n. U.S. Slang* **1.** A building, vehicle, etc. **2.** Matter; affair: tired of the whole *shebang*.

She·bat (shi·bät′) *n.* The fifth month of the Hebrew year. Also spelled *Sebat*. See (Hebrew) CALENDAR.

shed¹ (shed) *v.* **shed, shed·ding** *v.t.* **1.** To pour forth in drops; emit, as tears. **2.** To cause to pour forth. **3.** To send forth; radiate. **4.** To throw off without allowing to penetrate, as rain; repel. **5.** To cast off by natural process, as hair, etc. **6.** To rid oneself of. — *v.i.* **7.** To cast off or lose skin, etc., by natural process. **8.** To fall or drop, as leaves. — **to shed blood** To kill. — *n.* **1.** That which sheds, as a sloping surface or watershed. **2.** That which has been shed. [OE *scēadan* to separate, part]

shed² (shed) *n.* **1.** A small low building, often with front or sides open; also, a lean-to: a wagon *shed*. **2.** *Brit.* A barn.

she'd (shed) **1.** She had. **2.** She would.

shed·der (shed′ər) *n.* **1.** One who sheds. **2.** An animal that sheds or has lately shed its skin, as a snake.

sheen (shēn) *n.* **1.** A glistening brightness, as if from reflection. **2.** Shining attire. — *adj.* Shining; beautiful. — *v.i.* To shine; glisten. [OE *sciene* beautiful] — **sheen′y** *adj.*

sheep (shēp) *n. pl.* **sheep 1.** A medium-sized, domesticated, even-toed ruminant, bred in many varieties for its flesh, wool, and skin. ◆ Collateral adjective: *ovine*. **2.** Sheepskin. **3.** A meek, bashful, or timid person. [OE *scēap*]

sheep·cote (shēp′kōt′) *n.* A small enclosure for the protection of sheep; a sheepfold. Also **sheep′cot′** (-kot′).

sheep dip Any of several liquid disinfectants containing creosote, nicotine, arsenic, etc., used for dipping sheep.

sheep dog A dog trained to guard and control sheep, often a collie, but also an **old English sheep dog**, a rough-coated, heavy, bobtailed dog much used by drovers in England: also called *shepherd dog*, *shepherd's dog*.

sheep·fold (shēp′fōld′) *n.* A pen for sheep.

sheep·herd·er (shēp′hûr′dər) *n.* A herder of sheep. — **sheep′herd′ing** *n.*

sheep·ish (shē′pish) *adj.* Foolish, as a sheep; awkwardly diffident; abashed. — **sheep′ish·ly** *adv.* — **sheep′ish·ness** *n.*

sheep ranch A ranch where sheep are bred and raised. Also *Brit.* **sheep·walk** (shēp′wôk′), *Austral.* **sheep run.**

sheep's eyes (shēps) Bashful or amorous glances.

sheep·skin (shēp′skin′) *n.* **1.** The skin of a sheep, tanned or untanned, or anything made from it. **2.** A document written on parchment, as an academic diploma.

sheep sorrel An herb growing in dry places, and having leaves of an acrid taste.

sheer¹ (shir) *v.i.* To swerve from a course; turn aside. — *v.t.* To cause to swerve. — *n.* **1.** *Naut.* The rise, or the amount of rise from a level, of the lengthwise lines of a vessel's hull. **b** A position of a vessel that enables it to swing clear of a single anchor. **2.** A swerving course. [< SHEAR]

sheer² (shir) *adj.* **1.** Having no modifying conditions; unmitigated; absolute: *sheer* folly. **2.** Exceedingly thin and fine: said of fabrics. **3.** Perpendicular; steep. **4.** Pure; pellucid. — *n.* Any very thin fabric used for clothes. — *adv.* Steeply; perpendicularly. [ME *schere*] — **sheer′ness** *n.* — **sheer′ly** *adv.*

sheet (shēt) *n.* **1.** A very thin and broad piece of any substance; as: **a** A large rectangular piece of bed linen. **b** A piece of paper. **c** A newspaper. **d** A piece of metal or other substance hammered, rolled, fused, or cut very thin. **2.** A broad, flat surface; superficial expanse: a *sheet* of water. **3.** *Naut.* **a** A rope or chain from a lower corner of a sail to extend it or move it. **b** *pl.* In an open boat, the space at the bow and stern not occupied by the thwarts. **c** A sail. **4.** Any superficial deposit, as of gravel left by a glacier, or of soil or ice. **5.** The large, unseparated block of stamps printed by one impression of a plate. — **three sheets in the wind** *Slang* Tipsy; drunk. — *v.t.* **1.** To cover with a sheet. **2.** To furnish with sheets. [OE *scȳte* linen cloth]

sheet anchor 1. One of two anchors for use only in emergency. **2.** One who or that which can be depended upon in danger or an emergency.

sheet bend *Naut.* A knot used to join two ropes' ends.

sheet·ing (shē′ting) *n.* **1.** The act of sheeting, in any sense. **2.** Cotton, muslin, etc., used for making sheets for beds.

sheet lightning Lightning appearing in sheetlike form as a momentary and broadly diffused radiance in the sky, caused by the reflection of a distant lightning flash.

sheet metal Metal rolled and pressed into sheets.

sheet music Music printed on unbound sheets of paper.

sheik (shēk, *Brit.* shāk) *n.* **1.** A Moslem high priest or a venerable man; also, the chief or head of an Arab tribe or family. **2.** *Archaic Slang* A man who fascinates women. Also **sheikh.** [< Arabic *sheikh, shaykh*, lit., an elder, chief]

sheik·dom (shēk′dəm) *n.* The land ruled by a sheik. Also **sheikh′dom.**

shek·el (shek′əl) *n.* **1.** An Assyrian, Babylonian, and, later, Hebrew unit of weight and money; also, a coin having this weight. **2.** *pl. Slang* Money. [< Hebrew *shāqal* to weigh]

shel·drake (shel′drāk′) *n.* **1.** A large Old World duck of southeastern Europe and North Africa. **2.** A merganser. [< dial. E *sheld* piebald, dappled + DRAKE]

shelf (shelf) *n. pl.* **shelves** (shelvz) **1.** A board or slab set horizontally against a wall, in a bookcase, etc., to support articles, as books. **2.** Contents of a shelf. **3.** Any flat projecting ledge, as of rock. **4.** A reef; shoal. **5.** A stratum of bedrock. — **on the shelf** No longer in use; discarded. [< LG *schelf* set of shelves]

shell (shel) *n.* **1.** Any of various hard structures encasing an animal, as a mollusk or other shellfish. **2.** The hard, relatively fragile outer coat of an egg. **3.** The relatively hard covering of a fruit, seed, or nut. **4.** The material composing a shell. **5.** A hollow structure or vessel, generally thin and weak; also, a case or mold for holding something: a pie *shell*. **6.** A very light, long, and narrow racing rowboat. **7.** A hollow metallic projectile filled with an explosive or chemical. **8.** A metallic or paper cartridge case for small arms. **9.** A shape or outline that merely simulates a reality; hollow form; external semblance. **10.** A reserved or impersonal attitude: to come out of one's *shell*. — *v.t.* **1.** To divest of or remove from a shell. **2.** To separate from the cob, as corn. **3.** To bombard with shells, as a fort. **4.** To cover with shells. — *v.i.* **5.** To shed the shell or pod. **6.** To fall off, as a shell. — **to shell out** *Informal* To hand over, as money. [OE *sciell* shell] — **shell′er** *n.* — **shell′y** *adj.*

she'll (shēl) She will.

shel·lac (shə·lak′) *n.* **1.** A purified lac in the form of thin plates, extensively used in varnish, sealing wax, insulators, etc. **2.** A varnishlike solution of flake shellac dissolved in methylated spirit, used for coating floors, woodwork, etc. — *v.t.* **·lacked, ·lack·ing 1.** To cover or varnish with shellac. **2.** *Slang* To belabor; beat. **3.** *Slang* To defeat utterly. Also **shell′-lac′, shel·lack′.** [< SHELL + LAC¹]

shel·lack·ing (shə·lak′ing) *n. U.S. Slang* **1.** A beating; assault. **2.** A thorough defeat.

shell·back (shel′bak′) *n.* A veteran sailor; an old salt; esp., one who has crossed the equator. [Prob. with reference to the shell of the sea turtle]

shell·bark (shel′bärk′) *n.* The shagbark or one of its nuts.

shell·fire (shel′fīr′) *n.* The firing of artillery shells.

shell·fish (shel′fish′) *n. pl.* **·fish** or **·fish·es** Any aquatic animal having a shell, as a mollusk.

shell game 1. A swindling game in which the victim bets on the location of a pea covered by one of three nutshells. **2.** Any game in which the victim cannot win.

shell·proof (shel′proof′) *adj.* Built to resist the destructive effect of projectiles and bombs.

shell shock Formerly, combat fatigue. — **shell-shocked** (shel′shokt′) *adj.*

shel·ter (shel′tər) *n.* **1.** That which covers or shields from exposure or danger; a place of safety. **2.** The state of being sheltered or protected. — *v.t.* **1.** To provide protection or shelter for; shield, as from danger or inclement weather. — *v.i.* **2.** To take shelter. [? Alter. of ME *scheltrum* < OE *sceld-truma* a body of men armed with shields, phalanx, protection] — **shel′ter·er** *n.* — **shel′ter·less** *adj.*

shelter tent *Mil.* A tent for two men, divided into two sections, each of which, called a **shelter half**, is carried as part of a soldier's field equipment: also called *pup tent.*

shelve (shelv) *v.* **shelved, shelv·ing** *v.t.* **1.** To place on a shelf. **2.** To postpone indefinitely; put aside. **3.** To retire. **4.** To provide or fit with shelves. — *v.i.* **5.** To incline gradually; slope. [< SHELF] — **shelv′y** *adj.*

shelves (shelvz) Plural of SHELF.

shelv·ing (shel′ving) *n.* **1.** Shelves collectively. **2.** Material for shelves.

Shem (shem) The eldest son of Noah. *Gen.* v 32.

Shem·ite (shem′īt) See SEMITE.

she·nan·i·gan (shi·nan′ə·gən) *n. Often pl. Informal* Trickery; foolery; nonsense; also, treacherous action or a treacherous act. [? < Irish *sionnach* fox]

she·ol (shē′ōl) *n.* Hell. [< Hebrew *she'ōl* cave]

She·ol (shē′ōl) In the Old Testament, a place under the earth where the departed spirits were believed to go.

shep·herd (shep′ərd) *n.* **1.** A keeper or herder of sheep. **2.** A pastor, leader, or guide. — *v.t.* To watch and tend as a shepherd. [OE *scēaphyrde*] — **shep′herd·ess** (-is) *n.fem.*

shepherd dog A sheep dog. Also **shepherd's dog.**

shep·herd's-purse (shep′ərdz·pûrs′) *n.* A weed bearing small white flowers and notched triangular pods.

Sher·a·ton (sher′ə·tən) *adj.* Denoting the graceful, straight-lined, classically chaste style of English furniture developed by Thomas Sheraton, 1751–1806, English furniture designer.

sher·bet (shûr′bit) *n.* **1.** A flavored water ice. **2.** *Brit.* A drink made of sweetened fruit juice and sometimes cooled with snow. [< Turkish *sherbet*]

sherd (shûrd) *n.* A fragment of pottery: often in combination: *potsherd*: also called *shard*. [Var. of SHARD]

she·rif (she·rēf′) *n.* **1.** A descendant of Mohammed through his daughter Fatima. **2.** An Arab chief. Also **she·reef′**. [< Arabic *sharīf* noble]

sher·iff (sher′if) *n.* The chief administrative officer of a county, who executes the mandates of courts, enforces order, etc. [OE *scīr-gerēfa* shire reeve] — **sher′iff·dom** *n.*

she·root (shə·root′) See CHEROOT.

Sher·pa (shûr′pə) *n.* One of a Tibetan tribe living on the southern slopes of the Himalayas in Nepal.

sher·ry (sher′ē) *n.* *pl.* ·ries A fortified wine of Jerez, Spain; also, any similar wine. [after *Jerez*, Spain]

Sher·wood Forest (shûr′wŏŏd) A forest in Nottingham-shire, England, known as the home of Robin Hood.

she's (shēz) **1.** She is. **2.** She has.

Shet·land pony (shet′lənd) A small, hardy, shaggy breed of pony originally bred on the Shetland Islands.

shew (shō) *v.t. & v.i.* shewed, shewn, shew·ing *Archaic* To show. — **shew′er** *n.*

shew·bread (shō′bred′) *n.* Unleavened bread formerly dis-played in the Jewish temple: also spelled *showbread*.

Shi·ah (shē′ä) *n.* **1.** One of the two great sects of Islam. Compare SUNNI. **2.** A Shiite. [< Arabic *shi'i* follower, sect]

shib·bo·leth (shib′ə·leth) *n.* **1.** A test word or pet phrase of a party; a watchword: from the Hebrew word *shibboleth*, given by Jephthah (*Judges* xii 4–6) as a test to distinguish his own men from the Ephraimites, who used the pronuncia-tion *sibboleth*. **2.** A custom or use of language regarded as distinctive of a particular social class, profession, etc. [< Hebrew *shibbōleth* ear of grain]

shied (shīd) Past tense and past participle of SHY.

shield (shēld) *n.* **1.** A broad piece of defensive armor, com-monly carried on the left arm. **2.** Something that protects or defends. **3.** Any device for covering or protecting some-thing. **4.** *Heraldry* An escutcheon. **5.** A conventional figure having an oval bottom and a cusp at the top, used in flags, emblems, etc. — *v.t.* **1.** To protect from danger as with a shield; defend; guard. — *v.i.* **2.** To act as a shield or safeguard. [OE *scīld*] — **shield′er** *n.*

shi·er (shī′ər) Comparative of SHY. — *n.* A horse in the habit of shying. Also spelled *shyer*.

shift (shift) *v.t.* **1.** To change or move from one position, place, etc., to another. **2.** To change for another or others of the same class. **3.** To change (gears) from one arrange-ment to another. **4.** *Ling.* To alter as part of a systematic change. — *v.i.* **5.** To change position, place, etc. **6.** To evade; equivocate. **7.** To shift gears. — **to shift for oneself** To do the best one can to provide for one's needs. — *n.* **1.** The act of shifting. **2.** A dodge; artifice; trick; evasion; expedient: We made *shift* to get along. **3.** *Archaic* or *Dial.* An undergarment; chemise. **4.** A straight, loosely hanging woman's garment, as a dress. **5.** A change of position, place, direction, or form: a *shift* in the wind. **6.** A relay of work-ers; also, the working time of each group. **7.** *Physics* Any of various displacements of spectral lines caused by velocity of the light source, gravitational effect, etc. See DOPPLER EFFECT. **8.** *Geol.* The relative displacement of areas on op-posite sides of a rock fault. [OE *sciftan* to divide] — **shift′er** *n.*

shift·less (shift′lis) *adj.* **1.** Unable or unwilling to shift for oneself; inefficient or lazy. **2.** Showing lack of energy or re-source. — **shift′less·ly** *adv.* — **shift′less·ness** *n.*

shift·y (shif′tē) *adj.* shift·i·er, shift·i·est **1.** Artful; tricky; fickle. **2.** Full of expedients; alert; capable. — **shift′i·ly** *adv.* — **shift′i·ness** *n.*

Shi·ite (shē′īt) *n.* A Moslem of the Shiah sect: distinguished from *Sunnite*: also *Shiah*. Also **Shie′ite, Shi′ite**.

shill (shil) *n.* *Slang* The assistant of a sidewalk peddler or gambler, who makes a purchase or bet to encourage onlookers to buy or bet; a capper. [Origin unknown]

shil·le·lagh (shi·lā′lä, -lē) *n.* In Ireland, a stout cudgel made of oak or blackthorn. Also **shil·e′lah**. [after *Shille-lagh*, a town in Ireland famed for its oaks]

shil·ling (shil′ing) *n.* **1.** A British monetary unit, since the Norman Conquest equivalent to 12 pence or ¹⁄₂₀ pound; also, a coin of this value, first issued in 1504. **2.** A similar mone-tary unit of various other countries. **3.** A former coin of colonial America. [OE *scilling*]

shil·ly-shal·ly (shil′ē-shal′ē) *v.i.* ·lied, ·ly·ing **1.** To act with indecision; be irresolute; vacillate. **2.** To trifle. — *adj.* Weak; hesitating. — *n.* Weak or foolish vacillation; irresolution. — *adv.* In an irresolute manner. [Dissimilated reduplication of *shall I?*] — **shil′ly-shal′li·er** *n.*

shi·ly (shī′lē) See SHYLY.

shim (shim) *n.* A piece of metal or other material used to fill out space, for leveling, etc. — *v.t.* shimmed, shim·ming To wedge up or fill out by inserting a shim. [Origin un-known]

shim·mer (shim′ər) *v.i.* To shine faintly; glimmer. — *n.* A tremulous shining or gleaming; glimmer; gleam. [OE *sci-merian*] — **shim′mer·y** *adj.*

shim·my (shim′ē) *n.* *pl.* ·mies *U.S. Informal* A che-mise. **2.** A former jazz dance accompanied by shaking movements. **3.** Unusual vibration, as in automobile wheels. — *v.i.* ·mied, ·my·ing **1.** To vibrate or wobble. **2.** To dance the shimmy. [Alter. of CHEMISE]

shin (shin) *n.* **1.** The front part of the leg below the knee; also, the shinbone. **2.** The lower foreleg: a shin of beef. — *v.t. & v.i.* shinned, shin·ning **1.** To climb (a pole) by grip-ping with the hands or arms and the shins or legs: usu. with *up*. **2.** To kick (someone) in the shins. [OE *scinu*]

shin·bone (shin′bōn′) *n.* The tibia.

shin·dig (shin′dig) *n.* *U.S. Slang* A dance or noisy party. [< SHINDY, by folk etymology, suggesting *a dig on the shin*]

shine (shīn) *v.i.* shone or (*esp. for def. 5*) shined, shin·ing **1.** To emit light; beam; glow. **2.** To gleam, as by reflected light. **3.** To excel or be conspicuous in splendor, beauty, etc. — *v.t.* **4.** To cause to shine. **5.** To brighten by rubbing or polishing. — **to shine up to** *Slang* To try to please. — *n.* **1.** The state or quality of being bright or shining; radiance; luster; sheen. **2.** Fair weather; sunshine. **3.** *U.S. Informal* A liking or fancy. **4.** *U.S. Informal* A smart trick or prank. **5.** A shoeshine. — **to take a shine to** *U.S. Informal* To be-come fond of. [OE *scīnan*]

shin·er (shī′nər) *n.* **1.** One who or that which shines. **2.** One of various silvery fresh-water fishes related to the min-nows. **3.** A silverfish, an insect. **4.** *Slang* A black eye.

shin·gle¹ (shing′gəl) *n.* **1.** A thin, tapering, oblong piece of wood or other material, used in courses to cover roofs. **2.** A small sign bearing the name of a doctor, lawyer, etc., and placed outside his office. **3.** A short haircut. — *v.t.* ·gled, ·gling **1.** To cover (a roof, building, etc.) with or as with shingles. **2.** To cut (the hair) short. [ME < L *scandula* shingle] — **shin′gler** *n.*

shin·gle² (shing′gəl) *n.* **1.** Rounded, waterworn gravel, found on the seashore. **2.** A place strewn with shingle, as a beach. [Cf. Norw. *singl* coarse gravel] — **shin′gly** *adj.*

shin·gles (shing′gəlz) *n.pl.* (*construed as sing. or pl.*) *Pathol.* An acute inflammatory virus disease characterized by blist-ers along the course of the affected nerve ganglia and accom-panied by pain: also called *herpes zoster*. [Alter. of Med.L *cingulus* < L *cingulum* girdle < *cingere* to gird]

shin·ing (shī′ning) *adj.* **1.** Emitting or reflecting a continu-ous light; gleaming; luminous. **2.** Of unusual brilliance or excellence; conspicuous. — **shin′ing·ly** *adv.*

shin·ny¹ (shin′ē) *n.* **1.** A game resembling hockey; also, one of the sticks or clubs used by the players. **2.** *Canadian* Pond hockey. Also **shin′ney**. [< *shin ye*, a cry used in the game]

shin·ny² (shin′ē) *v.i.* ·nied, ·ny·ing *U.S. Informal* To climb using one's shins: usually with *up*.

shin·plas·ter (shin′plas′ter, -plås′-) *n.* **1.** *U.S.* Fractional currency issued by other than the constituted authorities. **2.** Any paper money issued by private enterprises. **3.** A plaster for a sore shin.

Shin·to (shin′tō) *n.* A religion of Japan, consisting chiefly in ancestor worship, nature worship, and, formerly, a belief in the divinity of the Emperor. Also **Shin′to·ism**. [< Japanese, way of the gods] — **Shin′to·ist** *n.*

shin·y (shī′nē) *adj.* shin·i·er, shin·i·est **1.** Glistening; glossy; polished. **2.** Bright; clear.

ship (ship) *n.* **1.** Any vessel suitable for deep-water naviga-tion; also, its personnel. **2.** A large seagoing sailing vessel with at least three masts, carrying square-rigged sails on all three. **3.** An airship or airplane. — **when one's ship comes in** (or **home**) When one's fortune has been made or hopes realized. — *v.* shipped, ship·ping *v.t.* **1.** To trans-port by ship or other mode of conveyance. **2.** To hire and receive for service on board a vessel, as sailors. **3.** *Naut.* To receive over the side, as in rough weather: to *ship* a wave. **4.** *Informal* To get rid of. **5.** To set or fit in a prepared place on a boat or vessel, as a mast, or a rudder. — *v.i.* **6.** To go on board ship; embark. **7.** To undergo shipment: Raspberries do not *ship* well. **8.** To enlist as a seaman: usually with *out*. [OE *scip*]

-ship *suffix of nouns* **1.** The state, condition, or quality of: *friendship*. **2.** Office, rank, or dignity of: *kingship*. **3.** The art or skill of: *marksmanship*. [OE *-scipe*]

ship·board (ship′bôrd′, -bōrd′) *n.* **1.** The side or deck of a ship. **2.** A vessel: used only in the phrase **on shipboard**.

ship·build·er (ship′bil′dər) *n.* One whose work is the build-ing of vessels. — **ship′build′ing** *adj. & n.*

ship canal A waterway deep enough for seagoing vessels.

ship chandler One who deals in supplies for vessels.

ship·load (ship′lōd′) *n.* The quantity that a ship carries or can carry; a cargo.

ship·mas·ter (ship′mas′tər, -mäs′-)   *n.* The captain or master of a merchant ship.

ship·mate (ship′māt′)   *n.* A fellow sailor.

ship·ment (ship′mənt)   *n.* **1.** The act of shipping. **2.** That which is shipped.

ship of the line   Formerly, a man-of-war large enough to take a position in a line of battle.

ship·owner (ship′ō′nər)   *n.* One owning a ship or ships.

ship·pa·ble (ship′ə·bəl)   *adj.* That can be shipped or transported.

ship·per (ship′ər)   *n.* One who ships goods.

ship·ping (ship′ing)   *n.* **1.** Ships collectively; also, tonnage. **2.** The act of shipping.

ship·shape (ship′shāp′)   *adj.* Well arranged, orderly, and neat, as on a ship.   — *adv.* In an orderly manner; neatly.

ship's papers   The documents required by international law to be carried by a ship.

ship·worm (ship′wûrm′)   *n.* Any of various marine bivalves, resembling worms, that burrow into the timbers of ships, piers, wharfs, etc.

ship·wreck (ship′rek′)   *n.* **1.** The partial or total destruction of a ship at sea. **2.** Utter or practical destruction; ruin. **3.** Scattered remnants, as of a wrecked ship; wreckage. — *v.t.* **1.** To wreck, as a vessel. **2.** To bring to disaster; ruin.

ship·wright (ship′rīt′)   *n.* One who builds or repairs ships.

ship·yard (ship′yärd′)   *n.* A place where ships are built or repaired.

shire (shīr)   *n.* A territorial division of Great Britain; a county. [OE *scīr*]

shirk (shûrk)   *v.t.* **1.** To avoid the doing of; evade doing (something that should be done). — *v.i.* **2.** To avoid work or evade obligation. — *n.* One who shirks: also **shirk′er.** [? < G *schürke* rascal]

shirr (shûr)   *v.t.* **1.** To draw (material) into three or more parallel rows of gathers. **2.** To bake with crumbs in a buttered dish, as eggs. — *n.* **1.** A drawing of material into three or more parallel rows of gathers. **2.** A rubber thread woven into a fabric to make it elastic. [Origin unknown]

shirt (shûrt)   *n.* **1.** A garment for the upper part of the body, usu. having collar and cuffs and a front closing. **2.** A closely fitting undergarment. **3.** A shirtwaist. — **to keep one's shirt on** *Slang* To remain calm. — **to lose one's shirt** *Slang* To lose everything. [OE *scyrte* shirt, short garment] — **shirt′less** *adj.*

shirt·ing (shûr′ting)   *n.* Closely woven material of cotton, linen, silk, etc., used for making shirts, blouses, dresses, etc.

shirt·waist (shûrt′wāst′)   *n.* **1.** A woman's tailored, sleeved blouse or shirt, usu. worn tucked in under a skirt or slacks. **2.** A woman's tailored dress having a bodice like a shirtwaist: also **shirtwaist dress.**

shish ke·bab (shish′kə·bob′)   Meat roasted or broiled in small pieces on skewers and served with condiments. [< Turkish *shish* skewer + *kebap* roast meat]

shist (shist)   See SCHIST.

Shi·va (shē′və)   Siva, a Hindu god.

shiv·a·ree (shiv′ə·rē′)   *n. U.S.* A charivari. [Alter. of CHARIVARI]

shiv·er¹ (shiv′ər)   *v.i.* **1.** To tremble; shake; quiver. — *v.t.* **2.** *Naut.* To cause to flutter in the wind, as a sail. — *n.* The act of shivering; a tremble. [ME *chivere*] — **shiv′er·y** *adj.*

shiv·er² (shiv′ər)   *v.t. & v.i.* To break suddenly into fragments; shatter. — *n.* A splinter; sliver. [ME *schivere*] — **shiv′er·y** *adj.*

shoal¹ (shōl)   *n.* **1.** A shallow place in any body of water. **2.** A sandbank or bar, esp. one seen at low water. Compare REEF¹. — *v.i.* **1.** To become shallow. — *v.t.* **2.** To make shallow. **3.** To sail into a lesser depth of (water): said of a ship. — *adj.* Shallow. [OE *sceald* shallow]

shoal² (shōl)   *n.* **1.** An assemblage or multitude; throng. **2.** A school of fish. — *v.i.* **1.** To throng in multitudes. **2.** To school: said of fish. [OE *scolu* troop, multitude]

shoal·y (shō′lē)   *adj.* **shoal·i·er, shoal·i·est** Abounding in shoals. — **shoal′i·ness** *n.*

shock¹ (shok)   *n.* **1.** A violent collision or concussion; impact; blow. **2.** A sudden and violent sensation: a *shock* of paralysis. **3.** A sudden and severe agitation of the mind or emotions, as in horror or great sorrow. **4.** *Pathol.* Prostration of bodily functions, as from sudden injury. **5.** The physical reactions produced by the passage of a strong electric current through the body, as involuntary muscular contractions. — *v.t.* **1.** To shake by sudden collision; jar. **2.** To disturb the emotions or mind of; horrify; disgust. **3.** To give an electric shock to. [< F < *choquer* < Gmc.] — **shock′er** *n.*

shock² (shok)   *n.* A number of sheaves of grain, stalks of maize, or the like, stacked for drying upright in a field. — *v.t. & v.i.* To gather (grain) into a shock or shocks. [ME *schokke* < Gmc. Cf. MLG *schok.*] — **shock′er** *n.*

shock³ (shok)   *adj.* Shaggy; bushy. — *n.* A coarse, tangled mass, as of hair. [Back formation < *shock dog*]

shock absorber   *Mech.* A device designed to absorb the force of shocks, as the springs of an automobile.

shock·ing (shok′ing)   *adj.* **1.** Causing a mental or emotional shock, as with horror or disgust. **2.** *Informal* Terrible; awful. — **shock′ing·ly** *adv.* — **shock′ing·ness** *n.*

shock therapy   *Psychiatry* The treatment of certain psychotic disorders by the injection of drugs, or by electrical shocks, both methods inducing coma, with or without convulsions.

shock troops   *Mil.* Seasoned men selected to lead an attack.

shock wave   *Physics* A compression wave following a sudden and violent disturbance of the transmitting medium, through which it is propagated with a velocity equal to or greater than that of sound.

shod (shod)   Past tense and alternative past participle of SHOE.

shod·dy (shod′ē)   *n. pl.* **·dies 1.** Wool obtained by shredding discarded woolens or worsteds; also, cloth made of such wool. **2.** Any inferior goods made to resemble those of better quality. — *adj.* **shod·di·er, shod·di·est 1.** Made of or containing shoddy. **2.** Sham; inferior. [Origin uncertain] — **shod′di·ly** *adv.* — **shod′di·ness** *n.*

shoe (shoō)   *n. pl.* **shoes 1.** An outer covering, usu. of leather, for the human foot. **2.** Something resembling a shoe in position or use. **3.** A rim or plate of iron to protect the hoof of an animal. **4.** A strip of iron, steel, etc., fitted under a sleigh runner to receive friction. **5.** The part of the brake that presses upon a wheel or drum. **6.** The tread or outer covering of a pneumatic tire, as for an automobile. **7.** The sliding contact plate on an electric car or locomotive by which it obtains current from the third rail. — *v.t.* **shod, shod** or **shod·den, shoe·ing 1.** To furnish with shoes or the like. **2.** To furnish with a guard of metal, wood, etc., for protection, as against wear. [OE *scōh*]

shoe·black (shoō′blak′)   *n.* One who cleans or polishes shoes as an occupation.

shoe·horn (shoō′hôrn′)   *n.* A smooth curved implement of horn, metal, etc., used to help put on a shoe.

shoe·lace (shoō′lās′)   *n.* A lace or cord for fastening shoes.

shoe·mak·er (shoō′mā′kər)   *n.* One who makes or repairs shoes, boots, etc. — **shoe′mak′ing** *n.*

sho·er (shoō′ər)   *n.* One who shoes horses.

shoe·shine (shoō′shīn′)   *n.* **1.** The waxing and polishing of a pair of shoes. **2.** The polished look of shined shoes.

shoe·string (shoō′string′)   *n.* A shoelace. — **on a shoestring** With a small sum of money with which to begin a business, etc.

shoe·tree (shoō′trē′)   *n.* A form for inserting in a shoe to preserve its shape or to stretch it.

sho·far (shō′fär)   *n.* A ram's horn used in Jewish ritual, sounded on solemn occasions and in war: also spelled *shophar.* [< Hebrew *shōphār*]

sho·gun (shō′gun, -goōn)   *n.* Any of the hereditary military dictators who ruled Japan until the 19th century and under whom the emperor was a figurehead. [< Japanese < Chinese *chiang-chün* leader of an army]

sho·ji (shō′jē)   *n.* A translucent paper screen forming a partition, door, etc., in a Japanese house. [< Japanese]

shone (shōn, shon)   Past tense and past participle of SHINE.

shoo (shoō)   *interj.* Begone! be off!: used in driving away fowls, etc. — *v.t.* **1.** To drive away, as by crying "shoo." — *v.i.* **2.** To cry "shoo." [Imit.]

shoo·fly (shoō′flī)   *n. pl.* **·flies** *U.S.* **1.** An enclosed child's rocker with sides representing horses, swans, etc. **2.** A kind of pie with a syrupy filling made with molasses and brown sugar.

shoo-in (shoō′in′)   *U.S. Informal n.* A contestant, candidate, etc., who is certain to win.

shook (shoōk)   Past tense of SHAKE.

shoot (shoōt)   *v.* **shot, shoot·ing** *v.t.* **1.** To hit, wound, or kill with a missile discharged from a weapon. **2.** To discharge (a missile) from a bow, rifle, etc. **3.** To discharge (a weapon): often with *off*: to *shoot* a cannon. **4.** To take the altitude of with a sextant, etc.: to *shoot* the sun. **5.** To send forth as if from a weapon, as questions, glances, etc. **6.** To pass over or through swiftly: to *shoot* rapids. **7.** To go over (an area) in hunting game. **8.** To emit, as rays of light. **9.** To photograph; film. **10.** To cause to stick out or protrude; extend. **11.** To put forth in growth; send forth (buds, leaves, etc.). **12.** To push into or out of the fastening, as the bolt of a door. **13.** To propel, discharge, or dump, as down a chute or from a container. **14.** To variegate, as with streaks of color: usually in the past participle: His paintings are *shot* with pink and brown. **15.** In games: **a** To score (a goal, point, etc.) by kicking or otherwise forcing the ball, etc., to the objective. **b** To play (golf, craps, pool, etc.). **c**

To play (marbles). d To cast (the dice). **16.** *Slang* To inject (a drug, esp. a narcotic). — *v.i.* **17.** To discharge a missile from a bow, firearm, etc. **18.** To go off; discharge. **19.** To move swiftly; dart. **20.** To hunt game. **21.** To jut out; extend or project. **22.** To put forth buds, leaves, etc.; germinate; sprout. **23.** To take a photograph. **24.** To start the cameras, as in motion pictures. **25.** In games, to make a play by propelling the ball, puck, etc., in a certain manner. — **to shoot at** (or **for**) *Informal* To strive for; attempt to attain or obtain. — **to shoot down** To bring to earth by shooting. — **to shoot off one's mouth** *Slang* To talk too freely or too much. — *n.* **1.** A young branch or sucker of a plant; offshoot. **2.** A narrow passage in a stream; a rapid. **3.** An inclined passage down which anything may be shot; a chute. **4.** The act of shooting; a shot. **5.** A shooting match, hunting party, etc. **6.** *U.S. Informal* A rocket or missile launching. **7.** The thrust of an arch. **8.** Any new growth, as a new antler. **9.** Shooting distance; range. [OE *scēotan*] — **shoot'er** *n.*

shoot·ing (shoo′ting) *n.* The act of one who or that which shoots.

shooting gallery A place, usu. enclosed, where one can shoot at targets.

shooting star 1. A meteor. **2.** Any of certain small perennial herbs, having clusters of white, rose, or crimson flowers.

shoot-out (shoot′out′) *n.* An exchange of gunfire.

shop (shop) *n.* **1.** A place for the sale of goods at retail. Also **shoppe. 2.** A place for making or repairing any article, or the carrying on of any artisan craft: a blacksmith's *shop*. **3.** One's own craft or business as a subject of conversation: to talk *shop*. — *v.i.* **shopped, shop·ping** To visit shops or stores to purchase or look at goods. [OE *sceoppa* booth]

shop·girl (shop′gûrl′) *n.* A girl who works in a shop.

sho·phar (shō′fär) *See* SHOFAR.

shop·keep·er (shop′kē′pər) *n.* One who runs a shop or store; a tradesman.

shop·lift·er (shop′lif′tər) *n.* One who steals goods exposed for sale in a shop. — **shop′lift′ing** *n.*

shop·per (shop′ər) *n.* **1.** One who shops. **2.** An employee of a store who compares the merchandise of competitors as to quality, price, etc. — **shop′ping** *n.*

shopping center A group of retail stores, restaurants, etc., including an ample parking area, usu. built as a unit.

shop steward A union worker chosen by fellow workers to represent them to management in seeking redress of grievances, etc. Also **shop chairman.**

shop·talk (shop′tôk′) *n.* Conversation limited to one's job or profession.

shop·walk·er (shop′wô′kər) *n. Brit.* A floorwalker.

shop·worn (shop′wôrn′, -wōrn′) *adj.* **1.** Soiled or otherwise deteriorated from having been handled or on display in a shop. **2.** Worn out, as from overuse; stale.

shore¹ (shôr, shōr) *n.* **1.** The coast or land adjacent to an ocean, sea, lake, or large river. ◆ Collateral adjective: *littoral.* **2.** Land: to be on *shore.* — **in shore** Near or toward the shore. — *v.t.* **shored, shor·ing 1.** To set on shore. **2.** To surround as with a shore. [ME *schore*]

— **Syn.** (noun) **1.** *Shore, coast, beach,* and *bank* denote the land adjacent to a body of water. *Shore* is the general term; we speak of the *shore* of the sea, of a lake, or of a river. *Coast* is the ocean *shore,* especially along a great extent of land: the *coast* of Florida. A *beach* is a low, gently sloping expanse of sand or gravel; a *bank* is a more or less steep slope: the *banks* of the Red River.

shore² (shôr, shōr) *v.t.* **shored, shor·ing** To prop, as a wall, by a vertical or sloping timber: usu., with *up.* — *n.* A beam set endwise as a prop or temporary support against the side of a building, a ship in drydock, etc. [Cf. Du. *schoor* prop, ON *skortha* stay]

shore·less (shôr′lis, shōr′-) *adj.* **1.** Having no shore. **2.** Boundless.

shore·line (shôr′līn′, shōr′-) *n.* The contour of a shore.

shore patrol A detail of the U.S. Navy, Coast Guard, or Marine Corps assigned to police duties ashore.

shore·ward (shôr′wərd, shōr′-) *adj. & adv.* Toward the shore. Also **shore′wards** (-wərdz).

shor·ing (shôr′ing, shōr′ing) *n.* **1.** The operation of propping, as with shores. **2.** Shores, collectively.

shorn (shôrn, shōrn) Alternative past participle of SHEAR.

short (shôrt) *adj.* **1.** Having little linear extension; not long; of no great distance. **2.** Being below the average stature; not tall. **3.** Having little extension in time; of limited duration; brief. **4.** Abrupt in manner or spirit; cross. **5.** Not reaching or attaining a requirement, result, or mark; inadequate: often with *of.* **6.** Having a scant or insufficient amount: followed by *on.* **7.** Having little scope or breadth: a *short* view. **8.** In commerce: **a** Not having in possession when selling, but having to procure in time to deliver as contracted. **b** Of or pertaining to stocks or commodities not in possession of the seller: *short* sales. **9.** Not comprehensive or retentive; in error: a *short* memory. **10.** Breaking easily; crisp. **11.** *Phonet.* Denoting the vowel sounds of *Dan, den,*

din, don, duck, as contrasted with those of *Dane, dean, dine, dome, dune.* **12.** In English prosody, unaccented. **13.** Less than: with *of.* **14.** Concise; compressed. — *n.* **1.** Anything that is short. **2.** A deficiency, as in a payment. **3.** A short syllable or vowel. **4.** A short contract or sale; one who has sold short; a bear. **5.** *pl.* Bran mixed with coarse meal or flour. **6.** *pl.* Trousers with legs extending part way to the knees. **7.** *pl.* A man's undergarment covering the loins and often a portion of the legs. **8.** In baseball slang, shortstop. **9.** *Electr.* A short circuit. **10.** A short subject. — **for short** For brevity: Edward was called Ed *for short.* — **in short** In a word; briefly. — *adv.* **1.** Abruptly: to stop *short.* **2.** Curtly; crossly. **3.** So as not to reach or extend to a certain point, condition, etc.: to fall *short.* **4.** Without having in actual possession that which is sold: to sell *short.* — *v.t. & v.i.* To short-circuit. [OE *sort*] — **short′ness** *n.*

short·age (shôr′tij) *n.* The amount by which anything is short; deficiency.

short·bread (shôrt′bred′) *n.* A rich, dry cake or cooky made with shortening.

short·cake (shôrt′kāk′) *n.* **1.** A cake made short and crisp with butter or other shortening. **2.** Cake or biscuit served with fruit; strawberry *shortcake.*

short·change (shôrt′chānj′) *v.t.* **-changed, -chang·ing** *Informal* To give less change than is due to; also, to cheat or swindle. — **short′chang′er** *n.*

short-cir·cuit (shôrt′sûr′kit) *v.t. & v.i.* To make a short circuit (in).

short circuit *Electr.* **1.** A path of low resistance established between any two points in an electric circuit, thus shortening the distance traveled by the current. **2.** Any defect in an electric circuit or apparatus that may result in a dangerous leakage of current.

short·com·ing (shôrt′kum′ing) *n.* A failure or deficiency in character, action, etc.

short cut 1. A byway or path between two places that is shorter than the regular way. **2.** Any means or method that saves distance or time.

short·en (shôr′tən) *v.t.* **1.** To make short or shorter; curtail. **2.** To reduce; diminish; lessen. **3.** To furl or reef (a sail) so that less canvas is exposed to the wind. **4.** To make brittle or crisp, as pastry, by adding shortening. — *v.i.* **5.** To become short or shorter. — **short′en·er** *n.*

short·en·ing (shôr′tən·ing) *n.* **1.** A fat, such as lard or butter, used to make pastry crisp. **2.** An abbreviation. **3.** The act of one who shortens.

short·hand (shôrt′hand′) *n.* Any system of rapid writing, usu. employing symbols other than letters, words, etc. — *adj.* **1.** Written in shorthand. **2.** Using shorthand.

short-hand·ed (shôrt′han′did) *adj.* Not having a sufficient or the usual number of assistants, workmen, etc.

short·horn (shôrt′hôrn′) *n.* One of a breed of cattle with short horns, originally from northern England.

short-lived (shôrt′līvd′, -livd′) *adj.* Living or lasting but a short time.

short·ly (shôrt′lē) *adv.* **1.** In a short time; quickly; soon. **2.** In few words; briefly. **3.** Curtly; abruptly.

short order Food requiring little time to prepare. — **in short order** Without any delay; quickly; abruptly.

short shrift 1. A short time in which to confess before dying. **2.** Little or no mercy or delay, as in dealing with a person. — **to make short shrift of** To dispose of quickly.

short-sight·ed (shôrt′sī′tid) *adj.* **1.** Unable to see clearly at a distance; myopic; near-sighted. **2.** Lacking foresight. **3.** Resulting from or characterized by lack of foresight. — **short′-sight′ed·ly** *adv.* — **short′-sight′ed·ness** *n.*

short-spo·ken (shôrt′spō′kən) *adj.* Characterized by shortness or curtness of speech or manner; abrupt; gruff.

short·stop (shôrt′stop′) *n.* In baseball, an infielder stationed between second and third bases; also, his position.

short story A narrative prose story shorter than a novel.

short subject A motion picture of relatively short duration, often displayed between showings of the feature attraction on a program: also called *short.*

short-tem·pered (shôrt′tem′pərd) *adj.* Easily angered.

short-term (shôrt′tûrm′) *adj.* In finance, due or payable within a short time, usu. one year: said of loans, etc.

short ton See under TON¹.

short waves Electromagnetic waves that are 60 meters or less in length. — **short-wave** (shôrt′wāv′) *adj.*

short-wind·ed (shôrt′win′did) *adj.* Affected with difficulty of breathing; becoming easily out of breath.

Sho·sho·ne (shō·shō′nē) *n.* **1.** One of a large tribe of North American Indians of northern Shoshonean stock of the Uto-Aztecan family, formerly occupying parts of Wyoming, Idaho, Nevada, and Utah. **2.** The Shoshonean language of this tribe. Also **Sho·sho′ni.**

Sho·sho·ne·an (shō·shō′nē·ən, shō′shə·nē′ən) *n.* The largest branch of the Uto-Aztecan family of North American Indians, including the Comanche, Ute, and Shoshone plateau tribes, and the Hopi Indians. — *adj.* Of or pertaining to this linguistic branch. Also **Sho·sho′ni·an.**

shot[1] (shot) *n. pl.* **shots;** *for def.* **1 shot 1.** A solid missile, as a ball of iron, or a bullet or pellet of lead, to be discharged from a firearm; also, such pellets collectively. **2.** The act of shooting; any stroke, hit, or blow. **3.** One who shoots; a marksman. **4.** The distance traversed or that can be traversed by a projectile; range. **5.** *U.S. Informal* The firing of a rocket, etc., that is directed toward a specific target: a moon *shot.* **6.** A blast, as in mining. **7.** A stroke, esp. in certain games, as in billiards. **8.** A conjecture; guess. **9.** An attempted performance or try. **10.** A metal sphere that a competitor puts, pushes, or slings, in a distance contest. **11.** *Informal* A hypodermic injection of a drug. **12.** *Informal* A drink of liquor. **13.** A single action or scene recorded on motion-picture or television film or tape. **14.** A photograph or a snapshot. **15.** *Naut.* A unit of chain length: in the U.S., 15 fathoms; in Great Britain, 12½ fathoms. — *v.t.* **shot·ted, shot·ting 1.** To load or weight with shot. **2.** To clean, as bottles, by partially filling with shot and shaking. [OE *scot*]

shot[2] (shot) Past tense and past participle of SHOOT. — *adj.* **1.** Of changeable color, as when warp and weft are of different colors; also, streaked or mixed irregularly with other colors: a sky *shot* with pink. **2.** *Informal* Completely done for; ruined; also, worn out; completely broken.

shot[3] (shot) *n. Brit. & Canadian* A reckoning or charge, or a share of such a reckoning; scot. [Var. of SCOT]

shot effect *Electronics* The background noise resembling the patter of small shot, developed in an electron tube by the fluctuating emission of electrons from the heated filament. Also **shot noise.**

shot·gun (shot′gun′) *n.* A light, smoothbore gun, either single or double barreled, adapted for the discharge of shot at short range. — *adj.* **1.** Having a clear passageway straight through: a *shotgun* house. **2.** Coerced with, or as with, a· shotgun: a *shotgun* wedding.

shot-put (shot′pŏŏt′) *n.* **1.** An athletic contest in which a shot is thrown, or put, for distance. **2.** A single put of the shot. — **shot′-put′ter** *n.*

shot·ten (shot′n) *adj.* Having spawned: said of a fish, esp. a herring. [Obs. pp. of SHOOT]

should (shŏŏd) Past tense of SHALL, but rarely a true past, rather chiefly used as a modal auxiliary that, while conveying varying shades of present and future time, expresses a wide range of subtly discriminated feelings and attitudes: **1.** Obligation or propriety in varying degrees, but milder than *ought:* You *should* write that letter; *Should* we tell him the truth about his condition? **2.** Condition: **a** Simple contingency, but involving less probability than *shall* or the present with future sense: If I *should* go, he would go too. **b** Assumption: *Should (Assuming that)* the space platform prove practicable, as seems almost certain, a trip to the moon will be easy. **3.** Surprise at an unexpected event in the past: When I reached the station, whom *should* I run into but the detective! **4.** Expectation: I *should* be at home by noon. **5.** *U.S. Informal* Irony, in positive statement with negative force: He'll be fined heavily, but with all his money he *should* (*need not*) worry! ◆ In American usage the first person may be followed by either *should* or *would* in such expressions as I *should/would* be glad to see you. [OE *scolde,* pt. of *sculan* to owe]

shoul·der (shōl′dər) *n.* **1.** The part of the trunk between the neck and the free portion of the arm or forelimb; also, the joint connecting the arm or forelimb with the body. **2.** Anything that supports, bears up, or projects like a shoulder. **3.** The forequarter of various animals. **4.** An enlargement, projection, or offset, as for keeping something in place, or preventing movement past the projection. **5.** Either edge of a road or highway. **6.** The angle of a bastion included between a face and the adjacent flank; also **shoulder angle.** — **shoulder to shoulder 1.** Side by side and close together. **2.** With united effort; in cooperation. — **straight from the shoulder** *Informal* Candidly; straightforwardly. — **to cry on (one's) shoulder** To seek sympathy and understanding from (one). — **to give the cold shoulder to 1.** To treat with scorn, contempt, or coldness. **2.** To ignore, shun, or avoid. — **to put (one's) shoulder to the wheel** To work with great vigor and purpose. — *v.t.* **1.** To assume as something to be borne; sustain; bear. **2.** To push with or as with the shoulder or shoulders. **3.** To fashion with a shoulder or abutment. — *v.i.* **4.** To push with the shoulder or shoulders. — **to shoulder arms** To rest a rifle against the shoulder, holding the butt with the hand. [OE *sculdor*]

shoulder blade *Anat.* The scapula.

shoulder patch A cloth insignia worn on the upper part of the sleeve of a uniform to indicate one's branch or unit.

shoulder strap 1. A strap worn on or over the shoulder

to support an article of dress. **2.** A strap of cloth marked with insignia of rank, worn by army and navy officers.

should·n't (shŏŏd′nt) Should not.

shouldst (shŏŏdst) Archaic second person singular of SHALL: used with *thou.* Also **should·est** (shŏŏd′ist).

shout (shout) *n.* A sudden and loud outcry, often expressing joy, anger, etc., or used as a call or command. — *v.t.* **1.** To utter with a shout; say or express loudly. — *v.i.* **2.** To utter a shout. [Cf. ON *skūta* a taunt] — **shout′er** *n.*

shove (shuv) *v.t. & v.i.* **shoved, shov·ing 1.** To push, as along a surface. **2.** To press forcibly (against); jostle. — **to shove off 1.** To push along or away, as a boat. **2.** *Informal* To depart. — *n.* The act of pushing or shoving. [OE *scūfan*] — **shov′er** *n.*

shov·el (shuv′əl) *n.* A somewhat flattened scoop with a handle, as for digging, lifting earth, rock, snow, etc.; also, any large, usu. toothed device for extensive, heavy digging. — *v.* **shov·eled** or **·elled, shov·el·ing** or **·el·ling** *v.t.* **1.** To take up and move with a shovel. **2.** To toss hastily or in large quantities as if with a shovel. **3.** To clear with a shovel, as a path. — *v.i.* **4.** To work with a shovel. [OE *scofl*]

shov·el·board (shuv′əl-bôrd′, -bōrd′) *n.* Shuffleboard.

shov·el·er (shuv′əl-ər, shuv′lər) *n.* **1.** One who or that which shovels. **2** A large river duck with a spatulate bill: also called *spoonbill:* also **shov·el·bill** (shuv′əl-bil′). Also **shov′el·ler.**

show (shō) *v.* **showed, shown** or, sometimes **showed, show·ing** *v.t.* **1.** To cause or permit to be seen; exhibit, display. **2.** To give in a marked or open manner; bestow: to *show* favor. **3.** To cause or allow (something) to be understood or known; reveal; tell. **4.** To cause (someone) to understand or see; teach. **5.** *Law* To advance an allegation; plead: to *show* cause. **6.** To make evident by logical process; demonstrate. **7.** To guide; introduce, as into a room or building: with *in* or *up;* to *show* a caller in. **8.** To indicate: The thermometer *shows* the temperature. **9.** To enter in a show or exhibition. — *v.i.* **10.** To become visible or known. **11.** To seem. **12.** To make one's or its appearance; be present. **13.** *Informal* To give a theatrical performance; appear. **14.** In racing, to finish third: distinguished from *place, win.* Also, *Archaic,* **shew.** — **to show off 1.** To exhibit proudly or ostentatiously. **2.** To make an ostentatious display of oneself, or of one's accomplishments. — **to show up 1.** To expose or be exposed, as faults. **2.** To be evident or prominent. **3.** To make an appearance. **4.** *Informal* To be better than; outdo. — *n.* **1.** An entertainment or performance: a Broadway *show.* **2.** Anything shown or manifested. **3.** An elaborate display: a *show* of wealth. **4.** A pretense or semblance: a *show* of piety. **5.** Any public exhibition, contest, etc.: an art *show.* **6.** An appearance: a bad *show.* **7.** An indication; promise: a *show* of ore. **8.** The third position among the first three winners of a race. **9.** The act of showing. — **show of hands** A display of raised hands indicating the vote of a group. [OE *scēawian*] — **show′er** *n.*

show bill A poster announcing a play or show.

show·boat (shō′bōt′) *n.* A boat on which a traveling troupe gives a theatrical performance.

show·bread (shō′bred′) See SHEWBREAD.

show business The entertainment arts, esp. the theater, motion pictures, television, etc., collectively considered as an industry or profession.

show·case (shō′kās′) *n.* A glass case for exhibiting and protecting articles for sale.

show·down (shō′doun′) *n.* **1.** In poker, the play in which the hands are laid on the table face up. **2.** Any action or disclosure that brings an issue to a head.

show·er (shou′ər) *n.* **1.** A fall of rain, hail, or sleet, esp. heavy rain of short duration within a local area. **2.** A copious fall, as of tears, sparks, etc. **3.** A shower bath. **4.** An abundance or profusion of something. **5.** A variety of fireworks for simulating a shower of stars. **6.** A party for the bestowal of gifts, as to a bride; also, the gifts. — *v.t.* **1.** To sprinkle or wet with or as with showers. **2.** To discharge in a shower; pour out. **3.** To bestow with liberality. — *v.i.* **4.** To fall as in a shower. **5.** To take a shower bath. [OE *scūr*] — **show′er·y** *adj.*

shower bath A bath in which water is sprayed on the body from an overhead, perforated nozzle; also, the area or room in which this is done.

show·ing (shō′ing) *n.* **1.** A show or display, as of a quality. **2.** A presentation or statement, as of a subject.

show·man (shō′mən) *n. pl.* **·men** (-mən) **1.** One who exhibits or owns a show. **2.** One who is skilled in presenting something. — **show′man·ship** *n.*

Show Me State Nickname of Missouri.

shown (shōn) Past participle of SHOW.

show·off (shō′ôf′, -of′) *n. Informal* **1.** The act of showing off; ostentatious display. **2.** One who shows off.

show·piece (shō′pēs′) *n.* **1.** A prized object considered worthy of special exhibit. **2.** An object on display.

show place A place exhibited for its beauty, historic interest, etc.

show room A room in which things, as merchandise, are displayed for sale or advertising.

show·y (shō′ē) *adj.* **show·i·er, show·i·est 1.** Making a great or brilliant display. **2.** Given to cheap display; gaudy; ostentatious. — **show′i·ly** *adv.* — **show′i·ness** *n.*

shrank (shrangk) Past tense of SHRINK.

shrap·nel (shrap′nəl) *n. pl.* **·nel** *Mil.* **1.** A field artillery projectile for use against personnel, containing a quantity of metal balls and a time fuse and base charge that expel the balls in mid-air. **2.** Shell fragments. [after Henry *Shrapnel*, 1761–1842, British artillery officer]

shred (shred) *n.* **1.** A small irregular strip torn or cut off. **2.** A bit; fragment; particle. — *v.t.* **shred·ded** or **shred, shred·ding** To tear or cut into shreds. [OE *scrēade*] — **shred′der** *n.*

shrew (shrōō) *n.* **1.** Any of numerous diminutive, chiefly insectivorous mammals having a long pointed snout and soft fur, as the **long-tailed shrew** of North America. Also **shrew′mouse′** (-mous′). **2.** A woman of vexatious, scolding, or nagging disposition. [OE *scrēawa*]
— **Syn. 2.** scold, vixen, termagant, virago.

shrewd (shrōōd) *adj.* **1.** Sharp or wise; sagacious. **2.** Artful; sly. [ME < *shrew* malicious person] — **shrewd′ly** *adv.* — **shrewd′ness** *n.*

shrew·ish (shrōō′ish) *adj.* Like a shrew; ill-tempered; nagging. — **shrew′ish·ly** *adv.* — **shrew′ish·ness** *n.*

shriek (shrēk) *n.* A sharp shrill outcry or scream. — *v.i.* **1.** To utter a shriek. — *v.t.* **2.** To utter with or in a shriek. [ME] — **shriek′er** *n.*

shrift (shrift) *n.* **1.** The act of shriving. **2.** Confession or absolution, as to or from a priest. [OE *scrift*]

shrike (shrīk) *n.* Any of numerous predatory birds with hooked bill, short wings, and long tail. [OE *scrīc* thrush]

shrill (shril) *adj.* **1.** Having a high-pitched and piercing tone quality. **2.** Emitting a sharp, piercing sound. — *v.t.* **1.** To cause to utter a shrill sound. — *v.i.* **2.** To make a shrill sound. — *adv.* Shrilly. [< Gmc.] — **shril′ly** *adv.* — **shrill′ness** *n.*

shrimp (shrimp) *n. pl.* **shrimp** or **shrimps** *for def. 1,* **shrimps** *for def. 2* **1.** Any of numerous small, long-tailed, principally marine animals, some species of which are used as food. **2.** *Slang* A small or unimportant person. [Akin to OE *scrimman* to shrink, G *schrimpfen*]

shrine (shrīn) *n.* **1.** A receptacle for sacred relics. **2.** A place, as a tomb or a chapel, sacred to some holy personage. **3.** A thing or spot made sacred by historic or other association. — *v.t.* **shrined, shrin·ing** *Rare & Poetic* To enshrine. [OE < L *scrinium* case, chest]

SHRIMP
a Cephalothorax. *b* Abdomen. *c* Tail. *t* Telson.

shrink (shringk) *v.* **shrank** or **shrunk, shrunk** or, sometimes, **shrunk·en, shrink·ing** *v.i.* **1.** To draw together; contract, as from heat, cold, etc. **2.** To diminish. **3.** To draw back, as from disgust, horror, or timidity; recoil: with *from.* **4.** To flinch; wince. — *v.t.* **5.** To cause to shrink, contract, or draw together. — *n.* **1.** The act of shrinking. **2.** *Slang* A psychiatrist. [OE *scrincan*] — **shrink′a·ble** *adj.*

shrink·age (shringk′ij) *n.* **1.** The act or fact of shrinking; contraction. **2.** The amount lost by such shrinking. **3.** Decrease in value; depreciation.

shrive (shrīv) *v.* **shrove** or **shrived, shriv·en** or **shrived, shriv·ing** *v.t.* **1.** To receive the confession of and give absolution to. **2.** To obtain absolution for (oneself) by confessing one's sins and doing penance. — *v.i.* **3.** To make confession. **4.** To hear confession. [OE *scrīfan*, ult. < L *scribere* to write, prescribe] — **shriv′er** *n.*

shriv·el (shriv′əl) *v.t. & v.i.* **shriv·eled** or **·elled, shriv·el·ing** or **·el·ling 1.** To contract into wrinkles; shrink and wrinkle: often with *up.* **2.** To make or become impotent; wither. [Origin uncertain]

shriv·en (shriv′ən) Alternative past participle of SHRIVE.

Shrop·shire (shrop′shir, -shər) *n.* A breed of black-faced, hornless sheep, noted for heavy fleece and superior mutton, originating in Shropshire.

shroud[1] (shroud) *n.* **1.** A dress or garment for the dead. **2.** Something that envelops or conceals like a garment: the *shroud* of night. — *v.t.* **1.** To dress for the grave; clothe in a shroud. **2.** To envelop, as with a garment. [OE *scrūd* garment] — **shroud′less** *adj.*

shroud[2] (shroud) *n.* **1.** *Naut.* One of a set of ropes, often of wire, stretched from a masthead to the sides of a ship, serving as means of ascent and as a support for the masts. **2.** *Usu. pl.* A guy, as a support for a smokestack. **3.** One of the supporting ropes attached to the edges of a parachute canopy. [< SHROUD[1]]

shrove (shrōv) Alternative past tense of SHRIVE.

Shrove·tide (shrōv′tīd′) *n.* The three days immediately preceding Ash Wednesday, **Shrove Sunday** (Quinquagesima Sunday), **Shrove Monday, Shrove Tuesday,** on which confession is made in preparation for Lent. [ME *schroftide*]

shrub (shrub) *n.* A woody perennial plant of low stature, characterized by persistent stems and branches springing from the base. [OE *scrybb* brushwood]

shrub·ber·y (shrub′ər·ē) *n. pl.* **·ber·ies 1.** Shrubs collectively. **2.** A collection of shrubs, as in a garden.

shrub·by (shrub′ē) *adj.* **·bi·er, ·bi·est 1.** Containing many shrubs; covered with shrubs. **2.** Of, pertaining to, or like a shrub. — **shrub′bi·ness** *n.*

shrug (shrug) *v.t. & v.i.* **shrugged, shrug·ging** To draw up (the shoulders), as in displeasure, doubt, surprise, etc. — *n.* **1.** The act of shrugging the shoulders. **2.** A very short sweater or jacket, open in front. [ME *schrugge*]

shrunk (shrungk) Alternative past tense and past participle of SHRINK.

shrunk·en (shrungk′ən) Alternative past participle of SHRINK. — *adj.* Contracted and atrophied.

shuck (shuk) *n.* **1.** A husk, shell, or pod. **2.** A shell of an oyster or a clam. — *v.t.* **1.** To remove the husk or shell from (corn, oysters, etc.). **2.** *Informal* To take off or cast off, as clothes. [Origin unknown] — **shuck′er** *n.*

shucks (shuks) *interj.* *U.S. Informal* A mild ejaculation expressing annoyance, disgust, etc.

shud·der (shud′ər) *v.i.* To tremble or shake, as from fright or cold; shiver; quake. — *n.* The act of shuddering; a convulsive shiver, as from horror or fear; tremor. [ME *shodder*]

shuf·fle (shuf′əl) *n.* **1.** A mixing or changing of the order of things, as of cards in a pack before each deal. **2.** A hesitating, evasive, or tricky action; artifice. **3.** A scraping of the feet, as in walking; a slow, dragging gait. **4.** A dance, or the step used in it, where the dancer pushes his foot along the floor at each step. — *v.* **·fled, ·fling** *v.t.* **1.** To shift this way and that; mix; confuse; disorder; esp. to change the order of by mixing, as cards in a pack. **2.** To move (the feet) along the ground or floor with a dragging gait. **3.** To change from one place to another. **4.** To make up or remove fraudulently or hastily; also, to put aside carelessly: with *up, off,* or *out.* — *v.i.* **5.** To change position. **6.** To resort to indirect methods. **7.** To dance the shuffle. **8.** To scrape the feet along. **9.** To scrape or struggle along awkwardly. [Prob. < LG *schuffeln* to move with dragging feet, mix cards, etc.] — **shuf′fler** *n.*

shuf·fle·board (shuf′əl·bôrd′, -bōrd′) *n.* **1.** A game in which wooden or composition disks are slid by means of a pronged cue along a smooth surface toward numbered spaces. **2.** The board or surface on which the game is played. Also called *shovelboard.*

shun (shun) *v.t.* **shunned, shun·ning** To keep clear of; avoid; refrain from. [OE *scunian*] — **shun′ner** *n.*

shunt (shunt) *n.* **1.** The act of shunting. **2.** A railroad switch. **3.** *Electr.* A conductor joining two points in a circuit and serving to divert part of the current to an auxiliary circuit: also called *by-pass.* — *v.t.* **1.** To turn aside. **2.** To switch, as a train or car, from one track to another. **3.** *Electr.* To distribute by means of shunts. **4.** To evade by turning away from; put off on someone else, as a task. — *v.i.* **5.** To move to one side. **6.** *Electr.* To be diverted by a shunt: said of current. **7.** To shift or transfer one's views or course. [ME *schunten*] — **shunt′er** *n.*

shunt-wound (shunt′wound′) *adj. Electr.* Designating a type of direct-current motor in which the armature circuit and field circuit are connected in parallel.

shush (shush) *v.t.* To quiet, as by making the sound "sh."

shut (shut) *v.* **shut, shut·ting** *v.t.* **1.** To bring into such position as to close an opening or aperture; close, as a door, lid, or valve. **2.** To close (an opening, aperture, etc.) so as to prevent ingress or egress. **3.** To close and fasten securely, as with a latch or lock. **4.** To forbid entrance into or exit from. **5.** To keep from entering or leaving: with *in, out, from,* etc. **6.** To close, fold, or bring together, as extended, expanded, or unfolded parts: to *shut* an umbrella. **7.** To hide from view; obscure. — *v.i.* **8.** To be or become closed or in a closed position. — **to shut down 1.** To cease from operating, as a factory or mine; close up; stop work. **2.** To lower; come down close: the fog *shut down.* **3.** *Informal* To suppress: with *on.* — **to shut one's eyes to** To ignore. — **to shut out** In sports, to keep (an opponent) from scoring during the course of a game. — **to shut up 1.** *Informal* To stop talking or cause to stop talking. **2.** To close all the entrances to, as a house. **3.** To imprison; confine. — *adj.* **1.** Made fast or closed. **2.** Not sonorous; dull: said of sound. — *n.* **1.** The act of shutting. **2.** The time or place of shutting or closing. [OE *scyttan*]

shut·down (shut′doun′) *n.* The closing of or ceasing of work in a mine, mill, factory, or other industrial plant.

shut·eye (shut′ī) *n. Slang* Sleep.

shut-in (shut′in′) *n.* An invalid who is unable to go out. — *adj.* Obliged to stay at home.

shut·off (shut′ôf′, -of′) *n. Mech.* A device for shutting something off.

shut·out (shut′out′) *n.* 1. A shutting out; esp., a lockout. 2. In sports, a game in which one side is prevented from scoring.

shut·ter (shut′ər) *n.* 1. One who or that which shuts. 2. That which shuts out or excludes; esp., a cover or screen, usu. hinged, for closing a window. 3. *Photog.* Any of various mechanisms for momentarily admitting light through a camera lens to the film or plate. — *v.t.* To furnish, close, or divide off with shutters.

shut·tle (shut′l) *n.* 1. A device used in weaving to carry the weft to and fro between the warp threads. 2. A similar rotating or other device in a sewing machine or used in tatting. 3. A transport system operating between two nearby points. — *v.t. & v.i.* **·tled, ·tling** To move to and fro, like a shuttle. [OE *scytel* missile]

shut·tle·cock (shut′l·kok′) *n.* A rounded piece of cork, with a crown of feathers, used in badminton and battledore; also, the game of battledore. — *v.t.* To send or knock back and forth like a shuttlecock.

shy[1] (shī) *v.i.* **shied, shy·ing** 1. To start suddenly aside, as in fear: said of a horse. 2. To draw back, as from doubt or caution: with *off* or *away*. — *adj.* **shi·er** or **shy·er, shi·est** or **shy·est** 1. Easily frightened or startled; timorous. 2. Bashful; coy. 3. Circumspect, as from motives of caution; wary: with *of*. 4. Not easy to perceive, seize, or secure; elusive. 5. Not prolific: said of plants, trees, or, rarely, birds. 6. *Informal* Having less money than is called for or required: to be *shy* a dollar. 7. *Informal* Short; lacking: often with *on*. — *n.* A starting aside, as in fear. [OE *scēoh* timid] — **shy′ness** *n.*

shy[2] (shī) *v.t. & v.i.* **shied, shy·ing** To throw with a swift sidelong motion. — *n. pl.* **shies** A careless throw or fling. [Origin unknown]

shy·er (shī′ər) *n.* 1. One who shies. 2. See SHIER.

Shy·lock (shī′lok) In Shakespeare's *Merchant of Venice*, a revengeful usurer. — *n. Slang* Any relentless creditor.

shy·ly (shī′lē) *adv.* In a shy manner: also spelled *shily*.

shy·ster (shīs′tər) *n. Slang* Anyone, esp. a lawyer, who conducts his business in an unscrupulous or tricky manner. [Origin uncertain]

si[1] (sē) *n. Music* Formerly ti[1].

si[2] (sē) *adv.* Italian, Portuguese, Spanish, and sometimes French, for "yes." [< L *sic* thus]

Si *Chem.* Silicon.

sialo- *combining form* Saliva; pertaining to saliva. Also, before vowels, **sial-**. [< Gk. *sialon* saliva]

Si·a·mese (sī′ə·mēz′, -mēs′) *adj.* 1. Pertaining to Thailand (Siam), its people, or their language. 2. Closely connected; twin. — *n.* 1. *pl.* **·mese** A native of Siam, belonging to the Thai stock. 2. The Thai language of the people of Siam, now officially called *Thai*.

Siamese cat A breed of short-haired cat, typically fawn-colored, with dark-tipped ears, tail, feet, and face, and blue, gently slanting eyes.

Siamese twins Any twins joined together at birth. [after the two Chinese males, Eng and Chang, 1811–74, born in Siam, whose bodies were joined by a fleshy band]

sib (sib) *Rare n.* 1. A blood relation; kinsman. 2. Kinsmen collectively; relatives. — *adj.* 1. Related by blood; akin. 2. Related; similar. Also **sibb.** [OE *sibb*]

sib·bo·leth (sib′ə·leth) See SHIBBOLETH.

sib·i·lant (sib′ə·lənt) *adj.* 1. Hissing. 2. *Phonet.* Denoting those consonants produced by the fricative passage of breath through a very narrow orifice, in the front part of the mouth, as (s), (z), (sh), and (zh). — *n. Phonet.* A sibilant consonant. [< L *sibilans, -antis*, ppr. of *sibilare* to hiss] — **sib′i·lance, sib′i·lan·cy** *n.* — **sib′i·lant·ly** *adv.*

sib·ling (sib′ling) *n.* A brother or sister. [OE, a relative]

sib·yl (sib′əl) *n.* 1. In ancient Greece and Rome, any of several women who prophesied under the supposed inspiration of some deity. 2. A fortuneteller; sorceress. [< F < L *sibylla* < Gk.] — **sib′yl·line** (-īn, -ēn, in), **si·byl·ic** (si·bil′ik), **si·byl′lic** *adj.*

sic[1] (sik) *adv.* So; thus: inserted in brackets after a quotation to indicate that it is accurately reproduced even though it may seem questionable or incorrect. [< L]

sic[2] (sik) *v.t.* **sicked, sick·ing** To sick. See SICK[2].

Si·cil·i·an (si·sil′ē·ən, -sil′yən) *adj.* Of or pertaining to Sicily or its people: also **Si·ca′ni·an** (-ka/nē·ən). — *n.* An inhabitant or native of Sicily.

sick[1] (sik) *adj.* 1. Affected with disease; ill. 2. Of or used by ill persons: often used in combination: *sickroom*. 3. Affected by nausea; desiring to vomit. 4. Expressive of or experiencing disgust or unpleasant emotion. 5. Impaired or unsound from any cause. 6. Mentally unsound. 7. Pallid; wan. 8. Depressed and longing: *sick* for the sea. 9. Disinclined by reason of satiety or disgust; surfeited: with *of*. 10. Sadistic or macabre; morbid: *sick* jokes. — *n.* Sick people collectively: with *the*. [OE *sēoc*]
— **Syn.** 2, 3. In U.S. usage, *sick* is a general term that may refer to a slight ailment or the most severe illness; it may also mean nauseated, the sense it always bears in British usage. *Ill* is a close synonym but may refer to a greater variety of symptoms. *Unwell* is similar to *ill*, but is sometimes felt to be affected. *Ailing* and *indisposed* refer to slight illnesses. *Ailing* implies a minor, but chronic, condition; *indisposed* suggests a trivial or temporary illness that prevents normal activity.

sick[2] (sik) *v.t.* 1. To attack: used in the imperative as an order to a dog. 2. To urge to attack: I'll *sick* the dog on you. Also spelled *sic*. [Var. of SEEK]

sick·bay (sik′bā′) *n.* That part of a ship or of a naval base set aside for the care of the sick.

sick·bed (sik′bed′) *n.* The bed a sick person lies on.

sick call *Mil.* 1. The daily period during which all non-hospitalized sick or injured personnel report to the medical officer. 2. The call or signal that announces this.

sick·en (sik′ən) *v.t. & v.i.* To make or become sick or disgusted. — **sick′en·er** *n.*

sick·en·ing (sik′ən·ing) *adj.* Disgusting; revolting; nauseating. — **sick′en·ing·ly** *adv.*

sick headache Headache with nausea, esp., migraine.

sick·ish (sik′ish) *adj.* 1. Somewhat sick. 2. Slightly nauseating. — **sick′ish·ly** *adv.* — **sick′ish·ness** *n.*

sick·le (sik′əl) *n.* An implement with a curved or crescent-shaped blade mounted on a short handle, used for cutting tall grass, grains, etc. — *v.t.* **·led, ·ling** To cut with a sickle, as grass. [OE < L *secare* to cut]

sickle cell A crescent-shaped red blood corpuscle containing a genetically transmitted type of hemoglobin in which the oxygen concentration is below normal, and causing an anemia (**sickle cell anemia**) occurring chiefly among Negroes.

sick·ly (sik′lē) *adj.* **·li·er, ·li·est** 1. Habitually indisposed; ailing; unhealthy. 2. Marked by the prevalence of sickness: a *sickly* summer. 3. Nauseating; disgusting. 4. Pertaining to or characteristic of sickness: a *sickly* appearance. 5. Weak; faint. — *adv.* In a sick manner; poorly: also **sick/li·ly.** — *v.t.* **·lied, ·ly·ing** To make sickly, as in color or complexion. — **sick′li·ness** *n.*

sick·ness (sik′nis) *n.* 1. The state of being sick. 2. A particular form of disease. 3. Nausea.

sick·room (sik′rōōm, -rōōm′) *n.* A room in which a sick person lies or stays.

side (sīd) *n.* 1. Any one of the bounding lines of a surface or of the bounding surfaces of a solid object; also, a particular line or surface other than top or bottom: the *side* of a mountain. 2. A lateral part of a surface or object, usu. designated as *right* or *left*. 3. Either of the two surfaces of a piece of paper, cloth, etc.; also, a specific surface of something: the rough *side* of sandpaper. 4. One of two or more contrasted directions, parts, or places: the east *side* of town. 5. A distinct party or body of competitors or partisans. 6. An opinion, aspect, or point of view: my *side* of the question. 7. Family connection, esp. by descent through one parent. 8. The lateral half of a slaughtered animal. 9. Either half of the human body. 10. The space beside someone. 11. In billiards, a lateral spin given to the cue ball. 12. In sports, a team. — **side by side** Beside or next to each other. — **to take sides** To support a particular opinion, point of view, etc. — **Syn.** See PHASE. — *adj.* 1. Situated at or on one side: a *side* window. 2. Being or viewed as if from one side: a *side* glance. 3. Directed towards one side: a *side* blow. 4. Not primary; subordinate: a *side* issue. — *v.t.* **sid·ed, sid·ing** To provide with sides, as a building. — **to side with** To support or take the part of. [OE *sīde*]

side·arm (sīd′ärm′) *adj.* Executed with the hand level with the elbow, as a pitch. — *adv.* In a sidearm manner.

side arms Weapons worn at the side, as pistols, etc.

side·band (sīd′band′) *n. Telecom.* One of the two bands immediately adjacent to a carrier frequency, corresponding to the band-width of the modulating signal.

side·board (sīd′bôrd′, -bōrd′) *n.* A piece of dining-room furniture for holding tableware.

side·burns (sīd′bûrnz′) *n.pl. Chiefly U.S.* The hair growing on the sides of a man's face below the hairline, esp. when worn as whiskers. [Alter. of BURNSIDES]

side·car (sīd′kär′) *n.* A small, one-wheeled passenger car attached to the side of a motorcycle.

sid·ed (sī′did) *adj.* Having or characterized by (a specified kind or number of) sides: used in combination: *one-sided*.

SIAMESE CAT
(About 11 inches high at shoulder)

side effect A secondary, usu. injurious effect, as of a drug.

side·kick (sīd′kik′) *n. U.S. Slang* A close friend; buddy.

side·light (sīd′līt′) *n.* 1. A side window. 2. A light coming from the side. 3. Incidental facts or information.

side·line (sīd′līn′) *n.* 1. An auxiliary line of goods sold by a store or a commercial traveler. 2. Any additional or secondary work differing from one's main job. 3. In sports: a One of the lines bounding the two sides of a football field, tennis court, etc. b *Often pl.* The area just outside these lines. Also **side line.** — *v.t.* **·lined, ·lin·ing** To prevent or remove (someone) from active participation.

side·long (sīd′lông′, -long′) *adj.* 1. Inclining, tending or directed to one side. 2. Indirect; sly. — *adv.* In a lateral or oblique direction.

side·piece (sīd′pēs′) *n.* A piece at or forming a side.

si·de·re·al (sī·dîr′ē·əl) *adj.* 1. Of or pertaining to stars. 2. Measured by means of the stars: *sidereal* year. [< L < *sidus* star] — **si·de·re·al·ly** *adv.*

sidereal year The period of 365 days, 6 hours, 9 minutes, and 9 seconds in which the sun apparently returns to the same position among the stars.

sidero-¹ *combining form* Iron; of or pertaining to iron. Also, before vowels, **sider-.** [< Gk. *sidēros* iron]

sidero-² *combining form* Star; stellar. Also, before vowels, **sider-.** [< L *sidus* star]

sid·er·o·lite (sīd′ər·ə·līt′) *n.* A meteorite consisting of iron containing embedded grains of certain minerals.

side·sad·dle (sīd′sad′l) *n.* A woman's saddle having one stirrup and designed so that both legs of the rider are on the same side of the horse. — *adv.* On or as on a sidesaddle.

side show 1. A small show incidental to but connected with a larger or more important one: a circus *side show.* 2. Any subordinate issue or attraction.

side·slip (sīd′slip′) *v.i.* **·slipped, ·slip·ping** To slip or skid sideways. — *n.* 1. A lateral skid. 2. *Aeron.* A downward, sideways slipping of an airplane along the lateral axis.

side·split·ting (sīd′split′ing) *adj.* 1. Hearty and uproarious, as laughter. 2. Causing great laughter or hilarity.

side·step (sīd′step′) *v.* **·stepped, ·step·ping** *v.i.* 1. To step to one side. 2. To avoid responsibility, conflict, etc. — *v.t.* 3. To avoid, as an issue, or postpone, as a decision; evade.

side step 1. A step to one side, as of a pugilist. 2. *Usu. pl.* One of a series of steps at the side of a building, etc.

side·swipe (sīd′swīp′) *n.* A sweeping blow along the side. — *v.t. & v.i.* **·swiped, ·swip·ing** To strike or collide with such a blow.

side·track (sīd′trak′) *v.t. & v.i.* 1. To move to a siding, as a railroad train. 2. To divert or distract from the main issue or subject. — *n.* A railroad siding; also, a branch line.

side·walk (sīd′wôk′) *n. U.S.* A path or pavement at the side of the street, for the use of pedestrians.

side·ward (sīd′wərd) *adj.* Directed or moving toward or from the side; lateral. — *adv.* Toward or from the side; laterally: also **side′wards** (-wərdz).

side·ways (sīd′wāz′) *adv.* 1. From the side. 2. So as to incline toward the side, or with the side forward: Hold it *sideways.* 3. Toward one side; obliquely. — *adj.* Moving to or from one side. Also **side′way′, side′wise′** (-wīz′).

side wheel A wheel at the side; esp., one of two paddle wheels on either side of a steamboat. — **side-wheel** (sīd′hwēl′) *adj.* — **side′-wheel′er** *n.*

sid·ing (sī′ding) *n.* 1. A railway track by the side of the main track. 2. The boarding that covers the side of a wooden house, etc.

si·dle (sīd′l) *v.i.* **·dled, ·dling** To move sideways, esp. in a cautious or stealthy manner. — *n.* A sideways movement. [Back formation < obs. *sidling* sidelong] — **si′dler** *n.*

siege (sēj) *n.* 1. The act of surrounding any fortified area with the intention of capturing it. 2. A steady attempt to win something. 3. The time during which one undergoes a protracted illness or difficulty. — **to lay siege to** To attempt to capture or gain; besiege. — *v.t.* **sieged, sieg·ing** To lay siege to. [< OF < L < *sedere* to sit]

Sieg·fried (sēg′frēd, *Ger.* zēkh′frēt) The hero of the *Nibelungenlied* and several other Germanic legends.

si·en·na (sē·en′ə) *n.* 1. A brownish yellow clay containing oxides of iron and manganese, used as a pigment. 2. The brownish yellow color of this pigment. [< Ital. (*terra di*) *Siena* (earth of) Siena]

si·er·ra (sē·er′ə) *n.* A mountain range or chain, esp. one having a jagged outline. [< Sp. < L *serra* saw]

si·es·ta (sē·es′tə) *n.* A midday or afternoon nap. [< Sp. < L *sexta* (*hora*) sixth (hour), noon]

sieve (siv) *n.* A utensil for straining or sifting, consisting of a frame with a bottom of wire mesh, etc. — *v.t. & v.i.* **sieved, siev·ing** To pass through a sieve. [OE *sife* sieve]

sift (sift) *v.t.* 1. To pass through a sieve in order to separate the fine parts from the coarse. 2. To scatter as by a sieve. 3. To examine carefully. 4. To separate; distinguish: to *sift* fact from fiction. — *v.i.* 5. To use a sieve. 6. To fall through or as through a sieve. [OE *siftan*] — **sift′er** *n.*

sigh (sī) *v.i.* 1. To draw in and exhale a deep, audible breath, as in expressing sorrow, weariness, etc. 2. To make a sound suggestive of a sigh, as the wind. 3. To yearn; long. — *v.t.* 4. To express with a sigh. — *n.* The act or sound of sighing. [Back formation < ME *sighte* < OE *sīcan* to sigh]

sight (sīt) *n.* 1. The act or fact of seeing. 2. That which is seen; a view. 3. *pl.* Things worth seeing: the *sights* of the town. 4. The faculty of seeing; vision. 5. The range or scope of vision. 6. A device to assist aim, as on a gun, etc. 7. An aim or observation taken with a telescope or other sighting instrument. 8. *Informal* Something unusual or ugly to look at: He was a *sight.* 9. *Dial.* A great quantity or number: a *sight* of people. — **at** (or **on**) **sight** As soon as seen. — **not by a long sight** 1. Never; not at all. 2. Not nearly. — **sight unseen** Without ever having seen the object in question. — *v.t.* 1. To perceive with the eyes; observe. 2. To take a sight of. 3. To furnish with sights, or adjust the sights of, as a gun. — *v.i.* 4. To take aim. 5. To make an observation or sight. [OE *gesiht*]

sight draft A draft or bill payable on presentation.

sight·less (sīt′lis) *adj.* 1. Lacking sight; blind. 2. Invisible. — **sight′less·ly** *adv.* — **sight′less·ness** *n.*

sight·ly (sīt′lē) *adj.* **·li·er, ·li·est** 1. Pleasant to the view; comely. 2. Affording a fine view. — **sight′li·ness** *n.*

sight·see·ing (sīt′sē′ing) *n.* The visiting of places of interest. — **sight·seer** (sīt′sēr′) *n.*

sig·ma (sig′mə) *n.* The 18th letter in the Greek alphabet, written Σ (capital), σ (small initial or medial), or ς (small final), and corresponding to English *s* in *so.* See ALPHABET.

sig·moid (sig′moid) *adj.* Shaped like the Greek capital letter sigma (Σ), or like the letter S. Also **sig·moi·dal** (sig·moid′l). [< Gk. *sigmoeidēs*]

sign (sīn) *n.* 1. A motion or action indicating a thought, desire, command, etc. 2. A board, placard, etc., generally bearing an inscription conveying information of some kind: a street *sign*; an advertising *sign.* 3. Any arbitrary mark, symbol, or token used to indicate a word, etc., or having its own specific meaning: a *sign* of mourning. 4. Any indication, trace, or evidence: *signs* of poverty. 5. A vestige; trace. 6. Any omen or miraculous occurrence. 7. One of the twelve equal divisions of the zodiac. — *v.t.* 1. To write one's signature or initials on. 2. *Law* To acknowledge an instrument by affixing a mark or seal to. 3. To mark or consecrate with a sign, esp. with a cross. 4. To engage by obtaining the signature of a contract; also, to hire (oneself) out for work: often with *on.* 5. To dispose of or transfer title to by signature: with *off, over,* or *away.* 6. To express or indicate with a sign. — *v.i.* 7. To make signs or signals. 8. To write one's signature or initials. — **to sign off** *Telecom.* To announce the close of a program from a broadcasting station and stop transmission. — **to sign up** To enlist, as in a military service. [< OF < L *signum*] — **sign′er** *n.*

sig·nal (sig′nəl) *n.* 1. A sign or means of communication agreed upon or understood, and used to convey information, a command, etc. 2. *Telecom.* An electromagnetic impulse that transmits information, whether direct or in code. 3. Anything that incites to action or movement. 4. In some card games, a lead or play that conveys certain information to one's partner. — *adj.* 1. Notable; conspicuous. 2. Used to signal. — *v.* **sig·naled** or **·nalled, sig·nal·ing** or **·nal·ling** *v.t.* 1. To make signals to. 2. To communicate by signals. — *v.i.* 3. To make a signal or signals. [< F < L *signum* sign] — **sig′nal·er** or **sig′nal·ler** *n.*

Signal Corps A branch of the U.S. Army responsible for communications equipment and systems, photography, electronic reconnaissance devices, and related matters.

sig·nal·ize (sig′nəl·īz) *v.t.* **·ized, ·iz·ing** 1. To render noteworthy. 2. To point out with care.

sig·nal·ly (sig′nəl·ē) *adv.* In a signal manner; eminently.

sig·nal·man (sig′nəl·mən) *n. pl.* **·men** (-mən) One who makes or interprets signals, esp. railroad signals.

sig·na·to·ry (sig′nə·tôr′ē, -tō′rē) *adj.* Bound by the terms of a signed document; having signed: *signatory* powers. — *n.* One who has signed or is bound by a document; esp., a nation so bound. [< L < *signum* sign]

sig·na·ture (sig′nə·chər) *n.* 1. The name of a person written by himself; also, the act of signing one's name. 2. A distinctive mark, characteristic, etc. 3. *Printing* a A distinguishing mark, letter, or number on the first page of each form or sheet of a book, as a guide to the binder. b The form or sheet on which this mark is placed. c A large printed sheet that, when folded, forms four, or a multiple of four, pages of a book. 4. *Music* A symbol or group of symbols at the beginning of a staff, indicating meter or key. 5. *Telecom.* The musical number or sound effect that introduces or closes a program. [< F < Med.L < L *signum* sign]

sign·board (sīn′bôrd′, -bōrd′) *n.* A board on which a sign, direction, or advertisement is displayed.

sig·net (sig′nit) *n.* 1. A seal, esp. one used to authenticate documents, etc. 2. An impression made by or as by a seal. [< F *signe* sign < L *signum*]

signet ring A seal ring.

sig·nif·i·cance (sig-nif′ə-kəns) *n.* **1.** The character or state of being significant. **2.** Meaning. **3.** Importance; consequence. Also **sig·nif′i·can·cy.**

sig·nif·i·cant (sig-nif′ə-kənt) *adj.* **1.** Having or expressing a meaning; bearing or embodying a meaning. **2.** Conveying or having some covert meaning: a *significant* look. **3.** Important; weighty; momentous. [< L < *signum* sign + *facere* to do, make] — **sig·nif′i·cant·ly** *adv.*

sig·ni·fi·ca·tion (sig′nə-fə-kā′shən) *n.* **1.** Meaning; sense; import. **2.** The act of signifying; communication. — **sig·nif′i·ca·tive** (sig-nif′ə-kā′tiv, -kə-tiv) *adj.*

sig·ni·fy (sig′nə-fī) *v.* **·fied, ·fy·ing** *v.t.* **1.** To make known by signs or words; express. **2.** To betoken in any way; import. **3.** To amount to; mean. — *v.i.* **4.** To have some meaning or importance; matter. — **sig′ni·fi′er** *n.*

sign language A system of communication by means of signs, largely manual.

si·gnor (sēn′yôr) *n.* An anglicized form of the Italian title *signore.* Also **si′gnior.**

si·gno·ra (sē-nyô′rä) *n. pl.* **·re** (-rā) *Italian* The Italian title of courtesy for a married woman, equivalent to *Mrs.*

si·gno·re (sē-nyô′rē) *n. pl.* **·ri** (-rē) The Italian title of courtesy for a man, equivalent to *Mr., sir.*

si·gno·ri·na (sē′nyô-rē′nä) *n. pl.* **·ne** (-nā) The Italian title of courtesy for an unmarried woman, equivalent to *Miss.*

sign·post (sīn′pōst′) *n.* **1.** A post bearing a sign. **2.** Any sign, clue, or indication.

Sig·urd (sig′ŏŏrd) In German mythology, a hero who corresponds to Siegfried, the hero of the *Nibelungenlied.*

Sikh (sēk) *n.* One of a religious and military sect founded in India early in the 16th century. — *adj.* Of or pertaining to the Sikhs. [< Hind., lit., disciple] — **Sikh′ism** *n.*

si·lage (sī′lij) *n.* Ensilage. [< ENSILAGE]

si·lence (sī′ləns) *n.* **1.** The state or quality of being silent. **2.** Absence of sound or noise; stillness. **3.** A failure to mention or take note of something. — *v.t.* **·lenced, ·lenc·ing** **1.** To make silent. **2.** To stop the motion or activity of. **3.** To force (guns, etc.) to cease firing, as by bombing, etc. — *interj.* Be silent. [< F < L *silere* to be silent]

si·lenc·er (sī′lən-sər) *n.* **1.** A tubular device attached to the muzzle of a firearm to reduce the sound of the report. **2.** *Chiefly Brit.* A muffler (def. 1). **3.** One who or that which silences.

si·lent (sī′lənt) *adj.* **1.** Not making any sound or noise; noiseless; still; mute. **2.** Not given to speech; taciturn. **3.** Making no mention or allusion. **4.** Unspoken or unuttered: *silent* grief. **5.** Free from activity, motion, or disturbance; calm; quiet: a *silent* retreat. [< L *silere* to be silent] — **si′lent·ly** *adv.* — **si′lent·ness** *n.*

silent butler A small receptacle with a handle and hinged lid, used for collecting refuse from ashtrays, etc.

silent partner One who has invested money in a business but does not participate in its management or its affairs.

si·lex (sī′leks) *n.* **1.** Silica. **2.** Glass that is resistant to heat. [< L, flint]

Si·lex (sī′leks) *n.* A coffee maker: a trade name. Also **si′lex.**

sil·hou·ette (sil′ŏŏ-et′) *n.* **1.** A profile drawing or portrait having its outline filled in with uniform color, commonly black, and often cut out of paper, etc. **2.** The figure cast by a shadow; also, the outline of a solid figure. — *v.t.* **·et·ted, ·et·ting** To cause to appear in silhouette; outline; make a silhouette profile of. [after Étienne de *Silhouette*, 1709–67, French minister of finance]

silic- Var. of SILICO-.

sil·i·ca (sil′i·kə) *n.* A white or colorless, very hard, crystalline silicon dioxide, SiO₂, the principal constituent of quartz and sand: also called *silex.* [< NL < L *silex, silicis* flint]

sil·i·cate (sil′i·kit) *n.* A salt or ester of silicic acid.

si·li·ceous (si-lish′əs) *adj.* **1.** Pertaining to, resembling, or containing silica. **2.** Growing or living on soil rich in silica. Also **si·li′cious.** [< L *silex, silicis* flint]

si·lic·ic (si-lis′ik) *adj.* Of, pertaining to, or derived from silica or silicon. [< SILIC- + -IC]

silicic acid *Chem.* Any of several gelatinous and easily decomposed compounds of silica and water; esp., H₄SiO₄, associated in the formation of many metallic silicates.

silico- *combining form* Silicon; of, related to, or containing silicon. Also, before vowels, *silic-.* [< L *silex, silicis* flint]

sil·i·con (sil′ə-kən, -kon) *n.* A widely distributed nonmetallic element (symbol Si) prepared as a dull brown amorphous powder, as shining metallic scales, or as a steel-gray crystalline mass. See ELEMENT. [< L *silex, silicis* flint]

sil·i·cone (sil′ə-kōn) *n. Chem.* Any of various compounds containing a silicon-carbon bond, used as lubricants, insulating resins, waterproofing materials, etc. [< SILICON]

sil·i·co·sis (sil′ə-kō′sis) *n. Pathol.* A pulmonary disease caused by the inhalation of finely powdered silica or quartz.

silk (silk) *n.* **1.** The creamy-white or yellowish, very fine natural fiber produced by the larvae of silkworms. **2.** A similar filamentous material spun by other insects. **3.** Cloth, thread, or garments made of silk. **4.** Anything resembling silk. — **to hit the silk** *Slang* To descend from an aircraft by parachute. — *adj.* **1.** Consisting of silk. **2.** Resembling silk. **3.** Of or pertaining to silk. — *v.t.* **1.** To clothe or cover with silk. — *v.i.* **2.** To produce the portion of the flower called silk: said of corn. [OE < L *sericus* silken]

silk cotton The silky seed covering of various tropical American trees; esp., kapok fiber.

silk·en (sil′kən) *adj.* **1.** Made of silk. **2.** Like silk; glossy; delicate; smooth. **3.** Dressed in silk. **4.** Luxurious.

silk hat A high cylindrical hat covered with fine silk plush, worn by men in dress clothes.

silk-screen process (silk′skrēn′) A stencil process that prints designs by forcing ink through the open meshes of a silk screen.

silk-stock·ing (silk′stok′ing) *adj.* **1.** Wearing silk stockings. **2.** Wealthy; luxurious. — *n.* One who wears silk stockings; a member of the wealthy class.

silk·worm (silk′wûrm′) *n.* The caterpillar of certain moths that spin a dense silken cocoon; esp., the **common silkworm,** yielding commercial silk.

silk·y (sil′kē) *adj.* **silk·i·er, silk·i·est** **1.** Made of or resembling silk; soft; lustrous. **2.** Long and fine, as hairs, or covered with such hairs, as leaves. **3.** Gentle or insinuating in manner. — **silk′i·ly** *adv.* — **silk′i·ness** *n.*

sill (sil) *n.* **1.** *Archit.* A horizontal, lower member of something, as the bottom of a door or window casing. **2.** A timber in the frame of the floor of a railroad car: end *sill.* [OE *syll*]

sil·ly (sil′ē) *adj.* **·li·er, ·li·est** **1.** Destitute of ordinary good sense; foolish. **2.** Stupid; absurd. **3.** *Informal* Stunned, as by a blow. — *n. pl.* **·lies** *Informal* A silly person. [OE *sæsig* happy] — **sil′li·ly** *adv.* — **sil′li·ness** *n.*

si·lo (sī′lō) *n. pl.* **·los** A pit or tower in which fodder, grain, or other food is stored green to be fermented and used as feed for cattle, etc. — *v.t.* **·loed, ·lo·ing** To put or preserve in a silo; turn into ensilage. [< Sp. < L < Gk. *siros* pit for corn]

silt (silt) *n.* An earthy sediment consisting of fine particles of rock and soil suspended in and carried by water. — *v.i.* **1.** To become filled or choked with silt: usu. with *up.* **2.** To ooze; drift. — *v.t.* **3.** To fill or choke with silt or mud: usually with *up.* [ME *cylte*] — **silt′y** *adj.*

Si·lu·ri·an (si-lŏŏr′ē-ən, sī-) *adj. Geol.* Of the period or rock system of the Paleozoic era. See chart for GEOLOGY. — *n. Geol.* The Silurian period or system.

sil·ver (sil′vər) *n.* **1.** A white, ductile, and very malleable metallic element (symbol Ag) of high electric conductivity, found native as well as in combination, and used in medicine, industry, and the arts: also called *argentum.* See ELEMENT. **2.** Silver regarded as a commodity or as a standard of currency. **3.** Silver coin; cash or change; money in general. **4.** Articles for domestic use made of silver or silver plate; silverware. **5.** A lustrous, pale gray color resembling that of silver. — *adj.* **1.** Made of or coated with silver. **2.** Of, containing, or producing silver. **3.** Having a silvery lustre. **4.** Having the soft, clear tones of a silver bell. **5.** Persuasive; eloquent. **6.** White or hoary, as the hair. **7.** Favoring the use of silver as a monetary standard. — *v.t.* **1.** To coat or plate with silver or with a silver-like substance. **2.** To make silvery. — *v.i.* **3.** To become silver or white. [OE *seolfor*] — **sil′ver·er** *n.*

SILO
(Showing interior and pit)

silver anniversary A 25th anniversary.

silver certificate *U.S.* Paper currency representing one dollar in silver bullion on deposit in the U.S. treasury, and valid as full legal tender.

sil·ver·fish (sil′vər-fish′) *n. pl.* **·fish** or **·fish·es** **1.** A silvery-white variety of the goldfish. **2.** Any of numerous flat-bodied, wingless insects that damage books, papers, etc.

silver fox **1.** A color phase of the red fox of North America, having fur that is interspersed with white-tipped hairs. **2.** The fur of this animal.

silver gray A light, slightly bluish gray, the color of silver.

silver nitrate *Chem.* A crystalline, poisonous compound, AgNO₃, obtained by treating silver with nitric acid, widely used in industry, photography, and medicine.

silver plate Articles, as table utensils, made of silver or metal plated with silver.

sil·ver·smith (sil′vər-smith′) *n.* A worker in silver; a maker of silverware.

silver standard A monetary standard or system based on silver.

Silver Star A U.S. military decoration, first issued in 1932, awarded for gallantry in action. See DECORATION.

Silver State Nickname of Nevada.

sil·ver-tongued (sil′vər·tungd′) *adj.* Eloquent.

sil·ver·ware (sil′vər·wâr′) *n.* Articles, esp., for table use, made of silver.

sil·ver·y (sil′vər·ē) *adj.* 1. Containing or adorned with silver. 2. Resembling silver, as in luster or hue. 3. Soft and clear in sound. **— sil′ver·i·ness** *n.*

s'il vous plait (sēl vōō plē′) *French* If you please; please.

Sim·chath To·rah (sim′khäs tō′rə) A Jewish holiday; literally, the rejoicing over the Law. Also **Sim′hath To′rah.**

Sim·e·on (sim′ē·ən) In the Old Testament, a son of Jacob and Leah. *Gen.* xxix 33. **—** *n.* The tribe of Israel descended from him.

sim·i·an (sim′ē·ən) *adj.* Pertaining to, resembling, or characteristic of apes and monkeys. **—** *n.* An ape or monkey. [< L *simia* ape]

sim·i·lar (sim′ə·lər) *adj.* 1. Bearing resemblance to one another or to something else; like, but not completely identical. 2. Of like characteristics, nature, or degree; of the same scope, order, or purpose. 3. *Geom.* Shaped alike, as figures that may become congruent by the alteration of linear dimensions, the angles remaining unchanged. [< F < L *similis* like] **— sim′i·lar·ly** adv.

sim·i·lar·i·ty (sim′ə·lar′ə·tē) *n. pl.* **·ties** 1. The quality or state or being similar. 2. The point in which the objects compared are similar. 3. *pl.* Things that coincide with or resemble each other. **— Syn.** See ANALOGY.

sim·i·le (sim′ə·lē) *n.* A figure of speech expressing comparison or likeness by the use of such terms as *like, as, so,* etc.: distinguished from *metaphor*. [< L, neut. of *similis* similar] **— Syn.** Simile is a literary device to conjure up a vivid picture; "an Alpine peak like a frosted cake" is a *simile*. A *metaphor* omits "like" or "as", the words of comparison; "the silver pepper of the stars" is a *metaphor*. A *comparison* brings together things of the same kind or class.

si·mil·i·tude (si·mil′ə·tōod, -tyōod) *n.* 1. Similarity. 2. A counterpart or likeness. [< OF < L < *similis* like]

sim·mer (sim′ər) *v.i.* 1. To boil gently or with a subdued sound; be or stay at or just below the boiling point. 2. To be on the point of breaking forth, as with rage. **—** *v.t.* 3. To keep at or just below the boiling point. **— to simmer down** 1. To reduce liquid content by boiling gently. 2. *Informal* To subside from a state of anger or excitement. **—** *n.* The state or process of simmering. [< obs. *simper* to boil]

Si·mon Le·gree (sī′mən li·grē′) 1. A cruel overseer of slaves in Harriet Beecher Stowe's *Uncle Tom's Cabin*. 2. Any brutal master.

Simon Peter See PETER.

si·mon-pure (sī′mən·pyōor′) *adj.* Real; genuine; authentic. [after *Simon Pure*, a character in the comedy *A Bold Stroke for a Wife* (1718), who is impersonated by a rival]

si·mo·ny (sī′mə·nē, sim′ə-) *n.* Traffic in sacred things; the purchase or sale of ecclesiastical preferment. [< Med.L < *Simon (Magus)*, who offered Peter money for the gift of the Holy Spirit] **— si′mon·ist** *n.*

si·moom (si·mōom′, sī-) *n. Meteorol.* A hot dry wind of the desert in northern Africa, Arabia, etc. Also **si·moon′** (-mōon′). [< Arabic < *samma* poison]

sim·per (sim′pər) *v.i.* 1. To smile in a silly, self-conscious manner; smirk. **—** *v.t.* 2. To say with a simper. **—** *n.* A silly, self-conscious smile. [< Scand. Cf. Sw. and Norw. *semper* coy.] **— sim′per·er** *n.* **— sim′per·ing·ly** adv.

sim·ple (sim′pəl) *adj.* **·pler, ·plest** 1. Consisting of one thing; single; uncombined. 2. Not complex or complicated; easy. 3. Without embellishment; plain; unadorned. 4. Free from affectation; sincere; artless. 5. Of humble rank; lowly. 6. Silly; feeble-minded. 7. Insignificant; trifling. 8. Lacking luxury; frugal. 9. Having nothing added; mere. 10. *Chem.* Of one element; also, unmixed. 11. *Bot.* Not divided; entire. **—** *n.* 1. That which is simple; an uncomplex, or natural thing. 2. A simpleton. [< OF < L *simplex*]

simple fraction *Math.* A fraction in which both numerator and denominator are integers.

simple interest Interest computed on the original principal alone.

simple machine Any of certain elementary mechanical contrivances, as the lever, the wedge, the inclined plane, the screw, the wheel and axle, and the pulley.

sim·ple-mind·ed (sim′pəl·mīn′did) *adj.* 1. Artless or unsophisticated. 2. Mentally defective. 3. Stupid; foolish. **— sim′ple-mind′ed·ly** adv. **— sim′ple-mind′ed·ness** *n.*

simple sentence See under SENTENCE.

sim·ple·ton (sim′pəl·tən) *n.* A weak-minded or silly person.

simplici- *combining form* Simple. Also, before vowels, **simplic-.** [< L *simplex, simplicis* simple]

sim·plic·i·ty (sim·plis′ə·tē) *n. pl.* **·ties** 1. The state of being simple; freedom from admixture, ostentation, subtlety, difficulty, etc. 2. Sincerity; unaffectedness. 3. Lack of intelligence or good sense. [< OF < L *simplicitas*]

sim·pli·fy (sim′plə·fī) *v.t.* **·fied, ·fy·ing** To make more simple or less complex. [< F < Med.L < L *simplex* simple + *facere* to make] **— sim′pli·fi·ca′tion** *n.* **— sim′pli·fi′er** *n.*

sim·plis·tic (sim·plis′tik) *adj.* Tending to ignore complications or details. **— sim′plism** *n.* **— sim·plis′ti·cal·ly** adv.

sim·ply (sim′plē) *adv.* 1. In a simple manner; intelligibly. 2. Without ostentation or extravagance. 3. Without subtlety or affectation; unassumingly. 4. Merely. 5. Without sense or discretion; foolishly. 6. Really; absolutely: *simply charming*: sometimes used ironically.

sim·u·la·crum (sim′yə·lā′krəm) *n. pl.* **·cra** (-krə) 1. An image. 2. An imaginary, visionary, or shadowy semblance. 3. A sham. [See SIMULATE.]

sim·u·late (*v.* sim′yə·lāt; *for adj., also* -lit) *v.t.* **·lat·ed, ·lat·ing** 1. To have the appearance or form of, without the reality; counterfeit; imitate. 2. To make a pretense of. **—** *adj.* Pretended. [< L < *similis* like] **— sim′u·la′tor** *n.*

sim·u·la·tion (sim′yə·lā′shən) *n.* 1. The act of simulating; counterfeit; sham. 2. The taking on of a particular aspect or form. **— sim′u·la·tive, sim′u·la·to·ry** (-lə·tôr′ē, -tō′rē) *adj.* **— sim′u·la·tive·ly** adv.

si·mul·cast (sī′məl·kast′, -käst′) *v.t.* **·cast, ·cast·ing** To broadcast by radio and television simultaneously. **—** *n.* A broadcast transmitted by radio and television simultaneously. [< SIMUL(TANEOUS) + (BROAD)CAST]

si·mul·ta·ne·ous (sī′məl·tā′nē·əs, sim′əl-) *adj.* Occurring, done, or existing at the same time. [< LL < L *simul* at the same time] **— si′mul·ta·ne·ous·ly** adv. **— si′mul·ta·ne·ous·ness, si′mul·ta·ne′i·ty** (-nə·ē·ə·tē) *n.*

sin (sin) *n.* 1. A transgression, esp., when deliberate, of a law having divine authority. 2. A particular instance of such transgression. 3. Any offense against a standard: a literary *sin*. **—** *v.* **sinned, sin·ning** *v.i.* 1. To commit sin; transgress the divine law. 2. To violate any requirement of right, duty, etc.; do wrong. **—** *v.t.* 3. To commit or do wrongfully. [OE *synn*]

Si·nai (sī′nī, -nē·ī′), Mount The mountain where Moses received the law from God. *Ex.* xix.

since (sins) *adv.* 1. From a past time, mentioned or referred to, up to the present. 2. At some time between a certain past time or event and the present. 3. In time before the present; ago; before now. **—** *prep.* 1. During or within the time after or later than: *since* you left. 2. Continuously throughout the time after: *since* noon. **—** *conj.* 1. During or within the time after which. 2. Continuously from the time when. 3. Because of or following upon the fact that; inasmuch as. [ME < OE *siththan* afterwards]

sin·cere (sin·sir′) *adj.* 1. Being in reality as it is in appearance; genuine. 2. Free from hypocrisy; honest. [< L < *sin-* without + *carus* (of *caries* decay] **— sin·cere′ly** adv.

sin·cer·i·ty (sin·ser′ə·tē) *n. pl.* **·ties** The state or quality of being sincere; honesty of purpose or character; freedom from hypocrisy, deceit, or simulation. Also **sin·cere′ness.**

sine¹ (sīn) *n. Trig.* In a right triangle, a function of an acute angle, equal to the ratio of the side opposite the angle to the hypotenuse. [< L *sinus* a bend]

si·ne² (sī′nē) *prep. Latin* Without.

si·ne·cure (sī′nə·kyōor, sin′ə-) *n.* 1. An office or position for which recompense is received, but involving few or no duties. 2. *Eccl.* A benefice without cure of souls. [< L *sine* without + *cura* care] **— si′ne·cur·ism** *n.* **— si′ne·cur·ist** *n.*

si·ne di·e (sī′nē dī′ē) *Latin* Without setting a day for reassembling; literally, without a day.

si·ne qua non (sī′nē kwä non′) *Latin* That which is indispensable; an essential; literally, without which not.

sin·ew (sin′yōo) *n.* 1. A tendon or similar fibrous cord. 2. Strength, or that which supplies strength. **—** *v.t.* To strengthen or knit together. [OE *seono*] **— sin′ew·less** *adj.*

sin·ew·y (sin′yōo·ē) *adj.* 1. Characteristic or consisting of a sinew or sinews. 2. Well supplied with sinews; strong; brawny. 3. Forceful; vigorous: a *sinewy* style.

sin·ful (sin′fəl) *adj.* Characterized by, suggestive of, or tainted with sin; wicked; immoral. [OE *synfull*] **— sin′ful·ly** adv. **— sin′ful·ness** *n.*

sing (sing) *v.* **sang** or (*less commonly*) **sung, sung, sing·ing** *v.i.* 1. To produce word sounds that differ from speech in that vowels are lengthened and pitches are clearly defined. 2. To use the voice in this manner for musical rendition or performance. 3. To produce melodious sounds, as a bird. 4. To make a melodious sound suggestive of singing, as a teakettle. 5. To buzz or hum; ring. 6. To be suitable for singing. 7. To relate something in verse. **—** *v.t.* 8. To produce (a tone or tones) with the voice. 9. To render (a song, etc.) by singing. 10. To chant, intone, or utter in a songlike manner. 11. To bring to a specified condition by singing: *Sing* me to sleep. 12. To relate in or as in song; acclaim: they *sing* his fame. **— to sing out** *Informal* To call out loudly; shout. **—** *n.* 1. A humming sound, as of a bullet in flight. 2. *Informal* A gathering for general participation in singing. [OE *singan*] **— sing′a·ble** *adj.*

singe (sinj) *v.t.* **singed, singe·ing** 1. To burn slightly or superficially; scorch. **2.** To remove bristles or feathers from by passing through flame. **3.** To burn the ends of (hair, etc.). — *n.* **1.** The act of singeing, esp. as performed by a barber. **2.** A superficial burn; scorch. [OE *sengan* to scorch, hiss, causative of *singan* to sing]

sing·er¹ (sing′ər) *n.* **1.** One who sings, esp. as a profession. **2.** That which produces a songlike utterance, as a songbird.

sing·er² (sin′jər) *n.* One who or that which singes.

Sin·gha·lese (sing′gə·lēz′, -lēs′) *adj.* Of or pertaining to Ceylon, to a people constituting the majority of the inhabitants of Ceylon, or to their language. — *n.* **1.** One of the Singhalese people. **2.** The Indic language of the Singhalese. Also *Sinhalese.* [< Skt. *Sinhala* Ceylon]

sin·gle (sing′gəl) *adj.* **1.** Consisting of one only; individual. **2.** Having no companion or assistant; alone. **3.** Unmarried. **4.** Pertaining to the unmarried state. **5.** Consisting of only one part. **6.** Unswerving in purpose, intention, etc.; sincere. **7.** Designed for use by only one person or individual: a *single* bed. **8.** Engaged in by individuals in opposition to one another: *single* combat. — *n.* **1.** One who or that which is single; a unit. **2.** In baseball, a base hit that enables the batter to reach first base. **3.** A hotel room for one person. **4.** A golf match between two players only: opposed to *foursome.* **5.** In cricket, a hit that scores one run. **6.** *pl.* In tennis, etc., a game having one player on each side. — *v.* **-gled, ·gling** *v.t.* **1.** To choose or select (one) from others: usu. with *out.* — *v.i.* **2.** To single-foot. **3.** In baseball, to make a one-base hit. [< OF < L *singulus*] — **sin′gle·ness** *n.*

single bed A bed wide enough for one person.

sin·gle-breast·ed (sing′gəl·bres′tid) *adj.* Having only one thickness of cloth over the breast and fastening in front with a single set of buttons, loops, etc., as a coat or jacket.

single file A line of people, animals, etc., disposed one behind the other, with no two abreast.

sin·gle-hand·ed (sing′gəl·han′did) *adj.* **1.** Having no assistance; unaided. **2.** Having or using but one hand. **3.** Capable of being used with a single hand. **4.** Having only one workman. — **sin′gle-hand′ed·ly** *adv.*

sin·gle-heart·ed (sing′gəl·här′tid) *adj.* Sincere; straightforward; loyal. — **sin′gle-heart′ed·ly** *adv.*

sin·gle-mind·ed (sing′gəl·mīn′did) *adj.* **1.** Having but one purpose or aim. **2.** Free from duplicity; ingenuous; sincere. — **sin′gle-mind′ed·ly** *adv.* — **sin′gle-mind′ed·ness** *n.*

sin·gle-phase (sing′gəl·fāz′) *adj. Electr.* Designating an alternating-current circuit having one phase at any given instant.

sin·gle·stick (sing′gəl·stik′) *n.* **1.** A cudgel. **2.** A stick with a basket-shaped hilt, used in fencing. **3.** The art or practice of fencing with singlesticks.

single tax A tax to be obtained from a single source, esp. from a levy on land and natural resources, as a substitute for all other forms of taxation.

sin·gle·ton (sing′gəl·tən) *n.* **1.** In a hand of cards dealt to one player, a single card of a suit. **2.** Any single thing or individual, as distinguished from a pair or larger group.

sin·gle·tree (sing′gəl·trē′) *n.* A whiffletree.

sin·gly (sing′glē) *adv.* **1.** Without companions or associates; unaided, as an individual. **2.** One by one; one at a time.

sing·song (sing′sông′, -song′) *n.* **1.** Monotonous cadence in speaking or reading. **2.** Inferior verse; doggerel. — *adj.* Monotonous; droning, as verse, speech, etc.

sin·gu·lar (sing′gyə·lər) *adj.* **1.** Extraordinary; remarkable; uncommon. **2.** Odd; peculiar; not customary or usual. **3.** Representing the only one of its type; unique. **4.** *Gram.* Of or designating a word form that denotes one person or thing, or a class considered as a unit: distinguished from *dual, plural.* — *n. Gram.* The singular number, or a singular word form. [< OF < L *singulus* single] — **sin′gu·lar′i·ty** (-lar′ə·tē) *n.* — **sin′gu·lar·ly** *adv.* — **sin′gu·lar·ness** *n.*

sin·gu·lar·ize (sing′gyə·lə·rīz′) *v.t.* **·ized, ·iz·ing** To make or designate as singular.

Sin·ha·lese (sin′hə·lēz′, -lēs′) *adj. & n.* Singhalese.

sin·is·ter (sin′is·tər) *adj.* **1.** Underhandedly or suspiciously wrong or wicked. **2.** Malevolent; evil. **3.** Boding, tending toward, or attended with disaster; unlucky: often with *to.* **4.** *Heraldry* Being on the wearer's left, and hence on the observer's right: opposed to *dexter.* [< F < L *sinister* left] — **sin′is·ter·ly** *adv.* — **sin′is·ter·ness** *n.*

sin·is·tral (sin′is·trəl) *adj.* **1.** Of, pertaining to, or turned toward the left. **2.** Left-handed. — **sin′is·tral·ly** *adv.*

sin·is·trorse (sin′is·trôrs, sin′is·trôrs′) *adj. Bot.* Twining spirally toward the left, as certain climbing plants: opposed to *dextrorse.* Also **sin′is·tror′sal.** [< L, ult. < *sinister* left + *versum* turned] — **sin′is·tror′sal·ly** *adv.*

sink (singk) *v.* **sank** or (*less commonly*) **sunk, sunk** (*Obs.* **sunk·en**), **sink·ing** *v.i.* **1.** To go beneath the surface or to the bottom, as of a liquid. **2.** To descend to a lower level; go down, esp. slowly or by degrees. **3.** To descend toward or below the horizon, as the sun. **4.** To incline downward;

slope, as land. **5.** To pass into a specified state: to *sink* into a coma. **6.** To fail, as from ill health or lack of strength; approach death. **7.** To become less in force, volume, or degree: His voice *sank* to a whisper. **8.** To become less in value, price, etc. **9.** To decline in moral level, prestige, wealth, etc. **10.** To permeate: The oil *sank* into the wood. **11.** To become hollow; cave in, as the cheeks. **12.** To be impressed or fixed, as in the mind: with *in.* — *v.t.* **13.** To cause to go beneath the surface or to the bottom. **14.** To cause to fall or drop; lower. **15.** To force or drive into place: to *sink* a fence post. **16.** To make (a mine shaft, well, etc.) by digging or excavating. **17.** To reduce in force, volume, or degree. **18.** To debase or degrade, as one's character or honor. **19.** To suppress, hide, or omit. **20.** To defeat; ruin. **21.** To invest. **22.** To invest and subsequently lose. — *n.* **1.** A box-shaped or basinlike porcelain or metal receptacle with a drainpipe and usu. with a water supply. **2.** A cesspool, etc. **3.** A place where corruption and vice gather or are rampant. **4.** A natural pool, marsh, or basin in which a river terminates by evaporation or percolation. [OE *sincan*] — **sink′a·ble** *adj.*

sink·er (singk′ər) *n.* **1.** One who or that which sinks, or causes to sink. **2.** A weight for sinking a fishing line.

sink·hole (singk′hōl′) *n.* A natural cavity, esp. a drainage cavity, as a hole worn by water through a rock along a joint.

sinking fund A fund established and invested so that its gradual accumulations will wipe out a debt.

sin·less (sin′lis) *adj.* Having no sin; guiltless; innocent. — **sin′less·ly** *adv.* — **sin′less·ness** *n.*

sin·ner (sin′ər) *n.* One who has sinned; esp., one who has transgressed against religious laws or moral principles.

Sinn Fein (shin fān) An Irish political society that originated about 1905, having as its aims both independence and the cultural development of the Irish people. [< Irish, we ourselves] — **Sinn Fein′er** — **Sinn Fein′ism**

Sino- *combining form* Chinese; of or pertaining to the Chinese people, language, etc. Compare CHINO-. [< LL *Sinae* the Chinese]

Si·no-Ti·bet·an (sī′nō·ti·bet′n) *n.* A putative family of languages spoken over a wide area in central and SE Asia, comprising the two established subfamilies Sino-Thai (sī′nō·tī′) and **Tibeto-Burman:** also called *Indochinese.* — *adj.* Of these languages or the people who speak them.

sin·ter (sin′tər) *n. Metall.* Metal particles made cohesive by sintering. — *v.t. & v.i. Metall.* To make or become cohesive by the combined action of heat and pressure. [< G, dross of iron]

sin·u·ate (*adj.* sin′yōo·it, -āt; *v.* sin′yōo·at) *adj.* **1.** Winding in and out; sinuous. **2.** *Bot.* Having a wavy or undulating margin, as a leaf. Also **sin′u·at′ed.** — *v.i.* **·at·ed, ·at·ing** To curve in and out; wind. [< L *sinuatus,* pp. of *sinuare* to turn, wind] — **sin′u·ate·ly** *adv.* — **sin′u·a′tion** *n.*

sin·u·ous (sin′yōo·əs) *adj.* **1.** Characterized by bends, curves, or folds; winding; undulating. **2.** *Bot.* Sinuate. **3.** Devious; erring. [< L *sinus* bend] — **sin′u·os′i·ty** (-os′ə·tē) *n.* — **sin′u·ous·ly** *adv.* — **sin′u·ous·ness** *n.*

si·nus (sī′nəs) *n.* **1.** A recess formed by a bending or folding; an opening or cavity. **2.** *Anat.* **a** Any of the air-filled cavities in the cranial bones, communicating with the nostrils. **b** A channel or receptacle for venous blood. **c** A dilated part of a blood vessel. **3.** *Pathol.* Any narrow opening leading to an abscess. **4.** *Bot.* A recess or rounded curve between two projecting lobes or teeth of a leaf. [< L]

si·nu·si·tis (sī′nə·sī′tis) *n. Pathol.* Inflammation of a sinus or sinuses, esp. in the cranial bones.

-sion Var. of -TION.

Si·on (sī′ən) See ZION.

Siou·an (sōo′ən) *n.* A large family of North American Indian languages formerly spoken from the west banks of the Mississippi to the Rocky Mountains. — *adj.* Of or pertaining to this family of languages.

Sioux (sōo) *n. pl.* **Sioux** One of a group of North American Indian tribes formerly occupying the Dakotas and parts of Minnesota and Nebraska: also called *Dakota.*

sip (sip) *v.* **sipped, sip·ping** *v.t.* **1.** To drink by swallowing small quantities at a time. **2.** To drink from by sips. **3.** To imbibe. — *v.i.* **4.** To drink in sips. — *n.* **1.** A small amount of liquid swallowed at one time. **2.** The act of sipping. [ME < OE *sypian* to absorb] — **sip′per** *n.*

si·phon (sī′fən) *n.* **1.** A bent or flexible tube through which liquids may be passed from a higher to a lower level over an intervening elevation by making use of atmospheric pressure. **2.** A siphon bottle. **3.** *Zool.* A tubular structure in certain aquatic animals, as the squid, for drawing in or expelling liquids: for illus. see SQUID. — *v.t.* **1.** To draw off or cause to pass through or as through a siphon. — *v.i.* **2.** To pass through a siphon. Also spelled *syphon.* [< F < L < Gk. *siphōn*] — **si′phon·al** *adj.*

siphon bottle A bottle containing aerated or carbonated water that can be expelled by pressure on a valve through a bent tube in the neck of the bottle.

sir (sûr) *n.* The conventional term of respectful address to men, used absolutely, and not followed by a proper name. [< SIRE]

Sir (sûr) *n.* A title of baronets and knights, used before the Christian name or the full name.

sire (sīr) *n.* **1.** A father; begetter: sometimes used in combination: *grandsire.* **2.** The male parent of a mammal. **3.** A form of address to a superior, now used in addressing a king or sovereign. — *v.t.* **sired, sir·ing** To beget: now used chiefly of domestic animals. [< OF < L *senior* older]

si·ren (sī′rən) *n.* **1.** In Greek legend, one of a group of nymphs living on an island, who lured sailors to destruction by their sweet singing. **2.** A fascinating, dangerous woman. **3.** An acoustical device having a perforated rotating disk or disks through which sharp puffs of steam or compressed air are permitted to escape so as to produce a continued musical note or a loud whistle, often used as a warning signal. **4.** *Zool.* Any of a family of eellike amphibians, as the mud eel. — *adj.* **1.** Of or pertaining to a siren. **2.** Alluring; dangerously fascinating. [< OF < L < Gk. *seirēn*]

Sir·i·us (sir′ē-əs) The brightest star, −1.58 magnitude; Alpha in the constellation Canis Major: also called *Dog Star.* [< Gk. *seirios* hot, scorching]

sir·loin (sûr′loin) *n.* A loin of beef, esp. the upper portion. [< OF < *sur-* over, above + *longe* loin]

si·roc·co (si-rok′ō) *n.* *pl.* **·cos** *Meteorol.* **1.** A hot, dry, and dusty southerly wind blowing from the African coast to Italy, Sicily, and Spain. **2.** A warm, sultry wind blowing from a warm region toward a center of low barometric pressure. [< Ital. < Arabic *sharq* the east, the rising sun]

sir·rah (sir′ə) *n.* *Archaic* Fellow; sir: a term of address expressing contempt or annoyance. [Var. of SIR]

sir·up (sir′əp) See SYRUP.

sis (sis) *n.* *Informal* Sister.

si·sal (sī′səl, sī′zəl, sis′əl, sē′səl) *n.* **1.** A strong fiber obtained from the leaves of an agave of the West Indies. **2.** The plant yielding this fiber. Also **sisal grass, sisal hemp.** [after *Sisal,* town in Yucatán, Mexico]

sis·si·fied (sis′i-fīd) *adj.* *U.S. Informal* Effeminate.

sis·sy (sis′ē) *n.* *pl.* **·sies** *U.S. Informal* **1.** An effeminate man or boy; a milksop. **2.** A coward or weakling. [< SIS] — **sis′sy·ish** *adj.*

sis·ter (sis′tər) *n.* **1.** A female having the same parents as another or others of either sex. **2.** Something characterized as female, and closely associated with another of the same kind. **3.** A member of a sisterhood; a nun. **4.** *Brit.* A head nurse in the ward of a hospital; also, popularly, any nurse. — *adj.* Bearing the relationship of a sister or one suggestive of sisterhood. [OE *sweostor*]

sis·ter-ger·man (sis′tər-jûr′mən) *n.* *pl.* **sis·ters-ger·man** A full sister.

sis·ter·hood (sis′tər-hŏŏd) *n.* **1.** The relationship of or state of being sisters, esp. by blood. **2.** A body of women or girls united by some bond of fellowship or sympathy. **3.** A community of women bound by monastic vows or pledged to works of mercy and faith.

sis·ter-in-law (sis′tər-in-lô′) *n.* *pl.* **sis·ters-in-law 1.** A sister of a husband or wife. **2.** A brother's wife. **3.** The wife of a wife's or husband's brother.

sis·ter·ly (sis′tər-lē) *adj.* Pertaining to or characteristic of a sister. — *adv.* As a sister. — **sis′ter·li·ness** *n.*

Sis·y·phus (sis′ə-fəs) In Greek mythology, a crafty, greedy king of Corinth, condemned in Hades forever to roll uphill a huge stone that always rolled down again.

sit (sit) *v.* **sat** (*Archaic* **sate**), **sat, sit·ting** *v.i.* **1.** To rest with the buttocks on a supporting surface, with the body bent at the hips, and the spine nearly vertical. **2.** To occupy a chair, bench, etc., in such a position. **3.** To perch or roost, as a bird; also, to cover eggs so as to give warmth for hatching. **4.** To be or remain in a seated or settled position. **5.** To remain passive or inactive, or in a position of idleness or rest. **6.** To assume an attitude or take a position for a special purpose; pose, as for a portrait. **7.** To meet in assembly; hold a session. **8.** To occupy or be entitled to a seat in a deliberative body. **9.** To have or exercise judicial authority. **10.** To fit or be adjusted; suit: That hat *sits* well. **11.** To be suffered or borne, as a burden. **12.** To be situated or located: The wind *sits* in the east. **13.** To baby-sit, serve as company for someone ill, etc. — *v.t.* **14.** To have or keep a seat or a good seat upon: to *sit* a horse. **15.** To seat (oneself, etc.). — **to sit in** (**on**) *U.S.* To join or take part. — **to sit out 1.** To sit or remain quietly till the end of: to *sit out* an entertainment. **2.** To sit aside during: They *sat out* a dance. **3.** To stay longer than. — **to sit tight** *Informal* To wait for the next move. [OE *sittan*]

si·tar (si·tär′) *n.* An East Indian stringed instrument resembling a guitar. [< Hind. *sitār*]

sit-down strike (sit′doun′) A strike during which strikers refuse to leave their place of employment until agreement is reached. Also **sit′-down′.**

site (sīt) *n.* **1.** Place of location. **2.** A plot of ground set apart for some specific use. [< F < L *situs* position]

sit-in (sit′in′) *n.* A demonstration of protest, as by Negroes in the southern U.S., in which participants enter and remain seated in a public place, commercial establishment, etc., from which they are customarily excluded.

sito- *combining form* Food. [< Gk. *sitos* food]

sit·ter (sit′ər) *n.* **1.** One who sits. **2.** A baby sitter. **3.** A person posing as a model. **4.** A setting hen.

sit·ting (sit′ing) *adj.* **1.** Being in a seated position. **2.** Used for sitting: *sitting* room. — *n.* **1.** The act or position of one who sits. **2.** A seat; also, the place of or the right to a seat. **3.** A single period of remaining seated for a specific purpose. **4.** A session or term. **5.** A period of hatching. **6.** The number of eggs on which a bird sits at one incubation.

sitting duck *Informal* Any easy target.

sitting room A parlor; living room.

sit·u·ate (sich′ŏŏ-āt) *v.t.* **·at·ed, ·at·ing 1.** To fix a site for; locate. **2.** To place in a certain position or under certain conditions or circumstances. [< Med.L *situatus,* pp. of *situare* to place]

sit·u·at·ed (sich′ŏŏ-ā′tid) *adj.* **1.** Having a fixed place or location; placed. **2.** Placed in (usu. specified) circumstances or conditions: He is *well* situated.

sit·u·a·tion (sich′ŏŏ-ā′shən) *n.* **1.** Condition as modified or determined by surroundings or attendant circumstances; status. **2.** A combination of circumstances, often leading to a complication, climax, or crisis. **3.** The place in which something is situated; locality. **4.** A salaried post of employment, usu. subordinate. — **sit′u·a′tion·al** *adj.*

Si·va (sē′və, shē′-) The Hindu god of destruction and reproduction, forming with Brahma and Vishnu the Hindu trinity: also *Shiva.* [< Hind. < Skt. *śivás* propitious] — **Si′va·ism** *n.* — **Si′va·is′tic** *adj.*

Si·van (sē·vän′) *n.* The ninth month of the Hebrew year. See (Hebrew) CALENDAR. Also **Si·wan′** (-vän′).

six (siks) *n.* **1.** The sum of five and one: a cardinal number. **2.** Any symbol of this number, as 6, vi, VI. **3.** Anything consisting of or representing six units. — **at sixes and sevens 1.** In a state of confusion. **2.** At odds; estranged. — **six of one, half-dozen of another** A situation offering no obvious choice. — *adj.* Being one more than five. [OE]

six·pence (siks′pəns) *n.* A British silver coin of the value of six pennies, equivalent to half a shilling.

six·pen·ny (siks′pen′ē, -pən·ē) *adj.* **1.** Worth or sold for sixpence. **2.** Paltry; trashy. **3.** Denoting a size of nails.

six-shoot·er (siks′shŏŏ′tər) *n.* *Informal* A revolver that may be fired six times without reloading.

six·teen (siks′tēn′) *n.* **1.** The sum of fifteen and one: a cardinal number. **2.** Any symbol of this number, as 16, xvi, XVI. **3.** Anything consisting of or representing sixteen units. — *adj.* Being one more than fifteen. [OE *sixtÿne*] — **six′teenth′** *adv.* & *n.*

six·teen·mo (siks·tēn′mō) *adj.* & *n.* Sextodecimo.

sixteenth note *Music* A note having one sixteenth the time value of a whole note: also, *chiefly Brit.,* semiquaver.

sixth (siksth) *adj.* **1.** Next after the fifth: the ordinal of *six.* **2.** Being one of six equal parts. — *n.* **1.** One of six equal parts. **2.** That which follows the fifth. **3.** *Music* a The interval between any tone and another tone five steps from it in a diatonic scale. **b** A tone separated by this interval from any other, considered with reference to that other; esp., the sixth above the keynote. — *adv.* In the sixth order, place, or rank: also, in formal discourse, **sixth′ly.**

sixth sense Intuitive perception supposedly independent of the five senses.

six·ty (siks′tē) *n.* *pl.* **·ties 1.** The sum of fifty and ten: a cardinal number. **2.** Any symbol of this number, as 60, lx, LX. **3.** Anything consisting of or representing sixty units. — *adj.* Being ten more than fifty. [OE *sixtig*] — **six′ti·eth** *adj.* & *n.*

six·ty-fourth note (siks′tē-fôrth′, -fōrth′) *Music* A note having one sixty-fourth the time value of a whole note: also, *chiefly Brit.,* hemidemisemiquaver.

siz·a·ble (sī′zə-bəl) *adj.* Of comparatively large size. Also **size′a·ble.** — **siz′a·ble·ness** *n.* — **siz′a·bly** *adv.*

size¹ (sīz) *n.* **1.** Measurement or extent of a thing as compared with some standard. **2.** Comparative magnitude or bulk. **3.** One of a series of graded measures, as of hats, shoes, etc. **4.** A standard of measurement; specified quantity. **5.** *Informal* State of affairs; true situation: That's the *size* of it. — *v.t.* **sized, siz·ing 1.** To estimate the size of. **2.** To distribute or classify according to size. **3.** To cut or otherwise shape (an article) to the required size. — **to size up** *Informal* **1.** To form an estimate, judgment, or opinion of. **2.** To meet specifications. [< F *assise* to assize]

size² (sīz) *n.* A solution of gelatinous material, usu. glue, casein, wax, or clay, used to glaze paper, coat wall surfaces, etc. — *v.t.* **sized, siz·ing** 1. To treat with size. 2. To make plastic, as clay. [< OItal. *sisa* painter's glue]

sized (sīzd) *adj.* Being of a definite or specified size: often used in combination: *good-sized.*

siz·ing (sī′zing) *n.* 1. Size[2]. 2. The process of adding or applying size to a fabric, surface, etc.

siz·y (sī′zē) *adj.* **siz·i·er, siz·i·est** Glutinous. [< SIZE[2]]

siz·zle (siz′əl) *v.i.* **·zled, ·zling** 1. To burn, fry, quench, etc., with or as with a hissing sound; emit a hissing sound under the action of heat. 2. To be extremely hot. — *n.* A hissing sound as from frying or effervescence. [Imit.]

siz·zler (siz′lər) *n. Informal* Something extremely hot, as a summer day. [< SIZZLE]

skate[1] (skāt) *n.* 1. A device consisting of a metal runner attached to the sole of a boot or shoe, enabling the wearer to glide over ice; also, such a runner. 2. A roller skate. — *v.i.* **skat·ed, skat·ing** To glide or move over ice or some other smooth surface on or as on skates. [< earlier *skates* < Du. < OF *escache* stilt < Gmc.] — **skat′er** *n.*

skate[2] *n.* Any of various ray fishes having large pectoral fins and a pointed snout. [< ON *skata*]

ske·dad·dle (ski-dad′l) *Informal v.i.* **·dled, ·dling** To flee in haste. — *n.* Hasty flight. [Origin unknown]

skeet (skēt) *n.* A variety of trapshooting in which a succession of targets simulating the flight of birds are fired at from various angles by the shooter. [Ult. < ON *skjota* to shoot]

skein (skān) *n.* 1. A quantity of yarn, thread, etc., wound in a loose, elongated coil. 2. Something resembling or suggestive of this. 3. A flight of geese, etc. [< OF *escaigne*]

skel·e·ton (skel′ə·tən) *n.* 1. The supporting or protective framework of a human or animal body, consisting of the bones and connective cartilage (endoskeleton) in man and the vertebrates, or of a hard outer structure (exoskeleton), as in crustaceans, insects, etc. 2. A sketch or outline, as of a written work. 3. A very thin or emaciated person or animal. 4. A structure, group, etc., consisting of few parts, reduced numbers, or bare essentials. — **skeleton in the closet** A secret source of shame or discredit. — *adj.* 1. Consisting merely of a framework, outline, or few parts or members. 2. Resembling a skeleton in nature or appearance; meager; emaciated. [< NL < Gk. *skeleton* (sōma) dried (body), mummy < *skeletos* dried up] — **skel′e·tal** *adj.*

Cranium

Mandible

Cervical Vertebrae

Clavicle

Scapula

Sternum

Humerus

Ribs

Thoracic Vertebrae

Olecranon

Lumbar Vertebrae

Radius

Ilium

Ulna

Sacrum

Coccyx

Carpus

Pubis

Metacarpus

Ischium

Phalanges

Femur

Patella

Fibula

Tibia

Tarsus

Metatarsus

Phalanges

HUMAN SKELETON

skeleton crew A work crew barely sufficient for the job.

skel·e·ton·ize (skel′ə·tən·īz′) *v.t.* **·ized, ·iz·ing** 1. To reduce to a skeleton, framework, or outline by removing soft tissues,

extraneous parts, etc. 2. To reduce greatly in size or numbers. 3. To draft in outline.

skeleton key A key filed to a slender shape, and used to open a number of different locks.

skep·tic (skep′tik) *n.* 1. One who doubts, disbelieves, or disagrees with generally accepted ideas. 2. One who by nature doubts or questions what he hears, reads, etc. 3. One who questions the fundamental doctrines of a religion, esp. the Christian religion. 4. *Sometimes cap.* An adherent of any philosophical school of skepticism. Also spelled *sceptic.* [< F < L < LGk. *skeptikos* reflective]
— **Syn.** *Skeptic* is a general term, and refers to a person who does not feel that the state of human knowledge, or the evidence available, is sufficient to establish the doctrine. A *freethinker* is one who refuses to accept a doctrine, especially a religious doctrine, simply on authority, and demands empiric proof. An *agnostic* rejects a doctrine because he believes that human knowledge is, and always will be, incapable of determining its truth or falsity.

Skep·tic (skep′tik) *n.* In ancient Greek philosophy, a member of a school of skepticism. [< SKEPTIC]

skep·ti·cal (skep′ti·kəl) *adj.* 1. Doubting; questioning; disbelieving. 2. Of, pertaining to, or characteristic of a skeptic or skepticism. Also spelled *sceptical.* — **skep′ti·cal·ly** *adv.* — **skep′ti·cal·ness** *n.*

skep·ti·cism (skep′tə·siz′əm) *n.* 1. A doubting or incredulous state of mind; disbelieving attitude. 2. *Philos.* The doctrine that absolute knowledge is unattainable and that judgments must be continually questioned and doubted. Also spelled *scepticism.*

sketch (skech) *n.* 1. A rapid, incomplete, or hasty delineation or presentation, intended to give a general impression of a work, study, etc., to be completed; an outline. 2. An artist's rough or rapid drawing or study. 3. A short, slight, or unpretentious literary or dramatic composition. 4. A short scene, play, or musical act in a revue, musical comedy, etc. 5. *Informal* An amusing person; joker. — *v.t.* 1. To make a sketch or sketches of; outline. — *v.i.* 2. To make a sketch or sketches. — **to sketch in** To present or explain (details) in a rapid summary, way. — **to sketch out** To present or explain in a rapid, summary way. [< Du. < Ital. < L < Gk. *schedios* improvisation] — **sketch′a·ble** *adj.* — **sketch′er** *n.*

sketch·book (skech′bŏŏk′) *n.* 1. A book of paper used for sketching. 2. A set or collection of literary sketches. Also **sketch book.**

sketch·y (skech′ē) *adj.* **sketch·i·er, sketch·i·est** 1. Resembling or consisting of a sketch; roughly suggested without detail. 2. Incomplete. — **sketch′i·ly** *adv.* — **sketch′i·ness** *n.*

skew (skyōō) *v.i.* 1. To take an oblique direction; swerve. 2. To look obliquely or askance; squint. — *v.t.* 3. To give an oblique position, direction, or form to; make lopsided. 4. To shift or twist the meaning or significance of; distort. — *adj.* 1. Placed or turned obliquely; twisted to one side; lopsided. 2. Distorted in effect or meaning. — *n.* A deviation from symmetry or straightness; oblique direction or position. [< AF *eskiuer*, OF *eschiuver* to shun < Gmc.]

skew·er (skyōō′ər) *n.* 1. A long pin of wood, or metal, thrust into meat to hold it or keep it in shape while roasting or broiling. 2. Any of various articles of similar shape or use. — *v.t.* To run through or fasten with or as with a skewer. [Var. of SKIVER]

ski (skē, *Norw.* shē) *n. pl.* **skis** or **ski** One of a pair of wooden or metal runners with turned-up points, attached to the feet and used in sliding over snow, esp. on slopes. — *v.i.* **skied** (skēd), **ski·ing** 1. To glide or travel on skis. 2. To engage in the sport of gliding over snow-covered inclines on skis. [< Norw. < ON *skith* snowshoe]

skid (skid) *n.* 1. The act of skidding or slipping. 2. A small frame or platform upon which merchandise is stacked to be moved about or temporarily stored. 3. One of a pair of timbers used to support a heavy tilting or rolling object, or a log used as a track in sliding heavy articles about, or forming an inclined plane to ease their descent. 4. In lumbering, one of several logs used to make a skid road or skidway. 5. A shoe or drag on a wagon wheel. 6. *Aeron.* A runner in an airplane's landing gear. — **on the skids** *U.S. Slang* Rapidly declining in prestige or power. — *v.* **skid·ded, skid·ding** *v.i.* 1. To slide instead of revolving, as a wheel that does not rotate. 2. Of a wheel, vehicle, etc., to slide or slip sideways because of loss of traction. 3. *Aeron.* To move sideways, because of insufficient banking. — *v.t.* 4. To furnish with skids; put, drag, or haul on skids. 5. To brake or hold back with a skid. [? < ON *skith* piece of wood]

skid road A road or track along which logs are hauled.

skid row *U.S. Slang* An urban section inhabited by vagrants and derelicts. [< SKID ROAD]

ski·er (skē′ər) *n.* One who skis.

skiff (skif) *n.* A light rowboat or small, open sailing vessel light enough to be rowed with ease. [< F < Ital. < OHG *scif* ship, boat]

ski·ing (skē′ing) *n.* The act or sport of one who skis.

ski jump 1. A jump or leap made by a person wearing skis. 2. A course prepared for making such jumps.

ski lift Any of various devices, usu. an endless cable running on towers, with attached bars or chairs, used to transport skiers to the top of a slope or trail.

skill (skil) *n.* 1. Proficiency or technical ability in any art, science, handicraft, etc. 2. A specific art, trade, or technique. — **Syn.** See DEXTERITY. [< ON *skil* knowledge]

skilled (skild) *adj.* 1. Possessing or showing skill; proficient. 2. Having specialized ability or training, as a worker. 3. Requiring specialized ability or training, as a job.

skil·let (skil′it) *n.* A frying pan or similar cooking pot having a long handle. [ME *skelet*, ? < OF *esculette* dish]

skill·ful (skil′fəl) *adj.* 1. Having skill; clever; dexterous; able. 2. Characterized by or requiring skill. Also *Brit.* **skil′·ful.** — **skill′ful·ly** *adv.* — **skill′ful·ness** *n.*

skim (skim) *v.* **skimmed, skim·ming** *v.t.* 1. To remove floating matter from the surface of, as with a ladle: to *skim* milk. 2. To remove thus: to *skim* cream. 3. To cover with a thin film, as of ice. 4. To move lightly and quickly across or over. 5. To cause to pass swiftly and lightly, as a flat stone across a pond. 6. To read or glance over hastily or superficially. — *v.i.* 7. To move quickly and lightly across or near a surface; glide. 8. To make a hasty and superficial perusal; glance: with *over* or *through*. 9. To become covered with a thin film. — *n.* 1. The act of skimming. 2. That which has been skimmed, as skim milk. 3. A thin film or layer. — *adj.* Skimmed: *skim* milk. [Var. of SCUM]

skim·mer (skim′ər) *n.* 1. A flat ladle or other utensil for skimming. 2. One who or that which skims. 3. A hat having a shallow crown and a wide, round brim.

skim milk Milk from which the cream has been removed.

skimp (skimp) *v.t. & v.i.* To scrimp or scamp. — *adj.* Scant; meager. [Prob. < ON *skemma* to shorten]

skimp·y (skim′pē) *adj.* **skimp·i·er, skimp·i·est** 1. Insufficient in size, amount, etc. 2. Excessively saving or sparing. — **skimp′i·ly** *adv.* — **skimp′i·ness** *n.*

skin (skin) *n.* 1. The membranous tissue covering the body of an animal; the integument. ◆ Collateral adjectives: *cutaneous, dermal.* 2. The pelt of a small animal, removed from its body, whether raw or dressed. 3. A vessel for holding liquids, made of skin. 4. An outside layer, coat, or covering as the rind of a fruit, etc. 5. One's life: to save one's *skin*. — **by the skin of one's teeth** Very closely or narrowly; barely. — **to get under one's skin** 1. To be provoking or irritating. 2. To be an obsession. — **under the skin** In a close but not apparent figurative relationship: sisters *under the skin*. — *v.* **skinned, skin·ning** *v.t.* 1. To remove the skin of; flay; peel. 2. To cover with or as with skin. 3. To remove or peel off hastily. 4. *Slang* To cheat or swindle. — *v.i.* 5. To shed the skin. [< ON *skinn*]

skin-deep (skin′dēp′) *adj.* Superficial. — *adv.* Superficially.

skin-dive (skin′dīv′) *v.i.* **-dived** (*U.S. Informal* **-dove**), **-dived, -div·ing** To engage in skin diving.

skin diving Underwater swimming or exploration in which the swimmer is equipped with goggles and foot fins, and sometimes with a scuba or snorkel. — **skin diver**

skin-flint (skin′flint) *n.* A miser or niggardly person.

skin game 1. A crooked or rigged gambling game in which the players have no chance. 2. Any swindle.

skink (skingk) *n.* One of a group of lizards having smooth scales and short limbs. [< L < Gk. *skinkos* kind of lizard]

skin·ner (skin′ər) *n.* 1. One who flays or sells the skins of animals. 2. *U.S. Slang* A mule driver.

skin·ny (skin′ē) *adj.* **-ni·er, -ni·est** 1. Very thin or emaciated; lean. 2. Consisting of or resembling skin. — **skin′·ni·ness** *n.*

skin-tight (skin′tīt′) *adj.* Fitting tightly to the skin.

skip (skip) *v.* **skipped, skip·ping** *v.i.* 1. To move with light springing steps; caper. 2. To bounce over, ricochet from, or skim a surface. 3. To pass from one point to another omitting or not noticing what lies between. 4. *Informal* To leave or depart hurriedly; flee. 5. To be advanced in school beyond the next grade in order. — *v.t.* 6. To leap lightly over. 7. To cause to skim or ricochet. 8. To pass over or by; omit. 9. *Informal* To leave (a place) hurriedly. — *n.* 1. A light bound or hop. 2. A passing over without notice. [Prob. < Scand. Cf. Sw. *skuppa* to skip.]

ski pants Long trousers that fit snugly, esp. at the ankles, worn for skiing, etc.

skip·jack (skip′jak′) *n.* Any of various fishes that leap from or skip along the surface of the water, as the bonito.

skip·per¹ (skip′ər) *n.* 1. One who or that which skips. 2. Any of a family of small butterflies.

skip·per² (skip′ər) *n.* 1. The captain of a ship. 2. One in a position of leadership. [< Du. *schip* ship]

skirl (skûrl, skirl) *Scot. v.i.* To produce a shrill sound, as a bagpipe. — *n.* A shrill cry or sound. [ME *scrille*]

skir·mish (skûr′mish) *v.i.* To fight in a preliminary or desultory way. — *n.* 1. A light engagement, as between small parties or groups. 2. Any encounter or action that evades the main contention or business. — **Syn.** See BATTLE. [< OF *eskermir* to fence, fight] — **skir′mish·er** *n.*

skirt (skûrt) *n.* 1. The part of a dress, gown, or robe that hangs from the waist downward. 2. A separate garment hanging from the waist and covering the lower portion of the body. 3. *pl.* The border, fringe, or edge of a particular area: on the *skirts* of the town. 4. One of the flaps or loose, hanging parts of a saddle. 5. *Slang* A woman or girl. — *v.t.* 1. To lie along or form the edge of; to border. 2. To surround or border: with *with*. 3. To pass around or about. 4. To evade or avoid (a subject, issue, etc.). — *v.i.* 5. To pass or be near the edge or border of something. [ON *skyrt* shirt]

skit (skit) *n.* 1. A short, usu. humorous dramatic scene or presentation. 2. A brief, humorous, often satirical piece of writing. [< Scand. Cf. ON *skjota* to shoot]

ski tow A type of ski lift consisting of an endless rope.

skit·ter (skit′ər) *v.i.* 1. To glide or skim along, touching a surface at intervals. — *v.t.* 2. To cause to skitter.

skit·tish (skit′ish) *adj.* 1. Easily frightened, as a horse. 2. Capricious; uncertain; unreliable. 3. Tricky; deceitful. [< dial. E *skit* to caper, as a horse] — **skit′tish·ly** *adv.* — **skit′·tish·ness** *n.*

skit·tle (skit′l) *n.* 1. *pl.* A game of ninepins, in which a flattened ball or thick rounded disk is thrown to knock down the pins. 2. One of the pins used in this game. — **beer and skittles** Carefree existence; drink and play. [Prob. < Dan. *skyttel* a child's earthen ball]

skiv·vy (skiv′ē) *n.* *pl.* **·vies** *U.S. Slang* 1. A man's short-sleeved undershirt. Also **skivvy shirt.** 2. *pl.* Men's underwear. [Origin uncertain]

skoal (skōl) *interj.* To your good health: a toast in drinking, used esp. by Scandinavians. [< Scand.]

sku·a (skyōō′ə) *n.* A predatory gull-like bird of northern regions. [< Faroese *skúgver* < ON *skúfr*]

skul·dug·ger·y (skul·dug′ər-ē) *n.* *U.S.* Trickery; underhandedness. [Var. of dial. *sculduddery*; origin uncertain]

skulk (skulk) *v.i.* 1. To move about furtively; lie close or keep hidden. 2. To shirk; evade work or responsibility. — *n.* One who skulks. [< Scand.] — **skulk′er** *n.*

skull (skul) *n.* 1. The bony framework of the head of a vertebrate animal; the cranium. 2. The head considered as the seat of brain; the mind. [< Scand.]

skull and crossbones A representation of the human skull over two crossed bones, used as a symbol of death, as a warning label on poison, and as an emblem of piracy.

skull·cap (skul′kap′) *n.* A small, snug, brimless cap.

skunk (skungk) *n.* 1. A carnivorous mammal of North America, usu. black with a white stripe and a bushy tail, and ejecting at will a malodorous liquid. 2. *Informal* A hateful or contemptible person. — *v.t. Slang* To defeat utterly in a game or contest. [< Algonquian *seganku*]

skunk cabbage A perennial plant of the arum family, emitting a strong odor. Also **skunk-weed** (skungk′wēd′).

sky (skī) *n.* *pl.* **skies** 1. The region of the upper air seen as a high vault or arch over the earth; the firmament. 2. *Often pl.* Atmospheric condition or appearance of the upper air: cloudy *skies*. 3. The celestial regions; heaven. — *v.t.* **skied, sky·ing** *Informal* To bat or throw (a ball, etc.) high into the air. [< ON *sky* cloup]

sky blue A blue like the color of the sky on a clear day. — **sky-blue** (skī′blōō′) *adj.*

sky·div·ing (skī′dī′ving) *n.* The sport of jumping from an airplane and performing various maneuvers and assuming various positions before opening the parachute.

Skye terrier (skī) A small terrier having a long body, short legs, and long, straight hair.

sky-high (skī′hī′) *adj. & adv.* Extremely high.

sky·jack (skī′jak′) *v.t.* To seize control of (an aircraft) while in flight and redirect it to a different destination. [< SKY + (HI)JACK] — **sky′jack′er** *n.* — **sky′jack′ing** *n.*

sky·lark (skī′lärk) *n.* A lark of the Old World that sings as it rises in flight. — *v.i.* To indulge in hilarious or boisterous frolic. — **sky′lark′er** *n.*

sky·light (skī′līt′) *n.* A window in a roof or ceiling, admitting daylight from above.

sky·line (skī′līn′) *n.* 1. The visible horizon. 2. The outline of a group of buildings, etc., seen against the sky.

sky pilot *Slang* A clergyman or a chaplain.

sky·rock·et (skī′rok′it) *n.* A rocket, as in a fireworks display, projected so as to explode high in the air. — *v.i.* To rise rapidly or suddenly.

sky·sail (skī′sāl, -səl) *n. Naut.* A light sail above the royal in a square-rigged vessel.

sky·scrap·er (skī′skrā′pər) *n.* A very high building.

sky·ward (skī′wərd) *adv.* Toward the sky. Also **sky′·wards.** — *adj.* Moving or directed toward the sky.

sky·way (skī′wā′) *n.* **1.** An air travel route. **2.** An elevated highway.

sky·writ·ing (skī′rī′tǐng) *n.* **1.** The forming of words in the air by the release of vapor from an airplane. **2.** The words or letters thus formed. **— sky′writ′er** *n.*

slab (slăb) *n.* **1.** A flat plate, piece, mass, or slice, as of metal, stone, etc. **2.** The outside piece of a log sawed for lumber, often with the bark remaining on it. **3.** *U.S. Slang* In baseball, the pitcher's plate. **— v.t. slabbed, slab·bing 1.** To make or form into slabs. **2.** To cover with slabs. **3.** To saw slabs from, as a log. [ME. Origin uncertain.]

slack¹ (slăk) *adj.* **1.** Hanging or extended loosely. **2.** Loose or careless in performance; remiss; slovenly. **3.** Flaccid; loose: a *slack* mouth. **4.** Lacking activity; not busy: a *slack* season. **5.** Listless; limp: a *slack* grip. **6.** Flowing or moving sluggishly, as wind, water, etc. **— v.t. 1.** To slacken. **2.** To slake, as lime. **— v.i. 1.** To be or become slack. **— to slack off** To slow down; be less diligent. **— n. 1.** A part of a rope, sail, etc., that is slack or loose. **2.** Slack condition; looseness. **3.** A period of inactivity. **4.** An extent of water where there is no current. **— adv.** In a slack manner. [OE *sleac*] **— slack′ly** *adv.* **— slack′ness** *n.*

slack² (slăk) *n.* Screenings or small pieces of coal. [Cf. Flemish *slecke*, LG *slacke*]

slack·en (slăk′ən) *v.i.* **1.** To become less active, productive, etc. **2.** To become less tense or tight. **3.** To become slow or less intense. **— v.t. 4.** To become slow, negligent, or remiss in: to *slacken* one's efforts. **5.** To make slack.

slack·er (slăk′ər) *n.* One who shirks his duties or avoids military service in wartime; shirker.

slack-off (slăk′ôf′) *n. Informal* A slowdown; abatement.

slacks (slăks) *n.pl.* Trousers worn by men or women for casual or sports wear.

slag (slăg) *n.* **1.** *Metall.* The fused residue separated in the reduction of metals from their ores. **2.** Volcanic lava in small, cinderlike pieces. **— v.t. & v.i. slagged, slag·ging** To form into slag. [< MLG *slagge*] **— slag′gy** *adj.*

slain (slān) Past participle of SLAY.

slake (slāk) *v.* **slaked, slak·ing** *v.t.* **1.** To quench or satisfy, as thirst or an appetite. **2.** To lessen the force or intensity of. **3.** To moisten or refresh. **4.** To mix with water or moist air, as in the preparation of slaked lime. **— v.i. 5.** To become disintegrated and hydrated, as lime. [OE *slacian* to retard < *sleac* slack¹]

slaked lime See under LIME¹.

sla·lom (slä′ləm, slä′-) *n.* In skiing, a race or descent over a winding downhill course laid out between posts and marked with flags. **— v.i.** To ski in such a course. [< Norw.]

slam¹ (slăm) *v.* **slammed, slam·ming** *v.t.* **1.** To shut or push to with violence and a loud noise. **2.** To put, dash, throw, etc., with violence and a loud noise; bang. **3.** *Slang* To hit or strike violently. **4.** *Slang* To disparage or criticize harshly. **— v.i. 5.** To close, swing, etc., with force and noise. **6.** To make a noisy entrance. **— n. 1.** The act or noise of slamming. **2.** *Slang* Harsh criticism; abuse. [< Scand. Cf. dial. Norw. *slamra* slam.]

slam² (slăm) *n.* In bridge, the winning of all (grand slam) or all but one (little or small slam) of the tricks in a round of play; also, a bid to do so. [Origin uncertain]

slam-bang (slăm′băng′) *adv.* Violently; noisily. **— v.i.** To move with noise and violence.

slan·der (slăn′dər) *n.* **1.** *Law* An oral statement of a false, malicious, or defamatory nature, tending to damage another's reputation, means of livelihood, etc. **b** The utterance of such a statement. **2.** A maliciously false tale or report. **— v.t. 1.** To injure by maliciously uttering a false report. **— v.i. 2.** To utter slander. [< AF < L *scandalum* cause of stumbling] **— slan′der·er** *n.*

slan·der·ous (slăn′dər·əs) *adj.* **1.** Uttering or containing slander. **2.** Characterized by slander; calumnious. **— slan′der·ous·ly** *adv.* **— slan′der·ous·ness** *n.*

slang (slăng) *n.* **1.** Language, words, or phrases of a vigorous, colorful, facetious, or taboo nature, invented for specific occasions or uses, or derived from the unconventional use of the standard vocabulary. **2.** The special vocabulary of a certain class, group, or profession: college *slang.* **3.** Formerly, the argot or jargon of thieves and vagrants. **— v.t. & v.i.** To address with or use slang. [Origin uncertain]

slang·y (slăng′ē) *adj.* **slang·i·er, slang·i·est 1.** Like or consisting of slang. **2.** Using slang. **— slang′i·ly** *adv.* **— slang′i·ness** *n.*

slant (slănt) *v.t.* **1.** To give an oblique or sloping direction to; incline. **2.** To write or edit (news or other literary matter) so as to express a special attitude, bias, or opinion. **— v.i. 3.** To have or take an oblique direction; slope. **4.** To have a certain bias or attitude. **— Syn.** See TIP¹. **— adj.** Lying at an angle; sloping. **— n. 1.** A slanting direction, course, or plane; slope. **2.** A bent, bias, or leaning. **3.**

Point of view; attitude. [< earlier *slent* < Scand. Cf. Norw. *slenta* slope.] **— slant′ing·ly** *adv.*

slant·wise (slănt′wīz′) *adj.* Slanting; oblique. **— adv.** At a slant or slope; obliquely. Also **slant′ways′** (-wāz′).

slap (slăp) *n.* **1.** A blow delivered with the open hand or with something flat. **2.** A sharp rebuke; insult; slur. **— v. slapped, slap·ping** *v.t.* **1.** To hit or strike with the open hand or with something flat. **2.** To rebuff; insult. **3.** To put or place violently or carelessly. **— v.i. 4.** To strike or beat as if with slaps. **— adv. 1.** Suddenly and forcibly; abruptly. **2.** *Informal* Directly; straight. [< LG *slapp*] **— slap′·per** *n.*

slap·dash (slăp′dăsh′) *adj.* Done or acting in a dashing or reckless way; impetuous; careless. **— n.** Offhand or careless work, behavior, etc. **— adv.** In a careless manner.

slap·hap·py (slăp′hap′ē) *adj.* **·pi·er, ·pi·est** *Slang* **1.** Dazed or giddy from or as from repeated blows. **2.** Silly; irresponsible. **— slap′hap′pi·ness** *n.*

slap·jack (slăp′jak′) *n. U.S.* A griddlecake; flapjack.

slap·stick (slăp′stick′) *n.* **1.** Boisterous, loud comedy. **2.** A flexible paddle formerly used in farces and pantomimes to make a loud report when an actor was struck with it. **— adj.** Using or suggestive of slapstick: *slapstick* humor.

slash (slăsh) *v.t.* **1.** To strike or cut violently with or as with an edged instrument. **2.** To whip; lash. **3.** To make long gashes, cuts, or slits in. **4.** To cut slits in, as a garment, so as to expose lining. **5.** To criticize severely. **6.** To reduce sharply, as prices, wages, etc. **— v.i. 7.** To make sweeping, violent, or haphazard strokes with or as with something sharp. **— n. 1.** The act or result of slashing. **2.** A slit or gash, esp. an ornamental slit in a garment. **3.** An opening or gap left in a forest after logging, a destructive fire, or a high wind. **4.** *Printing* A virgule. [? < OF *esclachier* to break] **— slash′er** *n.*

slash·ing (slăsh′ing) *adj.* **1.** Aggressively or destructively severe; violent. **2.** *Informal* Very fine; splendid. **— n.** A slash. **— slash′ing·ly** *adv.*

slat (slăt) *n.* A thin, narrow strip of wood or metal, as one of those in a crate, window blind, etc. **— v.t. slat·ted, slat·ting** To provide or make with slats. [< OF *esclat* splinter]

slate (slāt) *n.* **1.** A compact, fine-grained rock that splits readily into thin and even layers. **2.** A piece, slab, or plate of slate used for roofing, writing upon, etc. **3.** A record of one's past performance or behavior: a clean *slate.* **4.** A prearranged list, as of political candidates before their nomination or election. **5.** A dull bluish gray color resembling slate. **— adj. 1.** Made of slate. **2.** Having the color of slate. **— v.t. slat·ed, slat·ing 1.** To roof with slate. **2.** To put on a political slate or a list of any sort. **3.** To designate or mark, as for a specific change in condition. [< OF *esclate*, fem. of *esclat* chip, splinter] **— slat′er** *n.* **— slat′y** *adj.*

slath·er (slath′ər) *Informal* or *Dial.* *v.t.* **1.** To daub thickly. **2.** To spend or use profusely. [Origin uncertain]

slat·tern (slăt′ərn) *n.* An untidy or slovenly woman. **— adj.** Untidy; slovenly. [< dial. E *slatter* to slop, spill] **— slat′tern·li·ness** *n.* **— slat′tern·ly** *adj. & adv.*

slaugh·ter (slô′tər) *n.* **1.** The act of killing; esp. the butchering of cattle and other animals for market. **2.** Wanton or savage killing, esp. of human beings; massacre; carnage. **Syn.** See MASSACRE. **— v.t. 1.** To kill for the market; butcher. **2.** To kill wantonly or savagely. [< ON *slátr* butcher's meat] **— slaugh′ter·er** *n.* **— slaugh′ter·ous** *adj.* **— slaugh′ter·ous·ly** *adv.*

slaugh·ter·house (slô′tər·hous′) *n.* A place where animals are butchered; a scene of carnage.

Slav (släv, slav) *n.* A member of any of the Slavic-speaking peoples of northern or eastern Europe, comprising the Russians, Poles, Czechs, Moravians, Wends, Slovaks, Bulgarians, Serbians, Croats, Slovenes, etc.

slave (slāv) *n.* **1.** A person over whose life, liberty, and property someone has absolute control. **2.** A person in mental or moral subjection to a habit, vice, or influence. **3.** One who labors like a slave; a drudge. **— v.i. slaved, slav·ing** To work like a slave. [< F < Med.L *slavus, sclavus*]

slave driver 1. A person who oversees slaves at work. **2.** Any severe or exacting employer.

slave·hold·er (slāv′hōl′dər) *n.* An owner of slaves. **— slave′hold′ing** *adj. & n.*

slav·er¹ (slav′ər) *v.t.* **1.** To dribble saliva over. **— v.i. 2.** To dribble saliva; drool. **— n.** Saliva issuing or dribbling from the mouth. [Prob. < ON *slafra*] **— slav′er·er** *n.*

slav·er² (slā′vər) *n.* A person or a vessel engaged in the slave trade.

slav·er·y (slā′vər·ē, slāv′rē) *n.* **1.** The holding of human beings as property or chattels; also, the condition of a slave. **2.** Mental, moral, or spiritual bondage. **3.** Slavish toil.

slave trade The business of dealing in slaves; esp. the bringing of Negro slaves to America. **— slave trader**

slav·ey (slā′vē, slav′ē) *n. pl.* **slav·eys** *Brit. Informal* A female servant, esp. a maid of all work.

Slav·ic (slä′vik, slav′ik) *adj.* Of or pertaining to the Slavs or their languages. — *n.* A branch of the Balto-Slavic subfamily of the Indo-European language family, consisting of the following groups: **East Slavic** (Russian, including Great Russian, Ukrainian, and Byelorussian); **West Slavic** (Czech, Slovak, Polish, Wendish); **South Slavic** (Serbo-Croatian, Bulgarian, Slovenian, Macedonian). — **Church Slavic** or **Church Slavonic** The liturgical language of the Eastern Orthodox Slavs and of certain Uniats: also called *Old Church Slavic, Old Church Slavonic, Old Slavic.*

slav·ish (slā′vish) *adj.* **1.** Pertaining to or befitting a slave; servile; base. **2.** Extremely hard or laborious. **3.** Dependent; imitative. — **slav′ish·ly** *adv.* — **slav′ish·ness** *n.*

Sla·von·ic (slə-von′ik) *adj. & n.* Slavic.

slaw (slô) *n.* Cole slaw.

slay (slā) *v.t.* **slew, slain, slay·ing** To kill, esp. by violence. [OE *slēan*] — **slay′er** *n.*

slea·zy (slē′zē, slā′-) *adj.* **·zi·er, ·zi·est 1.** Lacking firmness of texture or substance; poorly made. **2.** Cheap; shoddy. [Origin uncertain] — **slea′zi·ly** *adv.* — **slea′zi·ness** *n.*

sled (sled) *n.* **1.** A vehicle on runners, designed for carrying people or loads over snow and ice; a sledge. **2.** A small, light frame mounted on runners, used by children for sliding on snow and ice. — *v.* **sled·ded, sled·ding** *v.t.* **1.** To convey on a sled. — *v.i.* **2.** To ride on a sled. [< MLG *sledde*] — **sled′der** *n.*

sled·ding (sled′ing) *n.* **1.** The condition of roads for sleds. **2.** The act of using a sled. **3.** State or circumstances of progress, work, etc.: *hard sledding.*

sledge[1] (slej) *n.* A vehicle or sled for moving loads over snow and ice. — *v.t. & v.i.* **sledged, sledg·ing** To travel or convey on a sledge. [< MDu. *sleedse*]

sledge[2] (slej) *n.* A heavy hammer wielded with one or both hands, for blacksmiths' use, or for breaking stone, coal, etc.: also **sledge hammer.** — *v.t.* **sledged, sledg·ing** To hammer, break, or strike with a sledge. [OE *slecg*]

sleek (slēk) *adj.* **1.** Smooth and glossy; polished. **2.** Smooth-spoken; flattering; unctuous. — *v.t.* **1.** To make smooth, even, or glossy. **2.** To soothe; mollify. [Var. of SLICK] — **sleek′ly** *adv.* — **sleek′ness** *n.* — **sleek′y** *adj.*

sleep (slēp) *n.* **1.** A state or period of reduced activity, accompanied by a complete or partial unconsciousness. **2.** A period of slumber. **3.** Any condition of inactivity, torpor, or rest. — *v.* **slept, sleep·ing** *v.i.* **1.** To be or fall asleep; slumber. **2.** To be dormant, inactive or quiet, or to rest in death. — *v.t.* **3.** To rest or repose in: to *sleep* the sleep of the dead. **4.** To provide with sleeping quarters; lodge. — **to sleep away** (or **off** or **out**) To pass or get rid of by or as by sleep: to *sleep off* a hangover. — **to sleep on** To postpone a decision upon. [OE *slǣp*]

sleep·er (slē′pər) *n.* **1.** One who or that which sleeps. **2.** A railroad sleeping car. **3.** *U.S. Informal* A play, motion picture, or book that achieves unexpected and striking success.

sleeping bag A large bag with a warm lining, used for sleeping, esp. out of doors.

sleeping car A passenger railroad car with accommodations for sleeping.

sleeping pill *Med.* A sedative; esp., one of the barbiturates taken to relieve acute or persistent insomnia.

sleeping sickness *Pathol.* The final stage of a disease prevalent in tropical Africa, marked by lethargy, fever and headaches and terminating in death.

sleep·less (slēp′lis) *adj.* Unable to sleep; wakeful; restless; unquiet. — **sleep′less·ly** *adv.* — **sleep′less·ness** *n.*

sleep·walk·ing (slēp′wô′king) *n.* The act or practice of one who walks while asleep. — **sleep′walk′er** *n.*

sleep·y (slē′pē) *adj.* **sleep·i·er, sleep·i·est 1.** Inclined to sleep. **2.** Drowsy; sluggish; dull; heavy. **3.** Conducive to sleep. — **sleep′i·ly** *adv.* — **sleep′i·ness** *n.*

sleep·y·head (slē′pē-hed′) *n.* A sleepy person. — **sleep′y·head′ed** *adj.*

sleet (slēt) *n.* **1.** A mixture of snow or hail and rain. **2.** A drizzle or shower of partly frozen rain. **3.** A thin coating of ice. — *v.i.* To pour or shed sleet. [Akin to MLG *slōte* hail] — **sleet′y** *adj.*

sleeve (slēv) *n.* **1.** The part of a garment that serves as a covering for the arm. **2.** *Mech.* A tube surrounding something, as a shaft, for protection or connection. — **up one's sleeve** Hidden but at hand. — *v.t.* **sleeved, sleev·ing** To furnish or fit with a sleeve or sleeves. [OE *slīefe*] — **sleeve′less** *adj.*

sleigh (slā) *n.* A light vehicle, usu. drawn by a horse with runners for use on snow and ice. — *v.i.* To ride or travel in a sleigh. [< Du. *slee*, contr. of *slede* sledge] — **sleigh′er** *n.* — **sleigh′ing** *n.*

SLEIGH

sleight (slīt) *n.* **1.** The quality of being skillful in manipulation. **2.** Craft; cunning. [< ON *slǣgth* slyness]

sleight of hand **1.** A juggler's or magician's trick so deftly done that the manner of performance escapes observation: also called *legerdemain.* **2.** The performance of such tricks.

slen·der (slen′dər) *adj.* **1.** Having a small diameter or circumference in proportion to the length or height; slim; thin. **2.** Having little strength or vigor; feeble; frail. **3.** Having slight basis or foundation; of little validity. **4.** Small or inadequate; moderate; insignificant. [ME *slendre*] — **slen′der·ly** *adv.* — **slen′der·ness** *n.*

slen·der·ize (slen′də-rīz) *v.t. & v.i.* **·ized, ·iz·ing** To make or become slender.

slept (slept) Past tense and past participle of SLEEP.

sleuth (slooth) *n.* **1.** *U.S. Informal* A detective. **2.** A bloodhound. — *v.t.* **1.** To follow; track. — *v.i.* **2.** To play the detective. [< ON *slōth* track, trail]

slew[1] (sloo) Past tense of SLAY.

slew[2] (sloo) See SLOUGH (def. 2).

slew[3] (sloo) *n. U.S. Informal* A large number, crowd, or amount; a lot: also spelled *slue.* [Cf. Irish *sluagh* crowd]

slew[4] (sloo) See SLUE[1].

slice (slīs) *n.* **1.** A thin, broad piece cut off from a larger piece. **2.** Any of various tools or devices having a broad, flat blade. **3.** In golf, a stroke that causes the ball to veer to the right. — *v.* **sliced, slic·ing** *v.t.* **1.** To cut or remove from a larger piece: often with *off.* **2.** To cut into broad, thin pieces; divide; apportion. **3.** In golf, to hit (the ball) with a slice. — *v.i.* **4.** In golf, to slice a ball. [< OF < OHG *slīzan* to slit] — **slic′er** *n.*

slick (slik) *adj.* **1.** Smooth; slippery; sleek. **2.** Flattering; obsequious. **3.** *Informal* Dexterously done; cleverly said. **4.** Smart and clever, but often of little depth. **5.** Smooth; oily, as the surface of water. **6.** Glazed, as paper; also, printed on glazed paper: *slick* magazines. **7.** *Slang* Agreeable; excellent. — *n.* **1.** A smooth place on a surface of water, as from oil. **2.** A broad chisel for paring or slicking: also **slick chisel. 3.** *Usu. pl. U.S.* A magazine printed on glazed paper: distinguished from *pulp.* — *adv. Slang* In a slick or smooth manner; deftly. — *v.t.* **1.** To make smooth, trim, glossy, or oily. **2.** *Informal* To trim up; make presentable: often with *up.* [ME *slike,* ? < OE *nīgslȳcod* glossy]

slick·er (slik′ər) *n.* **1.** *U.S.* A waterproof overcoat of oilskin, plastic, etc. **2.** *Informal* A clever, shifty person.

slide (slīd) *v.* **slid** (slid), **slid** or **slid·den** (slid′n), **slid·ing** *v.i.* **1.** To pass along over a surface with a smooth, slipping movement. **2.** To move easily or smoothly; pass gradually or imperceptibly. **3.** To proceed without being acted upon or directed: to let the matter *slide.* **4.** To lose one's equilibrium or foothold; slip. **5.** In baseball, to throw oneself along the ground toward a base. — *v.t.* **6.** To cause to slide, as over a surface. **7.** To move, put, enter, etc., with quietness or dexterity: with *in* or *into.* — *n.* **1.** An act of sliding. **2.** The slipping of a mass of earth, snow, etc., from a higher to a lower level; avalanche. **3.** An inclined plane or channel for sliding, as for children to slide upon. **4.** A small plate of glass on which a specimen is mounted and examined through a microscope. **5.** A small plate bearing a single image for projection on a screen. **6.** *Music* In a trumpet or trombone, a U-shaped portion of the tubing that is pushed in and out to vary the pitch. **7.** *Mech.* A sliding part. [OE *slīdan*] — **slid′er** *n.*

slide fastener A zipper.

slide projector An optical device for projecting magnified images from transparent slides onto a wall or screen.

slide rule A device consisting of a rigid ruler with a central sliding piece, both ruler and slide being graduated in a similar logarithmic scale to permit rapid calculations.

sliding door A door that opens and closes by moving sidewise along grooves.

sliding scale A schedule affecting imports, prices, or wages, varying under conditions of consumption, demand, or the market price of some article.

slight (slīt) *adj.* **1.** Of small importance; trifling. **2.** Small in quantity, intensity, or degree; inconsiderable. **3.** Slender; frail; delicate; flimsy. — *v.t.* **1.** To manifest neglect of or disregard for; ignore. **2.** To do imperfectly or thoughtlessly; shirk. **3.** To treat as trivial or insignificant. — *n.* An act or omission involving failure in courtesy or respect toward another. [ME] — **slight′ing** *adj.* — **slight′ing·ly** *adv.* — **slight′ly** *adv.* — **slight′ness** *n.*

sli·ly (slī′lē) See SLYLY.

slim (slim) *adj.* **slim·mer, slim·mest 1.** Small in thickness in proportion to height or length, as a human figure or a tree. **2.** Insufficient; meager: a *slim* attendance. — *v.t. & v.i.* **slimmed, slim·ming** To make or become thin or thinner. [< Du. *slim* bad] — **slim′ly** *adv.* — **slim′ness** *n.*

slime (slīm) *n.* **1.** Any soft, sticky, or dirty substance. **2.** Soft, moist, adhesive mud or earth; muck. **3.** A mucous exudation from the bodies of certain animals, as fishes and snails, and certain plants. — *v.* **slimed, slim·ing** *v.t.* **1.** To smear or cover with or as with slime. **2.** To remove slime from. [OE *slīm*]

slim·y (slī′mē) *adj.* **slim·i·er, slim·i·est** **1.** Covered or bedaubed with slime. **2.** Containing slime. **3.** Slimelike; foul. — **slim′i·ly** *adv.* — **slim′i·ness** *n.*

sling[1] (sling) *n.* **1.** A strap or pocket usu. with a string attached to each end, for hurling a stone or other missile by whirling the whole and releasing one of the strings. **2.** Any of various ropes, straps, etc., for suspending or hoisting something, as for holding up an injured limb, carrying a rifle, etc. **3.** The act of slinging; a sudden throw; cast; fling. — *v.t.* **slung, sling·ing** **1.** To fling from or as from a sling; hurl. **2.** To place or hang up in or as in a sling; move or hoist, as by a rope or tackle. [OE *slingan*] — **sling′er** *n.*

sling[2] (sling) *n.* *U.S.* A drink of brandy, whisky, or gin, with sugar and nutmeg, lemon juice, and ice.

sling·shot (sling′shot′) *n.* A weapon or toy consisting of a forked stick with an elastic strap attached to the prongs for catapulting small missiles: also called *catapult.*

slink (slingk) *v.i.* **slunk, slunk, slink·ing** To creep or steal along furtively or stealthily, as in fear. [OE *slincan* to creep] — **slink′ing·ly** *adv.*

slink·y (slingk′ē) *adj.* **slink·i·er, slink·i·est** **1.** Sneaking; stealthy. **2.** *Slang* Sinuous or feline in movement or form.

slip[1] (slip) *v.* **slipped** or **slipt, slip·ping** *v.t.* **1.** To cause to move smoothly and easily; cause to glide or slide. **2.** To put on or off easily, as a loose garment. **3.** To convey slyly or secretly. **4.** To free oneself or itself from, as a fetter or bridle. **5.** To let loose; unleash, as hounds. **6.** To escape or pass unobserved: It *slipped* my mind. **7.** To overlook; omit negligently. — *v.i.* **8.** To slide so as to cause harm or inconvenience; lose one's footing; become misplaced by failing to hold. **9.** To fall into an error or fault; err. **10.** To escape, as a ship. **11.** To move smoothly and easily. **12.** To get free of restraint. **13.** To go or come stealthily or unnoticed: often with *off, away,* or *from.* — **to let slip** To say without intending to. — **to slip one over on** *Informal* To cheat; hoodwink. — *n.* **1.** An act of slipping; a sudden slide. **2.** A lapse or error in speech, writing, or conduct; a slight mistake. **3.** *U.S.* A narrow space between two wharves. **4.** An artificial pier sloping down to the water, serving as a landing place. **5.** An inclined plane leading down to the water, on which vessels are repaired or constructed. **6.** A woman's undergarment, usu. the length of a dress. **7.** A pillow case: also **pillow slip.** **8.** A leash that permits quick release of the dog. **9.** *Geol.* A joint or fissure where two rock strata have moved upon each other. — **to give (someone) the slip** To elude (someone). [< MLG *slippen*]

slip[2] (slip) *n.* **1.** A cutting from a plant for planting or grafting; a cion. **2.** A small, slender person, esp. a youthful one. **3.** A small piece of something, as of paper or cloth, rather long relative to its width; a strip. **4.** A small piece of paper for jotting down memoranda, a record, etc. — *v.t.* **slipped, slip·ping** To cut off for planting; make a slip or slips of. [< MDu. *slippen* to cut]

slip·cov·er (slip′kuv′ər) *n.* A fitted cloth cover for a chair, sofa, etc., that can be readily removed.

slip·knot (slip′not′) *n.* **1.** A knot having part of the material drawn through in a loop so that it is easily untied. For illus. see KNOT. **2.** A running knot.

slip-on (slip′on′, -ôn′) *adj.* Easily donned or taken off. — *n.* A slip-on garment, as a blouse.

slip·o·ver (slip′ō′vər) *adj.* Easily donned by drawing over the head: a *slipover* shirt. — *n.* A slipover garment.

slip·per (slip′ər) *n.* A low, light shoe that is easily slipped on or off the foot. — **slip′pered** *adj.*

slip·per·y (slip′ər·ē) *adj.* **·per·i·er, ·per·i·est** **1.** Having a surface so smooth that objects slip or slide easily on it. **2.** That evades one's grasp; tricky; elusive. **3.** Unreliable; undependable. — **slip′per·i·ly** *adv.* — **slip′per·i·ness** *n.*

slippery elm **1.** A tree of eastern North America. **2.** Its mucilaginous inner bark, used in medicine.

slip·shod (slip′shod′) *adj.* **1.** Carelessly done or wrought; negligent; slovenly. **2.** Down at the heel; ragged; seedy.

slip-stream (slip′strēm′) *n.* *Aeron.* The stream of air driven backwards by the propeller of an aircraft.

slip-up (slip′up′) *n.* *Informal* A mistake; error.

slit (slit) *n.* A cut that is relatively straight and long; also, a long, narrow opening. — *v.t.* **slit, slit·ting** **1.** To make a long incision in; slash. **2.** To cut lengthwise into strips. [ME *slitten* to cut] — **slit′ter** *n.*

slith·er (slith′ər) *v.i.* **1.** To slide; slip, as on a surface where footing is insecure. **2.** To glide, as a snake. — *v.t.* **3.** To cause to slither. [OE *slīdan* to slide] — **slith′er·y** *adj.*

sliv·er (sliv′ər) *n.* **1.** A slender piece cut or torn off lengthwise; a splinter. **2.** Corded textile fibers drawn into a fleecy strand. — *v.t. & v.i.* To cut or split into long thin pieces. [< dial. E *slive* to cleave < OE *tōflīfan*] — **sliv′er·er** *n.*

slob (slob) *n.* **1.** *Informal* A stupid, careless, or unclean person. **2.** *Irish* Mud; mire. [< Irish *slab*]

slob·ber (slob′ər) *v.t.* **1.** To wet and foul with, or as if with, liquids oozing from the mouth. — *v.i.* **2.** To drivel; slaver. **3.** To talk or act gushingly. — *n.* **1.** Liquid spilled as from the mouth; slaver. **2.** Gushing, sentimental talk. [Var. of SLABBER] — **slob′ber·er** *n.* — **slob′ber·y** *adj.*

sloe (slō) *n.* **1.** The blackthorn (defs. 1 & 2). **2.** Any of various related plants. [OE *slāh*]

sloe-eyed (slō′īd′) *adj.* Having dark, velvety eyes.

sloe gin A cordial with a gin base, flavored with sloes.

slog (slog) *v.t. & v.i.* **slogged, slog·ging** **1.** To strike hard; slug. **2.** To plod (one's way), as through deep mud. — *n.* A heavy blow. [Var. of SLUG] — **slog′ger** *n.*

slo·gan (slō′gən) *n.* **1.** A battle or rallying cry, originally of the Highland clans. **2.** A catchword or motto adopted by a group, as a political party. [< Scottish Gaelic *sluagh* army + *gairm* yell]

sloop (slōōp) *n.* *Naut.* A single-masted, fore-and-aft rigged sailing vessel carrying at least one jib, now used principally as a racing vessel. [< Du. *sloep*]

SLOOP

slop (slop) *v.* **slopped, slop·ping** *v.i.* **1.** To splash or spill. **2.** To walk or move through slush. — *v.t.* **3.** To cause (a liquid) to spill or splash. **4.** To spill a liquid upon. — **to slop over** **1.** To overflow and splash. **2.** To do or say more than is necessary, because of excess zeal, sentimentality, etc. — *n.* **1.** Slush; watery mud. **2.** A puddle of liquid that has been slopped. **3.** An unappetizing liquid or watery food. **4.** Refuse liquid. **5.** *pl.* Waste food or swill, used to feed pigs, etc. [ME < OE *-sloppe*]

slope (slōp) *v.* **sloped, slop·ing** *v.i.* **1.** To be inclined from the level or the vertical; slant. — *v.t.* **2.** To cause to slope. — *Syn.* See TIP. — *n.* **1.** Any slanting surface or line. **2.** The degree of inclination of a line or surface from the plane of the horizon. [OE *āslūpan* to slip away] — **slop′er** *n.* — **slop′ing·ly** *adv.* — **slop′ing·ness** *n.*

slop·py (slop′ē) *adj.* **·pi·er, ·pi·est** **1.** Slushy; splashy; wet. **2.** Watery or pulpy. **3.** Splashed with liquid or slops. **4.** *Informal* Messy; slovenly; untidy. **5.** *Informal* Slipshod; careless. — **slop′pi·ly** *adv.* — **slop′pi·ness** *n.*

slops (slops) *n.pl.* **1.** Articles of clothing, bedding, etc., supplied to sailors on shipboard. **2.** Cheap, ready-made clothes. [ME < OE *-slop*]

slosh (slosh) *v.t.* **1.** To throw about, as a liquid. — *v.i.* **2.** To splash; flounder: to *slosh* through a pool. — *n.* Slush. [Var. of SLUSH] — **slosh′y** *adj.*

slot (slot) *n.* **1.** A long narrow groove or opening; notch or slit: the coin *slot* of a vending machine; the *slot* of a mailbox. **2.** A job opening or a place in a sequence. — *v.t.* **slot·ted, slot·ting** To cut a slot in; groove. [< OF *esclot* the hollow between the breasts]

sloth (slōth, slôth, sloth) *n.* **1.** Disinclination to exertion; habitual indolence; laziness. **2.** A slow-moving, tree-dwelling mammal of tropical America. [ME < OE *slǣwth*]

sloth·ful (slōth′fəl, slôth′-, sloth′-) *adj.* Sluggish; lazy; indolent. — **sloth′ful·ly** *adv.* — **sloth′ful·ness** *n.*

slot machine A vending machine or gambling machine having a slot in which a coin is dropped to cause operation.

slouch (slouch) *v.i.* **1.** To have a downcast or drooping gait, look, or posture. **2.** To hang or droop in a careless manner, as a hat. — *v.t.* **3.** To cause to droop or hang down. — *n.* **1.** A drooping of the head and shoulders caused by depression, fatigue, etc. **2.** A drooping of the brim of a hat. **3.** An awkward, heavy, or incompetent person: usu. in the negative: He's no *slouch* at baseball. [Origin uncertain] — **slouch′y** *adj.* — **slouch′i·ness** *n.*

slough[1] (slou *for defs. 1 & 3;* slōō *for def. 2*) *n.* **1.** A place of deep mud or mire; bog. **2.** A stagnant swamp, backwater, bayou, inlet, or pond in which water backs up: also spelled *slew, slue.* **3.** A state or moral depravity or despair. [OE *slōh*] — **slough′y** *adj.*

slough[2] (sluf) *n.* **1.** Dead tissue separated and thrown off from the living parts, as in gangrene. **2.** The skin of a serpent that has been or is about to be shed. — *v.t.* **1.** To cast off, as dead from living tissue: with *off.* **2.** To discard; shed, as a habit: with *off.* — *v.i.* **3.** To be cast off. **4.** To cast off a slough or tissue. [ME *slouh*] — **slough′y** *adj.*

slough of despond (slōō) Deep despair or dejection; despondency. [after the *Slough of Despond* in John Bunyan's *Pilgrim's Progress*]

Slo·vak (slō′vak, slō-vak′) *n.* **1.** One of a Slavic people of eastern Czechoslovakia. **2.** The West Slavic language of the Slovaks. — *adj.* Of or pertaining to the Slovaks or to their language. Also **Slo·vak·i·an** (slō-vak′ē-ən, -vä′kē-ən). [< Czech *slovák* Slav]

slov·en (sluv′ən) *n.* One who is careless of dress or of cleanliness; one habitually untidy.

Slo·vene (slō′vēn, slō·vēn′) *n.* One of a group of southern Slavs now living in NW Yugoslavia. — *adj.* Of or pertaining to the Slovenes or to their language. [< G *Slovene*]

Slo·ve·ni·an (slō·vē′nē·ən) *adj.* Of or pertaining to Slovenia, its people, or their language. — *n.* The South Slavic language of the Slovenes.

slov·en·ly (sluv′ən·lē) *adj.* **·li·er, ·li·est** **1.** Having the habits of a sloven. **2.** Careless or slipshod in manner of work, etc. — *adv.* In a slovenly manner. — **slov′en·li·ness** *n.*

slow (slō) *adj.* **1.** Having relatively small velocity; not quick in motion, performance, or occurrence. **2.** Behind the standard time: said of a timepiece. **3.** Not precipitate or hasty: *slow* to anger. **4.** Dull or tardy in comprehending; mentally sluggish. **5.** Lacking promptness, spirit, or liveliness. **6.** *Informal* Dull or tedious in character: a *slow* party. **7.** Being in a condition that is not conducive to speed: a *slow* track. **8.** Inactive: Business is *slow* today. — *v.t.* **1.** To make slow or slower: often with *up* or *down.* — *v.i.* **2.** To go or become slow or slower: often with *up* or *down.* — *adv.* In a slow or cautious manner or speed. [OE *slāw*] — **slow′ly** *adv.* — **slow′ness** *n.*

slow-mo·tion (slō′mō′shən) *adj.* Pertaining to or designating a motion picture filmed at greater than standard speed so that the action appears slow in normal projection.

slow·poke (slō′pōk′) *n. Informal* A person who works or moves at an exceedingly slow pace; a laggard.

sludge (sluj) *n.* **1.** Soft, water-soaked mud; mire. **2.** A slush of snow or broken ice. **3.** Muddy or pasty refuse, as that produced by sewage purification. **4.** The sediment in a water tank or boiler. [Earlier *slutch*] — **sludg′y** *adj.*

slue[1] (slōō) *v.* **slued, slu·ing** *v.t.* **1.** To cause to move sideways, as if some portion were pivoted. — *v.i.* **2.** To move sideways. — *n.* The act of sluing around sideways; also, the position of a body that has slued. Also spelled *slew.* [Origin unknown]

slue[2] (slōō) See SLEW[3].

slue[3] (slōō) See SLOUGH[1] (def. 2).

slug[1] (slug) *n.* **1.** A bullet or shot of irregular or oblong shape. **2.** *Printing* **a** A strip of type metal for spacing matter, etc. **b** A metal strip used as a compositor's mark. **3.** Any often counterfeit small chunk of metal; esp., one used as a coin in automatic machines. [Origin uncertain]

slug[2] (slug) *n.* **1.** Any of various mollusks related to the snail, having an elongated body and a rudimentary shell. **2.** The larva of a sawfly or other insect, resembling a slug. **3.** A sluggard. [ME *slugge* sluggard]

slug[3] (slug) *Informal n.* **1.** A heavy blow, as with the fist or a baseball bat. **2.** A drink of undiluted liquor. — *v.t.* **slugged, slug·ging** To strike heavily or brutally, as with the fist or a baseball bat. [Origin uncertain] — **slug′ger** *n.*

slug·gard (slug′ərd) *n.* A person habitually lazy or idle; a drone. — *adj.* Lazy; sluggish.

slug·gish (slug′ish) *adj.* **1.** Slow; inactive; torpid. **2.** Habitually idle and lazy. **3.** Not active; slow; stagnant: a *sluggish* season. — **slug′gish·ly** *adv.* — **slug′gish·ness** *n.*

sluice (slōōs) *n.* **1.** An artificial channel for conducting water, equipped with a valve or gate (**sluice gate**) to regulate the flow. **2.** The body of water so channeled. **3.** Any artificial channel, esp. one for excess water. **4.** A trough through which water is run to separate gold ore, to float logs, etc. **5.** That through which anything issues or flows. — *v.* **sluiced, sluic·ing** *v.t.* **1.** To wet, water, or irrigate by or as by means of a sluice. **2.** To wash in or by a sluice. **3.** To draw out or conduct by or through a sluice. **4.** To send (logs) down a sluice. — *v.i.* **5.** To flow out or issue from a sluice. [< OF < L *excludere* to shut out]

slum (slum) *n. Often pl.* A squalid, dirty, overcrowded section of a city, marked by poverty and poor living conditions. — *v.t.* **slummed, slum·ming** To visit slums for amusement or curiosity. [< cant, room] — **slum′mer** *n.*

slum·ber (slum′bər) *v.i.* **1.** To sleep, esp. lightly or quietly. **2.** To be inactive; stagnate. — *v.t.* **3.** To spend or pass in sleeping. — *n.* **1.** Sleep. **2.** A state of inactivity or quiescence. [OE *slūma* slumber] — **slum′ber·er** *n.* — **slum′ber·ing·ly** *adv.* — **slum′ber·less** *adj.*

slum·ber·ous (slum′bər·əs) *adj.* **1.** Inducing sleep. **2.** Sleepy; drowsy. **3.** Suggesting or resembling sleep. Also **slum′ber·y, slum·brous** (slum′brəs). — **slum′ber·ous·ly** *adv.* — **slum′ber·ous·ness** *n.*

slum·lord (slum′lôrd′) *n. U.S.* A landlord of slum property. [< SLUM + (LAND)LORD]

slump (slump) *v.i.* **1.** To break through a crust and sink. **2.** To slide with perceptible motion down a declivity: said of rock, etc. **3.** To fall or fail suddenly, as in value or quality. **4.** To stand or walk with a stooping posture. — *n.* The act of slumping; a collapsing fall; a failure; a decline.

slung (slung) Past tense and past participle of SLING.

slunk (slungk) Past tense and past participle of SLINK.

slur (slûr) *v.t.* **slurred, slur·ring** **1.** To slight; disparage; depreciate. **2.** To pass over lightly or hurriedly. **3.** To weaken and elide (speech sounds) by hurried articulation.

4. *Music* **a** To sing or play as indicated by the slur. **b** To mark with a slur. — *n.* **1.** A disparaging remark or insinuation. **2.** *Music* **a** A curved line (‿ or ⌢) indicating that tones so tied are to be sung to the same syllable or performed without a break between them. **b** The legato effect indicated or produced by this mark. **3.** A blur. **4.** A slurred articulation. [< dial. E, orig., fluid mud]

slush (slush) *n.* **1.** Soft, sloppy material, as melting snow or soft mud. **2.** Grease. **3.** Overly sentimental talk or writing; drivel. [? Scand. origin] — **slush′y** *adj.*

slush fund *U.S.* Money collected or spent for corrupt purposes, as bribery, etc.

slut (slut) *n.* **1.** A slatternly woman. **2.** A woman of loose character; hussy. **3.** A female dog. [ME *slutte*] — **slut′tish** *adj.* — **slut′tish·ly** *adv.* — **slut′tish·ness** *n.*

sly (slī) *adj.* **sli·er** or **sly·er, sli·est** or **sly·est** **1.** Artfully dexterous in doing things secretly; cunning in evading detection. **2.** Playfully clever; mischievous. **3.** Meanly or stealthily clever. **4.** Done with or marked by artful secrecy: a *sly* trick. **5.** Skillful; wise. — **on the sly** In a stealthy way; with concealment. [< ON *slǣgr*] — **sly′ness** *n.*

sly·ly (slī′lē) *adv.* In a sly manner: also spelled *slily*.

smack[1] (smak) *n.* **1.** A quick, sharp sound, as of the lips when separated rapidly. **2.** A sounding blow or slap. **3.** The sound of a blow, esp. with something flat. — *v.t. & v.i.* To give or make a smack, as in tasting, kissing, etc.

smack[2] (smak) *v.i.* **1.** To have a taste or flavor, esp. as tested by smacking: usu. with *of.* **2.** To have or disclose a slight suggestion: with *of.* — *n.* **1.** A suggestive taste, or flavor. **2.** A mere taste; smattering. [OE *smǣc* the taste]

smack[3] (smak) *n.* A small, decked or half-decked vessel of various rig used chiefly for fishing, esp. one having a well for fish in its hold. [< Du. *smak*]

smack·ing (smak′ing) *adj.* Brisk; lively: a *smacking* breeze.

small (smôl) *adj.* **1.** Comparatively less in size, quantity, extent, etc.; diminutive. **2.** Being of slight moment, weight, or importance. **3.** Narrow; ignoble; mean; paltry. **4.** Lacking in the qualities of greatness. **5.** Acting or transacting business in a limited way. **6.** Weak in characteristic properties: said of liquors: *small* beer. **7.** Slender; fine; soft, as a voice. **8.** Of low degree; obscure. **9.** Lacking in power or strength. — *adv.* **1.** In a low or faint tone. **2.** Into small pieces. **3.** In a small way; trivially; also, timidly. — *n.* **1.** A small or slender part: the *small* of the back. **2.** A small thing or quantity. [OE *smæl*] — **small′ness** *n.*

small arms Firearms of small caliber, as pistols, rifles, and machine guns.

small capital A capital letter cut slightly larger than the lower-case letters of a specified type size.

small change Coins of small denomination.

small craft Small boats or vessels collectively.

small fry **1.** Small, young fish. **2.** Young children. **3.** Small or insignificant people or things.

small hours The early hours of the morning.

small letter A lower-case letter, as *a* in Ra.

small-mind·ed (smôl′mīn′did) *adj.* **1.** Having a trivial, petty mind. **2.** Narrow; intolerant; ungenerous. — **small′-mind′ed·ly** *adv.* — **small′-mind′ed·ness** *n.*

small potatoes *U.S. Informal* Insignificant persons or things.

small·pox (smôl′poks′) *n. Pathol.* An acute, highly contagious virus disease, characterized by inflammatory fever and the eruption of deep-seated pustules that usu. leave permanent scars: also called *variola*.

small talk Unimportant or trivial conversation.

small-time (smôl′tīm′) *adj. U.S. Slang* Petty; unimportant: a *smalltime* hoodlum.

smart (smärt) *v.i.* **1.** To experience a stinging sensation, generally superficial, either bodily or mental. **2.** To cause a stinging sensation. **3.** To experience remorse. **4.** To have one's feelings hurt. — *v.t.* **5.** To cause to smart. — *adj.* **1.** Quick in thought or action; bright; clever. **2.** Impertinently witty: often used contemptuously. **3.** Vigorous; emphatic; severe; brisk. **4.** Causing a smarting sensation; stinging; pungent. **5.** Sharp, as at trade; shrewd. **6.** *Dial.* Large; considerable: a *smart* crop of wheat. **7.** Sprucely dressed; showy. **8.** Belonging to the stylish classes; fashionable. — *n.* **1.** An acute stinging sensation, as from a scratch or an irritant. **2.** Any distress; poignant mental suffering. [OE *smeortan*] — **smart′ly** *adv.* — **smart′ness** *n.*

smart al·eck (al′ik) *Informal* A cocky, offensively conceited person. — **smart-al·eck·y** (smärt′al′ik·ē) *adj.*

smart·en (smär′tən) *v.t.* **1.** To improve in appearance; make smart: with *up.* **2.** To make more alert or clever.

smart set Fashionable society.

smart·weed (smärt′wēd′) *n.* Any of several species of widely distributed marsh plants whose leaves cause itching.

smash (smash) *v.t.* **1.** To break in many pieces suddenly, as by a blow, pressure, or collision. **2.** To flatten; crush. **3.** To dash or fling violently so as to crush or break. **4.** To strike with a sudden, forceful blow. **5.** To make bankrupt.

6. To destroy, as a theory. **7.** In tennis, etc., to strike (the ball) with a hard, swift, overhand stroke. — *v.i.* **8.** To go bankrupt; fail, as a business, etc. **9.** To come into violent contact so as to crush or be crushed; collide. — **to go to smash** *Informal* To be ruined; fail. — *n.* **1.** An act or instance of smashing, or the state of being smashed. **2.** Any disaster or sudden breakup: a *smash* in business. **3.** In tennis, etc., a strong overhand shot. **4.** *Informal* Something acclaimed by the public: a **smash hit**. [Prob. imit. Cf. Norw. *smaska*.] — **smash′er** *n.*

smash·ing (smash′ing) *adj. Informal* Extremely impressive; overwhelmingly good: a *smashing* success.

smash-up (smash′up′) *n.* A smash; a disastrous collision.

smat·ter (smat′ər) *v.t.* To talk of, dabble in, study, or use superficially. — *n.* A smattering. [ME *smateren*, ? < Scand.] — **smat′ter·er** *n.*

smat·ter·ing (smat′ər·ing) *n.* A superficial knowledge of something. — **smat′ter·ing·ly** *adv.*

smear (smir) *v.t.* **1.** To spread, rub, or cover with grease, paint, dirt, etc.; bedaub. **2.** To spread or apply in a thick layer or coating: to *smear* grease on an axle. **3.** To defame; slander. **4.** *U.S. Slang* To defeat utterly. — *v.i.* **5.** To be or become smeared. — *n.* **1.** A soiled spot; stain. **2.** A small quantity of material, as blood, sputum, etc., placed on a microscope slide for analysis. **3.** A substance to be smeared on something, as a glaze for pottery. **4.** A slanderous attack; defamation. [OE < *smeoru* grease]

smear·y (smir′ē) *adj.* **smear·i·er, smear·i·est** Greasy, viscous, or staining; also, smeared. — **smear′i·ness** *n.*

smell (smel) *v.* **smelled** or **smelt, smell·ing** *v.t.* **1.** To perceive by means of the nose and its olfactory nerves. **2.** To perceive the odor of; scent. **3.** To test by odor or smell. **4.** To discover or detect as if by smelling: often with *out*. — *v.i.* **5.** To emit an odor or perfume: frequently with *of*; also, to give indications of, as if by odor: to *smell* of treason. **6.** To be malodorous. **7.** To use the sense of smell. **8.** To pry; investigate: with *about*. — *n.* **1.** The special sense by means of which odors are perceived. **2.** The sensation excited through the olfactory nerves. **3.** That which is directly perceived by this sense; an odor. **4.** A hint; trace. **5.** An act of smelling. [ME *smellen*] — **smell′er** *n.*

— **Syn.** (noun) **3.** *Smell* often suggests a strong and slightly unpleasant sensation, and *odor*, a more delicate and pleasing one. *Scent* is always delicate. *Aroma*, *fragrance*, and *perfume* are pleasant. *Stench* and *stink* are sickening and unpleasant.

smelling salts Pungent or aromatic salts, or mixtures of such, often scented, used as stimulants by smelling.

smel·ly (smel′ē) *adj.* **·li·er, ·li·est** *Informal* Having an unpleasant smell; malodorous.

smelt[1] (smelt) *v.t. Metall.* **1.** To reduce (ores) by fusion in a furnace. **2.** To obtain (a metal) from the ore by a process including fusion. — *v.i.* **3.** To melt or fuse, as a metal. [< MDu. *smelten* to melt]

smelt[2] (smelt) *pl.* **smelts** or **smelt** Any of various small silvery food fishes of north Atlantic and Pacific waters. [OE]

smelt[3] (smelt) Alternative past tense and past participle of SMELL.

smelt·er (smel′tər) *n.* **1.** One engaged in smelting ore. **2.** An establishment for smelting: also **smelt′er·y.**

smidg·en (smij′ən) *n. U.S. Informal* A tiny bit or part.

smi·lax (smī′laks) *n.* **1.** Any of various shrubby or herbaceous plants of the lily family, having thorny stems, flowers in umbels, and globular fruit, esp. one yielding sarsaparilla. **2.** A delicate twining greenhouse plant of the lily family, with greenish flowers. [< L < Gk. *smilax* yew]

smile (smīl) *n.* **1.** A pleased or amused expression of the face, characterized by a raising up of the corners of the mouth. **2.** A pleasant aspect: the *smile* of spring. **3.** Propitious disposition; favor; blessing: the *smile* of fortune. — *v.* **smiled, smil·ing** *v.i.* **1.** To give a smile; wear a cheerful aspect. **2.** To show approval or favor: often with *upon*. — *v.t.* **3.** To express by means of a smile. [ME *smilen*, prob. < LG] — **smil′er** *n.* — **smil′ing·ly** *adv.* — **smil′ing·ness** *n.*

— **Syn.** (noun) **1.** In a *smile*, the mouth is closed or slightly opened; in a *grin* it is opened wide, displaying the teeth. A *smile* suggests pleasure, satisfaction, approval, or amity. A *grin* may denote amusement, triumph, or irony.

smirch (smûrch) *v.t.* **1.** To soil, as with grime; smear. **2.** To defame; degrade: to *smirch* a reputation. — *n.* The act of smirching, or the state of being smirched; a smear; a moral stain or defect. [ME < OF *esmorcher* to hurt]

smirk (smûrk) *v.i.* To smile in a silly, self-complacent, or affected manner. — *n.* An affected or artificial smile. [OE *smearcian*] — **smirk′er** *n.* — **smirk′ing·ly** *adv.*

smite (smīt) *v.* **smote, smit·ten** or **smit** or **smote, smit·ing** *v.t.* **1.** To strike (something). **2.** To strike a blow with (something); cause to strike. **3.** To cut, sever, or break by a blow: usually with *off* or *out*. **4.** To strike with disaster;

afflict. **5.** To affect powerfully with sudden feeling. **6.** To cause to feel regret or remorse. **7.** To affect as if by a blow: The thought *smote* him. **8.** To kill by a sudden blow. — *v.i.* **9.** To come with sudden force; also, to knock against something. [OE *smītan*] — **smit′er** *n.*

smith (smith) *n.* **1.** One who shapes metals by hammering: *goldsmith, tinsmith.* **2.** A blacksmith. [OE]

smith·er·eens (smith′ə·rēnz′) *n.pl. Informal* Fragments produced as by an explosion. Also **smith′ers** (-ərz). [Cf. dial. E (Irish) *smidirin* fragment]

smith·y (smith′ē, smith′ē) *n. pl.* **smith·ies** A blacksmith's shop; a forge. [< ON *smithja*]

smit·ten (smit′n) Alternative past participle of SMITE. — *adj.* **1.** Struck with sudden force; gravely afflicted. **2.** Having the affections suddenly attracted.

smock (smok) *n.* A loose outer garment of light material worn to protect one's clothes. — *v.t.* **1.** To clothe in a smock. **2.** To decorate with smocking. [OE *smoc*]

smock·ing (smok′ing) *n.* Needlework in which the material is stitched into very small pleats or gathers, forming a kind of honeycomb ornamentation.

smog (smog) *n.* A combination of smoke and fog, esp. as seen in thickly populated industrial and manufacturing areas. [Blend of SM(OKE) and (F)OG]

smoke (smōk) *n.* **1.** The volatilized products of the combustion of organic substances, as coal, wood, etc., forming a suspension of carbon particles in a gas. **2.** Anything transient and unsubstantial; a useless or ephemeral result. **3.** The act of smoking a pipe, cigar, etc. **4.** A period of time during which one smokes tobacco. **5.** *Informal* A cigarette, cigar, or pipeful of tobacco. — *v.* **smoked, smok·ing** *v.i.* **1.** To emit or give out smoke. **2.** To inhale and exhale the smoke from a pipe, cigarette, etc. — *v.t.* **3.** To inhale and exhale the smoke of (tobacco, opium, etc.); also, to use (a pipe, etc.) for this purpose. **4.** To cure (meat, fish, etc.) by treating with smoke. **5.** To apply smoke to (animals) in order to drive away: with *out*. **6.** To force out of hiding (a criminal, etc.) or secrecy (information): with *out*. [OE *smoca*]

smoke·house (smōk′hous′) *n.* A building or closed room in which meat, fish, hides, etc., are cured by smoke.

smoke·less (smōk′lis) *adj.* Having or emitting little or no smoke: *smokeless* powder.

smok·er (smō′kər) *n.* **1.** One who or that which smokes. **2.** A smoking car. **3.** A social gathering of men.

smoke screen A dense cloud of smoke used to prevent enemy observation of a place, force, or operation. Also **smoke blanket, smoke curtain.**

smoke·stack (smōk′stak′) *n.* **1.** An upright pipe, usu. of sheet or plate iron, through which combustion gases from a furnace are discharged into the air. **2.** The funnel of a steamboat or locomotive, or the chimney of a factory, etc.

smoking jacket A short coat worn instead of a regular suit coat as a lounging jacket.

smok·y (smō′kē) *adj.* **smok·i·er, smok·i·est** **1.** Giving forth smoke. **2.** Mixed with smoke: *smoky* air. **3.** Emitting smoke improperly and unpleasantly, as from bad draft. **4.** Discolored with smoke. **5.** Smoke-colored; dark gray. **6.** Covered with mist. — **smok′i·ly** *adv.* — **smok′i·ness** *n.*

smol·der (smōl′dər) *v.i.* **1.** To burn and smoke with little smoke and no flame. **2.** To exist in a latent state; to manifest suppressed feeling. — *n.* Smoke. [ME *smoldren*]

smolt (smōlt) *n.* A young salmon on its first descent from the river to the sea. [? Akin to SMELT[2]]

smooth (smooth) *adj.* **1.** Having a surface without irregularities; not rough; continuously even. **2.** Having no impediments or obstructions; easy; free from shocks or jolts. **3.** Calm and unruffled; bland; mild. **4.** Flowing melodiously: a *smooth* style. **5.** Suave, as in speech; flattering: often implying deceit. **6.** Free from hair; beardless. **7.** Without lumps; having the elements perfectly blended. **8.** Offering no resistance to a body sliding along its surface; without friction. — *adv.* Calmly; evenly. — *v.t.* **1.** To make smooth or even on the surface. **2.** To make easy or less difficult: to *smooth* one's path. **3.** To free from or remove obstructions. **4.** To render less harsh or softer and more flowing. **5.** To soften the worst features of; palliate: usu. with *over*. **6.** To make calm; mollify. — *v.i.* **7.** To become smooth. — **to smooth (someone's) ruffled feathers** To mollify. — *n.* **1.** The smooth portion or surface of anything. **2.** The act of smoothing. [OE *smōth*] — **smooth′er** *n.* — **smooth′ly** *adv.* — **smooth′ness** *n.*

smooth·bore (smooth′bôr′, -bōr′) *n.* A firearm with an unrifled bore. Also **smooth bore.** — **smooth′bored′** *adj.*

smooth breathing In classical Greek: **a** The absence of an aspirated sound. **b** The symbol (′) indicating this.

smooth·en (smoo′thən) *v.t. & v.i.* To smooth.

smör·gås·bord (smôr′gəs·bôrd, *Sw.* smœr′gös·bôrd) *n.* **1.** Scandinavian hors d'oeuvres. **2.** A buffet supper consisting of such hors d'oeuvres. **3.** A restaurant serving **smörgåsbord.** Also **smor'gas·bord.** [< Sw.]

smote (smōt) Past tense of SMITE.

smoth·er (smuth'ər) *v.t.* **1.** To prevent the respiration of; suffocate; stifle. **2.** To cover, or cause to smolder, as a fire. **3.** To hide or suppress: to *smother* one's feelings. **4.** To cook in a covered dish or under some other substance. — *v.i.* **5.** To suffocate, as from lack of air, etc. **6.** To be covered without air, as a fire. **7.** To be hidden or suppressed, as wrath. — *n.* **1.** That which smothers, as stifling vapor or dust. **2.** The state of being smothered; suppression. [Earlier *smorther*] — **smoth'er·y** *adj.*

smoul·der (smōl'dər) See SMOLDER.

smudge (smuj) *v.* **smudged, smudg·ing** *v.t.* **1.** To smear; soil. **2.** To protect (from frost, insects, etc.) by a heavy, smoky pall. — *v.i.* **3.** To cause a smudge. **4.** To be smudged. — *n.* **1.** A soiling, as of dry dirt or soot; smear; stain. **2.** A smoky fire or its smoke for driving away insects, preventing frost, etc. [Var. of SMUTCH]

smudg·y (smuj'ē) *adj.* **smudg·i·er, smudg·i·est** Full of or causing smudges. — **smudg'i·ly** *adv.* — **smudg'i·ness** *n.*

smug (smug) *adj.* **smug·ger, smug·gest** **1.** Characterized by a self-satisfied or complacent air. **2.** Trim; spruce. [Cf. LG *smuk* neat] — **smug'ly** *adv.* — **smug'ness** *n.*

smug·gle (smug'əl) *v.* **·gled, ·gling** *v.t.* **1.** To take (goods) into or out of a country without payment of lawful duties. **2.** To bring in illicitly. — *v.i.* **3.** To practice smuggling. [< LG *smuggeln*] — **smug'gler** *n.* — **smug'gling** *n.*

smut (smut) *n.* **1.** The blackening made by soot, smoke, etc. **2.** Obscenity; obscene language. **3.** Any of various fungus diseases of plants, in which the affected parts change into a dusty black powder. **4.** Any of the fungi causing such a disease. — *v.* **smut·ted, smut·ting** *v.t.* **1.** To blacken or stain, as with soot or smoke. **2.** To affect with smut, as growing grain. **3.** To pollute; defame. — *v.i.* **4.** To give off smut. **5.** To be or become stained. [< LG *schmutt* dirt]

smutch (smuch) *v.t.* To smudge; soil. — *n.* A smear; smudge. [Cf. MHG *smutzen* to smear] — **smutch'y** *adj.*

smut·ty (smut'ē) *adj.* **·ti·er, ·ti·est** **1.** Soiled with smut; black; stained. **2.** Affected with smut: *smutty* corn. **3.** Obscene; coarse; indecent. — **smut'ti·ly** *adv.* — **smut'ti·ness** *n.*

snack (snak) *n.* **1.** A slight, hurried meal. **2.** A share of something. [< MDu. *snacken* to bite]

snaf·fle (snaf'əl) *n.* A horse's bit without a curb, jointed in the middle. Also **snaf'fle·bit** ('-bit'). — *v.t.* **·fled, ·fling** To control with a snaffle. [Cf. Du. *snavel* muzzle]

sna·fu (sna·fōō', sna'fōō) *Slang adj.* In a state of utter confusion. — *v.t.* **·fued, ·fu·ing** To put into confusion. [Acronym for "Situation normal, all fouled up"]

snag (snag) *n.* **1.** A jagged or stumpy knot or protuberance, esp. the stumpy base of a branch. **2.** A broken or projecting tooth. **3.** The trunk of a tree fixed in the bottom of a river, etc., by which boats are sometimes pierced. **4.** Any obstacle or difficulty. — *v.* **snagged, snag·ging** *v.t.* **1.** To injure, destroy, or impede by or as by a snag. **2.** To clear of snags. — *v.i.* **3.** To run upon a snag: said esp. of river craft. [Prob. < Scand.] — **snag'gy** *adj.*

snag·gle·tooth (snag'əl·tōōth') *n.* *pl.* **·teeth** A tooth that is broken, projecting, or out of alignment with the others. — **snag'gle·toothed'** ('-tōōtht', -tōōthd') *adj.*

snail (snāl) *n.* **1.** Any of a large class of slow-moving mollusks of aquatic and terrestrial habits and having a spiral shell. **2.** A slow or lazy person. [OE *snægl*]

snail pace A very slow gait or forward movement. Also **snail's pace.** — **snailpaced** (snāl'pāst') *adj.*

snake (snāk) *n.* **1.** Any of a large order of scaly, legless reptiles with long, slim bodies and tapering tails; some kinds inject venom into the victim through tubular fangs. **2.** A treacherous person. **3.** A flexible, resilient wire used to clean clogged drains, etc. — *v.* **snaked, snak·ing** *v.t.* **1.** To drag by pulling forcibly from one end, as a log. **2.** To pull with jerks. — *v.i.* **3.** To move like a snake. [OE *snaca*]

snake·bite (snāk'bīt') *n.* **1.** The bite of a snake. **2.** Poisoning caused by the venom of a snake.

snake charmer An entertainer who charms venomous snakes by rhythmic motions of his body and by music.

snake dance **1.** A ceremonial dance of the Hopi Indians of Arizona. **2.** A procession of persons moving in a winding or zigzag line to celebrate an athletic victory, etc.

snake·root (snāk'rōōt', -rŏōt') *n.* **1.** Any of various plants having roots reputed to be effective against snakebite. **2.** The root of any of these plants.

snak·y (snā'kē) *adj.* **snak·i·er, snak·i·est** **1.** Of or like a snake; serpentine; winding. **2.** Insinuating; cunning; treacherous. **3.** Full of snakes. — **snak'i·ly** *adv.* — **snak'i·ness** *n.*

snap (snap) *v.* **snapped, snap·ping** *v.i.* **1.** To make a sharp, quick sound. **2.** To break suddenly with a cracking noise. **3.** To fly off or give way quickly, as when tension is suddenly

SNAIL

relaxed. **4.** To make the jaws come suddenly together in an effort to bite: often with *up* or *at.* **5.** To seize or snatch suddenly: often with *up* or *at.* **6.** To speak sharply, harshly, or irritably: often with *at.* **7.** To emit, or seem to emit, a spark or flash of light: said of the eyes. **8.** To close, fasten, etc., with a click. **9.** To move or act with sudden, neat gestures: He *snapped* to attention. — *v.t.* **10.** To seize suddenly or eagerly, with or as with the teeth: often with *up.* **11.** To sever with a snapping sound. **12.** To utter, address, or interrupt harshly, abruptly, or irritably. **13.** To cause to make a sharp, quick sound: to *snap* one's fingers. **14.** To close, fasten, etc., with a snapping sound. **15.** To cause to move suddenly, neatly, etc. **16.** To photograph with a camera. **17.** In football, to put in play. — **to snap one's fingers at** To be unimpressed or unintimidated by. — **to snap out of it** *Informal* **1.** To recover quickly, as from a state of depression. **2.** To change one's attitude. — *n.* **1.** The act of snapping, or a sharp, quick sound produced by it. **2.** A sudden breaking of anything, or the sound so produced. **3.** Any catch, fastener, or other similar device. **4.** A sudden seizing or effort to seize with or as with the teeth. **5.** A quick blow of the thumb sprung from the finger or of the finger from the thumb. **6.** The sudden release of the tension of a spring or elastic cord. **7.** A small, thin, crisp cake or cooky. **8.** Brisk energy; vigor; vim; zip. **9.** A brief spell; a sudden turn: said chiefly of cold weather. **10.** *Informal* Any task or duty easy to perform. **11.** A bit: It is not worth a *snap.* **12.** A snapshot. — *adj.* **1.** Made or done suddenly and without consideration; offhand. **2.** Fastening with a snap. **3.** *Informal* Easy; requiring little work. — *adv.* With a snap; quickly. [< MDu. *snappen* to bite at]

snap·drag·on (snap'drag'ən) *n.* A plant of the figwort family having solitary flowers likened to dragons' heads.

snap·per (snap'ər) *n.* **1.** One who or that which snaps. **2.** A large food fish of the Gulf Coast, as the **red snapper.** **3.** A snapping turtle.

snapping turtle A large, voracious, fresh-water turtle of North America, much used as food.

snap·pish (snap'ish) *adj.* **1.** Apt to speak crossly or tartly. **2.** Disposed to snap, as a dog. — **snap'pish·ly** *adv.* — **snap'pish·ness** *n.*

snap·py (snap'ē) *adj.* **·pi·er, ·pi·est** **1.** *Informal* Brisk; energetic; vivacious. **2.** *Informal* Smart or stylish in appearance. **3.** Snappish. — **make it snappy** *Informal* Hurry up! — **snap'pi·ly** *adv.* — **snap'pi·ness** *n.*

snap·shot (snap'shot') *n.* **1.** A photograph taken with a small camera without timing. **2.** A shot made without aim.

snare¹ (snâr) *n.* **1.** A device, as a noose, for catching birds or other animals; a trap. **2.** Anything by which one is entangled or entrapped. **3.** *Surg.* A loop of wire used to remove tumors and other growths from the body. — *v.t.* **snared, snar·ing** **1.** To catch with a snare. **2.** To capture by trickery; entice. [OE < ON *snara*] — **snar'er** *n.*

snare² (snâr) *n.* **1.** One of the cords or wires stretched across one of the heads of a snare drum to increase the resonance. **2.** A snare drum. [< MDu., a string]

snare drum A small drum having snares on one head.

snarl¹ (snärl) *n.* A sharp, harsh, angry growl; harsh or quarrelsome utterance. — *v.i.* **1.** To growl harshly, as a dog. **2.** To speak angrily and resentfully. — *v.t.* **3.** To utter or express with a snarl. [Freq. of obs. *snar* to growl] — **snarl'er** *n.* — **snarl'ing·ly** *adv.* — **snarl'y** *adj.*

snarl² (snärl) *n.* **1.** A tangle, as of hair or yarn. **2.** Any complication or entanglement. **3.** *Informal* A quarrel. — *v.i.* **1.** To get into a snarl or tangle. — *v.t.* **2.** To put into a snarl or tangle. **3.** To confuse; entangle mentally. [< SNARE¹] — **snarl'er** *n.* — **snarl'y** *adj.*

snatch (snach) *v.t.* **1.** To seize or lay hold of suddenly, hastily, or eagerly. **2.** To take or remove suddenly. **3.** To take or obtain as the opportunity arises. **4.** *Slang* To kidnap. — *v.i.* **5.** To attempt to seize swiftly and suddenly: with *at.* **6.** To be eager to accept: with *at.* — *Syn.* See STEAL. — *n.* **1.** An act of snatching. **2.** A brief period. **3.** A small amount. **4.** *Slang* A kidnaping. **5.** In weightlifting, a bringing of the weight from the floor to above the head in one motion. [ME *snacchen*] — **snatch'er** *n.*

snatch block *Naut.* A single block having an opening in one cheek to receive a rope. For illus. see BLOCK¹.

snatch·y (snach'ē) *adj.* **snatch·i·er, snatch·i·est** Interrupted; spasmodic.

sneak (snēk) *v.i.* **1.** To move or go in a stealthy manner. **2.** To act with cowardice or servility. — *v.t.* **3.** To put, give, transfer, move, etc., secretly or stealthily. **4.** *Informal* To pilfer. — *n.* **1.** One who sneaks. **2.** An act of sneaking. — *adj.* Stealthy; covert. [OE *snīcan* to creep]

sneak·er (snē'kər) *n.* **1.** A sneak. **2.** *pl. U.S. Informal* Rubber-soled canvas shoes esp. for sports.

sneak·ing (snē'king) *adj.* **1.** Acting in an underhand way. **2.** Secret: a *sneaking* suspicion. — **sneak'ing·ly** *adv.*

sneak preview *U.S.* The showing of a new motion picture before its date of release.

sneak·y (snē′kē) *adj.* **sneak·i·er, sneak·i·est** Like a sneak; sneaking. **— sneak′i·ly** *adv.* **— sneak′i·ness** *n.*

sneer (snir) *n.* **1.** A grimace of contempt or derision made by slightly raising the upper lip. **2.** A mean insinuation. — *v.i.* **1.** To make or show a sneer. **2.** To express derision or contempt in speech, writing, etc. — *v.t.* **3.** To utter with a sneer or in a sneering manner. [ME *sneren*] **— sneer′er** *n.* **— sneer′ing·ly** *adv.*

sneeze (snēz) **sneezed, sneez·ing** *v.i.* To drive air forcibly and audibly out of the mouth and nose by a spasmodic involuntary action caused by irritation of the mucus membranes. **— not to be sneezed at** *Informal* Worthy of consideration. **—** *n.* An act of sneezing. [Alter. of ME *fnese*, OE *fnēosan* to sneeze] **— sneez′er** *n.* **— sneez′y** *adj.*

snell (snel) *n.* A short line of gut, horsehair, etc., bearing a fish hook, to be attached to a longer line. [Origin unknown]

snick (snik) *n.* A small cut; nick; snip. **—** *v.t.* To cut a nick in. [See SNICKERSNEE.]

snick·er (snik′ər) *n.* A half-suppressed or smothered laugh, often in derision. **—** *v.i.* **1.** To utter a snicker. **—** *v.t.* **2.** To utter or express with a snicker. [Imit.]

snick·er·snee (snik′ər·snē′) *n.* A swordlike knife. [Alter. of earlier *snick* or *snee* to thrust or cut]

snide (snīd) *adj.* Malicious or derogatory; nasty: *snide* comments. [Origin unknown]

sniff (snif) *v.i.* **1.** To breathe through the nose in short, quick, audible inhalations. **2.** To express contempt, etc., by or as by sniffing: often with *at*. **—** *v.t.* **3.** To breathe in through the nose; inhale. **4.** To smell with sniffs. **5.** To perceive as if by sniffs: to *sniff* peril. **6.** To express (contempt) by sniffs. **—** *n.* **1.** An act or the sound of sniffing. **2.** Perception by or as by sniffing. **3.** That which is inhaled by sniffing. [Appar. back formation < SNIVEL]

snif·fle (snif′əl) *v.i.* **·fled, ·fling** **1.** To breathe through the nose noisily. **2.** To snivel or whimper. **—** *n.* A snuffle. **— the sniffles** *Informal* A head cold or the sniffling that results. [Freq. of SNIFF]

snif·ter (snif′tər) *n.* **1.** A pear-shaped liquor glass. **2.** *U.S. Slang* A small drink of liquor. [< *snift*, var. of SNIFF]

snig·ger (snig′ər) *n.* A snicker. **—** *v.t. & v.i.* To snicker. [Var. of SNICKER] **— snig′ger·er** *n.*

snip (snip) *v.* **snipped, snip·ping** *v.t.* **1.** To clip, remove, or cut with a light stroke of shears: often with *off*. **—** *v.i.* **2.** To cut with small, quick strokes. **—** *n.* **1.** An act of snipping. **2.** A small piece snipped off. **3.** *U.S. Informal* A small or insignificant person or thing. [< Du. *snippen*]

snipe (snīp) *n.* *pl.* **snipe** or **snipes** Any of various long-billed shore or marsh birds, allied to the woodcock. **—** *v.i.* **sniped, snip·ing** **1.** To hunt or shoot snipe. **2.** To shoot at or pick off individual enemies from hiding. [< ON *snipa*]

snip·er (snī′pər) *n.* One who shoots an enemy from hiding.

snip·pet (snip′it) *n.* **1.** A small piece snipped off. **2.** A small portion or share.

snip·py (snip′ē) *adj.* **·pi·er, ·pi·est** *Informal* **1.** Pert; impertinent. **2.** Fragmentary; scrappy. Also **snip′pet·y** (-it·ē).

snitch (snich) *Slang* *v.t.* **1.** To grab quickly; steal; swipe. **—** *v.i.* **2.** To turn informer: often with *on*. [Origin unknown]

sniv·el (sniv′əl) *v.* **·eled** or **·elled, ·el·ing** or **·el·ling** *v.i.* **1.** To cry in a snuffling manner. **2.** To whine. **3.** To run at the nose. **—** *v.t.* **4.** To utter with sniveling. **—** *n.* **1.** The act of sniveling. **2.** Nasal mucus. [OE *snyflung* mucus from the nose] **— sniv′el·er** or **sniv′el·ler** *n.*

snob (snob) *n.* **1.** One who makes birth, wealth, education, or intelligence the sole criterion of worth. **2.** Any pretender to gentility. [Origin uncertain] **— snob′ber·y** *n.*

snob·bish (snob′ish) *adj.* Characteristic of or befitting a snob or snobs. **— snob′bish·ly** *adv.* **— snob′bish·ness** *n.*

Sno·cat (snō′kat′) *n.* A trucklike vehicle used for traveling in arctic conditions: a trade name. Also **sno′cat.**

snood (snood) *n.* A small, meshlike cap or bag, worn by women to keep the hair in place. **—** *v.t.* To bind (hair) with a snood. [OE *snōd*]

snoop (snoop) *Informal* *v.i.* To look or pry into things with which one has no business. **—** *n.* One who snoops: also **snoop′er.** [< Du. *snoepen* to eat goodies on the sly]

snoop·y (snoo′pē) *adj.* **snoop·i·er, snoop·i·est** *Informal* Given to snooping.

snoot (snoot) *n.* *Informal* **1.** The nose or face. **2.** A wry face; a grimace. [Var. of SNOUT]

snoot·y (snoo′tē) *adj.* **snoot·i·er, snoot·i·est** *U.S. Informal* Conceited or supercilious.

snooze (snooz) *Informal* *v.i.* **snoozed, snooz·ing** To sleep lightly; doze. **—** *n.* A short nap. [Origin uncertain]

snore (snôr, snōr) *v.i.* **snored, snor·ing** To breathe in sleep with a hoarse, rough noise, usu. with an open mouth. **—** *n.* An act or the noise of snoring. [ME *snoren*] **— snor′er** *n.*

snor·kel (snôr′kəl) *n.* **1.** A mouth tube permitting a skin diver to breathe while swimming on the surface with his face under water. **2.** A tubelike apparatus for the ventilation of a submerged submarine. [< G *schnörkel*, lit., spiral]

snort (snôrt) *v.i.* **1.** To force air violently and noisily through the nostrils, as a horse. **2.** To express indignation, ridicule, etc., by a snort. **3.** *Informal* To laugh with a boisterous outburst. **—** *v.t.* **4.** To utter or express by snorting. **—** *n.* **1.** The act or sound of snorting. **2.** *Slang* A small drink. [ME *snorten*] **— snort′er** *n.*

snot (snot) *n.* **1.** Mucus from or in the nose: a vulgar term. **2.** *Slang* A low or mean fellow. [OE *gesnot*]

snot·ty (snot′ē) *adj.* **·ti·er, ·ti·est** **1.** Dirtied with snot: a vulgar term. **2.** *Slang* Contemptible; mean; paltry. **3.** *Slang* Impudent; proudly conceited; saucy.

snout (snout) *n.* **1.** The forward projecting part of a beast's head. **2.** Something resembling a hog's snout. **3.** A person's nose: a contemptuous or humorous term. **—** *v.t.* To provide with a snout. [ME *snūte*] **— snout′ed** *adj.*

snow (snō) *n.* **1.** Water vapor in the air precipitated in the form of minute flakes when the temperature is below 32° F. ◆ Collateral adjective: *nival.* **2.** Anything resembling snow. **3.** A fall of snow; snowstorm. **4.** *Slang* Heroin or cocaine. **5.** The pattern of snowlike flecks appearing on a television screen. **—** *v.i.* **1.** To fall as snow. **—** *v.t.* **2.** To scatter or cause to fall as or like snow. **3.** To cover, enclose, or obstruct with or as with snow. **4.** *U.S. Slang* To subject to a snow job. [OE *snāw*]

snow·ball (snō′bôl′) *n.* **1.** A small round mass of snow compressed to be thrown, as in sport. **—** *v.i.* **1.** To throw snowballs. **2.** To gain in size, importance, etc., as a snowball that rolls over snow. **—** *v.t.* **3.** To throw snowballs at.

snow·bank (snō′bangk′) *n.* A large mound of snow.

snow·ber·ry (snō′ber′ē) *n.* *pl.* **·ries** A bushy American shrub having white berries: also called *waxberry.*

snow·bird (snō′bûrd′) *n.* **1.** The junco. **2.** *Slang* A cocaine or heroin addict.

snow blindness A temporary dimming of the sight caused by light reflected by snow. **— snow-blind** (snō′blīnd′) *adj.*

snow·bound (snō′bound′) *adj.* Hemmed in or forced to remain in a place because of heavy snow; snowed in.

snow bunting Any of various finches, the male of which in the breeding season is snow-white with black markings.

snow·cap (snō′kap′) *n.* A crest of snow, as on a mountain peak. **— snow′-capped′** *adj.*

snow·clad (snō′klad′) *adj.* Covered with snow.

snow·drift (snō′drift′) *n.* A snowbank made by the wind.

snow·drop (snō′drop′) *n.* A low, European, early-blooming bulbous plant, bearing a single, white, drooping flower.

snow·fall (snō′fôl′) *n.* **1.** A fall of snow. **2.** The amount of snow that falls in a given period.

snow fence *U.S. & Canadian* Portable fencing of thin, closely placed slats, used to prevent the drifting of snow over roads, fields, etc., by causing it to drift elsewhere.

snow·flake (snō′flāk′) *n.* **1.** One of the small, feathery masses in which snow falls. **3.** Any of certain plants allied to and resembling the snowdrop.

snow job *U.S. Slang* An elaborate, insincere speech contrived to impress or persuade.

snow line The limit of perpetual snow on the sides of mountains. Also **snow limit.**

snow·mo·bile (snō′mō·bēl) *n.* An enclosed vehicle used for traveling over snow, ice, etc., often equipped with caterpillar treads. [< SNOW + (AUTO)MOBILE]

snow·plow (snō′plou′) *n.* Any plowlike device for turning fallen snow aside from a road or railroad, or for the removal of snow from buildings. Also **snow′plough′.**

snow·shoe (snō′shoo′) *n.* A device, usu. a network of thongs in a wooden frame, fastened on the foot and worn in walking over snow. **—** *v.i.* **·shoed, ·shoe·ing** To walk on snowshoes. **— snow′sho′er** (-shoo′ər) *n.*

snow·storm (snō′stôrm′) *n.* A storm with a fall of snow.

snow·y (snō′ē) *adj.* **snow·i·er, snow·i·est** **1.** Abounding in or full of snow. **2.** Pure; unblemished; spotless: *snowy* linen. **— snow′i·ly** *adv.* **— snow′i·ness** *n.*

snub (snub) *v.t.* **snubbed, snub·bing** **1.** To treat with contempt or disdain, esp. by ignoring; slight. **2.** To rebuke with a cutting remark. **3.** To stop or check, as a rope in running out, by taking a turn about a post, etc.; also, to make fast (a boat, etc.) thus. **—** *adj.* Short; pug: said of the nose. **—** *n.* **1.** An act of snubbing; deliberate slight. **2.** A sudden checking, as of a running rope or cable. [< ON *snubba* to snub] **— snub′ber** *n.*

snub-nosed (snub′nōzd′) *adj.* Having a pug or snub nose.

snuff¹ (snuf) *v.t.* **1.** To draw in (air, etc.) through the nose. **2.** To smell: sniff. **—** *v.i.* **3.** To snort; sniff. **—** *n.* An act of snuffing. [< MDu. *snuffen*]

snuff² (snuf) *n.* The charred portion of a wick. **—** *v.t.* **1.** To extinguish: with *out.* **2.** To crop the snuff from (a wick). [Cf. G *schnuppe* snuff of a candle] **— snuf′fer** *n.*

---

snuff³ (snuf) *n.* Pulverized tobacco to be inhaled into the nostrils. **— up to snuff** *Informal* Meeting the usual standard, as in quality, health, etc. **—** *v.i.* To take snuff. [< Du. *snuf*] **— snuf′fer** *n.* **— snuff′y** *adj.* **— snuf′fi·ness** *n.*

snuff·box (snuf′boks′) *n.* A small box for carrying snuff.

snuf·fle (snuf′əl) *v.* **·fled, ·fling** *v.t.* **1.** To sniffle. **2.** To breathe noisily, as a dog following a scent. **3.** To talk through the nose; snivel. **—** *v.t.* **4.** To utter in a nasal tone. **—** *n.* **1.** An act of snuffing, or the sound made by it. **2.** An affected nasal or emotional voice or twang. [Freq. of SNUFF] **— snuf′fler** *n.* **— snuf′fly** *adj.*

snug (snug) *adj.* **snug·ger, snug·gest 1.** Closely and comfortably sheltered, covered, or situated. **2.** Close or compact; comfortable; cozy. **3.** Having everything closely secured; trim: said of a ship. **4.** Fitting closely but comfortably. **—** *v.* **snugged, snug·ging** *v.t.* **1.** To make snug. **—** *v.i.* **2,** To snuggle; move close. **— to snug down** To make a vessel ready for a storm by reducing sail, etc. [Prob. < LG. Cf. Du. *snugger* clean, smooth.] **— snug′ly** *adv.* **— snug′ness** *n.*

snug·gle (snug′əl) *v.t. & v.i.* **·gled, ·gling** To lie or draw close; cuddle: often with *up* or *together.*

so¹ (sō) *adv.* **1.** To this or that or such a degree; to this or that extent. **2.** In this, that, or such a manner; in the same way: often following a clause beginning with *as,* or preceding one beginning with *that:* As the twig is bent, *so* is the tree inclined. **3.** Just as said, directed, suggested or implied: Do it *so;* I will do *so.* **4.** According to fact: That is not *so.* **5.** *Informal* To an extreme degree; very. **6.** About as many or as much stated: I shall stay a day or *so.* **7.** According to the truth of what is sworn or averred: *So* help me God. **8.** To such an extent: used elliptically for *so much:* I love him *so!* **9.** Too: used in emphatic contradiction of a negative statement: You can *so!* **10.** Consequently; thus; therefore. **11.** *Informal* It seems that; can it be that; apparently: *So* you don't like it here! **12.** Let it be that way; very well. **— conj. 1.** With the purpose that; usu. with *that:* They left early *so* that they would avoid meeting him. **2.** As a consequence of which: He consented, *so* they left. **— interj. 1.** Is that so! **2.** Hold still! [OE *swā*]
♦ Careful writers use *so that* rather than the informal *so* (conj. def. 1) to introduce clauses of result or purpose, as in "I want to leave now *so that* I won't be late."

so² (sō) *n. Music* Sol.

soak (sōk) *v.t.* **1.** To place in liquid until thoroughly saturated; steep. **2.** To wet thoroughly; drench. **3.** To suck up; absorb: with *in* or *up.* **4.** To take in eagerly or readily: with *up:* to *soak* up knowledge. **5.** *Informal* To drink, esp. to excess: with *up.* **6.** *U.S. Slang* To overcharge. **7.** *U.S. Slang* To strike hard. **—** *v.i.* **8.** To remain or be placed in liquid till saturated. **9.** To penetrate; pass: with *in* or *into.* **10.** *U.S. Slang* To drink to excess. **—** *n.* **1.** The act of soaking, or state of being soaked. **2.** Liquid in which something is soaked. **3.** *Slang* A hard drinker. [OE *socian*] **— soak′er** *n.*

so-and-so (sō′ən·sō′) *n.* **1.** An unnamed person or thing. **2.** *Informal* A euphemism for many offensive epithets.

soap (sōp) *n.* **1.** A cleansing agent made by decomposing the glyceryl esters of fats and oils with alkalis. **2.** A metallic salt of one of the fatty acids. **3.** *U.S. Slang* Money used for bribery. **— no soap** *U.S. Slang* **1.** No; not a chance. **2.** Futile. **—** *v.t.* To rub or treat with soap. [OE *sāpe*]

soap·ber·ry (sōp′ber′ē) *n.* *pl.* **·ries 1.** The fruit of any of mostly tropical trees and shrubs, sometimes used as a substitute for soap. **2.** A tree or shrub bearing this fruit.

soap·box (sōp′boks′) *n.* **1.** A box or crate for soap. **2.** Any box or crate used as a platform by street orators. Also **soap box.** **— soapbox oratory** Impromptu or crude oratory.

soapbox derby *U.S.* A race among unpowered racing cars, steered down a slope by the boys who have built them.

soap opera A daytime television or radio serial drama usu. dealing with highly emotional domestic themes.

soap·stone (sōp′stōn′) *n.* Steatite.

soap·suds (sōp′sudz′) *n. pl.* Suds of water and soap.

soap·y (sō′pē) *adj.* **soap·i·er, soap·i·est 1.** Resembling or consisting of soap. **2.** Smeared with soap. **3.** *Slang* Flattering; unctuous. **— soap′i·ly** *adv.* **— soap′i·ness** *n.*

soar (sôr, sōr) *v.i.* **1.** To rise high into the air. **2.** To sail through the air without perceptibly moving the wings, as a hawk or vulture. **3.** *Aeron.* To fly without power while gaining or holding altitude. **4.** To rise sharply above the usual level: Prices *soared.* **5.** To attain a lofty or exalted state. **—** *n.* The act of soaring; also, the height or range reached in soaring. [< F < L *ex* out + *aura* breeze, air] **— soar′er** *n.*

sob (sob) *v.* **sobbed, sob·bing** *v.i.* **1.** To weep with audible, convulsive catches of the breath. **2.** To make a sound like a sob. **—** *v.t.* **3.** To utter with sobs. **4.** To bring to a specified condition by sobbing: to *sob* oneself to sleep. **—** *n.* The act of sobbing. [ME *sobben*] **— sob′bing·ly** *adv.*

so·be·it (sō·bē′it) *conj. Archaic* If so; if only; provided.

so·ber (sō′bər) *adj.* **1.** Possessing or characterized by properly controlled faculties; well-balanced. **2.** Grave, sedate. **3.** Not drunk. **4.** Moderate or abstinent. **5.** Subdued or modest in color, manner of dress, etc. **—** *v.t. & v.i.* To make or become sober. [< OF < L *sobrius*] **— so′ber·ly** *adv.* **— so′ber·ness** *n.*

so·bri·e·ty (sō·brī′ə·tē) *n.* *pl.* **·ties 1.** The state or quality of being sober. **2.** Moderateness in temper or conduct.

so·bri·quet (sō′bri·kā) *n.* A fanciful or humorous appellation; a nickname: also *soubriquet.* [< F]

sob story *Slang* A sad personal narrative told to elicit pity.

so-called (sō′kôld′) *adj.* Called as stated; generally styled thus: often implying a doubtful or incorrect designation.

soc·cer (sok′ər) *n.* A form of football in which the ball is propelled toward the opponents' goal by kicking or by striking with the body or head: officially called *association football.* [Alter. of ASSOCIATION]

so·cia·ble (sō′shə·bəl) *adj.* **1.** Inclined to seek company; social. **2.** Agreeable in company; genial. **3.** Characterized by or affording occasion for agreeable conversation and friendliness. **—** *n. U.S.* An informal social gathering: also called *social.* [< F < L *sociabilis* friend] **— so′cia·bil′i·ty, so′cia·ble·ness** *n.* **— so′cia·bly** *adv.*

so·cial (sō′shəl) *adj.* **1.** Of or pertaining to society or its organization. **2.** Disposed to hold friendly intercourse with others; sociable; also, promoting friendly intercourse: a *social* club. **3.** Constituted to live in society: *social* beings. **4.** Of or pertaining to public welfare: *social* insurance. **5.** Of, pertaining to, or characteristic of persons considered aristocratic, fashionable, etc.: *social* register. **6.** Of animals or insects, living in communities. **7.** Venereal: *social* disease. **—** *n.* A sociable. [< L *socius* ally]

social disease A venereal disease.

so·cial·ism (sō′shəl·iz′əm) *n.* **1.** Public collective ownership or control of the basic means of production, distribution, and exchange, with the avowed aim of operating for use rather than for profit, and of assuring to each member of society an equitable share of goods, services, etc. **2.** The doctrines of those advocating this system.

so·cial·ist (sō′shəl·ist) *n.* An advocate of socialism. **—** *adj.* Socialistic.

so·cial·is·tic (sō′shəl·is′tik) *adj.* **1.** Of, pertaining to, or practicing socialism. **2.** Like or tending toward socialism.

Socialist Party The U.S. political party of socialism, formed in 1901 under the leadership of Eugene V. Debs.

so·cial·ite (sō′shəl·īt) *n. Informal* One who is prominent in fashionable society.

so·ci·al·i·ty (sō′shē·al′ə·tē) *n.* *pl.* **·ties** The state or character of being social; sociability.

so·cial·ize (sō′shəl·īz) *v.* **·ized, ·iz·ing** *v.t.* **1.** To place under group or government control. **2.** To make friendly, cooperative, or sociable. **3.** To convert or adapt to the needs of a social group. **—** *v.i.* **4.** *Informal* To take part in social activities. Also *Brit.* **so′cial·ise.** **— so′cial·i·za′tion** *n.*

socialized medicine A system proposing to supply the public with medical care at nominal cost, by regulating services and fees, by government subsidies to physicians, etc.

social register A directory of persons prominent in fashionable society.

social science 1. Sociology. **2.** Any field of knowledge dealing with human society, as economics, history, sociology, education, politics, ethics, etc.

social security *U.S.* A Federal program of old-age and unemployment insurance, public assistance to the blind, disabled, and dependent, and maternal and child welfare services.

social service Organized activity intended to advance human welfare. **— so·cial-ser·vice** (sō′shəl·sûr′vis) *adj.*

social studies *U.S.* In elementary and secondary schools, a course or unit of study based upon the social sciences.

social work Any clinical, social, or recreational service for improving community welfare, as through health clinics, recreational facilities, aid to the poor and the aged, etc.

so·ci·e·ty (sə·sī′ə·tē) *n.* *pl.* **·ties 1.** The system of community life in which individuals form a continuous and regulatory association for their mutual benefit and protection. **2.** The body of persons composing such a community; also, all people collectively. **3.** A number of persons regarded as having certain common interests, similar status, etc. **4.** The fashionable or aristocratic portion of a community. **5.** Association based on friendship or intimacy; companionship; also, one's friends or associates. [< OF *societe* < L *societas, -tatis* < *socius* friend] **— so·ci·e·tal** (sō·sī′ə·təl) *adj.*

Society of Friends A Christian religious group founded in England by George Fox about 1650, and characterized by the doctrine of "waiting upon the Spirit", for direct guidance and the repudiation of ritual, formal sacraments, oaths, and violence: commonly known as *Quakers.*

Society of Jesus The religious organization of the Jesuits.

socio- *combining form* **1.** Society; social. **2.** Sociology; sociological. [< F < L *socius* companion]

so·ci·o·ec·o·nom·ic (sō′sē·ō·ek′ə·nom′ik, sō′shē, -ē′kə-) *adj.* Social and economic: considered as a single factor: an upper *socioeconomic* group. — **so′ci·o·ec′o·nom′i·cal·ly** *adv.*

so·ci·ol·o·gy (sō′sē·ol′ə·jē, sō′shē-) *n.* The science that treats of the origin and evolution of human society and social phenomena. — **so·ci·o·log·ic** (sō′sē·ə·loj′ik) or **-i·cal** *adj.* — **so′ci·o·log′i·cal·ly** *adv.* — **so′ci·ol′o·gist** *n.*

so·ci·om·e·try (sō′sē·om′ə·trē, sō′shē-) *n.* The study of the interrelationships of individuals within a social group.

sock¹ (sok) *n. pl.* **socks;** *for def. 1 also* **sox** 1. A short stocking reaching above the ankle or just below the knee. 2. The light shoe worn by comic actors in the Greek and Roman drama. [OE < L *soccus* slipper]

sock² (sok) *Slang v.t.* To strike or hit, esp. with the fist; to punch. — *n.* A hard blow. [Origin unknown]

sock·et (sok′it) *n.* 1. *Mech.* A cavity or an opening adapted to receive and hold some corresponding piece or fixture. 2. *Anat.* A cavity or hollowed depression for the reception of an organ or part. — *v.t.* To furnish with, hold by, or put into a socket. [< AF *soket*, dim. of OF *soc* plowshare]

sock·eye (sok′ī′) *n.* A salmon of the Pacific coast, highly valued as a food fish. [Alter. of Salishan *sukkegh*]

So·crat·ic (sō·krat′ik) *adj.* Pertaining to or characteristic of Socrates: also **So·crat′i·cal.** — **So·crat′i·cal·ly** *adv.*

Socratic method The dialectic method of instruction by questions and answers, as adopted by Socrates.

sod (sod) *n.* 1. A piece of grassy surface soil held together by the matted roots of grass and weeds; a turf or divot. 2. The surface of the earth. — *v.t.* **sod·ded, sod·ding** To cover with sod. [< MDu. *sode* piece of turf]

so·da (sō′də) *n.* 1. Any of several white, alkaline compounds widely used in medicine, industry, and the arts. 2. A soft drink containing soda water and flavoring: also **soda pop.** 3. A drink made from soda water, ice cream, and, sometimes, flavoring. [< Med.L, ? < Ital. *soda* (*cenere*) solid (ash) < L *solidus*]

soda ash Crude sodium carbonate, widely used in the manufacture of glass, soaps, paper, etc.

soda cracker A thin, crisp cracker made with yeast-leavened dough containing soda.

soda fountain 1. An apparatus from which soda water is drawn, usu. containing receptacles for syrups, ice cream, etc. 2. A counter at which soft drinks, etc., are dispensed.

soda jerk *U.S. Slang* A clerk at a soda fountain.

so·dal·i·ty (sō·dal′ə·tē) *n. pl.* **·ties** 1. Companionship. 2. A society; association. 3. In the Roman Catholic Church, a society organized for devotional and charitable purposes. [< L < *sodalis* companion]

soda water An effervescent drink consisting of water charged under pressure with purified carbon dioxide gas.

sod·den (sod′n) *adj.* 1. Soaked with moisture. 2. Doughy; soggy, as bread, biscuits, etc. 3. Flabby and pale, esp. from dissipation. 4. Dull; dreary. — *v.t. & v.i.* To make or become sodden. [ME *soden*, orig. pp. of SEETHE] — **sod′den·ly** *adv.* — **sod′den·ness** *n.*

so·di·um (sō′dē·əm) *n.* A silver-white, highly reactive, alkaline, metallic element (symbol Na) that is soft and malleable, and forms many compounds: also called *natrium.* See ELEMENT. [< NL < SODA]

sodium bicarbonate *Chem.* A white crystalline compound of alkaline taste, used in medicine and cookery: also called *baking soda, bicarbonate of soda.*

sodium carbonate *Chem.* A strongly alkaline compound that in crystalline hydrated form is known as washing soda, and in the anhydrous form as soda ash.

sodium chloride Common salt.

sodium hydroxide *Chem.* A strongly basic compound, NaOH, used for bleaching, etc.: also called *caustic soda.*

sodium nitrate *Chem.* A white compound used as a fertilizer and in explosives.

sodium Pen·to·thal (pen′tə·thôl, -thal) Proprietary name for a brand of thiopental sodium: also called *Pentothal sodium.* Also **sodium pent′o·thal.**

sodium thiosulfate *Chem.* A crystalline salt used industrially and medicinally and in photography as a fixing agent: also called *hypo.* Also **sodium hyposulfite.**

Sod·om (sod′əm) In the Bible, a city on the Dead Sea, destroyed with the city of Gomorrah because of the wickedness of the people. *Gen.* xiii 10. — **Sod′om·ite** *n.*

sod·om·y (sod′əm·ē) *n.* Unnatural sexual relations, esp. between male persons or between a human being and an animal. [< OF < LL *Sodoma* Sodom, to whose people this practice was imputed] — **sod′om·ite** *n.*

so·ev·er (sō·ev′ər) *adv.* To or in some conceivable degree: often added to *who, which, what, when, how,* etc.

so·fa (sō′fə) *n.* A wide seat, upholstered and having a back and raised ends. [< F < Arabic *soffah* a part of a floor raised to form a seat]

soft (sôft, soft) *adj.* 1. Being or composed of a substance whose shape is changed easily by pressure, but without fracture; pliable, or malleable; easily worked: *soft* wood. 2. Smooth and delicate to the touch. 3. Gentle in its effect upon the ear; not loud or harsh. 4. Mild in any mode of physical action; bland: a *soft* breeze. 5. Of subdued coloring or delicate shading. 6. Expressing mildness, sympathy, etc.; gentle: *soft* words. 7. Giving or enjoying rest; placid: *soft* sleep. 8. Easily or too easily touched in feeling; tender: a *soft* heart. 9. Incapable of bearing hardship, strain, etc.; delicate: *soft* muscles. 10. Of yielding character; weak; effeminate. 11. *Informal* Involving little effort; easy: a *soft* job. 12. Free from mineral salts that prevent the detergent action of soap: said of water. 13. Bituminous, as opposed to anthracite: said of coal. 14. *Phonet.* a Describing *c* and *g* when articulated fricatively as in *cent* and *gibe:* opposed to *hard.* b Voiced and weakly articulated. 15. *Physics* Having relatively weak penetrating power: *soft* X-rays. — *n.* 1. That which is soft; a soft part or material. 2. *Informal* One who is soft or foolish; a softy. — *adv.* 1. Softly. 2. Quietly; gently. [OE *sōfte*] — **soft′ly** *adv. & interj.* — **soft′ness** *n.*

soft·ball (sôft′bôl′, soft′-) *n.* 1. A variation of baseball, requiring a smaller diamond and a larger ball. 2. The ball used in this game.

soft-boiled (sôft′boild′) *adj.* Boiled, as an egg, to an extent of incomplete coagulation of the albumen.

soft coal Bituminous coal.

soft drink A nonalcoholic drink, as ginger ale, etc.

sof·ten (sôf′ən, sof′-) *v.t. & v.i.* To make or become soft or softer. — **sof′ten·er** *n.*

soft·heart·ed (sôft′här′tid, soft′-) *adj.* Tender-hearted; merciful. — **soft′heart′ed·ly** *adv.* — **soft′heart′ed·ness** *n.*

soft-ped·al (sôft′ped′l, soft′-) *v.t.* **·aled** or **·alled, ·al·ing** or **·al·ling** 1. To mute the tone of by depressing the soft pedal. 2. *Informal* To render less emphatic; moderate.

soft pedal A pedal that mutes the tone, as in a piano.

soft-shell (sôft′shel′, soft′-) *adj.* Having a soft shell, as certain clams, or a crab or lobster after shedding its shell: also **soft′-shelled′** (-sheld′). — *n.* A soft-shelled crab.

soft-shelled crab A crab of North America after it has molted.

soft-shelled turtle Any member of a family of turtles having a long snout and a soft, leathery shell.

soft-soap (sôft′sōp′, soft′-) *v.t. Informal* To flatter; cajole. — **soft′-soap′er** *n.*

soft soap 1. Fluid or semifluid soap. 2. *Informal* Flattery.

soft-spo·ken (sôft′spō′kən) *adj.* 1. Speaking with a soft, low voice. 2. Ingratiating; suave: said of speech.

soft·ware (sôft′wâr′, soft′-) *n.* Any of the programs used in operating a digital computer, as input and output programs: distinguished from *hardware* (def. 3).

soft·wood (sôft′wood′, soft′-) *n.* 1. A coniferous tree or its wood. 2. Any soft wood, or any tree with soft wood.

soft·y (sôf′tē, sof′-) *n. pl.* **soft·ies** *Informal* 1. An extremely sentimental person. 2. A sissy.

sog·gy (sog′ē) *adj.* **·gi·er, ·gi·est** 1. Saturated with water or moisture; wet and heavy; soaked. 2. Heavy: said of pastry. 3. Soft; boggy: said of land. Also **sog·ged** (sog′id). [< dial. E *sog* a swamp, bog < Scand.] — **sog′gi·ly** *adv.* — **sog′gi·ness** *n.*

soil¹ (soil) *n.* 1. Finely divided rock mixed with vegetable or animal matter, constituting that portion of the surface of the earth in which plants grow. 2. Land; country: native *soil.* 3. A particular kind of earth. 4. A medium for development or growth: Slums are fertile *soil* for disease. [< OF < L < *solum* the ground]

soil² (soil) *v.t.* 1. To make dirty; smudge. 2. To disgrace; defile. — *v.i.* 3. To become dirty. — *n.* 1. The act of soiling or the state of being soiled. 2. A spot or stain. 3. Filth; sewage. 4. Manure used as fertilizer. [< OF, ult. < L *suculus,* dim. of *sus* pig]

soil·age (soi′lij) *n.* Green crops for feeding animals.

soi·ree (swä·rā′, *Fr.* swä·rā′) *n.* A party or reception given in the evening. Also **soi·rée′.** [< F < *soir* evening]

so·ja (sō′jə, sō′yə) *n.* The soybean. [< NL < Du. *soya*]

so·journ (*v.* sō′jûrn, sō·jûrn′; *n.* sō′jûrn) *v.i.* To stay or dwell temporarily; abide for a time. — *n.* A temporary residence or stay, as of one in a foreign land. [< OF, ult. < L *sub-* under + *diurnus* daily] — **so′journ·er** *n.*

sol¹ (sōl) *n. Music* The fifth of the syllables used in solmization; the fifth tone of a major scale; also, the tone G: also *so.* [See GAMUT.]

sol² (sol, sōl) *n.* A colloidal suspension of a solid in a liquid.

Sol (sol) 1. The sun. 2. In Roman mythology, the god of the sun. [< L]

sol·ace (sol′is) *n.* Comfort in grief, trouble, or calamity; also, that which supplies such comfort: also **sol′ace·ment.**

—*v.t.* **·aced, ·ac·ing** **1.** To comfort or cheer in trouble, grief, or calamity. **2.** To alleviate, as grief; soothe. — **Syn.** See CONSOLE[1]. [< OF < L *solacium* comfort] — **sol'ac·er** *n.*

so·lar (sō'lər) *adj.* **1.** Pertaining to, proceeding from, or connected with the sun. **2.** Affected, determined, or measured by the sun. **3.** Operated by the action of the sun's rays: a *solar* engine. [< L *sol* sun]

solar battery An assembly of photovoltaic cells for the direct conversion of solar energy into electricity.

so·lar·i·um (sō·lâr'ē·əm) *n. pl.* **·i·a** (-ē·ə) or **·i·ums** A room or enclosed porch exposed to the sun's rays. [< L]

solar plexus **1.** *Anat.* The large network of nerves found behind the stomach, and serving the abdominal viscera. **2.** *Informal* The pit of the stomach.

solar system The sun together with the heavenly bodies that revolve about it.

sold (sōld) Past tense and past participle of SELL.

sol·der (sod'ər) *n.* **1.** A fusible metal or alloy used for joining metallic surfaces or margins, applied in a melted state. **2.** Anything that unites or cements. —*v.t.* **1.** To unite or repair with solder. **2.** To join together. —*v.i.* **3.** To work with solder. **4.** To be united by or as by solder. [< OF < L *solidus* firm, hard] — **sol'der·er** *n.*

sol·dier (sōl'jər) *n.* **1.** A person serving in an army. **2.** An enlisted man, as distinguished from a commissioned officer. **3.** A brave, skillful, or experienced warrior. **4.** One who serves loyally in any cause. **5.** *Entomol.* An asexual form of a termite or of certain ants, in which the head and jaws are largely developed to defend the colony. —*v.i.* To be a soldier. [< OF *soude* wages < LL *solidus* a gold coin] — **sol'dier·ly** *adj.*

soldier of fortune An adventurous, restless person who is willing to serve wherever his services are well paid.

Soldier's Medal A U.S. military decoration awarded to any member of the army, or of a military organization connected with it, for heroism not involving actual conflict with the enemy. See DECORATION.

sol·dier·y (sōl'jər·ē) *n. pl.* **·dier·ies** **1.** Soldiers collectively. **2.** Military service.

sole[1] (sōl) *n.* **1.** The bottom surface of the foot. ◆ Collateral adjective: *plantar*. **2.** The bottom surface of a shoe, boot, etc. **3.** The lower part of a thing, or the part on which it rests when standing; esp., the bottom part of a plowshare. **4.** The bottom part of the head of a golf club. —*v.t.* **soled, sol·ing** To furnish with a sole; resole, as a shoe. [< OF < Med.L *sola*, var. of L *solea* sandal]

sole[2] (sōl) *n.* **1.** Any of a family of flatfishes allied to the flounders, many of which are highly esteemed as food. **2.** One of various flounders of the Pacific coast of the U.S. [< OF < L *solea*]

sole[3] (sōl) *adj.* Being alone or the only one; only; individual. [< OF < L *solus* alone]

so·le·cism (sol'ə·siz'əm) *n.* **1.** A violation of grammatical rules or of the approved idiomatic usage of language. **2.** Any impropriety or incongruity. [< L < Gk. < *soloikos* speaking incorrectly < *Soloi*, a Cilician town whose people spoke a substandard Attic dialect] — **sol'e·cist** *n.* — **sol'e·cis'tic** or **·ti·cal** *adj.*

sole·ly (sōl'lē) *adv.* **1.** By oneself or itself alone; singly. **2.** Completely; entirely. **3.** Without exception; exclusively.

sol·emn (sol'əm) *adj.* **1.** Characterized by majesty, mystery, or power; impressive; awe-inspiring. **2.** Marked by gravity; serious. **3.** Characterized by ceremonial observances; sacred. **4.** *Law* Done in due form of law: a *solemn* protest. [< OF < L *solemnis*] — **sol'emn·ness, sol'emn·ness** *n.* — **sol'emn·ly** *adv.*

so·lem·ni·ty (sə·lem'nə·tē) *n. pl.* **·ties** **1.** The state or quality of being solemn; gravity; reverence. **2.** A rite expressive of religious reverence; also, any ceremonious observance. **3.** A thing of a solemn or serious nature.

sol·em·nize (sol'əm·nīz) *v.t.* **·nized, ·niz·ing** **1.** To perform as a ceremony or solemn rite, or according to legal or ritual forms: to *solemnize* a marriage. **2.** To dignify, as with a ceremony; celebrate. **3.** To make solemn, grave, or serious. Also *Brit.* **sol'em·nise.** — **Syn.** See CELEBRATE. — **sol'em·ni·za'tion** *n.* — **sol'em·niz'er** *n.*

so·le·noid (sō'lə·noid) *n.* *Electr.* A conducting wire in the form of a helix, capable of setting up a magnetic field by the passage through it of an electric current. [< F < Gk. *sōlēn* a channel + -OID] — **so'le·noi'dal** *adj.*

so·lic·it (sə·lis'it) *v.t.* **1.** To ask for earnestly; seek to obtain by persuasion or entreaty. **2.** To beg or entreat (a person) persistently. **3.** To tempt; esp., to entice (one) to an unlawful or immoral act. —*v.i.* **4.** To make petition or solicitation. — **Syn.** See ASK. [< OF < L *sollicitare* to agitate] — **so·lic'i·ta'tion** *n.*

so·lic·i·tor (sə·lis'ə·tər) *n.* **1.** A person who solicits; esp., one who solicits gifts of money or subscriptions to magazines. **2.** The legal advisor to certain branches of the public service. **3.** In England, a lawyer who may advise clients or prepare cases for presentation in court, but who may appear as an advocate in the lower courts only: distinguished from *barrister*. Also **so·lic'i·ter.** — **so·lic'i·tor·ship'** *n.*

Solicitor General *pl.* **Solicitors General** **1.** In the U.S., an officer who ranks after the Attorney General. **2.** The principal law officer in some States, corresponding to the Attorney General in others.

so·lic·i·tous (sə·lis'ə·təs) *adj.* **1.** Full of anxiety or concern, as for the attainment of something: *solicitous* of our good will. **2.** Full of eager desire; willing. — **so·lic'i·tous·ly** *adv.* — **so·lic'i·tous·ness** *n.*

so·lic·i·tude (sə·lis'ə·tōōd, -tyōōd) *n.* **1.** The state of being solicitous; anxiety or concern. **2.** *Usu. pl.* That which makes one solicitous.

sol·id (sol'id) *adj.* **1.** Having definite shape and volume; not fluid. **2.** Substantial; firm and stable. **3.** Filling the whole of; not hollow. **4.** Having no aperture or crevice; compact. **5.** Manifesting strength and firmness; sound. **6.** Characterized by reality; substantial or satisfactory. **7.** Exhibiting united and unbroken characteristics, opinions, etc.; unanimous: a *solid* vote. **8.** Financially sound or safe. **9.** *U.S. Informal* Certain and safe in approval and support: They were *solid* with the boss. **10.** Having or relating to the three dimensions of length, breadth, and thickness. **11.** Written without a hyphen: said of a compound word. **12.** Cubic in shape: a *solid* yard. **13.** Unadulterated; unalloyed: *solid* gold. **14.** Carrying weight or conviction: a *solid* argument. **15.** Serious; reliable: a *solid* citizen. **16.** *Printing* Having no leads or slugs between the lines; not open. — *n.* **1.** A state of matter characterized by definite shape and volume. **2.** A magnitude that has length, breadth, and thickness, as a cone, cube, sphere, etc. [< F < L *solidus*] — **sol'id·ly** *adv.* — **sol'id·ness** *n.*

sol·i·dar·i·ty (sol'ə·dar'ə·tē) *n. pl.* **·ties** Coherence and oneness in nature, relations, or interests, as of a class.

solid fuel *Aerospace* A rocket fuel in solid, rather than liquid or gaseous, form. Also, **solid propellant.**

solid geometry The geometry that includes all three dimensions of space in its reasoning.

so·lid·i·fy (sə·lid'ə·fī) *v.t. & v.i.* **·fied, ·fy·ing** **1.** To make or become solid, hard, firm, or compact. **2.** To bring or come together in unity. — **so·lid'i·fi·ca'tion** *n.*

so·lid·i·ty (sə·lid'ə·tē) *n. pl.* **·ties** **1.** The quality or state of being solid; extension in the three dimensions of space. **2.** Mental, moral, or financial soundness; stability.

solid state physics The branch of physics that deals with the properties of solids, esp. at the atomic and molecular levels.

sol·i·dus (sol'ə·dəs) *n. pl.* **·di** (-dī) The sign (/) used to divide shillings from pence: 10/6 (10*s.* 6*d.*): sometimes also used to express fractions: 3/4. [< LL]

so·lil·o·quize (sə·lil'ə·kwīz) *v.i.* **·quized, ·quiz·ing** To talk to oneself; utter a soliloquy. Also *Brit.* **so·lil'o·quise.**

so·lil·o·quy (sə·lil'ə·kwē) *n. pl.* **·quies** A talking or discourse to oneself, as in a drama; a monologue. [< LL < L *solus* alone + *loqui* to talk]

sol·ip·sism (sol'ip·siz'əm) *n.* *Philos.* The theory that the self is the only thing really existent. [< L *solus* alone + *ipse* self] — **sol'ip·sist** *n.*

sol·i·taire (sol'ə·târ') *n.* **1.** A diamond or other gem set alone. **2.** *Chiefly U.S.* One of many games, esp. of cards, played by one person: also, *Brit.*, patience. **3.** *Brit.* Pegboard. [< F < L *solitarius* solitary]

sol·i·tar·y (sol'ə·ter'ē) *adj.* **1.** Living, being, or going alone. **2.** Made, done, or passed alone: a *solitary* life. **3.** Unfrequented by human beings; secluded. **4.** Lonesome; lonely. **5.** Single; sole: Not a *solitary* soul was there. — *n. pl.* **·tar·ies** **1.** One who lives alone; a recluse. **2.** *Informal* Solitary confinement. [< L < *solus* alone] — **sol'i·tar'i·ly** *adv.* — **sol'i·tar'i·ness** *n.*

solitary confinement The confining of a prisoner apart from other prisoners, usu. as punishment.

sol·i·tude (sol'ə·tōōd, -tyōōd) *n.* **1.** The state of being solitary; seclusion. **2.** A deserted or lonely place.

sol·mi·za·tion (sol'mə·zā'shən) *n.* *Music* The use of syllables, most commonly *do, re, mi, fa, sol, la, ti* (*si*), as names for the tones of a major scale, with vowel changes to indicate chromatic tones. [< SOL[1] + MI]

so·lo (sō'lō) *n. pl.* **·los** or **·li** (-lē) **1.** A musical composition or passage for a single voice or instrument, with or without accompaniment. **2.** Any of several card games, esp. one in which one player may play alone against the other three. **3.** Any performance accomplished alone or without assistance. — *adj.* **1.** Composed or written for, or executed by, a single voice or instrument. **2.** Done by a single person alone: a *solo* flight. —*v.i.* **·loed, ·lo·ing** To fly an airplane alone, esp. for the first time. [< Ital. < L *solus* alone] — **so'lo·ist** *n.*

Sol·o·mon (sol'ə·mən) Tenth-century B.C. king of Israel; son of David and Bathsheba; noted for his wisdom.

Sol·o·mon's-seal (sol'ə·mənz·sēl') *n.* Any of several rather large perennial herbs having tubular flowers and rootstocks marked at intervals by circular scars.

sol·stice (sol′stis) *n.* **1.** *Astron.* The time of year when the sun is at its greatest distance from the celestial equator; either the **summer solstice**, about June 22 in the northern hemisphere, or the **winter solstice**, about Dec. 22. **2.** Either of the two points on the ecliptic marking these distances. **3.** A culminating or high point. [< F < L < *sol* sun + *sistere* to cause to stand] — **sol·sti·tial** (sol·stish′əl) *adj.*

sol·u·bil·i·ty (sol′yə·bil′ə·tē) *n.* *pl.* **·ties** The state of being soluble; capability of being dissolved. Also **sol′u·ble·ness**.

sol·u·ble (sol′yə·bəl) *adj.* **1.** Capable of being dissolved in a liquid. **2.** Susceptible of being solved or explained. [< OF < L < *solvere* to solve, dissolve] — **sol′u·bly** *adv.*

sol·ute (sol′yōōt, sō′lōōt) *n.* The substance dissolved in a solution. — *adj.* Dissolved; in solution.

so·lu·tion (sə·lōō′shən) *n.* **1.** A homogeneous mixture formed by dissolving one or more substances, whether solid, liquid, or gaseous, in another substance. **2.** The act or process by which such a mixture is made. **3.** The act or process of explaining, settling, or disposing, as of a difficulty, problem, or doubt. **4.** The answer to a problem; also, the method of finding the answer. **5.** Separation; disruption. [< OF < L *solutus*, pp. of *solvere* to dissolve]

So·lu·tre·an (sə·lōō′trē·ən) *adj.* *Anthropol.* Pertaining to or characteristic of a Paleolithic culture preceding the Magdalenian and typified by a skilled technique in the making of flint implements. Also **So·lu′tri·an**. [after *Solutré*, a village in central France, where remains were found]

solv·a·ble (sol′və·bəl) *adj.* **1.** That may be solved. **2.** That may be dissolved. — **solv′a·bil′i·ty, solv′a·ble·ness** *n.*

solve (solv) *v.t.* **solved, solv·ing** To arrive at or work out the correct explanation or solution of; find the answer to; resolve. [< L *solvere* to solve, loosen] — **solv′er** *n.*

sol·vent (sol′vənt) *adj.* **1.** Having means sufficient to pay all debts. **2.** Having the power of dissolving. — *n.* **1.** That which solves. **2.** A substance, generally a liquid, capable of dissolving other substances. [< L *solvens, -entis*, ppr. of *solvere* to solve, loosen] — **sol′ven·cy** *n.*

-soma See -SOME².

So·ma·li (sō·mä′lē) *n.* **1.** A member of one of certain Hamitic tribes of Somalia, Kenya, Ethiopia, and French Somaliland. **2.** Their Hamitic language. Also **So·mal** (sō·mal′).

so·mat·ic (sō·mat′ik) *adj.* *Biol.* **1.** Of or relating to the body; physical; corporeal. **2.** Of or pertaining to the framework or walls of a body. [< Gk. *sōma* body]

somato- *combining form* Body; of, pertaining to, or denoting the body. Also, before vowels, **somat-**. [< Gk. *sōma, sōmatos* the body]

som·ber (som′bər) *adj.* **1.** Partially deprived of light or brightness; dusky; murky; gloomy. **2.** Somewhat melancholy; depressing. Also *Brit.* **som′bre**, *Archaic* **som′brous**. [< F *sombre*]

som·bre·ro (som·brâr′ō) *n.* *pl.* **·ros** A broad-brimmed hat, usu. of felt, much worn in Spain, Latin America, and the southwestern U.S. [< Sp. < *sombra* shade]

some (sum) *adj.* **1.** Of indeterminate or limited quantity, number, or amount. **2.** Conceived or thought of, but not definitely known: *some* person. **3.** Part (at least one) but not all of a class. **4.** *U.S. Informal* Worthy of notice: That was *some* cake. — *pron.* **1.** A certain undetermined quantity or part. **2.** Certain particular ones not definitely known or not specifically designated. — *adv.* **1.** In an approximate degree; about: *Some* eighty people were present. **2.** *Informal* or *Dial.* Somewhat. [OE *sum*]

-some¹ *suffix of adjectives* Characterized by, or tending to be (what is indicated by the main element): *blithesome, frolicsome*. [OE -*sum* like, resembling]

-some² *suffix of nouns* A body: *chromosome*. Also spelled **-soma**. [< Gk. *sōma* a body]

-some³ *suffix of nouns* A group consisting of (a specified number): *twosome, foursome*. [< SOME]

some·bod·y (sum′bod′ē, -bəd·ē) *pron.* A person unknown or unnamed. — *n.* *pl.* **·bod·ies** A person of consequence.

some·day (sum′dā′) *adv.* *U.S.* At some future time.

some·how (sum′hou′) *adv.* In some manner not explained.

some·one (sum′wun′, -wən) *pron.* Some person; somebody. — *n.* A somebody.

some·place (sum′plās′) *adv.* *Informal* Somewhere.

som·er·sault (sum′ər·sôlt) *n.* **1.** An acrobatic stunt in which a person either leaps or rolls from a sitting posture, turning heels over head. **2.** A complete reversal of opinion, attitude, etc. — *v.i.* To perform a somersault. Also spelled *summersault*. Also **som′er·set** (-set). [< OF, ult. < L *supra* above + *saltus* leap]

some·thing (sum′thing) *n.* **1.** A particular thing indefinitely conceived or stated. **2.** Some portion or quantity. **3.** A person or thing of importance. — *adv.* Somewhat: now only in the phrase **something like**.

some·time (sum′tīm′) *adv.* **1.** At some future time not precisely stated; eventually. **2.** At some indeterminate time or occasion. — *adj.* Former; quondam: a *sometime* student.

some·times (sum′tīmz′) *adv.* At times; occasionally.

some·way (sum′wā′) *adv.* In some way or other; somehow. Also **some way, some′ways′** (-wāz′).

some·what (sum′hwot′, -hwət) *n.* **1.** An uncertain quantity or degree; something. **2.** An individual or thing of consequence. — *adv.* In some degree.

some·where (sum′hwâr′) *adv.* **1.** In, at, or to some place unspecified or unknown. **2.** In one place or another. **3.** In or to some existent place. **4.** Approximately: with *about*. — *n.* An unspecified or unknown place.

some·wheres (sum′hwârz′) *adv.* *Chiefly Dial.* Somewhere.

som·nam·bu·late (som·nam′byə·lāt) *v.i.* **·lat·ed, ·lat·ing** To walk or wander about while asleep. [< L *somnus* sleep + AMBULATE]

som·nam·bu·lism (som·nam′byə·liz′əm) *n.* The act or state of walking during sleep; sleepwalking. Also **som′nam′·bu·la′tion**. — **som·nam′bu·lant** (-lənt) *adj.* — **som·nam′·bu·list** *n.* — **som·nam′bu·lis′tic** *adj.*

somni- *combining form* Sleep; of or pertaining to sleep: *somniferous*. [< L *somnus* sleep]

som·nif·er·ous (som·nif′ər·əs) *adj.* Tending to produce sleep; soporiferous; narcotic. Also **som·nif′ic**.

som·no·lence (som′nə·ləns) *n.* Oppressive drowsiness or inclination to sleep. Also **som′no·len·cy**.

som·no·lent (som′nə·lənt) *adj.* **1.** Inclined to sleep; drowsy. **2.** Tending to induce drowsiness. [< F < L < *somnus* sleep] — **som′no·lent·ly** *adv.*

son (sun) *n.* **1.** A male child considered with reference to either parent or to both parents. **2.** Any male descendant. **3.** One who occupies the place of a son, as by adoption, marriage, or regard. **4.** A person regarded as a native of a particular country or place. **5.** A male person representing some quality or character. [OE *sunu*] — **son′ship** *n.*

-son A descendant of: English and Scandinavian patronymic suffix: *Anderson*.

Son (sun) Jesus Christ; the second person of the Trinity.

so·nant (sō′nənt) *adj.* **1.** Sounding; resonant. **2.** *Phonet.* Voiced. — *n.* *Phonet.* **1.** A voiced speech sound. **2.** A syllabic sound. [< L *sonans, -antis*, ppr. of *sonare* to resound] — **so′nance** *n.*

so·nar (sō′när) *n.* A device using underwater sound waves for navigation, range finding, detection of submerged objects, communication, etc. — *adj.* Of, or pertaining to this device. [< SO(UND) NA(VIGATION) and R(ANGING)]

so·na·ta (sə·nä′tä) *n.* *Music* A composition for one, two, or in older music, three or more instruments. [< Ital. < *sonare* to sound]

sonata form *Music* The outline upon which a movement, esp. the first, of a sonata, quartet, symphony, etc., is based.

so·na·ti·na (son′ə·tē′nə) *n.* *pl.* **·ti·nas** or **·ti·ne** (-tē′nā) *Music* A short or easy sonata. [< Ital., dim. of SONATA]

song (sông, song) *n.* **1.** A musical composition for one or more voices. **2.** The rendering of vocal music; more widely, any melodious utterance, as of a bird. **3.** A lyric or ballad. **4.** Poetry; verse. — **for a song** At a very low price. [OE]

song·bird (sông′bûrd′, song′-) *n.* A bird that utters a musical call.

song·ful (sông′fəl, song′-) *adj.* Full of song or melody.

Song of Solomon A book of the Old Testament consisting of a Hebrew dramatic love poem attributed to Solomon: also, in the Douai Bible, *Canticle of Canticles*. Also **Song of Songs**.

song sparrow A common sparrow of the eastern U.S. noted for its song.

song·ster (sông′stər, song′-) *n.* **1.** A person or bird given to singing. **2.** A poet. — **song′stress** *n.fem.*

song thrush A bird of the thrush family, native in Europe and having brown wings and a spotted breast.

song·wri·ter (sông′rī′tər) *n.* One who writes music or lyrics, or both, for songs, esp. popular songs. Also **song writer**.

son·ic (son′ik) *adj.* **1.** Of, pertaining to, determined or affected by sound. **2.** Having a speed approaching that of sound. [< L *sonus* sound]

sonic barrier *Aeron.* The transonic barrier.

son-in-law (sun′in·lô′) *n.* *pl.* **sons-in-law** The husband of one's daughter.

son·net (son′it) *n.* A poem usu. of fourteen decasyllabic lines, properly expressing two successive phases of a single thought or idea. — *v.t.* **1.** To celebrate in sonnets. — *v.i.* **2.** To compose sonnets. [< F < Ital. < Provençal *sonet*, dim. of *son* sound < L *sonus*]

son·net·eer (son′ə·tir′) *n.* A composer of sonnets. — *v.i.* To compose sonnets.

son·ny (sun′ē) *n.* *Informal* Youngster: a familiar form of address to boys.

so·nor·ant (sə·nôr′ənt, -nō′rənt) *n.* *Phonet.* A voiced consonant of relatively high sonority, as (l), (r), (m), (n).

so·nor·i·ty (sə-nôr′ə·tē, -nor′-) *n. pl.* **·ties 1.** Sonorous quality or state; resonance; also **so·no′rous·ness. 2.** A sound.

so·no·rous (sə-nôr′əs, -nō′rəs, son′ər-əs) *adj.* **1.** Productive or capable of sound vibrations. **2.** Loud and full-sounding; resonant. [< L *sonare* to resound] — **so·no′rous·ly** *adv.*

soon (soon) *adv.* **1.** At a future or subsequent time not long distant; shortly. **2.** Without delay; in a speedy manner. **3.** With ease; readily. **4.** With willingness or readiness: usu. preceded by *would as, had as,* etc. **5.** In good season; early. [OE *sōna* immediately]

Soon·er State (soo′nər) Nickname for Oklahoma.

soot (soot, soot) *n.* A black substance, essentially carbon from the incomplete combustion of wood, coal, natural gas, etc., as deposited on the inside of chimneys and other surfaces. — *v.t.* To soil or cover with soot. [OE *sōt*]

sooth (sooth) *Archaic adj.* True. — *n.* Truth. — **in sooth** In truth. [OE *sōth*] — **sooth′ly** *adv.*

soothe (sooth) *v.* **soothed, sooth·ing** *v.t.* **1.** To restore to a quiet or normal state; calm. **2.** To mitigate, soften, or relieve, as pain or grief. — *v.i.* **3.** To have a calming or relieving effect. [OE *sōthian* to verify] — **sooth′er** *n.* — **sooth′ing** *adj.* — **sooth′ing·ly** *adv.*

sooth·say·er (sooth′sā′ər) *n.* One who claims to be able to foretell events. — **sooth′say·ing** *n.*

soot·y (soot′ē, soo′tē) *adj.* **soot·i·er, soot·i·est 1.** Blackened or stained by soot. **2.** Producing or consisting of soot. **3.** Black like soot. — **soot′i·ly** *adv.* — **soot′i·ness** *n.*

sop (sop) *v.* **sopped, sop·ping** *v.t.* **1.** To dip or soak in a liquid. **2.** To drench. **3.** To take up by absorption: often with *up.* — *v.i.* **4.** To be absorbed; soak in. **5.** To be or become drenched. — *n.* **1.** Anything softened in liquid, as bread. **2.** Anything given to pacify, as a bribe. [OE *sopp*]

soph·ism (sof′iz·əm) *n.* **1.** A false argument intentionally used to deceive. **2.** The doctrine or method of the sophists. [< F or L < Gk., ult. < *sophos* wise]

soph·ist (sof′ist) *n.* **1.** A philosopher; a learned man. **2.** One who argues cleverly but fallaciously or unnecessarily minutely. — *adj.* Pertaining to the art or method of sophists, or to sophistry. [< L < Gk., ult. < *sophos* wise]

Soph·ist (sof′ist) *n.* **1.** A member of a school of early Greek philosophy, preceding the Socratic school. **2.** One of the later Greek teachers of philosophy and rhetoric, who showed great skill in subtle disputation under logical forms.

so·phis·tic (sə·fis′tik) *adj.* Pertaining to a Sophist, sophists, or sophistry. — *n.* The art or method of the Sophists. Also **so·phis′ti·cal.** — **so·phis′ti·cal·ly** *adv.* — **so·phis′ti·cal·ness** *n.*

so·phis·ti·cate (*v.* sə·fis′tə·kāt; *n.* sə·fis′tə·kit, -kāt) *v.* **·cat·ed, ·cat·ing** *v.t.* **1.** To make less simple or ingenuous in mind or manner; render worldly-wise. **2.** *Rare* To mislead or corrupt (a person). **3.** To increase the complexity and capability of. — *v.i.* **4.** To indulge in sophistry; be sophistic. — *n.* A sophisticated person. [< Med.L < L *sophisticus* sophistic] — **so·phis′ti·ca′tor** *n.*

so·phis·ti·cat·ed (sə·fis′tə·kā′tid) *adj.* **1.** Having fine or subtle perceptions; cultured. **2.** Appealing to the intellect; not suited to popular tastes. **3.** Worldly-wise; deprived of natural simplicity. **4.** Very complicated in design, capabilities, etc.: said of mechanical and electronic devices.

so·phis·ti·ca·tion (sə·fis′tə·kā′shən) *n.* **1.** Sophisticated ideas, attitudes, etc., derived from education and culture. **2.** The act of sophisticating. **3.** Adulteration; falsification.

soph·is·try (sof′is·trē) *n. pl.* **·tries 1.** Subtly fallacious reasoning or disputation. **2.** The art or methods of the Greek Sophists.

soph·o·more (sof′ə·môr, -mōr) *n.* In American high schools, colleges, and universities having a four-year course, a second-year student. [Earlier *sophumer* one who uses sophisms; later infl. in meaning by Gk. *sophos* wise + *mōros* fool]

soph·o·mor·ic (sof′ə·môr′ik, -mōr′-) *adj.* **1.** Of, pertaining to, or like a sophomore. **2.** Marked by a shallow assumption of learning or by empty grandiloquence; immature; callow. Also **soph′o·mor′i·cal.** — **soph′o·mor′i·cal·ly** *adv.*

Soph·o·ni·as (sof′ə·nī′əs) The Douai Bible name for ZEPHANIAH.

-sophy *combining form* Knowledge pertaining to a (specified) field: *theosophy.* [< Gk. *sophia* wisdom]

so·po·rif·ic (sō′pə·rif′ik, sop′ə-) *adj.* **1.** Causing or tending to cause sleep. **2.** Drowsy; sleepy. — *n.* A medicine that produces sleep. [< L *sopor* deep sleep]

sop·ping (sop′ing) *adj.* Wet through; drenched; soaking.

sop·py (sop′ē) *adj.* **·pi·er, ·pi·est 1.** Very wet. **2.** Rainy. **3.** *Brit. Slang* Mawkish; sentimental.

so·pra·no (sə·pran′ō, -prä′nō) *n. pl.* **so·pran·os** or **so·pra·ni** (sə·prä′nē) **1.** A voice of the highest range. **2.** The music intended for such a voice. **3.** A person having a treble or high-range voice, or singing such a part. — *adj.* Of or pertaining to a soprano voice, part, etc. [< Ital. *sopra* above]

so·ra (sôr′ə, sō′rə) *n.* A small North American rail, esteemed as food. Also **sora rail.** [? < N.Am.Ind.]

Sorb (sôrb) *n.* A Wend.

Sor·bi·an (sôr′bē·ən) *adj.* Of or pertaining to the Sorbs or Wends or to their language. — *n.* **1.** A Sorb or Wend. **2.** The West Slavic language of the Sorbs; Wendish.

Sor·bonne (sôr·bôn′) The faculties of literature and science of the University of Paris.

sor·cer·er (sôr′sər·ər) *n.* A wizard; conjurer; magician. — **sor′cer·ess** *n.fem.*

sor·cer·y (sôr′sər·ē) *n. pl.* **·cer·ies** Alleged employment of supernatural agencies; witchcraft. [< OF < L *sors* fate] — **sor′cer·ous** *adj.* — **sor′cer·ous·ly** *adv.*

sor·did (sôr′did) *adj.* **1.** Filthy; dirty. **2.** Mercenary. **3.** Of degraded character; vile; base. [< L *sordes* filth] — **sor′did·ly** *adv.* — **sor′did·ness** *n.*

sore (sôr, sōr) *adj.* **sor·er, sor·est 1.** Painful or tender to the touch as an inflamed or injured part of the body. **2.** Grieved; distressed: a *sore* heart. **3.** Arousing painful feelings; irritating: a *sore* point. **4.** Extreme or severe: *sore* need. **5.** *Informal* Offended; aggrieved. — *n.* **1.** A place on the body where the skin or flesh is bruised, broken, or inflamed. **2.** A painful memory; grief. — *adv. Archaic* Sorely. [OE *sār*] — **sore′ness** *n.*

sore·head (sôr′hed′, sōr′-) *U.S. Slang n.* A disgruntled or offended person. — **sore′head·ed** *adj.*

sore·ly (sôr′lē, sōr′-) *adv.* **1.** Grievously; distressingly. **2.** Greatly; in high degree: His aid was *sorely* needed.

sor·ghum (sôr′gəm) *n.* **1.** Any of various stout, canelike tropical grasses cultivated for their saccharine juices and as fodder. **2.** Syrup prepared from their sweet juices of the plant. [< NL < Ital. *sorgo*]

so·ror·i·ty (sə·rôr′ə·tē, -ror′-) *n. pl.* **·ties** A sisterhood; esp., a women's national or local association having chapters in a secondary school, college, or university. [< Med.L < L *soror* sister]

sorp·tion (sôrp′shən) *n.* Any process by which one substance takes up and holds the molecules of another substance, as by absorption or adsorption. [< NL < L *sorbere*]

sor·rel¹ (sôr′əl, sor′-) *n.* Any of several herbs with acid leaves used in salads. [< F < OHG *sur* sour]

sor·rel² (sôr′əl, sor′-) *n.* **1.** A reddish or yellowish brown color. **2.** An animal of this color. [< OF *sor* hawk with red plumage]

sor·row (sôr′ō, sōr′ō) *n.* **1.** Pain or distress of mind because of loss, injury, or misfortune. **2.** An event that causes pain or distress of mind. **3.** The expression of grief. — *v.i.* To feel sorrow; grieve. [OE *sorg*] — **sor′row·er** *n.*

sor·row·ful (sôr′ə·fəl, sōr′-) *adj.* Sad; unhappy; mournful. — **sor′row·ful·ly** *adv.* — **sor′row·ful·ness** *n.*

sor·ry (sôr′ē, sōr′ē) *adj.* **·ri·er, ·ri·est 1.** Grieved or pained; affected by sorrow from any cause. **2.** Causing sorrow; dismal. **3.** Pitiable or worthless; paltry. **4.** Painful; grievous. [OE *sār* sore] — **sor′ri·ly** *adv.* — **sor′ri·ness** *n.*

sort (sôrt) *n.* **1.** Any number or collection of persons or things characterized by the same or similar qualities; a kind; species; class; set. **2.** Form of being or acting; character; nature; quality; also, manner; style. **3.** *Usu. pl. Printing* A character or type considered as a portion of a font. — **of sorts** Originally, of various or different kinds; now, of a poor or unsatisfactory quality: an actor *of sorts.* — **out of sorts** *Informal* In an ill humor; irritable. — **sort of** *Informal* Somewhat. — *v.t.* To arrange or separate into grades, kinds, or sizes. [< OF < L *sors* lot, condition] — **sort′a·ble** *adj.* — **sort′a·bly** *adv.* — **sort′er** *n.*

sor·tie (sôr′tē) *n. Mil.* **1.** A sally of troops from a besieged place to attack the besiegers. **2.** A single trip of an aircraft on a military or naval mission. [< F *sortir* to go forth]

S O S (es′ō′es′) **1.** The code signal of distress adopted by the Radiotelegraphic Convention in 1912, and used by airplanes, ships, etc. **2.** Any call for assistance.

so-so (sō′sō′) *adj.* Passable; mediocre. — *adv.* Tolerably.

sot (sot) *n.* A habitual drunkard. [OE < OF < LL *sottus* drunkard] — **sot′tish** *adj.* — **sot′tish·ly** *adv.* — **sot′tish·ness** *n.*

sot·to vo·ce (sot′ō vō′chē, *Ital.* sôt′tō vō′chā) Softly; in an undertone; privately. [< Ital., under the (normal) voice]

sou (soo) *n.* A former French coin of varying value. [< F < LL *solidus* a gold coin]

sou·brette (soo·bret′) *n.* **1.** In light opera or comedy, the role of a pert, intriguing lady's maid. **2.** An actress playing such a role. **3.** Any frivolous or coquettish young woman character. [< F < Provençal *soubret* shy, coy] — **sou·bret′ish** *adj.*

sou·bri·quet (soo′bri·kā) *n.* A sobriquet.

souf·flé (soo·flā′) *adj.* Made light and frothy, and fixed in that condition by heat: also **souf·fléed′** (-flād′). — *n.* A light, baked dish made fluffy with beaten egg whites. [< F < L < *sub-* under + *flare* to blow]

sough (suf, sou) *v.i.* To make a sighing sound, as the wind. — *n.* A deep, murmuring sound. [OE *swōgan* to sound]

sought (sôt) Past tense and past participle of SEEK.

soul (sōl) *n.* **1.** The rational, emotional, and volitional faculties in man, conceived of as forming an entity distinct from the body. **2.** *Theol.* **a** The divine principle of life in man. **b** The moral or spiritual part of man as related to God. **3.** The emotional faculty of man as distinguished from the intellect: He puts his *soul* into his acting. **4.** Fervor; emotional force; heartiness; vitality. **5.** An essential or vital element: Justice is the *soul* of law. **6.** The leading figure or inspirer of a cause, movement, etc. **7.** A person considered as the embodiment of a quality or attribute: He is the *soul* of generosity. **8.** A living person: Every *soul* trembled at the sight. **9.** Among U.S. Negroes: **a** The awareness of a black African heritage. **b** A strongly emotional pride and solidarity based on this awareness. **c** The qualities that arouse such feelings. [OE *sāwol*] — **souled** *adj.*

soul food Any of various Southern foods or dishes popular with American Negroes, as fried chicken, ham hocks, etc.

soul·ful (sōl'fəl) *adj.* Full or expressive of deep feeling: a *soulful* gaze. — **soul'ful·ly** *adv.* — **soul'ful·ness** *n.*

soul·less (sōl'lis) *adj.* **1.** Heartless; unemotional. **2.** Having no soul. — **soul'less·ly** *adv.* — **soul'less·ness** *n.*

sound[1] (sound) *n.* **1.** Any of a class of waves consisting of mechanical disturbances in an elastic system, esp. in air. **2.** The auditory stimulation produced by waves of this type having frequencies between about 20 and 20,000 cycles per second. **3.** An instance of this stimulation. **4.** A speech sound. **5.** Significance; implication: The story has a sinister *sound.* **6.** Sounding or hearing distance; earshot. **7.** Noise. — *v.i.* **1.** To give forth a sound or sounds. **2.** To give a specified impression; seem: The story *sounds* true. — *v.t.* **3.** To cause to give forth sound. **4.** To signal, order, announce or celebrate: to *sound* retreat, someone's praises, etc. **5.** To utter audibly; pronounce. **6.** To articulate a letter: to *sound* the *r* in *park.* **7.** To test or examine by sound; auscultate. [< OF < L *sonus*]
— **Syn.** (noun) **3.** *Sound* is the general term embracing aural sensations of all qualities. A *tone* is a *sound* of definite pitch, caused by vibrations, predominantly of one frequency. *Noise* is a *sound* lacking pitch, caused by vibrations of dissonant frequencies.

sound[2] (sound) *adj.* **1.** Having all the organs or faculties complete and in normal action and relation; healthy. **2.** Free from injury, flaw, mutilation, or decay: *sound* timber. **3.** Founded in truth; valid; legal. **4.** Correct in views or processes of thought. **5.** Solvent. **6.** Profound, as rest; deep; unbroken. **7.** Complete and effectual; thorough. **8.** Solid; stable; safe; also, trustworthy. **9.** Based on good judgment. [OE *gesund*] — **sound'ly** *adv.* — **sound'ness** *n.*

sound[3] (sound) *n.* **1.** A long and narrow body of water, more extensive than a strait, connecting larger bodies. **2.** The air bladder of a fish. [Fusion of OE and ON *sund*]

sound[4] (sound) *v.t.* **1.** To test or measure the depth of (water, etc.), esp., by means of a lead weight at the end of a line. **2.** To explore or examine (the bottom of the sea, etc.) by means of a sounding lead adapted for bringing up adhering particles. **3.** To discover or try to discover the views, beliefs, etc., of (a person) by means of conversation and roundabout questions: usu. with *out.* — *v.i.* **4.** To sound depth. **5.** To dive down suddenly and deeply. **6.** To investigate; inquire. — *n. Surg.* An instrument for exploring a cavity. [< OF < L *sub-* under + *unda* a wave] — **sound'a·ble** *adj.*

sound barrier *Aeron.* The transonic barrier.

sound effects In motion pictures, radio, etc., the incidental and often mechanically produced sounds, as of rain, hoofbeats, etc., used to give the illusion of reality.

sound·ing[1] (soun'ding) *adj.* **1.** Giving forth a full sound; sonorous. **2.** Having much sound with little significance.

sound·ing[2] (soun'ding) *n.* **1.** The act of one who or that which sounds. **2.** Measurement of the depth of water. **3.** *pl.* The depth of water as sounded; also, water of such depth that the bottom may be reached by sounding.

sounding board A structure or dome over a pulpit or speaker's platform to amplify and clarify the speaker's voice.

sound·less (sound'lis) *adj.* Having or making no sound; silent. — **sound'less·ly** *adv.* — **sound'less·ness** *n.*

sound·proof (sound'proof') *adj.* Resistant to the penetration or spread of sound. — *v.t.* To make soundproof.

sound track The portion along the edge of a motion-picture film that carries the sound record.

soup (soop) *n.* **1.** Liquid food made by boiling meat, vegetables, etc., in water. **2.** *Slang* A thick overcast or fog. — **in the soup** *U.S. Slang* In difficulties. — **to soup up** *U.S. Slang* To supercharge or otherwise modify (an automobile) for high speed. [< F *soupe* < Gmc.]

soup·çon (soop·sôn') *n. French* A minute quantity; a taste; literally, a suspicion.

sour (sour) *adj.* **1.** Sharp to the taste; acid; tart, like vinegar. **2.** Having an acid or rancid taste as the result of fermentation. **3.** Having a rancid, acrid smell or vapor; dank. **4.** Misanthropic and crabbed; cross; morose: a *sour* person.

5. Cold and wet; unpleasant. **6.** Acid: said of soil. — *v.t. & v.i.* To become or make sour. — *n.* **1.** Something sour or distasteful. **2.** An acid solution used in bleaching, etc. **3.** A sour or acid beverage: a whisky *sour.* [OE *sūr*]
— **sour'ly** *adv.* — **sour'ness** *n.*
— **Syn.** (adj.) *Sour* and *acid* refer to the taste of vinegar, but *acid* stresses the natural composition and *sour* the result of fermentation or decay. *Bitter* suggests the taste of quinine or gall.

source (sôrs, sōrs) *n.* **1.** That from which any act, movement, or effect proceeds; a creator; origin. **2.** A place where something is found or whence it is taken or derived. **3.** The spring from which a stream of water proceeds; a fountain. **4.** A person, writing, or agency from which information is obtained. [< OF < L *surgere*]

sour·dough (sour'dō') *n.* **1.** *Dial.* Fermented dough for use as leaven in making bread. **2.** *U.S. & Canadian Slang* A pioneer or prospector.

sour grapes The attitude of affecting to despise something one cannot do or have: an allusion to a fable of Aesop.

sour·puss (sour'poos') *n. Slang* A person with a sullen, peevish expression or character.

souse (sous) *v.t. & v.i.* **soused, sous·ing 1.** To dip or steep in a liquid. **2.** To pickle. **3.** *Slang* To make or get drunk. — *n.* **1.** The act of sousing. **2.** Something steeped in pickle, esp., the feet and ears of a pig. **3.** A liquid used in pickling; brine. **4.** *Slang* A drunkard. [< OF < OHG *sulza* brine]

sou·tane (soo·tän') *n.* A Roman Catholic priest's cassock. [< F < Ital. < *sotto* under < L *subtus*]

south (south) *n.* **1.** The direction along a meridian that falls to the right of an observer on earth facing the sun at sunrise. **2.** One of the four cardinal points of the compass, directly opposite *north* and 90° clockwise from *east.* See COMPASS CARD. **3.** Any direction near this point. **4.** *Sometimes cap.* Any region south of a specified point. — **the South** In the U.S.: **a** The population or territory of the southern or southeastern States. **b** The Confederacy. — *adj.* **1.** To, toward, facing, or in the south; southern. **2.** Coming from the south: the *south* wind. — *adv.* In or toward the south; southward. [OE *sūth*]

south·east (south'ēst', *Naut.* sou'ēst') *n.* **1.** The direction midway between south and east. **2.** A point on the mariner's compass, 12 points or 135° clockwise from due north. See COMPASS CARD. **3.** Any region lying in or toward this point. — *adj.* **1.** To, toward, facing, or in the southeast. **2.** Coming from the southeast. — *adv.* In or toward the southeast. — **south'east'ern** *adj.*

south·east·er (south'ēs'tər, *Naut.* sou'ēs'tər) *n.* A gale or storm from the southeast.

south·east·er·ly (south'ēs'tər·lē, *Naut.* sou'ēs'tər·lē) *adj.* **1.** In, of, or toward the southeast. **2.** From the southeast, as a wind. — *adv.* Toward or from the southeast.

south·east·ward (south'ēst'wərd, *Naut.* sou'ēst'wərd) *adv.* Toward the southeast. Also **south'east'wards.** — *adj.* To, toward, facing, or in the southeast. — *n.* Southeast.

south·east·ward·ly (south'ēst'wərd·lē, *Naut.* sou'ēst'wərd·lē) *adj. & adv.* Toward or from the southeast.

south·er (sou'thər) *n.* A gale or storm from the south.

south·er·ly (suth'ər·lē) *adj.* **1.** In, of, toward, or pertaining to the south. **2.** From the south, as a wind. — *adv.* Toward or from the south.

south·ern (suth'ərn) *adj.* **1.** To, toward, or in the south. **2.** Native to or inhabiting the south. **3.** *Sometimes cap.* Of, pertaining to, or characteristic of the south or South. **4.** From the south, as a wind. [OE *sūtherne*] — **south'ern·most** *adj.*

Southern Cross A southern constellation having four bright stars in the form of a cross.

south·ern·er (suth'ərn·ər) *n.* **1.** One who is native to or lives in the south. **2.** *Usu. cap.* One who lives in or comes from the southern United States.

Southern Hemisphere See under HEMISPHERE.

southern lights The aurora australis.

south·land (south'land') *n. Sometimes cap.* A land or region in the south or South. — **south'land'er** *n.*

south·paw (south'pô') *Informal n.* **1.** In baseball, a left-handed pitcher. **2.** Any left-handed person or player. — *adj.* Left-handed.

South Pole The southern extremity of the earth's axis.

south-south·east (south'south'ēst', *Naut.* sou'sou'ēst') *n.* **1.** The direction midway between south and southeast. **2.** A point on the mariner's compass, 14 points or 157° 30' clockwise from due north. See COMPASS CARD. — *adj. & adv.* In, toward, or from the south-southeast.

south-south·west (south'south'west', *Naut.* sou'sou'west') *n.* **1.** The direction midway between south and southwest. **2.** A point on the mariner's compass, 18 points or 202° 30' clockwise from due north. See COMPASS CARD. — *adj. & adv.* In, toward, or from the south-southwest.

south·ward (south′wərd, *Naut.* suth′ərd) *adv.* Toward the south. Also **south′wards.** — *adj.* To, toward, facing, or in the south. — *n.* A southward direction or point. — **south′ward·ly** *adj. & adv.*

south·west (south′west′, *Naut.* sou′west′) *n.* **1.** The direction midway between south and west. **2.** A point on the mariner's compass, 20 points or 225° clockwise from due north. See COMPASS CARD. **3.** Any region lying in or toward this point. — *adj.* **1.** To, toward, facing, or in the southwest. **2.** Coming from the southwest: a *southwest* wind. — *adv.* In or toward the southwest. — **south′west′ern** *adj.*

south·west·er (south′wes′tər, *Naut.* sou′wes′tər) *n.* **1.** A gale or storm from the southwest. **2.** A waterproof hat with a broad brim over the neck. Also **sou′′west′er.**

south·west·er·ly (south′wes′tər-lē, *Naut.* sou′wes′tər-lē) *adj.* **1.** In, of, or toward the southwest. **2.** From the southwest, as a wind. — *adv.* Toward or from the southwest.

south·west·ward (south′west′wərd, *Naut.* sou′west′wərd) *adv.* Toward the southwest. Also **south′west′wards.** — *adj.* To, toward, facing, or in the southwest. — *n.* Southwest. — **south′west′ward·ly** *adj. & adv.*

sou·ve·nir (sōō′və-nir′, sōō′və-nir′) *n.* A token of remembrance; memento. [< F < L *subvenire* to come to mind]

sov·er·eign (sov′rən, suv′-) *n.* **1.** A person, governing body, etc., in whom the supreme power or authority is vested; monarch; ruler. **2.** An English gold coin equivalent to one pound sterling or twenty shillings. — *adj.* **1.** Exercising or possessing supreme authority or jurisdiction. **2.** Independent, and free from external authority or influence: a *sovereign* state. **3.** Possessing supreme excellence or efficacy. [< OF, ult. < L *super* above] — **sov′er·eign·ly** *adv.*

sov·er·eign·ty (sov′rən-tē, suv′-) *n. pl.* **·ties 1.** The state of being sovereign; supreme authority. **2.** The supreme power in a state. **3.** A sovereign state, kingdom, etc. **4.** The status or dominion of a sovereign.

so·vi·et (sō′vē·et, -ət, sō′vē·et′) *n.* **1.** In the Soviet Union, any of the legislative bodies existing at various governmental levels. See SUPREME SOVIET. **2.** Any of various similar legislative bodies. [< Russian *sovyet* council]

So·vi·et (sō′vē·et, -ət, sō′vē·et′) *adj.* Of or pertaining to the Union of Soviet Socialist Republics.

so·vi·et·ism (sō′vē·ə·tiz′əm) *n.* The policies of or government by soviets, esp., as practiced in the Soviet Union. — **so′vi·et·ist** *n.* — **so′vi·et·is′tic** *adj.*

so·vi·et·ize (sō′vē·ə·tīz′) *v.t.* **·ized, ·iz·ing** To bring under a soviet form of government. — **so′vi·et·i·za′tion** *n.*

sow¹ (sō) *v.* **sowed, sown** or **sowed, sow·ing** *v.t.* **1.** To scatter (seed) over land for growth. **2.** To scatter seed over (land). **3.** To spread abroad; disseminate; implant: to *sow* the seeds of distrust. **4.** To cover or sprinkle. — *v.i.* **5.** To scatter seed. [OE *sāwan*] — **sow′er** *n.*

sow² (sou) *n.* A female hog. [OE *sū, sugu*]

sow·bel·ly (sou′bel′ē) *n. U.S. Dial.* Salt pork.

soy (soi) **1.** The soybean. **2.** An Asian sauce prepared from soybeans fermented and steeped in brine: also **soy sauce.** [< Japanese, short for *shōyū*]

soy·bean (soi′bēn′) *n.* **1.** An erect, leguminous herb native to China and India, and cultivated for forage. **2.** Its bean, a source of oil, flour, and other products. Also called *soy:* also **soy·a** (soi′ə). [< SOY + BEAN]

spa (spä) *n.* **1.** Any locality frequented for its mineral springs. **2.** A mineral spring. [from the Belgian town, *Spa*]

space (spās) *n.* **1.** That which is characterized by dimensions extending indefinitely in all directions from any given point, and within which all material bodies are located. **2.** An interval or area between or within points or objects. **3.** Area, room, or extent, as for some purpose: parking *space*. **4.** Outer space. **5.** An interval of time; period; while. **6.** An occasion or opportunity. **7.** *Printing* A piece of type metal used for spacing between words. **8.** A part of a musical staff included between two lines. **9.** Reserved accommodations, as on a train. **10.** Pages, linage, broadcasting time, etc., available for advertisements. — *v.t.* **spaced, spac·ing 1.** To separate by spaces. **2.** To divide into spaces. [< OF < L *spatium*] — **space′less** *adj.* — **spac′er** *n.*

space·craft (spās′kraft′, -kräft′) *n. Aerospace* Any vehicle, manned or unmanned, designed for research, exploration, or travel in outer space. Also **space·ship** (spās′ship′).

space·flight (spās′flīt′) *n.* Flight in outer space by a man-made object or vehicle.

space·man (spās′mən) *n. pl.* **·men** (-mən) *Aerospace* One who travels in outer space; an astronaut.

space medicine *Aerospace* Medicine.

space·port (spās′pôrt′, -pōrt′) *n. Aerospace* A base for rockets and other spacecraft, with supporting equipment.

space probe *Aerospace* An artificial satellite or other spacecraft equipped to obtain data in outer space.

space-time (spās′tīm′) *n.* A four-dimensional continuum consisting of three spatial coordinates and one coordinate of time. Also **space-time continuum.**

spa·cial (spā′shəl) See SPATIAL.

spac·ing (spā′sing) *n.* **1.** The act, process, or result of arrangement by spaces. **2.** A space or spaces, as in print.

spa·cious (spā′shəs) *adj.* **1.** Of indefinite or vast extent. **2.** Affording ample room; capacious. — **spa′cious·ly** *adv.* — **spa′cious·ness** *n.*

spade¹ (spād) *n.* **1.** An implement used for digging, cutting turf, etc., heavier than a shovel and having a flatter blade. **2.** Any of various tools or implements resembling a spade. — **to call a spade a spade** To speak the plain, uncompromising truth. — *v.t.* **spad·ed, spad·ing** To dig or cut with a spade. [OE *spadu*] — **spad′er** *n.*

spade² (spād) *n.* **1.** A figure on playing cards, resembling a heart with a stalk or handle at the juncture of the lobes. **2.** A card so marked. **3.** *Usu. pl.* The suit of cards so marked. [< Sp. < L < Gk. *spathē* sword]

spade·work (spād′wûrk′) *n.* **1.** Work done with a spade. **2.** Preliminary work necessary to get a project under way.

spa·dix (spā′diks) *n. pl.* **spa·di·ces** (spā·dī′sēz) *Bot.* A spike or head of flowers with a fleshy axis, usu. enclosed within a spathe. [< Gk. < *spaein* to break]

spa·ghet·ti (spə·get′ē) *n.* A food consisting of cordlike strands of flour paste. [< Ital., pl. dim. of *spago* cord]

spake (spāk) Archaic past tense of SPEAK.

span¹ (span) *v.t.* **spanned, span·ning 1.** To measure, esp. with the hand with thumb and little finger extended. **2.** To encircle or grasp with the hand, as in measuring. **3.** To stretch across: This road *spans* the continent. **4.** To provide with something that stretches across or extends over. — *n.* **1.** The extreme space over which the hand can be expanded, usu. considered as nine inches. **2.** Distance or extent between any two extremities. **3.** Any small interval or distance, in space or in time. **4.** That which spans, as a bridge. [OE *spann*] — **span′less** *adj.*

span² (span) Archaic past tense of SPIN.

span·drel (span′drəl) *n. Archit.* **a** The triangular space between the outer curve of an arch and the rectangular figure formed by the moldings or framework surrounding it. **b** The space between the shoulders of two adjoining arches. Also **span′dril.** [Dim. of AF *spaundre*, prob. < OF *espandre* to expand]

spang (spang) *adv. U.S. Informal* Directly; exactly; straight: He ran *spang* into the wall. [Origin uncertain]

span·gle (spang′gəl) *n.* **1.** A small bit of sparkling metal, plastic, etc., used for decoration in dress, as in theatrical costume. **2.** Any small sparkling object. — *v.* **·gled, ·gling** *v.t.* **1.** To adorn with or as with spangles; cause to glitter. — *v.i.* **2.** To sparkle as spangles; glitter. [Dim. of MDu. *spang* clasp, brooch] — **span′gly** *adj.*

Span·iard (span′yərd) *n.* A native or citizen of Spain.

span·iel (span′yəl) *n.* **1.** Any of various breeds of small or medium-sized dogs having large pendulous ears and usu. long silky hair. **2.** One who follows like a dog; an obsequious follower. [< OF *espaignol* Spanish (dog)]

Span·ish (span′ish) *adj.* Of or pertaining to Spain, its people, or their language. — *n.* **1.** The Romance language of Spain, Spanish America, and the Philippine Islands. **2.** The inhabitants of Spain collectively: with *the.*

Span·ish-A·mer·i·can (span′ish·ə·mer′ə·kən) *adj.* **1.** Of or pertaining to Spanish America. **2.** Designating or pertaining to the war between the U.S. and Spain, 1898. — *n.* One of Spanish origin living in America, esp. Central or South America; a citizen of a Spanish-American country.

Spanish-American War See table for WAR.

Spanish Main Loosely, the part of Caribbean through which Spanish merchant vessels formerly sailed.

Spanish moss A long, pendent plant that grows on trees of the southern U.S. near the seacoast.

spank (spangk) *v.t.* **1.** To slap or strike, esp. on the buttocks with the open hand as a punishment. — *v.i.* **2.** To move briskly. — *n.* A smack on the buttocks. [Imit.]

spank·er (spangk′ər) *n.* **1.** One who or that which spanks. **2.** *Naut.* A fore-and-aft sail extended by a boom and a gaff from the mizzenmast of a ship or boat. **3.** Any person or thing uncommonly large or fine.

spank·ing (spangk′ing) *adj.* **1.** Moving or blowing rapidly; swift; dashing; lively; strong. **2.** *Brit. Informal* Uncommonly large or fine. — *n.* A series of slaps on the buttocks given as punishment. — *adv. Informal* Very: *spanking* clean.

span·ner (span′ər) *n.* **1.** One who or that which spans. **2.** *Brit.* A hand tool used to turn nuts, bolts, etc. [< G]

spar¹ (spär) *n.* **1.** *Naut.* A round timber or pole for extending a sail, as a mast, yard, or boom. **2.** A similar pole forming part of a derrick, crane, etc. **3.** *Aeron.* Any principal lateral member of an airplane wing. — *v.t.* **sparred, spar·ring** To furnish with spars. [Cf. ON *sparri*, MDu. *sparre* beam]

spar² (spär) *v.i.* **sparred, spar·ring 1.** To box, esp. with care and adroitness. **2.** To bandy words; wrangle. — *n.* The act or practice of boxing. [? < OF < Ital. *sparare* to kick < L *parare* to prepare]

spar³ (spär) *n.* A vitreous, crystalline, easily cleavable, lustrous mineral of varied composition. [< MDu.]

Spar (spär) *n.* A member of the women's reserve of the U.S. Coast Guard. Also **SPAR**. [< L *s(emper) par(atus)* always ready, the motto of the U.S. Coast Guard]

spar deck *Naut.* The light upper deck of a vessel, extending from bow to stern.

spare (spär) *v.* **spared, spar·ing** *v.t.* **1.** To refrain from injuring, molesting, or killing. **2.** To free or relieve (someone) from (pain, expense, etc.). **3.** To refrain from using or exercising; use frugally. **4.** To part with; do without: Can you *spare* a dime? — *v.i.* **5.** To be frugal. **6.** To be lenient or forgiving; show mercy. — *adj.* **spar·er, spar·est 1.** That can be spared or used at will; disposable; available. **2.** Held in reserve; extra. **3.** Having little flesh; lean. **4.** Not lavish or abundant; scanty. **5.** Economical; parsimonious. — *n.* **1.** That which has been saved or stored away. **2.** A duplicate item kept as a substitute in case the original breaks down, as an automobile tire. **3.** In bowling, the knocking down by a player of all the pins with the two bowls in any frame; also, the score so made. [OE *sparian*] — **spare'ly** *adv.* — **spare'ness** *n.* — **spar'er** *n.*

spare·rib (spär'rib') *n.* A cut of meat, esp. pork, consisting of closely trimmed ribs. [? Alter. of MLG *ribbespēr*]

spar·ing (spâr'ing) *adj.* **1.** Scanty; slight. **2.** Frugal. **3.** That spares. — **spar'ing·ly** *adv.* — **spar'ing·ness** *n.*

spark (spärk) *n.* **1.** An incandescent particle thrown off from a red-hot or burning substance or struck from a flint. **2.** Any glistening or brilliant point or transient luminous particle. **3.** Anything that kindles or animates. **4.** *Electr.* **a** The luminous effect of a disruptive electric discharge, or the discharge itself. **b** A small transient arc or an incandescent particle thrown off from such an arc. **5.** A small diamond or bit of diamond, as for cutting glass. **6.** A small trace or indication. — *v.i.* **1.** To give off sparks; scintillate. — *v.t.* **2.** To activate or cause: to *spark* a revolution. [OE *spearca*] — **spark'er** *n.*

spar·kle (spär'kəl) *v.i.* **·kled, ·kling 1.** To give off flashes of light; scintillate; glitter. **2.** To emit sparks. **3.** To bubble; effervesce. **4.** To be brilliant or vivacious. — *n.* A spark; gleam. [Freq. of SPARK[1]]

spar·kler (spär'klər) *n.* **1.** Something that sparkles. **2.** A sparkling gem. **3.** A thin, rodlike firework that emits sparks.

spar·kling (spär'kling) *adj.* **1.** Giving out sparks or flashes; glittering. **2.** Brilliant; vivacious. — **spar'kling·ly** *adv.*

spark plug An electrical device for igniting the explosive gases in an internal-combustion engine by means of a spark passing between two terminals. Also *Brit.* **spark'ing plug.**

spar·ling (spär'ling) *n.* **1.** A smelt, parr, or other young fish. **2.** A young herring. [< OF *esperlinge* < Gmc.]

spar·row (spar'ō) *n.* **1.** A small hardy bird related to the finches, grosbeaks, and buntings, introduced into the U.S., where it is known as the **English sparrow. 2.** Any of several related North American birds. [OE *spearwa*]

sparrow hawk 1. A small American falcon that preys on other birds, mice, insects, etc. **2.** A small European hawk that preys on birds.

sparse (spärs) *adj.* Scattered at considerable distances apart; not dense. [< L *sparsus*, pp. of *spargere* to scatter] — **sparse'ly** *adv.* — **sparse'ness, spar'si·ty** *n.*

Spar·ta (spär'tə) An ancient city in the Peloponnesus, southern Greece; capital of ancient Laconia.

Spar·tan (spär'tən) *adj.* **1.** Of or pertaining to Sparta or the Spartans. **2.** Resembling the Spartans in character; courageous, hardy, austere, stoical, and rigorous. — *n.* **1.** A native or citizen of Sparta. **2.** A person of Spartan character. — **Spar'tan·ism** *n.*

spasm (spaz'əm) *n.* **1.** Any sudden, transient burst of energy or activity. **2.** *Pathol.* Any involuntary convulsive muscular contraction. When manifested by alternate contractions and relaxations it is a **clonic spasm;** when persistent and steady, it is a **tonic spasm.** [< L < Gk. < *span* to draw, pull]

spas·mod·ic (spaz·mod'ik) *adj.* **1.** Of the nature of a spasm; convulsive. **2.** Violent, impulsive, and transitory. Also **spas·mod'i·cal.** — **spas·mod'i·cal·ly** *adv.*

spas·tic (spas'tik) *adj.* Of, pertaining to, or characterized by spasms; spasmodic. — *n.* A person afflicted with cerebral palsy. — **spas'ti·cal·ly** *adv.*

spat[1] (spat) Past tense and past participle of SPIT[1].

spat[2] (spat) *n.* **1.** Spawn of shellfish; esp., spawn of the oyster. **2.** A young oyster, or young oysters collectively. — *v.i.* **spat·ted, spat·ting** To spawn, as oysters. [? Akin to SPIT[1]]

spat[3] (spat) *n.* **1.** A slight blow; slap. **2.** A splash, as of rain; spatter. **3.** A petty dispute. — *v.* **spat·ted, spat·ting** *v.i.* **1.** To strike with a slight sound; slap. **2.** To engage in a petty quarrel. — *v.t.* **3.** To slap. [Prob. imit.]

spat[4] (spat) *n.* *Usu. pl.* A short gaiter worn over a shoe and fastened beneath with a strap. [Short for SPATTERDASH]

spate (spāt) *n.* *Chiefly Brit.* A sudden or vigorous outpouring, as of words, feeling, etc. Also **spait.** [Origin uncertain]

spathe (spāth) *n.* *Bot.* A large bract or pair of bracts sheathing a flower cluster, spadix, etc. [< L < Gk. *spathē* broadsword] — **spa·those** (spā'thōs, spath'ōs) *adj.*

spa·tial (spā'shəl) *adj.* Pertaining to, involving, or having the nature of space. Also spelled *spacial.* [< L *spatium* space] — **spa·ti·al·i·ty** (spā'shē·al'ə·tē) *n.* — **spa'tial·ly** *adv.*

spa·ti·o·tem·po·ral (spā'shē·ō·tem'pər·əl) *adj.* Of or pertaining to both space and time.

spat·ter (spat'ər) *v.t.* **1.** To scatter in drops or splashes, as mud or paint. **2.** To splash with such drops. **3.** To defame; slander. — *v.i.* **4.** To throw off drops or splashes. **5.** To fall in a shower, as raindrops. — *n.* **1.** The act of spattering, or the matter spattered. **2.** A pattering noise, as of falling rain. [Cf. Frisian *spatterje,* Du. *spatten* to spatter]

spat·ter·dash (spat'ər·dash') *n.* A legging or puttee.

spat·u·la (spach'ōō·lə) *n.* **1.** A knifelike instrument with a flat, flexible blade, used to spread plaster, cake icing, etc. **2.** *Med.* An instrument used to press the tongue down or aside, as in examinations. [< L, dim. of *spatha* spathe] — **spat'u·lar** *adj.*

spawn (spôn) *n.* **1.** *Zool.* The eggs of fishes, amphibians, mollusks, etc., esp. in masses. **2.** The offspring of any animal. **3.** Outcome or results; yield. **4.** The spat of the oyster. **5.** Very small fish; fry. **6.** *Bot.* The mycelium of mushrooms or other fungi. — *v.i.* **1.** To produce spawn; deposit eggs or roe. **2.** To come forth as or like spawn. — *v.t.* **3.** To produce (spawn). **4.** To give rise to. **5.** To bring forth abundantly or in great quantity. **6.** To plant with spawn or mycelium. [< AF, OF < L *expandere*]

spay (spā) *v.t.* To remove the ovaries from (a female animal). [< AF, OF < L *spatha* sword]

speak (spēk) *v.* **spoke** (*Archaic* **spake**), **spo·ken** (*Archaic* **spoke**), **speak·ing** *v.i.* **1.** To employ the vocal organs in ordinary speech; utter words. **2.** To express or convey ideas, opinions, etc., in or as in speech. **3.** To make a speech. **4.** To talk together; converse. **5.** To make a sound; also, to bark, as a dog. — *v.t.* **6.** To express or make known in or as in speech. **7.** To utter in speech. **8.** To use or be capable of using (a language) in conversation. **9.** To speak to. — **to speak for 1.** To speak in behalf of; represent officially. **2.** To lay claim to; engage. [OE *specan, sprecan*] — **speak'a·ble** *adj.*

speak·eas·y (spēk'ē'zē) *n.* *pl.* **·eas·ies** *Slang* A place where liquor is sold illegally.

speak·er (spē'kər) *n.* **1.** One who speaks. **2.** The presiding officer in any one of various legislative bodies. **3.** A loudspeaker. — **speak'er·ship** *n.*

speak·ing (spē'king) *adj.* **1.** Having the power of effective speech. **2.** Expressive; telling. — *n.* **1.** The act of utterance; vocal expression. **2.** Oratory; public declamation. — **speak'ing·ly** *adv.*

spear (spir) *n.* **1.** A weapon consisting of a pointed head on a long shaft. **2.** A similar instrument, barbed and usu. forked, as for use in spearing fish. **3.** A leaf or slender stalk, as of grass. — *v.t.* **1.** To pierce or capture with a spear. — *v.i.* **2.** To pierce as a spear does. **3.** To send forth spears or spires, as a plant. [OE *spere* spear] — **spear'er** *n.*

spear·head (spir'hed') *n.* **1.** The point of a spear. **2.** One who or that which leads, influences, or directs an action, etc.; esp., a military force leading an attack on enemy positions. — *v.t.* To be in the lead of (an attack, etc.).

spear·man (spir'mən) *n.* *pl.* **·men** (-mən) A man armed with a spear. Also **spears'man** (spirz'-).

spear·mint (spir'mint') *n.* An aromatic herb similar to peppermint.

spe·cial (spesh'əl) *adj.* **1.** Having some peculiar or distinguishing characteristic or characteristics; particular. **2.** Designed for or assigned to a specific purpose; limited or specific in range, aim, or purpose. **3.** Of, pertaining to, constituting, or designating a species; differential. **4.** Unique; exceptional. **5.** Extra or additional, as a dividend. **6.** Intimate; beloved. — *n.* A person or thing made, detailed for, or appropriated to a specific service or occasion, as a train, a newspaper edition, etc. [< OF < L *species* kind, species] — **spe'cial·ly** *adv.* — **spe'cial·ness** *n.*

special delivery *U.S.* Mail delivery by special courier, a service obtained for an additional fee.

spe·cial·ist (spesh'əl·ist) *n.* **1.** A person devoted to some one line of study, occupation, or professional work; esp., a physician who restricts his practice to one branch of medicine. **2.** In the U.S. Army, an enlisted person in a technical or administrative position, with pay equal to that of a noncommissioned officer in the same grade, but ranking below a corporal and above a private first class. See table at GRADE. — **spe'cial·ism** *n.* — **spe'cial·is'tic** *adj.*

spe·ci·al·i·ty (spesh'ē·al'ə·tē) *n.* *pl.* **·ties 1.** A specific or individual characteristic. **2.** Specialty (defs. 3, 4, 5). ◆ In British usage, this form is preferred to *specialty*.

spe·cial·i·za·tion (spesh/əl·ə·zā/shən, -ī·zā/-) *n.* **1.** The act or process of specializing; also, the state of being or becoming specialized. **2.** *Biol.* The development of a plant or animal organ or part in adaptation to environmental influences or for a special function.

spe·cial·ize (spesh/əl·īz) *v.* **·ized, ·iz·ing** *v.i.* **1.** To concentrate on one particular activity or subject; engage in a specialty. **2.** *Biol.* To take on a special form or forms by specialization. **—** *v.t.* **3.** To adapt for some special use or purpose. **4.** *Biol.* To modify or adapt by specialization. **5.** To endorse, as a check, to a particular payee. **6.** To mention specifically. Also *Brit.* **spe/cial·ise.**

spe·cial·ty (spesh/əl·tē) *n. pl.* **·ties 1.** A special occupation, craft, or study. **2.** The state of being special or of having peculiar characteristics. **3.** An individual characteristic or peculiarity; distinguishing mark. **4.** An article dealt in exclusively or chiefly, or having a special character.

spe·cie (spē/shē) *n.* Coined money; coin. **— in specie 1.** In coin. **2.** *Law* In kind. [< L (*in*) *specie* (in) kind]

spe·cies (spē/shēz, -shiz, -sēz) *n. pl.* **·cies 1.** *Biol.* A category of animals or plants subordinate to a genus but above a breed, race, strain, or variety. **2.** A group of individuals or objects agreeing in some common attribute or attributes and designated by a common name. **3.** *Eccl.* The visible form of bread or of wine retained by the eucharistic elements after consecration. **4.** A kind, sort, or variety. **5.** An image, form, or appearance. [< L, form, kind]

spec·i·fi·a·ble (spes/ə·fī/ə·bəl) *adj.* Such as can be specified.

spe·cif·ic (spi·sif/ik) *adj.* **1.** Distinctly and plainly set forth; definite or determinate. **2.** *Biol.* Of, pertaining to, or distinguishing a species. **3.** Peculiar or special, as characteristics, qualities, etc. **4.** Characteristic of or proper to a given substance or phenomenon, esp. in relation to some arbitrary but constant standard of comparison: *specific gravity.* **5.** *Med.* **a** Curing or alleviating a special disease or pathological condition: said of a remedy or medicine. **b** Caused by a particular condition, germ, etc.: said of a disease. **—** *n.* **1.** Anything specific or adapted to effect a specific result. **2.** A special medicine for a particular disease. **3.** *Usu. pl. U.S. Informal* A particular; item; instance. [< L < *species* kind, class + *facere* to make] **— spec·i·fic·i·ty** (spes/ə·fis/ə·tē) *n.*

spe·cif·i·cal·ly (spi·sif/ik·lē) *adv.* **1.** In a specific manner; explicitly; particularly; definitely. **2.** As to or in respect to species. **3.** In a particular sense or case.

spec·i·fi·ca·tion (spes/ə·fə·kā/shən) *n.* **1.** The act of specifying. **2.** Something specified, as in a contract, plans, etc.; also, one detail in such a statement. **3.** *Usu. pl.* A specific description of certain dimensions, types of material, etc., to be used in a manufacturing or engineering project.

specific gravity *Physics* The ratio of the mass of a body to that of an equal volume of some standard substance, water in the case of solids and liquids, and air or hydrogen in the case of gases; a measure of density.

spec·i·fy (spes/ə·fī) *v.t.* **·fied, ·fy·ing 1.** To mention specifically; state in full and explicit terms. **2.** To embody in a specification. [< OF < L < *species* species + *facere* to make]

spec·i·men (spes/ə·mən) *n.* **1.** One of a class of persons or things regarded as representative of the class; an example; sample. **2.** *Med.* A sample of body tissue or exudates taken for analysis and diagnosis. **3.** *Informal* A person of pronounced or curious type. [< L < *specere* to look at]

spe·ci·os·i·ty (spē/shē·os/ə·tē) *n. pl.* **·ties** One who or that which is plausible at first view but actually is not.

spe·cious (spē/shəs) *adj.* **1.** Apparently good or right, but actually not so; plausible: *specious* reasoning. **2.** Pleasing or attractive in appearance, but deceptive. **3.** Beguiling, but lacking in sincerity. [< L *speciosus* fair] **— spe/cious·ly** *adv.* **— spe/cious·ness** *n.*

speck (spek) *n.* **1.** A small spot, stain, or discoloration. **2.** Any very small thing; a particle. **—** *v.t.* To mark with spots or specks; speckle. [OE *specca*]

speck·le (spek/əl) *v.t.* **·led, ·ling** To mark with specks or speckles. **—** *n.* A small spot; speck. **— speck/led** *adj.*

specs (speks) *n.pl. Informal* **1.** Eyeglasses; spectacles. Also **specks. 2.** Specifications (def. 3).

spec·ta·cle (spek/tə·kəl) *n.* **1.** That which is exhibited to public view, esp. something grand or showy. **2.** An unwelcome or deplorable exhibition. **3.** *pl.* A pair of eyeglasses. [< F < L < *spectare*, freq. of *specere* to see]

spec·ta·cled (spek/tə·kəld) *adj.* **1.** Wearing spectacles. **2.** Having markings resembling a pair of spectacles.

spec·tac·u·lar (spek·tak/yə·lər) *adj.* **1.** Characterized by or displaying unusual, exciting, or unexpected qualities, conditions, etc.: a *spectacular* rescue. **2.** Of, pertaining to, or like a spectacle. **—** *n.* **1.** In television, a lavish dramatic or musical production. **2.** An elaborate, illuminated sign. **— spec·tac/u·lar·ly** *adv.* **— spec·tac/u·lar/i·ty** (-lar/ə·tē) *n.*

spec·ta·tor (spek/tā·tər, spek·tā/-) *n.* **1.** One who beholds;

eyewitness; onlooker. **2.** One who is present at and views a show, game, spectacle, etc. [< L < *spectare* to look at]

spec·ter (spek/tər) *n.* **1.** A ghost or apparition. **2.** Anything of a fearful or horrible nature. Also *Brit.* **spec/tre.** [< F < L *spectrum* vision]

spec·tra (spek/trə) Plural of SPECTRUM.

spec·tral (spek/trəl) *adj.* **1.** Of, pertaining to, or like a specter; ghostly. **2.** Pertaining to a spectrum or spectra. **— spec·tral·i·ty** (spek·tral/ə·tē) *n.* **— spec/tral·ly** *adv.*

spectro- *combining form* **1.** Radiant energy, as exhibited in the spectrum. **2.** Spectroscope; spectroscopic. [< SPECTRUM]

spec·tro·gram (spek/trə·gram) *n.* A photograph made by a spectrograph.

spec·tro·graph (spek/trə·graf, -gräf) *n.* **1.** An apparatus for photographing or forming a representation of the spectrum. **2.** A spectrogram.

spec·tro·scope (spek/trə·skōp) *n.* An optical instrument for forming and analyzing the spectrum emitted by bodies or substances. **— spec/tro·scop/ic** (-skop/ik) or **·i·cal** *adj.* **— spec/tro·scop/i·cal·ly** *adv.*

SIMPLE SPECTROSCOPE

a Prism. *b* Telescope for viewing prism through eyepiece (*e*). *c* Collimator with slit (*d*).

spec·tros·co·py (spek·tros/kə·pē) *n.* The study and analysis of the phenomena observed with the spectroscope. **— spec·tros/co·pist** *n.*

spec·trum (spek/trəm) *n. pl.* **·tra** (-trə) **1.** *Physics* **a** The band of color observed when a beam of white light is passed through a prism that separates each component of the light according to wavelengths, ranging from long for red to short for violet. **b** An image formed by radiant energy directed through a spectroscope and brought to a focus, and in which each wavelength corresponds to a specific band or line in a progressive series characteristic of the emitting source. **2.** Any range of characteristics, values, activities, etc. **3.** An afterimage. [< L, vision]

spec·u·la (spek/yə·lə) Plural of SPECULUM.

spec·u·late (spek/yə·lāt) *v.i.* **·lat·ed, ·lat·ing 1.** To form conjectures regarding anything without experiment; theorize; conjecture. **2.** To make an investment involving a risk, but with hope of gain. [< L *speculatus*, pp. of *speculari* to look at] **— spec/u·la/tor** *n.*

spec·u·la·tion (spek/yə·lā/shən) *n.* **1.** The act of theorizing or conjecturing; speculating. **2.** A theory or conjecture. **3.** A conclusion reached by or based upon conjecture. **4.** An investment involving risk with hope of large profit. **5.** The act of engaging in risky business transactions that offer a possibility of large profit.

spec·u·la·tive (spek/yə·lā/tiv, -lə·tiv) *adj.* **1.** Of, pertaining to, engaged in, or given to speculation, meditation, etc. **2.** Strictly theoretical or purely scientific. **3.** Engaging in or involving financial speculation. **4.** Involving risk. **— spec/u·la/tive·ly** *adv.* **— spec/u·la/tive·ness** *n.*

spec·u·lum (spek/yə·ləm) *n. pl.* **·la** (-lə) or **·lums 1.** A mirror of polished metal or of glass coated with a metal film, used for telescope reflectors, etc. **2.** *Med.* An instrument that dilates a passage of the body for examination. [< L, mirror < *specere* to see] **— spec/u·lar** *adj.*

sped (sped) Alternative past tense and past participle of SPEED.

speech (spēch) *n.* **1.** The faculty of expressing thought and emotion by spoken words. **2.** The act of speaking. **3.** That which is spoken; a saying or remark. **4.** A public address or talk. **5.** A characteristic manner of speaking. **6.** A particular language, idiom, or dialect: American *speech.* **7.** Any audible or visible method of communication, including cries, gestures, and sign language. **8.** The study of oral communication. [OE < *specan, sprecan* to speak]

speech clinic A place where speech disorders are treated.

speech disorder Disorganization or impairment of speech caused either by physical defect or by mental disorder.

speech·i·fy (spēch/ə·fī) *v.i.* **·fied, ·fy·ing** To make speeches: a derisive or dialectal term. **— speech/i·fi/er** *n.*

speech·less (spēch/lis) *adj.* **1.** Unable to speak or temporarily deprived of speech because of physical weakness, strong emotion, etc. **2.** Mute; dumb. **3.** Silent; reticent. **4.** Unable to be expressed in words: *speechless* joy. **— speech/less·ly** *adv.* **— speech/less·ness** *n.*

speed (spēd) *n.* **1.** The act or state of moving or progressing swiftly; rapidity of motion; swiftness. **2.** Rate of motion, esp., in physics, as considered without reference to direction. **3.** Rate of performance, as shown by the ratio of work done to time spent. **4.** *Mech.* A transmission gear in a motor vehicle. **5.** *Photog.* In a camera lens, the minimum time required for an effective exposure. **—** *v.* **sped** or **speed·ed, speed·ing** *v.t.* **1.** To move or go with speed. **2.** To exceed a speed limit. **—** *v.t.* **3.** To promote the forward progress of; cause to move or go with speed. **4.** To promote the success of. **5.** To wish Godspeed to: *Speed the parting guest.* **— to speed up** To accelerate in speed or action. **— adj.** Having, pertaining to, characterized by, regulating, or indicating speed. [OE *spēd* prosperity, power]

speed·boat (spēd/bōt/) *n.* A motorboat capable of high speed.

speed·er (spē/dər) *n.* One who or that which speeds; esp., a motorist who exceeds a safe or legally specified limit.

speed·om·e·ter (spi·dom/ə·tər) *n.* A device for indicating the speed of a vehicle, often combined with an odometer.

speed·ster (spēd/stər) *n.* One who speeds.

speed·up (spēd/up/) *n.* An acceleration in work, output, movement, etc.

speed·way (spēd/wā/) *n.* A specially reserved or prepared road for vehicles traveling at high speed.

speed·well (spēd/wel/) *n.* One of various low herbs of the figwort family, bearing blue or white flowers.

speed·y (spē/dē) *adj.* **speed·i·er, speed·i·est 1.** Characterized by speed; rapid. **2.** Without delay; prompt. **— Syn.** See SWIFT. **— speed/i·ly** *adv.* **— speed/i·ness** *n.*

spe·le·an (spi·lē/ən) *adj.* **1.** Of, or like a cave. **2.** Dwelling in a cave or caves. [< L < Gk. *spēlaion* cave]

speleo- *combining form* Cave. [< L *spelaeum* cave < Gk. *spēlaion*]

spe·le·ol·o·gy (spē/lē·ol/ə·jē) *n.* **1.** The scientific study of caves in their physical, geological, and biological aspects. **2.** The exploration of caves as a sport or profession. **— spe/le·o·log/i·cal** (-ə·loj/i·kəl) *adj.* **— spe/le·ol/o·gist** *n.*

spell[1] (spel) *v.* **spelled** or **spelt, spell·ing** *v.t.* **1.** To name or write the letters of (a word); esp., to do so correctly. **2.** To form or be the letters of: C-a-t *spells* cat. **3.** To compose; make up. **4.** To signify; mean. **— v.i. 5.** To form words out of letters, esp. correctly. **— to spell out 1.** To read with difficulty. **2.** To puzzle out and learn. **3.** To make clear and explicit. [< OF *espeler* < Gmc.]

spell[2] (spel) *n.* **1.** A word formula used as a charm. **2.** An irresistible fascination or attraction. **— v.t.** **spelled, spell·ing** To cast a spell upon. [OE, statement.]

spell[3] (spel) *n.* **1.** A period of time, usu. of short length. **2.** *Informal* A continuous period characterized by a certain type of weather. **3.** *Informal* A short distance. **4.** *Informal* A fit of illness, debility, etc. **5.** A turn of duty in relief of another. **6.** A period of work or employment. **— v.t. 1.** To relieve temporarily from some work or duty. **— v.i. 2.** To take a rest. [OE *gespelia* substitute]

spell·bind (spel/bīnd/) *v.t.* **·bound, ·bind·ing** To bind or enthrall, as if by a spell. **— spell/bind/er** *n.*

spell·bound (spel/bound/) *adj.* Fascinated; enchanted.

spell·er (spel/ər) *n.* **1.** One who spells. **2.** A spelling book.

spell·ing (spel/ing) *n.* **1.** The act of one who spells. **2.** The art of correct spelling; orthography. **3.** The way in which a word is spelled.

spelling bee A gathering at which contestants engage in spelling words, those who spell wrongly usu. being retired until only one remains.

spelt[1] (spelt) Alternative past tense and past participle of SPELL.

spelt[2] (spelt) *n.* A species of wheat or any of its winter or spring varieties. [OE]

spe·lunk·er (spē·lung/kər) *n.* An enthusiast in the exploration and study of caves; a speleologist. [< L *spelunca* cave] **— spe·lunk/ing** *n.*

spend (spend) *v.* **spent, spend·ing** *v.t.* **1.** To pay out or disburse (money). **2.** To expend by degrees; use up. **3.** To apply or devote, as thought or effort, to some activity, purpose, etc. **4.** To pass: to *spend* one's life in jail. **— v.i. 5.** To pay out or disburse money, etc. [OE < L *expendere* to expend] **— spend/er** *n.*

spend·thrift (spend/thrift/) *n.* One who spends money lavishly or wastefully. **— adj.** Excessively lavish; prodigal.

spent (spent) Past tense and part participle of SPEND. **— adj. 1.** Worn out or exhausted. **2.** Deprived of force.

sperm[1] (spûrm) *n.* **1.** The male fertilizing fluid; semen. **2.** A male reproductive cell; spermatozoon. [< OF < L < Gk. *sperma* seed]

sperm[2] (spûrm) *n.* **1.** A sperm whale. **2.** Spermaceti. **3.** Sperm oil. [Short for SPERMACETI]

-sperm *combining form Bot.* A seed (of a specified kind): *gymnosperm.* [< Gk. *sperma, spermatos* seed]

sper·ma·ce·ti (spûr/mə·sē/tē, -set/ē) *n.* A white, waxy substance separated from the oil contained in the head of the sperm whale, used for making candles, ointments, etc. [< L *sperma ceti* head of a whale]

sper·mat·ic (spûr·mat/ik) *adj.* Of, pertaining to, or like sperm; generative.

spermato- *combining form* **1.** Seed; pertaining to seeds. **2.** Spermatozoa; of or related to spermatozoa. Also *spermo-.*

Also, before vowels, **spermat-.** [< Gk. *sperma, spermatos* seed]

sper·ma·to·phyte (spûr/mə·tə·fīt/, spər·mat/ə·fīt) *n. Bot.* Any of a phylum or division of flowering and seed-bearing plants. **— sper/ma·to·phyt/ic** (-fit/ik) *adj.*

sper·ma·to·zo·on (spûr/mə·tə·zō/on) *n. pl.* **·zo·a** (-zō/ə) *Biol.* The male fertilizing element of an animal, usu. in the form of a highly motile cell with a long flagellate process or tail: also called *zoosperm.* [< SPERMATO- + Gk. *zōion* animal] **— sper/ma·to·zo/al, sper/ma·to·zo/ic** *adj.*

sper·mic (spûr/mik) *adj.* Spermatic.

spermo- See SPERMATO-.

-spermous *combining form* Having (a specified number or kind of) seeds; seeded. Also **-spermal, -spermic.** [< -SPERM + -OUS]

sperm whale A large, toothed whale of warm seas, having a huge truncate head containing a reservoir of sperm oil.

spew (spyōō) *v.t. & v.i.* To vomit; throw up. **— n.** That which is spewed; vomit. Also spelled *spue.* [OE *spīwan*]

sphag·num (sfag/nəm) *n.* Any of a genus of whitish gray mosses found in damp places; the bog or peat mosses, used as packing and in surgical dressings. [< L < Gk. *sphágnos,* kind of moss] **— sphag/nous** *adj.*

sphal·er·ite (sfal/ər·īt) *n.* A resinous to adamantine native zinc sulfide, ZnS, with traces of iron and cadmium; a principal ore of zinc: also called *zinc blende.* [< Gk. *sphaleros* deceptive + -ITE]

sphe·noid (sfē/noid) *n.* **1.** *Mineral.* A crystal form enclosed by four faces, each of which cuts all three axes. **2.** *Anat.* The sphenoid bone. **— adj.** Wedge-shaped. [< Gk. *sphēn* wedge + -OID] **— sphe·noi/dal** (sfi·noid/l) *adj.*

sphenoid bone *Anat.* An irregular, compound bone situated at the base of the skull.

sphere (sfir) *n.* **1.** The surface described by a semicircle making one complete rotation on its diameter. **2.** A solid or hollow figure enclosed by a surface every point of which is equidistant from the center. **3.** A globe; ball. **4.** Compass or field of activity, endeavor, influence, etc.; range; scope; province. **5.** A particular social rank or position. **6.** The apparent outer dome of the heavens on which the heavenly bodies appear to lie. **— v.t.** **sphered, spher·ing 1.** To place in or as in a sphere. **2.** To set among the celestial spheres. **3.** To make spherical. [< OF < L < Gk. *sphaira* ball]

-sphere *combining form* **1.** Denoting an enveloping spherical mass: *atmosphere.* **2.** Denoting a spherical form: *planisphere.* [< Gk. *sphaira* ball, sphere]

spher·i·cal (sfir/i·kəl, sfer/-) *adj.* **1.** Shaped like a sphere; globular. **2.** Pertaining to a sphere or spheres. **3.** Pertaining to the heavenly bodies; celestial. Also **spher/ic.** **— spher/i·cal·ly** *adv.* **— spher/i·cal·ness** *n.*

sphe·ric·i·ty (sfi·ris/ə·tē) *n. pl.* **·ties** The state of being a sphere; spherical form; roundness.

sphe·roid (sfir/oid) *n. Geom.* A body having nearly the form of a sphere. **— sphe·roi/dal** (sfi·roid/l), **sphe·roi·dic** or **·di·cal** *adj.* **— sphe·roi/dal·ly** *adv.*

sphe·roi·dic·i·ty (sfir/oi·dis/ə·tē) *n.* The state or character of being a spheroid. Also **sphe·roi/di·ty** (sfi·roi/də·tē).

sphinc·ter (sfingk/tər) *n. Anat.* A band of muscle that surrounds an opening or tube in the body and serves to close it. [< LL < Gk. < *sphingein* to bind fast] **— sphinc/ter·al** *adj.*

sphinx (sfingks) *n. pl.* **sphinx·es** or **sphin·ges** (sfin/jēz) **1.** In Egyptian mythology, a wingless monster with a lion's body and the head of a man, a ram, or hawk. **2.** In Greek mythology, a winged monster with a woman's head and breasts and a lion's body, that destroyed those unable to guess her riddle. **3.** A mysterious or enigmatical person. **— the Sphinx** The colossal sphinx at Gizeh, having the body of a lion. [< L < Gk. < *sphingein* to close, strangle]

sphyg·mo·ma·nom·e·ter (sfig/mō·ma·nom/ə·tər) *n.* An instrument for measuring blood pressure in the arteries. [< Gk. *sphygmos* pulse + MANOMETER]

Spi·ca (spī/kə) *n.* A star, one of the 20 brightest, 1.21 magnitude; Alpha in the constellation Virgo.

spi·cate (spī/kāt) *adj.* **1.** *Bot.* Arranged in spikes: said of flowers. **2.** *Ornithol.* Having a spur, as the legs of some birds. Also **spi/cat·ed.** [< L *spicatus* < *spica* spike]

spic·ca·to (spēk·kä/tō) *Music n. pl.* **·tos** A method of producing rapid, detached notes on a stringed instrument, by allowing the bow to rebound slightly. [< Ital.]

spice (spīs) *n.* **1.** An aromatic, pungent vegetable substance, as cinnamon, cloves, etc., used to flavor food and beverages. **2.** Such substances collectively. **3.** That which gives zest or adds interest. **4.** An aromatic odor. **— v.t.** **spiced, spic·ing 1.** To season with spice. **2.** To add zest to. [< OF *espice* < L *species*] **— spic/er** *n.*

spice·bush (spīs/bŏŏsh/) *n.* An aromatic American shrub of the laurel family. Also **spice/wood/** (-wŏŏd/).

spick (spik) *n. U.S. Slang* A Spanish-speaking person: an offensive term. Also **spic**.

spick-and-span (spik/ən-span/) *adj.* **1.** Neat and clean. **2.** Perfectly new, or looking as if new. [Prob. < *spick*, var. of SPIKE[1] +dial. E *span-new*, really or freshly new]

spic·ule (spik/yōol) *n.* **1.** A small, slender, sharp-pointed body; a spikelet. **2.** *Zool.* One of the small, needlelike, growths supporting the soft tissues of certain invertebrates, as sponges. Also **spic·u·la** (spik/yə-lə). [< L *spicum* point, spike] — **spic/u·lar, spic/u·late** (-lāt, -lit) *adj.*

spic·u·lum (spik/yə-ləm) *n. pl.* **·la** (-lə) A spicule.

spic·y (spī/sē) *adj.* **spic·i·er, spic·i·est** **1.** Containing, flavored with, or fragrant with spices. **2.** Producing spices. **3.** Having zest or piquancy. **4.** Somewhat improper; risqué. — **spic/i·ly** *adv.* — **spic/i·ness** *n.*

spi·der (spī/dər) *n.* **1.** Any of a large number of eight-legged wingless arachnids having an unsegmented abdomen and capable of spinning webs for the capture of flies or other insects. **2.** A long-handled iron frying pan, often having legs. **3.** A trivet. [OE *spinnan* to spin] — **spi/der·y** *adj.*

spider crab Any of a genus of crustaceans with long legs, common on the Atlantic coast of North America.

spider monkey An arboreal South American monkey with very long limbs and a long prehensile tail.

spi·der·wort (spī/dər-wûrt/) *n.* Any of a genus of plants, esp., an American perennial with deep blue flowers.

spied (spīd) Past tense and past participle of SPY.

spiel (spēl, shpēl) *U.S. Slang v.i.* To talk; orate. — *n.* A speech; esp., a noisy, high-pressure sales talk. [< G, game, play < *spielen* to play] — **spiel/er** *n.*

spi·er (spī/ər) *n.* A spy; scout.

spif·fy (spif/ē) *adj.* **·fi·er, ·fi·est** *Slang* Smartly dressed; spruce. — **spif/fi·ness** *n.* [< dial. E *spiff* a dandy]

spig·ot (spig/ət) *n.* **1.** A faucet. **2.** A plug or valve for the bunghole of a cask. **3.** A turning plug fitting into a faucet. [ME *spigote*]

spike[1] (spīk) *n.* **1.** A long, thick metal nail. **2.** A projecting, pointed piece of metal, as in the soles of shoes to prevent slipping. **3.** A very narrow high heel, used on women's shoes. — *v.t.* **spiked, spik·ing** **1.** To fasten with spikes. **2.** To set or provide with spikes. **3.** To block; put a stop to. **4.** To pierce with or impale on a spike. **5.** *Informal* To add alcoholic liquor to. [ME < Scand.] — **spik/y** *adj.*

spike[2] (spīk) *n.* **1.** An ear of corn, barley, wheat, or other grain. **2.** *Bot.* A flower cluster having numerous flowers arranged closely on an elongated common axis. [< L *spica* ear of grain]

spike·let (spīk/lit) *n. Bot.* A small spike bearing few flowers.

spike·nard (spīk/nərd, -närd) *n.* **1.** A fragrant ointment of ancient times: also called *nard.* **2.** The East Indian herb that yields it. **3.** An American perennial herb having an aromatic root. [< L *spica* spike + *nardus* nard]

spile (spīl) *n.* **1.** A post or supporting timber; pile. **2.** A wooden pin or plug used as a vent in a cask; a spigot. **3.** A spout driven into a sugar maple to lead the sap to a bucket. — *v.t.* **spiled, spil·ing** **1.** To pierce for and provide with a spigot. **2.** To drive spiles into. [< MDu., skewer, splinter]

spill[1] (spil) *v.* **spilled** or **spilt, spill·ing** *v.t.* **1.** To allow or cause to fall or run out or over, as a liquid or a powder. **2.** To shed, as blood. **3.** *Naut.* To empty (a sail) of wind. **4.** To cause to fall, as from a horse. **5.** *Informal* To divulge; make known, as a secret. — *v.i.* **6.** To fall or run out or over: said of liquids, etc. — **to spill the beans** *Informal* To divulge a secret. — *n.* **1.** A fall to the ground, as from a horse; tumble. **2.** The act of spilling. [OE *spillan* to destroy] — **spill/er** *n.*

spill[2] (spil) *n.* **1.** A thin strip of wood or rolled paper, used for lighting fires, etc. **2.** A peg or plug. [< SPILE]

spill·way (spil/wā/) *n.* A passageway, as in a dam, to release the water in a reservoir.

spilt (spilt) Alternative past tense and past participle of SPILL[1].

spin (spin) *v.* **spun** (*Archaic* **span**), **spun, spin·ning** *v.t.* **1.** To draw out and twist into threads; also, to draw out and twist fiber into (threads, yarn, etc.). **2.** To make or produce as if by spinning. **3.** To form (a web, etc.): said of spiders, silkworms, etc. **4.** To tell, as a story or yarn. **5.** To protract; prolong, as a period of time: with *out.* **6.** To cause to whirl rapidly: to *spin* a top. — *v.i.* **7.** To make thread or yarn. **8.** To make a web or thread: said of spiders, etc. **9.** To whirl rapidly; rotate. **10.** To seem to be whirling, as from dizziness. **11.** To move rapidly. — *n.* **1.** An act or instance of spinning; a rapid whirling. **2.** Any rapid movement. **3.** *Informal* A ride or drive. **4.** *Aeron.* The descent of an airplane in a spiral about a vertical axis, with its nose steeply inclined. [OE *spinnan*]

spin·ach (spin/ich, -ij) *n.* **1.** A pot herb of the goosefoot family. **2.** Its fleshy leaves, used as a vegetable. [< OF *espinage* < LL *spinacia*]

spi·nal (spī/nəl) *adj.* **1.** Of or pertaining to the backbone;

vertebral. **2.** Resembling a spine, spines, or spinous processes. — *n.* An injection for spinal anesthesia.

spinal anesthesia *Surg.* Anesthesia produced by the injection of an anesthetic into the spinal cord.

spinal column *Anat.* The series of articulated vertebrae that enclose and protect the spinal cord and provide dorsal support for the ribs; the backbone.

spinal cord *Anat.* That portion of the central nervous system enclosed by the spinal column.

spin·dle (spin/dəl) *n.* **1.** A rod having a slit or catch in the top and a whorl of wood or metal at its lower end, on which thread is wound from the distaff in hand spinning. **2.** The slender rod in a spinning wheel, containing a spool or bobbin on which the thread is twisted and wound; also, a similar device on a spinning machine or shuttle. **3.** *Mech.* A rotating rod, axis, or shaft; esp. when small and bearing something that rotates: the *spindle* of a lathe. **4.** A needlelike rod mounted on a weighted base, used for impaling bills, checks, etc.: also **spindle file. 5.** Any narrow, tapering object resembling a spindle. **6.** A small shaft passing through the lock of a door and bearing the knobs or handles. — *v.* **dled, ·dling** *v.i.* **1.** To grow into a long, slender stalk or body. — *v.t.* **2.** To form into a spindle. **3.** To provide with a spindle. **4.** To impale on a spindle. [OE *spinnan* to spin]

spin·dle-leg·ged (spin/dəl-leg/id, -legd/) *adj.* Having long, slender legs. Also **spin/dle-shanked/** (-shangkt/).

spin·dle·legs (spin/dəl-legz/) *n. pl.* (construed as sing. in def. 2) **1.** Long, slender legs. **2.** *Informal* A person having long, slender legs. Also **spin/dle-shanks/** (-shangks/).

spin·dling (spind/ling) *adj.* Long and thin; disproportionately slender. — *n.* A spindling person or plant shoot.

spin·dly (spind/lē) *adj.* **·dli·er, ·dli·est** Of a slender, lanky growth or form.

spin·drift (spin/drift) *n.* Blown sea spray: also called *spoondrift.* [Alter. of *spoondrift* < *spoon*, var. of SPUME + DRIFT]

spine (spīn) *n.* **1.** The spinal column of a vertebrate; backbone. **2.** *Zool.* Any of various hard, pointed outgrowths on the bodies of certain animals, as the fin ray of a fish. **3.** *Bot.* A stiff, pointed woody process on the stems of certain plants; thorn. **4.** The back of a bound book, usu. inscribed with the title and name of the author. **5.** A projecting eminence or ridge. [< OF < L *spina* spine]

spi·nel (spi·nel/, spin/əl) *n.* Any of a class of hard, variously colored minerals, some of which, as the **ruby spinel**, are used as gemstones. [< F < Ital. < L *spina* spine]

spine·less (spīn/lis) *adj.* **1.** Having no spine or backbone; invertebrate. **2.** Lacking spines. **3.** Lacking firmness of will or steadfastness; cowardly. — **spine/less·ness** *n.*

spin·et (spin/it) *n.* **1.** A small musical keyboard instrument of the harpsichord class. **2.** A small upright piano. [? after G. *Spinetti*, 16th c. Venetian inventor]

spin·na·ker (spin/ə-kər) *n. Naut.* A large, bellying jib sometimes carried on the mainmast of a racing vessel opposite the mainsail, used when sailing before the wind. [? < a mispronunciation of *Sphinx*, the name of the first yacht to carry this kind of sail, 1866]

spin·ner (spin/ər) *n.* **1.** One who or that which spins. **2.** In angling, a whirling spoon bait.

spin·ner·et (spin/ə-ret) *n.* **1.** An organ by which spiders or silkworms produce the filament for webs, cocoons, etc. **2.** A pierced metal plate through which plastic material is forced so as to make rayon fibers.

spin·ning (spin/ing) *n.* The act of one who or that which spins. — *adj.* **1.** That spins. **2.** Of, belonging to, or used in the process of spinning.

spinning jenny A framed mechanism for spinning more than one strand of yarn at a time.

spinning wheel A device used for spinning yarn or thread, a rotating spindle operated by a treadle and flywheel.

spin-off (spin/ôf/, -of/) *n.* An off-shoot or by-product.

spi·nose (spī/nōs) *adj.* Having many spines. — **spi/nose·ly** *adv.* — **spi·nos·i·ty** (-nos/ə-tē) *n.*

spin·ster (spin/stər) *n.* **1.** A woman who has remained unmarried, esp. one no longer young; an old maid. **2.** A woman who spins; a spinner. [ME < SPIN + -STER] — **spin/ster·hood** *n.* — **spin/ster·ish** *adj.*

spin·y (spī/nē) *adj.* **spin·i·er, spin·i·est** **1.** Having spines; thorny. **2.** Difficult; perplexing. — **spin/i·ness** *n.*

spiny anteater The echidna.

spiny lobster Any of various marine crustaceans having spiny shells but lacking large claws, valued as seafood: also called *crayfish, rock lobster.*

spir- Var. of SPIRO-.

spir·a·cle (spir/ə-kəl, spī/rə-) *n. Zool.* **1.** An aperture for the passage of air or water in the respiration of various animals, as sharks, rays, tadpoles, and insects. **2.** A breathing hole, as the nostril of a cetacean. [< OF < L *spiraculum* airhole]

spi·rae·a (spī-rē/ə) *n.* Any of a genus of shrubs of the rose family, having clusters of small, white or pink flowers. Also **spi·re/a.** [< L, meadowsweet]

spi·ral (spī′rəl) *n.* **1.** *Geom.* Any plane curve formed by a point that moves around a fixed center and continually increases or decreases its distance from it. **2.** A curve winding like a screw thread. **3.** Something spirally wound or having a spiral shape, as a spring. **4.** A flight of an airplane in a spiral path. — *adj.* **1.** Pertaining to or resembling a spiral. **2.** Winding and advancing; helical. **3.** Winding and rising in a spire, as some springs. — *v.* **·raled** or **·ralled, ·ral·ing** or **·ral·ling** *v.t.* **1.** To cause to take a spiral form or course. — *v.i.* **2.** To take a spiral form or course. **3.** To rise sharply or disproportionately, as prices, costs, etc. [< Med.L < L *spira* coil] — **spi′ral·ly** *adv.*

spire[1] (spīr) *n.* **1.** The tapering or pyramidal roof or top of a tower. **2.** Any similar high, pointed formation; a pinnacle. **3.** A slender stalk or blade. — *v.* **spired, spir·ing** *v.t.* **1.** To furnish with a spire or spires. — *v.i.* **2.** To shoot or point up in or as in a spire. **3.** To put forth a spire or spires; sprout. [OE *spīr* stalk, stem]

spire[2] (spīr) *n.* A spiral or a single turn of one; whorl; twist. [< F < L *spira* < Gk. *speira* coil]

spi·ril·lum (spī-ril′əm) *n. pl.* **·la** (-lə) Any of a genus of rigid, spirally twisted flagellate bacteria. [< NL, dim. of L *spira* coil]

spir·it (spir′it) *n.* **1.** The vital essence or animating force in living organisms, esp. man, often considered divine in origin. **2.** The part of a human being characterized by intelligence, personality, self-consciousness, and will; the mind. **3.** The substance or universal aspect of reality, regarded as opposed to matter. **4.** *Often cap.* In the Bible, the creative, animating power of God. **5.** A supernatural or immaterial being, as an angel, ghost, specter, etc. **6.** A person regarded with reference to any particular activity, characteristic, or temper: a leading *spirit* in the community. **7.** *Usually pl.* A state of mind; mood; temper. **8.** Vivacity or energy; ardor. **9.** Ardent loyalty or devotion: school *spirit*. **10.** True intent or meaning as opposed to outward, formal observance: the *spirit* of the law. **11.** The characteristic temper or disposition of a period or movement: the *spirit* of the Reformation. **12.** *pl.* Strong alcoholic liquor. **13.** *Usually pl. Chem.* The essence or distilled extract of a substance: *spirits* of turpentine. **14.** *Often pl.* In pharmacy, a solution of a volatile principle in alcohol: *spirits* of ammonia. — *v.t.* **1.** To carry off secretly: with *away, off,* etc. **2.** To infuse with spirit or animation; inspirit; encourage: often with *up*. — *adj.* **1.** Of or pertaining to ghosts; spiritualistic. **2.** Operated by the burning of alcohol: a *spirit* lamp. [< OF < L *spiritus* breath, spirit]

Spir·it (spir′it) *n.* In Christian theology, the Holy Spirit.

spir·it·ed (spir′it·id) *adj.* **1.** Full of spirit; animated. **2.** Having a (specified kind of) spirit or nature: *high-spirited*. — **spir′it·ed·ly** *adv.* — **spir′it·ed·ness** *n.*

spirit gum A quick-drying solution of a gum in ether.

spir·it·less (spir′it·lis) *adj.* Lacking enthusiasm, energy, etc.; listless. — **spir′it·less·ly** *adv.* — **spir′it·less·ness** *n.*

spirit level An instrument used to determine any deviation from the horizontal or perpendicular by reference to the position of a bubble of air in a tube of liquid.

spir·i·tu·al (spir′i·chōō·əl) *adj.* **1.** Of, pertaining to, like, or consisting of spirit, as distinguished from matter; incorporeal. **2.** Affecting the immaterial nature or soul of man. **3.** Of or pertaining to God; holy. **4.** Sacred or religious; not lay or temporal; ecclesiastical: *spiritual* authorities: distinguished from *secular*. **5.** Marked or characterized by the highest moral or intellectual qualities. — *n.* A religious folk song originating among the Negroes of the southern U.S.; also, any similar song. — **spir′i·tu·al·ly** *adv.* — **spir·i·tu·al·i·ty** (spir′i·chōō·al′ə·tē), spir′i·tu·al·ness** *n.*

spir·i·tu·al·ism (spir′i·chōō·əl·iz′əm) *n.* **1.** The belief that the spirits of the dead communicate with and manifest their presence to the living, usually through the agency of a medium. **2.** *Philos.* A form of idealism that identifies the spirit as the only ultimate reality. **3.** The state or character of being spiritual. — **spir′i·tu·al·ist** *n.* — **spir′i·tu·al·is′tic** *adj.*

spir·i·tu·al·ize (spir′i·chōō·əl·īz′) *v.t.* **·ized, ·iz·ing 1.** To make spiritual; free of grossness or materialism. **2.** To treat as having a spiritual meaning or sense. Also *Brit.* **spir·i·tu·al·ise′.** — **spir′i·tu·al·i·za′tion** *n.* — **spir′i·tu·al·iz′er** *n.*

spir·i·tu·el (spir′i·chōō·el′, *Fr.* spē·rē·tü·el′) *adj.* Characterized by wit and by the higher and finer qualities of the mind generally. [< F] — **spir′i·tu·elle′** *adj. fem.*

spir·i·tu·ous (spir′i·chōō·əs) *adj.* Containing alcohol, as distilled liquors; intoxicating. — **spir′i·tu·ous·ness** *n.*

spiro-[1] *combining form* Breath; respiration. Also, before vowels, **spir-.** [< L *spirare* to breathe]

spiro-[2] *combining form* Spiral; coiled. Also, before vowels, **spir-.** [< Gk. *speira* coil]

spi·ro·chete (spī′rə·kēt) *n.* **1.** Any of various motile bacteria having a corkscrewlike form and commonly found in water and sewage. **2.** Any similar bacteria including those that cause syphilis, trench mouth, and yaws. Also **spi·ro·chaete.** [< Gk. *speira* coil + *chaitē* bristle]

spir·y (spīr′ē) *adj.* **1.** Pertaining to or having the form of a spire. **2.** Abounding in spires, as a city.

spit[1] (spit) *v.* **spat** or **spit, spit·ting** *v.t.* **1.** To eject (saliva, etc.) from the mouth. **2.** To eject or utter with violence. **3.** To light, as a fuse. — *v.i.* **4.** To eject saliva, etc., from the mouth. **5.** To make a hissing or sputtering noise. **6.** To fall in scattered drops or flakes, as snow. — *n.* **1.** Spittle; saliva. **2.** An act of spitting or expectorating. **3.** A light, scattered fall of snow or rain. **4.** *Informal* Exact likeness; counterpart. [OE *spittan*] — **spit′ter** *n.*

spit[2] (spit) *n.* **1.** A pointed rod on which meat is turned and roasted before a fire. **2.** A point of low land extending from a shore into the water. — *v.t.* **spit·ted, spit·ting** To transfix or impale with or as with a spit. [OE *spitu*]

spit and image *Informal* An exact likeness; counterpart. Also **spitting image.** [See SPIT[1], *n.* (def. 4)]

spit·ball (spit′bôl) *n.* **1.** Paper chewed and shaped into a ball for use as a missile. **2.** In baseball, a pitched ball, now no longer legal, that is wet on one side with saliva, and deviates deceptively in its course.

spite (spīt) *n.* **1.** Malicious bitterness or hatred; grudge. **2.** That which is done in spite. — **in spite of** Notwithstanding. — **Syn.** See NOTWITHSTANDING. — *v.t.* **spit·ed, spit·ing** To show one's spite toward. [Short for DESPITE]

spite·ful (spīt′fəl) *adj.* **1.** Filled with spite. **2.** Prompted by spite. — **spite′ful·ly** *adv.* — **spite′ful·ness** *n.*

spit·fire (spit′fīr′) *n.* A quick-tempered person who is given to saying spiteful things.

spit·tle (spit′l) *n.* **1.** The fluid secreted by the mouth; saliva; spit. **2.** The salivalike matter in which the larvae of spittle insects live. [OE *spātl*; infl. in form by SPIT[1]]

spit·toon (spi·tōōn′) *n.* A receptacle for spit; a cuspidor.

spitz (spits) *n.* A small dog, a variety of Pomeranian, having long silky hair and a tapering muzzle. Also **spitz dog.** [< G, short for *spitzhund* < *spitz* pointed + *hund* dog]

splash (splash) *v.t.* **1.** To dash or spatter (a liquid, etc.) about. **2.** To spatter, wet, or soil with a liquid dashed about. **3.** To make (one's way) with splashes. **4.** To decorate or mark by or as by splashing. — *v.i.* **5.** To make a splash or splashes. **6.** To move, fall, or strike with a splash or splashes. — *n.* **1.** The act or noise of splashing. **2.** The result of splashing, as a spot. **3.** *Informal* A striking or ostentatious impression, action, success, etc.: to make a *splash*. [Var. of PLASH[1]] — **splash′er** *n.*

splash·down (splash′doun′) *n.* The setting down of a spacecraft or a part of it in the seas following its flight.

splash·y (splash′ē) *adj.* **splash·i·er, splash·i·est 1.** Slushy; wet. **2.** Marked by or as by splashes; blotchy. **3.** *Informal* Sensational; showy: They made a *splashy* appearance.

splat (splat) *n.* A thin, broad piece of wood, as that forming the middle of a chair back. [Origin uncertain]

splat·ter (splat′ər) *v.t. & v.i.* To splash or splash. — *n.* A spatter; splash. [Blend of SPLASH and SPATTER]

splay (splā) *adj.* **1.** Spread out; broad. **2.** Clumsily formed; awkward. — *n.* A slanted surface or beveled edge, as the sides of a doorway. — *v.t.* **1.** To make with a splay. **2.** To spread out; expand. — *v.i.* **3.** To spread out; open. **4.** To slant; slope. [Aphetic var. of DISPLAY]

splay·foot (splā′fŏŏt′) *n. pl.* **·feet** (-fēt′) **1.** Abnormal flatness and turning outward of the feet. **2.** A foot so deformed. — **splay′foot′ed** *adj.*

spleen (splēn) *n. Anat.* **1.** A highly vascular, flattened, ductless organ located on the upper left side of the abdominal cavity, and effecting certain modifications in the blood. **2.** Ill temper; spitefulness: to vent one's *spleen*. **3.** *Archaic* Low spirits; melancholy. [< OF < L < Gk. *splēn*] — **spleen′ful, spleen′ish, spleen′y** *adj.* — **spleen′ful·ly** *adv.*

splen·did (splen′did) *adj.* **1.** Magnificent; imposing. **2.** Inspiring to the imagination; glorious; illustrious. **3.** Giving out or reflecting brilliant light; shining. **4.** *Informal* Very good; excellent: a *splendid* offer. [< L *splendere* to shine] — **splen′did·ly** *adv.* — **splen′did·ness** *n.*

splen·dif·er·ous (splen·dif′ər·əs) *adj. Informal* Exhibiting great splendor; very magnificent: a facetious usage.

splen·dor (splen′dər) *n.* **1.** Exceeding brilliance from emitted or reflected light. **2.** Magnificence. **3.** Conspicuous greatness of achievement. Also *Brit.* **splen′dour.** [< L, brightness] — **splen′dor·ous, splen′drous** *adj.*

sple·net·ic (spli·net′ik) *adj.* **1.** Pertaining to the spleen. **2.** Fretfully spiteful; peevish. Also **sple·net′i·cal.** — *n.* A peevish person. — **sple·net′i·cal·ly** *adv.*

splen·ic (splen′ik, splē′nik) *adj.* Of, in, near, or pertaining to the spleen.

spleno- *combining form Anat. & Med.* The spleen; of or related to the spleen. Also, before vowels, **splen-.** [< Gk. *splēn, splēnos* spleen]

splice (splīs) v.t. **spliced, splic·ing 1.** To unite, as by twisting or intertwining the ends of rope, wires, etc. **2.** To connect, as timbers, by beveling, scarfing, or overlapping at the ends. **3.** *Slang* To join in marriage. — n. **1.** A union made by splicing. **2.** The place at which two parts are spliced. [< MDu. *splissen*] — **splic′er** n.

splint (splint) n. **1.** A thin, flat piece split off; a splinter. **2.** A thin, flexible strip of split wood used for basketmaking, chair bottoms, etc. **3.** *Surg.* An appliance, as of wood or metal, used for keeping a fractured limb or other injured part in a fixed or proper position. **4.** A splint bone. — v.t. To confine, support, or brace, as a fractured limb, with or as with splints. [< MDu. *splinte*]

splin·ter (splin′tər) n. A thin, sharp piece of wood, glass, metal, etc., split or torn off lengthwise; a sliver. — v.t. & v.i. To split into thin sharp pieces or fragments; shatter; shiver. [< MDu.] — **splint′er·y** adj.

split (split) v. **split, split·ting** v.t. **1.** To separate into parts by force, esp. into two approximately equal parts. **2.** To break or divide lengthwise or along the grain; separate into layers. **3.** To divide into groups or factions; disrupt, as a political party. **4.** To divide and distribute by portions or shares. — v.i. **5.** To break apart; divide lengthwise or along the grain. **6.** To become divided through disagreement, etc. **7.** To share something with others. — **to split hairs** To make fine distinctions; be unnecessarily precise. — **to split off 1.** To break off by splitting. **2.** To separate by or as by splitting. — **to split the difference** To divide equally a sum in dispute. — **to split up 1.** To separate into parts and distribute. **2.** To cease association; separate. — n. **1.** The act of splitting; also, the result of splitting, as a cleft or rent. **2.** Separation into factions; schism: a *split* in the church. **3.** A sliver; splinter. **4.** A share or portion, as of booty. **5.** *Informal* A bottle or a drink half the usual size. **6.** A confection made of a split banana, ice cream, syrup, chopped nuts, and whipped cream. **7.** In bowling, the position of two or more pins left standing on such spots so that a spare is nearly impossible. **10.** An acrobatic trick in which the legs are extended upon the floor in a straight line at right angles to the body: also **the splits.** — adj. **1.** Cleft, esp. longitudinally; fissured. **2.** Divided: a *split* ticket. [< MDu. *splitten*] — **split′ter** n.

split infinitive *Gram.* An infinitive in which the sign *to* is separated from the verb, generally by an adverb, as in "to really believe."

split level house A dwelling in which the floors of the several levels are less than a story above or below the adjoining one.

split ticket 1. A ballot on which the voter has distributed his vote among candidates of different parties. **2.** A ballot containing names of candidates of more than one party or party faction. Compare STRAIGHT TICKET.

split·ting (split′ing) adj. **1.** Acute or extreme: a *splitting* shriek. **2.** That aches severely: a *splitting* head.

splotch (sploch) n. A discolored spot, as of ink, etc.; a daub; splash; spot. — v.t. To soil or mark with a splotch or splotches. [Cf. OE *splott* spot] — **splotch′y** adj.

splurge (splûrj) *Informal* n. **1.** An ostentatious display. **2.** An extravagant expenditure. — v.i. **splurged, splurg·ing 1.** To show off; be ostentatious. **2.** To spend money lavishly or wastefully. [Origin uncertain] — **splurg′y** adj.

splut·ter (splut′ər) v.i. **1.** To make a series of slight, explosive sounds, or throw off small particles, as meat frying. **2.** To speak hastily, confusedly, or incoherently. — v.t. **3.** To utter excitedly or confusedly; sputter. **4.** To bespatter. — n. A noise as of spluttering; bustle; confused stir. [Blend of SPLASH and SPUTTER] — **splut′ter·er** n.

spoil (spoil) v. **spoiled** or **spoilt, spoil·ing** v.t. **1.** To impair or destroy the value, usefulness, or beauty of. **2.** To impair the character of, esp., by overindulgence: to *spoil* a child. **3.** *Obs.* To take property from by force; despoil. — v.i. **4.** To lose normal or useful qualities; esp., to become tainted or decayed, as food. — **Syn.** See DECAY. — **to be spoiling for** To long for; crave: He is *spoiling* for a fight. — n. **1.** *Often pl.* Plunder seized by violence; loot. **2.** *pl. Chiefly U.S.* The emoluments of public office. **3.** The act of pillaging; spoliation. [< OF < L < *spolium* booty] — **spoil′er** n.

spoil·age (spoi′lij) n. **1.** Spoiled material collectively. **2.** Something that is or has been spoiled. **3.** The process of spoiling. **4.** The state of being spoiled.

spoil·sport (spoil′spôrt′, -spôrt′) n. A person whose actions or attitudes spoil the pleasures of others.

spoils system *U.S.* In a political party after a victorious campaign, the system or practice of making public offices the rewards of partisan services.

spoke¹ (spōk) n. **1.** One of the rods or bars that serve to support the rim of a wheel by connecting it to the hub. **2.** A stick or bar for insertion in a wheel to prevent its turning. **3.** A rung of a ladder. — v.t. **spoked, spok·ing 1.** To provide with spokes. **2.** To fasten (a wheel) with a stick or spoke to prevent its turning. [OE *spāca*]

spoke² (spōk) Past tense and archaic past participle of SPEAK.

spo·ken (spō′kən) Past participle of SPEAK. — adj. **1.** Uttered orally, as opposed to written. **2.** Speaking or having (a specified kind of) speech: *smooth-spoken.*

spoke·shave (spōk′shāv′) n. A planing tool having a blade set between two handles, used in rounding and smoothing wooden surfaces; originally used for shaping spokes.

spokes·man (spōks′mən) n. pl. **·men** (-mən) One who speaks in the name and behalf of another or others. — **spokes′wom′an** (-wŏŏm′ən) n. fem..

spo·li·a·tion (spō′lē·ā′shən) n. The act of despoiling; esp., the authorized seizure of neutral ships by a belligerent. [< L < *spoliare* to despoil] — **spo′li·a′tor** n.

spo·li·a·tive (spō′lē·ā′tiv) adj. Tending to abstract from or lessen.

spon·dee (spon′dē) n. A metrical foot consisting of two long syllables or accented syllables. [< F < L < Gk. < *spondē* libation; because used in the solemn chants accompanying a libation] — **spon·da·ic** (-dā′ik) adj.

sponge (spunj) n. **1.** Any of a varied group of aquatic, usu. marine organisms, characterized by a highly porous body without specialized internal organs and incapable of free movement. **2.** The skeleton or network of elastic fibers that remains after the removal of the living matter from certain sponges and that readily absorbs liquids, used as an absorbent for bathing, etc. **3.** Any spongelike substance used as an absorbent. **4.** Leavened dough, or dough in the process of leavening. **5.** *Surg.* An absorbent pad, as of sterilized gauze. **6.** A sponge bath. **7.** *Informal* One who lives at the expense of another or others; a parasite. — **to throw** (or **toss**) **up** (or **in**) **the sponge** *Informal* To give up; abandon the struggle. — v. **sponged, spong·ing** v.t. **1.** To wipe, wet, or clean with a sponge. **2.** To wipe out; expunge; erase. **3.** To absorb; suck in. **4.** *Informal* To get without cost or at another's expense. — v.i. **5.** To be absorbent. **6.** *Informal* To live or get something at the expense of others. [OE < L < Gk. *spongos.*] — **spong′er** n. — **spong′i·ness** n. — **spong′y** adj.

sponge bath A bath taken by washing oneself with a cloth or sponge rather than in a bathtub or shower.

sponge cake A cake of sugar, eggs, and flour, containing no shortening and beaten very light.

spon·son (spon′sən) n. **1.** A curved projection from the hull of a vessel or seaplane, to give greater stability or increase the surface area. **2.** A similar protuberance on a ship or tank, for storage purposes or for the training of a gun. **3.** An air tank built into the side of a canoe, to improve stability and prevent sinking. [Appar. alter. of EXPANSION]

spon·sor (spon′sər) n. **1.** One who makes himself responsible for a statement by, or the debt or duty of, another; a surety. **2.** A godfather or godmother. **3.** A business enterprise that finances a broadcast program that advertises its product or service. — v.t. To act as sponsor for; vouch for. [< L < *spondere* to be a security] — **spon·so·ri·al** (spon·sôr′ē·əl, -sō′rē) adj. — **spon′sor·ship** n.

spon·ta·ne·i·ty (spon′tə·nē′ə·tē) n. pl. **·ties 1.** The quality or fact of being spontaneous. **2.** A spontaneous act.

spon·ta·ne·ous (spon·tā′nē·əs) adj. **1.** Done or resulting from one's own impulse or desire; not premeditated; unrestrained. **2.** Arising from inherent qualities without external cause; self-generated. **3.** *Biol.* Growing without cultivation; wild; indigenous. [< LL < *sponte* of free will] — **spon·ta′ne·ous·ly** adv. — **spon·ta′ne·ous·ness** n.
— **Syn. 1.** A *spontaneous* act seems to be prompted by inner feeling, rather than external stimulus: a *spontaneous* outburst of applause. An *impulsive* action comes from sudden inclination, and lacks deliberation: an *impulsive* gesture of welcome.

spontaneous combustion The burning of a substance through the generation of sufficient internal heat to ignite it, as masses of oiled rags, finely powdered ores, coal, etc.

spontaneous generation *Biol.* The doctrine of the generation of new organisms from putrid or decomposing organic matter assumed to be entirely devoid of life.

spoof (spōōf) *Informal* v.t. & v.i. To deceive or hoax; joke; parody. — n. Deception; parody; hoax. [after a game invented by Arthur Roberts, 1852–1933, English comedian]

spook (spōōk) *Informal* n. A ghost; an apparition; specter. — v.t. *Informal* To haunt (a person or place). [< Du.] — **spook′i·ly** adv. — **spook′ish, spook′y** adj.

spool (spōōl) n. **1.** A small cylinder with a flange at each end and an axial bore, upon which thread or yarn is or may be wound. **2.** The quantity of thread held by a spool. **3.** Anything resembling a spool in shape or purpose. — v.t. To wind on a spool. [< MLG *spole*]

spoon (spōōn) n. **1.** A utensil having a shallow, generally ovoid bowl and a handle, used in preparing, serving, or eating food. **2.** Something resembling a spoon or its bowl. **3.** A metallic lure attached to a fishing line: also **spoon bait, trolling spoon. 4.** A wooden golf club with lofted face and comparatively short, stiff shaft. — v.t. **1.** To lift up or out with a spoon. **2.** To hollow out like the bowl of a spoon. — *v.i.* **3.** *Informal* To make love, as by caressing or kissing. [OE spōn sliver, chip]

spoon·bill (spoon'bil) *n.* **1.** Any of various wading birds related to the ibises, having the bill broad and flattened. **2.** The shoveler. — **spoon'-billed'** *adj.*

spoon·drift (spoon'drift') *n.* Spindrift.

spoon·er·ism (spoon'nə·riz'əm) *n.* The unintentional transposition of sounds or of parts of words in speaking, as in "half-*w*armed *f*ish" for "half-*f*ormed *w*ish." [after William A. Spooner, 1844–1930, of New College, Oxford]

spoon·fed (spoon'fed') *adj.* **1.** Fed with a spoon. **2.** Pampered; over-indulged. **3.** Not given the opportunity to act or think for oneself.

spoon·ful (spoon'fool') *n.* *pl.* **·fuls** As much as a spoon will hold.

spoon·y (spoo'nē) *Informal adj.* **spoon·i·er, spoon·i·est** Sentimental or silly, as in lovemaking; soft. — *n.* *pl.* **spoon·ies** A foolish, sentimental lover. Also **spoon'ey.**

spoor (spoor) *n.* Footprint or other trace of a wild animal. — *v.t. & v.i.* To track by or follow a spoor. [< Du.]

spo·rad·ic (spô·rad'ik, spō-) *adj.* **1.** Occurring here and there; occasional. **2.** Separate; isolated. **3.** Neither epidemic nor endemic: said of disease. Also **spo·rad'i·cal.** [< Med.L < Gk. < *sporas* scattered] — **spo·rad'i·cal·ly** *adv.*

spo·ran·gi·um (spô·ran'jē·əm, spō-) *n.* *pl.* **·gi·a** (-jē-ə) *Bot.* A sac in which asexual spores are produced, as in certain algae and fungi: also called *spore case.* [< SPOR(O)- + Gk. *angeion* vessel] — **spo·ran'gi·al** *adj.*

spore (spôr, spōr) *n.* **1.** *Bot.* The reproductive body in cryptogams, analogous to the seeds of flowering plants, but able to develop asexually into an independent organism or individual. **2.** *Bacteriol.* A strongly resistant body developed in some bacilli, able to become active under suitable conditions. **3.** *Biol.* Any cell or minute body capable of developing into a new organism; a germ, seed, etc. — *v.i.* **spored, spor·ing** To develop spores: said of plants. [< NL < Gk. *seed, sowing*] — **spo·ra·ceous** (spô-rā'shəs, spō-) *adj.*

spore case A sporangium.

sporo- *combining form* Seed; spore. Also, before vowels, **spor-.** [< Gk. *spora* seed]

spo·ro·phyte (spôr'ə·fīt, spō'rə-) *n.* *Bot.* The stage in which spores are produced in certain plants that reproduce by alternation of generations.

-sporous *combining form* Having (a specified number or kind of) spores. [< SPOR(O)- + -OUS]

spo·ro·zo·an (spôr'ə·zō'ən, spō'rə-) *adj.* *Zool.* Designating or belonging to a class of parasitic protozoans reproducing by spores, as the malaria parasite. — *n.* A member of this class. [< SPORO- + Gk. *zōion* animal]

spor·ran (spor'ən) *n.* A purse, generally of fur, worn in front of the kilt by Highlanders. For illus. see KILT. [< Scottish Gaelic < LL *bursa* purse]

sport (spôrt, spōrt) *n.* **1.** That which amuses in general; diversion; pastime. **2.** A particular game or play pursued for diversion; esp., an outdoor or athletic game, as baseball, tennis, swimming, etc. **3.** A spirit of jesting. **4.** That with which one sports; a toy; plaything. **5.** Mockery; an object of derision: to make *sport* of someone; also, a laughingstock; butt. **6.** *Biol.* An animal or plant that exhibits sudden and spontaneous variation from the normal type; a mutation. **7.** *Informal* One who lives a fast, gay, or flashy life. **8.** A person characterized by his observance of the rules of fair play, or by his ability to get along with others: a good *sport.* — *v.i.* **1.** To amuse oneself; play; frolic. **2.** To participate in games. **3.** To make sport or jest; trifle. **4.** *Biol.* To vary suddenly or spontaneously from the normal type; mutate. — *v.t.* **5.** *Informal* To display or wear ostentatiously; show off. — *adj.* Of, pertaining to, or fitted for sports; also, appropriate for informal wear: a *sport* coat: also *sports.* [Aphetic var. of DISPORT] — **sport'er** *n.* — **sport'ful** *adj.* — **sport'ful·ly** *adv.* — **sport'ful·ness** *n.*

sport·ing (spôr'ting, spōr'-) *adj.* **1.** Of, engaged in, or connected with athletic games or field sports. **2.** Characterized by the spirit of sportsmanship; conforming to the codes or standards of sportsmanship. **3.** Associated with sports for gambling or betting: a *sporting* man. — **sport'ing·ly** *adv.*

sporting chance *Informal* A chance involving the risk of loss or failure.

sport·ive (spôr'tiv, spōr'-) *adj.* **1.** Relating to or fond of sport or play; frolicsome. **2.** Interested in, active in, or related to sports. — **spor'tive·ly** *adv.* — **spor'tive·ness** *n.*

sports car A low, rakish automobile, usu. seating two persons, and built for high speed and maneuverability.

sports·man (spôrts'mən, spōrts'-) *n.* *pl.* **·men** (-mən) **1.** One who pursues field sports, esp., hunting and fishing. **2.** One who abides by a code of fair play in games or in daily practice. — **sports'man·like** *adj.* — **sports'man·ship** *n.*

sports·wear (spôrts'wâr', spōrts'-) *n.* Clothes made for informal or outdoor activities.

sports·wom·an (spôrts'woom'ən, spōrts'-) *n.* *pl.* **·wom·en** (-wim'in) A woman who participates in sports.

sport·y (spôr'tē, spōr'-) *adj.* **sport·i·er, sport·i·est** *Informal* **1.** Relating to or characteristic of a sport. **2.** Gay, loud, or dissipated. — **sport'i·ly** *adv.* — **sport'i·ness** *n.*

spor·ule (spôr'yool, spor'-) *n.* A spore; esp., a little spore. [< F < NL < *spora* spore]

spot (spot) *n.* **1.** A particular place of small extent; a definite locality. **2.** Any small portion of a surface differing as in color from the rest; blot. **3.** A stain or blemish on character; a fault. **4.** *Slang* A currency note having a specified value: a ten *spot.* **5.** *U.S. Slang* A spotlight. — **in a spot** *Slang* In a difficult or embarrassing situation; in trouble. — **to hit the spot** *Slang* To gratify an appetite or need. — **to touch a** (or **one's**) **sore spot** To mention a topic that is painful to one. — **on the spot 1.** At once; immediately. **2.** At the very place. **3.** *Slang* In danger of death or of being held accountable for some action. — *v.* **spot·ted, spot·ting** *v.t.* **1.** To mark or soil with spots. **2.** To decorate with spots; dot. **3.** To place on a designated spot; locate; station. **4.** *Informal* To recognize or detect; see. — *v.i.* **5.** To become marked or soiled with spots. **6.** To make a stain or discoloration. — *adj.* **1.** Being on the place or spot. **2.** Paid or prepared for payment on delivery; spot cash. **3.** Made at random: a *spot* check. [ME < LG. Cf. MDu. *spotte.*] — **spot'less** *adj.* — **spot'ta·ble** *adj.*

spot check An inspection of one or a few typical things out of many, to insure quality and maintenance of standards.

spot·light (spot'līt') *n.* **1.** A circle of powerful light thrown on the stage to bring an actor or actors into clearer view. **2.** The apparatus that produces such a light. **3.** A pivoted automobile lamp. **4.** Notoriety; publicity.

spot·ted (spot'id) *adj.* **1.** Discolored in spots; stained; soiled. **2.** Characterized or marked by spots.

spotted fever *Pathol.* **1.** An epidemic form of cerebrospinal meningitis. **2.** Typhus.

spot·ter (spot'ər) *n.* **1.** *U.S. Informal* A detective; esp., one employed to discover dishonesty among employees. **2.** In civil defense, one who watches for enemy aircraft. **3.** In dry cleaning, one who removes spots.

spot·ty (spot'ē) *adj.* **·ti·er, ·ti·est 1.** Having many spots. **2.** Lacking uniformity. — **spot'ti·ly** *adv.* — **spot'ti·ness** *n.*

spous·al (spou'zəl) *adj.* Pertaining to marriage. — *n.* Often *pl.* Marriage; espousal.

spouse (spouz, spous) *n.* A partner in marriage; one's husband or wife. [< OF < L *spondere* to promise, betroth]

spout (spout) *v.t.* **1.** To pour out copiously and forcibly, as a liquid under pressure. **2.** To discharge a fluid either continuously or in jets. **3.** *Informal* To speak or orate pompously; declaim. — *v.t.* **4.** To cause to pour or shoot forth. **5.** To utter grandiloquently or pompously. — *n.* **1.** A tube, trough, etc., for the discharge of a liquid. **2.** A continuous stream of fluid. [ME *spoute*] — **spout'er** *n.*

sprain (sprān) *n.* **1.** A violent straining or twisting of the ligaments surrounding a joint. **2.** The condition due to such strain. — *v.t.* To cause a sprain in; wrench the muscles of (a joint). [? < OF *espreindre* to squeeze]

sprang (sprang) Alternative past tense of SPRING.

sprat (sprat) *n.* **1.** A herringlike fish found in shoals on the Atlantic coast of Europe. [OE *sprot*]

sprawl (sprôl) *v.i.* **1.** To sit or lie with the limbs stretched out ungracefully. **2.** To be stretched out ungracefully, as the limbs. **3.** To move with awkward motions of the limbs. **4.** To spread out in a straggling manner, as handwriting, vines, etc. — *v.t.* **5.** To cause to spread or extend awkwardly or irregularly. — *n.* The act or position of sprawling. [OE *sprēawlian* to move convulsively] — **sprawl'er** *n.*

spray¹ (sprā) *n.* **1.** Liquid dispersed in fine particles. **2.** An instrument for discharging such particles. — *v.t.* **1.** To disperse (a liquid) in fine particles. **2.** To apply spray to. — *v.i.* **3.** To send forth spray. **4.** To go forth as spray. [Akin to MDu. *sprayen* to sprinkle] — **spray'er** *n.*

spray² (sprā) *n.* **1.** A small branch bearing dependent branchlets or flowers. **2.** Any ornament, pattern, etc., having a similar form. [ME]

spray gun A device that ejects liquids such as paint or insecticides in a fine spray by means of air pressure.

spread (spred) *v.* **spread, spread·ing** *v.t.* **1.** To open or unfold to full width or extent, as wings, sail, etc. **2.** To distribute over a surface, esp. in a thin layer; scatter or smear. **3.** To cover with a layer of something: to *spread* toast with marmalade. **4.** To force apart or farther apart. **5.** To extend over a period of time. **6.** To make more widely known, active, etc.: to *spread* a rumor; to *spread* contagion. **7.** To set (a table, etc.), as for a meal. **8.** To place on a table, etc., as a meal. — *v.i.* **9.** To be extended or expanded. **10.** To be distributed. **11.** To become more widely known, active, etc. **12.** To be forced farther apart. — *n.* **1.** The act of spreading. **2.** An open extent or expanse. **3.** The limit of expansion of some designated object. **4.** A cloth or covering for a bed, table, etc. **5.** *Informal* An informal feast or banquet. **6.** Anything used to spread on bread or crackers. **7.** Two pages of a magazine or newspaper facing each other and covered by related material; also, print spread across two or more columns or on facing pages. — *adj.* Expanded; outstretched. [OE *sprædan*] — **spread'er** *n.*

spread-ea·gle (spred'ē'gəl) *adj.* **1.** Resembling the figure of an eagle with extended wings. **2.** *U.S. Informal* Bombastic: applied esp. to patriotic oratory. — *v.t.* **-ea·gled, -ea·gling** To lash to the mast or shrouds in spread-eagle position as a punishment.

spree (sprē) *n.* **1.** A drinking spell. **2.** A gay frolic. **3.** Excessive indulgence in an activity. [Origin uncertain]

sprig (sprig) *n.* **1.** A shoot or sprout of a tree or plant. **2.** An ornament in this form. **3.** A young man; a youth. — *v.t.* **sprigged, sprig·ging** To ornament with a design of sprigs. [ME *sprigge*] — **sprig'ger** *n.* — **sprig'gy** *adj.*

spright·ly (sprīt'lē) *adj.* **·li·er, ·li·est** Full of animation; lively. — *adv.* Spiritedly; briskly; gaily. — **spright'li·ness** *n.*

spring (spring) *v.* **sprang** or **sprung, sprung, spring·ing** *v.i.* **1.** To move or rise suddenly and rapidly; leap; dart. **2.** To move suddenly as by elastic reaction. **3.** To move as if with a leap: An angry retort *sprang* to his lips. **4.** To work or snap out of place, as a mechanical part. **5.** To become warped or bent, as boards. **6.** To rise above surrounding objects. **7.** To come into being: New towns have *sprung* up. **8.** To originate; proceed, as from a source. **9.** To develop; grow. — *v.t.* **10.** To cause to spring or leap. **11.** To cause to act, close, open, etc., suddenly, as by elastic reaction: to *spring* a trap. **12.** To cause to happen, become known, or appear suddenly: to *spring* a surprise. **13.** To leap over; vault. **14.** To warp or bend; split. **15.** To cause to snap or work out of place. **16.** To undergo (a leak). **17.** *Slang* To obtain the release of (a person) from prison. — *n.* **1.** *Mech.* An elastic body or contrivance, as a coiled steel wire, that yields under stress, and returns to its normal form when the stress is removed. **2.** Elastic quality or energy. **3.** The act of flying back from a position of tension. **4.** A cause of action. **5.** The act of leaping up or forward suddenly; a jump. **6.** The season in which vegetation starts anew, occurring between winter and summer. ◆ Collateral adjective: *vernal.* **7.** A flow, as of water. **8.** Any source or origin. **9.** A crack or break, as of a plank, etc., or a thing sprung or warped. — *adj.* **1.** Pertaining to the season of spring. **2.** Acting like or having a spring. **3.** Hung on springs. [OE *springan*] — **spring'er** *n.*

a b c
SPRINGS
a Compression coil.
b Double spiral.
c Extension coil.

spring·board (spring'bôrd', -bōrd') *n.* **1.** A flexible, resilient board used by athletes and acrobats as an aid in leaping or tumbling. **2.** A diving board.

spring·bok (spring'bok') *n.* A small South African gazelle noted for its ability to leap high in the air. Also **spring'buck'** (-buk'). [< Afrikaans]

spring chicken 1. A young chicken, 10 weeks to 10 months old, esp. tender for cooking. **2.** *Informal* A young, immature, or unsophisticated person.

spring fever The listlessness and restlessness that overtakes many people during the first warm days of spring.

spring lock A lock that fastens automatically by a spring.

spring tide 1. The tide occurring at or shortly after the new or full moon, when the rise and fall are greatest. **2.** Any great wave or flood, as of emotion.

spring·time (spring'tīm') *n.* The season of spring. Also **spring'tide'** (-tīd').

spring·y (spring'ē) *adj.* **spring·i·er, spring·i·est 1.** Elastic; resilient. **2.** Having many springs of water. — **spring'i·ly** *adv.* — **spring'i·ness** *n.*

sprin·kle (spring'kəl) *v.* **·kled, ·kling** *v.t.* **1.** To scatter in drops or small particles. **2.** To besprinkle. — *v.i.* **3.** To fall or rain in scattered drops. — *n.* **1.** A falling in drops or particles, or that which so falls; a sprinkling. **2.** A small quantity. [ME *sprenkelen*] — **sprin'kler** *n.*

sprin·kling (spring'kling) *n.* **1.** That which is sprinkled. **2.** A small number or quantity. **3.** A mottling. **4.** The act of scattering drops of liquid.

sprint (sprint) *n.* A short race run at top speed. — *v.i.* To run fast, as in a sprint. [< Scand.] — **sprint'er** *n.*

sprit (sprit) *n. Naut.* A spar reaching diagonally from a mast to the peak of a fore-and-aft sail. [OE *sprēot* pole]

sprite (sprīt) *n.* A fairy, elf, or goblin. [< OF < L *spiritus* breath, spirit]

sprit·sail (sprit'səl, sprit'sāl') *n. Naut.* A sail extended by a sprit.

sprock·et (sprok'it) *n. Mech.* **1.** A projection, as on the rim of a wheel, for engaging with the links of a chain. **2.** A wheel bearing such projections: also **sprocket wheel.** [Origin uncertain]

sprout (sprout) *v.i.* **1.** To put forth shoots; begin to grow; germinate. **2.** To develop or grow rapidly. — *v.t.* **3.** To cause to sprout. **4.** To remove shoots from. — *n.* **1.** A new shoot or bud on a plant. **2.** Something like or suggestive of a sprout. **3.** *pl.* Brussels sprouts. [OE *sprútan*]

spruce¹ (sproos) *n.* **1.** Any of a genus of evergreen trees of the pine family, having a pyramidal crown, needle-shaped leaves, and pendulous cones. **2.** The wood of these trees. **3.** Any of certain coniferous trees, as the Douglas fir.

spruce² (sproos) *adj.* **1.** Having a smart, trim appearance. **2.** Fastidious. — *v.* **spruced, spruc·ing** *v.t.* **1.** To make spruce: often with *up.* — *v.i.* **2.** To make oneself spruce: usu. with *up.* — **spruce'ly** *adv.* — **spruce'ness** *n.*

sprung (sprung) Past participle and alternative past tense of SPRING.

spry (sprī) *adj.* **spri·er** or **spry·er, spri·est** or **spry·est** Quick and active; agile; brisk; energetic. [< dial. E *sprey* < Scand.] — **spry'ly** *adv.* — **spry'ness** *n.*

spud (spud) *n.* **1.** A spadelike tool for removing the roots of weeds. **2.** *Informal* A potato. — *v.t.* **spud·ded, spud·ding** To remove with a spud. [ME *spudde* < Scand.]

spue (spyoo) See SPEW.

spume (spyoom) *n.* Froth, as on an agitated or effervescing liquid; foam; scum. — *v.i.* **spumed, spum·ing** To foam; froth [< F < L *spuma* foam] — **spu'mous, spum'y** *adj.*

spu·mo·ne (spə·mō'nē, *Ital.* spoo·mō'nā) *n. pl.* **·ni** (-nē) A dessert of ice cream or water ice containing fruit, nuts, etc. Also **spu·mo'ni.** [< Ital. < L *spuma* foam]

spun (spun) Past tense and past participle of SPIN.

spunk (spungk) *n.* **1.** Punk or other tinder. **2.** A small fire, spark, or flame; also, a match. **3.** *Informal* Mettle; pluck; courage. [< Irish < L *spongia* sponge]

spunk·y (spungk'ē) *adj.* **spunk·i·er, spunk·i·est** *Informal* Spirited; courageous; also, touchy. — **spunk'i·ly** *adv.* — **spunk'i·ness** *n.*

spur (spûr) *n.* **1.** A pricking or goading instrument worn on a horseman's heel. **2.** Anything that incites or urges; incentive. **3.** A part or attachment projecting like or suggestive of a spur, as a crag or mountain peak. **4.** A stiff, sharp spine, as on the legs of some insects and birds. **5.** *Bot.* A tubular extension of some part of a flower, as in the larkspur. **6.** A spur track. **7.** A pointed, curved cutting instrument fastened to each leg of a gamecock. — **on the spur of the moment** Hastily; prompted by an impulse. — *v.* **spurred, spur·ring** *v.t.* **1.** To prick or urge with or as with spurs. **2.** To furnish with spurs. — *v.i.* **3.** To spur one's horse. **4.** To hurry. [OE *spura*] — **spur'rer** *n.*

spurge (spûrj) *n.* A plant, euphorbia. [< OF < L < *ex- out* + *purgare* to cleanse]

spur gear *Mech.* **1.** A spur wheel. **2.** Spur gearing.

spur gearing *Mech.* Gearing composed of spur wheels.

spu·ri·ous (spyoor'ē·əs) *adj.* **1.** Not proceeding from the source pretended; not genuine; false. **2.** Illegitimate. [< L *spurius*] — **spu'ri·ous·ly** *adv.* — **spu'ri·ous·ness** *n.*

spurn (spûrn) *v.t.* **1.** To reject with disdain; refuse contemptuously; scorn. **2.** To strike with the foot; kick. — *v.i.* **3.** To reject something with disdain. — *n.* The act of spurning; also, a kick. [OE *spurnan*] — **spurn'er** *n.*

spurred (spûrd) *adj.* **1.** Wearing or having spurs. **2.** Having sharp spikes, claws, or shoots.

spurt (spûrt) *n.* **1.** A sudden gush of liquid. **2.** Any sudden outbreak, as of anger. **3.** An extraordinary effort of brief duration. — *v.i.* **1.** To come out in a jet; gush forth. **2.** To make a sudden and extreme effort. — *v.t.* **3.** To force out in a jet; squirt. [< OE *spryttan* to come forth]

spur track A short side track connecting with the main track of a railroad: also called *spur.*

spur wheel *Mech.* A wheel having radial teeth on the rim, with their edges parallel to the axis; also called *spur gear.*

sput·nik (sput'nik, spoot'-; *Russ.* spoot'nyik) *n.* A Soviet artificial earth satellite, the first of which, **Sputnik I,** was launched in 1957. [< Russian, satellite]

sput·ter (sput'ər) *v.i.* **1.** To throw off solid or fluid particles in a series of slight explosions. **2.** To emit particles of saliva from the mouth, as when speaking excitedly. **3.** To speak rapidly or confusedly. — *v.t.* **4.** To emit in small particles. **5.** To utter in a confused or excited manner. — *n.* **1.** The act or sound of sputtering; esp., excited talk. **2.** That which is ejected in sputtering. — **sput'ter·er** *n.*

spu·tum (spyoo'təm) *n. pl.* **·ta** (-tə) Saliva; spittle; expectorated matter. [< L *spuere* to spit]

spy (spī) *n. pl.* **spies 1.** One who enters an enemy's military lines covertly to get information. **2.** One who watches others secretly. — *v.* **spied, spy·ing** *v.i.* **1.** To keep watch closely or secretly; act as a spy. **2.** To make careful examination; pry: with *into.* — *v.t.* **3.** To observe stealthily and with hostile intent: usu. with *out.* **4.** To catch sight of; see.

5. To discover by careful or secret investigation: with *out*. [< OF *espier* to espy < Gmc.]
spy·glass (spī′glas′, -gläs′) *n.* A small telescope.
squab (skwob) *n.* **1.** A young pigeon, esp. when an unfledged nestling. **2.** A fat, short person. **3.** A soft, stuffed cushion. **4.** A sofa; couch. — *adj.* **1.** Fat and short; squat. **2.** Unfledged or recently hatched. [< dial. E < Scand.]
squab·ble (skwob′əl) *v.* ·bled, ·bling *v.i.* **1.** To engage in a petty wrangle or scuffle; quarrel. — *v.t.* **2.** *Printing* To disarrange (composed type). — *n.* A petty wrangle. — **Syn.** See QUARREL. — **squab′bler** *n.*
squad (skwod) *n.* **1.** A small group of persons organized for the performance of a specific function. **2.** A small detachment of troops or police; esp., the smallest tactical unit in the infantry of the U.S. Army. **3.** A team: a football *squad*. — *v.t.* **squad·ded, squad·ding 1.** To form into a squad or squads. **2.** To assign to a squad. [< F < OF < Ital. < L *quattuor* four]
squad car An automobile used by police for patrolling, and equipped with radiotelephone: also called *patrol car*.
squad·ron (skwod′rən) *n.* **1.** In the U.S. Navy, two or more divisions of vessels or flights of naval aircraft. **2.** In the U.S. Air Force, a unit composed of two or more flights. **3.** A subordinate unit of a cavalry regiment. **4.** Any regularly arranged or organized body. [< Ital. < L *quattuor* four]
squadron leader In the Royal, Royal Canadian, and other Commonwealth air forces, a commissioned officer ranking next below a wing commander. See table at GRADE.
squal·id (skwol′id) *adj.* Having a foul appearance; dirty and wretched. [< L *squalere* to be foul] — **squal′id·ly** *adv.* — **squal′id·ness, squa·lid·i·ty** (skwo·lid′ə·tē) *n.*
squall¹ (skwôl) *n.* A loud, screaming outcry. — *v.i.* To cry loudly; scream; bawl. — **squall′er** *n.*
squall² (skwôl) *n.* **1.** A sudden, violent burst of wind, often accompanied by rain or snow. **2.** *Informal* A commotion. — *v.i.* To blow a squall. — **squall′y** *adj.*
squal·or (skwol′ər) *n.* The state of being squalid; filth and wretched poverty. [< L *squalere* to be foul]
squa·ma (skwā′mə) *n.* *pl.* ·mae (-mē) *Biol.* A thin, scalelike structure; a scale. [< L] — **squa′mate** (-māt), **squa′·mose** (-mōs), **squa′mous** *adj.*
squan·der (skwon′dər) *v.t.* To spend (money, time, etc.) wastefully. — *n.* Prodigality; wasteful expenditure. [Origin unknown] — **squan′der·er** *n.* — **squan′der·ing·ly** *adv.*
square (skwâr) *n.* **1.** A parallelogram having four equal sides and four right angles. **2.** Any object, part, or surface that has this form, or nearly so. **3.** An instrument having an L- or T-shape by which to measure or lay out right angles. **4.** An open area in a city or town formed by the intersection of several streets. **5.** An open area in a city or town formed by the intersection of four or more streets, often planted with trees, flowers, etc. **6.** A section in a town bounded on four sides by streets; also, the distance between one street and the next. **7.** *Math.* The product of a number multiplied by itself. **8.** Formerly, a body of troops formed in a four-sided array. **9.** *Slang* One not conversant with the latest trends or fads. — **on the square 1.** At right angles. **2.** *Informal* In a fair and honest manner. — **out of square 1.** Not at right angles. **2.** Incorrectly; askew; out of order. — *adj.* **1.** Having four equal sides and four right angles; also, resembling a square in form. **2.** Formed with or characterized by a right angle; rectangular. **3.** Adapted to forming squares or computing in squares: a *square* measure. **4.** Direct; fair; just; honest. **5.** Having debit and credit balanced. **6.** Absolute; complete; unequivocal. **7.** Having a broad, stocky frame; strong, sturdy. **8.** *Informal* Solid; full; satisfying: a *square* meal. — **square peg in a round hole** A misfit. — *v.* **squared, squar·ing** *v.t.* **1.** To make or form like a square. **2.** To shape or adjust so as to form a right angle. **3.** To mark with or divide into squares. **4.** To test for the purpose of adjusting to a straight line, right angle, or plane surface. **5.** To bring to a position suggestive of a right angle: *Square* your shoulders. **6.** To make satisfactory settlement or adjustment of: to *square* accounts. **7.** To make (the score of a game, etc.) equal. **8.** To cause to conform; adapt; reconcile. **9.** *Math.* **a** To multiply (a number) by itself. **b** To determine the area of. — *v.i.* **10.** To be at right angles. **11.** To conform; agree; harmonize. **12.** In golf, to make the scores equal. — **to square away 1.** *Naut.* To set (the yards) at right angles to the keel. **2.** To square up. — **square off** To prepare to fight. — **to square the circle 1.** To construct a square equal in area to a given circle, an insoluble problem. **2.** To attempt something impossible. — *adv.* **1.** So as to be square, or at right angles. **2.** *Informal* Honestly; fairly. **3.** Directly; firmly. [< OF < L *quattuor* four] — **square′ness** *n.* — **squar′er** *n.*
square-dance (skwâr′dans′) *v.i.* **-danced, -danc·ing** *U.S.* To perform a square dance.

square dance *U.S.* Any dance, as a quadrille, in which the couples form sets in squares.
square deal *Informal* **1.** In card games, an honest deal. **2.** Fair or just treatment.
square knot A common knot, formed of two overhand knots: also called *reef knot*. For illus. see KNOT.
square·ly (skwâr′lē) *adv.* **1.** In a direct or straight manner. **2.** Honestly; fairly. **3.** *U.S.* Plainly; unequivocally. **4.** In a square form. **5.** At right angles (to a line or plane).
square meal *Informal* A full and substantial meal.
square measure A unit or system of units for measuring areas. See table inside back cover.
square-rigged (skwâr′rigd′) *adj. Naut.* Fitted with square-rigged sails as the principal sails.
square root *Math.* A number that, multiplied by itself, produces the given number: 4 is the *square root* of 16.
square shooter *Informal* An upright person.
squash¹ (skwosh) *v.t.* **1.** To beat or press into a pulp or soft mass; crush. **2.** To quell or suppress. — *v.i.* **3.** To be smashed or squashed. **4.** To make a splashing or sucking sound. — *n.* **1.** A soft or overripe object; also, a crushed mass. **2.** The sudden fall of a heavy, soft body; also, the sound made by such a fall. **3.** A sucking, oozy sound. **4.** Either of two games played on an indoor court with rackets and a ball. **5.** A beverage of which one ingredient is a fruit juice. — *adv.* With a squelching, oozy sound. [< OF < L *ex-* thoroughly + *quassare* to crush] — **squash′er** *n.*
squash² (skwosh) *n.* **1.** The edible fruit of various trailing annuals of the gourd family. **2.** The plant that bears it. [< Algonquian]
squash·y (skwosh′ē) *adj.* **squash·i·er, squash·i·est** Soft and moist. — **squash′i·ly** *adv.* — **squash′i·ness** *n.*
squat (skwot) *v.* **squat·ted** or **squat, squat·ting** *v.i.* **1.** To sit on the heels or hams, or with the legs near the body. **2.** To crouch or cower down. **3.** To settle on a piece of land without title or payment. **4.** To settle on government land in accordance with certain government regulations that will eventually give title. — *v.t.* **5.** To cause (oneself) to squat. — *adj.* **1.** Short and thick; squatty. **2.** Being in a squatting position. — *n.* **1.** A squatting attitude or position. **2.** The act of squatting. [< OF < *es-* thoroughly + *quatir* to press down] — **squat′ter** *n.*
squat·ty (skwot′ē) *adj.* Disproportionately short and thick.
squaw (skwô) *n.* **1.** An American Indian woman or wife. **2.** *Informal* Any woman or girl. [< Algonquian, woman]
squawk (skwôk) *v.i.* **1.** To utter a shrill, harsh cry, as a parrot. **2.** *Slang* To utter loud complaints or protests. — *n.* **1.** The harsh cry of certain birds; also, the act of squawking. **2.** *Slang* A loud protest or complaint. [Prob. imit.] — **squawk′er** *n.*
squeak (skwēk) *n.* A thin, sharp, penetrating sound. — **narrow (or near) squeak** *Informal* A narrow escape. — *v.i.* **1.** To make a squeak. **2.** *Slang* To let out information; squeal. — *v.t.* **3.** To utter or effect with a squeak. **4.** To cause to squeak. [ME *squeke*] — **squeak′er** *n.*
squeak·y (skwē′kē) *adj.* **squeak·i·er, squeak·i·est** Making a squeaking noise. — **squeak′i·ly** *adv.* — **squeak′i·ness** *n.*
squeal (skwēl) *v.i.* **1.** To utter a sharp, shrill, somewhat prolonged cry. **2.** *Slang* To turn informer; betray an accomplice or a plot. — *v.t.* **3.** To utter with a squeal. — *n.* A shrill, prolonged cry, as of a pig. [Imit.] — **squeal′er** *n.*
squeam·ish (skwē′mish) *adj.* **1.** Easily disgusted or shocked; modest; prudish. **2.** Overly fastidious. **3.** Easily nauseated. [< earlier *squaymisch* < AF *escoymous*; ult. origin unknown] — **squeam′ish·ly** *adv.* — **squeam′ish·ness** *n.*
squee·gee (skwē′jē) *n.* **1.** An implement having a stout, straight crosspiece edged with rubber or leather, used for removing water from decks or floors, window panes, etc. **2.** *Photog.* A smaller similar implement. — *v.t.* **1.** To smooth down, as a photographic film, with a squeegee. **2.** To cleanse with a squeegee. [< SQUEEZE]
squeeze (skwēz) *v.* **squeezed, squeez·ing** *v.t.* **1.** To press hard upon; compress. **2.** To extract something from by pressure: to *squeeze* oranges. **3.** To draw forth by pressure; express: to *squeeze* juice. **4.** To force or push; cram. **5.** To oppress, as with burdensome taxes. **6.** To exert pressure upon (someone) to act as one desires. **7.** To make a facsimile impression of. — *v.i.* **8.** To apply pressure. **9.** To force one's way; push: with *in, through*, etc. **10.** To be pressed; yield to pressure. — **to squeeze out** To force out of business, or ruin financially. — *n.* **1.** The act or process of squeezing; pressure. **2.** A firm grasp of someone's hand; also, an embrace; hug. **3.** Something, as juice, extracted or expressed. **4.** A facsimile, as of a coin or inscription, produced by pressing some soft substance upon it. **5.** *Informal* Pressure exerted for the extortion of money or favors; also, financial pressure. [? < OF *es-* thoroughly + ME *queisen* to crush] — **squeez′a·ble** *adj.* — **squeez′er** *n.*

squeeze play In baseball, a play in which the batter tries to bunt the ball so that a man on third base may score by starting while the pitcher is about to deliver the ball.

squelch (skwelch) *v.t.* **1.** To crush; squash. **2.** *Informal* To silence, as with a crushing reply. — *v.i.* **3.** To make a splashing or sucking noise, as when walking in deep mud. **4.** To walk with such a sound. — *n.* **1.** A squelching sound. **2.** A squelched or crushed mass of anything. **3.** *Informal* A crushing reply. [Prob. imit.] — **squelch′er** *n.*

squib (skwib) *n.* **1.** A firework to be thrown or rolled swiftly, finally exploding like a rocket. **2.** A broken firecracker that burns with a spitting sound. **3.** A short speech or writing in a satirical vein. — *v.* **squibbed, squib·bing** *v.i.* **1.** To write or use squibs. **2.** To fire a squib. **3.** To explode or sound like a squib. **4.** To move quickly or restlessly. — *v.t.* **5.** To attack with squibs; lampoon. **6.** To fire or use as a squib. [Origin unknown]

squid (skwid) *n.* Any of various ten-armed mollusks having a slender conical body, ink sac, and broad tail flukes, used as food and for bait. [Origin uncertain]

squig·gle (skwig′əl) *Informal n.* A meaningless scrawl. — *v.i.* To wriggle. [Blend of SQUIRM and WRIGGLE] **squig·gly** (skwig′lē) *adj.* **·gli·er, ·gli·est** Twisty; crooked.

squill (skwil) *n.* **1.** The bulb of a plant of the lily family, found in the Mediterranean region, used chiefly as an expectorant: also called *sea onion.* **2.** The plant itself. [< L < Gk. *skilla* sea onion]

SQUID

a Arm. *b* Body. *c* Caudal fin. *d* Eye. *e* Mouth. *f* Siphon. *g* Tentacles

squint (skwint) *v.i.* **1.** To look with half-closed eyes, as into bright light. **2.** To look with a side glance. **3.** To be cross-eyed. **4.** To incline or tend: with *toward,* etc. — *v.t.* **5.** To hold (the eyes) half-shut, as in glaring light. **6.** To cause to squint. — *adj.* **1.** Cross-eyed. **2.** Looking obliquely or askance; indirect. — *n.* **1.** *Pathol.* Strabismus. **2.** The act or habit of squinting. **3.** An indirect leaning, tendency, or drift. [Origin uncertain] — **squint′er** *n.*

squire (skwīr) *n.* **1.** In England a landed proprietor or country gentleman. **2.** *U.S.* A title often used in rural areas for justices of the peace, judges, lawyers, etc. **3.** A young aspirant to knighthood serving as an attendant. **4.** A man who escorts a woman in public; gallant. — *v.t. & v.i.* **squired, squir·ing** To attend or serve (someone) as a squire or escort. [Aphetic var. of ESQUIRE]

squirm (skwûrm) *v.i.* **1.** To bend and twist the body; wriggle; writhe. **2.** To show signs of pain or distress. — *n.* A squirming motion; a wriggle. [Origin uncertain] — **squirm′er** *n.* — **squirm′y** *adj.*

squir·rel (skwûr′əl, *Brit.* skwir′əl) *n.* **1.** Any of various arboreal rodents having a long bushy tail and feeding chiefly on nuts, as the **red squirrel,** the **gray squirrel,** and the **fox squirrel** of North America. **2.** Any of various related animals, as the chipmunk, flying squirrel, etc. **3.** The fur of a squirrel. [< OF < LL < Gk. < *skia* shadow + *oura* tail]

squirt (skwûrt) *v.i.* **1.** To come forth in a thin stream or jet; spurt out. **2.** To eject water, etc., thus. — *v.t.* **3.** To eject (water or other liquid) forcibly and in a jet. **4.** To wet or bespatter with a squirt or squirts. — *n.* **1.** The act of squirting; also, a jet of liquid squirted forth. **2.** A syringe or squirt gun. **3.** *Informal* A small, impudent, or presumptuous person. [Cf. LG *swirtjen.*] — **squirt′er** *n.*

squirt gun A child's toy gun used for squirting water.

squish (skwish) *v.t. & v.i. Informal* To squash. — *n.* A squashing sound. [Var. of SQUASH¹] — **squish′y** *adj.*

stab (stab) *v.* **stabbed, stab·bing** *v.t.* **1.** To pierce with or as with a pointed weapon; wound. **2.** To thrust (a dagger, etc.), as into a body. **3.** To penetrate; pierce. — *v.i.* **4.** To thrust or lunge with a knife, sword, etc. **5.** To inflict a wound thus. — **to stab in the back** To slander or injure in a treacherous, stealthy manner. — *n.* A thrust made with any pointed weapon. — **to have** (or **make**) **a stab at** To make an attempt at. [? < Scot. & dial. E *stob* to push, thrust, fix a stake < *stob* stake] — **stab′ber** *n.*

sta·bil·i·ty (stə·bil′ə·tē) *n. pl.* **·ties 1.** The condition of being stable. **2.** Steadfastness of purpose or resolution. **3.** Continued existence; permanence. [See STABLE.¹]

sta·bi·lize (stā′bə·līz) *v.t.* **·lized, ·liz·ing 1.** To make firm or stable. **2.** To keep steady; keep from changing or fluctuating: to *stabilize* prices. Also *esp. Brit.* **sta′bi·lise.** [< L *stabilis* steady + -IZE] — **sta′bi·li·za′tion** *n.*

sta·bi·liz·er (stā′bə·lī′zər) *n.* **1.** One who or that which stabilizes. **2.** *Aeron.* An airfoil serving to give an aircraft stability in flight. **3.** A device in a ship or boat, as a gyroscope, to keep it from rolling. **4.** *Chem.* A substance that increases the stability of another substance or compound.

sta·ble¹ (stā′bəl) *adj.* **1.** Standing firmly in place; not easily moved, shaken, or overthrown; fixed. **2.** Marked by fixity of purpose; steadfast. **3.** Having durability or perma-

nence; abiding. **4.** *Chem.* Not easily decomposed: said of compounds. [< F < L *stabilis* < *stare* to stand] — **sta′bly** (-blē) *adv.* — **sta′ble·ness** *n.*

sta·ble² (stā′bəl) *n.* **1.** A building set apart for lodging and feeding horses or cattle; also, the animals. **2.** Race horses belonging to a particular owner; also, the owner and personnel collectively. **3.** *U.S.* A group of writers, artists, athletes, etc., under a single manager. — *v.t. & v.i.* **·bled, ·bling** To put or lodge in a stable. [< OF < L *stare* to stand]

stac·ca·to (stə·kä′tō) *adj.* **1.** *Music* Having or producing silence through most of the written time value of each note; very short and detached. **2.** Marked by abrupt, sharp emphasis. — *adv.* In a staccato manner. — *n. pl.* **·tos 1.** *Music* A staccato style or passage. **2.** An abrupt, emphatic manner or sound. [< Ital., pp. of *staccare* to detach]

stack (stak) *n.* **1.** A large, orderly pile of unthreshed grain, hay, or straw, usu. conical. **2.** Any systematic pile or heap, as a pile of poker chips. **3.** A group of rifles (usu. three) set upright and supporting one another. **4.** A case composed of several rows of bookshelves one above the other. **5.** *pl.* That part of a library where most of the books are shelved. **6.** A chimney; smokestack. **7.** *Informal* A great amount; plenty. — *v.t.* **1.** To pile up in a stack. **2.** To load (a vehicle, etc.) with stacks of a material. — **to stack the cards** (or **deck**) **1.** To arrange cards secretly in the pack in a manner favorable to the dealer. **2.** To have an advantage secured beforehand. [< ON *stakkr*] — **stack′er** *n.*

sta·di·um (stā′dē·əm) *n. pl.* **·di·a** (-dē·ə), *for def. 2* **·di·ums 1.** In ancient Greece, a course for foot races, with banked seats for spectators. **2.** A similar modern structure in which athletic games are played. [< L < Gk. *stadion,* measure of length]

staff (staf, stäf) *n. pl.* **staffs;** *for defs. 1, 2, & 3, also* **staves** (stāvz) **1.** A stick or piece of wood carried for some special purpose. **2.** A shaft or pole that forms a support or handle. **3.** A stick used in measuring or testing. **4.** *Mil.* A body of officers not having command but assigned in an executive or advisory capacity. **5.** A body of persons associated in carrying out some special enterprise. **6.** *Music* The five horizontal lines and four spaces used to represent the pitches of tones: also called *stave.* — *v.t.* To provide (an office, etc.) with a staff. [OE *stæf* stick]

staff officer 1. An officer on the staff of a military commander. **2.** In the U.S. Navy, an officer without command or operational functions, as a doctor, dentist, chaplain, etc.

stag (stag) *n.* **1.** The male of the red deer. **2.** The male of other large deer, as the caribou. **3.** A swine castrated after maturity. **4.** A man who attends a social function unaccompanied by a woman. **5.** A social gathering for men only. — *adj.* Of or for men only. — *v.i.* **stagged, stag·ging** To attend a social affair unaccompanied by a woman. [OE *stagga*]

stage (stāj) *n.* **1.** A raised platform, with its scenery and mechanical appliances, on which the performance in a theater or hall takes place. **2.** The theater: to write for the *stage.* **3.** The drama; also, the dramatic profession. **4.** The field or plan of action of some event: to set the *stage* for war. **5.** A definite portion of a journey. **6.** A step in some development, progress, or process. **7.** A water level: The river rose to flood *stage.* **8.** A horizontal section or story of a building. **9.** *Aerospace* One of the separate propulsion units of a rocket vehicle, each of which becomes operational after the preceding one reaches burnout and is jettisoned. **10.** Any raised platform or floor. **11.** One of the regular stopping places on the route of a stagecoach or postrider. — **by easy stages** Traveling or acting without hurry and with frequent stops. — *v.t.* **staged, stag·ing 1.** To put or exhibit on the stage. **2.** To conduct; carry on. [< OF < L *status,* pp. of *stare* to stand]

stage·coach (stāj′kōch′) *n.* A large, horse-drawn, four-wheeled vehicle having a regular route from town to town.

stage·craft (stāj′kraft′, -kräft′) *n.* Skill in writing or staging plays.

stage door A door to a theater used by actors and stage-hands that leads to the stage or behind the scenes.

stage fright A sudden panic that sometimes attacks those appearing before an audience.

stage·hand (stāj′hand′) *n.* A worker in a theater who handles scenery and props, operates lights, etc.

stage manager One who superintends the stage during the performance of a play.

stage-struck (stāj′struk′) *adj.* Struck with the idea of becoming an actor or an actress; enamored of theatrical life.

stage whisper 1. Any loud whisper intended to be overheard. **2.** A direction by a prompter in the wings to an actor on the stage, intended not to be heard by the audience.

stag·y (stā′jē) See STAGY.

stag·fla·tion (stag′flā′shən) *n.* An economic condition in which inflation is combined with slow buying and high unemployment. [<STAG(NANT) + (IN)FLATION]

stag·ger (stag′ər) *v.i.* **1.** To walk or run unsteadily; totter;

reel. **2.** To become less confident or resolute; waver; hesitate. — *v.t.* **3.** To cause to stagger. **4.** To affect strongly; overwhelm, as with grief. **5.** To place in alternating rows or groups. **6.** To arrange so as to prevent congestion or confusion: to *stagger* lunch hours. — *n.* The act of staggering or the condition of being staggered. [< ON *stakra*] — **stag'ger·er** *n.* — **stag'ger·ing·ly** *adv.*

stag·gers (stag'ərz) *n.pl.* (construed as sing.) **1.** *Vet.* Any of various diseases of domestic animals, as horses, characterized by staggering and sudden falling, due to disorder of the brain and spinal cord. **2.** A reeling sensation.

stag·ing (stā'jing) *n.* **1.** A scaffolding or temporary platform. **2.** The act of putting a play upon the stage. **3.** The business of driving or running stagecoaches.

stag line *U.S. Informal* A group of males at a dance who are without partners.

stag·nant (stag'nənt) *adj.* **1.** Standing still; not flowing: said of water or air. **2.** Foul from long standing, as water. **3.** Lacking briskness or activity; dull; sluggish. — **stag'nan·cy** *n.* — **stag'nant·ly** *adv.*

stag·nate (stag'nāt) *v.i.* **·nat·ed, ·nat·ing 1.** To be or become stagnant. **2.** To become dull or inert; vegetate. [< L *stagnare* to stagnate] — **stag·na·tion** (stag·nā'shən) *n.*

stag·y (stā'jē) *adj.* **stag·i·er, stag·i·est** Having a theatrical manner; of or suited to the stage: also spelled *stagey.* — **stag'i·ly** *adv.* — **stag'i·ness** *n.*

staid (stād) *adj.* **1.** Steady and sober. **2.** Fixed; established. [Orig. pt. and pp. of STAY¹] — **staid'ly** *adv.* — **staid'ness** *n.*

stain (stān) *n.* **1.** A spot; smirch; blot. **2.** The act of discoloring, or the state of being discolored. **3.** A dye or thin pigment used in staining. **4.** A moral taint; tarnish. — *v.t.* **1.** To make a stain upon; discolor; soil. **2.** To color by the use of a dye or stain. **3.** To bring a moral stain upon; blemish. — *v.i.* **4.** To take or impart a stain. [Aphetic var. of DISDAIN] — **stain'a·ble** *adj.* — **stain'er** *n.* — **stain'less** *adj.* — **stain'less·ly** *adv.*

stained glass (stānd) Glass colored by the addition of pigments in the form of metallic oxides, used in church windows, etc. — **stained-glass** (stānd'glas', -gläs') *adj.*

stainless steel A steel alloy made resistant to corrosion and atmospheric influences by the addition of chromium and other ingredients.

stair (stâr) *n.* **1.** A step, or one of a series of steps, for mounting or descending from one level to another. **2.** *Usually pl.* A series of steps. [OE *stæger*]

stair·case (stâr'kās') *n.* A flight or series of flights of stairs, usually from one floor to another.

stair·way (stâr'wā') *n.* A flight of stairs; staircase.

stake (stāk) *n.* **1.** A stick or post sharpened at one end for driving into the ground, used as a boundary mark, support for a fence, etc. **2.** A post to which a person is bound, to be executed by being burned alive; also, execution in this manner. **3.** Something wagered or risked, as money bet on a race. **4.** *Often pl.* A prize in a contest. **5.** An interest in an enterprise. **6.** A grubstake. — **at stake** In hazard or jeopardy; in question: My whole future was *at stake.* — **to pull up stakes** To wind up one's business in a place and move on. — *v.t.* **staked, stak·ing 1.** To fasten or support by means of a stake. **2.** To mark the boundaries of with stakes: often with *off* or *out.* **3.** *Informal* To put at hazard; wager; risk. **4.** *Informal* To grubstake; also, to supply with working capital; finance. [OE *staca*]

sta·lac·tite (stə·lak'tīt, stal'ək·tīt') *n.* A long, tapering formation hanging from the roof of a cavern, produced by continuous watery deposits containing certain minerals. [< NL < Gk. *stalassein* to trickle, drip] — **stal·ac·tit·ic** (stal'ək·tit'ik) or **·i·cal** *adj.*

sta·lag·mite (stə·lag'mīt, stal'əg·mīt') *n.* An incrustation, usu. cylindrical or conical, on the floor of a cavern, the counterpart of a stalactite. [< NL < Gk. < *stalassein* to drip] — **stal·ag·mit·ic** (stal'əg·mit'ik) or **·i·cal** *adj.*

STALACTITE (a) AND STALAGMITE (b)

stale (stāl) *adj.* **stal·er, stal·est 1.** Having lost freshness; slightly changed or deteriorated, as air, beer, bread, etc. **2.** Lacking in interest from age or familiarity; worn out; trite. **3.** Being in poor condition from prolonged activity or overstrain. **4.** Inactive; dull, as after a period of overactivity. — *v.i.* **staled, stal·ing** To become stale or trite. [Origin uncertain.] — **stale'ly** *adv.* — **stale'ness** *n.*

stale·mate (stāl'māt') *n.* **1.** In chess, a draw resulting when a player can make no move without placing his king in check. **2.** Any tie or deadlock. — *v.t.* **·mat·ed, ·mat·ing 1.** To put into a condition of stalemate. **2.** To bring to a standstill. [< AF *estale* fixed position + MATE²]

stalk¹ (stôk) *n.* **1.** The stem or axis of a plant. **2.** A supporting or connecting part of a plant. **3.** *Zool.* Any support on which an organ is borne. **4.** Any stem or main axis, as of a goblet. [ME *stalke*] — **stalked** (stôkt) *adj.* — **stalk'less** *adj.* — **stalk'y** *adj.*

stalk² (stôk) *v.i.* **1.** To approach game, etc., stealthily. **2.** To walk in a stiff, dignified manner. — *v.t.* **3.** To approach (game, etc.) stealthily. **4.** To hover over. — *n.* **1.** The act of stalking game. **2.** A stately step or walk. [OE *bestealcian* to move stealthily] — **stalk'er** *n.*

stalk·ing-horse (stô'king·hôrs') *n.* **1.** Anything serving to conceal one's intention. **2.** In politics, a candidate put forth to divide the opposition or to hide another candidacy. **3.** A horse behind which a hunter conceals himself.

stall (stôl) *n.* **1.** A compartment in which a horse or bovine animal is confined and fed. **2.** A small sales booth or compartment in a street, market, etc. **3.** A pew, as in a church. **4.** A space set aside for the parking of an automobile. **5.** *Aeron.* The condition of an airplane that, from loss of speed or excessive angle of attack, begins to drop. **6.** *Informal* An evasion. — *v.t.* **1.** To place or keep in a stall. **2.** To bring to a standstill; stop the progress or motion of, esp. unintentionally. — *v.i.* **3.** To come to a standstill; stop, esp. unintentionally. **4.** To stick fast in mud, snow, etc. **5.** *Informal* To make delays; be evasive. **6.** To live or be kept in a stall. **7.** *Aeron.* To go into a stall. [OE *steall*]

stall-feed (stôl'fēd') *v.t.* **-fed, -feed·ing** To feed (cattle) in a stall or stable; fatten. — **stall-fed** (-fed') *adj.*

stal·lion (stal'yən) *n.* An uncastrated male horse. [< OF *estalon* < OHG *stal* stable]

stall shower A small enclosed place, with a glass door or curtain, for taking a shower bath.

stal·wart (stôl'wərt) *adj.* **1.** Strong and brawny; robust. **2.** Resolute; determined; unwavering. **3.** Brave; courageous. — *n.* **1.** A brave or stalwart person. **2.** An uncompromising partisan, as in politics. [OE < *stæl* place + *wierthe* worth] — **stal'wart·ly** *adv.* — **stal'wart·ness** *n.*

sta·men (stā'mən) *n. pl.* **sta·mens** or *Rare* **stam·i·na** (stam'ə·nə) *Bot.* The pollen-bearing organ of a flower. For illus. see FLOWER. [< L, warp, thread]

stam·i·na (stam'ə·nə) *n.* Physical or moral capacity to endure or withstand hardship or difficulty; vitality; vigor. [< L, pl. of *stamen* warp, thread] — **stam'i·nal** *adj.*

stam·i·nate (stam'ə·nit, -nāt) *adj. Bot.* **1.** Having stamens. **2.** Having stamens but no pistils.

stam·mer (stam'ər) *v.t. & v.i.* To speak or utter haltingly, with involuntary repetitions or prolongations of a sound or syllable. — *n.* The act or condition of stammering. [OE *stamerian*] — **stam'mer·er** *n.*

stamp (stamp) *v.t.* **1.** To strike heavily with the sole of the foot. **2.** To bring down (the foot) heavily and noisily. **3.** To affect in a specified manner by or as by stamping with the foot: to *stamp* a fire out. **4.** To make marks or figures upon by means of a die, stamp, etc. **5.** To imprint or impress with a die, stamp, etc. **6.** To fix or imprint permanently: The deed was *stamped* on his memory. **7.** To assign a specified quality to; characterize; brand: to *stamp* a story false. **8.** To affix an official seal, stamp, etc., to. **9.** To crush, break, or pulverize, as ore. — *v.i.* **10.** To strike the foot heavily on the ground. **11.** To walk with heavy, resounding steps. — *n.* **1.** A die or block having a pattern or design for impressing upon a surface. **2.** The pattern, impression, design, etc., so made. **3.** A weight or block for crushing ore. **4.** Any characteristic mark, as a label or imprint; a brand. **5.** Characteristic quality or form; kind; sort: men of his *stamp.* **6.** The act of stamping. **7.** A printed device prepared and sold by a government, for attachment to a letter, commodity, etc., as proof that the tax or fee has been paid. [ME *stampen*] — **stamp'er** *n.*

stam·pede (stam·pēd') *n.* **1.** A sudden starting and rushing off through panic, as a herd of cattle, horses, etc. **2.** Any sudden, tumultuous running movement of a crowd or mob. **3.** Any sudden mass movement. — *v.* **·ped·ed, ·ped·ing** *v.t.* **1.** To cause a stampede or panic in. — *v.i.* **2.** To rush or flee in a stampede. [< Am. Sp. *estampida* crash] — **stam·ped'er** *n.*

stamp·ing ground (stam'ping) A favorite or habitual gathering place, for people or animals.

stance (stans) *n.* **1.** Mode of standing; posture. **2.** In golf, the relative positions of the player's feet and the ball, when making a stroke. [< OF < L *stare* to stand]

stanch (stanch, stänch) *v.t.* **1.** To stop or check the flow of (blood, etc.). **2.** To stop the flow of blood from (a wound). Also spelled *staunch.* — *adj.* See STAUNCH. [< OF *estanchier* to halt] — **stanch'er** *n.*

stan·chion (stan'shən) *n.* **1.** An upright bar forming a principal support. **2.** A vertical bar or pair of bars used to confine cattle in a stall. —*v.t.* To provide or confine with stanchions. [< OF *estanchon* < *estance* situation, position]

stand (stand) *v.* **stood, stand·ing** *v.i* **1.** To assume or maintain an erect position on one's feet. **2.** To be in a vertical position; be erect. **3.** To measure a specified height when standing. **4.** To assume a specified position: to *stand* aside. **5.** To assume or have a definite opinion, position, or attitude: How do you *stand* on civil rights? **6.** To be situated; have position or location; lie. **7.** To remain unimpaired, unchanged, or valid: My decision still *stands*. **8.** To have or be in a specified state, condition, or relation: He *stood* in fear of his life. **9.** To be of a specified rank or class: He *stands* third. **10.** To assume an attitude for defense or offense: *Stand* and fight. **11.** To be or remain firm or resolute, as in determination. **12.** To be consistent; accord; agree. **13.** To collect and remain; also, to be stagnant, as water. **14.** To stop or pause; halt. **15.** To scruple; hesitate. **16.** *Naut.* To take a direction; steer: The brig *stood* into the wind. **17.** To point, as a hunting dog. **18.** *Brit.* To be a candidate, as for election. —*v.t.* **19.** To place upright; set in an erect position. **20.** To put up with; endure; tolerate. **21.** To be subjected to; undergo: He must *stand* trial. **22.** To withstand; resist. **23.** *Informal* To pay for; bear the expense of: to *stand* a treat. **— to stand a chance (or show)** To have a chance or likelihood, as of success. **— to stand by 1.** To stay near and be ready to help, operate, or begin. **2.** To help; support. **3.** To abide by; make good. **4.** To remain passive and watch, as when help is needed. **— to stand clear** To remain at a safe distance. **— to stand for 1.** To represent; symbolize. **2.** To put up with; tolerate. **— to stand in** *Informal* To cost. **— to stand in for** To act as a substitute for. **— to stand off** *Informal* **1.** To keep at a distance. **2.** To fail to agree or comply. **— to stand on 1.** To be based on or grounded in; rest. **2.** To insist on or demand observance of: to *stand on* ceremony. **3.** *Naut.* To keep on the same tack or course. **— to stand on one's own (two) feet (or legs)** To manage one's own affairs. **— to stand out 1.** To stick out; project or protrude. **2.** To be prominent; appear in relief or contrast. **3.** To refuse to consent or agree; remain in opposition. **— to stand over 1.** To remain near and watch, as a subordinate. **2.** To be postponed. **— to stand pat 1.** In poker, to play one's hand as dealt, without drawing new cards. **2.** To resist change. **— to stand to reason** To conform to reason. **— to stand up 1.** To stand erect. **2.** To withstand wear, criticism, analysis, etc. **3.** *Slang* To fail to keep an appointment with. **— to stand up for** To side with; take the part of. **— to stand up to** To confront courageously; face. **— to stand up with** To be best man or bridesmaid for. —*n.* **1.** The act of standing, esp. of standing firmly: to make a *stand* against the enemy. **2.** An opinion, attitude, or position, as in a controversy. **3.** A structure or platform upon which persons or things may sit or stand, or on which articles may be kept or displayed. **4.** A small table. **5.** A rack or other piece of furniture on which hats, canes, etc. may be hung or placed. **6.** A stall, counter, or the like, where merchandise is displayed. **7.** Any place where or in which something or someone stands. **8.** In the theater, a stop made while on tour to give a performance: a one-night *stand*. **9.** The growing trees in a forest. **— to take a stand** To have or reveal an opinion or attitude, as on a controversial issue. **— stand'er** *n.*

stan·dard (stan'dərd) *n.* **1.** A flag, ensign, or banner, used as a distinctive emblem of a government, body of men, military unit, etc. **2.** Any established measure of extent, quantity, quality, or value: a *standard* of weight. **3.** Any type, model, or example for comparison; a criterion of excellence: a *standard* of conduct. **4.** An upright timber, post, pole, or beam, esp. as a support. —*adj.* **1.** Serving as a gauge or model: a *standard* weight. **2.** Of recognized excellence or authority: a *standard* book or author. **3.** *Ling.* Designating or belonging to those usages or varieties of a language that have gained literary, cultural, and social acceptance and prestige: *standard* English. [< OF *estandard* banner]

stan·dard-bear·er (stan'dərd·bâr'ər) *n.* **1.** The member of a military unit who carries the flag or ensign. **2.** A leader or a candidate for a leading position, as for a presidency.

stan·dard·bred (*n.* stan'dərd·bred'; *adj.* stan'dərd·bred') *n.* A breed of horse notable for its trotters and pacers. —*adj.* Bred so as to be of a required strain, quality, or pedigree, as poultry, horses, etc.

standard candle *Physics* A candle (def. 3).

standard English *Ling.* Those usages in English that have gained literary, cultural, and social acceptance and prestige, and are considered appropriate for educated speakers of the language. See LEVEL OF USAGE.

standard gauge A railroad having a track width of 56½ inches, considered as standard. **— stan·dard-gauge** (stan'dərd·gāj') *adj.*

stan·dard·ize (stan'dər·dīz) *v.t.* **·ized, ·iz·ing** To make to

or regulate by a standard. **— stan'dard·i·za'tion** *n.* **— stan'dard·iz'er** *n.*

standard of living The average quantity and quality of goods, services, luxuries, etc., that a person or group uses or consumes in daily living.

standard time Time as reckoned from a meridian officially established as standard over a large area. In the conterminous U.S. the four standard time zones are the **Eastern** (E.S.T.), **Central** (C.S.T.), **Mountain** (M.S.T.), and **Pacific** (P.S.T.), using respectively the mean local time of the 75th, 90th, 105th, and 120th meridians west of Greenwich, and being 5, 6, 7, and 8 hours slower (or earlier) than Greenwich time. Canada has a fifth zone, the **Atlantic** (or **Provincial**), based on the local time of the 60th meridian, 4 hours slower than Greenwich time.

stand·by (stand'bī') *n.* *pl.* **·bys** A person or thing on call for emergency use.

stand·ee (stan·dē') *n.* *Informal* A person who must stand for lack of chairs or seats, as at a theater or on a train.

stand·in (stand'in') *n.* **1.** A position of influence or favor; a pull. **2.** A person who takes the place of a motion-picture player, as during waiting intervals or in hazardous actions.

stand·ing (stan'ding) *adj.* **1.** Remaining erect; not prostrated or cut down, as grain. **2.** For regular or permanent use; not special or temporary: a *standing* army. **3.** Stagnant; not flowing. **4.** Begun while standing: a *standing* high jump. **5.** Established; permanent. —*n.* **1.** High grade or rank; good reputation: a man of *standing*. **2.** Time in which something goes on; duration: a feud of long *standing*. **3.** The act of one who stands; erectness; stance.

standing army An army that is prepared at all times for action, esp. during peacetime, and that consists of the regular army plus reservists and conscripts.

standing room Place in which to stand, as in a building, theater, etc., where the seats are all occupied.

stand·off (stand'ôf', -of') *n.* *Informal* **1.** A draw or tie, as in a game. **2.** A counterbalancing or neutralization. **3.** Indifference or coldness; aloofness. **4.** A postponement; delay.

stand·off·ish (stand'ôf'ish, -of'-) *adj.* Aloof; coolly reserved. **— stand·off'ish·ness** *n.*

stand·pat (stand'pat') *adj.* Characterized by or pertaining to the policy of opposition to change; conservative. **— stand·pat'ter** *n.*

stand·pipe (stand'pīp') *n.* A vertical pipe into which the water is pumped to give it a head; a water tower.

stand·point (stand'point') *n.* A position from which things are viewed or judged; point of view.

stand·still (stand'stil') *n.* A cessation; halt; rest. —*adj.* In a state of rest or inactivity; standing still.

stand·up (stand'up') *adj.* **1.** Having an erect position: a *standup* collar. **2.** Done, consumed, etc., while standing.

stank (stangk) Past tense of STINK.

stan·nic (stan'ik) *adj.* *Chem.* Of, pertaining to, or containing tin, esp. in its higher valence. [< L *stannum* tin + -IC]

stan·nous (stan'əs) *adj.* *Chem.* Of, pertaining to, or containing tin, esp. in its lower valence. [< L *stannum* tin + -OUS]

stan·num (stan'əm) *n.* Tin. [< L]

stan·za (stan'zə) *n.* A certain number of lines of verse grouped in a definite scheme of meter and sequence; a metrical division of a poem. [< Ital., room, stanza < L *stans, stantis* standing] **— stan·za·ic** (stan·zā'ik) *adj.*

sta·pes (stā'pēz) *n.* *pl.* **sta·pes** or **sta·pe·des** (stə·pē'dēz) *Anat.* The innermost ossicle of the middle ear of mammals: also called *stirrup bone.* For illus. see EAR. [< LL *stapes* stirrup] **— sta·pe·di·al** (stə·pē'dē·əl) *adj.*

staph (staf) *n.* *Informal* Staphylococci; also, an infection caused by staphylococci.

staph·y·lo·coc·cus (staf'ə·lō·kok'əs) *n.* *pl.* **·coc·ci** (-kok'sī) Any of a genus of typically pathogenic bacteria occurring singly, in pairs, or in irregular clusters; esp. an infective agent in boils and suppurating wounds. [< NL < Gk. *staphylos* bunch of grapes + *kokkos* berry] **— staph'y·lo·coc'cic** (-kok'sik) *adj.*

sta·ple¹ (stā'pəl) *n.* **1.** *Usu. pl.* A basic food or other ordinary item of household use. **2.** A principal commodity or production of a country or region. **3.** A main constituent of something. **4.** The carded or combed fiber of cotton, wool, or flax. **5.** Raw material. —*adj.* **1.** Regularly and constantly produced, used, or sold. **2.** Main; chief. **3.** Having regular commercial channels; marketable. —*v.t.* **pled, ·pling** To sort or classify according to length, as wool fiber. [< OF *estaple* market, support < Gmc.] **— sta'pler** *n.*

sta·ple² (stā'pəl) *n.* **1.** A U-shaped piece of metal with pointed ends, driven into a surface to secure a bolt, hook, hasp, etc. **2.** A thin piece of wire usu. shaped like a bracket (⊓), driven into paper, fabrics, etc., to serve as a fastening. —*v.t.* **pled, ·pling** To fix or fasten by a staple or staples. [OE *stapol* post, prop] **— sta'pler** *n.*

star (stär) *n.* **1.** Any of the heavenly bodies visible from earth on clear nights as apparently fixed points of light. **2.**

Astron. One of a class of self-luminous celestial bodies, exclusive of comets, meteors, and nebulae, but including the sun. ◆ Collateral adjectives: *astral, sidereal, stellar.* **3.** A conventional figure usu. having five or more radiating points, used as an emblem or device, as on the shoulder strap of a general. **4.** An actor or actress who plays the leading part. **5.** Anyone who shines prominently in a calling or profession: a sports *star.* **6.** An asterisk (*). **7.** A heavenly body considered as influencing one's fate. **8.** *Often pl.* Fortune; destiny. **— to see stars** *Informal* To see bright spots before the eyes, as from a sharp jolt to the head. **—** *v.* **starred, star·ring** *v.t.* **1.** To set or adorn with spangles or stars. **2.** To mark with an asterisk. **3.** To present as a star in a play or motion picture. **—** *v.i.* **4.** To shine brightly as a star. **5.** To play the leading part; be the star. **—** *adj.* **1.** Of or pertaining to a star or stars. **2.** Prominent; brilliant: a *star* football player. [OE *steorra*] **— star′less** *adj.* **— star′·like′** *adj.*

star·board (stär′bərd) *Naut. n.* The right-hand side of a vessel as one faces the front or bow. **—** *adj.* Being on or toward the starboard. Opposed to *larboard, port.* [OE *steorbord* steering side]

starch (stärch) *n.* **1.** *Biochem.* A white, odorless, tasteless, granular carbohydrate ($C_6H_{10}O_5$)n, found in most plants: also called *amylum.* **2.** A preparation of this substance, used for stiffening linen, and for many industrial purposes. **3.** Stiffness or formality; a formal manner. **4.** *U.S. Slang* Energy; vigor. **—** *v.t.* To apply starch to; stiffen with or as with starch. [OE *stercan* to stiffen < *stearc* stiff]

Star Chamber **1.** Formerly, in England, a secret high court, abolished in 1641 because of abuses. **2.** Any court engaged in arbitrary or illegal procedure.

starch·y (stär′chē) *adj.* **starch·i·er, starch·i·est** **1.** Stiffened with starch; stiff. Also **starched** (stärcht). **2.** Prim; formal; precise. **3.** Formed of or combined with starch; farinaceous. **— starch′i·ly** *adv.* **— starch′i·ness** *n.*

star·dom (stär′dəm) *n.* The status of a star (defs. 4 & 5).

stare (stâr) *v.* **stared, star·ing** *v i* **1.** To gaze fixedly, as from admiration, fear, or insolence. **2.** To be conspicuously or unduly apparent; glare. **3.** To stand on end, as hair. **—** *v.t.* **4.** To stare at. **5.** To affect in a specified manner by staring: to *stare* a person into silence. **—** *n.* The act of staring; an intense gaze. [OE *starian*] **— star′er** *n.*

star·fish (stär′fish′) *n.* *pl.* **·fish** or **·fish·es** Any of various radially symmetrical marine animals, commonly with a star-shaped body having five or more arms.

star·gaze (stär′gāz′) *v.i.* **·gazed, ·gaz·ing** **1.** To gaze at or study the stars. **2.** To engage in reverie; daydream. **— star′gaz·er** *n.* **— star′·gaz·ing** *n. & adj.*

STARFISH
(Ventral view showing tube feet)

stark (stärk) *adj.* **1.** Without ornamentation; blunt; simple: the *stark* truth. **2.** Complete; utter: *stark* misery. **3.** Stiff or rigid, as in death. **4.** Severe; tempestuous, as weather. **5.** Strict or grim, as a person. **—** *adv.* **1.** In a stark manner. **2.** Completely; utterly: *stark* mad. [OE *stearc* stiff] **— stark′ly** *adv.*

star·let (stär′lit) *n.* **1.** A small star. **2.** *U.S. Informal* A young movie or television actress represented as a future star.

star·light (stär′līt′) *n.* The light given by a star or stars. **—** *adj.* Lighted by or only by the stars: also **star′lit′** (-lit′).

star·ling (stär′ling) *n.* Any of various birds native to Europe and naturalized in North America, having a metallic purple and green luster. [OE *stærling* < *stær* starling]

star-of-Beth·le·hem (stär′əv-beth′lē-əm, -lə-hem) *n.* A European plant of the lily family having white stellate flowers, naturalized in the eastern U.S.

star of Bethlehem The large star by which the three Magi were guided to Jesus's manger in Bethlehem.

starred (stärd) *adj.* **1.** Spangled with stars. **2.** Presented or advertised as the star of a play, motion picture, etc. **3.** Marked with an asterisk. **4.** Affected by astral influence: chiefly in combination: *ill-starred.*

star·ry (stär′ē) *adj.* **·ri·er, ·ri·est** **1.** Set with stars or starlike spots or points; abounding in stars. **2.** Lighted by the stars. **3.** Shining as or like the stars. **4.** Shaped like a star. **5.** Of, pertaining to, proceeding from, or connected with stars. **6.** Consisting of stars; stellar. **— star′ri·ness** *n.*

star·ry-eyed (stär′ē-īd′) *adj.* Given to fanciful wishes or yearnings.

Stars and Bars, The The first flag of the Confederacy, consisting of a field of three bars and a circle of white stars.

Stars and Stripes, The The flag of the U.S. of America, a field of thirteen horizontal stripes, alternately red and white, and a blue union with 50 stars.

star-span·gled (stär′spang′gəld) *adj.* Spangled with stars or starlike spots or points.

Star-Spangled Banner, The **1.** The flag of the U.S. **2.** The national anthem of the U.S. The poem was written by Francis Scott Key in 1814 during the bombardment by the British of Fort McHenry, Md.

start (stärt) *v.i.* **1.** To make a beginning or start; set out. **2.** To begin; commence. **3.** To make an involuntary, startled movement, as from fear or surprise. **4.** To move suddenly, as with a spring, leap, or bound; jump. **5.** To seem to bulge or protrude: His eyes *started* from his head. **6.** To be displaced or loosened. **—** *v.t.* **7.** To set in motion or circulation: to *start* an engine. **8.** To begin; commence: to *start* a lecture. **9.** To set up; establish. **10.** To introduce (a subject) or propound (a question). **11.** To displace or loosen, etc. **12.** To rouse from cover; cause to take flight; flush, as game. **13.** To draw the contents from; tap, as a cask. **— to start in** To begin; undertake. **— to start off** To begin a journey; set out. **— to start out** To make a beginning or start, as of a journey. **— to start up** **1.** To rise or appear suddenly. **2.** To begin or cause to begin operation, as an engine. **—** *n.* **1.** A setting out or going forth; beginning. **2.** A quick, startled movement, as at something unexpected. **3.** A temporary or spasmodic action or attempt; a brief, intermittent effort: by fits and *starts.* **4.** Advantage or distance in advance at the outset; lead. **5.** Impetus at the beginning of motion or course of action: to get a *start* in business. **6.** A loosened place or condition; crack. [ME *sterten* to start, leap]

start·er (stär′tər) *n.* **1.** One who or that which starts. **2.** One who sees to it that buses, etc., leave on schedule. **3.** A mechanism for starting an internal combustion engine without manual cranking: also called *self-starter.* **4.** A competitor at the start of a race. **5.** A person who gives the signal for the start of a race.

star·tle (stär′təl) *v.* **·tled, ·tling** *v.t.* **1.** To arouse or excite suddenly; cause to start involuntarily; alarm. **—** *v.i.* **2.** To be aroused or excited suddenly; take alarm. **—** *n.* A sudden fright or shock; a scare. [OE *steartlian* to kick, struggle] **— star′tler** *n.*

star·tling (stärt′ling) *adj.* Rousing sudden surprise, alarm, or the like. **— star′tling·ly** *adv.*

star·va·tion (stär-vā′shən) *n.* The act of starving, or the state of being starved.

starve (stärv) *v.* **starved, starv·ing** *v.i.* **1.** To perish from lack of food. **2.** To suffer from extreme hunger. **3.** To suffer from lack or need: to *starve* for friendship. **—** *v.t.* **4.** To cause to die of hunger; deprive of food. **5.** To bring to a specified condition by starving: to *starve* an enemy into surrender. [OE *steorfan* to die] **— starv′er** *n.*

starve·ling (stärv′ling) *n.* A person or animal that is starving, starved, or emaciated. **—** *adj.* **1.** Starving; emaciated; hungry. **2.** Failing to meet needs; inadequate.

stash (stash) *v.t. Slang* To hide or conceal (money, valuables, etc.), for storage and safekeeping: often with *away.* [? Blend of STORE + CACHE]

sta·sis (stā′sis, stas′is) *n.* *pl.* **·ses** (-sēz) *Pathol.* **1.** Stoppage in the circulation of any of the body fluids. **2.** Retarded movement of the intestinal contents. [< NL < Gk., a standing < *histanai* to stand]

stat- Var. of STATO-.

-stat *combining form* A device that stops or makes constant: *thermostat; rheostat.* [< Gk. *-statēs* causing to stand]

state (stāt) *n.* **1.** Mode of existence as determined by circumstances, external or internal; nature; condition; situation. **2.** Frame of mind; mood. **3.** Mode or style of living; station. **4.** Grand and ceremonious style; pomp; formality. **5.** A sovereign political community organized under a distinct government recognized and conformed to by the people as supreme, and having jurisdiction over a given territory; a nation. **6.** *Usu. cap.* One of a number of political communities or bodies politic united to form one sovereign state; esp. one of the United States. **7.** *pl.* The legislative bodies of a nation; estates. **8.** The territorial, political, and governmental entity constituting a state or nation; authority of government. **— Syn.** See NATION. **— Department of State** An executive department of the U.S. government (established in 1789), headed by the Secretary of State, that supervises the conduct of foreign affairs, directs the activities of all diplomatic and consular representatives, protects national interests abroad, and assists in the formulation of policies in relation to international problems. Also **State Department. — to lie in state** To be placed on public view, with ceremony and honors, before burial. **—** *adj.* **1.** Of or pertaining to the state, nation, or government: *state* papers. **2.** Intended for use on occasions of ceremony. **—** *v.t.* **stat·ed, stat·ing** **1.** To set forth explicitly in speech or writing; assert; declare. **2.** To fix; determine; settle. [Aphetic var. of OF *estat* < L *status* condition, state] **— sta·tal** (stā′tal) *adj.*

state bank **1.** *U.S.* A bank that has a charter from a State government. **2.** Any bank that is owned or controlled by a state, esp. one that issues currency.

state·craft (stāt′kraft′, -kräft′) *n.* The art or practice of conducting affairs of state.

stat·ed (stā′tid) *adj.* **1.** Announced; specified. **2.** Established; regular; fixed. — **stat′ed·ly** *adv.*

State·hood (stāt′hŏod) *n.* The status of one of the United States, as distinguished from that of a Territory.

State House A building used for sessions of a State legislature and for other public purposes; State capitol.

state·less (stāt′lis) *adj.* **1.** Without nationality: a *stateless* person. **2.** Without a state or community of states.

state line In the U.S., any boundary between States.

state·ly (stāt′lē) *adj.* **·li·er, ·li·est** Dignified; lofty. — *adv.* Loftily: also **state′li·ly** (-lə·lē). — **state′li·ness** *n.*

state·ment (stāt′mənt) *n.* **1.** The act of stating. **2.** That which is stated. **3.** A summary of the assets and liabilities of a bank or firm, showing the balance due. **4.** A report sent, usu. monthly, to a debtor of a business firm or to a depositor in a bank.

state park *U.S.* A tract of land provided and maintained by a State for conservation and recreation.

State policeman *U.S.* A member of the separate police force of a State; also called *State trooper, trooper.*

state·room (stāt′rōom′, -rŏom′) *n.* **1.** A private room having sleeping accommodations on a passenger ship. **2.** A private sleeping compartment on a railroad car.

state's evidence **1.** Evidence produced by the State in criminal prosecutions. **2.** One who confesses himself guilty of a crime and testifies as a witness against his accomplices. — **to turn state's evidence** To become a witness for the state and inculpate one's accomplices.

state·side (stāt′sīd′) *adj.* Of or in the continental U.S. — *adv.* In or to the continental U.S.

states·man (stāts′mən) *n. pl.* **·men** (-mən) **1.** One who is skilled in government; a political leader of distinguished ability. **2.** One engaged in government, or influential in state affairs. — **states′man·like′, states′man·ly** *adj.* — **states′·man·ship** *n.* — **states′wom′an** (-wŏom′ən) *n.fem.*

state socialism A political theory advocating government ownership of utilities and industries.

States' rights **1.** The rights and powers not delegated to the U.S. by the Constitution nor prohibited by it to the respective States. **2.** An interpretation of the Constitution that makes these rights and powers as large as possible. Also **State rights.**

State trooper *U.S.* A State policeman.

state-wide (stāt′wīd′) *adj.* Throughout a state.

stat·ic (stat′ik) *adj.* **1.** At rest; dormant; not active, moving, or changing. **2.** Pertaining to bodies at rest or forces in equilibrium: opposed to *dynamic.* **3.** *Physics* Acting as weight, but not moving: *static* pressure. **4.** *Electr.* Pertaining to electricity at rest, or to stationary electric charges. Also **stat′i·cal.** — *n. Telecom.* A disturbance of a carrier wave caused by atmospheric or man-made sources; also, the noise caused by this. [< NL < Gk. *statikos* causing to stand] — **stat′i·cal·ly** *adv.*

stat·ics (stat′iks) *n.pl.* (*construed as sing.*) The branch of mechanics dealing with bodies at rest and with the interaction of forces in equilibrium.

sta·tion (stā′shən) *n.* **1.** The headquarters of some official person or body of men: a police *station.* **2.** An established building or place serving as a starting point, stage, stopping place, or post; terminal; depot. **3.** A place where a person or thing usu. stands or is; an assigned location. **4.** Social condition; rank. **5.** *Mil.* The place to which an individual, unit, or ship is assigned for duty; post. **6.** The offices, studios, and technical installations of a radio or television broadcasting unit. **7.** *Mining* A recess in a shaft or passage of a mine. **8.** *Austral.* A cattle or sheep ranch. — *v.t.* To assign to a station; place in a post or position. [< F < L < *stare* to stand]

sta·tion·ar·y (stā′shən·er′ē) *adj.* **1.** Remaining in one place; fixed. **2.** Not portable or not easily portable. **3.** Exhibiting no change of character or condition. — *n. pl.* **·ar·ies** One who or that which is stationary.

sta·tion·er (stā′shən·ər) *n.* A dealer in stationery and related articles. [< Med.L *stationarius* stationary]

sta·tion·er·y (stā′shən·er′ē) *n.* **1.** Writing paper and envelopes. **2.** Writing materials, as pencils, notebooks, etc.

sta·tion·mas·ter (stā′shən·mas′tər, -mäs′-) *n.* The person having charge of a bus or railroad station.

Stations of the Cross The fourteen images or pictures representing successive scenes of the Passion of Christ, and before which devotions are performed.

station wagon A large automobile with one or more rows of removable or folding seats and a hinged tailgate.

stat·ism (stā′tiz·əm) *n.* **1.** A theory of government holding that the returns from group or individual enterprise are vested in the state. **2.** Loosely, adherence to state sovereignty, as in a republic. — **stat′ist** *n. & adj.*

sta·tis·tic (stə·tis′tik) *adj.* Statistical. — *n.* Any element entering into a statistical statement or array.

sta·tis·ti·cal (stə·tis′tə·kəl) *adj.* Of, pertaining to, consisting of, or derived from statistics: also *statistic.* — **sta·tis′ti·cal·ly** *adv.*

sta·tis·ti·cian (stat′is·tish′ən) *n.* One skilled in collecting and tabulating statistical data.

sta·tis·tics (stə·tis′tiks) *n.pl.* (*construed as sing. in def. 2*) **1.** Quantitative data, pertaining to any subject or group, esp. when systematically gathered and collated. **2.** The science that deals with the collection, tabulation, and systematic classification of quantitative data, esp. as a basis for inference and induction. [< G < Med.L, ult. < L *status* state, condition]

stato- *combining form* Position. Also, before vowels, *stat-.* [< Gk. *statos* standing, fixed < *histanai* to stand]

sta·tor (stā′tər) *n. Mech.* The stationary portion of a dynamo, turbine, motor, etc.: distinguished from *rotor.* [< NL < L, supporter < *stare* to stand]

stat·u·ar·y (stach′ŏo·er′ē) *n. pl.* **·ar·ies** **1.** Statues collectively. **2.** The art of making statues. — *adj.* Of or suitable for statues.

stat·ue (stach′ŏo) *n.* A representation of a human or animal figure in marble, bronze, etc., esp. when nearly life-size or larger, and preserving the proportions in all directions. [< F < L < *status*, pp. of *stare* to stand]

Statue of Liberty A giant bronze statue on Liberty Island, depicting a crowned woman holding aloft a burning torch; presented to the U.S. by France and unveiled in 1886.

stat·u·esque (stach′ŏo·esk′) *adj.* Resembling a statue, as in grace, pose, or dignity. — **stat′u·esque′ly** *adv.* — **stat′u·esque′ness** *n.*

stat·u·ette (stach′ŏo·et′) *n.* A small statue. [< F]

stat·ure (stach′ər) *n.* **1.** The natural height of an animal body, esp. of a human body. **2.** The height of anything, esp. of a tree. **3.** Development; growth: moral *stature.* [< OF < L < *status* state]

sta·tus (stā′təs, stat′əs) *n.* **1.** State, condition, or relation. **2.** Relative position or rank. [< L < *stare* to stand]

sta·tus quo (stā′təs kwō, stat′əs) The condition or state in which (a person or thing is or has been): often used with *the:* to maintain the *status quo.* Also **status in quo.** [< L]

stat·ute (stach′ŏot) *n.* **1.** A legislative enactment duly sanctioned and authenticated by constitutional rule; act of Parliament, Congress, etc. **2.** Any authoritatively declared rule, ordinance, decree, or law. — *adj.* Consisting of or regulated by statute. [< F < LL *statuere* to constitute]

statute law The law as set forth in statutes.

statute mile A mile (def. 1).

statute of limitations A statute that imposes time limits upon the right of certain actions, as by obliging a creditor to demand payment of a debt within a specified time.

stat·u·to·ry (stach′ə·tôr′ē, -tō′rē) *adj.* **1.** Pertaining to a statute. **2.** Created by or dependent upon legislation.

statutory rape The crime of having sexual relations with a girl who is under the age of consent.

staunch (stônch, stänch) *adj.* **1.** Firm and dependable; constant; loyal: a *staunch* friend. **2.** Having firm constitution or construction: a *staunch* ship. **3.** Strong and vigorous. Also spelled *stanch.* — *v.t.* See STANCH. [< OF *estanchier* to make stand.] — **staunch′ly** *adv.* — **staunch′ness** *n.*

stauro- *combining form* Cross. [< Gk. *stauros* cross]

stave (stāv) *n.* **1.** A curved strip of wood, forming a part of the sides of a barrel, tub, or the like. **2.** Any narrow strip of material used for a like purpose. **3.** *Music* A staff. **4.** A stanza; verse. **5.** A rod, cudgel, or staff. **6.** A rung of a rack or ladder. — *v. staved* or **stove, stav·ing** *v.t.* **1.** To break in the staves of (a cask or a boat). **2.** To crush the shell or surface of; smash. **3.** To make (a hole) by crushing or collision. **4.** To furnish with staves. **5.** To ward off, as with a staff: usu. with *off:* to *stave* off hunger. — *v.i.* **6.** To be broken in, as a vessel's hull. [Back formation < *staves*]

staves (stāvz) **1.** Alternative plural of STAFF. **2.** Plural of STAVE.

stay¹ (stā) *v.i.* **1.** To cease motion; stop; halt. **2.** To continue in a specified place, condition, or state: to *stay* healthy. **3.** To remain temporarily as a guest, resident, etc. **4.** To pause; wait; tarry. **5.** *Informal* To have endurance; last. **6.** *Informal* To keep pace with a competitor, as in a race. **7.** In poker, to remain in a round by meeting an ante, bet, or raise. — *v.t.* **8.** To bring to a stop; halt; check. **9.** To hinder; delay. **10.** To postpone. **11.** To satisfy the demands of temporarily; to allay the pangs of hunger. **12.** To remain for the duration of: I will *stay* the night. **13.** To remain till or beyond the end of: with *out:* to *stay* out one's welcome. — **to stay put** *U.S. Informal* To remain or hold in spite of everything. — *n.* **1.** The act or time of staying; sojourn; visit. **2.** That which checks or stops; esp., a suspension of judicial proceedings. **3.** Staying power; endurance. **4.** A state of rest; standstill. [< AF *estaier*, OF *ester* < L *stare* to stand] — **stay′er** *n.*

stay² (stā) *v.t.* **1.** To be a support to; prop or hold up. **2.** To support mentally; sustain. **3.** To cause to depend or rely, as for support: with *on* or *upon*. — *n.* **1.** Anything that props or supports. **2.** A strip of plastic or metal, used to stiffen corsets, girdles, etc. **3.** *pl.* Formerly, a corset. [< OF *estayer*]

stay³ (stā) *Naut. n.* **1.** A strong rope, often of wire, used to support, steady, or fasten a mast or spar. **2.** Any rope supporting a mast or funnel. — *v.t.* **1.** To support with a stay or stays, as a mast. **2.** To put (a vessel) on the opposite tack. — *v.i.* **3.** To tack: said of vessels. [OE *stæg*]

stay·ing power (stā'ing) The ability to endure.

stay·sail (stā'səl, -sāl') *n. Naut.* A sail, usu. triangular, extended on a stay.

stead (sted) *n.* **1.** Place of another person or thing: preceded by *in*: Serfdom came in the *stead* of slavery. Compare INSTEAD. **2.** Place or attitude of support; service: chiefly in the phrase **to stand one in (good) stead. 3.** A steading or farm: used chiefly in compounds: *homestead.* [OE *stede*]

stead·fast (sted'fast', -fäst', -fəst) *adj.* **1.** Firmly fixed in faith or devotion to duty; constant; unchanging. **2.** Directed fixedly or purposefully; steady. [OE *stedefæst*] — **stead'fast'ly** *adv.* — **stead'fast'ness** *n.*

stead·y (sted'ē) *adj.* **stead·i·er, stead·i·est 1.** Stable in position; firmly supported; fixed. **2.** Moving or acting with uniform regularity; unfaltering: a *steady* light. **3.** Not readily disturbed or upset: *steady* nerves. **4.** Free from intemperance and dissipation: *steady* habits. **5.** Constant in mind or conduct; steadfast. **6.** Regular; reliable: a *steady* customer. **7.** Uninterrupted; continuous. **8.** *Naut.* Having the direction of the ship's head unchanged. — *v.t. & v.i.* **stead·ied, stead·y·ing** To make or become steady. — *interj.* Not so fast; keep calm: an order enjoining self-control or composure. — *n. Slang* One's regular sweetheart. — **to go steady** *Informal* To date only one person of the opposite sex. [< STEAD + -Y³] — **stead'i·er** *n.* — **stead'i·ly** *adv.* — **stead'i·ness** *n.*

steady-state theory *Astron.* A theory that matter is continuously created in the universe, balancing the matter dissipated by the expansion of the universe. Compare BIG-BANG THEORY, OSCILLATING UNIVERSE.

steak (stāk) *n.* **1.** A slice of meat, esp. beef, or fish, usu. broiled or fried. **2.** Meat chopped for cooking like a steak. [< ON *steik*]

steal (stēl) *v.* **stole, sto·len, steal·ing** *v.t.* **1.** To take from another without right, authority, or permission, and usu. in a secret manner. **2.** To take or obtain in a surreptitious, artful, or subtle manner. **3.** To move, place, or convey stealthily: with *away, from, in, into,* etc. **4.** In baseball, to reach (second base, third base, or home plate) without the aid of a hit, error, passed ball, or wild pitch: said of a baserunner. — *v.i.* **5.** To commit theft. **6.** To move secretly or furtively. **7.** In baseball, to steal a base. — *n.* **1.** The act of stealing. **2.** That which is stolen. **3.** *U.S. Slang* A bargain. [OE *stelan*] — **steal'er** *n.*

stealth (stelth) *n.* **1.** The quality or habit of acting secretly; a concealed manner of acting. **2.** A secret or clandestine act, movement, or proceeding. [ME < OE *stelan* to steal]

stealth·y (stel'thē) *adj.* **stealth·i·er, stealth·i·est** Moving or acting secretly or slyly; done or characterized by stealth; furtive. — **stealth'i·ly** *adv.* — **stealth'i·ness** *n.*

— **Syn.** Anything *stealthy* seeks to avoid notice; it may be applied to a worthy act or purpose. *Furtive* suggests the actions or manner of a thief; we speak of a *furtive* act, a *furtive* face. *Surreptitious* suggests quickness as well as concealment in acting illegally or improperly: a *surreptitious* glance into a neighbor's window. *Clandestine* describes that which is concealed because morally offensive or socially and politically dangerous: a *clandestine* love affair, a *clandestine* rally.

steam (stēm) *n.* **1.** Water in the form of vapor. **2.** The gas or vapor into which water is changed by boiling, esp. when used under pressure as a source of energy. **3.** The visible mist into which aqueous vapor is condensed by cooling. **4.** Any kind of vaporous exhalation. **5.** *Informal* Vigor; force; speed. — **to let (or blow) off steam** *Informal* To give expression to pent-up emotions or opinions. — *v.i.* **1.** To give off or emit steam or vapor. **2.** To rise or pass off as steam. **3.** To become covered with condensed water vapor: often with *up.* **4.** To generate steam. **5.** To move or travel by the agency of steam. — *v.t.* **6.** To treat with steam, as in softening, cooking, cleaning, etc. — *adj.* **1.** Of, driven, or operated by steam. **2.** Containing or conveying steam: a *steam* boiler. **3.** Treated by steam. [OE *stēam*]

steam·boat (stēm'bōt') *n.* A steamship.

steam engine An engine that derives its motive force from the action of steam, usu. by pressure against a piston sliding within a closed cylinder.

steam·er (stē'mər) *n.* **1.** A ship propelled by steam. **2.** A vessel in which something is steamed, as for cooking.

steamer trunk A trunk small enough to fit under a berth in a ship's cabin.

steam·fit·ter (stēm'fit'ər) *n.* A man who sets up or repairs steam pipes and their fittings. — **steam'fit'ting** *n.*

steam organ A calliope.

steam·roll·er (stēm'rō'lər) *n.* **1.** A road-rolling machine driven by steam. **2.** Any force that ruthlessly overcomes opposition. Also **steam roller.** — *v.t.* **1.** To work (a road, etc.) with a steamroller. **2.** To suppress; crush. **3.** To provide a path for by crushing opposition. — *v.i.* **4.** To work with or as with a steamroller. — *adj.* Resembling the action of a steamroller; aggressive: *steamroller* tactics.

steam·ship (stēm'ship') *n.* A large vessel used for ocean traffic and usu. propelled by steam; a steamer.

steam shovel A steam-powered machine for excavating.

steam table *U.S.* A long table, as in restaurants, with openings in which containers of food are placed to be kept warm by hot water or steam circulating beneath them.

steam turbine A turbine operated by steam power.

steam·y (stē'mē) *adj.* **steam·i·er, steam·i·est** Consisting of, like, or full of steam. — **steam'i·ly** *adv.* — **steam'i·ness** *n.*

ste·ar·ic (stē·ar'ik, stir'ik) *adj. Chem.* Of, pertaining to, or derived from stearin. [< F < Gk. *stear* suet]

stearic acid *Chem.* A white fatty acid, $C_{17}H_{35}COOH$, found in animal fats and in many vegetable oils.

ste·a·rin (stē'ə·rin, stir'in) *n. Chem.* **1.** A white, crystalline compound $(C_{17}H_{35}COO)_3C_3H_5$, obtained from various animal and vegetable fats. **2.** Stearic acid, esp. as prepared for making candles, etc. **3.** Fat in solid form. Also **ste'a·rine** (-rin, -rēn). [< F < Gk. *stear* suet]

ste·a·tite (stē'ə·tīt) *n.* Massive talc found in extensive beds and quarried for hearths, sink linings, coarse utensils, etc.: also called *soapstone.* [< L < Gk. *stear, steatos* suet, tallow]

steed (stēd) *n.* A horse; esp., a spirited war horse: now chiefly a literary term. [OE *stēda* studhorse]

steel (stēl) *n.* **1.** A tough alloy of iron containing carbon in variable amounts, malleable under proper conditions, and greatly hardened by sudden cooling. The addition of other components, as chromium and nickel, gives a large range of alloys having special properties. **2.** Something made of steel, as a sword. **3.** Hardness of character. **4.** A strip or band of steel, as for stiffening a corset. — *adj.* **1.** Made or composed of steel. **2.** Resembling steel, as in hardness. **3.** Adamant; unyielding. — *v.t.* **1.** To cover with steel; plate, edge, point, or face with steel. **2.** To make hard or strong like steel. **3.** To make unfeeling; harden. [OE *style, stēle*]

steel blue A metallic blue, as of certain steels.

steel engraving 1. The art and process of engraving on a steel plate. **2.** The impression made from such a plate.

steel gray Any of several dark shades of gray.

steel·head (stēl'hed') *n. U.S. & Canadian* The rainbow trout, esp. in its migratory stage to and from the sea, highly esteemed as a game fish: also called *salmon trout.*

steel wool Steel fibers matted together for use as an abrasive, as in cleaning, polishing, etc.

steel·work (stēl'wûrk') *n.* **1.** Any article or construction of steel. **2.** *pl.* A shop or factory where steel is made or fabricated. — **steel'work'ing** *n.*

steel·work·er (stēl'wûr'kər) *n.* A worker in a steel mill.

steel·y (stē'lē) *adj.* **steel·i·er, steel·i·est 1.** Made of, containing, resembling, or suggesting steel. **2.** Having a steel-like hardness: a *steely* gaze. — **steel'i·ness** *n.*

steel·yard (stēl'yärd', -yərd, stil'yərd) *n.* A weighing device consisting of a scaled beam, counterpoise, and hooks. Also **steel'yards.** [< *Steelyard*, formerly, the London headquarters for Hanseatic traders]

steen·bok (stān'bok, stēn'-) *n.* A small, fawn-colored African antelope: also called *steinbok.* [< Du. < *steen* stone + *bok* buck]

steep¹ (stēp) *adj.* **1.** Making a large angle with the plane of the horizon; precipitous. **2.** *Informal* Exorbitant; excessive; high, as a price. — *n.* A precipitous place, as a cliff or hill. [OE *stēap*] — **steep'ly** *adv.* — **steep'ness** *n.*

steep² (stēp) *v.t.* **1.** To soak in a liquid, as for softening, cleansing, etc. **2.** To imbue thoroughly; saturate: *steeped* in crime. — *v.i.* **3.** To undergo soaking in a liquid. — *n.* **1.** The process of steeping or the state of being steeped. **2.** A liquid or bath for steeping something; esp., a fertilizing liquid for seeds. [ME *stepen*, ? < Scand.] — **steep'er** *n.*

steep·en (stē'pən) *v.t. & v.i.* To make or become steep or steeper.

stee·ple (stē'pəl) *n.* A lofty, usu. tapering structure rising above the tower of a church; a spire. [OE *stīpel*]

stee·ple·chase (stē'pəl·chās') *n.* **1.** A race on horseback across country, in which obstacles are to be leaped. **2.** A

---

race over a course artificially prepared, as with hedges, rails, etc. **3.** Any cross-country run. [So called because originally the goal of the racers was a distant church steeple] — **stee'ple·chas'er** n. — **stee'ple·chas'ing** n.

stee·ple·jack (stē'pəl·jak') n. A man whose occupation is to climb steeples and other tall structures to inspect or make repairs. [< STEEPLE + obs. jack workman]

steer[1] (stir) v.t. **1.** To direct the course of (a vessel or vehicle) by means of a rudder, steering wheel, etc. **2.** To follow (a course). **3.** To direct; guide. — v.i. **4.** To direct the course of a vessel, vehicle, etc. **5.** To undergo guiding or steering. **6.** To follow a course: to steer for land. — **to steer clear of** To avoid. — n. U.S. Slang A piece of advice. [OE stīeran] — **steer'a·ble** adj. — **steer'er** n.

steer[2] (stir) n. **1.** A male bovine animal, esp. when castrated and from two to four years old. **2.** An ox of any age raised for beef. [OE stēor]

steer·age (stir'ij) n. **1.** Formerly, the part of an ocean passenger vessel in the forward lower decks. **2.** Any markedly inferior, overcrowded, third-class accommodations. **3.** The act of steering. **4.** The effect of the helm on a vessel.

steer·age·way (stir'ij·wā') n. Naut. The lowest speed at which a vessel can be accurately steered.

steer·ing committee (stir'ing) A committee in a legislature or other assemblage that arranges or directs the course of the business to be considered.

steering gear The coordinated mechanism that steers a ship, automotive vehicle, aircraft, bicycle, etc.

steering wheel A wheel turned by the driver or pilot of a vehicle, ship, etc., to change its direction.

steers·man (stirz'mən) n. pl. ·men (-mən) One who steers a boat; a helmsman.

steg·o·my·ia (steg'ə·mī'ə) n. Aedes, a type of mosquito: a former name. [< NL < Gk. stegos roof + myia fly]

stein (stīn) n. A beer mug, esp. of earthenware. [< G]

stein·bok (stīn'bok) n. A steenbok.

stel·lar (stel'ər) adj. **1.** Of or pertaining to the stars; astral. **2.** Of or pertaining to a prominent actor or actress or to other persons in the arts. [< LL < L stella star]

stel·late (stel'it, -āt) adj. Star-shaped or starlike. Also **stel·lat·ed** (stel'ā·tid). [< L stella star] — **stel'late·ly** adv.

stelli- combining form Star. [< L stella star]

St. El·mo's fire (sānt el'mōz) A luminous charge of atmospheric electricity sometimes appearing on the masts of ships, on church steeples, etc. Also **St. Elmo's light.**

stem[1] (stem) n. **1.** The main body or stalk of a tree, shrub, or other plant, rising above the ground. **2.** The relatively slender growth supporting the fruit, flower, or leaf of a plant. **3.** The long, slender, usu. cylindrical portion of an instrument, drinking vessels, etc. **4.** In a watch, the small, projecting, knobbed rod used for winding the mainspring. **5.** Printing The upright stroke of a type face or letter. **6.** Music The line attached to the head of a written musical note. **7.** Ling. A root plus a thematic vowel, as the Latin stem luci- ("light") in lucifer ("light-bearer"), composed of the root luc- plus the thematic vowel -i-. — v. stemmed, stem·ming v.t. **1.** To remove the stems of or from. **2.** To supply with stems. — v.i. **3.** To grow out of; develop or arise: usually with from. [OE stemn, stefn stem of a tree, prow of a ship] — **stem'mer** n. — **stem'less** adj.

stem[2] (stem) n. Naut. **1.** A nearly upright timber or metal piece uniting the two sides of a vessel at the bow. **2.** The bow or prow of a vessel. — **from stem to stern** From end to end; thoroughly. — v. stemmed, stem·ming v.t. **1.** To resist or make progress against, as a current: said of a vessel. **2.** To stand firm or make progress against (any opposing force): to stem the tide. [< STEM[1]]

stem[3] (stem) v.t. stemmed, stem·ming **1.** To stop, hold back, or dam up, as a current; stanch. **2.** To make tight, as a joint; to plug. [< ON stemma to stop]

stem·ware (stem'wâr') n. Drinking vessels with stems, as goblets, taken collectively.

stem-wind·er (stem'wīn'dər) n. A watch wound by turning the crown of the stem. — **stem'-wind'ing** adj.

stench (stench) n. A foul odor; stink. [OE stenc]

sten·cil (sten'səl) n. **1.** A sheet of paper, etc., in which a pattern is cut by means of spaces or dots, through which applied paint or ink penetrates to a surface beneath. **2.** A decoration or the like produced by stenciling. — v.t. sten·ciled or ·cilled, sten·cil·ing or ·cil·ling To mark with a stencil. [Prob. ME stansel to decorate with many colors < OF, ult. < L scintilla spark] — **sten'cil·er** or **sten'cil·ler** n.

steno- combining form Tight; narrow; contracted. Also, before vowels, **sten-**. [< Gk. stenos narrow]

ste·nog·ra·pher (stə·nog'rə·fər) n. One who writes stenography or is skilled in shorthand.

ste·nog·ra·phy (stə·nog'rə·fē) n. The art of writing by the use of contractions or arbitrary symbols; shorthand. — **sten·o·graph·ic** (sten'ə·graf'ik) or **·i·cal** adj. — **sten'o·graph'i·cal·ly** adv.

sten·o·type (sten'ə·tīp) n. **1.** A letter or combination of

letters representing a sound, word, or phrase, esp. in shorthand. **2.** A Stenotype.

sten·o·type (sten'ə·tīp) n. A keyboard-operated machine used in stenotypy: a trade name. Also stenotype.

sten·o·typ·y (sten'ə·tī'pē) n. A system of shorthand employing ordinary letters alone or in various combinations to represent specific sounds, words, or phrases.

sten·tor (sten'tôr) n. One who possesses an uncommonly strong, loud voice. [< Stentor]

Sten·tor (sten'tôr) In the Iliad, a herald with a loud voice.

sten·to·ri·an (sten·tôr'ē·ən, -tō'rē-) adj. Extremely loud.

step (step) n. **1.** An act of progressive motion that requires one of the supporting limbs of the body to be thrust in the direction of the movement, and to reassume its function of support; a pace. **2.** The distance passed over in making such a motion. **3.** Any short distance; a space easily traversed. **4.** That which the foot rests upon in ascending or descending, as a stair or ladder rung. **5.** A single action or proceeding regarded as leading to something: a step toward emancipation. **6.** An advance or promotion that forms one of a series; grade. **7.** The manner of stepping; gait. **8.** The sound of a footfall. **9.** A footprint; track. **10.** pl. Progression by walking; walk. **11.** A patterned combination of foot movements in dancing: the tango step. **12.** Music An interval corresponding to one degree of a scale or staff; a major or minor second. **13.** Something resembling a step, as a socket, supporting framework, etc.: the step of a mast. — **in step 1.** Walking, dancing, marching, etc., in accord with the proper rhythm or cadence, or in conformity with others. **2.** Informal In agreement or conformity. — **out of step** Not in step. — **to take steps** To adopt measures, as to attain an end. — v. stepped, step·ping v.i. **1.** To move forward or backward by taking a step or steps. **2.** To walk a short distance: to step across the street. **3.** To move with measured, dignified, or graceful steps. **4.** To move or act quickly or briskly. **5.** To pass into a situation, circumstance, etc., as if in a single step: He stepped into a fortune. — v.t. **6.** To take (a pace, stride, etc.). **7.** To perform the steps of: to step a quadrille. **8.** To place or move (the foot) in taking a step. **9.** To measure by taking steps: often with off. **10.** To cut or arrange in steps. **11.** Naut. To place the lower end of (a mast) in its step. — **to step down 1.** To decrease gradually, or by steps or degrees. **2.** To resign from an office or position. — **to step in** To begin to take part; intervene. — **to step on (or upon) 1.** To put the foot down on. **2.** To put the foot on so as to activate, as a brake or treadle. **3.** Informal To reprove or subdue. — **to step on it** Informal To hurry; hasten. — **to step out 1.** To go outside, esp. for a short while. **2.** Informal To go out for fun or entertainment. **3.** To quit; resign. **4.** To walk vigorously and with long strides. — **to step up** To increase; accelerate. [OE stæpe]

step- combining form Related through the previous marriage of a parent or spouse, but not by blood. [OE < stem of āstȳpan, āstēpan to bereave, orphan]

step·broth·er (step'bruth'ər) n. The son of one's stepparent by a former marriage.

step·child (step'chīld') n. The child of one's husband or wife by a former marriage.

step·daugh·ter (step'dô'tər) n. A female stepchild.

step-down (step'doun') adj. **1.** Decreasing by stages. **2.** Electr. Converting a high voltage into a low voltage, as a transformer. **3.** Mech. Designating a gear that transfers motion at a reduced rate. Opposed to step-up.

step·fa·ther (step'fä'thər) n. The husband of one's mother, other than one's own father.

step-in (step'in') n. **1.** A woman's brief underpants: also **step'-ins.** **2.** A pumplike shoe.

step·lad·der (step'lad'ər) n. A set of portable steps with, usu., a hinged frame at the back, that may be extended to support the steps in an upright position.

step·moth·er (step'muth'ər) n. The wife of one's father, other than one's own mother.

step·par·ent (step'pâr'ənt) n. A stepfather or stepmother.

steppe (step) n. A vast plain devoid of forest; esp., one of the extensive plains in Russia and Siberia. [< Russian step']

step·per (step'ər) n. **1.** One who or that which steps: The horse is a high stepper. **2.** Slang A dancer.

step·ping-stone (step'ing·stōn') n. **1.** A stone affording a footrest, as for crossing a stream. **2.** A preliminary step or stage in the fulfillment of a goal: steppingstones to success.

step·sis·ter (step'sis'tər) n. The daughter of one's stepparent by a former marriage.

step·son (step'sun') n. A male stepchild.

step-up (step'up') adj. **1.** Increasing by stages. **2.** Electr. Converting a low voltage into a high voltage, as a transformer. **3.** Designating a gear that transfers motion at an increased rate. Opposed to step-down.

-ster suffix of nouns **1.** One who makes or is occupied with: often pejorative: songster, prankster. **2.** One who belongs or is related to: gangster. **3.** One who is: youngster. [OE -estre, fem. suffix expressing the agent]

stere (stir) *n.* In the metric system, a measure of capacity equal to one cubic meter. See table inside back cover. [< F < Gk. *stereos* solid]

ster·e·o (ster'ē·ō, stir'-) *n.* A stereophonic system. — *adj.* Stereophonic.

stereo- *combining form* Solid; firm; hard; three-dimensional. Also, before vowels, **stere-**. [< Gk. *stereos* hard]

ster·e·o·chem·is·try (ster'ē·ō·kem'is·trē, stir'-) *n.* The branch of chemistry that treats of the spatial arrangement of atoms and molecules.

ster·e·o·phon·ic (ster'ē·ə·fon'ik, stir'-) *adj.* **1.** Pertaining to, designed for, or characterized by the perception of sound by both ears; binaural. **2.** *Electronics* Designating a system of sound reproduction in which two or more receivers or loudspeakers are so placed as to give the effect of hearing the sound from more than one direction. Also *stereo*. — **ster'e·o·phon'i·cal·ly** *adv.* — **ster·e·o·phon·y** (ster'ē·of'ə·nē, stir'-, ster'ē·ə·fō'nē, stir'-) *n.*

ster·e·op·ti·con (ster'ē·op'ti·kon, stir'-) *n.* A double magic lantern arranged to combine two images of the same object or scene, or used to bring one image after another on the screen. [< STEREO- + Gk. *optikos* of sight]

ster·e·o·scope (ster'ē·ə·skōp, stir'-) *n.* An instrument for blending into one image two pictures of an object from slightly different points of view, so as to produce the impression of relief and solidity. — **ster'e·o·scop'ic** (-skop'ik) or **-i·cal** *adj.* — **ster'e·o·scop'i·cal·ly** *adv.*

ster·e·os·co·py (ster'ē·os'kə·pē, stir'-) *n.* **1.** The art of making or using stereoscopes and stereoscopic slides. **2.** The viewing of objects as in three dimensions. — **ster'e·os'co·pist** *n.*

ster·e·o·type (ster'ē·ə·tīp', stir'-) *n.* **1.** A plate cast in type metal from a matrix and reproducing on its surface the composed type or other material impressed upon the matrix. **2.** Anything made or processed in this way. **3.** Stereotypy. **4.** A conventional or hackneyed expression, custom, mental image, etc. **5.** A person possessing characteristics that typify a particular group. — *v.t.* **·typed, ·typ·ing 1.** To make a stereotype of. **2.** To fix firmly or unalterably. — **ster'e·o·typ'er,** **ster'e·o·typ'ist** *n.*

ster·e·o·typed (ster'ē·ə·tīpt', stir'-) *adj.* **1.** Formalized; hackneyed; trite. **2.** Produced from a stereotype.

ster·e·o·typ·y (ster'ē·ə·tī'pē, stir'-) *n.* The art or act of making stereotypes: also called *stereotype*.

ster·ile (ster'əl, *esp. Brit.* -īl) *adj.* **1.** Having no reproductive power; barren. **2.** *Bot.* Incapable of germinating. **3.** Lacking productiveness: *sterile* soil. **4.** Containing no bacteria or other microorganisms. **5.** Lacking in vigor or imagination: *sterile* verse. [< L *sterilis* barren] — **ster'ile·ly** *adv.* — **ster'ile·ness, ste·ril·i·ty** (stə·ril'ə·tē) *n.*

ster·il·ize (ster'əl·īz) *v.t.* **·ized, ·iz·ing 1.** To free from infective or pathogenic microorganisms. **2.** To deprive of productive or reproductive power. **3.** To make barren. Also *Brit.* **ster'il·ise.** — **ster'il·i·za'tion** (-ə·zā'shən, -ī·zā'-) *n.* — **ster'il·iz'er** *n.*

ster·ling (stûr'ling) *n.* **1.** The official standard of fineness for British coins: for silver, 0.500; for gold, 0.91666. **2.** Sterling silver, 0.925 fine, as used in manufacturing articles; also, articles made of it. **3.** A former silver penny of England and Scotland. — *adj.* **1.** Made of or payable in sterling. **2.** Made of sterling silver. **3.** Genuine. **4.** Valuable; esteemed: *sterling* qualities. [Prob. OE *steorra* star + -LING, because a star was stamped on some of the coins]

stern[1] (stûrn) *adj.* **1.** Marked by severity or harshness; unyielding. **2.** Strict; severe. **3.** Inspiring fear; awesome. **4.** Resolute; stout: a *stern* resolve. [OE *styrne*] — **stern'ly** *adv.* — **stern'ness** *n.*

stern[2] (stûrn) *n.* **1.** *Naut.* The aft part of a ship, boat, etc. **2.** The hindmost part of any object. — *adj.* Situated at or belonging to the stern. [< ON *stýra* to steer]

stern·most (stûrn'mōst', -məst) *adj.* Farthest to the rear or stern.

sterno- *combining form Anat.* The sternum. Also, before vowels, **stern-**. [< L *sternum* or Gk. *stérnon* breast]

stern·post (stûrn'pōst') *n. Naut.* The main vertical post of the stern frame of a vessel, to which the rudder is attached.

ster·num (stûr'nəm) *n.* *pl.* **·na** (-nə) or **·nums** *Anat.* The breastbone that forms the ventral support of the ribs in vertebrates. [< L < Gk. *stérnon* breast] — **ster'nal** *adj.*

stern·ward (stûrn'wərd) *adj. & adv.* Toward the stern.

stern·way (stûrn'wā') *n. Naut.* Backward movement of a vessel.

stern-wheel·er (stûrn'hwē'lər) *n.* A steamboat propelled by one large paddle wheel at the stern.

ster·oid (ster'oid) *n. Biochem.* Any of a large group of fat-soluble organic compounds, including the sterols, the bile acids, and the sex hormones.

ster·ol (ster'ōl, -ol) *n. Biochem.* Any of a class of complex, chiefly unsaturated solid alcohols, widely distributed in plant and animal tissue, as cholesterol. [Contr. of CHOLESTEROL]

ster·tor·ous (stûr'tər·əs) *adj.* Characterized by snoring or accompanied by a snoring sound. [< NL < L *stertere* to snore] — **ster'tor·ous·ly** *adv.* — **ster'tor·ous·ness** *n.*

stet (stet) Let it stand: a direction used in proofreading to indicate that a word, letter, etc., marked for omission or correction is to remain. — *v.t.* **stet·ted, stet·ting** To cancel a former correction or omission of by marking with the word *stet*. Compare DELE. [< L < *stare* to stand, stay]

stetho- *combining form* The breast or chest; pectoral. Also, before vowels, **steth-**. [< Gk. *stéthos* breast]

steth·o·scope (steth'ə·skōp) *n. Med.* An apparatus for auscultation, adapted for conveying the sounds of the body to the examiner's ear or ears. — **steth'o·scop'ic** (-skop'ik), **steth'o·scop'i·cal** *adj.* — **steth'o·scop'i·cal·ly** *adv.* — **ste·thos·co·py** (ste·thos'kə·pē) *n.*

ste·ve·dore (stē'və·dôr, -dōr) *n.* One whose business is stowing or unloading the holds of vessels. — *v.t. & v.i.* **·dored, ·dor·ing** To load or unload (a vessel). [< Sp. < L *stipare* to compress, stuff]

stew (stoo, styoo) *v.t. & v.i.* **1.** To boil slowly and gently; seethe; keep or be at the simmering point. **2.** *Informal* To worry. — *n.* **1.** Stewed food, esp. a preparation of meat or fish and vegetables cooked together by stewing. **2.** *Informal* Mental agitation; worry. [< OF, prob. ult. < L *ex-* out + Gk. *typhos* steam, vapor]

stew·ard (stoo'ərd, styoo'-) *n.* **1.** One who is entrusted with the management of property, finances, or other affairs not his own. **2.** One who has charge of buying provisions, managing servants, etc., in a private residence or in a club, hotel, etc. **3.** One in charge of provisions and usu. of the tables on a ship. **4.** On an airplane, ship, or bus, one who waits on the passengers. **5.** One who manages any affair: *steward* of the races. [OE < *stī* hall, sty + *weard* ward, keeper] — **stew'ard·ess** *n.fem.* — **stew'ard·ship** *n.*

stewed (stood, styood) *adj.* **1.** Cooked by stewing. **2.** *Slang* Drunk.

stew·pan (stoo'pan, styoo'-) *n.* A cooking vessel used for stewing.

stib·i·um (stib'ē·əm) *n.* Antimony. [< L < Gk. *stibi*] — **stib'i·al** *adj.*

-stichous *combining form* Having (a specified number of) rows. [< Gk. *stichos* row, line]

stick (stik) *n.* **1.** A slender piece of wood, as a branch cut from a tree or bush, a baton or wand, etc. **2.** *Brit.* A cane. **3.** Anything resembling a stick in form: a *stick* of candy or dynamite. **4.** A piece of wood of any size, cut for fuel, lumber, or timber. **5.** *Aeron.* The control lever of an airplane, that operates the elevators and ailerons. **6.** A poke, stab, or thrust with a pointed instrument. **7.** The state of being stuck together; adhesion. **8.** In sports, a baseball bat, hockey stick, etc. **9.** *Informal* A stiff, inert, or dull person. **10.** A stalk, as of asparagus. — **the sticks** *Informal* An obscure rural district; the backwoods or country. — *v.* **stuck** or (*for def. 15*) **sticked, stick·ing** *v.t.* **1.** To pierce, stab, or penetrate with a pointed object. **2.** To kill or wound by piercing; stab. **3.** To thrust or force, as a sword or pin, into or through something else. **4.** To force the end of (a nail, etc.) into something so as to be fixed in place. **5.** To fasten in place with or as with pins, nails, etc.: to *stick* a ribbon on a dress. **6.** To cover with objects piercing the surface. **7.** To impale; transfix. **8.** To put or thrust: He *stuck* his hand into his pocket. **9.** To fasten to a surface by or as by an adhesive substance. **10.** To bring to a standstill; obstruct; halt: usu. in the passive: We were *stuck* in Rome. **11.** *Informal* To smear with something sticky. **12.** *Informal* To baffle; puzzle. **13.** *Slang* To impose upon; cheat. **14.** *Slang* To force great expense, an unpleasant task, etc., upon. **15.** To provide with sticks or brush on which to grow, as a vine. — *v.i.* **16.** To be or become fixed in place by being thrust in: to *stick* in a cushion. **17.** To become or remain attached or close to something by or as by adhesion; adhere; cling. **18.** To come to a standstill; become blocked or obstructed. **19.** To be baffled or disconcerted. **20.** To hesitate; scruple: with *at* or *to*. **21.** To persist; persevere: with *at* or *to*. **22.** To remain firm or resolute; be faithful. **23.** To be extended; protrude: with *from, out, through, up*, etc. — **to stick around** *Slang* To remain near or near at hand. — **to stick by** To remain faithful to; be loyal to. — **to stick it out** To persevere to the end. — **to stick up** *Slang* To detain and rob. — **to stick up for** *Informal* To take the part of; defend. [OE *sticca*]

stick·er (stik'ər) *n.* **1.** A gummed label, sign, etc. **2.** One who or that which fastens with or as with paste. **3.** One who holds tenaciously to anything. **4.** *Informal* A puzzle. **5.** A prickly stem, thorn, or bur.

stick·ing plaster (stik′ing) Adhesive tape.
stick·le (stik′əl) *v.i.* **·led, ·ling 1.** To contend or argue about trifling matters. **2.** To insist or hesitate for petty reasons. [ME *stightlen*, freq. of OE *stihtan* to arrange]
stick·le·back (stik′əl·bak′) *n.* A small fresh- or salt-water fish, having sharp dorsal spines.
stick·ler (stik′lər) *n.* One who contends over or insists upon something: usu. with *for*: a *stickler* for details.
stick·pin (stik′pin′) *n. U.S.* An ornamental pin for a necktie.
stick-to-it·ive (stik·tōō′it·iv) *adj. Informal* Persevering. **— stick-to′-it·ive·ly** *adv.* **— stick-to′-it·ive·ness** *n.*
stick·up (stik′up′) *n. Slang* A robbery or holdup.
stick·y (stik′ē) *adj.* **stick·i·er, stick·i·est 1.** Adhering to a surface; adhesive. **2.** Covered with something adhesive. **3.** Warm and humid. **— stick′i·ly** *adv.* **— stick′i·ness** *n.*
stiff (stif) *adj.* **1.** Resisting the action of a bending force; rigid. **2.** Not easily moved: *stiff* brakes; also, moving or functioning painfully or without suppleness: a *stiff* neck. **3.** Not natural, graceful, or easy; constrained and awkward; formal. **4.** Not liquid or fluid, thick; viscous. **5.** Taut; tightly drawn. **6.** Having a strong, steady movement: a *stiff* breeze. **7.** Firm in resistance; stubborn. **8.** Harsh; severe: a *stiff* penalty. **9.** High; dear: a *stiff* price. **10.** Strong or potent, as in alcoholic content: a *stiff* drink. **11.** Difficult; arduous: a *stiff* climb. **—** *n. Slang* **1.** A corpse. **2.** An awkward or unresponsive person; esp., a bore. **3.** A man; fellow: working *stiff*; also, a roughneck. [OE *stīf*] **— stiff′ly** *adv.* **— stiff′ness** *n.*
stiff·en (stif′ən) *v.t. & v.i.* To make or become stiff or stiffer. **— stiff′en·er** *n.*
stiff-necked (stif′nekt′) *adj.* Not yielding; stubborn.
sti·fle (stī′fəl) *v.* **·fled, ·fling** *v.t.* **1.** To keep back; suppress or repress; check: to *stifle* sobs. **2.** To suffocate; choke. **—** *v.i.* **3.** To die of suffocation. **4.** To experience difficulty in breathing, as in a stuffy room. [ME < OF *estouffer* to smother] **— sti′fler** *n.* **— sti′fling** *adj.* **— sti′fling·ly** *adv.*
stig·ma (stig′mə) *n. pl.* **stig·ma·ta** (stig′mə·tə, stig·mä′tə) or *(for defs. 1–3, usu.)* **stig·mas 1.** A mark of infamy, or token of disgrace. **2.** A mark indicating a defect or something not normal. **3.** *Bot.* The part of a pistil that receives the pollen. For illus. see FLOWER. **4.** *Biol.* **a** A mark or spot. **b** An aperture or opening, as a pore. **5.** *pl.* The wounds that Christ received during the Passion and Crucifixion. **6.** Formerly, a brand made on slaves and criminals. [< L < Gk. *stizein* to prick, brand] **— stig·mat′ic** (-mat′ik), **stig·mat′i·cal** *adj.*
stig·ma·tize (stig′mə·tīz) *v.t.* **·tized, ·tiz·ing 1.** To characterize or brand as ignominious. **2.** To mark with a stigma. [< Med.L < Gk. *stigma* pointed end, mark] **— stig′ma·ti·za′tion** *n.* **— stig′ma·tiz′er** *n.*
stile (stīl) *n.* **1.** A step, or series of steps, on each side of a fence or wall to aid in surmounting it. **2.** A turnstile. [OE *stīgan* to climb]
sti·let·to (sti·let′ō) *n. pl.* **·tos** or **·toes** A small dagger with a slender blade. **—** *v.t.* **·toed, ·to·ing** To pierce with a stiletto; stab. [< Ital. < L *stilus* writing instrument]
still[1] (stil) *adj.* **1.** Making no sound; silent. **2.** Peaceful; tranquil. **3.** Without movement; motionless. **4.** Low in sound; quiet; hushed. **5.** Subdued; soft. **6.** Dead; inanimate. **7.** Having no effervescence: said of wines. **8.** *Photog.* Of or designating a single photograph, as contrasted with a motion picture. **— Syn.** See CALM. **—** *n.* **1.** *Poetic* Stillness; calm. **2.** A still-life picture. **3.** *Photog.* A still photograph. **—** *adv.* **1.** Now as previously; up to this or that time: He is *still* here. **2.** All the same: nevertheless. **3.** Even; yet: *still* more. **4.** *Poetic & Dial.* Always; constantly. **—** *conj.* Nevertheless; and yet. **—** *v.t.* **1.** To cause to be still or calm. **2.** To silence or hush. **3.** To quiet or allay, as fears. **—** *v.i.* **4.** To become still. [OE *stille*] **— still′ness** *n.*
still[2] (stil) *n.* **1.** An apparatus in which a substance is vaporized by heat, and the vapor then liquefied in a condenser, used esp. for distilling alcoholic liquors. **2.** A distillery. **—** *v.t. & v.i.* To distill. [< L < *stilla* drop]
still·born (stil′bôrn′) *adj.* Dead at birth. **— still′birth′** *n.*
still life 1. In painting, the representation of objects, as tables, flowers, fruit, etc. **2.** A picture of such a subject.
Still·son wrench (stil′sən) A wrench closely resembling a monkey wrench, but with serrated jaws, one of which is capable of slight angular movement, so that the grip is increased by pressure on the handle: a trade name.

STILLSON WRENCH

still·y (*adj.* stil′ē; *adv.* stil′lē) *adj.* Still; silent; calm. **—** *adv.* Calmly; quietly; without noise.
stilt (stilt) *n.* **1.** One of a pair of long, slender poles made with a projection to support the foot some distance above the ground in walking. **2.** A tall post or pillar used as a support, as for a dock. **3.** Any of several long-legged, wading birds. **—** *v.t.* To raise on stilts. [ME *stilte*, ? < LG]

stilt·ed (stil′tid) *adj.* **1.** Artificially formal or elevated in manner; pompous. **2.** Raised or built on or as on stilts. **— stilt′ed·ly** *adv.* **— stilt′ed·ness** *n.*
stim·u·lant (stim′yə·lənt) *n.* **1.** Anything that quickens or promotes the activity of some physiological process, as a drug. **2.** An alcoholic beverage. **—** *adj.* Acting as a stimulant; serving to stimulate. [See STIMULATE.]
stim·u·late (stim′yə·lāt) *v.* **·lat·ed, ·lat·ing** *v.t.* **1.** To rouse to activity or to quickened action; spur. **2.** *Physiol.* To excite (an organ or tissue) by applying some form of stimulus. **3.** To affect by alcoholic beverages. **—** *v.i.* **4.** To act as a stimulant. [< L < *stimulus* goad] **— stim′u·lat′er, stim′u·la·tor** *n.* **— stim′u·la′tion** *n.* **— stim′u·la·tive** *adj. & n.*
stim·u·lus (stim′yə·ləs) *n. pl.* **·li** (-lī) **1.** Anything that rouses the mind or spirits; an incentive. **2.** *Physiol.* Any agent or form of excitation that influences the activity of an organism as a whole or in any of its parts. [< L]
sti·my (stī′mē) See STYMIE.
sting (sting) *v.* **stung, stung, sting·ing** *v.t.* **1.** To pierce or prick painfully, as with a sharp, sometimes venomous organ. **2.** To cause to suffer sharp, smarting pain from or as from a sting. **3.** To cause to suffer mentally; pain: His heart was *stung* with remorse. **4.** To stimulate; goad; spur. **5.** *Slang* To get the better of; also, to overcharge. **—** *v.i.* **6.** To have or use a sting, as a bee. **7.** To suffer or cause a sharp, smarting pain. **8.** To suffer or cause mental distress; pain. **—** *n.* **1.** *Zool.* A sharp, pointed organ, as of a bee, able to inflict a wound. **2.** The act of stinging; also, the wound or the pain caused by a sting. **3.** Any sharp, smarting sensation: the *sting* of remorse. **4.** A spur; goad. **5.** *Bot.* One of the sharp-pointed hairs of a nettle, charged with an irritating fluid: also **stinging hair.** [OE *stingan*] **— sting′er** *n.* **— sting′ing·ly** *adv.* **— sting′y** *adj.*
sting ray Any of a family of flat-bodied fishes having broad pectoral fins and a whiplike tail capable of inflicting wounds: also called **sting·a·ree** (sting′ə·rē, sting′ə·rē′) *n.*
stin·gy (stin′jē) *adj.* **·gi·er, ·gi·est 1.** Unwilling to spend or give; miserly. **2.** Scanty; inadequate; meager. [< dial. E *stinge* sting + -Y[1]] **— stin′gi·ly** *adv.* **— stin′gi·ness** *n.* **— Syn. 1.** niggardly, parsimonious, close, closefisted, tight.
stink (stingk) *n.* A strong, foul odor; stench. **— Syn.** See SMELL. **—** *v.* **stank** or **stunk, stunk, stink·ing** *v.i.* **1.** To give forth a foul odor. **2.** To be extremely offensive or hateful. **3.** *Informal* To be of bad quality. **—** *v.t.* **4.** To cause to stink. **— to make (or raise) a stink** *Slang* To protest vehemently. **— to stink out** To drive out by a foul or suffocating odor. [OE *stincan* to smell] **— stink′ing·ly** *adv.*
stink·bug (stingk′bug′) *n.* Any of various large, flattened bugs that emit an unpleasant odor if disturbed.
stink·weed (stingk′wēd′) *n.* Any of various plants having a disagreeable odor, as the jimsonweed.
stint (stint) *v.t.* **1.** To limit, as in amount or share; be stingy with. **—** *v.i.* **2.** To be frugal or sparing. **—** *n.* **1.** A fixed amount, as of work to be performed within a specified time. **2.** A bound; restriction; limit. **3.** A small sandpiper. [ME *stynten* to cause to stop] **— stint′er** *n.*
stipe (stīp) *n.* **1.** *Zool.* A stalk or support. **2.** *Bot.* A stalk-like support or stem, as that supporting a fern's frond, etc. [< F < L *stipes* branch]
sti·pend (stī′pend) *n.* An allowance, salary, or pension; esp., money paid under a scholarship. [< L < *stips* coin, payment in coin + *pendere* to weigh, pay out]
sti·pen·di·ar·y (stī·pen′dē·er′ē) *adj.* **1.** Receiving or performing services for a stipend. **2.** Of or like a stipend. **3.** Paid for by a stipend, as services. **—** *n. pl.* **·ar·ies** One who receives a stipend. See STIPEND.
stip·ple (stip′əl) *v.t.* **·pled, ·pling** To draw, paint, or engrave with dots or short touches instead of lines. **—** *n.* **1.** A method of painting, etc., by stippling. **2.** A painting produced by stippling; also the effect of stippling. [< Du. < *stip* dot] **— stip′pler** *n.*
stip·u·late (stip′yə·lāt) *v.* **·lat·ed, ·lat·ing** *v.t.* **1.** To specify as the terms or condition for an agreement, contract, etc. **2.** To promise; guarantee. **—** *v.i.* **3.** To demand something as a requirement: with *for*. **4.** To make an agreement. [< L < *stipulari* to bargain] **— stip′u·la′tor** *n.*
stip·u·la·tion (stip′yə·lā′shən) *n.* **1.** The act of stipulating, or the state of being stipulated. **2.** That which is stipulated; a condition. **— stip′u·la·to′ry** (-lə·tôr′ē, -tō′rē) *adj.*
stip·ule (stip′yool) *n. Bot.* One of a pair of leaflike appendages at the base of the petiole of certain leaves. [< L *stipula* stalk] **— stip·u·late** (stip′yə·lit, -lāt) *adj.*
stir[1] (stûr) *v.* **stirred, stir·ring** *v.t.* **1.** To agitate so as to alter the relative position of the particles or components of, as soup with a spoon. **2.** To cause to move, esp., slightly or irregularly; disturb. **3.** To move vigorously; bestir. **4.** To rouse, as from sleep, indifference, or inactivity; stimulate. **5.** To incite; provoke: often with *up*. **6.** To affect strongly; move with emotion. **—** *v.i.* **7.** To move, esp., slightly. **8.** To be active; move about. **9.** To happen. **10.** To undergo

stirring: This molasses *stirs* easily. — *n.* **1.** The act of stirring, or state of being stirred; activity. **2.** General interest or commotion. **3.** Excitement or agitation. **4.** A poke; nudge. [OE *styrian*] — **stir′rer** *n.*

stir² (stûr) *n. Slang* A jail; prison. [Origin uncertain]

stir·ring (stûr′ing) *adj.* **1.** Stimulating; inspiring. **2.** Full of activity or stir; lively. — **stir′ring·ly** *adv.*

stir·rup (stûr′əp, stir′-) *n.* **1.** An inverted U-shaped support hung from either side of a saddle to hold the rider's foot in and after mounting. **2.** Any similarly shaped supports, as for a beam. [OE *stigrāp* mounting rope]

stirrup bone *Anat.* The stapes.

stitch (stich) *n.* **1.** A single passage of a threaded needle through fabric and back again, as in sewing or embroidery, or, in surgery, through skin or flesh. **2.** A single turn of thread or yarn around a needle, as in knitting or crocheting; also, the link or loop resulting from such a turn. **3.** Any particular arrangement of a thread used in sewing, crocheting, etc.: a chain *stitch.* **4.** A sharp sudden pain, esp. in the back or side. **5.** *Informal* The smallest bit or fragment: not a *stitch* of work. — *v.t.* **1.** To join together or ornament with stitches. — *v.i.* **2.** To make stitches; sew. [OE *stice* a prick, stab] — **stitch′er** *n.*

sti·ver (stī′vər) *n.* **1.** A small Dutch coin, ¹⁄₂₀ of a guilder. **2.** Anything of little value. [< Du. *stuiver*]

St. Johns·wort (sānt jonz′wûrt′) A hardy perennial with deep yellow flowers. Also **St.-John's-wort.**

stoat (stōt) *n.* The ermine, esp. in its brown summer coat. [ME *stote*; origin uncertain]

stock (stok) *n.* **1.** A quantity of something acquired or kept for future use. **2.** The total merchandise or goods that a commercial establishment has on hand. **3.** Livestock. **4.** In finance: **a** The capital or fund raised by a corporation through the sale of shares. **b** The proportional part of this capital credited to an individual stockholder and represented by the number of shares he owns. **c** A certificate showing ownership of shares. **5.** The trunk or main stem of a tree or other plant. **6.** A line of familial descent. **7.** The original progenitor of a family line. **8.** An ethnic group; race. **9.** A family of languages. **10.** A related group or family of plants or animals; also, a type of animal or plant from which others are derived. **11.** *Bot.* **a** A rhizome. **b** In horticulture, a stem upon which a graft is made; also, a plant, tree, etc. that provides cuttings and slips. **12.** The broth from boiled meat or fish used in preparing soups, etc. **13.** Raw material: paper *stock.* **14.** *pl.* A timber frame with holes for confining the ankles, formerly used in punishing petty offenders. **15.** *pl.* The timber frame on which a vessel rests during construction. **16.** In firearms: **a** The rear wooden portion of a rifle etc., to which the barrel and mechanisms are secured. **b** The arm on rapidfire guns connecting the shoulder piece to the slide. **c** The handle of a pistol or similar firearm. **17.** The handle of certain instruments, as of a whip or fishing rod. **18.** A theatrical stock company; also, its repertoire. **19.** A broad, stiffened band, formerly worn as a cravat. **20.** An ornamental garden plant, as the gillyflower. — **in stock** On hand and available for sale or use. — **to take stock** To take an inventory. **2.** To estimate or appraise. — *v.t.* **1.** To furnish with livestock or with merchandise. **2.** To keep for sale. **3.** To put aside for future use. **4.** To provide with a handle or stock. — *v.i.* **5.** To lay in supplies or stock: often with *up.* — *adj.* **1.** Kept continually ready or constantly brought forth, like old goods: a *stock* joke. **2.** Kept on hand: a *stock* size. **3.** Banal; commonplace: a *stock* phrase. **4.** Used for breeding purposes. **5.** Employed in handling or caring for the stock. — *adv.* Motionlessly; like a stump: used in combination: *stock-still.* [OE *stocc*]

stock·ade (sto·kād′) *n.* **1.** A line of stout posts, stakes, etc., set upright in the earth to form a fence or barrier; also, the area thus enclosed, used as a prison, etc. **2.** Any similar area. — *v.t.* **·ad·ed, ·ad·ing** To surround or fortify with a stockade. [< OF < Sp. < *estaque* stake < Gmc.]

stock·breed·er (stok′brē′dər) *n.* One who breeds and raises livestock. — **stock′breed′ing** *n.*

stock·bro·ker (stok′brō′kər) *n.* One who buys and sells stocks or securities for others. — **stock′bro′ker·age** (-ij) **stock′bro′king** *n.*

stock car An automobile, often a sedan, modified for racing.

stock company **1.** An incorporated company that issues stock. **2.** A more or less permanent dramatic company under one management, that presents a series of plays.

stock exchange **1.** A place where stocks and bonds are bought and sold. **2.** An association of stockbrokers who transact business in stocks, bonds, etc.

stock farm A farm that specializes in breeding livestock.

stock·fish (stok′fish′) *n.* Cod, haddock, or the like, cured by splitting and drying in the air, without salt.

stock·hold·er (stok′hōl′dər) *n.* One who holds certificates of ownership in a company or corporation. — **stock′hold′ing** *adj. & n.*

stock·i·net (stok′i·net′) *n.* An elastic knitted fabric, machine-made and used for undergarments, stockings, etc. Also **stock′i·nette′.** [Alter. of *stockinet* < STOCKING + -ET]

stock·ing (stok′ing) *n.* **1.** A close-fitting woven or knitted covering for the foot and leg. **2.** Something resembling such a covering. — **in one's stocking feet** Wearing one's stockings or socks, but no shoes. [< STOCK, in obs. sense of "a stocking" + -ING³] — **stock′inged** (-ingd) *adj.*

stock·man (stok′mən) *n. pl.* **·men** (-mən) **1.** One who raises, owns, or has charge of livestock; a cattleman. **2.** One who works in a stockroom, warehouse, etc.

stock market **1.** A stock exchange. **2.** The business transacted in such a place: The *stock market* was active. **3.** The rise and fall of prices of stocks and bonds.

stock·pile (stok′pīl) *n.* A storage pile of materials or supplies. Also **stock pile.** — *v.t. & v.i.* **·piled, ·pil·ing** To accumulate a supply or stockpile (of).

stock raising Breeding and raising of livestock.

stock·room (stok′rōōm′) *n.* A room where reserve stocks of goods are stored. Also **stock room.**

stock·still (stok′stil′) *adj.* Still as a post; motionless.

stock·y (stok′ē) *adj.* **stock·i·er, stock·i·est** Solidly built, thickset, and usu. short. — **stock′i·ly** *adv.* — **stock′i·ness** *n.*

stock·yard (stok′yärd′) *n.* A large yard where cattle, sheep, pigs, etc., are kept ready for shipping or slaughter.

stodg·y (stoj′ē) *adj.* **stodg·i·er, stodg·i·est** **1.** Dull, stupid, and commonplace. **2.** Crammed full; distended; bulky. **3.** Indigestible and heavy: said of food. **4.** Thickset; stocky. — **stodg′i·ly** *adv.* — **stodg′i·ness** *n.*

sto·gy (stō′gē) *n. pl.* **·gies 1.** A long, slender, inexpensive cigar. **2.** A stout, heavy boot or shoe. Also **sto′gey, sto′gie.** [Earlier *stoga* < (CONE)STOGA (WAGON), because their drivers wore heavy boots and smoked coarse cigars]

sto·ic (stō′ik) *n.* A person apparently unaffected by pleasure or pain. — *adj.* Indifferent to pleasure or pain; impassive. Also **sto′i·cal.** — **sto′i·cal·ly** *adv.* — **sto′i·cal·ness** *n.*

Sto·ic (stō′ik) *n.* A member of a school of Greek philosophy founded by Zeno about 308 B.C., holding that wisdom lies in being superior to passion, joy, grief, etc. and in unperturbed submission to the divine will. — *adj.* Of the Stoics or Stoicism. [< L < Gk. < *Stoa (Poikilē)* (Painted) Porch, the colonnade at Athens where Zeno taught]

sto·i·cism (stō′ə·siz′əm) *n.* Indifference to pleasure or pain; stoicalness.

Sto·i·cism (stō′ə·siz′əm) *n.* The doctrines of the Stoics.

stoke (stōk) *v.t. & v.i.* **stoked, stok·ing** To supply (a furnace) with fuel; stir up or tend (a fire or furnace). [Back formation < STOKER]

stoke·hold (stōk′hōld′) *n. Naut.* The furnace room of a steamship.

stoke·hole (stōk′hōl′) *n.* **1.** The space about the mouth of a furnace or the mouth itself. **2.** A stokehold.

stok·er (stō′kər) *n.* **1.** One who supplies fuel to a furnace; a fireman on a locomotive, etc. **2.** A device for feeding coal to a furnace. [< Du. < *stoken* to stir a fire]

stole¹ (stōl) *n.* **1.** *Eccl.* A long, narrow band of decorated cloth worn about the shoulders by officiating clergymen. **2.** A long scarf worn about the shoulders by women. [OE < L < Gk. *stolē* garment] — **stoled** (stōld) *adj.*

stole² (stōl) Past tense of STEAL.

sto·len (stō′lən) Past participle of STEAL.

stol·id (stol′id) *adj.* Having or showing little feeling or perception; impassive; dull. [< L *stolidus* dull] — **sto·lid·i·ty** (stə·lid′ə·tē), **stol′id·ness** — **stol′id·ly** *adv.*

sto·ma (stō′mə) *n. pl.* **sto·ma·ta** (stō′mə·tə, stom′ə·tə) **1.** *Bot.* A minute orifice or pore in the epidermis of plants, esp. of leaves and stems. **2.** *Biol.* **a** An aperture in the walls of blood vessels or in serous membranes. **b** A mouthlike opening in nematodes. [< NL < Gk. *stoma* mouth]

-stoma See -STOME.

stom·ach (stum′ək) *n.* **1.** The pouchlike, highly vascular enlargement of the alimentary canal, situated in man and vertebrates between the esophagus and the small intestine, and serving as one of the principal organs of digestion. ◆ Collateral adjective: *gastric.* **2.** Any digestive cavity. **3.** Loosely, the abdomen or belly. **4.** Desire for food; appetite. **5.** Any desire or inclination. — *v.t.* **1.** To put up with; endure. **2.** To take into and retain in the stomach; digest. [< OF < L < Gk. < *stoma* mouth]

stom·ach·er (stum′ək·ər) *n.* A former ornamental article of dress, worn over the breast and stomach.

sto·mach·ic (stō·mak′ik) *adj.* **1.** Pertaining to the stomach. **2.** Beneficial to or stimulating the activity of the stomach. Also **stom·ach·al** (stum′ək·əl), **sto·mach′i·cal.** — *n.* Any medicine strengthening or stimulating the stomach.

sto·ma·ta (stō′mə·tə, stom′ə·tə) Plural of STOMA.

stomato- *combining form* Of, like, or pertaining to the mouth. Also, before vowels, **stomat-**. [< Gk. *stoma, stomatos* mouth]

sto·ma·tous (stō′mə·təs, stom′ə-) *adj.* Having a stoma or stomata.

-stome *combining form* Mouth; mouthlike opening: *peristome*. Also spelled **-stoma**. [< Gk. *stoma* mouth]

-stomous *combining form* Having a (specified kind of) mouth: *microstomous*. Also **-stomatous**. [< Gk. *stoma, stomatos* mouth]

stomp (stomp) *v.t. & v.i.* 1. To tread heavily or violently (upon); press down. 2. *Dial.* To stamp. — *n.* A dance involving a heavy and lively step. [Var. of STAMP]

-stomy *combining form Surg.* An operation to form an artificial opening for or into (a specified organ or part): *colostomy*. [< Gk. *stoma* mouth]

stone (stōn) *n.* 1. The hard, nonmetallic mineral or earthy matter of which rock is composed. 2. A small piece of rock, as a pebble. 3. Rock, or a piece of rock that has been hewn or shaped. 4. A precious stone; gem. 5. Anything resembling a stone in shape or hardness: a *hailstone*. 6. A gravestone. 7. A grindstone or millstone. 8. *Pathol.* A stony concretion in the bladder, or a disease characterized by such concretions. 9. *Bot.* The hard covering of the kernel in a fruit. 10. (*pl.* **stone**) In England, 14 pounds avoirdupois. — *adj.* 1. Made of stone: a *stone* ax. 2. Made of coarse hard earthenware: a *stone* bottle. — *v.t.* **stoned, ston·ing** 1. To hurl stones at; pelt or kill with stones. 2. To remove the stones or pits from. 3. To furnish or line, as a well, with stone. [OE *stān*] — **ston′er** *n.*

Stone Age The earliest known period in human culture when stone implements and weapons were used.

stone-blind (stōn′blīnd′) *adj.* Totally blind.

stone-broke (stōn′brōk′) *adj. Informal* Without any money; having no funds. Also **ston′y-broke′** (stō′nē-).

stone·crop (stōn′krop′) *n.* Any of various plants having small fleshy leaves and yellow flowers, often grown in rock gardens.

stone·cut·ter (stōn′kut′ər) *n.* One who or that which cuts stone; especially, a machine for facing stone.

stone-deaf (stōn′def′) *adj.* Completely deaf.

Stone·henge (stōn′henj) A prehistoric structure on Salisbury Plain, England, consisting primarily of great circles of huge, dressed stones.

stone·ma·son (stōn′mā′sən) *n.* One who prepares and lays stones in building. — **stone′ma′son·ry** (-rē) *n.*

STONEHENGE

stone's throw A short distance.

stone·ware (stōn′wâr′) *n.* A variety of very hard pottery, made from siliceous clay or clay mixed with flint or sand.

stone·work (stōn′wûrk′) *n.* 1. Work concerned with cutting or setting stone; also, something made of stone. 2. *pl.* A place where stone is prepared for masonry. — **stone′work′er** *n.*

ston·y (stō′nē) *adj.* **ston·i·er, ston·i·est** 1. Abounding in stone. 2. Made or consisting of stone. 3. Hard as stone. 4. Unfeeling or inflexible. 5. Converting into stone; petrifying. — **ston′i·ly** *adv.* — **ston′i·ness** *n.*

stood (stood) Past tense and past participle of STAND.

stooge (stooj) *Informal n.* 1. An actor placed in the audience to heckle a comedian on the stage. 2. An actor who feeds lines to the principal comedian, acts as a foil for his jokes, etc. 3. Anyone who acts as or is the tool or dupe of another. — *v.i.* **stooged, stoog·ing** To act as a stooge: usually with *for*. [Origin unknown]

stool (stool) *n.* 1. A backless and armless seat, high or low, for one person. 2. A low bench or support for the feet or for the knees in kneeling. 3. A seat used in defecating; a privy. 4. The matter evacuated from the bowels at each movement. 5. *Bot.* **a** A stump or root from which suckers or sprouts shoot up. **b** The shoots from such a root or stump. 6. A decoy. — *v.i.* 1. To send up shoots or suckers. 2. To decoy wild fowl with a stool. 3. To void feces. 4. *U.S. Slang* To be a stool pigeon. [OE *stōl*]

stool pigeon 1. A living or artificial pigeon attached to a perch to decoy others. 2. *U.S. Slang* An informer or spy, esp. for the police.

stoop[1] (stoop) *v.i.* 1. To bend or lean the body forward and down; bow; crouch. 2. To stand or walk with the upper part of the body habitually bent forward; slouch. 3. To bend; lean; sink, as a tree. 4. To lower or degrade oneself: to *stoop* to cheating. 5. To swoop, as a hawk on prey. — *v.t.* 6. To bend (one's head, shoulders, etc.) forward. — *n.* 1. An act of stooping; a slouch. 2. A habitual forward inclination of the head and shoulders. 3. A decline from dignity or superiority. 4. A swoop. [OE *stūpian*]

stoop[2] (stoop) *n. U.S.* 1. Originally, a platform at the door of a house approached by steps and having seats. 2. A small porch at the entrance to a house. [< Du. *stoep*]

stoop[3] (stoop) See STOUP.

stop (stop) *v.,* **stopped** or (*Chiefly Poetic*) **stopt, stop·ping** *v.t.* 1. To bring (something in motion) to a halt; arrest the progress of. 2. To prevent the doing or completion of. 3. To prevent (a person) from doing something; restrain. 4. To keep back, withhold, or cut off, as wages or supplies. 5. To cease doing; desist from. 6. To intercept in transit, as a letter. 7. To block up, obstruct, or clog (a passage, road, etc.): often with *up*. 8. To cover over, or otherwise close, as a hole, cavity, etc. 9. To close (a bottle, barrel, etc.) with a cork, plug, or other stopper. 10. To stanch (a wound, etc.). 11. To defeat; also, to kill. 12. *Music* To press down (a string) on the finger board, or to close (a hole) in order to vary the pitch produced by an instrument; finger. 13. To punctuate. 14. In boxing, etc., to parry. — *v.i.* 15. To come to a halt; cease progress or motion. 16. To cease doing something; pause or desist. 17. To come to an end. — **to stop off** *U.S. Informal* To cease traveling temporarily before reaching one's destination. — **to stop over** *U.S. Informal* 1. To stay at a place temporarily. 2. To interrupt a journey; make a stopover. — *n.* 1. The act of stopping, or the state of being stopped; a halt; pause; end. 2. That which stops or limits the range or time of a movement: a camera *stop*. 3. An obstruction or obstacle. 4. *Music* **a** The stopping of a string or hole of an instrument. **b** In an organ or harpsichord, a knob controlling a register of pipes or strings; also the register so controlled. 5. *Brit.* A punctuation mark, as a period. 6. In telegrams and cablegrams, the word *stop* spelled out to indicate a punctuation mark. 7. In joinery, a block, pin, or the like to check sliding motion, as of a drawer. 8. *Phonet.* **a** Complete blockage of the breath stream (implosion), as with the lips or tongue, followed by a sudden release (plosion). **b** A consonant so produced, as *p, b, t, d, k,* and *g.* [OE -*stoppian,* as in *forstoppian* to stop up]

stop·cock (stop′kok′) *n.* A faucet or short pipe having a valve for stopping or regulating the passage of fluids.

stope (stōp) *Mining n.* An excavation from which the ore is removed in a series of steps. — *v.t. & v.i.* **stoped, stop·ing** To excavate in stopes. [Appar. akin to STEP]

stop·gap (stop′gap′) *n.* 1. That which stops a gap. 2. Something improvised to fill a need temporarily; an expedient. — *adj.* That serves as a stopgap.

stop·light (stop′līt′) *n.* 1. The red light on a traffic light. 2. A red light on the rear of a motor vehicle that shines upon application of the brakes.

stop order An order to an agent or broker to buy or sell a stock at the market only when it reaches a specified price.

stop·o·ver (stop′ō′vər) *n.* 1. The act of staying in a place for a brief period, esp. while traveling. 2. The act of interrupting a journey without paying additional fare, as by taking a later train. Also **stop′-off′** (-ôf′, -of′).

stop·page (stop′ij) *n.* 1. The act of stopping, or the state of being stopped. 2. An obstruction of some kind; block.

stop payment An order to a bank to refuse payment on a certain check.

stop·per (stop′ər) *n.* 1. Something that stops up or closes, as a plug or cork. 2. One who or that which stops or checks a movement, action, etc. — *v.t.* To close with a stopper.

stop·ple (stop′əl) *n.* A stopper, plug, cork, or bung. — *v.t.* **·pled, ·pling** To close with or as with a stopple. [ME *stoppel,* prob. < *stoppen* to stop]

stopt (stopt) Alternative, chiefly poetic, past tense and past participle of STOP.

stop·watch (stop′woch′) *n.* A watch that has a hand indicating fractions of a second and that may be instantaneously started or stopped, used for timing races, etc.

stor·age (stôr′ij, stō′rij) *n.* 1. The depositing of articles in a warehouse for sakekeeping. 2. Space for storing goods. 3. A charge for storing. 4. The charging of a storage battery.

storage battery One or more secondary cells arranged as a single source of direct current and capable of being recharged on reversal of the current.

storage cell *Electr.* A secondary cell.

store (stôr, stōr) *v.t.* **stored, stor·ing** 1. To put away for future use; accumulate. 2. To furnish or supply; provide. 3. To place in a warehouse or other place of deposit for safekeeping. — *n.* 1. *U.S.* A place where merchandise of any kind is kept for sale. 2. That which is stored or laid up against future need. 3. *pl.* Supplies, as of arms, or clothing. 4. A place where commodities are stored; warehouse. — **in store** Set apart for the future; forthcoming; impending. — **to set store by** To value or esteem; regard. [< OF < L *instaurare* to restore, erect]

store·house (stôr′hous′, stōr′-) *n.* 1. A building in which goods are stored. 2. A large or inexhaustible fund; reservoir: a *storehouse* of ideas.

store·keep·er (stôr′kē′pər, stōr′-) *n.* 1. A person who keeps a retail store or shop; shopkeeper. 2. One who has charge of stores or supplies.

store·room (stôr'rōōm', -rŏŏm', stôr'-) *n.* A room in which things are stored, as supplies.

sto·rey (stôr'ē, stō'rē) See STORY².

sto·ried¹ (stôr'ēd, stō'rēd) *adj.* Having or consisting of stories, as a building: usu. in compounds: a six-*storied* house. Also **sto'reyed.**

sto·ried² (stôr'ēd, stō'rēd) *adj.* 1. Having a notable history. 2. Related in a story. 3. Ornamented with designs representing scenes from history or story.

stork (stôrk) *n.* Any of a family of large wading birds with long necks and long legs. [OE *storc*]

storm (stôrm) *n.* 1. A disturbance of the atmosphere, generally a great whirling motion of the air, accompanied by rain, snow, etc. 2. *Meteorol.* In the Beaufort scale, a wind force of the 11th degree. 3. A furious flight or shower of objects, esp. of missiles. 4. A violent outburst, as of passion or excitement: a *storm* of applause. 5. *Mil.* A violent and rapid assault on a fortified place. 6. A violent commotion, as in politics, society, or domestic life. — *v.i.* 1. To blow with violence; rain, snow, hail, etc., heavily: used impersonally: It *stormed* all day. 2. To be very angry; rage. 3. To move or rush with violence or rage. — *v.t.* 4. *Mil.* To take or try to take by storm. [OE]

storm·bound (stôrm'bound') *adj.* Delayed, confined, or cut off from communications because of a storm.

storm center 1. *Meteorol.* The center or area of lowest pressure and comparative calm in a cyclonic storm. 2. The central point of a heated argument; the focus of any trouble.

storm door A strong outer door for added protection during storms and inclement weather.

storm petrel Any of certain small petrels of the North Atlantic, thought to portend storm; Mother Carey's chicken: also called *stormy petrel.*

storm trooper In Germany, a member of the Nazi party militia unit, the *Sturmabteilung:* also called *Brown Shirt.*

storm warning A signal, as a flag or light, used to warn mariners of coming storm. Also **storm signal.**

storm window An extra window outside the ordinary one as a protection against storms or for greater insulation.

storm·y (stôr'mē) *adj.* **storm·i·er, storm·i·est** 1. Characterized by or subject to storms; tempestuous. 2. Characterized by violent emotions or actions: a *stormy* life. — **storm'i·ly** *adv.* — **storm'i·ness** *n.*

stormy petrel 1. The storm petrel. 2. One who portends trouble or discord, as by rebelling against accepted ideas, practices, etc.

sto·ry¹ (stôr'ē, stō'rē) *n.* *pl.* **·ries** 1. A narrative or recital of an event or series of events, whether real or fictitious. 2. A narrative, usu. of fictitious events, intended to entertain a reader or hearer. 3. A short story. 4. A report. 5. A news article in a newspaper or magazine; also, the material for such an article. 6. An anecdote. 7. *Informal* A lie. 8. The series of events in a novel, play, etc. — **Syn.** See LIE². — *v.t.* **·ried, ·ry·ing** 1. To relate as a story. 2. To adorn with designs representing scenes from history, legend, etc. [< OF < L *historia* an account]

STORM WARNINGS
A Daylight. *B* Night. *a* Small-craft warning. *b* Gale. *c* Whole gale. *d* Hurricane.

Red ☐ White ■ Black

sto·ry² (stôr'ē, stō'rē) *n.* *pl.* **·ries** 1. A horizontal division in a building comprising the space between two successive floors. 2. Habitable rooms on the same level. Also, *Chiefly Brit., storey.* [Special use of STORY¹; ? from earlier sense of "a tier of painted windows or sculptures that narrated an event"]

story line The rough plot of a film, play, novel, etc.

sto·ry·tell·er (stôr'ē·tel'ər, stō'rē-) *n.* 1. One who relates stories. 2. *Informal* A liar. — **sto'ry·tell'ing** *n.* & *adj.*

stoup (stōōp) *n.* 1. *Eccl.* A basin for holy water at the entrance of a church. 2. *Scot.* A pail, cup, etc.; also, its contents. Also spelled *stoop, stowp.* [< ON *staup* bucket]

stout (stout) *adj.* 1. Strong or firm of structure or material; sound; tough. 2. Determined; resolute. 3. Fat. 4. Substantial; solid: *stout* fare. 5. Having muscular strength; robust. 6. Proud; stubborn. — *n.* 1. A stout person. 2. A very dark porter or ale. [< OF *estout* bold, strong] — **stout'ly** *adv.* — **stout'ness** *n.*

stout·heart·ed (stout'här'tid) *adj.* Brave; courageous. — **stout'heart'ed·ly** *adv.* — **stout'heart'ed·ness** *n.*

stove¹ (stōv) *n.* 1. An apparatus, usu. of metal, in which gas, oil, electricity, etc., is consumed for heating or cooking. 2. A pottery kiln. [OE *stofa* heated room]

stove² (stōv) Alternative past tense and past participle of STAVE.

stove·pipe (stōv'pīp') *n.* 1. A pipe, usu. of thin sheet iron, for conducting the smoke and gases of combustion from a stove to a chimney flue. 2. *U.S. Informal* A tall silk hat: also **stovepipe hat.**

stow (stō) *v.t.* 1. To place or arrange compactly; pack. 2. To fill by packing. 3. To have room for; hold: said of a room, receptacle, etc. 4. *Slang* To stop; cease. — **to stow away** 1. To put in a place of safekeeping, hiding, etc. 2. To be a stowaway. [ME < OE *stōw* place]

stow·age (stō'ij) *n.* 1. The act or manner of stowing, or the state of being stowed. 2. Space for stowing goods; also, the goods stowed. 3. Charge for stowing goods.

stow·a·way (stō'ə·wā') *n.* One who conceals himself, as on a vessel, to obtain free passage or evade officials.

stowp (stōōp) See STOUP.

stra·bis·mus (strə·biz'məs) *n.* *Pathol.* A condition in which the eyes cannot be simultaneously focused on the same spot. When one or both eyes turn inward, the patient is *crosseyed,* when outward, *walleyed.* [< NL < Gk. *strabizein* to squint] — **stra·bis'mal, stra·bis'mic** or **·mi·cal** *adj.*

strad·dle (strad'l) *v.* **·dled, ·dling** *v.i.* 1. To stand, walk, or sit with the legs spread apart. 2. To stand wide apart: said of the legs. 3. *Informal* To appear to favor both sides of an issue. — *v.t.* 4. To stand, walk, or sit with the legs on either side of. 5. To spread (the legs) wide apart. 6. *Informal* To appear to favor both sides of (an issue). 7. *Mil.* To fire shots both beyond and in front of (a target) so as to determine the range — *n.* 1. The act of straddling. 2. The space between the feet or legs of one who straddles. 3. A noncommittal or vacillating position on any issue. 4. In the securities trade, a transaction in which the holder obtains the option of either delivering or buying a certain amount of stock or other commodity at a fixed price within a stipulated period. — **strad'dler** *n.*

Strad·i·var·i·us (strad'i·vâr'ē·əs) *n.* One of the violins produced by Antonio Stra·di·va·ri (strä'dē·vä'rē), 1644?–1737, Italian violinmaker.

strafe (strāf, sträf) *v.t.* **strafed, strafing** 1. To attack (troops, emplacements, etc.) with machine-gun fire from low-flying airplanes. 2. To bombard or shell heavily. 3. *Slang* To punish. — *n.* A heavy bombardment. [< G *strafen* to punish] — **straf'er** *n.*

strag·gle (strag'əl) *v.i.* **·gled, ·gling** 1. To stray from or lag behind the main body. 2. To wander aimlessly about. 3. To occur at irregular intervals. [? Freq. of obs. *strake* to move, go about] — **strag'gler** *n.*

strag·gly (strag'lē) *adj.* **·gli·er, ·gli·est** Scattered or spread out irregularly.

straight (strāt) *adj.* 1. Extending uniformly in one direction without curve or bend. 2. Free from kinks; not curly. 3. Not stooped or inclined; erect, as in posture. 4. Not deviating from truth, fairness, or honesty. 5. Clear; frank; direct. 6. Free from obstruction; uninterrupted; unbroken. 7. Correctly kept, ordered, or arranged: Are the facts *straight* in your mind? 8. Sold without discount for number or quantity taken. 9. *Informal* Strictly adhering to a particular party or policy: a *straight* Democrat. 10. In poker, consisting of five cards forming a sequence: a *straight* flush. 11. Having nothing added; undiluted. 12. *Slang* Conforming to normal or conventional standards. 13. *Slang* Heterosexual. — *n.* 1. A straight part or piece. 2. The part of a racecourse between the winning post and the last turn. 3. In poker, a numerical sequence of five cards not of the same suit, or a hand containing this. 4. A straight line. 5. *Slang* A conventional person. 6. *Slang* A heterosexual. — *adv.* 1. In a straight line or a direct course. 2. Closely in line; correspondingly. 3. At once; straightway. — **to go straight** To reform after a criminal career. [ME < OE *streccan* to stretch] — **straight'ly** *adv.* — **straight'ness** *n.*

straight angle *Geom.* An angle of 180°.

straight·a·way (strāt'ə·wā') *adj.* Having no curve or turn. — *n.* A straight course or track. — *adv.* At once.

straight·edge (strāt'ej') *n.* A bar of wood or metal having one edge true to a straight line, used for ruling, etc.

straight·en (strāt'n) *v.t.* 1. To make straight. 2. To lay out (a corpse). — *v.i.* 3. To become straight. — **to straighten out** To restore order to; set right; rectify. — **to straighten up** 1. To make neat; tidy. 2. To stand in erect posture. — **straight'en·er** *n.*

straight face A face that betrays no emotion, esp. amusement. — **straight-faced** (strāt'fāst') *adj.*

straight flush See under FLUSH³.

straight·for·ward (strāt'fôr'wərd) *adj.* 1. Proceeding in a straight course. 2. Honest; frank. — *adv.* In a straight course or direct manner: also **straight'for'wards.** — **straight'for'ward·ly** *adv.* — **straight'for'ward·ness** *n.*

straight man *U.S. Informal* An entertainer who acts as a foil for a comedian.

straight-out (strāt'out') *adj.* *Informal* 1. Showing the true sentiments or feelings; unreserved. **2.** Real; genuine. **3.** Uncompromising; all-out: a *straight-out* Republican.

straight ticket 1. A political party ballot or ticket that presents the regular party candidates without addition or change. **2.** A ballot cast for all the candidates of one party.

straight·way (strāt/wā/) *adv.* Immediately; straightaway.

strain[1] (strān) *v.t.* **1.** To exert to the utmost. **2.** To injure by overexertion; sprain. **3.** To pull or draw tight; stretch. **4.** To stretch beyond the true intent, proper limit, etc.: to *strain* a point. **5.** To pass through a filtering agent or strainer. **6.** To remove by filtration. **7.** To alter or deform in structure or shape as a result of pressure or stress. **8.** To embrace tightly; hug. — *v.i.* **9.** To make violent efforts; strive. **10.** To be or become wrenched or twisted. **11.** To filter, trickle, or percolate. — **to strain at 1.** To push or pull with violent efforts. **2.** To strive for. **3.** To scruple or balk at accepting. — *n.* **1.** An act of straining, or the state of being strained. **2.** The injury resulting from excessive tension or effort. **3.** Severe mental or emotional tension. [< OF < L *stringere* to bind tight]

strain[2] (strān) *n.* **1.** Line of descent, or the individuals, collectively, in that line; race; stock. **2.** Inborn or hereditary tendency; trace; element. **3.** *Biol.* A special line of animals or plants bred from a certain species or variety. **4.** *Often pl.* A passage of music or other sound when heard. **5.** Prevailing tone, style, or manner; mood. [? Var. of ME *strene*, OE *strēon* offspring]

strain·er (strā/nər) *n.* A utensil or device, containing meshes or porous parts, through which liquids are strained.

strait (strāt) *n.* **1.** *Often pl.* A narrow passage of water connecting two larger bodies of water. **2.** *Often pl.* A position of perplexity or distress. — *adj.* **1.** *Archaic* Narrow. **2.** *Archaic* Righteous; strict. **3.** Difficult. [< OF < L *stringere* to bind tight] — **strait/ly** *adv.* — **strait/ness** *n.*

strait·en (strāt/n) *v.t.* **1.** To make strait or narrow. **2.** To embarrass, as in finances; also, to distress.

strait·ened (strāt/nd) *adj.* **1.** Contracted; narrowed. **2.** Suffering privation or hardship, as from lack of money.

strait·jack·et (strāt/jak/it) *n.* **1.** A tight jacket of strong canvas, for confining the arms of violent patients. **2.** Anything that unduly confines or restricts. — *v.t.* To confine in or as if in a straitjacket.

strait-laced (strāt/lāst/) *adj.* Strict, esp. in morals.

strake (strāk) *n.* *Naut.* A breadth of planking or line of plating on a vessel's hull from stem to stern: also called *streak*. [Appar. akin to STRETCH; infl. in meaning by STREAK]

strand[1] (strand) *n.* A shore or beach, esp. that portion between high and low tides — *v.t. & v.i.* **1.** To drive or run aground. **2.** To leave or be left in straits or difficulties: usu. in the passive. [OE *strand*]

strand[2] (strand) *n.* **1.** One of the principal twists or members of a rope. **2.** A fiber, hair, or the like. **3.** Anything plaited or twisted. **4.** A string of beads or pearls — *v.t.* **1.** To break a strand of (a rope). **2.** To make by twisting strands. [? < OF *estran* < Gmc.]

strange (strānj) *adj.* **strang·er, strang·est 1.** Previously unknown, unseen, or unheard of; unfamiliar. **2.** Not according to the ordinary way; unaccountable; remarkable. **3.** Of a different class, character, or kind. **4.** Foreign; alien. **5.** Distant in manner; reserved; shy. **6.** Inexperienced; unaccustomed. — *adv.* In a strange manner. [< OF < L *extraneus* foreign] — **strange/ly** *adv.* — **strange/ness** *n.*

stran·ger (strān/jər) *n.* **1.** One who is not an acquaintance. **2.** An unfamiliar visitor; guest. **3.** A foreigner. **4.** One unversed in or unfamiliar with something specified: with *to*.

stran·gle (strang/gəl) *v.* **·gled, ·gling** *v.t.* **1.** To choke to death; throttle; suffocate. **2.** To repress; suppress. **3.** To inhibit the action or development of — *v.i.* **4.** To suffer or die from strangulation. [< F < L < Gk. *strangalē* halter < *strangos* twisted] — **stran/gler** *n.*

strangle hold 1. In wrestling, a usu. illegal hold that chokes one's opponent. **2.** Any influence or power that chokes freedom or progress.

stran·gu·late (strang/gyə·lāt) *v.t.* **·lat·ed, ·lat·ing 1.** To strangle. **2.** *Pathol.* To compress, contract, or obstruct, esp. so as to cut off flow of a fluid. — *adj.* Strangulated. [See STRANGLE.] — **stran/gu·la/tion** *n.*

strap (strap) *n.* **1.** A long, narrow, and flexible strip of leather, etc., usu. having a buckle or other fastener, for binding about objects. **2.** A razor strop. **3.** Something resembling a strap and used as a fastening or support. **4.** A thin metal band. — *v.t.* **strapped, strap·ping 1.** To fasten or bind with a strap. **2.** To beat with a strap. **3.** To embarrass financially. **4.** To sharpen or strop. [Var. of STROP] — **strap/less** *adj.* — **strap/per** *n.*

strap·hang·er (strap/hang·ər) *n.* A standee on a bus, etc., esp. one who holds on to an overhead strap.

strap·ping (strap/ing) *adj. Informal* Large and robust.

stra·ta (strā/tə, strat/ə) Alternative plural of STRATUM.

strat·a·gem (strat/ə·jəm) *n.* **1.** A maneuver designed to deceive or outwit an enemy in war. **2.** A device for obtain-

ing advantage; trick. [< F < L < Gk. < *stratos* army + *agein* to lead]

stra·te·gic (strə·tē/jik) *adj.* **1.** Of or pertaining to strategy. **2.** Characterized by, used in, or having relation to strategy. Also **stra·te/gi·cal, strat·e·get·ic** (strat/ə·jet/ik) or **·i·cal.** — **stra·te/gi·cal·ly, strat/e·get/i·cal·ly** *adv.*

strat·e·gist (strat/ə·jist) *n.* One versed in strategy.

strat·e·gy (strat/ə·jē) *n. pl.* **·ties 1.** The science and art of conducting a military campaign on a broad scale: distinguished from *tactics*. **2.** The use of stratagem or artifice, as in politics. **3.** A plan for achieving some end. [See STRATAGEM]

strat·i·fy (strat/ə·fī) *v.* **·fied, ·fy·ing** *v.t.* **1.** To form or arrange in strata. **2.** To preserve (seeds) by spreading in alternating layers of earth and sand. — *v.i.* **3.** To form in strata. **4.** *Geol.* To be formed in strata, as rocks. **5.** *Sociol.* To form social groups at different levels as determined by class, caste, or status. [< F < Med.L < L *stratum* layer + *facere* to make] — **strat/i·fi·ca/tion** *n.*

stra·to·cu·mu·lus (strā/tō·kyōō/myə·ləs) *n. pl.* **·li** (-lī) *Meteorol.* Large globular masses of cloud (Symbol Sc), gray to black in color, disposed in waves, groups, or bands, and often covering the whole sky: also called *cumulostratus.* [< *strato-* (< STRATUS) + CUMULUS]

strat·o·pause (strat/ə·pôz) *n. Meteorol.* The zone of transition between the stratosphere and the mesosphere.

strat·o·sphere (strat/ə·sfir, strā/tə-) *n. Meteorol.* That portion of the atmosphere beginning at a height of about seven miles and characterized by a more or less uniform temperature. — **strat·o·spher·ic** (-sfir/ik, -sfer/-) or **·i·cal** *adj.*

stra·tum (strā/təm, strat/əm) *n. pl.* **·ta** (-tə) or **·tums 1.** A natural or artificial layer, bed, or thickness. **2.** *Geol.* A more or less homogeneous layer of rock, serving to identify a geological group, system or series. **3.** Something corresponding to a layer, bed, or grade: a low *stratum* of society. [< L]

stra·tus (strā/təs, strat/əs) *n. pl.* **·ti** (-tī) *Meteorol.* A cloud of foglike appearance, low-lying and arranged in a uniform layer. [< L, orig. pp. of *sternere* to spread]

straw (strô) *n.* **1.** A slender tube of paper, glass, etc., used to suck up a beverage. **2.** Stems or stalks of grain, collectively, after the grain has been thrashed out. **3.** A dry or ripened stalk. **4.** A mere trifle. — **the last straw** The final test of patience or endurance: from the phrase **the straw that broke the camel's back.** — **to clutch (grasp, catch, etc.) at a straw** To try in desperation any solution or expedient. — *adj.* **1.** Like or of straw. **2.** Of no value; worthless; sham. **3.** Made of straw. **4.** Yellowish. [OE *strēaw*]

straw·ber·ry (strô/ber/ē, -bər·ē) *n. pl.* **·ries 1.** The edible fruit of a stemless perennial herb of the rose family. **2.** The plant bearing this fruit. [ME *strauberi*]

strawberry blond A person having reddish blond hair.

straw vote An unofficial vote to test the strength of opposing candidates, determine group opinion, etc.

straw·y (strô/ē) *adj.* **straw·i·er, straw·i·est 1.** Of or like straw. **2.** Covered or thatched with straw.

stray (strā) *v.i.* **1.** To wander from the proper course, an area, group, etc.; straggle; roam. **2.** To wander about; rove. **3.** To fail to concentrate; digress. **4.** To deviate from right or goodness; go astray. — *adj.* **1.** Having strayed; straying. **2.** Irregular; occasional; casual; unrelated. — *n.* **1.** A domestic animal that has strayed. **2.** A person who is lost or wanders aimlessly. **3.** The act of straying or wandering. [< OF *estraier* to wander about, ult. < L *extra vagare* to wander outside] — **stray/er** *n.*

streak (strēk) *n.* **1.** A long, narrow, somewhat irregularly shaped mark, line, or stripe: a *streak* of lightning. **2.** A vein or trace; dash: a *streak* of meanness; also, a transient mood; whim. **3.** A period of time; a spell. **4.** A strake. **5.** A layer or strip: meat with a *streak* of fat. **6.** *Slang* The act of streaking (*v.* def. 2). — *v.t.* **1.** To mark with a streak; form streaks in or on; stripe. **2.** *Slang* To appear naked in (a public place), usu. briefly and esp. while running, as for a thrill. — *v.i.* **3.** To form a streak or streaks. **4.** To move at great speed. **5.** *Slang* To appear naked in a public place, usu. briefly and esp. while running, as for a thrill. [OE *strica*] — **streaked** (strēkt) *adj.* — **streak/er** *n.*

streak·y (strē/kē) *adj.* **streak·i·er, streak·i·est 1.** Marked with or occurring in streaks. **2.** Of variable quality or character. — **streak/i·ly** *adv.* — **streak/i·ness** *n.*

stream (strēm) *n.* **1.** A current or flow of water or other fluid. **2.** Anything continuously flowing, moving, or passing, as people. **3.** A trend; drift. **4.** Anything issuing out or flowing from a source. — *v.i.* **1.** To pour forth or issue in a stream. **2.** To pour forth a stream: eyes *streaming* with tears. **3.** To move in continuous succession. **4.** To float with a waving movement, as a flag. **5.** To move with a trail of light, as a meteor. — *v.t.* **6.** To emit or exude. **7.** To cause (a flag, etc.) to stretch forth; display. [OE *strēam*]

stream·er (strē/mər) *n.* **1.** An object that streams forth, or hangs extended. **2.** A long, narrow flag or standard. **3.** A shaft of light, such as shoots up from the horizon. **4.** A newspaper headline that runs across the whole page.

stream·let (strēm′lit) *n.* A small stream; rivulet.

stream·line (strēm′līn′) *n.* **1.** *Physics* **a** The course of a fluid in which every particle maintains an identical speed and direction of flow; esp., a course free of turbulence or eddies. **b** The path traversed by one particle in such a course. **2.** Any shape or contour designed to offer minimum resistance to fluid flow. — *adj.* Designating an uninterrupted flow or drift. — *v.t.* **lined, lin·ing** **1.** To design with a streamlined shape. **2.** To make more simple, efficient, or up to date. — **stream′lined′** *adj.*

stream of consciousness *Psychol.* The series of individual conscious states moving continuously on in time.

street (strēt) *n.* A public way in a city or town, with buildings on one or both sides; also. the roadway for vehicles, between sidewalks. [OE *strǣt* < LL *strata* (*via*) paved (road)]

street·car (strēt′kär′) *n.* A public passenger car of an electric railway that runs on tracks set into the streets: also called *trolley, trolley car,* Brit., *tramcar.*

street people People, esp. young people, usu. without a permanent home and having a life style like that of hippies.

street·walk·er (strēt′wô′kər) *n.* A prostitute who solicits in the streets. — **street′walk′ing** *n. & adj.*

strength (strengkth, strength) *n.* **1.** Muscular power; vigor. **2.** Durability; toughness. **3.** Power in general, or a source of power. **4.** Binding force or validity, as of a law. **5.** Vigor or force of intellect, moral power, style, etc. **6.** Available numerical force in a military unit or other organization. **7.** Degree of intensity; vehemence: *strength* of passion. **8.** The degree of intensity or concentration, as of a color, odor, etc. **9.** Potency, as of a drug, chemical, or liquor. — **on the strength of** Based on or in reliance or dependence on. [OE *strengthu* < *strang* strong]

strength·en (strengk′thən, streng′-) *v.t.* **1.** To make strong. **2.** To encourage; hearten; animate. — *v.i.* **3.** To become or grow strong or stronger. — **strength′en·er** *n.*

stren·u·ous (stren′yōō·əs) *adj.* **1.** Necessitating or characterized by strong effort or exertion. **2.** Vigorously active or zealous. [< L *strenuus*] — **stren′u·ous·ly** *adv.* — **stren′u·os′i·ty** (-os′ə·tē), **stren′u·ous·ness** *n.*

strep·to·coc·cus (strep′tə·kok′əs) *n.* *pl.* **·coc·ci** (-kok′sī) Any of a genus of typically ovoid or spherical bacteria, grouped in long chains, including species causing many diseases. [< NL < Gk. *streptos* twisted + COCCUS] — **strep′to·coc′cal** (-kok′əl), **strep′to·coc′cic** (-kok′sik) *adj.*

strep·to·my·cin (strep′tō·mī′sin) *n.* A potent antibiotic isolated from a moldlike organism. [< Gk. *streptos* twisted + *mykēs* fungus]

stress (stres) *n.* **1.** Special weight, importance, or significance: to lay *stress* on the classics. **2.** In prosody, an emphasis given to a specific word or syllable to indicate the metrical pattern. **3.** *Mech.* A force exerted between contiguous portions of a body or bodies and generally expressed in pounds per square inch. **b** A force or system of forces that tends to produce deformation in a body. **4.** Influence exerted forcibly; pressure; compulsion. **5.** Emotional or intellectual strain or tension. **6.** *Phonet.* The relative force with which a sound, syllable, or word is uttered. — *v.t.* **1.** To subject to mechanical stress. **2.** To put stress or emphasis on; accent, as a syllable. **3.** To put into straits or difficulties; distress. [< OF < L *strictus*, pp. of *stringere* to draw tight] — **stress′ful** *adj.* — **stress′less** *adj.*

-stress *suffix of nouns* Feminine form of -STER: *songstress.*

stretch (strech) *v.t.* **1.** To extend or draw out, as to full length or width. **2.** To extend or draw out forcibly, esp. beyond normal or proper limits. **3.** To cause to reach, as from one place to another or over an area; extend. **4.** To put forth, hold out, or extend (the hand, an object, etc.): often with *out.* **5.** To tighten. **6.** To strain or exert to the utmost: to *stretch* every nerve. **7.** To make do with: to *stretch* one's salary with economies. — *v.i.* **8.** To reach or extend over an area or from one place to another. **9.** To become extended, esp. beyond normal or proper limits. **10.** To extend one's body or limbs, esp. to relieve stiffness. **11.** To lie down and extend one's limbs to full length: usu. with *out.* — *n.* **1.** The act of stretching, or the state of being stretched. **2.** Extent or reach of that which stretches. **3.** A continuous extent of space or time. **4.** In racing, the part of the track that, being straight, permits the greatest speed. **5.** A particular direction or course. **6.** *Slang* A term of imprisonment. — *adj.* Capable of stretching or of being stretched; elastic: *stretch* pants. [OE *streccan*] — **stretch′a·ble** *adj.*

stretch·er (strech′ər) *n.* **1.** One who or that which stretches. **2.** Any device for stretching, as for loosening the fit of gloves or shoes, for drying curtains, etc. **3.** A frame, as of stretched canvas, for carrying the wounded, sick, or dead; a litter. **4.** In masonry, a brick or stone lying lengthwise of a course. **5.** A tie beam in the frame of a building.

stretch·out (strech′out′) *n.* **1.** A system of industrial op-

eration in which employees do more work without proportionate increase in pay. **2.** A slowdown practiced by employees so as to make the work last longer.

strew (strōō) *v.t.* **strewed, strewed** or **strewn, strew·ing** **1.** To spread about loosely or at random; scatter; sprinkle. **2.** To cover with something scattered or sprinkled. **3.** To be scattered over (a surface). [OE *strewian*]

stri·a (strī′ə) *n.* *pl.* **stri·ae** (strī′ē) **1.** A narrow streak, stripe, or band of distinctive color, structure, or texture, often parallel with others. **2.** *Geol.* A small groove, channel, or ridge on a rock surface, due to the action of glacier ice. [< L, groove]

stri·ate (strī′āt) *adj.* **1.** Having fine linear markings; striped or grooved. **2.** Constituting a stria or striae. Also **stri′at·ed.** — *v.t.* **·at·ed, ·at·ing** To mark with striae. [< L < *stria* groove] — **stri·a′tion** *n.*

strick·en (strik′ən) Alternative past participle of STRIKE. ◆ *Stricken* is current in American English in certain senses: *stricken* with grief; a remark *stricken* from the record. — *adj.* **1.** Strongly affected or afflicted; overcome, as by calamity or disease. **2.** Wounded, esp. by a missile. [OE *stricen*, pp. of *strican* to strike]

strict (strikt) *adj.* **1.** Observing or enforcing rules exactly; severe. **2.** Containing exact or severe rules or provisions; exacting. **3.** Rigorously enjoined, maintained, and observed. **4.** Exactly defined, distinguished, or applied. **5.** Complete; absolute: *strict* attention. [< L *strictus*, pp. of *stringere* to draw tight] — **strict′ly** *adv.* — **strict′ness** *n.*

stric·ture (strik′chər) *n.* **1.** Severe criticism. **2.** *Pathol.* An abnormal contraction of some duct or channel.

stride (strīd) *n.* **1.** A long and sweeping or measured step. **2.** The space passed over by such a step. **3.** A progressive movement by an animal, completed when all the feet are returned to the same relative positions they occupied at the beginning of the movement. **4.** A stage of progress. — **to hit one's stride** To attain one's normal speed. — **to make rapid strides** To make quick progress. — **to take (something) in one's stride** To do or react to (something) without undue effort or disturbance, as if part of one's normal activity. — *v.* **strode, strid·den, strid·ing** *v.i.* **1.** To walk with long steps, as from haste or pride. — *v.t.* **2.** To walk through, along, etc., with long steps. **3.** To pass over with a single stride. **4.** To straddle. [OE *strīdan*] — **strid′er** *n.*

stri·dent (strīd′nt) *adj.* Having or making a high, harsh sound; shrill; grating. [< L *stridens, -entis,* ppr. of *stridere* to creak] — **stri′dence, strid′den·cy** *n.* — **stri′dent·ly** *adv.*

strid·u·late (strij′ōō·lāt) *v.i.* **·lat·ed, ·lat·ing** To make a shrill, creaking noise, as a cicada or cricket. [< NL *stridere* to rattle, rasp] — **strid′u·la′tion** *n.* — **strid′u·la·to′ry** (-lə·tôr′ē, -tō′rē) *adj.* — **strid′u·lous** *adj.*

strife (strīf) *n.* **1.** Angry contention; fighting. **2.** Any contest for advantage or superiority. [< OF *estriver* to strive]

strike (strīk) *v.* **struck, struck** or, sometimes, **strick·en, strik·ing** *v.t.* **1.** To come into violent contact with; hit. **2.** To hit with a blow; smite. **3.** To deal (a blow, etc.). **4.** To cause to hit forcibly: He *struck* his hand on the table. **5.** To attack; assault. **6.** To remove, separate, or take off by or as by a blow or stroke: with *off, from,* etc.: *Strike* it from the record. **7.** To ignite (a match, etc.); also, to produce (a light, etc.) thus. **8.** To form by stamping, printing, etc. **9.** To indicate (a specified time) by the sound of a stroke, bell, etc. **10.** To fall upon; reach: A sound *struck* his ear. **11.** To arrive at; come upon: to *strike* a trail. **12.** To find: to *strike* oil. **13.** To affect suddenly or in a specified manner: He was *struck* speechless. **14.** To come to the mind of; occur to: An idea *strikes* me. **15.** To impress in a specified manner: He *strikes* me as an honest man. **16.** To attract the attention of; impress: The dress *struck* her fancy. **17.** To assume; take up: to *strike* an attitude. **18.** To cause to enter or penetrate deeply or suddenly: to *strike* dismay into one's heart. **19.** To lower or haul down, as a sail, or a flag in token of surrender. **20.** To cease working at in order to compel compliance to a demand, etc. **21.** In the theater, to dismantle (a set or scene). **22.** To make level (a measure of grain, etc.) **23.** To make and confirm, as a bargain. **24.** To harpoon (a whale). **25.** To hook (a fish that has taken the lure) by a sharp pull on the line. **26.** To arrive at by reckoning: to *strike* a balance. — *v.i.* **27.** To come into violent contact; hit. **28.** To deal or aim a blow or blows. **29.** To make an assault or attack. **30.** To make a sound by or as by means of a blow or blows. **31.** To be indicated by the sound of blows or strokes: Noon has just *struck.* **32.** To ignite. **33.** To run aground, as on a reef or shoal. **34.** To lower a flag in token of surrender or in salute. **35.** To come suddenly or unexpectedly; chance: with *on* or *upon.* **36.** To start and proceed: to *strike* for home. **37.** To move quickly; dart. **38.** To cease work in order to enforce demands, etc. **39.** To snatch at or swallow the lure: said of fish. ◆ See note under STRICKEN. **— to strike camp** To take down the tents of a camp. **— to strike down 1.** To fell with a blow. **2.** To affect disastrously; incapacitate completely. **— to strike dumb** To astonish; amaze. **— to strike home 1.** To deal an effective blow. **2.** To have telling effect. **— to strike it rich** *Informal* **1.** To find a valuable vein or pocket of ore. **2.** To come into wealth or good fortune. **— to strike off 1.** To remove or take off by or as by a blow or stroke. **2.** To cross out or erase by or as by a stroke of the pen. **3.** To deduct. — **to strike out 1.** To strike off (def. 2). **2.** To aim a blow or blows. **3.** To make a start: *to strike out* on one's own. **4.** To originate; hit upon. **5.** In baseball: **a** To put out (the batter) by pitching three strikes. **b** To be put out because of having three strikes counted against one during a single turn at bat. **6.** In bowling, to complete a game by bowling three consecutive strikes. **— to strike up 1.** To begin to play, sing, or sound, as a band or musical instrument. **2.** To start up; begin, as a friendship. *— n.* **1.** An act of striking or hitting; a blow. **2.** In baseball: **a** An unsuccessful attempt by the batter to hit the ball. **b** A pitched ball that passes over home plate not lower than the level of the batter's knees and not above that of his shoulders. **c** A foul bunt or any foul tip held by the catcher. **d** Any ball hit foul except when there have been two strikes. **3.** In bowling, the knocking down by a player of all the pins with the first bowl in any frame; also, the score so made: also called *ten-strike*: distinguished from *spare*. **4.** The quitting of work by a body of workers to enforce some demand. **5.** A new or unexpected discovery, as of oil or ore. **6.** Any unexpected or complete success. **7.** An air attack on a surface target. **8.** In fishing, a bite. [OE *strīcan* to stroke, move]

strike·bound (strīk′bound′) *adj.* Closed or immobilized by a strike: said of companies, equipment, workers, etc.

strike·break·er (strīk′brā′kər) *n.* One who takes the place of a workman on strike or who supplies workmen to take the place of strikers. **— strike′break′ing** *n.*

strike·out (strīk′out′) *n.* In baseball, an instance of striking out.

strik·er (strī′kər) *n.* **1.** One who or that which strikes. **2.** An employee who is on strike. **3.** The clapper of a bell, etc.

strik·ing (strī′king) *adj.* Notable; impressive. **— strik′ing·ly** *adv.* **— strik′ing·ness** *n.*

string (string) *n.* **1.** A slender line or strip, as of twine, cloth, leather, etc., thinner than a cord and thicker than a thread. **2.** The cord of a bow. **3.** Prepared wire or catgut for musical instruments. **4.** A stringlike organ or formation, as a vegetable fiber or fibers or an animal nerve or tendon. **5.** A thin cord upon which anything is strung; a row or series of things connected by a small cord: a *string* of pearls. **6.** A connected series or succession, as of things, acts, or events. sometimes implying unusual length: a *string* of lies. **7.** *U.S. Informal* A small collection of animals, esp. of racehorses. **8.** *pl.* Stringed instruments, esp. those of an orchestra; also, those who play on these. **9.** *Archit.* **a** A stringcourse. **b** A ramp or sidepiece supporting the steps of a stairway. **10.** In sports, a group of contestants ranked as to skill. **11.** *Usu. pl. Informal* A condition, limitation, or restriction attached to a proposition, gift, or donation. **— to pull strings** To manipulate or influence others to gain some advantage. *— v.* **strung, string·ing** *v.t.* **1.** To thread, as beads, on or as on a string. **2.** To fit with a string or strings, as a guitar. **3.** To cover, drape, or adorn with things attached to a string or strings. **4.** To tune the strings of (a musical instrument). **5.** To brace; strengthen. **6.** To make tense or nervous. **7.** To arrange or extend in a line or series. **8.** To remove the strings from (vegetables). **9.** *U.S. Informal* To hang: usu. with *up.* **10.** *Slang* To fool or deceive; hoax: often with *along. — v.i.* **11.** To extend, stretch, or proceed in a line or series. **12.** To form into strings. **— to string along (with)** *Informal* To follow with trust or confidence. [OE *streng*]

string bean 1. Any of several varieties of beans cultivated for their edible pods. **2.** The pod itself.

string·board (string′bôrd′, -bōrd′) *n. Archit.* A board serving as a support for the ends of steps in a staircase.

string·course (string′kôrs′, -kōrs′) *n. Archit.* A horizontal molding or ornamental course, as of brick or stone, usu. projecting along the face of a building.

stringed instrument (stringd) A musical instrument that produces its tones by means of one or more vibrating strings, as a violin, cello, etc. Also **string instrument.**

strin·gent (strin′jənt) *adj.* **1.** Requiring or compelling adherence to strict requirements; severe, as regulations. **2.** Hampered by obstructions or scarcity of money. **3.** Convincing; forcible. [< L *stringens, -entis,* ppr. of *stringere* to draw tight] **— strin′gen·cy** *n.* **— strin′gent·ly** *adv.*

string·er (string′ər) *n.* **1.** One who or that which strings. **2.** *Archit.* A heavy timber, generally horizontal, supporting other members of a structure. **3.** A lengthwise timber on which rails are laid, as distinguished from a crosstie. **4.** *Informal* One having a specified numerical rank or degree of proficiency, as on a team: a second *stringer.*

string·piece (string′pēs′) *n. Archit.* A heavy supporting timber forming the margin or edge of a framework.

string tie A very narrow necktie, often tied in a bow with the ends hanging loosely.

string·y (string′ē) *adj.* **string·i·er, string·i·est 1.** Containing fibrous strings. **2.** Forming in strings; ropy. **3.** Having tough sinews. **— string′i·ly** *adv.* **— string′i·ness** *n.*

strip¹ (strip) *n.* **1.** A narrow piece, comparatively long, as of cloth, wood, etc. **2.** A number of stamps attached in a row. **3.** A narrow piece of land. **4.** An airstrip or landing strip. *— v.t.* **stripped, strip·ping** To cut or tear into strips. [? < MLG *strippe* strap]

strip² (strip) *v.* **stripped** (*Rare* **stript), strip·ping** *v.t.* **1.** To pull the covering, clothing, etc., from; lay bare. **2.** To pull off (the covering or clothing). **3.** To rob or plunder. **4.** To make bare or empty. **5.** To remove; take away. **6.** To divest: He was *stripped* of his rank. **7.** *Mech.* To damage or break the teeth, thread, etc., of (a gear, bolt, or the like). **—** *v.i.* **8.** To remove one's clothing; undress. **9.** To undergo stripping. [ME < OE *-strīepan,* as in *bestrīepan* to despoil, plunder] **— strip′per** *n.*

stripe¹ (strīp) *n.* **1.** A line, band, or strip of different color, material, texture, etc., from the adjacent surface. **2.** Striped cloth. **3.** A piece of material or braid on the sleeve of a uniform to indicate rank, service, an award, etc.; a chevron. **4.** Distinctive quality or character; sort: a man of his *stripe.* **—** *v.t.* **striped, strip·ing** To mark with a stripe or stripes. [< MDu.] **— striped** *adj.*

stripe² (strīp) *n.* A blow struck with a whip or rod, as in flogging. [Prob. < LG]

strip·ling (strip′ling) *n.* A mere youth.

strip mining The mining of coal by stripping off soil, etc., to expose and dig out a vein.

strip·tease (strip′tēz′) *n.* In burlesque, etc., a gradual disrobing, interspersed with various movements of the torso. Also **strip tease.** **— strip′teas′er** *n.*

strip·y (strī′pē) *adj.* **strip·i·er, strip·i·est** Being in or suggesting stripes or streaks; having or marked with stripes.

strive (strīv) *v.i.* **strove** or (*less commonly*) **strived, striv·en** (striv′ən) or **strived, striv·ing 1.** To make earnest effort. **2.** To engage in strife; contend; fight. **3.** To vie; emulate. [< OF *estriver,* prob. < Gmc.] **— striv′er** *n.*

strob·o·scope (strob′ə·skōp, strō′bə-) *n.* An instrument for observing the motion of a body or object by rendering it visible only at intervals or at certain points of its path. [< Gk. *strobos* twisting + -SCOPE] **— strob′o·scop′ic** (-skop′ik) or **·i·cal** *adj.* **— strob·os′co·py** (-os′kə·pē) *n.*

strode (strōd) Past tense of STRIDE.

stroke (strōk) *n.* **1.** The act or movement of striking; impact. **2.** A single movement, as of the hand, arm, or some instrument, by which something is made or done. **3.** A blow or any ill effect caused as if by a blow. **4.** An attack of paralysis or apoplexy. **5.** A blow or the sound of a blow of a striking mechanism, as of a clock. **6.** A sudden or brilliant act; coup: a *stroke* of wit. **7.** A pulsation, as of the heart. **8.** A mark or dash of a pen or tool. **9.** A light, caressing movement; a stroking. **10.** A manner or technique of swimming. **11.** *Informal* A portion or stint, as of work: usu. with the negative. **12.** *Mech.* **a** One of a series of alternating linear movements from one extreme position to another, as by the piston of an internal-combustion engine. **b** The distance covered by such a movement. *— v.* **stroked, strok·ing** *v.t.* **1.** To pass the hand over gently or caressingly, or with light pressure. **2.** To set the pace for (a rowboat or its crew); act as stroke for. *— v.i.* **3.** To perform strokes, as in swimming. [ME < OE *strācian* to strike]

stroll (strōl) *v.i.* **1.** To walk in a leisurely or idle manner; saunter. **2.** To go from place to place; wander. *— v.t.* **3.** To walk idly or wander over or through. *— n.* An idle or leisurely walk. [Origin uncertain]

stroll·er (strō′lər) *n.* **1.** One who strolls. **2.** A light, often collapsible, carriage in which a baby or child may sit upright. **3.** A wandering showman or player. **4.** A tramp.

strong (strông, strong) *adj.* **1.** Powerful in physique; muscular; vigorous. **2.** Healthy; robust: a *strong* constitution. **3.** Morally powerful; firm; resolute; courageous. **4.** Mentally powerful or vigorous. **5.** Especially competent or able in a specified subject or field: *strong* in mathematics. **6.** Abundantly or richly supplied with something: often with *in.* **7.** Solidly made or constituted: *strong* walls. **8.** Powerful as a rival or combatant: a *strong* team. **9.** Easy to defend or difficult to capture: a *strong* military position. **10.** Having (a specified) numerical force: an army 20,000 *strong.* **11.** Capable of exerting influence, authority, etc.: a *strong* government. **12.** Financially sound: a *strong* bank. **13.** Powerful in effect: *strong* poison, medicine, etc. **14.** Concentrated; not diluted or weak: *strong* coffee. **15.** Containing much alcohol: *strong* drink. **16.** Powerful in flavor or odor; also, rank; unpleasant: a *strong* breath. **17.** Intense in degree or quality; not faint or mild: a *strong* pulse. **18.** Loud and firm: a *strong* voice. **19.** Firm; tenacious: a *strong* grip.

20. Deeply earnest; fervid: a *strong* desire. **21.** Cogent; convincing: *strong* evidence. **22.** Distinct; marked: a *strong* resemblance. **23.** Extreme; forceful: *strong* measures. **24.** Emphatic; not moderate: *strong* language. **25.** Moving with great force: said of a wind, stream, or tide. **26.** *Meteorol.* Designating a breeze or gale on the Beaufort scale. **27.** Characterized by steady or rising prices: a *strong* market. **28.** *Gram.* In Germanic languages, denoting a strong verb. — *adv.* In a strong manner; so as to be strong. [OE *strang, strong*] — **strong'ly** *adv.*

strong-arm (strông'ärm', strong'-) *Informal adj.* Violent; having and depending on physical power. — *v.t.* To use physical force upon; assault.

strong·box (strông'boks', strong'-) *n.* A strongly built chest or safe for keeping valuables.

strong·hold (strông'hōld', strong'-) *n.* **1.** A strongly fortified place; fortress. **2.** A place of security or refuge.

strong·man (strông'man', strong'-) *n. pl.* **·men** (-men') A political leader having considerable or preeminent power, often derived from extralegal means, as a coup d'état.

strong-mind·ed (strông'mīn'did, strong'-) *adj.* Having a determined, vigorous mind. — **strong'-mind'ed·ly** *adv.* — **strong'-mind'ed·ness** *n.*

strong verb A verb that forms its past tense and past participle by internal vowel change, as *swim, swam, swum.*

strong-willed (strông'wild', strong'-) *adj.* Having a strong will; decided; obstinate.

stron·ti·um (stron'shē·əm, -shəm, -tē·əm) *n.* A hard, yellowish, metallic element (symbol Sr) of the calcium group, known chiefly through its salts, which burn with a red flame and are used largely in pyrotechnics, but also in medicine and ceramics. See ELEMENT. [< NL, from *Strontian,* Argyll, Scotland, where first discovered] — **stron'tic** (-tik) *adj.*

strontium 90 *Physics* A radioactive isotope of strontium chemically resembling calcium and with a half life of about 28 years. Also called *radiostrontium.*

strop (strop) *n.* **1.** A strip of leather, canvas, etc., on which to sharpen a razor. **2.** A strap. — *v.t.* **stropped, strop·ping** To sharpen on a strop. [OE < L < Gk. *strophos* band]

stro·phe (strō'fē) *n.* **1.** In ancient Greek poetry, the verses sung by the chorus in a play while moving from right to left. **2.** In classical prosody, the lines of an ode constituting a stanza and alternating with the antistrophe. **3.** The first of two alternating metrical systems in a poem. [< Gk. *strephein* to turn] — **stroph·ic** (strof'ik, strō'fik) or **·i·cal** *adj.*

strove (strōv) Past tense of STRIVE.

strow (strō) *v.t.* **strowed, strowed** or **strown, strow·ing** *Archaic* To strew.

struck (struk) Past tense and past participle of STRIKE. — *adj.* Closed down or affected by a strike, as a factory.

struck measure A measure having the contents level with the edge of the container, rather than heaping.

struc·tur·al (struk'chər·əl) *adj.* Of, pertaining to, characterized, or caused by structure. — **struc'tur·al·ly** *adv.*

structural steel Rolled steel of considerable toughness and strength, esp. adapted for use in construction.

struc·ture (struk'chər) *n.* **1.** That which is constructed; a combination of related parts, as a building or machine. **2.** The position and arrangement of parts, as of tissues in an organism, atoms within a molecule, etc. **3.** The manner of construction or organization: the social *structure* of a primitive society. — *v.t.* **·tured, ·tur·ing 1.** To form into an organized structure; build. **2.** To conceive as a structural whole; ideate. [< L < *structus,* pp. of *struere* to build]

stru·del (strood'l, *Ger.* shtroo'dəl) *n.* A kind of pastry made of a thin sheet of dough, spread with fruit or cheese, nuts, etc., rolled, and baked. [< G, lit., eddy]

strug·gle (strug'əl) *n.* **1.** A violent effort or series of efforts; a labored contest. **2.** Conflict; strife; battle. — *v.* **·gled, ·gling** *v.i.* **1.** To contend with an adversary in physical combat; fight. **2.** To put forth violent efforts; strive: to *struggle* against odds. **3.** To make one's way by violent efforts. — *v.t.* **4.** To accomplish with a struggle. [ME *strogelen*] — **strug'gler** *n.* — **strug'gling·ly** *adv.*

strum (strum) *v.t. & v.i.* **strummed, strum·ming** To play (a stringed instrument, a tune, etc.) idly, monotonously, or without technical skill. — *n.* The act of strumming. [Prob. imit.] — **strum'mer** *n.*

strum·pet (strum'pit) *n.* A whore; harlot. [? Ult. < OF *strupe* concubinage < L *stuprum* dishonor]

strung (strung) Past tense and past participle of STRING.

strut (strut) *n.* **1.** A proud or pompous step or walk. **2.** A member in a framework, designed to relieve weight or pressure in the direction of its length. For illus. see ROOF. — *v.* **strut·ted, strut·ting** *v.i.* **1.** To walk pompously, conceitedly, and affectedly. — *v.t.* **2.** To brace or support, as a framing or structure, with or as with struts. [OE *strūtian* to be rigid, stand stiffly] — **strut'ter** *n.* — **strut'ting·ly** *adv.*

strych·nine (strik'nin, -nēn, -nīn) *n.* A white, crystalline, bitter, extremely poisonous alkaloid, $C_{21}H_{22}N_2O_2$, contained in certain plants. Its salts are used in medicine, chiefly as a neural stimulant. Also **strych'nin** (-nin). [< F < L *strychnos* < Gk., nightshade]

Stu·art (stoo'ərt, styoo'-) The royal family of Scotland, 1371–1603, and of England, 1603–1714.

stub (stub) *n.* **1.** Any short projecting part or piece. **2.** The part of a tree trunk, bush, etc., that remains when the main part is cut down. **3.** A short or broken remnant, as of a pencil, cigarette, or broken tooth. **4.** *U.S.* In a checkbook, one of the inner ends upon which a memorandum is entered, and which remains when the check is detached; also, the detachable portion of a theater ticket, etc. **5.** Anything blunt, short, or stumpy, as a pen with a broad point. — *v.t.* **stubbed, stub·bing 1.** To strike, as the toe, against a low obstruction or projection. **2.** To grub up, as roots. **3.** To clear or remove the stubs or roots from. [OE *stubb*]

stub·ble (stub'əl) *n.* **1.** The stubs of grain stalks, sugar cane, etc., covering a field after the crop has been cut. **2.** The field itself. **3.** Any surface or growth resembling stubble, as short bristly hair or beard. [< OF *stuble,* ult. < L *stipula* stalk] — **stub'bled** *adj.* — **stub'bly** *adj.*

stub·born (stub'ərn) *adj.* **1.** Inflexible in opinion or intention; unreasonably obstinate. **2.** Difficult to handle, manage, or work with; resistant. **3.** Characterized by perseverance or persistence: *stubborn* fighting. [ME, ? < OE *stubb* stump] — **stub'born·ly** *adv.* — **stub'born·ness** *n.*

stub·by (stub'ē) *adj.* **·bi·er, ·bi·est 1.** Short, stiff, and bristling: a *stubby* beard. **2.** Resembling or of the nature of a stub: a *stubby* pencil. **3.** Stocky; thickset. **4.** Full of stubs. — **stub'bi·ly** *adv.* — **stub'bi·ness** *n.*

stuc·co (stuk'ō) *n. pl.* **·coes** or **·cos 1.** A fine plaster for walls or their relief ornaments, usu. of Portland cement, sand, and a small amount of lime. **2.** Any plaster or cement used for the external coating of buildings. **3.** Ornamental work made from stucco: also **stuc'co·work'** (-wûrk'). — *v.t.* **·coed, ·co·ing** To apply stucco to; decorate with stucco. [< Ital. < Gmc.] — **stuc'co·er** *n.*

stuck (stuk) Past tense and past participle of STICK.

stuck-up (stuk'up') *adj. Informal* Conceited; snobbish.

stud¹ (stud) *n.* **1.** A short intermediate post, as in a building frame; a post to which laths are nailed. **2.** A knob, round-headed nail, or small protuberant ornament. **3.** A removable button used to fasten a shirt front, etc. **4.** A crosspiece in a link, as in a chain cable. **5.** A small pin such as is used in a watch. — *v.t.* **stud·ded, stud·ding 1.** To set thickly with small points, projections, or knobs. **2.** To be scattered or strewn over. **3.** To support or stiffen by means of studs or upright props. [OE *studu* post]

stud² (stud) *n.* **1.** A collection of horses and mares for breeding. **2.** The place where they are kept. **3.** A collection of horses for riding, hunting, or racing. **4.** A studhorse or other male animal used for breeding purposes. **5.** Stud poker. — **at stud** Of a male animal, used or available for breeding purposes. — *adj.* **1.** Of or pertaining to a stud. **2.** Kept for breeding: a *stud* mare. [OE *stōd*]

stud·book (stud'book') *n.* A record of the pedigree of thoroughbred stock.

stud·ding (stud'ing) *n.* **1.** Studs or joists collectively. **2.** The material from which they are made.

stud·ding·sail (stun'səl, stud'ing·sāl') *n. Naut.* A light auxiliary sail set out beyond one of the principal sails by extensible booms during a following wind.

stu·dent (stood'nt, styood'nt) *n.* **1.** One engaged in a course of study, esp. in a secondary school, college or university. **2.** One devoted to study. **3.** One who makes a thorough study of a particular subject. [< OF < L *studens, -entis,* ppr. of *studere* to be eager, study] — **stu'dent·ship** *n.*

— **Syn.** A *student* is one who studies, not necessarily under a teacher: this is the common term for one enrolled in a secondary school or college. A *pupil* is one under close supervision of a teacher; children in elementary schools are called *pupils,* but the term is not synonymous with beginner. A concert violinist may be called the *pupil* of some great master under whom he has studied.

student body All the students attending a school.

stud·horse (stud'hôrs') *n.* A stallion kept for breeding. Also **stud horse.**

stud·ied (stud'ēd) *adj.* **1.** Deliberately designed or undertaken: a *studied* insult. **2.** Lacking freshness, naturalness, or spontaneity. — **stud'ied·ly** *adv.* — **stud'ied·ness** *n.*

stu·di·o (stoo'dē·ō, styoo'-) *n. pl.* **·os 1.** The workroom of an artist, photographer, etc. **2.** A place where motion pictures are filmed. **3.** A room or rooms where radio or television programs are broadcast or recorded. [< Ital., a study]

studio couch A backless couch with a bed frame underneath that may be drawn out to form a double bed.

stu·di·ous (stoo'dē·əs, styoo'-) *adj.* **1.** Given to study; de-

---

voting oneself to the acquisition of knowledge. **2.** Earnest in effort. **3.** Done with deliberation; studied: *studious politeness.* — **stu′di·ous·ly** *adv.* — **stu′di·ous·ness** *n.*

stud poker A game of poker in which the cards of the first round are dealt face down and the rest face up, betting opening on the second round. [< STUD²]

stud·y (stud′ē) *v.* **stud·ied, stud·y·ing** *v.t.* **1.** To apply the mind in acquiring a knowledge of. **2.** To examine: to *study* a problem. **3.** To look at attentively; scrutinize. **4.** To endeavor to memorize, as a part in a play. **5.** To give thought and attention to, as something to be done or devised. — *v.i.* **6.** To apply the mind in acquiring knowledge. **7.** To follow a regular course of instruction. **8.** To meditate. — *n.* *pl.* **stud·ies 1.** The act of studying; the process of acquiring information. **2.** A particular instance or form of mental work. **3.** Something to be studied; a branch of knowledge. **4.** A specific product of or work resulting from studious application. **5.** In art, a first sketch, exercise, etc. **6.** A carefully elaborated literary treatment of a subject. **7.** A room devoted to study, reading, etc. **8.** A state of deep thought or absent-mindedness. **9.** Earnest endeavor; thoughtful attention or care. **10.** Something worthy of close attention. **11.** *Music* An étude. [< OF < L < *studere* to apply oneself, be diligent]

stuff (stuf) *v.t.* **1.** To fill completely; pack; cram full. **2.** To fill (an opening, etc.) with something forced in; plug. **3.** To obstruct or stop up; choke. **4.** To fill or expand with padding, as a cushion. **5.** To fill (a fowl, roast, etc.) with stuffing. **6.** In taxidermy, to fill the skin of (a bird, animal, etc.) with a material preparatory to mounting. **7.** To fill too full; distend. **8.** To fill or cram with food. **9.** To fill with knowledge, ideas, or attitudes, esp. unsystematically. **10.** To force or cram, as into a small space. **11.** To put fraudulent votes into (a ballot box). — *v.i.* **12.** To eat to excess. — *n.* **1.** The material out of which something may be shaped or made; raw or unwrought material. **2.** The fundamental element or basic material of anything: the *stuff* of dreams. **3.** *Informal* Possessions generally, esp., household goods. **4.** A worthless collection of things; rubbish. **5.** Worthless ideas: often used as an interjection: *Stuff* and nonsense! **6.** Woven material, esp. of wool; also, any textile fabric. **7.** *Informal* Any unspecified or vaguely defined substance, activity, etc. [< OF *estoffe*, ? < L *stuppa* tow] — **stuff′er** *n.*

stuffed shirt (stuft) *Informal* A pompous person.

stuff·ing (stuf′ing) *n.* **1.** The material with which anything is stuffed. **2.** A mixture, as of bread or cracker crumbs with meat and seasoning, used in stuffing fowls, etc. **3.** The act or process of one who or that which stuffs.

stuff·y (stuf′ē) *adj.* **stuff·i·er, stuff·i·est 1.** Badly ventilated. **2.** Impeding respiration. **3.** *Informal* Pompous; smugly self-important. **4.** *Informal* Old-fashioned; stodgy; straight-laced. — **stuff′i·ly** *adv.* — **stuff′i·ness** *n.*

stul·ti·fy (stul′tə·fī) *v.t.* **·fied, ·fy·ing 1.** To cause to appear absurd; give an appearance of foolishness to. **2.** To make worthless or ineffectual. [< LL < L *stultus* foolish + *facere* to make] — **stul′ti·fi·ca′tion** *n.* — **stul′ti·fi′er** *n.*

stum·ble (stum′bəl) *v.* **·bled, ·bling** *v.i.* **1.** To miss one's step in walking or running; trip. **2.** To walk or proceed unsteadily. **3.** To speak, read, etc., falteringly. **4.** To happen upon something by chance: with *across, on, upon,* etc. **5.** To err. — *v.t.* **6.** To cause to stumble. — *n.* **1.** The act of stumbling. **2.** A blunder; false step. [Cf. Norw. *stumla* to stumble in the dark] — **stum′bler** *n.* — **stum′bling·ly** *adv.*

stumbling block Any obstacle, hindrance, or impediment, as to the achievement of some end.

stump (stump) *n.* **1.** That portion of the trunk of a tree left standing when the tree is felled. **2.** The part of anything, as of a limb, tooth, pencil, etc., that remains when the main part has been removed; a stub. **3.** *pl. Informal* The legs: chiefly in the phrase **to stir one's stumps. 4.** A place or platform from which a political speech is made. **5.** In cricket, any one of the three posts forming the wicket. **6.** A pencil-like soft leather or rubber bar, with conical ends, used to shade drawings of crayon or charcoal or to apply powdered pigments. **7.** A short, thickset person or animal. **8.** A heavy step; a clump; also, the sound made by such a step. — **to take the stump** To electioneer in a political campaign. — *adj.* **1.** Being or resembling a stump; stumpy. **2.** Of or pertaining to political oratory or campaigning: a *stump* speaker. — *v.t.* **1.** To reduce to a stump. **2.** To remove stumps from (land). **3.** To canvass (a district) by making political speeches: The candidate *stumped* the State. **4.** *Informal* To bring to a halt by real or fancied obstacles; baffle. **5.** To strike against an obstacle; stub, as one's toe. — *v.i.* **6.** To go about on or as on stumps; also, to walk heavily, noisily, and stiffly. **7.** To go about making political speeches. [< MLG] — **stump′er** *n.*

stump·y (stum′pē) *adj.* **stump·i·er, stump·i·est 1.** Full of stumps. **2.** Like a stump; short and thick. — **stump′i·ness** *n.*

stun (stun) *v.t.* **stunned, stun·ning 1.** To render unconscious or incapable of action by a blow, fall, etc. **2.** To astonish; astound. **3.** To daze or overwhelm by loud or explosive noise. — *n.* A stupefying blow, shock, or concussion; also, the condition of being stunned. [< OF < L *ex- thoroughly + tonare* to thunder, crash]

stung (stung) Past tense and past participle of STING.

stunk (stungk) Past participle and alternative past tense of STINK.

stun·ner (stun′ər) *n.* **1.** One who or that which stuns. **2.** *Informal* A person of extraordinary beauty, etc.

stun·ning (stun′ing) *adj.* **1.** Rendering unconscious. **2.** *Informal* Impressively beautiful, etc. — **stun′ning·ly** *adv.*

stunt¹ (stunt) *v.t.* To check the natural development of; dwarf; cramp. — *n.* **1.** A check in growth, progress, or development. **2.** A stunted animal or thing. [OE *stunt* dull, foolish] — **stunt′ed** *adj.* — **stunt′ed·ness** *n.*

stunt² (stunt) *U.S. Informal n.* **1.** A sensational feat, as of bodily skill. **2.** Any thrilling or unusual feat or undertaking. — *v.i.* **1.** To perform stunts. — *v.t.* **2.** To perform stunts with (an airplane, etc.). [? < G *stunde* lesson]

stunt man In motion pictures, a man employed to substitute for an actor in dangerous acts or situations.

stu·pe·fac·tion (stōō′pə·fak′shən, styōō′-) *n.* The act of stupefying or the state of being stupefied.

stu·pe·fy (stōō′pə·fī, styōō′-) *v.t.* **·fied, ·fy·ing 1.** To dull the senses or faculties of; stun. **2.** To amaze; astound. [< F < L < *stupere* to be stunned + *facere* to make] — **stu′pe·fied** *adj.* — **stu′pe·fi′er** *n.*

stu·pen·dous (stōō·pen′dəs, styōō-) *adj.* **1.** Of or characterized by any highly impressive or astonishing feature. **2.** Of prodigious size or bulk. [< L *stupere* to be stunned] — **stu·pen′dous·ly** *adv.* — **stu·pen′dous·ness** *n.*

stu·pid (stōō′pid, styōō′-) *adj.* **1.** Very slow of apprehension or understanding. **2.** Affected with stupor; stupefied. **3.** Marked by, or resulting from, lack of understanding, reason, or wit; senseless. **4.** Tedious; dull. — *n. Informal* A stupid person. [< L < *stupere* to be stunned] — **stu·pid′i·ty** *n.* — **stu′pid·ly** *adv.* — **stu′pid·ness** *n.*

stu·por (stōō′pər, styōō′-) *n.* **1.** A condition in which the senses and faculties are suspended or greatly dulled, as by drugs or liquor. **2.** Mental or moral dullness; gross stupidity. [< L *stupere* to be stunned] — **stu′por·ous** *adj.* — **Syn. 1.** lethargy, torpor.

stur·dy (stûr′dē) *adj.* **·di·er, ·di·est 1.** Possessing rugged health and strength; hardy; vigorous. **2.** Firm and unyielding; resolute: a *sturdy* defense. [< OF *estourdir* to stun, amaze] — **stur′di·ly** *adv.* — **stur′di·ness** *n.*

stur·geon (stûr′jən) *n.* A large, fresh-water and marine fish of northern regions, with coarse, edible flesh. It is valued as a source of isinglass and caviar. [< OF < Med.L < OHG *sturjo*]

Sturm·ab·teil·ung (shtōōrm′äp·tī′lŏŏngk) *n.* *pl.* **·teil·ung·en** A Nazi political militia: also called *Brown Shirts, storm troopers.* [< G, storm detachment]

stut·ter (stut′ər) *v.t. & v.i.* To utter or speak with spasmodic repetition, blocking, and prolongation of sounds, esp. those in initial position in a word. — *n.* The act or habit of stuttering. [Freq. of ME *stutten* to stutter] — **stut′ter·er** *n.* — **stut′ter·ing** *adj. & n.* — **stut′ter·ing·ly** *adv.*

St. Vi·tus's dance (sānt vī′təs·iz) *Pathol.* Chorea. Also **St. Vi′tus′ dance, St. Vi·tus dance** (vī′təs).

sty¹ (stī) *n.* *pl.* **sties 1.** A pen for swine. **2.** Any filthy place of bestiality or debauchery. — *v.t. & v.i.* **stied, sty·ing** To keep or live in a sty or hovel. [ME < OE *sti*]

sty² (stī) *n.* *pl.* **sties** *Pathol.* A small, inflamed swelling of a sebaceous gland on the edge of the eyelid. Also **stye.** [< OE < *stigan* to rise + *ye* eye]

styg·i·an (stij′ē·ən) *adj. Often cap.* **1.** Of or pertaining to the river Styx. **2.** Infernal; dark and gloomy.

style (stīl) *n.* **1.** Manner of expressing thought, in writing or speaking. **2.** A distinctive, characteristic, or suitable mode of expression: His writing lacks *style.* **3.** A particular or characteristic mode of composition, construction, or appearance, as in art, music, etc.: the Gothic *style.* **4.** The manner in which some action or work is performed: The horse ran in fine *style.* **5.** A good or exemplary manner of performing: a team with *style.* **6.** A mode of conduct; a way of living: to live in makeshift *style.* **7.** A fashionable manner or appearance: to live in *style.* **8.** A particular fashion in clothing. **9.** A particular type or fashion suitable for a person. **10.** The conventions of typography, design, usage, punctuation, etc., observed by a given publishing house, printing office, or publication. **11.** The legal or official title or appellation of a person, organization, etc. **12.** A stylus. **13.** The gnomon of a sundial. **14.** *Surg.* A slender probe with a blunt point. **15.** *Bot.* The prolongation of a carpel or ovary, bearing the stigma. For illus. see FLOWER. **16.** A system of arranging the length of the calendar years so as to average that of the true solar year. See OLD STYLE, NEW STYLE under CALENDAR. — *v.* styled, styl·ing *v.t.* **1.** To name; give a title to.   **2.** To make consistent in typography, spelling, punctuation, etc.   **3.** To give form, fashion, or style to.   [< OF < L *stilus* writing instrument] — **styl′er** *n.*

style book A book containing rules of spelling, punctuation, typography, etc., used by printers, editors, etc.

styl·ish (stī′lish) *adj.* Having style or fashionableness in clothes, etc. — **styl′ish·ly** *adv.* — **styl′ish·ness** *n.*

styl·ist (stī′list) *n.* **1.** One who is a master of literary or rhetorical style.   **2.** A designer or adviser of style in clothes, interior decoration, etc. — **sty·lis′tic** *adj.* — **sty·lis′ti·cal·ly** *adv.*

styl·ize (stī′līz) *v.t.* **·ized, ·iz·ing** To make conform to a distinctive mode or style; conventionalize. — **styl′i·za′tion** *n.* — **styl′iz·er** *n.*

stylo- *combining form* **1.** A pillar.   **2.** *Bot.* A style; of or related to a style. Also, before vowels, **styl-**.   [< Gk. *stylos* column, pillar]

sty·lus (stī′ləs) *n.* *pl.* **·lus·es** (-iz) or **·li** (-lī) **1.** An ancient writing instrument, having one end pointed for writing on wax tablets.   **2.** A pointed instrument for marking or engraving.   **3.** The needle of a record player or of a recording instrument. Also called *style*.   [< L] — **sty′lar** *adj.*

sty·mie (stī′mē) *n.* A condition in golf when an opponent's ball lies directly between the player's ball and the hole. — *v.t.* **·mied, ·my·ing** **1.** To block or hinder by or as by a stymie.   **2.** To baffle or perplex. Also spelled *stimy*. Also **sty′my.** [Prob. use of earlier Scot. *styme*, to be unable to see]

styp·tic (stip′tik) *adj.* **1.** Causing contraction of tissues, as blood vessels.   **2.** Stopping hemorrhage or bleeding. Also **styp′ti·cal.** — *n.* A styptic substance or agent.   [< L < Gk. *styphein* to contract] — **styp·tic′i·ty** (stip·tis′ə·tē) *n.*

Styx (stiks) *n.* In Greek mythology, the river of hate, one of the five rivers surrounding Hades.

sua·sion (swā′zhən) *n.* Persuasion: archaic except in the phrase **moral suasion.** [< L *suadere* to persuade] — **sua·sive** (swā′siv), **sua·so·ry** (swā′sər·ē) *adj.*

suave (swäv, swāv) *adj.* Smoothly pleasant and ingratiating in manner; blandly polite; urbane.   [< F < L *suavis* sweet] — **suave′ly** *adv.* — **suave′ness, suav·i·ty** (swä′və·tē) *n.*

sub (sub) *n.* *Informal* Short for any of various words beginning with *sub*-, as: **a** A substitute. **b** A subordinate or subaltern. **c** A submarine.

sub- *prefix* Used to form words meaning: **a** Under; beneath; below: *substratum.* **b** *Anat.* Situated under or beneath: *subcutaneous.* **c** Almost; nearly; slightly; imperfectly: chiefly in scientific terms: *subconical.* **d** Lower in rank or grade; secondary; subordinate: *subaltern, subcontract.* **e** Forming a subdivision: *subsection.* **f** *Chem.* Present (in a compound) in less than normal amount: *subchloride, suboxide.* Also: *suc-* before *c*, as in *succumb;* *suf-* before *f*, as in *suffer;* *sug-* before *g*, as in *suggest;* *sum-* before *m*, as in *summon;* *sup-* before *p*, as in *support;* *sur-* before *r*, as in *surrogate;* *sus-* before *c, p, t*, as in *susceptible, suspect, sustain.* [< L *sub* under]

sub·ac·id (sub·as′id) *adj.* Slightly sour or acid. — **sub′a·cid′i·ty** (-ə·sid′ə·tē) *n.*

sub·al·tern (sub·ôl′tərn) *adj.* **1.** *Brit. Mil.* Ranking below a captain.   **2.** Of inferior rank or position; subordinate. — *n.* **1.** A person of subordinate rank or position.   **2.** *Brit. Mil.* An officer ranking below a captain.   [< LL < L *sub-* under + *alternus* alternate]

sub·ant·arc·tic (sub′ant·ärk′tik, -är′tik) *adj.* Of or pertaining to the region surrounding the Antarctic Circle.

sub·arc·tic (sub·ärk′tik, -är′tik) *adj.* Denoting or pertaining to the region surrounding the Arctic Circle.

sub·a·tom·ic (sub′ə·tom′ik) *adj.* Within the atom: *subatomic* particle.

sub·base·ment (sub′bās′mənt) *n.* An underground story, or any one of several below the first or true basement.

sub·clin·i·cal (sub·klin′i·kəl) *adj.* Having no symptoms apparent in clinical tests, as in the early stages of a disease.

sub·com·mit·tee (sub′kə·mit′ē) *n.* A subordinate committee appointed from the members of the original committee for special work.

sub·con·scious (sub·kon′shəs) *adj.* **1.** Not clearly or wholly conscious.   **2.** *Psychol.* Denoting such phenomena of mental life as are not attended by full consciousness. — *n. Psychol.* That portion of mental activity not directly in the focus of consciousness but sometimes susceptible to recall by the proper stimulus. — **sub·con′scious·ly** *adv.* — **sub·con′scious·ness** *n.*

sub·con·ti·nent (sub·kon′tə·nənt) *n. Geog.* A great land mass forming part of a continent but having considerable geographical independence, as India.

sub·con·tract (*n.* sub·kon′trakt; *v.* sub′kən·trakt′) *n.* A contract subordinate to another contract and assigning part or all of the work to another party. — *v.t. & v.i.* To make a subcontract (for). — **sub′con·trac′tor** (-kən·trak′tər, -kon′·trak-) *n.*

sub·crit·i·cal (sub′krit′i·kəl) *adj. Physics* Of, pertaining to, or containing fissionable material in a quantity not sufficient to start or sustain a chain reaction: *subcritical* mass.

sub·cu·ta·ne·ous (sub′kyoo·tā′nē·əs) *adj.* **1.** Situated, found, or lying beneath the skin.   **2.** Introduced or applied beneath the skin, as an injection.   [< LL < L *sub-* under + *cutis* skin] — **sub′cu·ta·ne·ous·ly** *adv.*

sub·deb (sub′deb′) *n. Informal* **1.** A subdebutante.   **2.** Any girl of this age. — *adj.* In a style suitable for girls of this age.

sub·deb·u·tante (sub′deb·oo·tänt′, -deb′yoo·tant) *n.* A young girl the year before she becomes a debutante.

sub·di·vide (sub′di·vīd′) *v.t. & v.i.* **·vid·ed, ·vid·ing 1.** To divide (a part) resulting from a previous division; divide again.   **2.** To divide (land) into lots for sale or improvement.   [< LL < L *sub-* under + *dividere* to separate]

sub·di·vi·sion (sub′di·vizh′ən) *n.* **1.** Division following upon division.   **2.** A part, as of land, resulting from subdividing.   **3.** An area of land composed of subdivided lots.

sub·dom·i·nant (sub·dom′ə·nənt) *n. Music* The fourth tone or degree of a major or minor scale.

sub·due (sub·doo′, -dyoo′) *v.t.* **·dued, ·du·ing 1.** To gain dominion over: subjugate; vanquish.   **2.** To overcome by training, influence, or persuasion; tame.   **3.** To repress (emotions, impulses, etc.).   **4.** To reduce the intensity of; soften, as a color or sound.   [< OF < L *subducere* to withdraw] — **sub·du′a·ble** *adj.* — **sub·du′al** *n.* — **sub·du′er** *n.*
   — Syn. 1. conquer. **2.** master, control, bridle. **3.** check, restrain. **4.** moderate, temper.

sub·fam·i·ly (sub·fam′ə·lē, -fam′lē) *n. pl.* **·lies 1.** *Biol.* A division of plants or animals next below a family but above the genus.   **2.** *Ling.* A division of languages below a family and above a branch.

sub·ge·nus (sub·jē′nəs) *n. pl.* **·gen·e·ra** (-jen′ər·ə) or, less commonly, **·ge·nus·es** *Biol.* A primary subdivision of a genus including one or more species with common characters. — **sub′ge·ner′ic** (-ji·ner′ik) *adj.*

sub·head (sub′hed′) *n.* A heading or title of a subdivision. Also **sub′head′ing.**

sub·hu·man (sub·hyoo′mən) *adj.* **1.** Less than or imperfectly human.   **2.** Below the level of *Homo sapiens.*

sub·ja·cent (sub·jā′sənt) *adj.* **1.** Situated directly underneath.   **2.** Lower than but not directly below.   [< L < *sub-* under + *jacere* to lie] — **sub·ja′cen·cy** *n.*

sub·ject (*adj.* sub′jikt; *v.* səb·jekt′) *adj.* **1.** Being under the power of another; owing or yielding obedience to sovereign authority.   **2.** Liable to be affected by: with *to*: *subject* to disease.   **3.** Likely to bring about or incur: with *to*: *subject* to severe criticism.   **4.** Dependent on; contingent on: with *to*: a treaty *subject* to ratification. — *n.* **1.** One who is under the governing power of another, as of a ruler or government, esp. of a monarch.   **2.** One who or that which is employed or treated in a specified way, as a body for dissection, or a person used in psychological experiments.   **3.** A topic or main theme, as of a discussion, written work, etc.   **4.** Something represented by or serving as the basic idea for an artistic work.   **5.** A branch of learning or course of study.   **6.** An originating cause; motive.   **7.** *Gram.* The word, phrase, or clause of a sentence about which something is stated or asked in the predicate.   **8.** *Music* A melody on which a composition or a part of it is based.   **9.** *Philos.* The ego or self.   **10.** *Logic* In a proposition, that term about which something is affirmed or denied. See PROPOSITION. — *v.t.* **1.** To bring under dominion or control.   **2.** To cause to undergo some experience or action.   **3.** To offer for consideration or approval.   **4.** To make liable; expose: His inheritance was *subjected* to heavy taxation.   [< OF < L < *sub-* under + *jacere* to throw] — **sub·jec′tion** *n.*

sub·jec·tive (səb·jek′tiv) *adj.* **1.** Relating to, proceeding from, or taking place within an individual's mind, emotions, etc.: opposed to *objective.*   **2.** Originating from or influenced by one's personal interests, prejudices, etc.   **3.** Introspective.   **4.** Of the mind or emotions only; illusory.   **5.** In literature and art, giving prominence to the subject or author as treating of his inner experience and emotion.   **6.** *Gram.* Designating the nominative case. — **sub·jec′tive·ly** *adv.* — **sub·jec′tive·ness, sub·jec·tiv·i·ty** (sub′jek·tiv′ə·tē) *n.*

sub·join (sub·join′) *v.t.* To add at the end; attach; affix.   [< MF < L < *sub-* in addition + *jungere* to join]

sub·join·der (sub·join′dər) *n.* Something subjoined.

sub·ju·gate (sub′joo·gāt) *v.t.* **·gat·ed, ·gat·ing 1.** To bring under dominion; conquer; subdue.   **2.** To make subservient in any way.   [< L < *sub-* under + *jugum* yoke] — **sub′ju·ga′tion** *n.* — **sub′ju·ga′tor** *n.*

sub·junc·tive (səb·jungk′tiv) *Gram. adj.* Of or pertaining to that mood of the finite verb that is used to express a future contingency, a supposition implying the contrary, a mere supposition with indefinite time, or a wish or desire.   ◆ In

---

English the forms of the subjunctive mood are usu. introduced by conjunctions of condition, doubt, contingency, possibility, etc., as *if*, *though*, *lest*. *unless*, *that*, *till*, or *whether*, but verbs in conditional clauses are not always in the subjunctive mood, for the use of these conjunctions with the indicative is very common. — *n*. 1. The subjunctive mood. 2. A verb form or construction in this mood. [See SUBJOIN.]

sub·lease (v. sub·lēs′; n. sub′lēs′) *v.t.* ·leased, ·leas·ing To obtain or let (property) on a sublease. — *n*. A lease of property from a tenant or lessee. — **sub′les·see′** (-les-ē′), **sub·les·sor** (sub′les·ôr, sub′les·ôr′) *n*.

sub·let (sub·let′, sub′let′) *v.t.* ·let, ·let·ting 1. To let (property one holds on a lease) to another. 2. To let (work that one has contracted to do) to a subordinate contractor.

sub·li·mate (sub′lə·māt) *v.* ·mat·ed, ·mat·ing *v.t.* 1. *Chem.* To cause (a substance) to convert from the solid to the gaseous state by the application of heat or pressure, and then to solidify again. 2. To refine; purify. 3. *Psychol.* To convert the energy of (instinctual drives) into acceptable social manifestations. — *v.i.* 4. To undergo sublimation. — *adj.* Sublimated; refined. — *n. Chem.* The product of sublimation, esp., when regarded as purified. [See SUBLIME.] — **sub′li·ma′tion** *n*.

sub·lime (sə·blīm′) *adj.* 1. Characterized by elevation, nobility, etc.; grand; solemn. 2. Inspiring awe, deep emotion, etc.; moving. 3. Being of the highest degree; utmost. — *n*. That which is sublime; height, as of emotion, grandeur, etc.: often with *the*. — *v.* ·limed, ·lim·ing *v.t.* 1. To make sublime; ennoble. 2. *Chem.* To sublimate. — *v.i.* 3. To become sublimated. [< L *sublimis* lofty, prob. < *sub-* up to, under + *limen* lintel] — **sub·lime′ly** *adv.* — **sub·lim′er** *n*. — **sub·lim·i·ty** (sə·blim′ə·tē), **sub·lime′ness** *n*.

sub·lim·i·nal (sub·lim′ə·nəl) *adj. Psychol.* Perceived below the threshold of consciousness, as images, etc., of too low an intensity to produce a clear awareness. [< SUB- + L *limen*, *liminis* threshold] — **sub·lim′i·nal·ly** *adv.*

sub·ma·chine gun (sub′mə·shēn′) A lightweight automatic weapon using pistol ammunition, designed to be fired from the shoulder or hip.

sub·mar·gin·al (sub·mär′jən·əl) *adj.* 1. Below the margin. 2. Of low fertility; unproductive: *submarginal land.*

sub·ma·rine (*adj.* sub′mə·rēn′; *n.* sub′mə·rēn) *adj.* Existing, done, or operating beneath the surface of the sea: a *submarine mine.* — *n*. A ship designed to operate below the surface of the sea. — **sub·mar·i·ner** (sub·mar′ə·nər) *n.*

sub·max·il·lar·y (sub·mak′sə·ler′ē) *Anat. adj.* 1. Of or situated beneath the lower jaw. 2. Of one of the salivary glands on either side of the lower jaw. — *n. pl.* ·lar·ies The lower jaw bone: also **sub·max·il·la** (sub′mak·sil′ə).

sub·merge (səb·mûrj′) *v.* ·merged, ·merg·ing *v.t.* 1. To place under or plunge into water or other liquid. 2. To cover; hide. — *v.i.* 3. To sink or dive beneath the surface of water, etc. Also **sub·merse′** (-mûrs′). [< L < *sub-* under + *mergere* to plunge] — **sub·mer′gi·bil′i·ty** *n.* — **sub·mer′gi·ble** *adj.*

sub·mersed (səb·mûrst′) *adj.* 1. *Bot.* Growing under water. 2. Submerged. [See SUBMERGE.]

sub·mer·sion (səb·mûr′shən, -zhən) *n.* The act of submerging something in a liquid or the state of being submerged. Also **sub·mer′gence** (-jəns).

sub·mis·sion (səb·mish′ən) *n.* 1. The act of submitting or yielding to the power or authority of another. 2. The state or quality of being submissive. 3. The act of presenting something for consideration, approval, decision, etc.

sub·mis·sive (səb·mis′iv) *adj.* Willing or inclined to submit; yielding; obedient; docile. — **sub·mis′sive·ly** *adv.* — **sub·mis′sive·ness** *n.*

sub·mit (səb·mit′) *v.* ·mit·ted, ·mit·ting *v.t.* 1. To place under or yield to the authority, or power of another; surrender. 2. To present for the consideration, decision, or approval of others; refer. 3. To present as one's opinion; suggest. — *v.i.* 4. To give up; surrender. 5. To be obedient, submissive or acquiescent. [< L < *sub-* underneath + *mittere* to send] — **sub·mit′tal** *n.* — **sub·mit′ter** *n.*

sub·nor·mal (sub·nôr′məl) *adj.* 1. Below the normal. 2. *Psychol.* Less than normal in intelligence. — *n.* A subnormal individual. — **sub·nor·mal·i·ty** (sub′nôr·mal′ə·tē) *n.*

sub·or·di·nate (*adj. & n.* sə·bôr′də·nit; *v.* sə·bôr′də·nāt) *adj.* 1. Belonging to an inferior or lower order in a classification; secondary; minor. 2. Subject or subservient to another; inferior. 3. *Gram.* **a** Of or designating a clause connected with and dependent upon another clause and functioning as a subject, object, or modifier. **b** Serving to introduce such a clause. — *n*. One who or that which is subordinate. — *v.t.* ·nat·ed, ·nat·ing 1. To make subordinate; also, to hold as of less importance. 2. To make subject or subservient. [< L < *sub-* under + *ordinare* to order] — **sub·or′di·nate·ly** *adv.* — **sub·or′di·nate·ness** *n.* — **sub·or′di·na′tion** *n.* — **sub·or′di·na·tive** *adj.*

subordinate clause *Gram.* A dependent clause. See under CLAUSE.

sub·orn (sə·bôrn′) *v.t.* 1. To bribe or procure (someone) to commit perjury. 2. To incite to an evil act, esp. a criminal act. [< L < *sub-* secretly + *ornare* to equip] — **sub·or·na·tion** (sub′ôr·nā′shən) *n.* — **sub·orn′er** *n.*

sub·plot (sub′plot′) *n.* A plot subordinate to the principal one in a novel, play, etc.

sub·poe·na (sə·pē′nə, səb-) *n.* A judicial writ requiring a person to appear in court to give testimony. — *v.t.* To notify or summon by writ or subpoena. Also **sub·pe′na**. [< Med.L < L < *sub* under + *poena* penalty]

sub·ro·gate (sub′rō·gāt) *v.t.* ·gat·ed, ·gat·ing 1. To substitute (one thing) for another. 2. To substitute (one person) for another when assigning rights or appointing to an office. [< L < *sub-* in place of + *rogare* to ask]

sub·ro·ga·tion (sub′rō·gā′shən) *n.* The substitution of one person, esp. a creditor, or thing for another.

sub ro·sa (sub rō′zə) *Latin* Confidentially; in secret: literally, under the rose, the emblem of an Egyptian god, mistakenly regarded by the Romans as the god of silence.

sub·scribe (səb·skrīb′) *v.* ·scribed, ·scrib·ing *v.t.* 1. To write, as one's name, at the end of a document; sign. 2. To sign one's name to as an expression of assent, etc.; attest to by signing. 3. To promise, esp., in writing, to pay (a sum of money). — *v.i.* 4. To write one's name at the end of a document. 5. To give sanction, support, or approval; agree. 6. To promise to pay or contribute money. 7. To agree to receive and pay for issues of a newspaper, periodical, etc.: with *to*. [< L < *sub-* underneath + *scribere* to write] — **sub·scrib′er** *n.*

sub·script (sub′skript) *adj.* Written below or lower and to the right or left. — *n.* A subscript character. [See SUBSCRIBE.]

sub·scrip·tion (səb·skrip′shən) *n.* 1. The act of subscribing; signature. 2. Consent, confirmation, or agreement. 3. That which is subscribed; a signed paper or statement. 4. A signature written at the end of a document. 5. The individual or total sum or number subscribed for any purpose. 6. A formal signed undertaking to pay for the receipt of a magazine, book, ticket, etc. — **to take up a subscription** To collect money (for some special cause) from a large number of people. — **sub·scrip′tive** *adj.* — **sub·scrip′tive·ly** *adv.*

sub·se·quent (sub′sə·kwənt) *adj.* Following in time, place, or order, or as a result. [< L < *sub-* next below + *sequi* to follow] — **sub′se·quence, sub′se·quen·cy** *n.* — **sub′se·quent·ly** *adv.* — **sub′se·quent·ness** *n.*

sub·serve (səb·sûrv′) *v.t.* ·served, ·serv·ing 1. To be of use or help in furthering (a process, cause, etc.); serve; promote. 2. To serve as a subordinate to (a person). [< L < *sub-* under + *servire* < *servus* slave]

sub·ser·vi·ent (səb·sûr′vē·ənt) *adj.* 1. Adapted to promote some end or purpose; being of service; useful as a subordinate. 2. Servile; obsequious. — *n.* One who or that which subserves. — **sub·ser′vi·ent·ly** *adv.* — **sub·ser′vi·ence, sub·ser′vi·en·cy** *n.*

sub·side (səb·sīd′) *v.i.* ·sid·ed, ·sid·ing 1. To become less violent or agitated; become calm or quiet; abate. 2. To sink to a lower level. 3. To sink to the bottom; settle. [< L < *sub-* under + *sidere* to settle < *sedere* to sit] — **sub·sid′ence** (səb·sīd′ns, sub′sə·dəns) *n.*

sub·sid·i·ar·y (səb·sid′ē·er′ē) *adj.* 1. Assisting or functioning in a lesser capacity; supplementary; secondary. 2. Of or in the nature of a subsidy; helping by a subsidy. — *n. pl.* ·ar·ies 1. One who or that which furnishes aid or support; an auxiliary. 2. A subsidiary company. [See SUBSIDE.]

subsidiary company A company controlled by another company that owns the greater part of its shares.

sub·si·dize (sub′sə·dīz) *v.t.* ·dized, ·diz·ing 1. To furnish with a subsidy; grant a regular allowance or pecuniary aid to. 2. To obtain the assistance of by a subsidy: often implying bribery. — **sub′si·di·za′tion** *n.* — **sub′si·diz′er** *n.*

sub·si·dy (sub′sə·dē) *n. pl.* ·dies 1. Pecuniary aid directly granted by government to a private commercial enterprise deemed beneficial to the public. 2. Any financial assistance afforded by one individual or government to another. [< AF < L *subsidium* auxiliary forces, aid]
— **Syn.** 1. A government *subsidy* supports a public service, as an airline. The word *subvention* is sometimes applied to a *subsidy* to an artistic enterprise. A *grant* is given by a government or a private institution to be spent for a specified purpose.

sub·sist (səb·sist′) *v.i.* 1. To have existence or reality; continue to exist. 2. To manage to live, often with *on* or *by*: to *subsist* on vegetables. 3. To continue unchanged; abide. 4. To have existence in or by virtue of something; inhere. [< L < *sub-* under + *sistere* to cause to stand]

sub·sis·tence (səb·sis′təns) *n.* 1. The act of subsisting. 2. That on which one subsists; sustenance; livelihood. 3. The state of being subsistent; inherent quality. 4. That which subsists; real being. Also **sub·sis′ten·cy**. — **sub·sis′tent** *adj.*

sub·soil (sub′soil′) *n.* The stratum of earth next beneath the surface soil: also called *undersoil*. — *v.t.* To plow so as to turn up the subsoil. — **sub′soil′er** *n.*

sub·son·ic (sub·son′ik) *adj.* **1.** Designating those sound waves beyond the lower limits of human audibility. **2.** *Aeron.* Having a speed less than that of sound.

sub·stance (sub′stəns) *n.* **1.** The material of which anything consists; also, a material object as contrasted with something intangible. **2.** Any type of matter or a specific chemical composition. **3.** Density; body. **4.** A substantial quality; solidity. **5.** The essential part of anything said or written; the gist. **6.** Material wealth; property. [< OF < L < *sub-* under + *stare* to stand]

sub·stan·dard (sub′stan′dərd) *adj.* **1.** Below the standard. **2.** Lower than the established rate or authorized requirements. **3.** *Ling.* Nonstandard.

sub·stan·tial (səb·stan′shəl) *adj.* **1.** Solid; strong; firm. **2.** Of real worth and importance; of considerable value. **3.** Considerable and real: *substantial* progress. **4.** Possessed of wealth and influence. **5.** Of or pertaining to substance; material. **6.** Containing or conforming to the essence of a thing; giving the correct idea; fundamental. **7.** Ample and nourishing. — *n.* **1.** That which has substance; a reality. **2.** The more important part. — **sub·stan′ti·al′i·ty** (-shē·al′ə·tē), **sub·stan′tial·ness** *n.* — **sub·stan′tial·ly** *adv.*

sub·stan·ti·ate (səb·stan′shē·āt) *v.t.* **·at·ed, ·at·ing** **1.** To establish, as a position or a truth, by substantial evidence; verify. **2.** To give form to; embody. **3.** To make substantial, existent, or real; give substance to. [See SUBSTANCE.] — **sub·stan′ti·a′tion** *n.* — **sub·stan′ti·a′tive** *adj.*

sub·stan·tive (sub′stən·tiv) *n.* **1.** A noun or anything that functions as a noun, as a verbal form, phrase, or clause. One who or that which is independent. — *adj.* **1.** Capable of being used as a noun. **2.** Expressive of or denoting existence. The verb "to be" is called the *substantive* verb. **3.** Having substance or reality; lasting. **4.** Essential. **5.** Individual. **6.** Independent; self-supporting. **7.** Of considerable amount; substantial. [< OF < LL < L. See SUBSTANCE.] — **sub·stan·ti′val** (-tī′vəl) *adj.* — **sub′stan·tive·ly** *adv.* — **sub′stan·tive·ness** *n.*

sub·sta·tion (sub′stā′shən) *n.* A subsidiary station, a branch post office, etc.

sub·sti·tute (sub′stə·toōt, -tyoōt) *v.* **·tut·ed, ·tut·ing** *v.t.* **1.** To put in the place of another person, constituent, or thing. — *v.i.* **2.** To act as a substitute. — *n.* One who or that which takes the place of or serves in lieu of another. [< L *sub-* in place of + *statuere* to set up]

sub·sti·tu·tion (sub′stə·toō′shən, -tyoō′-) *n.* **1.** The act or process of substituting, or the state of being substituted. **2.** Something substituted. — **sub′sti·tu′tion·al** *adj.* — **sub′sti·tu′tion·al·ly** *adv.*

sub·strate (sub′strāt) *n.* *Biochem.* The material or substance acted upon by an enzyme or ferment.

sub·stra·tum (sub·strā′təm, -strat′əm) *n.* *pl.* **·ta** (-tə) or **·tums** **1.** An underlying stratum or layer, as of earth or rock; also, subsoil. **2.** That which forms the foundation, groundwork, or basis. [< NL < L < *sub-* underneath + *sternere* to strew] — **sub·stra′tive** *adj.*

sub·struc·ture (sub′struk′chər, sub·struk′-) *n.* A structure serving as a foundation of a building, etc.

sub·ten·ant (sub′ten′ənt) *n.* A person who rents or leases from a tenant: also called *undertenant.* — **sub·ten′an·cy** *n.*

sub·tend (sub·tend′) *v.t.* **1.** *Geom.* To extend under or opposite to, as the side of a triangle opposite to an angle. **2.** *Bot.* To enclose in its axil: A leaf *subtends* a bud. [< L < *sub-* underneath + *tendere* to stretch]

subter- *prefix* Under; less than. [< L *subter* below]

sub·ter·fuge (sub′tər·fyooj) *n.* Any stratagem to avoid unpleasantness or difficulty. [< L < *subter-* below, in secret + *fugere* to flee]

sub·ter·ra·ne·an (sub′tə·rā′nē·ən) *adj.* **1.** Situated or occurring below the surface of the earth; underground. **2.** Hidden or secret. Also **sub′ter·ra′ne·al, sub′ter·ra′ne·ous.**

sub·tile (sut′l, sub′til) *adj.* **1.** Delicate or tenuous in form, character, etc.; ethereal. **2.** Penetrating; pervasive. **3.** Subtle; wily. [< OF *subtil*, alter. of *soutil* subtle] — **sub′tile·ly** *adv.* — **sub·til·i·ty** (sub·til′ə·tē), **sub′tile·ness** *n.*

sub·til·ize (sut′l·īz, sub′tə·līz) *v.* **·ized, ·iz·ing** *v.t.* **1.** To make subtle or subtile; refine. **2.** To make acute; sharpen, as the senses. **3.** To argue subtly. — *v.i.* **4.** To make subtle distinctions; use subtlety. — **sub′til·i·za′tion** *n.*

sub·ti·tle (sub′tīt′l) *n.* **1.** A subordinate or explanatory title, as in a book, play, or document. **2.** In motion pictures: **a** A running written translation of original dialogue usu. appearing at the bottom of the screen. **b** A written comment or record of dialogue, as in a silent film.

sub·tle (sut′l) *adj.* **1.** Characterized by cunning, or artifice; crafty. **2.** Keen; discriminating. **3.** Apt; skillful. **4.** Ingenious; clever; refined. **5.** Insidious; secretly active. **6.** Abstruse. **7.** Of delicate texture. [< OF < L *subtilis* orig., closely woven] — **sub′tle·ness** *n.* — **sub′tly** *adv.*

sub·tle·ty (sut′l·tē) *n.* *pl.* **·ties** **1.** The state or quality of being subtle. **2.** Something subtle, as a nice distinction.

sub·ton·ic (sub′ton′ik) *n.* *Music* The tone below the tonic; the seventh tone of a major or minor scale.

sub·tract (səb·trakt′) *v.t. & v.i.* To take away or deduct, as a portion from the whole, or one quantity from another. [< L < *sub-* away + *trahere* to draw] — **sub·tract′er** *n.*

sub·trac·tion (səb·trak′shən) *n.* **1.** The act or process of subtracting; a deducting. **2.** Something deducted. **3.** *Math.* The operation, indicated by the minus sign (−), of finding the difference between two quantities.

sub·tra·hend (sub′trə·hend) *n.* *Math.* The number to be subtracted from another. [See SUBTRACT.]

sub·treas·ur·y (sub′trezh′ər·ē) *n.* *pl.* **·ur·ies** A branch of a treasury.

sub·trop·i·cal (sub′trop′i·kəl) *adj.* **1.** Of, pertaining to, or designating regions adjacent to the Torrid Zone. **2.** Having characteristics intermediate between or common to both Torrid and Temperate Zones. Also **sub·trop′ic.**

sub·trop·ics (sub′trop′iks) *n.pl.* Subtropical regions.

sub·urb (sub′ûrb′) *n.* **1.** A place adjacent to a city, esp., a residential area. **2.** *pl.* Outlying residential districts; outskirts. [< OF < L < *sub-* near to + *urbs, urbis* city]

sub·ur·ban (sə·bûr′bən) *adj.* **1.** Of or pertaining to a suburb. **2.** Dwelling or located in a suburb. — *n.* One who lives in a suburb; suburbanite.

sub·ur·ban·ite (sə·bûr′bən·īt) *n.* A resident of a suburb.

sub·ur·bi·a (sə·bûr′bē·ə) *n.* Suburbs or suburbanites collectively and their social and cultural world.

sub·ven·tion (səb·ven′shən) *n.* **1.** Giving of succor; aid. **2.** A grant, as of money; subsidy. — **Syn.** See SUBSIDY. [< OF < LL < L < *sub-* up from under + *venire* to come] — **sub·ven′tion·ar·y** (-er′ē) *adj.*

sub·ver·sion (səb·vûr′shən, -zhən) *n.* **1.** The act of subverting, or the state of being subverted; a demolition; overthrow. **2.** A cause of ruin. Also **sub·ver′sal** (-səl). [< OF < LL < L. See SUBVERT.]

sub·ver·sive (səb·vûr′siv) *adj.* Tending to subvert or overthrow, as a government. — *n.* One who acts in accordance with subversive principles. — **sub·ver′sive·ly** *adv.*

sub·vert (səb·vûrt′) *v.t.* **1.** To overthrow; destroy utterly. **2.** To undermine the morals, character, or faith of; corrupt. [< OF < L < *sub-* up from under + *vertere* to turn] — **sub·vert′er** *n.* — **sub·vert′i·ble** *adj.* — **Syn.** **1.** uproot, upset, overturn.

sub·way (sub′wā) *n.* **1.** *U.S.* An underground railroad, usu. electrically operated; also, a tunnel for such a railroad. **2.** An underground passage, as for cables, etc.

suc- Assimilated var. of SUB-.

suc·ceed (sək·sēd′) *v.i.* **1.** To accomplish what is attempted or intended; be successful. **2.** To come next in order or sequence; follow; ensue. **3.** To come after another into office, etc.; be the successor: often with *to.* — *v.t.* **4.** To come after; follow. **5.** To be the successor or heir of. [< OF < L *succedere* to follow after] — **suc·ceed′er** *n.*

suc·cess (sək·ses′) *n.* **1.** A favorable or desired outcome of something attempted. **2.** A successful person, enterprise, etc. **3.** Attainment of wealth, etc. [< L. See SUCCEED.]

suc·cess·ful (sək·ses′fəl) *adj.* **1.** Obtaining what one desires or intends. **2.** Having reached a high degree of worldly prosperity. **3.** Terminating in success; resulting favorably. — **suc·cess′ful·ly** *adv.* — **suc·cess′ful·ness** *n.*

suc·ces·sion (sək·sesh′ən) *n.* **1.** The act of following in order, or the state of being successive; a following consecutively. **2.** A series; sequence. **3.** The act or right of legally or officially coming into a predecessor's office, possessions, etc.; also, that which is so acquired. **4.** The order by which an office, etc., changes hands. **5.** Descendants collectively; issue. — **suc·ces′sion·al** *adj.* — **suc·ces′sion·al·ly** *adv.*

suc·ces·sive (sək·ses′iv) *adj.* Following in sequence; consecutive. — **suc·ces′sive·ly** *adv.* — **suc·ces′sive·ness** *n.*

suc·ces·sor (sək·ses′ər) *n.* One who or that which succeeds or comes after; esp., a person who succeeds to a throne, property, or office.

suc·cinct (sək·singkt′) *adj.* Consisting of or characterized by brief and meaningful language; terse; concise. — **Syn.** See TERSE. [< L < *sub-* underneath + *cingere* to gird] — **suc·cinct′ly** *adv.* — **suc·cinct′ness** *n.*

suc·cor (suk′ər) *n.* **1.** Help or relief rendered in danger, difficulty, or distress. **2.** One who or that which affords relief. — *v.t.* To go to the aid of; help; rescue. Also *Brit.* **suc′cour.** [< OF < Med.L < L < *sub-* up from under + *currere* to run] — **suc′cor·a·ble** *adj.* — **suc′cor·er** *n.*

suc·co·tash (suk′ə·tash) *n.* A dish of corn kernels and beans, usu. lima beans, boiled together. [< Algonquian (Narraganset) *misickquatash* ear of corn]

Suc·coth (soōk′ōth, -ōs, -əs) See SUKKOTH.

suc·cu·bus (suk′yə·bəs) *n.* *pl.* **·bus·es** or **·bi** (bī) **1.** In folklore, a female demon that has sexual intercourse with sleeping men. Compare INCUBUS. **2.** Any evil spirit. [< Med.L < L < *sub-* underneath + *cubare* to lie]

suc·cu·lent (suk′yə·lənt) *adj.* **1.** Full of juice; juicy. **2.** *Bot.* Juicy; fleshy, as the tissues of certain plants. **3.** Rich or vigorous; a *succulent* theme. [< L < *succus* juice] — **suc′·cu·lence, suc′cu·len·cy** *n.* — **suc′cu·lent·ly** *adv.*

suc·cumb (sə·kum′) *v.i.* **1.** To give way; yield, as to force or persuasion. **2.** To die. [< OF < L < *sub-* underneath + *cumbere* to lie]

such (such) *adj.* **1.** Of that kind; of the same or like kind: often with *as* or *that* completing a comparison: *Such* wit as this is rare. **2.** Being the same as what has been mentioned or indicated: *Such* was the king's command. **3.** Being the same in quality: Let the truthful continue *such.* **4.** Being the same as something understood by the speaker or the hearer, or purposely left indefinite: the chief of *such* a clan. **5.** So extreme, unpleasant, or the like: We have come to *such* a pass. — **as such 1.** As being what is indicated or implied: An executive, *as such*, must take responsibility. **2.** In or by itself: Clothes, *as such*, do not make the man. — **such as 1.** For example. **2.** Of a particular kind or degree: The outcome of the trial was *such as* might be expected. — *pron.* **1.** Such a person or thing, or such persons or things: The friend of *such* as are in trouble. **2.** The same; the aforesaid: I bring good tidings, for *such* the general sent. — *adv. Informal* So: *such* awful manners. ◆ *Such* and *such a* are widely used in informal contexts to intensify the adjective or noun they precede: He was *such a* kind man; He had *such* wisdom. [OE *swelc, swilc, swylc*]

such and such Being a condition, person, thing, or time, not specifically named.

such·like (such′līk′) *adj.* Of a like or similar kind. — *pron.* Persons or things of that kind.

suck (suk) *v.t.* **1.** To draw into the mouth by means of a partial vacuum created by action of the lips and tongue. **2.** To draw in or take up in a manner resembling this; absorb. **3.** To draw liquid or nourishment from with the mouth. **4.** To take into and hold in the mouth. **5.** To consume by licking, or by holding in the mouth: to *suck* candy. **6.** To bring to a specified state or condition by sucking: He *sucked* the lemon dry. — *v.i.* **7.** To draw in liquid, air, etc., by suction. **8.** To suckle. **9.** To draw in air instead of water, as a defective pump does. **10.** To make the sound of sucking. — **to suck in** *Slang* To take advantage of. — *n.* **1.** The act of sucking; suction. **2.** That which is sucked or comes by sucking. **3.** A slight draft or drink. [OE *sūcan*]

suck·er (suk′ər) *n.* **1.** One who or that which sucks. **2.** A North American fresh-water fish, having the mouth usu. protractile with thick and fleshy lips adapted for sucking in food. **3.** *Zool.* An organ by which an animal adheres to other bodies by suction. **4.** *U.S. Slang* One who is easily deceived; a foolish or gullible person. **5.** A lollipop. **6.** *Bot.* A shoot or sprout arising from the root near or remote from the trunk of certain trees. — *v.t.* **1.** To strip of suckers or shoots. — *v.i.* **2.** To form or send out suckers or shoots. [< SUCK]

suck·le (suk′əl) *v.* **·led, ·ling** *v.t.* **1.** To allow or cause to take nourishment from the breast by sucking; nurse. **2.** To bring up; nourish. — *v.i.* **3.** To take nourishment at the breast: also *suck.* [ME *sucklen*, prob. back formation < SUCKLING] — **suck′ler** *n.*

suck·ling (suk′ling) *n.* **1.** An unweaned mammal. **2.** An infant. [ME < *soken* to suck + *-ling* -ling[1]]

su·crose (soo′krōs) *n. Biochem.* A crystalline disaccharide, $C_{12}H_{22}O_{11}$, forming the greater part of the sugar as obtained from the sugar cane, maple, beet, etc. Also called *saccharose.* [< F *sucre* sugar + *-ose* -ose[2]]

suc·tion (suk′shən) *n.* **1.** The act or process of sucking. **2.** The production of a partial vacuum in a space connected with a liquid or gas under pressure. **3.** The tendency of a fluid to occupy all or part of a vaccuum contiguous with it. [< OF < L *sugere* to suck]

suction pump A pump operating by suction, consisting of a piston working in a cylinder, both equipped with valves.

suc·to·ri·al (suk·tôr′ē·əl, -tō′rē·əl) *adj.* **1.** Adapted for sucking or for adhesion. **2.** *Zool.* Having organs for sucking.

Su·da·nese (soo′də·nēz′, -nēs′) *adj.* Of or pertaining to the Sudan or its people. — *n. pl.* **·nese** A native or inhabitant of the Sudan.

sud·den (sud′n) *adj.* **1.** Happening quickly and without warning. **2.** Hurriedly or quickly contrived, used, or done; hasty. **3.** Come upon unexpectedly; causing surprise. **4.** Quick-tempered; precipitate. — **all of a sudden** Without warning; suddenly. [< AF < OF < L *sub-* secretly + *ire* to go] — **sud′den·ly** *adv.* — **sud′den·ness** *n.*

sudden infant death syndrome See CRIB DEATH.

su·dor·if·ic (soo′də·rif′ik) *Med. adj.* Causing perspiration. — *n.* A medicine that produces or promotes sweating. [< NL < L *sudor, -oris* sweat + *facere* to make]

suds (sudz) *n.pl.* **1.** Soapy water, or bubbles and froth on its surface. **2.** Foam; lather. **3.** *Slang* Beer. [Prob. < MDu. *sudde, sudse* marsh water] — **suds′y** *adj.*

sue (soo) *v.* **sued, su·ing** *v.t.* **1.** *Law* **a** To institute proceedings against for the recovery of some right or the redress of some wrong. **b** To prosecute (an action). **c** To seek a grant from (a court). **2.** To endeavor to persuade by entreaty; petition — *v.i.* **3.** To institute legal proceedings. **4.** To make entreaty. [< AF *suer*, OF *sivre*, ult. < L *sequi* to follow] — **su′a·ble** *adj.* — **su′er** *n.*

suede (swād) *n.* **1.** A leather having a soft napped finish, usu. on the flesh side. **2.** A woven or knitted fabric finished to resemble this. Also **suede.** [< F *Suède* Sweden, in phrase *gants de Suède* Swedish gloves]

su·et (soo′it) *n.* The fatty tissues about the loins and kidneys of sheep, oxen, etc., used in cookery and to make tallow. [Dim. of AF *sue*, OF *seu* < L *sebum* fat] — **su′et·y** *adj.*

suf- Assimilated var. of SUB-.

suf·fer (suf′ər) *v.i.* **1.** To feel pain or distress. **2.** To be affected injuriously; experience loss or injury. **3.** To undergo punishment; esp., to be put to death. — *v.t.* **4.** To have inflicted on one; sustain, as an injury or loss. **5.** To undergo; pass through, as change. **6.** To bear; endure: to *suffer* more pain. **7.** To allow; permit: Will he *suffer* us to leave? [< AF *suffrir*, OF *sofrir*, ult. < L < *sub-* up from under + *ferre* to bear] — **suf′fer·er** *n.*

suf·fer·a·ble (suf′ər·ə·bəl, suf′rə-) *adj.* Such as can be suffered or endured; tolerable. — **suf′fer·a·bly** *adv.*

suf·fer·ance (suf′ər·əns, suf′rəns) *n.* **1.** Permission given or implied by failure to prohibit; passive consent. **2.** The act or state of suffering. **3.** Power to endure pain or evil. **4.** Patience or endurance under suffering; submissiveness.

suf·fer·ing (suf′ər·ing, suf′ring) *n.* **1.** The state of anguish or pain of one who suffers. **2.** The bearing of pain, injury, or loss. **3.** Pain or distress borne or endured; injury. — *adj.* Inured to pain and loss; submissive. — **suf′fer·ing·ly** *adv.*

— **Syn. 1.** *Suffering* is acute bodily or mental pain. *Distress* may be physical, but is more often mental, referring to any deep anxiety, or the external circumstances that may produce it. *Misery* is extreme *suffering* or abject hopelessness, as from sorrow, great loss, poverty, or the like.

suf·fice (sə·fīs′) *v.* **·ficed, ·fic·ing** *v.i.* **1.** To be sufficient or adequate; meet the requirements or answer the purpose. — *v.t.* **2.** To be satisfactory or adequate for; satisfy. [< OF < L < *sub-* under + *facere* to make] — **suf·fic′er** *n.*

suf·fi·cien·cy (sə·fish′ən·sē) *n. pl.* **·cies 1.** The state of being sufficient. **2.** That which is sufficient; esp., adequate pecuniary means or income. **3.** Full capability or qualification; efficiency. **4.** Conceit; self-sufficiency.

suf·fi·cient (sə·fish′ənt) *adj.* Being all that is needful; adequate; enough. — **Syn.** See ADEQUATE. [See SUFFICE.] — **suf·fi′cient·ly** *adv.*

suf·fix (suf′iks) *n.* **1.** *Gram.* A bound form affixed to the end of a base, stem, or root, functioning as a derivative or inflectional element. Compare COMBINING FORM, PREFIX. **2.** Any added title or the like. — *v.t.* To add as a suffix. [< NL < L < *sub-* underneath + *figere* to fix.] — **suf′fix·al** *adj.* — **suf·fix·ion** (sə·fik′shən) *n.*

suf·fo·cate (suf′ə·kāt) *v.* **·cat·ed, ·cat·ing** *v.t.* **1.** To kill by obstructing respiration in any manner. **2.** To obstruct or oppress, as by an inadequate supply of air. **3.** To stifle; smother, as a fire. — *v.i.* **4.** To become choked or stifled; die from suffocation. [< L < *sub-* under + *fauces* throat] — **suf′fo·cat·ing·ly** *adv.* — **suf′fo·ca′tion** *n.* — **suf′fo·ca′tive** *adj.*

Suf·folk (suf′ək) *n.* **1.** A hardy English breed of working horses, with a heavy body and rather short legs. Also **Suffolk punch.** **2.** A breed of hornless sheep producing mutton of high quality. [after *Suffolk*, England]

suf·frage (suf′rij) *n.* **1.** The right or privilege of voting; franchise. **2.** The act or process of voting. **3.** A vote in support of some measure or candidate. **4.** Approbation; assent. [< L *suffragium* voting tablet, vote]

suf·fra·gette (suf′rə·jet′) *n.* Formerly, a woman who advocated or agitated for female suffrage. — **suf′fra·get′tism** *n.*

suf·fra·gist (suf′rə·gist) *n.* An advocate of some particular form of suffrage, esp. of female suffrage.

suf·fuse (sə·fyooz′) *v.t.* **·fused, ·fus·ing** To overspread, as with a vapor, fluid, or color. [< L < *sub-* underneath, up from under + *fundere* to pour] — **suf·fu·sive** (sə·fyoo′siv) *adj.*

suf·fu·sion (sə·fyoo′zhən) *n.* **1.** The act of suffusing, or the state of being suffused. **2.** That which suffuses, as a blush.

sug- Assimilated var. of SUB-.

sug·ar (shoog′ər) *n.* **1.** *Biochem.* **a** A sweet, crystalline carbohydrate, $C_{12}H_{22}O_{11}$, obtained from the juice of various plants, as from the sugar cane, the sugar beet, and the sugar maple. ◆ Collateral adjective: *saccharine.* **b** Any of a large class of similar carbohydrates, widely distributed in plants and animals. **2.** Flattering or honeyed words. **3.** *Slang* Sweet one: a pet name. — *v.t.* **1.** To sweeten, cover, or coat with sugar. **2.** To make agreeable or less distasteful, as by flattery. — *v.i.* **3.** *Chiefly U.S.* To make maple sugar. **4.** To form or produce sugar; granulate. [< OF < Med.L, ult. < Arabic *sukkar*]

sugar beet A sugar-producing species of beet.

sug·ar·bush (shŏŏg′ər·bŏŏsh′) *n.* A grove of sugar maples.

sugar cane A tall, stout, perennial grass of tropical regions, having a solid jointed stalk constituting a major source of commercial sugar.

sug·ar-coat (shŏŏg′ər·kōt′) *v.t.* **1.** To cover with sugar. **2.** To cause to appear attractive or less distasteful, as with euphemisms or flattery.

sug·ar-cured (shŏŏg′ər·kyŏŏrd′) *adj.* Cured by using sugar in the curing process, as ham and pork.

sug·ared (shŏŏg′ərd) *adj.* **1.** Sweetened with sugar; sugarcoated. **2.** Honeyed; pleasant; sweetened.

sugar loaf 1. A conical mass of hard refined sugar. **2.** A conical hat or hill. — **sug·ar-loaf** (shŏŏg′ər·lōf′) *adj.*

sugar maple A maple of eastern North America, yielding a sap from which maple sugar is made.

sug·ar·plum (shŏŏg′ər·plum′) *n.* A small ball or disk of candy; a bonbon.

sug·ar·y (shŏŏg′ər·ē) *adj.* **1.** Composed of or as of sugar; sweet. **2.** Fond of sugar. **3.** Insincerely or cloyingly sweet. **4.** Consisting of grains; granular. — **sug′ar·i·ness** *n.*

sug·gest (səg·jest′, sə·jest′) *v.t.* **1.** To bring or put forward for consideration, action, or approval; propose. **2.** To bring to mind by association or connection; connote. **3.** To give a hint or indirect indication of; intimate: *The simple house suggested a modest income.* **4.** To act as or provide a motive for; prompt: *these events suggest a sequel.* [< L < *sub-* underneath + *gerere* to carry] — **sug·gest′er** *n.*

sug·gest·i·bil·i·ty (səg·jes′tə·bil′ə·tē, sə-) *n.* **1.** *Psychol.* Responsiveness to suggestion, esp. when heightened or abnormal, as in hypnosis and certain nervous conditions. **2.** Readiness to believe and agree without reflection.

sug·gest·i·ble (səg·jes′tə·bəl, sə-) *adj.* **1.** That can be suggested. **2.** Easily led; yielding: a *suggestible* patient.

sug·ges·tion (səg·jes′chən, sə·jes′-) *n.* **1.** The act of suggesting. **2.** Something suggested. **3.** A hint; insinuation. **4.** The spontaneous calling up of an idea in the mind by a connected idea.

sug·ges·tive (səg·jes′tiv, sə-) *adj.* **1.** Fitted or tending to suggest; stimulating to thought or reflection. **2.** Hinting at or arousing indecent thoughts; suggesting the improper. — **sug·ges′tive·ly** *adv.* — **sug·ges′tive·ness** *n.*

su·i·cide (sōō′ə·sīd) *n.* **1.** The intentional taking of one's own life. **2.** Self-inflicted political, social, or commercial ruin. **3.** One who has taken his own life. — *v.i.* **cid·ed, ·cid·ing** *Informal* To commit suicide. [< NL < L < *sui* of oneself + *caedere* to kill] — **su′i·ci′dal** *adj.*

su·i gen·e·ris (sōō′ī jen′ər·is) *Latin* Forming a kind by itself; unique; literally, of its (his, or her) particular kind.

suit (sōōt) *n.* **1.** A set of garments consisting of a coat and trousers or skirt, made of the same fabric. **2.** A group of things of like kind or pattern composing a series or set. **3.** In cardplaying, one of the four sets of thirteen cards each that make up a pack, as spades, hearts, diamonds, or clubs. **4.** *Law* A proceeding in a court of law or chancery in which a plaintiff demands the recovery of a right or the redress of a wrong. **5.** The courting or courtship of a woman. **6.** *Archaic* Entreaty; petition. — **to follow suit 1.** To play a card identical in suit to the card led. **2.** To do as somebody or something else has done. — *v.t.* **1.** To meet the requirements of, or be appropriate to. **2.** To please; satisfy. **3.** To render appropriate or accordant; accommodate; adapt. — *v.i.* **4.** To be befitting; agree. **5.** To be or prove satisfactory. [< AF < OF *sieute*, ult. < L *sequi* to follow]

suit·a·ble (sōō′tə·bəl) *adj.* Appropriate to a particular occasion, condition, etc.; proper. — **suit′a·bil′i·ty, suit′a·ble·ness** *n.* — **suit′a·bly** *adv.*

suit·case (sōōt′kās′) *n.* A flat, rectangular valise.

suite (swēt) *n.* **1.** A succession of things forming a series and usu. intended to go or be used together; a set. **2.** A number of connected rooms. **3.** A set of furniture designed to be used together in the same room. **4.** A company of attendants or followers; retinue. **5.** *Music* A form of instrumental composition formerly consisting of a series of dances, but now often varying freely in its construction. **6.** *Canadian* In the West, an apartment. [< F < OF *sieute*]

suit·ing (sōō′ting) *n.* Cloth from which to make suits.

suit·or (sōō′tər) *n.* **1.** A man who courts a woman; a wooer. **2.** One who institutes a suit in court. **3.** A petitioner. [< AF < LL < L *secutus*, pp. of *sequi* to follow]

su·ki·ya·ki (sōō′kē·yä′kē, -yak′ē; skē-) *n.* A Japanese dish made of meat in thin slices, vegetables, and condiments. [< Japanese *suki* spade + *yaki* roast]

Suk·koth (sŏŏk′ōth, -ōs, -əs) *n.* The feast of Tabernacles, a Jewish holiday beginning on the 15th of Tishri (late Septem-

ber–October), originally a harvest festival: also spelled *Succoth.* Also **Suk′kos, Suk′kot.** [< Hebrew *sukkōth* tabernacles]

sulfa- *combining form Chem.* Sulfur; related to or containing sulfur: also spelled *sulpha-.* Also, before vowels, **sulf-.** See also SULFO-. [< SULFUR]

sul·fa drug (sul′fə) *Chem.* Any of a large group of organic compounds consisting mainly of substituted sulfanilamide derivatives, some of which are effective in the treatment of certain bacterial infections.

sul·fa·nil·a·mide (sul′fə·nil′ə·mīd, -mid) *n. Chem.* A colorless, crystalline sulfonamide, $C_6H_8N_2O_2S$, used in the treatment of various bacterial infections.

sul·fate (sul′fāt) *n. Chem.* A salt of sulfuric acid. — *v.* **·fat·ed, ·fat·ing** *v.t.* **1.** To form a sulfate of; treat with a sulfate or sulfuric acid. **2.** *Electr.* To form a coating of lead sulfate on (the plate of a secondary battery). — *v.i.* **3.** To become sulfated. Also spelled *sulphate.*

sul·fide (sul′fīd) *n. Chem.* A compound of sulfur with an element or radical: also *sulphide, sulphid.* Also **sul′fid** (-fid).

sul·fite (sul′fīt) *n. Chem.* A salt or ester of sulfurous acid: also spelled *sulphite.* — **sul·fit′ic** (-fit′ik) *adj.*

sulfo- *combining form Chem.* Sulfur; containing sulfur. Also spelled *sulpho-.* [< SULFUR]

sul·fon·a·mide (sul·fon′ə·mīd, sul′fən·am′īd, -id) *n. Chem.* Any of a class of chemotherapeutic compounds containing the univalent radical SO_2N, esp. those derived from sulfanilamide: also spelled *sulphonamide.*

sul·fur (sul′fər) *n.* A pale yellow, nonmetallic element (symbol S), found both free and combined in the native state, and existing in several forms, of which the best known is a crystalline solid that burns with a blue flame and a suffocating odor. It is used for making matches, gunpowder, vulcanized rubber, and medicines. See ELEMENT. Also spelled *sulphur.* [< AF *sulfre,* OF *soufre* < L *sulfur, -uris*]

sulfur dioxide *Chem.* A colorless, water-soluble, suffocating gas, SO_2, formed by the burning of sulfur and used in the manufacture of sulfuric acid.

sul·fu·re·ous (sul·fyŏŏr′ē·əs) *adj.* Of or like sulfur: also spelled *sulphureous.*

sul·fu·ret (sul′fyə·ret) *v.t.* **·fu·ret·ed** or **·ret·ted, ·fu·ret·ing** or **·ret·ting** To sulfurize.

sul·fu·ric (sul·fyŏŏr′ik) *adj. Chem.* Pertaining to or derived from sulfur, esp. in its higher valence: also *sulphuric.*

sulfuric acid *Chem.* A colorless, exceedingly corrosive, oily liquid, H_2SO_4, extensively employed in the manufacture of soda, batteries, guncotton, and in a great variety of industrial operations: formerly called *oil of vitriol, vitriol.*

sul·fur·ize (sul′fyə·rīz, -fə-) *v.t.* **·ized, ·iz·ing 1.** To impregnate, treat with, or subject to the action of sulfur. **2.** To bleach or fumigate with sulfur. Also spelled *sulphurize.* Also **sul′fu·rate** (-rāt). — **sul′fur·i·za′tion** *n.*

sul·fur·ous (sul′fər·əs, sul·fyŏŏr′əs) *adj.* **1.** Of, pertaining to, derived from, or containing sulfur, esp. in its lower valence. **2.** Fiery; hellish. Also spelled *sulphurous.*

sulfurous acid *Chem.* A compound corresponding to the formula H_2SO_3, and known only in solution and by its salts.

sul·fur·y (sul′fər·ē) *adj.* Resembling or suggesting sulfur; sulfureous: also spelled *sulphury.*

sulk (sulk) *v.i.* To be sulky or morose. — *n.* **1.** *Often pl.* A sulky mood or humor. **2.** One who sulks. [Back formation < SULKY]

sulk·y¹ (sul′kē) *adj.* **sulk·i·er, sulk·i·est 1.** Sullenly cross; doggedly or resentfully ill-humored. **2.** Dismal; gloomy: said of weather. [? OE (ā)*solcen,* orig. pp. of (ā)*seolcan* to be weak, slothful] — **sulk′i·ly** *adv.* — **sulk′i·ness** *n.*

sulk·y² (sul′kē) *n. pl.* **sulk·ies** A light, two-wheeled, one-horse vehicle for one person. [< SULKY¹]

sul·len (sul′ən) *adj.* **1.** Obstinately and gloomily ill-humored; morose; glum; melancholy. **2.** Depressing; somber: *sullen* clouds. **3.** Slow; sluggish: a *sullen* tread. **4.** Ill-omened; threatening. [Earlier *solein,* appar. < AF < L *solus* alone] — **sul′len·ly** *adv.* — **sul′len·ness** *n.*

sul·ly (sul′ē) *v.* **·lied, ·ly·ing** *v.t.* **1.** To mar the brightness or purity of; soil; defile; tarnish. — *v.i.* **2.** To become soiled or tarnished. — *n. pl.* **·lies** Anything that tarnishes; a stain; spot; blemish. [< MF *souiller* to soil]

sulpha- Var. of SULFA-.

sul·phur (sul′fər), **sul·phu·re·ous** (sul·fyŏŏr′ē·əs), etc. See SULFUR, etc.

sulpho- Var. of SULFO-.

sul·tan (sul′tən) *n.* The ruler of a Moslem country. — **the Sultan** Formerly, the title of the sovereign of Turkey. [< F < Med.L *sultanus* < Arabic *sultān*]

sul·tan·a (sul·tan′ə, -tä′nə) *n.* **1.** A sultan's wife, daughter, sister, or mother. Also **sul·tan·ess** (sul′tən·is). **2.** A variety of raisin from around Smyrna, Asia Minor.

sul·tan·ate (sul′tən·āt, -it) *n.* The authority or territorial jurisdiction of a sultan. Also **sul′tan·ship.**

---

sul·try (sul′trē) *adj.* **·tri·er**, **·tri·est 1.** Hot, moist, and still; close: said of weather. **2.** Emitting an oppressive heat. **3.** Showing or suggesting passion; sensual. [< obs. *sulter*, var. of SWELTER] **— sul′tri·ly** *adv.* **— sul′tri·ness** *n.*

sum (sum) *n.* **1.** The result obtained by addition. **2.** The entire quantity, number, or substance. **3.** An indefinite amount, as of money. **4.** A problem in arithmetic propounded for solution. **5.** The topmost or highest point; also, the maximum. **6.** The pith or essence; summary. **—** *v.* **summed, sum·ming** *v.t.* **1.** To present in brief; recapitulate succinctly: usu. with *up.* **2.** To add into one total: often with *up.* **3.** To ascertain the sum of (the terms of a series). **—** *v.i.* **4.** To make a summation or recapitulation: usu. with *up.* [< AF, OF < L *summa* (*res*) highest (thing)]

sum- Var. of SUB-.

su·mac (soo′mak, shoo′-) *n.* **1.** Any of various woody, erect, or root-climbing plants, with panicles of small drupaceous fruits, and yielding a resinous or milky juice. **2.** The poison sumac. **3.** The dried and powdered leaves of certain species of sumac, used for tanning and dyeing. Also **su′mach.** [< OF < Med.L < Arabic *summāq*]

Su·mer (soo′mər) A region and ancient country of Mesopotamia, later the southern division of Babylonia.

Su·me·ri·an (soo·mir′ē·ən) *adj.* Of or pertaining to ancient Sumer, its people, or their language. **—** *n.* **1.** One of an ancient non-Semitic people formerly occupying a part of lower Babylonia. **2.** The unclassified language of these people, written in cuneiform characters and preserved on rocks and clay tablets that date from as early as 4000 B.C. Also **Su·mir′i·an.**

sum·mand (sum′and) *n.* That which is added; any of the numbers forming part of a sum.

sum·ma·rize (sum′ə·rīz) *v.t.* **·rized, ·riz·ing** To make a summary of; sum up. Also *Brit.* **sum′ma·rise. — sum′ma·rist** (-ə·rist), **sum′ma·riz′er** *n.* **— sum·ma·ri·za′tion** *n.*

sum·ma·ry (sum′ə·rē) *adj.* **1.** Giving the substance or sum; concise. **2.** Performed without ceremony or delay; informal. **—** *n.* *pl.* **·ries** An abridgment or abstract. [< Med.L < L *summa* sum] **— sum·ma·ri·ly** (sum′ər·ə·lē, *emphatic* sə·mer′ə·lē) *adv.* **— sum′ma·ri·ness** *n.*

sum·ma·tion (sum·ā′shən) *n.* **1.** The act or operation of obtaining a sum; the computation of an aggregate sum; addition. **2.** A speech or a portion of a speech summing up the principal points.

sum·mer (sum′ər) *n.* **1.** The warmest season of the year, occurring between spring and autumn. ◆ Collateral adjective: *estival.* **2.** A year of life, esp. of early or happy life. **3.** A bright and prosperous period. **—** *v.t.* **1.** To keep or care for through the summer. **—** *v.i.* **2.** To pass the summer. **—** *adj.* Of, pertaining to, or occurring in summer. [OE *sumor*] **— sum′mer·ly** *adj. & adv.* **— sum′mer·y** *adj.*

sum·mer·house (sum′ər·hous′) *n.* A rustic structure, as in a garden, for rest or shade.

sum·mer·sault (sum′ər·sôlt) See SOMERSAULT.

summer school A school, college, or university offering courses during the summer vacation period.

sum·mer·time (sum′ər·tīm′) *n.* Summer; the summer season. Also **sum′mer·tide′.**

sum·mit (sum′it) *n.* **1.** The highest part; the top; vertex. **2.** The highest degree; maximum. **3.** The highest level or rank, as of government officials: a meeting at the *summit.* **4.** A meeting or discussion among the highest executives of government, esp. chiefs of state; also, the place where such a meeting is held. **—** *adj.* Of, pertaining to, or characterized by diplomacy at the highest level. [< OF < L *summum*, neut. of *summus* highest] **— sum′mit·al** *adj.*

— Syn. 1. acme, climax, peak, pinnacle, apex, zenith.

sum·mit·ry (sum′ə·trē) *n.* The practice of conducting diplomacy by means of conferences between the highest executives of government, esp. chiefs of state.

sum·mon (sum′ən) *v.t.* **1.** To order to come; send for. **2.** To call together; cause to convene, as a legislative assembly. **3.** To order (a person) to appear in court by a summons. **4.** To call forth or into action; arouse: usu. with *up*: to *summon up courage.* **5.** To bid or call on for a specific act: The garrison was *summoned* to surrender. [< AF, OF < L *subsecretly + monere* to warn]

sum·mon·er (sum′ən·ər) *n.* **1.** One who summons. **2.** *Archaic* An officer who summons persons to appear in court.

sum·mons (sum′ənz) *n.* *pl.* **sum·mon·ses** (sum′ən·zəz) **1.** A call to attend or act at a particular place or time. **2.** *Law* A notice to a defendant summoning him to appear in court; any citation issued to a party to an action to appear before a court or judge at chambers. **3.** A notice to a person requiring him to appear in court as a witness or as a juror. **4.** A military demand to surrender. **5.** Any signal or sound that is a peremptory call.

sum·mum bo·num (sum′əm bō′nəm) *Latin* The chief, supreme, or highest good.

sump (sump) *n.* **1.** A small well, pit, or cavity to receive liquid wastes or serve as a reservoir for lubricating oil. **2.** A cesspool or other reservoir for drainage. [< MDu. *somp*, *sump* marsh]

sump·ter (sump′tər) *n.* A pack animal; beast of burden. [< OF *sometier* driver of a pack horse]

sump·tu·ar·y (sump′choo·er′ē) *adj.* Pertaining to expense; limiting or regulating expenditure, as some laws. [< L < *sumptus* expenditure]

sump·tu·ous (sump′choo·əs) *adj.* **1.** Involving or showing lavish expenditure. **2.** Luxurious; magnificent. [See SUMPTUARY.] **— sump′tu·ous·ly** *adv.* **— sump′tu·ous·ness** *n.*

sun (sun) *n.* **1.** The star that is the center of attraction and the main source of radiant energy in the solar system, with a mean distance from the earth of about 93 million miles, a diameter of 864,000 miles, and a mass 332,000 times that of the earth. ◆ Collateral adjectives: *heliacal, solar.* **2.** Any star, esp. one that is the center of a system revolving around it. **3.** Sunshine. **4.** Anything brilliant and magnificent. **5.** The time of the earth's revolution around the sun; a year. **6.** The daily appearance of the sun; a day; also, the time of its appearance or shining; sunrise. **— a place in the sun 1.** A dominant position in international affairs. **2.** A position in the spotlight; publicity. **—** *v.* **sunned, sun·ning** *v.t.* **1.** To expose to the light or heat of the sun. **2.** To warm or dry (something) in the sun. **—** *v.i.* **3.** To bask in the sun. [OE *sunne*]

Sun may appear as a combining form or as the first element in two-word phrases, with the following meanings:
1. Of the sun: of sunshine:

sun blaze	sunland	sun worship
sun-eclipsing	sun lover	sun worshiper
sun glare	sun-loving	sun-worshiping

2. By or with the sun:

sun-arrayed	sun-browned	sun-heated
sun-bake	sun-cracked	sun-kissed
sun-baked	sun-dappled	sunlit
sun-blanched	sun-dried	sun-scorched
sun-blind	sun-dry	sun-scorching
sun-blinded	sun-filled	sun-streaked
sun-blistered	sun-flooded	sun-warmed
sun-brown	sun-gilt	sun-withered

sun bath Exposure of the body to the direct rays of the sun.

sun·bathe (sun′bāth′) *v.i.* **-bathed, -bath·ing** To bask in the sun, esp., as a method of tanning the skin. **— sun′bath′er** *n.* **— sun′bath′ing** *n.*

sun·beam (sun′bēm′) *n.* A ray or beam of the sun; light from the sun in a visible path.

Sun·belt (sun′belt′) *n.* The southern part of the U.S. from Virginia to southern California: also **sun′belt′.**

sun·bon·net (sun′bon′it) *n.* A bonnet of light material with projecting brim and sometimes a cape over the neck.

sun·burn (sun′bûrn′) *n.* Discoloration or inflammation of the skin from exposure to the sun. **—** *v.t. & v.i.* **·burned or ·burnt, ·burn·ing** To affect or be affected with sunburn.

sun·burst (sun′bûrst′) *n.* **1.** A strong burst of sunlight, as through rifted clouds. **2.** A jewelled brooch, etc., with rays shooting forth in all directions from a central disk.

sun·dae (sun′dē, -dā) *n.* A refreshment made of ice cream, crushed fruit, syrup, nuts, etc. [Prob. < SUNDAY]

Sun·day (sun′dē, -dā) *n.* The first day of the week; the Christian Sabbath. [OE < *sunnan* of the sun + *dæg* day]

Sunday school A school in which religious instruction is given on Sunday, esp., to the young; also, the teachers and pupils collectively.

sun deck An exposed surface or platform suitable for sunbathing, as on a ship or building; sun roof.

sun·der (sun′dər) *v.t.* **1.** To break apart; disunite; sever. **—** *v.i.* **2.** To be parted or severed. **—** *n.* Division into parts; separation. **— in sunder** Separate from other parts; apart. [OE *syndrian sundrian*] **— sun′der·ance** *n.*

sun·di·al (sun′dī′əl) *n.* A device that shows the time of day by the shadow of a gnomon thrown on a dial.

SUNDIAL
g Gnomon.

sun·down (sun′doun′) *n.* *Chiefly U.S.* Sunset.

sun·down·er (sun′dou′nər) *n.* *Informal* A tramp.

sun·dries (sun′drēz) *n.pl.* Items or things too small or too numerous to be separately specified. [< SUNDRY]

sun·dry (sun′drē) *adj.* Of an indefinite small number; various; several; miscellaneous. [OE *syndrig* separate]

sun·fish (sun′fish′) *n.* *pl.* **·fish or ·fish·es 1.** Any of various large oceanic fishes having a deep, compressed body truncated in the rear, and tough, leathery flesh. **2.** Any of a family of North American fresh-water fishes.

sun·flow·er (sun′flou′ər) *n.* Any of various tall, stout herbs with large leaves and circular heads of bright yellow flowers.

Sunflower State Nickname of Kansas.

sung (sung) Past participle and occasional past tense of SING.

Sung (soong) *n.* A dynasty in Chinese history, 960 to 1280, noted for its achievements in art and philosophy.

sun·glass (sun′glas′, -gläs′) *n.* **1.** *pl.* Spectacles that protect the eyes from the glare of the sun by their colored lenses. **2.** A burning glass.

sunk (sungk) Past participle and alternative past tense of SINK.

sunk·en (sung′kən) Obsolete past participle of SINK. —*adj.* **1.** Deeply depressed or fallen in; hollow: a *sunken* cheek. **2.** Located beneath the surface of the ground or the water. **3.** At a lower level: *sunken* gardens.

sun lamp A lamp radiating ultraviolet rays, used for therapeutic treatments or to acquire a sun tan.

sun·less (sun′lis) *adj.* **1.** Lacking sun or sunlight; overcast; dark. **2.** Cheerless; gloomy. —**sun′less·ness** *n.*

sun·light (sun′līt) *n.* The light of the sun.

sun·ny (sun′ē) *adj.* ·ni·er, ·ni·est **1.** Filled with the light and warmth of the sun; also, exposed to the sun. **2.** Of or resembling the sun or sunlight. **3.** Bright; genial; cheery: a *sunny* smile. —**sun′ni·ly** *adv.* —**sun′ni·ness** *n.*

sunny side 1. The side, as of a hill, facing the sun. **2.** The cheerful view of any situation, question, etc.

sun parlor A room enclosed in glass and having a sunny exposure. Also **sun porch.**

sun·rise (sun′rīz′) *n.* **1.** The daily first appearance of the sun above the horizon, with the atmospheric phenomena just before and after. **2.** The time at which the sun rises.

sun·set (sun′set′) *n.* **1.** The apparent daily descent of the sun below the horizon. **2.** The time when the sun sets; the early evening. **3.** The colors in the sky at sunset.

sun·shade (sun′shād′) *n.* Something used as a shade or protection from the sun, as a parasol, an awning, etc.

sun·shine (sun′shīn′) *n.* **1.** The shining light of the sun; the direct rays of the sun. **2.** The warmth of the sun's rays. **3.** Brightness; cheerfulness. —**sun′shin·y** *adj.*

Sunshine State Nickname of Florida, New Mexico, and South Dakota.

sun·spot (sun′spot′) *n. Astron.* One of many dark irregular spots appearing periodically on the sun's surface.

sun·stroke (sun′strōk′) *n. Pathol.* A sudden onset of high fever induced by exposure to the sun and often marked by convulsions and coma. —**sun′struck′** (-struk′) *adj.*

sun tan A bronze-colored condition of the skin, produced by exposure to the sun. —**sun′-tanned′** (-tand′) *adj.*

sun·up (sun′up′) *n. Chiefly U.S.* Sunrise.

sup¹ (sup) *v.t. & v.i.* **supped, sup·ping** To take (fluid food) in successive mouthfuls, a little at a time; sip. —*n.* A mouthful or taste of liquid or semiliquid food. [OE *sūpan*]

sup² (sup) *v.* **supped, sup·ping** *v.i.* To eat supper. [< OF *soper, super*]

sup- Var. of SUB-.

su·per¹ (sōō′pər) *n. Informal* A superintendent (def. 2).

su·per² (sōō′pər) *n. Slang* A supernumerary (def. 2).

su·per³ (sōō′pər) *n.* An article of superior size or quality; also, such size or quality. —*adj. Slang* First-rate; superfine. [Short for SUPERIOR]

super- *prefix* **1.** Above in position; over: *superstructure.* **2.** Above or beyond; more than: *supersonic.* **3.** Excessively: *supersaturate.* **4.** Greater than or superior to others of its class: *superhighway.* **5.** Extra; additional: *supertax.* [< L *super- < super* above, beyond]

In the following list of words *super-* denotes excess or superiority, as *supercritical* excessively critical, *superexcellence* superior excellence.

superabhor	superconformity	superextension	superlenient	superreliance
superabominable	superconfusion	superfecundity	superlie	superremuneration
superabsurd	supercongestion	superfeminine	superlogical	superrespectable
superaccession	superconservative	superfervent	superloyal	superresponsible
superaccommodating	supercontrol	superfoliation	superlucky	superrestriction
superaccomplished	supercordial	superfolly	superluxurious	superreward
superaccumulate	supercritic	superformal	supermagnificently	superrighteous
superachievement	supercritical	superformation	supermanhood	superromantic
superacquisition	supercultivated	superformidable	supermarvelous	supersacrifice
superacute	supercurious	superfriendly	supermasculine	supersafe
superadaptable	supercynical	superfructified	supermechanical	supersagacious
superadequate	superdainty	superfulfillment	supermediocre	supersanguine
superadmiration	superdanger	supergaiety	supermental	supersarcastic
superadorn	superdeclamatory	supergallant	supermentality	supersatisfaction
superaffluence	superdeficit	supergenerosity	supermetropolitan	superscholarly
superagency	superdejection	superglorious	supermishap	superscientific
superaggravation	superdelicate	supergoodness	supermodest	supersensitive
superagitation	superdemand	supergovernment	supermoisten	supersensitiveness
superambitious	superdemonic	supergratification	supermorose	supersensuousness
superangelic	superdesirous	supergravitation	supermundane	supersentimental
superappreciation	superdevelopment	superhandsome	supermystery	superserious
superarbitrary	superdevilish	superhearty	supernecessity	supersevere
superarduous	superdevotion	superhero	supernegligent	supersignificant
superarrogant	superdiabolical	superheroic	supernotable	supersimplify
superaspiration	superdifficult	superhistorical	supernumerous	supersmart
superastonish	superdiplomacy	superhypocrite	superobedience	supersolemn
superattachment	superdistribution	superideal	superobese	supersolemnly
superattraction	superdividend	superignorant	superobjectionable	supersolicitation
superattractive	superdonation	superillustrate	superobligation	superspecialize
superbelief	supereconomy	superimpending	superobstinate	superspiritual
superbeloved	supereffective	superimpersonal	superoffensive	superspirituality
superbenefit	supereffluence	superimportant	superofficious	superstimulation
superbenevolent	superelastic	superimprobable	superofficiousness	superstoical
superbenign	superelated	superimproved	superopposition	superstrain
superbias	superelegance	superincentive	superoratorical	superstrenuous
superblessed	supereligible	superinclination	superordinary	superstrict
superblunder	supereloquent	superinclusive	superorganize	superstrong
superbold	superemphasis	superinconsistent	superornamental	superstylish
superbrave	superendorsement	superindependent	superoutput	supersufficient
superbusy	superendow	superindifference	superpatient	supersurprise
supercandid	superenforcement	superindignant	superpatriotic	supersweet
supercapable	superenrollment	superindividualism	superpatriotism	supertension
supercatastrophe	superestablishment	superindividualist	superperfection	superthankful
supercatholic	superesthetic	superindulgence	superpious	superthorough
supercaution	superethical	superindustrious	superplease	supertoleration
superceremonious	superevident	superinference	superpolite	supertragic
superchivalrous	superexacting	superinfinite	superpositive	supertrivial
supercivil	superexalt	superinfirmity	superpraise	superugly
supercivilized	superexaltation	superinfluence	superprecise	superunity
superclassified	superexcellence	superingenious	superpreparation	superurgent
supercolossal	superexcellent	superinitiative	superpressure	supervexation
supercombination	superexcitation	superinjustice	superproduce	supervigilant
supercommendation	superexcited	superinquisitive	superprosperous	supervigorous
supercommercial	superexcitement	superinsistent	superpublicity	supervirulent
supercompetition	superexiguity	superintellectual	superpure	supervital
supercomplex	superexpansion	superintolerable	superpurgation	supervolume
supercomprehension	superexpectation	superjurisdiction	superradical	superwise
supercompression	superexpenditure	superjustification	superrational	superworldly
superconfident	superexpressive	superknowledge	superrefined	superwrought
superconformist	superexquisiteness	superlaborious	superreform	superzealous

su·per·a·ble (sōō′pər·ə·bəl) *adj.* That can be surmounted, overcome, or conquered. [< L < *superare* to overcome]

su·per·a·bun·dant (sōō′pər·ə·bun′dənt) *adj.* More than sufficient; excessive. — **su′per·a·bun′dance** *n.* — **su′per·a·bun′dant·ly** *adv.*

su·per·an·nu·ate (sōō′pər·an′yōō·āt) *v.t.* **·at·ed, ·at·ing** 1. To permit to retire on a pension on account of age or infirmity. 2. To set aside or discard as obsolete or too old. [< Med.L < L < *super* beyond + *annus* year]

su·per·an·nu·at·ed (sōō′pər·an′yōō·ā′tid) *adj.* 1. Retired on account of age, esp. with a pension. 2. Too old to be useful or efficient. 3. Obsolete; outdated.

su·perb (sōō·pûrb′, sə-) *adj.* 1. Having grand, impressive beauty; majestic; imposing. 2. Luxurious; rich and costly; elegant. 3. Very good; supremely fine. [< L *superbus* proud] — **su·perb′ly** *adv.* — **su·perb′ness** *n.*

su·per·car·go (sōō′pər·kär′gō) *n. pl.* **·goes** or **·gos** An agent on board ship in charge of the cargo and its sale and purchase. [< L *super-* over + CARGO]

su·per·charge (*v.* sōō′pər·chärj′; *n.* sōō′pər·chärj′) *v.t.* **·charged, ·charg·ing** 1. To adapt (an engine) to develop more power by fitting with a supercharger. 2. To charge to excess; overload. — *n.* An excess charge.

su·per·charg·er (sōō′pər·chär′jər) *n. Mech.* A compressor for supplying air or combustible mixture to an internal-combustion engine at a pressure greater than that developed by the suction of the pistons alone.

su·per·cil·i·ous (sōō′pər·sil′ē·əs) *adj.* Exhibiting haughty contempt or indifference; arrogant. [< L < *supercilium* eyebrow] — **su′per·cil′i·ous·ly** *adv.* — **su′per·cil′i·ous·ness** *n.*

su·per·con·duc·tiv·i·ty (sōō′pər·kon′duk·tiv′ə·tē) *n. Physics.* The property, exhibited by certain substances, of becoming almost perfect conductors of electricity at temperatures close to absolute zero. — **su′per·con·duc′tive** (-kən·duk′tiv) *adj.* — **su′per·con·duc′tor** *n.*

su·per·e·go (sōō′pər·ē′gō, -eg′ō) *n. Psychoanal.* The part of the psyche that acts to secure the conformity of the ego to parental, social, and moral standards.

su·per·em·i·nent (sōō′pər·em′ə·nənt) *adj.* Excelling or surpassing others; of a superior or remarkable quality. [< L *supereminere* to rise above] — **su′per·em′i·nence** *n.*

su·per·er·o·gate (sōō′pər·er′ə·gāt) *v.i.* **·gat·ed, ·gat·ing** To do more than is required or ordered. [< L < *super-* over and above + *erogare* to pay out] — **su′per·er·o·ga′tion** *n.* — **su′per·e·rog′a·to′ry** (-ə·rog′ə·tôr′ē, -tō′rē) *adj.*

su·per·fi·cial (sōō′pər·fish′əl) *adj.* 1. Of, lying near, or forming the surface; affecting only the surface. 2. Of only the ordinary and the obvious; shallow: a *superficial* writer. 3. Marked by partial knowledge; cursory; hasty; slight: a *superficial* analysis. 4. Not real or genuine: a *superficial* likeness. 5. Square: said of measure. [< L < L *super-* over + *ficies* face] — **su′per·fi′ci·al′i·ty** (-fish′ē·al′ə·tē), **su′·per·fi′cial·ness** *n.* — **su′per·fi′cial·ly** *adv.*

su·per·fine (sōō′pər·fīn′) *adj.* 1. Of surpassing fineness; of the best quality. 2. Overrefined; unduly elaborate.

su·per·flu·id (*n.* sōō′pər·flōō′id; *adj.* sōō′pər·flōō′id) *n. Physics.* Matter, as helium, cooled to within a degree of absolute zero, and characterized by an exceptional heat conductivity, a ready permeation of very dense substances, and the ability to flow upward against gravity. — *adj.* Of or pertaining to such a state.

su·per·flu·i·ty (sōō′pər·flōō′ə·tē) *n. pl.* **·ties** 1. The state of being superfluous. 2. That which is superfluous. 3. Superabundance; plenty. [< OF < L < *super-* over + *fluere* to flow]

su·per·flu·ous (sōō·pûr′flōō·əs) *adj.* 1. Exceeding what is needed; excessively abundant; surplus. 2. Unnecessary; uncalled for; irrelevant: a *superfluous* question. — **su·per′·flu·ous·ly** *adv.* — **su·per′flu·ous·ness** *n.*

su·per·heat (*v.* sōō′pər·hēt′; *n.* sōō′pər·hēt′) *v.t.* 1. To heat to excess; overheat. 2. To raise the temperature of (a gas or vapor not in contact with water) above the saturation point for a given pressure. 3. To heat (a liquid) above the boiling point for a given pressure, but without conversion into vapor. — *n.* The degree to which steam has been superheated, or the heat so imparted. — **su′per·heat′er** *n.*

su·per·het·er·o·dyne (sōō′pər·het′ər·ə·dīn′) *adj. Electronics.* Pertaining to or designating a type of radio reception using heterodyne circuits between stages of amplification. Also **su′per·het′.** — *n.* A superheterodyne receiver. [< SUPER- (SONIC) + HETERODYNE]

su·per·high·way (sōō′pər·hī′wā′) *n.* A highway for high-speed traffic, generally with four or more divided traffic lanes.

su·per·hu·man (sōō′pər·hyōō′mən) *adj.* 1. Above the range of human power or skill; miraculous or divine. 2. Beyond normal human ability or power. — **su′per·hu·man′i·ty** (-hyōō·man′ə·tē) *n.* — **su′per·hu′man·ly** *adv.*

su·per·im·pose (sōō′pər·im·pōz′) *v.t.* **·posed, ·pos·ing** 1. To lay or impose upon something else. 2. To add to something else. — **su′per·im′po·si′tion** (-im′pə·zish′ən) *n.*

su·per·in·duce (sōō′pər·in·dōōs′, -dyōōs′) *v.t.* **·duced, ·duc·ing** To introduce additionally; bring in or cause as an addition. — **su′per·in·duc′tion** (-duk′shən) *n.*

su·per·in·tend (sōō′pər·in·tend′) *v.t.* To have the charge and direction of; manage; supervise. [< LL < *super-* over + *intendere* to aim at] — **su′per·in·tend′ence** *n.*

su·per·in·ten·dent (sōō′pər·in·ten′dənt) *n.* 1. One whose function is to superintend some particular work, office, or undertaking. 2. A person charged with supervising maintenance and repair in an office or apartment building. — *adj.* Of or pertaining to superintendence or a superintendent; superintending. [< LL < *superintendere* to superintend] — **su′per·in·ten′den·cy** *n.*

su·per·i·or (sə·pir′ē·ər, sōō-) *adj.* 1. Surpassing in quantity, quality, or degree; more excellent; preferable. 2. Of great worth or excellence; extraordinary. 3. Of higher grade, rank, or dignity. 4. Too great or dignified to be influenced; serenely indifferent: with *to: superior* to envy. 5. Affecting superiority; supercilious; disdainful. 6. Locally higher; more elevated; upper. 7. *Printing* Set above the line: In C⁴Dⁿ, 4 and n are *superior.* — *n.* 1. One who surpasses another in rank or excellence. 2. The ruler of an ecclesiastical order or house, as a convent, or monastery. [< OF < L < *super* above] — **su·per·i·or·i·ty** (sə·pir′ē·ôr′ə·tē, -or′-, sōō-) *n.* — **su·pe′ri·or·ly** *adv.*

su·per·la·tive (sə·pûr′lə·tiv, sōō-) *adj.* 1. Elevated to the highest degree; of supreme excellence or eminence. 2. *Gram.* Expressing the extreme degree of comparison of adjectives or adverbs. See COMPARISON (def. 3). 3. Excessive. — *n.* 1. That which is superlative. 2. *Gram.* **a** The highest degree of comparison of the adjective or adverb. **b** Any word or phrase in this degree. [< OF < LL < L < *super-* above + *latus,* pp. of *ferre* to carry] — **su·per′la·tive·ly** *adv.* — **su·per′la·tive·ness** *n.*

su·per·man (sōō′pər·man′) *n. pl.* **·men** (-men′) 1. A hypothetical superior being, regarded as the product of evolutionary survival of the fittest. 2. A man possessing superhuman powers. [Trans. of G *übermensch*]

su·per·mar·ket (sōō′pər·mär′kit) *n.* A large store selling food and household supplies and operating on a self-service, cash-and-carry basis. Also **super market.**

su·per·nal (sōō·pûr′nəl) *adj.* 1. Heavenly; celestial. 2. Placed or located above; lofty; overhead; towering. [< OF < L < *super* over] — **su·per′nal·ly** *adv.*

su·per·nat·u·ral (sōō′pər·nach′ər·əl) *adj.* 1. Existing or occurring through some agency beyond the known forces of nature. 2. Believed to be miraculous or caused by the immediate exercise of divine power. 3. Of the miraculous. — *n.* 1. That which is supernatural. 2. The action or intervention of something supernatural: with *the.* [< Med.L < L *super-* above + *natura* (< *nasci* to be born)] — **su′per·nat′u·ral·ly** *adv.* — **su·per·nat′u·ral·ness** *n.*
— **Syn.** (adj.) 1. A *supernatural* event is literally not bound or explainable by known natural laws. *Preternatural* refers to that which is superlative in degree, but not outside the known realm of nature: to display *preternatural* insight into a situation. Anything *miraculous* is so marvellous or extraordinary that it is usually attributed to divine agency.

su·per·nat·u·ral·ism (sōō′pər·nach′ər·əl·iz′əm) *n.* 1. The quality of being supernatural. 2. Belief in the doctrine that a supernatural power guides the natural order. — **su′per·nat′u·ral·ist** *adj. & n.* — **su′per·nat′u·ral·is′tic** *adj.*

su·per·nu·mer·ar·y (sōō′pər·nōō′mə·rer′ē, -nyōō′-) *adj.* 1. Being beyond a fixed or standard number. 2. Beyond a customary or necessary number; superfluous. — *n. pl.* **·ar·ies** 1. A supernumerary person or thing. 2. A stage performer, as in crowd scenes, without any speaking part. [< LL < L < *super* over + *numerus* number]

su·per·pose (sōō′pər·pōz′) *v.t.* **·posed, ·pos·ing** To lay over or upon something else, as one layer upon another. [< F < *super-* over + *poser* to put] — **su′per·pos′a·ble** *adj.* — **su′per·po·si′tion** (-pə·zish′ən) *n.*

su·per·pow·er (sōō′pər·pou′ər) *n.* One of a few great, dominant nations characterized by superior economic or military strength and by large population.

su·per·sat·u·rate (sōō′pər·sach′ōō·rāt) *v.t.* **·rat·ed, ·rat·ing** To saturate (a solution) beyond the point normal under a given temperature. — **su′per·sat′u·ra′tion** *n.*

su·per·scribe (sōō′pər·skrīb′) *v.t.* **·scribed, ·scrib·ing** 1. To write or engrave on the outside or upper part of. 2. To inscribe with a name or address, as a letter. [< LL < L *super-* over + *scribere* to write] — **su′per·scrip′tion** (-skrip′shən) *n.*

su·per·script (sōō′pər·skript′) *adj.* Written above or overhead. — *n.* 1. A superscript character. 2. *Math.* A character written above and to the right or left of a term to indicate a specific operation or characteristic of the term.

su·per·sede (sōō′pər·sēd′) *v.t.* **·sed·ed, ·sed·ing** 1. To take the place of, as by reason of superior worth, right, or appropriateness; replace; supplant. 2. To put something in the place of; set aside; suspend; annul. [< OF < L < *super-*

above, over + *sedere* to sit] — **su'per·sed'er** *n.* — **su'per·se'dure** (-sē'jər), **su'per·ses'sion** (-sesh'ən) *n.*

su·per·son·ic (sōō'pər·son'ik) *adj.* Of or characterized by a speed greater than that of sound.

su·per·son·ics (sōō'pər·son'iks) *n.pl.* (*construed as sing.*) The science that treats of supersonic speed.

su·per·star (sōō'pər·stär') *n.* A public performer, as an actor, singer, or professional athlete, regarded as one of the best or most popular. — **su'per·star'dom** *n.*

su·per·sti·tion (sōō'pər·stish'ən) *n.* 1. A belief founded on irrational feelings, esp. of fear, and marked by a trust in charms, omens, the supernatural, etc.; also, any rite or practice inspired by such belief. 2. Any unreasonable belief. [< OF < L < *super-* over + *stare* to stand still]

su·per·sti·tious (sōō'pər·stish'əs) *adj.* 1. Disposed to believe in superstitions. 2. Of or manifesting superstition. — **su'per·sti'tious·ly** *adv.* — **su'per·sti'tious·ness** *n.*

su·per·struc·ture (sōō'pər·struk'chər) *n.* 1. Any structure or part of a structure considered in relation to its foundation. 2. *Naut.* The parts of a ship's structure, as of a warship, above the main deck.

su·per·tax (sōō'pər·taks') *n.* An extra tax in addition to the normal tax; a surtax.

su·per·vene (sōō'pər·vēn') *v.i.* **·vened, ·ven·ing** 1. To follow closely upon something; come as something extraneous or additional. 2. To take place; happen. [< L < *super-* over and above + *venire* to come] — **su'per·ven'ient** (-vēn'yənt) *adj.* — **su'per·ven'tion** (-ven'shən) *n.*

su·per·vise (sōō'pər·vīz') *v.t.* **·vised, vis·ing** To have charge of directing (employees, an operation, etc.); superintend; oversee. [< Med.L < L *super-* over + *videre* to see]

su·per·vi·sion (sōō'pər·vizh'ən) *n.* 1. The act of supervising; superintendence. 2. The authority to supervise.

su·per·vi·sor (sōō'pər·vī'zər) *n.* 1. One who supervises or oversees; superintendent; inspector; administrative officer. 2. A person supervising teachers of special subjects in a school. — **su'per·vi'sor·ship** *n.* — **su'per·vi'so·ry** *adj.*

su·pine (sōō·pīn') *adj.* 1. Lying on the back, or with the face turned upward. 2. Inactive; indolent; listless. [< L *supinus*] — **su·pine'ly** *adv.* — **su·pine'ness** *n.*

sup·per (sup'ər) *n.* The last meal of the day; the evening meal. [< OF *soper* to sup, dine] — **sup'per·less** *adj.*

sup·plant (sə·plant', -plänt') *v.t.* 1. To take the place of; displace. 2. To take the place of (someone) by scheming, treachery, etc. 3. To replace (one thing) with another; remove; uproot. [< OF < L *supplantare* to trip up < *sub-* up from below + *planta* the sole of the foot]

sup·ple (sup'əl) *adj.* **sup·pler** (sup'lər), **sup·plest** (sup'ləst) 1. Easily bent; flexible; pliant. 2. Yielding to the humor or wishes of others; esp., servilely compliant. 3. Showing adaptability of mind. — *v.t. & v.i.* **·pled, ·pling** To make or become supple. [< OF < L < *sub-* under + stem of *plicare* to fold] — **sup'ple·ly** *adv.* — **sup'ple·ness** *n.*

sup·ple·ment (*v.* sup'lə·ment; *n.* sup'lə·mənt) *v.t.* To make additions to; provide for what is lacking in. — *n.* Something that supplements; esp. an addition to a publication.

sup·ple·men·tal (sup'lə·men'təl) *adj.* Additional.

sup·ple·men·ta·ry (sup'lə·men'tər·ē) *adj.* Functioning as a supplement; supplemental.

supplementary angle *Geom.* Either of two angles whose sum is 180°.

sup·pli·ant (sup'lē·ənt) *adj.* 1. Entreating earnestly and humbly; beseeching. 2. Manifesting entreaty or supplication. — *n.* One who supplicates. [< MF < L. See SUPPLICATE.] — **sup'pli·ant·ly** *adv.* — **sup'pli·ant·ness** *n.*

sup·pli·cant (sup'lə·kənt) *n.* One who supplicates. — *adj.* Entreating humbly; beseeching. [See SUPPLICATE.]

sup·pli·cate (sup'lə·kāt) *v.* **·cat·ed, ·cat·ing** *v.t.* 1. To ask for humbly or by earnest prayer. 2. To beg something of; entreat. — *v.i.* 3. To beg or pray humbly. [< L < *sub-* under + *plicare* to bend, fold] — **sup'pli·ca'tion** *n.* — **sup'pli·ca·to'ry** (-kə·tôr'ē, -tō'rē) *adj.*

sup·ply[1] (sə·plī') *v.* **·plied, ·ply·ing** *v.t.* 1. To give or furnish (something needful or desirable). 2. To furnish with what is needed: to *supply* an army with ammunition. 3. To provide for adequately; satisfy: to *supply* a demand. 4. To make good or compensate for, as a loss or deficiency. 5. To fill (the place of another); also, to fill (an office, etc.) or occupy (a pulpit) as a substitute. — *v.i.* 6. To take the place of another temporarily. — *n.*, *pl.* **·plies** 1. That which is or can be supplied. 2. An amount sufficient for a given use; store or quantity on hand. 3. *Usu. pl.* Accumulated stores reserved for distribution, as for an army. 4. *Econ.* The amount of a commodity offered at a given price or available for meeting a demand. 5. A substitute or temporary incumbent. 6. The act of supplying. [< OF < L < *sub-* up from under + *ple-*, root of *plenus* full]

sup·ply[2] (sup'lē) *adv.* In a supple manner; supplely.

sup·port (sə·pôrt', -pōrt') *v.t.* 1. To bear the weight of. 2. To hold in position. 3. To bear or sustain (weight, etc.). 4. To keep (a person, the mind, etc.) from failing or declining. 5. To serve to uphold or corroborate (a statement, etc.). 6. To provide (a person, institution, etc.) with maintenance. 7. To give approval or assistance to; uphold. 8. To tolerate: I cannot *support* his insolence. 9. To carry on; keep up: to *support* a war. 10. In the theater: **a** To act (a part). **b** To act in a subordinate role to. — *n.* 1. The act of supporting, or the state of being supported. 2. One who or that which supports. 3. Subsistence. [< OF < L < *sub-* up from under + *portare* to carry] — **sup·por'tive** *adj.*

sup·port·a·ble (sə·pôr'tə·bəl, -pōr'-) *adj.* Capable of being supported or endured; bearable; endurable. — **sup·port'a·ble·ness, sup·port'a·bil'i·ty** *n.* — **sup·port'a·bly** *adv.*

sup·port·er (sə·pôr'tər, -pōr'-) *n.* 1. One who or that which supports. 2. An adherent. 3. An elastic or other support for some part of the body. — **Syn.** See ADHERENT.

sup·pose (sə·pōz') *v.* **·posed, ·pos·ing** *v.t.* 1. To think or imagine to oneself as true. 2. To believe or believe probable; think. 3. To assume as true for the sake of argument or illustration: *Suppose* he comes late. 4. To expect or require: used in the passive: He is *supposed* to be on time. 5. To imply as cause or consequence; presuppose. — *v.i.* 6. To conjecture. [< OF < *sup-* under (< L *sub-*) + *poser* to put down] — **sup·pos'a·ble** *adj.* — **sup·pos'a·bly** *adv.* — **sup·pos'er** *n.*

— **Syn.** 1. We *suppose* something to be true in expectation of finding that it is true, or in order to ascertain what follows if it is not true. We *conjecture* or *surmise* when the evidence is admittedly insufficient for certainty: *surmise* suggests slighter grounds for a conclusion than *conjecture*. Also, *conjecture* suggests that the question is one of fact, while *surmise* may refer to questions of interpretation or evaluation.

sup·posed (sə·pōzd', -pō'zid) *adj.* Accepted as genuine or true, often erroneously. — **sup·pos·ed·ly** (sə·pō'zid·lē) *adv.*

sup·po·si·tion (sup'ə·zish'ən) *n.* 1. The act of supposing. 2. That which is supposed. — **Syn.** See HYPOTHESIS. [< Med.L < L < *sub-* under + *ponere* to place] — **sup'po·si'tion·al** *adj.* — **sup'po·si'tion·al·ly** *adv.*

sup·pos·i·to·ry (sə·poz'ə·tôr'ē, -tō'rē) *n. pl.* **·ries** *Med.* A solid, readily fusible, medicated preparation for introduction into the rectum, vagina, or urethra. [< LL < L < *sub-* under + *ponere* to place]

sup·press (sə·pres') *v.t.* 1. To put an end or stop to; quell; crush, as a rebellion. 2. To stop or prohibit the activities of; also, to abolish. 3. To withhold from knowledge or publication, as a book, news, etc. 4. To repress, as a groan or sigh. 5. To check or stop (a hemorrhage, etc.). [< L < *sub-* under + *premere* to press] — **sup·press'er** or **sup·pres'sor** *n.* — **sup·press'i·ble** *adj.* — **sup·pres'sive** *adj.*

sup·pres·sion (sə·presh'ən) *n.* 1. The act of suppressing, or the state of being suppressed. 2. *Psychoanal.* The deliberate exclusion from consciousness and action of an idea, emotion, or desire.

sup·pu·rate (sup'yə·rāt) *v.i.* **·rat·ed, ·rat·ing** To form or generate pus; maturate. [< L < *sub-* under + *pus* pus] — **sup'pu·ra'tion** *n.* — **sup'pu·ra'tive** *adj. & n.*

supra- *prefix* Above; beyond. [< L]

su·pra·re·nal (sōō'prə·rē'nəl) *Anat. adj.* 1. Situated above the kidneys. 2. Of or pertaining to the suprarenal glands. — *n.* A suprarenal gland. [< NL < L *supra-* above + *renes* kidneys]

suprarenal gland *Anat.* An adrenal gland.

su·prem·a·cy (sə·prem'ə·sē, sōō-) *n. pl.* **·cies** 1. The state of being supreme. 2. Supreme power or authority.

su·preme (sə·prēm', sōō-) *adj.* 1. Highest in power or authority. 2. Highest in degree, importance, quality, etc.; utmost: *supreme* devotion. 3. Ultimate; last; final. [< L < *super* above] — **su·preme'ly** *adv.* — **su·preme'ness** *n.*

Supreme Being God.

Supreme Court In the U.S. and in various States, a court of appellate jurisdiction and, in most cases, of last resort.

Supreme Soviet The highest legislative body of the Soviet Union, consisting of two chambers, the **Soviet of the Union** and the **Soviet of Nationalities.**

sur-[1] *prefix* Above; beyond; over: *surcharge; surcoat.* [< OF < L *super* above]

sur-[2] Assimilated var. of SUB-.

su·rah (sōōr'ə) *n.* A soft, usu. twilled fabric of silk or silk and rayon. Also **surah silk.** [after *Surat*, India]

sur·cease (sûr·sēs', sûr'sēs) *Archaic n.* Absolute cessation; end. — *v.t. & v.i.* **·ceased, ·ceas·ing** To cease; end. [< AF < L < *super-* above + *sedere* to sit]

sur·charge (*n.* sûr'chärj; *v.* sûr·chärj') *n.* 1. An excessive burden, load, or charge. 2. An additional or excessive amount charged; overcharge. 3. A new valuation or something additional printed on a postage stamp. — *v.t.*

·charged, ·charg·ing 1. To overcharge. 2. To overload. 3. To fill to excess. 4. To imprint a surcharge on (postage stamps). [< F < *sur-* over + CHARGE] — **sur·charg'er** *n.*

sur·cin·gle (sûr'sing·gəl) *n.* A girth or strap encircling the body of a horse, etc., as for holding a saddle. [< OF < *sur-* over + L *cingulum* belt]

sur·coat (sûr'kōt') *n.* 1. An outer coat. 2. A cloaklike garment worn over armor. [< OF < *sur-* over + *cot* coat]

surd (sûrd) *n.* 1. *Math.* An irrational number, as √2. 2. *Phonet.* A voiceless speech sound. — *adj.* 1. *Math.* Incapable of being expressed in rational numbers; irrational. 2. *Phonet.* Voiceless. [< L *surdus* deaf, silent]

sure (shŏŏr) *adj.* **sur·er, sur·est** 1. Free from doubt; certain; positive. 2. Certain of obtaining, attaining, or retaining something: with *of.* 3. Not liable to change; firm; stable. 4. Bound to happen; inevitable. 5. Not liable to fail or err; infallible. 6. Reliable; trustworthy. 7. *Rare* Secure; safe. — **to be sure** Indeed; certainly. — **to make sure** To make certain; secure. — *adv. Informal* Surely; certainly. [< OF < L *se-* without + *cura* care] — **sure'ness** *n.*

sure-e·nough (shŏŏr'i·nuf') *U.S. Informal adj.* Real; genuine. — *adv.* Really; surely.

sure-foot·ed (shŏŏr'fŏŏt'id) *adj.* 1. Not liable to fall or stumble. 2. Not liable to fail or err.

sure·ly (shŏŏr'lē) *adv.* 1. Certainly. 2. Securely; safely.

sure·ty (shŏŏr'tē, shŏŏr'ə·tē) *n. pl.* **·ties** 1. One who agrees to be responsible for another; esp., one who engages to be responsible for the debt or default of another. 2. A pledge or guarantee to secure against loss, damage, default, etc.; security. 3. That which gives or serves as a basis for security or confidence; a guarantee. 4. The state of being sure. [< OF < L *securus.* See SURE.] — **sure'ty·ship** *n.*

surf (sûrf) *n.* The swell of the sea that breaks upon a shore; also, the foam caused by such a swell. — *v.i.* To engage in surfing. — **surf'er** *n.* [Earlier *suff,* ? var. of SOUGH] — **surf'y** *adj.*

sur·face (sûr'fis) *n.* 1. The exterior part or face of anything. 2. A superficial aspect; outward appearance. 3. That which has length and breadth, but not thickness. — *adj.* 1. Of, pertaining to, or on a surface. 2. Superficial; exterior; apparent. — *v.* **·faced, ·fac·ing** *v.t.* 1. To put a surface on; esp., to make smooth. — *v.i.* 2. To rise to the surface, as a submarine. [< F < *sur-* above + FACE]

sur·face-ac·tive (sûr'fis-ak'tiv) *adj. Chem.* Pertaining to any of a class of substances that have the property of reducing the surface tension of a liquid in which they are dissolved: said esp. of detergents.

surface tension *Physics* That property of a liquid by virtue of which the surface molecules exhibit a strong inward attraction, thus forming an apparent membrane that tends to contract to the minimum area.

sur·fac·tant (sûr·fak'tənt) *n. Chem.* A surface-active agent.

surf·board (sûrf'bôrd', -bōrd') *n.* A long, narrow board used in surfing.

surf·boat (sûrf'bōt') *n.* A boat of extra strength and buoyancy, for launching and landing through surf.

sur·feit (sûr'fit) *v.t.* 1. To feed or supply to fullness or satiety; satiate. — *v.i.* 2. To partake of anything to excess; overindulge. — *n.* 1. Excess in eating or drinking; also, the excessive quantity partaken of. 2. The result of such excess; satiety. 3. Oppressive fullness caused by excess in eating or drinking. [< OF *surfaire* to overdo < *sur-* above + *faire* to make] — **sur'feit·er** *n.*

surf·ing (sûrf'ing) *n.* A water sport in which a person standing on a surfboard is borne by the surf toward the shore. Also **surf·rid·ing** (sûrf'rī'ding).

surf·rid·er (sûrf'rī'dər) *n.* One who engages in surfing.

surge (sûrj) *v.i.* **surged, surg·ing** 1. To rise high and roll onward, as waves; swell or heave. 2. To move or go in a manner suggestive of this. 3. To increase or vary suddenly, as an electric current. — *n.* 1. A large swelling wave; billow; also, such billows collectively. 2. A heaving and rolling motion, as of great waves. 3. *Electr.* A sudden fluctuation of voltage or current due to lightning, switching, etc. [< OF < L *surgere* to rise] — **surg'er** *n.* — **surg'y** *adj.*

sur·geon (sûr'jən) *n.* One who practices surgery, as distinguished from a physician. [See SURGERY.]

Surgeon General *pl.* **Surgeons General** or **Surgeon Generals** The chief officer of the Medical Department in the United States Army or Navy.

surgeon's knot A knot used in tying ligatures, stitching up wounds, etc. For illus. see KNOT.

sur·ger·y (sûr'jər·ē) *n. pl.* **·ger·ies** 1. The branch of medical science that relates to body injuries, deformities, and diseased conditions requiring treatment by operative procedures, with or without instruments. 2. A place where surgical treatment is given, as an operating room. 3. The work of a surgeon. [< OF, ult. < LL < Gk. < *cheir* hand + *ergon* work]

sur·gi·cal (sûr'ji·kəl) *adj.* Of, pertaining to, or used in surgery. — **sur'gi·cal·ly** *adv.*

sur·ly (sûr'lē) *adj.* **sur·li·er, sur·li·est** Characterized by rudeness, ill-humor, or gruffness. [Earlier *sirly* < *sir* a lord + *-ly* like] — **sur'li·ly** (-lə·lē) *adv.* — **sur'li·ness** *n.*

sur·mise (sər·mīz'; *for n., also* sûr'mīz) *v.* **·mised, ·mis·ing** *v.t.* 1. To infer on slight evidence; guess. — *v.i.* 2. To make a conjecture. — *Syn.* See SUPPOSE. — *n.* 1. A conjecture made on slight evidence. 2. The act of surmising. [< OF < *sur-* upon + *mettre* to put < L *mittere* to send]

sur·mount (sər·mount') *v.t.* 1. To overcome (a difficulty, etc.). 2. To mount to the top or cross to the other side of (an obstacle or mountain). 3. To be or lie over or above. 4. To place something on top of. [< OF < Med.L < L *super-* over + *mons* hill, mountain] — **sur·mount'a·ble** *adj.* — **sur·mount'a·ble·ness** *n.* — **sur·mount'er** *n.*

sur·name (sûr'nām'; *for v., also* sûr·nām') *n.* The name of a person's family; the last name of a person: also called *family name.* — *v.t.* **·named, ·nam·ing** To give a surname to; call by a surname. [Alter. of obs. *surnoun* < OF < *sur-* above, beyond + *nom* name < L *nomen*] — **sur'nam·er** *n.*

sur·pass (sər·pas', -päs') *v.t.* 1. To go beyond or past in degree or amount; excel. 2. To go beyond the reach or powers of; transcend. — *Syn.* See EXCEED. [< MF < *sur-* above + PASS] — **sur·pass'a·ble** *adj.*

sur·pass·ing (sər·pas'ing, -päs'-) *adj.* Preeminently excellent; exceeding. — *adv. Poetic* Exceedingly; excellently. — **sur·pass'ing·ly** *adv.* — **sur·pass'ing·ness** *n.*

sur·plice (sûr'plis) *n. Eccl.* A loose white vestment with full sleeves, worn over the cassock by the clergy and choir of some churches. [< AF or OF < Med.L < *super-* over + *pellicia* fur garment]

sur·plus (sûr'plus) *adj.* Being in excess of what is used or needed. — *n.* 1. That which remains over and above what has been used or is required; excess. 2. Assets in excess of liabilities. [< OF < Med.L < *super-* over and above + *plus* more]

sur·prise (sər·prīz') *v.t.* **·prised, ·pris·ing** 1. To cause to feel wonder or astonishment because unusual or unexpected. 2. To come upon suddenly or unexpectedly; take unawares. 3. To attack or capture suddenly and without warning. 4. To lead unawares, as into doing something not intended: with *into.* 5. To elicit in this manner: They *surprised* the truth from him. — *n.* 1. The act of surprising; a coming upon unawares. 2. The state of being surprised; astonishment. 3. That which causes surprise, as a sudden and unexpected event, fact, or gift. — **to take by surprise** 1. To come upon without warning or unexpectedly. 2. To astound or amaze; astonish. [< OF < Med.L < L *super-* over + *prehendere* to take] — **sur·pris'al** *n.* — **sur·pris'er** *n.*

sur·pris·ing (sər·prī'zing) *adj.* Causing surprise or wonder; amazing. — **sur·pris'ing·ly** *adv.* — **sur·pris'ing·ness** *n.*

sur·re·al·ism (sə·rē'əl·iz'əm) *n.* A modern movement in literature and art that attempts to express the workings of the subconscious mind, characterized by the incongruous arrangement and presentation of subject matter. [< F < *sur-* beyond, above + *réalisme* realism] — **sur·re'al·ist** *adj. & n.* — **sur·re'al·is'tic** *adj.* — **sur·re'al·is'ti·cal·ly** *adv.*

sur·ren·der (sə·ren'dər) *v.t.* 1. To yield possession of or power over to another; give up because of compulsion. 2. To give up; abandon, as hope. 3. To relinquish, esp. in favor of another. 4. To give (oneself) over to a passion, influence, etc. — *v.i.* 5. To give oneself up, as to an enemy in warfare. — *n.* The act of surrendering. [< OF < *sur-* over + RENDER]

sur·rep·ti·tious (sûr'əp·tish'əs) *adj.* 1. Accomplished by secret or improper means; clandestine. 2. Acting secretly or by stealth. — *Syn.* See STEALTHY. [< L < *sub-* secretly + *rapere* to snatch] — **sur'rep·ti'tious·ly** *adv.* — **sur'rep·ti'tious·ness** *n.*

sur·rey (sûr'ē) *n.* A light vehicle, having two seats, four wheels, and sometimes a top. [Prob. after *Surrey,* England]

sur·ro·gate (sûr'ə·gāt; *for n., also* sûr'ə·git) *n.* 1. A substitute; deputy. 2. A probate judge. — *v.t.* **·gat·ed, ·gat·ing** 1. To put in the place of another; substitute. 2. To appoint (another) to succeed oneself. [< L < *sub-* in place of another + *rogare* to ask] — **sur'ro·gate·ship** *n.*

sur·round (sə·round') *v.t.* 1. To extend around; be on all sides of; encircle; enclose. 2. To shut in or enclose, as enemy troops, so as to cut off retreat. [< OF < LL < *super-* over + *undare* to rise in waves < *unda* a wave]

sur·round·ing (sə·roun'ding) *n.* 1. *pl.* That which surrounds; environment; conditions of life. 2. The act of one who surrounds. — *adj.* Encompassing; enveloping.

sur·tax (sûr'taks') *n.* An extra tax; esp., a graduated income tax over and above the usual tax, levied on the amount by which net income exceeds a certain sum. — *v.t.* To assess with a surtax. [< F < *sur-* above + TAX]

sur·veil·lance (sər·vā'ləns, -vāl'yəns) *n.* 1. Close watch kept over one, as a suspect. 2. The act of watching, or the state of being watched. [< F < *sur-* over + *veiller* to watch < L *vigilare*] — **sur·veil'lant** *adj. & n.*

sur·vey (sər·vā'; *for n., also* sûr'vā) *v.t.* 1. To look at in its entirety; view in a general way. **2.** To look at carefully and minutely; scrutinize. **3.** To determine accurately the area, contour, or boundaries of (land) by measuring lines and angles according to the principles of geometry and trigonometry. — *v.i.* **4.** To survey land. — *n.* **1.** The operation, act, process, or results of finding the contour, area, boundaries, etc., of a surface. **2.** A general or comprehensive view. **3.** A scrutinizing view; inspection. [< AF < OF < Med.L < *super-* over + *videre* to look]

sur·vey·ing (sər·vā'ing) *n.* **1.** The science and art of determining the area and configuration of portions of the surface of the earth and representing them on maps. **2.** The act of one who surveys.

sur·vey·or (sər·vā'ər) *n.* **1.** One who surveys; esp., one who surveys land. **2.** One who examines a thing for the purpose of ascertaining its condition, quality, or character; esp., a customs officer.

surveyor's measure A system of measurement used in surveying and based on the chain as a unit.

sur·viv·al (sər·vī'vəl) *n.* **1.** The act of surviving, or the state of having survived. **2.** One who or that which survives; esp., a custom, belief, etc., persisting in society.

survival of the fittest The principle of natural selection as applied to living organisms, societies, etc.

sur·vive (sər·vīv') *v.* **·vived, ·viv·ing** *v.i.* **1.** To remain alive or in existence. — *v.t.* **2.** To live or exist beyond the death, occurrence, or end of; outlive; outlast. [< AF < OF < LL < *super-* above, beyond + *vivere* to live] — **sur·viv'·ing** *adj.* — **sur·viv'er, sur·vi'vor** *n.*

sus- Assimilated var. of SUB-.

sus·cep·ti·bil·i·ty (sə·sep'tə·bil'ə·tē) *n.* *pl.* **·ties 1.** The state or quality of being susceptible. **2.** The ability to receive or be impressed by deep emotions or strong feelings; sensibility. **3.** *pl.* Sensitive emotions; feelings. **4.** *Physics* The ratio of the magnetization of a material to the magnetic force producing it. — **Syn.** See SENSIBILITY.

sus·cep·ti·ble (sə·sep'tə·bəl) *adj.* **1.** Yielding readily; capable of being influenced, acted on, or determined; open; liable: usu. with *of* or *to.* **2.** Having delicate sensibility; impressionable. [< Med.L < L < *sub-* under + *capere* to take] — **sus·cep'ti·ble·ness** *n.* — **sus·cep'ti·bly** *adv.*

sus·pect (*v.* sə·spekt'; *adj. & n.* sus'pekt) *v.t.* **1.** To think (a person) guilty as specified on little or no evidence. **2.** To have distrust of; doubt. **3.** To have an inkling or suspicion of; think possible. — *v.i.* **4.** To have suspicions. — *adj.* Exciting, open to, or viewed with suspicion; suspected. — *n.* One who is under suspicion, esp. for a crime. [< F < L < *sub-* from under + *specere* to look]

sus·pend (sə·spend') *v.t.* **1.** To bar for a time from a privilege, office, or function as a punishment. **2.** To cause to cease for a time; withhold temporarily. **3.** To hold in a state of indecision; withhold or defer action on: to *suspend* a sentence. **4.** To hang from a support so as to allow free movement. **5.** To sustain in a body of nearly the same specific gravity; keep in suspension, as dust motes in the air. — *v.i.* **6.** To stop for a time. **7.** To fail to meet obligations; stop payment. [< OF < L *sub-* under + *pendere* to hang]

sus·pend·er (sə·spen'dər) *n.* **1.** *pl. U.S.* A pair of straps worn over the shoulders for supporting the trousers. **2.** *Brit.* A garter.

sus·pense (sə·spens') *n.* **1.** The state of being uncertain, undecided, or insecure, usu. accompanied by anxiety, apprehension, etc. **2.** An uncertain or doubtful situation. [< OF < Med.L < L *suspendere.* See SUSPEND.]

sus·pen·sion (sə·spen'shən) *n.* **1.** The act of suspending, or the state of being suspended. **2.** The state of deferment. **3.** *Physics* A uniform dispersion of small particles in a medium, either by mechanical agitation or by molecular forces. **4.** Cessation of payments in business. **5.** Any device on or from which something is suspended. **6.** *Mech.* A system of flexible members, as springs in a vehicle, intended to insulate the chassis and body against road shocks. **7.** *Music* The prolongation of a chord tone into the succeeding chord, where it forms a momentary dissonance; also, the tone so prolonged. **8.** The act of debarring from an office or its privileges.

suspension bridge A bridge in which the roadway is hung from cables anchored over towers and without intervening support from below.

sus·pen·sive (sə·spen'siv) *adj.* **1.** Tending to suspend or keep in suspense. **2.** Of or character-

SUSPENSION BRIDGE
(Brooklyn Bridge, New York)

ized by suspense. **3.** Having the power of suspending operation: a *suspensive* veto. — **sus·pen'sive·ly** *adv.* — **sus·pen'sive·ness** *n.*

sus·pen·so·ry (sə·spen'sər·ē) *adj.* Suspending; sustaining; delaying. — *n.* *pl.* **·ries** A truss, bandage, or supporter.

sus·pi·cion (sə·spish'ən) *n.* **1.** The act of suspecting, or the state of one who suspects; the imagining of something wrong without proof or clear evidence. **2.** *Informal* The least particle, as of a flavor. — *v.t.* *Dial.* To suspect: [< OF < Med.L < L < *sub-* from under + *specere* to look] — **sus·pi'cion·al** *adj.*
— **Syn.** (noun) **1.** distrust, dubiety, skepticism. See DOUBT. **2.** soupçon, dash, touch, tinge, shade.

sus·pi·cious (sə·spish'əs) *adj.* **1.** Inclined to suspect; distrustful. **2.** Apt to arouse suspicion. **3.** Indicating suspicion. — **sus·pi'cious·ly** *adv.* — **sus·pi'cious·ness** *n.*

sus·tain (sə·stān') *v.t.* **1.** To keep from sinking or falling; uphold; support. **2.** To endure without yielding; withstand. **3.** To undergo or suffer, as loss or injury. **4.** To keep up the courage, resolution, or spirits of; comfort. **5.** To keep up or maintain; keep in effect or being. **6.** To maintain by providing with food, drink, etc. **7.** To uphold or support as being true or just. **8.** To corroborate; confirm. [< OF < L < *sub-* up from under + *tenere* to hold] — **sus·tain'a·ble** *adj.* — **sus·tain'er** *n.* — **sus·tain'ment** *n.*

sustaining program (sə·stā'ning) A radio or television program that has no commercial sponsor but is paid for by the network or station.

sus·te·nance (sus'tə·nəns) *n.* **1.** The act of sustaining, or the state of being sustained; esp., maintenance of life. **2.** That which sustains; esp., that which supports life; food. **3.** Means of support; livelihood. [See SUSTAIN.]

sut·ler (sut'lər) *n.* A peddler who sells goods and food to an army. [< Du. *soetelen* to perform mean duties]

sut·tee (su·tē', sut'ē) *n.* Formerly, the sacrifice of a Hindu widow on the funeral pyre of her husband; also, the widow so immolated. [< Hind. *satī* < Skt., a faithful wife] — **sut·tee'ism** *n.*

su·ture (soō'chər) *n.* **1.** The junction of two contiguous surfaces or edges along a line by or as by sewing. **2.** *Anat.* The interlocking of two bones at their edges, as in the skull. **3.** *Surg.* **a** The operation of uniting the edges of a cut or wound by or as by stitching. **b** The thread, silver wire, or other material used in this operation. — *v.t.* **·tured, ·tur·ing** To unite by means of sutures; sew together. [< MF < L *suere* to sew] — **su'tur·al** *adj.* — **su'tur·al·ly** *adv.*

su·ze·rain (soō'zə·rin, -rān) *n.* **1.** Formerly, a feudal lord. **2.** A nation having paramount control over a locally autonomous region. [< F *sus* above < L *sursum* upwards; on analogy with *souverain* sovereign] — **su'ze·rain·ty** *n.*

svelte (svelt) *adj.* Slender; slim; willowy. [< F < Ital. < L *ex-* out + *vellere* to pluck]

swab (swob) *n.* **1.** A small stick having a wad of cotton wound about one or both ends, used for cleansing the mouth of a sick person, applying medicines, etc.; also, a specimen of mucus, etc., taken with such a stick. **2.** A mop for cleaning decks, floors, etc. **3.** A cylindrical brush for cleaning firearms. **4.** *Slang* An awkward fellow; lout. — *v.t.* **swabbed, swab·bing** To clean, apply, medicate, etc., with or as with a swab. [? < MDu. *swabbe*] — **swab'ber** *n.*

swad·dle (swod'l) *v.t.* **·dled, ·dling** To wrap with a bandage; esp., to wrap (an infant) with a long strip of linen or flannel; swathe. — *n.* A band used for swaddling. [OE *swathian* to swathe]

swaddling clothes Bands or strips of linen or other cloth wound around a newborn infant. Also **swaddling bands, swaddling clouts.**

swag (swag) *n.* **1.** *Slang* Property obtained by robbery or theft; plunder; booty. **2.** In Australia, a bundle or pack of personal belongings. [Prob. < Scand.]

swage (swāj) *n.* A tool or form, often one of a pair, for shaping metal by hammering or pressure. — *v.t.* **swaged, swag·ing** To shape (metal) with or as with a swage. [< OF *souage*]

swag·ger (swag'ər) *v.i.* **1.** To walk with a proud or insolent air; strut. **2.** To boast; bluster. — *n.* Expression of superiority in words or deeds; braggadocio. [Appar. freq. of SWAG] — **swag'ger·er** *n.* — **swag'ger·ing·ly** *adv.*

swagger stick A short, canelike stick carried by army personnel, esp. officers. Also **swagger cane.**

Swa·hi·li (swä·hē'lē) *n.* *pl.* **·li 1.** A language of East Africa, basically Bantu with an admixture of Arabic elements, used widely as a lingua franca. **2.** A member of a Swahili-speaking group or community. [< Arabic < *sāhil* coast] — **Swa·hi'li·an** *adj.*

swain (swān) *n.* *Poetic* **1.** A youthful rustic. **2.** A young rustic gallant. **3.** A lover. [< ON *sveinn* boy]

swal·low¹ (swol'ō) *v.t.* **1.** To cause (food, etc.) to pass from the mouth into the stomach by means of muscular action of the gullet or esophagus. **2.** To take in or engulf; absorb; envelop: often with *up.* **3.** To put up with or endure. **4.** *Informal* To believe credulously. **5.** To refrain from expressing; suppress. **6.** To take back; recant: to *swallow* one's words. — *v.i.* **7.** To perform the act or the motions of swallowing. — *n.* **1.** The amount swallowed at once. **2.** The gullet; throat. **3.** The act of swallowing. [OE *swelgan* to swallow] — **swal'low·a·ble** *adj.* — **swal'low·er** *n.*

swal·low² (swol'ō) *n.* **1.** Any of various small birds with short bills, long, pointed wings, and forked tails, noted for their swiftness of flight and migratory habits. **2.** A similar bird, as the swift. [OE *swealwe*]

swal·low·tail (swol'ō·tāl') *n.* **1.** The tail of a swallow, or a similar deeply forked tail. **2.** A butterfly having a taillike prolongation on each hind wing. **3.** *Informal* A swallow-tailed coat.

swal·low-tailed coat (swol'ō-tāld') A man's formal dress coat with two long, tapering tails in the back.

swam (swam) Past tense of SWIM.

swa·mi (swä'mē) *n. pl.* **·mis** **1.** Master; lord: used by Hindus as a title of respect. **2.** A Hindu religious teacher. Also **swa'my.** [< Hind. < Skt. *swāmin* lord]

swamp (swomp, swômp) *n.* A tract or region of lowland saturated with water; a wet bog. Also **swamp'land'** (-land'). ◆ Collateral adjective: *paludal.* — *v.t.* **1.** To drench or submerge with water or other liquid. **2.** To overwhelm with difficulties; crush; ruin. **3.** *Naut.* To sink or fill (a vessel) with water. — *v.i.* **4.** To sink in or as in a swamp. — **swamp'ish** *adj.* — **swamp'y** *adj.*

swamp fever Malaria.

swan (swon, swôn) *n.* **1.** A large, long-necked, aquatic bird, noted for its brilliant white plumage and for its grace on the water. **2.** A poet or singer. [OE]

Swan (swon, swôn) *n.* The constellation Cygnus.

swan dive A dive performed with head tilted back and arms extended until near the water.

swang (swang) Dialectal past tense of SWING.

swank (swangk) *adj. Slang* Ostentatiously fashionable; pretentious. Also **swank'y.** — *n. Slang* **1.** Behavior, speech, etc., that is pretentious and overly stylish. **2.** Swagger; bluster. — *v.i.* To act in a pretentious or swaggering manner; show off. [< dial. E. Appar. akin to MLG *swank* flexible] — **swank'i·ly** *adv.* — **swank'i·ness** *n.*

swan's-down (swonz'doun', swônz'-) *n.* **1.** The down of a swan, used for trimming, powder puffs, etc. **2.** A soft woolen cloth resembling down. Also **swans'down'.**

swan song A last or dying work, as of a poet or composer: from the fable that the swan sings only before dying.

swap (swop) *Informal v.t. & v.i.* **swapped, swap·ping** To trade (one thing for another). — *n.* An exchange or trade. Also spelled *swop.* [ME *swappen* to strike (a bargain)]

sward (swôrd) *n.* Land thickly covered with grass; turf: also called *swarth.* — *v.t. & v.i.* To cover or become covered with sward. [OE *sweard* skin]

swarm¹ (swôrm) *n.* **1.** A large number or body of insects or small living things of any kind. **2.** A hive of bees; also, a large number of bees leaving the parent stock at one time, to take up new lodgings, accompanied by a queen. **3.** A crowd or throng of persons, animals, or things. — **Syn.** See FLOCK. — *v.i.* **1.** To leave the hive in a swarm: said of bees. **2.** To come together, move, or occur in great numbers. **3.** To teem: with *with.* — *v.t.* **4.** To fill with a swarm or crowd; throng. [OE *swearm*] — **swarm'er** *n.*

swarm² (swôrm) *v.t. & v.i.* To climb (a tree, etc.) by clasping it with the arms and legs. [Prob. akin to SWARM¹.]

swart (swôrt) *adj. Dial.* or *Poetic* Swarthy. Also *swarth.* [OE *sweart*] — **swart'ness** *n.*

swarth¹ (swôrth) *n. Dial.* Sward. [OE *swearth*]

swarth² (swôrth) *adj.* Swart; swarthy. [? Var. of SWART]

swarth·y (swôr'thē) *adj.* **swarth·i·er, swarth·i·est** Having a dark hue; of dark or sunburned complexion; tawny: also *swart, swarth.* Also **swart'y.** [Var. of obs. *swarty* < SWART] — **swarth'i·ly** *adv.* — **swarth'i·ness, swarth'ness** *n.*

swash (swosh, swôsh) *v.i.* **1.** To move or wash noisily, as waves; splash. **2.** To swagger. — *v.t.* **3.** To splash (water, etc.). **4.** To splash or dash water, etc., upon or against. — *n.* **1.** The splash of a liquid. **2.** A narrow channel through which tides flow. **3.** A swaggerer or his behavior. [Imit.]

swash·buck·ler (swosh'buk'lər, swôsh'-) *n.* A swaggering or boasting soldier. [< SWASH + BUCKLER] — **swash'·buck'ler·ing** — **swash'buck'ling** *adj. & n.*

swas·ti·ka (swos'ti·kə) *n.* **1.** A primitive religious ornament or symbol, consisting of a Greek cross with the ends of the arms bent at right angles. **2.** The emblem of the Nazis. [< Skt. *svastika* < *svasti* well-being, fortune]

swat (swot) *v.t.* **swat·ted, swat·ting** To hit with a sharp blow. — *n.* A smart blow. Also spelled *swot.* [Var. of SQUAT, in dial. sense of "squash"] — **swat'ter** *n.*

swatch (swoch) *n.* A strip, as of cloth, esp. one cut off for a sample. [< dial. E (Northern), a cloth tally]

swath (swoth, swôth) *n.* **1.** A row or line of cut grass, grain, etc. **2.** The space or width of grass, grain, etc., cut by any of various mowing devices. **3.** A narrow belt or track; strip. Also called *swathe.* — **to cut a wide swath** To make a fine impression or display. [OE *swæth* a track]

swathe¹ (swāth) *v.t.* **swathed, swath·ing** **1.** To bind or wrap, as in bandages. **2.** To envelop; surround. — *n.* A bandage for swathing. [OE *swathian*] — **swath'er** *n.*

swathe² (swāth) *n.* A swath.

sway (swā) *v.i.* **1.** To swing from side to side or to and fro; oscillate. **2.** To bend or incline to one side; lean; veer. **3.** To tend in opinion, sympathy, etc. **4.** To have influence or control. — *v.t.* **5.** To cause to swing, bend, or incline. **6.** To influence (a person, opinion, etc.). **7.** To cause to swerve, as from a course of action. — *n.* **1.** Power exercised in governing; dominion; control. **2.** The act of swaying; a sweeping, swinging, or turning from side to side. **3.** Overpowering force or influence. [Prob. fusion of ON *sveigja* to bend and LG *swajen* to be moved to and fro by the wind]

sway·back (swā'bak') *n.* A hollow or unnaturally sagging condition of the back, as in a horse. — **sway'-backed'** *adj.*

swear (swâr) *v.* **swore** (*Obs.* **sware**), **sworn, swear·ing** *v.i.* **1.** To make a solemn affirmation with an appeal to God, some deity, etc., as in attestation of truth or proof of good intentions. **2.** To utter a solemn promise. **3.** To use profanity; curse. **4.** *Law* To give testimony under oath. — *v.t.* **5.** To affirm or assert solemnly by invoking sacred beings or things. **6.** To vow. **7.** To declare or affirm upon oath. **8.** To take or utter (an oath). **9.** To administer a legal oath to. — **to swear by 1.** To appeal to by oath. **2.** To have complete confidence in. — **to swear in** To administer a legal oath to. — **to swear off** *Informal* To promise to renounce or give up: to *swear off* drink. — **to swear out** To obtain (a warrant for arrest) by making a statement or charge under oath. [OE *swerian*] — **swear'er** *n.*

swear·word (swâr'wûrd') *n.* A word used in cursing.

sweat (swet) *v.* **sweat** or **sweat·ed, sweat·ing** *v.i.* **1.** To exude or excrete sensible moisture from the pores of the skin; perspire. **2.** To exude moisture in drops; ooze. **3.** To gather and condense moisture in drops, as on the outer surface of a glass. **4.** To pass through pores or interstices in drops. **5.** To ferment, as tobacco leaves. **6.** *Informal* To work hard; toil; drudge. **7.** *Informal* To suffer: You will *sweat* for that! — *v.t.* **8.** To exude (moisture) from the pores. **9.** To gather or condense drops of (moisture). **10.** To soak or stain with perspiration. **11.** To cause to sweat. **12.** To cause to work hard. **13.** *Informal* To force (employees) to work for low wages and under unfavorable conditions. **14.** *Slang* To extort money from. **15.** To heat (solder, etc.) until it melts. **16.** To join, as metal objects, by applying heat. **17.** *Metall.* To heat so as to extract an element that is easily fusible. **18.** *Slang* To subject to torture or rigorous interrogation for the purpose of extracting information. — **to sweat (something) out** *U.S. Slang* To wait through anxiously and helplessly. — *n.* **1.** The act or state of sweating. **2.** That which is excreted from the sweat glands; perspiration. **3.** Any gathering in minute drops of moisture on a surface. **4.** *Archaic* Hard labor; drudgery. **5.** *Informal* Fuming impatience; worry; hurry. — **no sweat** *U.S. Slang* No difficulty whatever. [OE < *swāt* sweat] — **sweat'i·ly** *adv.* — **sweat'i·ness** *n.* — **sweat'y** *adj.*

sweat·band (swet'band') *n.* A band, usu. of leather, inside the crown of a hat to protect it from sweat.

sweat·box (swet'boks') *n.* **1.** A device for sweating such products as hides and dried fruits. **2.** A narrow cell or box where an unruly prisoner is confined.

sweat·er (swet'ər) *n.* **1.** A knitted garment in the form of a jersey or jacket with or without sleeves. **2.** One who or that which sweats.

sweat gland *Anat.* One of the convoluted tubules that secrete sweat, found in subcutaneous tissue.

sweat shirt A collarless pullover, sometimes lined with fleece, used by athletes.

sweat·shop (swet'shop') *n.* A place where work is done for insufficient wages and for long hours.

Swede (swēd) *n.* A native or inhabitant of Sweden, or a person of Swedish descent.

Swe·den·bor·gi·an·ism (swē'dən·bôr'jē·ən·iz'əm) *n.* The system of philosophy or the theology developed by **Emanuel Swe·den·borg** (swēd'n·bôrg), 1688–1772, Swedish mystic theologian and philosopher. — **Swe·den·bor·gi·an** (swēd'·n·bôr'jē·ən) *adj. & n.*

Swed·ish (swē'dish) *adj.* Pertaining to Sweden, the Swedes, or their language. — *n.* **1.** The North Germanic language of Sweden. **2.** The inhabitants of Sweden collectively.

sweep (swēp) *v.* **swept, sweep·ing** *v.t.* **1.** To collect, remove, or clear away with a broom, brush, etc. **2.** To clear or clean with or as with a broom or brush: to *sweep* a floor. **3.** To touch or brush: Her dress *swept* the ground. **4.** To pass over or through swiftly, as in searching: His eyes *swept* the sky. **5.** To cause to move with an even, continuous action: He *swept* the cape over her shoulders. **6.** To move, carry, bring, etc., with strong or continuous force: The flood *swept* the bridge away. **7.** To move over or through with strong or steady force: The gale *swept* the bay. **8.** To drag the bottom of (a body of water, etc.). —*v.i.* **9.** To clean or brush a floor or other surface with a broom, etc. **10.** To move or go strongly and evenly, esp. with speed: The train *swept* by. **11.** To walk with or as with trailing garments: She *swept* into the room. **12.** To trail, as a skirt. **13.** To extend with a long reach or curve: The road *sweeps* along the lake shore. —*n.* **1.** The act or result of sweeping. **2.** A long stroke or movement: a *sweep* of the hand. **3.** The act of clearing out or getting rid of, as a removal from office or place. **4.** A turning of the eye or of optical instruments over the field of vision. **5.** A great victory or success, as in an election. **6.** The range, area, or compass reached by sweeping, as extent of stroke, range of vision, etc. **7.** A curve or bend, as of a scythe blade, etc. **8.** *Brit.* A chimney sweep. **9.** A long, heavy oar. **10.** A well sweep. **11.** *pl.* Sweepings, as of a place where precious metals are worked. **12.** *Informal* Sweepstakes. [ME *swopen* to brush away] — **sweep′er** *n.* — **sweep′y** *adj.*

sweep·back (swēp′bak′) *n. Aeron.* The backward inclination of the leading edge of an airplane wing.

sweep·ing (swē′ping) *adj.* **1.** Carrying off or clearing away with a driving movement. **2.** Carrying all before it; covering a wide area; comprehensive. **3.** General and thoroughgoing. —*n.* **1.** The action of one who or that which sweeps. **2.** *pl.* Things swept up; refuse. — **sweep′ing·ly** *adv.* — **sweep′ing·ness** *n.*

sweep·stakes (swēp′stāks′) *n. pl.* **·stakes** **1.** A gambling arrangement by which all the sums staked may be won by one or by a few of the betters, as in a horse race. **2.** A race or contest using this arrangement; also, the prize or prizes. Also **sweep′stake′.**

sweet (swēt) *adj.* **1.** Having an agreeable flavor of or like that of sugar. **2.** Containing or due to sugar in some form. **3.** Not fermented or decaying; fresh. **4.** Not salt or salty: *sweet* water. **5.** Gently pleasing to the senses. **6.** Arousing gentle, pleasant emotions. **7.** Having gentle, pleasing, and winning qualities. **8.** *Music Slang* **a** Designating jazz marked by blandness, moderate tempo, etc. **b** Playing or performing such jazz: a *sweet* trumpet. **9.** Sound; rich; productive: said of soil. **10.** Not dry: said of wines. —*n.* **1.** The quality of being sweet; sweetness. **2.** *Chiefly pl.* A confection, preserve, or piece of candy. **3.** A beloved person; darling. **4.** Something agreeable or pleasing; a pleasure. **5.** *Brit.* A dessert. [OE *swēte*] — **sweet′ly** *adv.* — **sweet′ness** *n.*

sweet alyssum A perennial Mediterranean herb having very fragrant white blossoms: also called *madwort.*

sweet bay A highly ornamental tree or shrub with large flowers.

sweet·bread (swēt′bred′) *n.* The pancreas (**stomach sweetbread**) or the thymus gland (**neck sweetbread** or **throat sweetbread**) of a calf or other animal, when used as food. [< SWEET + BREAD, in obs. sense of "a morsel"]

sweet·bri·er (swēt′brī′ər) *n.* A stout prickly rose native to Europe and Asia, with aromatic leaves: Also **sweet′bri′ar.**

sweet clover Any of several cloverlike herbs, used for fodder.

sweet corn Young ears of corn having sweet, milky kernels, boiled or roasted as food: also called *green corn.*

sweet·en (swēt′n) *v.t.* **1.** To make sweet or sweeter. **2.** To make more endurable; lighten. **3.** To make pleasant or gratifying. —*v.i.* **4.** To become sweet or sweeter. — **sweet′en·er** *n.*

sweet·en·ing (swēt′n·ing) *n.* **1.** The act of making sweet. **2.** That which sweetens.

sweet flag A marsh-dwelling plant, having long leaves and an aromatic rootstock: also called *calamus.*

sweet gum **1.** A North American tree, the wood of which is sometimes used to imitate mahogany. **2.** The balsam or gum yielded by it.

sweet·heart (swēt′härt′) *n.* One who is particularly loved by or as a lover; a lover: often used as a term of endearment.

sweet·ie (swē′tē) *n. U.S. Informal* Darling; dear; honey.

sweet·ish (swē′tish) *adj.* Somewhat or rather sweet. — **sweet′ish·ly** *adv.* — **sweet′ish·ness** *n.*

sweet·meat (swēt′mēt′) *n.* **1.** A confection, preserve, candy, etc. **2.** *pl.* Very sweet candy, cakes, etc.

sweet pea An ornamental annual climber of the bean family cultivated for its varicolored flowers.

sweet pepper A mild variety of capsicum whose unripe green fruit is used as a vegetable.

sweet potato **1.** A perennial tropical vine, with rose-violet or pink flowers and a fleshy tuberous root. **2.** The root itself, eaten as a vegetable. **3.** *U.S. Informal* An ocarina.

sweets (swēts) *n.pl.* **1.** Sweet things. **2.** *Brit.* Candy.

sweet tooth *Informal* A fondness for candy or sweets.

sweet william A perennial species of pink with closely clustered, showy flowers. Also **sweet William.**

swell (swel) *v.* **swelled, swelled** or **swol·len, swell·ing** *v.i.* **1.** To increase in bulk or dimension, as by inflation within; dilate; expand. **2.** To increase in size, amount, degree, etc. **3.** To grow in volume or intensity, as a sound. **4.** To rise in waves or swells, as the sea. **5.** To bulge, as a sail. **6.** To become puffed up with pride. **7.** To grow within one: My anger *swells* at the sight. —*v.t.* **8.** To cause to increase in size or bulk. **9.** To cause to increase in amount, extent, or degree. **10.** To cause to bulge; belly. **11.** To puff with pride. **12.** *Music* To crescendo and diminuendo in immediate succession. —*n.* **1.** The act, process, or effect of swelling; expansion. **2.** The long continuous body of a wave; a billow; also, a rise in the land. **3.** A bulge or protuberance. **4.** *Music* A crescendo and an immediate diminuendo; also, the signs (< >) indicating it. **5.** A device, as on an organ, by which the volume of a tone may be uninterruptedly varied. **6.** *Informal* A person of the ultrafashionable set. —*adj. Informal* **1.** Ultrafashionable; smart. **2.** First-rate; distinctive. [OE *swellan*]

swell·ing (swel′ing) *n.* **1.** The act of expanding, inflating, or augmenting. **2.** *Pathol.* Abnormal enlargement or protuberance of a part of the body. —*adj.* Increasing; bulging.

swel·ter (swel′tər) *v.i.* **1.** To suffer from oppressive heat; perspire from heat. —*v.t.* **2.** To cause to suffer or perspire from heat. —*n. Archaic* A hot, sweltering condition. [OE *sweltan* to die]

swel·ter·ing (swel′tər·ing) *adj.* **1.** Oppressive; overpoweringly hot. **2.** Overcome by or suffering with heat. Also **swel′try** (-trē). — **swel′ter·ing·ly** *adv.*

swept (swept) Past tense and past participle of SWEEP.

swept·back (swept′bak′) *adj. Aeron.* Having the leading edge inclined backward at an angle with the lateral axis of the airplane: said of a wing.

swerve (swûrv) *v.t. & v.i.* **swerved, swerv·ing** To turn or cause to turn aside from a course or purpose; deflect. —*n.* **1.** The act of swerving or turning aside. **2.** That which swerves. [OE *sweorfan* to file or grind away]

swift (swift) *adj.* **1.** Traversing space or performing movements in a brief time; rapid; quick. **2.** Capable of quick motion; fleet; speedy. **3.** Passing rapidly, as time or events; also, unexpected. **4.** Acting with readiness; prompt. —*n.* A bird of swallowlike form possessing extraordinary powers of flight; esp. the **chimney swift.** [OE] — **swift′ly** *adv.* — **swift′ness** *n.*
— **Syn.** (adj.) *Swift* and *fleet* are chiefly applied to moving persons or animals; *swift* suggests ease of motion, and *fleet*, nimbleness: a *swift* bird, a *fleet* horse. *Speedy* may be applied to that which moves or that which progresses: a *speedy* worker, *speedy* action. *Rapid* is applied to progress: *rapid* delivery of mail.

swig (swig) *Informal n.* A deep draft, as of liquor. —*v.t. & v.i.* **swigged, swig·ging** To drink deeply or greedily. [Origin unknown] — **swig′ger** *n.*

swill (swil) *v.t.* **1.** To drink greedily or to excess. **2.** *Brit.* To drench, as with water; rinse; wash. —*v.i.* **3.** To drink to excess; tope. —*n.* **1.** Liquid food for animals; esp., swine; slop. **2.** Any animal or vegetable refuse; garbage. **3.** A deep draft of liquor. [OE *swillan, swilian* to wash]

swim¹ (swim) *v.* **swam, swum, swim·ming** *v.i.* **1.** To propel oneself through water by organized bodily movement. **2.** To be supported on liquid; float. **3.** To move with a smooth or flowing motion, as if swimming. **4.** To be immersed in or covered with liquid; be flooded; overflow. —*v.t.* **5.** To traverse by swimming. **6.** To cause to swim. —*n.* **1.** The action, pastime, or period of swimming. **2.** A gliding, swaying movement. — **in the swim** *Informal* In the current of affairs. [OE *swimman*] — **swim′mer** *n.*

swim² (swim) *v.i.* **1.** To be dizzy; reel; have a giddy sensation. **2.** To seem to reel, whirl, or spin. —*n.* A sudden dizziness or swoon. [OE *swīma* dizziness]

swim bladder The air bladder of a fish.

swim·ming¹ (swim′ing) *n.* The act of one who or that which swims. —*adj.* **1.** Used for swimming. **2.** Having the capacity of swimming; natatorial. **3.** Watery; flooded with tears, as the eyes. [< SWIM¹]

swim·ming² (swim′ing) *adj.* Dizzy. [< SWIM²]

swim·ming·ly (swim′ing·lē) *adv.* Easily, rapidly, and successfully.

swimming pool *U.S.* An indoor or outdoor tank designed for swimming, usu., equipped to cleanse the water.

swim·suit (swim′sōōt′) *n.* A garment designed to be worn while swimming.

swin·dle (swin′dəl) *v.* **·dled, ·dling** *v.t.* **1.** To cheat of money or property by deliberate fraud; defraud. **2.** To obtain by such means. —*v.i.* **3.** To practice fraud or decep-

---

tion for gain. — *n.* **1.** The act of swindling. **2.** Anything that proves to be fraudulent or deceptive, esp., a deal or scheme. [Back formation < SWINDLER]
— **Syn.** (verb) 1. fleece, cozen, bamboozle, hoodwink. — (noun) imposition, imposture.

swin·dler (swind′lər) *n.* One who swindles or deceives. [< G < *schwindeln* to act thoughtlessly, be giddy]

swine (swīn) *n. pl.* **swine** **1.** A domesticated pig. **2.** Any of several related omnivorous mammals having a long mobile snout and cloven hoofs. **3.** A low, greedy, stupid, or vicious person. [OE *swīn*] — **swin′ish** *adj.*

swine·herd (swīn′hûrd′) *n.* A tender of swine.

swing (swing) *v.* **swung** (*Dial.* **swang**), **swung**, **swing·ing** *v.i.* **1.** To move to-and-fro or backward and forward rhythmically, as something suspended; oscillate. **2.** To ride in a swing. **3.** To move with an even, swaying motion. **4.** To turn; pivot. **5.** To be suspended; hang. **6.** *Informal* To be executed by hanging. **7.** *Slang* To be very up-to-date and sophisticated. **8.** *Informal* To sing or play with a compelling, usu. jazzlike rhythm. **9.** *Slang* To be sexually promiscuous. — *v.t.* **10.** To cause to move to and fro or backward and forward. **11.** To cause to move with a sweeping motion, as a sword, ax, etc.; brandish; flourish. **12.** To cause to turn on or as on a pivot. **13.** To lift or hoist. **14.** *Informal* To bring to a successful conclusion; manage successfully. — *n.* **1.** The act, process, or manner of swinging; also, the distance covered. **2.** A free swaying motion. **3.** A seat hanging from ropes or chains on which a person may move to and fro as a pastime. **4.** Free course or scope; full liberty or license. **5.** Compass; sweep. **6.** The rhythm characterizing certain styles of poetry or music. **7.** A sweeping blow or stroke. **8.** The course of a career or period of activity; main current of business. **9.** In jazz: a development after about 1935, characterized by large bands, contrapuntal styles, etc. **10.** *Informal* A trip; tour. [OE *swingan* scourge]

swing·er (swing′ər) *n. Slang* **1.** A lively and up-to-date person. **2.** A person who indulges freely in sex.

swin·gle·tree (swing′gəl·trē′) *n.* A whiffletree.

swing shift *U.S. Informal* An evening work shift, usu. lasting from about 4 p.m. to midnight.

swipe (swīp) *v.t.* **swiped**, **swip·ing** **1.** *Informal* To give a strong blow; strike with a full swing of the arm. **2.** *Slang* To steal; snatch. — *n. Informal* A hard, sweeping stroke.

swirl (swûrl) *v.i.* **1.** To move with a whirling or twisting motion; whirl. **2.** To be dizzy; swim, as the head. — *v.t.* **3.** To cause to move in a whirling or twisting motion. — *n.* **1.** A whirling along, as in an eddy; whirl. **2.** A curl or twist; spiral. [< dial. E (Scottish) *swyrle*] — **swirl′y** *adj.*

swish (swish) *v.i.* **1.** To move through the air with a hissing, whistling sound, as a slender, flexible rod. **2.** To rustle, as silk. — *v.t.* **3.** To cause to swish. **4.** To thrash; flog. — *n.* **1.** A hissing or rustling sound. **2.** A movement producing such a sound. [Imit.]

Swiss (swis) *adj.* Of or pertaining to Switzerland or its inhabitants. — *n. pl.* **Swiss** A native or naturalized inhabitant of Switzerland.

Swiss chard Chard.

Swiss cheese A pale yellow cheese with many large holes, made in, or similar to that made in, Switzerland.

Swiss steak A thick cut of steak floured and braised, often with a sauce of tomatoes and onions.

switch (swich) *n.* **1.** A small flexible rod, etc., used for whipping. **2.** A tress of false hair, used by women in building a coiffure. **3.** A mechanism for shifting a railway train from one track to another. **4.** The act or operation of shifting, or changing. **5.** The end of the tail in certain animals, as a cow. **6.** *Electr.* A device to make or break a circuit, or transfer a current from one conductor to another. — *v.t.* **1.** To whip with or as with a switch. **2.** To move, jerk, or whisk suddenly or sharply. **3.** To turn aside or divert; shift. **4.** To exchange: They *switched* plates. **5.** To shift (a railroad car) to another track by means of a switch. **6.** *Electr.* To connect or disconnect with a switch. — *v.i.* **7.** To turn aside; change; shift. **8.** To be shifted or turned. [Earlier *swits*] — **switch′er** *n.*

switch·back (swich′bak′) *n.* **1.** A railway or road ascending a steep incline in a zigzag pattern. **2.** *Brit.* A roller coaster.

switch·board (swich′bôrd′, -bōrd′) *n.* A panel or arrangement of panels bearing switches for connecting and disconnecting electric circuits, as a telephone exchange.

switch·yard (swich′yärd′) *n.* A railroad yard for the assembling and breaking up of trains.

swiv·el (swiv′əl) *n.* **1.** A coupling device, link, ring, or pivot that permits either half of a mechanism, as a chain, to rotate independently. **2.** A pivoted support on which a gun may be swung. **3.** A cannon that swings on a pivot: also **swivel gun.** — *v.* **swiv·eled** or **·elled**, **swiv·el·ing** or **·el·ling** *v.t.* **1.** To turn on or as on a swivel. **2.** To fit with or secure by a swivel. — *v.i.* **3.** To turn on or as on a swivel. [ME < OE < *swīfan* to revolve]

swivel chair A chair having a seat that turns horizontally on a swivel.

swob (swob), **swob·ber** (swob′ər) See SWAB, etc.

swol·len (swō′lən) Alternative past participle of SWELL.

swoon (swōōn) *v.i.* To faint. — *n.* A fainting fit. [ME < OE *geswōgen* unconscious] — **swoon′ing** *n.*

swoop (swōōp) *v.i.* **1.** To drop or descend suddenly, as a bird pouncing on its prey. — *v.t.* **2.** To take or seize suddenly: often with *up*. — *n.* The act of swooping. [< OE *swāpan* to sweep]

swop (swop) See SWAP.

sword (sôrd, sōrd) *n.* **1.** A weapon consisting of a long blade fixed in a hilt, as a rapier, etc. **2.** Power; esp., military power. **3.** War; destruction; slaughter. — **at swords' points** Hostile; ready for a fight. — **to put to the sword** To kill with a sword; slaughter in battle. [OE *sweord*]

sword·fish (sôrd′fish′, sōrd′-) *n. pl.* **·fish** or **·fish·es** A large marine fish having the bones of the upper jaw consolidated to form an elongated swordlike process.

sword grass **1.** Any of several varieties of grasses or sedges with sharp or serrated edges. **2.** The gladiolus.

sword·knot (sôrd′not′, sōrd′-) *n.* Formerly, a loop of leather used to fasten the hilt of a sword to the wrist; now, a tassel of cord or ribbon tied to a sword hilt.

sword·play (sôrd′plā′, sōrd′-) *n.* The act, art, or skill of using the sword, esp. in fencing. — **sword′·play·er** *n.*

swords·man (sôrdz′mən, sōrdz′-) *n. pl.* **·men** (-mən) One skilled in the use of or armed with a sword. Also **sword′·man.** — **swords′man·ship** or **sword′man·ship** *n.*

swore (swôr, swōr) Past tense of SWEAR.

sworn (swôrn, swōrn) Past participle of SWEAR.

swot (swot) See SWAT.

swounds (zwoundz, zoundz), **swouns** (zwounz, zounz) See ZOUNDS.

swum (swum) Past participle and dialectal past tense of SWIM.

swung (swung) Past tense and past participle of SWING.

sy- Var. of SYN-.

syb·a·rite (sib′ə·rīt) *n.* One given to pleasure and luxury; an epicure. [< L < Gk. < *Sybaris*, an ancient Greek city in southern Italy, famed for its luxury.] — **syb′a·rit′ic** (-rit′ik) or **·i·cal** *adj.* — **syb′a·rit′i·cal·ly** *adv.*

syc·a·more (sik′ə·môr, -mōr) *n.* **1.** A medium-sized bushy tree of Syria and Egypt allied to the common fig. **2.** Any of various plane trees of the U.S., esp., the **American sycamore**: also called *buttonwood.* **3.** An ornamental shade tree of Europe and Asia. [< OF < LL < Gk. < *sykon* fig + *moron* mulberry]

syc·o·phant (sik′ə·fənt) *n.* A servile flatterer. [< L < Gk. *sykophantēs* informer] — **syc′o·phan·cy** *n.* — **syc′o·phan′tic** (-fan′tik) or **·i·cal** *adj.* — **syc′o·phan′ti·cal·ly** *adv.*

syl·la·bar·y (sil′ə·ber′ē) *n. pl.* **·bar·ies** A list or table of syllables; esp., a list of characters representing syllables. [< NL < Med.L < L. See SYLLABLE.]

syl·lab·ic (si·lab′ik) *adj.* **1.** Of or consisting of a syllable or syllables. **2.** *Phonet.* Designating a consonant capable of forming a complete syllable, as *l* in *middle* (mid′l). **3.** Having every syllable distinctly pronounced. Also **syl·lab′i·cal.** — *n. Phonet.* A sound of high sonority, usu., a vowel. — **syl·lab′i·cal·ly** *adv.*

syl·lab·i·cate (si·lab′ə·kāt) *v.t.* **·cat·ed**, **·cat·ing** To form or divide into syllables. — **syl·lab′i·ca′tion, syl·lab′i·fi·ca′tion** *n.*

syl·lab·i·fy (si·lab′ə·fī) *v.t.* **·fied**, **·fy·ing** To syllabicate.

syl·la·ble (sil′ə·bəl) *n.* **1.** *Phonet.* A word or part of a word uttered in a single vocal impulse, usu. consisting of a vowel alone or with one or more consonants. **2.** A part of a written or printed word corresponding, more or less, to the spoken division. In this dictionary, syllable breaks are indicated by centered dots. **3.** The least detail, mention, or trace: Please don't repeat a *syllable* of what you've heard here. — *v.* **·bled**, **·bling** *v.t.* **1.** To pronounce the syllables of. — *v.i.* **2.** To pronounce syllables. [< AF, OF < L < Gk. < *syn-* together + *lambanein* to take]

syl·la·bus (sil′ə·bəs) *n. pl.* **·bus·es** or **·bi** (-bī) A concise statement of the main points of a course of study, subject, etc. [< NL < Med.L < L < *sittyba* label on a book < Gk.]

syl·lo·gism (sil′ə·jiz′əm) *n.* **1.** *Logic* **a** A formula of argument consisting of two propositions, called *premises*, and a *conclusion*, logically drawn from them. Example: All men are mortal (*major premise*); kings are men (*minor premise*); therefore, kings are mortal (*conclusion*). **b** Deductive reasoning. **2.** A subtle or crafty argument. [< OF < L < Gk. < *syn-* together + *logizesthai* to infer] — **syl′lo·gis′tic** *adj. & n.* — **syl′lo·gis′ti·cal** *adj.* — **syl′lo·gis′ti·cal·ly** *adv.*

sylph (silf) *n.* **1.** An imaginary being, mortal but without a soul, living in the air. **2.** A slender, graceful young woman or girl. [< NL *sylphes*, pl.] — **sylph′like** *adj.*

syl·van (sil′vən) *adj. Chiefly Poetic* **1.** Of or located in a forest or woods **2.** Composed of or abounding in trees or woods. **3.** Characteristic of a forest or wood; rustic. — *n.*

A spirit, person or animal dwelling in the woods. [< MF < L *silva* wood]

sym- Assimilated var. of SYN-.

sym·bi·o·sis (sim′bī·ō′sis, -bē-) *n. Biol.* The consorting together, usu., in mutually advantageous partnership, of dissimilar organisms, as of the algae and fungi in lichens. [< NL < Gk. ult. < *syn-* together + *bios* life] — **sym′bi·ot′ic** (-ot′ik) or **·i·cal** *adj.* — **sym′bi·ot′i·cal·ly** *adv.*

sym·bol (sim′bəl) *n.* **1.** Something chosen to represent something else; esp., an object used to typify a quality, abstract idea, etc.: The oak is a *symbol* of strength. **2.** A character, mark, etc., indicating something, as a quantity in mathematics. — *v.t.* To symbolize. — **Syn.** See EMBLEM. [< LL < Gk. < *syn-* together + *ballein* to throw]

sym·bol·ic (sim·bol′ik) *adj.* **1.** Of, pertaining to, or expressed by a symbol or symbols. **2.** Serving as a symbol: with *of.* **3.** Characterized by or involving the use of symbols: *symbolic* poetry. Also **sym·bol′i·cal.** — **sym·bol′i·cal·ly** *adv.* — **sym·bol′i·cal·ness** *n.*

sym·bol·ism (sim′bəl·iz′əm) *n.* **1.** Representation by symbols; treatment or interpretation of things as symbolic. **2.** The quality of being symbolic. **3.** A system of symbols. **4.** The theories and practice of a group of symbolists.

sym·bol·ist (sim′bəl·ist) *n.* One who uses symbols; esp., one skilled in the interpretation or use of symbols, as in literature and art.

sym·bol·is·tic (sim′bəl·is′tik) *adj.* **1.** Expressed by symbols; characterized by the use of symbols **2.** Of or pertaining to symbolism; symbolic. Also **sym·bol·is′ti·cal.**

sym·bol·ize (sim′bəl·īz) *v.* **·ized, ·iz·ing** *v.t.* **1.** To be a symbol of; represent symbolically; typify. **2.** To represent by a symbol or symbols. **3.** To treat as symbolic or figurative. — *v.i.* **4.** To use symbols. — **sym′bol·i·za′tion** *n.*

sym·me·try (sim′ə·trē) *n. pl.* **·tries** **1.** An exact correspondence between the opposite halves of a figure, form, line, pattern, etc., on either side of an axis or center; the condition whereby half of something is the mirror image of the other half. **2.** Beauty or harmony of form resulting from a symmetrical or nearly symmetrical arrangement of parts; due or right proportion. [< MF < LL < Gk. < *syn-* together + *metron* a measure] — **sym·met′ric** (-met′rik), **sym·met′ri·cal** (-met′ri·kəl) *adj.*

sym·pa·thet·ic (sim′pə·thet′ik) *adj.* **1.** Of, expressing, or proceeding from sympathy. **2.** Having a fellow feeling for others; sympathizing; compassionate. **3.** Being in accord or harmony; congenial. Also **sym′pa·thet′i·cal.** [< NL < Gk. See SYMPATHY.] — **sym′pa·thet′i·cal·ly** *adv.*

sym·pa·thin (sim′pə·thin) *n. Biochem.* A substance liberated by the stimulation of certain fibers of the sympathetic nervous system and acting as a chemical mediator in associated nerve impulses. [< SYMPATH(ETIC) + -IN]

sym·pa·thique (saṅ·pȧ·tēk′) *adj. French* Pleasant; nice; congenial: said of persons.

sym·pa·thize (sim′pə·thīz) *v.i.* **·thized, ·thiz·ing** **1.** To share the sentiments, feelings, or ideas of another: with *with.* **2.** To feel or express compassion, as for another's sorrow or affliction: with *with.* **3.** To be in harmony or agreement. — **sym′pa·thiz′er** *n.* — **sym′pa·thiz′ing·ly** *adv.*

sym·pa·thy (sim′pə·thē) *n. pl.* **·thies** **1.** The quality of being affected by the state of another with feelings correspondent in kind. **2.** A fellow feeling; esp., a feeling of compassion for another's sufferings; pity; commiseration. **3.** An agreement of affections, inclinations, or temperaments that makes persons agreeable to one another; congeniality; accord. — **Syn.** See PITY. [< L < Gk. < *syn-* together + *pathos* feeling]

sympathy strike A strike in which the strikers support the demands of another group of workers but demand nothing for themselves.

sym·pho·ny (sim′fə·nē) *n. pl.* **·nies** **1.** *Music* A composition for orchestra, consisting usu., of four movements, that are related by structure, key, etc. **2.** A symphony orchestra. **3.** A harmonious or agreeable mingling of sounds, colors, etc.: *symphony* in gray. [< OF < L < Gk. < *syn-* together + *phōnē* sound] — **sym·phon′ic** (fon′ik) *adj.* — **sym′pho·nist** *n.*

symphony orchestra A large orchestra composed usu. of the string, brass, woodwind, and percussion sections needed to present symphonic works: also called *symphony.*

sym·phy·sis (sim′fə·sis) *n. pl.* **·ses** (-sēz) *Anat.* A junction of two parts of the skeleton, formed either by a growing together of two bones or by the intervention of a layer of cartilage between them. [< NL < Gk. < *syn-* together + *phyein* to grow] — **sym·phyt′ic** (sim·fit′ik) *adj.* — **sym·phyt′i·cal·ly** *adv.*

sym·po·si·um (sim·pō′zē·əm) *n. pl.* **·si·ums** or **·si·a** (-zē·ə) **1.** A meeting for discussion of a particular subject. **2.** A collection of comments or opinions brought together; esp., a

series of brief essays or articles on the same subject, as in a magazine. Also **sym·po′si·on** (-zē·on). [< L < Gk. < *syn-* together + *posis* a drinking < *po-*, stem of *pinein* to drink] — **sym·po′si·ac** (-ak) *adj.*

symp·tom (sim′təm) *n.* **1.** A sign, token, or indication. **2.** *Med.* Any observable alteration in bodily functions or mental behavior arising from and indicating the presence of disease, esp. when regarded as an aid in diagnosis. [< L < Gk. < *syn-* together + *piptein* to fall]

symp·to·mat·ic (simp′tə·mat′ik) *adj.* **1.** Pertaining to, of the nature of, or constituting a symptom or symptoms. **2.** According to symptoms: a *symptomatic* classification of diseases. Also **symp′to·mat′i·cal.** — **symp′to·mat′i·cal·ly** *adv.*

syn- *prefix* With; together; associated with or accompanying: *syntax, syndrome.* Also: *sy-* before *sc, sp, st,* and *z,* as in *system; syl-* before *l,* as in *syllable; sym-* before *b, p,* and *m,* as in *sympathy; sys-* before *s.* [< L < Gk. < *syn* together]

syn·a·gogue (sin′ə·gôg, -gog) *n.* **1.** A place of meeting for Jewish worship and religious instruction. **2.** A Jewish congregation or assemblage for religious instruction and observances. **3.** The Jewish religion or communion. Also **syn′a·gog.** [< OF < LL < Gk. *synagōgē* assembly < *syn-* together + *agein* to lead, bring] — **syn′a·gog′i·cal** (-goj′i·kəl), **syn′a·gog′al** (-gôg′əl, -gog′əl) *adj.*

syn·apse (si·naps′) *n. Physiol.* The junction point of two neurons, across which a nerve impulse passes. Also called **syn·ap·sis** (si·nap′sis). [< NL < Gk. < *syn-* together + *hapsis* a joining]

syn·carp (sin′kärp) *n. Bot.* **1.** A fruit composed of several carpels, as the blackberry. **2.** A multiple fruit, as the fig. Also **syn·car·pi·um** (sin·kär′pē·əm). [< NL < Gk. *syn-* together + *karpos* fruit] — **syn·car′pous** *adj.*

syn·chro (sing′krō) *n.* Any of various electromagnetic devices for the remote control of complex operations.

syn·chro·mesh (sing′krə·mesh′) *n. Mech.* **1.** A gear system by which driving and driven members are brought to the same speed before engaging. **2.** Any gear in such a system. [< SYNCHRO(NIZED) + MESH]

syn·chro·nism (sing′krə·niz′əm) *n.* **1.** The state of being synchronous. **2.** Coincidence in time of different events or phenomena; simultaneousness. **3.** A tabular grouping of historic personages or events according to their dates. **4.** In art, representation in the same picture of events that occurred at different times. — **syn′chro·nis′tic** or **·ti·cal** *adj.* — **syn′chro·nis′ti·cal·ly** *adv.*

syn·chro·nize (sing′krə·nīz) *v.* **·nized, ·niz·ing** *v.i.* **1.** To occur at the same time; coincide. **2.** To move or operate in unison. — *v.t.* **3.** To cause (timepieces) to agree in keeping or indicating time. **4.** To cause to operate in unison. **5.** To assign the same date or period to. — **syn′chro·ni·za′tion** *n.* — **syn′chro·niz′er** *n.*

syn·chro·nous (sing′krə·nəs) *adj.* **1.** Occurring at the same time; coincident. **2.** Happening at the same rate. **3.** *Physics* Having the same period or rate of vibration, as waves or electric currents. Also **syn·chron′ic, syn′chro·nal.** [< LL < Gk. < *syn-* together + *chronos* time] — **syn′chro·nous·ly** *adv.* — **syn′chro·nous·ness** *n.*

syn·cli·nal (sin·klī′nal, sing-) *adj.* **1.** Sloping downward on each side toward a line or point. **2.** *Geol.* Inclining upward on each side from the axis of the fold, as rock strata. Also **syn·clin·i·cal** (sin·klin′i·kəl, sing-). — *n.* A syncline. [< Gk. < *syn-* together + *klinein* to incline]

syn·cline (sing′klīn) *n. Geol.* A trough or structural basin toward which rocks dip.

syn·co·pate (sing′kə·pāt) *v.t.* **·pat·ed, ·pat·ing** **1.** *Gram.* To contract (a word) by syncope. **2.** *Music* To treat or modify, as a tone, by syncopation. [< LL *syncopatus*, pp. of *syncopare* to affect with syncope] — **syn′co·pat′or** *n.*

syn·co·pa·tion (sing′kə·pā′shən) *n.* **1.** The act of syncopating or state of being syncopated. **2.** That which is syncopated, as a dance or rhythm. **3.** *Music* **a** The rhythmic placement of a tone so that its accent does not coincide with the metric accent, as by beginning it on a weak beat or a fraction of a beat and continuing it through the next strong beat. **b** A tone so treated. **c** Any music featuring syncopation, as ragtime, jazz, etc. **4.** *Gram.* Syncope.

syn·co·pe (sing′kə·pē) *n.* **1.** *Gram.* The elision of a sound or syllable in the middle part of a word, as *e'er* for *ever.* **2.** *Pathol.* A loss of consciousness caused by temporary cerebral anemia. [< OF, ult. < LL < Gk. < *syn-* together + *kop-*, stem of *koptein* to cut] — **syn′co·pal, syn·cop′ic** (sin·kop′ik) *adj.*

syn·cre·tize (sing′krə·tīz) *v.t. & v.i.* **·tized, ·tiz·ing** To attempt to blend and reconcile, as various philosophies. [< NL < Gk. *synkrētizein* to combine] — **syn′cre·tism** *n.*

syn·det·ic (sin·det′ik) *adj.* Serving to unite or connect; connective, as a word. Also **syn·det′i·cal.** [< Gk. < *syn-* together + *deein* to bind] — **syn·det′i·cal·ly** *adv.*

syn·dic (sin′dik) *n.* **1.** A civil magistrate or officer representing a government. **2.** One who is designated to transact business for others. [< Gk. *syndikos* defendant's advocate < syn- together + *dikē* judgment]

syn·di·cal·ism (sin′di·kəl·iz′əm) *n.* A social and political theory proposing the taking over of the means of production by syndicates of workers, preferably by means of the general strike, with consequent political control. **— syn′di·cal·ist** *adj. & n.* **— syn′di·cal·is′tic** *adj.*

syn·di·cate (*n.* sin′də·kit; *v.* sin′də·kāt) *n.* **1.** An association of individuals united to negotiate some business or to prosecute some enterprise requiring large capital. **2.** An agency that sells articles, etc., to a number of periodicals, as newspapers, for simultaneous publication. **3.** The office or jurisdiction of a syndic; also, syndics collectively. *— v.t.* **·cat·ed, ·cat·ing** **1.** To combine into or manage by a syndicate. **2.** To sell (an article, etc.) for publication in many newspapers or magazines. [See SYNDIC.]

syn·drome (sin′drōm) *n. Med.* An aggregate or set of concurrent symptoms indicating the presence and nature of a disease. [< NL < Gk. < *syn*- together + *dramein* to run] **— syn·drom·ic** (sin·drom′ik) *adj.*

sy·nec·do·che (si·nek′də·kē) *n.* A figure of speech in which a part is put for a whole or a whole for a part, an individual for a class, or a material for the thing, as a *roof* for a *house.* [< LL < Gk. < *syn*- together + *ekdechesthai* to take from] **— syn·ec·doch·ic** (sin′ek·dok′ik) or **·i·cal** *adj.*

synfuel (sin′fyoō·əl) *n.* Synthetic fuel.

syn·i·ze·sis (sin′ə·zē′sis) *n.* **1.** *Biol.* The contractile massing of the chromatin in meiosis. **2.** *Med.* Contraction of the pupil of the eye. Also **syn′e·zi′sis** (-zi′sis). [< LL < Gk. < *syn*- together + *izanein* to settle down, sit]

syn·od (sin′əd) *n.* **1.** An ecclesiastical council. **2.** Any deliberative assembly. [OE < LL < Gk. *synodos*, lit., a coming together < *syn*- together + *hodos* way]

sy·nod·i·cal (si·nod′i·kəl) *adj.* **1.** Of, pertaining to, or of the nature of a synod; transacted in a synod. **2.** *Astron.* Pertaining to the conjunction of two heavenly bodies, one of which revolves round the other, or to the interval between two successive conjunctions. Also **syn·od·al** (sin′ə·dəl), **sy·nod′ic.** **— sy·nod′i·cal·ly** *adv.*

syn·o·nym (sin′ə·nim) *n.* **1.** A word having the same or almost the same meaning as some other: opposed to *antonym.* **2.** The equivalent of a word in another language. Also **syn′·o·nyme.** [< LL < Gk. < *syn*- together + *onyma, onoma* name] **— syn′o·nym′ic** or **·i·cal** *adj.* **— syn′o·nym′i·ty** *n.*

sy·non·y·mize (si·non′ə·mīz) *v.t.* **·mized, ·miz·ing** To give the synonyms of; express by words of similar meaning.

sy·non·y·mous (si·non′ə·məs) *adj.* **1.** Being a synonym or synonyms; equivalent or similar in meaning. **2.** Closely related or alike in significance or effect. Also **syn·o·ny·mat·ic** (sin′ə·ni·mat′ik). **— sy·non′y·mous·ly** *adv.*

sy·non·y·my (si·non′ə·mē) *n. pl.* **·mies** **1.** The quality of being synonymous. **2.** The science or systematic collection and study of synonyms; also, the use and discrimination of synonyms. **3.** A written analysis discriminating the meaning of synonyms. **4.** An index, list, or collection of synonyms, as in scientific nomenclature.

sy·nop·sis (si·nop′sis) *n. pl.* **·ses** (-sēz) A general view, as of a subject or its treatment; an abstract; syllabus; summary. [< LL < Gk. < *syn*- together + *opsis* view]

sy·nop·tic (si·nop′tik) *adj.* **1.** Giving or constituting a synopsis or general view. **2.** *Often cap.* Presenting the same or a similar point of view: said of the first three Gospels (**Synoptic Gospels**). Also **sy·nop′ti·cal.** **— sy·nop′ti·cal·ly** *adv.*

sy·no·vi·a (si·nō′vē·ə) *n. Physiol.* The viscid, transparent, albuminous fluid secreted by the **synovial membranes** at points where lubrication is necessary, as in joints. [< NL, appar. < Gk. *syn*- together + L *ovum* egg < Gk. *ōon*.] **— sy·no′vi·al** *adj.*

syn·tax (sin′taks) *n.* **1.** The arrangement and interrelationship of words in phrases and sentences. **2.** The branch of linguistics dealing with such relationships. [< F < LL < Gk. < *syn*- together + *lassein* to arrange] **— syn·tac·tic** (sin·tak′tik) or **·ti·cal** *adj.* **— syn·tac′ti·cal·ly** *adv.*

syn·the·sis (sin′thə·sis) *n. pl.* **·ses** (-sēz) **1.** The assembling of separate or subordinate parts into a whole: opposed to *analysis.* **2.** A complex whole composed of originally separate parts. **3.** *Chem.* The building up of compounds from a series of reactions involving elements, radicals, or similar compounds. Compare ANALYSIS. [< L < Gk. < *syn*- together + *tithenai* to place] **— syn′the·sist** *n.*

syn·the·size (sin′thə·sīz) *v.t.* **·sized, ·siz·ing** **1.** To unite or produce by synthesis. **2.** To apply synthesis to.

syn·thet·ic (sin·thet′ik) *adj.* **1.** Pertaining to, of the nature of, or characterized by synthesis. **2.** Tending to reduce particulars to inclusive wholes. **3.** *Chem.* Produced artificially by the synthesis of simpler materials or substances rather than occurring naturally. **4.** Artificial; spurious. *— n.* Anything produced by synthesis. **— syn·thet′i·cal·ly** *adv.*

synthetic fuel Fuel obtained by processing, such as crude oil obtained from shale or tar sands by extraction and from coal by liquefaction, or natural gas obtained from coal by gasification.

syph·i·lis (sif′ə·lis) *n. Pathol.* An infectious, chronic, venereal disease caused by a spirochete transmissible by direct contact or congenitally, and usu..progressing by three stages of increasing severity. [after a Latin poem published in 1530, the hero of which, *Syphilus*, a shepherd, was the first sufferer from the disease]

syph·i·lit·ic (sif′ə·lit′ik) *adj.* Relating to or affected with syphilis. *— n.* A person suffering from syphilis.

Syr·i·ac (sir′ē·ak) *n.* The language of the Syrians, belonging to the eastern Aramaic subgroup of the Northwest Semitic languages. [< L < Gk. *Syriakos*]

Syr·i·an (sir′ē·ən) *adj.* Of or pertaining to ancient or modern Syria. *— n.* **1.** A native of Syria, esp. one of the Semitic people of Arabic, Phoenician, and Aramean descent. **2.** One who is a member of a Christian church in Syria. [< OF < L < Gk. *Syria* Syria]

sy·rin·ga (si·ring′gə) *n.* **1.** Any of various ornamental shrubs of the saxifrage family, having fragrant cream-colored flowers. **2.** The lilac. [< NL < Gk. *syrinx, -ingos* a pipe]

syr·inge (sir′inj, si·rinj′) *n.* **1.** *Med.* A small instrument of glass, metal, rubber, or plastic, consisting of a receptacle into which a liquid may be drawn for ejection in a fine jet or stream, used for cleaning wounds, affected parts, etc. **2.** A hypodermic syringe. *— v.t.* **·inged, ·ing·ing** To spray or inject by a syringe; cleanse or treat with injected fluid. [< Med.L < Gk. *syrinx, -ingos* tube, pipe]

syr·inx (sir′ingks) *n. pl.* **sy·rin·ges** (sə·rin′jēz) or **sy′rinx·es** **1.** *Ornithol.* A special modification of the windpipe serving as the song organ in birds. **2.** *Anat.* The Eustachian tube. [< Gk., pipe] **— sy·rin·ge·al** (si·rin′jē·əl) *adj.*

syr·up (sir′əp) · *n.* A thick, sweet liquid, as the boiled juice of fruits, sugar cane, etc.: also, *esp. U.S.,* sirup. [< OF < Arabic *sharāb*] **— syr′up·y** *adj.*

sys- Var. of SYN-.

sys·tal·tic (sis·tal′tik) *adj. Physiol.* Alternately contracting and dilating, as the motion of the heart; pulsatory. [< LL < Gk. < *syn*- together + *stellein* to send]

sys·tem (sis′təm) *n.* **1.** Orderly combination or arrangement of parts, elements, etc., into a whole; esp., such combination according to some rational principle; any methodical arrangement of parts. **2.** Any group of facts, concepts, and phenomena regarded as constituting a natural whole for purposes of philosophic or scientific investigation and construction: the Ptolemaic *system*; the solar *system*. **3.** The connection or manner of connection of parts as related to a whole, or the parts collectively so related: a railroad *system*. **4.** The state or quality of being in order or orderly; method. **5.** *Physiol.* **a** An assemblage of organic structures composed of similar elements and combined for the same general functions: the nervous *system*. **b** The entire body, taken as a functional whole. **6.** *Physics* An aggregate or region of matter considered as a unit with respect to specified factors such as mass, energy, gravitation, radioactivity, etc. **7.** *Chem.* A group of substances in one or more phases exhibiting, or tending to approach, equilibrium. **8.** *Mineral.* One of the primary divisions into which all crystal forms may be grouped, depending upon the relative lengths and mutual inclinations of the assumed crystal axes. **9.** *Geol.* A category of igneous and sedimentary rock strata corresponding with a period in the time scale. [< LL < Gk. < *syn*- together + *histanai* to stand, set up]

sys·tem·at·ic (sis′tə·mat′ik) *adj.* **1.** Of, pertaining to, of the nature of, or characterized by system. **2.** Characterized by system or method; methodical: a *systematic* person. **3.** Forming a system; systematized. **4.** Carried out with organized regularity. **5.** Taxonomic. Also **sys′tem·at′i·cal.** **— sys′tem·at′i·cal·ly** *adv.*

sys·tem·a·tism (sis′tə·mə·tiz′əm) *n.* **1.** Systematic arrangement or classification. **2.** Adherence to or reduction of principles, etc., to a system. **— sys′tem·a·tist** *n.*

sys·tem·a·tize (sis′tə·mə·tīz′) *v.t.* **·tized, ·tiz·ing** To reduce to a system. Also **sys′tem·ize,** *Brit.* **sys′tem·a·tise′.** **— sys′·tem·a·ti·za′tion** *n.* **— sys′tem·a·tiz′er** *n.*

sys·tem·ic (sis·tem′ik) *adj.* **1.** Of or pertaining to system or a system. **2.** *Physiol.* Pertaining to or affecting the body as a whole: a *systemic* poison. **— sys·tem′i·cal·ly** *adv.*

sys·to·le (sis′tə·lē) *n.* **1.** *Physiol.* The regular contraction of the heart, esp. of the ventricles, that impels the blood outward. Compare DIASTOLE. **2.** The shortening of a syllable that is naturally so by position long. [See SYSTALTIC.] **— sys·tol·ic** (sis·tol′ik) *adj.*

syz·y·gy (siz′ə·jē) *n. pl.* **·gies** *Astron.* **a** One of two opposite points in the orbit of a celestial body when it is in conjunction with or in opposition to the sun. **b** The points on the moon's orbit when the moon is most nearly in line with the earth and the sun. [< LL < Gk. < *syn*- together + *zeugnynai* to yoke] **— sy·zyg·i·al** (si·zij′ē·əl) *adj.*

T

t, T (tē) *n. pl.* **t's** or **ts, T's** or **Ts, tees** (tēz) **1.** The twentieth letter of the English alphabet. **2.** The sound represented by the letter *t*, the voiceless alveolar stop. **3.** Anything shaped like the letter T. — **to a T** Precisely; with exactness.

't Contraction for IT: used initially, as in *'tis* and finally, as in *on't.*

-t Inflectional ending used to indicate past participles and past tenses, and corresponding to *-ed*, as in *bereft, lost, spent.*

tab (tab) *n.* **1.** A flap, strip, tongue, or appendage of something, as a garment. **2.** A small, projecting part used as an aid in filing papers, etc. **3.** *Informal* Tally; total; bill: to pick up the *tab.* — **to keep tab** or **tabs** (**on**) **1.** To watch or supervise closely. **2.** To maintain a factual record (of). [Origin uncertain]

tab·ard (tab′ərd) *n.* **1.** Formerly, a short, sleeveless or short-sleeved outer garment. **2.** A knight's cape or cloak, worn over his armor; also, a similar garment worn by a herald. [< OF *tabart*, ult. < L *tapete* tapestry]

Ta·bas·co (tə·bas′kō) *n.* A pungent sauce made from red pepper: a trade name. Also **Tabasco sauce.**

tab·by (tab′ē) *n. pl.* **·bies 1.** A brindled or striped cat. **2.** Any domestic cat, esp. a female. **3.** A gossiping old maid. **4.** Any of various plain-woven fabrics, as a watered taffeta. — *adj.* **1.** Having dark, wavy markings; brindled, as a cat. **2.** Watered or mottled, as a fabric. **3.** Made of tabby. — *v.t.* **·bied, ·by·ing** To give a wavy or watered appearance to (silk, etc.). [< F < Arabic *'Attābi*, name of a quarter of Baghdad where the cloth was manufactured]

tab·er·nac·le (tab′ər·nak′əl) *n.* **1.** A tent or similar temporary structure or shelter. **2.** A Jewish house of worship; a temple. **3.** Originally, the portable sanctuary used by the Jews in the wilderness. **4.** Any house of worship, esp. one of large size. **5.** The human body as the dwelling place of the soul. **6.** *Eccl.* The ornamental receptacle for the consecrated Eucharistic elements, or for the pyx. **7.** An ornamental recess or structure sheltering something. — *v.i. & v.t.* **·led, ·ling** To dwell or place in or as in a tabernacle. [< OF < L *tabernaculum*, dim. of *taberna* shed] — **tab·er·nac·u·lar** (tab′ər·nak′yə·lər) *adj.*

tab·la·ture (tab′lə·chər) *n. Music* A notation for instrumental music that indicates rhythm and fingering, but not the pitches produced. [< F < L *tabula* board]

ta·ble (tā′bəl) *n.* **1.** An article of furniture with a flat horizontal top upheld by one or more supports. **2.** Such a table around which persons sit for a meal. **3.** The food served or entertainment provided at a meal or dinner. **4.** The company of persons at a table. **5.** A collection of related numbers, values, signs, or items of any kind, arranged for reference or comparison, often in parallel columns: a *table* of logarithms. **6.** A synoptical statement; list: *table* of contents. **7.** A tableland; plateau. **8.** A tablet or slab bearing an inscription; esp., one of those that bore the Ten Commandments or certain Roman laws. — **to turn the tables** To thwart an opponent's action and turn the situation to his disadvantage. — *v.t.* **·bled, ·bling 1.** To place on a table, as a playing card. **2.** To postpone discussion of (a resolution, bill, etc.) until a future time, or for an indefinite period. **3.** *Rare* To tabulate. [Fusion of OF *table* and OE *tabule*, both < L *tabula* board]

tab·leau (tab′lō, ta·blō′) *n. pl.* **·leaux** (-loz, -lō) or **·leaus** (-lōz) **1.** Any picture or picturesque representation; esp., a striking scene presented dramatically. **2.** A tableau vivant. [< F, dim. of *table* table]

ta·bleau vi·vant (ta·blō′ vē·vän′) *pl.* **ta·bleaux vi·vants** (ta·blō′ vē·vän′) *French* A picturelike scene represented by silent and motionless persons standing in appropriate attitudes: also called *tableau.*

ta·ble·cloth (tā′bəl·klôth′, -kloth′) *n.* A cloth covering a table, esp., at meals.

ta·ble d'hôte (tā′bəl dōt′, tä′bəl; *Fr.* ta·blə dōt′) *pl.* **ta·bles d'hôte** (tā′bəlz dōt′, tä′bəlz; *Fr.* ta·blə dōt′) A complete meal served at a restaurant or hotel, the price of the entire meal being determined by the price of the entrée one

chooses. Compare À LA CARTE. [< F, lit., table of the host, as at an inn]

ta·ble·land (tā′bəl·land′) *n.* A broad, level, elevated region, usu. treeless; a plateau.

table linen Tablecloths, napkins, doilies, etc.

ta·ble·spoon (tā′bəl·spōōn′, -spŏŏn′) *n.* **1.** A fairly large spoon used for serving food and in measuring for recipes, etc. **2.** A tablespoonful, equivalent to three teaspoons.

ta·ble·spoon·ful (tā′bəl·spōōn·fōŏl′, -spŏŏn-) *n. pl.* **·fuls** As much as a tablespoon will hold.

tab·let (tab′lit) *n.* **1.** A pad, as of writing paper or note paper. **2.** A small, flat surface, esp., one designed for or containing an inscription or design. **3.** A definite portion of a drug, etc., pressed into a solid form. **4.** A small, flat, or nearly flat piece of some prepared substance, as chocolate or soap. **5.** A thin sheet or slab of solid material, as stone, wood, etc., used for writing, painting, or drawing. [< OF *tablete*, dim. of *table* table]

table tennis A table game resembling tennis, played usu. indoors with a small celluloid ball and wooden paddles: also called *ping-pong.*

ta·ble·ware (tā′bəl·wâr′) *n.* Dishes, knives, forks, spoons, etc., for table use, collectively.

tab·loid (tab′loid) *n.* A newspaper consisting of sheets one half the size of those in an ordinary newspaper, in which the news is presented by means of pictures and concise reporting. — *adj.* **1.** Compact; concise; condensed. **2.** Sensational: *tabloid* journalism. [< TABL(ET) + -OID]

Tab·loid (tab′loid) *n.* Proprietary name for any of various medical preparations and drugs in concentrated or condensed tablet form.

ta·boo (tə·bōō′, ta-) *n.* **1.** Among primitive peoples, esp. the Polynesians, a religious and social interdict forbidding the mention of a certain person, thing, or place, the performance of a certain action, etc. **2.** The system or practice of such interdicts or prohibitions. **3.** Any restriction or ban founded on custom or social convention. **4.** The convention of avoiding certain words as profane, obscene, disagreeable, or otherwise socially unacceptable: compare EUPHEMISM. — *adj.* **1.** Consecrated or prohibited by taboo. **2.** Banned or forbidden by social authority or convention. — *v.t.* **1.** To place under taboo. **2.** To exclude; ostracize. Also **ta·bu′.** [< Tonga *tabu*]

ta·bor (tā′bər) *n.* A small drum or tambourine on which a fifer beats his own accompaniment. — *v.i.* To beat or play on a timbrel or small drum; beat lightly and repeatedly. Also **ta′bour.** [< OF *tabour*, prob. < Persian *tabīrah* drum] — **ta′bor·er** *n.*

tab·o·ret (tab′ər·it, tab′ə·ret′) *n.* **1.** A small tabor. **2.** A stool or small seat, usu. without arms or back. **3.** An embroidery frame. Also **tab·ou·ret** (tab′ər·it, tab′ə·ret′).

tab·u·lar (tab′yə·lər) *adj.* **1.** Pertaining to or consisting of a table or list. **2.** Computed from or with a mathematical table. **3.** Having a flat surface; tablelike. — **tab′u·lar·ly** *adv.*

tab·u·lar·ize (tab′yə·lə·rīz′) *v.t.* **·ized, ·iz·ing** To arrange in tabular form; tabulate. — **tab′u·lar·i·za′tion** *n.*

tab·u·late (tab′yə·lāt) *v.t.* **·lat·ed, ·lat·ing 1.** To arrange in a table or list: to *tabulate* results. **2.** To form with a tabular surface. — *adj.* Having a flat surface. — **tab′u·la′tion** *n.*

tab·u·la·tor (tab′yə·lā′tər) *n.* **1.** One who or that which tabulates. **2.** A device built into a typewriter, and used to present statistical matter in tabulated form. **3.** An automatic accounting machine for tabulating reports.

tac·a·ma·hac (tak′ə·mə·hak′) *n.* **1.** A yellowish, resinous substance with a strong odor, derived from various trees and used as incense. **2.** Any of the trees producing this substance. **3.** A tree of the U.S., having leaf buds exuding a gummy resin: also **tac′a·ma·hack′**, **tac·a·ma·hack′**, **tac′ca·ma·hac′.** [< Sp. < Nahuatl *tecomahca*, lit., fetid copal]

tace (tās) *n.* Tasset, a type of armor plate.

ta·chom·e·ter (te·kom′ə·tər) *n.* **1.** An instrument for measuring speed and velocity, as of a machine, the flow of a current, blood, etc. **2.** A device for indicating the speed of rotation of an engine, etc. [< Gk. *tachos* speed + -METER]

ta·chom·e·try (tə·kom′ə·trē) *n.* The art or science of using a tachometer. — **tach·o·met·ric** (tak′ə·met′rik) *adj.*

tachy- *combining form* Speed; swiftness. [< Gk. *tachys* swift]

tac·it (tas′it) *adj.* **1.** Existing, inferred, or implied without being directly stated. **2.** Making no sound; silent; noiseless. [< F < L *tacere* to be silent] — **tac′it·ly** *adv.* — **tac′· it·ness** *n.*

tac·i·turn (tas′ə·tûrn) *adj.* Habitually silent or reserved. — **tac′i·turn′i·ty** *n.* — **tac′i·turn·ly** *adv.*

tack¹ (tak) *n.* **1.** A small sharp-pointed nail, commonly with tapering sides and a flat head. **2.** *Naut.* **a** A rope that holds down the lower outer corner of certain sails. **b** The corner so held. **c** The direction in which a vessel sails when sailing close-hauled, considered in relation to the position of her sails. **d** The distance or the course run at one time in such direction. **e** The act of tacking. **f** Any veering of a vessel to one side, as to take advantage of a side wind. **3.** A change of policy; a new course of action. **4.** In sewing, a large, temporary stitch. — *v.t.* **1.** To fasten or attach with tacks. **2.** To secure temporarily, as with tacks or long stitches. **3.** To attach as supplementary; append. **4.** *Naut.* **a** To bring (a vessel) momentarily into the wind so as to go on the opposite tack. **b** To navigate (a vessel) to windward by making a series of tacks. — *v.i.* **5.** *Naut.* **a** To tack a vessel. **b** To go on the opposite tack, or sail to windward by a series of tacks. **6.** To change one's course of action; veer. [< AF *taque*, OF *tache* nail] — **tack′er** *n.*

tack² (tak) *n.* Food in general. [Origin uncertain]

tack·le (tak′əl) *n.* **1.** A rope, pulley, or combination of ropes and pulleys used for hoisting or moving objects. **2.** A windlass or winch, together with ropes and hooks. **3.** The equipment used in any work or sport; gear; fishing *tackle.* **4.** In football: **a** The act of tackling. **b** One of two linemen whose position is usu. between the guard and end. **5.** A ship's rigging. — *v.t.* **·led, ·ling 1.** To deal with; undertake to master, accomplish, or solve. **2.** In football, to seize and stop (an opponent carrying the ball). — *v.i.* **3.** In football, to tackle an opposing player. [< MLG *takel* < *taken* to seize] — **tack′ler** *n.*

tack·y¹ (tak′ē) *adj.* **tack·i·er, tack·i·est** Having adhesive properties; sticky, as a surface covered with partly dried varnish. Also **tack′ey.** [Prob. < TACK¹, v. (def. 2)]

tack·y² (tak′ē) *adj.* **tack·i·er, tack·i·est** *U.S. Informal* Shabby; neglected; shoddy. [Cf. dial. G *taklig* untidy]

tact (takt) *n.* A quick or intuitive appreciation of what is fit, proper, or right; esp., skill in avoiding what would offend or disturb. [< L *tactus* a touching]

tact·ful (takt′fəl) *adj.* Possessing or manifesting tact; considerate. — **tact′ful·ly** *adv.* — **tact′ful·ness** *n.*

tac·ti·cal (tak′ti·kəl) *adj.* **1.** Pertaining to or like tactics. **2.** Exhibiting adroit maneuvering. — **tac′ti·cal·ly** *adv.*

tac·ti·cian (tak·tish′ən) *n.* An expert in tactics.

tac·tics (tak′tiks) *n.pl.* (*construed as sing. in def. 1*) **1.** The science and art of handling troops in the presence of the enemy or for immediate objectives: distinguished from *strategy.* **2.** Any maneuvering to gain an objective. [< Gk. *taktikos* suitable for arranging or organizing]

tac·tile (tak′til, -təl, *esp. Brit.* -tīl) *adj.* **1.** Pertaining to the organs or sense of touch; caused by or consisting of contact. **2.** That may be touched; tangible. [< F < L *tactus* touch] — **tac·til′i·ty** *n.*

tact·less (takt′lis) *adj.* Lacking tact. — **tact′less·ly** *adv.* — **tact′less·ness** *n.*

tac·tu·al (tak′chōō·əl) *adj.* Tactile. — **tac′tu·al·ly** *adv.*

tad·pole (tad′pōl) *n.* The aquatic larva of an amphibian, as a frog or toad, breathing by external gills and having a tail: also called *polliwog.* [ME *taddepol* < *tadde* toad]

tael (tāl) *n.* **1.** An Oriental weight varying from 1 to 2⅓ ounces, commonly about 1⅓ ounces. **2.** A Chinese monetary unit of varying value. [< Pg. < Malay *tahil*]

ta'en (tān) *Scot.* Taken.

taf·fe·ta (taf′ə·tə) *n.* A fine, plain-woven, somewhat stiff fabric of silk, rayon, etc. — *adj.* Made of or resembling taffeta. [< OF < Med.L < Persian *tāftan* to twist]

taff·rail (taf′rāl′, -rəl) *n.* *Naut.* **1.** The rail around a vessel's stern. **2.** The upper part of a vessel's stern. [< MDu. *tafereel* panel, picture]

taf·fy (taf′ē) *n.* **1.** A confection made of brown sugar or molasses, mixed with butter, boiled down, and pulled: also called *toffee.* **2.** *Informal* Flattery. [Origin unknown]

tag¹ (tag) *n.* **1.** Something tacked on or attached to another thing else; an appendage. **2.** A label tied or attached loosely as to a piece of baggage. **3.** A loose, ragged edge of anything; tatter. **4.** The tail or tip of the tail of any animal. **5.** The final lines of a speech in a play; catchword; cue. — *v.* **tagged, tag·ging** *v.t.* **1.** To supply, adorn, fit, mark, or label with a tag. **2.** To shear away matted locks of wool from (sheep). **3.** To follow closely or persistently. — *v.i.* **4.** To follow closely at one's heels. [Prob. < Scand.]

tag² (tag) *v.t.* **tagged, tag·ging 1.** In baseball, to touch (a

player) with the ball or with the hand or glove in which the ball is held. **2.** To overtake and touch, as in the game of tag. **3.** *Informal* To make contact with; designate: *tagged* him for a loan. — *n.* **1.** In baseball, the act or instance of tagging a player, esp., a base runner, in an attempt to retire him. **2.** A children's running game in which a player who is touched or caught (usu., called "it") tries to touch or catch the others. [< TAG¹]

Ta·ga·log (tä·gä′log, tag′ə·log, -lôg) *n.* **1.** A member of a Malay people native to the Philippines, esp., Luzon. **2.** One of the principal native languages and, since 1940, the official language of the Philippines. Also **Ta·gal** (tä·gäl′).

tag day A day on which contributions are solicited for charitable and other institutions.

tag end 1. A loose end or tag of cloth, yarn, etc. **2.** The endmost part of anything.

tagged atom A tracer.

tag·ger (tag′ər) *n.* One who or that which tags.

Ta·hi·ti·an (tä·hē′tē·ən, tə-, -shən) *adj.* Of or relating to Tahiti, its people, or their language. — *n.* **1.** One of the native Polynesian people of Tahiti. **2.** The Polynesian language of the Tahitians.

Tai (tī) See THAI.

tail¹ (tāl) *n.* **1.** The hindmost part or rear end of an animal; esp., when prolonged beyond the rest of the body as a distinct, flexible member. ◆ Collateral adjective: *caudal.* **2.** Any slender, flexible, terminal extension of the main part of an object: the *tail* of a shirt. **3.** *Astron.* The luminous trail extending from the nucleus of a comet. **4.** The bottom, back, or inferior portion of anything. **5.** *pl. Informal* The reverse side of a coin. **6.** Anything of taillike appearance, as a number of persons in single file. **7.** A pigtail; braid. **8.** *Aeron.* The rear end of an aircraft; also, the stabilizer and control surfaces at the rear of an aircraft. **9.** The rear portion of a bomb, projectile, rocket, or guided missile. **10.** *pl. Informal* A man's full-dress suit; also, a swallow-tailed coat. — *v.t.* **1.** To furnish with a tail. **2.** To cut off the tail of. **3.** To be the tail or end of: to *tail* a procession. **4.** To insert and fasten by one end, as a beam into a wall: with *in* or *on.* **5.** *Informal* To follow secretly and stealthily; shadow. — *v.i.* **6.** To extend or proceed in a line. **7.** *Informal* To follow close behind. **8.** To be inserted and fastened at one end, as a beam. — **to tail off** To diminish or recede gradually. — *adj.* **1.** Rearmost; hindmost. **2.** Coming from behind; following: a *tail* wind. [OE *tægl*] — **tail′less** *adj.*

tail² (tāl) *Law adj.* Restricted in succession to particular heirs: an estate *tail.* — *n.* A cutting off, abridgment, or limitation of ownership; an entail. [< OF *taillier* to cut]

tail·gate (tāl′gāt′) *n.* A hinged or vertically sliding board or gate closing the back end of a truck, wagon, etc. Also **tail·board** (tāl′bôrd, -bōrd). — *v.t. & v.i.* **·gat·ed, ·gat·ing** To drive too close behind for safety.

tail·ing (tā′ling) *n.* **1.** *pl.* Refuse or residue from grain after milling, or from ground ore after washing. **2.** The inner, covered portion of a projecting brick or stone in a wall.

tail·light (tāl′līt′) *n.* A light attached to the rear of a vehicle. Also **tail lamp.**

tai·lor (tā′lər) *n.* One who makes to order or repairs men's or women's outer garments. — *v.i.* **1.** To do a tailor's work. — *v.t.* **2.** To fit with garments: He is well *tailored.* **3.** To work at or make by tailoring: to *tailor* a coat. ◆ Collateral adjective: *sartorial.* **4.** To make, adjust, or adapt for a specific purpose. [< OF < LL *taliare* to split, cut]

tai·lor·bird (tā′lər·bûrd′) *n.* A passerine bird of Asia and Africa, that stitches leaves together to hold and hide its nest.

tai·lored (tā′lərd) *adj.* **1.** Characterized by simple, severe style: said esp. of women's clothes. **1.** Made by a tailor.

tai·lor-made (tā′lər·mād′) *adj.* **1.** Made by a tailor. **2.** Made or as if made to order; perfectly right or suitable.

tail·piece (tāl′pēs′) *n.* **1.** Any endpiece or appendage. **2.** In a violin or similar instrument, a piece of wood, as ebony, at the soundboard end, having the strings fastened to it. For illus., see VIOLIN. **3.** *Printing* An ornamental design on the lower blank portion of a page.

tail pipe An exhaust (*n.* def. 2).

tail·race (tāl′rās′) *n.* **1.** That part of a millrace below the water wheel. **2.** The channel for water to remove tailings.

tail·spin (tāl′spin′) *n.* **1.** *Aeron.* The descent of a stalled airplane along a tight helical path at a steep angle. **2.** *Informal* An emotional upheaval often resulting in loss of control.

tail wind A wind blowing in the same general direction as the course of an aircraft, ship, or other vehicle.

taint (tānt) *v.t.* **1.** To imbue with an offensive, poisonous, or deteriorating quality or principle; infect with decay. **2.** To render morally corrupt. — *v.i.* **3.** To be or become tainted. — *n.* **1.** A trace or germ of decay. **2.** A moral stain or blemish; disgrace. [Fusion of ATTAINT and F *teint*, pp. of *teindre* to tinge, color]

Taj Ma·hal (täzh′ mə·häl′, täj′) A mausoleum of white marble built (1631–45) at Agra, India.

take (tāk) *v.* **took, tak·en, tak·ing** *v.t.* **1.** To lay hold of;

grasp. **2.** To get possession of; seize. **3.** To seize forcibly; capture. **4.** To catch in a trap or snare. **5.** To win in competition. **6.** To choose; select. **7.** To buy. **8.** To rent or hire. **9.** To subscribe to, as a periodical. **10.** To assume occupancy of: to *take* a chair. **11.** To assume the responsibilities or duties of: to *take* office. **12.** To bring or accept into some relation to oneself: He *took* a wife. **13.** To assume as a symbol or badge: to *take* the veil. **14.** To impose upon oneself: to *take* a vow. **15.** To remove or carry off: with *away.* **16.** To steal. **17.** To remove by death. **18.** To subtract or deduct. **19.** To undergo: to *take* a beating. **20.** To accept passively: to *take* an insult. **21.** To become affected with: He *took* cold. **22.** To affect: The fever *took* him at dawn. **23.** To captivate; charm or delight. **24.** To react to: How did she *take* the news? **25.** To undertake to deal with: to *take* an examination. **26.** To consider; deem. **27.** To understand; comprehend. **28.** To strike in a specified place; hit: The blow *took* him on the forehead. **29.** *Informal* To aim or direct: He *took* a shot at the target. **30.** To carry with one: He *took* a briefcase along. **31.** To lead: This road *takes* you to town. **32.** To escort; conduct: Who *took* her to the dance? **33.** To receive into the body, as by eating, inhaling, etc. **34.** To accept, as something offered, due, or given: to *take* a degree. **35.** To let in; admit: The car will *take* only six people. **36.** To indulge oneself in: to *take* a nap. **37.** To perform, as an action: to *take* a stride. **38.** To avail oneself of (an opportunity, etc.). **39.** To put into effect; adopt: to *take* measures. **40.** To use up or consume: The piano *takes* too much space. **41.** To make use of; apply: They *took* clubs to him. **42.** To travel by means of: to *take* a train. **43.** To go to; seek: to *take* cover. **44.** To ascertain or obtain by measuring, computing, etc.: to *take* a census. **45.** To obtain or derive from some source; adopt or copy. **46.** To obtain by writing; write down or copy: to *take* notes. **47.** To obtain a likeness or representation of, as by drawing or photographing; also, to obtain (a likeness, picture, etc.) in such a manner. **48.** To experience; feel: to *take* pride. **49.** To conceive: to *take* a dislike. **50.** To absorb: The cloth will not *take* the pattern. **51.** In baseball, to allow (a pitch) to pass without swinging at it: said of a batter. **52.** *Slang* To cheat; deceive. **53.** *Gram.* To require by construction or usage: The verb *takes* a direct object. — *v.i.* **54.** To get possession. **55.** To engage; catch, as mechanical parts. **56.** To begin to grow; germinate. **57.** To have the intended effect: The vaccination *took*. **58.** To become popular; gain favor or currency, as a play. **59.** To admit of being photographed: His face *takes* well. **60.** To detract: with *from*. **61.** To become (ill or sick). **62.** To make one's way; go. **63.** In baseball, to allow a pitch to pass without swinging at it: said of a batter. **— to take after 1.** To resemble. **2.** To follow as an example. **— to take amiss** To be offended by. **— to take at one's word** To believe. **— to take back 1.** To regain. **2.** To retract. **— to take breath** To pause, as from working. **— to take down 1.** To pull down, as a building. **2.** To dismantle; disassemble. **3.** To humble. **4.** To write down; make a record of. **— to take heart** To gain courage or confidence. **— to take in 1.** To admit; receive. **2.** To lessen in size or scope. **3.** To furl or haul in (sail). **4.** To include; embrace. **5** To understand; comprehend. **6.** To receive into one's home for pay, as lodgers or work. **7.** *Informal* To cheat or deceive. **8.** *U.S. Informal* To visit, as on a trip or tour: Did you *take in* the Louvre? **— to take in vain** To use profanely or blasphemously, as the name of a deity. **— to take it 1.** To assume; understand. **2.** To endure hardship, abuse, etc. **— to take it out on** *U.S. Informal* To vent one's anger, frustration, etc., on. **— to take off 1.** To remove, as a coat. **2.** To carry away. **3.** To kill. **4.** To deduct. **5.** *Informal* To mimic; burlesque. **6.** To rise from the ground or water in starting a flight, as an airplane. **7.** *U.S. Informal* To leave; depart. **— to take on 1.** To hire; employ. **2.** To undertake to deal with; handle. **3.** *Informal* To exhibit violent emotion. **— to take out 1.** To extract; remove. **2.** To obtain from the proper authority, as a license or patent. **3.** To lead or escort. **— to take over 1.** To assume control. **2.** To convey. **— to take place** To happen. **— to take stock 1.** To make an inventory. **2.** To estimate probability, position, etc.; consider. **to take the field** To begin a campaign or game. **— to take to 1.** To have recourse to; go to: to *take* to one's bed. **2.** To develop the practice of, or an addiction to: He *took* to drink. **3.** To become fond of. **— to take to heart** To be deeply affected by. **— to take up 1.** To raise or lift. **2.** To make smaller or less; shorten or tighten. **3.** To pay, as a mortgage. **4.** To accept as stipulated: to *take up* an option. **5.** To begin or begin again. **6.** To reprove or criticize. **7.** To occupy, engage, or consume, as space or time. **8.** To acquire an interest in or devotion to: to *take up* a cause. **— to take up with** *Informal* To become friendly with. **— n. 1.**

The act of taking, or that which is taken. **2.** An uninterrupted run of a camera or recording apparatus in making a motion picture, television program, sound recording, etc. **3.** A quantity collected at one time: the *take* of fish. **4.** *U.S. Slang* Money collected, as the receipts of a sporting event. [OE *tacan* < ON *taka*]

take-down (tāk′doun′) *adj.* Fitted for being taken apart or easily down: a *takedown* rifle. — *n.* **1.** Any article so constructed as to be taken apart easily. **2.** *U.S. Informal* The act of humiliating anyone.

take-home pay (tāk′hōm′) *U.S.* The remainder of one's wages or salary after tax and other payroll deductions.

take-in (tāk′in′) *n. Informal* An act of cheating or hoaxing.

take-off (tāk′ôf′, -of′) *n.* **1.** The act of rising or leaping from the ground to begin flight; also, the spot where this happens. **2.** *Informal* A satirical imitation; caricature.

take-o-ver (tāk′ō-vər) *n.* An assuming or seizure of control, function, ownership, or rule.

tak-er (tā′kər) *n.* One who takes or collects.

tak-ing (tā′king) *adj.* **1.** Fascinating; captivating. **2.** *Informal* Contagious; infectious. — *n.* **1.** The act of one who takes. **2.** The thing or things taken. **3.** *pl.* Receipts. as of money. — **tak′ing-ly** *adv.* — **tak′ing-ness** *n.*

talc (talk) *n.* A soft, white or variously colored, hydrous magnesium silicate, $H_2Mg_3(SiO_3)_4$, used in making paper, soap, toilet powder, insulators, etc. Also **tal-cum** (tal′kəm). — *v.t.* **talcked** or **talced, talck-ing** or **talc-ing** To treat with talc. [< F < Med. L < Arabian *talq*]

talcum powder Finely powdered and purified talc, used as a dusting agent, filter, etc.

tale (tāl) *n.* **1.** That which is told or related; a story; recital. **2.** A piece of gossip. **3.** A lie; falsehood. [OE *talu* speech, narrative]

tale-bear-er (tāl′bâr′ər) *n.* One who carries gossip; a taleteller. — **tale′bear′ing** *adj. & n.*

tal-ent (tal′ənt) *n.* **1.** A particular and uncommon aptitude for some special work or activity. **2.** People of skill or ability, collectively. **3.** An ancient weight and denomination of money. [OE < L < Gk. *talanton* weight]

tal-ent-ed (tal′ən-tid) *adj.* Having great ability; gifted.

talent scout One whose business is to discover talented people, esp. for the performing arts.

ta-ler (tä′lər) *n.* A former German silver coin, the prototype of all dollars: also spelled *thaler*. [< G. See DOLLAR.]

ta-les (tā′lēz) *n. pl.* **tal-es** (-lēz) *Law* Persons to be summoned for jury duty to make up a deficiency when the regular panel is exhausted by challenges. [< L *tales* pl. of *talis* such a one]

tales-man (tālz′mən) *n. pl.* **-men** (-mən) *Law* One of the tales.

tale-tel-ler (tāl′tel′ər) *n.* **1.** One who tells stories, etc.; a raconteur. **2.** A talebearer. — **tale′tell′ing** *adj. & n.*

tal-i-pes (tal′ə-pēz) *n. Pathol.* Clubfoot. [< NL < L *talus* ankle + *pes, pedis* foot] — **tal-i-ped** (tal′ə-ped) *adj.*

tal-i-pot (tal′ə-pot) *n.* A stately East Indian palm crowned by large leaves used as fans, umbrellas, writing material, and as coverings for houses. [< Bengali *tālipāt* palm leaf]

tal-is-man (tal′is-mən, -iz-) *n. pl.* **-mans 1.** Something supposed to produce extraordinary or magical effects; a charm or amulet. **2.** An astrological charm or symbol supposed to benefit or protect the possessor. [< F < Sp. < Arabic *tilsam, tilasm* magic figure] — **tal′is-man′ic** (-man′ik) or **-i-cal** *adj.*

talk (tôk) *v.i.* **1.** To express or exchange thoughts in audible words; communicate by speech. **2.** To make a speech. **3.** To communicate by means other than speech: to *talk* with one's fingers. **4.** To speak irrelevantly; prate; chatter. **5.** To confer; consult. **6.** To spread rumor; gossip. **7.** To make sounds suggestive of speech. **8.** *U.S. Informal* To give information, as to the police; inform. **9.** *Informal* To be effective or influential: money *talks*. — *v.t.* **10.** To express in words; utter. **11.** To use in speaking; converse in: to *talk* Spanish. **12.** To converse about; discuss: to *talk* business. **13.** To bring to a specified condition or state by talking: to *talk* one into doing something. **14.** To pass or spend, as time, in talking: usu. with *away*. **— to talk back** To answer impudently. **— to talk big** *Slang* To brag; boast. **— to talk down 1.** To silence by talking; outtalk. **2.** To direct (an aircraft) to a landing, in darkness, fog, etc., by giving oral instructions to the pilot over the radio. **— to talk down to** To speak to in a condescending manner. **— to talk shop** To talk about one's work. **— to talk up 1.** To discuss, esp. so as to promote; praise; extol. **2.** *Informal* To speak loudly or boldly. — *n.* **1.** The act of talking; conversation; speech. **2.** A speech or lecture, usu. informal. **3.** Report; rumor: We heard *talk* of war. **4.** That which is talked about; a topic; theme. **5.** A conference for discussion or deliberation; a council. **6.** Mere words; verbiage. **7.** A language, dialect, or lingo: baseball *talk*. [ME *talken*, prob. freq. of OE *talian* to reckon, speak] **— talk'er** *n.*

talk·a·tive (tô'kə·tiv) *adj.* Given to much talking. **— talk'a·tive·ly** *adv.* **— talk'a·tive·ness** *n.*

talking picture A motion picture with spoken words, music, sound effects, etc. Also *Informal* **talk·ie** (tô'kē).

talk·ing-to (tô'king-tōō') *n.* *pl.* **-tos** *Informal* A scolding.

talk·y (tô'kē) *adj.* **talk·i·er, talk·i·est** Talkative.

tall (tôl) *adj.* **1.** Having more than average height; high or lofty. **2.** Having specified height: He is six feet *tall*. **3.** *Informal* Extravagant; boastful; also, unbelievable: a *tall* story. **4.** *Informal* Large; excellent; grand: a *tall* dinner. **— adv.** *Informal* Proudly: to stand *tall*. [OE *getæl* swift, prompt] **— tall'ness** *n.*

tall·ish (tô'lish) *adj.* Rather tall.

tal·lith (tal'ith, tä'lis) *n.* A fringed scarf or mantle worn around the shoulders by Orthodox and Conservative Jewish men when praying. [< Hebrew *tallīth* cover, robe]

tal·low (tal'ō) *n.* A mixture of the harder animal fats, as of beef or mutton, refined for use in candles, soaps, oleomargarine, etc. **— v.t.** To smear with tallow. [ME *talgh*] **— tal'low·y** *adj.*

tal·ly (tal'ē) *n.* *pl.* **·lies** **1.** A piece of wood on which notches or scores are cut as marks of number. **2.** A score or mark. **3.** A reckoning; account. **4.** A counterpart; duplicate. **5.** A mark indicative of a quantity or number, used to denote one in a series. **6.** A label; tag. **— v.** **·lied, ·ly·ing** *v.t.* **1.** To score on a tally; record. **2.** To reckon; count; estimate: often with *up*. **3.** To mark or cut corresponding notches in; cause to correspond. **— v.i.** **4.** To correspond; fit: The stories *tally*. **5.** To keep score. [< AF < L *talea* rod, cutting] **— tal'li·er** *n.*

tal·ly·ho (tal'ē·hō') *interj.* A huntsman's cry to hounds when the quarry is sighted. **— n.** *pl.* **·hos** **1.** The cry of "tallyho." **2.** A four-in-hand coach. **— v.t.** **1.** To urge on, as hounds, with the cry of "tallyho." **— v.i.** **2.** To cry "tallyho." [Alter. of F *taïaut*, a hunting cry]

tal·ly·man (tal'ē·mən) *n.* *pl.* **·men** (-mən) **1.** One who keeps a count or a tally, esp., of votes. **2.** One who records number, volume, and measurement, as of timber.

Tal·mud (tal'mud, täl'mŏŏd) *n.* The body of Jewish civil and religious law and related commentaries) not included in the Pentateuch. [< Hebrew *talmūdh* instruction] **— Tal·mud'ic** or **·i·cal** *adj.* **— Tal'mud·ist** *n.*

tal·on (tal'ən) *n.* **1.** The claw of a bird or other animal, esp. of a bird of prey. **2.** Anything resembling or suggesting a claw, as a grasping human hand. **3.** A projection on the bolt of a lock on which the key presses in shooting the bolt. [< OF < L *talus* heel] **— tal'oned** (-ənd) *adj.*

ta·lus (tā'ləs) *n.* *pl.* **·li** (-lī) **1.** *Anat.* The bone of the foot just above the heel bone: also called *anklebone, astragalus.* **2.** A slope, as of a tapering wall. **3.** *Geol.* The sloping mass of rock fragments below a cliff. [< L, ankle, heel]

tam (tam) *n.* A tam-o'-shanter.

ta·ma·le (tə·mä'lē) *n.* A Mexican dish made of crushed corn and meat, seasoned with red pepper, wrapped in corn husks, dipped in oil, and cooked by steam. Also **ta·mal** (tə·mäl'). [< Am. Sp. *tamales*, pl. of *tamal* < Nahuatl *tamalli*]

tam·a·rack (tam'ə·rak) *n.* **1.** The American larch, a tree common in northern North America. **2.** Its wood. Also called *hackmatack.* [< Algonquian]

tam·a·rind (tam'ə·rind) *n.* **1.** A tropical tree of the bean family, with hard yellow wood and showy yellow flowers striped with red. **2.** The fruit of this tree, a flat pod with soft acid pulp used in preserves and as a laxative. [< Sp. < Arabic *tamr hindi* Indian date]

tam·bour (tam'bŏŏr) *n.* **1.** A drum. **2.** A round wooden frame on which material for embroidering may be stretched; also, the fabric embroidered. **— v.t. & v.i.** To embroider on a tambour. [< F < Arabic *tambūr* a stringed instrument]

tam·bou·rin (tam'bə·rin) *n.* **1.** A long, narrow drum, originating in Provence. **2.** A gay, 18th-century Provençal dance, or the music for it. [< F < Provençal]

tam·bou·rine (tam'bə·rēn') *n.* A musical instrument like the head of a drum, with jingles in the rim, played by striking it with the hand; a timbrel. [< F]

tame (tām) *adj.* **tam·er, tam·est** **1.** Having lost its native wildness or shyness; domesticated. **2.** In agriculture, brought under or produced by cultivation. **3.** Docile; tractable. **4.** Subdued or subjugated. **5.** Gentle; harmless. **6.** Lacking in effectiveness; uninteresting; dull. **— v.t.** **tamed, tam·ing** **1.** To domesticate. **2.** To bring into subjection or obedience; render spiritless. **3.** To tone down; soften, as glaring colors. [OE *tam*] **— tam'a·ble** or **tame'a·ble** *adj.* **— tame'ly** *adv.* **— tame'ness** *n.* **— tam'er** *n.*

tame·less (tām'lis) *adj.* Untamed or untamable. **— tame'less·ness** *n.*

Tam·il (tam'əl, tum'əl) *n.* **1.** One of an ancient Dravidian people, and still the most numerous of the inhabitants of southern India and northern Ceylon. **2.** Their language.

Tam·ma·ny (tam'ə·nē) *n.* A fraternal society in New York City (founded 1789) serving as the central organization of the city's Democratic party. Also called **Tammany Hall, Tammany Society.** [Alter. of *Tamanend*, name of a 17th c. Delaware Indian chief friendly toward white men]

Tam·muz (täm·mōōz', täm'mōōz) The tenth month of the Hebrew year. See (Hebrew) CALENDAR. Also spelled *Thammuz*: also **Tam·uz.** [< Hebrew]

tam-o'-shan·ter (tam'ə·shan'tər) *n.* A Scottish cap with a tight headband and a full, flat top, sometimes with a pompon or tassel. [after *Tam o' Shanter*, a poem by Robert Burns]

tamp (tamp) *v.t.* **1.** To force down or pack closer by firm, repeated blows. **2.** To ram down, as dirt, etc., on top of the charge in a blasthole. [Back formation < TAMPION]

tam·per (tam'pər) *v.i.* **1.** To meddle; interfere: usu. with *with*. **2.** To make changes, esp., so as to damage or corrupt: with *with*. **3.** To use corrupt measures, as bribery; scheme or plot. [Var. of TEMPER] **— tam'per·er** *n.*

tam·pi·on (tam'pē·ən) *n.* *Mil.* A stopper, as the plug put into the mouth of a cannon to keep out moisture, etc. [< F *tampon*, nasal var. of *tapon*, *tape* bung < Gmc]

tam·pon (tam'pon) *n.* *Med.* A plug of cotton or lint for insertion in a wound or body cavity. **— v.t.** To plug up, as a wound, with a tampon. [See TAMPION]

tan (tan) *v.* **tanned, tan·ning** *v.t.* **1.** To convert into leather, as hides or skins, by treating with tannin. **2.** To turn brown, as the skin, by exposure to sunlight. **3.** *Informal* To thrash; flog. **— v.i.** **4.** To become tanned, as hides or the skin. **— n.** **1.** A yellowish brown color tinged with red. **2.** A dark or brown coloring of the skin, resulting from exposure to the sun. **3.** Tanbark. **— adj.** **1.** Of the color tan; light brown. **2.** Used in or pertaining to tanning. [OE < Med.L *tanum* tanbark, prob. < Celtic.]

tan·a·ger (tan'ə·jər) *n.* Any of a family of American songbirds noted for the brilliant plumage of the male. [< NL < Pg. *tangara* < Tupi] **— tan'a·grine** (-grēn) *adj.*

tan·bark (tan'bärk') *n.* **1.** The bark of certain trees, esp. oak or hemlock, containing tannin, and used in tanning leather. **2.** Spent bark from the tan vats, used on circus arenas, racetracks, etc.

tan·dem (tan'dəm) *adv.* One in front of or before another. **— n.** **1.** Two or more horses harnessed in single file. **2.** A two-wheeled carriage drawn by a tandem of horses. **3.** A bicycle with seats for two persons, one behind the other: also **tandem bicycle.** **4.** Any arrangement of two or more persons or things placed one before another. **— adj.** Arranged in tandem, or including parts so arranged. [< L, at length (of time); used in puns in sense of "lengthwise"]

tang (tang) *n.* **1.** A penetrating taste, flavor, or odor. **2.** A trace; hint. **3.** Any distinct taste, odor, quality, etc., other than one that is sweet. **4.** A slender shank or tongue projecting from some metal part, as the end of a sword blade or chisel, for inserting in or fixing upon a handle. **— v.t.** To provide with a tang. [< ON *tangi* point, dagger]

tan·gen·cy (tan'jən·sē) *n.* *pl.* **·cies** The state of being tangent. Also **tan'gence.**

tan·gent (tan'jənt) *adj.* Being in contact at a single point or along a line; touching. **— n.** **1.** *Geom.* **a** A straight line in contact with a curve at one point. **b** A straight line, curve, or surface touching another curve or surface at one or more consecutive points. **2.** *Trig.* A function of an acute angle, equal to the ratio of the side opposite the angle to the side adjacent to the angle when the angle is included in a right triangle. **— to fly** (or **go**) **off on a tangent** *Informal* To make a sharp or sudden change in direction or course of action. [< L *tangens, -entis*, ppr. of *tangere* to touch]

tan·gen·tial (tan·jen'shəl) *adj.* **1.** Of, pertaining to, or moving in the direction of a tangent. **2.** Touching slightly. **3.** Only partially relevant to a subject. Also **tan·gen'tal** (-jen'təl). **— tan·gen'ti·al·i·ty** (-shē·al'ə·tē) *n.* **— tan·gen'·tial·ly** *adv.*

tan·ger·ine (tan'jə·rēn') *n.* **1.** A small, juicy orange with a loose, easily removed skin: also called *mandarin.* **2.** A slightly burnt orange color. [after *Tangier*]

tan·gi·ble (tan'jə·bəl) *adj.* **1.** Perceptible by touch; also, within reach by touch. **2.** Capable of being apprehended by the mind; of definite shape; real: *tangible* evidence. **3.** *Law* Perceptible to the senses; corporeal; material: *tangible* property. **— n.** **1.** That which is tangible. **2.** *pl.* Material assets. [< F < L *tangere* to touch] **— tan'gi·bil'i·ty, tan'·gi·ble·ness** *n.* **— tan'gi·bly** *adv.*

tan·gle (tang'gəl) *v.* **·gled, ·gling** *v.t.* **1.** To twist or involve in a confused and not readily separable mass. **2.** To ensnare as in a tangle; enmesh. **— v.i.** **3.** To be or become entangled. **— to tangle with** *Informal* To come to blows with. **— n.** **1.** A confused intertwining, as of threads or hairs; a snarl. **2.** A state of confusion or complication; a jumbled mess. **3.** A state of perplexity or bewilderment. [Nasalized var. of obs. *tagle* < Scand.] **— tan'gler** *n.*

tan·gly (tang'glē) *adj.* Consisting of or being in a tangle.

tan·go (tang'gō) *n.* *pl.* **·gos** **1.** Any of several Latin-American dances in 2/4 time, characterized by deliberate gliding steps and low dips. **2.** Any syncopated tune or melody to which the tango may be danced. — *v.i.* To dance the tango. [< Am.Sp., fiesta, Negro drum dance]

tang·y (tang′ē) *adj.* **tang·i·er, tang·i·est** Having a tang in taste or odor; pungent.

tank (tangk) *n.* **1.** A large vessel, basin, or receptacle for holding a fluid. **2.** Any natural or artificial pool or pond. **3.** *Mil.* A heavily armored combat vehicle, moving on caterpillar treads and mounting guns of various calibers. — *v.t.* To place or store in a tank. [< Pg. *tanque,* aphetic var. of *estanque* < L *stagnum* pool]

tank·age (tangk′ij) *n.* **1.** The act, process, or operation of putting in tanks. **2.** The price for storage in tanks. **3.** The capacity or contents of a tank. **4.** Slaughterhouse waste, bones and entrails, used when dried as a fertilizer or feed.

tank·ard (tangk′ərd) *n.* A large, one-handled drinking cup, usu. made of pewter or silver, often with a cover. [< MDu. < Med.L *tancardus* large goblet]

tank·er (tangk′ər) *n.* A cargo vessel specially constructed for the transport of liquids, esp. oil and gasoline.

tank farm *U.S.* An area near a refinery, factory, port, etc., occupied by large storage tanks.

tank·ful (tangk′fool′) *n.* The quantity that fills a tank.

tank town *U.S. Informal* A small town where trains formerly stopped to refill from a water tank.

tan·nage (tan′ij) *n.* The act or operation of tanning.

tan·ner (tan′ər) *n.* One who tans hides.

tan·ner·y (tan′ər-ē) *n. pl.* **·ner·ies** A place where leather is tanned.

tan·nic (tan′ik) *adj.* Pertaining to or derived from tannin or tanbark.

tannic acid *n. Chem.* Any of a group of brownish astringent compounds extracted from gallnuts, sumac, etc., used in the preparation of ink and in the manufacture of leather.

tan·nin (tan′in) *n.* Tannic acid.

tan·ning (tan′ing) *n.* **1.** The art or process of converting hides into leather. **2.** A bronzing, as of the skin, by exposure to the sun, wind, etc. **3.** *Informal* A beating or thrashing.

tan·sy (tan′zē) *n. pl.* **·sies** Any of various coarse perennial herbs with yellow flowers and an aromatic, bitter taste, used in medicine for its tonic properties. [< OF *tanesie,* aphetic var. of *athanasie* < LL < Gk., immortality]

tan·ta·lize (tan′tə-līz) *v.t.* **·lized, ·liz·ing** To tease or torment by repeated frustration of hopes or desires. Also *Brit.* **tan·ta·lise.** [< TANTALUS] — **tan′ta·li·za′tion** *n.* — **tan′ta·liz′ing·ly** *adv.*

tan·ta·lum (tan′tə-ləm) *n.* A silver-white, very heavy, ductile, metallic element (symbol Ta), forming alloys with tungsten, molybdenum, and iron. See ELEMENT. [< TANTALUS; from its inability to absorb water]

Tan·ta·lus (tan′tə-ləs) In Greek mythology, a rich king, who was punished in Hades by being made to stand in water that receded when he tried to drink, and under fruit-laden branches he could not reach.

tan·ta·mount (tan′tə-mount) *adj.* Having equivalent value, effect, or import; equivalent: with *to.* [< AF < L *tantus* as much + OF *amonter* to amount]

tan·trum (tan′trəm) *n.* A petulant fit of rage. [Origin unknown]

Tao·ism (dou′iz-əm, tou′-) *n.* One of the principal religions or philosophies of China, founded by Lao-tse, who taught that happiness could be acquired through obedience to the requirements of man's nature in accordance with the **Tao** (dou, tou), or Way, the basic principle of all nature. [< Chinese *tao* way, road] — **Tao′ist** *adj. & n.* — **Tao·is′tic** *adj.*

tap¹ (tap) *n.* **1.** An arrangement for drawing out liquid, as beer from a cask. **2.** A faucet or cock; spigot. **3.** A plug or stopper to close an opening in a cask or other vessel. **4.** Liquor drawn from a tap; also, a particular liquor or quality of liquor contained in casks. **5.** *Brit.* A place where liquor is served; taproom. **6.** A tool for cutting internal screw threads. **7.** A point of connection for an electrical circuit. — **on tap 1.** Contained in a cask; ready for tapping: beer *on tap.* **2.** Provided with a tap. **3.** *Informal* Available; ready. — *v.t.* **tapped, tap·ping 1.** To provide with a tap or spigot. **2.** To pierce or open so as to draw liquid from. **3.** To draw (liquid) from a container. **4.** To make connection with: to *tap* a gas main. **5.** To make connection with secretly: to *tap* a telephone wire. **6.** To make an internal screw thread with a tap. [OE *tæppa*]

tap² (tap) *v.* **tapped, tap·ping** *v.t.* **1.** To touch or strike gently. **2.** To make or produce by tapping. **3.** To apply leather to (the sole or heel of a shoe) in repair. — *v.i.* **4.** To strike a light blow or blows, as with the finger tip. — *n.* **1.** A gentle or playful blow; also, the sound made by such a blow. **2.** Leather, etc., affixed to a shoe sole or heel; also, a metal plate on the toe or heel of a shoe. [< OF *taper*] — **tap′per** *n.*

ta·pa (tä′pä) *n.* **1.** The inner bark of an Asian mulberry tree used in making a kind of cloth. **2.** The cloth. [< native Polynesian name]

tap-dance (tap′dans′, -däns′) *v.i.* **-danced, -danc·ing** To dance or perform a tap dance.

tap dance A dance in which the dancer emphasizes his steps by tapping the floor with the heels or toes of shoes designed to make the rhythm audible. — **tap dancer**

tape (tāp) *n.* **1.** A narrow strip of strong woven fabric. **2.** Any long, narrow, flat strip of paper, metal, etc. **3.** A magnetic tape. **4.** A tapeline. **5.** A string stretched breast-high across the finishing point of a racing track and broken by the winner of the race. — *v.t.* **taped, tap·ing 1.** To wrap or secure with tape. **2.** To apply a tape to; bandage: to *tape* a boxer's hands. **3.** To measure with or as with a tapeline. **4.** To record on magnetic tape. [OE *tæppe* strip of cloth]

tape·line (tāp′līn′) *n.* A tape for measuring distances. Also **tape measure.**

ta·per¹ (tā′pər) *n.* One who or that which tapes.

ta·per² (tā′pər) *n.* **1.** A small candle. **2.** A burning wick or other light substance giving but feeble illumination. **3.** A gradual diminution of size in an elongated object: the *taper* of a mast. **4.** Any tapering object, as a cone. — *v.t. & v.i.* **1.** To make or become smaller or thinner toward one end. **2.** To lessen gradually; diminish: with *off.* — *adj.* Growing small by degrees in one direction; slender and conical or pyramidal. [OE, dissimilated var. of Med.L *papur* taper, wick < L, papyrus] — **ta′per·ing·ly** *adv.*

tape-re·cord (tāp′ri-kôrd′) *v.t.* To tape (*v.* def. 4).

tape recorder A device that converts sound into magnetic patterns stored on a tape, reversing the process for playback.

tape recording 1. The process of transcribing music, speech, etc., on a tape recorder. **2.** A transcription so made.

tap·es·try (tap′is-trē) *n. pl.* **·tries** A woven, ornamental fabric, used for hangings, in which the woof is supplied by a spindle, the design being formed by stitches across the warp. — *v.t.* **·tried, ·try·ing 1.** To hang or adorn with tapestry. **2.** To make or weave as tapestry. [< OF < L < Gk. *tapētion,* dim. of *tapēs* rug]

tape·worm (tāp′wûrm′) *n.* Any of various worms with segmented, ribbonlike bodies, parasitic on the intestines of vertebrates and often infesting man.

tap·i·o·ca (tap′ē-ō′kə) *n.* A nutritious starchy substance having irregular grains, obtained by drying cassava starch. [< Sp. < Tupi < *ty* juice + *pýa* heart + *oco* to be removed]

ta·pir (tā′pər) *n.* A large nocturnal mammal, having short limbs and a flexible snout, native to South and Central America and to the Malay Peninsula. [< Sp. < Tupi *tapy′ra*]

tap·pet (tap′it) *n. Mech.* A lever or projecting arm of a mechanism that moves or is moved intermittently by automatically touching another part. [< TAP²]

tap·ping (tap′ing) *n.* **1.** The act of one who or that which taps. **2.** Something taken by tapping, or running from a tap.

tap·room (tap′room′, -room′) *n.* A bar or barroom.

tap·root (tap′root′, -root′) *n. Bot.* The principal descending root of a plant. — **tap′root′ed** *adj.*

taps (taps) *n.pl.* (*usu.* construed as *sing.*) A military signal by bugle or beat of drum, regularly sounded after tattoo for the extinguishing of all lights and sometimes played after a military burial.

tap·ster (tap′stər) *n.* One who draws and serves liquor; a bartender. [OE *tæppestre* barmaid]

tar¹ (tär) *n.* **1.** A dark, oily, viscid mixture of hydrocarbons, obtained by the destructive distillation of resinous woods, coal, etc. **2.** Coal tar. — *v.t.* **tarred, tar·ring** To cover with or as with tar. — **to tar and feather** To smear (a person) with tar and then cover with feathers as a punishment. — *adj.* Made of, derived from, or resembling tar. [OE *teoru*]

tar² (tär) *n. Informal* A sailor. [Short for TARPAULIN]

tar·an·tel·la (tar′ən-tel′ə) *n.* A lively Neapolitan dance in 6/8 time; also, the music written for it. [< Ital., dim. of *Taranto* Taranto]

ta·ran·tu·la (tə-ran′chŏō-lə) *n. pl.* **·las** or **·lae** (-lē) **1.** A large, hairy spider of southern Europe. **2.** Any of various related spiders known for their painful but not dangerous bite. [< Med.L < Ital. < *Taranto* Taranto]

tar·boosh (tär-boosh′) *n.* A brimless, usu. red, felt cap with colored silk tassel, worn by Moslem men. Also **tar·bush′.** [< Arabic *tarbūsh*]

tar·di·grade (tär′də-grād) *adj.* Slow in motion or action. [< F < L *tardus* slow + *gradi* to walk]

tar·dy (tär′dē) *adj.* **·di·er, ·di·est 1.** Not coming at the appointed time; late. **2.** Moving slowly. [< F < L *tardus* slow] — **tar′di·ly** *adv.* — **tar′di·ness** *n.*

tare¹ (tär) *n.* **1.** An unidentified weed that grows among wheat. **2.** A seed of wickedness. *Matt.* xiii 25. **3.** Any of various species of vetch. [MDu. *tarwe* wheat]

tare² (târ) *n.* An allowance made to a buyer of goods by deducting from the gross weight of his purchase the weight of the container. — *v.t.* **tared, tar·ing** To weigh, as a package, in order to determine the amount of tare. [< F < Arabic < *taraha* to reject, throw away]

tar·get (tär'git) *n.* **1.** An object presenting a surface that may be used as a mark or butt, as in rifle or archery practice. **2.** Anything that is shot at. **3.** A person or thing made an object of attack or center of attention; a butt. — **on target 1.** Headed or aimed so as to hit a target. **2.** *Informal* Aptly directed or placed; to the point: The quip was right *on target.* [ME *targette, targuete,* dim. of *targa* shield]

Tar·heel (tär'hēl') *n. Informal* A native of North Carolina. Also **Tar Heel.**

Tarheel State Nickname of North Carolina.

tar·iff (tar'if) *n.* **1.** A schedule of articles of merchandise with the rates of duty to be paid for their importation or exportation. **2.** A duty, or duties collectively. **3.** The law or principles governing the imposition of duties. **4.** Any schedule of charges. — *v.t.* **1.** To make a list or table of duties or customs on. **2.** To fix a price or tariff on. [< Ital. < Arabic *ta'rif* information]

tar·mac (tär'mak) *n. Brit. & Canadian* **1.** *Aeron.* **a** A hangar apron. **b** An asphalt runway. **2.** An asphalt road.

tarn (tärn) *n.* A small mountain lake. [ME < ON *tjörn*]

tar·na·tion (tär-nā'shən) *interj. & n. U.S. Dial.* Damnation: a euphemism.

tar·nish (tär'nish) *v.t.* **1.** To dim the luster of. **2.** To dim the purity of; stain; disgrace. — *v.i.* **3.** To lose luster, as by oxidation. — *n.* **1.** Loss of luster. **2.** A blemish or stain. **3.** The thin film of color on the exposed surface of a metal or mineral. [< OF < *terne* dull, wan] — **tar'nish·a·ble** *adj.*

ta·ro (tä'rō) *n. pl.* **·ros 1.** Any of several tropical plants of the arum family, grown for their edible, cornlike rootstocks. **2.** The rootstock of this plant. [< native Polynesian name]

tar·ot (tar'ō, -ət) *n.* One of a set of playing cards with grilled or checkered backs employed by fortunetellers and gypsies in foretelling future events. [< F < Ital. < *tarocco* to wrangle, play at cards]

tar·pau·lin (tär-pô'lin, tär'pə-) *n.* **1.** A waterproof canvas impregnated with tar, used to cover merchandise, athletic fields, etc. **2.** A sailor's wide-brimmed storm hat. Also *Informal* **tarp.** [< TAR¹ + PALL¹ + -ING¹]

tar·pon (tär'pon, -pən) *n. pl.* **·pon** or **·pons** A large marine game fish of the West Indies and the coast of Florida, having conspicuous silvery scales. [Origin unknown]

tar·ra·gon (tar'ə-gon) *n.* **1.** A European perennial plant allied to wormwood. **2.** The aromatic leaves of this plant, used as seasoning. [< Sp. < Arabic < Gk. *drakōn* dragon]

tar·ri·er (tar'ē-ər) *n.* One who or that which tarries.

tar·ry¹ (tar'ē) *v.* **·ried, ·ry·ing** *v.i.* **1.** To put off going or coming; linger. **2.** To remain in the same place, esp. longer than one expected. **3.** To wait; stay. — *n.* Sojourn; stay. [ME *tarien* to vex, hinder, delay, fusion of OE *tirgan* to vex + OF *targer* to delay, < LL < *tardare* to delay]

tar·ry² (tär'ē) *adj.* **·ri·er, ·ri·est** Covered with tar; like tar.

tar·sal (tär'səl) *adj.* Of, relating to, or situated near the tarsus or ankle.

tarso- *combining form* The tarsus; pertaining to the tarsus. Also, before vowels, **tars-.** [< Gk. *tarsos* flat of the foot, edge of the eyelid]

tar·sus (tär'səs) *n. pl.* **·si** (-sī) **1.** *Anat.* The ankle, or, in man, the group of seven bones of which it is composed. **2.** *Zool.* **a** The shank of a bird's leg. **b** The distal part of the leg in insects. [< NL < Gk. *tarsos* flat of the foot, any flat surface]

tart¹ (tärt) *adj.* **1.** Having a sharp, sour taste. **2.** Severe; cutting; caustic: a *tart* remark. [OE *teart*] — **tart'ly** *adv.* — **tart'ness** *n.*

tart² (tärt) *n.* **1.** A small pastry shell with fruit or custard filling and without a top crust. **2.** In England, an uncovered fruit pie. **3.** *Slang* A girl or woman of loose morals, as a prostitute. [< OF *tarte*]

tar·tan (tär'tən) *n.* **1.** A woolen fabric having varicolored lines or stripes at right angles, forming a distinctive pattern, the characteristic dress of the Scottish Highlanders, each clan having its particular pattern or patterns. **2.** Any similar pattern; a plaid. **3.** A garment made of tartan. For illus. see KILT. — *adj.* **1.** Made of tartan. **2.** Striped or checkered in a manner similar to the Scottish tartans. [? < OF *tiretaine* linsey-woolsey]

tar·tar¹ (tär'tər) *n.* **1.** An acid substance deposited from grape juice during fermentation as a pinkish sediment; crude bitartrate of potassium. **2.** *Dent.* A yellowish incrustation on the teeth, chiefly calcium phosphate. [< F < LL < Med.Gk. *tartaron,* ? < Arabic]

tar·tar² (tär'tər) *n. Often cap.* **1.** A person of intractable or savage temper. **2.** An unexpectedly formidable opponent. — **to catch a tartar** To take on or be matched with an unexpectedly strong opponent. [< TARTAR]

Tar·tar (tär'tər) *n.* A Tatar. — *adj.* Of or pertaining to

the Tatars or Tartary: also **Tar·tar·i·an** (tär-târ'ē-ən). [< F < LL < Persian *Tātar* Tatar]

Tar·tar·e·an (tär-târ'ē-ən) *adj.* Of or pertaining to Tartarus.

tartar emetic *Chem.* A white, crystalline, poisonous derivative of tartaric acid, used in medicine and in dyeing.

tar·tare sauce (tär'tər) A fish sauce made of mayonnaise, capers, chopped olives, and pickles. Also **tar'tar sauce.**

tar·tar·ic (tär-tar'ik, -tär'ik) *adj.* Pertaining to or derived from tartar or tartaric acid.

tartaric acid *Chem.* Any one of four organic compounds, $C_4H_6O_6$, occurring in the free state or as a potassium or calcium salt, as in grape juice, various unripe fruits, etc.

tar·tar·ize (tär'tə-rīz) *v.t.* **·ized, ·iz·ing** To impregnate or treat with tartar, cream of tartar, or tartar emetic. — **tar'· tar·i·za'tion** *n.*

Tartar mink The kolinsky. Also **Tartar sable.**

tar·tar·ous (tär'tər-əs) *adj.* Of or derived from tartar.

Tar·ta·rus (tär'tər-əs) **1.** In Greek mythology, the abyss below Hades where Zeus confined the Titans. **2.** Hades.

Tar·ta·ry (tär'tər-ē) A region of Asia and eastern Europe, ruled by the Tatars, under Mongol leadership, in the 13th and 14th centuries.

tart·let (tärt'lit) *n.* A small pastry tart.

tar·trate (tär'trāt) *n. Chem.* A salt or ester of tartaric acid.

task (task, täsk) *n.* **1.** A specific amount of labor or study imposed by authority or required by duty or necessity. **2.** Any work voluntarily undertaken. **3.** An exhausting or bothersome job or duty. **4.** A specific military mission. — **to take to task** To reprove; lecture. — *v.t.* **1.** To assign a task to. **2.** To overtax with labor; burden. **3.** To reprimand. [< AF < L *taxare* to appraise]

task force *Mil.* A tactical unit consisting of elements drawn from different branches of the armed services and assigned to execute a specific mission.

task·mas·ter (task'mas'tər, täsk'mäs'tər) *n.* **1.** One who assigns tasks, esp. severe ones. **2.** One who or that which loads with heavy burdens.

Tass (täs, tas) *n.* A Soviet news agency. [< Russian *T(e)- legrafnoe) A(gentstvo) S(ovetskovo) S(oyuza)*]

tas·sel (tas'əl) *n.* **1.** A dangling ornament for curtains, cushions, etc., consisting of a tuft of loose threads or cords. **2.** Any of various similar objects, as the inflorescence on a stalk of Indian corn. **3.** Formerly, a clasp for holding a cloak. — *v.* **tas·seled** or **·selled, tas·sel·ing** or **·sel·ling** *v.t.* **1.** To provide or adorn with tassels. **2.** To form in a tassel or tassels. **3.** To remove the tassels from (Indian corn). — *v.i.* **4.** To put forth tassels, as Indian corn. [< OF, clasp < Med.L *tasselus,* var. of L *taxillus*]

taste (tāst) *v.* **tast·ed, tast·ing** *v.t.* **1.** To perceive the flavor of (something) by taking into the mouth or touching with the tongue. **2.** To take a little of (food or drink); eat or drink a little of. **3.** To test the quality of (a product) thus: His business is *tasting* tea. — *v.i.* **4.** To have specified flavor: Sugar *tastes* sweet. **5.** To take a small quantity into the mouth; take a taste: usu. with *of.* **6.** To have experience or enjoyment; with *of:* to *taste* of great sorrow. — *n.* **1.** *Physiol.* Any of the four fundamental sensations, salt, sweet, bitter, or sour, excited by the sole action of the gustatory nerves. **2.** A small quantity tasted, eaten, or sipped. **3.** A slight experience or sample of anything. **4.** Special fondness and aptitude for a pursuit; bent; inclination: a *taste* for music. **5.** The faculty of discerning and appreciating what is beautiful, appropriate, or correct, as in nature, art, clothes, etc. **6.** Style or form with respect to the rules of propriety. **7.** Individual preference: That tie suits my *taste.* **8.** The act of tasting. [< OF *taster* to taste, try, feel] — **tast'a·ble** *adj.*

taste bud *Physiol.* One of the clusters of cells situated in the epithelial tissue, chiefly of the tongue, and containing sensitive receptors for the discriminatory perception of taste.

taste·ful (tāst'fəl) *adj.* **1.** Conforming to taste. **2.** Possessing good taste. — **taste'ful·ly** *adv.* — **taste'ful·ness** *n.*

taste·less (tāst'lis) *adj.* **1.** Having no flavor; insipid; dull. **2.** Lacking in, or showing a lack of, good taste. **3.** Devoid of esthetic taste. — **taste'less·ly** *adv.* — **taste'less·ness** *n.*

tast·er (tās'tər) *n.* One who tastes; esp., one who tests the quality of as an occupation: a *teataster.*

tast·y (tās'tē) *adj.* **tast·i·er, tast·i·est** *Informal* **1.** Having a fine flavor; savory. **2.** Tasteful. — **tast'i·ly** *adv.* — **tast'· i·ness** *n.*

tat (tat) *v.* **tat·ted, tat·ting** *v.t.* **1.** To make, as an edging, by tatting. — *v.i.* **2.** To make tatting. [Back formation < TATTING] — **tat'ter** *n.*

Ta·tar (tä'tər) *n.* **1.** One belonging to any of the Turkic peoples of west central and southwest central U.S.S.R. **2.** Any of the Turkic languages of the Tatars, as Uzbek. — *adj.* Of or pertaining to the Tatars. Also *Tartar.* [< Persian] — **Ta·tar'i·an** (-tär'ē-ən) *adj.*

tat·ter (tat'ər) *n.* **1.** A torn and hanging shred; rag. **2.** *pl.* Ragged clothing. — *v.t.* **1.** To make ragged; tear into tatters. —*v.i.* **2.** To become ragged. [< Scand. Cf. ON *tö-turr* rags] — **tat′tered** *adj.*

tat·ter·de·mal·ion (tat′ər·di·māl′yən, -mal′-) *n.* A person wearing ragged clothes; a raggamuffin. [Origin unknown]

tat·ting (tat′ing) *n.* A lacelike threadwork, made by hand; also, the act or process of making it. [Origin unknown]

tat·tle (tat′l) *v.* **·tled, ·tling** *v.i.* **1.** To talk idly; prate; chatter. **2.** To tell tales about others. — *v.t.* **3.** To reveal by gossiping. — *n.* **1.** Idle talk or gossip. **2.** Prattling speech. [Prob. < MDu. *tatelen*] — **tat′tling·ly** *adv.*
— **Syn.** (verb) **1.** prattle. **2.** blab, inform.

tat·tler (tat′lər) *n.* One who tattles; a talebearer.

tat·tle·tale (tat′l·tāl′) *n.* A talebearer; tattler.

tat·too[1] (ta·tōō′) *v.t.* **1.** To prick and mark (the skin) with indelible pigments. **2.** To mark the skin with (designs, etc.) in this way. — *n. pl.* **·toos** A pattern or picture so made. [< Polynesian] — **tat·too′er** *n.* — **tat·too′ing** *n.*

tat·too[2] (ta·tōō′) *n.* **1.** A continuous beating or drumming. **2.** In military or naval usage, a signal by drum or bugle to repair to quarters, usu., occurring about 9 P.M. [< Du. < *tap* tap, faucet + *toe* to shut]

tau (tou) *n.* The nineteenth letter in the Greek alphabet (T, τ), corresponding to the English *t.* See ALPHABET.

taught (tôt) Past tense and past participle of TEACH.

taunt (tônt) *n.* A sarcastic, biting speech or remark; scornful reproach. — *v.t.* **1.** To reproach with sarcastic or contemptuous words; mock; upbraid. **2.** To tease in any way; provoke with taunts. [? < OF < L *temptare, tentare* to test, try] — **taunt′er** *n.* — **taunt′ing·ly** *adv.*

taupe (tōp) *n.* The color of moleskin; dark gray, often tinged with brown, purple, or yellow. [< F < L *talpa* mole]

tauro- *combining form* Bull; ox; bovine. Also, before vowels, **taur-.** [< Gk. *tauros* bull]

Tau·rus (tôr′əs) *n.* A constellation, the Bull, containing the bright star Aldebaran; also, the second sign of the zodiac. See CONSTELLATION, ZODIAC. [< L]

taut (tôt) *adj.* **1.** Stretched tight; not loose or slack. **2.** Tense; tight: *taut* muscles. **3.** In proper shape; tidy. [ME *togt, toht*] — **taut′ly** *adv.* — **taut′ness** *n.*

tau·ten (tôt′n) *v.t. & v.i.* To make or become taut; tighten.

tauto- *combining form* Same; identical. Also, before vowels, **taut-.** [< Gk. *tauto* the same]

tau·tog (tô·tôg′, -tog′) *n.* A blackish, edible, fish of the North American Atlantic coast. Also **tau·taug′.** [< Algonquian pl. of *tautau*, a blackfish]

tau·tol·o·gy (tô·tol′ə·jē) *n. pl.* **·gies** Unnecessary repetition of the same idea in different words; pleonasm: *He is writing his own autobiography.* [< LL < Gk. < *tauto* the same + *logos* discourse] — **tau·to·log·ic** (tô′tə·loj′ik) or **·i·cal** *adj.* — **tau′to·log′i·cal·ly** *adv.*

tav·ern (tav′ərn) *n.* **1.** A place licensed to retail liquors to be drunk on the premises. **2.** A public house providing lodging, food, and drink. [< OF < L *taberna* hut, booth]

taw (tô) *n.* **1.** A game of marbles. **2.** The line from which marble-players shoot. **3.** A marble used for shooting. [< Scand. ON *taug* string.]

taw·dry (tô′drē) *adj.* **·dri·er, ·dri·est** Showy and cheap; tastelessly ornamental. [< *St. Audrey's lace,* a type of neckpiece sold at St. Audrey's Fair at Ely, England] — **taw′dri·ly** *adv.* — **taw′dri·ness** *n.*

taw·ny (tô′nē) *adj.* **·ni·er, ·ni·est** Tan-colored; brownish yellow. Also **taw′ney.** [< AF < OF < *tanner* to tan] — **taw′ni·ness** *n.*

tax (taks) *n.* **1.** A compulsory contribution levied upon persons, property, or business for the support of government. **2.** Any proportionate assessment, as on the members of a society. **3.** A heavy demand on one's powers or resources; an onerous duty; a burden. — *v.t.* **1.** To impose a tax on. **2.** *Law* To settle or fix (costs) in any judicial matter. **3.** To subject to a severe demand; impose a burden upon: He *taxes* my patience. **4.** To accuse; charge; blame: usu. with *with.* [< OF < L *taxare* to estimate, appraise] — **tax′a·bil′i·ty, — tax′a·ble·ness** *n.* — **tax′a·ble** *adj.* — **tax′a·bly** *adv.* — **tax′er** *n.*
— **Syn.** (noun) **1.** assessment, custom, duty, excise, impost, levy, rate, tariff, tithe, toll, tribute.

Tax may appear as a combining form with the meaning of def. 1, as in the following list:

tax assessor	tax evader	tax payment
tax burden	tax-evading	tax proposal
tax-burdened	tax-exempt	tax receipt
tax claim	tax-free	tax repeal
tax collecting	tax-laden	tax revenue
tax collector	tax law	tax-ridden
tax cut	tax levy	tax-supported
tax dodger	taxman	tax system
tax-dodging	taxpaid	taxwise

tax·a·tion (tak·sā′shən) *n.* **1.** The act of taxing. **2.** The amount assessed as a tax.

tax-de·duct·i·ble (taks′di·duk′tə·bəl) *adj.* Legally deductible from that portion of one's income or assets subject to taxes: Medical expenses are *tax-deductible.*

tax·i (tak′sē) *n. pl.* **tax·is** A taxicab. — *v.* **tax·ied, tax·i·ing** or **tax·y·ing** *v.i.* **1.** To ride in a taxicab. **2.** To move along the ground or on the surface of the water under its own power, as an airplane before taking off. — *v.t.* **3.** To cause (an airplane) to taxi. [< TAXI(CAB)]

tax·i·cab (tak′sē·kab′) *n.* An automobile available for hire, usually fitted with a taximeter. [Short for *taximeter cab*]

tax·i·der·my (tak′sə·dûr′mē) *n.* The art of stuffing and mounting the skins of dead animals for preservation or exhibition. [< Gk. *taxis* arrangement + *derma* skin] — **tax′i·der′mal, tax′i′der′mic** *adj.* — **tax′i·der′mist** *n.*

tax·i·me·ter (tak′si·mē′tər) *n.* An instrument for measuring distances and recording fares, used in taxicabs. [< F < *taxe* tariff + *mètre* meter]

-taxis *combining form* Order; disposition; arrangement: *thermotaxis.* Also spelled **-taxy.** [< Gk. *taxis* arrangement]

tax·on·o·my (tak·son′ə·mē) *n.* **1.** The department of knowledge that embodies the laws and principles of classification. **2.** *Biol.* The systematic arrangement of plant and animal organisms according to established criteria in the following major groups, beginning with the most inclusive: kingdom, phylum or division, class, order, family, genus, and species. [< F < Gk. *taxis* arrangement + *nomos* law] — **tax·o·nom·ic** (tak′sə·nom′ik) or **·i·cal** *adj.* — **tax′o′nom′i·cal·ly** *adv.* — **tax·on′o·mer, tax·on′o·mist** *n.*

tax·pay·er (taks′pā′ər) *n.* One who pays a tax or is subject to taxation.

T-bone (tē′bōn) *n.* A beefsteak containing a T-shaped bone, taken from the loin. Also **T-bone steak.**

tea (tē) *n.* **1.** An evergreen Asian shrub having leathery, toothed leaves and white or pink flowers. **2.** The prepared leaves of this plant, or an infusion of them used as a beverage. **3.** Any infusion, preparation, or extract used as a beverage or medicinally: beef *tea,* senna *tea.* **4.** *Brit.* A light evening or afternoon meal. **5.** A social gathering at which tea is served. [< dial. Chinese *t'e*]
Tea may appear as a combining form, as in **teacart, teataster, teaware.**

tea bag A small porous sack of cloth or paper containing tea leaves, immersed in water to make tea: also called *tea ball.*

tea ball **1.** A perforated metal ball that is filled with tea leaves and placed in hot water to make tea. **2.** A tea bag.

tea ceremony A ritual preparation and serving of tea, practiced by the Japanese.

teach (tēch) *v.* **taught, teach·ing** *v.t.* **1.** To impart knowledge by lessons; give instruction to: to *teach* a class. **2.** To give instruction in; communicate the knowledge of: to *teach* French. **3.** To train by practice or exercise. — *v.i.* **4.** To follow the profession of teaching. **5.** To impart knowledge or skill. [OE *tǣcan*] — **teach′a·bil′i·ty** *n.* — **teach′a·ble** *adj.* — **teach′a·bly** *adv.*
— **Syn. 1.** *Teach* embraces all methods of imparting knowledge, information, guidance, or counsel. To *instruct* is to give specific directions about a subject: to *instruct* recruits in the use of a rifle. *Educate* usu., means to instruct in a school or college. Both *school* and *discipline* refer to the teaching of certain patterns of behavior; they both connote authority: to *school* a child to obey promptly, to *discipline* oneself to eat sparingly. *Train* suggests the fitting of a person for a particular work; of all these words, *train* is preferred when reference is made to an animal.

teach·er (tē′chər) *n.* One who teaches; esp., one whose occupation is to teach others; an instructor.

teach·ing (tē′ching) *n.* **1.** The act or occupation of a teacher. **2.** That which is taught.

tea cozy A cozy.

tea·cup (tē′kup′) *n.* **1.** A small cup suitable for serving tea. **2.** As much as a teacup will hold, usu., four fluid ounces: also **tea′cup·ful′** (-fŏŏl′).

teak (tēk) *n.* **1.** A large East Indian tree, yielding a very hard, durable timber highly prized for shipbuilding. **2.** The wood of this tree: also **teak′wood** (-wŏŏd). [< Malayalam *tēkka*]

tea·ket·tle (tē′ket′l) *n.* A kettle with a spout, used for boiling water.

teal (tēl) *n.* **1.** Any of various small, short-necked river ducks of the Old World and North America. **2.** A dull blue color with a greenish cast: also **teal blue.** [ME *tele*]

team (tēm) *n.* **1.** Two or more beasts of burden harnessed together, often including harness and vehicle; also, a single horse and vehicle. **2.** A set of workers, or players competing in a game: a baseball *team.* — *v.t.* **1.** To convey with a team. **2.** To harness together in a team. — *v.i.* **3.** To drive a team as a business. **4.** To form a team; work as a team: to *team* up. — *adj.* Of or pertaining to a team: *team* spirit. [OE *tēam* offspring, succession, row]

---

team·mate (tēm′māt′) *n.* A fellow player on a team.

team·ster (tēm′stər) *n.* **1.** One who drives or owns a team. **2.** One who drives a truck or other commercial vehicle.

team·work (tēm′wûrk′) *n.* **1.** Concerted action or effort by the members of a group to achieve some common end, as the coordinated play of an athletic team. **2.** Work done or requiring to be done by or with a team.

tea party A social gathering at which tea and light sandwiches or cakes are the principal refreshments.

tea·pot (tē′pot′) *n.* A vessel with a spout and handle in which tea is made and from which it is served.

tear[1] (târ) *v.* **tore, torn, tear·ing** *v.t.* **1.** To pull apart, as cloth; separate by pulling; rip; rend. **2.** To make by rending or tearing: to *tear* a hole in a dress. **3.** To injure or lacerate, as skin. **4.** To divide; disrupt: a party *torn* by dissension. **5.** To distress or torment: The sight *tore* his heart. — *v.i.* **6.** To become torn or rent. **7.** To move with haste and energy. — **to tear into** *Informal* To charge into or attack without restraint. — *n.* **1.** A fissure made by tearing; a rent; an act of tearing. **2.** *Slang* A spree; frolic. **3.** A rushing motion: to start off with a *tear*. **4.** Any violent outburst, as of anger, enthusiasm, etc. [OE *teran*]

tear[2] (tir) *n.* **1.** A drop of the saline liquid secreted by the lachrymal gland, serving to moisten the eye, and stimulated to a flow by emotional distress. **2.** Something resembling or suggesting a tear. **3.** A drop of any liquid. **4.** A droplike portion, as of glass, amber, etc. **5.** *pl.* Sorrow; lamentation. — **in tears** Weeping; crying. — *v.i.* To shed or fill with tears. [OE *tēar*] — **tear·less** *adj.* — **tear′y** *adj.*

tear·drop (tir′drop′) *n.* A tear or tear-shaped object.

tear·ful (tir′fəl) *adj.* **1.** Weeping abundantly. **2.** Causing tears. — **tear′ful·ly** *adv.* — **tear′ful·ness** *n.*

tear gas (tir) Any of various chemicals that provoke a copious flow of tears, with irritation of the eyes.

tear·ing (târ′ing) *adj.* *Informal* **1.** Violent; hasty; headlong. **2.** *Chiefly Brit.* Tremendous; mighty.

tear-jerk·er (tir′jûr′kər) *n.* *U.S. Slang* A story, play, etc., full of sentimental sadness.

tea·room (tē′rōōm′, -rŏŏm′) *n.* A restaurant serving tea and other refreshments: also called *teashop.*

tease (tēz) *v.* **teased, teas·ing** *v.t.* **1.** To annoy or harass with continual importunities, raillery, etc.; pester. **2.** To scratch or dress in order to raise the nap, as cloth with teasels. **3.** To comb or card, as wool or flax; also, to shred, as tobacco. **4.** To comb (hair) so as to form fluffy layers and give an effect of fullness. — *v.i.* **5.** To annoy a person in a facetious or petty manner. — *n.* **1.** One who or that which teases. **2.** The act of teasing, or the state of being teased. [OE *tǣsan* to tease] — **teas′er** *n.* — **teas′ing·ly** *adv.*

tea·sel (tē′zəl) *n.* **1.** A coarse, prickly Old World herb of which the flower head is covered with hooked bracts. **2.** The rough bur of such a plant, or a mechanical substitute, used in dressing cloth. — *v.t.* **tea·seled** or **·selled, tea·sel·ing** or **·sel·ling** To raise the nap of with a teasel. Also **tea′zel, tea′zle.** [OE *tǣsel*] — **tea′sel·er** or **tea′sel·ler** *n.*

tea·spoon (tē′spōōn′, -spŏŏn′) *n.* **1.** A small spoon used for stirring tea, etc. **2.** A teaspoonful.

tea·spoon·ful (tē′spōōn·fŏŏl′, -spŏŏn-) *n.* *pl.* **·fuls** As much as a teaspoon will hold, ⅓ of a tablespoon.

teat (tēt, tit) *n.* The protuberance on the breast or udder of most female mammals, through which the milk is drawn; a nipple; pap; dug. [< OF *tete* < Gmc.]

tea wagon A table on wheels for use in serving tea, etc.

Te·bet (tā·vāth′, tā′ves) *n.* The fourth month of the Hebrew year. See (Hebrew) CALENDAR. Also **Te·beth′.**

tech·ne·ti·um (tek·nē′shē·əm) *n.* A chemical element (symbol Tc), artificially produced by the bombardment of molybdenum with neutrons or deuterons. It displaces the hypothetical element *masurium.* See ELEMENT. [< NL < Gk. *technētos* artificial]

tech·ni·cal (tek′ni·kəl) *adj.* **1.** Pertaining to some particular art, science, or trade. **2.** Peculiar to or used in a specialized field of knowledge. **3.** Of or pertaining to the mechanical arts. **4.** Considered in terms of an accepted body of rules: a *technical* defeat. [< Gk. < *technē* art] — **tech′ni·cal·ly** *adv.* — **tech′ni·cal·ness** *n.*

tech·ni·cal·i·ty (tek′ni·kal′ə·tē) *n.* *pl.* **·ties 1.** The state of being technical. **2.** The use of technical terms. **3.** A technical point peculiar to some profession, art, trade, etc. **4.** A petty distinction; quibble. Also **tech·nism** (tek′niz′əm).

technical knockout In boxing, a victory awarded when one fighter has been beaten so severely that the referee discontinues the fight.

tech·ni·cian (tek·nish′ən) *n.* One skilled in the handling of instruments or in the performance of tasks requiring specialized training.

Tech·ni·col·or (tek′ni·kul′ər) *n.* A motion-picture photographic process that reproduces the colors of the original scene: a trade name. Also **tech′ni·col·or.**

tech·nics (tek′niks) *n.pl.* (*construed as sing.*) **1.** Practical method; technique. **2.** The theory of an art or the arts; esp.,

the study of the techniques of an art. **3.** Technical rules, methods, etc. **4.** Technology. — *adj.* Technical.

tech·nique (tek·nēk′) *n.* Working methods or manner of performance, as in art, science, etc. [< F < Gk. See TECHNICAL.]

techno- *combining form* **1.** Art; skill; craft. **2.** Technical; technological. Also, before vowels, **techn-.** [< Gk. *technē* art, skill]

tech·noc·ra·cy (tek·nok′rə·sē) *n.* *pl.* **·cies** A theory of society and government that advocates control by an organized body of experts to achieve minimum waste and maximum efficiency. — **tech′no·crat** (tek′nə·krat) *n.* — **tech′·no·crat′ic** *adj.*

tech·no·log·i·cal (tek′nə·loj′i·kəl) *adj.* Of, pertaining to, associated with, produced or affected by technology. Also **tech′no·log′ic.** — **tech′no·log′i·cal·ly** *adv.*

technological unemployment Unemployment brought about by technical advances, as automation, etc.

tech·nol·o·gy (tek·nol′ə·jē) *n.* *pl.* **·gies 1.** Theoretical knowledge of industry and the industrial arts. **2.** The application of science and of technical advances in industry, the arts, etc. **3.** The technical language of an art, science, etc. **4.** The means by which material things are produced, as in a particular civilization. — **tech·nol′o·gist** *n.*

ted (ted) *v.t.* **ted·ded, ted·ding** To turn over and strew about, or spread loosely for drying, as newly mown grass. [Prob. < Scand.] — **ted′der** *n.*

ted·dy bear (ted′ē) A toy bear, usu. covered with plush. Also **Teddy bear.** [after *Teddy,* a nickname of Theodore Roosevelt]

Te De·um (tē dē′əm) **1.** An ancient Christian hymn beginning with these words. **2.** The music to which this hymn is set. **3.** Any thanksgiving service in which this hymn is sung. [< L *Te Deum* (*laudamus*) (we praise) Thee, O God]

te·di·ous (tē′dē·əs) *adj.* Causing weariness; boring. [See TEDIUM.] — **te′di·ous·ly** *adv.* — **te′di·ous·ness** *n.* — **Syn.** tiresome, tiring, fatiguing, wearisome, irksome, dull.

te·di·um (tē′dē·əm) *n.* The state of being tiresome or wearisome; tediousness. [< L *taedere* to vex, weary]

tee[1] (tē) *n.* **1.** A small peg with a concave top on which a golf ball is placed in making the first play to a hole. **2.** A designated area within which the golf tee must be placed. — *v.t. & v.i.* **teed, tee·ing** To place (the golf ball) on a tee. — **to tee off** To strike (the golf ball) in starting play.

tee[2] (tē) *n.* In certain games, a mark toward which the balls, quoits, etc., are directed, as in curling. — **to a tee** As precisely as possible; exactly.

teem[1] (tēm) *v.i.* To be full, as if at the point of producing; to be full to overflowing; abound. [OE *tēam* progeny] — **teem′er** *n.* — **teem′ing** *adj.*

teem[2] (tēm) *v.i.* To come down heavily; pour: said of rain. [< ON *tǣma* empty]

-teen *suffix* Plus ten: used in cardinal numbers from 13 to 19 inclusive: *fifteen.* [OE < *tīen* ten]

teen age The age from 13 to 19 inclusive; adolescence. — **teen-age** (tēn′āj), **teen′-aged** (-ājd′) *adj.*

teen-ag·er (tēn′ā′jər) *n.* A person of teen age.

teens (tēnz) *n.pl.* **1.** The numbers that end in *-teen.* **2.** The years of one's age from 13 to 19 inclusive.

tee·ny (tē′nē) *adj.* **·ni·er, ·ni·est** *Informal* Tiny.

tee·pee (tē′pē) See TEPEE.

tee·ter (tē′tər) *v.i.* **1.** To walk or move with a tottering motion. **2.** To seesaw; waver; vacillate. — *v.t.* **3.** To cause to teeter. — *n.* **1.** An oscillating motion. **2.** A seesaw. [< dial. E *titter,* prob. < ON *titra* to tremble, shiver]

teeth (tēth) Plural of TOOTH.

teethe (tēth) *v.i.* **teethed, teeth·ing** To cut or develop teeth.

teeth·ing ring (tē′thing) A ring of hard rubber, bone, plastic, etc., for a teething baby to bite on.

tee·to·tal (tē·tōt′l) *adj.* **1.** Pertaining to total abstinence from intoxicants. **2.** Total; entire. **3.** *TOTAL,* with emphatic repetition of initial letter] — **tee·to′tal·ism** *n.*

tee·to·tal·er (tē·tōt′l·ər) *n.* One who abstains totally from alcoholic drinks. Also **tee·to′tal·ist,** *Brit.* **tee·to′tal·ler.**

teg·u·ment (teg′yə·mənt) *n.* A covering or envelope; an integument. [< L < *tegere* to cover] — **teg·u·men·ta·ry** (teg′yə·men′tər·ē) *adj.* — **teg′u·men′tal** *adj.*

tel- Var. of TELO-[1].

tele- *combining form* **1.** Far off; at a distance: *telegraph.* **2.** Related to or transmitted by television: *telecast.* Also spelled *telo-.* Also, before vowels, **tel-.** [< Gk. *tēle* far]

tel·e·cast (tel′ə·kast, -käst) *v.t. & v.i.* **·cast** or **·cast·ed, ·cast·ing** To broadcast by television. — *n.* A program broadcast by television.

tel·e·com·mu·ni·ca·tion (tel′ə·kə·myōō′nə·kā′shən) *n.* **1.** The art and science of communicating at a distance, as in radio, radar, television, telegraphy, telephony, etc. Also **tel′e·com·mu′ni·ca′tions. 2.** Any message so transmitted.

tel·e·gram (tel′ə·gram) *n.* A message sent by telegraph.

tel·e·graph (tel′ə·graf, -gräf) *n.* Any of various devices, or systems, using a code; esp., one using coded impulses transmitted by wire or radio. — *v.t.* **1.** To send (a message) by telegraph. **2.** To communicate with by telegraph. — *v.i.* **3.** To transmit a message by telegraph. — **te·leg·ra·pher** (tə·leg′rə·fər), **te·leg′ra·phist** *n.*

tel·e·graph·ic (tel′ə·graf′ik) *adj.* Of or pertaining to the telegraph; transmitted by means of telegraphy. Also **tel′e·graph′i·cal.** — **tel′e·graph′i·cal·ly** *adv.*

te·leg·ra·phy (tə·leg′rə·fē) *n.* **1.** The process of conveying messages by telegraph. **2.** The art or science of the construction and operation of telegraphs.

Te·lem·a·chus (tə·lem′ə·kəs) In Greek legend, son of Odysseus and Penelope.

te·lem·e·ter (tə·lem′ə·tər) *n.* Any of various electronic devices for indicating, measuring, recording, or integrating various quantities and for transmitting the data to a distant point.

te·lem·e·try (tə·lem′ə·trē) *n.* The theory and practice of using telemeters, esp. in relation to rockets, space probes, guided missiles, etc. Also **tel·e·me·ter·ing** (tel′ə·mē′tər·ing). — **tel′e·met′ric** (-met′rik) or **·ri·cal** *adj.* — **tel′e·met′ri·cal·ly** *adv.*

teleo- Var. of TELO-[1].

te·le·ol·o·gy (tel′ē·ol′ə·jē, tē′lē-) *n. pl.* **·gies 1.** The branch of cosmology that treats of final causes. **2.** *Biol.* The doctrine that the phenomena of organic life and development can be fully explained only by the action of design and purpose and not by mechanical causes. Compare VITALISM. **3.** The explanation of nature in terms of utility or purpose, esp. divine purpose. [< NL < Gk. *telos* end + *logos* discourse] — **tel′e·o·log′i·cal** (-ə·loj′i·kəl) or **tel′e·o·log′ic** *adj.* — **tel′e·o·log′i·cal·ly** *adv.* — **tel′e·ol′o·gist** *n.*

te·lep·a·thy (tə·lep′ə·thē) *n.* The supposed communication of one mind with another at a distance by other than normal sensory means. — **tel·e·path·ic** (tel′ə·path′ik) *adj.* — **tel′e·path′i·cal·ly** *adv.* — **te·lep′a·thist** *n.*

tel·e·phone (tel′ə·fōn) *n.* A device or system for transmitting sound over a wire or other communication channel. — *v.* **·phoned, ·phon·ing** *v.t.* **1.** To communicate with by telephone. **2.** To send by telephone, as a message. — *v.i.* **3.** To communicate by telephone. — **tel′e·phon′er** *n.* — **tel·e·phon·ic** (tel′ə·fon′ik) *adj.* — **tel′e·phon′i·cal·ly** *adv.*

te·leph·o·ny (tə·lef′ə·nē) *n.* The science of designing, constructing, and operating telephones.

tel·e·pho·to (tel′ə·fō′tō) *adj.* **1.** Designating a lens system used in connection with a camera to produce a large image of a distant object. **2.** Pertaining to telephotography.

tel·e·pho·to·graph (tel′ə·fō′tə·graf, -gräf) *n.* A picture transmitted by telephotography. **2.** A picture made with a telephoto lens. — **tel′e·pho′to·graph′ic** *adj.*

tel·e·pho·tog·ra·phy (tel′ə·fə·tog′rə·fē) *n.* **1.** The art of producing photographic images of distant objects on a larger scale than is possible with an ordinary camera. **2.** The facsimile reproduction of photographs or other pictures by radio or telegraphic communication; phototelegraphy.

Tel·e·promp·er (tel′ə·promp′tər) *n.* A prompting device for television whereby a prepared script, unseen by the audience, is shown to a speaker or performer, enlarged line by line: a trade name. Also **tel′e·prompt′er.**

tel·e·ran (tel′ə·ran) *n. Telecom.* A system of air navigation that combines the principles of television and radar to transmit information gathered by ground stations to all aircraft within range. [< TELE(VISION) + R(ADAR) + A(IR) N(AVIGATION)]

tel·e·scope (tel′ə·skōp) *n.* An optical instrument for enlarging the image of a distant object, consisting of an object glass or concave mirror for collecting the light rays and a magnifying eyepiece for viewing the image. — *v.* **·scoped, ·scop·ing** *v.t.* **1.** To drive or slide together so that one part fits into another in the manner of the sections of a small telescope. **2.** To crush by driving something into or upon. — *v.i.* **3.** To crash into one another, as railroad cars.

tel·e·scop·ic (tel′ə·skop′ik) *adj.* **1.** Pertaining to the telescope. **2.** Visible only through a telescope. **3.** Farseeing. **4.** Having sections that slide within or over one another. Also **tel′e·scop′i·cal.** — **tel′e·scop′i·cal·ly** *adv.*

te·les·co·py (tə·les′kə·pē) *n.* The art of using or making telescopes. — **te·les′co·pist** *n.*

tel·e·type (tel′ə·tīp) *v.t. & v.i.* **·typed, ·typ·ing** To communicate (with) by teletypewriter or Teletype. — **tel′e·typ′er** *n.*

Tel·e·type (tel′ə·tīp) *n.* A teletypewriter: a trade name. Also **tel′e·type.**

tel·e·type·writ·er (tel′ə·tīp′rī′tər) *n.* A telegraph system transmitting by means of a typewriter keyboard in which each key produces a coded signal that activates a specific character in a typewriterlike receiver.

tel·e·view (tel′ə·vyōō) *v.t. & v.i.* To observe by means of television. — **tel′e·view′er** *n.*

tel·e·vise (tel′ə·vīz) *v.t. & v.i.* **·vised, ·vis·ing** To transmit or receive by television.

tel·e·vi·sion (tel′ə·vizh′ən) *n.* **1.** The transmission of continuous visual images as a series of electrical impulses or a modulated carrier wave, restored to visual form on the cathode-ray screen of a receiver, often with accompanying sound. **2.** The television broadcasting industry. **3.** A television receiving set. Also called *TV.*

tel·ex (tel′eks) *n.* **1.** A system for sending messages by teletypewriter. **2.** A teletypewriter. **3.** A message sent by telex. — *v.t.* To send (a message) by telex. [< TEL-(ETYPEWRITER) + EX(CHANGE)]

tell (tel) *v.* **told, tell·ing** *v.t.* **1.** To relate in detail; narrate, as a story. **2.** To communicate. **3.** To reveal: to *tell* secrets. **4.** To decide; ascertain: I cannot *tell* who is to blame. **5.** To express in words: to *tell* a lie. **6.** To give a command to; order: I *told* him to go home. **7.** To let know; inform. **8.** *Informal* To inform or assure emphatically: It's cold out, I *tell* you! **9.** To say (a rosary): to *tell* one's beads. — *v.i.* **10.** To give an account or description: usu. with *of.* **11.** To serve as indication or evidence: with *of.* **12.** To produce a marked effect: Every blow *told.* — **all told** In all. — **to tell off 1.** To count and set apart. **2.** *Informal* To reprimand severely. — **to tell on 1.** To tire; weary. **2.** *Informal* To inform against. [OE *tellan*] — **tell′a·ble** *adj.*

Tell (tel), **William** A legendary Swiss hero in the struggle for independence from Austria, forced to shoot an apple off his son's head with bow and arrow.

tell·er (tel′ər) *n.* **1.** One who relates or informs. **2.** A person who receives or pays out money, as in a bank. **3.** A person appointed to collect and count ballots in a legislative body or other assembly. — **tell′er·ship′** *n.*

tell·ing (tel′ing) *adj.* Producing a great effect; impressive; effective; striking. — **tell′ing·ly** *adv.*

tell·tale (tel′tāl′) *n.* **1.** One who improperly gives information concerning the private affairs of others; a tattler. **2.** That which conveys information, esp. in an involuntary way. **3.** An instrument or device for giving or recording information. — *adj.* That is or serves as a telltale.

tel·lu·ric (te·loor′ik, tel·yoor′-) *adj.* Of or pertaining to the earth; terrestrial; earthly.

tel·lu·ri·um (te·loor′ē·əm, tel·yoor′-) *n.* A rare nonmetallic element (symbol Te) resembling sulfur and selenium in chemical properties, occasionally found native as white crystals, but usu. combined with metals. See ELEMENT. [< NL < L *tellus* the earth]

tel·ly (tel′ē) *n. pl.* **·lies** *Brit. informal* Television.

telo-[1] *combining form* Final; complete; perfect: also, before vowels, *tel-.* Also *teleo-.* [< Gk. *telos* end]

telo-[2] Var. of TELE-.

tel·son (tel′sən) *n. Zool.* The last abdominal segment of the body of an arthropod, as of a lobster, shrimp, or scorpion. For illus. see SHRIMP. [< Gk. *telson* boundary]

Tel·star (tel′stär′) The first artificial satellite for global communication, launched from Cape Canaveral, July 10, 1962.

Tel·u·gu (tel′oo·goo) *n. pl.* **·gu 1.** A Dravidian language used in NW Andhra Pradesh, India, and important in literary culture. **2.** One of a Dravidian people of Telugu speech. — *adj.* Of or pertaining to the Telugu or to Telugu.

te·mer·i·ty (tə·mer′ə·tē) *n.* Venturesome or foolish boldness; rashness. [< L *temere* rashly]

— **Syn.** *Temerity* is the quality of one who underestimates danger, or overrates his chances for success. *Audacity* refers (in its bad sense) to going beyond the decent restraints of social behavior. *Foolhardiness* characterizes the man who rushes into peril from lack of sense. — **Ant.** caution, wariness, timidity.

tem·per (tem′pər) *n.* **1.** Heat of mind or passion; disposition to become angry. **2.** Frame of mind; mood: to be in a bad *temper.* **3.** Composure of mind; self-command: to lose one's *temper.* **4.** *Metall.* The condition of a metal as regards hardness and elasticity, esp. when due to heating and sudden cooling. **5.** Something mixed with a substance to alter its properties or qualities. — *v.t.* **1.** To bring to a state of moderation or suitability, as by addition of another quality; moderate: to *temper* justice with mercy. **2.** To bring to the proper consistency, etc., by moistening and working: to *temper* clay. **3.** *Metall.* To bring (metal) to a required hardness and elasticity by heating and suddenly cooling. **4.** *Music* To adjust the tones of (an instrument) by temperament; tune. — *v.i.* **5.** To be or become tempered. [OE and OF < L *temperare* to combine in due proportion] — **tem′per·a·bil′i·ty** *n.* — **tem′per·a·ble** *adj.* — **tem′per·er** *n.*

— **Syn.** (noun) **2.** temperament, mood, humor. — (verb) moderate, modify, qualify.

tem·per·a (tem′pər·ə, *Ital.* tem′pä·rä) *n.* **1.** A painting medium consisting of an emulsion prepared from a mixture of water and egg yolks, glue, gum, or casein solutions, etc.;

also, a method of painting with such a medium. **2.** Paint prepared by adding pigment to the medium of tempera. Also called *distemper*. [< Ital. *temperare* to temper < L]

tem·per·a·ment (tem′pər·ə·mənt, -prə-) *n.* **1.** The physical and mental peculiarities of an individual; nature. **2.** An intense, moody, and often rebellious nature. **3.** *Music* The tuning of an instrument or scale so that each semitone is a twelfth of an octave: also **equal temperament**. [< L *temperamentum* proper mixture]

tem·per·a·men·tal (tem′pər·ə·men′təl, -prə-) *adj.* **1.** Of or pertaining to temperament. **2.** Sensitive; easily excited. — **tem′per·a·men′tal·ly** *adv.*

tem·per·ance (tem′pər·əns) *n.* **1.** The state or quality of being temperate; habitual moderation. **2.** The principle or practice of total abstinence from intoxicants. [< OF < L < *temperare* to mix in due proportions]

tem·per·ate (tem′pər·it) *adj.* **1.** Observing moderation in the indulgence of an appetite, esp. in the use of intoxicating liquors. **2.** Moderate as regards temperature. **3.** Characterized by moderation; not excessive. **4.** Calm; restrained; self-controlled. **5.** *Music* Tempered: said of an interval or scale. [< L < *temperare* to mix in due proportions] — **tem′per·ate·ly** *adv.* — **tem′per·ate·ness** *n.*

tem·per·a·ture (tem′pər·ə·chər, -prə-) *n.* **1.** Condition as regards heat or cold. **2.** The degree of heat in a body or substance, as measured on the graduated scale of a thermometer. **3.** The degree of heat of an animal, esp. the human body; also, excess of this above the normal (which for the human body is 98.6° F, or about 37° C). [< L *temperatura* due measure]

tem·pered (tem′pərd) *adj.* **1.** Having temper or a specified disposition: used mainly in compounds: quick-*tempered*. **2.** *Music* Adjusted in pitch so as to produce or conform to temperament. **3.** Moderated by admixture. **4.** Having the right degree of hardness and elasticity.

tem·pest (tem′pist) *n.* **1.** A violent wind, usu. attended with rain, snow, or hail. **2.** A violent commotion or agitation; a fierce tumult. — **tempest in a teapot** A considerable uproar over a trivial matter. [< OF < L *tempestas* weather]

tem·pes·tu·ous (tem·pes′chōō-əs) *adj.* Stormy; turbulent; violent. — **tem·pes′tu·ous·ly** *adv.* — **tem·pes′tu·ous·ness** *n.*

tem·plate (tem′plit′) *n.* **1.** A pattern or gauge, as of wood or metal, used as a guide in shaping something accurately. **2.** In building, a stout stone or timber for distributing weight or thrust. Also **tem·plet** (tem′plit). [< F < L *templum* small timber]

tem·ple[1] (tem′pəl) *n.* **1.** A stately edifice consecrated to the worship of one or more deities. **2.** In the U.S., a Reform synagogue. **3.** In France, a Protestant church. **4.** Any place considered as occupied by God. — **the Temple** Any of three sacred edifices built in Jerusalem for the worship of Jehovah. [OE < L *templum* temple]

tem·ple[2] (tem′pəl) *n.* The region on each side of the head above the cheek bone. [OF, ult. < L *tempus* temple]

tem·po (tem′pō) *n.* *pl.* **·pos** or **·pi** (-pē) **1.** *Music* Relative speed at which a composition is rendered. **2.** Characteristic manner or style. [< Ital. < L *tempus* time]

tem·po·ral[1] (tem′pər·əl) *adj.* **1.** Pertaining to affairs of the present life; earthly. **2.** Pertaining or related to time. **3.** Temporary; transitory. **4.** Civil; lay; secular. [< L < *temporis* time] — **tem′po·ral·ly** *adv.* — **tem′po·ral·ness** *n.*

tem·po·ral[2] (tem′pər·əl) *adj.* *Anat.* Of, pertaining to, or situated at the temple or temples.

temporal bone *Anat.* A compound bone situated at either side of the head, and containing the organ of hearing.

tem·po·ral·i·ty (tem′pə·ral′ə·tē) *n.* *pl.* **·ties 1.** *Usu. pl.* A temporal or material matter, interest, revenue, etc. **2.** The state of being temporal or temporary.

tem·po·ra·ry (tem′pə·rer′ē) *adj.* Lasting or intended to be used for a short time only; transitory. [< L < *tempus, temporis* time] — **tem′po·ra·ri·ly** (tem′pə·rer′ə·lē, tem′pə·rer′-) *adv.* — **tem′po·rar′i·ness** *n.*

tem·po·rize (tem′pə·rīz) *v.i.* **·rized, ·riz·ing 1.** To act evasively so as to gain time or put off decision or commitment. **2.** To give real or apparent compliance to the circumstances; comply. **3.** To effect a compromise; negotiate: with *with* or *between*. Also *Brit.* **tem′po·rise.** [< F < L *tempus, temporis* time] — **tem′po·ri·za′tion** *n.* — **tem′po·riz′er** *n.* — **tem′po·riz′ing·ly** *adv.*

tempt (tempt) *v.t.* **1.** To attempt to persuade (a person) to do something evil or unwise. **2.** To be attractive to; invite: Your offers do not *tempt* me. **3.** To provoke or risk provoking: to *tempt* fate. [< OF < L *temptare, tentare* to test] — **tempt′a·ble** *adj.* — **tempt′er** *n.* — **tempt′ress** *n.fem.*

temp·ta·tion (temp·tā′shən) *n.* **1.** The act of tempting, or the state of being tempted. **2.** That which tempts.

tempt·ing (temp′ting) *adj.* Alluring; attractive; seductive. — **tempt′ing·ly** *adv.* — **tempt′ing·ness** *n.*

tem·pus fu·git (tem′pəs fyōō′jit) *Latin* Time flies.

ten (ten) *n.* **1.** The sum of nine and one: a cardinal number. **2.** Any symbol of this number, as 10, x, X. **3.** Anything

consisting of or representing ten units, as a playing card, bill, etc. — *adj.* Being one more than nine. [OE *tīen*] — **tenth** (tenth) *adj. & n.*

ten- Var. of TENO-.

ten·a·ble (ten′ə·bəl) *adj.* Capable of being held, maintained, or defended. [< F < L *tenere* to hold] — **ten′a·bil′i·ty, ten′a·ble·ness** *n.* — **ten′a·bly** *adv.*

te·na·cious (ti·nā′shəs) *adj.* **1.** Having great cohesiveness of parts; tough. **2.** Adhesive; sticky. **3.** Holding or tending to hold strongly, as opinions, rights, etc. **4.** Stubborn; obstinate. **5.** Apt to retain; strongly retentive, as memory. [< L < *tenere* to hold, grasp, embrace] — **te·na′cious·ly** *adv.* — **te·na′cious·ness** *n.*

te·nac·i·ty (ti·nas′ə·tē) *n.* The state or quality of being tenacious.

ten·an·cy (ten′ən·sē) *n.* *pl.* **·cies 1.** The holding of lands, houses, offices, etc.; occupancy. **2.** The period of holding lands, houses, etc. **3.** The houses, lands, etc. so held.

ten·ant (ten′ənt) *n.* **1.** One who holds or possesses lands or property by the payment of rent or other fee. **2.** A dweller in any place; an occupant. — *v.t.* **1.** To hold as tenant; occupy. — *v.i.* **2.** To be a tenant. [< F, orig. ppr. of *tenir* to hold < L *tenere*] — **ten′ant·a·ble** *adj.* — **ten′ant·less** *adj.* — **ten′ant·ship** *n.*

tenant farmer One who farms land owned by another and pays rent, usu. in a share of the crops.

ten·ant·ry (ten′ən·trē) *n.* *pl.* **·ries 1.** Tenants collectively. **2.** The state of being a tenant; tenancy.

ten-cent store (ten′sent′) A five-and-ten-cent store.

Ten Commandments The set of injunctions given by God to Moses on Mount Sinai, constituting the moral code of the Mosaic Law: also called *Decalogue*. *Ex.* xx 1–17.

tend[1] (tend) *v.i.* **1.** To have an aptitude, tendency, or disposition; incline. **2.** To have influence toward a specified result: Education *tends* to refinement. **3.** To go in a certain direction. [< OF < L *tendere* to extend, tend]

tend[2] (tend) *v.t.* **1.** To attend to the needs or requirements of; take care of; minister to: to *tend* a fire. **2.** To watch over; look after. — *v.i.* **3.** To be in attendance; serve or wait: with *on* or *upon*. **4.** *Informal* To give attention or care: with *to*. [Aphetic var. of ATTEND]

ten·den·cy (ten′dən·sē) *n.* *pl.* **·cies 1.** An inclination toward some purpose, end, or result; bent; aptitude. **2.** That which tends to produce some specified effect. **3.** Bias; propensity. [< Med.L < *tendere* to extend, tend]

ten·den·tious (ten·den′shəs) *adj.* Having a tendency to favor a particular point of view; biased. Also **ten·den′cious.** [See TENDENCY.] — **ten·den′tious·ly** *adv.* — **ten·den′tious·ness** *n.*

ten·der[1] (ten′dər) *adj.* **1.** Yielding easily to force that tends to crush, bruise, break, or injure. **2.** Easily chewed or cut: said of food. **3.** Delicate or weak; not strong, rough, or hardy. **4.** Youthful and delicate: a *tender* age. **5.** Kind; affectionate; gentle. **6.** Capable of arousing sensitive feelings; touching: *tender* memories. **7.** Susceptible to spiritual or moral feelings: a *tender* conscience. **8.** Painful if touched: a *tender* sore. **9.** Of delicate effect or quality; soft: a *tender* light. **10.** Requiring deft or delicate treatment; ticklish; touchy: a *tender* subject. — *v.t.* To make tender; soften. [< OF < L *tener, teneris* soft] — **ten′der·ly** *adv.* — **ten′der·ness** *n.*

ten·der[2] (ten′dər) *v.t.* **1.** To present for acceptance, as a resignation; offer. **2.** *Law* To proffer, as money, in discharge of an obligation. — *n.* **1.** The act of tendering; an offer. **2.** *Law* A formal offer of satisfaction. **3.** That which is offered as payment: legal *tender*. [< F < L *tendere* to extend, tend] — **ten′der·er** *n.*

tend·er[3] (ten′dər) *n.* **1.** *Naut.* **a** A vessel used to bring supplies, passengers, etc. back and forth between a larger vessel and shore. **b** A vessel that services another at sea. **2.** A vehicle attached to the rear of a steam locomotive to carry fuel and water. **3.** One who ministers to. [< TEND[2]]

ten·der·foot (ten′dər·fŏŏt′) *n.* *pl.* **·foots** or **·feet** (-fēt) *U.S.* **1.** In the West, one not yet inured to the hardships of the plains, the mining camp, etc.; a greenhorn. **2.** Any inexperienced person. **3.** A boy scout in the beginning class or group.

ten·der·heart·ed (ten′dər·här′tid) *adj.* Having deep or quick sensibility, as to love, pity, etc.; compassionate. — **ten′der·heart′ed·ly** *adv.* — **ten′der·heart′ed·ness** *n.*

ten·der·ize (ten′də·rīz) *v.t.* **ized, iz·ing** To make tender, as meat.

ten·der·iz·er (ten′də·rī′zər) A substance for softening the tough fibers and connective tissues of meat.

ten·der·loin (ten′dər·loin′) *n.* The tender part of the loin of beef, pork, etc., lying close to the ventral side of the lumbar vertebrae. — **the tenderloin district** Any urban district noted for its night life, crime, etc.

ten·don (ten′dən) *n.* *Anat.* One of the bands of tough, fibrous connective tissue forming the termination of a muscle and serving to transmit its force to some other part; a sinew. [< Med.L < Gk. *tenōn* sinew < *tenein* to stretch]

ten·dril (ten′dril) *n. Bot.* One of the slender, filamentous organs that serve a climbing plant as a means of attachment to a wall, tree trunk, or other surface. [< F < *tendron* sprout] — **ten′dril·lar, ten′dril·ous** *adj.*

ten·e·brae (ten′ə·brē) *n.pl. Eccl. Usu. cap.* The matins and lauds sung on the afternoons or evenings of Thursday, Friday, and Saturday of Holy Week. [< L, darkness]

ten·e·ment (ten′ə·mənt) *n.* 1. An urban apartment building or rooming house that is poorly constructed or maintained, typically overcrowded and often part of a slum: also **tenement house.** 2. A room or set of rooms designed for one family. 3. *Law* Property held by one person of another, as land, houses, offices, etc. 4. Any dwelling place; abode. [< OF < LL *tenementum* tenure] — **ten′e·men′tal** (-men′təl), **ten′e·men′ta·ry** (-men′tə·rē) *adj.*

ten·et (ten′it, tē′nit) *n.* An opinion, principle, dogma, etc., that a person or organization believes or maintains as true. — **Syn.** See DOCTRINE. [< L, he holds < *tenere* to hold]

ten·fold (ten′fōld′) *n.* An amount or number ten times as great as a given unit. — *adv.* So as to be ten times as many or as great. — *adj.* 1. Consisting of ten parts. 2. Ten times as many or as great.

ten-gal·lon hat (ten′gal′ən) *U.S.* A wide-brimmed felt hat with a tall crown, traditionally worn by cowboys.

Ten·nes·se·an (ten′ə·sē′ən) *n.* A native or inhabitant of Tennessee. — *adj.* Of or pertaining to Tennessee.

ten·nis (ten′is) *n.* A game played by striking a ball back and forth with rackets over a net stretched between two equal areas that together constitute a court. It has two forms, **court tennis,** played indoors, and **lawn tennis,** played out-of-doors on a court of grass, clay, concrete, etc. [< AF *tenetz* take, receive]

Ten·ny·so·ni·an (ten′ə·sō′nē·ən) *adj.* Relating to or characteristic of Alfred Tennyson, or his verse or style.

teno- *combining form Med.* Tendon; related to a tendon, or to tendons: also **ten-.** Also **tenonto-.** [< Gk. *tenōn* tendon]

ten·on (ten′ən) *n.* A projection on the end of a timber, etc., for inserting in a socket to form a joint. For illus. see MORTISE. — *v.t.* 1. To form a tenon on. 2. To join by a mortise and tenon. [< F < *tenir* to hold]

ten·or (ten′ər) *n.* 1. The adult male voice intermediate in range between baritone and countertenor; also, a singer having such a voice, or a part to be sung by it. 2. *Music* An instrument playing the part intermediate between the bass and the alto. 3. Course of thought; general purport. 4. A settled course or manner of progress. 5. General character and tendency; nature. — *adj.* 1. Of or pertaining to a tenor. 2. Having a relation to other instruments as the tenor bears to other musical parts. [< OF < L *tenor* course]

ten·pen·ny (ten′pen′ē, -pə·nē) *adj.* 1. Valued at tenpence. 2. Designating the size of nails three inches long. See PENNY.

ten·pin (ten′pin′) *n.* One of the pins used in tenpins.

ten·pins (ten′pinz′) *n.pl. (construed as sing.)* A game played in a bowling alley in which the players attempt to bowl down ten pins set up at the far end of the alley.

tense[1] (tens) *adj.* **tens·er, tens·est** 1. Stretched tight; taut. 2. Under mental or nervous strain; strained. 3. *Phonet.* Produced with the tongue and its muscles taut, as (ē) and (ōō). — *v.t. & v.i.* **tensed, tens·ing** To make or become strained or drawn tight. [< L *tendere* to stretch] — **tense′·ly** *adv.* — **tense′ness** *n.*

tense[2] (tens) *n.* A form of a verb that relates it to time viewed either as finite past, present, or future, or as non-finite. — **sequence of tenses** In inflected languages, the customary choice of tense for a verb that follows another in a sentence, particularly in reported or indirect discourse. [< OF < L *tempus* time, tense]

ten·si·ble (ten′sə·bəl) *adj.* Tensile.

ten·sile (ten′sil, *Brit.* ten′sīl) *adj.* 1. Of or pertaining to tension. 2. Capable of being drawn out or extended. 3. Producing tones from stretched strings: said of instruments. [See TENSE[1].] — **ten·sil·i·ty** (ten·sil′ə·tē) *n.*

tensile strength *Physics* The resistance of a material to forces of rupture and stress in the direction of length: usually expressed in pounds per square inch.

ten·sion (ten′shən) *n.* 1. The act of stretching or the condition of being stretched tight. 2. Mental strain; intense nervous anxiety. 3. Any strained relation, as between governments. 4. *Physics* **a** Stress on a material caused by a force pulling or stretching in one direction. **b** The condition of a body when acted on by such a force. 5. A device for regulating the tension of something. 6. *Electr.* Electromotive force; also, electric potential. — **Syn.** See STRESS. — **ten′sion·al** *adj.*

ten·si·ty (ten′sə·tē) *n.* The state of being tense; tension.

ten·sive (ten′siv) *adj.* Of, like, or causing tension.

ten·sor (ten′sər, -sôr) *n. Anat.* A muscle that stretches a part. [< NL < L *tensus.* See TENSE[1].]

ten-strike (ten′strīk′) *n.* 1. In bowling, a strike (def. 3). 2. *U.S. Informal* A totally successful stroke or act.

tent (tent) *n.* A shelter of canvas or the like, supported by poles and fastened by cords to pegs driven into the ground. — *v.t.* To cover with or as with a tent. — *v.i.* To pitch a tent; camp out. [< F < LL *tenta,* orig. neut. pl. of *tentus,* pp. of *tendere* to stretch]

TENTS
a Pup. *b* Pyramid. *c* Wall.

ten·ta·cle (ten′tə·kəl) *n.* 1. *Zool.* A protruding flexible process or appendage of invertebrate animals, functioning as an organ of touch or motion, as the arms of a cuttlefish. 2. *Bot.* A sensitive glandular hair, as on the leaves of some plants. [< L < *tentare* to touch, try] — **ten·tac′u·lar** *adj.*

tent·age (ten′tij) *n.* 1. The supply of tents available for any purpose. 2. Tents collectively.

ten·ta·tive (ten′tə·tiv) *adj.* Provisional or conjectural; subject to change; experimental. [< Med.L < L *tentare* to try, probe] — **ten′ta·tive·ly** *adv.* — **ten′ta·tive·ness** *n.*

tent caterpillar Any of the larvae of several North American moths that spin silken webs to shelter the colony in which they live.

ten·ter (ten′tər) *n.* A frame or machine for stretching cloth to prevent shrinkage while drying. — *v.t.* 1. To stretch on or as on a tenter. — *v.i.* 2. To be or admit of being so stretched. [< L *tentus* extended]

ten·ter·hook (ten′tər·hŏŏk′) *n.* A sharp hook for holding cloth while being stretched on a tenter. — **to be on tenterhooks** To be in a state of anxiety or suspense.

ten·u·ous (ten′yŏŏ·əs) *adj.* 1. Thin; slim; delicate; also, weak; flimsy; unsubstantial. 2. Having slight density; rare. [< L *tenuis* thin] — **ten′u·ous·ly** *adv.* — **ten′u·ous·ness, ten·u·i·ty** (te·nyŏŏ′ə·tē, ti·nŏŏ′-) *n.*

ten·ure (ten′yər) *n.* 1. A holding, as of land. 2. The act of holding in general, or the state of being held. 3. The term during which a thing is held. 4. The conditions or manner of holding. 5. Permanent status granted to an employee, usu. after a trial period. [< OF < L *tenere* to hold] — **ten·u·ri·al** (ten·yŏŏr′ē·əl) *adj.* — **ten·u′ri·al·ly** *adv.*

te·nu·to (te·nŏŏ′tō) *adj. Music* Sustained; held for the full time. [< Ital. < L *tenere* to hold]

te·pee (tē′pē) *n.* A conical tent of the North American Plains Indians, usu. covered with skins: also spelled *teepee.* [< Dakota < *ti* to dwell + *pi* used for]

tep·id (tep′id) *adj.* Moderately warm; lukewarm, as a liquid. [< L *tepere* to be lukewarm] — **te·pid·i·ty** (tə·pid′ə·tē), **tep′id·ness** *n.* — **tep′id·ly** *adv.*

te·qui·la (tə·kē′lə) *n.* 1. A Mexican alcoholic liquor distilled from the juices yielded by the roasted stems of an agave plant. 2. The plant itself. [after *Tequila,* Jalisco, Mexico]

ter- *combining form* Three; third; threefold; three times: *tercentenary.* [< L *ter* thrice]

ter·a·tism (ter′ə·tiz′əm) *n.* A monstrosity; esp., a malformed human or animal fetus. [< Gk. *teras* monster]

terato- *combining form* A wonder; monster. Also, before vowels, **terat-.** [< Gk. *teras* wonder]

ter·bi·um (tûr′bē·əm) *n.* A metallic element (symbol Tb) belonging to the lanthanide series, found in rare-earth minerals. See ELEMENT. [< NL < *Ytterby,* town in Sweden] — **ter′bic** *adj.*

ter·cen·te·nar·y (tûr·sen′tə·ner′ē, tûr′sen·ten′ər·ē) *adj.* Of or pertaining to a period of 300 years or to a 300th anniversary. — *n. pl.* **·nar·ies** A 300th anniversary. Also *tricentennial.* Also **ter·cen·ten′ni·al** (tûr′sen·ten′ē·əl).

ter·cet (tûr′sit, tûr′set′) *n.* 1. A group of three lines rhyming together or connected with adjacent triplets by rhyme. 2. *Music* A triplet. [< F < Ital. < L *tertius* third]

ter·gi·ver·sate (tûr′ji·vər·sāt′) *v.i.* **·sat·ed, ·sat·ing** 1. To be evasive; equivocate. 2. To change sides, attitudes, etc.; apostatize. [< L *tergum* back + *versare* to turn] — **ter′gi·ver·sa′tion** *n.* — **ter′gi·ver·sa′tor** *n.*

term (tûrm) *n.* 1. A word or expression used to designate some definite thing: a scientific *term.* 2. Any word or expression conveying some conception or thought: to speak in general *terms.* 3. *pl.* The conditions or stipulations according to which something is to be done or acceded to: the *terms* of sale. 4. *pl.* Mutual relations: usu. preceded by *on* or *upon:* England was on friendly *terms* with France. 5. *Math.* **a** The numerator or denominator of a fraction. **b** One of the quantities of an algebraic expression that are connected by the plus and minus signs. **c** One of the quantities that compose a series or progression. **6.** *Logic* Either the subject or predicate of a proposition. **7.** A fixed period or definite length of time: a *term* of office. **8.** One of the periods of the school year. **9.** *Law* **a** One of the prescribed periods during which a court may hold a session. **b** A specific extent of time for which an estate is granted. **c** An interval allowed a debtor to meet his obligation. **10.** *Med.* The time for childbirth. — **at term** At the end of a definite time. — **in terms of** With reference to; concerning. — **to bring to terms** To force to accede or agree. — **to come to terms** To reach an agreement. — *v.t.* To designate by means of a term; name or call. [< OF < L *terminus* limit] — **term/less** *adj.*

ter·ma·gant (tûr/mə·gənt) *n.* A scolding or abusive woman; shrew. — *adj.* Violently abusive and quarrelsome; vixenish. [after *Termagant*, an imaginary Moslem deity of overbearing character] — **ter/ma·gan/cy** *n.*

term·er (tûr/mər) *n. Informal* A prisoner serving a certain term: a first *termer.*

ter·mi·na·ble (tûr/mə·nə·bəl) *adj.* That may be terminated; limitable; not perpetual. — **ter/mi·na·bil/i·ty, ter/·mi·na·ble·ness** *n.* — **ter/mi·na·bly** *adv.*

ter·mi·nal (tûr/mə·nəl) *adj.* **1.** Of, pertaining to, or forming a boundary, limit, or end: a *terminal* railroad station. **2.** Pertaining to the delivery or storage of freight or baggage: *terminal* charges. **3.** Pertaining to a term or name. **4.** Situated at the end of a series or part. **5.** *Bot.* Borne at the end of a stem or branch. **6.** Of, pertaining to, or occurring in or at the end of a period of time. **7.** Ending in death: said of a disease. — *n.* **1.** That which terminates; a terminating point or part; end. **2.** *Electr.* A point at which a circuit element, as a battery, generator, resistor, capacitor, transistor, etc., may be connected to other elements. **3.** A railroad terminus. [< LL < L *terminus* boundary] — **ter/mi·nal·ly** *adv.*

ter·mi·nate (tûr/mə·nāt) *v.* **·nat·ed, ·nat·ing** *v.t.* **1.** To put an end or stop to. **2.** To form the conclusion of; finish. **3.** To bound or limit. — *v.i.* **4.** To have or come to an end. [< L *terminus* limit] — **ter/mi·na/tive** *adj.* — **ter/mi·na/·tor** *n.* — **ter/mi·na·to/ry** (-nə·tôr/ē, -tō/rē) *adj.*

ter·mi·na·tion (tûr/mə·nā/shən) *n.* **1.** The act of setting bounds or limits. **2.** The act of ending or concluding. **3.** That which bounds or limits; close; end. **4.** Outcome; result; conclusion. **5.** The final letters or syllable of a word; a suffix. — **ter/mi·na·tion·al** *adj.*

ter·mi·nol·o·gy (tûr/mə·nol/ə·jē) *n. pl.* **·gies** The technical terms used in a science, art, trade, etc.; nomenclature. [< L *terminus* + -LOGY] — **ter/mi·no·log/i·cal** (-nə·loj/i·kəl) *adj.* — **ter/mi·no·log/i·cal·ly** *adv.*

ter·mi·nus (tûr/mə·nəs) *n. pl.* **·nus·es** or **·ni** (-nī) **1.** The final point or goal; end. **2.** The farthermost station on a railway. **3.** A boundary or border. [< L]

ter·mite (tûr/mīt) *n.* Any of various small, whitish social insects native in warm regions, several species of which are very destructive of wooden structures, furniture, etc.: also, loosely, *white ant.* [< L *termes*]

tern (tûrn) *n.* Any of several birds allied to the gulls, but having a smaller bill and body, with wings more pointed, and the tail usu. deeply forked. [< Scand.]

ter·na·ry (tûr/nər·ē) *adj.* Formed or consisting of three; grouped in threes. — *n. pl.* **·ries** A group of three; a triad. [< L *terni* by threes]

ter·nate (tûr/nāt) *adj.* Arranged in threes. [< NL < L *terni* by threes] — **ter/nate·ly** *adv.*

ter·pene (tûr/pēn) *n. Chem.* Any of a class of isomeric hydrocarbons, $C_{10}H_{16}$, contained chiefly in the essential oils of coniferous plants. [< *terp(entin)*, earlier form of TURPENTINE + -ENE]

Terp·sich·o·re (tûrp·sik/ə·rē) The Muse of dancing. [< Gk. < *terpsis* enjoyment + *choros* dance] — **Terp·si·cho·re·an** (tûrp/si·kə·rē/ən) *adj.*

terp·si·cho·re·an (tûrp/si·kə·rē/ən) *adj.* Of or relating to dancing: also **terp/si·cho/re/al.** — *n. Informal* A dancer.

ter·race (ter/is) *n.* **1.** An artificial, raised, level space, as of lawn, having one or more vertical or sloping sides; also, such levels collectively. **2.** A raised level supporting a row of houses, or the houses occupying such a position. **3.** The flat roof of an Oriental or Spanish house. **4.** An unroofed, usu. paved area near a house. **5.** An open gallery. — *v.t.* **·raced, ·rac·ing** To form into or provide with a terrace or terraces. [< OF < Ital. < L *terra* earth]

ter·ra cot·ta (ter/ə kot/ə) **1.** A hard, durable clay, reddish brown in color and usu. unglazed, widely used as a structural material and in pottery, tiles, building façades, etc. **2.** Its brownish orange color. [< Ital., cooked earth]

ter·ra fir·ma (ter/ə fûr/mə) Solid ground. [< L]

ter·rain (te·rān/, ter/ān) *n.* A piece or plot of ground; esp., a region or territory viewed with regard to its suitability for some particular purpose. [< F < L < *terra* earth]

Ter·ra·my·cin (ter/ə·mī/sin) *n.* Proprietary name for an antibiotic isolated from a soil mold and used in the treatment of a wide variety of bacterial infections. Also **ter/ra·my/cin.**

ter·ra·pin (ter/ə·pin) *n.* Any of several North American edible tortoises of fresh and brackish waters; esp., the diamond back. [< Algonquian]

ter·rar·i·um (te·râr/ē·əm) *n. pl.* **·rar·i·ums** or **·rar·i·a** (-râr/ē·ə) A place or enclosure for keeping land animals, plants, etc. [< L *terra* earth + -ARIUM, on analogy with *aquarium*]

ter·res·tri·al (tə·res/trē·əl) *adj.* **1.** Of, pertaining to, or consisting of earth or land. **2.** Of, belonging to, or representing the earth. **3.** *Biol.* Living on or growing in the earth or land. **4.** Belonging to or consisting of land, as distinct from water, trees, etc. **5.** Worldly; mundane. — *n.* An inhabitant of the earth. [< L *terra* land] — **ter·res/tri·al·ly** *adv.* — **ter·res/tri·al·ness** *n.*

ter·ret (ter/it) *n.* One of two metal rings projecting from the saddle of a harness, through which the reins are passed. [ME < F *touret*, dim. of *tour* turn]

terri- *combining form* Earth; ground. [< L *terra* earth]

ter·ri·ble (ter/ə·bəl) *adj.* **1.** Of a nature to excite terror; appalling. **2.** *Informal* Characterized by excess; severe; extreme. **3.** Inspiring awe. **4.** *Informal* Inferior. [< F < L *terrere* to terrify] — **ter/ri·ble·ness** *n.* — **ter/ri·bly** *adv.*

ter·ri·er (ter/ē·ər) *n.* Any of various small, active, wiry dogs of several breeds, formerly used to hunt burrowing animals. [< OF < L *terra* earth]

ter·rif·ic (tə·rif/ik) *adj.* **1.** *Informal* **a** Extreme; intense; tremendous. **b** Wonderful; great; splendid. **2.** Arousing or calculated to arouse great terror or fear. — **ter·rif/i·cal·ly** *adv.*

ter·ri·fy (ter/ə·fī) *v.t.* **·fied, ·fy·ing** To fill with extreme terror. [< L < *terrere* to frighten + *facere* to make]

ter·ri·to·ri·al (ter/ə·tôr/ē·əl, -tō/rē-) *adj.* **1.** Of or pertaining to a territory or territories. **2.** Limited to or within the jurisdiction of a particular territory or region. **3.** Designating military forces intended for territorial defense. **4.** Belonging to a particular locality. **5.** *Often cap.* Organized or intended primarily for national defense: the British *Territorial* Army. — **ter/ri·to/ri·al·ism** *n.* — **ter/ri·to/ri·al·ist** *n.* — **ter/ri·to/ri·al/i·ty** (-al/ə·tē) *n.* — **ter/ri·to/ri·al·ly** *adv.*

Ter·ri·to·ri·al (ter/ə·tôr/ē·əl, -tō/rē-) *adj.* Of any or all of the Territories of the U.S., Great Britain, etc. — *n.* A member of the Territorial Army in Great Britain.

ter·ri·to·ry (ter/ə·tôr/ē, -tō/rē) *n. pl.* **·ries 1.** The domain over which a sovereign state exercises jurisdiction. **2.** Any considerable tract of land; a region; also, a sphere, province. **3.** An area assigned for a special purpose. [< L *terra* earth]

Ter·ri·to·ry (ter/ə·tôr/ē, -tō/rē) *n. U.S.* A region having a certain degree of self-government but not having the status of a State, as American Samoa.

ter·ror (ter/ər) *n.* **1.** An overwhelming impulse of fear; extreme fright or dread. **2.** A person or thing that causes extreme fear. **3.** *Informal* An intolerable nuisance. [< F < L *terrere* to frighten]

ter·ror·ism (ter/ə·riz/əm) *n.* **1.** The act of terrorizing or the state of being terrorized. **2.** Unlawful acts of violence committed in an attempt to overthrow a government. **3.** A system of government that rules by intimidation. — **ter/·ror·ist** *n.* — **ter·ror·is/tic** *adj.*

ter·ror·ize (ter/ə·rīz) *v.t.* **·ized, ·iz·ing 1.** To reduce to a state of terror; terrify. **2.** To coerce through intimidation. — **ter/ror·i·za/tion** *n.* — **ter/ror·iz/er** *n.*

ter·ry (ter/ē) *n. pl.* **·ries** A pile fabric in which the loops are uncut: also **terry cloth.** [Prob. < F *tirer* to draw]

terse (tûrs) *adj.* **ters·er, ters·est** Short and to the point; concise: a *terse* comment. [< L < *tergere* to rub off, rub down] — **terse/ly** *adv.* — **terse/ness** *n.*

— **Syn.** Terse, concise, pithy, and *succinct* characterize speech or writing that says much in relatively few words. *Terse* emphasizes the finish and cogency of the result; *concise* suggest that all unnecessary words have been pruned away. *Pithy* describes something both brief and forceful, while *succinct* characterizes that which is highly compact because all extraneous detail has been removed. — **Ant.** diffuse, prolix, wordy.

ter·tial (tûr/shəl) *Ornithol. adj.* Tertiary. — *n.* A tertiary feather. [< L *tertius* third]

ter·tian (tûr/shən) *adj.* Recurring every other day, or if reckoned inclusively, every third day. — *n. Pathol.* A tertian disease or fever. [< L *tertius* third]

ter·ti·ar·y (tûr/shē·er/ē, -shə·rē) *adj.* **1.** Third in point of time, number, degree, etc. **2.** *Ornithol.* Denoting one of the flight feathers attached to a bird's wing: also called *tertial.* — *n. pl.* **·ar·ies** *Ornithol.* A tertiary feather. [< L < *tertius* third]

Ter·ti·ar·y (tûr/shē·er/ē, -shə·rē) *Geol. adj.* Of the earlier of the two geological periods or systems comprising the Cenozoic era, following the Cretaceous and succeeded by the Quaternary. — *n.* The Tertiary period or system, characterized by the rise of mammals. See table for GEOLOGY.

tes·sel·late (tes/ə·lāt) *v.t.* **·lat·ed, ·lat·ing** To construct in the style of checkered mosaic; lay or adorn with squares or tiles. [< L < dial. Gk. (Ionic) *tesseres* four] — **tes/sel·lat/·ed** *adj.* — **tes/sel·la/tion** *n.*

test[1] (test) v.t. **1.** To subject to a test or trial; try. **2.** Chem. **a** To assay or refine (a precious metal). **b** To examine by means of some reagent. — v.i. **3.** Chem. **a** To undergo testing. **b** To show specified qualities or properties under testing. — n. **1.** Subjection to conditions that disclose the true character of a person or thing in relation to some particular quality. **2.** An examination made for the purpose of proving or disproving some matter in doubt: a sobriety test. **3.** A series of questions, problems, etc., intended to measure the extent of knowledge, aptitudes, intelligence, and other mental traits. **4.** A criterion or standard of judgment. **5.** Chem. **a** A reaction by means of which the presence and identity of a compound or one of its constituents may be determined. **b** The agent or result of such a reaction. [< OF, vessel used in assaying metals < L testum earthen vessel] — test′a·ble adj. — test′er n.

test[2] (test) n. **1.** Zool. A rigid external case or covering of many invertebrates, as a sea urchin or mollusk: a shell: also called testa. **2.** Bot. A testa. [< L testa shell]

tes·ta (tes′tə) n. pl. ·tae (-tē) **1.** Bot. The outer, usu. hard and brittle coat or integument of a seed: also called test. **2.** Zool. A test. [See TEST[2].]

tes·ta·ceous (tes·tā′shəs) adj. **1.** Of or derived from shells or shellfish. **2.** Having a hard shell. [< L < testa shell]

tes·ta·ment (tes′tə·mənt) n. **1.** Law The written declaration of one's last will: chiefly in the phrase last will and testament. **2.** In Biblical use, a covenant. [< F < L < testis witness] — tes′ta·men′tal adj.

Tes·ta·ment (tes′tə·mənt) n. **1.** One of the two volumes of the Bible, distinguished as the Old and the New Testament. **2.** A volume containing the New Testament.

tes·ta·men·ta·ry (tes′tə·men′tər·ē) adj. **1.** Derived from, bequeathed by, or set forth in a will. **2.** Appointed or provided by, or done in accordance with, a will. **3.** Pertaining to a will, or to the administration or settlement of a will.

tes·tate (tes′tāt) adj. Having made a will before decease. [< L testis witness]

tes·ta·tor (tes·tā′tər, tes′tā·ter) n. **1.** The maker of a will. **2.** One who has died leaving a will. [< L] — tes·ta′trix (-triks) n.fem.

tes·tes (tes′tēz) Plural of TESTIS.

tes·ti·cle (tes′ti·kəl) n. Biol. One of the two male sex glands enclosed in the scrotum and in which the spermatozoa and certain secretions are formed: also called testis. [< L, dim. of testis testicle]

tes·ti·fy (tes′tə·fī) v. ·fied, ·fy·ing v.i. **1.** To make solemn declaration of truth or fact. **2.** Law To give testimony; bear witness. **3.** To serve as evidence or indication: Her rags testified to her poverty. — v.t. **4.** To bear witness to; affirm positively. **5.** Law To state or declare on oath or affirmation. **6.** To be evidence or indication of. **7.** To make known publicly; declare. [< L < testis witness + facere to make] — tes′ti·fi·ca′tion (-fə·kā′shən) n. — tes′ti·fi′er n.

tes·ti·mo·ni·al (tes′tə·mō′nē·əl) n. **1.** A formal token or statement of regard. **2.** A written acknowledgment of services or worth; also, a letter of recommendation. — adj. Pertaining to or constituting testimony or a testimonial.

tes·ti·mo·ny (tes′tə·mō′nē) n. pl. ·nies **1.** A statement or affirmation of a fact, as before a court. **2.** Evidence; proof; also, the aggregate of proof offered in a case. **3.** The act of testifying; attestation. **4.** Public declaration regarding some experience. [< L < testis witness]

— **Syn.** Testimony is the oral statements made by a witness under examination. A deposition or affidavit is testimony put into writing; depositions are made under formal questioning, and may be subject to cross-examination, while an affidavit is a sworn document that may be accepted when the testifier cannot appear in court in person.

tes·tis (tes′tis) n. pl. ·tes (-tēz) A testicle. [< L]

tes·tos·ter·one (tes·tos′tə·rōn) n. Biochem. A male sex hormone, $C_{19}H_{28}O_2$, isolated as a white crystalline substance from the testes, and also made synthetically. [< TESTIS + STER(OL) + -ONE]

test pilot An aviator who tests aircraft of new design.

test tube A glass tube, open at one end and usu. with a rounded bottom, used in making chemical or biological tests.

tes·tu·do (tes·tōō′dō, -tyōō′-) n. pl. ·di·nes (-də·nēz) **1.** A shed or screen used by the Romans for the protection of soldiers in siege operations. **2.** A protecting cover formed by soldiers in ranks by overlapping their shields above their heads. [< L testa shell]

tes·ty (tes′tē) adj. ·ti·er, ·ti·est Irritable in manner or disposition; touchy. [< AF testif heady < OF < L testa skull] — tes′ti·ly adv. — tes′ti·ness n.

te·tan·ic (ti·tan′ik) adj. Relating to or productive of tetanus. Also te·tan′i·cal. — n. A drug capable of causing convulsions, as strychnine or nux vomica.

tet·a·nus (tet′ə·nəs) n. **1.** Pathol. An acute infectious disease caused by a bacillus and characterized by rigid spasmodic contraction of various voluntary muscles, esp. those of the neck and jaw. Compare LOCKJAW. **2.** Physiol. A state of contraction in a muscle excited by a rapid series of shocks. [< L < Gk. tetanos spasm]

tetarto- combining form Four; fourth. Also, before vowels, tetart-. [< Gk. tetartos fourth < tettares fourth]

tetch·y (tech′ē) adj. tetch·i·er, tetch·i·est Peevishly sensitive; irritable; touchy. [< OF teche mark, quality] — tetch′i·ly adv. — tetch′i·ness n.

tête-à-tête (tāt′ə·tāt′, Fr. tet·à·tet′) adj. Confidential, as between two persons only. — n. **1.** A confidential interview between two persons; a private chat. **2.** An S-shaped sofa on which two persons may face each other. — adv. In or as in intimate conversation. [< F, lit. head to head]

teth·er (teth′ər) n. **1.** Something used to check or confine, as a rope for fastening an animal. **2.** The range, scope, or limit of one's powers or field of action. — at the end of one's tether At the extreme end or limit of one's resources, patience, etc. — v.t. To fasten or confine by a tether. [ME tethir < Scand.]

tetra- combining form Four; fourfold. Also, before vowels, tetr-. [< Gk.]

tet·ra·chord (tet′rə·kôrd) n. Music Four contiguous tones, of which the extreme tones are a perfect fourth apart. [< Gk. < tetras group of four + chordē string] — tet′ra·chor′dal adj.

tet·rad (tet′rad) n. A group or collection of four. [< Gk. tetras, -ados group of four]

tet·ra·eth·yl lead (tet′rə·eth′il led) Chem. A colorless, heavy, flammable, poisonous, liquid hydrocarbon $Pb(C_2H_5)_4$, used as an antiknock agent in internal-combustion engines.

tet·ra·he·dron (tet′rə·hē′drən) n. pl. ·drons or ·dra (-drə) Geom. A polyhedron bounded by four plane triangular faces. [< Gk. < tetra- four + hedra base] — tet′ra·he′dral adj.

TETRAHEDRON

te·tral·o·gy (te·tral′ə·jē) n. pl. ·gies **1.** A group of four dramas, including three tragedies and one satyr play, presented together at the festivals of Dionysus at Athens. **2.** Any series of four related dramatic, operatic, or literary works. [< Gk. < tetra- four + logos word]

te·tram·e·ter (te·tram′ə·tər) n. **1.** In prosody, a line of verse consisting of four metrical feet: Fŭll fā | thŏm fīve | thў fā | thĕr lĭes. **2.** Verse consisting of lines of four metrical feet. — adj. Consisting of four metrical feet or of lines containing four metrical feet. [< LL < Gk. < tetra- four + metron measure]

tet·rarch (tet′rärk, tē′trärk) n. **1.** The governor of one of four divisions of a country or province. **2.** A tributary prince under the Romans; a subordinate ruler. **3.** In ancient Greece, an army commander of a subdivision of a phalanx. [< LL < Gk. < tetra- four + archos ruler]

tet·rar·chy (tet′rär·kē, tē′trär-) n. pl. ·chies **1.** The rule, territory, or jurisdiction of a tetrarch. **2.** Government by a group of four; also, the four members of such a group. Also tet′rar·chate (-kāt, -kit).

tet·ra·stich (tet′rə·stik) n. A poem or stanza of four lines. [< TETRA- + Gk. stichos row, line] — tet′ra·stich′ic adj.

tet·ra·va·lent (tet′rə·vā′lənt) adj. Chem. Quadrivalent.

Teu·ton (tōōt′n, tyōōt′n) n. **1.** One of the Teutons. **2.** One belonging to any of the Teutonic peoples; esp., a German.

Teu·to·nes (tōō′tə·nēz, tyōō′-) n.pl. An ancient German tribe that dwelt in Jutland north of the Elbe.

Teu·ton·ic (tōō·ton′ik, tyōō-) adj. **1.** Of, pertaining to, or designating the peoples of northern Europe, formerly the Angles, Saxons, Danes, Normans, Goths, etc., now embracing also the English, Germans, Dutch, etc. **2.** Of or pertaining to the Germanic languages. **3.** Of or pertaining to the Teutones. — n. The Germanic subfamily of languages.

Teu·ton·ism (tōōt′n·iz′əm, tyōōt′n-) n. **1.** A custom or mode of expression peculiar to Germans or Teutons; Germanism. Also Teu·ton·i·cism (tōō·ton′ə·siz′əm, tyōō-). **2.** A belief in the superiority of the Teutonic peoples. **3.** Teutonic character and civilization. — Teu′ton·ist n.

Teu·ton·ize (tōōt′n·īz, tyōōt′n-) v.t. & v.i. ·ized, ·iz·ing To make or become Teutonic or German. — Teu′ton·i·za′tion n.

Texas fever A destructive cattle disease caused by a blood parasite transmitted by a tick.

Texas leaguer U.S. Informal In baseball, a fly ball that falls between an infielder and an outfielder for a base hit.

text (tekst) n. **1.** The body of matter on a written or printed page, as distinguished from notes, commentary, illustrations, etc. **2.** The actual or original words of an author. **3.** A written or printed version of the matter of an author's works: the folio text of Shakespeare. **4.** Any one of various recensions that are taken to represent the authentic words, or portion of the words, of the original Scriptures. **5.** A verse of Scripture, particularly when cited as the basis of a discourse or sermon. **6.** Any subject of discourse; a topic. **7.** A textbook. [< OF < L *textus* fabric < *texere* to weave]

text·book (tekst′bŏŏk′) *n.* A book used as a standard work or basis of instruction in any branch of knowledge.

tex·tile (teks′til, -tīl) *adj.* **1.** Pertaining to weaving or woven fabrics. **2.** Such as may be woven; manufactured by weaving. — *n.* **1.** A woven fabric. **2.** Material capable of being woven. [< L < *textus* fabric.]

tex·tu·al (teks′chŏŏ-əl) *adj.* **1.** Pertaining to, contained in, or based on the text of a book. **2.** Word for word; literal. **3.** Versed in texts. — **tex′tu·al·ly** *adv.*

tex·tu·al·ism (teks′chŏŏ-əl-iz′əm) *n.* Rigid adherence to a text. — **tex′tu·al·ist** *n.*

tex·ture (teks′chər) *n.* **1.** The arrangement or character of the threads, etc., of a woven fabric. **2.** The mode of union or disposition of elementary constituent parts, as in a photograph, surface of paper, etc. **3.** The structure of the surface of a painting, sculpture, etc.; also, the apparent surface structure of an object or part represented in a work of art, as skin, fur, etc. **4.** Any woven fabric; a web. — *v.t.* **·tured, ·tur·ing** To give a particular texture to. [< L < *textus* fabric] — **tex′tur·al** *adj.* — **tex′tur·al·ly** *adv.*

tex·tured (teks′chərd) *adj.* **1.** Having a distinctive texture. **2.** Having (a specified kind of) texture: used in combination: *rough-textured.*

-th¹ *suffix of nouns* **1.** The act or result of the action expressed in the root word: *growth.* **2.** The state of being what is indicated in the root word: *health.* [OE *-thu, -th*]

-th² *suffix* Used in ordinal numbers: *tenth.* Also, after vowels, *-eth,* as in *fortieth.* [OE *-tha, -the*]

-th³ See -ETH¹.

Thai (tī) *n.* **1.** The people collectively of Thailand, Laos, and parts of Burma: preceded by *the.* **2.** A family of languages spoken by these people, considered by some to be a branch of the Sino-Tibetan family and by others to be affiliated with the Austronesian Polynesian family. **3.** The language of Thailand. — *adj.* Of or pertaining to the Thai, their culture, or their languages. Also spelled *Tai.*

tha·lam·ic (thə-lam′ik) *adj.* Of or pertaining to a thalamus, esp. to the thalamus of the brain.

thal·a·mus (thal′ə-məs) *n. pl.* **·mi** (-mī) **1.** *Anat.* A large, ovoid mass of gray matter at the base of the brain, the chief center for transmission of sensory impulses to the cerebral cortex: also called *optic thalamus.* **2.** *Bot.* The receptacle of a flower. [< L < Gk. *thalamos* chamber]

tha·las·sic (thə-las′ik) *adj.* **1.** Of or pertaining to the seas, as distinguished from the oceans. **2.** Pelagic; oceanic. [< F < L *thalassa* sea]

thalasso- *combining form* The sea; of the sea. Also, before vowels, **thalass-, thalassi-.** [< Gk. *thalassa* sea]

tha·ler (tä′lər) See TALER.

thal·i·do·mide (thə-lid′ə-mīd) *n. Chem.* An organic compound, $C_{13}H_{10}N_2O_4$, originally a mild sedative and later withdrawn because its use by pregnant women was suspected of causing serious malformations in newborn children.

thal·li·um (thal′ē-əm) *n.* A soft, white, crystalline metallic element (symbol Tl), whose salts are used in rat poison, insecticides, and in making optical glass. See ELEMENT. [< NL < Gk. *thallos* green shoot; from the bright green line in its spectrum that led to its discovery]

thal·lo·phyte (thal′ə-fīt) *n.* Any of various plants belonging to a division including forms without true roots, stems, or leaves, comprising the bacteria, fungi, algae, and lichens. — **thal′lo·phyt′ic** (-fit′ik) *adj.*

thal·lus (thal′əs) *n. pl.* **·lus·es** or **·li** (-lī) *Bot.* A plant body without true root, stem, or leaf, as in thallophytes. [< L, shoot < Gk. < *thallein* to bloom]

Tham·muz (täm′mŏŏz, tam′uz) See TAMMUZ.

than (than, *unstressed* thən) *conj.* **1.** When, as, or if compared with: after an adjective or adverb to express comparison between what precedes and what follows: I am stronger *than* he (is). **2.** Except; but: used after *other, else,* etc.: no other *than* you. [OE *thonne* then]

◆ *Than* is usu. taken as a conjunction; as such, it may be followed by the nominative or the objective, depending on the nature of the ellipsis: You struck him harder *than I* (struck him) or You struck him harder *than* (you struck) *me.* A minority of grammarians and writers have accepted *than* as a preposition, in which case it is regularly followed by the objective: He is stronger *than me.*

thanato- *combining form* Death; of or pertaining to death. Also, before vowels, **thanat-.** [< Gk. *thanatos* death]

than·a·top·sis (than′ə-top′sis) *n.* A meditation upon death. [< THANAT(O)- + Gk. *opsis* appearance, sight]

thane (thān) *n.* **1.** A warrior companion of an English king before the Conquest. **2.** A man who ranked above an ordinary freeman or ceorl (churl) but below an earl or nobleman. **3.** *Scot.* The chief of a clan. Also *thegn.* [OE *thegn*]

thank (thangk) *v.t.* **1.** To express gratitude to. **2.** To hold

responsible; blame: often used ironically. — **thank you** I thank you. [OE *thancian* < *thanc* thanks, thought]

thank·ful (thangk′fəl) *adj.* **1.** Appreciative of favors received; grateful. **2.** Expressing thanks. — **thank′ful·ly** *adv.* — **thank′ful·ness** *n.*

thank·less (thangk′lis) *adj.* **1.** Not feeling or showing gratitude; ungrateful. **2.** Not gaining or likely to gain thanks; unappreciated. — **thank′less·ly** *adv.* — **thank′less·ness** *n.*

thanks (thangks) *n.pl.* Expressions of gratitude; grateful acknowledgment. — *interj.* Thank you. — **thanks to 1.** Thanks be given to. **2.** Because of.

thanks·giv·ing (thangks′giv′ing) *n.* **1.** The act of giving thanks, as to God; an expression of gratitude. **2.** A public celebration in recognition of divine favor.

Thanksgiving Day 1. *U.S.* The fourth Thursday in November, set apart as an annual festival of thanksgiving. **2.** *Canadian* The second Monday in October, a statutory holiday. Also **Thanksgiving.**

that (that, *unstressed* thət) *pl.* for *adj.* and *pron. def.* 1 **those** (thōz) *adj.* **1.** Pertaining to some person or thing previously mentioned, understood, or specifically designated. **2.** Denoting something more remote, or something contrasted with another thing: distinguished from *this:* This house is brown, *that* one is red. — *pron.* **1.** As a demonstrative, the person or thing implied, mentioned, or understood; the person or thing there or as distinguished from one already designated: *That* is the dress I like; Keep this and discard *that.* **2.** As a relative pronoun, who, whom, or which: the person *that* I saw. — *adv.* **1.** To that extent: I can't see *that* far. **2.** *Informal* In such a manner or degree; so: He's *that* simple, he can hardly read. — *conj.* **1.** As a fact: introducing a fact: I tell you *that* it is so. **2.** As a result: introducing a result, consequence, or effect: He bled so profusely *that* he died. **3.** At which time; when: It was only yesterday *that* I saw him. **4.** So that: I tell you *that* you may know. **5.** For the reason that; because. **6.** Introducing an exclamation: O *that* he would come: — **so that 1.** To the end that. **2.** With the result that. [OE *thæt,* neut. of *se* the, that]

thatch (thach) *n.* **1.** A covering of reeds, straw, etc., arranged on a roof so as to shed water. **2.** Anything resembling such a covering. **3.** Any of various palms whose leaves are used for thatching. — *v.t.* To cover with or as with thatch. [OE *thæc* cover] — **thatch′er** *n.* — **thatch′y** *adj.*

thatch·ing (thach′ing) *n.* **1.** The act or process of covering a roof with thatch. **2.** Material used for thatch.

thaumato- *combining form* A wonder; a miracle. Also, before vowels, **thauma-.** [< Gk. *thauma, -atos* wonder]

thau·ma·tur·gy (thô′mə-tûr′jē) *n.* Magic; the working of wonders or miracles. — **thau′ma·tur′gic** or **·gi·cal** *adj.*

thaw (thô) *v.i.* **1.** To melt or dissolve; become liquid or semiliquid, as snow or ice. **2.** To rise in temperature so as to melt ice and snow: said of weather and used impersonally. **3.** To become less cold and unsociable. — *v.t.* **4.** To cause to thaw. — *n.* **1.** The act of thawing, or the state of being thawed. **2.** Warmth of weather above the freezing point, following a colder period. **3.** A state of warmer feeling or expression. [OE *thawian*] — **thaw′er** *n.*

the¹ (*stressed* thē; *unstressed* before a consonant thə; *unstressed* before a vowel thē or thi) *definite article* or *adj. The* is opposed to the indefinite article *a* or *an,* and is used, esp. before nouns, to render the modified word more particular or individual. It is used specifically: **1.** When reference is made to a particular person, thing, or group: He left *the* room. **2.** To give an adjective substantive force, or render a notion abstract: *the* doing of the deed; *the* quick and *the* dead. **3.** Before a noun to make it generic: *The* dog is a friend of man. **4.** With the force of a possessive pronoun: He kicked me in *the* (my) leg. **5.** To give distributive force: equivalent to *a, per, each,* etc.: a dollar *the* volume. **6.** To designate a particular one as emphatically outstanding: usu. stressed in speech and italicized in writing: He is *the* officer for the command. [OE, later form of *sē*]

the² (thə) *adv.* By that much; by so much; to this extent: used to modify words in the comparative degree: *the* more, *the* merrier. [OE *thȳ,* instrumental case of *sē* the¹]

the- Var. of THEO-.

the·a·ter (thē′ə-tər) *n.* **1.** A building especially adapted to present dramas, operas, motion pictures, etc.; playhouse. **2.** The theatrical world and everything relating to it. **3.** A room or hall arranged with seats that rise as they recede from a platform, esp. adapted to lectures, demonstrations, etc. **4.** Any place of semicircular form with seats rising by easy gradations. **5.** Any place or region that is the scene of events: a *theater* of operations in war. Also *esp. Brit.* **the′a·tre.** [< OF < L < Gk. < *theasthai* to behold]

the·a·ter·go·er (thē′ə-tər-gō′ər) *n.* One who goes often or regularly to the theater. Also *esp. Brit.* **the′a·tre·go′er.**

the·a·ter-in-the-round (thē′ə-tər-in-thə-round′) *n.* Arena theater.

the·at·ri·cal (thē-at′ri-kəl) *adj.* **1.** Pertaining to the theater or to dramatic performances. **2.** Designed for show, display, or effect; showy; artificial. **3.** Suited to dramatic presentation. **4.** Resembling the manner of actors; histrionic. Also **the·at'ric.** — *n.pl.* Dramatic performances, esp. by amateurs. — **the·at'ri·cal·ly** *adv.* — **the·at'ri·cal·ness** *n.*

the·at·ri·cal·ism (thē·at'ri·kəl·iz'əm) *n.* Theatrical or melodramatic manner or style.

the·at·rics (thē·at'riks) *n.pl.* (*construed as sing.*) **1.** The staging of plays. **2.** The art of creating effects appropriate to dramatic performances.

Thebes (thēbz) **1.** The ancient capital of Upper Egypt; Luxor and Karnak occupy part of its site on the Nile. **2.** The chief city of ancient Boeotia, Greece: also **The·bae** (thē'bē). — **The·ban** (thē'bən) *adj. & n.*

the·ca (thē'kə) *n. pl.* **·cae** (-sē) **1.** *Biol.* A protective sheath or case for an organ or part, as of the spinal cord, a follicle, an insect pupa, etc. **2.** *Bot.* A spore case, sac, or capsule. [< L < Gk. *thēkē* case] — **the'ca** *adj.* — **the·cate** (thē'kit, -kāt)

thee (thē) *pron.* **1.** *Archaic* The objective case of the pronoun *thou.* **2.** Thou: used by some Quakers with a verb in the third person singular: *Thee* knows my mind. [OE *thē,* orig. dative, later accusative case of *thū* thou]

theft (theft) *n.* **1.** The act or crime of thieving; larceny. **2.** *Rare* That which is stolen. [OE *thēoft, thīefth*]
— **Syn. 1.** *Theft* is the general term for the crime of stealing. In law, *larceny* includes many forms of stealing, but not embezzlement and swindling. *Burglary* is the crime of breaking into and entering another's home, place of business, or other property with intent to commit a felony. *Robbery* is stealing from the person, or in the presence of, the victim.

thegn (thān) See THANE.

the·ine (thē'ēn, -in) *n. Chem.* The alkaloid found in the tea plant, chemically identical with caffeine. Also **the'in** (-in). [< F < NL *thea* tea < dial. Chinese *t'e*]

their (thâr) *pronominal adj.* The possessive case of the pronoun *they,* used attributively: *their* homes. [ME < ON *theirra* of them]

theirs (thârz) *pron.* **1.** The possessive case of the pronoun *they,* used predicatively: That house is *theirs.* **2.** The one or ones belonging or relating to them: our country and *theirs.* — **of theirs** Belonging or pertaining to them.

the·ism (thē'iz·əm) *n.* **1.** Belief in, or in the existence of, God, a god, or gods. **2.** Belief in a personal God as creator and supreme ruler of the universe, who transcends his creation but works in and through it in revealing himself to men. **3.** Belief in one god; monotheism. [< Gk. *theos* god] — **the'ist** *n.* — **the·is'tic** or **·ti·cal** *adj.* — **the·is'ti·cal·ly** *adv.*

them (them, *unstressed* thəm) *pron.* The objective case of the pronoun *they.* [ME *theim* < ON, to them]

the·mat·ic (thē·mat'ik) *adj.* **1.** Of, constituting, or pertaining to a theme or themes. **2.** *Ling.* Constituting a stem. Also **the·mat'i·cal.** — **the·mat'i·cal·ly** *adv.*

thematic vowel *Ling.* A vowel added to a root to form a stem.

theme (thēm) *n.* **1.** A topic to be discussed or developed in speech or writing; a subject of discourse. **2.** Any topic. **3.** A brief composition, esp. one written as an exercise as part of a course of instruction. **4.** *Music* **a** A melody that is subjected to variation or elaboration; subject. **b** A musical feature, as a chordal sequence, rhythm, melody, etc. that forms the basis of a composition. [< OF < L < Gk. *the-,* stem of *tithenai* to place]

theme song 1. A melody used throughout a dramatic presentation to establish or maintain a mood. **2.** A strain of music that identifies a radio program, a dance band, etc.

them·selves (them·selvz', *unstressed* thəm-) *pron.* A form of the third person plural pronoun, used: **1.** As a reflexive or as object of a preposition in a reflexive sense: They laughed at *themselves.* **2.** As an emphatic or intensive form of *they:* They *themselves* are at fault. **3.** As a designation of a normal, proper, or usual state: They were not *themselves* then.

then (then) *adv.* **1.** At that time. **2.** Soon or immediately afterward; next in space or time. **3.** At another time: often introducing a sequential statement following *now, at first,* etc. **4.** For that reason; as a consequence. **5.** In that case. — *adj.* Being or acting in, or belonging to, that time: the *then* secretary of state. — *n.* A specific time already mentioned or understood; that time. [OE *thanne*]

thence (thens) *adv.* **1.** From that place. **2.** From the circumstance, fact, or cause; therefore. **3.** From that time; after that time. [ME < OE *thanon* from there + -s³]

thence·forth (thens'fôrth', -fôrth', thens'fôrth', -fôrth') *adv.* From that time on; thereafter.

thence·for·ward (thens'fôr'wərd) *adv.* **1.** Thenceforth. **2.** From that place or time forward. Also **thence'for'wards.**

theo- *combining form* God; of or pertaining to God, a god, or gods. Also, before vowels, **the-.** [< Gk. *theos* a god]

the·oc·ra·cy (thē·ok'rə·sē) *n. pl.* **·cies 1.** A state, polity,

or group of people that claims a deity as its ruler. **2.** Government of a state by a priesthood claiming divine authority, as in the Papacy. [< Gk. < *theos* god + *krateein* to rule] — **the·o·crat'ic** (thē'ə·krat'ik) or **·i·cal** *adj.*

the·o·crat (thē'ə·krat) *n.* **1.** A theocratic or divine ruler. **2.** An advocate of theocracy.

the·od·o·lite (thē·od'ə·līt) *n.* In surveying, an instrument for measuring horizontal and vertical angles by means of a small telescope turning on a horizontal and a vertical axis. [An arbitrary formation] — **the·od'o·lit'ic** (-lit'ik) *adj.*

the·o·lo·gi·an (thē'ə·lō'jē·ən, -jən) *n.* One versed in theology, esp. that of the Christian church.

the·o·log·i·cal (thē'ə·loj'i·kəl) *adj.* Of or pertaining to theology or to divine revelation. Also **the'o·log'ic.** — **the'o·log'i·cal·ly** *adv.*

the·ol·o·gize (thē·ol'ə·jīz) *v.* **·gized, ·giz·ing** *v.t.* **1.** To devise or fit (something) into a system of theology. — *v.i.* **2.** To reason theologically. Also *Brit.* **the·ol'o·gise.**

the·ol·o·gy (thē·ol'ə·jē) *n. pl.* **·gies 1.** The study of religion, culminating in a synthesis or philosophy of religion; also, a critical survey of religion, esp. of the Christian religion. **2.** A body of doctrines as set forth by a particular church or religious group. [< OF < LL < Gk. < *theos* god + *logos* discourse]

the·oph·a·ny (thē·of'ə·nē) *n. pl.* **·nies** A manifestation or appearance of a deity or of the gods to man. [< L < Gk. < *theos* god + *phainein* to show]

the·o·rem (thē'ər·əm, thir'əm) *n.* **1.** A proposition demonstrably true or acknowledged as such. **2.** *Math.* **a** A proposition setting forth something to be proved. **b** A proposition that has been proved or assumed to be true. **c** A rule or statement of relations formulated in symbols. [LL < Gk. *theōrēma* sight, theory < *theōreein* to look at] — **the·o·re·mat·ic** (thē'ər·ə·mat'ik), **the'o·rem'ic** (-ə·rem'ik) *adj.*

the·o·ret·i·cal (thē'ə·ret'i·kəl) *adj.* **1.** Of, relating to, or consisting of theory. **2.** Relating to knowledge or science without reference to its application. **3.** Existing only in theory; hypothetical. **4.** Addicted to theorizing; impractical; visionary. Also **the·o·ret'ic.** — **the'o·ret'i·cal·ly** *adv.*

the·o·re·ti·cian (thē'ər·ə·tish'ən) *n.* One who deals with the speculative, hypothetical, or ideal rather than with the practical and executive aspects of a subject.

the·o·ret·ics (thē'ə·ret'iks) *n.pl.* (*construed as sing.*) The theoretical aspect of a science.

the·o·rist (thē'ər·ist) *n.* One who theorizes.

the·o·rize (thē'ə·rīz) *v.i.* **·rized, ·riz·ing** To form or express theories; speculate. Also *Brit.* **the'o·rise.** — **the'o·ri·za'tion** *n.* — **the'o·riz'er** *n.*

the·o·ry (thē'ər·ē, thir'ē) *n. pl.* **·ries 1.** A plan or scheme existing in the mind only; a speculative or conjectural view of something. **2.** An integrated group of the fundamental principles underlying a science or its practical applications: the atomic *theory.* **3.** Abstract knowledge of any art as opposed to the practice of it. **4.** A closely reasoned set of propositions, derived from and supported by established evidence and intended to serve as an explanation for a group of phenomena: the quantum *theory.* — **Syn.** See DOCTRINE, HYPOTHESIS. [< LL < Gk. *theoria* view, speculation]

the·os·o·phy (thē·os'ə·fē) *n. pl.* **·phies 1.** Any of various religious systems that aim at establishing a direct relation between the individual soul and the divine principle through contemplation and speculation. **2.** *Often cap.* The doctrines of a modern religious sect (**Theosophical Society**), resembling those of Buddhism and Brahmanism. [< Med.L < Gk. < *theos* god + *sophos* wise] — **the·o·soph'ic** (thē'ə·sof'ik) or **·i·cal** *adj.* — **the'o·soph'i·cal·ly** *adv.* — **the·os'o·phist** *n.*

ther·a·peu·tic (ther'ə·pyōō'tik) *adj.* **1.** Having healing qualities; curative. **2.** Pertaining to therapeutics. Also **ther'a·peu'ti·cal.** [< NL < Gk. < *therapeuein* take care of < *therapōn* an attendant] — **ther'a·peu'ti·cal·ly** *adv.*

ther·a·peu·tics (ther'ə·pyōō'tiks) *n.pl.* (*construed as sing.*) The branch of medical science dealing with the treatment of disease. — **ther'a·peu'tist** *n.*

ther·a·py (ther'ə·pē) *n. pl.* **·pies 1.** The treatment of disease: often used in combination: *chemotherapy.* **2.** Treatment, activity, etc., intended to remedy or alleviate a disorder or undesirable condition. **3.** Healing or curative quality. — **ther'a·pist** *n.*

there (thâr) *adv.* **1.** In, at, or about that place: opposed to *here.* Also used to indicate or emphasize: John *there* is a good student. **2.** To, toward, or into that place; thither. **3.** At that stage or point of action or time. — *n.* That place: Are you from *there,* too? — *interj.* An exclamation of triumph, relief, etc.: *There!* It's finished. ♦ The adverb *there* cannot, in standard English, appear in the adjective position, as that *there* girl. That girl *there* is the accepted order. *There* is very often used as an expletive introducing a clause or sentence, the subject usu. following the verb: *There* once were three bears. It is also used as an equivalent of the pronoun *that* in expressions of encouragement, approval, etc.: *There's* a good boy. [OE *thær*]

there·a·bout (thâr′ə·bout′) *adv.* Near that number, quantity, degree, place, or time. Also **there′a·bouts′.**

there·af·ter (thâr′af′tər, -äf′-) *adv.* Afterward; from that time on.

there·at (thâr′at′) *adv.* At that event, place, or time; at that incentive; upon that.

there·by (thâr′bī′) *adv.* **1.** Through the agency of that. **2.** Connected with that. **3.** Conformably to that. **4.** *Archaic* Nearby; thereabout.

there·for (thâr′fôr′) *adv.* For this, that, or it.

there·fore (thâr′fôr′, -fōr′) *adv. & conj.* For that or this reason; on that ground or account; consequently: He did not run fast enough; *therefore* he lost the race.

there·from (thâr′frum′, -from′) *adv.* From this, that, or it; from this or that time, place, state, event, or thing.

there·in (thâr′in′) *adv.* **1.** In that place. **2.** In that time, matter, or respect.

there·in·af·ter (thâr′in·af′tər, -äf′-) *adv.* In a subsequent part of that (book, document, speech, etc.).

there·in·to (thâr′in·tōō′) *adv.* Into this, that, or it.

there·of (thâr′uv′, -ov′) *adv.* **1.** Of or relating to this, that, or it. **2.** From or because of this or that cause or particular.

there·on (thâr′on′, -ôn′) *adv.* **1.** On this, that, or it. **2.** Thereupon; thereat.

there's (thârz) There is.

there·to (thâr′tōō′) *adv.* **1.** To this, that, or it. **2.** In addition; furthermore. Also **there′un·to′** (-un·tōō′).

there·to·fore (thâr′tə·fôr′, -fōr′) *adv.* Before this or that; previously to that.

there·un·der (thâr′un′dər) *adv.* **1.** Under this or that. **2.** Less in number; fewer than that. **3.** In accordance with that; by that authority.

there·up·on (thâr′ə·pon′, -ə·pôn′) *adv.* **1.** Upon that; upon it. **2.** Following upon or in consequence of that. **3.** Immediately following; at once.

there·with (thâr′with′, -with′) *adv.* **1.** With this, that, or it. **2.** Thereupon; thereafter; immediately afterward.

there·with·al (thâr′with·ôl′) *adv.* With all this or that; besides.

therm- Var. of THERMO-.

therm. Thermometer.

ther·mal (thûr′məl) *adj.* **1.** Pertaining to, determined by, or measured by heat. **2.** Caused by, using, or producing heat. **3.** Hot or warm. Also **ther′mic.** **— ther′mal·ly** *adv.*

thermo- *combining form* Heat; of or caused by heat. Also, before vowels, *therm-.* [< Gk. *thermos* heat, warmth]

ther·mo·cou·ple (thûr′mə·kup′əl) *n.* A device for temperature measurement that depends upon the electric current or potential produced when joined conductors of two different metals have their ends at different temperatures. Also **thermoelectric couple.**

ther·mo·dy·nam·ics (thûr′mō·dī·nam′iks, -di-) *n.pl.* (*construed as sing.*) The branch of physics dealing with the relations between heat and other forms of energy. **— ther′mo·dy·nam′ic** or **·i·cal** *adj.* **— ther′mo·dy·nam′i·cist** (-ə·sist) *n.*

ther·mo·e·lec·tric (thûr′mō·i·lek′trik) *adj.* **1.** Designating or associated with changes of electrical potential between two dissimilar metals in contact with each other as temperature varies. **2.** Designating or associated with the ability of an electric current to cause a flow of heat in a wire. Also **ther′·mo·e·lec′tri·cal.** **— ther′mo·e·lec′tri·cal·ly** *adv.*

ther·mo·e·lec·tric·i·ty (thûr′mō·i·lek′tris′ə·tē) *n.* Electricity generated by thermoelectric phenomena.

ther·mom·e·ter (thər·mom′ə·tər) *n.* An instrument for measuring temperature, usu. by means of a graduated glass capillary tube with a bulb containing a liquid, as mercury or alcohol, that expands or contracts as the temperature rises or falls. [< THERMO- + METER]

ther·mom·e·try (thər·mom′ə·trē) *n.* **1.** The measurement of temperature. **2.** The design and construction of thermometers. **— ther·mo·met·ric** (thûr′mō·met′rik) or **·ri·cal** *adj.* **— ther′mo·met′ri·cal·ly** *adv.*

ther·mo·nu·cle·ar (thûr′mō·nōō′klē·ər, -nyōō′-) *adj. Physics* Pertaining to or characterized by reactions involving the fusion of atomic nuclei at very high temperatures, esp. in stars and in the hydrogen bomb.

ther·mo·pile (thûr′mō·pīl) *n.* A group of thermocouples acting jointly to produce an electric current, esp. when used with a galvanometer to measure heat.

ther·mo·plas·tic (thûr′mō·plas′tik) *adj.* Plastic in the presence of or under the application of heat, as certain synthetic molding materials. **— n.** A thermoplastic substance.

Ther·mop·y·lae (thər·mop′ə·lē) A narrow mountain pass in Greece; scene of a battle, 480 B.C., in which the Spartans under the command of Leonidas held off the Persians under Xerxes and finally died to the last man rather than yield.

ther·mos bottle (thûr′məs) A bottle that keeps the con-

tents hot or cold, consisting of two containers with a vacuum between, the whole usu. enclosed in a metal cylinder. [< Gk. *thermos* hot]

ther·mo·set·ting (thûr′mō·set′ing) *adj.* Having the property of assuming a fixed shape after being molded under heat, as certain plastics and urea resins.

ther·mo·stat (thûr′mə·stat) *n.* A device for the automatic regulation of temperature, used for actuating fire alarms, starting or stopping heating plants, etc. [< THERMO- + Gk. *statos* standing] **— ther′mo·stat′ic** *adj.* **— ther′mo·stat′i·cal·ly** *adv.*

ther·mot·ro·pism (thər·mot′rə·piz′əm) *n. Biol.* The property whereby growing plants or other organisms turn toward or away from a source of heat. **— ther·mo·trop·ic** (thûr′mō·trop′ik) *adj.*

the·sau·rus (thə·sôr′əs) *n.* *pl.* **·sau·ri** (-sôr′ī) **1.** A book containing a store of words, esp., of synonyms and antonyms arranged in categories. **2.** A storehouse; treasury. [< L < Gk. *thesauros* treasure house]

these (thēz) *adj. & pron.* Plural of THIS.

The·seus (thē′sōōs, -sē·əs) In Greek mythology, the king of Athens, celebrated for killing the Minotaur and for unifying Attica with Athens as its capital. See ARIADNE, PHAEDRA.

the·sis (thē′sis) *n.* *pl.* **·ses** (-sēz) **1.** A proposition. **2.** A formal proposition, advanced and defended by argumentation. **3.** A formal treatise on a particular subject; esp., a dissertation presented by a candidate for an academic degree. **4.** *Logic* An affirmative proposition; a premise or postulate. [< L < Gk. < *tithenai* to put, place]

Thes·pi·an (thes′pē·ən) *adj.* Of or relating to drama; dramatic; tragic. **— n.** An actor or actress. [after *Thespis*, Greek poet and actor, 6th century B.C.]

Thes·sa·lo·ni·an (thes′ə·lō′nē·ən) *n.* **1.** A native or inhabitant of ancient Thessalonica. **2.** *pl.* (*construed as sing.*) Either of two books in the New Testament consisting of epistles written by St. Paul to the Christians of Thessalonica. **— adj.** Of or pertaining to Thessalonica.

the·ta (thā′tə, thē′tə) *n.* **1.** The eighth letter in the Greek alphabet (Θ, ϑ, θ). See ALPHABET. **2.** *Math.* A symbol for an angle of unknown value. [< Gk. *thēta*]

thew (thyōō) *n.* **1.** A sinew or muscle, esp., when strong or well-developed. **2.** *pl.* Bodily strength. [ME < OE *thēaw* habit, characteristic quality] **— thew′y** *adj.*

they (thā) *pron. pl., possessive* **their** or **theirs**, *objective* **them** **1.** The nominative plural of *he, she,* and *it,* used of the persons, beings, or things previously mentioned or understood. **2.** People in general: *They* say this is his best book. [ME *thei, thai* < ON *their,* pl. of *sā* this, that]

they'd (thād) **1.** They had. **2.** They would.

they'll (thāl) They will.

they're (thâr) They are.

they've (thāv) They have.

thi- Var. of THIO-.

thi·a·mine (thī′ə·mēn, -min) *n. Biochem.* A white crystalline compound, $C_{12}H_{18}ON_4SCl_2$, vitamin B_1, found in various natural sources and also made synthetically. Also **thi′a·min** (-min). [< THI- + -AMINE]

Thi·bet·an (ti·bet′ən) See TIBETAN.

thick (thik) *adj.* **1.** Having relatively large depth or extent from one surface to its opposite; not thin. **2.** Having a specified dimension of this kind, whether great or small: an inch *thick.* **3.** Arranged compactly; close: a *thick* forest; also, following at brief intervals; frequent, as blows, raindrops, etc. **4.** Set or furnished closely or abundantly with objects; abounding. **5.** Having considerable density or consistency; dense; heavy. **6.** Having the component particles closely packed together, as smoke, fog, etc. **7.** Dull; stupid. **8.** Indistinct; muffled: a *thick* sound; also, guttural; husky. **9.** *Informal* Very friendly; intimate. **10.** *Brit. Informal* Excessive; beyond what is tolerable. **— adv.** So as to be thick; thickly: bread sliced *thick.* **— to lay it on thick** *Informal* **1.** To overstate; exaggerate. **2.** To flatter excessively. **— n.** **1.** The dimension of thickness; the thickest part. **2.** The thickest or most intense time or place of anything: the *thick* of the fight. **— through thick and thin** Through good times and bad; loyally. [OE *thicce*] **— thick′ish** *adj.* **— thick′ly** *adv.* **— thick′ness** *n.*

thick·en (thik′ən) *v.t. & v.i.* **1.** To make or become thick or thicker. **2.** To make or become more intricate or intense: The plot *thickens.* **— thick′en·er** *n.*

thick·en·ing (thik′ən·ing) *n.* **1.** The act of making or becoming thick. **2.** Something added to a liquid to increase its consistency. **3.** A thickened place or part.

thick·et (thik′it) *n.* A thick, dense growth, as of underbrush; a coppice. [OE < *thicce* thick]

thick·head (thik′hed′) *n.* A stupid person; numskull. **— thick′head′ed** *adj.* **— thick′head′ed·ness** *n.*

thick·set (thik′set′) *adj.* **1.** Having a short, thick body; stout. **2.** Planted closely together. **— n.** A thicket.

thick-skinned (thik′skind′) *adj.* **1.** Having a thick skin; pachydermatous. **2.** Insensitive; callous to hints or insults.

thick·wit·ted (thik′wit′id) *adj.* Stupid; obtuse; dense.

thief (thēf) *n.* *pl.* **thieves** (thēvz) One who takes something belonging to another; one who steals. [OE *thēof*]

thieve (thēv) *v.* **thieved, thiev·ing** *v.t.* 1. To take by theft; steal. — *v.i.* 2. To be a thief; commit theft. [OE *thēofian*] — **thiev′ish** *adj.* — **thiev′ish·ly** *adv.* — **thiev′ish·ness** *n.*

thiev·er·y (thē′vər·ē) *n.* *pl.* **·er·ies** The practice or act of thieving; theft.

thigh (thī) *n.* The leg between the hip and the knee of man or the corresponding portion in other animals. ◆ Collateral adjective: *femoral.* [OE *thēoh*]

thigh·bone (thī′bōn′) *n.* The femur.

thill (thil) *n.* Either of the shafts of a vehicle, between which a horse is harnessed. [OE *thille* board]

thim·ble (thim′bəl) *n.* 1. A caplike cover with a pitted surface, worn in sewing to protect the end of the finger that pushes the needle. 2. *Mech.* A sleeve through which a bolt passes. 3. *Naut.* **a** A metal antichafing ring forming a guard over a loop or eye in a sail. **b** The metal piece about which a rope is bent and spliced. [OE < *thūma* thumb]

thim·ble·ful (thim′bəl·fŏŏl) *n.* 1. As much as a thimble will hold. 2. Any very small quantity.

thim·ble·rig (thim′bəl·rig′) *n.* A swindling trick in which a pea is shifted from one to another of three inverted cups. — *v.t.* **rigged, ·rig·ging** To cheat by or as by thimblerig. — **thim′ble·rig′ger** *n.*

thin (thin) *adj.* **thin·ner, thin·nest** 1. Having opposite surfaces relatively close to each other; being of little depth or width; not thick. 2. Lacking roundness or plumpness of figure; slender. 3. Having the parts or particles scattered or diffused; sparse: *thin* ranks, *thin* gas. 4. Small in number: The audience was *thin.* 5. Having little substance: *thin* clothing. 6. Having little or no consistency, as a liquid. 7. Lacking in essential ingredients: *thin* blood. 8. Having little volume or richness, as a voice. 9. Not abundantly supplied; scant: a *thin* table. 10. Having little intensity; pale: *thin* colors. 11. *Photog.* Not having sufficient contrast to print well: said of a negative. 12. Feeble; superficial: *thin* wit. — *adv.* So as to be thin; thinly: butter spread *thin.* — *v.t.* & *v.i.* **thinned, thin·ning** To make or become thin or thinner. [OE *thynne*] — **thin′ly** *adv.* — **thin′ner** *n.* — **thin′ness** *n.*

thine (thīn) *pron.* *Archaic* 1. The possessive case of the pronoun *thou:* used predicatively. 2. The one or ones belonging or relating to thee: thou and *thine.* — *pronominal adj.* Thy: used before a vowel or *h:* thine eyes. [OE *thīn*, genitive of *thū* thou]

thing (thing) *n.* 1. That which exists as a separate entity; an inanimate object. 2. That which is designated, as contrasted with the word or symbol used to denote it. 3. A matter or circumstance; an affair; concern: *Things* have changed. 4. An act or deed; transaction. 5. A statement; utterance: to say the right *thing.* 6. An idea; opinion: Stop putting *things* in her head. 7. A quality; attribute; characteristic. 8. An organic being: usu. with a qualifying word: Every living *thing* dies. 9. An object that is not or cannot be described or particularized: The *thing* disappeared in the shadows. 10. A person, regarded in terms of pity, affection, or contempt: that poor *thing.* 11. *pl.* Possessions. 12. The proper or befitting act or result: with *the:* That was not the *thing* to do. 13. The important point: with *the:* The *thing* we learned from the war was this. — **to see things** To have hallucinations. [OE, thing, cause, assembly]

thing·a·ma·bob (thing′ə·mə·bob′) *n.* *Informal* A thing the specific name of which is unknown or forgotten; a dingus. Also **thing′um·a·bob′, thing′um·bob, thing′a·ma·jig.**

think¹ (thingk) *v.* **thought** (thôt), **think·ing** *v.t.* 1. To produce or form in the mind; conceive mentally. 2. To examine in the mind; determine by reasoning: to *think* a plan through. 3. To believe; consider: I *think* him guilty. 4. To expect; anticipate: They did not *think* to meet us. 5. To remember; recollect: I cannot *think* what he said. 6. To bring about by thinking: to *think* oneself sick. 7. To intend: Do they *think* to rob me? — *v.i.* 8. To use the mind in exercising judgment, forming ideas, etc.; reason. 9. To have a particular opinion or feeling: I don't *think* so. — **to think better of** 1. To abandon or change a course of action. 2. To form a better opinion of. — **to think fit (proper, right, etc.)** To regard as worth doing. — **to think nothing of** 1. To consider of no importance; ignore. 2. To consider easy to do. — **to think of** 1. To bring to mind; remember. 2. To invent; imagine. 3. To have a specified opinion or attitude toward; regard. 4. To be considerate of; have regard for. — **to think out** To devise, invent, or solve by thinking. — **to think over** To reflect upon. — **to think the world of** 1. To have a high opinion of. 2. To love very much. — **to think twice** To consider carefully. — **to think up** To devise, arrive at, or invent by thinking. — *n.* An act of thinking; a thought. [OE *thencean*] — **think′a·ble** *adj.* — **think′er** *n.*

think² (thingk) *v.i.* **thought** (thôt), **think·ing** To seem; appear: now obsolete except in the combinations *methinks, methought.* [OE *thyncan* to seem]

think·ing (thingk′ing) *adj.* 1. Exercising the mental capacities. 2. Capable of such exercise; rational. — *n.* 1. Mental action; thought. 2. The product of such action, as an idea. — **think′ing·ly** *adv.*

thin-skinned (thin′skind′) *adj.* 1. Having a thin skin. 2. Easily hurt or offended; sensitive.

thio- *combining form Chem.* Containing sulfur; denoting a compound of sulfur, esp., one in which sulfur has displaced oxygen. [< Gk. *theion* sulfur]

thi·o·pen·tal sodium (thī′ō·pen′tal) A yellowish white powder, $C_{11}H_{17}N_2O_2SNa$, of the barbiturate group, used intravenously as a general anesthetic: also called *sodium pentothal.* Also *Chiefly Brit.* **thi·o·pen/tone sodium.**

thi·o·sul·fate (thī′ō·sul′fāt) *n.* *Chem.* A salt of thiosulfuric acid.

thi·o·sul·fu·ric acid (thī′ō·sul·fyŏŏr′ik) *Chem.* An unstable acid, $H_2S_2O_3$, known chiefly by its salts, which have extensive applications in bleaching and photography.

third (thûrd) *adj.* 1. Next after the second: the ordinal of *three.* 2. Being one of three equal parts. 3. Pertaining to the forward gears with the third highest ratio in an automobile transmission. — *n.* 1. That which follows the second. 2. One of three equal parts. 3. A unit of time or of an arc, equal to one sixtieth of a second. 4. *Music* **a** The interval between a tone and another tone two steps from it in a diatonic scale. **b** A tone separated by this interval from any other, considered in relation to that other; esp., the third above the keynote. 5. In baseball, the third base. 6. *Mech.* The forward gears with the third highest ratio in an automobile transmission. — *adv.* In the third order, rank, or place: also, in formal discourse, **third/ly.** [OE *thridda* < *thrī* three]

third base In baseball, the third base reached by the runner, at the left-hand angle of the infield.

third base·man (bās′mən) *n.* *pl.* **·men** (-mən) A baseball player stationed at or near third base.

third class 1. In the U.S. postal system, a classification of mail that includes all miscellaneous printed matter but not newspapers and periodicals legally entered as second class. 2. A classification of accommodations on some ships and trains, usu. the cheapest and least luxurious available. — **third-class** (thûrd′klas, -kläs) *adj.* & *adv.*

third degree *Informal* Severe or brutal examination of a prisoner by the police for the purpose of securing information.

third estate The third political class of a kingdom, following the nobility and the clergy.

third rail A rail that supplies current to the trains of an electric railway. — **third-rail** (thûrd′rāl′) *adj.*

third-rate (thûrd′rāt′) *adj.* 1. Of the third rate or class. 2. Of poor quality; very inferior.

third world Any or all of the underdeveloped countries in the world. Also **Third World.**

thirst (thûrst) *n.* 1. An uncomfortable feeling of dryness in the throat and mouth, accompanied by an increasingly urgent desire for liquids. 2. The physiological condition that produces this feeling. 3. Any longing or craving. — *v.i.* 1. To be thirsty. 2. To have an eager desire or craving. [OE *thurst, thyrstan*] — **thirst′er** *n.*

thirst·y (thûrs′tē) *adj.* **thirst·i·er, thirst·i·est** 1. Affected with thirst. 2. Lacking moisture; arid; parched. 3. Eagerly desirous. 4. *Informal* Causing thirst. [OE *thurstig*] — **thirst′i·ly** *adv.* — **thirst′i·ness** *n.*

thir·teen (thûr′tēn′) *n.* 1. The sum of twelve and one: a cardinal number. 2. Any symbol of this number, as 13, xiii, XIII. 3. Anything consisting of or representing thirteen units. — *adj.* Being one more than twelve. [OE *thrēotīne*] — **thir′teenth′** *adj.* & *n.*

thir·ty (thûr′tē) *n.* *pl.* **·ties** 1. The sum of twenty and ten: a cardinal number. 2. Any symbol of this number, as 30, xxx, XXX. 3. Anything consisting of or representing thirty units. — *adj.* Being ten more than twenty. [OE *thrītig*] — **thir′ti·eth** *adj.* & *n.*

thir·ty-sec·ond (thûr′tē·sek′ənd) *adj.* 1. Being the second after the thirtieth. 2. Being one of thirty-two equal parts. — *n.* A thirty-second note.

thirty-second note *Music* A note having a time value, equal to one thirty-second of a whole note: also, *Chiefly Brit.*, *demisemiquaver.*

thir·ty-two·mo (thûr′tē·tōō′mō) *n.* *pl.* **·mos** 1. The page size (3⅛ x 4¾ inches) of a book made up of printer's sheets folded into thirty-two leaves. 2. A book consisting of pages of this size. Also written **32mo** — *adj.* Consisting of pages of this size.

Thirty Years' War See table for WAR.

this (this) *pl. for adj. and pron. def. 2* **these** (thēz) *adj.* **1.** That is near or present, either actually or in thought: *This* house is for sale; I shall be there *this* evening. **2.** That is understood or has just been mentioned: *This* offense justified my revenge. **3.** Denoting something nearer than or contrasted with something else: distinguished from *that*: *This* tree is still alive, but that one is dead. **4.** These: used of a number or collection considered as a whole: He has been dead *this* ten years. — *pron.* **1.** The person or thing near or present, being understood or just mentioned: *This* is where I live. **2.** The person or thing nearer than or contrasted with something else: opposed to *that*: *This* is a better painting than that. **3.** The idea, statement, etc., about to be made clear: I will say *this*: he is a hard worker. — *adv.* To this degree: I was not expecting you *this* soon. [OE]

this·tle (this'əl) *n.* One of various prickly plants of the composite family, with cylindrical or globular heads of purple flowers; esp., the **bull thistle**, the national emblem of Scotland. **2.** Any of several other prickly plants. [OE *thistel*] — **this'tly** *adj.*

this·tle·down (this'əl·doun') *n.* The ripe silky fibers from the dry flower of a thistle.

thith·er (thith'ər, thith'-) *adv.* To or toward that place; in that direction. — *adj.* Situated or being on the other side; farther: the *thither* bank of the river. [OE *thider*]

thith·er·to (thith'ər·tōo', thith'-) *adv.* Up to that time.

thith·er·ward (thith'ər·wərd, thith'-) *adv.* In that direction; toward that place. Also **thith'er·wards.**

tho (thō) See THOUGH.

thole (thōl) *n. Naut.* A peg or pair of pegs serving as a fulcrum for an oar in rowing. Also **thole pin.** [OE *thol* pin]

Thom·as (tom'əs) One of the twelve apostles, known for his doubting disposition: called **Saint Thomas.** Also *Didymus. John* xx 25.

Tho·mism (tō'miz·əm, thō'-) *n.* The system of dogmatic theology of St. Thomas Aquinas and his followers that formed the basis of 13th-century scholasticism. — **Tho'·mist** *adj. & n.* — **Tho·mis'tic** or **·ti·cal** *adj.*

Thomp·son submachine gun (tomp'sən) A type of .45 caliber submachine gun: a trade name: also called *Tommy gun.*

thong (thông, thong) *n.* **1.** A narrow strip of leather, as for tying or fastening. **2.** A whiplash. [OE *thwang*]

Thor (thôr, tôr) In Norse mythology, the god of war, thunder, and strength. — *n.* An intermediate range, liquid-fueled ballistic missile of the U.S. Air Force.

tho·rac·ic (thô·ras'ik, thō-) *adj.* Of, relating to, or situated in or near the thorax. [< F < NL < Gk. *thōrax* chest]

thoraco- *combining form Med. & Surg.* The thorax or the chest; of or related to the thorax. Also, before vowels, **thorac-.** [< Gk. *thōrax* chest]

tho·rax (thôr'aks, thō'-) *n. pl.* **tho·rax·es** or **tho·ra·ces** (thôr'ə·sēz, thō'rə-) **1.** *Anat.* The part of the body between the neck and the abdomen, enclosed by the ribs and containing the lungs, heart, etc.; the chest. **2.** The corresponding part in other animals. **3.** *Entomol.* The middle region of the body of an insect. [< L < Gk. *thōrax*]

tho·ri·um (thôr'ē·əm, thō'rē-) *n.* A gray, radioactive, metallic element (symbol Th), found only in small quantities in certain rare minerals. See ELEMENT. [after *Thor*]

thorn (thôrn) *n.* **1.** A hard, leafless spine or sharp-pointed process from a branch. **2.** One of various other sharp processes, as the spine of a porcupine. **3.** Any of various thorn-bearing shrubs or trees; esp., a rosaceous plant, as the hawthorn. **4.** Anything or anyone that causes discomfort, pain, or annoyance. **5.** The name of the Old English rune þ; also, the corresponding Icelandic character. It was used originally to represent both voiceless and voiced *th*, as in *thin, then,* but finally only the voiceless sound. [OE] — **thorn'less** *adj.* — *v.t.* To pierce or prick with a thorn.

thorn apple 1. The jimsonweed. **2.** The fruit of the hawthorn; a haw.

thorn·y (thôr'nē) *adj.* **thorn·i·er, thorn·i·est 1.** Full of thorns; spiny. **2.** Sharp like a thorn. **3.** Presenting difficulties or trials; painful; vexatious. — **thorn'i·ness** *n.*

tho·ron (thôr'on, thō'ron) *n.* A gaseous, radioactive isotope of radon, produced during the disintegration of thorium. [< NL < THOR(IUM) + -ON]

thor·ough (thûr'ō) *adj.* **1.** Carried to completion; thoroughgoing: a *thorough* search; also, persevering, accurate, and painstaking: a very *thorough* worker. **2.** Marked by careful attention throughout; complete. **3.** Completely (such and such); through and through: a *thorough* nincompoop. **4.** Painstakingly conforming to a standard. **5.** *Rare* Going or passing through. — *adv. & prep. Obs.* Through. Also *Rare* **thor'o.** [Emphatic var. of THROUGH] — **thor'ough·ly** *adv.* — **thor'ough·ness** *n.*

thor·ough·bred (thûr'ō·bred', thûr'ə-) *n.* **1.** Pure and unmixed stock. **2.** *Informal* A person of culture and good breeding. — *adj.* **1.** Bred from pure stock. **2.** Possessing the traits of a thoroughbred; elegant; graceful.

thor·ough·fare (thûr'ō·fâr', thûr'ə-) *n.* A road or street

through which the public has unobstructed passage; highway. [ME < OE *thurh* through + *faru* going]

thor·ough·go·ing (thûr'ō·gō'ing, thûr'ə-) *adj.* **1.** Characterized by extreme thoroughness or efficiency. **2.** Unmitigated: a *thoroughgoing* scoundrel.

those (thōz) *adj. & pron.* Plural of THAT. [OE *thās,* pl. of *this*]

thou (thou) *pron., possessive* **thy** or **thine,** *objective* **thee;** *pl. nominative* **you, ye,** *possessive* **your** or **yours,** *objective* **you, ye** *Archaic* The nominative singular pronoun of the second person: formerly a familiar form, it has been replaced by the more formal singular *you,* and is no longer used except in religious, elevated, or poetic language. [OE *thū*]

though (thō) *conj.* **1.** Notwithstanding the fact that: introducing a clause expressing an actual fact. **2.** Conceding or granting that; even if. **3.** And yet; still; however: introducing a modifying clause or statement: I am well, *though* I do not feel very strong. **4.** Notwithstanding what has been done or said; nevertheless. ♦ As used in this sense, *though* is sometimes regarded as a conjunctive adverb. Also spelled *tho.* [Prob. fusion of OE *thēah* and ON *tho*]

thought¹ (thôt) *n.* **1.** The act or process of using the mind actively and deliberately; meditation; cogitation. **2.** The product of thinking; an idea, concept, judgment, etc. **3.** Intellectual activity of a specific kind: Greek *thought.* **4.** Consideration; attention. **5.** Intention or plan: All *thought* of returning was abandoned. **6.** Expectation: He had no *thought* of finding her there. — **Syn.** See IDEA. [OE *thōht*]

thought² (thôt) Past tense and past participle of THINK.

thought·ful (thôt'fəl) *adj.* **1.** Full of thought; meditative. **2.** Showing, characterized by, or promotive of thought: a *thoughtful* book. **3.** Attentive; careful; esp., considerate of others. — **thought'ful·ly** *adv.* — **thought'ful·ness** *n.*

thought·less (thôt'lis) *adj.* **1.** Manifesting lack of thought or care; heedless. **2.** Lacking capacity for thought; stupid. — **thought'less·ly** *adv.* — **thought'less·ness** *n.*

thou·sand (thou'zənd) *n.* The product of ten and a hundred; ten hundreds, written as 1,000 or M: a cardinal number. — *adj.* Being a thousand in number. [OE *thūsend*] — **thou·sandth** *adj. & n.*

thou·sand·fold (thou'zənd·fōld') *n.* An amount or number a thousand times as great as a given unit. — *adv.* So as to be a thousand times as many or as great. — *adj.* **1.** Consisting of one thousand parts. **2.** One thousand times as many or as great.

Thra·cian (thrā'shən) *adj.* Pertaining to Thrace or its people. — *n.* **1.** One of the people of Thrace. **2.** The Indo-European language of the ancient Thracians.

thrall (thrôl) *n.* **1.** A person in bondage; a slave; serf. **2.** The condition of bondage; thralldom. [OE *thrǣl* < ON]

thrall·dom (thrôl'dəm) *n.* **1.** The state of being a thrall. **2.** Any sort of bondage or servitude. Also **thral'dom.**

thrash (thrash) *v.t.* **1.** To beat as if with a flail; flog; whip. **2.** To defeat utterly. — *v.i.* **3.** To move or swing about with flailing, violent motions. — **to thrash out** To discuss fully and to a conclusion. — *n.* The act of thrashing. [Dial. var. of THRESH]

thrash·er¹ (thrash'ər) *n.* **1.** One who or that which thrashes or threshes. **2.** A thresher (def. 2), a shark.

thrash·er² (thrash'ər) *n.* Any of several long-tailed American songbirds resembling the thrushes and related to the mockingbirds. [< dial. E *thresher* < THRUSH¹]

thrash·ing (thrash'ing) *n.* A sound beating or whipping.

thread (thred) *n.* **1.** A very slender cord composed of two or more filaments, as of flax, cotton, or silk, twisted together; also, such twisted fibers used in sewing. **2.** A filament of any ductile substance, as of metal, glass, etc. **3.** A fine stream or beam: a *thread* of light. **4.** A fine line of color. **5.** Anything conceived of as serving to give sequence to the whole, as the course of existence represented by the ancient Greeks as a thread spun and cut off by the three Fates. **6.** *Mech.* The spiral ridge of a screw. — *v.t.* **1.** To pass a thread through the eye of (a needle). **2.** To arrange or string on a thread, as beads. **3.** To cut a thread on or in, as a screw. **4.** To make one's way through or over: to *thread* a maze. **5.** To make (one's way) carefully. — *v.i.* **6.** To make one's way carefully. **7.** To drop from a spoon in a fine thread, as boiling syrup. [OE *thrǣd*] — **thread'er** *n.*

thread·bare (thred'bâr') *adj.* **1.** Worn so that the threads show, as a rug or garment. **2.** Clad in worn garments. **3.** Commonplace; hackneyed. — **thread'bare'ness** *n.*

thread·y (thred'ē) *adj.* **thread·i·er, thread·i·est 1.** Resembling a thread; stringy. **2.** Consisting of, containing, or covered with thread. **3.** *Med.* Weak and feeble: said of the pulse. **4.** Weak and thin like a thread: a *thready* voice.

threat (thret) *n.* **1.** A declaration of an intention to inflict injury or pain. **2.** An indication of impending danger or harm. **3.** A person or thing regarded as endangering the lives, peace of mind, etc., of others; menace. [OE *thrēat*]

threat·en (thret'n) *v.t.* **1.** To utter threats against. **2.** To be menacing or dangerous to. **3.** To be ominous or portentous of.   **4.** To utter threats of (injury, vengeance, etc.). — *v.i.* **5.** To utter threats. **6.** To have a menacing aspect; lower: The rising waters seemed to *threaten*. [OE *thrēatnian* to urge, compel] — **threat·en·er** *n.* — **threat′en·ing·ly** *adv.*

three (thrē) *n.* **1.** The sum of two and one: a cardinal number. **2.** Any symbol of this number, as 3, iii, III. **3.** Anything consisting of or representing three units. — *adj.* Being one more than two; ternary. [OE *thrīe*]

three-base hit (thrē′bās′) In baseball, a base hit that enables the batter to reach third base; a triple.

three-D (thrē′dē′) *adj.* Three-dimensional. — *n.* A three-dimensional representation; esp., a motion picture that gives the illusion of depth. Often written **3-D.**

three-deck·er (thrē′dek′ər) *n.* **1.** A vessel having three decks or gun decks. **2.** Any structure having three levels. **3.** A sandwich made with three slices of bread.

three·fold (thrē′fōld′) *n.* An amount or number three times as great as a given unit. — *adv.* So as to be three times as many or as great. — *adj.* **1.** Consisting of three parts. **2.** Three times as many or as great.

three-mile limit (thrē′mīl′) A distance of three nautical miles from the shoreline seaward, allowed by international law for territorial jurisdiction.

three·pence (thrip′əns, threp′-, thrup′-) *n. Brit.* **1.** The sum of three pennies. **2.** A small coin of Great Britain, worth three pennies: also **threepenny bit.**

three·pen·ny (thrip′ə-ni, threp′-, thrup′-, thrē′pen′ē) *adj. Brit.* **1.** Worth or costing threepence. **2.** Of little value.

three-ply (thrē′plī′) *adj.* Consisting of three thicknesses, strands, layers, etc.

three-point landing (thrē′point′) **1.** *Aeron.* A perfect airplane landing. **2.** Any successful outcome.

three-ring circus (thrē′ring′) **1.** A circus in which separate acts are carried on simultaneously in three ringlike enclosures. **2.** Any situation characterized by simultaneous activities, esp. of bewildering variety.

three·score (thrē′skôr′, -skōr′) *adj. & n.* Sixty.

three·some (thrē′səm) *adj.* **1.** Consisting of three. **2.** Performed by three. — *n.* **1.** A group of three persons. **2.** That which is played by three persons.

three-square (thrē′skwâr′) *adj.* Having a triangular cross section, as some files.

threm·ma·tol·o·gy (threm′ə-tol′ə-jē) *n.* The science of breeding domestic animals and plants. [< Gk. *thremma, -matos* nursling + -LOGY]

thren·o·dy (thren′ə-dē) *n. pl.* **·dies** An ode or song of lamentation; a dirge. Also **thren′ode** (-ōd). [< Gk. < *thrēnos* lament + *ōidē* song] — **thre·no·di·al** (thri-nō′dē-əl), **thre·nod·ic** (thri-nod′ik) *adj.* — **thren′o·dist** *n.*

thresh (thresh) *v.t.* **1.** To beat stalks of (ripened grain) with a flail or machine so as to separate the grain from the straw or husks. — *v.i.* **2.** To thresh grain. **3.** To move or thrash about. — *n.* The act of threshing. [OE *therscan*]

thresh·er (thresh′ər) *n.* **1.** One who or that which threshes; esp., a machine for threshing. **2.** A large shark of warm seas, having the dorsal lobe of the tail extremely long: also **thresher shark.**

thresh·old (thresh′ōld, -hōld, -əld) *n.* **1.** The plank, timber, or stone lying under the door of a building. **2.** The entrance, entering point, or beginning of anything. **3.** *Physiol. & Psychol.* **a** The point at which a stimulus just produces a response. **b** The minimum degree of stimulation necessary for conscious perception: the *threshold* of consciousness. [OE *therscold*]

threw (thrōō) Past tense of THROW.

thrice (thrīs) *adv.* **1.** Three times. **2.** In a threefold manner. **3.** Extremely; very. [ME < OE *thriwa* + -s²]

thrift (thrift) *n.* **1.** Care and wisdom in the management of one's resources; frugality. **2.** Vigorous growth, as of a plant. **3.** Any of a genus of tufted herbs, growing on mountains and the seashore and having white or pink flowers. [< ON] — **thrift′less** *adj.*

thrift·y (thrif′tē) *adj.* **thrift·i·er, thrift·i·est** **1.** Displaying thrift or good management; economical; frugal. **2.** Prosperous; thriving. **3.** Growing vigorously. — **thrift′i·ly** *adv.* — **thrift′i·ness** *n.*

thrill (thril) *v.t.* **1.** To cause to feel a sudden wave of emotion; move to great or tingling excitement. **2.** To cause to vibrate or tremble. — *v.i.* **3.** To feel a sudden wave of emotion or excitement. **4.** To vibrate or tremble. — *n.* **1.** A tremor of feeling or excitement. **2.** A pulsation. [Var. of dial. *thirl*] — **thrill′ing** *adj.* — **thrill′ing·ly** *adv.*

thrill·er (thril′ər) *n.* **1.** One who or that which thrills. **2.** *Informal* A sensational book, play, or motion picture.

thrive (thrīv) *v.i.* **throve** (thrōv) or **thrived, thrived** or **thriv·en** (thriv′ən), **thriv·ing** **1.** To prosper; be successful. **2.** To grow with vigor; flourish. [< ON *thrīfast*, orig. reflexive of *thrīfa* to grasp] — **thriv′er** *n.* — **thriv′ing·ly** *adv.*

thro (thrōō) See THROUGH. Also **thro′.**

throat (thrōt) *n.* **1.** The passage leading from the back of the mouth to the stomach and lungs. **2.** The front of the neck, extending from below the chin to the collarbones. **3.** Any narrow passage resembling the throat, as the entrance to a chimney. — **to jump down one's throat** *Informal* To criticize or berate one severely. — **to ram (something) down one's throat** *Informal* To force one to accept or hear something against his will. — **to stick in one's throat** To be difficult to utter, as from unwillingness or fear. [OE *throte*]

throat·y (thrō′tē) *adj.* **throat·i·er, throat·i·est** Uttered in the throat; guttural. — **throat′i·ly** *adv.* — **throat′i·ness** *n.*

throb (throb) *v.i.* **throbbed, throb·bing** **1.** To beat rapidly or violently, as the heart from exertion or excitement. **2.** To pulsate. **3.** To feel or show great emotion. — *n.* **1.** The act or state of throbbing. **2.** A pulsation or beat, esp. one caused by excitement or emotion. [? Imit.] — **throb′ber** *n.* — **throb′bing·ly** *adv.*

throe (thrō) *n.* **1.** A violent pang or pain. **2.** *pl.* The pains of childbirth or of death. **3.** *pl.* Any agonizing or violent activity. [ME *throwe*, prob. fusion of OE *thrōwian* to suffer and *thrāwan* to twist, throw]

throm·bin (throm′bin) *n. Biochem.* The enzyme present in blood serum that reacts with fibrinogen to form fibrin in the process of clotting. [< THROMBUS]

throm·bo·cyte (throm′bə-sīt) *n.* A blood platelet. [< Gk. *thrombos* clot + -CYTE]

throm·bo·sis (throm-bō′sis) *n. pl.* **·ses** (sēz) *Pathol.* Local coagulation of blood in the heart or blood vessels, forming an obstruction to circulation. — **throm·bot·ic** (-bot′ik) *adj.*

throm·bus (throm′bəs) *n. pl.* **·bi** (-bī) *Pathol.* The blood clot formed in thrombosis. [< NL < Gk. *thrombos* clot]

throne (thrōn) *n.* **1.** The royal chair occupied by a sovereign on state occasions. **2.** The chair of state of a pope or of some other dignitary, as a cardinal, bishop, etc. **3.** Royal estate or dignity; sovereign power. **4.** One who occupies a throne. — *v.t. & v.i.* **throned, thron·ing** To place or sit on a throne; exalt. [< OF < L < Gk. *thronos* seat]

throng (thrông, throng) *n.* **1.** A multitude of people crowded closely together. **2.** Any numerous collection. — *v.t.* **1.** To crowd into; jam. **2.** To press or crowd upon. — *v.i.* **3.** To collect or move in a throng. [OE *gethrang*] — **Syn.** (noun) **1.** crowd, concourse, mob, host, horde, press.

thros·tle (thros′əl) *n.* The song thrush. [OE]

throt·tle (throt′l) *n. Mech.* **a** A valve controlling the supply of steam to a steam engine, or of vaporized fuel to the cylinders of an internal-combustion engine: also **throttle valve. b** The lever that operates the throttle: also **throttle lever.** — *v.t.* **·tled, ·tling** **1.** To press or constrict the throat of; strangle; choke. **2.** To silence, stop, or suppress by or as by choking. **3.** *Mech.* **a** To reduce or shut off the flow of steam or fuel (in a steam or internal-combustion engine). **b** To reduce the speed of by means of a throttle. — *v.i.* **4.** To choke. [Dim. of ME *throte*] — **throt′tler** *n.*

through (thrōō) *prep.* **1.** Into one side, end, or point, and out of the other. **2.** Covering, entering, or penetrating all parts of; throughout. **3.** From the first to the last of; during the time or period of. **4.** In the midst of; among. **5.** By way of: He departed *through* the door. **6.** By means of; by the instrumentality or aid of. **7.** Having reached the end of, esp. with success: He got *through* his examinations easily. **8.** On account of; because or as a result of. — *adv.* **1.** From one end, side, surface, etc., to or beyond another. **2.** From beginning to end. **3.** To a termination or conclusion, esp. a successful one: to pull *through*. **4.** Completely; entirely: He is wet *through*. — **through and through** Thoroughly. — *adj.* **1.** Going from beginning to end without stops or with very few stops: a *through* train. **2.** Extending from one side or surface to another. **3.** Unobstructed; open; clear: a *through* road. **4.** Arrived at an end; finished. **5.** At the end of all relations or dealings: He is *through* with school. Also spelled *thro, thru*. [OE *thurh*]

through·out (thrōō-out′) *adv.* Through or in every part: The house was searched *throughout*. — *prep.* All through; everywhere in: *throughout* the nation.

through·way (thrōō′wā′) See THRUWAY.

throve (thrōv) *v.* Past tense of THRIVE.

throw (thrō) *v.* **threw** (thrōō), **thrown, throw·ing** *v.t.* **1.** To launch through the air by means of a sudden straightening or whirling of the arm. **2.** To propel or hurl. **3.** To put hastily or carelessly: He *threw* a coat over his shoulders. **4.**

HUMAN THROAT

a Palate. *b* Tongue. *c* Nasal cavity. *d* Uvula. *e* Tonsils. *f* Pharynx. *g* Epiglottis. *h* Esophagus. *i* Larynx. *j* Vocal cords. *k* Trachea.

To direct or project (light, a glance, etc.). **5.** To bring to a specified condition or state by or as by throwing: to *throw* the enemy into a panic. **6.** To cause to fall; overthrow: The horse *threw* its rider. **7.** In wrestling, to force the shoulders of (an opponent) to the ground. **8.** To cast (dice). **9.** To make (a specified cast) with dice. **10.** To cast off or shed; lose. **11.** *Informal* To lose purposely, as a race, contest, etc., in accordance with a prearranged plan. **12.** To give birth to (young): said of domestic animals. **13.** To move, as a lever or switch, in connecting or disconnecting a circuit, mechanism, etc. **14.** *Slang* To give (a party, etc.). **15.** In card games, to play or discard. **16.** In ceramics, to shape on a potter's wheel. **17.** To spin (filaments, as of silk) into thread. — *v.i.* **18.** To cast or fling something. — **to throw away 1.** To discard. **2.** To waste; squander. — **to throw back 1.** To return by throwing. **2.** To revert to ancestral characteristics. — **to throw cold water on** To discourage. — **to throw in 1.** To cause (gears or a clutch) to mesh or engage. **2.** To contribute; add. **3.** To join with others. — **to throw in the towel** (or **sponge**) *Slang* To accept defeat; surrender. — **to throw off 1.** To cast aside; reject; spurn. **2.** To rid oneself of. **3.** To do or utter in an offhand manner. **4.** To disconnect, as a machine. — **to throw oneself at** To strive to engage or take part in vigorously. — **to throw oneself into** To engage or take part in vigorously. — **to throw oneself on** (or **upon**) To entrust oneself to; rely on. — **to throw open 1.** To open suddenly or completely, as a door. **2.** To free from restrictions or obstacles. — **to throw the book at** *Slang* **1.** To sentence to the maximum penalty. **2.** To reprimand or castigate severely. — **to throw out 1.** To put forth; emit. **2.** To cast out or aside; discard; reject. **3.** To utter as if accidentally: to *throw out* hints. **4.** In baseball, to retire (a runner) by throwing the ball to the base toward which he is advancing. — **to throw over 1.** To overturn. **2.** To discard. — **to throw (something) up to (someone)** *Informal* To mention or repeat as a reproach. — **to throw together** To put together hastily or roughly. — **to throw up 1.** To construct hastily. **2.** To give up; relinquish. **3.** To vomit. — *n.* **1.** An act of throwing or hurling; a fling. **2.** The distance over which a missile may be thrown: a stone's *throw*. **3.** A cast of dice, or the resulting number. **4.** *Mech.* The radius of the circle described by a crank, cam, or the like. **5.** A scarf used for draping an easel or picture frame; also, a woman's scarf. **6.** *Geol.* **a** A faulting, or dislocation of rock strata. **b** The amount of vertical displacement produced by dislocation of strata. [OE *thrāwan* to turn, twist, curl] — **throw'er** *n.*

throw·a·way (thrō'ə·wā') *n.* A free broadside or leaflet handed out for advertising or propaganda purposes.

throw·back (thrō'bak') *n.* **1.** Reversion to an ancestral type or condition; also, an example of such reversion. **2.** A throwing back.

thru (thrōō) See THROUGH.

thrum¹ (thrum) *v.* **thrummed, thrum·ming** *v.t.* **1.** To play on or finger (a stringed instrument) idly and without expression. **2.** To drum or tap monotonously or listlessly. **3.** To recite or repeat in a droning, monotonous way. — *v.i.* **4.** To thrum a stringed instrument. **5.** To sound when played thus, as a guitar. — *n.* Any monotonous drumming. [Imit.]

thrum² (thrum) *n.* **1.** The fringe of warp threads remaining on a loom beam after the web has been cut off; also, one of such threads. **2.** Any loose thread or fringe, or a tuft of filaments or fibers; a tassel. — *v.t.* **thrummed, thrum·ming 1.** To cover or trim with thrums or similar appendages. **2.** *Naut.* To insert bits of rope yarn in (canvas) to produce a rough surface or mat to be used to prevent chafing. [OE -*thrum* ligament, as in *tungethrum* the ligament of the tongue]

thrush¹ (thrush) *n.* Any of numerous migratory birds having a long and slightly graduated tail, long wings, and spotted underparts, as the hermit thrush, wood thrush, and the song thrush of Europe. ◆ Collateral adjective: *turdine.* [OE *thrysce*]

thrush² (thrush) *n. Pathol.* A vesicular disease of the mouth, lips, and throat of infants caused by a fungus. [Cf. Dan. *tröske,* Sw. *trosk* mouth disease]

thrust (thrust) *v.* **thrust, thrust·ing** *v.t.* **1.** To push or shove with force or sudden impulse. **2.** To pierce or stab, as with a sword or dagger. **3.** To put (a person) forcibly into some condition or situation. **4.** To interpose; put in: to *thrust* in a remark. — *v.i.* **5.** To make a sudden push against something. **6.** To force oneself on or ahead: push one's way: with *through, into, on,* etc. — *n.* **1.** A sudden, forcible push, esp. with a pointed weapon. **2.** A vigorous attack. **3.** *Archit.* A stress or strain tending to push a member of a structure outward or sidewise: the *thrust* of an arch. **4.** *Mech.* The driving force exerted by a steam engine, motor, propeller, jet engine, etc. **5.** Salient force or meaning: the *thrust* of his remarks. [< ON *thrysta*] — **thrust'er** *n.*

thru·way (thrōō'wā') *n. U.S.* A long-distance express highway: also spelled *throughway.*

thud (thud) *n.* **1.** A dull, heavy sound, as of a hard body

striking upon a comparatively soft surface. **2.** The blow causing such a sound; a thump. — *v.i.* **thud·ded, thud·ding** To make a thud. [OE *thyddan* to strike, thrust, press]

thug (thug) *n.* **1.** A cutthroat or ruffian. **2.** Formerly, one of an organization of religious, professional assassins in northern India. [< Hind. *thag* < Skt. *sthaga* swindler] — **thug'ger·y** *n.* — **thug'gish** *adj.*

Thu·le (thōō'lē) In ancient geography, the northernmost limit of the habitable world.

thu·li·um (thōō'lē·əm) *n.* A metallic element (symbol Tm) of the erbium group in the lanthanide series. See ELEMENT. [after *Thule*]

thumb (thum) *n.* **1.** The short, thick digit next to the forefinger of the human hand. **2.** The corresponding digit in certain other animals, esp. primates. **3.** The division in a glove or mitten that covers the thumb. — **all thumbs** *Informal* Clumsy with the hands. — **thumbs down** *Informal* No; nix: from a sign used to indicate negation or disapproval. — **under one's thumb** Under one's influence or power. — *v.t.* **1.** To press, rub, soil, or wear with the thumb in handling, as the pages of a book. **2.** To perform clumsily with or as with the thumbs. **3.** To run through the pages of (a book, manuscript, etc.) rapidly and perfunctorily. **4.** *Informal* To solicit (a ride in an automobile) by signaling with the thumb. — *v.i.* **5.** To hitchhike. — **to thumb one's nose** To show defiance or disgust by raising the thumb to the nose with the fingers extended. [OE *thūma*]

thumb·in·dex (thum'in'deks) *v.t.* To provide with a thumb index.

thumb index A series of scalloped indentations cut along the right-hand edge of a book and labeled to indicate its various sections.

thumb·nail (thum'nāl') *n.* **1.** The nail of the thumb. **2.** Anything as small and essentially complete as a thumbnail. — *adj.* Small and essentially complete: a *thumbnail* sketch.

thumb·screw (thum'skrōō') *n.* **1.** A screw to be turned by thumb and fingers. **2.** An instrument of torture for compressing the thumb or thumbs: also **thumb'kin** (-kin).

thumb·tack (thum'tak') *n. U.S.* A broad-headed tack that may be pushed in with the thumb.

thump (thump) *n.* **1.** A blow with a blunt or heavy object. **2.** The sound made by such a blow; a dull thud. — *v.t.* **1.** To beat or strike so as to make a heavy thud or thump. **2.** *Informal* To beat or defeat severely. — *v.i.* **3.** To strike with a thump. **4.** To make a thump or thumps; pound or throb. [Imit.] — **thump'er** *n.*

thump·ing (thum'ping) *adj.* **1.** That thumps. **2.** *Informal* Huge; whopping.

thun·der (thun'dər) *n.* **1.** The sound that accompanies lightning, caused by the sudden heating and expansion of the air along the path of the electrical discharge. **2.** Any loud, rumbling or booming noise, suggestive of thunder. **3.** A denunciation or threat; a vehement utterance. — **to steal one's thunder** To take for one's own use anything popular or effective originated by another: said esp. of an argument. — *v.i.* **1.** To give forth a peal or peals of thunder: used impersonally: It *thunders.* **2.** To make a noise like thunder. **3.** To utter vehement denunciations or threats. — *v.t.* **4.** To utter or express with a noise like or suggestive of thunder. [OE *thunor*] — **thun'der·er** *n.*

thun·der·bolt (thun'dər·bōlt') *n.* **1.** An electric discharge accompanied by a clap of thunder. **2.** An imaginary molten ball or bolt hurled by the lightning flash. **3.** One who or that which acts with or as with the force and speed or destructiveness of lightning.

thun·der·clap (thun'dər·klap') *n.* **1.** A sharp, violent detonation of thunder. **2.** Anything having the violence or suddenness of a clap of thunder.

thun·der·cloud (thun'dər·kloud') *n.* A dark, heavy mass of cloud highly charged with electricity.

thun·der·head (thun'dər·hed') *n. Meteorol.* A rounded mass of cumulus cloud, either silvery white or dark with silvery edges, often developing into a thundercloud.

thun·der·ing (thun'dər·ing) *adj.* **1.** Giving forth, or accompanied by, thunder. **2.** Resembling thunder in force or effect; extremely violent. **3.** *Informal* Unusually great or extreme; superlative. — **thun'der·ing·ly** *adv.*

thun·der·ous (thun'dər·əs) *adj.* Producing a noise like thunder. Also **thun'drous** (-drəs). — **thun'der·ous·ly** *adv.*

thun·der·peal (thun'dər·pēl') *n.* A clap of thunder.

thun·der·show·er (thun'dər·shou'ər) *n.* A shower of rain with thunder and lightning.

thun·der·storm (thun'dər·stôrm') *n.* A local storm accompanied by lightning and thunder.

thun·der·struck (thun'dər·struk') *adj.* **1.** Struck by lightning. **2.** Amazed, astonished, or confounded, as with fear, surprise, etc. Also **thun'der·strick'en** (-strik'ən).

thun·der·y (thun'dər·ē) *adj. Informal* **1.** Indicative of or accompanied by thunder. **2.** Ominous.

thu·ri·ble (thōōr'ə·bəl, thûr'-) *n.* A censer. [< L < *thus, thuris* frankincense]

Thu·rin·gi·an (thŏŏ·rin′jē·ən) *adj. Geol.* Denoting the upper division of the Permian in Europe. — *n.* One of a Teutonic tribe occupying central Germany until the sixth century.

Thurs·day (thûrz′dē, -dā) *n.* The fifth day of the week. [Fusion of OE *Thunres dæg* day of Thunor and ON *Thōrsdagr* day of Thor; trans. of LL *dies Jovis* day of Jove]

thus (thus) *adv.* 1. In this, that, or the following way of manner. 2. To such degree or extent; so: *thus* far. 3. In these circumstances or conditions; therefore. [OE]

thwack (thwak) *v.t.* To strike with something flat; whack. — *n.* A blow with a flat or blunt instrument. [Prob. OE *thaccian* to smack; infl. in form by *whack*] — **thwack′er** *n.*

thwart (thwôrt) *v.t.* To prevent the accomplishment of, as by interposing an obstacle; also, to prevent (one) from accomplishing something; foil; frustrate; balk. — *n.* 1. An oarsman's seat extending across a boat. 2. A crosspiece or transverse member in a boat. — *adj.* Lying, moving, or extending across something; transverse. — *adv. & prep.* Athwart; across. [< ON *thvert*, neut. of *thverr* transverse] — **thwart′er** *n.*

thy (thī) *pronominal adj. Archaic* The possessive case of the pronoun *thou*, used attributively: *Thy* kingdom come. [Apocopated var. of THINE]

thyme (tīm) *n.* Any of various small shrubby plants of the mint family, having aromatic leaves and used in cookery. [< F < L < Gk. *thymon*] — **thym′y** *adj.*

thym·ic[1] (tī′mik) *adj.* Pertaining to or derived from thyme.

thy·mic[2] (thī′mik) *adj.* Of, pertaining to, or derived from the thymus.

thy·mus (thī′məs) *n. Anat.* A glandular organ of man and some other vertebrates, found behind the top of the breast-bone. [< NL < Gk. *thymos*]

thyro- *combining form Med. & Surg.* The thyroid; of or related to the thyroid. Also, before vowels, **thyr-**. Also **thyreo-**. [< Gk. *thyreoeidēs* thyroid]

thy·roid (thī′roid) *adj. Physiol.* Relating or pertaining to the thyroid cartilage or the thyroid gland. — *n.* 1. The thyroid cartilage or gland. 2. The dried and powdered thyroid gland of certain domesticated food animals, used in the treatment of hypothyroid disorders. [< Gk. < *thyreos* large shield + *eidos* form]

thyroid cartilage *Anat.* The largest cartilage of the larynx, composed of two blades whose juncture in front forms the Adam's apple.

thyroid gland *Anat.* An endocrine gland situated in front of and on each side of the trachea, and secreting thyroxin, important in the regulation of metabolism and body growth.

thy·rox·in (thī·rok′sin) *n. Biochem.* An odorless, crystalline amino acid, $C_{15}H_{11}O_4NI_4$, obtained as the hormone of the thyroid gland and also made synthetically, used to treat thyroid disorders. Also **thy·rox′ine** (-sēn, -sin). [< THYR(O)- + OX(Y)- + -IN] — **thy·rox·in·ic** (thī′rok·sin′ik) *adj.*

thyr·soid (thûr′soid) *adj. Bot.* Resembling or shaped like a thyrsus. Also **thyr·soi·dal** (thûr·soid′l).

thyr·sus (thûr′səs) *n. pl.* **·si** (-sī) A staff wreathed in ivy and crowned with a pine cone or a bunch of ivy leaves, as carried by Dionysus and the satyrs. [< L < Gk. *thyrsos*]

thy·self (thī·self′) *pron. Archaic* A form of the second person singular pronouns *thee* and *thou*, used: 1. As a reflexive: Know *thyself*. 2. As an emphatic or intensive form: I love thee for *thyself*.

ti (tē) *n. Music* In solmization, a syllable representing the seventh tone of the diatonic scale. [See GAMUT]

ti·ar·a (tī·âr′ə, tē·är′ə, -ar′ə) *n.* 1. The pope's triple crown; also, the papal dignity. Compare MITER. 2. An ornamental, semicircular band of jewels, etc., worn by women for formal occasions. [< L < Gk. *tiara* Persian headdress]

Ti·bet·an (ti·bet′n) *adj.* Of or pertaining to Tibet, the Tibetans, or to their language, religion, or customs. — *n.* 1. One of the native Mongoloid people of Tibet, now intermixed with Chinese and various peoples of India. 2. The Sino-Tibetan language of Tibet. Also *Thibetan.*

tib·i·a (tib′ē·ə) *n. pl.* **tib·i·ae** (tib′i·ē) or **tib·i·as** 1. *Anat.* The inner and larger of the two bones of the leg below the knee; the shin bone. 2. The corresponding bone in the hind limb of other animals. [< L] — **tib′i·al** *adj.*

tic (tik) *n.* An involuntary spasm or twitching of muscles, usu. of the face and sometimes of neurotic origin. [< F]

tick[1] (tik) *n.* 1. A light, recurring sound made by a watch, clock, or similar mechanism. 2. A mark, as a dot or dash, used in checking off something. — *v.i.* 1. To make a recurrent clicking sound, as a running watch or clock. — *v.t.* 2. To mark or check with ticks. [Prob. imit.]

tick[2] (tik) *n.* 1. One of numerous flat, bloodsucking arachnids that attack the skin of man and other animals. 2. Any of certain two-winged or wingless insects, parasitic on sheep, horses, cattle, bats, and other animals. [OE *ticia*]

tick[3] (tik) *n.* 1. The stout outer covering of a mattress or pillow. 2. *Informal* Ticking. [Earlier *teke, tyke,* ult. < L < Gk. *thēke* case]

tick[4] (tik) *n. Brit. Informal* Credit; trust: to buy something on *tick*. [Short for TICKET]

tick·er (tik′ər) *n.* 1. One who or that which ticks. 2. A telegraphic instrument that records stock quotations on a paper ribbon. 3. *Slang* A watch. 4. *Slang* The heart.

ticker tape A paper ribbon that receives the printed information on a ticker. — **tick·er·tape** (tik′ər·tāp′) *adj.*

tick·et (tik′it) *n.* 1. A card showing that the holder is entitled to something, as transportation in a public vehicle, admission to a theater, etc. 2. A label or tag for attachment or identification. 3. A certificate or license, as of an airplane pilot or the captain of a ship. 4. In politics: **a** A list of candidates of a single party on a ballot. **b** The group of candidates running for the offices of a party. 5. *Informal* A legal summons, as for a traffic violation. — *v.t.* 1. To fix a ticket to; label. 2. To present or furnish with a ticket or tickets. [< MF < OF < *estiquer* to stick < OLG *stekan*]

ticket of leave Formerly, in Great Britain and Australia, a written permit granted to a penal convict to be at large before the expiration of his sentence.

tick·ing (tik′ing) *n.* A strong, closely woven cotton or linen fabric, used for ticks, awnings, etc. [< TICK[3] + -ING[1]]

tick·le (tik′əl) *v.* **·led, ·ling** *v.t.* 1. To touch or scratch (someone) so as to produce a sensation resulting in spasmodic laughter or twitching; titillate. 2. To arouse or excite agreeably; please: Compliments *tickle* our vanity. 3. *Informal* To amuse or entertain; delight. 4. To move, stir, or get by or as by tickling. — *v.i.* 5. To have or experience a thrilling or tingling sensation. — *n.* 1. The act of tickling or of being tickled; also the sensation produced. 2. *Canadian* In Newfoundland, a narrow strait. [ME *tikelen*]

tick·ler (tik′lər) *n.* 1. One who or that which tickles. 2. A memorandum book or file, as of bills or notes due, etc.

tick·lish (tik′lish) *adj.* 1. Sensitive to tickling. 2. Liable to be upset or easily offended. 3. Attended with risk; difficult; delicate. — **tick′lish·ly** *adv.* — **tick′lish·ness** *n.*

tick·tack·toe (tik′tak·tō′) *n.* A game for two players who alternately put circles or crosses in the spaces of a figure formed by two parallel lines crossing at right angles two other parallel lines, each player trying to get a row of three circles or three crosses before his opponent does: also called *tit-tat-toe.* Also **tick′tack·too′** (-tōō′), **tic′tac·toe′** (-tō′).

tick·tock (tik′tok′) *n.* The sound of a clock or watch. — *v.i.* To make this sound. [Imit.]

tid·al (tīd′l) *adj.* 1. Of, pertaining to, or influenced by the tides. 2. Dependent on the rise of the tide as to time of starting or leaving: a *tidal* steamship.

tidal wave 1. Any great incoming rise of waters along a shore, caused by windstorms at sea or by excessively high tides. 2. A great movement in popular feeling, opinion, action, etc. 3. A tsunami.

tid·bit (tid′bit′) *n.* A choice bit, as of food. Also, *Brit., titbit.* [< dial. E *tid* small object + BIT[1]]

tid·dly·winks (tid′lē·wingks′) *n.* A game in which the players attempt to snap little disks of bone, ivory, or the like, from a plane surface into a cup. Also **tid·dle·dy·winks** (tid′l·dē·wingks′). [Prob. < *tiddly* child's word for *little*]

tide (tīd) *n.* 1. The periodic rise and fall of the surface waters of the oceans, caused by the attraction of moon and sun. In each lunar day of 24 hours and 51 minutes there are two high tides and two low tides, alternating at equal intervals of flood and ebb. 2. Anything that rises and falls like the tide; also, the time at which something is most flourishing. 3. A natural drift or tendency of events, opinions, etc. 4. Season; time; esp., a season of the ecclesiastical year: used chiefly in combination: *Christmastide.* — *v.* **tid·ed, tid·ing** *v.i.* 1. To ebb and flow like the tide. 2. To float with the tide. — *v.t.* 3. To carry or help like a boat buoyed up by the tide: Charity *tided* us over the depression. 4. To survive; endure, as a difficulty: with *over*: to *tide* over hard times. [OE *tīd* period, season] — **tide′less** *adj.*

tide·land (tīd′land′) *n.* Land alternately covered and uncovered by the tide.

tide·rip (tīd′rip′) *n.* Riptide. [< TIDE[1] + RIP[2]]

tide·wait·er (tīd′wā′tər) *n.* A customs officer who boards vessels entering port, to enforce customs regulations.

tide·wa·ter (tīd′wô′tər, -wot′ər) *n.* 1. Water that inundates land at high tide. 2. Water affected by the tide on the seacoast or in a river. 3. Any area, as a seacoast, whose waters are affected by tides. — *adj.* Pertaining to the tidewater; also, situated on the seacoast: the *tidewater* country.

ti·dings (tī′dingz) *n.pl.* (*sometimes construed as sing.*) A report or information; news. [OE *tīdung*]

ti·dy (tī′dē) *adj.* **·di·er, ·di·est** 1. Marked by neatness and order; trim. 2. Of an orderly disposition. 3. *Informal*

Moderately large; considerable: a *tidy* sum. **4.** *Informal* Tolerable; fairly good. — *v.t.* & *v.i.* **·died, ·dy·ing** To make (things) tidy; put (things) in order. — *n.* *pl.* **·dies** A light, detachable covering, as of lace or embroidery, to protect the back or arms of a chair or sofa. [ME < OE *tīd* time] — **ti′di·ly** *adv.* — **ti′di·ness** *n.*

tie (tī) *v.* **tied, ty·ing** *v.t.* **1.** To fasten with cord, rope, etc., the ends of which are then drawn into a knot. **2.** To draw the parts of together or into place by a cord or band fastened with a knot: to *tie* one's shoes. **3.** To form (a knot). **4.** To form a knot in, as string. **5.** To fasten, attach, or join in any way. **6.** To restrain or confine; bind. **7.** In sports, games, etc.: **a** To equal (a competitor) in score or achievement. **b** To equal (a competitor's score). **8.** *Informal* To unite in marriage. **9.** *Music* To unite by a tie. — *v.i.* **10.** To make a tie or connection. **11.** To make the same score; be equal. — **to tie down** To hinder; restrict. — **to tie in** *Informal* To have a certain relationship or connection; often with *with*. — **to tie (something) in** *Informal* To bring into a certain relationship or connection. — **to tie up 1.** To fasten with rope, string, etc. **2.** To moor (a vessel). **3.** To block; hinder. **4.** To have or be already committed, in use, etc., so as to be unavailable. — *n.* **1.** A string, cord, etc., with which something is tied. **2.** Any bond or obligation, mental, moral, or legal: *ties* of affection. **3.** An exact equality in number, as of a score, votes, etc.; esp., a contest which neither side wins; a draw. **4.** A necktie. **5.** A structural member fastening parts of a framework together and receiving tensile stress. **6.** *Music* A curved line placed over or under two musical notes of the same pitch on the staff to make them represent one tone length. **7.** *pl.* Low shoes fastened with lacings. **8.** *U.S.* One of a set of timbers laid crosswise on the ground as supports for railroad tracks; a sleeper. [OE *tīegan* to bind]

tie·back (tī′bak′) *n.* A piece of fabric, metal, etc., by which curtains are draped or tied back at the sides.

tie beam A timber that serves as a tie in a roof, etc. For illus. see ROOF.

tie-in (tī′in′) *n.* A connection; association; relation.

tie-in sale A sale in which the buyer, in order to get the article he wants, is required to buy a second article.

tier (tir) *n.* A rank or row of things, as seats, placed one above another. — *v.t.* & *v.i.* To place or rise in tiers. [Earlier *tire* < OF, sequence < *tirer* to draw, elongate]

tierce (tirs) *n.* **1.** A former liquid measure equivalent in the U.S. to 42 wine gallons; a third of a pipe or butt. **2.** A cask holding this amount. **3.** *Often cap. Eccl.* Prescribed prayers constituting the third of the seven canonical hours: often called *undersong*. [< OF *tierce, terce* a third < L *tertia*]

tie-up (tī′up′) *n.* **1.** A situation, resulting from a strike, mechanical breakdown, etc., in which progress or operation is impossible. **2.** *Informal* A connection or relation.

tiff (tif) *n.* **1.** A peevish display of irritation; a pet; huff. **2.** A light quarrel; a spat. — *v.i.* To be in or have a tiff. [Origin unknown]

ti·ger (tī′gər) *n.* **1.** A large carnivorous feline of Asia, with vertical black wavy stripes on a tawny body and black bars or rings on the limbs and tail. **2.** One of several other animals resembling the tiger. **3.** A fierce, cruel person. [OE *tiger* or OF *tigre*, both < L < Gk. *tigris*]

ti·ger-eye (tī′gər-ī′) *n.* A gemstone showing a changeable luster. Also **ti′gers-eye′.**

ti·ger·ish (tī′gər-ish) *adj.* Of or resembling the tiger or its habits; predacious; bloodthirsty: also **ti′grish** (-grish)

tiger lily A tall cultivated lily, with nodding orange flowers spotted with black.

tiger moth A stout-bodied moth with striped or spotted wings.

tight (tīt) *adj.* **1.** So closely held together or constructed as to be impervious to fluids, air, etc.: a *tight* vessel. **2.** Firmly fixed or fastened in place; secure. **3.** Fully stretched; taut: *tight* as a drum. **4.** Closely drawn, packed, fastened, etc.: a *tight* weave. **5.** Strict; stringent: to keep a *tight* rein over us. **6.** Fitting closely; esp., fitting too closely. **7.** *Informal* Difficult to cope with; troublesome: a *tight* spot. **8.** *Informal* Parsimonious; tightfisted. **9.** Characterized by a feeling of constriction: a *tight* cough. **10.** *Slang* Drunk; intoxicated. **11.** Evenly matched: said of a contest. **12.** *Econ.* **a** Difficult to obtain. **b** Straitened from lack of money or commodities: a *tight* market. **13.** Yielding very little or no profit: said of a bargain. **14.** *Dial.* Well-built; compact. **15.** *Dial.* Neat; tidy. — *adv.* **1.** Firmly; securely. **2.** Closely; with much constriction. — **to sit tight** To remain firm in one's position; refrain from taking action. [ME *thight*] — **tight′ly** *adv.* — **tight′ness** *n.*

-tight *combining form* Impervious to: *watertight.*

tight·en (tīt′n) *v.t.* & *v.i.* To make or become tight or tighter. — **tight′en·er** *n.*

tight·fist·ed (tīt′fis′tid) *adj.* Stingy; parsimonious.

tight·lipped (tīt′lipt′) *adj.* **1.** Having the lips held tightly together. **2.** Unwilling to talk; reticent or secretive.

tight·rope (tīt′rōp′) *n.* A rope or cable stretched out tight above the ground, on which acrobats do balancing acts, etc.

tights (tīts) *n.pl.* Skintight garments, commonly for the legs and lower torso, worn by dancers, acrobats, etc.

tight·wad (tīt′wod′) *n.* *U.S. Slang* A parsimonious person; miser. [< TIGHT + WAD¹]

ti·gress (tī′gris) *n.* **1.** A female tiger. **2.** A cruel, fierce woman.

til·bur·y (til′ber-ē) *n.* *pl.* **·bur·ies** A form of gig for two persons. [after *Tilbury*, a 19th c. London coachmaker]

til·de (til′də, -dē) *n.* A sign (~); used esp., in Spanish over *n* to represent the palatal nasal (roughly equivalent to *ny*) as in *cañon.* [< Sp. < L *titulus* superscription, title]

tile (tīl) *n.* **1.** A thin piece of baked clay or other material, as asbestos, linoleum, etc., used for covering roofs, floors, etc., and as an ornament. **2.** A short earthenware pipe, used in forming sewers. **3.** Tiles collectively; tiling. **4.** Any of the counters used in mahjong. **5.** *Informal* A high silk hat. — *v.t.* **tiled, til·ing** To cover with tiles. [OE, ult. < L < *tegere* to cover] — **til′er** *n.*

til·ing (tī′ling) *n.* **1.** The act, operation, or system of using tiles for roofing, drainage, etc. **2.** Tiles collectively. **3.** Something made of or faced with tiles.

till¹ (til) *v.t.* & *v.i.* To work (soil) for the production of crops, as by plowing, harrowing, hoeing, sowing, etc.; cultivate. [OE *tilian* to strive, acquire] — **till′a·ble** *adj.*

till² (til) *prep.* **1.** To the time of; until. **2.** Before: with the negative: I can't go *till* noon. — *conj.* **1.** Up to such time as; until: *till* death do us part. **2.** Before: with the negative: They couldn't go *till* he came. [OE *til* < ON, to]

till³ (til) *n.* A drawer or tray in which money or valuables are kept, as at a bank, store, etc. [Origin uncertain]

till·age (til′ij) *n.* The cultivation of land. [< TILL¹ + -AGE]

till·er¹ (til′ər) *n.* One who or that which tills. [< TILL¹]

till·er² (til′ər) *n. Naut.* A lever to turn a rudder when steering. [< OF < Med.L *telarium* weaver's beam]

tilt (tilt) *v.t.* **1.** To cause to rise at one end or side; incline at an angle; slant; tip. **2.** To aim or thrust, as a lance. **3.** To charge or overthrow in a tilt or joust. — *v.i.* **4.** To slope; lean. **5.** To engage in a joust. — **Syn.** See TIP¹. — *n.* **1.** A slant; slope. **2.** The act of inclining, or the state of being inclined. **3.** A medieval sport in which mounted knights, charging with lances, endeavored to unseat each other. **4.** Any similar encounter, as a quarrel. **5.** A thrust or blow, as with a lance. **6.** A seesaw. — **at full tilt** At full speed. [ME < OE *tealt* unsteady] — **tilt′er** *n.*

tilth (tilth) *n.* **1.** The act of tilling; cultivation of soil; tillage. **2.** Cultivated land. [OE < *tilian* to till]

tim·bal (tim′bəl) *n.* A kettledrum. [< F < Sp. < Arabic *at-tabl* a drum]

tim·bale (tim′bəl, *Fr.* tan-bål′) *n.* **1.** A custardlike dish made of chicken, fish, cheese, or vegetables, cooked in a drum-shaped mold. **2.** A small cup made of fried pastry, in which food may be served. [< F. See TIMBAL.]

tim·ber (tim′bər) *n.* **1.** Wood suitable for building or structural purposes. **2.** Growing or standing trees; also, woodland. **3.** A single piece of prepared wood for use in a structure. **4.** *Naut.* Any principal beam of a vessel. **5.** Personal character, talent, potentiality: presidential *timber.* — *v.t.* To provide or shore with timber. [OE] — **tim′bered** *adj.*

timber hitch *Naut.* A knot by which a rope is fastened around a spar.

tim·ber·land (tim′bər-land′) *n.* Land covered with forests.

timber line The upper limit of tree growth on mountains and in arctic regions. — **tim′ber-line′** (-līn′) *adj.*

timber wolf The large gray or brindled wolf of the forests of the northern U.S. and Canada: also called *lobo.*

tim·bre (tim′bər, tam′-; *Fr.* tan′br′) *n.* The attribute of a sound distinguishing one vowel from another, the tone of one musical instrument from another, etc.; quality; tone color. [< F < OF < L *tympanum* kettledrum]

TIMBER WOLF
(About 4 feet long)

tim·brel (tim′brəl) *n.* An ancient instrument resembling a tambourine. [< OF. See TIMBRE.]

time (tīm) *n.* **1.** The general concept, relation, or fact of continuous or successive existence, capable of division into measurable portions, and comprising the past, present, and future. **2.** Duration with reference to finite existence as distinguished from eternity. **3.** A system of measuring duration: solar *time.* **4.** A definite portion of duration; esp., a specific hour, day, season, year, etc.: The *time* is 2:35; Autumn is my favorite *time.* **5.** The moment or period in which something takes place, has taken place, or will take place: at the *time* of his marriage. **6.** That moment or portion of duration allotted to or sufficient for some special action, purpose, or event: *time* enough to catch the train. **7.** The period of duration generally allotted to human life. **8.** Leisure: no *time* to read. **9.** An instance or occasion of recurrence or repetition: next *time*; three *times* a day. **10.** A fit or proper moment or occasion: a *time* to plant. **11.** The period of pregnancy or gestation; also, the moment of childbirth. **12.** The moment of death. **13.** A period considered with reference to one's personal experience: to have a good *time*. **14.** *Usu. pl.* An era marked by some cultural, historical, or other special characteristics: ancient *times*; the *time* of Charlemagne. **15.** *Usu. pl.* The present period or era or the period or era under consideration. **16.** *Usu. pl.* A period of duration having some specific quality: *Times* are hard. **17.** *Informal* A period of imprisonment. **18.** The period during which work has been done or remains to be done by a worker; also, the pay given for this. **19.** *Music* Loosely, meter, tempo, or the duration of a note. See METER. **20.** Speed or rate of movement in marching, dancing, etc.: double *time*. **21.** *Usu. pl.* In arithmetic, an instance of being multiplied or added: How many *times* does three go into nine? **— against time** With an imminent time limit; as quickly as possible. **— ahead of time** Before the time stated or due; early. **— at the same time 1.** At the same moment or period. **2.** Despite that; however; nevertheless. **— at times** Now and then; occasionally. **— behind the times** Old-fashioned. **— behind time** After the time stated or due; late. **— for the time being** Temporarily. **— from time to time** Now and then; occasionally. **— in good time 1.** Quickly; fast. **2.** At the appropriate time; when properly due. **— in the nick of time** At just the right or critical moment. **— in time 1.** While time permits or lasts; before it is too late. **2.** In the progress of time; ultimately. **3.** In the proper rhythm, tempo, etc. **— on time 1.** Promptly; according to schedule. **2.** To be paid for, later or in installments. **— time and again** Frequently; repeatedly: also **time after time.** **— to gain time 1.** To run fast: said of a timepiece. **2.** To prolong an act or occasion so as to consider, decide, etc. **— to keep time 1.** To indicate time correctly, as a clock. **2.** To make rhythmic movements in unison with others. **3.** To render or conduct a musical composition in the desired tempo or rhythm. **— to lose time 1.** To run slow: said of a clock. **2.** To waste or miss opportunities; delay advancement. **— adj. 1.** Of or pertaining to time. **2.** Devised so as to operate at a specified time: a *time* bomb. **3.** Of purchases, paid for in installments or at a future date. **— v.t. timed, tim-ing 1.** To regulate as to time. **2.** To cause to correspond in time: They *timed* their steps to the music. **3.** To arrange the time or occasion for. **4.** To mark the rhythm or measure of. **5.** To ascertain or record the speed or duration of: to *time* a race. [OE *tīma*]

time-card (tīm'kärd') *n.* A card for recording the time of arrival and departure of an employee.

time clock A clock equipped for automatically recording times of arrival and departure.

time exposure *Photog.* **1.** A film exposure made for a relatively long interval. **2.** A picture made by such an exposure.

time-hon-ored (tīm'on'ərd) *adj.* Observed or honored because of long usage or existence. Also *Brit.* **time'-hon'oured.**

time-keep-er (tīm'kē'pər) *n.* **1.** One who or that which keeps time. **2.** One who declares the time in a race, game, athletic match, etc., or records the hours worked by employees. **3.** A railroad train starter. **4.** A timepiece.

time-less (tīm'lis) *adj.* **1.** Independent of or unaffected by time; unending; eternal. **2.** Not limited to any special time or era. **— time'less-ly** *adv.* **— time'less-ness** *n.*

time-ly (tīm'lē) *adj.* **-li-er, -li-est** Being or occurring in good or suitable time; opportune; seasonable; well-timed. **— adv.** Opportunely; seasonably; early. **— time'li-ness** *n.*

time-out (tīm'out') *n.* In sports, a short recess requested by a team during play. Also **time out.**

time-piece (tīm'pēs') *n.* Something that records or measures time, as a clock or watch.

tim-er (tī'mər) *n.* **1.** A timekeeper. **2.** A stopwatch, as for timing a race. **3.** A device attached to an internal-combustion engine so as to time the spark automatically. **4.** A clockwork or other device that signals the lapse of a time period, controls an operation, etc.

time-serv-er (tīm'sûr'vər) *n.* One who yields to the demands or opinions of the time, occasion, or authorities, without reference to principle. **— time'serv'ing** *adj. & n.*

time signature *Music* A symbol placed on a musical staff to indicate the meter.

time-ta-ble (tīm'tā'bəl) *n.* A tabular schedule of the times at which certain things are to take place, as arrivals and departures of trains, times of high and low tides, etc.

time-test-ed (tīm'tes'tid) *adj.* Having worth or efficiency proved by use over an extended period.

time-work (tīm'wûrk') *n.* Work paid for on the basis of a set wage per hour, day, week, etc. **— time'work'er** *n.*

time-worn (tīm'wôrn', -wōrn') *adj.* **1.** Showing the ravages or effects of time. **2.** Trite; overused.

time zone One of the 24 sectors of 15° each, or a time interval of one hour, into which the earth is divided for reckoning standard time from the meridian of Greenwich.

tim-id (tim'id) *adj.* **1.** Shrinking from danger or risk; fearful. **2.** Lacking self-confidence; shy. **3.** Characterized by fear or shyness: a *timid* voice. [< L < *timere* to fear] **— ti-mid-i-ty** (ti-mid'ə-tē), **tim'id-ness** *n.* **— tim'id-ly** *adv.*

tim-ing (tī'ming) *n.* The act or art of regulating the speed of performance, utterance, a blow, stroke, etc., so as to insure maximum effectiveness; also, the effect so produced.

tim-or-ous (tim'ər-əs) *adj.* **1.** Fearful of danger; timid. **2.** Indicating or produced by fear. [< OF < Med.L < *timor, -oris* fear] **— tim'or-ous-ly** *adv.* **— tim'or-ous-ness** *n.*

tim-o-thy (tim'ə-thē) *n.* A perennial fodder grass having long, cylindrical spikes. Also **timothy grass.** [after *Timothy* Hanson, who took the seed to the Carolinas about 1720]

Tim-o-thy (tim'ə-thē) A convert and companion of the apostle Paul. **— n.** Either of two books in the New Testament consisting of two epistles addressed to Timothy and attributed to Saint Paul.

tim-pa-ni (tim'pə-nē) *n. pl.* of **tim-pa-no** (-nō) Kettledrums: also spelled *tympani.* [< Ital. < L *tympanum* drum] **— tim'pa-nist** *n.*

tim-pa-num (tim'pə-nəm) See TYMPANUM.

tin (tin) *n.* **1.** A white, malleable, metallic element (symbol Sn) of low tensile strength: also called *stannum.* See ELEMENT. **2.** Tin plate. **3.** A container or box made of tin. **4.** *Brit.* A can. **— v.t. tinned, tin-ning 1.** To coat or cover with tin. **2.** To pack or put up in tins. **— adj.** Made of a tin. [OE]

tin-a-mou (tin'ə-mōō) *n.* Any of certain South American birds resembling the partridge and hunted as game birds. [< F < Carib *tinamu*]

tinc-ture (tingk'chər) *n.* **1.** A solution, usu., in alcohol, of some medicinal substance: *tincture* of iodine. **2.** A tinge of color; tint. **3.** A slight additional flavor, quality, etc. **— v.t. -tured, -tur-ing 1.** To impart a slight hue or tinge to. **2.** To imbue with flavor, odor, etc. **3.** To imbue with a specified quality. [< L *tingere* to dye, color]

tin-der (tin'dər) *n.* Any readily combustible substance, as charred linen or touchwood, that will ignite on contact with a spark. [OE *tynder*] **— tin'der-y** *adj.*

tin-der-box (tin'dər-boks') *n.* **1.** A portable metallic box containing tinder. **2.** Anything highly flammable, explosive, touchy, etc.

tine (tīn) *n.* A spike or prong, as of a fork or of an antler. [OE *tind*] **— tined** *adj.*

tin-foil (tin'foil') *n.* Tin or an alloy of tin made into thin sheets for use as wrapping material, etc. Also **tin foil.**

ting (ting) *n.* A single high metallic sound, as of a small bell. **— v.t. & v.i.** To give forth or cause to give forth a ting. [Imit.]

ting-a-ling (ting'ə-ling') *n.* The sound of a little bell.

tinge (tinj) *v.t.* **tinged, tinge-ing** or **ting-ing 1.** To imbue with a faint trace of color; tint. **2.** To impart a slight characteristic quality of some other element to. **— n. 1.** A faint trace of added color. **2.** A quality or peculiar characteristic imparted to something. [< L *tingere* to dye]

tin-gle (ting'gəl) *v.* **-gled, -gling** *v.i.* **1.** To experience a prickly, stinging sensation, as from cold, or from a sharp blow. **2.** To cause such a sensation. **— v.t. 3.** To cause to tingle. **— n.** A prickly, stinging sensation; a tingling. [Appar. var. of TINKLE] **— tin'gler** *n.* **— tin'gly** *adj.*

tin-horn (tin'hôrn') *U.S. Slang n.* One who is cheaply and noisily pretentious; esp., a flashy, small-time gambler.

tink-er (tingk'ər) *n.* **1.** An itinerant mender of domestic tin utensils, as pots and pans. **2.** Loosely, one who does repairing work of any kind; a jack-of-all-trades. **3.** A clumsy workman; a botcher. **4.** The act of roughly repairing; hasty workmanship. **— v.i. 1.** To work as a tinker. **2.** To work in a clumsy makeshift fashion. **3.** To potter; fuss. **— v.t. 4.** To mend as a tinker. **5.** To repair inexpertly. [Var. of earlier *tinekere* worker in tin]

tinker's damn *Slang* The smallest, most contemptible bit: not worth a *tinker's damn.* Also **tinker's dam.** [< TINKER + DAMN; with ref. to the reputed profanity of tinkers]

tin-kle (ting'kəl) *v.* **-kled, -kling** *v.i.* **1.** To produce slight, sharp, metallic sounds, as a small bell. **— v.t. 2.** To cause to tinkle. **3.** To summon or signal by a tinkling. **— n.** A tinkling sound. [Imit.] **— tin'kly** *adj.* **— tink'ling** *n.*

tin-ner (tin'ər) *n.* **1.** A miner employed in tin mines. **2.** A maker of or dealer in tinware; a tinsmith.

tin-ny (tin'ē) *adj.* **-ni-er, -ni-est 1.** Pertaining to, composed of, or abounding in tin. **2.** Resembling tin in lack of durability. **3.** Having a thin sound like that of tin being struck. **— tin'ni-ly** *adv.* **— tin'ni-ness** *n.*

tin-pan alley (tin'pan') **1.** A section of a city, esp., of New York, frequented by musicians and song writers and occupied by publishers of popular music. **2.** The composers and publishers of popular music, collectively.

tin-plate (tin′plāt′) *v.t.* **-plat·ed, -plat·ing** To plate with tin. — **tin′-plat′er** *n.*

tin plate Sheet iron or steel plated with tin.

tin·sel (tin′səl) *n.* **1.** Very thin, glittering bits of cheap metals used as decoration. **2.** A yarn containing gold or silver thread. **3.** Anything sparkling and showy, with little real worth. **4.** A fabric in which such spangles or bits of metal are woven. — *adj.* **1.** Made of, resembling, or covered with tinsel. **2.** Superficially brilliant; tawdry. — *v.t.* **·seled** or **·selled, sel·ing** or **·sel·ling 1.** To decorate with or as with tinsel. **2.** To give a showy or gaudy appearance to. [< MF < OF < L *scintilla* spark]

tin·smith (tin′smith′) *n.* One who works with tin or tin plate: also called *whitesmith.*

tint (tint) *n.* **1.** A variety of color; tincture; esp., a slight admixture of a different color; tinge. **2.** A gradation of a color made by dilution with white. **3.** Any pale or delicate hue. **4.** In engraving, an effect of light, shade, texture, etc., produced by the spacing of lines or by hatching. — *v.t.* **1.** To give a tint to; tinge. **2.** In engraving, to form a tint upon. [< L < *tingere* to dye, color] — **tint′er** *n.*

tin·tin·nab·u·la·tion (tin′ti·nab′yə·lā′shən) *n.* The pealing, tinkling, or ringing of bells. [< L < *tintinnare* to ring]

tin·type (tin′tīp′) *n.* A photograph taken on a sensitized film supported on a thin sheet of enameled tin or iron.

tin·ware (tin′wâr′) *n.* Articles made of tin plate.

ti·ny (tī′nē) *adj.* **·ni·er, ·ni·est** Very small; minute; wee. [< *obs. tine* small amount, bit + -Y³; ult. origin unknown]

-tion *suffix of nouns* **1.** Action or process of: *rejection.* **2.** Condition or state of being: *completion.* **3.** Result of: *connection.* Also **-ation, -cion, -ion, -sion, -xion.** [< F < OF < L *-tio, -tionis*]

tip¹ (tip) *n.* A slanting or inclined position; a tilt. — *v.* **tipped, tip·ping** *v.t.* **1.** To cause to lean by lowering or raising one end or side; tilt. **2.** To overturn or upset: often with *over.* **3.** To raise or touch (one's hat) in greeting. — *v.i.* **4.** To become tilted; slant. **5.** To overturn; topple: with *over.* [ME *tipen* to overturn; origin uncertain] — **tip′per** *n.* — **Syn. 1, 3.** Tilt, slant, slope.

tip² (tip) *n.* **1.** A small gift of money for services rendered, given to a servant, waiter, etc. **2.** A friendly, helpful hint; esp., information presumed to increase a better's or speculator's chance of winning. — *v.* **tipped, tip·ping** *v.t.* **1.** To give a small gratuity to. **2.** *Informal* To give secret information to, as in betting: often with *off.* — *v.i.* **3.** To give tips. [Orig. < thieves' cant, ? < TIP⁴] — **tip′per** *n.*

tip³ (tip) *n.* **1.** The point or extremity of anything tapering; end: the *tip* of the tongue. **2.** A piece or part made to form the end of anything, as a nozzle, ferrule, etc. **3.** The top or summit, as of a mountain. — *v.t.* **tipped, tip·ping 1.** To furnish with a tip. **2.** To form the tip of. **3.** To cover or adorn the tip of. [Prob. < MDu., point]

tip⁴ (tip) *v.t.* **tipped, tip·ping 1.** To strike lightly, or with something light; tap. **2.** In baseball, to strike (the ball) a light, glancing blow. — *n.* A tap; light blow. [Earlier *tippe*]

tip-off (tip′ôf′, -of′) *n. Informal* A hint or warning.

tip·pet (tip′it) *n.* **1.** An outdoor covering for the neck, or neck and shoulders, hanging well down in front. **2.** *Eccl.* A long scarf worn by Anglican clergymen. **3.** Formerly, a long, dangling part of a sleeve, hood, etc. [Prob. dim. of TIP³]

tip·ple (tip′əl) *v.t. & v.i.* **·pled, ·pling** To drink (alcoholic beverages) frequently and habitually. — *n.* Alcoholic liquor. — **tip′pler** *n.*

tip·ster (tip′stər) *n. Informal* One who sells tips, as for betting on a race. [< TIP³]

tip·sy (tip′sē) *adj.* **tip·si·er, tip·si·est 1.** Partially intoxicated; high. **2.** Apt to tip over; shaky; also, crooked; askew. [< TIP¹] — **tip′si·ly** *adv.* — **tip′si·ness** *n.*

tip·toe (tip′tō′) *v.i.* **·toed, ·toe·ing** To walk on tiptoe; go stealthily or quietly. — *n.* The tip of a toe. — **on tiptoe 1.** On one's tiptoes. **2.** Eagerly expectant. **3.** Stealthily; quietly. — *adj.* **1.** Standing or walking on tiptoe. **2.** Stealthy. **3.** Eager; excited. — *adv.* On tiptoe.

tip·top (tip′top′) *n.* **1.** The highest point; the very top. **2.** *Informal* The highest quality or degree. — *adj.* **1.** Located at the very top. **2.** *Informal* Best of its kind; first-rate. — *adv.* In a tiptop manner. [< TIP³ + TOP¹] — **tip′top′per** *n.*

ti·rade (tī′rād, tə·rād′) *n.* A prolonged declamatory outpouring, as of censure. [< F < Ital. *tirare* to fire, pull]

tire¹ (tīr) *v.* **tired, tir·ing** *v.t.* **1.** To reduce the strength of, as by toil; weary; fatigue. **2.** To reduce the interest or patience of, as with tediousness. — *v.i.* **3.** To become weary or exhausted. **4.** To lose patience, interest, etc. — **to tire of** To become weary of or impatient with. — **to tire out** To weary completely. [OE *tīorian*]

tire² (tīr) *n.* **1.** A pneumatic, doughnut-shaped structure, as of rubber, forming the outer part of the wheels of vehicles, serving to absorb shock and provide traction. **2.** A band or hoop of metal, etc. fixed tightly around the rim of a wheel.

— *v.t.* **tired, tir·ing** To furnish with a tire; put a tire on. [Aphetic var. of ATTIRE]

tired (tīrd) *adj.* Weary; exhausted; jaded; fatigued. — **tired′ly** *adv.* — **tired′ness** *n.*

tire·less (tīr′lis) *adj.* Proof against fatigue; untiring. — **tire′less·ly** *adv.* — **tire′less·ness** *n.*

tire·some (tīr′səm) *adj.* Tending to tire, or causing one to tire; tedious. — **tire′some·ly** *adv.* — **tire′some·ness** *n.*

ti·ro (tī′rō) See TYRO.

'tis (tiz) *Archaic or Poetic* It is.

Tish'ah b'Ab (tish′ə·bäb) *n.* In Judaism, a day of fasting, held on the 9th of Ab (July-August), to commemorate the destruction of the Temple.

Tish·ri (tish·rē′, tish′rē) *n.* The first month of the Hebrew calendar. Also **Tis·ri.** See (Hebrew) CALENDAR. [< Hebrew < Aramaic *tishrī* < *sherā* to begin]

tis·sue (tish′ōō) *n.* **1.** *Biol.* One of the elementary aggregates of cells and their products, developed by plants and animals for the performance of a particular function: connective *tissue.* **2.** A light, absorbent piece of paper, usu. consisting of two or more layers, used as a disposable towel, handkerchief, etc. **3.** Tissue paper. **4.** A tissuelike typewriting paper, as onionskin, commonly used for making carbon copies. **5.** A connected or interwoven series; chain: a *tissue* of lies. **6.** Any light or gauzy textile fabric. [< OF < *tistre* to weave]

tissue paper Very thin, unsized, almost transparent paper for wrapping delicate articles, protecting engravings, etc.

tit¹ (tit) *n.* **1.** A titmouse. **2.** Any of various small birds, as a titlark. [Short for TITMOUSE, TITLARK, etc.]

tit² (tit) *n.* Teat; breast; nipple. [OE *titt*]

ti·tan (tīt′n) *n.* A person of gigantic size and strength. [< TITAN]

Ti·tan (tīt′n) *n.* **1.** In Greek mythology, one of a race of giant gods who were vanquished and succeeded by the Olympian gods. **2.** Helios: so called by some Latin poets. **3.** A liquid-fueled intercontinental guided missile of the U.S. Air Force. — *adj.* Titanic. — **Ti′tan·ess** *n.fem.*

Ti·ta·ni·a (ti·tā′nē·ə, tī-) Queen of fairyland and wife of Oberon in Shakespeare's *A Midsummer Night's Dream.*

ti·tan·ic (tī·tan′ik) *adj.* Of great size; huge.

Ti·tan·ic (tī·tan′ik) *adj.* Of or resembling the Titans.

ti·ta·ni·um (tī·tā′nē·əm, ti-) *n.* A widely distributed dark gray metallic element (symbol Ti), found in small quantities in many minerals and used to toughen steel alloys. See ELEMENT. [< NL < L < Gk. *Titanes* the Titans]

tit·bit (tit′bit′) *n. Brit.* A tidbit.

tit for tat Retaliation in kind; blow for blow. [? Alter. of *tip for tap*]

tithe (tīth) *n.* **1.** A tax or assessment of one tenth; loosely, any ratable tax. **2.** In England, a tenth part of the yearly proceeds arising from lands and from the personal industry of the inhabitants, for the support of the clergy and the church. **3.** The tenth part of anything. **4.** A small part. — *v.t.* **tithed, tith·ing 1.** To give or pay a tithe, or tenth part of. **2.** To tax with tithes. [ME *tithe*, OE *teogotha* tenth] — **tith′a·ble** *adj.* — **tith′er** *n.*

ti·tian (tish′ən) *n.* A reddish yellow color much used by Titian, esp. in painting women's hair. — *adj.* Having or pertaining to the color titian. [after *Titian*]

tit·il·late (tit′ə·lāt) *v.t.* **·lat·ed, ·lat·ing 1.** To cause a tickling sensation in. **2.** To excite pleasurably in any way. [< L *titillare* to tickle] — **tit′il·la′tion** *n.* — **tit′il·la′tive** *adj.*

tit·i·vate (tit′ə·vāt) *v.t. & v.i.* **·vat·ed, ·vat·ing** *Informal* To put on decorative touches; dress up: also spelled *tittivate.* [? < TIDY, on analogy with *cultivate*] — **tit′i·va′tion** *n.*

tit·lark (tit′lärk′) *n.* A pipit. [ME *tit* little thing + LARK]

ti·tle (tīt′l) *n.* **1.** The name of a book, play, poem, motion picture, etc. **2.** An appellation significant of office, rank, etc.; esp., a designation of nobility. **3.** A characteristic or descriptive name; epithet. **4.** A claim based on an acknowledged or alleged right. **5.** In some sports, a championship. **6.** The subtitle in a motion picture. **7.** *Law* The means whereby the owner of lands has the just possession of his property; the union of possession, the right of possession, and the right of property in lands and tenements; also, the legal evidence of one's right of property, or the means by or source from which one's right to property has accrued: *title* by purchase. — *v.t.* **ti·tled, ti·tling** To give a name or title to; entitle; call. [< OF < L *titulus* label, inscription] — **ti′tled** *adj.*

title page A page containing the title of a work and the names of its author and publisher.

title role The role of the character in a play, opera, or motion picture for whom it is named.

tit·mouse (tit′mous′) *n.* *pl.* **·mice** (-mīs′) Any of several small birds related to the nuthatches; esp., the tufted titmouse of the U.S., having a conspicuous crest. [Alter. of ME *titmuse* < *tit-* little + OE *mase* titmouse]

ti·trate (tī′trāt, tit′rāt) *v.i. & v.t.* **·trat·ed, ·trat·ing** *Chem.* To determine the strength of (a solution) by means of standard solutions or by titration. [< F *titre* the fineness of gold or silver alloy]

ti·tra·tion (tī·trā′shən, ti-) *n. Chem.* The process of determining the strength or concentration of the ingredients of a solution by adding measured amounts of a suitable reagent until the desired chemical reaction has been effected.

tit-tat-toe (tĭt′tat-tō′) *n.* Ticktacktoe.

tit·ter (tĭt′ər) *v.i.* To laugh in a suppressed way, as from nervousness or in ridicule; snicker; giggle. — *n.* The act of tittering. [Imit.] **— tit′ter·er** *n.* **— tit′ter·ing·ly** *adv.*

tit·ti·vate (tĭt′ə·vāt) See TITIVATE.

tit·tle (tĭt′l) *n.* 1. The minutest quantity; iota. 2. Originally, a very small mark in writing, as the dot over an *i.* 3. Any diacritical mark. [< L *titulus* label, inscription]

tit·tle-tat·tle (tĭt′l·tat′l) *n.* 1. Foolish or trivial talk; gossip. 2. An idle, trifling, or tattling talker. — *v.i.* **·tled, ·tling** To talk foolishly or idly; gossip. [Reduplication of TATTLE]

tit·u·lar (tich′ŏŏ·lər, tĭt′yə-) *adj.* 1. Existing in name or title only; nominal. 2. Of, pertaining to, or like a title. 3. Bestowing or taking title. Also **tit′u·lar·y** (-ler′ē). [< L *titulus* title] **— tit′u·lar·ly** *adv.*

Ti·tus (tī′təs) A disciple of the apostle Paul. — *n.* A book in the New Testament consisting of an epistle addressed to Titus and attributed to Paul.

tiz·zy (tĭz′ē) *n. pl.* **·zies** *Slang* A bewildered or excited state of mind; a dither. [Origin unknown]

TNT (tē′en′tē′) *n.* 1. Trinitrotoluene. 2. *Informal* Any explosive and dangerous circumstance, force, or person.

to (tōō, *unstressed* tə) *prep.* 1. In a direction toward or terminating in: going *to* town. 2. Opposite, in contact with, or near: face *to* face. 3. Intending or aiming at; having as an object or purpose: Come *to* my rescue. 4. Resulting in; having as a condition or effect: frozen *to* death. 5. Belonging or used in connection with: the key *to* the door. 6. Accompanied by; in rhythm with: March *to* the music. 7. In honor of: Drink *to* me only with thine eyes. 8. In comparison, correspondence, or agreement with: often denoting ratio: four quarts *to* the gallon. 9. Approaching as a limit; until: five minutes *to* one. 10. For the utmost duration of; as far as: a miser *to* the end of his days. 11. In respect of; concerning: blind *to* her charms. 12. In close application toward: Buckle down *to* work. 13. For; with regard for: The contest is open *to* everyone. 14. Noting an indirect or limiting object after verbs, adjectives, or nouns, and designating the recipient of the action: taking the place of the dative case in other languages: Give the ring *to* me. 15. By: known *to* the world. 16. From the point of view of: It seems *to* me. 17. About; involved in: That's all there is *to* it. ♦ *To* also serves to indicate the infinitive, and is often used elliptically for it: You may come if you care *to.* — *adv.* 1. To or toward something. 2. In a direction, position, or state understood or implied; esp., shut or closed: Pull the door *to.* 3. Into a normal condition; into consciousness: She soon came *to.* 4. *Naut.* With head to the wind: said of a sailing vessel: to lie *to.* 5. Upon the matter at hand; into action or operation: They fell *to* with good will. 6. Nearby; at hand. [OE *tō*]

toad (tōd) *n.* 1. A tailless, jumping, insectivorous amphibian resembling the frog but without teeth in the upper jaw, and resorting to water only to breed. 2. A lizard, the horned toad. 3. Any person regarded scornfully or contemptuously. [OE *tāde*]

toad·fish (tōd′fish′) *n. pl.* **·fish** or **·fish·es** Any of various fishes of the Atlantic coast of the U.S., having scaleless skin, and a mouth and head resembling those of a toad.

toad·stool (tōd′stōōl′) *n.* 1. A mushroom. 2. *Informal* A poisonous mushroom.

toad·y (tōd′ē) *n. pl.* **toad·ies** An obsequious flatterer; a fawning, servile person. — *v.t. & v.i.* **toad·ied, toad·y·ing** To act the toady (to). [Short for *toadeater* an assistant to a charlatan, who ate, or pretended to eat, toads to show the efficacy of a patent medicine] **— toad′y·ish** *adj.* **— toad′y·ism** *n.*

to-and-fro (tōō′ən·frō′) *adj.* Moving back and forth.

to and fro In opposite or different directions.

toast¹ (tōst) *v.t.* 1. To brown before or over a fire; esp., to brown (bread or cheese) before a fire or in a toaster. 2. To warm thoroughly before a fire. — *v.i.* 3. To become warm or toasted. — *n.* Sliced bread browned in a toaster or at a fire. [< OF < L *tostus*, pp. of *torrere* to parch, roast]

toast² (tōst) *n.* 1. The act of drinking to someone's health or to some sentiment. 2. A person or sentiment named in so drinking. — *v.t.* 1. To drink to the health of or in honor of. — *v.i.* 2. To drink a toast. [< TOAST¹, in obs. sense of "a spiced piece of toast put in a drink to flavor it"]

toast·er¹ (tōs′tər) *n.* A device for making toast.

toast·er² (tōs′tər) *n.* One who proposes a toast.

toast·mas·ter (tōst′mas′tər, -mäs′tər) *n.* A person who, at public dinners, announces the toasts, calls upon the various speakers, etc. **— toast′mis′tress** (-mis′tris) *n.fem.*

to·bac·co (tə·bak′ō) *n. pl.* **·cos** or **·coes** 1. An annual plant of the nightshade family. 2. Its leaves prepared in various ways, as for smoking, chewing, etc. 3. The use of tobacco for smoking. 4. The various products prepared from tobacco leaves, as cigarettes, cigars, etc. [< Sp. *tabaco* < Carib, a tube or pipe used in smoking tobacco]

to·bac·co·nist (tə·bak′ə·nist) *n.* One who sells tobacco.

To·bit (tō′bit) A pious Hebrew captive in Nineveh, hero of the Apocryphal book of the Old Testament. — *n.* The Old Testament book bearing his name. Also **To·bi·as** (tə·bī′əs).

to·bog·gan (tə·bog′ən) *n.* A light sledlike vehicle, consisting of a long thin board or boards curved upward at the forward end, used for transporting goods or coasting. — *v.i.* 1. To coast on a toboggan. 2. To move downward swiftly: Wheat prices *tobogganed*. [< dial. F (Canadian) *tabagan* sleigh < Algonquian] **— to·bog′gan·er, to·bog′gan·ist** *n.*

to·by (tō′bē) *n. pl.* **·bies** A mug or jug for ale or beer, often made in the form of an old man wearing a three-cornered hat. [after *Toby*, dim. of *Tobias*, a personal name]

toc·ca·ta (tə·kä′tə, *Ital.* tôk·kä′tä) *n. Music* A free composition for a keyboard instrument, sometimes written to show virtuosity. [< Ital., orig. pp. fem. of *toccare* to touch]

toco- *combining form* Child; pertaining to children or to childbirth. Also, before vowels, **toc-**. [< Gk. *tokos* child]

to·coph·er·ol (tō·kof′ə·rōl, -rol) *n. Biochem.* Any of four closely related alcohols, widely distributed in nature and forming the active principle of vitamin E. [< TOCO- + Gk. *pherein* to bear + -OL¹]

toc·sin (tok′sin) *n.* 1. A signal sounded on a bell; alarm. 2. An alarm bell. [< MF < OF < Provençal < *tocar* to strike, touch + *senh* bell < L *signum* sign]

to·day (tə·dā′) *adv.* 1. On or during this present day. 2. At the present time; nowadays. — *n.* 1. The present day, time, or age. Also **to-day′**. [OE < *tō* to + *dæg* day]

tod·dle (tod′l) *v.i.* **·dled, ·dling** To walk unsteadily and with short steps, as a little child. — *n.* The act of toddling; also, a stroll. [Origin uncertain] **— tod′dler** *n.*

tod·dy (tod′ē) *n. pl.* **·dies** 1. A drink made with spirits, hot water, sugar, and a slice of lemon. 2. The sap or juice of certain East Indian trees, the **toddy palms.** 3. A spirituous liquor distilled from these palms. [< Hind. *tārī* toddy (def. 2) < *tār* palm tree]

to-do (tə·dōō′) *n. Informal* Confusion or bustle; fuss. [OE < *to-* asunder + *dōn* to do, put]

toe (tō) *n.* 1. One of the digits of the foot. 2. The forward part of the foot, as distinguished from the heel. The portion of a shoe, sock, stocking, skate, etc., that covers or corresponds in position with the toes. 3. The lower end or projection of something, resembling or suggestive of a toe. **— on one's toes** Alert; wide-awake. **— to tread on (someone's) toes** To trespass on (someone's) feelings, opinions, prejudices, etc. — *v.* **toed, toe·ing** *v.t.* 1. To touch with the toes: to *toe* the line. 2. To kick with the toe. 3. To furnish with a toe. 4. To drive (a nail or spike) obliquely; also, to attach (beams, etc.) end to end, by nails so driven. — *v.i.* 5. To stand or walk with the toes pointing in a specified direction: to *toe* out. **— to toe the mark (or line)** To abide by the rules; conform. [OE *tā*] **— toe′less** *adj.*

toed (tōd) *adj.* Having toes: chiefly in combination: *pigeon-toed*.

toe-dance (tō′dans′, -däns′) *v.i.* **-danced, -danc·ing** To dance on tiptoe; perform a toe dance. **— toe dancer**

toe dance A dance performed on tiptoe.

toe·hold (tō′hōld′) *n.* 1. A small space that supports the toes in climbing. 2. Any means of entrance, support, etc.; a footing: to gain a *toehold* on the island. 3. A hold in which a wrestler bends back the foot of his opponent.

toe·nail (tō′nāl′) *n.* 1. A nail growing on the toe. 2. A nail driven obliquely to hold the foot of a stud or brace. — *v.t.* To fasten with obliquely driven nails.

tof·fee (tôf′ē, tof′ē) *n.* Taffy. Also **tof′fy.**

tog (tog) *Informal n. pl.* Clothes; outfit. — *v.t.* **togged, tog·ging** To dress; clothe: often with *up* or *out.* [Short for vagabond's cant *togemans* < F < L *toga*]

to·ga (tō′gə) *n. pl.* **·gas** or **·gae** (-jē) 1. The distinctive outer garment worn in public by a citizen of ancient Rome. 2. Any gown or cloak characteristic of a calling or profession: the lawyer's *toga.* [< L *tegere* to cover] **— to′gaed** (-gəd) *adj.*

TOGA

to·geth·er (tōō·geth′ər, tə-) *adv.* 1. Into union or contact with each other. 2. In the same place or at the same spot; with each other; in company. 3. At the same moment of time; simultaneously. 4. Without cessation or intermission. 5. With one another; mutually. [OE < *tō* to + *gædre* together]

tog·ger·y (tog′ər·ē) *n. pl.* **·ger·ies** *Informal* 1. Togs collectively; clothes. 2. A clothing shop.

tog·gle (tog/əl) *n.* A pin, or short rod, properly attached in the middle, as to a rope, and designed to be passed through a hole or eye and turned. — *v.t.* **·gled, ·gling** To fix, fasten, or furnish with a toggle. [Prob. var. of *tuggle,* freq. of TUG]

toggle joint *Mech.* A joint having a central hinge like an elbow, and operable by applying the power at the junction, thus changing the direction of force and giving indefinite mechanical pressure.

toggle switch *Electr.* A switch in the form of a projecting lever whose movement through a small arc opens or closes an electric circuit.

toil¹ (toil) *n.* **1.** Fatiguing work; labor. **2.** Any oppressive task. **3.** Any notable work accomplished by labor. — *v.i.* **1.** To work arduously; labor painfully and tiringly. **2.** To progress or make one's way with slow and labored steps. [< AF < OF < L *tudicular* to stir about] — **toil/er** *n.*
— **Syn.** (noun) **1.** Work, labor, drudgery.

toil² (toil) *n.* **1.** *Usu. pl.* Something that binds or ensnares, as a net. **2.** *Archaic* A net, snare, or other trap. [< MF < OF < L *tela* web]

toile (twäl) *n.* A sheer linen fabric; also, a fine cretonne with scenic designs printed in one color. [< F. See TOIL².]

toi·let (toi/lit) *n.* **1.** *U.S.* **a** A room with a washbowl, water closet, etc.: sometimes called *bathroom.* **b** A hopper flushed and discharged by means of water, into which one urinates or defecates: also called *water closet.* **2.** The act of dressing oneself; formerly, esp. of dressing the hair. **3.** Attire. — *adj.* Used in dressing or grooming: *toilet* articles. [< F *toilette* orig., cloth dressing gown, dim. of *toile* cloth]

toi·let·ry (toi/lit·rē) *n. pl.* **·ries** Any of the several articles used in making one's toilet, as soap, comb, brush, etc.

toi·lette (toi·let/, *Fr.* twà·let/) *n.* **1.** The act or process of grooming oneself, usu. including bathing, hairdressing, etc. **2.** A person's actual dress or style of dress. [< F]

toilet water A scented liquid containing a small amount of alcohol, used in or after the bath, after shaving, etc.

toil·some (toil/səm) *adj.* Accomplished with fatigue; involving toil. — **toil/some·ly** *adv.* — **toil/some·ness** *n.*

toil·worn (toil/wôrn/, -wōrn/) *adj.* Exhausted by toil; showing the effects of toil.

To·kay (tō·kā/) *n.* **1.** A white or reddish blue grape. **2.** A wine made from it. [after *Tokay,* Hungary]

to·ken (tō/kən) *n.* **1.** Anything indicative of some other thing; a visible sign. **2.** A symbol: a *token* of my affection. **3.** Some tangible proof or evidence of a statement or of one's identity, etc. **4.** A memento; souvenir. **5.** A characteristic mark or feature. **6.** A piece of metal issued as currency and having a face value greater than its actual value. **7.** A piece of metal issued by a transportation company and good for one fare. — *v.t.* To evidence by a token; betoken. — *adj.* Done or given as a token, esp. in partial fulfillment of an obligation. [OE *tācen, tācn*]

to·ken·ism (tō/kən·iz·əm) *n.* The policy of attempting to meet certain conditions by symbolic or token efforts.

told (tōld) Past tense and past participle of TELL.

To·le·do (tə·lē/dō) *n. pl.* **·dos** A sword or sword blade from Toledo, Spain. Also **to·le/do.**

tol·er·a·ble (tol/ər·ə·bəl) *adj.* **1.** Passably good; commonplace. **2.** Endurable. **3.** Allowable; permissible. **4.** *Informal* In passably good health. [< OF < L *tolerare* to endure] — **tol/er·a·ble·ness** *n.* — **tol/er·a·bly** *adv.*

tol·er·ance (tol/ər·əns) *n.* **1.** The character, state, or quality of being tolerant. **2.** Freedom from bigotry or from racial or religious prejudice. **3.** The act of enduring, or the capacity for endurance. **4.** A small permissible allowance for variations from the specified weight, dimensions, etc. **5.** *Med.* Ability to tolerate, as a drug.

tol·er·ant (tol/ər·ənt) *adj.* **1.** Disposed to tolerate beliefs, views, etc. **2.** Indulgent; liberal. **3.** *Med.* Capable of taking with impunity unusual or excessive doses of dangerous drugs. — **tol/er·ant·ly** *adv.*

tol·er·ate (tol/ə·rāt) *v.t.* **·at·ed, ·at·ing 1.** To allow to be or be done without active opposition. **2.** To concede, as the right to opinions or participation. **3.** To bear, sustain, or be capable of sustaining. **4.** *Med.* To endure, as a poisonous amount or dose, with impunity. [< L *toleratus,* pp. of *tolerare* to endure] — **tol/er·a/tive** *adj.* — **tol/er·a/tor** *n.*

tol·er·a·tion (tol/ə·rā/shən) *n.* **1.** The act or practice of tolerance. **2.** The recognition of the rights of the individual to his own opinions and customs, as in religious worship.

toll¹ (tōl) *n.* **1.** A fixed compensation for some privilege granted or service rendered, as passage on a bridge or turnpike. **2.** The right to levy such charge. **3.** Something taken or elicited like a toll; price: The train wreck took a heavy *toll* of lives. **4.** A due charged for shipping or landing goods. **5.** A charge for transportation of goods, esp. by rail or canal. **6.** A charge for a long-distance telephone call. [OE < LL < L < Gk. *telōnion* customhouse < *telos* tax]

toll² (tōl) *v.t.* **1.** To cause (a bell) to sound slowly and at regular intervals. **2.** To announce by tolling, as a death or funeral. **3.** To call or summon by tolling. **4.** To decoy (game, esp. ducks). — *v.i.* **5.** To sound slowly and at regular intervals. — *n.* The act or sound of tolling a bell. [ME *tollen, tullen*]

toll·bar (tōl/bär/) *n.* A tollgate, esp. one with a single bar.

toll bridge A bridge at which a toll is charged for passage.

toll call A long-distance telephone call, the charge for which is higher than local rates.

toll collector A collector of tolls.

toll·er (tō/lər) *n.* **1.** One who tolls a bell. **2.** A bell used for tolling. **3.** A small dog trained to toll or decoy ducks.

toll·gate (tōl/gāt/) *n.* A gate at the entrance to a bridge, or on a road, at which toll is paid.

toll·house (tōl/hous/) *n.* A toll collector's lodge adjoining a tollgate: also **toll/booth/** (-bōōth/, -bōōth/).

toll·keep·er (tōl/kē/pər) *n.* One who keeps a tollgate.

toll line A long-distance telephone line or channel for the use of which a toll is charged.

toll road A road on which a toll is charged for each vehicle using it. Also **toll·way** (tōl/wā/).

Tol·tec (tol/tek, tōl/-) *n.* One of certain ancient Nahuatlan tribes that dominated central and southern Mexico about A.D. 900–1100 and through contact with Mayan culture founded the highly civilized Nahua culture of the Aztecs. — *adj.* Of or pertaining to the Toltecs. [< Nahuatl *Tolteca*] — **Tol/tec·an** *adj.*

tol·u·ene (tol/yōō·ēn) *n. Chem.* A colorless, flammable liquid hydrocarbon, $C_6H_5CH_3$, obtained from coal tar by distillation and used in making dyestuffs, explosives, etc.

tom (tom) *n.* The male of various animals, esp. the cat. [after *Tom,* a personal name. See TOMCAT.]

tom·a·hawk (tom/ə·hôk) *n.* **1.** An axlike weapon used by North American Indians, originally a carved club in which a piece of bone or metal was inserted. **2.** Any similar weapon, tool, etc. — *v.t.* To strike or kill with a tomahawk. [< Algonquian < *tamahaken* he uses for cutting]

tom·al·ley (tom/al·ē) *n.* The liver of the lobster, considered a delicacy. [Prob. < Carib]

Tom and Jer·ry (tom/ ən jer/ē) A drink made with brandy, rum, beaten egg, hot milk or water, sugar, and nutmeg. [after two main characters in *Life in London,* 1821, by Pierce Egan, 1772–1849]

to·ma·to (tə·mā/tō, -mä/-) *n. pl.* **·toes 1.** The large, pulpy, edible berry, yellow or red when ripe, of a perennial plant of the nightshade family, widely cultivated as a vegetable. **2.** The plant itself. **3.** *U.S. Slang* A girl or woman. [< Sp. < Nahuatl *tomatl*]

tomb (tōōm) *n.* **1.** A place for the burial of the dead, as a vault or grave. **2.** Any place or structure serving as a final repository for the dead. **3.** A monument, tombstone, etc., commemorating the dead. **4.** Death: often preceded by *the.* [< AF *tumbe,* OF *tombe* < LL < Gk. *tymbos* mound]

tom·boy (tom/boi/) *n.* A girl who prefers boyish activities, dress, etc. — **tom/boy/ish** *adj.* — **tom/boy/ish·ness** *n.*

tomb·stone (tōōm/stōn/) *n.* A stone, usu. inscribed, marking a place of burial.

tom·cat (tom/kat/) *n.* A male cat. [after *Tom,* a male cat, hero of *The Life and Adventures of a Cat,* 1760]

Tom Col·lins (tom kol/inz) A drink consisting of gin, lemon or lime juice, sugar, and carbonated water.

Tom, Dick, and Har·ry (dik/ har/ē) Any persons taken at random from the general public: used disparagingly, and often preceded by *every.*

tome (tōm) *n.* **1.** A volume; large book. **2.** One of a series of volumes. [< MF < L < Gk. *tomos* fragment]

-tome *combining form* A cutting instrument (of a specified kind). [< Gk. *tomos* a cutting < *temnein* to cut]

tom·fool (tom/fōōl/) *n.* An idiotic or silly person. — *adj.* Very stupid or foolish. [after *Tom Fool,* a name formerly applied to mental defectives]

tom·fool·er·y (tom/fōō/lər·ē) *n. pl.* **·er·ies 1.** Nonsensical or foolish behavior. **2.** Worthless or trivial stuff; frippery. Also **tom/fool/ish·ness** (-fōō/lish·nis).

tom·my (tom/ē) *n. pl.* **·mies** *Brit. Informal Often cap.* A British soldier.

Tommy gun A Thompson submachine gun.

tom·my·rot (tom/ē·rot/) *n. Informal* Utter nonsense.

to·mor·row (tə·môr/ō, -mor/ō) *adv.* On or for the next day after today. — *n.* **1.** The next day after today; the morrow. **2.** Some time in the future. Also **to·mor/row.** [ME < OE < *tō* to + *morgen* morning, morrow]

tom·pi·on (tom/pē·ən) See TAMPION.

Tom Thumb 1. In English folklore, a hero who was no bigger than his father's thumb. **2.** A tiny person.

tom·tit (tom/tit/) *n.* Any of various small birds, as a chickadee or a wren. [< TOM + TIT¹]

tom-tom (tom/tom/) *n.* A drum of India, Africa, etc., variously shaped and usu. beaten with the hands. [< Hind. *tamtam,* imit. of the instrument's sound]

-tomy *combining form* **1.** *Surg.* A cutting of a (specified) part or tissue. **2.** A (specified) kind of cutting or division: *dichotomy.* [< Gk. *tomē* a cutting < *temnein* to cut]

ton (tun) *n.* **1.** Any of several large measures of weight; esp.: **a** The **short ton** of 2000 pounds avoirdupois, commonly used in the U.S. and Canada. **b** The **long** or **gross ton** of 2240 pounds, used in Great Britain. See table inside back cover. **2.** A unit for reckoning the displacement or weight of vessels, 35 cubic feet of sea water weighing about one long ton: called in full a **displacement ton**. **3.** A unit for reckoning the freight-carrying capacity of a ship, usu. equivalent to 40 cubic feet of space but varying with the cargo: called in full a **freight ton** or **measurement ton**. **4.** A unit for reckoning the internal capacity of merchant vessels for purposes of registration, equivalent to 100 cubic feet or 2.8317 cubic meters: called in full a **register ton**. **5.** A metric ton. [Var. of TUN.]

ton- Var. of TONO-.

-ton *suffix* Town: used in place names: *Charleston*. [OE < *tūn*]

to·nal (tō′nəl) *adj.* Of or pertaining to tone or tonality. — **to′nal·ly** *adv.*

to·nal·i·ty (tō-nal′ə-tē) *n. pl.* **·ties** **1.** *Music* **a** The use of a system of tones so that one tone is the central or primary tone of the system. **b** Any particular arrangement of this type centering on a specific tone; key; mode. **2.** The general color scheme or collective tones of a painting.

tone (tōn) *n.* **1.** Sound in relation to quality, volume, duration, and pitch. **2.** A sound having a definite pitch. **3.** *Music* **a** The timbre, or characteristic sound, of a voice, instrument, etc. **b** The interval between the first two degrees of a major scale: also called *whole tone*. **4.** A predominating disposition; mood. **5.** Characteristic style or tendency; tenor. **6.** Style or distinction; elegance. **7.** Vocal inflection as expressive of feeling: a *tone* of pity. **8.** *Phonet.* **a** The acoustical pitch, or change in pitch, of a phrase or sentence. **b** Special stress or pitch accent given to a syllable or word. **9.** The prevailing impression of a picture, produced by effects of light and shadow, variations in color quality, etc. **10.** A shade, hue, tint, or degree of a particular color, or some slight modification of it: red with a purplish *tone*. **11.** *Physiol.* **a** The general condition of the body with reference to the vigorous and healthy discharge of its functions. **b** Firmness and resilience, as of a tissue. — **Syn.** See SOUND[1]. — *v.* **toned, ton·ing** *v.t.* **1.** To give tone to. **2.** To modify in tone. **3.** To alter the color or increase the brilliancy of (a photographic print) by a chemical bath. **4.** *Rare* To intone. — *v.i.* **5.** To assume a certain tone or hue. **6.** To blend or harmonize, as in tone or shade. — **to tone down 1.** To subdue the tone of (a painting). **2.** To moderate in quality or tone. — **to tone up 1.** To raise in quality or strength. **2.** To gain in vitality. [< OF < L < Gk. *teinein* to stretch]

tone color The timbre of a voice, musical instrument, etc.

tone-deaf (tōn′def′) *adj.* Unable to perceive fine distinctions in pitch, as musical intervals. — **tone′deaf′ness** *n.*

tone·less (tōn′lis) *adj.* **1.** Having no tone; without tone. **2.** Lacking spirit or vivacity; listless. — **tone′less·ly** *adv.* — **tone′less·ness** *n.*

tong[1] (tông, tong) *v.t.* **1.** To gather, collect, or seize with tongs. — *v.i.* **2.** To use tongs, as for fishing. [< TONGS]

tong[2] (tông, tong) *n.* A Chinese secret society or fraternal association; esp., such a group formerly active in the U.S. [< Chinese *t'ang* hall, meeting place]

Ton·ga (tong′gə) *n.* A Polynesian language spoken in the Tonga Islands.

tongs (tôngz, tongz) *n.pl.* (*sometimes construed as sing.*) An implement for grasping, holding, or lifting objects, consisting usu. of a pair of pivoted levers: sometimes called a **pair of tongs**. [OE *tang, tange*]

tongue (tung) *n.* **1.** A protrusile, freely moving organ situated in the mouth of most vertebrates, highly developed in mammals, where it serves as an organ of taste, and in man also as an organ of speech. ◆ Collateral adjective: *lingual*. For illus. see THROAT. **2.** *Zool.* An analogous organ or part of the mouth of various insects, fishes, etc. **3.** An animal's tongue, as of beef, prepared as food. **4.** The power of speech or articulation: to lose one's *tongue*. **5.** Manner or style of speaking: a smooth *tongue*. **6.** Mere speech, as contrasted with fact or deed. **7.** Utterance. **8.** A language, vernacular, or dialect. **9.** *Archaic* A people or race, regarded as having its own language: a Biblical use. **10.** Anything resembling an animal tongue in shape or function. **11.** A slender projection of land, as a cape or small promontory. **12.** A long narrow bay or inlet of water. **13.** A jet of flame. **14.** A strip of leather for closing the gap in the front of a shoe. **15.** *Music* The free or vibrating end of a reed in a wind instrument. **16.** The clapper of a bell. **17.** The harnessing pole of a horse-drawn vehicle. **18.** Any flange or projecting part of a machine or mechanical device. **19.** A projecting edge or tenon of a board for insertion into a corresponding groove of another board, thus forming a **tongue-and-groove joint.** — **on the tip of one's tongue** On the verge of being recalled. — **to**

hold one's tongue To keep silent. — **(with) tongue in cheek** With ironical or facetious intent. — *v.* **tongued, tongu·ing** *v.t.* **1.** *Music* In wind-instrument playing: **a** To separate the tones played on (an instrument) by means of the tongue. **b** To begin (a tone) using the tongue. **c** To tongue the notes of (a phrase, etc.). **2.** To touch or lap with the tongue. **3.** In carpentry: **a** To cut a tongue on (a board). **b** To join or fit by a tongue-and-groove joint. **4.** *Poetic* To utter; articulate. — *v.i.* **5.** To use the tongue in playing a wind instrument. **6.** To talk or prattle. **7.** To extend as a tongue. [OE *tunge*]

tongued (tungd) *adj.* **1.** Having a tongue or tongues. **2.** Having or characterized by a (specified kind of) tongue or (a specified number of) tongues: *sharp-tongued.*

tongue-lash·ing (tung′lash′ing) *n.* *Informal* A severe or thoroughgoing reprimand; scolding.

tongue·less (tung′lis) *adj.* **1.** Having no tongue. **2.** Speechless; dumb.

tongue-tie (tung′tī′) *n.* Abnormal shortness of the frenum of the tongue, whereby its motion is impeded or confined. — *v.t.* **-tied, -ty·ing** To deprive of speech or the power of speech, or of distinct articulation.

tongue-tied (tung′tīd′) *adj.* **1.** Speechless or halting in speech, as from shyness, etc. **2.** Impeded by tongue-tie.

tongue twister A word or phrase difficult to articulate quickly, as "Miss Smith's fish-sauce shop."

ton·ic (ton′ik) *adj.* **1.** Having power to invigorate or build up; bracing. **2.** Pertaining to tone or tones. **3.** *Music* Pertaining to or in the key of the keynote. **4.** In art, denoting the general effect of color or of light and shade. **5.** *Physiol.* **a** Of or pertaining to tension, especially muscular tension. **b** Rigid; unrelaxing: *tonic* spasm. **6.** *Phonet.* Stressed, as a syllable. — *n.* **1.** A medicine that gradually restores the normal tone of organs from a condition of debility. **2.** Something imparting animation, vigor, or tone. **3.** *Music* The basic tone of a key or mode. **4.** Quinine water: gin and tonic. **5.** *U.S.* In the Boston area, soda (def. 2). [< Gk. < *tonos* sound, tone]

tonic accent An accent that is spoken or pronounced rather than written.

to·nic·i·ty (tō-nis′ə-tē) *n.* The resilience and elasticity of healthy muscles, arteries, and other bodily tissues.

tonic sol-fa A system of musical notation that uses the initial letters of the solmization syllables to indicate pitch, and dots and lines to indicate rhythm.

to·night (tə-nīt′) *adv.* In or during the present or coming night. — *n.* **1.** The night that follows this day. **2.** The present night. Also **to-night′.** [OE < *tō* + *niht* night]

ton·nage (tun′ij) *n.* **1.** The cubic capacity of a merchant vessel expressed in tons of 100 cubic feet each. **2.** The total carrying capacity of a collection of vessels, esp. of a country's merchant marine. **3.** A tax levied on vessels at a given rate per ton. **4.** Total weight in tons, as of materials produced, mined, or transported.

ton·neau (tu-nō′) *n. pl.* **·neaus** (-nōz′) or **·neaux** (-nōz′) The rear part of an early type of automobile or vehicle, with seats enclosed by low sides. [< F, lit., barrel]

tono- *combining form* **1.** Tension; pressure. **2.** *Music* Tone; pitch. Also, before vowels, *ton-*. [< Gk. *tonos* tension < *teinein* to stretch]

ton·sil (ton′səl) *n. Anat.* One of two oval lymphoid organs situated on either side of the passage from the mouth to the pharynx. For illus. see THROAT. [< L *tonsillae* tonsils] — **ton′sil·lar** or **ton′sil·ar** *adj.*

ton·sil·lec·to·my (ton′sə-lek′tə-mē) *n. pl.* **·mies** *Surg.* Removal of a tonsil or tonsils.

ton·sil·li·tis (ton′sə-lī′tis) *n. Pathol.* Inflammation of the tonsils. — **ton′sil·lit′ic** (-lit′ik) *adj.*

ton·so·ri·al (ton-sôr′ē-əl, sō′rē) *adj.* Pertaining to a barber or barbering: chiefly in the humorous term **tonsorial artist**, a barber. [< L < *tonsus*, pp. of *tondere* to clip]

ton·sure (ton′shər) *n.* **1.** The shaving of the head, or of the crown of the head, as of a priest or monk. **2.** The state of being thus shaven. **3.** The part of a priest's or monk's head left bare by shaving. — *v.t.* **·sured, ·sur·ing** To shave the head of. [< OF < L. See TONSORIAL.]

ton·tine (ton′tēn, ton-tēn′) *n.* A form of collective life annuity, the individual profits of which increase as the number of survivors diminishes, the final survivor taking the whole. [< F, after Lorenzo *Tonti*, a Neopolitan banker who introduced it into France in about 1653]

ton·y (tō′nē) *adj.* **ton·i·er, ton·i·est** *Informal* High toned; fashionable; stylish. [< TONE (def. 6)]

too (too) *adv.* **1.** In addition; likewise; also. **2.** In excessive quantity or degree; more than sufficiently. **3.** *Informal* Very; extremely: That's not too likely. **4.** *Informal* Indeed: an intensive, often used to reiterate a contradicted statement: You are *too* going! [Stressed var. of OE *tō* to]

took (tŏŏk) Past tense of TAKE.

tool (tōōl) *n.* **1.** A simple mechanism or implement, as a hammer, saw, spade, or chisel, used chiefly in manual work. **2.** A power-driven apparatus, as a lathe, used for cutting and shaping the parts of a machine. **3.** The cutting or shaping part of such an apparatus. **4.** A bookbinder's hand stamp used in lettering or ornamenting book covers. **5.** A person used to carry out the designs of others or another; a dupe. **6.** Any instrument or means necessary to the efficient prosecution of one's profession or trade: Words are the writer's *tools.* — *v.t.* **1.** To shape, mark, or ornament with a tool. **2.** To provide with tools. **3.** To ornament or impress designs upon (leather, a book binding, etc.) with a roller bearing a pattern. — *v.i.* **4.** To work with a tool or tools. [OE *tōl*] — **tool′er** *n.*

tool·ing (tōō′ling) *n.* **1.** Ornamentation or work done with tools; esp., stamped or gilded ornamental designs on leather. **2.** The application of a tool or tools to any work.

tool·mak·er (tōōl′mā′kər) *n.* A maker of tools.

toot (tōōt) *v.i.* **1.** To blow a horn, whistle, etc., esp. with short blasts. **2.** To give forth a blast or toot, as a horn. **3.** To make a similar sound. — *v.t.* **4.** To sound (a horn, etc.) with short blasts. **5.** To sound (a blast, etc.). — *n.* **1.** A short note or blast on or as on a horn. **2.** *Slang* A spree; esp., a drinking spree. [? < MLG *tūten*; prob. orig. imit.] — **toot′er** *n.*

tooth (tōōth) *n. pl.* **teeth** (tēth) **1.** One of the hard structures in the mouth of most vertebrates, used for seizing and chewing food, as offensive and defensive weapons, etc. ◆ Collateral adjective: *dental.* **2.** One of various hard calcareous or chitinous bodies of the oral or gastric regions of invertebrates. **3.** Any small toothlike projection, as at the edge of a leaf. **4.** Something resembling a tooth in form or use; esp., a projecting point, tine, or cog, as on a saw, comb, fork, rake, or gearwheel. **5.** Appetite; liking: used chiefly in the expression *sweet tooth.* **6.** *pl.* Something that opposes in or as in a gnawing, biting, or piercing manner: the *teeth* of the wind. — **armed to the teeth** Completely or heavily armed. — **in the teeth of** Directly against, counter to, or in defiance of. — **to get one's teeth into** To achieve a solid grip or grasp of; engage completely with. — **to show one's teeth** To display a disposition to fight; threaten. — **to throw (cast, fling,** etc.**) (something) in one's teeth** To fling at one, as a challenge or taunt. — *v.t.* **1.** To supply with teeth, as a rake or saw. **2.** To give a serrated edge to; indent. — *v.i.* **3.** To become interlocked, as gear wheels. [OE *tōth*]

tooth·ache (tōōth′āk′) *n.* Pain in a tooth or teeth.

tooth and nail With all possible strength and effort; fiercely: to fight *tooth and nail.*

tooth·brush (tōōth′brush′) *n.* A small brush used for cleaning the teeth.

toothed (tōōtht, tōōthd) *adj.* **1.** Having teeth. **2.** Having or characterized by a (specified kind or number of) teeth: used in combination: *sharp-toothed.* **3.** Notched or indented.

tooth·less (tōōth′lis) *adj.* **1.** Being without teeth. **2.** Lacking effective power or force; ineffectual. — **tooth′less·ly** *adv.*

tooth·paste (tōōth′pāst′) *n.* A paste used to clean teeth.

tooth·pick (tōōth′pik′) *n.* A small sliver of wood, plastic, etc., used for removing particles of food from between the teeth.

tooth·pow·der (tōōth′pou′dər) *n.* A powder used in cleaning the teeth.

tooth·some (tōōth′səm) *adj.* **1.** Having a pleasant taste. **2.** Appetizing; attractive. — **tooth′some·ly** *adv.* — **tooth′some·ness** *n.*

tooth·y (tōō′thē) *adj.* **tooth·i·er, tooth·i·est** **1.** Having large or prominent teeth. **2.** Displaying the teeth: a *toothy* smile.

too·tle (tōōt′l) *v.t. & v.i.* **·tled, ·tling** To toot lightly or continuously, as on the flute. — *n.* The act or sound of tootling. [Freq. of TOOT]

top¹ (top) *n.* **1.** The uppermost or highest part, end, side, or surface of anything. **2.** The end or part regarded as the higher or upper extremity: the *top* of the street. **3.** A lid or cover: a bottle *top.* **4.** *U.S.* The roof of a vehicle, as an automobile. **5.** The crown of the head: from *top* to toe. **6.** *pl.* The aboveground part of a plant producing root vegetables. **7.** The highest degree or range: the *top* of one's ambition. **8.** The highest or most prominent place or rank. **9.** One who is highest in rank or position. **10.** The highest or loudest pitch: at the *top* of his voice. **11.** The choicest or best

TEETH OF ADULT HUMAN

A Section of a molar: *a* Crown, *b* Enamel, *c* Pulp cavity, *d* Dentine, *e* Cementum, *f* Roots.

B and *C* Left upper and lower jaws: *g* Incisors, *h* Canines, *i* Bicuspids, *j* Molars, *k* Wisdom teeth.

part: the *top* of the crop. **12.** In bridge, etc., the highest card in a suit. **13.** In tennis, golf, etc.: **a** A stroke in which the player hits the ball above the center or on the upper half. **b** The forward spinning motion thus imparted to the ball. **14.** *Naut.* A platform at the head of the lower section of a ship's mast, used as a place to stand for and for extending the topmast rigging. — **to blow one's top** *Slang* **1.** To break out in a rage; flare up. **2.** To go insane. — **on top 1.** At the highest point or position. **2.** In a situation of dominance or power. **3.** Highly successful. — **on top of 1.** On the highest point or upper surface of. **2.** In addition to; as a climax to. — **over the top 1.** In trench warfare, over the breastwork, as in an attack. **2.** Beyond a set goal, quota, etc. — *adj.* **1.** Of or pertaining to the top. **2.** Forming or comprising the top or upper part. **3.** Highest in rank or quality; chief: *top* authors. **4.** Greatest in amount or degree: *top* prices. — *v.* **topped, top·ping** *v.t.* **1.** To remove the top or upper end of. **2.** To provide with a top, cap, etc. **3.** To form the top of. **4.** To reach or pass over the top of; surmount. **5.** To surpass or exceed. **6.** In golf, tennis, etc., to hit the upper part of (the ball) in making a stroke. — *v.i.* **7.** To top someone or something. — **to top off 1.** To put something on the top of. **2.** To complete or finish with a final or crowning touch. [OE]

top² (top) *n.* A toy with a point on which it is made to spin, as by the unwinding of a string, spring, etc. [OE]

top- Var. of TOPO-.

to·paz (tō′paz) *n.* **1.** A native silicate of aluminum, occurring in prismatic crystals of various colors, but chiefly yellow to brownish, that are valued as gemstones. **2.** A yellow variety of sapphire. Also **Oriental topaz. 3.** A brownish or grayish yellow. [< OF < L < Gk. *topazos*]

top boot A boot with a high top that is sometimes bordered or decorated with material different from the rest of the boot.

top·coat (top′kōt′) *n.* A lightweight overcoat.

top dog *Informal* The leading or dominant individual or group; the head; chief. — **top-dog** (top′dôg′, -dog′) *adj.*

top·draw·er (top′drôr′) *adj. Informal* Of the highest standing, merit, excellence, etc.

top-dress (top′dres′) *v.t. Agric.* To apply top-dressing to.

top-dress·ing (top′dres′ing) *n.* A dressing of manure spread over the surface of a field. Also **top′dress′ing, top dressing.**

tope (tōp) *v.t.* **tope, top·ing** To drink (alcoholic beverages) excessively and frequently. [? Akin to earlier *top* to tilt]

top·er (tō′pər) *n.* A habitual drunkard; sot. [< TOPE]

top·flight (top′flīt′) *adj.* Of the highest quality; superior.

top gal·lant (tə-gal′ənt, top′gal′ənt) *n. Naut.* **1.** The mast, sail, yard, or rigging immediately above the topmast and topsail. **2.** The parts of a deck that are higher than the rest. — *adj.* Pertaining to the topgallants. [< TOP¹ + GALLANT; with ref. to "making a gallant show" compared with the lower tops]

top hat A man's hat, usu. made of silk, having a tall, cylindrical crown and a narrow brim: also called *high hat.*

top-heav·y (top′hev′ē) *adj.* **-heav·i·er, -heav·i·est 1.** Having the top or upper part too heavy for the lower part; ill-proportioned or precariously balanced. **2.** In finance, over-capitalized. — **top′heav′i·ly** *adv.* — **top′heav′i·ness** *n.*

to·pi (tō·pē′) *n.* A helmet made of pith, worn as protection against the sun: also called *pith helmet.* [< Hind., hat]

top·ic (top′ik) *n.* **1.** A subject of discourse or of a treatise. **2.** Any matter treated of in speech or writing; a theme for discussion. **3.** A subdivision of an outline or a treatise. [< L < Gk. (*ta*) *topika*, title of a work by Aristotle, neut. pl. of *topikos* of a place < *topos* place, commonplace]

top·i·cal (top′i·kəl) *adj.* **1.** Pertaining to a topic. **2.** Of the nature of merely probable argument. **3.** Belonging to a place or spot; local. **4.** Pertaining to matters of present interest: a *topical* song. **5.** *Med.* Local. — **top′i·cal·ly** *adv.*

top kick *Slang* A top sergeant.

top·knot (top′not′) *n.* **1.** A crest, tuft, or knot on the top of the head, as of feathers on the head of a bird. **2.** The hair of the human head when worn as a high knot.

top·less (top′lis) *adj.* **1.** Lacking a top. **2.** Nude above the waist, or designed to include such nudity, as a bathing suit. — **top′less·ness** *n.*

top·loft·y (top′lôf′tē, -lof′tē) *adj.* **·loft·i·er, ·loft·i·est 1.** Towering very high. **2.** Very proud or haughty; inflated; pompous. — **top′loft′i·ly** *adv.* — **top′loft′i·ness** *n.*

top·mast (top′məst, top′mast′, mäst′) *n. Naut.* The mast next above the lower mast.

top·most (top′mōst′) *adj.* Being at the very top.

top notch (top′noch′) *adj. Informal* Excellent; best.

topo- *combining form* A place or region; regional. Also, before vowels, **top-.** [< Gk. *topos* place]

to·pog·ra·pher (tə·pog′rə·fər) *n.* An expert in topography.

to·pog·ra·phy (tə·pog′rə·fē) *n. pl.* **·phies 1.** The detailed description of places. **2.** The art of representing on a map the physical features of a place. **3.** The physical features, collectively, of a region. **4.** Surveying with reference to the physical features of a region. **—top·o·graph·ic** (top/ə·graf/-ik) or **-i·cal** *adj.* **—top/o·graph/i·cal·ly** *adv.*

top·per (top/ər) *n.* **1.** One who or that which cuts off the top of something. **2.** *Slang* One who or that which is of supreme quality. **3.** *Slang* A top hat. **4.** A woman's short, usu. lightweight, coat.

top·ping (top/ing) *adj. Brit. Informal* Excellent; first rate. **—** *n.* **1.** That which forms the top of anything. **2.** A sauce, garnish, etc., put on a cake, portion of food, etc.

top·ple (top/əl) *v.* **·pled, ·pling** *v.t.* **1.** To push and cause to totter or fall by its own weight; overturn. **—** *v.i.* **2.** To totter and fall, as by its own weight. **3.** To lean or jut out, as if about to fall. [Freq. of TOP[1], v.]

tops (tops) *adj. Slang* Excellent; first-rate.

top·sail (top/səl, top/sāl/) *n. Naut.* **1.** In a square-rigged vessel, a square sail set next above the lowest sail of a mast. **2.** In a fore-and-aft-rigged vessel, a square or triangular sail carried above the gaff of a lower sail.

top-se·cret (top/sē/krit) *adj. U.S. Mil.* Denoting the highest category of security classification. Compare SECRET.

top sergeant *Informal* The first sergeant of a company, battery, or troop.

top·side (top/sīd/) *n. Naut.* The portion of a ship above the main deck. **—** *adv.* To or on the upper parts of a ship.

top·soil (top/soil/) *n.* The surface soil of land.

top·sy-tur·vy (top/sē·tûr/vē) *adv.* **1.** Upside-down; hind side before. **2.** In utter confusion. **—** *adj.* **1.** Being in an upset or disordered condition. **2.** Upside-down. **—** *n.* A state of confusion; disorder; chaos. [Prob. < TOP[1] + obs. *terve* to turn, overturn] **—top/sy-tur/vi·ly** *adv.* **—top/sy-tur/vi·ness** *n.* **—top/sy-tur/vy·dom** (-dəm) *n.*

toque (tōk) *n.* A close-fitting, brimless hat worn by women. [< F, cap < Sp. < Basque *tauka*, a kind of cap]

to·rah (tôr/ə, tō/rə) *n.* In Hebrew literature, a law; also, counsel or instruction proceeding from a specially sacred source. Also **to/ra.** [< Hebrew *tōrāh* instruction, law]

To·rah (tôr/ə, tō/rə) *n.* In Judaism, the Pentateuch: also called *the Law.*

torch (tôrch) *n.* **1.** A source of light, as from flaming pine knots, or from some material dipped in tallow, etc., and fixed at the end of a handle. **2.** Anything that illuminates: the *torch* of science. **3.** A portable device giving off an intensely hot flame and used for burning off paint, melting solder, etc. **4.** *Brit.* A flashlight. **—to carry a** (or the) **torch for** *Slang* To continue to love (someone), though the love is unrequited. [< OF *torche*, ult. < L *torquere* to twist]

torch-bear·er (tôrch/bâr/ər) *n.* **1.** One who carries a torch. **2.** One who imparts knowledge, truth, etc.

tor·chère (tôr·shâr/) *n.* A tall lamp giving light directed upward by a bowllike shade. [< F, candelabrum]

torch-light (tôrch/līt/) *n.* The light of a torch or torches. **—** *adj.* Lighted by torches: a *torchlight* rally.

torch song A popular love song expressing sadness and hopeless yearning. [< phrase *to carry a torch for*]

tore (tôr, tōr) Past tense of TEAR[1].

tor·e·a·dor (tôr/ē·ə·dôr/, Sp. tô/rä·ä·thôr/) *n.* A bullfighter. [< Sp. < *torear* to fight bulls < L *taurus* bull]

to·ri·i (tôr/i·ē, tō/ri·ē) *n.* The gateway of a Shinto temple, consisting of two uprights with one straight crosspiece, and another above with a concave lintel. [< Japanese]

tor·ment (*n.* tôr/ment; *v.* tôr·ment/) *n.* **1.** Intense bodily pain or mental anguish; agony; torture. **2.** One who or that which torments. **—** *v.t.* **1.** To subject to excruciating physical or mental suffering. **2.** To make miserable. **3.** To harass. [< OF < L *tormentum* rack < *torquere* to twist] **—tor·ment/er, tor·men/tor** *n.* **—tor·ment/ing·ly** *adv.*

torn (tôrn, tōrn) Past participle of TEAR[1].

tor·na·do (tôr·nā/dō) *n. pl.* **·does** or **·dos** *Meteorol.* **1.** A whirling wind of exceptional violence, accompanied by a pendulous, funnel-shaped cloud marking the narrow path of greatest destruction. **2.** Any whirlwind or hurricane. [Prob. alter. of Sp. *tronada* thunderstorm < L *tonare* to thunder] **—tor·nad/ic** (-nad/ik) *adj.*

tor·pe·do (tôr·pē/dō) *n. pl.* **·dos** or **·does** **1.** A device or apparatus containing an explosive to be fired by concussion or otherwise. **2.** An explosive, self-propelled, cigar-shaped underwater projectile, used to destroy enemy ships. **3.** A submarine mine. **4.** The electric ray, a fish. **—** *v.t.* **·doed, ·do·ing** To sink, damage, or wreck with or as with a torpedo. [< L, numbness < *torpere* to be numb]

torpedo boat A small, swift war vessel equipped with tubes for the discharge of torpedoes.

tor·pid (tôr/pid) *adj.* **1.** Inactive, as a hibernating animal. **2.** Dormant; numb. **3.** Sluggish; apathetic; dull. [< L *torpere* to be numb] **—tor·pid·i·ty** (tôr·pid/ə·tē), **tor/pid·ness** *n.* **—tor/pid·ly** *adv.*

tor·por (tôr/pər) *n.* **1.** Complete or partial insensibility; stupor. **2.** Apathy; torpidity. **—tor/po·rif/ic** *adj.*

torque (tôrk) *n. Mech.* Anything that causes or tends to cause torsion in a body; the rotary force in a mechanism. [< L *torquere* to twist]

tor·rent (tôr/ənt, tor/-) *n.* **1.** A stream, as of water, flowing with great velocity or turbulence. **2.** Any abundant or tumultuous flow: a *torrent* of abuse. [< OF < L *torrens*, boiling, burning, ppr. of *torrere* to parch]

tor·ren·tial (tô·ren/shəl, to-) *adj.* **1.** Of, resembling, or resulting from the action of a torrent. **2.** Suggestive of a torrent; overpowering. **—tor·ren/tial·ly** *adv.*

tor·rid (tôr/id, tor/-) *adj.* **1.** Exposed to or receiving the full force of the sun's heat. **2.** Very hot; scorching; burning. **3.** Impassioned; ardent. [< L *torrere* to parch] **—tor·rid·i·ty** (tô·rid/ə·tē, to-), **tor/rid·ness** *n.* **—tor/rid·ly** *adv.*

tor·sion (tôr/shən) *n.* **1.** The act of twisting, or the state of being twisted. **2.** *Mech.* Deformation of a body, as a thread or rod, by twisting around its length as an axis. **3.** The force with which a twisted cord or cable tends to return to its former position. [< OF < LL < L < *torquere* to twist] **—tor/sion·al** *adj.* **—tor/sion·al·ly** *adv.*

tor·so (tôr/sō) *n. pl.* **·sos** or **·si** (-sē) **1.** The trunk of a human body. **2.** A sculptured representation of a human body without the head or limbs. **3.** Any truncated or defective thing. [< Ital. < L < Gk. *thyrsos* stalk]

tort (tôrt) *n. Law* Any private or civil wrong by act or omission for which a civil suit can be brought, but not including breach of contract. [See TORSION.]

torte (tôrt, *Ger.* tôr/tə) *n.* A rich cake made with butter, eggs, and often fruit and nuts. [< G < Ital. *torta*]

tor·til·la (tôr·tē/yä) *n.* In Mexico, a flat cake made of coarse cornmeal baked on a hot sheet of iron or a slab of stone. [< Sp., dim. of *torta* cake < LL < L *torquere* to twist]

tor·toise (tôr/təs) *n.* **1.** A turtle; esp., one of a terrestrial species as distinguished from those that are aquatic. **2.** A slow-moving person or thing. [< Med.L *tortuca*, ? < L *tortus* twisted; so called from its crooked feet]

tor·toise-shell (tôr/təs·shel/) *adj.* Made of or variegated like tortoise shell. Also **tor/toise·shell/.**

tortoise shell The shell of a marine turtle, consisting of a mottled, brownish, hornlike substance used for combs, etc.

tor·tu·ous (tôr/chōō·əs) *adj.* **1.** Consisting of or abounding in irregular bends or turns; twisting. **2.** Not straightforward; devious. **3.** Morally twisted or warped. [< AF < L *torquere* to twist] **—tor·tu·os/i·ty** (-os/ə·tē) *n.* **—tor/tu·ous·ly** *adv.* **—tor/tu·ous·ness** *n.*

tor·ture (tôr/chər) *n.* **1.** Infliction of or subjection to extreme physical pain. **2.** Great mental suffering; agony. **3.** Something that causes severe pain. **—** *v.t.* **·tured, ·tur·ing** **1.** To inflict extreme pain upon, as from cruelty. **2.** To subject to judicial torture. **3.** To cause to suffer agony, extreme discomfort, etc. **4.** To twist or turn into an abnormal form, meaning, etc. [< OF < L *torquere* to twist] **—tor/tur·er** *n.* **—tor/tur·ous** *adj.*

to·rus (tôr/əs, tō/rəs) *n. pl.* **to·ri** (tôr/ī, tō/rī) **1.** *Archit.* A large convex molding used in bases as the lowest molding, or in columns above the plinth. **2.** *Bot.* The swollen end of a flower-stalk that bears the floral leaves. **3.** *Geom.* A solid figure usu. resembling a doughnut. [< L, lit., a swelling]

To·ry (tôr/ē, tō/rē) *n. pl.* **·ries** **1.** A member of an English political party, successor to the Cavaliers and opponent of the Whigs, since about 1832 called the Conservative Party. **2.** One who at the period of the American Revolution adhered to the cause of British sovereignty over the colonies. **3.** One having very conservative beliefs, esp. in politics. Also **to/ry.** [< Irish *tóir* to pursue] **—To/ry·ism** *n.*

toss (tôs, tos) *v.t.* **1.** To throw, pitch, or fling about. **2.** To agitate; disturb. **3.** To throw with the hand, esp. with the palm of the hand upward. **4.** To lift with a quick motion, as the head. **5.** *Informal* To toss up with: I'll *toss* you to see who pays. **—** *v.i.* **6.** To be flung to and fro, as a ship in a storm. **7.** To throw oneself from side to side restlessly, as in sleep. **8.** To go quickly or angrily, as with a fling of the head. **9.** To toss up a coin. **—to toss off** **1.** To drink at one draft. **2.** To utter, write, or do in an offhand manner. **—to toss up** To throw a coin into the air to decide a wager or choice, the outcome depending on the side on which the coin falls. **—** *n.* **1.** The act of tossing; a pitch; also, the distance over which a thing is tossed. **2.** A quick upward or backward movement, as of the head. **3.** A tossup or wager. [Prob. < Scand.] **—toss/er** *n.*

toss-up (tôs/up/, tos/-) *n. Informal* **1.** The throwing up of a coin to decide a bet, etc. **2.** An even chance.

tot[1] (tot) *n.* **1.** A little child; toddler. **2.** A small amount or portion, as of liquor. [Origin unknown]

tot[2] (tot) *v.t.* **tot·ted, tot·ting** *Informal* To add; total: usu. with *up.* [Short for TOTAL]

to·tal (tōt/l) *n.* The whole sum or amount. **—** *adj.* **1.** Constituting or comprising a whole. **2.** Complete; absolute: a *total* loss. — *v.* ·**taled** or ·**talled**, ·**tal·ing** or ·**tal·ling** *v.t.* **1.** To ascertain the total of. **2.** To come to or reach as a total. — *v.i.* **3.** To amount: often with *to*. [< OF < Med.L < L *totus* all] — **to′tal·ly** *adv.*

total eclipse *Astron.* An eclipse in which during some period the entire disk of a celestial body is hidden from view.

to·tal·i·tar·i·an (tō·tal′ə·târ′ē·ən) *adj.* Designating or characteristic of a government controlled exclusively by one party or faction, and maintained by political suppression. — *n.* An adherent of totalitarian government. — **to·tal′i·tar′i·an·ism** *n.*

to·tal·i·ty (tō·tal′ə·tē) *n.* *pl.* ·**ties** **1.** An aggregate of parts or individuals. **2.** The state of being total.

to·tal·i·za·tor (tōt′l·ə·zā′tər, -ī·zā′-) *n.* A pari-mutuel machine: also **to·tal·iz′er** (-ī′zər). Also *Brit.* **to′tal·i·sa′tor.**

tote (tōt) *U.S. Informal* *v.t.* **tot·ed, tot·ing** **1.** To carry about or bear on the person. **2.** To haul, as supplies. — *n.* **1.** The act of toting. **2.** A load or haul. [? < West African] — **tot′er** *n.*

tote board *Informal* A board at a racetrack, etc., showing the betting odds and results of races.

to·tem (tō′təm) *n.* **1.** Among many primitive peoples, an animal, plant, or other natural object believed to be ancestrally related to a tribe, clan, etc. **2.** The representation of such an animal, plant, or object taken as an emblem. **3.** The name or symbol of a person, clan, or tribe. [< Algonquian] — **to·tem·ic** (tō·tem′ik) *adj.* — **to′tem·ism** *n.* — **to′tem·ist** *n.* — **to′tem·is′tic** *adj.*

totem pole A tall post or pole carved or painted with totemic symbols, often erected outside a dwelling by North American Indians, esp. those of the NW coast.

toth·er (tuth′ər) *adj. & pron. Informal* The other; other. Also **t′oth′er.** [ME *the tother* < *thet other* the other]

toti- *combining form* Whole; wholly. [< L *totus* whole]

tot·ter (tot′ər) *v.i.* **1.** To walk feebly and unsteadily. **2.** To shake or sway, as if about to fall. — *n.* The act or condition of tottering. [Prob. < Scand.] — **tot′ter·er** *n.* — **tot′ter·y** *adj.*
— **Syn.** (verb) **2.** teeter, wobble, reel.

tou·can (tōō′kan, tōō·kän′) *n.* A large, fruit-eating bird of tropical America, with brilliant plumage and an immense, thin-walled beak. [< F < Pg. < Tupi *tucana*]

touch (tuch) *v.t.* **1.** To place the hand, finger, etc., in contact with. **2.** To be in or come into contact with. **3.** To bring into contact with something else. **4.** To hit or strike lightly. **5.** To lay the hand or hands on, esp. roughly. **6.** To border on; adjoin. **7.** To come to; reach. **8.** To attain to; equal. **9.** To mark or delineate lightly. **10.** To color slightly; tinge. **11.** To affect injuriously; taint: vegetables *touched* by frost. **12.** To affect by contact: The drill could not *touch* the steel. **13.** To affect the emotions of; move, esp. to pity, gratitude, etc. **14.** To relate to; concern. **15.** To treat or discuss in passing; deal with. **16.** To have to do with, use, or partake of: I will not *touch* this food. **17.** To handle or appropriate improperly. **18.** *Slang* To be successful in borrowing from: used with *for*: He *touched* me for a loan. **19.** *Geom.* To be tangent to. — *v.i.* **20.** To touch someone or something. **21.** To come into or be in contact. — **to touch at** To stop briefly at (a port or place) in the course of a journey or voyage. — **to touch off** **1.** To cause to explode; fire. **2.** To cause to happen or occur. — **to touch on** (or **upon**) **1.** To relate to; concern. **2.** To treat briefly or in passing. — **to touch up** To improve or alter by slight additions or corrections. — *n.* **1.** The act or process of touching. **2.** The state of being touched. **3.** *Physiol.* That sense by which external objects are perceived through direct contact with any part of the body. ◆ Collateral adjective: *tactile*. **4.** The sensation conveyed by touching something: a smooth *touch*. **5.** A stroke; hit; blow. **6.** A perceptible effect or influence: He felt the *touch* of her wit. **7.** Any slight or delicate execution or effect, as of a brush, etc.; a light stroke or mark. **8.** Any slight detail or effort given to anything, as to a literary work. **9.** The manner or style in which an artist, etc. executes his work: a master's *touch*. **10.** A trace; tinge: a *touch* of irony. **11.** A slight attack or twinge: a *touch* of rheumatism. **12.** A small quantity or dash. **13.** Close communication or contact: to keep in *touch* with someone. **14.** A test; trial. **15.** *Music* **a** The resistance made to the fingers by the keys of a piano, etc. **b** The manner in which a player presses the keyboard. **16.** *Slang* A sum of money obtained by borrowing or mooching. **17.** *Slang* A request for such a sum of money. **18.** *Slang* A person who is an easy mark for a loan: an easy *touch*. [< OF *tochier*; prob. ult. imit.] — **touch′a·ble** *adj.* — **touch′a·ble·ness** *n.* — **touch′er** *n.*

touch-and-go (tuch′ən-gō′) *adj.* Risky; precarious.

touch and go An uncertain or precarious situation.

touch·back (tuch′bak′) *n.* In football, the act of touching the ball to the ground behind the player's own goal line when it has been sent over the goal line by an opponent.

touch·down (tuch′doun′) *n.* In football, a scoring play, worth six points, in which the ball is held on or over the opponent's goal line and is there declared dead.

tou·ché (tōō·shā′) *French adj.* In fencing, touched by the point of an opponent's foil. — *interj.* You've scored a point!: an exclamation to indicate an opponent's success.

touched (tucht) *adj.* **1.** Emotionally moved. **2.** Slightly unbalanced in mind.

touch·hole (tuch′hōl′) *n.* The orifice in old-fashioned cannon or firearms through which the powder was ignited.

touch·ing (tuch′ing) *adj.* Appealing to the sympathies or emotions; affecting; pathetic. — *prep.* With regard to; concerning. — **touch′ing·ly** *adv.* — **touch′ing·ness** *n.*

touch-me-not (tuch′mē-not′) *n.* Any of various herbs whose ripe fruit bursts open on contact to discharge its seeds.

touch·stone (tuch′stōn′) *n.* **1.** A fine-grained dark stone formerly used to test the fineness of gold and silver by the color of the streak made on the stone. **2.** A criterion or standard by which the qualities of something are tested.

touch·wood (tuch′wŏŏd′) *n.* **1.** Punk¹ (def. 1). **2.** A tinder prepared from fungus.

touch·y (tuch′ē) *adj.* **touch·i·er, touch·i·est** **1.** Likely to take offense easily; irritable. **2.** Risky; delicate: a *touchy* subject. — **touch′i·ly** *adv.* — **touch′i·ness** *n.*

tough (tuf) *adj.* **1.** Capable of sustaining great tension or strain without breaking. **2.** Firm and resilient in substance or texture. **3.** Not easily separated, softened, etc.: *tough* meat. **4.** Possessing great physical endurance: a *tough* constitution. **5.** Possessing moral or intellectual endurance; steadfast; persistent. **6.** Unmanageably rough, unruly, or vicious. **7.** Difficult to accomplish; laborious. **8.** Severe; rigorous. **9.** *Informal* Unfortunate; unpleasant: *tough* luck. — *n.* A lawless person; a rowdy; ruffian. [OE *tōh*] — **tough′ly** *adv.* — **tough′ness** *n.*

tough·en (tuf′ən) *v.t. & v.i.* To make or become tough or tougher. — **tough′en·er** *n.*

tou·pee (tōō·pā′, -pē′) *n.* A wig worn to cover baldness or a bald spot. [< F < OF *toup* tuft of hair]

tour (tŏŏr) *n.* **1.** A trip or rambling excursion. **2.** A circuit or passing through, as for inspection or sightseeing, or for presenting a performance. **3.** A turn or shift, as of service. — **on tour** Traveling from place to place giving performances, as a theatrical company, etc. — *v.t.* **1.** To make a tour of. **2.** To present on a tour, as a play. — *v.i.* **3.** To go on a tour. [< MF < OF < L *tornus* lathe < Gk. *tornos*]

tour de force (tōōr′ də fôrs′) *French* A feat of remarkable strength or skill; esp., a work, performance, etc., that is merely ingenious rather than intrinsically excellent.

tour·ing car (tŏŏr′ing) A large, open automobile for five or more passengers and baggage. Also *Brit.* **tour′er.**

tour·ist (tŏŏr′ist) *n.* One who makes a tour or a pleasure trip. — *adj.* For or suitable for tourists.

tourist class A class of accommodations for steamship passengers, lower than cabin class.

tour·ma·line (tŏŏr′mə·lēn, -lin) *n.* A complex silicate of aluminum occurring in various colors, the transparent varieties being esteemed as gemstones. Also **tour′ma·lin** (-lin). [< F, ult. < Singhalese *tōramalli* carnelian]

tour·na·ment (tûr′nə·mənt, tŏŏr′-) *n.* **1.** Any contest of skill involving a number of competitors and a series of games: a chess *tournament*. **2.** In medieval times, a pageant in which two opposing parties of men in armor contended on horseback in mock combat. Also called *tourney*. [< OF < *torneier, tornoier* tourney]

tour·ney (tûr′nē, tŏŏr′-) *n.* A tournament. — *v.i.* To take part in a tournament; tilt. [See TOURNAMENT.]

tour·ni·quet (tŏŏr′nə·ket, -kā, tûr′-) *n.* *Surg.* A bandage, etc., for stopping the flow of blood through an artery by compression. [< F < *tourner* to turn]

tour of duty *Mil.* The hours or period of time during which a serviceman is on official duty; also, an extended period of duty on a given assignment or in a particular area.

tou·sle (tou′zəl) *v.t.* ·**sled,** ·**sling** To disarrange or disorder, as the hair or dress. — *n.* A tousled mass or mop of hair. Also **tou′zle.** [< ME *tusen, tousen*]

tout (tout) *Informal* *v.i.* **1.** To solicit patronage, customers, votes, etc., esp., in an obtrusive or importunate manner. **2.** To spy on a racehorse so as to gain information for betting. — *v.i.* **3.** To solicit; importune. **4.** In horse racing: **a** To spy on (a horse) to gain information for betting. **b** To sell information about (a horse). — *n.* One who touts. [ME, ? < OE *tōtian*, to peep, look out] — **tout′er** *n.*

tout de suite (tōōt′swēt′) *French* Immediately; at once.

tout en·sem·ble (tōō′tän säṅ′bl′) *French* **1.** All in all; everything considered. **2.** The general effect.

tow¹ (tō) *n.* Coarse, short hemp or flax fiber prepared for spinning. [Prob. OE *tow-* for spinning] — **tow′y** *adj.*

tow² (tō) *v.t.* To pull or drag, as by a rope, chain, etc. — *n.*

TOTEM POLE

1. The act of towing, or the state of being towed. **2.** That which is towed, as barges by a tugboat. **3.** That which tows. **4.** The rope used; towline. **— to take in tow 1.** To take in charge for or as for towing. **2.** To take under one's protection; take charge of. [OE *togian*]

tow·age (tō′ij) *n.* **1.** The service of or charge for towing. **2.** The act of towing. [< TOW²]

to·ward (tôrd, tōrd; *for prep., also* tə·wôrd′) *prep.* **1.** In the direction of; facing. **2.** With respect to; regarding: his attitude *toward* women. **3.** In anticipation of; for: He is saving *toward* his education. **4.** Near in point of time; approaching; about: arriving *toward* evening. **5.** Tending to result in; designed to achieve: an effort *toward* mutual understanding. Also **to·wards′.** *— adj.* [OE < *tō* to + -*weard* -ward] **— to·ward′ness** *n.*

tow·a·way (tō′ə·wā) *n.* The act of towing away a vehicle, esp. one illegally parked.

tow·boat (tō′bōt′) *n.* A tugboat.

tow·el (toul, tou′əl) *n.* A cloth or paper for drying anything by wiping. *— v.t.* **tow·eled** or **·elled, tow·el·ing** or **·el·ling** To wipe or dry with a towel. [< OF *toaille*]

tow·el·ing (tou′ling, tou′əl·ing) *n.* Material used for towels. Also **tow′el·ling.**

tow·er (tou′ər) *n.* **1.** A tall but relatively narrow structure, sometimes part of a larger building. **2.** Any similar tall structure or object, often erected for a specific use: a water *tower.* **3.** A place or thing of security or defense; citadel. *— v.i.* To rise or stand like a tower: often with *over* or *above.* [OE < OF < L *turris*] **— tow′er·y** *adj.*

tow·ered (tou′ərd) *adj.* Having a tower or towers.

tow·er·ing (tou′ər·ing) *adj.* **1.** Like a tower; lofty. **2.** Unusually high or great; outstanding. **3.** Intense.

tow·head (tō′hed′) *n.* A head of very light-colored or flaxen hair; also, a person having such hair. [< TOW¹ + HEAD] **— tow′-head′ed** *adj.*

tow·hee (tou′hē, tō′-) *n.* Any of various American birds related to the buntings and the sparrows; esp., the chewink. Also **towhee bunting.** [Imit. of one of its notes]

tow·line (tō′līn′) *n.* A towrope.

town (toun) *n.* **1.** Any considerable collection of dwellings and other buildings larger than a village, but not incorporated as a city. **2.** The inhabitants of such a community; townspeople. **3.** A township (def. 1). **4.** Any closely settled urban district. **5.** The downtown or business section of a city. **— on the town** *Slang* On a round of pleasure. **— to go to town** *Slang* To act with speed and efficiency. [OE *tūn* enclosure, group of houses]

town clerk An official who keeps the records of a town.

town crier Formerly, a person appointed to make proclamations through the streets of a town.

town hall The building containing the public offices of a town and used for meetings of the town council.

town house A residence in a town or city, as distinguished from one in the country.

town meeting 1. A general assemblage of the people of a town. **2.** An assembly of qualified voters for the purpose of transacting town business; also, the voters assembled.

town·ship (toun′ship) *n.* **1.** In the U.S.: **a** A territorial subdivision of a county with certain corporate powers of municipal government. **b** In New England, a local political unit governed by a town meeting. **2.** A unit of area in surveys of U.S. public lands, normally six miles square. **3.** *Brit.* Formerly, a parish. [OE < *tūn* village, group of houses]

towns·man (tounz′mən) *n. pl.* **·men** (-mən) **1.** A resident of a town; also, a fellow citizen. **2.** In New England, a town officer; a selectman.

towns·peo·ple (tounz′pē′pəl) *n.pl.* People who live in towns or in a particular town or city. Also **town′folk′** (-fōk′), **towns′folk′.**

tow·path (tō′path′, -päth′) *n.* A path along a river or canal used by draft animals, etc., for towing boats.

tow·rope (tō′rōp′) *n.* A heavy rope or cable used in towing.

tow truck A truck equipped to tow other vehicles.

tox·e·mi·a (tok·sē′mē·ə) *n. Pathol.* Blood poisoning. Also **tox·ae′mi·a.** [< NL < Gk. *toxicon* poison + *haima* blood] **— tox·e′mic, tox·ae′mic** *adj.*

tox·ic (tok′sik) *adj.* Of or caused by poison; poisonous. Also **tox′i·cal.** [< Med.L < L < Gk. *toxicon* (*pharmakon*) (poison) for arrows] **— tox·i·cal·ly** *adv.* **— tox·ic′i·ty** *n.*

toxico- *combining form* Poison; of or pertaining to poisons. Also, before vowels, **toxic-.** [< Gk. *toxicon* poison]

tox·i·col·o·gy (tok′sə·kol′ə·jē) *n.* The science that treats of the origin, nature, properties, etc., of poisons. [< F *toxicologie*] **— tox′i·co·log′i·cal** (-kō·loj′i·kəl) *adj.* **— tox′i·co·log′i·cal·ly** *adv.* **— tox′i·col′o·gist** *n.*

tox·in (tok′sin) *n.* **1.** Any of a class of more or less unstable poisonous compounds developed by animal, vegetable, or bacterial organisms and acting as causative agents in many

diseases. **2.** Any toxic matter generated in living or dead organisms. Also **tox·ine** (tok′sēn). [< TOX(IC) + -IN]

tox·oid (tok′soid) *n.* A toxin that has been specially treated to remove toxicity, often used in immunization.

toy (toi) *n.* **1.** A plaything for children. **2.** Any object of little importance or value; a trifle. **3.** A small ornament or trinket. **4.** Any diminutive object. **5.** A dog bred to extreme smallness: also **toy dog.** *— v.i.* To trifle; play. *— adj.* Resembling a toy; of miniature size. [< ME *toye* sport and Du. *tuig* tools] **— toy′er** *n.*

to·yon (tō′yən) *n.* An evergreen shrub of the Pacific coast of North America, having white flowers and bright red berries. [< Sp. *tollón* < N. Am. Ind. (Mexican)]

trace¹ (trās) *n.* **1.** A vestige or mark left by some past event or agent, esp., when regarded as a sign or clue. **2.** A barely detectable quantity, quality, token; or characteristic; touch. **3.** A proportion or ingredient too small to be weighed: a *trace* of soda. **4.** An imprint or mark indicating the passage of a person or thing, as a footprint, etc. **5.** A path or trail through woods or forest beaten down by men or animals. **6.** A lightly drawn line. *— v.* **traced, trac·ing** *v.t.* **1.** To follow the tracks, course, or development of. **2.** To follow (tracks, etc.). **3.** To discover by examination or investigation; determine. **4.** To draw; sketch. **5.** To copy (a drawing, etc.) on a superimposed transparent sheet. **6.** To form (letters, etc.) with careful strokes. **7.** To imprint (a pattern or design). **8.** To mark or record by a curved or broken line. **9.** To go or move over, along, or through. *— v.i.* **10.** To make one's way; proceed. **11.** To have its origin; go back in time. [< OF < L < *trahere* to draw] **— trace′a·ble** *adj.* **— trace′a·bil′i·ty, trace′a·ble·ness** *n.* **— trace′a·bly** *adv.*

trace² (trās) *n.* One of two side straps or chains for connecting the collar of a harness with the whiffletree. **— to kick over the traces** To throw off control; become unmanageable. *— v.t.* **traced, trac·ing** To fasten with or as with traces. [< OF < L. See TRACE¹.]

trace element *Biol.* Any of certain chemical elements found in very small amounts in plant and animal tissues and having a significant effect upon biochemical processes.

trac·er (trā′sər) *n.* **1.** One who or that which traces. **2.** One of various instruments used in tracing drawings, etc. **3.** An inquiry forwarded from one point to another, to trace missing mail matter, etc. **4.** *Mil.* A chemical incorporated in certain types of ammunition used for ranging, signaling, or incendiary purposes. **5.** A radioisotope introduced into the body for the purpose of following the processes of metabolism, the course of a disease, etc. [< TRACE¹]

tracer bullet A bullet that leaves a line of smoke or fire in its wake to indicate its course for correction of aim.

trac·er·y (trā′sər·ē) *n. pl.* **·er·ies 1.** Ornamental stonework formed of ramifying lines. **2.** Any work, ornamentation, etc., resembling this.

tra·che·a (trā′kē·ə) *n. pl.* **·che·ae** (-kē·ē) or **·che·as 1.** *Anat.* The duct by which air passes from the larynx to the bronchi and the lungs: also called *windpipe.* For illus. see LUNG, MOUTH, THROAT. **2.** *Zool.* One of the passages by which air is conveyed from the exterior in air-breathing arthropods, as insects and arachnids. [< Med.L < LL < Gk. (*artēria*) *tracheia* a rough (artery)] **— tra′che·al** *adj.*

tracheo- *combining form* The trachea; of or pertaining to the trachea. Also, before vowels, **trache-.** [< TRACHEA]

tra·che·ot·o·my (trā′kē·ot′ə·mē) *n. pl.* **·mies** *Surg.* The operation of cutting into the trachea.

tra·cho·ma (trə·kō′mə) *n. Pathol.* A contagious virus disease characterized by the formation of hard granular excrescences on the conjunctiva of the eyelids, with inflammation of the lining. [< NL < Gk. < *trachys* rough] **— tra·chom·a·tous** (trə·kom′ə·təs) *adj.*

trachy- *combining form* Rough; uneven. Also, before vowels, **trach-.** [< Gk. *trachys* rough]

trac·ing (trā′sing) *n.* **1.** The act of one who traces. **2.** A copy made by tracing on transparent paper. **3.** A record made by a self-registering instrument.

track (trak) *n.* **1.** A mark or trail left by the passage of anything, as footprints. **2.** Any regular path; course. **3.** Any kind of racecourse; also, sports performed on such a course; track athletics. **4.** A set of rails or a rail on which trains, etc., may travel. **5.** A trace or vestige. **6.** A sequence of events or ideas. **— to keep track of** To keep in touch with. **— in one's tracks** Right where one is; on the spot. **— to lose track of** To fail to keep in touch with; lose sight of. **— to make tracks** To hurry; run away in haste. *— v.t.* **1.** To follow, the tracks of; trail. **2.** To discover, pursue or follow by means of marks or indications. **3.** To make tracks upon or with. **4.** To traverse, as on foot. **5.** To furnish with rails or tracks. [< OF *trac*] **— track′er** *n.* **— track′a·ble** *adj.* **— track′less** *adj.*

track·age (trak′ij) *adj.* **1.** Railroad tracks collectively. **2.** The right of one company to use the track system of another company; also, the charge for this right.

track man An athlete who competes in a track or field event, as a runner, shot-putter, etc.

track meet An athletic contest made up of track and field events.

tract[1] (trakt) *n.* **1.** An extended area, as of land or water. **2.** *Anat.* An extensive region of the body, esp. one comprising a system of parts or organs: the alimentary *tract*. [< L < *trahere* to draw]

tract[2] (trakt) *n.* A short treatise; esp., a pamphlet on some question of religion or morals. [Short for L *tractatus* a handling, treatise]

tract·a·ble (trak′tə-bəl) *adj.* **1.** Easily led or controlled; manageable; docile. **2.** Readily worked or handled; malleable. [< L < *trahere* to draw] — **tract′a·ble·ness, tract′a·bil′i·ty** *n.* — **tract′a·bly** *adv.*

trac·tile (trak′til) *adj.* Capable of being drawn out; ductile. [< L < *trahere* to draw] — **trac·til′i·ty** *n.*

trac·tion (trak′shən) *n.* **1.** The act of drawing, as by motive power over a surface. **2.** The state of being drawn, or the power employed. **3.** Adhesive or rolling friction, as of wheels on a track. [< Med.L < L < *trahere* to draw] — **trac′tion·al** *adj.*

traction engine A locomotive for hauling on roads or ground, as distinguished from one used on a railway.

trac·tor (trak′tər) *n.* **1.** A powerful, motor-driven vehicle used, as on farms, to draw a plow, reaper, etc. **2.** An automotive vehicle with a driver's cab, used to haul trailers, etc. **3.** *Aeron.* An airplane with the propeller or propellers situated in front of the supporting surface: also **tractor airplane.** [< NL < L < *trahere* to draw]

trade (trād) *n.* **1.** A business; esp., a skilled handicraft; a craft. **2.** Mercantile traffic; commerce. **3.** An exchange, as in barter, buying and selling, etc.; also, a bargain or deal. **4.** The people following a particular calling. **5.** A firm's customers. **6.** Customary pursuit; occupation. **7.** *Usu. pl.* A trade wind. — **Syn.** See OCCUPATION. — *v.* **trad·ed, trad·ing** *v.t.* **1.** To exchange by barter, bargain and sale, etc. **2.** To exchange for something comparable. — *v.i.* **3.** To engage in commerce or in business. — **to trade in** To give in exchange as payment or part payment. — **to trade off** To get rid of by trading. — **to trade on** To make advantageous use of. [< MLG, track]

trade-in (trād′in′) *n.* Something given or accepted in payment or part payment for something else; an exchange.

trade journal A periodical publishing news and discussions of a particular trade or business.

trade-last (trād′last′, -läst′) *n. Informal* A favorable remark that one has heard and offers to repeat to the person complimented in return for a similar remark.

trade·mark (trād′märk′) *n.* **1.** A name, design, etc., often officially registered, used by a merchant or manufacturer to distinguish his goods from those made or sold by others. **2.** Any distinctive characteristic. — *v.t.* **1.** To label with a trademark. **2.** To register as a trademark.

trade name **1.** The name by which an article, process, service, or the like is designated in trade. **2.** A style or name of a business house.

trad·er (trā′dər) *n.* **1.** One who trades. **2.** Any vessel employed in a particular trade.

trade route A route, esp. a sea lane, used by traders.

trade school A school where a specific trade is taught.

trades·folk (trādz′fōk′) *n.pl.* People engaged in trade; esp., shopkeepers. Also **trades′peo′ple** (-pē′pəl).

trades·man (trādz′mən) *n. pl.* **·men** (-mən) A retail dealer; shopkeeper.

trade union A labor union. Also *Brit.* **trades union.**

trade wind *Meteorol.* Either of two steady winds blowing in the same course toward the equator from about 30° N and S latitude, one from the northeast on the north, the other from the southeast on the south side of the equator.

trading post A station for barter in unsettled territory set up by a trader or trading company.

trading stamp A stamp given by a tradesman to a purchaser, and exchangeable, in quantities, for merchandise.

tra·di·tion (trə·dish′ən) *n.* **1.** The knowledge, doctrines, customs, practices, etc., transmitted from generation to generation; also, the transmission of such knowledge, doctrines, etc. **2.** The body of unwritten Christian doctrine, handed down through successive generations. **3.** Among the Jews, an unwritten code said to have been handed down orally from Moses. **4.** The historic conceptions and usages of a school of art, literature, etc. A custom so long continued that it has almost the force of a law. [< OF < L < *trans-* across + *dare* to give]

tra·di·tion·al (trə·dish′ən·əl) *adj.* Relating or adhering to tradition. Also **tra·di′tion·ar′y** (-er′ē). — **tra·di′tion·al·ism** *n.* — **tra·di′tion·al·ist** *n.* — **tra·di′tion·al·ist′ic** *adj.* — **tra·di′tion·al·ly** *adv.* — **tra·di′tion·ist** *n.*

tra·duce (trə·dōōs′, -dyōōs′) *v.t.* **·duced, ·duc·ing** To defame; slander. [< L *traducere* to transport, bring into disgrace] — **tra·duc′er** *n.* — **tra·duc′i·ble** *adj.* — **tra·duc′ing·ly** *adv.* — **tra·duc·tion** (trə·duk′shən) *n.*

traf·fic (traf′ik) *n.* **1.** The movement or passage of vehicles, pedestrians, ships, etc., along a route; also, the vehicles, pedestrians, etc. **2.** Buying and selling; trade. **3.** The business of transportation; also, the freight or passengers carried. **4.** The messages, signals, etc., handled by a communications system. **5.** Unlawful or improper trade. — *v.i.* **·ficked, ·fick·ing** **1.** To engage in buying and selling; do business, esp., illegally: with *in.* **2.** To have dealings: with *with.* [< MF < Ital. < *trafficare* < L *trans-* across + Ital. *ficcare* to thrust in] — **traf′fick·er** *n.*

traffic light A signal light that, by changing color, directs the flow of traffic along a road or highway.

tra·ge·di·an (trə·jē′dē·ən) *n.* **1.** An actor in tragedy. **2.** A writer of tragedies.

tra·ge·di·enne (trə·jē′dē·en′) *n.* An actress of tragedy. [< F]

trag·e·dy (traj′ə·dē) *n. pl.* **·dies** **1.** An intensely sad, calamitous, or fatal event or course of events; disaster. **2.** A form of drama in which the protagonist comes to disaster through a flaw in his nature or is crushed by social and psychological forces. **3.** The branch of drama treating of such themes. **4.** The art or theory of acting or composing such drama. **5.** The sense of human life embodied in tragic drama. [< OF < L < Gk. *tragōidia*, appar. < *tragos* goat + *ōidē* song]

trag·ic (traj′ik) *adj.* **1.** Involving death, calamity, or suffering; fatal; terrible. **2.** Pertaining to or having the nature of tragedy. **3.** Appropriate to or like tragedy, esp., in drama. Also **trag′i·cal.** [< L < Gk. *tragikos* pertaining to tragedy] — **trag′i·cal·ly** *adv.* — **trag′i·cal·ness** *n.*

trag·i·com·e·dy (traj′i·kom′ə·dē) *n. pl.* **·dies** **1.** A drama in which tragic and comic scenes are intermingled. **2.** A situation or event suggestive of such a drama. [< MF < LL < L < *tragicus* tragic + *comoedia* comedy] — **trag′i·com′ic** or **·i·cal** *adj.* — **trag′i·com′i·cal·ly** *adv.*

trail (trāl) *v.t.* **1.** To draw along lightly over a surface; also, to drag or draw after: to *trail* a robe. **2.** To follow the track of; track. **3.** To follow or lag behind, esp., in a race. **4.** *Mil.* To carry, as a rifle, with the muzzle to the front and the butt nearly touching the ground. **5.** To tread or force down, as grass into a pathway. — *v.i.* **6.** To hang or float loosely so as to drag along a surface. **7.** To grow along the ground or over rocks, bushes, etc., in a loose, creeping way. **8.** To follow behind loosely; stream. **9.** To move along slowly, tiredly, or heavily. **10.** To lag behind; straggle. **11.** To follow or track game. — *n.* **1.** A path or track made by the passage of persons or animals. **2.** The spoor followed by a hunter. **3.** Anything drawn behind or in the wake of something. **4.** *Mil.* The inclined stock of a gun carriage, or extension of the stock that rests on the ground when the piece is not limbered up. — **to hit** (or **take**) **the trail** To set out on a journey. [< AF < L < *trahere* to draw]

trail·blaz·er (trāl′blā·zər) *n.* **1.** One who blazes a trail. **2.** A pioneer in any field. — **trail′blaz·ing** *n.*

trail·er (trā′lər) *n.* **1.** One who or that which trails. **2.** A vehicle drawn by another having motive power. **3.** A vehicle drawn by a car or truck and used as a temporary or permanent dwelling. **4.** A short motion-picture film made up of scenes from a coming feature picture, used for advertising.

trailer court A large area equipped with running water, electrical outlets, and other accommodations for the parking of trailers. Also **trailer park.**

trail·ing arbutus (trā′ling) A perennial bearing fragrant pink flowers: the State flower of Massachusetts.

train (trān) *n.* **1.** A continuous line of coupled railway cars. **2.** A series, or set of connected things; a sequence; esp., a procession of people or line of objects. **3.** A retinue or suite. **4.** Something pulled along with and in the track of another. **5.** An extension of a dress skirt, trailing behind the wearer. **6.** Proper order; due course. **7.** *Mech.* A series of parts acting upon each other, as for transmitting motion. **8.** *Mil.* The men, animals, and vehicles, transporting military supplies, ammunition, etc. **9.** A succession or line of wagons and pack animals en route. **10.** A line of gunpowder, etc., laid to conduct fire to a charge or mine. — *v.t.* **1.** To render proficient or qualified by instruction, drill, etc.; educate. **2.** To make obedient or capable of performing tricks, as an animal. **3.** To bring into a required physical condition by means of diet and exercise. **4.** To lead into taking a particular course; develop into a fixed shape: to *train* a plant on a trellis. **5.** To bring to bear; aim, as a cannon. — *v.i.* **6.** To undergo a course of training. **7.** To give a course of training; drill. — **Syn.** See TEACH. [OF < L *trahere* to draw] — **train′a·ble** *adj.* — **train′er** *n.*

train·ee (trā·nē′) *n.* One who undergoes training.

train·ing (trā′ning) *n.* **1.** The action of one who or that which trains. **2.** The state or condition of being trained.

train·man (trān′mən) *n. pl.* **·men** (-mən) A railway employee serving on a train; esp., a brakeman.

traipse (trāps) *v.i.* **traipsed, traips·ing** *Informal* To walk about in an idle or aimless manner. [Earlier *trapass*]

trait (trāt, *also Brit.* trā) *n.* A distinguishing feature or quality of character. — **Syn.** See CHARACTERISTIC. [< F < MF < L < *trahere* to draw]

trai·tor (trā′tər) *n.* One who betrays a trust; esp., one who commits treason. [< OF < L < *trans-* across + *dare* to give] — **trai′tress** (-tris) *n.fem.*

trai·tor·ous (trā′tər·əs) *adj.* 1. Of or characteristic of a traitor. 2. Pertaining to or of the nature of treason. — **trai′tor·ous·ly** *adv.* — **trai′tor·ous·ness** *n.*

tra·jec·to·ry (trə·jek′tər·ē) *n. pl.* **·ries** The path described by an object moving in space; esp., the path of a projectile. [< Med.L < L < *trans-* over + *jacere* to throw]

tram (tram) *n.* 1. *Brit.* A streetcar or street railway: also **tram′car** (-kär′). 2. A four-wheeled vehicle for conveying coals to or from a pit's mouth. [Short for *tramroad*, a road with metal tracks]

tram·mel (tram′əl) *n.* 1. *Usu. pl.* That which limits freedom or activity; an impediment; hindrance. 2. A fetter, shackle, or bond, esp., one used in teaching a horse to amble. 3. An instrument for describing ellipses. 4. A hook used to suspend cooking pots from a fireplace crane. — *v.t.* **tram·meled** *or* **·melled, tram·mel·ing** *or* **·mel·ling** 1. To hinder or obstruct; restrict. 2. To entangle in or as in a snare. Also **tram′el** *or* **tram′ell**. [< OF < LL < L *tri-* three + *macula* mesh] — **tram′mel·er** *or* **tram′mel·ler** *n.*

tramp (tramp) *v.i.* 1. To walk or wander, esp., as a vagrant or vagabond. 2. To walk heavily or firmly. — *v.t.* 3. To walk or wander through. 4. To walk on heavily; trample. — *n.* 1. An indigent wanderer; a vagrant; vagabond. 2. A heavy, continued tread. 3. The sound of continuous and heavy marching or walking. 4. A long walk; hike. 5. A steam vessel that picks up freight wherever it can be obtained: also **tramp steamer**. 6. *Informal* A sexually promiscuous girl or woman. [ME *trampen* < Gmc.]

tram·ple (tram′pəl) *v.* **·pled, ·pling** *v.t.* 1. To tread on heavily; injure, violate, or encroach upon by or as by tramping. — *v.i.* 2. To tread heavily or ruthlessly; tramp. — *n.* The act or sound of treading under foot. [ME < *trampen*]

tram·po·line (tram′pə·lin) *n.* A section of strong canvas stretched on a frame, on which an acrobat, athlete, etc., may bound or spring. [< Ital. *trampoli* stilts]

trance (trans, träns) *n.* 1. A condition intermediate between sleep and wakefulness, characterized by dissociation and automatisms of behavior, as in hypnosis and seances. 2. A dreamlike state marked by bewilderment and an insensibility to ordinary surroundings. 3. A state of deep abstraction. — *v.t.* **tranced, tranc·ing** To put into or as into a trance. [< OF < *transir* to pass, die]

tran·quil (trang′kwil) *adj.* **·quil·er** *or* **·quil·ler, ·quil·est** *or* **·quil·lest** 1. Free from mental agitation or disturbance; calm. 2. Quiet and motionless. — **Syn.** See CALM. [< L *tranquillus* quiet] — **tran′quil·ly** *adv.* — **tran′quil·ness** *n.*

tran·quil·ize (trang′kwəl·īz) *v.t. & v.i.* **·ized, ·iz·ing** To make or become tranquil. Also **tran′quil·lize**, *Brit.* **tran′quil·lise**. — **tran′quil·i·za′tion** *n.*

tran·quil·iz·er (trang′kwəl·ī′zər) *n.* 1. One who or that which tranquilizes. 2. *Med.* Any of a class of drugs having the property of reducing nervous tension and anxiety states. Also **tran′quil·liz′er**.

tran·quil·li·ty (trang·kwil′ə·tē) *n.* The state of being tranquil; calm; quiet. Also **tran′quil′i·ty**.

trans- *prefix* 1. Across; beyond; through; on the other side of; as in:

transarctic	transcontinental	transfrontier
transborder	transdesert	transisthmian
transchannel	transequatorial	transpolar

In adjectives and nouns of place, the prefix may signify "on the other side of" (opposed to *cis-*) or "across; crossing." Through long usage, certain of these are written as solid words, as *transalpine, transatlantic*; otherwise, words in this class are usually written with a hyphen, as in:

trans-African	trans-Baltic	trans-Iberian
trans-American	trans-Canadian	trans-Mediterranean
trans-Andean	trans-Germanic	trans-Scandinavian
trans-Arabian	trans-Himalayan	trans-Siberian

2. Through and through; changing completely; as in:

| transcolor | transfashion |

3. Surpassing; transcending; beyond; as in:

transconscious	transmaterial	transnational
transempirical	transmental	transphysical
transhuman	transmundane	transrational

4. *Anat.* Across; transversely; as in:

| transcortical | transfrontal | transthoracic |
| transduodenal | transocular | transuterine |

[< L < *trans* across, beyond, over]

trans·act (trans·akt′, tranz-) *v.t.* 1. To carry through; accomplish; do. — *v.i.* 2. *Rare* To do business. [< L < *trans-* through + *agere* to drive, do] — **trans·ac′tor** *n.*

trans·ac·tion (trans·ak′shən, tranz-) *n.* 1. The act of transacting, or the state of being transacted. 2. Something transacted; esp., a business deal. 3. *pl.* Published reports, as of a society. — **trans·ac′tion·al** *adj.*

trans·al·pine (trans·al′pin, -pīn, tranz-) *adj.* Of, pertaining to, or situated on the northern side of the Alps. — *n.* A native or a resident of Transalpine Gaul. [< L < *trans-* across + *alpinus* alpine < *Alpes* the Alps]

trans·at·lan·tic (trans′at·lan′tik, tranz′-) *adj.* 1. On the other side of the Atlantic. 2. Across the Atlantic.

tran·scend (tran·send′) *v.t.* 1. To rise above in excellence or degree. 2. To overstep or exceed as a limit. 3. *Philos. & Theol.* To be independent of or beyond (the universe, experience, etc.) — *v.i.* 4. To be transcendent; excel. [< L < *trans-* beyond, over + *scandere* to climb]

tran·scen·dent (tran·sen′dənt) *adj.* 1. Of very high and remarkable degree; surpassing; excelling. 2. *Theol.* Above and beyond the universe: said of God. [See TRANSCEND.] — **tran·scen′dence, tran·scen′den·cy, tran·scen′dent·ness** *n.* — **tran·scen′dent·ly** *adv.*

tran·scen·den·tal (tran′sen·den′təl) *adj.* 1. Of very high degree; transcendent. 2. Beyond or contrary to common sense or experience. — **tran′scen·den′tal·ly** *adv.*

tran·scen·den·tal·ism (tran′sen·den′təl·iz′əm) *n.* 1. *Philos.* Any of several doctrines holding that reality is essentially mental or spiritual in nature, and that knowledge of it can be attained by intuitive or a priori, rather than empirical, principles. 2. The state or quality of being transcendental. — **tran′scen·den′tal·ist** *n. & adj.*

tran·scribe (tran·skrīb′) *v.t.* **·scribed, ·scrib·ing** 1. To copy or recopy in handwriting or typewriting. 2. *Telecom.* To make an electrical recording of (a radio program). 3. To adapt (a musical composition) for a change of instrument or voice. [< L < *trans-* over + *scribere* to write] — **tran·scrib′a·ble** *adj.* — **tran·scrib′er** *n.*

tran·script (tran′skript) *n.* 1. That which is transcribed; esp., a written or typewritten copy. 2. Any copy. 3. A copy of a student's academic record, listing courses and grades.

tran·scrip·tion (tran·skrip′shən) *n.* 1. The act of transcribing. 2. A copy; transcript. 3. Phonetic notation of speech sounds, also, a text containing such symbols. 4. *Telecom.* A recording of a performance made for a later radio broadcast. 5. *Music* The adaptation of a composition for some instrument or voice other than that for which it was written. — **tran·scrip′tion·al, tran·scrip′tive** *adj.*

trans·duc·er (trans·dōō′sər, -dyōō′-, tranz-) *n. Physics* Any device whereby energy may be transmitted from one system to another system, whether of the same or a different type. [< L < *trans-* across + *ducere* to lead]

trans·sect (tran·sekt′) *v.t.* To dissect transversely. [< TRANS- + L *sectus*, pp. of *secare* to cut] — **tran·sec′tion** (-sek′shən) *n.*

tran·sept (tran′sept) *n. Archit.* One of the lateral projections between the nave and choir of a cruciform church. [< Med.L < L < *transversus* lying across + *septum* enclosure] — **tran·sep′tal** *adj.* — **tran·sep′tal·ly** *adv.*

trans·fer (trans′fər; *for v.*, *also* trans·fûr′) *v.* **·ferred, ·fer·ring** *v.t.* 1. To carry, or cause to pass, from one person, place, etc., to another. 2. To make over possession of to another. 3. To convey (a drawing) from one surface to another. — *v.i.* 4. To transfer oneself. 5. To be transferred. 6. To change from one vehicle to another on a transfer (def. 4). 7. To shift one's enrollment as a student from one school to another. — **Syn.** See CONVEY. — *n.* 1. The act of transferring, or the state of being transferred. Also **trans·fer′al** (-fûr′əl) *or* **trans·fer′ral**. 2. That which is transferred as a design. 3. A place, method, or means of transfer. 4. A ticket entitling a passenger to change to another public vehicle. 5. *Law* A delivery of title or property from one person to another. 6. An order transferring money or securities. [< OF < L < *trans-* across + *ferre* to carry] — **trans·fer′a·bil′i·ty** *n.* — **trans·fer′a·ble** *adj.* — **trans·fer′ence** (-fûr′əns) *n.* — **trans·fer′rer** (-fûr′ər) *n.*

trans·fer·or (trans·fûr′ər) *n. Law* One who executes a transfer of property, title, etc.

Trans·fig·ur·a·tion (trans′fig·yə·rā′shən) *n.* 1. The supernatural transformation of Christ on the mount as recorded in the Gospels. *Matt.* xvii 1–9. 2. A church festival commemorating this, observed on August 6.

trans·fig·ure (trans·fig′yər) *v.t.* **·ured, ·ur·ing** 1. To change the outward form or appearance of. 2. To make glorious; idealize. [< L < *trans-* across + *figura* shape] — **trans·fig′ur·a′tion, trans·fig′ure·ment** *n.*

trans·fix (trans·fiks′) *v.t.* 1. To pierce through; impale. 2. To fix in place by impaling. 3. To make motionless, as with horror, awe, etc. [< L < *trans-* through + *figere* to fasten] — **trans·fix′ion** (-fik′shən) *n.*

trans·form (trans-fôrm′) *v.t.* **1.** To give a different form or appearance to. **2.** To change the character, nature, condition, etc., of. **3.** *Math.* To change (one expression or operation) into another equivalent to it or similar. **4.** *Electr.* To change the potential or flow of (a current), as with a transformer. **5.** *Physics* To alter the energy form of, as electrical into mechanical. — *v.i.* **6.** To be or become changed. [< L < *trans-* over + *formare* to form] — **trans·form′a·ble** *adj.* — **trans·for·ma′tion** (-fər-mā′shən) *n.* — **trans·for′ma·tive** (-fôr′mə-tiv) *adj.*

trans·form·er (trans-fôr′mər) *n.* **1.** One who or that which transforms. **2.** *Electr.* A device for altering the ratio of current to voltage in alternating-current circuts, often consisting of two coils wound on the same iron core.

trans·form·ism (trans-fôr′miz·əm) *n.* *Biol.* The theory of the development of one species from another through successive gradual modifications.

trans·fuse (trans-fyōōz′) *v.t.* **·fused, ·fus·ing 1.** To pour, as a fluid, from one vessel to another. **2.** To cause to be imparted or instilled. **3.** *Med.* To transfer (blood) from one person or animal to another. [< L < *trans-* across + *fundere* to pour] — **trans·fus′er** *n.* — **trans·fus′i·ble** *adj.* — **trans·fu·sive** (trans-fyōō′siv) *adj.*

trans·fu·sion (trans-fyōō′zhən) *n.* **1.** The act of transfusing. **2.** *Med.* The transfer of blood from one person or animal to the veins or arteries of another.

trans·gress (trans-gres′, tranz-) *v.t.* **1.** To break (a law, oath, etc.); violate. **2.** To pass beyond or over (limits); exceed; trespass. — *v.i.* **3.** To break a law; sin. [Appar. < OF < L < *trans-* across + *gradi* to step] — **trans·gress′i·ble** *adj.* — **trans·gress′ing·ly** *adv.* — **trans·gres′sive** *adj.* — **trans·gres′sor** *n.*

trans·gres·sion (trans-gresh′ən, tranz-) *n.* **1.** A violation of a law, command, etc.; esp., a violation of a divine law; sin. **2.** The act of transgressing.

tran·ship (tran·ship′), **tran·ship·ment** (tran·ship′mənt) See TRANSSHIP, etc.

tran·sient (tran′shənt) *adj.* **1.** Passing away quickly; of short duration; brief. **2.** Not permanent; temporary; transitory. — *n.* One who or that which is transient; esp., a lodger or boarder who remains for a short time. [< L < *trans-* across + *ire* to go] — **tran′sience, tran′sien·cy** *n.* — **tran′sient·ly** *adv.* — **tran′sient·ness** *n.*

— **Syn.** (adj.) **1, 2.** Something *transient* actually passes soon, while a *transitory* has the quality of impermanence: a *transient* visitor, a *transitory* stage of development. *Passing* is close to *transitory* but less formal: a *passing* fad.

tran·sis·tor (tran-zis′tər, -sis′-) *n.* *Electronics* A miniature device for the control and amplification of an electron current, made of semiconducting materials, and having three or more electrodes, the current between one pair controlling the amplified current between another pair, one electrode being common to each pair. [< TRANS(FER) (RES)ISTOR]

tran·sit (tran′sit, -zit) *n.* **1.** The act of passing over or through; passage. **2.** The act of carrying across or through; conveyance. **3.** A transition or change. **4.** *Astron.* **a** The passage of one heavenly body across the disk of another. **b** The moment of passage of a celestial body across the meridian. **5.** A surveying instrument for measuring horizontal and vertical angles: also **transit theodolite.** — *v.t.* To pass through or across. [< L < *trans-* across + *ire* to go]

tran·si·tion (tran-zish′ən) *n.* **1.** The act or state of passing from one place, condition, or action to another; change **2.** The time, period, or place of such passage. **3.** A sentence, paragraph, etc., that leads from one subject to another, as in an essay. **4.** *Music* A modulation or a passage connecting two themes or subjects. — **tran·si′tion·al, tran·si′tion·ar′y** (-er′ē) *adj.* — **tran·si′tion·al·ly** *adv.*

tran·si·tive (tran′sə-tiv) *adj.* *Gram.* **1.** Of transitive verbs. **2.** Capable of passing; effecting transition. — *n.* *Gram.* A transitive verb. [< LL < L. See TRANSIT.] — **tran′si·tive·ly** *adv.* — **tran′si·tive·ness, tran′si·tiv′i·ty** *n.*

transitive verb A verb that requires a complement to complete its meaning.

tran·si·to·ry (tran′sə-tôr′ē, -tō′rē) *adj.* Existing for a short time only. — **Syn.** See TRANSIENT. [< OF < L. See TRANSIT.] — **tran′si·to′ri·ly** *adv.* — **tran′si·to′ri·ness** *n.*

trans·late (trans-lāt′, tranz-, trans′lāt, tranz′-) *v.* **·lat·ed, ·lat·ing** *v.t.* **1.** To express in another language; change into another language. **2.** To explain in other words; interpret. **3.** To change into another form; transform. — *v.i.* **4.** To act as translator. **5.** To admit of translation: This book *translates* easily. [? < OF *translater* < L < pp. of *transferre* < *trans-* across + *ferre* to carry] — **trans·lat′a·ble** *adj.* — **trans·lat′a·ble·ness** *n.* — **trans·la′tor** *n.*

trans·la·tion (trans-lā′shən, tranz-) *n.* **1.** The act of translating, or the state of being translated. **2.** That which is translated; esp., a work translated into another language; a version. — **trans·la′tion·al** *adj.*

trans·lit·er·ate (trans-lit′ə·rāt, tranz-) *v.t.* **·at·ed, ·at·ing** To represent (a letter or word) by the alphabetic characters of another language. [< TRANS- + L *litera* letter] — **trans·lit′er·a′tion** *n.*

trans·lu·cent (trans-lōō′sənt, tranz-) *adj.* Allowing the passage of light, but not permitting a clear view of any object; semitransparent. — **Syn.** See CLEAR. [< L < *trans-* through, across + *lucere* to shine] — **trans·lu′cence, trans·lu′cen·cy** *n.* — **trans·lu′cent·ly** *adv.*

trans·mi·grate (trans-mī′grāt, tranz-, trans′mə-, tranz′-) *v.i.* **·grat·ed, ·grat·ing 1.** To migrate from one place or condition to another, esp., from one country to another. **2.** To pass into another body, as the soul at death. [< L < *trans-* across + *migrare* to migrate] — **trans·mi′grant** *adj. & n.* — **trans′mi·gra′tion** *n.* — **trans′mi·gra′tor** *n.* — **trans·mi·gra·to·ry** (trans-mī′grə-tôr′ē, -tō′rē, tranz-) *adj.*

trans·mis·si·ble (trans-mis′ə-bəl, tranz-) *adj.* Capable of being transmitted. Also **trans·mit′ti·ble** (-mit′ə-bəl). — **trans·mis′si·bil′i·ty** *n.*

trans·mis·sion (trans-mish′ən, tranz-) *n.* **1.** The act of transmitting, or the state of being transmitted. **2.** That which is transmitted. **3.** *Mech.* **a** A device that transmits power from the engine of an automobile to the driving wheels. **b** The gears for changing speed. [See TRANSMIT.] — **trans·mis′sive** *adj.*

trans·mit (trans-mit′, tranz-) *v.t.* **·mit·ted, ·mit·ting 1.** To send from one place or person to another; forward or convey; dispatch. **2.** To pass on by heredity; transfer. **3.** To pass on or communicate (news, information, etc.). **4.** *Telecom.* To send out (information, radio and television broadcasts, etc.) by means of electromagnetic waves. **5.** *Physics* To cause (light, sound, etc.) to pass through a medium. **6.** *Mech.* To convey (force, motion, etc.) from one part or mechanism to another. [< L < *trans-* across + *mittere* to send] — **trans·mit′tal** *n.*

trans·mit·tance (trans-mit′ns, tranz-) *n.* The act or process of transmitting.

trans·mit·ter (trans-mit′ər, tranz-) *n.* **1.** One who or that which transmits. **2.** A telegraphic sending instrument. **3.** The part of a telephone that converts sound waves into electrical waves. **4.** *Telecom.* The part of a radio or television system that generates, modulates, and transmits electromagnetic waves to the antenna.

trans·mu·ta·tion (trans′myōō·tā′shən, tranz′-) *n.* **1.** The act of transmuting, or the state of being transmuted. **2.** *Physics* The change of one element into another through alteration of its nuclear structure, as by bombardment with high-energy particles in an accelerator. **3.** *Biol.* Successive change of form. **4.** In alchemy, the supposed change of a base metal into gold, silver, etc. — **trans′mu·ta′tion·al, trans·mut·a·tive** (trans-myōō′tə·tiv, tranz-) *adj.*

trans·mute (trans-myōōt′, tranz-) *v.t.* **·mut·ed, ·mut·ing** To change in nature, form, quality, etc.; transform. Also **trans·mu′tate.** [< L < *trans-* across + *mutare* to change] — **trans·mut′a·ble** *adj.* — **trans·mut·a·bil′i·ty, trans·mut′a·ble·ness** *n.* — **trans·mut′a·bly** *adv.* — **trans·mut′er** *n.*

trans·o·ce·an·ic (trans′ō·shē·an′ik, tranz′-) *adj.* **1.** Lying beyond or over the ocean. **2.** Crossing the ocean.

tran·som (tran′səm) *n.* **1.** A small window above a door or window, usu. hinged to a horizontal crosspiece; also, the crosspiece. **2.** A horizontal construction dividing a window into stages. **3.** *Naut.* A beam running across the stern frame of a ship. **4.** The horizontal crossbar of a gallows or cross. [< L *transtrum* crossbeam] — **tran′somed** *adj.*

tran·son·ic (tran-son′ik) *adj.* *Aeron.* Of or pertaining to conditions encountered when passing to supersonic speeds.

transonic barrier *Aeron.* A barrier to supersonic flight encountered by aircraft designed for subsonic speed, caused by turbulence of the airflow around different parts of the plane: also called *sonic barrier, sound barrier.*

trans·pa·cif·ic (trans′pə·sif′ik, tranz′-) *adj.* **1.** Crossing the Pacific Ocean. **2.** Situated across or beyond the Pacific.

trans·par·en·cy (trans-pâr′ən·sē, -par′-) *n.* *pl.* **·cies 1.** The quality of being transparent. Also **trans·par′ence. 2.** Something transparent; esp., a picture on a substance, as glass, intended to be viewed by shining a light through it.

trans·par·ent (trans-pâr′ənt, -par′-) *adj.* **1.** Admitting the passage of light, and permitting a clear view of objects beyond. **2.** Easy to see through or understand; obvious. **3.** Without guile; frank; candid. **4.** Diaphanous; sheer. — **Syn.** See CLEAR. [< Med.L < L *trans-* across + *parere* to appear, be visible] — **trans·par′ent·ly** *adv.* — **trans·par′ent·ness** *n.*

trans·pierce (trans-pirs′) *v.t.* **·pierced, ·pierc·ing** To pierce through; penetrate completely. [< MF < *trans-* (< L, across, through) + *percer* to pierce]

tran·spire (tran-spīr′) *v.* **·spired, ·spir·ing** *v.t.* **1.** To give off (waste products) from the surface of the body, leaves, etc.; exhale. — *v.i.* **2.** To give off waste products, as the surface of the body, leaves, etc. **3.** To become known. **4.** *Informal* To happen; occur. ◆ Although *transpire* is used widely in this last sense, this usage is considered erroneous by some. [< F < L *trans-* across, through + *spirare* to breathe] — **tran·spi·ra·tion** *n.*

trans·plant (*v.* trans·plant′, -plänt′; *n.* trans′plant′, -plänt′) *v.t.* **1.** To remove and plant in another place. **2.** To remove and settle or establish for residence in another place. **3.** *Surg.* To transfer (a portion of tissue) from its original site to another part of the same individual, or to another individual. — *n.* **1.** That which is transplanted. **2.** The act of transplanting. [< LL < L *trans-* across + *plantare* to plant] — **trans′plan·ta′tion** *n.* — **trans·plant′er** *n.*

trans·port (*v.* trans·pôrt′, -pōrt′; *n.* trans′pôrt, -pōrt) *v.t.* **1.** To carry or convey from one place to another. **2.** To carry away with emotion. **3.** To carry into banishment, esp. beyond the sea. — **Syn.** See BANISH. — *n.* **1.** A vessel used to transport troops, military supplies, etc. **2.** An aircraft used to transport passengers, mail, etc. **3.** The state of being transported with rapture; ecstasy. **4.** The act of transporting. **5.** A deported convict. [< MF < L < *trans-* across + *portare* to carry] — **trans·port′er** *n.*

trans·port·a·ble (trans·pôr′tə·bəl, -pōr′-) *adj.* Capable of being transported. — **trans·port′a·bil′i·ty** *n.*

trans·por·ta·tion (trans′pər·tā′shən) *n.* **1.** The act of transporting, or the state of being transported. **2.** A means of transporting, as a vehicle. **3.** A charge for conveyance. **4.** A ticket, pass, etc., for travel.

trans·pose (trans·pōz′) *v.t.* **·posed, ·pos·ing** **1.** To reverse the order or change the place of; interchange. **2.** To change in place or order, as a word in a sentence. **3.** *Math.* To transfer (a term) with a changed sign from one side of an algebraic equation to the other, so as not to destroy the equality of the members. **4.** *Music* To move (a chord, melody, composition, etc.) upward or downward in pitch while retaining its internal interval structure. — *v.i.* **5.** *Music* To play in a key other than the one notated: said of players or instruments. [< OF < L *trans-* over + OF *poser* to place] — **trans·pos′a·ble** *adj.* — **trans·pos′er** *n.* — **trans′po·si′tion, trans·po′sal** *n.*

trans·sex·u·al (trans-sek′shōō-əl, -sek′shəl) *n.* **1.** A person who is genetically and physically of one sex but who identifies psychologically with the other. **2.** One whose sex characteristics have been altered by surgery and hormone treatment.

trans·ship (trans-ship′) *v.t. & v.i.* **·shipped, ·ship·ping** To transfer from one conveyance or line to another: also spelled *tranship*. — **trans·ship′ment** *n.*

tran·sub·stan·ti·a·tion (tran′səb·stan′shē·ā′shən) *n.* **1.** *Theol.* The doctrine that the substance of the eucharistic elements is converted into that of the body and blood of Christ. **2.** A change of anything into something essentially different. [< Med.L < L *trans-* over + *substantia* substance] — **tran′sub·stan′ti·a′tion·al·ist** *n.*

trans·u·ra·ni·an (trans′yōō·rā′nē·ən, tranz′-) *adj. Physics* Of or pertaining to any of those radioactive elements having an atomic number greater than that of uranium. Also **trans′·u·ran′ic** (-ran′ik).

trans·ver·sal (trans·vûr′səl, tranz-) *adj.* Transverse. — *n. Geom.* A line intersecting a system of lines.

trans·verse (trans·vûrs′, tranz-) *adj.* Lying or being across or from side to side; athwart. — *n.* **1.** That which is transverse. **2.** *Geom.* That axis of a hyperbola that passes through its foci. [< L < *trans-* across + *vertere* to turn] — **trans·verse′ly** *adv.* — **trans·verse′ness** *n.*

trans·ves·tite (trans·ves′tīt, tranz-) *n.* One who wears the clothes of the opposite sex. [< L *trans-* over + *vestire* to clothe + -ITE] — **trans·ves′tism, trans·ves′ti·tism** *n.*

trap[1] (trap) *n.* **1.** A device for catching game or other animals, as a pitfall or snare. **2.** Any artifice or stratagem by which a person may be betrayed or taken unawares. **3.** *Mech.* A U- or S-bend in a pipe, etc., that fills with water or other liquid for sealing the pipe against a return flow, as of noxious gas. **4.** A contrivance for hurling clay pigeons or glass balls into the air for sportsmen to shoot at. **5.** In some games, esp. golf, an obstacle or hazard: a sand *trap.* **6.** A light, two-wheeled carriage suspended by springs. **7.** *pl.* Percussion instruments, as drums, cymbals, etc. **8.** A trap door. **9.** *U.S. Slang* The mouth: Shut your *trap.* — *v.* **trapped, trap·ping** *v.t.* **1.** To catch in a trap; ensnare. **2.** To stop or hold (a gas, liquid, etc.) by some obstruction. **3.** To provide with a trap. — *v.i.* **4.** To set traps for game. **5.** To be a trapper. [OE *treppe, træppe*]

trap[2] (trap) *n. Geol.* A dark, fine-grained igneous rock, often of columnar structure, as basalt, dolerite, etc. Also **trap′·rock′** (rok′). [< Sw. *trappa* stair; so called from the steplike arrangement of this rock in other rock]

trap door A door, hinged or sliding, to cover an opening, as in a floor or roof.

tra·peze (trə·pēz′, tra-) *n.* **1.** A short swinging bar, sus-

pended by two ropes, used by gymnasts, etc. **2.** *Geom.* A trapezium. [< F < NL *trapezium* trapezium]

tra·pe·zi·um (trə·pē′zē·əm) *n. pl.* **·zi·a** (-zē·ə) **1.** *Geom.* **a** A four-sided plane figure of which no two sides are parallel. **b** *Brit.* A trapezoid. **2.** *Anat.* The bone of the wrist situated at the base of the thumb. [< NL < Gk. *trapezion,* dim. of *trapeza* table, lit., four-footed (bench) < *tetra-* four, + *peza* foot]

TRAPEZIUM (*a*) AND TRAPEZOID (*b*)

trap·e·zoid (trap′ə·zoid) *n.* **1.** *Geom.* **a** A quadrilateral of which two sides are parallel. **b** *Brit.* A trapezium. **2.** *Anat.* An irregular bone near the base of the forefinger. [< NL < Gk. < *trapeza* table + *eidos* form] — **trap′e·zoi′dal** *adj.*

trap·per (trap′ər) *n.* One whose occupation is the trapping of fur-bearing animals.

trap·pings (trap′ingz) *n.pl.* **1.** An ornamental housing or harness for a horse. **2.** Adornments of any kind; embellishments; superficial dress. [< obs. *traps* < ME *trappe*]

Trap·pist (trap′ist) *n.* A member of an ascetic order of Cistercian monks, noted for silence and abstinence. — *adj.* Of or pertaining to the Trappists. [after *La Trappe* in Normandy, name of their first abbey, established 1664]

trap·shoot·ing (trap′shōō′ting) *n.* The sport of shooting clay pigeons sent up from spring traps. — **trap′shoot′er** *n.*

trash (trash) *n.* **1.** Worthless or waste matter of any kind; rubbish. **2.** A worthless or despicable individual or group of individuals. **3.** Worthless or foolish writing, ideas, etc.; nonsense. **4.** That which is broken or lopped off; esp., the loppings and trimmings of trees and plants. — *v.t.* **1.** To free from trash. **2.** To strip of leaves; prune; lop. [Cf. dial. Norw. *trask* lumber, trash, baggage]

trash·y (trash′ē) *adj.* **trash·i·er, trash·i·est** Resembling trash or rubbish; worthless; cheap: *trashy* poetry. — **trash′·i·ly** *adv.* — **trash′i·ness** *n.*

trau·ma (trô′mə, trou′-) *n. pl.* **·mas** or **·ma·ta** (-mə·tə) **1.** *Pathol.* **a** Any injury to the body caused by shock, violence, etc.; a wound. **b** The general condition of the system resulting from such an injury or wound. Also **trau′ma·tism** (-tiz′əm). **2.** *Psychiatry* A severe emotional shock having a deep, often lasting effect upon the personality. [< NL < Gk. *trauma, -atos* wound]

trau·mat·ic (trô·mat′ik) *adj.* Of, pertaining to, or caused by a trauma. — **trau·mat′i·cal·ly** *adv.*

tra·vail (trav′āl, trə·vāl′) *v.i.* **1.** To toil; labor. **2.** To suffer the pangs of childbirth. — *n.* **1.** Strenuous physical or mental labor. **2.** Anguish; pain. **3.** Labor in childbirth. [< OF < *travaillier* to toil, ult. < LL *trepalium* instrument of torture < *tres, tria* three + *palus* stake]

trav·el (trav′əl) *v.* **trav·eled** or **·elled, trav·el·ing** or **·el·ling** *v.i.* **1.** To go from one place to another; make a journey or tour. **2.** To proceed; advance. **3.** To go about from place to place as a traveling salesman. **4.** *U.S. Informal* To move with speed. **5.** To pass or be transmitted, as light, sound, etc. **6.** *Mech.* To move in a fixed path, as part of a mechanism. — *v.t.* **7.** To move or journey across or through; traverse. — *n.* **1.** The act of traveling. **2.** *pl.* A trip or journey. **3.** A movement or progress of any kind. **4.** *Mech.* **a** The full course of a moving part in one direction. **b** Length of stroke, as of a piston. [Var. of TRAVAIL]

trav·eled (trav′əld) *adj.* **1.** Having made many journeys. **2.** Experienced as the result of travel. **3.** Frequented or used by travelers. Also **trav′elled.**

trav·el·er (trav′əl·ər, trav′lər) *n.* **1.** One who travels or journeys. **2.** *Brit.* A traveling salesman. **3.** *Naut.* A metal ring or thimble running freely on a rope, rod, or spar; also, the rope, rod, or spar. Also **trav′el·ler.**

traveler's check A draft issued by a bank, express company, etc., having the bearer's signature, and payable when the bearer signs it again in order to cash it.

traveling salesman A salesman who travels to various places obtaining orders for his firm. Also **traveling man.**

trav·e·logue (trav′ə·lôg, -log) *n.* A lecture or film on travel. Also **trav′e·log.**

tra·verse (trav′ərs; *for v. & adv.,* also trə·vûrs′) *v.* **·versed, ·vers·ing** *v.t.* **1.** To pass over, across, or through. **2.** To move back and forth over or along. **3.** To examine carefully; survey or scrutinize. **4.** To oppose; thwart. **5.** To turn (a gun, lathe, etc.) to right or left; swivel. **6.** *Law* **a** In legal pleading, to deny (a matter of fact alleged by the opposite party). **b** To impeach (the validity of an inquest of office). **7.** *Naut.* To brace (a yard) fore and aft. — *v.i.* **8.** To move back and forth. **9.** To move across; cross. **10.** To turn; swivel. — *n.* **1.** A part, as of a machine or structure, placed across or traversing another, as a crosspiece, crossbeam, transom, etc. **2.** *Archit.* A gallery or loft communicating with opposite sides of a building. **3.** Something serving as a screen or barrier. **4.** *Geom.* A transversal. **5.** The act of traversing or crossing. **6.** A way or path across. **7.** *Mech.* Sidewise travel, as of the tool in a slide rest. **8.** *Law* A formal denial. **9.** *Naut.* A zigzag track of a vessel while beating to windward. —*adj.* Transverse; lying or being across. [< OF < LL < L *trans-* across + *vertere* to turn] — **trav·ers·a·ble** *adj.* — **trav·er·sal** (trav′ər·səl, trə·vûr′səl) *n.* — **trav·ers·er** *n.*

trav·er·tine (trav′ər·tin, -tēn, -tīn) *n.* A porous, light yellow, crystalline limestone deposited in solution from ground or surface waters, used for building purposes. Also **trav′er·tin** (-tin). [< Ital. < L *Tiburtinus* Tiburtine < *Tibur,* -*ur·tis* of Tibur]

trav·es·ty (trav′is·tē) *n.* *pl.* **·ties** **1.** A grotesque imitation; burlesque. **2.** In literature, a burlesque treatment of a lofty subject. —*v.t.* **·tied, ·ty·ing** To make a travesty on; parody. [< MF < Ital. < L *trans* across + *vestire* to dress]

trawl (trôl) *n.* **1.** A stout fishing line having many lines frequently spaced and bearing baited hooks: also called *trotline.* Also **trawl line. 2.** A great fishing net shaped like a flattened bag, for towing on the bottom of the ocean by a boat: also **trawl net.** —*v.t.* **1.** To catch (fish) with a trawl. —*v.i.* **2.** To fish with a trawl. [Cf. MDu. *traghel* dragnet]

trawl·er (trô′lər) *n.* **1.** A vessel used for trawling. **2.** One who is engaged in trawling.

tray (trā) *n.* A flat receptacle with a low rim, made of wood, metal, etc., used to carry, hold, or display articles: a sandwich *tray.* [OE *trīg, trēg* wooden board]

treach·er·ous (trech′ər·əs) *adj.* **1.** Traitorous; perfidious; disloyal. **2.** Having a deceptive appearance; unreliable; untrustworthy: a *treacherous* path. — **treach′er·ous·ly** *adv.* — **treach′er·ous·ness** *n.*

treach·er·y (trech′ər·ē) *n.* *pl.* **·er·ies** Violation of allegiance, confidence, or faith; perfidy; treason. [< OF < *tricher, trechier* to cheat]

trea·cle (trē′kəl) *n.* **1.** *Brit.* Molasses. **2.** Formerly, a compound used as an antidote. [< OF < L < Gk. *thēriakē* remedy for poisonous bites] — **trea′cly** *adj.*

tread (tred) *v.* **trod** (*Archaic* **trode**), **trod·den** or **trod, tread·ing** *v.t.* **1.** To step or walk on, over, along, etc. **2.** To press with the feet; trample. **3.** To accomplish in walking or in dancing: to *tread* a measure. **4.** To copulate with: said of male birds. —*v.i.* **5.** To step or walk. **6.** To trample: usually with *on.* — **to tread water** In swimming, to keep the body erect and the head above water by moving the feet up and down as if walking. —*n.* **1.** The act, manner, or sound of treading or walking. **2.** The flat part of a step in a staircase. **3.** The part of a wheel that bears upon the ground or rails. **4.** The outer, often grooved surface of an automobile tire. **5.** That part of the sole of a shoe that treads upon the ground. **6.** The part of a rail on which the wheels bear. [OE *tredan*] — **tread′er** *n.*

tread·le (tred′l) *n.* A lever operated by the foot, usu. to cause rotary motion. For illus. see POTTER'S WHEEL. —*v.i.* **·led, ·ling** To work a treadle. [OE < *tredan* to tread] — **tread′ler** *n.*

tread·mill (tred′mil′) *n.* **1.** A mechanism rotated by the walking motion of one or more persons. **2.** A similar mechanism operated by a quadruped. **3.** Any wearisome or monotonous work, activity, routine, etc.

trea·son (trē′zən) *n.* **1.** Betrayal or breach of allegiance or of obedience toward one's sovereign or government. **2.** *Rare* A breach of faith; treachery. [< AF *treyson,* OF *traison* < L *traditio,* -*onis* betrayal, delivery]

trea·son·a·ble (trē′zən·ə·bəl) *adj.* Of, involving, or characteristic of treason. Also **trea′son·ous.** — **trea′son·a·ble·ness** *n.* — **trea′son·a·bly** *adv.*

treas·ure (trezh′ər) *n.* **1.** Riches accumulated or possessed, esp. in the form of money, jewels, or precious metals. **2.** One who or that which is regarded as valuable, precious, or rare. —*v.t.* **·ured, ·ur·ing** **1.** To lay up in store; accumulate. **2.** To retain carefully, as in the mind. **3.** To set a high value upon; prize. [< OF < L < Gk. *thēsauros*]

treas·ur·er (trezh′ər·ər) *n.* An officer of a state, city, corporation, society, etc., who has charge of funds or revenues.

Treasure State Nickname of Montana.

trea·sure-trove (trezh′ər·trōv′) *n.* **1.** *Law* Any treasure found hidden in the earth, etc., the owner being unknown. **2.** Any discovery that proves valuable. [< AF < *tresor* + *trové,* pp., of *trover* to find]

treas·ur·y (trezh′ər·ē) *n.* *pl.* **·ur·ies** **1.** The place where private or public funds or revenues are received, kept, and disbursed. **2.** Any public or private funds or revenues. **3.** Any group or collection of treasures or things regarded as treasures. **4.** A place or receptacle where treasures are kept. — **Department of the Treasury** An executive department of the U.S. government that superintends and manages the national finances. Also **Treasury Department.**

treasury note *U.S.* A note issued by the Treasury as legal tender for all debts, public and private.

treat (trēt) *v.t.* **1.** To conduct oneself toward in a specified manner. **2.** To look upon or regard in a specified manner:

They *treat* the matter as a joke. **3.** To subject to chemical or physical action, as for altering or improving. **4.** To give medical or surgical attention to. **5.** To deal with in writing or speaking. **6.** To deal with or develop (a subject in art or literature) in a specified manner or style. **7.** To pay for the entertainment, food, or drink of. —*v.i.* **8.** To handle a subject in writing or speaking: usu. with *of.* **9.** To negotiate. **10.** To pay for another's entertainment or food. —*n.* **1.** Something that gives unusual pleasure. **2.** Entertainment furnished gratuitously to another. **3.** The act of treating; also, one's turn to treat. [< OF < L *tractare* to handle] — **treat′a·ble** *adj.* — **treat′er** *n.*

trea·tise (trē′tis) *n.* A formal and systematic written account of some subject. [< AF *tretiz,* OF *traitier* to treat]

treat·ment (trēt′mənt) *n.* **1.** The act, manner, or process of treating. **2.** The care of an illness, by drugs, surgery, etc. **3.** The manner of handling an artistic or literary subject.

trea·ty (trē′tē) *n.* *pl.* **·ties** A formal agreement or compact, duly concluded and ratified, between two or more states; also, the document containing such an agreement or compact. [< AF *treté,* OF *traitie,* pp. of *traitier* to treat]

treb·le (treb′əl) *v.t. & v.i.* **·led, ·ling** To multiply by three; triple. —*adj.* **1.** Threefold; triple. **2.** Soprano. —*n.* **1.** *Music* **a** A soprano voice, part, or instrument; also, the singer or player taking this part. **b** The highest register of an instrument. **2.** High, piping sound. [< OF < L *triplus*] — **treb′le·ness** *n.* — **treb′ly** *adv.*

tree (trē) *n.* **1.** A perennial woody plant having usu. a single self-supporting trunk of considerable height, with branches and foliage growing at some distance above the ground. ◆ Collateral adjective: *arboreal.* **2.** Any shrub or plant that assumes treelike shape or dimensions. **3.** Something resembling a tree in form or outline, as a clothes tree, crosstree, etc. **4.** A diagram or outline resembling a tree and showing family descent. **5.** A timber, post, pole, etc.: used in combination: *axletree.* — **up a tree** *Informal* In a position from which there is no retreat; cornered: also, in an embarrassing position. —*v.t.* **treed, tree·ing** **1.** To force to climb or take refuge in a tree: to *tree* an opossum. **2.** *Informal* To get the advantage of; corner. **3.** To stretch, as a boot, on a boot tree. [OE *trēow, trīow, trēo*]

tree fern Any of various ferns with large fronds and woody trunks that often attain a treelike size.

tree frog An arboreal amphibian, having the toes dilated with viscous, adhesive disks: also called *tree toad.*

tree of heaven The ailanthus.

tree of knowledge of good and evil In the Bible, a tree in Eden whose fruit Adam and Eve were forbidden to eat. *Gen.* iii 3, 6. Also **tree of knowledge.**

Tree-Plant·er State (trē′plan′tər, -plän′-) Nickname of Nebraska.

tree sparrow A North American sparrow that nests in Canada and migrates southward in winter.

tree surgery The treatment of disease conditions and decay in trees by operative methods. — **tree surgeon**

tree toad A tree frog.

tree·top (trē′top′) *n.* The highest part of a tree.

tre·foil (trē′foil) *n.* **1.** Any of a genus of leguminous plants, the clovers, with red, purple, pink, or yellow flowers and trifoliate leaflets. **2.** A three-lobed architectural ornamentation. [< AF, OF < L *trifolium*]

trek (trek) *v.* **trekked, trek·king** *v.i.* **1.** In South Africa, to travel by ox wagon. **2.** To travel, esp. slowly or arduously. —*v.t.* **3.** In South Africa, to draw (a vehicle or load): said of an ox. —*n.* **1.** In South Africa, a journey or any part of it; esp., an organized migration, as for the founding of a colony. **2.** A journey; esp., a slow or arduous journey. [< Du. < MDu. < OHG *trechan* to draw] — **trek′ker** *n.*

trel·lis (trel′is) *n.* **1.** A crossbarred structure or panel of wood, metal, or other material, used as a screen or a support for vines, etc. **2.** A summerhouse, archway, etc., made from or consisting of such a structure. —*v.t.* **1.** To interlace so as to form a trellis. **2.** To furnish with or fasten on a trellis. [< OF < L < *tri-* three + *licium* thread]

trel·lis·work (trel′is·wûrk′) *n.* Openwork made from, consisting of, or resembling a trellis.

trem·a·tode (trem′ə·tōd) *n.* One of a class of parasitic flatworms, including the liver flukes. [< NL < Gk. < *trēma,* -*atos* hole + *eidos* form] — **trem′a·toid** (-toid) *adj.*

trem·ble (trem′bəl) *v.i.* **bled, ·bling** **1.** To shake involuntarily, as with fear or weakness; be agitated. **2.** To have slight, irregular vibratory motion, as from some jarring force; shake. **3.** To feel anxiety or fear. **4.** To quaver, as the voice. —*n.* The act or state of trembling. [< OF < LL *tremulus* tremulous < *tremere* to tremble] — **trem′bler** *n.* — **trem′bling·ly** *adv.* — **trem′bly** *adj.*

tre·men·dous (tri·men′dəs) *adj.* **1.** *Informal* Extraordinarily large; huge; vast. **2.** *Informal* Unusual; amazing; wonderful. **3.** Causing astonishment by its magnitude, force, etc. [< L *tremendus* to be trembled at < *tremere* to tremble] — **tre·men′dous·ly** *adv.* — **tre·men′dous·ness** *n.*

trem·o·lo (trem′ə·lō) *n. pl.* **·los** *Music* **1.** In string instrument playing, a rapid reiteration of a tone caused by alternating movements of the bow. **2.** A rapid alternation of two tones, usu. a third or more apart. Compare TRILL. **3.** A device or stop for producing a vibrato effect on an organ tone. [< Ital. < L *tremulus*]

trem·or (trem′ər, trē′mər) *n.* **1.** A quick, vibratory movement; a shaking. **2.** Any involuntary and continued quivering or trembling of the body or limbs; a shiver. **3.** A quavering sound. **4.** Any trembling, quivering effect. [< OF, fear, a trembling < L < *tremere* to tremble]

trem·u·lous (trem′yə·ləs) *adj.* **1.** Characterized or affected by trembling: *tremulous* speech. **2.** Showing timidity or fear. — **trem′u·lous·ly** *adv.* — **trem′u·lous·ness** *n.*

trench (trench) *n.* **1.** A long narrow excavation in the ground; ditch. **2.** A long irregular ditch, lined with a parapet of the excavated earth, to protect troops. — *v.t.* **1.** To dig a trench or trenches in. **2.** To fortify with trenches. **3.** To cut deep furrows in; ditch. **4.** To confine in a trench, as water. — *v.i.* **5.** To cut or dig trenches. **6.** To cut; carve. **7.** To encroach. [< OF *trenchier* to cut, ult. < L *truncare* to lop off < *truncus* tree trunk] — **trench′er** *n.*

trench·ant (tren′chənt) *adj.* **1.** Cutting; incisive; keen: a *trenchant* remark. **2.** Forceful; vigorous; effective. **3.** Clearly defined; distinct. [< OF, ppr. of *trenchier* to cut] — **trench′an·cy** *n.* — **trench′ant·ly** *adv.*

trench coat A loose-fitting overcoat of rainproof fabric.

trench·er (tren′chər) *n.* Formerly, a wooden plate or board on which food was served or cut. [See TRENCH⁶]

trench·er·man (tren′chər·mən) *n. pl.* **·men** (-mən) A feeder; eater; esp., one who enjoys food.

trench fever *Pathol.* A remittent rickettsial fever transmitted by body lice and common among soldiers assigned to prolonged service in trenches during World War I.

trench foot *Pathol.* A disease of the feet caused by continued dampness and cold, and characterized by discoloration, weakness, and sometimes gangrene.

trench mouth *Pathol.* A disease of the mouth, gums, and sometimes the larynx and tonsils, caused by a soil bacillus.

trend (trend) *n.* A general course, inclination, or direction. — *v.i.* To have or take a particular trend. [OE *trendan* to roll]

tre·pan (tri·pan′) *n.* **1.** An early form of the trephine. **2.** A large rock-boring tool. — *v.t.* **·panned, ·pan·ning 1.** *Mech.* To cut circular disks from (a rock or metal plate) by a rotary tool. **2.** *Surg.* To trephine. [< OF, borer < Med.L < Gk. < *trypaein* to bore] — **trep·a·na·tion** (trep′ə·nā′shən) *n.* — **tre·pan′ner** *n.*

tre·pang (tri·pang′) *n.* An East Indian sea cucumber, used in China for making soup. [< Malay *trīpang*]

tre·phine (tri·fīn′, -fēn′) *n. Surg.* A crown saw for removing a piece of bone from the skull so as to relieve pressure, etc. — *v.t.* **·phined, ·phin·ing** To operate on with a trephine. [< earlier *trafine* < L *tres fines* three ends]

trep·i·da·tion (trep′ə·dā′shən) *n.* **1.** A state of agitation or alarm; perturbation. **2.** An involuntary trembling. Also **tre·pid·i·ty** (tri·pid′ə·tē). [< L < *trepidatus*, pp. of *trepidare* to hurry, be alarmed < *trepidus* alarmed]

trep·o·neme (trep′ə·nēm) *n.* Any of a group of bacteria including the causative agent of syphilis. [< NL < Gk. *trepein* to turn + *nēma* thread] — **trep′o·nem′a·tous** (-nem′ə·təs) *adj.*

tres·pass (tres′pəs, -pas′) *v.i.* **1.** *Law* To commit a trespass; esp., to enter wrongfully upon another's land: with *on* or *upon*. **2.** To pass the bounds of propriety or rectitude, to the injury of another; intrude offensively; encroach: with *on* or *upon*. **3.** To transgress or sin. — *n.* **1.** Any voluntary transgression of law or rule of duty; any offense done to another. **2.** *Law* Any wrongful act accompanied with force, either actual or implied, as wrongful entry on another's land. [< OF < Med.L < L *trans-* across, beyond + *to* pass] — **tres′pass·er** *n.*

tress (tres) *n.* **1.** A lock, or ringlet of human hair. **2.** *pl.* The hair of a woman or girl, esp. when worn loose. [< OF *tresce*] — **tress′y** *adj.*

-tress *suffix* Used to form many feminine nouns corresponding to masculine nouns in *-ter*, *-tor*: *actress*. [Var. of *-ESS*]

tressed (trest) *adj.* Wearing or arranged in tresses; braided.

tres·tle (tres′əl) *n.* **1.** A beam or bar supported by four divergent legs, for bearing platforms, etc. **2.** An open braced framework for supporting a railway bridge, etc. [< OF < L, dim. of *transtrum* crossbeam]

tres·tle·work (tres′əl·wûrk′) *n.* **1.** Trestles collectively. **2.** A bridge made of trestles. Also **tres′tling**.

trey (trā) *n.* A card, domino, or die having three spots or pips. [< OF *trei*, *treis* < L *tres* three]

tri- *prefix* **1.** Three; threefold; thrice. **2.** *Chem.* Containing three (specified) atoms, radicals, groups, etc.: *trioxide*.

3. Occurring every three (specified) intervals, or three times within an (assigned) interval: *tri-weekly*. [< L *tri-* threefold]

tri·a·ble (trī′ə·bəl) *adj.* **1.** That may be tried or tested. **2.** *Law* That may undergo a judicial examination or determination. — **tri′a·ble·ness** *n.*

tri·ad (trī′ad) *n.* **1.** A group of three persons or things. **2.** *Music* A chord of three tones formed of superimposed thirds. [< L < Gk. *trias*, *-ados* < *treis* three] — **tri·ad′ic** *adj.* & *n.*

tri·al (trī′əl, trīl) *n.* **1.** The examination before a court of the facts or law in a case in order to determine that case. **2.** The act of testing or proving by experience or use. **3.** The state of being tried or tested, as by suffering: hour of *trial*. **4.** Experimental treatment or action performed to determine a result: to learn by *trial* and error. **5.** An attempt or effort to do something; a try: to make a *trial*. — **on trial** In the process of being tried or tested. — *adj.* **1.** Of or pertaining to a trial or trials. **2.** Made, used, or performed in the course of trying or testing. [< AF *trier* to try]

trial and error Experimentation, investigation, learning, etc., in which various methods, theories, or alternatives are tried and faulty or erroneous ones are rejected.

trial balance In double-entry bookkeeping, a draft or statement of the debit and credit footings or balances of each account in the ledger.

trial balloon 1. A balloon released in order to test atmospheric and meteorological conditions. **2.** Any tentative plan or scheme advanced to test public reaction.

trial jury A petit jury.

tri·an·gle (trī′ang′gəl) *n.* **1.** *Geom.* A figure, esp. a plane figure, bounded by three sides, and having three angles. **2.** Something resembling such a figure in shape or arrangement. **3.** A flat drawing implement for making parallel or diagonal lines, etc. **4.** A group or set of three; a triad. **5.** A situation involving three persons: the eternal *triangle*. **6.** *Music* An instrument consisting of a metal bar bent into a triangle and sounded by being struck with a metal rod. [< OF < L < *tri-* three + *angulus* angle]

tri·an·gu·lar (trī·ang′gyə·lər) *adj.* **1.** Pertaining to, like, or bounded by a triangle. **2.** Concerned with or pertaining to three things, parties, or persons. — **tri·an′gu·lar′i·ty** (-lar′ə·tē) *n.* — **tri·an′gu·lar·ly** *adv.*

tri·an·gu·late (trī·ang′gyə·lāt) *v.t.* **·lated, ·lat·ing 1.** To divide into triangles. **2.** To survey by triangulation. **3.** To make triangular. — *adj.* Of or marked with triangles.

tri·an·gu·la·tion (trī·ang′gyə·lā′shən) *n.* **1.** The laying out and accurate measurement of a network of triangles. **2.** A method of determining a position by taking bearings to two fixed points of known distance apart and computing it on the resultant triangle.

Tri·as·sic (trī·as′ik) *adj. Geol.* Of or pertaining to the earliest of the three geological periods comprised in the Mesozoic era. — *n.* The Triassic period or rock system, following the Permian and succeeded by the Jurassic. Also **Tri·as** (trī′əs). See chart under GEOLOGY. [< LL *trias* triad]

tri·bal·ism (trī′bəl·iz′əm) *n.* Tribal organization, culture, or relations.

tribe (trīb) *n.* **1.** A division, class, or group of people, esp. a primitive or nomadic people, usu. characterized by common ancestry, leadership, customs, etc. **2.** In ancient states, an ethnic, hereditary, or political division of a united people; also, one of the twelve divisions of ancient Israel. **3.** A number of persons of any class or profession taken together: often an offensive term: the theatrical *tribe*. **4.** *Biol.* A group of plants or animals of indefinite rank. [< L *tribus* tribe] — **tri′bal** *adj.* — **tri′bal·ly** *adv.*

tribes·man (trībz′mən) *n. pl.* **·men** (-mən) A member of a tribe.

trib·u·la·tion (trib′yə·lā′shən) *n.* A condition of affliction and distress; suffering; also, that which causes it. [< OF < LL < L < *tribulum* threshing floor < *terere* to rub, grind]

tri·bu·nal (tri·byōo′nəl, trī-) *n.* **1.** A court of justice. **2.** The seat apart for judges, etc. [See TRIBUNE.]

trib·une¹ (trib′yōon) *n.* **1.** In Roman history, a magistrate chosen by the plebeians to protect them against patrician oppression. **2.** Any champion of the people. [< L *tribunus* < *tribus* tribe] — **trib′u·nar′y** (-yə·ner′ē), **trib′u·ni′cial** (-yə·nish′əl), **trib′u·ni′cian** *adj.* — **trib′u·nate** (-yə·nit, -nāt), **trib′·une·ship** *n.*

trib·une² (trib′yōon) *n.* A rostrum or platform. [< MF < Ital. < L *tribunal* tribunal]

trib·u·tar·y (trib′yə·ter′ē) *adj.* **1.** Bringing supply; contributory: a *tributary* stream. **2.** Offered or due as tribute: a *tributary* payment. **3.** Paying tribute, as a state. — *n. pl.* **·tar·ies 1.** A person or state paying tribute. **2.** A stream flowing into a larger stream or body of water. [See TRIBUTE.] — **trib′u·tar′i·ly** *adv.* — **trib′u·tar′i·ness** *n.*

trib·ute (trib′yōot) *n.* **1.** A speech, compliment, gift, etc., given in acknowledgment of admiration, gratitude, or respect. **2.** Money or other valuables paid by one state or ruler to another as an acknowledgment of submission or as the price of peace and protection; also, the taxes imposed to raise money to make such payment. **3.** Any enforced payment as by bribery. [< L *tribuere* to pay, allot]

trice (trīs) *v.t.* **triced, tric·ing** To raise with a rope; also, to tie or lash: usu. with *up.* — *n.* An instant: now only in the phrase **in a trice.** [< MDu. *trisen* to hoist]

tri·cen·ten·ni·al (trī/sen·ten/ē·əl) *adj. & n.* Tercentenary.

tri·ceps (trī/seps) *n. Anat.* A large muscle at the back of the upper arm, of which the function is to extend the forearm. [< L < *tri-* three + *caput* head]

tri·chi·na (tri·kī/nə) *n. pl.* **·nae** (-nē) A small nematode worm, parasitic in the intestines and muscles of man, swine, and other mammals. [< NL < Gk. *thrix* hair]

trich·i·no·sis (trik/ə·nō/sis) *n. Pathol.* The disease produced by trichinae in the intestines and muscles of the body, in man, usu. through eating improperly cooked meat, esp. pork. — **trich/i·nous** (-nəs) *adj.*

tricho- *combining form* Hair; of or resembling a hair or hairs. Also **trichi-**: also, before vowels, **trich-.** [< NL < Gk. *thrix* hair]

trick (trik) *n.* **1.** A device for getting an advantage by deception; a petty artifice; ruse. **2.** A malicious, injurious, or annoying act: a dirty *trick.* **3.** A practical joke; prank. **4.** A particular habit or manner; characteristic; trait. **5.** A peculiar skill or knack. **6.** An act of legerdemain or magic. **7.** In card games, the whole number of cards played in one round. — **to do** (or **turn**) **the trick** *Slang* To produce the desired result. — *v.t.* **1.** To deceive or cheat; delude. **2.** To dress or array: with *up* or *out.* — *v.i.* **3.** To practice trickery or deception. [< OF < *trichier* to cheat, prob. ult. < L < *tricae* trifles, tricks] — **trick/er** *n.* — **trick/less** *adj.*

trick·er·y (trik/ər·ē) *n. pl.* **·er·ies** The practice of tricks; artifice; stratagem; wiles.

trick·le (trik/əl) *v.* **·led, ·ling** *v.i.* **1.** To flow or run drop by drop or in a very thin stream. **2.** To move, come, go, etc., slowly or bit by bit. — *v.t.* **3.** To cause to trickle. — *n.* **1.** The act or state of trickling. **2.** Any slow and irregular movement. [ME *triklen*] — **trick/ly** *adj.*

trick·ster (trik/stər) *n.* One who plays tricks; a cheat.

trick·y (trik/ē) *adj.* **trick·i·er, trick·i·est** Disposed to or characterized by trickery; deceitful; wily. — **trick/i·ly** *adv.* — **trick/i·ness** *n.*

tri·col·or (trī/kul/ər) *adj.* Having or characterized by three colors: also **tri/col/ored.** — *n.* **1.** A flag of three colors. **2.** *Sometimes cap.* The French flag. Also *Brit.* **tri/col/our.** [< F < LL < L *tri-* three + *color* color]

tri·corn (trī/kôrn) *n.* A hat with the brim turned up on three sides. Also **tri/corne.** — *adj.* Having three hornlike processes. [< F < L < *tri-* three + *cornu* horn]

tri·cot (trē/kō, *Fr.* trē·kō/) *n.* **1.** A plain, knitted fabric, usu. machine made. **2.** A soft ribbed cloth. [< F < *tricoter* to knit]

tri·cus·pid (trī·kus/pid) *adj.* **1.** Having three cusps or points, as a molar tooth. **2.** *Anat.* Of the tricuspid valve. Also **tri·cus/pi·dal, tri·cus/pi·date.** — *n. Anat.* The tricuspid valve. [< L < *tri-* three + *cuspis* point]

tricuspid valve *Anat.* A three-segmented valve that controls the flow of blood from the right atrium to the right ventricle of the heart.

tri·cy·cle (trī/sik·əl) *n.* A three-wheeled vehicle; esp., such a vehicle with pedals. [< F < *tri-* three + Gk. *kyklos* circle]

tri·dent (trīd/nt) *n.* A three-pronged fork. — *adj.* Having three teeth or prongs: also **tri·den·tate** (trī·den/tāt), **tri·den/tat·ed.** [< L < *tri-* three + *dens* tooth]

tried (trīd) Past tense and past participle of TRY. — *adj.* Tested; trustworthy.

tri·en·ni·al (trī·en/ē·əl) *adj.* **1.** Taking place every third year. **2.** Lasting three years. — *n.* **1.** A third anniversary. **2.** A ceremony, etc., celebrated every three years. **3.** A plant lasting three years. — **tri·en/ni·al·ly** *adv.*

tri·er (trī/ər) *n.* One who or that which tries.

tri·fa·cial (trī·fā/shəl) *adj. Anat.* Trigeminal.

tri·fid (trī/fid) *adj.* Divided into three parts or sections. [< L < *tri-* three + *findere* to split]

tri·fle (trī/fəl) *v.* **·fled, ·fling** *v.i.* **1.** To treat something as of no value or importance; dally: with *with.* **2.** To act or speak frivolously. **3.** To play; toy. **4.** To idle. — *v.t.* **5.** To pass (time) in an idle and purposeless way. — *n.* **1.** Anything of very little value or importance. **2.** A confection, usu. made of alternate layers of macaroons or ladyfingers with sugared fruit, covered with a custard and topped with meringue or whipped cream. — **a trifle** Slightly: *a trifle* short. [< OF *trufe* cheating, mockery] — **tri/fler** *n.*

tri·fling (trī/fling) *adj.* **1.** Frivolous. **2.** Insignificant. — **tri/fling·ly** *adv.*

tri·fo·cal (trī·fō/kəl) *adj.* **1.** Having three foci. **2.** *Optics* Pertaining to or describing eyeglasses or a lens ground in three segments, for near, intermediate, and far vision. — *n. pl.* Eyeglasses having trifocal lenses.

tri·fo·li·ate (trī·fō/lē·it, -āt) *adj. Bot.* Having three leaves or leaflike processes. Also **tri·fo/li·at/ed.**

tri·fo·ri·um (trī·fôr/ē·əm, -fō/rē-) *n. pl.* **·fo·ri·a** (-fôr/ē·ə, -fō/rē·ə) *Archit.* A gallery above the arches of the nave in a church. [< Med.L < L *tri-* three + *foris* a door]

trig (trig) *adj.* **1.** Trim; neat. **2.** Strong; sound. — *v.t.* **trigged, trig·ging** To make trig or neat: often with *out* or *up.* [< ON *tryggr* true] — **trig/ly** *adv.* — **trig/ness** *n.*

tri·gem·i·nal (trī·jem/ə·nəl) *adj. Anat.* Of or pertaining to the trigeminus: also *trifacial.* — *n.* The trigeminus. [< L < *tri-* + *geminus* a twin]

tri·gem·i·nus (trī·jem/ə·nəs) *n. pl.* **·ni** (-nī) *Anat.* The double-rooted fifth cranial nerve, whose three divisions, mandibular, maxillary, and opthalmic, function as the great sensory nerve of the face. [See TRIGEMINAL.]

trig·ger (trig/ər) *n.* **1.** The lever or other device actuated manually to fire a firearm. **2.** Any lever, release, etc., that serves to initiate a process or operation. — **quick on the trigger 1.** Quick to shoot. **2.** Quick to act; alert. — *v.t.* To initiate; precipitate. [< Du. *trekken* to pull]

trigonometric functions Certain functions of an angle or arc, of which the most commonly used are the sine, cosine, tangent, cotangent, secant, and cosecant.

trig·o·nom·e·try (trig/ə·nom/ə·trē) *n.* The branch of mathematics that deals with the relations of the sides and angles of triangles. [< NL < Gk. *trigōnon* triangle + *metron* measure] — **trig·o·no·met·ric** (trig/ə·nə·met/rik) or **·ri·cal** *adj.* — **trig/o·no·met/ri·cal·ly** *adv.*

tri·he·dron (trī·hē/drən) *n. pl.* **·dra** (-drə) *Geom.* A figure having three plane surfaces meeting at a point. [< NL < Gk. *tri-* three + *hedra* a base] — **tri·he/dral** *adj.*

tri·lat·er·al (trī·lat/ər·əl) *adj.* Having three sides. [< L < *tri-* three + *latus* a side] — **tri·lat/er·al·ly** *adv.*

trill (tril) *v.t.* **1.** To sing or play in a tremulous tone. **2.** *Phonet.* To articulate with a trill. — *v.i.* **3.** To give forth a tremulous sound. **4.** *Music* To execute a trill. — *n.* **1.** A tremulous utterance of successive tones, as of birds; a warble. **2.** *Music* A rapid alternation of two tones either a tone or a semitone apart. **3.** *Phonet.* A rapid vibration of the tongue in the articulation of *rr* in Spanish, or of the uvula in the articulation of *r* in some varieties of German. **4.** A consonant so uttered. [< Ital. *trillare*]

tril·lion (tril/yən) *n.* **1.** *U.S.* A thousand billions, written as 1 followed by twelve zeros: a cardinal number: called a billion in Great Britain. **2.** *Brit.* A million billions (def. 2), written as 1 followed by eighteen zeros: a cardinal number. — *adj.* Being a trillion in number. [< MF < *tri-* three + (*mi*)*llion* million] — **tril/lionth** *adj. & n.*

tril·li·um (tril/ē·əm) *n.* Any of various herbs of the lily family, having a stout stem bearing a whorl of three leaves and a solitary flower. [< NL < L *tri-* three]

tri·lo·bate (trī·lō/bāt, trī/lə·bāt) *adj. Bot.* Having three lobes, as some leaves. Also **tri·lo/bal, tri·lo/bat·ed, tri/lobed.**

tri·lo·bite (trī/lə·bīt) *n. Paleontol.* Any of a group of extinct Paleozoic marine animals having a flattened body divided into a variable number of segments covered by a hard dorsal shield marked in three lobes. [< NL < Gk. *tri-* three + *lobos* a lobe] — **tri/lo·bit/ic** (-bit/ik) *adj.*

tril·o·gy (tril/ə·jē) *n. pl.* **·gies** A group of three literary or dramatic compositions, each complete in itself, but continuing the same general subject. [< Gk. < *tri-* three + *logos* a discourse]

trim (trim) *v.* **trimmed, trim·ming** *v.t.* **1.** To put in or restore to order; make neat by clipping, etc. **2.** To remove by cutting: usu. with *off* or *away.* **3.** To put ornaments on; decorate. **4.** In carpentry, to smooth; dress. **5.** *Informal* **a** To defeat. **b** To punish or thrash. **c** To rebuke. **d** To cheat. **6.** *Naut.* **a** To adjust (sails or yards) for sailing. **b** To balance (a ship) by adjusting cargo, etc. — *v.i.* **7.** To act so as to appear to favor both sides in a controversy. — *n.* **1.** State of adjustment or preparation; orderly disposition: All was in good *trim.* **2.** Condition as to general appearance; dress. **3.** *Naut.* **a** Fitness for sailing: said of a vessel in reference to disposition of ballast, masts, cargo, etc. **b** Degree of immersion. **4.** Particular character or nature. **5.** The moldings, etc., as about the doors of a building. **6.** Ornament; trapping; trimming; dress. — *adj.* **trim·mer, trim·mest 1.** Adjusted to a nicety; being in perfect order; handsomely equipped or of stylish and smart appearance; precise. **2.** Excellently fit; fine. — *adv.* In a trim manner: also **trim/ly.** [OE *trymman* to arrange, strengthen < *trum* strong] — **trim/mer** *n.* — **trim/ness** *n.*

trim·e·ter (trim/ə·tər) *n.* In prosody, a line of verse consisting of three metrical feet. — *adj.* In prosody, consisting of three metrical feet or of lines containing three metrical feet. [< L < Gk. < *tri-* three + *metron* measure] — **trim·et·ric** (trī·met/rik), **tri·met/ri·cal** *adj.*

tri·meth·yl·pen·tane (trī/meth·il·pen/tān) *n. Chem.* One of three isomeric hydrocarbon compounds, C_8H_{18}, one of which, often called isooctane, is used in rating motor fuels.

trim·ming (trim/ing) *n.* **1.** Something added for ornament.

2. *pl.* Articles or equipment; fittings, as the hardware of a house. **3.** *pl.* The usual or proper accompaniments or condiments of an article or food. **4.** *pl.* That which is removed by trimming. **5.** *Informal* A severe reproof; flogging; beating. **6.** *Informal* A defeat. **7.** The act of one who trims.

tri·month·ly (trī-munth'lē) *adj. & adv.* Done or occurring every third month.

tri·nal (trī'nəl) *adj.* Having three parts; threefold. Also *trine* (trīn). [< LL < L *tres* three]

tri·na·ry (trī'nər-ē) *adj.* Made up of three parts or proceeding by threes; ternary. [See TRINAL.]

Trin·i·tar·i·an (trin'ə-târ'ē-ən) *adj.* **1.** Of or pertaining to the Trinity. **2.** Holding or professing belief in the Trinity. Compare UNITARIAN. — *n.* A believer in the doctrine of the Trinity. — **Trin'i·tar'i·an·ism** *n.*

tri·ni·tro·tol·u·ene (trī'nī'trō-tol'yōō-ēn) *n. Chem.* A high explosive, $C_7H_5N_3O_6$, made by treating toluene with nitric acid, used in warfare, as a blasting agent, and as a base for measuring the explosive power of nuclear bombs: also called TNT, *trotyl.* Also **tri·ni'tro·tol'u·ol** (-yōō-ōl, -ol). [< TRI- + NITRO- + TOLUENE]

trin·i·ty (trin'ə-tē) *n. pl.* **·ties** Any union of three parts or elements in one; a trio. [< OF < LL < L < *trinus* triple]

Trin·i·ty (trin'ə-tē) *n. Theol.* A threefold personality existing in the one divine being or substance; the union in one God of Father, Son, and Holy Spirit.

Trinity Sunday *Eccl.* The eighth Sunday after Easter, observed as a festival in honor of the Trinity.

trin·ket (tring'kit) *n.* **1.** Any small ornament, as of jewelry. **2.** A trifle; a trivial object; a toy. [< AF *trenquet*, OF *trenchet* a toy knife, ornament]

tri·no·mi·al (trī-nō'mē-əl) *adj.* **1.** *Biol.* Of, having, or employing three terms or names in taxonomy, as the generic, the specific, and the subspecific or varietal, as *Lynx rufus texensis*, the Texas bobcat. **2.** *Math.* Consisting of three terms connected by plus or minus signs or both. — *n.* **1.** *Math.* A trinomial expression, as $3x + y - 27z$. **2.** *Biol.* A trinomial name. Also **tri·nom'i·nal** (-nom'ə-nəl), **tri·on'y·mal** (-on'ə-məl). [< L *trinominus* having three names]

tri·o (trē'ō; *for def. 1, also* trī'ō) *n. pl.* **tri·os 1.** Any three things grouped or associated together. **2.** *Music* **a** A composition for three performers. **b** The second part of a minuet, scherzo, etc. **c** A group of three musicians that plays trios. [< F < Ital. < L *tres* three]

-triol *suffix Chem.* Denoting an organic compound containing three hydroxyl radicals.

tri·ox·ide (trī-ok'sīd, -sid) *n. Chem.* An oxide containing three atoms of oxygen in combination. Also **tri·ox'id** (-sid).

trip (trip) *n.* **1.** A journey or voyage. **2.** A misstep or stumble caused by losing balance or striking the foot against an object. **3.** An active, nimble step or movement. **4.** *Mech.* A pawl or similar device that trips, or the action of such a device. **5.** A sudden catch, esp. of the legs and feet, as of a wrestler. **6.** A blunder; mistake. **7.** *Slang* The taking of a psychedelic drug, or the resulting mental experience. — *v.* **tripped, trip·ping** *v.i.* **1.** To stumble. **2.** To move quickly with light or small steps. **3.** To commit an error. **4.** *Mech.* To be triggered, released, etc. — *v.t.* **5.** To cause to stumble: often with *up.* **6.** To detect and expose in an error; defeat the purpose of. **7.** To perform (a dance) lightly. **8.** *Mech.* To set free or in operation by releasing a stay, catch, trigger, etc. **9.** *Naut.* To loosen (an anchor) from the bottom. [< OF *treper, triper* to leap, trample]

tri·par·tite (trī-pär'tīt) *adj.* **1.** Divided into three parts or divisions; threefold: a *tripartite* leaf: also **tri·part·ed** (trī'pär'tid). **2.** Pertaining to or executed between three parties. [< L < *tri-* three + *partiri* to divide] — **tri·par'tite·ly** *adv.*

tri·par·ti·tion (trī'pär·tish'ən) *n.* Division into three parts, into thirds, or among three.

tripe (trīp) *n.* **1.** A part of the stomach of a ruminant, used for food. **2.** *Informal* Anything worthless; nonsense. [< OF < Arabic *tharb* entrails, a net]

trip hammer A heavy power hammer that is raised or tilted by a cam and then allowed to drop.

tri·ple (trip'əl) *v.* **·led, ·ling** *v.t.* **1.** To make threefold in number or quantity. — *v.i.* **2.** To be or become three times as many or as large. **3.** In baseball, to hit a triple. — *adj.* **1.** Consisting of three things united or of three parts; threefold. **2.** Multiplied by three; thrice said or done. — *n.* **1.** A set or group of three. **2.** In baseball, a base hit that enables the batter to reach third base. [< MF < L < Gk. *triplous* threefold] — **trip'ly** *adv.*

triple play In baseball, a play during which three men are put out.

trip·let (trip'lit) *n.* **1.** A group of three of a kind. **2.** One of three children born at one birth. **3.** A group of three rhymed lines. **4.** *Music* A group of three equal notes performed in the time of two: also called *tercet.*

triple threat *U.S. Informal* **1.** A football player expert at kicking, running, and passing. **2.** One skillful in three areas of activity. — **trip·le-threat** (trip'əl·thret') *adj.*

tri·plex (trī'pleks, trip'leks) *adj.* Having three parts. [< L < *tri-* three + *plicare* to fold]

trip·li·cate (adj. & n. trip'lə·kit; v. trip'lə·kāt) *adj.* Threefold; made in three copies. — *n.* One of or a set of three identical things. — *v.t.* **·cat·ed, ·cat·ing** To make three times as much or as many. [< L *triplicatus*, pp. of *triplicare* to triple] — **trip'li·cate·ly** *adv.* — **trip'li·ca'tion** *n.*

tri·plic·i·ty (trī-plis'ə·tē) *n. pl.* **·ties 1.** Threefold character. **2.** A group or combination of three. **3.** In astrology, a combination of three of the twelve signs of the zodiac.

tri·pod (trī'pod) *n.* **1.** A utensil or article having three feet or legs. **2.** A three-legged stand for supporting a camera, transit, etc. [< L < Gk. < *tri-* three + *pous* foot]

trip·o·dal (trip'ə-dəl) *adj.* **1.** Of the nature or form of a tripod. **2.** Having three feet or legs. Also **tri·po·di·al** (trī-pō'dē-əl, trī-), **tri·pod'ic** (trī-pod'ik).

trip·o·dy (trip'ə-dē) *n. pl.* **·dies** A verse or meter having three feet.

trip·per (trip'ər) *n.* **1.** One who trips. **2.** *Brit. Informal* A traveler; tourist. **3.** *Mech.* A trip or tripping mechanism.

trip·ping (trip'ing) *n.* The act of one who or that which trips. — *adj.* Nimble. — **trip'ping·ly** *adv.*

trip·tych (trip'tik) *n.* **1.** A triple tablet; esp., a Greek or Roman hinged triple writing tablet. **2.** A triple picture or carving on three hinged panels, often depicting a religious subject. Also **trip·ty·ca** (-ti·kə), **trip·ty·chon** (-ti·kon). [< LL < Gk. < *tri-* thrice + *ptyssein* to fold]

tri·reme (trī'rēm) *n.* An ancient Greek or Roman warship with three banks of oars. [< L < *tri-* three + *remus* oar]

tri·sect (trī-sekt') *v.t.* To divide into three parts, esp. as in geometry, into three equal parts. [< TRI- + L *sectus*, pp. of *secare* to cut] — **tri·sect'ed** *adj.* — **tri·sec'tion** (-sek'shən) *n.* — **tri·sec'tor** *n.*

tri·seme (trī'sēm) *n.* A syllable or foot consisting of or equivalent to three short syllables, as the trochee. — *adj.* Consisting of or equal to three short syllables: also **tri·se'mic.** [< Gk. < *tri-* three + *sēma* a sign]

tris·mus (triz'məs, tris'-) *n. Pathol.* Lockjaw. [< NL < Gk. *trismos* gnashing of teeth] — **tris'mic** *adj.*

Tris·tan (tris'tän, -tən) In medieval legend and Richard Wagner's *Tristan und Isolde*, a knight sent to Ireland to bring back the princess Iseult the Beautiful as a bride for his uncle, King Mark of Cornwall. Iseult and Tristan drink a magic love potion, and ultimately die together. Also **Tris·tram** (tris'trəm).

triste (trēst) *adj. French* Sorrowful; sad.

tris·tesse (trēs·tes') *n. French* Sadness; melancholy.

tris·tich (tris'tik) *n.* A strophe or system of three lines; triplet. Compare COUPLET, DISTICH. [< TRI- + (DI)STICH]

tri·syl·la·ble (trī-sil'ə-bəl) *n.* A word of three syllables. — **tri·syl·lab·ic** (trī'si·lab'ik) *or* **·i·cal** *adj.* — **tri'syl·lab'i·cal·ly** *adv.*

trite (trīt) *adj.* Used so often as to be hackneyed; made commonplace by repetition. [< L *tritus*, pp. of *terere* to rub] — **trite'ly** *adv.* — **trite'ness** *n.*
— **Syn.** **1.** *Trite* suggests merely a lack of freshness or originality. *Hackneyed* is stronger, suggesting something worn out from overuse; the extreme of *hackneyed* is *threadbare.* We speak of *hackneyed* expressions, and of *threadbare* subjects. *Stereotyped* describes that which uses clichés instead of seeking to evoke new images and ideas. — **Ant.** fresh, original, vivid, striking.

trit·i·cum (trit'ə·kəm) *n.* Any of a widely distributed genus of cereal grasses, the wheats, cultivated in many varieties. [< NL < L, wheat]

trit·i·um (trit'ē-əm, trish'ē-əm) *n. Physics* The isotope of hydrogen having the atomic weight 3. [< NL < Gk. *tritos* third]

tri·ton[1] (trīt'n) *n.* Any of a genus of marine gastropods having many gills and a trumpet-shaped shell. [< L < Gk. *Tritōn*]

tri·ton[2] (trī'ton) *n. Physics.* The nucleus of an atom of tritium. [< TRIT(IUM) + (ELECTR)ON]

Tri·ton (trīt'n) In Greek mythology, a son of Poseidon (Neptune) and Amphitrite, represented with a man's head and upper body and a dolphin's tail. — *n.* In Greek mythology, one of a race of attendants of the sea gods.

trit·u·rate (trich'ə-rāt) *v.t.* **·rat·ed, ·rat·ing** To reduce to a fine powder or pulp by grinding or rubbing; pulverize. — *n.* That which has been triturated. [< LL < L *tritura* a rubbing, threshing < *terere* to rub] — **trit·u·ra·ble** (trich'ər·ə·bəl) *adj.* — **trit'u·ra'tion** *n.* — **trit'u·ra'tor** *n.*

TRITON[1]

tri·umph (trī'əmf) *v.i.* **1.** To win a victory; be victorious. **2.** To be successful. **3.** To rejoice over a victory; exult.

4. To celebrate a triumph, as a victorious Roman general. — *n.* **1.** In Roman antiquity, the religious pageant of the entry of a victorious consul, dictator, or praetor into Rome. **2.** Exultation over victory. **3.** The condition of being victorious; victory. [< OF < L < Gk. *thriambos* a processional hymn to Dionysus] — **tri′umph·er** *n.*

tri·um·phal (trī·um′fəl) *adj.* **1.** Of, pertaining to, or of the nature of a triumph. **2.** Celebrating a victory.

triumphal arch A monumental arch erected to commemorate a great victory or achievement.

tri·um·phant (trī·um′fənt) *adj.* **1.** Exultant for or as for victory. **2.** Victorious. — **tri·um′phant·ly** *adv.*

tri·um·vir (trī·um′vər) *n. pl.* **·virs** or **·vi·ri** (-və·rī) One of three men united in public office or authority, as in ancient Rome. [< L < *tres, trium* three + *vir* a man] — **tri·um′vi·ral** *adj.*

tri·um·vi·rate (trī·um′vər·it, -və·rāt) *n.* **1.** A group or coalition of three men who unitedly exercise authority or control; government by triumvirs. **2.** The office of a triumvir. **3.** A group of three men; trio.

tri·une (trī′yoon) *adj.* Three in one: said of God. — *n.* A group of three things united; triad; trinity in unity. [< TRI- + L *unus* one] — **tri·u′ni·ty** *n.*

tri·va·lent (trī·vā′lənt, triv′ə·lənt) *adj. Chem.* Having a valence or combining value of three. [< TRI- + L *valens*, ppr. of *valere* to be worth] — **tri·va′lence, tri·va′len·cy** *n.*

triv·et (triv′it) *n.* A stand, usu. three-legged, for holding cooking vessels in a fireplace, a heated iron, or a hot dish on a table. [OE < L < *tri-* three + *pes, pedis* a foot]

triv·i·a (triv′ē·ə) *n.pl.* Insignificant or unimportant matters; trifles. [See TRIVIAL.]

triv·i·al (triv′ē·əl) *adj.* **1.** Of little value or importance; trifling; insignificant. **2.** Such as is found everywhere or every day; commonplace. **3.** Occupied with trifles. [< L *trivialis* of the crossroads, commonplace < *tri-* three + *via* road] — **triv′i·al·ism** *n.* — **triv′i·al·ly** *adv.*

triv·i·al·i·ty (triv′ē·al′ə·tē) *n. pl.* **·ties** **1.** The state or quality of being trivial: also **triv′i·al·ness.** **2.** A trivial matter.

tri·week·ly (trī·wēk′lē) *adj.* **1.** Occurring three times a week. **2.** Done or occurring every third week. — *adv.* **1.** Three times a week. **2.** Every third week. — *n.* A publication appearing triweekly.

-trix *suffix* A feminine termination of agent nouns the masculine form of which is *-tor: testatrix.* See **-OR¹.** [< L]

tro·cha·ic (trō·kā′ik) *adj.* Pertaining to, containing, or composed of trochees: a *trochaic* foot or verse. — *n.* A trochaic verse or line. [See TROCHEE.]

tro·chal (trō′kəl) *adj.* Shaped like a wheel; rotiform. [< Gk. *trochos* a wheel]

tro·che (trō′kē) *n.* A medicated lozenge, usu. circular: also called *pastille.* [Alter. of obs. *trochisk* < MF < L < Gk. *trochos* wheel]

tro·chee (trō′kē) *n.* **1.** In prosody, a metrical foot consisting of one long or accented syllable followed by one short or unaccented syllable (—◡). **2.** A line of verse made up of or characterized by such feet: Nōw thĕ| līght hăs| fāllĕn| frŏm thĕ| hēavĕns. [< L < Gk. < *trechein* to run]

trod (trod) Past tense and alternative past participle of TREAD.

trod·den (trod′n) Past participle of TREAD.

trog·lo·dyte (trog′lə·dīt) *n.* **1.** A cave man. **2.** A hermit; anyone of primitive habits. **3.** An anthropoid ape, as the chimpanzee. [< L < Gk. < *trōglē* hole + *dyein* to go into] — **trog′lo·dyt′ic** (-dit′ik) or **·i·cal** *adj.*

tro·gon (trō′gon) *n.* A tropical American bird noted for its resplendent plumage. [< NL < Gk. *trōgein* to gnaw]

troi·ka (troi′kə) *n.* A Russian vehicle drawn by a team of three horses driven abreast. [< Russian < *troie* three]

Tro·jan (trō′jən) *n.* **1.** A native of Troy. **2.** One who works earnestly or suffers courageously. — *adj.* Of or pertaining to ancient Troy. [< L < *Troja* Troy]

Trojan horse **1.** In classical legend, a large, hollow wooden horse, filled with Greek soldiers and left at the Trojan gates. When it was brought within the walls the soldiers emerged at night and admitted the Greek army, who burned the city: also called *wooden horse.* **2.** A person, device, etc., intended to disrupt or undermine a plan.

Trojan War In Greek legend, the ten years' war waged by the confederated Greeks under their king, Agamemnon, against the Trojans to recover Helen, the wife of Menelaus, who had been abducted by Paris: celebrated esp. in the *Iliad* and the *Odyssey.*

troll¹ (trōl) *v.t.* **1.** To fish for with a moving lure, as from a slowly moving boat. **2.** To move (the line or lure) in fishing. **3.** To sing in succession, as in a round or catch. **4.** To sing in a full, hearty manner. **5.** To cause to roll; revolve. — *v.i.* **6.** To fish with a moving lure. **7.** To sing a tune, etc., in a full, hearty manner. **8.** To be uttered in such a way. **9.** To roll; turn. — *n.* **1.** A catch or round. **2.** A rolling movement or motion; also, repetition or routine.

3. In fishing, a spoon or other lure. [? < OF *troller* to quest, wander < Gmc.] — **troll′er** *n.*

troll² (trōl) *n.* In Scandinavian folklore, a giant; later, a mischievous dwarf. Also **trold** (trōld). [< ON]

trol·ley (trol′ē) *n. pl.* **·leys** **1.** *U.S.* A streetcar. **2.** A grooved metal wheel for rolling in contact with a conductor (the **trolley wire**), to convey the current to an electric vehicle. **3.** In a subway system, a device adapted to the same purpose attached to a current taker operating through a third rail. **4.** A small truck or car for conveying material, as in a factory, mine, etc. **5.** The mechanism of a traveling crane. **6.** A small car running on tracks and worked by a manually operated lever, used by workmen on a railway. — *v.t. & v.i.* To travel by trolley. Also **trol′ly.** [< TROLL¹]

trolley bus A bus propelled electrically by current from an overhead wire by means of a trolley. Also **trolley coach.**

trolley car A car with a trolley for use on an electric railway; esp., *U.S.*, a streetcar.

trol·ling (trō′ling) *n.* The method or act of fishing by dragging a hook and line, as behind a boat and near the surface. [< TROLL¹]

trolling rod A strong fishing rod for trolling.

trol·lop (trol′əp) *n.* **1.** A slatternly woman. **2.** A prostitute. [< dial. E (Scottish) < ME *trollen* to roll about] — **trol′lop·ish, trol′lop·y, trol′lop·ing** *adj.*

trom·bone (trom·bōn′, trom′bōn′) A brass instrument of the trumpet family, but larger and lower in pitch than the trumpet. A **slide trombone** changes pitch by means of a U-shaped slide that can lengthen or shorten the air column, a **valve trombone** changes pitch by means of valves. [< Ital., aug. of *tromba* trumpet < Gmc.] — **trom·bon′ist** *n.*

trompe l'oeil (trônp lœ′y′) In art and decoration, the accurate representation of details, scenes, etc., to create an illusion of reality. [< F, lit., fool the eye]

-tron *suffix* **1.** Vacuum tube: *magnetron.* **2.** Device for the manipulation of subatomic particles: *cyclotron.* [< Gk., instrumental suffix]

troop (troop) *n.* **1.** An assembled company; gathering; a herd or flock. **2.** *Usu. pl.* A body of soldiers; soldiers collectively. **3.** The cavalry unit corresponding to a company of infantry. **4.** A body of Boy Scouts consisting of four patrols of eight scouts each. — *v.i.* **1.** To move along or gather as a troop or as a crowd. — *v.t.* **2.** To form into troops. **3.** *Brit. Mil.* To carry ceremonially before troops: to *troop* the colors. [< OF < LL *troppus* a flock < Gmc.]

troop carrier **1.** A transport aircraft for carrying troops and equipment. **2.** An armored vehicle for carrying troops.

troop·er (troo′pər) *n.* **1.** A cavalryman. **2.** A mounted policeman. **3.** A troop horse; charger. **4.** A troopship. **5.** A state policeman.

troop·ship (troop′ship′) *n.* A ship for carrying troops.

trope (trōp) *n.* **1.** The figurative use of a word. **2.** Loosely, a figure of speech; figurative language in general. [< F < L < Gk. *tropos* a turn < *trepein* to turn]

-trope *combining form* **1.** One who or that which turns or changes: *allotrope.* **2.** Turning; turned in a (specified) way: *hemitrope.* [< Gk. *tropos* a turning < *trepein* to turn]

troph·ic (trof′ik) *adj.* Pertaining to nutrition and its processes. Also **troph′i·cal.** [< Gk. < *trephein* to nourish] — **troph′i·cal·ly** *adv.*

tro·phied (trō′fēd) *adj.* Adorned with trophies.

tropho- *combining form* Nutrition; nourishment; of or pertaining to food or nutrition. Also, before vowels, **troph-.** [< Gk. *trophē* food, nourishment < *trephein* to feed, nourish]

tro·phy (trō′fē) *n. pl.* **·phies** **1.** Something symbolizing victory or success; as: **a** A cup, statuette, etc., awarded for athletic or other achievement. **b** A mounted fish, animal's head, etc. **c** A weapon, etc., captured from an enemy. **2.** An ornamental symbolic group of objects hung together on a wall. **3.** A memento or memorial. [< MF < L < Gk. *tropē* a defeat < *trepein* to turn, rout]

-trophy *combining form* A (specified) kind of nutrition or development: *hypertrophy.* Corresponding adjectives end in *-trophic.* [< Gk. *trophē.* See TROPHO-.]

trop·ic (trop′ik) *n. Geog.* Either of two parallels of latitude 23° 27′ north and south of the equator, on which the sun is seen in the zenith on the days of its greatest declination, called respectively **tropic of Cancer** and **tropic of Capricorn.** **2.** *pl.* The regions of the earth's surface between the tropics of Cancer and Capricorn; the Torrid Zone. — *adj.* Of or pertaining to the tropics; tropical. [< L < Gk. *tropikos (kyklos)* the tropical (circle) < *tropē* a turning]

TROPICS

-tropic *combining form* Having a (specified) tropism; turning or changing in a (particular) way, or in response to a (given) stimulus: *phototropic.* Also *-tropal.*

trop·i·cal (trop′i·kəl) *adj.* **1.** Of, pertaining to, or characteristic of the tropics. **2.** Of the nature of a trope or metaphor. — **trop′i·cal·ly** *adv.*

tropic bird A long-winged, oceanic bird, allied to the pelicans, found mostly in the tropics, having the two middle tail feathers elongated.

tro·pism (trō′piz·əm) *n. Biol.* 1. The involuntary response of an organism to an external stimulus. 2. Any automatic reaction to a stimulus. [< Gk. *tropē* a turning] — **tro·pis·tic** (trō·pis′tik) *adj.*

-tropism *combining form* A (specified) tropism: *phototropism.* Also *-tropy.* [< TROPISM]

trop·o·pause (trop′ə·pôz) *n. Meteorol.* A transition zone in the atmosphere between the troposphere and the stratosphere. [< TROPO(SPHERE) + Gk. *pausis* a ceasing]

trop·o·sphere (trop′ə·sfir) *n. Meteorol.* The region of the atmosphere beneath the stratosphere; it is characterized by turbulence and by decreasing temperature with increasing altitude. [< F < Gk. *tropos* a turning + F *sphère* < L *sphaera* sphere] — **trop·o·spher′ic** (-sfir′ik, -sfer′-) *adj.*

trot (trot) *n.* 1. A gait of a quadruped, esp. a horse, in which diagonal pairs of legs are lifted, thrust forward, and placed down almost simultaneously, also, the sound of this gait. 2. A race for trotters. 3. A reasonably rapid run. 4. *Informal* A pony (def. 3). — *v.* **trot·ted, trot·ting** *v.i.* 1. To go at a trot. 2. To hurry. — *v.t.* 3. To cause to trot. 4. To ride at a trotting gait. — **to trot out** To bring forth for inspection, approval, etc. [< OF < OHG *trottōn* to tread]

troth (trôth, trōth) *n.* 1. Good faith; fidelity. 2. The act of pledging fidelity; esp., betrothal. 3. Truth; verity. — *v.t. Archaic* To betroth; pledge. [ME *trowthe, trouthe,* var. of OE *trēowth* truth; faith]

Trot·sky·ism (trot′skē·iz′əm) *n.* The doctrines of Trotsky and his followers; esp., his theory that Communism to succeed must be international. — **Trot′sky·ist, Trot′sky·ite** *n. & adj.*

trot·ter (trot′ər) *n.* One who or that which trots; esp., a horse trained to trot for speed.

tro·tyl (trō′til) *n.* Trinitrotoluene. [< (TRINI)TROT(O-LUENE) + -YL]

trou·ba·dour (trōō′bə·dôr, -dōr, -dŏŏr) *n.* 1. One of a class of lyric poets, originating in Provence in the 11th century and flourishing in southern France, northern Italy, and eastern Spain during the 12th and 13th centuries. 2. A singer, esp., of love songs. [< MF < Provençal < *trobar* to compose, invent, find]

trou·ble (trub′əl) *n.* 1. The state of being distressed, annoyed, upset, afflicted, or confused. 2. A difficulty, perplexity, annoyance, disturbance, etc. 3. Toilsome exertion; pains: Take the *trouble* to do it correctly. 4. A diseased condition: lung *trouble.* — **in trouble** 1. Enmeshed in threatening difficulties. 2. *Informal* Pregnant and unmarried. — *v.* **·led, ·ling** *v.t.* 1. To cause mental agitation to; distress; worry. 2. To agitate or disturb; stir up or roil, as water. 3. To inconvenience or incommode. 4. To bother. 5. To cause physical pain or discomfort to. — *v.i.* 6. To take pains; bother. 7. To worry. [< OF < L *turbula* dim. of *turba* crowd] — **troub′ler** *n.* — **troub′ling·ly** *adv.*

troub·led (trub′əld) *adj.* 1. Beset with trouble. 2. Distressed. 3. Agitated, disturbed, or roiled, as water. — **troub′led·ly** *adv.* — **troub′led·ness** *n.*

troub·le-shoot·er (trub′əl·shōō′tər) *n.* One who locates difficulties and seeks to remove them, esp., in the operation of a machine, in an industrial process, etc. — **troub′le-shoot′ing** *n.*

troub·le·some (trub′əl·səm) *adj.* 1. Causing trouble; vexatious; burdensome; trying. 2. Marked by violence; tumultuous. 3. Greatly agitated or disturbed; troublous. — **troub′le·some·ly** *adv.* — **troub′le·some·ness** *n.*

troub·lous (trub′ləs) *adj.* 1. Marked by commotion or tumult; full of trouble: *troublous* times. 2. Uneasy; restless.

trough (trôf, trof) *n.* 1. A long, narrow, open receptacle for conveying a fluid or for holding food or water for animals. 2. A long, narrow channel or depression, as between ridges on land or waves at sea. 3. A gutter (def. 3). 4. *Meteorol.* A long, usu., narrow area having a low barometric pressure. 5. *Econ.* A low or the lowest point reached in a business cycle. [OE *trog*]

trounce (trouns) *v.t.* **trounced, trounc·ing** 1. To beat or thrash severely; punish. 2. *Informal* To defeat. [Ult. origin uncertain]

troupe (trōōp) *n.* A company of actors or other performers. — *v.i.* **trouped, troup·ing** To travel as one of a theatrical company. [< MF < OF *trope* troop]

trou·per (trōō′pər) *n.* 1. A member of a theatrical company. 2. An actor of long experience.

trou·sers (trou′zərz) *n.pl.* A garment, esp. for men and boys, covering the body from the waist to the ankles and divided so as to make a separate covering for each leg. Also **trow′sers.** [Blend of obs. *trouse* breeches and DRAWERS]

trous·seau (trōō′sō, trōō·sō′) *n. pl.* **·seaux** (-sōz, -sōz′) or

·seaus A bride's outfit, esp. of clothing, linens, etc. [< F *trousse* a packed collection of things]

trout (trout) *n.* 1. A fish of the salmon family mostly found in fresh waters and highly esteemed as a game and food fish. The **brown** or **salmon trout** is common in Europe; the **cut-throat trout** and the **rainbow trout** or steelhead are species of western North America; the **speckled trout** or **brook trout** is common in eastern North America. 2. A fish resembling, or supposed to resemble, the above, as the greenling. [OE < LL < Gk. *trōktēs* nibbler < *trōgein* to gnaw]

trove (trōv) *n.* Something, esp. of value or pleasing quality, found or discovered. [< (TREASURE-)TROVE]

trow (trō) *v.t. & v.i. Archaic* To suppose; think; believe. [Fusion of OE *truwian* (< *truwa* faith) and *trēowan* to believe < *trēowe* true]

trow·el (trou′əl, troul) *n.* 1. A flat-bladed, sometimes pointed implement having an offset handle, used to smooth plaster, mortar, etc. 2. A small concave scoop with a handle, used in digging about small plants, potting them, etc. — *v.t.* **trow·eled** or **·elled, trow·el·ing** or **·el·ling** To apply, dress, or form with a trowel. [< OF < LL < L *trulla,* dim. of *trua* stirring spoon, ladle] — **trow′el·er** or **trow′el·ler** *n.*

troy (troi) *n.* A system of weights in which 12 troy ounces make a pound, used by jewelers in England and the U.S. See table inside back cover. Also **troy weight.** [after *Troyes,* a city in France]

Troy (troi) An ancient city in NW Asia Minor of perhaps about 1200 B.C., the scene of the *Iliad:* also called *Ilium, Ilion.*

tru·an·cy (trōō′ən·sē) *n. pl.* **·cies** The state or habit of being truant; also, an act of being truant. Also **tru′ant·ry.**

tru·ant (trōō′ənt) *n.* One who absents himself, esp., from school, without leave. — *v.i.* To be truant. — *adj.* 1. Being truant; idle. 2. Relating to or characterizing a truant. [< OF, vagabond, prob. < Celtic]

truant officer *U.S.* An official who investigates truancy from school.

truce (trōōs) *n.* 1. An agreement between belligerents for a temporary suspension of hostilities; an armistice. 2. Temporary cessation or intermission. [Plural of ME *trew,* OE *trūwa* faith, a promise]

truck[1] (truk) *n.* 1. *U.S. & Canadian* Any of various automotive vehicles designed to carry loads, freight, etc.: also, *Brit., lorry.* 2. A two-wheeled barrowlike vehicle with a forward lip and no sides, used for moving barrels, boxes, etc., by hand. 3. A vehicle used about railway stations, for moving trunks, etc. 4. *Brit.* An open or platform freight car. 5. *Naut.* A disk at the top of a mast or flagpole through which the halyards of signals are run. 6. One of the pivoting sets of wheels on a railroad car or engine. — *v.t.* 1. To carry on a truck. — *v.i.* 2. To carry goods on a truck. 3. To drive a truck. [Appar. < L < Gk. *trochos* wheel]

truck[2] (truk) *v.t. & v.i.* To exchange or barter; also, to peddle. — *n.* 1. Commodities for sale. 2. *U.S.* Garden produce for market. 3. *Informal* Rubbish; worthless articles collectively. 4. Barter. 5. *Informal* Dealings: I will have no *truck* with him. [< OF *troquer* to barter]

truck·age[1] (truk′ij) *n.* 1. Money paid for conveyance of goods on trucks. 2. Such conveyance.

truck·age[2] (truk′ij) *n.* Exchange; barter.

truck·er[1] (truk′ər) *n.* One who drives or supplies trucks or moves commodities in trucks. Also **truck′man** (-mən).

truck·er[2] (truk′ər) *n.* 1. *U.S.* A market gardener; truck farmer. 2. One who barters or sells commodities; hawker.

truck farm *U.S.* A farm on which vegetables are produced for market. Also **truck garden.** — **truck farming**

truck·ing[1] (truk′ing) *n.* The act or business of transportation by trucks.

truck·ing[2] (truk′ing) *n.* 1. Exchanging or bartering; dealings. 2. *U.S.* Cultivation of vegetables for market.

truck·le (truk′əl) *v.* **·led, ·ling** *v.i.* 1. To yield meanly or weakly: with *to.* 2. To roll on truckles or casters. — *v.t.* 3. To cause to roll on truckles or casters. — *n.* A small wheel. [< AF < L *trochlea* a pulley] — **truck′ler** *n.* — **truck′ling·ly** *adv.*

truc·u·lence (truk′yə·ləns) *n.* Savageness of character, behavior, or aspect. Also **truc′u·len·cy.**

truc·u·lent (truk′yə·lənt) *adj.* 1. Of savage character; awakening terror; cruel; ferocious. 2. Scathing; harsh; violent: said of writing or speech. [< L < *trux, trucis* fierce] — **truc′u·lent·ly** *adv.*

trudge (truj) *v.i.* **trudged, trudg·ing** To walk wearily or laboriously; plod. — *n.* A tiresome walk or tramp. [Earlier *tredge, tridge*] — **trudg′er** *n.*

trudg·en (truj′ən) In swimming, a former racing stroke similar to the crawl but performed with a frog kick or a scissors kick. Also **trudgen stroke, trudg′eon.** [after John *Trudgen,* 19th c. British swimmer]

true (trōō) *adj.* **tru·er, tru·est** **1.** Faithful to fact or reality; not false. **2.** Being real or natural; genuine: *true* gold. **3.** Faithful; loyal; steadfast. **4.** Conformable to an existing standard type or pattern; exact: a *true* copy. **5.** Required by justice; legitimate: the *true* king. **6.** Truthful; honest. **7.** Indicating or predicting correctly: a *true* sign. **8.** *Biol.* **a** Of pure strain or pedigree. **b** Conformed to the structure of the type of a plant or animal: a *true* locust. **9.** In perfect tune: His voice is *true.* — *n.* Truth; pledge. — **in** (or **out of**) **true** In (or not in) line of adjustment: said of a mark or part. — *adv.* **1.** In truth; truly. **2.** In a true and accurate manner: The wheel runs *true.* — *v.t.* **trued, tru·ing** To bring to conformity with a standard; adjust: to *true* a frame. [OE *trēowe*] — **true′ness** *n.*
true bill *Law* **1.** The endorsement by a grand jury on a bill of indictment that the jurors find to be sustained by the evidence. **2.** A bill so endorsed.
true-blue (trōō′blōō′) *adj.* Staunch; faithful; genuine.
true·born (trōō′bôrn′) *adj.* Being such by birth or inheritance: a *trueborn* Scot.
true-lov·ers′ knot (trōō′luv′ərz) A complicated double knot, a symbol of fidelity in love.
truf·fle (truf′əl, trōō′fəl) *n.* Any of various edible fleshy underground fungi. [< OF *trufe, truffe*]
tru·ism (trōō′iz·əm) *n.* An obvious or self-evident truth.
trull (trul) *n.* *Archaic* A prostitute. [< G *trulle, trolle*]
tru·ly (trōō′lē) *adv.* **1.** In conformity with fact. **2.** With accuracy. **3.** With loyalty or fidelity. **4.** Legally.
trump[1] (trump) *n.* **1.** In various card games, a card of the suit selected to rank above all others temporaril ... **2.** *Usu.*, *pl.* The suit thus determined. **3.** A powerful or decisive stroke, resource, etc. **4.** *Informal* A good fellow. — *v.t.* **1.** To top (another card) with a trump. **2.** To surpass; excel; beat. — *v.i.* **3.** To play a trump. — **to trump up** To make up or invent for a fraudulent purpose. [Alter. of TRIUMPH]
trump[2] (trump) *n.* *Poetic* A trumpet. [< OF *trompe*]
trump·er·y (trum′pər·ē) *n.* *pl.* **·er·ies** **1.** Worthless finery. **2.** Rubbish; nonsense. **3.** Deceit; trickery. — *adj.* Showy but valueless. [< OF < *tromper* to deceive]
trum·pet (trum′pit) *n.* **1.** A soprano brass wind instrument with a flaring bell and a long, narrow-bored metal tube. **2.** Something resembling a trumpet in form; an ear trumpet. **3.** A loud penetrating sound like that of a trumpet; trumpeting. — *v.t.* **1.** To sound or proclaim by or as by a trumpet; publish abroad. — *v.i.* **2.** To blow a trumpet. **3.** To give forth a sound as if from a trumpet. [< OF *trompe*]
trumpet creeper A woody vine of the southern U.S., with scarlet, trumpet-shaped flowers. Also **trumpet vine.**
trum·pet·er (trum′pit·ər) *n.* **1.** One who plays a trumpet. **2.** One who publishes something loudly abroad. **3.** A large South American bird related to the cranes. **4.** A large North American wild swan, having a clarionlike cry: also **trumpeter swan.**
trun·cate (trung′kāt) *v.t.* **·cat·ed, ·cat·ing** To cut the top or end from. — *adj.* **1.** Truncated. **2.** *Biol.* Appearing as though cut or broken squarely off. [< L < *truncus* trunk] — **trun·ca·tion** (trung·kā′shən) *n.*
trun·cat·ed (trung′kā·tid) *adj.* **1.** Cut off; shortened. **2.** Describing a cone or pyramid whose vertex is cut off by a plane.
trun·cheon (trun′chən) *n.* **1.** A short, heavy stick; a club; staff. **2.** *Brit.* A policeman's club. — *v.t.* To beat as with a truncheon; cudgel. [< OF ult. < L *truncus* trunk]

TRUNCATED PYRAMID

trun·dle (trun′dəl) *n.* **1.** A small, broad wheel, as of a caster. **2.** The act, motion, or sound of trundling. **3.** A trundle bed. **4.** *Obs.* A small, low-wheeled truck. — *v.t.* & *v.i.* **·dled, ·dling** **1.** To roll along. **2.** To rotate. [ME < OE *trendel* circle] — **trun′dler** *n.*
trundle bed A bed with a very low frame resting upon casters, so that it may be rolled under another bed.
trunk (trungk) *n.* **1.** The main stem of a tree. **2.** A large box or case for carrying clothes, etc., as for a journey. **3.** *U.S. & Canadian* A large compartment of an automobile for storing luggage, etc., often at the rear. **4.** The human body, apart from the head, neck, and limbs; the torso. **5.** *Entomol.* The thorax. **6.** *Anat.* The main stem of a nerve, blood vessel, or lymphatic. **7.** The main line of a transportation system. **8.** The circuit connecting two telephone exchanges. **9.** The main body, line, or stem of anything. **10.** A proboscis, as of an elephant. **11.** *pl.* A close-fitting garment covering the loins, worn by male swimmers, etc. — *adj.* Being or belonging to a trunk or main body: a *trunk* railroad. [< OF < L *truncus* stem, trunk]
trunk·fish (trungk′fish′) *n.* *pl.* **·fish** or **·fish·es** A fish of warm seas, characterized by a covering of hard, bony plates.
trunk hose Full breeches extending to the middle of the thigh, worn by men in the 16th and early 17th centuries.
trunk line The main line of a transportation or communication system, as distinguished from a branch line.

trun·nion (trun′yən) *n.* One of two opposite cylindrical studs on a cannon, forming an axis on which it is elevated or depressed. [< F *trognon* stump, trunk]
truss (trus) *n.* **1.** *Med.* A bandage or support for a rupture. **2.** A braced framework of ties, beams, or bars, as for the support of a roof, bridge, etc. **3.** A package, bundle, esp., of hay (usu. 56 or 60 pounds) or straw (usu. 36 pounds). **4.** *Naut.* A heavy iron piece by which a lower yard is attached to a mast. — *v.t.* **1.** To tie or bind; fasten: often with *up.* **2.** To support by a truss; brace, as a roof. **3.** To fasten the wings of (a fowl) before cooking. **4.** To fasten, tighten, or tie around one, as a garment. [< OF < *trousser, trusser* to pack up, bundle] — **truss′er** *n.*
truss bridge A bridge supported chiefly by trusses.
trust (trust) *n.* **1.** A confident reliance on the integrity, honesty, or justice of another; faith. **2.** Something committed to one's care; a charge; responsibility. **3.** The state or position of one who has received an important charge. **4.** A confidence in the reliability of persons or things without careful investigation. **5.** Credit, in the commercial sense. **6.** Custody; care; keeping. **7.** *Law* **a** The confidence, reposed in a person to whom the legal title to property is conveyed for the benefit of another; also, the beneficial title or ownership of property of which the legal title is held by another. ◆ **Collateral adjective:** *fiducial.* **b** The property or thing held in trust. **8.** A permanent combination, now illegal, for the purpose of controlling the production, price, etc., of some commodity or the management, profits, etc., of some business. **9.** A trust company. **10.** One who or that which is trusted. **11.** Confident expectation; belief; hope. — *v.t.* **1.** To have trust in; rely upon. **2.** To commit to the care of another; entrust. **3.** To commit something to the care of: with *with.* **4.** To allow to do something without fear of the consequences. **5.** To expect with confidence or with hope. **6.** To believe. **7.** To allow business credit to. — *v.i.* **8.** To place trust or confidence; rely: with *in.* **9.** To hope: with *for.* **10.** To allow business credit. — **to trust to** To depend upon; confide in. — *adj.* Held in trust: *trust* money. [< ON *traust,* lit., firmness] — **trust′er** *n.*
trust·bust·er (trust′bus′tər) *n.* *U.S. Informal* One who advocates or works for the dissolution of a trust (def. 8) or trusts, as by antitrust legislation. Also **trust buster.**
trust company An incorporated institution formed to accept and execute trusts, to manage money and property, and to lend money.
trus·tee (trus·tē′) *n.* **1.** One who holds property in trust. **2.** One of a body of men, often elective, who manage the affairs of a college, church, foundation, etc. — *v.t.* **·teed, ·tee·ing** To place (property) in the care of a trustee.
trus·tee·ship (trus·tē′ship) *n.* **1.** The post or function of a trustee. **2.** Supervision and control of a Trust Territory by a country or countries commissioned by the United Nations; also, the Territory so controlled.
trust·ful (trust′fəl) *adj.* Disposed to trust. — **trust′ful·ly** *adv.* — **trust′ful·ness** *n.*
trust fund Money, securities, etc., held in trust.
trust·ing (trus′ting) *adj.* Having trust; trustful. — **trust′ing·ly** *adv.* — **trust′ing·ness** *n.*
Trust Territory A dependent area administered by a nation under the authority of the United Nations.
trust·wor·thy (trust′wûr′thē) *adj.* Worthy of confidence; reliable. — **trust′wor′thi·ly** (-wûr′thə·lē) *adv.* — **trust′wor′thi·ness** *n.*
trust·y (trus′tē) *adj.* **trust·i·er, trust·i·est** **1.** Faithful to duty or trust. **2.** Staunch; firm. — *n.* *pl.* **trust·ies** A trustworthy person; esp., a convict who has been found reliable and to whom special liberties are granted. — **trust′i·ly** *adv.* — **trust′i·ness** *n.*
truth (trōōth) *n.* *pl.* **truths** (trōō*th*z, trōōths) **1.** The state or character of being true in relation to being, knowledge, or speech. **2.** Conformity to fact or reality. **3.** Conformity to rule, standard, pattern, or ideal. **4.** Steadfastness; sincerity. **5.** That which is true; a statement or belief that corresponds to the reality. **6.** Fact; reality. **7.** A disposition to tell only what is true; veracity. **8.** Fidelity; constancy. [OE < *trēowe* true] — **truth′less** *adj.*
truth·ful (trōōth′fəl) *adj.* **1.** Habitually telling the truth. **2.** Corresponding to the facts or to reality; true. — **truth′ful·ly** *adv.* — **truth′ful·ness** *n.*
try (trī) *v.* **tried, try·ing** *v.t.* **1.** To make an attempt to do or accomplish; undertake; endeavor. **2.** To make experimental use or application of: often with *out.* **3.** *Law* **a** To determine the guilt or innocence of by judicial trial. **b** To examine or determine judicially, as a case. **4.** To subject to a test; put to proof. **5.** To put severe strain upon; tax, as the eyes. **6.** To subject to trouble or tribulation; afflict. **7.** To extract by rendering or melting; refine: often with *out:* to *try* out oil. — *v.i.* **8.** To make an attempt; put forth effort. **9.** To make an examination or test. — **to try on** To put on (a garment) to test it for fit or appearance. — **to try out** To attempt to qualify: He *tried* out for the

football team. — *n. pl.* **tries** The act of trying; trial; experiment. [< OF *trier* to sift, pick out]

try·ing (trī′ing) *adj.* Testing severely; hard to endure.

try·out (trī′out′) *n. U.S. Informal* A test of ability, as of an actor or athlete, often in competition with others.

tryp·a·no·some (trip′ə·nə·sōm′, tri·pan′ə-) *n.* Any of a genus of protozoans parasitic in the blood of man and some lower animals and often causing serious and even fatal diseases, as sleeping sickness. Also **tryp′a·no·so′ma** (-sō′mə). [< Gk. *trypanon* borer + -SOME (< Gk. *sōma* a body)]

tryp·sin (trip′sin) *n. Biochem.* A digestive enzyme contained in the pancreatic juice. [< Gk. *tripsis* a rubbing (< *tribein* to rub) + (PEP)SIN] — **tryp′tic** (-tik) *adj.*

try·sail (trī′səl, -sāl′) *n. Naut.* A small sail bent to a gaff abaft the foremast and mainmast of a ship: also called *spencer.* [< nautical phrase (*at*) *try* lying to in a storm + SAIL]

try square A carpenter's square having usu. a wooden stock and a steel blade.

tryst (trist, trīst) *n.* **1.** An appointment, as between lovers, to meet at a designated time and place; also, the meeting place agreed upon; rendezvous. **2.** A prearranged meeting, as of lovers. [< OF *triste, tristre* an appointed station in hunting] — **tryst′er** *n.*

tryst·ing place (tris′ting) A meeting place, as of lovers.

tset·se (tset′sē) *n.* **1.** A small bloodsucking fly of southern Africa, whose bite transmits disease in cattle, horses, etc. **2.** A related species, that transmits the causative agent of sleeping sickness. Also spelled *tzetze.* Also **tsetse fly.** [< Afrikaans < Bantu]

T-shirt (tē′shûrt′) *n.* A cotton undershirt or sweater with short sleeves. Also **T shirt.**

T-square (tē′skwâr′) *n.* An instrument by which to measure or lay out right angles or parallel lines, consisting usu. of a flat strip with a shorter head at right angles to it.

tsu·na·mi (tsōō·nä′mē) *n.* An extensive and often very destructive ocean wave caused by a submarine earthquake: also loosely called *tidal wave.* [< Japanese, a storm wave]

tub (tub) *n.* **1.** A broad, open-topped vessel with handles on the side. **2.** A bathtub. **3.** *Brit. Informal* A bath taken in a tub. **4.** The amount that a tub contains. **5.** *Informal* Anything resembling a tub, as a broad, clumsy boat. — *v.t. & v.i.* **tubbed, tub·bing** To wash, bathe, or place in a tub. [< MDu. *tubbe*] — **tub′ba·ble** *adj.* — **tub′ber** *n.*

tu·ba (tōō′bə, tyōō′-) *n. pl.* **·bas** or **·bae** (-bē) Any of various wide-bored, bass brass instruments whose pitch is varied by means of valves. [< Ital. < L, a war trumpet]

tub·by (tub′ē) *adj.* **·bi·er, ·bi·est** **1.** Resembling a tub in form. **2.** Short and fat; corpulent.

tube (tōōb, tyōōb) *n.* **1.** A long, hollow, cylindrical body of metal, glass, rubber, etc., generally used for the conveyance of something through it; a pipe. **2.** An electron tube. **3.** A collapsible metal cylinder for containing paints, toothpaste, glue, etc. **4.** A thing or device having a tube or tubelike part, as a telescope. **5.** *Zool.* Any elongated hollow part or organ: a bronchial *tube.* **6.** A subway or tunnel. — *v.t.* **tubed, tub·ing** **1.** To fit or furnish with a tube. **2.** To enclose in a tube or tubes. **3.** To make tubular. [< F < L *tubus*] — **tub′al** *adj.*

tu·ber (tōō′bər, tyōō′-) *n.* **1.** *Bot.* A short, thickened portion of an underground stem, as in the potato. **2.** *Anat.* A swelling or prominence; tubercle. [< L, a swelling]

tu·ber·cle (tōō′bər·kəl, tyōō′-) *n.* **1.** A small rounded eminence or nodule. **2.** *Bot.* A minute swelling on the roots of leguminous plants. **3.** *Pathol.* **a** A small granular nodule or swelling formed within an organ or plant. **b** The lesion of tuberculosis. **4.** *Anat.* A small knoblike excrescence, esp., on the skin or on a bone. [< L < *tuber* a swelling] — **tu·ber′cu·loid** (tōō·bûr′kyə·loid, tyōō-) *adj.*

tubercle bacillus The rod-shaped bacterium that causes tuberculosis in man.

tu·ber·cu·lar (tōō·bûr′kyə·lər, tyōō-) *adj.* **1.** Covered with tubercles; nodular. **2.** Tuberculous. — *n.* One affected with tuberculosis. — **tu·ber′cu·late** *adj.*

tuberculo- *combining form* **1.** Tuberculosis; of tuberculosis. **2.** Tuberculous. Also, before vowels, **tubercul-.** [< L < *tuber* a swelling]

tu·ber·cu·lo·sis (tōō·bûr′kyə·lō′sis, tyōō-) *n. Pathol.* **1.** A communicable disease caused by infection with the tubercle bacillus, characterized by the formation of tubercles within some organ or tissue. **2.** Tuberculosis affecting the lungs: also called *consumption, phthisis, pulmonary tuberculosis.* [< NL < L (See TUBERCLE) + -OSIS]

tu·ber·cu·lous (tōō·bûr′kyə·ləs, tyōō-) *adj.* Of, pertaining to, or affected with tuberculosis.

tube·rose (tōōb′rōz′, tyōōb-, -tōō·bə·rōs′, tyōō′-) *n.* A bulbous plant of the amaryllis family, bearing fragrant white flowers. [< NL < L *tuber* a swelling]

tu·ber·ous (tōō′bər·əs, tyōō′-) *adj.* **1.** Bearing projections

or prominences. **2.** Resembling tubers. **3.** *Bot.* Bearing tubers. Also **tu′ber·ose.** — **tu′ber·os′i·ty** (-bə·ros′ə·tē) *n.*

tub·ing (tōō′bing, tyōō′-) *n.* **1.** Tubes collectively. **2.** A piece of tube or material for tubes. **3.** Material for pillowcases. **4.** The act of making tubes.

tu·bu·lar (tōō′byə·lər, tyōō′-) *adj.* **1.** Having the form of a tube. **2.** Made up of or provided with tubes. Also **tu′bu·lous, tu′bu·lose** (-lōs). [< L *tubus* tube]

tu·bu·late (tōō′byə·lāt, tyōō′-) *v.t.* **·lat·ed, ·lat·ing 1.** To shape or fashion into a tube. **2.** To furnish with a tube. — *adj.* **1.** Shaped like or into a tube. **2.** Provided with a tube: also **tu′bu·lat′ed.** [< L *tubus* tube] — **tu′bu·la′tion** *n.*

tuck (tuk) *v.t.* **1.** To fold under; press in the ends or edges of. **2.** To wrap or cover snugly. **3.** To thrust or press into a close place; cram; hide. **4.** To make tucks in, by folding and stitching. — *v.i.* **5.** To contract; draw together. **6.** To make tucks. — *n.* **1.** A fold stitched into a garment for a better fit or for decoration. **2.** Any tucked piece or part. [Fusion of OE *tūcian* to tug and MDu. *tucken* to pluck]

tuck·er[1] (tuk′ər) *n.* **1.** One who or that which tucks. **2.** A covering of linen, lawn, etc., formerly worn over the neck and shoulders by women.

tuck·er[2] (tuk′ər) *v.t. Informal* To weary completely; exhaust: usu. with *out.* [Freq. of TUCK, v.]

-tude *suffix of nouns* Condition or state of being: *gratitude.* [< F < L *-tudo*]

Tu·dor (tōō′dər, tyōō′-) A royal family of England descended from **Sir Owen Tudor,** died 1461, a Welshman who married the widow of Henry V. — *adj.* Designating or pertaining to the architecture, poetry, etc., developed during the reigns of the Tudors.

Tues·day (tōōz′dē, -dā, tyōōz′-) *n.* The third day of the week. [OE *tīwesdæg* day of Tiw < *Tīw,* ancient Teutonic deity + *dæg* day]

tu·fa (tōō′fə, tyōō′-) *n.* **1.** A porous calcium carbonate, deposited from springs and streams. **2.** Tuff. [< Ital. < L *tofus*] — **tu·fa·ceous** (tōō·fā′shəs, tyōō-) *adj.*

tuff (tuf) *n.* A fragmentary volcanic rock composed of material varying in size from fine sand to coarse gravel. [< MF < Ital. *tufo.* See TUFA.] — **tuff·a′ceous** *adj.*

tuft (tuft) *n.* **1.** A collection or bunch of small, flexible parts, as hair, grass, or feathers, held together at the base. **2.** A clump or knot, as a cluster of threads drawn tightly through a quilt, mattress, or upholstery to secure the stuffing. — *v.t.* **1.** To separate or form into tufts. **2.** To cover or adorn with tufts. — *v.i.* **3.** To form tufts. [< OF *tuffe,* prob. < Gmc.] — **tuft′ed** *adj.* — **tuft′er** *n.* — **tuft′y** *adj.*

tug (tug) *v.* **tugged, tug·ging** *v.t.* **1.** To pull at with effort; strain at. **2.** To pull, draw, or drag with effort. **3.** To tow with a tugboat. — *v.i.* **4.** To pull strenuously: to *tug* at an oar. **5.** To strive; toil. — *n.* **1.** An act of tugging; a violent pull. **2.** A strenuous contest. **3.** A tugboat. **4.** A trace of a harness. [ME < OE < *tēon* to tow] — **tug′ger** *n.*

tug·boat (tug′bōt′) *n.* A small, compact, ruggedly built vessel designed for towing: also called *towboat, tug.*

tug of war **1.** A contest in which a number of persons at one end of a rope pull against a like number at the other end, each side endeavoring to drag the other across a line marked between. **2.** A hard struggle for supremacy.

tu·i·tion (tōō·ish′ən, tyōō-) *n.* **1.** The charge or payment for instruction, esp. formal instruction. **2.** Teaching; instruction. [< AF & OF < L *tueri* to look at, watch] — **tu·i′tion·al, tu·i′tion·ar′y** (-er′ē) *adj.*

tu·la·re·mi·a (tōō′lə·rē′mē·ə) *n.* A plaguelike disease of rodents, esp. rabbits, that may be transmitted to man: also called *rabbit fever.* Also **tu′la·rae′mi·a.** [< NL, after *Tulare* County, California + Gk. *haima* blood]

tu·lip (tōō′lip, tyōō′-) *n.* **1.** Any of numerous hardy, bulbous herbs of the lily family, cultivated in many varieties for their large, variously colored, bell-shaped flowers. **2.** A bulb or flower of this plant. [< F < OF < Turkish < Persian *dulband* turban]

tulip tree **1.** A large tree of the magnolia family of the eastern U.S., with greenish cup-shaped flowers. **2.** Any of various other trees having tuliplike flowers.

tu·lip·wood (tōō′lip·wŏŏd′, tyōō′-) *n.* **1.** The wood of the tulip tree. **2.** Any of several ornamental cabinet woods yielded by various trees. **3.** Any of the trees themselves.

tulle (tōōl, *Fr.* tül) *n.* A fine, silk, open-meshed material, used for veils, etc. [< F, after *Tulle,* city in France]

tum·ble (tum′bəl) *v.* **·bled, ·bling** *v.i.* **1.** To roll or toss about. **2.** To perform acrobatic feats, as somersaults, etc. **3.** To fall violently or awkwardly. **4.** To move in a careless or headlong manner; stumble. **5.** *Informal* To understand: with *to.* — *v.t.* **6.** To toss carelessly; cause to fall. **7.** To throw into disorder or confusion; disturb; rumple. — *n.* **1.** The act of tumbling; a fall. **2.** A state of disorder or confusion. [ME < OE *tumbian* to fall, leap]

tum·ble·bug (tum′bəl·bug′) *n.* A beetle that rolls up a ball of dung to enclose its eggs.

tum·ble-down (tum′bəl·doun′) *adj.* Rickety, as if about to fall in pieces; dilapidated.

tum·bler (tum′blər) *n.* **1.** A drinking glass with a flat bottom. **2.** One who or that which tumbles; esp., an acrobat or gymnast. **3.** One of a breed of domestic pigeons noted for the habit of turning forward somersaults during flight. **4.** In a lock, a latch that prevents a bolt from being shot in either direction until it is raised by the key bit. For illus. see LOCK[1]. **5.** In a firearm lock, a piece attached to the hammer and receiving the thrust of the mainspring.

tum·ble·weed (tum′bəl·wēd′) *n.* Any of various plants that, when withered, break from the root and are driven by the wind, scattering their seed.

tum·brel (tum′bril) *n.* **1.** A farmer's cart; esp., a boxlike cart for carrying and dumping dung. **2.** A rude cart in which prisoners were taken to the guillotine during the French Revolution. Also **tum′bril.** [< OF *tomber* to fall, ult. < Gmc.]

tu·me·fy (tōō′mə·fī, tyōō′-) *v.t. & v.i.* **·fied, ·fy·ing** To swell or puff up; become tumid. [< MF < L < *tumere* to swell + *facere* to make] — **tu′me·fac′tion** (-fak′shən) *n.*

tu·mes·cent (tōō·mes′ənt, tyōō-) *adj.* **1.** Swelling; somewhat tumid. **2.** Beginning to swell. [< L *tumere* to swell] — **tu·mes′cence** *n.*

tu·mid (tōō′mid, tyōō′-) *adj.* **1.** Swollen; enlarged, as a part of the body. **2.** Inflated or pompous in style. **3.** Bursting; teeming. [< L < *tumere* to swell] — **tu·mid′i·ty** *n.* — **tu′mid·ly** *adv.* — **tu′mid·ness** *n.*

tu·mor (tōō′mər, tyōō′-) *n. Pathol.* A local swelling on or in any part of the body, esp. from some abnormal growth of tissue that may or may not become malignant. Also *Brit.* **tu′mour.** [< L *tumere* to swell] — **tu′mor·ous** *adj.*

tu·mult (tōō′mult, tyōō′-) *n.* **1.** The commotion, disturbance, or agitation of a multitude; an uproar; turbulence; hubbub. **2.** Any violent commotion or agitation, as of the mind. [< L *tumere* to swell]

tu·mul·tu·ous (tōō·mul′chōō·əs, tyōō-) *adj.* **1.** Characterized by tumult; disorderly. **2.** Causing or affected by tumult or agitation; agitated or disturbed. Also **tu·mul′tu·ar·y** (-er′ē). — **tu·mul′tu·ous·ly** *adv.* — **tu·mul′tu·ous·ness** *n.*

tun (tun) *n.* **1.** A large cask. **2.** A varying measure of capacity, usu. equal to 252 gallons. — *v.t.* **tunned, tun·ning** To put into a cask or tun. [OE *tunne*]

tu·na (tōō′nə) *n. pl.* **·na** or **·nas 1.** Any of several large marine food fishes of the mackerel family. **2.** Any of various similar or related fishes. **3.** The flesh of any of these fishes processed and eaten as food: also **tuna fish.** Also called *tunny.* [< Am. Sp., ult. < L < Gk. *thynnos*]

tun·dra (tun′drə, tōōn′-) *n.* A treeless, often marshy plain of Siberia, arctic North America, etc. [< Russian < Lapp]

tune (tōōn, tyōōn) *n.* **1.** A melody or air, usu. simple and easy to remember. **2.** The state or quality of being at the proper pitch, or, loosely, in the proper key: out of *tune.* **3.** Concord or unison. **4.** Suitable temper or humor. — **to change one's tune** To assume a different manner, style, or attitude. — **to sing a different (or another) tune** To assume a different manner or attitude; change one's tune. — **to the tune of** To the price of. — *v.* **tuned, tun·ing** *v.t.* **1.** To adjust the pitch of to a standard. **2.** To adapt to a particular tone, expression, or mood. **3.** To bring into harmony. **4.** To express musically. — *v.i.* **5.** To be in harmony. — **to tune in** To adjust a radio receiver to the frequency of (a station, broadcast, etc.). — **to tune out** To adjust a radio receiver to exclude (interference, a station, etc.). — **to tune up 1.** To bring (musical instruments) to a standard or common pitch. **2.** To adjust (an engine, etc.) to proper working order. [Var. of TONE] — **tun′a·ble** or **tune′a·ble** *adj.*

tune·ful (tōōn′fəl, tyōōn′-) *adj.* **1.** Melodious; musical. **2.** Producing musical sounds. — **tune′ful·ly** *adv.* — **tune′ful·ness** *n.*

tune·less (tōōn′lis, tyōōn′-) *adj.* **1.** Not employed in making music; silent. **2.** Lacking in rhythm, melody, etc. — **tune′less·ly** *adv.* — **tune′less·ness** *n.*

tun·er (tōō′nər, tyōō′-) *n.* **1.** One who or that which tunes. **2.** *Telecom.* A radio receiver without amplifiers.

tune-up (tōōn′up′, tyōōn′-) *n. Informal* An adjustment to bring a motor, etc., into proper operating condition.

tung oil (tung) A yellow to brown oil extracted from the seeds of a Chinese tree, used in paints, varnishes, etc. and also for waterproofing. [< Chinese *t'ung* tung tree]

tung·sten (tung′stən) *n.* A steel-gray, brittle, heavy metallic element of the chromium group (symbol W), having a high melting point and much used in the manufacture of filaments for electric lamps and high-speed cutting tools: also called *wolfram.* See ELEMENT. [< Sw. < *tung* weighty + *sten* stone] — **tung·sten·ic** (tung·sten′ik) *adj.*

tu·nic (tōō′nik, tyōō′-) *n.* **1.** In ancient Greece and Rome, a garment with or without sleeves, reaching to the knees and usu. worn without a belt. **2.** A modern outer garment gathered at the waist, as a short overskirt or blouse. **3.** *Biol.* Any loose membranous skin or mantle of tissue enveloping an organ or part. [< L < Semitic]

tu·ni·cate (tōō′nə·kit, -kāt, tyōō′-) *adj.* **1.** *Zool.* Of or pertaining to a group of small marine chordates, having in the adult stage a cylindrical saclike body covered with a transparent membrane or tunic, as the ascidians. **2.** *Zool.* Having a tunic. — *n.* A tunicate animal. [< NL < L < *tunicare* to clothe with a tunic < *tunica* tunic]

tun·ing fork (tōō′ning, tyōō′-) A fork-shaped piece of steel that produces a tone of definite pitch when struck.

Tu·ni·sian (tōō·nish′ən, -nē′zhən, tyōō-) *adj.* Of or relating to Tunisia, or Tunis, or their inhabitants. — *n.* **1.** An inhabitant or native of Tunisia or Tunis. **2.** The speech of Tunisia, a North Arabic dialect.

tun·nel (tun′əl) *n.* **1.** An artificial subterranean passageway or gallery, esp. one under a hill, etc., as for a railway. **2.** Any similar passageway under or through something, as in a mine. — *v.* **tun·neled** or **·nelled, tun·nel·ing** or **·nel·ling** *v.t.* **1.** To make a tunnel through. **2.** To shape or make in the form of a tunnel: to *tunnel* a passage. — *v.i.* **3.** To make a tunnel. [Fusion of OF *tonnelle* partridge net and dim. of *tonne* cask] — **tun′nel·er** or **tun′nel·ler** *n.*

tun·ny (tun′ē) *n. pl.* **·ny** or **·nies** The tuna, a fish. [< OF < L < Gk. *thynnos*]

tup (tup) *n.* **1.** A ram, or male sheep. **2.** The striking part of a power hammer. — *v.t. & v.i.* **tupped, tup·ping** To copulate with (a female): said of the ram. [ME *tupe*]

Tu·pi (tōō·pē′) *n. pl.* **·pis** or **·pi 1.** A member of any of a group of South American Indian tribes, comprising the northern branch of the Tupian stock. **2.** The language spoken by the Tupis, used as a lingua franca along the Amazon. [< Tupi, comrade]

Tu·pi·an (tōō·pē′ən) *adj.* Of or pertaining to the Tupis or their language. — *n.* A large stock of South American Indians of some one hundred tribes of the Tupis and Guaranis: also **Tu·pi′-Gua′ra·ni′** (-gwä′rä·nē′).

tup·pence (tup′əns) *n. Brit. Informal* Twopence.

tuque (tōōk, tyōōk) *n. Canadian* A knitted cap, worn for tobogganing, etc. [< dial. F (Canadian) < *toque* cap]

Tu·ra·ni·an (tōō·rā′nē·ən, tyōō-) *adj.* **1.** Of or pertaining to a hypothetical nomadic people who antedated the Aryans in Europe and Asia. **2.** Pertaining to the non-Indo-European Ural-Altaic family of languages. [< Persian *Tūrān*, country north of the Oxus River]

tur·ban (tûr′bən) *n.* **1.** An Oriental head covering consisting of a sash or shawl, twisted about the head or about a cap. **2.** Any similar headdress. **3.** A round-crowned brimless hat for women or children. [< F < Ital. < Turkish < Persian < *dul* turn + *band* band] — **tur′baned** (-bənd) *adj.*

tur·bid (tûr′bid) *adj.* **1.** Opaque or cloudy, as a liquid with a suspension of foreign particles. **2.** Thick and dense, like heavy smoke or fog. **3.** Being in a state of confusion. [< L < *turbare* to trouble < *turba* crowd] — **tur′bid·ly** *adv.* — **tur′bid·ness, tur·bid′i·ty** (tûr·bid′ə·tē) *n.*

tur·bi·nate (tûr′bə·nit, -nāt) *adj.* **1.** Top-shaped; also, spinning like a top. [< L *turbo* whirlwind]

tur·bine (tûr′bin, -bīn) *n.* Any of various motors consisting of one or more rotary units, mounted on a shaft and provided with a series of curved vanes, actuated by the impulse of steam, water, gas, or other fluid under pressure. [< F < L *turbo* whirlwind, top]

turbo- *combining form* A turbine; related to or operated by a turbine or turbines. [< L *turbo* top]

tur·bo·gen·er·a·tor (tûr′bō·jen′ə·rā′tər) *n.* An electric power-generating machine adapted for direct coupling to a steam turbine.

tur·bo·jet engine (tûr′bō·jet′) *n. Aeron.* A type of jet engine using a gas turbine to drive an air compressor.

tur·bo·prop (tûr′bō·prop′) *n. Aeron.* A turbojet engine connecting directly with a propeller. Also called *propjet.*

tur·bot (tûr′bət) *n. pl.* **·bot** or **·bots 1.** A large European flatfish, esteemed as food. **2.** One of various related flatfishes. [< AF *turbut*, OF *tourbout*, or MDu. *turbot*]

tur·bu·lence (tûr′byə·ləns) *n.* **1.** The state or condition of being violently disturbed, restless, or confused. **2.** *Physics* The irregular eddying flow of a gas or other fluid, esp. as caused by an obstacle or by friction, as of a ship or airplane in rapid motion. Also **tur′bu·len·cy.**

tur·bu·lent (tûr′byə·lənt) *adj.* **1.** Being in violent agitation or commotion. **2.** Inclined to rebel; insubordinate. **3.** Having a tendency to disturb or throw into confusion. [< MF < L *turbare.* See TURBID.] — **tur′bu·lent·ly** *adv.* — **Syn. 1.** agitated, boisterous, disorderly, disturbed, riotous, tumultuous, wild. **2.** insurgent, mutinous, refractory.

tur·dine (tûr′din, -dīn) *adj.* Belonging or pertaining to a large and widely distributed family of singing birds, including thrushes and bluebirds. [< NL < L *turdus* thrush]

tu·reen (tŏŏ·rēn′, tyŏŏ-) *n.* A deep, covered dish, as for holding soup to be served. [< F < LL < L *terra* earth]

turf (tûrf) *n.* *pl.* **turfs** (*Archaic* **turves**) 1. The grass or other fine plants with their matted roots filling the upper stratum of certain soils; sod. 2. A piece of peat for burning as fuel. — **the turf** 1. A racetrack for horses. 2. The practice of racing horses. [OE] — **turf′y** *adj.*

turf·man (tûrf′mən) *n.* *pl.* **·men** (-mən) A man who is devoted to or connected with horse racing.

tur·ges·cence (tûr·jes′əns) *n.* The process of swelling up. [< Med.L < L *turgere* to swell] — **tur·ges′cent** *adj.*

tur·gid (tûr′jid) *adj.* 1. Unnaturally distended, as by contained air or liquid; swollen. 2. Inflated; bombastic, as language, etc. [< L *turgere* to swell] — **tur·gid′i·ty, tur′gid·ness** (tûr′jid·nis) *n.* — **tur′gid·ly** *adv.*

tur·gor (tûr′gər) *n.* The state of being turgid; turgidity.

Turk (tûrk) *n.* 1. A native or inhabitant of Turkey: sometimes called *Ottoman.* 2. One of any of the peoples speaking any of the Turkic languages. 3. A Moslem.

tur·key (tûr′kē) *n.* *pl.* **·keys** 1. A large American bird related to the pheasant, having the head naked and the tail extensible; esp., the American domesticated turkey, much esteemed as food. 2. *U.S. Slang* A play that is a failure. — **to talk turkey** To discuss in a practical and direct manner. [Short for *turkey cock* the guinea fowl, after *Turkey*; later applied erroneously to the American bird]

turkey buzzard A sooty black vulture of tropical America and the southern U.S., having a naked red head.

Tur·ki (tŏŏr′kē) *adj.* 1. Of or pertaining to Turkic. 2. Of or pertaining to any of the peoples speaking a Turkic language, as the Osmanlis. — *n.* *pl.* **·kis** 1. The Turkic languages. 2. A member of any of the Turki peoples.

Turk·ic (tûr′kik) *n.* A subfamily of the Altaic family of languages, including Osmanli or Turkish, Uzbek, etc. — *adj.* Pertaining to this linguistic subfamily, or to any of the peoples speaking these languages.

Turk·ish (tûr′kish) *adj.* 1. Of or pertaining to Turkey or the Turks. 2. Of or relating to the Turkic subfamily of Altaic languages, esp. to Osmanli. — *n.* Osmanli.

Turkish bath A bathing establishment where sweating is induced by exposure to high temperature, usu. in a room heated by steam, followed by washing, massage, etc.

Turkish towel A heavy, rough towel with loose, uncut pile. Also **turkish towel.**

tur·mer·ic (tûr′mər·ik) *n.* 1. The root of an East Indian plant, used as a condiment, aromatic stimulant, dyestuff, etc. 2. The plant yielding this root. — *adj.* Of, pertaining to, or saturated with turmeric. [? < F < Med.L *terra merita* deserving earth]

tur·moil (tûr′moil) *n.* Confused motion; disturbance; tumult. [? < OF < L *tremere* to tremble]

turn (tûrn) *v.t.* 1. To cause to rotate, as about an axis. 2. To change the position of, as by rotating: to *turn* a trunk on its side. 3. To move so that the upper side becomes the under and the under side becomes the upper: to *turn* a page; to *turn* the soil; to *turn* a shirt collar. 4. To reverse the arrangement or order of. 5. To cause to rotate in order to tighten, loosen, open, etc.: to *turn* a screw. 6. To revolve mentally; ponder: often with *over.* 7. To sprain or strain: to *turn* one's ankle. 8. To nauseate (the stomach). 9. To give rounded or curved form to, as by turning in a lathe. 10. To give graceful or finished form to: to *turn* a phrase. 11. To perform by revolving: to *turn* cartwheels. 12. To bend, curve, fold, twist, or blunt. 13. To change or transform: to *turn* water into wine. 14. To translate. 15. To exchange for an equivalent: to *turn* stocks into cash. 16. To adapt to some purpose; apply: to *turn* information to good account. 17. To cause to become as specified: The sight *turned* him sick. 18. To change the color of. 19. To make sour or rancid. 20. To change the direction or focus of. 21. To direct or aim; point. 22. To deflect or divert: to *turn* a blow. 23. To repel: to *turn* a charge. 24. To go around or to the other side of: to *turn* a corner. 25. To pass or go beyond: to *turn* twenty-one. 26. To cause to go; send; drive: to *turn* a beggar from one's door. — *v.i.* 27. To move around an axis; rotate; revolve. 28. To move partially on or as if on an axis: He *turned* and ran. 29. To change position; also, to roll from side to side. 30. To reverse position; become inverted. 31. To change or reverse direction or flow: We *turned* north. The tide has *turned.* 32. To change the direction or focus of one's thought, attention, etc. 33. To depend; hinge: with *on* or *upon.* 34. To whirl, as the head. 35. To become nauseated, as the stomach. 36. To become hostile: to *turn* on one's neighbors. 37. To change one's position in order to act in retaliation: The worm *turns.* 38. To become transformed: The water *turned* into ice. 39. To become as specified: His hair *turned* gray. 40. To change color: said esp. of leaves. 41. To become sour, rancid, or fermented. — **to turn against** To become or cause to become opposed or hostile to. — **to turn down** 1. To diminish the flow, volume, etc., of. 2. *Informal* To reject or refuse, as a request; also, to refuse the request, etc., of. — **to turn in** 1. To fold or double. 2. To bend or incline inward. 3. To deliver; hand over. 4. *Informal* To go to bed. — **to turn loose** *Informal* To set free. — **to turn off** 1. To stop the operation, flow, etc., of. 2. To leave the direct road. — **to turn on** 1. To set in operation, flow, etc. 2. *Slang* To take or experience the effects of taking a psychedelic drug, as marijuana. 3. *Slang* To evoke in (someone) a rapt response, as though under the influence of a psychedelic drug: Baroque music really *turned* him *on.* — **to turn out** 1. To turn inside out. 2. To eject or expel. 3. To dismiss. 4. To stop the operation, flow, etc., of. 5. To bend or incline outward. 6. To produce; make. 7. To come or go out, as for duty or service. 8. To prove (to be). 9. To become or result. 10. To equip: dress. 11. *Informal* To get out of bed. — **to turn over** 1. To change the position of; invert. 2. To upset; overturn. 3. To hand over; transfer or relinquish. 4. To do business to the amount of. 5. To invest and get back (capital). 6. To buy and then sell: to *turn over* merchandise. — **to turn to** 1. To set to work. 2. To seek aid from. 3. To refer or apply to. 4. To open a book, etc., to (a specified page). — **to turn up** 1. To bring or fold the under side upward. 2. To bend or incline upward. 3. To find or be found. 4. To increase the flow, volume, etc. of. 5. To put in an appearance; arrive. — *n.* 1. The act of turning, or the state of being turned. 2. A change to another direction, motion, or position. 3. A deflection or deviation from a course; change in trend. 4. The point at which a change takes place: a *turn* for the better. 5. A rotation or revolution. 6. A bend, as in a road. 7. A regular time or chance in some succession: It's my *turn* to play. 8. A round; spell: a *turn* at painting. 9. Characteristic form, shape, or style: the *turn* of a phrase. 10. A knack or special ability: a *turn* for study. 11. Tendency; direction: The talk took a serious *turn.* 12. A deed performed: a good *turn.* 13. An advantage: It served his *turn.* 14. A walk, drive, or trip to and fro: a *turn* in the park. 15. A round in a skein, coil, etc.; also, a twist. 16. *Music* An ornament formed by a group of four rapid notes, the first a degree above and the third a degree below the principal tone, that occupies the second and fourth positions. In an **inverted turn** the tones are reversed in order. 17. *Informal* A shock to the nerves, as from alarm. 18. A short theatrical act. — **at every turn** On every occasion; constantly. — **by turns** 1. In alternation or sequence. 2. At intervals. — **in turn** One after another; in proper order or sequence. — **out of turn** Not in proper order or sequence. — **to a turn** Just right: said esp. of cooked food. — **to take turns** To act, play, etc., one after another in proper order. [Fusion of OE *tyrnan* and *turnian* and OF *turner,* all < L *tornare* to turn in a lathe]

turn·a·bout (tûrn′ə·bout′) *n.* The act of turning completely about and taking the opposite direction, opinion, etc.

turn·a·round (tûrn′ə·round′) *n.* The act of unloading a ship, aircraft, etc., and loading it to begin its next trip.

turn·buck·le (tûrn′buk′əl) *n.* *Mech.* A form of coupling so threaded that when connected lengthwise between two metal rods or wires it may be turned so as to regulate the distance or tension between them.

TURNBUCKLES
a Insulated, for electric wires. *b* For metal tie rods. *c* For window shutters.

turn·coat (tûrn′kōt′) *n.* One who goes over to the opposite side or party; a renegade.

turn·down (tûrn′doun′) *adj.* Folded down, as a collar; also, capable of being turned down.

turn·er¹ (tûr′nər) *n.* One who turns; esp. one who fashions objects with a lathe.

turn·er² (tûr′nər) *n.* A gymnast; a member of a turnverein. [< G < *turnen* to engage in gymnastics < F *tourner*]

turn·ing (tûr′ning) *n.* 1. The act of one who or that which turns. 2. The art of shaping wood, metal, etc., in a lathe. 3. Any deviation from a straight or customary course; a winding; bend. 4. The point where a road forks. 5. Fashioning or shaping, as of a literary work.

turning point 1. The point of a decisive change in direction of action; a crisis. 2. The point at which the direction of a motion is reversed.

tur·nip (tûr′nip) *n.* 1. The fleshy, globular, edible root of either of two biennial herbs, of the mustard family, the **white turnip,** and the rutabaga. 2. Either of the plants yielding this root. [Earlier *turnepe,* ? < F *tour* turn (< L *turnus* lathe) + ME *nepe* < OE *nǣp* < L *napus* turnip]

turn·key (tûrn′kē) *n.* One who has charge of the keys of a prison; a jailer.

---

turn·off (tûrn′ôf′, -of′) *n. Informal* A road, path, or way branching off from a main thoroughfare.

turn·out (tûrn′out′) *n.* **1.** An act of turning out or coming forth. **2.** An assemblage of persons; attendance. **3.** A quantity produced; output. **4.** Array; equipment; outfit. **5.** A railroad siding. **6.** A carriage or wagon with its horses and equipage. **7.** *Brit.* A labor strike; also, a striker.

turn·o·ver (tûrn′ō′vər) *n.* **1.** The act or process of turning over; an upset or overthrow, as of a vehicle. **2.** The rate at which persons hired by a given establishment within a given period are replaced by others; also, the number of persons hired. **3.** A change or revolution. **4.** A small pie or tart made by covering half of a circular crust with fruit, jelly, or the like, and turning the other half over on top. **5.** The amount of business accomplished, or of work achieved. **6.** A completed commercial transaction or course of business; also, the money receipts of a business for a given period: also called *overturn.* — *adj.* **1.** Designed for turning over or reversing. **2.** Capable of being turned over or folded down. **3.** Made with a part folded down: a *turnover* collar.

turn·pike (tûrn′pīk′) *n.* **1.** A road, now esp. a superhighway, on which there are tollgates. **2.** Loosely, any highway: also **turnpike road. 3.** A tollbar or tollgate. [ME *turnpyke* spiked road barrier < TURN + *pyke* pike¹]

turn·stile (tûrn′stīl′) *n.* A gate, having revolving horizontal arms, that admits passengers to subways, buses, etc., on the deposit of fares, or registers the number of persons entering a building, or restricts passage to one direction only.

turn·stone (tûrn′stōn′) *n.* A ploverlike migratory bird of northern regions: so called from its habit of turning over stones to obtain its food.

turn·ta·ble (tûrn′tā′bəl) *n.* **1.** A rotating disk, as one that carries a phonograph record. **2.** A rotating platform arranged to turn a section of a bridge in order to open a passage for ships. **3.** Such a platform to turn a locomotive, car, etc. Also *Brit.* **turn′plate′** (-plāt′).

turn·up (tûrn′up′) *n.* **1.** That which is turned up, as part of a garment. **2.** A particular card or die turned up in gambling. **3.** Pure chance; a tossup. — *adj.* Turned up.

turn·ver·ein (tōórn′fə·rīn, tûrn′və·rīn) *n. Sometimes cap.* An athletic club. [< G < *turnen* to exercise + *verein* club]

tur·pen·tine (tûr′pən·tīn) *n.* An oleoresin obtained from any of several coniferous trees, esp. pines. — **oil of turpentine** The colorless essential oil formed when turpentine is distilled with steam; chiefly used to thin paint: also called *spirits of turpentine.* — *v.t.* **·tined, ·tin·ing 1.** To put turpentine with or upon; saturate with turpentine. **2.** To obtain crude turpentine from (a tree). [< OF < L < Gk. *terebinthos,* a tree from which it was originally obtained]

tur·pi·tude (tûr′pə·tōod, -tyōod) *n.* Inherent baseness; vileness; depravity, or any action showing depravity. [< MF < L < *turpis* vile]

tur·quoise (tûr′koiz, -kwoiz) *n.* **1.** A blue or green aluminum phosphate, colored by copper, found massive, and in its highly polished blue varieties esteemed as a gemstone. **2.** A light greenish blue, the color of the turquoise: also **turquoise blue.** [< MF (*pierre*) *turquoise* Turkish (stone)]

tur·ret (tûr′it) *n.* **1.** *Mil.* **a** A rotating armored housing, large enough to contain a powerful gun or guns and gunners, forming part of a warship or of a fort. **b** A similar structure in a tank or a bombing or combat airplane. **2.** *Archit.* A small tower rising above a larger structure, as on a castle. **3.** *Mech.* In a lathe, a cylinder fitted with sockets or chucks for the reception of various tools, any one of which may be presented in the axial line of the work: also **turret head.** [< OF *torete,* dim. of *tor* tower] — **tur·ri·cal** (tûr′i·kəl) *adj.*

tur·ret·ed (tûr′it·id) *adj.* **1.** Provided with turrets. **2.** Having the form of a turret.

turret lathe A lathe having a turret.

tur·tle¹ (tûr′təl) *n.* **1.** Any of numerous reptiles having a horny, toothless beak, and a short, stout body enclosed within a carapace and plastron, into which all the members may be drawn for protection. **2.** A marine species as distinguished from a terrestrial or fresh-water species. **3.** The flesh of certain varieties of turtle, served as food. — **green turtle** An important food turtle of wide distribution in tropical and semitropical seas: so called from the greenish color of its flesh. — **to turn turtle** To capsize. — *v.i.* **·tled, ·tling** To hunt or catch turtles. [Appar. alter. of F *tortue* or Sp. *tortuga* < Med.L *tortuca* tortoise; infl. in form by TURTLE²]

tur·tle² (tûr′təl) *n. Archaic* A turtledove. [OE < L *turtur*]

tur·tle·back (tûr′təl·bak′) *n.* **1.** *Naut.* An arched covering, resembling the shell of a turtle, built over the bow or stern of a ship as protection against heavy seas. Also **turtle deck. 2.** *Archeol.* A chipped stone implement rounded on one side.

tur·tle·dove (tûr′təl·duv′) *n.* A small Old World dove conspicuous for its white-edged black tail and soft, mournful coo. [< TURTLE² + DOVE]

turtle neck A high collar that fits snugly about the neck, usu. rolled or turned over double, used esp. on athletic sweaters. — **tur·tle·neck** (tûr′təl·nek′) *adj.*

Tus·can (tus′kən) *adj.* Pertaining to Tuscany. — *n.* **1.** A native or inhabitant of Tuscany. **2.** Any Italian dialect used in Tuscany; esp. the one spoken in Florence.

Tus·ca·ro·ra (tus′kə·rôr′ə, -rō′rə) *n. pl.* **·ra** or **·ras** One of a tribe of North American Indians of Iroquoian stock formerly living in North Carolina, now surviving in New York and Ontario.

tush (tush) *interj.* An exclamation expressing disapproval, impatience, etc. [ME *tussch*]

tusk (tusk) *n.* **1.** A long, pointed tooth, generally one of a pair, as in the boar, walrus, or elephant. **2.** A sharp, projecting, toothlike point. **3.** A shoulder on a tenon, to strengthen it at its base; also, a tenon having such a shoulder. — *v.t.* **1.** To gore with the tusks. **2.** To root up with the tusks. [Metathetic var. of OE *tūx*] — **tusked** (tuskt) *adj.* — **tusk′less** *adj.*

tusk·er (tus′kər) *n.* A tusked elephant or boar.

tus·sah (tus′ə) *n.* **1.** An Asian silkworm that spins large cocoons yielding a coarse, brownish or yellowish silk. **2.** The silk, or the durable fabric woven from it. Also **tus·sar** (tus′ər), **tus·sore** (tus′ôr, -ōr). [< Hind. < Skt. *tasara, trasara,* lit., shuttle]

tus·sis (tus′is) *n. Pathol.* A cough. [< NL < L] — **tus′sal, tus′sive** *adj.*

tus·sle (tus′əl) *v.t. & v.i.* **·sled, ·sling** To fight or struggle in a vigorous, determined way; scuffle; wrestle. — *n.* A disorderly struggle, as in sport; scuffle. [Var. of TOUSLE]

tus·sock (tus′ək) *n.* **1.** A tuft or clump of grass or sedge. **2.** A tuft, as of hair or feathers. Also **tus′suck.** [Prob. dim. of obs. *tusk* tuft of hair, ? < TUSK] — **tus′sock·y** *adj.*

tut (tut) *interj.* An exclamation to check rashness or express impatience. Also **tut tut.**

tu·te·lage (tōō′tə·lij, tyōō′-) *n.* **1.** The state of being under a tutor or guardian. **2.** The act or office of a guardian; guardianship. **3.** The act of tutoring; instruction. [< L < *tueri* to watch, guard]

tu·te·lar·y (tōō′tə·ler′ē, tyōō′-) *adj.* **1.** Invested with guardianship. **2.** Pertaining to a guardian. Also **tu′te·lar** (-lər).

tu·tor (tōō′tər, tyōō′-) *n.* **1.** One who instructs another in one or more branches of knowledge; a private teacher. **2.** A college teacher who gives individual instruction. **3.** *Brit.* A college official entrusted with the tutelage and care of undergraduates assigned to him. **4.** *Law* A guardian of a minor or of a woman. — *v.t.* **1.** To act as tutor to; instruct; teach; train. **2.** To have the guardianship of. **3.** To treat severely or sternly, as a tutor might; discipline. — *v.i.* **4.** To do the work of a tutor. **5.** To be tutored or instructed. [< AF, OF < L < *tueri* to watch, guard] — **tu·to·ri·al** (tōō·tôr′ē·əl, -tō′rē, tyōō-) *adj.*

tu·tor·ship (tōō′tər·ship, tyōō′-) *n.* **1.** The office of a tutor or of a guardian. Also **tu′tor·age** (-ij). **2.** Tutelage.

tut·ti (tōō′tē) *Music adj.* All: a term used to indicate that all performers are to take part. — *n. pl.* **·tis** A composition, piece, movement, or passage for all the voices and instruments together. [< Ital., pl. of *tutto* all < L *totus*]

tut·ti-frut·ti (tōō′tē·frōō′tē) *n.* A confection, chewing gum, ice cream, etc., made with a mixture of fruits. — *adj.* Having fruit flavors. [< Ital., all fruits]

tu·tu (tū·tū′) *n. French* A short, full, projecting skirt consisting of many layers of sheer fabric, worn by ballet dancers.

tu-whit tu-whoo (tōō·hwit′, tōō·hwōō′) The cry of an owl.

tux·e·do (tuk·sē′dō) *n. pl.* **·dos** **1.** *U.S.* A man's semiformal dinner coat without tails: also called *dinner coat, dinner jacket.* **2.** *U.S.* The suit of which the coat is a part. Also **Tux·e′do.** [after *Tuxedo* Park, N.Y.]

TV (tē′vē′) *n. pl.* **TVs** or **TV's** Television. — *adj.* Of or pertaining to television.

twad·dle (twod′l) *v.t. & v.i.* **·dled, ·dling** To talk foolishly and pretentiously. — *n.* Pretentious, silly talk. [Prob. alter. of TWATTLE] — **twad′dler** *n.*

twain (twān) *adj. Archaic & Poetic* Two. — *n.* **1.** A couple; two. **2.** In river navigation, two fathoms or twelve feet. [OE *twēgen,* masculine of *twā* two]

twang (twang) *v.t. & v.i.* **twanged, twang·ing 1.** To make or cause to make a sharp, vibrant sound, as a bowstring. **2.** To utter or speak nasally. — *n.* **1.** A sharp, vibrating sound, as of a tense string plucked. **2.** Excessive nasality of the voice. **3.** A sound resembling either of the foregoing. [Imit.] — **twang′y** *adj.*

twat·tle (twot′l) *v.t. & v.i.* **·tled, ·tling** *n.* Twaddle. [Short for *twittle-twattle,* var. of TITTLE-TATTLE]

tweak (twēk) *v.t.* To pinch and twist sharply; twitch. — *n.* A twisting pinch; twitch. [Var. of dial. *twick,* OE *twiccian* to twitch] — **tweak′y** *adj.*

tweed (twēd) *n.* **1.** A soft woolen fabric with a homespun surface, often woven in two or more colors to effect a check or plaid pattern. **2.** *pl.* Clothing of tweed. — **Harris tweed** A homespun woolen cloth, usu. of mixed colors, made at Harris in the Hebrides. [Alter. of dial. E (Scottish) *tweel,* var. of TWILL]

twee·dle (twēd′l) *v.* **·dling, ·dling** *v.t.* **1.** To play (a musical instrument) casually or carelessly. **2.** To wheedle; cajole. — *v.i.* **3.** To produce a series of shrill tones. **4.** To play a musical instrument casually or carelessly. — *n.* A sound resembling the tones of a violin. [Imit.]

twee·dle·dum and twee·dle·dee (twēd/l·dum', twēd/l·dē') Two things between which there is only the slightest possible distinction. [Orig. imit. of low- and high-pitched musical instruments, respectively]

'tween (twēn) Contraction of BETWEEN.

tweet (twēt) *v.i.* To utter a thin, chirping note. — *n.* A twittering or chirping. Also **tweet'-tweet'**. [Imit.]

tweet·er (twē/tər) *n. Electronics* A small loudspeaker used to reproduce high-pitched sounds in high-fidelity sound equipment. Compare WOOFER. [< TWEET]

tweeze (twēz) *v.t.* **tweezed, tweez·ing** *Informal* To handle, pluck, etc., with tweezers. [Back formation < TWEEZERS]

tweez·ers (twē/zərz) *n.pl.* Small pincers for grasping and holding small objects. Also called **pair of tweezers**. [Alter. of *tweezes*, pl. of *tweeze*, earlier *etweese* case of small instruments < F *étuis*, pl. of *étui*.]

Twelfth-day (twelfth/dā') *n.* Epiphany.

Twelfth-night (twelfth/nīt') *n.* The evening (Jan. 5th) before Epiphany; sometimes, the evening (Jan. 6th) of Epiphany. — *adj.* Of or pertaining to Twelfth-night.

twelve (twelv) *n.* **1.** The sum of eleven and one: a cardinal number. **2.** Any symbol of this number, as 12, xii, XII. **3.** Anything consisting of or representing twelve units. — **the Twelve** The twelve apostles. — *adj.* Being one more than eleven. [OE *twelf*] — **twelfth** (twelfth) *adj. & n.*

Twelve Apostles The twelve disciples of Jesus: more commonly *the Twelve*.

twelve·mo (twelv/mō) *adj. & n.* Duodecimo.

twelve·month (twelv/munth') *n.* A year.

twelve-tone (twelv/tōn') *adj. Music* **1.** Of, using, or composed in the technique developed by Arnold Schönberg, in which the tones of the chromatic scale are arranged in an arbitrary series, which is used as the basis of the composition. **2.** In 20th-century music, using or composed in a freely chromatic style.

twen·ty (twen/tē) *n. pl.* **·ties 1.** The sum of nineteen and one: a cardinal number. **2.** Any symbol of this number, as 20, xx, XX. **3.** Anything consisting of or representing twenty units. — *adj.* Being one more than nineteen. [OE *twēntig*] — **twen'ti·eth** *adj. & n.*

twen·ty-one (twen/tē-wun') *n.* A card game in which each player bets against the dealer, the object being to draw cards whose value will equal or approach twenty-one without exceeding that amount: also called *blackjack, vingt-et-un*.

twi- *prefix* Two; double; twice: *twibil*. Also spelled *twy-*. [OE, double < *twā* two]

twi·bil (twī/bil) *n.* **1.** A battle-ax with two cutting edges. **2.** A mattock having one blade like an ax and the other an adz. Also **twi/bill**. [OE < *twi-* two + *bill* ax]

twice (twīs) *adv.* **1.** Two times. **2.** In double measure; doubly. [OE *twiges*, gen. of *twiga* twice]

twice-told (twīs/tōld) *adj.* Told more than once.

twid·dle (twid/l) *v.* **·dled, ·dling** *v.t.* **1.** To twirl idly; toy or play with. — *v.i.* **2.** To revolve or twirl. **3.** To toy with something idly. **4.** To be busy about trifles. — **to twiddle one's thumbs 1.** To rotate one's thumbs idly around one another. **2.** To pass time in doing nothing. — *n.* A gentle twirling, as of the fingers. [Origin unknown] — **twid'dler** *n.*

twig (twig) *n.* A small shoot or branchlet of a tree. [OE *twigge*] — **twigged** *adj.* — **twig'less** *adj.*

twig·gy (twig/ē) *adj.* **·gi·er, ·gi·est** Like, or full of, twigs.

twi·light (twī/līt') *n.* **1.** The light diffused over the sky when the sun is below the horizon, esp. in the evening; also, the period during which this light is prevalent. **2.** Any faint light. **3.** A condition following the waning of past glory, achievement, etc. — *adj.* Pertaining to, resembling, or characteristic of twilight. [ME < OE *twi-* (< *twa* two) + LIGHT; used in the sense of "the light between the two," i.e., between day and night]

twilight sleep *Med.* A light or partial anesthesia as by injection of morphine and scopolamine, sometimes used to relieve childbirth pains. [Trans. of G *dämmerschlaf*]

twill (twil) *n.* **1.** A weave characterized by diagonal ribs or lines in fabrics. **2.** A fabric woven with a twill. — *v.t.* To weave (cloth) so as to produce diagonal lines or ribs on the surface. [Var. of ME *twile*, OE < *twa* two, partial trans. of L *bilix* having a double thread]

twilled (twild) *adj.* Woven so as to produce a diagonal rib or line; ribbed or ridged.

twin (twin) *n.* **1.** One of two young produced at the same birth. **2.** The counterpart or exact mate of another. — *adj.* **1.** Being, or standing in the relation of, a twin or twins. **2.** Consisting

TWILL
(Enlarged to show weave)

of, forming, or being one of a pair of similar and closely related objects; twofold. — *v.* **twinned, twin·ning** *v.i.* **1.** To bring forth twins. **2.** To be matched or equal; agree. — *v.t.* **3.** To bring forth as twins. **4.** To couple; match. [OE *twinn*]

twine (twīn) *v.* **twined, twin·ing** *v.t.* **1.** To twist together, as threads. **2.** To form by such twisting. **3.** To coil or wrap about something. **4.** To encircle by winding or wreathing. **5.** To enfold; embrace. — *v.i.* **6.** To interlace. **7.** To proceed in a winding course; meander. — *adj.* Of or like twine. — *n.* **1.** A string composed of two or more strands twisted together: loosely, any small cord. **2.** The act of twining or entwining. **3.** A form or conformation produced by twining. **4.** An interweaving or interlacing. [OE *twin* twisted double thread < *twā* two] — **twin'er** *n.*

twinge (twinj) *n.* **1.** A sharp, darting, local pain. **2.** A mental or emotional pang. — *v.t. & v.i.* **twinged, twing·ing** To affect with or suffer a sudden pain or twinge. [OE *twengan* to pinch]

twin·kle (twing/kəl) *v.* **·kled, ·kling** *v.i.* **1.** To shine with fitful, intermittent gleams, as a star. **2.** To be bright, as with amusement: Her eyes *twinkled*. **3.** To move rapidly to and fro; flicker: *twinkling* feet. — *v.t.* **4.** To emit or cause to flash out, as gleams of light. — *n.* **1.** A tremulous gleam of light; sparkle; glimmer. **2.** A wink or sparkle of the eye. **3.** An instant; a twinkling. [OE *twinclian*] — **twin'kler** *n.*

twin·kling (twing/kling) *n.* **1.** The act of scintillating. **2.** A wink or twinkle. **3.** The act of winking, or the time required for it. **4.** A moment.

twin-screw (twin/skrōō') *adj. Naut.* Having two propeller shafts, one on each side of a vessel's keel, and two propellers, normally turning in opposite directions.

twin·ship (twin/ship') *n.* **1.** The character or condition of being a twin. **2.** The relation of a twin or twins.

twirl (twûrl) *v.t. & v.i.* **1.** To whirl or rotate. **2.** In baseball, to pitch. — *n.* **1.** A whirling motion. **2.** A quick twisting action, as of the fingers. **3.** A curl; coil. [Alter. of ME *tirlen*, var. of *trillen* to roll] — **twirl'er** *n.*

twist (twist) *v.t.* **1.** To wind (strands, etc.) around each other. **2.** To form by such winding: to *twist* thread. **3.** To give spiral, circular, or semicircular form to, as by turning at either end. **4.** To force out of natural shape; distort or contort. **5.** To distort the meaning of. **6.** To confuse; perplex. **7.** To wreathe, twine, or wrap. **8.** To cause to revolve or rotate. **9.** To impart spin to (a ball) so that it moves in a curve. — *v.i.* **10.** To become twisted. **11.** To move in a winding course. **12.** To squirm; writhe. **13.** To dance the twist. — *n.* **1.** The act, manner, or result of twisting or turning on an axis. **2.** The state of being twisted. **3.** A curve; turn; bend. **4.** A contortion or twisting of a facial or bodily feature: a smile with a certain *twist*. **5.** A wrench; strain, as of a joint or limb. **6.** A peculiar or perverted inclination or attitude: the *twist* of a criminal's mind. **7.** A deviation, variation, or distinctive difference: a *twist* of meaning. **8.** Thread or cord made of tightly twisted strands; also, one of the strands. **9.** A twisted roll or loaf of bread. **10.** Tobacco twisted in the form of a large cord. **11.** In baseball, tennis, etc.: **a** A spin or whirling motion given to a ball by a certain stroke or throw. **b** The stroke or throw producing such a spin. **12.** A dance characterized by a twisting or turning movement from side to side. [ME *twisten* to divide in two, combine two, prob. < OE *-twist* rope]

twist·er (twis/tər) *n.* **1.** One who or that which twists. **2.** A ball, as in cricket, bowled with a twist. **3.** In baseball, a curve; also, one who pitches a curve. **4.** *U.S.* A tornado.

twit (twit) *v.t.* **twit·ted, twit·ting** To taunt, reproach, or annoy by reminding of a mistake, fault, etc. — *n.* A taunting allusion; reproach. [Aphetic var. of ME *atwite*, OE *æwītan* to taunt < *æt-* at + *witan* to accuse]

twitch (twich) *v.t.* **1.** To pull sharply; pluck with a jerky movement. **2.** In lumbering, to drag or skid (logs) along the ground with a chain. — *v.i.* **3.** To move with a quick, spasmodic jerk. — *n.* **1.** A sudden involuntary contraction of a muscle. **2.** A sudden jerk or pull. [ME *twicchen*] — **twitch'ing·ly** *adv.*

twit·ter (twit/ər) *v.i.* **1.** To utter a series of light chirping or tremulous notes, as a bird. **2.** To titter. **3.** To be excited; tremble. — *v.t.* **4.** To utter or express with a twitter. — *n.* **1.** The act of twittering. **2.** A succession of light, tremulous sounds. **3.** A state of nervous agitation. [Imit.] — **twit'ter·er** *n.* — **twit'ter·y** *adj.*

twixt (twikst) *prep. Poetic* Betwixt. Also **'twixt**.

two (tōō) *n.* **1.** The sum of one and one: a cardinal number. **2.** Any symbol of this number, as 2, ii, II. **3.** Anything consisting of or representing two units. **4.** A couple; pair. — **in two** So as to be in two parts or pieces; asunder. — **to put two and two together** To reach the obvious conclusion. — *adj.* Being one more than one. [OE *twā, tū*]

---

two-base hit (tōō′bās′) In baseball, a base hit that enables the batter to reach second base; a double.

two-bit (tōō′bit′) *adj. U.S. Slang* Cheap; small-time.

two bits *U.S. Informal* 1. Twenty-five cents. 2. A trifling or insignificant sum.

two-by-four (*adj.* tōō′bī-fôr′, -fōr; *n.* tōō′bī-fôr′, -fōr′) *adj.* 1. Measuring two inches by four inches. 2. *U.S. Slang* Of trifling size or significance. — *n.* A piece of lumber actually measuring 1⅝ inches by 3⅝ inches, much used in building.

two-edged (tōō′ejd′) *adj.* 1. Having an edge on each side, as a sword or knife blade. 2. Having two meanings, effects, etc., as an argument, supposed compliment, etc.

two-faced (tōō′fāst′) *adj.* 1. Having two faces. 2. Double-dealing. — **two′-fac′ed·ly** (-fā′sid·lē, -fāst′lē) *adv.*

two-fist·ed (tōō′fis′tid) *adj. U.S. Informal* Vigorous and aggressive.

two-fold (tōō′fōld′) *n.* An amount or number two times as great as a given unit. — *adv.* So as to be two times as many or as great. — *adj.* 1. Consisting of two parts. 2. Two times as many or as great.

two-hand·ed (tōō′han′did) *adj.* 1. Requiring both hands at once. 2. Constructed for use by two persons. 3. Ambidextrous. 4. Having two hands.

two-mas·ter (tōō′mas′tər, -mäs′-) *n.* A ship with two masts.

two·pence (tup′əns) *n. Brit.* 1. Money of account of the value of two pennies. 2. A silver coin of the same value, now issued only for alms money, distributed on Maundy Thursday. Also, *Informal,* tuppence.

two·pen·ny (tup′ən·ē) *adj. Brit.* 1. Of the price or value of twopence. 2. Cheap; worthless. Also, *Informal,* tuppenny.

two-ply (tōō′plī′) *adj.* 1. Made of two united webs; woven double: a *two-ply* carpet. 2. Made of two strands, layers, or thicknesses of material.

two·some (tōō′səm) *n.* 1. Two persons together; a couple. 2. A match with one player on each side.

two-spot (tōō′spot′) *n.* 1. A playing card having two pips; a deuce. 2. *U.S. Slang* A two-dollar bill.

two-step (tōō′step′) *n.* A ballroom dance consisting of a sliding step in 2/4 meter; also, the music for it.

two-time (tōō′tīm′) *v.t.* -timed, -tim·ing *Slang* To be unfaithful to in love; deceive. — **two′-tim′er** *n.*

two-way (tōō′wā′) *adj.* 1. Characterized by or permitting movement or communication in two directions. 2. Of cocks and valves, having an arrangement that will permit a fluid to be directed in either of two channels.

twy- See TWI-.

-ty[1] *suffix of nouns* The state or condition of being: *sanity.* [< F *-té* < L *-tas*]

-ty[2] *suffix* Ten; ten times: used in numerals, as *thirty, forty,* etc. [OE *-tig* ten]

ty·coon (tī-kōōn′) *n. U.S. Informal* A wealthy and powerful industrial or business leader. [< Japanese *taikun* mighty lord < Chinese *ta* great + *kiun* prince]

tyke (tīk) *n.* 1. *Informal* A small child. 2. A mongrel dog.

tym·bal (tim′bəl) See TIMBAL.

tym·pan (tim′pən) *n. Printing* A thickness of paper placed on the platen of a press to improve the quality of the presswork.

tym·pa·ni (tim′pə·nē) See TIMPANI.

tym·pan·ic (tim·pan′ik) *adj.* 1. Of or resembling a drum. 2. Of or pertaining to a tympanum or to the middle ear. Also **tym·pa·nal** (tim′pə·nəl).

tympanic membrane *Anat.* The membrane separating the middle ear from the external ear: also called *eardrum.* For illus. see EAR.

tym·pa·nist (tim′pə·nist) *n.* One who plays a kettledrum.

tym·pa·num (tim′pə·nəm) *n., pl.* **·na** (-nə) or **·nums** 1. *Anat.* a The middle ear. b The tympanic membrane. 2. *Archit.* An ornamental space, as over a doorway, enclosed by an arch or the coping of a pediment. 3. A drumlike membrane or part. Also spelled *timpanum.* [< NL < L, drum < Gk. < *typtein* to beat]

typo- Var. of TYPO-.

ty·pal (tī′pəl) *adj.* Of or pertaining to a type; typical.

type (tīp) *n.* 1. Class; category; kind; sort. 2. One who or that which has the characteristics of a group or class; embodiment. 3. *Biol.* a An organism whose structural and functional characteristics make it representative of a group, species, class, etc. b A taxonomic group considered as representative of the next higher category in a system of classification: the *type* genus. 4. *Printing* A piece or block of metal or of wood, bearing on its upper surface, usu. in relief, a letter or character for use in printing; also, such pieces collectively. 5. Printed or typewritten characters. 6. *Informal* A person. ◆ In business English and in informal speech, *type* is often used for *type of,* as in *This type car is very popular.* — *v.* typed, typ·ing *v.t.* 1. To typewrite (something). 2. To determine the type of; identify: to *type* a blood sample. 3. To assign to a particular type. 4. To represent; typify. 5. To prefigure. — *v.i.* 6. To typewrite. [< MF < L < Gk. < *typtein* to strike]

-type *combining form* 1. Representative form; type: *prototype.* 2. Printing; duplicating or photographic process; type: *Linotype, collotype.* [< Gk. *typos* stamp]

type·cast (tīp′kast′, -käst′) *v.t.* **-cast, -cast·ing** To cast, as an actor, in a role suited to his appearance, personality, etc.

type foundry An establishment in which metal type is made. — **type founder** — **type founding**

type genus *Biol.* A genus that combines the essential characteristics of the family or higher group to which it belongs.

type metal *Printing* The alloy of which type is made, usu. of lead, tin, and antimony, in various proportions.

type·script (tīp′skript′) *n.* Typewritten matter.

type·set·ter (tīp′set′ər) *n.* 1. One who sets type. 2. A machine for composing type. — **type′set′ting** *n.*

type species *Biol.* The species regarded as most typical of the genus to which its name is given.

type·write (tīp′rīt′) *v.t. & v.i.* **·wrote, ·writ·ten, ·writ·ing** To write with a typewriter: also *type.*

type·writ·er (tīp′rī′tər) *n.* A machine equipped with a keyboard, that produces printed characters by impressing type upon paper through an inked ribbon.

type·writ·ing (tīp′rī′ting) *n.* 1. The act or operation of one who uses a typewriter. 2. Typescript.

typhlo- *combining form* 1. Blindness. 2. *Anat. & Med.* The cecum. Also, before vowels, **typhl-.** [< Gk. *typhlos* blind]

typho- *combining form* Typhus; typhoid. Also, before vowels, **typh-.** [< Gk. *typhos* smoke, stupor]

ty·phoid (tī′foid) *n.* Typhoid fever. — *adj.* Of or like typhoid fever: also **ty·phoi′dal, ty′phose** (-fōs). [< TYPH(US) + -OID]

typhoid bacillus A motile, flagellated bacterium, the pathogen of typhoid fever.

typhoid fever *Pathol.* An acute, infectious fever caused by the typhoid bacillus and characterized by severe intestinal disturbances, an eruption of rose-red spots on the chest and abdomen, and physical prostration.

ty·phoon (tī-fōōn′) *n. Meteorol.* A hurricane originating over tropical waters in the western Pacific and the China Sea. [< dial. Chinese *tai feng,* lit., big wind]

ty·phus (tī′fəs) *n. Pathol.* An acute, contagious rickettsial disease, marked by high fever, with eruption of red spots, cerebral disorders, and extreme prostration. Also called *spotted fever.* Also **typhus fever.** [< NL < Gk. *typhein* to smoke] — **ty′phous** (-fəs) *adj.*

typ·i·cal (tip′i·kəl) *adj.* 1. Having the nature or character of a type; constituting a type or pattern. 2. Conforming to the essential features of a species, group, class, pattern of action or behavior, etc. Also *typ′ic.* [< Med.L < L < Gk. < *typos* type] — **typ′i·cal·ly** *adv.* — **typ′i·cal·ness** *n.*

typ·i·fy (tip′ə·fī) *v.t.* **·fied, ·fy·ing** 1. To represent by a type; signify, as by an image or token. 2. To constitute a type or serve as a characteristic example of. — **typ′i·fi·ca′tion** *n.* — **typ′i·fi′er** *n.*

typ·ist (tī′pist) *n.* 1. One whose occupation is operating a typewriter. 2. One who is able to operate a typewriter.

ty·po (tī′pō) *n. Informal* A typographical error.

typo- *combining form* Type; of or related to type. Also, before vowels, *typ-.* [< Gk. *typos* stamp, type]

ty·pog·ra·pher (tī·pog′rə·fər) *n.* A printer.

ty·po·graph·i·cal (tī′pə·graf′i·kəl) *adj.* Of or relating to typography or printing. Also **ty′po·graph′ic.** — **ty′po·graph′i·cal·ly** *adv.*

ty·pog·ra·phy (tī·pog′rə·fē) *n., pl.* **·phies** 1. The arrangement of composed type. 2. The style and appearance of printed matter. 3. The act or art of composing and printing from type.

ty·pol·o·gy (tī·pol′ə·jē) *n., pl.* **·gies** 1. The study of types, as in systems of classification. 2. A set or listing of types.

Tyr (tūr, tir) In Norse mythology, the god of war and son of Odin: also **Tyrr.**

ty·ran·ni·cal (ti-ran′i·kəl, tī-) *adj.* Of or characteristic of a tyrant; harsh; despotic. Also **ty·ran′nic.** — **ty·ran′ni·cal·ly** *adv.* — **ty·ran′ni·cal·ness** *n.*

ty·ran·ni·cide (ti-ran′ə-sīd, tī-) *n.* 1. The killing of a tyrant. 2. One who has killed a tyrant.

tyr·an·nize (tir′ə·nīz) *v.* **·nized, ·niz·ing** *v.i.* 1. To exercise power cruelly or unjustly: often with *over.* 2. To rule as a tyrant. — *v.t.* 3. To treat tyrannically. Also *Brit.* **tyr′an·nise.** — **tyr′an·niz′er** *n.*

tyr·an·nous (tir′ə·nəs) *adj.* Despotic; tyrannical. — **tyr′an·nous·ly** *adv.* — **tyr′an·nous·ness** *n.*

tyr·an·ny (tir′ə·nē) *n., pl.* **·nies** 1. Absolute power arbitrarily or unjustly administered; despotism. 2. An arbitrarily cruel exercise of power; a tyrannical act. 3. In Greek history, the office or the administration of a tyrant. 4. Severity; roughness. [< OF < L < *tyrannus* tyrant]

ty·rant (tī′rənt) *n.* 1. One who rules oppressively or cruelly; a despot. 2. One who exercises absolute power without legal warrant, whether ruling well or badly. [< OF < L < Gk. *tyrannos* master, usurper]

tyre (tīr) See TIRE².

Tyr·i·an purple (tir′ē·ən) 1. A purple or crimson dyestuff obtained by the ancient Greeks and Romans from certain species of the murex. 2. A violet purple color of high sauturation and low brightness. Also **Tyrian dye.** [after *Tyre*, the capital of ancient Phoenicia]

ty·ro (tī′rō) *n. pl.* **·ros** A beginner; novice: also spelled *tiro*. — **Syn.** See NOVICE. [< Med.L < L *tiro* recruit]

tzar (tsär) See CZAR.

tzet·ze (tset′sē) See TSETSE.

tzi·gane (tsē·gän′) *n. Sometimes cap.* A Gypsy, esp. a Hungarian Gypsy. [< F, < Hung. *czigány*]

U

u, U (yoo) *n. pl.* **u's, us, U's** or **Us** (yooz) 1. The twenty-first letter of the English alphabet. 2. Any sound represented by the letter *u*. — *symbol.* 1. Anything shaped like a U. 2. *Chem.* Uranium (symbol U).

u·biq·ui·tous (yoo·bik′wə·təs) *adj.* Existing, or seeming to exist, everywhere at once; omnipresent. Also **u·biq′ui·tar′y** (-ter′ē). — **u·biq′ui·tous·ly** *adv.* — **u′nar** *adj.*

u·biq·ui·ty (yoo·bik′wə·tē) *n.* 1. The state of being in an indefinite number of places at once; omnipresence. 2. The state of existing always without beginning or end. [< L *ubique* everywhere]

U-boat (yoo′bōt′) *n.* A German submarine. [< G *U-boot*, contr. of *Unterseeboot* undersea boat]

ud·der (ud′ər) *n.* A large, pendulous gland, secreting milk and provided with nipples or teats for the suckling of offspring, as in cows. [OE *üder*]

UFO 1. Unidentified flying object: an official U.S. Air Force designation. 2. *Informal* A flying saucer.

ugh (ukh, u, ōōkh, ōō) *interj.* An exclamation of repugnance or disgust. [Imit.]

ug·li·fy (ug′lə·fī) *v.t.* **·fied, ·fy·ing** To make ugly. — **ug′li·fi·ca′tion** (-fə·kā′shən) *n.*

ug·ly (ug′lē) *adj.* **·li·er, ·li·est** 1. Displeasing to the esthetic feelings; distasteful in appearance; ill-looking; unsightly. 2. Repulsive to the moral sentiments; revolting. 3. Bad in character or consequences, as a rumor, wound, etc. 4. *Informal* Ill-tempered; quarrelsome. 5. Portending storms; threatening: said of the weather. [< ON *uggligr* dreadful < *uggr* fear] — **ug′li·ly** *adv.* — **ug′li·ness** *n.*

ugly duckling Any ill-favored or unpromising child who unexpectedly grows beautiful or remarkable, as did the little swan in Hans Christian Andersen's story.

U·gri·an (ōō′grē·ən, yōō′-) *n.* 1. A member of any of the Finno-Ugric peoples of Hungary and western Siberia. 2. Ugric. — *adj.* Of or pertaining to the Ugrians, their culture, or their languages.

U·gric (ōō′grik, yōō′-) *n.* A branch of the Finno-Ugric subfamily of Uralic languages, comprising Magyar, Ostyak, and Vogul. — *adj.* Of or pertaining to any of these languages.

U·gro-Fin·nic (ōō′grō-fin′ik, yōō-) See FINNO-UGRIC.

uh·lan (ōō′län, ōō·län′, yōō′lən) *n.* 1. A cavalryman and lancer of a type originating in eastern Europe, formerly prominent in European armies, notably the German. 2. One of a body of Tatar militia. Also **u′lan.** [< G < Polish < Turkish *öghlän* lad, servant]

u·kase (yōō′kās, yōō·kāz′) *n.* 1. Any official decree. 2. Formerly, an edict or decree of the imperial Russian government. [< Russian *ukaz*]

U·krain·i·an (yōō·krā′nē·ən, -krī′-) *adj.* Of or pertaining to the Ukraine, its people, or their language. — *n.* 1. A native or inhabitant of the Ukraine. 2. The East Slavic language of the Ukrainians. Also *Little Russian, Ruthenian.*

u·ku·le·le (yōō′kə·lā′lē, *Hawaiian* ōō′kōō·lā′lä) *n.* A small guitarlike musical instrument having four strings. [< Hawaiian, flea < *uku* insect + *lele* to jump]

ul·cer (ul′sər) *n.* 1. *Pathol.* An open sore on an external or internal surface of the body, usu. accompanied by disintegration of tissue with the formation of pus. 2. A corroding fault or vice; corruption; evil. [< L *ulcus, ulceris*]

ul·cer·ate (ul′sə·rāt) *v.t. & v.i.* **·at·ed, ·at·ing** To make or become ulcerous. [< L < *ulcus, ulceris* ulcer] — **ul′cer·a′tion** *n.* — **ul′cer·a·tive** *adj.*

ul·cer·ous (ul′sər·əs) *adj.* 1. Like an ulcer. 2. Affected with ulcers. — **ul′cer·ous·ly** *adv.* — **ul′cer·ous·ness** *n.*

-ule *suffix of nouns* Small; little: used to form diminutives: *granule.* [< F < L *-ulus, -ula, -ulum*, diminutive suffix]

-ulent *suffix of adjectives* Abounding in; full of: *opulent, truculent.* Corresponding nouns are formed in **-ulence**, as in *opu-lence, truculence.* [< L *-ulentus*]

ul·na (ul′nə) *n. pl.* **·nae** (-nē) or **·nas** *Anat.* 1. That one of the two long bones of the forearm that is on the same side as the little finger. 2. The corresponding bone in the forelimb of other vertebrates. [< L, elbow] — **ul′nar** *adj.*

-ulose *suffix of adjectives* Marked by or abounding in: used in scientific and technical terms: *ramulose.* [< L *-ulosus*]

-ulous *suffix of adjectives* 1. Tending to do or characterized by (what is indicated by the root): *tremulous, ridiculous.* 2. Full of: *meticulous, populous.* [< L *-ulus* and *-ulosus*]

ul·ster (ul′stər) *n.* A very long, loose overcoat, sometimes belted at the waist. [after *Ulster*, Ireland]

ul·te·ri·or (ul·tir′ē·ər) *adj.* 1. More remote; not so pertinent as something else: *ulterior* considerations. 2. Intentionally unrevealed; hidden: *ulterior* motives. 3. Later in time or secondary in importance; following; succeeding. 4. Lying beyond or on the farther side of a certain bounding line. [< L < *ulter* beyond] — **ul·te′ri·or·ly** *adv.*

ul·ti·mate (ul′tə·mit) *adj.* 1. Beyond which there is no other; last of a series; final. 2. Not susceptible of further analysis; fundamental or essential. 3. Most distant; farthest; extreme. — *n.* 1. The final result; last step; conclusion. 2. A fundamental or final fact. [< LL < *ultimus* farthest, last] — **ul′ti·mate·ly** *adv.* — **ul′ti·mate·ness** *n.*

ul·ti·ma Thu·le (ul′tə·mə thōō′lē, tōō′lē) 1. Farthest Thule; in ancient geography, the northernmost habitable regions of the earth. 2. Any distant, unknown region. 3. The farthest possible point, degree, or limit.

ul·ti·ma·tum (ul′tə·mā′təm, -mä′-) *n. pl.* **·tums** or **·ta** (-tə) A final statement, as concerning terms, conditions or concessions, esp., in diplomatic negotiations, the final terms offered. [< NL < LL. See ULTIMATE.]

ul·ti·mo (ul′tə·mō) *adv. Archaic* In the last month. [< L *ultimo* (*mense*) in the last (month)]

ul·tra (ul′trə) *adj.* Going beyond the bounds of moderation; extreme. — *n.* One who goes to extremes. [< L, beyond]

ultra- *prefix* 1. On the other side of; beyond in space, as in: **ultra-Arctic, ultrastellar.** 2. Going beyond the limits of; surpassing, as in: **ultra-atomic, ultrahuman.** 3. Beyond what is usual or natural; excessively, as in: **ultra-ambitious, ultrafashionable.**

ul·tra·cen·tri·fuge (ul′trə·sen′trə·fyōōj) *n.* A centrifuge whose rotor will operate at extremely high velocities. — *v.t.* **·fuged, ·fug·ing** To subject to the action of an ultracentrifuge. — **ul′tra·cen′tri·fu·ga′tion** (-fyōō·gā′shən) *n.*

ul·tra·con·ser·va·tive (ul′trə·kən·sûr′və·tiv) *adj.* Unusually or excessively conservative. — *n.* An ultraconservative person; a reactionary.

ul·tra·high frequency (ul′trə·hī′) *Telecom.* A band of wave frequencies between 300 and 3,000 megacycles per second.

ul·tra·ism (ul′trə·iz′əm) *n.* 1. The policies or opinions of those who are in favor of extreme measures. 2. An extreme view or action. — **ul′tra·ist** *n. & adj.* — **ul′tra·is′tic** *adj.*

ul·tra·ma·rine (ul′trə·mə·rēn′) *n.* 1. A deep blue, permanent pigment made from powdered lapis lazuli. 2. A similar pigment made artificially, as from kaolin, etc. 3. A deep blue. — *adj.* Being beyond or across the sea. [< Med.L < L *ultra* beyond + *marinus* marine]

ul·tra·mi·crom·e·ter (ul′trə·mī·krom′ə·tər) *n.* A micrometer designed for measurements requiring a high order of precision and accuracy.

ul·tra·mi·cro·scope (ul′trə·mī′krə·skōp) *n.* An optical instrument for detecting objects too small to be seen with an ordinary microscope.

ul·tra·mi·cro·scop·ic (ul′trə·mī′krə·skop′ik) *adj.* 1. Too minute to be seen by an ordinary microscope. 2. Relating to the ultramicroscope. Also **ul′tra·mi·cro·scop′i·cal.**

ul·tra·mod·ern (ul′trə·mod′ərn) *adj.* Extremely modern. — **ul′tra·mod′ern·ism** *n.* — **ul′tra·mod′ern·ist** *n.* — **ul′tra·mod′ern·is′tic** *adj.*

ul·tra·na·tion·al·ism (ul′trə·nash′ən·əl·iz′əm) *n.* Extreme devotion to or support of national interests or considerations. — **ul′tra·na′tion·al** *adj.* — **ul′tra·na′tion·al·ist** *n. & adj.* — **ul′tra·na′tion·al·is′tic** *adj.*

ul·tra·son·ic (ul′trə·son′ik) *adj. Physics* Pertaining to or designating sound waves having a frequency above the limits of human audibility, or in excess of about 20 kilocycles per second.

ul·tra·vi·o·let (ul′trə·vī′ə·lit) *adj. Physics* Lying beyond the violet end of the visible spectrum: said of high-frequency wavelengths ranging from about 3,900 to below 400 angstroms, the lower limit of X-rays. Compare INFRARED.

ul·u·late (yool′yə·lāt, ul′-) *v.i.* **·lat·ed, ·lat·ing** To howl, hoot, or wail. [< L < *ululare* to howl] — **ul′u·lant** *adj.*

U·lys·ses (yoo·lis′ēz) The Latin name for Odysseus.

um·bel (um′bəl) *n. Bot.* A flower cluster spreading outward from a small area at the top of a very short axis, giving an umbrellalike appearance. [< L *umbella* parasol] — **um′bel·lar, um′bel·late, um′bel·lat′ed.**

um·ber (um′bər) *n.* **1.** A brown ferric oxide, containing some manganese oxide and clay, and used as a pigment. **2.** The color of such a pigment. — *adj.* Of or pertaining to umber; of a dusky hue; brownish. — *v.t.* To color with umber. [< F (*terre d'*)*ombre* or Ital. *ombra*]

um·bil·i·cal (um·bil′i·kəl) *adj.* **1.** Pertaining to or situated near the umbilicus. **2.** Placed near the navel; central. [< LL < L *umbilicus* navel]

umbilical cord *Anat.* A ropelike tissue connecting the navel of the fetus with the placenta and serving to transmit nourishment to and remove wastes from the fetus.

um·bil·i·cus (um·bil′ə·kəs, um·bə·lī′kəs) *n.* *pl.* **·ci** (-sī) **1.** *Anat.* The navel. **2.** *Bot.* A hilum. [< L]

um·ble pie (um′bəl) See HUMBLE PIE.

um·bles (um′bəlz) *n.pl.* The entrails of a deer; humbles. [Var. of NUMBLES]

um·bra (um′brə) *n.* *pl.* **·brae** (-brē) **1.** A shadow or dark area; esp., the portion of a shadow from which direct light is entirely cut off. **2.** *Astron.* In an eclipse, that part of the shadow of the earth or moon within which the moon or the sun is entirely hidden. [< L, shadow]

um·brage (um′brij) *n.* **1.** Resentment; a sense of injury; offense: now usu., in **to take umbrage. 2.** That which gives shade, as a leafy tree. **3.** *Poetic* Shade. [< F < L < *umbra* shade] — **um·bra′geous** (-brā′jəs) *adj.*

um·brel·la (um·brel′ə) *n.* A light, round, portable screen or shade on a folding frame, carried as a protection against sun or rain. [< Ital. < L *umbella* parasol]

umbrella tree 1. A small magnolia of the southern U.S., with fragrant white flowers and oval leaves crowded in umbrellalike whorls. **2.** Any of several other trees.

u·mi·ak (oo′mē·ak) *n. U.S. & Canadian* A large, open boat made by drawing skins over a wooden frame, used by Eskimos. Also **u′mi·ack.** [< Eskimo]

um·laut (oom′lout) *n.* **1.** *Ling.* **a** The change in quality of a vowel sound caused by its partial assimilation to a vowel or semivowel (often later lost) in the following syllable, esp. in the Germanic languages. **b** A vowel so altered. **2.** In German, the two dots (¨) put over a vowel modified by umlaut: Short for **umlaut-mark.** — *v.t.* To modify by umlaut. [< G, change of sound < *um* about + *laut* sound]

um·pire (um′pīr) *n.* **1.** In various games, as baseball, a person chosen to enforce the rules of the game and settle disputed points. **2.** A person called upon to settle a disagreement in opinion. — **Syn.** See JUDGE. — *v.t. & v.i.* **·pired, ·pir·ing** To decide as umpire; act as umpire (of or in). [< ME < OF < *non* not + *per* even, equal]

un-[1] *prefix* Not; opposed to. [OE] ◆ *Un-*[1] is used to express negation, lack, incompleteness or opposition. It is freely attached to adjectives and adverbs, less often to nouns. See UN-[2].

un-[2] *prefix* Back. [OE *un-, on-,* and-] ◆ *Un-*[2] is used to express reversal of the action of verbs, or to form verbs from nouns indicating removal from the state or quality expressed by the noun, or sometimes to intensify the force of negative verbs. At the bottom of this page and of following pages is a partial list of words that are formed with *un-*[1] and *un-*[2]. Other compounds of these prefixes, with strongly positive, specific, or special meanings, will be found in vocabulary place. In the verbs in the list, *un-* gives the sense of reversal: *unchain* "to loose the chains of." In the nouns and the adjectives it usually has negative or privative force. Thus, *unburdened* may be regarded as an adjective meaning "not burdened," or as a participle of the verb *unburden*, meaning "relieved of a burden."

◆ **un-, in-** *In-* as a prefix of adjectives expresses in usage more of negation, *un-* more of mere lack or privation: a child's *unartistic* speech, a writer's *inartistic* diction.

---

unabashed
unabated
unabetted
unabolished
unabsolved
unacademic
unaccented
unacceptable
unaccepted
unacclimated
unacclimatized
unaccommodating
unaccounted
unaccredited
unacknowledged
unacquainted
unacquitted
unadaptable
unadjustable
unadjusted
unadorned
unadulterated
unadvisable
unadvisably
unaesthetic
unaffiliated
unafraid
unaggressive
unagitated
unaided
unaimed
unalike
unalleviated
unallied
unallowable
unalloyed
unalterable
unaltered
unaltering
unambiguous
unambitious
unamiable
unamplified
unamusing
unanalytic
unanalyzable
unanimated
unannealed
unannounced

unanswerably
unanswerable
unanswered
unapologetic
unappalled
unapparent
unappeasable
unappeased
unappetizing
unappreciated
unappreciative
unapproached
unapproved
unarmored
unarrested
unartful
unartistic
unashamed
unasked
unaspirated
unaspiring
unassailed
unassignable
unassigned
unassumed
unattainable
unattained
unattempted
unattended
unattested
unattired
unattracted
unattractive
unauspicious
unauthentic
unauthentical
unauthenticated
unauthorized
unavailability
unavailable
unavailably
unavenged
unavouched
unavowed
unavowedly
unawaked
unawakened
unawed
unbaptized

unbarbed
unbeatable
unbeaten
unbefitting
unbeloved
unbeneficed
unbenighted
unbenign
unbeseeming
unbesought
unbespoken
unbetrayed
unbetrothed
unbewailed
unblamable
unblamably
unblamed
unbleached
unblemished
unblissful
unboastful
unbookish
unborrowed
unbottomed
unbought
unbox
unboxed
unbraid
unbranched
unbranded
unbreakable
unbreathable
unbreech
unbreeched
unbribable
unbridgeable
unbridged
unbridle
unbrotherly
unbruised
unbrushed
unburied
unburned
unburnt
unbusinesslike
unbuttoned
uncage
uncalculate
uncalculating

uncalendered
uncanceled
uncandid
uncandidly
uncanonic
uncanonical
uncarbureted
uncarpeted
uncastrated
uncaught
unceasing
uncelebrated
uncensored
uncensured
uncertified
unchainable
unchained
unchallenged
unchambered
unchangeable
unchanged
unchanging
unchaperoned
uncharged
uncharted
unchartered
unchary
unchaste
unchastened
unchastised
unchastity
unchecked
uncheerful
uncheerfully
uncheerfulness
unchewed
unchilled
unchivalrous
uncholeric
unchosen
unchristened
unclaimed
unclarified
unclassed
unclassifiable
unclassified
uncleaned
uncleansed

uncleared
uncleavable
unclipped
unclog
unclogged
uncloud
unclouded
uncloyed
uncoagulable
uncoagulated
uncoated
uncocked
uncoerced
uncoffined
uncollectable
uncollected
uncollectible
uncolonized
uncolored
uncombed
uncombinable
uncombined
uncomely
uncomforted
uncomforting
uncommanded
uncommissioned
uncompanionable
uncomplaining
uncomplaisant
uncomplaisantly
uncompleted
uncompliable
uncompliant
uncomplicated
uncomplimentary
uncomplying
uncompounded
uncomprehended
uncomprehending
uncomprehensible
uncomprehensibly
uncompressed
uncompromised
uncomputed
unconcealable
unconcealed
unconceded
unconcerted

unconciliated
unconcluded
uncondemned
uncondensed
unconfined
unconfinedly
unconfirmed
unconfused
unconfusedly
unconfuted
uncongeal
uncongealable
uncongealed
uncongenial
uncongeniality
uncongenially
unconquerable
unconquered
unconscientious
unconsecrated
unconsenting
unconsidered
unconsoled
unconsonant
unconstant
unconstituted
unconstrained
unconstricted
unconsumed
uncontaminated
uncontemplated
uncontending
uncontested
uncontradictable
uncontradicted
uncontrite
uncontrolled
uncontrolledly
uncontroverted
uncontrovertible
uncontrovertibly
unconversant
unconvinced
unconvincing
unconvincingly
uncooked
uncooperative
uncoordinated
uncordial

un·a·ble (un-ā'bəl) *adj.* **1.** Lacking the necessary power or resources; not able: usu. used with an infinitive: *unable to walk.* **2.** Lacking mental capacity; incompetent.

un·a·bridged (un'ə-brijd') *adj.* Not abridged or condensed; original and complete: an *unabridged* dictionary.

un·ac·com·mo·dat·ed (un'ə-kom'ə-dā'tid) *adj.* **1.** Not made suitable; ill-adapted or -adjusted. **2.** Being without accommodations or conveniences.

un·ac·com·pa·nied (un'ə-kum'pə-nēd) *adj.* **1.** Proceeding, acting, or accomplished without an escort or companion. **2.** *Music* Performing or intended to be performed without accompaniment.

un·ac·com·plished (un'ə-kom'plisht) *adj.* **1.** Having fallen short of accomplishment; not done or finished. **2.** Lacking accomplishments.

un·ac·count·a·ble (un'ə-koun'tə-bəl) *adj.* **1.** Impossible to be accounted for; inexplicable. **2.** Remarkable; extraordinary. **3.** Not accountable; irresponsible. — **un'ac·count'a·ble·ness** *n.* — **un'ac·count'a·bly** *adv.*

un·ac·count·ed-for (un'ə-koun'tid-fôr') *adj.* Unexplained.

un·ac·cus·tomed (un'ə-kus'təmd) *adj.* **1.** Not accustomed or habituated: *unaccustomed* to hardship. **2.** Not familiar or well known; strange: an *unaccustomed* sight.

un·ad·vised (un'əd-vīzd') *adj.* **1.** Not advised; not having received advice. **2.** Rash or imprudent; ill-considered. — **un'ad·vis'ed·ly** (-vī'zid-lē) *adv.* — **un'ad·vis'ed·ness** *n.*

un·af·fect·ed (un'ə-fek'tid) *adj.* **1.** Not showing affectation; natural; sincere; real. **2.** Not influenced or changed. — **un'af·fect'ed·ly** *adv.* — **un'af·fect'ed·ness** *n.*

un-A·mer·i·can (un'ə-mer'ə-kən) *adj.* **1.** Not American in character, style, etc. **2.** Not consistent with the ideals, objectives, spirit, etc., of the U.S.; lacking patriotism or national feeling; a derogatory term.

u·na·nim·i·ty (yōō'nə-nim'ə-tē) *n.* The state of being unanimous; complete agreement in opinion, etc.

u·nan·i·mous (yōō-nan'ə-məs) *adj.* **1.** Sharing the same views or sentiments; harmonious. **2.** Showing or resulting from the assent of all concerned. [< L < *unus* one + *animus* mind] — **u·nan'i·mous·ly** *adv.* — **u·nan'i·mous·ness** *n.*

un·ap·proach·a·ble (un'ə-prō'chə-bəl) *adj.* **1.** Not easy to know or make personal contact with; aloof. **2.** Inaccessible. — **un'ap·proach'a·ble·ness** *n.* — **un'ap·proach'a·bly** *adv.*

un·arm (un-ärm') *v.t.* To deprive of weapons; disarm. — **un·armed'** *adj.*

un·as·sail·a·ble (un'ə-sāl'ə-bəl) *adj.* **1.** Not capable of being disproved, denied, or contested; incontrovertible. **2.** Proof against attack or destruction; impregnable. — **un'as·sail'a·ble·ness** *n.* — **un'as·sail'a·bly** *adv.*

un·as·sum·ing (un'ə-sōō'ming) *adj.* Unpretentious; modest. — **un'as·sum·ing·ly** *adv.*

un·at·tached (un'ə-tacht') *adj.* **1.** Not attached. **2.** Not engaged or married.

un·a·vail·ing (un'ə-vā'ling) *adj.* Futile; unsuccessful; ineffective. — **un'a·vail'ing·ly** *adv.*

un·a·void·a·ble (un'ə-voi'də-bəl) *adj.* That cannot be avoided; inevitable. — **un'a·void'a·bil'i·ty, un'a·void'a·ble·ness** *n.* — **un'a·void'a·bly** *adv.*

un·a·ware (un'ə-wâr') *adj.* **1.** Not aware or cognizant, as of something specified. **2.** Carelessly unmindful; inattentive; heedless. — *adv. Archaic* Unawares.

un·a·wares (un'ə-wârz') *adv.* **1.** Unexpectedly; without warning. **2.** Without premeditation; unwittingly.

un·bal·ance (un-bal'əns) *v.t.* ·anced, ·anc·ing **1.** To deprive of balance. **2.** To disturb or derange, as the mind. — *n.* The state or condition of being unbalanced.

un·bal·anced (un-bal'ənst) *adj.* **1.** Not in a state of equilibrium. **2.** In bookkeeping, not adjusted so as to balance. **3.** Lacking mental balance; unsound; erratic.

un·bar (un-bär') *v.* ·barred, ·bar·ring *v.t.* **1.** To remove the bar from. — *v.i.* **2.** To become unlocked or unbarred; open.

un·bear·a·ble (un'bâr'ə-bəl) *adj.* That cannot be borne or tolerated; unendurable. — **un'bear'a·ble·ness** *n.* — **un'bear'a·bly** *adv.*

un·be·com·ing (un'bi·kum'ing) *adj.* **1.** Not becoming; unsuited. **2.** Not befitting. **3.** Not decorous; improper. — **un'be·com'ing·ly** *adv.* — **un'be·com'ing·ness** *n.*

un·be·known (un'bi·nōn') *adj.* Unknown: used with *to.* Also **un'be·knownst'** (-nōnst').

un·be·lief (un'bi·lēf') *n.* **1.** Absence of positive belief; incredulity. **2.** A refusal to believe; disbelief, as in religion.

un·be·liev·er (un'bi·lē'vər) *n.* **1.** One who withholds belief. **2.** One who has no religious faith. **3.** One having a religion different from that of the speaker or writer.

un·be·liev·ing (un'bi·lē'ving) *adj.* **1.** Doubting; skeptical; incredulous. **2.** Disbelieving, esp., in religious matters. — **un'be·liev'ing·ly** *adv.* — **un'be·liev'ing·ness** *n.*

un·bend (un-bend') *v.* ·bent, ·bend·ing *v.t.* **1.** To relax, as from exertion or formality. **2.** To straighten (something bent or curved). **3.** To relax, as a bow, from tension. — *v.i.* **4.** To become free of restraint or formality; relax. **5.** To become straight or nearly straight again.

un·bend·ing (un·ben'ding) *adj.* **1.** Not bending easily; stiff. **2.** Unyielding, as in character; resolute. — *n.* Relaxation; ease. — **un·bend'ing·ly** *adv.* — **un·bend'ing·ness** *n.*

un·bi·ased (un·bī'əst) *adj.* Having no bias; not prejudiced or warped; impartial; fair. Also **un·bi'assed.** — **un·bi'ased·ly** *adv.* — **un·bi'ased·ness** *n.*

un·bid·den (un·bid'n) *adj.* **1.** Not commanded; not invited. **2.** Not called forth: *unbidden* thoughts.

un·bind (un·bīnd') *v.t.* ·bound, ·bind·ing **1.** To free from bindings; undo; also, to release. **2.** To remove, as something that binds; unfasten. [OE *unbindan*]

un·blessed (un·blest') *adj.* **1.** Deprived of a blessing. **2.** Unhallowed or unholy; evil. **3.** Deprived of good fortune; wretched. Also **un·blest'.**

un·blush·ing (un·blush'ing) *adj.* **1.** Not blushing. **2.** Immodest; shameless. — **un·blush'ing·ly** *adv.*

un·bolt (un·bōlt') *v.t.* To release, as a door, by withdrawing a bolt; unlock; open.

un·bolt·ed[1] (un·bōl'tid) *adj.* Not fastened by bolts.

un·bolt·ed[2] (un·bōl'tid) *adj.* Not sifted: *unbolted* flour.

un·born (un·bôrn') *adj.* **1.** Not yet born; being of a future time or generation; future. **2.** Not in existence.

un·bos·om (un·bŏŏz'əm, -bōō'zəm) *v.t.* **1.** To reveal, as one's thoughts or secrets; disclose or give vent to: often used reflexively. — *v.i.* **2.** To say what is troubling one; tell one's thoughts, feelings, etc. — **un·bos'om·er** *n.*

un·bound·ed (un·boun'did) *adj.* **1.** Having no bounds; of unlimited extent; very great; boundless. **2.** Having no boundary, as a closed surface. **3.** Going beyond bounds; unrestrained. — **un·bound'ed·ly** *adv.* — **un·bound'ed·ness** *n.*

un·bowed (un·boud') *adj.* **1.** Not bent or bowed. **2.** Not subdued; proud in defeat or adversity.

un·brace (un·brās') *v.t.* ·braced, ·brac·ing **1.** To free from braces. **2.** To free from tension; loosen. **3.** To weaken.

un·bri·dled (un·brīd'ld) *adj.* **1.** Having no bridle on: an *unbridled* horse. **2.** Without restraint; unruly: an *unbridled* tongue. — **un·bri'dled·ly** *adv.* — **un·bri'dled·ness** *n.*

un·bro·ken (un·brō'kən) *adj.* **1.** Not broken; whole; entire. **2.** Unviolated. **3.** Uninterrupted; regular; smooth:

uncorked	uncrystalline	undebatable	undelivered	undesignated	undignified
uncorrected	uncrystallizable	undecayed	undemocratic	undesigned	undilated
uncorroborated	uncrystallized	undecaying	undemonstrable	undesignedly	undiluted
uncorrupt	uncultivable	undeceived	undemonstrably	undesired	undiminishable
uncorrupted	uncultivated	undecipherable	undenied	undesirous	undiminished
uncorruptly	uncultured	undeciphered	undenominational	undesisting	undimmed
uncorruptness	uncumbered	undeclared	undenounced	undespairing	undiplomatic
uncountable	uncurable	undeclinable	undependable	undestroyed	undisbanded
uncourteous	uncurb	undeclined	undeplored	undetachable	undiscerned
uncourtliness	uncurbed	undecomposable	undeposed	undetached	undiscernedly
uncourtly	uncurdled	undecomposed	undepraved	undetectable	undiscernible
uncovered	uncured	undecorated	undepreciated	undetected	undiscernibly
uncrate	uncurious	undefaceable	undepressed	undetectible	undiscerning
uncrated	uncurl	undefaced	undeputed	undeterminable	undischarged
uncredited	uncurled	undefeated	underived	undetermined	undisciplined
uncrippled	uncurrent	undefended	underogating	undeterred	undisclosed
uncritical	uncursed	undefensible	underogatory	undeveloped	undisconcerted
uncriticizable	uncurtained	undefiled	undescribable	undeviating	undiscordant
uncropped	uncushioned	undefinable	undescribed	undevoured	undiscouraged
uncross	uncustomary	undefined	undescried	undevout	undiscoverable
uncrossed	undamaged	undeformed	undeserved	undifferentiated	undiscoverably
uncrowded	undated	undelayed	undeservedly	undiffused	undiscovered
uncrown	undaughterly	undelineated	undeservedness	undigested	undiscredited
uncrushable	undazzled	undeliverable	undeserving	undigestible	undiscriminating

unbroken sleep. **4.** Not weakened; firm. **5.** Not broken to harness or service, as a draft animal. **6.** Not disarranged. — **un·bro′ken·ly** *adv.* — **un·bro′ken·ness** *n.*

un·buck·le (un·buk′əl) *v.t. & v.i.* **·led, ·ling** To unfasten the buckle or buckles (of).

un·bur·den (un·bûr′dən) *v.t.* To free from a burden.

un·but·ton (un·but′n) *v.t. & v.i.* To unfasten the button or buttons (of).

un·caged (un·kājd′) *adj.* **1.** Not locked up in a cage; free. **2.** Released from a cage; freed.

un·called-for (un·kôld′fôr′) *adj.* Not justified by circumstances; improper; unnecessary; gratuitous.

un·can·ny (un·kan′ē) *adj.* **1.** Strange and inexplicable, esp. so as to excite wonder or dismay; weird; unnatural. **2.** So good as to seem almost supernatural in origin: *uncanny accuracy.* — **un·can′ni·ly** *adv.* — **un·can′ni·ness** *n.*

un·cap (un·kap′) *v.* **·capped, ·cap·ping** *v.t.* **1.** To take off the cap or covering of. — *v.i.* **2.** To remove the hat or cap, as in respect.

un·cer·e·mo·ni·ous (un′ser·ə·mō′nē·əs) *adj.* Informal; abrupt; discourteous. — **un′cer·e·mo′ni·ous·ly** *adv.*

un·cer·tain (un·sûr′tən) *adj.* **1.** That cannot be certainly predicted; doubtful. **2.** Not having certain knowledge or assured conviction. **3.** Not capable of being relied upon; variable. **4.** Not surely or exactly known: a lady of *uncertain* age. **5.** Having no exact or precise significance. — **un·cer′tain·ly** *adv.* — **un·cer′tain·ness** *n.*

un·cer·tain·ty (un·sûr′tən·tē) *n. pl.* **·ties 1.** The state of being uncertain; doubt. **2.** A doubtful matter.

un·chain (un·chān′) *v.t.* To release from a chain; set free.

un·char·i·ta·ble (un·char′ə·tə·bəl) *adj.* Not charitable; harsh in judgment; censorious. — **un·char′i·ta·ble·ness** *n.* — **un·char′i·ta·bly** *adv.*

un·chris·tian (un·kris′chən) *adj.* **1.** Unbecoming to a Christian. **2.** Contrary to Christian precepts; uncharitable, ungracious, rude, etc. **3.** Non-Christian; pagan.

un·church (un·chûrch′) *v.t.* **1.** To deprive of membership in a church; expel from a church. **2.** To deny the validity of the sacraments and order of, as a sect.

un·cial (un′shəl, -shē·əl) *adj.* Pertaining to or consisting of a form of letters found in manuscripts from the fourth to the eighth century, and resembling rounded modern capitals. — *n.* **1.** An uncial letter. **2.** An uncial manuscript. [< L < *uncia* inch, ounce]

un·ci·nate (un′sə·nit, -nāt) *adj.* Hooked or bent at the end. Also **un′ci·nal, un′ci·nat′ed.** [< L < *uncus* hook]

un·cir·cum·cised (un·sûr′kəm·sīzd) *adj.* **1.** Not circumcised. **2.** Not Jewish; Gentile. **3.** Heathen; pagan. — *n.* Gentiles or heathens collectively: used with *the.*

un·civ·il (un·siv′əl) *adj.* Wanting in civility; discourteous; ill-bred. — **un·civ′il·ly** *adv.*

un·civ·i·lized (un·siv′ə·līzd) *adj.* Not civilized; barbarous.

un·clad (un·klad′) Alternate past tense and past participle of UNCLOTHE. — *adj.* Being without clothes; naked.

un·clasp (un·klasp′, -kläsp′) *v.t.* **1.** To release from a clasp. **2.** To release the clasp of. — *v.i.* **3.** To become released from a clasp.

un·cle (ung′kəl) *n.* The brother of one's father or mother; also, the husband of one's aunt. ◆ Collateral adjective: *avuncular.* [< F < L *avunculus* mother's brother]

un·clean (un·klēn′) *adj.* **1.** Not clean; foul. **2.** Characterized by impure thoughts; unchaste; depraved. **3.** Ceremonially impure. — **un·clean′ness** *n.*

un·clean·ly[1] (un·klen′lē) *adj.* **1.** Lacking cleanliness. **2.** Impure; indecent; not chaste. — **un·clean′li·ness** *n.*

un·clean·ly[2] (un·klēn′lē) *adv.* In an unclean manner.

un·clear (un′klir′) *adj.* **1.** Not clear. **2.** Not easily understandable; confused or muddled: *unclear* reasoning.

Uncle Sam (sam) The personification of the government or the people of the U.S., represented as a tall, lean man with chin whiskers, wearing a plug hat, a blue swallow-tailed coat, and red-and-white striped pants. [Nickname of *Samuel Wilson,* 1766–1854, businessman]

Uncle Tom (tom) *U.S. Slang* A Negro who is servile to white men: a contemptuous term. [After the chief character in Harriet Beecher Stow's *Uncle Tom's Cabin,* a faithful, elderly Negro slave] — **Uncle Tom′ism**

un·cloak (un·klōk′) *v.t.* **1.** To remove the cloak or covering from. **2.** To unmask; expose. — *v.i.* **3.** To remove one's cloak or outer garments.

un·close (un·klōz′) *v.t. & v.i.* **·closed, ·clos·ing 1.** To open or set open. **2.** To reveal; disclose.

un·clothe (un·klōth′) *v.t.* **·clothed** or **·clad** (klad), **·cloth·ing 1.** To remove clothes from; undress. **2.** To uncover.

un·coil (un·koil′) *v.t. & v.i.* To unwind or become unwound.

un·com·fort·a·ble (un·kum′fər·tə·bəl, -kumpf′tə·bəl) *adj.* **1.** Not at ease; feeling discomfort. **2.** Causing physical or mental uneasiness; disquieting. — **un·com′fort·a·ble·ness** *n.* — **un·com′fort·a·bly** *adv.*

un·com·mit·ted (un′kə·mit′id) *adj.* Not committed; esp., not pledged to a particular action, viewpoint, etc.

un·com·mon (un·kom′ən) *adj.* Not common or usual; remarkable. — **un·com′mon·ly** *adv.* — **un·com′mon·ness** *n.*

un·com·mu·ni·ca·tive (un′kə·myōō′nə·kə·tiv, -nə·kā′tiv) *adj.* Not communicative; silent; reserved. — **un′com·mu′ni·ca·tive·ly** *adv.* — **un′com·mu′ni·ca·tive·ness** *n.*

un·com·pro·mis·ing (un·kom′prə·mī′zing) *adj.* Making or admitting of no compromise; inflexible; strict. — **un·com′pro·mis′ing·ly** *adv.* — **un·com′pro·mis′ing·ness** *n.*

un·con·cern (un′kən·sûrn′) *n.* Absence of or freedom from concern or anxiety; indifference.

un·con·cerned (un′kən·sûrnd′) *adj.* Undisturbed; not anxious; indifferent. — **un′con·cern′ed·ly** (-sûr′nid·lē) *adv.* — **un′con·cern′ed·ness** *n.*

un·con·di·tion·al (un′kən·dish′ən·əl) *adj.* Limited by no conditions; absolute. — **un′con·di′tion·al·ly** *adv.*

un·con·di·tioned (un′kən·dish′ənd) *adj.* **1.** Not restricted; unconditional, absolute. **2.** *Psychol.* Not acquired; natural. **3.** Admitted without condition.

un·con·form·i·ty (un′kən·fôr′mə·tē) *n. pl.* **·ties** Want of conformity; nonconformity.

un·con·scion·a·ble (un·kon′shən·ə·bəl) *adj.* **1.** Going beyond reasonable bounds; unjustifiable. **2.** Not governed by prudence; unconscientious. — **un·con′scion·a·ble·ness** *n.* — **un·con′scion·a·bly** *adv.*

un·con·scious (un·kon′shəs) *adj.* **1.** Temporarily deprived of consciousness. **2.** Unaware: with *of: unconscious* of his charm. **3.** Not known or felt to exist; not produced by conscious effort. **4.** Not endowed with consciousness or a mind. — *n. Psychoanal.* That extensive area of the psyche that is not in the immediate field of awareness. — **un·con′scious·ly** *adv.* — **un·con′scious·ness** *n.*

un·con·sti·tu·tion·al (un′kon·sti·tōō′shən·əl, -tyōō′-) *adj.* Contrary to the constitution or basic law of a state. — **un′·con·sti·tu′tion·al·i·ty** *n.* — **un′con·sti·tu′tion·al·ly** *adv.*

un·con·ven·tion·al (un′kən·ven′shən·əl) *adj.* **1.** Not adhering to conventions. **2.** Not usual or ordinary. — **un′·con·ven′tion·al·i·ty** *n.* — **un′con·ven′tion·al·ly** *adv.*

un·cork (un·kôrk′) *v.t.* To draw the cork from.

un·count·ed (un·koun′tid) *adj.* **1.** Not counted. **2.** Beyond counting; innumerable.

un·cou·ple (un·kup′əl) *v.* **·led, ·ling** *v.t.* **1.** To disconnect or unfasten. **2.** To set loose. — *v.i.* **3.** To break loose.

un·couth (un·kōōth′) *adj.* **1.** Rough; crude; unrefined. **2.** Awkward or odd; ungainly. [OE *uncūth* unknown] — **un·couth′ly** *adv.* — **un·couth′ness** *n.*

undiscriminatingly	undistinguishing	undreamed	unemancipated	unengaging	unerased
undiscussed	undistracted	undreamt	unembarrassed	unengagingly	unescapable
undisguised	undistraught	undressed	unembellished	un-English	unessayed
undisguisedly	undistressed	undried	unemotional	unenjoyable	unessential
undisheartened	undistributed	undrilled	unemotionally	unenjoyed	unestablished
undishonored	undisturbed	undrinkable	unemphatic	unenlightened	unesthetic
undisillusioned	undisturbedly	undutiful	unemphatically	unenlivened	unestimated
undismantled	undiversified	undutifully	unemptied	unenriched	unethical
undismayed	undiverted	undutifulness	unenclosed	unenrolled	unetymological
undismembered	undivested	undyed	unencumbered	unenslaved	unexacting
undismissed	undivided	unearned	unendangered	unentangled	unexaggerated
undispatched	undivorced	uneatable	unendeared	unentered	unexalted
undispelled	undivulged	uneaten	unendearing	unenterprising	unexamined
undispensed	undomestic	unecclesiastic	unendearingly	unentertaining	unexcavated
undisputable	undomesticated	uneclipsed	unended	unenthralled	unexcelled
undisputed	undoubting	uneconomic	unending	unenthusiastic	unexchangeable
undissected	undrained	uneconomical	unendorsed	unenthusiastically	unexcited
undissembling	undramatic	unedible	unendowed	unentitled	unexciting
undisseminated	undramatical	unedifying	unendurable	unenviable	unexcluded
undissolved	undramatically	uneducable	unenduring	unenvied	unexcused
undissolving	undramatized	uneducated	unenforceable	unenvious	unexecuted
undistilled	undrape	uneffaced	unenforced	unenvying	unexercised
undistinguishable	undraped	uneliminated	unenfranchised	unequipped	unexhausted
undistinguished	undreaded	unelucidated	unengaged	unerasable	unexorcised

un·cov·er (un·kuv′ər) *v.t.* **1.** To remove the covering from. **2.** To make known; disclose. — *v.i.* **3.** To remove a covering. **4.** To raise or remove the hat, as in respect.

unc·tion (ungk′shən) *n.* **1.** The state or quality of being unctuous. **2.** *Eccl.* **a** A ceremonial anointing with oil. **b** The sacramental rite of anointing those in danger of death: also called *extreme unction.* **3.** The act of anointing. **4.** The unguent used in anointing. [< F < L < *ungere* to anoint]

unc·tu·ous (ungk′chōō·əs) *adj.* **1.** Characterized by affected emotion; oily-tongued; unduly suave. **2.** Characterized by deep sympathetic feeling. **3.** Greasy; slippery to the touch, as an unguent [< Med.L < L < *ungere* to anoint] — **unc′tu·ous·ly** *adv.* — **unc′tu·os′i·ty** (-chōō·os′ə·tē), **unc′tu·ous·ness** *n.*

un·cut (un·kut′) *adj.* **1.** Not cut. **2.** In bookbinding, having untrimmed margins. **3.** Unground, as a gem.

un·daunt·ed (un·dôn′tid, -dän′-) *adj.* Not daunted or intimidated; fearless; intrepid. — **un·daunt′ed·ly** *adv.*

un·de·ceive (un′di·sēv′) *v.t.* **·ceived, ·ceiv·ing** To free from deception, error, or illusion.

un·de·cid·ed (un′di·sī′did) *adj.* **1.** Not having the mind made up. **2.** Not decided upon; not determined.

un·de·ni·a·ble (un′di·nī′ə·bəl) *adj.* **1.** That cannot be denied; indisputably true; obviously correct. **2.** Unquestionably good; excellent. — **un′de·ni′a·bly** *adv.*

un·der (un′dər) *prep.* **1.** Beneath, so as to have something directly above; covered by: layer *under* layer. **2.** In a place lower than; at the foot or bottom of: *under* the hill. **3.** Beneath the shelter of. **4.** Beneath the guise or assumption of: *under* a false name. **5.** Less than in number, degree, etc.: *under* 10 tons. **6.** Inferior to in quality, character, or rank. **7.** Dominated by; owing allegiance to; subordinate to. **8.** Subject to the guidance or tutorship of. **9.** Subject to the moral sanction of: *under* oath. **10.** With the liability of incurring: *under* penalty of the law. **11.** Subject to the pressure of; swayed by: *under* the circumstances. **12.** Driven or propelled by: *under* sail. **13.** In the group or class of: included *under* History. **14.** Being the subject of: *under* treatment. **15.** During the period of; in the reign of. **16.** By virtue of; attested or warranted by: *under* his own signature. **17.** In conformity to or in accordance with. **18.** Planted or sowed with. — *adv.* **1.** In or into a position below something; underneath. **2.** In or into a lower degree or rank. **3.** So as to be covered or hidden. **4.** So as to be less than the required amount. — **to go under** To fail, as a business. — *adj.* **1.** Situated or moving under something else; lower or lowermost. **2.** *Zool.* Ventral. **3.** Lower in rank; subordinate. **4.** Less than usual, standard, or prescribed; insufficient.

under- *combining form* **1.** Below in position; situated or directed beneath; on the underside, as in: **underlip, undersole.** **2.** Below a surface or covering; lower, as in: **underflooring, underpainting. 3.** Inferior in rank or importance; subordinate; subsidiary, as in: **underofficer, undertreasurer. 4.** Insufficient or insufficiently; less than is usual or proper, as in: **underdone, underpaid, underpopulated. 5.** Subdued; hidden, as in: **underemphasis, underplot.**

un·der·a·chieve (un′dər·ə·chēv′) *v.i.* **·chieved, ·chiev·ing** To fail to achieve the approximate level of performance, esp. in school studies, commensurate with one's abilities. — **un′der·a·chieve′ment** *n.* — **un′der·a·chiev′er** *n.*

un·der·age (un′dər·āj′) *adj.* Not of a requisite age; immature. Also **un′der·age′.**

un·der·arm¹ (un′dər·ärm′) *adj.* Situated, placed, or used under the arm. — *n.* The armpit.

un·der·arm² (un′dər·ärm′) *adj.* In various sports, as tennis, baseball, etc., executed with the hand lower than the elbow. — *adv.* In an underarm manner. Also *underhand.*

un·der·bid (un′dər·bid′) *v.t.* **·bid, ·bid·ding** To bid lower than, as in a competition. — **un′der·bid′der** *n.*

un·der·brush (un′dər·brush′) *n.* Small trees and shrubs growing beneath forest trees; undergrowth. Also **un′der·bush′** (-bŏŏsh′).

un·der·buy (un′dər·bī′) *v.t.* **·bought, ·buy·ing 1.** To buy at a price lower than that paid by (another). **2.** To pay less than the value for.

un·der·car·riage (un′dər·kar′ij) *n.* **1.** The framework supporting the body of a structure, as an automobile. **2.** The principal landing gear of an aircraft.

un·der·charge (*v.* un′dər·chärj′; *n.* un′dər·chärj′) *v.t.* **·charged, ·charg·ing 1.** To make an inadequate charge for. **2.** To load with an insufficient charge, as a gun. — *n.* An inadequate or insufficient charge.

un·der·class·man (un′dər·klas′mən, -kläs′-) *n. pl.* **·men** (-mən) A freshman or sophomore in a school or college.

un·der·clothes (un′dər·klōz′, -klō͟thz′) *n.pl.* Clothes designed for underwear, or to be worn next to the skin. Also **un′der·cloth′ing** (-klō͟th′ing).

un·der·coat (un′dər·kōt′) *n.* **1.** A coat worn under another coat. **2.** Underfur. **3.** A layer of paint, varnish, etc., beneath another layer: also **un′der·coat′ing.** — *v.t.* To provide with an undercoat (def. 3).

un·der·cov·er (un′dər·kuv′ər) *adj.* Secret; surreptitious; esp., engaged in spying or secret investigation.

un·der·cur·rent (un′dər·kûr′ənt) *n.* **1.** A current, as of water or air, below another or below the surface. **2.** A hidden drift or tendency, as of popular sentiments.

un·der·cut (*n. & adj.* un′dər·kut′; *v.* un′dər·kut′) *n.* **1.** The act or result of cutting under. **2.** The tenderloin. **3.** Any part that is cut away below. **4.** In sports, a cut or backspin imparted to the ball. — *v.t.* **·cut, ·cut·ting 1.** To cut under. **2.** To cut away a lower portion of. **3.** To work or sell for lower payment than (a rival). **4.** In sports, to give an undercut to (the ball). **5.** To lessen or destroy the effectiveness of; undermine. — *adj.* Done by undercutting.

un·der·de·vel·oped (un′dər·di·vel′əpt) *adj.* **1.** Not sufficiently developed. **2.** Below a normal or adequate standard in the development of industry, resources, etc.

un·der·dog (un′dər·dôg′, -dog′) *n.* **1.** One who is at a disadvantage in a struggle; a probable loser. **2.** One who is victimized or downtrodden by society.

un·der·es·ti·mate (*v.* un′dər·es′tə·māt; *n.* un′dər·es′tə·mit) *v.t.* **·mat·ed, ·mat·ing** To put too low an estimate upon. — *n.* An estimate that is too low. — **un′der·es′ti·ma′tion** *n.*

un·der·ex·pose (un′dər·ik·spōz′) *v.t.* **·posed, ·pos·ing** *Photog.* To expose (a film) less than is required for proper development. — **un′der·ex·po′sure** (-spō′zhər) *n.*

un·der·feed (un′dər·fēd′) *v.t.* **·fed, ·feed·ing 1.** To feed insufficiently. **2.** To fuel (an engine) from beneath.

un·der·foot (un′dər·fŏŏt′) *adv.* **1.** Beneath the feet; down on the ground; immediately below. **2.** In the way.

un·der·fur (un′dər·fûr′) *n.* The coat of dense, fine hair forming the main part of a pelt, as in seals.

un·der·gar·ment (un′dər·gär′mənt) *n.* A garment to be worn under the outer garments.

un·der·go (un′dər·gō′) *v.t.* **·went, ·gone, ·go·ing 1.** To be subjected to; have experience of; suffer. **2.** To endure.

un·der·grad·u·ate (un′dər·graj′ŏŏ·it) *n.* A university or college student who has not received a bachelor's degree.

un·der·ground (*adj.* un′dər·ground′; *adv.* un′dər·ground′)

unexpanded	unfaded	unfetter	unforeseeable	unfreezable	ungirded
unexpectant	unfading	unfettered	unforeseeing	unfreeze	ungladdened
unexpended	unfallen	unfilial	unforeseen	un-French	unglazed
unexpendible	unfaltering	unfilled	unforested	unfrequent	unglossed
unexpert	unfashionable	unfilmed	unforetold	unfrequented	unglove
unexpiated	unfashioned	unfiltered	unforfeited	unfrequently	ungloved
unexpired	unfastened	unfired	unforged	unfrozen	unglue
unexplainable	unfatherly	unfittingly	unforgetful	unfruitful	ungoverned
unexplained	unfathomable	unfixed	unforgetting	unfulfilled	ungowned
unexplicit	unfathomed	unfixedness	unforgivable	unfunded	ungraced
unexploded	unfatigued	unflagging	unforgiven	unfurnished	ungraceful
unexploited	unfavored	unflaggingly	unforgiving	unfurrowed	ungracefully
unexplored	unfeared	unflattered	unforgot	ungallant	ungraded
unexported	unfearing	unflattering	unforgotten	ungalled	ungrafted
unexposed	unfeasible	unflavored	unformulated	ungarnished	ungrained
unexpressed	unfed	unflickering	unforsaken	ungartered	ungratified
unexpunged	unfederated	unfoiled	unfortified	ungathered	ungrounded
unexpurgated	unfeignedly	unforbearing	unfought	ungenerous	ungrudging
unextended	unfelt	unforbidden	unfound	ungenial	ungrudgingly
unexterminated	unfeminine	unforced	unframed	ungenteel	unguided
unextinguishable	unfenced	unforcedly	unfranchised	ungentle	unhackneyed
unextinguished	unfermented	unfordable	unfraternal	ungentlemanly	unhailed
unextraditable	unfertile	unforeboding	unfraught	ungently	unhalved
unfadable	unfertilized	unforeknown	unfree	ungifted	unhammered

adj. **1.** Situated, done, or operating beneath the surface of the ground. **2.** Done in secret; clandestine. — *n.* **1.** That which is beneath the surface of the ground. **2.** A group secretly organized to oppose those in control of a government or country. **3.** *Brit.* A subway (def. 1). — *adv.* **1.** Beneath the surface of the ground. **2.** Secretly.

Underground Railroad A system of cooperation among antislavery people, before 1861, for assisting fugitive slaves to escape to Canada and the free States.

un·der·growth (un′dər-grōth′) *n.* **1.** A growth of smaller plants among larger ones; esp., a thicket or copse in or as in a forest. **2.** The condition of being undergrown.

un·der·hand (un′dər-hand′) *adj.* **1.** Done or acting in a treacherously secret manner; sly. **2.** In sports, underarm. — *adv.* **1.** Underhandedly; slyly. **2.** Underarm².

un·der·hand·ed (un′dər-han′did) *adj.* **1.** Underhand. **2.** Short-handed. — **un′der·hand′ed·ly** *adv.* — **un′der·hand′ed·ness** *n.*

un·der·lay (*v.* un′dər-lā′; *n.* un′dər-lā) *v.t.* **laid, lay·ing** **1.** To place (one thing) under another. **2.** To furnish with a base or lining. **3.** *Printing* To support or raise by underlays. — *n.* **1.** *Printing* A piece of paper, etc., placed under certain parts of a printing form.

un·der·lie (un′dər-lī′) *v.t.* **lay, lain, ly·ing 1.** To lie below or under. **2.** To be the basis or support of: the principle that *underlies* a scheme. [OE *underlicgan*]

un·der·line (un′dər-līn′) *v.t.* **lined, lin·ing 1.** To mark with a line underneath. **2.** To emphasize.

un·der·ling (un′dər-ling) *n.* A subordinate; an inferior.

un·der·ly·ing (un′dər-lī′ing) *adj.* **1.** Lying under. **2.** Fundamental. **3.** Prior in claim or lien.

un·der·mine (un′dər-mīn′, un′dər-mīn) *v.t.* **mined, min·ing 1.** To excavate beneath; dig a mine or passage under: to *undermine* a fortress. **2.** To weaken by wearing away at the base. **3.** To weaken or impair secretly or by degrees: to *undermine* one's health. — **un′der·min′er** *n.*

un·der·most (un′dər-mōst′) *adj.* Having the lowest place or position.

un·der·neath (un′dər-nēth′, -nēth′) *adv.* **1.** In a place below. **2.** On the under or lower side. — *prep.* **1.** Beneath; under; below. **2.** Under the form or appearance of. **3.** Under the authority of; in the control of. — *adj.* Lower. — *n.* The lower or under part or side. [OE *underneothan*]

un·der·nour·ish (un′dər-nûr′ish) *v.t.* To provide with nourishment insufficient in amount or quality for proper health and growth. — **un′der·nour′ish·ment** *n.*

un·dern·song (un′dərn-sông′, -song′) *n.* Tierce (def. 3). [OE *undern* midday, midday meal + SONG]

un·der·pants (un′dər-pants′) *n.pl. U.S.* An undergarment worn over the loins.

un·der·pass (un′dər-pas′, -päs′) *n. U.S.* A passage beneath; esp., the section of a way or road that passes under railway tracks or under another road.

un·der·pay (un′dər-pā′) *v.t.* **paid, pay·ing** To pay insufficiently.

un·der·pin·ning (un′dər-pin′ing) *n.* **1.** Material or framework used to support a wall or building from below. **2.** *pl. Informal* The legs.

un·der·pitch vault (un′dər-pich′) *Archit.* A vault formed by the intersection of two vaults that spring from the same level but are of uneven widths. For illus. see VAULT¹.

un·der·priv·i·leged (un′dər-priv′ə-lijd) *adj.* Not privileged to enjoy certain rights to which everyone is theoretically entitled, as because of poverty, illiteracy, etc.

un·der·pro·duc·tion (un′dər-prə-duk′shən) *n.* Production below capacity or below requirements.

un·der·proof (un′dər-prōōf′) *adj.* Having less strength than proof spirit.

un·der·quote (un′dər-kwōt′) *v.t.* **quot·ed, quot·ing** To undersell or offer to undersell, as goods or stocks.

un·der·rate (un′dər-rāt′) *v.t.* **rat·ed, rat·ing** To rate too low; underestimate. — **Syn.** See UNDERESTIMATE.

un·der·run (un′dər-run′) *v.t.* **ran, run, run·ning 1.** To run or pass beneath. **2.** *Naut.* To examine (a line, hawser, etc.) from below by drawing a boat along beneath it.

un·der·score (*v.* un′dər-skôr′, -skōr′; *n.* un′dər-skôr′, -skōr′) *v.t.* **scored, scor·ing** To underline. — *n.* A line drawn beneath a word, etc., as for emphasis.

un·der·sea (un′dər-sē′) *adj.* Existing, carried on, or adapted for use beneath the surface of the sea. — *adv.* Beneath the surface of the sea: also **un′der·seas′** (-sēz′).

un·der·sec·re·tar·y (un′dər-sek′rə-ter′ē) *n. pl.* **·tar·ies** In a government department, the official who ranks next below the secretary.

un·der·sell (un′dər-sel′) *v.t.* **sold, sell·ing 1.** To sell at a lower price than. **2.** To sell for less than the real value. — **un′der·sell′er** *n.*

un·der·set (un′dər-set′) *n.* An undercurrent in the ocean.

un·der·sher·iff (un′dər-sher′if) *n.* A deputy sheriff, esp. one upon whom the sheriff's duties devolve in his absence.

un·der·shirt (un′dər-shûrt′) *n.* A garment worn beneath the shirt, generally of cotton.

un·der·shoot (un′dər-shōōt′) *v.* **shot, shoot·ing** *v.t.* **1.** To shoot short of or below (the mark, target, etc.). **2.** *Aeron.* To land an airplane or deliver a bomb short of (the mark). — *v.i.* **3.** To shoot or land short of the mark.

un·der·shot (un′dər-shot′) *adj.* **1.** Propelled by water that flows underneath: said of a water wheel. **2.** Projecting, as the lower jaw or teeth; also, having a projecting lower jaw or teeth.

un·der·side (un′dər-sīd′) *n.* The lower or under side or surface.

un·der·sign (un′dər-sīn′) *v.t.* To sign at the foot, end, or bottom of: used chiefly in the past participle.

un·der·signed (un′dər-sīnd′) *adj.* **1.** Having one's signature at the foot of a document. **2.** Signed at the foot of a document. — *n.* The subscriber or subscribers to a document: with *the.*

un·der·sized (un′dər-sīzd′) *adj.* Of less than the normal or average size. Also **un′der·size′.**

un·der·slung (un′dər-slung′) *adj. Mech.* Having the springs fixed to the axles from below, instead of resting upon them: said of certain automobiles: also *underhung.*

un·der·soil (un′dər-soil′) *n.* Subsoil.

un·der·stand (un′dər-stand′) *v.* **stood, stand·ing** *v.t.* **1.** To come to know the meaning or import of; apprehend. **2.** To comprehend the nature or character of. **3.** To have comprehension or mastery of: Do you *understand* German? **4.** To be aware of; realize: She *understands* her position. **5.** To have been told: I *understand* that she went home. **6.** To infer the meaning of: How am I to *understand* that remark? **7.** To accept as a condition or stipulation: It is *understood* that the tenant will provide his own heat. **8.** To supply in thought when unexpressed. **9.** To be in agreement with; be privately in sympathy with. — *v.i.* **10.** To have understanding; comprehend. **11.** To be informed; believe. — **Syn.** See APPREHEND. [OE < *under-* under + *standan* to stand] — **un′der·stand′a·ble** *adj.* — **un′der·stand′a·bly** *adv.*

un·der·stand·ing (un′dər-stan′ding) *n.* **1.** The act of one who understands, or the resulting state; comprehension. **2.** The power by which one understands. **3.** The sum of the mental powers by which knowledge is acquired, retained, and extended. **4.** The facts or elements of a case as apprehended by any one individual. **5.** An informal or confidential compact; also, the thing agreed on. **6.** An arrangement

unhampered	unheeding	unhuman	unimpeached	uninformed	unintentionally
unhandicapped	unheedingly	unhumanize	unimpeded	uninfringed	uninteresting
unhandled	unhelped	unhung	unimplored	uningenious	uninterestingly
unhang	unhelpful	unhurt	unimportant	uningenuous	unintermitted
unhanged	unheralded	unhurtful	unimposing	uninhabitable	unintermittent
unharassed	unheroic	unhygienic	unimpregnated	uninhabited	unintermitting
unharbored	unheroically	unhygienically	unimpressed	uninhibited	uninterpolated
unhardened	unhesitant	unhyphenated	unimpressible	uninitiated	uninterpreted
unharmed	unhesitantly	unhyphened	unimpressionable	uninjured	uninterrupted
unharmful	unhesitating	unideal	unimpressive	uninspired	unintimidated
unharmfully	unhesitatingly	unidentified	uninaugurated	uninspiring	unintoxicated
unharming	unhewn	unidiomatic	uninclosed	uninspiringly	uninvaded
unharmonious	unhindered	unilluminated	unincorporated	uninstructed	uninvented
unharnessed	unhired	unillumined	unincubated	uninstructive	uninventive
unharrowed	unhistoric	unillustrated	unincumbered	uninsurable	uninventively
unharvested	unhistorical	unimaginable	unindemnified	uninsured	uninverted
unhastily	unhistorically	unimaginably	unindicated	unintellectual	uninvested
unhasty	unhomogeneous	unimaginative	unindorsed	unintelligent	uninvited
unhatched	unhonored	unimaginatively	uninfected	unintelligibility	uninviting
unhealed	unhood	unimagined	uninfested	unintelligible	uninvitingly
unhealthful	unhoped	unimbued	uninflammable	unintelligibleness	uninvoked
unheated	unhostile	unimitated	uninflected	unintelligibly	uninvolved
unheeded	unhouse	unimpaired	uninfluenced	unintended	unissued
unheedful	unhoused	unimpassioned	uninfluential	unintentional	unjacketed

or settlement of differences, or of disputed points. — *adj.*
1. Possessing comprehension and good sense. 2. Tolerant or sympathetic. — **un·der·stand·ing·ly** *adv.* — **un'der·stand'ing·ness** *n.*
— **Syn.** (noun) 2. reason, intelligence, intuition, judgment.

un·der·state (un'dər·stāt') *v.* **·stat·ed, ·stat·ing** *v.t.* 1. To state with less force than the truth warrants or allows. 2. To state, as a number or dimension, as less than the true one. — *v.i.* 3. To make an understatement.

un·der·state·ment (un'dər·stāt'mənt) *n.* A statement that is deliberately unemphatic or restrained in tone.

un·der·stood (un'dər·stŏŏd') Past tense and past participle of UNDERSTAND. — *adj.* 1. Assumed; agreed upon by all. 2. Assumed when unexpressed, as the subject of a sentence.

un·der·stra·tum (un'dər·strā'təm, -strat'əm) *n.* *pl.* **·stra·ta** (-strā'tə, -strat'ə) or **·stra·tums** A substratum.

un·der·stud·y (un'dər·stud'ē) *v.t. & v.i.* **stud·ied, ·stud·y·ing** 1. To study (a part) in order to be able, if necessary, to take the place of the actor playing it. 2. To act as an understudy (to another actor). — *n.* *pl.* **·stud·ies** 1. An actor or actress who can take the place of another actor in a given role when necessary. 2. A person prepared to perform the work or fill the position of another.

un·der·take (un'dər·tāk') *v.* **took, ·tak·en, ·tak·ing** *v.t.* 1. To take upon oneself; agree or attempt to do; begin. 2. To contract to do; pledge oneself to. 3. To guarantee or promise. 4. To take under charge or guidance. — *v.i.* 5. To make oneself responsible or liable: with *for.*

un·der·tak·er (un'dər·tā'kər *for def. 1*; un'dər·tā'kər *for def. 2*) *n.* 1. One who undertakes any work or enterprise. 2. One whose business it is to arrange for the cremation or burial of the dead and to oversee funerals.

un·der·tak·ing (un'dər·tā'king; *for def. 3* un'dər·tā'king) *n.* 1. The act of one who undertakes any task or enterprise. 2. The thing undertaken; a task. 3. The business of an undertaker (def. 2). 4. An engagement, promise, or guaranty.

un·der·ten·ant (un'dər·ten'ənt) *n.* A subtenant.

un·der·tone (un'dər·tōn') *n.* 1. A tone of lower pitch or loudness than is usual; esp., the tone of a subdued voice or a whisper. 2. A subdued shade of a color; also, a color upon which other colors have been imposed and which is seen through them. 3. An implicit meaning or suggestion.

un·der·took (un'dər·tŏŏk') Past tense of UNDERTAKE.

un·der·tow (un'dər·tō') *n.* 1. The flow of water beneath and in a direction opposite to the surface current. 2. The seaward undercurrent below the surf.

un·der·val·ue (un'dər·val'yōō) *v.t.* **·ued, ·u·ing** To value too highly; underrate; underestimate. — **Syn.** See UNDERESTIMATE. — **un'der·val'u·a'tion** *n.*

un·der·wa·ter (un'dər·wô'tər, -wot'ər) *adj. & adv.* Below the surface of a body of water; also, below the water line of a ship. — *n.* The region below the surface of water.

un·der·way (un·dər·wā') *adv.* In progress or into operation: The meeting was already *underway.* Also **under way.**

un·der·wear (un'dər·wâr') *n.* Garments worn underneath the ordinary outer garments; underclothes.

un·der·weight (un'dər·wāt') *adj.* Having less than the normal weight. — *n.* Insufficiency of weight; also, weight below normal.

un·der·went (un'dər·went') Past tense of UNDERGO.

un·der·wood (un'dər·wŏŏd') *n.* Underbrush.

un·der·world (un'dər·wûrld') *n.* 1. In Greek and Roman mythology, the abode of the dead; Hades. 2. The part of society engaged in crime or vice; esp., organized criminals.

un·der·write¹ (un'dər·rīt') *v.* **wrote, ·writ·ten, writ·ing**

---

v.t. 1. To write beneath; subscribe. 2. In finance, to execute and deliver (a policy of insurance on specified property); insure; assume (a risk) by way of insurance. 3. To engage to buy, at a determined price and time, all or part of the stock in (a new enterprise or company) that is not subscribed for by the public. 4. Loosely, to assume responsibility for, as an enterprise. 5. To undertake to pay, as a written pledge of money. — **un'der·writ'er** *n.*

un·der·write² (un'dər·rīt') *v.t. & v.i.* **wrote, ·writ·ten, ·writ·ing** To write in a deliberately restrained style.

un·de·sir·a·ble (un'di·zīr'ə·bəl) *adj.* Not desirable; objectionable. — *n.* An objectionable person. — **un'de·sir'a·bil'i·ty, un'de·sir'a·ble·ness** *n.* — **un'de·sir'a·bly** *adv.*

un·did (un·did') Past tense of UNDO.

un·dies (un'dēz) *n. pl. Informal* Women's or children's underwear.

un·do (un·dōō') *v.t.* **did, ·done, ·do·ing** 1. To cause to be as if never done; reverse; annul. 2. To loosen or untie, as a knot, etc. 3. To unfasten and open, as a parcel. 4. To bring to ruin; destroy. [OE *undōn*] — **un·do'er** *n.*

un·do·ing (un·dōō'ing) *n.* 1. Reversal, cancellation, etc., of what has been done. 2. Destruction; ruin; also, the cause of ruin. 3. The act or process of unfastening, etc.

un·done¹ (un·dun') *adj.* 1. Untied; unfastened. 2. Ruined. [Orig. pp. of UNDO]

un·done² (un·dun') *adj.* Not done. [< UN- + DONE]

un·doubt·ed (un·dou'tid) *adj.* Assured beyond question; being beyond a doubt; indubitable. — **un·doubt'ed·ly** *adv.*

un·draw (un·drô') *v.t. & v.i.* **drew, ·drawn, ·draw·ing** To draw open, away, or aside.

un·dreamed-of (un·drēmd'uv', -ov') *adj.* Not conceived of in the mind; unimaginable. Also **un·dreamt'-of** (-dremt'-).

un·dress (*v. & n.* un·dres'; *adj.* un'dres') *v.t.* 1. To divest of clothes; strip. 2. To remove the dressing or bandages from, as a wound. — *v.i.* 3. To remove one's clothing. — *n.* 1. Ordinary attire, as distinguished from formal dress. 2. Comfortable, informal clothing. — *adj.* Informal.

un·due (un·dōō', -dyōō') *adj.* 1. Excessive; disproportionate. 2. Not justified by law; illegal. 3. Not due; not yet demandable. 4. Not appropriate; improper.

un·du·lant (un'dyə·lənt, -də-) *adj.* Undulating; waving.

undulant fever *Pathol.* A disease transmitted to man in the milk of infected cows and goats, and characterized by recurrent fever, swelling of the joints, neuralgic pains, etc.

un·du·late (*v.* un'dyə·lāt, -də-; *adj.* un'dyə·lit, -lāt, -də-) *v.* **·lat·ed, ·lat·ing** *v.t.* 1. To cause to move like a wave or in waves. 2. To give a wavy appearance to. — *v.i.* 3. To move like waves. 4. To have a wavy appearance. — *adj.* 1. Having a wavy margin, as a leaf. 2. Having wavelike markings, as of color: also **un'du·lat'ed** (-lā'tid). [< L *undulatus* having wavelike markings < *unda* wave]

un·du·la·tion (un'dyə·lā'shən, -də-) *n.* 1. The act of undulating. 2. A waving or sinuous motion. 3. A wave. 4. An appearance as of waves; a gentle rise and fall. — **un'du·la·to'ry** (-lə·tôr'ē, -tō'rē), **un'du·lous** (-ləs) *adj.*

un·du·ly (un·dōō'lē, -dyōō-) *adv.* 1. Excessively. 2. In violation of a moral or of a legal standard; unjustly.

un·dy·ing (un·dī'ing) *adj.* Immortal; everlasting.

un·earth (un·ûrth') *v.t.* 1. To dig or root up from the earth. 2. To reveal by or as by searching.

un·earth·ly (un·ûrth'lē) *adj.* 1. Not earthly; sublime. 2. Weird; terrifying; supernatural. 3. *Informal* Ridiculously unconventional or inconvenient. — **un·earth'li·ness** *n.*

un·eas·y (un·ē'zē) *adj.* **eas·i·er, eas·i·est** 1. Lacking ease, assurance, or security; disturbed. 2. Not affording ease or

---

unjaded	unlashed	unlocated	unmannishly	unmenaced	unmoistened
unjoined	unlaundered	unlocked	unmanufacturable	unmendable	unmold
unjointed	unleased	unlovable	unmanufactured	unmended	unmolded
unjoyful	unled	unloved	unmarked	unmensurable	unmolested
unjoyfully	unlessened	unloveliness	unmarketable	unmentionability	unmollified
unjudged	unlessoned	unloverlike	unmarketed	unmentioned	unmolten
unjudicial	unlet	unloving	unmarred	unmercenary	unmortgaged
unjustifiable	unletted	unlovingly	unmarriageable	unmerchantable	unmotivated
unjustifiably	unlevel	unlubricated	unmarried	unmerited	unmounted
unkept	unlevied	unmagnified	unmastered	unmeriting	unmourned
unkindled	unlibidinous	unmaidenliness	unmatched	unmethodical	unmovable
unkindliness	unlicensed	unmaidenly	unmated	unmilitary	unmoved
unkingly	unlifelike	unmailable	unmaternal	unmilled	unmoving
unkissed	unlighted	unmalleable	unmatted	unmingle	unmown
unknelled	unlikable	unmanageable	unmatured	unmingled	unmurmuring
unknightly	unlikeable	unmanful	unmeant	unmirthful	unmusical
unknowing	unlined	unmanfully	unmeasurable	unmirthfully	unmuzzle
unknowingly	unlink	unmanfulness	unmeasurably	unmistaken	unmuzzled
unknowingness	unliquefiable	unmangled	unmeasured	unmitigable	unmystified
unlabeled	unliquefied	unmanifested	unmechanical	unmixed	unnail
unlabelled	unliquidated	unmanipulated	unmediated	unmixt	unnamable
unladylike	unlit	unmanned	unmedicated	unmodified	unnameable
unlamented	unliveliness	unmannered	unmelodious	unmodish	unnamed
unlash	unlively	unmannish	unmelted	unmodishly	unnaturalized

---

rest; causing discomfort. **3.** Showing embarrassment or constraint; strained. — **un·eas′i·ly** adv. — **un·eas′i·ness** n.

un·em·ploy·a·ble (un′əm·ploi′ə·bəl) adj. Not employable. — n. A person who, because of illness, age, mental or physical incapacity, etc., cannot be employed.

un·em·ployed (un′əm·ploid′) adj. **1.** Having no remunerative employment; out of work. **2.** Not being put to use; idle. — n. A jobless person. — **the unemployed** Unemployed persons collectively. — **un′em·ploy′ment** n.

unemployment insurance U.S. A system of insurance authorized by the Federal Social Security Act of 1935, providing those who are involuntarily out of work with temporary compensation. Also **unemployment compensation.**

un·e·qual (un·ē′kwəl) adj. **1.** Not having equal extension, duration, proportions, amounts, etc. **2.** Not equal in strength, ability, status, etc. **3.** Inadequate for the purpose: with to. **4.** Inequitable; unfair. **5.** Varying; irregular. **6.** Not balanced; unsymmetrical. — **un·e′qual·ly** adv.

un·e·qualed (un·ē′kwəld) adj. Not equaled or matched; unrivaled; supreme. Also **un·e′qualled.**

un·e·quiv·o·cal (un′i·kwiv′ə·kəl) adj. Understandable in only one way; not equivocal. — **un′e·quiv′o·cal·ly** adv.

un·err·ing (un·ûr′ing, -er′-) adj. **1.** Making no mistakes; not erring. **2.** Certain; accurate. — **un·err′ing·ly** adv.

UNESCO (yōō·nes′kō) The United Nations Educational, Scientific and Cultural Organization. Also **U·nes′co.**

un·e·ven (un·ē′vən) adj. **1.** Not even, smooth, parallel, or level; rough. **2.** Not divisible by two without remainder; odd: said of numbers. **3.** Not uniform; variable; spasmodic. — **un·e′ven·ly** adv. — **un·e′ven·ness** n.

un·e·vent·ful (un′i·vent′fəl) adj. Devoid of noteworthy events; quiet. — **un′e·vent′ful·ly** adv.

un·ex·am·pled (un′ig·zam′pəld) adj. Having no precedent.

un·ex·cep·tion·a·ble (un′ik·sep′shən·ə·bəl) adj. That cannot be objected to; irreproachable. — **un′ex·cep′tion·a·ble·ness** n. — **un′ex·cep′tion·a·bly** adv.

un·ex·cep·tion·al (un′ik·sep′shən·əl) adj. **1.** Not exceptional; ordinary. **2.** Subject to no exception.

un·ex·pect·ed (un′ik·spek′tid) adj. Not expected; unforeseen. — **un′ex·pect′ed·ly** adv. — **un′ex·pect′ed·ness** n.

un·fail·ing (un·fā′ling) adj. **1.** Giving or constituting a supply that never fails; inexhaustible: an unfailing spring. **2.** Not falling short of need, hope, or expectation. **3.** Sure; infallible. — **un·fail′ing·ly** adv. — **un·fail′ing·ness** n.

un·fair (un·fâr′) adj. **1.** Characterized by partiality or prejudice; not fair or just. **2.** Dishonest; fraudulent. — **un·fair′ly** adv. — **un·fair′ness** n.

un·faith·ful (un·fāth′fəl) adj. **1.** Not having kept faith; unworthy of trust; faithless. **2.** Not true to marriage vows; adulterous. **3.** Not accurate or exact. — **un·faith′ful·ly** adv. — **un·faith′ful·ness** n.

un·fa·mil·iar (un′fə·mil′yər) adj. **1.** Not having acquaintance: with with. **2.** Not known or recognizable. — **un′fa·mil′i·ar′i·ty** (-mil′ē·ar′ə·tē) n. — **un′fa·mil′iar·ly** adv.

un·fa·vor·a·ble (un·fā′vər·ə·bəl) adj. Not favorable; unpropitious; adverse. Also Brit. **un·fa′vour·a·ble.** — **un·fa′vor·a·ble·ness** n. — **un·fa′vor·a·bly** adv.

un·feel·ing (un·fē′ling) adj. **1.** Not sympathetic; hard; cruel. **2.** Devoid of feeling or sensation. — **un·feel′ing·ly** adv. — **un·feel′ing·ness** n.

un·feigned (un·fānd′) adj. Not feigned; not pretended; sincere; genuine. — **un·feign·ed·ly** (un·fā′nid·lē) adv.

un·fin·ished (un·fin′isht) adj. **1.** Not finished; incomplete. **2.** Having no finish or special surface treatment, as wood. **3.** Of fabrics: **a** Not bleached. **b** Having a slight nap.

un·fit (un·fit′) adj. **1.** Having no fitness; unsuitable. **2.** Not appropriate; improper. **3.** Not in sound physical condition. — v.t. **·fit·ted** or **·fit, ·fit·ting** To make unfit; dis-

qualify. — **un·fit′ly** adv. — **un·fit′ness** n.

un·fix (un·fiks′) v.t. **1.** To unfasten. **2.** To unsettle.

un·flap·pa·ble (un·flap′ə·bəl) adj. Characterized by unshakable composure; imperturbable. — **un·flap′pa·bil′i·ty** n.

un·fledged (un·flejd′) adj. **1.** Not yet fledged, as a young bird. **2.** Immature; inexperienced.

un·flesh·ly (un·flesh′lē) adj. Ethereal; spiritual.

un·flinch·ing (un·flin′ching) adj. Not shrinking from danger, pain, etc.; brave. — **un·flinch′ing·ly** adv.

un·fold (un·fōld′) v.t. **1.** To open or spread out (something folded). **2.** To lay open to view. **3.** To make clear by detailed explanation; explain: to unfold a plan. **4.** To evolve; develop. — v.i. **5.** To become opened; expand. **6.** To become manifest. [OE unfealdan] — **un·fold′er** n.

un·for·get·ta·ble (un′fər·get′ə·bəl) adj. Not forgettable; memorable. — **un′for·get′ta·bly** adv.

un·formed (un·fôrmd′) adj. **1.** Devoid of shape or form. **2.** Not fully developed in character. **3.** Unorganized.

un·for·tu·nate (un·fôr′chə·nit) adj. **1.** Not fortunate; unhappy, unsuccessful, etc. **2.** Causing or attended by ill fortune; disastrous. — n. One who is unfortunate. — **un·for′tu·nate·ly** adv. — **un·for′tu·nate·ness** n.

un·found·ed (un·foun′did) adj. **1.** Having no foundation; groundless; baseless. **2.** Not founded or established. — **un·found′ed·ly** adv. — **un·found′ed·ness** n.

un·friend·ly (un·frend′lē) adj. **1.** Unkindly disposed; inimical; hostile. **2.** Not favorable or propitious. — adv. In an unfriendly manner. — **un·friend′li·ness** n.

un·frock (un·frok′) v.t. **1.** To depose, as a monk or priest, from ecclesiastical rank. **2.** To divest of a frock or gown.

un·furl (un·fûrl′) v.t. & v.i. **1.** To unroll, as a flag. **2.** To spread out; expand; unfold.

un·gain·ly (un·gān′lē) adj. Lacking grace; awkward. — adv. In an awkward manner. — **un·gain′li·ness** n.

un·gird (un·gûrd′) v.t. **1.** To divest of or free from a belt, girdle, or confining band. **2.** To loosen or unfasten by or as by removing a belt, etc.

un·god·ly (un·god′lē) adj. **1.** Having no reverence for God; impious. **2.** Wicked; sinful. **3.** Informal Outrageous; unseemly. — **un·god′li·ness** n.

un·gov·ern·a·ble (un·guv′ər·nə·bəl) adj. **1.** Not capable of being governed or controlled. **2.** Refractory; unruly. — **un·gov′ern·a·ble·ness** n. — **un·gov′ern·a·bly** adv.

un·gra·cious (un·grā′shəs) adj. **1.** Lacking in graciousness of manner; unmannerly. **2.** Not pleasing; offensive; unacceptable. — **un·gra′cious·ly** adv. — **un·gra′cious·ness** n.

un·gram·mat·i·cal (un′grə·mat′i·kəl) adj. **1.** Not in accordance with the rules of grammar. **2.** Characterized by or using grammar at variance with the rules. — **un′gram·mat′i·cal·ly** adv.

un·grate·ful (un·grāt′fəl) adj. **1.** Not feeling or showing gratitude; not thankful. **2.** Not pleasant; disagreeable. **3.** Unrewarding. — **un·grate′ful·ly** adv. — **un·grate′ful·ness** n.

un·guard·ed (un·gär′did) adj. **1.** Having no guard; being without protection. **2.** Characterized by lack of caution or discretion: unguarded speech. — **un·guard′ed·ly** adv. — **un·guard′ed·ness** n.

un·guent (ung′gwənt) n. Any ointment or salve. [< L < unguere to anoint]

un·gu·la (ung′gyə·lə) n. pl. **·lae** (-lē) **1.** Zool. A hoof, claw, or nail. **2.** Geom. That which is left of a cone or cylinder when the top is cut off by a plane oblique to the base. **3.** Bot. An unguis. [< L < unguis nail] — **un′gu·lar** adj.

un·gu·late (ung′gyə·lit, -lāt) adj. **1.** Having hoofs. **2.** Designating, pertaining to, or belonging to a large group of hoofed mammals, including the elephant, rhinoceros, horse, hog, and all the ruminants. **3.** Hoof-shaped. — n. A hoofed mammal. [< LL < L ungula hoof]

---

unnavigable	unobtainable	unorthodoxy	unpatented	unphilological	unplowed
unnavigated	unobtained	unostentatious	unpatriotic	unphilosophic	unplucked
unneeded	unobtruding	unostentatiously	unpatriotically	unphilosophical	unplug
unneedful	unobtrusive	unostentatiousness	unpaved	unphonetic	unplugged
unnegotiable	unobtrusively	unowned	unpeaceable	unpicked	unpoetic
unneighborliness	unobtrusiveness	unoxidized	unpeaceful	unpicturesque	unpoetical
unneighborly	unoccasioned	unpacified	unpedigreed	unpierced	unpointed
unnoted	unoffended	unpaid	unpen	unpile	unpoised
unnoticeable	unoffending	unpainful	unpenetrated	unpitied	unpolarized
unnoticeably	unoffensive	unpainfully	unpensioned	unpitying	unpolished
unnoticed	unoffensively	unpainfulness	unperceivable	unpityingly	unpolitical
unnurtured	unoffered	unpaired	unperceived	unplaced	unpolluted
unobjectionable	unofficial	unpalatable	unperceiving	unplagued	unpondered
unobliged	unofficious	unpalatably	unperfected	unplait	unpopulated
unobliging	unofficiously	unparagraphed	unperformed	unplanned	unposted
unobligingly	unoiled	unpardonable	unperplexed	unplanted	unpractical
unobnoxious	unopen	unpardonably	unpersuadable	unplayed	unpracticality
unobscured	unopened	unpardoned	unpersuaded	unpleased	unpractically
unobservable	unopposed	unparental	unpersuasive	unpleasing	unpredictable
unobservant	unoppressed	unparted	unpersuasively	unpledged	unpredictably
unobservantly	unordained	unpartisan	unpersuasiveness	unpliable	unpreoccupied
unobserved	unoriginal	unpartizan	unperturbed	unpliant	unprepared
unobserving	unornamental	unpasteurized	unperused	unplighted	unprepossessing
unobstructed	unornate	unpatched	unphilanthropic	unploughed	unprepossessingly

un·hal·lowed (un·hal′ōd) *adj.* 1. Not consecrated or made holy. 2. Unholy; wicked.

un·hand (un·hand′) *v.t.* To remove one's hand from; release from the hand or hands; let go.

un·hand·y (un·han′dē) *adj.* **·hand·i·er, ·hand·i·est** 1. Inconvenient; hard to handle. 2. Clumsy; lacking in manual skill. — **un·hand′i·ly** *adv.* — **un·hand′i·ness** *n.*

un·hap·py (un·hap′ē) *adj.* **·pi·er, ·pi·est** 1. Sad; miserable; depressed. 2. Unlucky; unfortunate. 3. Not tactful or appropriate. — **un·hap′pi·ly** *adv.* — **un·hap′pi·ness** *n.*

un·har·ness (un·här′nis) *v.t.* 1. To remove the harness from; unyoke; release. 2. To remove the armor from.

un·health·y (un·hel′thē) *adj.* **·health·i·er, ·health·i·est** 1. Lacking health or vigor; sickly; unsound: *unhealthy* animals or plants; also, indicating such a condition: *unhealthy* signs. 2. Injurious to health. 3. Morally unsound; unwholesome. — **un·health′i·ly** *adv.* — **un·health′i·ness** *n.*

un·heard (un·hûrd′) *adj.* 1. Not perceived by the ear. 2. Not granted a hearing. 3. Obscure; unknown.

un·heard-of (un·hûrd′uv′, -ov′) *adj.* Not known of before; unknown or unprecedented.

un·hinge (un·hinj′) *v.t.* **·hinged, ·hing·ing** 1. To take from the hinges. 2. To remove the hinges of. 3. To detach; dislodge. 4. To throw into confusion; disorder. 5. To make unstable; unsettle, as the mind.

un·hitch (un·hich′) *v.t.* To unfasten.

un·ho·ly (un·hō′lē) *adj.* **·ho·li·er, ·ho·li·est** 1. Not sacred or hallowed. 2. Lacking purity; wicked; sinful. 3. *Informal* Terrible; dreadful: an *unholy* hour. [OE *unhālig*] — **un·ho′li·ly** *adv.* — **un·ho′li·ness** *n.*

un·hook (un·hŏŏk′) *v.t.* 1. To remove from a hook. 2. To unfasten the hook or hooks of. — *v.i.* 3. To become unhooked.

un·hoped-for (un·hōpt′fôr′) *adj.* Not expected or hoped for: an *unhoped-for* solution.

un·horse (un·hôrs′) *v.t.* **·horsed, ·hors·ing** 1. To throw from a horse. 2. To dislodge; overthrow. 3. To remove a horse or horses from: to *unhorse* a vehicle.

un·hur·ried (un·hûr′ēd) *adj.* Leisurely; not hurried.

uni- *combining form* Having or consisting of one only. [< L *unus* one]

U·ni·at (yōō′nē·at) *n.* A member of the Uniat Church. — *adj.* Of or pertaining to the Uniats or the Uniat Church. Also **U′ni·ate** (-it, -āt). [< Russian < *uniya* union < L *unus* one; from union with the Roman Catholic Church]

Uniat Church Any body of Eastern Christians forming a church that acknowledges the Pope as its supreme head and that has its own distinctive liturgy: also called *Eastern Church*. Also **Uniate Church**.

u·ni·ax·i·al (yōō′nē·ak′sē·əl) *adj.* Having one axis.

u·ni·cam·er·al (yōō′nə·kam′ər·əl) *adj.* Consisting of but one legislative chamber.

u·ni·cel·lu·lar (yōō′nə·sel′yə·lər) *adj. Biol.* Consisting of a single cell, as a protozoan; one-celled.

u·ni·col·or (yōō′nə·kul′ər) *adj.* Of one color.

u·ni·corn (yōō′nə·kôrn) *n.* A mythical horselike animal with one horn. [< OF < L < *unus* one + *cornu* horn]

u·ni·cy·cle (yōō′nə·sī′kəl) *n.* A vehicle consisting of a metal frame mounted on one wheel and propelled by means of pedals.

u·ni·di·rec·tion·al (yōō′nə·di·rek′shən·əl, -dī-) *adj.* 1. Having or moving in only one direction. 2. *Telecom.* Designed or equipped to operate best in only one direction, as a radio antenna.

UNICORN

u·ni·fi·a·ble (yōō′nə·fī′ə·bəl) *adj.* That can be unified.

u·ni·fi·ca·tion (yōō′nə·fə·kā′shən) *n.* The act of unifying, or the state of being unified. — **u′ni·fi·ca′tion·ist** *n.*

unified command *Mil.* An armed force of two or more U.S. military services under a single commander.

u·ni·form (yōō′nə·fôrm) *adj.* 1. Being always the same or alike, as in form, appearance, quality, degree, etc.; not varying: *uniform* temperature. 2. Agreeing or identical with each other; alike: *uniform* tastes. — *n.* 1. A distinctive form of dress having a uniform style and appearance and worn by members of the same organization or service, as soldiers, sailors, etc. 2. A single suit of such clothes. — *v.t.* 1. To put into or clothe with a uniform. 2. To make uniform. [< F < *unus* one + *forma* form] — **u′ni·form·ly** *adv.* — **u′ni·form·ness** *n.*

u·ni·formed (yōō′nə·fôrmd) *adj.* Dressed in uniform.

u·ni·form·i·ty (yōō′nə·fôr′mə·tē) *n. pl.* **·ties** 1. The state or quality of being uniform; also, an instance of it. 2. Conformity, as in opinions or religion. 3. Monotony; sameness.

u·ni·fy (yōō′nə·fī) *v.t. & v.i.* **·fied, ·fy·ing** To combine into a unit; become or cause to be one. [< F or LL < L *unus* one + *facere* to make] — **u′ni·fi′er** *n.*

u·ni·lat·er·al (yōō′nə·lat′ər·əl) *adj.* 1. Of, pertaining to, or existing on one side only. 2. Made, undertaken, done, or signed by only one of two or more people or parties. 3. One-sided. 4. Relating to or concerned with only one side of a question, dispute, etc. 5. Turned to or showing only one side. — **u′ni·lat′er·al·ly** *adv.* — **u′ni·lat′er·al·ism, u′ni·lat′er·al′i·ty** (-al′ə·tē) *n.*

un·im·peach·a·ble (un′im·pē′chə·bəl) *adj.* Not to be called into question as regards truth, honesty, etc.; faultless; blameless. — **un′im·peach′a·bly** *adv.*

un·im·proved (un′im·prōōvd′) *adj.* 1. Not improved, bettered, or advanced. 2. Having no improvements; not cleared, cultivated, or built upon: *unimproved* land. 3. Not made anything of; unused: *unimproved* opportunities.

un·in·ter·est·ed (un·in′tər·is·tid, -tris-) *adj.* 1. Having no interest in, as in property. 2. Taking no interest in; unconcerned. — **un·in′ter·est·ed·ly** *adv.* — **un·in′ter·est·ed·ness** *n.*

un·ion (yōōn′yən) *n.* 1. The act of uniting, or the state of being united; also, that which is so formed. 2. A combining or joining of nations, states, parties, etc., for some mutual interest or purpose. 3. The harmony, agreement, or concord that results from such a combining or joining. 4. The joining of two persons in marriage; also, the state of wedlock. 5. A labor union. 6. *Mech.* A device for connecting parts of machinery; esp., a coupling or connection for pipes or rods. 7. A device emblematic of union, used in a flag or emblem and found in the corner near the staff or occupying the entire field. — *adj.* Of, pertaining to, or adhering to a union, esp. a labor union. [< F < LL < L *unus* one]

PIPE UNION

Un·ion (yōōn′yən) *n.* 1. The U.S. regarded as a national unit: with *the.* 2. The former Union of South Africa. — *adj.* Of, pertaining to, or loyal to the U.S.; esp., the Federal government during the Civil War: a *Union* soldier.

union catalogue A library catalogue that contains the contents of more than one library.

un·ion·ism (yōōn′yən·iz′əm) *n.* 1. The principle of combining for unity of purpose and action. 2. The principle or the support of trade unions. 3. *Usu. cap.* Adherence to the federal union during the Civil War. — **un′ion·is′tic** *adj.*

un·ion·ist (yōōn′yən·ist) *n.* 1. An advocate of union or unionism. 2. A member of a trade union.

unprescribed	unprogressive	unpunishable	unreachable	unrecorded	unrelievable
unpresentable	unprohibited	unpunished	unreached	unrecounted	unrelieved
unpresentably	unpromising	unpurchasable	unreadable	unrecoverable	unrelished
unpreserved	unpromisingly	unpure	unrealizable	unrecruited	unremarkable
unpressed	unprompted	unpurged	unrealized	unrectified	unremarked
unpresumptuous	unpronounced	unpurified	unreasoned	unredeemed	unremedied
unpretending	unpropitiable	unpurposed	unrebukable	unredressed	unremembered
unpretentious	unpropitiated	unpursuing	unrebuked	unreelable	unremittable
unpretentiously	unpropitious	unpuzzle	unreceipted	unrefined	unremitted
unpretentiousness	unpropitiously	unquaffed	unreceivable	unreflected	unremorseful
unprevailing	unproportionate	unquailing	unreceived	unreflecting	unremorsefully
unpreventable	unproportioned	unquaking	unreceptive	unreformed	unremorsefulness
unprevented	unproposed	unqualifying	unreceptively	unrefreshed	unremovable
unprimed	unprosperous	unquelled	unreceptiveness	unrefreshing	unremoved
unprincely	unprotected	unquenchable	unreciprocated	unregarded	unremunerated
unprinted	unproved	unquenched	unreclaimable	unregistered	unremunerative
unprivileged	unproven	unquestioning	unreclaimed	unregretted	unrendered
unprized	unprovoked	unquotable	unrecognizable	unregulated	unrenewed
unprobed	unprovoking	unraised	unrecognizably	unrehearsed	unrenounced
unprocessed	unpruned	unransomed	unrecognized	unrelated	unrenowned
unprocurable	unpublishable	unrated	unrecommended	unrelatedness	unrent
unprocured	unpublished	unratified	unrecompensed	unrelaxed	unrented
unprofaned	unpucker	unravaged	unreconcilable	unrelaxing	unrepaid
unprofited	unpunctual	unrazed	unreconciled	unreliable	unrepairable

Un·ion·ist (yōōn′yən·ist) *n.* During the U.S. Civil War, one who supported the Union cause and opposed secession.
un·ion·ize (yōōn′yən·īz) *v.* **·ized, ·iz·ing** *v.t.* **1.** To cause to join, or to organize into a union, especially a labor union. **2.** To make conform to the rules, etc., of a union. — *v.i.* **3.** To become a member of or organize a labor union. — **un′ion·i·za′tion** *n.*
union jack A flag consisting of the union only.
Union Jack The British national flag, a combination of the flags of England, Scotland, and Ireland.
union shop An industrial establishment that hires only members of a labor union or those who promise to join a union within a specified time.
union suit A one-piece undergarment for men and boys consisting of shirt and drawers.
u·nip·a·rous (yōō·nip′ər·əs) *adj.* **1.** *Biol.* Bringing forth but one offspring at a time, or not having borne more than one. **2.** *Bot.* Having but one axis or stem at each branching.
u·ni·po·lar (yōō′nə·pō′lər) *adj.* *Physics* Showing only one kind of polarity.
u·nique (yōō·nēk′) *adj.* **1.** Being the only one of its kind; sole. **2.** Being without or having no equal or like. **3.** Loosely, unusual, rare, or notable: a *unique* opportunity. [< F < L < *unus* one] — **u·nique′ly** *adv.* — **u·nique′ness** *n.*
u·ni·sex (yōō′nə·seks′) *Informal adj.* For, appropriate to, or having characteristics of both sexes: *unisex* fashions. — *n.* The embodiment of qualities, etc., of both sexes.
u·ni·sex·u·al (yōō′nə·sek′shōō·əl) *adj.* *Biol.* **1.** Of only one sex; also, having sexual organs of one sex only. **2.** *Informal* Unisex.
u·ni·son (yōō′nə·sən, -zən) *n.* **1.** A speaking or sounding the same words, tones, etc., simultaneously: with *in*: they answered in *unison*. **2.** Complete accord or agreement: harmony. **3.** *Music* **a** A state in which instruments or voices perform identical parts simultaneously, in the same or different octaves. **b** The interval formed by two tones of the same pitch. [< L < *uni-* one + *sonus* sound]
u·nit (yōō′nit) *n.* **1.** A single person or thing regarded as an individual but belonging to an entire group. **2.** A body or group, as of soldiers, considered as a subdivision of a similar but larger body or group. **3.** An apparatus or piece of equipment, usu. part of a larger object and having a specific function: the cooling *unit* of a freezer. **4.** A standard quantity with which others of the same kind are compared for purposes of measurement and in terms of which their magnitude is stated. **5.** *Math.* A quantity whose measure is represented by the number 1; a least whole number. **6.** *Med.* The quantity of a drug, vaccine, serum, or antigen required to produce a given effect. [Back formation < UNITY]
u·ni·tar·i·an (yōō′nə·târ′ē·ən) *n.* One who rejects the doctrine of the Trinity; a non-Trinitarian monotheist. — *adj.* Of or pertaining to a unit. [< NL *unitarius* unitary]
U·ni·tar·i·an (yōō′nə·târ′ē·ən) *n.* A member of a religious denomination that rejects the doctrine of the Trinity and emphasizes complete freedom of religious opinion, the importance of personal character, and the independence of each local congregation. — *adj.* Of or pertaining to the Unitarians, or to their teachings. — **U′ni·tar′i·an·ism** *n.*
u·ni·tar·y (yōō′nə·ter′ē) *adj.* **1.** Of or pertaining to a unit. **2.** Characterized by or based on unity, as a system of government. **3.** Having the nature of a unit; whole.
u·nite (yōō·nīt′) *v.* **u·nit·ed, u·nit·ing** *v.t.* **1.** To join together so as to form a whole; combine; compound. **2.** To bring into close connection, as by legal, physical, social, or other tie; join in action, interest, etc. **3.** To join in marriage. **4.** To attach permanently or solidly; cause to adhere; bond. **5.** To show or possess (characteristics, etc.) in combination: to *unite* wit and beauty. — *v.i.* **6.** To become or be merged into one; combine. **7.** To join together for action; concur. [< LL *unitus,* pp. of *unire* to make one < L *unus* one]
— **Syn. 1.** consolidate, amalgamate, merge, blend, fuse. **2.** connect, join, link, associate. — **Ant.** divide, separate, disconnect.
u·nit·ed (yōō·nī′tid) *adj.* Incorporated into one; allied; combined. — **u·nit′ed·ly** *adv.* — **u·nit′ed·ness** *n.*
United Church of Canada A church made up of former denominational Methodists, Presbyterians, and others.
United Nations 1. A coalition to resist the aggression of the axis powers in World War II, formed of 26 nations in January, 1942. **2.** An organization of sovereign states, having its permanent headquarters in an enclave of international territory in New York City since 1951, created by the **United Nations Charter** drafted in September–October, 1944. Formerly **United Nations Organization.** *Abbr. UN, U.N.*
United Nations Trust Territory See TRUST TERRITORY.
United Press International An organization for collecting and distributing news, formed in 1958 by a merger of two similar organizations, the International News Service and the United Press. *Abbr. UPI, U.P.I.*
unit modifier A conventional or improvised compound used adjectively before a substantive. Examples: *blue-green* algae, *bitter-sweet* chocolate, *suit-coat* pattern.
◆ The use of the hyphen in the unit modifier is to avoid ambiguity in a word sequence where the relationship is not immediately apparent from context: The house had faded *red-brick* walls (faded walls of red brick, *not* faded red walls of brick). The hyphen here is to be considered a nonce use and not a spelling form or variant.
u·ni·ty (yōō′nə·tē) *n.* *pl.* **·ties 1.** The state or fact of being one. **2.** Something that is wholly united and complete within itself. **3.** A state or quality of general concord and mutual understanding; harmony. **4.** The harmonious agreement of parts or elements into one united whole. **5.** The condition or fact of being free from variety or diversity. **6.** Singleness or constancy of purpose, action, etc. **7.** In art and literature, the arrangement of parts into a homogeneous whole exhibiting oneness of purpose, thought, spirit, and style. **8.** *Math.* **a** The number one. **b** The element of a number system that leaves any number unchanged under multiplication, that is, a number *e* such that $ex = xe = x$ for all x. [< OF < L < *unus* one]
u·ni·va·lent (yōō′nə·vā′lənt) *adj.* *Chem.* Having a valence or combining value of one; monovalent. — **u′ni·va′lence, u′ni·va·len·cy** *n.*
u·ni·valve (yōō′nə·valv′) *adj.* Having only one valve, as a mollusk. Also **u′ni·valved′, u′ni·val′vu·lar** (-val′vyə·lər). — *n.* **1.** A mollusk having a univalve shell; a gastropod. **2.** A shell of a single piece.
u·ni·ver·sal (yōō′nə·vûr′səl) *adj.* **1.** Of, pertaining to, or typical of all or the whole: a *universal* reaction. **2.** Including, involving, or intended for all: a *universal* law. **3.** Applicable to everyone or to all cases: a *universal* cure. **4.** That can be used or understood by all: a *universal* language. **5.** Accomplished or interested in all or many subjects, activities, etc.: a *universal* genius. **6.** Of, pertaining to, or occurring throughout the universe. **7.** Common to all in any specific group or field: a *universal* practice of politicians. **8.** *Mech.* **a** Adapted or adaptable to a great variety of uses, shapes, etc., as certain machine parts. **b** Permitting free movement within fixed extremes, as a joint. **9.** *Logic* **a** Including all the individuals of a class or genus; generic. **b** In a proposition, predicable of all the individuals denoted by the subject: opposed to *particular*: "All men are mortal" is a *universal* proposition. — *n.* **1.** *Logic* A universal proposition. **2.** Any general or universal notion, condition, principle, etc. — **u′ni·ver′sal·ly** *adv.* — **u′ni·ver′sal·ness** *n.*
U·ni·ver·sal·ism (yōō′nə·vûr′səl·iz′əm) *n.* *Theol.* The doc-

unrepaired	unrespectful	unrighted	unsaleability	unscarred	unseeded
unrepealed	unrespectfully	unrightful	unsaleable	unscented	unseeing
unrepentant	unrespited	unrightfully	unsalted	unsceptical	unseeingly
unrepented	unrested	unrimed	unsanctified	unscheduled	unsegmented
unrepenting	unresting	unripened	unsanctioned	unscholarly	unseized
unrepining	unrestrainable	unrisen	unsanitarily	unschooled	unselected
unreplaced	unrestraint	unroasted	unsanitary	unscientific	unselective
unreplenished	unrestricted	unrobe	unsated	unscientifically	unselectively
unreported	unretarded	unromantic	unsatiable	unscorched	unsensitive
unrepresentative	unretentive	unromantically	unsatiated	unscorned	unsent
unrepresented	unretracted	unroof	unsatiating	unscoured	unsentimental
unrepressed	unretrieved	unroofed	unsatisfactorily	unscourged	unsentimentally
unreprievable	unreturned	unrough	unsatisfactory	unscraped	unserved
unreprieved	unrevealed	unrounded	unsatisfied	unscratched	unserviceable
unreprovable	unrevenged	unrulable	unsatisfying	unscreened	unserviceableness
unrequested	unreversed	unruled	unsatisfyingly	unscriptural	unserviceably
unrequited	unrevised	unsafe	unsaved	unsculptured	unset
unresented	unrevoked	unsafely	unsawed	unsealed	unsevered
unresigned	unrewarded	unsaid	unsawn	unseated	unsew
unresistant	unrhetorical	unsaintliness	unsayable	unseaworthiness	unsewn
unresisted	unrhymed	unsaintly	unscabbarded	unseaworthy	unsexual
unresisting	unrhythmic	unsalability	unscaled	unseconded	unshaded
unresolved	unrhythmical	unsalable	unscanned	unsectarian	unshadowed
unrespectable	unrhythmically	unsalaried	unscarified	unsecured	unshaken

trine that all souls will finally be saved and that good will triumph universally. — **U'ni·ver'sal·ist** *adj. & n.*

u·ni·ver·sal·i·ty (yōō'nə·vər·sal'ə·tē) *n. pl.* **·ties** **1.** The state or quality of being universal. **2.** Unrestricted fitness or adaptability. **3.** An all-embracing range of knowledge, abilities, etc.

u·ni·ver·sal·ize (yōō'nə·vûr'səl·īz) *v.t.* **·ized, ·iz·ing** To make universal.

universal joint *Mech.* A joint that permits connected parts of a machine to be turned in any direction within definite limits. Also **universal coupling.**

u·ni·ver·sal·ly (yōō'nə·vûr'sə·lē) *adv.* In a universal manner; on all occasions or in all places; without exception.

u·ni·verse (yōō'nə·vûrs) *n.* **1.** The aggregate of all existing things; the whole creation embracing all celestial bodies and all of space; the cosmos. **2.** In restricted sense, the earth. **3.** Human beings collectively; mankind. [< F < L < *unus* one + *versus,* pp. of *vertere* to turn]

u·ni·ver·si·ty (yōō'nə·vûr'sə·tē) *n. pl.* **·ties** **1.** An institution for higher instruction that includes one or more schools or colleges for graduate or professional study, as well as an undergraduate division, and grants master's and doctor's degree. **2.** The faculty and students of a university. **3.** The buildings and grounds of a university. [< OF < L *universitas* the whole, entire number]

u·niv·o·cal (yōō·niv'ə·kəl) *adj.* Having but one proper sense or meaning. — *n.* A word that has but one meaning. [< LL < L *unus* one + *vox, vocis* voice]

un·just (un·just') *adj.* **1.** Not legitimate, fair, or just; wrongful. **2.** Acting contrary to right and justice; unrighteous. — **un·just'ly** *adv.* — **un·just'ness** *n.*

un·kempt (un·kempt') *adj.* **1.** Not combed. **2.** Not clean or neat; untidy. **3.** Without polish or refinement; rough. [< UN-¹ + *kempt* combed, pp. of dial. *kemb,* var. of COMB]

un·kind (un·kīnd') *adj.* Showing lack of kindness; unsympathetic; cruel. — **un·kind'ly** *adv.* — **un·kind'ness** *n.*

un·knit (un·nit') *v.* **·knit** or **·knit·ted, ·knit·ting** *v.t.* **1.** To untie or unravel (something tied or knit). **2.** To smooth out (something wrinkled). — *v.i.* **3.** To become unknitted.

un·known (un·nōn') *adj.* **1.** Not known or apprehended; not recognized, as a fact or person. **2.** Not ascertained, discovered, or established: an *unknown* element. — *n.* An unknown person or quantity.

Unknown Soldier One of the unidentified dead of World War I who is honored as a symbol of all his compatriots who died in action, extended to include unknown dead of World War II and the Korean conflict.

un·la·bored (un·lā'bərd) *adj.* **1.** Produced without strain or effort; seemingly free and easy; natural. **2.** Uncultivated by labor; unworked; untilled. Also *Brit.* **un·la'boured.**

un·lace (un·lās') *v.t.* **·laced, ·lac·ing** **1.** To loosen or unfasten the lacing of; untie. **2.** To loosen or remove (armor or clothing) in this way.

un·lade (un·lād') *v.t. & v.i.* **·lad·ed, ·lad·ing** **1.** To unload the cargo of (a ship). **2.** To unload or discharge (cargo, etc.).

un·laid (un·lād') *adj.* **1.** Not laid or placed; not fixed. **2.** Not allayed or pacified. **3.** Not twisted, as the strands of a rope.

un·latch (un·lach') *v.t.* **1.** To open or unlock by releasing the latch. — *v.i.* **2.** To come open or unlocked.

un·law·ful (un·lô'fəl) *adj.* **1.** Contrary to or in violation of law; illegal. **2.** Born out of wedlock; illegitimate. — **un·law'ful·ly** *adv.* — **un·law'ful·ness** *n.*

un·lay (un·lā') *v.t. & v.i.* **·laid, ·lay·ing** To untwist: said of the strands of a rope.

un·learn (un·lûrn') *v.t. & v.i.* **·learned** or **·learnt, ·learn·ing** To dismiss from the mind; forget.

un·learn·ed (un·lûr'nid; *for def. 3* un·lûrnd') *adj.* **1.** Not possessed of or characterized by learning; illiterate; ignorant. **2.** Unworthy of or unlike a learned man. **3.** Not acquired by learning or study. — **un·learn'ed·ly** *adv.*

un·leash (un·lēsh') *v.t.* To set free from or as from a leash.

un·leav·ened (un·lev'ənd) *adj.* Not leavened: said esp. of the bread used at the feast of the Passover.

un·less (un·les') *conj.* If it be not a fact that; supposing that . . . not; except that: *Unless* we persevere, we shall lose. — *prep.* Save; except; excepting: with an implied verb: *Unless* a miracle, he'll not be back in time. [Earlier *onlesse (that)* (than) in a less case < ON + LESS]

un·let·tered (un·let'ərd) *adj.* Not educated; illiterate.

un·like (un·līk') *adj.* Having little or no resemblance; different. — *prep.* Dissimilar to or different from; not like: It was *unlike* him to go. — **un·like'ness** *n.*

un·like·ly (un·līk'lē) *adj.* **1.** Not likely; improbable. **2.** Not inviting or promising success. — *adv.* Improbably. — **un·like'li·ness, un·like'li·hood** *n.*

un·lim·ber (un·lim'bər) *v.t. & v.i.* To disconnect (a gun or caisson) from its limber; prepare for action.

un·lim·it·ed (un·lim'it·id) *adj.* **1.** Having no limits in space, number, or time; unbounded. **2.** Not limited by restrictions. **3.** Not limited by qualifications; undefined. — **un·lim'it·ed·ly** *adv.* — **un·lim'it·ed·ness** *n.*

un·load (un·lōd') *v.t.* **1.** To remove the load or cargo from. **2.** To take off or discharge (cargo, etc.). **3.** To relieve of something burdensome or oppressive. **4.** To withdraw the charge of ammunition from. **5.** *Informal* To dispose of. — *v.i.* **6.** To discharge freight, cargo, or other burden. — **un·load'er** *n.*

un·lock (un·lok') *v.t.* **1.** To unfasten (something locked). **2.** To open or undo; release. **3.** To lay open; reveal or disclose. — *v.i.* **4.** To become unlocked.

un·looked-for (un·lŏŏkt'fôr') *adj.* Not anticipated.

un·loose (un·lōōs') *v.t.* **·loosed, ·loos·ing** To release from fastenings; set loose or free.

un·loos·en (un·lōō'sən) *v.t.* To loose; unloose.

un·luck·y (un·luk'ē) *adj.* **·luck·i·er, ·luck·i·est** **1.** Not favored by luck; unfortunate. **2.** Resulting in or attended by ill luck. **3.** Ill-omened; inauspicious: an *unlucky* day. — **un·luck'i·ly** *adv.* — **un·luck'i·ness** *n.*

un·make (un·māk') *v.t.* **·made** (-mād'), **·mak·ing** **1.** To reduce to the original condition or form. **2.** To ruin; destroy. **3.** To depose, as from a position of authority.

un·man (un·man') *v.t.* **·manned, ·man·ning** **1.** To cause to lose courage or fortitude; dishearten. **2.** To render unmanly or effeminate. **3.** To deprive of virility; castrate.

un·man·ly (un·man'lē) *adj.* **1.** Not masculine or virile; effeminate. **2.** Not honorable. — **un·man'li·ness** *n.*

un·man·ner·ly (un·man'ər·lē) *adj.* Lacking manners; rude. — *adv.* Impolitely; rudely. — **un·man'ner·li·ness** *n.*

un·mask (un·mask', -mäsk') *v.t.* **1.** To remove a mask from. **2.** To reveal or disclose the truth about. — *v.i.* **3.** To remove one's mask or disguise.

un·mean·ing (un·mē'ning) *adj.* **1.** Having no meaning. **2.** Showing no expression of intelligence, interest, etc.; empty. — **un·mean'ing·ly** *adv.* — **un·mean'ing·ness** *n.*

un·meet (un·mēt') *adj.* Not meet or suitable; not proper; unbecoming. — **un·meet'ly** *adv.* — **un·meet'ness** *n.*

un·men·tion·a·ble (un·men'shən·ə·bəl) *adj.* Not proper to be mentioned or discussed; embarrassing; shameful. — **un·men'tion·a·ble·ness** *n.* — **un·men'tion·a·bly** *adv.*

unshamed	unsisterly	unsolved	unsprinkled	unstripped	unsusceptible
unshapely	unsized	unsoothed	unsprung	unstuffed	unsuspicious
unshared	unskeptical	unsophistication	unsquandered	unstung	unsuspiciously
unshaved	unslacked	unsorted	unsquared	unsubdued	unsustainable
unshaven	unslaked	unsought	unstack	unsubmissive	unsustained
unshed	unsleeping	unsounded	unstainable	unsubscribed	unswayed
unshelled	unslumbering	unsoured	unstained	unsubsidized	unsweetened
unsheltered	unsmiling	unsowed	unstalked	unsubstantiated	unswept
unshielded	unsmilingly	unsown	unstamped	unsuccess	unswerving
unshod	unsmirched	unspecified	unstandardized	unsuccessful	unsworn
unshorn	unsmoked	unspeculative	unstarched	unsuggestive	unsymmetrical
unshrinkable	unsoaked	unspeculatively	unstarred	unsuited	unsymmetrically
unshrinking	unsober	unspelled	unstated	unsullied	unsympathetic
unshriven	unsocial	unspent	unstatesmanlike	unsunk	unsympathetically
unshrouded	unsoftened	unspilled	unsteadfast	unsupportable	unsympathizing
unshrunk	unsoiled	unspilt	unstemmed	unsupportably	unsympathizingly
unshunned	unsold	unspiritual	unsterile	unsupported	unsystematic
unshut	unsoldierly	unspirituality	unsterilized	unsupportedly	unsystematically
unsifted	unsolicited	unspiritually	unstick	unsuppressed	unsystematized
unsigned	unsolicitous	unspiritualness	unstigmatized	unsure	untack
unsilenced	unsolid	unspoiled	unstinted	unsurmountable	untactful
unsimilar	unsolidly	unspoilt	unstitched	unsurpassable	untactfully
unsingable	unsoluble	unspoken	unstrained	unsurpassed	untactfulness
unsinkable	unsolvable	unsportsmanlike	unstressed	unsurprised	untainted

un·men·tion·a·bles (un-men′shən-ə-bəlz) *n.pl.* Things not ordinarily mentioned; usu., undergarments.

un·mer·ci·ful (un-mûr′sə-fəl) *adj.* Showing no mercy; pitiless. **— un·mer′ci·ful·ly** *adv.* **— un·mer′ci·ful·ness** *n.*

un·mind·ful (un-mīnd′fəl) *adj.* Neglectful; inattentive; careless. **— un·mind′ful·ly** *adv.* **— un·mind′ful·ness** *n.*

un·mis·tak·a·ble (un′mis-tā′kə-bəl) *adj.* That cannot be mistaken; evident; clear. **— un′mis·tak′a·bly** *adv.*

un·mit·i·gat·ed (un-mit′ə-gā′tid) *adj.* 1. Not mitigated or lightened in effect: *unmitigated* sorrow. 2. Absolute: an *unmitigated* rogue. **— un·mit′i·gat′ed·ly** *adv.*

un·mor·al (un-môr′əl, -mōr′-) *adj.* Having no moral sense; neither moral nor immoral. **— un·mo·ral·i·ty** (un′mə-ral′ə-tē) *n.* **— un·mor′al·ly** *adv.*

un·nat·u·ral (un-nach′ər-əl) *adj.* 1. Contrary to the laws of nature. 2. Monstrous; inhuman: *unnatural* crimes. 3. Not having, or inconsistent with, those attitudes, feelings, etc., considered normal; abnormal. 4. Artificial; affected. **— un·nat′u·ral·ly** *adv.* **— un·nat′u·ral·ness** *n.*

un·nec·es·sar·y (un-nes′ə-ser′ē) *adj.* Not required or necessary; not essential. **— un·nec′es·sar′i·ly** *adv.*

un·nerve (un-nûrv′) *v.t.* **·nerved, ·nerv·ing** To deprive of strength; firmness, self-control, or courage; unman.

un·num·bered (un-num′bərd) *adj.* 1. Not counted. 2. Innumerable. 3. Not marked with or assigned a number.

un·oc·cu·pied (un-ok′yə-pīd) *adj.* 1. Empty; not dwelt in; uninhabited: an *unoccupied* house. 2. Idle; unemployed.

un·or·gan·ized (un-ôr′gən-īzd) *adj.* 1. Not organized in structure, system, government, etc. 2. Not living; inorganic. 3. Not unionized. Also *Brit.* **un·or′gan·ised.**

un·or·tho·dox (un-ôr′thə-doks) *adj.* Not orthodox in doctrine, manner, method, etc. **— un·or′tho·dox′ly** *adv.*

un·pack (un-pak′) *v.t.* 1. To open and take out the contents of. 2. To take out of the container, as something packed. **— v.i.** 3. To unpack a trunk, etc. **— un·pack′er** *n.*

un·paged (un-pājd′) *adj.* Having the pages unnumbered: said of a book, magazine, etc.

un·par·al·leled (un-par′ə-leld) *adj.* Without parallel; unmatched; unprecedented.

un·par·lia·men·ta·ry (un′pär-lə-men′tər-ē) *adj.* Contrary to the rules that govern parliamentary bodies. **— un′par·lia·men′ta·ri·ly** *adv.* **— un′par·lia·men′ta·ri·ness** *n.*

un·peg (un-peg′) *v.t.* **·pegged, ·peg·ging** To open or unfasten by removing a peg or pegs.

un·peo·ple (un-pē′pəl) *v.t.* **·pled, ·pling** To take or remove people from; depopulate. **— un·peo′pled** *adj.*

un·pin (un-pin′) *v.t.* **·pinned, ·pin·ning** 1. To remove the pins from. 2. To unfasten by removing pins.

un·pleas·ant (un-plez′ənt) *adj.* Disagreeable; objectionable; not pleasing. **— un·pleas′ant·ly** *adv.* **— un·pleas′ant·ness** *n.*

un·plumbed (un-plumd′) *adj.* 1. Not sounded or explored fully; unfathomed. 2. Not furnished with plumbing.

un·polled (un-pōld′) *adj.* 1. Not registered: an *unpolled* vote or voter. 2. Not having voted at an election.

un·pop·u·lar (un-pop′yə-lər) *adj.* Having no popularity; generally disliked or condemned. **— un·pop′u·lar·ly** *adv.* **— un·pop·u·lar·i·ty** (-lar′ə-tē) *n.*

un·prac·ticed (un-prak′tist) *adj.* 1. Being without practice, experience, or skill. 2. Not carried out in practice; not used. 3. Not yet tried.

un·prec·e·dent·ed (un-pres′ə-den′tid) *adj.* Being without precedent; unheard-of. **— un·prec′e·dent′ed·ly** *adv.*

un·prej·u·diced (un-prej′ŏŏ-dist) *adj.* 1. Free from prejudice or bias; impartial. 2. Not impaired, as a right.

un·priced (un-prīst′) *adj.* Having no fixed price.

un·prin·ci·pled (un-prin′sə-pəld) *adj.* Lacking in moral principles; unscrupulous. **— un·prin′ci·pled·ness** *n.*

un·print·a·ble (un-prin′tə-bəl) *adj.* Not fit to be printed.

un·pro·fes·sion·al (un′prə-fesh′ən-əl) *adj.* 1. Having no profession or no professional status. 2. Violating the rules or ethical code of a profession. **— un′pro·fes′sion·al·ly** *adv.*

un·qual·i·fied (un-kwol′ə-fīd) *adj.* 1. Being without the proper qualifications; unfit. 2. Without limitation or restrictions; absolute; entire: *unqualified* approval. **— un·qual′i·fied·ly** *adv.* **— un·qual′i·fied′ness** *n.*

un·ques·tion·a·ble (un-kwes′chən-ə-bəl) *adj.* Too certain or sure to admit of question; being beyond a doubt; indisputable. **— un·ques′tion·a·bil′i·ty, un·ques′tion·a·ble·ness** *n.* **— un·ques′tion·a·bly** *adv.*

un·qui·et (un-kwī′ət) *adj.* 1. Not at rest; disturbed; restless. 2. Causing unrest or discomfort. 3. Uneasy; disturbing. **— un·qui′et·ly** *adv.* **— un·qui′et·ness** *n.*

un·quote (un-kwōt′) *v.t. & v.i.* **·quot·ed, ·quot·ing** To close (a quotation).

un·rav·el (un-rav′əl) *v.* **·eled** or **·elled, ·el·ing** or **·el·ling** *v.t.* 1. To separate the threads of, as a tangled skein or knitted article. 2. To free from entanglement; unfold; explain, as a mystery or a plot. **— v.i.** 3. To become unraveled.

un·read (un-red′) *adj.* 1. Not informed by reading; ignorant. 2. Not yet perused.

un·read·y (un-red′ē) *adj.* 1. Being without readiness or alertness. 2. Not in a condition to act effectively; unprepared. **— un·read′i·ly** *adv.* **— un·read′i·ness** *n.*

un·real (un-rēl′, -rē′əl) *adj.* 1. Having no reality or substance. 2. Artificial; insincere; also, fanciful. **— un·re·al·i·ty** (un′rē-al′ə-tē) *n.* **— un·re′al·ly** *adv.*

un·rea·son·a·ble (un-rē′zən-ə-bəl) *adj.* 1. Acting without or contrary to reason. 2. Not according to reason; irrational. 3. Immoderate; exorbitant. **— un·rea′son·a·bil′i·ty, un·rea′son·a·ble·ness** *n.* **— un·rea′son·a·bly** *adv.*

un·rea·son·ing (un-rē′zən-ing) *adj.* Not accompanied by reason or control. **— un·rea′son·ing·ly** *adv.*

un·reck·on·a·ble (un-rek′ən-ə-bəl) *adj.* That cannot be reckoned or computed; unlimited.

un·re·con·struct·ed (un-rē′kən-struk′tid) *adj.* 1. Not reconstructed. 2. Not reconciled to or accepting the conditions of the Reconstruction.

un·reel (un-rēl′) *v.t. & v.i.* To unwind, as from a reel.

un·re·gen·er·ate (un′ri-jen′ər-it) *adj.* 1. Not having been changed spiritually; remaining unreconciled to God. 2. Sinful; wicked. Also **un′re·gen′er·at′ed** (-ā′tid). **— un′re·gen′er·a·cy** (-ə-sē) *n.* **— un′re·gen′er·ate·ly** *adv.*

un·re·lent·ing (un′ri-len′ting) *adj.* 1. Not relenting; pitiless; inexorable. 2. Not diminishing, or not changing, in pace, effort, speed, etc. **— un′re·lent′ing·ly** *adv.*

un·re·li·gious (un′ri-lij′əs) *adj.* 1. Irreligious; hostile to religion. 2. Not connected in any way with religion.

un·re·mit·ting (un′ri-mit′ing) *adj.* Not relaxing or stopping; incessant. **— un′re·mit′ting·ly** *adv.* **— un′re·mit′ting·ness** *n.*

un·re·served (un′ri-zûrvd′) *adj.* 1. Given or done without reserve; full; unlimited. 2. Having no reserve of manner; informal; open; frank. **— un·re·serv·ed·ly** (un′ri-zûr′vid-lē) *adv.* **— un′re·serv′ed·ness** *n.*

un·rest (un-rest′) *n.* 1. Restlessness, esp. of the mind. 2.

untaken	unthriftily	untrimmed	unveiled	unwatched	unwomanish
untalented	unthriftiness	untroubled	unventilated	unwavering	unwomanishly
untamable	unthrifty	untrustful	unveracious	unwaveringly	unwomanly
untame	unthrone	untrustiness	unveraciously	unweakened	unwon
untameable	untillable	untrusty	unveraciousness	unweaned	unwooded
untamed	untilled	untuck	unverifiable	unwearable	unwooed
untangled	untilted	untufted	unverifiableness	unwearily	unworkability
untanned	untinged	untunable	unverifiably	unweary	unworkable
untapped	untired	untuned	unverified	unwearying	unworkableness
untarnished	untiring	untuneful	unversed	unwearyingly	unworkmanlike
untasted	untiringly	unturned	unvexed	unweathered	unworn
untaxable	untouched	untwilled	unvext	unweave	unworshiped
untaxed	untraceable	untwisted	unvisited	unwed	unworshipped
unteachable	untraced	untypical	unvitiated	unwedded	unwound
untechnical	untracked	untypically	unvitrified	unweeded	unwounded
untempered	untractable	untypicalness	unvocal	unwelcome	unwoven
untenanted	untrained	ununiform	unvocally	unwelded	unwreathe
untended	untrammeled	ununiformly	unvolatilized	unwetted	unwrought
unterrified	untrammelled	ununited	unvulcanized	unwhetted	unwrung
untested	untransferable	unurged	unwakened	unwhipped	unyielding
untether	untransferred	unusable	unwalled	unwifely	unyieldingly
untethered	untranslatable	unutilizable	unwanted	unwincing	unyieldingness
unthanked	untranslated	unuttered	unwarlike	unwinking	unyouthful
unthatched	untransmitted	unvaccinated	unwarmed	unwinning	unyouthfully
untheatrical	untrapped	unvacillating	unwarped	unwisdom	unyouthfulness
unthinkable	untraversable	unvacillatingly	unwarranted	unwished	unzealous
unthinkably	untraversed	unvalidated	unwashed	unwithered	unzealously
unthought	untreasured	unvanquished	unwasted	unwithering	unzip
unthoughtful	untrim	unvaried	unwasting	unwitnessed	

Trouble; turmoil, esp. with regard to public or political conditions and suggesting premonitions of revolt.

un·rid·dle (un·rid'l) *v.t.* **·dled, ·dling** To solve, as a mystery.

un·ri·fled[1] (un·rī'fəld) *adj.* Smoothbored, as a gun.

un·ri·fled[2] (un·rī'fəld) *adj.* Not rifled, seized or plundered.

un·right·eous (un·rī'chəs) *adj.* **1.** Not righteous; wicked; sinful. **2.** Contrary to justice; unfair. — **un·right'eous·ly** *adv.* — **un·right'eous·ness** *n.*

un·ripe (un·rīp') *adj.* **1.** Not arrived at maturity; not ripe; immature. [OE *unrīpe* untimely] — **un·ripe'ness** *n.*

un·ri·valed (un·rī'vəld) *adj.* Having no rival or competitor; unequaled; matchless. Also *Brit.* **un·ri'valled.**

un·roll (un·rōl') *v.t.* **1.** To spread or open (something rolled up). **2.** To exhibit to view. — *v.i.* **3.** To become unrolled.

un·ruf·fled (un·ruf'əld) *adj.* Not disturbed or agitated emotionally; calm.

un·ru·ly (un·rōō'lē) *adj.* **·li·er, ·li·est** Disposed to resist rule or discipline; intractable; ungovernable. — **un·ru'li·ness** *n.*

un·sad·dle (un·sad'l) *v.t.* **·dled, ·dling** **1.** To remove a saddle from. **2.** To throw from the saddle; unhorse.

un·sat·u·rat·ed (un·sach'ə·rā'tid) *adj.* **1.** Containing less of a solute required for equilibrium, as a solution. **2.** *Chem.* Capable of uniting with elements or radicals without loss of the original constituents.

un·sa·vor·y (un·sā'vər·ē) *adj.* **1.** Having a disagreeable taste or odor. **2.** Suggesting something disagreeable, offensive, or unclean; also, morally bad. Also *Brit.* **un·sa'vour·y.** — **un·sa'vor·i·ly** *adv.* — **un·sa'vor·i·ness** *n.*

un·say (un·sā') *v.t.* **·said, ·say·ing** To retract (something said).

un·scathed (un·skāthd') *adj.* Uninjured.

un·scram·ble (un·skram'bəl) *v.t.* **·bled, ·bling** *Informal* To resolve the confused or disordered condition of.

un·screw (un·skrōō') *v.t.* **1.** To remove the screw or screws from. **2.** To remove or detach by withdrawing screws, or by turning. — *v.i.* **3.** To permit of being unscrewed.

un·scru·pu·lous (un·skrōō'pyə·ləs) *adj.* Not scrupulous; having no scruples or morals; unprincipled. — **un·scru'pu·lous·ly** *adv.* — **un·scru'pu·lous·ness** *n.*

un·seal (un·sēl') *v.t.* **1.** To break the seal of. **2.** To open.

un·search·a·ble (un·sûr'chə·bəl) *adj.* That cannot be searched or explored; hidden; mysterious. — **un·search'a·ble·ness** *n.* — **un·search'a·bly** *adv.*

un·sea·son·a·ble (un·sē'zən·ə·bəl) *adj.* **1.** Not being in or characteristic of the season. **2.** Inappropriate; ill-timed. — **un·sea·son·a·ble·ness** *n.* — **un·sea'son·a·bly** *adv.*

un·seat (un·sēt') *v.t.* **1.** To remove from a seat or fixed position. **2.** To unhorse. **3.** To deprive of office or rank; depose.

un·seem·ly (un·sēm'lē) *adj.* **·li·er, ·li·est** Not seemly or proper; unbecoming; indecent. — *adv.* In an unseemly fashion. — **un·seem'li·ness** *n.*

un·self·ish (un·sel'fish) *adj.* Not selfish; generous. — **un·self'ish·ly** *adv.* — **un·self'ish·ness** *n.*

un·set·tle (un·set'l) *v.* **·tled, ·tling** *v.t.* **1.** To change or move from a fixed or settled condition. **2.** To confuse; disturb. — *v.i.* **3.** To become unsteady or unfixed.

un·sex (un·seks') *v.t.* To deprive of the distinctive qualities of a sex; esp., to render unfeminine or unwomanly.

un·shack·le (un·shak'əl) *v.t.* **·led, ·ling** To unfetter; free from or as from shackles.

un·sheathe (un·shēth') *v.t.* **·sheathed, ·sheath·ing** To take from or as from a scabbard or sheath; bare.

un·ship (un·ship') *v.t.* **·shipped, ·ship·ping** **1.** To unload from a ship or other vessel. **2.** To remove from the place where it is fixed or fitted, as a rudder or oar.

un·sight·ly (un·sīt'lē) *adj.* **·li·er, ·li·est** Offensive to the sight; ugly. — **un·sight'li·ness** *n.*

un·skilled (un·skild') *adj.* **1.** Destitute of skill or dexterity. **2.** Not requiring special skill or training: *unskilled* labor.

un·skill·ful (un·skil'fəl) *adj.* Lacking or not evincing skillfulness; awkward. Also *Brit.* **un·skil'ful.** — **un·skill'ful·ly** *adv.* — **un·skill'ful·ness** *n.*

un·snap (un·snap') *v.t.* **·snapped, ·snap·ping** To undo the snap or snaps of; unfasten.

un·snarl (un·snärl') *v.t.* To disentangle.

un·so·cia·ble (un·sō'shə·bəl) *adj.* **1.** Not sociable; not inclined to seek the society of others. **2.** Not congenial or in accord. **3.** Not encouraging social intercourse. — **un·so'cia·bil·i·ty, un·so'cia·ble·ness** *n.* — **un·so'cia·bly** *adv.*

un·sol·der (un·sod'ər) *v.t.* **1.** To disunite or take apart (something soldered). **2.** To separate; sunder.

un·so·phis·ti·cat·ed (un'sə·fis'tə·kā'tid) *adj.* **1.** Not sophisticated; artless; simple. **2.** Free from adulteration; genuine; pure. — **un'so·phis'ti·cat'ed·ly** *adv.* — **un'so·phis'ti·cat'ed·ness** *n.*

un·sound (un·sound') *adj.* **1.** Lacking in soundness; not strong or solid; weak. **2.** Not sound in health; diseased. **3.**

Not logically valid; erroneous. **4.** Disturbed; not profound: said of sleep. — **un·sound'ly** *adv.* — **un·sound'ness** *n.*

un·spar·ing (un·spâr'ing) *adj.* **1.** Not sparing or saving; lavish; liberal. **2.** Showing no mercy. — **un·spar'ing·ly** *adv.* — **un·spar'ing·ness** *n.*

un·speak·a·ble (un·spē'kə·bəl) *adj.* **1.** That cannot be expressed; unutterable. **2.** Extremely bad or objectionable. — **un·speak'a·ble·ness** *n.* — **un·speak'a·bly** *adv.*

un·sta·ble (un·stā'bəl) *adj.* **1.** Lacking in stability or firmness; not stable. **2.** Having no fixed purposes; easily influenced; inconstant. **3.** *Chem.* Readily decomposable, as certain compounds. — **un·sta'ble·ness** *n.* — **un·sta'bly** *adv.*

un·stead·y (un·sted'ē) *adj.* **1.** Not steady or firm; shaky. **2.** Not regular or constant; wavering: the motor's *unsteady* movement. **3.** Inconstant and erratic in behavior, habits, etc. — **un·stead'i·ly** *adv.* — **un·stead'i·ness** *n.*

un·stop (un·stop') *v.t.* **·stopped, ·stop·ping** **1.** To remove a stopper from. **2.** To open by removing obstructions; clear.

un·strap (un·strap') *v.t.* **·strapped, ·strap·ping** To unfasten or loosen the strap or straps of.

un·string (un·string') *v.t.* **·strung, ·string·ing** **1.** To remove from a string. **2.** To take the string or strings from. **3.** To loosen the string or strings of. **4.** To weaken: usu., in the passive: Her nerves were *unstrung.*

un·strung (un·strung') *adj.* **1.** Having the strings removed or relaxed. **2.** Unnerved; emotionally upset; weakened.

un·stud·ied (un·stud'ēd) *adj.* **1.** Not planned; unpremeditated. **2.** Not stiff or artificial; natural. **3.** Not acquainted through study; unversed: with *in.*

un·sub·stan·tial (un'səb·stan'shəl) *adj.* **1.** Lacking solidity, strength, or weight. **2.** Having no valid basis. **3.** Having no bodily existence; unreal; fanciful. — **un'sub·stan'tial·ly** *adv.* — **un'sub·stan'ti·al'i·ty** (-shē·al'ə·tē) *n.*

un·suit·a·ble (un·sōō'tə·bəl) *adj.* Not suitable; unfitting. — **un·suit·a·bil·i·ty** (un'sōō·tə·bil'ə·tē), **un·suit'a·ble·ness** *n.* — **un·suit'a·bly** *adv.*

un·sung (un·sung') *adj.* **1.** Not celebrated in song or poetry; obscure. **2.** Not yet sung, as a song.

un·tan·gle (un·tang'gəl) *v.t.* **·gled, ·gling** **1.** To free from entanglement or snarls. **2.** To clear up; resolve.

un·taught (un·tôt') *adj.* **1.** Not instructed; ignorant. **2.** Acquired without training or instruction; natural.

un·ten·a·ble (un·ten'ə·bəl) *adj.* That cannot be maintained or defended: *untenable* theories. — **un·ten'a·bil·i·ty, un·ten'a·ble·ness** *n.*

un·thank·ful (un·thangk'fəl) *adj.* **1.** Not grateful. **2.** Not received with thanks; unwelcome. — **un·thank'ful·ly** *adv.* — **un·thank'ful·ness** *n.*

un·think·ing (un·thingk'ing) *adj.* **1.** Not having the power of thought. **2.** Thoughtless; careless; heedless; inconsiderate. — **un·think'ing·ly** *adv.* — **un·think'ing·ness** *n.*

un·thought-of (un·thôt'uv') *adj.* **1.** Not remembered or called to mind. **2.** Not conceived of; not discovered.

un·thread (un·thred') *v.t.* **1.** To remove the thread from, as a needle. **2.** To find one's way out of, as a maze.

un·ti·dy (un·tī'dē) *adj.* **·di·er, ·di·est** Showing lack of tidiness. [ME *untīdi*] — **un·ti'di·ly** *adv.* — **un·ti'di·ness** *n.*

un·tie (un·tī') *v.* **·tied, ·ty·ing** *v.t.* **1.** To loosen or undo, as a knot. **2.** To free from restraint. **3.** To clear up or resolve. — *v.i.* **4.** To become untied. [OE *untīgan*]

un·til (un·til') *prep.* **1.** Up to the time of; till: We will wait *until* midnight. **2.** Before: used with a negative: The music doesn't begin *until* nine. — *conj.* **1.** To the time when: *until* I die. **2.** To the place or degree that: Walk east *until* you reach the river. **3.** Before: with a negative: He couldn't leave *until* noon. [ME < *un-* up to, as far as + TILL]

un·time·ly (un·tīm'lē) *adj.* **1.** Before the proper or expected time; premature. **2.** At the wrong time; ill-timed. — *adv.* Inopportunely. — **un·time'li·ness** *n.*

un·to (un·tōō) *prep.* **1.** *Poetic & Archaic* To. **2.** *Archaic* Until. [ME *un-* up to, as far as + TO]

un·told (un·tōld') *adj.* **1.** That cannot be revealed or described; inexpressible: *untold* misery. **2.** That cannot be numbered or estimated: *untold* numbers. **3.** Not told.

un·touch·a·ble (un·tuch'ə·bəl) *adj.* **1.** Inaccessible to the touch; out of reach. **2.** Intangible; unrivaled; unapproachable. **3.** Forbidden to the touch. **4.** Unpleasant, vile, or dangerous to touch. — *n.* In India, a member of the lowest caste, whose touch was formerly counted as pollution by Hindus of higher station. — **un·touch·a·bil·i·ty** (-bil'ə·tē) *n.*

un·to·ward (un·tôrd', -tōrd') *adj.* **1.** Causing hindrance; vexatious. **2.** Refractory; perverse. **3.** Unseemly; uncouth. — **un·to'ward·ly** *adv.* — **un·to'ward·ness** *n.*

un·trod·den (un·trod'n) *adj.* Not having been trodden upon; also, unfrequented. Also **un·trod'.**

un·true (un·trōō') *adj.* **1.** Lacking truth; not true; not corresponding with fact. **2.** Not conforming to rule or standard. **3.** Not faithful; disloyal. — **un·tru'ly** *adv.*

un·truss (un·trus′) *v.t.* **1.** To unfasten. **2.** *Obs.* To undress.

un·truth (un·trooth′) *n. pl.* **truths** (-trooths′, -troothz′) **1.** The quality or character of being untrue; want of veracity. **2.** A lie. — *Syn.* See LIE². [OE *untrēowth*]

un·truth·ful (un·trooth′fəl) *adj.* **1.** Not truthful; untrue. **2.** Given to telling lies. — **un·truth′ful·ly** *adv.* — **un·truth′ful·ness** *n.*

un·tu·tored (un·too′tərd, -tyoo′-) *adj.* **1.** Having had no tutor or teacher. **2.** Naive; simple.

un·twine (un·twīn′) *v.* **twined, twin·ing** *v.t.* **1.** To undo (something twined); unwind by disentangling. — *v.i.* **2.** To become untwined.

un·twist (un·twist′) *v.t. & v.i.* To unwind or untwine.

un·used (un·yoozd′ *for def. 1*; un·yoost′ *for def. 2*) *adj.* **1.** Not made use of; also, never having been used. **2.** Not accustomed or wont: with *to.*

un·u·su·al (un·yoo′zhoo·əl) *adj.* Not usual, common, or ordinary; rare. — **un·u′su·al·ly** *adv.* — **un·u′su·al·ness** *n.*

un·ut·ter·a·ble (un·ut′ər·ə·bəl) *adj.* **1.** Too great or deep for verbal expression; ineffable. **2.** Unpronounceable. — **un·ut′ter·a·ble·ness** *n.* — **un·ut′ter·a·bly** *adv.*

un·var·nished (un·vär′nisht) *adj.* **1.** Having no covering of varnish. **2.** Having no embellishment; plain.

un·veil (un·vāl′) *v.t.* **1.** To remove the veil from; reveal. — *v.i.* **2.** To remove one's veil; reveal oneself.

un·voiced (un·voist′) *adj.* **1.** Not expressed. **2.** *Phonet.* **a** Voiceless. **b** Rendered voiceless: The final (v) in "have" is often heard *unvoiced* in "have to."

un·war·y (un·wâr′ē) *adj.* Not careful or cautious; imprudent; rash; careless. — **un·war′i·ly** *adv.* — **un·war′i·ness** *n.*

un·well (un·wel′) *adj.* Not well; ailing; sick. — *Syn.* See SICK¹. — **un·well′ness** *n.*

un·wept (un·wept′) *adj.* **1.** Not lamented or wept for, as a deceased person. **2.** Not shed, as tears.

un·whole·some (un·hōl′səm) *adj.* **1.** Harmful to physical or mental health. **2.** Unsound in condition; diseased or decayed: *unwholesome* provisions. **3.** Suggestive of illness or disease: an *unwholesome* look. **4.** Morally bad; pernicious. — **un·whole′some·ly** *adv.* — **un·whole′some·ness** *n.*

un·wield·y (un·wēl′dē) *adj.* Moved or managed with difficulty, as from great size or awkward shape; bulky; clumsy. — **un·wield′i·ly** *adv.* — **un·wield′i·ness** *n.*

un·will·ing (un·wil′ing) *adj.* **1.** Not willing; reluctant; loath. **2.** Done, said, etc., with reluctance. — **un·will′ing·ly** *adv.* — **un·will′ing·ness** *n.*

un·wind (un·wīnd′) *v.* **wound, wind·ing** *v.t.* **1.** To reverse the winding of; untwist or wind off; uncoil. **2.** To disentangle. — *v.i.* **3.** To become unwound.

un·wise (un·wīz′) *adj.* Showing a lack of wisdom; imprudent; foolish. [OE *unwīs*] — **un·wise′ly** *adv.*

un·wit·ting (un·wit′ing) *adj.* **1.** Having no knowledge or consciousness of the thing in question. **2.** Unintentional. [OE *unwitende*] — **un·wit′ting·ly** *adv.*

un·wont·ed (un·wun′tid, -wōn′-) *adj.* **1.** Not according to habit or custom; unusual. **2.** *Obs.* Not accustomed; unfamiliar. — **un·wont′ed·ly** *adv.* — **un·wont′ed·ness** *n.*

un·wor·thy (un·wûr′thē) *adj.* **1.** Not deserving: usu., with *of.* **2.** Not befitting or becoming: often with *of;* improper. **3.** Lacking worth or merit. **4.** Shameful; contemptible. — **un·wor′thi·ly** *adv.* — **un·wor′thi·ness** *n.*

un·wound (un·wound′) Past tense and past participle of UNWIND.

un·wrap (un·rap′) *v.* **wrapped, wrap·ping** *v.t.* **1.** To take the wrapping from. — *v.i.* **2.** To become unwrapped.

un·wrin·kle (un·ring′kəl) *v.t.* **kled, ·kling** To free from wrinkles; smooth.

un·writ·ten (un·rit′n) *adj.* **1.** Not written or in writing. **2.** Not reduced to writing; traditional; customary. **3.** Having no writing upon it; blank.

unwritten law 1. A rule or custom established by general usage. **2.** Common law (which see). **3.** A custom in some communities granting a measure of immunity to those who commit criminal acts of revenge in support of personal or family honor, esp., in cases of adultery, etc.

un·yoke (un·yōk′) *v.* **yoked, yok·ing** *v.t.* **1.** To release from a yoke. **2.** To separate; part. — *v.i.* **3.** To become unyoked. **4.** To stop work; cease. [OE *ungeocian*]

up (up) *adv.* **1.** From a lower to a higher place, level, position, etc.: Come *up.* **2.** In, on, or to a higher place, level, position, etc. **3.** Toward that which is figuratively or conventionally higher; as: **a** To or at a higher price. **b** To or at a higher place, rank, etc. **c** To or at a greater size or amount: to swell *up.* **d** To or at a place that is locally or arbitrarily regarded as higher: *up* north. **e** Above the surface or horizon. **f** From an earlier to a later period. **g** To a source, conclusion, etc.: Follow *up* this lead. **4.** To a vertical position; standing; also, out of bed. **5.** So as to be compact or secure: Tie *up* the boxes. **6.** So as to be even with in space, time, degree, etc.: *up* to date. **7.** In or into an excited state or some specific action: They were stirred *up* to mutiny. **8.** In or into view or existence: to draw *up* a will. **9.** In or into prominence; under consideration: *up* for debate. **10.** In or into a place of safekeeping; aside: Fruits are put *up* in jars. **11.** At an end: Your time is *up.* **12.** Completely; totally: The house was burned *up.* **13.** In baseball and cricket, at bat. **14.** In tennis and other sports: **a** In the lead; ahead. **b** Apiece; alike: said of a score. **15.** Running for as a candidate. **16.** *Naut.* Shifted to windward, as a tiller. ◆ In informal usage *up* is often added to a verb without affecting the meaning of the sentence: to light *up* a room. — **to be all up with** To be all over for. — **to be up against** *Informal* To meet with; confront. — **to be up against it** *Informal* To be in difficulty. — **to be up in** (or **on**) *Informal* To be well informed in or skilled at something. — **to be up to 1.** *Informal* To be doing or plotting. **2.** To be equal to; be capable of. **3.** To be incumbent upon; be dependent upon: It's *up* to him to save us. — *adj.* **1.** Moving, sloping, or directed upward. **2.** At stake, as in gambling. **3.** *Informal* Going on; taking place: What's *up*? **4.** *Informal* Acquainted (with), equal (to): He is *up* in that subject. **5.** In golf, in advance of an opponent by a specified number of holes. **6.** Rising, risen, overflowing, or at flood. **7.** In an active or excited state: His temper was *up.* — **up and around** *Informal* Sufficiently recovered to walk. — **up to no good** Engaged in or contemplating some mischief. — *prep.* **1.** From a lower to a higher point or place of, on, or along. **2.** Toward a higher condition or rank on or in. **3.** To or at a point farther above or along: *up* the road. **4.** From the coast toward the interior of (a country). **5.** From the mouth toward the source of (a river). **6.** At, on, or near the height or top of. — *n.* **1.** A rise or ascent. **2.** A period of prosperity, etc.: chiefly in the phrase **ups and downs.** — **to be on the up and up 1.** *Slang* To be honest. **2.** *Informal* Rising and improving. — *v.* **upped, up·ping** *Informal v.t.* **1.** To *increase.* **2.** To put or take up. — *v.i.* **3.** To rise. [OE *ūp*]

up- *combining form* As a combining element *up* has adverbial force with various meanings: **1.** To a higher place or level, as in: **upgaze, uprise. 2.** To a greater size or larger amount, as in: **upflooding, upswell. 3.** To a vertical position, as in: **upprop, upstand. 4.** In or into commotion or activity, as in: **upboil, upstir. 5.** Completely; wholly, as in: **upbind, upgather.**

up-and-com·ing (up′ən·kum′ing) *adj.* Enterprising; energetic; promising.

up-and-down (up′ən·doun′) *adj.* **1.** Alternately rising and falling; fluctuating; varying: an *up-and-down* motion; an *up-and-down* career. **2.** Vertical; perpendicular.

u·pas (yoo′pəs) *n.* **1.** A tall evergreen Javanese tree of the mulberry family, having an acrid, poisonous sap. **2.** This sap. [< Malay (*pohon*) *upas* poison (tree)]

up·beat (up′bēt′) *n. Music* The relatively unaccented beat that precedes the downbeat. — *adj. Slang* Characterized by a lively, swinging rhythm.

up·braid (up·brād′) *v.t.* **1.** To reproach for some wrongdoing; scold or reprove. — *v.i.* **2.** To utter reproaches. [OE < *up-* up + *bregdan* to weave, twist] — **up·braid′er** *adj.* — **up·braid′ing** *n.* — **up·braid′ing·ly** *adv.*

up·bring·ing (up′bring′ing) *n.* The rearing and training received by a person during childhood.

up·coun·try (*n. & adj.* up′kun′trē; *adv.* up′kun′trē) *Informal n.* Country remote from the coast or from lowlands; inland country. — *adj.* Living in, from, or characteristic of inland places. — *adv.* In or toward the interior.

up·date (up·dāt′) *v.t.* **dat·ed, ·dat·ing** To bring up to date; to revise, with corrections, additions, etc., as a textbook.

up·end (up′end′) *v.t. & v.i.* To set or stand on end.

up·grade (*n.* up′grād′; *v.* up·grād′; *adv.* up′grād′) *n.* An upward incline or slope. — *v.t.* **·grad·ed, ·grad·ing** To raise to a higher grade, rank, post, etc. — *adv.* Up a hill or slope. — **on the upgrade 1.** Improving. **2.** Rising.

up·heav·al (up·hē′vəl) *n.* **1.** The act of upheaving, or the state of being upheaved. **2.** A violent disturbance or change.

up·heave (up·hēv′) *v.* **·heaved** or **·hove, ·heav·ing** *v.t.* **1.** To heave or raise up. — *v.i.* **2.** To be raised or lifted.

up·held (up·held′) Past tense and past participle of UPHOLD.

up·hill (*adv. & adj.* up′hil′; *n.* up′hil′) *adv.* Up or as up a hill or an ascent; against difficulties. — *adj.* **1.** Going up an ascent; sloping upward. **2.** Attended with difficulty or exertion. **3.** At a high place. — *n.* An upward slope.

up·hold (up·hōld′) *v.t.* **·held, ·hold·ing 1.** To hold up; raise. **2.** To keep from falling. **3.** To support; agree with; encourage. **4.** To regard with approval. — **up·hold′er** *n.*

up·hol·ster (up·hōl′stər) *v.t.* To fit, as furniture, with coverings, cushioning, etc. [Back formation < UPHOLSTERER]

up·hol·ster·er (up·hōl′stər·ər) *n.* One who upholsters. [alter. of < ME *upholder* tradesman]

up·hol·ster·y (up·hōl′stər·ē, -strē) *n. pl.* **·ster·ies 1.** Fabric and fittings used in upholstering. **2.** The act, art, or business of upholstering.

up·keep (up′kēp′) *n.* The act or state of maintaining something; also, the cost of maintenance.

up·land (up′lənd, -land′) *n.* **1.** The higher portions of a region, district, farm, etc. **2.** The country in the interior. — *adj.* Pertaining to or situated in an upland.

up·lift (*v.* up·lift′; *adj., n.* up′lift′) *v.t.* **1.** To lift up; elevate. **2.** To raise the tone of; put on a higher plane, mentally or morally. — *n.* **1.** The act of raising, or the fact of being raised. **2.** A movement upward. **3.** Mental or spiritual stimulation or elevation. **4.** A movement aiming to improve the condition of the underprivileged. **5.** A brassiere designed to lift and support the breasts. — **up·lift′er** *n.*

up·most (up′mōst′) *adj.* Uppermost.

up·on (ə·pon′, ə·pôn′) *prep.* On, in all its meanings. — *adv.* On: completing a verbal idea: *The paper has been written upon.* [ME]

◆ **upon, on** *Upon* now differs little in use from *on*, the former being sometimes used for reasons of euphony and also when motion into position is involved. When *upon* means *up* and *on*, it is written as two words: *Let's go up on the roof.*

up·per (up′ər) *adj.* **1.** Higher than something else; being above. **2.** Higher or further inland in location, place, etc. **3.** Higher in station, rank, dignity, etc.; superior. — *n.* **1.** That part of a boot or shoe above the sole; the vamp. **2.** *Informal* An upper berth. **3.** *Slang* Any of various drugs that stimulate the central nervous system, as amphetamine. — **on one's uppers** *Informal* **1.** Having worn out the soles of one's shoes. **2.** At the end of one's resources.

Up·per (up′ər) *adj. Geol.* Designating a later period or a later formation of a specified period: the *Upper* Cambrian.

upper berth The top berth in a ship, railroad sleeping car, etc., where two bunks or beds are built one above the other.

up·per-brack·et (up′ər·brak′it) *adj.* Of or belonging to a higher bracket or level: an *upper-bracket* income.

upper case *Printing* **1.** Type for capital letters. See CASE². **2.** The capital letters of the alphabet.

up·per-case (up′ər·kās′) *Printing adj.* Of, in, or indicating capital letters, as distinguished from small letters. — *v.t.* **-cased, -cas·ing** To set as or change to capital letters.

upper class The socially or economically superior group in society. — **up′per-class′** (up′ər·klas′, -kläs′) *adj.*

up·per-class·man (up′ər·klas′mən, -kläs′-) *n. pl.* **-men** (-mən) A junior or senior in a school or college.

up·per·cut (up′ər·kut′) *n.* In boxing, a swinging blow upward, delivered under or inside the opponent's guard. — *v.t. & v.i.* **·cut, ·cut·ting** To strike with an uppercut.

upper hand Advantage: to get the *upper hand.*

Upper House The branch, in a bicameral legislature, where membership is usu., smaller and more restricted, as the British House of Lords. Also **upper house.**

up·per·most (up′ər·mōst′) *adj.* **1.** Highest in place, rank, authority, influence, etc. **2.** First to come into the mind: one's *uppermost* thoughts. Also *upmost.* — *adv.* In the highest place, rank, authority, etc.; also, first, as in time.

up·pish (up′ish) *adj. Informal* Inclined to be self-assertive, pretentious, or snobbish. Also **up·pi·ty** (up′ə·tē). — **up′·pish·ly** *adv.* — **up′pish·ness** *n.*

up·raise (up·rāz′) *v.t.* **·raised, ·rais·ing** To lift up; elevate.

up·right (up′rīt′) *adj.* **1.** Being in a vertical position; straight up; erect. **2.** Just and honest. — *n.* **1.** Something having a vertical position, as an upright piano. **2.** The state of being upright. **3.** In football, one of the goal posts. — *adv.* In an upright position; vertically. [OE < *ŭp-* up + *riht* right] — **up′right·ly** *adv.* — **up′right′ness** *n.*

upright piano A piano smaller than a grand piano, having strings arranged vertically in a rectangular case.

up·ris·ing (up·rī′zing, up′rī′zing) *n.* **1.** The act of rising. **2.** A revolt or insurrection. **3.** An ascent; a slope.

up·roar (up′rôr′, -rōr′) *n.* A violent disturbance, noise, or tumult. [< Du. < *op-* up + *roeren* to stir]

up·roar·i·ous (up·rôr′ē·əs, -rōr′ē-) *adj.* **1.** Accompanied by or making an uproar. **2.** Loud and noisy; tumultuous. **3.** Very funny: an *uproarious* play. — **up·roar′i·ous·ly** *adv.* — **up·roar′i·ous·ness** *n.*

up·root (up·rōōt′, -rŏŏt′) *v.t.* **1.** To tear up by the roots. **2.** To destroy utterly; eradicate. — **up·root′er** *n.*

up·set (*v.* up·set′; *adj.* up·set′, up′set′; *n.* up′set′) *v.* **·set, ·set·ting** *v.t.* **1.** To overturn. **2.** To throw into confusion or disorder. **3.** To disconcert, derange, or disquiet. **4.** To defeat, esp., unexpectedly. — *v.i.* **5.** To become overturned. — *adj.* **1.** Tipped or turned over. **2.** Mentally or physically disturbed or ill. **3.** Confused; disordered. — *n.* **1.** The act of upsetting, or the state of being upset. **2.** *Informal* An unexpected defeat. **3.** A mental or physical disturbance or disorder. — **up·set′ter** *n.*

up·shot (up′shot′) *n.* The final outcome; result.

up·side (up′sīd′) *n.* The upper side or part.

up·side-down (up′sīd′doun′) *adj.* Having the upper side down; in disorder. — *adv.* With the upper side down. Also **upside down.** [< ME *up so down* up as if down]

up·si·lon (yōōp′sə·lon, up′sə·lon, *Brit.* yōōp·sī′lən) *n.* The twentieth letter and sixth vowel in the Greek alphabet (Υ, υ). See ALPHABET, Υ. [< Gk. < *u* u + *psilon* smooth]

up·stage (up′stāj′) *adj.* **1.** Of the back half of a stage. **2.** *Informal* Haughty; supercilious. — *adv.* Toward or on the back of a stage. — *v.t.* **staged, stag·ing 1.** To steal a scene from. **2.** *Informal* To treat in a haughty manner.

up·stairs (up′stârz′) *adj.* Pertaining to an upper story. — *n.* An upper story; esp., the part of a building above the ground floor. — *adv.* In, to, or toward an upper story. — **to kick upstairs** To promote so as to get out of the way.

up·stand·ing (up·stan′ding) *adj.* **1.** Honest; upright; straightforward. **2.** Standing up; erect.

up·start (*v.* up·stärt′; *adj. & n.* up′stärt′) *v.t.* To start or spring up suddenly. — *adj.* **1.** Suddenly raised to prominence, wealth, or power. **2.** Characteristic of an upstart; vulgar; pretentious. — *n.* **1.** One who or that which springs up suddenly. **2.** One who has suddenly risen from a humble position to one of wealth or importance and is usu. arrogant.

up·state (up′stāt′) *U.S. adj.* Of, from, or designating that part of a State lying outside, usu. north, of the principal city. — *n.* The outlying, usu. northern, sections of a State; esp., the northern part of New York State. — *adv.* In or toward the outlying or northern sections of a State. — **up′stat′er** *n.*

up·stream (up′strēm′) *adv.* Toward or at the source or upper part of a stream; against the current.

up·stretched (up′strecht′) *adj.* Stretched or extended upward: *upstretched* arms.

up·stroke (up′strōk′) *n.* An upward stroke, as of a pen.

up·surge (*v.* up·sûrj′; *n.* up′sûrj′) *v.i.* **·surged, ·surg·ing** To surge up. — *n.* A surge or swell upward.

up·sweep (*n.* up′swēp′; *v.* up·swēp′) *n.* A sweeping up or upward; esp., a hairdo that is swept upward smoothly in the back and piled high on the top of the head. — *v.t. & v.i.* **·swept, ·sweep·ing** To brush or sweep upward or up.

up·swing (*n.* up′swing′; *v.* up·swing′) *n.* **1.** A swinging upward. **2.** An improvement. — *v.i.* **·swung, ·swing·ing 1.** To swing upward. **2.** To improve.

up·take (up′tāk′) *n.* **1.** The act of lifting or taking up. **2.** A boiler flue that unites the combustion gases and carries them toward the smokestack. **3.** An upward ventilating shaft in a mine. — **to be on** (or **in**) **the uptake** *Informal* To demonstrate mental comprehension or perception.

up·throw (up′thrō′) *n.* **1.** An upheaval. **2.** *Geol.* An upward displacement of the rock on one side of a fault.

up·thrust (up′thrust′) *n.* **1.** An upward thrust. **2.** *Geol.* An upheaval of rocks in the earth's crust.

up·tight (up′tīt′) *adj. U.S. Slang* Uneasy, anxious, or tense; nervous. Also **up′-tight′.** — **up′tight′ness** *n.*

up-to-date (up′tə-dāt′) *adj.* **1.** Having the latest information, improvements, etc.: an *up-to-date* dictionary. **2.** Modern in manner, fashion, or style.

up to date To the present time.

up·town (up′toun′) *adv.* In or toward the upper part of a town. — *adj.* Of, pertaining to, or resident in the upper part of a town or city, or the part that is regarded as the upper part. — *n.* The upper part of a town or city.

up·turn (*v.* up·tûrn′; *n.* up′tûrn′) *v.t.* **1.** To turn up or over, as sod with the plow. **2.** To overturn; upset. — *n.* A turning upward; an increase; an improvement.

up·ward (up′wərd) *adv.* **1.** In, to, or toward a higher place or position. **2.** To or toward the source, origin, etc.: to trace a stream *upward.* **3.** Toward a higher rank, amount, age, etc. **4.** Toward that which is better, nobler, etc. **5.** In excess; more. Also **up′wards.** — **upward** (or **upwards**) **of** Higher than; in excess of. — *adj.* In, on, turned, or directed toward a higher place. — **up′ward·ly** *adv.*

ur-¹ Var. of URO-¹.

ur-² Var. of URO-².

Ur (ûr) An ancient city of Sumer, southern Mesopotamia, the site of which is on the Euphrates in SE Iraq. Old Testament **Ur of the Chal·dees** (kal·dēz′, kal′dēz).

u·rae·mi·a (yōō·rē′mē·ə), **u·rae·mic** (yōō·rē′mik) See URE-MIA, etc.

U·ral-Al·ta·ic (yōōr′əl·al·tā′ik) *n.* A hypothesized family of languages comprising the Uralic and Altaic subfamilies. — *adj.* **1.** Of or pertaining to the Ural and Altai mountain ranges. **2.** Of, pertaining to, or designating the Ural-Altaic languages or the peoples speaking these languages.

U·ral·ic (yōō·ral′ik) *n.* A family of languages comprising the Finno-Ugric and Samoyedic subfamilies: sometimes classified with Altaic in a Ural-Altaic family. — *adj.* Of or pertaining to this family. Also **U·ra·li·an** (yōō·rā′lē·ən).

u·ra·nal·y·sis (yōōr′ə·nal′ə·sis) See URINALYSIS.

U·ra·ni·a (yōō·rā′nē·ə) The Muse of astronomy. [< L < Gk. *ouranos* heaven]

U·ra·ni·an (yōō·rā′nē·ən) *adj.* **1.** Of or pertaining to the planet Uranus. **2.** Celestial.

---

u·ra·ni·um (yŏŏ·rā'nē·əm) *n.* A heavy, white, radioactive, metallic element (symbol U), found only in combination. It is important in the generation of atomic energy. See ELEMENT. [< URANUS]

urano- *combining form* Astron. The heavens; of or pertaining to the heavens, or to celestial bodies. Also, before vowels, **uran-.** [< Gk. *ouranos* heaven]

U·ra·nus (yŏŏr'ə·nəs) In Greek mythology, the son and husband of Gaea (Earth) and father of the Titans, Furies, and Cyclopes, overthrown by his son Cronus. — *n.* The third largest planet of the solar system and seventh in order from the sun. See PLANET. [< L < Gk. < *ouranos* heaven]

u·ra·re (yŏŏ·rä'rē) *n.* Curare. Also **u·ra·ri.** [Var. of CURARE]

ur·ban (ûr'bən) *adj.* 1. Pertaining to, characteristic of, including, or constituting a city. 2. Situated or dwelling in a city. [< L *urbanus.* See URBANE.]

urban district An administrative subdivision of a county of England, Wales, or Northern Ireland, usu. comprising several thickly populated communities.

ur·bane (ûr·bān') *adj.* Characterized by or having refinement or elegance, esp. in manner; suave. [< L *urbs, urbis* city] — **ur·bane'ly** *adv.* — **ur·bane'ness** *n.*

ur·ban·ism (ûr'bən·iz'əm) *n.* The character or condition of the life of people living in urban areas.

ur·ban·ite (ûr'bən·īt) *n.* One who lives in a city.

ur·ban·i·ty (ûr·ban'ə·tē) *n. pl.* ·**ties** 1. The character or quality of being urbane; refined or elegant courtesy. 2. *pl.* Amenities or courtesies. [< F or L < *urbs, urbis* city]

ur·ban·ize (ûr'bən·īz) *v.t.* ·**ized, ·iz·ing** To render urban, as in character or manner. — **ur'ban·i·za'tion** *n.*

urban renewal The planned upgrading of a deteriorating urban area, usu. using public funds.

ur·chin (ûr'chin) *n.* 1. A roguish, mischievous boy. 2. A cylinder in a carding machine. 3. A sea urchin. [ME < OF < L *ericius* hedgehog < *er* hedgehog]

Ur·du (ōōr'dōō, ōōr·dōō', ûr'dōō) *n.* A variety of Hindustani spoken by Moslems in India, containing many Persian and Arabic elements and written in a Persian-Arabic script: the official language of Pakistan. [< Hind. < Turkish *ordū* camp < Persian *urdū*]

-ure *suffix of nouns* 1. The act, process, or result of: *pressure.* 2. The function, rank, or office of: *prefecture.* 3. The means or instrument of: *ligature.* [< F < L *-ura*]

u·re·a (yŏŏ·rē'ə) *n.* Biochem. A colorless crystalline compound, $CO(NH_2)_2$, formed in the body, and also made synthetically, used in medicine and in the making of plastics and fertilizers. [< NL < F < Gk. *ouron*] — **u·re'al** *adj.*

u·re·mi·a (yŏŏ·rē'mē·ə) *n.* Pathol. A condition of the blood due to the presence of urinary constituents ordinarily excreted by the kidneys. Also *uraemia.* — **u·re'mic** *adj.*

-uret *suffix* Chem. Used to denote a compound: now replaced by *-ide.* [< F < *-ure.* See *-URE.*]

u·re·ter (yŏŏ·rē'tər) *n.* Anat. The duct by which urine passes from the kidney to the bladder or the cloaca. For illus. see KIDNEY. [< NL < Gk. < *ourein* to urinate] — **u·re'ter·al, u·re·ter·ic** (yŏŏr'ə·ter'ik) *adj.*

u·re·thra (yŏŏ·rē'thrə) *n.* Anat. The duct by which urine is discharged from the bladder of most mammals, and which, in males, carries the seminal discharge. — **u·re'thral** *adj.*

urethro- *combining form* Med. The urethra; of or pertaining to the urethra. Also, before vowels, **urethr-.** [< Gk. *ourēthra* the urethra]

u·ret·ic (yŏŏ·ret'ik) *adj.* Med. Of or pertaining to the urine; urinary. [< LL *ureticus* < Gk. *ourētikos* < *ouron* urine]

urge (ûrj) *v.* **urged, urg·ing** *v.t.* 1. To drive or force forward; impel; push. 2. To plead with or entreat earnestly, as with arguments or explanations. 3. To press or argue the doing, consideration, or acceptance of. 4. To move or force to some course or action. 5. To stimulate or excite. 6. To ply or use vigorously, as oars. — *v.i.* 7. To present or press arguments, claims, etc. 8. To exert an impelling or prompting force. — Syn. See ACTUATE. — *n.* 1. A strong impulse to perform a certain act. 2. The act of urging; the state of being urged. [< L *urgere* to drive, urge]

ur·gen·cy (ûr'jən·sē) *n. pl.* ·**cies** 1. The quality of being urgent. 2. Pressure by entreaty; pressure of necessity. 3. The act of urging. 4. Something urgent.

ur·gent (ûr'jənt) *adj.* 1. Characterized by urging or importunity; requiring prompt attention; pressing. 2. Eagerly importunate or insistent. — **ur'gent·ly** *adv.*

-urgy *combining form* Development of or work with a (specified) material or product: *metallurgy, chemurgy.* [< Gk. *-ourgia* < *ergon* work]

-uria *combining form* Pathol. A (specified) condition of the urine: usu. used to indicate disease or abnormality. [< NL < Gk. *-ouria* < *ouron* urine]

U·ri·ah (yŏŏ·rī'ə) A Hittite captain in the Israelite army, husband of Bathsheba, treacherously sent to his death by David, II *Sam.* xi 15–17.

u·ric (yŏŏr'ik) *adj.* Of, pertaining to, or derived from urine.

uric acid Biochem. A colorless dibasic acid, $C_5H_4N_4O_3$, of varying crystalline forms and slight solubility, found in the urine of man and animals and, in man, forming the nucleus of most urinary and renal calculi.

u·ri·nal (yŏŏr'ə·nəl) *n.* 1. An upright wall fixture with facilities for flushing, for men's use in urination; also the room containing such a fixture. 2. A glass receptacle for urine.

u·ri·nal·y·sis (yŏŏr'ə·nal'ə·sis) *n. pl.* ·**ses** (-sēz) Chemical analysis of the urine: also spelled *uranalysis.*

u·ri·nar·y (yŏŏr'ə·ner'ē) *adj.* Of, pertaining to, or involved in the production and excretion of urine: the *urinary* organs. — *n. pl.* ·**nar·ies** 1. A reservoir for storing urine, etc., for use as manure. 2. A urinal.

u·ri·nate (yŏŏr'ə·nāt) *v.i.* ·**nat·ed, ·nat·ing** To void or pass urine. [< Med.L *urinatus,* pp. of *urinare* to pass urine < *urina* urine] — **u'ri·na'tion** *n.*

u·rine (yŏŏr'in) *n.* A liquid containing body wastes, secreted by the kidneys, stored in the bladder, and voided through the urethra. [< F < L *urina*]

urino- *combining form* Urine. Also, before vowels, **urin-,** as in *urinalysis.* [< L *urina* urine]

u·ri·no·gen·i·tal (yŏŏr'ə·nō·jen'ə·təl) *adj.* Urogenital.

u·ri·nos·co·py (yŏŏr'ə·nos'kə·pē) *n. pl.* ·**pies** Med. Uroscopy.

u·ri·nous (yŏŏr'ə·nəs) *adj.* Of, pertaining to, containing, or resembling urine. Also **u'ri·nose** (-nōs).

urn (ûrn) *n.* 1. A rounded or angular vase having a foot, variously used in antiquity as a receptacle for the ashes of the dead, a water vessel, etc. 2. A vessel for preserving the ashes of the dead. 3. In ancient Rome, a receptacle used to hold lots drawn in voting. 4. A vase-shaped receptacle having a faucet, and designed for keeping tea, coffee, etc., hot, as by means of a spirit lamp. [< L *urna*]

uro-[1] *combining form* Urine; pertaining to urine or to the urinary tract: *urology.* Also, before vowels, **ur-.** [< Gk. *ouron* urine]

uro-[2] *combining form* A tail; of or related to the tail; caudal. Also, before vowels, **ur-.** [< Gk. *oura* tail]

u·ro·gen·i·tal (yŏŏr'ō·jen'ə·təl) *adj.* Of or pertaining to the urinary and genital organs and their functions.

u·rol·o·gy (yŏŏ·rol'ə·jē) *n.* The branch of medicine that deals with the urine and the genitourinary tract. — **u·ro·log·ic** (yŏŏr'ə·loj'ik) or ·**i·cal** *adj.* — **u·rol'o·gist** *n.*

u·ros·co·py (yŏŏ·ros'kə·pē) *n. pl.* ·**pies** Med. Diagnosis by examination of the urine: also *urinoscopy.* — **u·ro·scop·ic** (yŏŏr'ə·skop'ik) *adj.* — **u·ros'co·pist** *n.*

ur·sa (ûr'sə) *n.* Latin A she-bear: used in the phrases *Ursa Major* and *Ursa Minor.*

Ursa Major A constellation, the Great Bear, containing seven bright stars: also called *Big Dipper, Charles's Wain.* [< L]

Ursa Minor A constellation, the Lesser Bear, containing the polestar Polaris: also called *Cynosure, Little Bear, Little Dipper.* [< L]

URSA MAJOR (*a*) AND URSA MINOR (*b*)
c Polestar.
d,d Pointers.

ur·sine (ûr'sīn, -sin) *adj.* 1. Pertaining to or like a bear. 2. Clothed with dense bristles, as certain caterpillars. [< L *ursinus* < *ursus* bear]

Ur·su·line (ûr'syə·lin, -sə-, -līn) *adj.* Pertaining to Saint Ursula or to an order of nuns founded in 1537, and engaged chiefly in the education of girls. — *n.* An Ursuline nun. [after Saint *Ursula,* 4th-c. Cornish princess and martyr]

ur·ti·car·i·a (ûr'tə·kâr'ē·ə) *n.* Pathol. A disease of the skin, characterized by transient eruptions and attended with itching. Also called *hives, nettle rash.* [< NL < L *urtica* nettle] — **ur'ti·car'i·al** or ·**i·ous** *adj.*

us (us) *pron.* The objective case of the pronoun *we.* [OE]

us·a·ble (yŏŏ'zə·bəl) *adj.* 1. Capable of being used. 2. That can be used conveniently. Also **use'a·ble.** — **us'a·ble·ness** *n.* — **us'a·bly** *adv.*

us·age (yŏŏ'sij, -zij) *n.* 1. The manner of using or treating a person or thing; treatment; also, the act of using. 2. Customary or habitual practice, or something permitted by it or done in accordance with it. 3. Uniform practice. 4. The customary way of using words, sounds, and grammatical forms in a language. 5. A particular verbal or written expression or application of such an expression: a contemptuous *usage.*

us·ance (yŏŏ'zəns) *n.* 1. A period of time, variable as between various countries, that, by commercial usage, is allowed, exclusive of days of grace, for payment of bills of exchange, esp. foreign. 2. Econ. An income derived from the possession of wealth, as by investment.

use (*v.* yŏŏz; *n.* yŏŏs) *v.* **used** (yŏŏzd; yŏŏst for defs. 5, 7), **us·ing** *v.t.* 1. To employ for the accomplishment of a purpose; make use of. 2. To put into practice or employ habitually; make a practice of: to *use* diligence in business. 3. To expend the whole of; consume: often with *up.* 4. To conduct oneself toward; treat: to *use* one badly. **5.** To make familiar by habit or practice; inure: now only in the past participle: He is *used* to exposure. **6.** To partake of; smoke or chew: He does not *use* tobacco. — *v.i.* **7.** To do something customarily or habitually: now only in the past tense as an auxiliary to form a phrase equivalent to a frequentative past tense: I *used* to go there. — *n.* **1.** The act of using; the fact or condition of being employed. **2.** Suitableness or adaptability to an end: the *uses* of adversity. **3.** Way or manner of using. **4.** Occasion or need to employ; purpose. **5.** Habitual practice or employment; custom. **6.** Any special form, ceremony, or ritual, or any individual service that arose in or was perpetuated by a church, diocese, or branch of a church: Roman *use*. **7.** *Law* The permanent equitable right that a beneficiary has to the enjoyment of the rents and profits of lands and tenements of which the legal title and possession are vested in another in trust for the beneficiary. — **to have no use for 1.** To have no need of. **2.** *Informal* To have a contempt or dislike for; want nothing to do with. [< OF < L *usus*, pp. of *uti* to use]

use·ful (yōōs′fəl) *adj.* Serviceable; serving a use or purpose, esp. a valuable one. — **use′ful·ly** *adv.* — **use′ful·ness** *n.*

use·less (yōōs′lis) *adj.* **1.** Unserviceable; being of no use; not capable of serving any beneficial purpose. **2.** Futile; in vain. — **use′less·ly** *adv.* — **use′less·ness** *n.*

us·er (yōō′zər) *n.* **1.** One who or that which uses. **2.** *Law* The exercise or enjoyment of a right.

ush·er (ush′ər) *n.* **1.** One who acts as doorkeeper, as of a court or other assembly room. **2.** An officer whose duty it is to introduce strangers or walk before a person of rank. **3.** One who conducts persons to seats, etc., as in a church or theater. **4.** *Brit.* An assistant or subordinate teacher in a school. — *v.t.* **1.** To act as an usher to; escort; conduct. **2.** To precede as a harbinger; be a forerunner of: usu. with *in*. [< OF < L *ostiarius* doorkeeper < *ostium* door]

ush·er·ette (ush′ə·ret′) *n.* A female usher, as in a theater.

us·nic acid (us′nik) A yellow, crystalline substance, $C_{18}H_{16}O_7$, derived from lichens, used as an antibiotic.

u·su·al (yōō′zhōō·əl) *adj.* Such as occurs in the ordinary course of events; frequent; common. [< OF < LL < L *usus* use] — **u′su·al·ly** *adv.* — **u′su·al·ness** *n.*

u·su·fruct (yōō′zyōō·frukt, yōō′syōō-) *n. Law* The right of using the property of another and of drawing the profits it produces without wasting its substance. [< LL < L < *usus et fructus* use and fruit]

u·su·fruc·tu·ar·y (yōō′zyōō·fruk′chōō·er′ē, yōō′syōō-) *n. pl.* **·ar·ies** One who holds property for use by usufruct, as a tenant. — *adj.* Of or pertaining to a usufruct.

u·su·rer (yōō′zhər·ər) *n.* One who practices usury; one who lends money, esp. at an exorbitant or illegal rate.

u·su·ri·ous (yōō·zhōōr′ē·əs) *adj.* Practicing usury; having the nature of usury. — **u·su′ri·ous·ly** *adv.* — **u·su′ri·ous·ness** *n.*

u·surp (yōō·zûrp′, -sûrp′) *v.t.* **1.** To seize and hold (the office, rights, or powers of another) without right or legal authority; take possession of by force. **2.** To take arrogantly, as if by right. — *v.i.* **3.** To practice usurpation; encroach: with *on* or *upon*. [< OF < L, ? < *usus* use + *rapere* to seize] — **u·surp′er** *n.* — **u·surp′ing·ly** *adv.*

u·sur·pa·tion (yōō′zər·pā′shən, -sər-) *n.* The act of usurping: said esp. of unlawful or forcible seizure of kingly power.

u·su·ry (yōō′zhər·ē) *n. pl.* **·ries 1.** The act or practice of exacting a rate of interest beyond what is allowed by law. **2.** A premium paid for the use of money beyond the rate of interest established by law. [< OF < L < *usus* used]

ut (ōot) *n. Music* The first syllable in the Guido solmization system: now commonly *do*. [See GAMUT.]

Ute (yōot, yōo′tē) *n.* One of a group of tribes of North American Indians of Shoshonean stock living in Colorado and Utah.

u·ten·sil (yōo·ten′səl) *n.* A vessel, tool, implement, etc., serving a useful purpose, esp. for domestic or farming use. [< OF < L *utensilis* fit for use < *utens*, ppr. of *uti* to use]

u·ter·ine (yōō′tər·in, -īn) *adj.* **1.** Pertaining to the uterus. **2.** Born of the same mother, but having a different father. [< LL *uterinus* born of the same mother]

utero- *combining form* The uterus; of or pertaining to the uterus. Also, before vowels, **uter-**. [< L *uterus* uterus]

u·ter·us (yōō′tər·əs) *n. pl.* **u·ter·i** (yōō′tər·ī) *Anat.* The organ of a female mammal in which the young are protected and developed before birth; the womb. [< L]

u·tile (yōō′til) *adj. Rare* Useful. [< OF < L *uti* to use]

u·til·i·dor (yōō·til′i·dôr) *n. Canadian* A system of pipes,

cables, etc., raised and insulated to provide utilities to communities on the permafrost.

u·til·i·tar·i·an (yōō·til′ə·târ′ē·ən) *adj.* **1.** Relating to utility; esp., placing utility above beauty or the amenities of life. **2.** Pertaining to or advocating utilitarianism. — *n.* **1.** An advocate of utilitarianism. **2.** One devoted to mere material utility.

u·til·i·tar·i·an·ism (yōō·til′ə·târ′ē·ən·iz′əm) *n.* **1.** *Philos.* **a** The doctrine that actions derive their moral quality from their usefulness as means to some end, as happiness. **b** The ethical theory, held by Jeremy Bentham and John Stuart Mill, that the greatest human happiness determines the highest moral good. **2.** Devotion to mere material interests.

u·til·i·ty (yōō·til′ə·tē) *n. pl.* **·ties 1.** Fitness for some desirable, practical purpose; also, that which is necessary. **2.** Fitness to supply the natural needs of man. **3.** A public service, as gas, water, etc. **4.** *pl.* Shares of utility company stocks. **5.** In utilitarianism, the greatest happiness for the greatest number of people. [< F < L *utilis* useful]

u·til·ize (yōō′təl·īz) *v.t.* **·ized**, **·iz·ing** To make useful; turn to practical account; make use of. Also *Brit.* **u′til·ise.** — **u′til·iz·a·ble** *adj.* — **u·til·i·za′tion** *n.* — **u′til·iz′er** *n.*

ut·most (ut′mōst) *adj.* **1.** Of the highest degree or the largest amount or number; greatest. **2.** Being at the farthest limit or point. — *n.* The greatest possible extent; the most possible. Also *uttermost*. [OE *ūtmest, ȳtemest*]

U·to-Az·tec·an (yōō′tō·az′tek·ən) *n.* **1.** One of the chief stocks of North and Central American Indians, formerly occupying two large regions of the NW and SW U.S., comprising three branches (Shoshonean, Piman, and Nahuatlan) and embracing about fifty tribes, still surviving in the U.S. and Mexico. **2.** The family of languages spoken by these peoples. — *adj.* Of or pertaining to the Uto-Aztecans or their languages.

u·to·pi·a (yōō·tō′pē·ə) *n.* **1.** Any state, condition, or place of ideal perfection. **2.** A visionary, impractical scheme for social improvement. [after *Utopia*]

U·to·pi·a (yōō·tō′pē·ə) An imaginary island described as the seat of a perfect social and political life in a romance by Sir Thomas More, published in 1516. [< NL < Gk. *ou* not + *topos* place] — **U·to′pi·an** *n. & adj.*

u·to·pi·an (yōō·tō′pē·ən) *adj.* Excellent, but existing only in fancy or theory; ideal. — *n.* One who advocates impractical reforms; a visionary. — **u·to′pi·an·ism** *n.*

u·tri·cle (yōō′tri·kəl) *n. Anat.* The larger of two saclike cavities found in the bony vestibule of the inner ear. [< L *utriculus*, dim. of *uter* skin bag]

u·tric·u·lar (yōō·trik′yə·lər) *adj.* **1.** Resembling a utricle or small sac. **2.** Bladderlike; bearing or provided with utricles. Also **u·tric′u·late** (-lit, -lāt).

ut·ter¹ (ut′ər) *v.t.* **1.** To give out or send forth with audible sound; say. **2.** *Law* To put in circulation; now, esp. to deliver or offer (something forged or counterfeit) to another. [ME *outre*, freq. of obs. *out* to say, speak out < OE *ūt*] — **ut′ter·a·ble** *adj.* — **ut′ter·er** *n.*

ut·ter² (ut′ər) *adj.* **1.** Absolute; total: *utter* misery. **2.** Being or done without conditions or qualifications; final; absolute: *utter* denial. [OE *ūtera*, orig. compar. of *ūt* out]

ut·ter·ance (ut′ər·əns) *n.* **1.** The act of uttering; vocal expression; manner of speaking; also, the power of speech. **2.** A thing uttered or expressed. **3.** *Ling.* Any stretch of speech capable of being isolated from the flow of connected discourse, as a word, phrase, or sentence.

ut·ter·ly (ut′ər·lē) *adv.* Thoroughly; entirely.

ut·ter·most (ut′ər·mōst′) *adj. & n.* Utmost.

U-turn (yōō′tûrn′) *n. Informal* A continuous turn that reverses the direction of a vehicle on a road.

u·vu·la (yōō′vyə·lə) *n. pl.* **·las** or **·lae** (-lē) *Anat.* The pendent fleshy portion of the soft palate. For illus. see MOUTH, THROAT. [< LL, dim. of *uva* grape]

u·vu·lar (yōō′vyə·lər) *adj.* **1.** Pertaining to or of the uvula. **2.** *Phonet.* Produced by vibration of, or with the back of the tongue near or against, the uvula. — *n. Phonet.* A uvular sound.

ux·o·ri·al (uk·sôr′ē·əl, -sō′rē-, ug·zôr′ē·əl, -zō′rē-) *adj.* **1.** Of, pertaining to, characteristic of, or becoming to a wife. **2.** Uxorious. [< L *uxor* wife]

ux·o·ri·ous (uk·sôr′ē·əs, -sō′rē-, ug·zôr′ē-, -zō′rē-) *adj.* Fatuously or foolishly devoted to one's wife. [< L *uxor* wife] — **ux·o′ri·ous·ly** *adv.* — **ux·o′ri·ous·ness** *n.*

Uz·bek (ōoz′bek, uz′-) *n.* **1.** A member of a Turkic people dominant in Turkestan; a native or inhabitant of the Uzbek S.S.R. **2.** The Turkic language of the Uzbeks. Also **Uz′beg.**

V

v, V (vē) *n. pl.* **v's** or **vs, V's** or **Vs, vees** (vēz) 1. The twenty-second letter of the English alphabet. 2. The sound represented by the letter *v*, the voiced, labiodental fricative. 3. Anything shaped like a V. — *symbol* 1. *Informal* A five-dollar bill. 2. The Roman numeral five. 3. *Chem.* Vanadium (symbol V).

va·can·cy (vā′kən·sē) *n. pl.* **·cies** 1. The state of being vacant; vacuity; emptiness. 2. That which is vacant or unoccupied; empty space. 3. An unoccupied post, place, or office; a place destitute of an incumbent.

va·cant (vā′kənt) *adj.* 1. Containing or holding nothing; esp. devoid of occupants; empty. 2. Occupied with nothing; unemployed; unencumbered; free. 3. Being or appearing without intelligence; inane. 4. Having no incumbent; unfilled: a *vacant* office. 5. *Law* Unoccupied or unused, as land; also, abandoned; having neither claimant nor heir, as an estate. 6. Free from cares. 7. Devoid of thought. [< F < L *vacare* to be empty] — **va′cant·ly** *adv.* — **va′cant·ness** *n.*

va·cate (vā′kāt) *v.* **·cat·ed, ·cat·ing** *v.t.* 1. To make vacant; surrender possession of by removal. 2. To set aside; annul. 3. To give up (a position or office); quit. — *v.i.* 4. To leave an office, position, place, etc. 5. *Informal* To go away; leave. — **Syn.** See ANNUL.

va·ca·tion (vā·kā′shən) *n.* 1. An interlude, usu. of several days or weeks, from one's customary duties, as for recreation or rest. 2. *Law* The period of time between stated terms of court. 3. The intermission of the course of studies and exercises in an educational institution. 4. The act of vacating. — *v.i.* To take a vacation. [< F < L *vacatio, -onis* freedom from duty] — **va·ca′tion·er** *n.*

va·ca·tion·ist (vā·kā′shən·ist) *n.* One who is taking a vacation or staying at a resort; a tourist.

vac·ci·nate (vak′sə·nāt) *v.* **·nat·ed, ·nat·ing** *Med. v.t.* 1. To inoculate with a vaccine as a preventive measure; esp. to inoculate against smallpox. — *v.i.* 2. To perform vaccination. — **vac′ci·na′tor** *n.*

vac·ci·na·tion (vak′sə·nā′shən) *n. Med.* The act or process of vaccinating, esp. against smallpox.

vac·cine (vak′sēn, -sin) *n.* 1. The virus of cowpox, as prepared for or introduced by vaccination. 2. Any preparation containing bacteria or viruses so treated as to give immunity from specific diseases when injected into the subject. [< L *vaccinus* pertaining to a cow] — **vac′ci·nal** (sə·nəl) *adj.*

vac·cin·i·a (vak·sin′ē·ə) *n. Vet.* Cowpox.

vac·il·late (vas′ə·lāt) *v.i.* **·lat·ed, ·lat·ing** 1. To sway one way and the other; totter; waver. 2. To fluctuate. 3. To waver in mind; be irresolute. [< L *vacillare* to waver] — **vac′il·lan·cy** (-lən·sē) *n.* — **vac′il·lant** (-lənt) *adj.* — **vac′il·la·to·ry** (-lə·tôr′ē, -tō′rē) *adj.*
— **Syn.** 3. To *vacillate* is to incline to one alternative and then another, without coming to a decision. To *waver* is to be undecided whether to embark on a chosen course. *Falter* suggests failure to act through weakness, timidity, or fright.

vac·u·a (vak′yōō·ə) Alternative plural of VACUUM.

va·cu·i·ty (va·kyōō′ə·tē) *n. pl.* **·ties** 1. The state of being a vacuum: emptiness. 2. Vacant space; a void. 3. Freedom from mental exertion. 4. Lack of intelligence. 5. An inane or idle thing or statement. [< L *vacuus* empty]

vac·u·ole (vak′yōō·ōl) *n. Biol.* A minute cavity containing air, a watery fluid, or a chemical secretion of the protoplasm, found in an organ, tissue, or cell. For illus. see CELL. [< F < L *vacuus* empty] — **vac′u·o·lar** *adj.*

vac·u·ous (vak′yōō·əs) *adj.* 1. Having no contents; empty. 2. Lacking intelligence; blank. 3. Idle; unoccupied. [< L *vacuus*] — **vac′u·ous·ly** *adv.* — **vac′u·ous·ness** *n.*

vac·u·um (vak′yōō·əm, -yōōm) *n. pl.* **·u·ums** or **·u·a** (-yōō·ə) 1. A space absolutely devoid of matter. 2. A space from which air or other gas has been exhausted to a very high degree. 3. A void; an empty feeling. 4. A condition of isolation from environmental influences. — *adj.* 1. Of, or used in the production of, a vacuum. 2. Exhausted or partly exhausted of gas, air, or vapor. 3. Operated by suction to produce a vacuum. — *v.t. & v.i. Informal* To clean with a vacuum cleaner: to *vacuum* a rug. [< L, neut. of *vacuus* empty]

vacuum bottle A thermos bottle. Also **vacuum flask.**

vacuum cleaner A machine for cleaning carpets, furnishings, etc., by suction. — **vacuum cleaning**

vacuum pump A pulsometer.

vacuum tube *Electronics* 1. A glass tube exhausted of air to a high degree and containing electrodes between which electric discharges may be passed. 2. An electron tube.

vacuum valve *Brit.* A vacuum tube.

va·de me·cum (vā′dē mē′kəm) *Latin* Anything carried for constant use, as a guidebook, manual, or bag; literally, go with me. Also **va′de·me′cum, va′de·me′cum.**

vag·a·bond (vag′ə·bond) *n.* 1. One who wanders from place to place without visible means of support; a tramp. 2. One without a settled home; a wanderer; nomad. 3. A worthless fellow; rascal. — *adj.* 1. Pertaining to a vagabond; nomadic. 2. Having no definite residence; wandering; irresponsible. 3. Driven to and fro; aimless. [< F < L *vagus* wandering] — **vag′a·bond′age** (-ij) *n.* — **vag′a·bond′ish** *adj.* — **vag′a·bond·ism** *n.*

va·gar·y (və·gâr′ē, vā′gər·ē) *n. pl.* **·gar·ies** A wild fancy; extravagant notion. [< L *vagari* to wander]

va·gi·na (və·jī′nə) *n. pl.* **·nas** or **·nae** (-nē) *Anat.* The canal leading from the external genital orifice in female mammals to the uterus. [< L, sheath] — **vag′i·nal** (vaj′ə·nəl, və·jī′-) *adj.*

vag·i·nate (vaj′ə·nit, -nāt) *adj.* 1. Having a sheath. 2. Formed into a sheath; tubular. Also **vag′i·nat′ed** (-nā′tid). [< NL < L *vagina* sheath]

vagino- *combining form Med.* The vagina; of or pertaining to the vagina. Also, before vowels, **vagin-.** [< L *vagina* sheath, vagina]

va·gran·cy (vā′grən·sē) *n. pl.* **·cies** The state of being a vagrant. Also **va′grant·ness.**

va·grant (vā′grənt) *n.* 1. A person without a settled home; an idle wanderer; vagabond; tramp. 2. A roving person. — *adj.* 1. Wandering about as a vagrant. 2. Pertaining to one who or that which wanders; nomadic. 3. Having a wandering course; capricious; wayward. [ME, alter. of AF *wakerant* < OF *wacrer* to walk, wander < Gmc.; infl. in form by L *vagari* to wander] — **va′grant·ly** *adv.*

vague (vāg) *adj.* **va·guer, va·guest** 1. Lacking definiteness or precision. 2. Of uncertain source or authority: a *vague* rumor. 3. Not clearly recognized, understood, stated, or felt. 4. Shadowy; hazy. [< F < L *vagus* wandering] — **vague′ly** *adv.* — **vague′ness** *n.*

va·gus (vā′gəs) *n. pl.* **·gi** (-jī) *Anat.* Either of the tenth pair of cranial nerves sending branches to the lungs, heart, stomach, and most of the abdominal viscera. Also **vagus nerve.** [< L, wandering]

vain (vān) *adj.* 1. Filled with or showing undue admiration for oneself, one's appearance, etc.; conceited. 2. Unproductive; worthless; fruitless: a *vain* attempt. 3. Having no real basis or worth; empty: *vain* hopes. 4. Ostentatious; showy. — **in vain** To no purpose; without effect. [< F < L *vanus* empty] — **vain′ly** *adv.* — **vain′ness** *n.*
— **Syn.** 1. proud, vainglorious. 2. abortive. See FUTILE.

vain·glo·ry (vān·glôr′ē, -glō′rē) *n. pl.* **·ries** Excessive or groundless vanity; also, vain pomp; boastfulness. — **Syn.** See PRIDE. [< OF < Med.L *vana gloria* empty pomp, show] — **vain·glo′ri·ous** (-glôr′ē·əs, -glō′rē-) *adj.* — **vain·glo′ri·ous·ly** *adv.* — **vain·glo′ri·ous·ness** *n.*

val·ance (val′əns, vā′ləns) *n.* 1. A hanging drapery, as from the framework of a bed to the floor, from a shelf, etc. 2. A short drapery, board, or plate across the top of a window. — *v.t.* **·anced, ·anc·ing** To furnish with or as with a valance. [< OF *avaler* to descend, or after *Valence*, textile-manufacturing commune in France] — **val′anced** *adj.*

vale[1] (vāl) *n. Chiefly Poetic* A valley. [< OF < L *vallis*]

va·le[2] (vā′lē) *interj. Latin* Farewell.

val·e·dic·tion (val′ə·dik′shən) *n.* A bidding farewell. [< L < *valere* to be well + *dicere* to say]

val·e·dic·to·ri·an (val′ə·dik·tôr′ē·ən, -tō′rē-) *n.* A student who delivers a valedictory at graduating exercises, usu. the graduating student ranking highest in scholarship.

val·e·dic·to·ry (val′ə·dik′tər·ē) *adj.* Pertaining to a leave-taking. — *n. pl.* **·ries** A parting address, as by a member of a graduating class.

va·lence (vā′ləns) *n. Chem.* 1. The property possessed by an element or radical of combining with or replacing other elements or radicals in definite and constant proportion. 2.

The number of atoms of hydrogen (or its equivalent) with which an atom or radical can combine, or which it can replace. Also **va/len·cy.** [< LL < L *valere* to be strong]

val·en·tine (val/ən-tīn) *n.* 1. A greeting card or token of affection sent on Saint Valentine's Day. 2. A sweetheart.

va·le·ri·an (və-lir/ē-ən) *n.* Any of various perennial herbs; esp., one species with small pink or white flowers and a strong odor: also called *heliotrope.* [< OF < Med.L, appar. ult. < *Valerius*, a personal name]

val·et (val/ā, val/it; *Fr.* vå·le/) *n.* 1. A gentleman's personal servant. 2. A manservant in a hotel who performs personal services for patrons. — *v.t. & v.i.* To serve or act as a valet. [< F, a groom < OF *vaslet, varlet,* dim. of *vasal* vassal]

val·e·tu·di·nar·i·an (val/ə·tōō/də·nâr/ē·ən, -tyōō/-) *n.* A chronic invalid; one unduly solicitous about his health. — *adj.* Seeking to recover health; infirm. Also **val/e·tu/di·nar/y.** [< L *valetudo* health, ill health < *valere* to be well] — **val/e·tu/di·nar/i·an·ism** *n.*

Val·hal·la (val·hal/ə) In Norse mythology, the great hall into which the souls of heroes fallen bravely in battle were borne by the valkyries and received and feasted by Odin. [< NL < ON *valr* the slain + *höll* hall]

val·iant (val/yənt) *adj.* 1. Strong and intrepid; powerful and courageous. 2. Performed with valor; bravely conducted; heroic. [< OF < L *valere* to be strong] — **val/iant·ly** *adv.* — **val/iance, val/ian·cy, val/iant·ness** *n.*

val·id (val/id) *adj.* 1. Based on evidence that can be supported; acceptable; convincing. 2. Legally binding; effective; warranted. 3. Properly derived from accepted premises by the rules of logic. [< F < L *validus* powerful < *valere* to be strong] — **val/id·ly** *adv.* — **val/id·ness** *n.*

val·i·date (val/ə·dāt) *v.t.* **·dat·ed, ·dat·ing** 1. To make valid; ratify and confirm. 2. To declare legally valid; legalize. — Syn. See RATIFY. — **val/i·da/tion** *n.*

va·lid·i·ty (və·lid/ə·tē) *n.* *pl.* **·ties** 1. The state or quality of being valid; soundness, as in law or reasoning; efficacy.

va·lise (və·lēs/) *n.* A portable case or bag for clothes, etc., used when traveling; a suitcase. [< F < Ital. *valigia*]

val·kyr·ie (val·kir/ē, val/kir·ē) *n.* Often *cap.* In Norse mythology, one of the maidens who ride through the air and choose heroes from among those slain in battle, and carry them to Valhalla. Also **val/kyr.** [< ON < *valr* the slain + stem of *kjósa* to choose, select] — **val·kyr/i·an** *adj.*

val·ley (val/ē) *n.* *pl.* **·leys** 1. A depression of the earth's surface, as one through which a stream flows; level or low land between mountains, hills, or high lands. 2. Any depression or hollow like a valley. [< OF < L *vallis* valley]

val·or (val/ər) *n.* Courage; personal bravery. Also *Brit.* **val/our.** [< OF < LL < L *valere* to be strong] — **val/or·ous** *adj.* — **val/or·ous·ly** *adv.* — **val/or·ous·ness** *n.*

val·or·i·za·tion (val/ər·ə·zā/shən, -ī·zā/-) *n.* The maintenance by governmental action of an artificial price for any product. [< Pg. *valorização* < *valor* value < LL. See VALOR.]

val·or·ize (val/ə·rīz) *v.t.* **·ized, ·iz·ing** To subject to valorization. Also **val/or·ise.**

val·u·a·ble (val/yōō·ə·bəl, val/yə·bəl) *adj.* 1. Having relatively great financial worth, price, or value; costly. 2. Of a nature or character capable of being valued or estimated. 3. Having moral worth, value, or importance; worthy. — *n.* *Usu. pl.* An article of worth or value, as a piece of jewelry. — **val/u·a·ble·ness** *n.* — **val/u·a·bly** *adv.*

val·u·a·tion (val/yōō·ā/shən) *n.* 1. The act of valuing. 2. Estimated worth or value. 3. Personal estimation; judgment of merit or character. — **val/u·a/tion·al** *adj.*

val·ue (val/yōō) *n.* 1. The desirability or worth of a thing; intrinsic worth; utility. 2. Often *pl.* Something regarded as desirable, worthy, or right, as a belief, standard, or moral precept. 3. The rate at which a commodity is potentially exchangeable for others; a fair return in service, goods, etc.; worth in money; market price; also, the ratio of utility to price; a bargain. 4. Attributed or assumed valuation; esteem or regard. 5. Exact meaning. 6. *Music* The relative length of a tone as signified by a note. 7. *Math.* The quantity, magnitude, or number an algebraic symbol or expression is supposed to denote. 8. Rank in a system of classification. 9. In the graphic arts, the relation of the elements of a picture, as light and shade, to one another. 10. *Phonet.* The special quality of the sound represented by a written character. — *v.t.* **·ued, ·u·ing** 1. To estimate the value or worth of; appraise. 2. To regard highly; esteem; prize. 3. To place a relative estimate of value or desirability upon. 4. To give a (specified) value to. [< OF *valoir* to be worth < L *valere*] — **val/ue·less** *adj.* — **val/u·er** *n.*

val·ued (val/yōōd) *adj.* 1. Regarded or estimated; much or highly esteemed. 2. Having a (specified) value.

val·vate (val/vāt) *adj.* 1. Serving as or resembling a valve; having a valve; valvular. 2. *Bot.* Meeting without overlapping, as petals. [< L *valvatus* with folding doors]

valve (valv) *n.* 1. *Mech.* Any contrivance or arrangement that regulates the amount and direction of flow of a liquid, gas, vapor, or loose material. 2. *Anat.* A structure formed by one or more loose folds of the lining membrane of a vessel or other organ, allowing flow of a fluid in one direction only, as blood to and from the heart. 3. *Zool.* One of the parts of a shell, as of a mollusk. 4. A device in certain brass instruments for lengthening the air column and lowering the pitch of the instrument's scale. — *v.t.* **valved, valv·ing** To furnish with valves; control the flow of by means of a valve. [< L *valva* leaf of a door] — **val/val** (-vəl), **val/var** (-vər) *adj.* — **valve/less** *adj.*

val·vu·lar (val/vyə·lər) *adj.* 1. Pertaining to or of the nature of a valve, as of the heart. 2. Having valves.

va·moose (va·mōōs/) *v.t. & v.i.* **·moosed, ·moos·ing** *U.S. Slang* To leave hastily or hurriedly; quit. Also **va·mose/** (-mōs/). [< Sp. *vamos* let us go < L *vadere* to go]

vamp[1] (vamp) *n.* 1. The piece of leather forming the upper front part of a boot or shoe. 2. Something added to give an old thing a new appearance. 3. *Music* A simple improvised accompaniment. — *v.t.* 1. To provide with a vamp. 2. To repair or patch. 3. *Music* To improvise an accompaniment to. — *v.i.* 4. *Music* To improvise accompaniments. [< OF < *avant* before + *pied* foot] — **vamp/er** *n.*

vamp[2] (vamp) *Informal* *v.t.* 1. To seduce (a man) by utilizing one's feminine charms. — *v.i.* 2. To play the vamp. — *n.* An unscrupulous flirt. [Short for VAMPIRE] — Syn. (noun) siren, temptress, gold-digger, femme fatale.

vam·pire (vam/pīr) *n.* 1. In folklore, a corpse that rises from its grave at night to feed upon the living, usu. by sucking the blood. 2. A man or woman who victimizes persons of the opposite sex; esp., a woman who brings her lover to a state of poverty or degradation. 3. A large bat of South or Central America, that drinks the blood of horses, cattle, and, sometimes, men. 4. An insectivorous or frugivorous bat formerly supposed to suck blood. [< F < G *vampir* < Slavic] — **vam·pir·ic** (vam·pir/ik), **vam/pir·ish** (-pīr·ish) *adj.* — **vam/pir·ism** (-pī·riz/əm, -pə-) *n.*

van[1] (van) *n.* 1. A large covered vehicle for transporting furniture, livestock, etc. 2. *Brit.* A closed railway car for luggage, etc. [Short for CARAVAN]

van[2] (van) *n.* 1. The portion of an army, fleet, etc., that is nearest or in advance of the front: opposed to *rear.* 2. The leaders of a movement; those at the front of any line or unit. [Short for VANGUARD]

va·na·di·um (və·nā/dē·əm) *n.* A rare, silver-white metallic element (symbol V), used in steel alloys to increase tensile strength. See ELEMENT. [< NL < ON *Vanadis,* a name of the Norse goddess Freya]

Van Al·len radiation (van al/ən) A high-intensity radiation consisting of charged atomic particles believed to circle the earth in an inner and outer belt conforming to the earth's magnetic field. Also **Van Allen belts.** [after James A. *Van Allen,* born 1914, U.S. physicist]

van·dal (van/dəl) *n.* One who willfully destroys or defaces property, esp. anything artistic. — *adj.* Wantonly destructive. [< VANDAL] — **van·dal·ic** (van·dal/ik) *adj.*

Van·dal (van/dəl) *n.* One of a Germanic people who ravaged Gaul and overran Spain and North Africa in the early part of the fifth century, and pillaged the city of Rome in 455. — **Van·dal·ic** (van·dal/ik) *adj.* — **Van/dal·ism** *n.*

van·dal·ism (van/dəl·iz/əm) *n.* Willful destruction or defacement of artistic works, or of property in general.

Van·dyke beard (van·dīk/) A short pointed beard resembling those depicted in the paintings of Anthony Van Dyck.

vane (vān) *n.* 1. A thin plate of metal or wood that pivots on a vertical rod to indicate the direction of the wind; weather vane. 2. An arm or blade extending from a rotating shaft, as of a windmill, propeller, turbine, etc. 3. *Ornithol.* The web of a feather. [OE *fana* flag] — **vaned** *adj.*

van·guard (van/gärd) *n.* 1. The advance guard of an army; the van. 2. Those in the forefront of a movement, as in art, etc. [< OF < *avant* before + *garde* guard]

WINDMILL VANES

va·nil·la (və·nil/ə) *n.* 1. A flavoring extract made from the podlike seed capsules of a climbing tropical orchid. 2. The seed capsule of this plant: also **vanilla bean.** 3. A food, as ice cream, flavored with vanilla. [< NL < Sp. dim. of *vaina* sheath, pod < L *vagina* sheath] — **va·nil/lic** (-ik) *adj.*

va·nil·lin (və·nil/in) *n.* *Chem.* A colorless, fragrant, crystalline compound, $C_8H_8O_3$, contained in vanilla, and also made synthetically. Also **va·nil·line** (və·nil/in, -ēn)

van·ish (van/ish) *v.i.* 1. To disappear from sight; fade away; depart. 2. To pass out of existence; be annihilated. [< OF < L *evanescere* to fade away] — **van/ish·er** *n.*

van·ish·ing point (van′ish·ing) In perspective, the point at which parallel lines appear to converge.

van·i·ty (van′ə·tē) *n. pl.* **·ties** 1. The condition or character of being vain; excessive personal pride; conceit. 2. Ambitious display; ostentation; show. 3. The quality or state of being fruitless, useless, or destitute of reality, etc. 4. That which is vain or unsubstantial. 5. A bag or box containing cosmetics, comb, mirror, etc.: also **vanity case**. 6. A dressing table. [< OF < L *vanus* empty, vain]

van·quish (vang′kwish, van′-) *v.t.* 1. To defeat in battle; overcome; conquer. 2. To suppress or overcome (a feeling). 3. To defeat, as in argument. [< OF < L *vincere* to conquer] **—van′quish·a·ble** *adj.* **—van′quish·er** *n.*

van·tage (van′tij) *n.* 1. Superiority over a competitor or opponent; advantage. 2. Advantage (def. 4). 3. An opportunity; chance. [OF < L *ab ante* from before]

vantage ground A position or condition that gives one an advantage.

vantage point A strategic position affording perspective; point of view.

van·ward (van′wərd) *adj.* Of or situated in the van or front. **—** *adv.* To or toward the van or front.

vap·id (vap′id) *adj.* 1. Having lost sparkling quality and flavor. 2. Flat; dull; insipid. [< L *vapidus* insipid] **—va·pid·i·ty** (ve·pid′ə·tē), **vap′id·ness** *n.* **—vap′id·ly** *adv.*

va·por (vā′pər) *n.* 1. Moisture in the air; esp., visible floating moisture, as light mist. 2. Any light, cloudy substance in the air, as smoke or fumes. 3. Any substance in the gaseous state, that is usu. a liquid or solid. 4. A gas below its critical temperature. 5. That which is fleeting and unsubstantial. **—** *v.t.* 1. To vaporize. **—** *v.i.* 2. To emit vapor. 3. To evaporate. 4. To brag. Also *Brit.* **va′pour**. [< AF < OF < L *vapor* steam] **—va·por·a·bil′i·ty** *n.* **—va′por·a·ble** *adj.* **—va′por·er** *n.* **—va′por·ish** *adj.*

vapori- *combining form* Vapor; of or related to vapor, steam, etc. Also, before vowels, **vapor-**. [< L *vapor* steam]

va·por·ize (vā′pə·rīz) *v.t. & v.i.* **·ized, ·iz·ing** To convert or be converted into vapor. **—va′por·iz′a·ble** *adj.* **—va′por·i·za·tion** (-ə·zā/shən, -ī·zā′-) **va′por·iz′er** *n.*

va·por·ous (vā′pər·əs) *adj.* 1. Of or like vapor; foggy; misty. 2. Full of or producing vapors. 3. Diaphanous; ethereal. 4. Vainly imaginative; whimsical. Also **va′por·y**. **—va·por·os·i·ty** (vā′pə·ros′ə·tē) *n.* **—va′por·ous·ly** *adv.* **—va′por·ous·ness** *n.*

vapor pressure *Physics* The pressure of a confined vapor in equilibrium with its liquid at any specific temperature. Also **vapor tension**.

vapor trail *Aeron.* A contrail.

va·que·ro (vä·kā′rō) *n. pl.* **·ros** (-rōz, *Sp.* -rōs) A herdsman; cowboy. [< Sp. < L *vacca* cow]

vari- *combining form* Various; different: *variform, varicolored.* Also **vario-**. [< *varius* varied]

var·i·a·ble (vâr′ē·ə·bəl) *adj.* 1. Having the capacity of varying; alterable; mutable. 2. Having a tendency to change; not constant; fickle. 3. Having no definite value as regards quantity. 4. *Biol.* Prone to variation from a normal or established type. **—** *n.* 1. That which varies or is subject to change. 2. *Math.* A quantity susceptible of fluctuating in value or magnitude under different conditions. [< OF < L < *varius* various, diverse] **—var′i·a·bil′i·ty, var′i·a·ble·ness** *n.* **—var′i·a·bly** *adv.*

variable star *Astron.* Any of several groups of stars whose apparent magnitude varies at different times.

var·i·ance (vâr′ē·əns) *n.* 1. The act of varying, or the state of being variant; difference; discrepancy. 2. Dissension; discord. **—at variance** 1. Disagreeing or conflicting, as facts. 2. In a state of dissension or discord.

var·i·ant (vâr′ē·ənt) *adj.* 1. Having or showing variation; differing. 2. Tending to vary; changing. 3. Restless; fickle; inconstant. 4. Differing from a standard or type. **—** *n.* A thing that differs from another in form only; esp., a different spelling or pronunciation of a word. [See VARIABLE]

var·i·a·tion (vâr′ē·ā′shən) *n.* 1. The act, process, state, or result of varying; modification; diversity. 2. The extent to which a thing varies. 3. A repetition with its essential features intact and other features modified. 4. *Music* A modification of the rhythm, harmony, melodic pattern, etc., of a basic theme. 5. *Biol.* Deviation in structure or function from the type or parent form of an organism. [< F < L *variatio, -onis*] **—var′i·a′tion·al** *adj.*

varico- *combining form Med.* A varicose vein; varix. Also, before vowels, **varic-**. [< L *varix, -icis* varicose vein]

var·i·col·ored (vâr′i·kul′ərd) *adj.* Variegated in color; parti-colored; of various colors. Also *Brit.* **var′i·col′oured**.

var·i·cose (var′ə·kōs) *adj. Pathol.* Abnormally dilated, as veins. [< L *varix, -icis* varicose vein] **—var′i·cos′i·ty** (-kos′ə·tē) *n.*

var·ied (vâr′ēd) *adj.* 1. Consisting of differing parts; diverse. 2. Partially or repeatedly altered, modified, etc. 3. Varicolored. **—var′ied·ly** *adv.*

var·i·e·gate (vâr′ē·ə·gāt′) *v.t.* **·gat·ed, ·gat·ing** 1. To mark

with different colors or tints; dapple; spot; streak. 2. To make varied; diversify. [< LL < *varius* various + *agere* to drive, do] **—var′i·e·ga′tion** *n.*

var·i·e·gat·ed (vâr′ē·ə·gā′tid) *adj.* 1. Having diverse colors; varied in color, as with streaks or blotches. 2. Having or exhibiting different forms, styles, or varieties.

va·ri·e·tal (və·rī′ə·təl) *adj.* Of, pertaining to, or of the nature of a variety. **—va·ri·e·tal·ly** *adv.*

va·ri·e·ty (və·rī′ə·tē) *n. pl.* **·ties** 1. The state or character of being various or varied; diversity. 2. A collection of diverse things. 3. The possession of different characteristics by one individual. 4. A limited class of things that differ in certain common peculiarities from a larger class to which they belong. 5. *Biol.* An individual or a group that differs from the type species in certain characters; a subdivision of a species. [< MF < L < *varius* various]

variety show A theatrical show, as in vaudeville, consisting of a series of short, diversified acts or numbers.

vario- Var. of VARI-.

va·ri·o·la (və·rī′ə·lə) *n. Pathol.* Smallpox. [< Med.L, pustule < L *varius* speckled] **—va·ri′o·lar, va·ri′o·lous** *adj.*

var·i·om·e·ter (vâr′ē·om′ə·tər) *n. Electr.* A variable inductance device composed of a fixed and a movable coil connected in series, and capable of controlling the strength of a current. [< VARIO- + -METER]

var·i·o·rum (vâr′ē·ôr′əm, -ō′rəm) *adj.* Having notes or comments by different critics or editors. **—** *n.* An edition containing various versions of a text, usu. with notes and commentary: also **variorum edition**. [< L (*cum notis*) *variorum* (with the notes) of various persons]

var·i·ous (vâr′ē·əs) *adj.* 1. Characteristically different from one another; diverse. 2. More than one; several. 3. Many-sided; varying. 4. Having a diversity of appearance; variegated. 5. *Rare* Changeable; inconstant. [< L *varius*] **—var′i·ous·ly** *adv.* **—var′i·ous·ness** *n.*

var·ix (vâr′iks) *n. pl.* **var·i·ces** (vâr′ə·sēz) *Pathol.* **a** Permanent dilatation of a vein or other vessel of circulation. **b** A vessel thus distorted, as a varicose vein. [< L, a varicose vein]

var·let (vär′lit) *n. Archaic* 1. A menial or subordinate; also, a page. 2. A knave or scoundrel. [< OF, groom]

var·mint (vär′mənt) *n. Dial.* Any obnoxious or pestiferous person or animal. [Alter. of VERMIN]

var·nish (vär′nish) *n.* 1. A solution of certain gums or resins in alcohol, linseed oil, etc., used to produce a shining, transparent coat on a surface. 2. Any natural or artificial product or surface resembling varnish. 3. Outward show, or any superficial polish, as of politeness. **—** *v.t.* 1. To cover with varnish. 2. To give a smooth or glossy appearance to. 3. To improve the appearance of; polish. 4. To hide by a deceptive covering or appearance; gloss over. [< OF < Med.L *vernicium* a resin] **—var′nish·er** *n.*

var·si·ty (vär′sə·tē) *n. pl.* **·ties** *Informal* The highest ranking team that represents a university, college, or school in sports, debating, etc. [< UNIVERSITY]

var·y (vâr′ē) *v.* **var·ied, var·y·ing** *v.t.* 1. To change the form, nature, substance, etc., of; modify. 2. To cause to be different from one another. 3. To impart variety to; diversify. 4. *Music* To modify (a melody) by changes of rhythm, harmony, etc. **—** *v.i.* 5. To become changed in form, nature, substance, etc. 6. To be diverse; differ. 7. To deviate: with *from.* 8. *Math.* To be subject to continual change. 9. *Biol.* To undergo variation. [< OF < L < *varius* diverse] **—var′i·er** *n.*

vas (vas) *n. pl.* **va·sa** (vā′sə) *Biol.* A blood vessel or duct. [< L, vessel, dish]

vas- Var. of VASO-.

vas·cu·lar (vas′kyə·lər) *adj. Biol.* **a** Of, or consisting of, or containing ducts for the transport of body liquids, as blood, lymph, etc. **b** Richly supplied with blood vessels. Also **vas·cu·lose** (-lōs), **vas·cu·lous** (-ləs). [< L *vas* vessel] **—vas·cu·lar·i·ty** (-lar′ə·tē) *n.* **—vas′cu·lar·ly** *adv.*

vas def·er·ens (vas def′ər·enz) *Anat.* The duct by which semen is conveyed from the testicles to the seminal vesicles. [< NL < L *vas* vessel + *deferens* leading down]

vase (vās, vāz, väz) *n.* A decorative container, usu., rounded and of greater height than width, used as an ornament or for holding flowers. [< F < L *vas* vessel]

Vas·e·line (vas′ə·lēn, -lin) *n.* Proprietary name for a brand of petrolatum. Also **vas′e·line**.

vaso- *combining form Physiol.* 1. A vessel, esp., a blood vessel. 2. The vas deferens. Also, before vowels, **vas-**. [< L *vas* vessel]

vas·o·mo·tor (vas′ō·mō′tər) *adj. Physiol.* Producing contraction or dilatation in the walls of vessels.

vas·sal (vas′əl) *n.* 1. In the feudal system, one who held land of a superior lord by a feudal tenure; a liegeman or feudal tenant. 2. A dependent, retainer, or servant; a slave or bondman. **—** *adj.* 1. Of or like a vassal. 2. Servile. [< OF < Med.L < LL *vassus* servant < Celtic]

vas·sal·age (vas′əl·ij) *n.* 1. The state of being a vassal;

also, the duties, and obligations of a vassal. **2.** The feudal system. **3.** Servitude in general. **4.** Land held by feudal tenure; a fief. **5.** Vassals collectively.

vast (vast, väst) *adj.* **1.** Of great extent or size; immense; enormous; huge. **2.** Very great in number, quantity, or amount. **3.** Very great in degree, intensity, etc. [< L *vastus* waste, empty, vast] — **vast′ly** *adv.* — **vast′ness** *n.*

vat (vat) *n.* A large vessel, tub, etc., for holding liquids, as dyeing materials. — *v.t.* **vat·ted, vat·ting** To put into a vat; treat in a vat. [OE *fæt*]

Vat·i·can (vat′ə·kən) *n.* **1.** The papal palace in Vatican City, Rome. **2.** The papal government: distinguished from the *Quirinal*. [< L *Vaticanus (mons)* Vatican (hill) in Rome]

vaude·ville (vôd′vil, vô′də·vil) *n.* A miscellaneous theatrical entertainment, as a variety show; also, a theater presenting such shows. [< F < *Vau de Vire* the valley of the Vire river (in Normandy)]

vault[1] (vôlt) *n.* **1.** An arched chamber; also, any subterranean compartment; cellar. **2.** An arched structure, as a ceiling or roof esp., of a cavity. **3.** Any vaultlike covering, as the sky. **4.** An underground room or compartment for storing wine, etc. **5.** A strongly protected place for keeping valuables, as in a bank. **6.** A burial chamber. — *v.t.* **1.** To form with a vaulted roof; cover with or as with a vault. **2.** To construct in the form of a vault. [< OF < L < *volvere* to roll]

VAULTS

a Cove or cloister. *b* Groin.
c Underpitch or Welsh.

vault[2] (vôlt) *v.t.* **1.** To leap over, esp. with the aid of a pole or with the hands resting on something. **2.** To mount (a horse, etc.) with a leap. — *v.i.* **3.** To leap; spring. **4.** To do a curvet. — *n.* **1.** A leap or bound, as one made with the aid of a pole. **2.** The curvet of a horse. [< OF *volter* to leap, gambol, ? ult. < L *volutus*] — **vault′er** *n.*

vault·ing[1] (vôl′ting) *n.* **1.** Vaulted work, or vaults collectively. **2.** The work or art of building a vault.

vault·ing[2] (vôl′ting) *adj.* **1.** That overleaps. **2.** Unduly confident or presumptuous: *vaulting* ambition.

vaunt (vônt, vänt) *v.i.* **1.** To speak boastfully. — *v.t.* **2.** To boast of. — *n.* Boastful assertion or ostentatious display. [< OF < LL *vanitare* to brag < L *vanus* empty, vain] — **vaunt′er** *n.* — **vaunt′ing·ly** *adv.*

Ve·a·dar (vē·ä·där′, vē′ä·där, vā′-) *n.* An intercalary month of the Hebrew year. See (Hebrew) CALENDAR.

veal (vēl) *n.* The flesh of a calf considered as food. — **bob veal** The flesh of a calf too young to be eaten. [< OF < L *vitellus*, dim. of *vitulus* calf]

vec·tor (vek′tər) *n.* **1.** *Math.* A physical quantity that has magnitude and direction in space, as velocity and acceleration. **2.** *Med.* A carrier of pathogenic microorganisms from one host to another. [< L, carrier < *vehere* to carry] — **vec·to·ri·al** (vek·tôr′ē·əl, -tō′rē-) *adj.*

Ve·da (vā′də, vē′-) *n.* **1.** One of the collections of Indian sacred writings, dating from the second millennium B.C., that form the Hindu scriptures. **2.** The Vedas collectively. [< Skt., knowledge] — **Ve·da·ic** (vi·dā′ik) *adj.* — **Ve·da·ism** (vā′də·iz′əm, vē′-) *n.*

Ve·dan·ta (vi·dän′tə, -dan′-) *n.* Any of several schools of Hindu religious philosophy based on the Upanishads; esp., a monistic system that teaches the worship of Brahma as the creator and soul of the universe. [< Skt. < *Veda* Veda + *anta* end] — **Ve·dan′tic** *adj.* — **Ve·dan′tism** *n.*

V-E Day (vē′ē′) May 8, the date of victory of the United Nations in Europe in World War II, 1945.

ve·dette (vi·det′) *n.* **1.** A mounted sentinel placed in advance of an outpost. **2.** A small vessel used to watch the movements of the enemy: also **vedette boat.** Also spelled *vidette.* [< F < Ital. *vedetta*, alter. (after *vedere* to see) of *veletta*, dim. of Sp. *vela* vigil < L *vigilare* to watch]

Ve·dic (vā′dik, vē′-) *adj.* Of or pertaining to the Vedas or the language in which they were written.

veep (vēp) *n.* *U.S. Slang* A vice president, esp. of the United States. [< V.P., abbr. of vice president]

veer (vir) *v.i.* **1.** *Naut.* To turn to another course. **2.** To change direction by a clockwise motion, as the wind. **3.** To shift from one position to another; be variable or fickle. — *v.t.* **4.** To change the direction of. — *n.* A change in direction; a swerve. [< F *virer* to turn]

veer·y (vir′ē) *n. pl.* **veer·ies** A melodious, tawny thrush of eastern North America. [Prob. imit.]

Ve·ga (vē′gə, vā′-) *n.* One of the 20 brightest stars, 0.14 magnitude; Alpha in the constellation Lyra. [< Med.L < Arabic (*al-Nasr*) *al-Waqi* the falling (vulture)]

veg·e·ta·ble (vej′ə·tə·bəl, vej′tə-) *n.* **1.** The edible part of any herbaceous plant, raw or cooked. **2.** Any member of the vegetable kingdom; a plant. **3.** *Informal* A person who is apathetic or passive. — *adj.* **1.** Pertaining to plants, esp. garden or farm vegetables. **2.** Derived from, of the nature of, or resembling plants. **3.** Made from or consisting of vegetables. **4.** Dull; passive. [< OF < LL < L *vegetare* to animate < *vegere* to be lively] — **veg′e·ta·bly** *adv.*

vegetable kingdom The division of nature that includes all organisms classified as plants.

vegetable oil Any of various oils expressed from the seeds or fruits of plants and used in cooking, medicine, paints, and as lubricants, as corn oil, olive oil, linseed oil, etc.

veg·e·tal (vej′ə·tal) *adj.* **1.** Of or pertaining to plants or vegetables. **2.** Characterizing those vital processes that are common to plants and animals, esp., as distinguished from sensation and volition. [< L *vegetus* lively, vigorous]

veg·e·tant (vej′ə·tənt) *adj.* **1.** Invigorating; vivifying; stimulating growth. **2.** Of the nature of plant life.

veg·e·tar·i·an (vej′ə·târ′ē·ən) *adj.* **1.** Pertaining to or advocating vegetarianism. **2.** Exclusively vegetable, as a diet. — *n.* One who holds or practices vegetarianism.

veg·e·tar·i·an·ism (vej′ə·târ′ē·ən·iz′əm) *n.* The theory or practice of eating only vegetables and fruits.

veg·e·tate (vej′ə·tāt) *v.i.* **·tat·ed, ·tat·ing 1.** To grow, as a plant. **2.** To live in a monotonous, passive way. **3.** *Pathol.* To increase abnormally in size.

veg·e·ta·tion (vej′ə·tā′shən) *n.* **1.** The process of vegetating. **2.** Plant life in the aggregate. **3.** *Pathol.* An abnormal growth on the body. — **veg′e·ta′tion·al** *adj.*

veg·e·ta·tive (vej′ə·tā′tiv) *adj.* **1.** Of, pertaining to, or exhibiting the processes of plant life. **2.** Growing or capable of growing, as plants; productive. **3.** Having a mere physical or passive existence; showing little mental activity. **4.** Concerned with growth and nutrition. Also **veg·e·tive** (vej′ə·tiv). — **veg′e·ta′tive·ly** *adv.* — **veg′e·ta′tive·ness** *n.*

ve·he·ment (vē′ə·mənt) *adj.* **1.** Arising from or marked by impetuosity of feeling or passion; ardent. **2.** Acting with great force or energy; energetic; violent; furious. [< OF < L *vehemens, -entis* impetuous, rash; ult. origin uncertain] — **ve′he·mence, ve′he·men·cy** *n.* — **ve′he·ment·ly** *adv.*

ve·hi·cle (vē′ə·kəl) *n.* **1.** Any contrivance fitted with wheels or runners for carrying something; a conveyance, as, a car or sled. **2.** *Med.* An innocuous medium, as a liquid, with which is mixed some therapeutic substance that may be applied or administered more easily; an excipient. **3.** A liquid, as oil, with which pigments are mixed in painting. **4.** Anything by means of which something else, as power, thought, etc., is transmitted or communicated. **5.** In the performing arts, anything, as a play, musical composition, etc., that permits the performer to display his particular powers or talents. [< F < L < *vehere* to carry, ride] — **ve·hic·u·lar** (vi·hik′yə·lər) *adj.*

veil (vāl) *n.* **1.** A piece of thin and light fabric, worn over the face or head for concealment, protection, or ornament. **2.** Any piece of fabric used to conceal an object; a screen; curtain; mask. **3.** Anything that conceals from inspection; a disguise; pretext. **4.** The life of a nun; also, vows made by a nun. — **to take the veil** To become a nun. — *v.t.* **1.** To cover with a veil. **2.** To hide; disguise. [< OF < L *velum* piece of cloth, sail] — **veil′er** *n.*

veil·ing (vā′ling) *n.* **1.** Material for veils. **2.** A veil.

vein (vān) *n.* **1.** *Anat.* One of the muscular, tubular vessels that convey blood to the heart. **2.** Loosely, any blood vessel. **3.** *Entomol.* One of the radiating supports of an insect's wing. **4.** *Bot.* One of the slender vascular bundles that form the framework of a leaf. **5.** In mining, a lode. **6.** A long, irregular, colored streak, as in wood; marble, etc. **7.** A distinctive trait, tendency, or disposition. **8.** A temporary state of mind; humor; mood. — *v.t.* **1.** To furnish or fill with veins. **2.** To streak or ornament with veins. **3.** To extend over or throughout as veins. [< OF < L *vena* blood vessel] — **vein′y** *adj.*

veined (vānd) *adj.* **1.** Having, marked with, or abounding in veins. **2.** Marked with streaks of another color.

vein·ing (vā′ning) *n.* A network of veins.

vein·let (vān′lit) *n.* A small vein.

ve·lar (vē′lər) *adj.* **1.** Of or pertaining to a velum, esp. to the soft palate. **2.** *Phonet.* Formed with the back of the tongue touching or near the soft palate, as (k) in *cool*, (g) in *go*: sometimes *guttural.* — *n. Phonet.* **a** A velar consonant. **b** A back vowel. [< L *velum* a sail, curtain]

ve·lar·ize (vē′lə·rīz) *v.* **·ized, ·iz·ing** *Phonet. v.t.* To modify (a sound) by raising the back of the tongue toward the soft palate. — *v.i.* To be modified to a velar sound.

veldt (velt, felt) *n.* In South Africa, open country or grassland having few shrubs or trees. Also **veld.** [< Afrikaans *veld* < Du., field]

vel·lum (vel′əm) *n.* **1.** Fine parchment made from the skins of calves, used for expensive binding, printing, etc. **2.** A manuscript written on such parchment. **3.** Paper made to resemble parchment. [< OF < *veel, viel* calf]

ve·loc·i·pede (və·los′ə·pēd) *n.* **1.** An early form of bicycle or tricycle. **2.** A child's tricycle. **3.** A type of handcar. [< F < L *velox, velocis* swift + *pes, pedis* foot]

ve·loc·i·ty (və·los′ə·tē) *n. pl.* **·ties 1.** The state of moving or developing swiftly; rapidity; celerity; speed. **2.** The distance traveled by an object in a specified time. **3.** The time rate of motion in a stated direction; a vector quantity. [< L < *velox* swift]

ve·lours (və·loor′) *n. pl.* **·lours** (-loorz) A soft, velvetlike, closely woven cotton or wool fabric having a short, thick pile. Also **ve·lour′.** [< F. See VELURE.]

ve·lum (vē′ləm) *n. pl.* **·la** (-lə) **1.** *Biol.* A thin membranous covering or partition. **2.** *Anat.* The soft palate: see under PALATE. [< L]

ve·lure (və·loor′) *n.* **1.** Velvet, or a fabric resembling velvet. **2.** A velvet or silk pad for smoothing a silk hat. —*v.t.* **·lured, ·lur·ing** To smooth with a velure. [< F < L *villus* shaggy hair]

vel·vet (vel′vit) *n.* **1.** A fabric of silk, rayon, cotton, etc., having on one side a thick, short, smooth pile, formed either of loops (**pile velvet**) or of single threads (**cut velvet**). **2.** Anything resembling such a fabric in softness, smoothness, etc. **3.** The furry skin covering a growing antler. —*adj.* **1.** Made of velvet. **2.** Smooth and soft to the touch; velvety. [< Med.L *velvetum,* ult. < L *villus* shaggy hair]

vel·vet·een (vel′və·tēn′) *n.* **1.** A cotton fabric with a short, close pile like velvet. **2.** *pl.* Clothes, esp. trousers, made of this material. [< VELVET]

vel·vet·y (vel′vit·ē) *adj.* **1.** Smooth and soft like velvet. **2.** Mild and smooth to the taste: *velvety* liqueur.

ve·na ca·va (vē′nə kā′və) *pl.* **ve·nae ca·vae** (vē′nē kā′vē) *Anat.* Either of the two great venous trunks emptying into the right atrium of the heart. For illus. see HEART. [< L, hollow vein]

ve·nal (vē′nəl) *adj.* **1.** Ready to sell honor or principle, or to accept a bribe; mercenary; purchasable. **2.** Subject to sordid bargaining or to corrupt influences; salable. **3.** Characterized by corruption. [< L *venum* sale] —**ve·nal′i·ty** (-nal′ə·tē) *n.* —**ve′nal·ly** *adv.*

ve·na·tion (vē·nā′shən) *n. Biol.* The arrangement of veins, as in a leaf, an insect wing, etc.

vend (vend) *v.t.* **1.** To sell. **2.** To utter (an opinion); publish. —*v.i.* **3.** To be a vender. **4.** To be sold. [< F *vendre* < L < *venum* sale + *dare* to give] —**ven·di·tion** (ven·dish′ən) *n.*

ven·dee (ven·dē′) *n. Law* The person or party to whom something is sold; a buyer.

vend·er (ven′dər) *n.* One who sells, as a hawker or peddler. Also **ven′dor** (-dər).

ven·det·ta (ven·det′ə) *n.* A blood feud in which the relatives of the killed or injured person take vengeance on the offender or his relatives. [< Ital. < L *vindicta* vengeance]

vend·i·ble (ven′də·bəl) *adj.* Capable of being vended or sold; marketable. —*n.* A vendible thing. —**vend′i·bil′i·ty, vend′i·ble·ness** *n.* —**vend′i·bly** *adv.*

vend·ing machine (ven′ding) A coin-operated device that dispenses some product or packaged article.

ve·neer (və·nir′) *n.* **1.** A thin layer, as of choice wood, upon a commoner surface. **2.** Any of the thin layers glued together to strengthen plywood. **3.** Mere outside show or elegance. —*v.t.* **1.** To cover (a surface) with veneer; overlay for decoration or finer finish. **2.** To glue together to form plywood. **3.** To conceal, as something disagreeable or coarse, with an attractive or deceptive surface. [Earlier *fineer* < G < F *fournir* to furnish] —**ve·neer′er** *n.*

ve·neer·ing (və·nir′ing) *n.* **1.** The art of applying veneer. **2.** Material used for veneer. **3.** A surface of veneer.

ven·er·a·ble (ven′ər·ə·bəl) *adj.* **1.** Meriting or commanding veneration; worthy of reverence: now usu. implying age. **2.** Exciting reverential feelings because of sacred or historic associations. **3.** Revered: used as a title for an archdeacon in Anglican churches, and in the Roman Catholic Church, for one past the first stage of canonization, prior to beatification. [< OF < L *venerari* to revere] —**ven′er·a·ble·ness, ven′er·a·bil′i·ty.** *n.* —**ven′er·a·bly** *adv.*

ven·er·ate (ven′ə·rāt) *v.t.* **·at·ed, ·at·ing** To look upon or regard with respect and deference; revere. [< L *veneratus,* pp. of *venerari* to revere]

—**Syn.** We *venerate* that which we judge objectively to be of great worth, as a great man, our ancestors, a holy person, or a sacred object. *Revere* and *reverence* imply respect, to which have been added personal affection and awe; *revere* is chiefly applied to persons or to a deity, and *reverence,* to places or objects: to *revere* God and the saints, to *reverence* a holy shrine. In strict usage, we *worship* or *adore* only that which we consider divine; *worship* refers to participation in religious ceremonies, and *adore,* to the sense of personal gratitude for divine favor which the worshiper feels.

ven·er·a·tion (ven′ə·rā′shən) *n.* **1.** The act of venerating, or the state of being venerated. **2.** A feeling of profound respect and awe; reverence.

ve·ne·re·al (və·nir′ē·əl) *adj.* **1.** Pertaining to or proceeding from sexual intercourse. **2.** Communicated by sexual relations with an infected person: a *veneral* disease. **3.** Pertaining to or curative of diseases so communicated. **4.** Infected with venereal disease. [< L < *Venus*]

venereal disease *Pathol.* One of several diseases communicated by sexual intercourse, as syphilis, gonorrhea, and chancroid.

ven·er·y¹ (ven′ər·ē) *n. pl.* **·er·ies** *Archaic* Sexual indulgence, esp. when excessive. [< L *Venus*]

ven·er·y² (ven′ər·ē) *n. pl.* **·er·ies** *Archaic* The hunting of game. [< F < L *venari* to hunt]

Ven·e·ti (ven′ə·tī) *n.pl.* **1.** An ancient Celtic people of NW Gaul, conquered by Caesar in 56 B.C. **2.** An ancient people of NE Italy, friendly to Rome.

Ve·ne·tian (və·nē′shən) *adj.* Pertaining to Venice, its inhabitants, art etc. —*n.* A native of Venice.

Venetian blind A flexible window screen that may be raised or lowered, having overlapping horizontal slats so connected with a cord as to permit opening and closing.

Venetian carpet A worsted carpet for stairs and hallways, commonly of a simple striped pattern.

Venetian glass A delicate and fine glassware made at or near Venice.

ven·geance (ven′jəns) *n.* The act of revenging; retribution for a wrong or injury. —**Syn.** See REVENGE. —**with a vengeance** With great force or violence; to an unusual extent. [< AF < OF < L *vindicare* to defend, avenge]

venge·ful (venj′fəl) *adj.* **1.** Seeking to inflict vengeance; vindictive. **2.** Serving to inflict vengeance. —**venge′ful·ly** *adv.* —**venge′ful·ness** *n.*

veni- *combining form* Vein; also, vein in the earth. [< L *vena* vein]

ve·ni·al (vē′nē·əl, vēn′yəl) *adj.* **1.** *Theol.* That may be easily pardoned or forgiven: distinguished from *mortal: venial* sin. **2.** Excusable; pardonable. [< OF < L *venia* forgiveness, mercy] —**ve′ni·al′i·ty** (-al′ə·tē), **ve′ni·al·ness** *n.* —**ve′ni·al·ly** *adv.*

ve·ni·re (vi·nī′rē) *n. Law* A writ issued to the sheriff for summoning persons to serve as a jury. Also **ve·ni′re fa·ci·as** (fā′shi·as′) [< L *venire facias,* that you cause to come]

ve·ni·re·man (vi·nī′rē·mən) *n. pl.* **·men** (-mən) One summoned to serve on a jury under a venire.

ven·i·son (ven′ə·zən, -sən; *Brit.* ven′zən) *n.* Deer flesh used for food. [< OF < L *venatus,* pp. of *venari* to hunt]

ve·ni, vi·di, vi·ci (vē′nī, vī′dī, vī′sī; wā′nē, wē′dē, wē′kē) *Latin* I came, I saw, I conquered: words used by Julius Caesar to report a victory in Asia Minor.

ven·om (ven′əm) *n.* **1.** The poisonous liquid secreted by certain animals, as serpents and scorpions, and introduced into the victim by a bite or sting. **2.** Malice; malignity; spite. [< OF < L *venenum* poison]

ven·om·ous (ven′əm·əs) *adj.* **1.** Having glands secreting venom. **2.** Able to give a poisonous sting. **3.** Malignant; spiteful. —**ven′om·ous·ly** *adv.* —**ven′om·ous·ness** *n.*

ve·nous (vē′nəs) *adj.* **1.** Of, pertaining to, or marked with veins. **2.** *Physiol.* Designating the blood carried by the veins, distinguished from arterial blood by its darker color and presence of carbon dioxide. [< L *venosus* < *vena* vein] —**ve′nous·ly** *adv.* —**ve′nous·ness** *n.*

vent (vent) *n.* **1.** An opening, commonly small, for the passage of liquids, gases, etc. **2.** Utterance; expression: chiefly in the phrase **to give vent to. 3.** *Zool.* The external opening of the alimentary canal, esp. of animals below mammals; the anus. —*v.t.* **1.** To give expression to: often with *on:* to *vent* one's rage on the cat. **2.** To relieve, as by giving vent to emotion. **3.** To permit to escape from an opening. [ME < OF *fente* cleft < L *findere* to split] —**vent′er** *n.*

vent·age (ven′tij) *n.* **1.** A small opening. **2.** A finger hole in a musical instrument. [< VENT]

ven·tail (ven′tāl) *n.* The lower adjustable front of a medieval helmet. [< OF < *vent* wind]

ven·ti·late (ven′tə·lāt) *v.t.* **·lat·ed ·lat·ing 1.** To produce a free circulation of air in; admit fresh air into. **2.** To provide with a vent. **3.** To make widely known; expose to examination and discussion. **4.** To oxygenate, as blood. [< L *ventilatus,* pp. of *ventilare* to fan < *ventus* wind] —**ven′ti·la′tion** *n.* —**ven′ti·la·tive** *adj.*

ven·ti·la·tor (ven′tə·lā′tər) *n.* A device or arrangement for supplying fresh air. —**ven′ti·la·to′ry** (-lə·tôr′ē, -tō′rē) *adj.*

ven·tral (ven′trəl) *adj. Anat.* **a** Of, pertaining to, or situated on or near the abdomen. **b** On or toward the lower or anterior part of the body. [< L < *venter, ventris* belly] —**ven′tral·ly** *adv.*

ven·tri·cle (ven′trə·kəl) *n. Anat.* **1.** One of the two lower chambers of the heart, from which blood received from the atria is forced into the arteries. **2.** Any of various cavities in the body, as of the brain, the spinal cord, etc. For illus. see HEART. [< L *ventriculus,* dim. of *venter, ventris* belly]

ven·tric·u·lar (ven-trik′yə-lər) *adj.* **1.** Of, pertaining to, or of the nature of a ventricle. **2.** Swollen and distended.

ven·tril·o·quism (ven-tril′ə·kwiz′əm) *n.* The art of speaking in such a manner that the sounds seem to come from some source other than the person speaking. Also **ven·tril′o·quy** (-kwē). [< L < *venter* belly + *loqui* to speak] — **ven·tril′o·quist** *n.* — **ven·tril′o·quis′tic** *adj.*

ven·tril·o·quize (ven-tril′ə-kwīz) *v.t. & v.i.* ·quized, ·quiz·ing To speak as a ventriloquist. Also *Brit.* **ven·tril′o·quise.**

ventro- *combining form Anat.* The abdomen; related to or near the abdomen; ventral. [< L *venter, ventris* belly]

ven·ture (ven′chər) *v.* ·tured, ·tur·ing *v.t.* **1.** To expose to chance or risk; hazard; stake. **2.** To run the risk of; brave. **3.** To express at the risk of denial or refutation: to *venture* a suggestion. — *v.i.* **4.** To take a risk; dare. — *n.* **1.** An undertaking attended with risk or danger; a risk; hazard; esp., a business investment. **2.** That which is ventured; esp., property risk. — **at a venture** At hazard; offhand. [Aphetic form of ADVENTURE] — **ven′tur·er** *n.*

ven·ture·some (ven′chər·səm) *adj.* **1.** Bold; daring. **2.** Involving hazard; risky. — **ven′ture·some·ly** *adv.* — **ven′· ture·some·ness** *n.*

ven·tur·ous (ven′chər·əs) *adj.* **1.** Adventurous; willing to take risks and brave dangers; bold. **2.** Hazardous; risky; dangerous. — **ven′tur·ous·ly** *adv.* — **ven′tur·ous·ness** *n.*

ven·ue (ven′yōō) *n. Law* The place where a crime is committed or a cause of action arises; also, the county or political division from which the jury must be summoned and in which the trial must be held. — **change of venue** The change of the place of trial. [< OF, orig. fem. pp. of *venir* to come < L *venire*]

Ve·nus (vē′nəs) In Roman mythology, the goddess of love, spring, bloom, and beauty: identified with the Greek *Aphrodite.* — *n.* **1.** The sixth largest planet of the solar system and second in order from the sun. See PLANET. **2.** A statue or painting of Venus. **3.** A lovely woman. [< L]

Venus of Mi·lo (mē′lō) A marble statue of Venus, with the arms missing, discovered in 1820 on the island of Milo and later placed in the Louvre. Also **Venus de Milo.**

Ve·nus's flytrap (vē′nəs·iz flī′trap′) *n.* A plant with clustered leaves whose spiked blades instantly close upon insects lighting upon them, found native chiefly in the sandy bogs of eastern North and South Carolina.

ve·ra·cious (və-rā′shəs) *adj.* **1.** Habitually disposed to speak the truth; truthful. **2.** Conforming to or expressing truth; true; accurate. [< L *verax, veracis* < *versus* true] — **ve·ra′cious·ly** *adv.* — **ve·ra′cious·ness** *n.*

ve·rac·i·ty (və-ras′ə·tē) *n. pl.* ·ties **1.** The habitual regard for truth; truthfulness; honesty. **2.** Agreement with truth; accuracy. **3.** That which is true; truth.

ve·ran·da (və-ran′də) *n.* An open portico or balcony, usu. roofed, along the outside of a building; a porch or stoop. Also **ve·ran′dah.** [< Hind. < Pg. *varanda* railing, balustrade]

verb (vûrb) *n. Gram.* **1.** The part of speech that expresses existence, action, or occurrence, as the English words *be, collide, think.* **2.** Any word or construction functioning similarly. [< F < L *verbum* word]

ver·bal (vûr′bəl) *adj.* **1.** Of, pertaining to, or connected with words. **2.** Concerned with words rather than the ideas they convey: *verbal* distinctions. **3.** Expressed orally; not written: a *verbal* contract. **4.** Having word corresponding with word; literal: a *verbal* translation. **5.** *Gram.* **a** Partaking of the nature of or derived from a verb: a *verbal* noun. **b** Used to form verbs: a *verbal* prefix. — *n. Gram.* A verb form that functions as a substantive (gerund and infinitive) or as a modifier (present and past participles and infinitive), but retains some of the characteristics of a verb. [< F < LL < L *verbum* word] — **ver′bal·ly** *adv.*

— **Syn.** (adj.) **2.** In strict usage, *verbal* refers to spoken or written words, and *oral,* to spoken words only: a *verbal* dispute, an *oral* examination. However, the distinction is often blurred, so that we speak of a *verbal* agreement, rather than of an *oral* agreement. *Oral* and *verbal* always imply communication: *vocal* refers to the use of the voice, whether for communicating thought or not: a *vocal* exercise, a *vocal* defect.

ver·bal·ism (vûr′bəl·iz′əm) *n.* **1.** A verbal expression. **2.** A meaningless form of words. **3.** Wordiness; verbiage.

ver·bal·ist (vûr′bəl·ist) *n.* **1.** One who deals with words rather than facts or ideas. **2.** One who is skilled in the use and meaning of words.

ver·bal·ize (vûr′bəl·īz) *v.* ·ized, ·iz·ing *v.t.* **1.** To express in words. **2.** *Gram.* To make a verb of; change into a verb. — *v.i.* **3.** To speak or write verbosely. **4.** To express oneself in words. — **ver′bal·i·za′tion** *n.* — **ver′bal·iz′er** *n.*

ver·ba·tim (vûr·bā′tim, -təm) *adj. & adv.* In the exact words; word for word. [< LL < L *verbum* word]

ver·be·na (vər·bē′n *n.* Any of various American garden plants having dense terminal spikes of showy flowers. [< L, foliage, vervain]

ver·bi·age (vûr′bē·ij) *n.* **1.** Excess of words. **2.** Wordiness; verbosity. [< F *verbier* to gabble < L *verbum* word]

ver·bose (vər·bōs′) *adj.* Using or containing a wearisome and unnecessary number of words; wordy. [< L *verbosus* < *verbum* word] — **ver·bose′ly** *adv.* — **ver·bose′ness** *n.*

— **Syn.** Diffuse, prolix. Compare CIRCUMLOCUTION.

ver·bos·i·ty (vər·bos′ə·tē) *n. pl.* ·ties The state or quality of being verbose; wordiness.

ver·bo·ten (fer·bōt′n) *adj. German* Forbidden.

verb phrase *Gram.* A finite verb form, consisting of a principle verb and an auxiliary or auxiliaries.

ver·dant (vûr′dənt) *adj.* **1.** Green with vegetation; covered with grass or green leaves; fresh. **2.** Unsophisticated. [< F < L *viridis* green] — **ver′dan·cy** *n.* — **ver′dant·ly** *adv.*

ver·dict (vûr′dikt) *n.* **1.** The decision of a jury in an action. **2.** A conclusion expressed; judgment. [< AF *verdit,* OF *voirdit* < L < *verus* true + *dictum,* pp. of *dicere* to say]

ver·di·gris (vûr′də·grēs, -gris) *n.* The green or bluish patina formed on copper, bronze, or brass surfaces after long exposure to the air. [< OF *verd de Grice, vert de Grece,* lit., green of Greece]

ver·dure (vûr′jər) *n.* The fresh greenness of growing vegetation; also, such vegetation itself. [< F < L *viridis* green]

ver·dur·ous (vûr′jər·əs) *adj.* Covered with verdure; verdant. — **ver′dur·ous·ness** *n.*

Ver·ein (fer·īn′) *n. German* A society; association.

verge¹ (vûrj) *n.* **1.** The extreme edge of something having defined limits; brink; margin. **2.** The point at which some action, condition, or state is likely to occur: on the *verge* of bankruptcy. **3.** A bounding or enclosing line; a boundary; also, the space enclosed. **4.** A rod, wand, or staff as a symbol of authority or emblem of office. — *v.i.* **verged, verg·ing 1.** To come near; approach; border; usu. with *on:* His speech *verges* on the chaotic. **2.** To form the limit or verge. [< F, rod, stick < L *virga* twig]

verge² (vûrj) *v.i.* **verged, verg·ing** To slope; tend; incline. [< L *vergere* to bend, turn]

Ver·gil·i·an (vər·jil′ē·ən) *adj.* Pertaining to or in the style of Vergil: also spelled *Virgilian.*

ver·i·fi·a·ble (ver′ə·fī′ə·bəl) *adj.* Capable of being verified. — **ver′i·fi′a·ble·ness** *n.* — **ver′i·fi′a·bly** *adv.*

ver·i·fi·ca·tion (ver′ə·fə·kā′shən) *n.* **1.** The act of verifying, or the state of being verified. **2.** *Law* An oath appended to an account, petition, or plea, as to the truth of the facts stated in it.

ver·i·fy (ver′ə·fī) *v.t.* ·fied, ·fy·ing **1.** To prove to be true or accurate; substantiate; confirm. **2.** To test or ascertain the accuracy or truth of. **3.** *Law* **a** To affirm under oath. **b** To add a confirmation to. [< OF < Med.L < *verus* true + *facere* to make] — **ver′i·fi′er** *n.*

ver·i·ly (ver′ə·lē) *adv. Archaic* In truth; really. [< VERY]

ver·i·sim·i·lar (ver′ə·sim′ə·lər) *adj.* Appearing or seeming to be true; likely; probable. [< L < *verus* true + *similis* like] — **ver′i·sim′i·lar·ly** *adv.*

ver·i·si·mil·i·tude (ver′ə·si·mil′ə·tōōd, -tyōōd) *n.* **1.** Appearance of truth. **2.** That which resembles truth.

ver·i·ta·ble (ver′ə·tə·bəl) *adj.* Properly so called; unquestionable: a *veritable* villain. [< F *vérité* verity] — **ver′i·ta·ble·ness** *n.* — **ver′i·ta·bly** *adv.*

ver·i·ty (ver′ə·tē) *n. pl.* ·ties **1.** The quality of being correct or true. **2.** A true or established statement, principle, etc.; a fact; truth. [< F < L *veritas* truth]

ver·juice (vûr′jōōs) *n.* **1.** The sour juice of green fruit, as unripe grapes. **2.** Sharpness or sourness of disposition or manner; acidity. [< OF < *vert* green + *jus* juice]

ver·meil (vûr′mil) *n.* **1.** Silver or bronze gilt. **2.** *Poetic* Vermilion, or the color of vermilion. — *adj.* Of a bright-red color. [< OF < L *vermiculus,* dim. of *vermis* worm, the cochineal insect]

vermi- *combining form* A worm; of or related to a worm. [< L *vermis* worm]

ver·mi·cel·li (vûr′mə·sel′ē, *Ital.* ver′mē·chel′lē) *n.* A food paste made into slender cords thinner than spaghetti or macaroni. [< Ital., lit., little worms, pl. of *vermicello*]

ver·mi·cide (vûr′mə·sīd) *n.* Any substance that kills worms; esp., any drug destructive of intestinal worms. — **ver·mi·ci·dal** (vûr′mə·sīd′əl) *adj.*

ver·mic·u·lar (vər·mik′yə·lər) *adj.* **1.** Having the form or motion of a worm. **2.** Like the wavy tracks of a worm. [< L < *vermis* worm] — **ver·mic′u·lar·ly** *adv.*

ver·mic·u·late (vər·mik′yə·lāt) *adj.* **1.** Covered with wormlike markings. **2.** Having the motions of a worm. **3.** Insinuating; tortuous. **4.** Worm-eaten.

ver·mi·form (vûr′mə·fôrm) *adj.* Like a worm in shape. [< Med.L < L *vermis* worm + *forma* form]

vermiform appendix *Anat.* A slender, wormlike vestigial structure, protruding from the end of the cecum in man and certain other mammals. For illus. see INTESTINE.

ver·mi·fuge (vûr′mə·fyōōj) *n.* Any remedy that destroys intestinal worms. —*adj.* Acting as a vermifuge. [< F < L *vermis* worm + *fugare* to expel]

ver·mil·ion (vər·mil′yən) *n.* 1. A brilliant, durable red pigment, obtained naturally by grinding cinnabar to a fine powder, or made synthetically. 2. The color of the pigment, an intense orange red. —*adj.* Of a bright-red color. —*v.t.* To color with vermilion; dye bright red. [See VERMEIL.]

ver·min (vûr′min) *n. pl.* **·min** 1. Noxious small animals or parasitic insects, as lice, fleas, worms, rats, mice, etc. 2. *Brit.* Certain animals injurious to game, as weasels, owls, etc. 3. A repulsive or obnoxious human being; also, such persons collectively. [< OF < L *vermis* worm]

ver·min·ous (vûr′mən·əs) *adj.* 1. Infested with vermin, esp. parasites. 2. Relating to or caused by vermin. 3. Of the nature of or resembling vermin. —**ver′min·ous·ly** *adv.* —**ver′min·ous·ness** *n.*

ver·mouth (vûr′mōōth, vər·mōōth′) *n.* A liqueur made from white wine flavored with aromatic herbs. Also **ver′·muth.** [< F < G *wermuth* wormwood]

ver·nac·u·lar (vər·nak′yə·lər) *n.* 1. The native language of a locality. 2. The common everyday speech of the people, as opposed to the literary language. 3. The vocabulary or jargon of a particular profession or trade. 4. An idiomatic word or phrase. 5. The common name of a plant or animal as distinguished from its scientific designation. —*adj.* 1. Originating in or belonging to one's native land; indigenous: said of a language, idiom, etc. 2. Using everyday speech rather than the literary language. 3. Written in the native language. 4. Characteristic of a specific locality or country: *vernacular* arts. 5. Designating the common name of a plant or animal. [< L *vernaculus* native < *verna* home-born slave, native] —**ver·nac′u·lar·ly** *adv.*

ver·nal (vûr′nəl) *adj.* 1. Belonging to, appearing in, or appropriate to spring. 2. Youthful; fresh. [< L *vernus* belonging to spring < *ver* spring] —**ver′nal·ly** *adv.*

ver·nal·ize (vûr′nəl·īz) *v.t.* **·ized, ·iz·ing** To accelerate the growth of (a plant) by subjecting the seeds to low temperatures. —**ver′nal·i·za′tion** *n.*

ver·na·tion (vər·nā′shən) *n. Bot.* The disposition of leaves within the leaf bud. [< NL < *vernare* to flourish]

ver·ni·er (vûr′nē·ər) *n.* 1. The small, movable, auxiliary scale for obtaining fractional parts of the subdivisions of a fixed scale on a barometer, sextant, gauge, or other measure. Also **vernier scale.** 2. *Mech.* An auxiliary device to insure fine adjustments in precision instruments. [after Pierre *Vernier,* 1580?–1637, French mathematician]

Ve·ro·nal (ver′ə·nəl) *n.* Proprietary name for a brand of barbital.

ver·sa·tile (vûr′sə·til) *adj.* 1. Having an aptitude for various occupations; many-sided. 2. Subject to change; variable. 3. *Bot.* Attached so as to be freely swinging or turning. 4. *Zool.* Capable of being turned forward or backward, as the toe of a bird. [< F < L < *vertere* to turn] —**ver′sa·tile·ly** *adv.* —**ver′sa·til′i·ty, ver′sa·tile·ness** *n.*

verse (vûrs) *n.* 1. A single metrical or rhythmical line. 2. Metrical composition; poetry: distinguished from *prose.* 3. A poem. 4. A specified type of meter or metrical structure: iambic *verse.* 5. One of the short divisions of a chapter of the Bible. 6. A short division of any metrical composition, song, etc., esp., a stanza. —*v.t. & v.i.* **versed, vers·ing** *Rare* To versify. [OE and OF < L < *vertere* to turn]

versed (vûrst) *adj.* Thoroughly acquainted; adept; proficient: with *in.* [< L < *versari* to occupy oneself]

versed sine *Trig.* A function of an angle, equal to one minus the cosine. Also **ver·sine** (vûr′sīn).

ver·si·cle (vûr′si·kəl) *n.* One of a series of lines said or sung alternately by minister and congregation. [< L. See VERSE.]

ver·si·fy (vûr′sə·fī) *v.* **·fied, ·fy·ing** *v.t.* 1. To change from prose into verse. 2. To narrate or treat in verse. —*v.i.* 3. To write poetry. [< OF < L < *versus* verse + *facere* to make] —**ver′si·fi·ca′tion** (-fə·kā′shən) *n.* —**ver′si·fi′er** *n.*

ver·sion (vûr′zhən, -shən) *n.* 1. A description or account as modified by a particular point of view. 2. A translation. 3. *Usu. cap.* A translation of the whole or part of the Bible: the Douai *version.* [< MF < Med.L < L *vertere* to turn] —**ver′sion·al** *adj.*

vers li·bre (ver lē′br′) *French* Free verse.

ver·so (vûr′sō) *n. pl.* **·sos** 1. A left-hand page of a book, or sheet of folded paper: opposed to *recto.* 2. The reverse of a coin or medal. [< L *verso* (*folio*) a turned (leaf)]

verst (vûrst) *n.* A Russian measure of distance, about two thirds of a mile, or 1.067 kilometers. [< F and G < Russian *versta,* orig. a line]

ver·sus (vûr′səs) *prep.* 1. In law and sports, against: Dempsey *versus* Tunney. 2. Considered as the alternative of: free trade *versus* tariffs. [< L, toward, *vertere* to turn]

ver·te·bra (vûr′tə·brə) *n. pl.* **·brae** (-brē) or **·bras** *Anat.* Any of the segmented bones of the spinal column in man and the higher vertebrates. [< L, joint < *vertere* to turn] —**ver′te·bral** *adj.*

ver·te·brate (vûr′tə·brāt, -brit) *adj.* 1. Having a backbone or spinal column. 2. Pertaining to or characteristic of vertebrates. —*n.* Any of a primary division of animals, characterized by a segmented spinal column, as fishes, birds, reptiles, and mammals.

ver·tex (vûr′teks) *n. pl.* **·tex·es** or **·ti·ces** (-tə·sēz) 1. The highest point of anything; apex; top. 2. *Astron.* The point in the sky toward or from which a group of stars appears to be moving. 3. *Geom.* **a** The point of intersection of the sides of an angle. **b** The point of a triangle opposite to, and farthest from, the base. [< L, the top < *vertere* to turn]

ver·ti·cal (vûr′ti·kəl) *adj.* 1. Perpendicular to the plane of the horizon, extending up and down; upright. 2. Directly above or overhead. 3. Of or at the vertex or highest point. 4. *Econ.* Of or pertaining to a group of business concerns that handle all the stages of the manufacture and distribution of a product. —*n.* 1. A vertical line, plane, or circle. 2. An upright beam or rod in a truss. [< MF < L. See VERTEX.] —**ver′ti·cal′i·ty** (-kal′ə·tē), **ver′ti·cal·ness** *n.* —**ver′ti·cal·ly** *adv.*

vertical union An industrial union.

ver·ti·ces (vûr′tə·sēz) Plural of VERTEX.

ver·ti·cil (vûr′tə·sil) *n. Biol.* 1. A set of organs, as leaves or tentacles, disposed in a circle around an axis; whorl. 2. A volution of a spiral shell. [< L *verticillus* whorl]

ver·ti·cil·late (vər·tis′ə·lit, -lāt, vûr′tə·sil′it, -āt) *adj.* 1. Arranged in a verticil. 2. Having parts so arranged. Also **ver·tic′il·lat·ed.** —**ver·tic′il·late·ly** *adv.* —**ver·tic′il·la′tion** *n.*

ver·tig·i·nous (vər·tij′ə·nəs) *adj.* 1. Affected by vertigo; dizzy. 2. Turning round; whirling; revolving. 3. Liable to cause dizziness. [See VERTIGO.] —**ver·tig′i·nous·ly** *adv.* —**ver·tig′i·nous·ness** *n.*

ver·ti·go (vûr′tə·gō) *n. pl.* **·goes** or **ver·tig·i·nes** (vər·tij′ə·nēz) *Pathol.* Any of a group of disorders in which a person feels as if he or his surroundings are whirling around; dizziness. [< L < *vertere* to turn]

ver·tu (vər·tōō′, vûr′tōō) See VIRTU.

ver·vain (vûr′vān) *n.* Any of a family of herbs, shrubs, and trees, including many cultivated ornamental verbenas. [< OF < L *verbena*]

verve (vûrv) *n.* 1. Enthusiasm or energy, esp., as manifested in artistic production. 2. Spirit; vigor. [< F]

ver·y (ver′ē) *adv.* In a high degree; extremely: *very* generous. —*adj.* **ver·i·er, ver·i·est** 1. Absolute; actual; simple: the *very* truth. 2. Identical: my *very* words. 3. The (thing) itself: used as an intensive equivalent to *even:* The *very* stones cry out. 4. Unqualified; utter; complete: a *very* rogue. [< AF or OF < L *verus* true]

very high frequency *Telecom.* A band of radio wave frequencies ranging from 30 to 300 megacycles.

very low frequency *Telecom.* A band of radio wave frequencies ranging from 10 to 30 kilocycles.

ves·i·cant (ves′i·kənt) *adj.* Producing blisters. —*n.* That which produces blisters. [< NL < L *vesica* blister, bladder]

ves·i·cate (ves′i·kāt) *v.t. & v.i.* **·cat·ed, ·cat·ing** To blister. —**ves′i·ca′tion** *n.*

ves·i·ca·to·ry (ves′i·kə·tôr′ē, və·sik′ə·tôr′ē, -tō′rē) *adj.* Capable of producing blisters; vesicant. —*n. pl.* **·ries** Any substance, as an ointment or plaster, that causes a blister.

ves·i·cle (ves′i·kəl) *n.* 1. Any small bladderlike cavity, cell, or cyst. 2. *Anat.* A small sac, containing gas or fluid. 3. *Pathol.* A blister. [< L < *vesica* bladder] —**ve·sic·u·lar** (və·sik′yə·lər) *adj.*

vesico- *combining form Med.* The urinary bladder; of or pertaining to the urinary bladder. Also, before vowels, **vesic-.** [< L *vesica* bladder]

ve·sic·u·late (*v.* və·sik′yə·lit; *adj.* və·sik′yə·lit, -lāt) *v.t. & v.i.* **·lat·ed, ·lat·ing** To make or become vesicular. —*adj.* Having vesicles; vesicular. —**ve·sic′u·la′tion** *n.*

ves·per (ves′pər) *n.* 1. A bell that calls to vespers. 2. An evening service, prayer, or song. 3. *Obs.* Evening. —*adj.* Of evening or vespers. [< L, the evening star]

Ves·per (ves′pər) *n.* The evening star; Hesperus; the planet Venus when an evening star. [< OF < L]

ves·pers (ves′pərz) *n.pl. Often cap. Eccl.* 1. The sixth of the seven canonical hours. 2. A service of worship in the evening. [< OF < Med.L < L *vespera* evening]

ves·sel (ves′əl) *n.* 1. A hollow receptacle, esp. one capable of holding a liquid, as a bowl, pitcher, etc. 2. A craft designed to float on the water, usu. one larger than a rowboat; a ship or boat. 3. *Anat.* A duct or canal for transporting a body fluid, as a vein. [< OF < L < *vas* vessel]

vest (vest) *n.* 1. *Chiefly U.S.* A man's short, sleeveless garment, buttoning in front, commonly worn underneath a suit coat: also, *esp. Brit., waistcoat.* —*v.t.* 1. To confer (ownership, authority, etc.) upon some person or persons: usu., with *in*. **2.** To place ownership, or authority with (a person or persons). **3.** To clothe, as with vestments. — *v.i.* **4.** To clothe oneself, as in vestments. **5.** To become vested; devolve. [< F < Ital. < L *vestis* garment]

Ves·ta (ves′tə) *n.* In Roman mythology, the goddess of the hearth and the hearth fire.

ves·tal (ves′təl) *n.* **1.** One of the virgin priestesses of Vesta. Also **vestal virgin**. **2.** A woman of pure character; a virgin. **3.** A nun. — *adj.* **1.** Pertaining to Vesta. **2.** Chaste; pure.

vest·ed (ves′tid) *adj.* **1.** *Law* Held by fixed tenure. Established by law as a permanent right. **2.** Dressed; robed, esp. in church vestments.

vested interest 1. A strong commitment to a system or institution whose existence serves one's self-interest. **2.** *Usu. pl.* A financially powerful or influential group.

vest·ee (ves·tē′) *n.* An imitation blouse-front worn in the front of a suit or dress. [Dim. of VEST]

ves·ti·bule (ves′tə·byōōl) *n.* **1.** A small antechamber behind the outer door of a building; an entrance hall; lobby. **2.** The enclosed passage between railway passenger cars. **3.** *Anat.* Any of several chambers or channels adjoining or communicating with others: the *vestibule* of the ear. — *v.t.* **·buled, ·bul·ing** To provide with a vestibule. [< L *vestibulum* entrance hall] — **ves·tib′u·lar** (-tib′yə-lər) *adj.*

ves·tige (ves′tij) *n.* **1.** A visible trace, impression, or sign, of something absent or lost; trace. **2.** *Biol.* A part or organ, small or degenerate, but well developed and functional in ancestral forms of organisms. [< F < L *vestigium* footprint] — **ves·tig′i·al** *adj.* — **ves·tig′i·al·ly** *adv.*

ves·tig·i·um (ves·tij′ē·əm) *n. pl.* **·tig·i·a** (-tij′ē-ə) *Biol.* A vestigial part; vestige. [< L, footprint]

vest·ment (vest′mənt) *n.* **1.** An article of dress; esp., a robe of office. **2.** *Eccl.* One of the ritual garments of the clergy. [< OF < L < *vestire* to clothe] — **vest′ment·al** *adj.*

vest-pock·et (vest′pok′it) *adj.* Small enough to fit in a vest pocket; very small; diminutive: a *vest-pocket* edition.

ves·try (ves′trē) *n. pl.* **·tries 1.** A room, as in a church, where vestments and sacred vessels are kept: often called *sacristy*. **2.** A room in a church used for Sunday School, meetings, as a chapel, etc. **3.** In the Anglican Church, a body administering the affairs of a parish or congregation; also, a meeting of such a body. [< OF *vestiarie* < Med.L *vestiarium* wardrobe]

ves·try·man (ves′trē·mən) *n. pl.* **·men** (-mən) A member of a vestry.

ves·ture (ves′chər) *n.* **1.** *Archaic* Garments; clothing; a robe. **2.** *Archaic* A covering or envelope. — *v.t.* **·tured, ·tur·ing** *Archaic* To cover or clothe with vesture. [< OF < *vestir* cloth < L *vestire* to clothe]

vet¹ (vet) *Informal n.* A veterinarian. — *v.* **vet·ted, vet·ting** *v.t.* **1.** To treat as a veterinarian does. — *v.i.* **2.** To treat animals medically. [Short for VETERINARIAN]

vet² (vet) *n. Informal* A veteran. [Short for VETERAN]

vetch (vech) *n.* **1.** Any of various climbing herbaceous vines of the bean family; esp., the common broad bean, grown for fodder. **2.** A leguminous European plant yielding edible seeds. [< AF *veche, vecce* < L *vicia*]

vet·er·an (vet′ər·ən, vet′rən) *n.* **1.** One who is much experienced in any service. **2.** A former member of the armed forces. — *adj.* **1.** Having had long experience or practice; old in service. **2.** Of or pertaining to veterans. [< MF < L *veteranus* < *vetus, veteris* old]

Veterans Administration An agency of the U.S. government that administers all federal laws relating to the relief of former members of the military and naval services.

Veterans Day A U.S. national holiday honoring veterans of the armed forces, November 11, the anniversary of the armistice in World War I: formerly called *Armistice Day*.

Veterans of Foreign Wars A society of ex-servicemen who have served in the U.S. armed forces in a war with and in a foreign country; founded 1899.

vet·er·i·nar·i·an (vet′ər·ə·nâr′ē·ən, vet′rə-) *n. Chiefly U.S.* A practitioner of veterinary medicine or surgery.

vet·er·i·nar·y (vet′ər·ə·ner′ē, vet′rə-) *adj.* Pertaining to the diseases or injuries of animals, and to their treatment by medical or surgical means. — *n. pl.* **·nar·ies** A veterinarian. [< L *veterinarius* pertaining to beasts of burden]

veterinary medicine The branch of medicine that deals with the prevention, treatment, and cure of animal diseases.

ve·to (vē′tō) *v.t.* **·toed, ·to·ing 1.** To refuse executive approval of (a bill passed by a legislative body). **2.** To forbid or prohibit authoritatively. — *n. pl.* **·toes 1.** The prerogative of a chief executive to refuse to approve a legislative enactment by withholding his signature; also, the exercise of such a prerogative: also *veto power*. **2.** The official communication containing a refusal to approve a bill and the reasons for refusing: also *veto message*. **3.** Any authoritative prohibition. [< L, I forbid] — **ve′to·er** *n.*

vex (veks) *v.t.* **1.** To provoke to anger or displeasure by small irritations; annoy. **2.** To trouble or afflict. **3.** To make a subject of dispute. [< OF < L *vexare* to shake] — **vexed** *adj.* — **vex′er** *n.*

vex·a·tion (vek·sā′shən) *n.* **1.** A vexing or being vexed. **2.** That which vexes.

vex·a·tious (vek·sā′shəs) *adj.* **1.** Causing vexation. **2.** Harassing; annoying. — **vex·a′tious·ly** *adv.* — **vex·a′tious·ness** *n.*

vi·a (vī′ə, vē′ə) *prep.* By way of; by a route passing through: He went to Boston *via* New Haven. ◆ In informal usage, *via* can refer to the means of travel as well as the route: We went *via* train. [< L, ablative sing. of *via* way]

vi·a·ble (vī′ə·bəl) *adj.* **1.** Capable of developing normally, as a newborn infant, a seed, etc. **2.** Workable; practicable. [< F < *vie* life < L *vita*] — **vi′a·bil′i·ty** *n.*

vi·a·duct (vī′ə·dukt) *n.* A bridgelike structure, esp. a large one of arched masonry, to carry a roadway or the like over a valley or ravine. [< L *via* way + (AQUE)-DUCT]

vi·al (vī′əl) *n.* A small bottle for liquids: also *phial*. — **to pour out the vials of wrath upon** To inflict retribution or vengeance on. See *Rev.* xvi. — *v.t.* **vi·aled** or **·alled, ·vi·al·ing** or **·al·ling** To put or keep in or as in a vial. [< OF < L < Gk. *phialē* shallow cup]

VIADUCT
(Pont du Gard, a Roman aqueduct at Nîmes, France)

vi·and (vī′ənd) *n.* **1.** An article of food, esp. meat. **2.** *pl.* Victuals; provisions; food. [< OF *viande*, ult. < L *vivenda*, neut. pl. gerundive of *vivere* to live]

vi·at·i·cum (vī·at′ə·kəm) *n. pl.* **·ca** (-kə) or **·cums 1.** *Eccl.* The Eucharist, as given on the verge of death. **2.** Provisions for a journey. [< L, traveling money, neut. sing. of *viaticus* < *via* way]

vibes¹ (vībz) *n.pl. Informal* A vibraphone.

vibes² (vībz) *n.pl. Slang* Vibration (def. 3).

vi·bran·cy (vī′brən·sē) *n. pl.* **·cies** The state or character of being vibrant; resonance.

vi·brant (vī′brənt) *adj.* **1.** Vibrating. **2.** Throbbing; pulsing: *vibrant* with enthusiasm. **3.** Rich and resonant, as a sound: *vibrant* tones. **4.** Energetic; vigorous. **5.** *Phonet.* Voiced. — *n. Phonet.* A voiced sound. [< L ppr. of *vibrare* to shake] — **vi′brant·ly** *adv.*

vi·bra·phone (vī′brə·fōn) *n.* A type of marimba in which a pulsating sound is produced by valves in the resonators. Also **vi′bra·harp** (-härp′). [< VIBRA(TO) + -PHONE]

vi·brate (vī′brāt) *v.* **·brat·ed, ·brat·ing** *v.i.* **1.** To move back and forth rapidly; quiver. **2.** To move or swing back and forth, as a pendulum. **3.** To sound: The note *vibrates* on the ear. **4.** To be emotionally moved; thrill. **5.** To vacillate; waver, as between choices. — *v.t.* **6.** To cause to quiver or tremble. **7.** To cause to move back and forth. **8.** To send forth (sound, etc.) by vibration. [< L *vibratus*, pp. of *vibrare* to shake]

vi·bra·tile (vī′brə·til, -tīl) *adj.* **1.** Adapted to, having, or used in vibratory motion. **2.** Pertaining to or resembling vibration. — **vi·bra·til′i·ty** (vī′brə·til′ə·tē) *n.*

vi·bra·tion (vī·brā′shən) *n.* **1.** The act of vibrating or the state of being vibrated. **2.** *Physics* **a** Any physical process characterized by cyclic variations in amplitude, intensity, or the like, as wave motion or an electric field. **b** A single complete oscillation. **3.** *pl.* The atmosphere of a place or the mood of a person as perceived by another person. — **vi·bra′tion·al** *adj.* — **vi·bra·to·ry** *adj.*

vi·bra·to (vē·brä′tō) *n. pl.* **·tos** *Music* A trembling or pulsating effect caused by rapid but minute variations in pitch during the production of a tone. [< Ital. < L, pp. of *vibrare* to shake]

vi·bra·tor (vī′brā·tər) *n.* **1.** That which vibrates. **2.** An electrically operated massaging apparatus.

vib·ri·o (vib′rē·ō) *n. pl.* **·ri·os** Any of various comma-shaped bacteria. [< L *vibrare* to shake] — **vib·ri·on′ic** *adj.*

vi·bur·num (vī·bûr′nəm) *n.* Any of a genus of shrubs or small trees related to the honeysuckle, bearing small flowers and berrylike fruit. [< L, the wayfaring tree]

vic·ar (vik′ər) *n.* **1.** In the Anglican Church, the priest of a parish of which the main revenues are appropriated or impropriated by a layman, the priest himself receiving but a stipend. **2.** In the Roman Catholic Church, a substitute or representative of an ecclesiastical person. **3.** In some parishes of the Protestant Episcopal Church, the clergyman who is the head of a chapel. **4.** One authorized to perform functions in the stead of another; deputy. [< AF, OF < L *vicarius* substitute < *vicis* change]

vic·ar·age (vik′ər·ij) *n.* **1.** The benefice, office, or duties of a vicar. **2.** A vicar's residence or household.

vicar general *pl.* **vicars general 1.** In the Roman Catholic Church, a functionary appointed by the bishop as assistant or representative in certain matters of jurisdiction. **2.** In the Church of England, an official assisting the bishop or archbishop in ecclesiastical causes.

vi·car·i·al (vī·kâr′ē·əl, vi-) *adj.* **1.** Vicarious; delegated. **2.** Of, relating to, or acting as a vicar.

vi·car·i·ate (vī·kâr′ē·it, -āt, vi-) *n.* A delegated office or power; esp., the office or authority of a vicar. Also **vic·ar·ate** (vik′ər·it).

vi·car·i·ous (vī·kâr′ē·əs, vi-) *adj.* **1.** Made or performed by substitution; suffered or done in place of another: a *vicarious* sacrifice. **2.** Enjoyed, felt, etc., by a person as a result of his imagined participation in an experience not his own: *vicarious* gratification. **3.** Filling the office of or acting for another. [< L *vicarius* substitute] —**vi·car′i·ous·ly** *adv.* —**vi·car′i·ous·ness** *n.*

Vicar of Christ The Pope.

vic·ar·ship (vik′ər·ship) *n.* The office or position of a vicar.

vice¹ (vīs) *n.* **1.** An immoral habit or trait. **2.** A slight personal fault; foible. **3.** Habitual indulgence in degrading or harmful practices. **4.** Something that mars; a blemish or imperfection. [< OF < L *vitium* fault]

vice² (vīs) See VISE.

vice³ (*adj. & n.* vīs; *prep.* vī′sē) *adj.* Acting in the place of; substitute; deputy: *vice* president. —*n.* One who acts in the place of another; a substitute; deputy. —*prep.* Instead of; in the place of. [< L, ablative of *vicis* change]

vice admiral *Naval* A commissioned officer ranking next below an admiral. Also *Brit. & Canadian* **vice-ad·mi·ral** (vīs′ad′mər·əl). See tables at GRADE.

vice-ad·mir·al·ty (vīs′ad′mər·əl·tē) *n. pl.* **·ties** The office of a vice admiral.

vice consul One who exercises consular authority, either as the substitute or as the subordinate of a consul. —**vice-con·su·lar** (vīs′kon′sə·lər) *adj.* —**vice-con·su·late** (vīs′·kon′sə·lit) *n.* —**vice′-con′sul·ship** *n.*

vice-ge·ren·cy (vīs·jir′ən·sē) *n. pl.* **·cies 1.** The office or authority of a vicegerent. **2.** A district ruled by a vicegerent.

vice-ger·ent (vīs·jir′ent) *n.* One duly authorized to exercise the powers of another; a deputy; vicar. —*adj.* Acting in the place of another, usu. in the place of a superior. [< Med.L < L *vice* in place + *gerens, -entis,* ppr. of *gerere* to carry, manage] —**vice·ge′ral** *adj.*

vi·ce·nar·y (vis′ə·ner′ē) *adj.* **1.** Consisting of or pertaining to twenty. **2.** Relating to a system of notation based upon twenty. [< L < *viceni* twenty each < *viginti* twenty]

vi·cen·ni·al (vī·sen′ē·əl) *adj.* **1.** Occurring once in twenty years. **2.** Lasting or existing twenty years.

vice president An officer ranking next below a president, and acting, on occasion, in his place. —**vice-pres·i·den·cy** (vīs′prez′ə·dən·sē) *n.* —**vice′-pres′i·den′tial** (-prez′ə·den′shəl) *adj.*

vice-re·gal (vīs·rē′gəl) *adj.* Of or relating to a viceroy, his office, or his jurisdiction. Also **vice-roy′al** (-roi′əl). —**vice·re′gal·ly** *adv.*

vice regent A deputy regent. —**vice-re·gen·cy** (vis′rē′jən·sē) *n.* —**vice′-re′gent** *adj.*

vice·roy (vīs′roi) *n.* **1.** One who rules a country, colony, or province by the authority of his sovereign or king. **2.** A North American nymphalid butterfly, orange red with black markings and a row of white marginal spots. [< MF < *vice-, vis-* in place + *roy* king, ult. < L *rex, regis*]

vice·roy·al·ty (vīs·roi′əl·tē) *n. pl.* **·ties 1.** The office or authority of a viceroy. **2.** The term of office of a viceroy. **3.** A district governed by a viceroy. Also **vice′roy·ship.**

vice squad A police division charged with combating prostitution, gambling, etc.

vi·ce ver·sa (vī′sē vûr′sə, vīs′) The order being changed; conversely. [< L]

vi·chy·ssoise (vē′shē·swäz′) *n.* A potato cream soup, usu. served cold. [< F, of Vichy]

Vi·chy water (vish′ē, vē·shē′) The effervescent mineral water from the springs at Vichy, France; also, any mineral water resembling it. Also **Vi′chy, vi′chy.**

vic·i·nage (vis′ə·nij) *n.* **1.** Neighboring places collectively; vicinity. **2.** The state of being a neighbor or neighbors. [< OF < L *vicinus* nearby]

vic·i·nal (vis′ə·nəl) *adj.* Neighboring; adjoining; near.

vi·cin·i·ty (vi·sin′ə·tē) *n. pl.* **·ties 1.** A region adjacent or near; neighborhood. **2.** Nearness in space or relationship; proximity. [< L *vicinus* nearby]

vi·cious (vish′əs) *adj.* **1.** Characterized by malice or spite; malicious. **2.** Characterized by violence and fierceness: a *vicious* blow. **3.** Addicted to vice; corrupt in conduct or

habits. **4.** Morally injurious, vile. **5.** Unruly or dangerous; refractory, as an animal. **6.** Defective or faulty. **7.** *Informal* Intense; severe; extreme: a *vicious* storm. [< OF < L *vitium* fault] —**vi′cious·ly** *adv.* —**vi′cious·ness** *n.*

vicious circle 1. The process or predicament that arises when the solution of a problem creates a new problem and each successive solution adds another problem. **2.** *Med.* The accelerating effect of one disease upon another when the two are coexistent.

vi·cis·si·tude (vi·sis′ə·tōōd, -tyōōd) *n.* **1.** *pl.* Irregular changes or variations, as of fortune: the *vicissitudes* of life. **2.** A change; esp., a complete change; mutation or mutability. **3.** Alternating change or succession, as of the seasons. [< MF < L < *vicis* turn, change]

vi·cis·si·tu·di·nar·y (vi·sis′ə·tōō′də·ner′ē, -tyōō′-) *adj.* Marked by or subject to change. Also **vi·cis′si·tu′di·nous.**

vic·tim (vik′tim) *n.* **1.** One who is killed, injured, or subjected to suffering. **2.** One who is swindled or tricked; a dupe. **3.** A living creature sacrificed to some deity or as a religious rite. [< L *victima* beast for sacrifice]

vic·tim·ize (vik′tim·īz) *v.t.* **·ized, ·iz·ing** To make a victim of, esp. by defrauding or swindling; dupe; cheat. —**vic′tim·i·za′tion** *n.* —**vic′tim·iz′er** *n.*

vic·tor (vik′tər) *n.* **1.** One who vanquishes an enemy. **2.** One who wins any struggle or contest. —*adj.* Pertaining to a victor; victorious: the *victor* nation. [< AF *victor, victour,* OF *victeur* < L *victus,* pp. of *vincere* to conquer]

vic·to·ri·a (vik·tôr′ē·ə, -tō′rē·ə) *n.* A low, light, four-wheeled carriage, with a calash top, a seat for two persons, and a raised driver's seat. [after Queen *Victoria*]

Vic·to·ri·a (vik·tôr′ē·ə, -tō′rē·ə) *n.* In Roman mythology, the winged goddess of victory: identified with the Greek *Nike.*

Victoria Cross A British military and naval decoration in the form of a bronze Maltese cross, awarded for conspicuous bravery. *Abbr. V.C.*

Victoria Day In Canada, the Monday next before May 24, commemorating the birthday of Queen Victoria.

Vic·to·ri·an (vik·tôr′ē·ən, -tō′rē-) *adj.* **1.** Of or relating to Queen Victoria, or to her reign. **2.** Pertaining to or characteristic of the ideals and standards of morality and taste prevalent during the reign of Queen Victoria; prudish; conventional; narrow. —*n.* Anyone, esp. an author, contemporary with Queen Victoria. —**Vic·to′ri·an·ism** *n.*

vic·to·ri·ous (vik·tôr′ē·əs, -tō′rē-) *adj.* **1.** Having won victory; triumphant. **2.** Relating to or characterized by victory. —**vic·to′ri·ous·ly** *adv.* —**vic·to′ri·ous·ness** *n.*

vic·to·ry (vik′tər·ē) *n. pl.* **·ries** The overcoming of an enemy, opponent, or any difficulty; triumph. [See VICTOR.]

vict·ual (vit′l) *n.* Food for human beings, as prepared for eating: used in the plural. —*v.* **vict·ualed** or **·ualled, vict·ual·ing** or **·ual·ling** *v.t.* **1.** To furnish with victuals. —*v.i.* **2.** To lay in supplies of food. [< OF < LL *victualia* provisions < L *victus* food]

vi·cu·ña (vi·kōōn′yə, -kyōō′nə) *n.* **1.** A small ruminant of the high Andes related to the llama and alpaca, having fine and valuable wool. **2.** A textile made from this wool, or some substitute. Also **vi·cu′gna.** [< Sp. < Quechua]

vi·de (vī′dē) See: used to make a reference or direct attention to: *vide* p. 36. [< L, imperative sing. of *videre* to see]

vi·de an·te (vī′dē an′tē) *Latin* See before.

vi·de in·fra (vī′dē in′frə) *Latin* See below.

vi·de·li·cet (vi·del′ə·sit) *adv.* To wit; that is to say; namely. *Abbr. viz.* [< L < *videre licet* it is permitted to see]

vid·e·o (vid′ē·ō) *adj.* **1.** Of or pertaining to television, esp. to the picture. **2.** Producing a signal convertible into a television picture: a *video* cassette. —*n.* A television image. [< L, I see]

vid·e·o·tape (vid′ē·ō·tāp′) *n.* A recording of a television program on magnetic tape. —*v.t.* **·taped, ·tap·ing** To make such a recording.

vi·de post (vī′dē pōst′) *Latin* See after; see what follows.

vi·de su·pra (vī′dē sōō′prə) *Latin* See above.

vi·dette (vī·det′) See VEDETTE.

vi·de ut su·pra (vī′dē ut sōō′prə) *Latin* See what is written above.

vie (vī) *v.* **vied, vy·ing** *v.i.* **1.** To strive for superiority; compete, as in a race: with *with* or *for.* —*v.t.* **2.** *Rare* To put forth in competition. [< MF < L *invitare* to invite]

Vi·en·nese (vē′ə·nēz′, -nēs′) *adj.* Of or relating to Vienna, or its inhabitants. —*n. pl.* **·nese** A native or citizen of Vienna.

Vi·et·nam·ese (vē·et′näm·ēz′, -ēs′) *n. pl.* **Vi·et·nam·ese 1.** A native or inhabitant of Vietnam. **2.** The language of Vietnam: formerly called *Annamese.* —*adj.* Of or pertaining to Vietnam, its inhabitants, or their language.

view (vyōō) *n.* **1.** The act of seeing; survey; inspection. **2.** Mental examination or inspection. **3.** Power or range of vision. **4.** That which is seen; outlook; prospect. **5.** A representation of a scene; esp., a landscape. **6.** The object of action; aim; intention; purpose. **7.** Manner of looking at things; opinion; judgment. **8.** A general summary or account. **— in view 1.** In range of vision. **2.** Under consideration. **3.** As a goal or end. **— in view of** In consideration of. **— on view** Open to the public; set up for public inspection. **— with a view to 1.** With the aim or purpose of. **2.** With a hope of. *— v.t.* **1.** To look at; see; behold. **2.** To look at carefully; observe. **3.** To survey mentally; consider. [< OF *veoir* to see < L *videre*] **— view'er** *n.*

view finder *Photog.* A finder (def. 3).

view·less (vyōō'lis) *adj.* **1.** Devoid of a view; that cannot be viewed. **2.** Having no views or opinions. **3.** Invisible; unseen. **— view'less·ly** *adv.* **— view'less·ness** *n.*

view·point (vyōō'point') *n.* Point of view.

vi·ges·i·mal (vī·jes'ə·məl) *adj.* **1.** Twentieth. **2.** Of or pertaining to twenty; proceeding by twenties. [< L *viginti* twenty]

vig·il (vij'əl) *n.* **1.** The act of staying awake in order to observe, protect, etc.; watch. **2.** *Eccl.* **a** The eve of a holy day. **b** *pl.* Religious devotions on such an eve. [< OF < Med.L < L *vigil* wide-awake]

vig·i·lance (vij'ə·ləns) *n.* The quality of being vigilant; alertness; watchfulness in guarding against danger.

vigilance committee *U.S.* Formerly, a body of men self-organized for the maintenance of order and the administration of summary justice.

vig·i·lant (vij'ə·lənt) *adj.* Characterized by vigilance; being on the alert; watchful; heedful; wary. [< MF < L < *vigil* awake] **— vig'i·lant·ly** *adv.* **— vig'i·lant·ness** *n.*

— **Syn.** *Vigilant* suggests action as well as attention: a riot was averted by the *vigilant* police. *Watchful* suggests unremitting attention: his *watchful* eye caught the covert signal. *Alert* stresses the speed of a response to necessity or opportunity: *alert* traders made a killing on the stock market. **— Ant.** inattentive, heedless.

vig·i·lan·te (vij'ə·lan'tē) *n. U.S.* **1.** One of a group who take upon themselves the unauthorized responsibility of interpreting and acting upon matters of law, public morality, etc. **2.** A member of a vigilance committee: also **vigilance man.** [< Sp., vigilant < L. See VIGILANT.]

vi·gnette (vin·yet') *n.* **1.** A description, short literary work, etc., that depicts something subtly and delicately. **2.** Any charming, intimate scene, etc. **3.** A decorative design placed on or before the title page of a book, at the end or beginning of a chapter, etc. **4.** An engraving, photograph, or the like, having a background that shades off gradually. *— v.t.* **·gnet·ted, ·gnet·ting 1.** To make with a gradually shaded background, as a photograph. **2.** To ornament with vignettes. **3.** To depict in a vignette. [< F, dim. of *vigne* vine] **— vi·gnet'tist** *n.*

vig·or (vig'ər) *n.* **1.** Active strength or force, physical or mental. **2.** Vital or natural power, as in a healthy animal or plant. **3.** Forcible exertion of strength; energy; intensity. **4.** Effective force; validity. Also *Brit.* **vig'our.** [< AF, OF < L *vigere* to be lively, thrive]

vig·or·ous (vig'ər·əs) *adj.* **1.** Full of physical or mental vigor; robust. **2.** Performed or done with vigor. **3.** Showing or exemplifying vigor. **4.** Forceful and effective: a *vigorous* style. **— vig'or·ous·ly** *adv.* **— vig'or·ous·ness** *n.*

vi·king (vī'king) *n.* One of the Scandinavian warriors who harried the coasts of Europe from the eighth to the tenth centuries. Also **Vi'king.** [< ON *vikingr* pirate]

vile (vīl) *adj.* **vil·er, vil·est 1.** Morally base; shamefully wicked. **2.** Despicable; vicious. **3.** Loathsome; disgusting. **4.** Degrading; ignominious: *vile* treatment. **5.** Flagrantly bad or inferior. **6.** Unpleasant; disagreeable. [< AF, OF < L *vilis* cheap] **— vile'ly** *adv.* **— vile'ness** *n.*

vil·i·fy (vil'ə·fī) *v.t.* **·fied, ·fy·ing 1.** To abuse or characterize with defamatory language; malign; slander. **2.** To make base; degrade. [< LL < L *vilis* cheap + *facere* to make] **— vil'i·fi·ca'tion** (-fə·kā'shən) *n.* **— vil'i·fi'er** *n.*

vil·la (vil'ə) *n.* **1.** A comfortable or luxurious house in the country, at a resort, etc. **2.** *Chiefly Brit.* A modest suburban residence. [< Ital. < L, a country house, farm]

vil·lage (vil'ij) *n.* **1.** A collection of houses in a rural district, usu. smaller than a town but larger than a hamlet. **2.** *U.S.* In some States, a municipality smaller than a city, sometimes incorporated. **3.** Any comparatively small community. **4.** The inhabitants of a village, collectively. [< OF < L < *villa* a country house]

vil·lag·er (vil'ij·ər) *n.* One who lives in a village.

vil·lain (vil'ən) *n.* **1.** An egregiously wicked, evil, or malevolent man. **2.** Such a man represented as a leading character in a novel, play, etc., often in opposition to the hero. **3.** A rogue; scoundrel: often used humorously. **4.** A villein. [< AF, OF *vilein, vilain* farm servant < LL < L *villa* farm] **— vil'lain·ess** *n.fem.*

vil·lain·ous (vil'ən·əs) *adj.* **1.** Having the nature of a villain. **2.** Characteristic of a villain; evil. **3.** Very bad or unpleasant. **— vil'lain·ous·ly** *adv.* **— vil'lain·ous·ness** *n.*

vil·lain·y (vil'ən·ē) *n. pl.* **·lain·ies 1.** The quality of being villainous. **2.** Conduct characteristic of a villain.

vil·lein (vil'ən) *n.* In the feudal system, a member of a class of serfs who were regarded as freemen in respect to their legal relations with all persons except their lord: also *villain.* [See VILLAIN.] **— vil'lain·age, vil'lein·age, vil'len·age** *n.*

vil·lus (vil'əs) *n. pl.* **vil·li** (vil'ī) **1.** *Anat.* One of the short, hairlike processes found on certain membranes, as of the small intestine, where they aid in the digestive process. **2.** *Bot.* One of the long, close, rather soft hairs on the surface of certain plants. [< L, tuft of hair, shaggy hair, var. of *vellus* fleece, wool] **— vil'lous** *adj.* **— vil'lous·ly** *adv.*

vim (vim) *n.* Force or vigor; energy; spirit. [< L, accusative of *vis* power]

vin (vaṅ) *n. French* Wine.

vin- Var. of VINI-.

vi·na (vē'nä) *n.* An East Indian musical instrument with seven steel strings stretched on a long, fretted fingerboard over two gourds. [< Hind. *vīnā* < Skt.]

vi·na·ceous (vī·nā'shəs) *adj.* **1.** Of or pertaining to wine or grapes. **2.** Having the characteristic color of red wine. [< L *vinaceus* < *vinum* wine]

vin·ai·grette (vin'ə·gret') *n.* **1.** A small ornamental box or bottle, used for holding smelling salts, or a similar pungent restorative. **2.** Vinaigrette sauce. [< F, dim. of *vinaigre* vinegar]

vinaigrette sauce A sauce made from vinegar, savory herbs, etc., served with fish and cold meats.

vin·ci·ble (vin'sə·bəl) *adj. Rare* Capable of being conquered or overcome; conquerable. [< L *vincibilis* < *vincere* to conquer] **— vin'ci·bil'i·ty, vin'ci·ble·ness** *n.*

vin·cu·lum (vingk'yə·ləm) *n. pl.* **·la** (-lə) *Math.* A straight line drawn over several algebraic terms to show that all are to be operated on together. [< L < *vincire* to bind]

vin·di·ca·ble (vin'də·kə·bəl) *adj.* Capable of being vindicated; justifiable.

vin·di·cate (vin'də·kāt) *v.t.* **·cat·ed, ·cat·ing 1.** To clear of accusation, censure, suspicion, etc. **2.** To support or maintain, as a right or claim. **3.** To serve to justify. [< L *vindicatus*, pp. of *vindicare* to avenge, claim] **— vin'di·ca'tor** *n.*

vin·di·ca·tion (vin'də·kā'shən) *n.* **1.** A vindicating or being vindicated. **2.** Justification; defense.

vin·di·ca·to·ry (vin'də·kə·tôr'ē, -tō'rē) *adj.* **1.** Serving to vindicate; justificatory. **2.** Punitive; avenging.

vin·dic·tive (vin·dik'tiv) *adj.* **1.** Having a revengeful spirit. **2.** Revengeful or spiteful in quality, character, etc. [< L *vindicta* revenge] **— vin·dic'tive·ly** *adv.* **— vin·dic'tive·ness** *n.*

vine (vīn) *n.* **1.** Any of a large and widely distributed group of plants having a slender flexible stem that may twine about a support or clasp it by means of tendrils, petioles, etc.; also, the slender flexible stem itself. **2.** A grapevine. [< OF *vigne, vine* < L *vinea* vineyard < *vinum* wine]

vin·e·gar (vin'ə·gər) *n.* **1.** An acid liquid consisting chiefly of dilute acetic acid, obtained by the fermentation of cider, wine, etc., and used as a condiment and preservative. **2.** Sourness of manner, speech, etc. [< OF < *vin* wine + *aigre,egre* sour] **— vin'e·gar·y, vin'e·gar·ish** *adj.*

vin·er·y (vī'nər·ē) *n. pl.* **·er·ies 1.** A greenhouse for grapes; grapery. **2.** Vines collectively.

vine·yard (vin'yərd) *n.* An area planted with grapevines. [Earlier *wineyard*, OE *winegeard*]

vingt-et-un (vaṅ·tā·œn') *n.* Twenty-one, a card game. [< F, twenty-one]

vini- *combining form* **1.** Wine. **2.** Of or pertaining to wine grapes. Also *vin-* (before vowels): also **vino-**. [< L *vinum* wine]

vin·i·cul·ture (vin'ə·kul'chər) *n.* The cultivation of grapes for wine. **— vin'i·cul'tur·al** *adj.* **— vin'i·cul'tur·ist** *n.*

vin or·di·naire (vaṅ ôr·dē·nâr') *French* Cheap red wine; literally, ordinary wine.

vi·nous (vī'nəs) *adj.* **1.** Pertaining to, characteristic of, or having the qualities of wine. **2.** Caused by, affected by, or addicted to wine. **3.** Tinged with dark red. [< L < *vinum* wine] **— vi·nos'i·ty** (-nos'ə·tē) *n.*

vin·tage (vin'tij) *n.* **1.** The yield of a vineyard or wine-growing district for one season; also, the wine produced from this yield. **2.** The harvesting of a vineyard and the making of wine. **3.** Wine of high quality or of an exceptionally good year: also **vintage wine. 4.** *Informal* The type popular at a particular time of the past: a joke of ancient *vintage.* — *adj.* Of exceptional quality or excellence; choice: a *vintage* wine. [< AF, alter. of *vindage, vendage*, OF *vendaĝe* < L < *vinum* wine + *demere* to remove]

vint·ner (vint'nər) *n.* A wine merchant. [< OF *vinetier, vinotier* < *vinot*, dim. of *vin* wine < L *vinum*]

vin·y (vī'nē) *adj.* **vin·i·er, vin·i·est 1.** Of, pertaining to, or resembling a vine. **2.** Full of vines.

vi·nyl (vī′nəl, vin′əl) *n. Chem.* The univalent radical, CH₂:CH, derived from ethylene, and extensively used in organic synthesis. [< L *vinum* wine + -YL]

vi·ol (vī′əl) *n.* Any of a family of stringed musical instruments, predecessors of the violin family; also, any member of the violin family. [Earlier *vielle* < AF, OF < Med.L *vidula*, *vitula* < Gmc.]

vi·o·la (vē-ō′lə, vī-; *Ital.* vyō′lä) *n.* A musical instrument of the violin family, somewhat larger than the violin, and tuned a fifth lower, with a graver and less brilliant tone. [< Ital., orig., a viol < Med.L *vidula* < Gmc.]

vi·o·la·ble (vī′ə-lə-bəl) *adj.* Capable of being violated. [< L *violabilis* < *violare*. See VIOLATE.] — **vi′o·la·ble·ness, vi′o·la·bil′i·ty** *n.* — **vi′o·la·bly** *adv.* [< L *violaceus* < *viola* violet]

viola da gam·ba (dä gäm′bä) The bass of the viol family, held between the legs, and having a range similar to that of the cello, but with a thinner tone: also called *bass viol.* [< Ital., viol of the leg]

vi·o·late (vī′ə-lāt) *v.t.* **·lat·ed, ·lat·ing 1.** To break or infringe, as a law, oath, agreement, etc. **2.** To profane, as a holy place. **3.** To break in upon; disturb. **4.** To ravish; rape. **5.** To do violence to; offend grossly; outrage. [< L *violatus*, pp. of *violare* to use violence < *vis* force] — **vi′o·la′tive** *adj.* — **vi′o·la′tor** *n.*

vi·o·la·tion (vī′ə-lā′shən) *n.* **1.** The act of violating, or the state of being violated. **2.** Infringement or infraction, as of a law, regulation, etc. **3.** Profanation; desecration. **4.** Rape.

vi·o·lence (vī′ə-ləns) *n.* **1.** The quality or state of being violent; intensity; fury. **2.** An instance of violent action, treatment, etc. **3.** Violent or abusive exercise of power; injury; outrage. **4.** *Law* Physical force unlawfully exercised. **5.** Perversion or distortion of meaning, intent, etc. — **to do violence to 1.** To injure or damage by rough or abusive treatment. **2.** To distort the meaning of.

vi·o·lent (vī′ə-lənt) *adj.* **1.** Proceeding from or marked by great physical force or roughness; overwhelmingly forcible. **2.** Caused by or exhibiting intense emotional or mental excitement; passionate; impetuous; fierce. **3.** Characterized by intensity of any kind; extreme: *violent* heat. **4.** Marked by undue exercise of force; harsh; severe: to take *violent* measures. **5.** Resulting from unusual force or injury: a *violent* death. **6.** Tending to pervert the meaning or sense: a *violent* construction. [< OF < L *violentus* < *vis* force] — **vi′o·lent·ly** *adv.*

vi·o·let (vī′ə-lit) *n.* **1.** One of a widely distributed genus of herbaceous perennial herbs, bearing spurred flowers typically having a purplish blue color but sometimes yellow or white. The violet is the State flower of Illinois, New Jersey, Rhode Island, and Wisconsin. **2.** Any of several similar plants. **3.** A deep bluish purple color. — *adj.* Having a bluish purple color. [< OF < L *viola* violet]

violet rays 1. High-frequency radiation from the violet end of the visible spectrum. **2.** Loosely, ultraviolet rays.

vi·o·lin (vī′ə-lin′) *n.* A musical instrument having four strings and a sounding box of seasoned wood, held against the shoulder and played by means of a bow. It is the treble member of the **violin family,** which includes also the viola and cello: also called *fiddle.* [< Ital. *violino,* dim. of *viola*]

vi·o·lin·ist (vī′ə-lin′ist) *n.* One who plays the violin.

vi·o·list (vē-ō′list *for def. 1,* vī′ə-list *for def. 2*) *n.* **1.** One who plays the viola. **2.** One who plays a viol.

vi·o·lon·cel·list (vē′ə-lən-chel′ist) *n.* A cellist.

vi·o·lon·cel·lo (vē′ə-lən-chel′ō) *n. pl.* **·los** A cello. [< Ital., dim. of *violone* double bass]

VIP or **V.I.P.** Very important person.

vi·per (vī′pər) *n.* **1.** Any of a family of venomous Old World snakes, esp. a small, variously colored snake native to Europe. **2.** Any of various similar or related snakes. **3.** Loosely, a pit viper. **4.** Any allegedly poisonous snake. **5.** A treacherous or spiteful person. [< OF < L < *vivus* living + *parere* to bring forth] — **vi′per·ine** *adj.* — **vi′per·ish** *adj.*

vi·per·ous (vī′pər-əs) *adj.* **1.** Snakelike; viperine. **2.** Venomous; malicious. — **vi′per·ous·ly** *adj.*

vi·ra·go (vi-rä′gō, -rā′-, vī-) *n. pl.* **·goes** or **·gos** A noisy, sharp-tongued woman; a scold. [< L, mannish woman < *vir* man]

vi·ral (vī′rəl) *adj.* Of, pertaining to, caused by, or of the nature of a virus.

VIOLIN

a Scroll. *b* Peg box. *c* Peg. *d* Nut. *e* Fingerboard. *f* Neck plate. *g* Sound hole. *h* Bridge. *i* Tailpiece. *j* Chin rest. *k* Button.

vir·e·o (vir′ē·ō) *n. pl.* **·os** Any of various small, insectivorous birds having predominantly dull green and grayish plumage. [< L, a small bird, ? the greenfinch]

vi·res·cence (vī-res′əns) *n.* The state or condition of becoming green.

vi·res·cent (vī-res′ənt) *adj.* Greenish or becoming green. [< L *virescens, -entis,* ppr. of *virescere* to grow green]

vir·gin (vûr′jin) *n.* **1.** A person, esp. a young woman, who has never had sexual intercourse. **2.** A chaste young girl or unmarried woman. — *adj.* **1.** Being a virgin. **2.** Pertaining or suited to a virgin; chaste; maidenly. **3.** Uncorrupted; pure; undefiled: *virgin* whiteness. **4.** Not hitherto used, touched, tilled, or worked upon by man: *virgin* soil. **5.** Not previously processed: *virgin* rubber; *virgin* wool. [< OF < L *virgo, -inis* maiden]

Vir·gin (vûr′jin) *n.* **1.** Mary, the mother of Jesus: usu. preceded by *the:* also **Virgin Mary. 2.** The constellation and sign of the zodiac Virgo.

vir·gin·al¹ (vûr′jin·əl) *adj.* Pertaining to or characteristic of a virgin; chaste. [< OF < L *virginalis* < *virgo, -inis* virgin]

vir·gin·al² (vûr′jin·əl) *n. Often pl.* A small, legless harpsichord of the 16th and 17th centuries: sometimes called a **pair of virginals.** [< OF < VIRGINAL¹; ? so called from its use by young men and girls]

virgin birth *Theol.* The doctrine that Jesus Christ was divinely conceived without impairment of the virginity of his mother Mary. Also **Virgin Birth.**

Virginia cowslip A smooth perennial herb having clusters of tubular blue flowers. Also **Virginia bluebell.**

Virginia creeper A common American climbing vine of the grape family, with compound toothed leaves and dark blue berries: also called *five-fingers, woodbine.*

Vir·gin·ian (vər·jin′yən) *adj.* Of, pertaining to, or from Virginia. — *n.* A native or inhabitant of Virginia.

Virginia reel A country-dance in which the performers stand in two parallel lines and perform various figures.

vir·gin·i·ty (vər·jin′ə·tē) *n. pl.* **·ties 1.** The state or condition of being a virgin; maidenhood; virginal chastity. **2.** The state of being unsullied, unused, untouched, etc.

vir·gin·i·um (vər·jin′ē·əm) *n.* The former name of an element now identified as francium. [after the State of *Virginia*]

Virgin Mary Mary, the mother of Jesus: usu. with *the.*

vir·gin's-bow·er (vûr′jinz·bou′ər) *n.* A species of clematis bearing white flowers in leafy panicles.

Vir·go (vûr′gō) *n.* A constellation, the Virgin, containing the bright star Spica; also, the sixth sign of the zodiac. [< L, a virgin]

vir·gule (vûr′gyool) *n.* A slanting line (/) used to indicate two alternatives, as in *and/or,* to set off phoneme symbols, etc.: also called *slash.* [< L *virgula,* dim. of *virga* rod]

vir·i·des·cent (vir′ə·des′ənt) *adj.* Greenish, or becoming slightly green. [< LL < *viridescere* to become green] — **vir′i·des′cence** *n.*

vir·ile (vir′əl) *adj.* **1.** Having the characteristics of adult manhood; masculine. **2.** Having qualities considered typically masculine; vigorous; forceful. **3.** Capable of procreation. [< OF < L *virilis* < *vir* man]

vi·ril·i·ty (və·ril′ə·tē) *n. pl.* **·ties** The state, character, or quality of being virile.

vi·rol·o·gy (və·rol′ə·jē, vī-) *n.* The study of viruses, esp. in their relation to disease. [< *viro-* (< VIRUS) + -LOGY] — **vi·rol′o·gist** *n.*

vir·tu (vər·tōō′, vûr′tōō) *n.* **1.** Rare, curious, or beautiful quality: usu. in the phrase **objects** or **articles of virtu. 2.** A taste for such objects. **3.** Such objects collectively. Also spelled *vertu.* [< Ital. *virtù* merit < L *virtus* strength]

vir·tu·al (vûr′chōō·əl) *adj.* Having the effect but not the actual form of what is specified: a *virtual* usurpation. [See VIRTUE.] — **vir′tu·al′i·ty** (-al′ə·tē) *n.*

vir·tu·al·ly (vûr′chōō·ə·lē) *adv.* In effect; for all practical purposes.

vir·tue (vûr′chōō) *n.* **1.** The quality of moral righteousness or excellence; rectitude. **2.** The practice of moral duties and the abstinence from immorality and vice. **3.** Chastity, esp. in women. **4.** A particular type of moral excellence, esp. one of those considered to be of special importance in philosophical or religious doctrine. Compare CARDINAL VIRTUES. **5.** Any admirable quality or trait. **6.** Inherent or essential quality, power, etc. **7.** Efficacy; potency. — **by** (or **in**) **virtue of** By or through the fact, quality, force, or authority of. — **to make a virtue of necessity** To seem to do freely or from principle what is or must be done necessarily. [< OF < L *virtus* strength, bravery < *vir* man]

— **Syn.** We regard *virtue* as acquired through self-discipline, and predicate it of human beings only. *Goodness* is an innate quality, and so may be ascribed to God as well as to man. *Morality* involves conformity to an accepted code of right conduct; it is less elevated but more concrete than *virtue. Rectitude* also implies conformity to a moral code, but stresses intention or disposition; hence, a man's *morality* may arise from fear of punishment or of censure, but his *rectitude* can come only from a love of the right and a conscious desire to follow it. — **Ant.** vice, sin, evil.

vir·tu·os·i·ty (vûr′chōō·os′ə·tē) *n. pl.* **·ties** The skill, etc., of a virtuoso; technical mastery of an art, as music.

vir·tu·o·so (vûr′chōō·ō′sō) *n. pl.* **·si** (-sē) or **·sos** 1. A master of technique, as a skilled musician. 2. One who displays impressive or dazzling skill in any area of accomplishment. 3. A connoisseur; a collector or lover of curios or works of art. [< Ital., skilled, learned]

vir·tu·ous (vûr′chōō·əs) *adj.* 1. Characterized by, exhibiting, or having the nature of virtue. 2. Chaste: now said esp. of women. — **vir′tu·ous·ly** *adv.* — **vir′tu·ous·ness** *n.*

vir·u·lent (vir′yə·lənt, vir′ə-) *adj.* 1. Manifesting or characterized by malignity; exceedingly noxious, harmful, etc. 2. Bitterly rancorous; acrimonious. 3. *Med.* Actively poisonous or infective; malignant. 4. *Bacteriol.* Having the power to injure an organism by invasion of tissue and generation of internal toxins, as certain microorganisms. [< L *virus* poison] — **vir′u·lence** *n.* — **vir′u·lent·ly** *adv.*

vi·rus (vī′rəs) *n.* 1. Any of a class of filterable, submicroscopic pathogenic agents, chiefly protein in composition but often reducible to crystalline form, and typically inert except when in contact with certain living cells: also called *filterable virus*. 2. An illness caused by such an agent. 3. Any virulent substance developed within an animal body, and capable of transmitting a specific disease. 4. Venom, as of a snake. — **Syn.** See MICROBE. [< L, poison, slime]

vis (vis) *n. pl.* **vi·res** (vī′rēz) *Latin* Force; potency.

vi·sa (vē′zə) *n.* An official endorsement, as on a passport, certifying that it has been found correct and that the bearer may proceed. — *v.t.* **·saed, ·sa·ing** 1. To put a visa on. 2. To give a visa to. Also *visé.* [< F < L < *videre* to see]

vis·age (viz′ij) *n.* The face or facial expression of a person; countenance; distinctive aspect. [< OF < L *visus* look, appearance < *videre* to see] — **vis′aged** *adj.*

vis·ard (viz′ərd) See VIZARD.

vis-à-vis (vē′zə·vē′, *Fr.* vē·zà·vē′) *n. pl.* **vis-à-vis** 1. One of two persons or things that face each other from opposite sides. 2. One in a corresponding capacity, etc. — *adv.* Face to face. — *prep.* Regarding. [< F, face to face]

vis·cer·a (vis′ər·ə) *n. pl. of* **vis·cus** (vis′kəs) *Anat.* The internal organs, esp. those of the great cavities of the body, as the stomach, lungs, heart, intestines, etc. [< L, pl. of *viscus* internal organ] — **vis′cer·al** *adj.*

vis·cid (vis′id) *adj.* Sticky or adhesive; mucilaginous; viscous. [< LL < L *viscum* birdlime] — **vis·cid·i·ty** (vi·sid′ə·tē), **vis′cid·ness** *n.* — **vis′cid·ly** *adv.*

vis·cose (vis′kōs) *n. Chem.* A thick, honeylike substance produced by the action of caustic soda and carbon disulfide upon cellulose, and constituting an important source of rayon. — *adj.* 1. Viscous. 2. Of, pertaining to, containing, or made from viscose. [See VISCOUS.]

vis·cos·i·ty (vis·kos′ə·tē) *n. pl.* **·ties** 1. The state, quality, property, or degree of being viscous. 2. *Physics* That property of fluids by virtue of which they offer resistance to flow or to any change in the arrangement of their molecules.

vis·count (vī′kount) *n.* In England, a title of nobility ranking between those of earl and baron. [< AF, OF < *vis-* in place (< L *vice*) + *counte.* See COUNT².] — **vis′count·cy, vis′count·ship, vis′count·y** *n.*

vis·count·ess (vī′koun·tis) *n.* 1. The wife of a viscount. 2. A peeress holding a corresponding title in her own right.

vis·cous (vis′kəs) *adj.* 1. Glutinous; semifluid; sticky. 2. *Physics* Characterized by or having viscosity. [< LL < L *viscum* birdlime] — **vis′cous·ly** *adv.* — **vis′cous·ness** *n.*

vis·cus (vis′kəs) Singular of VISCERA.

vise (vīs) *n.* A clamping device, usu. of two jaws made to be closed together with a screw, lever, etc., used for grasping and holding objects being worked on, glued, etc. — *v.t.* **vised, vis·ing** To hold, force, or squeeze in or as in a vise. Also, *Brit.,* **vice.** [< OF < L *vitis* vine; with ref. to the spiral growth of vine tendrils]

vi·sé (vē′zā, vē·zā′) *v.t.* **·séed, ·sé·ing** To visa. — *n.* A visa.

Vish·nu (vish′nōō) In Hindu theology, a major deity, a member of the trinity also including Brahma and Siva, and having many incarnations, of which the most famous is as Krishna. — **Vish′nu·ism** *n.*

vis·i·bil·i·ty (viz′ə·bil′ə·tē) *n. pl.* **·ties** 1. Condition, capability, or degree of being visible. 2. The clarity of unaided vision as affected by distance, atmospheric conditions, etc.

vis·i·ble (viz′ə·bəl) *adj.* 1. Perceivable by the eye; capable of being seen. 2. Apparent; observable; evident. 3. At hand; available; manifest. [< OF < L *visibilis* < *videre* to see] — **vis′i·ble·ness** *n.* — **vis′i·bly** *adv.*

Vis·i·goth (viz′ə·goth) *n.* One of the western Goths, a Teutonic people that invaded the Roman Empire in the third and fourth centuries and settled in France and Spain. [< LL *Visigothus*] — **Vis′i·goth′ic** *adj.*

vi·sion (vizh′ən) *n.* 1. The faculty or sense of sight. 2. The ability to anticipate and make provision for future events; foresight. 3. Insight; imagination: a man of great *vision.* 4. A mental representation of or as of external objects, scenes, etc., as in a religious revelation, dream, etc. 5. A vividly imagined thing, state, occurrence, etc. 6. Something or someone very beautiful or pleasing. — *v.t. Rare* To see in or as in a vision. [< OF < L *visio* < *videre* to see] — **vi′sion·al** *adj.* — **vi′sion·al·ly** *adv.*

vi·sion·ar·y (vizh′ən·er′ē) *adj.* 1. Not founded on fact; imaginary; impracticable. 2. Affected by or tending toward fantasies; dreamy; impractical. 3. Having idealistic goals or aims incapable of realization. 4. Having or of the nature of apparitions, dreams, etc. — *n. pl.* **·ar·ies** 1. One who has visions. 2. A dreamer; an impractical schemer. 3. One who is impracticably idealistic. — **vi′sion·ar′i·ness** *n.*

vis·it (viz′it) *v.t.* 1. To go or come to see (a person) from friendship, on business, etc. 2. To go or come to (a place, etc.), as for touring, etc. 3. To be a guest of; stay with temporarily. 4. To go or come to so as to make official inspection or inquiry. 5. To come upon or afflict. 6. To inflict punishment upon or for. 7. To inflict (punishment, wrath, etc.). — *v.i.* 8. To make a visit; pay a call or calls. 9. *Informal* To chat or converse sociably. — *n.* 1. The act of visiting a person or thing. 2. A sojourn in a place or with a person. 3. *Informal* A talk or friendly chat. 4. An authoritative personal call for inspection and examination, or discharge of an official or professional duty. [< OF < L *visitare* to go to see < *videre* to see] — **vis′it·a·ble** *adj.*

vis·i·tant (viz′ə·tənt) *n.* 1. A visitor. 2. A migratory animal or bird stopping at a particular region.

vis·i·ta·tion (viz′ə·tā′shən) *n.* 1. The act or fact of visiting; a visit; also, the state or circumstance of being visited. 2. An official or authoritative inspection and examination. 3. In Biblical and religious use, a visiting of blessing or affliction. — **vis′i·ta′tion·al** *adj.* — **vis′i·ta·to′ri·al** (-tə·tôr′ē·əl, -tō′rē-) *adj.*

Vis·i·ta·tion (viz′ə·tā′shən) *n. Eccl.* 1. The visit of the Virgin Mary to Elizabeth. *Luke* i 39–42. 2. July 2, the church festival commemorating this visit.

vis·it·ing card (viz′i·ting) A calling card.

vis·i·tor (viz′ə·tər) *n.* One who visits.

vi·sor (vī′zər, viz′ər) *n.* 1. A projecting piece at the front of a cap, etc., serving as a shade for the eyes. 2. In armor, the movable front piece of a helmet, serving to protect the upper part of the face. 3. A movable piece or part serving as a shield against glare, etc., as on the windshield of an automobile. — *v.t.* To mask or cover with a visor. Also spelled *vizor.* [< AF & OF *vis* face]

vis·ta (vis′tə) *n.* 1. A view or prospect, as along an avenue; an outlook. 2. A mental view embracing a series of events. [< Ital. < L *ridere* to see]

vis·u·al (vizh′ōō·əl) *adj.* 1. Pertaining to, resulting from, or serving the sense of sight. 2. Perceptible by sight; visible. 3. Optical: the *visual* focus of a lens. 4. Produced or induced by mental images: a *visual* conception. [< MF < LL < L *visus* sight < *videre* to see] — **vis′u·al·ly** *adv.*

visual aid *Often pl.* In education, a device or method designed to convey information by visible representation, as motion pictures, charts, etc.

vis·u·al·ize (vizh′ōō·əl·īz′) *v.t. & v.i.* **·ized, ·iz·ing** To form a mental image (of). — **vis′u·al·ist** (-ist) *n.* — **vis′u·al·i·za′tion** *n.* — **vis′u·al·iz′er** *n.*

vi·ta·ceous (vī·tā′shəs) *adj. Bot.* Of or belonging to the grape family of mostly woody and climbing vines. [< NL, family name < L *vitis* vine]

vi·tal (vīt′l) *adj.* 1. Necessary to existence or continuance; essential. 2. Of or pertaining to life: *vital* statistics. 3. Essential to or supporting life. 4. Affecting the course of life or existence, esp. so as to be dangerous or fatal: a *vital* error. 5. Energetic; forceful; dynamic. 6. Having immediate interest or importance: a *vital* question. [< OF < L *vita* life] — **vi′tal·ly** *adv.* — **vi′tal·ness** *n.*

vi·tal·ism (vīt′l·iz′əm) *n. Biol.* The doctrine that life and its phenomena arose from and are the product of a hypothetical *vital force* (or *vital principle*) regarded as acting independently of all physical and chemical forces. — **vi′tal·ist** *n.* — **vi′tal·is′tic** *adj.*

vi·tal·i·ty (vī·tal′ə·tē) *n.* 1. The state or quality of being vital. 2. Vital or life-giving force, principle, etc. 3. Vigor; energy; animation. 4. Power of continuing in force or effect.

vi·tal·ize (vīt′l·īz) *v.t.* **·ized, ·iz·ing** To make vital; endow with life or energy. — **vi′tal·i·za′tion** *n.* — **vi′tal·iz′er** *n.*

vi·tals (vīt′lz) *n.pl.* 1. The parts or organs necessary to life. 2. The parts or qualities essential to the continued existence or well-being of anything.

vital statistics Quantitative data relating to certain aspects and conditions of human life.

---

vi·ta·min (vī′tə·min) *n. Biochem.* Any of a group of complex organic substances found in minute quantities in most natural foodstuffs, and closely associated with the maintenance of normal physiological functions in man and animals. Also **vi′ta·mine** (-mēn, -min). [< NL *vit-* (< L *vita* life) + AMINE] — **vi′ta·min′ic** *adj.*

vitamin A A fat-soluble vitamin derived from carotene and occurring naturally in animal tissues, esp. egg yolk and fish-liver oils, essential to the prevention of atrophy of epithelial tissue and night blindness.

vitamin B complex A group of water-soluble vitamins widely distributed in plants and animals, most members of which have special names.

vitamin B₁ Thiamine.

vitamin B₂ Riboflavin.

vitamin B₃ Pantothenic acid.

vitamin B₆ Pyridoxine.

vitamin B₁₂ A dark red, crystalline vitamin, $C_{63}H_{90}N_{14}O_{14}PCo$, extracted from liver and certain mold fungi, and active against pernicious anemia.

vitamin B_c Folic acid.

vitamin C Ascorbic acid.

vitamin D The antirachitic vitamin occurring chiefly in fish-liver oils.

vitamin D₁ An impure mixture of calciferol and irradiated ergosterol.

vitamin D₂ Calciferol.

vitamin D₃ A form of vitamin D₂ found principally in fish-liver oils.

vitamin E The antisterility vitamin, composed of three forms of tocopherol and found in whole grain cereals.

vitamin G Riboflavin.

vitamin H Biotin.

vitamin K₁ A vitamin, found in green leafy vegetables, that promotes the clotting of blood.

vitamin K₂ A form of vitamin K₁ prepared from fishmeal.

vitamin P complex A group of substances obtained from citrus fruits and promoting the normal permeability of capillary walls.

vi·ti·ate (vish′ē·āt) *v.t.* **·at·ed, ·at·ing 1.** To impair the use or value of; spoil. **2.** To debase or corrupt. **3.** To render legally ineffective. [< L *vitium* fault] — **vi·ti·a·ble** (vish′ē·ə·bel) *adj.* — **vi′ti·a′tion** *n.* — **vi′ti·a′tor** *n.*

vit·i·cul·ture (vit′ə·kul′chər, vī′tə-) *n.* The science and art of grape growing. [< L *vitis* vine + CULTURE] — **vit′i·cul′tur·al** *adj.* — **vit′i·cul′tur·er, vit′i·cul′tur·ist** *n.*

vit·re·ous (vit′rē·əs) *adj.* **1.** Pertaining to glass; glassy. **2.** Obtained from glass. **3.** Resembling glass. **4.** Pertaining to the vitreous humor. [< L < *vitrum* glass] — **vit′re·os′i·ty** (-os′ə·tē), **vit′re·ous·ness** *n.*

vitreous humor *Anat.* The transparent, jellylike tissue that fills the ball of the eye. Also **vitreous body.**

vitri- *combining form* Glass; of or pertaining to glass. Also, before vowels, **vitr-.** [< L *vitrum* glass]

vit·ri·fy (vit′rə·fī) *v.t. & v.i.* **·fied, ·fy·ing** To change into glass or a vitreous substance; make or become vitreous. [< MF < L *vitrum* glass + *facere* to make] — **vit′ri·fac′tion** (-fak′shən) *n.* — **vit′ri·fi·a·ble** *adj.* — **vit′ri·fi·ca′tion** (-fə·kā′shən) *n.*

vit·ri·ol (vit′rē·ōl, -əl) *n.* **1.** *Chem.* **a** Sulfuric acid. **b** Any sulfate of a heavy metal, as *green vitriol* from iron, *blue vitriol* from copper, or *white vitriol* from zinc. **2.** Anything sharp or caustic, esp. speech or writing. — *v.t.* **·oled** or **·olled, ·ol·ing** or **·ol·ling 1.** To injure (a person) with vitriol. **2.** To subject (anything) to the agency of vitriol. [< OF < Med.L < L *vitrum* glass]

vit·ri·ol·ic (vit′rē·ol′ik) *adj.* **1.** Derived from a vitriol. **2.** Corrosive, burning, or caustic.

vit·ri·ol·ize (vit′rē·əl·īz′) *v.t.* **·ized, ·iz·ing 1.** To corrode, injure, or burn with sulfuric acid. **2.** To convert into or impregnate with vitriol. — **vit′ri·ol·i·za′tion** *n.*

vit·tles (vit′əls) *n.pl. Informal* or *Dial.* Victuals.

vi·tu·per·ate (vī·tōō′pə·rāt, -tyōō′-, vi-) *v.t.* **·at·ed, ·at·ing** To find fault with abusively; rail at; berate; scold. [< L *vitium* fault + *parare* to prepare, make] — **vi·tu′per·a′tion** *n.* — **vi·tu′per·a·tive** (-pər·ə·tiv) *adj.* — **vi·tu′per·a·tive·ly** *adv.* — **vi·tu′per·a′tor** *n.*

vi·va (vē′vä) *interj.* Live! Long live!: a shout of applause; an acclamation or salute. [< Ital. *vivere* to live < L]

vi·va·ce (vē·vä′chā) *adv. Music* Lively; quickly; briskly. Also **vi·va·ce·men′te** (-män′tā). [< Ital.]

vi·va·cious (vi·vā′shəs, vī-) *adj.* Lively; active. [< L *vivere* to live] — **vi·va′cious·ly** *adv.* — **vi·va′cious·ness** *n.*

vi·vac·i·ty (vi·vas′ə·tē, vī-) *n., pl.* **·ties 1.** The state or quality of being vivacious. **2.** Sprightliness, as of temper or behavior; liveliness. **3.** A vivacious act, expression, etc.

vi·var·i·um (vī·vâr′ē·əm) *n., pl.* **·var·i·a** (-vâr′ē·ə) or **·var·i·ums** A place for keeping or raising live animals, fish, or plants, as a park, pond, aquarium, cage, etc. Also **viv·a·ry** (viv′ər·ē). [< L *vivere* to live]

vi·va vo·ce (vī′və vō′sē) *Latin* By spoken word; orally.

vive (vēv) *interj. French* Long live!: used in acclamation.

viv·id (viv′id) *adj.* **1.** Very bright; intense: said of colors. **2.** Producing or evoking lifelike imagery, freshness, etc.: *vivid* prose. **3.** Clearly felt or strongly expressed, as emotions. **4.** Full of life and vigor. **5.** Clearly seen in the mind, as a memory. **6.** Clearly perceived by the eye. [< L *vivere* to live] — **viv′id·ly** *adv.* — **viv′id·ness** *n.* — **Syn. 1.** brilliant, clear. **2.** lifelike. **4.** animated, lively.

viv·i·fy (viv′ə·fī) *v.t.* **·fied, ·fy·ing 1.** To give life to; animate; vitalize. **2.** To make more vivid or striking. [< OF < LL < L *vivus* alive + *facere* to make] — **viv′i·fi·ca′tion** (-fə·kā′shən) *n.* — **viv′i·fi′er** *n.*

vi·vip·a·rous (vī·vip′ər·əs) *adj.* **1.** *Zool.* Bringing forth living young, as most mammals: distinguished from *oviparous.* **2.** *Bot.* Producing bulbs or seeds that germinate while attached to the parent plant. [< L < *vivus* alive + *parere* to bring forth] — **vi·vip·a·rous·ly** *adv.* — **vi·vip′a·rism** (-riz′əm), **viv·i·par·i·ty** (viv′ə·par′ə·tē), **vi·vip′a·rous·ness** *n.*

viv·i·sect (viv′ə·sekt) *v.t.* **1.** To dissect or operate upon (a living animal), with a view to exposing its physiological processes. — *v.i.* **2.** To practice vivisection. — **viv′i·sec′tor** *n.*

viv·i·sec·tion (viv′ə·sek′shən) *n.* **1.** The act of cutting into or dissecting a living animal body. **2.** Experimentation on living animals by means of operations designed to promote knowledge of physiological and pathological processes. [< L *vivus* living, alive + SECTION.] — **viv′i·sec′tion·al** *adj.* — **viv′i·sec′tion·ist** *n.*

vix·en (vik′sən) *n.* **1.** A female fox. **2.** A turbulent, quarrelsome woman; shrew. [Alter. of ME *fixen* she-fox < OE fem. of *fox*] — **vix′en·ish** *adj.* — **vix′en·ly** *adj. & adv.*

viz·ard (viz′ərd) *n.* A mask; visor: also spelled *visard.* [Alter. of VISOR] — **viz′ard·ed** *adj.*

vi·zier (vi·zir′, viz′yər) *n.* A high official of a Moslem country; esp., a minister of state. Also **vi·zir′.** [< Turkish < Arabic *wazīr* counselor, orig., porter < *wazara* to carry]

vi·zier·ate (vi·zir′it, -āt, viz′yər·it, -yə·rāt) *n.* The office of a vizier. Also **vi·zier′al·ty, vi·zier′ship, vi·zir′ate, vi·zir′ship.**

vi·zor (vī′zər, viz′ər) See VISOR.

V-J Day (vē′jā′) September 2, the official date of the victory over Japan in World War II, 1945.

V-mail (vē′māl′) *n.* Mail written on special forms, transmitted overseas in World War II on microfilm, and enlarged for final delivery. [< V(ICTORY) + MAIL¹]

vo·ca·ble (vō′kə·bəl) *n.* **1.** A spoken or written word considered only as a sequence of sounds or letters, without regard to its meaning. **2.** A vocal sound. — *adj.* Capable of being spoken. [< F < L *vocabulum* name < *vocare* to call]

vo·cab·u·lar·y (vō·kab′yə·ler′ē) *n., pl.* **·lar·ies 1.** A list of words, esp. one arranged in alphabetical order and defined or translated; a glossary. **2.** All the words of a language. **3.** A sum or aggregate of the words used by a particular person, class, etc., or employed in some specialized field of knowledge. [< LL < L *vocabulum.* See VOCABLE.]

vocabulary entry A word or term given in a vocabulary. **2.** A word, term, or phrase entered in a dictionary.

vo·cal (vō′kəl) *adj.* **1.** Of or pertaining to the voice. **2.** Having voice; endowed with the power of utterance. **3.** Uttered or performed by the voice: *vocal* music. **4.** Concerned in the production of voice: the *vocal* organs. **5.** Full of voices or sounds. **6.** Freely expressing oneself in speech: the *vocal* segment. [< L *vocalis* speaking, sounding < *vox* voice] — **vo′cal·ly** *adv.* — **vo′cal·ness** *n.*

vocal cords Two membranous bands extending from the thyroid cartilage of the larynx and having edges that, when drawn tense, are caused to vibrate by the passage of air from the lungs, thereby producing voice. For illus. see THROAT.

vo·cal·ic (vō·kal′ik) *adj.* Consisting of, like, or relating to vowel sounds.

vo·cal·ist (vō′kəl·ist) *n.* A singer.

vo·cal·ize (vō′kəl·īz) *v.* **·ized, ·iz·ing** *v.t.* **1.** To make vocal; utter, say, or sing. **2.** To provide a voice for; render articulate. **3.** *Phonet.* **a** To change (a consonant) to a vowel by some shift in the articulatory process. **b** To voice. — *v.i.* **4.** To produce sounds with the voice, as in speaking or singing. — **vo′cal·i·za′tion** *n.* — **vo′cal·iz′er** *n.*

vo·ca·tion (vō·kā′shən) *n.* **1.** A stated or regular occupation; a calling. **2.** A call to or fitness for a certain career. **3.** The work or profession for which one has a sense of special fitness. — **Syn.** See OCCUPATION. [< L *vocare* to call] — **vo·ca′tion·al** *adj.* — **vo·ca′tion·al·ly** *adv.*

vocational guidance A systematic program of tests and interviews to help a person find the occupation for which he is best suited.

vocational school A school, usu. on the secondary level, that trains students for special trades.

voc·a·tive (vok′ə·tiv) *adj.* **1.** Pertaining to or used in the act of calling. **2.** *Gram.* In some inflected languages, denoting the case of a noun, pronoun, or adjective used in direct address. — *n. Gram.* **1.** The vocative case. **2.** A word in this case. [< F, fem. of *vocatif* < L *vocare* to call]

vo·ces (vō′sēz) Plural of VOX.

vo·cif·er·ant (vō-sif′ər-ənt) *adj.* Viciferous; clamorous. — *n.* A vociferous person. — **vo·cif′er·ance** *n.*

vo·cif·er·ate (vō-sif′ə-rāt) *v.t. & v.i.* **·at·ed, ·at·ing** To cry out with a loud voice; shout. [< L < *vox, vocis* voice + *ferre* to carry] — **vo·cif′er·a′tion** *n.* — **vo·cif′er·a′tor** *n.*

vo·cif·er·ous (vō-sif′ər-əs) *adj.* Making or characterized by a loud outcry; clamorous; noisy. — **vo·cif′er·ous·ly** *adv.* — **vo·cif′er·ous·ness** *n.*

vod·ka (vod′kə, *Russ.* vôd′kə) *n.* An alcoholic liquor, originally made in Russia from a fermented mash of wheat but now also from other cereals and potatoes. [< Russian, dim. of *voda* water]

vogue (vōg) *n.* **1.** The prevalent way or fashion; mode: often preceded by *in.* **2.** Popular favor; general acceptance. [< F, fashion, orig., rowing < Ital. *vogare* to row]

Vo·gul (vō′gōōl) *n.* **1.** One of a Finno-Ugric people of the Ural Mountains. **2.** The Ugric language of these people.

voice (vois) *n.* **1.** The sound produced by the vocal organs of a person or animal. **2.** The quality or character of such sound: a melodious *voice.* **3.** The power or faculty of vocal utterance; speech. **4.** A sound suggesting vocal utterance or speech: the *voice* of the wind. **5.** Opinion or choice expressed; also, the right of expressing a preference or judgment: to have a *voice* in the affair. **6.** Instruction; admonition: the *voice* of nature. **7.** A person or agency by which the thought, wish, or purpose of another is expressed. **8.** Expression of thought, opinion, feeling, etc.: to give *voice* to one's ideals. **9.** *Phonet.* The sound produced by vibration of the vocal cords in the production of most vowels and certain consonants. **10.** Musical tone produced by vibration of the vocal cords and resonating in the cavities of the throat and head; also, the ability to sing, or the state of the vocal organs with regard to this ability: to be in poor *voice.* **11.** *Music* A part (def. 11a), esp. as considered without regard to the particular instrument or human voice rendering it: also **voice part. 12.** *Gram.* The relation of the action expressed by the verb to the subject, or the form of the verb indicating this relationship. In most Indo-European languages, a distinction between an *active* and a *passive* voice is made, indicating, respectively, that the subject of the sentence is either performing the action or is being acted upon. (Active: *He wrote the letter.* Passive: *The letter was written by him.*) — **in voice** In proper condition for singing. — **with one voice** With one accord; unitedly; unanimously. — *v.t.* **voiced, voic·ing 1.** To put into speech; utter. **2.** *Music* To regulate the tones of; tune, as the pipes of an organ. **3.** *Phonet.* To utter with voice or sonance. [< OF < L *vox, vocis*]

voice box The larynx.

voiced (voist) *adj.* **1.** Having a voice; expressed by voice. **2.** *Phonet.* Uttered with vibration of the vocal cords, as (b), (d), (z); sonant: also *vocal.*

voice·less (vois′lis) *adj.* **1.** Having no voice, speech, or vote. **2.** *Phonet.* Produced without voice, as (p), (t), (s); surd. — **voice′less·ly** *adv.* — **voice′less·ness** *n.*

void (void) *adj.* **1.** No longer having force or validity, as a contract, license, etc., that has lapsed; invalid; null. **2.** Destitute; clear or free: with *of*: *void* of reason. **3.** Not occupied by matter; empty. **4.** Unoccupied, as a house or room. **5.** Producing no effect; useless. — *n.* **1.** An empty space; a vacuum. **2.** A breach of surface or matter; a disconnecting space. **3.** Empty condition or feeling; a blank. — *v.t.* **1.** To make void or of no effect; invalidate. **2.** To empty or remove (contents); evacuate, as urine. — **Syn.** See ANNUL. [< OF, ult. < LL *vocuus* empty < L *vacuus*] — **void′er** *n.*

void·a·ble (voi′də-bəl) *adj.* **1.** Capable of being made void. **2.** That may be evacuated. — **void′a·ble·ness** *n.*

void·ance (void′ns) *n.* **1.** The act of voiding, evacuating, ejecting, or emptying. **2.** The state or condition of being void; vacancy. [< AF < OF < *voider* to empty]

voi·là (vwå·lå′) *interj. French* There! behold!

voile (voil, *Fr.* vwàl) *n.* A fine, sheer fabric like heavy veiling, used for summer dresses and curtains. [< F, veil]

vo·lant (vō′lənt) *adj.* **1.** Flying, or able to fly. **2.** Nimble. [< OF, ppr. of *voler* to fly < L *volare*]

vo·lan·te (vō·län′tā) *adj. Music* Swift and light. [< Ital.]

vo·lar (vō′lər) *adj.* Pertaining to flight. [< L *volare* to fly]

vol·a·tile (vol′ə·til) *adj.* **1.** Evaporating rapidly at ordinary temperatures on exposure to the air. **2.** Capable of being vaporized. **3.** Easily influenced; changeable. **4.** Transient; ephemeral. [< OF < L *volare* to fly]

vol·a·til·i·ty (vol′ə·til′ə·tē) *n.* **1.** The state or quality of being volatile. **2.** The property of being freely or rapidly diffused in the atmosphere. Also **vol′a·tile·ness.**

vol·a·til·ize (vol′ə·til·īz′) *v.t. & v.i.* **·ized, ·iz·ing 1.** To make or become volatile. **2.** To pass off or cause to pass off in vapor; evaporate. — **vol′a·til·iz′a·ble** *adj.* — **vol′a·til·i·za′tion** *n.* — **vol′a·til·iz′er** *n.*

vol·can·ic (vol·kan′ik) *adj.* **1.** Of, pertaining to, or characteristic of a volcano or volcanoes. **2.** Produced by or emitted from a volcano. **3.** Eruptive. — **vol·can·ic·i·ty** (vol′kə·nis′ə·tē) *n.* — **vol·can′i·cal·ly** *adv.*

vol·can·ism (vol′kən·iz′əm) *n.* The conditions and phenomena associated with volcanoes or volcanic action.

vol·can·ize (vol′kən·īz) *v.t.* **·ized, ·iz·ing** To subject to the action and effects of volcanic heat. — **vol′can·i·za′tion** *n.*

vol·ca·no (vol·kā′nō) *n. pl.* **·noes** or **·nos** *Geol.* **1.** An opening in the crust of the earth from which steam, hot gases, ashes, etc., are expelled, forming a conical hill or mountain with a central crater. **2.** The formation itself. [< Ital. < L *Volcanus, Vulcanus* Vulcan]

vol·can·ol·o·gy (vol′kan·ol′ə·jē) *n.* The scientific study of volcanoes. — **vol′can·o·log′i·cal** (-ə·loj′i·kəl) *adj.* — **vol′can·ol′o·gist** *n.*

vole (vōl) *n.* Any of various short-tailed, mouselike or rat-like rodents; esp., the **European vole** or the **North American vole:** also called *field mouse, meadow mouse.* [Short for earlier *vole mouse* < *vole* field < Norw. *voll*]

vo·li·tion (və·lish′ən) *n.* **1.** The act or faculty of willing; exercise of the will; esp., the termination of reasoning or uncertainty by a decision. **2.** Strength of will. **2.** That which is willed or determined upon. [< F < Med.L < L *vol-*, stem of *velle* will] — **vo·li′tion·al** *adj.* — **vo·li′tion·al·ly** *adv.*

vol·i·tive (vol′ə·tiv) *adj.* **1.** Of, pertaining to, or originating in the will. **2.** Expressing a wish or permission.

vol·ley (vol′ē) *n. pl.* **·leys 1.** A simultaneous discharge of many missiles; also, the missiles so discharged. **2.** Any discharge of many things at once: a *volley* of oaths. **3.** In tennis, a return of the ball before it touches the ground. **4.** In soccer, a kick given the ball before its rebound. **5.** In cricket, a ball bowled so that it strikes the wicket before it touches the ground. — *v.t. & v.i.* **·leyed, ·ley·ing 1.** To discharge or be discharged in a volley. **2.** In tennis, to return (the ball) without allowing it to touch the ground. **3.** In soccer, to kick (the ball) before its rebound; in cricket, to bowl (a ball) full pitch. [< MF < L *volare* to fly]

vol·ley·ball (vol′ē·bôl′) *n.* A game in which two teams on either side of a high net strike a large ball with the hands in an attempt to send the ball over the net without letting it touch the ground; also, the ball used. Also **volley ball.**

vo·lost (vō′lost) *n.* In Russia, a district having one joint administrative assembly; a rural soviet. [< Russian *volost′*]

vol·plane (vol′plān) *Archaic v.i.* **·planed, ·plan·ing** To glide in an airplane. — *n.* An airplane glide. [< F *vol plané* gliding flight < *vol* flight + *plané,* pp. of *planer* to glide]

Vol·sci (vol′sī) *n.pl.* A warlike people of ancient Italy, subdued by the Romans about 350 B.C. — **Vol·scian** (vol′shən) *adj. & n.*

Vol·sun·ga Sa·ga (vol′sŏong·gə sä′gə) A prose version of the Icelandic legends of the dwarf race, the Nibelungs, and Sigurd, the grandson of Volsung. [< ON *Völsunga saga,* lit., saga of the Volsungs]

Vol·sungs (vol′sŏongz) *n.pl.* In Icelandic mythology, a race of warriors descended from the hero **Vol′sung.**

volt[1] (vōlt) *n.* The unit of electromotive force, or that difference of potential that, when steadily applied against a resistance of one ohm, will produce a current of one ampere. [after Alessandro *Volta,* 1745–1827, Italian physicist]

volt[2] (vōlt) *n.* **1.** In horse-training, a gait in which the horse moves partially sidewise round a center. **2.** In fencing, a sudden leap to avoid a thrust. [< F < Ital. *volta,* orig. pp. fem. of *volvere* to turn < L]

volt·age (vōl′tij) *n.* Electromotive force expressed in volts.

vol·ta·ic (vol·tā′ik) *adj.* Pertaining to electricity developed through chemical action or contact; galvanic.

voltaic battery *Electr.* A battery or primary cells.

voltaic cell *Electr.* A primary cell.

vol·ta·ism (vol′tā·iz′əm) *n.* Galvanism (def. 1).

volt·am·me·ter (vōlt′am′mē′tər) *n.* An instrument for measuring either volts or amperes.

volt·am·pere (vōlt′am′pir) *n.* The rate of work in an electric circuit when the current is one ampere and the potential one volt, equivalent to one watt.

volt·me·ter (vōlt′mē′tər) *n.* An instrument for determining the voltage between any two points, generally consisting of a calibrated galvanometer wound with a coil of high resistance.

vol·u·ble (vol′yə·bəl) *adj.* **1.** Having a flow of words or fluency in speaking; garrulous. **2.** Turning readily or easily; apt or formed to roll. **3.** Twining, as a plant. [< MF < L < *volutus,* pp. of *volvere* to turn] — **vol′u·bil′i·ty, vol′u·ble·ness** *n.* — **vol′u·bly** *adv.*

vol·ume (vol′yŏŏm, -yəm) *n.* **1.** A collection of sheets of paper bound together; book. **2.** A separately bound part of a work. **3.** Sufficient matter to fill a volume. **4.** Quantity of sound or tone; loudness. **5.** A large quantity; a considerable amount. **6.** Space occupied in three dimensions, as measured by cubic units. — **to speak volumes** To be full of meaning; express a great deal. [< OF < L *volumen* roll, scroll < *volvere* to turn]

vo·lu·me·ter (və·lōō′mə·tər) *n.* Any of several instruments for measuring the volume of gases, liquids, or solids under specified conditions. [< VOLU(ME) + -METER]

vol·u·met·ric (vol′yə·met′rik) *adj. Chem.* Of or pertaining to measurement of substances by comparison of volumes. Also **vol′u·met′ri·cal.** — **vol′u·met′ri·cal·ly** *adv.* — **vo·lu·me·try** (və·lōō′mə·trē) *n.*

vo·lu·mi·nous (və·lōō′mə·nəs) *adj.* 1. Having great quantity or volume. 2. Consisting of or capable of filling several volumes. 3. Writing or having written much; productive. 4. Having coils, folds, windings, etc. — **vo·lu′mi·nous·ly** *adv.* — **vo·lu′mi·nos′i·ty, vo·lu′mi·nous·ness** *n.*

vol·un·tar·y (vol′ən·ter′ē) *adj.* 1. Proceeding from the will or from one's own free choice; intentional; volitional. 2. Endowed with, possessing, or exercising will or free choice. 3. Effected by choice or volition. 4. *Law* a Unconstrained of will; done without compulsion. b Performed without legal obligation. — *n. pl.* **·tar·ies** 1. Any work or performance not compelled or imposed by another. 2. *Music* An organ solo, often improvised, played before, during, or after a service. [< OF < L *voluntas* will] — **vol′un·tar′i·ly** *adv.* — **vol′un·tar′i·ness** *n.*

vol·un·teer (vol′ən·tir′) *n.* One who enters into any service, esp. military service or a hazardous undertaking, of his own free will. — *adj.* 1. Pertaining to or composed of volunteers. 2. Springing up naturally or spontaneously, as from fallen or self-sown seed. — *v.t.* 1. To offer to give or do. — *v.i.* 2. To enter or offer to enter into some service or undertaking of one's free will; enlist. [< obs. F *voluntaire* < OF *voluntas*]

Volunteer State Nickname of Tennessee.

vo·lup·tu·ar·y (və·lup′chōō·er′ē) *adj.* Pertaining to or promoting sensual indulgence and luxurious pleasures. — *n. pl.* **·ar·ies** One addicted to sensual pleasures; a sensualist.

vo·lup·tu·ous (və·lup′chōō·əs) *adj.* 1. Belonging to, producing, exciting, or yielding sensuous gratification. 2. Pertaining to or devoted to the enjoyment of pleasures or luxuries; luxurious; sensual. 3. Having a full and beautiful form, as a woman. [< OF < L *voluptas* pleasure] — **vo·lup′tu·ous·ly** *adv.* — **vo·lup′tu·ous·ness** *n.*

vo·lute (və·lōōt′) *n.* 1. *Archit.* A spiral, scroll-like ornament, esp. one characteristic of the Ionic capital. 2. *Zool.* One of the whorls or turns of a spiral shell. — *adj.* 1. Rolled up; forming spiral curves. 2. Having a spiral form, as a machine part. [< F < L *voluta* scroll, orig. fem. pp. of *volvere* to turn] — **vo·lut′ed** *adj.* — **vo·lu′tion** *n.*

VOLUTE

vom·it (vom′it) *v.i.* 1. To throw up or eject the contents of the stomach through the mouth. 2. To issue with violence from any hollow place; be ejected. — *v.t.* 3. To throw up or eject from the stomach, as food. 4. To discharge or send forth copiously or forcibly: The volcano *vomited* smoke. — *n.* Matter that is ejected, as from the stomach in vomiting. [< L *vomitare*, freq. of *vomere* to vomit] — **vom′it·er** *n.*

vom·i·tive (vom′ə·tiv) *adj.* Causing vomiting. — *n.* An emetic.

vom·i·to·ry (vom′ə·tôr′ē, -tō′rē) *adj.* Efficacious in producing vomiting. — *n. pl.* **·ries** 1. An emetic. 2. An opening through which matter is discharged. 3. In a Roman amphitheater, one of the entrances from the encircling arcades to the passages leading to the seats: so called because of the numbers of people who flowed forth from it: also **vom·i·tor·i·um** (vom′ə·tôr′ē·əm, -tō′rē-).

von (von, *Ger.* fôn, *unstressed* fən) *prep. German* Of; from: used in German and Austrian family names as an attribute of nobility, corresponding to the French *de*.

voo·doo (vōō′dōō) *n. pl.* **·doos** 1. A primitive religion of West African origin characterized by belief in sorcery and the use of charms, fetishes, witchcraft, etc. 2. One who practices voodoo. 3. A voodoo charm or fetish. — *adj.* Of or pertaining to the beliefs, ceremonies, or practices of voodoo. — *v.t.* **·dooed, ·doo·ing** To put a spell upon after the manner of a voodoo. [< Creole < Ewe (a W. African language) *vodu*]

voo·doo·ism (vōō′dōō·iz′əm) *n.* 1. The religion of voodoo. 2. Belief in or practice of this religion. — **voo′doo·ist** *n.* — **voo′doo·is′tic** *adj.*

-vora *combining form Zool.* Used to denote orders or genera when classified according to their food: *Carnivora.* An individual member of such an order or genus is denoted by **-vore:** *carnivore.* [< NL < L *-vorus.* See -VOROUS.]

vo·ra·cious (vô·rā′shəs, vō-, və-) *adj.* 1. Eating with greediness; ravenous. 2. Greedy; rapacious. 3. Ready to swallow up or engulf. 4. Insatiable; immoderate. [< L *vorare* to devour] — **vo·ra′cious·ly** *adv.* — **vo·rac·i·ty** (vô·ras′ə·tē, vō-, və-), **vo·ra′cious·ness** *n.*

-vorous *combining form* Consuming; eating or feeding upon: *omnivorous, carnivorous.* [< L *-vorus* < *vorare* to devour]

vor·tex (vôr′teks) *n. pl.* **·tex·es** or **·ti·ces** (-tə·sēz) 1. A mass of whirling gas or liquid, esp. when sucked spirally toward a central axis; a whirlwind or whirlpool. 2. Any action or state of affairs that is similar to a vortex in violence, force, etc. [< L, var. of *vertex* top, point] — **vor′ti·cal** (-ti·kəl) *adj.* — **vor′ti·cal·ly** *adv.*

vo·ta·ry (vō′tər·ē) *n. pl.* **·ries** 1. One bound by a vow or promise, as a nun. 2. One devoted to some particular worship, pursuit, study, etc. Also **vo′ta·rist.** — **Syn.** See ENTHUSIAST. — *adj.* Consecrated by a vow or promise; votive. [< L *votus,* pp. of *vovere* to vow] — **vo·ta·ress** (vō′tə·ris) or **vo′tress** (vō′tris) *n.fem.*

vote (vōt) *n.* 1. A formal expression of will or opinion in regard to some question submitted for decision, as in electing officers, passing resolutions, etc. 2. That by which such choice is expressed, as a show of hands, or ballot. 3. The result of an election. 4. The number of votes cast; also, votes collectively: a light *vote;* the farm *vote.* 5. The right to vote. 6. A voter. — *v.* **vot·ed, vot·ing** *v.t.* 1. To enact or determine by vote. 2. To cast one's vote for: to *vote* a straight ticket. 3. *Informal* To declare by general agreement: to *vote* a concert a success. — *v.i.* 4. To cast one's vote; express opinion or preference by or as by a vote. — **to vote down** To defeat or suppress by voting against. — **to vote in** To elect. [< L *votum* vow, wish, orig. pp. neut. of *vovere* to vow] — **vot′a·ble** or **vote′a·ble** *adj.* — **vot′er** *n.*

vote getter 1. A person who can win votes. 2. A campaign slogan, etc., that draws votes. — **vote getting**

voting machine A device which enables the voter to indicate his choices by operating small levers and which registers and counts all votes.

vo·tive (vō′tiv) *adj.* Dedicated by a vow; performed in fulfillment of a vow. — **vo′tive·ly** *adv.* — **vo′tive·ness** *n.*

vouch (vouch) *v.i.* 1. To give one's own assurance or guarantee; bear witness: with *for:* I will *vouch* for them. 2. To serve as assurance or proof: with *for.* — *v.t.* 3. To bear witness to; attest or affirm. 4. To cite as support or justification. 5. To substantiate. — *n.* A declaration that attests; an assertion. [< OF < L *vocare* to call < *vox, vocis* voice]

vouch·er (vou′chər) *n.* 1. Any material thing, usu. a writing, that serves to vouch for the truth of something, or attest an alleged act, esp. the payment or receipt of money. 2. One who vouches for another; a witness.

vouch·safe (vouch·sāf′) *v.* **·safed, ·saf·ing** *v.t.* 1. To grant, as with condescension; permit; deign. — *v.i.* 2. To condescend; deign. — **vouch′safe′ment** *n.*

vous·soir (vōō·swär′) *n. Archit.* A stone in an arch shaped to fit its curve. [< OF *vausoir* < L *volvere* to turn]

vow (vou) *n.* 1. A solemn promise to God or to a deity or saint to perform some act or make some gift or sacrifice. 2. A solemn engagement to adopt a certain course of life, pursue some end, etc.; also, a pledge of faithfulness. 3. A solemn and emphatic affirmation. — **to take vows** To enter a religious order. — *v.t.* 1. To promise solemnly, esp. to God or to some deity. 2. To declare with assurance or solemnity. 3. To make a solemn promise or threat to do, inflict, etc. — *v.i.* 4. To make a vow. [< AF *vu,* OF *vo, vou* < L *votum*] — **vow′er** *n.*

vow·el (vou′əl) *n.* 1. *Phonet.* A speech sound produced by the relatively unimpeded passage of breath through the mouth, varying in quality according to the size, shape, and condition of the resonance cavities. Vowels may be characterized by length (long or short), the height of the tongue (high, mid, low), the place of articulation (front, central, back), the tension of the tongue muscles (tense, lax), and the presence of lip rounding. Thus (ōō) is a long, high, back, tense, rounded vowel. 2. A letter representing such a sound, as *a, e, i, o, u,* and sometimes *y.* — *adj* Of or pertaining to a vowel; vocal. [< OF < L *vox, vocis* voice, sound]

vox (voks) *n. pl.* **vo·ces** (vō′sēz) Voice; esp., in music, a voice; part. [< L]

vox po·pu·li (voks pop′yə·lī) *Latin* The voice of the people.

voy·age (voi′ij) *n.* 1. A journey by water, esp. by sea: commonly used of a somewhat extended journey by water. 2. Any journey. 3. A book describing a voyage or voyaging. 4. Any enterprise or project; also, course. — *v.* **·aged, ·ag·ing** *v.i.* 1. To make a voyage; journey by water. — *v.t.* 2. To travel over. [< OF < L *viaticum*] — **voy′ag·er** *n.*

voy·age·a·ble (voi′ij·ə·bəl) *adj.* Navigable.

voy·a·geur (vwä·yà·zhœr′) *n. pl.* **·geurs** (-zhœr′) *Canadian* A boatman of Hudson's Bay Company or another fur company, engaged in carrying men, supplies, etc., between remote trading posts; also, a Canadian boatman or fur trader. [< dial. F (Canadian)]

vo·yeur (vwä·yûr′) *n.* One who is sexually gratified by looking at sexual objects or acts. [< F < L *videre* to see] — **vo·yeur′ism** *n.*

VTOL (vē′tôl) *n. Aeron.* An aircraft that takes off and lands vertically.

Vul·can (vul′kən) In Roman mythology, the god of fire and of metallurgy. — **Vul·ca·ni·an** (-kā′nē·ən) *adj.*

vul·ca·ni·an (vul·kā′nē·ən) *adj.* Volcanic: also **vul·can·ic** (vul·kan′ik). [< L < *Vulcanus* Vulcan]

vul·can·ite (vul′kən·īt) *n.* A dark, hard variety of rubber that has been vulcanized: also called *ebonite, hard rubber.* — *adj.* Made of vulcanite. [after *Vulcan*]

vul·can·ize (vul′kən·īz) *v.t.* **·ized, ·iz·ing** To treat (crude rubber) with sulfur or sulfur compounds in varying proportions and at different temperatures, thereby increasing its strength and elasticity. — **vul′can·iz′a·ble** *adj.* — **vul′can·i·za′tion** *n.* — **vul′can·iz′er** *n.*

vul·can·ol·o·gy (vul′kən·ol′ə·jē) *n.* Volcanology. — **vul′can·o·log′i·cal** (-ə·loj′i·kəl) *adj.* — **vul′can·ol′o·gist** *n.*

vul·gar (vul′gər) *adj.* **1.** Lacking in refinement, good taste, sensitivity, etc.; coarse; crude; boorish; also, obscene; indecent. **2.** Of, pertaining to, or characteristic of the people at large, as distinguished from the privileged or educated classes; popular; common. **3.** Written in or translated into the common language or vulgate; vernacular. [< L < *vulgus* the common people] — **vul′gar·ly** *adv.*

vul·gar·i·an (vul·gâr′ē·ən) *n.* A person of vulgar tastes or manners.

vul·gar·ism (vul′gə·riz′əm) *n.* **1.** Vulgarity. **2.** A word, phrase, or expression that is in nonstandard or unrefined usage, though not necessarily coarse or gross.

vul·gar·i·ty (vul·gar′ə·tē) *n.* *pl.* **·ties 1.** The quality or character of being vulgar. **2.** Something vulgar, as an action, word, etc. Also **vul·gar·ness** (vul′gər·nis).

vul·gar·ize (vul′gə·rīz) *v.t.* **·ized, ·iz·ing 1.** To make vulgar. **2.** To express and diffuse (something abstruse or complex) in a more widely comprehensible form; popularize. Also *Brit.* **vul′gar·ise.** — **vul′gar·i·za′tion** *n.* — **vul′gar·iz′er** *n.*

Vulgar Latin See under LATIN.

vul·gate (vul′gāt) *adj.* Common; popular; generally accepted. — *n.* **1.** Everyday speech. **2.** Any commonly accepted text. [< L < *vulgus* the common people]

Vul·gate (vul′gāt) *n.* A Latin version of the Bible, translated between A.D. 383 and 405, now revised and used as the authorized version by the Roman Catholics. — *adj.* Belonging or relating to the Vulgate. [< Med.L *vulgata (editio)* the popular (edition), fem. of L *vulgatus* common]

vul·ner·a·ble (vul′nər·ə·bəl) *adj.* **1.** Capable of being hurt or damaged. **2.** Liable to attack; assailable. **3.** In contract bridge, having won one game of a rubber, and thus receiving increased penalties and increased bonuses. [< LL < L *vulnerare* to wound] — **vul′ner·a·bil′i·ty, vul′ner·a·ble·ness** *n.* — **vul′ner·a·bly** *adv.*

vul·pine (vul′pin, -pīn) *adj.* **1.** Of or pertaining to a fox. **2.** Like a fox; sly; crafty. [< L < *vulpes* fox]

vul·ture (vul′chər) *n.* **1.** Any of various large birds related to the eagles, hawks, and falcons, having the head and neck naked or partly naked, and feeding mostly on carrion. **2.** Someone or something disgustingly predatory. [< AF, OF < L *vultur, vulturius*] — **vul·tur·ine** (vul′chə·rīn, -chər·in), **vul′tur·ous** *adj.*

VULTURE
(To 55 inches long; wing-spread to 11 feet)

vul·va (vul′və) *n.* *pl.* **·vae** (-vē) *Anat.* The external genital parts of the female. [< L, a covering, womb] — **vul′val, vul′var** *adj.* — **vul′vi·form** (-və·fôrm) *adj.*

vy·ing (vī′ing) *adj.* Contending. — **vy′ing·ly** *adv.*

W

w, W (dub′əl·yōō, -yōō) *n.* *pl.* **w's** or **ws , W's** or **Ws, double·yous 1.** The twenty-third letter of the English alphabet; double u: a ligature of vv or uu. **2.** The sound represented by the letter *w*, a voiced bilabial velar semivowel before vowels (*we, wage, worry*), and a *u*-glide in diphthongs (*how, allow, dew, review*). It often has no phonetic value before *r* (*wrist, write, wrong*), and internally (*two, sword, answer*). ◆ The combination *wh-* (in Old English spelled *hw-*) is represented in this dictionary as (hw) because most Americans and probably most Canadians use that pronunciation. In some regions, however, *wh-* is consistently pronounced (w), and the use cannot be considered nonstandard. — *symbol Chem.* Tungsten (symbol W, for *wolfram*).

wab·ble (wob′əl) *v.t. & v.i.* **·bled, ·bling** To wobble. — *n.* A wobble. — **wab′bler** *n.* — **wab′bly** *adj.*

WAC or **W.A.C.** (wak) *n.* A member of the Women's Army Corps. [< W(OMEN'S) A(RMY) C(ORPS)]

wack·y (wak′ē) *adj.* **wack·i·er, wack·i·est** *Slang* Extremely irrational or impractical; erratic; screwy. [Prob. < WHACK; with ref. to damaging blows on the head]

wad (wod) *n.* **1.** A small compact mass of any soft or flexible substance, esp. as used for stuffing, packing, or lining; also, a lump; mass. **2.** A piece of paper, cloth, or leather used to hold in a charge of powder in a muzzleloading gun; also, a pasteboard or paper disk to hold powder and shot in place in a shotgun shell. **3.** Fibrous material for stopping up breaks, leakages, etc.; wadding. **4.** *Informal* A large amount. **5.** *Informal* A roll of banknotes; also, money or wealth. **6.** A chew of tobacco. — *v.* **wad·ded, wad·ding** *v.t.* **1.** To press (fibrous substances, as cotton) into a mass or wad. **2.** To roll or fold into a tight wad, as paper. **3.** To pack with wadding for protection, as valuables, or to stuff or line with wadding. **4.** To place a wad in, as a gun; hold in place with a wad. — *v.i.* **5.** To form into a wad. [Origin uncertain] — **wad′dy** *adj.*

wad·ding (wod′ing) *n.* **1.** Wads collectively. **2.** Any substance, as carded cotton, used as material for wads. **3.** The act of applying a wad or wads.

wad·dle (wod′l) *v.i.* **·dled, ·dling 1.** To walk with short steps, swaying from side to side. **2.** To move clumsily; totter. — *n.* A clumsy rocking walk, like that of a duck. [Freq. of WADE] — **wad′dler** *n.* — **wad′dly** *adj.*

wad·dy (wod′ē) *n.* *pl.* **·dies** *Austral.* A thick war club used by the aborigines. **2.** A walking stick; piece of wood. — *v.t.* **·died, ·dy·ing** To strike with a waddy. [< native Australian pronun. of *wood*]

wade (wād) *v.* **wad·ed, wad·ing** *v.i.* **1.** To walk through water or any substance more resistant than air, as mud, sand, etc. **2.** To proceed slowly or laboriously: to *wade* through a book. — *v.t.* **3.** To pass or cross, as a river, by walking on the bottom; ford. — **to wade in** (or **into**) *Informal* To attack or begin energetically or vigorously. — *n.* **1.** The act of wading. **2.** A ford. [OE *wadan* to go]

wad·er (wā′dər) *n.* **1.** One who wades. **2.** A long-legged wading bird, as a snipe, plover, or stork. **3.** *pl.* High waterproof boots, worn esp. by anglers.

wa·di (wä′dē) *n.* *pl.* **·dies 1.** In Arabia and northern Africa, a ravine containing the bed of a watercourse, usu. dry except in the rainy season; also, the watercourse. **2.** An oasis. Also **wa′dy.** [< Arabic *wādī*]

WAF or **W.A.F.** (waf, wäf) *n.* A member of the Women in the Air Force. [< W(OMEN IN THE) A(IR) F(ORCE)]

wa·fer (wā′fər) *n.* **1.** A very thin crisp biscuit, cooky, or cracker; also, a small disk of candy. **2.** *Eccl.* A small flat disk of unleavened bread stamped with a cross or the letters IHS, and used in the Eucharist in some churches. **3.** A thin disk of gelatin or other substance used for sealing letters, attaching papers, or receiving a seal. — *v.t.* To attach, seal, or fasten with a wafer. [< AF < MLG *wafel*]

waf·fle (wof′əl, wô′fəl) *n.* A batter cake, crisper than a pancake, baked between two hinged metal griddles marked with regular indentations (**waffle iron**). [< Du. *wafel* wafer]

waft¹ (waft, wäft) *v.t.* **1.** To carry or bear gently or lightly over air or water; float. **2.** To convey as if on air or water. — *v.i.* **3.** To float, as on the wind. — *n.* **1.** The act of one who or that which wafts. **2.** A current of air; also, something, as an odor, carried on a current of air. **3.** A wafting or waving motion or movement. [Back formation < *wafter*, in obs. sense, "an escort ship" < Du. *wachten* to guard]

waft² (waft, wäft) *n.* *Naut.* **1.** A signal flag or pennant, sometimes used to indicate wind direction. **2.** A signal made with a flag or pennant. Also called *weft.* [Alter. of dial. E *waff*, var. of WAVE]

waft·er (waf′tər, wäf′-) *n.* **1.** One who or that which wafts. **2.** A form of fan or revolving disk used in a blower.

wag¹ (wag) *v.* **wagged, wag·ging** *v.t.* **1.** To cause to move lightly and quickly from side to side or up and down; swing: The dog *wags* its tail. **2.** To move (the tongue) in talking. — *v.i.* **3.** To move lightly and quickly from side to side or up and down. **4.** To move busily in animated talk: said of the tongue. — *n.* The act or motion of wagging. [ME *waggen*, prob. < Scand.]

wag² (wag) *n.* A humorous fellow; wit; joker. [? Short for obs. *waghalter* gallows bird < WAG¹ + HALTER¹]

wage (wāj) *v.t.* **waged, wag·ing** To engage in and maintain vigorously; carry on: to *wage* war. — *n.* **1.** Payment for service rendered; esp., the pay of artisans or laborers receiving a fixed sum by the hour, day, week, or month, or for a certain amount of work; hire. **2.** *pl. Econ.* The remuneration received by labor as distinguished from that received by capital. **3.** *pl.* Recompense or yield: formerly, often construed as sing.: The *wages* of sin is death. [< AF *wagier*, OF *guagier* to pledge]

wage earner One who works for wages.

wa·ger (wā′jər) *v.t. & v.i.* To bet. — *n.* **1.** A bet (defs. 1, 2, & 3). **2.** The act of giving a pledge. [< AF *wagier* to pledge] — **wa′ger·er** *n.*

wage scale A scale or series of amounts of wages paid.

wage·work·er (wāj′wûr′kər) *n.* An employee receiving wages.

wag·ger·y (wag′ər·ē) *n. pl.* **·ger·ies 1.** Mischievous jocularity; drollery. **2.** A jest; joke.

wag·gish (wag′ish) *adj.* **1.** Being or acting like a wag. **2.** Said or done in waggery. — **wag′gish·ly** *adv.* — **wag′gish·ness** *n.*

wag·gle (wag′əl) *v.* **·gled, ·gling** *v.t.* **1.** To cause to move with rapid to-and-fro motions; wag: The duck *waggles* its tail. — *v.i.* **2.** To totter; wobble. — *n.* The act of waggling. [Freq. of WAG¹] — **wag′gling·ly** *adv.* — **wag′gly** *adj.*

Wag·ne·ri·an (väg·nir′ē·ən) *adj.* Relating to Richard Wagner or to his style, theory, or works. — *n.* An admirer, performer, or advocate of Wagnerian works.

wag·on (wag′ən) *n.* **1.** Any of various four-wheeled horse-drawn vehicles used for carrying crops, goods, freight, etc. **2.** A child's four-wheeled toy cart. **3.** A stand on wheels or casters for serving food or drink. **4.** *Brit.* A railway freight car. **5.** *Informal* A patrol wagon. **6.** A station wagon. — **on the (water) wagon** *Informal* Abstaining from alcoholic beverages. — **to fix (someone's) wagon** *U.S. Slang* To ruin or punish. — *v.t.* To carry or transport in a wagon. Also *Brit.* **wag′gon.** [< Du. *wagen*]

wag·on·er (wag′ən·ər) *n.* One whose business is driving wagons. Also *Brit.* **wag′gon·er.**

wag·on-head·ed (wag′ən-hed′id) *adj. Archit.* Having a round-arched roof.

wa·gon-lit (và·gôn·lē′) *n. pl.* **-lits** (-lē′) *French* A railway sleeping car.

wag·on·load (wag′ən·lōd′) *n.* The amount that a wagon can carry.

wagon train A train or line of wagons.

wag·tail (wag′tāl′) *n.* Any of several small singing birds having a long tail that is habitually wagged up and down.

Wa·ha·bi (wä·hä′bē) *n.* A member of an orthodox Moslem sect of Arabia. Also **Wa·ha′bee, Wah·ha·bi.**

wa·hoo (wä·hōō′, wä′hōō) *n.* A deciduous North American shrub or small tree with purple flowers and scarlet fruit. [< Siouan (Dakota) *wánhu,* lit., arrowwood]

waif (wāf) *n.* **1.** A homeless, neglected wanderer; a stray. **2.** Anything found and unclaimed, the owner being unknown. — *v.t.* To throw away; cast off, as a waif. — *adj.* Stray; wandering; homeless. [< AF *waif,* OF *gaif*]

wail (wāl) *v.i.* **1.** To grieve with mournful cries; lament. **2.** To make a sad, melancholy sound, as if in grief. — *v.t.* **3.** To grieve on account of. **4.** To cry out in sorrow. — *n.* **1.** A prolonged, high-pitched sound of lamentation or grief. **2.** Any mournful sound, as of the wind. [< ON < *væ, vei* woe] — **wail′er** *n.* — **wail′ful** *adj.*

wain (wān) *n.* An open, four-wheeled wagon for hauling heavy loads. [OE *wægn, wēn*]

wain·scot (wān′skət, -skot, -skōt) *n.* **1.** A facing for inner walls, usu. of paneled wood. **2.** The lower part of an inner wall, when finished with material different from the rest of the wall. — *v.t.* **wain·scot·ed** or **·scot·ted, wain·scot·ing** or **·scot·ting** To face or panel with wainscot. [< MLG < *wagen* wagon + *schot* wooden partition]

wain·scot·ing (wān′skət·ing, -skot-, -skōt-) *n.* Material for a wainscot; a wainscot. Also **wain′scot·ting.**

wain·wright (wān′rīt) *n.* A maker of wagons.

waist (wāst) *n.* **1.** The part of the body between the chest and the hips. **2.** The middle part of any object, esp. if narrower than the ends. **3.** That part of a woman's dress covering the body from the waistline to the shoulders; a bodice. **4.** A waistband. [ME *wast*]

waist·band (wāst′band′, -bənd) *n.* A band encircling the waist, esp., as part of a skirt or trousers.

waist·coat (wāst′kōt′, wes′kit) *n. Chiefly Brit.* A vest (def. 1).

waist·line (wāst′līn′) *n.* The line of the waist, between the ribs and the hips; in dressmaking, the line at which the skirt of a dress meets the waist.

wait (wāt) *v.i.* **1.** To stay or remain in expectation, as of an anticipated action or event: with *for, until,* etc. **2.** To be or remain in readiness. **3.** To remain temporarily neglected or undone. **4.** To perform duties of personal service or attendance; esp., to act as a waiter or waitress. — *v.t.* **5.** To stay or remain in expectation of; await. **6.** *Informal* To postpone; delay: Don't *wait* breakfast for me. — **to wait on** (or **upon**) **1.** To act as a servant or attendant to. **2.** To go to see; call upon; visit. **3.** To attend as a consequence. — **to wait up** To delay going to bed in anticipation of someone or something; delay. — *n.* **1.** The act of waiting, or the time spent in waiting; delay. **2.** An ambush or trap: to lie in *wait* for a victim. [< AF and OF < OHG < *wahta* guard]

wait·er (wā′tər) *n.* **1.** One who serves food and drink, as in a restaurant. **2.** One who awaits something. **3.** A tray for dishes, etc.

wait·ing (wā′ting) *n.* The act of one who waits. — **in waiting** In attendance, esp. at court. — *adj.* That waits; expecting.

waiting room A room for the use of persons waiting, as for a railroad train, a doctor, dentist, or the like.

wait·ress (wā′tris) *n.* A woman or girl employed to wait on guests at table, as in a restaurant.

waive (wāv) *v.t.* **waived, waiv·ing 1.** To give up or relinquish a claim to. **2.** To refrain from insisting upon or taking advantage of; forego. **3.** To put off; postpone; delay. [< AF *weyver,* OF *gaiver* to abandon]

waiv·er (wā′vər) *n. Law* The voluntary relinquishment of a right or privilege; also, the instrument that evidences such relinquishment. [< AF < *weyver* to abandon]

wake¹ (wāk) *v.* **woke** (*Rare* **waked**)**, waked** (*Dial.* and alternative *Brit.* **woke, wok·en**)**, wak·ing** *v.i.* **1.** To emerge from sleep. **2.** To be or remain awake. **3.** To become active or alert after being inactive or dormant. **4.** *Dial.* To keep watch at night; esp., to hold a wake (def. 1). — *v.t.* **5.** To rouse from sleep; awake. **6.** To stir up; excite: to *wake* evil passions. **7.** *Dial.* To keep a vigil over; esp., to hold a wake over. — *n.* **1.** A watch over the body of a dead person through the night, before burial. **2.** The act of refraining from sleep, as on a solemn occasion. [Fusion of OE *wacan* to awake and *wacian* to be awake]

wake² (wāk) *n.* **1.** The track left by a vessel passing through the water. **2.** The area behind any moving thing. — **in the wake of 1.** Following close behind. **2.** In the aftermath of; as a result of. [< ON *vök* an opening in ice]

wake·ful (wāk′fəl) *adj.* **1.** Remaining awake, esp. at the ordinary time of sleep; not sleeping or sleepy. **2.** Watchful; alert. **3.** Arousing from or as from sleep. — **wake′ful·ly** *adv.* — **wake′ful·ness** *n.*

wak·en (wā′kən) *v.t.* **1.** To rouse from sleep; awake. **2.** To rouse to alertness or activity. — *v.i.* **3.** To cease sleeping; wake up. [OE *wæcnan, wæcnian*]

wake-rob·in (wāk′rob′in) *n.* Any species of trillium.

Wal·dorf salad (wôl′dôrf) A salad of chopped celery, apples, and walnuts, garnished with lettuce and mayonnaise. [after the first *Waldorf*-Astoria Hotel, New York City]

wale (wāl) *n.* **1.** A welt (def. 3). **2.** *Naut.* One of certain strakes of outer planking running fore and aft on a vessel. **3.** A ridge on the surface of cloth. — *v.t.* **waled, wal·ing 1.** To raise wales on by striking, as with a lash; beat. **2.** To manufacture, as cloth, with a ridge or rib. **3.** To weave as wickerwork with several rods together. [OE *walu*]

walk (wôk) *v.i.* **1.** To advance on foot in such a manner that one part of a foot is always on the ground; of quadrupeds, to advance in such a manner that two or more feet are always on the ground. **2.** To move or go on foot for exercise or amusement. **3.** To proceed slowly. **4.** To act or live in some manner: to *walk* in peace. **5.** To return to earth and appear, as a ghost. **6.** In baseball, to achieve first base as a result of having been pitched four balls. — *v.t.* **7.** To pass through, over, or across at a walk: to *walk* the floor. **8.** To cause to go at a walk; lead, ride, or drive at a walk. **9.** To accompany on a walk. **10.** To bring to a specified condition by walking: She *walked* me to death. **11.** In baseball, to allow to advance to first base by pitching four balls. — **to walk off 1.** To depart; go abruptly or without warning. **2.** To get rid of (fat, etc.) by walking. — **to walk off with 1.** To win. **2.** To steal. — **to walk out** *Informal* **1.** To go out on strike. **2.** To keep company: with *with* or *together.* — **to walk out on** *Informal* To forsake; desert. — **to walk over** To defeat easily; overwhelm. — *n.* **1.** The act of walking, as for enjoyment; a stroll. **2.** Manner of walking; gait. **3.** Chosen profession or habitual sphere of action: the different *walks* of life. **4.** Distance as measured by the time taken by one who walks: an hour's *walk.* **5.** A place set apart for walking; a path or sidewalk. **6.** A piece of ground set apart for domestic animals; range; pasture. **7.** In baseball, an advancing to first base as a result of having been pitched four balls. [OE *wealcan* to roll, toss] — **walk'er** *n.*

walk·a·way (wôk'ə·wā') *n.* A contest won without serious opposition: also called *walkover.*

walk·ie-talk·ie (wô'kē·tô'kē) *n. Telecom.* A portable sending and receiving radio set light enough to be carried by one man: also spelled *walky-talky.*

walking papers *Informal* Notice of dismissal from employment, etc.

walking stick 1. A staff or cane. 2. Any of various insects having legs, body, and wings resembling a twig.

walk-on (wôk'on', -ôn') *n.* A performer having a very small part; also, the part.

walk·out (wôk'out') *n. Informal* A workmen's strike.

walk·o·ver (wôk'ō'vər) *n.* A walkaway.

walk·up (wôk'up') *Informal n.* An apartment house having no elevator. — *adj.* Having no elevator.

walk·y-talk·y (wô'kē·tô'kē) See WALKIE-TALKIE.

wall (wôl) *n.* 1. A continuous structure designed to enclose an area, to be the surrounding exterior of a building, to be a partition between rooms, etc.; also, a fence separating fields, etc. ◆ Collateral adjective: *mural.* 2. Something suggestive of a wall: a *wall* of bayonets. 3. A rampart for defense; in the plural, fortifications. 4. A sea wall; levee. — **to drive, push,** or **thrust to the wall** To force (one) to an extremity; crush. — **to go to the wall** To be driven to an extremity; be forced to yield. — *v.t.* 1. To provide, surround, etc., with or as with a wall. 2. To fill or block with a wall: often with *up.* — *adj.* Of, pertaining to, or on, a wall. [OE < L < *vallus* stake, palisade]

wal·la·by (wol'ə·bē) *n. pl.* **·bies** One of the smaller kangaroos. [< Australian *wolabā*]

wall·board (wôl'bôrd', -bōrd') *n.* A material composed of several layers of compressed wood chips and pulp, used as a substitute for wooden boards and plaster.

wal·let (wol'it) *n.* 1. A pocketbook, usu. of leather, for holding unfolded paper money, personal papers, etc.: also called *billfold.* 2. A leather or canvas bag for tools, etc. 3. A knapsack. [ME *walet*; ult. origin uncertain]

wall·eye (wôl'ī') *n.* 1. An eye in which the iris is light-colored or white. 2. Any of several walleyed fishes. [Back formation < WALLEYED]

wall·eyed (wôl'īd') *adj.* 1. Having a whitish or grayish eye. 2. Having large, staring eyes, as a fish. 3. *Slang* Drunk. [< ON < *vagl* film on the eye + *eygr* < *auga* eye]

walleyed pike A fresh-water game fish of the Great Lakes, having large eyes. Also **walleyed perch.**

wall·flow·er (wôl'flou'ər) *n.* 1. Any of various European herbs of the mustard family, having fragrant yellow, orange, or red flowers. 2. *Informal* A person, esp. a woman, at a party who stays by the wall for want of a dancing partner.

Wal·loon (wo·lōōn') *n.* 1. One of a people inhabiting southern and southeastern Belgium and the adjoining regions of France. 2. Their language, a dialect of French. — *adj.* Of or pertaining to the Walloons or their dialect.

wal·lop (wol'əp) *v.t. Informal* 1. To beat soundly; thrash. 2. To hit with a hard blow. 3. To defeat soundly. — *v.i. Dial.* or *Informal* 4. To gallop. — *n. Informal* A severe blow. [< AF *waloper,* OF *galoper*]

wal·lop·er (wol'əp·ər) *n. Informal* 1. One who or that which wallops. 2. A whopper.

wal·lop·ing (wol'əp·ing) *Informal adj.* Very large; whopping. — *n.* A beating; whipping.

wal·low (wol'ō) *v.i.* 1. To roll about; be pleasurably and actively immersed. 2. To thrash about; flounder. 3. To move with a heavy, rolling motion, as a ship in a storm. 4. To live self-indulgently: to *wallow* in sensuality. — *n.* 1. The act of wallowing. 2. A pool or hole in which animals wallow; also, any depression or hollow made by or suggesting such use. [OE *wealwian*] — **wal'low·er** *n.*

wall·pa·per (wôl'pā'pər) *n.* Paper specially prepared and printed in colors and designs, for covering walls and ceilings of rooms. — *v.t.* To cover or provide with wallpaper.

Wall Street 1. A street in the financial district of New York City. 2. The world of U.S. finance.

wal·nut (wôl'nut', -nət) *n.* 1. Any of various trees of the North temperate zone cultivated as ornamental shade trees and valued for their timber and their edible nuts. 2. The wood or nut of any of these trees, esp. the edible seed or kernel. 3. The shagbark hickory, or its nut. 4. The color of the wood of any of these trees, esp. of the black walnut, a very dark brown. [OE < *wealh* foreign + *hnutu* nut]

Wal·pur·gis Night (väl·pŏŏr'gis) The night before May 1, associated with a witches' Sabbath. [after St. *Walpurga* (or *Walburga*), whose feast day falls on this date]

wal·rus (wôl'rəs, wol'-) *n. pl.* **·rus·es** or **·rus** A large marine mammal of arctic seas, having flippers, tusks in the upper jaw, and a thick neck. [< Du. *walrus* < Scand.]

waltz (wôlts) *n.* 1. A dance for couples to music in triple time. 2. The music for such a dance, or any similar music in triple time. — *v.i.* 1. To dance a waltz. 2. To move quickly and boldly; flounce. 3. To move freely. — *v.t.* 4. To cause to waltz. — *adj.* Of, or typical of, the waltz: *waltz* time. [< G < *walzen* to waltz] — **waltz'er** *n.*

wam·pum (wom'pəm, wôm'-) *n.* 1. Beads made from shells, often worked into ornaments, formerly used as currency by North American Indians. 2. *Informal* Money. [< Algonquian *wampum(peage),* lit., a white string (of beads)]

wan (won) *adj.* **wan·ner, wan·nest** 1. Pale, as from sickness or anxiety; pallid. 2. Indicating illness, unhappiness, etc.: a *wan* smile. — *v.t.* & *v.i.* **wanned, wan·ning** *Poetic* To make or become wan. [OE *wann* dark, gloomy] — **wan'ly** *adv.* — **wan'ness** *n.*

wand (wond) *n.* 1. A slender rod waved by a magician; also, any rod indicating an office or function of the bearer, as a scepter. 2. A musician's baton. 3. A thin, flexible stick or twig; also, a willow shoot; osier. [< ON *vöndr*]

wan·der (won'dər) *v.i.* 1. To move or travel about without destination or purpose; roam; rove. 2. To go casually or indirectly; idle; stroll. 3. To twist or meander. 4. To stray. 5. To deviate in conduct or opinion; go astray. 6. To think or speak deliriously or irrationally. — *v.t.* 7. To wander through or across. — *n.* A ramble. [OE *wandrian*] — **wan'der·er** *n.* — **wan'der·ing·ly** *adv.*
— **Syn.** (verb) 1. *Wander* implies no more than the absence of purpose: to *wander* through the shops. *Ramble* tends to be deprecatory: the speaker *rambled* on for an hour. *Roam* and *rove* imply travel through a large area, and suggest an irregular rather than a purposeless course: the explorers *roamed* through the jungle, pirates *roved* the sea.

wan·der·lust (won'dər·lust', *Ger.* vän'dər·lŏŏst) *n.* An impulse to travel; restlessness combined with a sense of adventure. [< G < *wandern* to travel + *lust* joy]

wane (wān) *v.i.* **waned, wan·ing** 1. To diminish in size and brilliance: opposed to *wax.* 2. To decline or decrease gradually; draw to an end. — *n.* 1. Decrease, as of power, prosperity, or reputation. 2. The decrease of the moon's visible illuminated surface; also, the period of such decrease. — **on the wane** Waning. [OE *wanian*]

wan·gle (wang'gəl) *v.* **·gled, ·gling** *Informal v.t.* 1. To obtain or accomplish by indirect or irregular methods: to *wangle* an introduction. 2. To manipulate or adjust, esp., dishonestly. — *v.i.* 3. To resort to indirect, irregular, or dishonest methods. — *n.* An act of wangling. [? Alter. of WAGGLE] — **wan'gler** *n.*

Wan·kel engine (väng'kəl, wäng'-) A light, compact type of internal-combustion engine including a triangular piston that rotates in one direction within combustion chambers. Also **Wan'kel.** [< F. *Wankel,* born 1902, Ger. inventor]

want (wont, wônt) *v.t.* 1. To feel a desire or wish for. 2. To wish; desire: used with the infinitive: Your friends *want* to help you. 3. To be deficient in; lack; be without. 4. To be lacking to the extent of: He *wants* three inches of six feet. 5. *Brit.* To need; require. — *v.i.* 6. To have need: usu. with *for.* 7. To be needy or destitute. 8. *Rare* To be lacking or absent. — **to want for** To be in need of; lack. — **to want to** *Informal* Ought to: You *want* to eat well. — *n.* 1. A lack; scarcity; shortage. 2. Privation; poverty; need. 3. Something lacking; a need. 4. A conscious need of something; a craving. — **for want of** Because of the lack or absence of: The crop failed *for want* of rain. [Prob. < ON *vanta* to be lacking] — **want'er** *n.*

want ad *Informal* A classified advertisement for something wanted, as hired help, a job, a lodging, etc.

want·ing (won'ting, wôn'-) *adj.* 1. Not at hand; missing; lacking. 2. Not coming up to need or expectation: His work was found *wanting.* — **wanting in** Deficient in. — *prep.* 1. Without; lacking. 2. Minus; less.

wan·ton (won'tən) *adj.* 1. Licentious; lustful. 2. Unjust; malicious; *wanton* savagery; also, unprovoked: a *wanton* murder. 3. Of abundant growth; rank. 4. Extravagant; excessive; unrestrained: *wanton* speech. 5. *Poetic* Not bound or tied; loose: *wanton* curls; also, frolicsome. — *v.i.* 1. To act wantonly or playfully; revel or sport. 2. To grow luxuriantly. — *v.t.* 3. To waste wantonly. — *n.* 1. A licentious person, esp., a woman. 2. A playful or frolicsome person or animal. 3. A trifler; dallier. [ME < OE *wan* deficient + ME *towen* < OE < *tēon* to educate] — **wan'ton·ly** *adv.* — **wan'ton·ness** *n.*

wap·i·ti (wop'ə·tē) *n. pl.* **·tis** or **·ti** *U.S. & Canadian* A large North American deer; an elk. [< Algonquian]

war (wôr) *n.* 1. An armed conflict between nations or states, or between different parties in the same state. See table MAJOR WARS OF HISTORY. 2. Any act or state of hostility; enmity; also, a contest or conflict. 3. The science

MAJOR WARS OF HISTORY

Name	Contestants (victor shown first)	Notable Battles	Treaties
Greco-Persian Wars 499–478 B.C.	Greek states — Persia	Marathon, 490; Thermopylae, Salamis, 480; Plataea, 479	
Peloponnesian War 431–404 B.C.	Sparta — Athens	Syracuse, 415; Cyzicus, 410; Aegospotami, 405	Peace of Nicias, 421
First Punic War 264–241 B.C.; Second Punic War 218–201 B.C.; Third Punic War 149–146 B.C.	Rome — Carthage	Drepanum, 249; Aegates, 241; Lake Trasimene, 217; Cannae, 216; Zama, 202	
Norman Conquest 1066	Normandy — England	Hastings, 1066	
Crusades 1096–1291	Christianity — Islam (indecisive)	Jerusalem, 1099; Acre, 1191	
Hundred Years' War 1338–1453	England — France	Crécy, 1346; Poitiers, 1356; Agincourt, 1415; Siege of Orléans, 1428–39	
Wars of the Roses 1455–85	Lancaster — York (indecisive)	St. Albans, 1455	
Thirty Years' War 1618–48	Catholics — Protestants	Leipzig, Breitenfeld, 1631; Lützen, 1632	Westphalia, 1648
Civil War (English) 1642–46	Roundheads — Cavaliers	Marston Moor, 1643; Naseby, 1645	
Second Great Northern War 1700–1721	Russia — Sweden and Baltic allies	Poltava, 1709	Nysted, 1721
War of the Spanish Succession 1701–14	England, Austria, Prussia, Netherlands — France, Spain	Blenheim, 1704	Utrecht, 1713
War of the Austrian Succession 1740–48	France, Prussia, Sardinia, Spain — Austria, England	Dettingen, 1743; Fontenoy, 1745	Aix-la-Chapelle, 1748
French & Indian War 1755–63	England — France	Plains of Abraham, 1759; Montreal, 1760	
Seven Years' War 1756–63	Prussia — Austria, France, Russia	Rossbach, Leuthen, 1757	Hubertusberg, 1763
Revolutionary War 1775–83	American Colonies — England	Lexington, Concord, Bunker Hill, 1775; Saratoga, 1777; Yorktown, 1781	Paris, 1783
Napoleonic Wars 1796–1815	England, Austria, Russia, Prussia, etc. — France	Nile, 1798; Trafalgar, 1805; Jena, Auerstädt, 1806; Leipzig, 1813; Waterloo, 1815	Campoformio, 1797; Tilsit, 1807; Schönbrunn, 1809; Paris, 1814–15; Vienna, 1815
War of 1812 1812–15	United States — England	Lake Erie, 1813; New Orleans, 1815	Ghent, 1814
War of Independence (Greek) 1821–29	Greece, England, Sweden, Russia — Turkey	Navarino, 1827	London, 1827
Mexican War 1846–48	United States — Mexico	Resaca de la Palma, 1846; Chapultepec, 1847	Guadalupe Hidalgo, 1848
Crimean War 1854–56	Turkey, England, France, Sardinia — Russia	Sevastopol, 1854	Paris, 1856
Civil War (United States) 1861–65	Union (North) — Confederate States (South)	Bull Run, 1861; Antietam, 1862; Chancellorsville, Gettysburg, Vicksburg, Chattanooga, 1863; Wilderness, 1864	
Franco-Prussian War 1870–71	Prussia — France	Sedan, 1870	Versailles, 1871
Spanish-American War 1898	United States — Spain	Manila Bay, Santiago, 1898	Paris, 1898
Boer War 1899–1902	England — Transvaal Republic & Orange Free State	Ladysmith, 1899	Vereeniging, 1902
Russo-Japanese War 1904–1905	Japan — Russia	Port Arthur, Mukden, Tsushima, 1905	Portsmouth, 1905
First Balkan War 1912–13; Second Balkan War 1913	Bulgaria, Serbia, Greece, Montenegro — Turkey	Scutari, 1912; Salonika, 1912; Adrianople, 1912	London, 1913
World War I 1914–18	Allies — Central Powers	Dardanelles, 1915; Verdun, Somme, Jutland, 1916; Caporetto, 1917; Vittorio Veneto, Amiens, Marne, Ypres, 1918	Versailles, Saint-Germain, Neuilly, 1919; Trianon, Sèvres, 1920; Lausanne, 1923
Civil War (Spanish) 1936–39	Insurgents — Loyalists	Teruel, 1937; Ebro River, 1938	
World War II 1939–45	United Nations — Axis 1939–45	Dunkirk, 1940; Crete, 1941; El Alamein, 1942; Tunis, 1943; Stalingrad, 1942–43; Kharkov, 1943; Cassino, 1943–44; Saint-Lô, 1944; Rhine, Ruhr, Berlin, 1945	Potsdam, 1945
	United Nations — Japan 1941–45	Pearl Harbor, 1941; Bataan, 1941–1942; Singapore, Coral Sea, Midway Island, Guadalcanal, 1942; Bismarck Sea, Tarawa, 1943; Leyte Gulf, 1944; Philippines, 1944–45; Okinawa, 1945	San Francisco, 1951
Korean War 1950–52	United Nations — North Korea	Inchon, Pyongyang, 1950; Seoul, 1951	Panmunjom, 1953

of military operations; strategy. **—v.i. warred, war·ring** **1.** To wage war; fight or take part in a war. **2.** To be in any state of active opposition. **— adj.** Of, used in, or resulting from war. [OE < AF < OHG *werra* strife]

war belt Among certain North American Indians, a belt of wampum sent to declare war, to invoke aid in war, etc.

War between the States The U.S. Civil War: used esp., in the former Confederate States.

war·ble (wôr′bəl) *v.* **·bled, ·bling** *v.t.* **1.** To sing with trills and runs, or with tremulous vibrations. **2.** To celebrate in song. **—v.i. 3.** To sing with trills, etc. **4.** To make a liquid, murmuring sound, as a stream. **5.** *U.S.* To yodel. **—n.** The act of warbling: a carol; song. [< AF and OF < *werble* warble]

war·bler (wôr′blər) *n.* **1.** One who or that which warbles. **2.** Any of various plain-colored, mostly Old World birds noted for their song. **3.** Any of various small American insectivorous birds, usu. brilliantly colored.

war bonnet The ceremonial head dress of the North American Plains Indians.

war crime Any of various crimes considered in violation of the rules of warfare, as atrocities against civilians, slave labor, genocide, and the mistreatment of prisoners.

war cry A rallying cry used by combatants in a war, or by participants in any contest.

ward (wôrd) *n.* **1.** A large room in a hospital, usu. for six or more patients. **2.** An administrative or electoral division of a city. **3.** *Law* A person, often a minor, who is in the charge of a guardian. **4.** The act of guarding, or the state of being guarded; custody. **5.** A means of defense: a protection. **6.** A defensive attitude, as in fencing; guard. **7.** Any of the separate divisions of a prison. —*v.t.* **1.** To repel or turn aside, as a blow: usu., with *off.* **2.** To keep in safety. **3.** *Archaic* To guard. [OE < *weardian* to watch, guard]

-ward *suffix* Toward; in the direction of: *upward, homeward.* Also **-wards.** [OE *-weard, -weardes* at, toward]

war dance A dance of savage tribes before going to war or in celebration of a victory.

war·den[1] (wôr′dən) *n.* **1.** *U.S.* The chief officer of a prison. **2.** *Brit.* The head of certain colleges. **3.** In Connecticut, the chief executive of a borough. **4.** A churchwarden. **5.** A warder. [< AF *wardein*, OF *gardein, guarden* < Gmc] — **war′den·ry, war′den·ship** (-ship) *n.*

war·den[2] (wôr′dən) *n.* A variety of pear used chiefly for cooking. Also **War′den.** [ME *wardon*]

ward·er (wôr′dər) *n.* **1.** A keeper; guard; sentinel; watchman. **2.** An official staff or baton; a truncheon. **3.** *Chiefly Brit.* A prison official; warden. [< AF < *warder* to keep]

ward heel·er *U.S. Slang* A hanger-on of a political boss, who does minor tasks, canvasses votes, etc. [< WARD (def. 2) + HEELER (def. 1)]

ward·robe (wôrd′rōb′) *n.* **1.** All the garments belonging to any one person. **2.** An upright cabinet for clothes. **3.** Theatrical costumes; also, the room in which they are kept. [< AF < OF < *warder* to keep + *robe* dress]

ward·room (wôrd′rōōm′, -rŏŏm′) *n.* On a warship, the common recreation area and dining room for the commissioned officers; also, these officers as a group.

ward·ship (wôrd′ship) *n.* **1.** The state of being a ward or having a guardian. **2.** Custody; guardianship.

ware (wâr) *n.* **1.** Articles of the same class; esp., manufactured articles: used collectively, often in combination: *tableware, glassware.* **2.** *pl.* Articles of commerce; goods; merchandise. **3.** Pottery; earthenware. [OE *waru*]

ware·house (wâr′hous′) *n.* A storehouse for goods or merchandise. —*v.t.* **·housed** (-houzd′), **·hous·ing** (-hou′zing) To place or store in a warehouse.

ware·house·man (wâr′hous′mən) *n. pl.* **·men** (-mən) One who works in, manages, or owns a warehouse.

war·fare (wôr′fâr′) *n.* **1.** The waging or carrying on of war; conflict with arms; war. **2.** Struggle; strife.

war game *pl.* Practice maneuvers imitating the conditions of actual warfare.

war·head (wôr′hed′) *n. Mil.* The section at the nose of a guided missile, bomb, etc., containing the explosive.

war horse 1. *Informal* A veteran; esp., an aggressive or veteran politician. **2.** A horse used in combat; charger.

war·like (wôr′līk) *adj.* **1.** Disposed to engage in war; belligerent. **2.** Relating to, used in, or suggesting war; military. **3.** Threatening war; pugnacious; hostile.

war·lock (wôr′lok′) *n.* A wizard; sorcerer; also, a demon. [OE < *wǣr* covenant + *lēogan* to lie, deny]

warm (wôrm) *adj.* **1.** Moderately hot; having heat somewhat greater than temperate. **2.** Imparting warmth or heat. **3.** Preserving warmth; preventing loss of bodily heat: a *warm* coat. **4.** Having a feeling of heat greater than ordinary: *warm* from exertion. **5.** Affectionate; loving; warmhearted. **6.** Possessing ardor, liveliness, etc.: a *warm* argument. **7.** Excited; agitated; also, vehement; passionate: a *warm* temper. **8.** United by affection. **9.** Having predominating tones of red or yellow. **10.** Recently made; fresh: a *warm* trail. **11.** Near to discovering concealed fact or object. **12.** *Informal* Uncomfortable; dangerous. **13.** Characterized by brisk activity: a *warm* skirmish. —*v.t.* **1.** To heat slightly. **2.** To make ardent or enthusiastic; interest. **3.** To fill with kindly feeling. —*v.i.* **4.** To become warm. **5.** To become ardent or enthusiastic: often with *to.* **6.** To become kindly disposed or friendly: with *to* or *toward.* — **to warm up 1.** To warm. **2.** To exercise just before a game, etc. **3.** To run an engine until it reaches operating temperature. —*n. Informal* Warmth; a heating. [OE *wearm*] — **warm′er** *n.* — **warm′ly** *adv.* — **warm′ness** *n.*

warm-blood·ed (wôrm′blud′id) *adj.* **1.** *Zool.* Preserving a uniform body temperature, as man. **2.** Enthusiastic; ardent; passionate.

warm·heart·ed (wôrm′här′tid) *adj.* Kind; affectionate.

warm·ing pan (wôr′ming) A closed metal pan with a long handle, containing hot coals or water, for warming a bed.

war·mon·ger (wôr′mung′gər, -mong′-) *n.* One who propagates warlike ideas. — **war′mon′ger·ing** *adj. & n.*

warmth (wôrmth) *n.* **1.** The state, quality, or sensation of being warm. **2.** Ardor or fervidness of disposition or feeling; excitement of temper or mind. **3.** The effect produced by warm colors. [ME < OE *wearm* + *-thu, th* -th[1]]

warm-up (wôrm′up′) *n. Informal* The act of one who or that which warms up.

warn (wôrn) *v.t.* **1.** To make aware of possible harm; caution. **2.** To advise; admonish. **3.** To give notice in advance. **4.** To notify (a person) to stay away etc.: with *off, away,* etc. [OE *warnian*] — **warn′er** *n.*

warn·ing (wôr′ning) *n.* **1.** The act of one who warns; also, notice of danger. **2.** That which warns or admonishes. — *adj.* Serving as a warning. — **warn′ing·ly** *adv.*

War of 1812 See table for WAR.

War of American Independence *Brit.* The American Revolution.

War of Independence The American Revolution.

War of Secession The Civil War in the U.S.

War of the Spanish Succession See table for WAR.

warp (wôrp) *v.t.* **1.** To turn or twist out of shape, as by shrinkage or heat. **2.** To turn from a correct course; give a twist or bias to; corrupt. **3.** To stretch (yarn) so as to form a warp. **4.** *Naut.* To move (a vessel) by hauling on a rope fastened to a pier or anchor. —*v.i.* **5.** To become turned or twisted out of shape. **6.** To deviate from a proper course; go astray. **7.** *Naut.* To move by means of ropes fastened to a pier, etc. — *n.* **1.** The state of being warped; a distortion, esp. in wood. **2.** A mental or moral deviation; bias. **3.** The threads that run the long way of a fabric, crossing the woof. **4.** *Naut.* A cable used for warping a ship. [OE *weorpan* to throw] — **warp′er** *n.*

war paint 1. Paint applied to faces and bodies by primitive peoples in token of going to war. **2.** *Informal* Cosmetics; finery; also, official garb or regalia.

war·path (wôr′path′, -päth′) *n.* The route taken by American Indians going to war. — **on the warpath 1.** On a warlike expedition. **2.** Ready for a fight; angry.

war·plane (wôr′plān′) *n.* An airplane equipped for fighting.

war·rant (wôr′ənt, wor′-) *n.* **1.** *Law* A judicial writ or order authorizing arrest, search, seizure, etc. **2.** Something that assures or attests; evidence; guarantee. **3.** That which gives authority for some act; sanction; justification. **4.** A certificate of appointment given to army and navy warrant officers. **5.** A document giving a certain authority; esp., for receipt or payment of money. —*v.t.* **1.** To guarantee the quality, sufficiency, etc., of: to *warrant* a title to property. **2.** To guarantee the character of; pledge oneself for. **3.** To guarantee against injury, loss, etc. **4.** To be sufficient grounds for; justify. **5.** To give legal authority; to empower; authorize. **6.** To say confidently; feel sure. [< AF *warant*, OF *guarant*] — **war′rant·a·ble** *adj.* — **war′rant·a·bly** *adv.* — **war′rant·er** *n.*

war·ran·tee (wôr′ən·tē′, wor′-) *n. Law* The person to whom a warranty is given.

warrant officer *Mil.* An officer serving without a commission, but having authority by virtue of a certificate or warrant, with rank superior to that of a noncommissioned officer. See tables at GRADE.

war·rant·or (wôr′ən·tôr, wor′-) *n. Law* One who makes or gives a warranty to another.

war·ran·ty (wôr′ən·tē, wor′-) *n. pl.* **·ties 1.** *Law* **a** An assurance that facts regarding property, insurance risks, etc., are as they are stated to be. **b** A covenant securing a title of ownership. **2.** A guarantee (def. 1). **3.** Authorization; warrant. [< AF *warantie*, < OF *guarant* warrant]

war·ren (wôr′ən, wor′-) *n.* **1.** A place where rabbits live and breed in communities. **2.** An enclosure for keeping small game. **3.** An obscure, crowded place of habitation. [< AF < *warir* to preserve]

war·ri·or (wôr′ē·ər, -yər, wor′-) *n.* A man engaged in or experienced in warfare. [< AF < OHG *werra* strife]

war·ship (wôr′ship′) *n.* Any vessel used in naval combat.

Wars of the Roses See table for WAR.

wart (wôrt) *n.* **1.** A small, usu. hard and nonmalignant bump formed on and rooted in the skin. **2.** A hard glandular protuberance on a plant. [OE *wearte*] — **wart′y** *adj.*

wart hog An African wild hog having warty excrescences on the face and large tusks in both jaws.

war·time (wôr′tīm′) *n.* A time of war. — *adj.* Caused by or related to a war, or occurring during a period of war.

war whoop A yell, as that made by American Indians, uttered as a signal for attack or to terrify opponents in battle.

war·y (wâr′ē) *adj.* **war·i·er, war·i·est 1.** Carefully watching and guarding. **2.** Shrewd; wily. [< OE *warian*] — **war′i·ly** *adv.* — **war′i·ness** *n.*

was (wuz, woz, *unstressed* wəz) First and third person singular, past indicative of BE. [OE *wæs*]

wash (wosh, wôsh) *v.t.* **1.** To cleanse by immersing in or applying water or other liquid, often with rubbing. **2.** To purify from defilement or guilt. **3.** To wet or cover with liquid. **4.** To flow against or over: a beach *washed* by the ocean. **5.** To remove by the action of water: with *away, off, out,* etc. **6.** To form or wear by erosion: The storm *washed* gulleys in the hillside. **7.** To purify, as gas, by passing through a liquid. **8.** To coat with a thin layer of color or a thin coat of metal. **9.** *Mining* To subject (gravel, earth, etc.) to the action of water so as to separate the ore, etc. — *v.i.* **10.** To wash oneself. **11.** To wash clothes, etc. **12.** To withstand the effects of washing: That calico will *wash.* **13.** *Brit. Informal* To undergo testing successfully: That story won't *wash.* **14.** To flow with a lapping sound, as waves. **15.** To be removed by the action of water: with *away, off, out,* etc. **16.** To be eroded by the action of water. — **to wash down 1.** To drink liquid along with or right after (food) to facilitate swallowing. **2.** To scrub from top to bottom, as walls. — **to wash up 1.** To wash oneself. **2.** *Brit. Informal* To wash the dishes. — *n.* **1.** The act or process of washing; cleansing. **2.** A number of clothes, etc. set apart to be washed at one time; laundry. **3.** Liquid or semiliquid refuse; swill. **4.** A preparation used in washing or coating, as: **a** A mouthwash. **b** Water color spread on a picture. **5.** The breaking of a body of water upon the shore, or the sound made by waves breaking or surging against a surface; swash. **6.** Erosion of soil by the action of running water. **7.** Churned air, water, or other fluid resulting from the passage of an object through it. **8.** An area washed by a sea or river; a marsh; bog. — *adj.* Washable without injury: *wash* fabrics. [OE *wascan, wæscan*]

wash·a·ble (wosh′ə·bəl, wôsh′-) *adj.* That may be washed without fading or injury.

wash-and-wear (wosh′ən·wâr′, wôsh′-) *adj.* Designating or pertaining to a garment or fabric so treated as to require little or no ironing after washing.

wash·board (wosh′bôrd′, -bōrd′, wôsh′-) *n.* A board or frame having a corrugated surface on which to rub clothes while washing them.

wash·bowl (wosh′bōl′, wôsh′-) *n.* A basin or bowl used for washing the hands and face. Also **wash′ba·sin** (-bā′sən).

wash·cloth (wosh′klôth′, -kloth′, wôsh′-) *n.* A small cloth used for washing the body.

wash·day (wosh′dā′, wôsh′-) *n.* A day of the week set aside for doing household washing.

washed-out (wosht′out′, wôsht′-) *adj.* **1.** Faded; colorless; pale. **2.** *Informal* Exhausted; worn-out; tired.

washed-up (wosht′up′, wôsht′-) *adj.* **1.** *Slang* No longer successful, popular, etc.; finished. **2.** *Informal* Tired.

wash·er (wosh′ər, wô′shər) *n.* **1.** One who or that which washes. **2.** *Mech.* A small, flat, perforated disk of metal, leather, rubber, etc., used for placing beneath a nut or at an axle bearing or joint, to serve as a cushion, to prevent leakage, or to relieve friction. **3.** A washing machine.

wash·er·wom·an (wosh′ər·wŏom′ən, wô′shər-) *n. pl.* **·wom·en** (-wim′in) A laundress.

wash·ing (wosh′ing, wô′shing) *n.* **1.** The act of one who or that which washes. **2.** Things, as clothing, washed or to be washed on one occasion. **3.** That which is retained after being washed: a *washing* of ore. **4.** A thin coating of metal.

washing machine A machine for washing laundry.

washing soda Sodium carbonate in crystalline form, used for washing textiles and as a bleaching agent.

wash·out (wosh′out′, wôsh′-) *n.* **1.** A considerable erosion of earth by the action of water; also, the excavation thus made; a gully or gulch. **2.** *Slang* A failure. **3.** The act of one who or that which washes out.

wash·rag (wosh′rag′, wôsh′-) *n.* A washcloth.

wash·room (wosh′rōōm′, -rōōm′, wôsh′-) *n.* A lavatory.

wash·stand (wosh′stand′, wôsh′-) *n.* A stand for washbowl, pitcher, etc.

wash·tub (wosh′tub′, wôsh′-) *n.* A tub used for washing.

wash·wom·an (wosh′wŏom′ən, wôsh′-) *n. pl.* **·wom·en** (-wim′in) A washerwoman.

wash·y (wosh′ē, wô′shē) *adj.* **wash·i·er, wash·i·est 1.** Overly diluted; weak. **2.** Faded; wan. — **wash′i·ness** *n.*

was·n't (wuz′ənt, woz′-) Was not.

wasp (wosp, wôsp) *n.* Any of numerous stinging insects, including social wasps, that make nests of vegetable matter, and solitary wasps, living in mud or sand nests. [OE *wæsp*]

WASP (wosp, wôsp) *n. Slang* A white Protestant American: sometimes used contemptuously. Also **Wasp.** [Acronym formed from the initial letters of "white Anglo-Saxon Protestant"]

wasp·ish (wos′pish, wôs′-) *adj.* **1.** Having a nature like a wasp; irritable; irascible. **2.** Having a wasplike form or slender waist. — **wasp′ish·ly** *adv.* — **wasp′ish·ness** *n.*

wasp waist A waist so slender as to suggest that of a wasp. — **wasp-waist·ed** (wosp′wās′tid, wôsp′-) *adj.*

wasp·y (wos′pē, wôs′-) *adj.* **wasp·i·er, wasp·i·est** Like a wasp; waspish.

was·sail (wos′əl, was′-, wo·sāl′) *n.* **1.** An ancient salutation or toast to someone's health. **2.** The liquor, as spiced ale, prepared for a wassail. **3.** A festivity at which healths are drunk; a carousal. — *v.i.* **1.** To take part in a wassail; carouse. — *v.t.* **2.** To drink the health of; toast. [ME < ON *ves heill* be in good health] — **was′sail·er** *n.*

Was·ser·mann test (wos′ər·mən) A diagnostic test for syphi-lis, based on the reaction of the blood serum of an infected individual. Also **Wassermann reaction.** [after August von *Wassermann*, 1866–1925, German bacteriologist.]

wast (wost, *unstressed* wəst) *Archaic* second person singular, past indicative of BE: used with *thou.*

wast·age (wās′tij) *n.* That which is lost by wear, waste, etc.

waste (wāst) *v.* **wast·ed, wast·ing** *v.t.* **1.** To use or expend thoughtlessly, uselessly, or without return; squander. **2.** To cause to lose strength, vigor, or bulk. **3.** To use up; consume. **4.** To fail to use or take advantage of, as an opportunity. **5.** To lay waste; devastate. — *v.i.* **6.** To lose strength, vigor, or bulk: often with *away.* **7.** To diminish or dwindle gradually. **8.** To pass gradually: said of time. — *n.* **1.** The act or wasting or the state of being wasted; useless or unnecessary expenditure, consumption, etc. **2.** Misuse, neglect, or failure to take advantage of opportunity etc. **3.** A place or region that is devastated or made desolate; desert. **4.** A continuous, gradual diminishing of strength, vigor, or substance by use or wear. **5.** The act of laying waste or devastating. **6.** Something rejected as worthless or unneeded; esp., tangled spun cotton thread. **7.** Garbage; rubbish; trash. — **to lay waste** To turn into ruins; destroy utterly; devastate. — *adj.* **1.** Cast aside as worthless; worn out; discarded. **2.** Excreted, as undigested material, etc. **3.** Not under cultivation; unproductive; unoccupied. **4.** Made desolate; ruined. **5.** Containing or conveying waste products. **6.** Superfluous: *waste* energy. [< AF, ult. < L *vastare* to lay waste < *vastus* desert, desolate]

Waste, meaning containing or conveying refuse or waste, may appear as a combining form or as the first element in two-word phrases, as in:

    waste bin   **waste heap**
    waste pipe

waste·bas·ket (wāst′bas′kit, -bäs′-) *n.* An open container for paper scraps and other waste. Also **wastepaper basket.**

waste·ful (wāst′fəl) *adj.* **1.** Prone to waste; extravagant. **2.** Causing waste. — **waste′ful·ly** *adv.* — **waste′ful·ness** *n.*

waste·land (wāst′land′) *n.* A barren or desolate land.

waste·pa·per (wāst′pā′pər) *n.* Paper thrown away as worthless. Also **waste paper.**

wast·er (wās′tər) *n.* One who wastes; a wastrel.

wast·ing (wās′ting) *adj.* **1.** Producing emaciation; enfeebling: a *wasting* fever. **2.** Laying waste; devastating.

wast·rel (wās′trəl) *n.* **1.** A waster; spendthrift. **2.** An idler; loafer; vagabond. [Dim. of WASTER]

watch (woch) *v.i.* **1.** To look attentively. **2.** To wait expectantly: with *for.* **3.** To be constantly on the alert. **4.** To do duty as a guard or sentinel. **5.** To be an onlooker. **6.** To go without sleep; keep vigil. — *v.t.* **7.** To look at steadily and attentively; observe. **8.** To keep informed concerning. **9.** To be alert for: to *watch* one's opportunity. **10.** To keep watch over; guard; tend. — **to watch out** To be on one's guard. — *n.* **1.** The act of watching; close and continuous attention; careful observation. **2.** A small, portable timepiece worn or carried on the person, and usu. actuated by a coiled spring. **3.** Position or service as a guard. **4.** One or more persons set to watch. **5.** An act or period of wakefulness or attentive alertness, esp. during the night; vigil. **6.** The period of time during which a guard is on duty. **7.** *Naut.* **a** One of the two divisions of a ship's officers and crew, performing duty in alternation. **b** The period of time during which each division is on duty: usu. four hours. [OE *wæccan*] — **watch′er** *n.*

watch band A band to fasten a watch on the wrist.

watch·case (woch′kās′) *n.* The protecting case of a watch.

watch·dog (woch′dôg′, -dog′) *n.* **1.** A dog kept to guard property. **2.** One who acts as a vigilant guardian.

watch·ful (woch′fəl) *adj.* Vigilant. — **watch′ful·ly** *adv.* — **watch′ful·ness** *n.*

watch·mak·er (woch′mā′kər) *n.* One who makes or repairs watches. — **watch′mak′ing** *n.*

watch·man (woch′mən) *n. pl.* **·men** (-mən) Anyone who keeps watch or guard, as over a building at night.

watch night A religious service usu. held on New Year's Eve. Also **watch meeting.**

watch·tow·er (woch′tou′ər) *n.* A tower upon which a sentinel is stationed.

watch·word (woch′wûrd′) *n.* **1.** A password. **2.** A rallying cry or maxim.

wa·ter (wô′tər, wot′ər) *n.* **1.** A limpid, tasteless, odorless liquid compound of hydrogen and oxygen, H_2O, in the proportion by weight of approximately 2 parts of hydrogen to 16 of oxygen. When pure, water has its maximum density at 4° C. or 39° F.; at normal atmospheric pressure it freezes at 0° C. or 32° F., and boils at 100° C. or 212° F. **2.** Any body of water, as a lake, river, or a sea. **3.** Any one of the aqueous or liquid secretions of the body, as perspiration, tears, urine, etc. **4.** Any preparation of water holding a gaseous or volatile substance in solution. **5.** The transparency or luster of a precious stone or a pearl. **6.** Excellence; quality: first *water.* **7.** An undulating sheen given to certain fabrics, as silk, etc. **8.** In commerce and finance, stock issued without increase of paid-in capital to represent it. **— above water** Out of danger; secure. **— like water** Very freely or quickly: to spend money *like water*. **— of the first water** Of the highest degree. **— to hold water** To be valid or effective: His argument doesn't *hold water*. **— to make water** To urinate. **—** *v.t.* **1.** To pour water upon; moisten; sprinkle. **2.** To provide with water for drinking. **3.** To dilute with water: often with *down*. **4.** To give an undulating sheen to the surface of (silk, etc.). **5.** To enlarge the number of shares of (a stock company) without increasing the paid-in capital in proportion. **6.** To provide with streams or sources of water; irrigate. **—** *v.i.* **7.** To secrete or discharge water, tears, etc. **8.** To fill with saliva, as the mouth, from desire for food. **9.** To drink water. **10.** To take in water, as a locomotive. [OE *wæter*] **— wa′ter·er** *n.*

Water may appear as a combining form, or as the first element in two-word phrases, as in:

water meter	water right
water motor	water supply
water-repellant	water system

Water Bearer The constellation and sign of the zodiac Aquarius.

water bed A bed with a water-filled mattress.

wa·ter·borne (wô′tər·bôrn′, -bōrn′, wot′ər-) *adj.* **1.** Floating on water. **2.** Transported or carried by water.

wa·ter·buck (wô′tər·buk′, wot′ər-) *n.* Either of two large African antelopes frequenting the neighborhood of rivers and swimming with ease. [< Afrikaans *waterbok*]

water buffalo A large buffalo of Asia, India, and the Philippines, having a very wide spread of horns, and often domesticated for use as a draft animal: also called *water ox*, *carabao*.

WATER BUFFALO
(To 6 feet high at shoulder)

water chestnut **1.** The edible fruit of an aquatic plant contained in a hard, nutlike husk. **2.** The plant itself.

water clock An instrument for measuring time by the regulated flow of water.

water closet A toilet.

water color **1.** A color prepared for painting with water as the medium, as distinguished from one to be used with oil, tempera, etc. **2.** A picture or painting done in water colors. **— wa·ter-col·or** (wô′tər·kul′ər, wot′ər-) *adj.*

wa·ter-cool (wô′tər·kōōl′, wot′ər-) *v.t.* To cool by means of water, as by using a water jacket on an internal-combustion engine. **— wa′ter-cooled′** *adj.* **— wa′ter-cool′ing** *adj.*

water cooler A vessel or apparatus for cooling and dispensing drinking water.

wa·ter·course (wô′tər·kôrs′, -kōrs′, wot′ər-) *n.* **1.** A stream of water; river; brook. **2.** The course or channel of a stream or canal.

wa·ter·craft (wô′tər·kraft′, -kräft′, wot′ər-) *n.* **1.** Skill in sailing boats or in aquatic sports. **2.** Any boat or ship; also, sailing vessels collectively.

wa·ter·cress (wô′tər·kres′, wot′ər-) *n.* A perennial herb of the mustard family, growing in springs and clear, cool streams and having edible, pungent leaves used as salad.

water cure *Med.* Hydropathy.

wa·ter·fall (wô′tər·fôl′, wot′ər-) *n.* A steep fall of water, as of a stream over a dam or from a precipice; cascade.

wa·ter·fowl (wô′tər·foul′, wot′ər-) *n.* *pl.* **·fowl** or **·fowls** **1.** A bird that lives on or about the water; esp., a swimming game bird. **2.** Such birds collectively.

wa·ter·front (wô′tər·frunt′, wot′ər-) *n.* **1.** Real property abutting on or overlooking a natural body of water. **2.** That part of a town fronting on a body of water.

water gap A deep ravine in a mountain ridge, giving passage to a stream.

water gas A poisonous mixture, chiefly of hydrogen and carbon monoxide, produced by forcing steam over white-hot carbon, as coal or coke, and used for cooking, heating, and as an illuminant. **— wa·ter-gas** (wô′tər·gas′, wot′ər-) *adj.*

water gate A floodgate (def. 1)

water gauge A gauge indicating the level of water, as in a boiler. Also **water gage**.

water glass **1.** A drinking glass. **2.** Any glass vessel for holding water. **3.** Sodium silicate, a soluble silicate preparation; esp., an aqueous solution used in preserving eggs, etc. **4.** A water gauge on a steam boiler, etc.

water hole A small pond, pool, or depression containing water; esp., one used by animals as a drinking place.

water ice A frozen dessert made with water, sugar, and fruit juice.

wa·ter·ing (wô′tər·ing, wot′ər-) *n.* **1.** The act of one who or that which waters. **2.** The process of producing a wavy, ornamental effect on fabric, etc. **—** *adj.* **1.** That waters. **2.** Situated near the shore or near mineral springs.

watering can A container used for watering plants, etc., esp. one having a long spout. Also **watering pot**.

watering place **1.** A place where water can be obtained, as a spring. **2.** A health resort having mineral springs; also, a pleasure resort near the water.

water jacket A casing containing water and surrounding a cylinder or mechanism, esp. the cylinder block of an internal-combustion engine, for keeping it cool.

water jump A water barrier, as a pool, stream, or ditch, to be jumped over by the horses in a steeplechase.

water level **1.** The level of still water in the sea or in any other body of water. **2.** *Geol.* A water table. **3.** *Naut.* A ship's water line.

water lily **1.** Any of a genus of aquatic plants having showy flowers with numerous white or pinkish petals: also called *pond lily*. **2.** Any of various related plants.

water line **1.** *Naut.* The part of the hull of a ship that corresponds with the water level at various loads: also called *water level*. **2.** A line or demarcation corresponding to the height to which water has risen or may rise.

wa·ter·logged (wô′tər·lôgd′, -logd′, wot′ər-) *adj.* **1.** Heavy and unmanageable on account of the leakage of water into the hold, as a ship. **2.** Water-soaked; saturated with water.

Wa·ter·loo (wô′tər·lōō) *n.* A final and decisive defeat: usu. in the phrase **to meet one's Waterloo**. [after Napoleon's defeat at *Waterloo*, Belgium]

water main A large conduit for carrying water.

wa·ter·man (wô′tər·mən, wot′ər-) *n.* *pl.* **·men** (-mən) A man who works with a boat or small vessel on the water; a boatman. **— wa′ter·man·ship′** *n.*

wa·ter·mark (wô′tər·märk′, wot′ər-) *n.* **1.** A mark showing the extent to which water rises. **2.** In papermaking: **a** A marking in paper, usu. produced by pressure of a projecting design on a processing roll or in the mold. **b** The metal pattern that produces this marking. **—** *v.t.* **1.** To impress (paper) with a watermark. **2.** To impress as a watermark.

wa·ter·mel·on (wô′tər·mel′ən, wot′ər-) *n.* **1.** The large, edible fruit of a trailing plant of the gourd family, containing a many-seeded red or pink pulp and a watery juice. **2.** The plant on which this fruit grows.

water mill A mill operated by waterpower.

water moccasin A venomous pit viper of the southern U.S.: also called *cottonmouth*.

water nymph In classical mythology, any nymph or goddess living in or guarding a body of water.

water of crystallization *Chem.* Molecules of water forming part of certain crystallized salts. They may be eliminated by heat, often with apparent loss of crystalline structure.

water ouzel Any of various small birds adapted to feeding under water. Also **water ousel**.

water ox A water buffalo.

water pipe **1.** A hookah. **2.** A conduit for water.

water polo A game in which two teams of swimmers push or throw a buoyant ball toward opposite goals.

wa·ter·pow·er (wô′tər·pou′ər, wot′ər-) *n.* **1.** The power of water derived from its momentum, as applied to the driving of machinery. **2.** A fall in a stream, yielding kinetic energy from which motive power may be obtained.

wa·ter·proof (wô′tər·prōōf′, wot′ər-) *adj.* **1.** Permitting no water to enter or pass through; impervious to water. **2.** Coated with some substance, as rubber, that resists the passage of water. **—** *n.* **1.** Material or fabric rendered impervious to water. **2.** *Brit.* A raincoat or other garment made of such fabric. **—** *v.t.* To render waterproof.

water rat **1.** The muskrat. **2.** The European vole. **3.** Any aquatic rodent. **4.** *Slang* A waterfront thief or tough.

wa·ter·shed (wô′tər·shed′, wot′ər-) *n.* **1.** The line of separation between two contiguous drainage valleys. **2.** The region from which a river receives its supply of water.

wa·ter·side (wô′tər·sīd′, wot′ər-) *n.* The shore of a body of water; the water's edge. **—** *adj.* Of, pertaining to, or living, growing, or working by the water's edge.

wa·ter·ski (wô′tər·skē′, wot′ər-) *v.i.* **-skied**, **-ski·ing** To glide over water on water-skis, while being towed by a motorboat. **—** *n.* *pl.* **-skis** or **-ski** A broad, skilike runner with a fitting to hold the foot, worn when water-skiing: also **water ski**. **— wa′ter·ski′er** *n.* **— wa′ter·ski′ing** *n.*

water snake Any of various harmless snakes that live chiefly in or near fresh water.

wa·ter·soak (wô′tər·sōk′, wot′ər-) *v.t.* To fill the pores or crevices of with water; soak in water.

water softener A substance added to hard water to counteract the effect of its mineral content.

wa·ter·sol·u·ble (wô′tər·sol′yə·bəl, wot′ər-) *adj.* Soluble in water: said esp. of certain organic compounds.

water spaniel A large, reddish brown spaniel having a curly, waterproof coat, used primarily for retrieving ducks.

wa·ter·spout (wô′tər·spout′, wot′ər-) *n.* **1.** A moving, whirling column of spray and mist, with masses of water in the lower parts, generated at sea or on other large bodies of water. **2.** A pipe for the free discharge of water.

water sprite A sprite living in the water; water nymph.

water table *Geol.* The surface marking the upper level of a water-saturated zone extending beneath the ground to depths determined by the thickness of the permeable strata.

wa·ter·tight (wô′tər-tīt′, wot′ər-) *adj.* **1.** So closely made that water cannot enter or leak through. **2.** Having no loopholes; foolproof: *watertight* tax laws.

water tower **1.** A standpipe or tower, often of considerable height, used as a reservoir for a system of water distribution. **2.** A vehicular towerlike structure having an extensible vertical pipe from which water can be thrown on the upper floors of a burning building.

water vapor The vapor of water, esp. when below the boiling point, as in the atmosphere.

water wave An undulating effect of the hair, artificially produced when the hair is wet, and set by drying with heat.

wa·ter·way (wô′tər-wā′, wot′ər-) *n.* A river, channel, canal, etc., used as a means of travel.

water wheel A wheel so equipped with floats, buckets, etc., that it may be turned by flowing water, as a noria.

water wings A waterproof, inflatable device used as a support for the body while swimming or learning to swim.

wa·ter·works (wô′tər-wûrks′, wot′ər-) *n.pl.* A system of machines, buildings, and appliances for furnishing a water supply, esp. for a city.

wa·ter·worn (wô′tər-wôrn′, -wōrn′, wot′ər-) *adj.* Worn smooth by running or falling water.

wa·ter·y (wô′tər-ē, wot′ər-ē) *adj.* **1.** Containing or discharging water. **2.** Brimming; flowing. **3.** Resembling water; thin or liquid. **4.** Consisting of or pertaining to water. **5.** Diluted with water; weak. **— wa′ter·i·ness** *n.*

watt (wot) *n.* The practical unit of electric power, activity, or rate of work, equivalent to one joule per second, or one volt-ampere. [after James *Watt* 1736–1819, Scottish inventor]

watt·age (wot′ij) *n.* **1.** Amount of electric power in terms of watts. **2.** The total number of watts needed to operate an appliance.

watt-hour (wot′our′) *n.* Electrical energy equivalent to one watt acting for one hour.

wat·tle (wot′l) *n.* **1.** A structure of rods or twigs woven together. **2.** A twig or withe. **3.** A naked, fleshy process, often wrinkled and brightly colored, hanging from the throat of a bird or snake. **4.** Any of various acacias of Australia, Tasmania, and South Africa. **— *v.t.* ·tled, ·tling** **1.** To weave or twist, as twigs, into a network. **2.** To form, as baskets, by intertwining flexible twigs. **3.** To bind together with wattles. **— *adj.*** Made of or covered with wattles. [OE *watel, watul*] **— wat′tled** *adj.*

watt·me·ter (wot′mē′tər) *n.* An instrument for measuring electrical power in watts.

wave (wāv) *v.* **waved, wav·ing** *v.i.* **1.** To move freely back and forth or up and down, as a flag in the wind; fluctuate. **2.** To be moved back and forth or up and down as a signal; also, to make a signal by moving something thus. **3.** To have an undulating shape or form: Her hair *waves*. **— *v.t.* 4.** To cause to wave: to *wave* a banner. **5.** To form with an undulating surface or outline. **6.** To give a wavy appearance to; water, as silk. **7.** To form into waves: to *wave* one's hair. **8.** To signal by waving something: He *waved* me aside. **9.** To express by waving something: to *wave* farewell. **— *n.* 1.** A ridge or undulation moving on the surface of a liquid. **2.** One of the rising curves on an undulatory surface; one of a series of curves: *waves* of grain. **3.** Something that comes, like a wave, with great volume or power: a *wave* of enthusiasm. **4.** One of a series, as of events, occurring with wavelike fluctuations: He went ashore with the first *wave* of Marines. **5.** A progressive change in temperature or in barometrical condition: a heat *wave*. **6.** A wavelike tress or curl of hair. **7.** The act of waving; a sweeping or undulating motion, as with the hand. **8.** A wavelike stripe or undulation impressed on a surface. **9.** *Physics* One of the periodic vibratory impulses produced by a disturbance in and propagated through an elastic medium, as sound. **10.** *Usu. pl. Poetic* Any body of water, esp., the sea. [OE *wafian*] **— wav′er** *n.* **— wave′less** *adj.*

— Syn. (noun) **1.** *Wave* is the general term for an upheaval of the ocean's surface. A *ripple* is a very small *wave*, such as might be produced by a light breeze, or by an object dropping into still water. *Billow* is a poetic word for any *wave*, but esp., for a *wave* of great height. A *roller* is one of the long, irregular *waves* that move swiftly outward from a storm center.

Wave (wāv) *n.* A member of the WAVES.

wave band *Physics* A specified group of wave frequencies, esp. one assigned for radio or television broadcasting.

wave·length (wāv′length′) *n. Physics* The distance, measured along the line of propagation, between two points representing similar phases of two consecutive waves.

wave·let (wāv′lit) *n.* A little wave.

wave mechanics The branch of physics that investigates the wave characteristics ascribed to the atom and its associated particles, esp. with reference to the quantum theory.

wa·ver (wā′vər) *v.i.* **1.** To move one way and the other; sway; flutter. **2.** To be uncertain or undecided; show irresolution; vacillate. **3.** To show signs of falling back or giving way; falter. **4.** To flicker; gleam. **5.** To quaver; tremble. **— *n.*** A wavering. [< ME *waveren*] **— wa′ver·er** *n.* **— wa′ver·ing·ly** *adv.*

WAVES or **W.A.V.E.S.** (wāvz) *n.* A corps of women in the U.S. Navy; officially, Women in the United States Navy (1946). [< *W(omen) A(ccepted for) V(oluntary) E(mergency) S(ervice)*, an earlier name]

wave set A preparation put on the hair before setting to make waves and curls last.

wav·y (wā′vē) *adj.* **wav·i·er, wav·i·est** **1.** Full of waves; ruffled by or raised into waves. **2.** Undulatory; waving. **3.** Unstable; wavering. **— wav′i·ly** *adv.* **— wav′i·ness** *n.*

wax[1] (waks) *n. pl.* **wax·es** **1.** Beeswax. **2.** *Chem.* Any of various natural substances consisting of the esters of fatty acids and alcohols other than glycerol, including spermaceti and the secretions of certain plants and insects. **3.** A solid mineral substance resembling wax, as paraffin. **4.** Sealing wax. **5.** Earwax. **— *v.t.*** To coat or treat with wax. **— *adj.*** Made of or pertaining to wax. [OE *weax*]

wax[2] (waks) *v.i.* **waxed, waxed** (*Poetic* **wax·en**), **wax·ing** **1.** To become larger gradually; increase in size or numbers; grow: said esp., of the moon as it approaches fullness. **2.** To become: to *wax* angry. [OE *weaxan* to grow]

wax bean A variety of string bean of a pale yellow color, cultivated in the U.S.: also called *butter bean.*

wax·ber·ry (waks′ber′ē) *n. pl.* **·ries** **1.** The wax myrtle. **2.** Its wax-covered fruit. **3.** The snowberry.

wax·en (wak′sən) *adj.* **1.** Resembling wax. **2.** Consisting wholly or in part of wax; covered with wax. **3.** Pale; pallid: a *waxen* complexion; also, pliable or impressible as wax.

wax myrtle Any of various North American shrubs or small trees having fragrant leaves and small berries covered with wax, often used in making candles: also called *bayberry, candleberry, waxberry.*

wax palm **1.** A South American palm with pinnate leaves, having a lofty straight trunk covered with a waxy, whitish, resinous substance. **2.** A Brazilian palm whose young leaves yield a valuable wax.

wax paper Paper coated or treated with wax and used to retain or protect against moisture. Also **waxed paper.**

wax·weed (waks′wēd′) *n.* An annual, clammy, hairy herb of the loosestrife family with irregular purplish flowers.

wax·wing (waks′wing′) *n.* Any of various crested birds having soft, mainly brown plumage and wing feathers tipped with appendages resembling red or yellow sealing wax.

wax·work (waks′wûrk′) *n.* **1.** Work produced in wax; esp., ornaments or life-size figures of wax. **2.** *pl.* An exhibition of such figures. **— wax′work′er** *n.*

wax·y (wak′sē) *adj.* **wax·i·er, wax·i·est** **1.** Like wax in appearance, consistency, color, etc.; pliable; impressionable; pallid. **2.** Made of or abounding in wax; rubbed with wax. **— wax′i·ness** *n.*

way (wā) *n.* **1.** A manner or method of doing something; procedure. **2.** Direction; turn; route; line of motion: Which *way* is the city? **3.** A path, or track leading from one place to another or along which one goes. **4.** Space or room to advance or work: Make *way* for the king. **5.** Length of space passed over. **6.** Distance in general: a little *way* off: often popularly, **ways.** **7.** Passage from one place to another. **8.** Headway; progress. **9.** A customary style; a manner peculiar to certain people: the British *way* of doing things. **10.** A point of relation; particular: He erred in two *ways.* **11.** A course of life or experience: the *way* of sin. **12.** *Informal* State of health: to be in a bad *way.* **13.** A course wished for or resolved upon: Have it your *way.* **14.** The range of one's observation: An accident threw it in his *way.* **15.** *Naut. pl.* A tilted framework of timbers upon which a ship slides when launched. **16.** *Law* A right of way. **17.** *Informal* Neighborhood, or route home: He lives out of my *way.* **— by the way** In passing; incidentally. **— by way of 1.** With the purpose of; to serve as: *by way of* introduction. **2.** Through; via. **— out of the way 1.** Removed, as an obstruction. **2.** Remarkable; unusual. **3.** Improper; wrong. **4.** Out of place; lost; remote. **— the way** *Informal* In the manner that; as: Do it *the way* I told you to. **— under way** In motion; making progress. **— *adv. Informal* ** Away; very much or very far. [OE *weg*]

way back *Informal* Long ago. [Short for AWAY BACK]

way·bill (wā′bil′) *n.* A list describing or identifying goods or naming passengers carried by a train, steamer, etc.

way·far·er (wā′fâr′ər) *n.* One who journeys.

way·far·ing (wā′fâr′ing) *adj. & n.* Journeying; being on the road.

way·lay (wā′lā′, wā′lā′) *v.t.* **·laid, ·lay·ing** **1.** To lie in ambush for and attack, as in order to rob. **2.** To accost on the way. [< WAY + LAY¹] — **way′lay′er** n.

-ways suffix of adverbs In a (specified) manner, direction, or position: noways, sideways: often equivalent to -wise. Also **-way.** [< WAY + -S³]

ways and means Means or methods of accomplishing an end or defraying expenses; esp., in legislation, methods of raising funds for the use of the government.

way·side (wā′sīd′) adj. Standing or being near the side of a road. — n. The side or edge of the road or highway.

way station Any station between principal stations, esp. on a railroad; a local station.

way train A train stopping at way stations.

way·ward (wā′wərd) adj. **1.** Wanting its way; willful. **2.** Without definite course; unsteady; capricious. **3.** Unexpected or unwished for. [ME < awei away + -WARD] — **way′ward·ly** adv. — **way′ward·ness** n.

way·worn (wā′wôrn′, -wōrn′) adj. Fatigued by travel.

we (wē) pron. pl., possessive **our** or **ours,** objective **us** The nominative plural pronoun of the first person, used by the persons speaking or writing to denote themselves, by an individual to refer to himself or herself and one or more others, by an editor or other writer to give his words an impersonal character, or by a sovereign on formal occasions. [OE wē]

weak (wēk) adj. **1.** Lacking in physical strength; wanting in energy or activity; feeble. **2.** Insufficiently resisting stress: a weak link or bridge. **3.** Lacking in strength of will or stability of character; pliable. **4.** Ineffectual, as from deficient supply: weak artillery support. **5.** Lacking in power or sonorousness: a weak voice. **6.** Lacking a specified component or components in the proper amount; of less than customary potency: weak tea. **7.** Lacking the ability to function properly: a weak heart. **8.** Lacking in mental or moral strength. **9.** Showing or resulting from poor judgment: a weak plan; unable to convince: a weak argument. **10.** Lacking in influence or authority. **11.** Deficient in strength, skill, experience, or the like. **12.** Gram. In Germanic languages, denoting a weak verb. **13.** Phonet. Unstressed; unaccented, as a syllable or sound. **14.** In prosody, indicating a verse ending in which the accent falls on a word or syllable otherwise without stress. **15.** Wanting in impressiveness or interest: a weak play. [< ON veikr] — **weak′ly** adv. — **weak′ness** n.

Weak may appear as a combining form, as in the following self-explanatory compounds:

weak-backed	weak-looking	weak-stemmed
weak-bodied	weak-made	weak-tasting
weakbrained	weak-muscled	weak-throated
weak-brewed	weak-natured	weak-tinted
weak-built	weak-nerved	weak-toned
weak-colored	weak-seeming	weak-voiced
weak-eyed	weak-sided	weak-walled
weak-growing	weak-sighted	weak-willed
weakhanded	weak-smelling	weak-winged
weakhearted	weak-sounding	weak-witted
weak-limbed	weak-spirited	weak-woven

weak·en (wē′kən) v.i. v.t. & To make or become weak or weaker. — **weak′en·er** n.

weak·fish (wēk′fish′) n. pl. **·fish** or **·fish·es** Any of several marine food fishes of the coastal waters of the eastern U.S.

weak-kneed (wēk′nēd′) adj. **1.** Weak in the knees. **2.** Without resolution, strong purpose, or energy; spineless.

weak·ling (wēk′ling) n. A feeble person or animal. — adj. Having no natural strength or vigor.

weak·ly (wēk′lē) adj. **·li·er, ·li·est** Sickly; feeble; weak.

weak-mind·ed (wēk′mīn′did) adj. **1.** Indecisive; weakwilled. **2.** Feeble-minded. — **weak′mind′ed·ness** n.

weak·ness (wēk′nis) n. **1.** The state, condition, or quality of being weak. **2.** A characteristic indicating feebleness. **3.** A slight failing; a fault. **4.** A penchant or fondness: with for: a weakness for pastry.

weal¹ (wēl) n. Archaic A sound or healthy state; prosperity; welfare. [OE wela]

weal² (wēl) n. A welt (def. 3). [Var. of WALE]

weald (wēld) n. Chiefly Brit. An exposed forest area; waste woodland; also, an open region; down. [OE, a forest]

wealth (welth) n. **1.** A large aggregate of real and personal property; riches; also, the state of being rich. **2.** Econ. All material objects having economic utility; also, in the private sense, all property possessing a monetary value. **3.** Great abundance of anything: usu. preceded by a: a wealth of learning. [ME < wele weal]
— Syn. **1.** affluence, opulence. Compare PROPERTY.

wealth·y (wel′thē) adj. **wealth·i·er, wealth·i·est** **1.** Possessing wealth; affluent. **2.** More than sufficient; abounding. — **wealth′i·ly** adv. — **wealth′i·ness** n.

wean (wēn) v.t. **1.** To transfer (the young of any mammal) from dependence on its mother's milk to another form of nourishment. **2.** To estrange from former habits or associations: usu. with from. [OE wenian to accustom]

wean·ling (wēn′ling) adj. Freshly weaned. — n. A child or animal newly weaned.

weap·on (wep′ən) n. **1.** Any implement for fighting or warfare. **2.** Any means that may be used against an adversary: verbal weapons. **3.** The sting, claw, spur, etc., of an animal. — v.t. To furnish with a weapon or weapons. [OE wǣpen] — **weap′on·less** adj.

weap·on·ry (wep′ən·rē′) n. Weapons collectively.

wear¹ (wâr) v. **wore, worn, wear·ing** v.t. **1.** To carry or have on the person as a garment, ornament, etc. **2.** To bear on the person habitually: He wears a derby. **3.** To have in one's appearance; exhibit: He wears a scowl. **4.** To bear habitually in a specified manner; carry: She wears her hair long. **5.** To display or fly: A ship wears its colors. **6.** To impair, waste, or consume by use or constant action. **7.** To cause by rubbing, etc.: to wear a hole in a coat. **8.** To bring to a specified condition by wear: to wear a sleeve to tatters. **9.** To exhaust; weary. — v.i. **10.** To be impaired gradually by use, rubbing, etc. **11.** To withstand the effects of use, wear, etc.: The skirt wears well. **12.** To become as specified from use or attrition: His patience is wearing thin. **13.** To pass gradually or tediously: with on or away. — **to wear out 1.** To make or become worthless by use. **2.** To waste gradually; use up: He wears out patience. **3.** To tire. — n. **1.** The act of wearing, or the state of being worn. **2.** The material or clothes to be worn: silk for summer wear: also in compounds: footwear. **3.** The destructive effect of use, work, or time. **4.** Capacity for resistance to use or impairment; durability. [OE werian] — **wear′a·bil′i·ty** n. — **wear′a·ble** adj. — **wear′er** n.

wear² (wâr) v. **wore, worn, wear·ing** Naut. v.t. **1.** To turn (a vessel) through an arc in which its head points momentarily directly to leeward. — v.i. **2.** To go about with the wind astern. [Prob. alter. of VEER¹]

wear and tear Loss by the service, exposure, decay, or injury incident to ordinary use.

wear·ing (wâr′ing) adj. **1.** Fatiguing; exhausting; wasting: a wearing job. **2.** Capable of being, or designed to be, worn. — **wear′ing·ly** adv.

wearing apparel Clothing; garments.

wea·ri·some (wir′i·səm) adj. Causing fatigue; tiresome or tedious. — **wea′ri·some·ly** adv. — **wea′ri·some·ness** n.

wea·ry (wir′ē) adj. **·ri·er, ·ri·est** **1.** Tired; fatigued. **2.** Discontented or vexed by continued endurance, as of something disagreeable, tedious, etc.: often with of: weary of life. **3.** Indicating or characteristic of fatigue, boredom, etc. **4.** Wearisome. — v.t. & v.i. **·ried, ·ry·ing** To make or become weary; tire. [OE wērig] — **wea′ri·ness** adj. — **wea′ri·ly** adv. — **wea′ri·ness** n.

wea·sel (wē′zəl) n. **1.** Any of certain small, slender, predacious carnivores having brownish fur that in northern regions turns white in winter. **2.** A sneaky, treacherous person. — v.i. **·seled, ·sel·ing** U.S. Informal To speak or act evasively, etc. [OE wesle]

weasel word A word that weakens a statement by rendering it ambiguous or equivocal.

weath·er (weth′ər) n. **1.** Atmospheric condition as regards temperature, moisture, winds, or other meteorological phenomena. **2.** Bad weather; storm. — **to keep one's weather eye open** Informal To be alert. — **under the weather** Informal **1.** Ailing; ill. **2.** Somewhat intoxicated. — v.t. **1.** To expose to the action of the weather. **2.** To discolor, crumble, or otherwise affect by action of the weather. **3.** To pass through and survive, as a crisis. **4.** Naut. To pass to windward of: to weather Cape Horn. — v.i. **5.** To undergo changes resulting from exposure to the weather. **6.** To resist the action of the weather. — adj. Chiefly Naut. Facing the wind. [OE weder] — **weath′ered** adj.

Weather may appear as a combining form or as the first element in two-word phrases, as in weather report, weather-marked, weathertight.

weath·er·beat·en (weth′ər·bēt′n) adj. **1.** Bearing or showing the effects of exposure to weather. **2.** Toughened or tanned by or as by exposure to weather, as a face.

weath·er·board (weth′ər·bôrd′, bōrd′) n. A clapboard. — v.t. To fasten weatherboards on.

weath·er·bound (weth′ər·bound′) adj. Detained by unfavorable weather, as a vessel in port.

Weather Bureau A bureau of the Department of Commerce in Washington, D.C., serving as headquarters for meteorological observation, the diffusion of information concerning the weather, etc.

weath·er·cock (weth′ər·kok′) n. **1.** A weather vane in the form of a cock. **2.** A fickle person or variable thing.

WEASEL
(To 9 inches long; tail 2 inches)

weath·er·glass (weth′ər·glas′, -gläs′) *n.* An instrument for indicating the state of the weather; esp., a simple barometer showing falls in atmospheric pressure.

weath·er·man (weth′ər·man′) *n.* *pl.* **-men** (-men′) *n. Informal* A meteorologist, esp. one concerned with daily weather conditions and reports.

weather map A map or chart indicating weather conditions, as temperature, atmospheric pressure, wind velocity, precipitation, etc., for a given region and time.

weath·er·proof (weth′ər·prōōf′) *adj.* Capable of withstanding rough weather without appreciable deterioration. — *v.t.* To make weatherproof.

weather station A station or office where meteorological observations are taken and recorded.

weath·er·strip (weth′ər·strip′) *v.t.* **-stripped, -strip·ping** To equip or fit with weather strips.

weather strip A narrow strip of material placed over or in crevices, as at windows, to keep out drafts, rain, etc.

weather stripping 1. A weather strip. 2. Weather strips collectively.

weather vane A vane that indicates the direction from which the wind is blowing; weathercock.

weath·er·wise (weth′ər·wīz′) *adj.* 1. Experienced in observing or predicting the weather. 2. Skillful in predicting trends or shifts in public opinion, etc.

weave (wēv) *v.* **wove** or for *def.* 10 **weaved, wo·ven** or (*less common*) **wove, weav·ing** *v.t.* 1. To form, produce, or manufacture as a textile, by interlacing threads or yarns; esp., in a loom. 2. To form by interlacing strands, strips, twigs, etc.: to *weave* a basket. 3. To produce by combining details or elements: to *weave* a story. 4. To bring together so as to form a whole. 5. To twist into, about, or through: to *weave* ribbons through one's hair. 6. To spin (a web). 7. To make or effect by moving from side to side or in a winding or zigzag course: to *weave* one's way through a crowd. — *v.i.* 8. To make cloth, baskets, etc., by weaving. 9. To become woven or interlaced. 10. To move from side to side or with a zigzagging motion. — *n.* A particular method or style of weaving. [OE *wefan*]

weav·er (wē′vər) *n.* 1. One who weaves; esp., one whose occupation is the weaving of textiles, etc. 2. A weaverbird.

weav·er·bird (wē′vər·bûrd′) *n.* Any of various finchlike birds, native to Asia, Africa, etc., and constructing intricately woven nests.

web (web) *n.* 1. Any fabric, structure, etc., woven of or as of interlaced or interwoven strands. 2. Textile fabric, esp. in the piece or being woven in a loom. 3. The network of delicate threads spun by a spider to entrap its prey, by certain caterpillars, other insect larvae, etc.; a cobweb. 4. Any complex network: a *web* of highways. 5. Anything artfully contrived or elaborated into a trap or snare: a *web* of espionage. 6. *Zool.* A membrane or fold of skin connecting the digits of an animal, as in aquatic birds, otters, bats, frogs, etc. 7. *Ornithol.* The series of barbs on either side of the shaft of a feather: also called *vane.* 8. A plate or sheet, as of metal, connecting the heavier sections, ribs, frames, etc., of any structural or mechanical element. 9. *Archit.* The part of a ribbed vault between the ribs. — *v.t.* **webbed, web·bing** 1. To provide with a web. 2. To cover or surround with a web; entangle. [OE]

webbed (webd) *adj.* 1. Having a web. 2. Having the digits united by a membrane, as the foot of a goose or duck.

web·bing (web′ing) *n.* 1. A woven strip of strong fiber, used for safety belts, in upholstery, etc. 2. Any structure or material forming a web.

web·by (web′ē) *adj.* **·bi·er, ·bi·est** Resembling, having, or consisting of a web or membrane.

web·foot (web′fŏŏt′) *n.* *pl.* **·feet** 1. A foot with webbed toes. 2. A web-footed bird or animal.

web·foot·ed (web′fŏŏt′id) *adj.* Having the toes connected by a membrane, as many aquatic animals and birds.

Web·ste·ri·an (web·stir′ē·ən) *adj.* Of or pertaining to Daniel or Noah Webster.

wed (wed) *v.* **wed·ded, wed** or **wed·ded, wed·ding** *v.t.* 1. To take as one's husband or wife; marry. 2. To unite or give in matrimony; join in wedlock. 3. To join in a close relationship or attachment. — *v.i.* 4. To marry. [OE *wed·dian* to pledge]

we'd (wēd) 1. We had. 2. We would.

wed·ded (wed′id) *adj.* 1. Joined in wedlock; married. 2. Characteristic of marriage. 3. Having a close relationship or attachment: often with *to*: *wedded* to his work.

wed·ding (wed′ing) *n.* 1. The ceremony or celebration of a marriage. 2. The anniversary of a marriage: golden *wedding.* [OE *weddung* < *weddian* to pledge]

wedge (wej) *n.* 1. A piece of wood, metal, etc., that is V-shaped in longitudinal cross section, capable of being inserted into a narrow opening, and used as an aid in splitting substances, securing movable parts, raising weights, etc. 2. Anything in the form of a wedge, as a piece of pie, a formation of soldiers, etc. 3. An action, procedure, or idea constituting the earliest stage in a division of unity, change of policy, intrusive action, etc. — *v.* **wedged, wedg·ing** *v.t.* 1. To force apart or split with or as with a wedge. 2. To compress or fix in place with a wedge. 3. To crowd or squeeze (something) into a narrow or confined space. — *v.i.* 4. To jam or be forced in like a wedge. [OE *wecg*]

Wedg·wood (wej′wŏŏd) *n.* A type of fine, hard pottery, often of unglazed, tinted clay bearing small, white, finely detailed, classical figures in cameo relief. Also **Wedgwood ware.** [after Josiah *Wedgwood,* 1730–95, English potter]

wedg·y (wej′ē) *adj.* **wedg·i·er, wedg·i·est** Having the form or uses of a wedge.

wed·lock (wed′lok) *n.* The state or relationship of being married; matrimony. — **in wedlock** 1. With one's parents legally married to one another, as at the time of one's conception or birth. 2. In the married state. — **out of wedlock** With one's parents not married to one another, as at the time of one's conception or birth. [OE < *wed* pledge + *-lāc,* suffix of nouns of action]

Wednes·day (wenz′dē, -dā) *n.* The fourth day of the week. [OE *Wōdnesdæg* day of Woden]

wee (wē) *adj.* **we·er, we·est** Very small; tiny. — *n. Chiefly Scot.* A short time or space; a bit: bide a *wee.* [ME *wei* < OE *wæge* a quantity]

weed[1] (wēd) *n.* 1. Any common, unsightly, or troublesome plant that grows in abundance, esp. to injurious excess on cultivated ground. 2. *Informal* Tobacco: usu. with *the*; also, a cigarette or cigar. 3. Any worthless animal or thing. 4. The stem and leaves of any useful plant as distinguished from its flower and fruit: dill *weed.* 5. Thick, luxuriant growth, as of underbrush or shrubs. — *v.t.* 1. To pull up and remove weeds from. 2. To remove (a weed): often with *out.* 3. To remove (anything regarded as harmful or undesirable): with *out.* 4. To rid of anything harmful or undesirable. — *v.i.* 5. To remove weeds, etc. [OE *wēod*] — **weed′er** *n.* — **weed′less** *adj.*

weed[2] (wēd) *n.* 1. A token of mourning, as a band of crepe, worn as part of the dress. 2. *pl.* A widow's mourning garb. [OE *wæd* garment]

weed·y (wē′dē) *adj.* **weed·i·er, weed·i·est** 1. Having a growth of weeds; abounding in weeds. 2. Of or pertaining to a weed or weeds. 3. Resembling a weed; weedlike, as in rapid, ready growth. 4. *Informal* Gawky; awkward; ungainly: *weedy* youths. — **weed′i·ly** *adv.* — **weed′i·ness** *n.*

wee folk Fairies, elves, etc.

wee hours The hours after midnight; early morning.

week (wēk) *n.* 1. A period of seven days; esp., such a period beginning with Sunday. ◆ Collateral adjective: *hebdomadal.* 2. The period of time within a week devoted to work: a 35-hour *week.* 3. A period of seven days preceding or following any given day or date: a *week* from Tuesday. [OE *wucu, wicu, wice*]

week·day (wēk′dā′) *n.* Any day of the week except Sunday.

week·end (wēk′end′) *n.* The end of the week; esp., the time from Friday evening or Saturday to the following Monday morning. — *v.i. Informal* To pass the weekend: We *weekended* in the country. — **week′end′er** *n.*

week·long (wēk′lông′, -long′) *adj.* Continuing for a week; lasting all week.

week·ly (wēk′lē) *adv.* Once a week; esp., at regular seven-day intervals. — *adj.* 1. Of or pertaining to a week or to weekdays. 2. Done or occurring once a week. — *n.* *pl.* **·lies** A publication issued once a week.

ween (wēn) *v.t. & v.i. Archaic* To suppose; guess; fancy. [OE *wēnan* to think]

ween·ie (wē′nē) *n. U.S. Informal* A wiener.

weep (wēp) *v.* **wept, weep·ing** *v.i.* 1. To manifest grief or other strong emotion by shedding tears. 2. To mourn; lament: with *for.* 3. To ooze or shed liquid in drops. — *v.t.* 4. To weep for; mourn. 5. To shed (tears, or drops of other liquid). 6. To bring to a specified condition by weeping: to *weep* oneself to sleep. — *n.* The act of weeping, or a fit of tears. [OE *wēpan*] — **weep′er** *n.*

weep·ing (wē′ping) *adj.* 1. That weeps; crying; tearful. 2. Having slim, pendulous branches: *weeping* willow.

weeping willow A willow having long, slender, pendulous branches.

weep·y (wē′pē) *adj.* **weep·i·er, weep·i·est** *Informal* Inclined to weep; tearful.

wee·vil (wē′vəl) *n.* 1. Any of numerous small beetles, many of them serious pests, having snoutlike heads and strong, pincerlike jaws, and feeding on plants and plant products. 2. Any of a family of small beetles that feed principally on beans and seeds. [OE *wifel* beetle] — **wee′vil·y** or **wee′vil·ly** *adj.*

weft (weft) *n.* 1. The cross threads in a web of cloth; woof. 2. A woven fabric; web. 3. *Naut.* A waft. [OE]

Wehr·macht (vâr′mäkht) *n. German* The armed forces, collectively, of Germany; literally, defense force.

weigh[1] (wā) *v.t.* 1. To determine the weight of, as by measuring on a scale or balance. 2. To balance or hold in the hand so as to estimate weight or heaviness. **3.** To measure (a quantity or quantities of something) according to weight: with *out*. **4.** To consider carefully; estimate the worth or advantages of: to *weigh* a proposal. **5.** To press or force down by weight or heaviness; burden or oppress: with *down*. **6.** To raise or hoist: now only in the phrase **to weigh anchor**. — *v.i.* **7.** To have weight; be heavy to a specified degree: She *weighs* ninety pounds. **8.** To have influence or importance: The girl's testimony *weighed* heavily with the jury. **9.** To be burdensome or oppressive: with *on* or *upon*: What *weighs* on your mind? **10.** *Naut.* **a** To raise anchor. **b** To begin to sail. — **to weigh in** Of a prize fighter, etc., to be weighed before a contest. — **to weigh one's words** To consider one's words carefully before speaking. [OE *wegan* to weigh, carry, lift] — **weigh′er** *n.*

weigh² (wā) *n.* Way: used in the phrase **under weigh** by mistaken analogy with *aweigh*. [Var. of WAY]

weight (wāt) *n.* **1.** Any quantity of heaviness, expressed indefinitely or in terms of standard units. **2.** The measure of the force with which bodies tend toward the center of the earth or other celestial body, equal to the mass of the body multiplied by the acceleration due to gravitation; also, the quality so measured. **3.** Any object or mass that weighs a definite or specific amount. **4.** A definite mass of metal, etc., equal to a specified unit or amount of heaviness, and used in scales as a standard; also, any unit of heaviness, as a pound, ounce, etc. **5.** Any mass used as a counterpoise or to exert pressure by force of gravity: a *paperweight*. **6.** Burden; oppressiveness: the *weight* of care. **7.** The relative tendency of any mass toward a center of superior mass: the *weight* of a planet. **8.** A scale or graduated system of standard units of weight: avoirdupois *weight*. See tables inside back cover. **9.** Influence; importance; consequence: a man of *weight*. **10.** The comparative heaviness of clothes, as appropriate to the season: summer *weight*. — **by weight** Measured by weighing. — **to carry weight** To be of importance or significance. — **to pull one's weight** To do one's share; perform one's duty. — **to throw one's weight around** *Informal* To exercise one's authority more than is necessary or proper; make unwarranted use of position or power. — *v.t.* **1.** To add weight to; make heavy. **2.** To oppress or burden. **3.** To adulterate or treat (fabrics, etc.) with extraneous substances. [OE *wiht, gewiht*]

weight·less (wāt′lis) *adj.* **1.** Having or seeming to have no weight. **2.** *Aerospace* Being at zero gravity. — **weight′·less·ly** *adv.* — **weight′less·ness** *n.*

weight·y (wā′tē) *adj.* **weight·i·er, weight·i·est 1.** Having great weight; ponderous. **2.** Having power to move the mind; cogent. **3.** Of great importance. **4.** Influential, as in public affairs. **5.** Burdensome. — **weight′i·ly** *adv.* — **weight′i·ness** *n.*

Weimar Republic A German Republic formed by a constitutional assembly at Weimar, 1919; dissolved 1933.

weir (wir) *n.* **1.** An obstruction or dam placed in a stream to raise the water, divert it into a millrace or irrigation ditches, etc. **2.** An aperture in such an obstruction, used to determine the quantity of water flowing through it. **3.** A series of wattled enclosures in a stream to catch fish. [OE *wer* < *werian* to dam up]

weird (wird) *adj.* **1.** Concerned with the unnatural or with witchcraft; unearthly; uncanny. **2.** Strange; bizarre. **3.** Pertaining to or having to do with fate or the Fates. [OE *wyrd* fate] — **weird′ly** *adv.* — **weird′ness** *n.*

weird·ie (wir′dē) *n. pl.* **weird·ies** *U.S. Slang* A bizarre or freakish person, thing, or occurrence. Also **weird′y.**

weiss beer (vīs, wīs) A pale, effervescent beer, brewed usu. from wheat. [< G *weissbier*, lit., white beer]

welch (welch, welsh) *v.i.* To welsh. — **welch′er** *n.*

Welch (welch, welsh) See WELSH.

Welch·man (welsh′mən, welch-) See WELSHMAN.

wel·come (wel′kəm) *adj.* **1.** Admitted gladly to a place or festivity; received cordially: a *welcome* guest. **2.** Producing satisfaction or pleasure; pleasing: *welcome* tidings. **3.** Made free to use or enjoy: She is *welcome* to my purse. — **you are** (or **you're**) **welcome** You are under no obligation: a conventional response to "thank you." — *n.* The act of bidding or making welcome; a hearty greeting. — **to wear out one's welcome** To come so often or to linger so long as no longer to be welcome. — *v.t.* **·comed, ·com·ing 1.** To give a welcome to; greet hospitably. **2.** To receive with pleasure. [OE < *will-* will, pleasure + *cuma* guest] — **wel′come·ly** *adv.* — **wel′come·ness** *n.* — **wel′com·er** *n.*

welcome mat *Informal* **1.** A doormat. **2.** Any enthusiastic welcome or reception: chiefly in the phrase **to put** (or **roll**) **out the welcome mat.**

weld (weld) *v.t.* **1.** To unite, as two pieces of metal, usu. with hammering or pressure, by the application of heat along the area of contact. **2.** To bring into close association or

connection. — *v.i.* **3.** To be capable of being welded. — *n.* The consolidation of pieces of metal by welding; also, the closed joint so formed. [Alter. of WELL, v.] — **weld′a·bil′i·ty** *n.* — **weld′a·ble** *adj.* — **weld′er** *n.*

wel·fare (wel′fâr) *n.* **1.** The condition of faring well; prosperity. **2.** Welfare work. **3.** Aid, as money, food, or clothing, given to those in need. — **on welfare** Receiving money, food, clothing, etc., from a government because of need. [ME < *wel* well + *fare* a going]

welfare state A state or polity in which the government assumes a large measure of responsibility for the social welfare of its members, as through unemployment and health insurance, fair employment legislation, etc.

welfare work Organized efforts carried on by government or private organizations to improve the social and economic condition of a group or class. — **welfare worker**

wel·kin (wel′kin) *n. Archaic* or *Poetic* **1.** The vault of the sky; the heavens. **2.** The air. [OE *wolcen, wolcn* cloud]

well¹ (wel) *n.* **1.** A hole or shaft sunk into the earth to obtain a fluid, as water, oil, brine, or natural gas. **2.** A spring of water; a fountain. **3.** A source of continued supply, or that which issues forth continuously; a wellspring: a *well* of learning. **4.** A depression, cavity, or vessel used to hold a supply of liquid: an *inkwell*. **5.** *Archit.* A vertical opening descending through floors, or a deep enclosed space in a building for light, ventilation, etc.: a *stairwell*; an elevator *well*. **6.** *Naut.* The enclosed space in a vessel's hold, housing the pumps. — *v.i.* **1.** To pour forth or flow up, as water in a spring. — *v.t.* **2.** To gush: Her eyes *welled* tears. [OE < *weallan* to boil, bubble up]

well² (wel) *adv.* **bet·ter, best 1.** Satisfactorily; favorably; according to one's wishes: Everything goes *well*. **2.** In a good or correct manner; expertly: to speak *well*. **3.** Suitably; with reason or propriety: I cannot *well* remain here. **4.** In a successful manner; also, agreeably or luxuriously: He lives *well*. **5.** Intimately: How *well* do you know him? **6.** To a considerable extent or degree: *well* aware. **7.** Completely; wholly. **8.** Far; at some distance: He lagged *well* behind us. **9.** Kindly; generously; graciously. — **as well 1.** Also; in addition. **2.** With equal effect or consequence: He might just *as well* have sold it. — **as well as 1.** As satisfactorily as. **2.** To the same degree as. **3.** In addition to. — *adj.* **1.** Having good health. **2.** Satisfactory; right: All is *well*. **3.** Prosperous; comfortable. — *interj.* An exclamation used to express surprise, expectation, resignation, doubt, indignation, acquiescence, etc., or merely to preface a remark. [OE *wel*]

◆ *Well* may be used in combination, as in *well-chosen*, *well-informed*, etc. Such combinations are hyphenated before the words they modify, as in *well-aimed* shots, but not when used predicatively, as in: The shots were *well aimed*.

we'll (wel) **1.** We will. **2.** We shall.

well-ap·point·ed (wel′ə-poin′tid) *adj.* Properly equipped; excellently furnished.

well·a·way (wel′ə-wā′) *interj. Archaic* Woe is me! alas! Also **well′a·day′** (-dā′). [OE *wā lā wā* woe! lo! woe!]

well-bal·anced (wel′bal′ənst) *adj.* **1.** Evenly balanced or proportioned. **2.** Sensible; sane; sound.

well-be·ing (wel′bē′ing) *n.* A condition of health, happiness, or prosperity; welfare.

well-born (wel′bôrn′) *adj.* Of good birth or ancestry.

well-bred (wel′bred′) *adj.* **1.** Characterized by or showing good breeding; polite. **2.** Of good stock, as an animal.

well-curb (wel′kûrb«) *n.* The frame or stone ring around the mouth of a well.

well-dis·posed (wel′dis·pōzd′) *adj.* Disposed or inclined to be kind, favorable, etc.

well-do·er (wel′dōō′ər) *n.* One who performs good deeds. — **well′-do′ing** *n.*

well-done (wel′dun′) *adj.* **1.** Satisfactorily accomplished. **2.** Thoroughly cooked, as meat.

well enough Tolerably good or satisfactory. — **to let well enough alone** To leave things as they are lest the result of interference be worse.

well-fa·vored (wel′fā′vərd) *adj.* Of attractive appearance; comely; handsome. Also *Brit.* **well′-fa′voured.**

well-fed (wel′fed′) *adj.* **1.** Plump; fat. **2.** Properly nourished.

well-fixed (wel′fikst′) *adj. Informal* Affluent; well-to-do.

well-found (wel′found′) *adj.* Well equipped or supplied.

well-found·ed (wel′foun′did) *adj.* Based on fact, sound, evidence, etc.: *well-founded* suspicions.

well-groomed (wel′grōomd′) *adj.* **1.** Carefully dressed, combed, etc.; very neat. **2.** Carefully curried, as a horse.

well-ground·ed (wel′groun′did) *adj.* **1.** Adequately schooled in the elements of a subject. **2.** Well-founded.

well-head (wel′hed′) *n.* **1.** A natural source supplying water to a spring or well. **2.** Any source or fountainhead.

well-heeled (wel′hēld′) *adj. Slang* Plentifully supplied with money.

well-in·ten·tioned (wel′in·ten′shənd) *adj.* Having good intentions; well-meant: often with connotation of failure.

well-known (wel′nōn′) *adj.* **1.** Widely known; famous. **2.** Thoroughly or fully known.

well-man·nered (wel′man′ərd) *adj.* Characterized by good manners; courteous; polite.

well-mean·ing (wel′mē′ning) *adj.* **1.** Having good intentions. **2.** Done with or characterized by good intentions: also **well′-meant′** (-ment′).

well-nigh (wel′nī′) *adv.* Very nearly; almost.

well-off (wel′ôf′, -of′) *adj.* In comfortable or favorable circumstances; fortunate.

well-read (wel′red′) *adj.* Having a wide knowledge of literature or books; having read much.

well-round·ed (wel′roun′did) *adj.* **1.** Having or displaying diverse knowledge, interests, etc. **2.** Wide in scope; comprehensive: a *well-rounded* program. **3.** Fully formed or developed: a *well-rounded* figure.

well-spo·ken (wel′spō′kən) *adj.* **1.** Fitly or excellently said. **2.** Of gentle speech and manners.

well·spring (wel′spring′) *n.* **1.** The source of a stream or spring; fountainhead. **2.** A source of continual supply.

well sweep A device used for drawing water from a well, consisting of a pole swung on a pivot attached to a high post, and having a bucket suspended from one end.

well-thought-of (wel′thôt′uv′, -ov′) *adj.* In good repute; esteemed; respected.

well-to-do (wel′tə-dōō′) *adj.* Prosperous; affluent.

well-wish·er (wel′wish′ər) *n.* One who wishes well, as to another. — **well′-wish′ing** *adj. & n.*

welsh (welsh, welch) *v.i. Slang* **1.** To cheat by failing to pay a bet or debt: often with *on*. **2.** To avoid fulfilling an obligation: often with *on*. Also spelled *welch*. [? Back formation < *welsher*, prob. < *Welsher* Welshman, with ref. to supposed national traits] — **welsh′er** *n.*

Welsh (welsh, welch) *adj.* Pertaining to Wales, its people, or their language. — *n.* **1.** The Celtic people of Wales: with *the*: also called *Cymry*. **2.** The Celtic language of Wales, belonging to the Brythonic or Cymric group: also called *Cymric*. Also spelled *Welch*. [OE *wealh* foreigner]

Welsh·man (welsh′mən, welch′-) *n. pl.* **·men** (-mən) A man of Welsh birth or ancestry. Also spelled *Welchman*.

Welsh rabbit A concoction of melted cheese cooked in cream or milk, often with ale or beer added, and served hot on toast or crackers. ◆ The form *rarebit* was a later development and is the result of mistaken etymology.

Welsh terrier A black-and-tan terrier having a flat skull and wiry coat, used for hunting.

welt (welt) *n.* **1.** A strip of material, covered cord, etc., applied to a seam to cover or strengthen it. **2.** A strip of leather set into the seam between the edges of the upper and the outer sole of a shoe. **3.** A stripe raised on the skin by a blow: also called *wale, weal.* — *v.t.* **1.** To sew a welt on or in; decorate with a welt. **2.** *Informal* To flog severely, so as to raise welts. [ME *welte, walt*]

wel·ter (wel′tər) *v.i.* **1.** To roll about; wallow. **2.** To lie or be soaked in some fluid, as blood. **3.** To surge or move tumultuously, as the sea. — *n.* **1.** A rolling movement, as of waves. **2.** A commotion; turmoil. [< MDu. *welteren*]

wel·ter·weight (wel′tər-wāt′) *n.* A boxer or wrestler whose fighting weight is between 136 and 147 pounds. [< *welter* heavyweight horseman + WEIGHT]

Welt·schmerz (velt′shmârts′) *n. German* Melancholy pessimism over the state of the world; literally, world pain.

wen (wen) *n. Pathol.* Any benign tumor of the skin containing sebaceous matter, occurring commonly on the scalp. [OE *wenn, wænn*] — **wen′nish, wen′ny** *adj.*

wench (wench) *n.* **1.** A young woman; girl: a humorous term. **2.** *Archaic* A young peasant woman; also, a female servant; maid. **3.** *Archaic* A prostitute; strumpet. — *v.i. Archaic* To keep company with strumpets. [ME < OE *wencel* child, servant]

wend (wend) *Chiefly Poetic v.* **wend·ed** (*Archaic* went), **wend·ing** *v.t.* **1.** To direct or proceed on (one's course or way). — *v.i.* **2.** To travel; proceed; go. [OE *wendan*]

Wend (wend) *n.* One of a Slavic people now occupying the region between the Elbe and Oder rivers in eastern Germany: also called *Sorb, Sorbian.* [< G *Wende, Winde*]

Wend·ish (wen′dish) *adj.* Of or pertaining to the Wends or their language: also *Sorbian.* — *n.* The West Slavic language of the Wends; Sorbian. Also **Wend′ic.**

went (went) An archaic past tense and past participle of *wend*, now used as past tense of GO.

wept (wept) Past tense and past participle of WEEP.

were (wûr, *unstressed* wər) Plural and second person singular past indicative, and past subjunctive singular and plural of BE. [OE *wære, wæron*, pt. forms of *wesan* to be]

we're (wir) We are.

were·n't (wûr′ənt) Were not.

were·wolf (wir′wŏŏlf′, wûr′-) *n. pl.* **·wolves** (-wŏŏlvz′) In European folklore, a human being transformed into a wolf or one having power to assume the form of a wolf at will. Also **wer′wolf′.** [OE < *wer* man + *wulf* wolf]

wert (wûrt, *unstressed* wərt) Archaic second person singular, past tense of both indicative and subjunctive of BE: used with *thou*.

Wes·ley·an (wes′lē·ən, *Brit.* wez′lē·ən) *adj.* Of or pertaining to John Wesley or Methodism. — *n.* A disciple of John Wesley; a Methodist. — **Wes′ley·an·ism** *n.*

Wes·sex (wes′iks) The ancient kingdom of the West Saxons in southern England.

west (west) *n.* **1.** The direction of the sun in relation to an observer on earth at sunset. **2.** One of the four cardinal points of the compass, directly opposite *east* and 90° counterclockwise from *north*. See COMPASS CARD. **3.** Any direction near this point. **4.** *Sometimes cap.* Any region west of a specified point. — **the West 1.** The countries lying west of Asia and Turkey; the Occident. **2.** The western hemisphere. — *adj.* **1.** To, toward, facing, or in the west; western. **2.** Coming from the west: the *west* wind. — *adv.* In or toward the west; westward. [OE]

west·bound (west′bound′) *adj.* Going westward. Also **west′-bound′.**

west·er·ing (wes′tər·ing) *adj.* Moving or turning westward: the *westering* sun.

west·er·ly (wes′tər·lē) *adj.* **1.** In, toward, or pertaining to the west. **2.** From the west, as a wind. — *n. pl.* **·lies** A wind or storm from the west. — *adv.* Toward or from the west. — **west·er·li·ness** *n.*

west·ern (wes′tərn) *adj.* **1.** To, toward, or in the west. **2.** Native to or inhabiting the west: a *western* species. **3.** *Sometimes cap.* Of, pertaining to, or characteristic of the west or the West. **4.** From the west, as a wind. — *n.* **1.** A westerner. **2.** A type of fiction or motion picture using cowboy and pioneer life in the western U.S. as its material.

Western Church 1. The medieval church of the Western Roman Empire, now the Roman Catholic Church: distinguished from the church of the Eastern Empire, now the Eastern Orthodox Church. **2.** The Christian churches of western Europe and America.

west·ern·er (wes′tər·nər) *n.* **1.** One who is native to or lives in the west. **2.** *Usu. cap.* One who lives in or comes from the western U.S.

western frontier Formerly, the part of the U.S. bordering on the still unsettled regions of the west.

west·ern·ism (wes′tər·niz′əm) *n.* An expression or practice peculiar to the west, esp. the western U.S.

west·ern·ize (wes′tər·nīz′) *v.t.* **·ized, ·iz·ing** To make western in characteristics, habits, etc. — **west′ern·i·za′tion** *n.*

west·ern·most (wes′tərn·mōst′) *adj.* Farthest west.

Western Ocean In ancient geography, the ocean lying westward of the known world; the Atlantic Ocean.

Western (Roman) Empire The part of the Roman Empire west of the Adriatic that existed as a separate empire from A.D. 395 until the fall of Rome in A.D. 476.

West Highland white terrier A small, short-legged terrier having a stiff, white coat.

west-north·west (west′nôrth′west′) *n.* The direction midway between west and northwest, 26 points or 292° 30′ clockwise from due north. See COMPASS CARD. — *adj. & adv.* In, toward, or from the west-northwest.

West Saxon 1. One of a Saxon tribe that invaded England in the fifth and sixth centuries A.D. and settled in Wessex. **2.** The dialect of Old English spoken in Wessex.

west-south·west (west′south′west′) *n.* The direction midway between west and southwest, 22 points or 247° 30′ clockwise from due north. See COMPASS CARD. — *adj. & adv.* In, toward, or from the west-southwest.

west·ward (west′wərd) *adv.* Toward the west: also **west′wards.** — *adj.* To, toward, facing, or in the west. — *n.* A western part or region. — **west′ward·ly** *adv.*

wet (wet) *adj.* **wet·ter, wet·test 1.** Covered or saturated with water or other liquid. **2.** Not yet dry: *wet* varnish. **3.** Treated or separated by means of water or other liquids. **4.** Preserved in liquid; also, bottled in alcohol, as laboratory specimens. **5.** Marked by showers or by heavy rainfall; rainy. **6.** *Informal* Favoring or permitting the manufacture and sale of alcoholic beverages: a *wet* State. — **all wet** *Slang* Quite wrong; crazy. — **wet behind the ears** Inexperienced or unsophisticated. — *n.* **1.** Water; moisture; wetness. **2.** Showery or rainy weather; rain. **3.** *Informal* One opposed to prohibition. — *v.t. & v.i.* **wet** or **wet·ted, wet·ting** To make or become wet. — **to wet one's whistle** *Informal* To take a drink. [OE *wæt*] — **wet′ly** *adv.* — **wet′ness** *n.* — **wet′ta·ble** *adj.* — **wet′ter** *n.*

wet·back (wet′bak′) *n. U.S. Informal* A Mexican laborer who enters the U.S. illegally. [So called because many cross the border by swimming or wading across the Rio Grande]

wet blanket *Informal* One who or that which has a discouraging effect on enthusiasm, activity, etc.

weth·er (weth'ər) *n.* A castrated ram. [OE]
wet-nurse (wet'nûrs') *v.t.* **-nursed, -nurs·ing 1.** To act as a wet nurse to. **2.** To attend to with painstaking care.
wet nurse A woman who is hired to suckle the child of another woman.
wet·ting (wet'ing) *n.* **1.** The act of one who wets, or the state of being wetted. **2.** A liquid, as water, used in moistening something, as flour in breadmaking.
wetting agent *Chem.* Any of a class of substances that, by reducing surface tension, enable a liquid to spread more readily over a solid surface.
we've (wēv) We have.
whack (hwak) *v.t. & v.i.* **1.** *Informal* To strike sharply; beat; hit. **2.** *Slang* To share: often with *up.* — *n.* **1.** *Informal* A sharp, resounding stroke or blow. **2.** *Slang* A share; portion. — **to have a whack at** *Slang* To give a blow to. **2.** To have a chance or turn at. — **out of whack** *Slang* Out of order. [? Var. of THWACK]
whack·ing (hwak'ing) *Chiefly Brit. Informal adj.* Strikingly large; whopping. — *adv.* Very; extremely.
whale[1] (hwāl) *n.* **1.** A marine mammal of fishlike form, esp. one of the larger pelagic species, having the fore limbs developed as paddles, a broad, flat tail, and a thick layer of fat or blubber immediately beneath the skin. The principal types are the toothless or whalebone whales and the toothed whales. **2.** *Informal* Something extremely good or large: a *whale* of a party. — *v.i.* **whaled, whal·ing** To engage in the hunting of whales. [OE *hwæl*]
whale[2] (hwāl) *v.t.* **whaled, whal·ing** *Informal* To strike as if to produce wales or stripes; flog; wale. [? Var. of WALE[1], v.]
whale·back (hwāl'bak') *n.* A steamship having a rounded main deck, used on the Great Lakes.
whale·boat (hwāl'bōt') *n.* A long, deep rowboat, sharp at both ends, often steered with an oar, so called because first used in whaling, but now carried on steamers as lifeboats.
whale·bone (hwāl'bōn') *n.* **1.** The horny substance developed in plates from the upper jaw on either side of the palate of certain whales; baleen. **2.** A strip of whalebone, used in stiffening dress bodies, corsets, etc.
whal·er (hwā'lər) *n.* **1.** A person or a vessel engaged in whaling. **2.** A whaleboat.
whal·ing (hwā'ling) *n.* The industry of capturing whales. — *adj. Slang* Huge; whopping.
wham·my (hwam'ē) *n. pl.* **·mies** *U.S. Slang* A jinx; hex; to put the *whammy* on someone. [< *wham*, informal interjection imit. of the sound of a hard blow]
whang (hwang) *Informal v.t. & v.i.* To beat or sound with a resounding noise. — *n.* A heavy blow. [Imit.]
wharf (hwôrf) *n. pl.* **wharves** (hwôrvz) **or wharfs** A structure of masonry or timber erected on the shore of a harbor, river, etc., alongside which vessels may lie to load or unload cargo, passengers, etc.; also, any landing place for vessels, as a pier or quay. — *v.t.* **1.** To moor to a wharf. **2.** To provide or protect with a wharf or wharves. **3.** To deposit or store on a wharf. [OE *hwearf*]
— **Syn.** (noun) A *wharf* is usually a platform supported by wooden piles. A *pier* usually has a masonry foundation and projects into the water at right angles to the bank. A *dock* was originally the water between two *piers*, in which a vessel floated; by extension, any *pier* or *wharf* has come to be called a *dock.*
wharf·age (hwôr'fij) *n.* **1.** The use of wharves for unloading ships, storing goods, etc. **2.** Charge for the use of a wharf. **3.** Wharves collectively.
wharf·in·ger (hwôr'fin·jər) *n.* One who keeps a wharf for landing goods and collects wharfage fees. [Earlier *wharfager*]
wharf rat 1. A brown rat that inhabits wharves. **2.** *U.S. Slang* One who loiters about wharves, esp. with criminal intent.
wharf·side (hwôrf'sīd') *n.* The space on or at the side of a wharf. — *adj.* On or at the side of a wharf.
wharve (hwôrv) In spinning, a round piece on a spindle, serving as a pulley. [OE *hweorfa*]
what (hwot, hwut) *pron.* **1.** Which specific thing or things, action, etc.: *What* does he do? I don't know *what* to do. **2.** That which: He knew *what* he wanted. — **and what not** What need not be mentioned in addition; and so forth. — **what for** *Slang* A punishment; scolding: I'll give him *what for.* — **what have you** What need not be mentioned in addition; and so forth. — **what if** What would happen if; suppose that. — **what's what** *Informal* The actual situation or state of affairs. — **what with** As a result of taking into consideration. — *adj.* **1.** In interrogative construction: **a** Asking for information that will specify the person or thing qualified by it; which: Of *what* person do you speak? **b** How much; what money has he? **2.** How surprising, ridiculous, great, etc.: *What* genius! **3.** Whatever: *What* money he had left was soon spent. — *adv.* **1.** In what respect; to what extent: *What* are you profited? **2.** For what reason; why:

with *for*: *What* are you saying that for? — *conj. Informal* That: used only in negative expressions: I do not doubt but *what* he will come. [OE *hwæt*, neut. of *hwā* who]
what·ev·er (hwot/ev'ər, hwut/-) *pron.* **1.** As a compound relative, the whole that; anything that; no matter what: often added for emphasis to a negative assertion: *whatever* makes life dear; I do not want anything *whatever.* **2.** *Informal* What: usually interrogative: *Whatever* were you saying? Also *Poetic* **what'e'er** (-âr').
what·not (hwot'not', hwut'-) *n.* An ornamental set of shelves for holding bric-à-brac, etc.
what·so·ev·er (hwot/sō·ev'ər, hwut'-) *adj. & pron.* Whatever: a more formal usage. Also *Poetic* **what'so·e'er** (-âr').
wheat (hwēt) *n.* **1.** The grain of a cereal grass, widely cultivated and providing a flour used for bread, pastries, etc. **2.** The plant producing this grain, bearing at its summit a dense spike called the ear or head, sometimes with awns (**bearded wheat**) and sometimes without awns (**beardless** or **bald wheat**). **3.** A field of wheat; crop of wheat. [OE *hwǣte*]
wheat·en (hwēt'n) *adj.* Belonging to or made of wheat.
whee·dle (hwēd'l) *v.* **·dled, ·dling** *v.t.* **1.** To persuade or try to persuade by flattery, cajolery, etc.; coax. **2.** To obtain by cajoling or coaxing. — *v.i.* **3.** To use flattery or cajolery. [? OE *wǣdlian* to beg, be poor] — **whee'dler** *n.* — **whee'dling·ly** *adv.*

WHEAT
a Bearded.
b Beardless.
c,d Grain.

wheel (hwēl) *n.* **1.** A circular rim and hub connected by spokes or a disk, capable of rotating on a central axis, as in vehicles and machines. **2.** An instrument or device having a wheel or wheels as its distinguishing characteristic, as a steering wheel, water wheel, spinning wheel, etc. **3.** Anything resembling or suggestive of a wheel; any circular object or formation. **4.** *Informal* A bicycle. **5.** An old instrument of torture or execution, consisting of a wheel to which the limbs of the victim were tied and then broken with an iron bar. **6.** A turning; rotation; revolution. **7.** *pl.* That which imparts or directs motion or controls activity; the moving force: the *wheels* of democracy. — **at the wheel 1.** Driving or steering a vehicle, boat, etc. **2.** In control. — *v.t.* **1.** To move or convey on wheels. **2.** To cause to turn on or as on an axis; pivot or revolve. **3.** To perform with a circular movement. **4.** To provide with a wheel or wheels. — *v.i.* **5.** To turn on or as on an axis; rotate or revolve. **6.** To take a new direction or course of action: often with *about.* **7.** To move in a circular or spiral course. **8.** To move on wheels. — **to wheel and deal** *U.S. Slang* To act freely or independently, without restrictions, as in business. [OE *hwēol*]
wheel·bar·row (hwēl'bar'ō) *n.* A boxlike vehicle ordinarily with one wheel and two handles, for moving small loads. — *v.t.* To convey in a wheelbarrow.
wheel·base (hwēl'bās') *n.* The distance from the center of a back hub to the center of the front hub on the same side, as in an automobile.
wheel·chair (hwēl'châr') *n.* A mobile chair mounted between large wheels, for the use of invalids. Also **wheel chair.**
wheel·er (hwē'lər) *n.* **1.** One who wheels. **2.** A wheel horse or other draft animal working next to the wheel. **3.** Something furnished with a wheel or wheels: a *side-wheeler.*
wheel·er-deal·er (hwē'lər-dē'lər) *n. U.S. Slang* One who wheels and deals; a shrewd, quick-witted person.
wheel horse 1. A horse harnessed to the pole or shafts when there is a leader or leaders in front. **2.** One who does the heaviest work or assumes the greatest responsibility.
wheel·house (hwēl'hous') *n.* A pilothouse.
wheel of fortune The wheel represented as being turned in order to bring about changes in human destiny, and that symbolizes the uncertainty of fate.
wheel·wright (hwēl'rīt') *n.* A man whose business is making or repairing wheels.
wheeze (hwēz) *v.t. & v.i.* **wheezed, wheez·ing** To breathe or utter with a husky, whistling sound. — *n.* **1.** A wheezing sound. **2.** A loud whisper. **3.** *Informal* A popular tale, saying, or trick, esp. a trite one. [Prob. < ON *hvǣsa* hiss] — **wheez'er** *n.* — **wheez'ing·ly** *adv.*
wheez·y (hwē'zē) *adj.* **wheez·i·er, wheez·i·est** Affected with or characterized by wheezing. — **wheez'i·ly** *adv.* — **wheez'i·ness** *n.*
whelk[1] (hwelk) *n.* Any of various large marine mollusks having whorled shells, that burrow in sand, esp. the common whelk, much eaten in Europe. [OE *weoloc*]

whelk² (hwelk)   *n.* A swelling, protuberance, or pustule. [OE *hwylca* pustule]   —**whelk′y** *adj.*

whelm (hwelm)   *v.t.* **1.** To cover with water or other fluid; submerge; engulf. **2.** To overpower; overwhelm. — *v.i.* **3.** To roll with engulfing force. [Prob. blend of OE *helmian* to cover and *gehwielfan* to bend over]

whelp (hwelp)   *n.* **1.** One of the young of a dog, wolf, lion, or other beast. **2.** A dog. **3.** A young fellow: a contemptuous term. — *v.t. & v.i.* To give birth (to): said of dogs, lions, etc. [OE *hwelp*]

when (hwen)   *adv.* **1.** At what or which time: *When* did you arrive? I know *when* he arrived. **2.** At which: the time *when* we went on a picnic. — *conj.* **1.** At what or which time: They watched until midnight, *when* they fell asleep. **2.** As soon as: He laughed *when* he heard it. **3.** Although: He walks *when* he might ride. **4.** At the time that; while: *when* we were young. **5.** If; considering that: How can I buy it *when* I have no money? **6.** After which: We had just awakened *when* you called. — *pron.* What or which time: since *when*; until *when*. — *n.* The time; date: I don't know the *when* or the circumstances of it. [OE *hwanne, hwenne*]

whence (hwens)   *Archaic adv.* From what place or source: *Whence* and what are you? — *conj.* **1.** From what or which place, source, or cause; from which: the place *whence* these sounds arise. **2.** To the place from which. **3.** For which reason; wherefore. [ME < OE *hwanne* when]

whence·so·ev·er (hwens′sō·ev′ər)   *Archaic adv. & conj.* From whatever place, cause, or source.

when·e'er (hwen·âr′)   *adv. & conj. Poetic* Whenever.

when·ev·er (hwen′ev′ər)   *adv. & conj.* At whatever time.

when·so·ev·er (hwen′sō·ev′ər)   *adv. & conj.* Whenever.

where (hwâr)   *adv.* **1.** At or in what place, relation, or situation: *Where* is my book? **2.** To what place or end: *Where* are you going? **3.** From what place: *Where* did you get that hat? **4.** At or in which place: *where* men gather. **5.** To a place or situation in or to which: Let us go *where* the mountains are. — *conj.* **1.** At which place: Let us go home *where* we can relax. **2.** With the condition that: xy = 4 *where* x = 2 and y = 2. — *pron.* **1.** The place in which: The bear passed three yards from *where* we stood. **2.** The point at which: That's *where* you are wrong. — *n.* Place; locality. ◆ *Where* has absorbed completely the sense of *whither* but not of *whence*. We must use a preposition to express the idea of motion from a place: *Where* did you come from? We do not use a preposition to show place at which: *Where* is the dog *at*? is not accepted in standard usage. [OE *hwǣr*]

where·a·bouts (hwâr′ə·bouts′)   *adv.* Near or at what place; about where. — *n.pl. (construed as sing.)* The place in or near which a person or thing is.

where·as (hwâr·az′)   *conj.* **1.** Since the facts are such as they are; seeing that: used in the preamble of a resolution, etc. **2.** The fact of the matter being that; when in truth: implying opposition to a previous statement. — *n. pl.* **·as·es** A clause or item beginning with the word "whereas."

where·at (hwâr′at′)   *Archaic or Rare adv.* At what: *Whereat* are you angry? — *conj.* At which; for which reason.

where·by (hwâr·bī′)   *adv.* **1.** By means of which; through which: the gate *whereby* he entered. **2.** By what; how.

wher·e'er (hwâr·âr′)   *adv. Poetic* Wherever.

where·fore (hwâr′fôr′, -fōr′)   *Archaic adv.* For what reason; why: *Wherefore* do you doubt me? — *conj.* For which reason: It began to rain, *wherefore* we called off the picnic.

where·from (hwâr′frum′, -from′)   *Archaic adv.* Whence.

where·in (hwâr′in′)   *adv.* **1.** In what: *Wherein* is the error? **2.** In which: a marriage *wherein* there is discord.

where·of (hwâr′uv′, -ov′)   *Archaic adv.* **1.** Of or from what: *Whereof* did you partake? **2.** Of which or whom.

where·on (hwâr′on′, -ôn′)   *Archaic adv.* On what or on which.

where·so·ev·er (hwâr′sō·ev′ər)   *Archaic adv. & conj.* In or to whatever place; wherever.

where·to (hwâr′tōō′)   *Archaic adv.* To what place or end: *Whereto* serves avarice? — *conj.* To which or to whom.

where·up·on (hwâr′ə·pon′, -ə·pôn′)   *adv. Archaic* Upon what; whereon. — *conj.* Upon which or whom; in consequence of which; after which: *whereupon* they took in sail.

wher·ev·er (hwâr·ev′ər)   *adv. & conj.* In, at, or to whatever place; wheresoever.

where·with (hwâr′with′, -with′)   *Archaic adv.* Interrogatively, with what: *Wherewith* shall I do it? — *conj.* With which; by means of which: the food *wherewith* we abated hunger. — *pron.* That with or by which: with the infinitive: I have not *wherewith* to do it.

where·with·al (hwâr′with·ôl′)   *n.* The necessary means or resources; esp., the necessary money: with the definite article.

wher·ry (hwer′ē)   *n. pl.* **·ries** **1.** A light, fast rowboat used on inland waters. **2.** *Brit.* A fishing vessel with two sails. **3.** A rowboat for racing or exercise, built for one person. **4.** *Brit.* A very broad, light barge. — *v.t. & v.i.* **·ried, ·ry·ing** To transport in or use a wherry. [Origin unknown]

whet (hwet)   *v.t.* **whet·ted, whet·ting** **1.** To sharpen, as a knife, by friction. **2.** To make more keen or eager; excite; stimulate, as the appetite. — *n.* **1.** The act of whetting. **2.** Something that whets. [OE *hwettan*] —**whet′er** *n.*

wheth·er (hweth′ər)   *conj.* **1.** If it be the case that: used to introduce an indirect question, often with the negative being implied: Tell me *whether* you are considering our plan. **2.** In case; in either case: as the first alternative, followed by a correlative *or*, or *or whether*: *Whether* it rains or (*whether* it) snows, the roads become very slippery. **3.** Either: *Whether* by luck or sheer determination, he will probably succeed. — **whether or no** In any case. [OE *hwæther*]

whet·stone (hwet′stōn′)   *n.* A fine-grained stone for whetting knives, axes, etc.

whew (hwōō, hwyōō)   *interj.* An exclamatory sound, expressive of amazement, dismay, relief, admiration, etc.

whey (hwā)   *n.* A clear, straw-colored liquid that separates from the curd when milk is curdled, as in making cheese. [OE *hwæg*] —**whey′ey, whey′ish** *adj.*

whey·face (hwā′fās′)   *n.* A pale, sallow face; also, a person having such a face. —**whey′faced′** *adj.*

which (hwich)   *pron. & adj.* **1.** What particular person or thing or collection of persons or things of a certain class: *Which* (or *which* apples) do you want? We don't know *which* (or *which* story) to believe. **2.** The thing designated; it: a relative pronoun whose antecedents refer now only to animals or objects; that: the story *which* we preferred. ◆ *Which* sometimes has an entire clause or sentence as its antecedent: He raised his hand, *which* surprised me. See also usage note under WHO. [OE *hwilc*]

which·ev·er (hwich′ev′ər)   *pron.* One or another (of two or of several). — *adj.* No matter which. Also **which′so·ev·er.**

whiff (hwif)   *n.* **1.** Any sudden or slight gust or puff of air. **2.** A gust or puff of odor: a *whiff* of onions. **3.** A single expulsion or inhalation of breath or smoke from the mouth; puff. — *v.t.* **1.** To drive or blow with a whiff or puff. **2.** To exhale or inhale in whiffs. **3.** To smell or sniff. **4.** To smoke, as a pipe. — *v.i.* **5.** To blow or move in whiffs or puffs. **6.** To exhale or inhale whiffs. [Prob. ult. imit.] — **whiff′er** *n.*

whif·fet (hwif′it)   *n. Informal* **1.** A trifling, useless person. **2.** A small, snappish dog. [? Dim. of WHIFF]

whif·fle (hwif′əl)   *v.* **·fled, ·fling** *v.i.* **1.** To blow with puffs or gusts; shift about, as the wind. **2.** To vacillate; veer. — *v.t.* **3.** To blow or dissipate with or as with a puff. [Freq. of WHIFF] —**whiff′ler** *n.* — **whiff′ler·y** *n.*

whif·fle·tree (hwif′əl·trē′)   *n.* A horizontal crossbar to which the ends of the traces of a harness are attached: also called *singletree, swingletree, whippletree.* [Var. of WHIPPLE-TREE]

Whig (hwig)   *n.* **1.** An American colonist who supported the Revolutionary War in the 18th century in opposition to the Tories. **2.** A member of an American political party (1834–1855) formed in opposition to the Democratic Party, and in 1856 succeeded by the Republican Party. **3.** In England, a member of a more or less liberal political party in the 18th and 19th centuries, opposed to the Tories and later known as the Liberal Party. — *adj.* Consisting of or supported by Whigs. [< ? *Whiggamore* < dial. E (Scottish) < *Whig*, a cry to urge on a horse + *mere* horse] — **Whig′ger·y** *n.* — **Whig′gish** *adj.* — **Whig′gish·ly** *adv.* — **Whig′gish·ness** *n.* — **Whig′gism** *n.*

while (hwīl)   *n.* **1.** A short time; also, any period of time: Stay and rest a *while.* **2.** Time or pains expended on a thing: only in the phrase **worth while** or **worth one's while.** — **between whiles** From time to time. — **the while** At the same time. — *conj.* **1.** During the time that; as long as. **2.** At the same time that; although: *While* he found fault, he also praised. **3.** Whereas: This man is short, *while* that one is tall. ◆ This sense is widely used and is generally considered standard, although some authorities still disapprove of it. — *v.t.* **whiled, whil·ing** To cause (time) to pass lightly and pleasantly: usu. with *away.* [OE *hwil*]

whiles (hwīlz)   *Archaic or Dial. adv.* **1.** Occasionally. **2.** In the meantime. — *conj.* While; during the time that.

whi·lom (hwī′ləm)   *Archaic adj.* Former. — *adv.* Formerly. [OE *hwīlum* at times, dative pl. of *hwīl* a while]

whilst (hwīlst)   *conj. Chiefly Brit.* While.

whim (hwim)   *n.* A sudden or unexpected notion or fanciful idea; caprice. [Short for earlier *whim-wham* trifle]

whim·per (hwim′pər)   *v.i.* **1.** To cry or whine with plaintive broken sounds. — *v.t.* **2.** To utter with a whimper. — *n.* A low, broken, whining cry; whine. [Imit.] — **whim′per·er** *n.* — **whim′per·ing** *n.* — **whim′per·ing·ly** *adv.*

whim·si·cal (hwim′zi·kəl)   *adj.* **1.** Having eccentric ideas; capricious. **2.** Oddly constituted; fantastic; quaint. — **whim′si·cal·i·ty** (-kal′ə·tē) *n.* — **whim′si·cal·ly** *adv.* — **whim′si·cal·ness** *n.*

whim·sy (hwim′zē)   *n. pl.* **·sies** **1.** A whim. **2.** Quaint, fanciful humor, as in a literary work. Also **whim′sey.**

whin (hwin) *n.* Furze. [Prob. < Scand.]

whine (hwīn) *v.* **whined, whin·ing** *v.i.* **1.** To utter a low, plaintive sound expressive of grief, peevishness, etc. **2.** To complain in a tiresome or childish way. —*v.t.* **3.** To utter with a whine. —*n.* The act or sound of whining. [OE *hwīnan*] —**whin′er** *n.* —**whin′ing·ly** *adv.* —**whin′y** *adj.*

whin·ny (hwin′ē) *v.* **·nied, ·ny·ing** *v.i.* **1.** To neigh, esp. in a low or gentle way. —*v.t.* **2.** To express with a whinny. —*n., pl. ·nies* A neigh, esp. if low and gentle. [< WHINE]

whip (hwip) *v.* **whipped** or **whipt, whip·ping** *v.t.* **1.** To strike with a lash, rod, strap, etc. **2.** To punish by striking thus; flog. **3.** To drive or urge with lashes or blows: with *on, up, off,* etc. **4.** To strike in the manner of a whip: The wind *whipped* the trees. **5.** To beat, as eggs or cream, to a froth. **6.** To seize, move, jerk, throw, etc., with a sudden motion: with *away, in, off, out,* etc. **7.** In fishing, to make repeated casts upon the surface of (a stream, etc.). **8.** To wrap (rope, cable, etc.) with light line so as to prevent chafing or wear. **9.** To wrap or bind about something. **10.** To sew, as a flat seam, with a loose overcast or overhand stitch. **11.** *U.S. Informal* To defeat; overcome. —*v.i.* **12.** To go, come, move, or turn suddenly and quickly: with *away, in, off, out,* etc. **13.** To thrash about in a manner suggestive of a whip: pennants *whipping* in the wind. —**to whip up 1.** To excite; arouse. **2.** *Informal* To prepare quickly, as a meal. —*n.* **1.** An instrument consisting of a lash attached to a handle, used for driving draft animals or for administering punishment. **2.** One who handles a whip expertly, as a driver. **3.** A stroke, blow, or lashing motion with, or as with, a whip. **4.** In politics, a member of a legislative body, as Congress or Parliament, appointed unofficially to enforce the discipline and look after the interests of his party. **5.** A dish or dessert containing cream or eggs and usu. fruit, whipped to a froth. [ME *wippen*] —**whip′per** *n.*

whip·cord (hwip′kôrd′) *n.* **1.** A strong, hard-twisted or braided hempen cord, used in making whiplashes. **2.** A worsted fabric with a pronounced diagonal rib.

whip hand **1.** The hand that wields the whip in riding or driving. **2.** An instrument or means of mastery; advantage.

whip·lash (hwip′lash′) *n.* The lash of a whip.

whiplash injury An injury to the neck caused by a sudden jolting, as in an automobile collision.

whip·per·snap·per (hwip′ər-snap′ər) *n.* A pretentious but insignificant person, esp. a young one. [? Extension of *whipsnapper* a cracker of whips]

whip·pet (hwip′it) *n.* A small, swift breed of dog, probably a cross between a greyhound and a terrier, used esp. in racing and coursing. [Dim. of WHIP]

whip·ping (hwip′ing) *n.* **1.** The act of one who or that which whips; esp., a flogging. **2.** Cord or other material used to whip or lash parts together.

whipping boy Anyone who receives punishment deserved by another; scapegoat.

whipping post The post to which those sentenced to flogging are secured.

whip·ple·tree (hwip′əl-trē′) *n.* A whiffletree. [Prob. < WHIP]

whip·poor·will (hwip′ər-wil) *n.* A small nocturnal bird allied to the goatsuckers, common in the eastern U.S. [Imit. of its reiterated cry]

whip·saw (hwip′sô′) *n.* A long, narrow, tapering saw, mounted in a wooden frame. —*v.t.* **·sawed, ·sawed** or **·sawn, ·saw·ing 1.** To saw with a whipsaw. **2.** To get the best of (an opponent) in spite of every effort he makes.

whip·stitch (hwip′stich′) *v.t.* To sew or gather with overcast stitches. —*n.* A stitch made in this way.

whip·stock (hwip′stok′) *n.* The handle of a whip.

whir (hwûr) *v.t. & v.i.* **whirred, whir·ring** To fly, move, or whirl with a buzzing sound. —*n.* **1.** A whizzing, swishing sound, as that caused by the sudden rising of birds. **2.** Confusion; bustle. Also *Brit.* **whirr.** [Prob. < Scand.]

whirl (hwûrl) *v.i.* **1.** To turn or revolve rapidly, as about a center. **2.** To turn away or aside quickly. **3.** To move or go swiftly. **4.** To have a sensation of spinning: My head *whirls.* —*v.t.* **5.** To cause to turn or revolve rapidly. **6.** To carry or bear along with a revolving motion: The wind *whirled* the dust into the air. —*n.* **1.** A swift rotating or revolving motion. **2.** Something whirling. **3.** A state of confusion; turmoil. **4.** A rapid succession of events, social activities, etc. **5.** *Informal* A brief drive or trip. **6.** *Informal* A try. [Prob. < ON *hvirfla* to revolve] —**whirl′er** *n.*

whirl·i·gig (hwûr′lə-gig′) *n.* **1.** Any toy or small device that revolves rapidly on an axis. **2.** A merry-go-round. **3.** Anything that moves in a cycle. **4.** A whirling motion. [< *whirly* (< WHIRL) + obs. *gig,* a whirling toy]

whirl·pool (hwûrl′pool′) *n.* **1.** A vortex where water moves with a whirling motion, as from the meeting of two currents. **2.** Anything resembling the motion of a whirlpool.

whirl·wind (hwûrl′wind′) *n.* **1.** A funnel-shaped column of air, with a rapid, upward spiral motion and moving forward on the surface of the land or sea. **2.** Anything resembling a whirlwind, as rotary motion or violent activity. —*adj.* Extremely swift or impetuous: a *whirlwind* courtship.

whish (hwish) *v.i.* To move with a swishing, whistling sound. —*n.* A swishing sound. [Imit.]

whisk (hwisk) *v.t.* **1.** To bear along or sweep with light movements, as of a small broom: often with *away* or *off.* **2.** To cause to move with a quick sweeping motion. **3.** *Chiefly Brit.* To beat with a quick movement, as eggs, etc. —*v.i.* **4.** To move quickly and lightly. —*n.* **1.** A sudden, sweeping movement. **2.** A little broom or brush. **3.** *Chiefly Brit.* A small culinary instrument for rapidly whipping (cream, etc.) to a froth. [Prob. < Scand.]

whisk·broom (hwisk′broom′, -broom′) *n.* A small, short-handled broom for brushing clothing, etc.

whisk·er (hwis′kər) *n.* **1.** *pl.* The hair that grows on the sides of a man's face, as distinguished from that on his lips, chin, and throat; loosely, the beard or any part of the beard. **2.** A hair from the whiskers or beard. **3.** One of the long, bristly hairs on the sides of the mouth of some animals, as cats and rodents. —**whisk′ered, whisk′er·y** *adj.*

whis·key (hwis′kē) *n. pl. ·keys* **1.** An alcoholic liquor obtained by the distillation of certain fermented grains, as rye, barley, corn, etc., and containing about 40 to 50 per cent of alcohol. **2.** A drink of whiskey. —*adj.* Pertaining to or made of whiskey. Also **whis′ky.** [Short for *usquebaugh* < Irish, water of life < *uisge* water + *beatha* life]

whis·per (hwis′pər) *n.* **1.** A low, soft, breathy voice. **2.** A low, rustling sound. **3.** *Phonet.* The sound produced by the passage of breath through the partially closed glottis. **4.** A whispered utterance; secret communication; hint; insinuation. —*v.i.* **1.** To speak in a whisper. **2.** To talk cautiously or furtively; plot or gossip. **3.** To make a low, rustling sound. —*v.t.* **4.** To utter in a whisper. **5.** To speak to in a whisper. [OE *hwisprian*] —**whis′per·er** *n.* —**whis′per·ing** *adj. & n.* —**whis′per·ing·ly** *adv.*

whispering campaign A deliberate spreading of rumors in order to discredit a person or group.

whist[1] (hwist) *n.* A game of cards, the forerunner of bridge, played by four persons. [Alter. of earlier *whisk*]

whist[2] (hwist) *interj.* Hush! be still! —*adj.* Silent or quiet.

whis·tle (hwis′əl) *v.* **·tled, ·tling** *v.i.* **1.** To make a musical tone, usu. shrill, by sending the breath through the teeth or through a small orifice formed by contracting the lips. **2.** To emit a sharp, shrill cry, as some birds and animals. **3.** To cause a sharp, shrill sound by swift passage through the air, as wind, etc. **4.** To blow or sound a whistle. —*v.t.* **5.** To produce (a tune) by whistling. **6.** To call, manage, or direct by whistling. **7.** To send or move with a whistling sound. —**to whistle for** To go without; fail to get. —*n.* **1.** A device for producing a shrill tone by forcing a current of air, etc., through a pipe or tube with a narrowed aperture, or against a thin edge. **2.** A whistling sound. **3.** The act of whistling. **4.** *Slang* The mouth and throat: to wet one's *whistle.* [OE *hwistle* shrill pipe]

whis·tler (hwis′lər) *n.* **1.** One who or that which whistles. **2.** Any of various birds so called from the noise of their wings in flight. **3.** A radio signal of very low frequency generated by atmospheric electricity.

whistle stop *U.S. Informal* A small town, where a train stops only on signal. —**whis·tle-stop** (hwis′əl-stop′) *adj.*

whit (hwit) *n.* The smallest particle; speck: not a *whit* abashed. [Var. of *wight* < OE *wiht* a certain amount]

white (hwīt) *adj.* **whit·er, whit·est 1.** Having the color produced by reflection of all of the visible solar spectrum, as from a bed of new-fallen snow. **2.** Light or comparatively light in color. **3.** Bloodless; ashen: *white* with rage. **4.** Very fair; blond. **5.** Silvery or gray. **6.** Snowy. **7.** Habited in white clothing: *white* nuns. **8.** Not intentionally wicked; not harmful: a *white* lie. **9.** Free from spot or stain; innocent. **10.** Incandescent: *white* heat. **11.** Blank; unmarked by ink. **12.** Belonging to a racial group characterized by light-colored skin; esp., Caucasian. **13.** Of, pertaining to, or controlled by white men: the *white* power structure. **14.** *Informal* Fair and honorable; honest. **15.** Designating any of various wines ranging in color from pale yellow to deep amber. —*n.* **1.** The color seen when light is reflected without sensible absorption of any of the visible rays of the spectrum; the color of new-fallen snow. **2.** The state or condition of being white. **3.** *Biol.* The white or light-colored part of something, as the albumen of egg or the white part of the eyeball. **4.** A white or light-colored thing, as a white fabric, a white pigment, etc. **5.** *pl.* A white uniform or outfit: a sailor's summer *whites.* **6.** A member of the so-called white race. —*v.t.* **whit·ed, whit·ing** To make white; whiten. [OE *hwīt*] —**white′ly** *adv.* —**white′ness** *n.*

white ant Loosely, a termite.

white-bait (hwīt′bāt′) *n.* The young of various fishes, esp. of sprat and herring, netted in great quantities and much esteemed in Europe as a delicacy.

white bear The polar bear.

white birch 1. Birch. 2. The common European birch, having an ash-colored bark.

white-cap (hwīt′kap′) *n.* A wave with a crest of foam.

white cedar 1. An evergreen tree of the pine family, growing in moist places along the Atlantic coast: also called *cypress.* 2. Its soft, easily worked wood.

white clover A common variety of clover, with white flowers.

white coal Water considered as a source of power.

white-collar (hwīt′kol′ər) *adj.* Designating workers, jobs, attitudes, etc., associated with clerical, professional, and other nonmanual occupations.

whit-ed sepulcher (hwī′tid) A hypocrite. *Matt.* xxiii 27.

white elephant 1. A rare, pale gray variety of Asian elephant held sacred by the Burmese and Siamese. 2. Anything rare but expensive to keep. 3. Any burdensome possession.

white-faced (hwīt′fāst′) *adj.* 1. Pallid in countenance; pale. 2. Having a white mark or spot on the face or front of the head, as a horse. 3. Having a white facing or exposed surface.

white-fish (hwīt′fish′) *n.* *pl.* **·fish** or **·fish·es** 1. Any of various food fishes of North America, living mostly in lakes, some species of which are called chubs. 2. Any of various other fish having a silvery appearance, as the beluga. 3. A tropical marine food fish of California.

white flag 1. A flag of truce. 2. A white flag or cloth hoisted as a signal of surrender during a battle.

White Friar A Carmelite friar: so called from the color of his cloak.

white gold An alloy of gold with a white metal, usu. nickel and zinc, sometimes palladium and platinum.

white goods Household linens, such as sheets, towels, etc.

White-hall (hwīt′hôl) 1. A street in Westminster, London, where a number of government offices are located. 2. The British government.

white heat 1. The temperature at which a body becomes incandescent. 2. Great excitement, intense emotion, etc.

white horse A wave crested with foam; whitecap.

white-hot (hwīt′hot′) *adj.* 1. Exhibiting the condition of white heat. 2. *Informal* Extremely angry.

White House, The 1. The official residence of the President of the U.S., at Washington, D.C., a white, colonial style building: officially called the *Executive Mansion.* 2. The executive branch of the U.S. government.

white lead A heavy, white, poisonous mixture of lead carbonate and lead oxide, used as a pigment and in some medicinal ointments for burns.

white lie See under LIE.

white-liv·ered (hwīt′liv′ərd) *adj.* 1. Having a pale and unhealthy look. 2. Base; cowardly.

white man 1. A person belonging to a racial group characterized by light-colored skin. 2. A male member of the so-called white race.

white man's burden The alleged duty of the white peoples to spread culture among the so-called backward peoples of the world: phrase originated by Rudyard Kipling.

white matter *Anat.* The portion of the brain and spinal cord composed mainly of medullated nerve fibers, giving it a white appearance.

white meat The light-colored meat or flesh of animals, as veal or the breast of turkey.

whit·en (hwīt′n) *v.t.* & *v.i.* To make or become white; blanch; bleach. — **whit′en·er** *n.*
 — **Syn.** *Whiten, bleach,* and *blanch* mean to make nearly or completely white or colorless. *Whiten* implies overlay with a white paint or polish, while *bleach* and *blanch* refer to removal of color by sunlight, chemical agents, etc. Industrial products are *bleached,* while foodstuffs are *blanched.*

white oak 1. A North American oak of the eastern U.S. with long leaves having from five to nine entire, rounded lobes. 2. Any of several related species. 3. The wood of any species of white oak.

white pine 1. A pine widely distributed in eastern North America, with soft, bluish green leaves in clusters of five. The cone and tassel of this tree are the State emblem of Maine. 2. The light, soft wood of this tree. 3. Any of several similar species of pine.

white plague *Pathol.* Tuberculosis, esp. of the lungs.

white poplar A large, rapidly growing Old World tree, often planted in the U.S. for shade or for its ornamental green and silvery white leaves.

white potato The common potato.

white race The Caucasian ethnic division of mankind.

white rat One of a special breed of albino Norway rats much used in biological and medical experimentation.

White Russian Byelorussian.

white sale A sale of sheets, towels, etc., at reduced prices.

white sauce A sauce made of butter, flour, milk, etc., used for vegetables, meats, and fish.

white slave A girl forced into or held in prostitution. — **white-slave** (hwīt′slāv′) *adj.*

white slavery The business or practice of forced prostitution. — **white slaver**

white supremacy The doctrine arising from the belief that the white race is superior to the Negro race and that the latter must therefore be kept in an inferior economic and social position. — **white su·prem·a·cist** (sə·prem′ə·sist)

white-tailed deer (hwīt′tāld′) A common North American deer, having a moderately long tail white on the underside: also called *Virginia deer.*

white-throat·ed sparrow (hwīt′thrō′tid) A common North American sparrow, with a white patch on the throat.

white tie 1. A white bow tie, worn with men's formal evening attire. 2. A swallowtail coat and its correct accessories.

white-wash (hwīt′wosh′, -wôsh′) *n.* 1. A mixture of slaked lime and water, sometimes with salt, whiting, and glue added, used for whitening walls, etc. 2. *Slang* A covering up or glossing over of reprehensible actions or inefficiencies, esp. of a political figure; also, a suppression of adverse evidence, as in a legal matter. 3. *Informal* A failure to score in a game. — *v.t.* 1. To coat with whitewash. 2. *Slang* To gloss over; hide. 3. *Informal* In sports, to defeat without allowing the losing side to score. — **white′wash′er** *n.*

white water *U.S. & Canadian* Rapids in a river.

white whale The beluga.

whith·er (hwith′ər) *Archaic & Poetic adv.* 1. To what or which place? Where? 2. To what point, end, extent, etc.? — *conj.* To which or what place, end, etc. [OE *hwider*]

whith·er·so·ev·er (hwith′ər·sō·ev′ər) *adv.* Archaic To whatever place.

whit·ing (hwī′ting) *n.* A pure white chalk, powdered and washed, used in making putty and whitewash, as a pigment, and for polishing.

whit·ish (hwī′tish) *adj.* Somewhat white or, esp., very light gray. — **whit′ish·ness** *n.*

whit·low (hwīt′lō) *n.* *Pathol.* An inflammatory tumor, esp. on the terminal phalanx of a finger, seated between the epidermis and true skin; a felon. [ME *whitflaw*]

Whit·mon·day (hwīt′mun′dē, -dā) *n.* The Monday next following Whitsunday, observed in England as a holiday. Also **Whit-Monday, Whit′sun-Mon′day.**

Whit·sun (hwīt′sən) *n.* Whitsunday: frequently used in combination: *Whitsun-week.*

Whit·sun·day (hwīt′sun′dē, -dā, hwīt′sən·dā′) *n.* Pentecost (def. 1). [OE *Hwīta Sunnandæg,* lit., white Sunday]

Whit·sun·tide (hwīt′sən·tīd′) *n.* The week that begins with Whitsunday, esp. the first three days. Also **Whitsun Tide.**

whit·tle (hwīt′l) *v.* **·tled, ·tling** *v.t.* 1. To cut or shave bits from (wood, a stick, etc.). 2. To make or shape by carving or whittling. 3. To reduce or wear away by or as by paring a little at a time: with *down, off, away,* etc. — *v.i.* 4. To whittle wood, usu. as an aimless diversion. [Alter. of ME *thwitel* < OE *thwītan* to cut] — **whit′tler** *n.*

whit·tlings (hwīt′lingz) *n.pl.* The fine chips and shavings made by a whittler.

whiz (hwiz) *v.* **whizzed, whiz·zing** *v.i.* 1. To make a hissing and humming sound while passing through the air. 2. To move or pass with such a sound. — *v.t.* 3. To cause to whiz. — *n.* *pl.* **whiz·zes** 1. A whizzing sound. 2. *Slang* Any person or thing of extraordinary excellence or ability. Also **whizz.** [Imit.]

who (hōō) *pron. possessive case* **whose;** *objective case* **whom** 1. Which or what person or persons: *Who* said that? I know *who* he is. 2. That; a relative pronoun: used when the antecedent refers to a human being. 3. He, she, or they that; whoever: *Who* steals my purse steals trash. — **as who should say** As if one should say. [OE *hwā*]
 ◆ In modern usage, *who* as a relative is applied only to persons, *which* only to animals or to inanimate objects, *that* to persons or things indiscriminately. The use of *whom* as an interrogative pronoun in initial position, as in *Whom* did you see?, is supported by some grammarians, but the more natural *Who* did you see? *Who* did you give the book to? are in wider use and are now considered acceptable. However, when used after a verb or preposition, *whom* is still required, as in To *whom* did you give it? You saw *whom?*

whoa (hwō) *interj.* Stop! stand still! [Var. of HO]

who·dun·it (hōō·dun′it) *n.* *Informal* A type of mystery fiction or dramatic production that challenges the reader or spectator to detect the perpetrator of a crime.

who·ev·er (hōō·ev′ər) *pron.* Any one without exception; any person who.

whole (hōl) *adj.* 1. Containing all the parts necessary to make up a total; entire. 2. Having all the essential or original parts unbroken and uninjured; intact. 3. In or having regained sound health; hale. 4. Constituting the full extent, amount, quantity, etc.; total; entire. **5.** Having the same parents; full, as opposed to *half*: a *whole* brother. **6.** *Math.* Integral. **— as a whole** Completely; altogether. **— on the whole** Taking everything into consideration. **— out of whole cloth** Fabricated; made up, without foundation in truth or fact. **—** *n.* **1.** All the parts or elements entering into and making up a thing; totality. **2.** An organization of parts making a unity or system; an organism. [OE *hāl*] **— whole′ness** *n.*

whole blood Blood as taken directly from the body, esp. that used in transfusions.

whole·heart·ed (hōl′här′tid) *adj.* Done or experienced with earnestness, sincerity, etc.; earnest. **— whole′heart′ed·ly** *adv.* **— whole′heart′ed·ness** *n.*

whole hog *Slang* The whole of anything; completeness. **— to go the whole hog** *Slang* To do something thoroughly; become involved without reservation.

whole milk Milk containing all its constituents.

whole note *Music* A note having a time value equal to one half of a breve: also, *Chiefly Brit.*, *semibreve*.

whole number *Math.* An integer.

whole·sale (hōl′sāl′) *n.* The selling of goods in large bulk or quantity, esp. for resale: distinguished from *retail*. **—** *adj.* **1.** Pertaining to, involving, or engaged in the sale of goods at wholesale. **2.** Made or done on a large scale or indiscriminately: *wholesale* murder. **—** *adv.* **1.** In bulk or quantity. **2.** Indiscriminately. **—** *v.t. & v.i.* **-saled, -sal·ing** To sell at wholesale. [ME < *by hole sale* in large quantities] **— whole′sal′er** *n.*

whole·some (hōl′səm) *adj.* **1.** Tending to promote health; salubrious; healthful: *wholesome* air or food. **2.** Favorable to virtue and well-being; beneficial: *wholesome* entertainment. **3.** Indicative or characteristic of health: *wholesome* red cheeks. **4.** Safe; free from danger or risk. [ME *holsum*] **— whole′some·ly** *adv.* **— whole′some·ness** *n.*

whole tone *Music* A tone (def. 3b).

whole-wheat (hōl′hwēt′) *adj.* Made from wheat grain and bran.

who'll (hōōl) **1.** Who will. **2.** Who shall.

whol·ly (hō′lē, hōl′lē) *adv.* **1.** Completely; totally. **2.** Exclusively; only.

whom (hōōm) *pron.* The objective case of WHO.

whom·ev·er (hōōm′ev′ər), **whom·so** (hōōm′sō′), **whom·so·ev·er** (hōōm′sō·ev′ər) Objective cases of WHOEVER, WHOSO, etc.

whoop (hōōp, hwōōp, hwŏŏp) *v.i.* **1.** To utter loud cries, as of excitement, rage, or exultation. **2.** To hoot, as an owl. **3.** To make a loud, gasping inspiration, as after a paroxysm of coughing. **—** *v.t.* **4.** To utter with a whoop or whoops. **5.** To call, urge, chase, etc., with whoops; hoot. **— to whoop up** *Slang* To arouse enthusiasm in or for. **— to whoop it** (or **things**) **up** *Slang* **1.** To make noisy revelry. **2.** To arouse enthusiasm. **—** *n.* The cry, shout, or sound of one who or that which whoops. **— not worth a whoop** *Informal* Not worth anything. **—** *interj.* An exclamation of joy, enthusiasm, etc. [ME *whope*]

whoop·ee (hwōō′pē, hwōō′pē′) *interj. & n.* An exclamation of joy, excitement, etc. **— to make whoopee** To have a noisy, festive time. [< WHOOP]

whoop·er (hōō′pər, hwōō′pər, hwŏŏp′r) *n.* **1.** One who or that which whoops. **2.** A large Old World swan: so called from its loud cry.

whoop·ing cough (hōō′ping, hŏŏp′ing) *Pathol.* A contagious respiratory disease of bacterial origin chiefly affecting children, marked in its final stage by violent coughing.

whop (hwop) *Informal* A blow or fall, or the resulting noise. **—** *v.* **whopped, whop·ping** *v.t.* **1.** To strike or beat. **2.** To defeat convincingly. **—** *v.i.* **3.** To drop or fall suddenly; flop. [Prob. imit.]

whop·per (hwop′ər) *n. Informal* Something large or remarkable; esp., a big falsehood.

whop·ping (hwop′ing) *adj.* Unusually large; great.

whore (hōr, hôr) *n.* A prostitute. **—** *v.i.* **whored, whor·ing** **1.** To have illicit sexual intercourse, esp. with a prostitute. **2.** To be a whore. [OE *hōre*, prob. < ON *hōra*]

whore·house (hōr′hous′, hôr′-) *n.* A house of prostitution.

whore·mas·ter (hōr′mas′tər, -mäs′-, hôr′-) *n. Archaic* **1.** A procurer. **2.** A man who has intercourse with whores. Also **whore·mon·ger** (hōr′mung′gər, -mong′-, hôr′-).

whor·ish (hōr′ish, hôr′ish) *adj.* Characteristic of a whore; lewd. **— whor′ish·ly** *adv.* **— whor′ish·ness** *n.*

whorl (hwûrl, hwôrl) *n.* **1.** The flywheel of a spindle. **2.** *Bot.* A set of leaves, etc., on the same plane with one another, distributed in a circle. **3.** *Zool.* A turn or volution, as of a spiral shell. **4.** Any of the convoluted ridges of a fingerprint. [ME *wharwyl, whor-whil*]

WHORL (def. 2)

whorled (hwûrld, hwôrld) *adj.* Furnished with or arranged in whorls.

whor·tle·ber·ry (hwûr′təl·ber′ē) *n.* *pl.* **·ries 1.** A European variety of blueberry. **2.** Its blue-black fruit. Also called *bilberry*. [< OE *horta* + BERRY]

whose (hōōz) The possessive case of WHO and often of WHICH. [ME < OE *hwæs*, altered by analogy with nominative form *hwo*]

whose·so·ev·er (hōōz′sō·ev′ər) Possessive case of WHOSOEVER.

who·so (hōō′sō) *pron.* Whoever; any person who. [Reduced form of OE *swā hwā swā*]

who·so·ev·er (hōō′sō·ev′ər) *pron.* Any person whatever; who; whoever.

why (hwī) *adv.* **1.** For what cause, purpose, or reason? wherefore? **2.** The reason or cause for which: I don't know *why* he went. **3.** Because of which; for which: I know no reason *why* he went. **—** *n.* *pl.* **whys 1.** An explanatory cause; reason; cause. **2.** A puzzling problem; riddle; enigma. **—** *interj.* An introductory expletive, sometimes denoting surprise. ◆ The *why* in the expression *the reason why*, though sometimes condemned as a redundancy, is commonly used in standard written English. [OE *hwȳ, hwī*, instrumental case of *hwæt* what]

wich (wich) *n.* The wych-elm.

wich-elm (wich′elm) See WYCH-ELM.

wick (wik) *n.* A wand of loosely twisted or woven fibers, as in a candle or lamp, acting by capillary attraction to convey oil or other illuminant to a flame. [OE *wēoce*]

wick·ed (wik′id) *adj.* **1.** Evil in principle and practice; vicious; sinful; depraved. **2.** Mischievous; roguish. **3.** Noxious; pernicious. **4.** Troublesome; painful. **5.** *Informal* Done with great skill: a *wicked* game. [ME, alter. of *wikke, wicke*] **— wick′ed·ly** *adv.* **— wick′ed·ness** *n.*

wick·er (wik′ər) *adj.* Made of twigs, osiers, etc. **—** *n.* **1.** A pliant young shoot or rod; twig; osier. **2.** Wickerwork. [Prob. < Scand.]

wick·er·work (wik′ər·wûrk′) *n.* A fabric or texture, as a basket, made of woven twigs, osiers, etc.; basketwork.

wick·et (wik′it) *n.* **1.** A small door or gate subsidiary to or made within a larger entrance. **2.** A small opening in a door. **3.** A small sluice gate in a canal lock or at the end of a millrace. **4.** In cricket: **a** An arrangement of three stumps set near together, with two bails laid over the top. **b** The place at which the wicket is set up. **c** The right or turn of each batsman at the wicket. **d** The playing pitch between the wickets: a fast *wicket*. **e** An inning that is not finished or not begun. **5.** In croquet, any one of the arches, usu. of wire, through which the ball must be hit. [< AF *wiket*, OF *guichet*, prob. < Gmc.]

wick·et·keep·er (wik′it·kē′pər) *n.* In cricket, the fielder stationed behind the wicket that is being bowled at.

wide (wīd) *adj.* **wid·er, wid·est 1.** Having relatively great extent between sides; broad. **2.** Extended far in every direction; ample; spacious: a *wide* expanse. **3.** Having a specified degree of width or breadth: an inch *wide*. **4.** Distant from the desired or proper point by a great extent of space; remote; wild: *wide* of the mark. **5.** Having intellectual breadth; liberal: a man of *wide* views. **6.** Fully open; expanded or extended: *wide* eyes. **7.** Comprehensive; inclusive: *wide* learning. **8.** Loose; roomy: *wide* breeches. **—** *n.* **1.** In cricket, a ball bowled too far over or on either side of the wicket to be within the batsman's reach. **2.** Breadth of extent; also, a broad, open space. **—** *adv.* **1.** To a great distance; extensively. **2.** Far from the mark. **3.** To the greatest extent; fully open. [OE *wīd*] **— wide′ly** *adv.* **— wide′ness** *n.*

wide-an·gle lens (wīd′ang′gəl) *Photog.* A type of lens permitting an angle of view wider than that of the ordinary lens.

wide-a·wake (wīd′ə·wāk′) *adj.* **1.** Fully awake. **2.** Marked by vigilance and alertness; keen.

wide-eyed (wīd′īd′) *adj.* With the eyes wide open, as in wonder or surprise.

wid·en (wīd′n) *v.t. & v.i.* To make or become wide or wider. **— wid′en·er** *n.*

wide-o·pen (wīd′ō′pən) *adj.* **1.** Opened wide. **2.** *Informal* Remiss in the enforcement of laws that regulate various forms of vice, as gambling, etc.: a *wide-open* city.

wide-screen (wīd′skrēn′) *adj.* Designating a motion-picture process using an elongated screen designed to accommodate various systems of projection beyond 35 mm.

wide·spread (wīd′spred′) *adj.* **1.** Extending over a large space or territory. **2.** Occurring, accepted, etc., among many people; general: a *widespread* belief. Also **wide-spread′, wide′spread′ing**.

widg·eon (wij′ən) *n.* Any of various river ducks with short bill and wedge-shaped tail. [Cf. MF *vigeon* wild duck]

wid·ow (wid′ō) *n.* **1.** A woman who has lost her husband by death and has not remarried. **2.** In some card games, an additional hand dealt to the table; also, a kitty. **3.** *Printing* An incomplete line of type at the top of a page or column. — *v.t.* **1.** To make a widow of; deprive of a husband: usu. in the past participle. **2.** To deprive of something desirable; bereave. [OE *widewe, wuduwe*]

wid·ow·er (wid′ō·ər) *n.* A man whose wife is dead, and who has not married again. [ME < OE *widewe* widow]

wid·ow·hood (wid′ō·hŏŏd) *n.* The state or period of being a widow, or, rarely, of being a widower.

widow's mite A small but selfless contribution from one who can hardly afford it. *Mark xii* 42.

widow's peak A hairline growing in a V-shaped point from the forehead.

widow's walk A railed observation area built on the roof of a home near the sea giving the observer a clear view of incoming vessels: also called *captain's walk*.

width (width) *n.* **1.** Dimension or measurement of an object taken from side to side, and at right angles to the length. **2.** The state or fact of being wide; breadth. **3.** Something that has width; esp., one of the several pieces of material used in making a garment. [< WIDE]

width·wise (width′wīz′) *adv.* In the direction of the width; from side to side. Also **width′way′** (-wā′), **width′ways′**.

wield (wēld) *v.t.* **1.** To handle, as a weapon or instrument, esp. with full command and effect. **2.** To exercise (authority, power, etc.). [Fusion of OE *wealdan* to rule and OE *wieldan* to conquer] — **wield′a·ble** *adj.* — **wield′er** *n.*

wield·y (wēl′dē) *adj.* **wield·i·er**, **wield·i·est** Easily handled or managed; manageable.

wie·ner (wē′nər) *n.* *U.S.* A kind of sausage, often shorter than a frankfurter, made of beef and pork. Also **wie·nie** (wē′nē), **wie·ner·wurst** (wē′nər·wûrst′, *Ger.* vē′nər·vŏŏrst′). [Short for G *Wiener-wurst* Vienna sausage]

Wie·ner schnit·zel (vē′nər schnit′səl) A breaded veal cutlet, seasoned or garnished in any of several ways. [< G *Wiener* Viennese + *schnitzel* cutlet, dim. of *schnitz* slice]

wife (wīf) *n. pl.* **wives** (wīvz) **1.** A woman joined to a man in lawful wedlock. ◆ Collateral adjective: *uxorial.* **2.** *Archaic* A grown woman; adult female: now usu. in combination or in certain phrases: *housewife, old wives' tales.* — **to take (a woman) to wife** To marry (a woman). [OE *wīf*] — **wife′dom, wife′hood** *n.* — **wife′ly** *adj.*

wig (wig) *n.* An artificial covering of hair for the head. — *v.t.* **wigged, wig·ging** **1.** *Rare* To furnish with a wig or wigs. **2.** *Brit. Informal* To censure severely; berate or scold, esp. in public. [Short for PERIWIG]

wig·ging (wig′ing) *n. Brit. Informal* A rebuke; a scolding.

wig·gle (wig′əl) *v.t. & v.i.* **·gled, ·gling** To move or cause to move quickly and irregularly from side to side; squirm; wriggle. — *n.* A wiggling motion. — **to get a wiggle on** *Slang* To hurry up. [? < MLG *wiggelen*] — **wig′gly** *adj.*

wig·gler (wig′lər) *n.* **1.** One who or that which wiggles. **2.** The larva of a mosquito.

wig·wag (wig′wag′) *v.t. & v.i.* **·wagged, ·wag·ging** To send (a message) by moving hand flags, lights, etc., according to a code. — *n.* The act of wigwagging; also, a message so sent. [< dial. E *wig* to wiggle + WAG¹] — **wig′wag′ger** *n.*

wig·wam (wig′wom, -wôm) *n.* **1.** A dwelling or lodge of the North American Indians, commonly a conical framework of poles covered with bark, hides, etc. **2.** *U.S. Informal* A public building used for political gatherings, mass meetings, etc. [< Algonquian (Ojibwa) *wigwaum*, lit., their dwelling]

wild (wīld) *adj.* **1.** Inhabiting the forest or open field; not domesticated or tamed; living in a state of nature. **2.** Growing or produced without care or culture; not cultivated: *wild* flowers. **3.** Being without civilized inhabitants or cultivation; waste: *wild* prairies. **4.** Living in a primitive or savage way; uncivilized: the *wild* men of Borneo. **5.** Boisterous; unruly. **6.** Immoral; orgiastic: a *wild* affair. **7.** Affected with or originating violent disturbances; stormy; turbulent: a *wild* night, a *wild* crowd. **8.** Showing reckless want of judgment; extravagant: a *wild* speculation. **9.** Fantastically irregular or disordered; odd in arrangement or effect: a *wild* imagination, *wild* dress. **10.** Eager and excited, as by reason of joy, fear, desire, etc. **11.** Excited to frenzy or distraction; roused to fury or desperation; crazed or crazy: to drive one *wild*. **12.** Being or going far from the proper course or from the mark aimed at; erratic: a *wild* ball, a *wild* guess. **13.** In some card games, having its value arbitrarily determined by the dealer or holder. — **wild and wooly** *Informal* Untamed; reckless; boisterous. — *n. Often pl.* An uninhabited or uncultivated place; wilderness: the *wilds* of Africa. — **the wild** The wilderness; also, the free, natural, wild life: the call of *the wild*. — *adv.* In a wild manner: without control. [OE *wilde*] — **wild′ly** *adv.* — **wild′ness** *n.*

wild boar The native hog of continental Europe, southern Asia, North Africa, and formerly of Great Britain.

wild carrot An herb having filmy white flowers and from which the cultivated carrot is derived; also called *Queen Anne's lace.*

wild·cat (wīld′kat′) *n.* **1.** An undomesticated feline carnivore of Europe, resembling the domestic cat, but larger and stronger. **2.** The lynx. **3.** One of several other felines, as the ocelot and serval. **4.** An aggressive quick-tempered person, esp. a woman. **5.** An unattached locomotive and its tender, used on special work, as to haul trains, etc. **6.** A successful oil well drilled in an area previously unproductive. **7.** A tricky or unsound business venture; esp. a worthless mine: also **wildcat mine.** Also **wild cat.** — *adj.* **1.** Unsound; risky; esp. financially unsound or risky. **2.** Illegal; made or carried on without official sanction or authorization. **3.** Not running on a schedule; also, running wild or without control, as a railroad train or engine. — *v.t. & v.i.* **·cat·ted, ·cat·ting** To drill for oil in (an area not known to be productive). — **wild′cat′ting** *n. & adj.*

wildcat strike A strike unauthorized by regular union procedure.

wild·cat·ter (wīld′kat′ər) *n.* **1.** A promoter of mines of doubtful value. **2.** One who develops oil wells in unproved territory. **3.** One who manufactures illicit whisky.

wilde·beest (wīld′bēst, wil′də-; *Du.* vil′də·bāst) *n.* A gnu. [< Afrikaans < Du. *wild* wild + *beeste* beast]

wil·der·ness (wil′dər·nis) *n.* **1.** An uncultivated, uninhabited, or barren region. **2.** A waste, as of an ocean. **3.** A multitudinous and confusing collection: a *wilderness* of curiosities. [ME < OE *wilddēor* wild beast + -NESS]

wild·fire (wīld′fīr′) *n.* **1.** A raging, destructive fire: now generally in the phrase **to spread like wildfire.** **2.** A composition of flammable materials, or the flame produced by it, very hard to put out, as Greek fire. **3.** A phosphorescent luminousness; ignis fatuus.

wild·flow·er (wīld′flou′ər) *n.* Any uncultivated flowering plant; also, the flower of such a plant. Also **wild flower.**

wild·fowl (wīld′foul′) *n. pl.* **·fowl** (*esp. for def.* 2), or **fowls** **1.** A wild game bird, esp. a wild duck or goose. **2.** *pl.* Wild game birds collectively. Also **wild fowl.**

wild-goose chase (wīld′gōōs′) **1.** Pursuit of the unknown or unattainable. **2.** Any strenuous and fruitless task.

wild·life (wīld′līf′) *n.* Wild animals, trees, and plants collectively.

wild oat **1.** *Usually pl.* An uncultivated grass, esp. a common species of Europe. **2.** *pl.* Indiscretions of youth: usu. in the expression **to sow one's wild oats.**

wild pansy The pansy in its uncultivated state; esp., a European species from which the garden pansy is derived.

wild pitch In baseball, a misplay charged to the pitcher for allowing a runner to advance by throwing a pitch that the catcher does not and could not be expected to catch.

wild rice The grain of a tall aquatic grass of North America, esteemed as a table delicacy.

wild turkey A large North American turkey formerly ranging east of the Rocky Mountains from southern Canada to Florida and Mexico, and first domesticated in Mexico, now rare in the wild state.

Wild West The western U.S., esp. in its early period of Indian fighting, lawlessness, etc.

wild·wood (wīld′wŏŏd′) *n.* Natural forest land.

wile (wīl) *n.* **1.** An act or a means of cunning deception; also, any beguiling trick or artifice. **2.** Craftiness; cunning. — *v.t.* **wiled, wil·ing** **1.** To lure, beguile, or mislead. **2.** To pass divertingly, as time: usu. with *away*: by confusion with *while*. [ME *wil*, prob. < Scand.]

wil·ful (wil′fəl), **wil·ful·ly, wil·ful·ness** See WILLFUL, etc.

will¹ (wil) *n.* **1.** The power of conscious, deliberate action; the faculty by which the mind makes choices and acts to carry them out. **2.** The act or experience of exercising this faculty. **3.** Strong determination; also, self-control. **4.** That which has been resolved or determined upon; a purpose. **5.** Power to dispose of a matter arbitrarily; discretion. **6.** *Law* The legal declaration of a person's intentions as to the disposal of his estate after his death. **7.** A conscious inclination toward any end or course; a wish. **8.** A request or command. — **at will** As one pleases. — *v.* **willed, will·ing** *v.t.* **1.** To decide upon; choose. **2.** To resolve upon as an action or course; determine to do. **3.** To give, devise, or bequeath by a will. **4.** To control, as a hypnotized person, by the exercise of will. **5.** *Archaic* To have a wish for. — *v.i.* **6.** To exercise the will. [OE *willa*] — **will′a·ble** *adj.*

will² (wil) *v.* Present: *3rd person sing.*: **will**; *Archaic 2nd person sing.* **wilt**; past: **would**; *Archaic 2nd person sing.* **would·est** or **wouldst.** An auxiliary verb used with the infinitive without *to*, or elliptically without the infinitive, to express: **1.** Futurity: They *will* arrive by dark. **2.** Willingness or disposition: Why *will* you not tell the truth? **3.** Capability or capacity: The ship *will* survive any storm. **4.** Custom or habit: He *will* sit for hours and brood. **5.** *Informal* Probability or inference: I expect this *will* be the main street. ◆ See usage note under SHALL. — *v.t. & v.i.* To wish or have a wish; desire: As you *will*. [OE *willan*]

willed (wild) *adj.* Having a will, esp. one of a given character: usu. in combination: *self-willed*.

will·ful (wil′fəl) *adj.* **1.** Bent on having one's own way; headstrong. **2.** Resulting from the exercise of one's own will; voluntary; intentional. Also, *esp. Brit., wilful.* [Cf. OE *wilfullīce* willfully] — **will′ful·ly** *adv.* — **will′ful·ness** *n.*

wil·lies (wil′ēz) *n.pl. Slang* Nervousness; jitters: with *the.* [? < WILLY-NILLY; with ref. to a state of indecision]

will·ing (wil′ing) *adj.* **1.** Having the mind favorably inclined or disposed. **2.** Answering to demand or requirement; compliant. **3.** Gladly proffered or done; hearty. **4.** Of or pertaining to the faculty or power of choice; volitional. — **will′ing·ly** *adv.* — **will′ing·ness** *n.*

will-o′-the-wisp (wil′ə-thə-wisp′) *n.* **1.** Ignis fatuus. **2.** Any elusive or deceptive object. — *adj.* Deceptive; fleeting; misleading. [Earlier *Will with the wisp*]

wil·low (wil′ō) *n.* **1.** Any of various shrubs and trees, having generally smooth branches and often long, slender, pliant, and sometimes pendent branchlets. **2.** The soft white wood of the willow. **3.** *Informal* Something made of willow wood, especially a baseball or cricket bat. — *adj.* Of or pertaining to the willow; made of willow wood. [OE *welig*] — **wil′low·ish** *adj.*

wil·low·y (wil′ō-ē) *adj.* **1.** Abounding in willows. **2.** Having supple grace of form or carriage.

will power Ability to control oneself; determination; strength or firmness of mind.

wil·ly-nil·ly (wil′ē-nil′ē) *adj.* Having no decisiveness; uncertain; irresolute. — *adv.* Willingly or unwillingly. [Earlier *will I, nill I* whether I will or not]

wilt¹ (wilt) *v.i.* **1.** To lose freshness; droop or become limp, as a flower that has been cut or that has not been watered. **2.** To lose energy and vitality; become faint or languid: We *wilted* under the hot sun. **3.** To lose courage or spirit; subside suddenly. — *v.t.* **4.** To cause to droop or wither. **5.** To cause to lose vitality and energy. — *n.* **1.** The act of wilting. **2.** Languor; faintness. **3.** *Bot.* Any of several plant diseases marked by a wilting of the leaves. [Prob. dial. var. of obs. *welk* to wither]

wilt² (wilt) Archaic second person singular, present tense of WILL²: used with *thou.*

Wil·ton (wil′tən) *n.* A kind of carpet having the loops of the pile cut, thus giving it a velvety texture. [after *Wilton*, England, where first made] Also **Wilton carpet, Wilton rug.**

Wilt·shire (wilt′shir) *n.* One of a breed of long-horned sheep. [after *Wiltshire*, England, where raised]

Wiltshire cheese A variety of Cheddar cheese.

wi·ly (wī′lē) *adj.* **·li·er, ·li·est** Full of or characterized by wiles; sly; cunning. — **wi′li·ly** *adv.* — **wi′li·ness** *n.*

wim·ble (wim′bəl) *n.* Anything that bores a hole, esp. if turned by hand, as a brace and bit. — *v.t.* **·bled, ·bling** To bore or pierce, as with a wimble. [< AF, OF *quimbel* < MLG *wiemel*]

wim·ple (wim′pəl) *n.* **1.** A cloth, as of linen or silk, wrapped in folds around the neck close under the chin and over the head, exposing only the face, formerly worn as a protection by women outdoors, and still by nuns. **2.** *Scot.* A fold; plait; also, a curve; a winding turn, as in a river or road. — *v.* **·pled, ·pling** *v.t.* **1.** To cover or clothe with a wimple; veil. **2.** To make or fold into plaits, as a veil. **3.** To cause to move with slight undulations; ripple. — *v.i.* **4.** To lie in plaits or folds. **5.** To ripple. [OE *wimpel*]

win (win) *v.* **won, won, win·ning** *v.i.* **1.** To gain a victory; prevail, as in a contest. **2.** To succeed in an effort or endeavor. **3.** To succeed in reaching or attaining a specified end or condition; get: often with *across, over, through,* etc.: The fleet *won* through the storm. — *v.t.* **4.** To be successful in; gain victory in: to *win* an argument. **5.** To gain in competition or contest: to *win* the blue ribbon. **6.** To gain by effort, persistence, etc.: to *win* fame. **7.** To obtain the good will or favor of: often with *over.* **8.** To secure the love of; gain in marriage: He wooed and *won* her. **9.** To succeed in reaching; attain. **10.** To make (one's way), esp. with effort. **11.** To capture; take possession of. **12.** To earn or procure, as a living. — **to win out** *Informal* To succeed to the fullest extent. — *n.* **1.** A victory; success. **2.** Profit; winnings. **3.** The first position in a race. [OE *winnan* to contend]

wince (wins) *v.i.* **winced, winc·ing** To shrink back or start aside, as from a blow or pain; flinch. — *n.* The act of wincing. [< AF *wenchier*] — **winc′er** *n.*

winch (winch) *n.* **1.** A windlass used for hoisting, as on a crane, having usu., one or more hand cranks geared to a drum. **2.** A crank with a handle, used to impart motion to a grindstone or the like. [OE *wince*] — **winch′er** *n.*

Win·ches·ter (win′ches·tər) *n.* Originally, a repeating rifle, first produced in 1866: now a trade name applied to other firearms. [after Oliver F. *Winchester*, 1810–80, U.S. industrialist]

wind¹ (wind; *for n., also poetic* wīnd) *n.* **1.** Any movement of air, esp., a natural movement. **2.** Any powerful or destructive wind; a tornado; hurricane. **3.** Air in motion by artificial means. **4.** Air pervaded by a scent: The deer got *wind* of the hunter. **5.** A suggestion or intimation: to get *wind* of a plot. **6.** The power of breathing; breath. **7.** Idle chatter; also, vanity. **8.** *pl.* The wind instruments of an orchestra. **9.** The gaseous product of indigestion; flatulence. — **in the wind** Impending; astir; afoot. — **in the wind's eye** Directly opposed to the point from which the wind blows. — **to break wind** To expel gas through the anus. — **to get wind of** To receive a hint of. — **to have in the wind** To be on the track or scent of. — **to have the wind up** To be apprehensive or alarmed. — **to sail close to the wind 1.** To sail in a direction as near as possible to that from which the wind blows. **2.** To come near to the limit, as of a danger line. **3.** To live economically. — *v.t.* **1.** To follow by scent; to catch a scent of on the wind. **2.** To exhaust the breath of, as by running. **3.** To allow to recover breath by resting. **4.** To expose to the wind, as in ventilating. [OE]

wind² (wīnd) *v.* **wound** (*Rare* wind·ed), **wind·ing** *v.t.* **1.** To coil (thread, rope, etc.) around some object or fixed core; twine; wreathe. **2.** To cover with something by coiling or wrapping: to *wind* a spool with thread. **3.** To renew the motion of, as a clock, by coiling a spring, etc. **4.** To cause to turn and twist. **5.** To make (one's way) by a twisting course. **6.** To introduce carefully or deviously; insinuate: He *wound* himself into my confidence. **7.** To raise or hoist, as by means of a capstan or windlass. — *v.i.* **8.** To move in a twisting course; meander. **9.** To coil or twine about some central object or core. **10.** To move in a circular or spiral course. **11.** To proceed carefully, subtly, or deviously. — **to wind up 1.** To coil or wind round and round. **2.** To excite; arouse. **3.** To bring to conclusion or settlement: He *wound up* his affairs. **4.** In baseball, to swing the arm preparatory to pitching. **5.** To hoist. — *n.* The act of winding, or the condition of being wound; a winding, turn, or twist. [OE *windan*] — **wind′a·ble** *adj.* — **wind′er** *n.*

wind³ (wīnd, wind) *v.t.* **wind·ed** or **wound, wind·ing 1.** To blow, as a horn; sound. **2.** To give (a call or signal), as with a horn. [< WIND¹]

wind·age (win′dij) *n.* **1.** The rush of air caused by the rapid passage of an object, as a projectile or a railway train. **2.** Deflection of an object, as a bullet, from its natural course due to wind pressure. **3.** *Naut.* The surface offered to the wind by a vessel.

wind·bag (wind′bag′) *n. Informal* A wordy talker.

wind-blown (wind′blōn′) *adj.* **1.** Blown by the wind. **2.** Bobbed and brushed forward: said of a woman's hair.

wind-borne (wind′bôrn′, -bōrn′) *adj.* Carried or transported by the wind, as pollen.

wind·break (wind′brāk′) *n.* Something, as a hedge or fence, that protects from or breaks the force of the wind.

Wind·break·er (wind′brā′kər) *n.* A sports jacket with fitted waistband: a trade name. Also **wind′break′er.**

wind-bro·ken (wind′brō′kən) *adj.* Asthmatic; broken-winded: said of a horse.

wind·ed (win′did) *adj.* Breathless, as from exercise.

wind·fall (wind′fôl′) *n.* **1.** A piece of unexpected good fortune; esp., a sudden and substantial financial profit. **2.** Something, as ripening fruit, brought down by the wind.

wind·flaw (wind′flô) *n.* A sharp gust of wind.

wind·flow·er (wind′flou′ər) *n.* The anemone. [Trans. of Gk. *anemōnē* anemone < *anemos* the wind]

wind gauge A scale on a gunsight to allow for windage (def. 2). Also **wind gage.**

wind·hov·er (wind′huv′ər) *n. Brit.* The kestrel, a bird.

wind·ing (wīn′ding) *n.* **1.** The act or condition of one who or that which winds; a spiral turning or coiling. **2.** A bend or turn, or a series of them. — *adj.* **1.** Turning spirally about an axis or core. **2.** Having bends or lateral turns. — **wind′ing·ly** *adv.*

winding sheet (wīn′ding) The sheet that wraps a corpse.

wind instrument (wind) A musical instrument whose sounds are produced by vibrations of air injected by the lungs or by bellows. Compare ORGAN, WOODWINDS, etc.

wind·jam·mer (wind′jam′ər) *n.* **1.** *Naut.* A merchant sailing vessel. **2.** A member of its crew.

wind·lass (wind′ləs) *n.* Any of several devices for hauling or lifting, esp. one consisting of a drum or barrel on which the hoisting rope winds, and turned by means of cranking. — *v.t. & v.i.* To raise or haul with a windlass. [< ME < ON < *vinda* wind + *ass* beam]

wind·mill (wind′mil′) *n.* **1.** A mill that operates by the action of the wind against adjustable slats, wings, or sails attached to a horizontal axis and that transmit motion to a pump, millstone, or the like. **2.** An imaginary wrong, evil, or foe: usu. in the phrase **to fight** (or **tilt at**) **windmills**, in allusion to Don Quixote's combat with windmills, which he mistook for giants. [< WIND¹ + MILL¹]

PRONUNCIATION KEY: add, āce, câre, pälm; end, ēven; it, īce; odd, ōpen, ôrder; tŏŏk, pōōl; up, bûrn; ə = a in *above*, e in *sicken*, i in *flexible*, o in *melon*, u in *focus*; yōō = u in *fuse*; oil; pout; check; go; ring; thin; this; zh, vision. For å, œ, ü, kh, ṅ, see inside front cover.

win·dow (win'dō) *n.* **1.** An opening in the wall of a building to admit light and air, commonly equipped with movable sashes that enclose one or more panes of glass. **2.** A sash. **3.** A windowpane. **4.** Anything resembling or suggesting a window. — *v.t.* To provide with a window or windows. [< ON < *vindr* wind + *auga* eye]

window box A box, generally long and narrow, along a window ledge or sill, for growing plants.

win·dow-dress·ing (win'dō-dres'ing) *n.* **1.** The act or art of arranging merchandise attractively in store windows; also, the goods so displayed. **2.** An appearance, statement, etc., that gives an unduly favorable impression of reality. — **win'dow-dress'er** *n.*

win·dow-pane (win'dō-pān') *n.* A single sheet of glass for a window. Also **window pane.**

window seat A seat in the recess of a window.

window shade A flexible shade or screen, usu., mounted on a spring roller, used to regulate light at a window.

win·dow-shop (win'dō-shop') *v.i.* -**shopped, -shop·ping** To look at goods shown in store windows without buying them. — **win'dow-shop'per** *n.*

wind·pipe (wind'pīp') *n.* The trachea.

wind·row (wind'rō') *n.* **1.** A long ridge or pile of hay or grain raked together preparatory to building into cocks. **2.** A row of Indian corn made by setting two rows together. **3.** A wind-swept line of dust, surf, leaves, etc. — *v.t.* To rake or shape into a windrow. — **wind'row'er** *n.*

wind·shield (wind'shēld') *n.* A transparent screen, usu. of glass, attached in front of the occupants of an automobile as protection against wind and weather.

wind·sock (wind'sok') *n. Meteorol.* A large conical bag open at both ends, mounted on a pivot and indicating the direction of wind by the current of air that blows through it. Also **wind sleeve.**

Wind·sor chair (win'zər) A wooden chair, common in the 18th century, typically with a spindle back, slanting legs, and a flat or slightly depressed seat.

Windsor tie A wide, soft necktie knotted loosely in a double bow, usu. of black silk cut on the bias.

wind·storm (wind'stôrm') *n.* A violent wind, usu. with little or no precipitation.

wind tunnel *Aeron.* A large cylindrical structure in which the aerodynamic properties of airplane models, airfoils, etc., can be observed under the effects of artificially produced winds of varying velocities.

wind·up (wīnd'up') *n.* **1.** The act of concluding or closing. **2.** A final act or part; conclusion. **3.** In baseball, the swing of the arm preparatory to pitching the ball.

wind·ward (wind'wərd) *adj.* **1.** Of the direction from which the wind is blowing. **2.** Being on the side exposed to the wind. — *n.* The direction from which the wind blows. — *adv.* In the direction from which the wind blows. Opposed to *leeward.*

wind·y (win'dē) *adj.* **wind·i·er, wind·i·est** **1.** Of, consisting of, or abounding in wind; stormy; tempestuous. **2.** Exposed to the wind; wind-swept. **3.** Suggestive of wind; boisterous; swift. **4.** Producing, due to, or troubled with gas in the stomach or intestines; flatulent. **5.** Bombastic; pompous. [OE *windig*] — **wind'i·ly** *adv.* — **wind'i·ness** *n.*

wine (wīn) *n.* **1.** The fermented juice of the grape, commonly used as a beverage and in cooking. **2.** The fermented juice of some other fruit as the elderberry, or of a plant. **3.** A dark purplish red, the color of certain wines. — *v.* **wined, win·ing** *v.t.* **1.** To entertain with wine. — *v.i.* **2.** To drink wine. [OE < L *vinum*]

wine·bib·bing (wīn'bib'ing) *adj.* Addicted to excessive drinking of wine. — *n.* The habitual, excessive drinking of wine. — **wine'bib'ber** *n.*

wine cellar **1.** A storage place for wines; also, the wines stored. **2.** Any stock of wines.

wine-col·ored (wīn'kul'ərd) *adj.* Having the color of certain red wines; dark purplish red.

wine·glass (wīn'glas', -gläs') *n.* A small goblet for drinking wine.

wine·grow·er (wīn'grō'ər) *n.* One who cultivates a vineyard and makes wine. — **wine'grow'ing** *adj. & n.*

wine·press (wīn'pres') *n.* An apparatus or a place where the juice of grapes is expressed. Also **wine'press'er.**

win·er·y (wī'nər·ē) *n. pl.* **·er·ies** **1.** An establishment for making wine. **2.** A room for fining and storing wines.

Wine·sap (wīn'sap) *n.* A U.S. variety of red winter apple.

wine-skin (wīn'skin') *n.* The skin of a domestic quadruped kept as entire as possible and made into a tight bag for containing wine, much used in the Orient.

wing (wing) *n.* **1.** An organ of flight; esp., one of the anterior movable pair of appendages of a bird or bat, homologous with the forelimbs of vertebrates but adapted for flight. **2.** An analogous organ in insects and some other animals. **3.** Anything resembling or suggestive of a wing, as in form or function. **4.** Flight or passage by or as by wings; also, the means or act of flying: to take *wing.* **5.** Something

regarded as conferring the power of swift motion or flight: on *wings* of song. **6.** Either of two extremist groups in a political or other organization: the left *wing.* **7.** *Archit.* A part attached to a side; esp., an extension of a building. **8.** *Aeron.* One of the main sustaining surfaces of an airplane. **9.** One of the sides of a stage; also, a piece of scenery for the side. **10.** *Mil.* Either division of a military force on either side of the center. **11.** An analogous formation in certain sports, as football. **12.** A side section of something that shuts or folds, as a screen, etc. **13.** A tactical unit of the U.S. Air Force, larger than a group. **14.** *Slang* An arm; esp., in baseball. **15.** One of the pectoral fins of a flying fish. **16.** *Anat.* An ala: a *wing* of the nose. **17.** *Bot.* Any thin membranous or foliaceous expansion of an organ, as of certain stems, seeds, etc. — **Syn.** See FACTION. — **on** (or **upon**) **the wing 1.** In flight. **2.** Departing; also, journeying. — **to take wing** To fly away. — **under one's wing** Under one's protection. — *v.t.* **1.** To pass over or through in flight. **2.** To accomplish by flying: the bird *winged* its way south. **3.** To enable to fly. **4.** To cause to go swiftly; speed. **5.** To transport by flight. **6.** To provide with wings for flight. **7.** To supply with a wing body or part. **8.** To wound (a bird) in a wing. **9.** To disable by a minor wound. — *v.i.* **10.** To fly; soar. [< ON *vængr*] — **wing'less** *adj.*

wing chair A large armchair, upholstered throughout, with high back and side pieces designed as protection from drafts.

wing commander In the Royal, Royal Canadian, and other Commonwealth air forces, a commissioned officer ranking next below group captain. See table at GRADE.

winged (wingd; *for defs. 1, 2, & 3, also poetic* wing'id) *adj.* **1.** Having wings. **2.** Passing swiftly; soaring; lofty; rapt. **3.** Alive with creatures having wings. **4.** *Informal* Wounded or disabled in or as in the wing or arm.

wing·spread (wing'spred') *n.* The distance between the tips of the fully extended wings of a bird, insect, or airplane.

wink (wingk) *v.i.* **1.** To close and open the eye or eyelids quickly. **2.** To draw the eyelids of one eye together, as in conveying a hint or making a sign. **3.** To pretend not to see: usu. with *at.* **4.** To emit fitful gleams; twinkle. — *v.t.* **5.** To close and open (the eye or eyelids) quickly. **6.** To move, force, etc., by winking: with *away, off,* etc. **7.** To signify or express by winking. — *n.* **1.** The act of winking. **2.** The time necessary for a wink. **3.** A twinkle; gleam. **4.** A hint conveyed by winking. — **forty winks** *Informal* A short nap. [OE *wincian* to close the eyes]

wink·er (wing'kər) *n.* **1.** One who winks. **2.** A blinder for a horse.

win·ner (win'ər) *n.* One who or that which wins.

win·ning (win'ing) *adj.* **1.** Successful in achievement, esp., in competition. **2.** Charming; attractive; winsome. — *n.* **1.** The act of one who wins. **2.** *Usu. pl.* That which is won; esp., money won in gambling. — **win'ning·ly** *adv.* — **win'ning·ness** *n.*

win·now (win'ō) *v.t.* **1.** To separate (grain, etc.) from the chaff by means of wind or a current of air. **2.** To blow away (the chaff) thus. **3.** To examine; analyse minutely; sift. **4.** To select or eliminate; distinguish; sort: often with *out.* **5.** To blow upon; cause to flutter. **6.** To beat or fan (the air) with the wings. **7.** To scatter by blowing; disperse. — *v.i.* **8.** To separate grain from chaff. **9.** To fly; flap. — *n.* **1.** Any device used in winnowing grain. **2.** The act of winnowing; also, a vibrating motion caused by a current of air. [OE < *wind* the wind] — **win'now·er** *n.*

win·some (win'səm) *adj.* Having a winning appearance or manner; pleasing; attractive. [OE < *wyn* joy] — **win'some·ly** *adv.* — **win'some·ness** *n.*

win·ter (win'tər) *n.* **1.** The coldest season of the year, occurring between autumn and spring. ◆ Collateral adjectives: *hibernal.* **2.** A period of time marked by lack of life, coldness, or cheerlessness. **3.** *Chiefly Poetic* A year of life: a man of ninety *winters.* — *v.i.* **1.** To pass the winter. — *v.t.* **2.** To care for, feed, or protect during the winter: to *winter* animals. — *adj.* **1.** Of or taking place in winter; hibernal. **2.** Suitable to or characteristic of winter. [OE] — **win'ter·er** *n.* — **win'ter·less** *adj.*

win·ter·green (win'tər·grēn) *n.* **1.** A small evergreen plant of North America, bearing a cluster of bell-shaped flowers, and aromatic oval leaves that yield a colorless volatile oil (**oil of wintergreen**), used as a flavor. **2.** Any of various low evergreen herbs.

win·ter·ize (win'tə·rīz) *v.t.* **·ized, ·iz·ing** To prepare or equip (engines, etc.) for winter.

win·ter·kill (win'tər·kil') *v.t. & v.i.* To die or kill by exposure to extreme cold: said of plants and grains.

win·try (win'trē) *adj.* **·tri·er, ·tri·est** Belonging to winter; cold; frosty. Also **win'ter·y** (-tər·ē). [OE *wintrig*] — **win'tri·ly** (-trə·lē) *adv.* — **win'tri·ness** *n.*

win·y (wī'nē) *adj.* **win·i·er, win·i·est** Having the taste or qualities of wine.

wipe (wīp) *v.t.* **wiped, wip·ing** **1.** To subject to slight friction or rubbing, usu. with some soft, absorbent material. **2.**

To remove by rubbing lightly; brush: usu. with *away* or *off*. **3.** To move, apply, or draw for the purpose of wiping: He *wiped* his hand across his brow. — **to wipe out** To remove or destroy utterly. — *n.* **1.** The act of wiping or rubbing. **2.** *Slang* A blow; a swipe. **3.** *Slang* A handkerchief. **4.** *Slang* A jeer. [OE *wīpian*] — **wip'er** *n.*

wire (wīr) *n.* **1.** A slender rod, strand, or thread of ductile metal. **2.** Something made of wire, as a fence, a snare, etc. **3.** A telegraph or telephone cable. **4.** The telegraph system as a means of communication. **5.** A telegram. **6.** *pl.* A secret means of exerting influence. — **under the wire** Just in time or barely within the limits. — **under wire** Fenced. — *v.* **wired, wir·ing** *v.t.* **1.** To fasten with wire. **2.** To furnish or equip with wiring. **3.** To transmit or send by electric telegraph: to *wire* an order. **4.** To send a telegram to. **5.** To place on wire, as beads. **6.** To catch, as a rabbit, with a snare of wire. — *v.i.* **7.** To telegraph. [OE *wīr*]

wire-draw (wīr'drô') *v.t.* **-drew, -drawn, -draw·ing 1.** To draw, as a metal rod, through a series of holes of diminishing diameter to produce a wire. **2.** To treat (a subject) with excessive subtlety or overrefinement. — **wire'-draw'er** *n.*

wire gauge 1. A gauge for measuring the diameter of wire, usu. a round plate with calibrated numbered slots on its periphery, or a long graduated plate with a slot of diminishing width. **2.** A standard system of sizes for wire.

wire-haired terrier (wīr'hârd') A fox terrier having a wiry coat. Also **wire'hair'** (-hâr').

wire·less (wīr'lis) *adj.* **1.** Having no wire or wires. **2.** *Brit.* Radio. — *n.* **1.** The wireless telegraph or telephone system, or a message transmitted by either. **2.** *Brit.* Radio. — *v.t. & v.i. Brit.* To communicate (with) by wireless telegraphy.

wireless telegraphy Telegraphy without wires, the message being transmitted through space by electromagnetic waves.

wireless telephony The transmission and reception of vocal messages by radio.

Wire·pho·to (wīr'fō'tō) *n. pl.* **-tos** An apparatus and method for transmitting and receiving photographs by wire: a trade name. Also **wire'pho'to.**

wire·pull·er (wīr'pŏŏl'ər) *n.* **1.** One who pulls wires, as of a puppet. **2.** One who uses secret means to control others or gain his own ends; an intriguer. — **wire'pull'ing** *n.*

wire recorder *Electronics* A device for recording sounds by electromagnetic registration on a fine moving wire, the impulses being reconverted to sound as the magnetized wire is passed through a receiver.

wire service A news agency that collects and distributes news to subscribing newspapers, radio stations, etc.

wire-spun (wīr'spun') *adj.* **1.** Drawn out to form a wire. **2.** Spun or drawn out too fine; overrefined.

wire-tap (wīr'tap') *v.* **-tapped, -tap·ping** *v.t.* **1.** To intercept (information) by means of wiretapping. — *v.i.* **2.** To engage in wiretapping. — *n.* Wiretapping. [Back formation < WIRETAPPING] — **wire'tap'per** *n.*

wire·tap·ping (wīr'tap'ing) *n.* The act, process, or practice of tapping telephone or telegraph wires for the purpose of secretly securing information: also called *wiretap.*

wire·work (wīr'wûrk) *n.* **1.** Small articles made of wire cloth. **2.** Wire fabrics in general.

wir·ing (wīr'ing) *n.* An entire system of wire installed for the distribution of electric power.

wir·y (wīr'ē) *adj.* **wir·i·er, wir·i·est 1.** Having great resisting power; thin, but tough and sinewy: said of persons. **2.** Like wire; stiff. — **wir'i·ly** *adv.* — **wir'i·ness** *n.*

wis·dom (wiz'dəm) *n.* **1.** The power of true and right discernment; also, conformity to the course of action dictated by such discernment. **2.** Good practical judgment; common sense. **3.** A high degree of knowledge; learning. **4.** A wise saying. [OE *wīsdōm* < *wīs* wise]

Wisdom of Solomon A book of the Old Testament Apocrypha, consisting of a hymn in praise of wisdom, ascribed by tradition to Solomon.

wisdom tooth The last molar tooth on either side of the upper and lower jaws in man, usu. appearing between the 17th and 22d year. For illus. see TOOTH. — **to cut one's wisdom teeth** To acquire mature judgment.

wise¹ (wīz) *adj.* **wis·er, wis·est 1.** Possessed of wisdom; having sound judgment. **2.** Sagacious; shrewd. **3.** Marked by wisdom; sensible. **4.** Having great learning; erudite. **5.** *Informal* Aware of; onto: *wise* to his motives. **6.** *U.S. Slang* Arrogant or sarcastic in manner; also, impudent. — **to get wise** *Slang* To know the true facts. — *v.t.* **wised, wis·ing** *Slang* To make cognizant of; inform. — **to wise up** *Slang* To make or become aware, informed, or sophisticated. [OE *wīs*] — **wise'ly** *adv.* — **wise'ness** *n.*

wise² (wīz) *n.* Way of doing; manner; method: chiefly in the phrases **in any wise, in no wise,** etc. [OE *wīse* manner]

-wise *suffix of adverbs* In a (specified) way or manner: *no-*

wise, likewise: often equivalent to *-ways.* [OE *wīse* manner]

◆ The suffix *-wise,* long considered archaic, has recently come back into fashion, and is now freely added to nouns, with the general meaning "with reference to": *Weather-wise,* it will probably snow. Such compounds often add no further information to a statement, and should be used with discretion.

wise·a·cre (wīz'ā'kər) *n.* **1.** One who affects great wisdom. **2.** A wise man; sage. [< MDu. *wijsseggher* soothsayer]

wise·crack (wīz'krak') *Slang n.* A smart or supercilious remark. — *v.i.* To utter a wisecrack. — **wise'crack'er** *n.*

wish (wish) *n.* **1.** A desire or longing, usu. for some definite thing. **2.** An expression of such a desire; petition. **3.** Something wished for. — *v.t.* **1.** To have a desire or longing for; want: We *wish* to be sure. **2.** To desire a specified condition or state for (a person or thing): I *wish* this day were over. **3.** To invoke upon or for someone: I *wished* him good luck. **4.** To bid: to *wish* someone good morning. **5.** To request or entreat; also, to command: I *wish* you would be quiet. — *v.i.* **6.** To have or feel a desire; yearn; long: usu. with *for.* **7.** To make or express a wish. — **to wish on** To impose (something or someone) on a person. [OE *wȳscan*]

wish·bone (wish'bōn') *n.* The forked bone formed by the united clavicles in many birds. [from the old belief that when pulled apart by two persons, each making a wish, the one who gets the longer part will have his wish fulfilled]

wish·ful (wish'fəl) *adj.* Having a wish or desire; full of longing. — **wish'ful·ly** *adv.* — **wish'ful·ness** *n.*

wishful thinking Thinking characterized by a conscious or unconscious attempt to impose upon reality conditions that, if true, would make it more pleasant or tolerable.

wish·y-wash·y (wish'ē-wosh'ē, -wôsh'ē) *adj. Informal* **1.** Thin; diluted, as liquor. **2.** Lacking character or resolution; indecisive; weak.

wisp (wisp) *n.* **1.** A small bunch, as of hay, straw, or hair. **2.** A small bit; a mere indication: a *wisp* of vapor. **3.** Will-o'-the-wisp. — *v.t.* **1.** To dress, brush, or groom with a wisp or whisk. **2.** To fold and lightly twist into a wisp or wisplike form; crumple. [ME *wisp, wips*] — **wisp'y** *adj.*

wisp·ish (wis'pish) *adj.* Like or having the nature of a wisp.

wist (wist) Past tense and past participle of WIT².

wis·te·ri·a (wis-tir'ē-ə) *n.* Any of various woody twining shrubs of the bean family, with clusters of blue, purple, or white flowers. Also **wis·tar'i·a** (-târ'ē-ə). [after Caspar *Wistar,* 1761–1818, U.S. anatomist]

wist·ful (wist'fəl) *adj.* **1.** Wishful; longing. **2.** Musing; pensive. [Appar. < obs. *wistly* intently; infl. in form by WISHFUL] — **wist'ful·ly** *adv.* — **wist'ful·ness** *n.*

wit¹ (wit) *n.* **1.** The power of knowing or perceiving; intelligence; ingenuity. **2.** The power or faculty of rapid and accurate observation; the power of comprehending and judging. **3.** *pl.* The faculties of perception and understanding: to use one's *wits.* **4.** *pl.* The mental faculties with regard to their state of balance: out of her *wits.* **5.** The ready perception and happy expression of unexpected or amusing relations between apparently incongruous ideas. **6.** One who has a keen perception of the incongruous or ludicrous and makes skillful use of it in writing or speaking; also, a clever conversationalist. **7.** Significance; meaning. — **at one's wits' end** At the limit of one's devices and resources. [OE]

wit² (wit) *v.t. & v.i.* **wist, wit·ting** Present indicative: I **wot,** thou **wost,** he **wot,** we, you, they **wite(n)** *Archaic* To be or become aware (of); learn; know. — **to wit** That is to say; namely: used to introduce a detailed statement or explanation, especially in legal documents. [OE *witan* to know]

witch¹ (wich) *n.* **1.** A woman who practices sorcery; one having supernatural powers, esp. to work evil, and usu. by association with evil spirits or the devil. **2.** An ugly, malignant old woman; a hag. **3.** A bewitching or fascinating woman or girl. — *v.t.* **1.** To work an evil spell upon. **2.** To effect by witchcraft. **3.** To fascinate or bewitch; enchant. [OE *wicce* witch, fem. of *wicca* wizard]

witch² (wich) *n.* The wych-elm. [OE < *wīcan* to yield]

witch·craft (wich'kraft', -kräft') *n.* **1.** The practices or powers of witches or wizards, esp. when regarded as due to dealings with evil spirits or the devil: also called *black magic.* **2.** An instance of such practices. **3.** Extraordinary influence or fascination; witchery.

witch doctor 1. Among certain primitive peoples of Africa, a medicine man skilled in detecting witches and counteracting evil spells. **2.** Any medicine man or magician. **3.** One who professes to heal or cure by sorcery; a hex.

witch-elm (wich'elm') See WYCH-ELM.

witch·er·y (wich'ər·ē) *n. pl.* **·er·ies 1.** Witchcraft. **2.** Power to charm; fascination.

witches' Sabbath In medieval folklore, a midnight orgy of demons and witches, that in German folklore is believed to occur on Walpurgis Night.

---

witch hazel 1. A shrub of the U.S. and Canada, with several branching crooked trunks and small yellow flowers. 2. An ointment and extract derived from the bark and dried leaves of this shrub. Also *wychhazel*. [< WITCH² + HAZEL]

witch hunt *Informal* An investigation of persons ostensibly to uncover subversive activities, but intended for ulterior motives, such as harassing political opposition. — **witch·hunt·ing** (wich′hun′ting) *adj. & n.* — **witch·hunt·er** *n.*

witch·ing (wich′ing) *adj.* Having power to enchant; weird; fascinating. — *n.* Witchcraft; sorcery. — **witch′ing·ly** *adv.*

with (with, with) *prep.* 1. In the company of; as a member or associate of. 2. Next to; beside: Walk *with* me. 3. Having; bearing: a hat *with* a feather. 4. Characterized or marked by: the house *with* green shutters. 5. In a manner characterized by; exhibiting: to dance *with* grace. 6 Among: counted *with* the others. 7. During; in the course of: We forget *with* time. 8. From; so as to be separated from: to dispense *with* luxury. 9. Against: to struggle *with* an adversary. 10. In the opinion of: That is all right *with* me. 11. Because of; as a consequence of: faint *with* hunger. 12. In possession of: Leave the key *with* the janitor. 13. Using; by means or aid of: to write *with* a pencil. 14. By adding or having as a material or quality: trimmed *with* lace; endowed *with* beauty. 15. Under the influence of: confused *with* drink. 16. In spite of: *With* all his money, he could not buy health. 17. At the same time as: to go to bed *with* the chickens. 18. In the same direction as: to drift *with* the crowd. 19. In regard to; in the case of: I am angry *with* them. 20. Onto; to: Join this tube *with* that one. 21. In proportion to: His fame grew *with* his deeds. 22. In support of: He voted *with* the Left. 23. Of the same opinion as: I'm *with* you there! 24. Compared to; contrasted to: Consider this book *with* that one. 25. Immediately after: *With* that, he slammed the door. 26. Having received or been granted: *With* your consent I'll go. [OE]

with- *prefix* 1. Against: *withstand.* 2. Back; away: *withhold.* [OE *with-* < *with* against]

with·al (with-ôl′, with-) *Archaic adv.* With the rest; in addition. — *prep.* With: intensive form used after its object: a bow to shoot *withal.* [ME < *with* + *alle* all]

with·draw (with-drô′, with-) *v.* **·drew, ·drawn, ·draw·ing** *v.t.* 1. To draw or take away; remove. 2. To take back, as an assertion or a promise. 3. To keep or abstract from use. — *v.i.* 4. To draw back; retire.

with·draw·al (with-drô′əl, with-) *n.* The act or process of withdrawing. Also **with·draw′ment** (-mənt).

withdrawing room 1. A room behind another room for retirement. 2. A drawing room.

with·drawn (with-drôn′, with-) *adj. Psychol.* Lacking in responsiveness, esp. emotional responsiveness.

withe (with, with, with) *n.* 1. A willowy, supple twig. 2. A band made of twisted flexible shoots, straw, or the like. — *v.t.* **withed, with·ing** To bind with withes. [OE *withthe*]

with·er (with′ər) *v.i.* 1. To become limp or dry, as a plant when cut down or deprived of moisture. 2. To waste, as flesh. 3. To droop or languish. — *v.i.* 4. To cause to become limp or dry. 5. To abash, as by a scornful glance. [Appar. var. of WEATHER, v.]

with·ers (with′ərz) *n.pl.* 1. The highest part of the back of the horse between the shoulder blades. 2. The similar part in some other animals, as the deer and ox. [OE *wither* against; so called because the horse opposes this part against the load he pulls]

with·hold (with-hōld′, with-) *v.* **·held, ·hold·ing** *v.t.* 1. To hold back; restrain. 2. To keep back; decline to grant. — *v.i.* 3. To refrain; forbear. — **with·hold′er** *n.*

withholding tax A part of an employee's wages or salary that is deducted as an installment on his income tax.

with·in (with-in′, with-) *adj.* 1. In the inner part; interiorly. 2. Inside the body, heart, or mind. 3. Indoors. — *prep.* 1. In the inner or interior parts or parts of; inside. 2. In the limits, range, or compass of (a specified time, space, or distance). 3. Not exceeding (a specified quantity): Live *within* your means. 4. In the reach, limit, or scope of: *within* my power. [OE < *with* with + *innan* in]

with-it (with′it) *adj. Slang* 1. In touch with modern ways; hip. 2. Lively and fashionably up-to-date. Also **with it.**

with·out (with-out′, with-) *prep.* 1. Not having, as the result of loss, privation, negation, etc.; lacking: They are *without* a home. 2. In the absence of: We must manage *without* help. 3. Free from: *without* fear. 4. At, on, or to the outside of. 5. Outside of or beyond the limits of: living *without* the pale of civilization. 6. With avoidance of: He listened *without* paying attention. — *adv.* 1. In or on the outer part. 2. Out of doors. [OE < *with* with + *ūtan* out]

with·stand (with-stand′, with-) *v.* **·stood, ·stand·ing** *v.t.* 1. To oppose with any force; resist successfully. — *v.i.* 2. To endure. [OE < *with-* against + *standan* to stand]

with·y (with′ē, with′ē) *adj.* Made of withes; flexible and tough. — *n.* *pl.* **with·ies** 1. A rope made of withes. 2. A flexible twig; withe. [OE *wīthig*]

wit·less (wit′lis) *adj.* Lacking in wit; foolish. [OE *witlēas*] — **wit′less·ly** *adv.* — **wit′less·ness** *n.*

wit·ling (wit′ling) *n.* One who considers himself a wit.

wit·ness (wit′nis) *n.* 1. A person who has seen or knows something, and is therefore competent to give evidence concerning it; a spectator. 2. That which serves as or furnishes evidence or proof. 3. *Law* a One who has knowledge of facts relating to a given cause and is subpoenaed to testify. b A person who has signed his name to an instrument executed by another in order that he may testify to the genuineness of the maker's signature. 4. An attestation to a fact or an event; testimony: usu. in the phrase **to bear witness.** — *v.t.* 1. To see or know by personal experience. 2. To furnish or serve as evidence of. 3. To give testimony to. 4. To be the site or scene of: This spot has *witnessed* many heinous crimes. 5. *Law* To see the execution of (an instrument) and subscribe to it for the purpose of establishing its authenticity. — *v.i.* 6. To give evidence; testify. [OE *witnes* knowledge, testimony] — **wit′ness·er** *n.*

witness stand The place in a courtroom from which a witness gives evidence.

wit·ted (wit′id) *adj.* 1. Having wit. 2. Having (a specified kind of) wit: used in combination: quick-*witted.*

wit·ti·cism (wit′ə-siz′əm) *n.* A witty saying. [< WITTY, on analogy with *criticism*; coined by Dryden]

wit·ting (wit′ing) *adj.* Done consciously, with knowledge and responsibility; deliberate. [< WIT²] — **wit′ting·ly** *adv.*

wit·ty (wit′ē) *adj.* **·ti·er, ·ti·est** 1. Given to making original or clever speeches; quick at repartee; humorous. 2. Displaying or full of wit. — **Syn.** see HUMOROUS. [OE *wittig* wise] — **wit′ti·ly** *adv.* — **wit′ti·ness** *n.*

wives (wīvz) Plural of WIFE.

wiz (wiz) *n. Slang* A wizard (def. 2). [Short for WIZARD]

wiz·ard (wiz′ərd) *n.* 1. A male witch; sorcerer. 2. *Informal* A very skillful or clever person: He's a *wizard* with machinery. — *adj.* 1. Having magical powers. 2. Fascinating; enchanting. [ME < OE *wis* wise]

wiz·ard·ry (wiz′ərd-rē) *n.* The practice or methods of a wizard.

wiz·en (wiz′ən) *v.t. & v.i.* To become or cause to become withered; shrivel. — *adj.* Wizened; shrunken; shriveled. [OE *wisnian* to dry up, wither]

wiz·ened (wiz′ənd) *adj.* Shrunken; withered; dried up.

woad (wōd) *n.* 1. An Old World herb of the mustard family. 2. The blue dyestuff obtained from its leaves. [OE *wād*] — **woad′ed** *adj.*

wob·ble (wob′əl) *v.* **·bled, ·bling** *v.i.* 1. To move or sway unsteadily, as a top while rotating at a low speed. 2. To show indecision or unsteadiness; waver; vacillate. — *v.t.* 3. To cause to wobble. — *n.* An unsteady motion, as that of unevenly balanced rotating bodies. Also spelled **wabble.** [? < LG *wabbeln*] — **wob′bler** *n.* — **wob′bling·ly** *adv.* — **wob′bly** *adj.*

wob·bly (wob′lē) *n. pl.* **·blies** *U.S. Slang* A member of the Industrial Workers of the World (IWW).

Wo·den (wōd′n) The Old English name for Odin, the chief Norse god. Also **Wo′dan.**

woe (wō) *n.* 1. Overwhelming sorrow; grief. 2. Heavy affliction or calamity; disaster. — *interj.* Alas! Also *Archaic* **wo.** [OE *wā* misery]

woe·be·gone (wō′bi-gôn′, -gon′) *adj.* Overcome with woe; mournful; sorrowful. Also **wo′be·gone′.**

woe·ful (wō′fəl) *adj.* 1. Accompanied by or causing woe; direful. 2. Expressive of sorrow; doleful. 3. Paltry; miserable; mean. — **woe′ful·ly** *adv.* — **woe′ful·ness** *n.*

wok (wok) *n.* A bowl-shaped pan used esp. in Chinese cooking. [< Cantonese]

woke (wōk) Past tense of WAKE¹.

wok·en (wō′kən) Dialectal and alternative British past participle of WAKE¹.

wold (wōld) *n.* An undulating tract of open upland; down or moor. [OE *wald* forest]

wolf (woolf) *n. pl.* **wolves** (woolvz) 1. Any of numerous carnivorous mammals related to the dog, especially the common European species or the timber wolf of North America. ◆ Collateral adjective: *lupine.* 2. Any ravenous, cruel, or rapacious person or thing. 3. *Slang* A man who habitually and aggressively flirts with women; a philanderer. — **to cry wolf** To give a false alarm. — **to keep the wolf from the door** To avert want or starvation. — *v.t.* To devour ravenously; gulp down: He *wolfed* his food. [OE *wulf*]

wolf·ber·ry (woolf′ber′ē) *n. pl.* **·ries** A shrub of the honeysuckle family, with pinkish flowers and white berries.

wolf·hound (woolf′hound′) *n.* Either of two breeds of large dogs, the Russian wolfhound (or borzoi) and the Irish wolfhound, originally trained to hunt and kill wolves.

wolf·ish (woolf′ish) *adj.* 1. Having the qualities of a wolf; rapacious; savage. 2. *Informal* Ravenously hungry. — **wolf′ish·ly** *adv.* — **wolf′ish·ness** *n.*

wolf·ram (wool′frəm) *n.* 1. Wolframite. 2. Tungsten. [< G, prob. < *wolf* wolf + *rahm* cream, soot]

wolf·ram·ite (wŏŏl'frəm·īt) *n.* A grayish black or brown mineral of iron and magnesium, an important source of tungsten. [< G < *wolfram* tungsten]

wolf's-bane (wŏŏlfs'bān') *n.* **1.** Aconite. **2.** A species of European arnica, a perennial herb, used as a lotion for bruises. [Trans. of NL *lycoctonum* < Gk. < *lykos* wolf + *kteinein* to kill]

wolv·er (wŏŏl'vər) *n.* One who hunts wolves.

wol·ver·ine (wŏŏl'və·rēn') *n.* A rapacious carnivore of northern forests, with stout body and limbs and bushy tail. Also **wol'ver·ene'**. [Dim. of WOLF]

Wolverine State Nickname of Michigan.

wolves (wŏŏlvz) Plural of WOLF.

wom·an (wŏŏm'ən) *n. pl.* **wom·en** (wim'in) **1.** An adult human female. **2.** The female part of the human race; women collectively. **3.** Womanly character; femininity: usu. with *the*. **4.** As applied to a man, one who is effeminate, timid, or weak. **5.** A female attendant or servant. **6.** A paramour or kept mistress. **7.** *Informal* A wife. — **the little woman** *U.S. Informal* One's wife. — *adj.* **1.** Feminine; characteristic of women. **2.** Female: a *woman* doctor. **3.** Affecting or pertaining to women. [OE < *wīf* wife + *mann* human being]

wom·an·hood (wŏŏm'ən·hŏŏd) *n.* **1.** The state of a woman or of womankind. **2.** Women collectively.

wom·an·ish (wŏŏm'ən·ish) *adj.* **1.** Characteristic of a woman; womanly. **2.** Effeminate; unmanly. — **wom'an·ish·ly** *adv.* — **wom'an·ish·ness** *n.*

wom·an·ize (wŏŏm'ən·īz) *v.* **·ized, ·iz·ing** *v.t.* To make effeminate or womanish.

wom·an·kind (wŏŏm'ən·kīnd') *n.* Women collectively.

wom·an·ly (wŏŏm'ən·lē) *adj.* Having the qualities natural, suited, or becoming to a woman; feminine. — *adv.* Like a woman. — **wom'an·li·ness** *n.*

womb (wŏŏm) *n.* **1.** The organ in which the young of higher mammals are developed; the uterus. **2.** The place where anything is engendered or brought into life. **3.** A cavity viewed as enclosing something. [OE *wamb* the belly]

wom·bat (wom'bat) *n.* An Australian nocturnal marsupial resembling a small bear. [< Australian]

wom·en (wim'in) Plural of WOMAN.

wom·en·folk (wim'in·fōk') *n.pl.* Women collectively. Also **wom'en·folks'**.

won (wun) Past tense and past participle of WIN.

won·der (wun'dər) *n.* **1.** A feeling of mingled surprise and curiosity; astonishment. **2.** That which causes wonder; a strange thing; a miracle. — *v.t.* **1.** To have a feeling of doubt and strong curiosity in regard to. — *v.i.* **2.** To be affected or filled with wonder; marvel. **3.** To be doubtful; want to know. [OE *wundor*] — **won'der·er** *n.* — **won'der·ing** *adj.* — **won'der·ing·ly** *adv.*

won·der·ful (wun'dər·fəl) *adj.* Of a nature to excite wonder; marvelous. — **won'der·ful·ly** *adv.* — **won'der·ful·ness** *n.*

won·der·land (wun'dər·land') *n.* A realm of fairy-tale romance or wonders.

won·der·ment (wun'dər·mənt) *n.* **1.** The emotion of wonder; surprise. **2.** Something wonderful; a marvel.

Wonder State Nickname for Arkansas.

won·der·strick·en (wun'dər·strik'ən) *adj.* Suddenly smitten with wonder or admiration. Also **won'der·struck'** (-struk').

won·der·work (wun'dər·wûrk') *n.* A work inspiring wonder. — **won'der·work'er** *n.* — **won'der·work'ing** *adj.*

won·drous (wun'drəs) *adj.* Wonderful; marvelous. — *adv.* Surprisingly. — **won'drous·ly** *adv.* — **won'drous·ness** *n.*

wont (wunt, wōnt) *adj.* Accustomed; used: He is *wont* to smoke after dinner. — *n.* Ordinary manner of doing or acting; habit. [OE pp. of *gewunian* to be accustomed]

won't (wōnt) Will not. [ME *woll not*]

wont·ed (wun'tid, wōn'-) *adj.* **1.** Commonly used or done; habitual. **2.** Habituated; accustomed. — **wont'ed·ness** *n.*

woo (wŏŏ) *v.t.* **1.** To seek the love or affection of, esp. in order to marry; court. **2.** To entreat earnestly; beg. **3.** To invite; seek. — *v.i.* **4.** To pay court. [OE *wōgian*]

wood¹ (wŏŏd) *n.* **1.** The hard, fibrous material beneath the bark of a tree or shrub. **2.** Lumber; timber; firewood. **3.** Often *pl.* A large and compact collection of trees; a forest; grove. **4.** Something made of wood. **5.** *pl.* A rural district; backwoods. — **out of the woods** Clear of difficulties; safe after peril. — *adj.* **1.** Made of wood. **2.** Made for using or holding wood. **3.** Living or growing in woods. — *v.t.* **1.** To furnish with wood for fuel. **2.** To plant with trees. — *v.i.* **3.** To take on a supply of wood. [OE *wudu*] — **wood'ed** *adj.* — **wood'less** *adj.*

wood alcohol Methanol.

wood·bine (wŏŏd'bīn) *n.* **1.** The common honeysuckle of Europe. **2.** The Virginia creeper. Also called *bine*: also **wood'bind** (-bīnd). [OE < *wudu* wood + *bindan* to bind]

wood·block (wŏŏd'blok') *n.* **1.** A block of wood prepared for engraving. **2.** A woodcut.

wood·chuck (wŏŏd'chuk') *n.* A marmot of eastern North America, having a chunky body and a brown, bristly coat: also called *ground hog*. [By folk etymology < Ojibwa *wejack*]

wood·cock (wŏŏd'kok') *n.* **1.** A small European game bird having the thighs entirely feathered. **2.** A related North American bird. [OE *wuducocc*]

wood·craft (wŏŏd'kraft', -kräft') *n.* **1.** Skill in things pertaining to woodland life, as hunting and trapping. **2.** Skill in woodwork or in constructing articles of wood. — **wood'crafts'man** (-krafts'mən, -kräfts'-) *n.*

wood·cut (wŏŏd'kut') *n.* **1.** An engraved block of wood. **2.** A print from such a block. Also called *woodblock*.

wood·cut·ter (wŏŏd'kut'ər) *n.* One who cuts or chops wood. — **wood'cut'ting** *n.*

wood·en (wŏŏd'n) *adj.* **1.** Made of wood. **2.** Like a block of wood; stupid; mechanical; stiff; awkward. **3.** Dull; spiritless. — **wood'en·ly** *adv.* — **wood'en·ness** *n.*

wood engraving 1. The art of cutting designs on wood for printing. **2.** A woodcut. — **wood engraver**

wood·en·head (wŏŏd'n·hed') *n. Informal* A stupid person; blockhead. — **wood'en·head'ed** *adj.*

wooden horse Trojan horse.

wood·en·ware (wŏŏd'n·wâr') *n.* Dishes, vessels, bowls, etc., made of wood.

wood·house (wŏŏd'hous') *n.* A house or shed for storing firewood: also called *woodshed*.

wood·land (wŏŏd'lənd; *for n., also* wŏŏd'land') *n.* Land occupied by or covered with woods or trees. — *adj.* Belonging to or dwelling in the woods. — **wood'land·er** *n.*

wood louse Any of numerous small terrestrial flat-bodied crustaceans commonly found under old logs.

wood·man (wŏŏd'mən) *n. pl.* **·men** (-mən) A woodsman.

wood·note (wŏŏd'nōt') *n.* A simple, artless, or natural song, as of a wild bird.

wood nymph A nymph of the forest; a dryad.

wood·peck·er (wŏŏd'pek'ər) *n.* Any of various birds having stiff tail feathers for climbing, strong claws, and a sharp, chisellike bill for drilling holes in the wood of trees, etc., in search of insects.

wood·pile (wŏŏd'pīl') *n.* A pile of wood, esp. of wood cut for burning.

wood pulp Wood reduced to pulp, used for making paper.

RED-HEADED WOODPECKER (To 9½ inches long)

woods·man (wŏŏdz'mən) *n. pl.* **·men** (-mən) **1.** A woodcutter; lumberman. **2.** A forester; also, a dweller in forests. **3.** A man skilled in woodcraft. **4.** A hunter of forest game. Also called *woodman*.

wood sorrel A herb having purple, rose, or white flowers.

woods·y (wŏŏd'zē) *adj.* **woods·i·er, woods·i·est** *Informal* Of, like, or dwelling in the woods.

wood tar A tar produced by the dry distillation of wood and containing turpentine, resins, and other hydrocarbons.

wood thrush A large woodland thrush of North America, noted for the vigor and sweetness of its song.

wood·turn·ing (wŏŏd'tûr'ning) *n.* The process or art of shaping blocks of wood on a lathe. — **wood'turn'er** *n.*

wood·winds (wŏŏd'windz') *n.pl. Music* Instruments in which a player's breath sets an air column into vibration by passing through a reed or striking a sharp edge, as oboes, bassoons, clarinets, flutes, etc. — **wood'wind'** *adj.*

wood·work (wŏŏd'wûrk') *n.* **1.** The wooden parts of any structure, esp. interior wooden parts, as moldings or doors. **2.** Work made of wood. — **wood'work'er** *n.* — **wood'work'ing** *n.*

wood·y (wŏŏd'ē) *adj.* **wood·i·er, wood·i·est** **1.** Of the nature of or containing wood. **2.** Of or like wood. **3.** Wooded; abounding with woods. — **wood'i·ness** *n.*

woof (wŏŏf) *n.* **1.** The weft; the threads carried back and forth across the fixed threads of the warp in a loom. **2.** The texture of a fabric. [OE < *on* on + *wefan* to weave]

woof·er (wŏŏf'ər) *n. Electronics* A loudspeaker used to reproduce low frequencies in high-fidelity sound equipment. [< WOOF, imit. of a dog's growl]

wool (wŏŏl) *n.* **1.** The soft, curly or crisped hair obtained from the fleece of sheep and some allied animals. **2.** The underfur of a furbearing animal. **3.** Material or garments made of wool. **4.** A substance resembling wool. — **all wool and a yard wide** One hundred percent genuine. — **to pull**

the wool over one's eyes To deceive one. — *adj.* Of or made of wool or woolen material. [OE *wull*]

wool-clip (wŏŏl′klip′) *n.* The amount of wool clipped from the sheep in one year.

wool-en (wŏŏl′ən) *adj.* 1. Made of wool; like wool. 2. Of wool or its manufacture. — *n.pl.* Woolen cloth or clothing. Also **wool′len.** [OE *wullen, wyllen*]

wool-gath-er-ing (wŏŏl′gath′ər-ing) *n.* Any trivial or purposeless employment; esp., idle reverie. — *adj.* Idly indulging in fancies. — **wool′gath′er-er** *n.*

wool-grow-er (wŏŏl′grō′ər) *n.* A person who raises sheep for the production of wool. — **wool′grow′ing** *adj.*

wool-ly (wŏŏl′ē) *adj.* **·li-er, ·li-est** 1. Made of, covered with, or resembling wool; wool-bearing. 2. Soft and vaporous; lacking clearness; fuzzy; blurry. 3. Having a growth of woollike hairs. 4. Rough and exciting: usu. in the phrase **wild and woolly.** — *n. pl.* **·lies** A garment made of wool; esp., underwear. Also *esp. U.S.* **wool′y.** — **wool′li-ness** *n.*

wool-sack (wŏŏl′sak′) *n.* 1. A sack of wool. 2. The chair of the lord chancellor in the English House of Lords, a cushion stuffed with wool. 3. The office of lord high chancellor.

wooz-y (wŏŏ′zē) *adj.* **wooz-i-er, wooz-i-est** *Slang* Befuddled, esp. with drink; dazed. [*Prob.* < *wooze*, var. of OOZE] — **wooz′i-ly** *adv.* — **wooz′i-ness** *n.*

Worces-ter-shire sauce (wŏŏs′tər-shir) A piquant sauce made from vinegar and many other ingredients. Also **Worcestershire, Worcester sauce.** [after *Worcester*, England where originally made]

word (wûrd) *n.* 1. A linguistic form that can meaningfully be spoken in isolation. 2. The letters or characters that stand for such a linguistic form. 3. A mere sequence of sounds or letters; vocable: *words* rather than ideas. 4. *Usu. pl.* Conversation; talk: a man of few *words.* 5. A brief remark. 6. A short and pithy saying. 7. A communication or message; information: Send him *word.* 8. A command, signal, or direction: Give the *word* to start. 9. A promise; avowed intention: a man of his *word.* 10. A watchword. 11. *pl.* Language used in anger, rebuke, or otherwise emotionally: They had *words.* — **by word of mouth** Orally. — **in a word** In short; briefly. — **the Word** The Scriptures. — **to be as good as one's word** To keep one's promise. — **to break one's word** To violate one's promise. — **to eat one's words** To retract something that one has said. — **to have a word with** To have a brief conversation with. — **to mince words** To be evasive; avoid coming to the point. — **to take one at his word** To understand or deal with one literally in accordance with his own statement. — **to take the words out of one's mouth** To say what one was just about to say. — *v.t.* To express in a word or words, esp. in selected words; phrase. [OE]

word-age (wûr′dij) *n.* Words collectively.

word-book (wûrd′bŏŏk′) *n.* 1. A collection of words; vocabulary; lexicon; dictionary. 2. An opera libretto.

word for word In the exact words; literally; verbatim.

word-i-ness (wûr′dē-nis) *n.* The use of excessive words.

word-ing (wûr′ding) *n.* The act or style of expressing in words; phraseology; also, words used; expression.

word-less (wûrd′lis) *adj.* Having no words; inarticulate; silent. — **word′less-ly** *adv.* — **word′less-ness** *n.*

word order The sequence or order of words in a phrase, clause, or sentence.

word play 1. Fencing with words; repartee. 2. Subtle discussion on words and their meaning. 3. Play on words.

word square An arrangement of letters in rectangular form, so that they form the same words in either horizontal or vertical lines.

```
FRET
REAR
EASE
TREE
```
WORD SQUARE

word-y (wûr′dē) *adj.* **word-i-er, word-i-est** 1. Of the nature of words; verbal. 2. Expressed in many words. 3. Given to the use of words; verbose; prolix. [OE *wordig*] — **word′i-ly** *adv.*

wore (wôr, wōr) Past tense of WEAR[1] and WEAR[2].

work (wûrk) *n.* 1. Continued exertion or activity, whether physical or mental, directed to some purpose or end; labor. 2. The acts, obligations, etc., that one does or undertakes in return for something of value, as money; esp., the activities by which one earns one's livelihood; occupation. 3. A job or position; employment: to look for *work.* 4. A place of employment: Is he at home or at *work?* 5. That upon which labor is expended; task. 6. Exhausting or unrewarding effort; toil. 7. The matter at hand; the business that remains to be done: Get to *work.* 8. That which is produced by or as by labor, as an engineering structure, a design produced by a needle, etc.; also, a product of mental labor, as a book or opera. 9. A feat or deed. 10. *pl.* (*usu. construed as sing.*) A manufacturing or other industrial establishment, including buildings and equipment: a gas *works.* 11. *pl.* Running gear or machinery, as of a watch. 12. Manner of working, or style of treatment; workmanship. 13. *pl. Slang* The whole of anything: the whole *works.* 14. *pl. Theol.* Moral duties considered as external acts, especially as meritorious. 15. *Physics* A transference of energy from one body to another resulting in the motion or displacement of the body acted upon, expressed as the product of the force and the amount of displacement in the line of its action. — **in the works** *Informal* In progress or in preparation. — **to give (someone) the works** *Slang* 1. To maul or kill. 2. To be severe with. — **to shoot the works** *Slang* To make a supreme effort; risk one's all in a single attempt. — *v.* **worked** (*Archaic* **wrought**), **work-ing** *v.i.* 1. To perform work; labor; toil. 2. To be employed in some trade or business. 3. To perform a function; operate: The machine *works* well. 4. To prove effective; succeed: His stratagem *worked.* 5. To move or progress gradually or with difficulty: He *worked* up in his profession. 6. To become as specified, as by gradual motion: The bolts *worked* loose. 7. To have some slight improper motion in functioning: The wheel *works* on the shaft. 8. To move from nervousness or agitation: His features *worked* with passion. 9. To undergo kneading, hammering, etc.; be shaped: Copper *works* easily. 10. To ferment. 11. *Naut.* To labor in a heavy sea so as to loosen seams and fastenings: said of a ship. — *v.t.* 12. To cause or bring about; accomplish: to *work* a miracle. 13. To direct the operation of: to *work* a machine. 14. To make or shape by toil or skill. 15. To prepare, as by manipulating, hammering, etc.: to *work* dough. 16. To decorate, as with embroidery or inlaid work. 17. To cause to be productive, as by toil: to *work* a mine. 18. To cause to do work: He *works* his employees too hard. 19. To cause to be as specified, usu. with effort: We *worked* the timber into position. 20. To make or achieve by effort: He *worked* his way through the narrow tunnel. 21. To carry on some activity in (an area, etc.); cover: to *work* a stream for trout. 22. To solve, as a problem in arithmetic. 23. To cause to move from nervousness or excitement: to *work* one's jaws. 24. To excite; provoke: He *worked* himself into a passion. 25. To influence or manage, as by insidious means; lead. 26. *Informal* To make use of for one's own purposes; use. — **to work in** To put in; insert or be inserted. — **to work off** To get rid of, as extra flesh by exercise. — **to work on** (or **upon**) 1. To try to influence or persuade. 2. To influence or affect. — **to work out** 1. To make its way out or through. 2. To effect by work or effort; accomplish. 3. To exhaust, as a mineral vein or a subject of inquiry. 4. To discharge, as a debt, by labor rather than by payment of money. 5. To develop; form, as a plan. 6. To solve. 7. To prove effective or successful. 8. To result as specified: It *worked* out badly. — **to work over** 1. To do again; repeat. 2. *U.S. Slang* To beat up; maul. — **to work up** 1. To excite; rouse. 2. To form or shape by working; develop. [OE *weorc*]

-work *combining form* 1. A product made from a (specified) material: *paperwork, brickwork.* 2. Work of a (given) kind: *piecework.* 3. Work performed in a (specified) place: *housework.* [< WORK]

work-a-ble (wûr′kə-bəl) *adj.* 1. Capable of being worked. 2. Capable of being put into effect, as a plan; practicable. — **work′a-bil′i-ty, work′a-ble-ness** *n.*

work-a-day (wûrk′ə-dā′) *adj.* 1. Of, pertaining to, or suitable for working days; everyday. 2. Commonplace; prosaic. [Alter. of ME *werkeday* < OE *weorca* work + DAY]

work basket A basket for holding sewing materials.

work-bench (wûrk′bench′) *n.* A bench for work, as that of a carpenter or machinist.

work-book (wûrk′bŏŏk′) *n.* 1. A booklet based on a course of study and containing problems and exercises that a student works out directly on the pages. 2. A manual containing operating instructions. 3. A book for recording work performed or planned.

work-day (wûrk′dā′) *n.* 1. Any day not a Sunday or holiday; a working day. 2. The part of the day or number of hours of one day spent in work. — *adj.* Workaday.

work-er (wûr′kər) *n.* 1. One who or that which does work; esp., a laborer. 2. A female of an insect colony, as an ant, bee, or termite, with undeveloped sexual organs.

work force The total number of workers of a company, project, factory, region, etc.; staff. Also **working force.**

work-horse (wûrk′hôrs′) *n.* 1. A horse used for pulling loads, as a cart or plow. 2. A person who takes upon himself the hardest or most arduous part of an undertaking.

work-house (wûrk′hous′) *n.* 1. *Brit.* A house for paupers able to work. 2. An industrial prison for petty offenders.

work-ing (wûr′king) *adj.* 1. Engaged actively in some employment. 2. That works, or performs its function: This is a *working* model. 3. Sufficient for use or action: a *working* knowledge of French. 4. Relating to or occupied by work. 5. Throbbing with pain; also, twitching: said esp. of the face muscles. 6. Fermenting, as wine. — *n.* 1. The act or operation of one who or that which works. 2. *Usu. pl.* The part of a mine or quarry where excavation is going on or has gone on.

working capital 1. That part of the finances of a business available for its operation. 2. The amount of quick assets that exceed current liabilities.

working class The part of society consisting of working people paid in wages; esp., manual or industrial laborers. — **work·ing-class** (wûr′king·klas′, -kläs′) adj.

working day 1. A day on which work is normally done, as distinguished from a Sunday or holiday. 2. The number of hours constituting a day's work: a four-hour *working day*.

work·ing·man (wûr′king·man′) n. pl. **·men** (-men′) A male worker; laborer.

working papers An age certificate and other official papers certifying that a minor may be legally employed.

work·ing·wom·an (wûr′king·wŏŏm′ən) n. pl. **·wom·en** (-wim′in) A female worker; laborer.

work·less (wûrk′lis) adj. Jobless; unemployed.

work·load (wûrk′lōd′) n. The amount of work apportioned to a person, machine, or department over a given period.

work·man (wûrk′mən) n. pl. **·men** (-mən) One who earns his living by manual labor; an artisan; mechanic; workingman. — **work′man·ly** adv.

work·man·like (wûrk′mən·līk) adj. Like or befitting a skilled workman; skillfully done. — **work′man·ly** adv.

work·man·ship (wûrk′mən·ship) n. 1. The art or skill of a workman, or the quality of work. 2. The work or result produced by a worker.

workmen's compensation 1. Damages recoverable from an employer by an employee in case of accident. 2. Government insurance against illness, accident, or unemployment.

work of art 1. A product of the fine arts, esp. of the graphic arts and sculpture, but including literary and musical productions. 2. Anything likened to an artistic work, as because of great beauty, intricacy, etc.

work·out (wûrk′out′) n. Informal 1. A test, trial, practice performance, etc., to discover, maintain, or increase ability for some work or competition, as a practice boxing bout or race. 2. Any activity involving considerable effort or vigor.

work·room (wûrk′rōōm′, -rŏŏm′) n. A room where work is performed.

work·sheet (wûrk′shēt′) n. 1. A sheet of paper on which practice work or rough drafts of problems are written. 2. A sheet of paper used to record work schedules and operations.

work·shop (wûrk′shop′) n. A building or room where any work is carried on; workroom.

work stoppage A stopping of work, as in industry, because of a strike or layoff.

work·ta·ble (wûrk′tā′bəl) n. A table with drawers for use while working, esp. while sewing.

work·week (wûrk′wēk′) n. The number of hours worked in a week; also, the number of working hours in a week.

world (wûrld) n. 1. The earth. 2. A part of the earth: the Old *World*. 3. The universe. 4. A division of existing or created things belonging to the earth: the animal *world*. 5. The human inhabitants of the earth. 6. A definite class of people having certain interests or activities in common: the scientific *world*. 7. A sphere or domain: the *world* of letters. 8. Man regarded socially. 9. Public or social life and intercourse: to go out into the *world*. 10. The practices, usages, and ways of men: He knows the *world*. 11. A total of things as pertaining to or affecting an individual person: a child's private *world* of fantasy. 12. A great quantity, number, or size: a *world* of trouble. 13. A scene of existence or of affairs regarded from a moral or religious point of view; worldly aims, pleasures, or people collectively. 14. Earthly existence. — **for all the world** In every respect. — **on top of the world** Informal Elated. — **out of this world** Informal Very fine; extraordinarily good. — **to bring into the world** To give birth to. [OE *weorold, woruld*]

World Court 1. The Permanent Court of International Justice. 2. The International Court of Justice.

world·ling (wûrld′ling) n. One who lives merely for this world; a worldly-minded person.

world·ly (wûrld′lē) adj. **·li·er, ·li·est** 1. Pertaining to the world; mundane; earthly; not spiritual. 2. Devoted to temporal things; secular. 3. Sophisticated; worldly-wise. — adv. In a worldly manner. — **world′li·ness** n.

world·ly-mind·ed (wûrld′lē·mīn′did) adj. Absorbed in the things of this world. — **world′ly-min′ded·ly** adv. — **world′ly-mind′ed·ness** n.

world·ly-wise (wûrld′lē·wīz′) adj. Wise in the ways and affairs of the world; sophisticated.

world power A state or organization whose policy and action are of world-wide influence.

World Series In baseball, the games played at the finish of the regular schedule between the champion teams of the American and National Leagues, the first team to win four games being adjudged world champions. Also **world's series**.

world's fair An international exhibit of the folk crafts and arts, agricultural and industrial products, and scientific progress of various countries.

world-shak·ing (wûrld′shā′king) adj. Enormously significant or consequential; affecting the entire world.

World War See table for WAR.

world-wea·ry (wûrld′wir′ē) adj. **·ri·er, ·ri·est** Dissatisfied and weary with life and its conditions.

world-wide (wûrld′wīd′) adj. Extended or spread throughout the world.

worm (wûrm) n. 1. A small, limbless invertebrate with an elongated, soft, and usu. naked body, as a flatworm, roundworm, or annelid. ◆ Collateral adjective: *vermicular*. 2. Loosely, any small creeping animal having a slender body and short or undeveloped limbs, as an insect larva, a grub, etc. 3. That which suggests the action or habit of a worm as eating away or as an agent of decay, as remorse, death, etc. 4. A despicable, groveling, or abject person. 5. Something like a worm in appearance or movement. 6. pl. An intestinal disorder due to the presence of parasitic worms. — v.t. 1. To insinuate (oneself or itself) in a wormlike manner: with *in* or *into*. 2. To draw forth by artful means, as a secret: with *out*. 3. To free from intestinal worms. 4. Naut. To wind yarn, etc., along (a rope) so as to fill up the grooves between the strands. 5. To remove the worms from, as a dog. — v.i. 6. To move or progress slowly and stealthily. 7. To insinuate oneself by artful means: with *into*. [OE *wyrm*] — **worm′er** n.

worm-eat·en (wûrm′ēt′n) adj. 1. Eaten or bored through by worms. 2. Worn-out or decayed, as by time.

worm gear Mech. 1. A worm wheel. 2. The gear formed by a worm wheel together with a worm screw.

worm·hole (wûrm′hōl′) n. The hole made by a worm or termite, as in plants, timber, etc. — **worm′holed** adj.

worm screw Mech. A short threaded portion of a shaft constituting an endless screw formed to mesh with a worm wheel.

worm wheel Mech. A toothed wheel gearing with a worm screw.

worm·wood (wûrm′wŏŏd′) n. 1. Any of various European herbs or small shrubs related to the sagebrush; esp., a common species that is aromatic and bitter and is used in making absinthe. 2. That which embitters or makes bitter; bitterness. [Alter. of obs. *wermōd* < OE]

worm·y (wûr′mē) adj. **worm·i·er, worm·i·est** 1. Infested with or injured by worms. 2. Of or pertaining to worms. 3. Resembling a worm. 4. Mean; groveling. — **worm′i·ness** n.

worn (wôrn, wōrn) Past participle of WEAR. — adj. 1. Affected by use or any continuous action; as: a Threadbare: a *worn* suit. b Exhausted, as from worry, anxiety, etc.: a *worn* face. c Hackneyed: a *worn* phrase. 2. Used up; spent.

worn-out (wôrn′out′, wōrn′-) adj. 1. Used until without value or effectiveness. 2. Thoroughly tired; exhausted.

wor·ri·some (wûr′i·səm) adj. 1. Causing worry or anxiety. 2. Given to worry. — **wor′ri·some·ly** adv.

wor·ry (wûr′ē) v. **·ried, ·ry·ing** v.i. 1. To be uneasy in the mind; fret. 2. To pull or tear at something with the teeth: with *at*. 3. Informal To advance or manage despite difficulties: with *along* or *through*. — v.t. 4. To cause to feel uneasy in the mind; trouble. 5. To bother; pester. 6. To mangle or kill by biting, shaking, or tearing with the teeth. — n. pl. **·ries** 1. A state of anxiety or vexation. 2. Something that causes anxiety. 3. The act of worrying. [OE *wrygan* to strangle] — **wor′ri·er** n. — **wor′ri·ment** n.

worse (wûrs) Comparative of BAD and ILL. — adj. 1. Bad or ill in a greater degree; more evil, etc. 2. Physically ill in a greater degree. 3. Less favorably situated as to means and circumstances. — n. Something worse. — adv. In a manner more intense, severe, or evil. [OE *wiersa*]

wors·en (wûr′sən) v.t. & v.i. To make or become worse.

wor·ship (wûr′ship) n. 1. The adoration, homage, or veneration given to a deity. 2. The rites, ceremonial forms, prayers, etc., such adoration requires or assumes. 3. Excessive or ardent devotion or admiration. 4. The object of such devotion or admiration. 5. Chiefly Brit. A title of honor in addressing persons of rank or station: with *your, his,* etc. — v. **wor·shiped** or **·shipped, wor·ship·ing** or **·ship·ping** v.t. 1. To pay an act of worship to. 2. To have an intense or exaggerated admiration or devotion for. — v.i. 3. To perform acts or have sentiments of worship. [OE < *weorth* value] — **wor′ship·er, wor′ship·per** n.

wor·ship·ful (wûr′ship·fəl) adj. 1. Giving or feeling reverence or adoration. 2. Chiefly Brit. Worthy of or entitled to honor or respect: used as a title of respect for magistrates, etc. — **wor′ship·ful·ly** adv. — **wor′ship·ful·ness** n.

worst (wûrst) Superlative of BAD and ILL. — adj. Bad, ill, evil, harmful, etc., in the highest degree. — **in the worst way** Slang Very much. — n. That which is worst. — **at worst** By the most pessimistic estimate. — **if (the) worst comes to (the) worst** If the worst imaginable thing comes to pass. — **to get the worst of it** To be defeated or put at a disadvantage. — *adv.* In the worst or most extreme manner or degree. — *v.t.* To defeat; vanquish. [OE *wierrest*]

wors·ted (wŏŏs'tid, wûr'stid) *n.* **1.** Woolen yarn spun from long staple, with fibers combed parallel and twisted hard. **2.** A fabric made from worsted yarns. — *adj.* Consisting of or made from this yarn. [after *Worsted*, former name of a parish in Norfolk, north of Norwich, England]

wort (wûrt) *n.* **1.** A plant or herb: usu. in combination: *liverwort.* **2.** The unfermented infusion of malt that becomes beer when fermented. [OE *wyrt* root, plant]

worth (wûrth) *n.* **1.** Value or excellence of any kind. **2.** The exchangeable or market value of anything. **3.** The quality or combination of qualities that makes one deserving of esteem. **4.** Wealth. **5.** The amount of something that can be had for a specific sum: three cents' *worth* of candy. — *adj.* **1.** Equal in value (to); exchangeable (for). **2.** Deserving of: to be *worth* seeing. **3.** Having possessions to the value of: He is *worth* a million. — **for all it is worth** To the utmost. — **for all one is worth** With every effort possible: to the utmost of one's capacity. [OE *weorth*] — **Syn.** (noun) **1.** *Worth* and *value* relate to the merit or excellence of a person or thing. In pecuniary matters, the words are usually equivalent: to get one's money's *worth*, to receive good *value* in a purchase. *Worth* often implies some intangible merit or efficacy, while *value* has reference to a measurable or precisely definable quality: ideas of little *worth*, the *value* of a house and its lot.

-worth *combining form* Of the value of: *pennyworth.* [OE *weorth* worth]

worth·less (wûrth'lis) *adj.* Having no worth, value, dignity, virtue, etc. — **worth'less·ly** *adv.* — **worth'less·ness** *n.*

worth·while (wûrth'hwīl') *adj.* Sufficiently important to occupy the time; of enough value to repay the effort. — **worth'while'ness** *n.*

wor·thy (wûr'thē) *adj.* **·thi·er, ·thi·est 1.** Possessing worth or value; deserving of respect or honor. **2.** Having such qualities as to be deserving of or adapted to some specified thing; suitable: followed by *of* (rarely *for*) or sometimes by an infinitive: He is *worthy* of our prasie. — *n.* *pl.* **·thies 1.** A person of eminent worth. **2.** A person or character of local note: a humorous usage. [ME *wurthi, worthi*] — **wor'thi·ly** *adv.* — **wor'thi·ness** *n.*

-worthy *combining form* **1.** Meriting or deserving: *trustworthy.* **2.** Valuable as; having worth as: *newsworthy.* **3.** Fit for: *seaworthy.* [OE *wythe* worthy]

wot (wot) Present tense, first and third person singular, of WIT[2].

Wo·tan (vō'tän) In Wagner's *Ring of the Nibelung*, Woden.

would (wŏŏd) Past tense of WILL, but rarely a true past, rather chiefly used as a modal auxiliary expressing: **a** Desire or inclination: He *would* like to write. **b** Condition: He *would* give if he were able. **c** Futurity: He kept searching for something that *would* cure him. **d** Determination: He *would* not go. **e** Expectation or possibility: Letting him speak *would* have serious consequences. **f** Preference: We *would* have you succeed rather than fail. **g** Request: *Would* you give us a call? **h** Custom or habit: We *would* ride together each day. **i** Choice: He *would* never go if he could help it. **j** Uncertainty: It *would* seem to be wrong. ◆ See note under SHOULD. [OE *wolde*, pt. of *willan* to will]

would-be (wŏŏd'bē') *adj.* **1.** Desiring or professing to be: a *would-be* poet. **2.** Intended to be.

would·n't (wŏŏd'nt) Would not.

wouldst (wŏŏdst) Archaic or poetic second person singular of WOULD: used with *thou*.

wound[1] (wŏŏnd, *Poetic* wound) *n.* **1.** A hurt or injury to the body, usu. one in which the skin is cut or torn, as a stab, cut, etc. **2.** A similar injury to a tree or plant. **3.** Any injury or cause of pain or grief, as to the feelings, honor, etc. — *v.t. & v.i.* To inflict a wound or wounds (upon); cause injury or grief (to). [OE *wund*] — **wound'less** *adj.*

wound[2] (wound) Past tense and past participle of WIND[2].

wove (wōv) Past tense and alternative past participle of WEAVE.

wo·ven (wō'vən) Past participle of WEAVE.

wow (wou) *interj. Informal* An exclamation of wonder, surprise, pleasure, pain, etc. — *n. Slang* Something that is extraordinarily successful, amusing, etc. — *v.t. Slang* To be extraordinarily successful with.

wrack[1] (rak) *n.* **1.** Ruin; destruction: chiefly in the phrase **wrack and ruin. 2.** A wrecked ship; wreckage. **3.** Marine vegetation and floating material cast ashore by the sea, as seaweed or eelgrass. — *v.t. & v.i.* To wreck or be wrecked. [Fusion of OE *wræc* revenge and MDu. *wrak* wreck]

wrack[2] (rak) *n.* See RACK[3].

wraith (rāth) *n.* **1.** An apparition of a person thought to be alive, seen shortly before or shortly after his death. **2.** Any specter, ghost, or apparition. [Origin unknown]

wran·gle (rang'gəl) *v.* **·gled, ·gling** *v.i.* **1.** To argue or dispute noisily; brawl. — *v.t.* **2.** To argue; debate. **3.** *U.S.* To herd or round up (livestock). — *n.* An angry dispute. [Cf. LG *wrangeln* to quarrel] — **wran'gler** *n.*

wrap (rap) *v.* **wrapped** or **wrapt, wrap·ping** *v.t.* **1.** To surround and cover by something folded or wound about; swathe; enwrap. **2.** To cover with paper, etc., folded about and secured. **3.** To wind or fold (a covering) about something. **4.** To surround so as to obscure; blot out or conceal; envelop. **5.** To fold, wind, or draw together. — *v.i.* **6.** To be or become twined or coiled: with *about, around*, etc. — **to be wrapped up in 1.** To be clothed in or enveloped by (something). **2.** To be totally absorbed, involved, or interested in (something). — **to keep under wraps** To keep secret. — *n.* **1.** An article of dress drawn or folded about a person; a wrapper. **2.** *pl.* Outer garments collectively, as cloaks, scarfs, etc. **3.** A blanket. [ME *wrappen*]

wrap·a·round (rap'ə·round') *adj.* **1.** Designating a garment, as a skirt, dress, coat, etc., open down to the hem and made to fit by being wrapped around the body. **2.** Encircling or overlapping: a *wraparound* windshield.

wrap·per (rap'ər) *n.* **1.** A paper enclosing a newspaper, magazine, or similar packet for mailing or otherwise. **2.** A woman's dressing gown. **3.** One who or which wraps.

wrap·ping (rap'ing) *n.* Often *pl.* A covering; something in which an object is wrapped.

wrath (rath, räth; *Brit.* rôth) *n.* **1.** Extreme or violent rage or fury; vehement indignation. **2.** An act done in violent rage, esp. in vengeance or punishment. [OE < *wrath* wroth]

wrath·ful (rath'fəl, räth'-) *adj.* **1.** Full of wrath; extremely angry. **2.** Springing from or expressing wrath. — **wrath'ful·ly** *adv.* — **wrath'ful·ness** *n.*

wrath·y (rath'ē, räth'ē) *adj.* **wrath·i·er, wrath·i·est** *Informal* Wrathful. — **wrath'i·ly** *adv.* — **wrath'i·ness** *n.*

wreak (rēk) *v.t.* **1.** To inflict or exact, as vengeance. **2.** To give free expression to (anger, hatred, etc.); vent. [OE *wrecan* to drive, avenge]

wreath (rēth) *n.* *pl.* **wreaths** (rē*th*z) **1.** A band or circle of flowers or greenery, often worn on the head as a crown or placed on a grave or at a door, window, etc. **2.** Any curled band of circular or spiral shape, as of smoke. [OE < *writhan* to bind, tie] — **wreath'y** *n.*

wreathe (rē*th*) *v.* **wreathed, wreath·ing** *v.t.* **1.** To form into a wreath, as by twisting or twining. **2.** To adorn or encircle with or as with wreaths. **3.** To envelop; cover: His face was *wreathed* in smiles. — *v.i.* **4.** To take the form of a wreath. **5.** To twist, turn, or coil, as masses of cloud. [< ME *writhen* to writhe]

wreck (rek) *v.t.* **1.** To cause the destruction or wreck of, as a vessel. **2.** To bring ruin, damage, or destruction upon. **3.** To tear down, as a building; dismantle. — *v.i.* **4.** To suffer wreck; be ruined. — *n.* **1.** That which has been ruined or destroyed. **2.** Property cast upon land by the sea, either broken portions of a wrecked vessel or cargo from it. **3.** The accidental destruction or ruin of a ship; also, the ship so destroyed. **4.** One who is physically, mentally, or morally unsound or ruined. **5.** The act of wrecking, or the state of being wrecked. [< AF < OF < ON *wrekan* to drive]

wreck·age (rek'ij) *n.* **1.** The act of wrecking, or the state of being wrecked. **2.** Broken or disordered remnants or fragments from a wreck.

wreck·er (rek'ər) *n.* **1.** One who or that which causes wreck, destruction, or frustration of any sort. **2.** One employed in tearing down and removing old buildings. **3.** A person, train, car, or machine that clears away wrecks. **4.** One employed to recover disabled vessels or wrecked cargoes for the owners; also, a vessel employed in this service.

wreck·ing (rek'ing) *n.* The work or art of a wrecker. — *adj.* Of, engaged in, or used in pulling down buildings or in salvaging and clearing away wrecks.

wren (ren) *n.* **1.** Any of numerous small birds having short, rounded wings and a short tail, including the common house wren. **2.** Any of numerous similar birds. [OE *wrenna*]

wrench (rench) *n.* **1.** A violent twist. **2.** A sharp or violent twist or pull, as in the ankle, back, etc.; a sprain. **3.** Any sudden and violent emotion or grief. **4.** Any perversion or distortion of an original meaning. **5.** Any of various tools for twisting or turning bolts, nuts, pipe, etc. — *v.t.* **1.** To twist violently; turn suddenly by force; wrest. **2.** To twist forcibly so as to cause strain or injury; sprain. **3.** To twist from the proper meaning, intent, or use. **4.** To strain or force the feelings, thoughts, etc., of: to *wrench* oneself away from pleasure. — *v.i.* **5.** To give a twist or wrench. [OE *wrenc* trick]

wrest (rest) *v.t.* **1.** To pull or force away by violent twisting or wringing; wrench. **2.** To turn from the true meaning, character, intent, or application; distort. **3.** To seize forcibly by violence, extortion, or usurpation. **4.** To extract by toil and effort: to *wrest* a living from barren soil. — *n.* **1.** An act of wresting. **2.** A misapplication or perversion. **3.** A crooked act. **4.** A key for tuning a stringed instrument, as a harp. [OE *wræstan*] — **wrest'er** *n.*

wres·tle (res'əl) *v.* **·tled, ·tling** *v.i.* **1.** To engage in wrestling. **2.** To struggle, as for mastery; contend. — *v.t.* **3.** To engage in (a wrestling match), or wrestle with. **4.** To throw (a calf) and hold it down for branding. — *n.* **1.** A wrestling match. **2.** Any hard struggle. [OE *wrǣstlian*, freq. of *wrǣstan* to wrest] — **wres′tler** *n.*

wres·tling (res′ling) *n.* A sport or exercise in which each of two unarmed contestants endeavors to throw the other to the ground or force him into a certain fallen position.

wretch (rech) *n.* **1.** A base, vile, or contemptible person. **2.** A miserable or pitiable person. [OE *wrecca* outcast < *wrecan* to drive]

wretch·ed (rech′id) *adj.* **1.** Sunk in dejection; profoundly unhappy. **2.** Causing misery or grief. **3.** Unsatisfactory or worthless in ability or quality. **4.** Despicable; contemptible. — **wretch′ed·ly** *adv.* — **wretch′ed·ness** *n.*

wrig·gle (rig′əl) *v.* ·**gled,** ·**gling** *v.i.* **1.** To twist in a sinuous manner; squirm; writhe. **2.** To proceed as by twisting or crawling. **3.** To make one's way by evasive or indirect means. — *v.t.* **4.** To cause to wriggle. — *n.* The motion of one who or that which wriggles; a squirm. [< MLG *wriggeln,* freq. of *wriggen* to twist] — **wrig′gly** *adj.*

wrig·gler (rig′lər) *n.* **1.** One who or that which wriggles. **2.** A mosquito larva.

wright (rīt) *n.* One who constructs, contrives, or creates: used chiefly in compounds: *playwright.* [OE *wyrhta*]

wring (ring) *v.* **wrung** (*Rare* **wringed**), **wring·ing** *v.t.* **1.** To squeeze or compress by twisting. **2.** To squeeze or press out, as water, by twisting. **3.** To extort; acquire by extortion. **4.** To distress; torment. **5.** To twist or wrest violently out of shape or place: to *wring* his neck. — *v.i.* **6.** To writhe or squirm, as with anguish. — *n.* The act of wringing. [OE *wringan*]

wring·er (ring′ər) *n.* **1.** One who or that which wrings. **2.** A contrivance used to press water out of fabrics after washing; also, the operator of such a machine.

wrin·kle¹ (ring′kəl) *n.* **1.** A small ridge, crease, or fold, as on a smooth surface. **2.** A small fold or crease in the skin, usu. produced by age or by excessive exposure to the elements. — *v.* ·**kled,** ·**kling** *v.t.* **1.** To make a wrinkle or wrinkles in, as by creasing, folding, crumpling, etc. — *v.i.* **2.** To be or become contracted into wrinkles or ridges. [OE *gewrinclod,* pp. of *gewrinclian* to wind] — **wrin′kly** *adj.*

wrin·kle² (ring′kəl) *n. Informal* A curious or ingenious method, idea, device, etc. [Prob. dim. of OE *wrenc* trick]

wrist (rist) *n.* **1.** The part or joint of the arm that lies between the hand and the forearm. ◆ Collateral adjective: *carpal.* **2.** The part of a glove or garment that covers the wrist. **3.** A wrist pin. [OE, prob. < *wrīthan* to writhe]

wrist·band (rist′band, -bənd, riz′-) *n.* The band of a sleeve that covers the wrist or ends a shirt sleeve; a cuff.

wrist·let (rist′lit) *n.* **1.** A flexible band worn on the wrist for warmth. **2.** A bracelet. **3.** *Slang* A handcuff.

wrist pin *Mech.* **1.** A pin holding together the piston and connecting rod of a steam engine. **2.** A similar pin in the cross-head of an internal-combustion engine.

wrist watch A watch set in a band or strap and worn at the wrist.

writ¹ (rit) *n.* **1.** *Law* A mandatory precept, under seal, issued by a court, and commanding the person to whom it is addressed to do or not to do some act. **2.** That which is written: now chiefly in the phrase *Holy Writ,* meaning the Bible. [OE, a writing < *wrītan* to write]

writ² (rit) Archaic or dialectal past tense and past participle of WRITE.

write (rīt) *v.* **wrote** (*Archaic* or *Dial.* **writ**), **writ·ten** (*Archaic* or *Dial.* **writ**), **writ·ing** *v.t.* **1.** To trace or inscribe (letters, words, numbers, symbols, etc.) on a surface with pen or pencil, or by other means. **2.** To describe in writing. **3.** To communicate by letter. **4.** *Informal* To communicate with by letter: He *writes* her every day. **5.** To produce by writing; be the author or composer of. **6.** To draw up; draft: to *write* a check. **7.** To cover or fill with writing: to *write* two full pages. **8.** To leave marks or evidence of: Anxiety is *written* on his face. **9.** To spell or inscribe as specified: He *writes* his name with two *n*'s. **10.** To entitle or designate in writing: He *writes* himself "General." **11.** To underwrite: to *write* an insurance policy. — *v.i.* **12.** To trace or inscribe letters, etc., on a surface, as of paper. **13.** To communicate in writing. **14.** To be engaged in the occupation of a writer or author. **15.** To produce a specified quality of writing. — **to write down 1.** To put into writing. **2.** To injure or depreciate in writing. — **to write off 1.** To cancel or remove (claims, debts, etc.) from an open account. **2.** To acknowledge the loss or failure of. — **to write in 1.** To insert in writing, as in a document. **2.** To cast (a vote) for one not listed on a ballot by inserting his name in writing. — **to write out 1.** To put into writing. **2.** To write in full or complete form. — **to write up 1.** To describe fully in writing. **2.** To praise fully or too fully in writing. [OE *wrītan*]

write-in (rīt′in′) *adj. Informal* Designating a method of voting whereby a name not formally on the ballot is written in by the voter. — *n.* In voting, a name thus written.

write-off (rīt′ôf′, -of′) *n.* **1.** A cancellation. **2.** An amount canceled or noted as a loss.

writ·er (rī′tər) *n.* **1.** One who writes. **2.** One who engages in literary composition.

writer's cramp *Pathol.* Spasmodic contraction of the muscles of the fingers and hand, caused by excessive writing. Also **writer's palsy** or **spasm.**

write-up (rīt′up′) *n. Informal* A written description, record, or account, usu. laudatory, as of a town, manufacturing enterprise, or public institution.

writhe (rīth) *v.* **writhed, writhed, writh·ing** *v.t.* **1.** To cause to twist or bend; distort. — *v.i.* **2.** To twist or distort the body, face, etc., as in pain. **3.** To suffer acutely, as from embarrassment, anguish, etc. — *n.* An act of writhing. [OE *wrīthan*] — **writh′er** *n.*

writ·ing (rī′ting) *n.* **1.** The act of one who writes. **2.** The characters so made; handwriting. **3.** Anything written or expressed in letters; esp., a literary production. **4.** The profession or occupation of a writer. **5.** The practice, art, form, or style of literary composition.

writing paper Paper prepared to receive ink in writing.

writ·ten (rit′n) Past participle of WRITE.

wrong (rông, rong) *adj.* **1.** Not correct; mistaken; erroneous: a *wrong* estimate. **2.** Not suitable; inappropriate; improper: the *wrong* clothes; the *wrong* job. **3.** Not according to the right, proper, or correct method, standard, intention, etc.: the *wrong* way to do it. **4.** Not working or acting properly or satisfactorily: Something is *wrong* with the lock. **5.** Intended or made to be turned under, inward, or so as not to be seen: the *wrong* side of the cloth. **6.** Not desired or intended: the *wrong* road. **7.** Not favored by conventional social standards: the *wrong* side of town. **8.** Not morally right, proper, or just. **9.** Unsatisfactory: the *wrong* reply. — **to go wrong 1.** To lapse from the strict path of rectitude. **2.** To turn out badly; go astray. — *adv.* In a wrong direction, place, or manner; erroneously. — *n.* **1.** That which is wrong, as an evil or unjust action. **2.** The state or condition of being wrong: to be in the *wrong.* **3.** *Law* An invasion or violation of one's legal rights. — *v.t.* **1.** To violate the rights of; inflict injury or injustice upon. **2.** To impute evil to unjustly; malign: If you think so, you *wrong* him. **3.** To seduce or dishonor (a woman). [OE < ON *rangr* awry, unjust] — **wrong′er** *n.* — **wrong′ly** *adv.* — **wrong′ness** *n.*

wrong·do·er (rông′doo′ər, rong′-) *n.* One who does wrong. — **wrong′do′ing** *n.*

wrong·ful (rông′fəl, rong′-) *adj.* **1.** Characterized by wrong or injustice; injurious; unjust. **2.** Unlawful; illegal. — **wrong′ful·ly** *adv.* — **wrong′ful·ness** *n.*

wrong-head·ed (rông′hed′id, rong′-) *adj.* Stubbornly or perversely erring in judgment, action, etc. — **wrong′-head′ed·ly** *adv.* — **wrong′-head′ed·ness** *n.*

wrote (rōt) Past tense of WRITE.

wroth (rôth) *adj. Archaic* Filled with anger; furious; incensed. Also **wroth′ful** (-fəl). [OE *wrāth*]

wrought (rôt) *Archaic* past tense and past participle of WORK. — *adj.* **1.** Beaten or hammered into shape by tools: *wrought* gold. **2.** Worked; molded. **3.** Made with delicacy; elaborated carefully. **4.** Made; fashioned; formed: often in combination: *well-wrought.* — **wrought up** Excited; agitated. [ME < OE *geworht,* pp. of *wyrcan* to work]

wrought iron Commercially pure iron, prepared from pig iron and easily forged and welded into various shapes.

wrung (rung) Past tense and past participle of WRING.

wry (rī) *adj.* **wri·er** or **wry·er, wri·est** or **wry·est 1.** Bent to one side or out of position; contorted; askew: a *wry* smile. **2.** Deviating from that which is right or proper; warped. **3.** Perverse, ironic, or bitter: *wry* humor. — *v.t.* **wried, wry·ing** To twist; contort. [ME < OE *wrigian* to move, tend] — **wry′ly** *adv.* — **wry′ness** *n.*

wry·neck (rī′nek′) *n.* **1.** A bird allied to the woodpeckers, with the habit of twisting its head and neck. **2.** *Pathol.* A spasmodic affliction that twists the neck muscles. — **wry·necked** (rī′nekt′) *adj.*

Wy·an·dot (wī′ən·dot) *n. pl.* ·**dot** or ·**dots 1.** One of a tribe of North American Indians of Iroquoian stock and descendants of Hurons, presently settled in Oklahoma. **2.** An Iroquoian language. Also spelled *Wyandotte.*

Wy·an·dotte (wī′ən·dot) *n.* **1.** One of an American breed of domestic fowls. **2.** *pl.* ·**dotte** or ·**dottes** A Wyandot. **3.** The Wyandot language. [after the *Wyandot* Indians]

wych-elm (wich′elm′) *n.* A widespreading elm, common in the British Isles: also called *wich, witch:* also spelled *wich-elm, witch-elm.* Also **wych.** [< *wych,* var. of WITCH² + ELM]

wych-ha·zel (wich′hā′zəl) *n.* Witch hazel.

X

x, X (eks) *n. pl.* **x's** or **xs, X's** or **Xs, ex·es** (ek′siz) **1.** The twenty-fourth letter of the English alphabet. **2.** The sounds represented by the letter *x*, in English variously sounded as (ks), as in *axle, box, next;* (gz), as in *executive, exert;* (ksh), as in *noxious;* (gzh), as in *luxurious;* and initially, always (z), as in *xenophobe, xylophone.* **3.** Anything shaped like an X. **4.** An unknown quantity, factor, result, etc. — *symbol* **1.** The Roman numeral ten. **2.** A mark shaped like an X, representing the signature of one who cannot write. **3.** A mark used in diagrams, maps, etc., to place some event or substance, or to point out something to be emphasized. **4.** A symbol used to indicate a kiss. **5.** Christ: an abbreviation used in combination: *Xmas.*

xan·the·in (zan′thē·in) *n. Biochem.* The water-soluble portion of the yellow coloring matter found in the cell sap of some plants. [< F < Gk. *xanthos* yellow]

xan·thic (zan′thik) *adj.* Having a yellow or yellowish color. [< F < Gk. *xanthos* yellow]

xan·thine (zan′thĕn, -thin) *n. Biochem.* A crystalline nitrogenous compound, $C_5H_4N_4O_2$, contained in blood, urine, and other animal secretions, and in some plants.

xantho- *combining form* Yellow. Also, before vowels, **xanth-.** [< Gk. *xanthos* yellow]

xan·thous (zan′thəs) *adj.* **1.** Yellow. **2.** *Anthropol.* Of or pertaining to the yellow-skinned, or Mongoloid, ethnic division of mankind.

X-ax·is (eks′ak′sis) *n. pl.* **-ax·es** (-ak′sēz) The more nearly horizontal axis in a graph; the abscissa.

X-chro·mo·some (eks′krō′mə·sōm) *n. Genetics* One of the two types of chromosomes that determine the sex of an offspring.

xe·bec (zē′bek) *n.* A small, three-masted Mediterranean vessel, with both square and lateen sails, formerly used by Algerian pirates: also spelled *zebec.* [Earlier *chebec* < F < Sp. < Arabic *shabbāk*]

xeno- *combining form* Strange; foreign; different. Also, before vowels, **xen-.** [< Gk. *xenos* stranger]

xe·non (zē′non) *n.* A heavy, gaseous element (symbol Xe) occurring in extremely small quantities in the atmosphere and freezing at a very low temperature. See ELEMENT. [< Gk., neut. of *xenos* strange]

xen·o·phobe (zen′ə·fōb) *n.* One who hates or distrusts strangers or foreigners.

xen·o·pho·bi·a (zen′ə·fō′bē·ə) *n.* Hatred or distrust of foreigners or strangers. — **xen′o·pho′bic** (-fō′bik) *adj.*

xero- *combining form* Dry; dryness. Also, before vowels, **xer-.** [< Gk. *xēros* dry]

xe·rog·ra·phy (zi·rog′rə·fē) *n.* A method of printing in which a negatively charged ink powder is sprayed upon a positively charged metal plate, from which it is transferred to the printing surface by electrostatic attraction.

— **xe·ro·graph·ic** (zir′ō·graf′ik) *adj.* — **xe·rog′raph·er** *n.*

xe·roph·i·lous (zi·rof′ə·ləs) *adj. Biol.* Growing in or adapted to dry, hot climates.

xe·ro·phyte (zir′ə·fīt) *n. Bot.* A plant adapted to dry conditions of air and soil. — **xe·ro·phyt·ic** (-fit′ik) *adj.*

xe·ro·print·ing (zir′ō·prin′ting) *n.* A simplified variation of xerography, using a suitably prepared plate on a rotating cylinder.

Xer·ox (zir′oks) *n.* A xerographic process for reproducing printed or pictorial matter: a trade name. — *v.t.* To make or reproduce by Xerox: to *Xerox* 10 copies; to *Xerox* a document. Also **xer′ox.**

Xho·sa (kō′sä) *n.* The Bantu language of the Kaffirs, closely related to Zulu: also called *Kaffir:* also **Xosa.**

xi (zī, sī; *Gk.* ksē) *n.* The fourteenth letter in the Greek alphabet (Ξ, ξ), equivalent to the English *x.* See ALPHABET.

-xion Var. of -TION.

xiphi- *combining form* Sword. Also, before vowels, **xiph-.** [< Gk. *xiphos* sword]

xiph·oid (zif′oid) *adj.* Shaped like a sword.

Xmas Christmas: popular abbreviation. ◆ *Xmas,* though best avoided in formal contexts, has been used in written English since the sixteenth century and cannot be condemned as a modern commercialism. [< *X,* abbr. for *Christ* < Gk. *X,* chi, the first letter of *Christos* Christ + -MAS]

X-rat·ed (eks′rā′tid) *adj.* Of a motion picture, characterized by explicit sex.

X-ray (eks′rā′) *v.t.* To examine, photograph, diagnose, or treat with X-rays. — *n.* A picture made with X-rays; roentgenogram: also **X-ray photograph.**

X-rays (eks′rāz′) *n.pl.* Electromagnetic radiations of extremely short wavelength, emitted from a substance when it is bombarded by a stream of electrons moving in a vacuum at a sufficiently high velocity, as in an electron tube. Their ability to penetrate solids, to ionize gases, and to act on photographic plates has many useful applications, especially in the detection, diagnosis, and treatment of certain organic disorders, chiefly internal. Also called *Roentgen rays.* [Trans. of G *X-strahlen,* name coined by Roentgen, their discoverer, because their nature was unknown]

xy·lem (zī′ləm) *n. Bot.* The portion of a vascular bundle in higher plants that is made up of woody tissue, parenchyma, and associated cells, etc. [< G < Gk. *xylon* wood]

xylo- *combining form* Wood; woody. Also, before vowels, **xyl-.** [< Gk. *xylon* wood]

xy·lo·phone (zī′lə·fōn) *n.* A musical instrument consisting of a row of wooden bars graduated in length to form a chromatic scale, and sounded by being struck with mallets. — **xy·lo·phon·ist** (zī′lə·fō′-nist, zī·lof′ə·nist) *n.*

XYLOPHONE

Y

y, Y (wī) *n. pl.* **y's** or **ys, Y's** or **Ys, wyes** (wīz) **1.** The twenty-fifth letter of the English alphabet. **2.** The sounds represented by the letter *y.* Initial *y* (introducing either a vowel or a syllable) represents a voiced palatal semivowel, as in *yet, you, yonder, beyond.* Final *y* represents either a vowel, pronounced (ē), as in *honey, pretty, steady;* a diphthong, pronounced (ī), as in *fly, my;* or the final glide of a diphthong, as in *gray, obey, annoy.* Internal *y* represents a vowel (i), as in *lyric, myth, syllable;* a diphthong (ī), as in *lyre, type, psychic;* an r-colored central vowel·(ûr) or (ər), as in *myrtle, martyr.* **3.** Anything shaped like a Y, as: **a** A pipe coupling, connection, etc. **b** A forked piece serving as a rest or support, as for some part of a sighting instrument. — *symbol Chem.* Yttrium (symbol Y).

y- *prefix* Used in Middle English as a sign of the past participle, as an intensive, or without perceptible force: *yclad, yclept.* It survives (as a-) in such words as *alike, aware,* etc. Also spelled *i-.* [OE *ge-*]

-y[1] *suffix of adjectives* Being, possessing, or resembling what is expressed in the root: *stony, rainy.* Also *-ey,* when added to words ending in *y,* as in *clayey, skyey.* [OE *-ig*]

-y[2] *suffix* The equality or state of being: *victory:* often used in abstract nouns formed from adjectives in *-ous* and *-ic.* [< F *-ie* < L *-ia;* also < Gk. *-ia, -eia*]

-y[3] *suffix* Little; small: *kitty:* often used in nicknames or to express endearment, as in *Tommy.* [Prob. < dial. E (Scottish)]

yacht (yot) *n.* A vessel specially built or fitted for racing or for private pleasure excursions. — *v.i.* To cruise, race, or sail in a yacht. [< Du. *jaghte*, short for *jaghtschip* pursuit ship < *jaght* hunting + *schip* ship]

yacht·ing (yot′ing) *n.* The act, practice, or pastime of sailing a yacht.

yachts·man (yots′mən) *n. pl.* ·men (-mən) One who owns or sails a yacht. Also **yacht′er, yacht′man.** — **yachts′·wom′an** (-woŏm′ən) *n.fem.*

yachts·man·ship (yots′mən·ship) *n.* The art or skill of yachting. Also **yacht′man·ship.**

yah¹ (yä, ya) *interj.* An exclamation of disgust or contempt.

yah² (yä, yâ) *interj. Informal* Yes. [Alter. of YES]

ya·hoo (yä′hoŏ, yä′-, yä·hoŏ′) *n.* **1.** Any low, vicious person. **2.** An awkward fellow; a bumpkin. [< YAHOO]

Ya·hoo (yä′hoŏ, yä′-, yä·hoŏ′) *n.* In Swift's *Gulliver's Travels*, one of a race of brutish beings in human form.

Yah·weh (yä′we) In the Old Testament, the national god of Israel; God. See JEHOVAH. Also **Yah·ve** (yä′ve), **Yah·veh.** [< Hebrew *YHWH*]

yak¹ (yak) *n.* A large bovine ruminant of the higher regions of central Asia, having long hair fringing the shoulders, sides, and tail, and often domesticated. [< Tibetan *gyag*]

yak² (yak) *v.i.* **yakked, yak·king** *U.S. Slang* **1.** To chatter noisily or constantly. **2.** To laugh, esp. boisterously. [Imit.]

yam (yam) *n.* **1.** The fleshy, edible, tuberous root of any of various climbing tropical plants typical of a family of herbaceous or somewhat woody vines. **2.** Any of the plants growing this root. **3.** A large variety of the sweet potato. [< Pg. < Senegal *nyami* to eat]

yam·mer (yam′ər) *v.i. Informal* **1.** To complain peevishly; whimper. **2.** To howl; shout. — *v.t.* **3.** To utter peevishly; complain. — *n.* The act of yammering. [OE *gēomrian* to lament < *gēomor* sorrowful] — **yam′mer·er** *n.*

yang (yang) *n.* In Chinese philosophy and art, the male element, source of life and heat. Compare YIN. Also **Yang.** [< Chinese]

yank (yangk) *v.t.* **1.** To jerk or pull suddenly. — *v.i.* **2.** To give a pull or jerk. **3.** *Brit.* To be vigorously active. **4.** *Brit.* To jabber; scold. — *n. Informal* A sudden sharp pull. [? < dial. E (Scottish) *yank* a sharp sudden blow]

Yank (yangk) *n. & adj. Informal* Yankee.

Yan·kee (yang′kē) *n.* **1.** Originally, a native or inhabitant of New England. **2.** A Northerner; esp., a Union soldier during the Civil War, so called in the South. **3.** Any citizen of the U.S.: a chiefly foreign usage. — *adj.* **1.** Of, pertaining to, or characteristic of the Yankees. **2.** American. [? Back formation < *Jan Kees* (taken as a plural), John Cheese, orig. a nickname for a Hollander; later applied by Dutch colonists in New York to English settlers in Connecticut] — **Yan′kee·dom** *n.*

Yankee Doodle A song popular in pre-Revolutionary times and one of the national airs of the United States.

yap (yap) *n.* **1.** *Slang* Talk; jabber. **2.** A bark or yelp. **3.** *Slang* The mouth. — *v.t.* **yapped, yap·ping 1.** *Slang* To talk idly or emptily; jabber. **2.** *Informal* To bark or yelp, as a cur. [Imit. of a dog's bark]

Ya·qui (yä′kē) *n.* One of a tribe of North American Indians belonging to the Piman branch of the Uto-Aztecan stock, now living in southern Sonora, Mexico.

yard¹ (yärd) *n.* **1.** A standard English and American measure of length; 3 feet, or 36 inches, or 0.914 meter. See table inside back cover. **2.** A yardstick. **3.** *Naut.* A long, slender, tapering spar set crosswise on a mast and used to support sails. [OE *gierd* rod, measure of length]

yard² (yärd) *n.* **1.** A tract of ground, often enclosed, adjacent to a residence, church, school, or other building. **2.** An enclosure used for some specific work: often in combination: *brickyard; shipyard.* **3.** An enclosure or piece of ground adjacent to a railroad station, used for making up trains and for storing the rolling stock. **4.** The winter pasturing ground of deer and moose. **5.** An enclosure for animals, poultry, etc. — *v.t.* **1.** To put or collect into or as into a yard. — *v.i.* **2.** To gather into an enclosure or yard. [OE *geard* enclosure]

yard·age (yär′dij) *n.* **1.** The amount or length of something expressed in yards. **2.** Yard goods. [< YARD¹]

yard·arm (yärd′ärm′) *n. Naut.* Either end of a yard of a square sail.

yard goods Cloth that is sold by the yard.

yard·man¹ (yärd′mən) *n. pl.* ·men (-mən) *Naut.* A sailor who works on the yards.

yard·man² (yärd′mən) *n. pl.* ·men (-mən) A man employed in a yard, esp. on a railroad.

yard·mas·ter (yärd′mas′tər, -mäs′-) *n.* A railroad official having charge of a yard.

yard·stick (yärd′stik′) *n.* **1.** A graduated measuring stick a yard in length. **2.** Any measure or standard of comparison. Also *Archaic* **yard′wand′** (-wond′).

yarn (yärn) *n.* **1.** Any spun, threadlike material, natural or

synthetic, prepared for use in weaving, knitting, etc. **2.** Continuous strands of spun fiber, as wool, cotton, linen, silk, etc. **3.** A quantity of such material. **4.** *Informal* A long, exciting story of adventure, often of doubtful truth. — *v.i. Informal* To tell a yarn or yarns. [OE *gearn*]

yarn-dyed (yärn′dīd′) *adj.* Made of yarn dyed before being woven into material.

yar·row (yar′ō) *n.* Any of various perennial herbs of Europe and North America having finely dissected leaves, small white flowers, and a pungent odor. [OE *gearwe*]

yat·a·ghan (yat′ə·gan, -gən; *Turkish* yä′tä·gän′) *n.* A Turkish sword or scimitar with a double-curved blade and a handle without a guard. Also **yat′a·gan.** [< Turkish]

yaw (yô) *v.i.* **1.** *Naut.* To steer wildly, or out of its course, as a ship when struck by a heavy sea. **2.** To move unsteadily or irregularly. **3.** *Aeron.* To deviate from the flight path by angular displacement about the vertical axis; fishtail. — *v.t.* **4.** To cause to yaw. — *n.* **1.** A movement of a ship by which it temporarily alters its course. **2.** *Aeron.* The angular movement of an aircraft, projectile, etc., about its vertical axis. **3.** Any irregular, unsteady, or deviating motion. [Cf. ON *jaga* to move to and fro]

yawl¹ (yôl) See YOWL.

yawl² (yôl) *n.* **1.** A fore-and-aft rigged, two-masted vessel having the mizzenmast or jiggermast abaft the rudder post. **2.** A ship's small boat. **3.** A small fishing boat. [Appar. < Du. *jol*, orig. a boat used in Jutland]

yawn (yôn) *v.i.* **1.** To open the mouth wide, usu. involuntarily and with a long, full inspiration of the breath, often the result of drowsiness, fatigue, or boredom. **2.** To be or stand wide open, esp. as ready to engulf or receive something: A chasm *yawned* below. — *v.t.* **3.** To express or utter with a yawn. — *n.* **1.** The act of yawning. **2.** The act of opening wide. [Prob. fusion of OE *geonian* to yawn and *gānian* to gape] — **yawn′er** *n.*

yawp (yôp) *v.i.* **1.** To bark or yelp. **2.** *Informal* To gape; yawn audibly. **3.** *Brit. Informal* To shout; bawl; talk loudly. — *n.* **1.** A bark or yelp. **2.** A shout; noise; noisy talking; also, a loud, uncouth outcry. Also **yaup.** [ME *golpen*, pp. of *gelpen* to boast] — **yawp′er** *n.*

yaws (yôz) *n.pl. Pathol.* A contagious skin disease occurring in tropical and subtropical countries, caused by a spirochete and resembling syphilis. [< Carib *ydya*]

Y-ax·is (wī′ak′sis) *n. pl.* **-ax·es** (-ak′sēz) The more nearly vertical axis in a graph or coordinate system; the ordinate.

yay (yā) *U.S. Dial. adj.* **1.** This many; this much. **2.** Ever so many: for *yay* years. — *adv.* **1.** To this extent. **2.** Ever so: *yay* big. [Cf. G *je* ever]

Y-chro·mo·some (wī′krō′mə·sōm) *n. Genetics* One of the two types of chromosome that determine the sex of an offspring.

y·clept (i·klept′) *adj. Archaic* Called; named. Also **y·cleped′.** [OE *geclypod*, pp. of *clypian* to call]

ye¹ (the) The: a mistaken form resulting from the substitution of the character *y* for the thorn (þ) of the Old and Middle English alphabet.

ye² (yē) *pron. Archaic* A pronoun of the second person, originally nominative plural: "Blessed are *ye* when men shall revile you"; later, also nominative singular and objective singular and plural. [ME *ye, ȝe,* nominative pl. < OE *gē*]

yea (yā) *adv.* **1.** *Archaic* A term of affirmation or assent, now superseded by *yes.* **2.** *Archaic* Not only so, but more so: used to intensify or amplify: There were fifty, *yea,* a hundred archers. **3.** In reality; indeed; verily: used to introduce a sentence, etc. — *n.* **1.** An affirmative vote or voter: opposed to *nay.* **2.** An affirmation. [OE *gēa*]

yeah (yâ, ye′ə) *adv. Informal* Yes. [< YES]

yean (yēn) *v.t. & v.i.* To bear (young), as a goat or sheep. [OE (assumed) *geēanian*]

yean·ling (yēn′ling) *n.* The young of a goat or sheep. — *adj.* Young or newly born.

year (yir) *n.* **1.** The period of time in which the earth completes one revolution around the sun, consisting of 365 or 366 days divided into 12 months and now reckoned as beginning January 1 and ending December 31; also, a similar period in other calendars. **2.** Any period of 12 months, usu. reckoned from a specific date or time: a *year* from now. **3.** The period of time during which a planet revolves once around the sun. **4.** A specific period of time, usu. less than a year, given over to some special work or activity: the school *year.* **5.** *pl.* Age, esp. old age: active for his *years.* **6.** *pl.* Time: in *years* gone by and *years* to come. — **year after year** Every year. — **year by year** Each year; with each succeeding year. — **year in and out** From one year to the next; without cessation. [OE *gēar*]

year·book (yir′boŏk′) *n.* A book published annually, presenting information about the previous year.

year·ling (yir′ling) *n.* A young animal past its first year and not yet two years old; esp., a colt or filly a year old dating from January 1 of the year of foaling. — *adj.* Being a year old.

year·long (yir'lông', -long') *adj.* Continuing through a year.

year·ly (yir'lē) *adj.* 1. Occurring, done, payable, seen, etc., once a year; annual. 2. Continuing or lasting for a year: a *yearly* subscription. — *adv.* Once a year; annually.

yearn (yûrn) *v.i.* 1. To desire something earnestly; long; hanker; pine: with *for*. 2. To be deeply moved; feel sympathy. [OE *giernan, geornan*]

yearn·ing (yûr'ning) *n.* A strong emotion of longing or desire, esp. with tenderness. — **yearn'ing·ly** *adv.*

year-round (yir'round') *adj.* Open, operating, or continuing for the entire year: a *year-round* health resort.

yeast (yēst) *n.* 1. A substance consisting of minute cells of fungi that clump together in a yellow, frothy, viscous growth promoting fermentation in saccharine liquids, with the production of alcohol and carbon dioxide, as in the brewing of beer and the raising of bread. 2. Such a substance mixed with flour or meal, and sold commercially. 3. Froth or spume. 4. Mental or moral ferment or agitation. — *v.i.* To foam; froth. [OE *gist*]

yeast cake A mixture of living yeast cells and starch in compressed form, suitable for use in baking or brewing.

yeast plant Any of a group of fungi that form yeast.

yeast·y (yēs'tē) *adj.* **yeast·i·er, yeast·i·est** 1. Of, resembling, or containing yeast. 2. Causing or characterized by fermentation. 3. Restless; unsettled; frivolous. 4. Covered with or consisting mainly of froth or foam. 5. Light or unsubstantial. — **yeast'i·ness** *n.*

yegg (yeg) *n. Slang* A burglar or safe-cracker. Also **yegg'·man** (-mən) [Origin unknown]

yell (yel) *v.t. & v.i.* To shout; scream; roar; also, to cheer. — *n.* 1. A sharp, loud, inarticulate cry, as of pain, terror, anger, etc. 2. A rhythmic cheer composed of a series of words or nonsense syllables and shouted by a group in unison. [OE *giellan, gellan*] — **yell'er** *n.*

yel·low (yel'ō) *adj.* 1. Having the color of ripe lemons, or sunflowers. 2. Changed to a sallow color by age, sickness, or the like: a paper *yellow* with age. 3. Having a yellowish complexion, as a member of the Mongoloid ethnic group. 4. Melancholy or jealous. 5. Sensational, esp. offensively so: said of newspapers: *yellow* journalism. 6. *Informal* Cowardly; mean; dishonorable. — *n.* 1. The color of the spectrum between green and orange. 2. Any pigment or dyestuff having or producing such a color. 3. The yolk of an egg. 4. *pl. Bot.* Any of various unrelated plant diseases in which there is stunting of growth and yellowing of the foliage. 5. *pl.* Jaundice, esp. a variety that affects domestic animals. — *v.t. & v.i.* To make or become yellow. [OE *geolu*] — **yel'low·ly** *adv.* — **yel'low·ness** *n.*

yel·low-bel·lied (yel'ō-bel'ēd) *adj.* 1. *Slang* Cowardly; yellow. 2. Having a yellow underside, as a bird.

yel·low·bird (yel'ō-bûrd') *n.* Any of several yellow birds, as the American goldfinch or the yellow warbler.

yellow cake *Canadian Informal* Uranium ore; concentrated uranium oxide.

yel·low-dog contract (yel'ō-dôg', -dog') A contract with an employer, no longer legal, in which an employee agrees not to join a labor union during his term of employment.

yellow fever *Pathol.* An acute, infectious intestinal disease of tropical and semitropical regions, caused by a filterable virus transmitted by the bite of a mosquito and characterized by jaundice, vomiting, and fatty degeneration of the liver: also called *black vomit, vomito, yellow jack.*

yel·low·ham·mer (yel'ō-ham'ər) *n.* 1. An Old World bunting having in the male bright yellow plumage and blackish head and tail feathers. 2. The flicker, a bird. [prob. < OE *geolo* yellow + *amore*, a kind of bird]

yel·low·ish (yel'ō-ish) *adj.* Somewhat yellow. — **yel'low·ish·ness** *n.*

yellow jack 1. A fish of the West Indies and Florida. 2. The flag of the quarantine service. 3. Yellow fever.

yellow jacket Any of various social wasps having bright yellow markings.

yellow metal 1. A brass consisting of 60 parts copper and 40 parts zinc. 2. Gold.

yellow peril The alleged power, both political and numerical, of the Oriental peoples of Asia, conceived of as threatening white or Western supremacy.

yellow pine 1. Any of various American pines, as the loblolly pine. 2. Their tough, yellowish wood.

yellow race The Mongoloid ethnic division of mankind.

yellow streak A tendency to be cowardly, mean, etc.

yellow warbler A warbler of the southern U.S., bright yellow with brown streaks underneath.

yel·low·wood (yel'ō-wŏod') *n.* 1. The yellow or yellowish wood of a medium-sized tree of the southern U.S., having a smooth bark, showy white flowers, and yielding a yellow dye. 2. The tree. 3. Any of several other trees with yellowish wood, as the Osage orange, buckthorn, smoketree, etc.

yel·low·y (yel'ō·ē) *adj.* Yellowish.

yelp (yelp) *v.i.* 1. To utter a sharp, shrill cry or bark, as a dog. — *v.t.* 2. To express by a yelp or yelps. — *n.* A sharp, shrill cry or bark. [OE *gielpan* to boast] — **yelp'er** *n.*

yen[1] (yen) *Informal n.* An ardent longing or desire; intense want; infatuation. — *v.i.* **yenned, yen·ning** To yearn; long. [< Chinese, opium, smoke]

yen[2] (yen) *n. pl.* **yen** The standard monetary unit of Japan, equal to 100 sen: in 1960 worth about 3⁄10 U.S. cent. [< Japanese < Chinese *yüan* round, dollar]

yen·ta (yen'tə) *n.* A female gossip or meddler. [< Yiddish]

yeo·man (yō'mən) *n. pl.* **·men** (-mən) 1. A petty officer in the U.S. Navy or Coast Guard who performs clerical duties. 2. *Brit.* One who cultivates his own farm. 3. *Brit.* A yeoman of the guard. 4. Formerly, an attendant or servant in the service of a nobleman or of royalty. 5. Formerly, a freeholder next below the gentry who owned a small landed estate or farm. [ME *yeman, yoman*, prob. contr. of *yengman* young man < OE *geong* young + *mann* man]

yeo·man·ly (yō'mən·lē) *adj.* 1. Of, pertaining to, or resembling a yeoman. 2. Brave; rugged; staunch. — *adv.* Like a yeoman; bravely; staunchly.

yeoman of the (royal) guard A member of the special bodyguard of the English royal household, consisting of one hundred yeomen wearing medieval uniforms and first appointed by Henry VII: also called *beefeater.*

yeo·man·ry (yō'mən·rē) *n.* 1. The collective body of yeomen; freemen; farmers. 2. *Brit.* A home guard of volunteer cavalry.

yeoman's service Faithful and useful support or service; loyal assistance in need. Also **yeoman service.**

yep (yep) *adv. Informal* Yes. [Alter. of YES]

-yer Var. of -IER.

yes (yes) *adv.* As you say; truly; just so: a reply of affirmation or consent: opposed to *no*, and sometimes used to enforce by repetition or addition something that precedes. — *n. pl.* **yes·es** or **yes·ses** 1. A reply in the affirmative. 2. An affirmative vote or voter: often *aye.* — *v.t. & v i.* **yessed, yes·sing** To say "yes" (to). [OE *gēse*, prob. < *gēa* yea + *si*, third person sing. present subj. of *bēon* to be]

yes man *Informal* One who agrees without criticism; a servile, acquiescent assistant or subordinate; toady.

yester- *prefix* Pertaining to the day before the present; by extension of the preceding, used of longer periods than a day: *yesteryear.* [< YESTER(DAY)]

yes·ter·day (yes'tər·dē, -dā') *n.* 1. The day preceding today. 2. The near past. — *adv.* 1. On the day before today. 2. At a recent time. [OE < *giestran* yesterday + *dæg* day]

yes·ter·year (yes'tər·yir') *n.* Last year; yore. [Trans. of F *antan*; coined by D. G. Rossetti]

yet (yet) *adv.* 1. In addition; besides; further: often with a comparative: They had twenty miles *yet* to go. 2. Before or at some future time; eventually: He will *yet* succeed. 3. In continuance of a previous state or condition; still: I can hear him *yet.* 4. At the present time; now: Don't go *yet.* 5. After all the time that has or had elapsed: Are you not ready *yet*? 6. Up to the present time; before: commonly with a negative: He has never *yet* lied to me. 7. Than that which has been previously affirmed: with a comparative: It was hot yesterday; today it is hotter *yet.* 8. Nevertheless: It was hot, *yet* not unpleasant. 9. As much as; even: He did not believe the reports, nor *yet* the evidence. — **as yet** Up to now. — *conj.* 1. Nevertheless; notwithstanding: I speak to you peaceably, *yet* you will not listen. 2. But: He is willing, *yet* unable. 3. Although: active, *yet* ill. — **Syn.** See BUT[1]. [OE *gīet, gīeta*]

yew (yōō) *n.* 1. Any of several evergreen trees or shrubs, with flat, lanceolate leaves and a red berrylike fruit. 2. The hard, fine-grained, durable wood of the common yew. 3. A bow made from the wood of the yew tree. [OE *ēow, iw*]

Yid·dish (yid'ish) *n.* A Germanic language derived from the Middle High German spoken in the Rhineland in the thirteenth and fourteenth centuries, now spoken primarily by Jews in eastern Europe, and by Jewish immigrants from that region in other parts of the world. It contains elements of Hebrew and the Slavic languages, and is written in Hebrew characters. — *adj.* 1. Of or pertaining to Yiddish; written or spoken in Yiddish. 2. *Slang* Jewish. [< G *jüdisch* Jewish < *Jude* Jew]

yield (yēld) *v.t.* 1. To give forth by a natural process, or as a result of labor or cultivation. 2. To give in return, as for investment; furnish: The bonds *yield* five percent interest. 3. To give up, as to superior power; relinquish: often with *up*: to *yield* a fortress. 4. To concede or grant: to *yield* precedence. — *v.i.* 5. To provide a return; produce; bear. 6. To give up; surrender. 7. To give way, as to pressure or force; bend; collapse, etc. 8. To assent or comply, as under compulsion; consent: We *yielded* to their persuasion. 9. To give place, as through inferiority or weakness: with *to*: We will *yield* to them in nothing. — *n.* 1. The amount yielded; product, as of cultivation or mining. 2. The profit derived from invested capital. **3.** *Mil.* The explosive force of a nuclear bomb as expressed in kilotons or megatons of TNT. [OE *gieldan, geldan* to pay] — **yield′er** *n.*

yield·ing (yēl′ding) *adj.* Disposed to yield; flexible; obedient. — **yield′ing·ly** *adv.* — **yield′ing·ness** *n.*

yin (yin) *n.* In Chinese philosophy and art, the female element, that stands for darkness, cold, and death. Compare YANG. Also **Yin.** [< Chinese]

yip (yip) *n.* A yelp, as of a dog. — *v.i.* **yipped, yip·ping** To yelp. [Imit.]

yipe (yīp) *interj. Often pl.* An exclamation of fear, surprise, horror, etc.

-yl *suffix Chem.* Used to denote a radical: *ethyl, butyl.* [< Gk. *hylē* wood, matter]

yo·del (yōd′l) *n.* A melody or refrain sung to meaningless syllables, with abrupt changes from chest to falsetto tones, common among Swiss and Tyrolese mountaineers. — *v.t. & v.i.* **yo·deled** or **·delled, yo·del·ing** or **·del·ling** To sing with a yodel, changing the voice quickly from its natural tone to a falsetto and back. Also **yo′dle.** [< G *jodeln*, lit., to utter the syllable *jo*] — **yo′del·er, yo′del·ler, yo′dler** *n.*

yo·ga (yō′gə) *n.* **1.** A Hindu system of mystical and ascetic philosophy that involves certain physical and mental disciplines together with a withdrawal from the world and abstract meditation upon some spiritual principle or object. **2.** A related system of exercises, the purpose of which is to achieve both physical and spiritual well-being. [< Hind. < Skt., lit., union] — **yo·gic** (yō′gik) *adj.*

yogh (yōkh) *n.* The Middle English letter, ȝ, ȝ, that represented a voiced or voiceless palatal fricative, or a voiced velar fricative. It has been replaced in Modern English by *y*, as in *lay, w,* as in *law,* and *gh,* as in *daughter* and *enough.*

yo·gi (yō′gē) *n. pl.* **·gis 1.** One who practices yoga. **2.** Yoga. Also **yo′gee, yo′gin** (-gin). [< Hind. *yogi* < Skt.]

yo·gurt (yō′gŏort) *n.* A thick, curdled milk treated with bacteria, regarded as beneficial to the intestines. Also **yo′ghurt, yo′ghourt.** [< Turkish *yŏghurt*]

yoicks (yoiks) *interj.* Hoicks. [Earlier *hoik,* var. of HIKE]

yoke (yōk) *n. pl.* **yokes;** *for def. 3, often* **yoke 1.** A curved timber with attachments used for coupling draft animals, as oxen, usu. having a bow at each end to receive the neck of the animal. **2.** Any of various similar contrivances, as a frame fitted for a person's shoulders and designed to carry a burden at either end, as a pail. **3.** A pair of draft animals coupled with a yoke (def. 1). **4.** An oppressive force or influence: under the *yoke* of tyranny. **5.** That which binds or connects; a bond: the *yoke* of love. **6.** Servitude, or some visible sign of it; bondage. **7.** A part of a garment designed to support a plaited or gathered part, as at the hips or shoulders. **8.** *Naut.* A crosspiece on a rudderhead, carrying cables for steering. — *v.* **yoked, yok·ing** *v.t.* **1.** To put a yoke upon. **2.** To join with or as with a yoke; couple or link. **3.** To secure (a draft animal) to a plow, etc.; also, to secure a draft animal to (a plow, etc.). — *v.i.* **4.** To be joined or linked. [OE *geoc*]

YOKE (*def.* 1)

yoke·fel·low (yōk′fel′ō) *n.* A mate or companion in labor. Also **yoke′mate′** (-māt′).

yo·kel (yō′kəl) *n.* A countryman; country bumpkin: a contemptuous term. [? < dial. E, green woodpecker, yellowhammer] — **yo′kel·ish** *adj.*

yolk (yōk, yōlk) *n.* **1.** The yellow portion of an egg, as distinguished from the white portion, used for the formation and nourishment of the embryo. **2.** A fine yellow soapy exudation in sheep's wool. [OE *geol(o)ca,* lit., (the) yellow part < *geolu* yellow]

yolk·y (yō′kē, yōl′kē) *adj.* **yolk·i·er, yolk·i·est 1.** Of, like, or pertaining to yolk. **2.** Containing yolk: *yolky* wool.

Yom Kip·pur (yom kip′ər, *Hebrew* yōm ki·pŏŏr′) The Jewish Day of Atonement, the 10th of Tishri (September-October), marked by continuous prayer and fasting for 24 hours from sundown on the evening previous. [< Hebrew *yōm kipūr* day of atonement]

yon (yon) *adj. & adv. Archaic, Dial. & Poetic* Yonder; that or those over there: *yon* fine house. [OE *geon*]

yon·der (yon′dər) *adj.* Being at a distance indicated. — *adv.* In that place; there. [ME, prob. extension of *yone,* OE *geon* yon]

yore (yôr, yōr) *n.* Old time; time long past: in days of *yore.* [OE *gēara* formerly, prob. orig. genitive pl. of *gēar* year]

York boat *Canadian* A type of heavy cargo canoe used by the Hudson's Bay Company. [after *York* Factory on Hudson Bay]

York·shire pudding (yôrk′shir, -shər) A batter pudding baked under roasting meat to catch the drippings.

Yorkshire terrier A toy breed of terrier having a long, silky coat.

you (yōō) *pron., possessive* **your** or **yours 1.** The nominative and objective singular and plural pronoun of the second person, used in addressing one or more persons, animals, or things, and always taking a plural verb. **2.** An indefinite pronoun equivalent to *one: You* learn by trying. [OE *ēow,* dative and accusative pl. of *gē* ye]

you'd (yōōd, *unstressed* yŏŏd, yəd) **1.** You had. **2.** You would.

you'll (yōōl, *unstressed* yŏŏl, yəl) You will.

young (yung) *adj.* **young·er** (yung′gər), **young·est** (yung′gist) **1.** Being in the early period of life or growth; not old. **2.** Not having progressed far; newly formed: The day was *young.* **3.** Pertaining to youth or early life. **4.** Full of vigor or freshness. **5.** Being without experience; immature. **6.** Denoting the younger of two persons having the same name or title; junior. **7.** Radical or progressive in social or political aims: used with proper names: the *Young* Turks. — **Syn.** See YOUTHFUL. — *n.* **1.** Young persons as a group; youth. **2.** Offspring, esp. of animals. — **with young** With child; pregnant. [OE *geong*] — **young′ish** *adj.*

young·ber·ry (yung′ber′ē) *n. pl.* **·ries** A large dark red berry, hybridized from a trailing blackberry and a dewberry, of the western U.S. [after B. M. *Young,* U.S. horticulturist]

young blood Youth; young people.

young-eyed (yung′īd′) *adj.* Having youthful eyes or fresh vision; bright-eyed.

young·ling (yung′ling) *n.* **1.** A young person, animal, or plant. **2.** An inexperienced person. — *adj.* Young.

young·ster (yung′stər) *n.* **1.** A young person; a child or youth. **2.** A young animal, as a colt.

your (yŏŏr, yôr) *pronominal adj.* The possessive case of the pronoun *you,* used attributively: *your* fate. [OE *ēower,* genitive of *gē* ye]

you're (yŏŏr, yôr, *unstressed* yər) You are.

yours (yŏŏrz, yōrz) *pron.* **1.** The possessive case of the pronoun *you,* used predicatively: This room is *yours.* **2.** The one or ones belonging or relating to you: a home as quiet as *yours;* God bless you and *yours.* — **of yours** Belonging or relating to you: a double possessive. [ME *youres*]

your·self (yŏŏr·self′, yôr-) *pron. pl.* **·selves** (-selvz′) A form of the second person pronoun, used: **1.** As a reflexive or as object of a preposition in a reflexive sense: Did you hurt *yourself?* Look at *yourself* in the mirror. **2.** As an emphatic or intensive form of *you:* You said so *yourself.* **3.** As a designation of a normal, proper, or usual state: Why can't you be *yourself* instead of putting on airs?

yours truly 1. A formal phrase used to close a letter, before the signature. **2.** *Informal* I; me.

youth (yōōth) *n. pl.* **youths** (yōōths, yōō‖z) **1.** The state or condition of being young. **2.** The period when one is young; the part of life between childhood and manhood; adolescence. **3.** The early period of being or development, as of a movement. **4.** A young person, esp. a young man; also, young persons collectively. [OE *geoguth*]

youth·ful (yōōth′fəl) *adj.* **1.** Having youth; being still young. **2.** Characteristic of youth; fresh; vigorous. **3.** Of or pertaining to youth. **4.** Not far advanced; early; new. **5.** *Geol.* Young. — **youth′ful·ly** *adv.* — **youth′ful·ness** *n.*
— **Syn. 1.** *Youthful* describes character, manner, outlook, interests, appearance, and the like, while *young* refers merely to chronological age. A mature or old person may properly be described as *youthful,* though he is no longer *young. Juvenile* emphasizes immaturity and is therefore often disparaging; *puerile* is much the same, and is always uncomplimentary. *Adolescent* refers to the age close to maturity, and may be disparaging or not: *adolescent* pranks, *adolescent* energy and enthusiasm.

youth hostel A hostel.

you've (yōōv, *unstressed* yŏŏv, yəv) You have.

yowl (youl) *v.i.* To utter a yowl; howl; yell. — *n.* A loud, prolonged, wailing cry; a howl. Also spelled *yawl:* also **yow.** [Cf. ON *gaula* to howl, yell]

yo-yo (yō′yō′) *n. pl.* **-yos** A wheellike toy with a string wound about it in a deep groove, commonly attached to the operator's finger and spun up and down by manipulating the string. [Origin unknown]

Y·quem (ē·kem′) *n.* A highly esteemed Sauterne wine. [after Château *Yquem,* an estate in SW France]

yt·ter·bi·um (i·tûr′bē·əm) *n.* A rare metallic element (symbol Yb) of the lanthanide series, occurring in minute amounts in gadolinite and certain other minerals. See ELEMENT. [< NL, from *Ytterby,* a town in Sweden where gadolinite was first found] — **yt·ter′bic** *adj.*

yt·tri·um (it′rē·əm) *n.* A rare element (symbol Y) of the lanthanide series, found in gadolinite, samarskite, and other minerals. See ELEMENT. Abbr. *Yt* [< NL < YTTRIA]

yuc·ca (yuk′ə) *n.* **1.** Any of various liliaceous plants of the southern U.S., Mexico, and Central America, having a woody stem that bears a large panicle of white, bell-shaped, drooping flowers emerging from a crown of leaves. **2.** The flower of this plant, the State flower of New Mexico. [< NL < Sp. *yuca* < Taino]

Yu·go·slav (yōō'gō·släv, -slav) *adj.* Of or pertaining to Yugoslavia or its people. — *n.* A citizen or native of Yugoslavia. Also **Yu'go·sla'vi·an.**

yuk (yuk) *U.S. Slang n.* A loud, hearty laugh. — *v.i. & v.t.* **yukked, yuk·king** To laugh or cause to laugh loud and heartily.

Yule (yōōl) *n.* Christmas time, or the feast celebrating it. [OE *gēol* Christmas day, Christmastide]

yule log A large log or block of wood, brought in with much ceremony, and made the foundation of the Christmas Eve fire. Also **yule block, yule clog.**

Yule·tide (yōōl'tīd) *n.* Christmas time.

Yu·ma (yōō'mə) *n.* One of a tribe of North American Indians of Yuman stock, formerly living in northern Mexico and Arizona and in SE California.

Yu·man (yōō'mən) *n.* A North American Indian stock of the SW U.S. and NW Mexico, including the Mohave and Yuma tribes.

yum·my (yum'ē) *Slang adj.* **·mi·er, ·mi·est** Gratifying to the senses, esp. to the taste; delicious. — *n.* Something very gratifying; a delight. [from *yum-yum*, an exclamation expressing delight at an agreeable taste]

yurt (yûrt) *n.* A portable tent made of felt laid on a framework of branches, used by nomadic Mongols in central Asia. [< Russian *yurta* < Turkic]

Z

z, Z (zē, *Brit.* zed) *n.* *pl.* **z's** or **zs, Z's** or **Zs, zees** (zēz) **1.** The twenty-sixth letter of the English alphabet. Also, *Brit.,* **zed.** **2.** The sound represented by the letter *z,* a voiced alveolar fricative corresponding to the voiceless *s.* — *symbol* **1.** *Physics* Atomic number. **2.** *Math.* An unknown quantity.

Zach·a·ri·ah (zak'ə·rī'ə) The last king of Israel of Jehu's race. II *Kings* xiv 29.

Zach·a·ri·as (zak'ə·rī'əs) **1.** The father of John the Baptist. *Luke* i 5. **2.** The Douai Bible name for ZECHARIAH.

zai·bat·su (zī·bät·sōō) *n.* *Japanese* The wealthy clique of Japan, representing four or five dominant families.

za·mar·ra (zə·mär'ə, -mar'ə) *n.* A sheepskin coat worn by Spanish shepherds. Also **za·mar'ro** (-mär'ō). [< Sp.]

za·ny (zā'nē) *adj.* **·ni·er, ·ni·est** Odd and comical; outlandish; ludicrous. — *n.* *pl.* **·nies 1.** A simpleton; buffoon; fool. **2.** In old comic plays, one who imitated the other performers, esp. the clown, with ludicrous failure. [< F < Ital. *zanni* servants who act as clowns in early Italian comedy]

zap·ti·ah (zup·tē'ä) *n.* A Turkish policeman. Also **zap·ti'e, zap·ti'eh.** [< Turkish *dabtiyeh* < Arabic *dabt* administration, regulation]

za·ra·pe (sä·rä'pā) See SERAPE.

za·re·ba (zə·rē'bə) *n.* **1.** In the Sudan, a stockade or other palisaded enclosure for protecting a village or camp. **2.** A village or camp so protected; also, any village. Also **za·ree'ba.** [< Arabic *zarībah* pen for cattle < *zarb* sheepfold]

zarf (zärf) *n.* A metal cup-shaped holder, of open or ornamental filigree, for a hot coffee cup, used in the Levant. [< Arabic *zarf* vessel, sheath]

zar·zue·la (thär·thwā'lä) *n.* *Spanish* A form of lyrical theater in which song is intermingled with spoken dialogue.

za·yin (zä'yin) *n.* The seventh letter in the Hebrew alphabet. See ALPHABET.

zeal (zēl) *n.* Enthusiastic devotion; ardor, esp. for a cause. [< OF < L < Gk. *zēlos* < *zeein* to boil]

zeal·ot (zel'ət) *n.* **1.** An immoderate partisan; a fanatic. **2.** One who is zealous. [< LL < Gk. < *zēloein* to be zealous < *zēlos* zeal] — **zeal'ot·ry** *n.*

zeal·ous (zel'əs) *adj.* Filled with or incited by zeal; enthusiastic. — **zeal'ous·ly** *adv.* — **zeal'ous·ness** *n.*

ze·bec (zē'bek), **ze·beck** See XEBEC.

Zeb·e·dee (zeb'ə·dē) The father of James and John, disciples of Christ. *Matt.* iv 21.

ze·bra (zē'brə) *n.* Any of various African equine mammals resembling the ass, having a white or yellowish brown body fully marked with variously patterned, dark brown or blackish bands. [< Pg. < Bantu (Congo)] — **ze'brine** (-brēn, -brin), **ze'broid** (-broid) *adj.*

ze·bu (zē'byōō) *n.* The domesticated ox of India, China, and East Africa, having a hump on the withers, a large dewlap, and short horns. [< F *zébu* < Tibetan]

Zeb·u·lon (zeb'yə·lən) In the Old Testament, a son of Jacob and Leah. *Gen.* xxx 20. — *n.* The tribe of Israel descended from him. Also **Zeb'u·lun.**

Zech·a·ri·ah (zek'ə·rī'ə) Sixth-century B.C. Hebrew prophet who promoted the rebuilding of the Temple. — *n.* A book of the Old Testament bearing his name. Also, in the Douai Bible, *Zacharias.*

zed (zed) *n.* *Brit.* The letter Z. [< F < L < Gk. *zēta*]

zee (zē, *Du.* zā) *n.* *Dutch* Sea: used in geographic names: *Zuider Zee, Tappen Zee.*

Zeit·geist (tsīt'gīst) *n.* *German* The spirit of the time;

the intellectual and moral tendencies that characterize any age or epoch. [< G < *zeit* time + *geist* spirit]

zemst·vo (zem'stvō, *Russ.* zyem'stvō) *n.* Prior to 1917, a Russian elective district. [< Russian *semlya* land]

ze·na·na (zə·nä'nə) *n.* In India, the women's apartments; the East Indian harem: also spelled *zanana.* [< Hind. *zenāna* belonging to women < Persian *zanāna* < *zan* woman]

Zen Buddhism (zen) A form of contemplative Buddhism whose adherents believe in and work toward abrupt enlightenment. It originated in China, and later spread to Japan, where it greatly influenced Japanese culture. Also **Zen.** [< Japanese *zen* meditation < Chinese < Skt. *dhyana*]

Zend (zend) *n.* **1.** The ancient translation and commentary, in a literary form of Middle Persian (Pahlavi), of the Avesta, the sacred writings of the Zoroastrian religion. **2.** Erroneously, the language of the Avesta; Avestan. [< F < Persian, interpretation] — **Zend'ic** *adj.*

Zend-A·ves·ta (zend'ə·ves'tə) *n.* The Avesta, including the later translation and commentary called the Zend. — **Zend'-A·ves·ta'ic** (-ə·ves·tā'ik) *adj.*

ze·nith (zē'nith) *n.* **1.** The point of the celestial sphere that is exactly overhead, and opposite to the nadir. **2.** The highest or culminating point; peak: the *zenith* of one's career: opposed to *nadir.* [< OF *cenit,* ult. < Arabic *samt* (*ar-ras*) the path (over the head)]

ze·o·lite (zē'ə·līt) *n.* Any of a large class of secondary minerals found in cavities and veins in eruptive rocks, usu. a hydrous silicate of aluminum and sodium. [< Sw. < Gk. *zeein* to boil + *lithos* stone] — **ze·o·lit'ic** (-lit'ik) *adj.*

Zeph·a·ni·ah (zef'ə·nī'ə) Seventh-century B.C. Hebrew prophet. — *n.* A book of the Old Testament bearing his name. Also, in the Douai Bible, *Sophonias.*

zeph·yr (zef'ər) *n.* **1.** The west wind. **2.** Any soft, gentle wind. **3.** Worsted or woolen yarn of very light weight used for embroidery, shawls, etc.: also **zephyr worsted. 4.** Anything very light and airy. [< L < Gk. *zephyros*]

zephyr cloth Fine cassimere used for women's clothing.

zep·pe·lin (zep'ə·lin, *Ger.* tsep'ə·lēn') *n.* Often *cap.* A large dirigible having a rigid, cigar-shaped body. [after Count Ferdinand von *Zeppelin,* 1838–1917, German general and aviator who designed it]

ze·ro (zir'ō, zē'rō) *n.* *pl.* **ze·ros** or **ze·roes 1.** The numeral or symbol 0; a cipher. ◆ In nontechnical speech, this symbol is often pronounced (ō). **2.** *Math.* **a** A cardinal number indicating the absence of quantity. **b** The point where a continuous function changes its sign from plus to minus, or vice versa. **3.** The point on a scale, as of a thermometer, from which measures are counted; also, a temperature that registers zero on a thermometer. **4.** *Mil.* A setting for a gunsight that adjusts both for elevation and wind. **5.** The lowest point. **6.** Nothing. — *v.t.* **ze·roed, ze·ro·ing** To adjust (instruments) to an arbitrary zero point for synchronized readings. — **to zero in 1.** To adjust the sight of (a gun) by calibrated results of firings. **2.** To direct firepower exactly on target. **3.** To approach or give one's attention to as though directed to a target. — *adj.* Without value or appreciable change. [< F < Ital. < Arabic *sifr*]

zero gravity *Aerospace* A condition in which the gravitational attraction of the earth or other celestial body is nullified by inertial forces; weightlessness.

zero hour 1. H-hour. **2.** *Informal* The moment of undertaking something; any critical moment.

zest (zest) *n.* **1.** Invigorating excitement; keen enjoyment;

gusto: often with *for*: a *zest* for reading. **2.** That which imparts such excitement and relish. **3.** An agreeable and piquant flavor in anything tasted, esp. if added to the usual flavor. — *v.t.* To give zest or relish to; make piquant. [< F *zeste* lemon peel (for flavoring)]

zest·ful (zest′fəl) *adj.* Full of or marked by zest. Also **zest′y.** — **zest′ful·ly** *adv.* — **zest′ful·ness** *n.*

ze·ta (zā′tə, zē′-) *n.* The sixth letter (Z, ζ) in the Greek alphabet, corresponding to English *z*. See ALPHABET. [< Gk. *zēta*]

zeug·ma (zōōg′mə) *n.* A rhetorical figure in which an adjective is made to modify, or a verb to govern, two nouns, while applying properly only to one, as in *She was remembered but they forgotten.* [< NL < Gk. < *zeugnymi* to yoke]

Zeus (zōōs) In Greek mythology, the supreme deity, ruler of the celestial realm, son of Kronos and Rhea and husband of Hera: identified with the Roman *Jupiter.*

zib·et (zib′it) *n.* The Asian or Indian civet. Also **zib′eth.** [< Med.L < Arabic *zabād* civet]

zig·zag (zig′zag) *n.* **1.** A series of short, sharp turns or angles from one side to the other in succession. **2.** Something characterized by such angles, as a path or pattern. — *adj.* Having or proceeding in a zigzag. — *adv.* In a zigzag manner. — *v.t. & v.i.* **·zagged, ·zag·ging** To form or move in zigzags. [< F < G *zickzack,* prob. reduplication of *zacke* sharp point] — **zig′zag·ger** *n.*

zinc (zingk) *n.* A bluish white, metallic element (symbol Zn) occurring mostly in combination, widely used in industry, medicine, the arts, for roofing, and as the negative electrode in electric batteries. See ELEMENT. — *v.t.* **zincked** or **zinced, zinck·ing** or **zinc·ing** To coat or cover with zinc; galvanize. [< G *zink;* ult. origin unknown] — **zinc′ic** *adj.* — **zinck′y, zinc′y, zink′y** *adj.*

zinc blende Sphalerite.

zinc ointment A medicated ointment for skin affections, containing zinc oxide mixed with petrolatum.

zinc·ous (zingk′əs) *adj. Chem.* Pertaining to or derived from zinc.

zinc oxide *Chem.* A white pulverulent compound ZnO, used as a pigment, and in medicine as a mild antiseptic and astringent.

zinc white Zinc oxide used as a pigment in paints.

zin·fan·del (zin′fän·del) *n.* A dry, red or white claret-type wine made in California. [? after a European place name]

zing (zing) *Informal n.* **1.** A high-pitched buzzing or humming sound. **2.** Energy; vitality; vigor. — *v.i.* To make a shrill, humming sound. [Imit.]

zin·ga·ro (tsēng′gä·rō) *n. pl. ·ri* (-rē) *Italian* A gypsy. Also **zin′ga·no** (-nō). — **zin′ga·ra** (-rä) *n.fem.*

zin·ni·a (zin′ē·ə) *n.* Any of various American herbs, having showy flowers; esp., the common zinnia, the State flower of Indiana. [< NL, after J. G. *Zinn,* 1727–59, German professor of medicine]

Zi·on (zī′ən) **1.** A hill in Jerusalem, the site of the temple and the royal residence of David and his successors, regarded by the Jews as a symbol for the center of Jewish national culture, government, and religion. **2.** The Jewish people. **3.** Any place or community considered to be especially under God's rule. **4.** The heavenly Jerusalem; heaven. Also *Sion.* [OE < LL < Gk. < Hebrew *tsiyōn* hill]

Zi·on·ism (zī′ən·iz′əm) *n.* A movement for a resettlement of the Jews in Palestine. Also **Zion movement.** — **Zi′on·ist** *adj. & n.* — **Zi′on·is′tic** *adj.*

zip (zip) *n.* **1.** A sharp, hissing sound, as of a bullet passing through the air. **2.** *Informal* Energy; vitality; vim. — *v.* **zipped, zip·ping** *v.t.* **1.** To fasten with a zipper. — *v.i.* **2.** *Informal* To be very energetic. **3.** To move or fly with a zip. [Imit.]

ZIP Code (zip) A numerical code devised by the U.S. Post Office to aid in the distribution of domestic mail. Also **Zip Code.** [< Z(ONE) I(MPROVEMENT) P(LAN)]

zip gun *U.S. Slang* A homemade pistol consisting of a small pipe or other tube fastened to a block of wood and equipped with a firing pin actuated by a spring or rubber band.

zip·per (zip′ər) *n.* A fastener having two rows of interlocking teeth that may be closed or separated by a sliding device, used on clothing, boots, etc.: also called *slide fastener.*

zip·py (zip′ē) *adj.* **·pi·er, ·pi·est** *Informal* Brisk; energetic.

zir·con (zûr′kon) *n.* A crystalline, variously colored, zirconium silicate, ZrSiO₄; some translucent varieties of which are used as gems. [< G *zirken* or F *zircone* < Arabic *zarqūn* cinnabar < Persian < *zar* gold + *gūn* color]

zir·co·ni·um (zûr·kō′nē·əm) *n.* A metallic element (symbol Zr) chemically resembling titanium, used in alloys, as an opacifier of lacquers, and as an abrasive. See ELEMENT. [< NL < ZIRCON] — **zir·con′ic** (-kon′ik) *adj.*

zith·er (zith′ər) *n.* A simple form of stringed instrument, having a flat sounding board and from thirty to forty strings

that are played by plucking with a plectrum. Also **zith′ern** (-ərn). [< G < L < Gk. *kithara*]

zlo·ty (zlô′tē) *n. pl. ·tys* or **·ty** The standard monetary unit of Poland, equal to 100 groszy: in 1960 worth about 25 U.S. cents. [< Polish, lit., golden]

zo- Var. of ZOO-.

zo·di·ac (zō′dē·ak) *n.* **1.** An imaginary belt encircling the heavens and extending about 8° on each side of the ecliptic within which are the apparent orbits of the moon, sun, and larger planets. It is divided into twelve parts, called **signs of the zodiac,** that formerly corresponded to twelve constellations bearing the same names. **2.** A figure or diagram representing this belt and its signs, used in astrology. **3.** A complete circuit. [< OF < L < Gk. < *zōdiakos* (circle) of animals < *zōion* animal] — **zo·di·a·cal** (zō·dī′ə·kəl) *adj.*

SIGNS OF THE ZODIAC

A Vernal equinox: Aries, Taurus, Gemini. *B* Summer solstice: Cancer, Leo, Virgo. *C* Autumnal equinox: Libra, Scorpio, Sagittarius. *D* Winter solstice: Capricorn, Aquarius, Pisces.

zom·bie (zom′bē) *n.* **1.** The supernatural power by which a dead body is believed to be reanimated. **2.** A corpse reactivated by sorcery, but still dead. **3.** Loosely, a ghost. **4.** A large, strong cocktail made from several kinds of rum, fruit juices, and liqueur. **5.** *Slang* An unattractive person. Also **zom′bi.** [< West African] — **zom′bi·ism** *n.*

zo·nal (zō′nəl) *adj.* Of, pertaining to, exhibiting, or marked by a zone or zones; like a zone. Also **zo′na·ry** (-nər·ē).

zone (zōn) *n.* **1.** An area, tract, or section distinguished from other or adjacent areas by some special quality, purpose, or condition: a mountainous *zone;* a *zone* of disagreement. **2.** *Usu. cap.* Any of five divisions of the earth's surface, enclosed between two parallels of latitude and named for the prevailing climate: the **Torrid Zone,** extending on each side of the equator 23° 27′; the **Temperate Zones,** included between the parallels 23° 27′ and 66° 33′ on both sides of the equator, and the **Frigid Zones,** within the parallels 66° 33′ and the poles. **3.** An area of land designated as distinct from other areas because of its particular use or location: combat *zone;* school *zone.* **4.** *Ecol.* A belt or area delimited from others by the character of its plant or animal life, its climate, geological formations, etc. **5.** A concentric area or band; esp., any of a number of concentric areas used to determine the rate of charge for transporting something a specified distance, as in the U.S. parcel post system. **6.** A section of a city or town where only certain uses of the land or certain types of buildings are permitted by law: a residential *zone.* **7.** A section of a city designated with a number as an aid in the distribution of mail. **8.** A belt, band, stripe, etc., having a color or other characteristic that distinguishes it from the object it encircles. **9.** *Geom.* A portion of the surface of a sphere enclosed between two parallel planes. **10.** *Archaic* or *Poetic* A belt or girdle. — *v.t.* **zoned, zon·ing** **1.** To divide into zones; esp., to divide (a city, etc.) into zones that are restricted as to types of construction and use, as residential or industrial. **2.** To designate (an area, etc.) as a zone or part of a zone: to *zone* the waterfront district as commercial. **3.** To mark with or as with zones or stripes. **4.** To encircle with a zone or belt. [< L < Gk. *zōnē* girdle]

TERRESTRIAL ZONES

zoo (zōō) *n.* A park or garden in which wild animals are kept for exhibition. Also **zoological garden, zoological park.**

zoo- *combining form* Animal; of or related to animals, or to animal forms. Also, before vowels, **zo-.** [< Gk. *zōion* animal]

zo·o·ge·og·ra·phy (zō′ə·jē·og′rə·fē) *n.* The systematic study of the distribution of animals and of the relations between animal groups and the land or aquatic areas in which they predominate. **— zo·o·ge·og′ra·pher** *n*. **— zo′o·ge′o·graph′ic** (-jē′ə·graf′ik) or **·i·cal** *adj*. **— zo′o·ge′o·graph′i·cal·ly** *adv*.

zo·oid (zō′oid) *n*. **1.** *Biol*. Any animal or vegetable organism, usu. very small, capable of spontaneous movement and independent existence, as a spermatozoon, spermatozoid, etc. **2.** *Zool*. One of the distinct members of a compound or colonial organism. *— adj*. Having the nature of an animal: also **zo·oi·dal** (zō·oid′l).

zo·o·log·i·cal (zō′ə·loj′i·kəl) *adj*. **1.** Of or pertaining to zoology. **2.** Relating to or characteristic of animals. Also **zo′o·log′ic**. **— zo′o·log′i·cal·ly** *adv*.

zo·ol·o·gy (zō·ol′ə·jē) *n*. **1.** The science that treats of animals with reference to their structure, functions, development, evolution, and classification. **2.** The animal kingdom, or local examples of it, regarded biologically. [< NL < Gk. *zōion* animal + *logos* word, discourse] **— zo·ol′o·gist** *n*.

zoom (zōōm) *v.i*. **1.** To make a low-pitched but loud humming sound; also, to move with such a sound. **2.** To climb sharply in an airplane. *— v.t*. **3.** To cause to zoom. *— n*. The act of zooming. [Imit.]

zoom lens *Photog*. A lens, used chiefly on television and motion picture cameras, that permits the size of the image to be varied continuously without loss of focus.

zo·o·mor·phism (zō′ə·môr′fiz·əm) *n*. **1.** The conception, symbolization, or representation of a man or a god in the form of an animal; also, the attribution of divine or human qualities to animals. **2.** The representation of animals or animal forms in art or symbolism. **3.** Transformation into animals. Also **zo′o·mor′phy**. **·— zo′o·mor′phic** *adj*.

zo·o·phyte (zō′ə·fīt) *n*. An invertebrate animal resembling a plant, as a coral or sea anemone. **— zo′o·phyt′ic** (-fit′ik) or **·i·cal** *adj*.

zo·o·spore (zō′ə·spôr, -spōr) *n*. **1.** *Bot*. A spore, produced among some algae and fungi, that is provided with cilia by means of which it can move about. **2.** *Zool*. A flagellate or ameboid motile body in certain protozoa. **— zo′o·spor′ic** (-spôr′ik, -spor′ik), **zo·os·po·rous** (zō·os′pər·əs) *adj*.

Zo·ro·as·tri·an (zō′rō·as′trē·ən) *n*. A follower of Zoroaster; an adherent of Zoroastrianism. *— adj*. Of or pertaining to Zoroaster or to the religion he founded.

Zo·ro·as·tri·an·ism (zō′rō·as′trē·ən·iz′əm) *n*. The religious system founded by Zoroaster and taught in the Zend-Avesta. It recognizes two creative powers, one good and the other evil, includes the belief in life after death, and teaches the final triumph of good over evil. Also **Zo′ro·as′trism**.

Zou·ave (zōō·äv′, swäv) *n*. **1.** A light-armed French infantryman wearing a brilliant Oriental uniform, originally an Algerian recruit. **2.** In the Civil War, a member of a volunteer regiment assuming the name and part of the dress of the French Zouaves. **3.** A woman's short, gaily embroid-

ered jacket: also **Zouave jacket**. [< F < Arabic *Zouâoua*, a Kabyle tribe]

zounds (zoundz, zōōndz) *interj*. *Archaic* A mild oath used to express surprise or anger. [Short for *God's wounds*]

zuc·chet·to (tsōōk·ket′tō) *n*. A skullcap worn by ecclesiastics in the Roman Catholic Church, black for a priest, purple for a bishop, red for a cardinal, and white for the pope. Also **zuc·chet′ta** (-tä). [Var. of Ital. *zucchetta*, < LL *cucutia* a kind of wood]

zuc·chi·ni (zōō·kē′nē, *Ital*. dzōōk·kē′nē) *n*. A type of green summer squash of cylindrical shape. [< Ital., pl. of *zucchino*, dim. of *zucca* gourd, squash]

Zu·lu (zōō′lōō) *n*. *pl*. **Zu·lus** or **Zu·lu 1.** One of a Bantu nation of Natal, South Africa, sometimes included with the Kaffirs. **2.** The Bantu language of the Zulus. *— adj*. Of, pertaining to, or characteristic of the Zulus or their language.

Zu·ñi (zōō′nyē) *n*. **1.** One of a tribe of North American Indians of pueblo culture but comprising a distinct, ethnic stock, living in New Mexico. **2.** The language of this tribe. **— Zu′ñi·an** *adj. & n*.

zwie·back (zwī′bak, zwē′-, swī′, swē′-, -bäk; *Ger*. tsvē′bäk) *n*. A biscuit of wheaten breat or rusk baked yellow in the loaf and later sliced and toasted. [< G, twice baked < *zwie*-twice (< *zwei* two) + *backen* to bake]

zygo- *combining form* Yoke; pair; resembling a yoke, esp. in shape. Also, before vowels, **zyg-**. [< Gk. *zygon* yoke]

zy·gote (zī′gōt, zig′ōt) *n*. *Biol*. **1.** The product of the union of two gametes. **2.** A new organism developed from such a union. [< Gk. < *zygon* yoke] **— zy·got·ic** (zī·got′·ik) *adj*.

zy·mase (zī′mās) *n*. *Biochem*. An enzyme, obtained principally from yeast, that induces fermentation by breaking down glucose and related carbohydrates into alcohol and carbon dioxide. [< F < Gk. *zymē* leaven]

zyme (zīm) *n*. A disease germ or virus supposed to be the specific cause of a zymotic disease. [< Gk. *zymē* leaven]

zymo- *combining form* Fermentation; of or related to fermentation. Also, before vowels, **zym-**. [< Gk. *zymē* leaven]

zy·mol·o·gy (zī·mol′ə·jē) *n*. The study of fermentation and the action of enzymes. **— zy·mo·log·ic** (zī′mə·loj′ik) or **·i·cal** *adj*. **— zy·mol′o·gist** *n*.

zy·mol·y·sis (zī·mol′ə·sis) *n*. Fermentation or the action of enzymes. **— zy·mo·lyt·ic** (zī′mə·lit′ik) *adj*.

zy·mo·sis (zī·mō′sis) *n*. *pl*. **·ses 1.** Any form of fermentation. **2.** *Med*. A process resembling fermentation formerly supposed to give rise to a diseased condition. [< NL < Gk. < *zymoein* to leaven, ferment < *zymē* leaven] **— zy·mot′ic** (-mot′ik) *adj*.

zy·mur·gy (zī′mûr·jē) *n*. A branch of chemistry treating of processes in which fermentation takes place, as brewing, winemaking, etc.

SUPPLEMENT

A PRONOUNCING GAZETTEER

This gazetteer lists all of the more important political divisions and geographical features of the world, and all the urban localities in the United States and Canada having a population of 5,000 or more. The population figures given for places in the United States are from the census of 1970; those for Canada and Australia are from the censuses of 1966. All other population figures are rounded to the nearest thousand.

An additional feature of this section is the inclusion of the postal ZIP codes for places in the United States. These were not, however, available in all cases. The asterisk (*) following some ZIP codes indicates that the city is further divided into postal zones and that the number given does not adequately identify a post office. In such cases further information is available from local postal authorities.

To conserve space, the following abbreviations have been used throughout this section:

ab.	about	NW	northwest(ern)
adm.	administrative	penin.	peninsula
ASSR	Autonomous Soviet Socialist Republic	poss.	possession
		prot.	protectorate
boro.	borough	prov.	province
cap.	capital or county seat	reg.	region
		s	south(ern)
CEN.	central	SE	southeast(ern)
co.	county	SSR	Soviet Socialist Republic
col.	colony		
ctr.	center	SW	southwest(ern)
dept.	department	terr.	territory
dist.	district	twp.	township
div.	division	uninc.	unincorporated
E	east(ern)	urb.	urban
isl(s).	island(s)	USSR	Union of Soviet Socialist Republics
mtn(s).	mountain(s)		
N	north(ern)	vill.	village
NE	northeast(ern)	W	west(ern)

Aa·chen (ä′kən) city, W West Germany; 176,864.

Aar·hus (ôr′hōōs) co., E Denmark; 310 sq. mi.; 210,000. — city, E Aarhus co.; cap.; 119,000.

Ab·be·ville (ăb′ē·vil, -bi-) town, s Louisiana; 10,996; ZIP 70510.

— city, NW South Carolina; 5,515; ZIP 29620.

Ab·er·deen (ab·ər·dēn′) co., NE Scotland; 1,972 sq. mi.; 299,000. — city, SE Aberdeen co.; cap.; 183,463.

Ab·er·deen (ab′ər·dēn) town, NE Maryland; 12,375 (ZIP 21001); site of **Aberdeen Proving Ground**, a U.S. Army reservation; ZIP 21005.

— city, E Mississippi; 6,157; ZIP 39730.

— city, NE South Dakota; 26,476; ZIP 57401*.

— port city, W Washington; 18,489; ZIP 98520.

A·bi·djan (ä·bē·jän′) city, SE Ivory Coast; cap.; 500,000.

Ab·i·lene (ab′ə·lēn) city, E CEN. Kansas; 6,661; ZIP 67410.

— city, N CEN. Texas; 89,653; ZIP 79600.

Ab·ing·ton (ab′ing·tən) town, E Massachusetts; 12,334; ZIP 02351. — urb. twp., SE Pennsylvania; 8,594; ZIP 19001.

A·bu Dha·bi (ä′bōō dä′bē) city, N United Arab Emirates; cap.; 75,000

A·ca·pul·co (ä′kä·pōōl′kō) city, SW Mexico; 49,149.

Ac·cra (ä·krä′, ak′rə) city, s Ghana; cap.; 521,900.

A·chae·a (ə·kē′ə) dept., N Peloponessus, Greece; 1,146 sq. mi.; 229,000; cap. Patras.

A·con·ca·gua (ä′kôn·kä′gwä) extinct volcano, W CEN. Argentina; 22,834 ft.

A·cre (ä′kər, ä′kər) city, NE Israel; 24,000.

Ac·ton (ak′tən) town, NE Massachusetts; 14,770; ZIP 01720.

A·cush·net (ə·kōōsh′nit) town, NE Massachusetts; 7,767.

A·da (ā′də) city, NW Ohio; 5,309; ZIP 45810.

— city, s CEN. Oklahoma; 14,859; ZIP 74820*.

Ad·ams (ad′əmz) town, NW Massachusetts; 11,772; ZIP 01220.

Ad·dis Ab·a·ba (ä′dis ä′bə·bä, ad′is ab′ə·bə) city, CEN. Ethiopia; cap.; ab. 504,900.

Ad·di·son (ad′ə·sən) vill., NE Illinois; 24,482; ZIP 60101.

Ad·e·laide (ad′ə·lād) city, SE South Australia; cap.; 726,930.

A·den (äd′n, ād′n) port city, SW People's Democratic Republic of Yemen; cap.; 225,000.

Aden, Gulf of inlet of Arabian Sea betw. South Yemen and Somalia.

Aden Protectorate Formerly, group of Arab tribal districts comprising a British protectorate; now part of South Yemen; SW Arabian penin.; 150,000 sq. mi.; 650,000.

Ad·i·ron·dack Mountains (ad′ə·ron′dak) mtn. range, NE New York.

Ad·jun·tas (äd·hōōn′täs) town, CEN. Puerto Rico; 5,318; ZIP 00601.

A·dri·an (ā′drē·ən) city, SE Michigan; 20,382; ZIP 49221.

A·dri·at·ic Sea (ā′drē·at′ik) inlet of the Mediterranean Sea, E of Italy.

Ae·ge·an Sea (i·jē′ən) inlet of the Mediterranean Sea betw. Greece and Asia Minor.

Af·ghan·i·stan (af·gan′ə·stan) kingdom, s CEN. Asia; 250,000 sq. mi.; 12 million; cap. Kabul.

Af·ri·ca (af′ri·kə) second largest continent, s of Europe and W of Asia; 11,710,000 sq. mi.; 236 million.

Af·ton (af′tən) town, NE Missouri; 24,067; ZIP 63123.

A·ga·ña (ä·gä′nyä) city, W Guam; cap.; 1,642; ZIP 96910.

Ag·a·wam (ag′ə·wôm) town, W Massachusetts; 21,717; ZIP 01001.

A·gra (ä′grä, ä′grə) city, N India; site of Taj Mahal; 543,397.

A·gua·dil·la (ä′gwä·dē′yä) town, NW Puerto Rico; 15,943; ZIP 00603*.

A·guas·ca·lien·tes (ä′gwäs·kä·lyen′täs) state, CEN. Mexico; 2,499 sq. mi.; 237,000. — city, CEN. Aguascalientes state; cap.; 152,298.

A·gul·has (ə·gul′əs), **Cape** cape s South Africa; southernmost point of Africa.

Ah·med·a·bad (ä′məd·ä·bäd′) city, W India; temporary cap. of Gujarat; 1,347,999.

A·hos·kie (ə·hos′kē) city, NE North Carolina; 5,105; ZIP 27910.

Ai·bo·ni·to (ī·bō·nē′tō) town, CEN. Puerto Rico; 5,477; ZIP 00609.

A·ie·a (ä·yä′ə) town, s Oahu, Hawaii; 12,560; ZIP 96701.

Ai·ken (ā′kin) city, W South Carolina; 13,436; ZIP 29801*.

Aisne (ān) river, N France; 175 mi. long.

A·jac·cio (ä·yä′chō) city, W Corsica; cap.; birthplace of Napoleon; 41,006.

A·jax (ā′jaks) town, s Ontario, Canada; 9,412.

A·jo (ä′hō) vill., SW Arizona; 5,049; ZIP 85321.

Ak·ron (ak′rən) city, NE Ohio; 275,425; ZIP 44300*. = 3,444,165; cap. Montgomery.

Al·a·bam·a (al′ə·bam′ə) state, SE United States; 51,609 sq. mi.; 3,444,165; cap. Montgomery.

Al·a·me·da (al′ə·mē′də, -mä′-) city, W California; 70,968; ZIP 94501*.

Al·a·me·da (al′ə·mē′də) vill., SE Idaho; 40,036; ZIP see POCATELLO.

Al·a·mo·gor·do (al′ə·mə·gôr′dō) town, s New Mexico; site of the first atom bomb test; 23,035; ZIP 88310.

Al·a·mo Heights (al′ə·mō) city, s CEN. Texas; 6,933; ZIP see SAN ANTONIO.

Al·a·mo·sa (al′ə·mō′sə) city, s Colorado; 6,985; ZIP 81101.

A·las·ka (ə·las′kə) state of the United States, NW North America; 586,400 sq. mi.; 302,173; cap. Juneau.

Alaska, Gulf of inlet of the Pacific on the s coast of Alaska.

Alaska Highway road joining Dawson Creek, British Columbia and Fairbanks, Alaska; 1,527 mi.

Alaska Peninsula promontory of SW Alaska; ab. 400 mi. long.

Alaska Range mtn. range, s CEN. Alaska.

Al·ba·ni·a (al·bā′nē·ə, -bän′yə) Balkan republic s of Yugoslavia; 10,629 sq. mi.; 1,507,000; cap. Tirana.

Al·ba·ny (ôl′bə·nē) city, W California; 14,674; ZIP see BERKELEY.

— city, SW Georgia; 72,623; ZIP 31701*.

— city, E New York; cap.; 114,873; ZIP 12200*.

— city, W Oregon, 18,181; ZIP 97321.

Al·be·marle (al′bə·märl) town, s CEN. North Carolina; 11,126; ZIP 28001.

Albemarle Sound inlet of the Atlantic, NE North Carolina.

Al·ber·ta (al·bûr′tə) prov., W Canada; 255,285 sq. mi.; 1,463,203; cap. Edmonton.

Al·bert Lea (al′bûrt lē) city, s Minnesota; 19,418; ZIP 56007.

Al·bert·son (al′bûrt·sən) town, SE New York; 6,792; ZIP 11507.

Al·bert·ville (al′bûrt·vil) city, NE Alabama; 9,963; ZIP 35950.

Al·bi·on (al′bē·ən) city, s Michigan; 12,112; ZIP 49224.

— vill., W New York; 5,122; ZIP 14411.

Al·bu·quer·que (al′bə·kûr′kē) city, NW New Mexico; 243,751; ZIP 87100*.

Al·can Highway (al′kan) Alaska Highway: *unofficial name.*

Al·co·a (al·kō′ə) city, E Tennessee; 7,739; ZIP 37701.

Al·dan (ôl′dən) city, SE Pennsylvania; 5,001; ZIP 19018.

Al·der·ney (ôl′dər·nē) island, N Channel Islands; 3 sq. mi.

A·lep·po (ə·lep′ō) city, NE Syria; 528,618.

A·leu·tian Islands (ə·lōō′shən) island group, SW of the Alaska Peninsula.

Al·ex·an·der City (al′ig·zan′dər) city E Alabama; 12,358; ZIP 35010.

Al·ex·an·dri·a (al/ig·zan/drē·ə -zän-) city, N United Arab Republic; summer cap.; 1,513,000.
Al·ex·an·dri·a (al/ig·zan/drē·ə) city, E CEN. Indiana; 5,097; ZIP 46001.
— city, CEN. Louisiana; 41,557; ZIP 71301*.
— city, W CEN. Minnesota; 6,973; ZIP 56308.
— city, NE Virginia; 110,938; ZIP 22300*.
Al·ger·i·a (al·jir/ē·ə) republic, NW Africa; 919,352 sq. mi.; 10.9 million; cap. Algiers.
Al·giers (al·jirz/) city, N Algeria; cap.; 545,082.
Al·go·na (al·gō/nə) city, N Iowa; 6,032; ZIP 50511.
Al·ham·bra (al·ham/brə) city, SW California; 62,125; ZIP 91800*.
A·li·can·te (ä/lē·kän/tä) prov., E Spain; 2,264 sq. mi.; 696,000. — city, E Alicante prov.; cap.; 126,107.
Al·ice (al/is) city, S Texas; 20,121; ZIP 78332.
Al·i·quip·pa (al/ə·kwip/ə) boro., W Pennsylvania; 22,277; ZIP 15001.
A·li·sal (ä·lē·säl/) vill., W California; 16,473; ZIP see SALINAS.
Al·la·ha·bad (al/ə·hə·bad/, ä/lə·hä·bäd/) city N India; 475,098.
Al·le·ghe·ny Mountains (al/ə·gā/nē) mtn. range of Appalachian system; extends from Pennsylvania through Virginia.
Allegheny River river, W New York and Pennsylvania; 325 mi. long.
Al·len·dale (al/in·dāl) city, NE New Jersey; 6,240; ZIP 07401.
Al·len Park (al/ən) vill., SE Michigan; 40,747; ZIP 48101*.
Al·len·town (al/ən·toun/) city, E Pennsylvania; 109,527; ZIP 18100*.
Al·li·ance (ə·lī/əns) city, NW Nebraska; 6,862; ZIP 69301.
— city, NE Ohio; 26,547; ZIP 44601*.
Al·l·quez (ôl/kez) city, E CEN. Wisconsin; 13,753; ZIP 54301.
Al·ma (al/mə) city, CEN. Michigan; 9,790; ZIP 48801.
Al·ma (al/mə) city, S Quebec, Canada; 22,195.
Al·ma A·ta (äl/mä ä/tä) city, SE Kazakh SSR; cap.; 610,000.
Al·on·dra (al·on/drə) city, S California; 12,193.
Al·pe·na (al·pē/nə) city, NE Michigan; 13,805; ZIP 49707.
Al·pine (al/pīn) city, W Texas; 5,971; ZIP 79830.
Alps (alps) mtn. system, S Europe; extends from S coast of France to W coast of Yugoslavia.
Al·sace (al·sās/, al/sas) reg. and former prov., NE France.
Al·sace-Lor·raine (al/sās·lə·rān/, al/sas-) oft-disputed border reg., NE France; adjoins SW Germany.
Al·sip Village (al/sip) city, NE Illinois; 11,141; ZIP 60601.
Al·ta·de·na (al/tə·dē/nə) uninc. place, SW California; 42,380; ZIP 91001*.
Al·tai Mountains (al/tī, äl/-) mtn. system, CEN. Asia.
Al·ta·mont (al/tə·mont) uninc. place, S Oregon; 15,746.
Al·ton (ôl/tən) city, SW Illinois; 39,700; ZIP 62002*.
Al·too·na (al·tōō/nə) city, S CEN. Pennsylvania; 62,900; ZIP 16601*.
Al·tus (al/təs) city, SW Oklahoma; 23,302; ZIP 73521*.
Al·um Rock (al/əm) uninc. place SW California; 18,355.
Al·va (al/və) city, NW Oklahoma; 7,440; ZIP 73717.
Al·vin (al/vin) city, SE Texas; 10,671; ZIP 77511.
Am·a·ril·lo (am/ə·ril/ō) city, NW Texas; 127,010; ZIP 79100*.
Am·a·zon (am/ə·zon) river, N South America; 3,910 mi. long; carries the largest volume of water of all rivers.
Am·ber·ley (am/bər·lē) city, SW Ohio; 5,574; ZIP 45201.
Am·bler (am/blər) boro., SE Pennsylvania; 7,800; ZIP 19002.
Am·bridge (am/brij) boro., SE Pennsylvania; 11,324; ZIP 15003.
A·mer·i·ca (ə·mer/ə·kə) 1. The United States of America. 2. North and South America; the Western Hemisphere.
A·mer·i·can Fork (ə·mer/ə·kən) city, N CEN. Utah; 7,713; ZIP 84003.
American Samoa See SAMOA.
A·mer·i·cus (ə·mer/ə·kəs) city, SW CEN. Georgia; 16,091; ZIP 31709.
Ames (āmz) city, CEN. Iowa; 39,505; ZIP 50010*.
Ames·bur·y (āmz/ber/ē, -bûr/ē, -brē) uninc. place, NE Massachusetts; 11,388; ZIP 01913.
Am·herst (am/ərst) uninc. place, W CEN. Massachusetts; 26,331; ZIP 01002*.
— vill., N Ohio; 9,902; ZIP 44001.
Am·herst (am/ərst) town, N Nova Scotia, Canada; 10,551.
Am·i·ens (am/ē·əns) city, N France; 105,433.
Am·i·ty·ville (am/i·tē·vil) vill., SE New York; 9,857; ZIP 11701.
Am·man (äm/män) city, N CEN. Jordan; cap.; 330,000.
A·mo·ry (ā/mə·rē) city, E Mississippi; 7,236; ZIP 38821.
A·mos (ā/məs) town, W Quebec, Canada; 6,838.
A·moy (ə·moi/) isl. of China, Formosa Strait. — city, Amoy isl.; 224,300.
Am·rit·sar (um·rit/sər) city, W Punjab, India; 408,310.
Am·ster·dam (am/stər·dam) city, W Netherlands; cap.; 857,635.
Am·ster·dam (am/stər·dam) city, E CEN. New York; 25,524; ZIP 12010*.
A·mur (ä·mōōr/) river, E Asia; 2,700 mi. long.

An·a·con·da (an/ə·kon/də) city, SW Montana; 9,771; ZIP 59711.
An·a·cor·tes (an/ə·kôr/təs) city, NW Washington; 7,701; ZIP 98221*.
An·a·dar·ko (an/ə·där/kō) city, W CEN. Oklahoma; 6,682; ZIP 73005.
An·a·heim (an/ə·hīm) city, SW California; 166,701; ZIP 92800*.
An·a·to·li·a (an/ə·tō/lē·ə) penin. at W end of Asia; comprises most of Turkey.
An·chor·age (ang/kər·ij) city, S Alaska; 48,029; ZIP 99501*.
An·da·lu·sia (an/də·lōō/zhə, -shə) reg., S Spain.
An·da·lu·sia (an/də·lōō/zhə) city, S Alabama; 10,092; ZIP 36420.
An·der·son (an/dər·sən) city, N California; 5,492; ZIP 96007.
— city, E CEN. Indiana; 70,787; ZIP 46010*.
— city, NW South Carolina; 27,556; ZIP 29621*.
An·des (an/dēz) mtn. range, W South America; connects with the Rockies; over 4,000 mi. long.
An·dor·ra (an·dôr/ə, -dor/ə) republic betw. France and Spain; 179 sq. mi.; 6,000. — city, CEN. Andorra; cap.; 2,700.
An·do·ver (an/dō·vər, -də·vər) town, NE Massachusetts 23,-695; ZIP 01810*.
An·drews (an/drōōz) city, SW Maryland; 6,418.
— city, W Texas; 8,625; ZIP 79714.
An·gel Falls (ān/jəl) waterfall, SE Venezuela; over 3,300 ft.
An·gle·ton (ang/gəl·tən) city, S Texas; 9,770; ZIP 77515.
An·go·la (ang·gō /lə) Portuguese Overseas prov., W Africa; 481,351 sq. mi.; 4,833,000; cap. Luanda.
An·go·lan (ang/gə·lən) city, E Indiana; 5,117; ZIP 46703.
An·go·ra (ang·gō/rə, ang/gə·rə) Ankara: *former name.*
An·jou (an/jōō) former prov., W France.
An·jou (än/zhōō, an/-) town, S Quebec, Canada; 22,477.
An·ka·ra (äng/kə·rə, ang/-) city, CEN. Turkey; cap.; 902,218.
An·ke·ny (ang/kə·nē) city, SE Iowa; 9,151; ZIP 50021.
An·nam (ə·nam/, an/am) former French prot., E CEN. Indochina; now divided betw. North and South Vietnam.
An·nan·dale (an/ən·dāl) NE Virginia; 27,428; ZIP 22003.
An·nap·o·lis (ə·nap/ə·lis) city, CEN. Maryland; cap.; site of U.S. Naval Academy; 29,592; ZIP 21400*.
Ann Ar·bor (an/ är/bər) city, SE Michigan; 99,797; ZIP 48103*.
An·nis·ton (an/is·tən) city, NE Alabama; 31,533; ZIP 36201*.
A·no·ka (ə·nō/kə) city, E Minnesota; 13,489; ZIP 55303.
An·so·ni·a (an·sō/nē·ə) city, SW Connecticut; 21,160; ZIP 06401.
Ant·arc·ti·ca (ant·ärk/tə·kə, -är/-) continent surrounding the South Pole; over 5 million sq. mi.: also Antarctic Continent.
Antarctic Archipelago Palmer Archipelago: *alternative name.*
Antarctic Circle parallel of latitude at 66°33′ S; the boundary of the South Frigid Zone.
Antarctic Ocean parts of Atlantic, Pacific, and Indian oceans bordering on Antarctica.
Antarctic Zone region enclosed by the Antarctic Circle.
An·ti·go (an/ti·gō) city, NE Wisconsin; 9,005; ZIP 54409.
An·ti·gua (an·tē/gwə, -gə) British col. of the West Indies; 171 sq. mi.; 54,000; cap. St. John's.
An·til·les (an·til/ēz) islands of the West Indies excluding the Bahamas; comprises Greater Antilles: Cuba, Hispaniola, Jamaica, and Puerto Rico, and Lesser Antilles: Trinidad, the Windward Islands, the Leeward Islands, and other small islands.
An·ti·och (an/tē·ok) city, S Turkey; 37,000.
An·ti·och (an/tē·ok) city, W California; 28,060; ZIP 94509.
Ant·werp (ant/wûrp) city, N Belgium, 243,426.
Ap·en·nines (ap/ə·nīnz) mtn. range of Italy S of Po valley.
Ap·pa·la·chi·an Mountains (ap/ə·lā/chē·ən) mtn. system, E North America.
Ap·ple·ton (ap/əl·tən) city, E Wisconsin, 57,143; ZIP 54910*.
Ap·ple Valley (ap/əl) city, S CEN. California; 6,702; ZIP 92307. — city, SE Minnesota; 8,502; ZIP 55378.
Ap·ple·wood (ap/əl·wŏŏd) city, N CEN. Colorado; 8,214.
Ap·tos (ap/tōs) city, W California; 8,704; ZIP 95003.
Aq·ui·taine (ak/wə·tān) reg., SW France.
A·ra·bi·a (ə·rā/bē·ə) penin., SW Asia, betw. the Red Sea and Persian Gulf.
A·ra·bi·an Sea (ə·rā/bē·ən) part of the Indian Ocean betw. Arabia and India.
Arab Republic of Egypt See EGYPT.
Ar·a·gon (ar/ə·gon) reg., NE Spain.
Ar·al Sea (ar/əl) salt inland sea, S CEN. USSR.
Ar·an·sas Pass (ə·ran/zəs) city, S Texas; 5,813; ZIP 78336.
Ar·a·rat (ar/ə·rat), **Mount** mtn., E Turkey; 16,945 ft.; traditional landing place of Noah's ark.
Ar·bu·tus-Hale·thorpe-Re·lay (är/byōō/təs, hāl/thôrp, rē/lā) uninc. place, CEN. Maryland; 22,745.
Ar·ca·di·a (är·kā/dē·ə) dept., CEN. Peloponnesus, Greece; 1,168 sq. mi.; 154,000; cap. Tripolis.

Ar·ca·di·a (är·kā′dē·ə) city, sw California; 42,868; ZIP 91006*.
— city, s CEN. Florida; 5,658; ZIP 33821.
Ar·ca·ta (är·kä·tə) city, NW California; 8,985; ZIP 95521.
Arch·bald (ärch′bôld) boro., NE Pennsylvania; 6,118; ZIP 18403.
Arch·dale (ärch′dāl) city, CEN. North Carolina; 6,103; ZIP 27263.
Arc·tic Circle (ärk′tik, är′-) parallel of latitude at 66°33′ N; the boundary of the North Frigid Zone.
Arctic Ocean sea, N of Arctic Circle, surrounding North Pole.
Ar·den-Ar·cade (är′dən, är·kād′) uninc. place, CEN. California; 82,492; ZIP see SACRAMENTO.
Ar·den Hills (är′dən) city, CEN. Minnesota; 5,628.
Ard·more (ärd′mōr) city, s Oklahoma; 20,881; ZIP 73401.
— city, SE Pennsylvania; 5,801; ZIP 19003.
A·re·ci·bo (ä′rä·sē′bō) town, N Puerto Rico; 28,828; ZIP 00612*.
Ar·gen·ti·na (är′jən·tē′nə) republic, s South America; 1,084,362 sq. mi.; 20 million; cap. Buenos Aires.
Ar·gonne (är′gon) ridge, N France; site of battles in World War I and II.
Ar·i·zo·na (ar′ə·zō′nə) state, sw United States; 113,909 sq. mi.; 1,772,482; cap. Phoenix.
Ar·ka·del·phi·a (är′kə·del′fē·ə) city, s CEN. Arkansas; 9,841; ZIP 71923*.
Ar·kan·sas (är′kən·sô) state, s CEN. United States; 53,104 sq. mi.; 1,923,295; cap. Little Rock.
Ar·kan·sas City (är·kan′zəs) city, s Kansas; 13,216; ZIP 67005.
Ar·khan·gelsk (är·khän′gelsk) city, NW RSFSR; 256,000.
Ar·ling·ton (är′ling·tən) urb. co., NE Virginia; site of **Arlington National Cemetery**, containing tomb of the Unknown Soldier.
— town, E Massachusetts; 53,524; ZIP see BOSTON.
— vill., SE New York; 11,203; ZIP see POUGHKEEPSIE.
— city, N Texas; 90,643; ZIP 76010*.
— city, NE Virginia; 174,284; ZIP 22201.
Arlington Heights vill., NE Illinois; 64,884; ZIP 60004*.
Ar·me·ni·a (är·mē′nē·ə, -mēn′yə) 1. former country, sw Asia. 2. the Armenian SSR.
Ar·me·ni·an SSR (är·mē′nē·ən, -mēn′yən) republic, s USSR; 11,500 sq. mi.; 1,763,000; cap. Yerevan.
Arn·hem (ärn′hem) city, E Netherlands; 135,090.
Ar·nold (är′nəld) boro., sw Pennsylvania; 8,174; ZIP see NEW KENSINGTON.
Arn·pri·or (ärn·prī′ər) town, SE Ontario, Canada; 5,693.
Ar·ro·yo Grande (är·rôy′ō grand′) city, sw California; 7,454; ZIP 93420.
Ar·te·sia (är·tē′zhə) town, sw California; 14,751; ZIP 90701.
— city, SE New Mexico; 10,315; ZIP 88210.
Ar·va·da (är·va′də) town, N CEN. Colorado; 46,814; ZIP 80002*.
Ar·vi·da (är·vī′də, -vē′-) city, s CEN. Quebec, Canada; 15,342.
Ar·vin (är′vin) uninc. place, s CEN. California; 5,090; ZIP 93203.
As·bes·tos (as·bes′təs, az-) town, s Quebec, Canada; 10,534.
As·bur·y Park (az′ber′ē, -bər·ē) city, E New Jersey; 16,533; ZIP 07712*.
As·cen·sion (ə·sen′shən) isl. poss. of Great Britain, South Atlantic; 34 sq. mi.; 350.
Ashe·bor·o [ash′bûr·ə] town, CEN. North Carolina; 10,797; ZIP 27203.
Ashe·ville (ash′vil) city, w North Carolina; 57,681; ZIP 28800*.
Ash·land (ash′lənd) city, w California; 14,810; ZIP 94578.
— city, NE Kentucky; 29,245; ZIP 41101.
— city, NE Massachusetts; 8,882; ZIP 01721.
— city, N CEN. Ohio; 19,872; ZIP 44805.
— city, sw Oregon; 12,342; ZIP 97520.
— city, N Wisconsin; 9,615; ZIP 54806*.
Ash·ta·bu·la (ash′tə·byōō′lə) city, NE Ohio; 24,313; ZIP 44004*.
Ash·wau·be·non (ash·wô′bə·non) city, E CEN. Wisconsin; 9,323; ZIP 54304.
A·sia (ā′zhə, ā′shə) E part of Eurasian land mass; largest of the continents; 16.9 million sq. mi.; 1.6 billion.
Asia Minor penin. of extreme w Asia, comprising most of Turkey.
As·pen (as′pin) city, NW Maryland; 16,799; ZIP 20015.
As·to·ri·a (əs·tôr′ē·ə, -tō′rē·ə) city, NW Oregon; 10,244; ZIP 97103.
As·tra·khan (as′trə·kan, -kən) city, SE RSFSR; 332,000.
A·sun·ción (ä·sōōn·syôn′) city, sw Paraguay; cap.; 305,160.
As·wan (äs·wän′) city, s Arab Republic of Egypt; site of Aswan Dam, 1¼ mi. long; 46,218.

A·tas·ca·der·o (ə·tas′kə·dâr′ō) vill., sw California; 10,290; ZIP 93422.
Atch·i·son (ach′ə·sən) city, NE Kansas; 12,565; ZIP 66002.
Ath·ens (ath′enz) city, SE Greece; cap.; 627,564.
Ath·ens (ath′enz) city, N Alabama; 14,360; ZIP 35611.
— city, NE CEN. Georgia; 44,342; ZIP 30601*.
— city, SE Ohio; 23,310; ZIP 45701.
— city, SE Tennessee; 11,790; ZIP 37303.
— city, E Texas; 9,582; ZIP 74751.
Ath·er·ton (ath′ər·tən) town, w California; 8,085; ZIP see MENLO PARK.
Ath·ol (ath′ol, -əl) vill., N Massachusetts; 11,185; ZIP 01331.
At·lan·ta (at·lan′tə) city, NW CEN. Georgia; cap.; 496,973; ZIP 30300*.
— city, NE Texas; 5,007; ZIP 75551.
At·lan·tic (at·lan′tik) city, sw Iowa; 7,306; ZIP 50022.
Atlantic City city, SE New Jersey; 47,859; ZIP 08400*.
Atlantic Highlands city, E CEN. New Jersey; 5,102; ZIP 07716.
Atlantic Ocean ocean, extending from the Arctic to the Antarctic between the Americas and Europe and Africa.
At·las Mountains (at′ləs) mtn. range, NW Africa.
At·more (at′môr, -mōr) city, sw Alabama; 8,293; ZIP 36502.
At·ta·la (at′ə·le) city, NE Alabama; 7,510; ZIP 35954.
At·tle·bor·o (at′əl·bûr′ō) city, SE Massachusetts; 32,907; ZIP 02703.
At·wa·ter (at′wô·tər) city, CEN. California; 11,640; ZIP 95301.
Au·burn (ô′bûrn, -bərn) city, E CEN. Alabama; 22,767; ZIP 36830.
— city, CEN. California; 6,570; ZIP 95603.
— city, NE Indiana; 7,337; ZIP 46706.
— city, sw Maine; 24,151; ZIP 04210.
— town, s CEN. Massachusetts; 15,347; ZIP 01501.
— city, w CEN. New York; 34,599; ZIP 13021*.
— city, w CEN. Washington; 21,817; ZIP 98002*.
Au·burn·dale (ô′bərn·dāl) city, CEN. Florida; 5,386; ZIP 33823.
Auck·land (ôk′lənd) city, N North Island, New Zealand; 548,293.
Au·du·bon (ô′də·bon) boro., sw New Jersey; 10,802; ZIP see CAMDEN.
Augs·burg (ôgz′bûrg) city, s West Germany; 210,803.
Au·gus·ta (ô·gus′tə, ə-) city, E Georgia; 59,864; ZIP 30900*.
— city, s Kansas; 5,977; ZIP 67010.
— city, s Maine; cap.; 21,945; ZIP 04301*.
Augusta School Area city, w CEN. California; 6,293·
Au·ro·ra (ô·rôr′ə, ə-, -rō′rə) city, N CEN. Colorado; 74,974; ZIP 80010*.
— city, NE Illinois; 74,182; ZIP 60504*.
— city, sw Missouri; 5,359; ZIP 65605.
— city, NE Ohio; 6,549; ZIP 44202.
Au·ro·ra (ə·rôr′ə, ô-) town, s Ontario, Canada; 10,425.
Au·schwitz (ou′shvits) city, sw Poland; site of Nazi extermination camp in World War II; 14,000.
Aus·tin (ôs′tən) city, SE Minnesota; 25,074; ZIP 55912.
— city, CEN. Texas; cap.; 251,808; ZIP 78700*.
Aus·tin·town (ôs′tən·toun) city, NE Ohio; 29,393; ZIP 44515.
Aus·tral·a·sia (ôs′trəl·ā·zhə, -shə) isls. of the South Pacific, including Australia, New Zealand, and New Guinea.
Aus·tral·ia (ôs·trāl′yə) independent member of the Commonwealth of Nations, situated on an isl. continent in the South Pacific; 2,971,081 sq. mi.; 10.9 million; cap. Canberra.
Australian Capital Territory reg., SE Australia; 939 sq. mi.; contains Canberra, the capital· 58,828.
Aus·tri·a (ôs′trē·ə) republic, CEN. Europe; 32,375 sq. mi.; 7,060,000; cap. Vienna.
Aus·tri·a-Hun·ga·ry (ôs′trē·ə·hung′gə·rē) former monarchy, CEN. Europe
Av·a·lon (av′ə·lon) boro., sw Pennsylvania; 7,065; ZIP see PITTSBURGH.
A·vi·gnon (à·vē·nyôn′) city, SE France; 72,717.
Av·o·ca·do Heights (av′ə·kä′dō, ä′və-) city, s California; 9,810.
A·von (ā′von′) city, N CEN. Connecticut; 8,352; ZIP 06001.
— city, E CEN. Massachusetts; 5,295; ZIP 02322.
— city, N CEN. Ohio; 7,214; ZIP 44011.
A·von (ā′vən, av′ən) river, CEN. England; 96 mi. long.
Av·on·dale (av′ən·dāl) city, s CEN. Arizona; 6,304; ZIP 85323.
— city, sw Ohio; 5,195.
Av·on·dale-Moor·land (av′ən·dāl·mōōr′lənd) city, SE South Carolina; 5,236.
A·von Lake (ā′von′) vill., N Ohio; 12,761; ZIP 44012.
A·von Park (ā′von′) city, s CEN. Florida; 6,712; ZIP 33825.
Ayer (âr) city, NE Massachusetts; 7,393; ZIP 01432.
A·zal·ea (ə·zāl′yə) city, CEN. Florida; 7,367.
A·zer·bai·jan (ä′zər·bī·jän′, az′ər-) prov., NW Iran: **Eastern**

Azerbaijan; 28,488 sq. mi.; 2,138,000; cap. Tabriz: **Western Azerbaijan;** 13,644 sq. mi.; 721,000; cap. Rizaiyeh.

Azerbaijan SSR republic, sw USSR; 33,590 sq. mi.; 3,698,000; cap. Baku.

A·zores (ə·zōrz, ā′zōrz) three isl. groups of Portugal, E Atlantic; 922 sq. mi.; 320,000.

A·zov (ā·zôf′), **Sea of** inlet of the Black Sea; s USSR.

A·zu·sa (ə·zōō′zə) city, s California; 25,217; ZIP 91702.

Bab·y·lon (bab′ə·lən, -lon) vill., SE New York; 12,588 ZIP 11702*.

Ba·den (bäd′n, bãd′n) boro., w Pennsylvania; 5,536; ZIP 15005.

Ba·den-Ba·den (bäd′n·bäd′n) city, sw West Germany; site of famous mineral springs; 40,095.

Bad Lands arid plateau, South Dakota and Nebraska: also **Bad′lands.**

Bagh·dad (bag′dad, bäg·däd′) city, CEN. Iraq; cap.; 1,106,139.

Bag·ot·ville (bag′ət·vil) town, s Quebec, Canada; 5,876.

Ba·gu·o (bag′ē·ō, bä′gē·ō) city, Luzon, N Philippines; summer cap.; 50,436.

Ba·ha·mas (bə·hä′məz, -hä′-) isl. group SE of Florida; independent member of the Commonwealth of Nations; 4,404 sq. mi.; 136,000; cap. Nassau.

Bah·rain (bä·rän′) isl. group, Persian Gulf near Saudi Arabia; country; 213 sq. mi.; 143,000; cap. Manama. Also: **Bahrein.**

Baie-Co·meau (bā·kō′mō) town, E Quebec, Canada; 12,236.

Bai·kal (bī·käl′) freshwater lake, s USSR; 12,150 sq. mi.

Bain·bridge (bān′brij) city, sw Georgia; 10,887; ZIP 31717*. — city, NE Maryland; 5,257.

Ba·ker (bā′kər) city, NE Louisiana; 8,821; ZIP 70714. — city, NE Oregon; 9,354; ZIP 97814.

Baker, Mount mtn., Cascade range, N Washington; 10,750 ft.

Ba·kers·field (bā′kərz·fēld) city, s California; 64,515; ZIP 93300*.

Ba·ku (bä·kōō′) city, SE Azerbaijan SSR; cap.; 725,000.

Ba·la Cyn·wyd (ba′lə kin′wəd) city, SE Pennsylvania; 6,483; ZIP 19004.

Bal·bo·a (bal·bō′ə) town, E Canal Zone; 3,139.

Balboa Heights adm. ctr. of Canal Zone, near Balboa; 118.

Balch Springs (balch, bôlch) city, NE Texas; 10,464.

Bald·win (bôld′win) uninc. place, SE New York; 34,525; ZIP 11510*. — boro., sw Pennsylvania; 26,729.

Baldwin Park city, sw California; 47,285; ZIP 91706*.

Bald·wins·ville (bôld′winz·vil) vill., CEN. New York; 6,298; ZIP 13027.

Bal·e·ar·ic Islands (bal′ē·ar′ik, bə·lir′ik) isl. group, W Mediterranean; prov. of Spain; 1,935 sq. mi.; 443,000; cap. Palma.

Ba·li (bä′lē) isl. of Indonesia, E of Java; 2,243 sq. mi.

Bal·kan Mountains (bôl′kən) mtn. range, Balkan penin.

Balkan Peninsula large penin. of SE Europe.

Balkan States countries of Balkan penin.; Albania, Bulgaria, Greece, Rumania, Yugoslavia, and part of Turkey.

Ball·win (bôl′win) city, E Missouri; 10,656; ZIP 63011.

Bal·tic Sea (bôl′tik) inlet of the Atlantic in NW Europe.

Baltic States Estonian SSR, Latvian SSR, and Lithuanian SSR.

Bal·ti·more (bôl′tə·môr, -mōr) city, N Maryland; 905,759; ZIP 21200*.

Bal·ti·more Highlands See LANSDOWNE-BALTIMORE HIGHLANDS.

Ba·ma·ko (bä·mä·kō′) city, s CEN. Mali; cap.; 130,000.

Ba·na·ras (bə·nä′rəs) Hindu sacred city, NE India; 553,173.

Ban·dung (bän′dŏong) city, w Java, Indonesia; 972,566.

Ban·ga·lore (bang′gə·lôr, -lōr′) city, E Mysore, India; cap.; 985,035.

Bang·ka (bäng′kä, bang′kə) isl. of Indonesia, SE of Sumatra; 4,611 sq. mi.

Bang·kok (bang′kok) city, sw Thailand; cap.; 1,608,305.

Ban·gla·desh (bäng′glä·desh′) republic, s Asia; 54,501 sq. mi.; 53,460,000; cap. Dacca.

Ban·gor (bang′gôr, -gər) city, s CEN. Maine; 33,168; ZIP 04401*. — boro., E Pennsylvania; 5,425; ZIP 18013.

Ban·gui (bäng′gē) city, sw Central African Empire; cap.; 111,266.

Ban·ning (ban′ing) city, s California; 12,034; ZIP 92220.

Ba·ra·boo (bä′rə·bōō, bar′ə·bōō) city, s CEN. Wisconsin; 7,931; ZIP 53913.

Bar·ba·dos (bär·bä′dōz) isl., E Caribbean, British col. of the West Indies; 166 sq. mi.; 232,000; cap. Bridgetown.

Bar·ba·ry (bär′bər·ē) North Africa W of Egypt.

Barbary Coast **1.** coast of Barbary. **2.** former infamous waterfront reg. of San Francisco.

Barbary States formerly, states of the Barbary Coast: Tripolitania, Algeria, Tunisia, Morocco; centers of piracy until the 19th century.

Bar·ber·ton (bär′bər·tən) city, NE Ohio; 33,052; ZIP 44203.

Bar·ce·lo·na (bär′sə·lō′nə) prov., NE Spain; 2,985 sq. mi.;

2,878,000. — city, s Barcelona prov.; cap.; 1,633,921.

Bards·town (bärdz′toun) city, CEN. Kentucky; 5,816; ZIP 40004.

Barn·sta·ble (bärn′stə·bəl) town, SE Massachusetts; 19,842; ZIP 02630.

Bar·ran·quil·la (bär′äng·kē′yä) city, N Colombia; 493,034.

Bar·re (bar′ē) city, CEN. Vermont; 10,209; ZIP 05641.

Barre·town (bär′toun) town, N CEN. Vermont; 6,509; ZIP 05641.

Bar·rie (bar′ē) city, s Ontario, Canada; 24,016.

Bar·ring·ton (bar′ing·tən) vill., NE Illinois; 7,071; ZIP 60010. — boro., sw New Jersey; 8,409; ZIP 08007. — town, E Rhode Island; 17,554; ZIP 02806.

Bar·row (bar′ō), **Point** extreme N point of Alaska.

Bar·stow (bär′stō) city, s California; 17,442; ZIP 92310*.

Bar·tles·ville (bär′təlz·vil) city, NE Oklahoma; 29,638; ZIP 74003*.

Bar·ton·ville (bär′tən·vil) vill., CEN. Illinois; 7,221; ZIP see PEORIA.

Bar·tow (bär′tō) city, CEN. Florida; 12,891; ZIP 33830.

Ba·sel (bä′zəl) city, N Switzerland; 212,100.

Basque Provinces three provs. of N Spain, on the Bay of Biscay; inhabited largely by Basques.

Bas·trop (bas′trop, -trəp) city, NE Louisiana; 14,713; ZIP 71220.

Ba·su·to·land (bə·sōō′tō·land′) former British terr. in s Africa. See LESOTHO.

Ba·taan (bə·tan′, -tän′) prov., s Luzon, Philippines; 517 sq. mi.; 116,000; cap. Balanga; occupies **Bataan Peninsula,** scene of World War II surrender of U.S. and Philippine forces to the Japanese.

Ba·ta·vi·a (bə·tā′vē·ə, bə·tav′ē·ə) city, NE Illinois; 8,994; ZIP 60510.

Ba·ta·vi·a (bə·tā′vē·ə) city, w New York; 17,338; ZIP 14020*.

Bates·ville (bāts′vil, -vəl) city, NE CEN. Arkansas; 7,209; ZIP 72501.

Bath (bath, bäth) co. boro.; sw England; site of famous hot springs; 85,870.

Bath (bath) city, sw Maine; 9,679; ZIP 04530. — vill., sw New York; 6,053; ZIP 14810.

Bath·urst (bath′ûrst, -ərst) town, NE New Brunswick, Canada; 15,256.

Bath·urst (bath′ərst, bäth′-) city, w Gambia; cap.; 28,896.

Bat·on Rouge (bat′n rōōzh′) city, SE CEN. Louisiana; cap.; 165,963; ZIP 70800*.

Battle Creek city, s Michigan; 38,931; ZIP 49014*.

Ba·var·i·a (bə·vâr′ē·ə) state, SE West Germany; 27,235 sq. mi.; 9,731,000; cap. Munich.

Bay (bā) city, NE Ohio, 18,163.

Ba·ya·món (bä·yä·mōn′) town, N Puerto Rico; 15,109.

Bay City city, E CEN. Michigan; 49,449; ZIP 48706*. — city, s Texas; 11,733; ZIP 77414.

Bay Mi·nette (bā mi·net′) city, sw Alabama; 6,727; ZIP 36507.

Ba·yonne (bā·yōn′, bā′yōn) city, NE New Jersey; 72,743; ZIP 07002*.

Bay·ou Cane (bī′ōō kān) city, SE Louisiana; 9,077; ZIP 70360.

Bay·ou Vis·ta (bī′ōō vis′tə) city, SE Louisiana; 5,121; ZIP 70380.

Bay·port (bā′pôrt′) city, SE New York; 7,995; ZIP 11705.

Bay·shore (bā′shôr′) city, SE New York; 11,119; ZIP 11706.

Bay·shore Gardens (bā′shôr′, -shōr′) city, sw Florida; 9,255; ZIP 33902.

Bay St. Louis (bā sänt lōō′is) city, SE Mississippi; 6,752; ZIP 39520.

Bay·town (bā′toun′) city, s Texas; 43,980; ZIP 77520*.

Bay·ville (bā′vil) city, SE New York; 6,147; ZIP 11709.

Beach·wood (bēch′wŏod) vill., N Ohio; 9,631.

Bea·con (bē′kən) city, SE New York; 13,255; ZIP 12508.

Bea·cons·field (bē′kənz·fēld) town, s Quebec, Canada; 15,702.

Beale East (bēl ēst) city, N CEN. California; 7,029.

Beards·town (birdz′toun) city, w CEN. Illinois; 6,222; ZIP 62618.

Be·at·rice (bē·at′ris, bi-) city, SE Nebraska; 12,389; ZIP 68310.

Beau·fort (bō′fərt) city, s South Carolina; 9,434; ZIP 29902*.

Beau·har·nois (bō·här′nwä) city, sw Quebec, 8,810.

Beau·mont (bō′mont) city, SE California; 5,484; ZIP 92223. — city, SE Texas; 115,919; ZIP 77700*.

Beau·port (bō·pôr′) town, s CEN. Quebec, Canada; 11,742.

Bea·ver (bē′vər) boro., w Pennsylvania; 6,100; ZIP 15009*

Beaver Dam city, s CEN. Wisconsin; 14,265; ZIP 53916.

Beaver Falls city, w Pennsylvania; 14,375; ZIP 15010.

Bea·ver·ton (bē·vər·tən) city, NW Oregon; 18,577; ZIP 97005*.

Bech·u·a·na·land Protectorate (bech′ŏō·ä′nə·land, bek′/-)

former British terr. in s Africa. See BOTSWANA.
Beck·ley (bek′lē) city, s West Virginia; 19,884; ZIP 25801*.
Bed·ford (bed′fərd) city, s Indiana; 13,087; ZIP 47421.
— town, NE Massachusetts; 13,513; ZIP 01730.
— town, SW New Hampshire; 5,859; ZIP 03102.
— city, NE Ohio; 17,552; ZIP 44014.
— city, N Texas; 10,049; ZIP 76021.
— town, SW CEN. Virginia; 6,011; ZIP 24523.
Bedford Heights vill., NE Ohio; 13,063.
Beech Grove city, s CEN. Indiana; 13,468; ZIP 46107.
Bee·ville (bē′vil) city, s Texas; 13,506; ZIP 78102.
Bei·rut (bā′rōōt, bā-rōōt′) city, w Lebanon; cap.; 700,000.
Bel Air (bel âr) city, NE Maryland; 6,307; ZIP 21014.
Bel·cher·town (bel′chər·toun) town, w Massachusetts; 5,936; ZIP 01007.
Bel·ding (bel′ding) city, sw Michigan; 5,121; ZIP 48809.
Be·lém (be·leñ′) city, N Brazil; 319,000.
Bel·fast (bel′fast, -fäst) co. boro., and port, SE Northern Ireland; cap.; 402,900.
Bel·fast (bel′fast) city, s Maine; 5,957; ZIP 04915.
Bel·gium (bel′jəm, -jē·əm) kingdom, NW Europe; 11,775 sq. mi.; 9,129,000; cap. Brussels.
Bel·grade (bel′grād, bel·grād′) city E Yugoslavia; cap.; 612,000.
Be·lize (bə·lēz′) self-governing dependency of the United Kingdom, E CEN. Central America; 8865 sq. mi.; cap. Belmopan. Formerly *British Honduras.*
Bell (bel) city, s California; 21,836; ZIP 90201*.
Bell·aire (bel′âr′) city, E Ohio, 9,655; ZIP 43906.
Bell·aire (bə·lâr′) city, s Texas; 19,009; ZIP 77401*.
Belle·fon·taine (bel·foun′tin, -fon′-) city, w CEN. Ohio; 11,255; ZIP 43311.
Bellefontaine Neighbors city, E Missouri; 13,987.
Belle·fonte (bel·font′) boro., CEN. Pennsylvania; 6,828; ZIP 16823.
Belle Glade (bel·glād′) city, SE Florida; 15,494; ZIP 33430.
Belle·view (bel′vyōō′) city, NE Virginia; 8,298; ZIP 22307.
Belle·ville (bel′vil) city, sw Illinois; 41,699; ZIP 62220*.
— town, NE New Jersey; 34,643; ZIP see NEWARK.
Belle·ville (bel′vil) city, SE Ontario, Canada; 32,785.
Belle·vue (bel′vyōō) city, N Kentucky; 8,847; ZIP see NEWPORT.
— city, E Nebraska; 19,449; ZIP 68005.
— city, N Ohio; 8,604; ZIP 44811.
— boro., sw Pennsylvania; 11,586; ZIP see PITTSBURGH.
— city, CEN. Washington; 61,102; ZIP 98004.
Bell·flow·er (bel′flou′ər) city, sw California; 51,454; ZIP 90706*.
Bell Gardens uninc. place, sw California; 29,308; ZIP see BELL.
Bel·ling·ham (bel′ing·ham) town, NW Massachusetts; 13,967; ZIP 02019.
— city, NW Washington; 39,375; ZIP 98225.
Bell·mawr (bel′mär′) boro., sw New Jersey; 15,618; ZIP see GLOUCESTER CITY.
Bell·mead (bel′mēd) city, E CEN. Texas; 7,698; ZIP see WACO.
Bell·more (bel′môr) uninc. place, SE New York; 18,431; ZIP 11710*.
Bell·wood (bel′wŏŏd) vill., NE Illinois; 22,096; ZIP 60104.
Bel·mar (bel′mär) boro., E CEN. New Jersey; 5,782; ZIP 07719.
Bel·mont (bel′mont) city, w CEN. California; 23,667; ZIP 94002*.
— town, E Massachusetts; 28,285; ZIP see BOSTON.
Be·loeil (bə·lû′y′) town, s Quebec, Canada; 10,152.
Be·loit (bə·loit′) city, s Wisconsin; 35,729; ZIP 53511*.
Bel·pre (bel′prā) vill., SE Ohio; 7,189; ZIP 45714.
Bel·Ridge (bel′rij′) city, E Missouri; 5,561.
Bel·ton (bel′tən, belt′n) town, NW South Carolina; 5,257; ZIP 29627.
— city, CEN. Texas; 8,696; ZIP 76513*.
Belts·ville (belts′vil) city, sw Maryland; 8,912; ZIP 20705.
Bel·vi·dere (bel′vi·dir′, bel·vi·dir′) city, NE Illinois; 14,061.
Be·mid·ji (bə·mi′jē) city, N CEN. Minnesota; 11,490; ZIP 56601.
Ben·brook (ben′brŏŏk′) city, N Texas; 8,169; ZIP 76126.
Bend (bend) city, CEN. Oregon; 13,710; ZIP 97701.
Ben·gal (ben·gôl′, beng-, beng·gəl) former prov., NE British India; divided (1947) into: **East Bengal,** a part of East Pakistan, and **West Bengal,** a state of India; 33,928 sq. mi.; 34,968,000; cap. Calcutta.
Bengal, Bay of part of the Indian Ocean betw. E India and w Burma.
Ben·ga·si (ben·gä′zē, beng-) city, N Libya; one of two caps.; 136,641.
Be·nin (be·nēn′) republic, w Africa; 43,475 sq. mi.; 3,290,000; cap. Porto-Novo.

Ben·ning·ton (ben′ing·tən) vill., sw Vermont; 14,586; ZIP 05201.
Bennington Village vill., sw Vermont; 7,950.
Ben·sen·ville (ben′sən·vil) vill., NE Illinois; 12,833; ZIP 60106.
Ben·ton (ben′tən, bent′n) city, s CEN. Arkansas; 16,499; ZIP 72015.
— city, SE Illinois; 6,833; ZIP 62812.
Benton Central city, sw Michigan; 8,067.
Benton Harbor city, sw Michigan; 16,481; ZIP 49022*.
Benton Heights uninc. place, sw Michigan; 8,067.
Ben·ton·ville (ben′tən·vil) city, NW Arkansas; 5,508; ZIP 72712.
Be·re·a (bə·rē′ə) city, CEN. Kentucky; 6,956; ZIP 40403.
— city, NE Ohio; 22,395; ZIP 44017.
— city, NW South Carolina; 7,186; ZIP 29601.
Ber·gen (bûr′gən) city, sw Norway; 117,290.
Ber·gen·field (bûr′gən·fēld) boro., NE New Jersey; 33,131; ZIP 07621.
Ber·ing Sea (bâr′ing, bir′-) part of the North Pacific betw. Alaska and the USSR, joined to the Arctic by **Bering Strait.**
Berke·ley (bûrk′lē) city, w California; 116,716; ZIP 94700*.
— vill., NE Illinois; 6,152; ZIP see MELROSE PARK.
— city, E CEN. Missouri; 19,743; ZIP see ST. LOUIS.
Berk·ley (bûrk′lē) city, SE Michigan; 22,618; ZIP see ROYAL OAK.
Berk·shire Hills (bûrk′shər, -shir) wooded hill reg., w Massachusetts.
Ber·lin (bər·lin′) city, E CEN. Germany; cap. prior to 1945 when divided into the British, French, Soviet, and US sectors. In 1949 the Soviet sector, **East Berlin,** was designated capital of East Germany; 1,078,000. The remaining sectors formed **West Berlin,** associated with West Germany; 2,202,-000.
Ber·lin (bûr′lin) town, N CEN. Connecticut; 14,149; ZIP 06037.
— city, N New Hampshire; 15,256; ZIP 03570.
— city, s CEN. North Carolina; 5,217.
— city, CEN. Wisconsin; 5,338; ZIP 54923.
Ber·mu·da (bər·myōō′də) isl. group, w Atlantic; British col.; 21 sq. mi.; 56,000; cap. Hamilton.
Bern (bûrn, bern) city, w CEN. Switzerland; cap.; 166,800. Also **Berne.**
Ber·nards·ville (bûr′nərdz·vil) boro., N CEN. New Jersey 6,652; ZIP 07924.
Ber·wick (bûr′wick) boro., E CEN. Pennsylvania; 12,274; ZIP 18603.
Ber·wyn (bûr′win) city, NE Illinois; 52,502; ZIP 60402*.
Bes·sa·ra·bi·a (bes′ə·rā′bē·ə) reg., sw USSR.
Bes·se·mer (bes′ə·mər) city, CEN. Alabama; 33,428; ZIP 35020*.
Beth·al·to (beth·al′tō) city, sw Illinois; 7,074; ZIP 62010.
Beth·an·y (beth′ə·nē) city, CEN. Oklahoma; 21,785; ZIP 73008.
Beth·el (beth′əl) uninc. place, sw Connecticut; 10,945; ZIP 06801.
— boro., sw Pennsylvania; 34,791; ZIP 19507.
Be·thes·da (bə·thez′də) uninc. area, w Maryland; 71,621; ZIP see WASHINGTON, D.C.
Beth·le·hem (beth′lē·əm, -lə·hem) ancient town, w Jordan; birthplace of Jesus; 19,000.
Beth·le·hem (beth′lē·əm, -lə·hem) city, E Pennsylvania; 72,686; ZIP 18015*.
Beth·page-Old Beth·page (beth′pāj′) uninc. place, SE New York; 18,555; ZIP 11714.
Bet·ten·dorf (bet′n·dôrf) city, E CEN. Iowa; 22,126; ZIP 52722.
Bev·er·ly (bev′ər·lē) city, NE Massachusetts; 38,348; ZIP 01915.
Beverly Hills city, sw California; 33,416; ZIP 90210*.
— vill., SE Michigan; 13,598.
Bex·ley (beks′lē) city, CEN. Ohio; 14,888; ZIP see COLUMBUS.
Bhu·tan (bōō·tän′) kingdom, E Himalayas; ab. 16,000 sq. mi.; 1,235,000; cap. Thimbu.
Big Rapids city, w CEN. Michigan; 11,995; ZIP 49307.
Big Spring city, w Texas; 28,735; ZIP 79720*.
Bi·ki·ni (bi·kē′nē) atoll, Marshall Islands; 2 sq. mi.; site of US nuclear tests, July 1946.
Bille·ri·ca (bil′ri·kə) town, NE Massachusetts; 31,648; ZIP 01821.
Bil·lings (bil′ingz) city, s CEN. Montana; 61,581; ZIP 59101*.
Bi·lox·i (bi·luk′sē, -lok′-) city, SE Mississippi; 48,486; ZIP 39530*.
Bing·ham·ton (bing′əm·tən) city, CEN. New York; 64,123; ZIP 13990*.
Birch·wood (bûrch′wŏŏd′) city, sw Louisiana; 9,558.

Bir·ken·head (bûr′kən·hed) co. boro., NW England; 143,550.

Bir·ming·ham (bûr′ming·əm) co. boro., W CEN. England; 1,101,990.

Bir·ming·ham (bûr′ming·ham) city, N CEN. Alabama; 300,910; ZIP 35200*.

— city, SE Michigan; 26,170; ZIP 48008*.

Bis·bee (biz′bē) city, SE Arizona; 8,328; ZIP 85603.

Bis·cay (bis′kā, -kē) **Bay of** inlet of the Atlantic betw. W and SW France and N and NW Spain.

Bis·marck (biz′märk) city, S CEN. North Dakota; cap.; 34,703; ZIP 58501*.

Bismarck Archipelago isl. group, Trust Territory of New Guinea; 19,200 sq. mi.

Bi·zer·te (bi·zûr′tə), **bi·zûrt′**) city, N Tunisia; 44,721.

Black·foot (blak′fŏŏt′) city, SE Idaho; 8,716; ZIP 83221.

Black Forest wooded mtn. reg., SW West Germany.

Black Hills mtn. reg., SW South Dakota and NE Wyoming.

Black·lick (blak′lik) city, SW Ohio; 8,351.

Black Oak city, NW Indiana; 9,624; ZIP 46401.

Blacks·burg (blaks′bûrg) town, W Virginia, 9,384; ZIP 24060*.

Black Sea inland sea betw. Europe and Asia, connects with the Aegean via the Bosporus, the Sea of Marmara, and the Dardanelles.

Black·stone (blak′stōn′) town, CEN. Massachusetts; 6,566; ZIP 01504.

Black·well (blak′wel, -wəl) city, N CEN. Oklahoma; 8,645; ZIP 74631.

Bla·dens·burg (blā′dənz·bûrg) city, SW Louisiana; 7,488.

Blaine (blān) vill., E Minnesota; 20,640.

Blair (blâr) city, E CEN. Nebraska; 6,106; ZIP 68008.

Blake·ly (blāk′lē) city, SW Georgia; 5,267; ZIP 31723.

— boro., NE Pennsylvania; 6,391.

Blau·velt (blau′velt) city, SE New York; 5,426.

Bloom·field (blōōm′fēld) town, N CEN. Connecticut; 18,301; ZIP 06002.

— city, NE New Jersey; 52,029; ZIP 07003*.

Bloom·ing·dale (blōōm′ing·dāl) boro., N New Jersey; 7,797; ZIP 07403.

Bloom·ing·ton (blōōm′ing·tən) city, S CEN. California; 11,957; ZIP 92316.

— city, CEN. Illinois; 39,992; ZIP 61701*.

— city, S CEN. Indiana; 42,890; ZIP 47401*.

— city, E Minnesota; 81,970; ZIP see MINNEAPOLIS.

Blooms·burg (blōōmz′bûrg) town, NE Pennsylvania; 11,652; ZIP 17815.

Blue Ash vill., SW Ohio; 8,324.

Blue·field (blōō′fēld′) city, S West Virginia; 15,921; ZIP 24701*.

Blue Island city, NE Illinois; 22,958; ZIP 60406.

Blue Ridge Mountains, SW part of the Appalachians.

Blue Springs city, NE Missouri; 6,779; ZIP 64015.

Bluff Park (bluf) city, CEN. Alabama; 12,372; ZIP 35226.

Bluff·ton (bluf′tən) city, NE Indiana; 8,297; ZIP 46714.

Blythe (blīth, blĭth) city, SE California; 7,047; ZIP 92225.

Blythe·ville (blīth′vil, -vəl) city, NE Arkansas; 24,752; ZIP 72315*.

Board·man (bôrd′mən, bôrd′-) city, NE Ohio; 30,852; ZIP 44512.

Bo·ca Ra·ton (bō′ke rə·tōn′) city, SE Florida; 28,506; ZIP 33432.

Bo·ga·lu·sa (bō′gə·lōō′sə) city, SE Louisiana; 18,412; ZIP 70427.

Bo·go·tá (bō′gə·tä′) city, E CEN. Colombia; cap.; 1,661,935.

Bo·go·ta (bə·gō′tə) boro., NE New Jersey; 8,125; ZIP see HACKENSACK.

Bo·he·mi·a (bō·hē′mē·ə) former prov., W Czechoslovakia.

Bo·he·mi·a (bō·hē′mē·ə) city, SE New York; 8,718.

Boi·se (boi′zē, -sē) city, SW Idaho; cap.; 74,990; ZIP 83700*.

Bo·ling·brook (bō′ling·brŏŏk) city, NE Illinois; 7,275.

Bol·i·var (bol′ə·vər) city, SW Tennessee; 6,674; ZIP 38008.

Bo·liv·i·a (bə·liv′ē·ə) republic, W CEN. South America; 424,162 sq. mi.; 3,416,000; cap. Sucre (constitutional), La Paz (de facto).

Bo·lo·gna (bō·lō′nyä) prov., N CEN. Italy; 1,429 sq. mi.; 837,000. — city, cap. of Bologna prov.; 482,438.

Bom·bay (bom·bā′) city, W India; 4,146,000.

Bon Air (bon âr) city, CEN. Virginia; 10,562; ZIP 23235.

Bon·ham (bon′əm) city, NE Texas; 7,698; ZIP 75418.

Bonn (bon) city, W German Federal Republic (West Germany); cap.; 141,669.

Boone (bōōn) city, CEN. Iowa; 12,468; ZIP 50036.

— city, NW North Carolina; 8,754; ZIP 28607.

Boon·ton (bōōn′tən, bōōnt′n) town, NE New Jersey; 9,201; ZIP 07005.

Boon·ville (bōōn′vil) city, SW Indiana; 5,736.

— city, NE Mississippi; 5,895; ZIP 38829.

— city, CEN. Missouri; 7,514; ZIP 65233.

Bor·deaux (bôr·dō′) city, SW France; 244,688.

Bor·ger (bôr′gər, bôr′-) city, N Texas; 14,195; ZIP 79006*.

Bor·ne·o (bôr′nē·ō, bôr′-) isl., betw. Java and South China seas; comprising North Borneo, Sarawak, Brunei, and Indonesian Borneo; 286,969 sq. mi.

Bos·ni·a and Her·ze·go·vi·na (boz′nē·ə; hûr′tsə·gō·vē′nə) constituent republic, CEN. Yugoslavia; 19,745 sq. mi.; 3,347,000; cap. Sarajevo.

Bos·po·rus (bos′pə·rəs) strait, betw. the Black Sea and the Sea of Marmara.

Bos·sier City (bō′zhər) city, NW Louisiana; 41,595; ZIP 71010.

Bos·ton (bôs′tən, bos′-) city, E Massachusetts; cap.; 641,071; ZIP 02100*.

Bot·a·ny Bay (bot′ə·nē) inlet of the Pacific, S of Sydney, Australia.

Bot·swa·na (bot·swä·nä) independent member of the Commonwealth of Nations, S Africa; 222,000 sq. mi.; 368,000; cap. Gaberones: formerly *Bechuanaland Protectorate.*

Bouch·er·ville (bōō′shər·vil) town, S Quebec, Canada; 15,338.

Boul·der (bōl′dər) city, N CEN. Colorado; 66,870; ZIP 80301*.

— city, NE Mississippi; 5,895.

Boulder Dam Hoover Dam: *the former name.*

Bound Brook (bound′ brŏŏk′) boro., N CEN. New Jersey; 10,450; ZIP 08805.

Boun·ti·ful (boun′tə·fəl) city, N CEN. Utah; 27,853; ZIP 84010.

Bour·bon·nais (bŏŏr·bə·nā′) city, NE Illinois; 5,909; ZIP 60914.

Bourne (bôrn) town, E Massachusetts; 12,636; ZIP 02532.

Bow·ie (bōō′ē) city, SW Louisiana; 35,028.

— city, N CEN. Texas; 5,185; ZIP 76230.

Bowling Green city, S Kentucky; 36,253; ZIP 42101*.

— city, NW Ohio; 21,760; ZIP 43402.

Bow·man·ville (bō′mən·vil) town, S Ontario, Canada; 8,513.

Boyn·ton Beach (boin′tən, boint′n) city, SE Florida; 18,115; ZIP 33435.

Bo·za (bō′zə) city, NE Alabama; 5,621; ZIP 35957.

Boze·man (bōz′mən) city, SW Montana; 18,670; ZIP 59715.

Brad·dock (brad′ək) boro., SW Pennsylvania; 8,682; ZIP 15104*.

Bra·den·ton (brā′dən·tən) city, W Florida; 21,040; ZIP 33505*.

Brad·ford (brad′fərd) city, N Pennsylvania; 12,672; ZIP 16701.

Brad·ley (brad′lē) vill., NE Illinois; 9,881; ZIP 60915.

Bra·dy (brā′dē) city, CEN. Texas; 5,557; ZIP 76825.

Brai·nerd (brā′nərd) city, CEN. Minnesota; 11,667; ZIP 56401.

Brain·tree (brān′trē) town, E Massachusetts; 35,050; ZIP see BOSTON.

Bramp·ton (bram′tən, bramp′-) town, SE Ontario, Canada; 36,264.

Bran·don (bran′dən) city, SW Manitoba, Canada; 29,981.

Bran·don (bran′dən) city, CEN. Florida; 12,749; ZIP 33511.

Bran·dy·wine (bran′dē·wīn′) city, SE Pennsylvania; 11,411.

Bran·ford (bran′fərd) town, S CEN. Connecticut; 20,444; ZIP 06405.

Brant·ford (brant′fərd) city, SE Ontario, Canada; 59,548.

Bra·sí·li·a (brə·zē′lyə) city, CEN. Brazil; cap.; 453,000.

Brat·tle·bo·ro (brat′l·bûr′ō) uninc. place, SE Vermont; 12,239; ZIP 05301*.

Braw·ley (brô′lē) city, SE California; 13,146; ZIP 92227.

Bra·zil (brə·zil′) republic, NE and N CEN. South America; 3,287,951 sq. mi.; 66,302,000; cap. Brasília.

Bra·zil (brə·zil′) city, W Indiana; 8,163; ZIP 47834.

Braz·za·ville (braz′ə·vil) city, SE Republic of the Congo (Brazzaville) ; cap.; 136,200.

Bre·a (brā′ə, brē′-) city, SW California; 18,447; ZIP 92621.

Breck·en·ridge (brek′ən·rij) city, N CEN. Texas; 5,944; ZIP 76024.

Breckenridge Hills vill., E Missouri; 7,011.

Brecks·ville (breks′vil) vill., N Ohio; 9,137; ZIP see CLEVELAND.

Breed's Hill (brēdz) hill, near Bunker Hill. See BUNKER HILL.

Brem·en (brem′en) state, NW West Germany; 156 sq. mi. — port city, major part of Bremen state; 592,386.

Brem·er·ha·ven (brem′ər·hä′vən) city, part of Bremen state, NW West Germany; 145,419.

Brem·er·ton (brem′ər·tən) city, W Washington; 35,307; ZIP 98310*.

Bren·ham (bren′əm) city, E CEN. Texas; 8,922; ZIP 77833.

Bren·ner Pass (bren′ər) Alpine pass, Austrian-Italian border.

Brent·wood (brent′wŏŏd) city, E Missouri; 11,248; ZIP see ST. LOUIS.

— uninc. place, SE New York; 27,868.

— boro., SW Pennsylvania; 13,732; ZIP see PITTSBURGH.

Bres·lau (bres′lou, brez′-) Wrocław: *German name.*

Brest (brest) city, NW France; chief French naval station; 136,104.

Brest (brest) city, SW Byelorussian SSR; Russo-German peace treaty signed here, 1918; 85,000.

Bre·vard (brə·värd′) city, SW North Carolina; 5,243; ZIP 28712.

Brew·er (broō′ər) city, S CEN. Maine; 9,300.

Brew·ton (broōt′n) city, S Alabama; 6,747.

Bri·ar·cliff Man·or (brī′ər·klif′ man′ər) vill., SE New York; 6,521.

Bridge (brij) city, E CEN. Texas; 8,164; ZIP 77611.

Bridge·port (brij′pôrt, -pōrt) city, SW Connecticut; 156,542; ZIP 06600*.

— boro., SE Pennsylvania; 5,630; ZIP see NORRISTOWN.

Bridge·ton (brij′tən) town, E Missouri; 19,992; ZIP see HAZELWOOD.

— city, SW New Jersey; 20,435; ZIP 08302*.

Bridge·town (brij′toun′) town, SW Ohio; 13,352; ZIP 45201.

— port city, SW Barbados; cap.; 85,000.

Bridge View vill., NE Illinois; 12,522; ZIP see OAK LAWN.

Bridge·ville (brij′vil) boro., SW Pennsylvania; 6,717; ZIP 15017.

Bridge·wa·ter (brij′wô′tər, -wot′ər) town, E Massachusetts; 11,829; ZIP 02324.

Brig·an·tine (brig′ən·tēn) city, SE New Jersey; 6,741; ZIP 08203.

Brig·ham City (brig′əm) city, N Utah; 14,007; ZIP 84302.

Brigh·ton (brīt′n) co. boro. and resort, SW England; 162,160.

Brigh·ton (brīt′n) city, N CEN. Colorado; 8,309; ZIP 80601.

Brink·ley (bringk′lē) city, E Arkansas; 5,275; ZIP 72021.

Bris·bane (briz′bān, -bən) city, SE Queensland, Australia; cap.; 719,140.

Bris·tol (bris′təl) co. boro., SW England; 429,020.

Bris·tol (bris′təl) city, W CEN. Connecticut; 55,487; ZIP 06010*.

— boro., SE Pennsylvania; 12,085.

— urb. twp., SE Pennsylvania; 59,298; ZIP 19007.

— town, E Rhode Island; 17,860; ZIP 02809.

— city, NE Tennessee at Tennessee-Virginia line; 20,064; ZIP 37620*.

— city, SW Virginia; adjacent to, and integrated with Bristol, Tennessee; 14,857; ZIP 24201*.

Bristol Channel inlet of the Atlantic betw. Wales and SW England.

Brit·ain (brit′n) see GREAT BRITAIN.

British Columbia prov., W Canada; 366,255 sq. mi.; 1,873,674; cap. Victoria.

British Guiana Guyana: *the former name.*

British Honduras Belize: *the former name.*

British Isles isl. group of W Europe comprising Great Britain, Ireland, the Isle of Man, and the Channel Islands.

British Virgin Islands British col., E Greater Antilles; 59 sq. mi.; 7,000; cap. Road Town.

British West Indies see WEST INDIES.

Brit·ta·ny (brit′ə·nē) reg., W France; former prov.

Brno (bûr′nô) city, CEN. Czechoslovakia; 323,741.

Broad·view (brôd′vyoō) vill., NE Illinois; 9,307; ZIP see MAYWOOD.

Broadview Heights vill., N Ohio; 11,463; ZIP see CLEVE-LAND.

Brock·port (brok′pôrt, -pōrt) vill., W New York; 7,878; ZIP 14420.

Brock·ton (brok′tən) city, E Massachusetts; 89,040; ZIP 02401*.

Brock·ville (brok′vil) town, SE Ontario, Canada; 19,266.

Brod·er·ick-Bryte (brod′ər·ik-brīt′) city, NE California; 12,782; ZIP 95605.

Broken Arrow city, NE Oklahoma; 11,787; ZIP 74012.

Bronx (brongks) boro., N New York City; 1,471,701; also **the Bronx;** ZIP 10400*.

Bronx·ville (brongks′vil) vill., SE New York; 6,674; ZIP see YONKERS.

Brook·field (broŏk′fēld) town, SW Connecticut; 9,688; ZIP 06804.

— vill., NE Illinois; 20,284; ZIP 60513.

— city, N CEN. Missouri; 5,491; ZIP 64628.

— city, SE Wisconsin; 32,140; ZIP 53005.

Brook·ha·ven (broŏk·hā′vən) city, SW Mississippi; 10,100 ZIP 39601.

— boro., SE Pennsylvania; 7,370.

Brook·ings (broŏk′ingz) city, E South Dakota; 13,717; ZIP 57006*.

Brook·line (broŏk′līn) town, E Massachusetts; 58,886; ZIP see BOSTON.

Brook·lyn (broŏk′lin) city, NE Louisiana; 13,896.

— boro., SE New York City; 2,602,012; ZIP 11200*.

— city, NE Ohio; 13,896.

Brooklyn Center vill., SE Minnesota; 35,173; ZIP see MIN-NEAPOLIS.

Brooklyn Park vill., SE Minnesota; 26,230.

Brook Park vill., N Ohio; 30,774; ZIP see CLEVELAND.

Brook·side Park (broŏk′sīd′) city, NE Delaware; 7,856.

Broom·field (broōm′fēld′) city, N CEN. Colorado; 7,261; ZIP 80020.

Bros·sard (bro·sär′) city, S Quebec, Canada; 11,884.

Brow·ar·dale (brou′ər·dāl) city, SE Florida; 17,444.

Brown Deer vill., SE Wisconsin; 12,622; ZIP see MIL-WAUKEE.

Brown·field (broun′fēld) city, W Texas; 9,647; ZIP 79316.

Browns·burg (brounz′bûrg′) city, W CEN. Indiana; 5,186; ZIP 46112.

Browns Mills (brounz) city, CEN. New Jersey; 7,144; ZIP 08105.

Browns Village city, SE Florida; 23,442; ZIP 33101.

Browns·ville (brounz′vil, -vəl) uninc. place, NW Florida; 20,294.

— city, W Tennessee; 7,011.

— city, S Texas; 52,522; ZIP 78520*.

Brown·wood (broun′woŏd) city, CEN. Texas; 17,368; ZIP 76801*.

Bru·nei (broŏ·nī′) sultanate under British protection, NW Borneo; 2,226 sq. mi.; 84,000. — city, N Brunei; cap.; 38,000.

Bruns·wick (brunz′wik) city, NE West Germany; 52,030.

Bruns·wick (brunz′wik) city, SE Georgia; 19,585; ZIP 31520*.

— uninc. place, S Maine; 16,195; ZIP 04011.

— vill., N Ohio; 15,852; ZIP 44212.

Brus·sels (brus′əlz) city, CEN. Belgium; cap.; 170,086.

Bry·an (brī′ən) city, NW Ohio; 7,008; ZIP 43506.

— city, E CEN. Texas; 33,719; ZIP 77801*.

Bu·cha·rest (boō′kə·rest, byoō′-) city, S Rumania; cap.; 1,372,937.

Buck·han·non (buk/han′ən) city, N CEN. West Virginia; 7,261; ZIP 26201.

Buck·ing·ham (buk′ing·əm, -ham) town, SW Quebec, Canada; 7,227.

Bu·cy·rus (byoō·sī′rəs) city, N CEN. Ohio; 13,111; ZIP 44820.

Bu·da·pest (boō′də·pest) co. boro., CEN. Hungary; cap.; 1,919,700.

Bue·chel (byoō′kəl) city, NW Kentucky; 5,359; ZIP 40218.

Bue·na Park (bwā′nə) city, SW California; 63,646; ZIP 90620*.

Bue·na Vis·ta (byoō′nə vis′tə) city, W CEN. Virginia; 6,425; ZIP 24416.

Bue·nos Ai·res (bwā′nəs ī′riz, bō′nəs âr′ēz) city, E Argentina; cap.; 2,966,816.

Buf·fa·lo (buf′ə·lō) city, W New York; 462,768; ZIP 14200*.

Buffalo Grove city, NE Illinois; 11,799.

Bul·gar·i·a (bul·gâr′i·ə, boōl-) republic, SE Europe; 42,796 sq. mi.; 7,700,000; cap. Sofia.

Bull Run small stream, NE Virginia; site of Union defeats in the Civil War, 1861 and 1862.

Bunche Park (bunch) city, SE Florida; 5,773; ZIP 33054.

Bun·ker Hill (bung′kər) hill, Charlestown, Massachusetts, near which (on Breed's Hill) occurred the first organized engagement of the American Revolution, June 17, 1775.

Bun·kie (bung′kē) town, E CEN. Louisiana; 5,395; ZIP 71222.

Bur·bank (bûr′bangk) city, SW California; 88,871; ZIP 91500*.

Bur·gun·dy (bûr′gən·dē) reg., E CEN. France.

Burk·bur·nett (bûrk′bər·net′) city, N Texas; 9,230; ZIP 76354.

Bur·le·son (bûr′lə·sən) city, N Texas; 7,713; ZIP 76028.

Bur·ley (bûr′lē) city, S Idaho; 8,279; ZIP 83318.

Bur·lin·game (bûr′lin·gām, -ling·gām) city, W CEN. California; 27,320; ZIP 94010*.

Bur·ling·ton (bûr′ling·tən) city, SE Iowa; 32,366; ZIP 52601*.

— town, NE Massachusetts; 21,980; ZIP 01803.

— city, W New Jersey; 11,991; ZIP 08016.

— city, N CEN. North Carolina; 35,930; ZIP 27215*.

— city, NW Vermont; 38,633; ZIP 05401*.

— city, SE Wisconsin; 7,479; ZIP 53105.

Bur·ling·ton (bûr′ling·tən) town, SE Ontario, Canada; 65,941.

Bur·ma (bûr′mə) state, SE Asia, betw. East Pakistan and Thailand; 261,789 sq. mi.; 20,662,000; cap. Rangoon.

Burma Road road betw. N Burma and SW China; a World War II supply route.

Burns·ville (bûrnz′vil) city, SE Minnesota; 19,940; ZIP 55378.

Bur·rill·ville (bûr′əl·vil) town, N Rhode Island; 10,087.

PRONUNCIATION KEY: add, āce, câre, pälm; end, ēven; it, īce; odd, ōpen, ôrder; toōk, poōl; up, bûrn; ə = a in *above*, e in *sicken*, i in *flexible*, o in *melon*, u in *focus*; yoō = u in *fuse*; oil; pout; check; go; ring; thin; this; zh, vision. For å, œ, ü, kh, ṅ, see inside front cover.

Bu·run·di (boŏ·roōn′dē) kingdom, CEN. Africa; formerly part of Ruanda-Urundi; 10,747 sq. mi.; 2,400,000; cap. Usumbura. See RWANDA.

But·ler (but′lər) boro., N New Jersey; 7,051; ZIP 07405.

— city, w Pennsylvania; 18,691; ZIP 16001*.

Butte (byoōt) city, sw Montana; 23,368; ZIP 59701*.

Bye·lo·rus·sian SSR (bye′lə·rush′ən) constituent republic. w USSR; 80,154 sq. mi.; 8,055,000; cap. Minsk.

Cad·il·lac (kad′ə·lak) city, NW Michigan; 9,990; ZIP 49601.

Cá·diz (kā′diz, kə·diz′) city, sw Spain; 122,568.

Ca·guas (kä′gwäs) town, E CEN. Puerto Rico; 32,015; ZIP 00625*.

Ca·ho·ki·a (kə·hō′kē·ə) vill., sw Illinois; 20,649; ZIP see EAST ST. LOUIS.

Cai·ro (kī′rō) city, NE Arab Republic of Egypt; cap.; 3,518,200.

Cai·ro (kâr′ō, kā′rō) city, sw Georgia; 8,061; ZIP 31728.

— city, s Illinois; 6,277; ZIP 62914.

Cal·ais (kal′ā, ka·lā′, kal′is) city, N France; 70,372.

Cal·cut·ta (kal·kut′ə) city, NE India; 2,296,000.

Cald·well (kôld′wəl, -wel) city, sw Idaho; 14,219; ZIP 83605.

— boro., NE New Jersey; 8,719; ZIP 07006*.

Ca·lex·i·co (kə·lek′si·kō) city, SE California; 10,625; ZIP 92231.

Cal·ga·ry (kal′gə·rē) city, s Alberta, Canada; 330,575.

Cal·i·cut (kal′ə·kut) Kozhikode: *an alternate name.*

Cal·i·for·nia (kal/ə·fôr′nyə, -fôr′nē·ə) state, w United States; 158,693 sq. mi.; 19,953,134; cap. Sacramento.

— boro., sw Pennsylvania; 6,635; ZIP 15419.

California, Gulf of inlet of the Pacific, w Mexico, betw. Lower California and the rest of Mexico.

Cal·u·met City (kal′yə·met, -yoŏ-) city, NE Illinois; 32,956; ZIP 60409.

Calumet Park vill., NE Illinois; 10,069; ZIP see CHICAGO.

Cal·ver·ton (kal′vər·tən) city, sw Maryland; 6,543; ZIP 20705.

Cal·wa (kal′wə) city, CEN. California; 5,191; ZIP 93745.

Cam·a·ril·lo (kam/ə·ril′ō) city, sw California; 19,219; ZIP 93010.

Cam·as (kam′əs) city, sw Washington; 5,790; ZIP 98607.

Cam·bo·di·a (kam·bō′dē·ə) Kampuchea: *alternate name.*

Cam·bridge (kām′brij) city, SE England; site of Cambridge University; 100,340.

Cam·bridge (kām′brij) city, CEN. Maryland; 11,595; ZIP 21613.

— city, E Massachusetts; 100,361; ZIP see BOSTON.

— city, E Ohio; 13,656; ZIP 43725.

Cam·den (kam′dən) city, s Arkansas; 15,147; ZIP 71701.

— city, sw New Jersey; 102,551; ZIP 08100*.

— city, N CEN. South Carolina; 8,532; ZIP 29020.

Cam·e·ron (kam′rən) city, E Texas; 5,546; ZIP 76520.

Cam·e·roon (kam/ə·roōn′) republic, w equatorial Africa; 183,376 sq. mi.; 4,000,000; cap. Yaoundé. Also **Cam′e·roun′**.

Camp·bell (kam′bəl, -əl) city, w California; 24,770; ZIP 95008.

— city, E Ohio; 12,577.

Camp·bells·ville (kam′əlz·vil′, -bəlz-) city, s CEN. Kentucky; 7,598; ZIP 42718.

Camp·bell·ton (kam′bəl·tən, -əl-) city, N New Brunswick, Canada; 10,175.

Camp Hill boro., s Pennsylvania; 9,931; ZIP 17011.

Camp Le Jeune (lə joōn) city, SE North Carolina; 34,549.

Camp Springs city, sw Maryland; 22,776; ZIP 20031.

Cam·rose (kam′rōz) city, CEN. Alberta, Canada; 8,362.

Can·a·da (kan′ə·də) independent member of the Commonwealth of Nations, N North America; 3,851,809 sq. mi.; 16,080,791; cap. Ottawa.

Canal Zone US leased terr., CEN. Panama; extending five miles on either side of the Panama Canal; 648 sq. mi.; 41,684; adm. ctr. Balboa Heights.

Can·an·dai·gua (kan/ən·dā′gwə) city, w CEN. New York; 10,488; ZIP 14424.

Canary Islands isl. group of Spain near NW coast of Africa; 2,808 sq. mi.; 944,000.

Can·a·sto·ta (kan/ə·stō′tə) city, NW New York; 5,033; ZIP 13032.

Ca·nav·er·al (kə·nav′ər·əl), **Cape** Cape Kennedy: *the former name.*

Can·ber·ra (kan′bə·rə) city, SE Australia; cap.; 100,090.

Can·dle·wood (kan′dəl·woŏd) city, E CEN. New Jersey; 5,629; ZIP 08701.

Ca·ne·a (kä·nē′ä) city, NW Crete; cap.; 33,000.

Cannes (kan, kanz) city, SE France; 58,079.

Can·non (kan′ən) city, E CEN. New Mexico; 5,461.

Can·on City (kan′yən) city, s CEN. Colorado; 9,206; ZIP 81212.

Can·ons·burg (kan′ənz·bûrg) boro., sw Pennsylvania; 11,439; ZIP 15317.

Can·ter·bur·y (kan′tər·ber·ē, -brē, -ber·ə) co. boro., SE England; site of famous cathedral; 39,000.

Can·ton (kan·ton′) city, s China; 1,840,000.

Can·ton (kan′tən, kant′n) town, CEN. Connecticut; 6,868; ZIP 06019.

— city, w CEN. Illinois; 14,217; ZIP 61520.

— town, E Massachusetts; 17,100; ZIP 02021.

— city, w CEN. Mississippi; 10,503; ZIP 39046.

— town, w North Carolina; 5,158; ZIP 28716.

— vill., N New York; 6,398; ZIP 13617.

— city, NE Ohio; 110,053; ZIP 44700*.

Can·yon (kan′yən) city, NW Texas; 8,333; ZIP 79015.

Cap-de-la-Ma·de·leine (käp·də·lä·mäd·len′) city, s Quebec, Canada; 29,433.

Cape Cor·al (kôr′əl, kor′-) city, sw Florida; 10,193; ZIP 33904.

Cape E·liz·a·beth (i·liz/ə·bəth) city, SE Maine; 7,973.

Cape Gi·rar·deau (jə·rä′dō, jə·rär′-, -də) city, SE Missouri; 31,282; ZIP 63701.

Cape Town city, s South Africa; legislative cap.; 508,341. Also **Cape·town** (kāp′toun′).

Cape Verde (vûrd) republic, isl. group NW of Africa; 1,552 sq. mi.; 250,000; cap. Praia.

Cap·i·to·la (kap/ə·tō′lə) city, w CEN. California; 5,080; ZIP 95010.

Ca·pri (kä′prē, kə·prē′) isl., near the w coast of Italy; 4 sq. mi.

Ca·ra·cas (kə·rä′kəs, -rak′əs) city, N Venezuela; cap.; 786,710.

Car·bon·dale (kär′bən·dāl) city, s Illinois; 22,816; ZIP 62901.

— city, NE Pennsylvania; 12,808; ZIP 18407.

Car·diff (kär′dif) co. boro., sw Wales; 289,320.

Car·diff-by-the-Sea (kär′dif·bi·thə·sē′) city, sw California; 5,724; ZIP 92007.

Car·ib·be·an Sea (kar/ə·bē′ən, kə·rib′ē·ən) part of the Atlantic betw. the West Indies and Central and South America.

Car·i·bou (kar′i·boō) uninc. place, N Maine; 10,419; ZIP 04736.

Carle Place (kärl) city, SE New York; 6,326.

Car·lin·ville (kär′lin·vil) city, sw CEN. Illinois; 5,675; ZIP 62626.

Car·lisle (kär·lil′, kär′lil) boro., s Pennsylvania; 18,079; ZIP 17013.

Carls·bad (kärlz′bad) city, s California; 14,944; ZIP 92008.

— city, SE New Mexico; 21,297; ZIP 88220.

Carlsbad Caverns National Park area, SE New Mexico; contains **Carlsbad Caverns,** a series of limestone caves.

Carl·stadt (kärl′stat) boro., NE New Jersey; 7,974; ZIP see RUTHERFORD.

Car·mel (kär′məl) city, E CEN. Indiana; 6,568; ZIP 46032.

Car·mi (kär′mē) city, SE Illinois; 6,033; ZIP 62821.

Car·mi·chael (kär′mi·kəl) uninc. place, N CEN. California; 37,625; ZIP 95608.

Car·mo·dy Hills (kär′mə·dē) city, sw Maryland; 6,245.

Car·ne·gie (kär′nə·gē) boro., sw Pennsylvania; 15,864; ZIP 15106.

Carney See PARKVILLE-CARNEY.

Car·not-Moon (kär′nō·moōn′) city, sw Pennsylvania; 13,093.

Car·ol City (kar′əl) uninc. place, SE Florida; 27,361; ZIP see OPA-LOCKA.

Car·o·line Islands (kär/ə·lin) isl. group in the Pacific, E of the Philippines; 550 sq. mi.

Car·pa·thi·an Mountains (kär·pā′thē·ən) mtn. range, CEN. and E Europe.

Car·pen·ter·i·a (kär/pən·târ′ē·ə) city, sw California; 6,982; ZIP 93013.

Car·pen·ters·ville (kär′pən·tərz·vil) vill., NE Illinois; 24,059; ZIP 60110.

Car·ra·ra (kə·rä′rə) city, CEN. Italy; site of white marble quarries; 64,901.

Car·ri·zo Springs (kə·rē′zō) city, sw Texas; 5,374; ZIP 78834.

Car·roll (kar′əl) city, w CEN. Iowa; 8,716; ZIP 51401.

Car·roll·ton (kar′əl·tən) city, w Georgia; 13,520; ZIP 30117.

— city, NE Michigan; 7,300; ZIP 48724.

— city, N Texas; 13,855; ZIP 75006.

Car·son (kär′sən) uninc. place, sw California; 71,150; ZIP see WILMINGTON.

Carson City city, w Nevada; cap.; 15,468; ZIP 89701*.

Car·ter·et (kär′tər·et′, kär′tər·et) boro., NE New Jersey; 23,137; ZIP 07008.

Car·ters·ville (kär′tərz·vil, -vəl) city, NW Georgia; 9,929; ZIP 30120.

Car·thage (kär′thij, -thəj) city, sw Missouri; 11,035; ZIP 64836.

— city, E Texas; 5,392; ZIP 75633.

Ca·ruth·ers·ville (kə·ruth′ərz·vil) city, SE Missouri; 7,350; ZIP 63830.

Car·y (kâr′ē) city, CEN. North Carolina; 7,430; ZIP 27511.

Cas·a·blan·ca (kas/ə·blang′kə, kä/sə·bläng′kə) city, NW Morocco; 1,085,000.

Ca·sa Gran·de (kä′sə grän′dā) city, s Arizona; 10,536; ZIP 85222.

Cascade Range mtn. range in Oregon, Washington, and British Columbia.

Cash·mere (kash·mir′, kash′mir) See KASHMIR.

Cas·per (kas′pər) city, CEN. Wyoming; 39,361; ZIP 82601.

Cas·pi·an Sea (kas′pē·ən) salt-water lake in the s USSR and N Iran; 163,800 sq. mi.

Cas·sel·ber·ry City (kas′əl·ber′ē) city, sw Florida; 9,438; ZIP 32707.

Cas·tile (kas·tēl′) reg., N and CEN. Spain.

Castle Hills city, s CEN. Texas; 5,311.

Castle Shan·non (shan′ən) boro., sw Pennsylvania; 11,899; ZIP see PITTSBURGH.

Cas·tro Valley (kas′trō) uninc. place, w California; 44,760; ZIP see HAYWARD.

Cat·a·li·na Island (kat′ə·lē′nə) Santa Catalina: *an alternate name.*

Cat·a·lo·ni·a (kat′ə·lō′nē·ə) reg., NE Spain.

Ca·ta·nia (kä·tä′nyä) prov., E Sicily; 1,377 sq. mi.; 889,000.
— city, **Catania** prov.; cap.; 376,239.

Ca·ta·ño (kä·tä′nyō) town, N Puerto Rico; 25,208.

Cat·a·sau·qua (kat′ə·sô′kwə) boro., E Pennsylvania; 5,702; ZIP 18032.

Ca·tons·ville (kā′tənz·vil) uninc. place, N CEN. Maryland; 54,812; ZIP see BALTIMORE.

Cat·skill (kat′skil) vill., E New York; 5,317; ZIP 12414.

Catskill Mountains range of the Appalachians in SE New York.

Cau·ca·sus (kô′kə·səs) mtn. range betw. the Black and Caspian seas.

Cau·ca·sus (kô′kə·səs) reg., sw USSR, betw. the Black and Caspian seas. Also **Cau·ca·sia** (kô·kā′zhə, -shē, -kash′ə).

Cay·ce (kā′sē′) city, CEN. South Carolina; 9,967; ZIP 29033.

Ca·yey (kä·yā′) town, SE CEN. Puerto Rico; 38,061.

Ce·dar·brook-Mel·rose (sē′dər·brŏŏk′mel′rōz′) city, SE Pennsylvania; 9,980.

Ce·dar·burg (sē′dər·bûrg) city, E Wisconsin; 7,697.

Cedar City town, sw Utah; 8,946; ZIP 84720.

Cedar Falls city, E CEN. Iowa; 29,597; ZIP 50613.

Cedar Grove twp., NE New Jersey; 15,582; ZIP 07009.

Cedar Hammock-Brad·en·ton South (brad′ən·tən) city, W CEN. Florida; 10,820.

Cedar Heights city, SE Pennsylvania; 6,303.

Ce·dar·hurst (sē′dər·hûrst′) vill., SE New York; 6,941; ZIP 11516.

Cedar Lake uninc. place, NW Indiana; 7,589; ZIP 46303.

Cedar Rapids city, E Iowa; 110,642; ZIP 52400*.

Ce·dar·town (sē′dər·toun′) city, NW Georgia; 9,253.

Cel·e·bes (sel′ə·bēz, sə·lē′bēz) isl. of Indonesia, E of Borneo; 69,277 sq. mi.; 6,600,000.

Ce·li·na (sə·lī′nə) city, w Ohio; 7,779.

Cen·ter·each (sen′tər·rēch) uninc. place, SE New York; 9,427; ZIP 11720.

Center Line city, SE Michigan; 10,379.

Center Point city, CEN. Alabama; 15,675.

Cen·ter·ville (sent′tər·vil) city, s Iowa; 6,531; ZIP 52544*.
— city, sw Ohio; 10,333; ZIP 45459.

Central African Empire country, CEN. Africa; 238,224 sq. mi.; 2,370,000; cap. Bangui. Formerly, **Central African Republic.**

Central America s part of North America, betw. Mexico and Colombia, including the countries of Guatemala, El Salvador, Honduras, Nicaragua, Costa Rica, Panama, and Belize.

Central Falls city, NE Rhode Island; 18,716; ZIP see PAWTUCKET.

Central I·slip (ī′slip) city, SE New York; 36,369; ZIP 11722.

Cen·tra·li·a (sen·trä′lē·ə, -trä′lyə) city, s Illinois; 15,217; ZIP 62800.*
— city, sw Washington; 10,054.

Cen·tre·ville (sen′tər·vil) city, sw Illinois; 11,378; ZIP see EAST SAINT LOUIS.

Cer·es Point (sir′ēz) city, CEN. California; 6,029; ZIP 95307.

Cer·ri·tos (ser·ē′tōs) city, s California; 15,856; ZIP 90701.

Cey·lon (si·lon′) Sri Lanka: *the former name.*

Chad (chad), **Lake** lake, NW CEN. Africa; 8,000 sq. mi.

Chad, Republic of independent state of the French Community, CEN. Africa; 495,752 sq. mi.; 2,580,000; cap. Fort-Lamy.

Chad·ron (shad′rən) city, NW Nebraska; 5,853; ZIP 69337.

Cham·bers·burg (chăm′bərz·bûrg) boro., s Pennsylvania; 17,315; ZIP 17201.

Cham·blee (cham·blē′) city, NW CEN. Georgia; 9,727; ZIP 30005.

Cham·bly (shäm′blē) city, s Quebec, Canada; 10,798.

Cham·paign (cham·pān′) city, E CEN. Illinois; 56,532; ZIP 61820.

Cham·plain, Lake (sham·plān′) lake, betw. New York and Vermont, extending into Canada; 600 sq. mi.

Chan·dler (chand′dlər) city, s CEN. Arizona; 13,763; ZIP 85224*.

Chang·chun (chäng′chōōn′) city, NE China; 975,000.

Channel Islands British isl. group, English Channel near Normandy; includes Jersey, Guernsey, Alderney, and Sark; 75 sq. mi.; 104,000.

Cha·nute (shə·nōōt′) city, SE Kansas; 10,341; ZIP 66720.

Chapel Hill town, N CEN. North Carolina; 25,537; ZIP 27514*.

Chapel Oaks-Cedar Heights city, sw Maryland; 6,049.

Char·i·ton (shar′ət·n, shâr′-) city, s Iowa; 5,009; ZIP 50009.

Char·le·roi (shär·lə·roi′, shär′lə·roi) boro., sw Pennsylvania; 6,723; ZIP 15022.

Charles·bourg (shärl′bŏŏrg) city, s Quebec, Canada; 24,926.

Charles City (chärlz) city, N Iowa; 9,268; ZIP 50616.

Charles·ton (chärl′stən, chärlz′tən) city, E Illinois; 16,421; ZIP 61920.
— city, SE Missouri; 5,131; ZIP 63834.
— city, SE South Carolina; 66,945; ZIP 29400.
— city, CEN. West Virginia; cap.; 71,505; ZIP 25300.

Charleston Base town, SE South Carolina; 6,238.

Charleston Yard town, sw South Carolina; 13,565.

Charles·town (chärlz′toun) city, SE Indiana; 5,890; ZIP 47111.

Char·lotte (shär′lət) city, s Michigan; 8,244; ZIP 48813.
— city, s CEN. North Carolina; 241,178; ZIP 28200*.

Char·lot·te A·ma·li·e (shär·lot′ə ə·mä′lē·ə) city, s St. Thomas, Virgin Islands of the United States; cap.; 9,801; ZIP 00801.

Char·lottes·ville (shär′ləts·vil, -vəl) city, CEN. Virginia; 38,880; ZIP 22901.

Char·lotte·town (shär′lət·toun) city, CEN. Prince Edward Island, Canada; cap.; 18,427.

Châ·teau·guay (shä·tō·gā′) town, s Quebec, Canada; 12,460.

Châ·teau·guay-Cen·tre (shä·tō·gā′sänt·r′) town, s Quebec, Canada; 14,096.

Chat·ham (chat′əm) boro., NE New Jersey; 9,566; ZIP 07928.

Chat·ham (chat′əm) town, NE New Brunswick, Canada; 8,136.
— city, s Ontario, Canada; 32,424.

Chat·ta·hoo·chee (chat′ə·hōō′chē) town, NW Florida; 7,944; ZIP 32324.

Chat·ta·noo·ga (chat′ə·nōō′gə) city, SE Tennessee; 119,082; ZIP 37400.

Chat·wood (chat′wŏŏd′) city, SE Pennsylvania; 7,168; ZIP 19308.

Che·boy·gan (shi·boi′gən) city, N Michigan; 5,553; ZIP 49721.

Cheek·to·wa·ga (chēk·tə·wä′gə) uninc. place, w New York; 113,844; ZIP see BUFFALO.

Che·ha·lis (chi·hā′lis) city, sw Washington; 5,727; ZIP 98532.

Chelms·ford (chems′fərd, chemz′-) town, NE Massachusetts; 31,432; ZIP 01824.

Chel·sea (chel′sē) metropolitan boro., sw London, England; 47,000.

Chel·sea (chel′sē) city, E Massachusetts; 30,625; ZIP see BOSTON.

Chel·ten·ham (chel′tən·ham′) urb. twp., SE Pennsylvania; 40,238; ZIP 19012.

Che·ney (chē′nē) city, NE Washington; 6,358; ZIP 99004.

Cher·aw (cher′ô, chi·rô′) town, NE South Carolina; 5,627; ZIP 29520.

Cher·bourg (shĕr′bŏŏrg) city, N France; 39,000.

Cher·o·kee (cher′ə·kē, cher·ə·kē′) city, NW Iowa; 7,272; ZIP 51012.

Cher·ry·land (cher′ē·land) city, w California; 9,969; ZIP 94521.

Cherry Point city, SE North Carolina; 12,029.

Cher·ry·ville (cher′ē·vil) city, s CEN. North Carolina; 5,258; ZIP 28021.

Ches·a·peake (ches′ə·pēk) city, SE Virginia; 89,580.

Chesapeake Bay inlet of the Atlantic in Virginia and Maryland.

Chesh·ire (chesh′ər, -ir) co., w England; 1,105 sq. mi.; 1,368,000; cap. Chester.

Chesh·ire (chesh′ər, -ir) town, s CEN. Connecticut; 19,051; ZIP 06410.

Ches·ter (ches′tər) co. boro., w Cheshire, England; cap.; 60,360.

Ches·ter (ches′tər) city, SE Illinois; 5,310; ZIP 62233.
— city, SE Pennsylvania; 56,331; ZIP 19013*.
— city, N South Carolina; 7,045; ZIP 29706.
— city, CEN. Virginia; 5,556; ZIP 23831.

Ches·ter·ton (ches'tər·tən) city, NW Indiana; 6,177; ZIP 46304.

Chev·er·ly (shev'ər·lē) town, W Maryland; 6,696; ZIP see HYATTSVILLE.

Chev·i·ot (shiv'ē·ət, shev'-) city, SW Ohio; 11,135.

Chev·i·ot Hills (chev'ē·ət, chiv'-, chē'vē·ət, -yət, -vyət) mtn. range, on the border betw. England and Scotland.

Chey·enne (shī·an', -en') city, SE Wyoming; cap.; 40,914; ZIP 82001*.

Chi·ca·go (shə·kä'gō, -kô'-) city, NE Illinois; second largest city in the United States; 3,366,957; ZIP 60600*.

Chicago Heights city, NE Illinois; 40,900; ZIP 60411*.

Chicago Ridge vill., NE Illinois; 9,187; ZIP 60415.

Chick·a·saw (chik'ə·sô) city, SW Alabama; 8,447; ZIP see MOBILE.

Chick·a·sha (chik'ə·shā) city, S CEN. Oklahoma; 14,194; ZIP 73018*.

Chi·co (chē'kō) city, N CEN. California; 18,580; ZIP 95926*.

Chic·o·pee (chik'ə·pē) city, SW Massachusetts; 66,676; ZIP 01013*.

Chi·cou·ti·mi (shi·kōō'ti·mē) city, S Quebec, Canada; 32,526.

Chi·cou·ti·mi-Nord (shi·kōō'ti·mē·nôr') city, CEN. Quebec, Canada; 12,814.

Chi·hua·hua (chi·wä'wä) state, N Mexico; 94,830 sq. mi.; 1,236,000. — city, Chihuahua state; cap.; 209,632.

Chil·dress (chil'dris, chīl'-) city, N Texas; 5,408; ZIP 79201.

Chil·e (chil'ē) republic, W South America; 286,397; sq. mi.; 7,340,000; cap. Santiago.

Chil·li·coth·e (chil'i·koth'ē) city, N CEN. Missouri; 9,519; ZIP 64601.

— city, S CEN. Ohio; 24,842; ZIP 45601*.

Chil·li·wack (chil'ə·wak) city, SW British Columbia, Canada; 8,681.

Chil·lum (chil'əm) city, SW Maryland; 35,656; ZIP 20783.

Chi·na (chī'nə), **People's Republic of** republic, E and CEN. Asia; 3,760,000 sq. mi.; 700 million; cap. Peking.

Chi·na (chī'nə), **Republic of** republic on Taiwan and several smaller islands; 13,890 sq. mi.; 10 million; cap. Taipei.

China Sea part of the Pacific bordering on China. See EAST CHINA SEA, SOUTH CHINA SEA.

Chi·no (chē'nō) city, SW California; 20,411; ZIP 91710.

Chip·pe·wa Falls (chip'ə·wä', -wə, -wō') city, W CEN. Wisconsin; 12,351; ZIP 54729.

Chis·holm (chiz'əm) city, NE Minnesota; 5,913; ZIP 55719.

Chris·tia·ni·a (kris·tyä'nē·ä) Oslo: *a former name.*

Chris·tians·burg (kris'chənz·bûrg) city, S Virginia; 7,857; ZIP 24073.

Chu·la Vis·ta (chōō'lə vis'tə) city, SW California; 67,901; ZIP 92010*.

Chun·king (chōong'king') city, S CEN. China; cap. during World War II; 2,121,000.

Church·ill (chûrch'il) city, NE Ohio; 7,457.

Cic·e·ro (sis'ə·rō) city, NE Illinois; 67,058; ZIP see CHICAGO.

Cin·cin·nat·i (sin'sə·nat'ē, -nat'ə) city, SW Ohio; 452,524; ZIP 45200*.

Cir·cas·sia (sər·kash'ə, -kash'ē·ə) reg., NW Caucasus, RSFSR.

Cir·cle·ville (sûr'kəl·vil) city, S CEN. Ohio; 11,687; ZIP 43113.

Citrus Heights city, NE California; 21,760; ZIP 95610.

Ciu·dad Tru·jil·lo (syōō·thäth' trōō·hē'yō) Santo Domingo: from 1936–62.

Clair·ton (klâr'tən, klârt'n) city, SW Pennsylvania; 15,051; ZIP 15025.

Clan·ton (klant'n, klan'tən) city, CEN. Alabama; 5,868; ZIP 35045.

Clare·mont (klâr'mont) city, SW California; 23,464; ZIP 91711*.

— city, SW New Hampshire; 14,221; ZIP 03743.

Clare·more (klâr'môr, klâr'ə·môr) city, NE Oklahoma; 9,084; ZIP 74017.

Clar·en·don Hills (klar'ən·dən) vill., NE Illinois; 6,750; ZIP 60514.

Cla·rin·da (klə·rin'də) city, SW Iowa; 5,420; ZIP 51632.

Clar·i·on (klar'ē·ən) city, CEN. Pennsylvania 6,095; ZIP 16214.

Clark (klärk) twp., NE New Jersey; 18,829; ZIP see RAHWAY.

Clarks·burg (klärks'bûrg) city, N West Virginia; 24,864; ZIP 26301*.

Clarks·dale (klärks'dāl) city, NW Mississippi; 21,673; ZIP 38614.

Clarks Summit (klärks) city, NE Pennsylvania; 5,376; ZIP 18411.

Clarks·ton (klärks'tən) city, SE Washington; 6,312; ZIP 99403.

Clarks·ville (klärks'vil, -vəl) town, SE Indiana; 13,806; ZIP see JEFFERSONVILLE.

— city, N Tennessee; 31,719; ZIP 37040*.

Claw·son (klô'sən) city, SE Michigan; 17,617; ZIP 48017.

Clay·mont (klā'mont') city, CEN. Delaware; 6,584; ZIP 19703.

Clay·ton (klāt'n) city, E Missouri; 16,222; ZIP see SAINT LOUIS.

— city, SW New Jersey; 5,193; ZIP 08312.

Clear·field (klir'fēld) boro., W CEN. Pennsylvania; 8,176; ZIP 16830.

— city, N CEN. Utah; 5,193; ZIP 84015.

Clear Lake city, N Iowa; 6,430; ZIP 50428.

Clear·wa·ter (klir'wô'tər, -wot'ər) city, W Florida; 52,074; ZIP 33515*.

Cle·burne (klē'bərn) city, N CEN. Texas; 16,015; ZIP 76031.

Clem·son (klem'sən) city, NW South Carolina; 5,578; ZIP 29631.

Cleve·land (klēv'lənd) city, W Mississippi; 13,327; ZIP 38732.

— city, N Ohio; 750,903; ZIP 44100*.

— city, SE Tennessee; 20,651; ZIP 37311*.

— city, SE Texas; 5,627; ZIP 77327.

Cleveland Heights city, N Ohio; 60,767; ZIP see CLEVELAND.

Cliff·side Park (klif'sīd') boro., NE New Jersey; 14,387; ZIP 07010.

Cliff·wood-Cliff·wood Beach (klif'wood') city, E CEN. New Jersey; 7,056.

Clif·ton (klif'tən) city, NE Arizona; 5,087; ZIP 85533.

— city, NE New Jersey; 82,437; ZIP 07011*.

Clifton Forge city, W Virginia; 5,501; ZIP 24422.

Clifton Heights boro., SE Pennsylvania; 8,348; ZIP 19018*.

Clifton Knolls city, NE New York; 5,771.

Clin·ton (klint'n, klin'tən) town, SE Connecticut; 10,267; ZIP 06413.

— city, CEN. Illinois; 7,570; ZIP 61727.

— city, W Indiana; 5,340; ZIP 47842.

— city, E Iowa; 34,719; ZIP 52732.

— town, CEN. Massachusetts; 13,383; ZIP 01510.

— city, W Mississippi; 7,246; ZIP 39056.

— city, W Missouri; 7,504; ZIP 64735.

— town, S CEN. North Carolina; 7,157; ZIP 28328.

— city, W Oklahoma; 8,513; ZIP 73601.

— town, NW South Carolina; 8,138; ZIP 29325.

Clinton Center town, SE Connecticut; 5,957.

Clo·quet (klō·kā') city, E Minnesota; 8,699; ZIP 55720.

Clo·ster (klō'stər) boro., NE New Jersey; 8,604; ZIP 07624.

Clo·vis (klō'vis) city, CEN. California; 13,856; ZIP 93612.

— city, E New Mexico; 28,495; ZIP 88101.

Clute City (klōōt) city, SE Texas; 6,023; ZIP 77531.

Clyde (klīd) city, W CEN. Ohio; 5,503; ZIP 43410.

Co·a·chel·la City (kō'ə·chel'ə) city, SE California; 8,353; ZIP 92236.

Coal·in·ga (kō·ling'gə, kō'ə·ling'gə) city, CEN. California; 6,161; ZIP 93210.

Coa·mo (kwä'mō) town, S CEN. Puerto Rico; 12,146; ZIP 00640.

Coates·ville (kōts'vil) city, SE Pennsylvania; 12,331; ZIP 19320.

Co·at·i·cook (kō·at'i·kook) town, S Quebec, Canada; 6,984.

Co·bourg (kō'bûrg) town, S Ontario, Canada; 11,524.

Cock·ran (kok'rən) city, CEN. Georgia; 5,161; ZIP 31014.

Co·coa (kō'kō) city, E Florida; 16,170; ZIP 32922*.

Cocoa Beach city, E CEN. Florida; 9,952; ZIP 32931.

Cod, Cape (kod) penin., SE Massachusetts.

Co·dy (kō'dē) city, NW Wyoming; 5,161; ZIP 82414.

Coeur d'A·lene (kûr də·lān') city, N Idaho; 16,228; ZIP 83814.

Cof·fey·ville (kô'fē·vil, kof'ē-) city, SE Kansas; 15,116; ZIP 67337.

Co·has·set (kō·has'it) city, E Massachusetts; 6,954; ZIP 02025.

Co·hoes (kō·hōz') city, E New York; 18,613; ZIP 12047.

Col·ches·ter (kol'ches'tər) town, SE Connecticut; 6,603; ZIP 06415.

— town, NW Vermont; 8,776; ZIP 05446.

Cold Spring city, N Kentucky; 5,348; ZIP 41076.

— city, SE New York; 5,498; ZIP 10516.

Cold·wa·ter (kōld'wô'tər, -wot'ər) city, S Michigan; 9,099; ZIP 49036.

Cole·man (kōl'mən) city, CEN. Texas; 5,608; ZIP 76834.

Coles·ville (kōlz'vil) city, SW Maryland; 9,455.

College Park city, W Georgia; 18,203; ZIP 30022.

— city, W Maryland; 26,156; ZIP 20740*.

College Station city, E CEN. Texas; 17,676; ZIP 77840*.

Col·lier Man·or-Crest·ha·ven (kol'yər·man'ər·krest·hā'vən) city, SE Florida; 7,202.

Col·ling·dale (kol'ing·dāl) boro., SE Pennsylvania; 10,605; ZIP see DARBY.

Col·lings·wood (kol'lingz·wood) boro., W New Jersey; 17,422; ZIP see CAMDEN.

Col·ling·wood (kol'ing·wood) town, S Ontario, Canada; 8,471.

Col·lins·ville (kol'inz·vil) city, SW Illinois; 17,773; ZIP 62234.

— city, s CEN. Virginia; 6,015; ZIP 24078.

Col·lis·ter (kol′is·tər) uninc. place, sw Idaho; 5,436.

Co·logne (kə·lōn′) city, w West Germany; 780,000.

Co·lom·bi·a (kə·lum′bē·ə) republic, NW South America; 439,519 sq. mi.; 14.447.000; cap. Bogotá.

Co·lom·bo (kə·lum′bō) city, w Sri Lanka; cap.; 510,947.

Co·lón (kō·lōn′) city, Caribbean end of the Canal Zone; an enclave of Panama; 64,892.

Colonial Heights city, SE CEN. Virginia; 15,097; ZIP 23834.

Col·o·nie (kol·ə·nē′) vill., E CEN. New York; 8,701.

Col·o·ra·do (kol·ə·rad′ə, -ō, -rä′dō) state, w CEN. United States; 104,247 sq. mi.; 2,207,259; cap. Denver.

Col·o·ra·do City (kul′ə·rä′də) city, w CEN. Texas; 5,227; ZIP 79512.

Col·o·ra·do River (kol·ə·rad′ə, -ō, -rä′dō) river flowing through Colorado, Utah, Arizona, California, and Mexico to the Gulf of California; length ab. 1,400 mi.

Col·o·ra·do Springs (kol·ə·rad′ə, -ō, -rä′dō) city, E CEN. Colorado; site of US Air Force Academy; 135,060; ZIP 80900*.

Col·ton (kōl′tən, kōlt′n) city, s California; 19,974; ZIP 92324.

Co·lum·bi·a (kə·lum′bē·ə) city, s Mississippi; 7,587; ZIP 39429.

— city, CEN. Missouri; 58,804; ZIP 65201*.

— boro., SE Pennsylvania; 11,237; ZIP 17512.

— city, CEN. South Carolina; cap.; 113,542; ZIP 29200*.

— city, CEN. Tennessee; 21,471; ZIP 38401*.

Columbia Heights city, E Minnesota; 23,997; ZIP see MINNEAPOLIS.

Columbia River river, sw Canada and NW United States; 1,200 mi. long.

Co·lum·bus (kə·lum′bəs) city, w Georgia; 154,168; ZIP 31900*.

— city, SE CEN. Indiana; 27,141; ZIP 47201*.

— city, E Mississippi; 25,795; ZIP 39701*.

— city, E Nebraska; 15,471; ZIP 68601.

— city, CEN. Ohio; cap.; 539,677; ZIP 43200*.

Com·mack (kō′mak) uninc. place, SE New York; 22,507; ZIP 11725.

Com·merce (kom′ərs) city, sw California; 10,536.

— city, NE Colorado; 17,407; ZIP 80022.

— city, NE Texas; 9,534; ZIP 75428*.

Commerce Town town, NE CEN. Colorado; 17,407; ZIP 80022.

Com·o·ros (käm′ə·rōs) country, isl. group sw of Africa, 790 sq. mi.; 370,000; cap. Moroni. Also **Comoro Islands.**

Comp·ton (komp′tən) city, sw California; 78,611; ZIP 90220*.

Com·stock (kom′stok′) city, sw Michigan, 5,003; ZIP 49041.

Comstock Park city, sw Michigan; 5,766.

Co·na·kry (kô·nä·krē′) city, w Guinea; cap.; 43,000.

Con·cord (kong′kərd, kon′kôrd′) city, W California; 85,164; ZIP 94520*.

— town, NE Massachusetts; 16,148; ZIP 01742.

— city, NE Missouri; 21,217.

— city, s CEN. North Carolina; 18,464; ZIP 28025.

— city, s CEN. New Hampshire; cap.; 30,022; ZIP 03300*.

Con·cor·di·a (kən·kôr′dē·ə, kəng-) city, N Kansas; 7,221; ZIP 66901.

Con·go (kong′gō) republic, w CEN. Africa; 132,047 sq. mi.; 1,000,000; cap. Brazzaville.

Congo Zaire Republic: *former name.*

Con·go River (kong′gō) river, CEN. Africa; 2,720 mi. long.

Con·ne·aut (kō′nē·ôt′, -nē·ot′) city, NE Ohio; 14,552; ZIP 44030.

Con·nect·i·cut (kə·net′i·kət) state, NE United States; 5,009 sq. mi.; 3,032,217; cap. Hartford.

Con·nells·ville (kon′elz·vil) city, sw Pennsylvania; 11,643; ZIP 15425.

Con·ners·ville (kon′ərz·vil) city, E Indiana; 17,604; ZIP 47331.

Conning Towers-Nautilus Park city, SE Connecticut; 9,791.

Con·roe (kon′rō) city, E Texas; 11,969 ZIP 77301.

Con·sho·hock·en (kon′shə·hok′ən) boro., SE Pennsylvania; 10,195; ZIP 19428.

Con·stan·ti·no·ple (kon′stan·tə·nō′pəl) Istanbul: *the former name.*

Continental Divide ridge of the Rockies separating w flowing and E flowing streams in North America.

Con·way (kon′wā) city, CEN. Arkansas; 15,510; ZIP 72032.

— city, NE Florida; 8,642.

— town, E South Carolina; 8,151; ZIP 29526*.

Cooke·vill (kook′vil, -vəl) town, N CEN. Tennessee; 14,270. ZIP 38501*.

Coon Rapids (koon) vill., E Minnesota; 30,505; ZIP see MINNEAPOLIS.

Coop·er Road (koop′ər) city, NW Louisiana; 9,034.

Coos Bay (koos) city, sw Oregon; 13,466; ZIP 97420*.

Co·pen·ha·gen (kō′pən·hā′gən, -hä′-) city, E Denmark; cap.; 721,000.

Co·piague (kō′peg, -pāg) uninc. place, SE New York; 19,578; ZIP 11726.

Cop·per·as Cove (kop′ər·əs) city, CEN. Texas; 10,818; ZIP 76522.

Coral Gables city, SE Florida; 42,494; ZIP see MIAMI.

Coral Hills city, sw Maryland; 7,105; ZIP 20027.

Coral Sea part of the Pacific, E of Australia and New Guinea.

Cor·al·ville (kôr′əl·vil, kor′-) city, NE Iowa; 6,130; ZIP 52240.

Cor·a·op·o·lis (kôr′ē·op′ə·lis, kō′rē-) boro., sw Pennsylvania 8,435; ZIP 15108.

Cor·bin (kôr′bin) city, SE Kentucky; 7,317; ZIP 40701.

Cor·cor·an (kôr′kə·rən) city, CEN. California; 5,246; ZIP 93212.

Cor·dele (kôr′dēl′, kôr′dēl′) city, s CEN. Georgia; 10,733; ZIP 31015.

Cor·inth (kor′inth) city, NE Mississippi; 11,581; ZIP 38834.

Cork (kôrk) co., sw Ireland; 2,880 sq. mi.; 337,000. — co. boro., SE CEN. Cork co.; cap.; 122,146.

Corner Brook city, N Newfoundland, Canada; 27,116.

Cor·ning (kôr′ning) city, w New York; 15,792; ZIP 14830*.

Corn·wall (kôrn′wəl, -wôl) co., sw England; 1,357; sq. mi.; 342,000; cap. Bodmin.

Corn·wall (kôrn′wəl, -wôl) city, SE Ontario, Canada; 45,766.

Co·ro·na (kə·rō′nə) city, s California; 27,519; ZIP 91720.

Cor·o·na·do (kor′ə·nä′dō) city, s California; 20,910; ZIP see SAN DIEGO.

Corpus Chris·ti (kôr′pəs kris′tē) city, s Texas; 204,525; ZIP 78400*.

Cor·ry (kor′ē) city, NW Pennsylvania; 7,435; ZIP 16407.

Cor·si·ca (kôr′si·kə) isl., N Mediterranean; a dept. of France; 3,368 sq. mi.; 266,000; cap. Ajaccio.

Cor·si·can·a (kôr′si·kan′ə) city, NE CEN. Texas; 19,972; ZIP 75110*.

Cor·te Ma·der·a (kôr′tä mə·dâr′ə) town, w California; 8,464; ZIP 94925.

Cor·tez (kôr·tez′) city, sw Colorado; 6,039; ZIP 81321.

Cort·land (kôrt′lənd) city, CEN. New York; 19,621; ZIP 13045*.

Cor·val·lis (kôr·val′is) city, w Oregon; 35,153; ZIP 97330*.

Co·shoc·ton (kə·shok′tən) city E CEN. Ohio; 13,747; ZIP 43812.

Cos·ta Me·sa (kos′tə mā′sə) city, sw California; 72,660; ZIP 92626*.

Cos·ta Ri·ca (kos′tə rē′kə) republic, Central America; 19,690 sq. mi.; 1,119,000; cap. San José.

Côte-St-Luc (kōt·sañ·lük′) city, s Quebec, Canada; 20,546.

Cottage Grove city, NE Minnesota; 13,419; ZIP 55016.

— city, w CEN. Oregon; 6,004; ZIP 97424.

Cot·ton·wood (kot′n·wood′) city, NE Utah; 8,431.

Council Bluffs city, sw Iowa; 60,348; ZIP 51501*.

Country Club Hills city, NE Illinois; 6,920; ZIP 60477.

Cove·dale (kōv′dāl′) city, sw Ohio; 6,639; ZIP 45201.

Cov·en·try (kuv′ən·trē) city and co. boro.; CEN. England; 333,830.

Cov·en·try (kuv′ən·trē) town, NE Connecticut; 8,140; ZIP 06238.

— town, w CEN. Rhode Island; 22,947; ZIP 02816.

Co·vi·na (kō·vē′nə) city, sw California; 30,380; ZIP 91722*.

Cov·ing·ton (kuv′ing·tən) city, N CEN. Georgia; 10,267; ZIP 30209.

— city, N Kentucky; 52,535; 41011*.

— city, SE Louisiana; 7,170; ZIP 70433.

— town, w Tennessee; 5,801; ZIP 38019.

— city, NW Virginia; 10,060; ZIP 24426.

Cow·ans·ville (kou′anz·vil) town, s Quebec, Canada; 10,692.

Crac·ow (krak′ou, krā′kō) city, s Poland; 463,000.

Craf·ton (kraf′tən) boro. sw Pennsylvania; 8,233; ZIP see PITTSBURGH.

Cran·brook (kran′brook) city, SE British Columbia; Canada; 7,849.

Cran·ford (kran′fərd) urb. twp., E New Jersey; 27,391; ZIP 07016.

Cran·ston (kran′stən) city, E Rhode Island; 73,037; ZIP see PROVIDENCE.

Craw·fords·ville (krô′fərdz·vil) city, w Indiana; 13,842; ZIP 47933.

Cress·kill (kres′kil) boro., NE New Jersey; 7,164; ZIP 07626.

Crest Hill city, NE Illinois; 7,460; ZIP see JOLIET.

Crest·line (krest′līn) vill., N CEN. Ohio; 5,947; ZIP 44827.

Cres·ton (kres′tən) city, s Iowa; 8,234; ZIP 50801.

Crest·view (krest′vyoo′) city, NW Florida; 7,952; ZIP 32536*.

Crest·wood (krest′wŏŏd′) city, E Missouri; 15,398; ZIP see ST. LOUIS.

Crestwood Village city, NE Illinois; 5,543; ZIP 60445.

Crete (krēt) isl., E Mediterranean; adm. div. of Greece; 3,207 sq. mi.; 462,000; cap. Canea.

Creve Coeur (krĕv′ kŏŏr′) vill., CEN. Illinois; 6,440; ZIP see PEORIA. — city, E Missouri; 8,967; ZIP see ST. LOUIS.

Cri·me·a (krī·mē′ə) penin., SE Ukrainian SSR.

Cris·tó·bal (kris·tō′bəl) town, Panama; at the Atlantic end of the Panama Canal; 817.

Cro·a·tia (krō·ā′shə) constituent republic, W Yugoslavia; 21,719 sq. mi.; 4,218,000; cap. Zagreb.

Crock·ett (krok′it) city, E Texas; 6,616; ZIP 75835.

Crom·well (krom′wel) town, SE Connecticut; 7,400; ZIP 06416.

Crook·ston (krŏŏk′stən) city, NW Minnesota; 8,312; ZIP 56716*.

Cross·ett (kros′it) city, SE Arkansas; 6,191; ZIP 71635.

Cross·ville (krôs′vil, kros′-) city, CEN. Tennessee; 5,381; ZIP 38555.

Cro·ton·on-Hud·son (krō′tən·on·hud′sən) vill., SE New York; 7,523; ZIP 10520.

Crow·ley (krou′lē) city, S Louisiana; 16,104; ZIP 70526.

Crown Point city, NW Indiana; 10,931; ZIP 46307.

Croy·don (kroid′n) co. boro., SE England; 328,290.

Crys·tal (kris′təl) vill., SE Minnesota; 30,925; ZIP see MINNEAPOLIS.

Crystal City city, S Texas; 8,104; ZIP 78839.

Crystal Lake city, NE Illinois; 14,541; ZIP 60014. — city, W CEN. Ohio; 5,851; ZIP 45341.

Cu·ba (kyŏŏ′bə) isl. republic, Caribbean Sea; 44,217 sq. mi. (with the Isle of Pines); 6,743,000; cap. Havana.

Cu·ca·mon·ga (kyŏŏ′kə·mung′gə) city, S California; 5,796; ZIP 91730.

Cud·a·hy (kud′ə·hē) city, SW California; 16,998. — city, SE Wisconsin; 16,998; ZIP 53,110.

Cue·ro (kwâr′ō) city, SE Texas; 6,956; ZIP 77954.

Cull·man (kul′mən) city, N Alabama; 12,601; ZIP 35055.

Cul·pep·er (kul′pep·ər) city, N Virginia; 6,056; ZIP 22701.

Cul·ver City (kul′vər) city, SW California; 31,035; ZIP 90230*.

Cum·ber·land (kum′bər·lənd) city, NW Maryland; 29,724; ZIP 21501*. — town, NE Rhode Island; 26,605; ZIP see PAWTUCKET.

Cumberland Gap passage through Cumberland Mountains, betw. Tennessee and Virginia.

Cumberland Mountains range of the Appalachian Mountains between SW West Virginia and NW Alabama.

Cumberland River river, Kentucky and Tennessee; flows to Ohio River.

Cu·per·ti·no (kŏŏ′pər·tē′nō) city, W California; 18,216; ZIP 95014.

Cu·ra·çao (kyŏŏr′ə·sō′, kŏŏ′rä·sou′) isl., W Netherlands Antilles; 171 sq. mi.; 124,000; cap. Willemstad.

Cush·ing (kŏŏsh′ing) city, N CEN. Oklahoma; 7,529; ZIP 74023.

Cut·ler Ridge (kut′lər) uninc. place, SE Florida; 17,441; ZIP see MIAMI.

Cut·ler·ville (kut′lər·vil) city, SW Michigan; 6,267; ZIP 49501.

Cuy·a·ho·ga Falls (kə·hog′ə, kī′ə·hog′ə, -hôg′ə, -hō′gə) city, NE Ohio; 49,678; ZIP 44221*.

Cyc·la·des (sik′lə·dēz) isl. group, S Aegean; dept of Greece; 1,023 sq. mi.; 126,000; cap. Hermoupolis.

Cyn·thi·an·a (sin′thē·an′ə) city, N Kentucky; 6,356; ZIP 41031.

Cypress City city, SW California; 31,026; ZIP 90630.

Cy·prus (sī′prəs) isl. republic, E Mediterranean 3,572 sq. mi.; 562,000; cap. Nicosia.

Czech·o·slo·va·ki·a (chek′ə·slō·vä′ke·ə, -vak′ē·ə) republic, E CEN. Europe; 49,368 sq. mi.; 13,649,000; cap. Prague.

Dac·ca (dä′kä) city, E . CEN. Bangla Desh; cap.; 556,712.

Da·chau (dä′khou) town, SE West Germany; site of a Naz concentration camp; 25,000.

Da·ho·mey (də·hō′mē) Benin: the former name.

Dai·ren (dī′ren′) See LÜ-TA.

Da·kar (dä·kär′, də-) city, W Senegal; cap.; 374,700.

Da·ko·ta (də·kō′tə) former terr. comprising the present North and South Dakota.

Dale (dāl) city, NE Virginia; 13,857; ZIP 22172.

Dale·ville (dāl′vil) city, SE Alabama; 5,182; ZIP 36322.

Dal·hart (dal′härt) city, N Texas; 5,705; ZIP 79022.

Dal·hou·sie (dal·hou′zē, -sē, -hŏŏ′zē) town, N New Brunswick, Canada; 6,107.

Dal·las (dal′əs) city, NW Oregon; 6,361; ZIP 97338*. — city, N Texas; 844,401; ZIP 75200*.

Dalles, The (dalz) city, NW Oregon; 10,423.

Dal·ma·tia (dal·mā′shə) reg., Croatia, W Yugoslavia; 4,954 sq. mi.; 750,000; cap. Split.

Dal·ton (dôl′tən) city, NW Georgia; 18,872; ZIP 30720.

— town, W Massachusetts; 7,505; ZIP 01226.

Da·ly City (dā′lē) city, W California; 66,922; ZIP 94014*.

Da·mas·cus (də·mas′kəs) city, SW Syria; cap.; 532,000.

Dan·bur·y (dan′ber·ē, -bər·ē) city, SW Connecticut; 50,781; ZIP 06810*.

Da·ni·a (dā′nē·ə) city, SE Florida; 9,013; ZIP 33004.

Dans·ville (danz′vil) vill., W New York; 5,436; ZIP 14437.

Dan·ube (dan′yŏŏb) river, CEN. and E Europe; 1,770 mi. long.

Dan·vers (dan′vərz) town, NE Massachusetts; 26,151.

Dan·ville (dan′vil) city, E Illinois; 42,570; ZIP 61832*. — city, CEN. Kentucky; 11,542; ZIP 40422. — boro., E CEN. Pennsylvania; 6,176; ZIP 17821. — city, S Virginia; 46,391; ZIP 24540*.

Dan·zig (dan′sig, -tsig, -zig) city, N Poland; 308,700.

Dar·by (där′bē) boro., SE Pennsylvania; 13,726; ZIP 19023*.

Dar·da·nelles (där′də·nelz′) strait, NW Turkey; connects Sea of Marmara with the Aegean.

Dar·i·en (dar′ē·in, -en) town, NE Connecticut; 20,411; ZIP 06820. — city, NE Illinois; 8,077.

Dar·i·en (dâr′ē·en′, dâr′ē·en) Gulf of inlet of the Caribbean, E coast of Panama.

Darien, Isthmus of Isthmus of Panama: the former name.

Dar·ling·ton (där′ling·tən) town, NE South Carolina; 6,990; ZIP 29532.

Dart·mouth (därt′məth) town, SE Massachusetts; 18,800; ZIP 02714.

Dart·mouth (därt′məth) city, S Nova Scotia, Canada; 58,745.

Dau·phin (dô′fin) town, SW Manitoba, Canada; 8,655.

Dav·en·port (dav′ən·pôrt, -pōrt) city, E Iowa; 98,469; ZIP 52800*.

Da·vis (dā′vis) city, CEN. California; 23,488; ZIP 95616.

Da·vi·son (dā′və·sən) city, SE Michigan; 5,259; ZIP 48025.

Daw·son (dô′sən) city, SW Georgia; 5,383; ZIP 31742.

Dawson Creek (dô′sən) city, E British Columbia, Canada; 12,392.

Day·ton (dā′tən, dāt′n) city, N Kentucky; 8,691; ZIP see NEWPORT. — city, SW Ohio; 243,601; ZIP 45400*.

Day·to·na Beach (dā·tō′nə) city, E Florida; 45,327; ZIP 32014*.

Dead Sea large salt lake on Israel-Jordan border; 1,292 ft. below sea level.

Dear·born (dir′bôrn′, -bərn) city, SE Michigan; 104,199; ZIP 48120*.

Dear·born Heights (dir′bôrn′, -bərn) city, SE Michigan; 80,069; ZIP 48127.

Death Valley desert basin, SE California; maximum depth 280 ft. below sea level.

De·ca·tur (di·kā′tər) city, N Alabama; 38,044; ZIP 35601*. — city, NW CEN. Georgia; 21,943; ZIP 30030*. — city, CEN. Illinois; 90,397; ZIP 62521*. — city, E Indiana; 8,445; ZIP 46733.

Dec·can Plateau (dek′ən) triangular tableland covering most of the penin. of India.

De·cor·ah (di·kôr′ə) city, NE Iowa; 7,458; ZIP 52101.

Ded·ham (ded′əm) town, E Massachusetts; 26,938; ZIP 02026.

Deep River town, SE Ontario, Canada; 5,573.

Deer·field (dir′fēld) vill., NE Illinois; 18,949; ZIP 60015.

Deerfield Beach town, SE Florida; 17,130; ZIP 33441.

Deer Park uninc. place, SE New York; 31,120; ZIP 11729. — city, SW Ohio; 7,415; ZIP see CINCINNATI. — city, E CEN. Texas; 12,773; ZIP 77536.

Defense Heights city, SW Maryland; 6,775.

De·fi·ance (di·fī′əns) city, NW Ohio; 16,281; ZIP 43512.

De Kalb (dē kalb′) city, N Illinois; 32,949; ZIP 60115.

Del Aire (del âr) city, SW California; 11,930.

De Land (dē land′) city, E Florida; 11,641; ZIP 32720*.

De·la·no (də·lā′nō, del′ə·nō) city, S CEN. California; 14,559; ZIP 93215.

Del·a·van (del′ə·van) city, SE Wisconsin; 5,526; ZIP 53115.

Del·a·ware (del′ə·wâr) state, E United States; 1,978 sq. mi.; 548,104; cap. Dover. — city, CEN. Ohio; 15,008; ZIP 43015.

Delaware River river separating Pennsylvania and Delaware from New York and New Jersey; 315 mi. long.

Del City (del) city, CEN. Oklahoma; 27,133; ZIP see OKLAHOMA CITY.

Del·hi (del′ē) terr., NE CEN. India; 573 sq. mi.; 2,874,514; contains New Delhi. — city; Delhi terr.; cap.; 915,000.

Del·phos (del′fəs) city, W Ohio; 7,608; ZIP 45833.

Del·ray Beach (del·rā′) city, SE Florida; 19,366; ZIP 33444.

Del Rio (del rē′o) city, SW Texas; 21,330; ZIP 78840.

Dem·a·rest (dem′ə·rest) city, NE New Jersey; 6,262; ZIP 07627.

Dem·ing (dem′ing) vill., SW New Mexico; 8,343; ZIP 88030-

De·mop·o·lis (dē·mop′ə·lis) city, w Alabama; 7,651; ZIP 36732*.

Den·ham Springs (den′əm) town, SE Louisiana; 6,752; ZIP 70726.

Den·i·son (den′ə·sən) city, sw Iowa; 5,882; ZIP 51442.
— city, N Texas; 24,923; ZIP 75020.

Den·mark (den′märk) kingdom, NW Europe; 16,619 sq. mi.; 4,585,000; cap. Copenhagen.

Den·ton (dent′n, den′tən) city, N Texas; 39,874; ZIP 76201.

Den·ver (den′vər) city, CEN. Colorado; cap.; 514,678; ZIP 80200*.

De Pere (di pēr′, di pir′) city, E Wisconsin; 13,309; ZIP 54115.

De·pew (di·pyōō′) vill., w New York; 22,158; ZIP 14043.

Der·by (dûr′bē) uninc. place, N CEN. Colorado; 10,206.
— city, sw Connecticut; 12,599; ZIP 06418.
— city, s Kansas; 7,947; ZIP 67037.

De Rid·der (də rid′ər) city, w Louisiana; 8,030; ZIP 70634.

Der·ry (der′ē) city, SE New Hampshire; 11,712.

Derry Compact city, SE New Hampshire; 6,090.

Des Moines (də moin′) city, s CEN. Iowa; cap.; 200,587; ZIP 50300*.

De So·to (di sō′tō, də) city, E Missouri; 5,984; ZIP 63020.
— city, N CEN. Texas; 6,617; ZIP 75115.

Des Peres (dā pâr′) city, NE Missouri; 5,333; ZIP 63131.

Des Plaines (des plānz′) city, NE Illinois; 57,239; ZIP 60016*.

De·troit (di·troit′) city, SE Michigan; 1,511,482; ZIP 48200*.

Detroit Lakes city, w Minnesota; 5,797; ZIP 56501.

Devil's Island rocky isl. off the coast of French Guiana; formerly a penal colony.

Devils Lake City NE CEN. North Dakota; 7,078; ZIP 58301.

Dev·on·shire (dev′ən·shir) co.; sw England; 2,611 sq. mi.; 823,000; cap. Exeter.

De Witt (də wit) city, NW New York; 10,032; ZIP 13214.

Dex·ter (deks′tər) city, SE Missouri; 6,024; ZIP 63841.

Diamond Bar city, sw California; 12,234.

D'I·ber·ville (dē′bər·vil) city, NE Mississippi; 7,288; ZIP 39532.

Dick·in·son (dik′in·sən) city, w North Dakota; 12,405; ZIP 58601.

Dick·son (dik′sən) city, N Tennessee; 5,665; ZIP 37055.

Dil·lon (dil′ən) town, NE South Carolina; 5,991; ZIP 29536*.

Di·nu·ba (di·nōō′bə) city, CEN. California; 7,917; ZIP 93618.
— city, E Texas; 10,776; ZIP 77539.

Dish·man (dish′mən) city, NE Washington; 9,079; ZIP 99213.

District Heights town, sw Maryland; 8,424.

District of Columbia federal dist., E United States; co-extensive with Washington, the capital; 756,510.

Dix Hills (diks) city, SE New York; 9,840.

Dix·on (dik′sən) city, N Illinois; 18,147; ZIP 61021.

Dji·bou·ti (ji·bōō′tē) republic, NE Africa; 8,800 sq. mi.; 111,000; cap. Djibouti.

Dne·pro·pe·trovsk (dyne′prə·pə·trofsk′) city, sw Ukrainian SSR; 816,000. Also **Dnie′pro·pe·trovsk′**.

Dnie·per (dnye′pər, nē′pər) river, sw USSR; 1,420 mi. long. Also **Dne′pr**.

Dnies·ter (dnyes′tər, nē·stər) river, sw USSR; 876 mi. long. Also **Dnes′tr**.

Dobbs Ferry (dobz) vill., SE New York; 10,353; ZIP 10512.

Dock Junction uninc. place, SE Georgia; 6,009.

Do·dec·a·nese (dō·dek′ə·nēs′, -nēz′) isl. group, Aegean Sea; a dept. of Greece; 1,036 sq. mi.; 121,000; cap. Rhodes.

Dodge City city, s Kansas; 14,127; ZIP 67801.

Dol·beau (dol·bō′) town, s Quebec, Canada; 6,630.

Dol·o·mite Alps (dol′ə·mīt) E div. of the Alps, N Italy.

Dol·ton (dōlt′n, dōl′tən) vill., NE Illinois; 25,937; ZIP 60419.

Do·min·guez (dō·mēn·gez′) city, sw California; 5,980.

Do·min·i·can Republic (dō·min′i·kən) republic, E Hispaniola; 18,700 sq. mi.; 3,014,000; cap. Santo Domingo.

Don (don) river, sw RSFSR; 1,222 mi. long.

Don·ald·son·ville (don′əld·sən·vil, don′əl-) city, SE Louisiana; 7,367; ZIP 70346.

Don·el·son (don′əl·sən) uninc. place, N CEN. Tennessee; 17,195; ZIP see NASHVILLE.

Do·nets (do·nets′, -nyets′) river, sw USSR; 631 mi. long.

Don·na (don′ə) city, s Texas; 7,365; ZIP 78537.

Do·nor·a (də·nôr′ə) boro., sw Pennsylvania; 8,825; ZIP 15033.

Dor·a·ville (dôr′ə·vil, dôr′-) city, NW Georgia; 9,039; ZIP 30340.

Dor·mont (dôr′mont) boro., sw Pennsylvania; 12,856; ZIP see PITTSBURGH.

Dor·val (dôr·väl′) city, s Quebec, Canada; 20,905.

Do·than (dō′thən) city, SE Alabama; 36,733; ZIP 36301*.

Dou·ai (dōō·ā′) town, N France; ab. 49,187.

Doug·las (dug′ləs) city, SE Arizona; 12,462; ZIP 85607.
— city, SE CEN. Georgia; 10,195; ZIP 31533.

Doug·las·ville (dug′ləs·vil) city, w Georgia; 5,472; ZIP 30134.

Do·ver (dō′vər) municipal boro., SE England; 35,000.

Do·ver (dō′vər) city, CEN. Delaware; cap. 17,488; ZIP 19901.
— city, SE New Hampshire; 20,850; ZIP 03820.
— town, N New Jersey; 15,039; ZIP 07801.
— city, E Ohio; 11,516; ZIP 44622.

Dover Base city, CEN. Delaware; 8,106.

Dover, Strait of strait at the E end of the English Channel; width 21 mi.

Do·wa·giac (dō·wō′jak) city, sw Michigan; 6,583; ZIP 49047.

Down·ers Grove (doun′ərz) vill., NE Illinois; 32,751; ZIP 60515.

Down·ey (dou′nē) city, sw California; 88,445; ZIP 90240*.

Down·ing·town (doun′ing·toun) boro., SE Pennsylvania; 7,437; ZIP 19335.

Doyles·town (doilz′toun) boro., SE Pennsylvania; 8,270; ZIP 18901.

Dra·cut (drā′kut) town, NE Massachusetts; 18,214; ZIP 01826.

Dray·ton Plains (drā′tən) city, SE Michigan; 16,462; ZIP 48020.

Dres·den (drez′dən) city, s East Germany; 508,119.

Drum·mond·ville (drum′ənd·vil) city, s Quebec, Canada; 29,216.

Dry·den (drīd′n) town, NW Ontario, Canada; 6,732.

Du·ar·te (dwär′tē) city, sw California; 14,981; ZIP 91010.

Dub·lin (dub′lin) city, E Ireland; cap.; 568,772.

Dub·lin (dub′lin) city, w California; 13,641; ZIP 94566.
— city, CEN. Georgia; 15,143; ZIP 31021.

Du Bois (dōō′ bois, də bois′) city, w. CEN. Pennsylvania; 10,112; ZIP 15801.

Du·buque (də·byōōk′) city, E Iowa; 62,309; ZIP 52001*.

Dud·ley (dud′lē) town, CEN. Massachusetts; 8,087; ZIP 01570.

Duis·burg (düs′bōōkh) city, w West Germany; 490,310.

Du·luth (də·lōōth, dōō-) city, NE Minnesota; 100,578; ZIP 55800*.

Du·mas (dōō′məs) city, NW Texas; 9,771; ZIP 79029.

Du·mont (dōō′mont) boro., NE New Jersey; 17,534; ZIP 07628.

Dun·bar (dun′bär) city, w West Virginia; 9,151; ZIP 25064.

Dun·can (dung′kən) city, s Oklahoma; 19,718; ZIP 73533.

Dun·can·ville (dun′kən·vil, dung′kən-) city, N Texas; 14,105; ZIP 75116.

Dun·dalk (dun′dôk, -dôlk) uninc. place. CEN. Maryland; 85,377; ZIP see BALTIMORE.

Dun·das (dun′dəs) town, s Ontario, Canada; 15,501.

Dun·dee (dun·dē′) burgh, E Scotland.

Du·ne·din (də·nēd′n) city, w Florida; 17,639; ZIP 32528.

Du·nel·len (də·nel′ən) boro., E CEN. New Jersey; 7,072; ZIP 08812*.

Dun·kirk (dun′kûrk) town, N France; scene of evacuation of British forces in World War II, May–June 1940; ab. 21,000.

Dun·kirk (dun′kûrk) city, w New York; 16,855; ZIP 14048.

Dun·more (dun·môr′, dun′môr, -môr) boro., NE Pennsylvania; 17,300; ZIP see SCRANTON.

Dunn (dun) town, CEN. North Carolina; 8,302; ZIP 28334.

Dunn·ville (dun′vil) town, s Ontario, Canada; 5,402.

Du·quesne (də·kān′, dōō-, dyōō-) city, sw Pennsylvania; 11,410; ZIP 15110.

Du Quoin (dōō koin′, kwoin′) city, s Illinois; 6,691; ZIP 62832.

Du·ran·go (dōō·rang′gō) city, sw Colorado; 10,333; ZIP 81300*.

Du·rant (də·rant′) city, s Oklahoma; 11,118; ZIP 74701.

Dur·ban (dûr′bən) city, SE South Africa; 560,010.

Dur·ham (dûr′əm) city, SE New Hampshire; 8,869; ZIP 03824.

Dur·ham (dûr′əm, du′rəm) city, N CEN. North Carolina; 95,438; ZIP 27700*.

Durham Compact (dûr′əm) town, SE New Hampshire; 7,221; ZIP 03824.

Dur·yea (dōōr′yā, dər·yā′) boro., NE Pennsylvania; 5,264; ZIP see PITTSTON.

Düs·sel·dorf (düs′səl·dôrf) city, w West Germany; 700,080.

Dutch East Indies See NETHERLANDS EAST INDIES.

Dutch Guiana See SURINAM.

Dutch Harbor US Naval base in the Aleutian Islands.

Dutch West Indies Netherlands Antilles: *the former name.*

Dux·bur·y (duks′ber·ē) town, E Massachusetts; 7,636; ZIP 02332.

Dy·ers·burg (dī′ərz·bûrg) city, NW Tennessee; 14,523; ZIP 38024.

PRONUNCIATION KEY: add, āce, câre, pälm; end, ēven; it, īce; odd, ōpen, ôrder; tŏŏk, pōōl; up, bûrn; ə = a in *above*, e in *sicken*, i in *flexible*, o in *melon*, u in *focus*; yōō = u in *fuse*; oil; pout; check; go; ring; thin; this; zh, vision. For à, œ, ü, kh, n, see inside front cover

Eagle Pass city, sw Texas; 15,364; ZIP 78852.
Ea·gle·ton Village (ē′gəl·tən) uninc. place, E Tennessee; 5,348.
Eas·ley (ēz′lē) city, NW South Carolina; 11,175; ZIP 29640.
East Al·ton (ôl′tən, ôlt′n) vill., sw Illinois; 7,309; ZIP 62024.
East Au·ror·a (ə·rôr′ə) vill., w New York; 7,033; ZIP 14052.
East Berlin See BERLIN.
East Bridge·wa·ter (brij′wô′tər, -wot′ər) town, E Massachusetts; 8,347; ZIP 02333.
East·ches·ter (ēst′ches·tər) city, SE New York; 21,330.
East Chi·ca·go (shə·kä′gō, -kô′-) city, NW Indiana; 46,982; ZIP 46312*.
East Chicago Heights city, NE Illinois; 5,000; ZIP 60411.
East China Sea NE part of the China Sea
East Cleve·land (klēv′lənd) city, NE Ohio; 39,600; ZIP see CLEVELAND.
East Comp·ton (komp′tən) city, sw California; 5,853.
East De·troit (di·troit′) city, SE Michigan; 45,920; ZIP 48021.
Easter Island isl. of Chile, South Pacific; known for stone monuments found there; 45.5 sq. mi.
East Gar·y (gâr′ē) town, NW Indiana; 9,858; ZIP see GARY.
East Germany See GERMANY.
East Glen·ville (glen′vil) city, NE New York; 5,898.
East Grand Forks city, NW Minnesota; 7,607; ZIP 56721.
East Grand Rapids city sw Michigan; 12,565.
East Green·wich (gren′ich) city, sw Rhode Island; 9,577.
East Half Hollow Hills city, SE New York; 9,691.
East Hamp·ton (hamp′tən) city, sw Connecticut; 7,078; ZIP 06424.
East·hamp·ton (ēst′ham′tən, -hamp′-, -ham′-, -hamp′-) town, w Massachusetts; 13,012; ZIP 01027.
East Hart·ford (härt′fərd) town, N CEN. Connecticut; 57,583; ZIP see HARTFORD.
East Haven town, s Connecticut; 25,120; ZIP see NEW HAVEN.
East Hills city, NE New York; 8,675.
East I·slip (ī′slip) city, SE New York; 6,819.
East Kil·do·nan (kil·dō′nən) city, s Manitoba. Canada; 28,796.
East·lake (ēst′lāk) city, NE Ohio; 19,690; ZIP see WILLOUGHBY.
East La Mi·ran·da (lä mə·ran′də) city, sw California; 12,339.
East Lansing (lan′sing) city, s CEN. Michigan; 47,540; ZIP 48823*.
East Las Ve·gas (läs vā′gəs) city, SE Nevada; 6,501; ZIP 89112.
East Liv·er·pool (liv′ər·pool) city, E Ohio; 22,306; ZIP 43920.
East Long·mead·ow (lông′med′ō, long′-) town, N Massachusetts; 13,029; ZIP 01028.
East Los An·ge·les (lôs än′jə·lēz, ang′gə·les, los) uninc. place, sw California; 105,033; ZIP see Los ANGELES.
East Lyme (līm) town, SE Connecticut; 11,399; ZIP 06333.
East·man (ēst′mən) city, s CEN. Georgia; 5,416; ZIP 31023.
East Mas·sa·pe·qua (mas′ə·pē′kwə) city, SE New York; 15,926.
East Meadow city, SE New York; 46,252; ZIP 11554.
East Mill·creek (mil′krēk′) city, NE Utah; 26,579; ZIP 84101.
East Mo·line (mō·lēn′) city, NW Illinois; 20,832; ZIP 61244.
East Na·ples (nā′pəlz) city, sw Florida; 6,152; ZIP 33940.
East Neck city, SE New York; 5,144.
East North·port (nôrth′pôrt, -pōrt) city, SE New York; 12,292; ZIP 11731.
Eas·ton (ēs′tən) town, E Massachusetts; 12,157; ZIP 02334.
— city, E CEN. Maryland; 6,809; ZIP 21601.
— city, s Pennsylvania; 30,256; ZIP 18042*.
East Or·ange (ôr′inj, or′-) city, NE New Jersey; 75,471; ZIP 07017*.
East Pal·es·tine (pal′əs·tīn) city, E Ohio; 5,604; ZIP 44413.
East Pa·lo Al·to (pal′ō al′tō) city, w CEN. California; 7,873.
East Patch·ogue (pach′äg′, ôg′) city, SE New York; 8,092.
East Pat·er·son (pat′ər·sən) boro., NE New Jersey; 22,749; ZIP 07407.
East Pe·o·ri·a (pē·ō′rē·ə) city, CEN. Illinois; 18,455; ZIP see PEORIA.
East Point city, NW CEN. Georgia; 39,315; ZIP 30044.
East Providence town, E Rhode Island; 48,151; ZIP see PROVIDENCE.
East Prussia former prov. of Prussia, NE Germany.
East Ridge town, SE Tennessee; 21,799; ZIP see CHATTANOOGA.
East Roch·es·ter (roch′es·tər, -is-) vill., w New York; 8,347; ZIP 14445.
East Rock·a·way (rok′ə·wā′) vill., SE New York; 10,323; ZIP 11518.
East Ruth·er·ford (ruth′ər·fərd) boro., NE New Jersey; 8,536; ZIP see RUTHERFORD.
East Saint Lou·is (loo′is) city, sw Illinois; 69,996; ZIP 62201*.

East Strouds·burg (stroudz′bûrg) boro., E Pennsylvania; 7,894; ZIP 18301.
East Ves·tal (ves′təl) city, sw New York; 10,472.
East·view (ēst′vyoo′) town, SE Ontario, Canada; 24,269.
East Wind·sor (wind′zər) town, N CEN. Connecticut; 8,513; ZIP 06088.
East Wil·ming·ton (wil′ming·tən) uninc. place, SE North Carolina; 5,520.
East Wood city, sw Michigan; 9,682; ZIP 49001.
Ea·ton (ēt′n) vill., sw Ohio; 6,020; ZIP 45320.
Eat·on·town (ē′tən·toun) city, E CEN. New Jersey; 14,619; ZIP 07724.
Eau Claire (ō′ klâr′) city, w CEN. Wisconsin; 44,619; ZIP 54701*.
Eau Gal·lie (ō gal′ə) city, E Florida; 12,300; ZIP 32935*.
E·con·o·my (i·kon′ə·mē) boro., w Pennsylvania; 17,176.
E·corse (ē·kôrs′) city, SE Michigan; 17,515; ZIP see DETROIT.
Ec·ua·dor (ek′wə·dôr) republic, NW South America; 104,306 sq. mi.; 4,396,000; cap. Quito.
E·den (ē′dən) city, N CEN. North Carolina; 15,871; ZIP 27288.
Eden Prairie city, SE Minnesota; 6,938; ZIP 55343.
Edge·mere (ej′mir) city, NW Maryland; 10,352.
Edge·wood (ej′wood′) city, NE Maryland; 8,551; ZIP 21040.
— boro., sw Pennsylvania; 5,101; ZIP see PITTSBURGH.
E·di·na (i·dī′nə) city, SE Minnesota; 44,046; ZIP see MINNEAPOLIS.
Ed·in·burg (ed′in·burg) city, s Texas; 17,163; ZIP 78539.
Ed·in·burgh (ed′ən·bûr′ə) city, E Scotland; cap.; 466,464.
Ed·mond (ed′mənd) city, CEN. Oklahoma; 16,633; ZIP 73034.
Ed·monds (ed′məndz) city, NW Washington; 23,998; ZIP 98020.
Ed·mon·ton (ed′mən·tən) city, CEN. Alberta, Canada; cap.; 376,925.
Ed·munds·ton (ed′məndz·tən) city, NW New Brunswick, Canada; 12,517.
Ed·na (ed′nə) city, SE Texas; 5,332; ZIP 77957.
Ed·wards (ed′wərdz)·city, sw California; 10,331; ZIP 93523.
Ed·wards·ville (ed′wərdz·vil) city, sw Illinois; 11,070; ZIP 62025.
— boro., NE Pennsylvania; 5,633.
Ef·fing·ham (ef′ing·ham′) city, SE CEN. Illinois; 9,458; ZIP 62401.
Eg·lin (eg′lin) city, NE Florida; 7,769.
E·gypt (ē′jipt) republic, NE Africa; 386,198 sq. mi.; 26,059,-000; cap. Cairo: official name *Arab Republic of Egypt*.
E·gypt Lake (ē′jipt) city, E Florida; 7,556; ZIP 33601.
Ei·el·son (ī′əl·sən) city, E CEN. Alabama; 6,149.
Eir·e (âr′ə) Ireland: *the Irish Gaelic name*.
El A·la·mein (el ä′lə·mān′, al′ə-) vill., N Egypt; scene of a British victory over Axis forces in World War II.
El·ba (el′bə) isl. betw. Italy and Corsica; sovereign under the exiled Napoleon Bonaparte, 1814–15.
El·be (el′bə) river, CEN. Europe; 725 mi. long.
El·ber·ton (el′bər·tən) city, NE Georgia; 6,438; ZIP 30635.
El·brus, Mount (el′broos) mtn., NW Georgian SSR; 18,603 ft.
El·burz Mountains (el·boorz′) mtn. range, N Iran.
El Ca·jon (el kə·hōn′) city, sw California; 52,273; ZIP 92020*.
El Cam·po (el kam′pō) city, SE Texas; 8,563; ZIP 77437.
El Cen·tro (el sen′trō) city, s California; 19,272; ZIP 92243*.
El Cer·ri·to (el sə·rē′tō) city, w California; 25,190; ZIP 94530*.
El Do·ra·do (el də·rā′də, -dō) city, s Arkansas; 25,283; ZIP 71730*.
— city, s Kansas; 12,308; ZIP 67042.
El En·can·to Heights (el en·kän′tō) city, sw California; 6,625.
El·gin (el′jin) city, NE Illinois; 55,691; ZIP 60120*.
E·liz·a·beth (i·liz′ə·bəth) city, NE New Jersey; 112,654; ZIP 07200*.
Elizabeth City town, NE North Carolina; 14,069; ZIP 27909.
E·liz·a·beth·ton (i·liz′ə·beth′tən) city, NE Tennessee; 12,269; ZIP 37643.
E·liz·a·beth·town (i·liz′ə·beth·toun′) city, w CEN. Kentucky; 11,748; ZIP 42701.
— boro., SE Pennsylvania; 8,072; ZIP 17022.
Elk City (elk) city, w Oklahoma; 7,323; ZIP 73644.
Elk Grove Village vill., NE Illinois; 24,516; ZIP see ARLINGTON HEIGHTS.
Elk·hart (el′kärt, elk′härt′) city, N Indiana; 43,152; ZIP 46514*.
El·kins (el′kinz) city, E CEN. West Virginia; 8,287; ZIP 26241.
El·ko (el′kō) city, NE Nevada; 7,621; ZIP 89801.
Elk·ton (elk′tən) town, NE Maryland; 5,362; ZIP 21921.
El·lens·burg (el′ənz·bûrg) city, CEN. Washington; 13,568; ZIP 98926.
El·li·cott (el′ə·kot) city, NW Maryland; 9,506; ZIP 21043.
El·ling·ton (el′ing·tən) town, NE Connecticut; 7,707; ZIP 06029.
El·lis Island (el′is) isl., upper New York Bay; former site

of US immigration station.

Ells·worth (elz′wûrth′) city, N CEN. South Dakota; 5,805.

Ell·wood City (el′wŏŏd) boro., W Pennsylvania; 10,857; ZIP 16117.

El·men·dorf (el′mən-dôrf) S CEN. Alaska; 6,018.

Elm Grove city, SE Wisconsin; 7,201; ZIP 53122.

Elmhurst (elm′hûrst) city, NE Illinois; 50,547; ZIP 60126*.

El·mi·ra (el-mī′rə) city, S New York; 39,945; ZIP 14901*.

El·mont (el′mont) uninc. place, SE New York; 28,363; ZIP see FLORAL PARK.

El Mon·te (el mon′tē) city, SW California; 69,837; ZIP 91731*.

Elm·wood Park (elm′wŏŏd) vill., NE Illinois; 26,160; ZIP see CHICAGO.

E·loy (ē·loi′) city, S Arizona; 5,381; ZIP 85231.

El Pas·o (el pas′ō) city, W Texas; 322,261; ZIP 79900*.

El Pas·o de Ro·bles (el pä′sō də rō′bles, el pas′ō de rō′bəlz) city, SW California; 7,168.

El Re·no (el rē′nō) city, CEN. Oklahoma; 14,510; ZIP 73036.

El Ri·o (el rē′ō) uninc. place, SW California; 6,173; ZIP see OXNARD.

El Sal·va·dor (el sal′və-dôr) republic, W Central America; 8,260 sq. mi.; 2,511,000; cap. San Salvador.

El Se·gun·do (el si-gun′dō, -gŏŏn′dō) city, SW California; 15,620; ZIP 90245*.

Els·mere (elz′mir) town, NE Delaware; 8,415.

— city, N Kentucky; 5,161; ZIP 41018.

El To·ro (el tôr′ō, tō′rō) city, SW California; 8,654; ZIP 92630.

El Toro Station city, SW California; 6,970.

El·wood (el′wŏŏd) city, CEN. Indiana; 11,196; ZIP 46036.

— city, SE New York; 15,031.

E·lyr·i·a (i-lir′ē-ə) city, N Ohio; 53,427; ZIP 44035*.

Em·er·son (em′ər-sən) city, NE New Jersey; 8,428; ZIP 07630.

Em·ma·us (e-mā′əs, ĕ′mŏs) boro., E Pennsylvania; 11,511; ZIP 18049.

Em·por·ia (em·pôr′ē-ə, -pō′rē-) city, CEN. Kansas; 23,327; ZIP 66801*.

— town, S Virginia; 5,300; ZIP 23847.

En·ci·ni·tas (en′sə-nē′täs) city, SW California; 5,375; ZIP 92024.

En·di·cott (en′di·kət) vill., S New York; 16,556; ZIP 13760*.

End·well (end′wel′) city, SW New York; 15,999; ZIP 13762.

En·field (en′fēld) town, N Connecticut; 46,189; ZIP 06030.

Eng·land (ing′glənd) S part and largest political division of Great Britain: 50,237 sq. mi.; 43,431,000; cap. London.

En·gle·wood (eng′gəl-wŏŏd) city, CEN. Colorado; 33,695; ZIP 80110.

— city, NW Florida; 5,182; ZIP 35335.

— city, NE New Jersey; 24,985; ZIP 07631*.

Englewood Cliffs city, NE New Jersey; 5,938; ZIP 07632.

English Channel strait, betw. England and France; 20–100 mi. wide.

E·nid (ē′nid) city, N Oklahoma; 44,008; ZIP 73701*.

E·ni·we·tok (en′i-wē′tok, i-nē′wi-tŏk) atoll, Marshall Islands; U.S. nuclear weapons testing area.

En·nis (en′is) city, NE CEN. Texas; 11,046; ZIP 75119.

En·ter·prise (en′tər-prīz) city, SE Alabama; 15,591; ZIP 36330*.

— city, N California; 11,486; ZIP 96001.

Eph·ra·ta (ef′rə-tə) boro., SE Pennsylvania; 9,662; ZIP 17522.

E·phra·ta (ĕ-frä′tə) city, CEN. Washington; 5,255; ZIP 98823.

Ep·som (ep′səm) town, SE England; site of famous racecourse; 72,300.

Equatorial Guinea republic, W equatorial Africa; 10,825 sq. mi.; 325,000; cap. Malabo.

E·rie (ir′ē) city, NW Pennsylvania; 129,231; ZIP 16500*.

Erie, Lake southernmost of the Great Lakes; 9,940 sq. mi.

Erie Canal waterway, betw. Albany and Buffalo, New York; integrated with New York State Barge Canal.

E·ri·tre·a (er′i-trē′ə) state, E Africa; federated with Ethiopia, 45,000 sq. mi.; 1 million; cap. Asmara.

Er·i·van (yi-ryi-vän′) See YEREVAN.

Er·lang·er (ûr′lang′gər) city, N Kentucky; 12,676; ZIP 41018.

Es·ca·na·ba (es-kə-nä′bə) city, NW Michigan; 15,368; ZIP 49829.

Es·con·di·do (es-kən-dē′dō) city, SW California; 36,792; ZIP 92025*.

Es·sen (es′ən) city, W West Germany; 726,762.

Es·sex (es′iks, -əks, -eks) uninc. place, N Maryland; 38,193; ZIP see BALTIMORE.

— town, NW Vermont; 10,951; ZIP 05451.

Essex Junction vill., NW Vermont; 6,511; ZIP 05452.

Es·te·van (es′tə-van) city, SE Saskatchewan, Canada; 9,062.

Es·to·ni·an SSR (es-tō′nē-ən) constituent republic, W

USSR, 17,400 sq. mi.; 1,197,000; cap. Tallinn. Also **Es·to·ni·a** (es-tō′nē-ə).

Es·ther·ville (es′tər-vil) city, N Iowa; 8,108; ZIP 51334.

E·thi·o·pi·a (ē-thē-ō′pē-ə) empire, E Africa; 350,000 sq. mi.; 21,800,000; cap. Addis Ababa.

Et·na (et′nə) boro., SW Pennsylvania; 5,819; ZIP see PITTSBURGH.

Et·na, Mount (et′nə) volcano, E Sicily; 10,868 ft.

Eu·boe·a (yōō-bē′-ə) isl. of Greece in the Aegean; 1,457 sq. mi.

Eu·clid (yōō′klid) city, NE Ohio; 71,552; ZIP see CLEVELAND.

Eu·fau·la (yōō-fô′lə) city, SE Alabama; 9,102; ZIP 36027.

Eu·gene (yōō-jēn′) city, W Oregon; 76,346; ZIP 97401*.

Eu·less (yōō′lis) city, N Texas; 11,046; ZIP 75119.

Eu·nice (yōō′nis) town, S CEN. Louisiana; 11,390; ZIP 70535.

Eu·phra·tes (yōō-frā′tēz) river, SW Asia; 1,740 mi. long.

Eur·a·sia (yŏŏr-ā′zhə, -shə) large land mass comprising Europe and Asia.

Eu·re·ka (yŏŏ-rē′kə) city, NW California; 24,337; ZIP 95501*.

Eur·ope (yŏŏr′əp) W part of the Eurasian land mass; 1.9 million sq. mi.; excluding Turkey and the USSR.

Eus·tis (yŏŏs′tis) city, CEN. Florida; 6,722; ZIP 32726.

Eux·ine Sea (yōōk′sin, -sĭn) See BLACK SEA.

Ev·ans·dale (ev′ənz-dāl) town, E CEN. Iowa; 5,038; ZIP see WATERLOO.

Ev·ans·ton (ev′ən-stən, -ənz-tən) city, NE Illinois; 79,808; ZIP 60201*.

Ev·ans·ville (ev′enz-vil) city, SW Indiana; 138,764; ZIP 47700*.

Ev·er·est (ev′ər-ist, ev′rist) mtn., E Nepal; highest point of the earth's surface; 29,028 ft.

Ev·er·ett (ev′ər-it, ev′rit) city, E Massachusetts; 42,485; ZIP see BOSTON.

— city, W Washington; 53,622; ZIP 98201*.

Ev·er·glades (ev′ər-glādz) large swampy reg., S Florida.

Evergreen Park vill., NE Illinois; 25,487; ZIP see CHICAGO.

Ev·voia (ev-vyä′) Euboea: *the Greek name.*

E·wa Beach (e′və) city, S Oahu, Hawaii; 7,765; ZIP 96706.

Ex·cel·si·or Springs (ek-sel′sē-ər, ik-) city, NW Missouri; 9,411; ZIP 64024.

Ex·e·ter (ek′sə-tər) co. boro., CEN. Devonshire, England; cap; 93,010.

Ex·e·ter (ek′sə-tər) uninc. place, SE New Hampshire; 8,892; ZIP 03833.

Exeter Compact city, NE New Hampshire; 6,439.

Faer·oe Islands (fâr′ō) isl. group of Denmark, North Atlantic; 540 sq. mi.; 34,000; cap. Thorshain.

Fair·banks (fâr′bangks) town, E CEN. Alaska; 14,771; ZIP 99701*.

Fair·born (fâr′bôrn) city, SW Ohio; 32,267; ZIP 45324.

Fair·bur·y (fâr′ber-ē) city, SE Nebraska; 5,265; ZIP 68352*.

Fair·child (fâr′chīld) city, N Washington; 6,754.

Fair·fax (fâr′faks) town, CEN. California; 7,661; ZIP 94930.

— town, N Virginia; 21,970; ZIP 22030.

Fair·field (fâr′fēld) city, N CEN. Alabama; 14,369; ZIP 35064.

— city, W CEN. California; 44,146; ZIP 94533*.

— town, SW Connecticut; 56,487; ZIP 06430*.

— city, SE Illinois; 5,897; ZIP 62837.

— city, SE Iowa; 8,715; ZIP 52556.

— town, NW Maine; 5,684; ZIP 04937.

— city, NE New Jersey; 6,142; ZIP 07006.

— city, SW Ohio; 14,680; ZIP see HAMILTON.

Fair·ha·ven (fâr′hā′vən) town, SE Massachusetts; 16,332; ZIP 02719.

Fair Ha·ven (fâr′ hā′vən) boro., E New Jersey; 6,142; ZIP see RED BANK.

Fair·hope (fâr′hōp′) city, SW Alabama; 5,720; ZIP 36530.

Fair Lawn boro., NE New Jersey; 37,975; ZIP 07410*.

— city, NW Ohio; 6,102; ZIP 44313.

Fair·mont (fâr′mont) city, S Minnesota; 10,751; ZIP 56031.

— city, CEN. New York; 15,317.

— city, N West Virginia; 26,093; ZIP 26550*.

Fair Oaks uninc. place, NW CEN. Georgia; 11,256 ZIP see MARIETTA.

Fair·port (fâr′pôrt, -pōrt) vill., W New York; 6,474; ZIP 14450.

Fair·view (fâr′vyōō′) boro., NE New Jersey; 10,698; ZIP 07022.

— uninc. place, SE New York; 8,517.

Fairview Heights city, SW Illinois; 8,625; ZIP 62230.

Fairview Park city, N Ohio; 21,681; ZIP see CLEVELAND.

Fair·way (fâr′wā) city, E Kansas; 5,133.

Fa·jar·do (fä-här′dō) town, NE Puerto Rico; 12,409; ZIP 00648*.

Fal·con Heights (fal′kən, fôl′-) vill., E Minnesota; 5,507; ZIP see SAINT PAUL.

Fal·fur·ri·as (fal-fyōō′rē-əs) city, S Texas; 6,355; ZIP 78355.

Falk·land Islands (fôk′lənd) British col., South Atlantic; 4,618 sq. mi.; 2,000; cap. Stanley.

Fall·brook (fôl′brŏŏk′) city, sw California; 6,945; ZIP 92028.

Fall River city, se Massachusetts; 96,898; ZIP 02720*.

Falls (fôlz) urb. twp., NE Pennsylvania; 29,082; ZIP 18615.

Falls Church city, NE Virginia; 10,772; ZIP 22040.

Falls City city, se Nebraska; 5,444; ZIP 68355*.

Fal·mouth (fal′məth) town, E Massachusetts; 15,942; ZIP 02540.

Fan·wood (fan′wŏŏd) boro., NE New Jersey; 8,920; ZIP 07023.

Far·go (fär′gō) city, se North Dakota; 53,365; ZIP 58100*.

Far·i·bault (fär′i·bō) city, se Minnesota; 16,595; ZIP 55021.

Farmers Branch city, N Texas; 27,492; ZIP see DALLAS.

Far·ming·dale (fär′ming·dāl) vill., se New York; 9,297; ZIP 11735*.

Far·ming·ton (fär′ming·tən) city, N CEN. Connecticut; 14,390; ZIP 06032.
— city, se Maine, 13,337; ZIP 48024.
— city, se Michigan; 5,657; ZIP 48024.
— city, E Missouri; 6,590; ZIP 63640.
— town, NW New Mexico; 21,979.

Farn·ham (fär′nəm) city, s Quebec, Canada; 6,752.

Far·rell (far′əl) city, w Pennsylvania; 11,022; ZIP 16121.

Fay·ette·ville (fā′it·vil, -vəl) city, NW Arkansas; 30,729; ZIP 72701*.
— city, s CEN. North Carolina; 53,510; ZIP 28301*.
— town, s Tennessee; 7,030; ZIP 37334.

Federal Republic of Germany See GERMANY.

Fen·ton (fent′n, fen′tən) vill., se Michigan; 8,284; ZIP 48430.

Fer·gus Falls (fûr′gəs) city, w Minnesota; 12,443; ZIP 56537*.

Fer·gu·son (fûr′gə·sən) city, E Missouri; 28,915; ZIP see SAINT LOUIS.

Fer·nan·di·na Beach (fûr′nən·dē′nə, -nan-) city, NE Florida; 6,955.

Fern·dale (fûrn′dāl′) city, NW Maryland; 9,929; ZIP 21061.
— city, se Michigan; 30,850; ZIP see DETROIT.

Fer·ri·day (fer′ə·dā) city, NE Louisiana; 5,239; ZIP 71334.

Fes·tus (fes′təs) city, E Missouri; 7,530; ZIP 63028.

Fi·ji (fē′jē) British col., South Pacific; comprises **Fiji Islands** (7,039 sq. mi.) and Rotuma (18 sq. mi.); 388,000; cap. Suva.

Fill·more (fil′môr, -mōr) city, sw California; 6,285; ZIP 93015.

Find·lay (fin′lē, find′-) city, NW CEN. Ohio; 35,800; ZIP 45840*.

Fin·land (fin′lənd) republic, N Europe; 117,913 sq. mi.; 4,440,000; cap. Helsinki.

Finland, Gulf of part of the Baltic Sea betw. Finland and the USSR.

Fir·crest (fûr′krest) city, w CEN. Washington; 5,651; ZIP 98466.

Fitch·burg (fich′bûrg) city, N Massachusetts; 43,343; ZIP 21420*.

Fitz·ger·ald (fits·jer′əld) city, s CEN. Georgia; 8,015; ZIP 31750.

Fiu·me (fyōō′mā) Rijeka: *the Italian name.*

Flag·staff (flag′staf) city, N CEN. Arizona; 26,117; ZIP 86001*.

Flan·ders (flan′dərz) reg., N France and s Belgium.

Flat Rock city, se Michigan; 5,643; ZIP 48134.

Flat·woods (flat′wŏŏdz′) city, NE Kentucky; 7,380; ZIP 41139.

Flin Flon (flin′ flon′) town, w Manitoba, Canada; 10,201.

Flint (flint) city, E CEN. Michigan; 193,317; ZIP 48500*.

Flintridge See LA CANADA-FLINTRIDGE.

Flo·ra (flô′rə, flōr′ə) city, s CEN. Illinois; 5,283; ZIP 62839.

Floral Park city, sw Montana; 5,113; ZIP 59701.
— vill., se New York; 18,422; ZIP 11001*.

Flor·ence (flôr′əns, flor′-) city, CEN. Tuscany, Italy; cap.; 455,665.

Flor·ence (flôr′əns, flor′-) city, NW Alabama; 34,031; ZIP 35630*.
— city, N Kentucky; 11,457; ZIP 41042.
— city, E South Carolina; 25,997; ZIP 29501.

Flor·ence-Gra·ham (flôr′əns, flor′-; grā′əm) uninc. place, sw California; 42,895.

Flor·ence-Roeb·ling (flôr′əns·rō′bling, flor′-) city, w CEN. New Jersey; 7,551; ZIP 08518.

Flor·ham Park (flôr′əm) boro., N New Jersey; 8,094; ZIP 07932.

Flor·i·da (flor′ə·də, flôr′-) state, se United States; 58,560 sq. mi.; 6,789,443; cap. Tallahassee.

Florida City city, se Florida; 5,153; ZIP 33030.

Florida Keys isl. group sw of Florida.

Flor·in (flôr′ən) city, CEN. California; 9,646; ZIP 95828.

Flo·ris·sant (flôr′i·sənt) city, E Missouri; 65,908; ZIP 63031*.

Floss·moor Village (flôs′mŏŏr′, flos′-) city, NE Illinois; 7,846; ZIP 60422.

Flush·ing (flush′ing) city, CEN. Michigan; 7,190; ZIP 48433.

Fol·croft (fol′krôft) boro., se Pennsylvania; 9,610; ZIP 19032.

Fol·som (fōl′səm) city, CEN. California; 5,810; ZIP 95630.

Fond du Lac (fon′ də lak′, dyə lak′) city, E Wisconsin; 35,515; ZIP 54935*.

Fon·taine·bleau (fôn·ten·blō′) town, N CEN. France; site of a former royal residence; 20,000.

Fon·tan·a (fon·tan′ə) city, s CEN. California; 20,673; ZIP 92335*.

Foo·chow (fōō′chou′) city, se China; 616,000.

Forest Acres city, CEN. South Carolina, 6,808; ZIP 29206.

Forest City town, sw North Carolina; 7,179; ZIP 28043.

For·est·dale (fôr′est·dāl, for′-) city, CEN. Alabama; 6,091; ZIP 35214.

Forest Grove city, NW Oregon; 8,275; ZIP 97116.

Forest Hill vill., s Ontario, Canada; 23,135.

Forest Hill city, N Texas; 8,236; ZIP 75701.

Forest Hills boro., sw Pennsylvania; 9,561; ZIP see PITTSBURGH.

Forest Park town, NW CEN. Georgia; 19,994; ZIP 30050.
— vill., NE Illinois; 15,472; ZIP 60130.

Forest Park city, sw Ohio; 15,139; ZIP 45405.

For·est·ville (fôr′est·vil, for′-) city, sw Maryland; 16,152; ZIP 20028.

For·mo·sa (fôr·mō′sə) Taiwan: *a former name.*

For·rest City (for′ist, fôr′-) city, E Arkansas; 12,521; ZIP 72335.

Fort At·kin·son (at′kin·sən) city, s Wisconsin; 9,164; ZIP 53538.

Fort Bel·voir (bel′vôr′) city, NE Virginia; 14,591.

Fort Bliss (blis) city, sw Texas; 13,288.

Fort Ben·ning (ben′ing) city, w Georgia; 27,495.

Fort Bragg (brag) city, CEN. North Carolina; 46,995.

Fort Camp·bell (kam′bəl) city, N CEN. Tennessee; 9,279.

Fort Campbell North city, sw Kentucky; 13,616.

Fort Car·son (kär′sən) city, CEN. Colorado; 19,399.

Fort Col·lins (kol′inz) city, N Colorado; 43,337; ZIP 80521*.

Fort Dev·ens (dev′ənz) city, CEN. Massachusetts; 12,951.

Fort Dix (diks) city, w CEN. New Jersey; 26,290; ZIP 07024.

Fort Dodge (doj) city, N CEN. Iowa; 31,263; ZIP 50501.

Fort Er·ie (ir′ē) town, s Ontario, Canada; 9,793.

Fort Fran·ces (fran′ses, -sis) town, w Ontario, Canada; 9,524.

Fort Gor·don (gôr′dən) city, E Georgia; 15,589.

Forth River (fôrth, fôrth) river, se Scotland; 65 mi. long.

Forth, Firth of estuary of the Forth River; 51 mi. long.

Fort Hood (hŏŏd) city, CEN. Texas; 32,597.

Fort Howard See SPARROWS POINT-FORT HOWARD-EDGEMERE.

Fort Hua·chu·ca (wä·chōō′kə) city, se Arizona; 6,659; ZIP 85613.

Fort Knox (noks) military reservation, N Kentucky; site of the Federal gold bullion depository; ZIP 40120*.

Fort La·my (fôr·lä·mē′) city, N Chad; cap.; 100,000.

Fort Lau·der·dale (lô′dər·dāl) city, se Florida; 139,590; ZIP 33300*.

Fort Leav·en·worth (lev′ən·wûrth) city, NE Kansas; 8,060; ZIP 66027.
— city, se Virginia; 12,435.

Fort Lee (lē) boro., NE New Jersey; 30,631; ZIP 07024*.

Fort Leon·ard (len′ərd) city, se Missouri; 33,799.

Fort Lew·is (lōō′is) city, w CEN. Washington; 38,054.

Fort Mad·i·son (mad′ə·sən) city, se Iowa; 13,996; ZIP 52627.

Fort Mc·Clel·lan (mə·klel′ən) city, E Alabama; 5,334.

Fort Mc·Kin·ley (mə·kin′lē) city, sw Ohio; 11,536; ZIP 45401.

Fort Meade (mēd) city, NW Maryland; 16,699.

Fort Mitch·ell (mich′əl) city, N CEN. Kentucky; 41017.

Fort Mor·gan (môr′gən) city, NE Colorado; 7,594; ZIP 80701.

Fort My·ers (mī′ərz) city, sw Florida; 27,351; ZIP 33901.

Fort Payne (pān) city, NE Alabama; 8,435; ZIP 35967.

Fort Pierce (pirs) city, E Florida; 29,721; ZIP 33450*.

Fort Rich·ard·son (rich′ərd·sən) city, s CEN. Alaska; 8,960.

Fort Ruck·er (ruk′ər) city, se Alabama; 14,242.

Fort Sam Hous·ton (sam hyōōs′tən) city, CEN. Texas; 10,553.

Fort Scott (skot) city, se Kansas; 8,967; ZIP 66701.

Fort Sill (sil) city, sw Oklahoma; 21,217.

Fort Smith (smith) city, w Arkansas; 62,802; ZIP 72901*.

Fort Stock·ton (stok′tən) city, w Texas; 8,283; ZIP 79735.

Fort Thom·as (tom′əs) city, N Kentucky; 16,338; ZIP see NEWPORT.

Fort Val·ley (val′ē) city, w CEN. Georgia; 9,251; ZIP 31030.

Fort Wain·wright (wān′rīt) city, E CEN. Alaska; 9,097.

Fort Wal·ton Beach (wôlt′n, wôl′tən) city, NW Florida; 19,994; ZIP 32548.

Fort Wayne (wān) city, NE Indiana; 177,671; ZIP 46800.

Fort Wil·liam (wil′yəm) city, w Ontario, Canada; 48,208.

Fort Worth (wûrth) city, N Texas; 393,476; ZIP 76100*.

For·ty Fort (fôr′tē) boro., NE Pennsylvania; 6,114; ZIP see WILKES-BARRE.

Fos·ter (fôs′tər, fos′-) city, W CEN. California; 9,327; ZIP 94404.

Fos·tor·i·a (fos·tôr′ē·ə) city, N Ohio; 16,037; ZIP 44830.

Fountain City uninc. place, E Tennessee; 10,365; ZIP see KNOXVILLE.

Fountain Hill boro., E Pennsylvania; 5,384.

Fountain Valley city, SW California; 31,826; ZIP 92708.

Four Corners city, NW Oregon; 6,199; ZIP 97301.

Fox·bor·ough (foks′bûr′ō) city, CEN. Massachusetts; 14,218; ZIP 02035.

Fox Point vill., SE Wisconsin; 7,937.

Frack·ville (frak′vil) boro., E CEN. Pennsylvania; 5,445; ZIP 17931.

Fra·ming·ham (frā′ming·ham) town, E Massachusetts; 64,048; ZIP 01701.

France (frans, fräns) republic, W Europe; 212,974 sq. mi.; 45,730,000; cap. Paris.

Frank·fort (frangk′fərt) city, CEN. Indiana; 14,956; ZIP 46041.

— city, N CEN. Kentucky; cap.; 21,356; ZIP 40601.

Frank·fort on the Main (frangk′fərt on the mān) city, CEN. West Germany; 690,865.

Frankfort on the O·der (ō′dər) city, E East Germany; 58,866.

Frank·lin (frangk′lin) city, S CEN. Indiana; 11,477; ZIP 46131.

— city, S Kentucky; 6,553; ZIP 42134.

— town, S Louisiana; 9,325; ZIP 70538.

— town, E Massachusetts; 17,830; ZIP 02038.

— city, CEN. New Hampshire; 7,292; ZIP 03235.

— city, SW Ohio; 10,075; ZIP 45005*.

— city, NW Pennsylvania; 8,629; ZIP 16323.

— town, CEN. Tennessee; 9,404; ZIP 37064.

— town, SE Virginia; 6,880; ZIP 23851.

— city, SE Wisconsin; 12,247; ZIP see HALES CORNERS.

Frank·lin Lanes (frangk′lin) city, NE New Jersey; 7,550; ZIP 07417.

Franklin Park vill., NE Illinois; 20,497; ZIP 60131.

— city, SW Pennsylvania; 5,310.

Franklin Square uninc. place, SE New York; 32,156; ZIP 11010.

Fra·ser (frā′zər) city, SE Michigan; 11,868; ZIP 48026.

Fred·er·ick (fred′rik, fred′ə·rik) city, NW Maryland; 23,641; ZIP 21701.

— city, SW Oklahoma; 6,132; ZIP 73542.

— CEN. Texas; 5,326; ZIP 78624.

Fred·er·icks·burg (fred′riks·bûrg, -ər·riks-) city, NE Virginia; 14,450; ZIP 22401*.

Fred·er·ic·ton (fred′rik·tən, -ər·ik-) city, S CEN. New Brunswick, Canada; 22,460.

Fre·do·ni·a (frē·dō′nē·ə) vill., W New York; 10,226; ZIP 14063.

Freedom city, W CEN. California; 5,563; ZIP 95019.

Free·hold (frē′hōld′) boro., E CEN. New Jersey; 10,545; ZIP 07728.

Free·port (frē′pôrt, -pōrt) city, N Illinois; 27,736; ZIP 61032*.

— vill., SE New York; 40,374; ZIP 11520.

— city, SE Texas; 11,997; ZIP 77541.

Fre·mont (frē′mont) city, N California; 100,869; ZIP 94536.

— city, E Nebraska; 22,962; ZIP 68025.

— city, N Ohio; 18,490; ZIP 43420.

French Gui·an·a (gē·an′ə, -än′ə) French Overseas dept.; NE South America; 35,000 sq. mi.; 32,000; cap. Cayenne.

French Polynesia French Overseas terr., South Pacific; comprises the Society, Marquesas, Gambier, and other islands; 1,560 sq. mi.; 75,000; cap. Papeete.

French Republic France, with its overseas depts. and terrs.

French So·ma·li·land (sō·mä′lē·land) Djibouti: *the former name.*

French West Indies isls. comprising Guadaloupe and Martinique.

Fres·no (frez′nō) city, CEN. California; 165,972; ZIP 93700*.

Frid·ley (frid′lē) city, E Minnesota; 29,233; ZIP see MINNE-APOLIS.

Friends·wood (frendz′wŏŏd) city, E CEN. Texas; 5,675; ZIP 77546.

Fries·land (frēz′lənd, -land) prov., N Netherlands; 1,251 sq. mi.; 478,000; cap. Leeuwarden.

Frigid Zone See NORTH FRIGID ZONE, SOUTH FRIGID ZONE.

Fris·ian Islands (frizh′ən, frizh′ē·ən) isl. group, North Sea near Germany, Denmark, and the Netherlands.

Front Royal (roi′əl) town, N Virginia; 8,211; ZIP 22630.

Frost·burg (frôst′burg, frost′-) city, NW Maryland; 7,327; ZIP 21532.

Fruitridge See SOUTH SACRAMENTO.

Fu·ji (fōō·jē) extinct volcano, Honshu, Japan; 12,389 ft.

Ful·ler·ton (fŏŏl′ər·tən) city, SW California; 85,826; ZIP 92631*.

— city, NE Pennsylvania; 7,908.

Ful·ton (fŏŏlt′n, fŏŏl′tən) city, CEN. Missouri; 12,148; ZIP 65251.

— city, N CEN. New York; 14,003; ZIP 13069.

Ful·ton·dale (ful′tən·dāl) city, CEN. Alabama; 5,163; ZIP 35068.

Fun·dy (fun′dē), **Bay of** inlet of the Atlantic betw. Nova Scotia and New Brunswick and NE Maine.

Ga·bon (ga·bon′) republic, W CEN. Africa; 102,290 sq. mi.; 535,000; cap. Libreville. Formerly Ga·bo·nese Republic (gab·ə·nēz′).

Gads·den (gadz′dən) city, NE Alabama; 53,982; ZIP 35901*.

Gaff·ney (gaf′nē) city, N South Carolina; 13,253; ZIP 29340.

Ga·han·na (gə·han′ə) city, CEN. Ohio; 12,400; ZIP 43230.

Gaines·ville (gānz′vil, -vəl) city, N Florida; 64,510; ZIP 32601*.

— city, N CEN. Georgia; 15,459; ZIP 30501*.

— city, N Texas; 13,830; ZIP 76240.

Gai·thers·burg (gā′thərz·bûrg) city, NW Maryland; 8,344; ZIP 20760.

Ga·lá·pa·gos Islands (gä·lä′pä·gōs) isl. group of Ecuador, South Pacific.

Ga·lax (gā′laks) city, SW Virginia; 6,278; ZIP 24333.

Ga·le·na Park (gə·lē′nə) city, SE Texas; 10,479; ZIP 77547.

Gales·burg (gālz′bûrg) city, W Illinois; 36,290; ZIP 61401.

Ga·li·cia (gə·lish′ə) reg., SE Poland and NW Ukrainian SSR.

Ga·li·cia (gə·lish′ə) reg., N Spain.

Gal·i·lee (gal′ə·lē) reg., N Israel.

Galilee, Sea of fresh water lake; betw. NE Israel, SW Syria, and NW Jordan; 64 sq. mi.

Gal·ion (gal′yən) city, N CEN. Ohio; 13,123; ZIP 44833.

Gal·la·tin (gal′ət·n, -tən) city, N Tennessee; 13,093; ZIP 37066.

Gal·lip·o·li Peninsula (gə·lip′ə·lē) penin., NW Turkey.

Gal·li·po·lis (gal′ə·pə·lēs′) city, S Ohio; 7,490; ZIP 45631.

Gal·lup (gal′əp) town, NW New Mexico; 14,596; ZIP 87301.

Galt (gôlt) city, S Ontario, Canada; 33,491.

Gal·ves·ton (gal′vəs·tən) city, SE Texas; 61,809; ZIP 77550*.

Gam·bi·a (gam′bē·ə) British col. and prot., W Africa; 4,003 sq. mi.; 295,000; cap. Bathurst.

Gan·a·no·que (gan′ə·nok′wē, -wə) town, SE Ontario, Canada; 5,237.

Gan·der (gan′dər) town, E Newfoundland, Canada; 7,183.

Gan·ges (gan′jēz) river, N India and E Pakistan; 1,560 mi. long.

Gar·de·na (gär·dē′nə) city, SW California; 41,021; ZIP 90247*.

Garden Acres city, W CEN. California; 7,870.

Garden City town, SE Georgia; 5,741; ZIP see SAVANNAH.

— city, SW Kansas; 14,708; ZIP 67846.

— city, SE Michigan; 41,864; ZIP 48135.

— vill., SE New York; 25,373; ZIP 11530.

Garden City Park-Her·ricks (her′iks) uninc. place, SE New York; 7,488.

Gar·den·dale (gär′dən·dāl) city, CEN. Alabama; 6,502; ZIP 35071.

Garden Grove city, SW California; 122,524; ZIP 92640*.

Gard·i·ner (gärd′nər) city, S Maine; 6,685; ZIP 04345.

Gard·ner (gärd′nər) city, N Massachusetts; 19,748; ZIP 01440*.

Gar·field (gär′fēld) city, NE New Jersey; 30,722; ZIP 07026.

Garfield Heights city, NE Ohio; 41,417; ZIP see CLEVELAND.

Gar·land (gär′lənd) city, N Texas; 81,437; ZIP 75040*.

Gar·wood (gär′wŏŏd) boro., NE New Jersey; 5,260; ZIP 07027.

Gar·y (gâr′ē) NW Indiana; 175,415; ZIP 46400*.

Gas City city, N Indiana; 5,742; ZIP 46933.

Gas·co·ny (gas′kə·nē) reg., SW France.

Gas·to·ni·a (gas·tō′nē·ə, -tōn′yə) city, SW North Carolina; 47,142; ZIP 28052*.

Gat·in·eau (gat′in·ō) town, SW Quebec, Canada; 17,727.

Ga·za (gä′zə) city, SW Palestine; adm. by the United Arab Republic with the Gaza Strip, the surrounding area; 377,000.

Gdańsk (gdäny′sk) Danzig: *the Polish name.*

Gdy·nia (gdin′yä, gdin′ē·ə) city, NW Poland; 179,200.

General Wayne (wän) city, SE Pennsylvania; 5,368.

Gen·e·se·o (jen′ə·sē′ō, jen′ə·sōō) city, NW Illinois; 5,840; ZIP 61254.

— city, W New York; 5,714; ZIP 14454.

Ge·ne·va (jə·nē′və) city, SW Switzerland; 170,500.

Ge·ne·va (jə·nē′və) city, NE Illinois; 9,115; ZIP 60134.

— city, W CEN. New York; 16,793; ZIP 14456.

PRONUNCIATION KEY: add, āce, câre, pälm; end, ēven; it, īce; odd, ōpen, ôrder; tŏŏk, pōōl; up, bûrn; ə = a in *above*, e in *sicken*, i in *flex-ible*, o in *melon*, u in *focus*; yōō = u in *fuse*; oil; pout; check; go; ring; thin; this; zh, vision. For à, œ, ü, kh, n, see inside front cover.

— city, NE Ohio; 6,449; ZIP 44041.
Geneva, Lake of lake, sw Switzerland; 224 sq. mi.
Gen·o·a (jen'ō-ə) city, NW Italy; 842,732.
George (jôrj) city, s CEN. California; 7,404.
George·town (jôrj'toun) city, N Guyana; cap.; 162,000.
George·town (jôrj'toun, jôrj'-) city, N CEN. Kentucky; 8,629; ZIP 40324.
— city, NE Massachusetts; 5,290; ZIP 01830.
— city, E South Carolina; 10,449; ZIP 29440.
— city, CEN. Texas; 6,395; ZIP 78626.
— section of Washington, D. C., in w part of city.
George·town (jôrj'toun) town, s Ontario, Canada; 11,832.
Geor·gia (jôr'jə, jôr'-) state, SE United States; 58,876 sq. mi.; 4,589,515; cap. Atlanta.
Geor·gian SSR (jôr'jən, jôr'-) constituent republic, sw USSR; 26,900 sq. mi.; 4,044,000; cap. Tbilisi.
Ge·ring (gir'ing) city, w Nebraska; 5,639; ZIP 69341.
German Democratic Republic See GERMANY.
Ger·ma·ny (jûr'mə-nē) country, CEN. Europe; divided in 1949 into the Federal Republic of Germany (West Germany); 95,735 sq. mi.; 55,257,000; cap. Bonn; and the German Democratic Republic (East Germany); 41,479 sq. mi. (excluding East Berlin); 17,286,900 (excluding East Berlin); cap. East Berlin.
Get·tys·burg (get'iz-bûrg) boro., s Pennsylvania; site of a Union victory in the Civil War; July, 1863; 7,725; ZIP 17325.
Gha·na (gä'nə) republic of the Commonwealth of Nations, w Africa; 92,100 sq. mi.; 6,691,000; cap. Accra.
Ghent (gent) city, NW Belgium; 157,834.
Gi·bral·tar (ji-brôl'tər) British col. on the Rock of Gibraltar; 2.25 sq. mi.; 26,000.
Gibraltar, Rock of penin., s Spain; dominates the Strait of Gibraltar.
Gibraltar, Strait of strait, betw. Spain and Africa, w Mediterranean.
Gif·fard (zhē'fär) city, s CEN. Quebec, Canada; 12,585.
Gif·ford (gif'ərd) city, E CEN. Florida; 5,772; ZIP 32960.
Gil·bert and El·lice Islands (gil'bərt; el'is) British col., South Pacific; 369 sq. mi.; 45,000; headquarters on Tarawa.
Gil·lette (jə-let') city, NE Wyoming; 7,194; ZIP 82716.
Gil·roy (gil'roi) city, w California; 12,665; ZIP 95020.
Gi·rard (ji-rärd') city, NE Ohio; 14,119; ZIP 44420.
Glace Bay (glās) town, NE Nova Scotia, Canada; 23,516.
Glade·wa·ter (glād'wô'tər) city, E Texas; 5,574; ZIP 75647.
Glad·stone (glad'stōn) city, NW Michigan; 5,237; ZIP 49837.
— city, w Missouri; 23,128; ZIP see KANSAS CITY.
— city NW Oregon; 6,237; ZIP 97027.
Glas·gow (glas'gō, -kō, gläs'-) burgh, sw Scotland; 1,755,328.
Glas·gow (glas'gō, -kō) city, s Kentucky; 11,301; ZIP 42141.
— city, NE Montana; 6,398; ZIP 59230*.
Glass·bor·o (glas'bûr'ō) boro., sw New Jersey; 13,938; ZIP 08028.
Glass·port (glas'pôrt, -pōrt) boro., sw Pennsylvania; 7,450; ZIP 15045.
Glas·ton·bur·y (glas'tən·ber'ē) city, N CEN. Connecticut; 20,651; ZIP 06033.
Glen A·von (glen ā'vən) city, s CEN. California; 5,759; ZIP 92501.
Glen Bur·nie (glen bûr'nē) city, NE Maryland; 38,608; ZIP 21061.
Glencliff See WOODBINE-RADNOR-GLENCLIFF.
Glen·coe (glen'kō) vill., NE Illinois; 10,542; ZIP 60022.
Glen Cove (glen kōv) city, SE New York; 25,770; ZIP 11542.
Glen·dale (glen'dāl) city, s CEN. Arizona; 36,228; ZIP 85301.
— city, sw California; 132,752; ZIP 91200*.
— city, E Missouri; 6,891; ZIP 63122.
— city, SE Wisconsin; 13,436.
— See WOODMONT-GREEN HILLS-GLENDALE.
Glen·dale Heights (glen'dāl) city, NE Illinois; 11,406.
Glen·dive (glen'dīv) city, E Montana; 6,305; ZIP 59330.
Glen·do·ra (glen·dôr'ə, -dō'rə) city, sw California; 31,349; ZIP 91740.
Glen El·lyn (glen el'ən) vill., NE Illinois; 21,909; ZIP 60137*.
Glen·ol·den (glen·ōl'dən) boro., SE Pennsylvania; 8,697; ZIP 19036.
Glen Ridge boro., NE New Jersey; 8,518; ZIP 07028.
Glen Rock boro., NE New Jersey; 13,011; ZIP see RIDGEWOOD.
Glens Falls city, E New York; 17,222; ZIP 12801*.
Glen·side (glen'sīd) city, SE Pennsylvania; 17,353; ZIP 19038.
Glen·view (glen'vyōō) vill., NE Illinois; 24,880; ZIP 60025*.
Glen·wood Village (glen'wŏŏd) city, NE Illinois; 7,416; ZIP 60425.
Globe (glōb) city, E CEN. Arizona; 7,333; ZIP 85501.
Gloces·ter (glos'tər) city, sw Rhode Island; 5,160; ZIP 01930.
Gloces·ter (glos'tər, glôs'-) co. boro., CEN. Gloucestershire, England; cap.; 70,000.
Gloces·ter (glos'tər, glôs'-) city, NE Massachusetts; 27,941; ZIP 01930*.

Gloucester City city, sw New Jersey; 14,707; ZIP 08030*.
Glouces·ter·shire (glos'tər-shir, glôs'-) co., w CEN. England; 1,258 sq. mi.; 1 million; cap. Gloucester.
Glov·ers·ville (gluv'ərz·vil) city, E CEN. New York; 19,677; ZIP 12078*.
Go·a (gō'ə) former Portuguese terr., w India; annexed by India in 1961; 1,394 sq. mi.; 551,000; cap. New Goa.
Go·bi Desert (gō'bē) desert, CEN. Asia; 500,000 sq. mi.
Gode·rich (god'rich, gōd'-) town, s Ontario, Canada; 6,710.
Goffs·town (gofs'toun) city, sw New Hampshire; 9,294.
Gold Coast Colony former British col., w Africa; now part of Ghana.
Gol·den (gōl'dən) city, N CEN. Colorado; 9,817; ZIP 80401*.
Golden Gate strait betw. San Francisco Bay and the Pacific.
Golden Valley vill., SE Minnesota; 24,246; ZIP see MINNEAPOLIS.
Golds·bor·o (gōldz'bûr'ō, -bûr'ə) city, E CEN. North Carolina; 26,810; ZIP 27530.
Golf Manor city, sw Ohio; 5,170; ZIP 45201.
Gon·zal·es (gən-zal'is) city, s CEN. Texas; 5,584; ZIP 78629.
Good Hope, Cape of promontory, sw South Africa.
Good·land (gŏŏd'land') city, SE Kansas; 5,510; ZIP 67735.
Good·luck (gŏŏd'luk') city, sw Maryland; 10,584; ZIP 20715.
Gor·ham (gôr'əm) city, SE Maine; 7,839; ZIP 04038.
Gor·ki (gôr'kē) city, w CEN. RSFSR; 942,000. Also **Gor'kiy, Gor'ky.**
Go·shen (gō'shən) city, N Indiana; 17,171; ZIP 46526.
Gö·te·borg (yœ'tə-bôr'y') city, sw Sweden; 418,600.
Got·land (got'lənd) isl. of SE Sweden, Baltic Sea; 1,167 sq. mi.
Goulds (gŏŏldz) uninc. place, SE Florida; 6,690; ZIP 33170.
Graf·ton (graf'tən) city, CEN. Massachusetts; 11,659; ZIP 01519.
— city, NE North Dakota; 5,946; ZIP 58237.
— city, N West Virginia; 6,433; ZIP 26354.
— city, SE Wisconsin; 5,998; ZIP 53024.
Gra·ham (grā'əm) town, N CEN. North Carolina; 8,172; ZIP 27253.
— See FLORENCE-GRAHAM.
— city, N Texas; 7,477; ZIP 76046.
Gra·na·da (grə-nä'də) city, s Spain; 157,663.
Gran·by (gran'bē, gram'-) city, s Quebec, Canada; 34,349.
Gran·by (gran'bē) city, w Massachusetts; 5,473; ZIP 01033.
Grand Banks submarine shoal, North Atlantic; near Newfoundland.
Grand Canyon gorge of the Colorado River, NW Arizona; ab. 250 mi. long.
Grand Cou·lee (kŏŏ'lē) city, NE CEN. Washington; site of **Grand Coulee Dam**; 1,058.
Grande Prair·ie (grand prâr'ē) city, w Alberta, Canada; 11,417.
Grand Forks city, E North Dakota; 39,008; ZIP 58201*.
Grand Forks Base city, NE North Dakota; 10,474; ZIP 58201.
Grand Haven city, w Michigan; 11,844; ZIP 49417.
Grand Island city, SE CEN. Nebraska; 31,269; ZIP 68801.
Grand Junction city, w Colorado; 20,170; ZIP 81501*.
Grand Ledge city, s CEN. Michigan; 6,032; ZIP 48837.
Grand' Mère (grän·mâr') city, s CEN. Quebec, Canada; 16,407.
Grand Prairie (grand prâr'ē) city, N Texas; 50,904; ZIP 75050*.
Grand Rapids city, w Michigan; 197,649; ZIP 49500*.
— vill., N CEN. Minnesota; 7,247; ZIP 55744.
Grand Terrace city, s CEN. California; 5,901; ZIP 92324.
Grand·view (grand'vyōō') city, w Missouri; 17,456; ZIP 64030*.
Grandview Heights city, CEN. Ohio; 8,460; ZIP 45733.
Grand·ville (grand'vil) city, w Michigan; 10,764; ZIP 49418.
Grang·er-Hunt·er (grän'jər-hun'tər) city, NW Utah; 9,029.
Granite City city, sw Illinois; 40,440; ZIP 62040*.
Granite Park city, NW Utah; 9,573.
Grants (grants) town, w New Mexico; 8,768; ZIP 87020.
Grants Pass city, sw Oregon; 12,455; ZIP 97526.
Grape·vine (grāp'vīn) city, N CEN. Texas; 7,023; ZIP 76051.
Grass Valley city, sw California; 5,149; ZIP 95945.
Great Barrier Reef chain of coral reef off the coast of Queensland, Australia.
Great Bar·ring·ton (bar'ing·tən) city, w Massachusetts; 16,733; ZIP 01230.
Great Bend city, CEN. Kansas; 16,733; ZIP 67530.
Great Brit·ain (brit'n) principal isl. of the United Kingdom; comprises England, Scotland, and Wales; 88,748 sq. mi.; 51,295,000; cap. London.
Great Divide See CONTINENTAL DIVIDE.
Greater Antilles See ANTILLES.
Great Falls city, w CEN. Montana; 60,091; ZIP 59401*.
Great Lakes chain of five lakes, CEN. North America; on Canada-United States border; comprises Lakes Superior, Michigan, Huron, Ontario, and Erie; total 94,710 sq. mi.

Great Neck vill., SE New York; 10,724; ZIP 11020*.
Great Neck Plaza city, SE New York; 5,921.
Great Plains plateau, W North America; E of the Rockies.
Great Russia CEN. and NW reg. of the USSR.
Great Salt Lake salt lake, NW Utah; ab. 2,000 sq. mi.
Great Slave Lake lake, S Northwest Territories, Canada; 11,170 sq. mi.
Great Smoky Mountains mtn. range, North Carolina and Tennessee.
Greece (grēs) kingdom, SE Europe; 50,547 sq. mi.; 8,350,-000; cap. Athens.
Gree·ley (grē′lē) city, N Colorado; 38,902; ZIP 80630*.
Green Bay city, E Wisconsin; 87,809; ZIP 54300*.
Green·belt (grēn′belt′) city, W CEN. Maryland; 18,199; ZIP 20770*.
Green·cas·tle (grēn′kas′əl) city, W CEN. Indiana; 8,852; ZIP 46135.
Green·dale (grēn′dāl) vill., SE Wisconsin; 15,089; ZIP 53129.
Greene·ville (grēn′vil, -vəl) town, NE Tennessee; 13,722; ZIP 37743.
Green·field (grēn′fēld) city, E CEN. Indiana; 9,986; ZIP 46140.
— uninc. place, NW Massachusetts; 18,116; ZIP 01301.
— town, SE Wisconsin; 24,424; ZIP see MILWAUKEE.
Green·field Park (grēn′fēld) town, S Quebec, Canada; 12,288.
Green·hills (grēn′hilz′) vill., SW Ohio; 6,092; ZIP see CINCINNATI.
Green Hills See WOODMONT-GREEN HILLS-GLENDALE.
Green·land (grēn′lənd) isl. of Denmark near NE North America; 840,154 sq. mi.; 31,000.
Green·lawn (grēn′lôn) uninc. place, SE New York; 8,178; ZIP 11740.
Green Mountains mtn. range, CEN. Vermont.
Greens·boro (grēnz′bûr′ō, -ə) city, N CEN. North Carolina; 144,076; ZIP 27400*.
Greens·burg (grēnz′bûrg) city, SE Indiana; 8,620; ZIP 47240.
— city, SW Pennsylvania; 15,870; ZIP 15601*.
Green·tree (grēn′trē′) boro., SW Pennsylvania; 6,441.
Green·ville (grēn′vil, -vəl) city, S Alabama; 8,033; ZIP 36037.
— city, CEN. Michigan; 7,493; ZIP 48838.
— city, W Mississippi; 39,648; ZIP 63944.
— city, E North Carolina; 29,063; ZIP 27834*.
— city, W Ohio; 12,380; ZIP 45331.
— boro., N Pennsylvania; 8,704; ZIP 16125.
— city, NW South Carolina; 61,208; ZIP 29601*.
— city, NE Texas; 22,043; ZIP 75401*.
Green·wich (gren′ich, -ij, grin′-) boro., SE London; former site of the Royal Observatory; location of prime meridian; 229,700.
Green·wich (gren′ich, grin′-, grēn′wich) town, SW Connecticut; 59,755; ZIP 06830*.
Green·wich Village (gren′ich, grin′-) part of lower Manhattan, New York City; traditionally frequented by artists.
Green·wood (grēn′wŏŏd) town, S CEN. Indiana; 11,408; ZIP 46142.
— city, W CEN. Mississippi; 22,400; ZIP 38930*.
— city, W South Carolina; 21,069; ZIP 29646*.
Greer (grir) town, NW South Carolina; 10,642; ZIP 29651.
Gre·na·da (gri·nā′də) British col. in the West Indies; 133 sq. mi.; 89,000; cap. St. George's.
Gre·na·da (gri·nā′də) city, NW CEN. Mississippi; 9,944; ZIP 38901.
Gresh·am City (gresh′əm) city, NW Oregon; 9,875; ZIP 97030.
Gret·na (gret′nə) city, SE Louisiana; 24,875; ZIP 70053.
Gret·na Green (gret′nə) vill., S Scotland; former scene of runaway marriages.
Grif·fin (grif′in, -ən) city, W CEN. Georgia; 22,734; ZIP 30223.
Grif·fith (grif′ith) town, NW Indiana; 18,168; ZIP 46319.
Grims·by (grimz′bē) town, S Ontario, Canada; 6,634.
Grin·nell (gri·nel′) city, CEN. Iowa; 8,402; ZIP 50112.
Gris·wold (griz′wōld) city, SE Connecticut; 7,763.
Grosse Ile (grōs īl) city, SE Michigan; 7,799; ZIP 48138.
Grosse Pointe (grōs point′) city, SE Michigan; 6,637; ZIP see DETROIT.
Grosse Pointe Farms city, SE Michigan; 11,701.
Grosse Pointe Park city, SE Michigan; 15,585.
Grosse Pointe Woods city, SE Michigan; 21,878.
Grot·on (grot′n) town, SE Connecticut; 8,933; ZIP 06340*.
— city, NE Massachusetts; 5,109; ZIP 01490.
Grove City (grōv) vill., S CEN. Ohio; 13,911; ZIP 43123.
— boro., W Pennsylvania; 8,312; ZIP 16127.
Grove·land (grōv′lənd) city; NE Massachusetts; 6,382; ZIP 01830.

Groves (grōvz) city, SE Texas; 18,062; ZIP 77619.
Grove·ton (grōv′tən) city, NE Virginia; 11,750; ZIP 22301.
Gua·da·la·ja·ra (gwä′thä·lä·hä′rä) city, W CEN. Mexico; 1,124,018.
Gua·dal·ca·nal (gwä′dəl·kə·nal′) isl., British Solomons; scene of an Allied invasion in World War II, 1943.
Gua·de·loupe (gwä′də·lōōp′) French overseas dept., Lesser Antilles; 639 sq. mi.; 254,000; cap. Basse-Terre.
Guam (gwäm) uninc. terr. of the United States, an isl. in the Marianas; 209 sq. mi.; 67,041; cap. Agaña.
Guan·tá·na·mo (gwän·tä′nə·mō) city, SE Cuba, near **Guantánamo Bay**, site of a US naval station; 135,100.
Gua·te·ma·la (gwä′tə·mä′lä) republic, N Central America; 42,042 sq. mi.; 3,759,000. — city, CEN. Guatemala; cap.; 577,120.
Gua·ya·ma (gwä·yä′mä) town, SE Puerto Rico; 16,913.
Guay·a·quil (gwī′ä·kēl′) city, W Ecuador; 604,151.
Guelph (gwelf) city, S Ontario, Canada; 51,311.
Guer·ni·ca (ger·nē′kä) town, N Spain; object of a German bombing, 1937.
Guern·sey (gûrn′zē) one of the Channel Islands; 25 sq. mi.
Guil·ford (gil′fərd) city, SE Connecticut; 12,033; ZIP 06437.
Guin·ea (gin′ē) republic, W Africa; 94,925 sq. mi.; 2,727,000; cap. Conakry.
Guinea, Gulf of large bay of the Atlantic off W Africa.
Guin·ea-Bis·sau (gin′ē·bi·sou′) republic, W Africa; 13,948 sq. mi.; 545,000; cap. Bissau.
Gulf·port (gulf′pôrt, -pōrt) city, W Florida; 9,730; ZIP see St. PETERSBURG.
— port city, SE Mississippi; 40,791; ZIP 39501*.
Gun·ters·ville (gun′tərz·vil, -vəl) city, NE Alabama; 6,491; ZIP 35976.
Guth·rie (guth′rē) city, CEN. Oklahoma; 9,575; ZIP 73044.
Gut·ten·berg (gut′n·bûrg) town, NE New Jersey; 5,754; ZIP see WEST NEW YORK.
Guy·a·na (gī·an′ə, -än′ə) republic, NE South America; 83,000 sq. mi.; 830,000; cap. Georgetown.

Haar·lem (här′ləm) city, W Netherlands; 173,133.
Ha·ci·en·da Heights (hä·sē·en′də) city, S California; 35,969.
Hack·en·sack (hak′ən·sak) city, NE New Jersey; 35,911; ZIP 07601*.
Hack·etts·town (hak′əts·toun) town, NW New Jersey; 9,472; ZIP 07840.
Had·don (had′n) urb. twp., SW New Jersey; 17,099.
Had·don·field (had′n·fēld) boro., SW New Jersey; 13,118; ZIP 08033*.
Haddon Heights boro., SW New Jersey; 9,365; ZIP 08035.
Ha·gers·town (hā′gərz·toun) city, W Maryland; 35,862; ZIP 21740*.
Hague (hāg), **The** city, W Netherlands; cap; seat of the Hague Tribunal; 576,160.
Hai·fa (hī′fä) city, NW Israel; 204,500.
Haines City (hānz) city, CEN. Florida; 8,956; ZIP 33844.
Hai·ti (hā′tē) republic, W Hispaniola; 10,714 sq. mi.; 4 million; cap. Port-au-Prince.
Ha·la·wa Heights (hä·lä′və) city, S Oahu, Hawaii; 5,809; ZIP 96701.
Hale·don (hāl′dən) boro., NE New Jersey; 6,767.
Hales Corners (hālz) vill., SE Wisconsin; 7,771; ZIP 53130*.
Halethorpe See ARBUTUS-HALETHORPE-RELAY.
Half Hollow Hills city, SE New York; 12,055.
Half·way (haf′wā) city, SW Maryland; 6,106; ZIP 21740.
Hal·i·fax (hal′ə·fax) city, S Nova Scotia; Canada; cap.; 86,192.
Hal·lan·dale (hal′ən·dāl) city, SE Florida; 23,849; ZIP 33009.
Hal·le (häl′ə) city, SW East Germany; 276,421.
Hal·pine (hal′pīn) city, NW Maryland; 5,912; ZIP 20850.
Hal·tom City (hôl′təm) vill., N Texas; 28,127; ZIP see FORT WORTH.
Ham·burg (ham′bûrg) state and city, N West Germany; 288 sq. mi.; 1,856,953.
Ham·burg (ham′bûrg) vill., W New York; 10,215; ZIP 14075.
Ham·den (ham′dən) town, S Connecticut; 49,357; ZIP see NEW HAVEN.
Ham·il·ton (ham′əl·tən) city, CEN. Bermuda; cap.; 3,000.
Ham·il·ton (ham′əl·tən)
— city, NE Massachusetts; 6,373; ZIP 01936.
— city, SW Ohio; 67,865; ZIP 45010*.
Ham·il·ton (ham′əl·tən) city, S Ontario, Canada; 298,121.
Ham·mond (ham′ənd) city, NW Indiana; 107,790; ZIP 46320*.
— city, SE Louisiana; 12,487; ZIP 70401*.
Ham·mon·ton (ham′ən·tən) town, S New Jersey; 11,464; ZIP 08037.
Hamp·ton (hamp′tən) port city, SE Virginia; 120,779; ZIP 23360*.

Hampton Compact city, SE New Hampshire; 5,407; ZIP 03842.

Hampton Falls city, SE New Hampshire; 8,011; ZIP 03842.

Hampton Roads channel, SE Virginia; connects several rivers with Chesapeake Bay; scene of the Civil War engagement of the "Monitor" and the "Merrimack," 1862.

Ham·tramck (ham-tram′ik) city, SE Michigan; an enclave in Detroit; 27,245; ZIP see DETROIT.

Han·a·han (han′ə-han) city, SE South Carolina; 8,376; ZIP 29410.

Han·ford (han′fərd) city, S CEN. California; 15,179; ZIP 93230*.

Hang·chow (hang′chou′) city, E China; 784,000.

Han·kow (hang′kou′) See WUHAN.

Han·ni·bal (han′ə-bəl) city, NE Missouri; 18,609; ZIP 63401*.

Ha·noi (hä-noi′) city, N Vietnam; cap.; 414,620.

Han·o·ver (han′ō-vər) city, N CEN. West Germany; 572,000.

Han·o·ver (han′ō-vər) town, NE Massachusetts; 10,107; ZIP 02339.
— uninc. place, W New Hampshire; 6,147; ZIP 03755.
— boro., S Pennsylvania; 15,623; ZIP 17331.

Hanover Park Village city, NE Illinois; 11,916.

Han·son (han′sən) city, E Massachusetts; 7,148; ZIP 02341

Hape·ville (hāp′vil, -vəl) city, NW CEN. Georgia; 9,567; ZIP 30054.

Har·a·han (har′ə-han) city, SE Louisiana; 13,037; ZIP see NEW ORLEANS.

Har·bin (här′bin) city, NE China; 1,552,000.

Hardwick See MIDWAY-HARDWICK.

Har·lan (här′lən) city, NW Iowa; 5,049; ZIP 51537.

Har·lem (här′ləm) area, N Manhattan, New York City;
— river channel NE of Manhattan, New York.

Har·lin·gen (här′lin-jən, -ling-ən) city, S Texas; 33,503; ZIP 78550*.

Har·per Woods (här′pər) city, SE Michigan; 20,186; ZIP see DETROIT.

Har·ri·man (har′ə-mən) city, E Tennessee; 8,734; ZIP 37748.

Har·ris·burg (har′is-bûrg) city, S Illinois; 9,535; ZIP 62946.
— city, S CEN. Pennsylvania; cap.; 68,061; ZIP 17101*.

Har·ri·son (har′ə-sən) city, N Arkansas; 7,239; ZIP 72601.
— town, NE New Jersey; 11,811; ZIP 07029.
— urb. twp., SW Pennsylvania; 8,734; ZIP 15636.

Har·ri·son·burg (har′ə-sən-bûrg) city, N Virginia; 14,605; ZIP 22801*.

Har·rods·burg (har′ədz-bûrg) city, CEN. Kentucky; 6,741; ZIP 40330.

Hart·ford (härt′fərd) city, CEN. Connecticut; cap.; 158,017; ZIP 06100*.
— city, SW Vermont; 6,477; ZIP 05047.
— city, E Wisconsin; 6,499; ZIP 53027.

Hartford City city, E Indiana; 8,207; ZIP 47348.

Harts·dale (härts′dāl) city, SE New York; 12,226.

Hart·selle (härt′sel) city, N Alabama; 7,355; ZIP 35640.

Harts·ville (härts′vil, -vəl) town, NE South Carolina; 8,017; ZIP 29550.

Har·vard (här′vərd) city, NE Illinois; 5,177; ZIP 60033.
— city, CEN. Massachusetts; 13,426; ZIP 70058.

Har·vey (här′vē) city, NE Illinois; 34,636; ZIP 60426*.
— city, SW Louisiana; 6,347; ZIP 70058.

Har·wich (här′wich) city, E Massachusetts; 5,892; ZIP 02645.

Har·wood Heights (här′wŏŏd) vill., NE Illinois; 9,060.

Has·brouck Heights (haz′brŏŏk) boro., NE New Jersey; 13,651; ZIP see HACKENSACK.

Has·tings (hās′tingz) city, SW Michigan; 6,501; ZIP 49058.
— city, SE Minnesota; 12,195; ZIP 55033.
— city, S Nebraska; 23,580; ZIP 68901.

Has·tings-on-Hud·son (hās′tingz-on-hud′sən) vill., SE New York; 9,479; ZIP see YONKERS.

Hat·bor·o (hat′bûr′ō) boro., SE Pennsylvania; 8,880; ZIP 19040.

Hatboro West city, SE Pennsylvania; 13,542; ZIP 19040.

Hat·ties·burg (hat′iz-bûrg) city, SE Mississippi; 38,277; ZIP 39401*.

Haup·pauge (hou′pəj) city, SE New York; 13,957.

Haute·rive (ōt′rēv′) town, E Quebec, Canada; 11,366.

Ha·va·na (hə-van′ə) city, W Cuba; cap.; 1,008,500.

Have·lock (hav′lok′) city, SE North Carolina; 5,283; ZIP 28532.

Hav·er·ford (hav′ər-fərd) urb. twp., SE Pennsylvania; 55,732; ZIP 19041.

Ha·ver·hill (hā′vər-əl, -vril) city, NE Massachusetts; 46,120; ZIP 01830*.

Hav·er·straw (hav′ər-strô′) vill., SE New York; 8,199; ZIP 10927.

Hav·re (hav′ər) city, N Montana; 10,558; ZIP 59501.

Hav·re de Grace (hav′ər de gras′, gräs′) city, NE Maryland; 9,791; ZIP 21078.

Ha·wai·i (hə-wä′ē, hə-wī′yē) state of the United States, North Pacific; coextensive with the Hawaiian Islands; 6,435 sq. mi.; 769,913; cap. Honolulu. — largest of the Hawaiian Islands; 4,020 sq. mi.

Hawaiian Gardens city, S California; 8,811.

Hawkes·bur·y (hôks′ber′ē, -bûr′ē, -brē) town, SE Ontario, Canada; 9,188.

Haw·thorne (hô′thôrn) city, SW California; 53,304; ZIP 90250*.
— boro., NE New Jersey; 19,173; ZIP see PATERSON.

Hayes·ville (hāz′vil) city, NW Oregon; 5,518; ZIP 97301.

Hays (hāz) city, CEN. Kansas; 15,396; ZIP 67601*.

Hays·ville (hāz′vil) city, S Kansas; 6,483; ZIP 67060.

Hay·ward (hā′wərd) city, W California; 93,058; ZIP 94541.

Haz·ard (haz′ərd) city, SE Kentucky; 5,459; ZIP 41701.

Ha·zel Crest (hā′zəl) vill., NE Illinois; 10,329; ZIP 60429.

Hazel Park city, SE Michigan; 23,784; ZIP 48030.

Ha·zel·wood (hā′zəl-wŏŏd) vill., E Missouri; 14,082; ZIP 63042*.

Ha·zle·ton (hāz′əlt·n, hāz′əl·ten) city, E Pennsylvania; 30,462; ZIP 18201.

Healds·burg (hēldz′bûrg) city, W CEN. California; 5,438; ZIP 95448.

Heath (hēth) city, CEN. Ohio; 6,768; ZIP 43055.

Heb·ri·des (heb′ri-dēz) isl. group off W coast of Scotland; ab. 3,000 sq. mi.

Hei·del·berg (hīd′l-bûrg) city, SW West Germany; 125,445.

He·jaz (hē-jaz′, he-) div., W Saudi Arabia; 150,000 sq. mi.; 2 million; cap. Mecca.

Hel·en·a (hel′ə-nə) city, E Arkansas; 10,415; ZIP 72342.
— city, W CEN. Montana.; cap.; 22,730; ZIP 59601*.

Hel·i·con (hel′i-kon, -kən) mtn. range, E CEN. Greece.

Hel·ler·town (hel′ər-toun) boro., E Pennsylvania; 6,613; ZIP 18055.

Hel·les·pont (hel′əs-pont) the Dardanelles: *the ancient name.*

Hel·sin·ki (hel′sing-kē) city, S Finland; cap.; 496,193.

Hem·et (hem′it) city, S California; 12,252; ZIP 92343.

Hemp·field (hemp′fēld) urb. twp., SW Pennsylvania; 29,704.

Hemp·stead (hem′sted, hemp′-) vill., SE New York; 39,411; ZIP 11550*.

Hen·der·son (hen′dər·sən) city, NW Kentucky; 22,976; ZIP 42420.
— city, S Nevada; 16,395; ZIP 89015.
— city, N North Carolina; 13,896; ZIP 27536.
— city, E Texas; 10,187; ZIP 75652.

Hen·der·son·ville (hen′dər-sən-vil) city, W North Carolina; 6,443; ZIP 28739.

Hen·ry·et·ta (hen′rē-et′ə) city, E CEN. Oklahoma; 6,430; ZIP 74437.

Here·ford (hûr′fərd) city, NW Texas; 13,414; ZIP 79045.

Her·ki·mer (hûr′kə-mər) vill., CEN. New York; 8,960; ZIP 13350.

Her·mo·sa Beach (hər-mō′sə) city, SW California; 17,412; ZIP 90254.

Her·ricks (her′iks) city, SE New York; 9,112.

Her·rin (her′ən) city, S Illinois; 9,623; ZIP 62948.

Her·shey (hûr′shē) uninc. place, S CEN. Pennsylvania; 7,407; ZIP 17033.

Her·ze·go·vi·na (hûr′tsə-gō-vē′nə) See BOSNIA AND HERZE-GOVINA.

Hes·se (hes′ə) state, W West Germany; 8,150 sq. mi.; 4,703,000; cap. Wiesbaden.

Hew·lett (hyŏŏ′lit) city, SE New York; 6,796; ZIP 11557.

Hi·a·le·ah (hī′ə-lē′ə) city, SE Florida; site of a famous race-track; 102,297; ZIP 33010.

Hib·bing (hib′ing) vill., NE Minnesota; 16,104; ZIP 55746.

Hick·man Housing (hik′mən) city, S Oahu, Hawaii, 7,352; ZIP 96824.

Hick·o·ry (hik′ə-rē, hik′rē) city, W CEN. North Carolina; 20,569; ZIP 28601*.

Hickory Hills Village city, NE Illinois; 13,176; ZIP 60457.

Hicks·ville (hiks′vil) vill., SE New York; 48,075; ZIP 11800*.

High·land (hī′lənd) city, S CEN. California; 12,669; ZIP 92346.
— city, SW Illinois; 5,981; ZIP 62249.
— town, NW Indiana; 24,947; ZIP see HAMMOND.

Highland Heights city, N Ohio; 5,926; ZIP 44143.

Highland Park city, NE Illinois; 32,263; ZIP 60035*.
— city, SE Michigan; 35,444; ZIP see DETROIT.
— city, NE Pennsylvania; 5,500; ZIP 17044.
— boro., E New Jersey; 14,385; ZIP see NEW BRUNSWICK.
— town, N Texas; 10,133; ZIP 75205.

High·lands (hī′ləndz) mtn. reg., N and W Scotland.

Highland Springs city, SE Virginia; 7,345; ZIP 23075.

High Point city, N CEN. North Carolina; 63,204; ZIP 27260*.

Hights·town (hīts′toun) city, W CEN. New Jersey; 5,431; ZIP 08520.

Hill·crest (hil′krest′) city, SE New York; 5,357.

Hillcrest Heights uninc. place, S Maryland; 24,037.

Hill·grove (hil′grōv) uninc. place, SW California; 14,669.

Hil·liard (hil′yərd) vill., CEN. Ohio; 8,369; ZIP 43026.

Hills·boro (hilz′bûr′ō, -bûr′ə) city, S Ohio; 5,584; ZIP 45133.
— city, NW Oregon; 14,675; ZIP 97123*.

— city, NE CEN. Texas; 7,224; ZIP 76645.

Hills·bor·ough (hilz′bûr′ō, -bûr′ə) town, w California; 8,753; ZIP see BURLINGAME.

Hills·dale (hilz′dāl) city, s Michigan; 7,728; ZIP 49242.

— boro., NE New Jersey; 11.768; ZIP 07642.

Hill·side (hil′sīd) vill., NE Illinois; 8,888; ZIP see MELROSE PARK.

— urb. twp., NE New Jersey; 21,636; ZIP see ELIZABETH.

Hi·lo (hē′lō) city, E Hawaii, Hawaii; 26,353; ZIP 96720.

Hi·ma·la·yas (hi·mäl′yəz, -mä′lə·yəz, him′ə·lā′əz) mtn. range, CEN. Asia.

Hin·du·stan (hin′dŏŏ·stan′, -stän′) 1. loosely, the reg. of the Ganges where Hindi is spoken. 2. loosely, India.

Hing·ham (hing′əm) town, E Massachusetts; 18,845; ZIP 02043.

Hins·dale (hinz′dāl) vill., NE Illinois; 15,918; ZIP 60521*.

Hir·o·shi·ma (hir′ə·shē′mə, hi·rō′shē·mə) city, sw Honshu isl. Japan; devastated by the first atom bomb used in war, Aug. 6, 1945; 515,000.

His·pa·nio·la (his′pə·nyō′lə) isl., West Indies; ab. 30,000 sq. mi.; divided into Haiti and the Dominican Republic.

Hitch·cock (hich′kok) city, SE Texas; 5,565; ZIP 77563.

Hix·son (hik′sən) city, SE Tennessee; 6,188; ZIP 37343.

Ho·bart (hō′bərt, -bärt) city, SE Tasmania; cap.; 115,932.

Ho·bart (hō′bärt, -bərt) city, NW Indiana; 21,485; ZIP 46342.

Hobbs (hobz) city, SE New Mexico; 26,025; ZIP 88240.

Ho·bo·ken (hō′bō·kən) city, NE New Jersey; 45,380; ZIP 07030*.

Hoff·man Estates (hof′mən) city, NE Illinois; 22,238.

Hok·kai·do (hô·kī·dô) isl. of N Japan; ab. 29,000 sq. mi.

Hol·brook (hōl′brŏŏk′) city, E Massachusetts; 11,775; ZIP 02343.

— city, SE New York; 12,103.

Hol·den (hōl′dən) city, CEN. Massachusetts; 12,564; ZIP 02343.

Holden Heights city, NE Florida; 6,206.

Hol·den·ville (hōl′dən·vil) city, CEN. Oklahoma; 5,181; ZIP 74848.

Hold·redge (hōl′drij) city, s Nebraska; 5,635; ZIP 68949.

Hol·la·day (hol′ə·dā) city, NW Utah; 23,014; ZIP 84117.

Hol·land (hol′ənd) See NETHERLANDS.

Hol·land (hol′ənd) city, sw Michigan; 26,337; ZIP 49422*.

Hol·li·days·burg (hol′ə·dāz·bûrg′) boro., s CEN. Pennsylvania; 6,262; ZIP 16648.

Hol·lis·ter (hol′is·tər) city w California; 7,663; ZIP 95023.

Hol·lis·ton (hol′is·tən) city, NE Massachusetts; 12,069; ZIP 01746.

Hol·lo·man (hol′ə·mən) city, s CEN. New Mexico; 8,001.

Holly Hill city, NE Florida; 8,191; ZIP 32017.

Hol·ly Springs (hol′ē) city, N Mississippi; 5,728; ZIP 38635.

Hol·ly·wood (hol′ē·wŏŏd) city, SE Florida; 106,873; ZIP 33020*.

— area, NW Los Angeles, California, ctr. of US motion-picture industry; ZIP see LOS ANGELES.

Holt (hōlt) city, s CEN. Michigan; 6,980; ZIP 48842.

Hol·yoke (hol′yōk) city, W CEN. Massachusetts; 50,112; ZIP 01040*.

Holy Roman Empire empire, CEN. and W Europe; existed from 962–1806.

Home Acre·Lyn·do·ra (lin·dôr′ə, -dō′rə) city, NW Pennsylvania; 8,415.

Home Gardens city, SE California; 5,116; ZIP 91720.

Home·stead (hōm′sted) city, s Florida; 13,674; ZIP 33030*.

— boro., SW Pennsylvania; 6,309; ZIP 15120*.

Home·town (hōm′toun) city, NE Illinois; 6,729; ZIP see OAK LAWN.

Home·wood (hōm′wŏŏd) city, CEN. Alabama; 21,245; ZIP see BIRMINGHAM.

— vill., NE Illinois; 18,871; ZIP 60430.

Hon·do (hon′dō) city, s CEN. Texas; 5,487; ZIP 78861.

Hon·du·ras (hon·dŏŏr′əs, -dyŏŏr′-) republic, NE Central America; 43,277 sq. mi.; 1,950,000; cap. Tegucigalpa.

Hones·dale (hōnz′dāl) boro., NE Pennsylvania; 5,224; ZIP 18431.

Hong Kong (hong′kong′, hông′kông) British col., SE China; includes **Hong Kong Island** and some coastal terr.; 398 sq. mi.; 3 million; cap. Victoria.

Hon·o·lu·lu (hon′ə·lŏŏ′lŏŏ) port city, SE Oahu; cap. of Hawaii; 324,871; ZIP 96800*.

Hon·shu (hon·shŏŏ) isl. of CEN. Japan; 88,745; sq. mi.

Hood (hŏŏd), **Mount** volcanic peak, Cascade Range, NW Oregon; 11,245 ft.

Hook·sett (hŏŏk′set) city, SE New Hampshire; 5,564; ZIP 03106.

Hoope·ston (hŏŏp′stən) city, E Illinois; 6,461; ZIP 60942.

Hoo·ver Dam (hŏŏ·vər) dam, Colorado River at the Arizona-Nevada border; 727 ft. high; 1,282 ft. long.

Ho·pat·cong (hō·pat′kông) city, NW New Jersey; 9,052; ZIP 07843.

Hope (hōp) city, sw Arkansas; 8,810; ZIP 71801.

Hope·well (hōp′wel, -wəl) city, SE Virginia; 23,471; ZIP 23860.

Hop·kins (hop′kinz) city, SE Minnesota; 13,428; ZIP 55343.

Hop·kins·ville (hop′kinz·vil) city, sw Kentucky; 21,250; ZIP 42240.

Hop·kin·ton (hop′kin·tən) city, NE Massachusetts; 5,981; ZIP 01748.

— city, sw Rhode Island; 5,392; ZIP 02833.

Ho·qui·am (hō′kwim, hō′kwē·əm) city, W Washington; 10,466; ZIP 98550*.

Horn (hôrn), **Cape** s extremity of South America.

Hor·nell (hôr·nel′) city, sw New York; 12,144; ZIP 14843.

Horse·heads (hôrs′hedz′) vill., s New York; 7,989; ZIP 14845.

Hot Springs city, CEN. Arkansas; 35,631.

Hough·ton Village (hō′tən) city, NW Michigan; 6,067; ZIP 49931.

Houl·ton (hōlt′n, hōl′tən) uninc. place, E Maine; 8,111; ZIP 04730.

Hou·ma (hō′mə) city, SE Louisiana; 30,922; ZIP 70360*.

Hous·ton (hyŏŏs′tən) city, SE Texas; 1,232,802; ZIP 77000*.

How·ell (hou′əl) city, SE Michigan; 5,224; ZIP 48843.

Hub·bard (hub′ərd) vill., NE Ohio; 8,583; ZIP 44425.

Hu·ber (hyŏŏ′bər) city, sw Ohio; 18,943; ZIP 45424.

Hud·son (hud′sən) uninc. place, E CEN. Massachusetts; 16,084; ZIP 01749.

— city, SE New Hampshire; 10,638; ZIP 03051.

— city, E New York; 8,940; ZIP 12534.

— city, NW Wisconsin; 5,049; ZIP 54016.

Hudson Bay inland sea; N CEN. Canada; connected with the Atlantic by **Hudson Strait**; ab. 475,000 sq. mi.

Hudson Falls vill., E New York; 7,917; ZIP 12839.

Hudson River river, E New York; 306 mi. long.

Hu·ey·town (hyŏŏ′ē·toun) city, CEN. Alabama; 7,095; ZIP see BESSEMER.

Hu·go (hyŏŏ′gō) city, SE Oklahoma; 6,585; ZIP 74743.

Hull (hul) town, E Massachusetts; 9,961; ZIP 02045.

Hull (hul) city, sw Quebec, Canada; 60,176.

Hu·ma·cao (ŏŏ·mä·kou′) town, E Puerto Rico; 8,005.

Hum·boldt (hum′bolt) city, w Tennessee; 10,066; ZIP 38343.

Hun·ga·ry (hung′gə·rē) republic, CEN. Europe; 35,912 sq. mi.; 9,978,000; cap. Budapest.

Hunt·ing·don (hunt′ing·dən) boro., s CEN. Pennsylvania; 6,987; ZIP 16652*.

Hunt·ing·ton (hunt′ing·tən) city, NE Indiana; 16,217; ZIP 46750.

— uninc. place, SE New York; 12,130; ZIP 11743*.

— city, NE Virginia; 5,559.

— city, w West Virginia; 74,315; ZIP 25700*.

Huntington Beach city, sw California; 115,960; ZIP 94646*.

Huntington Park city, sw California; 33,744; ZIP 90255*.

Huntington Station uninc. place, SE New York; 28,817; ZIP 11746*.

Huntington Woods city, SE Michigan; 8,536; ZIP see ROYAL OAK.

Hunts·ville (hunts′vil, -vəl) city, N Alabama; 137,802; ZIP 35800*.

— city, E Texas; 17,610; ZIP 77340*.

Hur·on (hyŏŏ′rən) vill., N Ohio; 6,896; ZIP 44839.

— city, E CEN. South Dakota; 14,299; ZIP 57350.

Huron, Lake one of the Great Lakes; betw. Michigan and Ontario; 23,010 sq. mi.

Hurst (hûrst) city, N Texas; 27,215; ZIP 76053.

Hutch·in·son (huch′in·sən) city, CEN. Kansas; 36,885; ZIP 67501.

— city, s CEN. Minnesota; 8,031; ZIP 55350.

Hwang Ho (hwäng′ hō′) river, N China; 2,900 mi. long.

Hy·an·nis (hī·an′is) uninc. place, SE Massachusetts; 6,847; ZIP 02601*.

Hy·atts·ville (hī′əts·vil) city, w CEN. Maryland; 14,998; ZIP 20780*.

Hyde Park (hīd) public park, London, England.

Hyde Park (hīd) uninc. place, SE New York; site of the estate and grave of Franklin D. Roosevelt; 1,979; ZIP 12538.

Hy·der·a·bad (hī′dər·ə·bad′, -bäd′) city, s CEN. India; 1,250,000.

Hy·der·a·bad (hī′dər·ə·bad′, -bäd′) city, SE West Pakistan; 434,537.

I·ber·i·a (ī·bir′ē·ə) part of sw Europe containing Spain and Portugal.

I·ber·ville (ē′bər·vil) town, s Quebec, Canada; 8,400.

Ice·land (īs′lənd) isl., North Atlantic; a republic; 39,758 sq. mi.; 174,000; cap. Reykjavik.

I·da·bel (ī′də·bel) city, SE Oklahoma; 5,946; ZIP 74745.

I·da·ho (ī′də·hō) state, NW United States; 83,557 sq. mi.; 713,008; cap. Boise.
Idaho Falls city, SE Idaho; 36,776; ZIP 83401*.
If·ni (ēf′nē) Spanish overseas prov.; SW Morocco; 741 sq. mi.; 50,000; cap. Sidi Ifni.
Ijs·sel (ī′səl), **Lake** fresh-water lake, CEN. Netherlands; created by diking the Zuider Zee.
Il·i·on (il′ē·ən) vill., E CEN. New York; 9,808; ZIP 13357.
Il·lin·ois (il′ə·noi′, -noiz′) state, NE CEN. United States; 56,400 sq. mi.; 11,113,976; cap. Springfield.
Imperial Beach city, SW California; 20,244; ZIP 92032.
Imperial Valley agricultural reg., SE California.
In·de·pen·dence (in′di·pen′dəns) city, E Iowa; 5,910; ZIP 50644.
— city, SE Kansas; 10,347; ZIP 67301.
— city, W Missouri; 111,682; ZIP 64050*.
— vill., N Ohio; 7,034; ZIP see CLEVELAND.
In·di·a (in′dē·ə) republic of the Commonwealth of Nations; S Asia; 1,259,797 sq. mi.; 440,316,000; cap. New Delhi.
In·di·an·a (in′dē·an′ə) state, NE CEN. United States; 36,291 sq. mi.; 5,193,669; cap. Indianapolis.
— boro., W CEN. Pennsylvania; 16,100; ZIP 15701.
In·di·a·nap·o·lis (in′dē·ə·nap′ə·lis) city, CEN. Indiana; cap; 744,624; ZIP 46200*.
Indian Harbour Beach city, SE Florida; 5,371; ZIP 32935.
Indian Hill city, SW Ohio; 5,651; ZIP 45201.
Indian Ocean ocean betw. Africa, Asia, Australia, and Antarctica.
In·di·a·no·la (in′dē·ə·nō′lə) city, S CEN. Iowa; 8,852; ZIP 50125. — city, W Mississippi; 8,947; ZIP 38751.
In·dies (in′dēz) See EAST INDIES, INDIA, INDOCHINA, WEST INDIES.
In·di·o (in′dē·ō) city, SW California; 14,459; ZIP 92201*.
In·do·chi·na (in′dō·chī′nə) **1.** SE penin. of Asia. **2.** Cambodia, Laos, North and South Vietnam.
In·do·ne·sia (in′dō·nē′zhə, -shə) republic, SE Asia; comprises over 100 isls. of the Malay Archipelago; 735,268 sq. mi.; ab. 93 million; cap. Jakarta.
In·dus (in′dəs) river, Tibet, Kashmir, and West Pakistan; ab. 1,800 mi. long.
In·ger·soll (ing′gər·sol) town, S Ontario, Canada; 7,249.
In·gle·wood (ing′gəl·wŏod) city, SW California; 89,985; ZIP 90301*. — uninc. place, N CEN. Tennessee; 26,527.
Ink·ster (ingk′stər) vill., SE Michigan; 38,595; ZIP 48141.
Inner Mongolian Autonomous Region See MONGOLIA.
International Falls city, N Minnesota; 6,439; ZIP 56649.
In·ver Grove Heights (in′vər) city, SE Minnesota; 12,148; ZIP 55075.
In·wood (in′wŏod) uninc. place, SE New York; 8,433.
I·o·la (ī·ō′lə) city, SE Kansas; 6,493; ZIP 66749.
I·o·ni·a (ī·ō′nē·ə) city, CEN. Michigan; 6,361; ZIP 48846.
Ionian Sea part of the Mediterranean betw. Greece and Sicily.
I·o·wa (ī′ə·wə, ī′ə·wä) state, N CEN. United States; 56,280 sq. mi.; 2,825,041; cap. Des Moines.
Iowa City city, E Iowa; 46,850; ZIP 52240*.
Iowa Falls city, CEN. Iowa; 6,454; ZIP 50126.
Iowa Park city, NW Texas; 5,796; ZIP 76367.
Ip·swich (ip′swich) city, NE Massachusetts; 10,750; ZIP 01938.
I·ran (i·ran′, ē·rän′) country, SW Asia; ab. 630,000 sq. mi.; 20,678,000; cap. Teheran.
I·raq (i·rak′, ē·räk′) republic, SW Asia; 171,599 sq. mi.; 7,250,000; cap. Baghdad.
Ire·land (īr′lənd) westernmost of the British Isles; 31,838 sq. mi. — republic, S Ireland; 26,600 sq. mi.; 2,815,000; cap. Dublin. See NORTHERN IRELAND.
Irish Sea part of the Atlantic betw. Great Britain and Ireland.
Ir·kutsk (ir·kōotsk′) city, S USSR; 397,000.
I·ron·de·quoit (i·ron′də·kwoit, -kwot) city, W New York; 63,675; ZIP 14617.
Iron Mountain city, NW Michigan; 8,702; ZIP 49801*.
I·ron·ton (ī′ərn·tən) city, S Ohio; 15,030; ZIP 45638.
I·ron·wood (ī′ərn·wŏod) city, NW Michigan; 8,711; ZIP 49938.
Ir·ra·wad·dy (ir′ə·wä′dē) river, Tibet and Burma; 1,200 mi. long.
Ir·ving (ûr′ving) city, N Texas; 97,260; ZIP 75060*.
Ir·ving·ton (ûr′ving·tən) town, NE New Jersey; 59,743; ZIP see NEWARK.
— vill., SE New York; 5,878; ZIP 10533.
I·sa·bel·la (ē′sä·vä′lä, iz′ə·bel′ə) town, NW Puerto Rico; 7,302; ZIP 00662*.
Ish·pe·ming (ish′pə·ming) city, NW Michigan; 8,245; ZIP 49849.
Is·lam·a·bad (iz·läm′ə·bäd) city, NE Pakistan; cap.; 50,000.
Island Park city, SE New York; 5,396; ZIP 11558.
Is·la Vis·ta (ī′lə vis′tə) city, SW California; 13,441; ZIP 93017.

I·slip (ī′slip) city, SE New York; 7,692; ZIP 11751.
Is·ra·el (iz′rē·əl) republic, E end of the Mediterranean; 7,993 sq. mi.; 2,241,000; cap. Jerusalem.
Is·tan·bul (is′tan·bōōl′) city, NE Turkey; 1,750,642.
It·a·ly (it′ə·lē) republic, S Europe; 116,286 sq. mi.; 50,464,-000; cap. Rome.
Ith·a·ca (ith′ə·kə) isl. of Greece; Ionian Sea; 36 sq. mi.
Ith·a·ca (ith′ə·kə) city, CEN. New York; 26,226; ZIP 14850.
Ivory Coast republic of the French Community, W Africa; 128,364 sq. mi.; 3,300,000; cap. Abidjan.
I·vy·wild (ī′vē·wild) uninc. place, E CEN. Colorado; 12,000.
Iz·mir (ēz·mir′) Smyrna: *the Turkish name.*

Ja·cin·to City (jə·sin′tō) city, SE Texas; 9,563; ZIP see HOUSTON.
Jack·son (jak′sən) city, SW Alabama; 5,957; ZIP 36545.
— city, S Michigan; 45,484; ZIP 49201*.
— city, S CEN. Mississippi; cap.; 153,968; ZIP 39200*.
— city, SE Missouri; 5,896; ZIP 63755.
— city, S Ohio; 6,843; ZIP 45640.
— city, W Tennessee; 39,996; ZIP 38301*.
Jack·son·ville (jak′sən·vil, -vəl) city, E Alabama; 7,715; ZIP 36265.
— city, CEN. Arkansas; 19,832; ZIP 72076*.
— city, NE Florida; 528,865; ZIP 32200*.
— city, W CEN. Illinois; 20,553; ZIP 62650*.
— city, E North Carolina; 16,021; ZIP 28540*.
— city, E Texas; 9,734; ZIP 75766.
Jacksonville Beach city, NE Florida; 12,049; ZIP 32050.
Jacques-Car·tier (zhàk·kár·tyā′) city, S Quebec, Canada; 52,527.
Jaf·fa (jaf′ə, yaf′ə) port, W Israel; part of Tel Aviv.
Ja·kar·ta (jä·kär′tä) city, NW Java; cap. of Indonesia; 2,922,000.
Ja·mai·ca (jə·mā′kə) independent member of the Commonwealth of Nations, isl. of the Greater Antilles; 4,411 sq. mi.; 1,607,000; cap. Kingston.
James·town (jāmz′toun) town, NW St. Helena; cap.; ab. 1,600.
James·town (jāmz′toun) city, SW New York; 39,795; ZIP 14701.
— city, SE CEN. North Dakota; 15,385; ZIP 58401.
— restored vill., E Virginia; site of the first English settlement in the present limits of the United States, 1607; ZIP 23081.
Jam·mu and Kash·mir (jum′ōō, kosh′mir, kash·mir′) state, N India; subject of a territorial dispute with Pakistan; 86,024 sq. mi.; 4,750,000; caps. Srinagar and Jammu.
Janes·ville (jānz′vil) city, S Wisconsin; 46,426; ZIP 53545*.
Ja·pan (jə·pan′) constitutional empire; E Asia; situated on a chain of isls.; 142,720 sq. mi.; 93,407,000; cap. Tokyo.
Japan, Sea of part of the Pacific betw. Japan and the Asian mainland.
Jas·per (jas′pər) city, NW CEN. Alabama; 10,798; ZIP 35501.
— city, S Indiana; 8,641; ZIP 47546.
— city, E Texas; 6,251; ZIP 75951.
Ja·va (jä′və, jav′ə) isl. of Indonesia; SE of Sumatra; 48,842 sq. mi.
Jean·er·ette (jen′ər·et′) town, S Louisiana; 6,322; ZIP 70544.
Jean·nette (jə·net′) city, SW Pennsylvania; 15,209; ZIP 15644.
Jef·fer·son (jef′ər·sən) boro., S Pennsylvania; 8,512; ZIP 15344.
— city, NE Virginia; 25,432.
Jefferson City city, CEN. Missouri; cap.; 32,407; ZIP 65101*.
— city, SE Tennessee; 5,124; ZIP 37760.
— city, SE Wisconsin; 5,429; ZIP 53549.
Jefferson Heights uninc. place, SE Louisiana; 16,489.
Jef·fer·son·town (jef′ər·sən·toun′) city, NW Kentucky; 9,701; ZIP 40299.
Jefferson Trooper city, SE Pennsylvania; 13,022.
Jefferson Valley city, SE New York; 9,008.
Jef·fer·son·ville (jef′ər·sən·vil) city, SE Indiana; 20,008; ZIP 47130*.
Jen·i·son (jen′i·sən) city, SW Michigan; 11,266; ZIP 49428.
Jen·kin·town (jeng′kin·toun) boro., SE Pennsylvania; 5,990; ZIP 19046.
Jen·nings (jen′ingz) city, SW Louisiana; 11,783; ZIP 70546.
— city, E Missouri; 19,379; ZIP see SAINT LOUIS.
Jer·i·cho (jer′i·kō) vill., W Jordan; on the site of the ancient city.
Jer·i·cho (jer′i·kō) uninc. place, SE New York; 14,010; ZIP 11753.
Jer·sey (jûr′zē) one of the Channel Islands; 45 sq. mi.
Jer·sey City (jûr′zē) city, NE New Jersey; 260,545; ZIP 07300*.
Jersey Shore boro., N CEN. Pennsylvania; 5,322; ZIP 17740.
Jer·sey·ville (jûr′zē·vil) city, W Illinois; 7,446; ZIP 62052.
Je·ru·sa·lem (ji·rōō′sə·ləm, -lem) city, on the Israel-Jordan border; Israeli Sector; cap.; 160,000; Jordanian sector; 46,000.

Jes·up (jes′əp) city, SE Georgia; 9,091; ZIP 31545.
Jid·da (jid′ə) city, W Saudi Arabia; ab. 160,000.
Jim Thorpe (jim thôrp) boro., E Pennsylvania; 5,456; ZIP 18229.
Jof·fa·towne (jof′ə·toun) city, NE Maryland; 9,092; ZIP 21101.
Jo·han·nes·burg (jō·han′is·burg, jə-, yō·hän′is-) city, NE South Africa; cap.; 1,097,000.
John·son City (jon′sən) vill., S New York; 18,025; ZIP 13790.
— city, NE Tennessee; 33,770; ZIP 37601.
John·ston (jon′stən) town, NE Rhode Island; 22,037.
Johns·town (jonz′toun) city, E CEN. New York; 10,045; ZIP 12095.
— city, SW CEN. Pennsylvania; 42,476; ZIP 15901*.
Jo·hore (jə·hôr′, -hōr′) state, S Malaya; 7,330 sq. mi.; 1,010,000; cap. Johore Baru.
Jo·li·et (jō′lē·et′) city, NE Illinois; 80,378; ZIP 60431*.
Jo·liette (zhō·lyet′) city, S Quebec, Canada; 19,188.
Jones·bor·o (jōnz′bûr′ō, -ə) city, NE Arkansas; 27,050; ZIP 72401.
— city, NE Louisiana; 5,072; ZIP 71251.
Jon·quiere (zhôn·kyâr′) city, S CEN. Quebec, Canada; 29,633.
Jop·lin (jop′lən) city, SW Missouri; 39,256; ZIP 64801*.
Jor·dan (jôr′dən) constitutional monarchy, betw. Israel, Iraq, Saudi Arabia, and Syria; 37,300 sq. mi.; 1,690,000; cap. Amman.
Jordan River river, CEN. Palestine; over 200 mi. long.
Jun·cos (hŏŏng′kōs) town, E Puerto Rico; 6,247; ZIP 00666.
Junction City city, E CEN. Kansas; 19,018; ZIP 66441.
Ju·neau (jōō′nō) city, SE Alaska; cap.; 6,050; ZIP 99801.
Jung·frau (yŏŏng′frou) mtn. peak, S CEN. Switzerland; 13,653 ft.
Ju·ra Mountains (jŏŏr′ə) mtn. range, E France and W Switzerland.
Justice Village city, NE Illinois; 9,473; ZIP 60453.
Jut·land (jut′lənd) penin., N Europe; comprises continental Denmark and part of Germany.

Ka·bul (kä′bəl) city, E CEN. Afghanistan; cap.; 449,000.
Ka·hu·lu·i (kä′hŏŏ·lōō′ē) city, NW Maui, Hawaii; 8,280; ZIP 96732.
Ka·i·lu·a-La·ni·kai (kä′ē·lōō′ə·lä′nē·kī′) uninc. place, E Oahu, Hawaii, 33,783; ZIP 96734.
Kal·a·ma·zoo (kal′ə·mə·zōō′) city, SW Michigan; 85,555; ZIP 49001*.
Ka·li·nin·grad (kä·lē′nin·grad) city, extreme W USSR; 270,000.
Kal·i·spell (kal′i·spel′ -spel′) city, NW Montana; 10,526; ZIP 59901*.
Kam·chat·ka (kam·chat′kə) penin., E USSR, betw. the Bering and Okhotsk Seas.
Kam·loops (kam′lōōps) city, S British Columbia, Canada; 10,759.
Kam·pu·che·a (kam·pōō·chē′ə, -sē′ə) country, SW Indochina penin.; 69,844 sq. mi.; 8,890,000; cap. Phnom Penh.
Kane (kān) boro., N Pennsylvania; 5,001; ZIP 16735.
Ka·ne·o·he (kä′nā·ō′hā) uninc. place, E Oahu, Hawaii; 29,903; ZIP 96744.
Kan·ka·kee (kang′kə·kē) city, NE Illinois; 30,944; ZIP 60901.
Kan·nap·o·lis (kə·nap′ə·lis) uninc. place, S CEN. North Carolina; 36,293; ZIP 28081.
Kan·sas (kan′zəs) state, CEN. United States; 82,276 sq. mi.; 2,249,071; cap. Topeka.
Kansas City city, NE Kansas; 168,213; ZIP 66100*.
— city, W Missouri; 507,087; ZIP 64100*.
Kap·lan (kap′lən) town, S Louisiana; 5,540; ZIP 70548.
Kap·us·ka·sing (kap′əs·kā′sing, -zing) town, CEN. Ontario, Canada; 12,617.
Ka·ra·chi (kə·rä′chē) city, S Pakistan; former cap.; 1,912,-598.
Ka·re·li·an ASSR (kə·rē′lē·ən, -rē′lyən) adm. div., NW RSFSR; 66,560 sq. mi.; 651,000; cap. Petrozhavodsk.
Kar·nak (kär′nak) vill., S Egypt; near the site of ancient Thebes.
Kash·mir (kash′mir, kazh′-) See JAMMU AND KASHMIR.
Kat·man·du (kät′män·dōō′) city, CEN. Nepal; cap.; 122,507.
Kat·te·gat (kat′ə·gat) strait of the North Sea betw. Sweden and Jutland.
Kau·ai (kou′ī) one of the Hawaiian Islands; 551 sq. mi.
Kau·kau·na (kô·kô′nə) city, E Wisconsin; 11,292; ZIP 54130*.
Kau·nas (kou′näs) city, S CEN. Lithuanian SSR; 214,000.
Kays·ville (kāz′vil) city, NW Utah; 6,192; ZIP 84037.
Ka·zakh SSR (kä·zäk′) constituent republic, S CEN. USSR; 1,064,000 sq. mi.; 9,310,000; cap. Alma-Ata.
Ka·zan (kə·zäny′) city, NW Tatar ASSR; cap.; 643,000.

Keans·burg (kēnz′bûrg) boro., E New Jersey; 9,720; ZIP 07734.
Kear·ney (kär′nē) city, S CEN. Nebraska; 19,181; ZIP 68847.
Kearns (kûrnz, kärnz) uninc. place, N Utah; 17,071; ZIP see SALT LAKE CITY.
Kear·ny (kär′nē) town, NE New Jersey; 37,585; ZIP 07032.
Keene (kēn) city, SW New Hampshire; 20,467; ZIP 03431.
Kei·zer (kī′zər) uninc. place, NW Oregon; 11,405; ZIP see SALEM.
Ke·low·na (ki·lō′nə) city, S British Columbia, Canada; 17,006.
Kel·so (kel′sō) city, SW Washington; 10,296; ZIP 98626.
Kemp Mill (kemp) city, NE Maryland; 10,037.
Ken·dall (ken′dəl) city, SE Florida; 35,479; ZIP 33156.
— city, NE New Jersey; 7,412; ZIP 08824.
Ken·dall·ville (ken′dəl·vil) city, NE Indiana; 6,838; ZIP 46755.
Ken·il·worth (ken′əl·wûrth) boro., NE New Jersey; 9,165; ZIP 07033.
Ken·more (ken′môr) vill., W New York; 20,980; ZIP see BUFFALO.
Ken·ne·bunk (ken′ə·bungk) city, SW Maine; 5,646; ZIP 04043.
Ken·ne·dy (ken′ə·dē) **Cape** cape, E Florida (ZIP 32920); site of the **John F. Kennedy Space Center,** a space research and missiles installation.
Ken·ner (ken′ər) city, SE Louisiana; 29,858; ZIP 70062.
Ken·nett (ken′et, -it, -ət) city, SE Missouri; 9,852.
Ken·ne·wick (ken′ə·wik) city, S Washington; 15,212; ZIP 99336.
Ken·og·a·mi (ken·og′ə·mē) city, S CEN. Quebec, Canada; 11,534.
Ke·nor·a (kə·nôr′ə) town, W Ontario, Canada; 11,295.
Ke·no·sha (kə·nō′shə) city, SE Wisconsin; 78,805; ZIP 53140*.
Ken·sing·ton (ken′sing·tən) city, W CEN. California; 5,823; ZIP 94701.
Kent (kent) co., SE England; 1,525 sq. mi.; 171,000; cap. Maidstone.
Kent (kent) city, NE Ohio; 28,183; ZIP 44240*.
— city, W CEN. Washington; 21,510; ZIP 98031.
Kent·land (kent′lənd) city, SW Maryland; 9,649.
Ken·ton (kent′n, ken′tən) city, W CEN. Ohio; 8,315; ZIP 43326.
Ken·tuck·y (kən·tuk′ē) state, E CEN. United States; 40,395; sq. mi.; 3,219,311; cap. Frankfort.
Kentucky River river, N Kentucky; 259 mi. long.
Kent·wood (kent′wŏŏd′) city, SW Michigan; 20,310; ZIP 49508.
Ken·wood (ken′wŏŏd′) city, SW Ohio; 15,789.
Ken·ya (kēn′yə, ken′-) Independent member of the Commonwealth of Nations, E Africa; 224,960 sq. mi.; 6,550,000; cap. Nairobi.
Ke·o·kuk (kē′ə·kuk′) city, SE Iowa; 14,631; ZIP 52632.
Ker·mit (kûr′mit) city, W Texas; 7,884; ZIP 79745.
Kerr·ville (kûr′vil) city, S CEN. Texas; 12,672; ZIP 78028.
Ketch·i·kan (kech′i·kan) town, SE Alaska; 6,994; ZIP 99901*.
Ket·ter·ing (ket′ər·ing) city, SW Ohio; 69,599; ZIP see DAYTON.
Ke·wa·nee (kē·wä′nē) city, NW Illinois; 15,762; ZIP 61443
Key·port (kē′pôrt, -pōrt) boro., E New Jersey; 7,205; ZIP 07735.
Key·ser (kī′zər) city, NE West Virginia; 6,586; ZIP 26726.
Key West southwesternmost of the Florida Keys. — city, Key West Island; 27,563; ZIP 33040*.
Khar·kov (kär′kôf) city, NE Ukrainian SSR; 930,000.
Khar·toum (kär·tōōm′) city, CEN. Sudan; cap.; 250,000.
Khy·ber Pass (kī′bər) mtn. pass betw. Afghanistan and Pakistan; ab. 30 mi. long.
Kiel (kēl) city, N West Germany; 270,700.
Kiel Canal ship canal betw. Kiel and the mouth of the Elbe; ab. 61 mi. long.
Ki·ev (kē·ev′, kē′ev) city, N CEN. Ukrainian SSR; cap.; 1,104,000.
Ki·lau·e·a (kē′lou·ā′ə) active crater, Mauna Loa volcano, Hawaii.
Kil·gore (kil′gôr, -gōr) city, NE Texas; 9,495; ZIP 75662.
Kil·i·man·ja·ro (kil′ē·män·jär′ō) **Mount** mtn., NE Tanzania; highest in Africa; 19,565 ft.
Kil·lar·ney (ki·lär′nē) urb. dist., SW Ireland; ab. 6,300.
Killarney, Lakes of three small lakes near Killarney.
Kil·leen (ki·lēn′) city, CEN. Texas; 35,507; ZIP 76540*.
Kil·ling·ly (kil′ing·lē) city, NE Connecticut; 13,573; ZIP 06241.
Kim·ber·ley (kim′bər·lē) city, CEN. South Africa; 77,000.
Kim·ber·ley (kim′bər·lē) city, SE British Columbia, Canada; 6,013.

Kim·ber·ly (kim′bər-lē) vill., E Wisconsin; 6,131; ZIP 54136.
Kin·che·loe (kin′chə-lō) city, NE Michigan; 6,331.
King·man (king′mən) city, NW Arizona; 7,312; ZIP 86701.
Kings·ford (kingz′fərd) city, NW Michigan; 5,276. ZIP see IRON MOUNTAIN.
Kings Mountain city, SW North Carolina; 8,465; ZIP 28086.
Kings Park (kingz) city, SE New York; 5,555; ZIP 11754.
Kings Point vill., SE New York; 5,525; ZIP see GREAT NECK.
Kings·port (kingz′pôrt, -pōrt) city, NE Tennessee; 31,938; ZIP 37660*.
Kingsport North city, NE Tennessee; 13,118.
Kings·ton (kingz′tən, king′stən) city, SE Jamaica; cap.; 126,000.
Kings·ton (king′stən, kingz′tən) city, NE Massachusetts; 5,999; ZIP 02360.
— city, SE New York; 25,554; ZIP 12401.
— boro., NE CEN. Pennsylvania; 18,325 ZIP see WILKES-BARRE.
— city, SW Rhode Island; 5,601; ZIP 02881.
Kings·ton (kingz′tən, king′stən) city, SE Ontario, Canada; 59,004.
Kings·ville (kingz′vil, -vəl) city, S Texas; 28,711; ZIP 78363*.
Kin·loch (kin′lok) city, E Missouri; 5,629; ZIP see SAINT LOUIS.
Kin·ne·lon (kin′ə-lon) city, N New Jersey; 7,600; ZIP 07405.
Kin·sha·sa (kēn-shä′sä) city, W Zaire Republic; cap.; 402,000.
Kin·ston (kin′stən) city, SE CEN. North Carolina; 22,309; ZIP 28501.
Kir·ghiz SSR (kir-gēz′) constituent republic, S USSR; 76,640 sq. mi.; 2,066,000; cap. Frunze.
Kirk·land (kûrk′lənd) city, W CEN. Washington; 15,249; ZIP 98033.
Kirks·ville (kûrks′vil, -vəl) city, N Missouri; 15,560; ZIP 63501.
Kirk·wood (kûrk′wood) city, E Missouri; 31,890; ZIP see SAINT LOUIS.
Kirt·land (kûrt′lənd) city, NE Ohio; 5,530; ZIP 44094.
K I Saw·yer (kā ī sô′yər) city, NW Michigan; 6,679.
Kis·sim·mee (ki-sim′ē) city, CEN. Florida; 7,119; ZIP 32741.
Kitch·e·ner (kich′ə-nər) city, S Ontario, Canada; 93,255.
Kit·tan·ning (ki-tan′ing) boro., W Pennsylvania; 6,231; ZIP 16201.
Kit·ter·y (kit′ər-ē) uninc. place, SW Maine; 11,028; ZIP 03904.
Kitty Hawk vill., NE North Carolina; site of the first sustained airplane flight, by Wilbur and Orville Wright, 1903.
Klam·ath Falls (klam′əth) city, S Oregon; 15,775; ZIP 97601*.
Klon·dike (klon′dīk) reg., NW Canada in the basin of the Klondike River.
Knoll·wood (nōl′wood) city, SW Ohio; 5,513.
Knox·ville (noks′vil, -vəl) city, S CEN. Iowa; 7,775; ZIP 50138.
— city, E Tennessee; 174,578; ZIP 37900*.
Ko·be (kō′bē) city, S Japan; 1,086,000.
Ko·di·ak Island (kō′dē-ak) isl., S Alaska.
Ko·ko·mo (kō′kə-mō) city, N CEN. Indiana; 44,042; ZIP 46901*.
Kö·nigs·berg (kœ′nikhs-berkh) Kaliningrad: the former German name.
Ko·re·a (kō-rē′ə, kō-) penin., E Asia; 85,266 sq. mi.; divided into the Democratic People's Republic of Korea (North Korea); 46,812 sq. mi.; 8,430,000; cap. Pyongyang; and the Republic of Korea (South Korea); 38,542 sq. mi.; 26,106,-000; cap. Seoul.
Korea Strait strait, betw. the Sea of Japan and the East China Sea.
Kos·ci·us·ko (kos′ē-us′kō) city, CEN. Mississippi; 7,266; ZIP 39090.
Kras·no·dar (kraz′nə-där) city, SW USSR; 312,000.
Kron·stadt (krōn-shtät′) city, W USSR; 59,000.
Kua·la Lum·pur (kwä′lə loom′poor) city, CEN. Malaya; cap. of Malaya and Malaysia; 315,000.
Kun·ming (koon′ming′) city, SW China; 900,000.
Kur·di·stan (kûr′di·stan, koor′di·stän) reg., NW Iran, NE Iraq, and SE Turkey; peopled largely by Kurds.
Ku·re (koo′re) city, SW Japan; 209,000.
Ku·rile Islands (koo′ril, koo-rēl′) isl. group, SE USSR; 5,700 sq. mi.
Kutz·town (kutz′toun) city, SE Pennsylvania; 6,017; ZIP 19530.
Ku·wait (koo-wīt′) shiekdom, NE Arabia; 5,000 sq. mi.; 322,000. — city, E Kuwait; cap.; 151,000.
Kyo·to (kyō-tō) city, SW Japan; 1,285,000.
Kyu·shu (kyoo-shoo) isl., S Japan; 16,247 sq. mi.

Lab·ra·dor (lab′rə-dôr) terr., Newfoundland, Canada; ab. 110,000 sq. mi.; 10,750.

— the penin. of North America betw. the St. Lawrence River and Hudson Bay.
La Ca·na·da-Flint·ridge (lä kə-nä′də-flint′rij) uninc. place, SW California; 20,652.
La·cey (lā′sē) uninc. place, W CEN. Washington; 9,696; ZIP 98553.
La·chine (lə-shēn′) city, S Quebec, Canada; 34,155.
La·chute (lə-shoot′) town, SW Quebec, Canada; 10,215.
Lack·a·wan·na (lak′ə-won′ə) city, W New York; 28,657; ZIP see BUFFALO.
Lac-Mé·gan·tic (läk-mä-gän-tek′) town, S Quebec, Canada; 6,958.
La·co·ni·a (lə-kō′nē-ə, -kō′nyə) city, CEN. New Hampshire; 14,888; ZIP 03246.
La Crosse (lə krôs′, kros′) city, W Wisconsin; 51,153; ZIP 54601*.
La·der·a Heights (lä-dâr′ə) city, SW California; 6,079.
La·do·ga (lä′də-gə), Lake lake, NW RSFSR; 7,100 sq. mi.
La·drone Islands (lə-drōn′) Marianas Islands: the former name.
La·due (lə-doo′) city, E Missouri; 10,491; ZIP 64758.
La·fay·ette (läf′ē-et′) uninc. place, W California; 20,484; ZIP 94549.
La·fay·ette (lä′fē-et′, laf′ē-et′) city, W CEN. Indiana; 44,955; ZIP 47901*.
La·fay·ette (lä′fā-et′) city, S Louisiana; 68,908; ZIP 70501*.
La Fay·ette (lə fä′it) city, NW Georgia; 6,044; ZIP 30728.
La·fay·ette Hills (laf′ē-et′) city, SE Pennsylvania; 8,263.
La·fleche (lä-flesh′) town, S Quebec, Canada; 13,433.
La Fol·lette (lə fol′it) city, NE Tennessee; 6,902; ZIP 37766.
La·gos (lä′gōs, lā′-) city, SW Nigeria; cap.; 364,000.
La Grande (lä grand′) city, NE Oregon; 9,645; ZIP 97850*.
La Grange (lə gränj′) city, W Georgia; 23,301; ZIP 30240.
— vill., NE Illinois; 16,773; ZIP 60525*.
La Grange Highlands city, NE Illinois; 6,920.
La Grange Park vill., NE Illinois; 15,626; ZIP see LA GRANGE.
La Grange Village city, NE Illinois; 16,773; ZIP 60525.
La·gu·na Beach (lə-goo′nə) city, SW California; 14,550; ZIP 92651*.
Laguna Hills city, SW California; 13,676; ZIP 92653.
La Ha·ba·na (lä hä-vä′nä) Havana: the Spanish name.
La Hab·ra (lə häb′rə) city, SW California; 41,350; ZIP 90631*.
La·hore (lə-hôr′, -hōr) city, E West Pakistan; 1,297,000.
La Jun·ta (lə hoon′tə, hun′tə) city, SE Colorado; 7,938; ZIP 81050.
Lake Bar·croft (bär′krôft′, -kroft′) city, NE Virginia; 11,605.
Lake Car·roll (kar′əl) city, SW Florida; 5,577; ZIP 33601.
Lake Charles city, SW Louisiana; 77,998; ZIP 70601*.
Lake City city, N Florida; 10,757; ZIP 32055.
— town, E CEN. South Carolina; 6,247; ZIP 29560.
Lake District reg., NW England; contains 15 lakes.
Lake Forest city, NE Illinois; 15,642; ZIP 60045.
Lake Grove city, SE New York; 8,133.
Lake Hi·a·wath·a (hī-ə-wäth′ə) city, N New Jersey; 11,389; ZIP 07034.
Lake Hol·lo·way (hol′ə-wā) city, CEN. Florida; 6,227.
Lake Jack·son (jak′sən) city, SE Texas; 13,376; ZIP 77566.
Lake·land (lāk′lənd) city, CEN. Florida; 41,550; ZIP 33801.
Lake Mag·da·lene (mag-də-lēn′) city, SW Florida; 9,266; ZIP 33601.
Lake Mo·hawk (mō′hôk′) city, NW New Jersey; 6,262; ZIP 07871.
Lake Os·we·go (oz-wē′gō) city, NW Oregon; 14,573; ZIP 97034.
Lake Park city, SE Florida; 6,993; ZIP 33403.
Lake Par·sip·pa·ny (pär-sip′ə-nē) city, N New Jersey; 7,488.
Lake Prov·i·dence (prov′ə-dəns) town, NE Louisiana; 6,183; ZIP 71254.
Lakes District city, W CEN. Washington; 48,195.
Lake·side (lāk′sīd′) city, SW California; 11,991.
Lake·view (lāk′vyoo′) uninc. place, S Michigan; 11,391; ZIP 48850.
— city, SE New York; 5,471.
— city, SE Virginia; 11,137.
— See WEST HEMPSTEAD-LAKEVIEW.
Lake·ville (lāk′vil) city, SE Minnesota; 7,556; ZIP 55044.
Lake Wales (wālz′) city, CEN. Florida; 8,240; ZIP 33853.
Lake·wood (lāk′wood) city, SW California; 82,973; ZIP 90712*.
— uninc. place, CEN. Colorado; 92,787; ZIP see DENVER.
— uninc. place, E New Jersey; 17,874; ZIP 08701.
— city, N Ohio; 70,173; ZIP see CLEVELAND.
Lake Worth city, SE Florida; 23,714; ZIP 33460.
La·mar (lə-mär′) city, SE Colorado; 7,797; ZIP 81052.
La·marque (lə-märk′) city, SE Texas; 16,131; ZIP 77568.
Lam·bert·ville (lam′bûrt·vil) city, SE Michigan; 5,721; ZIP 48144.
La Me·sa (lə mā′sə) city, SW California; 39,178; ZIP 92041*.

La·me·sa (lə-mē′sə) city, NW Texas; 11,559; ZIP 79331.
La Mir·an·da (lä mi-ran′də) city, SW California; 30,808; ZIP 90638.
La·mont (lə-mont′) uninc. place, SW California; 7,007; ZIP 93241.
Lam·pas·as (lam-pas′əs) city, CEN. Texas; 5,922; ZIP 76550.
Lan·ca·shire (lang′kə-shir) co., NW England; 1,878 sq. mi.; 5,132,000; cap. Lancaster.
Lan·cas·ter (lan′kas′tər, lang′-) uninc. place, SW California; 30,948; ZIP 93534*.
Lan·cas·ter (lan′kas′tər) city, CEN. Massachusetts; 6,095; ZIP 01523.
  — vill., W New York; 13,365; ZIP 14086.
Lan·cas·ter (lan′kas′tər, lang′-) city, S CEN. Ohio; 32,911; ZIP 43130*.
Lan·cas·ter (lang′kis·tər) city, SE Pennsylvania; 57,690; ZIP 17600*.
  — town, N CEN. South Carolina; 9,186; ZIP 29720.
Lan·cas·ter (lang′kas′tər) city, N Texas; 10,522; ZIP 75146.
Lan·cas·ter (lang′kəs·tər) city, SE New Brunswick, Canada; 15,836.
Lan·chow (lan′chou′) city, NW China; 732,000.
Lan·der (lan′dər) city, NW Wyoming; 7,125; ZIP 82520.
Lan·do·ver (lan′dō·vər) city, SW Maryland; 6,597; ZIP 20785.
La·nett (lə·net′) city, E Alabama; 6,908; ZIP 36863.
Lang·ley Park (lang′lē) uninc. place, W CEN. Maryland; 11,564; ZIP see HYATTSVILLE.
Lan·ham-Sea·brook (län′əm-sē′brŏŏk′) city, SW Maryland; 13,244; ZIP 20801.
Lanikai See KAILUA-LANIKAI.
Lans·dale (lanz′dāl) boro., SE Pennsylvania; 18,451; ZIP 19446.
Lans·downe (lanz′doun) boro., SE Pennsylvania; 14,090; ZIP 19050*.
Lansdowne-Baltimore Highlands uninc. place, N CEN. Maryland; 16,976.
Lans·ford (lans′fərd, lanz′-) boro., E Pennsylvania; 5,168; ZIP 18232.
Lan·sing (lan′sing) vill., NE Illinois; 25,805; ZIP 60438.
  — city, S CEN. Michigan; cap.; 131,546; ZIP 48900*.
Lan·tan·a (lan-tan′ə) town, SE Florida; 7,126; ZIP see LAKE WORTH.
La·os (lä′os, lä′ōs, lous) constitutional monarchy, NW Indochina; 91,428 sq. mi.; 1,850,000; cap. Vientiane; royal residence Luang Prabang.
La Pal·ma (lə päl′mə) city, SW California; 9,687.
La Paz (lä päz) city, W Bolivia; de facto cap.; 347,000.
La·peer (lə·pir′) city, E Michigan; 6,270; ZIP 48446.
La·peer Heights (lə·pir′) city, SE Michigan; 7,130; ZIP 48446.
La·place (lə·pläs′) city, SE Louisiana; 5,953; ZIP 70068.
Lap·land (lap′land) reg., N Norway, Sweden, and Finland, and the NE USSR; inhabited by Lapps.
La Pla·ta (lä plä′tä) city, E Argentina; 357,000.
La Porte (lə pôrt′, pōrt′) city, NW Indiana; 22,140; ZIP 46350*.
La Porte (lä pōrt) city, E Texas; 7,149; ZIP 77571.
La·prair·ie (lä-prâr′ē) town, S Quebec, Canada; 8,122.
La Puen·te (lə pwen′tä) city, SW California; 31,092; ZIP 91743*.
Lar·a·mie (lar′ə·mē) city, SE Wyoming; 23,143; ZIP 82070*.
Larch·mont (lärch′mont′) vill., SE New York; 7,203; ZIP 10538.
La·re·do (lə·rā′dō) city, S Texas; 69,024; ZIP 78040*.
Lar·go (lär′gō) city, W Florida; 22,031; ZIP 33540*.
Lark·spur (lärk′spûr) city, W California; 10,487; ZIP 94939.
La Salle (lə sal′) city, N CEN. Illinois; 10,736; ZIP 61301.
La·salle (lə·sal′) city, S Quebec, Canada; 48,322.
Las Cru·ces (läs krōō′sis) city, S New Mexico; 37,857; ZIP 88001*.
Las Ve·gas (läs vā′gəs) city, SE Nevada; 125,787.
  — city, NE CEN. New Mexico; 7,528; ZIP 87701*.
  — town, NE CEN. New Mexico; 6,307.
La·tham (lā′thəm) city, E CEN. New York; 9,661.
La·trobe (lə·trōb′) boro., SW Pennsylvania; 11,749; ZIP 15650.
La Tuque (lä tük′) town, S Quebec, Canada; 13,554.
Lat·vi·an SSR (lat′vē·ən) constituent republic, NE USSR; 24,600 sq. mi.; 2,093,000; cap. Riga. Also **Lat′vi·a.**
Lau·der·dale Lakes (lô′dər·dāl) city, SE Florida; 10,577; ZIP 33301.
Lau·der·hill (lô′dər·hil) city, SE Florida; 8,465; ZIP 33313.
Laur·el (lôr′əl, lor′-) town, W CEN. Maryland; 10,525; ZIP 20810.
  — city, SE Mississippi; 24,145; ZIP 39440*.
Laur·ence Harbor (lor′əns) city, E New Jersey; 6,715; ZIP 08879.

Laur·ens (lor′əns) city, NW CEN. South Carolina; 10,298; ZIP 29360.
Lau·ren·tian Mountains (lô·ren′shən) mtn. range, E Canada.
Laur·in·burg (lor′in·burg) city, S North Carolina; 8,859; ZIP 28352.
Lau·sanne (lō·zàn′) city, W Switzerland; 127,000.
Lau·zon (lō·zôn′) town, S Quebec, Canada; 12,877.
La·val (lä·väl′) town, S Quebec, Canada; 196,088.
La Verne (lə vûrn′) city, SW California; 12,965; ZIP 91750.
Lawn·dale (lôn′dāl) city, SW California; 24,825; ZIP 90260.
Law·rence (lôr′əns, lor′-) town, CEN. Indiana; 16,646; ZIP see INDIANAPOLIS.
  — city, E Kansas; 45,698; ZIP 66044*.
  — city, NE Massachusetts; 66,915; ZIP 01840*.
  — vill., SE New York; 8,889; ZIP 11559.
Law·rence·berg (lôr′əns·bûrg, lor′-) city, S Tennessee; 8,889; ZIP 38464.
Lawr·ence·ville (lor′əns·vil) city, N Georgia; 5,115; ZIP 30245.
Law·rence·ville (lôr′əns·vil, lor′-) city, SE Illinois; 5,863; ZIP 62439.
Law·ton (lôt′n) city, SW Oklahoma; 74,470; ZIP 73501*.
Lay·ton (lāt′n) city, N Utah; 13,603; ZIP 84041.
Lead (lēd) city, W South Dakota; 5,420; ZIP 57754.
League City (lēg) city, E Texas; 10,818; ZIP 77573.
Leam·ing·ton (lēm′ing·ton, lem′-) town, S Ontario, Canada; 9,554.
Lea·side (lē′sīd) town, S Ontario, Canada; 21,250.
Leav·en·worth (lev′ən·wûrth) city, NE Kansas; 25,147; ZIP 66048.
Lea·wood (lē′wŏŏd) city, E Kansas; 10,349.
Leb·a·non (leb′ə·nən) republic, SW Asia; 3,400 sq. mi.; 1,782,000; cap. Beirut.
Leb·a·non (leb′ə·nən) city, CEN. Indiana; 9,766; ZIP 46052.
  — city, CEN. Kentucky; 5,528; ZIP 40033.
  — city, S CEN. Missouri; 8,616; ZIP 65536.
  — city, W New Hampshire; 9,725; ZIP 03766.
  — vill., SW Ohio; 7,934; ZIP 45036.
  — city, W Oregon; 6,636; ZIP 97355.
  — city, SE Pennsylvania; 28,572; ZIP 17042.
  — city, N CEN. Tennessee; 12,492; ZIP 37087.
Led·yard (led′yərd, lej′ərd) city, SE Connecticut; 14,558; ZIP 06339.
Lee (lē) city, W Massachusetts; 6,426; ZIP 01238.
Leeds (lēdz) city and co. boro., N CEN. England; 511,000.
Leeds (lēdz) city, CEN. Alabama; 6,991; ZIP 35094.
Lees·burg (lēz′bûrg) city, CEN. Florida; 11,869; ZIP 32748.
Lees Summit city, W Missouri; 16,230; ZIP 64063.
Lees·ville (lēz′vil) city, SW Louisiana; 8,928; ZIP 71446.
Lee·ward Islands (lē′wərd) N isl. group, Lesser Antilles.
Leg·horn (leg′hôrn) city, NW Italy; 160,000.
Le Ha·vre (lə hä′vər, -vrə) city, N France; 140,000.
Le·high·ton (lē·hī′tən) boro., E Pennsylvania; 6,095; ZIP 18235.
Leices·ter (les′tər) co. boro., CEN. England; 273,000.
Leices·ter (les′tər) city, CEN. Massachusetts; 9,140; ZIP 01524.
Lei·den (līd′n) city, W Netherlands; 96,000.
Leip·zig (līp′sik, -sig) city, S CEN. East Germany; 593,000.
Le·land (lē′lənd) city, W Mississippi; 6,000; ZIP 38756*.
Le·man (lē′mən), **Lake** See GENEVA, Lake of.
Le Mars (lə märz′) city, NW Iowa; 8,159; ZIP 51031.
Le·may (lə·mā′) city, E Missouri; 40,115; ZIP 63125.
Lem·berg (lem′bûrg) Lvov: the German name.
Lemon Grove uninc. place, SW California; 19,690; ZIP 92045.
Le·mont Village (lə·mont′) city, NE Illinois; 5,080; ZIP 60439.
Le Moore Station (lə·mŏŏr′) city, CEN. California; 8,512; ZIP 93245.
Le·Moyne (lə·moin′) town, S Quebec, Canada; 8,888.
Le·nex·a (lə·neks′ə) city, E Kansas; 5,242.
Len·in·grad (len′in·grad) city, NW RSFSR; 3,296,000.
Len·nox (len′əks) uninc. place, SW California; 16,121; ZIP see INGLEWOOD.
Le·noir (lə·nôr′) town, W North Carolina; 14,705; ZIP 28645.
  — city, SE Tennessee; 5,324; ZIP 37771.
Len·ox (len′iks) city, W Massachusetts; 5,804; ZIP 01240.
Leom·in·ster (lem′in·stər) city, N CEN. Massachusetts; 32,939; ZIP 01453.
Le·on·ia (lē·ōn′yə) boro., NE New Jersey; 8,847; ZIP see HACKENSACK.
Le·o·pold·ville (lē′ə·pōld·vil′) former name for KINSHASA.
Le Roy (lə·roi′) city, SE New York; 5,118; ZIP 14482.
Les·bos (lez′bəs, -bos) isl. of Greece off NW Turkey; 623 sq. mi.
Le·so·tho (lə·sōō′tōō, -sō′thō) independent member of the

Commonwealth of Nations; enclave in E South Africa; 11,716 sq. mi.; 858,000; cap. Maseru: formerly *Basutoland*.
Lesser Antilles See ANTILLES.
Leth·bridge (leth′brij) city, S Alberta, Canada; 37,186.
Le·to (lē′tō) city, SW Florida; 8,458; ZIP 33601.
Leu·ca·di·a (lyōō-kā′dē-ə, lōō-) uninc. place, SW California; 5,900; ZIP 92046.
Lev·el·land (lev′ə-land′) city, W Texas; 11,445; ZIP 79336.
Le·vis (lē′vis) city, S Quebec, Canada; 15,627.
Lev·it·town (lev′i-toun′) Willingboro, New Jersey: *the former name.*
— vill., SE New York; 65,440; ZIP 11756.
Lew·is·burg (lōō′is-bûrg) boro., CEN. Pennsylvania; 6,376; ZIP 17837.
— town, S CEN. Tennessee; 7,207; ZIP 37091.
Lew·is·ton (lōō′is-tən) city, W Idaho; 26,068; ZIP 83501.
— city, SW Maine; 41,779; ZIP 04240*.
Lewiston Orchards uninc. place, W Idaho; 26,068.
Lew·is·town (lōō′is-toun) city, CEN. Montana; 6,437; ZIP 59457.
— boro., CEN. Pennsylvania; 11,098; ZIP 17044.
Lew·is·ville (lōō′is-vil) city, N CEN. Texas; 9,264; ZIP 75067.
Lex·ing·ton (lek′sing-tən) city, N CEN. Kentucky; 108,137; ZIP 40500*.
— town, NE Massachusetts; 31,886; ZIP see BOSTON.
— NW Missouri; 5,388; ZIP 64067.
— city, S CEN. Nebraska; 5,618; ZIP 68850.
— city, W CEN. North Carolina; 17,205; ZIP 27292.
— town, W CEN. Virginia; 7,597; ZIP 24450*.
Lexington Park uninc. place, S Maryland; 9,136; ZIP 20653.
Ley·den (līd′n) See LEIDEN.
Ley·te (lā′tā) isl., E Philippines, 2,875 sq. mi.
Lha·sa (lä′sä) city, S Tibet, cap.; ab. 70,000.
Lib·er·al (lib′ər-əl) city, SW Kansas; 13,471; ZIP 67901.
Li·ber·i·a (lī-bir′ē-ə) republic, W Africa; ab. 43,000 sq. mi.; 1,290,000; cap. Monrovia.
Lib·er·ty (lib′ər-tē) city, W Missouri; 13,679; ZIP 64068.
— city, E Texas; 5,591; ZIP 77575.
Lib·er·ty·ville (lib′ər-tē-vil) vill., NE Illinois; 11,684; ZIP 60048.
Li·bre·ville (lē-brə-vēl′) city, W Gabon; cap.; 44,000.
Lib·y·a (lib′ē-ə) constitutional monarchy, N Africa; 679,358 sq. mi.; 1,216,000; caps. Tripoli and Benghazi.
Liech·ten·stein (lik′tən-stīn) principality, CEN. Europe; 61 sq. mi.; 16,000; cap. Vaduz.
Li·ège (lē-ezh′, lyezh) city, E Belgium; 155,420.
Lighthouse Point city, SE Florida; 9,071; ZIP 33064.
Lille (lēl) city, N France; 190,546.
Li·ma (lē′mə) city, W Peru; cap.; 1,436,231.
Li·ma (lī′mə) city, W Ohio; 53,734; ZIP 45801*.
Lim·er·ick (lim′rik, -ə-rik) co. boro., W Ireland; 55,912.
Limestone city, N Maine; 8,745; ZIP 04750.
Li·moges (lē-mōzh′) city, W CEN. France; 132,935.
Lin·coln (ling′kən) city, CEN. Illinois; 17,582; ZIP 62656.
— NE Massachusetts; 7,567; ZIP 01773.
— city, SE Nebraska; cap.; 149,518; ZIP 68500*.
— town, NE Rhode Island; 16,182; ZIP see PAWTUCKET.
Lincoln Heights city, SW Ohio; 6,099.
Lin·coln·i·a (ling-kō′nē-ə, lin-) city, NE Virginia; 10,355.
Lincoln Park city, SE Michigan; 52,984; ZIP 48146.
— boro., N New Jersey; 9,034; ZIP 07035.
Lin·coln·ton (ling′kən-tən) town, SW CEN. North Carolina; 5,293; ZIP 28092.
Lincoln Village city, W CEN. California; 6,722.
— city, CEN. Ohio; 11,215.
Lin·coln·wood (ling′kən-wōōd) vill., NE Illinois; 12,929; ZIP see CHICAGO.
Lin·da (lin′də) uninc. place, N CEN. California; 7,731.
Lin·den (lin′dən) city, NE New Jersey; 41,409; ZIP 07036*.
Lin·den·hurst (lin′dən-hûrst) vill., SE New York; 28,338; ZIP 11757.
Lin·den·wold (lin′dən-wōld′) boro., SW New Jersey; 12,199; ZIP see CLEMENTON.
Lind·say (lin′zē) city, S CEN. California; 5,206; ZIP 93247.
Lind·say (lin′zē) town, S Ontario, Canada; 12,090.
Lin·thi·cum (lin′thə-kum) vill., NE Maryland; 9,830; ZIP 21090.
Lin·ton (lint′n, lin′tən) city, SW Indiana; 5,450; ZIP 47441.
Lin·wood (lin′wōōd′) city, SE New Jersey; 6,159; ZIP 08221.
Lis·bon (liz-bən) city, W Portugal; 839,325 sq. mi.; 18,552,996.
Lis·bon (liz′bən) city, SE Maine; 6,544; ZIP 04250.
Lisle Village (līl) city, NE Illinois; 5,324.
Litch·field (lich′fēld) — NW Connecticut; 7,399; ZIP 06759.
— city, S CEN. Illinois; 7,190; ZIP 62056.
— city, S CEN. Minnesota; 5,262; ZIP 55355.
Lith·u·a·ni·an SSR (lith′ōō-ā′nē-ən) constituent republic, NW USSR; 25,200 sq. mi.; 2,711,000; cap. Vilna. Also **Lith′·u·a′ni·a.**
Lit·itz (lit′its) boro., SE Pennsylvania; 7,072; ZIP 17545.

Little Chute (shōōt) vill., E Wisconsin; 5,365; ZIP 54140.
Little Falls city, CEN. Minnesota; 7,467; ZIP 56345.
— urb. twp., NE New Jersey; 11,726; ZIP 07424*.
— city, E CEN. New York; 7,629; ZIP 13365.
Little Farms city, SW Louisiana; 15,713; ZIP 70052.
Little Ferry boro., NE New Jersey; 9,042; ZIP 07643.
Lit·tle·field (lit′əl-fēld) city, NW Texas; 6,738; ZIP 79339.
Little Rock city, CEN. Arkansas; cap.; 132,483; ZIP 72200*.
Little Silver boro., E New Jersey; 6,010; ZIP 07739.
Lit·tle·ton (lit′əlt-n, -əl-tən) town, N CEN. Colorado; 26,466; ZIP 80120*.
— city, NE Massachusetts; 6,380; ZIP 01460.
— city, NE New Hampshire; 5.290; ZIP 03561.
Live·oak (līv′ōk′) city, N CEN. California; 6,443; ZIP 95953.
Live Oak city, N Florida; 6,443; ZIP 32060.
Liv·er·more (liv′ər-môr) city, W California; 37,703; ZIP 94550*.
Liv·er·pool (liv′ər-pōōl) co. boro., W England; 688,010.
Liv·ing·ston (liv′ing-stən) city, S Montana; 6,883; ZIP 59457.
— urb. twp., NE New Jersey; 30,127; ZIP 07039.
Li·vo·ni·a (li-vō′nē-ə) city, SE Michigan; 110,109; ZIP 48150*.
Lloyd·min·ster (loid′min·stər) city, E Alberta and W Saskatchewan, Canada; 7,071.
Loch Ra·ven (lok rā′vən) uninc. place, N Maryland; 25,000; ZIP see BALTIMORE.
Lock·bourne Base (lok′bôrn) city, CEN. Ohio; 5,623.
Lock·hart (lok′härt) city, CEN. Florida; 5,809.
— city, S CEN. Texas; 6,489; ZIP 78644.
Lock·land (lok′lənd) city, SW Ohio; 5,288; ZIP see CINCINNATI.
Lock·port (lok′pôrt, -pōrt) city, NE Illinois; 9,985; ZIP 60441.
— city, NW New York; 25,399; ZIP 14094.
Locust Grove uninc. place, SE New York; 11,558.
Lo·di (lō′dī) city, CEN. California; 28,691; ZIP 95240*.
— boro., NE New Jersey; 25,213; ZIP 07644.
Łódź (lōōj) city, CEN. Poland; 747,700.
Lo·gan (lō′gən) city, S CEN. Ohio; 6,269; ZIP 43138.
— city, N Utah; 22,333; ZIP 84321.
Logan, Mount peak, SW Yukon Territory, Canada; 19,850.
Lo·gans·port (lō′gənz-pôrt, -pōrt) city, N CEN. Indiana; 19,255; ZIP 46947.
Loire (lwär) river, SE France; 620 mi. long.
Lo·ma Lin·da (lō′mə lin′də) city, S CEN. California; 9,797; ZIP 92354.
Lom·bard (lom′bärd) vill., NE Illinois; 35,977; ZIP 60148.
Lom·bar·dy (lom′bər-dē, lum′-) reg., N Italy; 9,190; sq. mi.; 7,390,000; cap. Milan.
Lo·mé (lō-mā′) city, S Togo; cap.; ab. 97,000.
Lo·mi·ta (lō-mē′tə) uninc. place, SW California; 19,784; ZIP 90717.
Lo·mond (lō′mənd), **Loch** lake, W CEN. Scotland; 23 mi. long.
Lom·poc (lom′pok) city, SW California; 25,284; ZIP 93436*.
Lon·don (lun′dən) city and co., SE England; cap.; 1 sq. mi.; 5,000 (the city proper): 117 sq. mi.; 3,195,000 (the co.): 693 sq. mi.; 7,764,000 (Greater London).
Lon·don (lun′dən) city, SW CEN. Ohio; 6,481; ZIP 43140.
Lon·don (lun′dən) city, Ontario, Canada; 194,416.
Lon·don·der·ry (lun′dən-der′ē) city, SE New Hampshire; 5,346; ZIP 03053.
Long Beach city, SW California; 358,633; ZIP 90800*.
— city, NE Mississippi; 6,170; ZIP 39560.
— city, SE New York; 33,127; ZIP 11561*.
Long Branch city, E New Jersey; 31,774; ZIP 07740*.
— city, NE Virginia; 21,634.
Long Branch vill., S Ontario, Canada; 12,980.
Long Island isl., SE New York; 1,723 sq. mi.
Long Island Sound inlet of the Atlantic betw. Long Island and Connecticut.
Long·mead·ow (lông′med′ō, long′-) town, S Massachusetts; 15,630; ZIP see SPRINGFIELD.
Long·mont (lông′mont, long′-) city, N Colorado; 23,209; ZIP 80501.
Lon·gueuil (lôn-gāl′, lôn-gü′y′) city, SW Quebec, Canada; 25,593.
Long·view (lông′vyōō, long′-) city, NE Texas; 45,547; ZIP 75601*.
— city, SW Washington; 28,373; ZIP 98632.
Lo·rain (lō′rān) city, N Ohio; 78,185; ZIP 44051*.
Lo·rette·ville (lō-ret′vil) town, S CEN. Quebec, Canada; 9,465.
Lor·ing (lôr′ing) city, N Maine; 6,266.
Lor·raine (lô-rān′, lō-, lə) reg., E France.
Los Al·a·mi·tos City (lōs äl′ə-mē′tōs) city, SW California; 11,346; ZIP 90720.
Los Al·a·mos (lôs al′ə-mōs, los) town, N CEN. New Mexico; site of the development of the atom bomb; 11,310; ZIP 87544.

Los Al·tos (los al′təs) city, w California; 24,956; ZIP 94022.
Los Altos Hills city, w California; 6,865; ZIP 94022.
Los An·ge·les (lôs an′jə-lēz, ang′gə-ləs, los) city, sw California; 2,816,061; ZIP 90000*.
Los Ban·os (los ban′əs) city, CEN. California; 9,188; ZIP 93635.
Los Gat·os (los gat′əs) city, w California; 23,735; ZIP 95030*.
Lou·don·ville (lou′dən-vil) city, E CEN. New York; 9,299.
Lou·i·si·an·a (lə-wē′zē-an′ə, loo′zē-) state, s United States; 48,523 sq. mi.; 3,643,180; cap. Baton Rouge.
Lou·is·ville (loo′ē-vil, lyoo′-, -vəl) city, N Kentucky; 361,472; ZIP 40200*.
— city, E CEN. Mississippi; 6,626; ZIP 39339.
— vill., NE CEN. Ohio; 6,298; ZIP 44641.
Lourdes (loord) town, sw France; site of a famous shrine; ab. 16,000.
Love·land (luv′lənd) city, N Colorado; 16,220; ZIP 80537.
— vill., sw Ohio; 7,144; ZIP 45140.
Loves Park city, N Illinois; 12,390; ZIP see ROCKFORD.
Lov·ing·ton (luv′ing-tən) town, SE New Mexico; 8,915; ZIP 88260.
Low·ell (lō′əl) city, NE Massachusetts; 94,239; ZIP 01850*.
Lower Bur·rell (bûr′el) city, sw Pennsylvania; 13,654; ZIP see NEW KENSINGTON.
Lower California penin., NW Mexico; betw. the Gulf of California and the Pacific.
Lower Mer·i·on (mer′ē-ən) urb. twp., SE Pennsylvania; 59,420.
Lower South·amp·ton (south-amp′tən, -hamp′-) urb. twp., SE Pennsylvania; 12,619.
Low·lands (lō′ləndz, -landz′) areas of low elevation, E and s Scotland; 5,045.
Lu·an·da (loo′än-də) city, NW Angola; cap.; 224,540.
Lub·bock (lub′ək) city, NW Texas; 149,101; ZIP 79400*.
Lü·beck (loo′bek) city, NE West Germany; 239,523.
Lu·cerne (loo-sûrn′), **Lake of** lake, CEN. Switzerland; 44 sq. mi.
Luck·now (luk′nou) city, CEN. Uttar Pradesh, India; cap.; 690,902.
Lud·ing·ton (lud′ing-tən) city, w Michigan; 9,021; ZIP 49431.
Lud·low (lud′lō) city, N Kentucky; 5,815; ZIP see COVINGTON.
— town, s Massachusetts; 17,580; ZIP 01056.
Luf·kin (luf′kin) city, E Texas; 23,049; ZIP 75901*.
Luke (look) city, s CEN. Arizona; 5,047.
Lum·ber·ton (lum′bərt-n, -bər-tən) city, s North Carolina; 16,961; ZIP 28358.
Lu·nen·burg (loo′nən-bûrg) city, N Massachusetts; 7,419; ZIP 01462.
Lü·ta (loo′tä′) city, NE China; site of a naval base operated jointly after 1945 by the USSR and China; 1,508,000.
Lu·ther·ville-Ti·mo·ni·um (loo′thər-vil-ti-mō′nē-əm) city, NE Maryland; 24,055; ZIP 21093.
Lux·em·bourg (luk′səm-bûrg) constitutional grand duchy; betw. Belgium, France, and Germany; 998 sq. mi.; 313,000.
— city, s CEN. Luxembourg; cap.; 77,254. Also **Lux′em·burg.**
Lux·or (luk′sôr, look′-) city, E Egypt; near the site of ancient Thebes; ab. 30,000.
Lu·zon (loo-zon′) isl., N Philippines; 40,420 sq. mi.
Lvov (ly′vôf) city, w Ukrainian SSR; 512,000.
Lyn·brook (lin′brook) vill., SE New York; 23,776; ZIP 11563.
Lynch·burg (linch′bûrg) city, s CEN. Virginia; 54,083; ZIP 24501*.
Lynd·hurst (lind′hûrst) urb. twp., NE New Jersey; 22,729; ZIP see RUTHERFORD.
— city, N Ohio; 19,749; ZIP see CLEVELAND.
Lynn (lin) city, NE Massachusetts; 90,294; ZIP 01901*.
Lynn·field (lin′fēld) city, NE Massachusetts; 10,826; ZIP 01940.
Lynn Gardens uninc. place, NE Tennessee; 5,261; ZIP see KINGSPORT.
Lyn·wood (lin′wood) city, sw California; 43,353; ZIP 90262*.
— city, N CEN. Washington; 16,919; ZIP 98036.
Ly·ons (lī′ənz) city, E CEN. France; 527,800.
Ly·ons (lī′ənz) vill., N Illinois; 11,124; ZIP 60534.

Mab·le·ton (māb′əlt-n, -əl·tən) uninc. place, NW CEN. Georgia; 9,500; ZIP 30059.
Ma·cao (mə-kou′, -kä′ō) isl., Canton river delta, China. — Portuguese overseas prov. comprising a penin. of Macao isl. and two small isls.; 6 sq. mi.; 188,000. — city; cap of Macao; 161,252.
Mac·e·do·ni·a (mas′ə-dō′nē-ə) reg., SE Europe; divided among Bulgaria, Greece, and Yugoslavia.
Mac·e·do·ni·a (mas′ə-dō′nē-ə) city, NE Ohio; 6,375; ZIP 44056.

Mac·ken·zie (mə-ken′zē) river, NW Canada; 2,640 mi. long.
Mack·i·nac (mak′ə-nô), **Straits of** channel betw. Lakes Michigan and Huron; ab. 4 mi. wide.
Mackinac Island isl., Straits of Mackinac.
Ma·comb (mə-kōm′) city, w Illinois; 19,643; ZIP 61455.
Ma·con (mā′kən) city, CEN. Georgia; 122,423 ZIP 31200*.
— city, NE Missouri; 5,301; ZIP 63552.
Mad·a·gas·car (mad′ə·gas′kər) republic, isl. in Indian Ocean off SE Africa; 227,602 sq. mi.; 8,520,000; cap. Tananarive.
Mad·a·was·ka (mad′ə·wäs′kə) city, NE Maine; 5,585; ZIP 04756.
Ma·dei·ra (mə-dir′ə) isl. group w of Morocco; an adm. dist. of Portugal; 308 sq. mi.; 267,000; cap. Funchal. — principal isl., Madeira; 286 sq. mi.
Ma·dei·ra (mə-dir′ə) vill., sw Ohio; 6,713; ZIP see CINCINNATI.
Ma·de·ra (mə-dâr′ə) city, CEN. California; 16,044; ZIP 93637.
Mad·i·son (mad′ə-sən) city, sw Illinois; 7,042; ZIP 62060.
— city, SE Indiana; 13,081; ZIP 47250*.
— boro., N New Jersey; 16,710 ZIP 07940.
— city, SE South Dakota; 6,315; ZIP 57042.
— uninc. place, N Tennessee; 13,583; ZIP 37115.
— city, s CEN. Wisconsin; cap.; 173,258; ZIP 53700.
Madison Center city, SE Connecticut; 9,768; ZIP 06443.
Madison Heights city, SE Michigan; 38,599; ZIP see ROYAL OAK.
Madison North city, NE Ohio; 6,882.
Mad·i·son·ville (mad′ə-sən-vil, -vəl) city, w Kentucky; 15,332; ZIP 42431.
Ma·dras (mə-dras′, -dräs′, mad′rəs) state, s India; 50,132 sq. mi.; 33,651,000. — city, NE Madras; cap.; 1,927,431.
Ma·drid (mə-drid′) city, CEN. Spain; cap.; 2,443,152.
Ma·du·ra (mä-doo′rä) isl. of Indonesia E of Java; 1,762 sq. mi.
Mag·de·burg (mag′də-bûrg) city, w CEN. East Germany; 267,783.
Ma·gel·lan (mə-jel′ən), **Strait of** channel betw. the Atlantic and Pacific, separating the South American mainland from Tierra del Fuego.
Mag·ni·to·gorsk (məg-nyi-to-gôrsk′) city, s RSFSR; 357,000.
Magnolia city, SE Arkansas; 11,303; ZIP 71753.
— city, sw New Jersey; 5,893; ZIP 08049.
Ma·gog (mā′gog) city, s Quebec, Canada; 13,797.
Ma·ha·noy City (mä-hə-noi′) boro., E CEN. Pennsylvania; 7,257; ZIP 17948.
Ma·ho·pac (mā′ō-pak) city, SE New York; 5,265; ZIP 10541.
Maili See LUALUALEI-MAILI.
Main River (mān) river, s CEN. West Germany; 305 mi. long.
Maine (mān) state, NE United States; 32,562 sq. mi.; 993,663; cap. Augusta.
Mait·land (māt′lənd) city, CEN. Florida; 7,157; ZIP 32751.
Ma·jor·ca (mə-jôr′kə, -yôr′-) largest of the Balearic Islands; 1,405 sq. mi.
Makaha See WAIANAE-MAKAHA.
Mal·a·bar (mal′ə-bar) coastal reg., sw India. Also **Malabar Coast.**
Ma·lac·ca (mə-lak′ə) city, w Malaya; ab. 69,848.
Malacca, Strait of strait betw. Sumatra and the Malay Peninsula.
Mál·a·ga (mal′ə-gə) city, s Spain; 307,162.
Mal·a·gas·y Republic (mal′ə-gas′ē) Madagascar: *the former name.*
Mal·ar·tic (mäl-är-tēk′) town, w Quebec, Canada; 6,606.
Ma·la·wi (mä′lä-wē) independent member of the Commonwealth of nations, SE Africa; 49,177 sq. mi.; 2,830,000; cap. Zomba.
Ma·lay·a (mə-lā′ə) federation of Malay states, SE Asia; ab. 50,700 sq. mi.; 7,137,000; cap. Kuala Lumpur; after 1963 part of Malaysia.
Ma·lay Archipelago (mā′lā, mə-lā′) isl. group off SE Asia; includes isls. of Indonesia, Malaysia, and the Philippines.
Malay Peninsula s penin. of Asia; includes Malaya, Singapore, and part of Thailand.
Ma·lay·sia (mə-lā′zhə, -shə) federation of Malaya, Sarawak, and North Borneo; a member of the Commonwealth of Nations; 127,334 sq. mi.; ab. 10 million; cap. Kuala Lumpur.
Mal·den (môl′dən) city, NE Massachusetts; 56,127; ZIP see BOSTON.
— city, SE Missouri; 5,374; ZIP 63863.
Mal·dives (mal′dīvz) republic, isl. group in Indian Ocean; 115 sq. mi.; 140,000; cap. Malé.
Ma·li (mä′lē) republic, w Africa; 464,872 sq. mi.; 4,307,000; cap. Bamako.
Mal·lor·ca (mä-lyôr′kä) Majorca: *the Spanish name.*

Malm·strom (malm′strum) city, CEN. Montana; 8,374.
Ma·lone (mə·lōn′) vill., NE New York; 8,048; ZIP 12953.
Mal·ta (môl′tə) British autonomous state, CEN. Mediterranean; comprises the islands of **Malta**, Gozo, Comino, and two islets; 122 sq. mi.; 327,218; cap. Valletta.
Mal·vern (mal′vûrn, -vərn) city, CEN. Arkansas; 8,739; ZIP 72104*.
Mal·verne (mal′vûrn) vill., SE New York; 10,036; ZIP 11565.
Ma·mar·o·neck (mə·mar′ə·nek) vill., SE New York; 18,909; ZIP 10543*.
Man (man), **Isle of** one of the British Isles, CEN. Irish Sea; 227 sq. mi.; 48,151; cap. Douglas.
Ma·na·gua (mä·nä′gwä) city, SW Nicaragua; cap.; 262,047.
Managua, Lake lake, SW Nicaragua; 390 sq. mi.
Ma·nas·sas (mə·nas′əs) city, NE Virginia; 9,164; ZIP 22110.
Manassas Park town, NE Virginia; 6,844; ZIP 22110*.
Ma·na·ti (mä·nä·tē′) town, N Puerto Rico; 9,682; ZIP 00701*.
Man·ches·ter (man′ches·tər, -chis-) co. boro. and city, SE Lancashire, England; 602,790.
Man·ches·ter (man′ches·tər, -chis-) town, N Connecticut; 47,994; ZIP 06040*.
— city, NE Massachusetts; 5,151; ZIP 01944.
— city, NE Missouri; 5,031.
— city, S New Hampshire; 87,754; ZIP 03100*.
— city, S CEN. Tennessee; 6,208; ZIP 37355.
Man·chu·ri·a (man·chŏŏr′ē·ə) former div., NE China.
Man·da·lay (man′də·lā, man′də·lā′) city, CEN. Burma; 195,348.
Man·dan (man′dan) city, S CEN. North Dakota; 11,093; ZIP 58554*.
Man·has·set (mən·has′it) city, SE New York; 8,541; ZIP 11030.
Man·hat·tan (man·hat′n, mən-) city, NE Kansas; 27,575; ZIP 66502*.
Man·hat·tan (mən·hat′ən, man-) isl., SE New York; 22 sq. mi.; boro. New York City; 1,539,233; ZIP 10000*.
Manhattan Beach city, SW California; 35,352; ZIP 90266*.
Man·heim (man′hīm) city, SE Pennsylvania; 5,434; ZIP 17545.
Ma·nil·a (mə·nil′ə) city, SW Luzon, Philippines; 1,356,000.
Man·is·tee (man·is·tē′) city, W Michigan; 7,723; ZIP 49660.
Man·i·to·ba (man′ə·tō′bə, -tō·bä′) prov., CEN. Canada; 246,512 sq. mi.; pop. 963,066; cap. Winnipeg.
Manitoba, Lake lake, SW Manitoba; 1,817 sq. mi.
Man·i·to·woc (man′ə·tə·wok′) city, E Wisconsin; 33,430; ZIP 54220*.
Man·i·wa·ki (man·i·wô′kē) town, SW Quebec, Canada; 6,404.
Man·ka·to (man·kā′tō) city, S Minnesota; 30,895; ZIP 56001*.
Man·or·ha·ven (man′ər·hā′vən) city, SE New York; 5,710.
Mans·field (manz′fēld′) city, NE Connecticut; 19,994; ZIP 06250.
Mans·field (mans′fēld, manz′-) city, NW Louisiana; 6,432; ZIP 71052.
— city, CEN. Massachusetts; 9,939; ZIP 02048.
— city, N CEN. Ohio; 55,047; ZIP 44900*.
Man·te·ca (man·tē′kə) city, CEN. California; 13,845; ZIP 95336.
Man·tu·a (man′tōō·ə) city, NE Virginia; 6,911.
Man·ville (man′vil) boro., N CEN. New Jersey; 13,029; ZIP 08835.
Maple Grove city, SE Minnesota; 6,275; ZIP 55369.
Maple Heights city, NE Ohio; 34,093; ZIP see CLEVELAND.
Maple Shade urb. twp., SW New Jersey; 16,464; ZIP 08052.
Ma·ple·wood (mā′pəl·wŏŏd) vill., E Minnesota; 25,222; ZIP see ST. PAUL.
— city, E Missouri; 12,785; ZIP see ST. LOUIS.
— urb. twp., NE New Jersey; 24,932; ZIP 07040.
Ma·quo·ke·ta (mə·kō′ki·tə) city, E Iowa; 5,677; ZIP 52060.
Ma·ra·cai·bo (mä·rä·kī′bō) city, NW Venezuela; 621,109.
Maracaibo, Lake lake, NW Venezuela; ab. 5,000 sq. mi.
Mar·ble·head (mär′bəl·hed′, -hed′) town, NE Massachusetts; 21,295; ZIP 01945*.
Mar·gate City (mär′gāt) city, SE Florida; 8,867; ZIP 33066.
— city, SE New Jersey; 10,576; ZIP see ATLANTIC CITY.
Ma·ri·a·nas Islands (mär′ē·ä′näs) isl. group, W Pacific; including Guam, Saipan, Tinian, and Rota; part of the UN Trust terr. of the Pacific Islands (excluding Guam); 246 sq. mi.
Mar·i·an·na (mâr′ē·an′ə, mar′-) city, E Arkansas; 6,196; ZIP 72360.
— city, NW Florida; 6,741; ZIP 32446*.
Mar·i·et·ta (mâr′ē·et′ə, mar′ē-) city, NW Georgia; 27,216; ZIP 30060*.
— city, SE Ohio; 16,861; ZIP 45750.
Ma·ri·na (mə·rē′nə) city, W California; 8,343.
Mar·i·nette (mar′i·net′) city, NE Wisconsin; 12,696; ZIP 54143*.

Mar·i·on (mar′ē·ən, mâr′-) city, S Illinois; 11,724; ZIP 62959.
— city, E CEN. Indiana; 39,607; ZIP 46952*.
— city, E Iowa; 18,028; ZIP 52302.
— city, CEN. Ohio; 38,646; ZIP 43301*.
— town, NE South Carolina; 7,435; ZIP 29571.
— town, W Virginia; 8,185; ZIP 24354.
Mark·ham (märk′əm) vill., NE Illinois; 15,987; ZIP see HARVEY.
Marl·bor·ough (märl′bûr′ō, môl′bə·rə, -brə) city, E CEN. Massachusetts; 27,936; ZIP 01752.
Mar·lin (mär′lin) city, E CEN. Texas; 6,351; ZIP 76661.
Marl·ton (märl′tən) city, W New Jersey; 10,180; ZIP 08053.
Mar·ma·ra (mär′mə·rə), **Sea of** sea betw. Europe and Asia, connecting the Bosporus and the Dardanelles. Also **Mar·mo·ra** (mär′mə·rə, mär·môr′ə, -mō·rə).
Marne (märn) river, NE France; 325 mi. long.
Mar·ple (mär′pəl) urb. twp., SE Pennsylvania; 19,722.
Mar·que·sas Islands (mär·kā′säs, -kē′-) isl. group, French Polynesia; 492 sq. mi.
Mar·quette (mär·ket′) city, NW Michigan; 21,967; ZIP 49855.
Mar·ra·kesh (mä·rä′kesh) city, SW Morocco; a traditional cap.; 255,000.
Mar·rer·o (mə·râr′ō) city, SW Louisiana; 29,015; ZIP 70072.
Mar·seille (mär·sā′y′) city, SE France; 889,029. Also **Mar·seilles** (mär·sā′, -sālz′).
Mar·shall (mär′shəl) city, S Michigan; 7,253; ZIP 49068.
— city, SW Minnesota; 9,886; ZIP 56258.
— city, CEN. Missouri; 11,847; ZIP 65340.
— city, NE Texas; 22,937; ZIP 75607*.
Mar·shall Islands (mär′shəl) isl. group in Pacific; an adm. dist. of the Trust Terr. of the Pacific Islands; 66 sq. mi.; 15,000; cap. Jaluit.
Mar·shall·town (mär′shəl·toun) city, CEN. Iowa; 26,219; ZIP 50158.
Marsh·field (märsh′fēld′) city, E Massachusetts; 15,223; ZIP 02050.
— city, CEN. Wisconsin; 15,619; ZIP 54449.
Mar·ti·nez (mär·tē′nəs) city, W California; 16,506; ZIP 94553*.
Mar·ti·nique (mär′ti·nēk′) isl., Lesser Antilles; French overseas dept.; 421 sq. mi.; 271,000; cap, Fort-de-France.
Mar·tins·burg (märt′nz·bûrg, mär′tinz-) city, NE West Virginia; 14,626; ZIP 25401.
Mar·tins Ferry (märt′nz, mär′tinz) city, E Ohio; 10,757; ZIP 43935.
Mar·tins·ville (märt′nz·vil, mär′tinz-) city, S CEN. Indiana; 9,723; ZIP 46151.
— city, S Virginia; 19,653; ZIP 24112*.
Mar·y·land (mâr′i·lənd, mer′i-) state, E United States; 10,577 sq. mi.; 3,922,399; cap. Annapolis.
Maryland City city, NE Maryland; 7,102.
Maryland Heights city, NE Missouri; 8,805.
Mar·ys·ville (mâr′ēz·vil) city, N CEN. California; 9,353; ZIP 95901*.
— city, W CEN. Ohio; 5,744; ZIP 43040.
Mar·y·ville (mâr′ē·vil, -vəl) city, NW Missouri; 9,970; ZIP 64468.
— city, E Tennessee; 13,808; ZIP 37801*.
Mas·cou·tah (mas·kōō′tə) city, SW Illinois; 5,045; ZIP 62258.
Mason City city, N Iowa; 30,491; ZIP 50401*.
— city, SE Michigan; 5,468; ZIP 48854.
Ma·son-Dix·on line (mā′sən·dik′sən) boundary betw. Pennsylvania and Maryland, surveyed by Charles Mason and Jeremiah Dixon in 1763; regarded as dividing the North from the South.
Mason Village city, SW Ohio; 5,677; ZIP 45040.
Mas·sa·chu·setts (mas′ə·chōō′sits) state, NE United States; 8,257 sq. mi.; 5,689,170; cap. Boston.
Mas·sa·pe·qua (mas′ə·pē′kwə) uninc. place, SE New York; 26,951; ZIP 11758*.
Massapequa Park vill., SE New York; 22,112; ZIP 11762.
Mas·se·na (mə·sē′nə) vill., N New York; 14,042; ZIP 13662.
Mas·sil·lon (mas′ə·lən) city, NE Ohio; 32,539; ZIP 44646.
Ma·tane (mə·tän′) town, E Quebec, Canada; 11,109.
Mat·a·wan (mat′ə·wän′) boro., E New Jersey; 9,136; ZIP 07747.
Ma·ther (ma′thər) city, CEN. California; 7,027.
Math·is (math′is) city, S Texas; 5,351; ZIP 78368.
Ma·tsu (mä′tsōō′) isl. of the Republic of China, Formosa Strait; 4 sq. mi..
Mat·ter·horn (mat′ər·hôrn) mtn. in the Alps on the Swiss-Italian border; 14,701 ft..
Mat·toon (mat′ōōn, mə·tōōn′) city, E CEN. Illinois; 19,681; ZIP 61938.
Mat·ty·dale (mat′ē·dāl) city, CEN. New York; 8,292.
Mau·i (mou′ē) isl. of the Hawaiian Islands; 728 sq. mi.
Mau·mee (mô·mē′) city, NW Ohio; 15,937; ZIP 43537.
Mau·na Lo·a (mou′nä lō′ä) active volcano, CEN. Hawaii (isl.); 13,675 ft.
Mau·na·wi·li (mô′nə·vē′lē) S Oahu, Hawaii; 5,303; ZIP 96744.

Mau·ri·ta·ni·a (môr/ə·tā/nē·ə) republic, w Africa; 419,229 sq. mi.; 727,000; cap. Nouakchott.

Mau·ri·ti·us (mô·rish/ē·əs) isl. E of Madagascar; with other dependencies, a dominion of the Commonwealth of Nations; 788 sq. mi.; 910,000; cap. Port Louis.

Ma·ya·güez (mä/yä·gwäs/) city, w Puerto Rico; 50,147.

May·field (mā/fēld) city, sw Kentucky; 10,724; ZIP 42066.

Mayfield Heights city, N Ohio; 22,139.

May·nard (mā/nərd) town, NE CEN. Massachusetts; 9,710; ZIP 01754.

Mays·ville (māz/vil, -vəl) city, NE Kentucky; 7,411; ZIP 41056.

May·wood (mā/wŏŏd) city, sw California; 16,996; ZIP 90270.
— vill., NE Illinois; 30,036; ZIP 60153*.
— boro., NE New Jersey; 11,087; ZIP see HACKENSACK.

Mc·Al·es·ter (mək·al/is·tər) city, SE CEN. Oklahoma; 18,802; ZIP 74501*.

Mc·Al·len (mək·al/ən) city, s Texas; 37,636; ZIP 78501*.

Mc·Guire (mə·gwīr/) city, w CEN. New Jersey; 10,933.

Mc·Hen·ry (mək·hen/rē) city, NE Illinois; 6,772; ZIP 60050.

Mc·Kees·port (mə·kēz/pôrt, -pōrt) city, sw Pennsylvania; 37,977; ZIP 15130*.

Mc·Kees Rocks (mə·kēz/) boro., sw Pennsylvania; 11,901; ZIP 15136.

Mc·Kin·ley (mə·kin/lē), **Mount** peak, CEN. Alaska, highest in North America; 20,300 ft.

Mc·Kin·ney (mə·kin/ē) city, N Texas; 15,193; ZIP 75069.

Mc·Lean (mək·lēn/) city, NE Virginia; 17,698; ZIP 22101.

Mc·Minn·ville (mək·min/vil, -vəl) city, NW Oregon; 10,125; ZIP 97128*.
— town, E CEN. Tennessee; 10,662; ZIP 37110*.

Mc·Pher·son (mək·fûr/sən) city, CEN. Kansas; 10,851; ZIP 67460.

Mead (mēd), **Lake** reservoir formed by Hoover Dam in the Colorado River, Arizona and Nevada; 246 sq. mi.

Mead·ville (mēd/vil) city, NW Pennsylvania; 16,573; ZIP 16335.

Mec·ca (mek/ə) city, w Saudi Arabia; one of the caps.; birthplace of Mohammed and holy city to which Moslems make pilgrimages; ab. 185,000.

Me·chan·ics·burg (mə·kan/iks·bûrg/) boro., s CEN. Pennsylvania; 9,385; ZIP 17055.

Me·chan·ic·ville (mə·kan/ik·vil) city, E New York; 6,247; ZIP 12118.
— city, SE Tennessee; 10,662.

Med·field (med/fēld) city, E Massachusetts; 9,821; ZIP 02052.

Med·ford (med/fərd) city, NE Massachusetts; 64,397; ZIP BOSTON.
— city, sw Oregon; 28,454; ZIP 97501*.

Me·di·a (mē/dē·ə) boro., SE Pennsylvania; 6,444; ZIP 19063*.

Medicine Hat city, SE Alberta, Canada; 25,574.

Me·di·na (mə·dē/nə) city, w Saudi Arabia; site of Mohammed's tomb; ab. 72,291.

Me·di·na (mə·dī/nə) vill., NW New York; 6,415; ZIP 14103.
— city, N Ohio; 10,913; ZIP 44256.

Med·i·ter·ra·ne·an Sea (med/ə·tə·rān/ē·ən) sea betw. Europe, Asia, and Africa; 965,000 sq. mi.

Med·way (med/wā) city, E Massachusetts; 7,938; ZIP 02053.

Mei·ners Oaks-Mi·ca Monte (mā/nərz ōks mī/kə mont) city, sw California; 7,025; ZIP 93023.

Me·kong (mā·kong/) river, SE Asia; 2,500 mi. long.

Mel·a·ne·sia (mel/ə·nē/zhə, -shə) isls. of the w Pacific s of the Equator; ab. 60,000 sq. mi.

Mel·bourne (mel/bərn) city, s Victoria, Australia; cap.; 1,991,895 (including suburbs).

Mel·bourne (mel/bərn) city, E Florida; 40,236; ZIP 32901*.

Mel·rose (mel/rōz) city, NE Massachusetts; 33,180; ZIP see BOSTON.

Melrose Park city, NE Illinois; 22,706; ZIP 60160*.

Mel·ville (mel/vil) city, SE Saskatchewan, Canada; 5,690.

Mel·ville (mel/vil) city, SE New York; 5,999.

Mel·vin·dale (mel/vin·dāl) city, SE Michigan; 13,862; ZIP see DEARBORN.

Mem·phis (mem/fis) city, sw Tennessee; 623,530; ZIP 38100*.

Me·nash·a (mə·nash/ə) city, E Wisconsin; 14,905; ZIP 54952.

Men·do·ta (men·dō/tə) city, N CEN. Illinois; 6,902; ZIP 61342.

Mendota Heights vill., SE Minnesota; 6,165.

Men·lo Park (men/lō) city, w California; 26,734; ZIP 94025*.
— locality, CEN. New Jersey; former site of Thomas Edison's laboratory; ZIP 08837.

Me·nom·i·nee (mə·nom/ə·nē) city, NW Michigan; 10,748; ZIP 49858.

Me·nom·o·nee Falls (mə·nom/ə·nē) vill., SE Wisconsin; 31,697; ZIP 53051*.

Me·nom·o·nie (mə·nom/ə·nē) city, w Wisconsin; 11,275; ZIP 54751.

Men·tor (men/tər) city, NE Ohio; 36,912; ZIP 44060.

Mentor-on-the-Lake city, NE Ohio; 6,517; ZIP 44060.

Meq·uon (mek/won) city, SE Wisconsin; 12,110; ZIP 53092.

Mer·ced (mər·sed/) city, CEN. California; 22,670; ZIP 95340*.

Mer·ce·des (mûr·sā/dēz) city, s Texas; 9,355; ZIP 78570.

Mer·cer Island (mûr/sər) city, NE Washington; 10,047; ZIP 98040.

Mer·cer·ville-Ham·il·ton Square (mûr/sər·vil·ham/il·tən) city, w CEN. New Jersey; 24,465.

Mer·i·den (mer/ə·dn, -e·dən) city, s CEN. Connecticut; 55,959; ZIP 06450*.

Me·rid·i·an (mə·rid/ē·ən) city, E Mississippi; 45,083; ZIP 39301*.

Mer·i·on (mer/ē·ən) city, SE Pennsylvania; 5,686; ZIP 19026.

Mer·i·am (mer/ē·əm) city, NE Kansas; 10,851.

Mer·rick (mer/ik) uninc. place, SE New York; 25,904; ZIP 11566.

Mer·rill (mer/əl) city, N CEN. Wisconsin; 9,502; ZIP 54452.

Mer·rill·ville (mer/il·vil) city, NW Indiana; 15,918; ZIP 46410.

Mer·ri·mack (mer/ə·mak) city, SE New Hampshire; 8,595; ZIP 03054.

Mer·ritt Island (mer/it) city, E CEN. Florida; 29,233; ZIP 32952.

Me·sa (mā/sə) city, s CEN. Arizona; 62,853; ZIP 85201*.

Me·sa·bi Range (mə·sä/bē) range of hills, NE Minnesota; site of iron ore deposits.

Mes·quite (mes·kēt/) city, N Texas; 55,131; ZIP 75149.

Mes·si·na (mə·sē/nə) city, NE Sicily; 258,110.

Me·tair·ie (me·târ/ē) city, sw Louisiana; 135,816; ZIP 70001.

Me·thu·en (mə·thyōō/ən) city, NE Massachusetts; 35,456; ZIP see LAWRENCE.

Me·trop·o·lis (mə·trop/ə·lis) city, s Illinois; 6,940; ZIP 62960.

Me·tuch·en (mə·tuch/ən) boro., NE New Jersey; 16,031; ZIP 08840*.

Meuse (myōōz) river, w Europe; 580 mi. long.

Me·xi·a (mə·hā/ə, -hē/-) city, E CEN. Texas; 5,943; ZIP 76667.

Mex·i·co (mek/sə·kō) republic, s North America; 760,373 sq. mi.; 37,233,000. — city, s CEN. Mexico; cap.; 3,269,335. Also **Mexico City**.

Mex·i·co (mek/sə·kō) city, NE CEN. Missouri; 11,807; ZIP 65265.

Mexico, Gulf of inlet of the Atlantic, betw. the United States, Mexico, and Cuba; 700,000 sq. mi.

Mi·am·i (mī·am/ē, -am/ə) city, SE Florida; 334,859; ZIP 33100.
— city, NE Oklahoma; 13,880; ZIP 74354*.

Miami Beach city, SE Florida; 87,072; ZIP see MIAMI.

Mi·am·is·burg (mī·am/ēz·bûrg) city, sw Ohio; 14,797; ZIP 45342.

Miami Shores vill., SE Florida; 9,425; ZIP see MIAMI.

Miami Springs town, SE Florida; 13,279; ZIP see MIAMI.

Mich·i·gan (mish/ə·gən) state, N United States; 58,216 sq. mi.; 8,875,083; cap. Lansing.

Michigan, Lake one of the Great Lakes; betw. Michigan and Wisconsin; 22,400 sq. mi.

Michigan City city, N Indiana; 39,369; ZIP 46360*.

Mi·cro·ne·sia (mī/krə·nē/zhə, -shə) isls. of the w Pacific N of the equator.

Mid·dle·bor·ough (mid/l·bûr/ō) uninc. place, E Massachusetts; 13,607; ZIP 02346.

Mid·dle·burg Heights (mid/l·bûrg) vill., N Ohio; 12,367; ZIP 43336.

Mid·dle·bur·y (mid/əl·ber/ē) city, CEN. Connecticut; 5,542; ZIP 06762.
— city, w CEN. Vermont; 6,523; ZIP 05753.

Middle River uninc. place, N Maryland; 19,935; ZIP see BALTIMORE.

Mid·dles·bor·ough (mid/lz·bûr/ō, -ə) city, SE Kentucky; 11,844; ZIP 40965.

Mid·dle·sex (mid/l·seks) boro., NE New Jersey; 15,038; ZIP 08846.

Mid·dle·ton (mid/əl·tən) city, s CEN. Wisconsin; 8,286; ZIP 53562.

Mid·dle·town (mid/l·toun/) city, s CEN. Connecticut; 36,924; ZIP 06457*.
— urb. twp., E New Jersey; 54,623; ZIP 07748*.
— city, SE New York; 22,607; ZIP 10940*.
— city, sw Ohio; 48,767; ZIP 45042*.
— urb. twp., SE Pennsylvania; 26,894; ZIP 17057.
— boro., SE Pennsylvania; 9,080.
— town, SE Rhode Island; 29,621; ZIP see NEWPORT.

Mid·field (mid/fēld) city, CEN. Alabama; 6,399; ZIP 35228.

Mi·di (mē·dē/) s reg. of France.

Mid·land (mid′lənd) city, E CEN. Michigan; 35,176; ZIP 48640*.
— boro., w Pennsylvania; 5,271; ZIP 15059.
— city, w Texas; 59,463; ZIP 79701*.
Mid·land (mid′lənd) town, s Ontario, Canada; 10,129.
Midland Park boro., NE New Jersey; 8,159; ZIP 07432.
Mid·lands (mid′ləndz) cos. of CEN. England.
Mid·lo·thi·an (mid·lō′thē·ən) vill., NE Illinois; 15,939; ZIP 60445*.
Mid·vale (mid′vāl) city, N Utah; 7,840; ZIP 84047.
Mid·way Islands (mid′wā) 2 isls. NW of Honolulu, under control of the U.S. Navy; 2 sq. mi.; scene of an important battle of World War II, June, 1942.
Mid·way-Hard·wick (mid′wā, härd′wik) uninc. place, CEN. Georgia; 14,047; ZIP 31320.
Midwest City city, CEN. Oklahoma; 48,114; ZIP see OKLAHOMA CITY.
Mi·lan (mi·lan′, -län′, mil′ən) city, N Italy; 1,666,300.
Mi·lan (mī′lən) town, w Tennessee; 7,313; ZIP 38358.
Miles City (mīlz) city, E Montana; 9,023; ZIP 59301.
Mil·ford (mil′fərd) city, SW Connecticut; 50,858; ZIP 06460*.
— city, E Delaware; 5,314; ZIP 19963.
— uninc. place, S CEN. Massachusetts; 19,352; ZIP 01757.
— city, SE New Hampshire; 6,622; ZIP 03055.
Mil·lard (mil′ərd) city, E CEN. Nebraska; 7,460; ZIP 68137.
Mill·brae (mil′brā) city, w California; 20,781; ZIP 94030*.
Mill·burn (mil′bərn) urb. twp., NE New Jersey; 21,307; ZIP 07041.
Mill·bur·y (mil′ber·ē, -bər·ē) town, S CEN. Massachusetts; 11,987; ZIP 01527.
Mill·creek (mil′krēk′) boro., S CEN. Pennsylvania; 28,441; ZIP 17060.
Mill·edge·ville (mil′ij·vil, -vəl) city, CEN. Georgia; 11,601; ZIP 31061*.
Mil·lers·ville (mil′ərz·vil) city, SE Pennsylvania; 6,396; ZIP 17551.
Millford Mills See WOODLAWN-ROCKDALE-MILLFORD MILLS
Mill·ing·ton (mil′ingt·n, -ing·tən) town, SW Tennessee; 21,106; ZIP 38053.
Mil·li·nock·et (mil′ə·nok′et, -it) uninc. place, CEN. Maine; 7,742; ZIP 04462.
Mil·lis (mil′is) city, E Massachusetts; 5,686; ZIP 02054.
Mill·town (mil′toun) boro., CEN. New Jersey; 6,470; ZIP 08850.
Mill·vale (mil′vāl) boro., SE Pennsylvania; 5,815; ZIP see PITTSBURGH.
Mill Valley city, w California; 12,942; ZIP 94941*.
Mill·ville (mil′vil) city, S New Jersey; 21,366; ZIP 08332.
Mil·pi·tas (mil′pi·təs) city, w California; 27,149; ZIP 95035.
Mil·ton (milt′n, mil′tən) city, SW Florida; 5,360; ZIP 32570.
— town, E Massachusetts; 27,190; ZIP see BOSTON.
— boro., E CEN. Pennsylvania; 7,723; ZIP 17847.
Mil·ton (milt′n, mil′tən) town, S Ontario, Canada; 6,601.
Mil·wau·kee (mil·wô′kē) city, SE Wisconsin; 717,099; ZIP 53200*.
Mil·wau·kie (mil·wô′kē) city, NW Oregon; 16,379; ZIP see PORTLAND.
Mim·i·co (mim′i·kō) town, s Ontario, Canada; 19,431.
Mims (mimz) city, SW Florida; 8,309; ZIP 32754.
Min·da·na·o (min′də·nä′ō) isl., S Philippines; 36,537 sq. mi.
Min·den (min′dən) city, NW Louisiana; 13,996; ZIP 71055.
Min·do·ro (min·dō′rō) isl., CEN. Philippines; 3,759 sq. mi.
Min·e·o·la (min′ē·ō′lə) vill., SE New York; 21,845; ZIP 11501*
Mineral Wells city, N CEN. Texas; 18,411; ZIP 76067.
Min·ers·ville (mīn′ərz·vil) boro., E CEN. Pennsylvania; 6,012; ZIP 17954.
Min·go Junction (ming′gō) city, E CEN. Ohio; 5,278; ZIP 43938.
Min·ne·ap·o·lis (min′ē·ap′ə·lis) city, E Minnesota; 434,400; ZIP 55400*.
Min·ne·so·ta (min′ə·sō′tə) state, N United States; 84,068 sq. mi.; 3,805,069; cap. St. Paul.
Min·ne·ton·ka (min′ə·tong′kə) vill., E Minnesota; 35,776; ZIP see HOPKINS.
Mi·nor·ca (mi·nôr′kə) one of the Balearic islands; 271 sq. mi.
Mi·not (mī′nət) city, N North Dakota; 32,290; ZIP 58701*.
Mi·not Base (mī′not) city, NW North Dakota; 12,077; ZIP 58701.
Minsk (minsk) city, CEN. Byelorussian SSR; cap.; 772,000.
Mi·ra·da Hills (mə·rä′də) city, SW California; 22,444.
Mi·ra Lo·ma (mir′ə lō′mə) city, SW California; 8,482; ZIP 91752.
Mir·a·mar (mir′ə·mär) city, SE Florida; 23,973; ZIP see HOLLYWOOD.
Mish·a·wa·ka (mish′ə·wô′kə) city, N Indiana; 35,517; ZIP 46544.
Mission city, NE Kansas; 8,376; ZIP 66222.
— city, s Texas; 13,043; ZIP 78572.
Mission Vi·e·jo (vē·ā′hō) city, SW California; 11,933; ZIP 92675.

Mis·sis·sip·pi (mis′ə·sip′ē) state, S United States; 47,716 sq. mi.; 2,216,912; cap. Jackson.
Mississippi River river, CEN. United States; 2,350 mi. long.
Mis·sou·la (mi·zōō′lə) city, w Montana; 29,497; ZIP 59801.
Missoula West city, w Montana; 9,148; ZIP 59801.
Mis·sou·ri (mi·zŏŏr′ē, -zŏŏr′ə) state, w CEN. United States; 69,674 sq. mi.; 4,677,399; cap. Jefferson City.
Missouri River river, NW CEN. United States; 2,470 mi. long.
Mitch·ell (mich′əl) city, SE CEN. South Dakota; 13,425; ZIP 57301.
Mo·ber·ly (mō′bər·lē) city, N CEN. Missouri; 12,988; ZIP 65270.
Mo·bile (mō·bēl′) city, SW Alabama; 190,026; ZIP 36600*.
Mobile Bay inlet of the Gulf of Mexico, SW Alabama.
Mo·des·to (mō·des′tō) city, CEN. California; 61,712; ZIP 95350*.
Mo·ja·ve Desert (mō·hä′vē) arid reg., S California; ab. 15,000 sq. mi.
Mo·ka·pu (mō·kä′pōō) city, E Oahu, Hawaii; 7,860; ZIP 96734.
Mol·da·vi·an SSR (mol·dā′vē·ən) constituent republic, SW USSR; 13,000 sq. mi.; 2,844,000; cap. Kishinev. Also **Mol·da′vi·a**.
Mo·line (mō·lēn′) city, NW Illinois; 46,237; ZIP 61265*.
Mo·lo·kai (mō′lə·kī′) isl., CEN. Hawaiian Islands; 259 sq. mi.
Mo·luc·ca Islands (mə·luk′ə) isl. group of Indonesia, betw. Celebes and New Guinea; 33,315 sq. mi.
Mon·a·ca (mon′ə·kə) boro., w Pennsylvania; 7,486; ZIP 15061.
Mon·a·co (mon′ə·kō, mə·nä′kō) independent principality, SE France; 368 acres; 22,000.
Mon·a·hans (mon′ə·hanz) city, w Texas; 8,333; ZIP 79756.
Monc·ton (mungk′tən) city, SE New Brunswick, Canada; 45,847.
Mo·nes·sen (mə·nes′ən) city, SW Pennsylvania; 15,216; ZIP 15062.
Mo·nett (mō′net, mō·net′) city, SW Missouri; 5,937; ZIP 65708.
Mon·go·li·a (mong·gō′lē·ə, mon-) reg., E CEN. Asia; ab. million sq. mi.; divided into the **Mongolian People's Republic** (formerly **Outer Mongolia**) in the N and W part; 590,966 sq. mi.; 954,000; cap. Ulan Bator; and **Inner Mongolia**, a reg., N China, most of which comprises the **Inner Mongolian Autonomous Region**; ab. 400,000 sq. mi.; 6,100,000; cap. Huhehot.
Mon·mouth (mon′məth) city, w Illinois; 11,022; ZIP 61462.
— city, NW Oregon; 5,237; ZIP 97361.
Mo·no·na (mə·nō′nə) city, S CEN. Wisconsin; 10,420; ZIP 53716.
Mo·non·ga·he·la (mə·nong′gə·hē′lə) city, SW Pennsylvania; 7,113; ZIP 15063.
Monongahela River river, West Virginia and w Pennsylvania; 128 mi. long.
Mon·roe (mən·rō′) city, SW Connecticut; 12,047; ZIP 06468.
— city, N CEN. Georgia; 8,071; ZIP 30655.
— city, N Louisiana; 56,374; ZIP 71201*.
— city, SE Michigan; 23,894; ZIP 48161.
— city, S North Carolina; 11,282; ZIP 28110.
— city, S Wisconsin; 8,654; ZIP 53566.
Mon·roe·ville (mən·rō′vil) boro., SW Pennsylvania; 29,011; ZIP see TURTLE CREEK.
Mon·ro·vi·a (mən·rō′vē·ə) city, E Liberia; cap.; ab. 80,992.
Mon·ro·vi·a (mən·rō′vē·ə) city, SW California; 30,015; ZIP 91016*.
Mon·sey (mon′zē) city, SW New York; 8,767.
Mon·son (mon′sən) city, W Massachusetts; 7,355; ZIP 01057.
Mon·ta·gue (mon′tə·gyōō) town, N Massachusetts; 8,451; ZIP 01351.
Mon·tan·a (mon·tan′ə) state, NW United States; 147,138 sq. mi.; 694,409; cap. Helena.
Mont Blanc (mont blangk′) highest mountain of the Alps, on the French-Italian border; 15,781 ft.
Mont·clair (mont·klâr′, mont′klâr) city, SW California; 22,546; ZIP see ONTARIO.
— town, NE New Jersey; 44,043; ZIP 07042*.
Mon·te·bel·lo (mon′ti·bel′ō) city, SW California; 42,807; ZIP 90640*.
Mon·te Car·lo (mon′tē kär′lō) city, Monaco; 10,000.
Mon·te·ne·gro (mon′tə·nē′grō) constituent republic, S Yugoslavia; 5,343 sq. mi.; 485,000; cap. Titograd.
Mon·te·rey (mon′tə·rā′) city, w California; 26,302; ZIP 93940*.
Monterey Park city, SW California; 49,166; ZIP 91754*.
Mon·ter·rey (mon′tə·rā′) city, NE Mexico; 875,578.
Mon·te·vid·e·o (mon′tə·vi·dā′ō, -vid′ē·ō) city, S Uruguay; cap.; 1,202,890.
Mon·te·vid·e·o (mon′tə·vid′ē·ō) city, SW Minnesota; 5,661; ZIP 56265.
Mont·gom·er·y (mont·gum′ər·ē, mənt-) city, E CEN. Ala-

bama; cap.; 133,386; ZIP 36100*.
— sw Ohio; 5,683; ZIP 45242.
Mon·ti·cel·lo (mon'tə·sel'ō, -chel'ō) estate and residence of Thomas Jefferson, near Charlottesville, Virginia.
Mon·ti·cel·lo (mon'ti·sel'ō) city, s Arkansas; 5,085; ZIP 71655.
— vill., SE New York; 5,991; ZIP 12701.
Mont-Jo·li (môn·shô·lē') town, E Quebec, Canada; 6,366.
Mont-Lau·ri·er (môn·lô·rē·ā') town, sw Quebec, Canada; 6,140.
Mont·ma·gny (môn·mà·nyē') town, SE Quebec, Canada; 12,241.
Mont·mar·tre (môn·mâr'tr') dist., N Paris; former artists' quarter.
Mont·mo·ren·cy (mont·mə·ren'sē, môn·môr·än·sē') town, s Quebec, Canada; 5,541.
Mont·ours·ville (mon·tōōrz'vil) boro., N CEN. Pennsylvania; 5,985; ZIP 17754.
Mont·pel·ier (mont·pēl'yər) city, N CEN. Vermont; cap.; 8,609; ZIP 05601*.
Mon·tre·al (mon'trē·ôl') city, s Quebec, Canada; 1,222,255.
Mon·tre·al-E. (mon'trē·ôl'ēst') town, s Quebec, Canada; 5,779. Also **Mon'tre·al'-East'**.
Mon·tre·al-N. (mon'trē·ôl'nôrth') city, s Quebec, Canada; 67,806. Also **Mon'tre·al'-North'**.
Mon·tre·al-O., **Mon·tre·al-W.** town, s Quebec, Canada; 6,612. Also **Mon'tre·al'-Ouest'**, **Mon'tre·al'-West'**.
Mon·trose (mon·trōz', mon'trōz) city, w Colorado; 6,496; ZIP 81401.
— city, NW Maryland; 6,140; ZIP 20850.
Mont-Roy·al (môn·rwà·yàl') town, s Quebec, Canada; 21,845.
Mont Saint Mi·chel (môn san mē·shel') isl. off NW France; site of an ancient fortress and abbey.
Mont·vale (mont'vāl) city, NE New Jersey; 7,327; ZIP 07645.
Mont·ville (mont'vil) city, SE Connecticut; 15,662; ZIP 06353.
Moore·head (mōr'hed, mōōr'-) city, CEN. Oklahoma; 18,761; ZIP 73852.
Moores·town-Len·o·la (mōōrz'toun·len·ō'lə) city, w CEN. New Jersey; 14,179; ZIP 08057.
Moores·ville (mōrz'vil, mōōrz'-) city, CEN. Indiana; 5,800; ZIP 46158.
— town, w CEN. North Carolina; 8,808; ZIP 28115.
Moor·head (mōr'hed, mōōr'-) city, w Minnesota; 29,687; ZIP 56560*.
Moose Jaw city, s Saskatchewan, Canada; 33,417.
Mo·ra·ga (mō·rä'gə) city, w California; 14,205; ZIP 94556.
Mo·ra·vi·a (mō·rä'vē·ə, mō-) reg., CEN. Czechoslovakia.
More·head City (mōr'hed, môr-) city, NE Kentucky; 7,191; ZIP 40351.
— town, E North Carolina; 5,233; ZIP 28557.
Mor·gan City (môr'gən) city, s Louisiana; 16,586; ZIP 70380.
Morgan Hill city, w California; 6,485; ZIP 95037.
Mor·gan·ton (môr'gən·tən) town, w North Carolina; 13,625; ZIP 28655.
Mor·gan·town (môr'gən·toun) city, N West Virginia; 29,431; ZIP 26500*.
Mo·roc·co (mə·rok'ō) kingdom, NW Africa; ab. 160,000 sq. mi.; 11,626,470; cap. Rabat.
Mor·ril·ton (mor'əl·tən, môr'əl·tən) city, CEN. Arkansas; 6,814; ZIP 72110.
Mor·ris (mor'is) city, NE Illinois; 8,194; ZIP 60450.
— city, sw Minnesota; 5,366; ZIP 56267.
Morris Plains city, N New Jersey; 5,540; ZIP 07950.
Mor·ris·town (mor'is·toun) town, N CEN. New Jersey; 17,662; ZIP 07960*.
— city, NE Tennessee; 20,318; ZIP 37813*.
Mor·ris·ville (mor'is·vil) boro., SE Pennsylvania; 11,309; ZIP 19067*.
Mor·ro Bay City (mô'rō, môr'ō) city, sw California; 7,109; ZIP 93442.
Mor·ton (môrt'n, môr'tən) vill., CEN. Illinois; 10,419; ZIP 61550.
Morton Grove vill., NE Illinois; 26,369; ZIP 60053.
Mos·cow (mos'kou, -kō) city, w USSR; cap. USSR and RSFSR; 6,507,000.
Mos·cow (mos'kō) city, NW Idaho; 14,146; ZIP 83843*.
Mo·selle (mō·zel') river, NE France, Luxembourg, and w West Germany; 320 mi. long.
Mo·ses Lake (mō'ziz, -zis) city, E CEN. Washington; 10,310; ZIP 98837*.
Moss Point city, SE Mississippi; 19,321; ZIP 39563.
Mo·sul (mō·sōōl') N Iraq; 243,311.
Moul·trie (mōl'trē) city, s Georgia; 14,302; ZIP 31768.
Mound vill., E Minnesota; 7,572; ZIP 55364*.
Mound Village city, SE Minnesota; 7,572; ZIP 55364.

Mounds View vill., E Minnesota; 9,988.
Mounds·ville (mounz'vil, moundz'-, -vəl) city, N West Virginia; 13,560; ZIP 26041.
Mountain Brook city, N CEN. Alabama; 19,474; ZIP see BIRMINGHAM.
Mountain Home city, sw Idaho; 6,451; ZIP 83647.
Mountain Home Base city, sw Idaho; 6,038; ZIP 83647.
Moun·tain·side (mount'n·sīd', moun'tən-) boro., NE New Jersey; 7,520; ZIP see WESTFIELD.
Mountain View city, w California; 51,092; ZIP 94040*.
Mount Air·y (âr'ē) town, NW North Carolina; 7,325; ZIP 27030*.
Mount Car·mel (kär'məl) city, SE Illinois; 8,096; ZIP 62863.
— boro., E CEN. Pennsylvania; 9,317; ZIP 17851.
Mount Clem·ens (klem'ənz) city, SE Michigan; 20,476; ZIP 48043*.
Mount Eph·ra·im (ef'rē·əm) boro., sw New Jersey; 5,625; ZIP 08056.
Mount Heal·thy (hel'thē) city, sw Ohio; 7,446; ZIP see CINCINNATI.
Mount Hol·ly (hol'ē) urb. twp., w New Jersey; 12,713; ZIP 08060.
— city, s CEN. North Carolina; 5,107; ZIP 28120.
Mount Joy city, sw Pennsylvania; 5,041; ZIP 17552.
Mount Kis·co (kis'kō) vill., SE New York; 8,172; ZIP 10549.
Mount·lake Terrace (mount'lāk) city, NW CEN. Washington; 16,600; ZIP 98043.
Mount Leb·a·non (leb'ə·nən) urb. twp., sw Pennsylvania; 39,956; ZIP see PITTSBURGH.
Mount Ol·i·ver (ol'ə·vər) boro., sw Pennsylvania; 5,487; ZIP see PITTSBURGH.
Mount O·lym·pus (ə·lim'pəs) city, NW Utah; 5,909.
Mount Pleas·ant (plez'ənt) city, SE Iowa; 7,007; ZIP 52641*.
— city, CEN. Michigan; 20,504; ZIP 48858.
— boro., sw Pennsylvania; 5,895; ZIP 15666.
— town, SE South Carolina; 6,155; ZIP 29464.
— city, NE Texas; 8,877; ZIP 75455.
Mount Pros·pect (pros'pekt) vill., NE Illinois; 34,995; ZIP 60056*.
Mount Rai·nier (rā'nir) city, w CEN. Maryland; 8,180; ZIP 20822.
Mount Ster·ling (stûr'ling) city, NE CEN. Kentucky; 5,083; ZIP 40353.
Mount Ver·non (vûr'nən) home and burial place of George Washington, near Washington, D.C.
— city, s Illinois; 15,980; ZIP 62864.
— city, sw Indiana; 6,770; ZIP 47620.
— city, SE New York; 72,778; ZIP 10550*.
— city, CEN. Ohio; 13,373; ZIP 43050.
— city, NW Washington; 8,804; ZIP 98273.
Mo·zam·bique (mō'zam·bēk') country, SE Africa; 297,731 sq. mi.; 6,575,000; cap. Maputo.
Muk·den (mōōk'den', mōōk'dən, mōōk'-) Shenyang: a former name.
Mul·lins (mul'inz) town, E South Carolina; 6,006; ZIP 29574.
Mun·cie (mun'sē) city, E Indiana; 69,080; ZIP 47301*.
Mun·de·lein (mun'də·līn) vill., NE Illinois; 16,128; ZIP 60060.
Mun·hall (mun'hôl) boro., sw Pennsylvania; 16,674; ZIP see HOMESTEAD.
Mu·nich (myōō'nik) city, SE West Germany; 1,210,465.
Mun·ster (mun'stər) town, NW Indiana; 16,514; ZIP see HAMMOND.
Mur·frees·bor·o (mûr'frēz·bûr'ō) city, CEN. Tennessee; 26,360; ZIP 37130*.
Mur·mansk (mōōr·mänsk') city, NW USSR; 287,000.
Mur·phys·bor·o (mûr'fēz·byr'ə) city, s Illinois; 10,013; ZIP 62966.
Mur·ray (mur'ē) city, sw Kentucky; 13,537; ZIP 42071*.
— city, N CEN. Utah; 21,206; ZIP see SALT LAKE CITY.
Murray River river, SE Australia; 1,600 mi. long.
Mus·cat and O·man (məs·kät' ənd ō·män') Oman: the former name.
Mus·ca·tine (mus'kə·tēn, mus'kə·tēn') city, E Iowa; 22,405; ZIP 52761.
Muscle Shoals former rapids in the Tennessee River, NW Alabama; site of the Wilson Dam; 6,907.
Mus·co·vy (mus'kə·vē) Ancient Russia.
Mus·coy (mus'koi) city, SE California; 7,091; ZIP 92405.
Mus·ke·go (mus·kē'gō) city, SE Wisconsin; 11,573; ZIP 53150.
Mus·ke·gon (mə·skē'gən) city, w Michigan; 44,631; ZIP 49440*.
Muskegon Heights city, w Michigan; 17,304; ZIP see MUSKEGON.
Mus·ko·gee (mus·kō'gē) city, E Oklahoma; 37,331; ZIP 74401*.

PRONUNCIATION KEY: add, āce, câre, pälm; end, ēven; it, īce; odd, ōpen, ôrder; tŏŏk, pōōl; up, bûrn; ə = a in *above*, e in *sicken*, i in *flexible*, o in *melon*, u in *focus*; yōō = u in *fuse*; oil; pout; check; go; ring; thin; this; zh, vision. For à, œ, ü, kh, ń, see inside front cover.

Myrtle Beach town, E South Carolina; 8,536; ZIP 29577.
Myrtle Grove city, CEN. Florida; 16,186; ZIP 32506.
My·sore (mī·sôr′, -sōr′) state, S India; 74,122 sq. mi.; 23,547,000; cap. Bangalore.
— city, S India; 259,907.

Nac·og·do·ches (nak′əg·dō′chis) city, E Texas; 22,544; ZIP 75961*.
Na·ga·sa·ki (nä·gä·sä·kē) city, NW Kyushu island, Japan; largely destroyed by a U.S. atomic bomb, Aug. 9, 1945; 420,000.
Na·go·ya (nä·gō·yä) city, S CEN. Honshu isl., Japan; 1,990,277.
Nag·pur (näg′pŏŏr) city, CEN. India; 745,847.
Nai·ro·bi (nī·rō′bē) city, SW Kenya; cap.; 266,794.
Na·mib·i·a (nə·mib′ē·ə) country, SW Africa; 317,877 sq. mi.; 852,000; cap. Windhoek.
Nam·pa (nam′pə) city, SW Idaho; 20,768; ZIP 83651.
Na·nai·mo (nə·nī′mō) city, SW British Columbia, Canada; 15,188.
Na·na Ku·li (nä′nä kōō′lē) city, W Oahu, Hawaii; 6,506; ZIP 96792.
Nan·king (nan′king′, nän′-) city, E China; cap. 1928–37; 1,419,000.
Nantes (nants) city, W France; 259,208.
Nan·ti·coke (nan′ti·kōk) city, NE CEN. Pennsylvania; 14,632; ZIP 18634.
Nan·tuck·et (nan·tuk′it) isl. off SE Massachusetts; 57 sq. mi.
Nan·u·et (nan·yōō·et′) city, SE New York; 10,447.
Na·pa (nap′ə) city, W California; 35,987; ZIP 94558*.
Na·per·ville (nā′pər·vil) city, NE Illinois; 23,885; ZIP 60540.
Na·ples (nā′pəlz) city, SW Italy; 1,220,639.
Na·ples (nā′pəlz) city, SW Florida; 12,042; ZIP 33940.
Na·po·le·on (nə·pō′lē·ən) city, NW Ohio; 7,791; ZIP 43545.
Nar·berth (när′bərth) boro., SE Pennsylvania; 5,151; ZIP 19072.
Nar·ra·gan·sett (nar′ə·gan′sit) city SW Rhode Island; 7,138; ZIP 02882.
Narragansett Bay inlet of the Atlantic, SE Rhode Island.
Nash·u·a (nash′ōō·ə) city, S New Hampshire; 55,820; ZIP 03060.
Nash·ville (nash′vil) city, N CEN. Tennessee; cap.; 447,877; ZIP 37200*.
Nas·sau (nas′ô) city, New Providence, Bahamas Islands; cap.; 80,907.
Na·tal (nə·täl′, nə·tal′) prov., E South Africa; 33,578 sq. mi. (including Zululand); 2,933,000; cap., Pietermaritzburg.
Natch·ez (nach′iz) city, SW Mississippi; 19,704; ZIP 39120*.
Natch·i·toches (nak′ə·tosh) city, NW CEN. Louisiana; 15,974; ZIP 71457.
Na·tick (nā′tik) town, NE Massachusetts; 31,057; ZIP 01760*.
National City city, SW California; 43,184; ZIP 92050*.
Nau·ga·tuck (nô′gə·tuk′) town, SW CEN. Connecticut; 23.034; ZIP 06770*.
Na·u·ru (nä·ōō′rōō) republic, W Pacific Ocean; 8 sq. mi.; 8,000; cap. Yaren.
Na·varre (nə·vär′) reg. and former kingdom, N Spain and SW France.
Nav·a·so·ta (nav′ə·sō′tə) city, E CEN. Texas; 5,111; ZIP 77868.
Naz·a·reth (naz′ə·rith) town, N Israel; scene of Christ's childhood; 22,000.
Naz·a·reth (naz′ə·rith) boro., E Pennsylvania; 5,815; ZIP 18064.
Ne·bras·ka (nə·bras′kə) state, CEN. United States; 77,237 sq. mi.; 1,483,791; cap. Lincoln.
Nebraska City city, SE Nebraska; 7,441; ZIP 68410.
Ne·der·land (nē′dər·lənd) city, SE Texas; 16,810; ZIP 77627.
Need·ham (nēd′əm) town, NE Massachusetts; 29,748; ZIP see BOSTON.
Nee·nah (nē′nə) city, E CEN. Wisconsin; 22,892; ZIP 54956*.
Neg·ev (neg′ev, ne·gev′) desert reg., S Israel; 4,700 sq. mi. Also **Neg·eb** (neg′eb, nə·geb′).
Nejd (nejd) prov., CEN. Saudi Arabia; ab. 450,000 sq. mi.; 4 million; cap. Riyadh.
Ne·pal (nə·päl′) kingdom betw. Tibet and India; 54,362 sq. mi.; 9,407,000; cap. Katmandu.
Nep·tune (nep′tōōn, -tyōōn) urb. twp., E New Jersey; 27,863; ZIP 07753.
Nes·con·set (nes·kon′sit) city, SE New York; 10,048.
Neth·er·lands (neth′ər·ləndz) country, NW Europe; 15,780 sq. mi.; 11,745,000; cap. Amsterdam; seat of government, The Hague.
Netherlands, Kingdom of the kingdom comprising the Netherlands, the Netherlands Antilles, and Surinam; cap. Amsterdam.
Netherlands Antilles 3 isls. N of Venezuela and 3 in the Leeward Islands group; 336 sq. mi.; 196,000; cap. Willemstad.
Netherlands East Indies former Netherlands possessions

in the Malay Archipelago. Also **Netherlands Indies**. See INDONESIA.
Netherlands Guiana See SURINAM.
Netherlands New Guinea West New Guinea: *the former name.*
Netherlands West Indies See NETHERLANDS ANTILLES.
Neth·er Prov·i·dence (neth′ər prov′ə·dəns) urb. twp., SE Pennsylvania; 10,380.
Ne·vad·a (nə·vad′ə, -vä′də) state, W United States; 110,540 sq. mi.; 488,738; cap. Carson City.
Ne·va·da (nə·vä′də) city, W Missouri; 9,736; ZIP 64772.
New Al·ba·ny (ôl′bə·nē) city, S Indiana; 38,402; ZIP 47150.
— city, N Mississippi; 6,426; ZIP 38652.
New·ark (nōō′ərk, nyōō′-) city, W California; 27,153; ZIP 94560.
New·ark (nōō′ärk′, nyōō′-) city, NW Delaware; 20,757; ZIP 19711*.
New·ark (nōō′ərk, nyōō′-, nôôrk) city, NE New Jersey; 382,417; ZIP 07100*.
New·ark (nōō′ärk, nyōō′-) vill., W New York; 11,644; ZIP 14513.
— city, CEN. Ohio; 41,836; ZIP 43055*.
New Bed·ford (bed′fərd) city, SE Massachusetts; 101,777; ZIP 02740*.
New·berg (nyōō′bûrg) city, NW Oregon; 6,507; ZIP 97132.
New Ber·lin (bûr′lin) city, SE Wisconsin; 26,937; ZIP 53151.
New Bern (nyōō′ bərn) city, E North Carolina; 14,660; ZIP 28560*.
New·ber·ry (nyōō′ber′ē, -bər·ē) town, NW CEN. South Carolina; 9,218; ZIP 29108.
New Braun·fels (broun′fəlz) city, S CEN. Texas; 17,859; ZIP 78130*.
New Brith·ton (brīt′n, brī′tən) vill., E Minnesota; 19,507; ZIP see ST. PAUL.
— boro., W Pennsylvania; 7,637; ZIP 15066.
New Brit·ain (brit′n) city, N CEN. Connecticut; 83,441; ZIP 06050*.
New Bruns·wick (brunz′wik) city, E CEN. New Jersey; 41,885; ZIP 08900*.
New Bruns·wick (brunz′wik) prov., SE Canada; 27,836 sq. mi.; 616,788; cap. Fredericton.
New·burgh (nōō′bûrg, nyōō′-) city, SE New York; 26,219; ZIP 12550*.
New·bury·port (nyōō′bər·ē·pôrt′, nōō′, -pōrt′) city, NE Massachusetts; 15,807; ZIP 01950*.
New Cal·e·don·i·a (kal′ə·dō′nē·ə, -nyə) isl. E of Australia; comprising with adjacent isls. a French overseas terr.; 9,401 sq. mi.; 69,000; cap. Nouméa.
New Ca·naan (kā′nən) city, SW Connecticut; 17,455; ZIP 06840.
New Car·lisle (kär′līl, kär·līl′) city, SW Ohio; 6,112; ZIP 45344.
New Car·roll·ton (kar′əl·tən) city, NE Maryland; 13,395.
New Cas·sel (kas′əl) city, SE New York; 8,554.
New Castle city, E Indiana; 21,215; ZIP 47362.
— city, W Pennsylvania; 35,559; ZIP 16101*.
New·cas·tle-up·on-Tyne (nōō′kas·əl·ə·pon′tīn′, nyōō′-) city, NE England; 269,000. Also **Newcastle, Newcastle-on-Tyne**.
New·cas·tle (nōō′kas·el, nyōō′-) town, NE New Brunswick, Canada; 5,911.
New City city, SE New York; 27,344; ZIP 10956.
New Cum·ber·land (kum′bər·lənd) boro., S Pennsylvania; 9,803; ZIP 17070.
New Del·hi (del′ē) city, Delhi terr., India; cap. of India; 324,283.
New England NE section of the United States, including Maine, New Hampshire, Vermont, Massachusetts, Rhode Island, and Connecticut.
New·found·land (nōō′fənd·land′, nyōō′-) prov., E Canada; comprising the island of **Newfoundland** (42,734 sq. mi.) and Labrador on the mainland; 152,734 sq. mi.; 493,396; cap. St. John's.
New Geor·gia (jôr′jə, jôr′-) isl. group, British Solomon Islands; ab. 2,000 sq. mi.
New Glas·gow (glas′gō, glaz′-, glas′kō) town, N Nova Scotia, Canada; 10,489.
New Guin·ea (gin′ē) isl., N of Australia; 304,200 sq. mi. See WEST NEW GUINEA, PAPUA AND NEW GUINEA.
New Guinea, Territory of trust terr. comprising NE New Guinea, the Bismarck Archipelago, and Bougainville and Buka in the Solomon Islands; governed administratively with the Territory of Papua; 93,220 sq. mi.; 1,400,000; adm. ctr. Port Moresby.
New·hall (nyōō′hôl, nōō′-) city, SW California; 9,651; ZIP 91321.
New Hamp·shire (hamp′shir) state, NE United States; 9,304 sq. mi.; 737,681; cap. Concord.
New Ha·ven (hā′vən) city, S Connecticut; 137,707; ZIP 06500*.
— city, NE Indiana; 5,728; ZIP 46774.

New Heb·ri·des (heb′ri·dēz) isl. group, sw Pacific; an Anglo-French condominium; ab. 5,700 sq. mi.; 59,000; cap. Vila.

New Hope city, se Minnesota; 23,180.

New Hyde Park (hīd) vill., se New York; 10,116; ZIP 11040*.

New I·ber·i·a (ī·bir′ē·ə) city, s Louisiana; 30,147; ZIP 70560*.

New·ing·ton (nyōō′ing·tən, nōō′-) city, CEN. Connecticut; 26,037; ZIP 06111.

New Jer·sey (jûr′zē) state, E United States; 7,836 sq. mi.; 7,168,164; cap. Trenton.

New Ken·sing·ton (ken′zing·tən) city, w Pennsylvania; 20,312; ZIP 15068*.

New Lon·don (lun′dən) city, se Connecticut; site of a naval base; 31,630; ZIP 06301*.

  — city, E CEN. Wisconsin; 5,801; ZIP 54961.

New·mar·ket (nyōō′mär′ket, -kit) town, s Ontario, Canada; 9,758.

New Mar·tins·ville (märt′nz·vil, mär′tənz-) city, NW West Virginia; 6,528; ZIP 26155.

New Mex·i·co (mek′sə·ko) state, sw United States; 121,666 sq. mi.; 1,016,000; cap. Santa Fé.

New Mil·ford (mil′fərd) city, NW Connecticut; 14,601; ZIP 06776.

  — boro., NE New Jersey; 20,201; ZIP 07646.

New·nan (nyōō′nən) city, w Georgia; 11,205; ZIP 30263.

New Or·le·ans (ôr′lē·ənz, ôr·lēnz′, ôr′lənz) city, se Louisiana; 593,471; ZIP 70100*.

New Paltz (pôltz) city, E CEN. New York; 6,058; ZIP 12561.

New Phil·a·del·phi·a (fil′ə·del′fē·ə, -fyə) city, E CEN. Ohio; 15,184; ZIP 44663.

New·port (nōō′pôrt, nyōō′-, -pōrt) city, NE Arkansas; 7,725; ZIP 72112*.

  — city, N Kentucky; 25,998; ZIP 41079*.

  — city, sw New Hampshire; 5,899; ZIP 03773.

  — city, w Oregon; 5,188; ZIP 97365*.

  — city, se Rhode Island; 34,562; ZIP 02840*.

  — town, E Tennessee; 7,328; ZIP 37821.

Newport Beach city, sw California; 49,422; ZIP 92660*.

Newport East city, s Rhode Island; 10,285.

Newport News city, se Virginia; 138,177; ZIP 23600*.

New Port Rich·ey (rich′ē) city, sw Florida; 6,098; ZIP 33552.

New Prov·i·dence (prov′i·dəns) boro., NE New Jersey; 13,796; ZIP 07974.

New River-Gie·ger (gī′gər) city, se North Carolina; 8,699.

New Ro·chelle (rə·shel′) city, se New York; 75,385.

New Shrews·bur·y (shrōōz′ber·ē) boro., E New Jersey; 5,925.

New Smyr·na Beach (smûr′nə) city, NE Florida; 10,580; ZIP 32069.

New South Wales state, se Australia; 309,433 sq. mi.; 4,000,000; cap. Sydney.

New·ton (nōōt′n, nyōōt′-, nōō′tən, nyōō′-) city, CEN. Iowa; 15,619; ZIP 50208.

  — city, s CEN. Kansas; 15,439; ZIP 67114.

  — city, E Massachusetts; 91,066; ZIP see BOSTON.

  — town, N New Jersey; 7,297; ZIP 07860.

  — town, w CEN. North Carolina; 7,857; ZIP 28658.

Newton Falls vill., NE Ohio; 5,378; ZIP 44444.

New To·ron·to (tə·ron′tō) town, s Ontario, Canada; 13,234.

New·town (nyōō′toun, nōō′-) city, sw Connecticut; 16,942; ZIP 06470.

New Ulm (ulm) city, s Minnesota; 13,051; ZIP 56073.

New Wa·ter·ford (wô′tər·fərd, wot′ər-) town, NE Nova Scotia, Canada; 9,725.

New West·min·ster (west′min′stər, wes′-) city, sw British Columbia, Canada; 38,013.

New Wind·sor (wind′zər) city, se New York; 8,803; ZIP 12550.

New York (yôrk) state, NE United States; 49,576 sq. mi.; 18,190,740; cap. Albany.

  — city, se New York; divided into the five boroughs of the Bronx, Brooklyn, Manhattan, Queens, and Richmond (Staten Island); 365 sq. mi.; 7,867,760; ZIP 10000*.

New York State Barge Canal waterway system, New York; connects the Hudson River with Lakes Erie, Champlain, and Ontario; 525 mi. long.

New Zea·land (zē′lənd) self-governing member of the Commonwealth of Nations, comprising a group of isls. se of Australia; 103,416 sq. mi., excluding island territories; 2,414,000; cap. Wellington.

Ni·ag·a·ra Falls (nī·ag′rə, -ər·ə) city, w New York; 85,615; ZIP 14300*.

Ni·ag·a·ra Falls (nī·ag′rə, -ə·rə) city, s Ontario, Canada; 56,891.

Niagara River river betw. Ontario, Canada, and New York

State, connecting Lake Erie and Lake Ontario; in its course occurs **Niagara Falls**, a cataract divided by Goat Island into the American Falls, ab. 167 ft. high and 1,000 ft. wide, and Horseshoe Falls on the Canadian side, ab. 160 ft. high and 2,500 ft. wide.

Nic·a·ra·gua (nik′ə·rä′gwə) republic, Central America; ab. 57,100 sq. mi.; 1,502,000; cap. Managua.

Nicaragua, Lake lake, sw Nicaragua; 3,100 sq. mi.

Nice (nēs) city, se France; 322,442.

Nich·o·las·ville (nik′ə·ləs·vil) city, CEN. Kentucky; 5,829; ZIP 40356.

Nic·o·si·a (nik′ə·sē′ə) city, N CEN. Cyprus; cap.; 47,000.

Ni·ger (nī′jər, -gər) river, w Africa; ab. 2,600 mi. long.

Niger, Republic of republic of the French Community, w CEN. Africa; 458,976 sq. mi.; 3,112,000; cap. Niamey.

Ni·ge·ri·a (nī·jir′ē·ə), **Federation of** independent member of the Commonwealth of Nations, w Africa; 339,168 sq. mi.; 35,752,000; cap. Lagos.

Nile (nīl) river, E Africa; 4,130 mi. long.

Niles (nīlz) vill., NE Illinois; 31,432; ZIP see CHICAGO.

  — city, sw Michigan; 12,988; ZIP 49120.

  — city, NE Ohio; 21,581; ZIP 44446.

Nis·ka·yu·na (nis′kə·yōō′nə) city, se New York; 6,186; ZIP 12309.

Ni·tro (nī′trō) city, w West Virginia; 8,019; ZIP 25143.

No·bles·ville (nō′bəlz·vil) city, CEN. Indiana; 7,548; ZIP 46060.

No·gal·es (nō·gal′is) city, s Arizona; 8,946; ZIP 85621.

Nor·an·da (nôr·an′də) city, w Quebec, Canada; 11,521.

Nor·co (nôr′kō) city, sw California; 14,511; ZIP 91760.

Nor·folk (nôr′fək, -fôk′) city, NE Nebraska; 16,607; ZIP 68701.

Nor·folk (nôr′fək) city, se Virginia; 307,951; ZIP 23500*.

Nor·mal (nôr′məl) town, CEN. Illinois; 26,396; ZIP 61761.

Nor·man (nôr′mən) city, CEN. Oklahoma; 52,117; ZIP 73069*.

Nor·man·dy (nôr′mən·dē) reg. and former prov., NW France.

Nor·man·dy (nôr′mən·dē) city, NE Missouri; 6,306; ZIP 63121.

Nor·ridge (nor′ij) vill., NE Illinois; 16,880.

Nor·ris·town (nôr′is·toun′, nor′-) boro., se Pennsylvania; 38,169; ZIP 19401*.

North Adams city, NW Massachusetts; 19,195; ZIP 01247*.

North America N continent of the w hemisphere; 9.3 million sq. mi. (including adjacent islands); 261,348,000.

North Am·i·ty·ville (am′i·tē·vil) city, se New York; 11,905.

North·amp·ton (nôr·thamp′tən) city, w Massachusetts; 29,664; ZIP 01060*.

Northampton boro., E Pennsylvania; 8,389; ZIP 18067.

North An·do·ver (an′dō·vər) town, NE Massachusetts; 16,284; ZIP see LAWRENCE.

North An·drews Terrace (an′drōōz) city, se Florida; 7,082.

North Ard·more (ärd′môr, -mōr) city, se Pennsylvania; 5,856.

North Ar·ling·ton (är′ling·tən) boro., NE New Jersey; 18,096.

North At·lan·ta (at·lan′tə) vill., N CEN. Georgia; 15,000; ZIP see ATLANTA.

North At·tle·bor·ough (at′əl·bər·ə) town, E Massachusetts; 18,665; ZIP 02760*.

North Au·gus·ta (ô·gus′tə) city, w South Carolina; 12,883; ZIP 29841.

North Bab·y·lon (bab′i·lon) city, se New York; 39,556.

North Bat·tle·ford (bat′əl·fərd) city, w Saskatchewan, Canada; 12,262.

North Bay city, se CEN. Ontario, Canada; 23,635.

North Bell·more (bel′môr) uninc. place, se New York; 22,893; ZIP see BELLMORE.

North Bel·mont (bel′mont) uninc. place, sw North Carolina; 10,759; ZIP see BELMONT.

North Bend city, sw Oregon; 8,553; ZIP 97459.

North Ber·gen (bûr′gən) urb. twp., NE New Jersey; 47,751; ZIP 07047*.

North Bor·ne·o (bôr′nē·o, bôr′-) reg., N Borneo; part of Malaysia; 29,338 sq. mi.; 429,000; cap. Jesselton.

North·bor·ough (nôrth′bûr′ō) city, CEN. Massachusetts; 9,218; ZIP 01532.

North Brad·dock (brad′ək) boro., sw Pennsylvania; 10,838.

North Bran·ford (bran′fərd) city, s Connecticut; 10,778; ZIP 06471.

North·bridge (nôrth′brij) city, CEN. Massachusetts; 11,795; ZIP 01536.

North·brook (nôrth′brŏŏk) vill., NE Illinois; 27,297; ZIP 60062.

North Cald·well (kôld·wel) city, NE New Jersey; 6,425; ZIP 07006.
North Can·ton (kan′tən, kant′n) vill., NE Ohio; 15,228; ZIP see CANTON.
North Cape promontory, N Norway.
North Car·o·li·na (kar′ə·lī′nə) state, SE United States; 52,712 sq. mi.; 5,082,059; cap. Raleigh.
North Chi·ca·go (shə·kä′gō, -kô′-) city, NE Illinois; 47,275; ZIP 60064*.
North College Hill city, SW Ohio; 12,363; ZIP see CINCINNATI.
North Da·ko·ta (də·kō′tə) state, N United States; 70,665 sq. mi.; 617,761; cap. Bismarck.
Northern Ire·land (īr′lənd) part of the United Kingdom in N reg. of Ireland; 5,238 sq. mi.; 1,425,000; cap. Belfast.
Northern Rho·de·sia (rō·dē′zhə,-shə) former British prot., S CEN. Africa. See ZAMBIA.
Northern Territory reg., N Australia; 523,620 sq. mi.; 27 095; cap. Darwin.
North Fair Oaks city, W CEN. California; 9,740.
North·field (nôrth′fēld) city, SE Minnesota; 10,235; ZIP 55057.
— city, SE New Jersey; 8,875; ZIP 08225.
North Fort My·ers (mī′ərz) city, CEN. Florida; 8,789; ZIP 33930.
North Fort Polk (pōk) city, SE Louisiana; 7,955.
North Fort Ri·ley (rī′lē) city, NE Kansas; 12,469.
North Glen city, E CEN. Colorado; 27,937; ZIP 80201.
North Great River city, SE New York; 12,080.
North Hale·don (hāl′dən) boro., NE New Jersey; 7,614.
North Ha·ven (hā′vən) city, S Connecticut; 22,194; ZIP 06501.
North Highlands uninc. place, CEN. California; 31,854; ZIP 95660.
North Island isl., N New Zealand; 44,281 sq. mi.
North Islands city, SW California; 6,002.
North Kam·loops (kam′lōōps) vill., S British Columbia, Canada; 11,319.
North Kan·sas City (kan′zəs) town, W Missouri; 5,183; ZIP see KANSAS CITY.
North Kings·ton (kingz′tən, king′stən) town, S Rhode Island; 27,673; ZIP 02852*.
North Korea See KOREA.
North·lake (nôrth′lāk′) city, NE Illinois; 14,212; ZIP see MELROSE PARK.
North Las Ve·gas (läs vā′gəs) city, SE Nevada; 36,216; ZIP 89030*.
North Lin·den·hurst (lin′din·hûrst) city, SE New York; 11,205.
North Little Rock, CEN. Arkansas; 60,040; ZIP 72114*.
North Man·ches·ter (man′ches′tər) city, NE Indiana; 6,791; ZIP 46962.
North Man·ka·to (man·kā′tō) city, S Minnesota; 7,347; ZIP see MANKATO.
North Mas·sa·pequ·ua (mas′ə·pēk′wə) city, SE New York; 23,101.
North Mer·rick (mer′ik) uninc. place, SE New York; 12,650.
North Mi·am·i (mī·am′ē, -am′ə) city, SE Florida; 34,767; ZIP see MIAMI.
North Miami Beach city, SE Florida; 30,723; ZIP see MIAMI.
North New Hyde Park (hīd) uninc. place, SE New York; 17,945; ZIP see NEW HYDE PARK.
North Og·den (og·din) city, NW Utah; 5,257; ZIP 84401.
North Olm·sted (um′sted, -stid) city, N Ohio; 34,861; ZIP 44070.
North Park city, NE Illinois; 15,679; ZIP 61101.
North Patch·ogue (pach′og) city, SE New York; 6,383.
North Pel·ham (pel′əm) vill., SE New York; 5,184.
North Plain·field (plān′fēld) boro., NE New Jersey; 27,796; ZIP see PLAINFIELD.
North Platte (plat) city, CEN. Nebraska; 19,447; ZIP 69101*.
North Pole N extremity of the earth's axis.
North·port (nôrth′pôrt, -pōrt) city, W CEN. Alabama; 9,435; ZIP 35476.
— vill., SE New York; 7,440; ZIP 11768.
North Po·to·mac (pə·tō′mək) city, NW Maryland; 12,546.
North Prov·i·dence (prov′i·dəns) town, NE Rhode Island; 24,337.
North Read·ing (red′ing) city, N Massachusetts; 11,264; ZIP 01864.
North Rich·land Hills (rich′lənd) town, N Texas; 16,514.
North·ridge (nôrth′rij) city, SW Ohio; 10,084.
North Ridge·ville (rij′vil) city, N CEN. Ohio; 13,152; ZIP 44035.
North Riv·er·side (riv′ər·sīd′) vill., NE Illinois; 8,097; ZIP see RIVERSIDE.
North Roy·al·ton (roi′əlt·n, roi′əl·tən) vill., N Ohio; 12,807; ZIP see CLEVELAND.
North Sac·ra·men·to (sak′rə·men′tō) city, CEN. California; 12,922; ZIP see SACRAMENTO.

North Saint Paul vill., E Minnesota; 11,950; ZIP see ST. PAUL.
North Sea part of the Atlantic betw. Great Britain and Europe.
North Scit·u·ate (sich′ōō·āt) city, NE Massachusetts; 5,507; ZIP 02060.
North Shreve·port (shrēv′pôrt, -pōrt) uninc. place, NW Louisiana; 7,701.
North Smith·field (smith′fēld′) city, SW Rhode Island; 9,349.
North Spring·field (spring′fēld′) city, NE Virginia; 8,631; ZIP 22151.
North Syd·ney (sid′nē) town, E Nova Scotia, Canada; 8,752.
North Syr·a·cuse (sir′ə·kyōōs, -kyōōz) vill., CEN. New York; 8,687; ZIP see SYRACUSE.
North Ta·ko·ma Park (tə·kō′mə) city, NE Maryland; 7,373.
North Tar·ry·town (tar′ē·toun) vill., SE New York; 8,334; ZIP see TARRYTOWN.
North Ton·a·wan·da (ton′ə·won′də) city, NW New York; 36,012; ZIP 14120*.
North·vale (nôrth′vāl) city, NE New Jersey; 5,177; ZIP 07647.
North Valley city, CEN. New Mexico; 10,366.
North Valley Stream uninc. place, SE New York; 14,881.
North Van·cou·ver (van·kōō′vər) city, SW British Columbia, Canada; 20,851.
North Ver·sailles (vər·sālz′) urb. twp., SW Pennsylvania; 13,583.
North Vietnam See VIETNAM.
North·ville (nôrth′vil) city, SE Michigan; 5,400; ZIP 48167.
North Wan·taugh (won′tô) city, SE New York; 15,053.
Northwest Territories adm. div., N Canada; 1,304,903 sq. mi.; 28,136.
Northwest Territory reg. awarded to the United States by Britain in 1783, extending from the Great Lakes S to the Ohio River and from Pennsylvania W to the Mississippi.
Nor·ton (nôr′tən) city, S Massachusetts; 9,487; ZIP 02766.
— city, NE Ohio; 12,308; ZIP 44203.
Norton Shores city, SW Michigan; 22,271; ZIP 49444.
Nor·walk (nôr′wôk) city, SW California; 91,872; ZIP 90650*.
— city, SW Connecticut; 79,113; ZIP 06850*.
— city, N Ohio; 13,386; ZIP 44857.
Nor·way (nôr′wā) kingdom, N Europe; 119,240 sq. mi.; 3,626,000; cap. Oslo.
Nor·well (nôr′wel) city, NE Massachusetts; 7,796; ZIP 02061.
Nor·wich (nor′ij, -ich) co. boro., E England; 120,000.
Nor·wich (nôr′wich, nor′ich) city, SE Connecticut; 41,433; ZIP 06360*.
Nor·wich (nôr′wich) city, CEN. New York; 8,843; ZIP 13815.
Nor·wood (nôr′wŏŏd) city, SE Florida; 14,973; ZIP 33054.
— town, E Massachusetts; 30,815; ZIP 02062.
— city, SW Ohio; 30,420; ZIP see CINCINNATI.
— boro., SE Pennsylvania; 7,229; ZIP 19074.
Not·ting·ham (not′ing·əm) co. boro., N CEN. England; 305,050.
No·va Sco·tia (nō′və skō′shə) prov., E Canada; 21,068 sq. mi.; 756,039; cap. Halifax.
No·va·to (nō·vä′tō) city, W California; 31,006; ZIP 94947.
No·vi (nō′vī) vill., SE Michigan; 9,668; ZIP 48050.
Nu·bi·a (nōō′bē·ə, nyōō′-) reg., NE Africa.
Nu·rem·berg (nŏŏr′əm·bûrg, nyŏŏr′-) city, SE CEN. West Germany; 471,997.
Nut·ley (nut′lē) town, NE New Jersey; 32,099; ZIP see NEWARK.
Ny·ack (nī′ak′) vill., SE New York; 6,659; ZIP 10960.
Nya·sa·land (nyä′sä·land, nī·as′ə-) former British prot., SE Africa. See MALAWI.

O·a·hu (ō·ä′hōō) isl., N CEN. Hawaiian Islands; 589 sq. mi.
Oak Creek city, SE Wisconsin; 13,901; ZIP 53154*.
Oak·dale (ōk′dāl) city, W CEN. California; 6,594; ZIP 95361.
— city, SW CEN. Louisiana; 7,301; ZIP 71463.
— city, NE Minnesota; 7,304.
— city, SE New York; 7,334.
Oak Forest Village city, NE Illinois; 17,870; ZIP 60452.
Oak Harbor city, NW Washington; 9,167; ZIP 98277.
Oak·hurst (ōk′hûrst) city, E CEN. New Jersey; 5,558; ZIP 07755.
Oak·land (ōk′lənd) city, W California; 361,561; ZIP 94600*.
— boro., NE New Jersey; 14,420; ZIP 07436.
Oakland Park city, SE Florida; 16,261; ZIP see FORT LAUDERDALE.
Oak Lane city, SE Pennsylvania; 6,192.
Oak Lawn vill., NE Illinois; 60,305; ZIP 60453*.
Oak·mont (ōk′mont) boro., SW Pennsylvania; 7,550; ZIP 15139.
Oak Park vill., NE Illinois; 62,511; ZIP 60300*.
— city, SE Michigan; 36,762; ZIP see DETROIT.
Oak Ridge city, E Tennessee; 28,319; ZIP 37830*.

Oak·ville (ōk'vil) town, S Ontario, Canada; 52,793.
Oak·ville (ōk'vil) city, E CEN. New Jersey; 7,503.
Oak·wood (ōk'wŏŏd) city, SW Ohio; 10,095; ZIP 45873.
O·ber·am·mer·gau (ō'bər·äm'ər·gou) vill., SE West Germany; noted for its decennial Passion play.
O·ber·lin (ō'bər·lin) city, N Ohio; 8,761; ZIP 44074.
O·cal·a (ō·kal'ə) city, N CEN. Florida; 22,583; ZIP 32670.
Ocean City city, SW Florida; 5,267.
— city, SE New Jersey; 10,575; ZIP 08226.
O·ce·an·i·a (ō'shē·an'ē·ə) isls. of Melanesia, Micronesia, and Polynesia, and sometimes the Malay Archipelago and Australasia.
O·cean·port (ō'shən·pôrt) city, E CEN. New Jersey; 7,503; ZIP 07757.
O·cean·side (ō'shən·sīd') city, SW California; 40,494; ZIP 92054*.
— vill., SE New York; 35,028; ZIP see ROCKVILLE CENTRE.
Ocean Springs town, SE Mississippi; 9,580; ZIP 39564.
O·con·o·mo·woc (ō·kon'ə·mō·wok') city, SE Wisconsin; 8,741; ZIP 53066.
O·den·ton (ō'din·tən) city, NW Maryland; 5,989; ZIP 21113.
O·der (ō'dər) river, CEN. Europe; 563 mi. long.
O·des·sa (ō·des'ə) city, S Ukrainian SSR; 776,000.
O·des·sa (ō·des'ə) city, W Texas; 78,380; ZIP 79760*.
Oel·wein (ōl'wīn) city, NE Iowa; 7,735; ZIP 50662.
O'·Fal·lon (ō·fal'ən) city, NE Illinois; 7,268; ZIP 62269.
Of·fut East (ŏf'ət, of'-) city, E CEN. Nebraska; 5,195.
Offut West city, E CEN. Nebraska; 8,445.
Og·den (og'dən) city, N Utah; 69,478; ZIP 84400*.
Og·dens·burg (og'dənz·bûrg) city, N New York; 14,554; ZIP 13669.
O·hi·o (ō·hī'ō) state, NE CEN. United States; 41,222 sq. mi.; 10,652,017; cap. Columbus.
Ohio River river, E CEN. United States; 981 mi. long.
Oil City city, NW Pennsylvania; 15,033; ZIP 16301*.
Oil·dale (oil'dāl) city, S CEN. California; 20,879; ZIP 93308.
O·jai (ō'hī) city, SW California; 5,591; ZIP 93023.
O·ke·mos (ō·kē'məs) city, SE Michigan; 7,770; ZIP 48864.
O·khotsk (ō·kotsk'), **Sea** of inlet of the Pacific w of Kamchatka and the Kurile Islands.
O·ki·na·wa (ō'ki·nä'wä) The largest of the Ryuku Islands; 467 sq. mi.; administered by US military government; 719,000.
O·kla·ho·ma (ō'klə·hō'mə) state, S CEN. United States; 69,919 sq. mi.; 2,559,253. — **Oklahoma City** city, CEN. Oklahoma; cap.; 366,481; ZIP 73100*.
Ok·mul·gee (ōk·mul'gē) city, E CEN. Oklahoma; 15,180; ZIP 74447.
O·ko·lo·na (ō·kə·lō'nə) city, NW Kentucky; 17,643; ZIP 40291.
O·la·the (ō·lā'thē) city, E Kansas; 17,917; ZIP 66061.
Old Bethpage See BETHPAGE.
Old Bridge city, E CEN. New Jersey; 25,176; ZIP 08857.
Old Forge boro., NE Pennsylvania; 9,522; ZIP see SCRANTON.
Old Orchard Beach city, NW Maine; 5,404; ZIP 04064.
Old Say·brook (sā'brŏŏk') city, CEN. Connecticut; 8,467; ZIP 06475.
Old Town city, S CEN. Maine; 9,057; ZIP 04468.
O·le·an (ō'lē·an') city, SW New York; 19,169; ZIP 14760*.
Ol·ive·hurst (ol'iv·hûrst) city, N CEN. California; 8,100.
Ol·i·vette (ol'i·vet) city, E Missouri; 9,341; ZIP see ST. LOUIS.
Ol·ney (ol'nē) city, SE Illinois; 8,974; ZIP 62450.
O·lym·pi·a (ō·lim'pē·ə) city, w Washington; cap.; 23,111; ZIP 98501*.
O·lym·pus (ō·lim'pəs), **Mount** mtn., N Greece; regarded in Greek mythology as the home of the gods; 9,570 ft.
Ol·y·phant (ol'i·fant, ō'li-) boro., NE Pennsylvania; 5,442; ZIP 18447.
O·ma·ha (ō'mə·hä, -hô) city, E Nebraska; 347,328; ZIP 68100*.
O·man (ō'man, ō·man', ō·män') sultanate, E Arabia, 82,000 sq. mi.; 820,000; cap. Muscat.
Omsk (ômsk) city, S RSFSR; 774,000.
O·nei·da (ō·nī'də) city, CEN. New York; 11,658; ZIP 13421*.
On·e·on·ta (on'ē·on'tə, ō'nē-) city, CEN. New York; 16,030; ZIP 13820.
On·tar·i·o (on·târ'ē·ō) city, SW California; 64,118; ZIP 91761*.
— city, E Oregon; 6,523; ZIP 97914.
On·tar·i·o (on·târ'ē·o) prov., SE Canada; 412,582 sq. mi.; 6,960,870; cap. Toronto.
Ontario, Lake easternmost of the Great Lakes; 7,540 sq. mi.
Opal Cliffs city, W CEN. California; 5,425; ZIP 95060.
O·pa·Lock·a (ō'pə·lok'ə) city, SE Florida; 11,902; ZIP 33054*.
O·pe·li·ka (ō'pə·lī'kə) city, E Alabama; 19,027; ZIP 36801.

Op·e·lou·sas (op'ə·lōō'səs) city, S CEN. Louisiana; 20,121; ZIP 70570.
O·por·to (ō·pôr'tō) city, W Portugal; 304,000.
Opp (op) city, S Alabama; 6,493; ZIP 36467.
Opportunity uninc. place, E Washington; 16,604; ZIP see SPOKANE.
O·ra·dell (ôr'ə·del) boro., NE New Jersey; 8,903; ZIP 07649.
Or·ange (ôr'inj, or'-) former principality, now part of SE France.
Or·ange (ôr'inj, or'-) city, SW California; 77,374; ZIP 92666*.
— city, S Connecticut; 13,524; ZIP 06477.
— city, NE Florida; 7,619; ZIP 32073.
— city, NW Massachusetts; 6,104; ZIP 01364.
— city, NE New Jersey; 32,566; ZIP 07050*.
— city, E Texas; 24,457; ZIP 77630*.
Or·ange·burg (ôr'inj·bûrg, or'-) city, CEN. South Carolina; 13,252; ZIP 29115.
Orange River river, S Africa; 1,300 mi. long.
Or·ange·vale (ôr'inj·vāl, or'-) city, CEN. California; 16,493.
Or·cutt (ôr'kut) city, SW California; 8,500; ZIP 93454.
Or·e·gon (ôr'ə·gon, -gən, or'-, ôr'ē·gən) state, NW United States; 96,981 sq. mi.; 2,091,385; cap. Salem.
— city, N Ohio; 16,563; ZIP see TOLEDO.
Oregon City city, NW Oregon; 9,176; ZIP 97045.
Ore·land (ôr'lənd) city, SE Pennsylvania; 9,114.
Or·em (ôr'əm) city, N CEN. Utah; 25,729; ZIP 84057.
O·ril·lia (ō·ril'yə) town, S Ontario, Canada; 15,295.
O·rin·da Village (ō·rin'də) uninc. place, W California; 6,790.
O·ri·no·co (ôr'ə·nō'kō, or'-) river, Venezuela ab. 1,700 mi. long.
Ork·ney Islands (ôrk'nē) isl. group, N of Scotland comprising **Orkney**; a co. of Scotland; 376 sq. mi.; 19,000; cap. Kirkwall.
Or·lan·do (ôr·lan'dō) city, E CEN. Florida; 99,006; ZIP 32800*.
Orland Park Village (ôr'lənd) city, NE Illinois; 6,391; ZIP 60462.
Or·lé·ans (ôr·lā·äⁿ') city, N CEN. France; 95,828.
Or·mond Beach (ôr'mənd, ōr'-) city, E Florida; 14,063; ZIP 32074*.
Or·o·moc·to (ôr'ō·mok'tō) town, S CEN. New Brunswick, Canada; 14,112.
Or·o·no (ôr'ə·nō) city, CEN. Maine; 9,989; ZIP 04473.
Or·o·no (ôr'ə·nō) vill., E Minnesota; 6,787.
O·ro·ville (ôr'ō·vil) city, N CEN. California; 7,536; ZIP 95965.
Orr·ville (ôr'vil) city, NE CEN. Ohio; 7,408; ZIP 44667.
O·sa·ka (ō·sä·kä) city, S Honshu, Japan; 3,012,000.
Os·ce·o·la (ō·se·ō'lə) city, NE Arkansas; 7,204; ZIP 72370.
Osh·a·wa (osh'ə·wə) city, S Ontario, Canada; 78,082.
Osh·kosh (osh'kosh) city, E Wisconsin; 53,221; ZIP 54901*.
Os·ka·loo·sa (os'kə·lōō'sə) city, S CEN. Iowa; 11,224; ZIP 52577.
Os·lo (os'lō, oz'-) city, SE Norway; cap.; 483,196.
Os·sa (ôs'ə) mtn., E Greece; 6,490 ft.
Os·si·ning (os'ə·ning) vill., SE New York; 21,659; ZIP 10562*.
Os·tend (os'tend, os·tend') city, NW Belgium; 57,359.
Os·we·go (os·wē'gō) city, N New York; 23,844; ZIP 13126.
O·tis (ō'tis) city, E Massachusetts; 5,596.
O·tran·to (ō·trän'tō), **Strait of** strait betw. the Adriatic and Ionian seas; ab. 43 mi. wide.
Ot·ta·wa (ot'ə·wə) city, N Illinois; 18,716; ZIP 61350.
— city, E Kansas; 11,036; ZIP 66067.
Ot·ta·wa (ot'ə·wə) city, SE Ontario, Canada; cap. of Canada; 290,741.
Ot·to·man Empire (ot'ə·mən) former empire (1300–1919) of the Turks in Asia Minor, NE Africa, and SE Europe.
Ot·tum·wa (o·tum'wə, ō-) city, SE Iowa; 29,610; ZIP 52501*.
Oua·ga·dou·gou (wä'gə·dōō'gōō) city, CEN. Upper Volta; cap.; 59,126.
Outer Mongolia See MONGOLIA.
Ou·tre·mont (ōō'trə·mont, ōō·trə·mäⁿ') city, S Quebec, Canada; 30,881.
O·ver·land (ō'vər·lənd) city, E Missouri; 24,949; ZIP see ST. LOUIS.
Overland Park uninc. place, NE Kansas; 76,623.
O·ver·lea (ō'vər·lē) uninc. place, N CEN. Maryland; 13,086; ZIP see BALTIMORE.
O·ver·look-Page Manor (ō'vər·lŏŏk·pāj) city, SW Ohio; 19,596.
O·wa·ton·na (ō'wə·ton'ə) city, S Minnesota; 15,341; ZIP 55060.
O·we·go (ō·wē'gō) vill., S New York; 5,152; ZIP 13827.
Ow·ens (ō'ənz, -inz) uninc. place, S CEN. North Carolina; 5,207.
Ow·ens·bor·o (ō'ənz·bûr'ō) city, NW Kentucky; 50,329; ZIP 42301*.
Ow·en Sound (ō'ən) city, S Ontario, Canada; 17,769.

O·wines Mills (ō′winz) city, N CEN. Maryland; 7,360; ZIP 21117.
O·wos·so (ō-wos′ō) city, S CEN. Michigan; 17,179; ZIP 48867.
Ox·ford (oks′fərd) co. boro., S CEN. England; 110,050.
Ox·ford (oks′fərd) uninc. place, S CEN. Massachusetts; 10,345; ZIP 01540.
— city, N Mississippi; 13,846; ZIP 38655.
— town, N North Carolina; 7,178; ZIP 27565.
— city, SW Ohio; 15,868; ZIP 45056.
Ox·nard (oks′närd) city, SW California; 71,255; ZIP 93030*.
Ox·on Hill (oks′ən) city, NW Maryland; 11,974; ZIP 20021.
O·zark (ō′zärk) city, SE Alabama; 13,555; ZIP 36360*.
Ozark Mountains hilly uplands, SW Missouri, NW Arkansas, and NE Oklahoma.

Pa·cif·i·ca (pə-sif′i·kə) city, W California; 36,020; ZIP 94044.
Pa·cif·ic Grove (pə-sif′ik) city, W California; 13,505; ZIP 93950.
Pacific Islands, Trust Territory of the U.S. Trust Territory, W Pacific, comprising the Marshall Islands, the Marianas (excluding Guam), and the Caroline Islands; ab. 700 sq. mi.; 101,600; administrative center Saipan. Also called *Micronesia.*
Pacific Ocean ocean betw. the American continents and Asia and Australia; extending betw. the Arctic and Antarctic regions; ab. 70 million sq. mi.
Pacific Palisades city, SE Oahu, Hawaii; 7,846; ZIP 96782.
Pad·u·a (paj′ōō-ə, pad′yōō-ə) city, NE Italy; 205,057.
Pa·du·cah (pə-dōō′kə) city, W Kentucky; 31,627; ZIP 42001*.
Page·dale (pāj′dāl) city, E Missouri; 5,571.
Pa·go Pa·go (päng′ō päng′ō) town, SE Tutuila, American Samoa; 1,251; ZIP 96920.
Pa·ho·kee (pə-hō′kē) city, SE Florida; 5,663; ZIP 33476.
Paines·ville (pānz′vil) city, NE Ohio; 16,536; ZIP 44077.
Paines·ville Southwest (pānz′vil) city, NE Ohio; 5,461.
Pa·ki·stan (päʹki-stän′, pak′i-stan) republic of the Commonwealth of Nations, S Asia; 311,406 sq. mi.; 59,140,000; cap. Islamabad.
Pal·a·tine (pal′ə-tīn) vill., NE Illinois; 25,904; ZIP 60067.
Pa·lat·ka (pə-lat′kə) city, N Florida; 9,310; ZIP 32077.
Pa·lau Islands (pä-lou′) isl. group, W Caroline Islands; 188 sq. mi.
Pa·ler·mo (pä-ler′mō) city, NW Sicily; cap.; 622,646.
Pal·es·tine (pal′is-tīn) terr., E Mediterranean; 10,434 sq. mi.; cap. Jerusalem; divided (1947) by the United Nations into Israel and a terr. that became part of Jordan.
Pal·es·tine (pal′əs-tēn) city, E Texas; 14,525; ZIP 75801.
Pal·i·sades Park (pal′ə-sādz′) boro., NE New Jersey; 13,357; ZIP 07650.
Pal·ma (päl′mä) city, W Majorca; cap. of the Balearic Islands; 164,963.
Palm Bay city, SW Florida; 6,927; ZIP 32901.
Palm Beach town, SE Florida; 9,086; ZIP 33480*.
Palm Desert city, SW California; 6,171; ZIP 92260.
Palm·dale (päm′dāl) uninc. place, SW California; 8,511; ZIP 93550.
Palm·er (päm′ər) city, W Massachusetts; 11,680; ZIP 01069.
Palmer Park city, NW Maryland; 8,172.
Palm·er·ton (pal′mər-tən) boro., E Pennsylvania; 5,620; ZIP 18071.
Pal·met·to (pal-met′ō) city, SW Florida; 7,422; ZIP 33561.
Palm Springs city, S California; 20,936; ZIP 92262*.
Pal·my·ra (pal-mī′rə) boro., W New Jersey; 6,969; ZIP 08065.
— boro., SE Pennsylvania; 7,615; ZIP 17078.
Pa·lo Al·to (pal′ō al′tō) city, W California; 55,966; ZIP 94300*.
Pal·o·mar (pal′ə·mär), **Mount** mtn., S California, 6,126 ft.; site of **Mount Palomar Observatory.**
Pal·os Heights (pal′ōs) city, NE Illinois; 9,915; ZIP 60463.
Palos Hills city, NE Illinois; 6,629; ZIP 60465.
Pal·os Ver·des Estates (pal′os vûr′dēz) city, SW California; 13,641.
Palos Verdes Peninsula city, SW California; 39,616; ZIP 90274.
Pam·pa (pam′pə) city, N Texas; 21,726; ZIP 79065*.
Pan·a (pan′ə) city, CEN. Illinois; 6,326; ZIP 62557.
Pan·a·ma (pan′ə·mä, -mô) republic, Central America; 28,575 sq. mi. (excluding Canal Zone); 1,084,000. — city, near the Pacific end of the Panama Canal; cap. of Panama; 358,559.
Panama, Isthmus of isthmus connecting North and South America.
Panama Canal ship canal connecting the Atlantic and the Pacific across Panama; completed (1914) by the United States on the leased Canal Zone; 40 mi. long.
Panama Canal Zone See CANAL ZONE.
Pan·a·ma City (pan′ə·mä, -mô) city, NW Florida; 32,096; ZIP 32401*.
Pa·nay (pä-nī′) isl., CEN. Philippines; 4,446 sq. mi.

Papal States STATES OF THE CHURCH.
Pa·pil·lion (pə-pil′yən) city, E CEN. Nebraska; 5,606; ZIP 68046.
Pap·u·a New Guinea (pä′pōō-ə, pap′ōō-ə, -yōō-ə) isl. N of Australia; independent member of the Commonwealth of Nations; 178,260 sq. mi.; 2,905,000; cap. Port Moresby. Formerly **Papua and New Guinea.**
Pa·rá (pə-rä′) Belém: *a former name.*
Paradise city, S CEN. Arizona; 7,155.
Par·a·dise (par′ə-dīs) uninc. place, N CEN. California; 14,539.
— uninc. place, CEN. California; 5,616.
— SE Nevada; 24,477; ZIP 89101.
Par·a·gould (par′ə-gōōld) city, NE Arkansas; 10,639.
Par·a·guay (par′ə-gwä, -gwī′) republic, S CEN. South America; 157,047 sq. mi.; 1,812,000; cap. Asunción.
Paraguay River river, S CEN. South America, ab. 1,300 mi. long.
Par·a·mar·i·bo (par′ə-mar′i·bō) city, N Surinam; cap.; 135,000.
Par·a·mount (par′ə·mount) city, SW California; 34,734; ZIP 90723*.
Par·a·mus (pə-ram′əs) boro., NE New Jersey; 29,495; ZIP 07652*.
Pa·ra·ná (pä′rä-nä′) river, S CEN. South America; ab. 2,800 mi. long.
Par·is (par′is) city, N France; cap.; 2,590,771.
Par·is (par′is) city, E Illinois; 9,971; ZIP 61944.
— city, NE CEN. Kentucky; 7,823; ZIP 40361.
— city, NW Tennessee; 9,892; ZIP 38242.
— city, NE Texas; 23,441; ZIP 75460*.
Par·is (par′is) town, S Ontario, Canada; 6,271.
Par·kers·burg (pä′kərz-bûrg) city, W West Virginia; 44,208; ZIP 26100*.
Park Forest vill., NE Illinois; 30,638; ZIP 60466.
Park·land (pärk′land′) city, W CEN. Washington; 21,012; ZIP 98444.
Park Ridge city, NE Illinois; 42,466; ZIP 60068.
— boro., NE New Jersey; 8,709; ZIP 07656.
Park·ville (pärk′vil) city, S CEN. Pennsylvania; 5,120; ZIP 17331.
Parkville-Car·ney (kär′nē) uninc. place, N Maryland; 33,897.
Par·ma (pär′mä) city, N CEN. Italy; 155,132.
Par·ma (pär′mə) city, N Ohio; 100,216; ZIP see CLEVELAND.
Parma Heights (pär′mə) city, NE Ohio; 27,192; ZIP 44129.
Par·nas·sus (pär-nas′əs), **Mount** mtn., CEN. Greece; anciently regarded as sacred to Apollo and the Muses; 8,062 ft.
Par·ris Island (par′is) city, SE South Carolina; 8,568.
Par·ry Sound (par′ē) town, S CEN. Ontario, Canada; 5,901.
Par·sip·pa·ny (pär-sip′ə-nē) urb. twp., N New Jersey; 55,112; ZIP 07054.
Par·sons (pär′sənz) city, SE Kansas; 13,015; ZIP 67357.
Pas·a·de·na (pas′ə-dē′nə) city, SW California; 113,327; ZIP 91100*.
— city, SE Texas; 89,277; ZIP 77501*.
Pas·ca·gou·la (pas′kə-gōō′lə) city, SE Mississippi; 27,264; ZIP 39567.
Pas·co (pas′ko) city, S Washington; 13,920; ZIP 99301.
Pas·o Ro·bles (pas′ō rō′bəlz, pä′sō rō′bles) El Paso de Robles: *an alternate name.*
Pas·sa·ic (pə-sä′ik) city, NE New Jersey; 55,124; ZIP 07055*.
Pat·a·go·ni·a (pat′ə-gō′nē-ə) reg. at the S tip of South America.
Patch·ogue (pach′äg′, -ôg′) vill., SE New York; 11,582; ZIP 11772*.
Pat·er·son (pat′ər-sən) city, NE New Jersey; 144,824; ZIP 07500*.
Pauls·bor·o (pôlz′bûr′ō) boro., W New Jersey; 8,084; ZIP 08066.
Pauls Valley (pôlz) city, S CEN. Oklahoma; 5,769; ZIP 73075.
Paw·ca·tuck (pô′kə·tuk) city, SE Connecticut; 5,255; ZIP 02891.
Paw·tuck·et (pô·tuk′it) city, NE Rhode Island; 76,984; ZIP 02860*.
Pea·bod·y (pē′bod′ē, -bəd·ē) city, NE Massachusetts; 48,080; ZIP 01960*.
Peacedale See WAKEFIELD-PEACEDALE.
Pearl (pûrl) uninc. place, S CEN. Mississippi; 9,623; ZIP see JACKSON.
Pear·land (pâr′land′) city, E Texas; 6,444; ZIP 77581.
Pearl City city, S Oahu, Hawaii; 19,552; ZIP 96782.
Pearl Harbor inlet, S Oahu, Hawaii; site of a U.S. naval base, bombed by Japanese, December 7, 1941.
Pearl River city, SE New York; 17,146; ZIP 10965.
Pear·sall (pir′sôl) city, S CEN. Texas; 5,545; ZIP 78061.
Pe·cos (pā′kəs) city, W Texas; 12,682; ZIP 79772.
Peeks·kill (pēks′kil) city, SE New York; 18,881; ZIP 10566*.
Pe·kin (pē′kin) city, CEN. Illinois; 31,375; ZIP 61554*.
Pe·king (pē′king′) city, N China (mainland); cap.; 4,010,-000.

Pel·ham (pel′əm) city, SE New Hampshire; 5,408; ZIP 03076.
Pelham Manor vill., SE New York; 6,673.
Pe·li·on (pē′lē·on) mtn. range; SE Thessaly.
Pel·la (pel′ə) city, SE CEN. Iowa; 6,668; ZIP 50219.
Pell City (pel) city, CEN. Alabama; 6,907; ZIP 35125.
Pel·o·pon·ne·sus (pel′ə·pə·nē′səs) penin. betw. Aegean and Ionian seas; one of the main divisions of S Greece; 8,603 sq. mi.; 1,129,000.
Pem·broke (pem′brŏk) town, SE Ontario, Canada; 16,262.
Pem·broke (pem′brŏk′) city, NE Massachusetts; 11,193; ZIP 02359.
Pembroke Pines city, SE Florida; 15,520; ZIP 33023.
Pem·coyd (pem′koid) city, SE Pennsylvania; 6,650.
Pe·nang (pē′nang′) state, NW Malaya; 398 sq. mi.; 616,000; cap. George Town.
Pen·dle·ton (pen′dəlt·n, -dəl·tən) city, NE Oregon; 13,197; ZIP 97801.
Pen·e·tan·gui·shene (pen′ə·tang′gə·shēn′, -gwə·shēn′) town, S Ontario, Canada; 5,349.
Penn Hills (pen) urb. twp., SW Pennsylvania; 51,512; ZIP see PITTSBURGH.
Pen·nine Alps (pen′īn, -īn) SW div. of the Alps on the Swiss-Italian border.
Penn·sau·ken (pen·sô′kən) urb. twp., W New Jersey; 36,394; ZIP see CAMDEN.
Penns Grove (penz) boro., SW New Jersey; 5,727; ZIP 08069.
Penn Square city, SE Pennsylvania; 20,238.
Penns·ville (penz′vil) city, SW New Jersey; 11,014; ZIP 08070.
Penn·syl·va·ni·a (pen·səl·vā′nē·ə, -văn′yə) state, E United States; 45,333 sq. mi.; 11,793,909; cap. Harrisburg.
Penn Wynne (pen win) city, SE Pennsylvania; 6,038; ZIP 19003.
Penn Yan (pen′ yan′) vill., W CEN. New York; 5,168; ZIP 14527.
Pen·sa·co·la (pen′sə·kō′lə) city, NW Florida; site of a U.S. naval and air base; 59,507; ZIP 32501*.
Pen·tic·ton (pen·tik′tən) city, S British Columbia; 15,330.
Pe·o·ri·a (pē·ôr′ē·ə) city, N CEN. Illinois; 126,963; ZIP 61600*.
Peoria Heights vill., CEN. Illinois; 7,943; ZIP see PEORIA.
Pep·per·ell (pep′ər·əl) city, NE Massachusetts; 6,887; ZIP 01463.
Pepper Pike city, NE Ohio; 5,933; ZIP 44124.
Per·ka·sie (pûr′kə·sē) city, SE Pennsylvania; 5,451; ZIP 18944.
Per·nam·bu·co (pûr′nəm·bōō′kō) Recife: *an alternate name.*
Per·rine (per′ēn) uninc. place, SE Florida; 10,257; ZIP see MIAMI.
Per·ry (per′ē) city, N Florida; 7,701; ZIP 32347.
— city, CEN. Georgia; 7,771; ZIP 31069.
— city, CEN. Iowa; 6,906; ZIP 50220.
— city, N Oklahoma; 5,341; ZIP 73077.
Perry Go Place (per′ē) city, SE Wisconsin; 5,912; ZIP 53511.
Perry Hall city, N CEN. Maryland; 5,446; ZIP 21128.
Per·rys·burg (per′ēz·bûrg) vill., N Ohio; 7,693.
Per·ry·ton (per′ēt·n, -ē·tən) city, N Texas; 7,810; ZIP 79070.
Per·ry·ville (per′ē·vil, -vəl) city, E Missouri; 5,149; ZIP 63775.
Per·sia (pûr′zhə, -shə) Iran: *the former name.*
Persian Gulf inlet of the Arabian Sea betw. Iran and Arabia.
Perth (pûrth) city, SW Western Australia; cap.; 499,494.
Perth (pûrth) town, SE Ontario, Canada; 5,559.
Perth Am·boy (pûrth am′boi) port city, E New Jersey; 38,798; ZIP 08861*.
Pe·ru (pə·rōō′) republic, W South America; 533,916 sq. mi.; 13,997,000; cap. Lima.
Pe·ru (pə·rōō′) city, N CEN. Illinois; 11,772; ZIP 61354.
— city, N CEN. Indiana; 14,139; ZIP 46970*.
Petal city, S Mississippi; 6,986; ZIP 39465.
Pet·a·lu·ma (pet′ə·lōō′mə) city, W California; 24,870; ZIP 94952*.
Pe·ter·bor·ough (pē′tər·bûr′ō, -bə·rə, -brə) city, S Ontario, Canada; 56,177.
Pe·ters·burg (pēt′ərz·bûrg) city, SE Virginia; scene of Civil War battles, 1864, 1865; 36,103; ZIP 23801*.
Pe·tos·key (pē·tos′kē) city, N Michigan; 6,342; ZIP 49770*.
Pet·ro·grad (pet′rə·grad) Leningrad: *a former name.*
Pharr (fär) city, S Texas; 15,829; ZIP 78577.
Phe·nix City (fē′niks) city, E Alabama; 25,281; ZIP 36867.
Phil·a·del·phi·a (fil′ə·del′fē·ə) city, E CEN. Mississippi; 6,274; ZIP 39350.
— city, SE Pennsylvania; 1,948,609; ZIP 19100*.
Phil·ip·pines (fil′ə·pēnz), **Republic of the** republic occupying the **Philippine Islands,** a Pacific archipelago SE of China; 115,707 sq. mi.; 39,906,000; cap. Quezon City; seat of administration, Manila.
Phil·lips·burg (fil′əps·bûrg) city, W New Jersey; 17,849;

ZIP 08865*.
Phnom Penh (nom′pen′) city, S CEN. Kampuchea; cap.; 40,000.
Phoe·nix (fē′niks) city, S CEN. Arizona; cap.; 581,562; ZIP 85000*.
Phoe·nix·ville (fē′niks·vil) boro., SE Pennsylvania; 14,823; ZIP 19460.
Pic·ar·dy (pik′ər·dē) reg. and former prov., N France.
Pic·a·yune (pik′i·yōōn′) city, S Mississippi; 10,467; ZIP 39466.
Pi·co Ri·ve·ra (pē′kō ri·vā′rə) city, SW California; 54,170; ZIP 90660*.
Pied·mont (pēd′mont) reg., N Italy; 9,817 sq. mi.; 3,890,000; cap. Turin.
Pied·mont (pēd′mont) reg., E United States; extends from New Jersey to Alabama E of the Appalachians; ab. 80,000 sq. mi.
— city, NE Alabama; 5,063; ZIP 36372.
— city, W California; 10,917; ZIP see OAKLAND.
Pierre (pir) city, CEN. South Dakota; cap.; 9,699; ZIP 57501.
Pierre·fonds (pyer·fôn′) town, S Quebec, Canada; 27,924.
Pike's Peak (pīks) mtn., CEN. Colorado; 14,110 ft.
Pikes·ville (pīks′vil) uninc. place, N CEN. Maryland; 25,395; ZIP see BALTIMORE.
Pillars of Hercules 2 promontories on opposite sides of the E end of the Strait of Gibraltar.
Pine Bluff city, CEN. Arkansas; 57,389; ZIP 71601*.
Pine Hill city, W New Jersey; 5,132; ZIP 08021.
Pine Hills city, NE Florida; 13,882.
Pine Lawn city, E Missouri; 5,773; ZIP see ST. LOUIS.
Pi·nel·las Park (pi·nel′əs) city, W Florida; 22,287; ZIP 33565.
Pine·ville (pīn′vil, -vəl) city, CEN. Louisiana; 8,951; ZIP 71360.
Pi·nole (pē·nōl′) city, W California; 15,850; ZIP 94564.
Pipe·stone (pīp′stōn) city, SW Minnesota; 5,328; ZIP 56164.
Piq·ua (pik′wə) city, W Ohio; 20,741; ZIP 45356.
Pi·rae·us (pī·rē′əs) city, S Greece; 183,877.
Pi·sa (pē′sä) city, NE Italy; noted for its leaning tower; 90,928.
Pit·man (pit′mən) boro., SW New Jersey; 10,257; ZIP 08071.
Pitts·burg (pits′bûrg) city, W California; 20,651; ZIP 94565.
— city, SE Kansas; 20,171; ZIP 66762*.
Pitts·burgh (pits′bûrg) city, SW Pennsylvania; 520,117; ZIP 15200*.
Pitts·field (pits′fēld) city, W Massachusetts; 57,020; ZIP 01200*.
Pitts·ton (pits′tən) city, NE CEN. Pennsylvania; 11,113; ZIP 18640*.
Pla·cen·tia (plə·sen′shə) city, SW California; 21,948; ZIP 92670.
Plain·edge (plān′ej) uninc. place, SE New York; 10,759.
Plain·field (plān′fēld) city, NE Connecticut; 11,957; ZIP 03674.
— town, CEN. Indiana; 8,211; ZIP 46168.
— city, NE New Jersey; 46,862; ZIP 07060.
Plains (plānz) urb. twp., NE CEN. Pennsylvania; 6,606; ZIP see WILKES-BARRE.
Plain·view (plān′vyōo) vill., SE New York; 32,195; ZIP see HICKSVILLE.
— city, NW Texas; 19,096; ZIP 79072*.
Plain·ville (plān′vil) city, CEN. Connecticut; 16,733; ZIP 06062.
Pla·no (plā′nō) city, CEN. Texas; 17,872; ZIP 75074.
Plantation city, NE Florida; 23,523; ZIP 33314.
Plant City city, W Florida; 15,451; ZIP 33566.
Plaque·mine (plak′ə·min, plak′min) town, S Louisiana; 7,739; ZIP 70764.
Plate (plāt), **River** Rio de la Plata: *the British name.*
Platte River (plat) river, S Nebraska; 310 mi. long.
Platts·burgh (plats′bûrg) city, NE New York; scene of a U.S. naval victory in the War of 1812; 18,715. Also **Platts′·burg;** ZIP 12901*.
Platts·mouth (plats′məth, -mouth) city, E Nebraska; 6,371; ZIP 68048.
Platte·ville (plat′vil) city, SW Wisconsin; 9,599; ZIP 53818.
Pleasant Grove city, CEN. Alabama; 5,090.
— city, NW Utah; 5,327; ZIP 84062.
Pleasant Hill uninc. place, W California; 24,610; ZIP see CONCORD.
Pleasant Hills boro., SW Pennsylvania; 10,409; ZIP see PITTSBURGH.
Plea·san·ton (plez′ənt·n, -ən·tən) city, W California; 18,328; ZIP 94566.
— city, S CEN. Texas; 5,407; ZIP 78064.
Pleas·ant·ville (plez′ənt·vil) city, SE New Jersey; 13,778; ZIP 08232.
— vill., SE New York; 7,110; ZIP 10570.

Pleasure Ridge Park uninc. place, N Kentucky; 28,566; ZIP 40158.
Ples·sis·ville (ples/ē·vil) town, s Quebec, Canada; 7,238.
Plum (plum) boro., sw Pennsylvania; 21,932.
Plym·outh (plim/əth) co. boro. and port, sw England; 246,290.
Plym·outh (plim/əth) city, NW Connecticut; 10,321; ZIP 06782.
— city, N Indiana; 7,661; ZIP 46563.
— town, E Massachusetts; site of the first settlement in New England; 18,606; ZIP 02360*.
— city, SE Michigan; 11,758; ZIP 48170.
— vill., E Minnesota; 17,593.
— boro., NE CEN. Pennsylvania; 9,536; ZIP 18651.
— city, E Wisconsin; 5,810; ZIP 53073.
Plymouth Colony colony on the shore of Massachusetts Bay founded by the Pilgrim Fathers in 1620.
Plymouth Rock rock at Plymouth, Massachusetts, on which the Pilgrim Fathers are said to have landed in 1620.
Po·ca·tel·lo (pō/kə·tel/ō, -tel/ə) city, Idaho; 40,036; ZIP 83201*.
Pointe-aux-Trem·bles (pwⱥnt·ō·trän/blə) city, s Quebec, Canada; 29,888.
Pointe-Claire (point·klâr/, pwⱥnt·klâr/) city, s Quebec, Canada; 26,784.
Pointe-Ga·ti·neau (pwⱥnt·gä·tē·nō/) town, sw Quebec, Canada; 11,053.
Point Pleasant boro., E New Jersey; 15,968.
— city, w West Virginia; 6,122; ZIP 25550.
Po·land (pō/lənd) republic, N CEN. Europe; 120,359 sq. mi.; 33,183,000; cap. Warsaw.
Pol·y·ne·sia (pol/i·nē/zhə, -shə) isls. of Oceania, CEN. and SE Pacific; E of Melanesia and Micronesia.
Pom·e·ra·ni·a (pom/ə·rā/nē·ə) reg., N CEN. Europe.
Po·mo·na (pə·mō/nə) city, sw California; 87,384; ZIP 91766*.
Pom·pa·no Beach (pom/pə·nō) city, SE Florida; 37,724; ZIP 33060*.
Pomp·ton Lakes (pom/tən, pomp/-) boro., NE New Jersey; 11,397; ZIP 07442.
Pon·ca City (pong/kə) city, N Oklahoma; 25,940; ZIP 74601*.
Pon·ce (pôn/sā) city, s Puerto Rico; 125,926.
Pon·ti·ac (pon/tē·ak) city, E CEN. Illinois; 9,031; ZIP 61764.
— city, SE Michigan; 82,279; ZIP 48053*.
Pont-Viau (pon·vyō/) city, s Quebec, Canada; 16,077.
Poo·na (pōō/nə) city, w India; 806,351.
Pop·lar Bluff (pop/lər) city, SE Missouri; 16,653; ZIP 63901.
Po·po·cat·e·pet·l (pō/pə·kat/ə·pet/l, pō·pō/kä·tā/pet/l) dormant volcano, CEN. Mexico; 17,887 ft.
Po·quo·son (pō·kwō/sən) city, SE Virginia; 5,441.
Po River river, N Italy; 405 mi. long.
Por·tage (pôr/tij) town, NW Indiana; 19,127; ZIP 46368.
— city, sw Michigan; 33,590; ZIP 49081.
— city, s CEN. Wisconsin; 7,821; ZIP 53901.
Por·tage la Prai·rie (pôr/tij lə prâr/ē) city, s Manitoba, Canada; 13,012.
Port Al·ber·ni (al·bûr/nē) city, sw British Columbia; 13,755.
Por·tal·es (pər·tal/is, pôr-) city, E New Mexico; 10,554; ZIP 88130.
Port Al·fred (al/fred, -frid) town, s CEN. Quebec, Canada; 9,551.
Port Al·len (al/ən, -in) town, SE CEN. Louisiana; 5,728; ZIP 70767.
Port An·ge·les (an/jə·ləs) city, NW Washington; 16,367; ZIP 98362.
Port Ar·thur-Dai·ren (är/thər1dī/ren/) China; Lu-ta: former name; 1,508,000.
Port Ar·thur (är/thər) city, SE Texas; 57,371; ZIP 77640*.
Port Ar·thur (är/thər) city, s Ontario, Canada; 48,340.
Port-au-Prince (pôrt/ō·prins/, pôrt/-) city, s Haiti; cap.; 240,000.
Port Char·lotte (shär/lət) city, sw Florida; 10,769; ZIP 33950.
Port Ches·ter (pôrt/ ches/tər, pôrt/) vill., SE New York; 25,803; ZIP 10573*.
Port Clin·ton (klint/n, klin/tən) city, N Ohio; 7,202; ZIP 43452.
Port Col·borne (kōl/bərn) town, s Ontario, Canada; 17,986.
Port Co·quit·lam (kō·kwit/ləm) city, sw British Columbia, Canada; 11,121.
Port Cred·it (kred/it) town, s Ontario, Canada; 8,475.
Por·ter·ville (pôr/tər·vil, pōr/-) city, s CEN. California; 12,602; ZIP 93257*.
Port Hope (hōp) town, s Ontario, Canada; 8,656.
Port Hue·ne·me (wī·nē/mē) city, sw California; 14,295; ZIP 93041.
Port Hu·ron (hyōō/rən) city, E Michigan; 35,794; ZIP 48060*.

Port Jef·fer·son (jef/ər·sən) city, SE New York; 7,403; ZIP 11777.
Port Jefferson Village city, SE New York; 5,094.
Port Jer·vis (jûr/vis) city, SE New York; 8,852; ZIP 12771.
Port·land (pôrt/lənd, pōrt/-) uninc. place, CEN. Connecticut; 8,812; ZIP 06480.
— city, E Indiana; 7,115; ZIP 47371.
— city, sw Maine; 65,116; ZIP 04100*.
— city, NW Oregon; 382,619; ZIP 97200*.
— city, SE Texas; 7,302; ZIP 78384.
Port La·vac·a (lə·vak/ə) city, s Texas; 10,491: ZIP 77979.
Port Lou·is (lōō/is, lōō/ē) port city, sw Mauritius; cap.; 137,650.
Port Nech·es (nech/iz) city, SE Texas; 10,894; ZIP 77651.
Port-of-Spain (pôrt/-ov-spān/, pōrt/-) city, NW Trinidad; cap. of Trinidad and Tobago; 93,954. Also **Port of Spain.**
Por·to-No·vo (pôrt/tō·nō/vō) port city, SE Benin; cap.; 69,500.
Por·to Ri·co (pôr/tō rē/kō) Puerto Rico: the former name.
Port Said (sä·ēd/) city, NE Egypt; at the Mediterranean end of the Suez Canal; 256,100.
Ports·mouth (pôrts/məth, pōrts/-) co. boro., s England; site of the chief British naval station; 218,790.
Ports·mouth (pôrts/məth, pōrts/-) city, SE New Hampshire; 25,717; ZIP 03801*.
— city, s Ohio; 27,633; ZIP 45662*.
— town, SE Rhode Island; 12,521; ZIP 02871.
— city, SE Virginia; 110,963; ZIP 23700*.
Port Town·send (toun/zənd) city, NW Washington; 5,241; ZIP 98368.
Por·tu·gal (pôr/chə·gəl, pōr/-) republic, sw Europe; 35,419 sq. mi.; 9,793,000; cap. Lisbon.
Portuguese East Africa Mozambique: the former name.
Portuguese Guin·ea (gin/ē) Portuguese overseas prov., w Africa; 13,948 sq. mi.; 532,000; cap. Bissau.
Portuguese India former Portuguese overseas prov., w India.
Portuguese West Africa Angola: an alternate name.
Port Vue (pôrt/ vyōō) boro., sw Pennsylvania; 5,862; ZIP see McKEESPORT.
Port Washington (wash/ing·tən) uninc. place, SE New York; 15,923; ZIP 11050.
— city, E Wisconsin; 8,752; ZIP 53074.
Po·sen (pō/zən) Poznań: the German name.
Po·sen (pō/zən) city, NE Illinois; 5,498; ZIP 60469.
Po·teau (pō/tō) city, SE Oklahoma; 5,500; ZIP 74953.
Po·to·mac River (pə·tō/mək) river betw. Maryland, West Virginia, and Virginia; 287 mi. long.
Potomac Valley city, NW Maryland; 5,094: ZIP 20854.
Pots·dam (pots/dam) city, CEN. East Germany; scene of a United Nations conference, 1945; 110,790.
Pots·dam (pots/dam) vill., N New York; 9,985; ZIP 13676.
Potts·town (pots/toun) boro., SE Pennsylvania; 25,355; ZIP 19464*.
Potts·ville (pots/vil) city, E CEN. Pennsylvania; 19,715; ZIP 17901*.
Pough·keep·sie (pə·kip/sē) city, SE New York; 32,029; ZIP 12600*.
Po·way (pō/wā) city, s California; 9,422; ZIP 92064.
Poz·nań (pôz/näny/) city, w Poland; 455,500.
Prague (präg) city, w Czechoslovakia; cap.; 1,034,785.
Prai·rie du Chien (prâr/ē də shēn/) city, sw Wisconsin; 5,540; ZIP 53821.
Prairie Village city, NE Kansas; 28,138.
Pratt (prat) city, s Kansas; 6,736; ZIP 67124.
Pratt·ville (prat/vil, -vəl) city, CEN. Alabama; 13,116; ZIP 36067.
Pres·cott (pres/kət) city, CEN. Arizona; 13,030; ZIP 86301.
Pres·cott (pres/kət) town, SE Ontario, Canada; 5,176.
Presque Isle (presk ïl/) city, NE Maine; 11,452; ZIP 04769.
Pres·ton (pres/tən) town, s Ontario, Canada; 13,380.
Pre·to·ri·a (pri·tôr/ē·ə, -tō/rē·ə) city, NE CEN. South Africa; adm. cap.; 303,684.
Price (prīs) city, E CEN. Utah; 6,218; ZIP 84501.
Prich·ard (prich/ərd) city, sw Alabama; 41,578; ZIP see MOBILE.
Prince Al·bert (al/bərt) city, CEN. Saskatchewan, Canada; 26,269.
Prince Ed·ward Island (ed/wərd) prov., NE Canada; 2,184 sq. mi.; 108,535; cap. Charlottetown.
Prince George (jôrj) city, CEN. British Columbia, Canada; 24,471.
Prince Ru·pert (rōō/pərt) city, w British Columbia, Canada; 14,677.
Prince·ton (prins/tən) city, N CEN. Illinois; 6,959; ZIP 61356.
— city, sw Indiana; 7,431; ZIP 47570.
— city, w Kentucky; 6,292; ZIP 42445.
— boro., CEN. New Jersey; 12,311; ZIP 08540*.
— city, s West Virginia; 7,253; ZIP 24740.
Princeton North city, CEN. New Jersey; 5,488.
Pros·pect (pros/pekt/) city, s Connecticut; 6,543; ZIP 06712.

Prospect Heights city, NE Illinois; 13,333; ZIP 60070.
Prospect Park boro., NE New Jersey; 5,176.
— boro., SE Pennsylvania; 7,250; ZIP 19076.
Pro·vence (prô·väns′) reg. and former prov., SE France.
Prov·i·dence (prov′ə·dəns) city, NE Rhode Island; cap.; 179,213; ZIP 02900*.
Pro·vo (prō′vō) city, N CEN. Utah; 53,131; ZIP 84601.
Prus·sia (prush′ə) former state, N Germany; dissolved, 1947.
Pry·or Creek (prī′ər) city, NE Oklahoma; 7,057.
Pueb·lo (pweb′lō) city, s CEN. Colorado; 97,453; ZIP 81000*.
Puer·to Ri·co (pwer′tō rē′kō, pôr′-) isl., Greater Antilles; a Commonwealth of the United States; 3,423 sq. mi.; 2,353,-297; cap. San Juan.
Pu·get Sound (pyōō′jit) inlet of the Pacific, NW Washington.
Pu·las·ki (pə·las′kē) city, s Tennessee; 6,989; ZIP 38478.
— town, sw Virginia; 16,279; ZIP 24301.
Pull·man (pōōl′mən) city, SE Washington; 20,509; ZIP 99163*.
Pum·pher·ey (pum′fər·ē) city, NW Maryland; 6,370.
Pun·jab (pun′jäb, pun·jäb′) reg., NW India and West Pakistan.
Punx·su·taw·ney (pungk′sə·tô′nē) boro., W CEN. Pennsylvania; 7,792; ZIP 15767*.
Put·nam (put′nəm) city, NE Connecticut; 6,918; ZIP 06260.
Puy·al·lup (pyōō·al′əp) city, W CEN. Washington; 14,742; ZIP 98371*.
Pyong·yang (pyông·yäng) city, W North Korea; cap.; ab. 653,100.
Pyr·e·nees (pir′ə·nēz) mtn. chain betw. France and Spain.

Qa·tar (kä′tär) independent emirate, on the w coast of the Persian Gulf; ab. 8,500 sq. mi.; 100,000; cap. Doha: also spelled **Katar.**
Quak·er·town (kwäk′ər·toun) city, SE Michigan; 7,101.
— boro., SE Pennsylvania; 7,216 ZIP 18951.
Quan·ti·co Station (kwon′tə·kō) city, NE Virginia; 6,213; ZIP 22134.
Que·bec (kwi·bek′) prov., E Canada; 594,860 sq. mi.; 5,780,-845.
— city, s Quebec prov.; cap.; 166,984.
Queens (kwēnz) boro., E New York City; 113 sq. mi.; 1,986,473.
Queens·land (kwēnz′lənd) state, NE Australia; 670,500 sq. mi.; 1,732,280; cap. Brisbane.
Que·moy Islands (ki·moi′) 2 isls. of the Republic of China in Formosa Strait; 54 sq. mi.
Que·zon City (kā′sôn, -thôn) city, N CEN. Philippines; cap.; 482,400.
Quin·cy (kwin′sē) city, NW Florida; 8,334; ZIP 32351*.
— city, W Illinois; 45,288 ZIP 62301*.
Quin·cy (kwin′zē) city, E Massachusetts; 87,966; ZIP see BOSTON.
Qui·to (kē′tō) city, N CEN. Ecuador; cap.; 409,967.
Qum (kōōm) city, NE Iran; 110,000. Also **Qom.**

Ra·bat (rä·bät′) city, N Morocco; cap.; 266,000.
Ra·cine (rə·sēn′) city, SE Wisconsin; 95,162; ZIP 53400*.
Rad·cliff (rad′klif) city, W Kentucky; 7,881; ZIP 40160.
Rad·ford (rad′fərd) city, sw Virginia; 11,596; ZIP 24141*.
Rad·nor (rad′nər) urb. twp., SE Pennsylvania; 21,697.
— See WOODBINE-RADNOR-GLENCLIFF.
Rah·way (rô′wā) city, NE New Jersey; 29,114; ZIP 07065*.
Rai·nier (rā′nir) Mount extinct volcano, Cascade Range, sw Washington; 14,408 ft.
Ra·leigh (rô′lē, rä′lē) city, CEN. North Carolina; cap.; 121,577; ZIP 27600*.
Ram·ble·wood (ram′bəl·wōōd) city, W New Jersey; 5,556; ZIP 08057.
Ram·sey (ram′zē) boro., NE New Jersey; 12,571; ZIP 07446.
Ran·cho Cor·do·va (ran′chō kôr·dō′və) uninc. place, CEN. California; 30,451; ZIP 95670.
Ran·cho Rin·co·na·da (ran′chō rēn·kō·nä′də) city, W California; 5,149.
Ran·dalls·town (ran′dəlz·toun) city, NE Maryland; 33,683; ZIP 21133.
Ran·dolph (ran′dolf, -dəlf) city, NW Maryland; 13,233; ZIP 20853.
— town, E Massachusetts; 27,035; ZIP 02368.
— city, s CEN. Texas; 5,329.
Ran·goon (rang·gōōn′) city, s Burma; cap.; 821,800.
Ran·toul (ran′tōōl′) vill., E CEN. Illinois; 25,526; ZIP 61866*.
Rapid City city, sw South Dakota; 43,836; ZIP 57701*.
Rar·i·tan (rar′i·tn, rar′i·tən) boro., N CEN. New Jersey; 6,691; ZIP 08869.
Rar·i·tan (rär′i·tən) twp., N CEN. New Jersey; 15,334; ZIP 08869.

Ra·ton (ra′tōōn′, rat′ōōn′) city, NE New Mexico; 6,962; ZIP 87740.
Ra·ven·na (ri·van′ə, rə·ven′ə) city, NE Ohio; 11,780; ZIP 44266.
Ra·wal·pin·di (rä′wəl·pin′dē, rôl·pin′dē) city, N Pakistan; 343,000.
Raw·lins (rô′linz) city, s CEN. Wyoming; 7,855; ZIP 82301.
Ray·mond·ville (rā′mənd·vil, -vəl, -mən-) city, s Texas; 7,987; ZIP 78580.
Rayne (rān) city, s Louisiana; 9,571; ZIP 70578.
Rayn·ham (rān′ham) city, s Massachusetts; 6,705; ZIP 02767.
Ray·town (rā′toun) city, W Missouri; 33,632; ZIP see KANSAS CITY.
Read·ing (red′ing) town, NE Massachusetts; 22,539; ZIP 01867.
— city, sw Ohio; 14,303; ZIP see CINCINNATI.
— city, SE Pennsylvania; 87,643; ZIP 19600*.
Re·ci·fe (rā·sē′fə) city, NE Brazil; 1,056,000.
Red Bank boro., E New Jersey; 12,847; ZIP 07701*.
Red Bank-White Oak city, SE Tennessee; 12,715.
Red Bluff city, N California; 7,676; ZIP 96080.
Red Deer city, s CEN. Alberta, Canada; 26,171.
Red·ding (red′ing) city, N California; 16,657; ZIP 96001*.
— city, sw Connecticut; 5,590; ZIP 06875.
Red·lands (red′ləndz) city, sw California; 36,355; ZIP 92373*.
Red Lion boro., s Pennsylvania; 5,645; ZIP 17356.
Red·mond (red′mənd) city, W CEN. Washington; 11,031; ZIP 98052.
Red Oak city, sw Iowa; 6,210; ZIP 51566.
Re·don·do Beach (rē′don′dō) city, sw California; 56,075; ZIP 90277*.
Red River river in Texas, Arkansas, and Louisiana; 1,018 mi. long.
— river in the United States and Canada; 540 mi. long.
Red Sea sea betw. Egypt and Arabia; 1,450 mi. long; ab. 170,000 sq. mi.
Red Wing city, SE Minnesota; 10,441; ZIP 55066.
Red·wood City (red′wōōd) city, W California; 55,686; ZIP 94061*.
Reed·ley (rēd′lē) city, CEN. California; 8,131; ZIP 93654.
Re·gi·na (ri·jī′nə) city, s Saskatchewan, Canada; cap.; 131,127.
Re·ho·both (rē·hō′bəth) city, s Massachusetts; 6,512; ZIP 02769.
Reids·ville (rēdz′vil, -vəl) city, N North Carolina; 13,636; ZIP 27320.
Reims (rēmz) city, NE France; site of a famous cathedral; 152,967.
Reis·ter·town (rīs′tər·toun) city, NE Maryland; 14,037; ZIP 21136.
Relay See ARBUTUS-HALETHORPE-RELAY.
Ren·frew (ren′frōō) town, SE Ontario, Canada; 9,502.
Re·no (rē′nō) city, W Nevada; 72,863; ZIP 89500*.
Rens·se·laer (ren′sə·lir′, rens·lir′, ren′sə·lər, rens′lər) city, E New York; 10,136; ZIP 12144.
Ren·ton (rent′n, ren′tən) city, W CEN. Washington; 25,258; ZIP 98055.
Re·pen·ti·gny (rə·pän·tē·nyē′) town, s Quebec, Canada; 14,976.
Re·serve (ri·zûrv′) uninc. place, SE Louisiana; 6,381; ZIP 70084.
Res·ton (res′tən) city, NE Virginia; 5,723; ZIP 22070.
Ré·un·ion (rē·yōōn′yən) French overseas dept.; isl., E of Malagasy; 970 sq. mi.; 330,000; cap. Saint-Denis.
Re·vere (ri·vir′) city, E Massachusetts; 43,159; ZIP see BOSTON.
Rex·bur·y (reks′bûr·ē) city, E Idaho; 8,272; ZIP 83440.
Rey·kja·vik (rā′kyə·vik) city, sw Iceland; cap.; 77,220.
Reyn·olds·burg (ren′əldz·bûrg) vill., CEN. Ohio; 13,921; ZIP 43068.
Rheims (rēmz) Reims: an alternate name.
Rhine (rīn) river W CEN. Europe; 810 mi. long.
Rhine·lan·der (rīn′lan′dər) city, N Wisconsin; 8,218; ZIP 54501.
Rhode Island (rōd) state, NE United States; 1,214 sq. mi.; 946,725; cap. Providence.
Rhodes (rōdz) isl. of the Dodecanese group; 545 sq. mi.
— city, Rhodes; cap. Dodecanese Islands; 24,000.
Rho·de·sia (rō·dē′zhə, -zhē·ə) See ZIMBABWE RHODESIA.
Rhodesia and Nyasaland, Federation of former political association of N. and S. Rhodesia and Nyasaland.
Rhône (rōn) river, Switzerland and SE France; 504 mi. long. Also **Rhone.**
Ri·al·to (ri·al′tō) city, s California; 28,370; ZIP 92376.
Rice Lake city, NW Wisconsin; 7,278; ZIP 54868.
Rich·ard·son (rich′ərd·sən) city, N Texas; 48,582; ZIP 75080*.

Rich·field (rich′fēld) vill., E Minnesota; 47,231; ZIP see MINNEAPOLIS.
Rich·land (rich′lənd) city, S Washington; 26,290; ZIP 99352.
Richland Center city, SW Wisconsin; 5,086; ZIP 53581.
Richland Hills town, N Texas; 8,865; ZIP see FORT WORTH.
Rich·mond (rich′mənd) city, W California; 79,043; ZIP 94800*.
— city, E Indiana; 43,999; ZIP 47374.
— city, CEN. Kentucky; 16,861; ZIP 40475*.
— boro., SE New York City; 295,443.
— city, E CEN. Texas; 5,777; ZIP 77469.
— city, E CEN. Virginia; cap.; cap. of the Confederacy 1861–65; 249,621; ZIP 93200*.
Richmond Heights city, SE Florida; 6,663; ZIP 33158.
— city, E Missouri; 13,802; ZIP see SAINT LOUIS.
— vill., N Ohio; 9,220; ZIP see CLEVELAND.
Richmond Hill town, S Ontario, Canada; 19,773.
Ridge·crest (rij′krest) uninc. place, S California; 7,629; ZIP 93555*.
Ridge·field (rij′fēld) boro., NE New Jersey; 11,308; ZIP 07657.
Ridgefield Center city, SW Connecticut; 5,878; ZIP 06877.
Ridgefield Park urb. twp., NE New Jersey; 14,453; ZIP 07660.
Ridge·wood (rij′wŏŏd) urb. twp., NE New Jersey; 27,547; ZIP 07450*.
Ridg·way (rij′wā) boro., N CEN. Pennsylvania; 6,022; ZIP 15853.
Rid·ley (rid′lē) urb. twp., SE Pennsylvania; 35,738.
Ridley Park boro., SE Pennsylvania; 9,025; ZIP 19078.
Rif (rif) mtn. range, N Morocco. Also **Riff**.
Ri·ga (rē′gə) city, CEN. Latvian SSR; cap.; 680,000.
Ri·je·ka (rē·ye′kä) city, NW Yugoslavia; including its SE suburb and officially called **Ri·je·ka-Su′šak** (-sōō′shäk); 106,000.
Ri·mou·ski (ri mōō′ski) town, E Quebec, Canada; 20,330.
Ring·wood (ring′wŏŏd) city, NE New Jersey; 10,393; ZIP 07456.
Ri·o de Ja·nei·ro (rē′ō də jə·nâr′ō, zhə·nâr′ō) city, SE Brazil; former cap.; 4,031,000. Also **Ri′o**.
Ri·o de la Pla·ta (rē′ō thä lä plä′tä) estuary of the Paraná and Uruguay rivers betw. Argentina and Uruguay; 170 mi. long.
Ri·o de O·ro (rē′ō thä ō′rō) terr., Spanish Sahara; 73,362 sq. mi.; ab. 157,000; cap. Villa Cisneros.
Ri·o Grande (rē′ō grand′) river betw. Texas and Mexico; 1,890 mi. long.
Ri·o Grande Cit·y (rē′ō grand′ sit′ē) uninc. place, S Texas; 5,676; ZIP 98582.
Ri·o Lin·da (rē′ō lin′də) city, CEN. California; 7,524; ZIP 95673.
Ri·o Mu·ni (rē′ō mōō′nē) Spanish overseas prov., W Africa; 10,039 sq. mi.; 185,000; cap. Bata.
Rip·on (rip′ən) city, E CEN. Wisconsin; 7,053; ZIP 54971.
Ritt·man (rit′mən) vill., NE CEN. Ohio; 6,308; ZIP 44270.
Riv·er·dale (riv′ər·dāl′) vill., NE Illinois; 15,806; ZIP see CHICAGO.
— city, SW Maryland; 5,724; ZIP 20840.
Riverdale Heights city, SW Maryland; 8,941.
River Edge boro., NE New Jersey; 12,850; ZIP 07661.
River Falls city, S CEN. Wisconsin; 7,238; ZIP 54022.
River Forest vill., NE Illinois; 13,402; ZIP see OAK PARK.
River Grove vill., NE Illinois; 11,465; ZIP 60171.
Riv·er·head (riv′ər·hed′) uninc. place, SE New York; 7,585; ZIP 11901*.
River Oaks city, N Texas; 8,193; ZIP See HOUSTON.
River Rouge (rōōzh) city, SE Michigan; 15,947; ZIP see DETROIT.
Riv·er·side (riv′ər·sīd′) city, SW California; 140,089; ZIP 92501*.
— vill., NE Illinois; 10,432; ZIP 60546*.
— urb. twp. W New Jersey; 8,616; ZIP 08075*.
Riv·er·ton (riv′ərt·n, -ər·tən) city, W CEN. Wyoming; 7,995; ZIP 82501.
Riv·er·view (riv′ər·vyōō) city, SE Michigan; 11,342; ZIP see WYANDOTTE.
Riv·i·er·a (riv′ē·âr′ə) coastal strip; on the Mediterranean from Hyères, France to La Spezia, Italy.
Ri·vier·a Beach (ri·vir′ə) town, SE Florida; 21,401; ZIP see WEST PALM BEACH.
— city, NE Maryland; 7,464; ZIP 21122.
Ri·viere-du-Loup (ri·vyâr′dü·lōō′) city, SE Quebec, Canada; 11,637.
Ro·a·noke (rō′ə·nōk) city, E Alabama; 5,251; ZIP 36274.
— city, W Virginia; 92,115; ZIP 24001*.
Roanoke Island isl. off North Carolina; 12 mi. long, 3 mi. wide.
Roanoke Rapids city, NE North Carolina; 13,508; ZIP 27870.
Rob·bins (rob′inz) vill., NE Illinois; 9,641; ZIP 60472.
Rob·bins·dale (rob′inz·dāl′) city, E Minnesota; 16,845; ZIP see MINNEAPOLIS.

Ro·ber·val (rō′bər·vəl) city, S CEN. Quebec, Canada; 8,552.
Rob·in·son (rob′in·sən) city, SE Illinois; 7,178; ZIP 62454*.
Robla See DEL PASO HEIGHTS-ROBLA.
Robs·town (robz′toun) city, S Texas; 11,217; ZIP 78380.
Ro·chelle (rō·shel′) city, N Illinois; 8,594; ZIP 61068.
Rochelle Park urb. twp., NE New Jersey; 6,380; ZIP 07662*.
Roch·es·ter (roch′es/tər, -is·tər) vill., SE Michigan; 7,054; ZIP 48063*.
— city, SE Minnesota; 53,766; ZIP 55901.
— city, SE New Hampshire; 17,938; ZIP 03867.
— city, W New York; 296,233; ZIP 14600*.
Rock·a·way (rok′ə·wā′) boro., N New Jersey; 6,383; ZIP 07866.
Rockdale See WOODLAWN-ROCKDALE-MILLFORD MILLS.
Rock Falls city, NW Illinois; 10,287; ZIP 61071.
Rock·ford (rok′fərd) city, N Illinois; 147,370; ZIP 61100.
Rock Hill city, E Missouri; 7,275; ZIP see ST. LOUIS.
— city, N South Carolina; 33,846; ZIP 29730*.
Rock·ing·ham (rok′ing·ham) town, S North Carolina; 5,852; ZIP 28379.
— city, SW Vermont; 5,501; ZIP 05101.
Rock Island city, NW Illinois; 50,166; ZIP 61201*.
Rock·land (rok′lənd) town, E Massachusetts; 15,674; ZIP 02370.
— city, S Maine; 8,505; ZIP 04841.
Rock·ledge (rok′lej) city, SE Florida; 10,523; ZIP 32955.
Rock·port (rok′pôrt′) city, NE Maine; 5,636; ZIP 04856.
Rock Springs city, SW Wyoming; 11,657; ZIP 82901.
Rock·ville (rok′vil) city, W CEN. Maryland; 41,564; ZIP 20850*.
Rockville Centre vill., SE New York; 27,444; ZIP 11570*.
Rock·wood (rok′wŏŏd) city, E Tennessee; 5,259; ZIP 37854.
Rocky Hill city, CEN. Connecticut; 11,103; ZIP 06067.
Rocky Mount city, E CEN. North Carolina; 34,284; ZIP 27801*.
Rocky Mountains mtn. system, W North America, extends from the Arctic to Mexico.
Rocky River city, N Ohio; 22,958; ZIP see CLEVELAND.
Rodeo city, W CEN. California; 5,356; ZIP 94572.
Rodgers Forge See STONELEIGH-RODGERS FORGE.
Roe·land Park (rō′lənd) city, E Kansas; 9,974.
Roes·sle·ville (res′əl·vil) city, NE New York; 5,476.
Rog·ers (roj′ərz) city, NW Arkansas; 11,050; ZIP 73756.
Roh·nert Park (rō′nərt) city, W California; 6,133; ZIP 94928.
Rol·la (rol′ə) city, CEN. Missouri; 13,245; ZIP 65401.
Rolling Hills Estates city, S California; 6,027; ZIP 90274.
Rolling Meadows city, NE Illinois; 19,178; ZIP see ARLINGTON HEIGHTS.
Rolling Mill Park See ONEIDA-ROLLING MILL PARK.
Ro·ma·nia (rō·mā′nyə) Rumania: *an alternate form.*
Rome (rōm) city, W Italy; cap.; site of the Vatican City; cap. of the former Roman republic, the Roman Empire, and the States of the Church; 2,455,302.
Rome (rōm) city, NW Georgia; 30,759; ZIP 30161*.
— city, CEN. New York; 50,148; ZIP 13440*.
Ro·me·o·ville (rō′mē·ō·vil) city, NE Illinois; 12,674; ZIP 60441.
Ron·kon·ko·ma (ron·kong′kə·mə, rong-) city, SE New York; 7,284; ZIP 11779.
Roo·se·velt (rō′zə·velt, -vəlt) uninc. place, SE New York; 15,008; ZIP 11575.
Ro·sa·rio (rō·sä′ryō) city, E CEN. Argentina; 671,852.
Rose·burg (rōz′bûrg) city, SW Oregon; 14,461; ZIP 97470.
Rose·dale (rōz′dāl) city, NW Maryland; 19,417; ZIP 21237.
Rose Hill city, NE Virginia; 14,692; ZIP 24281.
Rose·land (rōz′land′) city, W California; 5,105.
Ro·selle (rō·zel′) boro., NE New Jersey; 22,585; ZIP see ELIZABETH.
Roselle Park boro., NE New Jersey; 14,277; ZIP see ELIZABETH.
Rose·mead (rōz′mēd) city, SW California; 40,472; ZIP 91770*.
Rose·mere (rōz′mir) town, S Quebec, Canada; 6,429.
Ro·sen·berg (rō′zən·bûrg) city, SE Texas; 12,098; ZIP 77471.
Rose·ville (rōz′vil) city, CEN. California; 17,895; ZIP 95678.
— city, SE Michigan; 60,529; ZIP 48066.
— vill., SE Minnesota; 34,518; ZIP see SAINT PAUL.
Ros·lyn (roz′lin) city, SW Pennsylvania; 18,317.
Roslyn Heights city, SE New York; 7,140.
Ross (rôs) urb. twp., SW Pennsylvania; 25,952.
Ross·ford (rôs′fərd) city, NW Ohio; 5,302.
Ross·moor (rôs′mŏŏr) city, SW California; 12,922.
Ros·tov-on-Don (ros′tov·on·don′) city, SW RSFSR; 757,000.
Ros·well (roz′wəl) city, NW Georgia; 5,430; ZIP 30075.
— city, SE New Mexico; 33,908; ZIP 88201*.
Rot·ter·dam (rot′ər·dam) city, W Netherlands; 710,871.
Rot·ter·dam (rot′ər·dam) uninc. place, E New York; 25,153; ZIP see SCHENECTADY.
Rou·en (rōō·äñ′) city, N France; site of a famous cathedral;

scene of the burning of Joan of Arc; 120,471.

Rou·ma·nia (rōō·mā′nyə) Rumania: *an alternate form.*

Round Lake Beach vill., NE Illinois; 5,717.

Rou·yn (rōō′in) city, w Quebec, Canada; 18,581.

Rox·bor·o (roks′bûr′ō) city, N North Carolina; 5,370; ZIP 27573.

Rox·bor·o (roks′bûr′ō) town, S Quebec, Canada; 7,930.

Roy (roi) city, N Utah; 14,356; ZIP 84067.

Royal Oak city, SE Michigan; 85,499; ZIP 48067*.

Ru·an·da-U·run·di (rōō·än′də-ōō·rōōn′dē) former UN Trust terr., CEN. Africa. See BURUNDI, RWANDA.

Ru·bi·doux (rōō·bi·dōō′) city, SE California; 13,969; ZIP 92509.

Rug·by (rug′bē) municipal boro., CEN. England; site of a boys' school; 57,190.

Ruhr (rōōr) river, w West Germany; 142 mi. long.

— reg. S of the Ruhr; an industrial and coal-mining district.

Ru·ma·ni·a (rōō·mā′nē·ə, -mān′yə) republic, SE Europe; 91,671 sq. mi.; 20,250,000; cap. Bucharest.

Rum·ford (rum′fərd) uninc. place, SW Maine; 9,363; ZIP 04276.

Rum·son (rum′sən) boro., E New Jersey; 7,421; ZIP 07760*.

Run·ne·mede (run′i·mēd) boro., SW New Jersey; 10,475; ZIP 08078.

Rush·ville (rush′vil) city, E CEN. Indiana; 6,686; ZIP 46173.

Rus·sell (rus′əl) city, CEN. Kansas; 5,371; ZIP 67665.

Rus·sell·ville (rus′əl·vil, -vəl) city, NW Alabama; 7,814; ZIP 35653*.

— city, NE CEN. Arkansas; 11,750; ZIP 72801*.

— city, S Kentucky; 6,456; ZIP 42276.

Rus·sia (rush′ə) before 1917, an empire, E Europe and N Asia; cap. Saint Petersburg (Petrograd). See RUSSIAN SOVIET FEDERATED SOCIALIST REPUBLIC, UNION OF SOVIET SOCIALIST REPUBLICS.

Russian Soviet Federated Socialist Republic constituent republic, N USSR; 6,592,800 sq. mi.; 246,176,000; cap. Moscow.

Rus·ton (rus′tən) city, N Louisiana; 17,365; ZIP 71270*.

Ruth·er·ford (ruth′ər·fərd) boro., NE New Jersey; 20,802; ZIP 07070*.

Rut·land (rut′lənd) city, S CEN. Vermont; 19,293; ZIP 05701*.

Rwan·da (rwän′dä, rōō·än′dä) republic, CEN. Africa; 10,169 sq. mi.; 3,734,000; cap. Kigali.

Ry·dal (rī′dəl) city, SE Pennsylvania; 5,083.

Rye (rī) city, SE New York; 15,869; ZIP 10580.

Ryu·kyu Islands (ryōō·kyōō) isl. group betw. Kyushu and Taiwan; 2,046 sq. mi.; 984,000; chief isl. Okinawa; jointly adm. by Japan and the United States.

Saar (zär) river, NE France and W Germany; 152 mi. long.

Saar (zär), **The** state, W West Germany; 989 sq. mi.; 1,040,000; cap. Saarbrücken.

Sa·co (sô′kō) city, SW Maine; 11,678; ZIP 04072.

Sac·ra·men·to (sak′rə·men′tō) city, N CEN. California; cap.; 254,413; ZIP 95801*.

Sacramento River river, N CEN. California; 382 mi. long.

Saddle Brook urb. twp., NE New Jersey; 15,098; ZIP see ROCHELLE PARK.

Saf·ford (saf′ərd) city, SE Arizona; 5,333; ZIP 85546.

Sag·i·naw (sag′ə·nô) city, E CEN. Michigan; 91,849; ZIP 48601*.

Sa·har·a (sə·har′ə, -hâr′ə, -hä′rə) desert area, N Africa; ab. 3 million sq. mi. Also **Sahara Desert.**

Sai·gon (si·gon′, sī′gon) city, S South Vietnam; cap; 1,681,893.

Sai·pan (sī·pan′, -pan′, sī′pan) one of the Mariana isls.; 47 sq. mi.; captured from Japan by U.S. forces in World War II, 1944.

Saint, Sainte See entries beginning ST., STE.

Sa·kha·lin (sak′ə·lēn′) isl., SE RSFSR; 29,700 sq. mi.; 649,000; adm. ctr. Yuzhno-Sakhalinsk.

Sal·a·man·ca (sal′ə·mang′kə) city, SW New York; 7,877; ZIP 14779.

Sa·lem (sā′lem) city, S CEN. Illinois; 6,187; ZIP 62881.

— city, SE Indiana; 5,041; ZIP 47167.

— city, NE Massachusetts; 40,556; ZIP 01970*.

— city, SE New Hampshire; 20,142; ZIP 03079.

— city, SW New Jersey; 7,648; ZIP 08079.

— city, E Ohio; 14,186; ZIP 44460*.

— city, NW Oregon; cap.; 68,296; ZIP 97301*.

— town, SW CEN. Virginia; 21,982; ZIP 24153.

Salem Heights uninc. place, NW Oregon; 10,770.

Sa·ler·no (sä·ler′nō) city, SW Italy; scene of a battle in World War II betw. Germans and Allied landing forces, 1943; 123,589.

Sa·li·na (sə·lī′nə) city, CEN. Kansas; 37,714; ZIP 67401*.

Sa·li·nas (sə·lē′nəs) city, w California; 58,896; ZIP 93901*.

Salis·bur·y (sôlz′ber′ē, -bər·ē) city, SE Maryland; 15,252; ZIP 21801.

— city, W CEN. North Carolina; 22,515; ZIP 28144.

Sa·lo·ni·ka (sä′lō·nē′kä) city, NE Greece; 250,920.

Salt Lake City city, N CEN. Utah; cap.; 175,885; ZIP 84100*.

Sal·va·dor (sal′və·dôr′) city, E Brazil; 863,000.

Sal·va·dor (sal′və·dôr′) See EL SALVADOR.

Salz·burg (zälts′bŏŏrkh) city, w Austria; birthplace of Mozart; 115,720.

Sa·mar (sä′mär) one of the Visayan isls., Philippines; 5,050 sq. mi.

Sam·ar·kand (sam′ər·kand′) city, E Uzbek SSR; 248,000.

Sa·mo·a (sə·mō′ə) isl. group, SW Pacific; 1,209 sq. mi.; divided into **American (or Eastern) Samoa,** an uninc. terr. of the United States; 76 sq. mi.; 20,051; cap. Pago Pago; and **Western Samoa,** an independent state; 1,133 sq. mi.; 110,000; cap. Apia.

Sa·mos (sā′mos) isl. of Greece, E Aegean; 194 sq. mi.

Sam·o·thrace (sam′ə·thrās) isl. of Greece, NE Aegean; 71 sq. mi.

San An·ge·lo (san an′jə·lō) city, W CEN. Texas; 63,884; ZIP 76901*.

San An·sel·mo (san′ an·sel′mō) city, W California; 13,031; ZIP 94960.

San An·to·ni·o (san an·tō′nē·ō) city, S CEN. Texas; site of the Alamo; 654,153; ZIP 78200*.

San Be·ni·to (san′ bə·nē′tō) city, S Texas; 15,176; ZIP 78586.

San Ber·nar·di·no (san bûr′nər·dē′nō) city, SW California; 104,251; ZIP 92400*.

San Bru·no (san brōō′nō) city, W California; 36,254; ZIP 94066*.

San Car·los (san kär′lōs) city, w California; 25,924; ZIP 94070*.

San Cle·men·te (san kli·men′tē) city, S California; 17,063; ZIP 92672.

San·ders·ville (san′dərz·vil, -vəl) city, E CEN. Georgia; 5,546; ZIP 31082.

San·di·a (san′dē·ə) city, CEN. New Mexico; 6,867.

San Di·e·go (san dē·ā′gō) city, SW California; 696,769; ZIP 92100.

San Di·mas (sän dē·mäs′) city, SW California; 15,692; ZIP 91773.

Sand Springs city, NE Oklahoma; 11,519; ZIP 74063.

San·dus·ky (san·dus′kē) city, N Ohio; 32,674; ZIP 44870*.

Sandusky South city, N CEN. Ohio; 8,501; ZIP 44870.

Sand·wich (sand′wich) city, NE Illinois; 5,056; ZIP 60548.

— city, E Massachusetts; 5,239; ZIP 02563.

Sand·wich Islands (sand′wich) Hawaiian Islands: *the former name.*

Sandy City city, NW Utah; 6,438; ZIP 84070.

San Fer·nan·do (san′ fər·nan′dō) city, SW California; 16,571; ZIP 91340*.

San·ford (san′fərd) city, E CEN. Florida; 17,393; ZIP 32771.

— uninc. place, SW Maine; 15,812; ZIP 04073.

— city, CEN. North Carolina; 11,716; ZIP 27330*.

San Fran·cis·co (san′ frən·sis′kō) city, W California; 715,674; ZIP 94100*.

San Francisco Bay inlet of the Pacific, W California.

San Ga·bri·el (san gā′brē·əl) city, SW California; 29,176; ZIP 91775*.

Sang·er (sang′ər) city, CEN. California; 10,088; ZIP 93657.

San Ger·mán (sän′ her·män′) town, SW Puerto Rico; 7,779; ZIP 00753.

San Joa·quin River (san′ wô·kēn′, wä·kēn′) river, S CEN. California; 317 mi. long.

San Jo·sé (san′ hō·zā′) city, CEN. Costa Rica; cap; 182,961.

San Jo·se (san′ hō·zā′) city, W California; 445,779; ZIP 95100*.

San Juan (sän hwän) city, NE Puerto Rico; cap.; 432,508; ZIP 00900*.

San Juan (san hwän) city, S Texas; 5,070; ZIP 78289.

San Le·an·dro (san lē·an′drō) city, W California; 68,698; ZIP 94577*.

San Lo·ren·zo (san lə·ren′zō) uninc. place, W California; 24,633; ZIP 94580.

San Lo·ren·zo (sän lō·ren′sō) town, E Puerto Rico; 5,551; ZIP 00754.

San Lu·is O·bis·po (san lōō′is ō·bis′pō, ə·bis′pō) city, W California; 28,036; ZIP 93401*.

San Mar·cos (san mär′kəs) city, S CEN. Texas; 18,860; ZIP 78666.

San Ma·ri·no (mä·rē′nō) republic, an enclave in NE Italy; 23 sq. mi.; 16,000. — city, San Marino; cap.; 4,057.

San Ma·ri·no (san mə·rē′nō) city, SW California; 14,177; ZIP see PASADENA.

San Ma·te·o (san mə·tā′ō) city, W California; 78,991; ZIP 94400*.

PRONUNCIATION KEY: add, āce, câre, pälm; end, ēven; it, īce; odd, ōpen, ôrder; tŏŏk, pōōl; up, bûrn; ə = a in *above,* e in *sicken,* i in *flexible,* o in *melon,* u in *focus;* yōō = u in *fuse;* oil; pout; check; go; ring; thin; this; zh, vision. For à, œ, ü, kh, ṅ, see inside front cover.

San Pab·lo (san pab′lō) city, w California; 21,461; ZIP see RICHMOND.

San Pe·dro (san pā′drō) uninc. place, s Texas; 7,634.

San Ra·fael (san rə·fĕl′) city, w California; 38,977; ZIP 94901*.

San Re·mo (rē′mō) uninc. place, SE New York; 8,302.

San Sal·va·dor (san′ sal′və·dôr) city, s El Salvador; cap.; 281,122.

San Sal·va·dor (san′ sal′və·dôr) isl., CEN. Bahamas; site of Columbus′ first landing in the western hemisphere, 1492.

San·ta An·a (san′tə an′ə) city, sw California; 156,601; ZIP 92700*.

San·ta Bar·ba·ra (san′tə bär′bər·ə) city, sw California; 70,215; ZIP 93100*.

San·ta Cat·a·li·na (san′tə kat′ə·lē′nə) isl. off sw California; 70 sq. mi.

San·ta Clar·a (san′tə clar′ə) city, w California; 87,717; ZIP 95050*.

San·ta Cruz (san′tə krōōz′) city, w California; 32,076; ZIP 95060*.

San·ta Fe (san′tə fā′) city, N New Mexico; cap; 41,167; ZIP 87501*.

Santa Fe Springs city, sw California; 14,750; ZIP 90670.

Santa Fe Trail trade route, important from 1821–80, betw. Independence, Missouri, and Santa Fe, New Mexico.

San·ta Ma·ri·a (san′tə mə·rē′ə) city, sw California; 32,749; ZIP 93454*.

San·ta Mon·i·ca (san′tə mon′i·kə) city, sw California; 88,289; ZIP 90400*.

San·ta Pau·la (san′tə pô′lə) city, sw California; 18,001; ZIP 93060.

San·ta Ro·sa (san′tə rō′zə) city, w California; 50,006; ZIP 95401*.

San·tee (san·tē′) city, sw California; 21,107; ZIP 92071.

San·ti·a·go (sän′tē·ä′gō) city, CEN. Chile; cap; 2,447,741. Also **Santiago de Chi·le** (thä chē′lā).

San·to Do·min·go (sän′tō dō·ming′gō) city, s Dominican Republic; cap.; 367,053. — Dominican republic: *the former name.*

São Pau·lo (souṅ pou′lŏŏ) city, SE Brazil; 5,383,000.

São Sal·va·dor (souṅ säl′və·thôr′) Salvador: *the former name.*

São To·mé and Prin·ci·pe (souṅ·tə·mä′ənd print′sə·pə) democratic republic, isls. on the equator, w Africa, 372 sq. mi.; 82,000; cap. São Tomé.

Sap·ping·ton (sap′ing·tən) city, NE Missouri; 10,603.

Sa·pul·pa (sə·pul′pə) city, NE CEN. Oklahoma; 15,159; ZIP 74066.

Sa·ra·je·vo (sä′rä′ye·vô) city, CEN. Yugoslavia; scene of the assassination of Archduke Franz Ferdinand, June 28, 1914; 206,000.

Sar·a·land (sâr′ə·land, sar′-) city, sw Alabama; 7,840; ZIP 36571.

Sar·a·nac Lake (sar′ə·nak) vill., N New York; 6,086; ZIP 12983.

Sar·a·nap (sar′ə·nap) uninc. place, w California; 6,450.

Sar·a·so·ta (sar′ə·sō′tə) city, sw Florida; 40,237; ZIP 33577*.

Sar·a·to·ga (sar′ə·tō′gə) city, w California; 27,110; ZIP 95070.

Saratoga Springs city, E New York; 18,845; ZIP 12866.

Sa·ra·wak (sə·rä′wäk, -wä) part of Malaysia on NW Borneo; 47,071 sq. mi.; 1,019,000; cap. Kuching.

Sar·din·i·a (sär·din′ē·ə) isl., E CEN. Mediterranean; with adjacent isls. a reg. of Italy; 9,298 sq. mi.; 1,448,011; cap. Cagliari.

Sar·ni·a (sär′nē·ə) city, s Ontario, Canada; 54,552.

Sas·katch·e·wan (sas·kach′ə·won) prov., w CEN. Canada; 251,700 sq. mi.; 955,344; cap. Regina.

Sas·ka·toon (sas′kə·tōōn′) city, s CEN. Saskatchewan, Canada; 115,892.

Satellite Beach city, sw Florida; 6,558; ZIP 32935.

Sa·u·di Arabia (sä·ōō′dē) kingdom N and CEN. Arabia; 927,000 sq. mi.; 7,478,000; caps. Mecca and Riyadh.

Sau·gus (sô′gəs) town, NE Massachusetts; 25,110; ZIP see LYNN.

Sauk (sôk) city, NE Illinois; 7,479; ZIP 60411.

Sauk Rapids city, SE Minnesota; 5,051; ZIP 56379.

Sault Sainte Ma·rie (sōō′ sänt′ mə·rē′) city, N Michigan; 15,136; ZIP 49783*.

Sault Sainte Ma·rie (sōō′sänt′mə·rē′) city, s CEN. Ontario Canada; 79,594. Also **Sault Ste. Marie.**

Sau·sa·li·to (sô′sə·lē′tō) city, w California; 6,158; ZIP 94965.

Sa·van·nah (sə·van′ə) city, E Georgia; 118,349; ZIP 31400*.
— city, SE Tennessee; 5,576.

Sax·o·ny (sak′sə·nē) reg. and former duchy, electorate, kingdom and prov.; cen. Germany.

Sayre (sâr) boro., NE Pennsylvania; 7,473; ZIP 18840.

Sayre·ville (sâr′vil) boro., E New Jersey; 32,508; ZIP 08872.

Say·ville (sā′vil) city, SE New York; 11,680; ZIP 11782.

Scan·di·na·vi·a (skan′də·nā′vē·ə) reg., NW Europe; includes Sweden, Norway, and Denmark and sometimes Finland, Iceland, and the Faroe Islands.

Scapa Flow (skä′pə flō′, skap′ə) sea basin and British naval base in the Orkney Islands, Scotland; 50 sq. mi.

Scar·bor·ough (skär′bûr·ō) city, SE Maine; 7,845.

Scars·dale (skärz′dāl) town, SE New York; 19,229; ZIP 10583*.

Schaum·berg (shoum′bûrg) city, NE Illinois; 18,730; ZIP 60172.

Scheldt (skelt) river, N France, Belgium and the Netherlands; 270 mi. long.

Sche·nec·ta·dy (skə·nek′tə·dē) city, E New York; 77,859; ZIP 12300*.

Schil·ler Park (shil′ər) vill., NE Illinois; 12,712; ZIP 60176.

Schles·wig-Hol·stein (shläs′vikh·hōl′shtīn) state, NE West Germany; 6,052 sq. mi.; 2,309,000; cap. Kiel.

Scho·field Barracks (skō′fēld) city, Oahu, Hawaii; 13,516; ZIP 96786.

Schuyl·kill Haven (skōōl′kil′, skōō′kəl) boro., E CEN. Pennsylvania; 6,125; ZIP see PHILADELPHIA.

Schuylkill River river, SE Pennsylvania; 130 mi. long.

Scit·u·ate (sich′ōō·āt) city, NE Massachusetts; 16,973; ZIP 02066.
— city, sw Rhode Island; 7,489.

Scotch Plains (skoch) urb. twp., NE New Jersey; 22,279; ZIP 07076.

Sco·tia (skō′shə) vill., E New York; 8,224; ZIP see SCHENECTADY.

Scot·land (skot′lənd) A political div. and the N part of Great Britain; a separate kingdom until 1707; 30,405 sq. mi.; 5,124,000; cap. Edinburgh.

Scot·land·ville (skot′lənd·vil) city, SE Louisiana; 22,557; ZIP 70807.

Scott (skot) city, E Delaware; 5,537; ZIP 19973.
— urb. twp., sw Pennsylvania; 19,094.

Scott·dale (skot′dāl) boro., sw Pennsylvania; 5,818; ZIP 15683.

Scotts·bluff (skots′bluf′) city, w Nebraska; 14,507; ZIP 69361.

Scotts·bor·o (skots′bûr′ō) city, NE Alabama; 9,324; ZIP 35768*.

Scotts·dale (skots′dāl) city, SE CEN. Arizona; 67,823; ZIP 85251*.

Scran·ton (skran′tən) city, NE Pennsylvania; 103,564; ZIP 18500*.

Sea Cliff vill., SE New York; 5,890; ZIP 11579.

Sea·ford (sē′fərd) city, SE Illinois; 7,871.
— uninc. place, SE New York; 17,379; ZIP 11783.

Seal Beach city, sw California; 24,441; ZIP 90740.

Sear·cy (sûr′sē) city, CEN. Arkansas; 9,040; ZIP 72143*.

Sea·side (sē′sīd′) city, w California; 35,935; ZIP 93955.

Seat Pleasant town, s CEN. Maryland; 7,217; ZIP see WASHINGTON, D.C.

Se·at·tle (sē·at′l) city, w CEN. Washington; 530,831; ZIP 98100*.

Se·bas·to·pol (si·bas′tə·pōl) See SEVASTOPOL.

Se·bring (sē′bring) city, s CEN. Florida; 7,223; ZIP 33870.

Se·cau·cus (sēəkō′kəs) town, NE New Jersey; 13,228; ZIP see WEST NEW YORK.

Se·cur·i·ty (si·kyŏŏr′ə·tē) uninc. place, E CEN. Colorado; 15,297; ZIP see COLORADO SPRINGS.

Se·dal·ia (si·dāl′yə) city, w CEN. Missouri; 22,847; ZIP 65301*.

See·konk (sē′kongk) city, s Massachusetts; 11,116; ZIP 02771.

Se·guin (sə·gēn′) city, s CEN. Texas; 15,934; ZIP 78155.

Seine (sān) river, NE France; 482 mi. long.

Sel·den (sel′dən) city, SE New York; 11,613.

Sel·ins·grove (sel′inz·grōv) city, N CEN. Pennsylvania; 5,116; ZIP 17870.

Sel·kirk (sel′kûrk) town, SE Manitoba, Canada; 9,157.

Sel·ma (sel′mə) city, s CEN. Alabama; 27,379; ZIP 36701*.
— city, CEN. California; 7,459; ZIP 93662.

Se·ma·rang (sə·mä′räng) city, N Java, Indonesia; 503,153.

Sem·i·nole (sem′i·nōl) city, CEN. Oklahoma; 7,878; ZIP 74868.
— city, NW Texas; 5,007; ZIP 79360.

Sen·e·ca (sen′ə·kə) town, NW South Carolina; 6,027; ZIP 29678.

Seneca Falls vill., w CEN. New York; 7,794; ZIP 13148.

Sen·e·gal (sen′ə·gal, -gôl) river, NW Africa; ab. 1,000mi. long.

Sen·e·gal (sen′ə·gal, -gôl) **Republic of** republic of the French Community, NW Africa; 76,084 sq. mi.; 3,922,000; cap. Dakar.

Se·oul (sä·ōōl′, sōl) city, NW South Korea; cap.; 3,470,880.

Sept-Iles (set·ēl′) i Quebec, Canada; 18,950.

Ser·bi·a (sûr′bē·ə) constituent republic, E Yugoslavia; 34,107 sq. mi.; 4,814,000; cap.; Belgrade.

Se·vas·to·pol (sə·vas′tə·pōl, sev′əs·tō′pəl) city, s Crimea, USSR; 209,000.

Seven Corners city, NE Virginia; 5,590.

Seven Hills vill., N Ohio; 12,700.

Sev·ern (sev′ərn) river, N Wales and W England; 210 mi. long.

Se·ver·na (sə-vûr′nə) city, NE Maryland; 16,358; ZIP 21146.

Se·ville (sə-vil′) city, SW Spain; 459,786.

Sè·vres (se′vr′) city, N France; 17,000.

Sey·chelles (sā′shelz) isl. group in Indian Ocean, colony in the Commonwealth of Nations; 107 sq. mi.; 60,000; cap. Victoria.

Sey·mour (sē′môr) town, SW Connecticut; 12,776; ZIP 06483.
— city, S Indiana; 13,352; ZIP 47274.

Sey·mour-John·son (sē′môr-jon′sən) city, E CEN. North Carolina; 8,172.

Sha·dy·side (shā′dē-sīd′) vill., SE Ohio; 5,070; ZIP 43947.

Shaf·ter (shaf′tər) city, SE California; 5,327; ZIP 93263.

Shaker Heights city, N Ohio; 36,306; ZIP see CLEVELAND.

Sha·ko·pee (shā′kə-pē) city, SE Minnesota; 6,876; ZIP 55379.

Sha·ler (shā′lər) urb. twp., SW Pennsylvania; 24,939.

Sha·mo·kin (shə-mō′kin) boro., E CEN. Pennsylvania; 11,719; ZIP 17872.

Shang·hai (shang′hī) city, E China; 6,900,000.

Shan·non (shan′ən) river, CEN. Ireland; 224 mi. long.

Shan·non·town (shan′ən-toun) uninc. place, E CEN. South Carolina; 7,491.

Shan·tung (shan′tung′) province, NE China; 55,000 sq. mi.; 54,030,000; cap. Tsinan.

Shar·on (shâr′ən, shar′-) uninc. place, E Massachusetts; 12,367; ZIP 02067.
— city, W Pennsylvania; 22,653; ZIP 16146*.

Sharon Hill boro., SE Pennsylvania; 7,464; ZIP 19079*.

Shar·on·ville (shâr′ən-vil, shar′-) city. SW Ohio; 10,985; ZIP 45241.

Sharps·burg (shärps′bûrg) boro., SW Pennsylvania; 5,499; ZIP see PITTSBURGH.

Sharps·ville (shärps′vil) boro., W Pennsylvania; 6,126; ZIP 16150.

Shas·ta (shas′tə), **Mount** extinct volcano, Cascade Range, N California; 14,162 ft.

Shaw (shô) city, CEN. South Carolina; 5,819.

Sha·wa·no (shô′nō, shô′wə-nō) city, E Wisconsin; 6,488; ZIP 54166.

Sha·win·i·gan (shə-win′ə-gən) city, S Quebec, Canada; 30,777.

Shawinigan-S. vill., S Quebec, Canada; 12,250. Also **Shawinigan-South**.

Shaw·nee (shô′nē′) city, NE Kansas; 20,482.
— city, CEN. Oklahoma; 25,075; ZIP 74801*.

She·boy·gan (shə-boi′gən) city, E Wisconsin; 48,484; ZIP 53081*.

Shef·field (shef′ēld) co. boro., N CEN. England; 531,800.

Shef·field (shef′ēld) city, NW Alabama; 13,115; ZIP 35660.*

Sheffield Lake vill., N Ohio; 8,734; ZIP see LORAIN.

Shel·by (shel′bē) city, SW North Carolina; 16,328; ZIP 28150.
— city, N CEN. Ohio; 9,847; ZIP 44875.

Shel·by·ville (shel′bē-vil, -vəl) city, SE CEN. Indiana; 15,094; ZIP 46176.
— town, S CEN. Tennessee; 12,262; ZIP 37160.

Shel·ton (shelt′n, shel′tən) city, SW Connecticut; 27,165; ZIP 06484*.
— city, W Washington; 6,515; ZIP 98584.

Shen·an·do·ah (shen′ən-dō′ə) river, N Virginia and NE West Virginia; 55 mi. long.
— city, SW Iowa; 5,968; ZIP 51601.
— boro., E CEN. Pennsylvania; 8,287; ZIP 17976.

Shen·yang (shun′yäng′) city, NE China; 2,423,000.

Sher·brooke (shûr′brŏŏk) city, S Quebec, Canada; 75,690.

Sher·i·dan (sher′id-n, -i-dən) city, N Wyoming; 10,856; ZIP 82801.

Sher·man (shûr′mən) city, N Texas; 20,061; ZIP 75090*.

Sher·rel·wood (sher′əl-wŏŏd) city, E CEN. Colorado; 18,868.

Sher·wood Forest (shûr′wŏŏd) forest, NE CEN. England; known as the home of Robin Hood.

Shet·land Islands (shet′lənd) isl. group NE of the Orkney Islands, comprising **Shetland**, a co. of Scotland; 551 sq. mi.; 18,000; cap. Lerwick.

Shi·ko·ku (shē-kō′kōō) isl., SW Japan; 7,248 sq. mi.

Shil·ling·ton (shil′ingt-n, -ing-tən) boro., SE CEN. Pennsylvania; 6,249; ZIP see READING.

Shi·loh (shī′lō) national military park, SW Tennessee; scene of a Union victory in the Civil War, 1862; 6 sq. mi.; established 1884.
— city, SW Ohio; 11,368; ZIP 44878.

Ship·pens·burg (ship′ənz-bûrg) boro., S Pennsylvania; 6,536; ZIP 17257.

Shir·ley (shûr′lē) city, SE New York; 6,280.

Shive·ly (shīv′lē) city, N Kentucky; 19,223; ZIP see LOUISVILLE.

Shore·view (shôr′vyŏō′, shôr′-) vill., E Minnesota; 11,034.

Shore·wood (shôr′wŏŏd, shôr′-) vill., SE Wisconsin; 15,576; ZIP see MILWAUKEE.

Shreve·port (shrēv′pôrt, -pôrt) city, NW Louisiana; 182,064; ZIP 71100*.

Shrews·bur·y (shrōōz′ber′ē) city, CEN. Massachusetts; 19,196; ZIP 01545.
— city, NE Missouri; 5,896; ZIP 63101.

Shrop·shire (shrop′shir, -shər) co., W England; 1,347 sq. mi.; 297,000; cap. Shrewsbury.

Si·am (sī-am′) Thailand: *the former name.*

Siam, Gulf of part of the South China Sea betw. the Malay Peninsula and Indochina.

Si·be·ri·a (sī-bir′ē-ə) reg., E RSFSR; ab. 5 million sq. mi.

Sic·i·ly (sis′ə-lē) isl. of Italy, CEN. Mediterranean; comprises with neighboring islands a reg. 9,926 sq. mi.; 4,809,130; cap. Palermo.

Sid·ney (sid′nē) city, W Nebraska; 6,403; ZIP 69162.
— city, W Ohio; 16,332; ZIP 45365.

Si·er·ra Le·o·ne (sē-er′ə lē-ō′nē, lē-ōn′) independent member of the Commonwealth of Nations, W Africa; 27,925 sq. mi.; 2,588,000; cap. Freetown.

Si·er·ra Mad·re (sē-er′ə mad′rē) city, SW California; 12,140; ZIP 91024.

Si·er·ra Ne·vad·a (sē-er′ə nə-vad′ə, -vä′də) mtn. range, E California.

Si·er·ra Vis·ta (sē-er′ə vis′tə) city, SE Arizona; 6,689; ZIP 85635.

Signal Hill city, SW California; 5,582; ZIP 90806.

Sikes·ton (sīks′tən) city, SE Missouri; 14,699; ZIP 63801.

Si·le·sia (si-lē′shə, sī-) reg., E CEN. Europe; divided betw. Czechoslovakia and Poland.

Sil·ler·y (sil′ər-ē) city, S Quebec, Canada; 14,737.

Si·loam Springs (sī′lōm) city, NW Arkansas; 6,009; ZIP 72761.

Sils·bee (silz′bē) city, E Texas; 7,271; ZIP 77656.

Silver Bow Park (bō) city, SW Montana; 5,524; ZIP 59701.

Silver City town, SW New Mexico; 7,751; ZIP 88061

Silver Hills See SUITLAND-SILVER HILLS.

Silver Spring uninc. place, W Maryland; 77,496; ZIP 20900*.

Sil·ver·ton (sil′vərt-n, -vər-tən) city, SW Ohio; 6,588.

Sil·vis (sil′vis) city, NW Illinois; 5,907; ZIP 61282.

Sim·coe (sim′kō) town, S Ontario, Canada; 9,929.

Si·mi (sī′mē) city, SW California; 56,464; ZIP 93065.

Sim·la (sim′lə) city, N India; 42,597.

Sims·bur·y (simz′ber′ē) city, CEN. Connecticut; 17,475; ZIP 06070.

Si·nai (sī′nī, -nē-ī′) penin., E Egypt, betw. the Mediterranean and the Red Sea.

Sin·ga·pore (sing′ə-pôr, sing′gə-) isl. off the tip of the Malay Peninsula; comprises with adjacent isls. a part of Malaysia; 225 sq. mi.; 2,128,000. — city, S Singapore; cap.; 1,820,000.

Sing Sing (sing′sing′) state prison near Ossining, New York.

Sin·kiang-Ui·gur Autonomous Region (shin′jyäng′-wē′gŏŏr′) div., W China; 635,829 sq. mi.; 5,640,000; cap. Urumchi (Tihwa): also formerly **Sinkiang**.

Sin·ton (sint′n, sin′tən) town, S Texas; 5,563; ZIP 78387.

Sioux City (sōō) city, W Iowa; 82,925; ZIP 51100*.

Sioux Falls city, SE South Dakota; 72,488; ZIP 57100*.

Sko·kie (skō′kē) vill., NE Illinois; 68,627; ZIP 60076*.

Skow·he·gan (skou-hē′gən) uninc. place, SW Maine; 7,601; ZIP 04976.

Sla·ton (slāt′n, slā′tən) city, NW Texas; 6,583; ZIP 79364.

Sla·vo·ni·a (slə-vō′nē-ə) reg., N Yugoslavia.

Sli·dell (sli-del′) town, SE Louisiana; 16,101; ZIP 70458.

Sloan (slōn) vill., W New York; 5,216.

Slo·vak·i·a (slō-vak′ē-ə, -vä′kē-ə) reg. and former prov., E Czechoslovakia.

Slo·ve·ni·a (slō-vē′nē-ə) constituent republic, NW Yugoslavia; 7,717 sq. mi.; 1,584,000; cap. Ljubljana.

Smith Falls (smiths) town, SE Ontario, Canada; 9,876.

Smith·field (smith′fēld) town, E CEN. North Carolina; 6,677; ZIP 27577.
— city, SW Rhode Island; 13,468.
— city, CEN. Tennessee; 5,698.

Smoky Mountains See GREAT SMOKY MOUNTAINS.

Smyr·na (smûr′nə) city, W Turkey; 371,000.

Smyr·na (smûr′nə) town, NW CEN. Georgia; 19,157; ZIP 30080.

Sno·ho·mish (snə-hō′mish) city, N CEN. Washington; 5,174; ZIP 98290.

Sny·der (snī′dər) city, NW CEN. Texas; 11,171; ZIP 79549.

So·ci·e·ty Islands (sə-sī′ə-tē) isl. group, French Polynesia; ab. 650 sq. mi.

Sod·dy-Dai·sy (sod′ē-dā′sē) city, SE Tennessee; 7,569; ZIP 37379.

So·fi·a (sō′fē-ə, sō-fē′ə) city, W Bulgaria; cap.; 800,953.

PRONUNCIATION KEY: add, āce, câre, pälm; end, ēven; it, īce; odd, ōpen, ôrder; tŏŏk, pōōl; up, bûrn; ə = a in *above*, e in *sicken*, i in *flexible*, o in *melon*, u in *focus*; yōō = u in *fuse*; oil; pout; check; go; ring; thin; this; zh, vision. For á, œ, ü, kh, ṅ, see inside front cover.

So·la·na (sō·lä′nə) city, sw California; 5,023; ZIP 92075.

So·le·dad (sō′lə·dad) city, w CEN. California; 6,843; ZIP 93960.

Sol·o·mon Islands (sol′ə·mən) isl. group, sw Pacific; ab. 16,500 sq. mi.; including the **British Solomon Islands**, a prot.; ab. 11,500 sq. mi.; 156,000; cap. Honiara.

So·lon (sō′lən) vill., N Ohio; 11,519; ZIP see CLEVELAND.

Sol·vay (sol′vā) vill., CEN. New York; 8,280; ZIP see SYRACUSE.

So·ma·li·a (sō·mä′lyə, -lē·ə) republic, E Africa; 262,000 sq. mi.; ab. 3,026,000; cap. Mogadiscio.

Som·er·dale (sum′ər·dāl) city, w New Jersey; 6,510; ZIP 08876.

Som·ers (sum′ərz) city, NE Connecticut; 6,893; ZIP 06071.

Somers Point city, SE New Jersey; 7,919; ZIP 08244.

Som·er·set (sum′ər·set, -sit) city, s Kentucky; 10,436; ZIP 42501.
— town, SE Massachusetts; 18,088; ZIP see FALL RIVER.
— boro., sw Pennsylvania; 6,269; ZIP 15501.

Som·ers·worth (sum′ərz·wûrth) city, SE New Hampshire; 9,026; ZIP 03878.

Som·er·ville (sum′ər·vil) city, E Massachusetts; 88,779; ZIP see BOSTON.
— boro., N CEN. New Jersey; 13,652; ZIP 08876.

Somme (sôm) river, N France; 150 mi. long.

Soo Canals (sōō) *informal* Sault Sainte Marie Canals.

So·quel (sō·kel′) city, w California; 5,795; ZIP 95073.

Sor·el (sôr′əl) city, s Quebec, Canada; 19,021.

Sou·der·ton (sou′dərt·n, -dər·tən) boro., SE Pennsylvania; 6,366; ZIP 18964.

South Af·ri·ca (af′ri·kə), **Republic of** republic, s Africa; 472,359 sq. mi.; 20,580,000; seat of government Pretoria; seat of legislature Capetown.

South Am·boy (am′boi) city, E New Jersey; 9,338; ZIP 08879.

South America s continent, Western Hemisphere; ab. 6.9 million sq. mi.; 195 million.

South·amp·ton (south·hamp′tən, sou·thamp′-) co. boro., s England; 210,050.

South Australia state, s Australia; 380,070 sq. mi.; 969,340; cap. Adelaide.

South Ba·kers·field (bā′kərz·fēld) city, s CEN. California; 30,249.

South Bend city, N Indiana; 125,580; ZIP 46600*.

South·bor·ough (south′bûr·ə) city, CEN. Massachusetts; 5,798; ZIP 01772.

South Bos·ton (bôs′tən, bos′-) city, s Virginia; 6,889; ZIP 24592.

South·bridge (south′brij) uninc. place, s Massachusetts; 17,057; ZIP 01550*.

South Bur·ling·ton (bûr′ling·tən) city, NW Vermont; 10,032; ZIP 05401.

South·bur·y (south′ber′ē) city, sw Connecticut; 7,852; ZIP 06488.

South Car·o·li·na (kar′ə·lī′nə) state, SE United States; 31,055 sq. mi.; 2,590,516; cap. Columbia.

South Charles·ton (chärlz′tən, chärl′stən) city, w CEN. West Virginia; 16,333; ZIP see CHARLESTON.

South China Sea part of the Pacific betw. SE Asia and the Malay Archipelago.

South Cleve·land (klēv′lənd) city, SE Tennessee; 5,070; ZIP 37311.

South Dakota state, N CEN. United States; 77,047 sq. mi.; 665,507; cap. Pierre.

Southern Pines town, s CEN. North Carolina; 5,937; ZIP 28387*.

Southern Rho·de·sia (rō·dē′zhə, -zhē·ə) former British col., s CEN. Africa.

Southern Yemen See YEMEN, PEOPLE'S DEMOCRATIC REPUBLIC OF.

South El Mon·te (el mon′tē) city, SE California; 13,443; ZIP 91733.

South Eu·clid (yōō′klid) city, NE Ohio; 29,579; ZIP see CLEVELAND.

South Far·ming·dale (fär′ming·dāl) uninc. place, SE New York; 20,464; ZIP see FARMINGDALE.

South·field (south′fēld) city, SE Michigan; 69,285; ZIP 48075*.

South Fort Polk (pōk) city, sw Louisiana; 15,600.

South·gate (south′gāt) city, SE Michigan; 33,909; ZIP see WYANDOTTE.

South Gate city, sw California; 56,909; ZIP 90280*.
— city, NE Maryland; 9,356.

South Had·ley (had′lē) town, sw CEN. Massachusetts; 17,033; ZIP 01075.

South Ha·ven (hā′vən) city, sw Michigan; 6,471; ZIP 49090.
— city, NW Mississippi; 8,931.

South Hol·brook (hōl′brŏŏk′) city, SE Massachusetts; 6,700.

South Hol·land (hōl′ənd) vill., SE Illinois; 23,931; ZIP 60473.

South Hun·ting·ton (hun′ting·tən) uninc. place, SE New York; 8,946.

South·ing·ton (suth′ing·tən) uninc. place, CEN. Connecticut; 30,946; ZIP 06489.

South Island one of the two main isls. of New Zealand; 58,093 sq. mi.

South Ken·sing·ton (ken′sing·tən) city, NW Maryland; 10,289.

South Kings·ton (kingz′tən, king′stən) town, s Rhode Island; 16,913.

South Korea See KOREA.

South Lake Ta·hoe (tä′hō) city, SE California; 12,921; ZIP 95705.

South Laur·el (lôr′il) city, NW Maryland; 13,345.

South Mi·am·i (mī·am′ē, -am′ə) city, SE Florida; 19,571; ZIP see MIAMI.

South Mil·wau·kee (mil·wô′kē) city, SE Wisconsin; 23,297; ZIP 53172.

South Mo·des·to (mō·des′tō) uninc. place, CEN. California; 7,889; ZIP see MODESTO.

South Og·den (og′dən) city, N CEN. Utah; 9,991; ZIP see OGDEN.

South Or·ange (ôr′inj, or′-) vill., NE New Jersey; 16,971; ZIP 07079.

South Pas·a·de·na (pas′ə·dē′nə) city, sw California; 22,979; ZIP 91030*.

South Pat·rick Shores (pat′rik) city, sw Florida; 10,313.

South Plain·field (plān′fēld) boro., NE New Jersey; 21,142; ZIP 07080.

South Pole s extremity of the earth's axis.

South·port (south′pôrt, -pōrt) city, sw New York; 8,685; ZIP 14901.

South Port·land (pôrt′lənd) city, sw Maine; 23,267; ZIP see PORTLAND.

South River boro., E New Jersey; 15,428; ZIP 08882.

South Sac·ra·men·to-Fruit·ridge (sak′rə·men′tō, frōōt′·rij) uninc. place, CEN. California; 28,574.

South Salt Lake city, N Utah; 7,810; ZIP see SALT LAKE CITY.

South San Fran·cis·co (san′ frən·sis′kō) city, w California; 46,646; ZIP 94080*.

South San Ga·bri·el (san gā′brē·əl) uninc. place, sw California; 5,051; ZIP see SAN GABRIEL.

South San Jo·se (san hō·zā′) city, sw California; 12,386.

South Sea Islands isls. of the South Pacific.

South Seas waters of the Southern Hemisphere, esp. the South Pacific Ocean.

South Sioux City (sōō) city, NE Nebraska; 7,920; ZIP 68776.

South Stick·ney (stik′nē) city, NE Illinois; 29,900.

South Stony Brook city, SE New York; 15,329.

South St. Paul (pôl) city, E Minnesota; 25,016; ZIP 55075*.

South Tucson (tōō·son′, tōō′son) city, s Arizona; 6,220; ZIP see TUCSON.

South Valley city, CEN. New Mexico; 29,389.

South Valley Stream city, SE New York; 6,595.

South Vietnam See VIETNAM.

South-West Africa Namibia: *the former name.*

South West·bur·y (west′ber′ē, -bər′ē, -brē) uninc. place, SE New York; 10,978.

Southwest Little Rock city, CEN. Arkansas; 13,231.

South Whit·ti·er (hwit′ē·ər, wit′-) city, sw California; 46,641.

South·wick (south′wik) city, s Massachusetts; 6,330; ZIP 01077.

South Wil·liams·port (wil′yəmz·pôrt, -pōrt) boro., NE CEN. Pennsylvania; 7,153; ZIP see WILLIAMSPORT.

South Wind·sor (wind′zər) city, CEN. Connecticut; 15,553; ZIP 06074.

South Yar·mouth (yär′məth) city, E Massachusetts; 5,380; ZIP 02664.

South Yemen, People's Republic of republic, s coast of Arabian peninsula; 110,000 sq. mi.; 1,276,000; cap. Medina al-Eshaab.

Soviet Central Asia reg., CEN. Asia, comprising Kazakh, Kirghiz, Tadzhik, Turkmen, and Uzbek S.S.R.

So·vi·et Rus·sia (sō′vē·et, -ət, sō′vē·et′/ rush′ə) **1.** Russian Soviet Federated Socialist Republic. **2.** Union of Soviet Socialist Republics.

Soviet Union See UNION OF SOVIET SOCIALIST REPUBLICS.

Spain (spān) nominal monarchy, sw Europe; 194,368 sq. mi.; 33,195,000; cap. Madrid.

Span·a·way (span′ə·wā) city, N CEN. Washington; 5,768; ZIP 98387.

Spanish America parts of the w hemisphere where Spanish is the predominant language.

Spanish Equatorial Region Equatorial Guinea: *the former name.*

Spanish Lake city, NE Missouri; 15,647; ZIP 63101.

Sparks (spärks) city, w Nevada; 24,187; ZIP 89431.

Spar·rows Point-Fort How·ard-Edg·mere (spar′ōz point′, fôrt hou′ərd, ej′mir) uninc. place, CEN. Maryland; 11,775; ZIP see BALTIMORE.

Spar·ta (spär′tə) city, W Wisconsin; 6,258; ZIP 54656.

Spar·tan·burg (spär′tən-bûrg) city, NW South Carolina; 44,546; ZIP 29301*.

Speed·way (spēd′wā′) town, S Indiana; 15,056; ZIP see INDIANAPOLIS.

Spen·ard (spi·närd′, spen′ərd) uninc. place, S Alaska; 18,089; ZIP see ANCHORAGE.

Spen·cer (spen′sər) city, NW Iowa; 10,278; ZIP 51301.

— uninc. place, CEN. Massachusetts; 8,779; ZIP 01562.

Spice Islands Molucca Islands: *a former name.*

Spits·ber·gen (spits′bûr·gən) isl. group of Norway; Arctic Ocean; 23,658 sq. mi. Also **Spitz′ber·gen.**

Spo·kane (spō·kan′) city, E Washington; 170,516; ZIP 99200*.

Spots·wood (spots′wŏŏd) boro., E New Jersey; 7,891; ZIP 08884.

Spring·dale (spring′dāl) city, NW Arkansas; 16,783; ZIP 72764.

— city, SW Ohio; 8,127; ZIP 45246.

— boro., W Pennsylvania; 5,202; ZIP 15144.

Spring·field (spring′fēld) city, CEN. Florida; 5,949; ZIP 32401.

— city, CEN. Illinois; cap.; 91,753; ZIP 62700*.

— city, SW Massachusetts; 163,805; ZIP 01100*.

— city, SW Missouri; 120,096; ZIP 65800.

— urb. twp., NE New Jersey; 15,740; ZIP 07081.

— city, W CEN. Ohio; 81,926; ZIP 45500.

— city, W Oregon; 27,047; ZIP 97477.

— urb. twp., SE Pennsylvania (Delaware County); 26,733; ZIP see MEDIA.

— urb. twp., SE Pennsylvania (Montgomery County); 20,652.

— city, N Tennessee; 9,720; ZIP 37172.

— uninc. place, W Vermont; 10,063; ZIP 05156.

— uninc. place, NE Virginia; 11,613; ZIP 22150*.

Springfield Center city, SE Vermont; 5,632; ZIP 05156.

Spring Garden urb. twp., S Pennsylvania; 11,387; ZIP see PHILADELPHIA.

Spring·hill (spring′hil) town, N Nova Scotia, Canada; 5,380.

Spring·hill (spring′hil) city, NW Louisiana; 6,496; ZIP 71075.

Spring Lake Park city, E Minnesota; 6,417; ZIP 55432.

Spring Valley city, SE California; 29,742.

— city, N Illinois; 5,605; ZIP 61362.

— vill., SE New York; 18,112; ZIP 10977.

Sri Lan·ka (srē lang′kə), republic, isl. S of India, 25,332 sq. mi.; 13,970,000; cap. Colombo.

St. Al·bans (ôl′bənz) city, NW Vermont; 8,802; ZIP 05478.

— city, W West Virginia; 14,356; ZIP 25177.

Sta·lin·grad (stä′lin-grad) Volgograd: *the former name.*

Stam·ford (stam′fərd) city, SW Connecticut; 108,798; ZIP 06901*.

St. An·drews (an′drōōz) city, SE South Carolina; 9,202; ZIP 29407.

St. Ann (an) city, E Missouri; 18,215; ZIP 63074.

St. An·tho·ny (an′thə-nē) vill., SE Minnesota; 9,239.

Stan·ford (stan′fərd) city, W CEN. California; 8,691; ZIP 94305.

Stan·ton (stant′n, stan′tən) city, SW California; 17,947; ZIP 90680.

Stark·ville (stärk′vil, -vəl) city, E Mississippi; 11,369; ZIP 39759.

State College boro., CEN. Pennsylvania; 33,778; ZIP 16801*.

St-Bru·no-de-Mon·tar·ville (san brōō′nō də mōn′tər-vəl, sänt) town, CEN. Quebec, Canada; 10,712.

Stat·en Island (stat′n) isl, SE New York, at the entrance to New York Harbor; coextensive with Richmond boro.

States·bor·o (stāts′bûr′ō) city, E Georgia; 14,616; ZIP 30458*.

States of the Church part of CEN. Italy under the sovereignty of the pope until 1870.

States·ville (stāts′vil, -vəl) city, W CEN. North Carolina; 19,996; ZIP 28677.

St. Au·gus·tine (ô′gəs-tēn) city, NE Florida; 12,352; ZIP 32084.

Staun·ton (stant′n, stan′tən) city, NW CEN. Virginia; 24,504; ZIP 24401*.

St. Ber·nard (bər·närd′) city, SW Ohio; 6,080; ZIP see CINCINNATI.

St. Bon·i·face (bon′i·fãs) city, SE Manitoba, Canada; 43,214.

St. Cath·a·rines (kath′rinz, kath′ə-rīnz) city, S Ontario, Canada; 97,101.

St. Charles (chärlz) city, NE Illinois; 12,928; ZIP 60174.

— city, E Missouri; 31,834; ZIP 63301*.

St. Clair, Lake lake betw. S Ontario and SE Michigan; 460 sq. mi.

St. Clair Shores (shôrz, shōrz) vill., SE Michigan; 88,093; ZIP 48080*.

St. Cloud (kloud) city, CEN. Florida; 5,041; ZIP 32769.

— city, CEN. Minnesota; 39,691; ZIP 56301*.

St. Croix (kroi′) one of the Virgin Islands of the United States; 82 sq. mi.

Ste-A·gathe-des-Monts (sant·à·gä′dā-môn′) town, S Quebec, Canada; 6,010.

Steel·ton (stēlt′n, stēl′tən) boro., S Pennsylvania; 8,556; ZIP 17092.

Ste-Foy (sant·fwä′) city, S Quebec, Canada; 48,298.

Ste·ger (stēt·gər) vill., NE Illinois; 8,104; ZIP 60475.

Stel·lar·ton (stel′ərt-n, stel′ər-tən) town, N Novia Scotia, Canada; 5,191.

Ste·phen·ville (stē′vən-vil, -vəl) city, N CEN. Texas; 9,277; ZIP 76401*.

Ste·phen·ville (stē′vən-vil) town, SW Newfoundland, Canada; 5,910.

Ster·ling (stûr′ling) city, NE Colorado; 10,636; ZIP 80751.

— city, NW Illinois; 16,113; ZIP 61081.

Sterling Heights city, SE Michigan; 61,365; ZIP 48077.

Sterling Park city, NE Virginia; 8,321; ZIP 22170.

Ste-Thé·rèse (san·tā-rez′) city, S Quebec, Canada; 15,528.

Stet·tin (stet′in) city, NW Poland; 331,700.

Steu·ben·ville (styōō′bən-vil) city, E Ohio; 30,771; ZIP 43952.

St. Eus·tache (sant-yōōs-täch′) town, S Quebec, Canada; 7,319.

Ste·vens Point (stē′vənz) city, CEN. Wisconsin; 23,479; ZIP 54481*.

St. Fé·li·cien (san-fā-lē-syän′) town, S CEN. Quebec, Canada; 5,104.

St. Fran·cis (fran′sis) city, SE Wisconsin; 10,489; ZIP see MILWAUKEE.

St. George (jôrj, jōrj) city, SW Utah; 7,097; ZIP 84770.

St. Helens (hel′ənz) city, NW Oregon; 6,212; ZIP 97051*.

St. He·le·na (hə-lē′nə) isl., South Atlantic, British Colony with Ascension Island and the Tristan da Cunha group as dependencies; 133 sq. mi.; 5,745; cap. Jamestown; site of Napoleon's exile, 1815–21.

St. Hubert (sant-ü-bâr′) town, S Quebec, Canada; 17,215.

St. Hy·a·cinthe (hī′ə-sənth, san-tē-ä-sänt′) city, S Quebec, Canada; 23,781.

Stick·ney (stik′nē) vill., NE Illinois; 6,601; ZIP see BERWYN.

Still·wa·ter (stil′wŏ′tər, -wot′ər) city E Minnesota; 10,191; ZIP 55082.

— city, N CEN. Oklahoma; 31,126; ZIP 74074*.

St. James (jāmz) city, S Manitoba, Canada; 35,685.

St. James (jāmz) city, SE New York; 10,818.

St. Jean (san-zhän′) city, S Quebec, Canada; 27,784.

St. Jé·rôme (jə-rōm′, san-zhä-rôm′) city, S Quebec, Canada; 26,511.

St. John (jon) one of the Virgin Islands of the United States; 19 sq. mi.

St. John (jon) city, S New Brunswick, Canada; 51,567.

St. John (jon) vill., E Missouri; 8,960.

St. John's (jonz) city, SE Newfoundland, Canada; cap.; 79,884.

St. Johns (jonz) city, S CEN. Michigan; 6,672; ZIP 48879.

St. Johns·bur·y (jonz′bûr′ē, -ber′ē) vill., NE Vermont; 8,409; ZIP 05819.

St. Joseph (jōz′if) city, SW Michigan; 11,042; ZIP 49085.

— city, NW Missouri; 72,691; ZIP 64500*.

St. Lam·bert (lam′bərt, san-lan-bâr′) city, S Quebec, Canada; 16,003.

St. Laurent (san-lô-rän′) city, S Quebec, Canada; 59,479.

St. Law·rence River (lôr′əns, lôr′-) river, SE Canada; the outlet of the Great Lakes system; 1,900 mi. long.

St. Lawrence, Gulf of inlet of the Atlantic, E Canada.

St. Lawrence Seaway system of ship canals extending 114 miles along the St. Lawrence River from Montreal to Lake Ontario.

St. Leon·ard (len′ərd) city, CEN. Quebec, Canada; 17,215.

St. Lou·is (lōō′is, lōō′ē) city, E Missouri; 622,236; ZIP 63100*.

St. Louis Park vill., E Minnesota; 48,883; ZIP see MINNEAPOLIS.

St. Mar·tins·ville (märt′nz·vil, mär′tinz-, -vəl) town, S CEN. Louisiana; 7,153; ZIP 70582.

St. Mar·ys (mâr′ēz) city, W Ohio; 7,699; ZIP 45885.

— boro., NW CEN. Pennsylvania; 7,470; ZIP 15857.

St. Mat·thews (math′yōōs) city, N Kentucky; 13,152; ZIP see LOUISVILLE.

St. Mi·chel (san-mē-shel′) city, S Quebec, Canada; 71,446.

Stock·holm (stok′hōm) city, SE Sweden; cap.; 793,714.

Stock·ton (stok'tən) city, CEN. California; 107,644; ZIP 95200*.

Stone·ham (stōn'əm) town, NE Massachusetts; 20,725; ZIP see BOSTON.

Stone·leigh-Rod·gers Forge (stōn'lē, roj'ərz fôrj', fōrj') uninc. place, N Maryland; 15,645.

Sto·ney Creek (stō'nē) town, s Ontario, Canada; 7,243.

Ston·ing·ton (stōn'ing·tən) city, NE Connecticut; 15,940; ZIP 06378.

Sto·ny Brook (stō'nē) city, SE New York; 6,391; ZIP 11790.

Stony Point city, SE New York; 8,270; ZIP 10980.

Storm Lake city, NW Iowa; 8,591; ZIP 50588.

Storrs (stôrz, stōrz) uninc. place, N CEN. Connecticut; 10,691; ZIP 06268.

Stough·ton (stōt'n) town, E Massachusetts; 23,459; ZIP 02072.

— city, s Wisconsin; 6,081; ZIP 53589.

Stow (stō) vill., NE CEN. Ohio; 19,847; ZIP see CUYAHOGA FALLS.

St. Paul (pôl) city, SE Minnesota; cap.; 309,880; ZIP 55100*.

St. Paul Park city, SE Minnesota; 5,587; ZIP 55071.

St. Pe·ter (pē'tər) city, s Minnesota; 8,339; ZIP 56082.

St. Pe·ters·burg (pē'tərz·bûrg') Leningrad: *a former name.*

St. Pe·ters·burg (pē'tərz·bûrg') city, w Florida; 216,232.

St. Petersburg Beach city, w Florida; 8,024; ZIP 33700*.

St. Pierre (sănt pē·âr', saṅ pyâr') town, s Quebec, Canada; 7,066.

Stras·bourg (stras'bûrg, sträz'-) city, NE France; 249,396.

Strat·ford (strat'fərd) town, SE Connecticut; 49,775; ZIP 06497.

— sw New Jersey; 9,801; ZIP 08084.

Strat·ford (strat'fərd) city, s Ontario, Canada; 23,068.

Strat·ford-on-A·von (strat'fərd·on·ā'von) town, s CEN. England; birthplace and burial place of Shakespeare; 17,000.

Strath·more (strath'mōr) city, E CEN. New Jersey; 7,674; ZIP 07747.

Strath·roy (strath·roi') town, s Ontario, Canada; 5,786.

Strat·ton Meadows (strat'n) city, E CEN. Colorado; 6,223; ZIP 80901.

Stream·wood (strēm'wŏŏd') city, NE Illinois; 18,176; ZIP 60103.

Strea·tor (strē'tər) city, N CEN. Illinois; 15,600; ZIP 61364.

Streets·bor·o (strēts'bûr·ō) city, NE Ohio; 7,966; ZIP 44240.

Streets·ville (strēts'vil) vill., s Ontario, Canada; 5,884.

Strongs·ville (strôngz·vil, strongz'-) vill., N Ohio; 15,182; ZIP see CLEVELAND.

Strouds·burg (strouds'bûrg) boro., E Pennsylvania; 5,451; ZIP 18360.

Struth·ers (struth'ərz) city, E Ohio; 15,343; ZIP 44471.

St. Thom·as (sănt tom'əs) one of the Virgin Islands of the United States; 28 sq. mi.; 16,046.

St. Thom·as (tom'əs) city, s Ontario, Canada; 22,983.

Stur·geon Bay (stûr'jən) city, NE Wisconsin; 6,776; ZIP 54235*.

Stur·geon Falls (stûr'jən) town, E CEN. Ontario, Canada; 6,430.

Stur·gis (stûr'jis) city, s Michigan; 9,295; ZIP 49091.

Stutt·gart (stut'gärt) city, sw West Germany; 632,727.

Stutt·gart (stut'gärt, -gərt) city, E CEN. Arkansas; 10,477; ZIP 72160.

St. Vi·tal (vē·tal') city, s Manitoba, Canada; 29,528.

Su·cre (sōō'krā) city, s CEN. Bolivia; cap.; 59,701. See LA PAZ.

Su·dan (sōō'dan') reg., N Africa s of the Sahara.

Sudan, Republic of the republic, NE Africa; 967,500 sq. mi.; 16,093,000; cap. Khartoum.

Su·da·nese Republic (sōō'də·nēz', -nēs') See MALI.

Sud·bur·y (sud'ber'ē, -bûr'ē, -brē) city, SE CEN. Ontario, Canada; 84,888.

Sud·bur·y (sud'ber'ē) city, NE Massachusetts; 13,506; ZIP 01776.

Su·de·ten·land (sōō·dāt'n·land') border dists., w Czechoslovakia.

Su·ez (sōō·ez', sōō'ez) city, NE Egypt; 219,000.

Suez, Gulf of inlet of the Red Sea; NE Egypt.

Suez, Isthmus of strip of land joining Asia and Africa, betw. the Gulf of Suez and the Mediterranean.

Suez Canal ship canal across the Isthmus of Suez; 107 mi.

Suf·fern (suf'ərn) vill., SE New York; 8,273; ZIP 10901.

Suf·field (suf'ēld) city, CEN. Connecticut; 7,534; ZIP 06078.

Suf·folk (suf'ək) co., E England; divided into **East Suffolk**; 879 sq. mi.; 343,000; cap. Ipswich, and **West Suffolk**; 628 sq. mi.; 130,000; cap. Bury St. Edmonds.

Sugar Creek city, NW Pennsylvania; 5,944; ZIP 16323.

Suit·land-Silver Hills (sōōt'lənd) uninc. place, w CEN. Maryland; 30,355.

Sul·folk (suf'ək, -ôk) city, SE Virginia; 9,858; ZIP 23434*.

Sul·li·van (sul'ə·vən) city, NE Missouri; 5,100; ZIP 63080.

Sul·phur (sul'fər) city, sw Louisiana; 13,551; ZIP 70663.

— s CEN. Oklahoma; 5,158; ZIP 73086.

Sulphur Springs city, NE Texas; 10,642; ZIP 75482.

Su·lu Archipelago (sōō'lōō) isl. group, sw Philippines; 1,086 sq. mi.

Su·ma·tra (sōō·mä'trə) isl. of Indonesia s of the Malay Peninsula; 163,557 sq. mi.

Sum·mer·side (sum'ər·sīd) town, w CEN. Prince Edward Island, Canada; 10,042.

Sum·mer·ville (sum'ər·vil) city, NW Georgia; 5,043; ZIP 30747.

Sum·mit (sum'it) vill., NE Illinois; 11,569.

— city, NE New Jersey; 23,620; ZIP 07901.

Sum·ter (sum'tər) city, CEN. South Carolina; 24,435; ZIP 29150*.

Sun·bur·y (sun'ber·ē, -bər·ē, -brē) city, E CEN. Pennsylvania; 13,025; ZIP 17801.

Sun City city, s CEN. Arizona; 13,670; ZIP 85351.

— sw California; 5,519; ZIP 92381.

Sun·ny·mead (sun'ē·med) city, SE California; 6,708; ZIP 92388.

Sun·ny·side (sun'ē·sīd') city, s Washington; 6,751; ZIP 98944.

Sun·ny·vale sun'ē·vāl) city, w California; 95,408; ZIP 94086*.

Sun Prairie city, s CEN. Wisconsin; 9,935; ZIP 53590.

Sunrise Golf Village city, SE Florida; 7,403; ZIP 33313.

Sunrise Manor city, SE Nevada; 10,886; ZIP 89101.

Sunset city, NW Utah; 6,268; ZIP 84015.

Su·pe·ri·or (sə·pir'ē·ər, sōō-) city, NW Wisconsin; 32,237; ZIP 54880*.

Superior, Lake largest of the Great Lakes; 31,820 sq. mi.

Su·ra·ba·ya (sōō'rä·bä'yä) city, NE Java, Indonesia; 1,007,945.

Su·ri·nam (sōōr'ə·näm') overseas part of the Netherlands, NE South America; 55,129 sq. mi.; 416,000; cap. Paramaribo.

Su·san·ville (sōō'zən·vil) city, NE California; 6,608; ZIP 96130.

Sus·que·han·na (sus'kwə·han'ə) river, New York, Pennsylvania, and Maryland; 444 mi. long.

Su·wan·nee River (sōō·wô'nē, -won'ē) river, Georgia and Florida; 250 mi. long.

Swains·bor·o (swāns'bûr'ō, -bə·rə) city, E CEN. Georgia; 7,325; ZIP 30401.

Swamp·scott (swomp'skət) town, NE Massachusetts; 13,578; ZIP see LYNN.

Swan·sea (swon'zē, -sē) vill., s Ontario, Canada; 9,703.

Swan·sea (swon'sē, -zē) city, sw Illinois; 5,432; ZIP 62221.

— city, s Massachusetts; 12,640; ZIP 02777.

Swarth·more (swôrth'mōr, swoth'-) boro., SE Pennsylvania; 6,156; ZIP 19081.

Swa·zi·land (swä'zē·land) independent member of the Commonwealth of Nations; SE Africa; 6,704 sq. mi.; 429,000; cap. Mbabane.

Swe·den (swēd'n) kingdom, NW Europe; 173,577 sq. mi.; 8,103,000; cap. Stockholm.

Sweet·wa·ter (swēt'wô'tər, -wot'ər) city, w Texas; 12,020; ZIP 79556.

Sweetwater Creek city, NW Florida; 19,433; ZIP 33601.

Swift Current city, sw Saskatchewan, Canada; 14,485.

Swiss·vale (swis'val') boro., sw Pennsylvania; 13,821; ZIP see PITTSBURGH.

Swit·zer·land (swit'sər·lənd) republic, CEN. Europe; 15,940 sq. mi.; 6,353,000; cap. Bern.

Swoy·ers·ville (swoi'ərz·vil) boro., E CEN. Pennsylvania; 6,786.

Syc·a·more (sik'ə·môr, -mōr) city, N Illinois; 7,843; ZIP 60178.

Syd·ney (sid'nē) city, NE Nova Scotia, Canada; 32,767.

Syd·ney (sid'nē) city, E New South Wales, Australia; cap.; 2,444,735.

Sydney Mines town, E Nova Scotia, Canada; 9,171.

Syl·a·caug·a (sil'ə·kog'ə, -kôg'ə) city, E CEN. Alabama; 12,255; ZIP 35150.

Syl·van·i·a (sil·văn'ē·ə) vill., N Ohio; 12,031; ZIP 43560.

Sy·os·set (sī·os'it) city, SE New York; 9,970; ZIP 11791.

Syr·a·cuse (sir'ə·kyōōs) city, CEN. New York; 197,208; ZIP 13200*.

Syr·i·a (sir'ē·ə) republic, sw Asia; 72,234 sq. mi.; 6,252,000; cap. Damascus.

Ta·briz (tä·brēz') city, NW Iran; 403,413.

Ta·co·ma (tə·kō'mə) city, w Washington; 154,581; ZIP 98400*.

Ta·dzhik SSR (tə·jēk') constituent republic, s USSR; 55,043 sq. mi.; 2,654,000; cap. Dyushambe.

Ta·hi·ti (tä·hē'tē, tə-, tī'tē) isl., Society group; 600 sq. mi.

Tah·le·quah (tal'ə·kwô) city, E Oklahoma; 9,254; ZIP 74464.

Ta·hoe (tä'hō, tä'-), **Lake** lake, E California and w Nevada; ab. 195 sq. mi.

Tai·pei (tī'pā') city, N Taiwan; cap.; 1,221,112.

Tai·wan (tī'wän') isl. off SE China; comprises with the

Pescadores, the National Republic of China; 13,890 sq. mi.; 14,672,000; cap. Taipei.

Ta·ko·ma Park (tə-kō′ınə) city, w Maryland; 18,455; ZIP see WASHINGTON, D.C.

Tal·la·de·ga (tal′ə-dē′gə) city, E CEN. Alabama; 17,662; ZIP 35160.

Tal·la·has·see (tal′ə-has′ē) city, N Florida; cap.; 71,897; ZIP 32301*.

Tal·linn (täl′lin) city, N Estonian SSR; cap.; 340,000.

Tall·madge (tal′mij) city, NE Ohio; 15,274; ZIP 44278.

Tal·lu·lah (tə-loo′lə) vill., NE Louisiana; 9,643; ZIP 71282.

Ta·ma·qua (tə-mô′kwə) boro., E Pennsylvania; 9,246; ZIP 18252.

Tam·pa (tam′pə) city, w Florida; 277,767; ZIP 33600*.

Tam·pi·co (tam-pē′kō) city, E Mexico; 196,147.

Ta·na·na·rive (tä-nä′nä-rēv′) city, E CEN. Madagascar; cap.; 321,654.

Tanganyika, Lake lake, E CEN. Africa; 12,700 sq. mi.

Tan·gier (tan-jir′) city, N Morocco; 110,000.

Tan·za·ni·a (tän′zä-nē′ə) republic of the Commonwealth of Nations, E Africa, includes **Tanganyika** and **Zanzibar**; 362,820 sq. mi.; 1ξ 566,000; cap. Dar es Salaam.

Tap·pan (tap′n, tap′ən) city, SE New York; 7,424.

Ta·ran·to (tä′rän-tō) city, SE Italy; 197,716.

Tar·bor·o (tär′bûr′ō, -bə-rə) town, NE CEN. North Carolina; 9,425; ZIP 27886.

Ta·ren·tum (tə-ren′təm) boro., w Pennsylvania; 7,379; ZIP 15084.

Tar·pon Springs (tär′pən) city, w Florida; 7,118; ZIP 33589.

Tar·rant City (tar′ənt) city, N CEN. Alabama; 6,835; ZIP see BIRMINGHAM.

Tar·ry·town (tar′ē-toun) vill., SE New York; 11,115; ZIP 10591*.

Tash·kent (təsh-kyent′) city, E Uzbek SSR; cap.; 1,239,000.

Tas·ma·ni·a (taz-mā′nē-ə) isl., SE Australia; comprises a state; 26,216 sq. mi.; 350,340; cap. Hobart.

Taun·ton (tôn′tən) city, SE Massachusetts; 43,756; ZIP 02780*.

Tay·lor (tā′lər) city, SE Michigan; 70,020; ZIP 48180.

— boro., NE Pennsylvania; 6,977.

— city, CEN. Texas; 9,616; ZIP 76574.

Tay·lors (tā′lərz) city, NW South Carolina; 6,831; ZIP 29687.

Tay·lor·ville (tā′lər-vil) city, CEN. Illinois; 10,644; ZIP 62568.

Tbi·li·si (tbi/li·sē) city, SE Georgian SSR; cap.; 842,000.

Tea·neck (tē′nek) urb. twp., NE New Jersey; 42,355; ZIP 07666.

Te·cum·seh (ti·kum′sə) city, SE Michigan; 7,120; ZIP 49286.

Te·gu·ci·gal·pa (tā·gōō′sē·gäl′pä) city, S CEN. Honduras; cap.; 170,535.

Te·he·ran (tel′ə·rän′, -ran′) city, N CEN. Iran; cap.; 2,719,730.

Tel A·viv (tel′ä·vēv′) city, w Israel; includes Jaffa; 392,100.

Tell City (tel) city, S Indiana; 7,933; ZIP 47586.

Tem·pe (tem′pē) city, S CEN. Arizona; 62,907.

Tem·ple (tem′pəl) city, CEN. Texas; 33,431; ZIP 85281*.

Temple City uninc. place, SW California; 29,673; ZIP 91780*.

Temple Terrace city, NW Florida; 7,347; ZIP 33617.

Tem·ple·ton (tem′pəl·tən) city, N Massachusetts; 5,863; ZIP 01468.

Ten·a·fly (ten′ə·flī) boro., NE New Jersey; 14,827; ZIP 07670.

Ten·nes·see (ten/ə·sē′) state, SE CEN. United States; 42,246 sq. mi.; 3,924,164; cap. Nashville.

Tennessee River river, flowing through E Tennessee, N Alabama, w Tennessee, and SW Kentucky; 652 mi. long.

Terre·bonne (târ·bôn′) town, S Quebec, Canada; 7,480.

Terre Haute (ter′ə hōt′) city, w Indiana; 70,286; ZIP 47801*.

Ter·rell (ter′əl) city, NE Texas; 14,182; ZIP 75160.

Terrell Hills city, S CEN. Texas; 5,225.

Ter·ry (ter′ē) city, SE Louisiana; 13,862; ZIP 70053.

Ter·ry·ville (ter′ē·vil) uninc. place, w CEN. Connecticut; 6,900; ZIP 06786.

Tewks·bur·y (tōōks′ber′ē) city, NE Massachusetts; 22,755; ZIP 01876.

Tex·ar·kan·a (teks′är·kan′ə) city, SW Arkansas at the Arkansas-Texas line; 21,682.

— city, NE Texas; adjacent to and integrated with Texarkana, Arkansas; 30,497; ZIP 75501*.

Tex·as (tek′səs) state, S United States; 267,339 sq. mi.; 11,196,730; cap. Austin.

Texas City city, SE Texas; 38,908; ZIP 77590*.

Thai·land (tī′land) constitutional monarchy, SE Asia; 198,404 sq. mi.; 36,925,000; cap. Bangkok.

Thames (temz) river, S England; 209 mi. long.

Thes·sa·lon·i·ca (thes′ə·lon′i·kə) Salonika: *an ancient name.*

Thes·sa·ly (thes′ə·lē) div., N CEN. Greece; 5,399 sq. mi.

Thet·ford Mines (thet′fərd) city, S Quebec, Canada; 21,614.

The Village city, CEN. Oklahoma; 13,695; ZIP see OKLAHOMA CITY.

Thib·o·daux (tib′ə·dō) town, SE Louisiana; 14,925; ZIP 70301.

Thief River Falls city, NW Minnesota; 8,618; ZIP 56701.

Thom·as·ton (tom′əs·tən) city, NW Connecticut; 6,233; ZIP 06787.

— city, w CEN. Georgia; 10,024; ZIP 30286.

Thom·as·ville (tom′əs·vil, -vəl) city, S Georgia; 18,155; ZIP 31792.

— city, CEN. North Carolina; 15,230; ZIP 27360.

Thomp·son (tomp′sən) city, NE Connecticut; 7,580; ZIP 06277.

Thom·son (tom′sən) city, CEN. Georgia; 6,503; ZIP 30824.

Thorn·ton (thôrnt′n, thôrn′tən) vill., CEN. Colorado; 13,326; ZIP see DENVER.

Thorn·wood (thôrn′wood′) city, NE New York; 6,874.

Thor·old (thôr′ōld, -əld, thûr′) town, S Ontario, Canada; 8,843.

Thousand Islands group of ab. 1,500 isls. in the St. Lawrence River.

Thousand Oaks city, SE California; 36,334; ZIP 91360.

Thrace (thrās) reg., E Balkan Peninsula.

Three Rivers city, SW Michigan; 7,355; ZIP 49093.

Ti·ber (tī′bər) river, CEN. Italy; 125 mi. long.

Ti·bet (ti·bet′) adm. div., w China; ab. 470,000 sq. mi.; 1,270,000; cap. Lhasa; formerly independent.

Tib·u·ron (tib′ə·ron) city, w California; 6,209; ZIP 94920.

Tice (tīs) city, SW Florida; 7,254; ZIP 33905.

Ticonderoga, Fort historic fort, NE New York.

Tien·tsin (tin′tsin′) city, NE China; 3,220,000.

Tier·ra del Fue·go (tyer′ä del fwä′gō) isl. group, S South America, included in Chile and Argentina; 7,996 sq. mi. (Argentina), 19,480 sq. mi. (Chile).

Tif·fin (tif′in) city, N CEN. Ohio; 21,596; ZIP 44883.

Tif·lis (tif′lis) Tbilisi: *the former name.*

Tif·ton (tif′tən) city, S Georgia; 12,179; ZIP 31794.

Tig·ard (tig′ərd) city, NW Oregon; 5,302; ZIP 97223.

Ti·gris (tī′gris) river, SW Asia, ab. 1,150 mi. long.

Ti·jua·na (tē·hwä′nä) city, NW Lower California, Mexico; 268,175.

Till·son·burg (til′sən·bûrg) town, S Ontario, Canada; 6,526.

Tim·buk·tu (tim·buk′tōō, tim′buk·tōō′) town, CEN. Mali; 7,000.

Tim·mins (tim′inz) town, E CEN. Ontario, Canada; 29,303.

Ti·mon·i·um-Luth·er·ville (ti·mō′nē·əm; lōō′thər·vil, -vəl) uninc. place, N CEN. Maryland; 24,055; ZIP 21093.

Ti·mor (tē′môr, ti·môr′) isl., SE Malay Archipelago; divided into **Indonesian Timor** in the w part; 5,765 sq. mi., and **Portuguese Timor,** a Portuguese overseas prov. in the E part; 5,761 sq. mi. (including offshore isls.); 517,000; cap. Dili.

Tin·ley Park (tin′lē) vill., NE Illinois; 12,382; ZIP 60477*.

Tipp City (tip) city, NE Connecticut; 5,090.

Tip·ton (tip′tən) city, CEN. Indiana; 5,176; ZIP 46072.

Tip·per·ar·y (tip′ə·râr′ē) co., S CEN. Ireland; 1,643 sq. mi.; 124,000; cap. Clonmel.

Ti·ra·na (tē·rä′nä) city, CEN. Albania; cap.; 156,950.

Ti·rol (ti·rōl′, tir′ōl, tī′rōl) See TYROL.

Ti·ti·ca·ca (tē/tē·kä′kä), **Lake** lake betw. SE Peru and w CEN. Bolivia; 3,200 sq. mi.; elevation 12,500 ft.

Ti·tus·ville (tī′təs·vil, -vəl) city, E Florida; 30,515; ZIP 32780.

— city, NW Pennsylvania; 7,331; ZIP 16354.

Tiv·er·ton (tiv′ərt·n, -ər·tən) town, SE Rhode Island; 12,559; ZIP 02878.

To·ba·go (tō·bā′gō) See TRINIDAD AND TOBAGO.

Toc·co·a (tə·kō′ə) city, NE Georgia; 6,971; ZIP 30577.

To·go (tō′gō) republic, w Africa; ab. 21,500 sq. mi.; 1,908,000; cap. Lomé.

To·go·land (tō′gō·land) former German protectorate, w Africa.

To·ky·o (tō′kē·ō) city, E Japan; cap.; 9,018,633.

To·le·do (tō·lē′dō) city, CEN. Spain; 40,651.

To·le·do (tə·lē′dō) city, NW Ohio; 383,818; ZIP 43600*.

Tol·land (tol′ənd) city, NE Connecticut; 7,857; ZIP 06084.

To·mah (tō′mə) city, w CEN. Wisconsin; 5,647; ZIP 54660.

Tomsk (tômsk) city, S RSFSR; 324,000.

Toms River (tomz) uninc. place, E New Jersey; 7,303; ZIP 08753.

Ton·a·wan·da (ton′ə·won′də) city, w New York; 21,898; ZIP 14150*.

— uninc. place, w New York; 83,771.

Ton·ga Islands (tong′gə) isl. group, SE of Fiji; a Polynesian kingdom under British protection; ab. 270 sq. mi.; 90,000; cap. Nukualofa.

Too·e·le (tōō-il′ə) city, N CEN. Utah; 12,539; ZIP 84074.

To·pe·ka (tə-pē′kə) city, NE Kansas; cap.; 125,011; ZIP 66600*.

Top·pe·nish (top′ə-nish) city, s Washington; 5,744; ZIP 98948.

Tops·field (tops′fēld) city, N Massachusetts; 5,225; ZIP 01983.

Tops·ham (top′səm) city, sw Maine; 5,022; ZIP 04086.

To·ron·to (tə-ron′tō) city, E Ohio; 7,705; ZIP 43964.

Toronto (tə-ron′tō) city, s Ontario, Canada; 664,584.

Tor·rance (tor′əns, tôr′-) city, sw California; 134,584; ZIP 90500*.

Tor·ring·ton (tôr′ing-tən, tor′-) city, NW Connecticut; 31,952; ZIP 06790*.

To·to·wa (tō′tə-wə) boro., NE New Jersey; 11,580; ZIP see PATERSON.

Tou·lon (tōō-lôn′) city, s France; 174,746.

Tou·louse (tōō-lōōz′) city, s France; 370,796.

Town and Country city, NE Washington; 6,484.

Tow·son (tou′sən) uninc. place, N CEN. Maryland; 77,809; ZIP see BALTIMORE.

Tra·cy (trā′sē) city, CEN. California; 14,724; ZIP 95376.

Tra·cy (trā′sē) town, s Quebec, Canada; 10,918.

Tra·fal·gar (trə-fal′gər), **Cape** headland, sw Spain; scene of a naval battle in which Nelson defeated the French and Spanish fleets, 1805.

Trail (trāl) city, SE British Columbia, Canada; 11,600.

Trans·cau·ca·sia (trans′kô·kā′zhə, -shə) reg., SE USSR; betw. the Caucasus mountains and Iran and Turkey.

Trans·co·na (trans-kō′nə) town, SE Manitoba, Canada; 19,761.

Trans-Jor·dan (trans·jôr′dən, tranz-) former Arab terr., now part of Jordan.

Trans·vaal (trans-väl′, tranz-) province, NE South Africa; 110,450 sq. mi.; 6,225,000; cap. Pretoria.

Trav·erse (trav′ərs) city, NW Michigan; 18,048; ZIP 49684.

Treasure Island city, NW Florida; 6,120; ZIP 33740.

Tren·ton (trent′n, tren′tən) city, SE Michigan; 24,127; ZIP 48183.

— city, N Missouri; 6,063; ZIP 64683.

— city, w New Jersey; cap.; 104,638; ZIP 08600*.

— city, sw Ohio; 5,278; ZIP 45067.

Tren·ton (trent′n, tren′tən) town, SE Ontario, Canada; 13,746.

Tri·este (trē-est′) city, NE Italy; 276,046.

Trin·i·dad and To·ba·go (trin′ə-dad, tō-bā′gō) independent member of the Commonwealth of Nations off N Venezuela; comprises isls. of **Trinidad**; 1,864 sq. mi., and **Tobago**; 116 sq. mi. 1,099,000; cap. Port-of-Spain.

Trin·i·dad (trin′ə-dad) city, s Colorado; 9,901.

Trip·o·li (trip′ə-lē) city, NW Lebanon; ab. 100,000.

Trip·o·li (trip′ə-lē) city, NW Libya; one of the two caps.; 212,577.

Trois-Ri·vieres (twä·rē·vyâr′) city, s Quebec, Canada; 57,540.

Trot·wood (trot′wŏŏd′) city, sw Ohio; 6,938.

Troy (troi) city, SE Alabama; 11,482; ZIP 36081.

— city, SE Michigan; 39,419; ZIP 48084.

— city, E New York; 62,918; ZIP 12180*.

— city, w Ohio; 17,186; ZIP 45373.

Tru·cial O·man (trōō′shəl ō-män′) United Arab Emirates: *a former name.*

Trum·bull (trum′bəl) city, SE Connecticut; 31,394; ZIP 06611.

Trur·o (trŏŏr′ō) town, CEN. Nova Scotia, Canada; 13,009.

Tsing·tao (ching′dou′) city, E China; 1,121,000.

Tuck·a·hoe (tuk′ə-hō) vill., SE New York; 6,236; ZIP see YONKERS.

Tuc·son (tōō-son′, tōō′son) city, SE Arizona; 262,933; ZIP 85700*.

Tu·cum·car·i (tōō′kəm-kâr′ē) city, E New Mexico; 7,189; ZIP 88401.

Tu·lar·e (tōō-lâr′ē, tōō-lâr′) city, s CEN. California; 16,235; ZIP 93274.

Tu·li·a (tōō′lē-ə) city, NW Texas; 5,294; ZIP 79088.

Tul·la·ho·ma (tul-ə-hō′mə) city, s CEN. Tennessee; 15,311; ZIP 37388.

Tul·sa (tul′sə) city, NE Oklahoma; 331,638; ZIP 74100*.

Tum·wa·ter (tum′wô-tər, -wot-ər) city, sw Washington; 5,373; ZIP 98501.

Tu·nis (tōō′nis, tyōō′-) city, NE Tunisia; cap.; 662,000.

Tu·ni·sia (tōō-nish′ə, -nish′ē-ə, tyōō-) republic, N Africa; 48,195 sq. mi.; 4,974,000; cap. Tunis.

Tu·pe·lo (tōō′pə-lō, tyōō′-) city, NE Mississippi; 20,471; ZIP 38801*.

Tu·rin (tŏŏr′in, tyŏŏr′-, tōō′rin, tyōō-) city, NW Italy; 1,116,631.

Tur·ke·stan (tûr′kə-stan′, -stän′) reg., CEN. Asia; extends from the Caspian Sea to the Gobi Desert.

Tur·key (tûr′kē) republic, SE CEN. Eurasia; 296,108 sq. mi.; 36,144,000; cap. Ankara. See ANATOLIA.

Turkish Empire Ottoman Empire: *an alternate name.*

Turk·men SSR (tûrk′men) constituent republic, s USSR; 189,370 sq. mi.; 1,966,000; cap. Ashkhabad.

Tur·lock (tûr′lok) city, CEN. California; 13,992; ZIP 95380.

Tur·ners Falls (tûr′nərz) city, NW Massachusetts; 6,168; ZIP 01376.

Turtle Creek boro., sw Pennsylvania; 8,038; ZIP 15145*.

Tus·ca·loo·sa (tus′kə-lōō′sə) city, w CEN. Alabama; 65,773; ZIP 35401*.

Tus·ca·ny (tus′kə-nē) reg. and former duchy, w CEN. Italy; 8,876 sq. mi.; 3,267,000; chief city, Florence.

Tus·cum·bi·a (tus-kum′bē-ə) city, NW Alabama; 8,828; ZIP 35674.

Tus·ke·gee (tus-kē′gē) city, SE Alabama; 11,028; ZIP 36083.

Tus·tin (tus′tin) city, sw California; 21,178; ZIP 92680.

Tustin-Foothills city, sw California; 26,598.

Tu·tu·i·la (tōō′tōō-ē′lä) chief isl., American Samoa; 40 sq. mi.; 16,785.

Twen·ty·nine Palms (twen′tē-nīn′) city, s California; 5,667; ZIP 92277.

Twin Falls city, s Idaho, 29,914; ZIP 83301*.

Twins·bur·y (twinz′ber′ē) city, NE Ohio; 6,432; ZIP 44087.

Two Rivers city, E Wisconsin; 13,553; ZIP 54241.

Ty·ler (tī′lər) city, E Texas; 57,770; ZIP 75701*.

Ty·rol (ti-rōl′, tir′ōl, tī′rōl) reg., w Austria and N Italy.

Ty·rone (tī-rōn′, ti-) boro., CEN. Pennsylvania; 7,072; ZIP 16686.

U·ban·gi (ōō·bäng′gē) river, CEN. Africa; 1,400 mi. long.

U·gan·da (yōō·gan′də, ōō-gän′dä) independent member of the Commonwealth of Nations, E CEN. Africa; 93,981 sq. mi.; 8,758,000; cap. Kampala.

Uh·richs·ville (yŏŏr′iks·vil) city, E Ohio; 5,731; ZIP 44683.

U·ki·ah (yōō-kī′ə) city, NW California; 10,095; ZIP 95482.

U·krain·i·an SSR (yōō-krā′nē-ən, -krī′-) constituent republic sw USSR; 231,986 sq. mi.; 45,966,000; cap. Kiev. Also **U·kraine** (yōō-krān′, yōō′krān, yōō-krīn′).

U·lan Ba·tor (ōō′län bä′tôr) city, N CEN. Mongolian People's Republic; cap.; ab. 195,300.

Ul·ster (ul′stər) former prov., N Ireland, of which the N part became Northern Ireland, 1925. — prov., N Republic of Ireland; comprises the part of Ulster that remained after 1925; 3,093 sq. mi.; 217,000.

Un·ion (yōōn′yən) urb. twp., NE New Jersey; 53,077; ZIP 07083*.

— city, N South Carolina; 10,775; ZIP 29379*.

Union Beach boro., E New Jersey; 6,472; ZIP see KEYPORT.

Union City city, w California; 14,724; ZIP 94587.

— city, NE Missouri; 5,183; ZIP 63084.

— city, NE New Jersey; 58,537; ZIP 07087.

— city, NW Tennessee; 11,925; ZIP 38261.

Un·ion·dale (yōōn′yən-dāl) uninc. place, SE New York; 22,077; ZIP see HEMPSTEAD.

Union of Soviet Socialist Republics federal union of 15 constituent republics occupying most of N Eurasia; 8,646,400 sq. mi.; 246,176,000; cap. Moscow.

Un·ion·town (yōōn′yən-town) city, sw Pennsylvania; 16,282; ZIP 15401.

United Arab E·mir·ates (i·mir′its, -āts) federation of sheikdoms, E Arabia; 32,300 sq. mi.; 230,000; cap. Abu Dhabi.

United Arab Republic Egypt: *the former name.*

United Kingdom constitutional monarchy comprising Great Britain, Northern Ireland, the Isle of Man, and the Channel Islands; 94,284 sq. mi.; 56,284,000; cap. London: officially **United Kingdom of Great Britain and Northern Ireland.**

United States of America federal republic, North America including 50 states and the District of Columbia (3,615,222 sq. mi.; 179,323,175), and the Canal Zone, Puerto Rico, the Virgin Islands of the United States, American Samoa, and Guam, Wake, and other Pacific islands; total 3,720,407 sq. mi.; 212,161,000; cap. Washington, coextensive with the District of Columbia.

Universal City city, s CEN. Texas; 7,613.

University city, sw Florida; 10,039.

University City city, E Missouri; 46,309; ZIP see ST. LOUIS.

University Heights city, N Ohio; 17,055.

University Park city, N Texas; 23,498; ZIP see SAN ANTONIO.

University Place city, w CEN. Washington; 13,220.

Up·land (up′lənd) city, sw California; 32,551; ZIP 91786.

Upper Ar·ling·ton (är′lingt·n, är′ling·tən) city, CEN. Ohio; 38,630; ZIP see COLUMBUS.

Upper Dar·by (där′bē) urb. twp., SE Pennsylvania; 95,510; ZIP 19082*.

Upper More·land (môr′lənd, mōr′-) urb. twp., SE Pennsylvania; 21,032.

Upper Saddle River city, NE New Jersey; 7,949; ZIP 07458.

Up·per San·dus·ky (san·dusʹkē) city, N Ohio; 5,645; ZIP 43351.

Upper Vol·ta (volʹtə) independent republic of the French Community, W Africa; 105,900 sq. mi.; 5,508,000; cap. Ougadougou.

U·ral Mountains (yŏŏrʹəl) mtn. system in the RSFSR, extending from the Arctic Ocean to the Kazakh SSR.

U·ral River (yŏŏrʹəl) river, S RSFSR and W Kazakh SSR; 1,574 mi. long.

Ur·ban·a (ûr·banʹə) city, E Illinois; 32,800; ZIP 61801*.
— city, W CEN. Ohio; 11,237; ZIP 43078.

Ur·ban·dale (ûrʹban·dāl) town, S CEN. Iowa; 14,434; ZIP see DES MOINES.

U·ru·guay (yŏŏrʹə·gwā) republic, SE South America; 72,172 sq. mi.; 2,929,000; cap. Montevideo.

Uruguay River river, SE South America; 1,000 mi. long.

U·run·di (ŏŏ·rŏŏnʹdē) Burundi: *the former name.*

U·tah (yŏŏʹtô, -tä) state, W CEN. United States; 84,916 sq. mi.; 1,059,273; cap. Salt Lake City.

U·ti·ca (yŏŏʹtə·kə) city CEN. New York; 91,611.

U·trecht (yŏŏʹtrekt) prov., CEN. Netherlands; 511 sq. mi.; 687,000. — city, CEN. Utrecht prov., cap.; 274,388.

Ut·tar Pra·desh (ŏŏtʹər prə·dāshʹ) state, N India; 113,409 sq. mi.; 73,752,914; cap. Lucknow.

U·tua·do (ŏŏ·twäʹdō) town, W CEN. Puerto Rico; 9,901; ZIP 00761.

U·val·de (yŏŏ·valʹdə) city, SW CEN. Texas; 10,764; ZIP 78801.

Ux·bridge (uksʹbrij) city, CEN. Massachusetts; 8,253; ZIP 01569.

Uz·bek SSR (ŏŏzʹbek, uzʹ-) constituent republic S USSR; 154,014 sq. mi.; 10,896,000; cap. Tashkent.

Vac·a·ville (vakʹə·vil, väʹkə-) city, W CEN. California; 21,690; ZIP 95688.

Val-d'Or (väl′dôrʹ) town, W Quebec, Canada; 12,147.

Val·dos·ta (val·dosʹtə) city, S Georgia; 32,303; ZIP 31601*.

Va·len·ci·a (və·lenʹshē·ə, -shə) city, E Spain; 503,358.

Va·lin·da (və·linʹdə, ba-) city, SE California; 18,837.

Val·le·jo (və·lāʹō, -hō) city, W California; 66,733; ZIP 94590.*

Valley City city, SE North Dakota; 7,843; ZIP 58072.

Valley Cottage city, SE New York; 6,007.

Val·ley·field (valʹē·fēld) city, S Quebec, Canada; 29,111. Also **Sal·a·ber·ry de Valleyfield** (salʹə·ber′ē də)

Valley Forge locality, SE Pennsylvania, scene of Washington's winter encampment, 1777–78.

Valley Station uninc. place, N Kentucky; 24,471; ZIP 40172.

Valley Stream vill., SE New York; 40,413; ZIP 11580*.

Val·pa·rai·so (val′pə·rāʹzō, -sō, -rīʹ-) city, CEN. Chile; 286,108.

Val·pa·rai·so (val′pə·rāʹzō, -sō, -rīʹ-) city, NW Florida; 6,504; ZIP 32580.
— city, NW Indiana; 20,020; ZIP 46383.

Van Bur·en (van byŏŏrʹən) city, W Arkansas; 8,373; ZIP 72956.

Van·cou·ver (van·kŏŏʹvər) city, SW Washington; 42,493; ZIP 98660*.

Van·cou·ver (van·kŏŏʹvər) city, SW British Columbia, Canada; 410,375.

Vancouver Island isl., off SW British Columbia, Canada; 12,408 sq. mi.

Van·da·li·a (van·dāʹlē·ə) city, S CEN. Illinois; 5,160; ZIP 62471.
— city, SW Ohio; 10,796; ZIP 45377.

Van·den·burg (van·din·bûrg) city, SW California; 12,193.

Van·der·grift (vanʹdər·grift) boro., W Pennsylvania; 7,873; ZIP 15690.

Van Wert (van wûrtʹ) city, W Ohio; 11,320; ZIP 45891.

Vat·i·can City (vatʹə·kən) sovereign papal state within Rome; includes the Vatican and St. Peter's Church; established June 10, 1929; 108.7 acres; ab. 1,000.

Ve·gas Creek (väʹgəs) city, SE Nevada; 8,970.

Ven·e·zue·la (ven′ə·zwäʹlə, -zwēʹlə) republic, N South America; 352,143 sq. mi.; 10,771,000; cap. Caracas.

Ven·ice (venʹis) city, NE Italy; 360,241.

Ven·ice (venʹis) city, SW Florida; 6,648; ZIP 33595.

Venice, Gulf of N part of the Adriatic.

Vent·nor City (ventʹnər) city, SE New Jersey; 10,385; ZIP see ATLANTIC CITY.

Ven·tu·ra (ven·tŏŏʹrə) San Buenaventura: *an alternate name.*

Ven·tu·ra (ven·tŏŏrʹə) city, S California; 55,797; ZIP 93001.

Ve·ra·cruz (ver′ə·krŏŏzʹ) city, E Mexico; 179,652.

Verde (vûrd), **Cape** westernmost point of Africa; a peninsula; ab. 20 mi. long.

Ver·dun (vər·dunʹ) town, NE France; scene of several battles of World War I; 19,000.

Ver·dun (vər·dunʹ) city, S Quebec, Canada; 76,832.

Ver·mil·ion (vər·milʹyən) city, N CEN. Ohio; 9,872; ZIP 44089.
— city, SE South Dakota; 9,128; ZIP 57069.

Ver·mont (vər·montʹ) state, NE United States; 9,609 sq. mi.; 444,330; cap. Montpelier.

Ver·non (vûrʹnən) city, NE Connecticut; 27,237; ZIP 06086.
— city, N Texas; 11,454; ZIP 76384.

Ver·non (vûrʹnən) city, S British Columbia, Canada; 11,423.

Vernon Valley uninc. place, SE New York; 17,925.

Ver·o Beach (virʹō) city, E Florida; 11,908; ZIP 32960*.

Ve·ro·na (və·rōʹnə) city, NE Italy; 230,907.

Ve·ro·na (və·rōʹnə) boro., NE New Jersey; 15,067; ZIP see MONTCLAIR.

Ver·sailles (vər·sīʹ, -sālz′) city, N France; site of the palace of Louis XIV; scene of the signing of a treaty (1919) betw. the Allies and Germany after World War I; 90,829.

Ver·sailles (vər·sālz) city, CEN. Kentucky; 5,679.

Ves·tal-Twin Orchards (vesʹtəl-twin′) city, CEN. New York; 8,309.

Ves·ta·vi·a (ves·täʹvē·ə) city, CEN. Alabama; 8,311; ZIP 35216.

Ve·su·vi·us (və·sōōʹvē·əs) active volcano, W Italy; 3,891 ft.

Vi·chy (vē·shēʹ) city, CEN. France; provisional cap. during German occupation, World War II; 30,000.

Vicks·burg (viksʹbûrg) city, W Mississippi; besieged and taken by the Union Army in the Civil War, 1863; 25,478; ZIP 39180*.

Vic·to·ri·a (vik·tôrʹē·ə, -tōʹrē·ə) state, SE Australia; 87,844 sq. mi.; 2,930,113; cap. Melbourne.

Vic·to·ri·a (vik·tôrʹē·ə, -tōʹrē·ə) city, SW British Columbia, Canada; cap.; 57,453.

Vic·to·ri·a (vik·tôrʹē·ə, -tōʹrē·ə) city, S Hong Kong; cap.; 674,962.

Vic·to·ri·a (vik·tôrʹō·ə, -tōʹrē·ə) city, S Texas; 41,349; ZIP 77901*.

Victoria, Lake lake betw. Uganda, Tanganyika, and Kenya; 26,828 sq. mi. Also **Victoria Ny·an·za** (nī·anʹzə, nyänʹzə).

Victoria Falls cataract on the Zambesi River betw. Northern and Southern Rhodesia; 343 ft. high; over a mile wide.

Vic·tor·i·a·ville (vik·tôrʹē·ə·vil, -tōʹrē-) town, S Quebec, Canada; 21,320.

Vic·tor·ville (vikʹtər·vil) city, SW California; 10,845; ZIP 92392.

Vi·da·lia (vi·dāʹlyə, və-) city, SE CEN. Georgia; 9,507; ZIP 30474.
— city, NE Louisiana; 5,538; ZIP 71373.

Vi·dor (vīʹdər) city, E CEN. Texas; 9,738; ZIP 77662.

Vi·en·na (vē·enʹə) city, NE Austria; cap.; 1,640,106.

Vi·en·na (vē·enʹə) town, NE Virginia; 17,152; ZIP 22180.
— city, NW West Virginia; 11,549; ZIP see PARKERSBURG.

Vien·tiane (vyan·tyanʹ) city, NW CEN. Laos; adm. cap.; 162,300.

Vi·et·nam (vē·et·nämʹ) republic, SW Indochina, officially the Socialist Republic of Vietnam, comprising the former Democratic Republic of Vietnam, or North Vietnam, and the former Republic of Vietnam, or South Vietnam; 126,422 sq. mi.; 48,000,000; cap. Hanoi. Also spelled Viet-Nam or Viet Nam.

View Park-Wind·sor Hills (windʹzər) city, SE California; 12,268.

Vil·la Park (vilʹə) vill., NE Illinois; 25,891; ZIP 60181.

Ville Platte (vēlʹplat′) town, S CEN. Louisiana; 9,692; ZIP 70586.

Vil·nius (vēlʹnyəs) city, SE Lithuanian SSR; cap.; 316,000. Also **Vil·na** (vēlʹnə), **Vilʹnyus.**

Vin·cennes (vin·senzʹ, vinʹsənz) city, SW Indiana; 19,867; ZIP 47591.

Vine·land (vīnʹlənd) boro., S New Jersey; 47,399; ZIP 08360.

Vi·ni·ta (və·nēʹtə) city, NE Oklahoma; 5,847; ZIP 74301.

Vin·ton (vinʹtən) city, SW Virginia; 6,347; ZIP 24179.

Vi·o·la (vī·ōʹlə) city, SE New York; 5,136.

Vir·gin·ia (vər·jinʹyə) state, E United States; 40,815 sq. mi.; 4,648,494; cap. Richmond.
— city, NE Minnesota; 12,450; ZIP 55792.

Virginia Beach city, SE Virginia; 172,106; ZIP 23450*.

Virgin Islands isl. group, West Indies, E of Puerto Rico. See BRITISH VIRGIN ISLANDS.

Virgin Islands of the United States uninc. terr., Virgin Islands; 133 sq. mi.; 31,904; cap. Charlotte Amalie.

Vi·sa·lia (vi·sāʹlyə) city, S CEN. California; 27,268; ZIP 93277*.

Vi·sa·yan Islands (vē·säʹyən) isl. group, CEN. Philippines; 23,621 sq. mi.

Vis·ta (visʹtə) uninc. place, SW California; 24,688; ZIP 92083.

Vis·tu·la (visʹchŏŏ·lə) river, CEN. and N Poland; 678 mi. long.

Vla·di·vos·tok (vlad/ə·vos·tok′, -vos′tok) city, SE RSFSR; 397,000.
Vol·ga (vol′gə, vôl′gə) river, W RSFSR; 2,290 mi. long.
Vol·go·grad (vol′gə·grad) city, W RSFSR; scene of a Russian victory over German forces in World War II, Sept. 1942 to Jan. 1943; 743,000: from 1925–61 *Stalingrad*.
Vol·ta (vol′tä) river, E Ghana; 800 mi. long.
Vosges Mountains (võzh) mtn. chain, E France.

Wa·ban·a (wô·ban′ə) town, SE Newfoundland, Canada; 7,884.
Wa·bash (wô′bash) city, NE CEN. Indiana; 13,379; ZIP 46992.
Wabash river, W Ohio and Indiana; 475 mi. long.
Wa·co (wā′kō) city, CEN. Texas; 95,326; ZIP 76700*.
Wade-Hamp·ton (wād′hamp′tən) city, NW South Carolina; 17,152; ZIP 29607.
Wads·worth (wäds′wəth) city, NE CEN. Ohio; 13,142; ZIP 44281.
Wa·hi·a·wa (wä′hē·ə·wä′) city, CEN. Oahu, Hawaii; 17,598; ZIP 96786.
Wah·pe·ton (wô′pət·n, -pə·tən) city, SE North Dakota; 7,076; ZIP 58075.
Wai·ki·ki (wī′kē·kē, wī/kē·kē′) beach on Honolulu harbor, SE Oahu, Hawaii.
Wai·lu·ku (wī·lōō′kōō) city, NW Maui, Hawaii; 7,979; ZIP 96793.
Wai·pi·o (wī·pē′ō) city, Oahu, Hawaii; 22,798; ZIP 96786.
Wake·field (wāk′fēld) town, E Massachusetts; 25,402; ZIP 01880*.
Wake·field-Peace·dale (wāk′fēld, pēs′dāl) uninc. place, S Rhode Island; 6,331.
Wake Island (wāk) coral atoll in the North Pacific; 4 sq. mi.; site of a U.S. naval and air base.
Wal·den (wôl′dən) city, NE New York; 5,277; ZIP 12586.
Wal·dorf (wôl′dôrf) city, SW Maryland; 7,368; ZIP 20601.
Wal·dwick (wôl′dwik) boro., NE New Jersey; 12,213; ZIP 07463.
Wales (wālz) penin., SW Britain; a principality of England; 8,016 sq. mi.; 2,774,000.
Walk·er (wôk′ər) city, SW Michigan; 11,492; ZIP 49504.
Walker Mill city, NE Maryland; 6,322.
Wal·lace·burg (wol/əs·bûrg) town, S Ontario, Canada; 10,696.
Wal·la Wal·la (wol/ə wol/ə) city, SE Washington; 23,619; ZIP 99362.
Wal·ling·ford (wol′ing·fərd) town, S CEN. Connecticut; 35,714; ZIP 06492.
Wal·ling·ton (wol′ingt·n, -ing·tən) boro., NE New Jersey; 10,284; ZIP see PASSAIC*.
Walnut city, SE California; 5,992; ZIP 91789.
Walnut Creek city, W California; 39,844; ZIP 94596*.
Walnut Heights uninc. place, W California; 5,080.
Wal·pole (wôl′pōl) town, E Massachusetts; 18,149; ZIP 02081.
Wal·ter·bor·o (wôl′tər·bûr′ō) town, S South Carolina; 6,257; ZIP 29488.
Wal·tham (wôl′thəm) city, E Massachusetts; 61,582; ZIP see BOSTON.
Wa·na·que (wô′nə·kē) boro., N New Jersey; 8,638; ZIP 07465.
Wan·tagh (won′tô′) vill., SE New York; 21,873; ZIP 11793.
Wa·pa·ko·net·a (wô/pə·kə·net/ə, wop/ə-) city, W Ohio; 7,324; ZIP 45895.
Wap·pin·gers Falls (wop′in·jərz) city, CEN. New York; 5,607; ZIP 12590.
Ware (wâr) town, S CEN. Massachusetts; 8,187; ZIP 01082.
Ware·ham (wâr′əm) city, E Massachusetts; 11,492; ZIP 02571.
War·min·ster (wôr′min/stər) urb. twp., SE Pennsylvania; 15,994; ZIP 18974.
War·ner Rob·ins (wôr′nər rob′inz) city, CEN. Georgia; 33,491; ZIP 31093*.
Warr Acres (wôr) city, CEN. Oklahoma; 9,887; ZIP see OKLAHOMA CITY.
War·ren (wor′ən, -in) city, S Arkansas; 6,433; ZIP 71671.
— vill., SE Michigan; 179,260; ZIP 48089*.
— city, NE Ohio; 63,494; ZIP 44480*.
— boro., NW Pennsylvania; 12,998; ZIP 16365*.
— town, E Rhode Island; 10,523; ZIP 02885*.
War·rens·burg (wor/ənz·bûrg, -inz-) city, W Missouri; 13,125; ZIP 64093.
War·rens·ville Heights (wor/ənz·vil, -inz-) vill., N Ohio; 18,925; ZIP see CLEVELAND.
War·ring·ton (wor/ing·tən, -ingt·n) uninc. place, NW Florida; 15,848; ZIP see PENSACOLA.
War·saw (wôr′sô) city, E CEN. Poland; cap.; 1,273,600.
War·saw (wôr′sô) city, N Indiana; 7,506; ZIP 46792.
War·wick (wôr′wik, wor′ik) city, E CEN. Rhode Island; 83,694; ZIP 02886*.
Was·co (wäs′kō) city, S CEN. California; 8,269; ZIP 93280.
Wa·se·ca (wo·sē′kə) city, S Minnesota; 6,789; ZIP 56093.

Wash·ing·ton (wosh′ing·tən, wô′shing-) state, NW United States; 68,192 sq. mi.; 3,409,169; cap. Olympia.
— city, E United States; coextensive with the District of Columbia; cap.; 756,510; ZIP 20000*.
— city, CEN. Illinois; 6,790; ZIP 61571.
— city, SW Indiana; 11,358; ZIP 47501.
— city, SE Iowa; 6,317; ZIP 52353.
— city, E Missouri; 8,499; ZIP 63090.
— boro., NW New Jersey; 5,943; ZIP 07882.
— city, E North Carolina; 8,961; ZIP 27889.
— city, S CEN. Ohio; 12,495; ZIP 43160.
— city, SW Pennsylvania; 19,827; ZIP 15301.
Washington Park vill., SW Illinois; 9,424; ZIP 61571.
Washington Terrace city, N CEN. Utah; 7,241; ZIP see OGDEN.
Wa·ter·bur·y (wô′tər·ber/ē, wot′ər-) city, W Connecticut; 108,033; ZIP 06700*.
Wa·ter·ford (wô′tər·fərd, wot′-) city, NE Connecticut; 17,227; ZIP 06385.
Wa·ter·loo (wô′tər·lōō, wô′tər·lōō′) vill., CEN. Belgium; scene of Napoleon's final defeat, June 18, 1815; ab. 10,000.
Wa·ter·loo (wô′tər·lōō) city, NE CEN. Iowa; 75,533; ZIP 50700*.
— vill., W CEN. New York; 5,418; ZIP 13165.
Wa·ter·loo (wô′tər·lōō) city, S Ontario, Canada; 29,889.
Wa·ter·town (wô′tər·toun, wot′ər-) city, SW Connecticut; 18,610; ZIP 06795.
— town, E Massachusetts; 39,307; ZIP see BOSTON.
— city, N New York; 30,787; ZIP 13601*.
— city, NE South Dakota; 13,388; ZIP 57201*.
— city, SE Wisconsin; 15,683; ZIP 53094.
Wa·ter·ville (wô′tər·vil, wot′ər-) city, S CEN. Maine; 18,192; ZIP 04900*.
Wa·ter·vliet (wô′tər·vlēt, -və·lēt/, wot′ər-) city, E New York; 12,404; ZIP 12189.
Wat·se·ka (wot·sē′kə) city, E Illinois; 5,294; ZIP 60970.
Wat·son·ville (wät′sən·vil) city, W California; 14,569; ZIP 95076*.
Wau·con·da (wô·kon′də) city, NE Illinois; 5,460; ZIP 60084.
Wau·ke·gan (wô·kē′gən) city, NE Illinois; 65,269; ZIP 60085*.
Wau·ke·sha (wô′ki·shô) city, SE Wisconsin; 40,258; ZIP 53186*.
Wau·pun (wô·pun′) city, E CEN. Wisconsin; 7,946; ZIP 53963.
Wau·sau (wô′sô) city, CEN. Wisconsin; 32,806; ZIP 54401*.
Wau·wa·to·sa (wô·wə·tō′sə) city, SE Wisconsin; 58,676; ZIP see MILWAUKEE.
Wa·ver·ly (wā′vər·lē) city, NE Iowa; 7,205; ZIP 50677.
— vill., S New York; 5,261; ZIP 14892.
Wax·a·hach·ie (wok/sə·hach/ē, wôk/-) city, N Texas; 13,452; ZIP 75165.
Way·cross (wā′krôs) city, SE Georgia; 18,996; ZIP 31501.
Way·land (wā′lənd) city, N Massachusetts; 13,461; ZIP 01778.
Wayne (wān) vill., SE Michigan; 21,054; ZIP 48184.
— city, NE Nebraska; 5,379; ZIP 68787.
— urb. twp., N New Jersey; 49,141; ZIP 07470*.
Waynes·bor·o (wānz′bûr′ō) city, E Georgia; 5,530; ZIP 30830.
— boro., S Pennsylvania; 10,011; ZIP 17268.
— city, N CEN. Virginia; 16,707; ZIP 22980*.
Waynes·burg (wānz′bûrg) boro., SW Pennsylvania; 5,152; ZIP 15370.
Waynes·ville (wānz′vil, -vəl) town, SW North Carolina; 6,488; ZIP 28786.
Weath·er·ford (weth/ər·fərd) city, NW Oklahoma; 7,959; ZIP 73096.
— city, N Texas; 11,750; ZIP 76086.
Webb City (web) city, SW Missouri; 6,811; ZIP 64870.
Web·ster (web/stər) uninc. place, S Massachusetts; 14,917; ZIP 01578*.
— city, CEN. New York; 5,037; ZIP 14580.
Webster City city, CEN. Iowa; 8,488; ZIP 50595.
Webster Groves city, E Missouri; 26,995; ZIP see ST. LOUIS.
Wee·haw·ken (wē/hô/kən, wē/hô′kən) urb. twp., NE New Jersey; 13,383; ZIP see UNION CITY.
Wei·mar (vī′mär) city, SW East Germany; 64,300.
Weir·ton (wirt/n, wir/tən) city, NW West Virginia; 27,131; ZIP 26062*.
Wel·by (wel′bē) city, E CEN. Connecticut; 6,875.
Wel·land (wel/ənd) city, S Ontario, Canada; 36,960.
Welland Canal waterway betw. Lakes Erie and Ontario.
Welles·ley (wēlz/lē) town, E Massachusetts; 28,051; ZIP see BOSTON.
Wel·ling·ton (wel/ing·tən) city, CEN. New Zealand; cap.; 167,859.
Wel·ling·ton (wel/ing·tən) city, S Kansas; 8,072; ZIP 67152.
Wells·ton (wel/stən) city, E Missouri; 7,050; ZIP see ST. LOUIS.
— city, S Ohio; 5,410.

Wells·ville (welz′vil) vill., sw New York; 5,815; ZIP 14895.
— city, E Ohio; 5,891; ZIP 43968.
We·natch·ee (wi·nach′ē) city, CEN. Washington; 16,912; ZIP 98801*.
Wes·la·co (wes′li·kō) city, s Texas; 15,313; ZIP 78596.
West Al·lis (al′is) city, SE Wisconsin; 71,723; ZIP see MIL-WAUKEE.
West Am·i·ty·ville (am′ə·tē·vil) city, SE New York; 6,393.
West Ath·ens (ath′inz) city, SE California; 13,386.
West Bend city, SE Wisconsin; 16,555; ZIP 53095*.
West Berlin See BERLIN.
West·bor·ough (west′bûr′ō) city, N CEN. Massachusetts; 12,594; ZIP 01581.
West Boyls·town (boilz′tən) city, N CEN. Massachusetts; 6,369; ZIP 01583.
West Bra·den·ton (brā′dən·tən) city, W CEN. Florida; 6,162.
West Bridge·wa·ter (brij′wô·tər, -wot·ər) city, E Massachusetts; 7,152; ZIP 02379.
West·brook (wes′brŏŏk, west′-) city, sw Maine; 14,444; ZIP 04092.
West·bur·y (west′ber′ē) vill., SE New York; 15,362; ZIP 11590.
West Cald·well (kôld′wəl, -wel) boro., NE New Jersey; 11,887; ZIP see CALDWELL.
West Car·roll·ton (kar′əl·tən) city, sw Ohio; 10,748; ZIP 45449.
West Car·son (kär′sən) city, SE California; 15,501.
West·ches·ter (west′ches′tər, wes′-) vill., NE Illinois; 20,033; ZIP see MAYWOOD.
West Chester (west′ ches′tər) boro., SE Pennsylvania; 19,301; ZIP 19380.
West Chi·ca·go (shə·kä′gō, -kô′-) city, NE Illinois; 10,111 ZIP 60185.
West Co·lum·bi·a (kə·lum′bē·ə) city, CEN. South Carolina; 7,838; ZIP 29169.
West Comp·ton (komp′tən) city, SE California; 5,748.
West Con·cord (kon′kôrd) uninc. place, s CEN. North Carolina; 5,347; ZIP see CONCORD.
West Co·vi·na (cō·vē′nə) city, sw California; 63,034; ZIP 91790*.
West Des Moines (də moin′) city, CEN. Iowa; 16,441; ZIP 50265.
West El·mi·ra (el·mī′rə) uninc. place, s New York; 5,901.
West End city, NW Florida; 5,289.
— city, NW Illinois; 7,554.
West End-Cobb (kob) city, E Alabama; 5,515; ZIP 26201.
Wes·ter·ly (wes′tər·lē) uninc. place, sw Rhode Island; 17,248; ZIP 02891.
Westerly Center city, sw Rhode Island; 13,654; ZIP 02891.
Western Australia state, W Australia; 975,920 sq. mi.; 736,629; cap. Perth.
Western Samoa See SAMOA.
Western Springs vill., NE Illinois; 12,147; ZIP 60558.
Wes·ter·ville (wes′tər·vil) vill., CEN. Ohio; 12,530; ZIP 43081.
West Far·go (fär′gō) city, E North Dakota; 5,161; ZIP 58078.
West·field (west′fēld) city, sw Massachusetts; 31,433; ZIP 01085.
— town, E New Jersey; 33,720; ZIP 07090*.
West·ford (west′fərd) city, NE Massachusetts; 10,368; ZIP 01886.
West Frank·fort (frangk′fərt) city, s Illinois; 8,836; ZIP 62896.
West Germany See GERMANY.
West Glen Park (glen) city, NE Indiana; 6,602.
West Gulf·port (gulf′pôrt, -pōrt) city, SE Mississippi; 6,996; ZIP 39501.
West Hart·ford (härt′fərd) town, CEN. Connecticut; 68,031; ZIP see HARTFORD.
West Ha·ven (hā′vən) town, s Connecticut; 52,581; ZIP see NEW HAVEN.
West Hav·er·straw (hav′ər·strô′) vill., SE New York; 8,558; ZIP 10993.
West Haz·le·ton (hāz′əlt·n, hāz′əl·tən) boro., E Pennsylvania; 6,059; ZIP see HAZLETON.
West Hel·en·a (hel′ə·nə) city, E Arkansas; 11,007; ZIP 72360.
West Hemp·stead-Lake·view (hem′sted, hemp′-; lāk′·vyŏō) uninc. place, SE New York; 23,375; ZIP see HEMP-STEAD.
West Hol·ly·wood (hol′ē·wŏŏd) uninc. place, sw California; 29,448.
West Indies series of isl. groups separating the North Atlantic from the Caribbean.
West Indies the group of British cols. in the Caribbean.
West I·slip (ī′slip) city, SE New York; 16,711.

West Kil·do·nan (kil·dō′nən) city, s Manitoba, Canada; 22,240.
West La·fay·ette (lä′fē·et′) city, W CEN. Indiana; 19,157; ZIP see LAFAYETTE.
West·lake (west′lāk′) city, N Ohio; 15,689; ZIP 44091.
West·land (west′land) city, SE Michigan; 86,749; ZIP 48185.
West Linn (lin) city, NW Oregon; 7,091; ZIP 97068.
West Long Branch boro., E New Jersey; 6,845; ZIP 07764.
West Mem·phis (mem′fis) city, E Arkansas; 25,892; ZIP 72301.
West·mere (west′mir) city, NE New York; 6,364.
West Mi·am·i (mī·am′ē, -am′ə) town, SE Florida; 5,494.
West Miff·lin (mif′lin) boro., sw Pennsylvania; 28,070; ZIP see HOMESTEAD.
West·min·ster (west′min·stər, wes′-) city and metropolitan boro., London, England; site of the Houses of Parliament and Buckingham Palace; 85,000.
Westminster Abbey A Gothic church in Westminster, London; burial place of English kings and notables.
West·min·ster (west′min·stər, wes′-) city, sw California; 59,865; ZIP 92683.
— city, CEN. Colorado; 19,432; ZIP 80030.
— city, N Maryland; 7,207; ZIP 21157*.
West Mo·des·to (mō·des′tō) CEN. California; 6,135.
West Mon·roe (mən·rō) city, N Louisiana; 14,868; ZIP 71291.
West·mont (west′mont) city, SE California; 29,310.
— vill., NE Illinois; 8,482; ZIP 60559.
— boro., sw CEN. Pennsylvania; 6,673.
West·mount (west′mount) city, s Quebec, Canada; 24,107.
West New Guinea prov. of Indonesia comprising the W part of New Guinea and adjacent islands; 159,375 sq. mi.; 716,000; cap. Kotabaru. Also **West Ir·i·an** (ir′ē·an).
West New York town, NE New Jersey; 40,627; ZIP 07093*.
West Nor·ri·ton (nôr′it·n, nor′-, -i·tən) urb. twp., SE Pennsylvania; 8,342.
West Ny·ack (nī′ak) city, SE New York; 5,510.
Wes·ton (wes′n, wes′tən) city, sw Connecticut; 7,417; ZIP 06808.
— city, W Massachusetts; 10,870; ZIP 02193.
— city, N CEN.. West Virginia; 7,323; ZIP 26452.
Wes·ton (west′n, wes′tən) town, s Ontario, Canada; 11,047.
West Orange town, NE New Jersey; 43,715; ZIP see ORANGE.
West Palm Beach city, SE Florida; 57,375; ZIP 33401*.
West Pat·er·son (pat′ər·sən) boro., N New Jersey; 11,692; ZIP see LITTLE FALLS.
West Pen·sa·co·la (pen′sə·kō′lə) city, sw Florida; 20,924; ZIP 32505.
West Pe·or·i·a (pē·ôr′ē·ə) city, NW Illinois; 6,873.
West Pitts·burg (pits′bûrg) city, W California; 5,969; ZIP 94565.
West Pitt·ston (pit′stən) boro., NE Pennsylvania; 7,074; ZIP see PITTSTON.
West Plains city, s Missouri; 6,893; ZIP 65775*.
West Point U.S. military reservation, SE New York; seat of the U.S. Military Academy; ZIP 10996.
— city, E Mississippi; 8,714; ZIP 39773.
West·port (west′pôrt, -pōrt) city, sw Connecticut; 27,414; ZIP 06880.
— city, s Massachusetts; 9,791; ZIP 02790.
West Puen·te Valley (pwen′tä) city, SE California; 20,733.
West Sac·ra·men·to (sak′rə·men′tō) city, W California; 12,002; ZIP 95691.
West Saint Paul city, E Minnesota; 18,799; ZIP see ST. PAUL.
West Say·ville (sā′vil) city, NE New York; 7,386; ZIP 11796.
West Sen·e·ca (sen′əkə) uninc. place, w New York; 48,404; ZIP see BUFFALO.
West Spring·field (spring′fēld) town, s Massachusetts; 28,491; ZIP 01089.
West University Place city, SE Texas; 13,317.
West·vale (west′väl) city, NE New York; 7,253.
West View boro., sw Pennsylvania; 8,312; ZIP see PITTS-BURGH.
West·ville (west′vil) city, sw New Jersey; 5,170; ZIP 08093.
West Vir·gin·ia (vər·jin′yə) state, E United States; 24,181 sq. mi.; 1,744,237; cap. Charleston.
West War·wick (wôr′wik) town, CEN. Rhode Island; 24,323; ZIP 02893.
West Wau·sau (wô′sô) city, CEN. Wisconsin; 6,399.
West·we·go (west·wē′gō) town, SE Louisiana; 11,402; ZIP 70094.
West Whit·ti·er-Los Nie·tos (hwit′yər-lōs nyä′tōs, wit′-) city, SE California; 20,845.
West Winter Haven uninc. place, CEN. Florida; 7,716.
West·wood (west′wŏŏd) city, CEN. Massachusetts; 12,750; ZIP 02090.
— city, sw Michigan; 9,143.

PRONUNCIATION KEY: add, āce, câre, pälm; end, ēven; it, īce; odd, ōpen, ôrder; tŏŏk, pōōl; up, bûrn; ə = a in *above*, e in *sicken*, i in *flexible*, o in *melon*, u in *focus*; yōō = u in *fuse*; oil; pout; check; go; ring; thin; this; zh, vision. For å, œ, ü, kh, ṅ, see inside front cover.

— boro., NE New Jersey; 11,105; ZIP 07674.
Westwood Lakes uninc. place, SE Florida; 12,811.
West York (yôrk) boro., S Pennsylvania; 5.314.
West Yu·ma (yōō′mə) city, SW Arizona; 5,552; ZIP 85364.
We·tas·ki·win (we·tas′kə·win) city, CEN. Alberta, Canada; 6,008.
Weth·ers·field (weth′ərz·fēld) town, CEN. Connecticut; 26,662; ZIP see HARTFORD.
We·wo·ka (wə·wō′kə, wē-) city, CEN. Oklahoma; 5,284; ZIP 74884.
Wey·burn (wā′bərn) city, SE Saskatchewan, Canada; 9,000.
Wey·mouth (wā′məth) town, E Massachusetts; 54,610; ZIP see BOSTON.
Whar·ton (hwôrt′n, wôrt′-, hwôr′tən, wôr′-) boro., N New Jersey; 5,535; ZIP 07885.
— city, S Texas; 7,881; ZIP 77488.
Whea·ton (hwēt′n, wēt′-) city, NE Illinois; 31,168; ZIP 60187*.
— uninc. place, W CEN. Maryland; 66,247; ZIP see SILVER SPRINGS.
Wheat Ridge uninc. place, N CEN. Colorado; 29,795; ZIP 80033.
Whee·ling (hwē′ling, wē′-) vill., NE Illinois; 14,746; ZIP 60090.
— city, NW West Virginia; 48,188; ZIP 26000*.
Whit·by (hwit′bē, wit′-) town, S Ontario, Canada; 17,273.
White city, NW Utah; 6,402.
White Bear Lake city, E Minnesota; 23,313; ZIP see ST. PAUL.
White·fish Bay (hwīt′fish′, wīt-) vill., SE Wisconsin; 17,394; ZIP see MILWAUKEE.
White·hall (hwīt′hôl, wīt′) city, CEN. Ohio; 25,263; ZIP see COLUMBUS.
— boro., SW Pennsylvania; 16,551.
White·ha·ven (hwīt′hā′vən, wīt′-) uninc. place, SW Tennessee; 19,000; ZIP see MEMPHIS.
White·man (hwīt′mən, wīt′-) city, NW Missouri; 5,040.
White Meadow Lake city, N New Jersey; 8,499.
White Mountains range of the Appalachians, N CEN. New Hampshire.
White Oak city, NE Maryland; 19,769; ZIP 20901.
— boro., SW Pennsylvania; 9,304; ZIP see McKEESPORT.
White Plains city, SE New York; 50,220; ZIP 10600*.
White Rock city, SW British Columbia, Canada; 7,787.
White Russia See BYELORUSSIAN SSR.
White Sea inlet of the Barents Sea, NW RSFSR; 36,680 sq. mi.
White Settlement town, N Texas; 13,449; ZIP see FORT WORTH.
White·wa·ter (hwīt′wô′tər, wīt′-, -wot′ər) city, SE Wisconsin; 12,038; ZIP 53190.
White-Yard·ville (hwīt′yärd′vil, wīt′-) city, W CEN. New Jersey; 18,680.
Whit·ing (hwīt′ing, wīt′-) city, NW Indiana; 7,247; ZIP 46394.
Whit·ins·ville (hwīt′nz·vil, wīt′-) uninc. place, S Massachusetts; 5,210; ZIP 01588.
Whit·man (hwit′mən, wit′-) town, E Massachusetts; 13,059; ZIP 02382.
Whit·ney (hwit′nē, wit′-) uninc. place, SW Idaho; 13,603; ZIP see BOISE.
Whitney, Mount peak, E California; 14,496 ft.
Whit·ti·er (hwit′ē·ər, wit′-) city, SW California; 72,863; ZIP 90601*.
Wich·i·ta (wich′ə·tô) city, S CEN. Kansas; 276,554; ZIP 67200*.
Wichita Falls city, N Texas; 97,564; ZIP 76301*.
Wick·liffe (wik′lif) city, NE Ohio; 21,354; ZIP 44092.
Wight (wīt), **Isle of** isl. off the S coast of England; 147 sq. mi.
Wil·bra·ham (wil′brə·ham) city, SW Massachusetts; 11,984; ZIP 01095.
Wilkes-Bar·re (wilks′bar·ə) city, NE Pennsylvania; 58,856; ZIP 18700*.
Wil·kins (wil′kinz) urb . twp., SW Pennsylvania; 8,272.
Wil·kins·burg (wil′kinz·bûrg) boro., SW Pennsylvania; 26,780; ZIP see PITTSBURGH.
Wil·lard (wil′ərd) vill., N Ohio; 5,510; ZIP 44890.
Wil·liams·burg (wil′yəmz·bûrg) city, E Virginia; capital of Virginia (1699–1779); restored to colonial condition; 9,069; ZIP 23185.
Wil·liam·son (wil′yəm·sən) city, SW West Virginia; 5,831; ZIP 25661.
Wil·liams·port (wil′yəmz·pôrt, -pōrt) city, N CEN. Pennsylvania; 37,918; ZIP 17701*.
Wil·liam·ston (wil′yəm·stən) town E North Carolina; 6,570; ZIP 27892.
Wil·liams·town (wil′yəmz·toun) uninc. place, NW Massachusetts; 8,454; ZIP 01267.
Wil·liams·ville (wil′yəmz·vil) vill., W New York; 6,835; ZIP see BUFFALO.
Wil·li·man·tic (wil′i·man′tik) city, E CEN. Connecticut; 14,402; ZIP 06226.

Wil·lis·ton (wil′ist·n, -is·tən) city, NW North Dakota; 11,280; ZIP 58801.
— city, NW Vermont; 5,376; ZIP 05495.
Williston Park vill., SE New York; 9,154; ZIP 11596.
Will·mar (wil′mər) city, SW CEN. Minnesota; 12,869; ZIP 56201.
Wil·lough·by (wil′ō·bē, -ə-) city, NE Ohio; 18,634; ZIP 44094*.
Willoughby Hills city, NE Ohio; 5,247; ZIP 44094.
Wil·low·brook (wil′ō·brōōk) city, SE California; 28,706.
Willow Grove city, SE Pennsylvania; 16,494; ZIP 19090.
Wil·lo·wick (wil′ə·wik′) city, NE Ohio; 21,237; ZIP see WILLOUGHBY.
Wil·mette (wil·met′) vill., NE Illinois; 32,134; ZIP 60091.
Wil·ming·ton (wil′ming·tən) city, N Delaware; 80,386.
— city, NE Massachusetts; 17,102; ZIP 01887.
— city, SE North Carolina; 46,169; ZIP 19800*.
— city, SW Ohio; 10,051; ZIP 45177.
Wilmington Manor city, NE Delaware; 10,134.
Wil·son (wil′sən) town, E CEN. North Carolina; 29,347; ZIP 14172.
— boro., E Pennsylvania; 8,482; ZIP see CLAIRTON.
Wil·son (wil′sən), **Mount** peak, SW California; 5,710 ft.; site of a famous observatory.
Wilson Dam power dam in the Tennessee River at Muscle Shoals, NW Alabama; 137 ft. high, 4,862 ft. long.
Wil·ton (wilt′n, wil′tən) city, SE Connecticut; 13,572; ZIP 06897.
Wil·ton Man·or (wilt′n man′ər, wil′tən) town, SE Florida; 10,948; ZIP FORT LAUDERDALE.
Wim·ble·don (wim′bəl·dən) town and municipal boro.; S England; scene of international tennis matches; 20,000.
Win·chen·don (win′chən·dən) town, N Massachusetts; 6,635; ZIP 01457.
Win·ches·ter (win′ches·tər, -chis·tər) city, NE Connecticut; 11,106; ZIP 06094.
— city, E Indiana; 5,493; ZIP 47394.
— city, CEN. Kentucky; 13,402; ZIP 40391.
— town, E Massachusetts; 22,269; ZIP 01890.
— city, SE Nevada; 13,981; ZIP 89101.
— city, SE Tennessee; 5,211; ZIP 37398.
— city, N Virginia; 14,643; ZIP 22601.
Wind·ber (wind′bər, win′-) boro., S Pennsylvania; 6,332; ZIP 15963.
Win·der (win′dər) city, N CEN. Georgia; 6,605; ZIP 30680.
Wind·ham (wind′əm) city, NE Connecticut; 19,626; ZIP 06280.
— city, SW Maine; 6,593.
Wind·sor (win′zər) municipal boro., S England; site of **Windsor Castle**, a residence of the English sovereigns; 15,000. Officially **New Windsor**.
Wind·sor (win′zər) town, N CEN. Newfoundland, Canada; 6,692.
— city, SE Ontario, Canada; 192,544.
— town, S Quebec, Canada; 6,496.
Wind·sor Forest (win′zər) city, NE Georgia; 7,288.
Windsor Heights town, S CEN. Iowa; 6,303; ZIP see DES MOINES.
Windsor Locks city, CEN. Connecticut; 15,080; ZIP 06096.
Wind·ward Islands (wind′wərd) isl. group, S Lesser Antilles.
Win·field (win′fēld) city, S Kansas; 11,405; ZIP 67156.
Win·net·ka (wi·net′kə) vill., NE Illinois; 14,131; ZIP 60093*.
Winn·field (win′fēld) city, N CEN. Louisiana; 7,142; ZIP 71483.
Win·ni·peg (win′ə·peg) city, SE Manitoba, Canada; cap.; 257,005.
Winnipeg, Lake lake, S Manitoba, Canada; 9,398 sq. mi.
Winns·bor·o (winz′bûr·ō) city, NE Louisiana; 5,349; ZIP 71295.
Wi·no·na (wi·nō′nə) city, SE Minnesota; 26,438; ZIP 55987*.
— city, CEN. Mississippi; 5,521; ZIP 38967.
Wi·noos·ki (wi·nōōs′kē) city, NW Vermont; 7,309; ZIP see BURLINGTON.
Wins·low (winz′lō) city, E CEN. Arizona; 8,066; ZIP 86047.
— city, SW Maine; 7,299; ZIP 04901.
Winslow Center city, SW Maine; 5,389; ZIP 04901.
Win·sted (win′stəd, -stid) city, NW Connecticut; 8,954; ZIP 06098.
Win·ston-Sa·lem (win′stən-sā′ləm) city, NW CEN. North Carolina; 132,913; ZIP 27100*.
Winter Garden city, CEN. Florida; 5,153; ZIP 32787.
Winter Haven city, CEN. Florida; 16,136; ZIP 33880*.
Winter Park city, E CEN. Florida; 21,895; ZIP 32789*.
Win·throp (win′throp) town, E Massachusetts; 20,335; ZIP see BOSTON.
Wis·con·sin (wis·kon′sən) state, N United States; 56,154 sq. mi.; 4,417,933; cap. Madison.
Wisconsin Rapids city, CEN. Wisconsin; 18,587; ZIP 54494.
Wo·burn (wō′bərn, wōō′-) city, E Massachusetts; 37,406; ZIP 01801*.

Wol·cott (wŏŏl′kət) city, s Connecticut; 12,495; ZIP 06716.
Wood·bine-Rad·nor-Glen·cliff (wŏŏd′bīn, rad′nər, glen′-klif) uninc. place, N CEN. Tennessee; 14,485; ZIP see NASH-VILLE.
Wood·bridge (wŏŏd′brij) city, s Connecticut; 7,673; ZIP 06501.
— urb. twp., NE New Jersey; 98,944; ZIP 07095.
Woodbridge-Ma·rum·so (mə-rum′sō) city, NE Virginia; 25,412; ZIP 22191.
Wood·burn (wŏŏd′bûrn) city, NW Oregon; 7,495; ZIP 97071.
Wood·bur·y (wŏŏd′ber′ē, -bə-bē) city, NW Connecticut; 5,869; ZIP 06798.
— city, SE Minnesota; 6,184; ZIP 55798.
— city, SW New Jersey; 12,408; ZIP 08096*.
Wood·cliff (wŏŏd′klif) city, NE New Jersey; 5,506; ZIP 07675.
— city, NE Illinois; 8,831; ZIP 60191.
Wood·land (wŏŏd′lənd) city, CEN. California; 20,677; ZIP 95695*.
Wood·lawn-Woodmoor (wŏŏd′lôn) uninc. place, N Maryland; 28,811.
Wood·mere (wŏŏd·mir′) uninc. place, SE New York; 19,831; ZIP 11598.
Wood·mont-Green Hills-Glen·dale (wŏŏd′mont, glen′-dāl) uninc. place, N CEN. Tennessee; 23,161.
Wood·ridge (wŏŏd′rij′) city, NE Illinois; 11,028; ZIP 60515.
Wood-Ridge (wŏŏd′·rij′) boro., NE New Jersey; 8,311; ZIP see RUTHERFORD.
Wood River city, SW Illinois; 13,186; ZIP 62095.
Wood·son Terrace (wŏŏd′sən) city, E Missouri; 5,936.
Wood·stock (wŏŏd′stok) city, N Illinois; 10,226; ZIP 60098.
Wood·stock (wŏŏd′stok) city, s Ontario, Canada; 24,027.
Wood·ward (wŏŏd′wərd) city, NW Oklahoma; 8,710; ZIP 73801.
Woon·sock·et (wŏŏn·sok′it) city, NE Rhode Island; 46,820; ZIP 02895.
Woos·ter (wŏŏs′tər) city, N CEN. Ohio; 18,703; ZIP 44691*.
Worces·ter (wŏŏs′tər) city, CEN. Massachusetts; 176,572; ZIP 01600*.
Wor·land (wûr′lənd) city, N CEN. Wyoming; 5,055; ZIP 82401.
Worms (wûrmz, vôrms) city, SW West Germany; 63,545.
Worth (wûrth) vill., NE Illinois; 11,999; ZIP 60482.
Wor·thing·ton (wûr′thing·tən) city, SW Minnesota; 9,825; ZIP 56187.
— city CEN. Ohio; 15,326; ZIP 43085.
Wren·tham (ren′thəm) city, CEN. Massachusetts; 7,315; ZIP 02093.
Wright-Pat·ter·son (rīt′pat′ər·sən) city, SW Ohio; 10,151.
Wro·claw (vrô′tswäf, -tsläf) city, SW Poland; 509,400.
Wu·han (wŏŏ′hän′) city, E CEN. China; 2,146,000.
Wup·per·tal (vŏŏp′ər·täl) city, W West Germany; 422,906.
Wurt·smith (wûrt′smith) city, NE Michigan; 6,932.
Würt·tem·berg (wûr′təm·bûrg, vür′təm·berkh) former state, SW Germany.
Würz·burg (wûrts′bûrg, vürts′bŏŏrkh) city, s CEN. West Germany; 121,707.
Wy·an·dotte (wī′ən·dot, wīn′dot) city, SE Michigan; 41,061; ZIP 48192*.
Wyck·off (wī′kof) urb. twp., NE New Jersey; 16,039; ZIP 07481.
Wynne City (win) city, E CEN. Arkansas; 6,696; ZIP 72396.
Wy·o·ming (wī·ō′ming) state, NW United States; 97,914 sq. mi.; 332,416; cap. Cheyenne.
— city, W Michigan; 56,560; ZIP see GRAND RAPIDS.
— city, SW Ohio; 9,089.
Wy·o·mis·sing (wī′ō·mis′ing) boro., SE Pennsylvania; 7,136; ZIP see READING.
Wythe·ville (with′vil, -vəl) town, SW Virginia; 6,069; ZIP 24382.

Xe·ni·a (zē′nē·ə) city, SW CEN. Ohio; 25,373; ZIP 45385.

Yak·i·ma (yak′ə·mə) city, s Washington; 45,588; ZIP 98901*.
Yal·ta (yäl′tə, yôl′-) city, s Crimea; scene of a conference of Roosevelt, Churchill, and Stalin in February, 1945; 55,000.
Ya·lu (yä′lŏŏ) river forming part of the boundary betw. NE China and Korea; 500 mi. long.
Yang·tze (yang′tsē′) river flowing from Tibet to the East China Sea; 3,600 mi. long.
Yank·ton (yangk′tən) city, SE South Dakota; 11,919; ZIP 57078.
Yap·hank (yap′hangk) city, SE New York; 5,460.
Yar·mouth (yär′məth) town, SW Nova Scotia, Canada; 8,319.
Yar·mouth (yär′məth) city, E Massachusetts; 12,033; ZIP 02675.

Yellow River Hwang Ho: *an alternate name.*
Yellow Sea inlet of the Pacific betw. Korea and China; 400 mi. long, 400 mi. wide.
Yel·low·stone Falls (yel′ō·stōn) 2 waterfalls of the Yellowstone River in Yellowstone National Park: Upper Yellowstone Falls, 109 ft.; **Lower Yellowstone Falls,** 308 ft.
Yellowstone National Park largest and oldest of the US national parks, largely in NW Wyoming; 3,458 sq. mi.; established, 1872.
Yellowstone River river, NW Wyoming, SE Montana, and NW North Dakota; 671 mi. long.
Yem·en (yem′ən), People's Democratic Republic of country, s Arabian penin.; 111,000 sq. mi.; 1,800,000; cap. Aden. Also Southern Yemen.
Yemen Arab Republic country, SW Arabian penin.; 75,000 sq. mi.; 7,000,000; cap Sana. Also **Yemen.**
Yo·ko·ha·ma (yō′kə·hä′mə) city, CEN. Honshu, Japan; 1,976,111.
Yon·kers (yong′kərz) city, SE New York; 204,370; ZIP 10700*.
Yor·ba Lin·da (yôr′bə lin′də) city, SW California; 11,865
York (yôrk) co. boro., CEN. Yorkshire, England; cap.; 108,600.
York (yôrk) city, SW Maine; 5,690; ZIP 03909.
— city, SE Nebraska; 6,778; ZIP 68467*.
— city, s Pennsylvania; 50,335; ZIP 17400*.
York·shire (yôrk′shir, -shər) co., NE England, divided into East Riding, West Riding, and North Riding; 6,080 sq. mi.; 3,675,000; cap. York.
York·ton (yôrk′tən) city, SE Saskatchewan, Canada; 12,645.
York·town (yôrk′toun) city, N CEN. South Carolina; 5,081.
Yo·sem·i·te Valley (yō·sem′ə·tē) gorge in **Yosemite National Park** (1,183 sq. mi., established 1890), E CEN. California; 7 mi. long, 1 mi. wide; traversed by the Merced River that forms **Yosemite Falls,** Upper Fall, 1,430 ft.; Lower Fall, 320 ft.; with intermediate cascades, 2,425 ft.
Youngs·town (yungz′toun′) city, NE Ohio; 139,788; ZIP 44500*.
Y·pres (ē′pr′) town, NW Belgium; site of three major battles of World War I, 1914, 1915, 1917; ab. 18,000.
Yp·si·lan·ti (ip·si·lan′tē) city, SE Michigan; 29,538; ZIP 48197.
Y·re·ka City (wī·rē′kə) city, SW California; 19,284; ZIP 96097.
Yu·ba City (yōō′bə) city, N CEN. California; 13,986; ZIP 95991.
Yu·cai·pa (yōō·kī′pə) city, SW California; 19,284; ZIP 92399.
Yu·ca·tán (yōō′kə·tan′) penin., SE Mexico and NE Central America; 70,000 sq. mi.
Yu·go·sla·vi·a (yōō′gō·slä′vē·ə), **Federal People's Republic of** republic, SE Europe; 98,538 sq. mi.; 20,859,000; cap. Belgrade.
Yu·kon (yōō′kon) terr., NW Canada; 207,076 sq. mi.; 14,382; cap. Whitehorse.
Yu·kon (yōō′kon) city, CEN. Oklahoma; 8,411; ZIP 73099.
Yukon River river, NW Canada and CEN. Alaska; 2,300 mi. long.
Yu·ma (yōō′mə) city, SW Arizona; 29,007; ZIP 85364.

Za·greb (zä′greb) city, CEN. Croatia, Yugoslavia; cap.; 471,000.
Zaire Republic (zâr) republic, CEN. Africa; 904,754 sq. mi.; 13,653,000; cap. Kinshasa.
Zam·be·zi (zam·bē′zē) river, s Africa; 1,700 mi. long.
Zam·bi·a (zam′bē·ə) independent member of the Commonwealth of Nations, s CEN. Africa; 288,130 sq. mi.; 4,442,000; cap. Lusaka.
Zanes·ville (zānz′vil) city, SE CEN. Ohio; 33,045; ZIP 43701*.
Zan·zi·bar (zan′zə·bär, zan′zə·bär′) reg. of Tanzania off the coast of E Africa; comprises isls. of Zanzibar (640 sq. mi.) and Pemba (380 sq. mi.); 315,000. — city, W Zanzibar; cap.; 57,923.
Zea·land (zē′lənd) isl. of Denmark betw. the Kattegat and the Baltic Sea; 2,709 sq. mi.
Zim·ba·bwe Rho·de·sia (zim·bä′bwe rō·dē′zhə) republic, South Africa; 150,685 sq. mi.; 7,000,000; cap. Salisbury. Also Zim·ba′bwe.
Zi·on (zī′ən) city, NE Illinois; 17,268; ZIP 60099.
Zu·lu·land (zŏŏ′lŏŏ·land′) dist., NE Natal, South Africa; formerly a native kingdom; 10,362 sq. mi.
Zu·rich (zŏŏr′ik) canton, NE Switzerland; 667 sq. mi.; 952,000. — city, CEN. Zurich; cap.; 432,500.
Zuy·der Zee (zī′dər zē) former shallow inlet of the North Sea, NW Netherlands; drainage projects have reclaimed much of the land and formed Lake Ijssel. Also **Zui′der Zee.**

Ad·ams (ad′əmz) A prominent Massachusetts family, including **John,** 1735–1826, second president of the U.S. 1797–1801, signer of the Declaration of Independence; his son **John Quincy,** 1767–1848, sixth president of the U.S. 1825–1829; **Henry,** 1838–1918, historian and author; **Samuel,** 1722–1803, patriot, signer of the Declaration of Independence.

Ad·di·son (ad′ə·sən), **Joseph,** 1672–1719, Eng. essayist.

Ad·en·au·er (ad′n·ou′ər, *Ger.* ä′dən·ou′ər). **Konrad,** 1876–1967, Chancellor of the Federal Republic of Germany, 1949–1963.

Ad·ler (ad′lər), **Alfred,** 1870–1937, Austrian psychiatrist.

Aes·chy·lus (es′kə·ləs), 525–456 B.C., Gk. tragic dramatist.

Ae·sop (ē′səp, ē′sop), 6th-c. B.C. Gk. compiler of fables.

Ag·as·siz (ag′ə·sē, *Fr.* à·gà·sē′), **(Jean) Louis (Rodolphe)** 1807–73, U.S. naturalist born in Switzerland.

Al·a·ric (al′ə·rik), 370?–410, Visigoth king; sacked Rome.

Al·cott (ôl′kət, -kot), **Louisa May,** 1832–88, U.S. novelist.

Al·den (ôl′dən), **John,** 1599–1687, Pilgrim settler in Plymouth Colony (1620); a character in Longfellow's poem *The Courtship of Miles Standish.*

Al·ex·an·der VI (al′ig·zan′dər, -zän′-) See (Rodrigo) BORGIA.

Alexander Nev·ski (nev′skē, nef′-), 1220?–63, Russ. hero.

Alexander the Great, 356–323 B.C., king of Macedon 336–323; conqueror of the Persian Empire.

Al·fred (al′frid), 849–899, king of Wessex and overlord of England 871–899: called **the Great.**

Al·len (al′ən), **Ethan,** 1737–89, Amer. soldier.

Am·brose (am′brōz), **Saint,** 340?–397, bishop of Milan; one of the Latin church fathers.

Amerigo Vespucci See VESPUCCI.

A·mund·sen (ä′mŏŏn·sən), **Roald,** 1872–1928, Norw. explorer; discovered South Pole, 1911.

An·der·sen (an′dər·sən), **Hans Christian,** 1805–75, Dan. writer of fairy tales.

An·dre·a del Sar·to (än·drā′ä del sär′tō) See SARTO.

An·gel·i·co (än·jel′i·kō), **Fra,** 1387–1455, Giovanni da Fiesole, Florentine painter and monk: original name **Guido di Pi·e·tro** (dē pē·ā′trō).

Anne (an), 1665–1714, queen of Great Britain and Ireland 1702–14.

An·tho·ny (an′thə·nē, -tə-), **Saint,** 250?–356?, Egyptian hermit and monk; founder of monastic life.

An·tho·ny (an′thə·nē), **Susan Brownell,** 1820–1906, U.S. suffragist.

An·to·ni·nus (an′tə·nī′nəs) See AURELIUS.

An·to·ny (an′tə·nē), **Mark,** Anglicized name of **Marcus An·to·ni·us** (an·tō′nē·əs), 83–30 B.C., Roman general; triumvir.

A·qui·nas (ə·kwī′nəs), **St. Thomas,** 1225?–74, Ital. Dominican monk and theologian: called **the Angelic Doctor.**

Ar·chi·me·des (är′kə·mē′dēz), 287?–212 B.C., Gk. mathematician born in Sicily.

Ar·is·toph·a·nes (ar′is·tof′ə·nēz), 450?–380? B.C. Gk. comic dramatist.

Ar·is·tot·le (ar′is·tot′l), 384–322 B.C., Gk. philosopher; pupil of Plato and teacher of Alexander the Great.

Arm·strong (ärm′strông′), **Neil Alden,** born 1930, U.S. astronaut; first man to walk on the moon, July 20, 1969.

Ar·nold (är′nəld), **Matthew,** 1822–88, Eng. poet and critic.

A·rou·et (à·rwe′), **François Marie** See VOLTAIRE.

Ar·thur (är′thər), **Chester Alan,** 1830–86, 21st president of the U.S. 1881–85.

A·ta·türk (ä·tä·türk′) See KEMAL ATATÜRK.

At·ti·la (at′ə·lə, ə·til′ə), 406?–453, king of the Huns.

Attlee, Clement Richard, Earl, 1883–1967, Eng. statesman; prime minister 1945–51.

Au·den (ô′dən), **W(ystan) H(ugh),** 1907–1973, U.S. poet born in England.

Au·du·bon (ô′də·bon), **John James,** 1785–1851, U.S. ornithologist born in Haiti.

Au·gus·tine (ô′gəs·tēn, ô·gus′tin), **Saint,** 354–430, bishop of Hippo; one of the Latin church fathers.

Au·gus·tus Cae·sar (ô·gus′təs sē′zər), 63 B.C.–A.D. 14, Gaius Julius Caesar Octavianus, the first Roman emperor 27 B.C.–A.D. 14: before 27 B.C. called *Octavian.*

Au·re·li·us (ô·rē′lē·əs, ô·rēl′yəs), **Marcus,** 121–180, Roman emperor, 161–180, and Stoic philosopher: full name **Marcus Aurelius An·to·ni·nus** (an′tə·nī′nəs).

Aus·ten (ôs′tən), **Jane,** 1775–1817, Eng. novelist.

A·vo·ga·dro (ä′vō·gä′drō), **Amedeo,** 1776–1856, Conte de Quaregna, Ital. physicist.

Bach (bäkh) A family of Ger. musicians and composers, of whom the best known are **Johann Sebastian,** 1685–1750, and his sons, **Karl Philipp Emanuel,** 1714–88, and **Johann Christian,** 1735–82.

Ba·con (bā′kən), **Francis,** 1561–1626, first Baron Verulam, Viscount St. Albans, Eng. philosopher, essayist, and statesman. — **Roger,** 1214?–94, Eng. scientist and philosopher.

Bal·bo·a (bal·bō′ə, *Sp.* bäl·vō′ä), **Vasco Núñez de,** 1475–1517, Sp. explorer; discovered the Pacific Ocean, 1513.

Bal·zac (bal′zak, bôl′-; *Fr.* bàl·zàk′), **Honoré de,** 1799–1850, Fr. novelist.

Bar·ba·ros·sa (bär′bə·ros′ə) Nickname of FREDERICK I.

Bar·ber (bär′bər), **Samuel,** born 1910, U.S. composer.

Bar·num (bär′nəm), **P(hineas) T(aylor),** 1810–91, U.S. showman.

Barth (bärt), **Karl,** 1886–1968, Swiss theologian.

Bar·tók (bär′tôk), **Béla,** 1881–1945, Hung. composer.

Bar·ton (bär′tən), **Clara,** 1821–1912, U.S. founder of the Amer. Red Cross.

Baude·laire (bōd·lâr′), **Charles Pierre,** 1821–67, Fr. poet.

Beard (bird), **Charles Austin,** 1874–1948, U.S. historian.

Beau·har·nais (bō·àr·ne′), **Josephine de** See JOSEPHINE.

Beck·et (bek′it), **Saint Thomas à** See THOMAS À BECKET.

Beck·ett (bek′it), **Samuel,** born 1906, Irish poet, novelist, and playwright.

Becque·rel (bek·rel′), **Antoine Henri,** 1852–1908, Fr. physicist.

Bede (bēd), **Saint,** 673?–735, Eng. theologian and historian: called the Venerable Bede. Also **Be·da** (bē′də).

Bee·be (bē′bē), **(Charles) William,** 1877–1962, U.S. naturalist and explorer.

Bee·tho·ven (bā′tō·vən), **Ludwig van,** 1770–1827, Ger. composer.

Bell (bel), **Alexander Graham,** 1847–1922, U.S. scientist born in Scotland; inventor of the telephone.

Ben·e·dict of Nur·si·a (ben′ə·dikt əv nûr′se·ə, nur′shē·ə, -shə), **Saint,** 480?–543, Ital. monk; founder of the Benedictine Order.

Ben-Gur·i·on (ben gŏŏr′ē·ən), **David,** 1886–1973, Israeli statesman born in Poland; prime minister 1948–53, 1955–57, 1958–1963.

Ben·tham (ben′thəm), **Jeremy,** 1748–1832, Eng. jurist and philosopher.

Berg (berkh), **Alban,** 1885–1935, Austrian composer.

Berg·son (berg′sən, *Fr.* berg·sôn′), **Henri Louis,** 1859–1941, Fr. philosopher.

Berke·ley (bûrk′le, *Brit.* bärk′-), **George,** 1685–1753, Irish Anglican prelate and philosopher.

Ber·li·oz (ber′lē·ōz), **Hector,** 1803–69, Fr. composer.

Bern·hardt (bûrn′härt, *Fr.* ber·nàr′), **Sarah,** 1844–1923, Fr. actress: orig. name **Rosine Ber·nard** (ber·nàr′).

Ber·ni·ni (ber·nē′nē), **Giovanni Lorenzo,** 1598–1680, Ital. sculptor and architect.

Ber·noul·li (bûr·nōō′le, *Fr.* ber·nōō·ye′), **Daniel,** 1700–82, Swiss mathematician.

Ber·ze·li·us (bər·zē′lē·əs, *Sw.* ber·sä′lē·ōōs), **Baron Jöns Jacob,** 1779–1848, Sw. chemist.

Bes·se·mer (bes′ə·mər), **Sir Henry,** 1813–98, Eng. engineer.

Beyle (bāl), **Marie Henri** See STENDHAL.

Bis·marck (biz′märk) **Prince Otto Eduard Leopold von,** 1815–98, Ger. statesman; founder of the Ger. Empire: called **the Iron Chancellor.**

Bi·zet (bē·zā′), **Georges,** 1838–75, Fr. composer: orig. name **Alexandre César Léopold Bizet.**

Black·stone (blak′stōn′, -stən), **Sir William,** 1723–80, Eng. jurist.

Blake (blāk), **William,** 1757–1827, Eng. poet and artist.

Blas·co-I·bá·ñez (bläs′kō·ē·vä′nyäth), **Vicente,** 1867–1928, Sp. novelist.

Blé·riot (blā·ryō′), **Louis,** 1872–1936, Fr. aviator and inventor.

Boc·cac·ci·o (bō·kä′chē·ō, *Ital.* bōk·kät′chō), **Giovanni,** 1313–75, Ital. writer and poet; author of the *Decameron.*

Bohr (bōr), **Niels,** 1885–1962, Dan. physicist.

Bol·eyn (bŏŏl′in, bō·lin′), **Anne,** 1507–36, second wife of Henry VIII of England; beheaded.

Bol·ing·broke (bol′ing·brŏŏk, bŏŏl′-) See HENRY IV (of England).

Bol·i·var (bol′ə·vər, -vär; *Sp.* bō·lē′vär), **Simón,** 1783–1830, Venezuelan general and statesman; liberated South America.

Bo·na·parte (bō′nə·pärt) A prominent Corsican Fr. family including: **Napoleon,** 1769–1821, Fr. military leader and conqueror; emperor of France 1804–15 as **Napoleon I;** **Joseph,** 1768–1844, king of Naples 1806–08, of Spain 1808–1813; and **Louis Napoleon,** 1808–73, emperor of France 1852–70 as **Napoleon III.** Also **Buonaparte.**

Boone (bōōn), **Daniel,** 1735?–1820, Amer. frontiersman in Kentucky and Missouri.

Booth (bōōth), **William,** 1829–1912, Eng. religious leader, founder of the Salvation Army: called **General Booth.** — **Edwin Thomas,** 1833–93, U.S. actor; his brother **John Wilkes,** 1838–65, U.S. actor; assassinated Abraham Lincoln.

Bor·gia (bôr′jä) An Italian aristocratic family of Spanish origin, including **Rodrigo,** 1431?–1503, pope 1492–1503 as *Alexander VI:* his children, **Cesare,** 1475?–1507, soldier and statesman, and **Lucrezia,** 1480–1519, duchess of Ferrara.

Bor·o·din (bôr′ə·dĕn), **Aleksandr Porfirevich**, 1834–87, Russ. composer.

Bosch (bos), **Hieronymus**, 1450?–1516, Du. painter.

Bos·well (boz′wel, -wəl), **James**, 1746–95, Scot. lawyer and writer; biographer of Samuel Johnson.

Bot·ti·cel·li (bot′ə·chel′ē), **Sandro**, 1447?–1515, Florentine painter: orig. name **Alessandro di Mariano dei Fi·li·pe·pi** (fē·lē·pā′pē).

Boyle (boil), **Robert**, 1627–91, Eng. chemist and physicist, born in Ireland.

Boz (boz) See DICKENS.

Brahms (brämz, *Ger.* bräms), **Johannes**, 1833–97, Ger. composer.

Bra·man·te (brä·män′tā), **Donato d'Agnolo**, 1444–1514, Ital. architect and painter.

Braque (bräk), **Georges**, 1882–1963, Fr. painter.

Brecht (brekht), **Bertolt**, 1898–1956, Ger. playwright and poet.

Breu·ghel (broe′gəl) See BRUEGHEL.

Brezh·nev (bryezh·nyôf′), **Leonid Ilyich**, born 1906, Soviet statesman; first secretary of the Communist party 1964–; president 1977–.

Bron·të (bron′tē), **Anne**, 1820–49, and her sisters, **Charlotte**, 1816–55, and **Emily Jane**, 1818–48, Eng. novelists. Pseudonyms, respectively, **Acton**, **Currer**, and **Ellis Bell**.

Brown (broun), **John**, 1800–59, U.S. abolitionist; led raid on arsenal at Harper's Ferry; hanged for treason.

Brown·ing (brou′ning), **Elizabeth Barrett**, 1806–61, Eng. poet; wife of Robert. — **Robert**, 1812–89, Eng. poet.

Broz (brōz), **Josip** See TITO.

Brue·ghel (broe′gəl) A family of Flemish painters, esp., **Pieter**, 1520?–69, known as **the Elder**, and his sons, **Pieter**, 1564?–1638?, known as **the Younger**, and **Jan**, 1568–1625. Also spelled *Breughel*: also **Brue′gel**.

Bru·nel·les·chi (broō′nāl·les′kē), **Filippo**, 1377–1446, Florentine architect and sculptor. Also **Bru·nel·les′co** (-les′kō).

Bru·tus (broō′təs), **Marcus Junius**, 85?–42 B.C., Roman politician and general; one of Caesar's assassins.

Bry·an (brī′ən), **William Jennings**, 1860–1925, U.S. statesman and orator.

Bu·ber (boō′bər), **Martin**, 1878–1965, Austrian Jewish religious philosopher.

Buchanan (byoō·kan′ən), **James**, 1791–1868, 15th president of the U.S. 1857–61.

Bud·dha (boōd′ə, boō′də) **Gautama** or **Gotama Siddhartha**, 563?–483? B.C., the founder of Buddhism.

Buf·fa·lo Bill (buf′ə·lō) See CODY.

Bun·yan (bun′yən), **John**, 1628–88, Eng. preacher and author of *Pilgrim's Progress*.

Buo·na·par·te (bwô′nä·pär′tā) See BONAPARTE.

Buo·nar·ro·ti (bwô′när·rô′tē) See MICHELANGELO.

Bur·bank (bûr′bangk), **Luther**, 1849–1926, U.S. horticulturist.

Burg·er (bûr′gər), **Warren Earl**, born 1907, U.S. jurist; chief justice of the Supreme Court 1969–.

Bur·goyne (bər·goin′), **John**, 1722–92, Brit. general in the Amer. Revolution.

Burke (bûrk), **Edmund**, 1729–97, Brit. statesman, writer, and orator born in Ireland.

Burns (bûrnz), **Robert**, 1759–96, Scot. poet.

Burr (bûr), **Aaron**, 1756–1836, Amer. lawyer and statesman, vice president of the U.S. 1801–05.

But·ler (but′lər), **Samuel**, 1835–1902, Eng. novelist.

Byrd (bûrd), **Richard Evelyn**, 1888–1957, U.S. rear admiral, aviator, polar explorer, and writer.

By·ron (bī′rən), **Lord**, 1788–1824, George Gordon Noel, 6th Baron Byron, Eng. poet.

Cab·ot (kab′ət), **John**, Anglicized name of **Giovanni Ca·bo·to** (kä·bō′tō), 1451?–98, Venetian seafarer and explorer.

Cæd·mon (kad′mən), 7th-c. Eng. poet.

Cae·sar (sē′zər), **Gaius Julius**, 100–44 B.C., Roman general, statesman, and historian.

Cal·vin (kal′vin), **John**, 1509–64, Fr. Protestant reformer.

Ca·mus (kä·mü′), **Albert**, 1913–60, Fr. writer.

Ca·pet (kā′pit, kap′it, *Fr.* kȧ·pe′) See HUGH CAPET.

Ca·ra·vag·gio (kä′rä·väd′jō), **Michelangelo Amerighi da**, 1569–1609, Ital. painter.

Car·lyle (kär·līl′), **Thomas**, 1795–1881, Scot. essayist.

Car·ne·gie (kär·nā′gē, -neg′ē, kär′nə·gē), **Andrew**, 1835–1919, U.S. industrialist and philanthropist born in Scotland.

Car·roll (kar′əl), **Lewis** Pseud. of *Charles Lutwidge Dodgson*, 1832–98, Eng. mathematician; author of *Alice in Wonderland*.

Car·ter (kär′tər). **Jimmy (James Earl, Jr.)**, born 1924, 39th president of the U.S., 1977–.

Ca·ru·so (kä·roō′sō, *Ital.* kä·roō′zō), **Enrico**, 1873–1921, Ital. operatic tenor.

Car·ver (kär′vər), **George Washington**, 1864–1943, U.S. botanist and chemist.

Ca·sals (kä·säls′), **Pablo**, 1876–1973, Sp. violoncellist, conductor, and composer.

Cas·a·no·va (kas′ə·nō′və, kaz′-; *Ital.* kä′sä·nô′vä), **Giovanni Giacomo**, 1725–98, Ital. adventurer; known for his *Memoirs*; full surname **Casanova de Sein·galt** (dä sīn′gält).

Cas·tro (käs′trō, kas′-), **Fidel**, born 1926, Cuban revolutionary leader; premier 1959–: full name **Fidel Castro Ruz** (roōth).

Cath·e·rine II (kath′rin, -ər·in), 1729–96, empress of Russia: called **Catherine the Great**.

Ca·to (kā′tō), **Marcus Porcius**, 234–149 B.C., Roman statesman: called **the Elder** or **the Censor**. — **Marcus Porcius**, 95–46 B.C., Roman patriot and Stoic philosopher: called **U·ti·cen·sis** (yoō′ti·ken′səs) or **the Younger**.

Cav·en·dish (kav′ən·dish), **Henry**, 1731?–1810, Eng. chemist.

Cel·li·ni (chə·lē′nē, *Ital.* chel·lē′nē), **Benvenuto**, 1500–71, Ital. sculptor and goldsmith; known for his autobiography.

Cer·van·tes (sər·van′tēz, *Sp.* ther·vän′täs), **Miguel de**, 1547–1616, Sp. novelist and dramatist; author of *Don Quixote*: full surname **Cervantes Sa·a·ve·dra** (sä′ä·vä′thrä).

Cé·zanne (sā·zȧn′), **Paul**, 1839–1906, Fr. painter.

Chap·lin (chap′lən), **Charles Spencer**, 1889–1977, Eng. motion-picture actor and producer formerly active in the U.S.: called **Charlie Chaplin**.

Char·le·magne (shär′lə·mān), 742?–814, king of the Franks 768–814; emperor of the West as **Charles I** 800–814: called **Charles the Great**.

Charles I (chärlz), 1600–49, Charles Stuart, king of England 1625–49; beheaded.

Charles II, 1630–85, king of England 1660–85.

Chat·ham (chat′əm), **Earl of** See PITT.

Chau·cer (chô′sər), **Geoffrey**, 1340?–1400, Eng. poet.

Che·khov (chek′ôf), **Anton Pavlovich**, 1860–1904, Russ. dramatist and story writer: also *Tchekhov*. Also **Che′kov**.

Che·ops (kē′ops) Egyptian king of the 4th dynasty (about 2900 B.C.), builder of the Great Pyramid at Giza: also **Khu·fu** (koō′foō).

Chiang Kai-shek (chyäng′ kī′shek′, chang′; *Chinese* jyäng′), 1886–1975, Chinese generalissimo; head of the Republic of China: orig. name **Chiang Chung-cheng**.

Cho·pin (shō′pan, *Fr.* shō·pań′), **Frédéric François**, 1810–1849, Polish composer and pianist active in France.

Chou En-lai (jō′en′lī′), 1898–1976, Chinese statesman; foreign minister 1949–58; premier of the People's Republic of China 1949–1976.

Christ (krist) See JESUS.

Chris·to·pher (kris′tə·fər), **Saint**, 3rd-c. Christian martyr.

Church·ill (chûrch′il, -əl), **Sir Winston (Leonard Spencer)**, 1874–1965, Brit. statesman and author; prime minister 1940–45, 1951–55.

Cic·e·ro (sis′ə·rō), **Marcus Tullius**, 106–43 B.C., Roman statesman, orator, and author; also called *Tully*.

Cid (sid, *Sp.* thēth), **the**, 1044?–99, Rodrigo Díaz de Bivar, Sp. epic hero; champion in wars against the Moors. Also called **El Cid Cam·pe·a·dor** (kam′pā·ȧ·thôr′).

Ci·ma·bu·e (chē′mä·boō′ā), **Giovanni**, 1240?–1302?, Florentine painter.

Clark (klärk), **Charles Joseph**, born 1939, Canadian statesman; prime minister 1979.

Clau·se·witz (klou′zə·vits), **Karl von**, 1780–1831, Prussian general and military scientist.

Clay (klā), **Henry**, 1777–1852, U.S. statesman and orator.

Cle·men·ceau (klem′ən·sō′, *Fr.* kle·män·sō′), **Georges Eugène**, 1841–1929, Fr. statesman; premier 1906–09, 1917–20: called **the Tiger**.

Clem·ens (klem′ənz), **Samuel Langhorne** See MARK TWAIN.

Cle·o·pat·ra (klē·ə·pat′rə, -pā′trə, -pä′trə), 69–30 B.C.; queen of Egypt 51–49 B.C., 48–30 B.C.; committed suicide.

Cleve·land (klēv′lənd), **(Stephen) Grover**, 1837–1908, 22nd and 24th president of the U.S. 1885–89, 1893–97.

Co·dy (kō′dē), **William Frederick**, 1846–1917, U.S. plainsman, army scout, and showman: called *Buffalo Bill*.

Cœur de Li·on (kûr′ də lē′ən) See RICHARD I.

Cole·ridge (kōl′rij), **Samuel Taylor**, 1772–1834, Eng. poet and critic.

Co·lum·bus (kə·lum′bəs), **Christopher**, 1446?–1506, Genoese seafarer and explorer; discovered America for Spain Oct. 12, 1492. Sp. **Cristóbal Co·lón** (kō·lōn′), Ital. **Cristoforo Co·lom·bo** (kō·lōm′bō).

Comte (kônt, *Fr.* kônt), **Auguste**, 1798–1857, Fr. philosopher.

Con·fu·cius (kən·fyoō′shəs), 551?–478? B.C., Chinese philosopher and teacher. Chinese **K'ung Fu-tse** (koōng′ foō′tse′).

Con·rad (kon′rad), **Joseph**, 1857–1924, Eng. author born in

Poland: orig. name **Teodor Józef Konrad Kor·ze·niow·ski** (kôr'ze·nyôf'skē).

Con·stan·tine I (kon'stən·tēn, -tīn), 288?–337, first Christian emperor of Rome; founder of the Byzantine Empire: called **the Great.**

Cook (kŏŏk), **Captain James,** 1728–79, Eng. seafarer and explorer.

Coo·lidge (kōō'lij), **(John) Calvin,** 1872–1933, 30th president of the U.S. 1923–29.

Coop·er (kōō'pər, kŏŏp'ər), **James Fenimore,** 1789–1851, U.S. novelist.

Co·per·ni·cus (kō·pûr'nə·kəs), **Nicholas,** Lat. name of **Mikofaj Ko·per·nik** (kō·pûr'nĕk), 1473–1543, Polish astronomer.

Cop·land (kŏp'lənd), **Aaron,** born 1900, U.S. composer.

Cor·neille (kôr·nā', _Fr._ kôr·nā'y'), **Pierre,** 1606–84, Fr. dramatist.

Corn·wal·lis (kôrn·wôl'is, -wol'-), **Charles,** 1738–1805, first Marquis Cornwallis, Eng. general and statesman.

Co·ro·na·do (kôr'ə·nä'dō, _Sp._ kō'rō·nä'thō), **Francisco Vásquez de,** 1510–54, Sp. explorer.

Cor·tés (kôr·tez', _Sp._ kôr·tās'), **Hernando,** 1485–1547, Sp. conquistador; conqueror of Mexico. Also **Cor·tez'.**

Cra·nach (krä'näkh), **Lucas,** 1472–1533, Ger. painter.

Crane (krān), **(Harold) Hart,** 1899–1932, U.S. poet. — **Stephen,** 1871–1900, U.S. writer.

Crock·ett (krok'it), **David,** 1786–1836, Amer. frontiersman and politician; killed at the Alamo: called **Davy Crockett.**

Crom·well (krom'wel), **Oliver,** 1599–1658, Eng. general and statesman; lord protector of England 1653–58.

Crookes (krŏŏks), **Sir William,** 1832–1919, Eng. physicist and chemist.

Cu·rie (kyŏŏr'ē, kyŏŏr·ē'; _Fr._ kü·rē'), 1867–1934, **Marie,** _née_ Sklodowska, born in Poland, and her husband **Pierre,** 1859–1906, Fr. physicists, discoverers of radium.

Cu·vi·er (kōō'vē·ā, _Fr._ kü·vyā'), **Baron Georges,** 1769–1832, Fr. naturalist.

Cyr·il (sir'əl), **Saint,** 827–869, Christian scholar and missionary: called **Apostle of the Slavs.**

Dal·ton (dôl'ten), **John,** 1766–1844, Eng. chemist and physicist.

Dan·te A·li·ghie·ri (dän'tä ä'lē·gyä'rē, dan'tē), 1265–1321, Ital. poet; author of the _Divine Comedy_: orig. name **Durante Alighieri.**

Dar·win (där'win), **Charles Robert,** 1809–82, Eng. naturalist.

Dau·mier (dō·myā'), **Honoré,** 1808–79, Fr. painter and caricaturist.

da Vin·ci (də vin'chē, _Ital._ dä vēn'chē), **Leonardo,** 1452–1519, Florentine painter, sculptor, architect, and inventor.

Da·vis (dā'vis), **Jefferson,** 1808–89, U.S. statesman; president of the Confederacy 1862–65.

Da·vy (dā'vē), **Sir Humphry,** 1778–1829, Eng. scientist.

De·bus·sy (də·byōō'sē, _Fr._ də·bü·sē'), **Claude (Achille),** 1862–1918, Fr. composer.

De·foe (di·fō'), **Daniel,** 1660–1731, Eng. novelist and political journalist. Also **De Foe.**

De For·est (di fôr'est, for'-), **Lee,** 1873–1961, U.S. inventor; pioneer in radio transmission.

De·gas (də·gä'), **(Hilaire Germaine) Edgar,** 1834–1917, Fr. impressionist painter.

de Gaulle (də gôl', _Fr._ də gōl'), **Charles André Joseph Marie,** 1890–1970, Fr. general and statesman; president 1944–45, 1959–1969.

De·la·croix (də·là·krwä'), **(Ferdinand Victor) Eugène,** 1799–1863, Fr. painter.

del Sar·to (dāl sär'tō), **Andrea** See SARTO.

De Quin·cey (di kwin'sē), **Thomas,** 1785–1859, Eng. essayist.

Des·cartes (dā·kärt'), **René,** 1596–1650, Fr. mathematician and philosopher.

De So·to (də sō'tō), **Hernando,** 1500?–42, Sp. explorer; discovered the Mississippi River, 1541.

De Va·le·ra (dev'ə·lâr'ə, dä'və·lir'ə), **Eamon,** 1882–1975, Irish statesman born in the U.S.; prime minister 1937–48, 1951–54, 1957–59, president 1959–73.

Dew·ey (dōō'ē, dyōō'ē), **George,** 1837–1917, U.S. admiral in the Spanish-Amer. War. — **John,** 1859–1952, U.S. philosopher, psychologist, and educator.

Dí·az de Bi·var (dē'äth thä bē·vär') See CID.

Dick·ens (dik'ənz), **Charles (John Huffam),** 1812–70, Eng. novelist: pseud. **Boz** (boz).

Dick·in·son (dik'ən·sən), **Emily (Elizabeth),** 1830–86, U.S. poet.

Di·de·rot (dē·drō'), **Denis,** 1713–84, Fr. philosopher and encyclopedist.

Di·og·e·nes (dī·oj'ə·nēz), 412?–323 B.C., Gk. Cynic philosopher, reputed to have lived in a tub.

Dis·rae·li (diz·rā'lē), **Benjamin,** 1804–81, first Earl of Beaconsfield, Eng. statesman and novelist; prime minister 1868, 1874–80.

Dob·zhan·sky (dôb·zhän'skē), **Theodosius,** born 1900, U.S. geneticist born in Russia.

Dodg·son (doj'sən), **Charles Lutwidge** See (Lewis) CARROLL.

Dom·i·nic (dom'ə·nik), **Saint,** 1170–1221, Sp. friar; founded the Dominican Order: orig. name **Domingo de Guz·mán** (gōōth·män').

Don·a·tel·lo (don'ə·tel'ō, _Ital._ dō'nä·tel'lō), 1386?–1466, Florentine sculptor: orig. name **Donato di Niccolò di Bet·to Bar·di** (dē bät'tō bär'dē).

Donne (dun), **John,** 1573–1631, Eng. poet and clergyman.

Dop·pler (dôp'lər), **Christian Johann,** 1803–53, Ger. physicist and mathematician active in Austria.

Dos·to·ev·ski (dôs'tô·yef'skē), **Feodor Mikhailovich,** 1821–1881, Russ. novelist. Also **Dos'to·yev'sky.**

Doug·las (dug'ləs), **Stephen Arnold,** 1813–61, U.S. senator; opposed Lincoln in a series of debates, 1858. — **William Orville,** 1898–1980, U.S. jurist, associate justice of the Supreme Court 1939–1975.

Doyle (doil), **Sir Arthur Conan,** 1859–1930, Eng. physician and novelist; creator of detective Sherlock Holmes.

Drake (drāk), **Sir Francis,** 1540?–96, Eng. admiral; first Englishman to sail round the world.

Drei·ser (drī'sər, -zər), **Theodore (Herman Albert),** 1871–1945, U.S. novelist.

Drey·fus (drā'fəs, drī-; _Fr._ dre·füs'), **Alfred,** 1859–1935, Fr. army officer; wrongfully convicted of treason in 1894; vindicated in 1906.

Dry·den (drīd'n), **John,** 1631–1700, Eng. poet, critic, and dramatist; poet laureate 1670–88.

Dul·les (dul'əs), **John Foster,** 1888–1959, U.S. lawyer and diplomat; secretary of state 1953–59.

Du·mas (dōō·mä', dōō·mä'; _Fr._ dü·mä'), **Alexandre,** 1802–1870, **Dumas père,** and his son **Alexandre,** 1824–95, **Dumas fils,** Fr. novelists and dramatists.

Duns Sco·tus (dunz skō'təs), **John,** 1265?–1308, Scot. scholastic theologian: called **the Subtile Doctor.**

Dü·rer (dü'rər), **Albrecht,** 1471–1528, Ger. painter and engraver.

Dzhu·ga·shvi·li (jōō'gä·shvē'lē), **Iosif Vissarionovich.** See STALIN.

Ear·hart (âr'härt), **Amelia,** 1898–1937, Mrs. George Palmer Putnam, U.S. aviatrix.

Ed·dy (ed'ē), **Mary Baker,** 1821–1910, _née_ Mary Morse Baker, U.S. religious leader; founder of Christian Science.

Ed·i·son (ed'ə·sən), **Thomas Alva,** 1847–1931, U.S. inventor.

Ed·ward VII (ed'ward), 1841–1910, king of England 1901–10; called the Peacemaker.

Edward VIII See (Duke of) WINDSOR.

Ein·stein (īn'stīn), **Albert,** 1879–1955, U.S. physicist born in Germany; developed the theory of relativity.

Ei·sen·how·er (ī'zən·hou'ər), **Dwight David,** 1890–1969, U.S. general; 34th president of the U.S. 1953–61.

El Grec·o (el grek'ō, grä'ko), 1548?–1614, Sp. painter born in Crete: orig. name **Domenicos The·o·to·co·pou·los** (thä'ō·tō·kō'pōō·lôs).

E·li·a (ē·lyē'ä) See (Charles) LAMB.

El·i·ot (el'ē·ət), **George** Pseud. of _Mary Ann Evans,_ 1819–1880, Eng. novelist. — **T(homas) S(tearns),** 1888–1965, Brit. poet, dramatist, and critic born in the U.S.

E·liz·a·beth I (i·liz'ə·bəth), 1533–1603, queen of England 1558–1603.

Elizabeth II, born 1926, queen of England 1952–.

Em·er·son (em'ər·sən), **Ralph Waldo,** 1803–82, U.S. essayist, philosopher, and poet.

Eng·els (eng'əls), **Friedrich,** 1820–95, Ger. socialist and theoretician; collaborated with Karl Marx.

Ep·i·cu·rus (ep'ə·kyōōr'əs), 342?–270? B.C., Gk. philosopher.

E·ras·mus (i·raz'məs), **Desiderius,** 1466?–1536, Du. theologian, classical scholar, and humanist: orig. name **Geert Geerts** (gerts) or **Gerhard Ger·hards** (ger'harts).

Er·ic·son (er'ik·sən), **Lief,** 11th-c. Norse adventurer; son of Eric the Red; probably discovered North America about 1000. Also **Er'ics·son.**

Er·ic the Red (er'ik), 950?–?1003, Scandinavian adventurer; colonizer of Greenland.

Eu·clid (yōō'klid), Gk. mathematician of about the 3rd-c. B.C.; developed the basic principles of geometry.

Eu·ler (oi'lər), **Leonhard,** 1707–83, Swiss mathematician.

Eu·rip·i·des (yōō·rip'ə·dēz), 480?–406? B.C., Gk. dramatist.

Ev·ans (ev'əns), **Mary Ann** See (George) ELIOT.

Far·a·day (far'ə·dā), **Michael,** 1791–1867, Eng. chemist and physicist; discovered properties of electromagnetism.

Far·ra·gut (far'ə·gət), **David Glasgow,** 1801–70, Union admiral in the Amer. Civil War.

Faulk·ner (fôk'nər), **William,** 1897–1962, U.S. novelist. Also **Falk'ner.**

Fer·di·nand V (fûr'di·nand), 1452–1516, king of Spain; husband of Isabella I: called **the Catholic.**

Fer·mi (fer'mē), **Enrico**, 1901–54, Ital. nuclear physicist active in the U.S.

Fich·te (fikh'tə), **Johann Gottlieb**, 1762–1814, Ger. patriot and philosopher.

Fill·more (fil'môr), **Millard**, 1800–74, 13th president of the U.S. 1850–53.

Fitz·Ger·ald (fits'jer'əld), **Edward**, 1809–83, Eng. poet.

Fitzgerald, F(rancis) Scott (Key), 1896–1940, U.S. writer.

Flau·bert (flō-bâr'), **Gustave**, 1821–80, Fr. novelist.

Flem·ing (flem'ing), **Sir Alexander**, 1881–1955, Brit. physician and bacteriologist; discoverer with Florey of penicillin.

Flo·rey (flôr'ē, flō'rē), **Sir Howard Walter**, 1898–1968, Brit. pathologist born in Australia; collaborated with Fleming in the discovery of penicillin.

Foch (fôsh), **Ferdinand**, 1851–1929, Fr. general; commander in chief of the Allied armies, 1918.

Fok·ker (fok'ər), **Anthony Herman Gerard**, 1890–1939, Du. airplane designer.

Ford (fôrd, fōrd), **Gerald Rudolph**, born 1913, U.S. representative; 38th president of the United States 1974–77.

— **Henry**, 1863–1947, U.S. automobile manufacturer.

Fos·ter (fôs'tər, fos'-), **Stephen (Collins)**, 1826–64, U.S. songwriter.

Fou·cault (fōō-kō'), **Jean Bernard Léon**, 1819–68, Fr. physicist.

Fou·rier (fōō-ryā'), **Jean Baptiste Joseph**, 1768–1830, Fr. mathematician and physicist.

Fox (foks), **George**, 1624–91, Eng. preacher; founded the Society of Friends.

Fra (frä) **Angelico** See ANGELICO.

France (frans, fräns), **Anatole** Pseud. of **Jacques Anatole Thi·bault** (tē-bō'), 1844–1924, Fr. novelist and critic.

Fran·ces·ca (frän-ches/kä), **Piero della** See PIERO DELLA FRANCESCA.

Fran·cis of As·si·si (frän'sis, frän'-; ə-sē'zē), **St.**, 1182?–1226, Ital. friar and preacher: orig. name **Giovanni Francesco Ber·nar·do·ne** (bär'när-dō'nä).

Francis Xavier, Saint See XAVIER.

Franck (fränk), **César Auguste**, 1822–90, Fr. composer born in Belgium.

Fran·co (frang'kō, Sp. fräng'kō), **Francisco**, 1892–1975, Sp. political and military leader; chief of state 1939–1975; called **el Cau·dil·lo** (el kou-thē'lyō, -thē'yō): full surname **Fran·co·Ba·ha·mon·de** (-bä'ä·môn'dä).

Frank·lin (frangk'lin), **Benjamin**, 1706–90, Amer. patriot, writer, scientist, and diplomat: pseud. **Richard Saun·ders** (sôn'dərz, sän'-).

Fred·er·ick I (fred'ər·ik, fred'rik), 1123?–90, emperor of the Holy Roman Empire 1152–90: called *Barbarossa* (Redbeard).

Frederick II, 1712–86, king of Prussia 1740–86: called **Frederick the Great**.

Fres·nel (frā-nel'), **Augustin Jean**, 1788–1827, Fr. physicist.

Freud (froid), **Sigmund**, 1856–1939, Austrian neurologist; founded modern theory of psychoanalysis.

Frost (frôst, frost), **Robert (Lee)**, 1875–1963, U.S. poet.

Ful·ton (fōōl'tən), **Robert**, 1765–1815, U.S. engineer and inventor.

Funk (fungk), **Isaac Kauffman**, 1839–1912, U.S. publisher and lexicographer.

Ga·len (gā'lən), 130?–200?, Gk. physician and medical writer.

Gal·i·le·o (gal'ə·lē'ō, Ital. gä'lē·lā'ō), 1564–1642, Florentine astronomer and physicist: full name **Galileo Gal·i·le·i** (gal'·ə·lā'ē).

Gal·va·ni (gäl·vä'ne), **Luigi**, 1737–98, Ital. physiologist.

Ga·ma (gam'ə, Pg. Gä'mə), **Vasco da**, 1469?–1524, Pg. seafarer and explorer.

Gan·dhi (gän'de, gan'-), **Mohandas Karamchand**, 1869–1948, Indian politician and Hindu spiritual leader: called **Mahatma Gandhi**; — **In·di·ra** (in·dir'ə), born 1917, Indian stateswoman; prime minister 1966–77, 1980–.

Gar·cí·a Lor·ca (gär·thē'ä lôr'kä), **Federico**, 1899–1936, Sp. poet, dramatist, and essayist.

Gar·field (gär'fēld), **James Abram**, 1831–81, 20th president of the U.S. 1881; assassinated.

Gar·i·bal·di (gar'ə·bôl'dē, Ital. gä'rē·bäl'dē), **Giuseppe**, 1807–82, Ital. patriot and general; worked to unite Italy.

Gar·rick (gar'ik), **David**, 1717–79, Eng. actor, manager, and author.

Gau·guin (gō·gaṅ'), **Paul**, 1848–1903, Fr. painter: full name **Eugène Henri Paul Gauguin**.

Gauss (gous), **Karl Friedrich**, 1777–1855, Ger. mathematician and astronomer.

Gau·ta·ma (gō'tə·mə, gou'-) See BUDDHA.

Gay-Lussac (gā·lü·sàk'), **Joseph Louis**, 1778–1850, Fr. chemist and physicist.

Gen·ghis Khan (jen'giz kän', jeng'gis, geng'gis), 1167?–1227, Mongol conqueror: orig. name **Te·much·in** (tə·mōō'·chin). Also **Jen'ghiz Khan**.

George (jôrj), **St.**, died 303?, Christian martyr; patron of England.

George III, 1738–1820, king of England 1760–1820.

George VI, 1895–1952, king of England 1936–52.

Ge·ron·i·mo (jə·ron'ə·mo), 1829–1909, Apache Indian chief.

Gide (zhēd), **André**, 1869–1951, Fr. writer.

Gil·bert (gil'bərt), **Sir William Schwenck**, 1836–1911, Eng. librettist; collaborator with Sir Arthur Sullivan.

Gior·gio·ne (jôr·jō'nä), 1477?–1511, Venetian painter: orig. name **Giorgio Bar·ba·rel·li** (bär'bä·rel'lē).

Giot·to (jôt'tō), 1266?–1337, Florentine painter, architect, and sculptor: full name **Giotto di Bon·do·ne** (dē bōn·dō'nä).

Glad·stone (glad'stōn, -stən), **William Ewart**, 1809–98, Eng. statesman and political leader; prime minister 1868–1874, 1880–85, 1886, 1892–94.

Goe·thals (gō'thəlz), **George Washington**, 1858–1928, U.S. army engineer; builder of the Panama Canal.

Goethe (gœ'tə), **Johann Wolfgang von**, 1749–1832, Ger. poet, dramatist, and novelist.

Gogh (gō, gôk; Du. khôkh), **Vincent van** See VAN GOGH.

Go·gol (gō'gəl, Russ. gô'gôl), **Nikolai Vasilievich**, 1809–52, Russ. writer and dramatist.

Gom·pers (gom'pərz), **Samuel**, 1850–1924, U.S. labor leader.

Gor·ki (gôr'kē), **Maxim** Pseud. of **Alexei Maximovich Pyesh·kov** (pyesh'kôf), 1868–1936, Russ. author. Also **Gor'ky**.

Gou·nod (gōō·nō'), **Charles François**, 1818–93, Fr. composer.

Go·ya (gō'yə), **Francisco José de**, 1746–1828, Sp. painter and etcher: full surname **Goya y Lu·cien·tes** (ē lōō·thyen'täs).

Gra·ham (grā'əm), **William Franklin**, born 1918, U.S. evangelist: called **Billy Graham**.

Grant (grant), **Ulysses S(impson)**, 1822–85, U.S. general in the Civil War; 18th president of the U.S. 1869–77: orig. name **Hiram Ulysses Grant**.

Gray (grā), **Thomas**, 1716–71, Eng. poet.

Gre·co (grek'ō, grä'kō), **El**, See EL GRECO.

Gregory I (greg'ər·ē), St., 540?–604, pope 590–604; reformed the church service: called **Gregory the Great**.

Gregory XIII, 1502–85, pope 1572–85; reformed the calendar: orig. name **Ugo Buon·cam·pag·ni** (bwôn'cäm·pän'yē).

Grieg (grēg), **Edvard (Hagerup)**, 1843–1907, Norw. composer.

Grimm (grim), **Jakob (Ludwig Karl)**, 1785–1863, and his brother **Wilhelm (Karl)**, 1786–1859, Ger. collectors of fairy tales.

Gro·pi·us (grō'pē·əs), **Walter**, 1883–1969, Ger. architect active in the U.S.

Grü·ne·wald (grü'nə·vält), **Mathias**, 1480?–1530?, Ger. painter.

Gu·ten·berg (gōōt'n·bûrg), **Johann**, 1400?–68?, Ger. printer; inventor of movable type: orig. name **Johannes Gens·fleisch** (gens'flīsh).

Ha·ber (hä'bər), **Fritz**, 1868–1934, Ger. chemist.

Haeck·el (hek'el), **Ernst Heinrich**, 1834–1919, Ger. naturalist and philosopher.

Hai·le Se·las·sie (hī'lē sə·las'ē, -läs'ē), 1891–1975, emperor of Ethiopia 1930–74; in exile 1936–41: orig. name **Taffari Ma·kon·nen** (mä·kôn'nen).

Hal·dane (hôl'dān), **J(ohn) B(urdon) S(anderson)**, 1892–1964, Eng. geneticist.

Hale (hāl), **Nathan**, 1755–76, Amer. Revolutionary patriot; hanged as a spy by the British.

Hals (häls), **Frans**, 1580?–1666, Du. painter.

Hal·sey (hôl'zē), **William Frederick**, 1882–1959, U.S. admiral in World War II.

Ham·il·ton (ham'əl·tən), **Alexander**, 1757–1804, Amer. statesman born in the British West Indies.

Ham·mar·skjöld (häm'är·shüld), **Dag**, 1905–61, Sw. statesman; UN Secretary General 1953–61.

Ham·mu·ra·bi (hä'mōō·rä'bē, ham'ə-), king of Babylonia in the first dynasty, about 2000 B.C.; promulgator of a system of laws called the **Code of Hammurabi**.

Han·cock (han'kok), **John**, 1737–93, U.S. patriot; signer of the Declaration of Independence.

Han·del (han'dəl), **George Frideric**, 1685–1759, Ger. composer active in England and Italy: orig. name **Georg Friedrich Hän·del** (hen'dəl): called **George Frederick Handel**.

Han·ni·bal (han'ə·bəl), 247?–183? B.C., Carthaginian general; invaded Italy by crossing the Alps.

Har·ding (här'ding), **Warren Gamaliel**, 1865–1923, 29th president of the U.S. 1921–23.

Har·ri·son (har′ə·sən), **Benjamin**, 1833–1901, 23rd president of the U.S. 1889–93; his grandfather, **William Henry**, 1773–1841, military commander; ninth president of the U.S. for a month in 1841.

Harte (härt), **Bret**, 1836–1902, U.S. novelist and short-story writer: orig. name **Francis Brett Harte.**

Har·vey (här′vē), **William**, 1578–1657, Eng. physician; discovered the circulation of the blood.

Haw·thorne (hô′thôrn), **Nathaniel**, 1804–64, U.S. novelist and short-story writer.

Hay·dn (hīd′n), **Franz Joseph**, 1732–1809, Austrian composer.

Hayes (hāz), **Rutherford Birchard**, 1822–93, 19th president of the U.S. 1877–81.

Hearst (hûrst), **William Randolph**, 1863–1951, U.S. newspaper publisher.

He·gel (hā′gəl), **Georg Wilhelm Friedrich**, 1770–1831, Ger. philosopher.

Hei·ne (hī′nə), **Heinrich**, 1797–1856, Ger. lyric poet.

Helm·holtz (helm′hōlts), **Hermann Ludwig Ferdinand von**, 1821–94, Ger. physiologist and physicist.

Hé·lo·ise (ā·lō·ēz′), died 1164?, Fr. abbess, mistress and then wife of Abelard.

Hem·ing·way (hem′ing·wā), **Ernest**, 1899–1961, U.S. writer.

Hen·ry (hen′rē), **O.** See O. HENRY. — **Patrick**, 1736–99, Amer. revolutionary statesman and orator.

Henry II, 1133–89, king of England 1154–89; first Plantagenet king: called **Henry Plantagenet.**

Henry IV, 1367–1413, king of England 1399–1413.

Henry V, 1387–1422, king of England 1413–22.

Henry VIII, 1491–1547, king of England 1509–47, asserted royal supremacy over the Catholic Church in England.

Her·od An·ti·pas (her′əd an′ti·pas), died A.D. 39?, tetrarch of Galilee 4 B.C.–A.D. 39; the Herod of the Gospels.

He·rod·o·tus (hi·rod′ə·təs), 5th-c. B.C. Gk. historian: called **the Father of History.**

Her·rick (her′ik), **Robert**, 1591–1674, Eng. lyric poet.

Herzl (her′tsəl), **Theodor**, 1860–1904, Austro-Hung. journalist; founded the Zionist movement.

Hin·de·mith (hin′də·mit), **Paul**, 1895–1963, Ger. composer.

Hin·den·burg (hin′dən·bûrg, *Ger.* hin′dən·bŏŏrkh), **Paul von**, 1847–1934, Ger. general and statesman; president of the Weimar Republic 1925–34.

Hip·poc·ra·tes (hi·pok′rə·tēz), 460?–377? B.C., Gk. physician: called **the Father of Medicine.**

Hi·ro·hi·to (hir·ō·hē·tō), born 1901, emperor of Japan 1926–.

Hit·ler (hit′lər), **Adolf**, 1889–1945, Ger. Nazi dictator born in Austria; chancellor 1933–45: called **der Fuhrer** (the Leader).

Hobbes (hobz), **Thomas**, 1588–1679, Eng. philosopher.

Ho·garth (hō′gärth), **William**, 1697–1765, Eng. painter and engraver.

Hol·bein (hōl′bīn, *Ger.* hôl′bīn), **Hans**, 1465?–1524, **the Elder**, and his son **Hans**, 1497?–1543, **the Younger**, Ger. painters.

Holmes (hōmz), **Oliver Wendell**, 1809–94, U.S. physician, poet, and essayist. — **Oliver Wendell**, 1841–1935, U.S. jurist; associate justice of the Supreme Court 1902–32; son of the preceding.

Ho·mer (hō′mər), 9th-c. B.C. Gk. epic poet; trad. author of the *Iliad* and the *Odyssey.*

Hooke (hŏŏk), **Robert**, 1635–1703, Eng. physicist.

Hoo·ver (hŏŏ′vər), **Herbert Clark**, 1874–1964, U.S. mining engineer and statesman; 31st president of the U.S. 1929–33. — **J**(ohn) **Edgar**, 1895–1972, U.S. lawyer; director of the Federal Bureau of Investigation 1924–72.

Hor·ace (hôr′is, hor′-) Anglicized name of **Quintus Horatius Flac·cus** (flak′əs), 65–8 B.C., Roman poet.

Hou·di·ni (hŏŏ·dē′nē), **Harry**, 1874–1926, U.S. magician: orig. name **Erich Weiss** (wīs).

Hous·man (hous′mən), **A**(lfred) **E**(dward), 1859–1936, Eng. poet.

Hous·ton (hyŏŏs′tən), **Sam**, 1793–1863, U.S. general and politician; first president of the Republic of Texas 1836–38, 1841–44.

Hud·son (hud′sən), **Henry**, died 1611?, Eng. navigator and explorer: discovered the Hudson River for the Dutch, 1609, and Hudson Bay for the English, 1610.

Hugh Ca·pet (hyŏŏ kā′pit, kap′it; *Fr.* kà·pe′), 938?–996, king of France 987–996; founder of the Capetian dynasty.

Hu·go (hyŏŏ′gō, *Fr.* ü·gō′), **Victor** (**Marie**), 1802–85, Fr. poet, novelist, and dramatist.

Hume (hyŏŏm), **David**, 1711–76, Scot. historian and philosopher.

Hux·ley (huks′lē) An Eng. family prominent in science and literature, notably **T**(homas) **H**(enry), 1825–95, biologist and Darwinian; and his grandsons **Julian** (**Sorell**), born 1887, biologist, and **Aldous** (**Leonard**), 1894–1963, novelist and critic.

Huy·gens (hī′gənz), **Christian**, 1629–95, Du. mathematician, physicist, and astronomer. Also **Huy′ghens.**

I·bá·ñez (ē·vä′nyeth), **Vicente Blasco** See BLASCO-IBÁÑEZ.

Ib·sen (ib′sən), **Henrik**, 1828–1906, Norw. dramatist.

Ig·na·ti·us Loyola (ig·nā′shē·əs, -shəs), **Saint** See LOYOLA.

Ir·ving (ûr′ving), **Washington**, 1783–1859, U.S. writer, historian, and humorist.

Is·a·bel·la I (iz′ə·bel′ə), 1451–1504, queen of Castile; aided Christopher Columbus: called **Isabella the Catholic.**

I·van IV (ī′vən, *Russ.* i·vän′), 1530–84, first czar of Russia 1547–84: called **the Terrible.**

Jack·son (jak′sən), **Andrew**, 1767–1845, U.S. general; seventh president of the U.S. 1829–37: called **Old Hickory.** — **Thomas Jonathan**, 1824–63, Confederate general in the Civil War: called **Stonewall Jackson.**

James (jāmz), **Henry**, 1843–1916, U.S. writer and critic active in England. — **Jesse** (**Woodson**), 1847–82, U.S. outlaw. — **William**, 1842–1910, U.S. philosopher and psychologist; brother of Henry.

James I, 1566–1625, 1st Stuart king of England 1603–25; as **James VI** king of Scotland 1567–1625.

James II, 1633–1701, king of England 1685–88; deposed.

Jeanne d'Arc (zhän dark) See JOAN OF ARC.

Jeans (jēnz), **Sir James** (**Hopwood**), 1877–1946, Eng. astronomer, physicist, and philosopher.

Jef·fer·son (jef′ər·sən), **Thomas**, 1743–1826, Amer. statesman, diplomat, and writer; third president of the U.S. 1801–1809.

Jen·ner (jen′ər), **Edward**, 1749–1823, Eng. physician; discovered vaccination.

Je·sus (jē′zəs) Founder of Christianity, 6? B.C.–29? A.D., son of Mary; regarded in the Christian faith as Christ, the Messiah. Also **Jesus Christ, Jesus of Nazareth.**

Joan of Arc (jōn), 1412?–31, Fr. heroine and martyr; burned as a heretic; canonized 1920; also called **the Maid of Orléans.**

John (jon), 1167?–1216, king of England 1199–1216, signed the Magna Carta 1215: called **John Lack·land** (lak′land).

John XXIII, 1881–1963, pope 1958–63: orig. name **Angelo Giuseppe Ron·cal·li** (rōn·käl′lē).

John Paul I (jon pôl), 1912–78, pope Aug.–Sept. 1978: orig. name **Albino Lu·cia·ni** (lŏŏ·chä′nē).

John Paul II, born 1920, pope 1978–: orig. name **Karol Woj·ty·la** (voi′tē·vä, -tē·ä).

John·son (jon′sən), **Andrew**, 1808–75, 17th president of the U.S. 1865–69; impeached. — **Lyndon Baines**, 1908–1973, 36th president of the U.S. 1963–69. — **Samuel**, 1709–84, Eng. lexicographer, poet, man of letters: called **Dr. Johnson.**

Jones (jōnz), **John Paul**, 1747–92, Amer. Revolutionary naval officer born in Scotland: orig. name **John Paul.**

Jon·son (jon′sən), **Ben**, 1573?–1637, Eng. poet and dramatist.

Jo·seph·ine (jō′zə·fēn, Fr. zhô·zā·fēn′), **Empress**, 1763–1814, widow of Vicomte Alexandre de Beauharnais, married Napoleon Bonaparte 1796, divorced 1809.

Joule (joul, jŏŏl), **James Prescott**, 1818–89, Eng. physicist.

Joyce (jois), **James** (**Augustine Aloysius**), 1882–1941, Irish writer and poet active in Zurich and Paris.

Jul·ius (jŏŏl′yəs) **Caesar** See (**Gaius Julius**) CAESAR.

Jung (yŏŏng), **Carl Gustav**, 1875–1961, Swiss psychologist.

Jus·tin·i·an I (jus·tin′ē·ən), Anglicized name of **Flavius Anicius Jus·tin·i·a·nus** (jus·tin′ē·ā′nus), 483–565, Byzantine emperor 527–565; codified Roman laws.

Kaf·ka (käf′kä), **Franz**, 1883–1924, Austrian writer born in Prague.

Kant (känt), **Immanuel**, 1724–1804, Ger. philosopher.

Keats (kēts), **John**, 1795–1821, Eng. poet.

Ke·mal A·ta·türk (ke·mäl′ ä·tä·türk′), 1881–1938, Turkish general and statesman; founder of modern Turkey. Also **Mus·ta·fa Ke·mal** (mŏŏ′stä·fä ke·mäl′).

Ken·ne·dy (ken′ə·dē), **John Fitzgerald**, 1917–63, 35th president of the U.S. 1961–63; assassinated. — **Robert Francis**, 1925–68, U.S. senator and political leader; brother of the preceding; assassinated.

Kep·ler (kep′lər), **Johann**, 1571–1630, Ger. astronomer; formulated laws of planetary motion.

Key (kē), **Francis Scott**, 1779–1863, Amer. lawyer and poet; wrote *The Star-Spangled Banner.*

Keynes (kānz), **John Maynard**, 1883–1946, first Baron of Tilton, Eng. economist.

Khay·yám (kī·äm′), **Omar.** See OMAR KHAYYÁM.

Khrush·chev (krŏŏsh·chôf′, *Russ.* khrŏŏ·shchôf′), **Nikita Sergeyevich**, 1894–1971, Soviet statesman; first secretary of the Communist Party 1953–1964; premier 1958–1964.

Kidd (kid), **William**, 1645?–1701, Brit. sea captain and pirate; hanged: called **Captain Kidd.**

Kier·ke·gaard (kir′kə·gôr), **Søren Aabye**, 1813–55, Dan. philosopher and theologian.

King (king), **Martin Luther, Jr.**, 1929–68, U.S. leader of nonviolent civil rights movement for Negroes; assassinated.

Kip·ling (kip′ling), (**Joseph**) **Rudyard**, 1865–1936, Eng. author and poet.

Klee (klā, klē), **Paul**, 1879–1940, Swiss painter and etcher.
Knox (noks), **John**, 1505?–72, Scot. Calvinist reformer, theologian, and historian.
Koest·ler (kest′lər), **Arthur**, born 1905, Hung. writer active in England.
Kos·ci·us·ko (kos′ē·us′kō), **Thaddeus**, 1746–1817, Polish patriot and general born in Lithuania; fought in the Amer. Revolution. *Polish* **Koś·ciusz·ko** (kôsh·chōōsh′kô).
Ko·sy·gin (ko·sig′in), **Alexei Nikolayevich**, born 1904, Soviet statesman; premier 1964–.
Kra·nach (krä′näkh), **Lucas** See CRANACH.
Ku·blai Khan (kōō′blī kän′), 1216?–94, Mongol emperor, founder of the Mongol dynasty of China. Also **Kub·la Khan** (kōō′blə).

La·fay·ette (lä′fē·et′, laf′ē·et′; *Fr.* là·fà·yet′), **Marquis de**, 1757–1834, Fr. general, revolutionist, and statesman; fought in the Amer. Revolution. Also **La·Fay·ette′**.
La Fon·taine (lä fon·tān′, *Fr.* là fôn·ten′), **Jean de**, 1621–1695, Fr. writer, noted for his fables.
La·marck (là·märk′), **Chevalier de**, 1744–1829, Fr. naturalist; orig. name **Jean Baptiste Pierre Antoine de Mo·net** (də mō·ne′).
Lamb (lam), **Charles**, 1775–1834, Eng. essayist: pseud. *Elia*.
Lao·tse (lou′dzu′), 604?–531? B.C., Chinese philosopher and mystic; founder of Taoism. Also **Lao·tze, Lao·tzu**.
Lard·ner (lärd′nər), **Ring**, 1885–1933, U.S. journalist and short-story writer: full name **Ringgold Wilmer Lardner**.
La Roche·fou·cauld (lä rôsh·fōō·kō′), **Duc François de**, 1613–80, Prince de Marcillac, Fr. moralist and writer.
La Salle (là sàl′), **Sieur Robert Cavelier de**, 1643–87, Fr. explorer in America.
Lau·trec (lō·trek′) See TOULOUSE-LAUTREC.
Law·rence (lôr′əns, lor′-), **D(avid) H(erbert)**, 1885–1930, Eng. novelist and poet. — **T(homas) E(dward)**, 1885–1935, Eng. archaeologist, soldier, and writer; led Arab revolt against Turkey in World War I; after 1927 changed his name to Shaw (shô): called **Lawrence of Arabia**.
Lee (lē), **Robert E(dward)**, 1807–70, Confederate commander in chief in the Civil War.
Leeu·wen·hoek (lā′vən·hōōk), **Anton van**, 1632–1723, Du. naturalist; pioneer in microscopy.
Leib·nitz (līb′nits), **Baron Gottfried Wilhelm von**, 1646–1716, Ger. philosopher and mathematician. Also **Leib′niz**.
Leif Er·ic·son (lēf er′ik·sən) See ERICSON.
Le·nin (len′in), **Vladimir Ilyich**, 1870–1924, Russ. statesman; chief leader and theorist of the Bolshevik Revolution; head of the U.S.S.R. 1917–24: original name **Vladimir Ilyich Ul·ya·nof** (ōōl′ya·nəf). Also, erroneously, **Nikolai Lenin**.
Leo X, 1475–1521, pope 1513–21: orig. name *Giovanni de′ Medici*.
Le·o·nar·do da Vin·ci (lē′ə·när′dō də vin′chē, *Ital.* lā′ō·när′dō dä vēn′chē) See DA VINCI.
Les·seps (les′əps, *Fr.* le·seps′), **Vicomte Ferdinand Marie de**, 1805–94, Fr. engineer and diplomat; supervised building of the Suez Canal.
Lew·is (lōō′is), **Sinclair**, 1885–1951, U.S. novelist.
Lie (lē), **Trygve Halvdan**, 1896–1968, Norw. statesman; first secretary general of the U.N., 1946–53.
Lil·i·en·thal (lē′lē·ən·täl′), **Otto**, 1848–98, Ger. inventor.
Lin·coln (ling′kən), **Abraham**, 1809–65, U.S. statesman; 16th president of the U.S. 1861–65; assassinated.
Lind·bergh (lind′bûrg), **Charles Augustus**, 1902–74, U.S. aviator.
Lin·nae·us (li·nē′əs), **Carolus**, Latinized name of **Karl von Lin·né** (lē·nā′), 1707–78, Sw. botanist and taxonomist.
Lis·ter (lis′tər), **Joseph**, 1827–1912, first Baron Lister of Lyme Regis, Eng. surgeon; founder of antiseptic surgery.
Liszt (list), **Franz**, 1811–86, Hung. composer and pianist.
Lloyd George (loid jôrj), **David**, 1863–1945, first Earl of Dwyfor, Brit. statesman; prime minister 1916–22.
Locke (lok), **John**, 1632–1704, Eng. philosopher.
Lon·don (lun′dən), **Jack**, 1876–1916, U.S. author: orig. name **John Griffith London**.
Long (lông, long), **Huey Pierce**, 1893–1935, U.S. politician; assassinated.
Long·fel·low (lông′fel·ō, long′-), **Henry Wadsworth**, 1807–1882, U.S. poet.
Lo·pe de Ve·ga (lō′pā thä vā′gä) See (Lope de) VEGA.
Lor·ca (lôr′kä), **Federico Garcia** See GARCIA LORCA.
Lo·rentz (lō′rents), **Hendrik Antoon**, 1853–1928, Du. physicist.
Lou·is XIV (lōō′ē, lōō′is; *Fr.* lwē), 1638–1715, king of France 1643–1715; called *le Roi Soleil* (the Sun King).
Louis XV, 1710–74, king of France 1715–74.
Louis XVI, 1754–93, king of France 1774–92, dethroned by the French Revolution; guillotined.
Louis Napoleon See (Louis Napoleon) BONAPARTE.

Louis Phi·lippe (fē·lēp′), 1773–1850, king of France 1830–1848; abdicated: called **le Roi Ci·toy·en** (lə rwä sē·twà·yań′) (the Citizen King).
Lo·yo·la (loi·ō′lä), **St. Ignatius**, 1491–1566, Sp. soldier, priest, and mystic; founder of the Society of Jesus: original name **Inigo de Oñez y Loyola**.
Lu·cre·tius (lōō·krē′shəs, -shē·əs), 96–55 B.C., Roman poet: full name **Titus Lucretius Car·us** (kâr′əs).
Lu·ther (lōō′thər), **Martin**, 1483–1546, Ger. monk, theologian, and reformer; leader of the Reformation; excommunicated 1520.

Mac·Ar·thur (mək·är′thər), **Douglas**, 1880–1964, U.S. general.
Mach·i·a·vel·li (mäk′ē·ə·vel′ē, *Ital.* mä′kyä·vel′lē), **Niccoló**, 1469–1527, Florentine statesman and writer on politics.
Mac·mil·lan (mak·mil′ən), **Harold**, born 1894, Brit. statesman; prime minister 1957–63.
Mad·i·son (mad′ə·sən), **James**, 1751–1836, 4th president of the U.S. 1809–17: called **the Father of the Constitution**.
Ma·gel·lan (mə·jel′ən), **Ferdinand**, 1480?–1521, Pg. navigator in the service of Spain.
Mah·ler (mä′lər), **Gustav**, 1860–1911, Austro-Hung. composer and conductor active in Austria and Germany.
Ma·hom·et (mə·hom′it) See MOHAMMED.
Mai·mon·i·des (mī·mon′ə·dēz), 1135–1204, Sp. rabbi, physician, and philosopher: orig. name **Moses ben Mai·mon** (mī′· mōn). Called **RaM·BaM** (ram·bam′).
Mal·colm X (mal′kəm eks) Name adopted by *Malcolm Little*, 1925–65, U.S. political and religious leader, active in the Black Muslim movement; assassinated.
Mal·o·ry (mal′ər·ē), **Sir Thomas**, died 1470, Eng. author and translator.
Mal·pi·ghi (mäl·pē′gē), **Marcello**, 1628–94, Ital. anatomist.
Mal·raux (màl·rō′), **André**, 1901–1967, Fr. novelist, art critic, and politician: full name **Georges André Malraux**.
Mal·thus (mal′thəs, môl′-), **Thomas Robert**, 1766–1834, Eng. political economist.
Mann (män), **Thomas**, 1875–1955, Ger. novelist active in the U.S.
Mao Tse·tung (mou′dzu′dōong′), 1893–1976, Chinese Communist leader; chairman of the People's Republic of China 1949–59.
Marc Antony (märk) See (Mark) ANTONY.
Mar·co·ni (mär·kō′nē), **Marchese Guglielmo**, 1874–1937, Ital. inventor; developed a system of wireless telegraphy.
Mar·co Po·lo (mär′kō pō′lō) See POLO.
Ma·rie An·toi·nette (mà·rē′ àn·twà·net′), 1755–93, queen of France; wife of Louis XVI; guillotined.
Ma·ri·tain (mà·rē·tań′), **Jacques**, 1882–1973, Fr. philosopher.
Mark Twain (märk twān) Pseud. of Samuel Langhorne Clemens, 1835–1910, U.S. humorist and novelist.
Mar·lowe (mär′lō), **Christopher**, 1564–93, Eng. poet.
Mar·ti (mär·tē′), **José Julian**, 1853–95, Cuban patriot.
Mar·vell (mär′vəl), **Andrew**, 1621–78, Eng. poet.
Marx (marks), **Karl (Heinrich)**, 1818–83, Ger. philosopher and theorist of modern socialism.
Ma·ry (mâr′ē) **I**, 1516–58, queen of England 1553–58: called **Mary Tudor, Bloody Mary**.
Mary, Queen of Scots, 1542–87, queen of Scotland 1542–1567; beheaded. Also **Mary Stuart**.
Ma·sac·cio (mä·sät′chō), 1401–29?, Florentine painter: orig. name **Tommaso Gui·di** (gwē′dē).
Ma·tisse (mà·tēs′) **Henri**, 1869–1954, Fr. painter.
Mau·pas·sant (mō·pà·sän′), **(Henri René Albert) Guy de**, 1850–93, Fr. writer.
Max·well (maks′wel), **James Clerk**, 1831–79, Scot. physicist.
Maz·zi·ni (mät·tsē′nē), **Giuseppe**, 1805?–72, Ital. patriot and revolutionary.
Mc·Cor·mick (mə·kôr′mik), **Cyrus (Hall)**, 1809–84, U.S. inventor; developed the reaping machine.
Mc·Kin·ley (mə·kin′le), **William**, 1843–1901, 25th president of the U.S. 1897–1901; assassinated.
Mead (mēd), **Margaret**, 1901–78, U.S. anthropologist.
Med·i·ci (med′ə·chē, *Ital.* mä′dē·chē) A family of Florentine bankers and statesmen, notably **Giovanni de′ Medici**, died 1429, and his sons **Cosimo**, 1389–1464, and **Lorenzo**, 1395–1440; **Lorenzo**, 1449?–92, grandson of Cosimo, patron of the arts, called **the Magnificent**; his son **Giovanni**, 1475–1521 (see LEO X); **Cosimo**, 1519–74, grand duke of Tuscany: called **the Great**.
Me·ir (mä·ir′), **Golda**, 1898–1978, Israeli politician and stateswoman; prime minister 1969–74; born **Golda Mabovitz** in Kiev, Russia.
Mel·ville (mel′vil), **Herman**, 1819–91, U.S. novelist.
Mem·ling (mem′ling), **Hans**, 1430?–95?, Flemish painter.

Menck·en (meng′kən), **H(enry) L(ouis)**, 1880–1956, U.S. author and editor.

Men·del (men′dəl), **Gregor Johann**, 1822–84, Austrian monk and botanist; formulated laws of genetics.

Men·de·ley·ev (men′də·lā′əf), **Dmitri Ivanovich**, 1834–1907, Russ. chemist; developed the periodic law. Also **Men·de·le′ev**.

Men·dels·sohn (men′dəl·sən, *Ger.* men′dəl·zōn), **Felix**, 1809–47, Ger. composer: full name **Jakob Ludwig Felix Men′dels·sohn-Bar·thol·dy** (-bär·tōl′dē).

Mer·ca·tor (mər·kā′tər, *Flemish* mer·kà′tôr), **Gerardus**, 1512–94, Flemish geographer and cartographer: orig. name **Gerhard Kre·mer** (krā′mər).

Mes·sa·li·na (mes′ə·lī′nə), **Valeria**, died 48 A.D., Roman empress; notorious for profligacy; executed. Also **Mes′sal·li′na**.

Metch·ni·koff (mech′ni·kôf), **Élie**, 1845–1916, Russ. physiologist and bacteriologist active in France: orig. name **Ilya Ilich Mechnikov**.

Met·ter·nich (met′ər·nikh), **Prince von**, 1773–1859, Klemens Wenzel Nepomuk Lothar von Metternich-Winneburg, Austrian statesman and diplomat.

Mi·chel·an·ge·lo (mī′kəl·an′jə·lō, *Ital.* mē′kel·än′je·lō), 1475–1564, Ital. sculptor, painter, architect, and poet: full name **Michelangelo Buo·nar·ro·ti** (bwô′när·rô′tē).

Mi·chel·son (mī′kəl·sən), **Albert Abraham**, 1852–1931, U.S. physicist born in Germany.

Mill (mil), **John Stuart**, 1806–73, Eng. philosopher and political economist.

Mil·lay (mi·lā′), **Edna St. Vincent**, 1892–1950, U.S. poet.

Mil·ler (mil′ər), **Arthur**, born 1915, U.S. novelist and playwright. — **Henry**, born 1891, U.S. author.

Mil·li·kan (mil′ə·kən), **Robert Andrews**, 1868–1955, U.S. physicist.

Mil·ton (mil′tən), **John**, 1608–74, Eng. poet and essayist.

Mo·ham·med (mō·ham′id), 570?–632, Arabian founder and prophet of Islam whose revelations are collected in the Koran: also *Mahomet*, *Muhammad*.

Mo·lière (mō·lyâr′), Pseud. of **Jean Baptiste Po·que·lin** (pō·klàn′), 1622–73, Fr. dramatist and actor.

Mon·dri·an (môn′drē·än), **Piet**, 1872–1944, Du. painter. Also **Mon′dri·aan**.

Mo·net (mō·ne′), **Claude**, 1840–1926, Fr. painter.

Mon·roe (mən·rō′), **James**, 1758–1831, 5th president of the U.S. 1817–25.

Mon·taigne (mon·tān′, *Fr.* môn·ten′y′), **Michel Eyquem de**, 1533–92, Fr. essayist.

Mon·tes·quieu (mon′təs·kyōō′, *Fr.* môn·tes·kyœ′), **Baron de la Brede et de**, 1689–1755, Charles de Secondat, Fr. jurist, political philosopher and man of letters.

Mon·te·ver·di (mon′tə·vûr′dē, *Ital.* môn′tā·ver′dē), **Claudio** **(Giovanni Antonio)**, 1567–1643, Ital. composer.

Mon·te·zu·ma II (mon′tə·zu′mə), 1479?–1520, last Aztec Emperor of Mexico, dethroned by Cortés. Also **Moctezuma**.

Moore (mōōr, môr, mōr), **Henry**, born 1898, Eng. sculptor. — **Marianne (Craig)**, 1887–1972, U.S. poet.

More (môr, mōr), **Sir Thomas**, 1478?–1535, Eng. statesman and author; beheaded by Henry VIII; canonized 1935.

Mor·gan (môr·gən), **John Pierpont**, 1837–1913, U.S. banker, art collector and philanthropist.

Mor·ris (môr′is, mor′-), **William**, 1834–96, Eng. poet, painter, and socialist writer.

Morse (môrs), **Samuel Finley Breese**, 1791–1872, U.S. artist and inventor; constructed the first practical telegraph.

Mose·ley (mōz′lē), **Henry Gwyn-Jefferys**, 1887–1915, Eng. physicist.

Mous·sorg·sky (mōō·sôrg′skē), **Modest Petrovich**, 1835–1881, Russ. composer. Also **Mus·sorg′sky**.

Mo·zart (mō′tsärt, -zärt), **Wolfgang Amadeus**, 1756–91, Austrian composer.

Mus·so·li·ni (mōōs′ə·lē·nē), **Benito**, 1883–1945, Ital. Fascist leader; premier 1922–43; executed: called **Il Du·ce** (ēl dōō′chä).

Mu·ham·mad (mōō·ham′əd) See MOHAMMED.

Na·pi·er (nā′pē·ər, nə·pir′), **John**, 1550–1617, Scot. mathematician.

Na·po·le·on I (nə·pō′lē·ən; *Fr.* nà·pô·lā·ôn′) See under BONAPARTE.

Napoleon III See under BONAPARTE.

Nas·ser (näs′ər, nas′-), **Gamal Abdel**, 1918–1970, Egyptian army officer and political leader; chief of state 1954–1970; president of the United Arab Republic 1958–1970.

Neb·u·chad·nez·zar (neb′yōō·kəd·nez′ər), died 562 B.C., king of Babylonia 605–562 B.C.; conquered Judea and destroyed Jerusalem. Also **Neb′u·chad·rez′zar** (-rez′ər).

Neh·ru (nā′rōō), **Ja·wa·har·lal** (jə·wä′har·läl), 1889–1964, Indian nationalist leader and statesman; 1st prime minister 1947–64.

Nel·son (nel′sən), **Viscount Horatio**, 1758–1805, Eng. admiral; killed at the battle of Trafalgar.

Ne·ro (nir′ō), 37–68, Nero Claudius Caesar Drusus Germanicus, Roman emperor 54–68; committed suicide: orig. name Lucius Domitius A·he·no·bar·bus (ə·hē·nō·bär′bus).

New·man (nyōō′mən, nōō′-), **John Henry**, 1801–90, Eng. cardinal and theologian.

New·ton (nōō′tən, nyōō′-), **Sir Isaac**, 1642–1727, Eng. philosopher and mathematician.

Nei·buhr (nē′bōōr), **Reinhold**, 1892–1971, U.S. Protestant theologian.

Nie·tzsche (nē′chə), **Friedrich Wilhelm**, 1844–1900, Ger. philosopher.

Night·in·gale (nī′tən·gāl, nī′ting-), **Florence**, 1820–1910, Eng. pioneer of modern nursing, born in Italy.

Nix·on (nik′sən), **Richard Milhous**, born 1913; 37th president of the U.S. 1969–74; resigned.

No·bel (nō·bel′), **Alfred Bernhard**, 1833–96, Sw. industrialist; inventor of dynamite; founded the Nobel Prizes.

Nos·tra·da·mus (nos′trə·dā′məs), 1503–66, Fr. astrologer: orig. name Michel de No·tre·dame (də nō′trə·däm′).

O′Ca·sey (ō·kā′sē), **Sean** (shôn), 1880–1964, Irish playwright.

Ock·ham (ok′əm), **William of**, 1300?–49?, Eng. Franciscan and scholastic philosopher; opponent of Duns Scotus: called **the Invincible Doctor**. Also spelled **Oc′cam**.

Oc·ta·vi·an (ok·tā′vē·ən) See AUGUSTUS CAESAR.

O. Henry (ō hen′rē) Pseud. of *William Sydney Porter*, 1862–1910, U.S. short-story writer.

Ohm (ōm), **Georg Simon**, 1787–1854, Ger. physicist.

O·li·vi·er (ō·liv′ē·ā), **Sir Laurence (Kerr)**, born 1907, Eng. actor.

O·mar Khay·yám (ō′mär kī·äm′, ō′mər), died 1123?, Persian poet and astronomer; author of the *Rubáiyát*.

O′Neill (ō·nēl′), **Eugene (Gladstone)**, 1888–1953, U.S. playwright.

Or·te·ga y Gas·set (ôr·tā′gä ē gä·set′), **José**, 1883–1955, Sp. philosopher, writer, and statesman.

Or·well (ôr′wel), **George**, pseud. of **Eric Blair** (blâr), 1903–1950, Brit. novelist and essayist.

Ov·id (ov′id), 43 B.C.–A.D. 18, Roman poet: full name **Publius O·vid·i·us Na·so** (ō·vid′i·əs nā′sō).

Ow·en (ō′in), **Robert**, 1771–1858, Brit. manufacturer and social reformer.

Paine (pān), **Thomas**, 1737–1809, Amer. patriot, author, and political philosopher born in England.

Pa·les·tri·na (pä′les·trē′nä), **Giovanni Pierluigi da**, 1524?–1594, Ital. composer: called **Prin·ceps Mu·si·cae** (prin′seps myōō′zi·sē) (Prince of Music).

Pas·cal (pas·kal′, pas·kal; *Fr.* pås·kàl′), **Blaise**, 1623–62, *Fr.* mathematician, philosopher, and author.

Pas·teur (päs·tœr′), **Louis**, 1822–95, Fr. chemist; founder of modern bacteriology.

Pat·rick (pat·rik), **St.**, 389?–461?, Christian missionary; patron of Ireland: called **the Apostle of Ireland**.

Paul VI (pôl), 1897–1978, pope 1963–78: orig. name Giovanni Battista Mon·ti·ni (môn·tē′nē).

Pav·lov (päv′lôf), **Ivan Petrovich**, 1849–1936, Russ. physiologist.

Pearson, **Lester Bowles**, 1897–1972, Can. statesman; prime minister of Canada 1963–68.

Pea·ry (pir′ē), **Robert Edwin**, 1856–1920, U.S. Arctic explorer; first to reach the North Pole, April 6, 1909.

Penn (pen), **William**, 1644–1718, Eng. Quaker; founder of Pennsylvania.

Pepys (pēps, pep′is), **Samuel**, 1633–1702, Eng. diarist.

Per·i·cles (per′ə·klēz), died 429 B.C., Athenian statesman, orator, and general.

Pe·rón (pā·rôn′), **Juan Domingo**, 1895–1974, Argentine politician; president 1946–55, 1973–74.

Per·ry (per′ē), **Oliver Hazard**, 1785–1819, U.S. naval commander during Amer. Revolution.

Per·shing (pûr′shing), **John Joseph**, 1860–1948, U.S. General of the Armies: called **Black Jack**.

Peter I (pē′tər), 1672–1725, czar of Russia 1682–1725: called **Peter the Great**.

Pe·trarch (pē′trärk), **Francesco**, 1304–74, Ital. poet and scholar. Also **Pe·trar·ca** (pā·trär′kä).

Phid·i·as (fid′ē·əs), 5th-c. B.C. Gk. sculptor and architect.

Pi·cas·so (pē·kä′sō), **Pablo**, 1881–1973, Sp. painter and sculptor active in France: full surname **Ru·iz y Picasso** (rōō·ēth′ē).

Pierce (pirs), **Franklin**, 1804–69, 14th president of the U.S. 1853–57.

Pie·ro del·la Fran·ces·ca (pyä′rō del′lä fran·ches′kä) 1420?–92, Ital. painter.

Pis·sar·ro (pē·sà·rō′), **Camille**, 1830–1903, Fr. painter born in West Indies.

Pitt (pit), **William**, 1708–78, first Earl of Chatham, Eng. statesman, prime minister 1766–68: called **the Elder, the Great Commoner**. — **William**, 1759–1806, Eng. statesman, prime minister 1783–1801, 1804–1806, son of the preceding: called **the Younger**.

Pi·us V, Saint, 1504–72, pope 1566–72: orig. name **Michele Ghis·lie·ri** (gēz·lyä′rē).

Pius IX, 1792–1878, pope 1846–78; orig. name **Giovanni Maria Ma·stai-Fer·ret·ti** (mäs·tä′ē·fer·ret′te).

Pius XII, 1876–1958, pope 1939–58: orig. name **Eugenio Pa·cel·li** (pä·chel′lē).

Pi·zar·ro (pi·zär′ō, *Sp.* pē·thär′rō), **Francisco,** 1471?–1541, Sp. conquistador, conqueror of Peru.

Planck (plängk), **Max (Karl Ernst Ludwig),** 1858–1947, Ger. physicist; formulated the quantum theory.

Pla·to (plā′tō), 427?–347? B.C., Gk. philosopher.

Plu·tarch (ploō·tärk), A.D., 46?–120?, Gk. biographer.

Po·ca·hon·tas (pō·ka·hon′tas), 1595?–1617. Amer. Indian princess in Virginia; reputedly saved the life of Captain John Smith.

Poe (pō), **Edgar Allan,** 1809–49, U.S. writer and critic.

Polk (pōk), **James Knox,** 1795–1849, 11th president of the U.S. 1845–49.

Pol·lock (pol′ək), **Jackson,** 1912–56, U.S. painter.

Po·lo (pō′lō), **Marco,** 1254?–1323?, Venetian traveler.

Pom·pey (pom′pē) Anglicized name of **Gnaeus Pompeius Mag·nus** (mag·nəs), 106–48 B.C., Roman general and statesman; defeated by Julius Caesar: called **the Great.**

Ponce de Le·ón (pons′ də· lē′ən, *Sp.* pôn′thä thä lā·ôn′), **Juan,** 1460?–1521, Sp. explorer; discovered Florida, 1513.

Pon·tius Pilate (pon′shəs, -tē·əs), Roman procurator of Judea 26–36 A.D., condemned Jesus to be crucified. Also called **Pilate** (pī′lət).

Pope (pōp), **Alexander,** 1688–1744, Eng. poet and satirist.

Por·ter (pôr′tər, pōr′-), **William Sydney** See O. HENRY.

Pound (pound), **Ezra (Loomis),** 1885–1972, U.S. poet.

Priest·ley (prēst′lē), **Joseph,** 1733–1804, Eng. clergyman, philosopher, and chemist; discovered oxygen.

Pro·kof·iev (prô·kôf′yəf), **Sergei Sergeyevich,** 1891–1953, Soviet composer. Also **Pro·kof′ieff.**

Ptol·e·my (tol′ə·mē) 2nd-c. Gk. astronomer, mathematician, and geographer in Alexandria: full name **Claudius Ptol·e·mae·us** (tol′ə·mē′əs).

Puc·ci·ni (pōōt·chē′nē), **Giacomo,** 1858–1924, Ital. operatic composer.

Pu·las·ki (pōō·las′kē, pə-; *Polish* pōō·läs′kē), **Casimir,** 1748–1779, Polish general in the Amer. Revolution.

Pur·cell (pûr′səl), **Henry,** 1658?–95, Eng. composer.

Push·kin (pōōsh′kin), **Aleksander Sergeyevich,** 1799–1837, Russ. poet.

Py·thag·o·ras (pi·thag′ər·əs) 6th-c. B.C. Gk. philosopher and mathematician.

Rab·e·lais (rab′ə·lā, *Fr.* rả·ble′), **François,** 1494?–1553?, Fr. humorist and satirist: pseud. **Al·co·fri·bas Na·sier** (ȧl·kô·frē·bas′ nả·zyā′).

Rach·ma·ni·noff (räkh·mä′ni·nôf), **Sergei Vassilievich,** 1873–1943, Russ. pianist and composer.

Ra·cine (rả·sēn′), **Jean Baptiste,** 1639–99, Fr. dramatist.

Ra·leigh (rô′lē), **Sir Walter,** 1552–1618, Eng. courtier, colonizer, admiral, and poet; beheaded. Also *Brit.* **Ra′legh.**

Ram·e·ses II (ram′ə·sēz), 1292–1225 B.C., Egyptian king; allegedly the pharaoh who oppressed the Israelites. Also **Ram·ses II** (ram′sēz).

Ran·dolph (ran′dolf), **A(sa) Philip,** 1889–1979, U.S. labor leader.

Raph·a·el (raf′ē·əl, rä′fē-), 1483–1520, Ital. painter: full name **Raphael (or Raffaello) San·zio** (sän′tsyō).

Ra·vel (rả·vel′), **Maurice Joseph,** 1875–1937, Fr. composer.

Reed (rēd), **Walter,** 1851–1902, U.S. army surgeon.

Rem·brandt (rem′brant), 1606–69, Du. painter: full name **Rembrandt Harmenszoon van Rijn** (vän rīn) or **van Ryn.**

Re·noir (rə·nwàr′), **Pierre Auguste,** 1840–1919, Fr. Impressionist painter.

Re·vere (ri·vir′), **Paul,** 1735–1818, Amer. Revolutionary patriot and silversmith; famous for his ride the night of April 18, 1775, to warn of the approach of British troops.

Rhee (rē), **Syngman,** 1875–1965, Korean statesman; president of the Republic of Korea 1948–60.

Rhodes (rōdz), **Cecil John,** 1853–1902, Brit. colonial statesman, financier, and philanthropist, active in S. Africa.

Rich·ard I (rich′ərd), 1157–99, king of England 1189–99: called **the Lion-Heart.** Also called *Coeur de Lion.*

Richard III, 1452–85, duke of Gloucester, king of England 1483–85: killed at Bosworth Field: called **Crouch·back** (krouch′bak′).

Ri·che·lieu (rē·shə·lyœ′), **Duc de,** 1585–1642, Armand Jean du Plessis, Fr. cardinal and statesman: called **E·mi·nence Rouge** (ā·mē·näns′ rōōzh′).

Rie·mann (rē′män), **George Friedrich Bernhard,** 1826–66, Ger. mathematician.

Ril·ke (ril′kə), **Rainer Maria,** 1875–1926, Austrian poet born in Prague.

Rim·baud (ran·bō′), **Arthur,** 1854–91, Fr. poet: full name **Jean Nicholas Arthur Rimbaud.**

Rim·sky-kor·sa·kov (rim/skē·kôr′sə·kôf), **Nicholas Andreievich,** 1844–1908, Russ. composer.

Ri·ve·ra (rē·vä′rä), **Diego,** 1886–1957, Mexican painter.

Robes·pierre (rōbz′pē·âr), 1758–94, Fr. Revolutionary leader; guillotined: full name **Maximilien François Marie Isidore de Robespierre:** called the **Incorruptible.**

Rock·e·fel·ler (rok′ə·fel′ər), **John D(avison),** 1839–1937, U.S. industrialist and philanthropist.

Ro·din (rō·dan′), **Auguste,** 1840–1917, Fr. sculptor.

Roent·gen (rent′gən, runt′-; *Ger.* rœnt′gən), **Wilhelm Konrad,** 1845–1923, Ger. physicist. Also **Rönt′gen.**

Rog·ers (roj′ərz), **Will,** 1879–1935, U.S. actor and humorist: full name **William Penn Adair Rogers.**

Roi So·leil (rwả sô·lå′) is see LOUIS XIV.

Rom·u·lo (rom′yōō·lō), **Carlos Pena,** born 1899, Philippine statesman, general and writer.

Ron·sard (rôn·sàr′), **Pierre de,** 1524–85, Fr. poet.

Roo·se·velt (rō′zə·velt, rōz′velt, -vəlt), **(Anna) Eleanor,** 1884–1962, *née* Roosevelt, U.S. lecturer, writer, and diplomat; wife of Franklin Delano. — **Franklin Delano,** 1882–1945, U.S. statesman, 32nd president of the U.S. 1933–45. — **Theodore,** 1858–1919, U.S. army officer and statesman; 26th president of the U.S. 1901–09.

Ross (rôs), **Betsy,** 1752–1836, *née* Griscom, Amer. patriot; reputed to have made the first American flag.

Ros·si·ni (rôs·sē′nē), **Gioacchino Antonio,** 1792–1868, Ital. composer.

Roth·schild (rôth′child, *Ger.* rōt′shilt), **Mayer Anselm,** 1743–1812, founder of the worldwide banking enterprise **(House of Rothschild)** at Frankfort on the Main, Germany.

Rou·get de Lisle (roo·zhē′ də lēl′), **Claude Joseph,** 1760–1836, Fr. army officer and composer; wrote the *Marseillaise,* 1792.

Rous·seau (rōō·sō′), **Henri,** 1844–1910, Fr. painter: called **le Dou·an·ier** (lə· dwȧ·nyā′) (the customs officer). — **Jean Jacques,** 1712–78, Fr. philosopher and author, born in Switzerland.

Ru·bens (rōō′bənz. *Flemish* rü′bəns), **Peter Paul,** 1577–1640, Flemish painter.

Rus·kin (rus′kin), **John,** 1819–1900, Eng. art critic and author.

Rus·sell (rus′əl), **Bertrand (Arthur William),** 1872–1970, 3rd Earl Russell, Eng. mathematician and philosopher.

Ruth (rōōth), **George Herman,** 1895–1948, U.S. baseball player: called **Babe Ruth.**

Ruth·er·ford (ruth′ər·fərd), **Sir Ernest,** 1871–1937, first Baron Rutherford, Brit. physicist born in New Zealand.

Sade (sȧd), **Comte Donatien Alphonse François de,** 1740–1814, Fr. novelist and libertine: called **Marquis de Sade.**

Sal·a·din (sal′ə·din), 1137?–93, sultan of Egypt and Syria, 1174?–93: full name **Sa·lah-al-Din Yusuf ibn-Ayyud** (sə·lä′ä·dēn′).

Salk (sôk, sôlk), **Jonas,** born 1914, U.S. bacteriologist; developed injected vaccine for poliomyelitis.

Sand·burg (sand′bûrg, san′-), **Carl,** 1878–1967, U.S. poet and biographer.

Sang·er (sang′ər), **Margaret,** 1883–1966, *née* Higgins, U.S. leader in birth-control education.

San·ta·ya·na (sän′tä·yä′nä), **George,** 1863–1952, U.S. philosopher and author born in Spain.

Sap·pho (saf·ō) 6th-c. B.C. Gk. lyric poetess.

Sar·to (sär′tō), **Andrea del,** 1486–1531, Florentine painter: orig. name **Andrea d'Angelo di Fran·ces·co** (frän·ches′kō).

Sar·tre (sär′tr′). **Jean Paul,** born 1905, Fr. philosopher, novelist, and dramatist.

Scar·lat·ti (skär·lät′tē), **Alessandro,** 1659–1725, and his son, **Domenico,** 1685–1757, Ital. composers.

Schil·ler (shil′ər), **Johann Christoph Friedrich von,** 1759–1805, Ger. poet and dramatist.

Schlie·mann (shlē′män), **Heinrich,** 1822–90, Ger. merchant and archaeologist.

Schön·berg (shoen′berkh), **Arnold,** 1874–1951, Austrian composer and conductor active in the U.S.

Scho·pen·hau·er (shō′pən·hou′ər), **Arthur,** 1788–1860, Ger. philosopher.

Schrö·ding·er (shroe′ding·ər), **Erwin,** 1887–1961, Austrian physicist.

Schu·bert (shōō′bərt), **Franz Peter,** 1797–1828, Austrian composer.

Schu·mann (shōō′män), **Robert,** 1810–56, Ger. composer.

Schwann (shvän), **Theodor,** 1810–82, Ger. physiologist.

Schweit·zer (shvī′tsər), **Albert,** 1875–1965, Fr. (Alsatian) clergyman, physician, missionary, philosopher, and musicologist; founder and director of the hospital at Lambaréné, Gabon.

Scott (skot), **Sir Walter**, 1771–1832, Scot. novelist and poet.

Se·go·via (sā·gō′vyä), **Andrés**, born 1893, Sp. classical guitarist.

Sen·e·ca (sen′ə·kə), **Lucius Annaeus**, 4? B.C.–A.D. 65, Roman Stoic philosopher, statesman and dramatist: called **Seneca the Younger.**

Shake·speare (shāk′spir), **William**, 1564–1616, Eng. poet and dramatist. Also **Shake′spere, Shak′speare, Shak′spere.**

Shaw (shô), **George Bernard**, 1856–1950, Brit. dramatist, critic, and novelist born in Ireland.

Shel·ley (shel′ē), **Mary Wollstonecraft**, 1797–1851, *née* Godwin, Eng. novelist; wife of Percy Bysshe. — **Percy Bysshe**, 1792–1822, Eng. poet.

Sher·man (shûr′mən), **William Tecumseh**, 1829–91, Union general in the Civil War.

Shos·ta·ko·vich (shos′tə·kō′vich), **Dimitri**, 1906–75, Soviet composer.

Si·be·li·us (si·bā′lē·əs, -bāl′yəs), **Jean**, 1865–1957, Finnish composer.

Sitting Bull, 1834?–90, Sioux Indian chief; won battle of Little Big Horn in 1876.

Sit·well (sit′wel, -wəl), **Edith**, 1887–1964, Eng. poet.

Smith (smith), **Adam**, 1723–90, Scot. moralist and political economist. — **Alfred E(manuel)**, 1873–1944, U.S. political leader. — **Captain John**, 1580–1631, Eng. adventurer; president of the Virginia colony 1608–1609. — **Joseph**, 1805–1844, founder and first prophet of the Mormon Church; assassinated.

Smuts (smuts), **Jan Christiaan**, 1870–1950, S. African general and statesman; prime minister 1919–24, 1939–48.

Soc·ra·tes (sok′rə·tēz), 469?–399 B.C., Gk. philosopher; forced to commit suicide by drinking hemlock.

Soph·o·cles (sof′ə·klēz), 496?–406 B.C., Athenian tragic poet.

Spal·lan·za·ni (späl′län·dzä′nē), **Lazzaro**, 1729–99, Ital. biologist.

Spen·cer (spen′sər), **Herbert**, 1820–1903, Eng. philosopher.

Speng·ler (speng′glər), **Oswald**, 1880–1936, Ger. philosopher and historian.

Spen·ser (spen′sər), **Edmund**, 1552?–99, Eng. poet.

Spi·no·za (spi·nō′zə), **Baruch**, 1632–77, Du. philosopher. Also **Benedict Spinoza.**

Sta·lin (stä′lin), **Joseph**, 1879–1953, Soviet statesman; chief of state 1924–53: orig. name *Iosif Vissarionovich Dzhugashvili.*

Stein (stīn), **Gertrude**, 1874–1946, U.S. writer active in France.

Sten·dhal (stän·dàl′) Pseud. of *Marie Henri Beyle*, 1783–1842, Fr. novelist and critic.

Sterne (stûrn), **Laurence** 1713–68, Brit. novelist, born in Ireland.

Steu·ben (stoō′bən, *Ger.* shtoi′bən), **Baron Friedrich Wilhelm Ludolph Gerhard Augustin von**, 1730–94, Prussian general, served under Washington in the Amer. Revolutionary War.

Ste·ven·son (stē′vən·sən), **Adlai Ewing**, 1900–65, U.S. lawyer and political leader. — **Robert Louis (Balfour)**, 1850–94, Scot. novelist and essayist active in the U.S. and Samoa.

Stowe (stō), **Harriet Beecher**, 1811–96, U.S. novelist and humanitarian: orig. name **Harriet Elizabeth Bee·cher** (bē′·chər).

Stra·di·va·ri (strä′dē·vä′rē), **Antonio**, 1644?–1737, Ital. violinmaker. Also **Strad·i·var·i·us** (strad/i·vâr′ē·əs).

Strauss (strous), **Johann**, 1804–49, Austrian composer. — **Johann**, 1825–99, Austrian composer; son of Johann: called **the Waltz King.** — **Richard**, 1864–1949, Ger. composer.

Stra·vin·sky (strə·vin′skē), **Igor Fëdorovich**, 1882–1971, U.S. composer born in Russia.

Strind·berg (strind′bûrg), **August**, 1849–1912, Sw. dramatist and novelist.

Sul·li·van (sul′ə·vən), **Sir Arthur (Seymour)**, 1842–1900, Eng. composer.

Sun Yat-sen (soōn′ yät′sen′), 1866–1925, Chinese political leader; founder of the Kuomintang 1912.

Swift (swift), **Jonathan**, 1667–1745, Eng. clergyman, satirist, and man of letters born in Ireland: called **Dean Swift.**

Swin·burne (swin′bûrn), **Algernon Charles**, 1837–1909 Eng. poet and critic.

Tac·i·tus (tas′ə·təs), **Cornelius**, 55?–117?, Roman historian.

Taft (taft), **Robert Alphonso**, 1899–1953, U.S. legislator; son of William Howard. — **William Howard**, 1857–1930, U.S. statesman and jurist, 27th president of the U.S. 1909–13.

Tal·ley·rand-Pe·ri·gord (tà·le·rän′pā·rē·gôr′), **Charles Maurice de**, 1754–1838, Prince de Bénévent, Fr. statesman and diplomat: often called **Tal·ley·rand** (tal′ē·rand).

Tam·er·lane (tam′ər·lān), 1336?–1405, Mogul conqueror: also called **Tam·bur·laine** (tam′bər·lān).

Tar·king·ton (tär′king·tən), **Booth**, 1869–1946, U.S. novelist: full name **Newton Booth Tarkington.**

Tay·lor (tā′lər), **Zachary**, 1784–1850, U.S. general, 12th president of the U.S. 1849–50: called **Old Rough and Ready.**

Tchai·kov·sky (chī·kof′skē), **Pëtr Ilich**, 1840–93, Russ. composer.

Tche·khov (chek′ôf), **Anton** See CHEKHOV.

Ten·ny·son (ten′ə·sən), **Alfred**, 1809–92, 1st Baron Tennyson, Eng. poet; poet laureate 1850–92: called **Alfred, Lord Tennyson.**

Ter·ence (ter′əns), 185?–159? B.C., Roman comic playwright born in Africa: full name **Publius Terentius A·fer** (ā′fər).

Thack·er·ay (thak′ə·rē), **William Makepeace**, 1811–63, Eng. author.

Thant (thont), **U**, 1909–74, Burmese statesman; secretary general of the United Nations 1961–71.

Thatch·er (thach′er), **Margaret Hilda**, born 1925, Brit. stateswoman; prime minister 1979–.

Tho·mas (tom′əs), **Dylan (Marlais)**, 1914–53, Brit. poet and author born in Wales. — **Norman (Mattoon)**, 1884–1968, U.S. socialist leader and writer.

Thomas à Becket, St., 1118–70, Eng. prelate; archbishop of Canterbury 1162–70; murdered for opposing Henry II; called **Saint Thomas Becket, Saint Thomas of London.**

Tho·reau (thôr′ō, thō′rō, thə·rō′), **Henry David**, 1817–62, U.S. author: orig. name **David Henry Thoreau.**

Thu·cyd·i·des (thoō·sid′ə·dēz, thyoō-), 471?–401? B.C., Gk. historian.

Til·lich (til′ik, -ikh), **Paul**, 1886–1965, Ger. Protestant theologian and philosopher active in the U.S.

Tin·to·ret·to (tin′tə·ret′ō, *Ital.* tēn′tô·ret′tō), 1518–94, Venetian painter: orig. name **Jacopo Ro·bus·ti** (rō·boōs′tē).

Ti·tian (tish′ən), 1477?–1576, Venetian painter: orig. name **Ti·zia·no Ve·cel·lio** (tē·tsä′nō vā·chel′lyō).

Ti·to (tē′tō), **Marshal**, 1892–1980, Yugoslav Communist statesman and leader; prime minister 1945–53; president 1953–80: orig. name **Josip Broz.**

Tocque·ville (tōk·vēl′), **Alexis Charles Henri Maurice Clérel de**, 1805–59, Fr. statesman and political writer.

Tol·stoy (tōl′stoi, tol′-), **Count Leo Nikolaevich**, 1828–1910, Russ. novelist and social reformer. Also **Tol′stoi.**

Tor·que·ma·da (tôr′kwə·mä′də, *Sp.* tôr′kä·mä′thä), **Tomás de**, 1420?–98, Dominican monk; head of the Inquisition in Spain.

Tos·ca·ni·ni (tos′kə·nē′nē; *Ital.* tôs′kä·nē′nē), **Arturo**, 1867–1957, Ital. orchestra conductor active in the U.S.

Tou·louse-Lau·trec (toō·loōz′lō·trek′), **Henri Marie Raymond de**, 1864–1901, Fr. painter and lithographer.

Tra·jan (trā′jən), 53?–117, Roman emperor 98–117: full name **Marcus Ulpius Tra·ja·nus** (trā·jā′nəs).

Trot·sky (trot′skē), **Leon**, 1879–1940, Russ. Revolutionist and Bolshevist leader; banished 1929; murdered: orig. name **Lev Davidovitch Bron·stein** (brun′shtīn).

Tru·deau (troō·dō′), **Pierre Elliott**, born 1919, Canadian statesman; prime minister 1968–79, 1980–: full name **Joseph Phillippe Pierre Ives Elliotte Trudeau.**

Tru·man (troō′mən), **Harry S**, 1884–1972, 33rd president of the U.S. 1945–53.

Tul·ly (tul′ē) See CICERO.

Tur·ge·nev (toōr·gā′nyef), **Ivan Sergeyevich**, 1818–83, Russ. novelist. Also **Tur·ge′niev.**

Tut-ankh-a·men (toōt′ängk·ä′min), 14th-c. B.C. Egyptian pharaoh. Also **Tut′ankh·a′mon.**

Twain (twān), **Mark** See MARK TWAIN.

Ty·ler (tī′lər), **John**, 1790–1862, 10th president of the U.S. 1841–45.

U·na·mu·no (oō′nä·moō′nō), **Miguel de**, 1864–1936, Sp. philosopher, novelist and poet.

U·rey (yoōr′ē), **Harold Clayton**, born 1893, U.S. chemist.

U·tril·lo (oō·trē′lyō, oō·tril′ō; *Fr.* ü·trē·lō′), **Maurice**, 1883–1955, Fr. painter.

Val·en·tine (val′ən·tīn), **St.** 3rd-c. Christian martyr.

Va·le·ra (və·ler′ə), **Eamon De** See DE VALERA.

Van Bu·ren (van byoōr′ən), **Martin** 1782–1862, 8th president of the U.S. 1837–{1.

Van Dyck (van dīk′), **Sir Anthony**, 1599–1641, Flemish painter active in England. Also **Van·dyke′.**

van Eyck (van īk′), **Jan**, 1385?–1440, Flemish painter.

van Gogh (van gō′, gôkh), **Vincent**, 1853–90, Du. painter.

Va·sa·ri (vä·zä′rē), **Giorgio**, 1511–74, Ital. painter, architect, and biographer of artists.

Veb·len (veb′lən), **Thorstein Bunde**, 1857–1929, U.S. economist and sociologist.

Ve·ga (vā′gə, *Sp.* bā′gä), **Lope de**, 1562–1635, Sp. dramatist and poet. Full name **Lope Félix de Vega Car·pio** (kär′pyo).

Ve·lás·quez (və·las′kwiz, *Sp.* bä·läs′käth), **Diego**, 1599–1660, Sp. painter: full name **Diego Rodriguez de Silva y Velásquez.** Also **Ve·láz′quez** (bä·läth′käth).

Ver·di (ver′dē), **Giuseppe**, 1813–1901, Ital. composer.

Ver·gil (vûr′jil) Anglicized name of **Publius Vergilius Ma·ro** (mä′rō), 70–19 B.C., Roman epic poet. Also *Virgil.*

Ver·laine (ver·len′), **Paul**, 1844–96, Fr. poet.

Ver·meer (vər·mâr′), **Jan**, 1632–75, Du. painter. Also **Jan van der Meer van Delft** (vän dər mâr vän delft′).

Verne (vûrn, *Fr.* vern), **Jules**, 1828–1905, Fr. novelist.

Ve·ro·ne·se (vā′rō·nā′zā), **Paolo**, 1528–88, Venetian painter: orig. name **Paolo Ca·glia·ri** (kä′lyä·rē).

Ve·sa·li·us (vi·sā′lē·əs), **Andreas**, 1514–64, Belgian physician; founder of modern anatomy.

Ves·puc·ci (ves·pōōt′chē), **Amerigo**, 1451–1512, Ital. explorer for whom America was named.

Vic·to·ri·a (vik·tôr′ē·ə, -tō′rē·ə), 1819–1901, queen of England 1837–1901: full name **Alexandrina Victoria**.

Vin·ci (vēn′chē), **Leonardo da** See DA VINCI.

Vir·gil (vûr′jəl) See VERGIL.

Vi·val·di (vē·väl′dē), **Antonio**, 1675?–1743, Ital. violinist and composer: called **the Red Priest**.

Vol·taire (vol·târ′; *Fr.* vôl·târ′) Pseud. of *François Marie Arouet*, 1694–1778, Fr. author and philosopher.

Wag·ner (väg′nər), **Richard**, 1813–83, Ger. composer, poet, and critic: full name **Wilhelm Richard Wagner**.

Waks·man (waks′mən), **Selman Abraham**, 1888–1973, U.S. biochemist and microbiologist born in Russia.

Wald·heim (vält′hīm), **Kurt**, born 1918, Austrian statesman; secretary general of the United Nations 1972–.

War·ren (wôr′ən, wor′-), **Earl**, 1891–1974, U.S. administrator and jurist; chief justice of the Supreme Court 1953–1969.

Wash·ing·ton (wosh′ing·tən, wô′shing-), **Booker T(aliaferro)**, 1856–1915, U.S. educator. — **George**, 1732–99, Amer. Revolutionary patriot, general, and statesman; 1st president of the U.S. 1789–97.

Watt (wot), **James**, 1736–1819, Scot. inventor and engineer.

Web·ster (web′stər), **Daniel**, 1782–1852, U.S. statesman and orator. — **Noah**, 1758–1843, U.S. lexicographer.

Wel·ling·ton (wel′ing·tən), **Duke of**, 1769–1852, Arthur Wellesley, Brit. general and statesman born in Ireland; prime minister 1828–30: called **the Iron Duke**.

Wells (welz), **H(erbert) G(eorge)**, 1866–1946, Eng. author.

Wes·ley (wes′lē, *Brit.* wez′lē), **John**, 1703–91, Eng. clergyman; founder of Methodism.

Whis·tler (hwis′lər), **James Abbott McNeill**, 1834–1903, U.S. painter and etcher, active in England.

White·head (hwīt′hed), **Alfred North**, 1861–1947, Eng. mathematician and philosopher active in the U.S.

Whit·man (hwit′mən), **Walt**, 1819–92, U.S. poet: full name **Walter Whitman**.

Whit·ney (hwit′nē), **Eli**, 1765–1825, U.S. inventor and manufacturer; devised the cotton gin.

Wie·ner (wē′nər), **Norbert**, 1894–1964, U.S. mathematician.

Wilde (wīld), **Oscar**, 1856–1900, Irish poet, dramatist, and novelist: full name **Oscar Fingal O'Flahertie Wills Wilde.**

Wil·kins (wil′kinz), **Roy**, born 1901, U.S. civil rights leader for Negroes.

Wil·liam I (wil′yəm), 1027?–87, Duke of Normandy; invaded England 1066; king of England 1066–87: called **William the Conqueror, William the Norman.**

Wil·liams (wil′yəms), **Roger**, 1603?–83, Eng. clergyman in New England; founded Rhode Island. — **Tennessee**, born 1916, U.S. playwright: orig. name **Thomas Lanier Williams.**

Wil·son (wil′sən), **(Thomas) Woodrow**, 1856–1924, U.S. educator and statesman; 28th president of the U.S. 1913–21.

Wind·sor (win′zər), **Duke of**, 1894–1972; King of England as *Edward VIII* 1936; abdicated.

Witt·gen·stein (wit′gən·stīn, *Ger.* vit′gen·shtīn), **Ludwig Joseph Johann**, 1889–1951, Brit. philosopher, born in Austria.

Words·worth (wûrdz′wûrth), **William**, 1770–1850, Eng. poet; laureate 1843–50.

Wren (ren), **Sir Christopher**, 1632–1723, Eng. architect.

Wright (rīt), **Frank Lloyd**, 1869–1959, U.S. architect. — **Orville**, 1871–1948, U.S. pioneer in aviation. — **Wilbur**, 1867–1912, U.S. pioneer in aviation; brother of Orville.

Wyc·liffe (wik′lif), **John**, 1324?–84, Eng. religious reformer; first translator of entire Bible into English. Also **Wyc′lif.**

Xa·vi·er (zā′vē·ər, zav′ē-), **Saint Francis**, 1506–52, Sp. Jesuit missionary in the orient; one of the founders of the society of Jesus: called **the Apostle of the Indies.**

Yeats (yāts), **William Butler**, 1865–1939, Irish poet, dramatist, and essayist.

Young (yung), **Brigham**, 1801–77, U.S. Mormon leader.

Za·ra·thus·tra (zä′rä·thōōs′trä, zar′ə·thōōs′trə) See ZOROASTER.

Zeng·er (zeng′ər), **John Peter**, 1697–1746, Amer. printer and newspaper publisher born in Germany; noted as the central figure in a lawsuit that helped establish the freedom of the press.

Ze·no of Elea (zē′nō) 5th c. B.C. Gk. philosopher.

Zeno the Stoic, died 264? B.C., Gk. philosopher; founder of the Stoic school.

Zo·la (zō′lə, zō·lä; *Fr.* zō·lä′), **Émile**, 1840–1902, Fr. novelist and journalist.

Zo·ro·as·ter (zō′rō·as′tər) 6th- or 7th-c. B.C. Iranian religious reformer; founder of Zoroastrianism. Also *Zarathustra.*

ABBREVIATIONS

A *Chem.* Argon.
a. 1. About. 2. Accepted. 3. Acre(s). 4. Acting. 5. Active. 6. Ad (L, at). 7. Adjective. 8. After. 9. Afternoon. 10. *Music* Alto. 11. Amateur. 12. *Electr.* Ampere. 13. Anno (L, in the year). 14. *Electr.* Anode. 15. Anonymous. 16. Ante (L, before). 17. Approved. 18. Are (measure). 19. Area. 20. Assist(s) (baseball).
A or Å *Physics* Angstrom unit(s).
A. 1. Absolute (temperature). 2. Academy. 3. Acre. 4. America; American.
AA or A.A. *Mil.* Antiaircraft.
AAA or A.A.A. 1. Amateur Athletic Association. 2. American Automobile Association. 3. Automobile Association of America.
AAAA or A.A.A.A. 1. Amateur Athletic Association of America. 2. Associated Actors and Artists of America.
A.A.A.L. American Academy of Arts and Letters.
AAAS or A.A.A.S. 1. American Academy of Arts and Sciences. 2. American Association for the Advancement of Science.
AAF or A.A.F. Formerly, Army Air Forces.
A. and M. Agricultural and Mechanical (College).
A.A.U. Amateur Athletic Union.
A.A.U.P. American Association of University Professors.
A.A.U.W. American Association of University Women.
ab. or a.b. In baseball, (times) at bat.
Ab *Chem.* Alabamine.
A.B. Bachelor of Arts (L *Artium Baccalaureus*).
A.B. or a.b. Able-bodied seaman.
abbr. or abbrev. Abbreviation.
abl. *Gram.* Ablative.
abn. Airborne.
Abp. or abp. Archbishop.
abr. 1. Abridged. 2. Abridgment.
abs. 1. Absent. 2. Absolute (temperature). 3. Absolutely.
ac. 1. Account. 2. Acre.
a/c or A/C (*pl.* **a/cs** or **A/Cs**) Account; account current.
Ac *Chem.* Actinium.
AC or A.C. Air Corps. 2. Army Corps.
AC or A.C. or a.c. *Electr.* Alternating current.
A.C. 1. After Christ. 2. Athletic Club.
acad. Academic; academy.
acc. 1. Account. 2. *Gram.* Accusative.
accel. 1. *Music* Accelerando. 2. Accelerate.
accus. *Gram.* Accusative.
ack. Acknowledge; acknowledgment.
A.C.P. American College of Physicians.
acpt. Acceptance (in banking).
ACS or A.C.S. American Chemical Society.
A/Cs Pay. Accounts payable.
A/Cs Rec. Accounts receivable.
Act *Chem.* Actinium.
actg. Acting.
ad. 1. Adapted; adaptor. 2. Add. 3. Advertisement.
a.d. After date.
AD *Mil.* Active duty.
A.D. In the year of our Lord (L *anno domini*).
A.D.A. 1. American Dental Association. 2. Americans for Democratic Action.
A.D.C. or ADC or a.d.c. Aide-de-camp.
add. 1. Addenda; addendum. 2. Addition. 3. Address.
ad fin. At, to, or toward the end (L *ad finem*).
adj. 1. Adjacent. 2. Adjective. 3. Adjourned. 4. Adjunct. 5. Adjustment (in banking). 6. Adjutant.
ad loc. At or to the place (L *ad locum*).
adm. 1. Administrative; administrator. 2. Admitted.
ADM or Adm. Admiral.
admin. Administration; administrator.
admrx. or admx. Administratrix.
ads or A.D.S. Autograph document signed.
A.D.S. American Dialect Society.
adv. 1. Ad valorem (L). 2. Advance. 3. *Gram.* Adverb; adverbial. 4. Advertisement. 5. Advise. 6. Advocate. 7. Against (L *adversus*).
advt. Advertisement.
ae. At the age of; aged (L *aetatis*).
A.E.A. Actors' Equity Association.
A.E. and P. Ambassador Extraordinary and Plenipotentiary.
AEC Atomic Energy Commission.
AEF or A.E.F. American Expeditionary Force(s).
aeron. Aeronautic; aeronautics.
AF 1. Air Force. 2. Anglo-French; also **A.F.**
AF or A.F., a.f., or a-f Audio frequency.
AFB Air Force Base.
AFL or A.F.L. or A.F. of L. American Federation of Labor.
AFL-CIO or A.F.L.-C.I.O. American Federation of Labor and the Congress of Industrial Organizations.

AFNC Air Force Nurse Corps.
AFRes. Air Force Reserve.
AFROTC Air Force Reserve Officers Training Corps.
Ag *Chem.* Silver (L *argentum*).
Ag. August.
AG Adjutant General.
A.G. 1. Attorney General. 2. Joint-stock company (G *Aktiengesellschaft*).
agcy. Agency.
agr. Agricultural; agriculture; agriculturist.
agric. Agricultural; agriculture; agriculturist.
A.H. In the year of Hegira (L *anno* the *Hegirae*).
AI Aircraft interception.
AKC or A.K.C. American Kennel Club.
al. 1. Other things (L *alia*). 2. Other persons (L *alii*).
Al *Chem.* Aluminum.
AL or AL. or A.L. Anglo-Latin.
Ala. Alabama.
ALA or A.L.A. American Library Association.
Alas. Alaska (unofficial).
Ald. or, as title, Aldm. Alderman.
alg. *Math.* Algebra.
Alg. 1. Algeria; Algerian. 2. Algiers.
ALP or A.L.P. American Labor Party.
als or A.L.S. Autograph letter signed.
alt. 1. Alternate; alternating; alternation(s); alternative. 2. Altitude. 3. *Music* Alto.
alter. Alteration.
alum. Aluminum.
am. Ammeter.
Am *Chem.* Americium.
Am. America; American.
AM or A.M., or a-m Amplitude modulation.
A.M. 1. Master of Arts (L *Artium Magister*). 2. Associate member.
A.M. or a.m. Ante meridiem; before noon.
AMA or A.M.A. 1. American Management Association. 2. American Medical Association.
Amb. Ambassador.
AMC Air Materiel Command.
AMDG or A.M.D.G. To the greater glory of God (L *ad majorem Dei gloriam*).
A.M.E. African Methodist Episcopal.
Amer. America; American.
AMG Allied (or American) Military Government.
Am. Ind. American Indian.
amp. *Electr.* Amperage; ampere(s).
amp.-hr. *Electr.* Ampere-hour.
amt. Amount.
Am·vets (am′vets′) American Veterans of World War II and Korea.
an. Anno (L, in the year).
AN or A.N. or A.-N. Anglo-Norman.
anal. 1. Analogous; analogy. 2. Analysis; analytic(al).
anat. Anatomical; anatomist; anatomy.
ANC or A.N.C. Army Nurse Corps.
and. Andante.
Angl. 1. Anglican. 2. Anglicized.
ANGUS Air National Guard of the United States.
anim. Animato.
ann. 1. Annals. 2. Anni (L, years). 3. Annual. 4. Annuity.
anon. Anonymous.
ans. Answer; answered.
ant. 1. Antenna. 2. Antiquarian. 3. Antiquity. 4. Antonym(s).
ANTA American National Theatre and Academy.
antiq. 1. Antiquarian. 2. Antiquities.
ANZAC or A.N.Z.A.C. Australian and New Zealand Army Corps.
A/O or a/o Account of.
AOL or A.O.L. or a.o.l. *Mil.* Absent over leave.
ap. Apothecaries' (weight or measure).
Ap. 1. Apostle. 2. April.
AP *Mil.* 1. Air Police. 2. Armor-piercing.
AP or A.P. Associated Press.
apmt. Appointment.
APO Army Post Office.
Apoc. 1. Apocalypse. 2. Apocrypha; Apocryphal.
app. 1. Apparent(ly): also **appar.** 2. Appended. 3. Appendix. 4. Appointed. 5. Apprentice.
approx. Approximate(ly).
Apr or Apr. April.
apt. (*pl.* **apts.**) Apartment.
aq. or Aq. Aqua.
ar. 1. Aromatic. 2. Arrival; arrive.
a.r. In the year of the reign (L *anno regni*).
Ar *Chem.* Argon.
Ar. 1. Arabia; Arabic. 2. Aramaic. 3. Silver (L *argentum*).

ARC or **A.R.C.** American Red Cross.
arch. 1. Archaic; archaism. 2. Archery. 3. Archipelago. 4. Architect; architectural; architecture.
Arch. Archbishop.
Archbp. Archbishop.
Archd. 1. Archdeacon. 2. Archduke.
archeol. Archeology.
archit. Architecture.
archt. Architect.
arg. Silver (L *argentum*).
arith. Arithmetic(al).
Ariz. Arizona.
Ark. Arkansas.
Ar.M. Master of Architecture (L *Architecturae Magister*).
Armen. Armenian.
arr. 1. Arrange; arranged; arrangement(s). 2. Arrival; arrive; arrived.
art. 1. Article. 2. Artificial. 3. Artist.
Arty. Artillery.
A.R.V. American (Standard) Revised Version (of the Bible).
As *Chem.* Arsenic.
AS *Mil.* Antisubmarine.
AS or **AS.**, **A.S.**, or **A.-S.** Anglo-Saxon.
ASA or **A.S.A.** American Standards Association.
asb. Asbestos.
ASCAP or **A.S.C.A.P.** American Society of Composers, Authors and Publishers.
asgd. Assigned.
ASN *Mil.* Army Service Number.
A.S.P.C.A. American Society for the Prevention of Cruelty to Animals.
ass. 1. Assistant. 2. Association.
assd. Assigned.
assn. Association.
assoc. 1. Associate. 2. Association.
asst. Assistant.
astr. Astronomer; astronomical; astronomy.
astrol. Astrologer; astrological; astrology.
astron. Astronomer; astronomical; astronomy.
at. 1. *Physics* Atmosphere. 2. Atomic.
At *Chem.* Astatine.
AT *Mil.* Antitank.
ATC Air Traffic Control.
athl. Athlete; athletic; athletics.
atm. *Physics* Atmosphere; atmospheric.
at. no. Atomic number.
att. 1. Attention. 2. Attorney.
atten. Attention.
attn. Attention.
attrib. 1. Attribute. 2. Attributive.
atty. Attorney.
Atty. Gen. Attorney General.
a.u. or **å.u.**, **A.U.** or **A.U.** *Physics* Angstrom unit(s).
Au *Chem.* Gold (L *aurum*).
aud. Auditor.
aug. Augmentative.
Aug. or **Aug** 1. August. 2. Augustan; Augustus.
AUS or **A.U.S.** Army of the United States.
auth. 1. Author. 2. Authority. 3. Authorized.
Auth. Ver. Authorized Version (of the Bible).
auto. 1. Automatic. 2. Automotive.
aux. or **auxil.** Auxiliary.
av. 1. Average. 2. Avoirdupois: also **avdp.**
av. or **Av.** Avenue.
A.V. Authorized Version (of the Bible).
ave. or **Ave.** Avenue.
avg. Average.
avn. Aviation.
avoir. Avoirdupois.
A/W 1. Actual weight. 2. All water.
AWOL (*as an acronym pronounced* ā′wôl) *Mil.* Absent or absence without leave. Also **awol, A.W.O.L., a.w.o.l.**
ax. 1. Axiom. 2. Axis.
az. Azimuth.

B *Chem.* Boron.
b Base.
B Bishop (chess).
B– Bomber.
B. 1. Bacillus. 2. Bible. 3. Boston. 4. British. 5. Brotherhood.
B. or **b.** 1. Bachelor. 2. Balboa (coin). 3. Base. 4. *Music* Bass; basso. 5. Bat. 6. Bay. 7. Bench. 8. *Dent.* Bicuspid. 9. Bolivar (coin). 10. Boliviano. 11. Book. 12. Born. 13. Brass. 14. Breadth. 15. Brother.
B/– 1. Bag. 2. Bale.
Ba *Chem.* Barium.
B.A. 1. Bachelor of Arts (L *Baccalaureus Artium*). 2. British Academy.
bach. Bachelor.
bacteriol. or **bact.** Bacteriological; bacteriology.

B.A.E. 1. Bachelor of Aeronautical Engineering. 2. Bachelor of Arts in Education.
B.Agr. or **B.Ag.** Bachelor of Agriculture (L *Baccalaureus Agriculturae*)
B.Ag.Sc. Bachelor of Agricultural Science.
bal. Balance; balancing.
Balt. Baltic.
bap. or **bapt.** Baptized.
Bapt. or **Bap.** Baptist.
bar. 1. Barometer; barometric. 2. Barrel. 3. Barrister.
B.Ar. Bachelor of Architecture.
BAR *Mil.* Browning automatic rifle.
B.Arch. Bachelor of Architecture.
barit. *Music* Baritone.
Bart. Baronet.
B.A.S. or **B.A.Sc.** 1. Bachelor of Agricultural Science. 2. Bachelor of Applied Science.
b.b. or **bb** Base(s) on balls.
B.B.A. or **B.Bus.Ad.** Bachelor of Business Administration.
BBC or **B.B.C.** British Broadcasting Corporation.
bbl. (*pl.* **bbls.**) Barrel.
B.C. 1. Bachelor of Chemistry. 2. Bachelor of Commerce. 3. Before Christ. 4. British Columbia.
B.C.E. 1. Bachelor of Chemical Engineering. 2. Bachelor of Civil Engineering.
bch. (*pl.* **bchs.**) Bunch.
B.Ch.E. Bachelor of Chemical Engineering.
B.C.L. Bachelor of Civil Law.
B.C.P. Book of Common Prayer.
B.C.S. Bachelor of Chemical Science.
bd (*pl.* **bds.**) 1. Board. 2. Bond. 3. Bound. 4. Bundle.
B/D or **b.d.** 1. Bank draft. 2. Bills discounted.
B.D. 1. Bachelor of Divinity. 2. Bills discounted.
bd.ft. Board feet.
bdg. Binding.
bdl. or **bdle.** Bundle.
bds. 1. Bundles. 2. (Bound in) boards.
B.D.S. Bachelor of Dental Surgery.
B.E. 1. Bachelor of Education. 2. Bachelor of Engineering. 3. Bank of England. 4. Board of Education.
B.E. or **B/E** or **b.e.** Bill of exchange.
B.E.E. Bachelor of Electrical Engineering.
B.E.F. British Expeditionary Force(s).
B. ès L. Bachelor of Letters (Fr. *Bachelier ès Lettres*).
bev or **BEV** Billion electron volts.
bf or **b.f.** *Printing* Boldface.
B/F Brought forward.
B.F. 1. Bachelor of Finance. 2. Bachelor of Forestry.
B.F.A. Bachelor of Fine Arts.
bg. (*pl.* **bgs.**) Bag.
B.G. Brigadier General.
Bi *Chem.* Bismuth.
Bib. Bible; Biblical.
bibl. Bibliographical.
Bibl. Biblical.
bibliog. Bibliographer; bibliography.
bicarb. Sodium bicarbonate.
b.i.d. *Med.* Twice a day (L *bis in die*).
biog. Biographer; biographical; biography.
biol. Biological; biologist; biology.
B.J. Bachelor of Journalism.
bk. 1. Bank. 2. Block. 3. Book.
Bk *Chem.* Berkelium.
bkg. Banking.
bkkpg. Bookkeeping.
bks. 1. Barracks. 2. Books.
bkt. 1. Basket(s). 2. Bracket.
bl. 1. Bale(s). 2. Barrel(s). 3. Black. 4. Blue.
b.l. or **B/L** Bill of Lading.
B.L. Bachelor of Laws.
B.L.A. Bachelor of Liberal Arts.
bld. *Printing* Boldface.
bldg. Building.
B.Lit. or **B.Litt.** Bachelor of Letters (Literature) (L *Baccalaureus Litterarum*).
blk. 1. Black. 2. Block. 3. Bulk.
B.LL. Bachelor of Laws (L *Baccalaureus Legum*).
bls. 1. Bales. 2. Barrels.
BLS Bureau of Labor Statistics.
B.L.S. Bachelor of Library Science.
blvd. Boulevard.
b.m. Board measure.
BM Bureau of Mines.
B.M. 1. Bachelor of Medicine (L *Baccalaureus Medicinae*). 2. Bachelor of Music (L *Baccalaureus Musicae*).
B.M.E. 1. Bachelor of Mechanical Engineering. 2. Bachelor of Mining Engineering.
B.Mech.E. Bachelor of Mechanical Engineering.
BMEWS *Mil.* Ballistic Missile Early Warning System.
BMR *Physiol.* Basal metabolic rate.
B.Mus. Bachelor of Music.

bn. or **Bn.**   Battalion.
B.N.   Bank note.
B.N.A.   1. Basel Anatomical Nomenclature (L *Basel Nomina Anatomica*).   2. British North America.
b.o.   1. Back order.   2. Bad order.   3. Box office.   4. Branch office.   5. Broker's order.   6. Buyer's option.   7. Body odor.
B/O   Brought over (bookkeeping).
bor.   Borough.
bot.   1. Botanical; botanist; botany.   2. Bottle.
B.O.T.   Board of Trade.
bp.   1. Birthplace.   2. Bishop.
b.p. or **bp.**   1. Below proof.   2. Boiling point.
B.P.   Bachelor of Pharmacy (L *Baccalaureus Pharmaciae*).
B.P. or **B.Ph.** or **B.Phil.**   Bachelor of Philosophy (L *Baccalaureus Philosophiae*).
B/P or **b.p.**   1. Bill of parcels.   2. Bills payable.
B.Pd. or **B.Pe.**   Bachelor of Pedagogy.
B.P.E.   Bachelor of Physical Education.
B.P.H.   Bachelor of Public Health.
br.   1. Branch.   2. Brand.   3. Bronze.   4. Brother.
Br   *Chem.* Bromine.
B/R or **b.r.**   Bills receivable.
B/R or **B.R.**   Bill of Rights.
B.Rec. or **b. rec.**   Bills receivable.
brev.   Brevet; brevetted.
Brig.   *Mil.* 1. Brigade.   2. Brigadier.
Brig. Gen.   Brigadier General.
Brit.   1. Britain; British.   2. Britannia.
bro. (pl. **bros.**)   Brother.
b.s.   1. Balance sheet.   2. Bill of sale.
B/s   1. Bags.   2. Bales.
B.S. or **B.Sc.**   Bachelor of Science (L *Baccalaureus Scientiae*).
B.S.A.   1. Bachelor of Scientific Agriculture.   2. Bibliographical Society of America.   3. Boy Scouts of America.
B.S.Ed.   Bachelor of Science in Education.
bsh.   Bushel(s).
Bs/L   Bills of lading.
BSM   Bronze Star Medal.
B.S.S. or **B.S.Sc.** or **B.S. in S.S.**   Bachelor of (Science in) Social Sciences.
Bt.   Baronet.
B.T. or **B.Th.**   Bachelor of Theology (L *Baccalaureus Theologiae*).
btry.   *Mil.* Battery.
BTU or **B.T.U.**, **B.Th.U.**, **b.t.u.**, or **btu**   British thermal unit.
bu. or **bu**   1. Bureau.   2. Bushel(s).
buck.   Buckram.
bul.   Bulletin.
bull.   Bulletin.
B.V.   1. Blessed Virgin (L *Beata Virgo*).   2. Farewell (L *bene vale*).
B.V.M.   Blessed Virgin Mary (L *Beata Virgo Maria*).
bvt.   Brevet; brevetted.
bx. (pl. **bxs.**)   Box.
Bz.   *Chem.* Benzene.

C   *Chem.* Carbon.
c. or **C.**   1. About (L *circa*).   2. Calends.   3. Candle.   4. *Electr.* Capacity.   5. Cape.   6. Carbon.   7. Carton.   8. Case.   9. Catcher (baseball).   10. Cathode.   11. Cent(s).   12. Center.   13. Centigrade.   14. Centime(s).   15. Centimeter(s).   16. Century.   17. Chancery.   18. Chapter.   19. Chief.   20. Child.   21. Church.   22. City.   23. Cloudy.   24. Consul.   25. Copper.   26. Copy.   27. Copyright.   28. Corps.   29. Cost.   30. Cubic.   31. *Electr.* Current.   32. Gallon (L *congius*).   33. Hundredweight.
C   *Math.* Constant.
C.   1. Catholic.   2. Celsius.   3. Celtic.   4. Chancellor.   5. Congress.   6. Conservative.   7. Court.
ca.   1. About (L *circa*).   2. Cathode.   3. Centare(s).
Ca   *Chem.* Calcium.
CA or **C.A.**   *Psychol.* Chronological age.
C.A.   1. Catholic Action.   2. Central America.   3. Confederate Army.   4. Court of Appeal.
C.A. or **c.a.**   1. Chartered accountant.   2. Chartered agent.   3. Chief accountant.   4. Claim agent.   5. Commercial agent.   6. Consular agent.   7. Controller of accounts
C/A   1. Capital account.   2. Credit account.   3. Current account.
CAB or **C.A.B.**   1. Civil Aeronautics Board.   2. Consumers Advisory Board.
C.A.F. or **c.a.f.**   1. Cost and freight.   2. Cost, assurance, and freight.
cal.   1. Calendar; calends.   2. Caliber.   3. Calorie(s) (small).
Cal.   1. California (unofficial).   2. Large calorie(s).
Calif.   California.
can.   1. Canon.   2. Canto.
canc.   Cancel; cancellation; canceled.
Cant.   1. Canterbury.   2. Canticles.   3. Cantonese.
Cantab.   Of Cambridge (L *Cantabrigiensis*).

cap.   1. Capacity.   2. (*pl.* **caps.**) Capital.   3. Capitalize.   4. Chapter (L *caput*).
CAP or **C.A.P.**   Civil Air Patrol.
CAPT or **Capt.**   *Mil.* Captain.
CAR or **C.A.R.**   Civil Air Regulations.
Car.   Carat(s).
Card. (title)   Cardinal.
CARE   Cooperative for American Remittances Everywhere.
cat.   1. Catalogue.   2. Catechism.
cath.   Cathedral.
Cath.   Catholic.
cav.   1. Cavalier.   2. Cavalry.
CAVU   *Aeron.* Ceiling and visibility unlimited.
c.b.   1. Center of buoyancy.   2. Confined to barracks.
Cb   1. *Chem.* Columbium.   2. *Meteorol.* Cumulonimbus.
CB   *Mil.* Construction Battalion.
C.B.   1. Bachelor of Surgery (L *Chirurgiae Baccalaureus*).   2. *Brit.* Companion of the Bath.   3. *Brit.* County borough.
C.B.D. or **c.b.d.**   Cash before delivery.
cc.   1. Chapters.   2. Cubic centimeter(s): also **c.c.**, **cc**
Cc   *Meteorol.* Cirrocumulus.
C.C. or **c.c.**   1. Carbon copy.   2. Cashier's check.   3. Chief clerk.   4. Circuit court.   5. City council; city councilor.   6. Common councilman.   7. Consular clerk.   8. Contra credit.   9. County clerk.   10. County commissioner.   11. County council.   12. County court.   13. Current account (F *compte courant*).
CCA   Commission for Conventional Armaments.
C.C.A.   1. Chief Clerk of the Admiralty.   2. Circuit Court of Appeals.
CCC   1. Civilian Conservation Corps.   2. Commodity Credit Corporation.
C.C.F.   Cooperative Commonwealth Federation.
cd.   Cord.
c.d.   Cash discount.
Cd   *Chem.* Cadmium.
C.D.   Civilian Defense.
cd. ft.   Cord foot (feet).
CDMB   Civil and Defense Mobilization Board.
CDR or **Cdr.**   *Mil.* Commander.
Ce   *Chem.* Cerium.
CE   1. Corps of Engineers.   2. Council of Europe.
C.E.   1. Chemical Engineer.   2. Chief Engineer.   3. Christian Endeavor.   4. Church of England.   5. Civil Engineer.
CEA   Council of Economic Advisers.
Celt.   Celtic.
cen.   1. Central.   2. Century.
cent.   1. Centered.   2. Centigrade.   3. Centimeter(s).
CERN   European Council for Nuclear Research (F *Centre Européen des Recherches Nucléaires*).
cert. or **certif.**   Certificate; certificated.
Cey.   Ceylon.
Cf   *Chem.* Californium.
cf.   1. Calif.   2. Compare (L *confer*).
c/f   Carried forward (bookkeeping).
c.f. or **cf**   Center field; center fielder (baseball).
C.F. or **c.f.**   Cost and freight.
C.F.I. or **c.f.i.**   Cost, freight, and insurance.
c.f.m. or **cfm**   Cubic feet per minute.
c.f.s. or **cfs**   Cubic feet per second.
cg or **cg.** or **cgm.**   Centigram(s).
CG   1. Commanding general.   2. Coast Guard: also **C.G.**
C.G. or **c.g.**   1. Center of gravity.   2. Consul general.
cgs   The centimeter-gram-second system of measurement in which the unit of length is the centimeter, the unit of mass is the gram, and the unit of time is one second. Also **c.g.s.**, CGS, C.G.S.
ch. or **Ch.**   1. Chain.   2. Champion.   3. Chancery.   4. Chaplain.   5. (*pl.* **chs.**) Chapter.   6. Check (in chess).   7. Chestnut.   8. Chief.   9. Child; children.   10. Church.   11. Of surgery (L *chirurgiae*).
C.H.   *Brit.* Companion of Honor.
C.H. or **c.h.**   1. Clearing-house.   2. Courthouse.   3. Customhouse.
Ch.B.   Bachelor of Surgery (L *Chirurgiae Baccalaureus*).
Ch.Clk.   Chief Clerk.
Ch.E.   Chemical Engineer.
chem.   Chemical; chemist; chemistry.
chg. (*pl.* **chgs.**)   Charge.
chgd. (*pl.* **chgs.**)   Charge.
Ch.J.   Chief Justice.
chm.   1. Checkmate.   2. Chairman: also **chmn.**
Ch.M.   Master of Surgery (L *Chirurgiae Magister*).
Chr.   1. Christ.   2. Christian.
chron. or **chronol.**   Chronological; chronology.
Chron.   Chronicles.
chs.   Chapters.
Ci.   *Meteorol.* Cirrus.
Cia. or **cia.**   Company (Sp. *compañia*).
CIA   Central Intelligence Agency.
CIC   *Mil.* Counterintelligence Corps.

C.I.D. *Brit.* Criminal Investigation Dept.

Cie. or **cie.** Company (F *compagnie*).

C.I.F. or **c.i.f.** Cost, insurance, and freight.

CINC or **C in C** *Mil.* Commander in Chief.

CIO or **C.I.O.** Congress of Industrial Organizations.

circ. or **cir.** 1. About (L *circa, circiter, circum*). 2. Circular. 3. Circulation. 4. Circumference.

cit. 1. Citation; cited. 2. Citizen.

civ. 1. Civil. 2. Civilian.

C.J. 1. Corpus juris (L, body of law). 2. Chief Judge. 3. Chief Justice.

ck. (*pl.* **cks.**) 1. Cask. 2. Check. 3. Cook.

cl. 1. Claim. 2. Class. 3. Classification. 4. Clause. 5. Clearance. 6. Clergyman. 7. Clerk. 8. Cloth.

cl. or **cl** Centiliter(s).

c.l. 1. Carload; carload lots. 2. Center line. 3. Civil law. 4. Craft loss (insurance).

Cl *Chem.* Chlorine.

clar. *Music* Clarinet.

class. 1. Classic; classical. 2. Classification. 3. Classified; classify.

clk. 1. Clerk. 2. Clock.

C.L.U. Chartered Life Underwriter.

Cm *Chem.* Curium.

cm. or **cm** Centimeter(s).

c.m. 1. Church missionary. 2. Circular mil. 3. Common meter. 4. Corresponding member.

CM *Mil.* Court martial.

C.M. Master of Surgery (L *Chirurgiae Magister*).

Cmdr. Commander.

C.M.G. Companion (of the Order) of St. Michael and St. George.

cml. Commercial.

CmlC *Mil.* Chemical Corps.

Cn *Meteorol.* Cumulonimbus.

C/N or **c.n.** 1. Circular note. 2. Credit note.

CNO *Mil.* Chief of Naval Operations.

CNS or **C.N.S.** *Med.* Central nervous system.

Co *Chem.* Cobalt.

c.o. or **c/o** 1. Care of. 2. Carried over.

Co. or **co.** (*pl.* **cos.**) 1. Company. 2. County.

CO or **C.O.** 1. *Mil.* Commanding Officer. 2. Conscientious objector.

C/O Cash order.

Cod. or **cod.** (*pl.* **Codd.** or **codd.**) Codex.

C.O.D. or **c.o.d.** 1. Cash on delivery. 2. Collect on delivery.

coef. or **coeff.** Coefficient.

C. of C. Chamber of Commerce.

C of S Chief of Staff.

col. 1. Collected; collector. 2. College. 3. Colonial; colony. 4. Color; colored. 5. Column.

Col. 1. Colombia. 2. Colonel. 3. Colorado (unofficial). 4. Colossians. 5. Columbia.

coll. 1. Colleague. 2. Collect; collection; collector. 3. College; collegiate. 4. Colloquial.

collab. Collaborated; collaboration; collaborator.

collat. Collateral.

colloq. Colloquial; colloquialism; colloquially.

Colo. Colorado.

Coloss. Colossians.

com. 1. Comedy; comic. 2. Comma. 3. Commentary. 4. Commerce; commercial. 5. Common; commonly. 6. Commune. 7. Communication(s).

Com. 1. Commission. 2. Commissioner. 3. Committee. 4. Communist.

comb. Combination; combining.

comdg. *Mil.* Commanding.

Comdr. *Mil.* Commander.

Comdt. *Mil.* Commandant.

coml. Commercial.

comm. 1. Commerce. 2. Commissary. 3. Commission. 4. Committee. 5. Commonwealth.

COMO or **Como.** *Mil.* Commodore.

comp. 1. Companion. 2. Comparative. 3. Compare. 4. Comparison. 5. Compilation; compiled; compiler. 6. Complete. 7. Composition. 8. Compositor. 9. Compound; compounded. 10. Comprising.

compar. Comparative.

Comr. Commissioner.

Com. Ver. Common Version (of the Bible).

con. 1. Against (L *contra*). 2. *Music* Concerto. 3. Conclusion. 4. Condense. 5. Connection. 6. Consolidate. 7. Continued. 8. Wife (L *conjunx*).

Con. 1. Conformist. 2. Consul.

conc. 1. Concentrate; concentrated; concentration. 2. Concerning.

cond. 1. Condition. 2. *Music* Conducted. 3. Conductivity. 4. Conductor.

conf. 1. Compare (L *confer*). 2. *Med.* Confection. 3. Conference. 4. Confessor.

Confed. 1. Confederate. 2. Confederation.

cong. Gallon (L *congius*).

Cong. 1. Congregational. 2. Congress; Congressional.

conj. 1. Conjugation. 2. Conjunction. 3. Conjunctive.

Conn. Connecticut.

cons. 1. Consecrated. 2. Conserve. 3. Consigned; consignment. 4. Consolidated. 5. Consonant. 6. Construction. 7. Consulting.

cons. or **Cons.** 1. Constable. 2. Constitution; constitutional. 3. Consul.

consol. Consolidated.

Const. or **const.** 1. Constable. 2. Constant. 3. Constitution.

constr. Construction.

cont. 1. Containing. 2. Contents. 3. Continent. 4. Continue; continued. 5. Contract; contraction. 6. Contrary.

Cont. Continental.

contd. Continued.

contemp. Contemporary.

contg. Containing.

contin. 1. Continued. 2. Let it be continued. (L *continuetur*).

contr. 1. Contract; contraction. 2. *Music* Contralto. 3. Control.

contrib. Contribution; contributor.

CONUS *Mil.* Continental United States.

co-op. or **coop.** Cooperative.

cop. 1. Copper. 2. Copyright; copyrighted.

cor. 1. Corner. 2. Coroner. 3. Corpus. 4. Correct; corrected. 5. Correlative. 6. Correspondence; correspondent; corresponding. 7. Corrupt.

Cor. Corinthians.

corol. or **coroll.** Corollary.

corp. or **corpn.** Corporation.

corr. 1. Correct; corrected. 2. Correspondence; correspondent; corresponding. 3. Corrupt; corrupted; corruption.

corresp. Correspondence.

C.O.S. or **c.o.s.** Cash on shipment.

cosec *Trig.* Cosecant.

cot *Trig.* Cotangent.

cp or **c.p.** Candlepower.

cp. Compare.

CP *Mil.* Command Post.

C.P. 1. Cape Province. 2. Chief Patriarch. 3. Common Prayer. 4. Communist Party.

C.P. or **c.p.** 1. Chemically pure. 2. Court of probate.

CPA or **C.P.A.** Certified Public Accountant.

cpd. Compound.

Cpl. *Mil.* Corporal.

cpm or **c.p.m.** Cycles per minute.

CPO or **C.P.O.** Chief Petty Officer.

cps or **c.p.s.** Cycles per second.

cps. Coupons.

CQ *Mil.* Charge of Quarters.

cr. 1. Created. 2. Credit; creditor. 3. Creek. 4. Crown(s).

Cr *Chem.* Chromium.

cres. or **cresc.** *Music* Crescendo.

crim. con. *Law* Criminal conversation.

crit. 1. Critic; criticism; criticize. 2. Critical.

crs. Credits; creditors.

Cs 1. *Chem.* Cesium. 2. *Meteorol.* Cirrostratus.

C/S or **cs.** Case(s).

C.S. Christian Science; Christian Scientist.

C.S. or **c.s.** 1. Capital stock. 2. Civil service.

C.S.A. Confederate States of America.

csc *Trig.* Cosecant.

CSC Civil Service Commission.

csk. 1. Cask. 2. Countersink.

CST or **C.S.T.** or **c.s.t.** Central Standard Time.

ct. 1. Cent(s). 2. County. 3. Court. 4. One hundred (L *centum*).

Ct. 1. Connecticut. 2. Count.

CT or **C.T.** or **c.t.** Central Time.

ctn *Trig.* Cotangent.

ctr. Center.

cts. 1. Centimes. 2. Cents. 3. Certificates.

cu. or **cu** Cubic.

Cu 1. *Chem.* Copper (L *cuprum*). 2. *Meteorol.* Cumulus.

cu. cm. Cubic centimeter(s).

cu. ft. Cubic foot or feet.

cu. in. Cubic inch(es).

cur. 1. Currency. 2. Current.

cu. yd. Cubic yard(s).

c/v Catalogue value.

C.V. Common Version (of the Bible).

CWO *Mil.* 1. Chief Warrant Officer. 2. Commissioned Warrant Officer.

C.W.O. or **c.w.o.** Cash with order.

cwt. Hundredweight.

cyc. Cyclopedia; cyclopedic.

cyl. Cylinder; cylindrical.

D *Chem.* Deuterium.
d. or **D.** 1. Dam (in animal pedigrees). 2. Date. 3. Daughter. 4. Day(s). 5. Dead. 6. Decree. 7. Degree. 8. Democrat(ic). 9. Deputy. 10. Diameter. 11. Died. 12. Director. 13. Dollar. 14. Door (stage). 15. Dose. 16. Dowager. 17. Drachma. 18. Dyne. 19. *Med.* Give (L *da*).
D. 1. December. 2. Department. 3. Deus. 4. Doctor. 5. Dominus. 6. Don (Sp.). 7. Duchess. 8. Duke.
da 1. Daughter. 2. Day(s). 3. Deciare.
D.A. District Attorney.
Dak. Dakota.
dal. or **dal** Decaliter.
Dan. 1. Daniel. 2. Danish.
Danl. Daniel.
DAR or **D.A.R.** Daughters of the American Revolution.
dat. *Gram.* Dative.
dau. Daughter.
db or **db.** Decibel(s).
d.b.a. Doing business as.
D.B.E. Dame (Commander, Order) of the British Empire.
d.b.h. In forestry, diameter at breast height.
D.Bib. Douai Bible.
dbl. Double.
DC *Mil.* Dental Corps.
DC or **D.C.** or **d.c.** *Electr.* Direct current.
D.C. 1. District of Columbia. 2. Doctor of Chiropractic. 3. Da capo.
D.C.L. 1. Doctor of Canon Law. 2. Doctor of Civil Law.
D.C.M. *Brit.* Distinguished Conduct Medal.
D.C.S. 1. Deputy Clerk of Sessions. 2. Doctor of Christian Science. 3. Doctor of Commercial Science.
dd. or **d/d** Delivered.
D/D or **D/d** or **d.d.** 1. Days after date. 2. Day's (or days') date.
D.D. Doctor of Divinity (L *Divinitatis Doctor*).
D.D. or **D/D** Demand draft.
D.D.S. Doctor of Dental Surgery.
D.D.Sc. Doctor of Dental Science.
DE *Mil.* Destroyer Escort.
deb. or **deben.** Debenture.
dec. 1. Deceased. 2. Declaration. 3. Declension. 4. Declination. 5. Decrease. 6. Decrescendo.
dec. Decimeter.
Dec. or **Dec** December.
decd. Deceased.
decim. Decimeter.
decl. Declension.
def. 1. Defective. 2. Defendant. 3. Defense. 4. Deferred. 5. Defined. 6. Definite. 7. Definition.
deg. Degree(s).
del. 1. Delegate. 2. Delete. 3. Deliver.
Del. Delaware.
Dem. Democrat; Democratic.
demon. Demonstrative.
dent. Dental; dentist; dentistry.
dep. 1. Department. 2. Departs; departure. 3. Deponent. 4. Depot. 5. Deputy.
dept. 1. Department. 2. Deputy.
der. Derivation; derivative; derived.
desc. Descendant.
D. ès L. Doctor of Letters (F *Docteur ès Lettres*).
De ès S. Doctor of Sciences (F *Docteur ès Sciences*).
det. 1. Detach; detachment. 2. Detail.
Deut. Deuteronomy.
devel. Development.
DF or **D/F** or **D.F.** *Telecom.* Direction finding; direction finder.
DFC *Mil.* Distinguished Flying Cross.
dg or **dg.** Decigram(s).
D.G. Dei gratia.
d.h. 1. Deadhead. 2. That is to say; i.e. (G *das heisst*).
di. or **dia.** Diameter.
Di *Chem.* Didymium.
diag. Diagram.
dial. Dialect; dialectal.
diam. Diameter.
dict. 1. Dictation. 2. Dictator. 3. Dictionary.
diff. Difference; different.
dim. Dimension(s).
dim. or **dimin.** 1. *Music* Diminuendo. 2. Diminutive.
din. Dinar.
dioc. Diocesan; diocese.
dipl. Diplomat; diplomatic.
dir. Director.
dist. 1. Distance; distant. 2. Distinguish(ed). 3. District.
dist. atty. or **Dist. Atty.** District attorney.
distr. Distribute; distribution; distributor.
div. 1. Divided. 2. Dividend. 3. Division; divisor. 4. Divorce(d).
dkg or **dkg.** Dekagram(s).

dkl or **dkl.** Decaliter(s).
dkm or **dkm.** Dekameter(s).
dks or **dks.** Dekastere(s).
dl or **dl.** Deciliter(s).
D/L Demand loan.
D.Lit. or **D.Litt.** Doctor of Letters (or Literature) (L *Doctor Lit(t)erarum*).
dlr. Dealer.
D.L.S. Doctor of Library Science.
dlvy Delivery.
dm or **dm.** 1. Decameter(s). 2. Decimeter(s).
DM. or **Dm.** Deutschemark.
D.M. Deputy Master.
D.M.D. Doctor of Dental Medicine (L *Dentariae Medicinae Doctor*).
DME Distance Measuring Equipment.
D.Mus. Doctor of Music.
DMZ Demilitarized zone.
D.N. Our Lord (L *Dominus Noster*).
DNA *Biochem.* Deoxyribonucleic acid.
DNB or **D.N.B.** *Brit.* Dictionary of National Biography.
do. Ditto.
D.O. Doctor of Osteopathy.
doc. document.
DOD or **DoD** Department of Defense.
dol. Dollar(s).
dom. 1. Domain. 2. Domestic. 3. Dominion.
Dom. Dominican.
DO-VAP Doppler navigation. [< *Do(ppler) v(elocity) a(nd) p(osition)*]
Dow. or **dow.** Dowager.
doz or **doz.** Dozen(s).
DP or **D.P.** 1. *Chem.* Degree of polymerization. 2. Diametrical pitch. 3. Displaced person.
D.Ph. or **D.Phil.** Doctor of Philosophy.
D.P.H. Doctor of Public Health.
D.P.Hy. Doctor of Public Hygiene.
dpt. 1. Department. 2. Deponent.
D.P.W. Department of Public Works.
dr. 1. Debit. 2. Debtor. 3. Drachma. 4. Dram(s). 5. Drawer.
Dr. 1. Doctor. 2. Drive.
D.R. or **d.r.** or **D/R** 1. Dead reckoning. 2. Deposit receipt.
d.s. Decistere.
d.s. or **D.S.** *Music* Dal segno.
D.S. or **D.Sc.** Doctor of Science (L *Doctor Scientiae*).
DSC *Mil.* Distinguished Service Cross.
DSM *Mil.* Distinguished Service Medal.
D.S.O. *Brit.* 1. (Companion of the) Distinguished Service Order. 2. District Staff Officer.
d.s.p. Died without issue (L *decessit sine prole*).
DST or **D.S.T.** Daylight Saving Time.
D.S.T. Doctor of Sacred Theology.
d.t. 1. Delirium tremens. 2. Double time.
D.Th. or **D.Theol.** Doctor of Theology.
Du. 1. Duke. 2. Dutch.
dup. or **dupl.** Duplicate.
D.V. Douai Version (of the Bible).
D.V.M. Doctor of Veterinary Medicine.
D.V.M.S. Doctor of Veterinary Medicine and Surgery.
D/W Dock warrant.
dwt. Pennyweight.
DX or **D.X.** Distance; distant.
Dy *Chem.* Dysprosium.
dyn. or **dynam.** Dynamics.
dz. Dozen(s).

e 1. *Physics* Erg. 2. Error(s) (baseball).
e. 1. East; eastern. 2. Eldest. 3. Engineer; engineering. 4. Entrance (theater). 5. Error(s) (baseball).
E 1. East; eastern. 2. *Physics* Energy. 3. English. 4. Excellent.
E. 1. Earl. 2. Earth. 3. East; eastern. 4. Engineer; engineering. 5. English.
ea. Each.
E. & O.E. or **e. and o.e.** Errors and omissions excepted.
EbN East by north.
EbS East by south.
eccl. or **eccles.** Ecclesiastical.
Eccles. or **Eccl.** 1. Ecclesiastes. 2. Ecclesiastical.
Ecclus. Ecclesiasticus.
ecol. Ecological; ecology.
econ. Economic; economics; economy.
ECOSOC Economic and Social Council (of the UN).
ECSC European Coal and Steel Community.
ed. (*pl.* **eds.**) 1. Edited. 2. Edition. 3. Editor.
Ed.B. Bachelor of Education.
Ed.D. Doctor of Education.
edit. 1. Edited. 2. Edition. 3. Editor.
Ed. M. Master of Education.

EDP Electronic data processing.
EDT or **E.D.T.** or **e.d.t.** Eastern daylight time.
educ. Education; educational.
e.e. Errors excepted.
E.E. 1. Early English. 2. Electrical Engineer; electrical engineering.
E.E. & M.P. Envoy Extraordinary and Minister Plenipotentiary.
EEG *Med.* Electroencephalogram.
e.g. For example.
EIB or **E.I.B.** Export-Import Bank.
EKG *Med.* Electrocardiogram.
el. Elevation.
elec. or **elect.** or **electr.** Electric; electrical; electrician.
elem. 1. Element(s). 2. Elementary.
elev. Elevation.
E. long or **e. long.** East longitude.
Em. *Physics* Emanation.
EM *Mil.* Enlisted man (men).
E.M.F. or **e.m.f.** or **emf** Electromotive force.
Emp. 1. Emperor; Empress. 2. Empire.
E.M.U. or **e.m.u.** or **emu** Electromagnetic unit(s).
enc. Enclosed; enclosure(s).
ency. or **encyc.** or **encycl.** Encyclopedia.
ENE or **ene, E.N.E.** or **e.n.e.** East-Northeast.
eng. 1. Engine; engineer; engineering. 2. Engraved; engraver; engraving.
Eng. D. Doctor of Engineering.
engin. Engineering.
engr. 1. Engineer. 2. Engraved; engraver; engraving.
enl. 1. Enlarge(d). 2. Enlisted.
ENS or **Ens.** *Mil.* Ensign.
env. Envelope.
e.o. Ex officio (L).
Ep. Epistle(s).
Eph. Ephesians: also **Ephes.**
Epis. 1. Episcopal: also **Episc.** 2. Epistle(s).
Epist. Epistle(s).
eq. 1. Equal. 2. Equation. 3. Equator. 4. Equivalent
Er *Chem.* Erbium.
E.R. King Edward (L *Eduardus Rex*) or Queen Elizabeth (L *Elizabeth Regina*).
erron. Erroneous; erroneously.
E.R.V. English Revised Version (of the Bible).
Es *Chem.* Einsteinium.
Esd. Esdras.
ESE or **ese, E.S.E.,** or **e.s.e.** East-southeast.
esp. or **espec.** Especially.
ESP Extrasensory perception.
Esq. or **Esqr.** Esquire.
est. 1. Established. 2. Estate. 3. Estimated. 4. Estuary.
EST or **E.S.T.** or **e.s.t.** Eastern standard time.
estab. Established.
Esth. Esther.
e.s.u. or **esu** Electrostatic unit(s).
ETA Estimated time of arrival.
ethnol. Ethnology.
ETO European Theater of Operations.
ety. or **etym.** or **etymol.** Etymological; etymology.
Eu *Chem.* Europium.
ev or **e.v.** Electron volt(s).
E.V. English Version (of the Bible).
ex. 1. Examination; examined. 2. Example. 3. Except; excepted; exception. 4. Exchange. 5. Excursion.
Ex. Exodus.
exam. Examination; examined.
exc. 1. Excellent. 2. Except; excepted; exception. 3. Exchange. 4. Excursion.
Exc. Excellency.
exch. 1. Exchange. 2. Exchequer.
excl. 1. Exclamation: also **exclam.** 2. Exclusive.
exec. 1. Executive. 2. Executor.
ex int. Without (L *ex*) interest.
Exod. Exodus.
exp. 1. Expenses. 2. Expiration; expired. 3. Export; exported; exporter. 4. Express.
expt. Experiment.
exptl. Experimental.
exr. Executor.
ext. 1. Extension. 2. External; externally. 3. Extinct. 4. Extra. 5. Extract.
Ez. or **Ezr.** Ezra.

F *Chem.* Fluorine.
f or **f.** 1. Foul(s). 2. *Math.* Function (of).
F *Math.* Function.
F, F/, F:, f, f/, or **f:** *Photog.* F number.
F or **F.** 1. Fahrenheit. 2. French.
F or **F.** or **f** 1. *Electr.* Farad. 2. Fathom.
F. 1. February. 2. Fellow. 3. France. 4. Friday. 5. Son (L *filius*).

F. or **f.** 1. Farthing. 2. Feminine. 3. Fine. 4. Fluid (ounce). 5. Folio. 6. Following. 7. Franc. 8. Frequency.
FA *Mil.* Field Artillery.
F.A. Fine Arts.
F.A. or **f.a.** 1. Free alongside. 2. Freight agent.
F.A.A.A.S. Fellow of the American Association for the Advancement of Science.
fac. 1. Facsimile. 2. Factor. 3. Factory.
F.A.C.P. Fellow of the American College of Physicians.
F.A.C.S. Fellow of the American College of Surgeons.
Fah. or **Fahr.** Fahrenheit.
fam. 1. Familiar. 2. Family.
FAO or **F.A.O.** Food and Agriculture Organization (of the United Nations).
F.A.S. or **f.a.s.** Free alongside ship.
fasc. Bundle; fascicle (L *fasciculus*).
fath. Fathom.
f.b. 1. Freight bill. 2. Fullback: also **fb.**
FBI or **F.B.I.** Federal Bureau of Investigation.
f.c. *Printing* Follow copy.
FC *Mil.* Finance Corps.
FCA Farm Credit Administration.
FCC or **F.C.C.** Federal Communications Commission.
F.D. 1. Fidei Defensor. 2. Fire Department.
FDA or **F.D.A.** Food and Drug Administration.
FDIC or **F.D.I.C.** Federal Deposit Insurance Corporation.
Fe *Chem.* Iron (L *ferrum*).
Feb. or **Feb** February.
fed. 1. Federal. 2. Federated; federation.
fem. Feminine; female.
ff *Music* Fortissimo.
ff. 1. Folios. 2. Following.
F.F.A. or **f.f.a.** 1. Free foreign agent. 2. Free from alongside.
FHA Federal Housing Administration.
FHLBB Federal Home Loan Bank Board.
FICA Federal Insurance Contributions Act.
fid. 1. Fidelity. 2. Fiduciary.
fig. 1. Figurative(ly). 2. Figure(s).
fl. 1. Floor. 2. Florin(s). 3. Flower. 4. Fluid. 5. *Music* Flute.
Fl *Chem.* Fluorine.
Fla. Florida.
fld. Field.
fl. dr. Fluid dram(s).
flex. Flexible.
Flor. Florida (unofficial).
fl. oz. Fluid ounce(s).
fm. 1. Fathom. 2. From.
Fm *Chem.* Fermium.
FM *Mil.* Field manual.
FM or **F.M., f-m,** or **f.m.** *Telecom.* Frequency modulation.
F.M. 1. Field Marshal. 2. Foreign Missions.
FMB Federal Maritime Board.
FMCS Federal Mediation and Conciliation Service.
FNMA Federal National Mortgage Association.
F.O. Foreign Office.
f.o.b. or **F.O.B.** Free on board.
fol. 1. Folio. 2. Following.
foll. Following.
for. 1. Foreign. 2. Forestry.
fort. Fortification; fortified.
fp *Music* Forte piano (Ital.).
fp. Foolscap.
f.p. or **fp** Forward pass.
F.P. or **f.p.** 1. Fireplug. 2. Fire policy. 3. Floating policy. 4. Fully paid.
F.P. or **f.p.** or **fp** 1. Foot-pound(s). 2. Freezing point.
FPA or **F.P.A.** Foreign Press Association.
FPC or **F.P.C.** Federal Power Commission.
fpm or **f.p.m.** Feet per minute.
FPO *Mil.* Fleet post office.
fps or **f.p.s.** 1. Feet per second. 2. Foot-pound-second (system).
fr. 1. Fragment. 2. Franc. 3. From.
Fr *Chem.* Francium.
Fr. 1. Brother (L *Frater*). 2. *Eccl.* Father. 3. France. 4. French. 5. Friar. 6. Friday. 7. Wife (G *Frau*).
FRB Federal Reserve Board.
F.R.C.P. Fellow of the Royal College of Physicians.
F.R.C.S. Fellow of the Royal College of Surgeons.
freq. 1. Frequency. 2. Frequentative. 3. Frequent(ly).
F.R.G.S. Fellow of the Royal Geographical Society.
Fri. Friday.
Frl. Fräulein.
FRS Federal Reserve System.
frt. Freight.
f.s. Foot-second.
ft. 1. Feet; foot. 2. Fort. 3. Fortification; fortified.
FTC or **F.T.C.** Federal Trade Commission.

fth. or **fthm.** Fathom.
ft-lb Foot-pound(s).
furn. Furnished; furniture.
fut. Future.
f.v. On the back of the page (L *folio verso*).
FWA, F.W.A. Federal Works Agency.
fwd. Forward.
FY Fiscal year.

g. or **g** 1. Goalie; goalkeeper. 2. Gram(s).
G 1. German: also G. 2. Gravitational force. 3. *Mil.* Gun.
G. 1. Specific gravity. 2. Gulf.
G. or **g.** 1. *Electr.* Conductance. 2. Gauge. 3. Grain(s). 4. Guilder(s). 5. Guinea(s).
Ga *Chem.* Gallium.
Ga or **G.A.** 1. General Agent. 2. General Assembly (of the United Nations).
Ga. 1. Gallic. 2. Georgia.
G.A. or **G/A** or **g.a.** General average.
Gal. Galatians.
gall. Gallon(s).
gals. Gallons.
galv. Galvanic; galvanism; galvanized.
GAO General Accounting Office.
GAR or **G.A.R.** Grand Army of the Republic.
gaz. 1. Gazette. 2. Gazetteer.
G.B.E. (Knight or Dame) Grand (Cross or Order) of the British Empire.
GCA or **G.C.A.** Ground control approach.
G.C.B. (Knight) Grand Cross of the Bath.
G.C.L.H. Grand Cross of the Legion of Honor.
GCM *Mil.* General Court Martial.
G.C.M. or **g.c.m.** or **gcm** Greatest common measure.
GCT or **G.C.T.** Greenwich civil time.
G.C.V.O. (Knight) Grand Cross of the (Royal) Victorian Order.
Gd *Chem.* Gadolinium.
G.D. Grand Duchess; Grand Duchy; Grand Duke.
gds. Goods.
Ge Germanium.
geb. Born (G *geboren*).
gel. Gelatinous.
gen. 1. Gender. 2. Genera. 3. General; generally. 4. Generator. 5. Generic. 6. Genitive. 7. Genus.
Gen. 1. *Mil.* General. 2. Genesis. 3. Geneva; Genevan.
geneal. Genealogical; genealogy.
genit. Genitive.
genl. General.
gent. Gentleman; gentlemen.
geod. Geodesy; geodetic.
geog. Geographer; geographic(al); geography.
geol. Geologic(al); geologist; geology.
geom. Geometrician; geometric(al); geometry.
ger. Gerund.
Ger. German; Germany.
gest. Died (G *gestorben*).
g.gr. Great gross.
GHA Greenwich hour angle.
GHQ, G.H.Q. *Mil.* General Headquarters.
GI or **G.I.** 1. General issue. 2. Government issue.
gi. Gill(s).
G.I. or **g.i.** *Anat.* Gastrointestinal.
Gk. Greek
gl. 1. Glass. 2. Gloss (sheen).
gld. Guilder(s).
gloss. Glossary.
glt. Gilt (bookbinding).
gm. Gram(s).
G.M. 1. General manager. 2. *Brit.* George Medal. 3. Grand Master.
GMT or **G.M.T.** or **G.m.t.** Greenwich mean time.
GNP or **G.N.P.** Gross national product.
GO *Mil.* General Order.
GOP or **G.O.P.** Grand Old Party: the Republican Party.
Gov. or **gov.** Governor.
Govt. or **govt.** Government.
G.P. 1. General paresis. 2. General practitioner. 3. Graduate in Pharmacy.
GPM or **gpm** or **g.p.m.** Gallons per minute.
GPO or **G.P.O.** 1. General Post Office. 2. Government Printing Office.
G.P.U. The OGPU.
GQ or **G.Q.** or **g.q.** *Mil.* General quarters.
gr. 1. Grade. 2. Grain(s). 3. Gram(s). 4. Grammar. 5. Great. 6. Gross. 7. Group.
gro. Gross (unit of quantity).
gr.wt. Gross weight.
GS 1. *Mil.* General Staff. 2. German silver.
G.S. 1. General Secretary. 2. Girl Scouts.
GSA General Services Administration.
GSC *Mil.* General Staff Corps.

G.S.U.S.A. Girls Scouts of the U.S.A.
gt. 1. Gilt (bookbinding). 2. Great.
G.T.C. or **g.t.c.** Good till canceled (or countermanded).
gtd. Guaranteed.
g.u. *Anat.* Genitourinary.
guar. Guaranteed.
guttat. *Med.* By drops (L *guttatim*).
g.v. Gravimetric volume.
gym. Gymnasium; gymnastics.
gyn. or **gynecol.** Gynecological; gynecology.

H *Chem.* Hydrogen.
h. or **h** Hit(s) (baseball).
H. or **h.** 1. Harbor. 2. Hard; hardness. 3. Heavy sea. 4. Height. 5. Hence. 6. High. 7. *Music* Horns. 8.Hour(s). 9. Hundred. 10. Husband.
ha. Hectare(s).
Hal. *Chem.* Halogen.
hb. or **hb** Halfback.
H.B.M. His (or Her) Britannic Majesty.
H.C. House of Commons.
hd. 1. Hand. 2. Head.
hdbk. Handbook.
hdkf. Handkerchief.
He *Chem.* Helium.
HE or **H.E.** High explosive.
H.E. 1. His Eminence. 2. His Excellency.
Heb. or **Hebr.** Hebrew(s).
her. Heraldic; heraldry.
hf. Half.
Hf *Chem.* Hafnium.
HF or **H.F.**, **hf** or **h.f.** High frequency.
hg. 1. Hectogram(s). 2. Heliogram.
Hg *Chem.* Mercury (L *hydrargyrum*).
HG High German.
H.G. 1. His (or Her) Grace. 2. *Brit.* Home Guard.
hgt. Height.
H.H. 1. His (or Her) Highness. 2. His Holiness.
hhd. Hogshead.
H.I.H. His (or Her) Imperial Highness.
H.I.M. His (or Her) Imperial Majesty.
Hind. 1. Hindi. 2. Hindu. 3. Hindustan. 4. Hindustani.
hist. 1. Histology. 2. Historian; historical; history.
H.J. Here lies (L *hic jacet*).
H.J.S. Here lies buried (L *hic jacet sepultus*).
hkf. Handkerchief.
hl. or **hl** Hectoliter(s).
H.L. House of Lords.
hm. or **hm** Hectometer(s).
H.M. His (or Her) Majesty.
H.M.S. 1. His (or Her) Majesty's Ship (or Steamer). 2. His (or Her) Majesty's Service.
ho. House.
Ho *Chem.* Holmium.
hon. Honorably; honorary.
Hon. Honorable.
hor. Horizon; horizontal.
horol. Horology.
hort. Horticulture; horticultural.
Hos. Hosea.
hosp. Hospital.
HP or **hp, H.P.** or **h.p.** 1. High pressure. 2. Horsepower.
HQ or **hq, H.Q.** or **h.q.** Headquarters.
hr. (*pl.* **hrs.**) Hour.
h.r. or **hr** Home run(s).
Hr. Mister (G *Herr*).
H.R. 1. Home Rule. 2. House of Representatives.
H.R.H. His (or Her) Royal Highness.
H.R.I.P. Here rests in peace (L *hic requiescat in pace*)
h.s. 1. Here is buried (L *hic sepultus* or *situs*). 2. High school. 3. In this sense (L *hoc sensu*).
H.S. 1. High School. 2. *Brit.* Home Secretary.
H.S.H. His (or Her) Serene Highness.
H.S.M. His (or Her) Serene Majesty.
ht. 1. Heat. 2. Height.
Hts. Heights.
H.V. or **h.v.** or **hv** High voltage.
h.w. High water.
hypoth. Hypothesis; hypothetical.

I *Chem.* Iodine.
i. 1. Incisor. 2. Interest. 3. Intransitive. 4. Island.
I. 1. Island(s); Isle(s). 2. Iowa (unofficial).
Ia. Iowa (unofficial).
IAEA International Atomic Energy Agency (of the United Nations).
IAS Indicated air speed.
ib. or **ibid.** In the same place (L *ibidem*).
IBRN International Bank for Reconstruction and Development.
IBT International Brotherhood of Teamsters.

IC Immediate constituent.
ICAO International Civil Aviation Organization.
ICBM The intercontinental ballistic missile.
ICC or **I.C.C.** Interstate Commerce Commission.
ICJ International Court of Justice.
id. The same (L *idem*).
Id. Idaho (unofficial).
ID or **I.D.** or **i.d.** Inside diameter.
Ida. Idaho (unofficial).
i.e. That is (L *id est*).
IF or **I.F.**, **i.f.** or **i-f** Intermediate frequency.
I.G. 1. Amalgamation (G *Interessengemeinschaft*). 2. Indo-Germanic. 3. Inspector General: also **IG**
ign. 1. Ignites; ignition. 2. Unknown (L *ignotus*).
IGY or **I.G.Y.** International Geophysical Year.
IHP or **ihp**, **I.H.P.** or **i.h.p.** Indicated horsepower.
IHS A monogram of the name Jesus, derived from the Greek IH(ΣΟΥ)Σ, Jesus.
Ill. Illinois.
illus. Illustrated; illustration; illustrator.
illust. Illustrated; illustration; illustrator.
ILO or **I.L.O.** International Labor Organization (of the United Nations).
I.L.P. *Brit.* Independent Labour Party.
ILS Instrument landing system.
imit. Imitation; imitative.
imp. 1. Imperative. 2. Imperfect. 3. Imperial. 4. Impersonal. 5. Import; imported; importer. 6. Important. 7. Imprimatur. 8. Improper.
imper. Imperative.
imperf. 1. Imperfect. 2. Imperforate.
impers. Impersonal.
impf. Imperfect.
imp. gal. Imperial gallon.
impv. Imperative.
in. Inch(es).
In *Chem.* Indium.
inbd. Inboard.
inc. 1. Inclosure. 2. Including. 3. Inclusive. 4. Income. 5. Incorporated. 6. Increase.
inch. or **incho.** Inchoative.
incl. 1. Inclosure. 2. Including.
incog. Incognito.
incor. or **incorp.** Incorporated.
incr. Increased; increasing.
ind. 1. Independent. 2. Index. 3. Indicated; indicative. 4. Indigo. 5. Indirect. 6. Industrial.
Ind. Indiana.
I.N.D. In the name of God (L *in nomine Dei*).
indecl. *Gram.* Indeclinable.
indef. Indefinite.
indent. *Printing* Indention.
indic. Indicating; indicative; indicator.
inf. 1. Below (L *infra*). 2. Inferior. 3. Infinitive. 4. Information.
Inf. or **inf.** Infantry.
infl. Influence(d).
init. 1. Initial. 2. In the beginning (L *initio*).
in.-lb. Inch-pound.
inorg. Inorganic.
I.N.R.I. Jesus of Nazareth, King of the Jews (L *Iesus Nazarenus, Rex Iudaeorum*).
ins. 1. Inches. 2. Inspector. 3. Insular. 4. Insulated; insulation. 5. Insurance.
insol. Insoluble.
insp. Inspected; inspector.
inst. 1. *Archaic* Instant (this month). 2. Instantaneous. 3. Instrument(al).
Inst. Institute; Institution.
instr. 1. Instructor. 2. Instrument(al).
int. 1. Intelligence. 2. Interest. 3. Interior. 4. Interjection. 5. Internal. 6. International. 7. Interval. 8. Intransitive.
inter. Intermediate.
internat. International.
Interpol International Police Organization.
interrog. Interrogative.
intr. Intransitive.
introd. Introduction; introductory.
inv. 1. Invented; invention; inventor. 2. Invoice.
Io Ionium.
Io. Iowa (unofficial).
IOU A written acknowledgment of indebtedness having on it these letters (meaning *I owe you*). Also **I.O.U.**
i.p. 1. Innings pitched: also **ip** 2. In passing (chess).
IPA or **I.P.A.** International Phonetic Alphabet (or Association)
i.q. The same as (L *idem quod*).
IQ or **I.Q.** Intelligence quotient.
Ir *Chem.* Iridium.
I.R.A. Irish Republican Army.

IRBM The intermediate range ballistic missile, having a range between 200 and 1500 miles. Compare *ICBM*.
irreg. Irregular(ly).
IRS Internal Revenue Service.
Is. 1. Isaiah. 2. Island(s); isle: also **is.**
Isa. Isaiah.
isl. Island(s).
iso. Isotropic.
isom. Isometric.
isoth. Isothermal.
isth. Isthmus.
it. or **ital.** Italic(s).

J *Physics* Joule.
J. 1. Journal. 2. Judge. 3. Justice.
Ja. January.
JA Judge Advocate.
JAG Judge Advocate General.
J.C.D. 1. Doctor of Canon Law (L *Juris Canonici Doctor*). 2. Doctor of Civil Law (L *Juris Civilis Doctor*).
JCS Joint Chiefs of Staff.
jct. or **jctn.** Junction.
J.D. Doctor of Laws (L *Juris Doctor*).
Je. June.
Jer. Jeremiah.
j.g. or **jg** Junior grade.
Jl. July.
Jon. Jonah.
Josh. Joshua.
jour. 1. Journal. 2. Journeyman.
J.P. Justice of the Peace.
Jr. or **jr.** Junior.
Ju. Judges.
Judg. Judges.
Jul. July.
Jun. or **jun.** Junior.
Junc. or **junc.** Junction.
Jur.D. Doctor of Law (L *Juris Doctor*).
jurisp. Jurisprudence.
jus. or **just.** Justice.
juv. Juvenile.
j.v. Junior varsity.
Jy. July.

K *Chem.* Potassium.
k Kilo.
k. 1. *Electr.* Capacity. 2. Carat or karat. 3. *Math.* Constant.
K 1. *Physics* Kelvin (temperature scale). 2. King (chess). 3. Koruna.
K. or **k.** 1. Calends (L *kalendae*). 2. Kilogram. 3. King. 4. Knight. 5. Kopeck(s). 6. Krone.
ka. Cathode or kathode.
kal. Calends (L *kalendae*).
Kan. Kansas (unofficial).
Kas. Kansas (unofficial).
KB King's bishop (chess).
K.B. 1. King's Bench. 2. Knight Bachelor.
KBP King's bishop's pawn (chess).
kc. or **kc** Kilocycle(s).
K.C. 1. King's Counsel. 2. Knights of Columbus.
kcal. Kilocalorie.
K.C.B. Knight Commander (of the Order) of the Bath.
K.C.V.O. Knight Commander of the (Royal) Victorian Order.
Ken. Kentucky (unofficial).
kg. or **kg** 1. Keg(s). 2. Kilogram(s).
K.G. Knight (of the Order) of the Garter.
K.G.B. In the Soviet Union, the Commission of State Security.
KIA *Mil.* Killed in action.
kilo 1. Kilogram(s): also **kilog.** 2. Kilometer(s): also **kilom.**
kilol. Kiloliter.
KKK or **K.K.K.** Ku Klux Klan.
KKt King's knight (chess).
KKtP King's knight's pawn (chess).
kl. or **kl** Kiloliter(s).
km. or **km** Kilometer(s).
KO or **K.O.** or **k.o.** Knockout (boxing).
kop. Kopeck(s).
KP King's pawn (chess).
KP or **K.P.** Kitchen police.
kr Krone.
Kr *Chem.* Krypton.
KR King's rook (chess).
KRP King's rook's pawn (chess).
kt. Karat or carat.
Kt. Knight (chess).
kv. or **kv** Kilovolt(s).
kva or **kv.-a.** Kilovolt-ampere.

kw. or **kw** Kilowatt(s).
K.W.H., kw-h, kwh, kw-hr., kw-hr Kilowatt-hour(s).
Ky. Kentucky.

l- or **l** *Chem.* Levo-.
l. or **l** Liter.
L 1. Latin. 2. *Physics* Length. 3. Longitude.
L or **l** *Electr.* Coefficient of inductance.
L or **£** or **l.** Pound (sterling) (L *libra*).
L. 1. Latin. 2. Licentiate. 3. Linnaeus.
L. or **l.** 1. Book (L *liber*). 2. Lake. 3. Latitude. 4. Law. 5. Leaf. 6. Left. 7. Length. 8. Line. 9. Link. 10. Lira; lire. 11. Low.
La *Chem.* Lanthanum.
La. Louisiana.
L.A. 1. Legislative Assembly. 2. Library Association. 3. Local Agent. 4. Los Angeles.
lab. Laboratory.
lam. Laminated.
Lam. Lamentations.
L.A.M. Master of Liberal Arts (L *Liberalium Artium Magister*).
lang. Language.
lat. Latitude.
lb. Pound(s) (L *libra, librae*).
L.B. 1. Bachelor of Letters (L *Litterarum Baccalaureus*). 2. Local Board.
lbs. Pounds.
l.c. 1. Left center. 2. In the place cited (L *loco citato*). 3. *Printing* Lower case.
L/C or **l/c** Letter of credit.
L.C. Library of Congress.
L.C.D. or **l.c.d.** or **lcd** Least (or lowest) common denominator.
LCDR or **LCdr** *Mil.* Lieutenant Commander.
L.C.L. or **l.c.l.** Less than carload lot.
L.C.M. or **l.c.m.** or **lcm** Least (or lowest) common multiple.
ld. *Printing* Lead.
Ld. 1. Limited. 2. Lord.
L.D. or **LD** Low Dutch.
L.D.S. Licentiate in Dental Surgery.
l.e. or **le** Left end.
lea. 1. League. 2. Leather.
lect. Lecture; lecturer.
leg. 1. Legal. 2. Legate. 3. Legato. 4. Legislation; legislature.
legis. Legislation; legislature.
L. ès S. Licentiate in Sciences (F *licencié ès sciences*).
Lev. Leviticus.
Levit. Leviticus.
lex. Lexicon.
l.f. or **lf** 1. Left field(er). 2. Left forward.
l.f. or **lf.** *Printing* Lightface.
L.F. or **LF, l.f.** or **l-f** Low frequency.
lg. or **lge.** Large.
l.g. or **lg** Left guard.
LG or **LG.** or **L.G.** Low German.
LGk. or **L.Gk.** Late Greek.
l.h. or **L.H.** or **LH** Left hand.
l.h.b. or **lhb** Left halfback.
L.H.D. Doctor of Humanities (L *Litterarum Humaniorum Doctor*).
li Link(s) (unit of measurement).
Li *Chem.* Lithium.
L.I. Long Island.
lib. 1. Book (L *liber*). 2. Librarian; library.
Lib. 1. Liberal. 2. Liberia.
Lieut. Lieutenant.
lin. 1. Lineal. 2. Linear.
ling. Linguistics.
liq. 1. Liquid. 2. Liquor.
lit. 1. Liter. 2. Literal(ly). 3. Literary; literature.
Lit.B. Bachelor of Letters (or Literature) (L *Lit(t)erarum Baccalaureus*).
Lit.D. Doctor of Letters (or Literature) (L *Lit(t)erarum Doctor*).
lith. Lithograph; lithography.
litho. or **lithog.** Lithograph; lithography.
Litt.B. Bachelor of Letters (or Literature) (L *Lit(t)erarum Baccalaureus*).
Litt.D. Doctor of Letters (or Literature) (L *Lit(t)erarum Doctor*).
ll. Lines.
LL or **LL.** or **L.L.** 1. Late Latin. 2. Legal Latin. 3. Low Latin.
LL.B. Bachelor of Laws (L *Legum Baccalaureus*).
LL.D. Doctor of Laws (L *Legum Doctor*).
LL.M. Master of Laws (L *Legum Magister*).
LM *Mil.* Legion of Merit.
L.M. Licentiate in Medicine (or Midwifery).
loc. cit. In the place cited (L *loco citato*)

long. Longitude.
L.O.O.M. Loyal Order of Moose.
L.P.S. *Brit.* Lord Privy Seal.
L.S. 1. Licentiate in Surgery. 2. Place of the seal (L *locus sigilli*).
LSS or **L.S.S.** Lifesaving Service.
l.t. Left tackle: also **lt.**
LT or **Lt.** *Mil.* Lieutenant.
Lt.Col. or **LtCol.** *Mil.* Lieutenant Colonel.
ltd. or **Ltd.** Limited.
Lt.Gen. or **LtGen** *Mil.* Lieutenant General.
L.Th. Licentiate in Theology.
Ltjg. *Mil.* Lieutenant, Junior Grade.
Lu *Chem.* Lutetium.
Luth. Lutheran.
lv. Leave(s).

m or **m.** Meter(s).
M 1. Medieval. 2. Middle.
M. 1. Handful (L *manipulus*). 2. Master (L *magister*). 3. Monday. 4. (*pl.* **MM.**) Monsieur.
M. or **m.** 1. Majesty. 2. Male. 3. Manual. 4. Mark. 5. Marquis. 6. Married. 7. Masculine. 8. Mass. 9. Medicine. 10. Medium. 11. Meridian. 12. Mile. 13. Mill. 14. Minim. 15. Minute. 16. Month. 17. Moon. 18. Morning. 19. Mountain. 20. Noon (L *meridies*).
Ma *Chem.* Masurium.
M.A. 1. Master of Arts (L *Magister Artium*). 2. Military Academy. 3. *Psychol.* Mental age.
mach. Machine; machinery; machinist.
mag. 1. Magazine. 2. Magnet; magnetism. 2. *Astron.* Magnitude.
M.Agr. Master of Agriculture.
Mal. Malachi.
Man. 1. Manila (paper). 2. Manitoba.
manuf. Manufacture(d); manufacturer; manufacturing.
mar. 1. Marine. 2. Maritime. 3. Married.
Mar. March.
marg. Margin; marginal.
Marq. Marquis.
mas. or **masc.** Masculine.
Mass. Massachusetts.
mat. 1. Matinée. 2. Matins. 3. Maturity.
math. Mathematical; mathematics.
MATS Military Air Transport Service.
Matt. Matthew.
max. Maximum.
M.B. Bachelor of Medicine (L *Medicinae Baccalaureus*).
M.B.A. Master in (or of) Business Administration.
mc or **m.c.** or **mc** Megacycle.
M.C. 1. Maritime Commission. 2. Master of Ceremonies. 3. Medical Corps. 4. Member of Congress.
M.Ch. Master of Surgery (L *Magister Chirurgiae*).
M.C.L. Master of Civil Law.
Md *Chem.* Mendelevium.
Md. or **M.D.** Middle Dutch.
Md. Maryland.
M/D or **m/d** 1. Memorandum of deposit. 2. Months' date.
M.D. 1. Doctor of Medicine (L *Medicinae Doctor*). 2. Medical Department. 3. Mentally deficient.
Mdme. (pl. **Mdmes.**) *Brit.* Madame.
M.D.S. Master of Dental Surgery.
mdse. Merchandise.
MDu. Middle Dutch.
m.e. Marbled edges (bookbinding).
Me *Chem.* Methyl.
Me. Maine (unofficial).
ME or **ME.** or **M.E.** Middle English.
M.E. 1. Mechanical Engineer. 2. Methodist Episcopal. 3. Mining Engineer.
meas. Measure.
mech. 1. Mechanical; mechanics. 2. mechanism.
med. 1. Medical; medicine. 2. Medieval. 3. Medium.
M.Ed. Master of Education.
Med.Gk. Medieval Greek.
Med.L. or **Med.L** Medieval Latin.
meg. 1. megacycle. 2. Megohm.
mem. 1. Member. 2. Memoir. 3. Memorandum. 4. Memorial.
memo. Memorandum.
mer. 1. Meridian. 2. Meridional.
Messrs. or **Messrs** Messieurs.
met. 1. Metaphor. 2. Metaphysics. 3. Meteorological. 4. Metronome. 5. Metropolitan.
metal. or **metall.** Metallurgical; metallurgy.
metaph. 1. Metaphor; metaphorical. 2. Metaphysics.
metath. Metathesis; metathetic(al).
meteorol. or **meteor.** Meteorologic(al); meteorology.
Meth. Methodist.
mev or **Mev** or **m.e.v.** Million electron volts.

mf or **mfd** Microfarad(s).
mf. or **mf** 1. *Music* Moderately loud (Ital. *mezzo forte*). 2. Millifarad.
MF or **MF.** or **M.F.** Middle French.
mfg. Manufacturing.
mfr. Manufacture; manufacturer.
mg. or **mg** or **mgm** Milligram(s).
Mg *Chem.* Magnesium.
Mgr. 1. Manager. 2. Monseigneur. 3. Monsignor.
MH *Mil.* Medal of Honor.
MHG or **MHG.** or **M.H.G.** Middle High German.
mi. 1. Mile(s). 2. Mill(s).
Mich. Michigan.
micros. Microscopy.
mid. 1. Middle. 2. Midshipman.
mil. 1. Mileage. 2. Military. 3. Militia. 4. Million.
milit. Military.
min. 1. Mineralogical; mineralogy. 2. Minim(s). 3. Minimum. 4. Mining. 5. Minor. 6. Minute(s).
mineral. Mineralogy.
Minn. Minnesota.
misc. 1. Miscellaneous. 2. Miscellany.
Miss. Mississippi.
mk. 1. Mark(s). 2. Markka(s).
Mk. Mark.
mks The meter-kilogram-second system of measurement in which the unit of length is the meter, the unit of mass is the kilogram, and the unit of time is one second. Also **m.k.s., MKS, M.K.S.**
mkt. Market.
ml. 1. Mail. 2. Milliliter(s).
ML or **ML.** or **M.L.** Medieval (or Middle) Latin.
M.L.A. 1. Member of the Legislative Assembly. 2. Modern Language Association.
MLG or **MLG.** or **M.L.G.** Middle Low German.
Mlle. or **Mlle** Mademoiselle.
Mlles. or **Mlles** Mesdemoiselles.
M.L.S. Master of Library Science.
mm. or **mm** 1. Millimeter(s). 2. Thousands (L *millia*).
m.m. With the necessary changes (L *mutatis mutandis*).
MM. Messieurs.
Mme. or **Mme** Madame.
Mmes. or **Mmes** Mesdames.
Mn *Chem.* Manganese.
mo. Month(s).
Mo *Chem.* Molybdenum.
Mo. 1. Missouri. 2. Monday.
M.O. 1. Medical Officer. 2. Money order: also **m.o.**
mod. 1. Moderate. 2. *Music* Moderato. 3. Modern.
Mod. Gr. Modern Greek.
mon. 1. Monastery. 2. Monetary.
Mon. 1. Monday. 2. Monsignor.
Monsig. Monsignor.
Mont. Montana.
mor. Morocco (bookbinding).
mos. Months.
MOS Military occupational specialty.
MP *Mil.* Military Police.
M.P. 1. Melting point: also **m.p.** 2. Member of Parliament.
M.Pd. Master of Pedagogy.
M.P.E. Master of Physical Education.
m.p.h. or **mph** Miles per hour.
Mr. (mĭs′tər) *n.* The contracted form of MISTER.
MR or **M.R.** Motivation Research.
Mrs. (mĭs′iz) *n.* A title prefixed to the name of a married woman: a contracted form of *Mistress*.
MS. or **MS, ms.** or **ms** Manuscript.
M.S. 1. Master of Science: also **M.Sc.** 2. Master in Surgery.
msg. Message.
Msgr. Monsignor.
M.Sgt. or **M/Sgt** *Mil.* Master Sergeant.
m.s.l. or **M.S.L.** Mean sea level.
MSS. or **MSS, mss.** or **mss** Manuscripts.
MST or **M.S.T.** or **m.s.t.** Mountain standard time.
MSTS Military Sea Transportation Service.
Mt. or **mt.** (pl. **mts.**) Mount; mountain.
M.T. 1. Metric ton. 2. Mountain time; also **m.t.**
mtg. 1. Meeting. 2. Mortgage: also **mtge.**
mtn. Mountain.
Mt.Rev. Most Reverend.
mun. Municipal; municipality.
mus. 1. Museum. 2. Music; musician.
Mus.B. or **Mus.Bac.** Bachelor of Music (L *Musicae Baccalaureus*).
Mus.D. or **Mus.Doc.** or **Mus.Dr.** Doctor of Music (L *Musicae Doctor*).
Mus.M. Master of Music (L *Musicae Magister*).
m.v. *Music* Softly (Ital. *mezzo voce*).
MVD The Ministry of Internal Affairs of the Soviet Union;

the secret police: formerly called *Cheka, OGPU, NKVD.* Also **M.V.D.**
M.W. 1. Most Worshipful. 2. Most worthy.
myth. or **mythol.** Mythology.

N *Chem.* Nitrogen.
n. 1. Born (L *natus*). 2. Name. 3. Nephew. 4. Net. 5. Neuter. 6. New. 7. Nominative. 8. Noon. 9. *Chem.* Normal. 10. Note. 11. Number.
N 1. Knight (chess). 2. North; northern.
N. 1. Nationalist. 2. Navy. 3. Noon. 4. *Chem.* Normal (strength solution). 5. Norse. 6. North; northern. 7. November.
Na *Chem.* Sodium (L *natrium*).
NAACP or **N.A.A.C.P.** National Association for the Advancement of Colored People.
Nah. Nahum.
NASA National Aeronautics and Space Administration.
natl. National.
NATO (nā′tō) North Atlantic Treaty Organization.
nav. 1. Naval. 2. Navigation.
navig. Navigation.
Nb *Chem.* Niobium.
N.B. Note well (L *nota bene*): also **n.b.**
NbE North by east.
NBS or **N.B.S.** National Bureau of Standards.
NbW North by west.
N.C. North Carolina: also **N.Car.** (unofficial).
NCAA or **N.C.A.A.** National Collegiate Athletic Association.
NCO Noncommissioned Officer.
Nd *Chem.* Neodymium.
N.D. or **n.d.** No date.
N.Dak. North Dakota: also **N.D.** (unofficial).
N.D.P. New Democratic Party (Canada).
Ne *Chem.* Neon.
NEA National Education Association.
NEB or **N.E.B.** New English Bible.
NED or **N.E.D.** New English Dictionary (Oxford English Dictionary).
neg. Negative(ly).
Neh. Nehemiah.
neut. Neuter.
Nev. Nevada.
New Test. New Testament.
N.F. 1. National Formulary. 2. Newfoundland (unofficial). 3. No funds: also **n.f.** 4. Norman French: also **NF.**
NG or **N.G.** National Guard.
N.G. or **n.g.** No good.
NGk. or **N.Gk.** New Greek.
N.H. New Hampshire.
Ni *Chem.* Nickel.
N.J. New Jersey.
NKVD Formerly, the MVD. Also **N.K.V.D.**
n.l. 1. *Printing* New line. 2. North latitude. 3. Not clear (L *non liquet*). 4. Not far (L *non longe*). 5. Not lawful (L *non licet*).
NL or **NL.** or **N.L.** New Latin.
N. lat. North latitude.
NLRB or **N.L.R.B.** National Labor Relations Board.
N.Mex. New Mexico: also **N.M.** (unofficial).
NNE or **nne, N.N.E.,** or **n.n.e.** North-northeast.
NNW or **nnw, N.N.W.,** or **n.n.w.** North-northwest.
No *Chem.* Nobelium.
No. 1. North; northern. 2. Number: also **no.**
nol. pros. Nolle prosequi.
nom. Nominative.
noncom. Noncommissioned (officer).
non pros. Non prosequitur.
non seq. Non sequitur.
Nos. or **nos.** Numbers.
nov. Novelist.
Nov. or **Nov** November.
n.p. No place (of publication).
n.p. or **d.** No place or date (of publication.)
Np *Chem.* Neptunium.
NP Neuropsychiatric.
N.P. Notary Public.
n.p.t. Normal pressure and temperature.
nr. Near.
NRA or **N.R.A.** National Recovery Administration.
Ns *Meteorol.* Nimbostratus.
N.S. 1. New Style. 2. Not specified: also **n.s.** 3. Nova Scotia.
N.S.F. or **N/S/F** Not sufficient funds.
NSLI National Service Life Insurance.
N.S.P.C.A. National Society for the Prevention of Cruelty to Animals.
N.S.P.C.C. National Society for the Prevention of Cruelty to Children.
Nt *Chem.* Niton.

N.T. 1. New Testament: also **NT.** 2. Northern Territory.
nt.wt. Net weight.
num. Numeral(s).
Num. Numbers.
NW or **nw, N.W.** or **n.w.** Northwest; northwestern.
N.Y. New York.
N.Y.C. New York City.

O *Chem.* Oxygen.
o Ohm.
o. 1. Octavo. 2. Off. 3. Old. 4. Only. 5. Order. 6. Out(s) (baseball). 7. Pint (L *octarius*).
O. 1. Ocean. 2. Octavo. 3. October. 4. Ohio (unofficial). 5. Old. 6. Ontario (unofficial).
OAS 1. Organization of American States. 2. Secret Army Organization (F *Organisation de l'armée secrète*).
ob. 1. He (or she) died (L *obiit*). 2. Incidentally (L *obiter*). 3. *Music* Oboe.
Obad. Obadiah.
obb. *Music* Obbligato.
obdt. Obedient.
O.B.E. Officer (of the Order) of the British Empire.
obit. Obituary.
obj. 1. Object. 2. Objection. 3. Objective.
obl. 1. Oblique. 2. Oblong.
obs. 1. Observation. 2. Observatory. 3. Obsolete.
obstet. Obstetrical; obstetrics.
obt. Obedient.
o/c Overcharge.
o.c. In the work cited (L *opere citato*).
Oc. or **oc.** Ocean.
OCDM Office of Civil and Defense Mobilization.
OCS *Mil.* Officer Candidate School.
oct. Octavo.
Oct. October.
O.D. 1. Doctor of Optometry. 2. Officer of the Day. 3. Olive drab: also **OD, o.d.** 4. Overdraft; overdrawn.
OE or **Œ** or **O.E.** Old English.
O.E.C.D. Organization for Economic Cooperation and Development.
O.E.D. Oxford English Dictionary.
OEEC or **O.E.E.C.** Organization for European Economic Cooperation.
OF or **OF.** or **O.F.** Old French.
off. 1. Offered. 2. Office. 3. Officer. 4. Official.
O.G. 1. Officer of the Guard. 2. Original gum (philately): also **o.g.**
OGPU (og'pōō) *n.* A former name of the MVD: also called *Gay-Pay-Oo.*
OHG or **OHG.** or **O.H.G.** Old High German.
O.H.M.S. On His (or Her) Majesty's Service.
O.C. Officer in Charge.
Okla. Oklahoma.
O.M. *Brit.* Order of Merit.
ON or **ON.** or **O.N.** Old Norse.
ONI Office of Naval Intelligence.
op. 1. Opera. 2. Operation. 3. Opposite. 4. Work(s) (L *opus, opera*).
OP *Mil.* Observation post.
OPA or **O.P.A.** Office of Price Administration.
op. cit. In the work cited (L *opere citato*).
opp. 1. Opposed. 2. Opposite.
OR or **O.R.** Operating room.
orch. Orchestra(l).
ord. 1. Ordained. 2. Order. 3. Ordinal. 4. Ordinance. 5. Ordinary. 6. Ordnance.
ordn. Ordnance.
Oreg. Oregon: also **Ore.** (unofficial).
org. 1. Organic. 2. Organism. 3. Organized.
orig. Original(ly).
Orth. Orthodox.
OS *Chem.* Osmium.
OS or **OS.** or **O.S.** Old Saxon.
O.S. or **O/S** or **o/s** Old Style.
O.S.A. Order of St. Augustine.
O.S.B. Order of St. Benedict.
OSD Office of the Secretary of Defense.
O.S.D. Order of St. Dominic.
O.S.F. Order of St. Francis.
OSS or **O.S.S.** Office of Strategic Services.
OT or **OT.** or **O.T.** Old Testament.
OWI or **O.W.I.** Office of War Information.
Oxon. 1. Oxford. 2. Oxfordshire. 3. Oxonian.
oz. Ounce(s).
ozs. Ounces.

P *Chem.* Phosphorus.
p or **p.** 1. *Music* Piano. 2. Pitcher (baseball).
p- *Chem.* Para-.
p. 1. After (L *post*). 2. By (L *per*). 3. By weight (L *pondere*). 4. First (L *primus*). 5. For (L *pro*). 6. Page.

7. Part. 8. Participle. 9. Past. 10. Penny. 11. Perch (measure). 12. Peseta. 13. Peso. 14. Pint. 15. Pole (measure). 16. Population.
P 1. Pawn (chess). 2. *Physics* Pressure. 3. *Mil.* Prisoner.
P- *Mil.* Pursuit.
P 1. Father (F *père*; L *pater*). 2. Pastor. 3. President. 4. Priest. 5. Prince. 6. Prompter (theater).
pa. Paper.
p.a. 1. Participial adjective. 2. Per annum (L, yearly).
Pa. *Chem.* Protactinium.
Pa. Pennsylvania.
PA 1. Press agent. 2. Public-address (system).
P.A. 1. Passenger Agent. 2. Power of attorney: also **P/A.** 3. Private account: also **P/A.** 4. Purchasing Agent.
Pac. Pacific.
par. 1. Paragraph. 2. Parallel. 3. Parenthesis. 4. Parish.
Parl. 1. Parliament. 2. Parliamentary: also **parl.**
part. 1. Participle. 2. Particular.
pass. 1. Passage. 2. Passenger. 3. Passive.
pat. 1. Patent(ed). 2. Patrol. 3. Pattern.
patd. Patented.
path. or **pathol.** Pathological; pathology.
Pat. Off. Patent Office.
payt. Payment.
Pb *Chem.* Lead (L *plumbum*).
P.B. 1. Pharmacopoeia Britannica. 2. Prayer Book.
PBX or **P.B.X.** Private branch (telephone) exchange.
pc. 1. (*pl.* **pcs.**) Piece. 2. Price(s).
p.c. 1. Percent. 2. Petty cash. 3. Postal card. 4. Price(s) current.
P/C or **p/c** 1. Petty cash. 2. Prices current.
P.C. 1. *Brit.* Police Constable. 2. Post Commander. 3. Privy Council.
pct. Percent.
pd. Paid.
p.d. 1. Per diem. 2. Potential difference.
Pd *Chem.* Palladium.
P.D. 1. Per diem. 2. Police Department.
Pd.B. Bachelor of Pedagogy (L *Pedagogiae Baccalaureus*).
Pd.D. Doctor of Pedagogy (L *Pedagogiae Doctor*).
Pd.M. Master of Pedagogy (L *Pedagogiae Magister*).
P.E. 1. Petroleum Engineer. 2. Presiding Elder. 3. *Printing* Printer's error. 4. *Stat.* Probable error. 5. Protestant Episcopal.
ped. 1. Pedal. 2. Pedestal.
Pen. or **pen.** Peninsula.
per. 1. Period. 2. Person.
perf. 1. Perfect. 2. Perforated. 3. Performer.
perh. Perhaps.
perm. Permanent.
pert. Pertaining.
Pet. Peter.
pf. Pfennig.
p.f. 1. *Music* Louder (Ital. *più forte*). 2. Power factor.
Pfc or **Pfc.** *Mil.* Private, first class.
pfg. Pfennig.
pg. Page.
PH *Mil.* Purple Heart.
PHA Public Housing Administration.
Phar. or **phar., Pharm.,** or **pharm.** 1. Pharmaceutical. 2. Pharmacopoeia. 3. Pharmacy.
Phar. B. Bachelor of Pharmacy (L *Pharmaciae Baccalaureus*).
Phar. D. Doctor of Pharmacy (L *Pharmaciae Doctor*).
Ph.B. Bachelor of Philosophy (L *Philosophiae Baccalaureus*).
Ph.C. Pharmaceutical Chemist.
Ph.D. Doctor of Philosophy (L *Philosophiae Doctor*).
phil. Philosopher; philosophical; philosophy.
Phil. 1. Philippians. 2. Philippine.
Phila. Philadelphia.
Philem. Philemon (bible).
philol. Philology.
philos. Philosopher; philosophical; philosophy.
phon. 1. Phonetic(s). 2. Phonology.
phonol. Phonology.
phot. Photograph; photographic; photography.
photog. Photograph; photographic; photography.
photom. Photometrical; photometry.
phr. Phrase.
PHS Public Health Service.
phys. 1. Physical. 2. Physician. 3. Physicist; physics.
physiol. Physiological; physiology.
pk. (*pl.* **pks.**) 1. Pack. 2. Park. 3. Peak. 4. Peck.
pkg. Package(s).
pkt. Packet.
pl. 1. Place. 2. Plate. 3. Plural.
plat. 1. Plateau. 2. Platoon.
plu. Plural.
plupf. Pluperfect.
plur. 1. Plural. 2. Plurality.

Pm *Chem.* Promethium.
P.M. 1. Afternoon (L *post meridiem*): also **p.m.** 2. Past Master. 3. Paymaster. 4. Police Magistrate. 5. Postmaster: also **PM.** 6. Post-mortem: also **p.m.** 7. Prime Minister. 8. *Mil.* Provost Marshal: also **PM.**
P.M.G. 1. Postmaster General. 2. Provost Marshal General.
P/n or **p.n.** Promissory note.
pnxt. He (or she) painted (L *pinxit*).
p.o. or **po** Put-out(s).
Po *Chem.* Polonium.
P.O. or **p.o.** 1. Personnel officer. 2. Petty officer. 3. Postal order. 4. Post office.
P.O.D. Pay on delivery: also **p.o.d.**
P.O.E. 1. *Mil.* Port of Embarkation. 2. Port of Entry.
pol. Political; politics.
pol. econ. Political economy.
polit. Political; politics.
pop. 1. Popular(ly). 2. Population.
POP Point of purchase.
pos. 1. Positive. 2. Possessive.
poss. 1. Possession; possessive. 2. Possible; possibly.
pot. Potential.
POW or **P.O.W.** Prisoner of War.
pp. 1. Pages. 2. Past participle. 3. *Music* Pianissimo: also **pp** 4. Privately printed.
p.p. 1. Parcel post. 2. Past participle. 3. Postpaid.
P.P. 1. Parcel post. 2. Parish Priest. 3. Postpaid.
P.P.C. or **p.p.c.** To take leave (F *pour prendre congé*).
ppd. 1. Postpaid. 2. Prepaid.
pph. Pamphlet.
ppl. Participial.
p.p.m. or **ppm.** or **ppm** Parts per million.
ppr. or **p.ppr.** Present participle.
P.P.S. or **p.p.s.** Additional postscript (L *post postscriptum*).
p.q. Previous question.
pr. 1. Pair(s). 2. Paper. 3. Power. 4. Present. 5. Price. 6. Priest. 7. Prince. 8. Printing. 9. Pronoun.
Pr *Chem.* Praseodymium.
Pr. 1. Prince. 2. Provençal.
PR Public relations.
P.R. Puerto Rico.
prec. Preceding.
precanc. Precanceled.
pred. Predicate.
pref. 1. Preface. 2. Prefatory. 3. Preference. 4. Prefix.
pres. 1. Present. 2. Presidency; presidential.
Pres. President.
Presb. Presbyterian.
pret. Preterit.
prim. 1. Primary. 2. Primitive.
print. Printing.
PRO or **P.R.O.** Public Relations Officer.
prod. 1. Produce(d). 2. Product.
Prof. or **prof.** Professor.
Prog. Progressive.
prom. 1. Promenade. 2. Promontory.
prop. 1. Proper(ly). 2. Property. 3. Proposition. 4. Proprietor. 5. Proprietary.
pros. Prosody.
Prot. Protestant.
prov. 1. Province. 2. Provincial. 3. Provisional. 4. Provost.
Prov. 1. Provençal. 2. Proverbs.
prs. Pairs.
ps. Pieces.
Ps. Psalms.
P.S. 1. Passenger Steamer. 2. Postscript: also **p.s.** 3. Privy Seal. 4. Public sale. 5. Public School.
p.s.f. or **psf** Pounds per square foot.
p.s.i. or **psi** Pounds per square inch.
P.SS. or **p.ss!** Postscripts.
PST or **P.S.T.** or **p.s.t.** Pacific Standard time.
psychol. Psychological; psychologist; psychology.
pt. 1. Part. 2. Payment. 3. Pint(s). 4. Point(s). 5. Port. 6. Preterit.
p.t. For the time being (L *pro tempore*).
Pt *Chem.* Platinum.
P.T. 1. Pacific Time. 2. Physical Training.
PTA or **P.T.A.** Parent-Teacher Association.
ptas. Pesetas.
ptg. Printing.
P.T.O. or **p.t.o.** Please turn over (page).
pts. 1. Parts. 2. Payments. 3. Pints. 4. Points. 5. Ports.
Pu *Chem.* Plutonium.
pub. 1. Public. 2. Publication. 3. Published; publisher; publishing.
Pvt. *Mil.* Private.
pwt. Pennyweight.
PX *Mil.* Post Exchange.
pxt. He (or she) painted (L *pinxit*).

q. 1. Farthing (L *quadrans*). 2. Quart(s). 3. Quarter(ly). 4. Quarto. 5. Quasi. 6. Query. 7. Question. 8. Quetzal 9. Quintal. 10. Quire.
Q Queen (chess).
Q. 1. (*pl.* **Qq.**) Quarto. 2. Quebec (unofficial). 3. Queen. 4. Question.
q.b. or **qb** Quarterback.
QB Queen's bishop (chess).
Q.B. *Brit.* Queen's Bench.
QBP Queen's bishop's pawn (chess).
Q.C. Queen's Counsel.
Q.E.D. Which was to be demonstrated (L *quod erat demonstrandum*).
Q.E.F. Which was to be done (L *quod erat faciendum*).
QKt Queen's knight (chess).
QKtP Queen's knight's pawn (chess).
ql. Quintal.
QM Quartermaster.
QMC Quartermaster Corps.
QMG Quartermaster General.
QP Queen's pawn (chess).
q.pl. or **Q.P.** As much as you please (L *quantum placet*).
Qq. Quartos.
qq.v. Which see (L *quae vide*).
qr. (*pl.* **qrs.**) 1. Farthing (L *quadrans*). 2. Quarter(ly). 3. Quire.
QR Queen's rook (chess).
QRP Queen's rook's pawn (chess).
q.s. 1. As much as suffices (L *quantum sufficit*). 2. Quarter section.
qt. 1. Quantity. 2. Quart(s).
q.t. or **Q.T.** *Slang* Quiet: chiefly in the phrase **on the q.t.**
qto. Quarto.
qu. 1. Quart. 2. Quarterl(y). 3. Queen. 4. Query. 5. Question.
Que. Quebec (unofficial).
ques. Question.
q.v. Which see. (L *quod vide*).
qy. Query.

r 1. Roentgen(s). 2. Ruble. 3. Rupee.
r or **r.** Run(s) (baseball).
r. 1. Radius. 2. Rare. 3. Received. 4. Recipe. 5. Residence; resides. 6. Retired. 7. Right-hand page (L *recto*). 8. Rises. 9. Rod. 10. Rubber. 11. Ruble.
R 1. Radius. 2. Ratio. 3. *Eccl.* Respond or response. 4. Rook (chess). 5. Rupee.
R. 1. Rabbi. 2. Radical. 3. Railroad. 4. Rector. 5. Redactor. 6. Republican. 7. Response. 8. Rex. 9. Right (theater). 10. River. 11. Road. 12. Royal.
Ra *Chem.* Radium.
RA *Mil.* Regular Army.
R.A. 1. *Mil.* Rear Admiral. 2. *Astron.* Right ascension. 3. Royal Academician; Royal Academy.
RAdm. *Mil.* Rear Admiral.
RAF or **R.A.F.** Royal Air Force.
RA·TO (rā′tō) *n.* An airplane takeoff assisted by an auxiliary rocket motor or unit; also, the rocket motor or unit used. Also **ra′to.** [< *r*(*ocket*) + *a*(*ssisted*) + *t*(*ake*)*o*(*ff*)]
Rb *Chem.* Rubidium.
RBI or **r.b.i.** or **rbi** Run(s) batted in (baseball).
R.C. 1. Red Cross. 2. Reserve Corps. 3. Roman Catholic.
RCAF or **R.C.A.F.** Royal Canadian Air Force.
R.C.Ch. Roman Catholic Church.
rcd. Received.
R.C.M.P. Royal Canadian Mounted Police.
RCN or **R.C.N.** Royal Canadian Navy.
Rct. *Mil.* Recruit.
rd. 1. Road. 2. Rod(s). 3. Round.
Rd. Road.
R.D. Rural Delivery.
r.e. or **re** Right end.
Re *Chem.* Rhenium.
R.E. 1. Real estate. 2. Reformed Episcopal. 3. Right Excellent. 4. Royal Engineers.
REA Rural Electrification Administration.
rec. 1. Receipt. 2. Received. 3. Recipe. 4. Record; recorded; recorder; recording.
recit. Recitative.
rec. sec. Recording secretary.
rect. 1. Receipt: also **rec't.** 2. Rector. 3. Rectory.
redupl. Reduplicated; reduplication.
ref. 1. Referee. 2. Reference. 3. Referred. 4. Reformation; reformed. 5. Refunding.
Ref. Ch. Reformed Church.
refl. 1. Reflection. 2. Reflective(ly). 3. Reflex. 4. Reflexive.
Ref. Sp. Reformed Spelling.
reg. 1. Regent. 2. Regiment. 3. Region. 4. Register(ed). 5. Registrar. 6. Registry. 7. Regular(ly). 8. Regulation.
Regt. 1. Regent. 2. Regiment.

rel. 1. Relating. 2. Relative(ly). 3. Released. 4. Religion; religious.
rep. 1. Report; reporter. 2. Representative. 3. Republic.
Rep. 1. Representative. 2. Republic. 3. Republican.
repr. 1. Representing. 2. Reprinted.
req. 1. Required. 2. Requisition.
res. 1. Research. 2. Reserve. 3. Residence. 4. Resides. 5. Residue. 6. Resigned. 7. Resolution.
resp. 1. Respective(ly). 2. Respondent.
retd. 1. Retained. 2. Returned.
rev. 1. Revenue. 2. Reverse(d). 3. Review(ed). 4. Revise(d); revision. 5. Revolution. 6. Revolving.
Rev. 1. Revelation. 2. Reverend.
rf. Right fielder (baseball).
r.f. 1. Radio frequency. 2. Rapid-fire.
RFC Royal Flying Corps.
RFD or **R.F.D.** Rural Free Delivery.
r.g. or **rg** Right guard.
r.h. 1. Relative humidity. 2. Right hand.
r.h. or **rh** Right halfback.
Rh 1. *Chem.* Rhodium. 2. *Biochem.* See RH FACTOR.
R.H. Royal Highness.
r.h.b. or **rhb** Right halfback.
rhet. Rhetoric(al).
R.I. 1. King and Emperor (L *Rex et Imperator*). 2. Queen and Empress (L *Regina et Imperatrix*). 3. Rhode Island.
R.I.P. May he (she, or they) rest in peace (L *requiescat, or requiescant, in pace*).
rit. or **ritard.** *Music* Ritardando.
riv. River.
rm. (*pl.* **rms.**) 1. Ream. 2. Room.
RM or **R.M., Rm.,** or **r.m.** Reichsmark(s).
Rn *Chem.* Radon.
R.N. 1. Registered nurse. 2. Royal Navy.
RNA *Biochem.* Ribonucleic acid.
R.N.A.S. Royal Naval Air Service.
R.N.R. Royal Naval Reserve.
R.N.V.R. Royal Naval Volunteer Reserve.
R.N.W.M.P. Royal Northwest Mounted Police.
ROK (rok) *n.* 1. The Republic of Korea (South Korea). 2. A soldier in the South Korean army.
rom. *Printing* Roman (type).
Rom. 1. Roman. 2. Romance. 3. Romans.
ROTC or **R.O.T.C.** Reserve Officers' Training Corps.
R.P. 1. Reformed Presbyterian. 2. Regius Professor.
R.P.D. Doctor of Political Science (L *Rerum Politicarum Doctor*).
rpm or **r.p.m.** Revolutions per minute.
rps or **r.p.s.** Revolutions per second.
rpt. Report.
R.R. 1. Railroad: also **RR** 2. Right Reverend. 3. Rural route.
R.S.F.S.R. or **RSFSR** Russian Soviet Federated Socialist Republic (Russian *Rossiyskaya Sovetskaya Federativnaya Sotsialisticheskaya Respublika*).
RSV or **R.S.V.** Revised Standard Version (of the Bible).
R.S.V.P. or **r.s.v.p.** Répondez s'il vous plaît. (F, please reply).
rt. Right.
r.t. or **rt** Right tackle.
Rt. Hon. Right Honorable.
Rt. Rev. Right Reverend.
Ru *Chem.* Ruthenium.
Russ. Russia; Russian.
RV or **R.V.** Revised Version (of the Bible).
R.W. 1. Right Worshipful. 2. Right Worthy.
Ry. Railway.

S *Chem.* Sulfur.
s. 1. *Anat.* Sacral. 2. Second. 3. Section. 4. See. 5. Semi-. 6. Shilling. 7. Singular. 8. Sire. 9. Son. 10. South; southern. 11. Stem; stem of. 12. Substantive. 13. Sun. 14. Surplus.
S 1. In chess, a knight (G *springer*). 2. Saxon. 3. South; southern.
S. 1. Fellow (L *Socius*). 2. Sabbath. 3. Saint. 4. Saturday. 5. Saxon. 6. School. 7. Sea. 8. Senate. 9. September. 10. South; southern. 11. Sunday.
Sa *Chem.* Samarium.
Sab. Sabbath.
SAC Strategic Air Command.
SAE or **S.A.E.** Society of Automotive Engineers.
S.Afr. South Africa; South African.
Sam. Samuel.
SANE Committee for a Sane Nuclear Policy.
Sat. 1. Saturday. 2. Saturn.
sb. Substantive.
s.b. or **sb** Stolen base(s).
Sb *Chem.* Antimony (L *stibium*).
S.B. Bachelor of Science (L *Scientiae Baccalaureus*).
SbE South by east.

SbW South by west.
sc. 1. He (or she) carved or engraved it (L *sculpsit*). 2. Namely (L *scilicet*). 3. Scale. 4. Scene. 5. Science(s). 6. Screw. 7. Scruple (weight).
s.c. 1. *Printing* Small capitals. 2. Supercalendered.
Sc 1. *Chem.* Scandium. 2. Stratocumulus.
SC Security Council (of the United Nations).
s. caps. *Printing* Small capitals.
Sc.B. Bachelor of Science (L *Scientiae Baccalaureus*).
Sc.D. Doctor of Science (L *Scientiae Doctor*).
sci. Science; scientific.
Sc.M. Master of Science. [L *Scientiae Magister*).
Scot. Scotch; Scotland; Scottish.
scr. Scruple (weight).
Script. Scriptural; Scripture(s).
sd. Sound.
s.d. Sine die.
S.D. 1. Doctor of Science (L *Scientiae Doctor*). 2. *Stat.* Standard deviation: also **s.d.**
S.Dak. South Dakota: also **S.D.** (unofficial).
Se *Chem.* Selenium.
SE or **se, S.E.,** or **s.e.** Southeast; southeastern.
SEATO (sē′tō) Southeast Asia Treaty Organization.
sec. 1. According to (L *secundum*). 2. Secant. 3. Second(s). 4. Secondary. 5. Secretary. 6. Section(s). 7. Sector.
SEC or **S.E.C.** Securities and Exchange Commission.
sect. Section; sectional.
secy Secretary: also **sec'y.**
Sem. 1. Seminary. 2. Semitic.
Sen. or **sen.** 1. Senate; senator. 2. Senior.
sep. 1. Sepal(s). 2. Separate.
Sep. 1. September. 2. Septuagint.
Sept. 1. September. 2. Septuagint.
seq. 1. Sequel. 2. The following (one) (L *sequens*)
seqq. The following (ones) (L *sequentia*).
ser. 1. Serial. 2. Series. 3. Sermon.
sf or **sf., sfz,** or **sfz.** *Music* With emphasis (Ital. *sforzando, sforzato*).
SF or **sf** Science fiction.
SFC *Mil.* Sergeant First Class.
s.g. Specific gravity.
sgd. Signed.
sh. 1. Share(s). 2. Sheep. 3. Sheet. 4. Shilling(s).
SHAEF (shāf) In World War II, Supreme Headquarters Allied Expeditionary Forces.
SHAPE Supreme Headquarters Allied Powers Europe.
SHF or **shf** Superhigh frequency. Also **S.H.F., s.h.f.**
shpt. Shipment.
Si *Chem.* Silicon.
Sig. or **sig.** 1. Signature. 2. Signor; signore.
SigC *Mil.* Signal Corps.
sing. Singular.
S.J. Society of Jesus.
S.J.D. Doctor of Juridical Science (L *Scientiae Juridicae Doctor*).
sk. Sack.
Skt. Sanskrit: also **Skr.**
s.l. Without place (of publication) (L *sine loco*).
S.lat. South latitude.
Slav. Slavic.
Sm *Chem.* Samarium.
S.M. 1. Master of Science (L *Scientiae Magister*). 2. Soldier's Medal.
SMaj. *Mil.* Sergeant Major.
sm.c. or **sm. cap(s).** *Printing* Small capital(s).
Sn *Chem.* Tin (L *stannum*).
s.o. or **so** Struck out; strike-out.
So. South; southern.
soc. 1. Socialist. 2. Society.
S. of Sol. Song of Solomon.
sol. 1. Soluble. 2. Solution.
Sol. 1. Solicitor. 2. Solomon.
sop. *Music* Soprano.
SOP or **S.O.P.** *Mil.* Standard operating procedure.
sos. or **sost.** or **sosten.** Sostenuto.
sp. 1. Special. 2. Species. 3. Specific. 4. Specimen. 5. Spelling. 6. Spirit(s).
s.p. 1. Sine prole (L, without issue). 2. Single phase.
Sp. Spain; Spaniard; Spanish.
SP *Naval* Shore patrol (or police).
spp. Species (plural).
S.P.Q.R. The Senate and People of Rome (L *Senatus Populusque Romanus*).
spt. Seaport.
sq. 1. Sequence. 2. The following one (L *sequens*). 3. Square.
Sq. Squadron.
sq. ft. Square foot (or feet).
sq. in. Square inch(es).
sq. m. or **sq. mi.** Square mile(s).

sqq. The following ones (L *sequentia*).
sq. yd. Square yard(s).
Sr *Chem.* Strontium.
Sr. 1. Senior. 2. Señor. 3. Sir. 4. Sister.
SR *Mil.* Seaman Recruit.
Sra. Señora.
S.R.O. Standing room only.
Srta. Señorita.
SS or **S.S.** or **S/S** Steamship.
SS. 1. Saints. 2. The Schutzstaffel: also **SS**
S.S. 1. Sunday School. 2. Written above (L *supra Scriptum*).
SSA or **S.S.A.** Social Security Act (or Administration).
SSE or **sse, S.S.E.** or **s.s.e.** South-southeast.
SSS Selective Service System.
SST supersonic transport.
SSW or **ssw, S.S.W.**, or **s.s.w.** South-southwest.
st. 1. Stanza. 2. Statute(s). 3. Stere. 4. Stet. 5. Stitch. 6. Stone (weight). 7. Street. 8. Strophe.
St *Meteorol.* Stratus.
St. 1. Saint. 2. Statute(s). 3. Strait. 4. Street.
St. For entries not found under ST., see under SAINT.
sta. 1. Station. 2. Stationary. 3. Stator.
Sta. 1. Santa. 2. Station.
stacc. *Music* Staccato.
S.T.B. 1. Bachelor of Sacred Theology (L *Sacrae Theologiae Baccalaureus*). 2. Bachelor of Theology (L *Scientiae Theologicae Baccalaureus*).
stbd. Starboard.
std. Standard.
S.T.D. Doctor of Sacred Theology (L *Sacrae Theologiae Doctor*).
Ste. Sainte.
ster. Sterling.
St. Ex. Stock Exchange.
stg. Sterling.
stge. Storage.
stk. Stock.
STOL Short takeoff and landing.
str. 1. Steamer. 2. Strait. 3. *Music* String(s).
sub. 1. Subaltern. 2. Subscription. 3. Substitute. 4. Suburb; suburban.
subj. 1. Subject. 2. Subjective(ly). 3. Subjunctive.
subst. 1. Substantive. 2. Substitute.
suf. or **suff.** Suffix.
Sun. or **Sund.** Sunday.
SUNFED Special United Nations Fund for Economic Development.
sup. 1. Above (L *supra*). 2. Superior. 3. Superlative. 4. Supine. 5. Supplement; supplementary. 6. Supply. 7. Supreme.
super. 1. Superfine. 2. Superintendent. 3. Superior. 4. Supernumerary.
superl. Superlative.
supp. or **suppl.** Supplement; supplementary.
supr. Supreme.
Supt. or **supt.** Superintendent.
sur. 1. Surcharged. 2. Surplus.
Sur. Surrey.
surg. Surgeon; surgery; surgical.
surv. 1. Survey; surveying; surveyor. 2. Surviving.
s.v. Under this word (L *sub verbo, sub voce*).
S.V. Holy Virgin (L *Sancta Virgo*).
SW or **sw, S.W.** or **s.w.** Southwest; southwestern.
syl. or **syll.** 1. Syllable. 2. Syllabus.
sym. 1. Symbol. 2. *Chem.* Symmetrical: also **sym-**. 3. Symphony. 4. Symptom.
synop. Synopsis.
syr. Syrup (pharmacy).
syst. System; systematic.

t. 1. In the time of (L *tempore*). 2. Tare. 3. Target. 4. Teaspoon(s). 5. Telephone. 6. Temperature. 7. Tempo. 8. Tenor. 9. *Gram.* Tense. 10. Terminal. 11. Territorial; territory. 12. Time. 13. Tome. 14. Ton(s). 15. Town; township. 16. Transit. 17. *Gram.* Transitive. 18. Troy (weight). 19. Volume (L *tomus*).
T 1. *Chem.* Tantalum. 2. Technician. 3. Temperature (absolute scale). 4. (Surface) tension. 5. Time.
T. 1. Tablespoon(s). 2. Territory. 3. Testament. 4. Tuesday. 5. Turkish.
Ta *Chem.* Tantalum.
TAA Technical Assistance Administration.
tab. Table(s).
TAB Technical Assistance Board.
TAC 1. *Mil.* Tactical Air Command. 2. Technical Assistance Committee.
TAG The Adjutant General.
tan or **tan.** Tangent.
Tb *Chem.* Terbium.
t.b. Trial balance.

TB or **T.B., Tb, Tb., t.b.** or **tb** Tuberculosis.
tbs. or **tbsp.** Tablespoon(s).
Tc. *Chem.* Technetium.
TC 1. Transportation Corps. 2. Trusteeship Council (of the United Nations).
TD 1. Touchdown: also **td** or **td.** 2. Treasury Dept.
Te *Chem.* Tellurium.
technol. Technology.
tel. 1. Telegram. 2. Telegraph; telegraphic. 3. Telephone.
teleg. Telegram; telegraph; telegraphic; telegraphy.
temp. 1. In the time of (L *tempore*). 2. Temperature. 3. Temporary.
ten. *Music* 1. Tenor. 2. Tenuto.
Tenn. Tennessee.
ter. 1. Terrace. 2. Territorial; territory.
term. 1. Terminal. 2. Termination. 3. Terminology.
test. 1. Testamentary. 2. Testator.
Test. Testament.
Tex. Texas; Texan.
Th *Chem.* Thorium.
Th. Thursday.
Th.B. Bachelor of Theology (L *Theologiae Baccalaureus*).
Th.D. Doctor of Theology (L *Theologiae Doctor*).
theol. Theologian; theological; theology.
theos. Theosophical; theosophy.
T.H.I. or **T.-H.I.** Temperature-humidity index.
Thur. or **Thurs.** Thursday.
Ti *Chem.* Titanium.
Tim. Timothy.
Tit. Titus.
TKO or **T.K.O.** or **t.k.o.** Technical knockout.
Tl *Chem.* Thallium.
TL or **T.L.** Trade-last.
Tm *Chem.* Thulium.
tn. 1. Ton. 2. Train.
Tn *Chem.* Thoron.
tng. Training.
TNT Trinitrotoluene.
top. Topographical; topography.
tp. Township.
tr. 1. Trace. 2. Train. 3. Transitive. 4. Translated; translation; translator. 5. Transpose. 6. Treasurer. 7. Trust.
Tr *Chem.* Terbium.
trans. 1. Transaction(s). 2. Transferred. 3. *Gram.* Transitive. 4. Translated; translation; translator. 5. Transportation. 6. Transpose. 7. Transverse.
transl. Translated; translation.
transp. 1. Transparent. 2. Transportation.
treas. Treasurer; treasury.
trfd. Transferred.
trig. or **trigon.** Trigonometric; trigonometry.
tripl. Triplicate.
TSgt *Mil.* Technical Sergeant.
Tu. Tuesday.
Tues. Tuesday.
TV (tē′vē) *n. pl.* **TVs** or **TV's** Television.
TV or **tv** Terminal velocity.
TVA or **T.V.A.** Tennessee Valley Authority.
twp. Township.
Ty. Territory.
typ. Typographic(al); typography.
typo. or **typog.** Typographic(al); typography.

U *Chem.* Uranium.
u. And (G *und*).
U. or **u.** 1. Uncle. 2. University. 3. Upper.
UAW or **U.A.W.** 1. United Auto, Aircraft and Agricultural Implements Workers. 2. United Automobile Workers of America.
u.c. 1. *Music* Soft pedal (Ital. *una corda* one string). 2. *Printing* Upper case.
UCMJ *Mil.* Uniform Code of Military Justice.
UFO Unidentified flying object.
U.J.D. Doctor of Civil and Canon Law (L *Utriusque Juris Doctor*).
ult. 1. Ultimate(ly). 2. Ultimo: also **ulto.**
UMT Universal Military Training.
UMTS Universal Military Training and Service.
UN or **U.N.** United Nations.
UNEF United Nations Emergency Force.
UNESCO (yōō·nes′kō) The United Nations Educational, Scientific and Cultural Organization. Also **U·nes′co.**
UNICEF (yōō′nə·sef) United Nations Children's Fund. Also **U′ni·cef.**
Unit. Unitarian.
univ. 1. Universal(ly). 2. University.
Univ. University.
UNKRA United Nations Korean Reconstruction Agency.
unpub. Unpublished.

UNREF United Nations Refugee Emergency Fund.
UNRRA United Nations Relief and Rehabilitation Administration.
UNRWA United Nations Relief and Works Agency for Palestine Refugees in the Near East.
UNSCOB United Nations Special Committee on the Balkans.
UNTSO United Nations Truce Supervision Organization.
UP or **U.P.** 1. Union Pacific (Railroad). 2. United Press.
UPI or **U.P.I.** United Press International.
Ur *Chem.* Uranium.
U.S. or **US** United States.
USA United States Army.
U.S.A. or **USA** United States of America.
USAF United States Air Force.
USAFI United States Armed Forces Institute.
USAR United States Army Reserve.
U.S.C. & G.S. United States Coast and Geodetic Survey.
USCG or **U.S.C.G.** United States Coast Guard.
USES or **U.S.E.S.** United States Employment Service.
USIA or **U.S.I.A.** United States Information Agency.
USIBA United States International Book Association.
U.S.M. 1. United States Mail. 2. United States Mint.
USMA or **U.S.M.A.** United States Military Academy.
USMC or **U.S.M.C.** United States Marine Corps.
USMCR United States Marine Corps Reserve.
USMS United States Maritime Service.
USN or **U.S.N.** United States Navy.
USNA or **U.S.N.A.** United States Naval Academy.
USNR or **U.S.N.R.** United States Naval Reserve.
USO or **U.S.O.** United Service Organizations.
USP or **U.S.P.** United States Pharmacopoeia: also **U.S. Pharm.**
USPHS or **U.S.P.H.S.** United States Public Health Service.
USS or **U.S.S.** 1. United States Senate. 2. United States Ship (or Steamer or Steamship).
USSB United States Shipping Board.
U.S.S.R. or **USSR** Union of Soviet Socialist Republics.
usw or **u.s.w.** And so forth (G *und so weiter*).
u.t. Universal time.
Ut. Utah (unofficial).
ux. Wife (L *uxor*)

v Volt.
v. 1. Valve. 2. Ventral. 3. *Gram.* **a** Verb. **b** Vocative. 4. Verse. 5. Version. 6. Versus. 7. Vice-. 8. Vide. 9. Village. 10. Voice. 11. Volt; voltage. 12. Volume. 13. Von.
V 1. *Math.* Vector. 2. Velocity. 3. *Electr.* Volt. 4. Volume. 5. *Chem.* Vanadium.
V. 1. Venerable. 2. Viscount.
v.a. *Gram.* 1. Active verb. 2. Verbal adjective.
Va. Virginia.
V.A. 1. Veterans' Administration: also **VA** 2. Vicar Apostolic. 3. Vice Admiral. 4. (Order of) Victoria and Albert.
V.Adm. Vice Admiral.
var. 1. Variant. 2. Variation. 3. Variety.
Vat. Vatican.
v. aux. *Gram.* Auxiliary verb.
vb. Verb; verbal.
V.C. 1. Veterinary Corps. 2. Vice Chairman. 3. Vice Chamberlain. 4. Vice Chancellor. 5. Vice Consul. 6. Victoria Cross.
Vd *Chem.* Vanadium.
v.d. Various dates.
VD or **V.D.** Venereal disease.
vel. Vellum.
Ven. 1. Venerable. 2. Venice.
ver. 1. Verse(s). 2. Version.
Ver. St. United States (G *Vereinigte Staaten*).
V.G. Vicar General.
VHF or **vhf, V.H.F.,** or **v.h.f.** Very high frequency.
v.i. 1. See below (L *vide infra*). 2. *Gram.* Intransitive verb.
Vi *Chem.* Virginium.
V.I. Virgin Islands.
vil. Village.
v. imp. *Gram.* Impersonal verb.
VIP or **V.I.P.** Very important person.
Vis. or **Visc.** Viscount; Viscountess.
Visct. Viscount; Viscountess.
viv. *Music* Lively (Ital. *vivace*).
viz. Namely (L *videlicet*).
VL or **V.L.** Vulgar Latin.
VLF or **vlf, V.L.F.,** or **v.l.f.** Very low frequency.
V.M.D. Doctor of Veterinary Medicine (L *Veterinariae Medicinae Doctor*).
v.n. *Gram.* Neuter verb: also **v. neut.**
vo. Verso.
vocab. Vocabulary.
vol. 1. Volcano. 2. Volume. 3. Volunteer.
vols. Volumes.

v.p. 1. Various pagings. 2. Various places. 3. *Gram.* Verb passive. 4. Voting pool (stocks).
V.P. Vice President: also **V.Pres.**
v.r. *Gram.* Reflexive verb.
V.R. Queen Victoria (L *Victoria Regina*).
V.Rev. Very Reverend.
vs. 1. Verse. 2. Versus.
V.S. Veterinary Surgeon.
VSS Versions.
v.t. *Gram.* Transitive verb.
Vt. Vermont.
VTOL Vertical takeoff and landing.
Vul. Vulgate.
vv. 1. Verses. 2. *Music* Violins.
v.v. Vice versa.

w. 1. Wanting. 2. Warehousing. 3. Week(s). 4. Weight. 5. West; western. 6. Wide; width. 7. Wife. 8. With. 9. Won: also **w** 10. *Physics* Work.
W *Chem.* Tungsten (L *wolfram*).
W or **w** 1. *Electr.* Watt(s). 2. West; western.
W. 1. Wales; Welsh. 2. Wednesday. 3. West; western. 4. *Physics* Work.
WAC or **W.A.C.** Women's Army Corps.
WAF or **W.A.F.** Women in the Air Force.
Wash. Washington.
Wat. Waterford.
WAVES or **W.A.V.E.S.** Women in the United States Navy.
w.b. 1. Warehouse book. 2. Waybill. 3. Westbound.
W.B. or **W/B, W.b.,** or **W/b** Waybill.
WbN West by north.
WbS West by south.
w.c. or **W.C.** 1. Water closet. 2. Without charge.
Wed. Wednesday.
wf or **w.f.** *Printing* Wrong font.
WFTU or **W.F.T.U.** World Federation of Trade Unions.
wh. Watt-hour(s).
whf. Wharf.
WHO World Health Organization.
w.i. When issued (stocks).
Wis. Wisconsin: also **Wisc.** (unofficial).
wk. (*pl.* **wks.**) 1. Week. 2. Work.
wkly. Weekly.
w.l. or **WL** 1. Water line. 2. Wave length.
W. long. West longitude.
wmk. or **w/m** Watermark.
WNW or **wnw, W.N.W., w.n.w.** West-northwest.
WO or **W.O.** 1. Wait order. 2. *Mil.* Warrant Officer.
WPA or **W.P.A.** Work Projects Administration.
WRAC or **W.R.A.C.** Women's Royal Army Corps.
WRAF or **W.R.A.F.** Women's Royal Air Force.
W.R.N.S. Women's Royal Naval Service.
WSW or **wsw, W.S.W.,** or **w.s.w.** West-southwest.
wt. Weight.
W.Va. West Virginia.
WVS or **W.V.S.** *Brit.* Women's Voluntary Service.
Wy. Wyoming (unofficial).
Wyo. Wyoming.

x-cp. Ex coupon. Also **X.C., x.c.**
x-div. Ex dividend. Also **X.D., x.d.**
Xe *Chem.* Xenon.
Xn. Christian.
Xnty. or **Xty.** Christianity.
x-ref. Cross-reference.
X-rts. Ex rights.
Xtian. Christian.

Y *Chem.* Yttrium.
y. 1. Yard(s). 2. Year(s).
Y. Young Men's (or Women's) Christian Association.
Yb *Chem.* Ytterbium.
yd. Yard (*pl.* **yd.** or **yds.**)
YHWH Yahweh.
YMCA or **Y.M.C.A.** Young Men's Christian Association.
YMHA or **Y.M.H.A.** Young Men's Hebrew Association.
yr. 1. Year(s). 2. Your.
yrs. 1. Years. 2. Yours.
Yt *Chem.* Yttrium.
YWCA or **Y.W.C.A.** Young Women's Christian Association.
YWHA or **Y.W.H.A.** Young Women's Hebrew Association.

Z *Astron.* Zenith distance.
Z. or **z.** Zone.
Zech. Zechariah.
Zeph. Zephaniah.
Z/F *Mil.* Zone of fire.
Zn *Chem.* Zinc.
zool. Zoological; zoologist; zoology.
Zr *Chem.* Zirconium.

SECRETARIAL HANDBOOK

SECRETARIAL HANDBOOK

by Alice Ottun

Secretaries, even though well-educated and experienced, encounter problems in their everyday dictation, transcription, and office work. It is the purpose of this Secretarial Handbook to help solve these problems by presenting clear, concise statements, along with recommendations on preferred usage, about traditionally troublesome areas of language.

The author of this Handbook, Alice Ottun, is a leading authority on secretarial and office procedures. For twenty years the Administrative Dean of Pace College, she is at present the Director of Business Education of the Middle Country School District in Centereach, Long Island. Miss Ottun has served as President of the Commercial Education Association of New York City, of the Business Institutes of the State of New York, and of the Private Schools Association of New York City. She is listed in *Who's Who in American Education* and in *Who's Who of American Women*. She has for many years taught business subjects and English and has an intimate knowledge of the type of information that secretaries and other office workers need and want.

Throughout the years Funk & Wagnalls' Dictionary Department has been called upon to answer a great many inquiries, many of them from secretaries, about various problems relating to language. Records have been kept of these inquiries, and a report based upon them has been made available to the author of this Handbook, thus providing her with original, practical data to aid her in selecting the categories that secretaries and others will find most useful.

WORD USAGE AND WORD RELATIONSHIPS

Agreement of Subject and Verb

It may seem needless to say that a singular subject takes a singular verb, while a plural subject takes a plural verb; however, many errors occur in this respect.

> The small table *was* in the hall.
> The small tables *were* in the hall.

In some instances, when phrases or other elements come between the subject and the verb, the agreement may not be so clear.

> The small table around which the children play *was* in the hall.
> The small tables owned by the church *were* in the hall.
> The men, as well as the policeman, *were* aghast at the sight.

The following words are generally considered singular and take the singular form of the verb: *each, either, neither, one, someone, anyone, everybody, nobody, somebody, much, anybody, everyone.*
The following words are plural and take the plural form of the verb: *both, few, many, several.*
The following pronouns may be singular or plural depending on the meaning intended: *all, most, some, every, none, any, half, more.*
When one is referring to two or more persons who are of different sexes, or to a group of people whose gender one has no way of determining, the pronouns *they, them,* and *their* are often used to refer to *anyone, each, everybody,* etc., in order to avoid the awkward *he or she, him or her, his or her.* Strictly speaking, one should use the masculine singular pronouns (*he, him, his*) in such cases, but in practice they are used consistently only in formal usage. Which procedure you follow will depend on how formal a style you wish to employ.

Either—Or; Neither—Nor

Neither always takes *nor; either* takes *or.*
When a subject is compounded with *neither . . . nor* or *either . . . or,* the verb is normally singular if the nouns joined are singular, and plural if they are plural. If, however, one noun is singular and one plural, the verb agrees with the second or nearer subject.

> Either Bill or Ralph *is* lying.
> Neither she nor her sisters *skate* well.

A collective noun, such as *class, company, club, crew, jury, committee,* takes a singular verb when the whole is considered as a unit, and a plural verb when part of the whole is considered separately.

> The jury *has* deliberated for six hours.
> The crew *were* near exhaustion after their many hours of exposure.

Some collective nouns, as *police* and *cattle,* are used only in the plural form; others, as *mankind* and *wildlife,* are generally used in the singular form.

> The cattle *were* almost destroyed by the severe storm.
> The New England wildlife *has* been protected.

Agreement of Pronoun with Its Antecedent

If the antecedent is singular, the pronoun is singular; if the antecedent is plural, the pronoun is likewise plural.

> The *boy* did *his* best in the contest.
> The *boys* in the school did *their* best.
> The *boy* and the *girl* did *their* best.
> *Neither one* of the boys did *his* best.

PUNCTUATION

For practical purposes, it is best to keep in mind that too much punctuation is as confusing as too little. The current trend is toward a minimum of punctuation, just enough to make the writer's meaning clear. This can best be accomplished by cultivating a simple, straightforward style that flows as naturally as ordinary speech.

Where a sentence is so complicated that no amount of punctuation seems adequate, a writer would be wise to reorganize his thoughts. Punctuation can help to guide a reader to the meaning of a sentence; it cannot, however, make order out of confused thinking and expression.

End Punctuation

Because the sentence is a grammatically complete and separate unit of utterance, it is necessary to show where one sentence ends and another begins. In speech, this is accomplished by falling pitch, intonation, and a full pause. In written discourse, the reader is guided by a period, a question mark, or an exclamation point, depending on the nature of the sentence.

The Period [.] The period is used at the end of a declarative sentence, an imperative sentence, an indirect question, and after a polite request that resembles a question. It is also used after initials and most abbreviations.

> Mrs. Morris placed the book on the table.
> The members of the committee asked when the meeting would take place.
> Will you open the door for me, please.

If a sentence ends in an abbreviation, only one period is needed.

> The bus will arrive at 8:30 A.M.

Do not use a period and two zeros after even amounts of money, except in tabulation.

> $25, not $25. or $25.00

The period should not be used in centered headings, such as manuscript and chapter headings; in the various elements in an outline; or in the items in a tabulation.
Do not use periods between the call numbers of broadcasting stations: WABC, WQXR; or between the letters indicating government agencies: FBI, CIA, FAA, IRS.
Three dots (. . .), called an *ellipsis,* are used to indicate an omission in quoted matter. When the omission comes at the end of the line, use the three dots together with the sentence period, making a total of four dots. If one or more paragraphs are omitted in the quoted matter, show the omission by using seven dots across the page.

The Question Mark [?] The question mark signifies that the sentence preceding it does not make a statement, but asks a question. This punctuation serves the same purpose in writing that rising or sustained pitch intonation of the voice does in speaking.

> When may we expect to receive your check?

If a sentence consists of several questions, the question mark should appear at the close of each question within the sentence and also at the close. The separate questions within the sentence do not begin with a capital since they are part of the larger and complete question.

> Who will attend the conference—the president? the vice president? or the secretary?

The Exclamation Point [!] This is used at the end of a statement denoting a strong emotional experience or a sense of urgency or excitement. If spoken, it would be gasped, shouted, groaned, or cried. Written, the exclamation point, and the reader's imagination, must suffice.

Watch out!
Oh, my head!

An interjection at the beginning of a sentence is usually followed by a comma, and the sentence is ended with an exclamation point. The interjection may, however, be immediately followed by an exclamation mark, and the following sentence punctuated without reference to it.

Oh, what a day this is!
Oh! How could you do that?

Exclamation points should be used with discretion and for particular emphasis. Excessive use tends to lessen the impact of this device.

Internal Punctuation

When sentences become more complex and deal with two or more closely related ideas, internal punctuation is necessary to show the relation between the various parts. Authorities differ in some respects on the rules applying to the use of the comma and the semicolon. Since this Handbook is a secretarial guide, however, some specific rules should be laid down, but with the understanding that research may indicate differences of opinion.

The Comma [,] The comma is used to separate the various elements in a series—either words, phrases, or clauses—when there are at least three units.

The torn, tattered, soaking flag was lowered.
The dog jumped up, barked ferociously, bared his teeth, and took off after the rabbit.

Formal punctuation requires that a comma be inserted between the last two elements of a series even when a conjunction is used; this rule is generally followed in letter writing. An informal style of writing, such as newspaper and editorial work, does not require the comma before the conjunction.

The flag is red, white and blue.

Sometimes the conjunction is used with each element in the series. When this occurs, no comma is used to separate the elements.

The banner will be red or blue or white or a combination of these colors.

When *etc.* is the concluding element in a series, it should be preceded by a comma. A comma should also follow *etc.* when it is not the last word in a sentence.

She stopped off at the supermarket to get some fruit, vegetables, etc., on the way home.

Use the comma to set off an introductory sentence element (word, phrase, clause) which is out of its natural order. Of all the comma rules, this is probably the most difficult to master. Some words, like *however*, are not always used as introductory words and would not then be followed by the comma.

Obviously, we cannot meet your request.
In order to meet the deadline, we shall have to work overtime.
When you go to see him in the hospital, bring along a few magazines.
However well you meant, it was the wrong thing to do.

When the main clause in the sentence comes first, do not use the comma between the main clause and the dependent clause.

Bring along a few magazines when you go to visit him in the hospital.

As a general rule, an introductory phrase which contains a verb should be followed with a comma.

After *making* the survey, the committee will publish the report.
To *complete* the survey, the officers worked overtime.

If the introductory phrase does not contain a verb, it should not be followed by a comma unless the phrase is parenthetical or explanatory.

After much debate the meeting was adjourned.
As an act of mercy the sick animal was killed.
Under separate cover we are sending you a catalogue.
On the contrary, I believe the President was absolutely right.

For example, consider the boy's attitude toward his parents.
In the second place, watch his behavior with his peers.

Use the comma to set off introductory *yes* or *no* or light exclamations in a sentence.

No, we shall not be ready on time.
Oh, what a wonderful day this has been!

A parenthetical expression (word, phrase, or clause) that can be omitted without changing the meaning of the sentence should be set off by commas.

The king, who was very ill, was not present at the ceremony.
Something may, of course, turn up to change what seems now to be the obvious outcome.

Note: When the information has little connection with the thought expressed in the main clause, it is usually enclosed in parentheses rather than in commas.

The strike (which began on the President's birthday) completely paralyzed the nation.

Dashes may also be used to set off any sort of nonrestrictive or parenthetical matter. Some writers feel that dashes lend a more personal dramatic effect to their writing.

The earth—all parched and dry—yearns for moisture.

Use the comma before short, direct quotations.

She asked, "Is the train on time?"

Use the comma to set off words in direct address.

We are certain, Mr. Long, that you will be satisfied with our product.

The comma or commas should be used to set off an identifying or explanatory word or phrase (called an *appositive*) which helps to make the meaning of the sentence clearer. This rule applies to a person's title or degree and to the abbreviation "Inc." when used in a company name.

Our salesman, Mr. Brown, will call on you tomorrow.
We shall write a letter to Ray Smith & Company, Inc., in New York City.
Harold Brown, Ph.D., has been appointed to the faculty.

Separate contrasting expressions—word, phrase, or clause—by using the comma.

We shall leave today, not tomorrow.

Use the comma to separate two or more parallel adjectives.

Their sleeping bags kept them warm during the long, cold nights.

Note: If the word *and* can be inserted between the two adjectives or if the two adjectives can be reversed, they are parallel and the comma should be used.

The comma is *not* used when the order of the adjectives helps to determine the meaning of the sentence.

They built the building with wide open stairways.

The comma should be used before a conjunction (*but, and, or,* etc.) that connects two independent clauses.

We have had the pleasure of counting you as one of our members for many years, but we notice that you have not yet renewed your membership.

If the clauses are short and uncomplicated, the comma may be omitted.

We were drenched but arrived safely.

The Semicolon [;] The semicolon is used to separate two independent clauses when the conjunction is omitted.

We are enclosing an envelope for your convenience; it requires no postage.

Use the semicolon to separate the members of a compound sentence when one or both members contain other punctuation marks.

If he is nominated, he will run; but his chances seem dim.

Use the semicolon to separate the members of a compound sentence when the clauses are connected by such words as *however, nevertheless, consequently,* etc.

He paid little attention to details; consequently, he failed to be promoted.

Phrases or clauses in a series are separated by the semicolon when any one or more of the phrases or clauses contain a comma.

Our profits for the three successive years were: 1960, $2,345,000; 1961, $2,070,400; 1962, $2,545,000.

The Colon [:] The colon is used most often to indicate that a list, example, strong assertion, or the like will follow to complete or fulfill some introductory statement.

The bride takes three vows: to love, honor, and obey.
We have only one goal: to win.

The colon is also used outside the sentence in certain purely conventional ways: after the salutation of a formal letter; between elements of a Biblical or bibliographical citation; after the name or other identification of the speaker in a dialogue or in a transcript of speech.

Use the colon to separate hours and minutes when time is expressed in figures. When no minutes are expressed, it is not necessary to use two zeros with the number designating the hour. When the word *o'clock* is used, do not indicate the time in figures but express the time in words.

We shall be there at 3:30 P.M.
We shall be there at 3 P.M.
We shall be there at three o'clock.

The Apostrophe [']

To Indicate Possession Apostrophes are employed most commonly to form the possessive of nouns and pronouns. In words not ending with an *s* or *z* sound, *'s* is added; in those ending with an *s* or *z* sound, the common practice is to add only an apostrophe at the end. Most singular nouns take the *'s*, and most plural forms add only '.

Words not ending in s *or* z:	*Words ending in* s *or* z:
the children's playroom	the babies' bottles
somebody's hat	for goodness' sake

Exceptions may be found in the possessive form of proper names ending in *s* or *z*. There is a growing tendency to add *'s* to a name having one syllable even though it ends with an *s* sound, thus making James *James's*, Marx *Marx's*, and Schultz *Schultz's*. With names of more than one syllable, either form may be used unless the additional *s* makes the word difficult to pronounce. Then only the apostrophe is used.

Thomas's *or* Thomas'	*but only* Genesis'
Adams's *or* Adams'	Exodus'
Titus's *or* Titus'	Moses'

Personal pronouns do not take the apostrophe in the possessive form.

my, mine	our, ours
your, yours	their, theirs
her, hers	his, its, whose

To Indicate Omission An apostrophe is also used to show that one or more letters have been omitted from a word, or that numerals have been omitted from a number.

it's—it is; can't—cannot; you're—you are;
we'll—we will; where'er—wherever; '29—1929

Plurals of Letters or Numbers The plural of a letter or a number is formed by adding 's, although it should be noted that there is a growing trend to drop the apostrophe where years are concerned. Abbreviations form the plural by adding 's.

Dot your i's and cross your t's.
There are four s's, four i's, and two p's in Mississippi.
Watch your ABC's.
6's and 7's
a company of GI's
a carload of VIP's

Quotation Marks [" "] [' ']

There are two classes of quotations: *direct* and *indirect*. Quotation marks are required at the beginning and end of a word or words spoken in direct discourse.

Roy said, "I am reading a good book."

Indirect quotations require no quotation marks, and are commonly introduced by the word *that*.

Roy said that he was reading a good book.

If a direct quotation is interrupted by one or more words, the quotation marks are placed around the quoted matter only and not around the interrupting words.

"Hurry along," said the coach, "or we shall not make the game in time."

When quoting material, be careful to include every detail of punctuation even though you may not wholly agree with the details involved.

"Stir not up agitation! Give us peace!"

The use of slang, humor, and colloquial expressions is unsuited to formal speech or writing. If used, such words should be enclosed in quotation marks.

It was a "whale" of a story.

Translations of foreign words and phrases should be enclosed in quotations marks.

Au revoir means "till we meet again" or "good-bye."
Laissez faire means "noninterference."

In manuscripts and business correspondence, the title of a book, a booklet, a magazine, or a newspaper should be typed in capital and small letters (or all in capitals) and underlined. Enclose in quotation marks and type in capital and small letters the titles of essays, magazine articles, lectures, term papers, and the titles of chapters. The first letter of the first word and the first letter of every important word following is capitalized.

I have just finished reading Why England Slept.

The "Foreword to the Memorial Edition," written by Robert F. Kennedy, shows great depth of feeling and love for his brother, John F. Kennedy.
Did you read the article "One Man's Opinion" in this morning's New York Times?

When a lengthy quotation of two or more paragraphs is used, beginning or opening quotation marks are used at the start of each paragraph, and closing quotation marks appear only at the very end of the quoted passage.

No quotation marks are necessary in interviews, dramatic dialogues, or legal testimony where the name of the speaker or other identification precedes the speech, or where question and answer are clearly marked.

Judge: How do you plead, guilty or not guilty?
Defendant: Not guilty, Your Honor.
Q.: Where were you on the night of June 26?
A.: I don't remember.

Quotation marks are used to set off words or phrases that the writer wishes not to claim as his own. These may be the words of other persons, or they may be jargon, slang, barbarisms, figures of speech, and the like, which he "decontaminates" by using quotation marks.

Let my opponent produce his "incontrovertible evidence."
The young men apparently did it "for kicks."

A quotation within a quotation is enclosed by single quotation marks.

Jack remarked, "I believe Patrick Henry said, 'Give me liberty or give me death.'"

Note: The period within the quotation marks serves as end punctuation both for the sentence spoken by Jack and that spoken by Patrick Henry. The period is never doubled at the end of a quotation within a quotation.

The rule for punctuating quoted matter is quite simple. The period and comma are always *inside* the closing quotation marks; the colon and semicolon are always *outside* the closing quotation marks; the question mark and exclamation point will be inside or outside the closing quotation marks depending on whether they are or are not part of the quoted matter.

He said, "Call the police."
He said, "Who called the police?"
Who said, "Call the police"?
He said, "Call the police"; but the sirens were already wailing.

The Hyphen [-]

The hyphen is used primarily for end-of-line word divisions and for hyphenation of compound words.
Words may be divided *only* between syllables.
Words pronounced as one syllable may never be divided.
Words may not be divided in groups of fewer than three letters.
Abbreviations should never be carried over from one line to the next, and every attempt should be made to include the initials or first name of a person's name on the same line with his surname.

For book editing, and when preparing a manuscript, hyphens should not be used at the end of more than two successive lines. (This rule should also be followed for letter writing.) Breaking the last word of a paragraph is also considered bad form.

Do not hyphenate a word at the end of a page.

Dividing a compound word or a word already hyphenated should be avoided.

If numbers must be divided, the break should be made after a comma: There are 35,675,-
545 chickens in Nebraska.

The general rule in the hyphenation of compound words is this: When two or more words precede a noun and together form a single idea modifying the noun, they should be hyphenated; they are usually not hyphenated if they follow the noun. In many instances only the context of the sentence will determine whether a hyphenated compound is required, or whether the words should remain separate.

He said it in a very matter-of-fact way.
He knew that to be true as a matter of fact.
As a matter of fact, he knew that to be true.
Her dress was green and white.
Her green-and-white dress was pretty.

Note: Do not confuse the adverb and the adjective when they precede a noun—these are not hyphenated.

The beautifully illustrated book was enjoyed by the membership.

Hyphens are used to separate prefixes from words where the writer's meaning would otherwise be distorted.

The upholsterer re-covered the chair.
The police recovered the typewriter.

The hyphen is also used to separate a prefix from a proper noun, or to simplify a confusing combination.

anti-American, pre-Renaissance, mid-ocean

Hyphens are also used in all numbers ranging from twenty-one to ninety-nine, and in fractions: one-half, three-quarters. Hyphens are also used in designating years: nineteen-sixties, nineteen sixty-two (*not* nineteen-sixty-two).

The hyphen is used in titles when combined with *elect* or *ex*.

President-elect
ex-President

The hyphen is generally used when words are compounded with the prefix *self*.

self-satisfied, self-confident, self-possessed, self-starter

The Dash [—]

A word of caution against confusing the hyphen (-) and the dash (—). The hyphen connects, while the dash separates. The dash is formed on the typewriter with two hyphens, no space before, between, or after.

If properly used, the dash is effective to secure emphasis but has only a few legitimate uses in business letters. It may be used in place of the comma and parentheses in handling appositive and parenthetical expressions. It is also used to mark intentional repetition.

Exercise every day—*every* day—and find out for yourself how beneficial it is to your health and well being.

The dash may be used to show an abrupt change in thought.

We do not know when we shall go—here is the bus.

Parentheses [( )]

Parentheses are used to enclose words which give additional information but have little, if any, direct connection with the main thought expressed. Commas and dashes have already been discussed in this relationship. Material enclosed in commas or separated from the rest of the sentence by dashes adds something to the main thought expressed, although not something essential; material enclosed in parentheses adds nothing to the main thought and has no direct relationship to the rest of the sentence.

If we win the contest (and I feel certain we will), we shall compete in the national contest in Chicago.

Parentheses are widely used to enclose references to statements, authors, etc.

"How to Express Thoughts Properly" is outlined in full in our text (see page 124).
We are using *Effective Business English* (Jones and Smith) for reference.

The Underscore

Underscoring a word or a group of words may be done for emphasis, but this device should be used with caution. There are a few fundamental rules, however, which should be followed.

Underline the title of a book, a booklet, essay, play, magazine, or newspaper. (Full capitals are also acceptable.)

Note: This rule is discussed more fully under the subject of Quotation Marks.

When preparing copy for the printer, underline material which is to be printed in italics.

Do not use underscoring for emphasis in the body of the letter.

Do not break the underscoring when underscoring headings.

Do not break the underscoring of parts of the text unless each part or each word is intended to be emphasized separately.

Do not include the punctuation at the end of the sentence in the underscoring.

CAPITALIZATION

Conventions governing the use of capital letters are quite clear.

Capitalize the first word of every sentence.

The first person singular pronoun *I* and the vocative *O* are generally capitalized.

Unless style requires a different form, *a.m.* and *p.m.* are set in small letters without a space between them. Capital letters are used for B.C. and A.D. but, again, there is no space between them.

9:30 a.m.   10:30 p.m.
A.D. 1760 *or* 1760 A.D.
76 B.C.

Note: Although A.D. should technically precede the number of the year, popular usage permits it to follow the date. In printed matter B.C., A.D., a.m., and p.m. usually appear in small capitals (B.C., A.D., A.M., P.M.).

The first letter of a line of conventional poetry is capitalized. Much modern poetry, however, ignores this convention.

Hickory, dickory, dock
The mouse ran up the clock.

The first word after a colon should be capitalized only when it begins a complete sentence.

The candidate made only one promise: If elected, he would fight for better conditions.

The list contained these items: five pounds of flour, two dozen eggs, and a pound of butter.

Every direct quotation should begin with a capital, except where the quoted passage is grammatically woven into the text preceding it.

The announcer shouted, "There it goes, over the back wall for a home run!"

The announcer saw the ball going "over the back wall for a home run."

Capitalize the first letters of all important words in the titles of books, newspapers, magazines, chapters, poems, articles. Short conjunctions and prepositions are generally not capitalized.

How to Win Friends and Influence People

Geographical divisions and regions require capitals.

Arctic Circle   the Atlantic Seaboard
the Orient   the Great Plains

Compass points are capitalized when they are part of a generally accepted name, but not when they denote direction, or are used with common nouns.

Middle East   eastern New York
Old South   Head west for twenty-five miles.

Capitalize names of streets, parks, buildings, but not the general categories into which they fall.

General Post Office *but* We went to the *post office*.
Metropolitan Museum of Art *but* Some *museums* are open until five.
Empire State Building *but* Which is the tallest *building* in New York City?

Religions, religious leaders, the various appellations for God and the Christian Trinity require capitalization, as do all names for the Bible and its parts.

the Father, the Son, and the Holy Ghost
Virgin Mary, the Immaculate Virgin
Yahweh, Jehovah, Saviour, Messiah

Buddhism, Shintoism, Taoism
New Testament
Exodus
Sermon on the Mount
Ten Commandments

Capitalize the names of political parties, classes, clubs, organizations, movements, and their adherents. Use small letters for the terms that refer generally to ideology (bolshevism, fascism, socialism).

Democratic Party
the Right Wing
Farm Bloc
Boy Scouts of America

Political divisions are capitalized.

Holy Roman Empire	the Colonies
French Republic	Suffolk County
the Dominion	Eighth Congressional District

Government bodies, departments, bureaus, and courts are capitalized.

the Supreme Court	the Cabinet
House of Representatives	Census Bureau
Department of Labor	British Parliament

Capitalize the titles of all high-ranking government officials, and all appellations of the President of the United States. Many publishers, it should be pointed out, prefer small letters for titles that are not accompanied by the name of the official.

President	Commander-in-Chief
Secretary of State	Chief Justice
Undersecretary	Prime Minister
Ambassador to India	Minister of War

Capitalize the names of treaties, documents, and important events.

Second World War	Declaration of Independence
Treaty of Versailles	Boston Tea Party

Family designations, when used without a possessive pronoun, take a capital letter.

I sent Mother home by taxi.
I sent my mother home by taxi.

Capitalize seasons only when they are personified. All personifications require capitals.

The frosty breath of Winter settled on the land.
The voice of Envy whispered in her ear.
The mother of Invention is Necessity.
When Headquarters commands, we jump.
He saw Mother Nature's grim visage.

Names and epithets of peoples, races, and tribes are capitalized.

Caucasian	Sioux
Negro	Cliff Dwellers

Articles and prepositions are generally capitalized in the names of Englishmen and Americans, and are not capitalized in French, Italian, Spanish, German, and Dutch names, unless otherwise specified by family usage.

Thomas De Quincey	Ludwig van Beethoven
Martin Van Buren	Leonardo da Vinci
Fiorello La Guardia	San Juan de la Cruz

Capitalize the names of holidays and festivals.

Christmas Eve	Shrove Tuesday
Yom Kippur	New Year's Day

Capitalize such parts of a book as the Glossary, Contents, Index, and Preface.
Capitalize the first and last words in the salutation in business letters, and all titles.

My dear Sir	Dear Doctor Brown
My dear Reverend Lothrop	Dear Reverend Father

Capitalize only the first word of the complimentary close of a letter.

Very truly yours	Sincerely yours

SPELLING

General Suggestions

When in doubt as to the correct spelling of a word, consult the dictionary; do not take anything for granted.

Keep a list of your spelling errors and study them.
Learn the available lists of the most commonly misspelled words—there are many such lists.
Learn to spell by syllables, carefully pronouncing each syllable. Faulty spelling is often due to faulty pronunciation.
Use newly acquired words and make them part of your oral and written vocabulary.
Do not use the simplified or modern forms of spelling in business correspondence, as *thru* for *through*.
Learn some basic spelling rules such as the following.

cede, ceed, and sede endings According to the Government Style Manual, there is only one word which ends in *sede*—*supersede*, and three that end in *ceed*—*proceed* (but *procedure*), *exceed*, *succeed*. All other words using this combination end in *cede*—*precede*, *secede*, *recede*.

ie and ei a. After *c*, when the sound is long *e* (ē), the *e* usually precedes the *i*: rece*i*ve, dece*i*ve, ce*i*ling, rece*i*pt.
b. After most other letters, the *i* precedes the *e* (*ie*): th*ie*f, gr*ie*f, bel*ie*ve, ach*ie*ve, l*ie*n.
The exceptions must be learned, since they follow no rule: n*ei*ther, l*ei*sure, w*ei*rd, s*ei*ze.
c. When the sound is *not* long *e* (ē), and especially if the sound is long *a* (ā), the *e* precedes the *i* (*ei*): sl*ei*gh, v*ei*l.

Beginnings and Endings of Words (Prefixes and Suffixes)

a. As a general rule, drop the final *e* in the base word when a suffix beginning with a vowel is added: decide—deciding; write—writing; type—typing. (When in doubt, use the dictionary.)
b. As a rule, retain the final *e* in the base word when a suffix beginning with a consonant is added: remote—remotely; care—carefully; adverse—adversely.
c. In applying the rule for adding *ed* or *ing*, the accent (or lack of it) may serve as a guide. Words of one syllable (and most words of more than one syllable) that end in a single consonant (except *f*, *h*, or *x*), preceded by a single vowel, double the final consonant *if the accent falls on the last syllable*.

plan—planned, planning; whet—whetted, whetting; bet—betting; can—canning
transfer—transferred, transferring; excel—excelled, excelling
omit—omitted, omitting; begin—beginning

d. When the word is *not* accented on the last syllable, the consonant is usually not doubled.

travel—traveled, traveling; benefit—benefited, benefiting; profit—profited, profiting; gossip—gossiped, gossiping

e. When the endings *ness* and *ly* are added to a word not ending in *y*, the base word rarely changes. In most words ending in *y*, the *y* changes to *i* when *ly* is added.

natural—naturally; similar—similarly; genuine—genuineness; blessed—blessedness; hazy—hazily; body—bodily

If the base word ends in *n* and the suffix *ness* is added, the *n* is doubled: sudden—suddenness; mean—meanness; vain—vainness.
f. In regard to the word endings *ise*, *ize*, *yze*, the most common form is *ize*, but here again the dictionary should be consulted if there is doubt.

legalize, fraternize, criticize, jeopardize
advertise, merchandise, surmise, enterprise
paralyze, analyze

◆ In British English *ise* is sometimes used for *ize*, as *realise* for *realize*. See the note under -IZE in the dictionary.
g. When the word beginnings (prefixes) *in*, *en*, *im*, *em*, *un*, *dis*, *mis*, *be*, *de*, *re*, *il*, and *over* are added to a word, the spelling of the base word is not changed.

inactive, enjoy, impending, embrace, uneasy
dismiss, mistrust, beguile, degrade, retreat, illegal, overhaul

h. When adding the suffix *ful*, the *l* is single except when *ly* is also added (*fully*): care—careful—carefully; hope—hopeful—hopefully.

Forming the Plurals of Nouns

a. Most nouns form the plural by simply adding *s*: table—tables; house—houses.
b. Some nouns, especially those ending in *s*, form the plural by adding *es*: class—classes; glass—glasses.
c. Words ending in *y* preceded by a consonant form the plural by changing the *y* to *i* and adding *es*: candy—candies; study—studies; secretary—secretaries.

d. Words ending in *y* preceded by a vowel form the plural without any change in the word: key—keys; boy—boys; money—moneys (monies when referring to "sums of money").

e. Nouns ending in *o* preceded by a vowel form the plural by adding *s*: rodeo—rodeos; radio—radios.

When the *o* is preceded by a consonant, the plural is formed by adding *es*: hero—heroes; torpedo—torpedoes.

f. Nouns referring to music which end in *o* preceded by a consonant form the plural by simply adding *s*: piano—pianos; oratorio—oratorios; contralto—contraltos; soprano—sopranos.

g. Some few nouns follow none of the above rules but form the plural in an unusual way: child—children; tooth—teeth; mouse—mice; ox—oxen.

h. Compound nouns (more than one noun) form the plural from the main word: notary public—notaries public; trade-union—trade-unions; father-in-law—fathers-in-law; court-martial—courts-martial.

i. When a solid compound ends in *ful*, the plural is formed at the end of the solid compound and not within the word: basketfuls, spoonfuls, pocketfuls.

j. Words taken from another language sometimes form the plural as they would in the original language: stratum—strata; addendum—addenda; datum—data.

k. When the words in compounds are of almost equal importance, both parts of the compound are pluralized: heads of departments; women operators.

◆ For further information, see the note under PLURAL in the body of this dictionary.

CONFUSING WORDS
[Including words that have different meanings but are pronounced the same (*homophones*) or similarly]

accept See EXCEPT.

addition, edition *addition* means the process of joining together or finding the sum of. *edition* refers to the form in which a book, magazine, or other literary work is published: first *edition*.

advice, advise *advice* is the noun: to give *advice*. *advise* is the verb: to *advise* a person.

affect See EFFECT.

all ready See ALREADY.

all right, alright *all right* is the only spelling to be used: It is *all right* to do so. The spelling *alright* is not yet considered acceptable and should not be used.

allude, elude *allude* means to make indirect or casual reference: He *alluded* to one of Shakespeare's sonnets. *elude* means to avoid or escape: The meaning *eludes* me.

already, all ready *already* means before or by this time or the time mentioned: The group has *already* gone. *all ready* (two words) means that everyone is ready to do a given thing: We are *all ready* to go.

among, between *among* is used when referring to more than two persons or things. *between* is usually preferable when referring to only two persons or things.

appraise, apprise *appraise* means to make an official valuation of. *apprise* means to notify or inform.

ascent, assent *ascent* means rising, soaring, or climbing: the *ascent* of the mountain. *assent* means to express agreement, consent, sanction: to *assent* to a course of action.

between See AMONG.

can See MAY.

capital, capitol *capital* means (*n.*) property, chief city: Albany is the *capital* of New York; and (*adj.*) of chief importance. *capitol*, always a noun, means a building in which a State legislature meets: The *capitol* is on Chamber Street.

censor, censure *censor* means (*n.*) an official examiner of manuscripts, plays, etc.; (*v.*) to act as a censor; delete; suppress. *censure* means (*v.*) to express disapproval of; condemn; (*n.*) the expression of disapproval or blame.

census See SENSES.

cite, sight, site *cite* means to quote or to summon: to *cite* an incident. *sight* means a view, a vision: a beautiful *sight*. *site* means a place or location: the *site* of the church.

compliment, complement *compliment* means praise or congratulation. *complement* means one of two parts that mutually complete each other.

consul See COUNCIL.

correspondents, correspondence *correspondents* refers to people who communicate by means of letters. *correspondence* refers to the letters written.

council, counsel, consul *council* means an assembly convened for consultation. *counsel* means guidance, advice; also, a lawyer. *consul* means an officer residing in a foreign country to protect his own country's interests.

creditable, credible *creditable* means deserving credit or esteem; praiseworthy: a *creditable* project for reducing poverty. *credible* means capable of being believed, reliable: a *credible* alibi.

decent, descent, dissent *decent* means proper; respectable. *descent* means the act of descending or going downward. *dissent* means (*v.*) to disagree; (*n.*) a disagreement.

device, devise *device* is the noun: a handy *device* for opening bottles. *devise* is the verb: He *devised* a new way to open bottles.

dissent See DECENT.

edition See ADDITION.

effect, affect *effect*, both a noun and a verb, means (*v.*) to bring about; to cause or achieve: The treatments will *effect* an early cure; and (*n.*) result, outcome. *affect*, a verb only, means to influence or act upon: Fear *affects* the mind.

effective, effectual *effective* means producing a desired result: *Effective* action averted the strike. *effectual* means having the power to produce a desired result: *effectual* legal steps.

elicit, illicit *elicit* means to bring to light: to *elicit* the truth. *illicit* means unlawful or unauthorized.

elude See ALLUDE.

eminent, imminent *eminent* means high in station; distinguished; prominent: an *eminent* statesman. *imminent* means about to happen (said especially of danger): an *imminent* calamity.

except, accept *except* means with the exclusion or omission of. *accept* means to receive or agree to; acknowledge: to *accept* an invitation.

farther, further *farther* refers to distance. *further* means to a greater degree; more; in addition.

formerly, formally *formerly* means some time ago; once: He was *formerly* a judge. *formally* means with formality or with regard to form: *formally* dressed.

further See FARTHER.

illicit See ELICIT.

imminent See EMINENT.

lay, lie See below, under CONSISTENCY OF TENSE AND PERSON OF VERBS.

learn See TEACH.

lesson, lessen *lesson* refers to instructive or corrective example. *lessen* means to make less; decrease.

loose, lose *loose* means not fastened or attached. *lose* means to part with; to be deprived of.

may, can *may* expresses permission: The child *may* play in the yard. *can* expresses ability to do: The child *can* do better than he is doing at present.

past, passed *past* means (*adj.*) ended or finished: His hopes are *past*; and (*n.*) time gone by: He dreams of the *past*. *passed*, the past tense and past participle of *pass*, means went (or gone) beyond or farther than: The car, which was going at high speed, *passed* him easily.

persecute, prosecute *persecute* means to maltreat or oppress; to harass. *prosecute* is generally used in a legal sense—to bring suit against.

personal, personnel *personal* pertains to a person: *personal* matters, *personal* opinions. *personnel* pertains to a body or group of persons: *personnel* problems, *personnel* department.

practical, practicable *practical* pertains to actual use and experience. *practicable* means feasible or usable. A *practicable* plan is a workable plan, but a *practical* plan is one based on experience rather than theory, or one that can easily be put into effect.

principal, principle *principal* means (*n.*) head or leader: The *principal* of the school will give the order; and (*adj.*) highest in rank; chief: The *principal* member of an orchestra is the concertmaster. *principle*, always a noun, means a fundamental truth or law: We cannot sacrifice the *principle* for which we stand.

prosecute See PERSECUTE.

rise, raise See below, under CONSISTENCY OF TENSE AND PERSON OF VERBS.

senses, census *senses*, the plural of *sense*, refers to the faculty of sensation, as through taste, touch, hearing, smell, or sight. *census* refers to an official count of the people of a country or district, etc.

sight See CITE.

sit, set See below, under CONSISTENCY OF TENSE AND PERSON OF VERBS.

site See CITE.

stationery, stationary *stationery* refers to writing supplies. *stationary* means remaining in one place.

sweet, suite *sweet* means agreeable to the sense of taste. *suite* refers to a set or series of things intended to be used together: *suite* of rooms, *suite* of furniture.

teach, learn The teacher *teaches*; the student *learns*.

CONSISTENCY OF TENSE AND PERSON OF VERBS

Care should be given not to change the *tense* or *form* of the verb or the *person* of a pronoun in the middle of a sentence. Such violation is generally due to carelessness.

The *tense* of a verb indicates the time when something took place; and the three main tenses are *present*, *past*, and *future*.

> I *eat* my dinner.
> I *ate* my dinner.
> I *shall eat* my dinner.

The form of the verb indicates *active voice* when the subject of the verb is acting, and the *passive voice* when the subject of the verb is acted upon.

> I *am helping*.
> I *am being helped*.

The *person* of a pronoun denotes the speaker (*first person* I, we); the person spoken to (*second person* you); and the person spoken of (*third person* he, she, it, they). The writer of the letter should never refer to himself in the third person (as "the writer" or "the undersigned") but should use the first person.

Some verbs cause confusion in both writing and speaking because of the similarity in spelling and in principal parts.

The most common verbs in this group are: **lie—lay; rise—raise;** and **sit—set.**

The principal parts of these verbs are as follows:

lie—meaning to rest or recline
lay—meaning to place or put
Present: lie—I *lie* down to rest at ten o'clock each morning.
 lay—I *lay* the wood for the fire each day.
Past: lay—I *lay* in bed too long.
 laid—I *laid* the book on the table.
Past Participle: lain—She has *lain* there for an hour.
 laid—She has *laid* the book on the table.
◆ For further information, see the note under LAY¹ in the body of this dictionary.

rise—meaning to move upward
raise—meaning to cause to rise up, to arouse or awaken
Present: rise—I *rise* at six o'clock in the morning.
 raise—I *raise* the flag each morning.
Past: rose—I *rose* at six o'clock today.
 raised—I *raised* the flag this morning.
Past Participle: risen—I shall have *risen* by six o'clock.
 raised—I shall have *raised* the prices on these articles by then.

sit—meaning to seat oneself
set—meaning to fix firmly or make fast or place
Present: sit—I like to *sit* in the sun.
 set—I plan to *set* the table for six persons.
Past: sat—I *sat* in the sun.
 set—He *set* the alarm for four o'clock.
Past Participle: sat—I have *sat* in the sun one hour.
 set—The sun has *set* in a bright glow.

shall—will ◆ See the note under SHALL in the body of this dictionary.

BUSINESS CORRESPONDENCE

Let it be stated at the outset that there are no unimportant letters. Good letters help to increase business, make friends, and influence people favorably; sloppy letters have the opposite effect.

Good letters are not written in haste. Often, they are written, revised, and rewritten until they express clearly the meaning the writer wishes to convey to his reader. As one authority puts it: "You must write not so that you can be understood but so that you cannot possibly be misunderstood."

The formalities of letter writing are definite and rigid. Brevity and clarity are the prime virtues. Carbon copies are made to give the sender an up-to-date file of his correspondence. The number of copies made will depend on the number of persons concerned with the information, but one office copy must be made of every letter or document sent out, either interoffice or through the mail.

Letter Styles The most common letter styles are the Block, Modified Block with Paragraph Indentions, Modified Block without Paragraph Indentions, and the Indented; but there are also the Inverted Paragraph style and the NOMA Simplified. (NOMA stands for National Office Management Association.)

Forms of Punctuation—Open, Closed, and Mixed

When the (Strictly) Open punctuation is used, no punctuation is used after the date line, after the inside address (unless there is an abbreviation), after the salutation, or after the complimentary close.

When Closed punctuation is used, place a period after the date line, and a comma (unless there is an abbreviation) after each line in the inside address except the last, where there is a period. Place a colon after the salutation and a comma after the complimentary close. Closed punctuation is generally used with the Indented letter style and rarely ever used with the Block style.

When Mixed punctuation is used, only two marks are involved unless abbreviations in the inside address dictate otherwise—a colon goes after the salutation and a comma after the complimentary close.

Letter Placement on the Standard-Size Letterhead

Letters are classified as short, average, and long. Short letters generally have wider side margins and are placed lower on the page than the long letters. The side (horizontal) margins should not vary by more than two or four spaces. The top and bottom (vertical) spacing should not vary by more than six lines to look well on the page.

In determining the placement of the letter on the page, the size of the typewriter type (pica or elite) must be considered. Pica type has ten spaces to the inch, whereas elite type has twelve spaces to the inch.

The following letter is in the Modified Block style. The date line is to the right and the complimentary close begins at or about the center of the letter. (The close may begin at the center of the horizontal line, five spaces to the left of center, or five spaces to the right of center, depending on the signature and title of the sender. Try to begin at the center, if possible.)

SAMPLE LETTER

(The address of the sender or merely the date line should begin eighteen or fewer spaces from the top of the page, depending on the depth of the letterhead and the length of the letter.)

> 811 Cedar Street (*Heading*)
> San Francisco, California 94125
> July 21, 1963 (*Date line*)

(leave 3 or more lines blank)

Mr. Jack Armstrong, President (*Inside Address*)
American Steel Foundation
355 Lexington Avenue
New York, New York 10017 (leave 2 spaces between State
(leave 1 line blank)   and ZIP Code)
Attention: Transportation Manager
(leave 1 line blank)
Dear Mr. Armstrong: (*Salutation*)
(leave 1 line blank)

Two spaces below the Salutation begins the body of the letter, which is single-spaced, with a double space between paragraphs. Each paragraph including the first begins flush with the left-hand margin. The spacing between the Heading and the Inside Address, and also between the top of the page and the Date Line, may be expanded if the letter is short so as to improve the appearance of the page. The Attention line is used to alert a particular member of the company, as the personnel manager, the purchasing agent, etc. Where it is customary to cite the subject of the correspondence separately from the text, it may appear on the same line with the Salutation, flush against the margin on the right; or it may be centered between the Salutation and the Body of the letter; or it may be placed flush with the left-hand margin between the Salutation and the Body of the letter, depending on the style of letter used.

(leave 1 line blank between paragraphs)

Two spaces below the body of the letter, centered, or five spaces to the right or left of center (depending on the signature and title of the sender), is placed the Complimentary Close. In formal correspondence this is *Yours truly, Very truly yours;* for a person of sufficient rank, *Respectfully yours* is appropriate.

(leave 1 line blank)

    Yours truly, (*Complimentary Close*)

(leave 1 line blank)
(full caps) J & B BOILER CORPORATION

(leave 3 lines blank)

(capitals and small letters) John J. Little (*Signature*)
(capitals and small letters) Chairman (*Title*) (no space
    between name and title)
(leave 1 line blank)
JJL: bp (*Identifying Initials*)
(leave 1 line blank)
Enclosure (*Enclosures*)
(leave 1 line blank)
cc: Mr. George Phipps (*Notation of Copies Sent*)

Elements of a Business Letter

Heading This consists of the address of the sender (often part of the letterhead) and the date of the letter. The date line ends flush with the right-hand margin except in the strictly Block and the NOMA styles.

Inside Address This identifies the recipient of the letter, and enables the sender to identify the file copy. It includes the name of the recipient, his title, if any, and the address.

Salutation For letters addressed to a company, *Gentlemen* is a suitable greeting. Where an individual is addressed, any one of the following may be appropriate: *Dear Sir, Dear Madam, Dear Mr.* (or *Mrs.* or *Miss*) (name of the person specifically addressed). When the marital status of a woman is unknown, she is addressed as *Miss* or simply by the letter *M*. The Salutation in business letters is always followed by a colon except in the Strictly Open form. The NOMA form uses no Salutation.

Complimentary Close The flowery close that was considered good form at one time, and is still used in many European countries, is a thing of the past in this country. The most-used closings are: Yours very truly, Very truly yours, Yours truly, Sincerely yours, Very sincerely yours. Except in extremely formal contexts, it is *not* considered good form to run the Body of the letter into the Complimentary Close, such as: Awaiting your decision, I remain, Very truly yours, etc. (The NOMA style letter uses no Close.)

Signature The name of the sender is usually typed in capitals and small letters, but sometimes in full capitals, four spaces below the Complimentary Close. On the line following is typed, always in capitals and small letters, the position he occupies in the firm, unless, of course, this information is included in the letterhead. When the company name is typed at the bottom of the letter, as well as the name and title of the writer, the company name is typed in full capitals two spaces below the Complimentary Close. Four spaces below this is the name of the writer in capitals and small letters; the writer's title appears on the line below the writer's name, always typed in capitals and small letters.

Identifying Initials In the lower left-hand corner of the letter, two spaces below the writer's title or name, it is customary to put the initials or name of the sender and the initials of the secretary. Full capitals or capital and small letters may be used, and the identification of the writer and secretary separated by the colon or diagonal (: /).

Enclosures Enclosures, if any, are indicated two spaces below the identification letters. If there is only one enclosure, the word "Enclosure" or merely "Enc." may be used. If more than one enclosure is being sent, the number must be indicated (Enclosures 4). Identifying the enclosure or enclosures may also be done (as Enclosure: Invoice, Number 642).

Postcript Generally, postcripts are not used in routine business correspondence. They are, however, used in sales letters for emphasis or to call attention to matters which, if placed in the body of the letter, might be overlooked. When a postcript is used, it should be prefaced by the letters P.S. (two spaces follow) and be placed two spaces below the Identification, or the Enclosure, if there is one. If the Block style is used, the letters P.S. are flush with the left-hand margin. If the Indented form of letter is used, the letters P.S. are indented five spaces from the left margin. The second and following lines are flush with the left margin, even with the lines in the body of the letter. The Postscript is not generally signed but should be initialed by the writer.

Notation of Copies Sent When a copy of a letter is sent to one or more persons, notation of this fact is usually made on the original letter and on all carbons. In this way, all parties concerned with the original letter know what other person or persons received copies. The notation is made two spaces below the Identification initials or two spaces below the last item in the letter, such as Enclosure or Postscript. The words "Copy to" or "Copies to" or the abbreviation "cc" may be used. If for some reason the writer does not wish to make known to whom copies were sent, the notation may be made only on the office file copy and is usually placed in a position other than the lower left—it may be placed in the upper left corner, which is not used for any other part of the letter. This position of the carbon notation signifies that the distribution of the carbon(s) is confidential but the notation keeps the information in the office files for future reference.

Business Envelopes The address on the envelope will coincide in all particulars with the Inside Address. Double spacing is preferred in order to expedite the mailman's task, even in the four-line address. The size of the envelope to be used (regular or legal—No. 6¾ or No. 10 being the most common with the standard 8½ by 11 inch paper) will be determined by the material to be sent. Letters of two pages or longer, or a one-page letter with an enclosure, should be sent in the larger envelope. The first line of the address should be written one or two lines below the horizontal center and five spaces to the left of the vertical center on the No. 6¾ envelope and at the center of the No. 10 envelope. If one or more of the lines in the address are particularly long or short, some adjustment should be made in placing the address properly on the envelope. The style of punctuation must agree with the inside address in the letter. The ZIP Code number is typed two spaces below the state (two spaces after the state in the inside address of the letter with no punctuation between the state and the ZIP Code number), whereas the Zone number is written between the city and state with a comma after the number (San Diego 3, California). Names of states must always be written in full as in the inside address. The words *Street, Court, Boulevard, Avenue*, etc., must always be written in full. Do not use *th, st, rd* with street numbers; write the address as follows: 125 East 45 Street.

Paragraphing in Business Letters There is no one rule for paragraphing in business letters. Most letters are of the short or medium length; therefore, plan on a short opening paragraph which states the purpose of the letter, or reason for writing, in clear, concise English. Avoid trite expressions. One or two paragraphs will probably be needed to carry the message, and a short closing should suggest action. Avoid overparagraphing; on the other hand, the busy executive has to absorb the substance of the letter as quickly as possible, and the long, involved paragraph tends to lose the reader. It is better to break up one main thought into two or three paragraphs than to make it difficult for the reader to grasp your message. Enumerations and quotations should be indented at the right of the letter as well as at the left-hand margin; enumerations may be numbered as well, and each enumeration should be treated as a paragraph. If numbers are used with the enumerations, two spaces are left after the period following the number, except in the NOMA letter, where no period follows the number.

Spacing in Business Letters The single-spaced letter is almost invariably used, with two spaces between paragraphs. In the first place, single spacing gives a better appearance; in the second place, it saves expensive stationery, tissues, and carbon, as well as filing space, since many of the single-spaced letters would go to two or more pages if they were double-spaced. If other than the Block paragraph is used, the indention may be five or ten spaces, but most writers prefer five spaces. When the Inverted Paragraph style is used, the overhang is also five spaces.

When a letter requires two or more pages, the second and subsequent pages must be identified with the first. There are various methods of doing this, but the two neatest and quickest styles are as follows:

Acme Products 　　　　-2-　　　　　　　Date
or
Acme Products—Page 2—Date

Spacing for Rough Drafts When preparing technical or otherwise difficult and important matter for printing or mailing, the copy should be double- or triple-spaced to leave room for corrections. Single-spaced copy is very difficult to correct.

Stationery Sizes The different sizes of letterheads can be identified by name. The common terms and dimensions are as follows:

Standard	8½ x 11 inches
Half-sheet	8½ x 5½ "
Monarch	7¼ x 10½ "
Baronial	5½ x 8½ "

The Standard and Half-sheet size stationery take the No. 10 and No. 6¾ envelopes respectively.

The Monarch and Baronial, which are used for personal letters and frequently by top executives in the firm, take their own special size envelopes—7½ x 3⅞ inches and 6 x 4⅝ inches, respectively.

Having various sizes of stationery is costly and time-consuming in handling, and the pages that are smaller than the standard file-folder size are troublesome in the files.

Carbon Paper and Carbon Packs To produce good clear carbon copies, care must be given to the selection of the weight and grade of the original copy, the tissue sheets, and the carbon paper. Most typewriters have a "copy set" which makes provision for space and pressure with respect to the cylinder, and the adjustment should be made to produce the best copies.

When only one copy is required for the files and the letter will be only one page in length, many offices use the back of the incoming letter for the file copy of the reply in order to save filing space as well as time.

In offices where it is standard procedure to make many carbons, ready-made carbon packs are used. The carbon paper and tissue sheets are fastened together at the bottom and save a great deal of time because the typist does not have to collate the papers. The carbons are thrown away after one using, since an inexpensive grade of carbon paper is used. The packs may be purchased in any number of sheets.

Making Corrections by Spreading and Squeezing Letters
Stenographers should learn the device for making corrections by spreading or squeezing letters instead of retyping the page containing the error. This is a difficult matter and takes a little skill. By erasing all or part of the word containing the error, and by manipulating the spacer, the word can be contracted or spread, thus concealing the insertion or deletion of a letter.

Erasing
If there is a movable carriage on the machine, move the carriage to the right or to the left to prevent the erasure particles from falling into the interior of the machine. If the carriage is stationary, move the writing unit away from the place in the copy containing the error in order to avoid having the erasure particles fall into the writing unit. Use the eraser shield, which has various slots to protect the typed words not to be erased. Be careful not to smudge the paper, particularly when correcting errors on carbon copies. A softer eraser should be used on the carbon tissues than the eraser used on the original.

FORMS OF ADDRESS

President of the United States
Address: Business: The President
The White House
Washington, D.C.
Social: The President
and Mrs. Washington
The White House
Washington, D.C.
Salutation: Formal: Sir:
Informal: My dear Mr. President:
Closing: Formal: I have the honor to remain,
Most respectfully yours,
Informal: Very respectfully yours,
In Conversation: Mr. President *or* Sir
Title of Introduction: *Only the name of the person being introduced is spoken*

Vice President of the United States
Address: Business: The Vice President
United States Senate
Washington, D.C.
Social: The Vice President
and Mrs. Hope
Home Address
Salutation: Formal: Sir
Informal: My dear Mr. Vice President:
Closing: Formal: Very truly yours,
Informal: Sincerely yours, *or* Faithfully yours,
In Conversation: Mr. Vice President *or* Sir
Title of Introduction: The Vice President

Chief Justice of the United States
Address: Business: The Chief Justice
The Supreme Court
Washington, D.C.
Social: The Chief Justice
and Mrs. Page
Home Address
Salutation: Formal: Sir
Informal: My dear Mr. Chief Justice
Closing: Formal: Very truly yours,
Informal: Sincerely yours, *or* Faithfully yours,
In Conversation: Mr. Chief Justice *or* Sir
Title of Introduction: The Chief Justice

Associate Justice of the Supreme Court
Address: Business: Mr. Justice Katsaros
The Supreme Court
Washington, D.C.
Social: Mr. Justice Katsaros
and Mrs. Katsaros
Home Address
Salutation: Formal: Sir:
Informal: My dear Mr. Justice Katsaros:
Closing: Formal: Very truly yours,

Informal: Sincerely yours,
In Conversation: Mr. Justice *or* Mr. Justice Katsaros *or* Sir
Title of Introduction: Mr. Justice Katsaros

Cabinet Officer
Address: Business: The Honorable Gary George Gussin
The Secretary of the Treasury
or The Attorney General
or The Postmaster General
Washington, D.C.
Social: The Honorable
The Secretary of the Treasury
and Mrs. Gussin
Home Address
or (for a woman cabinet member)
Mr. and Mrs. Henry Leo Woods
Salutation: Formal: Sir: *or* Dear Sir: *or* Madam:
Informal: My dear Mr. Secretary:
or My dear Mr. Attorney General:
or My Dear Mr. Postmaster General:
or Madam Secretary:
Closing: Formal: Very truly yours,
Informal: Sincerely yours,
In Conversation: Mr. Secretary *or* Madam Secretary *or*
Mr. Attorney General *or*
Mr. Postmaster General *or* Sir
Title of Introduction: The Secretary of the Treasury *or*
The Attorney General

Former President
Address: Business: The Honorable
Alfred Edward Work
Office Address
Social: The Honorable
Alfred Edward Work
and Mrs. Work
Home Address
Salutation: Formal: Sir:
Informal: My dear Mr. Work:
Closing: Formal: Very truly yours,
Informal: Sincerely yours,
In Conversation: Mr. Work *or* Sir
Title of Introduction: The Honorable Alfred Edward Work

United States Senator
Address: Business: The Honorable
John Wandzilak
United States Senate
Washington, D.C.
Social: The Honorable
John Wandzilak
and Mrs. Wandzilak
Home Address
or (for a woman senator)
Mr. and Mrs. John Row Doe
Salutation: Formal: Sir: *or* Madam:
Informal: My dear Senator Wandzilak:
Closing: Formal: Very truly yours,
Informal: Sincerely yours,
In Conversation: Senator *or* Senator Wandzilak *or* Sir
Title of Introduction: Senator Wandzilak of Alaska

Speaker of the House of Representatives
Address: Business: The Honorable
Walter Grevesmuhl
The Speaker of the House of
Representatives
Washington, D.C.
Social: The Speaker
and Mrs. Grevesmuhl
Home Address
Salutation: Formal: Sir:
Informal: My dear Mr. Speaker:
Closing: Formal: Very truly yours,
Informal: Sincerely yours,
In Conversation: Mr. Speaker *or* Sir
Title of Introduction: The Speaker of the House of
Representatives

Member of the House of Representatives
Address: Business: The Honorable
Henry Cobb Wellcome
United States House of Representatives
Washington, D.C.

Social: The Honorable
         Henry Cobb Wellcome
         and Mrs. Wellcome
         Home Address
         or (for a woman member)
         Mr. and Mrs. John Knox Jones
Salutation: Formal: Sir: or Madam:
         Informal: My dear Mr. Wellcome:
Closing: Formal: Very truly yours,
         Informal: Sincerely yours,
In Conversation: Mr. Wellcome or Mrs. Jones or Sir
         or Madam
Title of Introduction: Representative Wellcome from
         Nebraska

Ambassador of the United States
Address: Business: The Honorable
         John Wilson Smith
         The Ambassador of the United States
         American Embassy
         London, England
         Social: The Honorable
         John Wilson Smith
         and Mrs. Smith
         Home Address
         or (for a woman ambassador)
         Mr. and Mrs. Joseph Leeds Walker
         Home Address
Salutation: Formal: Sir: or Madam:
         Informal: My dear Mr. Ambassador: or My dear
         Madam Ambassador:
Closing: Formal: Very truly yours,
         Informal: Sincerely yours,
In Conversation: Mr. Ambassador or Madam Ambassa-
         dor or Sir or Madam
Title of Introduction: The American Ambassador or (if neces-
         sary) Our Ambassador to England

Minister Plenipotentiary of the United States
Address: Business: The Honorable
         James Lee Row
         The Minister of the United States
         American Legation
         Oslo, Norway
         Social: The Honorable
         James Lee Row
         and Mrs. Row
         Home Address
         or (for a woman minister)
         Mr. and Mrs. Arthur Johnson
         Home Address
Salutation: Formal: Sir: or Madam:
         Informal: My dear Mr. Minister or My dear
         Madam Minister:
Closing: Formal: Very truly yours,
         Informal: Sincerely yours,
In Conversation: Mr. Row or Mrs. Johnson
Title of Introduction: Mr. Row, the American Minister or
         (if necessary) Mrs. Johnson, the
         American Minister to Denmark

Consul of the United States
Address: Business: Mr. John Smith
         American Consul
         Rue de Quelque Chose
         Paris, France
         Social: Mr. and Mrs. John Smith
         Home Address
Salutation: Formal: Sir: or My dear Sir:
         Informal: Dear Mr. Smith:
Closing: Formal: Sincerely yours,
         Informal: Sincerely yours,
In Conversation: Mr. Smith
Title of Introduction: Mr. Smith

Ambassador of a Foreign Country
Address: Business: His Excellency
         Juan Luis Ortega
         The Ambassador of Mexico
         Washington, D.C.
         Social: His Excellency
         The Ambassador of Mexico
         and Señora Ortega
         Home Address

Salutation: Formal: Excellency:
         Informal: My dear Mr. Ambassador:
Closing: Formal: Very truly yours,
         Informal: Sincerely yours, or Faithfully yours,
In Conversation: Mr. Ambassador or Excellency or Sir
Title of Introduction: The Ambassador of Mexico

Minister of a Foreign Country
Address: Business: The Honorable
         Carluh Matti
         The Minister of Kezeah
         Washington, D.C.
         Social: The Honorable
         Carluh Matti
         and Mrs. Matti
         Home Address
Salutation: Formal: Sir:
         Informal: My dear Mr. Minister:
Closing: Formal: Very truly yours,
         Informal: Sincerely yours,
In Conversation: Mr. Minister or Sir
Title of Introduction: The Minister of Kezeah

Governor of a State
Address: Business: The Honorable
         Joseph L. Marvin
         Governor of Idaho
         Boise, Idaho
         Social: The Honorable
         Joseph L. Marvin
         and Mrs. Marvin
         Home Address
Salutation: Formal: Sir:
         Informal: Dear Governor Marvin:
Closing: Formal: Very truly yours,
         Informal: Sincerely yours,
In Conversation: Governor Marvin or Sir
Title of Introduction: The Governor or (if necessary) The
         Governor of Idaho

State Senators and Representatives are addressed like U.S.
Senators and Representatives, with appropriate addresses.

Mayor
Address: Business: His [or Her] Honor the Mayor
         City Hall
         Easton, Maryland
         Social: His Honor the Mayor
         and Mrs. Lake
         Home Address
         or (for a woman mayor)
         Mr. and Mrs. L. T. Wayne
         Home Address
Salutation: Formal: Sir: or Madam:
         Informal: Dear Mayor Lake:
Closing: Formal: Very truly yours,
         Informal: Sincerely yours,
In Conversation: Mr. Mayor or Madam Mayor
Title of Introduction: Mayor Lake

Judge
Address: Business: The Honorable
         Carson Little
         Justice, Appellate Division
         Supreme Court of the State of New York
         Albany, New York
         Social: The Honorable
         Carson Little
         and Mrs. Little
         Home Address
Salutation: Formal: Sir:
         Informal: Dear Judge Little:
Closing: Formal: Very truly yours,
         Informal: Sincerely yours,
In Conversation: Mr. Justice
Title of Introduction: The Honorable Carson Little, Judge of
         the Appellate Division of the Su-
         preme Court

Protestant Bishop
Address: Business: The Right Reverend John S. Bowman
         Bishop of Rhode Island
         Providence, Rhode Island
         Social: The Right Reverend John S. Bowman
         and Mrs. Bowman

Salutation: Formal: Right Reverend Sir:
    Informal: My dear Bishop Bowman:
Closing: Formal: Respectfully yours,
    Informal: Faithfully yours, *or* Sincerely yours,
In Conversation: Bishop Bowman
Title of Introduction: Bishop Bowman

Protestant Clergyman
Address: Business: The Reverend David Dekker
    Address of his church
    or (if he holds the degree)
    The Reverend David Dekker, D.D.
    Address of his church
Social: The Reverend David Dekker and Mrs.
    Dekker
    Home Address
Salutation: Formal: Sir: *or* My dear Sir:
    Informal: Dear Mr. [*or* Dr.] Dekker:
Closing: Formal: Sincerely yours, *or* Faithfully yours,
    Informal: Sincerely yours, *or* Faithfully yours,
In Conversation: Mr. [*or* Dr.] Dekker
Title of Introduction: Mr. [*or* Dr.] Dekker

Rabbi
Address: Business: Rabbi Paul Aaron Fine
    Address of his synagogue
    or (if he holds the degree)
    Dr. Paul Aaron Fine, D.D.
    Address of his synagogue
Social: Rabbi [*or* Dr.] and Mrs. Paul Aaron Fine
    Home Address
Salutation: Formal: Dear Sir:
    Informal: Dear Rabbi [*or* Dr.] Fine:
Closing: Formal: Sincerely yours,
    Informal: Sincerely yours,
In Conversation: Rabbi [*or* Doctor] Fine
Title of Introduction: Rabbi [*or* Doctor] Fine

The Pope
Address: His Holiness Pope Paul VI
    or His Holiness the Pope
    Vatican City
Salutation: Your Holiness:
Closing: Your Holiness' most humble servant,
In Conversation: Your Holiness

Cardinal
Address: His Eminence Alberto Cardinal Vezzetti
    Archbishop of Baltimore
    Baltimore, Maryland
Salutation: Your Eminence:
Closing: I have the honor to remain,
    Your Eminence's humble servant,
In Conversation: Your Eminence
Title of Introduction: *One is presented to:* His Eminence,
    Cardinal Vezzetti

Roman Catholic Archbishop
Address: The Most Reverend Preston Lowen
Salutation: Formal: Your Excellency: *or* Most Reverend Sir:
    Informal: Most Reverend and dear Sir:
Closing: I have the honor to remain,
    Your Excellency's humble servant,
In Conversation: Your Excellency
Title of Introduction: *One is presented to:* The Most Reverend
    The Archbishop of San Francisco

Roman Catholic Bishop
Address: The Most Reverend Matthew S. Borden
    Address of his church
Salutation: Formal: Most Reverend Sir:
    Informal: My dear Bishop Borden:
Closing: Formal: I have the honor to remain,
    Your obedient servant,
    Informal: Faithfully yours,
In Conversation: Your Excellency
Title of Introduction: Bishop Borden

Monsignor
Address: The Right Reverend Monsignor Ryan
    Address of his church
Salutation: Formal: Right Reverend and dear Monsignor
    Ryan:
    Informal: Reverend and dear Monsignor Ryan:

Closing: Respectfully yours,
    In Conversation: Monsignor Ryan
Title of Introduction: Monsignor Ryan

Priest
Address: The Reverend John Matthews [and the initials of
    his order]
    Address of his church
Salutation: Formal: Reverend Father:
    Informal: Dear Father Matthews:
Closing: Formal: I remain, Reverend Father, yours faith-
    fully,
    Informal: Faithfully yours,
In Conversation: Father *or* Father Matthews *or* Your
    Reverence
Title of Introduction: The Reverend Father Matthews

Member of Religious Order
Address: Sister Angelica [and initials of order] *or*
    Brother James [and initials]
    Address
Salutation: Formal: My dear Sister: *or* My dear Brother
    Informal: Dear Sister Angelica: *or* Dear Brother
    James
Closing: Formal: Respectfully yours,
    Informal: Faithfully yours,
In Conversation: Sister Angelica *or* Brother James
Title of Introduction: Sister Angelica [*or* Brother James],
    may I present Mrs. Jones

University Professor
Address: Business: Professor Robert Knowles
    Office Address
    or (if he holds the degree)
    Dr. Robert Knowles *or*
    Mr. Robert Knowles
    Office Address
Social: Professor [*or* Dr. *or* Mr.] and Mrs.
    Robert Knowles
    Home Address
Salutation: Formal: Dear Sir:
    Informal: Dear Professor [*or* Dr. *or* Mr.] Knowles:
Closing: Formal: Very truly yours,
    Informal: Sincerely yours,
In Conversation: Professor [*or* Doctor] Knowles (*within
    the college*); Mr. Knowles (*elsewhere*)
Title of Introduction: Professor [*or* Doctor] Knowles

Physician
Address: Business: William L. Barnes, M.D.
    Office Address
Social: Doctor and Mrs. William L. Barnes
    Home Address
Salutation: Formal: Dear Sir:
    Informal: Dear Doctor Barnes:
Closing: Formal: Very truly yours,
    Informal: Sincerely yours,
In Conversation: Doctor Barnes
Title of Introduction: Doctor Barnes

CANADA

Prime Minister
Address: Business: The Right Hon. John Smith, P.C., M.P.,
    Prime Minister of Canada
    Parliament Building
    Ottawa, Ontario
Social: The Hon. John Smith and Mrs. Smith
    Home Address
Salutation: Formal: Sir: *or* Dear Sir:
    Informal: Dear Mr. Prime Minister: *or*
    Dear Mr. Smith:
Closing: Formal: I am, Sir,
    Yours very truly,
    Informal: With kind regards,
    Yours very sincerely,
In Conversation: Sir *or* Mr. Smith *or* Mr. Prime Minister

Governor General—The Commonwealth
Address: Business: His Excellency
    John Smith (or his personal title)
    Government House
    Ottawa, Ontario

Social: Their Excellencies
      The Governor General and Mrs. John
      Smith
      Home Address
Salutation: Formal: Sir:
    Informal: My dear Mr. Smith:
Closing: Formal: I have the Honour to be, Sir,
      Your Excellency's obedient servant
    Informal: With kind regards,
      Yours very sincerely,
In Conversation: Your Excellency

Cabinet Officer
Address: Business: The Hon. John Smith, P.C., M.P.,
      Minister of Forestry
      Ottawa, Ontario
    Social: The Hon. John Smith and Mrs. Smith
      Home Address
      or (for a woman cabinet member)
      Mr. and Mrs. John Smith
Salutation: Formal: Sir: or Dear Sir: or Madam or Dear
    Madam:
    Informal: Dear Mr. Smith: or Dear Mrs. Smith
Closing: Formal: I am, Sir or Madam,
    Informal: Yours very sincerely,
In Conversation: Sir or Madam, formal; Mr. or Mrs. Smith
    or Mr. Minister; informal.

Former Prime Minister
Address: The Honourable (or Right Honourable)
    John Smith
    Home Address (or Office Address)

Judges
Judges of the following federal and provincial courts have the
title The Honourable, and are addressed as Mr. Justice:
  Supreme Court of Canada, Exchequer Court of Canada,
Courts of appeal of the provinces of British Columbia,
Manitoba, and Saskatchewan, Court of Chancery of the
province of Prince Edward Island, Courts of Queen's Bench
of the provinces of Manitoba, Quebec, and Saskatchewan,
Superior Court of the province of Quebec, Supreme courts of
the provinces of Alberta, British Columbia, New Brunswick,
Nova Scotia, Ontario, Prince Edward Island, and Newfound-
land; and the territorial courts.
Address: Business: The Hon. Mr. Justice John Smith
    Social: The Hon. Mr. Justice John Smith and
      Mrs. Smith
Salutation: Formal: Sir:
    Informal: Dear Mr. Justice Smith:
Closing: Formal: I am, Sir,
      Yours sincerely,
    Informal: Believe me,
      Dear Mr. Justice Smith,
      Yours very sincerely,
In Conversation: Sir (formal); Mr. Justice Smith (informal).

Mayor
Address: His Worship
    The Mayor of St. Lazare
Salutation: Formal: Dear Sir:
    Informal: Dear Mr. Mayor:
Closing: Formal: Yours sincerely,
    Informal: Believe me, Dear Mr. Mayor,
      Yours very sincerely,
In Conversation: Sir (formal); Mr. Mayor (informal).

Member of Parliament
Address: John Smith, Esq. M.P.
    House of Commons
    Ottawa, Ontario
Salutation: Formal: Dear Sir:
    Informal: Dear Mr. Smith
Closing: Formal: Yours sincerely,
    Informal: Believe me,
      Yours very sincerely,

MANUSCRIPT PREPARATION

A writer must bear in mind that strangers will be evaluating his manuscript. It is unreasonable to assume that editors
will take time out from a busy schedule to unscramble a poorly constructed manuscript when the author himself did not
care sufficiently to make it presentable. A carbon copy
smudged from handling and chewed around the edges is not
likely to encourage an editor to read very far into it. By exerting a little effort to learn the fundamental conventions of
style required by publishers and printers, a writer may save
himself much time and effort later.

Before a final copy is typed, the typewriter keys should be
thoroughly cleaned. A black, almost new ribbon is preferable,
because the ink is too dense on a brand new ribbon. Good
quality carbon paper will help to get the clearest possible impression. It is also common sense to submit the original copy
to the publisher, and a carbon copy if possible. One carbon
should always be retained by the author to protect against
loss in transit. Radical innovations in style should be avoided,
except where absolutely necessary to achieve a particular effect. More often than not, these innovations confuse the reader and distract him from the meaning of the text.

Paper Paper should be of a standard size, preferably
8½ x 11 inches, and of a good opacity, sixteen- or twenty-
pound weight. Onionskin is too flimsy to serve as a printer's
copy, and publishers are often put to the additional expense
of retyping a manuscript for the printer.

Margins Liberal margins on both sides of the sheet are es
sential. The copy editor needs this space to make corrections
to query the author, and to give instructions to the printer.
A six-inch line (seventy-two elite spaces, or sixty pica spaces)
centered on the page will insure sufficient margins. The lines
should be made as even as possible, without sacrificing the
rules governing word division. This will help the editor to estimate the length of the manuscript in its printed form.

Spacing Text, bibliography, and table of contents should
be double-spaced. Long footnotes also require double-spacing.
Shorter footnotes may be single-spaced with a double space
separating them. Single-spacing is also permitted for long excerpts, thereby setting them apart from the rest of the text.
The number of lines on a page should be uniform, generally
twenty-five for a standard eleven-inch sheet. Some brands of
carbon paper include a guide sheet which, when set in the plat-
en behind the paper, helps to achieve the desired uniformity.

Indentation All paragraphs start seven spaces from the
left-hand margin. This is true for quoted matter and footnotes. For long quotations, single-spaced, the opening line is
indented the same seven spaces, but then a new margin is set
four spaces from the left-hand side, and is maintained until
the excerpt is concluded.

SPECIAL SIGNS AND SYMBOLS

ASTRONOMY

ASTRONOMICAL BODIES

⊙ 1. the sun 2. Sunday
☿ 1. Mercury 2. Wednesday
♀ 1. Venus 2. Friday
⊕, ♁, ⊖ the earth
☽, ☾, ☽ 1. the moon 2. Monday
○, ☺ full moon
☽, ☽, ☾, ☽, ☽ the moon, first quarter
☾, ☾, ☾, ☾, ☾ the moon, last quarter
● new moon
♂ 1. Mars 2. Tuesday
①, ②, ③, etc. asteroids: in order of discovery, as ① Ceres, ② Pallas, etc.
♃ 1. Jupiter 2. Thursday
♄ 1. Saturn 2. Saturday
♅, ⛢, ♅ Uranus
♆ Neptune
♇, P Pluto
☄ comet
✳, ✶ star; fixed star
α, β, γ, etc. stars (of a constellation): in order of brightness, the Greek létter followed by the Latin genitive of the name of the constellation, as α Centauri

POSITION AND NOTATION

☌ in conjunction; having the same longitude or right ascension
✶ sextile; 60° apart in longitude or right ascension
□ quadrature; 90° apart in longitude or right ascension
△ trine; 120° apart in longitude or right ascension
☍ opposition; 180° apart in longitude or right ascension
☊ ascending node
☋ descending node
♈ vernal equinox
♎ autumnal equinox
α right ascension
β celestial latitude
δ declination
λ celestial or geographical longitude
Δ distance
θ sidereal time
a mean distance
v, ☊ longitude of ascending node
φ 1. angle of eccentricity 2. geographical latitude

SIGNS OF THE ZODIAC

♈	Aries, the Ram	Spring Signs
♉	Taurus, the Bull	
♊, ♊	Gemini, the Twins	
♋, ♋	Cancer, the Crab	Summer Signs
♌	Leo, the Lion	
♍	Virgo, the Virgin	
♎	Libra, the Balance	Autumn Signs
♏	Scorpio, the Scorpion	
♐, ♐	Sagittarius, the Archer	
♑, ♑	Capricorn, the Goat	Winter Signs
♒	Aquarius, the Water Bearer	
♓, ♓	Pisces, the Fishes	

BIOLOGY

○, ⊙, ① annual plant
⊙, ⊙, ♂ biennial plant
♃ perennial herb
△ evergreen plant
⊙ monocarpic plant
|w plant useful to wildlife
♂, ♂ 1. male organism or cell 2. staminate plant or flower
♀ 1. female organism or cell 2. pistillate plant or flower
☿ hermaphroditic or perfect plant or flower
♀ neuter organism or cell
○ individual organism, especially female
□ individual organism, especially male
∞ indefinite number
P parental generation
F filial generation
F_1, F_2, F_3, etc. first, second, third, etc., filial generation

BOOKS

f° folio
4mo, 4° quarto
8vo, 8° octavo
12mo, 12° duodecimo
18mo, 18° octodecimo
32mo, 32° thirty-twomo

CHEMISTRY

ELEMENTS

See table of ELEMENTS.

COMPOUNDS

Compounds are represented by the symbols for their constituent elements, each element followed by a subscript numeral if the number of atoms of it appearing in the compound is greater than one, as NaCl, H_2O, H_2SO_4, etc. If a radical appears more than once in a compound, the radical is enclosed in parentheses followed by a subscript numeral, as $Ca(OCl)_2$, $Al_2(SO_4)_3$, etc. Molecules consisting entirely of one element are represented by the symbol for the element followed by a subscript numeral indicating the number of atoms in the molecule, as H_2, O_2, O_3, etc. In addition:
· denotes water of crystallization or hydration, as $CaSO_4 \cdot 5H_2O$.
α, β, γ, etc., or 1, 2, 3, etc. (in names of compounds), indicate different positions of substituted atoms or radicals.
+ denotes dextrorotation, as + 120°.
− denotes levorotation, as − 113°.
[ ] include parentheses if one radical contains another, as $Fe_3[Fe(CN)_6]_2$.
In structural formulas:
−, =, ≡, etc., or ., :, ⁞, etc., denotes a single, double, or triple bond, etc.
R— denotes any alkyl radical.
◯ or ⬡ denotes a benzene ring.

IONS

Ions are represented by the symbols for their respective elements or by the symbols for the elements composing them, followed by a superscript symbol indicating the electric charge, as H^+, Cl^-, SO_4^{--}, etc. Thus:
⁻, ⁻⁻, ⁻⁻⁻, etc., or $^{-1}$, $^{-2}$, $^{-3}$, etc., denote a single, double, triple, etc., negative charge.
+, ++, +++, etc., or $^{+1}$, $^{+2}$, $^{+3}$, etc., denote a single, double, triple, etc., positive charge.
′, ″, ‴, etc., denote single, double, triple, etc., valence or charge (especially negative), as S''.

CHEMICAL REACTIONS

Chemical reactions are written in a form resembling equations, with reactants on the left and products on the right. If more than one equivalent of a compound appears, it is preceded by a coefficient. Conditions of temperature, pressure, catalysis, etc., are indicated above the arrow that shows direction. The following symbols are used:
→ or ← denotes "yields"; also indicates the direction of the reaction.
⇌ indicates a reversible reaction.
+ denotes "added to; together with."
↓ (written after a compound) denotes appearance as a precipitate.
↑ (written after a compound) denotes appearance as a gas.
△ denotes the presence of heat.
= or ≡ denotes equivalence of amounts in a quantitative equation.

COMMERCE AND FINANCE

@ 1. at: peaches @ $.39 per pound
   2. to: nails per pound $.50 @ $.60
$, $ dollar(s); peso(s): $100
¢ cent(s): 37¢
₱ peso(s) (Philippines)
/ shilling(s) (British): 3/
£ pound(s): £25
d penny, pence (British): 4d
¥, Y yen
₨, R rupee(s)

Rs rupees
₱ per: 50¢ ₱ dozen
number: #60 thread

MATHEMATICS

See table at MATHEMATICS.

MISCELLANEOUS

&, & and See AMPERSAND.
&c et cetera
7ber, 8ber, etc. September, October, etc.
† died
% percent
× by: used in expressing dimensions, as a sheet of paper 8½″ × 11″
© copyright; copyrighted
♠ spade
♥ heart
♦ diamond
♣ club

MUSIC

Music is generally written on one or more staves. The pitch of each staff is indicated by a clef. The forms of the various notes and their corresponding rests indicate relative duration. In addition the following are used:

♭ flat
♯ sharp
♭♭ double flat
※ double sharp
♮ natural
𝄴 common time; 4/4 meter
𝄵 alla breve; 2/2 or 4/2 meter
∿ turn
∿ inverted turn
∿ mordent
∿ inverted mordent
>, <, ∧ accent
˙ staccato
− tenuto
tr trill
⌒, ‿ slur or tie
′ phrase or breath mark
♪ grace note

〉 crescendo
〈 diminuendo; decrescendo
⊓ down-bow
V up-bow
8va all' ottava; at the octave (raises the pitch of a staff one octave when written above it, lowers it when written below)
⌢, ⌣ hold

PHYSICS

α alpha particle
β beta particle
c velocity of light
g acceleration due to gravity
h Planck's constant
λ wavelength
v frequency
j square root of minus one
∿ cycles (of alternating current or voltage)

RELIGION

☩, + 1. a sign of the cross used by bishops before their names 2. in some service books, an indication that the sign of the cross is to be made
* in some service books, a mark used to divide psalm verses into two parts
℞ response
℣, V′, V versicle
☧, ☧, ℞ a monogram for Christ [Gk. Χρ(ιστός)]

WEIGHTS AND MEASURES

See table inside back cover.

Experimental Behavioral Ecology and Sociobiology

In Memoriam KARL VON FRISCH 1886–1982

Edited by BERT HÖLLDOBLER and MARTIN LINDAUER

 Sinauer Associates, Inc. Sunderland · 1985

Unter Verantwortung der
Akademie der Wissenschaften und der Literatur, Mainz.

Gefördert durch
das Bundesministerium für Forschung und Technologie, Bonn
und das Bayerische Staatsministerium für Unterricht und Kultus, München
sowie durch die Stiftung Volkswagenwerk.

International Simposium of the Akademie der Wissenschaften und der Literatur, Mainz
October 17th–19th, 1983 at Mainz

Library of Congress Cataloging in Publication Data
Main entry under title:

Experimental behavioral ecology and sociobiology.

    Includes bibliographies and index.
    1. Animal behavior – Addresses, essays, lectures.
2. Animal ecology – Addresses, essays, lectures.
3. Sociobiology – Addresses, essays, lectures.
4. Zoology, Experimental – Addresses, essays, lectures.
I. Hölldobler, Bert, 1936–0000. II. Lindauer, Martin.
QL751.E96 1985   591.51   84–29807
ISBN 0-87893-460-X
ISBN 0-87893-461-8 (pbk.)

distributed in North America by Sinauer Associates Inc.,
Sunderland, Massachusetts 01375 U.S.A.

© Gustav Fischer Verlag · Stuttgart · New York · 1985
All rights reserved
Composed and printed by: Laupp & Göbel, Tübingen 3
Bound by: Großbuchbinderei Heinrich Koch, Tübingen
Printed in Germany
ISBN 0-87893-461-8   paper
ISBN 0-87893-460-X   cloth

In Memoriam Karl Ritter von Frisch

KARL RITTER VON FRISCH (Nobel Laureate 1973). A great biologist of the twentieth century. The pioneer and doyen of sensory physiology, experimental behavioral ecology, and sociobiology. He taught us respect and wonder for all living things. His friendship extended around the world.

Excerpt from the notebook of KARL v. FRISCH from the year 1949
Experiment No 178 of August 31, 1949

Die Bienen verkehren an einem Futterplatz im Westen.
Die Sternfolie als Modell des Bienenauges zeigt – zum Nordhimmel gerichtet – ein charakteristisches Muster. Beim Tanz auf horizontaler Wabe haben die Bienen Ausblick zu diesem Muster. Von 11.36 Uhr bis 11.44 Uhr wird über dem Tanzboden eine Polarisationsfolie so aufgelegt, daß dieses Muster 30° westlich von Nord verlagert erscheint. Die Tänze zeigen jetzt nicht mehr direkt zum Futterplatz nach Westen, sondern 32,5° nördlich von West (Fehler 2,5°).

Preface

The closely interlocked fields of behavioral ecology and sociobiology have experienced a tremendous revitalization during the past 10 to 15 years. They have been energized by the merging of ethology, population genetics, and modern evolutionary theory, in a manner that has proven effective in generating new hypotheses about the adaptiveness and evolution of behavior. We have now reached the phase where these theoretical concepts have to be put to the test by rigorous experimentation. It is here where we owe so much to KARL V. FRISCH. His way of asking questions and obtaining answers from the animals by ingenious experimentation, has been and will continue to be a major inspiration for experimental behavioral ecologists and sociobiologists.

This volume presents the papers which were read at a memorial symposium held in honor of KARL V. FRISCH and sponsored by the Mainzer Akademie der Wissenschaften und Literatur and the Stiftung Volkswagenwerk. We are most grateful to these institutions and to all contributors to this volume.

BERT HÖLLDOBLER   MARTIN LINDAUER

Contents

List of Authors

Dr. H. St. Bartz: Museum of Comparative Zoology, Harvard University, Cambridge, Massachusetts 02138, USA.

Prof. Dr. J. Bradbury: University of California, San Diego, Department of Biology, La Jolla, California 92039, USA.

Prof. Dr. J. Beetsma: Labor. of Entomology, Agricultural University, Wageningen, Netherlands.

Dr. J. R. Cheverton: Department of Zoology, Edward Grey Institute of Field Ornithology, South Park Road, Oxford OX1 3PS, United Kingdom.

Dr. F. C. Dyer: Department of Biology, Princeton University, Princeton, N.J. 08544, USA.

Prof. Dr. St. Emlen: Cornell University, Section of Neurobiology and Behavior, Division of Biological Sciences, Ithaca, N.Y. 14850, USA.

Dr. N. Franks: School of Biological Sciences, University of Bath, Bath BA2 7AY, United Kingdom.

Prof. Dr. J. L. Gould: Department of Biology, Princeton University, Princeton, N.J. 08544, USA.

Prof. Dr. D. Griffin: Rockefeller University, New York, N.Y. 10021, USA.

Prof. Dr. B. Heinrich: The University of Vermont, Department of Zoology, Marsh Life Science Bldg. Burlington, Vermont 05405, USA.

Prof. Dr. B. Hölldobler: Museum of Comparative Zoology, Harvard University, Cambridge, Massachusetts 02138, USA.

Prof. Dr. Warren Holmes: Department of Psychology, University of Michigan, Ann Arbor, Michigan 48109, USA.

Prof. Dr. D. v. Holst: Universität Bayreuth, Zoologisches Institut, Universitätsstr. 30, 8580 Bayreuth, FRG.

Dr. A. Kacelnik: Department of Zoology, Edward Grey Institute of Field Ornithology, South Park Road, Oxford OX1 3PS, United Kingdom.

Prof. Dr. J. Krebs: Department of Zoology, Edward Grey Institute of Field Ornithology, South Park Road, Oxford OX1 3PS, United Kingdom.

Prof. Dr. M. Lindauer: Zoologisches Institut II der Universität, Röntgenring 10, 8700 Würzburg, FRG.

Prof. Dr. K. Linsenmair: Zoologisches Institut III der Universität, Röntgenring 10, 8700 Würzburg, FRG.

Prof. Dr. H. Markl: Fachbereich Biologie der Universität, Postfach 733, 7750 Konstanz, FRG.

Prof. Dr. P. Marler: Rockefeller University, Center for Field Research, Tyrrel Road, Millbrook, N.Y. 12545, USA.

Prof. Dr. R. Menzel: Zoologisches Institut II der Freien Universität Berlin, Grunewaldstr. 34, 1000 Berlin 41, FRG.

Prof. Dr. C. Michener: Department of Entomology, University of Kansas, Lawrence, Kansas 66045, USA.

Prof. Dr. P.-F. Röseler: Zoologisches Institut II der Universität, Röntgenring 10, 8700 Würzburg, FRG.

Dr. S. Rossel: Zoologisches Institut der Universität, Winterthurer Str. 190, CH-8006 Zürich, Switzerland.

Prof. Dr. F. Ruttner: Institut für Bienenkunde, Universität Frankfurt, Im Rotkopf 5, 6370 Oberursel 1, FRG.

Prof. Dr. H. Scheich: Zoologisches Institut der Techn. Hochschule, Schnittspahnstr. 3, 6100 Darmstadt, FRG.

Prof. Dr. T. Seeley: Yale University, Department of Biology, Osborn Memorial Laboratory, P.O. Box 6666, New Haven, Conn. 06511, USA.

Prof. Dr. P. Sherman: Cornell University, Division of Biological Sciences, Section of Neurobiology and Behavior, Ithaca, N.Y. 14850, USA.

Dr. Barbara L. Thorne: Museum of Comparative Zoology, Harvard University, Cambridge, Mass. 02138, USA.

Dr. W. F. Towne: Department of Biology, Princeton University, Princeton, N.J. 08544, USA.

Prof. Dr. Sandra L. Vehrencamp: University of California, San Diego, Department of Biology, La Jolla, California 92039, USA.

Prof. Dr. H. Velthuis: Laboratorium voor vergleichende Fysiologie der Rijksuniversiteit Utrecht, Jan Van Galenstr. 40, 3572 La Utrecht, Netherlands.

Prof. Dr. Chr. Vogel: Lehrstuhl f. Anthropologie der Universität Göttingen, Bürgerstr. 50, 3400 Göttingen, FRG.

Prof. Dr. R. Wehner: Zoologisches Institut der Universität, Winterthurer Str. 190 Ch-8006 Zürich, Switzerland.

Prof. Dr. E. O. Wilson: Harvard University, Museum of Comparative Zoology, Cambridge, Mass. 02138, USA.

Fortschritte der Zoologie, Bd. 31 · Hölldobler/Lindauer (Hrsg.): Experimental Behavioral Ecology
G. Fischer Verlag · Stuttgart · New York · 1985

Karl von Frisch
and the beginning of experimental behavioral ecology

BERT HÖLLDOBLER

Department of Organismic and Evolutionary Biology, Harvard University, Cambridge, MA
02 138, USA

Experimental behavioral ecology can be said to have begun around 1911, when the young KARL VON FRISCH wondered why flowers are colorful. Like other biologists previously, he supposed that color attracts bees and other pollinators. However, this assumption was starkly at variance with the results obtained by the famous professor for ophthalmology CARL VON HESS, who by rigorously controlled laboratory experiments appeared to have demonstrated that honeybees as well as other invertebrates and fish, cannot perceive color. VON HESS placed honeybee workers into experimental chambers, where environmental factors could be controlled, and presented them with two light spots simultaneously, each of a different color and varying light intensity. In this situation the bees were invariably attracted to the brightest spot, whatever the color was, which seemed to prove that bees are color blind and react only to different light intensities.

KARL VON FRISCH reasoned that bees motivated to find a way out of a dark chamber obviously do not care for color, but aim for the brightes light spot which might indicate the exit hole. The question of whether or not bees perceive color has to be put to them when they are motivated to react to different colors, and this would be during foraging, when they visit flowers to collect nectar and pollen.

For the first time K. v. FRISCH introduced the powerful method of training animals by «associative learning» in the study of sensory physiology. In a series of ingeniously simple experiments, he let the bees remain free in their natural environment, and they gave him the correct answer: yes, they can perceive colors and readily associate color with rewards during foraging. These discoveries not only became an important milestone in the field of comparative sensory physiology, they also revealed for the first time the behavioral mechanisms by which the individual foraging bees maintain their remarkable fidelity to particular flower species, a crucial necessity for achieving effective pollination of the plants. Foraging bees associate a reward (nectar or pollen) with a whole array of stimuli (color, shape, scent and others) presented by the flower, and are thereby conditioned to visit flowers of the same kind repeatedly.

This is experimental behavioral ecology at its best! Behavioral ecology and sociobiology comprise the study of the evolutionary adaptiveness of behavior in general, including the most complicated social interactions. Any difference in structure, physiological process, behavioral pattern, or complex of traits that increase the inclusive fitness of one organism as compared to another organism of the same species is an evolutionary adaptation. But since the effect of specific traits on the inclusive fitness (or reproductive success) of organisms is very difficult if not impossible to measure directly, evolutionary adaptations are usually inferred from the organisms' good fit to their environment. It is one of the major tasks of experimental behavioral ecology to investigate and critically evaluate this particular correlation.

Niko Tinbergen, the great experimental behavioral ecologist, spoke of the «survival value» while Karl von Frisch referred to the «biological significance» or «function» of traits that are subject to experimental analysis. In 1971, on the occasion of the reprinting of his original papers, Tinbergen said that it is «my growing conviction that such ‹survival value› studies, if they are to outgrow the status of speculation about correlations, require experimentation». He continued, «Karl von Frisch's work had shown me the power of simple experiments in as natural conditions as possible». We know how imaginatively and effectively Niko Tinbergen has employed experiments to understand behavioral adaptations.

An excellent naturalist from childhood, Karl von Frisch believed that phenomena such as the colors and scents of flowers, or the Weberian ossicles of catfish must have an adaptive significance and he endeavoured to find it, not by telling adaptive stories, as some characterize the work of behavioral ecologists, but by ingenious experimentation. He consistently challenged the anthropocentric bias that animals have only a very limited sensory capacity. We learned from him that each species has its own unique sensory world, often vastly different from ours. Bees cannot see red, which we can, but perceive UV as color, which we do not.

I think James Gould recently expressed this contribution of Karl von Frisch extremely well when he said: «His pioneering work inspired the discovery of several otherwise unimaginable sensory systems in animals: infrared detectors in night-hunting snakes, ultrasonic sonar in dolphins and bats, infrasonic hearing in birds, and magnetic field sensitivity in a variety of animals. Doubtless, other systems are still to be discovered. The lesson is a melancholy one: We are blind to our own blindness, and must not try to read our own disabilities into the rest of animal kingdom«.

Karl von Frisch's discoveries laid the roots for many now flourishing scientific disciplines in zoology. Modern comparative sensory physiology has been built on his pioneering work. The discovery of an internal clock and sun compass in bees (at the same time independently discovered by Gustav Kramer in birds), with their supplementary employment of the polarized sky light for navigation, has led to alsmost uncountable studies of animal orientation in time and space. His work and that of his students on perceptual preferences in honeybee learning has foreshadowed the current intensive investigations of species differences in perceptual predispositions and their ecological significance. His discovery of a «Schreckstoff» in fish was the first demonstration of an alarm pheromone. Furthermore, von Frisch elaborated extensively on the role of environmental odors and chemical signals in the honeybees' orientation and communication during foraging long before «chemical ecology» became an established field. Although these latter experiments indicated that environmental odors and pheromones play a role in attracting honeybee newcomers to a rich food source, a series of controlled experiments suggested that the frequently observed massive recruitment response must be due to other, much more effective communication mechanisms. This finally led Karl von Frisch to the ingenious decoding of the dance language of the honeybees. In the view of most biologists this remains the single most fascinating discovery in the study of animal communiation.

How could such a sophisticated communication behavior have evolved in the first place? In a long sequence of comparative investigations, von Frisch and Martin Lindauer and their associates searched for more elementary forms of communication in other bee races and species, including the stingless bees, and they concluded from their findings that the waggle dance communication behavior in honeybees is in fact a miniature and highly ritualized replica of the flight to the target area. Simple motor displays, mechanical signals, and chemical cues of some stingless bees presumably represent the more primitive mechanisms from which the waggle dance originated.

KARL VON FRISCH had a broad interest in animals. He began his scientific career investigating the ability of fish to adapt to the color of their background, and he demonstrated color vision in fish. And in later years he always returned to the fish, especially during the winter months, when the bees were not active. He demonstrated that fish can hear, provided the first experimental support for the rod-cone theory of color vision, discovered chemical communication in fish, and more. Many of his students extended this work and laid the foundations for experimental behavioral research conducted today.

But KARL VON FRISCH's true scientific love must have been the honeybees, which he once compared to a magic well: «The more you draw from it, the more there is to draw». And this is still true today. Four academic generations of researches, all represented here today, have succeeded KARL VON FRISCH. The life of the honeybees continues to be a rich source of new scientific discoveries and an inspiration even for those of us who chose to study other organisms.

I would like to close with the first sentence of a laudatio HANS JOCHEM AUTRUM wrote on the occasion of KARL VON FRISCH's 90th birthday: «‹Simplicity is always a sign not only of truth, but of genius›. Anyone who has ever read one of KARL VON FRISCH's works, or heard him lecture or talked with him, can verify these words of SCHOPENHAUER».

Fortschritte der Zoologie, Bd. 31 · Hölldobler/Lindauer (Hrsg.): Experimental Behavioral Ecology
G. Fischer Verlag · Stuttgart · New York · 1985

Personal recollections of Karl von Frisch

Martin Lindauer

Zoologisches Institut der Universität Würzburg, F. R. Germany

Many of us had the chance to meet Karl von Frisch in his long life, which was enriched not only by an extraordinary scientific career but also by profound personal friendship. At the beginning of this symposium let me ask the question: «What was the real basis and background for his pioneer work in sensory physiology, behavioral ecology and sociobiology?»

In my personal recollections (from 1944 – 1982) I find 3 principles which may answer this question.

1. K. v. Frisch was inspired by a great *love of nature* and of the living organism. It was not a purely emotional love; its real origin was a *profound knowledge* of biology, morphology and physiology of the animal kingdom, something which nowadays has become a rare value. As a teacher K. v. Frisch had delivered in Munich and in Graz two lecture series in a masterly survey: «Allgemeine Zoologie» and «Vergleichende Anatomie der Wirbeltiere». None of his students will forget his fascinating demonstrations on the function of the fish swimbladder, of the cow-stomach etc. Teaching demands careful preparation, but the sympathy for the animals you have to deal with grows with the knowledge acquired.

K. v. Frisch's comprehensive knowledge of taxonomy, biology and ecology is demonstrated in an unique way by his *Museum in Brunnwinkl*, a private collection of the local fauna. It was started in 1910, and it has become a historical document, particularly in view of the fact that many species of butterflies, beetles, solitary bees, amphibia etc. have become extinct.

In his love of nature K. v. Frisch also enthusiastically supported the idea of «Naturschutz», the preservation of natural environment:

If a visitor comes to Brunnwinkl these days and can still drink in front of the Mühlhaus the clear cool water from the private spring, if he still can walk the romantic «Führberger Weg» along the Wolfgangsee, then this is only possible because K. v. Frisch was the advocate who fought against the project of a highway on the east side of the Wolfgangsee.

His *love of bees* is evident to all who have read his books or who assisted him in his so-called simple experiments in free nature (Fig. 1).

I will never forget that day in October, when the weather turned cold and the last forager bee on the feeding table 300 m away from the hive became stiff, so that she could not fly off:

K. v. Frisch warmed her up in the hollow of his hand and took her back into the hive.

Fig. 1: KARL V. FRISCH marking bees on the feeding table. In this quiet countryside of Brunnwinkl – preserved as natural environment – the most exciting discoveries were made.

2. Next to his love for animals was his overwhelming *enthusiasm for research*, an enthusiasm that has created many new ideas. K. V. FRISCH undertook his research not in

the hope of acquiring awards, but in order to elucidate and analyse the many mysteries of animal life. This enthusiasm was inspired by a powerful impetus to find the *truth*.

And as far as this was concerned he was inconsiderate towards himself, his co-workers and his students. «Die Wissenschaft ist eine strenge Göttin, die nichts neben sich duldet» he said.

In his attempts to find the truth in all details K. v. FRISCH always had a weakness for *little things*, for unexpected results, for so called *«singularities»*, which nowadays receive increasing attention in biophysics, in biochemistry and in biology.

«Nature never lies» he said and he always impressed on his students: «auch kleine Dinge muß man in der Biologie ernst nehmen» (in biology you also have to consider little things seriously).

Our publications «Himmel und Erde in Konkurrenz bei der Orientierung der Bienen» or «Richtungsweisung der Bienen bei Seitenwind» etc. originated from so called «unimportant observations». And the «Missweisung» in the beedance – small deviations in direction indication – was the starting point for his pioneer work concerning orientation by polarized light; last but not least the «Restmissweisung» gave me and my co-worker H. MARTIN the first inkling that the earth's magnetic field may be involved in the orientation of bees.

A personal comment may be added here:

The enthusiasm of K. v. FRISCH for research was not limited to his own work and his own discoveries. I remember when he reported to us in Graz immediately after World War II on GRIFFIN's work on echolocation in bats, or Pardi's sun compass orientation in *Talitrus* and later in Munich, when he reported MICHENER's manifold work on solitary bees, or WILSON's and HÖLLDOBLER's fine works on ants: he was as happy as if he had done all this research himself.

It was the same with BALTZER's, HADORN's, SCHARRER's, MÖHRES's work; and it was one of the high points in my life when I had given him the very first report on the debate of the scouts when they announce a new nesting site in the swarm cluster. With a smile on his face he said: «Congratulations! You have witnessed an ideal parliamentary debate; your bees can evidently change their decision when other scouts have to announce a better nesting site.»

3. A third principle that made the research work of K. v. FRISCH so successful was his unshakeable *optimism*.

When you start an experiment with bees you first have to look at the sky to see whether the sun will be shining that day. Even during the ill-famed «Salzburger Schnürlregen» K. v. FRISCH always saw a small bright spot somewhere between the dense clouds; «let's try again» he said, and we had to climb up the Schafberg. This went on day after day; even if it was raining and misty at the time; however (after 2 weeks) we were able to finish our experiments on the top of the mountain in bright sunshine. This incident is expressive of his typical optimism, which continued to prevail even when his hard work was not rewarded by clear or expected results. For example in a series of protracted experiments we wanted to find out immediately whether bees have included special information for a goal *up* and *down* in their dance. What was the result? «There is no vocabulary in the bee dance for up and down – which means – in an objective biological sense – it is of no use – the language of the bees is free of gossip.»

Let us cherish his love of nature
his enthusiasm for research
his optimism in all situations
as the legacy of a great biologist.

I. Orientation, Learning, Foraging

Fortschritte der Zoologie, Bd. 31 · Hölldobler/Lindauer (Hrsg.): Experimental Behavioral Ecology
G. Fischer Verlag · Stuttgart · New York · 1985

The bee's celestial compass – A case study in behavioural neurobiology

Rüdiger Wehner and Samuel Rossel

Department of Zoology, University of Zürich, Switzerland

Abstract

The scattering of sunlight within the earth's atmosphere produces an extensive pattern of polarization (Figs. 1 and 2) as well as coarse spectral gradients.

In 1949 Karl von Frisch showed that bees can use the celestial pattern of polarization as a compass, but how they manage to accomplish this task has remained elusive. In theory, there are a number of geometrical and non-geometrical ways of computing the exact position of the sun from single patches of polarized light in the sky. As shown in this paper, bees do not seem to resort to any of these methods. Instead, they use a very simple strategy in assuming that any particular e-vector orientation occurs at a fixed azimuthal position with respect to the solar and anti-solar meridian. In the real sky, these e-vector positions vary with the elevation of both the sun and the point observed, but in the bee's internal model of the sky they do not (Figs. 6, 7 a and 10). Thus, orientation errors must occur whenever e-vector positions in the sky do not coincide with the e-vector positions predicted by the bee's e-vector compass. It is on the basis of these orientation errors exhibited by the bees when viewing a single e-vector in the natural sky or a spot of artificially polarized light that the bee's e-vector compass has been derived (see e. g. Figs. 4 and 5).

Even when large parts of the natural blue sky are available, bees make mistakes exactly as large as predicted from their simple e-vector compass (Fig. 12). The prediction implies that the orientation error induced by any pattern of e-vectors is the mean of the orientation errors induced by individual «pixels» of sky within each of which the e-vector is approximately constant. Each e-vector is equally important, irrespective of its degree of polarization. Orientation errors do not occur when the patch of sky is positioned symmetrically with respect to the anti-solar meridian. Then the errors induced by the left and right halves of the pattern are equal in magnitude, but opposite in sign, and thus cancel each other out.

The bee's e-vector compass can be derived not only experimentally (from the bees) but also theoretically (from the sky) by referring exclusively to the most prominent feature of skylight polarization, the arc of maximum polarization. As it turns out, the bee's e-vector compass mimics the mean distribution of the maximally polarized e-vectors as they occur in the upper part of the sky (Figs. 7 c and 10 b).

Where does the e-vector compass reside within the bee's visual system? A crucial step in answering this question is our discovery that the ultraviolet receptors of a set of specialized ommatidia located at the dorsal margin of the bee's eye are necessary for the detection of polarized skylight. Over the entire region of this «POL area» the microvillar axes of the ultraviolet receptors vary in a fan-shaped array that resembles the distribution of the maximally polarized e-vectors in the sky. Thus, the geometry of the bee's e-vector compass as derived by behavioural experiments seems to reside in the utmost periphery of the bee's visual system – in the spatial arrangement of the retinal analysers (ultraviolet receptors). In addition to the fan-shaped array of the retinal analysers, the POL area exhibits a number of anatomical and physiological specialisations which can be expected to have functional consequences for the detection of polarized skylight.

How is the POL area used in deriving compass information from the celestial e-vector pattern? On the basis of both the neurophysiological and behavioural evidence mentioned above we propose the following model (Fig. 16): In the bee's eye the array of retinal analysers mimics the array of maximally polarized e-vectors in the sky. Equipped with such an array of analysers the bee can use a very simple strategy in determining the position of the solar or anti-solar meridian from any particular e-vector in the sky. If the bee scans the sky, i. e. rotates about its vertical body axis and thus sweeps its array of analysers across the celestial e-vector pattern, peak responses will occur whenever the bee faces the solar or anti-solar meridian. (There is a simple rule by which the bee can distinguish between these two possibilities.) To be exact, the former statement only holds when the e-vector observed is in its state of maximum polarization, because the design of the receptor array is based on the array of maximally polarized e-vectors in the sky. For other e-vectors peak responses will occur when the bee is not aligned exactly with the solar (or anti-solar) meridian. What then results are the orientation errors we have observed.

An important consequence of our model is that bees can derive compass information only from e-vector patterns that are designed according to the rules of Rayleigh scattering, because the retinal array of analysers is designed according to the celestial array of e-vectors. Furthermore, bees do not perceive polarized skylight as an extra quality of light. While scanning the sky, they translate e-vector orientations into modulations of perceived ultraviolet intensity. When peak responses occur, the bees are aligned with the solar or anti-solar meridian.

Bees use spectral information in addition to e-vector information when determining the position of the solar (or anti-solar) meridian. They interpret small unpolarized green and ultraviolet stimuli as lying along the solar meridian and within the anti-solar half of the sky, respectively (Figs. 13 and 14). The non-POL parts of the bee's dorsal retina are sufficient for the orientation by means of spectral cues: Bees in which the POL areas of both eyes have been painted out are able to derive compass information from unpolarized green and ultraviolet stimuli exactly as the untreated control bees do. When they view a polarized spot of ultraviolet light, they interpret it as if it were an unpolarized spot (Fig. 15). Furthermore, when large parts of the sky are available, they orient nearly as precisely (by referring to spectral cues) as the untreated controls do which can use the celestial e-vector pattern in addition. Possibly the polarization-sensitive ultraviolet channels interact with polarization-insensitive channels somewhere along the visual pathway.

The hasty reader is invited to take the figures and their legends as a short story of our hypotheses, results and conclusions.

1 Introduction: History and perspectives

No event did more to establish the fame and prestige of KARL VON FRISCH's work in the field of sensory physiology than his discovery that bees can perceive the polarized light in the sky and use it as a celestial compass. Actually, two decades earlier the myrmecologist FELIX SANTSCHI had already observed that ants could find their way even when they could see nothing but a small patch of blue sky. In an interesting but unfortunately neglected work almost forgotten in the Mémoires de la Société Vaudoise des Sciences Naturelles, SANTSCHI (1923) literally asked the question «What is it in this small patch of sky that guides the ants back home?» SANTSCHI, practising as a physician in North Africa, could not tell. In one experiment he had even used a ground glass disk (which depolarized the light from the sky) and put it above a homing ant. The ant instantly stopped and searched around at random, but SANTSCHI did not draw the right inferences from this important observation. Even if he had, at the time of his writing it would have been exceedingly difficult to perform behavioural experiments involving polarized light, simply because large polarizers such as sheets of polaroid filters were not yet available[1]. After a quarter of a century had passed, in 1947, VON FRISCH did an experiment with bees almost identical to the one SANTSCHI had performed with ants. He got the same result, asked the same question, and – *horribile dictu* – could not tell either. However, VON FRISCH, then Head of the Department of Zoology at the University of Graz, was in a better position to answer such questions than SANTSCHI had ever been. At one of the next Faculty Meetings he told the story to his colleague of the Physics Department, HANS BENNDORF. The physicist advised him to check for polarized light. Next summer, in 1948, VON FRISCH did the crucial experiment: He placed a polarizer above a bee which performed its recruitment dances on a horizontal comb, and as he rotated the polarizer, the direction of the bee's dances changed correspondingly (VON FRISCH, 1949). This was the first demonstration that an animal used skylight polarization for adjusting the direction of its course.

With this stirring discovery VON FRISCH has left to us two fascinating questions: How does the insect's polarization compass work, and what does it mean to the insect? These are the questions of neurobiology and behavioural ecology, respectively. Even though both questions call for quite different lines of experimentation, they are closely intertwined. In evolutionary terms, it is the role the celestial compass plays in the insect's overall system of navigation that has shaped the insect's visual system by deciding which information the insect's nervous system must extract from the sky, and which it can discard. In this chapter, we shall concentrate on the first question, but the answer we shall provide on how bees use polarized skylight will make full sense only when discussed in the context of other visual capacities and navigational strategies as well.

Are we to conclude from SANTSCHI's und VON FRISCH's early findings that insects can infer the position of the sun correctly from any particular patch of sky? Or in other words, does a bee place, in its mind, any patch of polarized light in the correct celestial position with respect to the sun? This would imply that the bee is informed exactly about all

---

[1] Nicol prisms were used by the first investigators who studied the responses of animals towards polarized light (CROZIER and MANGELSDORF, 1924; VERKHOVSKAYA, 1940). In these experiments a number of arthropods such as daphnids, blowfly and beetle larvae as well as drosophilid flies had to make phototactic choices between a polarized and an unpolarized beam of light with both beams adjusted for equal total intensity. The first study yielded negative, the second positive results.

geometrical properties of the extensive pattern of celestial polarization as well as about how this pattern varies during the course of the day. It has been assumed by VON FRISCH and many later workers in this field[2] that these questions can be answered in the affirmative, but the evidence for this conjecture is rather slim.

We tried to take a fresh look at the whole problem by starting with a series of rather straightforward experiments. Under the full blue sky bees were trained to a given compass course leading them to an artificial food source. Immediately thereafter they had to select this compass course solely by means of a small patch of blue sky. As was already apparent from these very first experiments, bees made mistakes in all but very few stimulus conditions. If this had not been surprising enough, the situation became more astounding when we presented the bees with large patches of sky. Even then consistent navigational errors occurred. Obviously, the bees were not informed exactly about where any particular patch of polarized skylight was positioned with respect to the sun. This was perplexing at first, but led us finally to the formulation of an extremely simple hypothesis of how bees could use skylight patterns as a compass. This hypothesis as first proposed by behavioural work was later substantiated by neuroanatomical and neurophysiological studies of the bee's peripheral visual system. According to this hypothesis bees do not take advantage of all visual information present in the sky, but resort to some principal features of their celestial world. Even though the skylight patterns are indeed rather complex, the bee's strategy is simple.

When first reported (ROSSEL, WEHNER and LINDAUER, 1978), our observations and conclusions were met with considerable doubt, and our hypothesis that the bee's model of the sky was a simplified rather than correct copy of the outside world, was treated with disbelief (WATERMAN, 1981, 1984; DYER and GOULD, 1983). In the meantime, a host of additional experiments has led to a confirmation of this apparently preposterous idea. We shall present in this article our principal conclusions and most of the critical evidence. Detailed documentation has already been provided (ROSSEL and WEHNER, 1982, 1984; WEHNER and ROSSEL, 1983; WEHNER, 1982, 1983) or will be published elsewhere (ROSSEL and WEHNER, in press; WEHNER and STRASSER, in prep.).

The following is organized so as to let the reader experience step by step how we arrived at our present understanding of the bee's celestial compass. We start with a short inquiry about the skylight cues used by the bees (Section 2). Then we derive the bee's celestial compass from behavioural experiments (Section 3). After the experimental techniques have been introduced (Section 3.1.1), the basic one-spot experiment, and its astonishing result, is described in detail (Section 3.1.2): Bees make mistakes. It is from these mistakes that we develop the hypothesis of the bee's stereotyped e-vector compass (Section 3.1.3). The spatial design of the bee's e-vector compass is derived first from the bees (by analyzing their navigational errors: Section 3.1.3., first part) and then from the sky (by referring to the most prominent feature of skylight polarization: Section 3.1.3., second part). Our hypothesis is later tested, and vindicated, by presenting the bees with more than one pixel of sky, artificial beams of polarized light, or large parts of the natural blue sky (Section 3.1.4). Finally, spectral information used by the bees alongside e-vector information is incorporated into the bee's celestial compass (Section 3.2). A discussion comparing our data with those of other authors (Section 3.3) rounds off the behavioural analysis of the bee's celestial compass. Next comes the crucial question: How does the bee's celestial compass work physiologically? Section 4 deals with this question. After a brief survey of

---

[2] One of us has recently summarized many aspects of skylight navigation in insects (WEHNER, 1982, 1984). The reader is referred to the extensive lists of references provided by these summaries.

some classical views (Section 4.1), a new approach is introduced (Section 4.2). Drawing upon neurobiological data (Section 4.2.1) and behavioural evidence (Section 4.2.2), a model is proposed according to which the bee adopts a global scanning strategy to determine the position of the solar and anti-solar meridian (Section 4.2.3). We end by inquiring about some of the more general implications of our results and conclusions (Section 5).

2 Celestial patterns: What skylight cues are used by the bees?

(i) *The scattering of sunlight within the earth's atmosphere creates e-vector patterns and spectral gradients.*

As *skylight polarization* arises from the scattering of sunlight by the air molecules within the earth's atmosphere (Fig. 1), the whole pattern of polarization is fixed relative to the sun. From the way it is portrayed in Fig. 2 a its main features are immediately apparent:

First, the *e-vector orientations (angles of polarization)*[3] form concentric circles around the sun. This simply follows from the laws of Rayleigh (primary) scattering, according to which light is always polarized perpendicularly to the plane of the scattering angle, i. e. the plane containing the sun, the observer, and the point observed (Fig. 1 a).

Second, the *degree of polarization* (per cent of polarized light relative to the total amount of light emanating from a given point in the sky) increases from the sun, where it is zero, to an angular distance of 90° from the sun. From there, it decreases towards the anti-solar point, where it is zero again (Fig. 2 a). In more detail, the laws of Rayleigh scattering imply that the degree of polarization is proportional to some sine function of the scattering angle, i. e. the angle which the earthbound observer forms with the direction of the sun and the celestial point observed (Fig. 1 a). Thus, direct light from the sun is unpolarized, while light emanating from celestial points that lie at an angular distance of 90° from the sun, are polarized maximally. As a consequence, the great circle[4] positioned 90° off the sun forms what can be called the *arc of maximum polarization*. During the course of the day, when the sun is above the horizon (see Fig. 1 a), this arc of maximum polarization passes across the anti-solar part of the sky. Generally speaking, a highly polarized (anti-solar) half of the sky can be distinguished from a less polarized (solar) half of the sky.

Third, there is a global *plane of symmetry* passing across the entire celestial hemisphere. It contains the solar and anti-solar meridian. The e-vector orientations at corresponding points on both sides of the solar and anti-solar meridian are mirror images of each other.

---

[3] Light can be described as a transverse electromagnetic wave characterized by a magnetic component (h-vector) and an electric component (e-vector). These vectors are perpendicular to each other and to the direction of propagation. It is the electric component that interacts with the electrons of atoms and molecules and thus is involved in optical phenomena such as the scattering of light. In a beam of unpolarized light, there is no preferred plane within which the e-vector vibrates, but in a beam of linearly polarized light, the e-vector vibrates in a fixed plane. The orientation of this plane with respect to the vertical is called the angle of polarization (or e-vector orientation, denoted by χ). For conventions see Figs. 1 b and 2 b.

[4] Great circles are defined as the largest possible circles which can be drawn on the surface of a sphere. The radius of a great circle is identical with the radius of the sphere. This implies that in the celestial sphere the plane formed by any great circle always includes the observer in the centre of the sphere.

of each other. Along this arc of symmetry, and nowhere else in the sky, the e-vectors are oriented parallel to the horizon.

Having described the static picture, let us now set it in motion. During the course of the day, the sun moves across the sky, and the e-vector pattern moves along with it. Of course, as mentioned earlier, the pattern remains fixed within a sun-related system of coordinates,

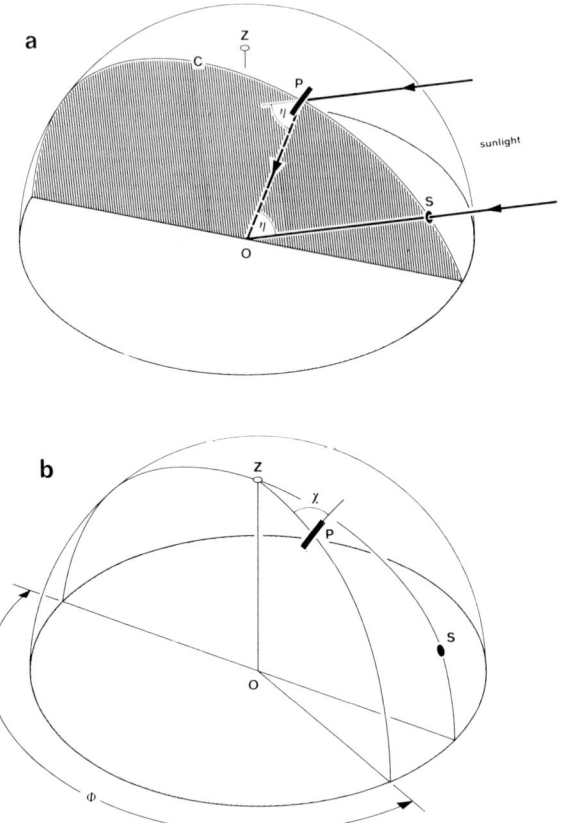

Fig. 1: Skylight optics: The scattering angle (η) and the angle of polarization (e-vector orientation, χ). *a* An observer (O) receives direct sunlight from S (the apparent position of the sun in the celestial hemisphere) and scattered light from the sky as shown here for the celestial point P. Scattered skylight is partially linearly polarized with the e-vector oriented perpendicularly to the plane of the scattering angle η. This plane *(hatched)* includes the direct rays from the sun *(heavy solid lines)* and the observer's line of sight *(heavy dashed line)*. The circle C in which the scattering plane intersects the celestial sphere is a meridian in a sun-related system of coordinates, in which the sun and the anti-solar point form the poles of the sphere (see Fig. 2 a). In the more conventional horizon-system of coordinates the zenith (Z) is the pole of the celestial hemisphere.
b The orientation of the e-vector (χ) is defined as the angle the e-vector forms with the vertical (see also Fig. 2 b). Throughout this paper the following convention is used: positive values of χ refer to angles measured clockwise from the vertical (as seen by the observer in the centre of the celestial hemisphere). Φ denotes the azimuth position of P relative to the anti-solar meridian.

but due to the sun's change in elevation, it changes within the horizon-system of coordinates. Just look at what happens to the arc of maximum polarization. As the sun moves up along the solar meridian, this arc tilts down across the anti-solar half of the sky. Concomitantly, all e-vectors change their positions with respect to the axis of symmetry of the pattern. A special situation exists at sunrise and sunset, when the sun is on the horizon. Then, the arc of maximum polarization passes through the zenith and forms a second axis of symmetry in the sky.[5]

A patch of sky is characterized not only by its state of polarization, but also by its spectral composition. Both parameters depend largely on the angular distance from the sun. Thus, the celestial straylight patterns provide *spectral gradients* alongside polarization gradients. As the radiant intensity of scattered light is inversely proportional to the fourth power of the wavelength, the relative intensity of short-wavelength (e.g. ultraviolet) radiation is higher in scattered skylight than in direct sunlight. More specifically, those parts of the sky that exhibit maximum polarization also exhibit the highest relative content of short-wavelength radiation. To sum up, all characteristics of sky radiation – intensity (radiance), colour, degree of polarization, and angle of polarization (e-vector orientation) – depend largely on the angular distance from the sun and thus can be used as cues for inferring the position of the sun from isolated patches of sky. If bees were able to detect and process all these parameters independently, they could determine the position of the sun from the skylight information available in a single patch of sky[6]. However, before we inquire about how this could be done in theory, and what the bee does in practice, let us have a look at the real sky.

(ii) *The real world is not so neat and tidy.*

All information presented above about skylight patterns applies to the simple case of the primary scattering of light within an ideal atmosphere. In such an atmosphere, the incoming unpolarized sunlight is scattered by molecules that are smaller than the wavelength of light, isotropic, and of low concentration, so that sunlight is scattered only once before it reaches the eye of the observer. In reality, however, these conditions are rarely met. Instead, the ideal Rayleigh pattern gets distorted by various kinds of pollution, haze or clouds as well as by reflections from the ground. Factors such as higher-order scattering, reflection, absorption and molecular anisotropy markedly affect the polarization and spectral gradients of the sky. What results is a celestial pattern in which the sun and the pattern of e-vector orientations provide the most reliable cues, whereas the degree of polarization, the radiant intensity and the spectral gradients often become subject to dramatic disturbances and variations. This is clearly borne out by the skylight measurements performed by BRINES and GOULD (1982) under a variety of atmospheric conditions.

---

[5] In a horizon system of coordinates, the pattern of polarization rotates about the zenith, due to the westward movement of the sun. Note, however, that the whole pattern does not merely rotate. Due to the sun's change in elevation mentioned above the pattern changes its intrinsic properties as it rotates about the zenith.

[6] This holds for all but one class of exceptions: At each elevation above the horizon there are, in general, two optically equivalent points in the sky, which coincide in all aspects of skylight radiation and thus are indistinguishable to any detector system. These are the points characterized by vertical e-vectors (see Figs. 2c and 2d).

(iii) *Bees cope amazingly well with the unreliabilities of their celestial world.*

If bees cannot see the sun, the most important skylight parameter on which they rely is the e-vector orientation. The degree of polarization is not used as a compass cue (VON FRISCH, 1965: 397; ZOLOTOV and FRANTSEVICH, 1973). It is important merely in the sense

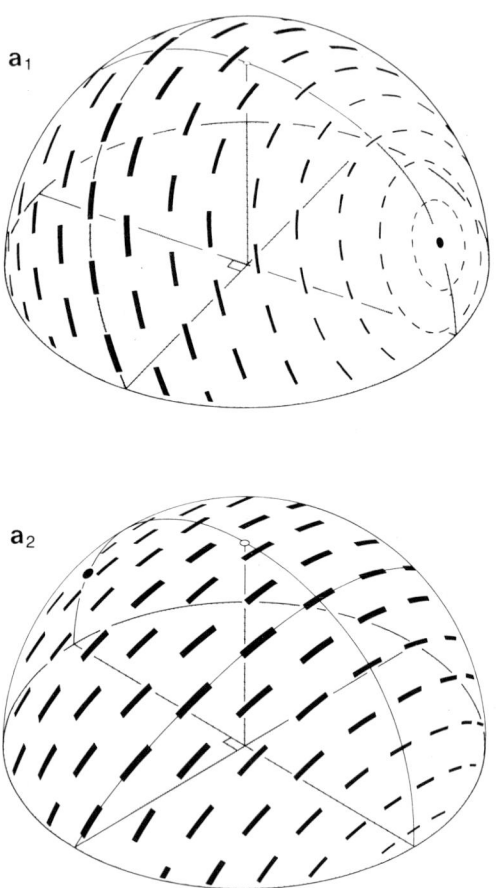

Fig. 2: The pattern of polarized light in the sky (e-vector pattern).
a Three dimensional representation of the celestial e-vector pattern. The two hemispheres are rotated relative to each other so that the reader faces either the solar (a_1) or the anti-solar meridian (a_2). The sun is shown as a black disk positioned at an elevation of 24° above the horizon. The electric vectors, or e-vectors, of light (*black bars*) form concentric circles around the sun. The e-vector pattern is further characterized by a global gradient of the degree (percentage) of polarization as indicated by the varying widths of the black bars. The direct light from the sun is unpolarized. Maximum polarization occurs at an angular distance of 90° from the sun. The arc of maximum polarization is depicted by the semicircle combining the widest bars. The other semicircle shown in either figure represents the symmetry plane of the e-vector pattern. It comprises the solar meridian and the anti-solar meridian. The zenith is marked by an *open circle*.

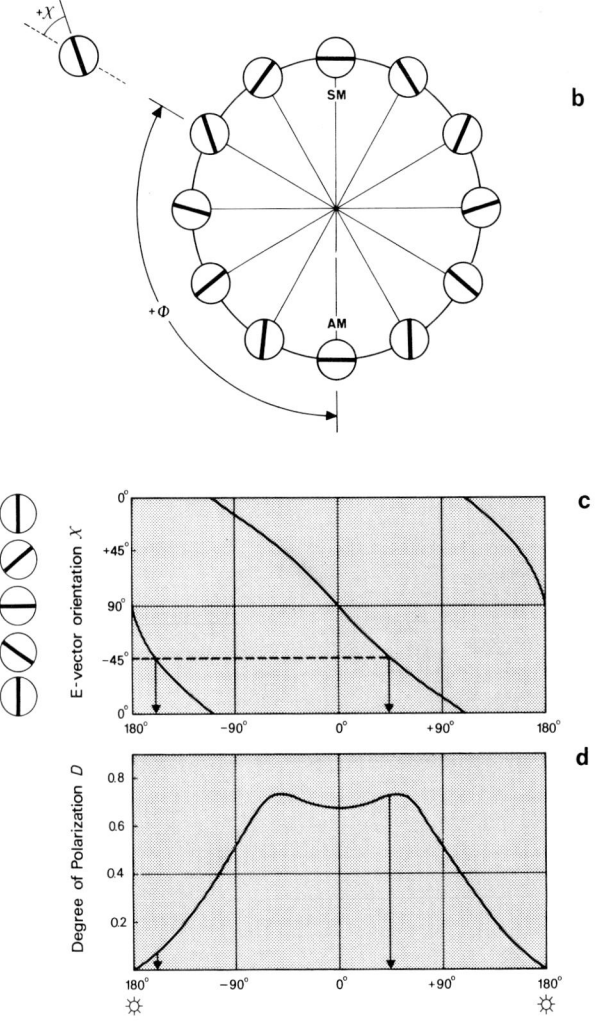

b E-vector orientations as they occur at an elevation of 60° when the sun is at an elevation of 24° above the horizon. To use e-vector patterns as a compass means to associate e-vector orientations (χ) with their corresponding azimuth positions (Φ, φ). Note definitions and sign conventions for χ and φ. *AM* anti-solar meridian, *SM* solar meridian. The correlation between χ and φ varies with both the parallel of altitude (here 60°) and the elevation of the sun (here 24°). It is a long-held view that bees are informed about all possible χ/φ correlations, so that they can assign the correct azimuth position to any particular e-vector occurring in the sky. This paper shows otherwise. Bees use a stereotyped rule of correlating χ and φ, no matter at what elevation and at what time of day an e-vector is presented.

c Correlation between e-vector orientation (χ) and azimuth direction (Φ, φ) as outlined schematically in Fig. 2 b. In the following this correlation is called the χ/φ function. As in Fig. 2 b it is depicted here for an elevation of 60° above the horizon (elevation of sun 24°). Note that each e-vector orientation that it must exceed a certain minimum value (about 0.1), before the bee is able to detect the orientation of an e-vector. Spectral cues are used to some extent (VAN DER GLAS, 1976, 1980), at least to discriminate between sun and sky (EDRICH, NEUMEYER and VON HELVERSEN, 1979; BRINES and GOULD, 1979). Direct sunlight contains less than 10 per cent of ultraviolet radiation, while in scattered skylight the relative amount of ultraviolet radiation is larger by a factor of up to four. Bees use this difference in the relative content of ultraviolet radiation to make the distinction between sun and sky. In this context, it is interesting to note that within the bee's visual system information about skylight polarization is mediated exclusively by the ultraviolet receptors[7]. Recall that those parts of the (anti-solar) sky that exhibit the most saturated ultraviolet tinge are also the ones that exhibit maximum polarization. Apparently, this important physical property of skylight patterns has been incorporated into the bee's visual system. In this context, it is attractive to assume that bees are able to distinguish between sun and sky by exploiting spectral gradients within the celestial hemisphere, and that they make finer spatial distinctions by using polarization gradients within the anti-solar half of the sky. We shall take up this idea after we have presented our experimental data. At present, it suffices to mention that the bee's celestial compass is based on the most reliable sources of celestial information – e-vector orientation and hue of colour.

(iv) *To understand the bee's celestial compass a less conventional model than hitherto suggested is required.*

Now that we have sketched out the skylight patterns, and discussed the skylight cues on which bees rely, let us again ask the crucial question: How do bees use these patterns as a compass? To what geometrical relationship between various parts of these patterns do they refer? This is the main topic of this paper. In more operational terms, the question can be phrased as follows: How do bees deduce the azimuthal position of the solar or anti-solar meridian from the information provided, for example, by a single patch of sky?[8] If

---

(e. g. χ = -45°, *dashed line*) is represented at two azimuth positions: one is closer to the solar meridian, the other closer to the anti-solar meridian.

d Correlation between degree (percentage) of polarization (*D*) and azimuth direction (Φ, φ), shown here for ultraviolet light. Note that any two points in the sky that are identical in e-vector orientation vary in degree of polarization. The member of a pair of identical e-vectors that is positioned farther from the sun is polarized more strongly than the member positioned closer to the sun. This difference holds for all but the vertical e-vectors (χ = 0°). As experimental evidence shows that bees do not rely on the degree of polarization, the intriguing question arises as to how they resolve the ambiguity inherent in the χ/φ function. The following figures provide the answer.

---

[7] Almost twenty years ago, VON FRISCH (1965: 408) showed that the e-vector orientation of bees depended upon the wavelength of light. He concluded from his experiments that only short-wavelength radiation (ultraviolet and blue lieght) was used in the detection of polarized skylight. More detailed studies later refined this conclusion (DUELLI and WEHNER, 1973; VON HELVERSEN and EDRICH, 1974): The ultraviolet receptors alone are necessary and sufficient for mediating e-vector orientation in both bees and ants. This is not to say, however, that the insect's celestial compass relies exclusively on ultraviolet input channels. As we shall see later, spectral cues are used as well, and the processing of such information requires some kind of interaction between ultraviolet and other spectral channels.

[8] There is a second problem not treated in this paper, the problem of time-compensation. As the azimuthal position of the solar and anti-solar meridian changes during the course of the day, the celestial compass must first be calibrated against a non-celestial system of references. For recent data and hypotheses see GOULD (1980) and WEHNER and LANFRANCONI (1981).

you stop and think about it, this is a rather tricky problem. Bees could remember the e-vector pattern last seen, and later try to match the memorized celestial image with whatever they experience in the sky. In this case it is not necessary to assume that bees know anything general about how these patterns are designed. They could form memory images of arbitrary celestial patterns just as they have been shown to form memory images of landmark panoramas which are unpredictable from one location to the other (WEHNER, 1981, 1983; CARTWRIGHT and COLLETT, 1983). Another possibility is that bees are informed about the spatial design of the celestial e-vector patterns. They could know, for example, that the e-vectors form concentric circles around the sun, or in other words: that the sun is positioned on the great circle oriented perpendicularly to the e-vector present in any given patch of sky. In following this rule, they could determine the orientations of at least two e-vectors, trace out the corresponding great circles, and compute the position of the sun as the point where the great circles intersect. However, a little careful thinking reveals the obvious fact that ambiguities arise when skylight vision is restricted to a single e-vector in the sky. None of these have been observed[9].

The two hypotheses outlined above are challenged by our experiments described below. Certainly, a less conventional model is required if one tries to understand how bees deduce compass information from skylight patterns.

3 Behavioural analysis: The bee's stereotyped celestial compass

3.1 Use of e-vector information

(i) *Experimental design: Bees perform their recruitment dances on a horizontal plane surrounded by an artificial sky vault.*

The design of the basic experiment is simple. Individually marked bees are trained to an artificial food source several hundred meters away from the hive. During training they are allowed to view the complete e-vector pattern in the sky, but in the subsequent test their view of the sky is restricted to a single e-vector, or a limited number of e-vectors. The direction which the bees now select, if they select any direction at all, should inform us about what knowledge they have of the celestial e-vector pattern.

All this is easier said than done. If a walking insect like an ant sets out for a foraging trip, it can easily be followed and its path recorded by the human observer. In addition, its visual environment can be manipulated experimentally by moving various kinds of optical equipment along with the insect as it walks (WEHNER, 1982). In the foraging bee, however, such experiments are not feasible. One cannot follow a flying bee, let alone put optical screens and filters on top of it as it flies. Bees could be trained to reach a food source by walking, but this is difficult to achieve experimentally (BISETZKY, 1957). Fortunately enough, when the bee has returned from a foraging flight, it indicates its foraging direction by the direction of its recruitment dance, the so-called waggle dance, by which it communicates information about the location of the food source to its nest mates.

---

[9] Most previous authors have agreed upon the assumption that bees determine individual e-vector orientations locally, but it is a little difficult to judge what they have assumed the bees to do next. Most workers including STOCKHAMMER (1959) and VON FRISCH (1965: 398) have certainly leaned towards the first hypothesis outlined above (that bees perform some kind of image matching), but KIRSCHFELD, MARTIN and LINDAUER (1975) have favoured the second (that bees possess some more general knowledge about the geometry of skylight patterns).

If the hive is put horizontally, and if the bee dancing on the horizontal comb has full view of the sky, or of a large circular patch of sky centred about the zenith (Fig. 3 b), the bee's waggle runs point exactly in the direction towards the food source. We can conclude from this kind of control experiment that the device used in our investigations does not disturb or misdirect the bees. In another control experiment, we surround the dancing bee by a translucent Plexiglass hemisphere which depolarizes the sky completely and provides the bee with nothing but homogeneously lit visual surroundings (Fig. 3 a). In this case, the bee's waggle runs are oriented randomly, as they are under a fully overcast sky, with no

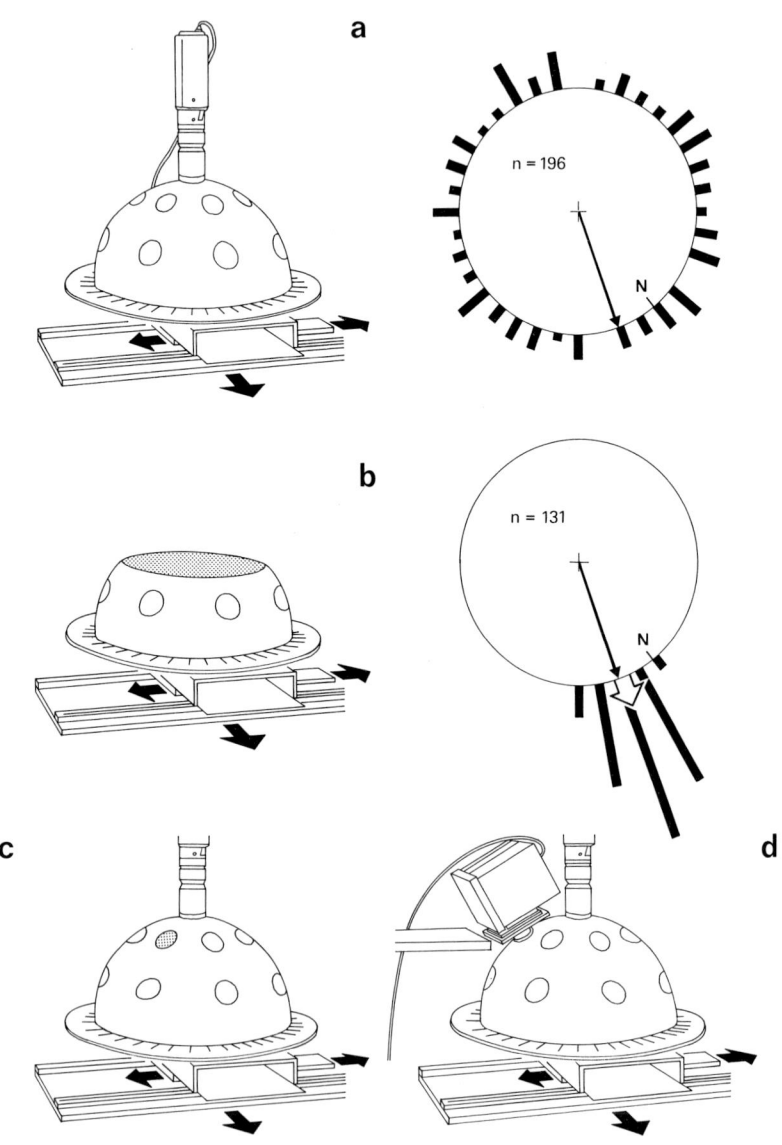

other visual cues available. This assures us that the diffuse illumination prevailing inside the Plexiglass dome does not offer visual cues that could guide the bees as they dance.

Now comes the crucial experiment. One of the apertures built into the Plexiglass hemisphere is opened, so that the bee can view the unobscured blue sky through a single small circular window (Fig. 3 c).

Before we describe in the next section how the bees behave in this potentially ambiguous situation (see p. 19), we must add some technical remarks. The diameter of the circular aperture through which the bees can see the sky is a mere $10°$, sometimes even $5°$. In additional experiments, artificially polarized light is displayed to the bees through one of the apertures (Fig. 3 d). In this case, the light entering the aperture is provided by a Xenon arc source (400 W). Before it reaches the eye of the dancing bee, it passes through a heat-absorbing filter (KG 2, Schott), a diffuser, spectral cutoff or broad-band interference filters (e. g. GG 400, UG 11, Schott), and a polarizer (HNP'B, Polaroid). In addition, two or more patches of artificially polarized light can be presented simultaneously by using more than one light source and more than one set of filters. This arrangement enables us not only to mimic stimulus conditions that occur in the natural sky, but also to display spatial configurations of e-vectors that do not occur in the natural sky and thus have never been experienced by any bee throughout its entire lifetime. Clearly, it is this kind of experiment which will finally provide a touchstone of any hypothesis about the bee's celestial compass. First, however, let us perform the basic experiment announced above and derive from it the hypothesis that will later be tested in more detail.

(ii) *The basic experiment: The bee's internal model of the sky is not a memory image of the e-vector pattern last seen.*

After the bees have been trained under the full blue sky (Fig. 4 a), they perform their recruitment dances underneath the translucent Plexiglass dome. In the first experiment, their skylight vision is restricted to a small patch of sky characterized by an e-vector orientation of $-45°$. The stimulus condition is sketched out in Fig. 4 b. In this and the following figures a heavy black arrow marks the foraging direction, which in this case points $15°$ to the left of the anti-solar meridian and $96°$ to the left of the skylight window opened within the Plexiglass dome. Much to our surprise, the mean direction of the bee's

---

Fig. 3: Experimental design. Bees trained to an artificial food source perform their recruitment dances (waggle runs) on a horizontal comb which is surrounded by a translucent Plexiglass hemisphere. The hive including the comb can be moved in x and y directions so as to centre the dancing bee with respect to the hemisphere *(black arrows)*. The dances are recorded by a video camera mounted in the zenith. In the data plots the directions of the recruitment dances are indicated by *black bars*. The *big open arrow* and the *small black arrow* mark the mean direction of the recruitment dances and the direction of the food source, respectively. N north, n number of recruitment dances recorded.

a Control experiment no. 1: Neither natural skylight nor artificially polarized light is displayed to the bees. As underneath a completely overcast sky, the dances of the bees are oriented at random.

b Control experiment no. 2: The bees view the entire upper half of the natural blue sky (elevation > $45°$), but the elevation of the sun is < $45°$. The dances of the bees point exactly in the direction of the food source.

c One of the apertures of the Plexiglass dome is opened enabling the bees to view a small patch of blue sky (diameter $10°$). The result of one of these experiments is described in Fig. 4.

d A precisely controlled artificial source of light (dimaeter $10°$) is displayed to the dancing bees. E-vector orientation, degree of polarization, spectral composition, and radiant intensity can be varied independently. In some experiments more than one patch of natural sky or more than one artificial source of light have been presented.

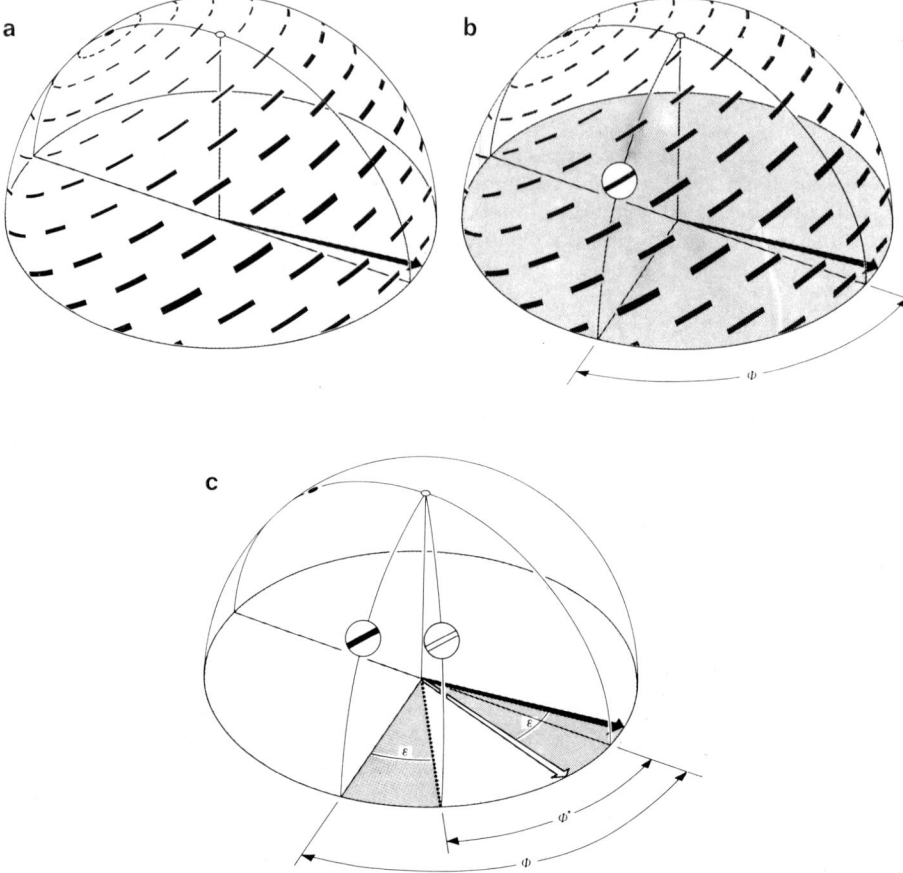

Fig. 4: The basic experiment. Bees are trained to fly under the full blue sky to a distant food source (*a*). The direction of the food source is marked by a *black arrow*. In the experiment described here the black arrow points 15° to the left of the anti-solar meridian. Having returned from the food source, the bees perform their recruitment dances underneath a translucent Plexiglass dome, under which their skylight vision is restricted to a small patch of sky (*b*). In the present experiment the orientation of the e-vector available in the patch of sky is -45° (elevation of patch 45°, elevation of sun 53°). The result (*c*) is astounding: The bees deviate considerably (*white arrow*) to the right of the foraging direction. The error angle ε is about 30°. Conclusion: Bees expect the -45° e-vector to occur nearer to the anti-solar meridian (*white bar*, azimuth position Φ^*) than it actually does (*black bar*, azimuth position Φ). Note that $\Phi^* = \Phi - \varepsilon$. When the -45° e-vector is presented at other times of day (when the sun is at other elevations), the values of Φ are different from the one shown here, but Φ^* turns out to be always the same. Obviously, bees expect the -45° e-vector to occur at a fixed azimuth position (Φ^*) relative to the symmetry line of the e-vector pattern. The same value of Φ^* holds for the -45° e-vector that is positioned closer to the sun (recall that at any given elevation each e-vector usually occurs twice; see Fig. 2 b, c). Hence, the e-vector closer to the sun is interpreted by the bees as if it is the one farther from the sun. This «misinterpretation» results in extremely large error angles ε.

recruitment dances as indicated by the open arrow deviates by as much as 30° to the right of the foraging direction.

Astounding as this result may appear, its tentative explanation is simple. Let us first assume that the bee while foraging has learned in what direction the food source is located with respect, say, to the anti-solar meridian[10]. Let us further assume that later, while dancing, the bee tries to infer the azimuth position of the anti-solar meridian from whatever information is available in the sky, in this case from a single e-vector (-45°) presented at a given elevation. To accomplish this task, the bee must somehow be informed about the spatial layout of the e-vector pattern. As noted earlier, it could have acquired this information during its previous foraging flight by building up in its mind a detailed image of the e-vector pattern in the sky as seen when heading for the food source. However, the errors made by the bees in the experiment described above show otherwise (Fig. 4c). Obviously, bees use an internal model of the sky in which the -45° e-vector is positioned closer to the anti-solar meridian (see open e-vector symbol) than it is in the real sky – closer by exactly that amount (ε) by which the bees deviate from their foraging direction towards the e-vector.

The experiment is outlined in more detail in Fig. 5. The main difference with respect to the experiment described in the former figure is that in the present case artificially polarized ultraviolet light rather than natural sky-light is presented. Nevertheless, as described in the next paragraph, the result is the same.

By now the reader will be so familiar with the design of the experiment that we will not lose him by switching from the three-dimensional representation used so far to the more convenient two-dimensional representation adopted in this and the following figures. The stimulus condition and the bee's dance directions are depicted in Figs. 5a and 5b, respectively. When the -45° e-vector is presented at an elevation of 60° above the horizon at a time of day when the sun is also at an elevation of 60° above the horizon, the bees deviate by 30° to the right of the true foraging direction. The conclusion drawn from this result is sketched out in Fig. 5c: In the bee's internal model of the sky (inner circle) the -45° e-vector lies 30° closer to the anti-solar meridian than it does in the outside world (outer circle). Now imagine that the bee turns until it has accomplished a match between its internal representation of the celestial e-vector pattern and what it actually experiences in our experimental set-up. To visualize what happens, the reader is invited to rotate – in his or her mind – the inner circle with respect to the outer one until both 45° e-vectors are aligned (lower graph of Fig. 5c). Then, the white arrow (indicating the direction in which the bee assumes the food source to occur) deviates from the black arrow (indicating the actual direction of the food source) by the error angle that has been observed under the experimental conditions mentioned above.

In conclusion, the bee's internal model of the sky cannot be a memory image of the actual e-vector pattern as experienced during the bee's previous foraging flight. The bee assumes the -45° e-vector to occur at a position which does not coincide with the real position of this e-vector in the sky. Another model is required whose precise formulation must await further evidence. Such evidence is presented in the following sections.

---

[10] In this and the following considerations we take the anti-solar meridian as the reference azimuth position. This is merely for the sake of convenience; we could have equally justifiably selected the solar meridian.

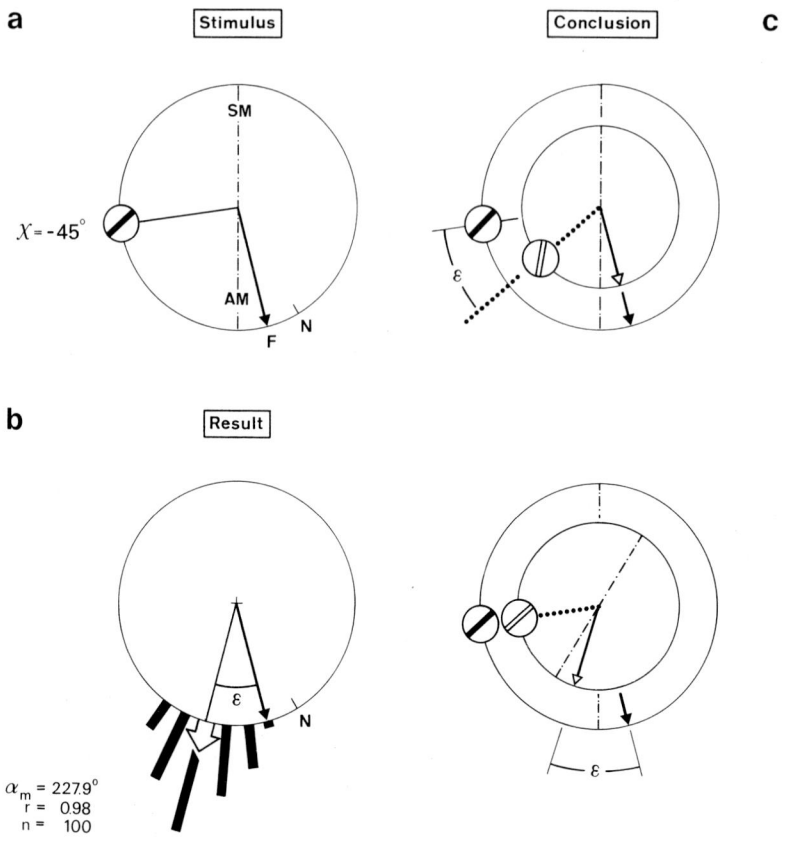

Fig. 5: Same experiment as in Fig. 4, but with the -45° e-vector presented by means of a beam of artificially polarized ultraviolet light (Fig. 3 d) rather than natural skylight (Fig. 3 c).

a The *black arrow* points towards the food source (*F*). N denotes north. *SM* solar meridian, *AM* anti-solar meridian. The e-vector is presented at an elevation of 60° above the horizon (elevation of sun 60°).

b The bees' waggle runs (*black bars*, mean value α_m indicated by *big white arrow*) deviate by about 30° (error angle ε) to the right of the foraging direction.

c The outer and the inner circles depict the position of the -45° e-vector in the real sky (*black bar*) and in the bee's model of the sky (*white bar*), respectively. The latter position is derived from the error angle ε observed in the experiment (see *b*). The *black arrow* marks the direction of the food source (as in *a*). Imagine that during its preceding foraging flight performed underneath the full blue sky, the bee has learned the direction of its food source with respect to the solar and anti-solar meridian (*white arrow*). Further imagine that the bee when confronted with a -45° e-vector alone tries to align the -45° e-vector of its internal compass with the -45° e-vector in the sky. Metaphorically, this can be done by rotating the inner circle relative to the outer one by the error angle ε. Then the *white arrow* points in the direction in which the bees actually dance (compare *b* and *c*, *lower figure*). See Appendix for definition of symbols.

(iii) *Outlining a hypothesis: The bee's e-vector compass reflects the mean azimuth positions of the maximally polarized e-vectors in the sky.*

The next logical step is to display to the bees different e-vectors presented at different elevations and at different times of day, to record the error angles exhibited by the bees, and to derive from these error angles where in the sky the bees assume any particular e-vector to occur. What has emerged from these tedious investigations during which more than ten thousand waggle runs have been recorded on videotape, is the bee's internal representation of the celestial e-vector pattern – the bee's e-vector compass. It is depicted at the inner circle of Fig. 6.

Let us just highlight the main features of this compass:

(a) The compass does not depend on the elevation at which a given e-vector is presented above the horizon. Each point of the compass is characterized invariably by its own e-vector orientation. In the real sky, at each azimuthal distance from the solar or anti-solar meridian the e-vector orientation varies with both the elevation of the point observed and the elevation of the sun (Fig. 6, outer circle), but in the bee's compass it does not. Referring back to Fig. 4c, we can rephrase this important statement as follows: The actual azimuth position Φ of a given e-vector varies with the elevation of both the e-vector and the sun, but the azimuth position the bee assumes (Φ^*) stays put. In conclusion, in the bee's e-vector compass e-vectors remain at fixed azimuth positions with respect to the solar and anti-solar meridian (see also Fig. 10a). This holds at least for elevations larger than 30° above the horizon.

(b) This stereotyped e-vector compass is used by the bee under all conditions tested so far. The following situation is especially intriguing. Depending on the elevation of the sun, and thus the time of day, certain e-vectors do not occur at a given elevation above the horizon. However, the bees are not disturbed when such an e-vector is presented by means of a beam of artificially polarized light. They expect this e-vector to occur exactly where it should according to their internal compass (see e.g. Fig. 9).

(c) The compass is restricted to the highly polarized half of the sky, that is the half centred around the anti-solar meridian. Recall that at each elevation above the horizon any particular e-vector usually occurs twice: once in the less polarized half of the sky (close to the sun) and another time in the highly polarized half of the sky (farther away from the sun). To assure oneself of this crucial point, one should consult again Figs. 2 b–d. However, the bee is not informed about this ambiguity. It indiscriminately expects all e-vectors to occur in the highly polarized half of the sky. This is one of the strongest arguments in favour of the previous statement that bees do not pay attention to the degree of polarization, which as noted earlier is highly variable in the natural sky. It further implies that the bee's e-vector compass does not cover all 360°, but only 180° of the points of the compass.

(d) In detail, the full range of e-vector orientations is spread along the points of the bee's e-vector compass in the following way:
Horizontal e-vectors are positioned along the anti-solar meridian ($\varphi = 0°$) forming the symmetry line of the bee's «demi-compass». This is the only case in which the bee's compass coincides with the real sky. Thus, no errors occur, if a patch of horizontally polarized skylight is displayed (Fig. 8).
Vertical e-vectors are positioned at right angles to the left and right of the symmetry line (at $\varphi = +90°$ and $\varphi = -90°$). When a vertical e-vector is presented, the bees usually exhibit bimodal orientation expecting the vertical e-vector at two positions lying opposite to each other and at right angles to the solar and anti-solar meridian (Fig. 9)[11].
All other e-vectors are spread out between the horizontal and vertical e-vectors in such

a way that the compass exhibits mirror-symmetry around the anti-solar meridian. Their exact positions can be inferred from Fig. 6 (inner circle) and in more detail from the *standard χ/φ function* shown in Fig. 7 a.

In conclusion, bees are not informed exactly about all intricacies of the celestial e-vector patterns. They follow a rather simple rule in assigning azimuth positions to e-vector orientations (Figs. 6 and 7 a).

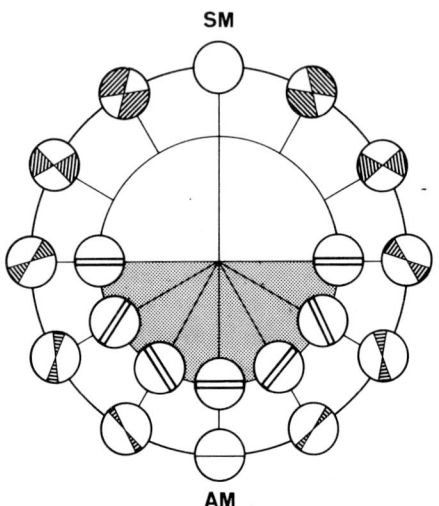

Fig. 6: The bee's e-vector compass *(inner circle)*.
SM solar meridian, *AM* anti-solar meridian. The two most striking features of the bee's e-vector compass are the following: (1) E-vector orientations occur at fixed azimuth positions as measured with respect to the symmetry plane of the skylight pattern *(SM-AM)*. (2) The bee's e-vector compass is restricted to the anti-solar half of the sky *(shaded semicircle)*. The *outer circle* depicts the azimuth positions at which the e-vectors displayed to the bees during the course of the experiments actually occurred in the sky. At each azimuth position marked by a small circle the range of e-vector orientations displayed in the experiments is indicated by the *hatched sectors*.

---

[11] While presenting vertical e-vectors, Brines and Gould (1979) usually observed unimodal dance orientation with a distinct preference for the e-vector to the right of the sun. This was thought to represent a dance convention used by the bees to avoid ambiguities. In contrast, we observed bimodal dance orientation throughout the day. However, when the sun was close to the horizon, one direction was sometimes selected more frequently than the other, but preference for either vertical e-vector could change from one day to the other. A close analysis of the dance directions revealed that in these cases, when there was a preference for one direction, the e-vectors presented were interpreted as being inclined by a few degrees relative to vertical. Thus we are not able to confirm the "right"-rule observed by Brines and Gould. Further work will be necessary to clarify this point. Note, however, that beyond this "right"-rule the major discrepancy between our results and those of Gould and his students is as follows. The latter workers have found that bees expect a vertical e-vector to occur exactly where it should according to its position in the sky. We find that bees expect vertical e-vectors to occur invariably at right angles to the solar and anti-solar meridian.

Now comes the poignant question we have pondered for quite some time: What properties of the actual e-vector patterns are hidden behind the bee's e-vector compass? Is there a rule by which the bee's compass strategy can be derived theoretically from the e-vector patterns in the sky? In evolutionary terms, the bee must have adopted such a rule, and so it

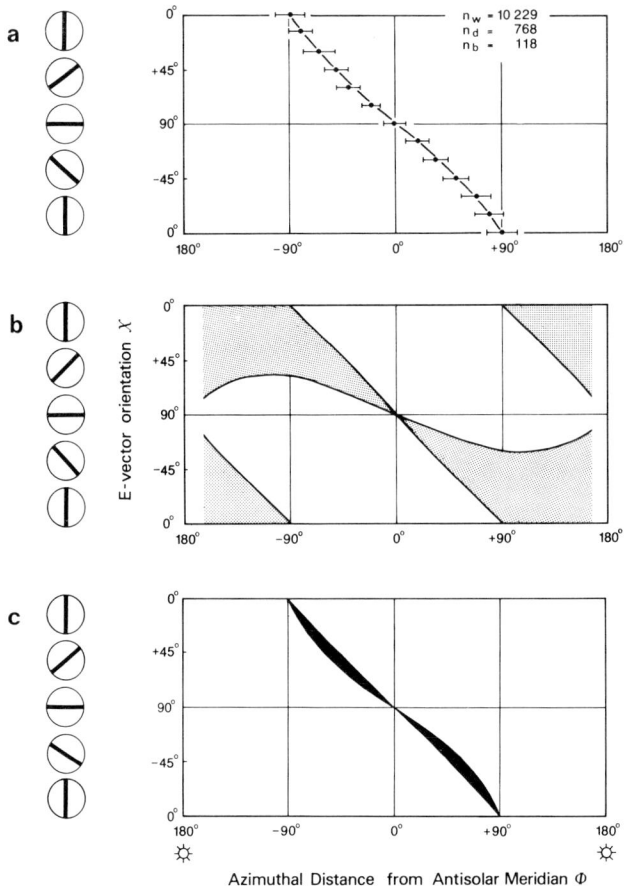

Fig. 7: *a* The bee's e-vector compass in detail: The *bee's standard χ/φ function* as derived from single-spot experiments (see Fig. 5). The figure demonstrates at which azimuth position (Φ, φ) the bee expects any particular e-vector orientation (χ) to occur. Mean values and standard deviations are given. For a more vivid representation see Fig. 6 (inner circle) and Fig. 10 a. n_w number of waggle runs recorded, n_d number of recruitment dances, n_b number of bees tested.
b Azimuth positions at which all e-vector orientations tested in *a* occurred in the sky during the time of the experiments *(celestial χ/φ functions)*. The elevations of the e-vectors displayed to the bees varied from 30° through 66°, and the elevation of the sun from 15° through 60°. In the figure the latter range is extended down to 0° (sun on horizon).
c Azimuth positions of the maximally polarized e-vectors in the sky *(celestial χ_{max}/φ functions)*. The range of elevations of both e-vector and sun for which the χ_{max}/φ functions have been determined is identical with the one shown in *b*. Note the close resemblance between the mean celestial χ_{max}/φ function *(c)* and the bee's standard χ/φ function *(a)*.

is a challenge to the human observer to inquire what the properties of the skylight patterns are that the bee has discovered and incorporated into its visual system.

The answer to this question is rather simple. The bee's e-vector compass can be derived theoretically by referring exclusively to the most prominent feature of skylight polariz-ation, the arc of maximum polarization (see Fig. 2 a). More specifically, the bee's e-vector compass reflects the mean distribution of the maximally polarized e-vectors as they occur across the sky during the course of the day.

What does this mean? The arguement can be understood easily by consulting Fig. 10 b. As we have seen before, the arc of maximum polarization passes across the sky vault at an angular distance of 90^0 from the sun. When the sun is on the horizon, the arc passes through the zenith. Consequently, at sunrise and sunset, the vertical e-vectors are part of the arc of maximum polarization. When this is the case, they occur at two azimuth positions which lie opposite to each other and at right angles to the solar and anti-solar

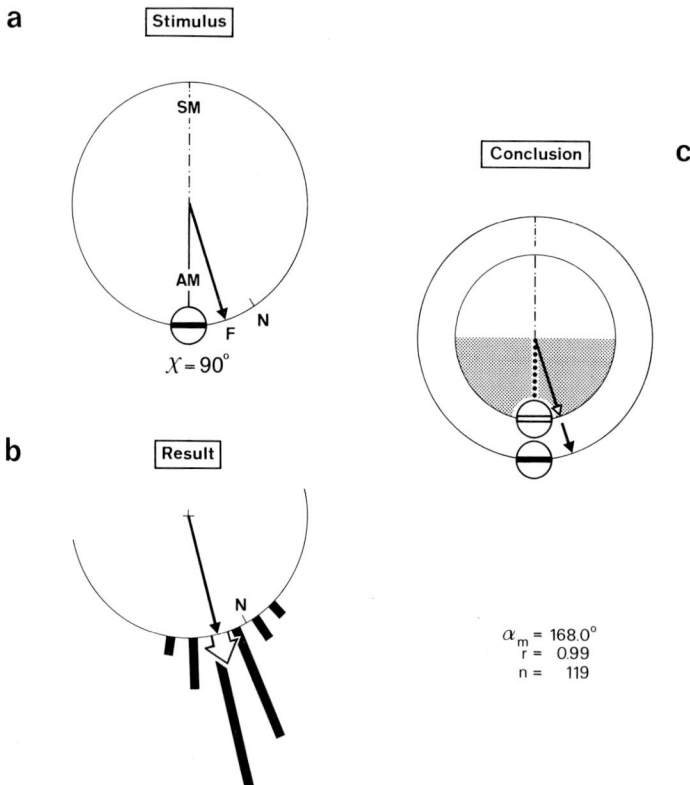

Fig. 8: In the sky, horizontal e-vectors ($\chi = 90°$) are positioned along both the solar and the anti-solar meridian. However, as borne out by the present experiment, bees expect horizontal e-vectors to occur exclusively along the anti-solar meridian. The experiment is as follows: An artificial beam of horizon-tally polarized ultraviolet light is presented to the bees at an elevation of 60°. The elevation of the sun is also 60°. The bees dance correctly in the direction of the food source F (see b) when the horizontal e-vector is presented at the azimuth position of the anti-solar meridian (see a). For explanation of symbols see Fig. 5 and Appendix.

meridian, exactly as described above for the bee's e-vector compass. When the sun moves up, the arc of maximum polarization tilts down. In Fig. 10 b the distribution of maximally polarized e-vectors as caused by the downward tilt of the arc of maximum polarization is shown for an elevation of 45°, but in fact it is very similar for all elevations > 30° above the horizon (Fig. 7 c). Furthermore, if one takes the mean of all these distributions, one arrives at the bee's celestial compass (compare Figs. 7 a and 7 c).

The similarity between what the bee uses as a compass (Fig. 7 a) and what is displayed in the sky by the maximally polarized e-vectors (Fig. 7 c) is striking. The bee's e-vector

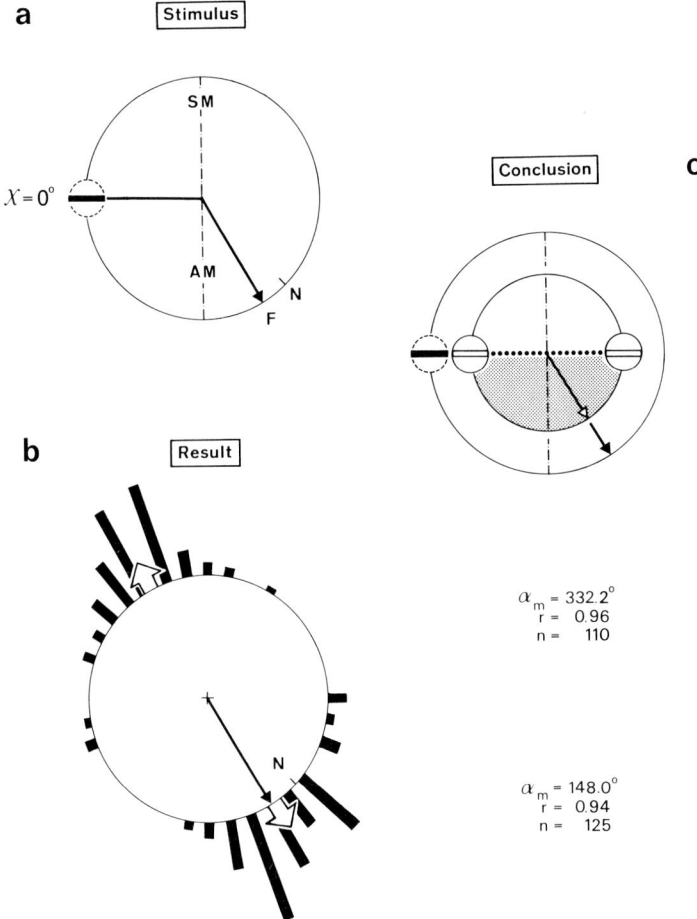

Fig. 9: Vertical e-vectors ($\chi = 0°$) are expected by the bees to occur at right angles to the left and right of the solar or anti-solar meridian. This follows from the experiment described in this figure. An artificially produced vertical e-vector is displayed to the bees at an elevation (60°) at which it does not occur in the sky at the time at which the experiment is performed (elevation of sun 60°). It is presented 90° to the right of the solar (and anti-solar) meridian (a). The bees dance bimodally in the direction of the food source and in the diametrically opposite direction (b). Note that in c there are two orientations of the inner circle in which the azimuth positions of the vertical e-vectors of both circles coincide.

compass and the maximally polarized e-vectors are restricted to the anti-solar half of the sky. With the only exception of the vertical e-vectors each maximally polarized e-vector is positioned at only one point of the compass. No ambiguities occur. Finally, the azimuth position of each maximally polarized e-vector in the sky is almost independent of the elevation of the e-vector above the horizon. This does not hold for all other (less polarized) e-vectors present in the sky. Their azimuth positions vary with the elevation above the horizon and, at each particular elevation, with the elevation of the sun (Fig. 7 b).

In conclusion, the bee's celestial compass can be derived not only experimentally as described in the former section, but also theoretically by referring to the arc of maximum

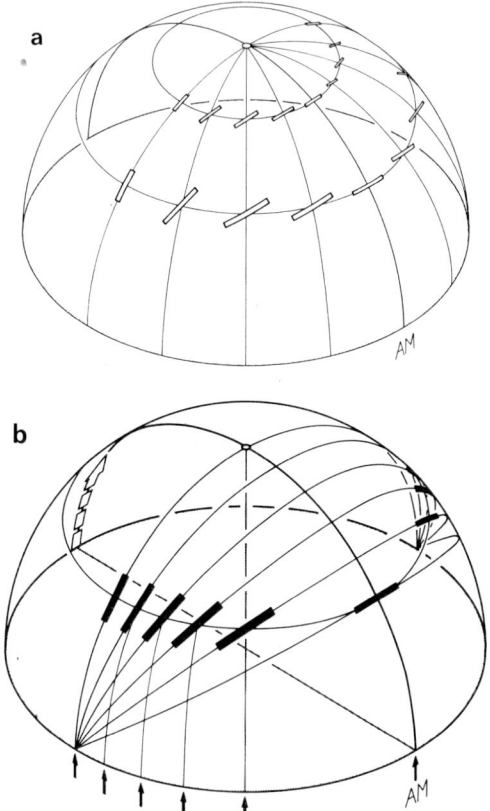

Fig. 10: *a* Three-dimensional representation of the bee's e-vector compass (compare Fig. 6, inner circle). The same distribution of e-vectors (the bee's standard χ/φ function, see Fig. 7 a) holds for all elevations > 30°. AM anti-solar meridian.

b The maximally polarized e-vectors shown for an elevation of 45° above the horizon. When the sun moves up *(white broken arrow)*, the arc of maximum polarization which is always positioned at an angular distance of 90° to the sun (Fig. 2 a) tilts down. As a consequence, the maximally polarized e-vectors are confined to the anti-solar half of the sky. This reflects an important aspect of the bee's e-vector compass. Moreover, the spatial distribution of the maximally polarized e-vectors is very similar for all elevations higher than about 30° above the horizon (Fig. 7 c), and is very similar to the spatial distribution of the e-vectors as assumed by the bees (Fig. 7 a).

polarization in the sky. What the bee has incorporated into its e-vector compass are the average azimuth positions of the maximally polarized e-vectors as they occur in the upper part of the sky.

(iv) *Testing and vindicating the hypothesis: Bees apply their simple compass rule even when large parts of the natural blue sky are available.*

The hypothesis outlined above implies that all the bee knows about skylight polarization is the simple compass rule depicted in Fig. 7 a. We have derived this compass empirically (from the bees) and theoretically (from the sky). Nevertheless, in all experiments described so far only a single e-vector, either natural or artificial, has been displayed to the bees. One may argue that the bees resort to their simple model of the sky only when such restrictive stimulus conditions prevail. Whenever they see large parts of the sky, they might exhibit more detailed knowledge of the natural e-vector patterns.

To cut a long story short, this is not the case. In the following we shall describe a number of experiments in which bees are confronted with more than one e-vector or with large parts of the natural blue sky. Even under such conditions the bees invariably apply their simple compass rule. Just as in the single spot experiments, each e-vector induces an orientation error, and the mean of these errors shows up as an angular deviation of the bees from the correct compass course.

Two-spot experiments: Only the most intriguing of a series of experiments will be described. In this experiment the horizontal and the vertical e-vector are presented simultaneously at an angular distance at which they occur in the natural sky (Fig. 11 a).

One might expect that in this situation no orientation errors would occur, because as described above (Fig. 8), the horizontal e-vector alone suffices for establishing the correct compass course. So it comes as a real surprise that the bees again make mistakes. They deviate by 21° from the correct course (Fig. 11 b). This is a really counter-intuitive observation: additional information is presented – a vertical e-vector in addition to the horizontal one – and orientation deteriorates. However, this is exactly what our hypothesis predicts.

A moment's thought helps to explain why this is so. Assume that the bee can do nothing but apply its simple compass rule even when there is more than one e-vector available. Then the bee should select a direction that is the mean of the directions it would take when confronted with each e-vector alone. This is exactly what we observe in the two-spot experiment described above. The error exhibited by the bees is the mean of the errors exhibited in each of the two one-spot experiments. When a horizontal or a vertical e-vector is presented alone, the error angles are 0° and 45°, respectively. These numbers can be read off Fig. 11 c by comparing where the two e-vectors occur in the bee's compass (inner circle) and the sky (outer circle). From these numbers a mean error angle of 22.5° is predicted for the two-spot experiment. The error angle actually observed (20.7°) is statistically indistinguishable from the predicted value.

What happens if the horizontal and vertical e-vector are presented at an angular distance of 90° rather than 135°, i. e. at an angular distance that is not found in the sky at the time of the experiment? In this case, the positions of the two stimuli exactly match the bee's celestial map. No orientation errors should occur, and none have been observed. This seems to contradict common sense: When the stimulus configuration coincides with the outside world, the bees make mistakes, but when an artificial configuration is presented which is not found in the natural sky, the bees are oriented correctly. However counter-intuitive this notion might appear, it is fully in accord with the assumption that the bee is inevitably bound to the simple compass strategy outlined in the previous section.

In conclusion, when any particular e-vector is presented in addition to a horizontal e-vector (which guarantees correct orientation when presented alone), the bees do not refer selectively to the latter. In their celestial compass, all e-vectors seem to be equally import-ant. The orientation errors observed in the two-spot experiments are the mean of the errors which the bees exhibit when they are confronted with the two e-vectors separately.

Large-field experiments: Now let us go one step further and display to the dancing bees large parts of the natural blue sky rather than sets of isolated e-vectors. Only two experi-ments of this kind will be described in Fig. 12, but a large number of similar experiments have all led to the same conclusion (WEHNER, 1983; ROSSEL and WEHNER, 1984). Even when large skylight windows are opened in the translucent Plexiglass dome, bees make mistakes exactly as large as predicted from their e-vector map. This holds irrespective of the size and position of the skylight window.

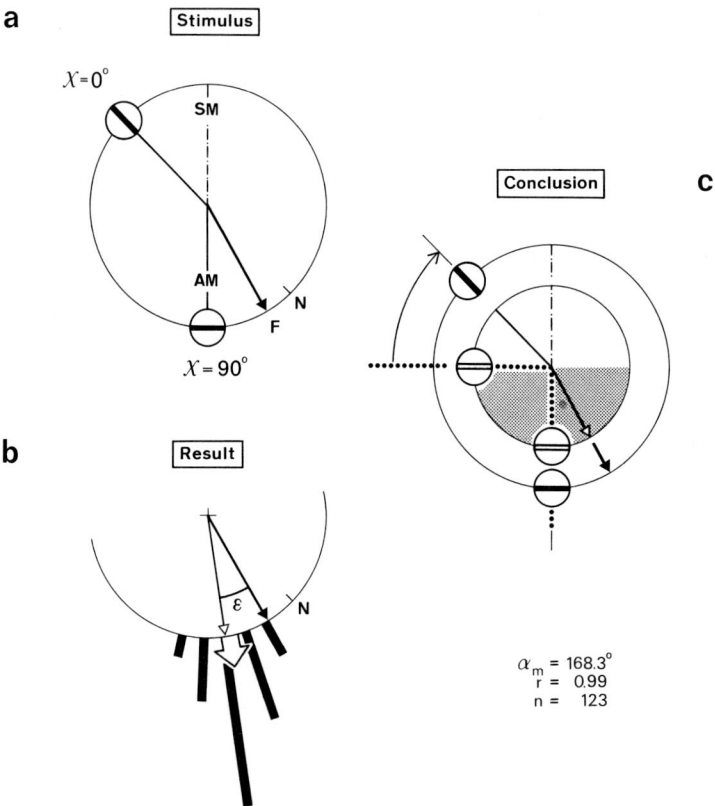

Fig. 11: Two-spot experiment. Horizontal and vertical e-vectors are presented simultaneously by two beams of ultraviolet light. The angular distance between the two e-vectors corresponds to the angular distance at which the two e-vectors occur in the sky at the time of day at which the experiment is performed. In spite of this correspondence, the directions of the bee's dances deviate from the direction of the food source *(b)*. The error angle observed can be predicted by assuming that the bees try to match their internal e-vector compass *(c: inner circle)* as closely as possible to the two stimuli displayed to them *(c: outer circle)*.

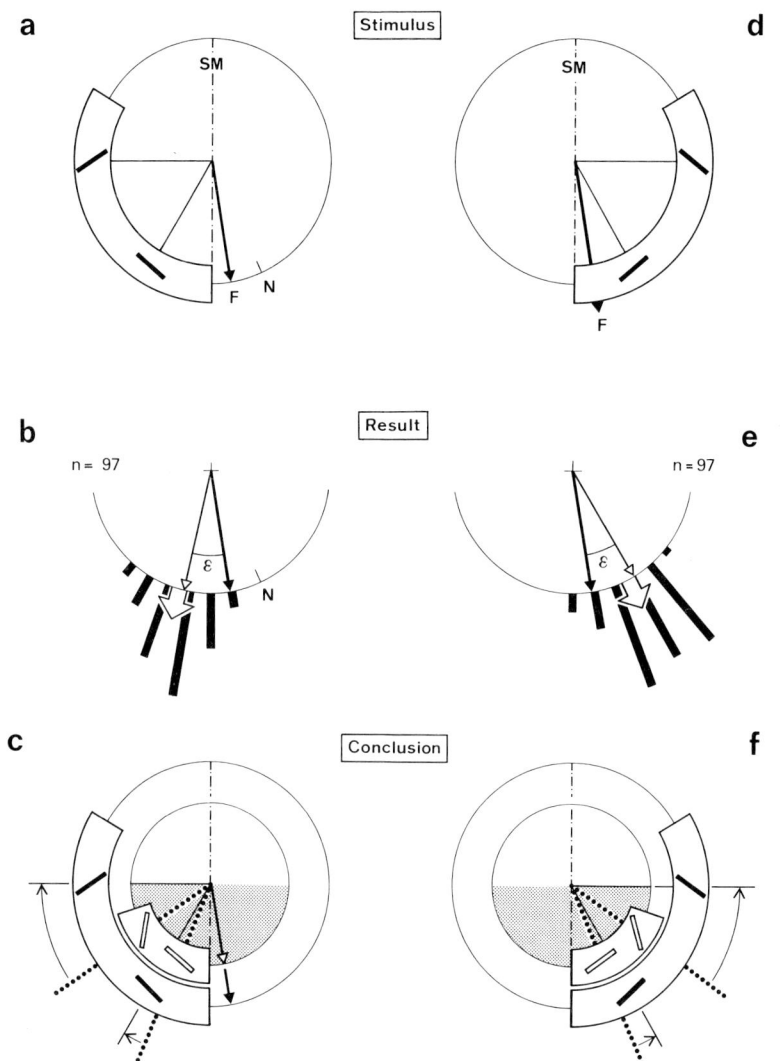

Fig. 12: Large-field experiments. The bees view a strip-like celestial window positioned 60° above the horizon either to the right *(a)* or to the left *(d)* of the anti-solar meridian. The window opened in the translucent Plexiglass dome is 135° wide and 10° high. The bees deviate to the right *(b)* and to the left *(e)* of the correct direction, respectively. As in the two-spot experiment of Fig. 11 the error angles observed *(large white arrows)* are statistically indistinguishable from the prediction *(small white arrows)* that the error induced by an e-vector pattern is the mean of the errors induced by each e-vector alone. In computing the mean error, the positions of individual e-vectors have been compared between the inner and outer circle in *c* and *f* at azimuthal distances of 10°, but only two such comparisons are shown in the figures. For the bees, each e-vector seems to be equally important, irrespective of its degree of polarization which decreases from the anti-solar side towards the solar side of the window.

A short description of one of the experiments will make the point. In this experiment (Fig. 12 a–c) the bees view a strip of blue skylight positioned to the right of the anti-solar meridian, at an elevation of 60° above the horizon (Fig. 12 a). Again, their waggle runs do not point exactly towards the food source, but deviate by 23.5° to the right (Fig. 12 b), and again this is to be expected if the bees apply the rule outlined above, i. e. calculate the mean of the error angles induced by each individual e-vector alone. For the sake of simplicity, only two of these e-vectors are shown in Fig. 12 c, but for the computation of the mean error angle e-vectors have been taken every 10°. The mean error angle computed this way is 22.1° (small open arrow in Fig. 12 b). It nicely coincides with the error angle actually observed in the experiment (23.5°, large open arrow in Fig. 12 b).

This coincidence finally disposes of the possibility that bees use the degree of polarization as an additional compass cue. The point is easy to grasp. The degree of polarization varies dramatically within the strip-like skylight window. In our experiment, it reaches its maximum near the anti-solar side of the strip and then decreases steadily towards the solar side of the strip. There, it is just high enough for the e-vectors to be detected by the bees (see p. 20). If the bees referred to the degree of polarization in addition to the e-vector orientation, the e-vectors should dwindle in importance on the way from the anti-solar to the solar side of the strip. This is not the case. As shown above, each e-vector is equally important for the bee, irrespective of its degree of polarization.

The error angles observed in the large-field experiments depend crucially on the position of the skylight window. In the experiment described above (Fig. 12 a–c), the window is positioned to the right of the anti-solar meridian. If it is positioned to the left, with all other things being equal (Fig. 12 d–f), the bees deviate to the left from the correct compass course by the same angular amount by which they deviated to the right in the former case (Figs. 12 a–c). It is only when the skylight window is positioned symmetrically with respect to the anti-solar meridian that no orientation errors occur. Then, the errors induced by the left and the right half of the pattern are equal in magnitude, but opposite in sign, and thus cancel each other out. As a consequence, the bees' waggle runs point towards the food source. Never have systematic errors been observed in such situations. This kind of experiment is not documented here, but described at length in Wehner (1983) and Rossel and Wehner (1984).

In conclusion, even when large parts of the natural blue sky are available, bees make mistakes exactly as large as predicted from their simple compass rule. The prediction implies that the orientation error induced by any e-vector pattern is the mean of the orientation errors induced by each e-vector alone. Each e-vector is equally important, irrespective of its degree of polarization (provided that the degree of polarization is high enough for the e-vector to be detected). Orientation errors do not occur when the patch of sky is positioned symmetrically to the anti-solar meridian, because then the errors induced by the left and the right half of the pattern neutralize each other.

3.2 Use of spectral information

How do bees behave if they view a patch of *unpolarized* light? In the full blue sky the only patch that is unpolarized is the sun and the area immediately around the sun. Therefore we would expect that bees take an unpolarized beam of light for the sun. However, bees behave according to this expectation only if the beam of unpolarized light is rich in long-wavelength radiation, so that the green receptors are stimulated predominantly (Fig. 13 b). If a beam of unpolarized ultraviolet light is presented instead, the bees expect this spot of light to lie within the anti-solar half of the sky (Fig. 13 c). The scatter within the data is much larger than in the former case (compare Figs. 13 b and 13 c).

Clearly, the mean vector of the directions plotted in Fig. 13 c points toward the anti-solar meridian. This is to be expected whenever the data are arranged symmetrically with respect to the anti-solar meridian, but it would be rash to conclude from this result that in the bee's internal image of the sky an unpolarized spot of ultraviolet light lies just along the anti-solar meridian rather than anywhere within the anti-solar half of the sky.

This is borne out by another set of experiments (Fig. 14). A polarized beam of ultraviolet light (e-vector orientation -45°) is presented in addition to an unpolarized beam of ultraviolet light (UV). The latter is positioned either 90° to the left (Fig. 14 a) or 90° to the right (Fig. 14 d) of the polarized beam. Even though the two stimulus conditions are completely symmetrical, the results are not (Figs. 14 b, e). In the first experiment, with the beam of unpolarized light to the left of the e-vector, the bees hehave as if the e-vector had been presented alone (compare Figs. 14 b and 5 b). They seem to disregard completely the

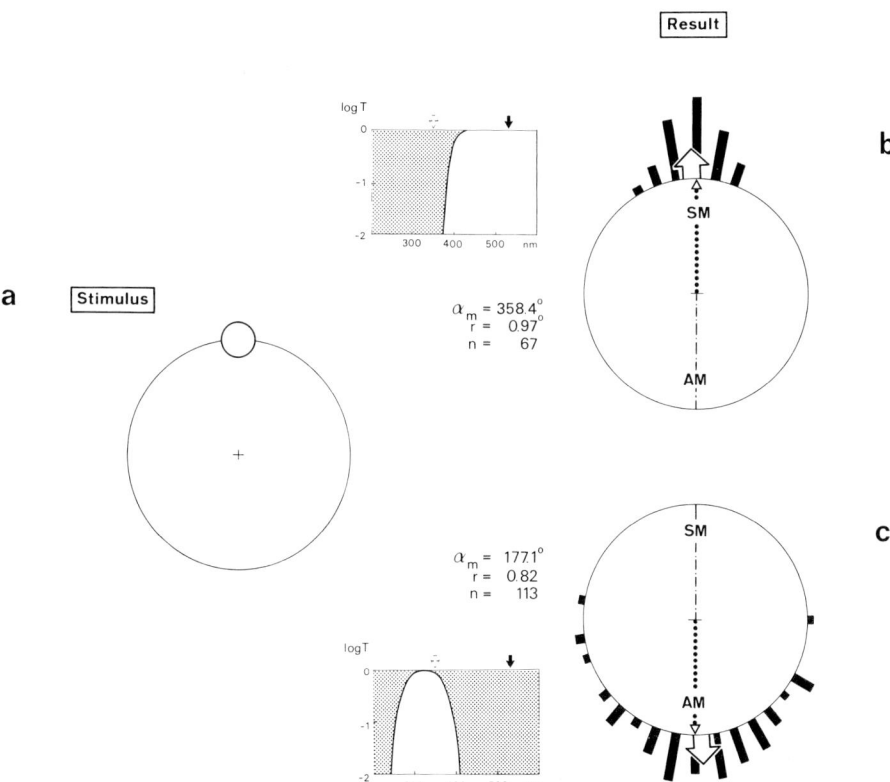

Fig. 13: Bees are presented with an unpolarized beam of green *(b)* or ultraviolet *(c)* light (diameter 10°, elevation 60°). In the first case they take the unpolarized stimulus for the sun, in the second for a celestial point lying anywhere within the anti-solar half of the sky. Note that in plotting the data the convention used in this and the following figures differs from the one used in the preceding figures. The *dotted line* with the *small white arrow* marks the direction in which the bees are expected to dance if they assume the stimulus to lie along the solar *(b)* or anti-solar *(c)* meridian. *Insets:* Spectral transmission *(T)* of the filters used. The black and white arrows point to the sensitivity peaks of the bee's green and ultraviolet receptors, respectively.

Fig. 14: Polarized and unpolarized beams of ultraviolet light are presented simultaneously. The unpolarized beam denoted by *UV* is positioned either to the left *(a)* or to the right *(d)* of the polarized beam ($\chi = -45°$). In the former case the bees behave as if the unpolarized beam were not present at all *(b)*, whereas in the latter case the directions of their dances scatter considerably *(e)*. In *b* and *e* the *heavily dotted line (with arrow)* indicates the direction in which the bees should dance when they refer to the -45° e-vector alone. The *lightly dotted lines (with arrows)* mark the range of dance directions expected when the bees use exclusively the unpolarized spot of ultraviolet light. Figures *c* and *f* show why the unpolarized stimulus greatly worsens the orientation towards the polarized stimulus when it is to the right *(f)* but not when it is to the left *(c)* of the polarized beam. This becomes immediately apparent if one recalls that bees expect an unpolarized patch of ultraviolet light to lie within the anti-solar rather than solar half of the sky (see Fig. 13).

unpolarized beam of ultraviolet light. This contrasts greatly to what happens in the second experiment, in which the unpolarized beam is presented to the right rather than the left of the polarized beam. As it appears, the bees are very disturbed when confronted with the latter stimulus configuration. They circle around hesitantly for long periods of time before they finally perform a waggle run. Successive waggle runs often point in different directions, and many times the course is changed even during a single waggle run. The casual observer might well get the impression that the bees are completely disoriented. When the directions of the waggle runs are finally plotted (Fig. 14 e), a peak shows up, roughly in the direction it should be in if the bee had used the -45° e-vector alone, but the angular distribution of the data is very broad covering nearly all points of the compass.

This result is perplexing at first, but once understood extremely rewarding. Do bees realize that there is any difference between the two stimulus conditions other than the mirror image symmetry? A comparison of Figs. 14 c and 14 f provides the answer. Imagine that the bees use the -45° e-vector to set their compass, i. e. to determine where the anti-solar meridian is in the sky. In the first experiment (Fig. 14c) they then would realize that the unpolarized beam of ultraviolet light lies within the anti-solar half of the sky where it really should (see Fig. 13 c). As a consequence, the unpolarized light adds nothing but redundant information. In the second experiment (Fig. 14 f), however, the stimulus condition is at variance with what the bees expect according to their celestial compass. The unpolarized beam of ultraviolet light lies outside the anti-solar half of the sky as defined by the polarized beam of light. For the bees, something must be wrong, and this explains the certain uneasiness we have observed in their behaviour. Taken at face value, the data of Fig. 14 e suggest that the bees respond alternatively to the polarized and the unpolarized beam of light, but, on closer scrutiny, one can see that more intricate interactions between the two responses are likely to occur.

One feature of Fig. 14 b deserves further comment. This is the close correspondence between this figure and Fig. 5 b. The only difference between the experiments described in the two figures is that in the one experiment (Fig. 14 a–c) an unpolarized beam of ultraviolet light is presented in addition to the -45° e-vector, whereas in the other (Fig. 5) the -45° e-vector is presented alone. The correspondence between the results of the two experiments finally assures us that bees do not interpret an unpolarized patch of ultraviolet light as lying exclusively along the anti-solar meridian. If they did, the stimulus condition shown in Fig. 14 a should introduce a certain ambiguity, because then the position of the anti-solar meridian as defined by the unpolarized beam of light would not coincide with the position of the anti-solar meridian as defined by the polarized beam of light. However, as mentioned above, no such ambiguities are observed.

In conclusion, when steering compass courses bees use spectral information in addition to e-vector information. A green spot of unpolarized light is taken for the sun, whereas an ultraviolet spot of unpolarized light is interpreted as lying anywhere whithin the anti-solar half of the sky.

3.3 Conclusion and implications

The most striking feature of the bee's celestial compass as described in this paper is its simplicity. Generally speaking, the compass consists of a green sun and an ultraviolet anti-solar half of the sky in which any particular point of the compass is further characterized by its own private e-vector orientation. The design of this compass is based on a few principal skylight features: a coarse spectral gradient extending over large parts of the sky and the more finely tuned spatial distribution of the maximally polarized e-vectors.

It is worth digressing here for the sake of perspective, to see how our data compare with those of other authors who have done similar experiments. This is particularly important since what we are finding runs counter to the prevailing view of how bees perceive and use polarized skylight. Since our first report (ROSSEL, WEHNER and LINDAUER, 1978) at least one feature of the bee's stereotyped *e-vector compass* has been confirmed by BRINES and GOULD (1979): At a given elevation above the horizon each e-vector orientation usually occurs at two azimuth positions, but bees invariably interpret either member of any such pair of e-vectors as the one farther from the sun. Beyond that rule BRINES and GOULD (1979) assume that the bees know exactly where a particular e-vector is positioned in the sky. The authors do not report that small navigational errors occur when individual e-vectors are displayed to the bees. These errors, however, are at the heart of the simple compass strategy we shall propose in the next section.

In fact, the errors exhibited by the bees under certain stimulus conditions are usually small and can be easily overlooked. We ourselves were convinced of them only after we had discovered their systematic nature by repeatedly varying the azimuthal positions of both food source and sun, and – most convincingly – by alternately presenting small patches of sky that were positioned symmetrically to the left and right of the anti-solar meridian. The latter set of experiments is especially convincing, because the error angles observed under these stimulus conditions are equal in magnitude but opposite in sign. It follows that the directions of the bees' dances induced by the two alternately presented patches of sky differ by an angle that is exactly twice as large as the individual error angle, and thus can be recognized easily even by the naked eye[12].

Apart from the difference between GOULD's and our data there is, more importantly, a major discrepancy between his and our point of view in interpreting the data. GOULD assumes that the «e-vector rule» mentioned above is an arbitrary convention applied by the bees only in the context of their dance language system of communication to ensure that both sender and receiver use the same reference system. The rule is «not necessary or even desirable for any of the vast number of social and nonsocial animals that .... lack a symbolic language» (BRINES and GOULD, 1979: 573).

In contrast, we assume that the «e-vector rule» reflects an integral and hard-wired property of the bee's navigational system used in steering compass courses in the field as well as performing recruitment dances in the hive. This is in accord with the hypothesis to be proposed shortly, that principal features of the bee's e-vector map are already laid down in the geometry of the receptor array. It is further borne out by the observation that desert ants, *Cataglyphis*, use essentially the same e-vector compass (work in preparation), but do not recruit.

With respect to *spectral cues*, EDRICH, NEUMEYER and VON HELVERSEN (1979) as well as BRINES and GOULD (1979) have reported that unpolarized spots of green or ultraviolet light are taken as the sun or the anti-solar point, respectively. Our data confirm the «green-rule», but in addition show that an unpolarized spot of ultraviolet light is expected by the bees to lie anywhere within the anti-solar half of the sky rather than exclusively along the anti-solar meridian. For statistical reasons, of course, the mean

---

[12] Long ago, VON FRISCH himself noticed that the mean dance directions of the bees sometimes did not coincide completely with the direction of the food source. However, he attributed such deviations to his "own inaccuracies in reading the directions of the dances rather than to the bees themselves" (personal communication). The verbal descriptions provided by him in his final summary (VON FRISCH, 1965: 393–397) are not detailed enough to allow any worthwhile generalization.

vector of the directions in which bees place an unpolarized spot of ultraviolet light would always point towards the anti-solar meridian.

Finally, let us return from this digression to the main story and inquire about some of the more general implications of our results. Certain overall impressions are inescapable. Bees operate underneath a complex celestial canopy, but do so by relying on some very simple rules. They adopt what can be called short-cut strategies or rules of thumb. Such short-cut strategies imply that under certain stimulus conditions navigational errors must occur – and, indeed, they do. Actually, it was from these errors that our concept of the bee's stereotyped celestial map was derived in the first place.

In the open, one usually does not observe such errors: first, because the errors only show up under certain stimulus conditions, and second, because the insect has at its disposal a number of back-up systems drawing upon non-celestial cues such as landmarks and including an efficient searching strategy when getting lost. What appears to us as unerring precision in an insect's foraging or homing path is in fact the result of some rather simple navigational rules, each relying on approximate rather than exact solutions of the underlying navigational problem and thus sacrificing absolute precision for a workable neural strategy (WEHNER, 1983). With respect to the bee's celestial compass, what is this neural strategy?

4 Model and neurobiological evidence: Scanning the sky

Until now we have been concerned with the question of where in the sky the bee expects any particular e-vector to occur. What resulted was the bee's stereotyped celestial compass. Next we ask, what does this compass mean in physiological terms. Where does it reside within the hardware of the bee's visual system, and how is it read and used?

4.1 The long-held view

It has been proposed by VON FRISCH (1965) and many later workers in this field that bees first determine the orientations of individual e-vectors available in the sky, and then use some knowledge about the celestial e-vector patterns to infer their compass course from the individually determined e-vector orientations. BRINES and GOULD (1979), for example, argue that a bee dancing on a horizontal comb and being provided with a single e-vector as the only navigational cue would first determine the orientation of the e-vector and then resort to memory information about the celestial pattern last seen as well as to a set of dance language conventions to avoid potential ambiguities. According to this concept, two separate questions have usually been asked. First, how does the bee determine the orientation of individual e-vectors in the sky, and second, how does it infer the position of the sun from a given e-vector or set of e-vectors?

By far the lion's share of recent publicity concerning the bee's e-vector compass has focused on the first question. Therefore it may seem strange that this fundamental topic should be discussed so late in this chapter, but at the time of this writing no agreed explanation is available on how bees solve this problem.

Nevertheless, some bits of information are at hand. We know from behavioural work done many years ago in both bees and ants (DUELLI and WEHNER, 1973; VON HELVERSEN and EDRICH, 1974) that it is only the ultraviolet type of receptor that mediates the analysis of polarized skylight. In the bee's eye the polarization sensitivity of such ultraviolet receptors reaches values as high as 10 (LABHART, 1980; WEHNER and BERNARD, 1981). We further know, as especially shown in this paper, that in a given patch of sky the orientation of the e-vector is detected independently of variations in intensity and degree of polarization. To accomplish this task three variables must be taken into account: e-vector orientation, degree of polarization, and radiant intensity. As a consequence, a set of three analysers (polarization-sensitive ultraviolet receptors), each characterized by its own analyser (microvillar) direction, is necessary to determine the orientation of an e-vector instantaneously. Alternatively, if the analysers are allowed to rotate about their optical axes, so that sequential readings can be taken, one analyser suffices for unambiguous e-vector detection (KIRSCHFELD, 1972; BERNARD and WEHNER, 1977).

In the strict sense mentioned above neither condition seems to be met in the bee's eye. Sets of ultraviolet receptors exhibiting three different microvillar directions have not yet been found either in individual ommatidia or in groups of adjacent ommatidia[13]. On the other hand, photoreceptors do not rotate within the eye. Nevertheless, as the foregoing suggests, bees are indeed able to rely on the orientation of the e-vector independently of the dedegree of polarization and the radiant intensity. Where do we go from here? In such complicated circumstances there is bound to be a certain uneasiness about the traditional way of posing the principal question. Thus, let us challenge the long-held view outlined above and entertain a new approach.

4.2 A new approach

The inconclusive nature of the neuroanatomical data presented at the end of the last paragraph drives home a major point: For all we know, there may be no *local* e-vector detectors[14] within the bee's visual system. However, there are *global* arrays of polarization-sensitive photoreceptors. Each individual photoreceptor is endowed with its own unique analyser direction[15], and the analyser directions of adjacent photoreceptors vary systematically. Even though a single photoreceptor ist not able to determine the orientation of an e-vector unambiguously, the whole array of photoreceptors certainly is. Just imagine what happens when the bee scans a small patch of polarized sky, i. e. turns about its vertical body axis and thus sweeps its array of retinal analysers through the patch of sky. While the bee turns, peak responses occur in that photoreceptor in which the analyser

---

[13] In all but the few specialized ommatidia located at the dorsal margin of the bee's eye there is only one polarization-sensitive photoreceptor per ommatidium. This polarization-sensitive photoreceptor is the short ninth cell. Referring to the three-channel hypothesis according to which the orientation of an e-vector is determined by the interaction of three polarization-sensitive photoreceptors (KIRSCHFELD, 1972), RIBI (1980) has claimed that the short ninth cells of adjacent ommatidia form a regular pattern of triplets each characterized by three separate microvillar directions (0° [= vertical], +40°, −40°). Other workers, however, have not been able to confirm these findings (MENZEL and SNYDER, 1974; WEHNER and MEYER, 1981). Furthermore, as will be shown later (p. 44), the parts of the eye for which such triplets of analysers have been described by RIBI (1980), are not at all able to detect the polarization of skylight.

[14] A *local e-vector detector* is defined as a local set of polarization-sensitive photoreceptors (e-vector analysers) that allows for detecting instantaneously and unambiguously the orientation of an e-vector.

[15] The *analyser direction* of a polarization-sensitive photoreceptor is the direction of maximum sensitivity for linearly polarized light: Maximum responses occur within the photoreceptor when light is polarized parallel to its analyser direction. In all rhabdomeric photoreceptors studied so far the analyser direction coincides with the microvillar direction of the rhabdomere. (unless the photoreceptor is twisted).

(microvillar) direction coincides with the orientation of the e-vector present in the patch of sky. This strategy sounds very simple indeed, but it has snags. For the model to work the bee must be informed about the analyser direction of the photoreceptor in which the maximal response occurs. Therefore, the ultimate usefulness of any such scanning model depends largely on how the analyser directions of adjacent photoreceptors are spatially arranged within the retina, and how well certain geometrical aspects of the skylight patterns are reflected by the array of the retinal analysers. Until the geometrical properties of the receptor array are well documented it seems premature to attempt to formulate specific hypotheses of how the scanning model proposed above actually works. Thus let us defer the full formulation of our hypothesis until later, and first have a closer look at the bee's eye.

(i) *Neurobiology: The ommatidia at the dorsal margin of the bee's eye exhibit striking structural specialisations which can be expected to have functional consequences for the detection of polarized light.*

At the uppermost dorsal margin of the bee's eye, the photoreceptors are arranged in a way that betokens specialization. All nine photoreceptors of each ommatidium are straight and of equal length. This is in stark contrast to what occurs in the remainder of the eye, where the photoreceptors are twisted and each ommatidium contains eight long photoreceptors and a short ninth cell (for details see WEHNER, BERNARD and GEIGER, 1975; WEHNER and MEYER, 1981). All ultraviolet receptors positioned a the dorsal margin of the eye are highly sensitive to polarized light. Measured values of polarization sensitivity[16] range up to 10, or even more. In all other ommatidia of the bee's eye the only photoreceptors that are sensitive to polarized light are the short ninth cells.

The most important thing of all to grasp from an anatomical reconstruction of this specialized area of the eye is the orderly, albeit somewhat curious, layout of microvillar directions. First, in each individual ommatidium the microvilli of the three ultraviolet receptors (cells R1, R5 and R9) are arranged in a mutually perpendicular way. The directions of the microvilli of R1 and R5 coincide and run at right angles to the microvilli of R9. Second, within the retina the ommatidial sets of orthogonally arranged photoreceptors form a striking fan-shaped pattern that spreads across the entire dorsal margin of the bee's eye (for details see WEHNER, 1982; MEYER, 1984).

When this pattern is projected into visual space, it reveals some gross geometrical properties of the bee's e-vector compass. Furthermore, as we have seen before, the bee's e-vector compass is based on the most prominent feature of skylight polarization – the distribution of the maximally polarized e-vectors. Taken together, these findings are extremely interesting, because they might imply that the bee's retina shares some important geometrical properties with the celestial patterns of polarization.

The structural and functional specilizations described so far[17] raise the intriguing question whether the ommatidia at the dorsal margin of the bee's eye are specialized for the

---

[16] Polarization sensitivity is defined as the sensitivity to light polarized parallel to the microvilli divided by the sensitivity to light polarized perpendicularly to the microvilli.

[17] In addition, there are other specializations that characterize the dorsal margin of the bee's eye. They refer to both the optics overlying the photoreceptors (MEYER and LABHART, 1981; WEHNER, 1982) and the visual neuropiles to which the photoreceptors project (MEYER, in press). Structural specializations similar to the ones described here for bees have been reported for ants (WEHNER, 1982), flies (WUNDERER and SMOLA, 1982; HARDIE, 1984), moths (MEINECKE, 1981) and crickets (BURGHAUSE, 1979; AEPLI et al., in press). A comparison between flies and bees is especially interesting because these two groups of insects differ strikingly in the structure of their rhabdoms,

detection of polarized skylight and, more specifically, whether the geometry of the fan-shaped receptor array tells us something about how this is done. Our curiosity was aroused even more by the fact that all specializations mentioned above were confined to an extremely small fraction of the bee's retina. The dorsal marginal ommatidia contribute 2.5 percent of the in total 5'600 ommatidia of the worker bee's eye. One may question whether such a small number of photoreceptors is really sufficient to handle and use all e-vector information available in the sky. On the other hand, it seems difficult to escape the conclusion that the geometrical similarities that exist between receptor array and skylight pattern are more than sheer coincidence. Furthermore, the fact that at the dorsal margin of the bee's eye each ommatidium contains two mutually perpendicular (crossed) analysers is clearly in favour of the view that this small marginal part of the eye has been shaped by natural selection to provide the bee with high-contrast e-vector signals. The reason behind this argument is that polarization-sensitivity can be enhanced by antagonistically comparing the outputs of two mutually perpendicular analysers (WATERMAN, 1981; WEHNER, 1982). Recent intracellular recordings from specialized marginal photoreceptors of the fly have shown that negative electrical interactions between orthogonally arranged ultraviolet receptors are likely to occur (HARDIE, 1984). Nevertheless, neurophysiological data and theoretical considerations are good as far as they go, but convincing evidence can be provided only by investigating the bee's behaviour. This is the topic to be discussed next.

(ii) *Behaviour: The ommatidia at the dorsal margin of the bee's eye are necessary for the detection of the polarized light in the sky.*

To test the hypothesis outlined in the preceding section the first crucial experiment to be performed is to anaesthetize a bee, paint out the specialized ommatidia at the dorsal margins of both its eyes, and let it dance again within the translucent Plexiglass dome. In the experiments described in Fig. 15 a a single beam of polarized ultraviolet light is displayed. When the specialized ommatidia of the two eyes have been occluded, the bees are no longer able to detect the e-vector. Instead, they behave as if the stimulus were an *unpolarized* beam of ultraviolet light, and place it anywhere within the anti-solar half of the sky (Fig. 15 c). This is immediately apparent from a comparison of Fig. 15 c and Fig. 13 c. In the latter case the beam of ultraviolet light is actually unpolarized, but the results of the two experiments are virtually the same. A number of additional experiments including those in which bees can view the sky only with the dorsal marginal ommatidia of their eyes (WEHNER, 1982; WEHNER and STRASSER, in prep.) are all in accord with the conclusion that these specialized ommatidia are indeed necessary for the detection of polarized skylight and thus comprise what can readily be called the POL area of the bee's eye.

which are open or fused, respectively. Yet the specializations of the rhabdoms that occur at the dorsal margin of the eye are strikingly similar. To make the point, let us briefly refer to the fly's eye. At the dorsal margin of the eye, the rhabdomeres of receptor cells R7 and R8 are greatly enlarged in diameter, reduced in length, and do not twist. Thus, high polarization sensitivity is to be expected, and has indeed been found (HARDIE, 1984). Furthermore, in contrast to the remainder of the eye in which R7 is the only type of ultraviolet receptor, at the dorsal margin of the fly's eye R7 and R8 are ultraviolet receptors. Due to this additional property R7 and R8 are similar in all respects except for their (mutually perpendicular) analyser directions. This makes such pairs of cells ideal input channels to any system used in the analysis of polarized light.

Finally, one example should be mentioned that looks like the exception to the rule. It is the water bug *Notonecta*. In this insect mutually perpendicular ultraviolet receptors occur in the ventral rather than dorsal part of the eye. However, when flying from one pond to another, *Notonecta* uses polarized light produced by reflections from water surfaces to decide where to descend and plunge into the water (SCHWIND, 1984).

Given this crucial role that the uppermost dorsal part of the eye plays in skylight vision, it may come as a surprise that bees are well oriented even when the POL areas of their eyes have been painted out – provided that large parts of the sky are available. We have already seen that bees treated this way can use the hue of colour to decide whether a small unpolarized stimulus belongs to the solar meridian or the anti-solar half of the sky (Fig. 13). Now, if we display to the bees the entire upper half of the sky (Fig. 3 b), the bees are oriented nearly as precisely as the controls in which the POL areas have been left open. In another experiment, a strip-like window, 90° wide and 10° high, is opened within the wall of the Plexiglass dome. In this case, the bees select the correct compass course when the

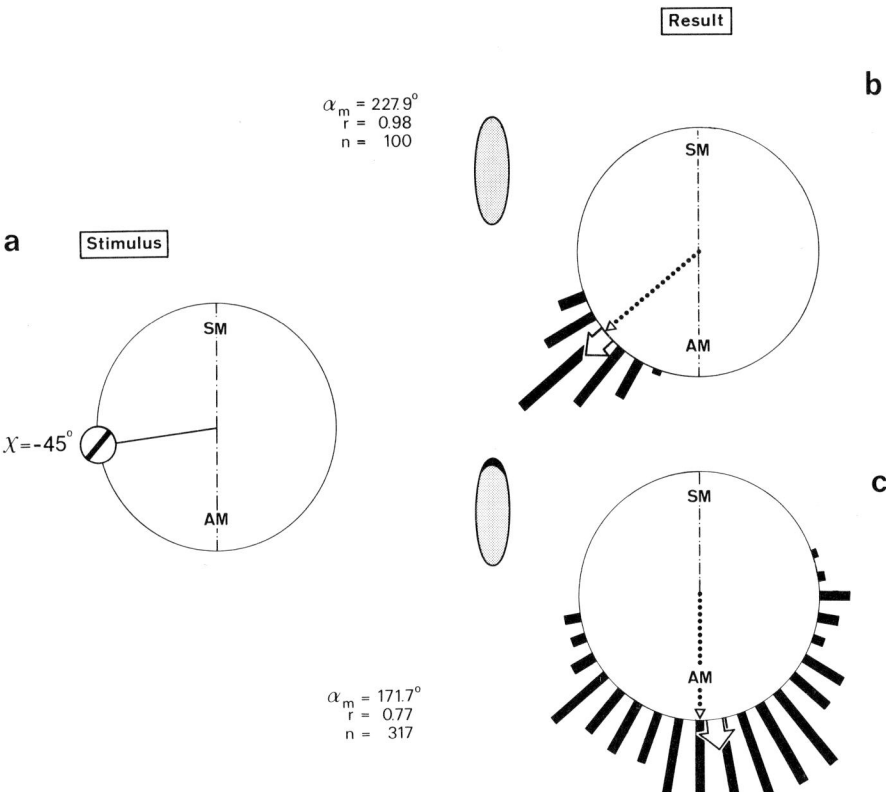

Fig. 15: Specialized ommatidia at the dorsal margin of the bee's eye are necessary for the detection of polarized skylight. In the present experiment, the stimulus is a polarized beam of ultraviolet light (a). The experimental data (black bars) plotted in b and c show where the bees expect the stimulus (a) to occur in the sky. The controls (b) behave as is to be expected if they use their stereotyped e-vector compass and place the −45° e-vector accordingly. Actually, the data are the same as the ones shown in Fig. 5. On the other hand, the bees in which the specialized ommatidia at the dorsal margins of the eyes have been painted out (c) place the stimulus anywhere within the anti-solar half of the sky. This means that they take it for an unpolarized patch of ultraviolet light (compare Fig. 13c). Conclusion: The ommatidia outside the uppermost dorsal part of the eye do not detect the polarization of light. They are used to interpret a celestial stimulus on the basis of its hue of colour.

skylight window is centred about the anti-solar meridian, but deviate by 45° to the left or right, when the sky-light window is shifted by 45° to the left or right, respectively. Obviously, they resort to spectral cues in the sky. If they had used the e-vector pattern available in the strip-like window, their orientation errors would have been much smaller than 45° (compare e. g. Fig. 12). In the mean, the bees with the uppermost dorsal ommatidia painted out take the centre of the patch of sky positioned to the left or right of the anti-solar meridian for the anti-solar meridian itself.

These and similar experiments are described and discussed in detail by ROSSEL and WEHNER (in press). What they show is that the uppermost dorsal part of the eye is necessary for the detection of polarized skylight (POL area). The remainder of the dorsal part of the eye is able to exploit spectral cues in the sky. The latter cues, however, are conveniently reliable only when large patches of the sky are available and when such large patches include the symmetry line of the skylight patterns.

(iii) *Model: Bees determine the position of the solar or anti-solar meridian by sweeping the POL areas of their eyes through the celestial e-vector pattern.*

Armed with the neurobiological and behavioural data just described, we now propose a model in which the POL area of the bee's eye is used in a rather direct way to determine the position of the solar or anti-solar meridian in the sky.

What information does the POL area of the eye extract from the celestial e-vector patterns? We had started with the conjecture, however vague, that understanding the receptor array within the POL area will go part of the way of understanding how the bee's celestial compass might work. Now that we have shown that this part of the eye is indeed necessary for analyzing polarized skylight, it is time to consider this possibility in greater detail.

As proposed earlier (p. 42), the bee could determine the orientation of an e-vector by sweeping its array of retinal analysers through the e-vector and detecting in which analyser (photoreceptor) the peak response occurs. Recall, however, that there is a problem. In order to read the orientation of the e-vector from the peak response, the bee must somehow know what the orientation of the analyser is within which the peak response occurs. It must further know where this e-vector is positioned in the sky with respect to the solar meridian. The whole problem could be solved most elegantly, if the geometry of the array of analysers mimicked the geometry of the celestial e-vector pattern to be analyzed. In the following, we shall propose a model eye in which this condition is met.

In the model eye, the spatial layout of the receptor array is assumed to match the spatial layout of the maximally polarized e-vectors in the sky. This is not a completely arbitrary assumption. We had seen that bees expect any e-vector to occur in its position of maximum polarization, and beyond that we had argued that within the POL area of the bee's eye the retinal array of ultraviolet receptors[18] shares some principal geometrical properties with the celestial array of the maximally polarized e-vectors. For our model to work, the bee must scan the sky with its model array of photoreceptors, and associate the occurrence

---

[18] For the sake of simplicity, we refer only to one analyser direction per ommatidium. Actually there are two (see p. 43), but the model works even if there were only one. Two mutually perpendicular analysers that interact antagonistically merely enhance the modulation of the signal that is mediated by a single analyser. Of course, such antagonistic interactions are an important improvement of the system, but they are not essential for understanding the rationale behind our scanning model.

of peak responses with being aligned with the solar or anti-solar meridian. To exemplify this point, let us select three stimulus conditions, which have been used before in the behavioural experiments, and discuss the bee's behaviour in terms of the scanning strategy proposed above.

First, the bee views a small patch of sky in which the e-vector is in its position of maximum polarization. In this stimulus condition, peak responses occur whenever the bee is aligned exactly with the solar or anti-solar meridian. This is because the array of analysers matches the celestial distribution of the maximally polarized e-vectors, and in the experiment described the e-vector is actually presented in its position of maximum polarization. Therefore, the bee can correctly assume that it faces the solar or anti-solar meridian whenever it experiences a peak response. No navigational errors should occur. Indeed, none have been observed.

Why do peak responses occur when the bee faces either the solar or the anti-solar meridian rather than only one of the two meridians? The reason for this ambiguity is that within the bee's receptor array each analyser direction occurs twice: once in the left (right) eye and once again in the diametrically opposite position in the right (left) eye. Owing to this peculiarity two peak responses are elicited whenever the bee performs a full turn

Celestial e-vector gradient	Retinal array of analysers (model)
Spatial distribution of maximally polarized e-vectors in the sky. *AM* anti-solar meridian, *SM* solar meridian. Compare Figs. 7c and 10b.	Spatial distribution of analyser (microvillar) directions within the retina. At the dorsal margin of the bee's eye (POL area) the microvilli of the ultraviolet receptors are arranged in a way similar to that shown here. *L, R* left and right visual field, respectively.

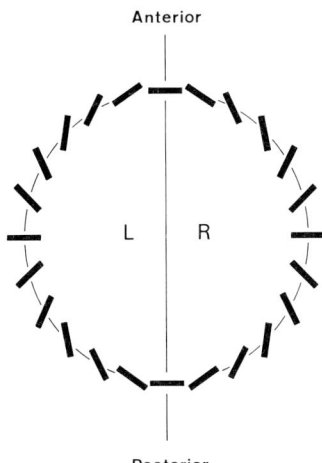

a   b

Fig. 16: Scanning model. When the model bee rotates about its vertical body axis and thus sweeps its array of analysers *(b)* through the sky *(a)*, peak responses occur whenever the bee is aligned with the solar or anti-solar meridian. A simple rule helps solve the ambiguity: When the peak response occurs in the anterior or posterior part of the visual field, the bee faces the anti-solar or solar meridian, respectively. How such a scanning system can be used as a celestial compass is described in detail in the text.

(scannning cycle). As our behavioural data suggest, bees use a very simple rule to solve this ambiguity. They associate peak responses invariably with the anti-solar meridian. Thus, when they experience a peak response in the anterior half of the visual field, they assume themselves to be facing the antisolar meridian, but when the peak response occurs in the posterior half of the visual field, they assume that they have the anti-solar meridian in their back and thus face the solar meridian. This simple rule applies to all but the vertical e-vectors. As the vertical analyser directions occur in the bee's lateral field of view, exactly at right angles to the forward and backward direction, the bee cannot distinguish the solar from the anti-solar meridian when it is confronted with a vertical e-vector alone. As a consequence, it orients in two preferred directions with one lying diametrically opposite to the other (Fig. 9).

Second, the bee views a small patch of sky in which the e-vector is not in its position of maximum polarization. Again, the bee while scanning the sky assumes that it is aligned with the solar or anti-solar meridian whenever a peak response occurs, but in this case the bee is mistaken. As the bee's receptor array reflects the celestial pattern of e-vectors only when the e-vectors are in their positions of maximum polarization, errors must occur whenever the e-vectors are not in this position, as is usually the case. Thus, the position of the solar or anti-solar meridian as assumed by the dancing bee deviates from the actual position of the corresponding meridian in the sky, and the directions of the bee's dances deviate by exactly that amount from the direction of the food source (Fig. 5). It was on the basis of these orientation errors that the bee's stereotyped e-vector compass was derived originally.

Third, the bee views a large part of the blue sky. Our hypothesis implies that even in this situation, with many e-vectors being provided, a bee is bound to use its simple scanning strategy. Of course, of the many e-vectors present in the patch of sky only a few will be in their positions of maximum polarization and only these few will simultaneously match the bee's receptor array whenever the bee faces the solar or anti-solar meridian. Any other e-vector will induce a peak response when the bee is not aligned exactly with the solar or anti-solar meridian, and thus will indicate an incorrect position of the corresponding reference meridian. How does the bee cope with this potentially ambiguous situation caused by the multitude of possible solar or anti-solar meridians? Our model proposes that the bee has no means of sorting out what peak response is induced by a maximally polarized e-vector and what by another one. A simple rule to apply is to take the mean of all possible positions of the solar or anti-solar meridian, and this is what the bee seems to do. In all our experiments in which bees were presented simultaneously with a number of e-vectors, the error angle exhibited by the bees coincided with the arithmetical mean of the error angles induced by each individual e-vector alone (see Figs. 11 and 12).

To sum up, in the three examples described above, as well as in all other experiments performed so far, the bee's behaviour is consonant with the scanning model. Although this model has been sketched out here rather hastily, it should have been possible for the reader to grasp the gist of the argument and to discover the rationale behind it. At the heart of the hypothesis is the assumption that while scanning the sky the bee translates e-vector orientations into temporal modulations of receptor responses. All that the bee derives from these responses is *when* during a scanning cycle it faces the solar (or anti-solar) meridian. A simple way of accomplishing this task is to use an array of analysers that, to a certain degree, reflects the spatial layout of the celestial e-vector patterns. In our model we have assumed that the array of analysers mimics the celestial distribution of the maximally polarized e-vectors. The gross features of the peculiar fan-shaped receptor array within the POL area of the bee's eye support this assumption.

In this context, a further peculiarity of the POL area must be mentioned, which might put the final piece of evidence in place. The visual fields of the photoreceptors at the dorsal margin of the eye are exceedingly wide but the polarization sensitivities of the photoreceptors do not decrease with off-axis stimulation (LABHART, 1980). The wide visual fields are mainly due to structural specializations of the corneal lenses, which contain dense arrays of rugged-walled pore canals widely scattering the incoming light (MEYER and LABHART, 1981; AEPLI, LABHART and MEYER, in press.). Consequently, the ultraviolet receptors of the POL area act as wide-field e-vector analysers. At first glance, the low acuity of this part of the eye seems to be a rather severe constraint on the general utility of the POL area as a means of deriving spatial information from the sky. On closer scrutiny, however, this may be just an interesting example of a constraint being turned into a virtue. First, the large visual fields of photoreceptors considerably increase the area of the sky that can be scanned by the rather limited number of POL ommatidia at the dorsal margin of the eye. Furthermore, wide-field sampling may be advantageous not only in rendering e-vector signals less susceptible to disturbances caused, for example, by clouds or the canopy of vegetation, but also in averaging out e-vector orientations. Finally, if wide-field sampling is accomplished by a corresponding degree of neural pooling, spatial irregularities within the array of receptors dwindle in importance. In any event, a wide-field, low-acuity detector system seems to be well suited for deriving *global* spatial information from the sky – such as information concerning the position of the solar or anti-solar meridian.

Once the bee has aligned itself with the solar or anti-solar meridian, it must turn about its vertical body axis until it faces the direction of the compass course intended. To accomplish this task it could resort to a number of strategies. Only one possibility shall be mentioned and discussed briefly: The bee could use any distant visual cue to select its final compass course.

To illustrate this point, take our basic experiment (Figs. 4 and 5) in which a single spot of polarized light is displayed within the otherwise featureless surroundings of the Plexiglass dome. The compass course intended by the bee is 15° to the left of the anti-solar meridian. First, the bee would align itself with, say, the anti-solar meridian by turning around and tuning in for peak responses to occur within the POL areas of its eyes. It is here that errors will occur (unless the e-vector presented to the bee is in its position of maximum polarization). Then, having aligned itself with the anti-solar meridian – or what it thinks is the anti-solar meridian – the bee must turn so as to shift the retinal image of the spot by 15° to the right, and lock on to it. Of course, outside the sterile visual world of our Plexiglass dome, there are usually many more visual cues available for selecting the final compass course than the single beam of light displayed in our basic experiment: Clouds, isolated patches of sky, or distant landmarks may be used. Setting its compass course by referring to such cues is very similar to what a bee would usually do when it uses the sun as a reference cue.

As we have seen before, there is no need for fine grain vision in accomplishing the first step of the task. Indeed, the POL area exhibits low visual acuity. However, fine grain vision is certainly required for accomplishing the second step of the task. Such fine grain vision is provided only by ommatidia lying outside the POL area. As the POL area of each eye looks contralaterally, it shares a common field of view with parts of the contralateral eye that lie outside the POL area and thus exhibit the high visual acuity afforded. Note, however, that in principle for setting the final compass course any non-POL part of the eye could be used, irrespective of whether it belongs to the monocular or binocular field of view.

A final point should be mentioned. Once the bee has selected its proper compass course, it again could use the pattern of polarized light in the sky for maintaining this course. The reason is that marked response modulations occur within the retinal image of the celestial e-vector pattern whenever the bee deviates from a straight course (see the sequence of false colour images in Wehner, 1982).

5 Epilogue: Speculation built on fact

What we have proposed in this paper is a rather simple solution to the long-standing puzzle of how bees analyse the polarized light in the sky. The most thought-provoking feature of our hypothesis is that bees are not able to determine e-vector orientations *locally* and *instantaneously* in any particular part of the sky. Instead, bees seem to use the celestial polarization merely to determine, in a rather direct way, the position of the solar (or anti-solar) meridian, and seem to do so by applying some kind of *global scanning* strategy.

More specifically, our hypothesis implies that in deriving compass information from the sky, bees use an array of photoreceptors within which the microvillar orientations vary systematically, and sweep this array of photoreceptors through the celestial e-vector pattern. This hypothesis is substantiated by our finding that a specialized small area at the dorsal margin of the bee's eye, termed POL area, is necessary for detecting polarized skylight, and that within this POL area the receptor array shares some principal geometrical properties with the e-vector patterns in the sky. Based on these observations, a model bee is designed, which uses e-vector patterns as a compass by following a rather simple rule: turn around, and whenever peak responses occur in the POL area of the eye, know that the solar (or anti-solar) meridian is straight ahead. While stationary, the bee would not know *where* the solar (or anti-solar) meridian is positioned in the sky, but while turning it would be able to determine *when* it faces the solar (or anti-solar) meridian.

Of course, our model owes its simplicity to its limitations. Unlike physicists, bees cannot determine the orientation of any arbitrary e-vector. They can derive useful information only from e-vector patterns that are designed according to the rules of Rayleigh scattering. This is because some principal design features of their receptor arrays have been adopted from these patterns. As receptor arrays are fixed, but celestial e-vector patterns are not (they vary with the elevation of the sun), navigational errors must occur under a variety of stimulus conditions – and they do exactly as predicted. In our model bee, however, they are minimized since we have allowed evolution to be intelligent: the retinal array of analysers mimics the most prominent feature of skylight polarization, that is the spatial distribution of the maximally polarized e-vectors. All behavioural data we have obtained so far under different experimental conditions are in full accord with the behaviour of the model bee.

We note in passing that our hypothesis disposes of the possibility that bees perceive polarized skylight as an extra quality of light. It is sufficient to assume that bees while scanning the sky translate e-vector orientations into modulations of perceived ultraviolet intensity (or saturation). Besides their polarization-sensitive ultraviolet channels bees use polarization-insensitive channels to read spectral information from the sky. The intriguing question remains as to whether and where along the visual pathway the polarization-sensitive and the polarization-insensitive channels interact.

Finally, a cautionary note must be added. The hypothesis outlined above is included in this chapter as the current best bet about how bees deduce compass information from the sky, not as received fact. Further research over the next few years will certainly shape and perhaps modify our present ideas. For example, the extent to which the array of receptors at the dorsal margin of the bee's eye really matches the bee's e-vector compass that we had deduced from our behavioural data, has still to be determined. For the proposed model to work, however, a complete match is not required. Another question relates to possible interactions between the dorsal marginal receptors (POL area) and the remainder of the dorsal retina. Of special interest is the contribution of those parts of the dorsal retina that share a common field of view with the POL area of the contralateral eye.

Notwithstanding many pieces of evidence that are still missing, the hypothesis meets the primary criterion of a successful explanation. It coordinates a series of observations that would otherwise remain unconnected and, in many cases, downright peculiar. Finally, the hypothesis is simple rather than complex and contrived. It implies that the bee's behaviour results from a set of simple rules deduced from and operating within a complex world.

For obvious reasons we have entitled our analysis of the bee's celestial compass a case study in behavioural neurobiology. It was only by keeping in line with von Frisch's early approach of combining behavioural studies alongside neurobiology that the bee's compass strategy could have been unravelled. In fact, we had discovered many optical, anatomical, and neurophysiological details of the ommatidia at the uppermost dorsal margin of the bee's eye long before the behavioural data enabled us to interpret these neurological idiosyncrasies in functional terms and to establish the concept of the bee's «POL area». Therefore let us conclude by referring to how the neurobiologist Gordon Shepherd (1983) has recently paraphrased to the point the well-known aphorism of the evolutionary biologist Ttheodosius Dobzhanski: «Nothing in neurobiology makes sense – except in the light of behaviour».

Appendix

Symbols and definitions used in the figures of this chapter.

(a) E-vector presented to the dancing bees either within a patch of natural blue sky (Fig. 3c) or by means of an artificially polarized beam of ultraviolet light (Fig. 3d).

(b) Artificially produced e-vector presented at an elevation at which it does not occur in the natural sky at the time of day at which the experiment is performed.

(c) E-vector shown at the azimuth position at which it occurs within the bee's e-vector compass (Fig. 6, inner circle; Fig. 7a).

(d) Direction of food source (F).

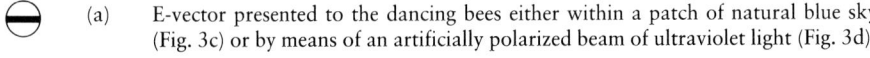
(e) Direction in which the bee expects the food source to occur when using the compass strategy outlined in this paper. This direction is not denoted by a separate symbol when (d) and (e) coincide.

(f) Mean direction of orientation as determined experimentally (α_m).

(g) Error angle (ε) observed in the experiments.

(h) Direction in which the bees expect a given celestial cue (e. g. a particular e-vector orientation, the solar or the anti-solar meridian) to occur in the sky. In Figs. 13–15 the directions of the bees' dances *(black bars)* are plotted so as to coincide with the *dotted line* when the bees behave according to the expectation, e. g. assume the stimulus to lie along the solar or anti-solar meridian, or in any other direction as predicted from the bee's celestial compass.

—·—·—·— (i)   Symmetry plane of the celestial patterns. It includes the solar and anti-solar meridian.

AM anti-solar meridian, F direction of food source, N north, n number of waggle runs recorded, r length of mean orientation vector (for statistical significance see Batschelet, 1981), SM solar meridian, α_m direction of mean orientation vector, ε error angle, η scattering angle, χ e-vector orientation (for conventions see Figs. 1 b and 2 b).

References

Aepli, F., Labhart, T., Meyer, E. P.: Structural specializations of the cornea and retina at the dorsal rim of the compound eyes in hymenopteran insects. In press.

Batschelet, E. (1981): Circular Statistics in Biology. Academic Press, London, New York.

Bernard, G. D., Wehner, R. (1977): Functional similarities between polarization vision and color vision. Vision Res., 17, 1019–1028.

Bisetzky, A. R. (1957): Die Tänze der Bienen nach einem Fußweg zum Futterplatz. Z. vergl. Physiol., 40, 264–288.

Brines, M. L., Gould, J. L. (1979): Bees have rules. Science, 206, 571–573.

Brines, M. L., Gould, J. L. (1982): Skylight polarization patterns and animal orientation. J. exp. Biol., 96, 69–91.

Burghause, F. (1979): Die strukturelle Spezialisierung des dorsalen Augenteils der Grillen (Orthoptera, Grylloidea). Zool. Jb. Physiol., 83, 502–525.

Cartwright, B. A., Collett, T. S. (1983): Landmark learning in bees. Experiments and models. J. Comp. Physiol., 151, 521–543.

Crozier, W. J., Mangelsdorf, A. F. (1924): A note on the relative photosensory effect of polarized light. J. gen. Physiol., 6, 703–709.

Duelli, P., Wehner, R. (1973): The spectral sensitivity of polarized light orientation in Cataglyphis bicolor (Formicidae, Hymenoptera). J. Comp. Physiol., 86, 37–53.

Dyer, F. C., Gould, J. L. (1983): Honey bee navigation. Amer. Scientist, 71, 587–597.

Edrich, W., Neumeyer, C., Helversen, O. von (1979): «Anti-sun orientation» of bees with regard to a field of ultraviolet light. J. Comp. Physiol., 134, 151–157.

Frisch, K. von (1949): Die Polarisation des Himmelslichts als orientierender Faktor bei den Tänzen der Bienen. Experientia, 5, 142–148.

Frisch, K. von (1965): Tanzsprache und Orientierung der Bienen. Springer, Berlin, Heidelberg, New York.

Glas, H. W. van der (1976): Polarization induced colour patterns: A model of the perception of the polarized skylight by insects. II. Experiments with direction trained dancing bees, Apis mellifera. Neth. J. Zool., 26, 383–413.

Glas, H. W. van der (1980): Orientation of bees, Apis mellifera, to unpolarized colour patterns, simulating the polarized zenith skylight pattern. J. Comp. Physiol., 139, 225–241.

Gould, J. L. (1980): Sun compensation in bees. Science, 207, 545–547.

Hardie, R. C. (1984): Properties of photoreceptors R7 and R8 in dorsal marginal ommatidia in the compound eyes of Musca and Calliphora. J. Comp. Physiol. A, 154, 157–165.

Helversen, O. von, Edrich, W. (1974): Der Polarisationsempfänger im Bienenauge: ein Ultraviolettrezeptor. J. Comp. Physiol., 94, 33–47.

Kirschfeld, K. (1972): Die notwendige Anzahl von Rezeptoren zur Bestimmung der Richtung des elektrischen Vektors linear polarisierten Lichtes. Z. Naturforsch., 27 c, 578–579.

Kirschfeld, K., Lindauer, M., Martin, H. (1975): Problems of menotactic orientation according to the polarized light of the sky. Z. Naturforsch., 30 c, 88–90.

Labhart, T. (1980): Specialized photoreceptors at the dorsal rim of the honeybee's compound eye: polarizational and angular sensitivity. J. Comp. Physiol., 141, 19–30.

Meinecke, C. C. (1981): The fine structure of the compound eye of the African armyworm moth, *Spodoptera exempta* (Lepidoptera: Noctuidae). Cell Tissue Res., *216*, 333–347.

Menzel, R., Snyder, A. W. (1974): Polarized light detection in the bee, *Apis mellifera*. J. Comp. Physiol., *88*, 247–270.

Meyer, E. P.: Retrograde labeling of photoreceptors in different regions of the compound eyes of bees and ants. J. Neurocytol. In press.

Meyer, E. P., Labhart, T. (1981): Pore canals in the cornea of a functionally specialized area of the honey bee's compound eye. Cell Tissue Res., *216*, 491–501.

Ribi, W. A. (1980): New aspects of polarized light detection in the bee in view of non-twisting rhabdomeric structures. J. Comp. Physiol., *137*, 281–285.

Rossel, S., Wehner, R. (1982): The bee's map of the e-vector pattern in the sky. Proc. Natl. Acad. Sci. USA, *79*, 4451–4455.

Rossel, S., Wehner, R. (1984): How bees analyse the polarization patterns in the sky. Experiments and model. J. Comp. Physiol. A, *154*, 607–615.

Rossel, S., Wehner, R.: Celestial orientation in bees: The use of spectral cues. J. Comp. Physiol. A. In press.

Rossel, S., Wehner, R., Lindauer, M. (1978): E-vector orientation in bees. J. Comp. Physiol., *125*, 1–12.

Santschi, F. (1923): L'orientation sidérale des fourmis, et quelques considérations sur leurs différentes possibilités d'orientation. I. Classification des diverses possibilités d'orientation chez les fourmis. Mém. Soc. Vaud. Sci. Nat., *4*, 137–175.

Schwind, R. (1984): Evidence for true polarization vision based on a two-channel analyser system in the eye of the water bug, *Notonecta glauca*. J. Comp. Physiol. A, *154*, 53–57.

Shepherd, G. M. (1983): Neurobiology. Oxford University Press, Oxford, New York.

Stockhammer, K. (1959): Die Orientierung nach der Schwingungsrichtung linear polarisierten Lichtes und ihre sinnesphysiologischen Grundlagen. Erg. Biol., *21*, 23–56.

Verkhovskaya, I. N. (1940): L'influence de la lumière polarisée sur la phototaxis de quelques organismes. Bull. Soc. Nat. Moscou, Sect. Biol., *49*, 101–113 [in Russian, French summary].

Waterman, T. H. (1981): Polarization sensitivity. In: Handbook of Sensory Physiology, Vol. VII/6B, ed. H. Autrum, pp. 281–469. Springer, Berlin, Heidelberg, New York.

Waterman, T. H. (1984): Natural polarized light and vision. In: Photoreception and Vision in Invertebrates, ed. M. A. Ali, pp. 63–114. Plenum Press, New York.

Wehner, R. (1981): Spatial vision in arthropods. In: Handbook of Sensory Physiology, Vol. VII/6C, ed. H. Autrum, pp. 287–616. Springer, Berlin, Heidelberg, New York.

Wehner, R. (1982): Himmelsnavigation bei Insekten. Neurophysiologie und Verhalten. Neujahrsbl. Naturforsch. Ges. Zürich, *184*, 1–132.

Wehner, R. (1983): Celestial and terrestrial navigation: human strategies – insect strategies. In: Neuroethology and Behavioral Physiology, eds. F. Huber and H. Markl, pp. 366–381. Springer, Berlin, Heidelberg, New York.

Wehner, R. (1984): Astronavigation in insects. Ann. Rev. Entomol., *29*, 277–298.

Wehner, R., Bernard, G. D. (1980): Intracellular optical physiology of the bee's eye. II. Polarizational sensitivity. J. Comp. Physiol., *137*, 205–214.

Wehner, R., Lanfranconi, B. (1981): What do the ants know about the rotation of the sky? Nature (Lond.), *293*, 731–733.

Wehner, R., Meyer, E. P. (1981): Rhabdomeric twist in bees – artefact or in vivo structure? J. Comp. Physiol., *142*, 1–17.

Wehner, R., Rossel, S. (1983): Polarized light navigation in bees: use of zenith and off-zenith e-vectors. Experientia, *39*, 642.

Wehner, R., Strasser, S.: The POL area of insect eyes: behavioural experiments with bees. In prep.

Wehner, R., Bernard, G. D., Geiger, E. (1975): Twisted and non-twisted rhabdoms and their significance for polarization detection in the bee. J. Comp. Physiol., *104*, 225–245.

Wunderer, H., Smola, U. (1982): Morphological differentiation of the central visual cells R 7/8 in various regions of the blowfly eye. Tissue and Cell, *14*, 341–358.

Zolotov, V. V., Frantsevich, L. I. (1973): Orientation of bees by the polarized light of a limited area of the sky. J. Comp. Physiol., *85*, 25–36.

Fortschritte der Zoologie, Bd. 31 · Hölldobler/Lindauer (Hrsg.): Experimental Behavioral Ecology
G. Fischer Verlag · Stuttgart · New York · 1985

RANDOLF MENZEL

Learning in honey bees in an ecological and behavioral context

Freie Universität Berlin, Fachbereich Biologie, F. R. Germany

Abstract

The search strategy of a generalist pollinator such as the honey bee is controlled to a great extent by individual experience at food sources. However, both learning of the features of a food source and choice behavior of potential food sources prior to any learning is guided by «prepared search images», which result from the coevolutionary adaptations between the signals of angiosperm plants and the sensory-neural capacity of the general pollinator. «Prepared search images» are hard to prove. Spontaneous choice behavior excluding prior learning has not yet been adequately analysed. More information comes from experiments which measure associative predispositions, signal preparedness and selectivity of associations in appetitive learning experiments. Useful behavioral measures are e. g. rate of acquisition, precision of learning or correctness of learned behavior, retention, sensitivity to extinction. The first example discussed in this paper is color learning. Bees learn any color, but violet is the color learned fastest and bluish-green the one learned slowest. The differential preparedness for color learning is not related to receptor or peripheral visual integration processes, but represents a central nervous weighting function. This function is not context specific, but applies both to learning at the feeding station and at the hive entrance. Other examples discussed in this paper are: learning of color patterns and learning of odors.

Another question relates to the species-specificity of color learning. Three hymenopteran species *(Apis mellifera, Melipona quadrifasciata, Osmia bicornis)* are compared. We find small but significant differences. Again, the general learning ability in all three species is the major effect and preparedness appears as an additional tuning factor.

Two other aspects of the honey bee's learning behavior are studied with respect to the neural basis of learning and memory and their ecological constraints. Reversal learning experiments demonstrate that bees are prepared to switch to new food signals after a certain number of initial trials. Short-term memory in bees has been found to be a neural strategy of fast adaptations to changing profitability of food sources, and not as a necessary mechanism to bridge time between the learning trial and the termination of slow processes establishing long-term memory. These two examples are used to demonstrate that learning both in the short and long term range is adapted to temporal and spatial features of natural food sources. «Prepared search images» include these features as well as the external signals for recognition.

It is concluded that the neural mechanisms of learning in the bee are controlled both by a strong inherent learning ability, and by species-specific preparedness, which result from the species evolutionary history.

1 Introduction

The two sources of information controlling behavior are the phylogenetic experience encoded in the genetically controlled wiring of the nervous system and the individual experience which modulates, alters, and adds neural pathways. It is common sense for the ethologist, but seemingly a quite recent revolutionary insight for the experimental psychologist that the effect of individual experience through learning is constrained by preprogrammed («prepared») combinations of stimuli and responses. As a result of selective pressure, certain adaptive responses to commonly encountered stimuli from the environment are genetically favored. This applies both to appetitve behavior – (responses to stimuli that in the history of the species have been associated with food, water, mating, safety, or relief of discomfort), and to aversive behavior (– responses to threatening or noxious stimuli).

In insects, the balance between phylogenetic and individual experience has long been thought to be on the side of phylogenetic experience; although insects are equipped with an astonishingly complex behavioral repertoire, they have been thought to act like robots following step by their instinctive guidance. Indeed, genetically programmed behavior can reach an unbelievably high degree of sophistication in insects, but in social hymenoptera indivual learning plays an important role. When a forager bee searches for food, for example, it may fly hundreds of meters in an irregular way until finding nectar or pollen producing flowers. In its flight back to the hive, the bee takes a straight path along the shortest distance, thereby integrating all the turns and using landmarks and the sun compass for orientation (v. Frisch, 1965). Obviously, the bee must learn the position of the landmarks, its relation to the wind, and its alignment to celestal cues, but programming tells the bee which signal should be attended to and stored at which time during its flight. The sun and the polarized light pattern are instinctively used as guides by the bee, but their changes in time have to be learned (Lindauer, 1959). Stimuli immediately surrounding the food source, such as colors, odors and shapes, are learned by the individual bee, and, as we shall see, the stimuli and the associations are ranked in a programmed hierarchy. I shall call those stimuli and those associations, which rank high in this hierachy «prepared stimuli» and «prepared associations». Preparedness, then, is used in this context with a wide ethological meaning, wider than the strict sense of preparedness as used in learning theory of experimental psychology (see Menzel, et al. in press).

Color and odor learning in bees at the feeding place has been a central theme in Karl von Frisch's work from the very beginning and was so through out his long and productive life. In his first and leading paper published in 1914 («Der Farbensinn und Formensinn der Biene, Zoologische Jahrbücher) he stressed the point that all the amazing sensory and learning capacities of bees have to be understood against the background of their biological adaptations. A good part of these adaptations are the result of a 80 million years long co-evolution of bees and angiosperm plants from which they obtain their carbohydrate (nectar) and protein (pollen) diet, and for which they, in turn function as species-specific fertilizing machines. As has been pointed out many times (e. g. Free, 1970, McGregor, 1976. Faegri, van der Pijl, 1978, Kevan and Baker, 1983, Proctor, Yeo, 1983) it is the discrepancy between the foraging behavior optimal for the plant and that optimal for the pollinator that has determined the evolution of features of plants and the sensory-neural capacities of the pollinators (see table 1 for a short summary).

On the side of the bee, color and odor perception and learning ability play a crucial role in the process of mutual adaptations. It should be advantageous for the bee not only to perceive the signal sent off by the flowers but also to «know» in advance what a potential food source looks like and how it may smell. In other words, the bee may have an «innate *search image»* for flowers (KEVAN and BAKER, 1983), which, through experience, develops into a precise *learned search image*.

Honey bees flying from flower to flower follow the search strategy of a generalist pollinator, which is not genetically bound to one or a few plants, but optimizes its profit by taking advantage of its social life style and relatively long individual life time. This means, that the individual bee changes its nectar and pollen sources frequently (see SEELEY, this Vol.) always trying to get the best out of the offerings available. Too strong «innate search images» are dangerous sources of information for the guidance of choices, since they may prevent the bee from finding a potentially better food source and from learning the features of that food source for later guidance. The bee, therefore, should be capable of both selecting a flower prior to any experience because it might be a potential food source *and* it should be able to learn very quickly the features fo that flower, if it indeed turns out to be a profitable food source.

The plant is involved in this ciritcal interplay of genetically prepared and individually experienced information too, because the plant wants to be both attractive to a pollinator prior to any individual experience *and* it wants to ensure a highly preferential choice of conspecific flowers after a visit of a pollinator. It should support the bee's behavior by both using common flower features and species specific features. As many flower species compete for adaptive *and* selective pollinators, each flower species should be mainly interested in being different from other flower species and still being recognized as a potential food source before any individual learning. This strategy should then put strong selective pressure on adaptive pollinators to improve their learning capacity within a framework of expected flower features (Tab. 1). In any case, we might expect a sensitive balance between «innate search images» and general learning capacity in such a general pollinator as the honey bee.

An «innate search image» not only allows the bee to select an object as a potential food source prior to learning, but also should facilitate learning of flower-like features and help to make the choice behavior more precise after learning.

The term «search image» is used here in a pragmatic sense without too many theoretical implications about its neural correlate. The term will be used as a short expression for an inferred neural representation of a compound of stimuli in a given behavioral context which has the potential of being compared with external stimuli. The addition «innate» has to be used in an even looser sense, since there is no direct evidence for the innateness of any of the «search images» which are thought to exist prior to a learning experiment. However, there is suggestive evidence in many experiments that what will be called «innate» exists prior to individual learning. The strongest evidence is that the results are independent of the age of the experimental bees, independent of the different experience of the bees and independent of the ecological conditions (e. g. seasons), at which the experiments were carried out.

When we ask the question of whether bees apply «innate search images» in their learning behavior of food sources, we look for associative predispositions, signal preparedness and selective associations in their appetitive learning. Do bees preferentially choose certain stimuli when they are searching for a food source? Are certain stimuli learned faster as food signals and do they acquire better control over the choice behavior? If there are such prepared stimuli, are they selective with respect to the behavioral context, e. g. prepared as food signals but not as signals for the hive entrance? Are such stimuli general features of flower visiting insects or are they species specific? We shall see that learning in bees is embedded in a contextual frame work which can be well understood against the background of the ecological adaptations mentioned above. However, compared with the powerful general learning ability both at the food source and at the hive

Table 1: Summary of factors in plant – pollinator coevolution

Bee	Plant
gain as much nectar and pollen with as little investment as possible; calculate net profit; adjust changes; communicate with comrades	gain as much specific pollen transfer with as little costs as possible. Keep pollinator long on the flower to increase chance of pollen deposit

The «Generalist – strategy»:

Social bees potentially active all year around;
They adapt to changes on the nectar/pollen
market and use a strategy to optimize net profit;
Flowers compete for individually adaptive pollinators;

Perceive the signals	Mark the flowers
– location – color, color pattern – odor, odor pattern – shape – timing of food supply	– conspicuous from background (color, odor, shape, location) – different from other competing flowers especially if plants grow in sparse population
Use innate search images	Support innate search images
– to locate flowers prior to learning – to fascillitate learning – to enhance the learning effect by making it more precise – to reduce handling time at each new flower	of pollinators by – large, contrasting inflorescence – apply common «flower features» color, odor, shape, nectar guides
Learn new search images effectively and adjust quickly to changes by	Support learned search images
– rapid acquisition – short-term memory and long-term memory – low sensitivity to extinction	– make your flower different from competing flowers – offer enough reward (more on rare plants) – signal drying up of nectar/pollen supply

entrance this framework gives guidance but does not restrict it to a preprogrammed machinery.

2 How can «innate search images» and prepared associations be proved

The simplest way to demonstrate the existence of «innate search images» might be to ask a bee on her first flight out, what signals she is choosing *spontaneously* in search of a food source. Although such experiments have been attempted (Oettingen-Spielberg, 1949, Butler, 1951, Lindauer, 1952, Ludwig, cited in v. Frisch, 1965, p. 250), they are practically not feasible, because (1) too few data are collected and (2) it can not be ruled out with certainty that a given bee did not have any experience in the field before or that she is not guided on her flight by information from other hive members. The results are thus quite inconsistent. For example, v. OETTINGEN-SPIELBERG (1949) claims that scout bees prefer yellow, BUTTLER (1951) maintains that blue and yellow are equally attractive, LUDWIG (cited in v. FRISCH, 1965) found blue to be most effective. The question of choice behavior prior to any experience and communicated guidance is a very important one, but as far as I can see it has not been adequately addressed yet.

Many data can be collected in learning experiments with experienced bees, and we are, therefore, bound to use indirect behavioral measures to demonstrate preparedness of learning. Two measures have been used successfully: (1) learning rate or acquisition of learning and (2) precision of learning or correctness of learned behavior, because learning should be quicker, more effective and more accurate for prepared signals than for others. We might even expect to find extreme cases of preparedness in so far as certain signals may not be learned at all, or that only certain stimuli are associated with each other and not others (selective association). But these are by no means the only useful behavioral measures. Others are: retention function, sensitivity to extinction, interference between consecutive learning events, multireversal effects, consolidation into long-term memory, compound vs single stimulus learning, specific differences in the association of different sensory modalities, etc. Some of these measures are used in the experiments described below.

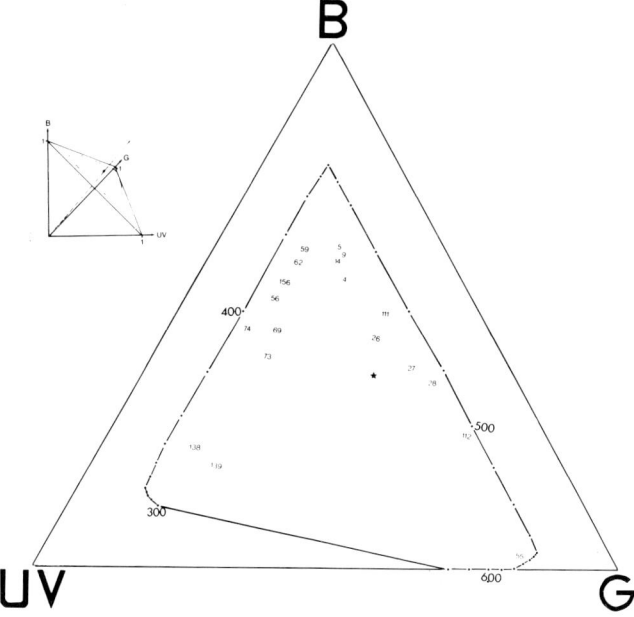

Fig. 1: The color vision of the honey bee can be appropriately described with a three-dimensional input model (see MENZEL, 1979, MENZEL and LIEKE, 1983). The three dimensions are the 3 color receptors UV, blue (B) and green (G). Their contributions define a space (upper left), in which each color is represented by a color locus. For simplicity, we refer to a two dimensional representation in a color triangle, which neglects the brightness of a color stimulus. All monochromatic colors lie along the dark line with dots showing the spectral colors at 10 nm intervals from 300 to 630 nm. The line connecting 300 and 630 nm is the purple line. The color loci of all the colors used in the experiments given in Fig. 6 and 7 are shown as numbers.

3 Bees show preparedness for learning «violet» as a flower color

Investigating preparedness for colors at the feeding place is an interesting approach to the question (v. FRISCH, 1914, MENZEL, 1967), since a lot is known about color vision in bees (AUTRUM and v. ZWEHL, 1964, DAUMER, 1956, MENZEL and BLAKERS, 1976, NEUMAYER, 1980, 1981, MENZEL, 1977, KIEN and MENZEL, 1977 a, b, HERTEL, 1980), and since the mutual adaptation of the bees' color vision and the coloration of flowers has attracted much attention (e. g. KEVAN, 1978). Color vision in bees is best described by means of a model calculation of the *color space* (Fig. 1, see MENZEL, 1977, 1979), which matches all our knowledge quite well. Bees have 3 color receptors with maxima of their spectral sensitivity functions at 350 nm, 440 nm, 540nm, respectively (Fig. 2 a). UV color

Fig. 2: Comparison of the spectral properties of color vision and color learning in bees. a. Spectral sensitivity of the 3 color receptor types (MENZEL, BLAKERS, 1976). b. Spectral threshold (dotted line) and spectral discrimination ($\Delta\lambda$) of bees in training experiment to spectral colors (v. Helversen, 1972). The left ordinate shows the relative spectral sensititity expressed for the maximal sensitivities in UV. The right ordinate shows the wavelength intervals which are separated by the bee by a criterion (70 %) of correct choices. c. Choice behavior after one reward on a spectral color λ_+) which is indicated at the abscissa. The ordinate shows the probability of choices of the trained color in a dual choice test (MENZEL, 1967). Two kinds of pretraining are used: ● three trials on an unilluminated ground glass, ○ three trials on a white illuminated ground glass. The two colors in the test situations are adjusted for each individually tested bee to induce equal choice probability (0.5) prior to training (from MENZEL, 1967).

around 360 nm appear brightest to medium-light adapted bees in a UV-free sorrounding (Fig. 2 b). Color discrimination is best for violet (around 440 nm) and bluish-green (490 nm) (Fig. 2 b). The mixture of the two ends of the visual spectrum (UV-Yellow) produces a unique color – bee purple – which is different from any other color (DAUMER, 1956, MENZEL, 1967). UV – bluish-green and blue-purple are complementary colors.

Color learning has been studied in a dual choice situation with free flying bees trained to spectral colors under constant background light conditions (MENZEL, 1967). It turns out that violet (400–420 nm) is learned fastest and is chosen most accurately. Bluish-green is learned most slowly and is chosen with least precision (Fig. 2 c, 3 c). Learning acquisition and level of correctness is a function only of the color learned (λ_+), not of the alternative color (λ_-) presented in the dual choice test (Fig. 3 a), provided that the colors can be discriminated. Neither is color learning a function of brightness (Fig. 3 b), if the color is sufficiently bright to be easily detected by the bee. Furthermore, color learning appears

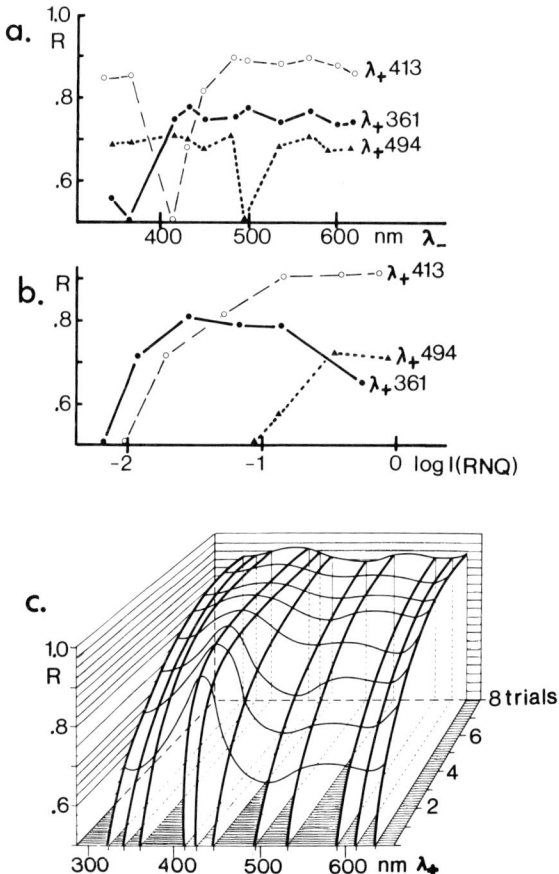

Fig. 3: *a*. Dependence of the alternative color (λ_-) on the learning of λ_+ and *b*. of the brightness of the color λ_+ on the learning of λ_+. In both cases the choice probability is given after two trials on λ_+ (see text). *c*. Acquisition functions for 10 different spectral colors and purple (P) (from MENZEL, 1967).

independent of the kind of pretraining which was necessary to introduce bees to the experimental training situation (Fig. 2 c). The sole dependence on λ_+, the color learned, is further supported by our finding that bees trained to white light choose white light equally well with various spectral lights as alternatives (LIEKE, unpubl.). Furthermore, there is evidence for an independence of the color-specific learning rate of the age of the bees and of the weather conditions (MENZEL, 1967).

We conclude from these results that color learning in the context of feeding follows a rank order of signal preparedness with violet ranking highest, followed by blue and purple, then green and UV and finally bluish-green. This rank order parallels the frequency of colors found in hymenopteran flowers, especially of those which grow in sparse populations (KEVAN, 1978, MENZEL and LIEKE, unpubl.). It well be pointed out, however, that proper spectral measurements have to be made of the flower colors as well as the calculations of their color loci in the bees' color space. Violet, the color learned best, is distinctive to the bee because it appears relatively bright *and* is highly discriminable. Furthermore, it contrasts very well with the greenish background of the foliage leaves and is less sensitive to changing UV-illumination than e. g. purple and UV in exposed versus shaded locations.

Although these results have shown that preparedness for the color of a foraging place exists, it is still a small effect compared with the strenght of the bees' learning ability, and can be demonstrated only in well-controlled, quantitative behavioral experiments. FOREL (1910) stated this correctly: «Die Farbe bildet ein Merkzeichen, aber keine Anziehung an und für sich für das Insekt» (p. 194) («Color is a learning signal but not an attractive signal in itself for this insect»).

4 Do bees show preparedness for particular color patterns?

VON FRISCH (1914) and WEHNER (1972) used a simple pattern of two vertically arranged half discs to study pattern recognition. Such a pattern has the advantage that the effect of the spatial arrangement of the pattern components can be tested easily. We used these discs to address the question of whether bees apply search images consisting of color patterns at the food source (MENZEL, LIEKE, 1983). The results we obtained are in partial agreement with the assumption of specific search images, but not all results fit into such an interpretation (Fig. 4).

Let us suppose that bees have a search image in which the UV component of the pattern is expected to appear in the upper portion and bluish-green in the lower portion of the visual field. Discrimination values should be high if the trained pattern has more overlap with the search image and low if the alternative test pattern shows more overlap. Indeed, this hypothesis is supported by experiments in which patterns with horizontal or vertical contrast lines have been trained (Fig. 4, upper left part, dark columns). If the trained pattern have either a 45 degree tilted contrast line between a UV and bluish-green sector or between a UV bright-dark sector, discrimination values contradict the hypothesis. The same is true for a search image in which the upper part of the visual field is orange and the lower part is blue (Fig. 4, second row). There are two ways of explaining these results (see MENZEL, LIEKE, 1983) by assuming either a selective change of the search image after training to tilted contrast line or by hypothesizing an additional color-selective position effect. In any case, if there is a search image for color patterns it cannot be very strong, because it is changed by a seemingly small difference in the trained pattern and/or is affected by additional parameters.

One might argue that search images for color patterns should show up more strongly in flower-like patterns e. g. in concentric UV-non-UV reflecting patterns, or purple-yellow configuration or star-like patterns with outer-inner color contrast and so on. We find it very difficult to interpret discrimination experiments using such patterns. At any rate, preliminary experiments do not support strong search images for such intuitively «flower-like» color patterns.

We have trained bees to the same half-disc color patterns at the hive entrance and – to our great surprise – found no discrimination with respect to the pattern component. Any flaws in the procedure can be excluded because the same bee colony discriminated colors at the hive entrance very well (see below). If this finding is confirmed in additional experiments, we have to conclude that learning of color patterns is context specific – a result very different from those obtained for color learning (see below). Furthermore, this result is one of the rare cases of selective association in bees. A signal, here the color pattern, is learned when sucrose solution is provided as a reward, but not learned when the reward is return into the hive.

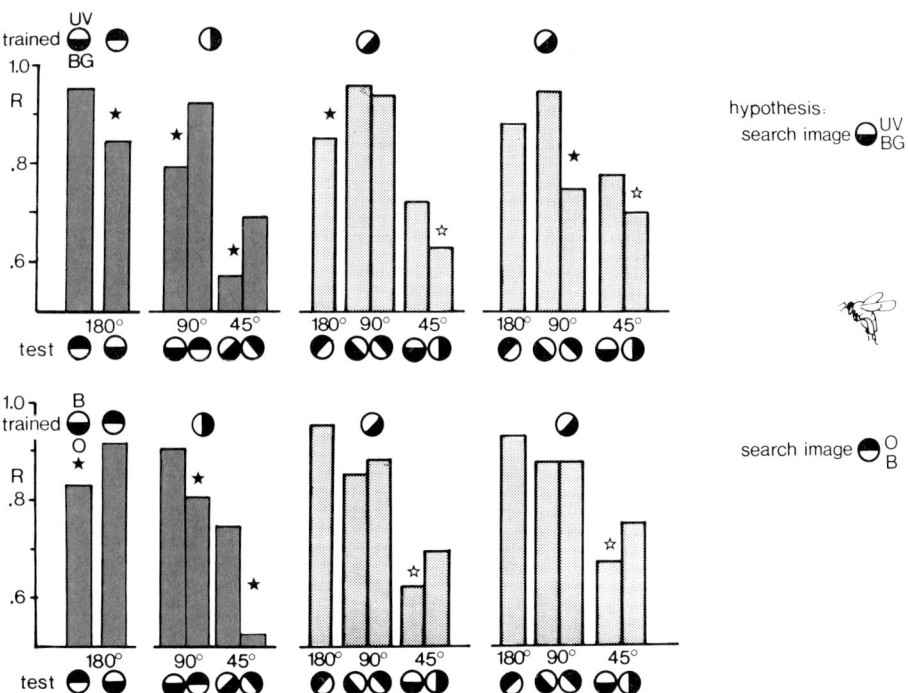

Fig. 4: Choice behavior of honey bees after training to patterns of two half circles of different colors (UV: ultra violet, No. 2 in Fig. 1, BG: bluish-green Nr. 14 B: blue No. 8 and O orange Nr. 17). The trained color pattern is given in the upper row of each set of experiments the alternative color pattern in the dual choice test is given below each column. The angular number of degrees indicate the angular deviation between test pattern and training pattern. The columns show the probability of correct choices for the respective pairs of color patterns. Heavy stars indicate highly significant differences between the two columns ($p \leq 0,01$, χ^2-test), light stars indicate weak statistical differences ($0,01 \leq p \leq 0.05$). The results given in dark columns are those which support the hypothesis of a search image shown at the right side, the grey columns do not support this hypothesis (see text) (from MENZEL, LIEKE, 1983).

5 Bees show preparedness for flower-like odors, but will learn any odor

Flower-like odors are learned faster than other odors (v. Frisch, 1919, Lauer, Lindauer, 1971, Schwarz, 1955, Kriston, 1971, 1973). Fig. 5 c,f shows a few examples. The odor learned fastest is geraniol, a component of the Nassanov gland which is used by the bee to mark productive food sources as well as the hive entrance. Von Frisch (1965 p. 506) found it surprising that bees can be conditioned to odors which cause obvious signs of discomfort. Lysol, for example, is used by bee keepers to prevent bees from approaching

Fig. 5: *a–c:* Average learning rate of free flying bees to different food signals. Choice behavior (ordinate) at trial O (left side of abscissa) indicates the probability of choices after pretraining (usually three trials on a neutral target). a. Acquisition functions for two spectral colors $\lambda_+ = 413$ nm, $\lambda_+ = 532$ nm (see Fig. 3). b. Acquisition functions for two color patterns of the kind described in Fig. 4. Note the different scale on the abscissa (number of trials). c. Acquisition functions for 2 different pairs of odors. The bees were pretrained by three trials to an unscented target (cardboard box). Ger + Carn −: Geraniol was the rewarded odor, Carnation the alternative odor; Prop + Oran −: Propanol trained, Orange alternative odor.

d–f: Conditioning of the proboscis-extension reflex of fixed bees to color and odor stimuli. d. Acquisition function to a flash of blue light to the right eye (trained eye). Note the different scale on the abscissa. Column: response probability. e. Side specificity of odor learning in free flying bees and fixed bees. The probability for the two kinds of experiments were so similar that only the numbers of the free flying bees are given (see text). The line around the antenna indicates covering of that antenna during learning in free flying bees or exclusion from odor stimulation during proboscis conditioning in fixed bees (Masuhr, Menzel, 1972). f. Acquisition functions for various odors during proboscis extension conditioning in fixed bees. Ger: geraniol, Carn: carnation, Iso: isoamylacetate, Prop: propanol (see text) (Experiments with Ger +, Carn +, Prop + from Bittermann et al., 1983, with Iso + from Salisbury, unpublished).

a location, and yet bees choose a feeding place marked with lysol preferentially when they have been rewarded there. Propanol is another example of an odor which has a repellent effect on bees and can still be conditioned (Fig. 5 c, f). During proboscis conditioning, bees may even retract the proboscis at the beginning of traning but later respond with conditioned proboscis extension. KRISTON (1971) found that bees even prefer butyric acid to thyme after pretraining to an unscented feeding place. Flower-like odors are more salient signals and, therefore, bees choose less salient odors after training to *no* odor. There is no evidence for an odor which cannot become a conditioned stimulus to the bee. Even CO_2, water vapor and the bee's own alarm pheromone can be conditioned. The latter is very interesting (Fig. 5 f). Isoamylacetate, the main component of the alarm pheromone, is even learned as fast as flower-like odors in proboscis extension conditioning, although a few bees after training put out their sting reflexively while extending their proboscis at the same time.

We learn from these experiments that as far as odor learning is concerned, bees are innately prepared for expected odor signals at the feeding place, but that the general learning ability is powerful enough to enable the bee to learn any odor as a food signal. Here again, «innate search images» seem to be relatively weak cues when compared with the general learning potential.

6 Comparison of color, color pattern and odor learning

In comparing the most salient visual and olfactory signals, we find that odors are learned fastest and are chosen more accurately than colors and color patterns (Fig. 5 a, b, c). However, a comparison of this kind is complicated by the fact that the same behavioral measures have been used to quantify choice behavior (approaches to the target or sitting down on the target), but visual and olfactory cues are known to guide the flight path of the bee at different distances from the target (v. FRISCH, 1965). In my view, the question of acquisition rate for different learning signals is open for more appropriate experimentation, which selects more appropriate behavioral measures for different learning signals.

In contrast to free bees, large differences between learning of visual and olfactory stimuli are found in the proboscis extension conditioning paradigm (Fig. 5 d, f). Flashes of colored light are turned into conditioned stimuli only with great difficulty (MASUHR, MENZEL, 1972). A moving-stripe pattern ist not much more effective as a conditioned stimulus (ERBER, SCHILDBERGER, 1980). Olfactory stimuli, however, are condtioned as quickly as in the free-flying paradigm (Fig. 5 c, f). These are strong hints for the existence of selective associations in the bee brain between certain stimuli and a well defined motor programm (proboscis extension). The biological background for such selective associations is obvious. Olfactory stimuli are always closely related to proboscis extension both at the flower and within the hive. They are used by the running and standing bee as food signals and not only in flight.

We found another difference in the processing of visual and olfactory stimuli during conditioning in bees which favors the notion of selective association. (Fig. 5 d, e): Color signals trained with one eye are responded to at the same rate when testing with the other eye. This is different in olfactory stimuli. Here stimulation of the unconditioned antenna does not elicit the conditioned response. We may suspect that the memory trace is limited to the side of the brain ipsilateral to the conditioned antenna and is not accessible by the contralateral antenna. This is, however, an inadequate explanation, because a conditioning by the initially covered antenna to the *same* odor gives a significantly *lower* response level than conditioning without pretraining of the contralateral antenna (Fig. 5 e). This result reminds us of FOREL's (1910) concept of the «topochemical sense» in bees (see v. FRISCH, 1965, p. 513). An odor perceived and learned with the *right* antenna is different from an odor perceived and learned with the left antenna. Therefore, training the initially covered antenna to the same odor is a reversal learning, which has to result in lower response levels. If this interpretation is correct, the side-specific effect is not related to the representation of the memory trace in the bee brain but is a result of the side-specific processing of odor information.

7 Color learning in different behavioral context

Search images have to be specific with respect to the behavioral context. Different behavioral contexts may work with different search images. The preparedness of an animal is, therefore, not only related to certain stimuli but also to the meaning of these stimuli in a given behavioral context. Bees are color-blind in certain behaviors (flight control through optomotor response, KAISER, LISKE, 1974; polarized light orientation, v. HELVERSEN, EDRICH, 1974; phototaxis, MENZEL, GREGGERS, unpubl.), but perceive and learn colors both for localising a food source and the hive entrance. The color signals marking a food source and the hive entrance are typically very different, although we should keep in mind that bees do feed also on greenish-brownish locations (e. g. aphids on

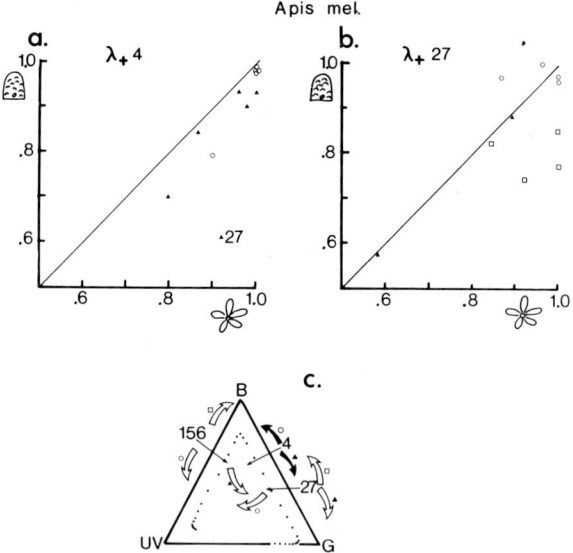

Fig. 6: Comparison of color learning of *Apis mellifera* at the feeding place and at the hive entrance. In a. the bees were trained to blue (No. 4, see c.), in b. to bluish-green (No. 27). The ordinates show the choice probability of the trained color at the hive entrance, the abscissa the choice probability of the same trained color at the feeding place. Each dot indicates identical dual choise tests in the two situations. If color discrimination were the same in the two situations all points would lie around the diagonal line (crossing through the graph). Triangles indicate color discrimination towards the bluish-green, open circles towards the UV and violet, and open squares towards the blue. c. gives the locations of the trained colors in the color triangle and explains the symbols used in a. and b.

leaves, extra-floral nectaries, phloem liquid squeezed out by leaves, and decomposing fruits). We may expect, therefore, different «innate search images» for color marks in the context of orientation at the hive entrance when compared with that of the foraging flight.

We have used identical test situations for color training at the feeding place and at the hive entrance (dual choice test, see MENZEL, LIEKE, 1983 and above). Two colors were trained: No. 4 (blue) and No. 27 (bluish-green). Discrimination was tested with alternative colors throughout the bee's color space. The results are presented in such a way that all points should lie around the line crossing the diagram (Fig. 6) if color learning is similar in both behavioral contexts. If bees learn colors better at the feeding place than at the hive entrance, the data points should lie below this line. Bees learn colors at the hive entrance very well, but most point lie somewhat below the crossing line, indicating a choice behavior at the hive entrance which is slighly less precisely controlled by learned color signals than at the feeding place. Most importantly, there is no selective effect with respect to color discrimination in the two behavioral contexts as we may have expected (see above). Some of the results are even contra-intuitive. Blusih-green is much better discriminated from blue at the feeding place than at the hive (Fig. 6 a, No. 27), and ultraviolet is equally well discriminated both from blue and bluish-green in the two test situations.

So far we have been unable to quantify the acquisitions process during hive-entrance training, but qualitative estimates indicate similar dependencies of acquisition on different colors as in appettitive training.

It is an intuitively attractive idea to expect context-specific preparedness for signal-reward aussociations, and, indeed, we have found such preparedness in the proboscis-extension-conditioning (see above). However, no selective preparedness has been found in color learning of the free-flying bees. This provides further evidence for the strength of the general learning ability in both behavioral contexts tested (feeding place and hive entrance).

8 Species-specificity of search images in color learning of hymenopterans

Flower visiting hymenopterans face the same problems in reliably indentifing and localising potential food sources and in relocating their nest sites. The specific adaptations may still differ according to the ecological conditions in which they collect nectar and pollen and relocate their nest sites. The overall conditions of light climate of the species-specific niche, for example, may influence the evolution of color perception and color learning. A comparative study may help us to identify the general properties of color vision and color learning of flower visiting hymenopterans and separate species-specific adaptations.

Such a study has been started in our laboratory, but is still in its infancy. The crucial point is that identical methods have to be used to characterize color discrimination. So far we have studied *Apis mellifera* (unpublished experiments by A. WERNER, S. MÜLLER, F. RRANK, S. MENZEL, K. WEBER and students of the course Neural Systems and Behavior at MBL in Woods Hol, Mass. 1983), *Melipona quadrifasciata* (in co-laboration with D. VENTURA, Sao Paulo) and *Osmia bicornis* (in co-laboration with E. STEINMANN, Chur) using the same methods of hive entrance training (see above).

Melipona discriminates colors in the bluish-green, green and yellow region better than *Apis*, and *Apis* is superior to *Melipona* in discriminating longer wavelength colors (bluish-green, green) from violet and UV (Fig. 7 a, b). Unfortunately, we have not yet trained *Apis* to violet (filter No. 156, Fig. 6 c) at the hive entrance, but let us compare color discrimination of *Melipona* after training to violet at the hive entrance with that of *Apis* trained to violet at the feeding place (Fig. 7 e). We may proceed in such a way, since we did not find color specific differences between discrimination of *Apis* at the food source and the hive entrance (Fig. 6 a, b). Here, too, we find *Melipona's* color discrimination to be best when bluish-green color are presented as alternatives and relatively weak when UV colors are the alternatives.

One possible explanation for these results may be, that the eye of *Melipona* quadrifasciata contains different color receptors. However, this is not the case. We have recorded intracellularly from many photoreceptors in the compound eye of Melipona (UV: λ_{max} = 350 nm, blue: λ_{max} = 440 nm, green: λ_{max} = 540 nm) and found the same three color receptor types as in *Apis mellifera* (Menzel, Ventura, unpubl.). Our conclusion then is that the processing of color information in the *Melipona* brain is adapted to an improvement of color discrimination in the bluish-green region and to a reduction of color discrimination in the violet-UV region. This may be a specific adaptation to the light conditions prevailing in the dense tropical rain forest. *Melipona* houses in hollow trees in the tropical forest and searches for nectar and pollen on flowering trees which are often overshadowed by the canopy of higher trees.

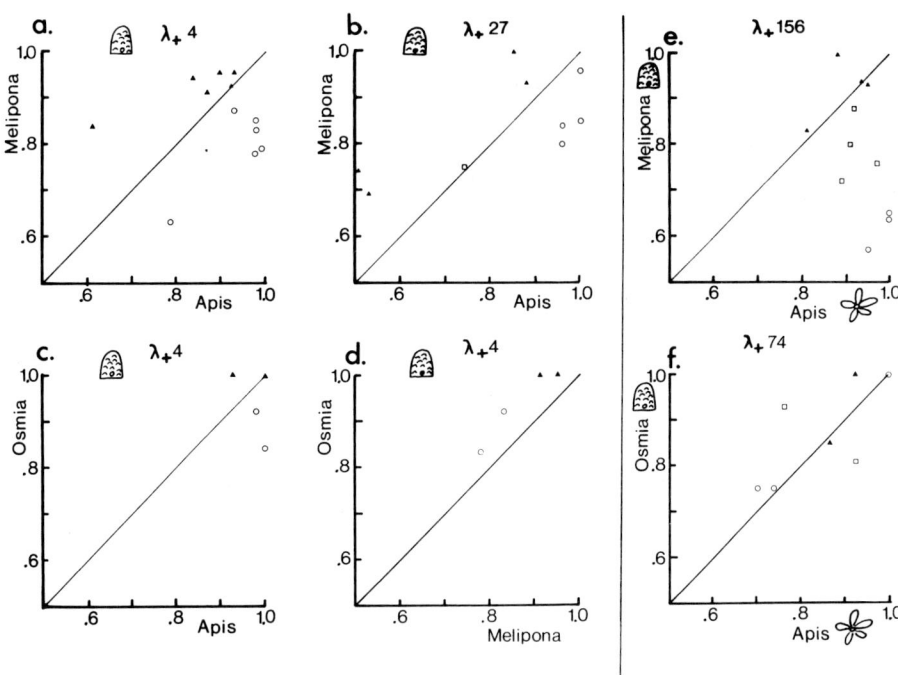

Fig. 7: A comparison of color discrimination of 3 hymenopteran species, the honey bee *Apis mellifera*, the stingless bee *Melipona quadrifasciata* and the solitary bee *Osmia bicornis*. a. and b.: Color discrimination of *Melipona* (ordinate) and *Apis* (abscissa) at the hive entrance after training to blue (No. 4) and bluish-green (No. 27). The same kind of plot and the same symbols are used as in Fig. 6. c. *Apis* compared with *Osmia* after training to blue (No. 4), d. *Melipona* compared with *Osmia* after training to blue (No. 4). e and f: A comparison between species and in different behavioral context. These plots are presented because most data we have collected so far are on *Apis* color discrimination at the feeding place, whereas *Melipona* and *Osmia* were tested only at the hive entrance. e. trained color is Violet (No. 156 see Fig. 1 and 6 c), f. trained color is Violet (No. 74 see Fig. 1) (see text).

The solitary bee *Osmia bicornis* has so far been tested with a few colors only and is found to discriminate colors in the bluish-green better or as well as *Apis* and not as well as *Apis* in the Violet-UV region (Fig. 7 c, f). It is, therefore, not surprising that *Osmia* is superior to *Melipona* (Fig. 7 d).

«Innate search images» are a product of the phyologenetic history of the species. We expect, therefore, species-specific preparedness for the association of certain stimuli with reward or reinforced behavior, and we expect more precisely controlled behavior for prepared stimuli. The species we have compared so far are phyolgenetically quite separate but relatively closely related with respect to their search behavior at the food source and at the nest-site. It is, therefore, not surprising that we find only marginal quantitative differences. Again, the general learning ability in all three species is the major effect and preparedness appears as an additional tuning factor.

9 Bees are prepared to switch to new food signals

The search strategy of a generalist is characterized by the ability to switch to new food sources when the old one becomes less attractive. As the typical food source of a generalist has a shorter duration than the life time of the animal, we might expect to find growing readiness of the animal to switch to new food sources when the old one has been visited throughout an extended period of time. Such a preparedness should be advantageous in so far as it tunes the animal to give up a food source when it exceeds an expected life time. From the learning point of view such a preparedness reflects a paradox, because ongoing

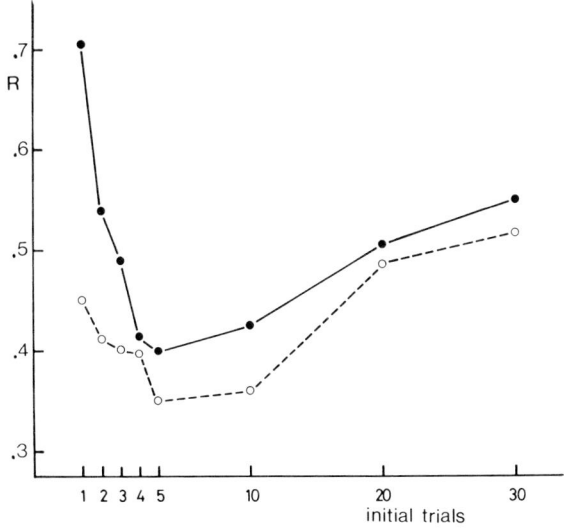

Fig. 8: Over-learning reversal effect in the honey bee (MENZEL, 1969). Bees were trained to a variing number of initial trials to one of two test colors (blue-yellow) and then rewarded once at the other color. The abscissa gives the number of initial trails on blue (○) or yellow (●), and the ordinate gives the choice probability after one reversal trial on blue (●) or on yellow (○). Choice probability below. 5 means preferred choice of the initially trained color, above. 5 preferred probability of the second trained color (see text) (from MENZEL, 1969).

reinforcement would not strengthen the learned behavior but, on the contrary, would actually weaken it.

We have found such an effect in the honey bee (Fig. 8). Bees are trained to one color out of a pair of colors by a variing number of rewards, each bee of a group of individually marked bees in consecutive experiments to a given number of initial rewards (ranging from 1–20 initial rewards). Then the alternative color is rewarded on several trials. The curves show the choice probability on a dual choice test after one reversal trial. Decreasing probability values give a decreasing choice of the second learned odor, increasing probability values reflect an increasing choice of the second learned color. Reversal learning is first slowed down with the number of initial trials as we would expect from the effect of strengthening a learned behavior by reinforcement. But ongoing reinforcement results in an increasing readiness to switch to the second color beyound 10 initial trials.

Such an effect is not unknown in learning psychology («overlearning reversal effect»), but there is little knowledge about what it may mean for animals under natural conditions. Our experimental conditions are not natural in a strict sense, since the bees could suck their fill during each landing, and the food source was always located at the same place. It is still tempting to interpret these results as an adaptation of a generalist pollinator to the expected temporal limits of its food sources and, therefore, as a temporal search image.

This effect is not related to any rhythm of learned behavior or time-linking of learning (Koltermann, 1971, Bogdany, 1978), because it is independent of the timing of the initial learning trials. We have looked into time-linked learning not only in this experiment but also in several other series of experiments (Menzel, 1968, 1969, Menzel, 1979, Menzel, Erber, Masuhr, 1974), and have not found any evidence for a periodicity of learning or a time-linking of learning and retrieval. Time-liking is the effect of an extended period of differential conditioning. During this long procedure timing of a signal-reward association is established through differential reinforcement (e. g. Bogdany, 1978). The positive outcome of such a training procedure proves that bees are able to learn that certain signal-reward associations are restricted to some time in the day and other signal-reward associations to another time of the day. These experiments do, however, not demonstrate a time-linking of signal-reward associations per se.

10 Short-term memory as a mechanism of fast adaptations to changing profitability of the food sources

In honey bees short-term memory (STM) traces are thought to be coded in an orderly neural activity, whereas long-term memory (LTM) appears to have some stable structural or biochemical substrate (Menzel, Erber, Masuhr, 1974). STM preceeds LTM, the time course of the STM-LTM transfer can be measured (Erber, 1975 a, b, 1976) by erasing STM with experimental procedures like narcosis, cooling or weak electronconvulsive shocks. At the beginning of our studies on STM in bees we thought that the time course of STM-LTM transfer with a half-life time of about 5 min is determined by slow biochemical processes transcribing neural activity into biochemical changes and viewed this process as an internal machinery of the nervous system necessary to establish LTM. This picture collapsed when Erber (1975 b) found that LTM can be established within less than a minute if several very short rewards follow each other quickly (Fig. 9). The time course of STM-LTM transfer, which we measured initially (Fig. 9 a, curve 1), may thus be an active process which prevents a memory trace from reaching LTM before it has been confirmed by additional associations (Menzel, 1979, 1983). If this concept is correct one might expect to find an adaptation of the actual time course of STM-LTM transfer on the expected interval between successive approaches to natural food sources. The underlying neural processes would then be under the control of phylogenetic adaptations which prepare these neural processes for expected time frequencies of associative events.

Evidence for this view comes from the following observations. (1) If two learning trials with two *different* conditioned stimuli follow each other within 30 sec, the memory trace for *both* is eliminated by subsequent eletroconvulsive shock (MENZEL, unpubl.). This result supports our assumption that only a confirming event establishes LTM quickly; (2) Unrewarded approaches to a trained visual target have a very weak extinction effect if the memory trace is in its longterm form (MENZEL, 1967). However, extinction trials are very effective in STM (MENZEL, 1968); (3) Reversal learning experiments after one initial trial on one color and a second trial on another color within a time interval ranging from 0,5 to 10 min demonstrate a biphasic time course (MENZEL, 1979, Fig. 9 b). This means that a second learning trial with competing information interferes with the memory trace of the first learning trial and erases the first memory trace effectively at two temporal windows: immediately after the initial learning trial and around 3 min after the initial learning trial.

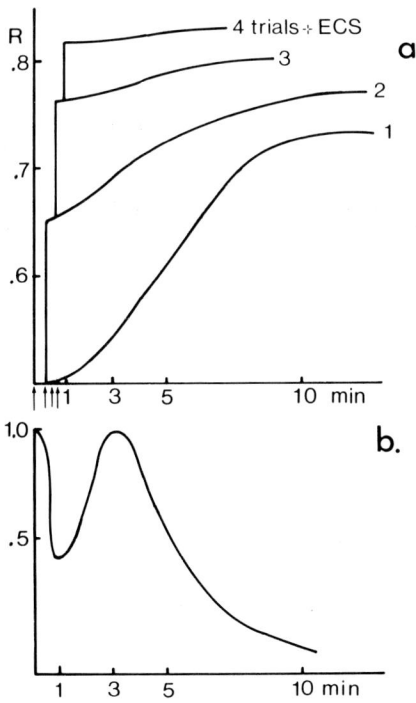

Fig. 9: Short-term memory and choice behavior in the honey bee. a. Bees were trained with 1 or 2 or 4 trials on blue and then treated with electroconvulsive shocks. The time course after one trial (lowest function) is supported by several points, those of 2–3 trials only by the beginning and endpoints (from ERBER, 1975 a, b). b. Thime course of the sensitivity of an initial learning trial to a reversal trial following the initial trial at a varying time interval (abscissa) (from MENZEL, 1979). The ordinate gives a normalized measure of the relative sensitivity of the initial memory trace to conflicting information coming from the new trial (reversal trial) (see text).

There are not enough data yet to allow any functional interpretation of this effect (see MENZEL, 1982, 1983 for discussion). Nevertheless, the biological meaning is that the establishment of a LTM trace is highly sensitive to the temporal sequence of associative experience. The temporal sequence of learning trials under natural conditions is a function of flight speed, sucking time (or pollen collecting time) and density of flowers, the latter being the most important factor. It is tempting to speculate that the time course of STM-LTM transfer is adapted to two categories of flower distribution: densely growing flowers (e. g. trees) and sparse distributed flowers. In the first case a just-established STM-trace is erased if a different experience is made within about 30 sec. Indeed, I have found an average sucking time per flower of 3 sec and an average landing interval of 10 sec in densely flowering orange trees (MENZEL, 1968). In sparsely growing flowers a just-established STM-trace should be sensitive to corrections at a longer time interval. An interval of three minutes seems quite long, and indeed we measured in widely distributed autumn flowers an average of 1 min interval between landings. However, many of these landings were unrewarded, so a time window of 3 mins for rewarded landings on sparsely growing flowers may be reasonable. These speculations have no further experimental support, but they can stimulate the design of a number of promising experiments.

11 Conclusion

Although all available evidence is indirect, it seems beyond doubt that bees have «innate search images» which guide their orientation and shape their learning processes. Does this mean that bees are little robots which carry prewired circuits in their brains with all possible subroutines ready to be switched on? My believe is that this view is too narrow and not supported by the experimental evidence at hand. In addition, such a mechanism would be maladaptive for a social insect following the search strategy of a generalist pollinator. Like FOREL (1910) and v. FRISCH (1965), I am overwhelmed by the power of the general learning ability of the bee, which allows her to learn pratically all perceived stimuli as food markers, at least under natural conditions. Comparative studies of learning in traditional paradigms have revealed great similarities between laboratory mammals and the bee (BITTERMANN at al., 1983, COUVILLON, BITTERMANN, 1980, 1982, 1983; MENZEL, 1983). Such findings support the notion of across-species rules of learning.

I conclude that the neural mechanisms of learning in the bee are controlled both by a strong inherent general learning ability following rules of interspecific applicability, and by species-specific preparedness for selective associations, which are the result of the species' evolutionary history. This concept advocates against an either – or of «general rules of learning» versus «selective associations of a preprogrammed switch board» and in favor of an integration of theories of learning psychology and ethology.

References

Autrum, H., Zwehl, V. von (1964): Spektrale Empfindlichkeit einzelner Sehzellen des Bienenauges. Z. vergl. Physiol. 48, 357–384.

Bitterman, M. E., Menzel, R., Fietz, A., Schäfer, S. (1983): Classical conditioning of proboscis extension in honeybees (Apis mellifera). J comp. Physiol. 97, 107–119.

Bogdany, F. J. (1978): Linking of learning signals in honey bee orientation. Behav. Ecol. Sociobiol. 3, 323–336.

Butler, C. G. (1951): The importance of perfume in the discovery of food by the worker honeybee. Proc. Roy. Soc. B. *138*, 403–413.

Daumer, K. (1956): Reizmetrische Untersuchungen des Farbensehens der Bienen. Z. vergl. Physiol. *38*, 413–478.

Erber, J. (1976): Retrograde amnesia in honey bees *(Apis mellifera carnica)*. J. comp. Physiol. Psychol. *90*, 41–46.

Erber, J., Schildberger, K. (1980): Conditioning of an antennal reflex to visual stimuli in bees *(Apis mellifera L:)*. J. comp. Physiol. *135*, 217–225.

Faegri, K. van der Pijl, L. (1978): The Principles of Pollination Ecology. Oxford, New York, Toronto, Sidney, Paris, Frankfurt: Pergamon, pp. 244, 3rd Ed.

Free, JB. (1970): Insect pollination of crops. New York, Academic, pp. 54.

Forel, A. (1910): Das Sinnesleben der Insekten. München.

Frisch, K. von (1914/1915): Der Farbensinn und Formensinn der Bienen. Zool. Jb. Physiol. *35*, 1–188.

Frisch, K. von (1965): Tanzsprache und Orientierung der Bienen. Springer Verlag, Berlin-Heidelberg-New York, pp. 1–567.

Helversen, O. von (1972): Zur spektralen Unterschiedsempfindlichkeit der Honigbiene. J. comp. Physiol. *80*, 372–439.

Helversen, O. von, Edrich, W. (1974): Der Polarisationsempfänger im Bienenauge: Ein Ultraviolett-rezeptor. J. comp. Physiol. *94*, 33–47.

Hertel, H. (1980–: Chromatic properties of identified interneuron in the optic lobes of the bee. J. comp. Physiol. *137*, 215–231.

Kaiser, W., Liske, E. (1974): Optomotor reactions of stationary flying bees during stimulation with spectral light. J. comp. Physiol. *89*, 391–408.

Kevan, P. G. (1978): Floral coleration, its colorimetric analysis and significance in anthecology. See Ref 24, pp. 51–78.

Kevan, P.G., Baker, H. G. (1983): Insects as flower visitors and pollinators. Ann. Rev. Entomol. *28*, 407–453.

Kien, J., Menzel, R. (1977): Chromatic properties of interneurons in the optic lobes of the bee. I. Broad band neurons. J. comp. Physiol. *113*, 17–34.

Kien, J., Menzel, R. (1977): Chromatic properties of interneurons in the optic lobes of the bees. II. Narrow band and color opponent neurons. J. comp. Physiol. *113*, 35–53.

Kolterman, R. (1971): 24-std-Periodik in der Langzeiterinnerung an Duft- und Farbsignale bei der Honigbiene. Z. vergl. Physiol. *75*, 49–68.

Kriston, I. (1971): Zum Problem des Lernverhaltens von *Apis mellifica* gegenüber verschiedenen Duftstoffen. Z. vergl. Physiol. *74*, 169–189.

Kriston, I. (1973): Zum Zusammenhang zwischen Signalbewertung und Lernprozess: Die Bewertung von Duft- und Farbsignalen an der Futterquelle durch *Apis* mellifica. J. compl Physiol. *84*, 77–94.

Lauer, J., Lindauer, M. (1971): Genetisch fixierte Lerndispositionen bei der Honigbiene. Akad. d. Wiss. u. Lit. Mainz, Wiesbaden, Fr. Steiner.

Lindauer, M. (1952): Ein Beitrag zur Frage der Arbeitsteilung im Bienenstaat. Z. vergl. Physiol. *34*, 299–345.

Lindauer, M. (1959): Angeborene und erlernte Komponenten in der Sonnenorientierung der Bienen. Z. vergl. Physiol. *42*, 43–62.

Masuhr, T., Menzel, R. (1972): Learning experiments on the use of side-specific information in the olfactory and visual system in the honey bee *(Apis mellifica)* In: Information Processing in the Visual Systems of Arthropods. (Ed. R. Wehner) pp 315–322, Berlin–Heidelberg–New York, Springer Verlag.

McGregor, S. E. (1976): Insect pollination of cultivated crop plants. Agriculture Handbook 496. ARS-USDA, Washington DC pp 411.

Menzel, R. (1967): Das Erlernen von Spektralfarben durch die Honigbiene. Z. vergl. Physiol. *56*, 22–62.

Menzel, R. (1968): Das Gedächtnis der Honigbiene für Spektralfarben. I. Kurzzeitiges und lang-zeitiges Behalten. Z. vergl. Physiol. *60*, 82–102.

Menzel, R. (1969): Das Gedächtnis der Honigbiene für Spektralfarben. II. Umlernen und Mehrfach-lernen. Z. vergl. Physiol. *63*, 290–309.

Menzel, R. (1977): Farbensehen bei Insekten – ein rezeptorphysiologischer und neurophysiologischer Problemkreis. Verh. Dtsch. Zool. Ges. pp 28–40.

Menzel, R. (1979): Behavioral access to short-term memory in bees. Nature 28, 368–369.

Menzel, R. (1979). Spectral sensitivity and color vision in invertebrates. In: Handbook of Sensory Physiology Vol. VII 6A (Ed. H. Autrum) pp 504–580, Berlin–Heidelberg–New York, Springer Verlag.

Menzel, R. (1982): Neurobiologie and behavior of social insects: An Introduction. In: The Biology of Social Insects (Eds. D. Breed, Ch. D. Michener, H. E. Evand), pp 335–337.

Menzel, R. (1983): Neurobiology of learning and memory: «The honey bee as a model system». Naturwiss. 70, 504–511.

Menzel, R. (in press): Report on: Biology of invertebrate learning. In: The Biology of Learning. (Eds. P. Marler, H. S. Terrace) Dahlem Konferenzen, Chemie Verlag Weinheim.

Menzel, R., Blakers, M. (1976): Colour rezeptors in the bee eye – morphology and spectral sensitivity. J. comp. Physiol. 108, 11–33.

Menzel, R., Erber, J., Masuhr, Th. (1974): Learning and memory in the honeybee. In: Experimental Analysis of Insect Behavior. (Ed. L. Barton-Browne) pp 195–217. Berlin–Heidelberg–New York, Springer Verlag.

Menzel, R., Lieke, E. (1983): Antagonistic color effects in spatial vision of honey bee. J. comp. Physiol. 151, 441–448.

Neumeyer, Ch. (1980): Simultaneous color contrast in the honey bee. J. comp. Physiol. 139, 165–176.

Neumeyer, Ch. (1981): Chromatic adaptation in the honey bee: Successive color contrast and color constancy. J. comp. Physiol. 144, 543–553.

Oettingen-Spielberg, Th. zu (1949): Über das Wesen der Suchbiene. Z. vergl. Physiol. 31, 454–489.

Proctor, M., Yeo, P. (1973): The pollination of flowers. London, Collins, pp 418.

Schwarz, R. (1955): Über die Richschärfe der Honigbiene. Z. vergl. Physiol. 37, 180–210.

Wehner, R. (1972): Dorso-ventral asymmetry in the visual field of the bee, Apis mellifica. J. comp. Physiol. 77, 256–277.

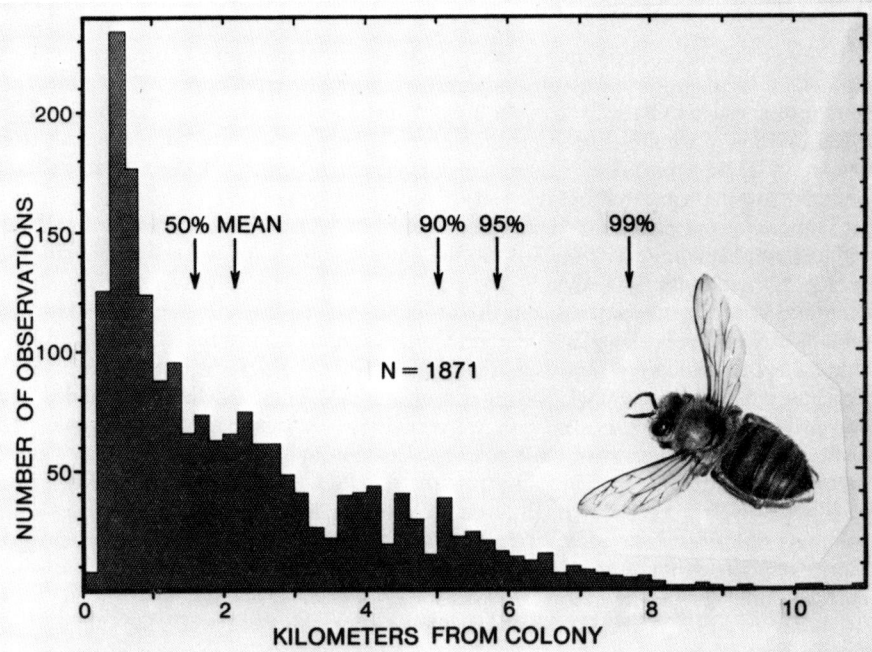

Fig. 3: Distribution of distances between a honeybee colony's nest and its forage patches.

The heart of this information-center hypothesis for the foraging strategy of honeybee colonies is the idea colonies organize their foraging so that on any given day a colony's foragers are focussed on the few best forage patches that the colony has found. This hypothesis is supported by the experiments of BOCH (1956). His studies demonstrate that a honeybee colony offered two feeding stations in various combinations of richness (concentration of sugar solution) and distance from the hive can evaluate the relative profitability of the two, allocate its forager labor accordingly, and shift its forager force from one to the other within hours of a reversal of their profitability. Further support for the hypothesis of information-center foraging comes from the observations by BUTLER (1945) and WEAVER (1979) of rapid shifts of foragers on to and later off of patches of flowers.

3 Mechanisms of forage patch selection

Obviously the mechanisms of patch choice which underlie a colony's shifts in forage sites are central to the foraging strategy of honeybee colonies. One possibility for the way that this decision-making works is that it reflects the joint operation of the following three processes:
1. workers abandon forage patches of relatively low profitability,
2. workers usually locate new patches by following recruitment dances,
3. workers only recruit to patches of relatively high profitability.
The net effect of these three processes working in concert is probably that workers are constantly leaving poor patches and moving onto good patches.

3.1 Assessing the relative profitability of forage patches

Processes 1 and 3 are probably correctly viewed as complementary processes, each one appropriate to an opposite extreme in the range of foraging experiences. When a forager's patch profitability is relatively low, she should abandon it to switch to a superior one. In contrast, when a forager's patch profitability is relatively high, she should recruit nest-mates to it. In the intermediate situation of average patch quality, the bee probably should continue working the patch but not recruit additional foragers.

The fundamental puzzle here is the mechanisms by which an individual bee can know the quality of her forage patch relative to the other patches being worked by her colony's foragers. One possibility is that honeybees, like bumblebees (Heinrich 1976), travel about and sample other patches. But this is unlikely given the immense distances which commonly occur between patches (see Fig. 1). Also arguing against the hypothesis of patch sampling are the numerous reports that labelled honeybee foragers will steadfastly work a particular patch for many days, leaving it only late in the day or when fully loaded with forage (Ribbands 1949, Singh 1950, Weaver 1957). A second possibility is that each worker possesses some sort of built-in scale of patch quality. By comparing her current patch profitability with the values on this scale, a forager could conclude whether her patch is relatively good or poor. (Built-in scales of quality are used by honeybees when ·evaluating nest sites [Lindauer 1955, 1961, Seeley 1977, 1982]. They enable bees with no prior experience in househunting to identify high-quality sites.) However, this possibility also is unlikely because large week-to-week or even day-to-day changes in forage availability (see Fig. 4) prevent bees from having a fixed definition of a top-quality food source. Thus, whereas a dish of 1.0 mol sugar syrup located 500 m from a hive attracts hordes of bees in New England in mid-August, a time when forage is poor, the same dish of sugar syrup is ignored by bees a few weeks later when the goldenrod plants (*Solidago* spp.) come into bloom.

One promising approach to solving the mystery of how honeybees assess the relative profitability of their forage patches is to explore certain ideas from optimal foraging theory (reviewed by Pyke et al. 1977, Krebs 1978, and various authors in Kamil and Sargent 1981). Within this literature, the ideas of central-place foraging theory (Orians and Pearson 1979, Orians 1980) are especially relevant to honeybee foraging. In this

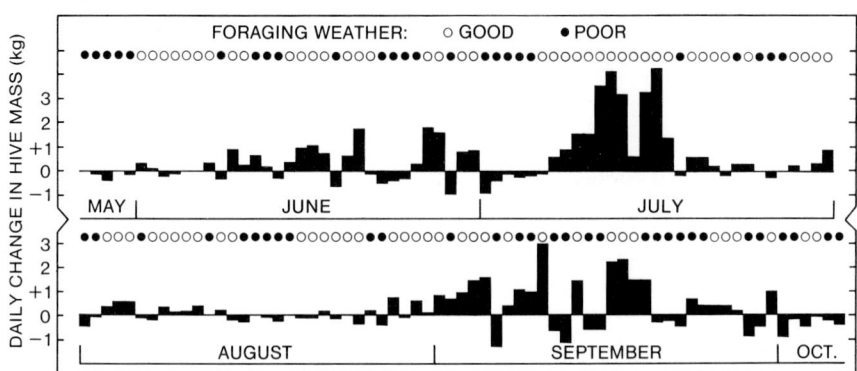

Fig. 4: Daily changes in mass of a hive of honeybees throughout a summer. «Good» foraging weather was defined here as a mean temperature above 14 °C during the hours 0600–1800 and no rain during the day.

discussion, I will apply these ideas to just one situation: bees foraging from patches of flowers producing just nectar.

It seems reasonable to assume that what a honeybee foraging for nectar would like to maximize is her rate of energy intake. PYKE (1981) reviews the validity of this assumption for nectarivores in general. Some of the justifications which apply specifically to honeybees are as follows. First, because the many foragers from a honeybee colony pool their forage, bees can specialize on either nectar or pollen collection and need not divide their time between foraging for these two types of food. Honeybee foragers do, in fact, frequently specialize in either nectar or pollen collection (reviewed by RIBBANDS 1953 and FREE 1970). Second, because of the division of labor between scouts and recruits in honeybee colonies (see below), nectar foragers working one patch need not sample alternative patches to track changes in patch profitability. Such sampling is performed by the colony's scout bees. Third, the risk of predation may be negligible for foraging honeybees and at least is probably not affected by the profitability of a bee's forage patch. And fourth, the ability of honeybee colonies to grow, reproduce, and survive winters is probably closely correlated with the total energy collected by a colony's foragers.

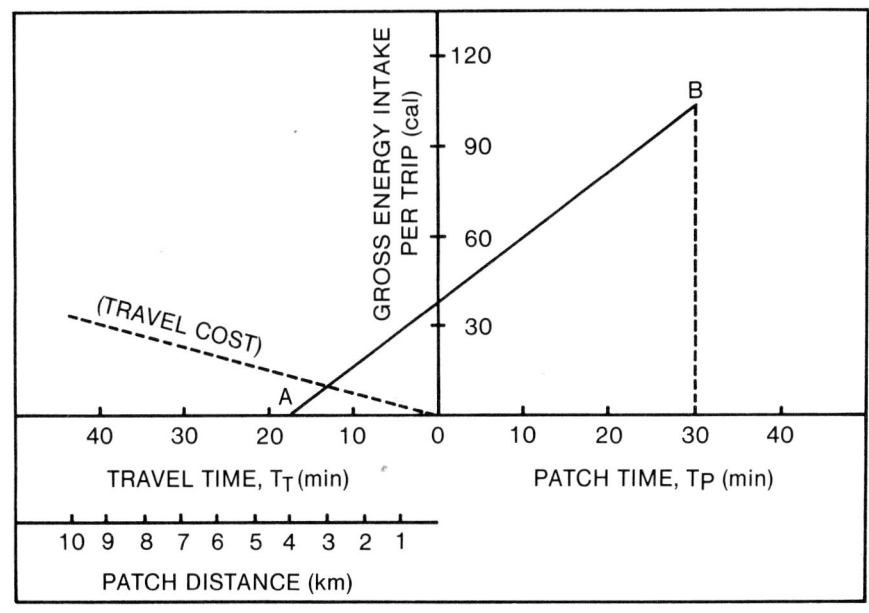

Fig. 5: Graphical representation of the calculation of a honeybee forager's gross rate of energy intake (indicated by the slope of the line AB) from a forage patch which is 4 km from the forager's nest, offers a 1.5 mol (= 43 %) sucrose solution, and requires 30 min of time at the patch for the forager to collect a full, 50 ul load of nectar. The dashed, sloping line on the left side denotes the cost, in calories, of a roundtrip flight between nest and forage patch for various distances, assuming foragers fly 7.7 m/sec (VON FRISCH and LINDAUER 1955, BOCH 1956), weigh 100 mg (OTIS 1982), and have a metabolic rate while flying of 1.42 ml $0_2 \cdot g^{-1} \cdot min^{-1}$ (HEINRICH 1979b). This line indicates that for forage patches up to about 5 km from the nest, the flight cost of a forage trip is only a tiny fraction of the trip's gross profit. In other words, for most forage flights by honeybees, the gross rate of energy intake closely approximates the net rate of energy intake.

I suggest that is is useful to think of a nectar-yielding patch as being characterized by 3 basic properties: (1) the time required to fly to and from the patch (travel time, T_T), (2) the time required to load up with nectar when in a patch (patch time, T_P), and (3) the sugar concentration of the nectar in the patch. Because all workers in a honeybee colony are roughly equivalent in size (Waddington 1981), and probably load similar volumes of nectar of a given sugar concentration (von Frisch 1967, Wells and Giacchino 1968, Nunez 1966, 1970)[1], it is probably also fair to characterize a patch by the gross energy acquired by a forager during a trip to the patch. Gross energy = (volume of nectar loaded) x (sugar concentration) x (4 calories/mg sugar).

One way of thinking about the relationship between the patch properties just mentioned and a patch's overall profitability to a foraging honeybee is shown in Fig. 5. The slope of the line AB denotes the gross rate of energy intake from the patch. According to this analysis, what a nectar forager needs to know in order to judge the profitability of her forage patch relative to other foragers' patches is the relative energy yield per trip to the patch and the relative duration ($T_T + T_P$) of her forage trips.

How might a bee perceive the relative energy intake per trip to her patch? If, as was argued above, all bees load equal volumes of nectar of a given sugar concentration, then the gross energy intake per trip to a patch can be deduced given knowledge of the value of just one variable – the sugar concentration of a patch's nectar. Thus a forager's problem of estimating the relative energy yield per trip to her patch may simplify to being able to perceive the relative sugar concentration of her patch's nectar.

Lindauer (1948, 1952, 1954) has already shown that honeybees apparently have a special communication system through which foragers exchange information about nectar concentration. Information transfer occurs during a forager's interactions with the bees in the nest which first receive her nectar, the so-called «receiver bees». These bees sample widely among in-coming foragers and thus know the range of sugar concentration in the available nectars (Nowogrodzki 1981). The receiver bees also scale the vigor of their reception of a forager in relation to the sugar concentration of the forager's nectar. Foragers bearing relatively concentrated nectar are quickly and vigorously unloaded whereas foragers returning with relatively dilute nectar are only slowly and seemingly unenthusiastically unloaded. By noting either the delivery time, or the intensity of antennal contacts, or some other variable aspect of the reception by receiver bees, a forager can apparently estimate the relative sugar concentration of her patch's nectar, and thus the relative energy yield per trip to her patch.

Recent studies (Seeley, unpublished) have revealed that this communication system enables colonies to preferentially allocate foragers to superior patches with high precision. If one offers a colony two food sources in opposite directions 500 m from the hive, with the two feeders identical except for the concentrations of their sugar solutions, and one compares the colony's recruitment rates to the two patches, one observes the pattern shown in Fig. 6. The recruitment rate to the poorer food source drops off exponentially as the difference in sugar concentration between the two feeders increases linearly. A difference in sugar concentration between the feeders as small as 0.125 mol elicits a significant ($p < 0.004$), approximately 30 %, difference in recruitment rate to the two food sources.

How might a bee perceive the relative duration of her forage trips? Unfortunately, there seems to be no way for foragers to exchange information about forage trip times the way they do about their patches' nectar concentrations. One possible alternative is that all

---

[1] When a bee works a nearby ($\leq$ 600 m away) patch, the volume of her nectar load appears to be influenced by patch distance (Núñez, 1982).

Fig. 6: Sensitivity of a honeybee colony to differences in sugar concentration between forage patches. Relative recruitment rate denotes the rate of recruitment to the patch with less concentrated nectar divided by the rate of recruitment to the patch with more concentrated nectar. A negative exponential describes a colony's response to linear increases in difference in sugar concentration between patches.

foragers possess a shared, innate scale of forage-trip times and that each forager compares the average of her own forage-trip times with the values on this scale to determine whether she is making relatively long, average, or short forage trips. Such a system would only work if the mean and variance of forage-trip durations do not vary widely throughout a summer. To my knowledge, no one has ever collected data on forage-trip times across a summer. Such data would provide a test of the plausibility of this hypothesis.

In summary, the hypothesis for how nectar foragers perceive the relative profitability of a patch is that a forager can estimate both the relative energy yield per trip to her patch and the relative duration of a trip to her patch, and can combine these two pieces of information to estimate the relative rate of energy intake available from the patch. Presumably it is this last piece of information which a nectar forager uses to decide whether to continue working or to abandon her patch. Although these ideas have yet to be tested, this situation should not last for long. Using artificial feeders, one can create forage patches whose sugar concentration, trip time, and patch time can be precisely controlled. Furthermore, by working with foragers from a colony living in an observation hive, one can easily observe the effects of changing the properties of a forage patch on a forager's behavior. Thus is should be possible to test the quantitative predictions outlined above about the relationship between patch properties and forager behavior.

3.2 Division of labor between scouts and recruits

In order for colonies to select forage patches by the method described earlier, most workers must locate new forage patches by following recruitment dances (as opposed to searching randomly on their own, i. e., scouting). Is this the case? It seems clear *a priori* that a colony needs some scouts among its foragers since it is the scout bees which discover new patches. Recruits are directed to known patches and sooner or later all of these known patches will cease yielding food. In other words, a colony needs some explorers as well as exploiters in order to achieve long-term foraging efficiency. But what sort of scout: recruit ratio prevails?

OETTINGEN-SPIELBERG (1949) made a preliminary measurement of the percent scouts among novice foragers by adding marked, newly-emerged bees to a hive kept in a flight room and observing what fraction of these bees began foraging by arriving at a feeding station, to which there was recruitment, or to a bouquet of flowers, to which no recruitment was allowed. Of 1062 bees, only 53 (5 %) found the flowers and so presumably were scouts. LINDAUER (1952) repeated this measurement using a far superior experimental technique. He observed which individuals within a large cohort of bees living in an observation hive started foraging without following any dances. He observed 13 % scouts (data analyzed in SEELEY 1983). I have recently extended these measurements to estimate the percent scouts among experienced foragers (SEELEY 1983). My basic experimental procedure was as follows: (1) train a small group of labelled foragers from an observation hive to a feeding station, (2) monitor the foraging tempo of each forager for 2 days, (3) shut off the feeding station and watch the labelled bees back in the observation hive to determine how each individual finds her next forage patch (whether by scouting or by following recruitment dances). This procedure was repeated 7 times to get data for 78 foragers, of which 18 (23 %) were scouts. Clearly, only a small minority of honeybee foragers, both novice and experienced, find patches without following recruitment dances.

The figure of 23 % scouts among experienced foragers is by no means a fixed percentage. Rather, the proportion of scouts apparently depends upon the foraging conditions. In trials when little forage was available, approximately 36 % of the bees found forage by scouting. In contrast, in trials when nectar-bearing plants were blooming profusely, only 5 % of the foragers scouted. Evidently the proportion of scouts is adjusted to the colony's needs. Probably a colony benefits by allocating more bees to scouting when forage is poor, and its foragers are underemployed, than when forage is rich, and the colony cannot fully exploit the many attractive sources discovered by its scouts.

What determines whether a forager serves as a scout or recruit, and how might this determination mechanism operate so that colonies can adjust the percent scouts in relation to changes in foraging conditions? The key to answering this question may be variation among individual foragers in tendency to perform as a scout or a recruit. According to this view, some bees always scout to find a new forage patch, other always follow recruitment dances, and still others can use either technique (see Fig. 7). What determines whether or not these intermediate, versatile foragers follow recruitment dances might be simply the ease of finding dancing bees to follow. If so, then as the availability of forage decreases, and the number of bees advertising underexploited forage patches dwindles, a colony will automatically allocate more bees to scouting. This in turn should boost the colony's probability of discovering new food sources. Because an exhaustive exploration of a colony's forage range probably requires only a fraction of a colony's forager force, it seems probable that there is an upper limit to the percent scouts among a colony's foragers.

At the heart of this hypothesis is the idea that foragers are not all equivalent, that there are scout and recruit specialists, and so instances of scouting and recruitment are distributed non-randomly among a group of foragers. Alternatively, all foragers are essentially equivalent, and random events determine whether a particular forager, at a given time, scouts or follows dances to find a forage patch. Careful observers of honeybee behavior have repeatedly concluded that individual bees differ markedly in foraging behavior (VON FRISCH 1923, 1967, 1969, LINDAUER 1952, OPFINGER 1949, RIBBANDS 1955, SCHMID 1964). One piece of quantitative evidence supporting the hypothesis of non-equivalent foragers emerged from my measurement of the scout: recruit ratio among experienced foragers (SEELEY 1983). A comparison of the foraging tempos of scouts and recruits during their two days of foraging from the feeding station revealed a significant difference. The scouts' foraging rates averaged higher than those of recruits (scouts, 95 ± 13; recruits, 75 ± 12 foraging trips $\cdot 8$ hr^{-1} $\cdot$ bee^{-1}; $p < 0.01$). Moreover, individual bees were moderately consistent from day to day in their foraging rates ($r = 0.65$ for the correlation between days in the number of forage trips made daily by each individual).

The origin of these differences among individuals remains unclear. Although foragers of a wide age range can become scouts (OETTINGEN-SPIELBERG 1949, VON FRISCH 1967), foraging experience may have some effect on a bee's scouting tendency since, as described above, experienced foragers seem more likely to scout than do beginning foragers. Genetic differences and differences in developmental conditions between individuals could, of course, also shape the differentiation of scouts and recruits, but there is no solid evidence for or against the role of these two factors.

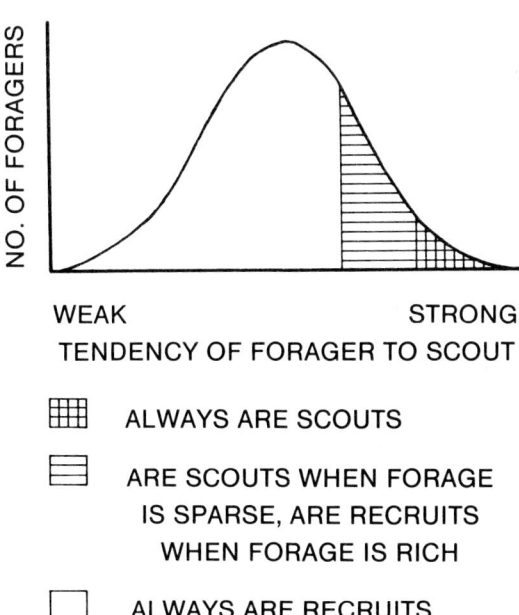

Fig. 7: Hypothetical distribution of foragers across a gradient of tendency to scout. By this scheme, the large majority of a colony's foragers have little inclination to scout and so are always recruits, a tiny minority have a strong tendency to scout and so are always scouts, and the remainder function either as scouts or recruits depending on whether the available forage is sparse or rich, respectively.

4 Foraging energetics

What is the impact on a colony's foraging energetics of the honeybee's elaborate forag-ing strategy, with its intricate intertwining of recruitment communication, scout-recruit division of labor, and selectivity in recruitment? A preliminary answer to this question has been made by comparing the cost to scouts and the cost to recruits of finding a new food source when the feeding station they had worked for the previous three days was shut off. Search cost comparisons were made by comparing the search times of scouts and recruits. Each bee's «search time» was the sum of the time periods spent outside the nest when searching for a new forage patch (see Seeley 1983 for details).

Initially, I thought that this comparison would reveal that a major payoff of the honey-bee's foraging strategy is a reduced cost of finding forage patches. My reasoning was that because it probably is easier for bees to find forage patches by following recruitment dances than by independently scouting, a colony with recruitment communication and a scout-recruit division of labor probably has lower search costs than one without this social organization of foraging.

Contrary to expectations, the recruits spent more time (and presumably energy) search-ing for a forage patch than did the scouts: recruits 138 ± 76 min; scouts, 85 ± 58 min ($p < 0.087$). The basis for this surprise is probably the fact that recruitment in the real world is much less automatic than previous studies under experimental conditions (von Frisch 1967, Esch and Bastian 1970, Mautz 1970, Gould 1976) had suggested. Whereas honeybee researchers usually study recruitment to conspicuous feeders a few hundred meters from a hive, in nature a typical situation for honeybee recruitment probably in-volves a small patch of flowers a few thousand meters from a nest. I observed that only rarely does a recruit locate her new patch on the first trip outside the nest after following a dancing bee. Recruits required on average 4.8 trips (range, 1–12 trips). Scouts, in contrast, seek any available forage patch, not particular patches, and so evidently expend less time and energy locating new food sources.

Apparently the payoff to recruits for their greater investment in finding a forage patch is that the patches found are unusually high in quality. This idea is supported by a compari-son between scouts and recruits in their behavior following the first trip to a new forage patch. The probability of again bringing back forage was higher for recruits than scouts: 95 % and 51 %, respectively. Clearly, the patches found by recruits had a higher probabili-ty of being worth returning to than did the patches found by scouts.

Although not enough data are yet available to provide a detailed picture of how the honeybee's social organization affects a colony's foraging energetics, the following picture is emerging. First, there is a spatial effect. The average rate of food collection per forager is raised because colonies, foraging as an integrated whole, can sample widely through the environment and focus their foragers on the best patches. In insect societies without recruitment communication, such as those of bumblebees (Heinrich 1979 a), each indi-vidual is limited to the information she herself collects when she chooses a work site. Inevitably, the area over which an individual bee can search is far smaller than the 100 or more square kilometers monitored by an entire honeybee colony. Secondly, there is a temporal effect. The honeybee's social organization also enhances foraging efficiency by facilitating the tracking of high-quality forage patches. Whenever a scout bee discovers a new rich food source, or there are changes in the relative rankings of known sources, foragers shift off the less profitable sources onto more rewarding ones. Such shifting of work sites does not depend on each forager making direct comparisons between her current and possible alternative food sources, but instead on the exchange of information among a colony's foragers. In contrast, the foragers in a bumblebee colony share little, if any, information about food sources. Thus each forager must periodically inspect alternative food sources in order to stay informed of changes in foraging opportunities.

5 Further studies

Future research on the social foraging strategy of honeybees will probably expand in two directions. One concerns foraging decisions other than patch choice, the second involves comparative studies within the genus *Apis*.

5.1 Foraging decisions besides patch choice

In collecting its food, a honeybee colony faces the following nested hierarchy of foraging decisions. First, what fraction of a colony's total work force should be devoted to food collection? Second, given a certain size forager force, how should a colony partition it between scouts and recruits? Third, given a certain number of recruits, how should they be divided between the tasks of pollen and nectar collection? And fourth, given a certain number of recruits for either pollen or nectar collection, how should they be distributed among the known patches yielding either pollen or nectar?

Anecdotal evidence suggests that colonies do make decisions at all four of these levels in the foraging process. The fraction of a colony's work force which is devoted to foraging apparently reflects forage availability. When forage is abundant, workers start foraging at an earlier age than when little forage is available (LINDAUER 1952, SEKIGUCHI and SAKAGAMI 1967), thereby creating a larger proportion of foragers in a colony during good times than bad times. Similarly, as we have seen above, the proportion of scout bees in a colony's forager force reflects forage availability. It may be affected by forage patch predictability as well. Current foraging theory (ORIANS 1981) predicts that animals should devote more effort to reconnaissance when the turnover rate of forage patches is high than when it is low. Labor allocation to pollen collection apparently also varies, depending on the relative magnitudes of pollen supply in the environment and demand in the colony. For example, colonies seem to devote a much larger fraction of their foragers to pollen collection in the early spring, when colonies need much pollen for brood rearing but still few flowers are available, than in the summer, when it is easy to balance a colony's collection and consumption of pollen (personal observations). It is also well known that equipping a beehive with a pollen trap (which scrapes the pollen loads from a proportion of the pollen collectors as they enter the hive) stimulates pollen collection (LINDAUER 1952). Finally, as was discussed above, colonies carefully distribute their foragers among patches in relation to profitability differences among patches.

Of these four decision-making processes, only one — forage patch selection — is understood in any detail.

5.2 Comparative studies of honeybee foraging strategies

One special attraction of honeybees for research on social foraging is that they provide a perfect opportunity for using the comparative approach to study the relationship between social organization and foraging ecology (KREBS and DAVIS 1981, SEELEY et al. 1982). On the one hand, the three honeybee species of southern Asia — *Apis florea*, *A. cerana*, and *A. dorsata* — are closely related and so share many features of their biology, such as their diet of nectar and pollen, their basic morphology, and the dance language system of recruitment communication. On the other hand, there are striking differences among the three species in such aspects of their foraging ecologies as habitat, worker size, flight range, aggressiveness in food source defense, and species diversity of food plants (Lindauer 1956, Singh 1962, Morse and Laigo 1969, Akratanakul 1977, Koeniger and Vorwohl 1979, Seeley et al. 1982). Because the three species are so closely related, differences among them probably represent a recent adaptive radiation within a monophyletic group rather than historical differences among phylogenetically distant species.

By carefully documenting these patterns of divergence in foraging behavior and ecology, it should be possible to identify the ecological pressures which have propelled the differentiation of the three species' foraging behaviors. So little is known about the foraging biologies of the Asian honeybees that it is hard to predict what general aspects of animal foraging behavior and ecology will be illuminated through study of the Asian *Apis*. One possibility is that the three species will display three distinct strategies of social foraging, all of which are based on recruitment communication, but which differ markedly in search area, forage patch selectivity, recruitment rate, vigor of patch defense, and total energy budget. Whatever story ultimately emerges, it is likely to provide a major contribution to our understanding of the ecology and evolution of cooperative foraging in animal societies.

References

Akratanakul, P. (1977): The natural history of the dwarf honey bee, *Apis florea* F., in Thailand. Ph. D. Thesis, Cornell Univ., Ithaca, New York, 1–91.

Alexander, R. D. (1974): The evolution of social behavior. Ann. Rev. Ecol. Syst. *5*, 325–383.

Aristotle (1956): Historia Animalium. Vol. IX, chapt. 40.

Boch, R. (1956): Die Tänze der Bienen bei nahen und fernen Trachtquellen. Z. vergl. Physiol. *38*, 136–167.

Butler, C. G. (1945): The influence of various physical and biological factors of the environment on honeybee activity and nectar concentration and abundance. J. exp. Biol. *21*, 5–12.

Esch, H. and J. A. Bastian (1970): How do newly recruited honeybees approach a food site? Z. vergl. Physiol. *68*, 175–181.

Free, J. B. (1970): Insect Pollination of Crops. Academic Press, New York.

Frisch, K. von (1923): Über die «Sprache» der Bienen, eine tierpsychologische Untersuchung. Zool. Jb. (Physiol.) *40*, 1–186.

Frisch, K. von (1967): The Dance Language and Orientation of Bees, Harvard Univ. Press, Cambridge, Ma.

Frisch, K. von (1969): The foraging bee. Bee World *50*, 141–152.

Frisch, K. von and M. Lindauer (1955): Über die Fluggeschwindigkeit der Bienen und ihre Richtungsweisung bei Seitenwind. Naturwissenschaften *42*, 377–385.

Gould, J. L. (1976): The dance-language controversy. Q. Rev. Biol. *51*, 211–244.

Heinrich, B. (1976): The foraging specializations of individual bumblebees. Ecol. Monogr. *46*, 105–128.

Heinrich, B. (1978): The economics of insect sociality. pp. 97–128. In: J. R. Krebs and N. B. Davies (Eds.): Behavioural Ecology. An Evolutionary Approach. Sinauer Assoc., Sunderland, Ma.

Heinrich, B. (1979 a): Bumblebee Economics. Harvard Univ. Press, Cambridge, Ma.

Heinrich, B. (1979 b): Keeping a cool head: honeybee thermoregulation. Science *205*, 1269–1271.

Kamil, A. C. and T. D. Sargent (1981): Foraging Behavior. Ecological, Ethological and Psychological Approaches. Garland STPM, New York.

Koeniger, N. and G. Vorwohl (1979): Competition for food among four sympatric species of Apini in Sri Lanka (*Apis dorsata, Apis cerana, Apis florea,* and *Trigona irridipennis*). J. Apic. Res. *18*, 95–109.

Krebs, J. R. (1978): Optimal foraging: decision rules for predators. pp. 23–63. In: J. R. Krebs and N. B. Davies (Eds.): Behavioural Ecology. An Evolutionary Approach. Sinauer Assoc., Sunderland, Ma.

Krebs, J. R. and N. B. Davies (1981): An Introduction to Behavioural Ecology. Sinauer Assoc., Sunderland, Ma.

Lindauer, M. (1948): Über die Einwirkung von Duft- und Geschmacksstoffen sowie anderen Faktoren auf die Tänze der Bienen. Z. vergl. Physiol. *31*, 348–412.

Lindauer, M. (1952): Ein Beitrag zur Frage der Arbeitsteilung im Bienenstaat. Z. vergl. Physiol. *34*, 299–345.

Lindauer, M. (1954): Temperaturregulierung und Wasserhaushalt im Bienenstaat. Z. vergl. Physiol. *36*, 391–432.

Lindauer, M. (1955): Schwarmbienen auf Wohnungssuche. Z. vergl. Physiol. *37*, 263–324.

Lindauer, M. (1956): Über die Verständigung bei indischen Bienen. Z. vergl. Physiol. *38*, 521–557.

Lindauer, M. (1961): Communication Among Social Bees. Harvard Univ. Press. Cambridge, Ma.

Mautz, D. (1971): Der Kommunikationseffekt der Schwanzeltänze bei *Apis mellifica carnica* (Pollm). Z. vergl. Physiol. *72*, 197–220.

Maynard Smith, J. (1976): Group selection. Q. Rev. Biol. *51*, 277–283.

Morse, R. A. and F. M. Laigo (1969): *Apis dorsata* in the Philippines. Monogr. Philippine Assoc. of Entomol. *1*, 1–96.

Nowogrodzki, R. (1981): Regulation of the number of foragers on a constant food source by honey bee colonies. M. S. thesis, Cornell Univ., Ithaca, New York, 1–131.

Núñez, J. A. (1966): Quantitative Beziehungen zwischen den Eigenschaften von Futterquellen und den Verhalten von Sammelbienen. Z. vergl. Physiol. *53*, 142–164.

Núñez, J. A. (1970): The relationship between sugar flow and foraging and recruiting behaviour of honey bees (*Apis mellifera* L.). Anim. Behav. *18*, 527–528.

Núñez, J. A. (1982): Honeybee foraging strategies at a food source in relation to its distance from the hive and the rate of sugar flow. J. Apic. Res. *21*, 139–150.

Oettingen-Spielberg, T. zu (1949): Über das Wesen der Suchbiene. Z. vergl. Physiol. *31*, 454–489.

Opfinger, E. (1949): Zur Psychologie der Duftdressuren bei Bienen. Z. vergl. Physiol. *31*, 441–453.

Orians, G. H. (1980): Some Adaptations of Marsh-nesting Blackbirds. Princeton Univ. Press, Princeton, New Jersey.

Orians, G. H. (1981): Foraging behavior and the evolution of discriminating abilities. pp. 389–405. In: A. C. Kamil and T. D. Sargent (Eds.): Foraging Behavior. Ecological, Ethological, and Psychological Approaches. Garland STPM, New York.

Orians, G. H. and N. E. Pearson (1979): On the theory of central place foraging. pp. 155–177. In: D. J. Horn, R. D. Mitchell, and G. R. Stairs (Eds.): Analysis of Ecological Systems. Ohio State Univ. Press, Columbus, Ohio.

Oster, G. F. and E. O. Wilson (1978): Caste and Ecology in the Social Insects. Princeton Univ. Press, Princeton, New Jersey.

Otis, G. W. (1982): Weights of worker honeybees in swarms. J. Apic. Res. *21*, 88–92.

Pyke, G. H. (1981): Optimal foraging in nectar-feeding animals and coevolution with their plants. pp. 19–38. In: A. C. Kamil and T. D. Sargent (Eds.): Foraging Behavior. Ecological, Ethological, and Psychological Approaches. Garland STPM, New York.

Pyke, G. H., H. R. Pulliam and E. L. Charnow (1977): Optimal foraging: a selective review of theory and tests. Q. Rev. Biol. *52*, 137–154.

Ribbands, C. R. (1949): The foraging method of individual honeybees. J. Anim. Ecol. *18*, 47–66.

Ribbands, C. R. (1953): The Behaviour and Social Life of Honeybees. Bee Research Assoc., Ltd., London.

Ribbands, C. R. (1955): The scent perception of the honeybee. Proc. Roy. Soc. London (B) *143*, 367–379.

Schmid, J. (1964): Zur Frage der Störung des Bienengedächtnisses durch Narkosemittel, zugleich ein Beitrag zur Störung der sozialen Bindung durch Narkose. Z. vergl. Physiol. *47*, 559–595.

Seeley, T. D. (1977): Measurement of nest cavity volume by the honey bee *(Apis mellifera)*. Behav. Ecol. Sociobiol. *2*, 201–227.

Seeley, T. D. (1982): How honeybees choose a home. Scien. Amer. *247*, 158–168.

Seeley, T. D. (1983): Division of labor between scouts and recruits in honeybee foraging. Behav. Ecol. Sociobiol. *12*, 253–259.

Seeley, T. D., R. H. Seeley and P. Akratanakul (1982): Colony defense strategies of the honeybees in Thailand. Ecol. Monogr. *52*, 43–63.

Sekiguchi, K. and S. F. Sakagami (1966): Structure of foraging population and related problems in the honeybee, with considerations on the division of labor in bee colonies. Hokkaido Nat. Agric. Expt. Sta. Rep. *69*, 1–65.

Singh, S. (1950): Behavior studies of honeybees in gathering nectar and pollen. Cornell Univ. Agric. Expt. Sta. Mem. *288*, 1–34.

Singh, S. (1962): Beekeeping in India. Indian Council of Agric. Res. Publ., New Delhi.

Visscher, P. K. and T. D. Seeley (1982): Foraging strategy of honeybee colonies in a temperate deciduous forest. Ecology *63*, 1790–1801.

Waddington, K. D. (1981): Patterns of size variation in bees and evolution of communication systems. Evolution *35*, 813–814.

Weaver, N. (1957): The foraging behavior of honeybees on hairy vetch. II. The foraging area and foraging speed. Insectes Soc. *4*, 43–57.

Weaver, N. (1979): Possible recruitment of foraging honeybees to high-reward areas of the same plant species. J. Apic. Res. *18*, 179–183.

Wells, P. H. and J. Giacchino (1968): Relationship between the volume and the sugar concentration of loads carried by honeybees. J. Apic. Res. *7*, 77–82.

Williams, G. C. (1966): Adaptation and Natural Selection. Princeton Univ. Press, Princeton, New Jersey.

Fortschritte der Zoologie, Bd. 31 · Hölldobler/Lindauer (Hrsg.): Experimental Behavioral Ecology
G. Fischer Verlag · Stuttgart · New York · 1985

Reproduction, foraging efficiency and worker polymorphism in army ants

NIGEL R. FRANKS

School of Biological Sciences, University of Bath, BA2 7AY England

Abstract

The size and growth rate of *Eciton burchelli*, army ant colonies has been determined by filming colony emigrations and by collecting the discarded pupal cases of their broods of new workers. Colonies of *Eciton burchelli* on Barro Colorado Island, Panama, have between 300,000 and 650,000 workers and they raise between 40,000 and 60,000 workers per 35 days. At one time of year the largest colonies produce a single brood of a few queens and about 4,000 males. These sexually reproductive colonies then undergo a process of binary fission to produce two daughter colonies. Parental colonies reproduce at approximately the size at which the combined growth rate of their daughter colonies just exceeds their own growth rate. This should minimize colony generation time.

There are four distinct physical castes of worker in *Eciton burchelli*, making this one of the most polymorphic of known ant species. I have evaluated the performance of these different worker castes during raids, because foraging efficiency is likely to be one of the key factors limiting colony growth rate. Of the four types of worker, submajors seem to specialise as porters; they are only 3 % of the worker population but they represent 26 % of the workers carrying prey items. Due to an unusual allometry submajors have the longest legs in proportion to their body size of any *Eciton burchelli* workers and they can run faster than any of their sisters and can carry disproportionately large items. Submajors probably also transport prey at a relatively low cost because they are the largest members of their colonies who retrieve prey items and transport costs decrease with increasing body size. The division of labour among *Eciton burchelli* workers may therefore serve to increase foraging efficiency and this should increase colony growth rate, decrease colony generation time and thereby contribute to the inclusive fitness of all members of the army ant colony.

1 Introduction

One of DARWIN's (1859) most penetrating insights was his suggestion that sterile forms evolved in social insects because they are «profitable to the community» and «selection may be applied to the family, as well as to the individual». He further suggested that once this colony-level selection had begun, the sterile forms could be molded into distinct castes: «Thus in *Eciton*, there are working and soldier neuters, with jaws and instincts extraordinarily different» (DARWIN, 1859). To evaluate this division of labour, which is a key to understanding the limits of social evolution (OSTER and WILSON, 1978, WILSON 1980 a, b), it is necessary to relate the size, shape and behaviour of individual workers to the growth and reproductive success of their colonies. Army ants of the genus *Eciton* are particularly suitable for this analysis because their workers are exceptionally polymorphic and yet their colony life-history strategies are relatively simple.

In this paper I examine one way in which the growth and reproductive rate of *Eciton burchelli* colonies is determined by their foraging efficiency and how this in turn is related to the distribution of labour and performance among their workers. *Eciton burchelli* is a good subject for this kind of study for two reasons. First, colonies of this species can be accurately sampled and their size determined, as they nest and raid above ground: and second, the production of both workers and new colonies follow extremely stereotyped patterns.

Colonies of *E. burchelli* alternate between 15 day nomadic phases when they raid during every day and emigrate at night, and 20 day statary phases when they raid less frequently and stay at the same nest site (SCHNEIRLA, 1971; WILLIS, 1967). This cyclical behaviour is correlated the production of discrete broods of eggs, larvae and pupae. These broods are generally of workers; however, at one time of year the largest colonies while maintaining their activity cycles produce a single brood of a few thousand males and about six queens. After such a sexual brood has completed its development the parental colony divides to produce two daughter colonies (RETTENMEYER, 1963; SCHNEIRLA, 1971). Because workers are produced in discrete broods it is relatively easy to estimate the growth rate of undisturbed colonies in the field. Furthermore, since new colonies are formed by binary fission it is possible to relate worker production and colony growth directly to reproductive success.

Recent studies (FRANKS and FLETCHER, 1983; FRANKS and BOSSERT, 1983) have shown that *Eciton burchelli* colonies have a distinct foraging strategy. In the statary phase these army ants separate neighbouring raids by using a pattern similar to that used by many plants in spiral phyllotaxis; and in the nomadic phase colonies navigate by raiding and emigrating in much the same direction from one day to the nest. This navigation lowers the probability that the nomadic raid path will cross itself and also separates the areas foraged in successive statary phases. These swarm raiding patterns will contribute to colony growth rate by increasing foraging efficiency. In this paper I examine the behaviour and morphology of individual workers within the raid system to determine how their design contributes to foraging efficiency. This paper also reports the first quantitative study of colony size, brood production, caste ratios, and reproduction in these army ants.

2 Methods

The study was conducted on Barro Colorado Island, Panama (LEIGH et al., 1982) during the dry season, January to May of 1979. The size of seven *Eciton burchelli* colonies was estimated by filming their emigrations. Colonies emigrate on almost every night of their nomadic phase and during these migrations the entire colony moves between bivouac sites where their nests take the form of hanging baskets of living workers. The route taken by an emigration can be predicted very accurately because the emigration column follows the exact path of the principal trail of the same day's raiding (RETTENMEYER, 1963). This is the trail that the ants used to go to the raiding swarm front and along which they returned with prey items. An emigration is signaled when the ants at the swarm raid no longer return to the old bivouac, but start to form a new bivouac towards the end of that day's raid system. When this is occurring return traffic to the old bivouac quickly diminishes, as does outward traffic to the swarm: then quite suddenly with the onset of dusk, movement becomes almost entirely outward and rapidly increases as the emigration begins. This moment was taken as the cue to begin filming the emigrations of the selected colonies.

The emigration from bivouac to bivouac is so orderly that it resembles a ribbon of ants unwinding from one spool and winding-up on another. The number of ants in a bivouac can be estimated from the following information: (1) the average velocity of the column, (2) the average number of ants per unit length of the trail, and (3) the duration of the emigration. The first was estimated by timing the progress of 20 burdened and unburdened ants of various sizes over a one metre section of trail, at various times during the emigration. The second was assessed by taking a picture of a known length of about one metre of trail every ¼ of an hour throughout the emigration. Finally the duration of the emigration, to the nearest ¼ of an hour, could also be estimated from the same series of pictures. The number of ants in the bivouac (B) was estimated from the relation B = T.V.N. where T is the duration of the emigration, V is the mean velocity of the column, and N is the average number of ants per unit length of the emigration column.

The photographs were taken automatically by a 35 mm single lens reflex camera fitted with a timer, an auto-winder and a flash. A fine grain, Kodak Pan-X monochrome film was used. The number of ants per unit length of trail, as sampled every 15 minutes throughout the emigration was counted directly from the film negatives. Members of the two largest worker castes could also be distinguished and counted from the films, to estimate possible changes in caste ratios with colony size (Table 1). The camera was stationed near the old bivouac site, so only the ants in the bivouac and none of the ants in the raid system were photographed.

The filmed colonies were all either forming or leaving a statary bivouac and I estimated the size of the brood each colony produced by collecting the pupal cases of either its worker brood or its predominantly male sexual brood. Pupal cases are sometimes also deposited at the first nomadic bivouac (RETTENMEYER, 1963) and these were also collected. A D-Vac suction sampler was used to collect all the pupal cases from even the most inaccessible recesses of the hollow trees in which the colonies had been bivouacing. The cases and the debris that were collected with them were later separated, after preliminary drying, by blowing them apart. The cases were then dried to constant weight in a 50 °C oven and weighed, as was a counted subsample, to provide an estimate of the number of workers or males produced by the filmed colonies.

To estimate the size of the workers that had emerged from the empty pupal cases, callow workers still in their pupal cases were collected from one of the first nomadic emigrations. I removed these callow workers from their cocoons and recorded both the dry weight of each ant and the width of its pupal case. Thus the size distribution in each worker brood was estimated by measuring the width of 100 pupal cases taken at random from those discarded by each colony.

In a separate series of measurements the raid lengths of the filmed colonies were also recorded by laying a 100 m tape along the principal trail of some of their nomadic phase foraging systems. These distances were measured when the raids were at their maximum length just before night fall.

Morphological measurements of ants, made by using a dissection microscope fitted with an eyepiece graticule, suggest that there are four distinct castes in *E. burchelli* (see results section). With practice, individual workers can be allocated to one of these four castes by visual sorting, and this can be done with a high degree of success as checked by subsequent measurement.

The relative abundance of these four worker castes in the foraging and bivouac populations were also estimated by using the suction sampler to make unbiased collections of
raiding ants and by pressing a beaker containing 70 % ethanol into the side of a pendulous
bivouac. In addition, to investigate the role of the different castes as porters of prey items,
just those ants engaged in this task were collected from raid trails. To ensure unbiased
sampling, a flag was placed by a trail and all the ants carrying prey past this marker were
collected individually. All samples of adult workers were taken from a series of different *E.
burchelli* colonies, which were not filmed, but which were judged to be of a wide range of
different sizes.

To analyse one aspect of foraging efficiency I measured the speed of workers running in
raid trails and the size of the prey items they carried. The velocity of various sizes of
workers was recorded as they ran in raid trails that passed along the length of fallen tree
trunks and other such obstacle-free courses. I followed and timed individual workers as
they ran over measured distances of 10 m and more and collected both the ants and any
prey items they were carrying. Burdened ants were only timed if they were carrying prey
items without the aid of other ants. Morphological measurements and dry weights of ants
and prey items were then obtained using the standard methods outlined above.

3 Results

3.1 Colony Size

Four of the filmed colonies had worker broods and three had sexual broods. The
colonies with sexual broods divided evenly at the end of their statary phase. This process is
described in detail by Schneirla (1956). One of these colonies (E.b. 11) was filmed before

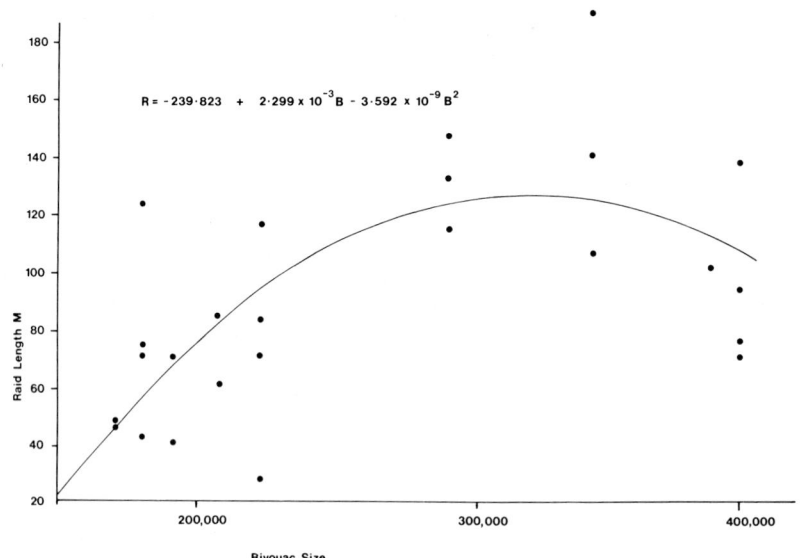

Fig. 1: Daily raid length (R) in metres as a function of bivouac size (B), with polynomial least squares
curve fit (r = 0.694, N = 25, p < 0.001).

it entered its last statary phase, whereas one daughter of each of the other sexual colonies (E.b. 14 and 16) was filmed and the size of their parental bivouac was estimated by doubling the estimated size of the filmed daughter bivouac (Table 1). The bivouacs studied ranged in size from about 180,000 to 450,000 ants and as the largest of these have swarm raids containing 200,000 ants (WILLIS, 1967) the maximum colony size of *Eciton burchelli* on Barro Colorado Island is about 650,000.

The larger bivouacs produced bigger and longer raids as described by $R = -239.82 + 2.29 \times 10^{-3} B - 3.59 \times 10^{-9} B^2$ ($r = 0.694$, $N = 25$, $p < 0.001$) where R is the raid length in metres and B is the number of ants in the bivouac (Fig. 1).

3.2 Castes

Four distinct castes can be recognized among *E. burchelli* workers, as can be seen in Figures 2 and 3 which depict aspects of their allometry. These graphs recorded data from a large sample of workers from a bivouac that was not filmed. A random sub-sample of 573 of these bivouac ants was used to obtain size-frequency data; (Figure 4) this shows the quadrimodal distribution of worker sizes in *Eciton burchelli*. From these data, the dry weight ranges of the different worker castes were estimated as follow; minims less than 1.5 mg, medium workers 1.6 to 5.5 mg, submajors 5.6 to 9.5 mg, majors 9.6 to 11.5 mg.

Majors and large submajors (those with heads of a lighter shade) could be distinguished from all other workers in the films of the emigrating colonies. This technique was used to obtain estimates of the relative abundance of these workers in the bivouacs of the filmed colonies (Table 1). These data suggest that the caste ratios of adult workers change little, or not at all, with increasing colony size.

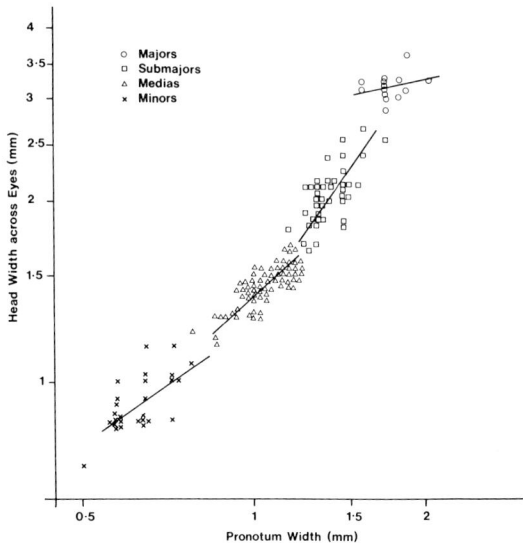

Fig. 2: Head width-pronotum width allometry, based on a sample of 150 ants. The ants were allocated to four castes before measurements were taken. Crosses indicate minims, triangles medium workers, squares submajors and circles majors. Curves have been fitted to each of the four castes by the least squares method.

In samples of dead workers, individuals can be accurately assigned to castes purely by visual sorting. This method was used to obtain caste ratios of raiding workers and those carrying prey (Table 2). It is clear from these data that the proportions of the different castes, present in raids and carrying prey are not the same as those in the bivouac as a whole.

Caste ratios of callow workers change as a function of colony size as shown in Figure 5, where the dry weights of 100 callows for each filmed colony, have been estimated from C $= 0.019 \, W^{3 \cdot 67}$ ($r = 0.99$, $N = 10$ $p < 0.001$) where Cmg is callow dry weight and Wmm is the maximum width of the ant's pupal case.

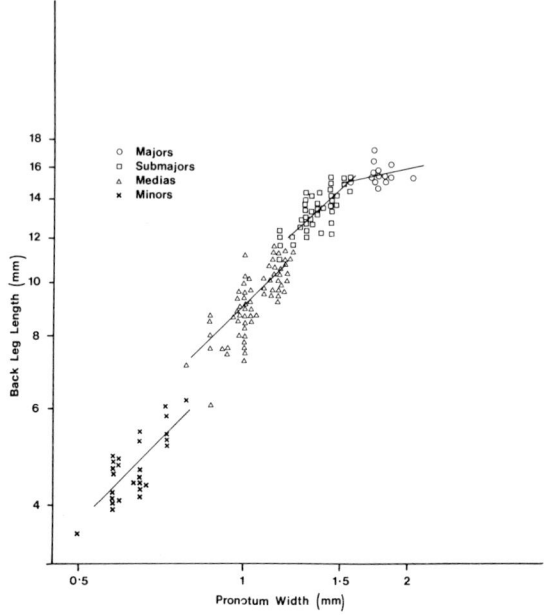

Fig. 3: Back leg length-pronotum width allometry (N = 150). The ants were allocated to four castes before measurements were taken. Crosses indicate minims, triangles medium workers, squares sub-majors and circles majors. Curves have been fitted to each of the four castes by the least squares method.

Table 1

Colony	Ants/M	Emigration data Velocity M/min	Duration min	Caste % Large Submajors	Majors	Bivouac size	Number of pupae
E.b.20	162	3.1	360	1.74%	0.99%	180,792	43,366 workers
E.b.19	145	3.2	450	1.80%	1.17%	208,800	44,982 workers
E.b.10	189	3.2	480	1.90%	1.48%	290,304	57,230 workers
E.b.18	219	3.0	600	1.68%	0.73%	394,200	60,112 workers
E.b.16*	154	2.9	390	1.53%	0.88%	348,348	3,798 males
E.b.14*	150	3.1	480	1.80%	1.20%	446,400	4,112 males
E.b.11	265	3.3	390	1.91%	1.70%	341,055	4,143 males

* Daughter colonies filmed

Fig. 4: The frequency-dry weight distribution of 573 bivouac workers, showing four modes at approximately 0.75 mg, 2.5 mg, 7 mg and 10.5 mg, corresponding to the mean weights of the four worker castes.

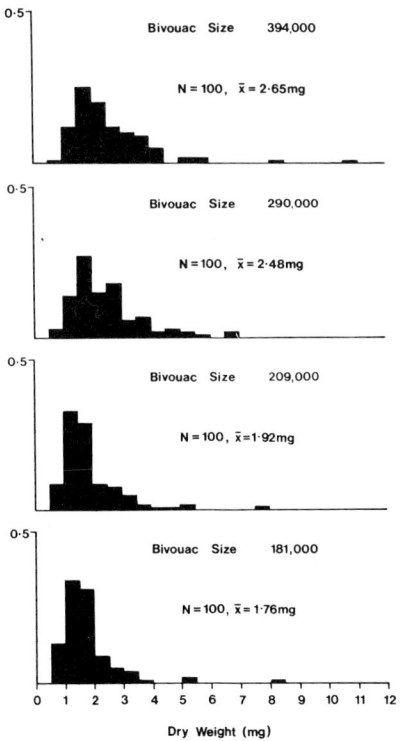

Fig. 5: Frequency – dry weight data of callow workers produced by four colonies. 100 pupal cases were measured from those produced by each colony and the weight of callows was estimated from these data (see text). The average dry weight of each colony's callows is given, as is the size of the bivouac.

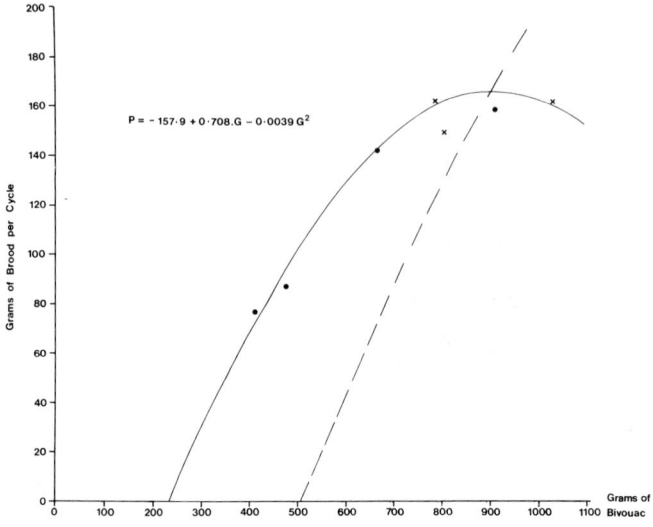

Fig. 6: Grams of brood produced per 35 days (P) as a function of bivouac dry weight (G grams). Circles indicate colonies that produced worker broods and crosses indicate colonies that produced sexual broods (see Table 1). The solid line shows a polynomial, least squares, curve fit based on all 7 colonies (r = 0.99, N = 7, p < 0.001). The broken line was derived from the formula of the solid line and represents the combined growth rate of two identical daughter colonies as a function of the size of their parental bivouac. The intersection of the solid and broken lines indicates the optimum size for colony division.

3.3 Colony Productivity

These data relating callow caste ratios to colony size have been used to calculate colony productivity, by estimating the dry weight of each colony's brood from its unique callow size distribution (Fig. 5) and the number of callows it produced (Table 1). The dry weight of sexual broods, which are more than 99.8 % male have been calculated from the average dry weight of males which is 39 mg. Bivouac dry weights have been estimated on the basis of the average dry weight of bivouac workers which is 2.32 mg (Fig. 4). The relationship between bivouac weight and the weight of brood produced per 35 day cycle is shown in Figure 6, which also shows a best fit line described by $P = -157.9 + 0.708 \, G - 0.0039 \, G^2$ (r = 0.99, N = 7, p < 0.001) where P is the dry weight of brood in grams and G is the dry weight of the bivouac in grams.

3.4 Foraging efficiency

Colony productivity is probably partly limited by foraging efficiency and one important aspect of raiding ergonomics is the ability of the workers to retrieve large prey items quickly and at low energetic cost. *Eciton burchelli* seems to have a specialist porter caste: submajors are engaged in the task of carrying prey items in much larger numbers than expected from their overall abundance in raid systems (Table 2). Furthermore, submajor morphology seems to be specially adapted for their role as porters. Submajors have the longest legs in proportion to their body size of any *E. burchelli* workers: the ratio of back

Table 2

	Minim	Caste populations Medium	Submajor	Major
Bivouac (N = 573)	33.68%	62.13%	3.14%	1.05%
Brood (N = 400)	29.75%	68.00%	2.00%	0.25%
Raid (N = 3314)	22.00%	74.55%	3.15%	0.30%
Carrying prey (N = 244)	7.38%	66.39%	26.23%	0%

leg length to body length (sting to occiput) is less than 1 for minims, between 1 and 1.3 for medium workers, between 1.4 and 1.5 for submajors and between 1.3 and 1.4 for majors (see also Fig. 3). Possibly as a consequence of their disproportionately long legs, submajors can run faster than any of their sisters. The velocity of unburdened running ants, excluding majors, is an exponential function of their leg length as described by: velocity = 0.038 exp 0.058L ($r = 0.79$, $N = 12$, $p < 0.005$) where velocity is in metres per second and L is back leg length in mm (Fig. 7). However, when minims, medium workers and submajors are carrying prey items they all run at much the same speed, as described by: velocity = 0.054–0.001 C ($r = 0.19$, $N = 24$ $P > 0.1$) where C is ant dry weight in mg and velocity is in metres per second. The reason the burdened ants run at the same speed is probably that the larger ants carry disproportionately large prey items, with the exception of majors who

Fig. 7: The velocity of individual unburdened workers in metres per second as a function of their back leg length (Lmm). The curve was fitted by the least squares method ($r = 0.79$, $N = 12$, $p < 0.005$).

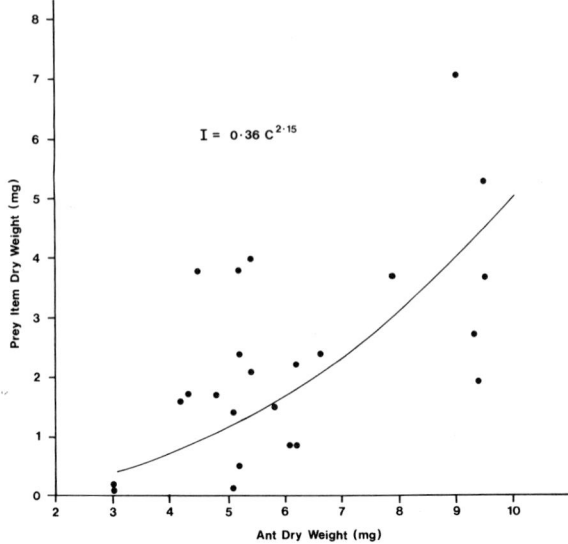

Fig. 8: The dry weight of prey items (Img) carried by individual workers as a function of worker dry weight (Cmg). Least squares curve fit ($r = 0.66$, N = 24, $p < 0.005$).

never carry anything (Rettenmeyer, 1963). Not only do submajors carry the largest items, but their burdens are so large that they also transport the greatest weight per unit of their own body weight: the relation between prey item dry weight I mg and ant dry weight C mg is $I = 0.36\,C^{2.15}$ ($r = 0.66$, N = 24 $p < 0.005$) (Fig. 8).

4. Discussion

To relate worker design to colony efficiency it is first necessary to consider the factors that limit the fitness of all the individuals within the colony. In army ants this problem is greatly simplified because new colonies are formed by the division of old ones (Schneirla, 1956; Schneirla and Brown, 1952). Hence the fitness of all members of an army ant colony will be largely determined by the rate at which the colony can divide and this will depend upon colony growth rate. Natural selection should act to minimize the generation time (Lewontin, 1965), by maximizing the rate of successive colony divisions. Colonies should therefore grow as quickly as possible and then divide at such a size that the average growth rate of their daughters is also maximized. For this reason we might expect army ant workers to be designed and allocated to castes in such a way as to maximize colony growth rate. To evaluate this hypothesis I will first test a simple model for the reproductive strategy of *Eciton burchelli*. This model highlights the importance of colony growth rate which is probably most limited by foraging costs. I will then go on to consider how worker design minimizes these foraging costs and contributes to colony productivity.

How and when should a colony divide? First, if the survival probabilities of the daughter colonies are the same, which is likely because at division the workers can chose the fittest queens (Franks and Hölldobler, in prep.), then the parental colony should divide its worker poupulation equally in two, as this will minimize the average generation time of its daughters (CALOW et al., 1979). Second, the timing of division should be determined by the growth rate of both parental and daughter colonies. Consider the growth rate of an established colony to be given by $y = f(S)$ which decelerates with colony size as in Figure 9. Now let each colony divide at $S_0 = 2.S_1$ to give two daughters of size S_1. So the generation time is given by:

$$T = \int_0^T dt = \int_{S_1}^{2S_1} \frac{dS}{S} = \int_{S_1}^{2S_1} \frac{dS}{f(S)}$$

which is a function of S_1. For a minimum $\frac{dT}{dS_1} = 0$ but $\frac{dT}{dS_1} = \frac{2}{f(2S_1)} - \frac{1}{f(S_1)}$. So $f(2S_1) = 2f(S_1)$ and $f(S_0) = 2f(S_1)$. Thus to maximize its fitness each colony should divide equally in two and at such a size that the combined growth rate of its daughters is equal to its own growth rate.

This seems to be the case in *Eciton burchelli*. Figure 6 shows the biomass of brood raised by different biomasses of bivouac in 35 days: the solid line in this figure can be taken to represent average colony growth rate as a function of colony size because both overall colony size and worker mortalities are likely to be proportional to bivouac size (FRANKS, 1982 a). The broken line in Figure 6 has been derived from the formula of the solid line, and represents the combined growth rate of two identical daughter colonies as a function of the size of their parental bivouac. For this reason the intersection of the solid and broken lines in this figure indicates the optimum bivouac size for division, which will be the best compromise between maximizing parental and daughter colony growth rates to minimize the generation time. Parental bivouacs quite closely approximate this optimum size (Fig. 6). Colony division occurs only in the dry season in Panama (SCHNEIRLA, 1971) and this seasonality must place an additional constraint on reproductive colony size. The decision whether to divide this year or next will inevitably mean that parental colony size can only be approximately optimized and this may account for the small scatter of parental colonies about the optimum size for division.

From this analysis it is clear that the shape of the colony growth function ultimately determines colony fitness. One of the most likely reasons for the fall in growth rate with

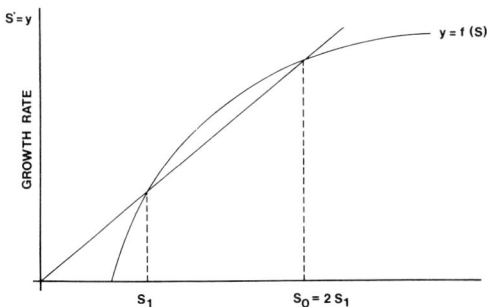

Fig. 9: A hypothetical model of colony growth rate as a function of colony size (see text for explanation). To minimize the generation time a colony should divide into two daughter colonies of equal size (S_1) whose combined growth rate is just equal to its own growth rate.

colony size is that foraging costs will increase for bigger colonies. A common assumption is that the size of social insect colonies is limited by the costs of central place foraging (HÖLLDOBLER and LUMSDEN, 1980; ORIANS and PEARSON, 1979). These costs result from the local depletion of resources which means that foragers must go further and further, at ever increasing costs, to retrieve less energy per unit time. Paradoxically these costs are perhaps most limiting for nomadic army ants because their foraging time is also limited by their need to make frequent emigrations which employ the entire colony (MIRENDA and TOPOFF, 1980). For example, nomadic *Eciton burchelli* colonies commonly spend 12 hours raiding and 8 hours emigrating each day. As large colonies have only the same time in which to forage as small colonies, but must produce more extensive raids (Fig. 1), it is reasonable to assume that raiding velocity is one of the key factors limiting colony growth. During the course of an average raid 30,000 prey items, which have been dismembered at the swarm front, are carried back to the bivouac (FRANKS, 1982 a). The ants carrying such prey items have to run considerable distances as the average raid length at the termination of foraging is 105 m (FRANKS, 1982 b) and only when these ants have delivered their burdens are they free to turn around and run back to join the swarm. Sometimes the army ants store prey items in booty caches situated along the raid system (RETTENMEYER, 1963), and these may help to reduce transport costs. Nevertheless, the progress of the swarm will be limited by the time the ants spend running from the raid to such prey stores and the bivouac, and back again. For this reason, foraging efficiency and colony growth rate will be both determined in part, by the ability of the ants to run fast and carry large prey items.

What design criteria should apply to workers that specialize in the role of prey transport? First, such workers should be relatively large, because the net cost of transport,

Fig. 10: A major on the right rears above a submajor who is carrying a fragment of a roach with the assistance of a medium worker.

defined as the quantity of energy used to transport one unit of body weight over one unit distance, is inversely proportional to body weight. For vertebrates the rapidly diminishing cost of transport with body size can be expressed by a negative linear relationship on a log log plot of cost versus weight (FEDAK and SEEHERMAN, 1979). Furthermore, JENSEN and HOLM-JENSEN (1980) have shown that ants have values for the cost of transport that are only slightly higher than those expected by extrapolation from vertebrates (ALEXANDER, 1982).

In addition to transporting items at low energetic cost the army ants also need to move their brood and booty quickly. This suggests that the large porter caste should have disproportionately long legs. The rationale for this prediction comes from an analysis of terrestrial locomotion by ALEXANDER (1976). He suggests that where inertia and gravity interact as with animals moving on land, the Froude number provides a good criterion for assessing the physical similarity of their movements. The Froude number is $u^2/g L$ where u is velocity, g the acceleration of free fall, and L is a characteristic dimension such as leg length. The theory of physical similarity suggests that relative stride length will be a function of the Froude number, even when animals are not geometrically similar and this implies that velocity is likely to be a positive function of leg lenght. These considerations of the cost and rate of transport therefore suggest that to be efficient porters workers should be both relatively large and disproportionately long legged. Remarkably, *Eciton burchelli* has a specialist porter caste with exactly these morphological adaptations.

Submajors clearly specialize in the role of prey transport as they are only 3 % of the workers population of the colony but represent 26 % of the ants carrying prey items (Table 2). Submajors are the largest *E. burchelli* workers that carry brood or booty: they are only marginally smaller than majors who never act as porters (RETTENMEYER, 1963). In addition to their relatively large size, submajors can run much faster than any of the other workers. The greater speed of submajors is unlikely to be purely a consequence of their larger size, because if all the workers were the same shape but of different sizes they would be expected to move at the same speed, since the power available and the power needed to run would both be proportional to body mass (ALEXANDER, 1971). As the Froude number analysis suggests, to move faster submajors should have relatively longer legs than their sisters. This is the case. Leg length is determined by a positive allometry for minims up to and including submajors, but in majors leg length is determined by a negative allometry (Fig. 3). A similar complex allometry of leg length is also found in *Eciton hamatum* (TOPOFF, 1971), but not in *Atta* (WILSON pers. comm.). This difference is expected because leaf cutting ants can forage from their sedentary nest for their immobile food for 24 hours a day. So in *Atta* running velocity will not limit foraging to the extent that it does in *Eciton*. Furthermore, *Eciton burchelli* workers run at much the same speed when they are carrying burdens; this may be due to the larger ants and submajors in particular carrying disproportionately large loads. This is itself may be an adaptation to prevent traffic congestion in the columns of ants returning to the bivouac. The speeds of burdened *Atta* workers seem to be similarly adjusted (WILSON, 1980 b). In *Eciton burchelli* the unladen workers move out to the swarm raid by running at great velocity down the sides of the foraging columns. Army ants are also unusual in that they carry prey items beneath their bodies, which enables teams of ants to co-operate efficiently when they carry very large prey items. An observation by RETTENMEYER (1963) further emphasizes the importance of this division of labour and the cost of transport. He observed that the frequency with which adult workers are carried varies inversely with their size, and increases near the ends of emigrations. It is probably less expensive for the colony as a whole, for a submajor to carry a minim than to have both ants move under their own power.

Submajors are specialists and so apparently are two of the other three castes in *Eciton burchelli*. Minim workers are disproportionately common in the bivouacs (Table 2) where they are believed to act as brood nurses (SCHNEIRLA, 1971; TOPOFF, 1971; DE SILVA, 1972) and majors are equipped with mandibles like ice-tongs and seem to be a specialist defensive caste against would-be vertebrate predators (SCHNEIRLA 1971). By contrast medium workers are a generalist caste and they seem to be equally abundant in all roles within the colony (Table 2).

The value of a particular worker caste will be determined not only by current performance but also by manufacturing and maintenance costs and by the rate at which the workers will need to be replaced as determined by their longevity. The manufacturing costs of workers are likely to be proprotional to adult dry weight (WILSON, 1980) and hence submajors with a dry weight of 7 mg will be much more expensive for the colony to grow than medium or minor workers with dry weight of 2.5 mg and 0.75 mg respectively. However, maintenance costs may not be much higher for larger workers as it is well known that in ants metabolic rate per gram of body tissue tends to fall rapidly with increasing body size (PEAKIN and JOSENS, 1977). Furthermore, majors and submajors may live longer than their smaller sister so their replacement rate will be less and their relative cost to the colony will also be reduced.

In army ants the importance of worker longevity is highlighted again by the phenomenon of reproduction by colony division. Worker longevity will not only affect colony growth rate directly but it will also determine the value of workers to the daughter colonies that receive them. The minimum average longevity of *Eciton burchelli* workers can be estimated from their rate of production in a colony of average size. Such a colony has about 400,000 workers and produces about 50,000 new workers everv 35 days, thus each worker must live at least 280 days for the colony to be able to grow at all.

Data are not available on caste specific death rates in *E. burchelli*, but differential mortality rates can be tentatively inferred from the rate of production of the various types of worker, and this can be estimated from the size of the pupal cases that the colonies deposited (Fig. 5). The most surprising thing about these data is that brood caste ratios change as a function of colony size, with larger colonies producing larger workers. Such shifts in the caste ratios of adult workers are known for many other ant species (OSTER and WILSON, 1978), but marked changes in the relative abundance of the four worker castes in *Eciton burchelli* are unlikely to occur for the following reasons. First, parental colonies provision their daughter colonies with their own workers; hence caste ratios must be very similar in mother and daughter colonies. Second, all colonies maintain similar nomadic and foraging life styles (FRANKS and FLETCHER, 1983; FRANKS and BOSSERT, 1983) and lastly, as a consequence of reproduction by binary fission the largest colonies are only twice as large as the smallest, whereas in many other non-doryline species mature colonies are thousands of times more populous than incipient ones (WILSON, 1971).

Submajors are the one caste that might be more useful in greater relative abundance in larger colonies, because bigger colonies forage further and will incur greater transport costs (Fig. 1). However, the proportion of even submajors does not appear to change markedly in the adult worker populations of the growing colonies (Table 1). For these reasons the data on callow worker production suggests that larger colonies are provisioning their daughter colonies with all, or most, of the submajors and majors they will need for a considerable period of time. This follows from the observation that small colonies are either not producing these larger worker castes or producing them at a very low rate. Furthermore, summed over all colony sizes the larger workers are produced at a much lower rate than their smaller sisters (Table 2). These findings suggest that submajors and majors live longer than their smaller sisters. This is important because if these larger castes do live longer then the relative costs of these workers to the colony will also be reduced.

Colony level selection is likely to determine the longevity of sterile workers and for this reason the demographic statistics of sterile workers are of great theoretical interest not least because workers are unlikely to suffer from conventional senescence (Wilson, 1975). This prediction stems from the hypothesis that conventional senescence is due to the accumulation of genes that are beneficial before, but detrimental after, the last age of reproduction (Medawar, 1957; Williams, 1957). Since sterile workers do not reproduce themselves they are unlikely to senesce in the conventional way.

Clearly, the realized longevity of workers will be determined in part by the risks they take, and colony level selection is likely to have caused the well known temporal division of labour, where young, and hence more valuable, workers are employed on such safe tasks as nursing brood while older workers take the hazardous roles of foraging and colony defense (Wilson, 1971). The much more speculative idea that I wish to discuss here is that colony level selection can alter the fundamental longevity of workers simply by altering their size.

If the same types of correlation apply to social insect workers as to a wide variety of other organisms then larger workers will tend to have inherently greater longevities. For a wide variety of oraganisms from *Escherichia coli* to *Sequoia* generation time is proportional to organism length to the power 0.9 (Bonner, 1965) which implies that generation time is proportional to body mass to the power 0.3. An equally all encompassing correlation is that within broad categories of organisms metabolic rate is proportional to body mass to the power 0.75 (Kleiber, 1961) although within more closely related groupings the relationship may be closer to the more theoretically satisfying proportionality of mass to the power 0.67 (Heusner, 1982). Furthermore, Pearl (1928) has suggested, in his hypothesis of a ‹rate of living› that these correlations are causally related, and that larger organisms live longer because they have a lower metabolic rate per unit of body mass. It should be noted that Pearl's hypothesis and Medawar's (1957) explanation for conventional senescence may be complimentary if for example the rate of metabolic activity per gram of body tissue is associated with the accumulation of gene replication errors that are only deleterious after the last age of reproduction (Grant, 1978).

The important point that I wish to draw from these hypotheses is that larger workers are likely to have greater physiological longevities than their smaller sisters if they have a lower metabolic rate per unit body weight. Most intriguingly, large ant workers do have lower respiratory rates per unit body weight than smaller workers (Peaking and Josens, 1977; Wilson, 1980 b), and in the harvester ant *Pogonomyrmex badius* this decline is so rapid that majors and minors have the same resting rate of oxygen consumption even though the larger caste is ten times heavier than the smaller (Golly and Gentry, 1964). Hence larger workers may have both relatively low maintenance costs and inherently greater longevities. Similar factors may contribute to the low replacement rate of submajors and majors in *Eciton burchelli*. Clearly worker longevity is not only of direct importance in social evolution but it may also shed light on the very nature of biological senescence (Wilson, 1975).

From Darwin onwards, studies of biological adaptation have been conducted by the comparative method. Social insects provide an unrivalled opportunity to refine this technique because colonies with polymorphic workers allow comparisons to be made not only with other species but also among the individuals within the same society. In species such as *Eciton burchelli* adaptations in behaviour, morphology, physiology and even longevity can be analysed in the context of the ecology of the society and the inclusive fitness of its individual members.

Acknowledgements

I wish to thank MARK HODSON for the anaylsis of allometry described in this paper. N. F. BRITTON for the optimum life history model and STUART REYNOLDS for his criticism of an earlier draft of this manuscript. R. MCNEILL ALEXANDER, E. BROADHEAD, B. HÖLLDO-BLER, S. D. PORTER, S. E. REYNOLDS and E. O. WILSON provided helpful advice and encouragement. Facilities were generously provided by the Smithsonian Tropical Research Institute, Republic of Panama. This research was supported in part by a Natural Environment Research Council Studentship and by a Fellowship from the Royal Commission for the Exhibition of 1851.

References

Alexander, R. McN. (1971): Size and shape. Arnold London.
Alexander, R. McN. (1976): Estimates of speeds of dinosaurs. Nature. *261*, 129–130.
Alexander, R. McN. (1982): Locomotion of Animals. Blackie Glasgow.
Bonner, J. T. (1965): Size and cycles: and essay on the structure of biology. Princeton University Press, Princeton.
Calow, P. Beveridge, M., Sibly, R. (1979): Heads and tails: adaptational aspects of asexual reproduction in freshwater triclands. Amer. Zool. *19*, 715–727.
Darwin, C. (1859): On the origin of species. Murray, London.
Fedak, M. A. Seeherman. H. J. (1979): Reappraisal of energetics of locomotion shows identical cost in bipeds and quadrupeds including ostrich and horse. Nature. *282*, 713–716.
Franks, N. R. (1982 a): Ecology and population regulation in the army ant *Eciton burchelli*. In: Leigh, E. G., Rand. A. S., Windsor, D. W. (eds) The ecology of a tropical forest: Seasonal rhythms and long-term changes. Smithsonian Institute Press. Washington DC pp. 389–395.
Franks, N. R. (1982 b): A new method for censusing animal populations: the number of *Eciton burchelli* army ant colonies on Barro Colorado Island. Panama. Oecologia (Berlin) *52*, 266–268.
Franks, N. R., Bossert, W. H. (1983): The influence of swarm raiding army ants on the patchiness and diversity of a tropical leaf litter ant community. In Sutton, S. L., Whitmore, T. C., Chadwick, A. C. (eds) Tropical rain forest: ecology and management. Blackwell, Oxford pp. 151–163.
Franks, N. R., Feltcher, C. R. (1983): Spatial patterns in army ant foraging and migration: *Eciton burchelli* on Barro Colorado Island, Panama. Behav. Ecol. Sociobiol. *12*, 261–270.
Golley, F. B., Gentry, J. B. (1964): Bioenergetics of the southern harvester ant *Pogonomyrmex badius*. Ecology *45*, 217–225.
Grant, P. (1978): Biology of Developing Systems. Holt, Rinehart and Winston, New York.
Heusner, A. A. (1982): Energy metabolism and body size. Is the 0.75 mass exponent of Kleiber's Equation a Statistical Artifact? Respiration Physiol. *48*, 1–12.
Hölldobler, B., Lumsden, C. J. (1970): Territorial strategies in ants. Science *210*, 732–739.
Jensen, T. F., Holm-Jensen, I. (1980): Energetic cost of running in workers of three ant species, *Formica fusca* L., *Formica rufa* L. and *Componotus herculeanus* L. (Hymenoptera, *Formicidae*). J. Comp. Physiol. B *137*, 151–156.
Kleiber, M. (1961): The fire of life. An introduction to animal energetics. John Wiley, New York.
Leigh, E. G., Rand, A. S., Windsor, D. W. (eds) (1982): The ecology of a tropical forest: Seasonal rhythms and long-term changes. Smithsonian Institute Press, Washington DC.
Lewontin, R. C. (1965): Selection for colonizing ability. In: Barker, H. G., Stebbins, G. L. (eds) The genetics of colonizing species. Academic Press, New York 79–94.
Medawar, P. B. (1957): The uniqueness of the individual. Methuen, London.
Mirenda, J. T., Topoff, H. (1980): Nomadic behaviour of army ants in a desert-grassland habitat. Behav. Ecol. Sociobiol. *7*, 129–135.
Orians, G. H., Pearson, N. E. (1979): On the theory of central place foraging. In: Horn, D. J., Mitchell, R. D., Stairs, G. R. (eds) Analysis of Ecological Systems. Ohio State University Press, Ohio pp. 155–177.

Oster, G. F., Wilson, E. O. (1978): Caste and ecology in the social insects. Princeton University Press, Princeton.

Peakings, G. J., Josens, G. (1978): Respiration and energy flow. In: Brian, M. V. (ed) Production ecology of ants and termites. Cambridge University Press, Cambridge pp. 111–163.

Pearl, R. (1928): The rate of living. Knopf, New York.

Rettenmeyer, C. W. (1963): Behavioural studies of army ants. Univ. Kans. Sci. Bull. *44*, 281–465.

Schneirla, R. C. (1956): A preliminary survey of colony division and related processes in two species of terrestrial army ants. Insectes Sociaux *3*, 49–69.

Schneirla, T. C. (1971): Army ants: a study in social organization. Topoff, H. R. (ed) Freeman, San Francisco.

Schneirla, T. C., Brown, R. Z. (1952): Sexual broods and the production of young queens in two species of army ants. *Zoologica 37*, 5–32.

Silva, M. M. T. G. da (1972): Contribucao ao estudo da biologia de *Eciton burchelli* Westwood (Hymenoptera, Formicidae) S. D. (Doutor em Ciencias) thesis. University of Sao Paulo, Brazil.

Topoff, H. (1971): Polymorphism in army ants related to the division of labour and colony cyclic behaviour. Am. Nat. *105*, 529–548.

Williams, G. C. (1957): Pleiotropy, natural selection, and the evolution of senescence. Evolution *11*, 398–411.

Willis, E. O. (1967): The behaviour of bicolored antbirds. Univ. Calif. Publ. Zool. *79*, 1–127.

Wilson, E. O. (1971): The insect societies. Belknap Press of Harvard University Press, Cambridge (Massachusetts).

Wilson, E. O. (1975): Sociobiology: The new synthesis. Belknap Press of Harvard University Press, Cambridge (Massachusetts).

Wilson, E. O. (1980 a): Caste and division of labor in leaf-cutter ants (Hymenoptera: Formicidae: *Atta*) 1. The overall pattern in *A. sexdens* Behav. Ecol. Sociobiol. *7*, 143–156.

Wilson, E. O. (1980 b): Caste and division of labor in leaf-cutter ants (Hymenoptera: Formicidae: *Atta*) II. The ergonomic optimization of leaf cutting. Behav. Ecol. Sociobiol. *7*, 157–165.

Fortschritte der Zoologie, Bd. 31 · Hölldobler/Lindauer (Hrsg.): Experimental Behavioral Ecology
G. Fischer Verlag · Stuttgart · New York · 1985

Optimal foraging: constraints and currencies

JOHN CHEVERTON, ALEJANDRO KACELNIK, JOHN R. KREBS

Edward Grey Institute of Field Ornithology, South Parks Road, Oxford, OXl 3PS England

Abstract

In order to construct an optimality model of behaviour, one has to identify constraints, and to identify constraints one has to know something about the mechanisms controlling behaviour. Thus optimality modelling implies a knowledge of mechanisms. By adding more constraints one modifies the model's predictions, but this does not mean that constrained animals are «suboptimal». We illustrate the idea of constraints and mechanisms with reference to the within-inflorescence movement rules of bumble bees. The bees' rule is dependent on both body posture and visibility of the next flower.

A second component of optimality models which may be modified in the light of experimental evidence is the currency. As an example of how currency assumptions affect predictions we consider the crop load of honey bees. If bees maximise gross energy gain they should fill the crop before flying home. If they maximise net gain (Gain − costs) or efficiency (Gain/costs) they should return to the hive from short distances with partially empty crops. The data are closer to the predictions of the second and third possibilities than to the first.

1 Introduction

To judge from its growth in the literature, optimal foraging theory (OFT), although not without its vigorous critics (e. g. GOULD and LEWONTIN 1979, LEWONTIN 1983, MYERS 1983), is a research topic of exponentially increasing interest (KREBS et. al. 1983). It is also a much reviewed area (e. g. PYKE et. al. 1977, WERNER and MITTELBACH 1981, KREBS et. al. 1983), and it is not our intention here to update or extend existing reviews of the literature. Nor do we set out to appraise the value of, and justification for, the optimality approach in general (ALEXANDER 1982, DENNETT 1983, MAYNARD SMITH 1978, OSTER and WILSON 1978). We will use examples from recent work in our laboratory to illustrate a discussion of two issues; the choice of appropriate *constraints* and *currencies* in foraging models.

To construct an optimality model one has to choose a currency (e. g. rate of energy intake in many but not all foraging models) and identify the constraints on the animals' performance. The constraints (for example, one might posit that the animal cannot eat and search at the same time) characterise the *strategy set* available to the animal (MAYNARD SMITH 1978, OSTER and WILSON 1978). A final component of optimality models, which we shall not discuss further, is the specification of how the currency relates to fitness (reproductive success or survival) (Schoener 1971). Modellers generally start off with assumptions based on intuition or natural history information about both constraints and currency. The currency is chosen on the basis of assumptions about what   contributes to fitness, and the constraints from knowledge about how animals behave; what they can and cannot do. Subsequently the model (assuming that it correctly defines the problem faced by the animal) may be refined either by incorporating more appropriate constraints, or by modifying the currency.

In this paper we will suggest that in order to develop optimality models in this way beyond their initial stage, a knowledge of behavioural and physiological mechanisms is essential (Heinrich 1983). In fact part of the optimality excercise itself can be seen as an attempt to unravel these mechanisms. In addition we will make two other general points: (a) The distinction between «optimal» and «suboptimal» animals proposed by some authors (e. g. Janetos and Cole 1981) can be reduced to a question of constraints. A suboptimal or satisficing animal is one operating under a larger set of constraints than initially assumed (Krebs et. al. 1983, Maynard Smith 1983). (b) Optimality models can be used at two levels in behavioural ecology; as a tool for investigating constraints and currencies and as a method for assessing quantitatively how well animals are adapted to their environment. In both kinds of analysis it is assumed that animals are designed by natural selection to fit their environment (an assumption questioned by some, e. g. Lewontin 1983). The former of the two levels is concerned with understanding *how* they are designed and the latter with how *well* they are designed.

2 Mechanisms and constraints

2.1 Constraints

The classical foraging models (e. g. MacArthur and Pianka 1966) were designed to be general and therefore include only the minimum number of assumptions about constraints. As we suggested in the Introduction, one way to improve upon these early models might be to include more realistic and accurate constraint assumptions. But where does the information on which to base these modifications come from? It comes from a detailed knowledge of behavioural and physiological mechanisms: once we know the cues used by the animal to detect its prey, its nutrient requirements, its capacity to remember past experiences and so on, we can accurately delineate the constraints and build a more refined optimality model. An example of this comes from work on prey selection by great tits *(Parus major)*. The classical diet model (MacArthur and Pianka 1966, Charnov 1976 a) assumes that prey types are perfectly discriminable, while a signal detection analysis of prey selection by great tits showed that they made discrimination errors in the set-up used for testing (Rechten et. al. 1983, Getty and Krebs in press). Incorporating this perceptual constraint into the diet model generated predictions (especially relating to partial perferences) which more closely matched the observed behaviour than those of the original model.

This suggests a cyclical procedure for testing, modifying, and retesting an optimality model which is summarized and extended in figure 1. The figure is meant to be in part a description of the way foraging studies have proceded to date, and in part as a prescription of what we see as one sensible way for foraging studies to proceed in the future. It is important to note, since there is still misunderstanding in the literature (Mazur 1983),

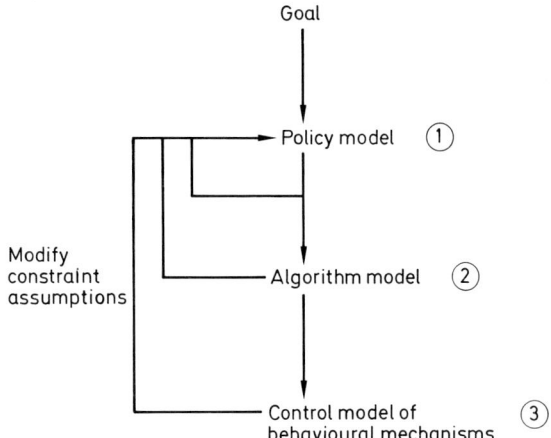

Figure 1: Levels of analysis in optimal foraging theory.

that the sequence in Figure 1, while cyclical, is not circular: modifications to the model in the form of constraint (or currency – section 4) assumptions can be independently verified. The concept of optimality itself is not under test, only the assumptions of the particular model studied (MAYNARD SMITH 1978), therefore one would not conclude, as did MAZUR (1983), that a frog starving to death while surrounded by dead flies is optimal, only that it has constraints in its visual system concerning the stimuli treated as food.

The bulk of the literature describing «tests» of optimal foraging theory has concerned itself only with the first level in Figure 1, namely tests of policy models. A policy model in our terminology is one which prescribes a general rule for maximising payoff (the goal), without identifying any specific procedure which would enable the animal to follow the rule. (A policy for maximising the goal of offspring production might, for example, be «Cross roads in a way that minimises the chance of being run over», and the procedure for doing this might be «Look in both directions and cross if clear»). A typical policy model in the literature is CHARNOV's (1976 b) marginal value theorem, which generates the intake-maximising rule for exploiting patches with resource depression (CHARNOV et. al. 1976) when the predator has perfect information. The policy, «leave a patch when the gain rate within the patch equals the average for the environment», can be used to predict a relationship between travel time and residence time within patches. This has been tested by measuring the appropriate variables by several authors (eg COWIE 1977, GIRALDEAU and KRAMER 1982, KACELNIK 1984).

The overall conclusion from studies of this sort is that provided a suitable study system is chosen, and the appropriate values measured correctly (not many supposed tests meet these requirements – KREBS et. al. 1983, KACELNIK and HOUSTON 1984), more often than not the predictions are qualitatively if not quantitatively supported (KRAMER and GIRAL-DEAU in prep).

Figure 1 suggests that one way to step from policy models to more specific models of a particular foraging problem is to construct *algorithms,* or procedures for solving the problem. An algorithm for patch use, for example, might be «leave patch if no prey items encountered within t seconds of arrival or since last capture». Obviously, there are a great number of possible algorithms for each foraging problem, and the criteria for choosing among them include the ability of the algorithm to describe accurately what the animal does (indeed, it may be derived inductively from the data) (Pyke 1979, Ydenberg 1982), and the performance of the algorithm in terms of payoff (i. e. how closely it approximates the optimal policy) (Iwasa et. al. 1981, Green 1980, Houston et. al. 1982, Janetos and Cole 1981). In the context of optimality modelling, the aim would be to see if there is an algorithm which both describes what the animal does and approximates the optimal policy in terms of payoff.

Such an algorithm will almost invariably contain implicit assumptions about the animal's behavioural mechanisms. The patch use algorithm above, for example, implies the ability to measure time. As a test of these assumptions it is appropriate to refine the algorithm by investigating the actual behavioural mechanisms used in prey detection, assessment of encounter rate, and so on. Some mechanisms may be analysable at the behavioural level by looking at moment to moment choices (e. g. molecular analyses of concurrent choice experiments – Staddon 1980), others may require physiological techniques. The information about mechanisms could be used, as Figure 1 indicates, either to modify the constraint assumptions in the policy model, or to develop more realistic algorithms. As this feedback progresses, information is incorporated from one level to another and the policy model, the algorithm model, and the behavioural mechanism model (we have called it the control model in Figure 1) lose their independence.

As the policy model is modified by incorporating new constraints, the optimal policy is automatically redefined with respect to these constraints. This suggests an alternative interpretation of Janetos' and Cole's (1981) distinction between optimal and imperfectly or suboptimal animals. An optimal animal according to these authors would be one following the predictions of a policy model, while a suboptimal one uses a rule of thumb which only approximates the optimal policy in terms of payoff (equivalent to what we have called an algorithm). Since a knowledge of the rules actually used by the animal can be incorporated as constraints in the policy model (figure 1) Janetos' and Cole's distinction disappears: it is simply a matter of how many constraints are recognised (Krebs et. al. 1983, Maynard Smith 1983). Houston and McNamara (in press) discuss a similar point in their distinction between local and global optima. A model of a global optimum in their terms is equivalent to our policy model, including as few constraints as possible. A local optimum is one subject to more constraints. As an example Houston and McNamara consider the effect of incorporating an additional constraint into the marginal value model. Animals in general appear to be unable to measure time without errors (Gibbon and Church 1981), the coefficient of variation being about 0.35, and if animals use time in their patch leaving decisions (e. g. Cowie and Krebs 1979), timing errors must be treated as a constraint. With this constraint, the marginal value model predicts a different optimal residence time from that of the usual version.

2.2 Proximate and ultimate causes

Baker (1938) was the first to clarify the distinction, now widely accepted, between accounts of biological phenomena in terms of their proximate or immediate causes, and those in terms of their ultimate causes or survival value. Where do optimality models lie in relation to this distinction?

The justification for using optimality models in biology is usually couched in terms of natural selection. Selection, it is argued, tends in the long term to maximise fitness (see Grafen 1984 for a discussion of fitness) and therefore it should maximise the performance of traits which contribute to fitness (Dennett 1983, Alexander 1982, Krebs and McCleery 1984). One way to study the performance of these traits (loosely referred to as adaptations) is to treat them as *design features* and use optimality models to analyse the design with respect to particular performance criteria. This view places optimality analysis firmly on the ultimate side of BAKER's distinction: ultimate explanations are concerned with how traits contribute to fitness, and optimality analyses help to elucidate exactly how certain traits are designed by selection, in other words, how they contribute to fitness.

But, as we have argued in the previous sections, optimality modelling cannot proceed beyond the initial stages without a knowledge of behavioural and physiological mechanisms. The cyclical process described in figure 1 shows that optimality models incorporate both proximate and ultimate causes of behaviour: they are about both mechanisms and survival value (this contrasts with the view of HEINRICH (1983), who sees optimality models as being concerned only with ultimate causes).

2.3 Built-in obsolescence?

Figure 1 suggests that testing a policy model is only the first step. The fact that most of the optimality literature has dealt only with this step may seem in retrospect as an attempt to test whether the optimality approach in general is of use. Some would accept that the evidence is now just about convincing enough to say that it *is* of use, and figure 1 offers a possible answer to the question «what next?». In giving this answer, we join McFARLAND (1976, 1977) and McFARLAND and HOUSTON (1981) in stressing the intimate relationship between ultimate and proximal accounts of behaviour.

Does the prescription in Figure 1 imply that policy models will gradually die of obsolescence? Ought we to get on with the analysis of mechanisms straight away, and not bother with the window dressing of optimality (HEINRICH 1983)? We believe not, for both theoretical and practical reasons. The theoretical reason is that optimal policy models offer greater generality than do models of mechanisms (KRAMER and GIRALDEAU in prep). This follows from the notion that regardless of how they do it, many or perhaps all foraging animals are designed to do the same thing: the policy models will reveal whether this is true or not. The practical reason is that optimality models can act as guides for investigating mechanisms. To put it at its simplest, understanding how a piece of machinery such as an animal works is made easier by having some idea of what it is designed to do.

We now turn to a specific example to illustrate some of the points brought up in the preceding sections, in particular the investigation of mechanisms of foraging.

3 Mechanisms in foraging bumblebees

In this section, we discuss the work done by one of us (J.C.), on foraging bumblebees. The stimulus for this was a paper by PYKE (1979), on the intra-inflorescence ‹movement rules› of bumblebees. Pyke recorded the movements of *Bombus appositus* workers on *Aconitum columbianum,* and proposed a movement rule as a summary and explanation of his data. He then proposed a strategy set of alternative movement rules, based on assumptions about the mechanisms likely to be used by the bees. He calculated the net rate of energy intake that the bees could achieve by using each of these rules. None of them gave a higher gain rate than the observed behaviour, two ot them gave equally high rates.

Compared with other optimality studies, PYKE's paper is unusual in that the ‹policy› level is skipped; PYKE goes straight from the ‹goal› of maximising the net rate of energy intake to a set of movement rules or algorithms which do not have generality beyond the *Bombus – Aconitum* system. However, the point of interest here is the status of these algorithms with respect to the mechanisms which may be used to implement them. They are worded so as to imply the existence of specific mechanisms. For example, ‹move to the closest flower not just visited› implies that the bees can discriminate distance and have memory of which flower has just been visited. CHEVERTON (1983) discusses in detail the implications of invoking mechanisms at this stage. Here, the important point is that PYKE's paper raises questions about mechanisms which it does not answer (HEINRICH 1983), so it is a natural sequel to PYKE's study to investigate these. The same approach could be taken with a great many optimality studies, for many of these also stop at the point where interesting questions about mechanisms are raised but not answered (OSTER & WILSON 1978).

An experimental system was used in which *B. lapidarius* workers, from a captive colony within a flight room, foraged freely from artificial flowers in two-dimensional arrays. Figure 2 shows the routes taken by the bees over four different patterns. PYKE's best movement rule would predict similar or identical paths, so the present system seems to be suitable for investigating the questions of mechanism raised by his paper. Seeking the simplest explanation of the bees' movements, we attempted to model them using a procedural algorithm that took account only of the position of other flowers relative to the present position of the bee. We found that such a model could be constructed, for movements on vertical arrays, using a series of lines of equal preference (‹iseclects›) around the

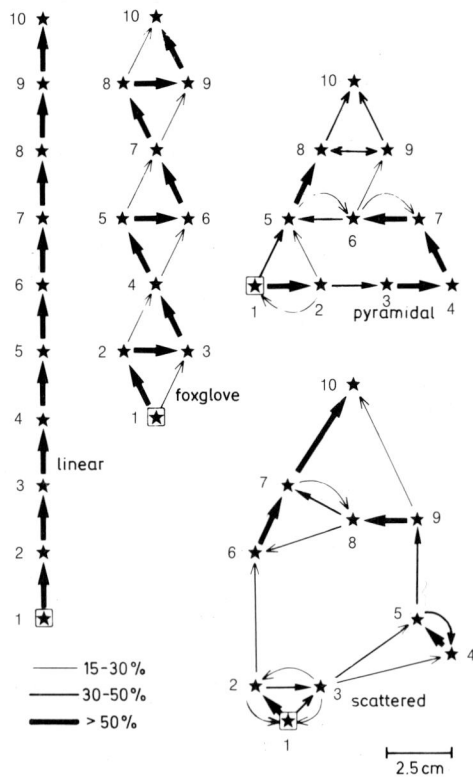

Figure 2: The movements of bumblebees over four experimental flower patterns. Filled arrow-heads represent significantly preferred choices ($p < 0.05$). Squared stars are starting points.

present position of the bee (Figure 4). The shape of these was adjusted to generate the same routes, over the four test patterns, as the preferred routes of the bees over the same patterns. Although this is no more than a description of the data, it is interesting that the same iseclects produce the preferred routes over all four patterns, suggesting that the bees use the same rule on each one. However, the success of this model depended on the inclusion of a ‹ratchet clause›, forbidding choice of the flower just visited (otherwise, for example, the model would make a revisit on 50 % of departures from flower 6 of the pyramidal array, and would alternate endlessly between flower 2 and 3 of the scattered array). This seemed to suggest that memory, at least of the most recently visited flower, was being used (HEINRICH 1983).

3.1 Memory

Several of PYKE's algorithms imply the ability to remember which flowers have already been visited on an inflorescence. Yet, PYKE expresses the opinion that:

«It is improbable that a bumblebee could have a memory and a sense of spatial geometry that would permit it to know exactly which flowers on an inflorescence it had already visited.»

This seems to contradict the implications of his strategy set. Also, it is well known that many insects have spatial memory (CARTWRIGHT and COLLETT 1982), and that bumb-lebees have excellent memory of the position of their nest (e. g. FREE and BUTLER, 1959), and that they can remember the position of individual inflorescences (MANNING, 1956).

Figure 3: Experimental set-up designed to test for spatial memory, and results.

This suggests that the question of memory is worth investigating. To do so, a ‹forced choice› experiment was used, conceptually similar to those used by Olton et. al. (1981) to demonstrate spatial memory in rats. In this experiment, a small horizontal array, 250 mm × 300 mm, was used, on which flowers could be exposed or concealed by means of a sliding shutter.

Figure 3 shows the hexagonal pattern of flowers used, three of which were exposed at first, the others being exposed in addition, when a bee was visiting the third of the original three flowers. All flowers had equal rewards, not replenished during the experiment. On the hypothesis that the bees use spatial memory to avoid revisiting previously emptied flowers, they should have skipped these, and visited only the newly exposed flowers (Figure 3, ‹expectation›). In fact, the proportion of moves which skipped adjacent flowers was lower (though not significantly) for this presentation than for the control presentation of the complete hexagon, the opposite of the prediction from spatial memory. In contrast with the papers mentioned above, the conclusion from this experiment, which was corroborated by other evidence, is either that the bees do not have spatial memory at this level, or that if they *do,* then it is not used to prompt them to skip previously-visited flowers. This is clearly a constraint which could be taken into account in any future optimality model of intra-inflorescence movements (illustrating the feedback in Figure 1). A more immediate problem was to seek an explanation for the ratchet clause of the iseclect model which did not require memory.

3.2 Posture

In conceiving the iseclet model, it was thought that the bees always sat on a flower facing directly upwards, so that their body axis, and the vertical axis of the iseclects were aligned. However, closer analysis revealed that the bees do not always orient vertically. The possible importance of posture was examined using the pyramidal array (see Figure 2). Flower ‹6› of this pattern may equally well be approached from flower ‹5› or flower ‹7›. Table 1 shows that the posture of the bees on flower ‹6› depended on which flower they had arrived from: they were tilted away from the direction of arrival.

Table 1: Contingency table demonstrating the dependence of posture on arrival direction for bees on flower 6 of the pyramidal pattern. The cells contain observed frequencies of visits.

| | Posture towards: | |
	Left	Right
Left:	4	37
Right:	18	0

Arrival from

$\chi_1^2 = 43.5 \quad p < 0.00001$

If the iseclects were tilted in the direction of the body axis, a ratchet clause was unnecessary to prevent choice of the previously-visited flower (Figure 4). To show that the posture was more than just an incidental variable, those few cases were examined where the posture was *not* as predicted from arrival direction (ie: where the bees were tilted towards

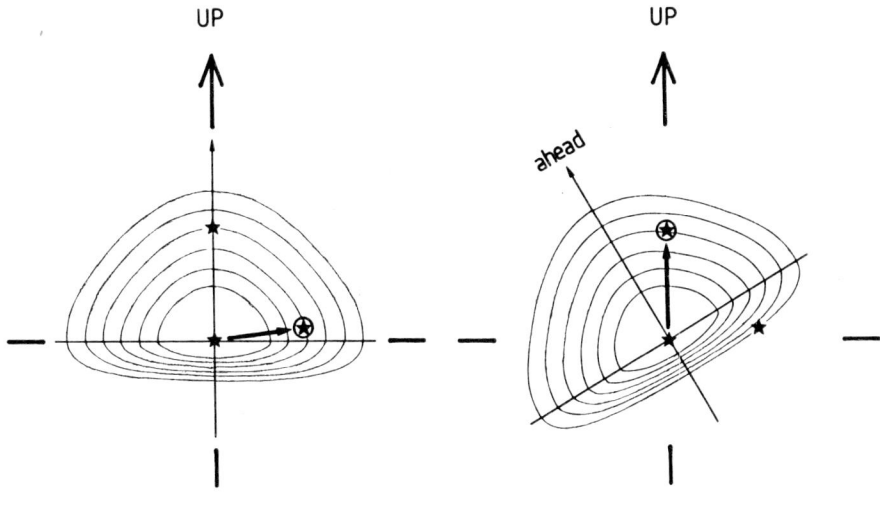

Flower cutting 'highest' iseclect is chosen

aligning iseclects with tilted body axis changes the choice

Figure 4: The ‹iseclect› model: Left: the means by which the next flower (circled star) is chosen. Preference values increase inwards. Right: the effect of aligning the iseclects with the body axis of a tilted bee.

the flower they had arrived from). In three out of four such occurences, these ‹mistakes› were carried through to the departure direction. On the hypothesis that departure mistakes were independent of posture mistakes, the probability of this occuring by chance was < 0.02 (binomial test), suggesting that departure *is* dependent on posture, rather than arrival direction *per se*. The posture variable allows for the influence of previous flowers on future choice in a simple way without the need to invoke memory, at least in the usual sense of the word.

The ‹tilting inseclect› model (Figure 4) which we have described is sub-optimal in the sense that it cannot cope with some artificial flower patterns without revisitation occurring, but once the constraints of this model are incorporated into the optimality analysis, this distinction disappears. What next? One approach (illustrating the interaction between OFT and control models shown in Figure 1) would be to pursue the question of the physiological basis of the iseclects. CHEVERTON (1983) has investigated the possibility that this is to be found in the distribution of ommatidia over the bees' visual field (cf. HEINRICH 1983). Measurements of ommatidial density showed that the shape of the iseclects cannot be explained on the simple hypothesis that the bees fly to the flower seen by most ommatidia from their position on the present flower. However, transformation of the ommatidial density map by a typical psychophysical function relating perceived to actual intensity of a stimulus (STEVENS 1961) renders much closer the fit between the behavioural and ommatidial isoclines. As an alternative approach, we could re-do the optimality analysis by accepting the iseclect model as a constraint, and trying to derive an optimum shape for the iseclects themselves.

4 Choosing the currency

Among the many examples of optimality modelling in behavioural ecology one can identify two contrasting approaches. Representing one of them, Sibly and McFarland (1976) (and also McFarland 1976, 1977) proposed that optimality models should ideally be based on a specification of how behaviour affects states and on direct measurements in the field of the fitness costs and benefits associated with each state and type of activity. For this research program the choice of an appropriate currency ought not to be a conceptual difficulty: the currency is fitness, measured directly. Having specified both constraints and currency, optimality models can be used to test whether or not the animal performs its behavioural repertoire in a sequence that maximises fitness. These optimality models do not have the goal of identifying constraints and how behaviour contributes to fitness (although investigation of these matters may be essential for the formulation of the models) but, in Sibly's and McFarland's words, their aim is to assess «... the extent to which behaviour maximises fitness.»

This route has not yet been successfully followed because of the difficulties posed by the field measurements required. Most optimality models in behavioural ecology, including OFT, have a much more limited aim. As discussed in the introduction, most models aim to gain insights into the constraints and currencies. They do this by formulating, testing and reformulating hypotheses based on particular constraint and currency assumptions, often in relation to only one or two kinds of activity. While this piecemeal approach cannot test whether observed behaviour is optimal (i. e. whether animals are optimally adapted, Maynard Smith 1978) it may, as knowledge of the constraints and currencies improves, develop towards a convergence with the use of optimality as proposed by Sibly and McFarland.

A major problem for the piecemeal approach is to establish the appropriate response to a discrepancy between predictions based on an optimality model and observed behaviour. How does one know whether to modify the constraint assumptions or the currency? There is no simple answer, but suitable choice of experimental systems may help to reduce this uncertainty. In general, when the primary interest lies in one of the themes, it is advisable to choose a system where the other factor offers little doubt. Thus, the study of constraints is best conducted in cases when animals have been shown to maximise a given currency (for example net energy gain) in a variety of other situations, while the study of currencies is ideally conducted when it is safe to assume that the necessary behavioural mechanisms to follow the optimal policy are available to the animal. As an example, consider the various attempts to test the choice of optimal patch residence time by animals foraging in a homogeneous environment. The usual rationale can be expressed as: if the foraging animal is subject to dimishing returns *in the relevant currency* while exploiting patches, then the optimal patch residence time is given by the marginal value rule. We will ignore here the problems arising from heterogeneous, stochastic and discontinuous environments, and refer only to cases when the instantaneous use of the marginal value rule does result in rate maximisation. If the animal can reasonably be assumed or shown to be capable of assessing marginal gain rate, failure to stay for the predicted time indicates the need for adjustements in the specification of currency. We shall discuss this in some detail in the framework of experimental work done by Nuñez (1982) with honey bees *(Apis mellifera)* and a theoretical extension of it elaborated by Kacelnik and Houston (in prep.).

4.1 Optimal crop load in honey bees

The prediction of the marginal value rule for cases when there is no depression in the relevant currency is trivial: the animal should never abandon a patch unless it has reached its maximum loading capacity (remember that we have excluded from our analysis all cases of patch heterogeneity, etc.).

NUÑEZ (1982) performed an experiment in which nectar collecting bees had access to an artificial dispenser placed at various distances from the hive. Flow of nectar in the dispenser was not subject to depression either during or between visits. NUÑEZ correctly predicted that if overall rate of nectar collection was the maximised currency, the bees ought to follow the marginal value rule and stay for as long as necessary to fill their crops before returning to the hive. The bees failed to do so. Instead, they abandoned the patch with various degrees of crop filling depending on the distance between the patch and the hive and the rate of flow of nectar while in the patch. Crop load was reduced at close distances and low flow rates.

Facing this discrepancy, the obvious step was to correct the assumption about the currency. Because both variables affecting crop filling are correlated with time away from the hive, NUÑEZ speculated that a possible reason for the discrepancy was to be found in the social nature of food gathering in this species. The long term advantages of exchanging information with other workers would affect individual behaviour, and the maximised currency could be thought of as a compromise between individual foraging efficiency and the advantage to the hive of information exchange between workers. The appeal of NUÑEZ' suggestion derives from its testability: if information exchange is responsible for departures from individual workers' optimal behaviour, then a solitary forager like the bumblebee ought not to show those discrepancies.

While this possibility has not been tested yet, KACELNIK and HOUSTON (in prep) took a different route, improving the expression of individual workers' energetic efficiency by refining the energetic currency. They reasoned that if one chose the *net* rate of delivery of nectar to the hive instead of the rate of extraction of nectar form the patch as the maximised currency the predictions might differ.

KACELNIK's and HOUSTON's rationale can best be followed by the graphical presentation in Figure 5. The ordinate in this figure represents quantities of sugar, and the abscisa is time, with the origin at the point of arrival at the patch. Costs and gains are analysed in three periods: the outward trip, the time in the patch and the return trip. Starting at the left hand side of the graph we can follow three trajectories, corresponding to gross nectar collection (F), cumulative energy expenditure (E) and resulting net gain or load (L). Cumulative nectar collection is represented by a rising linear function while the bee is in the patch (the slope of this line is the flow rate of the feeder) and remains unmodified while the bee is travelling from or to the hive. Expenditure is represented as a decreasing function for reasons of presentation. For the purposes of the graph the effect of a varying load during the journeys is ignored, and thus cumulative expenditure during them is represented by straight lines. Rate of expenditure during the outward trip (slope of E_o) depends on the initial load, which must itself be a function of the distance between the hive and the feeder, but only one distance is considered here. Rate of expenditure during the return trip (slope of E_r) depends on the load collected during the visit ot the patch, as will be analysed later on. Expenditure during the visit itself is an accelerating function of load, as shown by the convexity of E_p. Assuming an initial load large enough to pay for the anticipated cost of the outward journey, we can follow the net load by starting at point P, and ending at point Q, when the bee reaches the hive again. Notice that the net load curve while in the patch is curvilinear during patch time (L_p), due to the increasing cost of carrying the load. The position of Q depends on time in the patch in a way that combines the course of L_p with the slope and duration of L_r. This is because both expenditure during flight and flight velocity in bees are significantly affected by the range of loads normally carried.

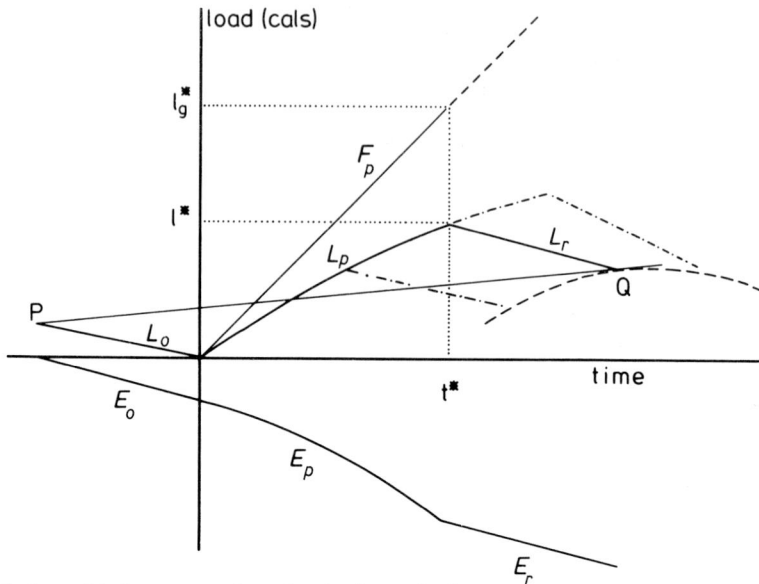

Figure 5: A graphical representation of optimal crop load.

The effect of staying for different patch times is shown by the broken lines. By leaving the patch earlier than indicated, the loss of time and energy during the return trip is reduced, but the net gain at departure from the patch is also lowered. The opposite (i. e. higher gain at departure but larger travel losses) would result from longer patch time. As result of these combined effects the position of point Q realised as a consequence of various patch times (or loads) describes an arc as shown by the broken line. Since this line represents the net load on arrival at the end of a foraging trip, the optimum patch time (t*) can be obtained by tracing the tangent to the broken line that passes through P. The optimal time corresponds to a net load of l*, and gross intake of lg*. It is immediately obvious that maximum load will not always be optimum if the maximised currency is net rate of delivery. In practice, the graphical method is inappropriate and unnecesary to calculate the optimum, and KACELNIK and HOUSTON used available information of rates of expenditure combined with suitable simplifications to find an analytical version of this model. The model states that optimal patch time (t) is that one that satisfies the equation:

$$(DCFe^{-mt} + l) [(F/m) (1 - e^{-mt}) + B/k - Be^{k\tau} ((l/k) + AD)]$$
$$=$$
$$[t + 2DA + (DCF/m) (1 - e^{-mt})] Fe^{-mt} [1 - kDC ((F/m) (1 - e^{-mt}) + B/k)]$$

where:
A : l/ unloaded velocity
B : Flight metabolism, unloaded
C : Slope for increase in travel time with load
D : Distance hive-feeder
k : Slope of increase in flight metabolism with load
m : Slope of increase in metabolism at the feeder with load
E : Metabolic rate in feeder, unloaded
F : feeder flow − E
τ : $D(A + Cl_0)$
l_0 : Net load at departure from patch

Their predicted crop loads for NUÑEZ' conditions do fit with the qualitative observation that the bees leave the patch with larger loads at greater distances and higher flows, but the quantitative details, as shown in Figure 6, still show interesting discrepancies. One important discrepancy between model and data is that at close distance (100 m) the bees did not wait for long enough to fill their crops even when the flow was high. This points to a structural problem of the model, rather than some error in the estimate of parameters.

This analysis is still in progress, and there is no reason why the informational view taken by NUÑEZ could not coexist with the energetic analysis presented here. The relevant question is whether by following this recursive process of proposal and modification of hypotheses about currencies we learn something about bees, and our belief is (as the reader might have guessed) that we do[1].

Figure 6: The relationship between nectar intake and flow-rate at four different distances from the hive. —·—·—·—: as observed by Nunez. ————: as predicted by the model.

[1] Further analyses and experiments (SCHMID-HEMPEL, KACELNIK, and HOUSTON in prep.) have shown that if the energetic losses while the bee is in the hive are included, a better fit is obtained by assuming that the maximised currency is the ratio of energy gained to energy spent.

5 Discussion

Our main general conclusions are as follows. (i) Optimality models include assumptions about constraints and specification of constraints requires a knowledge of behavioural and physiological mechanisms. We illustrate this point with work on foraging paths of bumblebees. (ii) The currency in an optimality model could in principle be measured directly as fitness, in which case the model could be used to test how well animals are adapted to their environment. Alternatively, optimality models can be used to evaluate different putative currencies which are thought to be related to fitness. The contrast between predictions based on gross and net energy intake as foraging currencies for honey bees illustrates this point. We now return in this concluding discussion to the question of constraints.

5.1 What are constraints?

Assumptions about constraints pose a problem: what at one time is treated as a fixed constraint may on another occassion be seen as subject to adaptive modification. How does one know, in other words, whether or not it is justifiable to treat *any* aspect of behaviour as a constraint? Is it acceptable, as would be the case for morphological or physiological properties, to infer the constraints simply from looking at the animal's behaviour?

The difficulties that may arise from inferring constraints by observing behaviour can be illustrated by two analyses of the courtship behaviour of the three-spined stickleback (*Gasterosteus aculeatus*). When a ripe female enters the territory of a male in breeding condition, he approaches and courts her in the well-known sequence culminating in egg laying described by ter Pelkwijk and Tinbergen (1937). Not infrequently, the normal courtship sequence is temporarily interrupted by the male, who leaves the female to visit the nest and performs a variety of nest-building or parental activities before resuming courtship. Wilz (1967, 1970) suggested that these activities are essential for the male to adjust his internal state from primarily territorial and aggressive to primarily sexually motivated. If the male is prevented from carrying out nest activities by being excluded from the nest, he subsequently tends to attack the female instead of courting her. Cohen and McFarland (1979) have a different interpretation. They argue that it is «very misleading to infer function simply on the basis of causal relationships». That is, Wilz's hypothesis is based entirely on the supposed motivational constraint that the stickleback cannot switch from aggression to sex in the presence of a ripe female without doing activities at the nest. (Many parallel examples can be found in the older ethological literature). Cohen and McFarland, instead of taking the motivational switch as a constraint, ask why sticklebacks are designed to have to visit the nest during courtship. They suggest that the courting male has to balance two needs: inducing the female to enter the nest and checking that the nest is in good order before the female arrives. It is the requirement to keep two balls in the water at once that has lead to the evolution of courtship interrupted by nesting activities. To the extent that visiting the nest is essential for the male to switch motivational states, this is an adaptive feature rather than a constraint. The failure of the male to continue courting after finding the nest entrance blocked is compatible with Cohen's and McFarland's interpretation: since the male is unable to complete fertilisation without an accessible nest, he would not be expected to continue courtship. Ridley and Rechten (1981) offer an additional functional hypothesis for interruptions to courtship. They show that females are more likely to spawn in nests with eggs than in those without, and suggest that the male, by visiting the nest to perform parental activities during courtship, indicates the presence (perhaps deceptively) of eggs in the nest.

The stickleback example serves to illustrate the fact that there can be alternative views about what constitutes a constraint. It can also be used to suggest a possible general procedure for identifying constraints: comparison between species. If it transpired that males of species closely related to the stickleback do *not* have courtship interruptions, this would indicate that the motivational switch is not a fixed constraint (DAWKINS 1982, p 43, p 49). If, on the other hand, a wide taxonomic range of fish show interruptions, whether or not the male tends a nest, a strong case would exist for a motivational constraint. This case would be further strengthened if the assumed constraint could be shown, perhaps by cladistic methods (RIDLEY 1983), to be primitive; that is, to have persisted in independent evolutionary lines. For example, the wide taxonomic applicability of equations relating metabolic rate to body size in endotherms (ASCHOFF und POHL 1970) and the similarity of maximum sustainable work rate in several taxa (DRENT and DAAN 1980) makes it likely that these are genuine constraints. Similarly many basic features of morphology and physiology would qualify as constraints under our proposed method. Parenthetically we note that a distinction can be made between constraints which exist here and now, but could change over evolutionary time – these are the ones we are mainly concerned with – and constraints which are so universal as to be, in effect, immutable.

Although the method outlined in the previous paragraph would in principle lead to a more accurate distinction between constraints and design features, in practice the information needed to use the method is often not available. Therefore the approach adopted by most workers is to identify constraints by observing mechanisms of behaviour; in doing this one should be aware of the pitfalls.

5.2 Variability in behaviour

Variance is a universal feature of behaviour and morphology, yet most foraging models do not predict variability and many do not take it into account in their assumptions. Two contrasting ways of treating variability have been suggested reflecting the problem outlined in the previous section of distinguishing between constraints and design features. HOUSTON and McNAMARA (in press) treat variance in a behavioural mechanism (timing ability) as a constraint subject to which an optimum can be calculated (see section 2.1). Since variance in timing has been shown in more than one taxon this seems to be a reasonable approach. In other cases the degree of variability in behaviour may differ between related taxa or may be flexible depending on costs, suggesting that it is not simply a fixed constraint. DENEUBOURG et. al. (1983), for example, show that different ant species differ in the variance about the mean recruitment directions of foragers: some species recruit accurately and others with a wide spread. These authors go on to suggest on the basis of simulation models that the different degrees of spread are adapted for exploiting different kinds of food – accurate recruitment for concentrated clumps and inaccurate recruitment for scattered food. KACELNIK (1984) noted that the distribution of deviations about the energy-maximising value of load size in Starlings *(Sturnus vulgaris)* bringing food to their young is related to the energetic costs of deviating. The loss in reward rate was asymmetric for deviations above and below the mean load and there were fewer deviations in the direction of higher loss, suggesting that variance is not entirely a fixed constraint. The question of variability would repay further study. Most tests of foraging models to date have considered only mean values and not even taken the first step of partitioning variance into components due to inter-, intra-individual differences and so on.

Finally, if variance is a universal feature of behaviour, is there any point in building models which predict deterministic behaviour? The answer depends on the purpose of the models. If the model is derived inductively as a description of behaviour (e. g. the matching law, Herrnstein 1970) then taking into account basic features of behaviour such as variability would seem to be important. On the other hand, foraging models, and optimality models in general, are justified primarily as *a priori* predictors of behaviour rather than inductive descriptors. In this case the tractability and simplicity of a deterministic model of the optimal policy outweighs the advantage of complete descriptive accuracy.

6 Summary

1. Optimality models contain assumptions about constraints and currencies.
2. Knowledge of appropriate constraints comes from understanding mechanisms of behaviour.
3. The investigation of behavioural mechanisms of foraging is illustrated by work on bumblebees collecting nectar from artificial inflorescences in a two-dimensional array. The bees avoid revisiting, but appear to do so without remembering which flowers they have visited. Their movement patterns can be explained by a model of preference isoclines and the effects of body posture.
4. If fitness is measured directly as the currency of an optimality model, the model can be used to evaluate how well an animal is adapted to its environment. More frequently a putative currency is proposed and the model used to investigate the predictive value of currency and constraint assumptions.
5. The comparison of alternative currencies is illustrated by the problem of crop load in honey bees. A model based on maximising net energy gain per unit time correctly predicted that bees return to the hive with partially loaded crops.

7 Acknowledgements

We thank the EGI foraging lunch group for valuable comments and the NERC for financial support.

References

Alexander, R. McN. (1982): Optima for animals. Arnold, London.
Aschoff, J. and Pohl, H. (1970): Rhythmic variations in energy metabolism. Federation Proceedings 29, 1541–1552.
Baker, J. R. (1938): The relation between latitude and breeeding season in birds. Proceedings of the Zoological Society of London 106, 557–582.
Cartwright, B. A. and Collett, T. S. (1982): How honeybees use landmarks to guide their return to a food source. Nature (London) 295, 560–564.
Charnov, E. L. (1976 a): Optimal foraging: attack strategy of a mantid. American Naturalist 110, 141–151.
Charnov, E. L. (1976 b): Optimal foraging: the marginal value theorem. Theoretical Population Biology 9, 129–136.
Charnov, E. L., Orians, G. H. and Hyatt, K. (1976): The ecological implications of resource depression. American Naturalist 110, 247–259.

Cheverton, J. (1983): Which flower next? Small scale foraging decisions in bumblebees. D. Phil. Thesis, Oxford University.

Cohen, S. and McFarland, D. J. (1979): Time-sharing as a mechanism for the control of behaviour sequences during the courtship of three-spined stickleback *Gasterosteus aculeatus*. Animal Behaviour *27*, 270–283.

Cowie, R. J. (1977): Optimal foraging in Great Tits *(Parus major)*. Nature *268*, 137–139.

Cowie, R. J., Krebs, J. R. (1978): Optimal foraging in patchy environments. Anderson, R. M., Taylor, L. R. and Turner, B. (eds): British Ecological Society Symposium on Population Dynamics. Blackwell's Scientific Publications, Oxford.

Dawkins, R. (1982): The extended phenotype. Freeman, Oxford.

Deneubourg, J. L., Pasteels, J. M. and Verhaege, J. C. (1983): Probabilistic behaviour in ants: a strategy of errors? Journal of Theoretical Biology. 105, 259–271.

Dennett, D. C. (1983): Intentional systems in cognitive ethology: «the Panglossian paradigm» defended. Brain and Behavioural Sciences 6, 343–390.

Drent, R. H. and Daan, S. (1980): The Prudent Parent: Energetic adjustements in avian breeding. Ardea *68*, 225–252.

Free, J. B. and Butler, C. G. (1959): Bumblebees. Collins New Naturalist Series, London.

Getty, T. W. and Krebs, J. R. (in press): Lagging partial preferences for cryptic prey: a signal detection analysis of great tit foraging. American Naturalist.

Gibbon, J. and Church, R. M. (1981): Time left: linear vs. logarithmic subjective time. J. exp. Psychol. *7*, 87–107.

Giraldeau, L. and Kramer, D. L. (1982): The marignal value theorem: a quantitative test using load size variation in a central place forager, the eastern chipmunk. Animal Behaviour *4*, 1036–1042.

Gould, S. J. and Lewontin, R. C. (1979): The spandrels of San Marco and the Panglossian Paradigm: a critique of the adaptationist programme. Proceedings of the Royal Society *205*, 581–598.

Green, R. F. (1980): Bayesian birds: a simple example of Oaten's stochastic model of optimal foraging. Theoretical Population Biology *18*, 244–256.

Heinrich, B. (1983): Do bumblebees forage optimally, and does it matter?. American Zoologist *23*, 273–282.

Herrnstein, R. J. (1970): On the law of effect. Journal of Experimental Analysis of Behaviour *13*, 243–266.

Houston, A. I., Kacelnik, A. and McNamara, J. (1982): Some learning rules for acquiring information. McFarland, D. J. (ed): Functional Ontogeny. Pitman Advanced Publishing Program, London.

Houston, A. I. and McNamara, J. (in press).: Variability of behaviour and constrained optimization. Journal of Theoretical Biology.

Iwasa, Y. Higashi, M. and Yamamura, N. (1981): Prey distribution as a factor determining the choice of optimal foraging strategy. American Naturalist *117*, 710–723.

Janetos, A. C. and Cole, B. J. (1981): Imperfectly optimal animals. Behavioral Ecology and Sociobiology 9, 203–210.

Kacelnik, A. (1984): Central place foraging in starlings *(Sturnus vulgaris)* I: patch residence time. Journal of Animal Ecology. 53, 283–299.

Kacelnik, A. and Houston, A. I. (1984): Some effects of energy costs on foraging strategies. Animal Behaviour.

Krebs, J. R. and McCleery, R. H. (1984): Optimization in behavioural ecology. Krebs J. R. and Davies N. B. (eds). Behavioural Ecology (2nd Edn.) Blackwell Scientific Publications, Oxford.

Krebs, J. R., Stephens, D. W. and Sutherland, W. J. (1983): Perspectives in optimal foraging. Clark G. A. and Brush, A. H. (eds) Perspectives in Ornithology. Cambridge University Press, New York.

Lewontin, R. C. (1983): Elementary errors about evolution. Brain and Behavioural Sciences *6*, 367–368.

MacArthur, R. H. and Pianka, E. R. (1966): On the optimal use of a patchy environment. American Naturalist *100*, 603–609.

McFarland, D. J. (1976): Form and function in the temporal organization of behaviour. Bateson, P. P. G. and Hinde, R. A. (eds): Growing points in theology. Cambridge University Press, Cambridge.

McFarland, D. J. (1977): Decision making in animals. Nature *269*, 15–21.

McFarland, D. J. and Houston, A. I. (1981): Quantitative ethology. Pitman, London.

MacNamara, J. M. (1982): Optimal patch use in a stochastic environment. Theoretical population biology 21, 269–288.

Manning, A. (1956): Some aspects of the foraging behaviour of bumblebees. Behaviour 9, 164–201.

Maynard Smith, J. (1978): Optimization theory in evolution. Annual Review of Ecology and Systematics 9, 31–56.

Maynard Smith, J. (1983): Adaptation and satisficing. Brain and Behavioral Sciences 6, 370–371.

Mazur, J. E. (1983): Optimization: result or mechanism. Science 221, 976–977.

Myers, J. P. (1983): Commentary on *Perspectives in Optimal Foraging* (Krebs, J. R., Stephens, D. W. and Sutherland, W. J.). Brush, A. H. and Clark, G. A. (eds): Perspectives in Ornithology. Cambridge University Press, Cambridge.

Nuñez, J. A. (1982): Honeybee foraging strategies at a food source in relation to its distance from the hive and the rate of sugar flow. Journal of Apicultural Research 21, 139–150.

Olton, D. S., Handelman, G. E. and Walker, J. A. (1981): Spatial memory and food searching strategies. Kamil, A. C. and Sargent, T. D. (eds): Foraging behaviour. Garland STPM Press, New York.

Oster, G. P. and Wilson, E. O. (1978): Caste and ecology in the social insects. Princeton University Press, Princeton, N. J.

Pyke, G. H. (1979): Optimal foraging in bumblebees: rule of movement between flowers in inflorescences. Animal Behaviour 27, 1167–1181.

Pyke, G. H., Pulliam, H. R. and Charnov, E. L. (1977): Optimal foraging: a selective review of theory and tests. Quarterly Review of Biology 52, 137–154.

Rechten, C., Avery, M. I. and Stevens, T. A. (1983): Optimal prey selection: why do great tits show partial preferences? Animal Behaviour 31, 576–584.

Ridley, M. (1983): The explanation of Organic diversity. Oxford University Press, Oxford.

Ridley, M. and Rechten, C. (1981): Female sticklebacks prefer to spawn in nests with eggs. Behaviour 76, 152–161.

Schoener, T. W. (1971): Theory of feeding strategies. Annual review of Ecology and Systematics 2, 369–404.

Sibly, R. M. and McFarland, D. J. (1976): On the fitness of behavior sequences. American Naturalist 110, 601–617.

Staddon, J. E. R. (1980): Optimality analyses of operant behaviour and their relation to optimal foraging. Staddon, J. E. R. (ed): Limits to action. The allocation of individual behaviour. Academic Press, New York.

Stevens, S. S. (1961). To honor Fechner and repeat his low. Science 133, 80–86.

ter Pelkwijk, J. J. and Tinbergen, N. (1937): Eine reizbiologische Analyse einiger Verhaltensweisen von *Gasterosteus aculeatus* L. Z. Tierpsychologie 1, 193–200.

Werner, E. E. and Mittelbach, G. G. (1981): Optimal foraging: field tests of diet choice and habitat switching. American Zoologist 21, 813–829.

Wilz, K. (1967): The organization of courtship in sticklebacks. Unpublished D. Phil Thesis, Oxford University.

Wilz, K. (1970): Causal and functional analysis of dorsal pricking and nest activity in the courtship of the three-spined stickleback. Animal Behaviour 18, 682–687.

Ydenberg, R. C. (1982): territorial vigilance and foraging, a study of tradeoffs. Unpublished D. Phil thesis, Oxford University.

II. The Analysis of Communication Signals

Fortschritte der Zoologie, Bd. 31 · Hölldobler/Lindauer (Hrsg.): Experimental Behavioral Ecology
G. Fischer Verlag · Stuttgart · New York · 1985

The dance language of honeybees: The history of a discovery

MARTIN LINDAUER

Zoologisches Institut der Universität Würzburg, F.R.Germany

Abstract

KARL V. FRISCH did not restrict his investigations on the beedance to its description of the symbolic code and its biological meaning. He encouraged studies on the evolution of this unique communication system. He was interested in what sensory performances were based on for each information, especially in indicating the distance and the direction towards the goal.

The world of the polarized light was detected, the complicated mechanism of sun compass orientation became understandable. His students of the 1., 2. and 3. generation are still working on unsolved problems raised from the beedance: e. g. the orientation of bees in the earth magnetic field and the information processing from one generation of bees to the next.

Preamble

The bee dance had already been discovered at least 3 times before KARL V. FRISCH published his first communication «Über die Sprache der Bienen» in 1920. ARISTOTLE observed that the forager bee after having thrown off her load returns to the crop and is followed by three or four companions – «but how they do it, has not been observed».

In 1788 Pastor ERNST SPITZNER, born in my own native country in Oberammergau, described the bee dances as «ballet of the bee»: «Full of joy they twirl in circles about those in the hive, from above downward and from below upward.

In a few minutes, after these had made it known to the others, they came in great numbers to the place!»

In 1823 UNHOCH gave an almost perfect description of the rounddance: «The dance mistresses twist and turn in something more than a semicircle, now to the right, then to the left, five or six times, and execute what is a genuine round dance. – What this dance really means I cannot yet comprehend. –»

1 The dance language of the forager bees

It was by no means a sudden and sensational discovery, when in 1919 for the first time KARL V. FRISCH saw in the Jesuit-Klosterhof of the old Zoological Institute in Munich the round dance of a returning forager bee. It was 26 years before the whole corpus of information was found. In small steps the mosaic stones were collected by himself and his students. (K. V. FRISCH 1920, 1923)

However the very first discovary already represented a breakthrough in sociobiology. In the year 1920 practically no biologist imagined that an animal

could communicate exact details about the flower-species visited and the quality and profitableness of a crop area by means of symbolic dance movements;

could deliver these pieces of information in the hive far away from the location of their origin

could successfully transmit a specific order to fellow-bees waiting near the entrance.

The philologists agree on «Semanticity», «Broadcast», «Displacement», and «Productivity» for these performances and some take them as elements of a proper language.

Twentysix years later, in 1945, an additional, almost unbelievable information code was detected:

the tailwagging dance, as the long distance dance, indicates the direction of and distance to the goal.

The distance is related to the rhythm of the wagging runs, the direction of the wagging line is related to the position of the sun, whereby the angle between sun and flight route is transposed on the vertical comb into the gravity-field. All these facts fascinating as they were in different ways, and which appear to us very clear nowadays, created some confusion for KARL v. FRISCH in the early years: precise data on the direction indication sometimes revealed deviations of up to 40° to the left or to the right; these deviations were not the same on the opposite side of the comb. Even more confusing were the dances on the horizontal surface, when the comb with the dancing bees was tilted: now the dances pointed directly towards the goal by their wagging line using the sun directly as a compass; but the dances were orientated even when the sun was covered by clouds – as long as a spot of blue sky was visible. (K. v. FRISCH 1965)

The only way to solve these riddles was to pick out single facts, isolate them, and test them again and agian. As we shall see later, pioneer work has been done in this way in the field of modern sensory physiology, opening new systems to detect parts of the environment to which our senses are blind.

This may be a useful priece of advice for the younger generation of biologists: not to throw in the sponge when a hopelessly complicated situation arises – something new and interesting may be awaiting discovery.

2 Communication in swarmbees

Of special interest was the finding that the bee dance uses its semantic code not only in foraging but also in house hunting. «Interchangeability» of semantics is another essential element in a genuine language.

Scout bees announce a suitable nesting site by the same wagging dances as successful nectar- or pollen-collectors. From the beginning quite new problems concerning sociobiology arose during our observations:

a) Scouts which are recruited from old experienced forager bees have to change their motivation radically when they move from collecting sweet nectar to inspection of dusty holes. They do this without any reward. Only social exigencies regulate this drastic psychological change in the dance mood.

b) Whereas in foraging the bees are attracted by the colour, odour, shape and pattern of flowers, now the same individual has to search for dark hollows in the ground, in a wall or even in a chimney.

c) If one follows for some time the dances of the scouting bees in the cluster and records their announcements of location, one comes to a very surprising conclusion: not just one nesting place is reported, but rather announcements are given of different directions and distances, and this means that several possible dwellings are announced at the same time.

We now have to answer the difficult question of how agreement is reached in the cluster about which of the nesting places offered should be chosen. Only one of them can be selected, for the entire swarm must move with its queen and cannot split itself up into small groups.

In fact only when the good fortune of agreement finally came about was the sign given to fly off, and the swarm moved out in the announced direction.

In any case, we arrived at the following conclusions: (1) the decision concerning the choice of a nesting place lies solely with the scouting bees; (2) the choice is always for the best nesting place offered.

The dancers in the cluster give information not only concerning the location of the new dwelling place, but also concerning its quality; this quality is indicated by the liveliness and the duration of the dance.

In this way it is not merely the interest of most novices in the swarm that is concentrated on the best nesting site offered; I have found – to my own surprise – that even the scouts which had previously announced mediocre sites later followed these lively dances, visited this new place and changed their mind, i. e. they voted for this new – better – nesting site. Only in this way can agreement in such a critical situation be reached.

d) How can the scouts judge so exactly the quality of a prospective bee home? We know that size, protection against wind, ants and rain, the distance from the mother hive etc. are decisive positive factors. We should realize, however, that they had no experience on house-hunting before; they cannot be informed in this matter by specialists, since generations can pass without any need for searching for new nesting sites.

But after swarming these old forager bees have to ensure the survival of the whole colony. Even if we suppose that the details of an optimal nesting site must be encoded as a fixed genetic information, we should admire such a radical change in motivation and in the orientation mechanism due to social demands (LINDAUER 1955).

3 Evolution of the bees dance

One day in 1954 K. v. FRISCH called me into his office to meet the director of the Rockefeller Foundation, Dr. POMERAT. To my great surprise I was asked: «Will you go – with a fund of the Rockefeller Foundation – to India in order to study the language of the Indian bees? Since we cannot believe», K. v. FRISCH explained, «that the bee dance of the European bees has come from heaven as it is, and since the Indian honeybees and the stingless bees there live in a more primitive social organisation, we should expect some phylogenetic primitive stages of the bee dance».

My stay afterwards in Sri Lanka and in Brazil confirmed the following:
1. that in all four species of the genus *Apis* essentially the same round- and tail-wagging dances are used in food gathering and in the search for housing
2. that in indicating the distance so called «dialects», which K. v. FRISCH has described for the different races in *Apis mellifera,* are even more pronounced
3. that in indicating the direction a more primitive stage in the dance of *Apis florea* is realised. This lovely dwarf honeybee is unable to transpose the direction towards the goal into the gravity field; she needs a horizontal platform on the top of her single comb, which is built on a branch right in the open air. Here the wagging line points directly towards the goal using the sun's position as the exclusive reference point (LINDAUER 1956). With this evolutionary aspect established it may be of interest for

future research to find out how, on a neurological basis, the increasing complexity in multimodal information processing should be understood. The stingless bees of Southeast Asia and of Brazil – there exist more than 400 species – in their still more primitive social organization use even more primitive means of communication: Meliponini newcomers are first alerted in the hive by excited but undirected wagging runs of the forager bees; then these alerted novices, waiting in a group in front of the hive are guided by scented trail marks previously laid down by the foraging pilot bees (Lindauer 1961).

There is a link to the odour marks of different ant species and this system may be a common root of the elaborate bee dance.

4 Sensory aspects of the bees' dance

Up to now hardly any other behavioural study has been analyzed in such careful detail and so comprehensively. Apart from sociobiology and evolution, *sensory physiology* in particular was promoted in an unique way. Let me demonstrate this in a few examples.

One of the most difficult problems v. Frisch had to face for years was the sun compass-orientation. To use the sun as reference point is fine in bright weather; but it was confusing indeed, when we had to state again and agian that the bees continued dancing even when the sun was covered by clouds. The famous «Ofenrohrversuch», whereby a small spot of blue sky through a stovepipe was visible for the dancers on a horizontal comb, pointed the way:

«Ich reinigte ein Ofenrohr von Russ, steckte es durch ein Zeltdach; dann zeigte ich den tanzenden Bienen auf horizontal gelegter Wabe ein Stück blauen Himmels durch die Öffnung dieses Rohres. Die Tänze waren sofort orientiert; mit einem Spiegel, der an der Öffnung des Rohres angebracht war, ließen sich die Tänze um 180° in die Gegenrichtung ablenken!»

Is there today any experimental setup in Biology which, by its «primitive arrangement» and by its simple but clear question, has brought a similar ingenious discovery and has opened to us human beings a new sensory world – the world of polarized light? The next decisive step which led to the discovery that polarized light was involved came about in a conversation with a friend in the physics department, Prof. Benndorf in Graz. His friend Krogh in Kopenhagen then provided for us a polaroid sheet from the US; by turning this sheet above a horizontal comb K. v. Frisch could deviate the wagging line of a dancing bee; a convincing demonstration that polarized light is used for orientation. Autrum suggested a model for the «Sternfolie», that could make visible the polarized pattern on the blue sky for the human eye. It opened the way in the search for the analysator in the bee's eye. But it was a stony search for the analysator until it was localized in the microvilli of the rhabdomeres based on the dichroitic absorption (for details see K. v. Frisch 1949, 1950, 1953, 1965).

The sun compass presents still another problem: As a reference point the sun changes its position from minute to minute. Do the bees calculate in their orientation this apparent sun movement? To clear up this question we had planned to train a group of bees in an unfamiliar countryside in the afternoon to a feeding place 180 m southwards. The next morning – displaced to another unknown area – these south-trained bees were to be tested on whether they prefered the eastern feeding place – which corresponded as «angle constant» with the sun (feeding table on the left side of the sun as in the afternoon before), or the true compass direction, i.e. the southern place – compensating the sunmovement

Fig. 1: In the afternoon of June 29th a group of bees was trained in an unfamiliar countryside to a feeding place 180 m NW.
The next morning 4 feeding tables in different compass directions were made available – again in an unknown area. The bees prefered the NW-place (15:2:2:0) (K. v. FRISCH 1965)

(Fig. 1) «Jeder wird uns für verrückt halten, wenn wir solche Leistung von den Bienen erwarten.»

«Everyone will think we are mad to expect the bees to achieve something like that» – v. FRISCH told me at that time, and I had to encourage both of us to risk the experiment; this was just a year before KRAMER reported on sun compass-orientation in starlings. In the last 30 years it has been proved that many animal species can orientate themselves by means of the sun compass. It has often happened that «strange» ideas, better to say «very improbable hypotheses» have prepared the way for important discoveries – provided that challenge, risk and courage are given free rein.

5 The detour and side wind experiment

«Kleine Dinge, große Wirkung» – little things but great consequences – this holds true for many «minor»-experiments of K. v. FRISCH: When the bees are forced to fly in a detour around a rock what angle will they indicate in their dance – the first or the second leg they have flown? Neither of them. Quite unexpectedly they indicate the *direct route;* only by this calculation can they avoid a mistake for the novices. Furthermore: if we move the hive and the feeding table towards the tip of the triangle so that the energy consumption in flight *over* the rock becomes lower than in the detour, the foragers choose the direct flight.

Even if we hesitate to call this calculation «intelligent» – it is an «ad hoc decision» which solves the problem – we should admire how a flying insect can have such a command of spatial coordinates. Related to this performance was the compensation performance in side wind. In such a situation the bees have to fly in an oblique body position to the goal, so that they see the sun at a wrong angle with regard to the direct route; nevertheless in the dance they keep this direct route, which is again the best solution for the novices since the wind can change from minute to minute (K. v. FRISCH u. M. LINDAUER 1955).

In conncetion with the «side wind problem» I should mention here again the great optimism and patience of K. v. FRISCH in facing experimental difficulties. For 3 summers we had arranged our setup expecting that the famous «Brunnwind» on sunny days would blow from 10:00 up to 14:00 from the Mondsee to the Wolfgangsee in an eastward direction. On some days we were happy indeed, but in other days there was no wind whatsoever; or suddenly the Föhn (a south-wind) came up or a thunderstorm offered a strong west-wind.

«We must try again» he said and this optimism eventually resulted in some fine successes for us.

6 Problems left as a challenge for future research

The history of the bees' dance can be completed only if we now deal with the many «seedlings» K. v. Frisch has planted during his life for his students in the 1., 2. and 3. generation – and over the whole world. (See Menzel, Wehner, Seeley, Gould, Dyer, Hölldobler as referees in this symposium).

6.1 Calculation of distance

When the dancing bees indicate distance by means of their rhythm then these bees must have measured the distance themselves before. K. v. Frisch already has found that the parameter is not the flight time but the consumption of energy. Heran and his group have confirmed this conclusion in fine experiments. (Scholze E., H. Pichler und H. Heran 1964) V. Neese, my co-worker in Würzburg went a step further by asking the question: how can the bee measure so exactly the consumption of energy during flight? It is the *decreasing tension* of the honeysac-wall, which is correlated with distance flown. Cutting the «nervus recurrens» or offering an artificial dense sugar solution with agar puts the system out of order (unpublished).

6.2 Orientation in the earth's magnetic field (EMF)

It was a great surprise indeed when we – after a long and tiresome analysis – had evidence that the earth's magnetic field influences the angle orientation in the wagging dance. In cooperation with H. Martin we registred regular deviations which follow a typical diurnal pattern.

These diurnal curves are correlated with the dynamic variation of the EMF according to the following function:

$$Mi \triangleq [(eA_2 \pm \frac{v}{2}) \cdot (eA_2 - eA_1)^2] \cdot \lambda$$

$Mi = (eA_2 \pm eA_1) \cdot \lambda$
eA = effective magnetic force = $\log (\Delta f + 1) .\mu. \sin\alpha$
v = Rayleigh-constant ($\approx$ 0,20–0,24)
ΔF = variation of EMF
μ = permeability
α = angle of dance in the gravity field
λ = scale factor.

Fig. 2 gives an example of the dynamic change of the «Missweisung» during the day, based on the above function. The data given so far show that bees are sensitive to variations of the magnetic field in the range from 0–300 γ. However, only dynamic changes are of importance.

Wabe N–S
Tanzboden W
Flugloch N
Futterplatz S

Temp. 25°-30°C,
windstill,
30 - 60% Himmelsblau,
stark wechselnde Bewölkung

4.8.69

Fig. 2: The «Missweisung» correlated with the dynamic diurnal change of the EMF (see text).

When the EMF is compensated the dancers orientate exclusively with respect to gravity. Also when the wagging line corresponds with the inclination (i. e. when it is parallel to the field line of the EMF; 65° in Würzburg) the dances show no deviation. (LINDAUER and MARTIN 1968, 1972, MARTIN, LINDAUER 1973, 1977). From the beginning we called in question whether these deviations are a «Missweisung» in the sense of true mistakes for the novices. LEUCHT (1982) in an extensive analysis, has confirmed our earlier hypothesis that the EMF has a stabilizing effect against disturbance of incident light. Only during the «Nulldurchgang» i. e. when the wagging line is parallel with the inclination (where the Missweisung is zero!) does the incident light considerably deviate.

There are however two situations where the EMF becomes a proper orientation parameter for the bees:

a) Swarming bees upon entering a new site have to select by unanimous decision the compass-orientation for the new combs. The bees prefer the main compass direction; in the natural magnetic field the north-south direction is preferred. (DE JONG 1982, KIRCHNER unpublished); in certain cases the swarms select the same orientation of the combs as in the mother hive.

b) The 24-hour periodicity of the EMF – as is shown in Fig. 3. is used by the bees as a *timer*, if other «Zeitgeber» such as light dark-change are excluded. In a disturbed aperiodic magnetic field the bees no longer orientate to the feeding time they were trained to in the preceding days. They are also disoriented in time when a colony is translocated to another geographic latitude, i. e. from Würzburg to the polarcircle. Here the 24-hour periodicity in intensity and the dynamic change in direction of the inclination and declination are quite different. (MARTIN and LINDAUER 1973).

Very recently it has been realized that in extreme situations, when all exogen «Zeitgeber», known up to now – including the periodicity of the EMF – are lacking, the bees still can use some astrophysical parameter for their orientation in time:

A group of foragers was fed continuously for 24 hours under so called «constant condition» (LL, constant temperature and humidity). In the natural EMF the bees display-

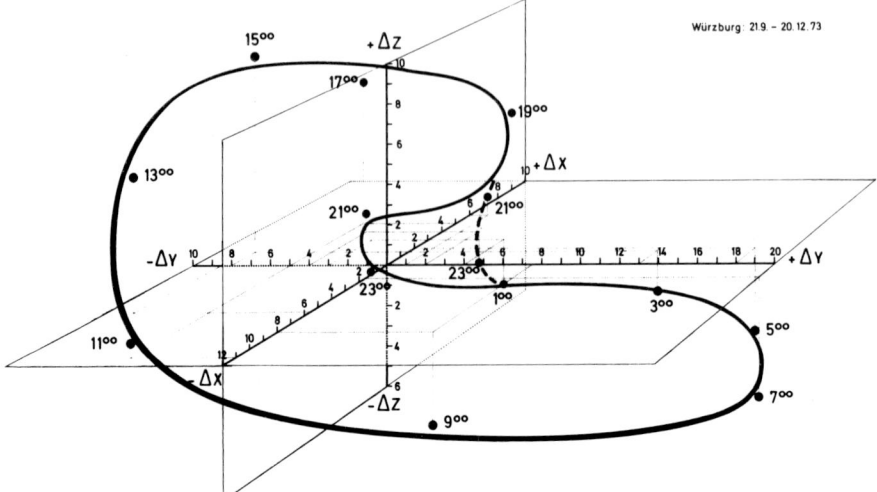

Fig. 3: The daily periodicity of the EMF in direction and intensity as a 3-Vector-Diagram.

Fig. 4: In an artificial disturbed magnetic field the bees – after long adaptation – show a free-running foraging activity, correlated with the sun-moon constellation (see text) ●—●—activity of the bees; ·—·—·· sun/moon constellation.

ed a preferential activity which corresponds with the dynmaic curve of the EMF. In the compensated or disturbed EMF the bees were totally disorientated in the first days, but after 2–3 weeks again the activity diagrams show a periodicity although a very smooth one. In detailed analysis MARTIN has found that besides the EMF – some additional events which originate form sun and moon affect the time sense of bees. (MARTIN, LINDAUER and MARTIN 1983) There is a nice correlation, when we take the azimuth of the sun and the moon, the altitude of both and the gravity constant of the sun.

Activity of the bees / time unit $\triangleq$ $[0,46 \times (\sin Az_S + \cos^2 h_S) + (\sin Az_M + \cos^2 h_M)]/ \Delta t$

Az_S = azimuth of the sun
Az_M = azimuth of the moon
h_S resp. H_M = altitude of the sun resp. moon (Fig. 4).

We have to conclude from these results, that at least in honeybees – the time sense has its basis on geophysical and astrophysical parameter as exogen «Zeitgeber».

6.3 Theories concerning the perception mechanism

In the last 15 years an increasing number of data were published which demonstrate that development, metabolism, information processing in animals are affected by the EMF; in addition as we have seen (p. 135) some parameters of the EMF are used for orientation and rhythmicity for establishing rhythm of activities. Therefore the question of the perception mechanism becomes urgent. Since up to now nobody has found magnetic receptors we can only offer some theories – which may encourage further research in this field.

Besides induction within a semiconductor moving within an external magnetic field (RUSSO and CALDWELL 1971) and besides the Josephson junction concept (1969) based on the change in the permeability of cell membranes due to alternating electromagnetic field, the theory of WALCOTT et al. (1979), GOULD et al. (1978, 1980) is favored by competent researchers today: in bacteria, in the abdomen of the honeybee, in some tissues of pigeons' head and in chitons magnetic crystals ($FeO \cdot Fe_2O_3$) have been detected, which should be involved in the orientation in the magnetic field. The mechanism may be well understood in bacteria, where the whole organism filled with crystals of magnetite reacts «magneto-tactically» as a single domain ferromagnet. In all other cases some morphological connection with the nervous system seems a prerequisite to us for special information processing coming from the magnetite crystals. Those connections have not be found.

Our own experiments, however, lead us close to the molecular niveau of perception:

As at first hand the orientation in the gravity field is affected by the EMF in bees, KORALL in our group has recorded the elementary transducer processes, i. e. the action potentials of a single gravity receptor in the neck organ of the honey bee under natural and artificial magnetic conditions (KORALL and MARTIN 1984).

The response of the receptor may be described as followed:

1. The frequency of impulses changes by tilting the vector of an artificial MF.
2. The frequency of impulses is correlated with the 24 hour periodicity of the EMF variations.
3. Early in the morning when the direction of the magnetic field vector changes very rapidly the EINSTEIN-DE HAAS-effect (gyromagnetic forces) is evident.

Some of these results and behavioural tests under distinct oscillating and static MF conditions lead us to the theory that unclear spin resonance (NMR) may be involved in the perception mechanism.

6.4 Tradition in the honeybee community?

I shall finish the history of the dance language in honeybees refering on a communication system which – as a *longterm* communication – is transmitted from one generation to the next. An essential information for the existence of a bee colony is their daily rhythm of collecting activity. I have found in the last years that besides the special collector group the whole colony is informed of such activity periods.

A group of about 300 bees was fed from April to July on a very inconventional time, from 5:00–6:00 every day. Three month later the whole group of these forager bees was removed and also all novices which had contact with the dances of this group before. Then a new group of 20 bees was trained to a feeding place for one day; however feeding time was not 5:00–6:00 but irregularly throughout the day. On the next day this group was tested – without food. Fig. 5 demonstrates clearly that these bees – as house bees – had taken over the activity period of the earlier collecting group.

This information was transmitted too the the next generation – the larvae and pupae. From the same colony I removed in July 3 combs with sealed brood. In a thermostat the young bees emerged and a new queen was added to the young colony. Two weeks later again a group of 20 bees was trained on an artificial feeding place for one day from morning to evening continuously every ½ hour for 10 minutes. Fig. 6 demonstrates that also

Fig. 5: From April to July ca. 300 bees could feed every morning from 5.30^h–7^h on a 2-molar sugar solution scented with Fenchel odour. After removing the whole forager group the remaining population still keeps the information concerning the odour and the activity period.

these bees – of the younger generation – were conditioned in their larval or pupal stage for the extraordinary collecting hour.

The same results we got in corresponding experiments, where the bees were trained for a feeding time 20:00–21:00.

We can only speculate how the information on the activity period is transmitted from the forager bees to all the house bees and to the larvae. No doubt in such an intense foraging activity some information is spreading out by the dances, due to food exchange and due to vibration over the combs produced by the sound in the wagging line (240 Hz). These vibrations should be perceived also by the larvae and the pupae in the brood cells. In this way the very long life period before the imago stage – 3 weeks is about ⅓ the total life span in honeybees – is used for an important communication between 2 generations (LINDAUER, unpublished).

Fig. 6: After eclosion from the pupal stage the next generation (of the mother colony in Fig. 5) also preferred the same odour and showed up as «early riser».

References

De Jong, D. (1982): Orientation of comb building by honeybees, J. comp. Physiol. *147*, 495–501.

Frisch, K. von (1920): Über die «Sprache» der Bienen. Münch. med. Wschr. 566–569.

Frisch, K. von (1923): Über die «Sprache» der Bienen, eine tierpsychologische Untersuchung. Zool. Jb. (Physiol.) *40*, 1–186.

Frisch, K. von (1949): Die Polarisation des Himmelslichtes als orientierender Faktor bei den Tänzen der Bienen. Experientia (Basel) *5*, 142–148.

Frisch, K. von (1950): Die Sonne als Kompaß im Leben der Bienen. Experientia (Basel) *6*, 210–221.

Frisch, K. von (1953): Die Richtungsorientierung der Bienen. Verhandl. d. Deutsch. Zool. Ges. in Freiburg 1952, 58–72, Leipzig.

Frisch, K. von u. M. Lindauer (1955): Über die Fluggeschwindigkeit der Bienen und ihre Richtungs-weisung bei Seitenwind. Naturwissenschaften *42*, 377–385.

Frisch, K. von (1961): Über die «Mißweisung» bei den richtungsweisenden Tänzen der Bienen. Naturwissenschaften *48*, 585–594.

Frisch, K. von (1965): Tanzsprache und Orientierung der Bienen. Springern, Berlin, Heidelberg, New York.

Gould, J. L.; Kirschvink, J. L.; Deffeyes, K. S. (1978): Bees have magnetic remanence. Science *201*, 1026–1028.

Gould, J. L.; Kirschvink, J. L.; Deffeyes, K. S.; Brines, M. L. (1980): Orientation of demagnetized bees. J. expl. Biol. *86*, 1–8.

Josephson, B. D. (1969): Weakly coupled superconductors, in: Superconductivity (R. D. Parks, ed), Vol. 1, pp. 423–447, Marcel Dekker, New York.

Korall, H. and H. Martin: The influence of Geomagnetic and Astrophysical Fields on the Impulse Responses of Mechanoreceptors in Apis mellifera. J. Comp. Physiol. (in Preparation).

Leucht, T. (1982): Responses to light under varying magnetic conditions in the honeybee, Apis mellifica. J. Comp. Physiol. A (1984) *154*: 865–870.

Lindauer, M. (1955): Schwarmbienen auf Wohnungssuche. Z. vergl. Physiol. *37*, 263–324.

Lindauer, M. (1956): Über die Verständigung bei indischen Bienen. Z. vergl. Physiol. *14*, 521–557.

Lindauer, M. (1961): Communication among social bees. Cambridge Mass., Harvard University Press.

Lindauer, M.; Martin, H. (1968): Die Schwereorientierung der Bienen unter dem Einfluß des Erdma-gnetfeldes. Z. vgl. Physiol. *60*, 219–243.

Lindauer, M.; Martin, H. (1972): Magnetic effect on dancing bees in: Animal orientation and navigation (Galler, S. R. et al., eds.) 559–567, Washington D. C.

Martin, H.; Lindauer, M. (1973): Orientierung im Erdmagnetfeld. Fortschr. Zool. *21*, 211–228.

Martin, H.; Lindauer, M. (1977): Der Einfluß des Erdmagnetfeldes auf die Schwereorientierung der Honigbiene (Apis mellifica). J. comp. Physiol. *122*, 145–187.

Martin, H.; Lindauer, M.; Martin, U.: Zeitsinn und Aktivitätsrhythmus der Honigbiene – endogen oder exogen gesteuert? Sitzungsbericht: Bayer. Akademie der Wissenschaft. Mathematisch Natur-wissenschaftliche Klasse. 1983. (Vorgelegt von Hansjochem Autrum in der Sitzung v. 7. Mai 1982)

Russo, F.; Caldwell, W. E. (1971): Biomagnetic Phenomena: some implications for the behavioural and neurophysiological sciences: Genetic Psychology Monographs *84*, 177–243.

Scholze, E.; H. Pichler, u. H. Heran (1964): Zur Entfernungsschätzung der Bienen nach dem Kraft-aufwand. Naturwissenschaften, *51*, 69–70.

Spitzner, M. J. E.: Ausführliche Beschreibung der Korbbienenzucht im sächsischen Churkreise, ihrer Dauer und ihres Nutzens, ohne künstliche Vermehrung nach den Gründen der Naturgeschichte und nach eigener langer Erfahrung. Leipzig 1788.

Unhoch, N.: Anleitung zur wahren Kenntnis und zweckmäßigsten Behandlung der Bienen. München 1823.

Walcott, C.; Gould, J. L.; Kirschvink, J. L. (1979): Pigeons have magnets. Science *205*, 1027–1029.

Fortschritte der Zoologie, Bd. 31 · Hölldobler/Lindauer (Hrsg.): Experimental Behavioral Ecology
G. Fischer Verlag · Stuttgart · New York · 1985

Recent progress in the study of the dance language

James, L. Gould, Fred C. Dyer, and William F. Towne

Department of Biology, Princeton University, Princeton, N. J. 08544, USA

Abstract

The dance language and orientation of honey bees is probably the best understood example of a complex, highly integrated behavior. Work over the past decade has revealed this remarkable behavioural system to be even more interesting than had been thought. Progress has been made on how the language works (both for the dancers and the recruits), on how bees recognize the cues used for orienting their flights and dances, and how bees can resolve ambiguities in these cues in order to communicate. Moreover, we now know that bees navigate and dance when both the sun and blue sky are obscured entirely by clouds by falling back on a time-linked memory of the sun's course with respect to landmarks. Recent comparative studies among the different races of *Apis mellifera,* and between *mellifera* and the three Asian species of bees have revealed much about the likely evolution and adaptation of the dance system to a variety of physical settings. For instance, the dance has been modified to suit such alternatives as a vertical dance surface, or the darkness of an enclosed nest, or the ambient light of exposed comb. It has also been modified to accommodate a wide range of habitat types. The modifications have taken place in the sensory channels used to transmit the dance information, in the dance distance dialects and divergence, and several other such parameters.

1 The dance and communication

The discovery and elucidation of the dance communication system of bees by von Frisch and his colleagues (rev. in von Frisch 1967) is probably the single most impressive accomplishment in ethology. The work set the standard for deftly combining observational and experimental techniques, and joining together mechanistic and ecological perspectives. Moreover, it was critical, thorough, clear, and fascinating. von Frisch once characterized the honey bee as a «magic well» which could never go dry, and only this hypothesis adequately accounts for there being anything left to discover about these remarkable insects.

1.1 The dance-language controversy

Interest in the dance communication of bees was rekindled in 1967 by the experiments of Wenner and his colleagues purporting to show that the distance and direction correlations in the dance did not convey any information to recruits (rev. in Gould 1976).

Briefly, their argument ran that since they could create conditions under which bees were recruited to odor alone, and since bees must use either odor or a language for communication, the dance correlations were not used. The flaw in this line of reasoning, of course, is the assumption that bees can communicate in only one way. In an analogous situation VON FRISCH's work had already shown that bees can use either the sun or patterns of polarized light in the sky for navigation, depending on the circumstances.

Initial attempts to pit the dance system against odor supported VON FRISCH (eg., 28, 39), but the possibility that recruits were using site-specific odors for locating food could not be excluded. GOULD (1974, 1975b,c) developed a technique for misdirecting recruits by painting over the ocelli of foragers, making them less sensitive to light. He then used a light as an artificial sun to reorient the dances (and interpretations) of untreated bees. Ocelli-covered bees, on the other hand, did not respond to this light, and continued to be oriented strictly to gravity. Thus the ocelli-painted dancers indicated a direction quite different from that read out by untreated dance attenders. As predicted by the dance language hypothesis, recruits did indeed fly preferentially to the distance and direction specified by the misdirected dances (Fig. 1).

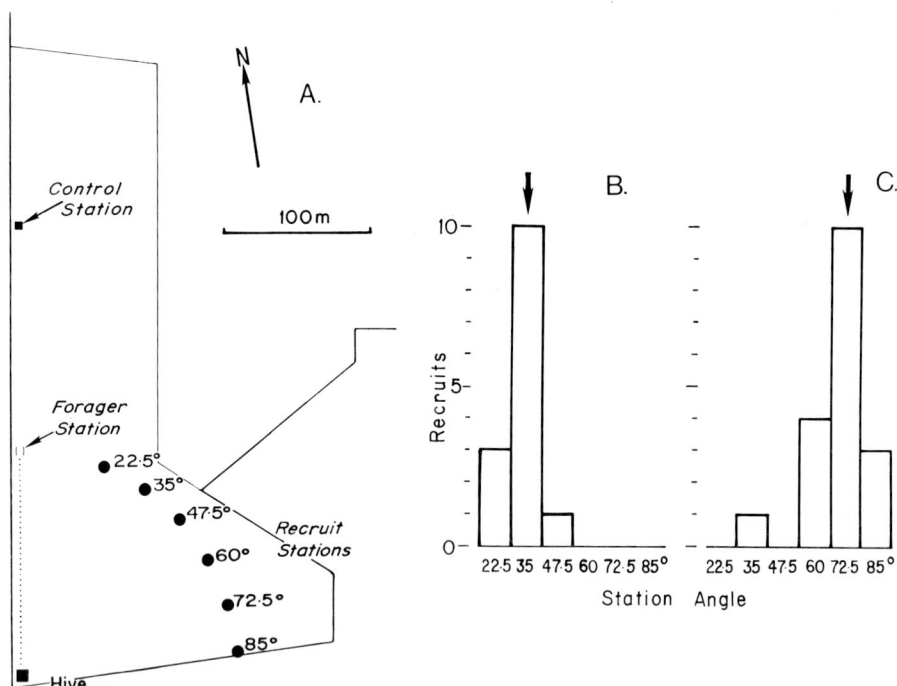

Fig. 1: Redirection experiments. a) Ocelli-painted foragers were trained to the forager station 150 m NNE of the hive. An array of recruit stations was set out offering the same food being collected at the forager station. A light was used to reorient the dance attenders (as judged by the reorientation of untreated foragers visiting the control station). In this example the redirection was first 35° clockwise and then 72.5° clockwise. b) Recruits during the first part of the experiment favored the 35° station, but c) recruitment shifted toward the 72.5° station after the light was moved. After GOULD (1975a, 1976).

At about the same time, SCHRICKER (1974) found that poisoning foragers with sublethal doses of parathion causes them to overestimate the distance to a food source. Recruits arrived preferentially at the (incorrect) distance specified by the dance.

1.2 Dance integration

From measurements of individual waggle runs, VON FRISCH and JANDER (1957) concluded that dance attenders must average over several runs to account for the accuracy of searching recruits. WENNER and his colleagues, in stressing the possible importance of odor cues, dismissed experiments in which the forager station was near the recruit array: the recruits could be using odors generated by the foragers at the forager station to increase their accuracy. LINDAUER (1971), on the other hand, suggested that the very poor accuracy of WENNER's bees might be accounted for if recruits attended and averaged together separate dances by different bees. GOULD's experiments (1975 b, c), in which the forager station is well away from the recruit array, showed that VON FRISCH's accuracy estimates were affected only slightly by the placement of the training station, but that recruits probably do not average separate dances. Instead, the poor accuracy of WENNER's bees seems mostly attributable to his training techniques.

2 The dance and navigation

When a forager reaches a food source, even if she has flown an indirect route, she knows the distance and direction of the hive and is able to fly directly home (rev. in VON FRISCH 1967). The dance is basically a readout of the information stored in a forager's navigational computer. VON FRISCH began almost immediately to exploit the dance to learn how bees orient to environmental cues and process the information they collect.

2.1 Sun recognition

By a series of ingenious mirror experiments, VON FRISCH showed that the sun is the primary celestial landmark for bee navigation as well as the standard reference point for the dance language (VON FRISCH 1967). He obtained some indirect evidence which suggested that the sun is recognized as a UV disc in the sky, but pointed out that this was physically implausible. BRINES and GOULD (1979) investigated this question further by offering a variety of artificial suns to trained foragers dancing on a horizontal surface. The bees would either orient to the pattern as though it were the sun, a patch of sky, or something to which they could not orient. The bees interpret virtually any patch of light low in UV and smaller than about 15° as the sun, regardless of its shape, color, or polarization. Hence a green, triangular, 100 %-polarized patch 10° across will substitute for the white, circular, unpolarized 0.5° disc of the sun. The low-UV requirement probably acts as a sign stimulus for the sun.

2.2 Sun compensation

The sun is a problematical landmark because it moves. Moreover, the rate at which the sun's azimuth changes depends on the latitude, date, and time of day. VON FRISCH showed very clearly that bees compensate for this movement, even when in the hive dancing, and pointed out that bees might 1) know how the sun moves innately, or 2) learn it, or 3) use a rough approximation (VON FRISCH 1967). LINDAUER (1959) showed that they have to learn that it moves, and in which direction, but the question of exactly what they learn about its movement remained open. GOULD (1980) attempted to discover the exact mechanism by training bees at one location, trapping them in the hive out of sight of the sun for two hours, and then releasing them at a new site. (It is essential to change locations since experienced foragers frequently ignore the sun and orient their outward flights to familiar landmarks (VON FRISCH and LINDAUER 1954)).

In one set of tests, the hive was closed from 11:00 to 13:00, near the summer solstice, while in the other the closing ran from 12:00 to 14:00. Around solar noon during this part of the year the sun's rate of azimuth movement changes rapidly (Fig. 2 a). Foragers trapped at 11:00 underestimated the subsequent change in sun azimuth, while those trapped at 12:00 overestimated (Fig. 2 b, c). The results most closely fit the hypothesis that bees can extrapolate the rate of movement of the sun.

A closer look at the data suggests that the extrapolation rate used is roughly 20 min out of date. This is reminiscent of LINDAUER's (1963) discovery that foragers dancing to a moving feeder never «catch up,» but instead dance toward the location of the food source

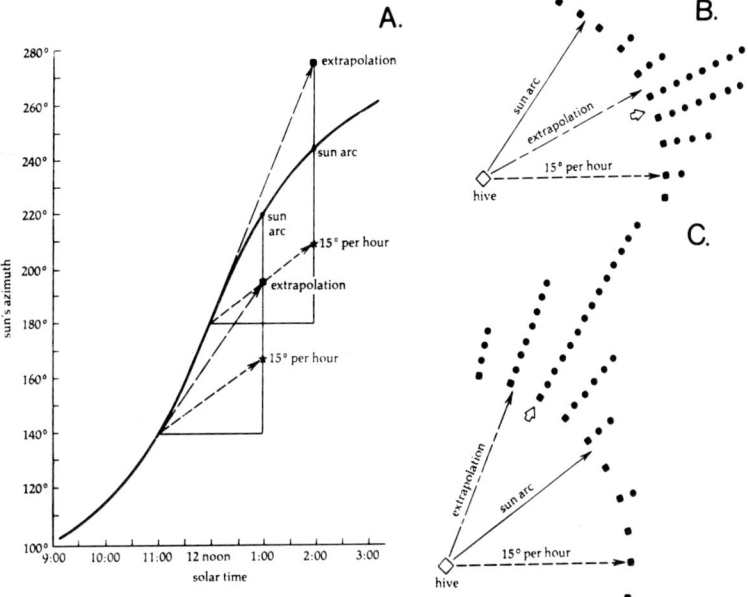

Fig. 2: Sun compensation. a) Near the solstice the sun moves very quickly in azimuth near noon, but more slowly both before and after. If foragers are prevented from seeing the sun for the two hours beginning at 11 : 00, their estimate of the azimuth of a training station after their incarceration will be in error if they have not memorized its course. For instance, simply extrapolating the sun's movement would lead to a moderate underestimate since the rate of azimuth movement increases after 11 : 00, whereas a 15°/hr approximation would be seriously in error. A bee unable to see the sun from 12 : 00 to 14 : 00, on the other hand, would overestimate the azimuth since the sun's rate of azimuth movement slows after 12 : 00. b) When the foragers are prevented from seeing the sun from 11 : 00 to 13 : 00, they tend to fly to stations near the extrapolation prediction, as though the rate used in extrapolation was measured at about 10 : 40. c) When the closing is from 12 : 00 to 14 : 00, foragers overestimate the sun's movement as though they were extrapolating the rate at about 11 : 40. After GOULD (1980).

several trips in the past. When LINDAUER moved the station direction in discrete steps to the west every 30 min, the dances first indicated the former site, and then gradually shifted toward the new location. They never fully compensated, however.

GOULD (1984) followed up this work by moving a feeder 30° east or west every hour. The dancers «caught up» with the move after about 41 min regardless of direction. Both this and the sun-compensation data are consistent with a running-average strategy of information processing. By using a sensory window of 40 min, inaccuracies in the inherently difficult task of measuring sun-azimuth movement (in which the location of an 0.5° disc must be measured with a visual system whose resolution is 2–3° at best) can be averaged out. The result is an extrapolation rate about 20 min slow and an ability to shift dances to compensate for the movement of a station over 40 min.

When bees have useful landmarks, they employ quite a different system of sun compensation: they memorize the azimuth of the sun with respect to prominent landmarks through the entire course of the day (DYER 1984 and DYER, GOULD 1981). Hence a recruit bee can correctly interpret a dance even on an overcast day (see below). It is not yet clear

Fig. 3: Resolving polarization ambiguities (left) the pattern of polarized light is the sky is centered on the sun and symmetrical about the solar meridian (only the right half is shown here). At most elevations the same e-vector angle is found at two distances from the sun (as indicated by the two points marked «A»). Vertical polarization, which is found at all elevations above the sun's, is present at two places equidistant from the sun (as, for instance, the two points marked «B»). The polarization at the zenith (marked «C») and all along the solar meridian is horizontal. a) When bees are presented an oblique pattern such as A, they orient their dances as though the pattern were the alternative more distant from the sun. The long line in the diagram is the direction expected for the dance if the patch of light were interpreted as the sun, while the short lines represent the two polarized light alternatives. Each circle is the dance of one bee. b) If the pattern is vertical, as for the points marked B, the bees interpret it as if it were the alternative to the right of the sun. (Note that the vertical patterns appear 60° from the sun, and that the dances of these bees are clearly more nearly oriented to 60° than 90°.) c) Dances to a zenith pattern (C) are ambiguous, with both alternatives being indicated. From BRINES and GOULD (1979).

whether bees using this system accurately compensate for the sun's changing rate of azimuth movement, or instead employ a time-averaged rate.

2.3 Polarized-light orientation

VON FRISCH discovered more than three decades ago that bees will orient their horizontal dances to the patterns of polarized light in blue sky (VON FRISCH 1967), using patches as small as 15° to deduce the sun's azimuth. He left open the question of how bees manage this deduction, and how they resolve the ambiguity which arises from the frequent existence of two polarization patterns with the same e-vector angle at most elevations (Fig. 3, left).

BRINES and GOULD (1979) found that dancers ignore many potentially useful cues such as color, degree of polarization, and intensity gradients, and instead interpret the patch arbitrarily as the one existing furthest from the sun (Fig. 3 a). When the e-vector is vertical – which, as a consequence of the geometry of scattering, occurs at points equidistant from the sun – bees choose the alternative to the right of the sun (Fig. 3 b). A zenith pattern, however, is ambiguous, and bees dance in both directions (Fig. 3 c).

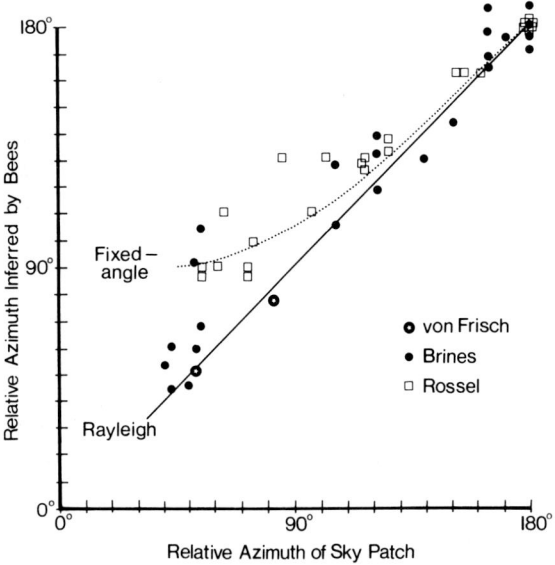

Fig. 4: Determining the sun's azimuth from polarized light. Both simple calculations based on Rayleigh scattering and a photograph-matching system would result in bees interpreting sky polarization relations accurately. In this case, dances should fall along the solid line marked «Rayleigh.» If bees use a system which ignores the elevation of the patch of sky, the dances should fall on the dotted line marked «Fixed-angle:» Data from VON FRISCH (only on two occasions does VON FRISCH report enough information to plot in this way), Brines, and Rossel are plotted, each based on a separate experiment. In general, the Brines and von Frisch data are more consistent with the Rayleigh line, while Rossel's better fit the Fixed-angle prediction. From DYER and GOULD (1983). (VON FRISCH's data comes from written reports and are of a qualitative nature – that is, he states that the dance angles correspond to the Rayleigh prediction – and so are not nearly as precise as other data; a ± 15° discrepancy would probably have gone unreported.)

Rossel et al (1978) performed similar experiments, and their data show a clear tendency for dancers to favour one direction, though they did not point this out. Subsequently they did report (Rossel and Wehner 1982) that their bees dance for the further alternative, but still dance bimodally for vertical e-vectors. It is not obvious why the dances to vertical polarization should be unambiguous for one group's bees and not for the other.

Rossel and Wehner (1982) have offered an intriguing explanation for how bees deduce the sun's position from polarization patterns. Whereas most researchers have concluded that bees take into account the elevation of the sky patch to either calculate the location of the sun or match an observed pattern against a stored one, Rossel and Wehner suggest that the bees ignore elevation altogether and simply interpret all vertical patterns to be 90° away, all horizontal patterns to be 180° away (which actually is the case) and all intermediate patterns to be some defined intermediate distance away (a 45° pattern, for instance, is roughly 135° from the sun). Their data (Fig. 4) fits this hypothesis relatively well, but data from Brines (1978) and von Frisch (1967) often does not fit, although von Frisch did sometimes report bimodal dances. Again, the source of this sometimes striking discrepancy is not clear.

Brines favors the idea that bees remember the polarization patterns as a photograph (analogous to the mechanism of canopy orientation in ants reported by Hölldobler (1980)) which they then match with the patch observed in the sky. The basis of this suggestion is his observation that dances to artificial polarization patterns on overcast days are more scattered than on clear days, even though the ability to calculate sun azimuth ought not to be affected. By using an artificial sun, Brines (1978) was able to show that the scatter did not arise from any uncertainty about the direction of the sun.

2.4 Cloudy-day orientation

Bees are able to orient and dance on overcast days when neither sun nor blue sky is visible (Brines, Gould 1982). Dyer and Gould (1981) discovered how bees know where the sun is when they cannot see it by taking advantage of von Frisch and Lindauer's (1954) observation that experienced foragers can be tricked into navigating along prominent landmarks in a new location if they resemble the landmarks the bees had become familiar with during training, even if the compass direction is different. Dyer and Gould trained bees along a tree line next to an open field, moved the hive overnight to a similar site where the tree line was was rotated 130° clockwise (Fig. 5 a), and recorded the dances of foragers visiting each of two foraging stations: one located along the landmarks and to which most bees flew, the other in the field in the actual compass direction used for training. On sunny days, the dances accurately reported the directions flown (Fig. 5 b) while under overcast the dances were oriented as though the bees were still at the former site (Fig. 5 c). Clearly the foragers could not see the sun or they would have oriented correctly as they did on clear days. Instead they relied on a time-linked memory of the sun's position relative to prominent landmarks. In more recent experiments, we have shown that this memory can persist through several days of cloudy weather (Dyer 1984).

Subsequently, Dyer (1984) has found that *Apis cerana* (the Asian hive bee which, like *A. mellifera,* lives in enclosed cavities, rather than on open branches like Asia's *A. dorsata* and the dwarf honey bee, *A. florea*) also orients its dances by means of a time-linked sun-vs-landmark system under overcast. *A. dorsata*, which also dances on a vertical surface, may well use the same system. As we shall see below, *A. florea* needs quite a different strategy for successful dance communication during cloudy weather.

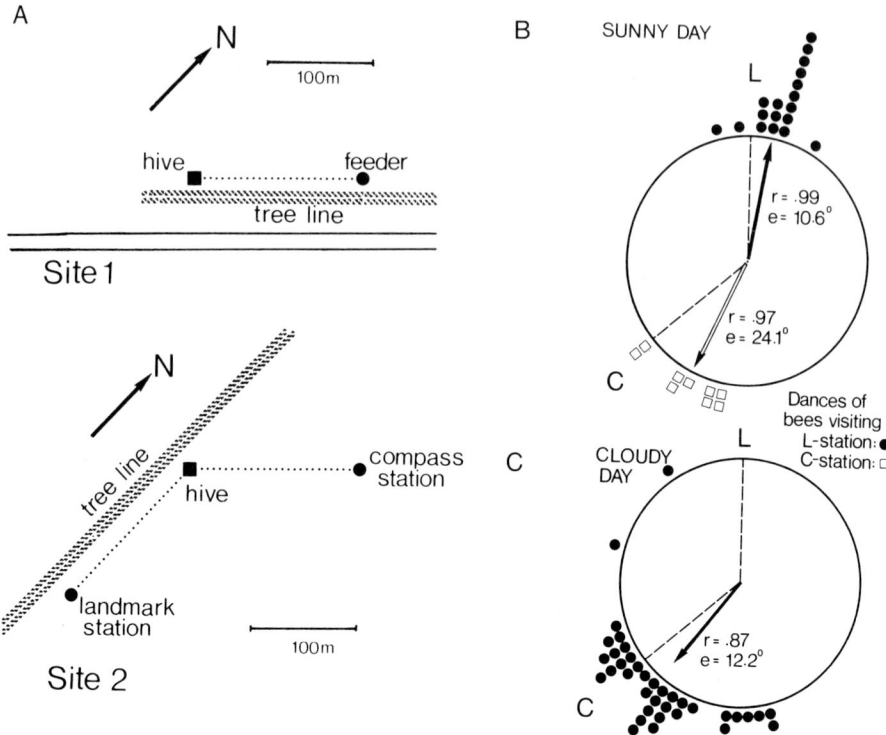

Fig. 5: Cloudy day orientation. a) Bees were trained to the feeder along a tree line at Site 1 and then moved overnight to Site 2 where the tree line was in a different direction. b) When the hive was opened under clear skies, eight of the ten foragers flew along the tree line and danced to indicate the true direction of the outward flight (marked «L» for landmark). The two foragers who found the compass station also danced relatively accurately (direction «C»). c) When the hive was opened at Site 2 under overcast, however, all foragers flew along the landmarks to find the landmark station, but danced as though they were still at Site 1, apparently relying on their memory of the sun's position relative to the direction of the tree line along which they were trained one day earlier. After DYER and GOULD (1981).

2.5 Nocturnal orientation

Apis dorsata, the large tropical honey bee, has often been reported to fly at night when the moon is sufficiently bright. DYER (1984), working in India, has confirmed this recently and at the same time observed vigorous and apparently normal dances to natural food sources. To determine whether these dances are oriented according to the moon or to the (unseen) sun, he chose nights when the sun set almost vertically, so that dances of bees flying to the same source over a given interval and using the sun as a reference (either the actual solar azimuth or the azimuth extrapolated from the sun's movement before sunset) would change only very slowly. The moon, on the other hand, was at a high elevation during the experiments so that its azimuth shifted very rapidly. If dances were oriented to the moon, they too should shift direction very quickly over the same period.

It was relatively easy to distinguish a group of foragers feeding on one source by sampling pollen loads carried by the dancers and measuring the distance they indicated. The dances of a group identified in this way would change very little over a period when the moon's azimuth shifted by as much as 160°; this implicates the invisible sun as the reference point for the dances. Bees might use the sun despite its absence by memorizing its setting azimuth relative to landmarks (by analogy with *A. mellifera's* cloudy day system (DYER, GOULD 1981)). However, DYER's observations of pre-dawn dances (under moonlight) which did not change after the sun came up (and so were presumably oriented by the sun all along), suggest that the bees might possess a knowledge of the entire nocturnal course of the sun, or be able to use their knowledge of the sun's azimuth at sunrise to anticipate the location. Given the very scattered orientation (not to mention the rarity) of marathon dances (rev. in VON FRISCH 1967), the nocturnal dances of *A. dorsata* are probably the best way to answer this question. Observations at times of year during which the sun's azimuth changes more rapidly at sunset, or observations near midnight will be necessary for clear-cut results.

2.6 Locale maps

VON FRISCH (1967) pointed out that bees trained along an indirect route would indicate the true straight line direction in their dance even if the topography prevented them from ever flying that route. Clearly bees are able to integrate two or more legs of a journey. VON

Fig. 6: Lake experiment. Dances indicating the lake station do not result in recruitment, whether the dancers are visiting that station or the one marked «feeder.» At the same time, dances to the equally distant shore station or feeder elicit heavy recruitment. One possible interpretation is that the recruits are able to «place» the location being advertised on the basis of the dance coördinates and judge its suitability without actually flying there. From GOULD (1984b).

Frisch also found that even when a direct flight is possible, many experienced foragers prefer using the training route on the outward journey, particularly if it is marked by prominent landmarks, though they often return directly. This suggests that a sequence of landmarks can be remembered. After reviewing a wide body of insect literature, Wehner (1981) concluded that bees must indeed store a series of «snapshots» of the landmarks along familiar routes, and consult these pictures as they fly.

Two recent results suggest that these snapshots or their equivalent may be integrated into the dance system (rev. in Gould 1984b). Von Frisch and his colleagues had shown that information gathered on the way to a food source is much more important to dancers than information collected on the way back. Brines (1967) attempted to see if experience from the return trip could be used in the absence of an outbound trip. He captured departing foragers at the hive entrance and transported them in darkness to feeders several hundred meters away and out of sight of the hive. Older bees (as judged by wing wear) were able to navigate directly to the hive, and some even performed accurate dances on their first return. Brines concluded that although the transported bees probably had never fed at the feeder site (frequently a large, asphalt parking lot 50 m from the nearest vegetation) they recognized their surroundings (perhaps by matching with an *en route* snapshot for some familiar but more distant natural food source) and so were able to «place» themselves with respect to home.

The second observation comes from an experiment in which Dyer (1984; rev. in Gould 1984b) trained foragers along the shore of a lake and redirected their dances to a spot in the lake (Fig. 6). Recruits did not turn up at a boat with a feeder located there, though when the redirection was set to zero, they turned up at the shore feeder in large numbers. Thinking a site odor might be involved, Dyer trained foragers to the boat itself, but still no recruits arrived. When he and the boat progressed to the far shore, however, recruits began ito arrive in substantial numbers. One (though by no means the only) interpretation is that the coordinates specified in the dance allowed recruits to consult a mental locale map or the appropriate «snapshot» in their collection, and see that the spot indicated was unsuitable. This flexibility, if it is real, may mean that the storage and organization of landmark memory is more fully integrated into the dance system than we had thought.

3 Dance divergence

Von Frisch was the first to notice that sequential waggling runs in a dance frequently alternate from left to right in direction, creating what he has called a divergence in the dance. In a divergent dance the bisector of the angle created by the two waggling directions points toward the food (Fig. 7, inset). The simplest explanation for the divergence is that it arises in some way as a result of the dancer's difficulty in determining the exact direction in which it should waggle. The divergence is greatest when the food source being indicated is nearby – that is, when the forager has only a brief flight during which to gather directional information (Fig. 7b) – and further , it is unusually large when the foragers are forced to fly a detour in reaching the food or when they are forced to dance on inclined rather than on vertical surfaces, weakening the gravity cues to which they orient (rev. in v. Frisch 1967).

Some recent evidence casts doubt on this simple explanation, however. One experiment, carried out by Towne (1984), was designed to test the hypothesis proposed by Edrich (1975) that under normal conditions the divergence depends upon the duration of the outward flight to the food. Using a manipulation invented by Heran (see von Frisch 1967, p. 115), Towne was able to hold the duration of the outward flight constant while

Fig. 7: Dance divergence. The inset shows the actual course followed by a dancer doing a divergent dance. The arrow indicates the true direction of the food (after VON FRISCH (1967)). The plot shows the relationship between the divergence and the distance to the food, the divergence being defined as the mean angle between consecutive waggling runs. Bars indicate standard error of the mean. N = 207 dances. Stars are data of VON FRISCH; filled squares are from EDRICH (1975). From TOWNE (48).

varying the bees' estimates of the distance flown as reflected in the durations of their waggling runs. (This confirms HERAN's original findings and supports VON FRISCH's conclusion that the bees do not use flight time to measure distance.) In addition TOWNE found that even though flight time was held constant throughout, the divergence decreased as the durations of the bees' waggling runs increased. Thus the decrease in divergence routinely observed in association with an increase in the distance to the food is most likely not a result of the increased flight time.

This result is further supported by some recent observations by TOWNE (1984a) on the three Asian honey bees. Although all four species of bees fly at roughly the same speed, they show strikingly different divergences for a given distance to the food. *A. dorsata* and *A. florea* show no noticeable divergence when the food source is 100 m from the nest, and *A. cerana* shows a divergence of only about 15° – one–half that observed in *A. mellifera*.

These observations taken together suggest that the divergence – at least under good navigating conditions (good dancing cues and no flight detours) – should not be viewed as unavoidable noise arising out of the bees' inability to learn, recall, and utilize their navigational cues with precision. Why, then, is it there? As it turns out, HALDANE and SPURWAY (1954) had suggested a possible function for the divergence almost 30 years ago. Their argument was simple: assuming that the divergence leads to imprecision in the communication and to the scattering of recruit bees around the particular flowers being visited by the dancer, it may nonetheless be adaptive if recruits that miss the mark are likely to encounter other open flowers of the species indicated. They hint further that there may be an optimal amount of scatter, the magnitude of which would presumably depend upon the spatial distribution of open flowers of the species being visited. (Since, however, the divergence is the same whether the goal is a single small feeder, a nest site, or a large patch of flowers (Towne 1984 a), this optimal amount of scatter would have to be a grand average which takes into account all of the resources typically used by a colony).

Gould (1975 a) has extended this line of reasoning by pointing out that if there is some average optimal amount of scatter, there is no reason to think it should change with the distance of the food source from the nest. These arguments lead to testable predictions. First, the divergence should indeed lead to a scatter of recruit bees around the food source being visited by the dancer. More specifically, the angular error of recruits should be greatest when the food source is nearby – that is, when the divergence is greatest. Second, as suggested by Gould, the error should be «tuned» so as to keep the absolute area over which recruit bees search roughly constant with changing distance to the food source. Finally, if the scatter of recruits has evolved in response to the type and distribution of flowers exploited by the bees, then bees which use different types of resources, say temperate vs. tropical, should show predictable differences in their divergences (Gould 1975 c).

The third prediction is clearly upheld by Towne's (1984 a) observations of the tropical bees mentioned earlier. All three species – at least in Puna, India where the observations were made – show little or no divergence compared to *A. mellifera carnica*, a temperate zone bee. This makes sense since the tropical bees most commonly frequent large, insect-pollinated trees which constitute massive and highly localized resources as compared to the more diffuse resources typically visited by *A. mellifera* (although exactly what we should consider to be a typical *A. mellifera* resource is, of course, problematic).

The first prediction, that the angular error of recruits should be greater for nearby food sources, is also upheld by the evidence. Both von Frisch (rev. in von Frisch 1967) and Gould (1976), using arc-shaped arrays of recruit stations, have performed experiments to determine recruit directional accuracy, and both found greater recruit errors for more nearby food sources. Because, however, the experiments of each involved only two distances and a relatively small number of recruit stations – von Frisch's widely spaced, and Gould's closely spaced so that the entire array was relatively narrow – Towne (1984 a) has recently extended these observations. Capturing recruits at a wide (300 m across) array of 26 traps baited with scent, he found that 50 % of recruits arrive within 16° of the correct direction when the food source being visited is 100 m from the hive. This error decreases to about 8° when the food source is 300 m distant and to about 6° when the food source is between 500 and 700 m from the hive. The second and most quantitative prediction, that the area searched by recruits should remain constant with changing distance to the food, is supported only roughly by these data, however. The angular errors just mentioned translate into absolute median errors of 30 m for food sources at a distance of 100 m from the hive, 40 m for food sources at 300 m, 52 m for food sources at 500 m, and 73 m for food sources 700 m distant. Thus there is a slow but steady increase in the area searched with increasing distance to the food.

Taken together we feel that these observations support the hypothesis that the divergence has evolved to increase the efficiency with which a colony collects its food. The reason for the slow increase in the area searched with increased distance to the food is not clear, but the increase is certainly much less dramatic than it would be if the angular error were to remain constant.

4 Dance dialects

BOCH (1957) demonstrated that most races of honey bees have different dialects, and VON FRISCH (1967) suggested that this dialect variation probably reflected racial differences in foraging range. Colonies living in regions where foraging most often takes place far from the hive would be better served by a longer-distance dialect (that is, one with fewer waggles per km) than those whose general habitat permits a more restricted flight range. GOULD (1982) demonstrated the likely correctness of VON FRISCH's guess by taking advantage of an observation by LINDAUER (1955). LINDAUER created an artificial swarm of German honey bees *(A. m. carnica)* and permitted it to choose between a nest box at 30 m and another at 250 m. The swarm flew to the more distant box. This makes sense because the swarm and the parent colony are relatively closely related, so for a swarm to move far enough to reduce the overlap of its own average foraging range with that of the parent hive would be adaptive. Indeed, LINDAUER (1955) found that among 22 natural swarms of German bees, none moved less than 300 m; while SEELEY and MORSE (1978) observed only one of 13 swarms to fly less than 300 m.

Considering the costs and benefits of swarming, then, it seems likely that moving too short a distance risks competing with relatives for resources, while moving too far has other risks, particularly in terms of the lower certainty that the abundance of resources which have served to sustain the parent hive exist in regions less familiar to the bees. If the dialects reflect the relative foraging ranges of the various races, we would expect that bees should have a preferred swarming distance which should be greater for the long-dialect German bees and shorter for the medium-dialect Italian race *(A. m ligustica)*.

GOULD (1982) tested this prediction by creating artificial swarms along forest edges and setting out a array of nest boxes at roughly 100 m intervals. German swarms invariably flew further than Italian swarms (690 ± 110 m, n = 7, vs 155 ± 50 m, n = 9) and, when offered a choice, always chose a 60 l hive box, while Italian swarms chose a 30 l box on five of the six occasions they were offered a choice. This led GOULD to suggest that colony size might be a relevant variable. The more bees in a hive, the farther a forager will have to fly on average to find an unexploited source. Noting the correlation between latitude and dialect – more northerly races tend to have longer dialects than more southerly ones – GOULD speculated that perhaps climate was the crucial parameter affecting dialect. Longer, colder winters probably require larger winter stores and winter clusters.

5 Horizontal dances

VON FRISCH discovered almost four decades ago that *Apis mellifera*, though it normally dances on the vertical sheets of comb in the darkness of the hive, will dance on a horizontal surface and orient to celestial cues when necessary (VON FRISCH 1967). Later LINDAUER (1956) reported that the dwarf honey bee *(A. florea)* always dances on the top of its exposed combs, while he was unable to persuade the giant honey bee *(A. dorsata)* to do the same. Although *dorsata* also lives on exposed combs, the comb is not built up and over tree limbs in the manner of *florea,* and so there is normally no opportunity to dance on a horizontal surface.

The dances of the three species of tropical bees are interesting because *Apis* almost certainly evolved there. One of the most plausible evolutionary sequences (rev. in GOULD 1982a) sees the movement into cavities as a response to predator pressure. As argued so cogently by SEELEY et al. (1982), predation has certainly been an important force in the evolution of tropical bee societies, and the move into cavities brought with it a two-fold advantage related to predation. First, the cavity walls of *A. cerana* nests provide excellent protection against both large and small predators. Second, as the walls protect the colony, they also emancipate a large fraction of the worker force from the task of hanging in the three- to six-bee thick protective curtain which can always be seen covering colonies of both *A. florea* and *A. dorsata* (SEELEY et al 1982). Regardless of the exact details of predator avoidance, the move into cavities necessitated changes in the dance; the communication now had to take place in the dark and in the absence of celestial orientation cues. We suspect that an understanding of how the dance orientation strategies of the four species compare will help us to understand how dancing, orientation, and nesting have evolved. We will consider horizontal dancing here, and the sounds and postures in the dance in a later section.

5.1 Dances of the dwarf honey bee

KOENIGER et al (1982) have recently showed that *A. florea* dancers orient their dances to the sun when it is available, and, in the absence of the sun, are reoriented by a polarized filter interposed between the dance area and the sky. They also reported that the dances remained oriented in the absence of celestial cues, suggesting yet another orientation system. This would be adaptive for a species which always dances on horizontal surfaces, and otherwise must depend on a view of celestial cues through forest canopy and, frequently, clouds.

DYER (1984) has carried this work further and shown that *A. florea* dancers rely heavily upon landmarks near the colony and visible from the dance floor as reference points for the dance. DYER positioned a striped card on one side of the dance floor, for instance, and in the absence of celestial cues was able to rotate the dances by moving the card. This stands in sharp contrast to *A. mellifera* which appears unable to use any non-celestial cue in its horizontal dances.

A. florea might have yet a further backup system. When DYER removed the striped card, leaving a view of only the circular arena around the dance floor and the white ceiling of the hut sheltering the colony, the dancers still showed a net orientation in one direction, though scatter was considerable and the dance direction did not always correspond to the direction of the food. This orientation was unaffected by rotation of the comb; thus comb topography (and therefore gravity) could not have served as the reference. Nor could the dances be changed by rotating the arena or by observing from a different direction. (DYER watched the bees through narrow slits cut in the arena.) The only manipulation that produced an effect was to cast a shadow on the ceiling above the dancers. This resulted in a random distribution of dances, and implies that the bees could orient relative to subtle gradients of reflected light that could not be totally eliminated. Another possibility that has not been excluded is that the dancers can refer to the earth's magnetic field as a last resort.

DYER has also been able to induce *A. florea* to dance on the vertical side of the colony by denying access to the horizontal and giving the bees on the vertical a clear view of the sky. In this situation the bees continue to try to point their dances directly toward the food using celestial cues, though this means that when the plane of the dancing surface is rotated they must adopt a different angle relative to gravity. Dances do not shift as the sun moves across the sky, supporting LINDAUER's (1956) proposal that *A. florea* lacks entirely the ability – shared by the other species – to transpose the horizontal angle into a vertical one in which gravity is taken to refer to the sun. Interestingly, dances on the vertical are the same whether or not the bees can see blue sky or the sun, but it is likely that landmarks visible from the colony could provide the reference points for these dances, as is true on a horizontal surface.

5.2 Dance of the giant honey bee

DYER (1984) has been able to induce *A. dorsata* foragers to dance on horizontal surfaces by preventing them from seeing any blue sky on the sides of the comb where they normally dance. Since his colony had been cut from its original site and suspended by a bamboo clip at ground level, the top of the colony was a large horizontal platform which the bees readily turned into a dance floor when it became the only part of the colony exposed to the sky. (Why *dorsata* should prefer a view of the sky for its normally vertical dances (LINDAUER 1956) is another question.) The horizontal dances were accurately oriented and could be rotated by a polarizer, confirming that *A. dorsata*, like the other three species, can use the polarization of blue sky for orientation. The horizontal dances are also interesting because there are no known natural circumstances under which horizontal dancing would be used by *A dorsata*. This behavior may, therefore, be an evolutionary holdover.

Fig. 8: Oscilloscope traces of the dance sounds (a) and «stop signals» (b) of all four species of *Apis*. In a), two waggling runs (indicated by lines under tracings) separated by a single circling return run are shown for the three sound-producing species. In the *A. mellifera* and *A. cerana* tracings, individual sound bursts produced within each waggling run can be clearly seen, while the individual sound cycles are just barely resolvable. The fundamental frequency and burst rate of the *A. mellifera* and *A. cerana* sounds are roughly the same for both species at 290 Hz and 30 bursts/sec, respectively. The fundamental frequency of the *A. florea* sound is about 250 Hz. In b), a single «stop signal» is shown for each species. The frequencies of the signals seem to vary even within species, but they are about 300 Hz in *A. mellifera*, 445 Hz in *A. cerana*, 475 Hz in *A. florea*, and 375 Hz in *A. dorsata*. The microphone was always held between about 5 and 10 mm from the bees during recording but since the amplification was varied in the face of varying levels of background noise, the relative amplitudes of the sounds as shown here should not be considered accurate. From TOWNE (1984b).

6 How the dance information is transmitted to recruits

Wenner (1959, 1962) and Esch (1961) independently discovered that *A. mellifera* dancers produce faint bursts of sound during the waggling run portion of their dances (see Fig. 8 a). Both have suggested that the sound carries the distance information used by recruits, but since the duration of sound production and the duration of waggling – both of which correlate extremely well with distance to the food (52, rev. in 15) – are so tightly intertwined, it has not been possible to separate them experimentally. In closing his review of the several correlates of distance in the dance, von Frisch (1967, p. 104) wrote, «... we regard the acoustically emphasized duration of waggling as the index of distance.» Although von Frisch is almost certainly correct, we still do not know the relative importance of the two cues. This applies to the transfer of directional as well as distance information.

6.1 The dance sounds

Esch (1963, 1964) observed that neither silent dances, which frequently occur when the sugar concentration of the food is low and dancing is not vigorous, nor the occasionally observed dances with continuous sound production were effective in inducing recruitment. He concluded from these observations that sound production during the waggling run is essential for successful recruitment, but von Frisch (1967) felt that the inefficacy of silent dances could be a result of their overall lack of vigor, and that the observations of dances with continuous sound were not extensive enough to permit a firm conclusion.

Some recent observations by Towne (1984b) on the dances of the Asian bees suggest that Esch's conclusions were essentially correct and, further, offer an explanation for exactly why the sounds are essential. *A. cerana,* the Asian cavity-nester, produces dance sounds just like those of *A. mellifera* (Fig. 8 a). The basic structure of the sounds is the same, and their production coincides precisely with waggling. Neither *A. florea* nor *A. dorsata,* the two open-nesting species, produce any detectable sounds as they waggle, though dance attenders of both species produce «stop signals» like those discovered by Esch (1964) in *A. mellifera* (Fig. 8 b). Sounds are produced by occasional (about one out of ten) *A. florea* dancers. These sounds, however, are produced almost exclusively during the *return run* of the dance (between waggles), and then only intermittently (Fig. 8 a). The frequency, burst duration, and amplitude of the *A. florea* sounds are roughly similar to those of *A. mellifera* and *A. cerana,* suggesting the possibility that *A. florea's* sounds represent evolutionary precursors of the highly structured and ritualized sounds of the cavity nesters.

6.2 Dance postures

The association between the production of sound during the information-rich waggling run and the habit of living in cavities strongly supports the hypothesis – hinted at by both Esch (1963, 1964) and Wenner (1962) – that the sounds have evolved to aid dance attenders in their efforts to extact the dance information while following dances in the dark. A second aspect of this hypothesis is the notion that both *A. florea* and *A. dorsata* dance attenders use vision in extracting the information from their dances. Another set of observations by Towne (1984b) is consistent with this idea.

As *A. mellifera* and *A. cerana* dancers waggle, their abdomens are depressed just slightly, and the waggling motion is strictly in the horizontal plane of the dancer's body (Fig. 9, top). The waggling postures of *A. florea* and *A. dorsata,* on the other hand, are quite different. In both species the abdomen is elevated and curved upward, causing it to protrude slightly above the mass of bees milling about the dance floor as the dancer waggles (Fig. 9 a). Immediately upon completion of a waggling run, dancers of both species quickly drop their abdomens to their normal resting postures. In addition, as observed by LINDAUER (1956, 1957) in *A. florea*, the abdomens of the dancers as they waggle show a dorso-ventral motion superimposed upon the normal side-to-side waggling of the rest of the body. Although LINDAUER describes the dorso-ventral excursions of the abdomens as «occasional,» TOWNE (1984b) found with the aid of video recordings that the dorso-ventral motion in both species is regular, with a frequency of several cycles per second. (The low resolution of TOWNE's video recordings does not allow precise measurements.)

The dance postures and waggling motions of both open-nesting species thus seem designed to help dance attenders to follow the dances visually. If this is true, it could explain LINDAUER's (1956) observation, confirmed by DYER (1984), that *A. dorsata* dancers prefer to dance on the most well-lit side of the comb. One additional observation made by TOWNE (1984 a), is that *A. dorsata* dance attenders, unlike those of the other three species, almost never turn with the dancer as she circles around in her figure-eight pattern on the dance floor. GOULD (1975 a) has described the circling behavior of *A. mellifera* dance attenders in detail. (*A. florea* and *A. cerana* attenders show basically the same pattern.) Groups of *A. dorsata* attenders instead usually form a more-or-less stationary semi-circle behind the dancer and «watch» as she performs her dance before them. In addition, although the attenders do step forward when the dancer starts to waggle, they

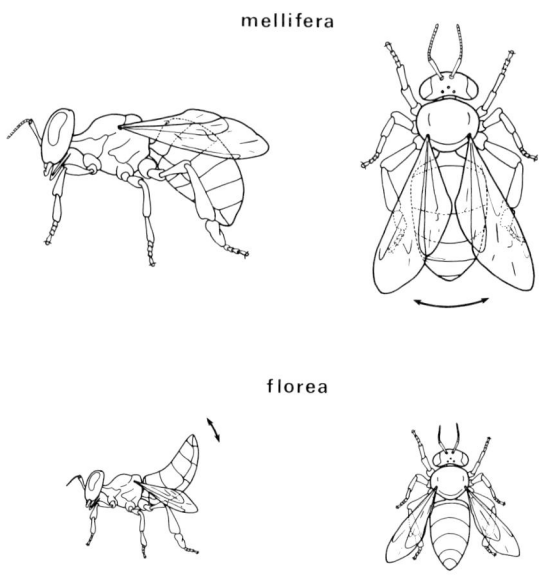

mellifera

florea

Fig. 9: The dance postures and waggling motions of *A. mellifera*, a cavity nester (top), and *A. florea*, an open nester (bottom). The drawings are to scale. The posture and motions of *A. cerana*, the Asian cavity nester, are the same as those of *A. mellifera*. Those of *A. dorsata*, the large Asian open nester, are similar to those of *A. florea* except that *A. dorsata*'s abdomen is relatively longer, and the amplitude of its dorso-ventral motions relatively greater. The upward curvatures of the abdomens of *A. florea* and *A. dorsata* are undoubtedly facilitated by their morphologies, which show a dorso-ventral flattening compared to those of the cavity nesters. From TOWNE (1984b).

rarely get close enough to make actual antennal contact with the dancer. This, too, is unlike the other species which routinely make antennal contact. Perhaps *A. dorsata* attenders are simply too big to wheel about after the dancer as the other species do.

In summary, there seem to be two different strategies for enhancing the ability of recruits to obtain the information from the waggling run. Bursts of sound are produced by the cavity nesting bees which normally dance in the dark. The open nesting species, which dance in the presence of the ambient light, instead employ exaggerated body postures which may facilitate the visual perception of waggling. The widely discussed notion that the duration of sound production is the indicator of distance in *A. mellifera* might still be correct, but we suspect that von FRISCH's (1967) more general interpretation of the sounds as «emphasis» upon the waggling run is closer to the truth.

7 The evolution of the dance language

Much of the progress we have just dicussed can best be summarized in the form of a brief, updated review of our ideas on the evolution of the dance. Previous reviews of this sort can be found in LINDAUER (1961), von FRISCH (1967), ESCH (1967), WILSON (1971), and MICHENER (1974).

7.1 Stingless bees

As pointed out by LINDAUER (1956) and ESCH et al. (1965) among others, the simplest and probably most primitive form of recruitment communication in the Apidae is the agitated jostling run, often accompanied by intermittent sound production, of several species of stingless bees (tribe Meliponini), such as *Trigona iridipennis* in Sri Lanka (LINDAUER 1956) and *T. silvestrii* in Brazil (KERR, ESCH 1965). In such species there is no communication regarding the location of the food source; their «dances» are merely invitations to go out searching for food of the same scent as that clinging to the «dancer's» body (31).

From this basic strategy at least two others have apparently arisen. The first, typified by *T. ruficrus* in Brazil (LINDAUER, KERR 1960), involves agitated running in the nest accompanied by the laying down of a pheromone trail by the foragers. Sometimes, perhaps always, recruits are led along the trail with the help of guiding flights by foragers (LINDAUER, KERR 1960).

The third and seemingly most advanced communication strategy among the stingless bees has been described by ESCH et al. (1965) for two species of *Melipona,* morphologically the most *Apis*-like of the Meliponines (MICHENER 1974). Dancers of these species, instead of producing intermittent and irregular sound bursts as they run, produce bursts that are evenly spaced and whose durations correlate well with the distance to the food. In addition, they seem to use only abbreviated guiding flights and no odor trails. ESCH et al. suggest that the sound burst duration symbolically communicates distance information to recruits, but, unfortunately, their observations are not conclusive on this point.

Both von FRISCH (1967) and MICHENER (1974) give excellent and more detailed reviews of stingless bee communication.

7.2 From *Melipona* to *Apis*

ESCH et al. (1965) have argued that symbolic communication in *Apis* has arisen from the simpler form they observed in *Melipona,* but even if communication in *Melipona* is symbolic, the two languages are probably not homologous. First, the «dance» sounds of stingless bees are substrate borne (1960). The *Apis* sounds on the other hand, are probably airborne (GOULD 1975 a). Second, the lack of regular sound production in *A. florea* and *A. dorsata* argues against the homology of the sounds of the two groups of bees. In any case, the homology between communication in stingless bees and honey bees is not well established, suggesting the interesting possibility that symbolic communication has arisen twice in the Apidae.

7.3 Changes within Apis

No one has yet discovered any forms of communication intermediate between the «dances» of *Melipona* and those of *Apis*, but it seems probable that the *Apis* dance first appeared in a bee with habits like *A. florea* (LINDAUER 1956, v. FRISCH 1967). Dances were on a horizontal surface, and agitated movements gave direction with reference to the sun or blue sky and distance in the duration of waggling. Although the use of polarized skylight occurs in many insects, the rules used to eliminate ambiguity in using these cues may have arisen first at an early stage in *Apis* because of the requirement that the bees dance on a platform where large parts of the sky might be blocked from view by clouds or vegetation. As far as we know, all that would need to be added to the behavioral repertoire thus assembled to produce the dance/orientation system of *A. florea* is the secondary backup system that resorts to landmarks when celestial cues are blocked entirely. Landmarks are important to bees during the flight (VON FRISCH, LINDAUER 1954, DYER, GOULD 1981) – and probably to most mobile animals – so the early *A. florea* might have been preadapted to incorporate landmarks into the dance.

The next step, which brings us to *A. dorsata*'s strategy, most likely involved the move from horizontal to vertical dance surfaces and the transition from celestial to gravity orientation (LINDAUER 1956). We can speculate that there was an intermediate step with vertical dances oriented to celestial cues (*A. mellifera* will still use celestial cues when dancing on the vertical if the cues are strong enough [VON FRISCH 1967]), but we cannot be certain. We can also make some reasonable guesses as to why the first vertical dances were necessary. The horizontal dance surfaces of *A. florea* are extensions of the comb which wrap around the relatively thin branches on which the colonies hang. Most likely as a result of increasing colony size, the need to avoid mammalian predators (SEELEY et al 1982), or both, the bees probably began to hang their single sheets of comb from the undersides of large branches or rock outcrops, the favored nest sites of *A. dorsata* today (LINDAUER 1956, SEELEY et al 1982). Since the comb could no longer wrap around the substrate, the only surfaces available to the dancing bees were vertical ones, and so dancing on the vertical became essential. Although *A. dorsata, A. cerana*, and *A. mellifera* now seem rarely (except in experiments) to have any use for their ability to dance on the horizontal – even *A. mellifera*'s nest-site dances on the swarm (LINDAUER 1955) normally occur on the more-or-less vertical sides of the hanging ball of bees – all three species have retained it (DYER 1984).

Regardless of exactly how it arose, gravity-oriented dancing brought with it the need for a new backup orientation system; dancers had only gravity for their orientation and so needed to know the position of the sun relative to the direction of their outward flights in order to communicate. This was probably made possible in a *dorsata*-like ancestor by the evolution of the ability to memorize the sun's course with respect to landmarks, creating a robust backup system that would allow normal activity under almost any weather conditions, or even at night.

Something else that dancing on the vertical brought with it was a preadaptation for the move into enclosed cavities. This move, most likely compelled by predator pressure

(Gould 1982a, Seeley et al 1982) eliminated the opportunity to use vision in the communication, thereby necessitating a change in the strategy used to transmit the dance information. The ancestors of *A. mellifera* and *A. cerana* seem to have responded with the introduction of sounds into the dance, the loss of their exaggerated dance postures, and the placement of a new emphasis on the side-to-side waggling motion (Towne 1984b). All the while the distance dialects probably drifted in accordance with changes in the colony sizes and foraging ranges of the bees (Gould 1982b), and the cloudy day back-up system, based on a memory of the sun's course with respect to landmarks (Dyer, Gould 1981), remained essentially unchanged.

The cavity-dwelling habit of *A. mellifera* and *A. cerana* was, in its turn, probably a preadaptation for the movement of these bees out of the tropics and into the temperate regions (of Europe and West Asia for *A. mellifera*, and East Asia for *A. cerana*). The former, because of the relatively broad and diffuse resources available in the temperate zones, and particularly intense selection for efficiency in exploiting them because of the necessity of storing sufficient honey to survive the brutal winters (Seeley 1983), may have led to selection for a certain amount of imprecision in the dance language, ultimately giving rise to the divergence in the dances of contemporary *A. mellifera*.

It remains to be seen what other adaptations may contribute to the efficiency and flexibility of this fascinating system. At least we can say with some certainly that von Frisch's magic well is still a long way from going dry.

References

Boch, R. (1957): Rassenmäßige unterschiede bei den Tanzen der Honigbiene. Z. vergl. Physiol. *40*, 289–320.

Brines, M. L. (1978): Skylight polarization patterns as cues for honey bee orientation: physical measurements and behavioral experiments. Ph. D. Thesis. New York, Rockefeller University.

Brines, M. L., Gould, J. L. (1979): Bees have rules. Science *206*, 571–573.

Brines, M. L., Gould, J. L. (1982): Skylight polarization patterns and animal orientation. J. Exp. Biol. *96*, 69–91.

Dyer, F. C. (1984): Ph. D. Thesis. Princeton University.

Dyer, F. C., Gould, J. L. (1981): Honey bee orientation: a backup system for cloudy days. Science *214*: 1041–1042.

Dyer, F. C., Gould, J. L. (1983): Honey bee navigation. Amer. Sci. *71*, 587–597.

Edrich, W. (1975): The waggle dance of the honey bee; a new formulation. Fortschr. Zool. *23*, (1), 20–30.

Esch, H. (1961): Ein neuer Bewegungstyp im Schwanzeltanz der Bienen. Naturwiss. *48*, 140–141.

Esch, H. (1961a): Über die Schallerzeugung beim Werbetanz der Honigbiene. Z. vergl. Physiol. *45*, 1–11.

Esch, H. (1963): Über die Auswirkung der Futterplatzqualität auf die Schallerzeugung im Werbetanz der Honigbiene. Verhandl. Deut. Zool. Ges. *26*, 302–309.

Esch, H. (1964): Beiträge zum Problem der Entfernungsweisung in den Schwanzeltänzen der Honigbiene. Z. vergl. Physiol. *44*, 534–546.

Esch, H. (1967): The evolution of bee language. Sci. Am. *216*, 96–104.

Esch, H., Esch, I., Kerr, W. E. (1965): Sound: an element common to communication of stingless bees and to dances of honey bees. Science *149*, 320–321.

Frisch, K. v. (1967): The Dance Language and Orientation of Bees. Cambridge, Mass., Harvard Univ. Press.

Frisch, K. v., Jander, R. (1957): Über den Schwanzeltanz der Bienen. Z. vergl. Physiol. *40*, 239–263.

Frisch, K. v., Lindauer, M. (1954): Himmel und Erde in Konkurrenz bei der Orientierung der Bienen. Naturwiss. *41*, 245–253.

Gould, J. L. (1974): Honey bee communication. Nature *252*, 300–301.

Gould, J. L. (1975 a): Honey bee communication: the dance-language controversy. Ph. D. Thesis. New York, Rockefeller University.

Gould, J. L. (1975 b): Communication of distance information by honey bees. J. Comp. Physiol. *104*, 161–173.

Gould, J. L. (1975 c): Honey bee recruitment: the dance-language controversy. Science *189*, 685–692.

Gould, J. L. (1976): The dance-language controversy. Quart. Rev. Biol. *51*, 211–244.

Gould, J. L. (1980): Sun compensation by bees. Science *207*, 545–547.

Gould, J. L. (1982 a): Ethology: The Mechanisms and Evolution of Behavior. New York, Nortons.

Gould, J. L. (1982 b) Why do honey bees have dialects? Behav. Ecol. Sociobiol. *10*, 53–56.

Gould, J. L. (1984 a): Processing of sun-azimuth information by honey bees. Anim. Behav. *32*, 149–152.

Gould, J. L. (1984 b): The natural history of honey bee learning. *In* The Biology of Learning, ed. P. Marler and H. Terrace. Berlin, Springer-Verlag (in press).

Gould, J. L., Henery, M., MacLeod. M. C. (1970): Communication of direction by the honey bee. Science *169*, 544–554.

Haldane, J. B. S., Spurway, H. (1954): A statistical analysis of communication in *Apis mellifera* and a comparison with communication in other animals. Insectes Sociaux *1*, 247–283.

Hölldobler, B. (1980): Canopy orientation: a new kind of orientation in ants. Science *210*, 86–88.

Kerr, W. E., Esch, H. (1965): Communicação entre as abelhas sociais brasileiras e sua contrabuicau para o entendimento da sua evolução. Ciencia e Cult. (Sao Paulo) *17*, 529–538.

Koeniger, N., Koeniger, G., Punchihewa, R. K. W., Fabritius, Mo., Fabritus, Mi. (1982): Observations and experiments on dance communication in *A. florea*. J. Apicult, Res. *21*, 45–52.

Lindauer, M. 1955): Schwarmbienen auf Wohnungssuche. Z. vergl. Physiol. *37*, 263–324.

Lindauer, M. (1956): Über die Verständigung bei indischen Bienen. Z. vergl. Physiol. *38*, 521–577.

Lindauer, M. (1957): Communication among the honeybees and stingless bees of India. Bee World *38*, 3–14, 34–39.

Lindauer, M. (1959): Angeborne und erlernte Komponenten in der Sonnenorientierung der Bienen. Z. vergl. Physiol. *42*, 43–62.

Lindauer, M. (1961): Communication among Social Bees. Cambridge, Mass., Harvard Univ. Press.

Lindauer, M. (1963): Kompaßorientierung. Ergebn. Biol. *26*, 158–181.

Lindauer, M. (1971): The functional significance of the honey bee waggle dance. Amer. Nat. *105*, 89–96.

Lindauer, M., Kerr, W. E. (1960): Communication between the workers of stingless bees. Bee World *41*, 29–41, 65–71.

Michener, M. C. (1974): The Social Behavior of the Bees. Cambridge, Mass., Harvard Univ. Press.

Rossel, S. R., Wehner, R. (1982): The bees' map of the e-vector pattern in the sky. P. N. A. S. *79*, 4451–4455.

Rossel, S. R., Wehner, R., Lindauer, M. (1978): E-vector orientation in bees, J. Comp. Physiol. *125*, 1–12.

Schricker, B. (1974): Der Einfluß subletaler Dosen von Parathion (E 605) auf die Entfernungsweisung bei der Honigbiene. Apidologie *5*, 149–175.

Seeley, T. D. (1983): The ecology of temperate and tropical honey bee societies. Am. Sci. *71*, (3), 264–272.

Seeley, T. D., Morse, R. A. (1978): Nest site selection by the honey bee. Insectes Sociaux *25*, 323–337.

Seeley, T. D., Seeley, R. H., Akratanakul, P. (1982): Colony defense strategies of the honeybees in Thailand. Ecol. Monogr. *52*, 43–63.

Towne, W. F. (1984 a): Ph. D. Thesis. Princeton University (in preparation).

Towne, W. F. (1984 b): Acoustic and visual cues in the dances of four honey bee species. Behav. Ecol. Sociobiol. (in press).

Wehner, R. (1981): Spatial vision in Arthropods. *In* Handbook of Sensory Physiology, ed. H. Autrum, pp. 287–616. Berlin, Springer-Verlag.

Wenner, A. M. (1959): The relationship of sound production during the waggle dance of honey bees to the distance to the food source (an abstract). Bull. Entomol. Soc. Am. *5*, 142.

Wenner, A. M. (1962): Sound production during the waggle dance of honey bees. Anim. Behav. *10*, 79–95.

Wilson, E. O. (1971): The Insect Societies. Cambridge, Mass., Harvard Univ. Press.

Fortschritte der Zoologie, Bd. 31 · Hölldobler/Lindauer (Hrsg.): Experimental Behavioral Ecology
G. Fischer Verlag · Stuttgart · New York · 1985

Manipulation, modulation, information, cognition: some of the riddles of communication

HuBERT MARKL

Fakultät für Biologie, Universität Konstanz – F.R.Germany

Abstract

Whether communicating animals exchange information for mutual benefit, or whether communication is actually a process of receiver exploitation by the manipulative powers of a sender's signals without any reliable information transfer, has recently been controversially discussed. This contribution argues that exploitative, unbalanced communicatory relationships between conspecifics should be transitory or only characteristic for special cases, while communication within social groups should be as a rule cooperative and mutually informative. In contrast, intrusion of third participants (e. g. mimics) into tuned sender-receiver relationships can more easily stay unilaterally exploitative (Tables 1,2). There are remarkable differences between signals used in manipulative relationships and those found in mutualistic communication. While the first often have the «classical» conspicuous releaser charcteristics, the latter are typically found to be unobtrusive, low-range, highly addressed, and exclusive. They frequently modulate receiver reactivity with respect to other contextual stimuli rather than triggering responses in all-or-none fashion. Ways of quantifying communication efficiency, and the meaning of different statistical information measures in a bidirectional communication loop (Fig. 1) are discussed. An analysis is made of how the ability for internal communication, which vastly expands the cognitive and therefore also behavioral powers of an organism, might derive from role-switching bidirectional social communication. Finally it is pointed out that mutualistic communication welds members of social groups into cooperative supersystems which develop all the properties of problemsolving, higher-order cognitive entities. In that respect, social communication processes can be profitably compared with functions of the central nervous system of individual organisms.

1 Introduction

It seems appropriate in a symposium dedicated to the memory of KARL VON FRISCH – a pioneer of the scientific investigation of communication in animals – to ask what animal communication is. Since «communio» means sharing, what is it that they share? What evolutionary and developmental conditions are necessary for them to participate in such a process? And if this process is the result of a history of coadaptive selection – be it through natural selection in the evolutionary history of a genepool or through selective learning by an individual – what are the advantages of this behavioral coadaptation, who receives the benefits payed out in fitness currency? Are they also equitably shared? Or do we also have to consider disadvantages and fitness costs of communicating, and how they are distributed between the communicating partners? Was KARL VON FRISCH right to summarize his astounding discovery of the «dance language» in honeybees by writing that they «können ... ein Ziel, das für *ihr Volk von Wichtigkeit ist,* den Kameraden mitteilen und seine Lage *so genau beschreiben,* daß es von den Stockgenossen in selbständigem Flug, ohne Geleit, auf kürzestem Wege gefunden wird – selbst in kilometerweiter Entfernung» (VON FRISCH 1965, p. 538, italics mine)? Or should we rather believe RICHARD DAWKINS and JOHN KREBS (1978, p. 309) who suggest quite categorically: «If information is shared at all it is likely to be false information, but it is probably better to abandon the concept of information altogether»? In the latter point they are at first glance even in full agreement with KARL VON FRISCH who seems not once to have used the word «information» in his authoritative 578 pages-magna summa of more than 40 years work on dance language and orientation in bees. This should, however, not be misread, because he readily speaks about the «Nachrichten», «Mitteilungen» and «Weisungen» contained in and transmitted by the dances – which is, of course, the very information language that DAWKINS and KREBS advise us against; even when they accept (p. 286) that in the bees' dances «the benefit is, in a sense, mutual», they «would still prefer to avoid «information terminology» and in fact even to abandon the word communication altogether» (p. 283). That this is not only an issue of semantic preferences, a disagreement about words, but relates to the very base of our understanding of animal communication, is abundantly clear from their lucid exposition and from the discussion it has aroused.

In this contribution I will further analyze this problem by first asking how we recognize communication in animals (i.e. how we define it operationally); second, why organisms communicate and who reaps the benefits and bears the costs involved; third, what determines the quality of communication processes (i.e. how we can quantify communication efficiency); finally, what is it that is communicated. I will then end with a somewhat daring comparison of communication between members of an animal society and that between neurons in a central nervous system. In doing this I will not only cast a metaphorical glimpse at the superorganism concept but argue that through the benefits of its communicatory powers a highly developed society is actually a higher level cognitive system with unpredictable (though not irreducible) emergent cognitive properties.

2 Manipulation – or the profit of communication

To communicate, it takes at least two; even if one communicates with oneself one somehow has to split into two roles: that of the *sender* and that of the *receiver* of messages. We don't know whether an animal can really communicate with itself (I will come back to that question later) therefore at least two of them have to participate as sender and receiver to make communication both possible and recognizable in animals. It is important to realize that sender and receiver of signals are temporary *roles* for most practical purposes (I will come to exceptions) and not immutable *characteristics* of individuals. Mostly, communication is bidirectional with interactants switching between these two roles (see MARKO 1983). I think it is important to emphasize this triviality because much of the argument about who is benefitting more or at all from the communicatory interaction, and who is selected to communicate, the sender or the receiver, becomes rather irrelevant in a bidirectional, role-alternating process.

There are scores of definitions of communication (see e.g. BURGHARDT 1970, TEM-BROCK 1971, SEBEOK 1977, CHERRY 1978, GREEN and MARLER 1979, LEWIS and GOWER 1980, HALLIDAY and SLATER 1983 for reviews). I am inclined to follow and slightly expand a version used by WILSON (1975), who maintains that *communication occurs when the action of or cue given by one organism is perceived by and thus alters the probability pattern of behavior in another organism in a fashion adaptive to either one or both of the participants.* DAWKINS and KREBS (1978) have argued – and I think one cannot disagree with them in this point – that the sender (whom they call the actor) of a signal is selected to manipulate the behavior of the receiver (their reactor) to the adavantage of the sender. In order to avoid the impression that a sender is a sender is a sender and never anything else it might be preferable to say that a *signal* is a trait that is selected to manipulate an addressee (which, however, may not be the only receiver, see below) to the advantage of the sender of this signal. That manipulation should be for the advantage of the manipulator follows not only straight from natural selection logic, it is also very much at the core of most serious communication theories. It is also the gist of GOFFMAN's influential «Strategic Interaction» (1969), oddly not cited by DAWKINS and KREBS, though it may be even more to their point than PACKARD's Hidden Pursuaders. However, GOFF-MAN never lost sight of the fact that manipulation to the benefit of the sender is only half the story of communication. Of course, addressees are not sitting around in extra-evolutionary space offering unmodifyable releasing mechanisms just waiting to be mani-pulated; in fact it is well known that there is hardly anything that can be more easily modified both by evolution and by individual experience – where we call it focussing of attention – than reaction thresholds and response selectivity of releasing mechanisms or sensory-neural pattern-recognition devices. Except in maladjusted transitory stages of communication, in cases of structural asymmetries of manipulative powers (e.g. between parents and offspring), and in exploitative communication triads (see below) nothing in the world can keep receivers dancing like puppets on the strings of the senders' signals – unless it is to their own advantage, too, to be manipulated: *mundus vult decipi,* successful manipulation begs the question about the sucker's interest in it.

Let me recall that sender and receiver are roles alternatingly taken over by the same individual in most processes of communication: how could we imagine the same individu-al being always overpowering in one role and a moment later overpowered in the next? Frequent change of sender – receiver roles between the interacting pair, the well-known intertwined communication chain of so many agonistic or sexual displays, could be *the* most important mechanism to avoid unilateral exploitation, just as exemplified by the simultaneously hermaphroditic serranid coral fish *Hypoplectus nigricans,* which takes turns in spawning and fertilizing eggs (FISCHER 1980).

Communicating animals have to be leninist: trust is good, control is better, but that holds for *both parties,* if the degeneration of manipulation into exploitation is to be avoided. If DAWKINS and KREBS dub their view of communication as cynical, I am afraid they have gone only half the way; it's like explaining the evolution of sex from the advantage for the male or, to borrow a metaphor from GREGORY BATESON, like clapping applause with one hand. We should be twice as cynical as they advise us to be: the receiver has to look at the matter just as cynically or rather realistically as the sender in order to stay in business. What is most important, half-cynicism may be unstable whereas full-cynics may open the door to a mutually satisfactory cooperative relationship even though, and even because, both partners continuously make every effort to manipulate each other. The agent behind this has been well known for over 200 years: it's ADAM SMITH's «invis-ible hand», and what's good for the marketplace may not be too bad for the genepool either: here we get a first glimpse of how communication produces social systems with emergent cognitive qualities: they «discover» that it can be good for others to be good to oneself. The «invisible hand» is, as it were, the hand of providence, and providence certainly is a cognitive capacity.

As Axelrod and Hamilton (1981; Axelrod 1984) have convincingly shown, in order to arrive at a stable situation of reliable mutual profit, communication partners should preferably not only interact once in their lives but repeatedly, so that common interest can prevail; this becomes particularly effective if the communicators recognize each other individually (van Rhijn and Vodegel 1980). This is typical for many important social interactions, e.g. between parents and offspring or between mates. The condition of common interest is of course no less well fulfilled in genetically closely related social groups, like insect societies, where individuals recognize each other as members of a joint family venture of investment for gaining fitness. Prolonged, addressed, role-switching partnership in communication is thus the gateway to the superior organizing powers and profitability of mutualism in complex organismal systems, be it in a lichen, a beehive, a family, or in Japan Incorporated. Whenever the profit in fitness for one partner is not decreased but rather increased by gains of the other, natural selection should drive the system up the hill of mutual social cooperation, manipulation, cynicism and selfish genes notwithstanding. It is, of course, fully appropriate to emphasize the potential for conflict and unilateral exploitation in all of these relations – as done from Trivers (1971, 1972, 1974) to Dawkins and Krebs (1978, 1979). There can also be no question that such unbalanced communicational relationships are not uncommon even in highly organized social systems which are always in danger of slipping into the trap of losing in the long run from gaining in the short run. To leave it at that and see conflict-solutions with unbalanced distribution of profits as almost paradigmatic for communication in animals, seems to be tantamount to stopping talking about communication where it actually becomes most interesting: namely, where it overcomes the more primitive stage of individuals striving in isolation for fitness, and organizes higher-order social entities with common interests and cooperative action to serve them. There is nothing suspiciously altruistic about ganging up to make a higher profit together instead of going it alone. It is the amazing adaptiveness, the astounding evolutionary success of cooperation between so many organisms that impresses us when we look into Nature. We see that this cooperation depends on sophisticated mechanisms of communication between the cooperating individuals. So it seems strange to denounce emphasis on cooperation in the study of communication as idealistic and obsolete.

The main reason why Dawkins and Krebs (1978) concentrated on non-cooperative solutions of communication problems is probably that they focussed predominantly on the example of aggressive competition for resources in developing their view. Evidently, that is not exactly the terrain to expect an outcome of mutual gain – much rather one of MAD, mutual assured destruction. As Maynard Smith and others (see Maynard Smith and Parker 1976, Maynard Smith 1982 a, b, Caryl 1979, 1981, 1982, van Rhijn 1980, van Rhijn and Vodegel 1980, Hinde 1981, Parker and Rubenstein 1981, Moynihan 1982) have discussed, an easy solution to decide such conflicts would be to use an asymmetry between the contenders, preferably one of Resource Holding Power (RHP Parker 1974): the more powerful wins, the weaker loses, rationalized as «der Klügere gibt nach», the rule of the dumb – literally, of those who cannot communicate – or rather, as Maynard Smith also pointed out, of those who, with brutal candour, project the message of their superior RHP. Although the loser at least avoids being damaged in such an asymmetrical fight, he certainly cannot gain resources by giving in, so to call this mutualism would really be at best a Brezhnev doctrine of cooperation.

Still, even there, second thoughts lead to second doubts: what if a subordinate can still profit somewhat by joining one whom he cannot beat, because battling alone would be even worse? We then arrive at a social system with a dominance hierarchy. If the winner in future contests can win even more with the loser in tow, the stage is set for mutual benefit, and even with intragroup competition for dominance continuing, intergroup competition might tend to favor cooperative solutions rather than disruptive competition, especially if the majority of group members invest in common family bonds. The facilitating importance of individual recognition in stable groups has in this connection been stressed by VAN RHIJN and VODEGEL (1980), van RHIJN (1980); see also BARNARD and BURK (1979).

With symmetry of RHP, the outcome is less transparent. First raised by game theorists, the argument goes that although the value of the contended resource and therefore the intention to fight for it may be different for both opponents, faithfully signalling by graded displays and thus accurately informing the opponent about one's motivation would not be a stable strategy since the expression of high interest could be too easily faked at little cost. «Bluff» and «deceit» would follow with the consequence that at the end of such a development all signals of intention would have to be disregarded in deciding a conflict – the symmetrically matched opponents would be back to fighting it out. This is the basic argument for rejecting the idea that any information – much less accurate information – about intentions and activity probabilities might be transmitted in animal communication.

Those who make that point confess, however, to find it a puzzle why in reality we often find gradually escalating pre-fight display in animal contests and why faked signals seem to be relatively uncommon in intraspecific communication. DAWKINS and KREBS (1978) have already suggested that if costs of fights are high – and they should be high in the RHP-symmetry case here considered – an inability to grade threat displays may be too costly for both parties to be stable. It should rather be to the advantage of the sender not to force the receiver to step up to violence immediately. Since in this match each of the opponents is playing the roles of sender and receiver simultaneously or in turn, this advantage accrues for both participants. This may not make them honest informers, but at least should lead them to make cautiously escalating threats.

The real problem with this case may be elsewhere, however, namely in the basic assumption of symmetry. If truly symmetrical matchings are sufficiently rare in reality, we might be looking at these homerian pre-fight displays from the wrong side in the first place. The problem is one of lack of sufficient information: if those who enter into a contest cannot assess at first glance the relative aggressive potential of the adversary, how should they best proceed?

Not enough emphasis may have been put on the fact that resource holding intention and resource holding power cannot be treated as completely independent variables, since intention determines how much of its available power an individual will be prepared to bring to bear in a given conflict; actual resource holding investment is thus a composite of motivation and available potential, as it were, of brains (or rather: guts) and brawns. There is a tradeoff between the two: the highly motivated weakling may prevail over the not sufficiently interested strong guy. Now, when entering into a contest, an individual may well gauge immediately the opponent's RHP and compare it to its own, but how should it gauge what is more decisive: how much of this RHP the adversary will mobilize in order to acquire the contended resource? As PARKER and RUBENSTEIN (1981), CARYL (1981) and others have emphasized, whatever happens will be strongly determined by the cost functions of different tactics and by the payoff-value of the resource: but the rating of both depends on «private» evaluation, the criteria of which are not fully accessible to the opponent. Thus we would expect each contestant to begin to find out at as low cost as possible how much the other one is prepared to invest in order to dominate. The lowest stage might be little more than indicating interest, like laying a claim. From that onwards we would expect a mutual probing of reactions at escalating costs for prober and reactor, before finally an all out fight sets in if no one withdraws from the highest level of probing. «Bluff» and «deceit» would thus be easily recognized and not pay out, because they forced the opponent to turn to an intensity of escalation which entailed the risk of serious damage to the «bluffer».

It may well be that a weaker individual – if not too badly mismatched – may be forced to step up escalation earlier and faster in a war of attrition since it can less afford to wait through, having fewer energy reserves and carrying higher opportunity costs, than the stronger, giving an observer a paradoxial impression of RHP relationships.

Rather than looking at graded escalation of displays as graded indications of a signaler's intentions, we might have to see in them a scale of (for both sides more and more costly) probes of the opponents' mobilizable aggressive potential, not only because probing can disclose «cheats» (Barnard and Burk 1979), but because it is necessary to check how much the opponent cares to become involved. Rather than informing the adversary of one's own intentions this would serve to inform oneself about the adversary's potential to resist by measuring the costs he shows himself prepared to pay. We would then also not be surprised to find displays poor indicators of what the displayer will do next (as shown by Caryl 1979), since what he will do next will have to be a function of the receiver's reaction to each move (see also Hinde 1981, Caryl 1982).

Maybe the occurrence of really symmetrical resource holding *potentials* (as defined above) are rare enough in the field to make the predictions about the advantages of «bluff» and «deceit», derived from a «war of attrition» model, only rarely applicable. Since in a scheme like this it must be dangerous to play «hawk» unless one is prepared to carry it through – forcing an opponent with unexpectedly high potential to react violently – this seems not only a way to understand why graded escalation in aggressive conflicts is common, but also a good reason to assume that «bluff» may not be a viable tactic and «honesty» in indicating the chances of one's potential paying out better. All these considerations apply with even more force if contestants know each other from previous fights and interact repeatedly (see Barnard and Burk 1979, van Rhijn 1980, Bossema and Burgler 1980) and even more so if genetic relatedness between them matters (Breed and Bekoff 1981).

This means that even in aggressive conflicts there are inherent selection pressures for arriving at arrangements which save costs for both sides. Communicative interactions may not establish perfect harmony, but they do at least create some kind of security partnership to mutual advantage, notwithstanding continuing competition for resources and for fitness. Although communication with unbalanced outcome during aggressive competition in species leading solitary lives may occur, I would argue that this is not the rule in more truly social interactions, such as between mates, between parents and offspring and in most kinds of interactions between members of a social group. In the latter cases we should rather expect strategies which yield the increased benefits of mutual cooperation for all participants. That cooperative social systems are ecologically extremely successful is abundantly clear from comparative sociobiology (see Wilson 1971, 1975) and of course from our own species. In that view, non-mutualistic interactions would be examples of more primitive stages or of transitory imbalances or of degenerative side tracks into blind alleys of the evolution of communication rather than paradigmatic for the real essence of communication.

Wiley (1983) has recently further developed a more balanced view of communication as manipulation by considering the possibilities of increase and decrease both of a signaler's and a receiver's fitness during communication. This approach can be further refined in two ways to cover animal communication as comprehensively as possible.

One should first distinguish – as has of course often been done before (see SEBEOK 1977, SMITH 1977 for review and examples) – between two types of traits of a *sender*. One type are *signals* (or *ritualized displays*) which can be assumed to have been selected to act on the perceptual mechanisms of specific addressees in order to influence their behavior. To produce such signals entails costs – e. g. of energy expenditure for signaling, of risks by making oneself conspicuous etc. – which have to be more than balanced by the fitness benefits derived from having them produced. The second type of a sender's traits are those properties of a sender which we might call *cues*. They also may make costs to acquire, but the costs are not incurred because these cues have been specifically selected to serve in communication. Examples would be unritualized intention (better: preparation) movements (e. g. getting ready for a jump), a flying bird's silhouette, the trampling of a stampeding herd, waves produced by a swimming fish, or the sheer impression of the body size and the quality of predatory weapons of a top carnivore.

On the *receiver's* side we can also discern between two kinds of conditions for reception. First, perceptual devices (releasing mechanisms or detectors) installed to allow a receiver to detect specific signals or cues. Though costs for developing these may be negligeable, they usually are combined in usage with quite important costs of search (i. e. selected appetitive behavior) for the appropriate stimuli and with costs of lost opportunities, (e. g., if a predator rejects an edible mimic) which again have to be more than compensated by the benefits accruing from being receptive. Second, a receiver can react to signals or cues without having to pay any costs for getting the opportunity to do this, e. g., because he encounters them by chance or because the sender has to pick up the bill for search risk and effort. Note that – in contrast to the approach of WILEY (1983) – the costs considered up to here – though ultimately also booked in fitness equivalents – are not the costs derived from the outcome of the communicatory interactions (e. g. from the loss of a territory or a mate), but the costs incurred in making preparations and efforts for being able to interact. These costs have then to be added to those of the outcome and to be put into balance with the benefits which only accrue from the outcome of a communicatory interaction.

The second refinement of argument should be always to make clear whether we are talking about a *dyadic* communicatory interaction, in which signals or cues act on receivers which have common interests (be it in getting the same resource or in cooperation), or a *triadic* relationship, in which a third party – as sender or as receiver – is involved that exploits such a dyadic signal-detector relationship (as first clearly expressed by WICKLER 1967). We could call the dyadic relationship bilaterally tuned, while the exploitative third participant in a triad is unilaterally tuning in to an existing dyadic relation. In dyadic mimesis a sender imitates stimuli to which the receiver is tuned *not* to react, e. g. inanimate background patterns.

Only if we consider all of these relationships, as done in Tables 1 and 2, do we see the whole universe of organismic communications and the richness of opportunities given there.

The triadic relationship is in some respects profoundly different in consequences from the dyadic one. In the dyadic system we have, as it were, a symmetry of evolutionary and developmental means. Selection acts in just the same way on the sender to manipulate the receiver more efficiently to the advantage of the sender, as on the receiver to be as discriminating as necessary to derive its own optimal profit from reacting. This makes unequal utilities (benefits – costs) for sender and receiver evolutionarily and developmentally unstable and favors balanced mutualistic relationships. Accordingly, outright receiver or sender exploitation (types 2, 3 in Table 1) should be *rare* in dyadic relationships.

The situation in the triad is quite different at least in the more common types 1 and 3 of

Table 1: *Communication dyads:* bilaterally tuned relationships between sender and receiver (or imitation by sender of stimuli which influence the receiver's behavior in a way advantageous for the sender: mimesis). The profit balance – total benefits minus total costs of interaction – of the participants is given as: gain (+) or loss (−) of fitness equivalents because of the communicative interaction of dyad members. Costs can be incurred for preparation and during interaction (sender: signaling effort, increased risks because of conspicuous signaling, search effort for receiver, lost opportunities because of signaling and searching; receiver: search effort for sender, lost opportunities from spending time on searching) and from the outcome of communication (e.g., loss of the contended resource). If the sender incurs no costs for preparation, the stimuli provided by the sender, to which the receiver reacts, are called *cues*; the receiver may incur no preparation costs if it encounters the sender by chance or if the sender carries the search costs. Benefits can be derived during interaction (receiver: avoided risk of injury by combat; sender and receiver: gain of experience) and from the outcome of the interaction (e.g. win of resource).

Type	Sender	Receiver	Examples of relationships
1	+	+	Intraspecific: mutualistic cooperation (e.g. male-female, parent-offspring, members of social group). Interspecific: symbiosis, aposematic signaling. Perfect, if gains are equal for sender and receiver; imperfect, if one gains more than the other (e.g. in agonistic communication).
2	+	−	Exploitation of receiver by sender. Intraspecific: ritualized combat (victory by threat) or social dominance hierarchy; cuckolded male investing alloparental care; immature males gaining experience by courting female who has to carry interference costs. Interspecific: mimesis, interspecific interference and dominance by threat.
3	−	+	Exploitation of sender by receiver. Intraspecific: kleptogamic interloper attracted by signals of male competitor. Interspecific: detector of palatability of mimetic prey which concentrates on hunting for the mimic.
4	−	−	Wasted efforts of sender and receiver. Intraspecific: disturbed and unsuccessful courtship; both opponents of fight – after undecided threat duel – severely damaged, none of them winning resource; fighting or courting pairs attracting predator. Interspecific: inexperienced predator suffering from killing dangerous aposematic prey.

Table 2, where the third party acts like a «parasite» or «predator» of the dyadic relationship. There the intruding participant derives benefit as a receiver from reacting to the signals of a sender I which are also under selective control in a mutual relationship with receiver I; or it derives that benefit from producing signals as sender II (mimic) that act on the detector devices of receiver I which are also under selective control in a relationship with sender I (the model). Since the mutually tuned communicators both derive fitness from their sender-receiver relationship – and only if so, which again demonstrates the importance of mutual benefits of communication – selection cannot make them completely unresponsive to the mimic's signals or stop producing their own signals in order to get rid of the parasitic or predatory exploiter, because they would at the same time jeopardize or even cut off the fitness derived from their own dyadic cooperation in system I.

Table 2: *Communication triads:* exploitation of communication dyad (I) by third participant (II) who can tune in as receiver II or as sender II. Profit balance of interactants: gain (+) or loss (−) of fitness equivalents because of communicative interaction between member of dyad and exploiter.

Type	Dyad		Participant II as		Examples of relationship
	Sender I	Receiver I	Sender II (Mimic)	Receiver II	
1	−	model		+	Sender I exploitation by predator or parasite which detect prey/host (= sender I) by their signals/cues which are selected to influence receiver I; food parasite/competitor attracted by «food calls».
2	+			+	Generalized cooperation, intraspecific in courtship chorus, lek displays (attraction of males by male displays); interspecific in mixed flocking or cross-specific alarm calls.
3	model	−	+		Mimicry, detrimental for receiver, e.g. Batesian mimicry (receiver loses opportunity, search effort) or aggressive mimicry.
4		+	+		Mimicry, advantageous for receiver, e.g., Müllerian mimicry or cichlid egg mimicry.

Clearly, the evolutionary means of the host/prey-dyad (I) and of the intruding exploiter (II) are not equal, since little can restrain the latter from becoming ever more perfectly tuned ot the dyad's signal-receiver system. Defence against exploitation by a third party can therefore not be selected as easily and as perfectly as can defence against mutual exploitation between the members of the dyadic set, unless the exploited one manages to embrace the exploiter at a point of common interest in a symbiotic relationship. This may also be the reason why intraspecific signal faking is more rare than that between species (see DAWKINS and KREBS (1979) for a lucid discussion of further aspects of this problem). The two types of relationships should therefore always be clearly kept apart and not be used interchangeably as exemplifying communication in animals.

It follows that persistently effective third party exploitation can take advantage of a dyadic communication system which is highly important for the dyad's fitness. Since this is also the condition most favoring selection against intradyadic exploitation and for intradyadic cooperation, we should expect to find such exploitative third party intrusion most spectacularly combined with very cooperative and mutually beneficial social relationships. Ant mimics and social parasites yield particularly impressive examples (HÖLL-DOBLER 1977,). We could also put this more simply: a cooperative system is more productive than comparable non-cooperative ones; a productive system is a valuable resource; any valuable resource will by itself select its skilled intruders and efficient exploiters, whether these are predators or parasites, whether interspecific or intraspecific ones.

Thus this section can be summed up by concluding that there are good reasons to see manipulation and counter-manipulation at work in communication of organisms. From this very fact it follows that there are also good reasons to expect the development of communication that enhances mutual cooperation between communicators both in their roles as senders and receivers. This should make «bluff» and «deceit» the exception rather than the rule in dyadic relationships at least in animals living in stable social groups. On the other hand «bluff» and «deceit» should be the rule rather than the exception in triadic communication – the exception being exemplified by types 2 and 4 of Table 2: mutual interest and common gain of members of dyad I and participant II. Finally, there are good reasons to assume that these cooperative communicators are under constant pressure from outside exploiters of their communicatory relationship (types 1 and 3 of Table 2).

In those highly developed forms of communication where mutual benefit for senders and receivers derives from communicating most efficiently in order to make the system most productive for common advantage – dance communication in honeybees being the paragon animal example – we would therefore expect a number of characteristics which enhance the efficiency of communication and make it as resistant as possible to un-cooperative parasitic cheaters from within the group and against exploitation by intruders from outside. A list of these might read like the exact opposite of what DAWKINS and KREBS have emphasized as characteristic features of exploitative communication. Mutualistic communication should be deictic, i. e. directed at specific addresses (GREEN and MARLER 1979) in the most economical way (optimizing the benefit/cost ratio), informing partners as accurately as necessary to achieve the communicative purpose (e. g. by indexing external referents), controlling (e. g. by frequent role change) for fair reciprocation and against in-group exploitation, keeping the whole exchange as private as possible so that unwelcome eavesdroppers and freeriders stay excluded. We therefore would expect such communication to be narrow-cast rather than broadcast, unobtrusive, difficult to discover and recognize by outsiders and unaddressed receivers (including observers).

That means, the very reasons that cause us to understand communication as manipulation force us to conclude that the most developed forms of cooperative communication should not be characterized by spectacular showiness but rather by finely adjusted subtlety (see MARKL 1983). Cooperative communication should express itself rather by delicate directed modulation of the receiver's behavioral tendencies by the sender's signals than by the overwhelming effects of conspicuous advertisement, which leads us to consider the efficiency of communicaton.

3 Modulation – or the efficiency of communication

Efficiency of communication is a vaguely defined and variably used concept. Quite evidently it cannot be measured by the number of kilowatts put into signal production. A lion's thundering roar, a howler monkey's sonorous bellow, a blackbird's resounding aria that precipitates me out of bed at dawn – they are impressive enough for an observer, but they may actually not have very much effect on the addressed receiver and therefore need so much volume to overcome «sales resistance» (see DAWKINS 1982). This reminds us once more that it needs a responsive receiver to be an impressive signaler and very little signal energy may have to be expended if it is awaited by an acutely sensitive detector.

MARKL (1983, see also WILSON 1975, SMITH 1977, SEBEOK 1977, MARLER and VAN-DENBERGH 1979) has considered four approaches to quantify the effectiveness of communication:

1. The *reach R* of a signal, as measured by the distance over which it can be perceived by the addressed receiver, defines the *active space* of communication with respect to that receiver. Since signals can have extremely variable persistance – from practically indefinite (light allowing) in visual badges, over more or less slowly decaying chemical signals to extremely rapidly fading acoustic ones – active space of animal communication has always to be also described in the time dimension. Environmental conditions – by providing the signal-transmitting channel and by loading it with noise – are as decisive for signal reach and detectability as source intensity and receiver sensitivity. The active space – which of course not only determines the area of reach for the addressed receiver but also for any «parasitic» eavesdropper – can for some signal modalities be actively set by the sender by varying radiation intensity (e. g. very easily for sound, hardly at all for visual signals). It can probably always be gradedly controlled by the receiver by modifying response threshold. Receiver-control is ultimately always decisive as every troubadour must doubt-lessly soon have found out. Thus we can say that active space is not only physically constrained but also motivationally controlled. Since sender and receiver motivations can also be under the influence of internal and external stimulation context, signal reach and active space are usually severely dependent on this context (see SMITH 1977 for thorough discussion).

2. Secondly, a signaling system may be rated according to how many receivers can be activated by one sender's signal: we could call this the amplification effect of communication or its *gain G*. It makes, for instance, quite a difference whether a dose of an alarm pheromone activates a dozen workers of an ant colony or whether it makes the whole nest-population pour over an intruder. Evidently this measure of effectiveness is as dependent on signal reach and active space as it is on the population structure of given receivers. This aspect has been quantitatively studied with respect to food or enemy alarm signals in social insects (see VON FRISCH 1965, WILSON 1971, HÖLLDOBLER 1977) or to predator alarm in rodents (e. g. SHERMAN 1981). It has to be emphasized that there must be no direct correlation between ultimate efficiency (see below) and communication gain (though there may be, as in evacuation alarm when social insect colonies are physically endangered).

3. Another aspect of effectiveness of communication – though closely related to the preceding measure – is the thightness of coupling between the occurrence of a signal and the receiver's reaction to it, a variable which is usually quantified by absolute or relative *transmission T* as defined in statistical communication theory (see SHANNON and WEAVER 1949, STEINBERG 1977, LOSEY 1978, MARKO 1983). Gain G quite clearly depends on T, a measure of the probability with which a sender's signal is followed by a change of be-havior in the receiver or of the decrease of uncertainty about the receiver's behavior for an observer if he knows that the signal has occurred (p. 181). Calculation of simple conditional probability of reaction will only do if there is only one clearly defined response to one clear-cut signal. Whenever we have probability distributions of signal and response fields, the influencing and constraining effect of the former on the latter is most easily quantified by T. At first glance this might seem like an ideal measure for signal effectiveness: what could more clearly show a signal's excellent quality than if all receivers without exception promptly react to it upon perception. I will come back to this question and show why this view can be erroneous. As pointed out for active space, transmission, too, is very much under the control of the receivers' motivation that sets reaction threshold and depends itself on internal and external context of stimulation and potentially also on previous experience (though this could be regarded as another internal context variable).

If these factors vary, transmission will hardly ever be all or none (0 or 1); it will depend on all these variables how effectively a signal can manipulate addressed receivers.

4. Though R, G and T quantify measures which can all be somehow related to real

effiency of communication there can be only one way to judge this on an ultimate scale, viz., by determining fitness increments and decrements Δ W for sender and receiver that are the result of their communicatory interactions. That means, we have to find out whether such interactions are of adaptive significance and if so, for whom: the sender, the receiver or for both. Although it is sometimes possible to measure the consequent change in fitness by severing the link between sender and receiver – e. g. if a muted cricket male fails to attract females – often the problem is not as easily solved: how does one eliminate a grin from a chimpanzee's repertoire, or chemical contact signals between bees? Nor will we as a rule be able to measure directly the resulting changes in reproductive success. The usual way to handle this is to select some intermediate indicator as fitness equivalent (e. g. amount of food collected or of weight gained) if it can be safely assumed that there is a monotonous relation between it and the real fitness effect. Once such a measure is available it can now be used to see how the other signs of effectiveness of communication (reach, gain and transmission) relate to it. To rate the efficiency of a particular mode of communication, one has to consider the profit ratio of benefits/costs. That means that communication is always under ergonomic control. Reach R, gain G and transmission T must be set by the selective forces optimizing fitness W (or its equivalent) and are not under selection to maximize R or G or T. Quite evidently there are cost functions of increasing active space (e. g. increased energy expenditure, increased risk of being detected by predators or of attracting competitors), of increasing gain (e. g. if more helpers than necessary to defend and exploit a food source are activated) and of increasing transmission (e. g. if a recruiting signal to one source of food detracts workforce engaged in exploiting another more valuable one). These cost functions have only rarely been estimated; they are specific for each kind of communication in a given species under given environmental conditions and only rarely can they be expected to be linear over their whole range; typically they should go through a minimum.

This allows me now to return to the question left at the end of the preceding section : how should different types of communication systems be most effectively organized? Clearly enough, if the effectiveness in attracting a mate, in deterring a competitor or in alarming from a predator depends on signal intensity and persuasiveness we would expect to find active space, gain and transmission maximized (at least as long as fitness effects for the receiver increase, too; beyond that limit the receiver will set resistive controls). However, even in these examples, signaling intensity will often come under the limiting constraint of exploitative eavesdroppers, as for example when frog-hunting bats or cricket-hunting parasitoids or firefly-hunting fireflies locate their prey by courtship signals (RYAN et al. 1981, TUTTLE et al. 1982, CADE 1979, LLOYD 1977, 1981). Not surprisingly, we often find that broadcast courtship displays are immediately replaced by low-range types of signals as soon as a mate has been attracted at close distance; lovers guard intimacy even in the «cynical» world of animals.

This brings us to the other extreme of communication. While broadcast communication has often been thoroughly analyzed (because it is easily observed, not because it is necessarily most important: ethologists tend to look for the key where the light is, too!) we know much less about that interesting realm of «private» communication which is at the very heart of complex and highly organized animal societies. I have already given the reasons why we should expect communication in such systems to be predominantly low-intensity, narrow-range, low-gain, low-transmission, but as accurately indexical and highly addressed as possible and altogether quite intimate and exclusive to guard from exploitation by unwelcome intruders. We can find *all* of these characteristics most impressively assembled in the honeybees' dances (see VON FRISCH 1965 and LINDAUER; GOULD et al, this volume).

I want to consider here another group of examples from social insects from our own work, which make the extremely different character of this type of communication as compared to broadcast displays even more strikingly evident: communication by *modulating signals* in ants (see Markl 1967, 1983, Markl and Fuchs 1972, Markl and Hölldobler 1978, Fuchs 1976 a, b, Lenoir 1982 for more details). The most typical example is communication by vibration signals which thousands of species of the subfamilies Ponerinae, Pseudomyrmecinae, Myrmicinae (and the living fossil *Nothomyrmecia*: Taylor 1978, Markl and Taylor, unpubl. observ.) produce by abdominal stridulation whenever they are prevented from moving freely. More rarely, stridulation has also been recorded in freely mobile ants, e. g. when in contact with food, enemies, during nest-disturbance or copulation.

The stridulation signal is a unitary signal, though message and meaning (Smith 1977) can vary exceedingly (see below). The *reach* of these signals is small because of their low intensity (10^{-8} W) and their exclusive transmission either in direct contact or as substrate vibrations over a few centimeters or maximally decimeters distance to the vibration-sensitive receivers. The *gain* depends on circumstances, in direct contact it is as low as one, usually less than 10 and only exceptionally does it exceed 100 (e. g. when acting as rescue signal of buried *Atta* queens). If *transmission* is measured by exposing workers, in a paired control situation either inside or outside the nest, to stridulation signals alone, without additional chemical signals, the effect of the signal on the workers' subsequent behavior – though somewhat dependant on the receivers' present occupation, e. g. as food collectors, diggers, scouts or brood attenders – is always exceedingly small. Normalized transmission values (corrected for bias according to Fagen 1978) range between 1 and a few percent (Markl and Hölldobler 1978, Markl unpubl.). That means that maximally a few percent of the information contained in the signal is actually transmitted to the receivers, or that the uncertainty of an observer (inversely related to his probability of guessing it correctly) about what the ants will do after having noticed the stridulation signal is only decreased by these few percent.

According to these three measures, ant stridulation would therefore have to be called a most inefficient way of communication. It barely makes the statistical significance level to qualify as a communication signal at all. This would, however, be a premature conclusion. If one sets up field experiments and lets the signal act in the relevant context of spontaneous usage, it can release quite remarkable behavioral effects in the receivers and can therefore clearly be interpreted as adaptive, i. e. as favoring the colony's fitness. Two points are of interest in this connection: first, the semantic contents (message-meaning) of stridulatory communication depend to a great extent on the appropriate situational context, in fact, they are almost completely determined by it; second, in some situations the effect becomes only fully evident if the stridulation signal is acting combined with other, especially chemical, signals. To give only three examples which have been more thoroughly analyzed up to now:

1. Leafcutting ants *(Atta)* stridulate persistently when trapped under soil in a cave-in of their ground nest. If such a catastrophe – which will destroy the whole colony if the single queen is also trapped and cannot be rescued – has occurred (e. g. after heavy rain or through a predator's attack) many nest mates which have not been caught react sensitively and promptly to soil-conducted stridulatory vibrations by approaching the epicentre of the vibrations and digging for the calling nest-members. This reaction depends not only much on the general stimulus context of the disaster but also on worker occupational «caste»: while soldiers contribute very little, the task class of workers who perform inside nest digging duties are most active at rescue digging, transmission values of signal effect on them sometimes coming close to 50 %. The reach of the signal hardly exceeds a few

decimeters even for the strongest source (the queen). Depending on location of the occurrence up to several hundred workers can be activated by one sender, but again a few tens is more typical. Accuracy of message and mutual benefit for sender and receiver are evident.

2. Some species of harvester ants *(Pogonomyrmex)* of southern US desert regions are exceptional for ants, in that they mate not on the wing but on the ground (HÖLLDOBLER 1976, MARKL et al 1977). While no stridulation signals seem to be involved in mate finding, courtship, and initiating copulation, stridulatory contact vibration of the female is an effective indicator of her unwillingness to accept further copulations after her spermatheca has been filled up; males who still try to lock up with her are thus discouraged and leave the no longer receptive female. Number of observations was not large enough to make a reliable estimate of transmission for this «female liberation signal», however, it is clearly much larger than if one exposes the males to the signals when they are not trying to mate a female. In this situation, the signal acts on the receivers only in direct contact (at minimal reach); the gain can range between the one and a few males that crowd around one female. It can be shown that this communication mutually benefits females and males (who are, as a rule, not genetically related) by saving the males time and thus lost mating chances, and by allowing the females to escape the rather dangerous grasp of overeager lovers. There are therefore also good reasons to assume that the female correctly informs about her lack of inclination for further copulations.

3. These two examples demonstrate that ant stridulation signals are extremely context-dependent as far as their semantic message-meaning contents are concerned. This is also true for the third example which introduces yet another aspect of a modulating signaling system. Workers of the American desert ant *Novomessor* have a remarkable ability to cooperate in retrieving prey which is too large to be dragged to the nest by a single ant. If a worker has for some time unsuccessfully tried to move an attractive piece of food, she begins to release a short-range recruiting pheromone and to stridulate while continuing with her efforts to dislodge the object.

If another nest mate is attracted traveling upwind towards the source of the chemical signal, it will upon contact with the prey and after receiving the stridulatory vibrations produced by the recruiting ant and transmitted through the prey, immediately join in chemical signaling (without being stimulated by vibrations this would take much longer), in stridulating and in trying to drag off the prey. Depending on the size of the object this process continues with rising effect until a large enough workforce is assembled to transport the bounty. Since competition for valuable food is fierce among ants of different species in the desert environment, it could be shown that the vibration-enhanced recruitment process can give *Novomessor* a decisive edge over their many competitors for prey. The reach of the vibration signal is again minimal, but through the combination with pheromones it is amplified up to several meters. The gain is small, from one to at most a dozen workers being activated at a time. Transmission, if measured without the accompanying chemical signal, is again only in the range of a few percent; however, in the relevant context of contact with a fixed prey-object, transmission rate immediately increases with a large proportion of receivers reacting fast to the signal by joining in stridulation, discharging additional recruitment pheromone and tearing wildly on the object.

The important point is here that a signal which by itself and in inappropriate contexts is almost completely unable to influence the behavior of the receivers, can strongly modulate their reaction probability to the contextual stimulation. We have therefore proposed to call such signals *modulating signals,* if they do not release a clear-cut response by themselves but rather alter (modulate) the responsiveness of receivers to other sources of stimulation, either facilitating or inhibiting reaction to them in a way which could be described as changing their state of arousal or attentiveness to other signals.

Mutuality of benefit is in the present example quite obvious. One could also conclude that the signal «informs» the receiver accurately, because signal production is stopped as soon as the prey-object is finally being moved, so that no more workers are attracted than are necessary for the task, an ergonomic measure of communicative efficiency. I have also never seen a finder calling for help and letting others do the carrying for her – as a rule she will be among the ones who drag off the prey.

From the last two examples it is also obvious that the limited reach and small gain of the signal are not signs of its inefficiency but seem rather well adapted to address exactly those receivers which ought to get the message without broadcasting further than necessary and useful.

Stridulatory vibrations are by no means the only mechanical communication signals produced by ants for modulating nestmates' reaction tendencies. In *Camponotus*, MARKL and FUCHS (1972), FUCHS (1976 a, b) have shown that drumming with mandibles and abdominal tip on the thin wooden shells of their tree-nests serves as modulating – facilitating or inhibiting – signal in a wide variety of conditions in highly context dependent ways, thus influencing different forms of alarm reactions, brood transport, colony removal (the latter function can also be taken over by stridulation signals in other species: MASCHWITZ and SCHÖNEGGE 1983, MASCHWITZ pers. comm.). Again, the limited reach, gain and transmission involved seem best suited for a signal that acts to organize limited numbers of workers in a contextually adaptive and ergonomic way. HÖLLDOBLER (1971) found that in *Camponotus socius* contact vibrations motivate workers to follow a recruiting leader to a food source. This is, of course, very similar to the more primitive forms of «dance» communication in bees (LINDAUER 1961, VON FRISCH 1965, MICHENER 1974). Modulating alarm by contact vibration is probably even more widespread in ants. In the primitive ponerine *Amblyopone* it is a prominent response to diverse kinds of disturbances (HÖLLDOBLER 1977, TRANIELLO 1982, HÖLLDOBLER and MARKL, unpubl.) and helps to organize defensive reactions in a variety of ways. In the Australian bulldog ant *(Myrmecia)* sham attacks – the most simple precursor of contact vibration signals – serve as a form of modulating alarm which sets colony members in a state of alert and distributes them over the territory to be defended in the fashion of a most economical random search pattern (MARKL unpubl.) as proven in computer models of these interactions (FREHLAND, KLEUTSCH and MARKL, in preparation), LENOIR (1982) found antennal palpations in *Myrmica* to be a modulating signal involved in controlling trophallactic food flow.

A particularly good example was found in *Oecophylla* by HÖLLDOBLER and WILSON (1978) where rectal gland secretion is combined with a variety of motor signals, depending on context. Most striking is the ritualized «attack-sequence» used as a signal in defence recruitment.

In all of these cases and a number of similar ones from other social insects (e. g. termites: HOWSE 1964) it is clear that the various forms of mechanical communication, often combined with contact- or close-range pheromonal ones, show all the characteristics listed above for an efficient, accurate and ergonomic means of coordinating behavior to the mutual benefit of senders and receivers (who need not even be closely related members of the same colony, see the *Pogonomyrmex* mating example!).

Although these examples have been picked only from social insects this should by no means suggest that modulatory communication as defined here is restricted to these groups. Quite to the contrary, even a cursory search of literature on communication both in animals and in man demonstrates that especially in species living in social groups, but also in solitary ones during more intimate social interactions (as e. g. during mating and broodcare) low-R, G, T-modulating signals for fine control of behavioral coordination are exceedingly common, though they have rarely been thoroughly investigated for obvious methodological reasons. All kinds of signal modalities can be involved with chemical, mimic-gestural, contact-mechanical and low-level acoustical ones predominating, and extreme context dependence seems always characteristic. What is most important, modulating signals are not the exception but rather the rule in communication during close interactions in exclusive social groups, and many examples leave the impression that mutuality of interests and fine-graded accuracy of information transmission may also be more typical than not. In the following, I pick only a small number of examples which can profitably be analyzed under this viewpoint (for sources see Hinde 1972, Ekman 1973, Krames et al. 1974, Weitz 1974, Argyle 1975, Wilson 1975, Argyle and Cook 1976, Sebeok 1977, Smith 1977, Brown 1979, Marler and Vandenbergh 1979, Morris et al. 1979, Pliner et al. 1979, Lewis and Gower 1979, Eibl-Eibesfeldt 1979, 1980, Peters 1980, de Waal 1982, Eisenberg and Kleiman 1983, Halliday and Slater 1983). Rather than referring to numerous specific examples, it may be more useful to try a rough and preliminary semantic classification of those message-meaning relationships in which modulating signal effects are most often to be found.

The «classical» examples are *social facilitation and social inhibition signals* (stigmergie, Stimmungsübertragung, see review by Clayton 1978), whenever the stimulating or inhibiting social influence is not only derived from perceiving other individuals perform «normal» maintenance routine (such as feeding, sleeping, walking, defecating, scratching) but comes from more specific behaviors which can be assumed to be performed or rather to have been selected for exerting a modifying influence on the behavior of receivers. Many mild alarm signals – both intra- and interspecific ones (often intention movements of escape behavior) – do not in fact release escape behavior in receivers by themselves but merely alert them and prepare them to react to additional stimuli, e. g. from an approching predator. For example according to the detailed analysis by Seyfarth et al. (1980, see also Cheney and Seyfarth 1982) the enemy markers of vervet monkeys serve primarily as such behavior modifying alerting signals notwithstanding their referential semantic significance, which makes them «specified» alerters.

Intention movements for leaving a place in group-living species are other typical examples for modulating signals, from jackdaws to baboons or hunting dogs. No less specific modulators can be found in social inhibition, e.g., if animals indicate by special sounds that they are in a socially «withdrawn state», i. e. want to be left alone and are unwilling to interact (see for example for rats Anisko et al. 1978). For a gregarious cricket, Boake and Capranica (1982) have described the function of «courtship» chirping as a comparable interference inhibitor signal.

A second group of modulating signals are *contact signals* which occur very commonly in nearly all kinds of social relationships (mates, parents-offspring, other members of social groups), sometimes in generalized form (e. g. colony odors), in vertebrates more often as individualized signals. They can be olfactory (group and individual odors), gestural («glancing,» see Chance 1967) or acoustical (see for primate examples Snowdon and Cleveland 1980, Cheney and Seyfarth 1982, and for bird duetting Wickler 1980, Wickler and Seibt 1980, 1982). The perception of familiar and regular contact signals keeps the animals in a socially connected and relaxed condition. Loss of contact, i.e., failure to perceive the familiar signals, can then effect behavioral changes, e. g. search. Evidently, there is a close similarity and partly even identity between such modulators and the signals used as familiarity cues which control kin-related behavioral preferences or aversions (see review in Markl 1980; and also Bateson 1980, 1982, McGregor and Krebs 1982, Holmes and Sherman 1983).

A third group of modulating signals is to be found in those cues and behaviors which regulate antagonistic relations in social groups by indicating *social status, dominance* and

submission. Though we often find threat or submission displays which immediately release defined behaviors in the receivers, this could be almost regarded as the breakdown of
the normal uninterrupted flow of more subtle status signals, in which mimic, gestural,
proxemic, acoustic and other expressions merge into a continuous multimedia show of
rank confidence and rank acceptance. Many or most of these elements have to be classified
as modulating signals which are as a rule extremely context dependent (see PRUSCHA and
MAURUS 1975 for one example of a detailed analysis). STAMM (1974) has even suggested
that in laughing gulls there may be a specific «codon» serving similar multi-purpose
pacifying functions as does «please» in human language. Olfactory scent marks, so prominent in mammals, may be regarded as sign posts exerting modulating influence during
spatial competition between different individuals or groups. As such they probably alert
for the detection of other more specific signals, as can introductory alerting notes of some
bird songs (similar to the familiar gong introducing a news broadcast).

A fourth category of modulating signals is difficult to define but may nevertheless be of
more than negligible importance in controlling behavioral tendencies: we may call them
self-communicatory signals (see e. g. GREEN and MARLER 1979, MILLER and INOUYE
1983). «Getting oneself into the mood» by acting as sender and receiver at the same time
is, of course, well known to us from introspection. There is suggestive evidence (e. g. from
acoustic selftutoring) that this also occurs in animals. Evidently, this is the ultimate example of sender-receiver mutuality!

Modulating signals as discussed here have some similarities with priming signals (BOS-
SERT and WILSON 1963), although these have primarily developmental influences, and
with signal modifiers (see e. g. JENSSEN 1979) which, however, qualify or grade displays
rather than modify a receiver's motivations, as modulating signals do. What VON FRISCH
(1965) described as the «vivacity» of the dances of bees which indicates nectar quality and
thus influences foraging motivations of recruits has every characteristic of a modulating
signal, the effects of which depend on the context of a colony's supplies and offers from
other sources.

While modulating signals in animals, though widely occurrent, are certainly only insufficiently understood in syntactic, semantic and pragmatic respects, the literature on human
non-language communication is full of thoroughly analyzed examples of signals that
continuously knit and mend the intricate web of human social relations: mimic, gestural,
postural, kinesic, proxemic, paralinguistic, prosodic and other cues permeate every human
interaction in all the semantic contexts just listed. As has been often pointed out, most
recently in relation to animal communication by DAWKINS and KREBS (1978) and EIBL-
EIBESFELDT (in press), all kinds of expressions of human art and ritual, most convincingly
manifested in music, song and dance, play the communicative roles of motivation modulators – to the extreme of hypnotic spell and trance. One need not, however, dive quite as
deeply into the arcana of the human mind to find suitable examples for modulating signals
in our life: traffic signs, to pick just one, demonstrate the whole gamut from high-effect
releasers to the most subtle and context-dependent modifiers of alertness and attention,
the communicative function of which – when studied in overt behavior and not in linguistic prescription! – is hardly different from some of the forms of alarming vibration signals
in ants.

This brings most forcefully back to our mind that efficiency of communication is only
rarely and under special circumstances a matter of maximizing reach, gain and transmission of signals, as so easily suggested by a purely information-technical approach to
animal communication. Conspicuous is not necessarily important, unobtrusive is not
negligible in animal (and human) communication. Setting R, G, and T rather low sets the
threshold for communicative effects accordingly high, but this avoids the trappings of false
alarm, of overreaction by exaggerated response and of parasitic intrusion.

To come back to the example of information transfer in agonistic display: a game-theoretical analysis of advantages and disadvantages of accurately signaling fighting potential and motivation or of concealing this information leads us to look at conspicuous agonistic displays from a different angle than has traditionally been the case (see Andersson 1980, Moynihan 1982, Maynard Smith 1982). However, one of the consequences of this is that what impresses us most by pompous conspicuousness in threat displays of animals may not be at all what most effectively influences the behavior of the receivers. These displays might well be examples of rather evacuated rhetoric which were formerly used to gauge a sender's potentials and intentions but which, because of this very reason, have been much devalued by imitation and bluff so that no experienced receiver cares for them much any more. At the same time the subtle, not yet ritualized, epiphenomenal indicators of behavioral intentions may be what actually counts in communication – and because this is so, will again stand a good chance of being made more conspicuous by ritualization and then devalued by imitation in due time.

Waves of rising and devaluating fashions of signals and displays would thus propagate through animal social systems just as in our social world propaganda campaigns and fashions become en vogue and fade again in public awareness and published opinion. If there is some truth to this view, theoretical and empirical ethologists alike would be well advised to pay more attention to those subtle signs – however unobtrusive they may seem – which are actually and presently employed to coordinate behavior, the informal ways of handling things, as it were, than to be too easily distracted by the empty rhetoric of highly formalized and stereotyped fossils of yesterday's communication.

4 Information – or transmission in communication

This brings us inevitably to ask once more what it is that is transmitted during communication. Is this a sharing of information as traditionally assumed, or is it the manipulative power of macchiavellian senders which lets receivers dangle on the strings of their mesmerizing signals? But if so, would this not mean too that controlling information has to be transferred to and exerted on the receiver's sensory-nervous-muscular system? Evidently, questions like these cannot be answered lest we first try to agree on how to use the word «information». Hundreds of publications have dwelt on this question. To avoid misunderstandings we have to distinguish between two different meanings of «information».

In one sense it designates, as in common usage, a semantic and pragmatic concept, describing the contents of the signal's message (as inferred from the sender's context-dependent behavior when emitting the signal) and its significance, the meaning for the receiver (as inferred from the receiver's context-dependent reactions upon perceiving the signal), and how both relate to the costs and benefits, i. e. to the fitness effects resulting for sender and receiver from their interaction (see Smith 1977 for details). In this sense information refers to the *biological importance* of the communicative process *for the communicators* under conditions in which it has evolved and developed and to which it is therefore adapted. Obviously, it is very much in the eye of the beholder how this semantic information is evaluated. Information in this sense is not «transferred» at all, it is *by definition* a property of every communicating system, because without adaptive significance for sender or receiver or for both we need not talk about communication at all. Semantic information refers to the coding and decoding rules of the communicators and why they use them. It is also evident that it does not make sense to discuss whether this interactional semantic property is true or false, because this could only be defined by interpretation from an *outside* observer or by postulating that the communicators have *subjective* expectations which can be fulfilled by true or disappointed by false informations, an assumption which not only cannot by proven for animals but mostly is quite unnecessary (see below). Finally, information in this sense must be discussed separately for each specific communication system. Specifically, there is no defined relation between how important a given signal is and how surprising, unexpected, uncertain it is for an observer and how easily he could have guessed its occurrence. If an opponent attacks after a particular highlevel threat display this may not be surprising at all, but it is nevertheless highly important and therefore certainly semantically very informative for the interactants. Just as well, a rare display of a rare animal may occur very unexpectedly and nevertheless be without much significance for a given receiver. As explained above (p. 173), the importance of a piece of information contained in a signal can also not simply be equated with the probability of reaction of a receiver to a signal: it is defined and it is only defined by the fitness consequences resulting from the communicatory interaction for the communicators.

The second sense in which information is used is that of *statistical information theory* (see SHANNON and WEAVER 1949, QUASTLER 1958, ATTNEAVE 1959, STEINBERG 1977, FAGEN 1978, LOSEY 1978, MARKO 1983). Here it is a measure of an *observer's uncertainty* about the occurrence of a particular signal event or of his probability of guessing this occurrence by chance: the more uncertain an observer is about the occurrence of the signal, the less probable it is that he can guess its occurrence, the more information he gains – about this question of non-occurrence or occurrence! – by receiving the signal. This is related to the surprise value of the signal for the observer and the evidence it provides for his decision between different hypotheses about it (PALM 1981). This gain of information in an observer, or the reduction of his uncertainty when observing the occurrence of an event x_i from a probabilistic event field X with k possible event states $(x_1, x_2 \ldots x_i \ldots x_k)$, is usually quantified as Shannon's statistical information measure

$$H(X) = - \sum_{i=1}^{k} p_i \log_2 p_i,$$

with p_i the probability of the ith event of X, which is estimated by n_i/N (n_i number of observations of x_i, N total number of observations of event field X). H(X) is often, though misleadingly, called the entropy of event field X. If A and B are two interacting individuals with – at a given moment – A being regarded as the sender emitting signal a_i from a signal repertoire with s signals $(a_1, a_2 \ldots a_i \ldots a_s)$ and B as the receiver, reacting with response b_j from a repertoire of r responses $(b_1, b_2 \ldots b_j \ldots b_r)$, the average reduction of uncertainty in an observer when signal a_i is produced is H(A), and that when response b_j occurs is H(B). The uncertainty for joint occurrence of a_i b_j is given by H(A, B). Communication can be said to occur if H(A,B) $\neq$ H(A) + H(B) or – as usually expressed – if T (A, B) = H(A) + H(B) – H(A,B) is significantly larger than zero.

For two interacting indiviudals, T measures the tightness of the connection between the probability fields of their signals and responses though it does not establish a causal link nor indicate whether A influences B or vice versa (they could both be dependent on a hidden third variable). To establish causal interdependence, the time relationship between a_i and b_j has to be observed as a first indication – if time relation is not significantly unidirectional, the connection cannot be causal. To really confirm a_i as cause of b_j, the occurrence of a_i should be given by experimental intervention and tested whether b_j follows as probabilistically expected.

The quantity t (A,B) = T (A,B)/H(B) is used to express in normalized fashion (in %) how much uncertainty about the response of B is reduced by knowing which signal A has produced. Unfortunately it has become customary to call the quantity T, which only indicates the tightness of correlation between two nominally scaled probabilistic variables, «transmission», «information transmitted» «transinformation», «shared information» or «synentropy», thus implying that T expresses the quantity of information flowing from sender to receiver, the higher T, the more informative the signal for the receiver. From what has been said it should be clear that it is misleading to thus look at this measure. What it really expresses is the reduction of uncertainty *in an observer of this interaction*, and in this sense the information thus gained by *him*, about the behavior of B upon knowing the behavior of A and viceversa in a given interaction. T says nothing about the significance of the interaction for A or B or both and therefore does not quantify the biological importance of their interaction; and it does not measure what B «gains» from receiving A's signal. It indicates how much the probability distribution of B's behavior changes in an average statistical sense in connection with A's signaling as compared to B's behavior in the absence of A's signal. The expressions «shared information» and «synentropy» if thus interpreted are somewhat less misleading. In fact it might be better to translate T as «tightness» (of correlation) rather than as «transmission».

These considerations seem at first glance to settle the question about whether information flows from sender to receiver: as far as the semantic contents are concerned it does not make much sense to say that the meaning comes from information flowing with the message from the sender to the receiver (except in the trivial sense that the signal precedes the reaction and has to travel – at best with the speed of light – from the first to the latter). As far as Shannon's statistical measure of covariance between the interactants' behavior is concerned, it is again quite misleading to state that y bits of information «flow from» A to B or are shared between them – the flow is in fact one to an outside observer, reducing *his* uncertainty about these joint events, and what is shared is the causal link between signal production and response to it that has been programmed – by evolution or experience – into this relationship. It should be emphasized that in both respects the concept «information» cannot be used without considering both sender and receiver involvement; it is in a semantic as well as in a statistical sense *an interactional property of a relationship between systems,* not some kind of «substance» which either of them can have, share, give, fake or deny.

It would be, however, premature to leave it at that. The reason is that A and B in a bidirectional communication loop really are not only sender and receiver but can also act as observers in the sense described above, thus really drawing information, i. e. reducing their uncertainty, about important aspects of their communicative relationship. This can be best explained by referring to a diagram (Fig. 1) which analyses the different kinds of possible information relations between A and B and their respective external and internal environments.

To understand this, it is important to realize that any probabilistic relationship between two event fields X and Y can be characterized by a T-value which indicates the tightness of correlation between the event states in the two connected fields or the informational, not necessarily causal constraints exerted by one on the other; if the connection is or can be assumed ot be a causal one $(X \rightarrow Y)$, an observer can draw particularly reliable information on what will occur in field Y upon observing event x_i in X, or what had occurred (but was unobservable) in X, from knowing the resultant event in Y (always referring to probabilistic conclusions). With animal A and B communicating (both alternatingly as senders and receivers) one has to consider the informational relationships indicated in Fig. 1, each represented by a T-value, with T significantly > 0 defining the possibility for the observer to

Fig. 1: Communicative relationships between animals A and B. EA, EB: overlapping external situations (environmental context) for A or B, with B's presence being part of EA and viceversa. IA, IB: Internal (motivational) states of A or B. A begins interaction by sending signal SA 1 at time 1; B responds with reaction RB 1 which is at the same time a signal SB 1 that influences response RA 2 of A at time 2; this again is the next signal action SA 2 of A etc. T: statistical information measure («transmission») for the tightness of coupling between the event states connected by lines. Lines with an arrow at one end indicate flow direction of a causal influence; lines without an arrow indicate a purely informational relationship. For the three different types of T see text.

extract useful information from T on the relationships between A, B, their external conditions and their internal constitutional and motivational states.

If A begins to act as a sender of signal SA 1 (e. g. a threat or alarm display), there is a causal relationship between his external situation EA (environment, stimulus context, which may also include the presence of B), his internal state of behavioral tendencies IA (motivation) and the signal selected for emission from an available repertoire. Therefore we can define the three informational relationships T_1, T_2, T_3. T_2 for example, being that between context and signal, i. e. what can be inferred about the external situation of A from knowing that A has produced signal SA 1, thus quantifying the reliability of connection between the signal and an external referent, e. g. the presence of a specific enemy or a mate. If A can monitor his own signal production and feed this back to his own internal state, we have another relation between SA 1 and IA, characterized by T_4, which in recurrent relationship with T_3 relates to what we might call «display management» of A or «self-communication» (see p. 186).

Assume that B perceives SA 1 and reacts by response RB 1 to it (e. g. a counter-threat display). This connection is represented by T_5, the classical «transmission» of statistical communication analysis, a measure of the constraint imposed on B's behavior by A's signaling. It need not be pointed out in detail that the relationships between B's environmental context EB (which may include A's presence again), its internal motivational state IB, the response RB 1 and its feedback on IB are all symmetrical to the conditions described for A and defined by their respective T-values (drawn but not numbered in Fig. 1 so as to avoid making the Figure even more complicated).

As a rule, response RB 1 will be monitored by A, thus closing the bidirectional communication loop («response monitoring»), influencing A's behavioral state (T_6), and allowing A to change its consecutive actions accordingly («impression or effect management», see Goffman 1959, Snyder 1979). In this respect, response RB 1 acts at the same time as a signal SB 1 which influences A's behavior. This influence adds at that stage to the combined action of EA and IA in determining the next action of A (represented by T_7) which can be regarded as a new signal SA 2 (e. g. a form of attack) or as response RA 2 to B's signal SB 1. The relationship between SB 1 and RA 2 is characterized by T_8 (which could be called «backward tranmission» if T_5 is seen as the «forward transmission»). Another important informational (not causal!) relationship is that between signals SA 1 and SA 2, given by T_9. SA 2 then can release response RB 2 (e. g. escape) in B, and so on.

Highly abstract as this may seem, all of these communicative or informational relationships are of importance in fully accounting for this simple, two-stage communication process between A and B. These 9 different relationships and T-values fall into 3 different groups according to whether and for which observer they are available from empirical evidence, reducing the observer's uncertainty.

1. T_1, T_3, T_4, T_6, T_7 all involve the «internal motivational state» of A which is not directly observable, let alone measurable, either for B or for an outside observer, who, however, may try to estimate it from presumed physiological correlates of IA. These T-values are therefore for principal reasons rather *theoretical constructs* than empirical variables. IA would, of course, be accessible for A himself: however, to treat $T_{1,3,4,6,7}$ as «real» for A, means postulating that A contains an «internal observer» as an own cognitive entity, separate from IA, that can compare the state of IA with those of other event fields to which IA is connected, and thus gain the information represented by $T_{1,3,4,6,7}$. This is an epistemologically critical issue and I will return to it in a moment.

2. T_5 and T_8 are only available to an *outside observer* – no wonder that they play a decisive role as «transmissions» in theory and practice of animal communication (see «transmission T», p. 173). They do not, to repeat it again, represent «pieces of information» flowing from A to B or back, but probabilistic constraints imposed upon each other's behavior by the communicating individuals. At first glance, T_5 and T_8 might be also regarded as being available for the interactants themselves (T_5 for B, T_8 for A). This need not imply «internal observers» in the same sense as just discussed. However, it seems fallacious for another reason: B cannot reduce any uncertainty from «observing» that it has responded with RB 1 to SA 1, because it already knows for certain that it has done so; therefore: no uncertainty reduced, no information gained, no transmission to talk about, – except in a rather schizophrenic view of animal B containing an «internal observer» which has no access to IB and therefore responds with surprise when noticing B (that is: itself!) produce RB 1 upon receiving SA 1.

3. Finally, T_2 and T_9 are most important, because they represent variables which are available from empirical observation to the *communicating animals* (at least in principle). Both represent informational, not direct causal links, since EA acts on SA 1, and SA 1 on SA 2, not directly but only through IA! From T_2 B can learn about the environmental context of A when producing SA 1, unless B itself shares this context completely with A; it is therefore representing *referential information* given by A on its external environment. With $T_2 > 0$ and B being able to extract this information from SA 1 (which is not proven by $T_2 > 0$, but has to be established *separetely* in suitable experiments, see for example the

honeybee dance language controversy about this, GOULD 1976), as has been demonstrated for honey bees, vervet monkeys (SEYFARTH et al. 1980) and chimpanzees (see review by RISTAU and ROBBINS 1982) this can be called *indexical* or even *descriptive communication*.

T_9 represents the reduction in uncertainty – for observer B if it is programmed to or has learned to extract this information, but of course also for an outside observer – about A's action SA 2 (RA 2) if its action SA 1 is known to the observer. It therefore represents *predictive information* about A for the observer. The discussion (referred to above, p. 168 f) about whether signals accurately inform about the sender's intentions (IA), and therefore are reliable predictors of the sender's future actions, refers to *this* information relationship only. As can be easily seen now, the first part of this question relates to T_3 and T_7 and is unanswerable because of the principal methodological constraints mentioned; it is therefore not a particularly useful question to ask at all (nor can it be regarded as useful to answer it in the affirmative from intuitional conviction) because it mixes statements pertaining to the subjective and the objective realms of experience. The second part is a useful and empirically answerable question – a CARYL (1979) has convincingly demonstrated – but, alas, there is no general theory which could predict that T_9 has to be either 0 (no predictive value of SA 1 for SA 2 whatsoever) or 1 (totally deterministic relation between the two). Much rather we would expect $0 < T_9 < 1$ (as CARYL has found indeed) with the actual values having to be determined for each particular communicative process. What we can expect from theory is that in some (e. g. agonistic) relationships T_9 should be smaller than in others (e. g. broodcare).

Evidently, whether SA 1 is accurate or «bluff» has actually nothing at all to do with the magnitude of T_9. In fact, this question pertains to an entirely different way of looking at the system. What could it mean to say that SA 1 is «deceptive»? Leaving the question of intention for a moment aside, the only way to sensibly introduce the concept of «deception» or «honesty» into the system represented in Fig. 1, would be to call an equality between T_7 and T_9 honesty and to speak of deception if T_9 is not equal to T_7, because the «honest informer» concept assumes that signal SA 1 given at time 1 accurately predicts the conditions in A (IA) at time 2 which will make A produce SA 2. However, simply for logical reasons, it cannot be assumed that $T_7 = T_9$, for instance because T_7 is the result of influences (represented by T_6) on A which occur *after* A has produced SA 1, not to mention other possible influences (e. g. from EA) and state changes of IA (e. g. represented by T_4) between times 1 and 2.

Does that mean that signal SA 1 cannot be an «honest predictor» and therefore must be «deceitful»? This would be a rash conclusion, mainly because it amounts to an entirely inappropriate usage of words and concepts. Even if A «honestly» expressed IA at time 1 by SA 1 and IA at time 2 in SA 2, and so on, SA 1 might still be a poor predictor of SA 2. Evidently, it is wrong to use the terms «honest» or «deceptive» at all in this connection. It is wrong, first, because neither B nor an outside observer can observe IA, T_3 or T_7 directly, thus making it impossible to empirically test the hypotheses $T_7 = T_9$ or $T_7 \neq T_9$. Second, and more important, because for any acceptable way of usage of the concept «deception» it seems impossible to not postulate an «internal observer» in A which not only has to be able to «extract» T_3 and T_7, but also to intervene in the production of signals by A so that not the true state IA is expressed by the signal but some virtual state, so that B's behavior is misled. Ascribing not only the cognitive entity «internal observer» to A but also giving it the power for deceitful intervention into signal production by A is tantamount to ascribing «intention» – namely to deceive – to A (which may imply to ascribe consciousness). Thus either one has to take this position and then may talk about «honest» or «deceptive» signaling – though without being able to operationally define and empirically test the correctness of these attributions – a standpoint which will be difficult to reconcile with accepted scientific procedure; or, one cannot apply these attributions; or, if one does so, must use the words relating to them incorrectly. The disclaimer that no assumption of conscious intent is meant to be implied with the usage of these terms, can thus only be regarded as pious self-deception. I would therefore suggest to regard the question of «honesty» or «deceptiveness» of displays as terminologically and epistemologically fallacious, a red herring of animal communication research at least as long as we deal with animals for which we are not compelled by convincing evidence to postulate an «internal observer».

The fully legitimate and important quenstion of whether signals should allow the prediction of future actions of a sender or not, cannot be answered theoretically in a general way. The answer depends, as discussed above (p. 168) on the ratio of benefit to cost of different values of T_9 for the sender, on the selective pressures exerted by the sender on the receiver and viceversa (via the ways represented by T_5, T_8) in communication, and thus ultimately on the fitness effects for the interactants. All this has nothing to do with one interactant informing the other more or less honestly; it rather means that all «transmission» values considered in Fig. 1 are under selection both on A and B for optimizing their fitness. If it increases the fitness of A to increase, e. g., the «referential information» T_2, or the «predictive information» T_9, selection will favor such increase; if not, not. If it increases the fitness of B to extract these informations from A's behaviors, selection will favor development of such observers' qualifications in B; if not, resistance in B will be favored against reacting to A's signals. Selection on the sender will favor exploitation of the receiver and selection on the receiver resistance against being exploited. If both parties gain from unexploitative, equitable communicative cooperation, such mutualism will be favored by selection on both of them.

The question posed in the beginning of what is being transferred, and, specifically, whether accurate information is transmitted by a signal in animal communication, thus resolves itself on close inspection into a series of separate questions about the manifold informational relationships in a communicative process. This leads to the hardly surprising general conclusion that the fitness effects of communication on both communicators determine how «informative» (in the sense of statistical information theory) these relationships will be for different types of observers. It does not make much sense to make a general statement that information is transmitted in communication; information is a property of the communicative interaction which cannot be treated in isolation from either of both interactants. Nor does this mean that no information can be transmitted under any circumstances. It all depends on what one is talking about.

5 Cognition – or the power of communication

To be critical about the unwarranted introduction of an «internal observer» in explaining animal communication in general should not, however, lead us to disregard the evident fact that at least in one species – our own – we know that such a conscious internal observer participates most influentially in communication. As the quip goes it makes all the difference whether «the brain has been switched on before operating the mouth» or not. Referring again to Fig. 1, where we only find the most parsimonious assumption about self-communication represented by the feedback-lopp $T_3 - T_4$, we have to expand this model in order to accommodate the participant mind by adding a separate entity – the internal observer – which stands in bidirectional informational relationship with IA, that we can call *internal communication*. In addition to the feedback from a partner's response

– which serves in *impression* or *signal effect management* – and the self-monitoring feedback from A's own signals – which serves in *display management* – we thus have a third level of communicative control, *self-image management*, which coordinates the mental representations of the actor, his theory of the self with its properties, abilities, fears and desires, with the mental representation of the environment, his theory of the outside world. Evidently, this additional level of internal communicative performance supplies us with the capacity to control our outward directed communication by experience gained from internal communication within our model of self and world representations.

Animals on the level of Fig. 1 can only cope with the challenges posed by interactions with other animals by communicating according to the present state of their programs – as introduced into them by evolutionary endowment or individual experience – at best correcting and adjusting these programs step by step according to the results of behavioral performance.

In contrast, a system that is capable of internal communication within conceptual models can self-instruct its programs according to internally pretested and thus anticipated consequences of using them. The vastly expanded power of this capability for behavior preconsidered by internal communication, whether resulting in deliberate altruism or premeditated felony, need not be pointed out. Honesty or deceit are no longer non-parsimonious modes of metaphorical parlance but real attributes of systems working with internally observing, thinking minds.

It is therefore only too natural that the «cognitive ethologist» should try to use the door opened by communication to an animal's inner world in order to find out whether the machine is inhabited by such an internal agent or only equipped to act out its programs (see GRIFFIN 1981 for the discussion of the aspirations and problems raised by this endeavour). Since the «perfected» state of mental development of our species is the result of a long evolutionary history, efforts have been made to trace the development of the way from animal mind to human mind (see CROOK 1980, GRIFFIN 1982). A most important step for giving a system the superior power provided by internal communication, is to enable it to put itself in the place of the external communication partner (empathy), or more correctly, to let it conceive an internal model of the partner's properties, intentions and behaviors and to interact cognitively with this model (see STENT 1978 for further discussions fo this view).

Now, even the most primitive forms of animal communication contain what may be the most decisive prerequisite for this development; the ability, even the necessity for each animal to function simultaneously and alternatingly as sender *and* as receiver of signals. This entails that – if the other with whom one communicates is not entirely different from oneself and it cannot be so, if at least some kind of reciprocal communication is to come about – the partner is in some respect already represented in oneself in the form of one's own alternate state of communicating. The animal that emits a specific signal contains at the same time at least some information on how to react to a similar signal which must overlap with that present in the receiving partner, and vice versa. The evolution of the «internal observer» could thus be viewed as the operational concentration of all the information that can represent the other interactant and the establishment of this representational unit in the central nervous system so that an *internal dialogue* can begin that precedes the overt external signal exchange. If there is some truth to this view this would mean that the development of the conscious mind is inseparable from the development of an internal operational representation of the communication partner in order to control more efficiently one's interaction with one's social environment. Thus the self could only define, i.e. demarcate itself by conceptually incorporating the interactant as partner of one's internal communication.

The development of advanced and intensive social cooperation would thus seem a prerequisite of the development of a conscious self. Just as – in the view of Ch. S. PEIRCE and C. W. MORRIS (see MORRIS 1946) nothing can be a sign without an object to which it refers and without an interpreter that responds to it, making the information contained in the sign a triadic relational quality, it could be that the power of the internal information processing that we call thinking could not develop without the internal representation of both communicators with the vis-à-vis being modeled from the ambivalent self-experience of a janus-headed sender-receiver-communicator. The ability to deceive the outside partner by a lie would then depend on the ability to tell its internal representation the truth, because only by internally rating the partner's presumed response to a signal can it become possible to change the display until the anticipated response suits one's own purposes.

This is, however, only one way of looking at the relationship between communication and cognition.

What is cognition? We may call it the ability to relate different unconnected informations in new ways and to apply the results of this in an adaptive manner, i. e. to solving one's problems. We know that (though hardly how) we do this by thinking in our minds. We are, however, also aware that there is a specific kind of thinking that is fueled by communicating with others. J. VON LIEBIG is said to have confessed to rarely having had a good idea, except if somebody else suggested anything: then he immediately had a better idea. This wellknown experience deserves further elaboration in the present context.

Communication in a social environment can not only sharpen an individual's acuity of cognition. The social organization can, by communicatory processes, itself develop the properties of a problem solving, cognitive system that transcends the cognitive capacities of individual participants even though it is entirely based on their contributions to the communicative interactions. To regard societies as supraorganismic systems with emergent properties is of course not new. We can find this view – in a sometimes more, sometimes less metaphorical fashion – in leading students of social insects (like W. M. WHEELER or A. E. EMERSON) as well as in many eminent observers of human sociology from ADAM SMITH to F. VON HAYEK, and even applied to the entire biosphere (see LOVELOCK 1979). What deserves emphasis in the present connection is that among the emergent properties of such supraindividual systems there is one that seems most intimately related to the communicative mechanisms that coordinate the complex workings of these systems: the invention of social adaptations which have all the characteristics of cognitive problem solving, of relating the information available to the single individuals in such a way as to produce novel solutions for the challenges and exigencies of life, not at the individual, but at the group level. The «invisible hand» that seems to guide the communal activities for the benefit of the whole system could then be seen as directed by an «invisible brain», the functional elements of which are the individual communicating members which are connected by a web of informational relationships, the most primitive core of which would be represented by the transmission-network in Fig. 1.

Ensemble performances are, of course, particularly evident in the amazing constructions of many social animals as KARL VON FRISCH so vividly described late in his life (1974). Although it could be argued that a honeybees' comb gives expression of the recognition of basic laws of material science, fluid and structural mechanics, and of solving the problems of storing large quantities of highly concentrated and perishable food over many months, we would ordinarily not be inclined to see more than metaphor in expressing these facts in a language inplying «cognition». However, there is a gradual, not categorical transition from these crystallized relics of behavior to behavioral processes, where we have to concede that the interaction group performs through communication and cooperation in a way that is not principally different from the outward behavioral expression of problem solving of a cognitive system (the assumption of conscious thinking being neither necessary in the one nor in the other case).

This idea can be elaborated by a few examples from social insects in an ascending scale of complexity:

– A most simple case is represented by the workers of the ant *Novomessor* which cooperatively transport large prey (see p. 176). Although the single worker is neither able to estimate the weight of a grasshopper, too large to be carried alone, nor to judge how many helpers would be needed to move the object, a complex communication system makes sure that the necessary workforce – and not much more – assembles fast and thus performs the transport at low cost and with high efficiency (HÖLLDOBLER et al. 1978, MARKL and HÖLLDOBLER 1978).

– Colonies of the bulldog ant *Myrmecia* have to guard an area of dozens of square meters around their nest against intruders with a workforce of only a few scores of individuals. They achieve this by a contact alarm system in combination with a random search technique that allows them to cover the area thoroughly with minimum personnel (MARKL, FREHLAND, KLEUTSCH unpubl.).

– Workers of different colonies of the honeypot ant *Myrmecocystus* engage in fighting tournaments in which they rate the strength of the enemy force in ritualized mass displays, thus gaining information on relative fighting strength (RHP) and deciding accordingly to attack, withstand or withdraw, an ensemble decision with all characteristics of a cognitive evaluation of the situation (HÖLLDOBLER 1983, LUMSDEN and HÖLLDOBLER 1983).

– One of the most complex achievements of an «ensemble cognitive process» is the decision finding about moving into a new home by a honeybee swarm: scouts that have discovered a suitable dwelling and investigated its quality according to well-defined bee public housing norms, return to the swarm and advertise their discovery in competition with other bidders, indicating the quality of their find by the vivacity and obstinacy of their dance. In an extended and sometimes even swarm-rending procedure, the receivers of these messages decide in ensemble fashion which offer to prefer (LINDAUER 1955, 1961, SEELEY 1977). It is hardly possible to describe what occurs in such a swarm without using vocabulary that implies that a higher-order cognitive performance is achieved during this process.

This brings us back once more to the importance of modulating signals in these communication processes. Many of the signal effects observed during these performances are not of the high-transmission, releaser kind, but rather ones that subtly modify the behavioral properties of the receivers, alerting them and focussing their attention to the situational context. It seems inevitable to compare the coordinating mechanisms active in such a «cognitive ensemble» with the interactive neuronal processes that presumably endow a central nervous system with its acknowledged cognitive capacities. It is remarkable that in the brain as in the social system we find mechanisms that set the overall level of arousal.

Tonic sensory input form a variety of sensory organs and spontaneous activity of neural arousal systems perform in the nervous system the functions that unspecific modulating alarm signals serve in social organizations.

In both forms of organization we further find more specific, as it were, regionalized or addressed mechanisms of focussing the attention to a specified subset of stimuli in a given context. Furthermore we find that within the larger systems mechanisms exist which modulate in graded fashion the activity probability of small dedicated subpopulations of neurons or individuals which are thus recruited to performing specified tasks. It is probably more than chance that the neurophysiologist arrives at describing these mechanisms as local modulating interactions between neurons just as the student of social communication in animals independently finds it appropriate to qualify basic processes of social organization in this way. It seems more convincing to accept that at the level of the highly organized, complex society we find a functional systemic correlate of what also occurs at the multicellular level of an individual organism (for a review of arousal and modulating mechanisms in nervous systems of invertebrates and vertebrates, see BULLOCK and HORRIDGE 1965, FLOREY 1967, SCHMITT et al. 1976, EVANS 1978, EVANS and O'SHEA 1978, HOYLE and DAGAN 1978, DISMUKES 1979, LAMING 1981, FREDERICKSON and GEARY 1982, JONES 1982, BLOOM 1983, IVERSEN 1983).

LUMSDEN (1982) has applied a very similar view to an explanation of the division of labor by dividing up the workforce of an insect society into distinct physical castes, and has shown that these supraorganismal achievements can be treated by rigorous theory (see also FRANKS and WILSON in this volume). This opens the even wider view of regarding one of the most basic elements of cooperation between members of an animal species – that between the sexes – as an expression of supraorganismal problem solving.

To view social systems as higher-level «organisms» characterized by emergent qualities notwithstanding the fact that each of their members strives to maximize its own (though inclusive) fitness, is – as was said before – not at all new.

The study of communication goes beyond the metaphor, however, by analysing the mechanisms that enable a society to achieve these ensemble performances and to unravel the mutualistic informational networks that are so tightly knit as to assume the properties of cognitive, problem-solving entities that process information in highly coordinated fashion and adapt to changes in the environment by discovering new solutions, by learning from experience and by establishing stores of knowledge in social traditions.

There is a long way to this stage of development from two solitary animals opposing each other over a desired resource, trying to arrive at their goal at minimal cost by employing browbeating signals rather than beating each other by violent force. There is, of course, nothing wrong about looking at animal communication from below, where it starts. Only one should not stop there. It would seem that one cannot get a comprehensive impression of what animal communication can be unless one also has looked at it from the top of achievement, where it is at its best in welding a cooperative whole out of numerous independently acting parts. It seems only appropriate to call this the KARL VON FRISCH-view of animal communication.

Acknowledgement

BERT HÖLLDOBLER and JOHN KREBS have read and commented on the manuscript. Their suggestions were highly appreciated.

References

Andersson, M. (1980): Why are there so many threat displays. J. theor. Biol. 86, 773–781.
Anisko, J. J., Suer, Sh. F., McClintock, M. K., Adler, N. T. (1978): Relation between 22-kHz ultrasonic signals and sociosexual behavior in rats. J. Comp. Physiol. Psychol. 92, 821–829.
Argyle, M. (1975): Bodily communication. Methuen, London.
Argyle, M., Cook, M. (1976): Gaze and mutual gaze. Cambridge Univ. Press, Cambridge.
Attneave, F. (1959): Applications of information theory to psychology. Holt, Rinehart, Winston, New York.
Axelrod, R., Hamilton, W. D. (1981): The evolution of cooperation. Science 211, 1390–1396.
Axelrod, R. (1984): The evolution of cooperation. Basic Books, New York.
Barnard, C. J., Burk, T. (1979): Dominance hierarchies and the evolution of «individual recognition». J. Theor. Biol. 81, 65–73.

Barnard, C. J., Burk, T. (1981): Individuals as assessment units. J. theor. Biol. 88: 595–598.

Bateson, P. P. (1980): Optimal outbreeding and the development of sexual preferences in Japanese quail. Z. Tierpsychol. 53, 231–244.

Bateson, P. P. (1982): Preferences for cousins in Japanese quail. Nature 295, 236–237.

Bloom, F. E. (1983): The endorphins: a growing family of pharmacologically pertinent peptides. Ann. Rev. Pharmakol. Toxicol. 23, 151–170.

Boake, Ch., Capranica, R. R. (1982): Aggressive signal in «courtship» chirps of a gregarious cricket. Science 218, 580–582.

Bossema, I., Burgler, R. R. (1980): Communication during monocular and binocular looking in European jays (Garrulus g. glandarius). Behaviour 74, 274–283.

Bossert, W. H., Wilson, E. O. (1963): The analysis of olfactory communication among animals. J. theor. Biol. 5, 443–469.

Breed, M. D., Bekoff, M. (1981): Individual recognition and social relationships. J. theor. Biol. 88, 589–594.

Brown, R. E. (1979): Mammalian social odors: a critical review. Adv. Study Behav. 10, 103–162.

Bullock, Th. H., Horridge, G. A. (1965): Structure and function in the nervous systems of invertebrates. 2 vol. Freeman, San Francisco.

Burghardt, G. M. (1970): Defining communication, p. 5–18, in: J. W. Johnston, D. G. Moulton, A. Turk (eds.) Communication by chemical signals. Appleton-Century-Crofts, New York.

Cade, W. (1979): The evolution of alternative male reproductive strategies in field crickets. p. 343–380 in: M. S. Blum, N. A. Blum (eds.) Sexual selection and reproductive competition in insects. Academic Press, New York.

Caryl, P. G. (1979): Communication by agonistic displays: what can games theory contribute to ethology? Behaviour 68, 136–169.

Caryl, P. G. (1981): Escalated fighting and the war of nerves: games theory and animal combat. p. 199–224 in: P. P. G. Bateson, P. H. Klopfer (eds.): Perspectives in Ethology 4, Plenum, New York.

Caryl, P. G. (1982): Animal signals: a reply to Hinde. Anim. Behav. 30, 240–244.

Chance, M. R. (1967): Attention structure as the basis of primate rank orders. Man 2, 503–518.

Cheney, D. L., Seyfarth, R. M. (1982 a): Recognition of individuals within and between groups of free ranging vervet monkeys. Amer. Zool. 22, 519–529.

Cheney, D. L., Seyfarth, R. M. (1982 b): How vervet monkeys perceive their grunts: field playback experiments. Anim. Behav. 30, 739–751.

Cherry, C. (1978): On human communication. MIT Press, Cambridge.

Clayton, D. A. (1978): Socially facilitated behavior. Quart. Rev. Biol. 53, 373–393.

Crook, J. H. (1980): The evolution of human consciousness. Clarendon Press, Oxford.

Dawkins, R. (1982): The extended phenotype. Freeman, San Francisco.

Dawkins, R., Krebs, J. R. (1978): Animal Signals: Information or manipulation? p. 282–309 in: J. R. Krebs, N. B. Davies (eds.) Behavioural Ecology. Blackwell, Oxford*.

Dawkins, R., Krebs, J. R. (1979): Arms races between and within species: Proc. R. Soc. Lond. B 205, 489–511.

de Waal, F. (1982): Chimpanzee Politics. Cape, London.

Dismukes, R. K. (1979): New concepts of molecular communication among neurons. Behav. Brain Sciences 2, 409–448.

Eibl-Eibesfeldt, I. (1979): Human ethology: concepts and implications for the sciences of man. Behav. Brain Sciences 2, 1–57.

Eibl-Eibesfeldt, I. (1980): Strategies of social interaction p. 57–80 in: Emotion. Theory, Research and Experience. Vol. 1, Theories of Emotion.

Eibl-Eibesfeldt, I.: The biological foundations of aesthetics (in press.).

Eisenberg, J. F., Kleiman, D. G. (eds.) (1983): Advances in the study of mammalian behavior. Amer. Soc. Mammal. Special Publ. No 7.

Ekman, P. (ed.) (1973): Darwin and facial expression. Acad. Press, New York.

Evans, P. D. (1978): Octopamine: from metabolic mistake to modulator. TINS 1, 154–157.

---

* Note added in proof: the revised 2nd edition (1984) of this book has not been available before this article was finished.

Evans, P. D., O'Shea, M. (1978): The identification of an octopaminergic neurone and the modulation of a myogenic rhythm in the locust. J. exp. Biol. 73, 235–260.

Fagen, R. M. (1978): Information measures: statistical confidence limits and inference. J. theor. Biol. 73, 61–79.

Fischer, E. A. (1980): The relationship between mating system and simultaneous hermaphroditism in the coral reef fish, Hypoplectus nigricans (Serranidae). Anim. Behav. 28, 620–633.

Florey, E. (1967): Neurotransmitters and modulators in the animal kingdom. Fed. Proc. 26, 1164–1178.

Frederickson, R. C., Geary, L. E. (1982): Endogenous opioid peptides: review of physiological, pharmacological and clinical aspects. Progr. Neurobiol. 19, 19–69.

Fuchs, S. (1976 a): The response to vibrations of the substrate and reactions to the specific drumming in colonies of carpenter ants (Camponotus, Formicidae, Hymenoptera) Behav. Ecol. Sociobiol. 1, 155–184.

Fuchs, S. (1976 b): An informational analysis of the alarm communication by drumming behavior in nests of carpenter ants (Camponotus, Formicidae, Hymenoptera). Behav. Ecol. Sociobiol. 1, 315–336.

Goffman, E. (1959): The presentation of self in everyday life. Doubleday Anchor, Garden City.

Goffman, E. (1969): Strategic Interaction. Basil Blackwell, Oxford.

Gould, J. L. (1976): The dance-language controversy. Quart. Rev. Biol. 51, 211–244.

Green, S., Marler, P. (1979): The analysis of animal communication, p. 73–158 in: P. Marler, J. G. Vandenbergh (eds.): Handbook of Behavioral Neurobiology 3. Social Behavior and Communication. Plenum, New York.

Griffin, D. R. (1981): Animal Mind-Human Mind. Dahlem Konferenzen 21 Springer, Berlin.

Griffin, D. R. (1982): The Question of Animal Awareness. Rockefeller Univ. Press, New York.

Halliday, T. R., Slater, P. J. B. (eds.) (1983): Animal Behavior. 2. Communication. Blackwell, Oxford.

Hinde, R. A. (ed.) (1972): Non-verbal Communication. Cambridge Univ. Press, Cambridge.

Hinde, R. A. (1981): Animal signals: ethological and games-theory approaches are not incompatible. Anim. Behav. 29, 535–542.

Hölldobler, B. (1971): Recruitment behavior in Camponotus socius (Hym. Formicidae). Z. vergl. Physiol. 75, 123–142.

Hölldobler, B. (1976): The behavioral ecology of mating in harvester ants (Hymenoptera: Formicidae: Pogonomyrmex). Behav. Ecol. Sociobiol. 1, 405–423.

Hölldobler, B. (1977): Communication in social hymenoptera p. 418–471 in: Th. A. Sebeok (ed.): How animals communicate. Indiana Univ. Press, Bloomington.

Hölldobler, B. (1983): Chemical manipulation, enemy specification and intercolony communication in ant communities. p. 354–365 in: F. Huber, H. Markl (eds.): Neuroethology and Behavioral Physiology. Springer, Berlin.

Hölldobler, B., Wilson, E. O. (1978): The multiple recruitment systems of the African weaver ant Oecophylla longinoda (Latreille) (Hymenoptera: Formicidae): Behav. Ecol. Sociobiol. 3, 19–60.

Holmes, W. G., Sherman, P. W. (1983): Kin recognition in animals. Amer. Sci. 71, 46–55.

Howse, P. E. (1964): The significance of the sound produced by the termite Zootermopsis angusticollis (Hagen). Anim. Behav. 12, 284–300.

Hoyle, G., Dagan, D. (1978): Physiological characteristics and reflex activation of DUM (octopaminergic) neurons of locust metathoracic ganglion. J. Neurobiol. 9, 59–79.

Jenssen, T. A. (1979): Display modifiers of Anolis opalinus (Lacertilia: Iguanidae) Herpetologica 35, 21–30.

Jones, R. S. G. (1982): Tryptamine: a neuromodulator or neurotransmitter in mammalian brain? Progr. Neurobiol. 19, 117–139.

Iversen, L. L. (1983): Nonopioid neuropeptides in mammalian CNS. Ann. Rev. Pharmacol. Toxicol. 23, 1–27.

Krames, L., Pliner, P., Alloway, Th. (eds.) (1974): Nonverbal communication. Plenum, New York.

Laming, P. R. (1981): The physiological basis of alert behavior in fish. p. 202–222 in: P. R. Laming (ed.) Brain mechanisms of behaviour in lower vertebrates. Soc. Exp. Biol. Sem. Ser. 9 Cambridge Univ. Press, Cambridge.

Lenoir, A. (1982): An informational analysis of antennal communication during trophallaxis in the ant *Myrmica rubra* L. Behav. Processes 7, 27–35.

Lewis, D. B., Gower, D. M. (1980): Biology of Communication. Blackie, Glasgow.

Lindauer, M. (1955): Schwarmbienen auf Wohnungssuche. Z. vergl. Physiol. 37, 263–324.

Lindauer, M. (1961): Communication among social bees. Harvard Univ. Press, Cambridge.

Lloyd, J. E. (1977): Bioluminescence and communication. p. 164–183 in: The. A. Sebeok: How Animals Communicate. Indiana Univ. Press, Bloomington.

Lloyd, J. E. (1981): Mimicry in the sexual signals of fireflies. Sci. Amer. 245, 111–117.

Losey, G. S. (1978): Information theory and communication. p. 43–78 in: P. W. Colgan (ed.): Quantitative Ethology. Wiley, New York.

Lovelock, J. E. (1979): Gaia. Oxford Univ. Press, Oxford.

Lumsden, Ch. J. (1982): The social regulation of physical caste: the superorganism revived. J. theor. Biol. 95, 749–781.

Lumsden, Ch. J., Hölldobler, B. (1983): Ritualized combat and intercolony communication in ants. J. theor. Biol. 100, 81–98.

Markl, H. (1967): Die Verständigung durch Stridulationssignale bei Blattschneiderameisen. I. Die biologische Bedeutung der Stridulation. Z. vergl. Physiol. 57, 299–330.

Markl, H. (1983): Vibrational Communication. p. 332–353 in: F. Huber, H. Markl (eds.): Neuroethology and Behavioral Physiology. Springer, Berlin.

Markl, H. Fuchs, S. (1972): Klopfsignale mit Alarmfunktion bei Roßameisen (*Camponotus*, Formicidae, Hymenoptera). Z. vergl. Physiol. 76, 204–225.

Markl, H., Hölldobler, B. (1978): Recruitment and food-retrieving behavior in *Novomessor* (Formicidae, Hymenoptera). II. Vibration signals. Behav. Ecol. Sociobiol. 4, 183–216.

Markl, H., Hölldobler, B., Hölldobler, T. (1977): Mating behavior and sound production in harvester ants (*Pogonomyrmex*, Formicidae): Insectes Sociaux 24, 191–212.

Marko, H. (1983): Information theory and communication theory. p. 788–794 in: W. Hoppe, W. Lohmann, H. Markl, H. Ziegler (eds.): Biophysics. Springer, Berlin.

Marler, P., Vandenberg, J. G. (1979): Handbook of Behavioral Neurobiology 3. Social Behavior and Communication. Plenum, New York.

Maschwitz, U., Schönegge, P. (1983): Forage communication, nest moving recruitment, and prey specialization in the oriental ponerine *Leptogenys chinensis*. Oecologia (Berlin) 57, 175–182.

Maynard Smith, J. (1982 a): Evolution and the theory of games. Cambridge Univ. Press, Cambridge.

Maynard Smith, J. (1982 b): Do animals convey information about their intentions? J. theor. Biol. 97, 1–5.

Maynard Smith, J., Parker, G. A. (1976): The logic of asymmetric contests. Anim. Behav. 24, 159–175.

McGregor, P. K., Krebs, J. R. (1982): Mating and song types in the great tit. Nature 297, 60–61.

Michener, Ch. D. (1974): The social behavior of the bees. Harvard Univ. Press, Cambridge.

Miller, S. J., Inouye, D. W. (1983): Roles of the wing whistle in the territorial behavior of the male broad-tailed humming-bird (*Selasphorus platycerus*). Anim. Behav. 31, 689–700.

Morris, C. W. (1946): Signs, language and behavior. Prentice-Hall, New York.

Morris, D., Collett, P. Marsh, P., O'Shaughnessy, M. (1979): Gestures. Their origins and distribution. Cape, London.

Moynihan, M. (1982): Why is lying about intentions rare during some kinds of contests? J. theor. Biol. 97, 7–12.

Palm, G. (1981): Evidence, information, and surprise. Biol. Cybern. 42, 57–68.

Parker, G. A. (1974): Assessment strategy and the evolution of animal conflicts. J. theor. Biol. 47, 223–243.

Parker, G. A., Rubenstein, D. J. (1981): Role assessment, reserve strategy, and acquisition of information in asymmetric animal conflicts. Anim. Behav. 29, 221–240.

Peters, R. (1980): Mammalian Communication. Brooks/Cole, Monterey.

Pliner, P., Blankstein, K. R., Spigel, I. M. (1979): Perception of emotion in self and others. Adv. Study of Communication and Affect. Vol. 5. Plenum, New York.

Pruscha, H., Maurus, M. (1976): The communicative function of some agonistic behavior patterns in squirrel monkeys: the relevance of social context. Behav. Ecol. Sociobiol. 1, 185–214.

Quastler, H. (1958): A primer in information theory. In: Symp. information theory in biology. Yockey, H. P., Platzman, R. L., Quastler, H. (eds.) p. 3–49. Pergamon, New York.

Ristau, C. A., Robbins, D. (1982): Language in the great apes: a critical review. Adv. Study Behav. 12, 141–255.

Ryan, M. J., Tuttle, M. D., Taft, L. K. (1981): The costs and benefits of frog chorusing behavior. Behav. Ecol. Sociobiol. 8, 273–278.

Schmitt, F. O., Dev, P., Smith, B. H. (1976): Electrotonic processing of information by brain cells. Science 193, 114–120.

Sebeok, Th. A. (1977) (ed.): How animals communicate. Indiana Univ. Press, Bloomington.

Seeley, Th. (1977): Measurement of nest cavity volume by the honey bee (Apis mellifera). Behav. Ecol. Sociobiol. 2, 201–227.

Shannon, C. E., Weaver, W. (1949): The mathematical theory of communication. Univ. of Illinois Press, Urbana.

Seyfarth, R. M., Cheney, D. L., Marler, P. (1980): Vervet monkey alarm calls: semantic communication in a free-ranging primate. Anim. Behav. 28, 1070–1094.

Sherman, P. W. (1981): Kinship, demography, and Belding's ground squirrel nepotism. Behav. Ecol. Sociobiol. 8, 251–259.

Smith, W. J. (1977): The behavior of communicating. Harvard Univ. Press, Cambridge.

Snowdon, Ch. T., Cleveland, J. (1980): Individual recognition of contact calls by pygmy marmosets. Anim. Behav. 28, 717–727.

Snyder, M. (1979): Cognitive, behavioral, and interpersonal consequences of self-monitoring, p. 181–201. In: Perception of emotion in self and others. Pliner, P., Blankstein, K. R., Spigel, I. M. (eds.) Plenum, New York.

Stamm, R. A. (1974): Ein Codon for «Bitte!» im Verständigungssystem der Lachmöve (Larus ridibundus Linnaeus; Aves, Laridae). Revue Suisse Zool. 81, 722–728.

Steinberg, J. B. (1977): Information theory as an ethological tool. p. 47–74. In: Quantitative methods in the study of animal behavior. Hazlett, B. A. (ed.) Academic Press, New York.

Stent, G. (ed.) (1978): Morality as a biological phenomenon. Dahlem Konferenz 9 Verlag Chemie, Weinheim.

Taylor, R. W. (1978): Nothomyrmecia macrops: a living-fossil ant rediscovered. Science 201, 979–985.

Tembrock, G. (1971): Biokommunikation I/II. Akademie-Verlag, Berlin.

Traniello, J. F. A. (1982): Population structure and social organization in the primitive ant Amblyopone pallipes (Hymenoptera: Formicidae). Psyche 89, 65–80.

Trivers, R. W. (1971): The evolution of reciprocal altruism. Quart. Rev. Biol. 46, 35–57.

Trivers, R. W. (1972): Parental investment and sexual selection. p. 136–179. In: Sexual selection and the descent of man. Campbell, B. (ed.) Heinemann, London.

Trivers, R. W. (1974): Parent-offspring conflict. Amer. Zool. 14, 249–264.

Tuttle, M. D., Taft, L. K., Ryan, M. J. (1982): Evasive behaviour of a frog in response to bat predation. Anim. Behav. 30, 393–397.

van Rhijn, J. G. (1980): Communication by agonistic displays: a discussion. Behaviour 74, 284–293.

van Rhijn, J. G., Vodegel, R. (1980): Being honest about one's intentions: an evolutionary stable strategy for animal conflicts. J. theor. Biol. 85, 623–641.

von Frisch, K. (1965): Tanzsprache und Orientierung der Bienen. Springer, Berlin.

von Frisch, K. (1974): Tiere als Baumeister. Ullstein, Frankfurt.

Weitz, Sh. (1974): Nonverbal communication, Oxford Univ. Press, New York.

Wickler, W. (1968): Mimikry. Kindler, München.

Wickler, W. (1980): Vocal dueting and the pair-bond: I. Coyness and partner commitment, a hypothesis. Z. Tierpsychol. 52, 201–209.

Wickler, W., Seibt, U. (1982): Song splitting in the evolution of dueting. Z. Tierpsychol. 59, 127–140.

Wiley, R. H. (1983): The evolution of communication: information and manipulation, p. 156–189. In: Animal Behaviour. 2. Communication. Halliday, T. R., Slater, P. J. B. (eds.) Blackwell, Oxford.

Wilson, E. O. (1971): The insect societies. Belknap Press of Harvard Univ. Press, Cambridge.

Wilson, E. O. (1975): Sociobiology. The new synthesis. Belknap Press of Harvard Univ. Press, Cambridge.

Fortschritte der Zoologie, Bd. 31 · Hölldobler/Lindauer (Hrsg.): Experimental Behavioral Ecology
G. Fischer Verlag · Stuttgart · New York · 1985

Auditory brain organization of birds and its constraints for the design of vocal repertoires

H. Scheich

Zoological Institute, Technical University Darmstadt, F. R. Germany

Abstract

Vocal repertoires of birds and mammals frequently contain a large number of calls with overlapping spectral components.In addition such calls may show meaningful variability. It is demonstrated in the Guinea fowl using the 2-deoxyglucose method how species-specific calls are represented in the tonotopically organized field L, the primary auditory projection area of the telencephalon. The main findings are 1. that calls are represented in restricted parts of the tonotopic map. The representation of calls with a wide-band spectrum is not according to the frequency bands which contain the largest energy but according to spectral bands with the largest intensity jump. This means that call analysis in field L chiefly relies on spectral contrasts. 2. the representation of spectral contrast was spatially separated in field L for the calls tested. 3. for frequency modulated calls the representation of the spectral contrast is enhanced by a special mechanism of lateral suppression. These results are at variance with previous postulates of environmental acoustics, namely that the strongest frequency components of calls are chosen according to optimal transmission in the atmosphere. Obviously atmospheric transmission of those parameters of complex calls which are most relevant for auditory analysis and recognition in the brain, namely spectral contrast, still awaits testing.

1 Introduction

Acoustic communication in birds and mammals commonly involves recognition of multiple sounds which together constitute the repertoire of a species. Some of these vocalizations may show a high degree of acoustic complexity and also meaningful variability comparing individuals or different situations (GREEN et al. 1977, MAIER 1982). It is *multiplicity* and *variability* of signals in a repertoire which pose a formidable problem for the organization of neuronal networks in the auditory system that has to recognize them. While recognition of a *unique* and *stereotyped signal,* even if acoustically complex, is a relatively trivial task for a specialized network, multiplicity and variability are not, especially if there is partial overlap of parameters among different sounds. This lesson has been learnt by all investigators trying to perform acoustic, or other signal recognition by auto-

Supported by the Deutsche Forschungsgemeinschaft, SFB 45.

mata (Schroeder 1977). The solution to this problem that the brain has found during evolution is the representation and analysis of a multiplicity of variable signals in *neuronal maps* (Mountcastle 1957, Hubel and Wiesel 1962). These maps are organized in such a way that neurons representing a continuum of important stimulus variables are laid out along spatial dimensions within the anatomical structure. I shall follow this hypothesis while describing some of the experiments carried out in this laboratory in order to elucidate the neuronal mechanisms of sound recognition in birds.

All available data from birds and mammals favor the view that a basic organizational feature of auditory maps is *tonotopy* which is projected from the cochlea onto most of the central auditory structures in the brain (Aitkin 1976, Scheich 1979). This tonotopy is a simple means of systematically monitoring and comparing frequencies. Implicitly tonotopy has consequences for the strategy of processing complex auditory signals. It has emerged from our studies of auditory maps in birds that there are important constraints on the analysis of vocal sounds of species once these auditory maps were formed during evolution, and consequently that there may be constraints on the design of these sounds.

2 Coding of vocal sounds and evolution

In communication messages can be encoded by various types of physical signals. In the domain of acoustic signals the three physical dimensions which together encode messages are: frequency, intensity of individual frequency components, and temporal structures of sounds. Even though all acoustic signals can be described by these general dimensions, more complex entities are useful to characterize the majority of communication sounds. This is because one of the dimensions or a combination of them may show the highest complexity and thus contain most of the information. Harmonic tones, noisy sounds, frequency or amplitude modulations and pulse sequences are some examples. It is obvious that such complex entities are most easily envisaged as *patterns* in a three-dimensional space of frequency, intensity and time. Displays like sonagrams or running power spectra (Fig. 1) facilitate visualizing these patterns.

Communication sounds of species were shaped as a result of evolutionary pressures. In other words, the rules of encoding particular messages may not be considered arbitrary. In following this idea it should be possible, in principle, to trace the external and internal factors which in each species have favored the use of particular sounds for certain messages. In reality there is no direct evidence of this evolution, since vocal records are lacking. Consequently, this approach relies entirely on comparative studies of extant species. Key factors for the use of particular sounds may then be derived from physical properties of biotopes and from the life style of species (Wiley and Richards 1978). There are also some attempts to relate the sounds in use to basic mechanisms of vocal organs (Dürrwang 1974).

In terms of one of the above acoustic dimensions, namely frequency, there is probably one concept which truly relates to the evolution of sound production (Scheich et al. 1983). The original forms of vocalization early in evolution were most likely sounds with a *wide-band spectrum*. In other words, it was only in the case of later specializations that vocal apparatus was capable of producing pure tones and controlled modulations of tones. Instead, the construction of primitive vocal organs may have permitted the generation of noisy sounds and harmonic tones. Similarly information bearing sounds from inanimate sources are never pure tones. The wide-band acoustic environment was most probably the reason for the evolution of a cochlea in higher vertebrates which permitted a systematic resolution of simultaneously occurring frequency components of sounds. The central auditory system in turn started to be capable of recognizing those components as a pattern in a three dimensional space of frequency, intensity and time. The possibility has not attracted considerable attention that the basic need for recognition of wide-band sounds may have favored particular mechanisms in the central auditory system which relate to tonotopy. These central mechanism of sound analysis, once they were established in phylogeny may subsequently have determined the design of the vocal repertoire in each species as much as physical and ecological constraints. It is the aim of the present paper to provide some evidence for this idea.

3 Physical and ecological constraints on acoustic communication

The strongest evidence that the choice of vocal sounds is critically dependent upon acoustic properties of the environment comes from studies in bats. Even though echo-location superficially has little bearing on communication, the physical constraints working on the choice of signals may be comparable.

In bats the sounds in use, i. e. tonal or harmonic ultrasounds with or without frequency modulations and short noise bursts, are probably adaptations for echo-location in various ecological niches. In studying bats, the concept of optimizing signals has been successfully exploited by showing that species with hunting grounds in open air, close to the surface or in dense foliage, all use different signals. In each case arguments can be found that echos from certain sounds contain relevant information about nature, speed or trajectories of targets or reduce sound scatter coming from the environment, i. e. improve signal to noise ratio (SIMMONS and STEIN 1980, NEUWEILER 1983, SCHNITZLER and OSTWALD 1983).

Following the same line of reasoning there have been attempts to explain the frequency content of long distance communication sounds of birds and mammals in various terrestrial habitats. Acoustic transmission within a few meters off the ground in open spaces or in forests favors the band between 1 and 4 kHz for distance communication. In spite of somewhat different mechanisms in both habitats this band is a compromise between *ground attenuation,* which effectively reduces frequencies lower than 1 kHz and *scattering* by plants and other obstacles, which strongly attenuates frequencies above 4 kHz (EMBLE-TON 1963, AYLOR 1971, LINSKEN et al. 1976, MARTEN and MARLER 1977, MARTEN et al. 1977, WILEY and RICHARDS 1978). This finding is in agreement with the general observation that the highest energy in bird calls is in this medium frequency range and that hearing in most birds (and mammals) has lowest thresholds in this band (KONISHI 1970, DOOLING et al. 1971, SACHS et al. 1978, KUHN et al. 1982, THEURICH et al. 1984).

More interesting in our context than this general match are reports on differences between birds of tropical forests and of open habitats. In accordance with the fact that forest scattering effectively attenuates high frequencies, birds in forests appear to use somewhat lower pitched calls than species in open spaces of the same area (CHAPPIUS 1971, MORTON 1975).

Similar observations on preference for lower pitched sounds stem from a comparison of African monkeys which keep different typical distances between social groups (WASER and WASER 1977). The lowest frequencies are used by the species with the largest typical distance. Note however that the frequencies involved are way below those which are used by the birds discussed above (around 500 Hz).

In summary there are several examples where physical constraints seem to have influenced the choice of frequencies in calls. In view of the fact that these examples cover only a small proportion of the repertoire of the species and that only an extremely small proportion of species has been studied, the evidence appears to be weak. It is also unfortunate that nobody has looked for counter examples where an apparent acoustic constraint has not led to an adaptation.

The use of complex parameters in long distance communication is even less understood than the choice of peak frequencies described above. There is good evidence that amplitude modulations become heavily distorted by so-called nonstationary heterogeneities such as air turbulence (WILEY and RICHARDS 1978). Nevertheless, amplitude modulations are characteristic of many bird and mammalian vocalizations (see GREENEWALT 1968, SEBEOK 1977). Among frequency modulations, slow modulations of a tone and fast repetitive modulations (trills) should be distinguished. Slow modulations between 1 and 4 kHz are not easily masked by any one of the discussed physical mechanisms. Therefore they are quite useful for long distance communication and are heard frequently from birds. Similarly trills are abundant in bird and mammalian repertoires. In theory, however, their usefulness is limited because they are masked by reverberations of the sound from dense arrays of obstacles such as leafs. It was claimed that birds of the *understory* in tropical forests avoid trills (MORTON 1975).

From these considerations it becomes apparent that so far there is only limited congruence between acoustic rules and preference or avoidance of certain parameters in vocalizations. One of the reasons may be that it is difficult to make a clear-cut distinction between long- and short distance communications. With all mechanisms discussed, the masking effect increases with distances and may be negligiable over a short range. In social animals the majority of sounds are short distance signals anyway.

There is a more fundamental objection to directly correlating the avoidance of some acoustic parameters with their vulnerability by physical influence in the environment. This has to do with the fact that there is little information on which parameters are actually used by the auditory system. As we shall see below, it is even doubtful that for the auditory system a prominent feature such as the peak frequency content (frequency with the highest energy) is an important parameter in all sounds. Similarly for more elaborate parameters such as amplitude or frequency modulations it is not intuitive in which way the system makes use of them and which kind of perturbations of these parameters the system is resistent to.

4 Functional organization of the auditory field L in the bird telencephalon

I shall describe here results which have been obtained in field L of the Guinea fowl. This field in the caudal neostriatum of the bird telencephalon was cytoarchitectonically distinguished from the sourrounding neostriatum by ROSE (1914) and later identified as the primary projection area of the thalamic auditory n. ovoidalis by KARTEN (1968) using degeneration technique. Trancing with labeled aminoacids in our laboratory has revealed that the extent of field L as shown by the earlier studies corresponds to only one layer, i. e. the chief input layer L_2 of terminals from n. ovoidalis (BONKE et al. 1979a). Two other layers, L_1 dorsal and L_3 ventral to L_2 were determined to be auitory as well, but to have little direct input. Microelectrode recordings showed that all three layers have a prominent and corresponding tonotopic organization with isofrequency contours oriented approximately perpendicular to the layering (BONKE et al. 1979b).

The 2-deoxyglucose method (SOKOLOFF et al. 1977) has enabled us to confirm this result and to demonstrate other features of field L (Fig. 1). The glucose analogue 2-deoxyglucose is incorporated into active neurons together with glucose proportional to its concentration in the blood. After phosphorylation it is not further metabolized and consequently accumulates. When animals injected with 14-C-2-deoxyglucose are stimulated, autoradiographs of brain sections show the spatial extent of neuronal ensembles which were activated by the stimulus. The three-dimensional organization of the field is visualized by the method. Each isofrequency contour extends into depth across the layers and with the second dimension rostro-caudally (SCHEICH et al. 1979a, SCHEICH and BONKE 1981). The crystalline structure of field L thus contains an orderly frequency representation, a map of isofrequency planes which is primarily excitatory.

Three questions arise from this type of organization. First, which mechanisms of processing or recognizing sounds benefit from the orderly representation of frequencies? Second, which is the significance of representing each frequency in a two-dimensional neuronal space. In other words, why is one locus along the one-dimensional cochlea represented in a plane? Third, what is the role of the different layers?

Fig. 1: 2-deoxyglucose autoradiographs of field L of Guinea fowls stimulated with pure tones. The sections were cut in the transverse plane and are taken from an intermediate rostrocaudal level of field L. The bird in the top figure was stimulated with 1 and 2 kHz alternatingly at the rate of 3/sec. Two tone-activated stripes of labeling are shown which cut perpendicularly across the three layers L_1, L_2 and L_3 and produce a focus of high intensity labeling in L_2. Note that the stripes reach into the auditory hyperstriatum ventrale (HV). The bottom figure was obtained with 1 and 3 kHz alternating tones. The 1 kHz stripe is at the same position along the L_2 layer as in the top experiment while the 3 kHz stripe is shifted towards the ventromedial end of L_2.

4.1 Representation of calls in field L

Experiments with complex stimuli including species specific calls have provided some preliminary answers to these questions. With respect to two-dimensional representation of frequencies in planes 2-deoxyglucose results with frequency modulated tones and species specific calls in comparison to simple tone burst have given the first clue for the second dimension. The representation of tone bursts diminishes in strenght along a gradient from caudal to rostral through field L. In the caudal and intermediate parts of L, tone bursts produce a stripe-like pattern across all three layers with a focus of higher optical density in the input layer L_2 (Fig. 1). Towards the rostral end of L the labeling in L_1 and L_3 becomes weaker. This demonstrates that the influence of the dominant frequency on neurons in the rostral part of isofrequency planes is small. In contrast more complex sounds which contain this dominant frequency label an isofrequency plane throughout (Scheich and Bonke 1981). These sounds may be frequency or amplitude modulated tones with small bandwidth or narrow band noise.

Similar 2DG results are obtained with calls of the Guinea fowl which contain such complex dimensions. Fig. 2 shows three calls of the Guinea fowl which were selected from the repertoire of the species (for a comprehensive review of the vocal ethology of the Guinea fowl see Maier 1982). One of the presented calls is the kecker, which is a harsh

Fig. 2: Analysis of three calls of the Guinea fowl in terms of average spectra, running spectra, and sonagrams. The sonagrams at the bottom show most clearly the large frequency overlap of the three wide-band calls (for explanation of the calls see text). The average spectra on top represent the average intensity in each frequency band for the full duration of each call shown in the sonagrams. The running spectra in the middle allow an appraisal of intensity fluctuations in all frequency bands with a time window of 30 ms for each profile. The time on the ordinate runs from bottom to top.

sounding utterance. It is used by males and females in a number of agonistic situations. The kecker has a noisy wide-band spectrum with quite variable frequency limits extending from less that 1 to more than 6 kHz. The spectrum is relatively flat but has energy peaks usually between 1.5 and 5 kHz. The group of trills covers calls which direct attention of group members towards food, strange objects and animals or strange conspecifics. The ee-trill used in the present experiment has a strong alarming connotation. Its frequency limits are between less that 100 Hz and 6 kHz. The chief bands of energy (formants) are below 400 Hz and between 2 and 3.5 kHz. The iambus is a hen call which serves to keep contact between a hen and her mate or the hen and her chicks. The spectral composition of the double-note iambus is quite complicated. It consists of a harmonic carrier with 1 kHz fundamental frequency and sidebands due to amplitude modulation at a rate of about 300 Hz. The spectrum is wide-band and overlaps with both that of the kecker and of the ee-trill. In contrast to the other calls, the iambus has several energy peaks of slightly different height, namely at 1, 2 and 3 kHz.

The exposure of Guinea fowls to calls of their repertoire produced several interesting effects in the 2-deoxyglucose autoradiographs of field L (BONKE 1982, BONKE and SCHEICH, in prep.). Figs. 3 and 4 provide an overview of the main results. 1. Stimulation with species-specific calls leads to labeling throughout the rostrocaudal extent of the field. There was also strong labeling in the rostral third where tones in previous experiments caused very little 2 DG incorporation (SCHEICH and BONKE 1981). 2. In spite of the large band-width of the calls, particularly of kecker and iambus, all calls produced stripe-like activation along isofrequency contours, similar to the effect of pure tones. 3. Some calls, namely the frequency modulated ee-trill, in addition to stripe-like zones of activation, produced adjacent zones of suppression of activity. 4. The calls not only produced stripes across all three layers of field L but also markedly enhanced the activity of the overlaying hyperstriatum ventrale (HV, see Fig. 3, B3). Note that this part of the HV was determined by physiological and anatomical methods (BONKE et al. 1979a, b) to be a higher order auditory field.

4.2 Representation of spectral contrast in field L

From these four main results several rules may be derived concerning how species-specific calls are processed in telencephalic auditory maps. Most important, it is evident that such calls activate only restricted frequency bands of the tonotopic map. This is astonishing in view of the fact that some of the calls have energy over a frequency range much wider than the tonotopic area which is activated by them. A detailed comparison of call spectra (Fig. 2) with the tonotopic organization known from microelectrode recordings (BONKE et al. 1979b) and 2 DG labeling with pure tones (Fig. 1) provides a frame for understanding this effect.

For instance, the spectrum of the iambus shows several sharp peaks of energy, namely at 1, 2 and 3 kHz. There are also several smaller peaks which are either harmonics of 1 kHz or sidebands due to the 300 Hz amplitude modulation of the harmonic carrier. The largest peak is at 2 kHz with the 1 kHz peak following next. The profiles of 2 DG labeling in Fig. 4 show two sharp peaks of labeling which on the tonotopic scale of the L_2 layer correspond to frequencies around 1 and 2 kHz. Similar to the iambus frequency spectrum the 2 kHz peak is the largest (Fig. 4, C1–5). Thus there is a very distinct representation of the band of highest energy in the call spectrum by the metabolic activity of neurons. Other bands of energy, even if only 10 dB waker lead to much smaller activation. For instance, the prominent band of energy at 3 kHz (Fig. 2) obtained very little representation in the profiles. Obviously the main issue in frequency representation of this call in field L is to kecker 1+2   ee-trill   iambus 1+2

B 7   B 3   B 4

emphasize the spectral peak. These 2 DG results closely correspond to the results of systematic microelectrode penetrations through field L while stimulating with a large number of natural variations of iambus calls. Most of these variations had spectral peaks between 1.7 and 2 kHz. We found that the tonotopic area around 1.8 kHz contained the largest number of units which responded to iambus calls or preferred them over calls (BONKE et al. 1979a, SCHEICH et al. 1979b, BONKE 1982). In view of the poor spatial resolution of microelectrode penetrations in a grid of 0.2 × 0.2 mm this is a very good match.

The iambus is a call which has a wide-band spectrum composed of relatively discrete lines with little energy in between. Other calls like the kecker or the ee-trill have a different type of spectrum. There the energy is more densely spaced. In the case of kecker, noise is the chief component while in the case of the ee-trill the frequency is modulated at a rate of about 100/s through the full bandwidth. Neither call has sharp peaks of energy.

For instance the spectrum of the kecker extends up to 6 kHz with a rather flat plateau of energy roughly between 2 and 4 kHz. In spite of this the profiles of 2 DG labeling (Fig. 4, B1–5) show one sharp peak of labeling which on the tonotopic scale of the L_2 layer corresponds to frequencies between 1 and 1.5 kHz. This is an extremely narrow band of tonotopic labeling with respect to the band-width of the kecker spectrum (see Fig. 2). In fact, the stripe of labeling is not wider than those obtained for pure tones (compare Fig. 1 with Fig. 3, B7/3). Obviously there is a special cue in the call spectrum which neither corresponds to the band-width nor to the spectral peak and yet determines the metabolic response of field L. Judging from Fig. 2 there is a 20 dB rise of average intensity in the kecker spectrum between 1 and 2 kHz. This is the largest rise of intensity in the whole spectrum. The preliminary conclusion which can be drawn from this result is that it is some kind of a spectral contrast which is represented in the case of wideband spectra lacking a clear spectral peak. The results from ee-trill stimulation further substantiate this idea.

The ee-trill has at least two bands of prominent energy. The main band is between 2 and 3.5 kHz and corresponds to the frequency modulated carrier. The other band is below 400 Hz and shows a first peak at 110 and a second at 220 Hz. These peaks correspond to that frequency (and its second harmonic) which modulates the carrier in the 2–3.5 kHz band. The 2 DG profiles in Fig. 4B show one prominent band of metabolic excitation with a peak at 2 kHz. Again, as in the case of kecker, it is not a prominent spectral frequency which is represented. Instead the steep rise of intensity at the low frequency end of the main spectral component elicits the largest metabolic response. In other words the system optimally reflects what I would like to call the *spectral contrast* of the call.

How can we now relate the results from the iambus experiment to those of ee-trill and kecker stimulation? In the first case the spectral peaks were represented, in the second a strong spectral contrast led to maximum labeling. There is no fundamental contradiction between these cases. As explained above the iambus has a line spectrum with strong tone-like frequency components separated by gaps with little or no energy. Consequently the

---

Fig. 3: 2-deoxyglucose autoradiographs of right and left field L of Guinea fowls stimulated with species-specific calls. Insets 1 through 6 are equidistant transverse sections from rostral to caudal through the field. Note that all three calls chiefly produce stripe-like activation which cuts across the three layers of field L similar to pure tones. This effect is most pronounced in the intermediate sections 2, 3 and 4. Autoradiographs from the frequency modulated ee-trill show marked suppression of metabolic activity in L_2 adjacent to the stripe of activation (arrow heads). The activation of the hyperstriatum ventrale (HV) in the rostral sections is most pronounced with this call.

ee–trill

kecker

iambus

largest spectral contrasts correspond to the largest spectral peaks. This is similar to pure tones where the spectral peaks and the maximum contrasts are identical. The fact that not the spectral peak but some frequency at the slope of this peak is chiefly represented in field L has been reported already by BONKE (1982) from both 2 DG results and microelectrode recordings. In summary it may be said that in terms of the largest metabolic response, field L appears to be interested chiefly in spectral contrasts of calls. This should be taken into account as an important point when speculating about the design of bird calls.

If this property of field L, of representing chiefly spectral contrasts, were a general property of telencephalic auditory maps which recognize auditory patterns, there are several basic implications for the optimal design of vocal patterns. First, if an animal uses a variety of different calls they should have their largest spectral contrast in different regions of the frequency scale. This would provide for an optimal distinction in the representational maps of the auditory system. It is implicit that the wide-band nature of calls with a considerable spectral overlap among different calls creates little complication as long as the contrasts are spaced out. It may also follow from this need to space out spectral contrasts of calls in a large repertoire that the species is not completely free to choose any suitable frequency for long distance calls. At least there may be pressures from physical constraints and perceptual constraints interacting to make this choice.

Second, if a call type is variable and thereby gradually shifts its meaning, the representation in the tonotopic map is affected only if the maximum contrast changes. In the case of the iambus which codes individual voices of females a detailed study of variability has shown that, in spite of considerable differences in terms of strength of harmonics and sideband, the energy peak was always between 1.5 and 2 kHz (SCHEICH et al. 1979b). With respect to the total band-width of the iambus this is a small range of variability. We shall see below that this variability may not be in conflict with the representation of the other calls.

4.3 Enhancement of spectral contrast in field L

Distribution of spectral constrasts of calls along the frequency scale and consequently separation in the neuronal space of field L is one basic strategy for the distinction of calls. There is another neuronal mechanism which enhances this effect. In Figs. 3 and 4 the 2 DG profiles of the ee-trill show an area of metabolic suppression in the L_2 layer adjacent to the large peak of labeling. This suppression is below the level of spontaneous labeling of L_2 which is obtained in animals kept in silence. It almost reaches down to the background labeling in the remainder of the brain sections. This type of suppression is typical for frequency modulated sounds (SCHEICH and BONKE 1981) and is related to inhibitory

Fig. 4: Densitometric profiles of 2-deoxyglucose labeling from the cases of Fig. 3. The autoradiographs of Fig. 3 were analyzed on X-rax film by a TV camera and transformed into a matrix of 256 × 256 picture points, each point with a relative intensity resolution of 256 grades. The average intensity of 8 rows of points respectively was integrated and transformed into an intensity profile. In that way 32 profiles represent the labeling in a given area. Note that the orientation of field L was rotated 45° with respect to Fig. 3. In A1 the midline between right and left field L is indicated by a line pointing dorsally (d) and ventrally (v). In that way the right field L (r) has a horizontal orientation and the perspective view of the profiles of labeling is from lateral. This allows a good overview of the layers L_3 and L_2. As indicated in B1 the left field L is seen from a medial aspect which unconvers mostly the layers L_1 and L_2. In A3, B3 and C3 a frequency scale of the tonotopic organization of the L_2 layer as obtained from tone experiments is fitted to the profiles. In that way the large peaks of labeling in L_2 (arrowheads) can be referred to frequencies.

sidebands of units in L_2 (Scheich et al. 1983). It is not seen in the other calls of Figs. 3 and 4. Only occasional weak suppression has been obtained with pure tone stimulation.

The net effect of suppression together with a large adjacent peak of activity corresponds to an enhancement of contrast. It may also be considered as an improvement of signal to noise ratio for the representation of a sound. There may be a fundamental implication of this effect for the design of vocal sounds in the repertoire of the Guinea fowl and of other animals. It is probably not a pure coincidence that all calls in the Guinea fowl repertoire which have an alerting connotation are frequency modulated sounds (see Maier 1982). Frequency modulations may be particularly suitable for this purpose because they increase signal to noise ratio in the auditory map and thereby facilitate recognition against a background of noise.

Frequency modulated sounds are widespread in the animal kingdom and their systematic study may subsequently disclose a common use as alerting signals. At least one such case of a fast modulated call has been describes for the dwarf mongoose (Maier et al. 1983). The well known cases of so called hawk alarm calls in European songbirds (Marler 1959), which are slow downward modulations of a tone, may be in the same category. Scheich and Bonke (1981) have shown that slowly modulated tones (3 Hz modulation frequency) also lead to sharp zones of suppression of metabolic activity. Finally the widespread use of frequency modulated sounds as alarm signals in our human civilization should be noted.

5 The mosaic pattern of call representation

We have seen that representation of spectral contrasts and enhancement of contrast by sideband-suppression are basic rules of operation of field L. For the three calls presented here and for a few others which have been tested these mechanism provide some rough distinction in the spatial map of the field. However, there are about 20 different call types in the repertoire of the Guinea fowl (Maier 1982), which all have to be distinguished. Some of these call types similar to the iambus show meaningful variations which among other cues may also involve small shifts of spectral contrast. Consequently there must be additional mechanisms which provide for a distinction of more subtle differences.

Close inspection of the 2 DG profiles in Fig. 4 shows that there are small secondary peaks of labeling beside the main peaks. The distribution of secondary peaks is uneven from rostral to caudal in the L_2 layer. In the intermediate third, i. e. particularly in A2, A3 the ee-trill produces small peaks below 500 Hz. They most probably correspond to a spectral contrast of the modulation frequencies in Fig. 1. In C3, C4 the already mentioned 1 kHz fundamental of the iambus or its spectral contrast produces a secondary peak of labeling. For the kecker the secondary peak is less pronounced but may be identified at the ventral high frequency end of L_2 in B2, B3. It probably reflects another intensity jump, i. e. the spectral contrast between 4 and 6 kHz (see Fig. 1). The representation of at least two separate spectral components in the tonotopic map may be the way to overcome the difficulty of identifying a great number of calls. In that way the combination of the strongest or primary representational component with a secondary one could easily lead to an unmistakable representational pattern. In other words the recognition of calls may reside in a mosaic of spatial excitation of neuronal ensembles in the map. It is not clear yet why the secondary component is most prominently represented in the intermediate third of the field.

The reader should be reminded here of the introductory statements about the three-dimensional organization of field L. So far I have focussed only on the tonotopy of the L_2

layer in the transverse plane and not mentioned differences of call representation along the rostrocaudal extent of this layer nor differences of call representation in L_1 and L_3. The description of these differences would be beyond the scope of this paper. I shall only mention that there are indeed such differences in the responsiveness and selectivity of neurons to calls along those spatial dimensions, some of which have been described in electrophysiological studies (SCHEICH et al. 1979b, BONKE et al. 1979b, SCHEICH et al. 1983). Their significance in terms of complex dimension, i.e. combination of frequency, intensity and time was clarified only in part.

6 Environmental acoustic versus neuronal call representation

The ultimate goals for the design of all communication sounds are a largely undisturbed transmission to and an optimal perception by the receiver. For long distance communication and to a lesser extent for short distance communication environmental acoustics impose certain constraints on transmission in the atmosphere and therefore may have influenced the choice of call frequency in species. This was claimed by a number of authors as discussed above and is best summarized in the article by RICHARDS and WILEY (1978). The results presented here on call representation in a forebrain auditory map of a bird are at variance with some of these claims or at least should make one cautions about the *consequences* of some results in environmental acoustics for auditory perception. Before drawing any conclusions from vocalizations it is important to determine first which parameters of a call the auditory system of the receiver is chiefly interested in. As we have seen, except for narrow band tonal stimuli, the bird system is interested in spectral contrasts. This means that in wideband calls the acoustic transmission of the strongest spectral components is not always the relevant parameter. I would like to propose therefore that future measurements of complex sound transmission in various biotopes should focus on spectral contrasts in order to elucidate physical constraints on this parameter.

Moreover, the discovery that frequency modulations produce extremely high contrast representations in the tonotopic map is important in the light of sound transmission. It suggests that in spite of a certain vulnerability of frequency modulated patterns by sound reverberation (RICHARDS and WILEY 1978), the representation of such a call may be preserved in the auditory map by the special mechanism of contrast enhancement. Again as in the case of other wide-band calls it is a spectral contrast and not the spectral peak which is represented. This should also be borne in mind when interpreting effects of environmental acoustics on frequency modulated calls.

References

Aitkin, L. M. (1976): Tonotopic organization at higher levels of the auditory pathway. Intern. Rev. Physiol. (Neurophysiology II) *10,* 249–279.

Aylor, D. (1971): Noise reduction by vegetation and ground. J. Acoust. Soc. Amer. *51,* 197–205.

Bonke, B. A., Bonke, D., Scheich, H. (1979): Connectivity of the auditory forebrain nuclei in the Guinea fowl (Numida meleagris). Cell Tissue Res. *200,* 101–121.

Bonke, D. (1982): Processing of species-specific calls in the field L in the Guinea fowl (Numida meleagris) demonstrated by the 2-deoxyglucose technique and y systematic electrophysiological recordings. Verh. Dtsch. Zool. Ges., Stuttgart, Gustav-Fischer-Verlag, *302.*

Bonke, D., Scheich, H., Langner, G. (1979): Responsiveness of units in the auditory neostriatum of the Guinea fowl (Numida meleagris) to species-specific calls and synthetic stimuli. I. Tonotopy and functional zones of field L. J. Comp. Physiol. *132*, 243–255.

Chappuis, C. (1971): Un exemple de l'influence du milieu sur les émissions vocales des oiseaux: l'évolution des chants en forêt équatoriale. Terre et Vie *118*, 183–202.

Dooling, R. J., Mulligan, Y. A., Miller, J. D. (1971): Auditory sensitivity and song spectrum of the common canary. J. Acoust. Soc. Am. *50*, 700–709.

Dürrwang, R. (1974): Funktionelle Biologie, Anatomie und Physiologie der Vogelstimme. Ph. D.-Thesis, University of Basel, Switzerland.

Embleton, T. F. W. (1963): Sound propagation in homogeneous deciduous evergreeen woods. J. Acoust. Soc. Amer. *35*, 1119–1125.

Green, S. M., Darwin, C. J., Evans, E. F., Fant, G. C. M., Fourcin, A. J., Fujimura, O., Fujisaki, H., Liberman, A. M., Markl, H. S., Marler, P. R., Miller, J. D., Milner, B. A., Nottebohm, F., Pisoni, D. B., Ploog, D., Scheich, H., Stevens, K. N., Studdert-Kennedy, M. G., Tallal, P. A. (1977): Comparative Aspects of Vocal Signals Including Speech (Group Report). In: Dahlem Workshop on Recognition of Complex Acoustic Signals (T. H. Bullock, Ed.), Berlin-Dahlem Konferenzen, pp. 209–237.

Greenewalt, C. H. (1968): Bird Song. Acoustics and Physiology. Washington D. C., Smithsonian Institution Press.

Hubel, D. H., Wiesel, T. N. (1962): Receptive fields, binocular interaction and functional architecture in the cat's visual cortex. J. Physiol. *160*, 106–154.

Karten, H. J. (1968): The ascending auditory pathway in the pigeon (Columba livia). II: Telencephalic projections of the nucleus ovoidalis thalami. Brain Res. *11*, 134–153.

Konishi, M. (1970): Comparative neurophysiological studies of hearing and vocalizations in songbirds. Z. Vergl. Physiol. *66*, 257–272.

Kuhn, A., Müller, Ch., Leppelsack, H.-J., Schwartzkopff, J. (1982): Heart-rate conditioning used for determination of auditory threshold in the starling. Naturwiss. *69*, 245.

Linskens, H. F., Martens, M. J. M., Hendricksen, H. J. G. M., Roestenberg-Sinnige, A. M., Brouwers, W. A. J. M., van der Staak, A. L. H. C., Strik-Jansen, A. M. J. (1976): The acoustic climate of plant communities. Oecologia (Berl.) *23*, 165–177.

Maier, V. (1982): Acoustic communication in the Guinea fowl (Numida meleagris): Structure and use of vocalizations and the principle of message coding. Z. Tierpsychol. *59*, 29–83.

Maier, V., Rasa, O. A. E., Scheich, H. (1983): Call-system similarity in a ground-living social bird and a mammal in the bush habitat. Behav. Ecol. Sociobiol. *12*, 5–9.

Marler, P. (1959): Developments in the study of animal communication. In: Darwin's Biological Work: Some Aspect Reconsidered (P. R. Bell, Ed.), Cambridge, Cambridge University Press.

Marten, K., Marler, P. (1977): Sound transmission and its significance for animal vocalization. I. Temperature habitats. Behav. Ecol. Sociobiol. *2*, 271–290.

Marten, K., Quine, D., Marler, P. (1977): Sound transmission and its significance for animal vocalization. II. Tropical forest habitats. Behav. Ecol. Sociobiol. *2*, 291–302.

Morton, E. S. (1975): Ecological sources of selection on avian sounds. Amer. Nat. *109*, 17–34.

Mountcastle, V. B. (1957): Modality and topographic properties of single neurons of cat's somatic sensory cortex. J. Neurphysiol. *20*, 408–434.

Neuweiler, G. (1983): Echolocation and adaptivity to ecological constraints. In: Neuroethology and Behavioral Physiology (F. Huber, H. Markl, Eds.), Springer, pp. 280–302.

Rose, M. (1914): Über die cytoarchitektonische Gliederung des Vorderhirns der Vögel. J. Physiol. Neurol. (Leipzig) *21*, 278–352.

Sachs, M. B., Sinott, J. M., Hienz, R. D. (1978): Behavioral and physiological studies of hearing in birds. Fed. Proc. *37*, 2329–2335.

Scheich, H. (1979): Common principles of organization in the central auditory pathway of vertebrates. Verh. Dtsch. Zool. Ges., Stuttgart, Gustav Fischer Verlag, pp. 155–166.

Scheich, H., Bock, W., Bonke, D., Langner, G., Maier, V. (1983): Acoustic communication in the Guinea fowl (Numida meleagris). In: Advances invertebrate neuroethology (J.-P. Ewert, R. R. Capranica, D. J. Igle, Eds.), Plenum Publishing Corp., 731–782.

Scheich, H., Bonke, B. A. (1981): Tone-versus FM-induced patterns of excitation and suppression in the 14-C-deoxyglucose labeled auditory «cortex» of the Guinea fowl. Exp. Brain Res. *44*, 445–449.

Scheich, H., Bonke, B. A., Bonke, D., Langner, G. (1979): Functional organization of some auditory nuclei in the Guinea fowl demonstrated by the 2-deoxyglucose technique, Cell Tissue Res. *204*, 17–27.

Schnitzler, H.-U., Ostwald, J. (1983): Adaptations for the detection of fluttering insects by echolocation in horseshoe bats. In: Advances in vertebrate neuroethology (J.-P. Ewert, R. R. Capranica, D. J. Ingle, Eds.), New York, London, Plenum Press, pp. 801–827.

Schroeder, M. R. (1977): Machine processing of acoustic signals: What mechanisms can do better than organisms (and vice versa). In: Dahlem Workshop on Recognition of Complex Acoustic Signals (T. H. Bullock, Ed.), Berlin-Dahlem-Konferenzen, pp. 183–207.

Sebeok, T. A. (Ed.) (1977): How animals communicate. Bloomington, London, Indiana University Press.

Simmons, J. A., Stein, R. A. (1980): Acoustic imaging in bat sonar: Echolocation signals and the evolution of echolocation. J. Comp. Physiol. *135*, 61–84.

Sokoloff, L. (1975): The coupling of function, metabolism and blood flow in the brain. In: Brain Work (H. D. Ingvar, N. A. Lassen, Eds.), Copenhagen-Munksgaard, pp. 385–388.

Waser, P., Waser, M. S. (1977): Experimental studies of primate vocalization: specializations for long-distance propagation. Z. Tierpsychol. *43*, 239–263.

Wiley, R. H., Richards, D. G. (1978): Physical constraints on acoustic communication in the atmosphere: Implications for the evolution of animal vocalizations. Behav. Ecol. Sociobiol. *3*, 69–94.

Fortschritte der Zoologie, Bd. 31 · Hölldobler/Lindauer (Hrsg.): Experimental Behavioral Ecology
G. Fischer Verlag · Stuttgart · New York · 1985

Representational vocal signals of primates

PETER MARLER

The Rockefeller University, Center for Field Research, Millbrook, N. Y., USA

Abstract

The prevailing view of the vocal signals of non-human primates is that they are signs of emotion and nothing more. A distinction is made between affective communication and symbolic communication, and the latter is thought to be a special human prerogative. Recent work on calls used by monkeys to signal alarm in the presence of predators, and to recruit aid from companions during agonistic encounters with other group members suggests that this view is incorrect. Vervet monkeys appear to use alarm calls as though they actually represent or symbolize particular predators. Rhesus macaques give screams while fighting that are usually thought of as addressed primarily to the opponent. In fact they are calls for help. The signals are discretely organized, and do not constitute a graded continuum as previously thought. Field experiments on responses to tape recorded vocalizations confirm the conclusions drawn from descriptive studies that each call appears to represent to other listening monkeys not only the severity of the fight but also the class of opponent present, as defined by rank and kin relationships to the caller. We conclude that the calls of non-human primates reflect both affective and cognitive processes. The signs of these two kinds of process are often intermingled and conveyed by different acoustic vehicles, as in human speech.

1 Introduction

The modern era of research on vocal signals and communication in non-human primates began in 1962, with the investigations by ROWELL and HINDE of rhesus monkeys in captivity (ROWELL 1962; ROWELL and HINDE 1962), followed soon afterwards by ANDREW's studies of a variety of captive primate species (ANDREW 1962, 1963). Prior to that time virtually nothing was known about non-human primate vocal behavior. The situation now is quite different. An impressive amount of descriptive information has been gathered on the physical structure of the vocalizations of monkeys and apes, and we are beginning to understand the relationships of vocal behavior to phylogeny, localizability and contexts of use (reviewed in STRUHSAKER 1970; GREEN 1975; GAUTIER and GAUTIER-HION 1977; MARLER and TENAZA 1977; SNOWDON, BROWN and PETERSEN 1982). The stage is now set for a more analytical approach, except for two serious gaps. We still know almost nothing about the ontogeny of primate vocal behavior (NEWMAN and SYMMES 1982) and perhaps most surprising of all, remarkably little is known about what is

Table 1: Interpretations of Monkey Signals as Manifestations Only of Affect, Emotion or Motivation

A. «Nonhuman primates can send complex messages about their motivational states; they communicate almost nothing about the state of their physical environments.» (Lancaster 1965, p. 64)

B. «... all signals appear to be clearly related to the immediate emotional states of the signaling individuals and their levels of arousal.» (Bastian 1965, p. 598)

C. «The use of both the face and the voice by rhesus monkeys in their natural habitat seems to be restricted to circumstances that connote emotion.» (Myers 1976, pp. 747–748)

D. «... the nonhuman primate does not use the auditory medium to communicate whatever conceptual knowledge it possesses. The vocal repertoire appears to relate to affective rather than cognitive dimensions, the nature of the signal reflecting the emotional disposition of the caller.» (Marin, et al. 1979, p. 184)

E. «... the signal emitted by an animal is an expression of its affective condition, and the reception of the signal indicates the infection of others by the same condition – nothing more.» (Luria 1982, p. 29)

F. «Man has both affective and symbolic communication. – All other species, except when tutored by man, have only the affective form.» (Premack 1975, p. 593)

actually being expressed in the calls of monkeys and apes and what they mean to other animals (Marler 1977, 1978a, b).

Rowell and Hinde (1962) made it clear that they view rhesus macaque calls as signs of affect or emotion. Their paper opens with the statement, «The noises made by monkeys express their mood, and are effective in communicating it to others». In their judgement the calls express not thoughts but affective moods. Until very recently this had been the prevailing view of animal vocal signals in general. To demonstrate how widespread and firmly rooted this interpretation has been over the past 20 years, I have assembled a series of quotations selected from different disciplines (Table 1). All take the position that there is nothing symbolic about primate vocalizations, and that the essential substrates for the calling behavior of non-human primates are to be found in the emotions. The present paper seeks to challenge that position by demonstrating that there is much more to primate vocal behavior than just affect.

The first quotation is from Lancaster (1965), a physical anthropologist. Bastian (1965) is a linguist, one of the few who has worked actively on animal communication. Myers (1976) is a neuroanatomist, representing another widely held view. Marin et al. (1979) presents the viewpoint of a clinician, and Luria (1982) that of a cognitive psychologist. Finally there is an expression of the same position from Premack (1975). The latter's viewpoint is especially important because of his demonstrations of the cognitive prowess of primates in the laboratory (Premack and Premack 1983). If we assume that nothing more than affect is involved in their vocal behavior, this raises the apparent paradox that there is a reserve of cognitive abilities that is simply not manifest in their normal communicative behavior.

2 Environmental representation: the alarm calls of monkeys

Some six years ago I decided to take a fresh look at this problem. As a starting point, I had already been preoccupied with the fascinating repertoire of alarm calls that Struhsaker (1967) had described in the vervet monkeys of Amboseli in Kenya while working as a student in my laboratory. Within a rather complicated vocal system there were three calls in particular that, if his data were valid, could provide the basis for a challenge to the «emotion» or «affect» interpretation of primate calls. According to Struhsaker, distinct alarm calls were employed for leopards, for snakes, and for eagles, used in ways that seemed to imply more than was compatible with a simple affect interpretation (MARLER 1977). Soon after, I invited DOROTHY CHENEY and ROBERT SEYFARTH to join forces with me to reexamine the natural patterns of use of vervet alarm calls, and then to conduct experiments under field conditions to study responses of the monkeys to playbacks of tape recordings of their alarm calls in the absence of predators.

The basic question was whether the alarm calling behavior of the vervets was indeed compatible with an affect interpretation. In this case different alarm calls would presumably reveal different degrees of fearfulness in the caller and evoke equivalent fearful states in other animals. Is this a sufficient explanation for what takes place, or is something more involved? As it turned out, the «something more» loomed larger and larger in our minds until we found ourselves entertaining a quite different interpretation.

The problem to be faced is the nature of the chain of events that intervenes between an eagle coming into view, a vervet giving a particular signal, and eliciting in another monkey the pattern of escape behavior appropriate for evading an eagle attack. In the case of a martial eagle the appropriate response would be to rush out of open areas and especially to drop rapidly from the treetops, into dense cover, which is the place where a monkey is safest from a stooping raptor. Field experiments in which alarm calls of animals of known identity were played back from concealed loudspeakers showed unequivocally that this behavior is triggered by the call when there is no predator present (SEYFARTH, CHENEY and MARLER 1980a, b). Note moreover that if the predator is a leopard, for which another alarm call is given, then a different escape reaction is appropriate, almost the opposite of that for an eagle. The safe response to a leopard is to rush out into the open or up into the tops of trees, away from dense cover which is where a leopard, which hunts by ambush, is most likely to be. If you play a recording of a leopard alarm call this is the behavior the signal evokes.

Note the difficulty that immediately confronts us if we try to explain these antithetical responses to predators on the basis of a simple affect interpretation of alarm calling behavior. In both cases the animals are clearly fearful, but in one situation they rush towards dense cover, and in the other they rush away from it. This contrast becomes comprehensible, however, if we propose that, in addition to the involvement of emotion, the alarm calls in some sense *represent* particular predators to other animals. What I am presuming here is that, after examination of the visual stimulus of an eagle while it is still only a silhouette in the sky and consulting schemata stored in the brain from past encounters with different species of flying birds, the calling monkey decides that this is indeed a martial eagle, serious enough as a threat, especially to infants in the group, to merit a signal. As I interpret the situation, the alarm call that is uttered elicits in monkeys hearing the call an equivalent mental concept to that experienced by the caller when it first saw the eagle. The appropriate sequel, on the basis of past experience, is to run for cover.

Fear will be of course a component in the response, galvanizing the animal into action, no doubt with all of the appropriate autonomic accompaniments. But although fearfulness plays a role, the essential key to this behavior must, I believe, be found in cognition rather than affect. The experimental result that convinced us more than any other that representation must be involved was to see the vervets, confronted with an alarm call played from a hidden speaker, but with no predator in sight, suddenly going bipedal when a snake alarm call was played and searching anxiously in the grass around them for a snake that the call told them must be there, or looking up into the sky for the non-existent eagle announced by playback of an eagle alarm call (SEYFARTH, CHENEY and MARLER loc cit.).

We are dealing of course with difficult problems that philosophers have argued about for centuries (GRIFFIN 1981). It is difficult to prove unequivocally that cognition is involved. At some point, the decision to adopt a cognitive interpretation hinges on an appeal to Occam's razor. You could, as some have suggested, invoke triggered reflexes of looking up or looking down. You could fractionate the categories of affect more and more finely so that distinct affective states would be evoked by different classes of predators, a solution that reduces the power of the concept of affect to a point where it loses all explanatory value. The fact is that the monkeys behave as though the alarm calls make them think that a predator is indeed present. I am using the term «think» advisedly, in the sense of evoking a mental concept. As a related accompaniment, there must be an expectation that a visual search will lead to detection of a member of a particular class of stimuli with specified properties, such as those of a soaring martial eagle.

The specificity of alarm calling behavior as manifest in adult animals is dramatized by the behavior of younger animals, who are prone to make mistakes. Inspection of the array of objects to which an infant vervet will give eagle alarm calls (Figure 1) reveals that, although martial eagles are occasionally responsible, they are no more common as a stimulus than a great variety of other birds, some predatory, others not (SEYFARTH, CHENEY and MARLER 1980a; SEYFARTH and CHENEY 1980). Similarly with leopard alarm calls, an infant will give this call to a lion or a hyena, or even to an impala or a warthog. As the Amboseli vervets mature, their calling behavior gradually becomes more and more focussed on very particular stimuli. Thus in adulthood the class of referents for the eagle

Fig. 1: A diagrammatic representation of data from SEYFARTH, CHENEY and MARLER (1980b) on stimulus objects evoking «eagle alarm» calls in wild vervet monkeys. Results for adult, juvenile and infant monkeys are given separately so that a developmental sequence can be discerned. Only the species connected by lines were effective. The width of the lines provides a rough index of the relative frequency of elicitation of alarm calling. In adult vervets, martial eagles were the major referent for eagle alarm calling, but a minor one for infants, along with many other non-raptorial birds as well.

alarm call consists not just of eagles in general, of which there are about 20 at Amboseli, but of one in particular, the martial eagle. The referents for other vervet alarm calls range from the general to the highly specific depending on the functional connotations of the situation.

Once it is mature, an adult vervet will display extraordinary visual acuity in identifying a soaring eagle long before a human observer is even aware that a raptor is present let alone able to identify the species. Thus in adulthood both the referents for calls and the responses that they evoke are specific. As arbitrary, non-iconic signals, the calls satisfy basic criteria for symbolic behavior. The calls seem to represent the predators to other animals that hear them for purposes of social communication. According to this view affect is indeed involved in this complicated predator situation that confronts vervets at Amboseli, but it plays a secondary role, more generalized than has been presumed in previous interpretations. By its very nature a purely affective system is unable to specify the particulars that are so crucial to vervets in making the right behavioral decisions both in selecting a signal for production and in choosing an appropriate response when a signal is received.

So we find ourselves in diametric opposition to the overwhelmingly prevalent view that affect is the crucial component of monkey vocal signals – even the only component – underlying their production and their interpretation by others. The question must be faced, are we dealing with an obscure special situation that arises because of peculiar selection pressures that confront the Amboseli vervets (SMITH 1977) or is representational signaling widespread, and perhaps undetected until now only because we have failed to investigate other cases in the right way? The case of the vervet monkey alarm calls was chosen because it was felt to be a relatively simple one. The notion of symbolic representation is difficult at best to submit to empirical investigation, but it is more manageable if that which is represented is a stable object in the environment, identifiable unequivocally by an observer, and subject to withholding or presentation by an experimenter. It is not inconceivable that representation of environmental referents, likely to be biologically salient objects such as predators, or perhaps in some cases food items, will prove to recur in non-human primates, and perhaps in other taxa as well. What of the possibility that animals might use their vocalizations to represent something more abstract than classes of objects, such as relationships? We can visualize this possibility most easily in social contexts, in the form of dominance relationships or kinship, engaging phenomena that are of interest in their own right as a challenge to the cognitive capacities of animals, and likely a special focus of their natural intelligence (CHENEY and SEYFARTH 1982a; HUMPHREY 1976).

3 Vocal representation of social relationships: agonistic recruitment calls of macaques

In a search for animal communication systems that are amenable to investigation of the possibilities of representational signaling about social relationships, my colleagues Harold and Sarah Gouzoules and I conducted an analysis of a system of vocal signals used by rhesus macaques to recruit help from relatives when they became embroiled in an agonistic encounter with a member of the social group. This pattern of social interaction proves to be peculiarly suitable for representational analysis. Macaques and baboons commonly display recruitment behavior during agonistic interactions. One animal gets into a fight and seeks help from another group member. If recruitment is successful, the two combine forces, so neutralizing or countering the aggressive threat (e. g. KAPLAN 1978).

Other investigators had already noted that there is commonly a lot of vocalization during recruitment, especially screaming. We set out to study the role of screams in the recruitment process, and to assess the adequacy of the classic «affect» view of primate calls in the interpretation of our findings. We knew already from the work of others that recruitment is by no means a random process. Recruits are much more likely to be drawn in if the opponent of the victim is a non-relative than if the altercation is between two members of the same family, for example. Thus one abstract dimension that is relevant in recruitment is kinship. It is also likely that dominance relationships between caller and opponent provide another dimension by which the potential severity of the threat could be assessed by other animals, and perhaps represented to them by a process of vocal encoding. An extended program of research was launched to explore the role, if any, of the calls in the recruitment process, and to see whether, if they are involved, they reflect any of these abstract aspects of social relationships. We also sought to establish what part affect plays, and whether something like the threat of the victim being hurt is sufficient to explain what takes place.

The subjects chosen were the rhesus macaques living in semi-natural conditions in Puerto Rico on the island of Cayo Santiago. The choice was also influenced by the fact that this is the species with which ROWELL and HINDE (1962) originally worked. They concluded that rhesus vocalizations do not form discrete categories, but rather are highly intergraded. This has since been widely cited as a classic case of graded vocal signals (e. g. MARLER 1965).

Our first undertaking was to assemble a catalogue of calls and the circumstances of use (GOUZOULES, GOUZOULES and MARLER 1984, in press). Contrary to expectations, it was found that the screams used by rhesus in recruitment are largely discrete. Five distinct classes of screams are used (Figure 2). More than 90 percent of the nearly 600 scream bouts that were analyzed contained only calls from one of these five types. Moreover, most bouts consisted only of a single type and only 9 percent included more than one of these five call types. Our data thus appear to indicate a discrete signaling system, contradicting earlier conclusions (ROWELL 1962). There is nevertheless a great deal of call variation. Individual differences occur and there are variations within a call class, but we found little or no intergradation between classes. This was reassuring for our purpose because the strategy of playback experimentation is more complicated with graded signals than with discrete ones.

Next we addressed the question of whether the different classes of calls were regularly associated with different probabilities of actual agonistic contact. This proved to be the case, as indicated in Figure 2. With one class, the noisy screams, there was a high probability that the caller would actually be contacted by the aggressor. With another call, the pulsed screams, the probability was also high, though significantly lower than for the first. Two scream types were associated with an intermediate probability of aggressive contact, tonal screams and undulated screams, and one with a low probability, the arched screams.

It is relatively straightforward to then rank the call types in an order that, on the basis of an «affect» interpretation of calling behavior, should predict the likelihood of an ally being recruited. If the primary issue is the likelihood of harm to the caller, translated into the degree to which the caller is aroused or fearful, and then manifest in one of the five scream types, we have a firm basis for predicting how likely each call type is to elicit recruitment. On the other hand, more abstract aspects of agonistic interaction, such as kinship and dominance, that are less bound up with the immediate arousal state of the caller, as will be discussed in a moment, also have potential significance to allies. If they proved to be involved, this might lend support to a representational interpretation of what is taking place. Our investigations in fact confirmed that different classes of calls are significantly associated with different kin and dominance rank relationships between caller and opponent, as well as with the probability of contact (Figure 2).

The next stage was to conduct playbacks of recorded calls to animals of known identity and descent. In early pilot studies we found these to be quite effective. If we recorded a sequence of screams from the victim of an aggressive encounter and subsequently played them back to a resting group of monkeys that included the caller's mother, she responded quickly and vigorously, looking towards the speaker, getting up and approaching, and even investigating the speaker box. However it also became clear that the response to a long string of calls was difficult to interpret, partly because of variation in call timing and quality, and partly because other animals sensed the disturbance of the mother and joined in. For this and other reasons, we decided to use the briefest samples of each call type possible, and to limit the responses studied to the viewing reaction of the mother. Re-

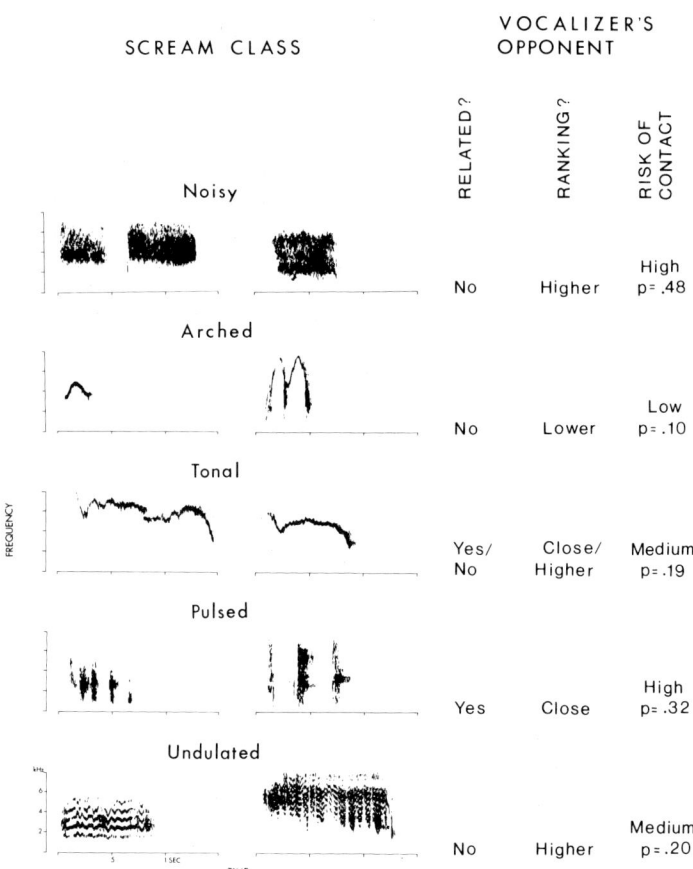

Fig. 2: Spectrograms of the five rhesus monkey scream classes used in recruiting the help of others in agonistic encounters. Degrees of relatedness and relative dominance rankings of typical opponents, and risks of contact are indicated for each scream type. (After GOUZOULES, GOUZOULES and MARLER, in preparation.)

sponse measures were looking at the speaker, the latency of the response, and the duration of looking.

As test sounds, good examples were recorded of several examples of four of the five scream classes, as given by the juvenile offspring of 11 adult female rhesus, all members of the same troop. We were unable to get adequate samples of undulated screams from juveniles for playback purposes. Effects of the playback were quite dramatic, with a strong response evoked from the mothers, as detected and measured by filming the animals before and after playback.

Analyses of the data revealed significant differences in the probability of responses to the different classes of call. When these were ranked, they did not fall out in the order predicted by the affect hypothesis. While the call that elicits the strongest response from mothers, the noisy scream, is the one with the highest probability of agonistic contact the call that ranked next, also evoking strong responses from mothers, was the one associated with the lowest probability of agonistic contact.

At this point more must be said about the organization of aggressive behavior in a rhesus group. While in the short term the likelihood of physical harm in aggressive encounters is obviously a serious issue, in the long term, what are called rank challenges are of equal if not more importance to other members of the group. If a lower ranking non-related animal, a member of some other matriline, challenges and intimidates a young animal, this defeat may have reverberations not only for the victim, but for the status of the entire matriline to which it belongs. Thus the security of a mother's rank might be endangered if such a challenge was not countered, even if the immediate risk of harm to the juvenile was minimal. Interestingly, this is the typical situation in which arched screams occur. With this call contact is rare, and the opponent is a lower ranking non-relative (Figure 2). According to the affect hypothesis, at least in simple form, the response of mothers should be weak. If on the other hand we are ready to admit that a mother can infer the nature of this challenge from the occurrence of arched screams, then her response should be strong. This is in fact what the playbacks show, requiring something more complex than a simple affect interpretation.

At this stage of the investigation we began to entertain the possibility that these calls actually encode abstract information about the nature of the victim's opponent, providing a secure basis on which the mother can judge whether she should respond strongly, or weakly, or not at all. It has already been mentioned that recruitment is less frequent if opponents are relatives, and the results of the playbacks conform to this finding. The two calls given when opponents are likely to be relatives, the likelihood being strong in one case and weaker in the other, are the same calls, tonal and pulsed screams, that evoked the weakest responses in the playbacks. This was the case despite the fact that one, the pulsed scream, is associated with a high probability of agonistic contact. Thus the kinship relationship between the victim and its opponent is reflected in the patterns of call use and in the response to the calls of potential recruits, in this case the mother.

As the experiments progressed, our skepticism about the adequacy of a simple affect interpretation of this recruitment signaling system increased. Thus we are more and more inclined to favor the notion that these calls do in some sense represent to a potential recruit information both about kinship and about dominance relationships between caller and attacker. There are things we need to know before we can be sure, such as how the system develops. It is conceivable, for example, that mothers teach young whom they should especially fear. On the other hand, a sequelae analysis failed to yield clear evidence of variations in fearfulness of the young across call types. The behaviors of callers were tallied while they were producing the different call classes, or immediately afterwards. If different calls were based on different levels of emotional arousal, we would expect the likelihood that call types would be accompanied by withdrawal, holding ground, or advancing on the opponent, to vary accordingly. In fact the sequelae to production of different scream types were remarkably similar, a further indication of the inadequacy of a simple affect interpretation of call production. The fact that calls tend to occur in bouts of one type even though the emotional state of a caller must be varying radically as a fight develops also argues against an affect interpretation, and is at least consistent with the representational hypothesis, as is the discreteness of call structure.

For all these reasons we favor the view that this is a system of representational signals that conveys information not just about classes of objects but about relationships between individuals. These are issues that we can be sure are very much on their minds, likely to be strong foci for their intelligence, and of great potential relevance for survival and reproduction in a species in which the social factors have a strong impact on the prospects of the individual.

4 Conclusions

The inadequacies of previous interpretations of primate vocal behavior are evident. The explanatory value of a simple affect interpretation as applied to rhesus recruitment calls, to vervet alarm calls and apparently to vervet signals with social connotations as well (CHENEY and SEYFARTH 1982a) is strictly limited. I am increasingly convinced that it will prove inadequate with other primate communication systems, though probably not with all. Monkeys surely do experience affect, and affect is surely sometimes manifest in certain aspects of their signaling behavior. We are forced to acknowledge, however, that in some non-human primate signaling behavior, as in our own speech, signs of affect and signs of cognitive activities must be intermingled, functioning as a synergistic blend in which different acoustic vehicles convey different kinds of information. Loudness, pitch, and rates of delivery are all features of monkey calls that are likely to reflect variations of affective arousal in the caller, with the potential to convey information of value to others (GREEN 1975). But the quality of the information, serving to shape the *nature* of the response, rather than its *intensity*, seems to be conveyed by other structural features of the vocalizations. As arbitrary, non-iconic signals these appear to function as symbols, in a representational fashion, involving some of the same powerful cognitive machinery that hitherto has been thought to be largely latent in the natural behavior of monkeys, unless revealed by the techniques of laboratory experimentation. We thus see the prospect of closure of the gap between the intelligence that monkeys display in the laboratory and the apparently simple, emotion-based automaticity of natural communicative behavior as it has previously been interpreted. These two studies on vocal communication in the vervet monkeys, and rhesus macaques invite us to contemplate a much richer view of the vocal behavior of primates, with profound implications both for cognitive ethology (GRIFFIN 1981) and for behavioral ecologists concerned with the functional implications of communicative behavior in animals. The occurrence of representational signaling in animals also bears on speculations about the origins of human language. It is self evident that these animals are not using language. But if they are indeed displaying symbolic behavior as our data indicate, this implies possession and use in their natural behavior of some of the cognitive underpinnings and cross-modal capabilities that are necessary prerequisites for the emergence of human language.

Acknowledgements

This paper is based on the research of four colleagues, Drs. DOROTHY CHENEY and ROBERT SEYFARTH, of the University of California, Los Angeles, and Drs. HAROLD and SARAH GOUZOULES of the Rockefeller University, New York. I am deeply indebted to them all for permission to quote this work, some of which is still unpublished. Research was supported by NIMH postdoctoral fellowship F32 MH08473 to S. G., NIMH postdoctoral fellowship F32 MH08533 to H. G., NSF grant BNS 8023423T to P. M., and Biomedical Research Support Grant PHS RR07065–15 to the Rockefeller University.

References

Andrew, R. J. (1962): The origin and evolution of the calls and facial expressions of the primates. Behaviour 20, 1–109.

Andrew, R. J. (1963): Trends apparent in the evolution of vocalization in the old world monkeys and apes. Symp. Zool. Soc. Lond. 10, 89–101.

Bastian, J. (1965): Primate signalling systems and human languages. In: Primate Behavior: Field Studies of Monkeys and Apes, I. DeVore (ed.). New York, Holt, Rinehart & Winston.

Cheney, D. L. and R. M. Seyfarth (1982a): How vervet monkeys perceive their grunts: field playback experiments. Anim. Behav. 30, 739–751.

Cheney, D. L. and R. D. Seyfarth (1982b): How monkeys see the world: a review of recent research on East African vervet monkeys. In: Primate Communication, C. T. Snowdon, C. H. Brown & M. R. Petersen (eds.). Cambridge, Cambridge University Press.

Gautier, J.-P. and A. Gautier-Hion (1977): Communication in old world monkeys. In: How Animals Communicate, T. A. Sebeok (ed.). Bloomington, Indiana, Indiana University Press.

Gouzoules, G., S. Gouzoules and P. Marler (in press): External reference in mammalian vocal communication. In: The Development of Expressive Behavior: Biology-Environment Interactions, G. Ziven (ed.). New York, Academic Press.

Gouzoules, S., H. Gouzoules and P. Marler (1984): Rhesus monkey (Macaca mulatta) screams: representational signalling in the recruitment of agonistic aid. Anim. Behav. 32: 182–193.

Green, S. (1975): Communication by a graded vocal system in Japanese monkeys. In: Primate Behavior, Vol. 4, L. A. Rosenblum (ed.). New York, Academic Press.

Griffin, D. R. (1981): The Question of Animal Awareness. New York, The Rockefeller University Press.

Humphrey, N. K. (1976): The social function of intellect. In: Growing Points in Ethology, P. P. G. Bateson and R. A. Hinde (eds.). Cambridge, Cambridge University Press.

Kaplan, J. R. (1978): Fight interference and altruism in rhesus monkeys. Am. J. Phys. Anthropol. 49, 241–250.

Lancaster, J. (1965): Primate Behavior and the Emergence of Human Culture. New York, Holt, Rinehart & Winston.

Luria, A. (1982): Language and Cognition. Cambridge, Mass., MIT Press.

Marin, O., M. F. Schwarz and E. M. Saffran (1979): Origins and distribution of language. In: Handbook of Behavioral Biology II. Neuropsychology, M. S. Gazzaniga (ed.). New York, Plenum Publ. Corp.

Marler, P. (1965): Communication in monkeys and apes. In: Primate Behavior, I. DeVore (ed.). New York, Holt, Rinehart & Winston.

Marler, P. (1977): Primate vocalization: Affective or symbolic? In: Progress in Ape Research, G. Bourne (ed.). New York, Academic Press.

Marler, P. (1978a): Affective and symbolic meaning: some zoosemiotic speculations. In: Sight, Sound and Sense, T. A. Sebeok (ed.). Bloomington, Indiana, Indiana University Press.

Marler, P. (1978b): Vocal ethology of primates: Implications for psychophysics and psychophysiology. In: Recent Advances in Primatology, Vol. 1, D. J. Chivers & J. Herbert (eds.). New York, Academic Press.

Marler, P. and R. Tenaza (1977): Signaling behavior of apes with special reference to vocalization. In: How Animals Communicate, T. A. Sebeok (ed.). Bloomington, Indiana, Indiana University Press.

Myers, R. E. (1976): Comparative neurology of vocalization and speech: proof of a dichotomy. In: Origins and Evolution of Language and Speech, S. R. Harnad, H. D. Steklis and J. Lancaster (eds.). New York, New York Academy of Sciences.

Newman, J. D. and D. Symmes (1982): Inheritance and experience in the acquisition of primate acoustic behavior. In: Primate Communication, C. T. Snowdon, C. H. Brown and M. R. Peterson (eds.). Cambridge, Cambridge University Press.

Premack, D. (1975): On the origins of language. In: Handbook of Psychobiology, M. S. Gazzaniga and C. B. Blakemore (eds.). New York, Academic Press.

Premack, D. and A. J. Premack (1983): The Mind of An Ape. New York, W. W. Norton & Co.

Rowell, T. E. (1962): Agonistic noises of the rhesus monkey (Macaca mulatta). Symp. Zool. Soc. Lond. 8, 91–96.

Rowell, T. E. and R. A. Hinde (1962): Vocal communication by the rhesus monkey, (Macaca mulatta). Proc. Zool. Soc. Lond. 138, 279–294.

Seyfarth, R. M. and D. L. Cheney (1980): The ontogeny of vervet monkey alarm calling behavior: A preliminary report. Z. Tierpsychol. 54, 37–56.

Seyfarth, R. M., D. L. Cheney and P. Marler (1980a): Vervet monkey alarm calls: semantic communication in a free-ranging primate. Anim. Behav. 28, 1070–1094.

Seyfarth, R. M., D. L. Cheney and P. Marler (1980b): Monkey responses to three different alarm calls: evidence of predator classification and semantic communication. Science 210, 801–803.

Smith, W. J. (1977): The Behavior of Communicating. Cambridge, Mass., Harvard University Press.

Snowdon, C. T., C. H. Brown and M. R. Peterson (eds.) (1982): Primate Communication. Cambridge, Cambridge University Press.

Struhsaker, T. T. (1967): Auditory communication among vervet monkeys (Cercopithecus aethiops). In: Social Communication Among Primates, S. A. Altmann (ed.). Chicago, University of Chicago Press.

Struhsaker, T. T. (1970): Phylogenetic implications of some vocalizations of Cercopithecus monkeys. In: Old World Monkeys, J. R. Napier and P. H. Napier (eds.). New York, Academic Press.

III. Communication and Reproductive Behaviour

Fortschritte der Zoologie, Bd. 31 · Hölldobler/Lindauer (Hrsg.): Experimental Behavioral Ecology
G. Fischer Verlag · Stuttgart · New York · 1985

Reproductive behaviour in honeybees

FRIEDRICH RUTTNER

Institut für Bienenkunde, Oberursel, F. R. Germany

Abstract

The reproductive behaviour of honey bees is very complex. Three points of major significance should be emphasized:
1. The course of reproduction is a concern of the whole colony with environmental
factors weighing heavily. Thus reproduction is the immediate subject of selection, as easily
shown by variation of the swarming impetus.
2. A sophisticated device is required to transfer semen in sterile conditions and to store
it for several years.
3. Specific characteristics of mating behaviour have the single goal of maintaining high
genetic variety for the purpose of the long term survival of the population – in spite of the
high individual risks for the queen and for the whole colony.

1 Introduction

Division of functions between worker and sexual castes in reproductive behaviour is a
definitive characteristic in eusocial insects.

In honeybees this division is developed to the highest level. No member of the honeybee
society can exist in isolation, even queen and drones during the mating period – except for
the short time of the mating flight itself. Thus reproduction in honeybees is strictly linked
with the process of fission of the colony, that is in most cases with swarming. The rate of
reproduction does not depend on the number of queens produced, but on the number of
swarms. The whole colony – primarily the worker bees – decide on swarming and production (and maintaining) of young queens and of drones. The interaction between queens
and workers is to be observed in various stages of the process of reproduction.

Another characteristic in honeybees which has to be considered in order to understand
the pecularities of reproductive behaviour is one of a genetic kind: The proneness of
honeybees to inbreeding. The rapid appearance of inbreeding effects in honeybees, well
known through apicultural experience, may be explained by the accumulation of two
different systems:
1. General inbreeding effects by increasing homozygosity, as found in other animals and
   plants. It is assumed that a decrease in fitness will occur as soon as the factor of
   inbreeding is 0,25 or more (R. MORITZ 1982). Decreased fitness of a bee colony is
   observed at two levels: in queens (and even in her haploid sons due to the insufficient
   equipment of the egg with maternal enzymes (MORITZ 1979), and in workers.

2. Loss of brood of queens after mating with related drones. This is due to the peculiar mechanism of «complementary sex determination» first described by WHITING (1943) in *Habrobracon hebetor*, and later on also in the honey bee by MACKENSEN (1951) and WOYKE (1963): The female sex is determined by heterozygosity in a certain locus («sex locus», «X»), the male sex by homozygosity or hemizygosity in the same locus. Homozygosity occurs after inbreeding (50 % after brother-sister mating with one drone, 25 % on average after mating with several drones).

Considering this double danger of inbreeding damages to fitness it is not surprising to find a number of behavioural characteristics of honeybees which seem to have only one single goal: the prevention of inbreeding as far as possible (e. g. obligatory mating during flight, great mating distance, multiple matings at drone congregation areas etc.).

All in all, mating behaviour is a complicated sequence of exactly determined elements. The peculiar complexity in this field is best illustrated by one unique morphological characteristic, the male genitalia. The endophallus of the drone is a complicated organ, not found elsewhere. The function of its different sections can only be partly explained. The structure is even more bizarre in the two species *A. dorsata* and *A. florea*.

A third very specific aspect of this field seems to be primarily inherent in human nature. That is the obvious irresistible stimulation of human fantasy and romantic imagination by certain phases of reproduction in honey bees, e. g. by the mating flight. This event was first correctly observed more than two hundred years ago by ANTON JANSCHA and FRANCOIS HUBER. In the following period of developing experimental research in biology scientists did not further the analysis of this phenomenon, However, poets such as MAETERLINCK and others gave a very romantic story and created the dogma of the honeybee queens monogamy, which was also accepted in the scientific world. We experienced ourselves 30 years ago how much evidence was needed to break this dogma.

This preference for hypothetizing before collecting experimental data in the field of honeybee reproduction still seems to be widespread nowadays.

It is true that experiments with honeybee sexuals are much more difficult to perform than those with worker bees: the sexuals can only be obtained in a restricted part of the season and in restricted numbers. All attempts to train them have so far been unsuccessful, and many experiments depend on the weather conditions. However, this alone cannot explain fully the scarcity of experimental data in certain sections of this field. As this symposium is being held in memory of KARL v. FRISCH, I am inclined to say we need more of his spirit, which can best be expressed by his own words: «The correctly planned experiment is the magic key that forces an animal to answer a given question and this answer will never be wrong». The following problems have to be borne in mind. First of all we have to consider the complexity of the subject. Secondly the level of research in this field. In my opinion it is inadequate compared to what has been accomplished concerning the behaviour of worker bees in orientation and communication. Thirdly the sensitiveness of honeybees to inbreeding.

The sequence in the reproductive behaviour of honeybees is as follows:

(1). Swarming
    1.1. Preparation for swarming and exodus of the prime swarm with the old queen.
    1.2. Hatching of one or several young queens in the residual part of the mother colony, eventual departure of one or several after-swarms with some virgin queens.
(2.) Premating phase of queens and drones
(3.) Mating
(4.) Behaviour and physiology in the postmating phase of the queen.

Emphasis will be put on the interactions of the sexuals with the whole bee colony, and with the environmental conditions.

2 Swarming

The process of swarming is the most spectacular event in the annual life cycle of a bee colony, and many studies have been made to analyse this behaviour (SIMPSON 1973). Here we will deal with this phenomenon as far as it is relevant to basic aspects of reproduction.

Many factors are involved in the swarming behaviour of a bee colony including over-crowding of the hive, especially of the brood nest, amount and quality of pollen collected, the age of the queen, microclimate and genetic disposition.

It is evident that these factors – except for genetic disposition – act only as releasers, not as causal agents. Swarming is an innate behavioural characteristic, obligatorily linked with reproduction: a colony can produce as many daughter colonies with mated young queens as it produces swarms (without considering supersedure of old queens).

The frequency of swarms varies from year to year, from region to region and from strain to strain. SEELEY (1978) found in feral colonies a minimum swarming frequency of 0.8–0.9 in the region of Ithaca, N. Y. A minimum average swarming frequency has to occur to maintain a given population size and to cover inevitable losses. In the temperate zones of Europe and America the average losses are as follows: during mating flight 20 %, during winter 10–20 % (in domestic hives). In feral colonies losses are probably sometimes much higher. Young feral colonies have a much higher loss rate than established ones (SEELEY 1978). The amount of loss due to enemies and diseases of a largely varying kind is not predictable.

2.1 Preparation to swarm

The first step in reproduction is the raising of sexuals. Drone brood appears prior to queen brood, exactly corresponding to the time of development from egg to the mature adult (40 versus 22 days). The production of drones and queens depends on a certain stage of development of the colony – a sufficient number of brood cells and nurse bees to raise and feed a large number of drones and – later on – to give viable divisions of the colony.

As soon as the first queen cell is capped, the prime swarm with the old queen leaves the nest. The earlier the swarm in the season, the better its chance of surviving.

2.2 Young queens in the mother colony after the departure of the prime swarm

Seven days after the first swarm, the decision is made on the further course of events. One virgin queen is hatched by this time, and it is again up to the worker bees whether she is allowd to destroy all other queens and queen cells. If so, the result of reproduction is one colony with a young queen and with old combs, and a colony with the old queen (which may be superseded later on) on a new site. If not, a second swarm with one or several virgin queens will issue. This incident may recur, depending on the number of bees left and the genetic disposition.

The chance of a secondary swarm to survive is worse than that of a prime swarm since mating of the virgin queen with its risks and loss of time to develop a wintering colony is involved. Thus a high selective pressure will act on the bee colony towards a swarming behaviour in a given climate which guarantees the necessary rate of reproduction and, at the same time, viable colonies.

Generally the tendency to swarm will be rather low in the temperate zones. However, a considerable genetic variability exists, corresponding to the variable conditions from year to year – swarming being either advantageous or disadvantageous to the population. Planned selection is feasible in both directions. There exist strains with a very low propensity to swarming (selected for modern apiculture). Other strains regularly give 2–3 swarms per season, a consequence of selection for centuries in a special environment (late honeyflow).

In warm climates with no wintering problems for the bees, though sometimes with heavy losses from drought, fire or enemies, extreme tendencies to swarming are observed during favorable conditions. This is well documented for the «Africanized bee» in South America. In an oasis of Algeria, BROTHER ADAM (1968) observed a colony of *A. mellifera intermissa* which yielded seven swarms in one single season. Finally only a cup of bees was left, which developed again to a full size colony. There is a clear correlation between environmental conditions and the degree of swarming tendency in various races of bees.

The principle of monogyny is abandoned for a short period during the act of swarming in all races of the temperate zone; at the moment of exodus of the secondary swarm several virgin queens hatch simultaneously from their cells and either join the swarm or stay in the mother colony. Monogyny, however, is restored within a few hours, since in each site one virgin kills all the other queens.

In several races of the southern Mediterranean *(A. mellifera lamarckii, intermissa, sicula)* the behaviour is quite different. Virgin queens are not aggressive towards each other. In one case we found more than 50 virgin queens in one swarm of *A. m. lamarckii*, and we were able to keep a dozen virgins together for several days in one cage. As soon as the first queen was mated, however, all the others were eliminated.

This behaviour is highly interesting. It seems excellently suited to reducing losses during mating to zero – a considerable advantage in selection. It is hard to understand why this characteristic has not been adopted by other races. This observation possibly indicates that the principle of monogyny is very important in the bee colony's life, even during the short period of mating.

3 Premating phase

3.1 Drones

In newly hatched drones the mucus gland consists of solid tissue; the semen is still in the testis. Neither mucus nor semen can be ejaculated. At least 12 days are needed for full sexual maturity. Six days after hatching, the mucus glands are transformed into thin walled sacs filled with a white liquid, which rapidly coagulates if exposed to air. The migration of the spermatozoa to the vesicula seminalis is nearly completed. At full sexual maturity semen mixed with the secretion of the vesicula is ejaculated after an adequate stimulus followed by the liquid mucus (RUTTNER and TRYASKO 1975).

In the first days of adult life drones depend to a large extent on feeding by worker bees. This explains the heavy influence of the colony's condition on the maintaining of drones. Flight activity of drones for orientation starts at the age of 8 days.

3.2 Queens

The freshly hatched queen is almost completely ignored by the worker bees, corresponding to the low quantity of 9-ODA produced by the still undeveloped mandibular glands (7 μg versus 135 μg in queens 5–10 days old, BUTLER and PATON 1962). Later on the first signs of a court around the queen are observed, but also an antagonistic behaviour of the workers towards the queen: the queen is attacked and chased through the hive. These attacks are obviously a part of the process of maturation (HAMANN 1956). The queen is only attacked by older bees, not by young bees. If the queen is kept permanently among young bees she will never show a tendeny to leave the hive for mating.

Generally the queen will not start earlier than the 6th day of adult life for the first short flight (orientation flight), having been suffering increasing attacks by worker bees. Longer flights, possibly with matings, start on the 7th day.

During the premating phase important physiologcial changes occur in the young queen: simultaneously with the mandibular glands, the tergite glands increase in size (RENNER and BAUMANN 1964). Both gland systems produce the sexual odour of the queen. High activity of the neurosecretory cells in the pars intercerebralis as well as a storage of neurosecretion in the corpora cardiaca and corpora allata is observed during sexual maturation (BIEDERMANN 1964, HERRMANN 1969). At the same time the yolk protein titre in the hemolymph of the queen and of workers is increasing (ENGELS 1980).

4 Mating

4.1 Time and number of mating flights and matings

It is a well known fact that A. *mellifera* queens never mate in the hive – all the later experiments confirmed the early observations by F. HUBER in 1814 –, and no really exact observation of a mating in confinement (in flight cages) is available.

Mature queens and drones can stay on the same comb in a hive without paying any attention to each other. However, it can be shown experimentally that the olfactory sensory cells of the drone respond to the queen in any situation, even when the drone is tethered (RUTTNER and KAISSLING 1968). On the other hand, the same drone will be strongly attracted by the same queen if she is tethered to a pole outside the hive at a height of 10 meters.

With A. *mellifera*, mating flights are restricted to the hours of early afternoon (13–16h local time) – the hours of highest average temperatures. The flight of the queen takes place only under the conditions of a warm, quiet, bright summer day, i. e. temperature not lower than 20°, bright sky (not necessarily sun), little air movement (under 4 on the meteorological scale).

Queens are inflexible in maintaining the mating flight time. This is important for behavioural isolation of sympatric species. N. KOENIGER (1976) found three different flight periods of drones of three species in Sri Lanka.

In regard to the queen's flight duration two groups are found:
(1.) Shorter than 10 min. The queen returns regularly without mating sign – orientation flights.
(2.) Longer than 10 min. (up to 45 min. and more). The queen returns with mating sign – effective mating flights.
The longer the duration of flight, the greater the number of spermatozoa in the queen (WOYKE 1956).

Half of the queens start egg laying after one single effective mating flight. The other half only after two or more (up to 5) effective mating flights, mostly on successive days (ROBERTS 1944, RUTTNER 1954, 1957). From data on the quantity of sperm in the oviducts of mated queens and on the analysis of the progeny after mating with genetically marked drones, it has to be concluded that the queen mates on average with 6–8 drones in one single flight (maximum observed 16 drones, WOYKE 1956; see also TABER 1954, TRYASKO 1956). According to RUTTNER et al. 1973 and WOYKE 1975, in A. *cerana* this figure is much higher – up to 30 drones per flight.

These relatively recent observations are of great significance for the genetics and the social structure of the bee colony. Assuming mating with 8 drones occurs, the average parentage of the progeny is reduced from 75 % (mating with one drone) to 53 % – that is approximately to the level of diploid organism. This diminishes the danger of inbreeding. Recently the consequences of multiple mating in regard to fitness were analysed by PAGE (1980) and PAGE and METCALF (1982).

However, there is another, very simple reason for multiple mating. To produce a large number of fertilized eggs during three or more years, the honeybee queen needs a) – a large number of spermatozoa in the spermatheca, b) a working device which regulates as exactly as possible the dosage of spermatozoa for fertilization of the individual egg (we calculated that on average only 15 spermatozoa are at the disposal of one egg).

Such an exact dosage is to be achieved only with a very narrow valve – as can be found in the ductus spermaticus of the queen ($\varnothing$ 20–25 μ). This narrow passage is a severe obstacle to the process of filling the spermatheca. Only 10 % of the spermatozoa deposited in the oviducts reach the spermatheca. To fill the spermatheca with 5 millions, 50 mill. spermatozoa have to be injected in the oviducts. Queens inseminated with a lower quantity of sperm will soon lay unfertilized eggs (WOYKE and RUTTNER 1976).

5 Drone congregation areas

The first approach to a closer study of the events during the mating flight was found by the observation of drone congregation areas in 1958 (P. JEAN-PROST). This term does not describe casual concentrations of drones in any location. A drone congregation area is an accumulation of flying drones in one and the same place during the whole flight season, year after year, independent of the presence of a queen (F. and H. RUTTNER 1963, 1965, 1966, 1968, 1972; GERIG 1975). Such places have been recorded during the last decades in many countries in different continents and climates. Some of the congregations were observed for more than 20 years without noticeable change. The height of maximum density of drones varies (in different regions and different seasons) from 2–4 m to as much as 20–40 m.

The evidence of a congregation area can be detected by ear (loud humming), by throwing a stone in the air (the stone will be followed by a couple of drones) or – best – by attracting drones to a tethered queen, to queen extract or synthetic 9-ODA.

It is strange to observe that evidently the drones are stronger attracted to a specific location than to the odour of a queen. If a tethered queen with a swarm of drones circling round her is moved beyond the borders of the congregation area, the drones will follow her only for a short distance, and then return to the area, leaving the queen alone. This behaviour allows the queen to terminate the mating process at any time.

It was observed that queens arrive at the congregation area about one hour later than the drones, and that they mate there (JEAN-PROST 1958). The assumption that queens mate mainly in drone areas is supported by the well known observation that the result of a mating flight follows the rule of «All or Nothing»: the queen returns either with the semen of many drones or without any (however very rarely with semen of one or two drones only).

6 Orientation

Direction and range of drone flights was studied by marking different drone populations in a region of the Austrian Alps and another in the Taunus Hills near Frankfurt.

More than 120 000 drones were marked during several years, and genetic markers were also used. It was shown that certain flight directions were clearly preferred to others, e. g. at the congregation area «Seekopf». This proved to be an excellent experimentation area, located on a saddle at the crossing of two valleys (Fig. 1A). At this heavily visited place drones were found from all but one bee yards of the region, in a radius of 5 km, corresponding to an area of 78 km² with several hundred colonies. A congregation area is the meeting place of all drones of the region – resulting in an effective prevention of inbreeding.

During these experiments it became evident that drones of certain apiaries visited this area more frequently than expected, in other cases less frequently. Apiaries located in the SW, NE and ENE from where a sharp mark on the mountain silhouette was clearly visible were overrepresented, those in the N with a less clear mark were underrepresented. From one apiary in NW with no visible horizon mark visible in this direction (Fig. 1B) not a single drone was found in two consecutive years in spite of the relatively short distance of 1700 m.

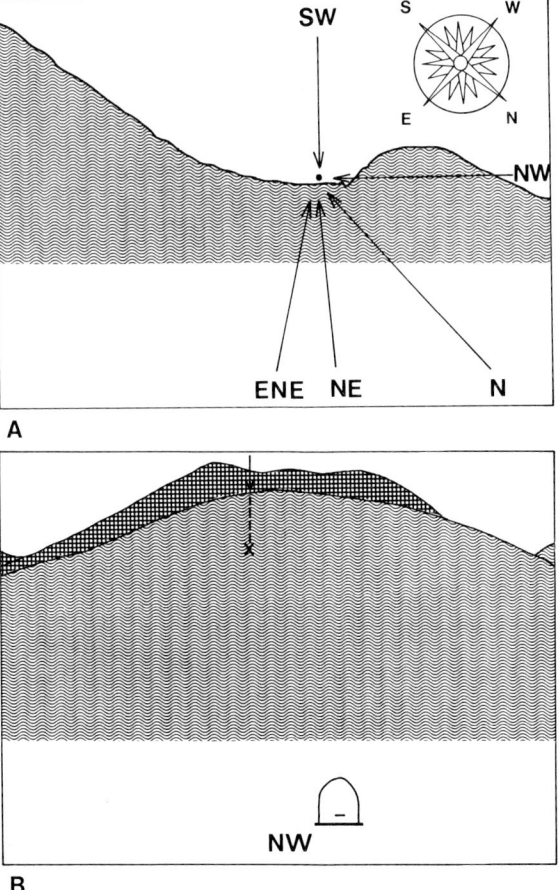

A

B

Fig. 1: *A* Drone congregation area «Seekopf». Lines indicate directions to apiaries with populations of marked drones. *B* View from NW – no horizon mark visible.

This orientation behaviour is not learned, it is present as an innate characteristic as the following experiment showed. We knew the frequency of drones arriving from one apiary ENE of the congregation area Seekopf. We transported 4 colonies with differently marked drones to a place 50 m away from this apiary. If the orientation behaviour were learned an increasing number of drones would have been expected during the following days. This was not the case. On the very first day we caught newcomer drones at just the frequency expected, without an increase on the following days (F. and H. Ruttner 1972).

In less mountainous regions other marks, e. g. trees may be used for orientation.

In the flight area of a bee colony several congregation places are found. Using three dominant genetic markers the approximate mating distance was determined. Maximum drone flight distance of more than 7 km, traversing a mountain ridge of 800 m was found in this case (H. Ruttner 1976) and a medium mating distance of queens of 2,5 km. The figures of flight distances of queens and drones added together give a maximum mating distance of 10–12 km. This corresponds exactly to the data of Peer (1957) from Canada, determined by a quite different method.

Thus good evidence exists regarding far distance orientation of drones and queens. However, the question remains unanswered concerning the orientation at the area itself. What makes drones circle at a certain location, within invisible boundaries, as if attracted to the area by magic powers? Several hypotheses have been discussed – condition of the ground, thermal upwind, distribution of radiation on the horizon – but not a single one can be applied to all cases observed. Thus an important question of orientation still remains to be solved.

7 Copula

From a greater distance drones are attracted by a moving object, irrespective of shape or size or odour. We have seen drones following other drones, butterflies, birds, leaves blown in the wind, or stones thrown upwards. The drone approaches the object upwind and at a closer distance it is attracted by the odour of the queen or synthetic 9-ODA, again irrespective of shape, size and movement.

Fig. 2: Genitalia of a freshly mated queen (G. Koeniger 1983) CH Chitinuous plates of the «mating sign», pressed into the bursa copulatrix (BC) of the queen; its sticky mucus (A) will adhere to the hairy part of the endophallus of the next drone during eversion, and thus the whole plug will be removed.

LO	lateral oviduct, filled with semen
MO	median oviduct
O	ovary
ST	sting

The copula itself will be described for the most frequent case, which is also the most complicated one, namely the mating of a queen with a mating sign, i. e. all the matings of a series but the very first one. Earlier it had been an enigma how a queen can mate again as long as the «mating sign» – a part of the male endophallus with mucus – is fixed in the sting chamber (Fig. 2; THORNHILL and ALCOCK 1983). This was fully understood only recently by a study of G. KOENIGER (1983). The drone clasps the queen from behind and below and brings the tip of the abdomen to the sting chamber of the queen. In all four *Apis* species the drones show brushes of sophisticated hairs on the metatarsus (RUTTNER 1976). The last stimulus – releasing eversion and ejaculation – is the contact to the opened sting chamber of the flying queen, that is to a tube 3,5 mm wide (GARY and MARSTON 1971). Tufts of sensory hairs with a peripheric ganglion on the parmeres serve as receptors (RUTTNER 1957, SCHLEGEL 1967).

In the first stages of eversion a field of soft brown hairs appears on the ventral side of the endophallus. These hairs glue to the mucus of the mating sign and extract it from the queen while the process of eversion proceeds. Thus the bulb of the endophallus can be inserted (Fig. 3) and the semen ejaculated into both oviducts. By detaching one part of the bulb the drone separates from the queen and falls dead to the ground.

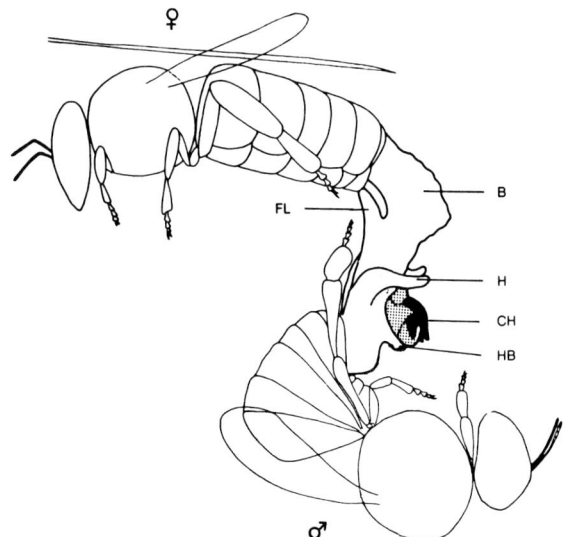

Fig. 3: Queen and drone during copula, as observed in experiments with tethered queens (G. KOENIGER 1983)

B   bulb of endophallus
CH   chitinuous plates of the mating sign (dotted) originating from the precedent drone, glued to a prominent hairy field (HB).
H   cornua
FL   fimbriate lobe of endophallus.

8 Postmating phase

The semen ejaculated into the lateral oviducts of the queen is transferred to the spermatheca within 24 hours. As shown by experiments at the laboratory at Oberursel, this is
a combined process of pressure by the queen and undulating locomotion of the spermatozoa (RUTTNER and G. KOENIGER 1972, GESSNER and RUTTNER 1976). The completely filled spermatheca of a queen of a European race contains 5–7 mill. spermatozoa
surviving for years in an isotonic and alkaline (p_H 8,5) liquid. A net of tracheae round the
receptaculum, a one-layer epithelium on its membrane and the secretion of the spermathecal gland are essential for their survival (G. KOENIGER 1970).

Oviposition starts as soon as 1½ days after the last mating. During the development of
the ovaries the neurosecretion is emitted from the neurosecretory cells and the corpora
allata (HERRMANN 1969). The external stimuli for the start of oviposition are certainly
linked to events during the mating flight. The perception mainly occurs in the sting
chamber and bursa copulatrix during the copula, but semen and mating sign do not have a
significant effect. Mere external contacts show a slight effect (G. KOENIGER 1985).

References

Adam, Brother (1968): In search of the best strains of bees. Walmar Verlag, Zell (BRD).

Alber, M., Jordan, R., Ruttner, F. and H. (1955): Von der Paarung der Honigbiene. Z. Bienenfor-
schung 3, 1–28.

Biedermann, M. (1964): Neurosekretion bei Arbeiterinnen und Königinnen von Apis mellifera L.
unter natürlichen und experimentellen Bedingungen. Z. wiss. Zool. 170, 256–308.

Butler, C. G., Paton, P. N. (1962): Inhibition of queen rearing by queen honeybees (Apis mellifera L.)
of different ages. Proc. R. Ent. Soc. London A 37, 114–116.

Engels, W. (1980): Control of fertility in bees. Int. Conf. on Regulation of Insect Development and
Behavior. Karpasz, Poland.

Gary, N., Marston, J. (1971): Mating behavior of drone honeybees with queen models (Apis mellifera
L.). Anim. Behav. 19, 229–304.

Gerig, L. (1971): Wie Drohnen auf Königinnen-Attrappen reagieren. Schweiz. Bienenz. 94, 558–562.

Gessner, B., Ruttner, F. (1977): Transfer der Spermatozoen in die Spermatheka der Bienenkönigin.
Apidologie 8, 1–18.

Hammann, E. (1956): Wer hat die Initiative bei den Ausflügen der Königin, die Königin oder die
Arbeitsbienen? Diss. Zool. Inst. der Freien Universität Berlin.

Herrmann, H. (1969): Die neurohormonale Kontrolle der Paarungsflüge und der Eilegetätigkeit bei
der Bienenkönigin. Z. f. Bienenforsch. 9, 509–544.

Jean-Prost, P. (1957): Observation sur le vol nuptial des reines d'abeilles. C. R. Acad. Sci. 245,
2107–2110.

Koeniger, G. (1985): Reproduction and mating behavior. In Rinderer, Genetics of honeybees.
Academic Press (in press).

Koeniger, G. (1970): Bedeutung der Tracheenhülle und der Anhangdrüse der Spermatheka für die
Befruchtungsfähigkeit der Spermatozoen in der Bienenkönigin (Apis mellifica L.). Apidologie 1,
55–71.

Koeniger, G. (1983): Die Entfernung des Begattungszeichens bei der Mehrfachpaarung der Bienenkönigin. Allg. Dtsch. Bienenztg. 17, 244–245.

Koeniger, N., Wijayagunasekera H. (1976): Time of drone flight in the three honeybee species (A.
cerana, A. florea, A. dorsata) of Sri Lanka. J. apic. Res. 15, 67–71.

Mackensen, O. (1951): Viability and sex determination in the honey bee (Apis mellifera L.). Genetics
36, 500–509.

Moritz, R. F. A. (1978): Einfluß der Inzuchtdepression auf die Fitness der Drohnen (Apis mellifera capensis). Apidologie 9, 156–158.

Moritz, R. F.A. (1982): Maternale Effekte bei der Honigbiene (Apis mellifera L.) Zeitschr. Tierzücht. Züchtungsbiol. 99, 139–148.

Page, R. E. (1980): The evolution of multiple mating behavior by honey bee queens (Apis mellifera L.). Genetics 96, 263–273.

Page, R. E., Metcalf, R. A. (1982): Multiple mating, sperm utilization, and social evolution. Amer. Naturalist 119, 263–281.

Peer, D. F. (1957): Further studies on the mating range of the honeybee, Apis mellifera. Can. Entom. 89, 108–110.

Pirchner, R., Ruttner, F. and H. (1961): Erbliche Unterschiede zwischen Ertragseigenschaften der Bienen. Proc. XIth Int. Congr. Entomol. II, 510–516.

Renner, M., Baumann, M. (1964): Über Komplexe von subdermalen Drüsenzellen (Duftdrüsen?) der Bienenkönigin. Naturwiss. 51, 68–69.

Roberts, W. C. (1944): Multiple mating of queen bees proved by progeny and flight tests. Glean. Bee Cult. 72, 281–283.

Ruttner, F. (1954): Mehrfache Begattung der Bienenkönigin. Zool. Anzeiger 153, 99–105.

Ruttner, F. (1957): Die Sexualfunktionen der Honigbienen im Dienste ihrer sozialen Gemeinschaft. Z. vergleich. Physiol. 39, 577–600.

Ruttner, F. (1962): Bau und Funktion des peripheren Nervensystems an den Fortpflanzungsorganen der Drohnen. Ann. Abeille 5, 5–58.

Ruttner, F. (1975): Ein metatarsaler Haftapparat bei den Drohnen der Gattung Apis (Hym.: Apidae). Ent. Germ. 2, 22–29.

Ruttner, F. (1979): Events during natural replacement of the queen in a bee colony. In «Queen Rearing», p. 5–18. Apimondia, Bucharest.

Ruttner, F., Kaissling, K.-E. (1968): Über die interspezifische Wirkung des Sexuallockstoffes von Apis mellifica und Apis cerana. Z. vergl. Phys. 59, 362–370.

Ruttner, F., Koeniger, G. (1971): Die Füllung der Spermatheka der Bienenkönigin. Aktive Wanderung oder passiver Transport der Spermatozoen? Z. vergl. Physiol. 72, 411–422.

Ruttner, F., Ruttner, H. (1963–1972): Untersuchungen über die Flugaktivität und das Paarungsverhalten der Drohnen. – I., 19. Int. Beekeeping Congr. Praha, 604–605. – II. Beobachtungen an Drohnensammelplätzen. Z. Bienenforsch. 8, 1–8. – III. Flugweite und Flugrichtung der Drohnen. Z. Bienenforsch. 8, 332–354. – IV. Zur Fernorientierung und Ortsstetigkeit der Drohnen auf ihren Paarungsflügen. Z. Bienenforsch. 9, 259–265. – V. Drohnensammelplätze und Paarungsdistanz. Apidologie 3, 1972, 203–232.

Ruttner, F., Woyke, J., Koeniger, N. (1972): Reproduction in Apis cerana. 1. Mating behaviour. J. apic. Res. 11, 141–146.

Ruttner, F., Woyke, J., Koeniger, N. (1973): Reproduction in Apis cerana. 2. Reproductive organs and natural insemination. J. apic. Res. 12, 21–34.

Ruttner, H. (1976): Untersuchungen über die Flugaktivität und das Paarungsverhalten der Drohnen. – VI. Flug auf und über Höhenrücken. Apidologie 7, 331–341.

Schlegel, P. (1967): Elektrophysiologische Untersuchungen an den Borstenfeld-Sensillen des äußeren Geschlechtsapparates der Drohnen (Apis mellifica). Naturwiss. 54, 26.

Seeley, T. (1978): Life history strategy of the honey bee, Apis mellifera. Oecologia 32, 109–118.

Simpson, J. (1973): Influence of hive space restriction on the tendency of honeybee colonies to rear queens. J. apic. Res. 12, 183–186.

Taber, S. III (1954): The frequency of multiple mating of queen honeybees. J. Econ. Entomol. 47, 995–998.

Thornhill, R., Alcock, J. (1983): The evolution of insect mating systems. Havard Univ. Press, New York.

Trjasko, V. V. (1956): Multiple matings of queen bees (in Russian). Pchelovodstvo 12, 29–31.

Whiting, P. (1943): Multiple alleles in complementary sex determination of Habrobracon. Genetics 28, 365–382.

Woyke, J. (1955): Multiple mating of the honeybee queen (Apis mellifica L.) in one nuptial flight. Bull. Acad. Polon. Sci II 3, 175–180.

Woyke, J. (1960): Natural and artifical insemination of queen honeybees. Pszczelinicze Zeszytyn Naukowe IV, 183–275.

Woyke, J. (1963): Drone larvae from fertilized eggs of the honeybee. J. apic. Res. 2, 19–24.

Woyke, J. (1975): Natural and instrumental insemination of *Apis cerana* indica in India. Journ. apic. Res. *14*, 153–159.

Woyke, J., Ruttner, F. (1958): An anatomical study of the mating process in the honeybee. Bee World *39*, 3–18.

Woyke, J., Ruttner, F. (1976): Results. In F. Ruttner, Instrumental Insemination of the Honeybee Queen. Apimondia Publ., Bucharest.

Fortschritte der Zoologie, Bd. 31 · Hölldobler/Lindauer (Hrsg.): Experimental Behavioral Ecology
G. Fischer Verlag · Stuttgart · New York · 1985

Sociobiology of reproduction in ants

BERT HÖLLDOBLER and STEPHEN H. BARTZ

Department of Organismic and Evolutionary Biology, MCZ-Laboratories, Harvard University, Cambridge, Mass. 02138, USA

Abstract

Two major components of the sociobiology of reproduction in ants are mating behavior and the division of reproductive labor in mature colonies. In this paper we review the facts and some of the theoretical issues associated with these major aspects of ant reproduction.

Mating behavior among ant species is quite diverse, but we recognize two major patterns which we have termed the «female calling syndrome» and the «male aggregation syndrome». In the female calling syndrome, new queens typically do not disperse widely, but tend to remain close to the natal nest, and secrete pheromones which attract males for mating. This syndrome has been found in several phylogenetically primitive species and in some socially parasitic, dulotic, and myrmecophylous species. Mature colonies are generally small and produce relatively few new reproductives each year. The male aggregation syndrome occurs among more phylogenetically advanced species that form large colonies and produce hundreds or thousands of alates in each reproductive season. Among these species, males congregate at mating sites and produce sex-attractant pheromones in concert. Females often come from considerable distances to these aggregations for mating. Differences between these syndroms in such features as the extent of synchronization of mating flights, the incidence of multiple insemination, and the potential for sexual selection are discussed both empirically and theoretically.

Conflict of interest between the queen and the workers in ant societies is expected to occur over the ratio of investment in male versus female reproductives and over the source of the reproductive males. The theoretical arguments concerning queen or worker control of colony reproduction are reviewed along with data suggesting that the queen has a powerful controlling influence. We argue that it is possible for workers to lose control of the colony's reproductive activities in the course of evolution.

1 Introduction

It has been estimated that there are 12,000–14,000 species of ants living on earth (WILSON 1971). With the exception of a few, clearly derived parasitic species, all form eusocial societies in which one or several individuals are aided in their reproductive effort by a much larger number of sterile or reproductively inactive individuals. The evolution and maintenance of these societies has been the subject of considerable theoretical interest (see STARR 1979, CROZIER 1979, 1980 for reviews). One issue that is still debated is whether colony reproduction is controlled, in a proximate as well as evolutionary sense, by workers or by the queen. We will review the facts and theoretical arguments concerning queen or worker control of reproduction in the second part of this paper.

Another important aspect in the reproductive biology of ants is the substantial diversity in mating behavior. This diversity is only now beginning to be explored in greater detail, and in the first part of this paper we will discuss some of the most distinct mating patterns in ants in the context of modern evolutionary theory.

2 Mating behavior

2.1 Two major mating syndromes

Although mating behavior among ant species is very diverse we can recognize two major syndromes. In one of these the females remain relatively stationary, they are often even wingless or have reduced wings and they attract males from distant nests by exhibiting a special calling behavior during which they release sex pheromones (Fig. 1). This

Fig. 1: Mating sequence in *Rhytidoponera metallica*. (1) Ergatoid female (black) in calling posture, during which the female releases a sex pheromone from the pygidial gland located between the 6th and 7th tergites. (2) A male (white) approaches a calling female, touching her with his antennae. (3) The male grasps the female at the thorax and mounts her. Simultaneously he extends his copulatory organ in search for the female's genitals. (4) This finally leads to copulation (from Hölldobler and Haskins 1977).

Fig. 2: *a Pogonomyrmex maricopa* females, emerging from the nest entrance in order to take flight.
b Mating aggregation of *Pogonomyrmex desertorum* at an acacia tree. Note the upwind flight of the
approaching males and females.
c Mating cluster of *P. desertorum*. A female is surrounded by two conspecific males (from HÖLL-
DOBLER 1976).

«female calling syndrome» has been found among several phylogenetically primitive species (Haskins 1978, Hölldobler and Haskins 1977, Janzen 1967), including perhaps the most primitive living ant species *Nothomyrmecia macrops* (Taylor 1978, Hölldobler and Taylor 1983) as well as in some phylogenetically more advanced species, especially in a number of socially parasitic, dulotic and myrmecophilic ants, including species of the genera *Leptothorax, Doronomyrmex, Harpagoxenus* and *Formicoxenus* (Buschinger 1968, 1971a, b, 1974a, 1975). As far as we know these females usually mate only once. Mature colonies of these species tend to be relatively small (on the order of 20–1000 workers) and produce relatively few new reproductives per year.

On the other hand, among species that form very large colonies (several thousands to more than a half million workers), another striking pattern of mating is observed. We call this the *«male-aggregation syndrome»*[1]. In these species males from many colonies gather at specific mating sites, usually marked out by conspicuous features in the landscape, like trees atop ridges, sunflecks, or tall buildings. Females fly in, also from considerable distances, to mate (Fig. 2). Multiple insemination is common among these species, and after mating females disperse widely before starting to build their founding nest chambers. Mature colonies of these species usually produce hundreds to thousands of reproductives every year.

2.2 Synchronization of mating

Nuptial flight activities in species with the *«female calling syndrome»* are inconspicuous and do not appear to be well coordinated or synchronized on the colony and population level (Buschinger 1975, Haskins 1978).

Male aggregation, however, requires precise synchronization of the mating flights within the colony as well as among conspecific colonies within a population. Indeed, most of these ant species exhibit strong seasonal periodicity in the production and release of alates, and the daily synchronicity of flights is often striking. Within minutes of one another, colonies in species like *Pogonomyrmex, Camponotus* or *Lasius* will release thousands of alates, literally filling the air with flying ants.

Experimental and observational evidence suggest that mating flight timing is, at least in part, controlled by endogenous rhythms (Kannowski 1963, 1969; McCluskey 1965). For example, McCluskey (1965) showed that male ants kept in the laboratory under constant illumination showed peaks in restlessness that corresponded in time to the hours at which mating flights occurred each day in the field. Virgin alate females of *Pogonomyrmex californicus* also displayed similar daily increases in activity corresponding to flight times in nature, but stopped exhibiting such behavior once mated (McCluskey 1967). In addition, environmental cues, or «Zeitgeber», and social synchronization signals can modulate and fine tune mating flight activities within colonies and across populations (Hölldobler and Maschwitz 1965). For example, for the carpenter ant *Camponotus herculeanus* it has been demonstrated that the mass take off of both sexes is controlled by the workers. Males and females attempting to depart prematurely are hindered by workers, either by warning signals or by physical restraint (Fig. 3). But once the workers stop interfering, it is usually the males that fly first, each discharging a pheromone from his mandibular gland. At the peak of male activity, the concentration of this pheromone is highest, and it appears that

---

[1]   We do not include here species which form polygynous unicolonial systems, or the special case of army ants, which reproduce by fission, but rather focus on species with monogynous-oligogynous societies which conduct massive nuptial flights.

this triggers the mass take-off of the females (Fig. 3) (HÖLLDOBLER and MASCHWITZ 1965).

It is interesting to note that in many ant species the males have well-developed mandibular glands which produce distinct mixtures of secretions (LAW et al 1965; PASTEELS et al 1980; for review see BLUM 1981), and in many species nuptial flights are well synchronized with the males leaving first and females following shortly afterwards. It is possible that this male synchronization pheromone is a more general phenomenon, but no experimental data exist as yet.

Such synchronization of mating flights may be the result of several important selective forces. In temperate and boreal species the annual periodicity of colony reproduction follows the distinct annual cycle of climatic changes (for reviews see BRIAN 1979; SCHMIDT 1974; WILSON 1971). With a few exceptions, reproductives are produced once a year and usually they depart from their natal colonies a few days or weeks after eclosion. But for some of the species that inhabit boreal regions with severe seasonality, the period available for raising large numbers of new reproductives, releasing them for the mating flight, and enabling the young queens to found incipient colonies might be too short within one year. In such a situation selection may have favored colonies that extended the reproductive cycle over two years. This is the case in some *Camponotus* species in which alates are produced in late summer, and only after having overwintered in the mother nest, do they become ready to take off for the nuptial flight, the temperature permitting (HÖLLDOBLER 1966). In the laboratory it has been demonstrated that the alates can stay through a second winter period in the mother colony provided the temperature remains below 18°C. This

a   b

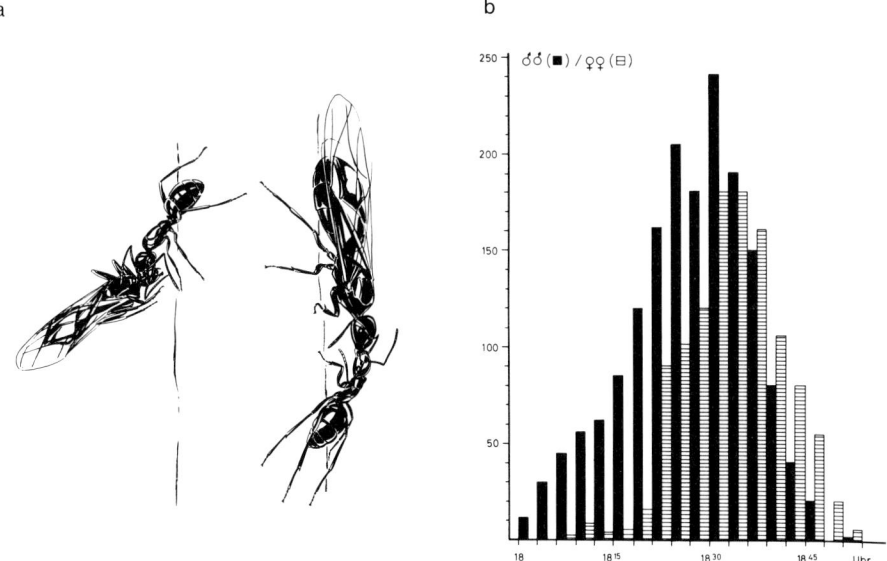

Fig. 3: *a* Males (left) and females (right) of *Camponotus herculeanus* attempting to depart prematurely are hindered by workers.
b Take off of males and females during the nuptial flight of *C. herculeanus*. At the peak of male activity (black columns), mass take off of the females (hatched columns) commences (from HÖLLDOBLER and MASCHWITZ 1965).

242 · B. Hölldobler and St. Bartz

«storage-system» of young reproductives makes *Camponotus* colonies very flexible in having young reproductives always ready for nuptial flights once the climatic conditions are suitable. Although the extended pressence of young male and female reproductives in the colony puts a considerable ergonomic burden on the society, this is alleviated by the unusually high degree of social behavior demonstrated in young *Camponotus* males (HÖLLDOBLER 1966).

The annual temperature cycle is clearly the dominant environmental timing factor in temperate and boreal regions. In more arid geographic areas the reproductive annual periodicity of ants appears to be synchronized with the seasonality of precipitation. But even in the tropics with relatively little annual climatic fluctuations, species specific peaks in the production of alates during the year have been reported (BALDRIDGE et al 1980).

Ecological factors may explain seasonal periodicity in nuptial flights, but many species also exhibit a remarkable daily periodicity in their mating activities. Among some closely related sympatric species this phenomenon is particularly evident, indicating that it may play a role in reproductive isolation. For example, four sympatric species of the harvester ant *Pogonomyrmex* in the Arizona desert tend to have nuptial flights on the same days, however the timing of their flights differ strongly. During a three years study *Pogonomyrmex maricopa* swarmed in the morning between 10:00 and 11:30 followed by *P. desertorum* (11:00–13:00) while the other two species flew in the afternoon (*P. barbatus* between 15:30 and 17:00, and *P. rugosus* from 16:30 to 18:00). Such timing was consistent from day to day (HÖLLDOBLER 1976). Another example is reported by KANNOWSKI (1959) for three sympatric species of *Myrmica* in which alates are released daily over a period of about six weeks from mid-July to September. *Myrmica emeryana* invariably flew between 6:00 and 8:00, *M. americana* between 12:30 and 16:30, and *M. fracticornis* between 18:00 and 19:30.

Finally, to the extent that selection favors outbreeding, it will also favor synchronization of mating flights and mating aggregations. The sparse data that has been collected so far on patterns of allozyme variation in ants (CRAIG and CROZIER 1979; PAMILO and VARVIO-AHO 1979; PEARSON 1983; WARD 1983a) indicates that inbreeding does not occur to any appreciable degree. Alates appear to mate preferentially with individuals from other colonies. This can only happen if the alates from several colonies are on their nuptial flights at the same time.

2.3 Mating aggregations and sexual selection

Mating aggregations and communal signalling occur in many insect groups. Among the more striking examples are communal chorusing in cicadas, crickets, and katydids (ALEXANDER 1975), synchronous flashing of males in some firefly species (LLOYD 1983), communal chemical calling in bark beetles (reviewed by ALCOCK 1981), and the assemblies of honeybee drones at traditional congregation places (see RUTTNER in this volume).

Many mating assemblies may be explained as the result of males congregating in places where females are likely to occur such as emergence or hibernation sites, feeding areas, or oviposition sites. This does not apply to the mating aggregations of most ant species, however. As in *Pogonomyrmex* which form large species-specific mating aggregations on bushes, small trees or on the ground, there is no competition among males for control of resources valuable to females, such as nesting sites or foraging areas, and males do not aggregate near nest entrances where females are likely to emerge. In fact, in *Pogonomyrmex* females fly off after they have mated, and only upon landing a second time, often hundreds of meters from the mating aggregation, do they break off their wings and begin to dig nest chambers in the soil (HÖLLDOBLER 1976).

Ant mating aggregations seem to be very similar to the situation described by ALEXAN-DER (1975) for some acoustical insects such as the periodical cicadas. He imagines that aggregations of males are the result of female choice. Females are selected to choose among males, and are thus attracted to places where males are dense. Once such a process is in operation, it is to the advantage of each male to participate in activities like synchron-ous calling because this increases the number of females attracted to his particular aggre-gation. Males attempting to «go it alone» simply fail to attract females. The evidence that *Pogonomyrmex* males release mandibular gland secretions in concert at their mating aggregations seems to suggest that this scenario describes the situation in these species.

As in other species, males far outnumber females in the mating aggregations of ants. When females arrive at the arena, there is often intense competition among the males for access to the females. In *Myrmecia*, for example, WHEELER (1916) describes the «balling behavior» at mating sites during which masses of males surround each female, often creating a ball of insects 15–20 cm in diameter. At some point, presumably when the female has been fully inseminated, the ball breaks up, the female leaves to establish a nesting chamber, and the males return to the swarm. In *Pogonomyrmex,* the males grapple

Fig. 4: *a* Behavioral sequences during mating in *Pogonomyrmex:* (1) A male (black) approaches a female (white) and touches her with his antennae. (2) The male grasps the female's thorax and attempts to insert copulatory organs into female's cloaca. (3) After successfully inserting copulatory organs the male releases the mandibular grip of the female's thorax. (4) The copulating male massages the female's gaster with his mandibles and forelegs; the female begins to gnaw at the male's gaster. A third male has arrived and grasps the second male's gaster.
b Mating cluster of *P. rugosus.* A female is surrounded by approximately ten males (from HÖLL-DOBLER 1976).

with the female and each other (Fig. 4). When one male has secured a female, he holds her tightly about the thorax with his large, heavily-muscled mandibles. Other males attempt to separate the pair and vie among themselves for position in a waiting line – ready to mount the female as soon as the first male is finished. HÖLLDOBLER (1976) attributes the large mandibles of males in these species to selection for holding onto females, rather than to selection favoring aptitude in male-male fighting. Watching females being surrounded by a frenzied cluster of powerful males, one wonders how the mated female can ever free herself in order to depart from the mating site. MARKL et al (1977) discovered that females, which are apparently fully charged with sperm and no longer motivated to mate, produce stridulation signals whenever they are assaulted by additional sexually excited males. The observational data indicate that males more readily release stridulating females than silent ones.

Many of these observations suggest that the mating aggregations, in *Pogonomyrmex* at least, may be similar to the mating aggregations in some other species of organisms like *Drosophila*, Sage Grouse, and Hammerheaded Bats, called leks (but see BRADBURY in this volume). Ant leks differ from other such mating aggregations, however, in at least one important aspect. Ant males are constrained in a way that Sage Grouse or fruit flies are not, because each male ant ecloses with all of the sperm that he is ever going to have. Dissections of sexually mature males from such phylogenetically diverse groups as *Formica, Camponotus, Lasius, Myrmica, Pogonomyrmex* and *Nothomyrmecia* (HÖLLDOBLER 1966, and unpublished data) reveal that the males' testes are degenerated and all the sperm is stored in the expanded vas deferens (Fig. 5). Thus, male reproductive success in ants does not necessarily increase with increasing number of copulations, as it can in other species in which males continually replenish their sperm supply. In addition, it does not appear, from the few cases that have been studied so far, that males typically have enough sperm to inseminate more than one female. Indeed, in *Atta sexdens* each newly eclosed male was found to contain between 40 and 80 million spermatozoans, while newly mated females contained between 200 and 310 million spermatozoans in their spermathecae

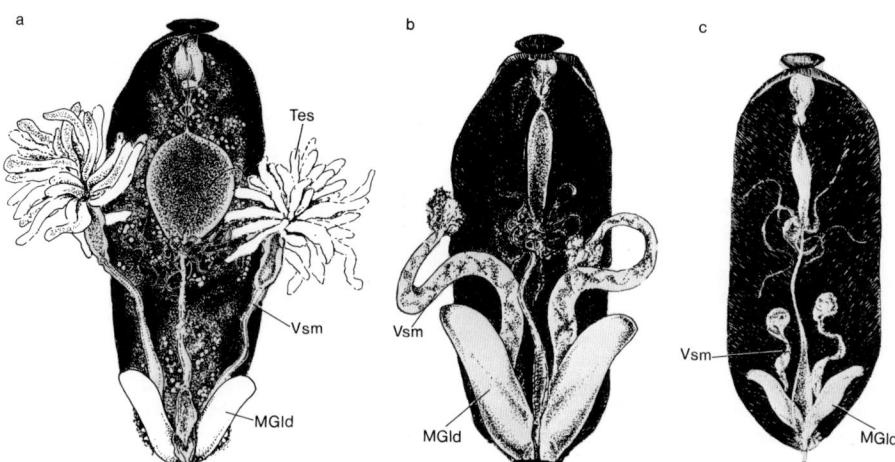

Fig. 5: Gasters of males of *Formica polyctena* were cut open to expose the gonads. (a) Freshly eclosed male; (b) eight days after eclosion; (c) after copulation. MGld = mucus gland; Tes = testis; Vsm = vesicula seminalis.

(KERR 1962). Male ants, therefore, should be under strong selection to be very particular about how they husband their sperm.

One obvious issue of concern for selection is whether it is better for a male, in terms of ultimate reproductive success, to invest all of his sperm in a single female or whether it is better to copulate with several females. Important to this issue is the fact that in ants, unlike other non-social species, a male's sperm does not all go towards effective reproduction. That is, in order for an ant colony to begin to produce any reproductive forms, it first must produce many workers. In most advanced ant societies it appears (claims to the contrary notwithstanding) that workers are rarely reproductive, and because workers are female, derived from fertilized eggs, a substantial portion of a male's sperm is used in colony growth and maintenance rather than in the direct production of new queens. So, the trade-off for a male is obvious. If he inseminates only a single female, and if she mates with no other male, then the male is certain to father any reproductives that she eventually produces. However, mortality of colony founding females is extremely high. Of the tens of thousands of female alates mated in a season's mating flight, at most only a few survive the colony founding phase and only a small portion of those will ever reach colony maturity. So, a male that inseminates only a single female puts all of his sperm in one basket. If he were to inseminate several females he increases the chance that his sperm will end up in a successful colony foundress. In this case, however, he might decrease the chance that his sperm is used by the female to make alates.

On the other hand, if males do inseminate several females, there may be selection favoring males whose sperm mixes with other males' sperm in the females' spermathecae. Mixing sperm increases the chance that each male will have at least some offspring among the new crop of alate queens. It appears indeed, from electrophoretic studies of allozyme variation in multiply-mating ant species (PAMILO 1982, PEARSON 1983, WARD 1983a), that workers in colonies have been fathered by several males.

Multiple insemination occurs relatively frequently among ant species. Of the 32 species for which COLE (1983) could find reliable accounts of the number of matings, in 22 species (69%) females typically mated more than once. As already pointed out, multiple mating is more common among species that form large colonies, and COLE attributes multiple mating to the founding queen's requirement for more than a single male's worth of sperm. It is obvious that females should be selected to acquire sufficient sperm to last the life of the colony. It is not obvious why, as colonies increased in size, this has led to the practice of multiple insemination rather than the evolution of males with more sperm. It could be, as DAVIDSON (1982) suggests, that there is some trade-off associated with the size of males such that larger males would not represent proportionally larger reproductive returns to the colonies producing them. This issue, and the other questions surrounding the sexual size dimorphism in ants (males are usually smaller, sometimes a tenth the size of females), are far from resolved.

In species that make large colonies where females apparently must mate with several males in order to acquire sufficient sperm, it has been noted (COLE 1983) that males seldom attempt to monopolize females. In many other insects, and other organisms as well, sperm competition is an important selective force, and males are often favored to ensure that no other male copulates with his mate (PARKER 1970). In multiply-mating ant species, however, a male that prevents his mate from mating again may well be preventing her from acquiring sufficient sperm to make a colony large enough to ever produce reproductives. Males in these species therefore should be selected to mate with females that are already mated. The active vying for position in the waiting lines behind copulating pairs in *Pogonomyrmex* species (HÖLLDOBLER 1976, DAVIDSON 1982) indicates at least that males do not discriminate against females that have mated before.

Some kind of discrimination seems to be practiced, however, by *Pogonomyrmex* females. Hölldobler (1976) suggested that the intense competition among males for females arriving at the mating arena in *Pogonomyrmex* may be the result of a form of female choice – only those aggressive or persistent males would achieve copulations. Davidson (1982) confirmed Hölldobler's suspicions by showing that larger females tended to mate disproportionately often with larger males. In fact, Davidson reports that there is significant variation in the copulatory success of males, and that variation is associated with male size. As support for this hypothesis of female choice, she points out that there is a weak but positive correlation between colony productivity (number of alates produced) and male size. In the absence of data on the heritability of male size, however, this only suggests that colonies in good reproductive condition produce bigger males.

A confounding bit of data reported by Davidson (1983) is that not only do larger females tend to mate with larger males, but smaller females tend to mate with *smaller* males! If sexual selection is operating such that females choose larger males, why do small females not also choose to mate with larger males? The answer to this question may be that males are selected to be choosy as well. Recall that unlike other lek-mating species, male ants have only so much sperm at their disposal. They cannot afford to be profligate, and selection may favor males who choose to mate with larger females because there is a better chance that large females will survive to produce a mature colony. It is not clear, among ant species, which sex represents a limiting resource to the other. This is especially true in multiply-mating species, even though males may outnumber females.

Mating is only the first phase in the complex process of reproduction in ants. After this phase the males die, but their sperm lives on in the females' spermathecae; it will be used to fertilize eggs in many years to come. For the freshly mated females colony founding follows the mating phase. Only after the colony has grown to maturity, that is, a large enough worker force has been produced to secure the resources needed to raise reproductive offspring, will the second phase of reproduction begin.

3 Reproduction division of labor

The reproductive interests of queens and workers in ant societies are not always identical. Specifically, there is expected to be conflict between the queen and the workers regarding two major aspects of reproduction: the relative investment in the sexes, and the source of reproductive males (Trivers and Hare 1976).

Because of the haplodiploid genetics of the Hymenoptera, a worker in a monogynous colony is three times as closely related to her sisters than to her brothers. The queen, however, is equally related to her sons and daughters. Consequently, workers will be selected to invest more of the colony's reproductive effort in the production of female sexuals than in male production, while the queen is selected to enforce equal investment in the sexes (Trivers and Hare 1976, Benford 1978, Oster et al. 1977).

With regard to the production of males, workers are more closely related to their sons and nephews than they are to their brothers, and selection acting on workers would favor the substitution of sons or nephews for brothers in the reproductive brood. The queen is more closely related to her sons than to her daughters' sons, and selection on the queen should favor any traits that ensure that her sons, rather than her grandsons, comprise the reproductive brood (Trivers and Hare 1976).

With several exceptions (see below) the data that exist point to a powerful and important role of the queen in controlling the reproductive activities in ant societies. In the following sections we will review these data, and discuss how these facts relate to current hypotheses regarding the evolution of eusociality in ants.

3.1 Evidence for the controlling effect of the queen

There are several facts that seem to indicate that the queens control the workers' reproductive activities. Pheromones, emanating from the queen, are usually highly attractive to workers (STUMPER 1956, WATKINS and COLE 1966, JOUVENAZ et al. 1974, VANDERMEER et al. 1980, COGLITORE and CAMMAERTS 1981, FOWLER and ROBERTS 1982, HÖLLDOBLER and WILSON 1983). These «queen tending pheromones» appear to play important roles in ensuring that the queens are always surrounded and protected by the workers (Fig. 6), and in directing the flow of high quality food to the queens (LANGE 1958, 1967). Indeed, queens seem to be the most powerful competitors for the best nutrients in the society. In some species it appears that this queen-ward direction of nutrients suppresses the rearing of sexuals by the workers. This was first demonstrated in *Formica polyctena* by GÖSSWALD and BIER (1954a, b).

In early spring, queens of *F. polyctena* cluster in the sun on top of the nest mounds. During this «sunning period» the queens' ovaries become activated and after a few days

Fig. 6: *a* The queen of *Oecophylla longinoda* during nest emigration is totally covered by a retinue of major workers. *b* Inside the nest chamber the queen is continuously licked and fed by workers (from HÖLLDOBLER and WILSON 1983).

thousands of eggs are deposited in the upper regions of the nest. These eggs appear to be blastogenically predisposed to become sexuals (BIER 1954), but the larvae must still be fed with high quality food in order to develop into reproductives. GÖSSWALD and BIER discovered that this is permitted because the queens move to the lower regions of the nest after egg-laying, where they rest until the first brood has been reared. This separation of queens and brood, the so-called «physiologische Weisellosigkeit» (physiological queenlessness) enables the workers to channel the high quality food to the developing reproductives. In the laboratory, if the larvae are forced to compete with the queen for these nutrients, they do not develop into reproductives. The females become workers, and the males are usually eaten in the larval stage (SCHMIDT 1972).

Similar inhibitory trophic effects caused by the queens have been reported for other ant species. PETERSEN-BRAUN (1977) discovered that in *Monomorium pharaonis* only queens in the period of their peak fecundity inhibit the rearing of reproductives. Very young queens and senile queens do not have such inhibitory effects. Earlier findings suggested that unmated as well as mated queens have an inhibitory effect (BUSCHINGER and KLOFT 1973), but more recent studies have shown that such effects emanate only from mated queens (PETERSEN-BRAUN 1977, BERNDT and NITSCHMANN 1979). BUSCHINGER and KLOFT (1973) and PETERSEN-BRAUN (1977, 1982) argue that this inhibition is due to the queen's high attractiveness to workers, which has the effect that workers preferentially feed the queens and not the brood. On the other hand, BERNDT (1975) and BERNDT and NITSCHMANN (1979) propose that the inhibition is not caused primarily by trophic effects, but rather by inhibitory pheromones emanating from the queens. The experimental results are ambiguous, however, and controlled feeding experiments (BUSCHINGER and KLOFT 1973) support the hypothesis of trophic inhibition. In other ant species, however, such as *Myrmica rubra* (for a review see BRIAN 1979) or *Pheidole pygmaea* (PASSERA 1980), strong circumstantial evidence indicates that queen pheromones can indeed directly inhibit the workers rearing of reproductives.

The fact that the queens in these ant species seem to regulate the reproductive activities of colonies is not necessarily an indication that it would be in the workers best interests to behave otherwise. Queens and workers, for example, should not be in conflict over such matters as the timing of the production of sexuals or the fraction of colony resources devoted to reproduction versus growth. Workers would clearly be selected to respond to influences emanating from the queen that regulate such matters.

The regulating power in the queen is especially striking in monogynous societies. Her presence seems to maintain a colony cohesiveness, and the behavioral changes among the workers after the queen has been removed are often remarkable. In some species the workers become indifferent, and after some time will readily accept a foreign queen in the old queen's place (K. HÖLLDOBLER 1928, GOETSCH 1953, HÖLLDOBLER 1962, SCHNEIRLA 1971, FLETCHER and BLUM 1983).

The fact that in many of these species workers will begin to lay viable, male-destined eggs after the removal of the queen is an indication that queen regulation may have become queen oppression. As mentioned earlier, workers ought to be selected to substitute sons or nephews for brothers in the reproductive brood. In species like *Novomessor cockerelli*, it appears that the presence of the queen prevents workers from reproducing. When the queen is removed, colony cohesion weakens, and workers sometimes become antagonistic towards one another. Correlated with the onset of this aggression is the production of viable, male-destined eggs (HÖLLDOBLER et al., unpublished data). In the presence of the queen, workers produce only trophic eggs, so it appears that the queen clearly affects workers' reproductive physiology.

Apparent reproductive dominance by the queen over other reproductive females or workers in functionally monogynous colonies (for definition see BUSCHINGER 1974) has been demonstrated for several ant species. FLETCHER and BLUM (1983) recently discovered that in *Solenopsis invicta* the presence of queens prevents alate virgin females from shedding their wings. Like in *Novomessor*, in *Plagiolepsis pygmaea* workers produce only trophic eggs in queenright colonies, but after removal of the queen they lay both trophic and viable eggs (PASSERA 1978). Some of the experimental results obtained by PASSERA suggest that the queen's effect in *Plagiolepis* is mediated pheromonally.

HÖLLDOBLER and WILSON (1983) recently obtained indirect evidence indicating that in the weaver ants *Oecophylla longinoda* and *O. smaragdina* the queen's reproductive dominance is based on pheromones. Weaver ant colonies are unusual among ants in combining very large size, extensive territories with multiple nests, and monogyny[2]. Therefore, if a queen control extends to the entire colony it must be of an especially potent form. Queens of *Oecophylla* have been demonstrated to exert an inhibitory influence on the workers' reproductive physiology. Like in the species mentioned above, in *Oecophylla* this effect is very specific. In the presence of a nest queen, the ovaries of young workers remain active and they produce trophic eggs which form an important part of the queen's diet. When the queen is removed, however, these same workers begin to produce viable, male-destined eggs in profusion.

Because the queen cannot be physically examined, seen, or heard by more than a small fraction of the worker population for substantial periods of time, it is reasonable to expect that the influence she exerts is mediated by pheromones rather than by signals in other sensory modalities. This assumption is strongly supported by the fact that the queen's suppressing effect on the workers' ovaries persists in the corpse of a dead queen for several month in the laboratory (HÖLLDOBLER and WILSON 1983). The presence of large complexes of exocrine glands in the head, mesosoma and gaster further suggests the existence of special queen pheromones. There are also exocrine glandular complexes associated with the queen's reproductive organs and it is possible that queen laid eggs are contaminated with queen pheromones. Workers usually carry the eggs to other leaf nests and in this way queen pheromones might also be spread in the colony.

The results of these laboratory experiments are at variance with previous findings reported by LEDOUX (1950, 1974). According to LEDOUX, groups of workers of *O. longinoda* depart from the territory of the mother colony and establish new colonies in the neighborhood. There, they produce workers and reproductive females by parthenogenesis. However, in our experimental series of 10 queenless colony fragments maintained in the laboratory, the broods produced by the workers were composed exclusively of males (HÖLLDOBLER and WILSON 1983). Thus, it seems unlikely that workers are producing viable diploid eggs by parthenogenesis.

Although there is ample circumstantial evidence that ant queens produce pheromones which affect the workers' behavior and reproductive activities, the anatomical source of the queen pheromones is largely unknown and no pheromone has been chemically identified. STUMPER (1956) was able to extract from queens of *Lasius alienus* and *Pheidole pallidula* secretions to which workers were attracted. VANDERMEER et al. (1980) found that workers of *Solenopsis invicta* are attracted to their queen's poison gland secretions, and BRIAN and HIBBLE (1963) found that in *Myrmica rubra* ethanol extracts of the queen heads, when applied to larvae inhibit their growth. Similar results were obtained with

---

[2] Monogyny can never be claimed with absolute certainty, as in some species so-called monogynous colonies can become oligogynous (HÖLLDOBLER 1962). But in all our field investigations during which we opened many leaf nests, we found only one queen per colony.

Pheidole pygmaea, where circumstantial evidence suggests that an inhibitory effect on the workers' sexual brood rearing behavior emanates from the queen's head (PASSERA 1980).

It is surprising that little attention has been given to the study of the ant queens' exocrine glandular repertory, although a previous histological investigation of *Eciton* by WHELDEN (1963) has shown that queens are much more richly endowed with exocrine glands than workers. Recently we found similar results in *Oecophylla* (HÖLLDOBLER and WILSON 1983) and in *Onychomyrmex* (HÖLLDOBLER and TAYLOR in prep.). In this context it is interesting to note that in some ecitonine army ants, where males have to enter a colony in order to get access to the wingless virgin females, the males are as richly endowed with abdominal tergal and sternal glands as reproductive females (HÖLLDOBLER and ENGEL-SIEGEL 1982).

As already indicated, there appears to be a fundamental difference in the mechanism of regulation of fertility in monogynous and truly polygynous ant societies. If a single queen is in «control», passing secretions around the colony, the reproductive behavior of workers can be regulated in a direct and relatively simple manner. In truly polygynous colonies, however, a very different circumstance pervails. Large numbers of queens are often found clustered together, and so far as known, all lay eggs and are not organized into dominance orders. BIER (1958) hypothesized that in these cases the suppression of fertility in the workers is not regulated by primer pheromones, but rather by a directed flow of «profertile» substances away from the workers toward the queens. Although queens of polygynous colonies produce attractants that mediate the directed social flow of profertile substances (LANGE 1958, 1967), these queen pheromones apparently do not function as primer pheromones in suppressing worker fertility.

Finally, it has been hypothesized that if a single queen is in «control», passing secretions around in the colony, the queen can also readily serve as the sole or primary source of the colony odor (HÖLLDOBLER and MICHENER 1980). It was reasoned that if genetic differences rather than environmental odors play the dominant role in the determination of colony odors in the large ant societies, the simplest procedure would appear to be for the queen to provide the essential ingredients. Monogyny would make such a system easily operable; polygyny would tend to break it down (HÖLLDOBLER and WILSON 1977).

Experimental evidence showing that ants recognize their own queen by odor supports these considerations. For example WATKINS and COLE (1966) discovered that workers of several army ant species of the genera *Labidus* and *Neivamyrmex* were attracted to spots of absorbent paper on which the queen had been previously confined. Spots that had been occupied by the mother queen were more attractive than spots occupied by foreign conspecific queens. Similar results were obtained by JOUVENAZ et al. (1974) with *Solenopsis invicta* and *S. geminata*.

Recently, CARLIN and HÖLLDOBLER (1983) have obtained the first experimental evidence that transferred queen discriminators serve as recognition cues in monogynous colonies of the ant genus *Camponotus*. These acquired odor labels are sufficiently powerful to cause non-preferential acceptance among unrelated workers of different species, raised in artificially mixed colonies, and rejection of genetic sisters reared by heterospecific queens.

3.2 Evidence for worker control of reproduction

Support for worker control of colony reproductive activities comes from data on the sex-ratios of alates in various ant species. TRIVERS and HARE (1976) pointed out that selection on workers would favor female-biassed investment ratios, while selection on queens would favor equal investment in the sexes. They produced data on investment ratios (dry weight was used as the measure of investment for several species of ants), and showed that, as they predicted, the sex-ratios exhibited by monogynous ants were normally female biassed. Such female biassed sex-ratios seem to indicate that, in the words of IWASA (1981), «the workers held hegemony in the nest». That is, that the workers are controlling the investment in the sexes. If the queen were controlling her workers in her own interests, one would expect sex-ratios nearer 50 : 50, but it appears that it is only in polygynous ant societies or in slave-making ant species that equal investment in the sexes is seen.

These observations, especially those indicating that some ant species that often serve as slaves for slave-making species produce female-biassed sex-ratios in their own nests, but 50 : 50 ratios in the slave makers' nests where it is not possible for selection on workers to counteract the evolution of control by heterospecific queens (TRIVERS and HARE 1976), suggest that eusocial colonies are maintained because of selection on workers, and not because of selection on queens.

However, the use of sex-ratio data to discriminate between worker and queen control is difficult because of several confounding effects. First, investment is extremely difficult to measure, and dry weights can only be viewed as rough approximations of total investment. For example, the males of some species like *Camponotus* (see HÖLLDOBLER 1966), contribute to colony maintenance by aiding in the distribution of food. If males' activities aid in the production of females, or in the production of workers, and if female alates do not engage in such activities (or at least not to the same extent as the males do), then males would represent a smaller «cost» to the colony than their dry weight would indicate.

Another major problem with using sex ratio data as an indication of queen or worker control of investment is that the relatednesses of the various actors represent only one of several powerful selective forces affecting the sex ratio. HAMILTON (1967) has shown that when family members expect to be competing with one another for access to the same mates, selection will favor decreasing the investment in the competing sex. If, for example, brothers often compete among themselves for access to the same females, then selection will favor a female-biassed sex-ratio. Small, viscous populations which, incidentally, are often inbreeding, will generally result in this kind of selection occurring. ALEXANDER and SHERMAN (1977) suggest that such local mate competition may be common for ant species and that the female biassed ratios reported by TRIVERS and HARE (1976) reflect only this, and say nothing about queen or worker control of investment. There is, however, no data suggesting that local mate competition is an important feature in ant populations. In fact, data on enzyme frequencies suggest that most populations of ants are relatively outbreeding, and that local mate competition is not likely to be occurring, even in polydomous ants like *Myrmecia pilosula* (CRAIG and CROZIER 1979). Data on *Rhytidoponera* (WARD 1983a, b) also suggest that inbreeding, and thus local mate competition, is not occurring. Finally, the species in which local mate competition would be most likely to be occurring are those polygynous species in which females mate in the near vicinity of their natal nests. In these species, however, the sex ratios are often nearly 50 : 50 (TRIVERS and HARE 1976).

Another factor affecting selection for a particular sex ratio strategy is the occurrence in many ant species of colonies that specialize in the production of one sex or the other. Among some species, colonies persist after the queen dies and continue to produce broods of reproductive males. In a population at equilibrium, the consistent proportion of such senescent nests producing males would favor production of excess females among queen-right colonies. In addition, extreme specialization in the production of the sexes seems to occur in polydomous species of ants. Data on alate production in *Harpagoxenus* (WESSON 1939) show the common polydomous pattern. Some nests produce almost exclusively males and some nests produce almost exclusively female alates. *Formica opaciventris*

(Scherba 1984) and *Formica exsectoides* (Talbot 1953) display similar patterns, and Herbers (1984) has shown that in the tiny acorn-nesting *Leptothorax* species, some nests produce excess females and others produce excess males. While it is not clear exactly whether this production data reflects the production of alates by one or several colonies, it does indicate that more than relatedness is important in determining particular sex-ratio strategies.

Finally, another confounding feature of sex ratio data collected to this point is that it describes alate production over only a very small portion of the life span of colonies. Relative investment at any one time is really irrelevant, because it is the total reproductive investment of a colony that must be measured in order to assess sex investment ratios. For example, many ant species seem to be protandrous (Wilson 1971, Bulmer 1983), that is, males are produced early in a colony's life and only later are alate females produced. Sampling that included only one or two seasons of production of alates would give a faulty impression of colonies' investment ratios.

Either of the factors, local mate competition or specialist male-producing colonies, could easily provide selection pressure sufficiently strong to neutralize any effect of queen-worker conflict, and at the very least, serve to complicate the interpretation of sex-ratio data.

Acknowledging these complications, there is one study of the sex-ratio in ants that indicates that Trivers and Hare's prediction about control of investment and the sex-ratio is correct. Ward (1983a, b) has studied populations in the *Rhytidoponera impressa* group in eastern Australia. He finds populations with mixtures of two kinds of colonies: «A» colonies which have only one queen, and «B» colonies which each have several queens. This situation was confirmed using electrophoretic techniques to assess the number of parents responsible for samples of workers taken from various colonies.

Using dry weights as estimates of investment, Ward has shown that type A colonies and type B colonies differ in the production of the sexes. Type A colonies tend to produce female biassed investment ratios while type B colonies tend to produce the sexes in about equal proportions. Remarkably, in populations with both A and B type colonies, the sex ratio produced by type A colonies depends on the frequencies of A and B type colonies in the population. As the frequency of type B colonies increases, the proportion of females in A colonies' broods increases. This is precisely the response that would be expected if the workers in the A type colonies were somehow assessing the population frequency of B colonies or the population sex ratio, and controlling the production of the sexes in their own interest. Incidentally, when the population consists of only type A colonies, the regression analysis predicts that there should be about three-to-one investment in favor of females. There seems to be no other way to account for A colonies changing their investment patterns with changing proportions of B colonies except on the view that workers are manipulating the sex ratio in their own interests.

3.3 Did the queen win in highly advanced species?

The data that has just been reviewed has been used to support one or the other of the two major hypotheses concerning the evolutionary origin of eusociality in the Hymenoptera. Trivers and Hare (1976) have argued that the female-biassed investment ratios in ant species support the hypothesis that eusociality evolved by kin selection increasing the inclusive fitness of workers. This «offspring consent» hypothesis (Charnov 1978) imagines that selection acts more effectively on offspring than on parents, and that when there is conflict between parents and offspring, it will be resolved in favor of the offspring.

If not completely resolved, at least the effects of selection on offspring will be manifest in those issues, like relative investment in the sexes, over which there is conflict (OSTER et al. 1977). On the other hand, the data on the controlling effects of the queen have been used by ALEXANDER (1974) and others (MICHENER and BROTHERS 1974) to support the hypothesis that eusociality arose by parental manipulation. On this view, parent-offspring conflict is always resolved in favor of the parents. This leads to the conclusion that offspring are essentially somatic extensions of the parents, and like any other organ of the parent's body, they can be modified by natural selection to function to increase parents' reproductive success, even if doing so decreases their own reproductive success. Thus, much as some vertebrate parents sacrifice one offspring of a brood so that the others may live, so the ancestors of the modern eusocial species could have forced offspring to remain on the natal nest, give up their own reproduction, and raise brothers and sisters instead. Important to this view is that there is no possibility for conflict between queens and workers, or among workers in eusocial colonies. The parent's reproductive interests are expected always to be realized.

It may, however, be inappropriate to use data on existing ant species to test hypotheses about the origins of eusociality. The oldest known ant, *Sphecomyrma freyi*, some 100 million years old, was undoubtably eusocial (WILSON et al. 1967a, b), and there are no solitary, subsocial, or presocial ant species that might represent transitional stages between solitary and eusocial states. Thus, all ant societies have a history of at least 100 million years of social evolution, and any traces of conditions affecting the origin of social behavior may be long lost. Furthermore, it is at least possible that the locus of control of reproductive activities has changed in the course of evolution, workers having lost, or perhaps gained control of various aspects of colony reproduction at different times.

A case appropriate to this point may be seen among species of ants that form especially large colonies, such as *Camponotus, Atta, Oecophylla, Acromyrmex, Lasius,* and *Pogonomyrmex*. It appears that the evolution of large colony size has been accompanied by, among other things, the evolution of multiple insemination (COLE 1983). Multiple insemination causes workers to be less closely related to the reproductives that they are working to raise, and selection might be expected to cause workers to treat more closely related reproductives preferentially. At least, there would be strong selection for workers in such colonies to produce sons rather than the more distantly related male issue of the queen or other workers. Yet, these colonies appear to be paragons of obedience to the queen. Reproducing workers appear to be rare in these species (at least they lay no viable eggs in the presence of the queen – see above), and colony investment ratios do not appear to be extremely female-biassed. The queen's presence is vital to some of these species like *Atta* in which, when the queen dies, the colony perishes as well. If not in any other species, among the phylogenetically highly advanced species that form large monogynous colonies the queen seems to be in control.

It is possible that, even if eusociality arose because of offspring consent, the workers in these species could have lost control in the course of their evolution. If workers had been selected to be responsive to organizing and regulating influences emanating from the queen, they may have lost the ability to evolve counteractive measures to the development of queen oppression. For example, in *Camponotus*, CARLIN and HÖLLDOBLER (1983) have shown that workers derive colony-specific recognition cues from the queen. In effect, she labels the workers, and unrelated individuals reared (in the lab) in single broods treat each other like full sister colony mates, and show aggression towards noncolony members regardless of closeness of relatedness. Once workers have «permitted» such a practice to evolve, they have lost substantial control within the colony.

Acknowledgement

The authors' personal research reproted in this review has been supported by a series of grants from the National Science Foundation, the latest of which is NSF BNS–82–19060 (to B. H.).

References

Alcock, J. (1981): Natural selection and communication among bark beetles. Florida Entomologist 65, 17–32.

Alexander, R. D. (1974): The evolution of social behavior. Ann. Rev. Ecol. Sys. 5, 325–383.

Alexander, R. D. (1975): Natural selection and specialized chorusing behavior. In: Insects, Science, and Society (D. Pimentel, ed.) pp. 35–77, Academic Press, London.

Alexander, R. D. and Sherman, P. W. (1977): Local mate competition and parental investment in social insects. Science 196, 494–500.

Baldridge, R., Rettenmeyer, C. and Watkins, J. (1980): Seasonal, nocturnal and diurnal flight periodicities of nearctic army ant males (Hymenoptera: Formicidae). J. Kansas Ent. Soc. 53, 189–204.

Benford, F. A. (1978): Fischer's theory of the sex ratio applied to the social Hymenoptera. J. Theor. Biol. 72, 701–727.

Berndt, K. P. (1975): Physiology of reproduction in the Pharaoh's ant (Monomorium pharaonis L.). 1. Pheromone mediated cyclic production of sexuals. Proc. 3rd Symp. med. vet. Acaroentomology, Gdansk, 25–28.

Berndt, K. P. and Nitschmann, J. (1979): The physiology of reproduction in the Pharao's ant (Monomorium pharaonis L.). 2. The unmated queens. Insect. Soc. 26, 137–145.

Bier, K. (1954): Über den Saisondimorphismus der Oogenese von Formica rufa rufo-pratensis minor Gössw. und dessen Bedeutung für die Kastendetermination. Biol. Zentralblatt 73, 170–190.

Bier, K. (1958): Die Regulation der Sexualität in den Insektenstaaten. Ergebn. Biol. 20, 97–126.

Blum, M. S. (1981): Sex pheromones in social insects: chemotaxonomic potential. In: Biosystematics of Social Insects (P. E. Howse and J. L. Clement, eds.), pp. 163–174, Academic Press, London.

Brian, M. V. (1979): Caste differentiation and division of labor. In: Social Insects Vol. I (H. R. Hermann ed.), pp. 121–222, Academic Press, London.

Brian, M. V. and Hibble, J. V. (1963): 9-Oxodec-trans-z-enoic acid and Myrmica queen extracts tested for influence on brood in Myrmica. J. Ins. Physiol. 9, 25–34.

Bulmer, M. G. (1983): The significance of protandry in social Hymenoptera. Am. Nat. 121, 540–551.

Buschinger, A. (1968): «Locksterzeln» begattungsbereiter ergatoider Weibchen von Harpagoxenus sublaevis Nyl. (Hymenoptera: Formicidae). Experientia 24, 297.

Buschinger, A. (1971a): «Locksterzeln» und Kopula der sozialparasitischen Ameise Leptothorax kutteri Buschinger (Hym. Form.) Zool. Anz. 186, 242–248.

Buschinger, A. (1971b): Weitere Untersuchungen zum Begattungsverhalten sozialparasitischer Ameisen (Harpagoxenus sublaevis Nyl. and Doronomyrmex pacis Kutter, Hym. Formicidae). Zool. Anz. 187, 184–198.

Buschinger, A. (1974a): Zur Biologie der sozialparasitischen Ameise Leptothorax goesswaldi Kutter (Hym. Formicidae). Insect. Soc. 21, 133–143.

Buschinger, A. (1974b): Monogynie und Polygynie in Insektensozietäten. In: Sozialpolymorphismus bei Insekten (G. H. Schmidt, ed.) pp. 862–896, Wissenschaftliche Verlagsgesellschaft Stuttgart.

Buschinger, A. (1975): Sexual pheromones in ants. International Union for the Study of Social Insects, Symposium on Pheromones and Defensive Secretions in Social Insects. pp. 225–233, Dijon.

Buschinger, A. and Kloft, W. (1973): Zur Funktion der Königin im sozialen Nahrungshaushalt der Pharaoameise Monomorium pharaonis (L). Forschungsber. Landes Nordrhein-Westfalen, No. 2306, 34 pp.

Sociobiology of reproduction in ants · 255

Carlin, N. F. and Hölldobler, B. (1983): Nestmate and kin recognition in interspecific mixed colonies of ants. Science, 222, 1027–1029.

Charnov, E. L. (1978): Sex-ratio selection in eusocial Hymenoptera. Am. Nat. 112, 317–326.

Coglitore, C. and Cammaerts, M. C. (1981): Étude du pouvoir agrégatif des reines de *Myrmica rubra* L. Insect. Soc. 4, 353–370.

Cole, B. J. (1983): Multiple mating and the evolution of social behavior in the Hymenoptera. Behav. Ecol. Sociobiol. 12, 191–201.

Craig, R. and Crozier, R. H. (1979): Relatedness in the polygynous ant *Myrmecia pilosula*. Evolution 33, 335–341.

Crozier, R. H. (1979): Genetics of sociality. In: Social Insects Vol I (H. R. Hermann ed.). pp. 223–286, Academic Press, London.

Crozier, R. H.: Genetical structure of social insect populations. In: Evolution of Social Behavior: Hypotheses and Empirical Tests (H. Markl ed.). pp. 129–146. Dahlem Konferenzen 1980. Verlag Chemie, Weinheim.

Davidson, D. W. (1982): Sexual selection in harvester ants (Hymenoptera: Formicidae: *Pogonomyrmex*). Behav. Ecol. Sociobiol. 10, 245–250.

Fletcher, D. J. C. and Blum, M. S. (1983): Regulation of queen number by workers in colonies of social insects. Science 219, 312–314.

Fowler, H. G. and Roberts, R. B. (1982): Entourage pheromone in carpenter ant *(Camponotus pennsylvanicus)* (Hymenoptera: Formicidae) Queens. J. Kansas Ent. Soc. 55, 568–570.

Goetsch, W. (1953): Vergleichende Biologie der Insektenstaaten. Geest & Portig, K. G. Leipzig, 482 pp.

Gösswald, K. and Bier, K. (1954a): Untersuchungen zur Kastendetermination in der Gattung *Formica*. 3. Die Kastendetermination von *Formica rufa rufopratensis* Gössw. Insect. Soc. 1, 229–246.

Gösswald, K. and Bier, K. (1954b): Untersuchungen zur Kastendetermination in der Gattung *Formica*. 4. Physiologische Weisellosigkeit als Voraussetzung der Aufzucht von Geschlechtstieren im polygynen Volk. Insect. Soc. 1, 305–318.

Hamilton, W. D. (1967): Extraordinary sex ratios. Science 156, 477–488.

Haskins, C. P. (1978): Sexual calling bahavior in highly primitive ants. Psyche 85, 407–415.

Herbers, J. (1984): Queen-worker conflict and eusocial evolution in a polygynous ant species. Evolution. 38, 631–643.

Hölldobler, B. (1962): Zur Frage der Oligogynie bei *Camponotus ligniperda* Latr. und *Camponotus herculeanus* L. (Hym. Formicidae). Z. angew. Entomol. 49, 337–352.

Hölldobler, B. (1966): Futterverteilung durch Männchen im Ameisenstaat. Z. vergl. Physiol. 52, 430–455.

Hölldobler, B. (1976): The behavioral ecology of mating in harvester ants (Hymenoptera: Formicidade: *Pogonomyrmex*). Behav. Ecol. Sociobiol. 1, 405–423.

Hölldobler, B. and Engel-Siegel, H. (1982): Tergal and sternal glands in male ants. Psyche 89, 113–132.

Hölldobler, B. and Haskins, C. P. (1977): Sexual calling in a primitive ant. Science 195, 793–794.

Hölldobler, B. and Maschwitz, U. (1965): Der Hochzeitsschwarm der Rossameise *Camponotus herculeanus* L. (Hym. Formicidae). Z. vergl. Physiol. 50, 551–568.

Hölldobler, B. and Michener, C. D.: Mechanisms of identification and discrimination in social Hymenoptera. In: Evolution of Social Behavior: Hypotheses and Empirical Tests (H. Mark, ed.) pp. 35–58, Dahlem Konferenzen 1980, Verlag Chemie, Weinheim.

Hölldobler, B. and Wilson, E. O. (1977): The number of queens: an important trait in ant evolution. Naturwissenschaften 64, 8–15.

Hölldobler, B. and Taylor, R. W. (1983): A behavioral study of the primitive ant *Nothomyrmecia macrops* Clark. Insect. Soc. 30, 384–401.

Hölldobler, B. and Wilson, E. O. (1983): Queen control in colonies of weaver ants (Hymenoptera: Formicidae). Ann. Ent. Soc. Amer. 76, 235–238.

Hölldobler, K. (1928): Zur Biologie der diebischen Zwergameise *(Solenopsis fugax)* und ihrer Gäste. Biol. Zentralbl. 48, 129–142.

Iwasa, Y. (1981): Role of the sex ratio in the evolution of eusociality in the haplodiploid social insects. J. Theor. Biol. 93, 125–142.

Janzen, D. H. (1967): Interaction of the bull's horn acacia (*Acadia cornigera* L.) with an ant inhabitant (*Pseudomyrmex ferruginea* F. Smith) in Eastern Mexico. Kansas University Science Bulletin 47, 315–558.

Jouvenaz, D. P., Banks, W. A. and Lofgren, C. S. (1974): Fire ants: attraction of workers to queen secretions. Ann. Entomol. Soc. Amer. 67, 442–444.

Kannowski, P. B. (1959): The flight activities and colony founding behavior in bog ants in Southeastern Michigan. Insect. Soc. 6, 115–162.

Kannowski, P. B. (1963): The flight activities of formicine ants. Symposia Genetica et Biologica Italica, 12, 74–102.

Kannowski, P. B. (1969): Daily and seasonal periodicities in the nuptial flights of neotropical ants. I. Dorylinae. Int. Union Study of Social Insectes, 6. Congress, Bern, pp. 77–83.

Kerr, W. E. (1962): Tendências evolutivas na reproducão dos himenópteros sociais. Arquivos do Musen Nacional, Rio de Janeiro, 52, 115–116.

Lange, R. (1958): Der Einfluß der Königin auf die Futterverteilung im Ameisenstaat. Naturwissenschaften 45, 196.

Lange, R. (1967): Die Nahrungsverteilung unter den Arbeiterinnen des Waldameisenstaates. Z. Tierpsychol. 24, 513–545.

Law, J. H., Wilson, E. O. and McCloskey, J. A. (1965): Biochemical polymorphism in ants. Science 149, 544–546.

Ledoux, A. (1950): Recherche sur la biologie de la fourmi fileuse (*Oecophylla longinoda* Latr.). Ann. Sci. Nat. Zool. 12, 313–461.

Ledoux, A. (1974): Polymorphismus und Kastendetermination bei den Weberameisen. In: Sozialpolymorphismus bei Insekten (G. H. Schmidt, ed.) pp. 533–541, Wissenschaftl. Verlagsgesellschaft, Stuttgart.

Lloyd, J. E. (1983): Bioluminescence and communication in insects. Ann. Rev. Entomol. 28, 131–160.

Markl, H., Hölldobler, B. and Hölldobler, T. (1977): Mating behavior and sound production in harvester ants (*Pogonomyrmex*, Formicidae). Insect. Soc. 24, 191–212.

McCluskey, E. S. (1965): Circadian rhythms in male ants of five diverse species. Science 150, 1037–1039.

McCluskey, E. S. (1967): Circadian rhythms in female ants and loss after mating flight. Comp. Biochem. Physiol. 23, 665–677.

Michener, C. D. and Brothers, D. J. (1974): Were workers of eusocial Hymenoptera initially altruistic or oppressed? Proc. Nat. Acad. Sci. USA 71, 671–674.

Oster, G., Eshel, I. and Cohen, D. (1977): Worker-queen conflict and the evolution of social insects. Theor. Pop. Biol. 12, 49–85.

Pamilo, P. (1982): Genetic evolution of sex ratios in eusocial Hymenoptera: allele frequency simulations. Am. Nat. 119, 638–696.

Pamilo, P. and Varvio-Aho, S. L. (1979): Genetic structure of nests of the ant *Formica sanguinea*. Behav. Ecol. Sociobiol. 6, 91–98.

Parker, G. A. (1970): Sperm competition and its evolutionary consequences in the insects. Biological Reviews 45, 525–568.

Passera, L. (1978): Demonstration of a pheromone inhibiting oviposition by workers in the ant *Plagiolepis pygmaea* Latr. (Hym. Formicidae). C. R. Acad. Sci. D 286, 1507–1509.

Passera, L. (1980): La fonction inhibitrice des reines de la fourmi *Plagiolepis pygmaea* Latr.: Rôle des pheromones. Insect. Soc. 27, 212–225.

Pasteels, J. M., Verhaeghe, J. C., Braekman, J. C., Daloze, D. and Tursch, B. (1980): Caste-dependent pheromones in the head of the ant *Tetramorium caespitum*. J. Chem. Ecol. 6, 467–472.

Pearson, B. (1983): Intra-colonial relatedness amongst workers in a population of nests of the polygynous ant *Myrmica rubra* Latreille. Behav. Ecol. Sociobiol. 12, 1–4.

Petersen-Braun, M. (1977): Untersuchungen zur sozialen Organisation der Pharaoameise *Monomorium pharaonis* (L.) (Hymenoptera, Formicidae). II. Die Kastendeterminierung. Insect. Soc. 24, 303–318.

Petersen-Braun, M. (1982): Intraspezifisches Aggressionsverhalten bei der Pharaoameise *Monomorium pharaonis* L. (Hymenoptera, Formicidae) Insect. Soc. 29, 25–33.

Scherba, G. (1961): Nest structure and reproduction in the mound-building ant *Formica opaciventris* emery in Wyoming. J. N. Y. Ent. Soc. *69*, 71–87.

Schmidt, G. H. (1972): Männchendetermination im polygynen Waldameisenstaat. Zool. Anz. *189*, 159–169.

Schmidt, G. H. (ed.) (1974): Sozialmorphismus bei Insekten, Wissenschaftl. Verlagsgesellschaft, Stuttgart.

Schneirla, T. C. (1971): Army Ants. W. H. Treeman & Comp., San Francisco.

Starr, C. K. (1979): Origin and evolution of insect sociality: a review of modern theory. In: Social Insects (H. R. Hermann, ed.) pp. 35–80. Academic Press, London.

Stumper, R. (1956): Sur les sécrétions des fourmis femelles. C. R. Acad. Sci. Paris *242*, 2487–2489.

Talbot, M. (1953): Ants of an old field community on the Edwin S. George Reserve, Livingston County, Michigan. Contrib. Lab. Vert. Biol. Univ. Mich. *63*, 1–13.

Taylor, R. W. (1978): *Nothomyrmecia macrops:* a living-fossil ant rediscovered. Science *201*, 979–985.

Trivers, R. L. and Hare, H. (1976): Haplodiploidy and the evolution of social insects. Science *191*, 249–263.

Vander Meer, R. K., Glancey, B. M., Lofgren, C. S., Glover, A., Tumlinson, J. H. and Rocca, J. (1980): The poison sac of red imported fire ant queens: source of a pheromone attractant. Ann. Entomol. Soc. Amer. *73*, 609–612.

Ward, P. S. (1983a): Genetic relatedness and colony organization in a species complex of ponerine ants. I. Phenotypic and genotypic composition of colonies. Behav. Ecol. Sociobiol. *12*, 285–299.

Ward, P. S. (1983b): Genetic relatedness and colony organization in a species complex of ponerine ants. II. Patterns of sex ratio investment. Behav. Ecol. Sociobiol. *12*, 301–307.

Watkins, J. F. and Cole, T. W. (1966): The attraction of army ant workers to secretions of their queens. Texas Journal of Science *18*, 254–265.

Wesson, L. G. (1939): Contribution to the natural history of *Harpagoxenus americanus* (Hymenoptera, Formicidae). Trans. Ann. Ent. Soc. *65*, 97–122.

Wheeler, W. M. (1916): The marriage-flight of a bull-dog ant (*Myrmecia sanguinea* F. Smith) J. Anim. Behav. *6*, 70–73.

Whelden, R. M. (1963): The anatomy of the adult queen and workers of the army ants *Eciton burchelli* Westwood and *Eciton hamatum* Fabricius. J. N. Y. Entomol. Soc. *71*, 246–261.

Wilson, E. O. (1971): The Insect Societies. Belknap Press of Harvard University Press, Cambridge.

Wilson, E. O., Carpenter, F. M. and Brown, W. L. (1967a): The first Mesocoic ants. Science *157*, 1038–1040.

Wilson, E. O., Carpenter, F. M. and Brown, W. L. (1967b): The first mesocoic ants, with the description of a new subfamily. Psyche (Cambridge) *74*, 1–19.

Fortschritte der Zoologie, Bd. 31 · Hölldobler/Lindauer (Hrsg.): Experimental Behavioral Ecology
G. Fischer Verlag · Stuttgart · New York · 1985

Endocrine basis of dominance and reproduction in polistine paper wasps

PETER-FRANK RÖSELER

Zoologisches Institut der Universität Würzburg, F.R.Germany

Abstract

In several *Polistes* wasps some overwintered females can cooperate in founding a colony. The females form a linear hierarchy: the dominant α – female becomes the principal egg-layer, whereas the others act as subordinate helpers and do not reproduce. The formation of multiple foundress associations results in a greater success of that colony and in an increased number of offspring per colony. Since reproduction is increased, the dominant egg-layer gains most by the association. Subordinates benefit by joining a group only if the egg-layer is a full sister. Correspondingly, in some species mechanisms are evolved to discriminate former nestmates.

After hibernation, differences in the endocrine activity among foundresses are used to rank them in dominance. Hormonal treatment gives an advantage in dominant behaviour and increases the probability of becoming dominant. After a dominance hierarchy is established the endocrine activity in subordinates is inhibited by the dominant. That mechanism for sorting foundresses ensures that only those females become dominant egg-layers which have a high endocrine activity and thereby a high reproductive capacity.

1 Introduction

Paper wasps *(Vespidae)* are social wasps. The family includes the *Vespinae* (hornets and yellow jackets) and the *Polistinae*. Formerly, the *Stenogastrinae* (social species found in Asian tropics) were also believed to be a subfamily of *Vespidae,* but now they are considered as a subfamily of the *Eumenidae.*

The biology of paper wasps is well illustrated in some books (KEMPER and DÖHRING, 1967; EVANS and WEST EBERHARD, 1973; SPRADBERY, 1973) and reviews (WEST EBERHARD, 1969; PARDI, 1980). The species are distributed in the tropics as well as in palaearctic and nearctic regions. Nests of *Vespinae* are characterized by an envelope built around the combs. In temperate zones, colonies are founded in the spring by a solitary queen. She is the only egg-layer and inhibits egg-formation in workers by a pheromone (ISHAY et al., 1965; IKAN et al., 1969; AKRE and REED, 1983). Only toward the end of the season or when the queen disappears can workers lay eggs. In temperate zones, the colonies are annual and the societies disintegrate during autumn. In the tropics, however, nests can persist. Young queens are recruited so that nests become polygynic. Such perennial colonies can have in excess of 100.000 individuals (Spradbery, 1973a).

The majority of the *Polistinae* genera are confined to the tropics, most of them found in Central- and South-America. *Polistes* is the only cosmopolitan genus (about 150 species) distributed in the tropics as well as in temperate zones. The nests of *Polistes* consist of a single comb without an envelope. Since a colony seldom contains more than one or two hundred individuals, observations on behaviour and experiments can be easily performed. «This visibility, and the fact that the range of temperate-zone *Polistes* happens to overlap that of university biologists, helps to explain why the biology of *Polistes* is relatively well known.» (Evans and West Eberhard, 1973). That situation has not yet changed. Thus, this review on endocrine activity and reproduction in wasps must be restricted to results obtained on some *Polistes* species.

2 Biology of *Polistes*

In the tropics, the colony cycle of *Polistes* species is asynchronous, so that all stages of colony development can be found around the year. In temperate zones the colonies have a seasonal cycle. Nests are started in the spring by overwintered females. Only the dominant female, the queen, lays eggs as long as she retains her dominant position. During colony development workers are produced at first, thereafter mainly future foundresses and males emerge. In autumn the colonies die out, only future foundresses are able to hibernate. They initiate new nests in the following spring.

Interestingly, there are certain *Polistes* species in which some overwintered females often cooperate in initiating a nest. The frequency of such multiple foundress associations is different in different species and also different in various localities for the same species (Table 1). The number of foundresses that cooperate is also different. An association mostly consists of between two and five females. Very large associations, some with more than twenty foundresses, were found in *P. annularis* (Strassmann, 1981).

An association is formed when foundresses meet at nesting sites or when a foundress joins an existing colony. Foundresses of a group are arranged in a linear dominance

Table 1: Frequency of multiple foundress colonies observed in different *Polistes* species.

Species	Percentage	Authors
P. annularis	100%	Strassmann, 1981
P. canadensis	98%	West Eberhard, 1969
P. exclamans	43%	Strassmann, 1981a
P. fuscatus	43%	Gibo, 1978
	50%	Noonan, 1981
	60%	West Eberhard, 1981
P. gallicus	30%	Turillazzi et al., 1982
	40%	Pardi, 1942
P. metricus	9%	Bohm and Stockhammer, 1977
	10–75%	Dropkin and Gamboa, 1981

hierarchy ($\alpha > \beta > \gamma > ...$) (PARDI, 1948). The dominant foundress subordinates the associated foundresses by a specific behaviour. In *Polistes*, pheromones are not known to be involved in domination. When two foundresses of *P. gallicus* meet for the first time after hibernation, they inspect each other by intensively antennating. Then they rise high on their hind-legs, try to climb the other with the fore-legs and to make the other akinetic by biting and mock-stinging it. But even severe fights seldom result in injuries. Finally, one female becomes the dominant, chewing on the other which itself behaves akinetically, that is, the body is pressed to the ground, and antennae and legs drawn nearest the body. In all further meetings the lower ranked female will immediately act subordinately in this way. After a hierarchy has been established, a change in the dominance order seldom occurs.

In the field, the associations are not confined to the first members. After a fight a subordinated female can escape and try to become a dominant in an other group; correspondingly, a dominant foundress can be subordinated by a usurper (YOSHIKAWA, 1955). Thus, in some species, foundresses can shift from nest to nest for the first time (GAMBOA, 1978).

The dominant foundress spends most of the time on the comb and seldom leaves the nest. The dangerous tasks are performed by the subordinated foundresses which behave as workers; they collect food, water and wood pulp for cell construction. In order to distinguish them from real workers (the first daughters), they are called co-foundresses or auxiliaries. A characteristic attribute of dominance is the trophic advantage of the dominant foundress by trophallaxis.

The dominant foundress lays all the eggs, or at least the majority of them; so the α-female is called the queen. Egg-formation in co-foundresses is inhibited. But at early stages of nest development co-foundresses of *P. gallicus* can occasionally lay some eggs which are immediately eaten by the dominant queen (differential oophagy, GERVET, 1964). Also in early nests of *P. annularis* with only eggs or larvae co-foundresses sometimes lay eggs, but it is not clear whether some eggs can develop (STRASSMANN, 1981). In *P. fuscatus* only a third of the eggs laid by co-foundresses are eaten by the queen, so that approximately 33 % of the offspring derives from subordinates (NOONAN, 1981). The situation in *P. metricus* is not clear. GAMBOA et al. (1978) reported that all eggs from co-foundresses are eaten by the queen, whereas METCALF and WHITT (1977) using electrophoretic analysis of isozymes estimated a 10–20 % contribution of subordinates to the offspring. In general, the dominance hierarchy of *Polistes* finally results in a reproductive dominance of the queen which inhibits reproduction of subordinates in two ways: by inhibition of oogenesis and by egg-eating.

In *Polistes* wasps there are several overwintered foundresses which renounce their own direct reproduction, join another foundress and help to raise its progeny, though they would be able to found their own nest. The percentage of non-reproductive females within a population can be very high. In *P. fuscatus* approximately 50 % (GIBO, 1978; NOONAN, 1981), in *P. canadensis* even 79 % (WEST EBERHARD, 1967a) of the females do not reproduce.

This system of multiple foundress colonies raises certain questions: are multiple foundress nests more successful than single foundress nests? What is the advantage for the dominant female? Why do other females join a dominant foundress instead of founding their own colony? Do different types of overwintered females exist, some of them probably predetermined to become subordinates? What factors control dominant behaviour and egg-formation and are possibly involved in ranking foundresses in dominance? Some of the problems have been extensively discussed in other papers and will be only briefly reviewed here (WEST, 1967; WEST EBERHARD, 1975; GIBO, 1978; PRATTE and GERVET 1980; PARDI, 1980; NOONAN, 1981; STRASSMANN, 1981, 1981b; et al.)

3 The advantage of multiple foundress colonies

3.1 The ecological advantage

The advantage of multiple foundress associations is commonly seen in the better protection of nests against predators, parasites, and usurpation by conspecific females. Multiple foundress nests are always attended by at least one female, whereas single foundresses must leave their nests unattended during the foraging trips. In P. *metricus,* for instance, three foundress nests are left unattended for only 0.7 % of the time, whereas single foundress nests are left unattended 29 % of the time (Gamboa, 1978).

Predators of *Polistes* wasps are mainly birds, which destroy nests or hunt females during their foraging trips. But several observations show that birds are not prevented from destroying nests by several foundresses on the comb. In P. *exclamans* many nests are regularly destroyed by birds which, on the other hand, do not attack P. *annularis* nests in the same region (Strassmann, 1981a). Probably, the aggressiveness of foundresses is different in different species. In general, foundresses were found to be less aggressive than workers. When workers are present, nests are not further attacked by birds. In P. *apachus* 60 % of nests (Gibo and Metcalf, 1978) and in P. *fuscatus* more than 80 % of nests (Gibo, 1978) were destroyed prior to the emergence of workers. Nest usurpation also exclusively occurs during that early period. Therefore, a good strategy to reduce predation is for a late foundress to join established nests which will produce workers early in the season. In P. *metricus,* nests with multiple foundresses are established earlier and, consequently, workers emerge earlier than in single foundress nests (Gamboa, 1980).

When nests are destroyed, they can be reestablished by the wasps. The probability for reestablishing was found to be greater in multiple foundress associations (40 % of the nests) than in single foundress nests (7 % of the nests) of P. *fuscatus* (Gibo, 1978). Also in P. *gallicus* the reestablishing activity tested in captivity is prolonged in multiple foundress associations (Pratte and Gervet, 1980).

The best strategy for survivorship, however, is to build the combs at protected sites. Only one of 32 protected nests of P. *fuscatus* was destroyed, in contrast to 59 of 68 non-protected nests (Gibo, 1978). In two nesting-sites of P. *gallicus* we observed that all nests were destroyed which could be reached by birds. Thus, the competition for suitable nesting sites can result in high densities of foundresses at that places. Gamboa (1978) found that in P. *metricus* multiple foundress associations are mainly established when densities are high. Single foundress nests were started at localities with low densities of foundresses.

Other strategies to reduce predation by birds or parasitism are the construction of satellite nests found in P. *exclamans* (Strassmann, 1981a, 1981b) and nest-sharing observed in P. *metricus* (Gamboa, 1981).

In temperate zones, weather conditions can frequently change in late spring. The nourishment of larvae seems to be better provided by multiple foundresses which can collect more food in warm periods, than by a single foundress. But this problem has never been investigated.

The ecological advantage of multiple foundress associations results in a higher success of those nests compared with single foundress nests. The reproductive success of a colony is the number of offspring which will again be reproductive, the future foundresses and the males. Workers do not pass their genes to the next generation, except when they occasionally produce males at the end of colony development. It is, therefore, necessary to estimate the production of future foundresses and males, and moreover to know whether the probability is the same for all future foundresses to survive the winter independent of their emergence early or late in the season. Since this is difficult to estimate in the field, a random sample is normally used. For instance, the number of cells before the emergence of the first brood is compared between nests (WEST EBERHARD, 1969; TURILLAZZI et al., 1982), or the number of offspring which emerge during the 24 days after the nests have been collected (METCALF and WHITT, 1977a), or the sizes of nests at the end of the season and the number of wasps counted biweekly on the nest during the season (GIBO, 1978), or the number of offspring emerged during August and September when only reproductives are produced (NOONAN, 1981).

Table 2: Production of cells or pupae at the late preemergence period in different size multiple foundress colonies. (1) WEST EEBERHARD, 1969; (2) GIBO, 1978; (3) TURILLAZZI et al., 1982.

Number of foundresses	P. canadensis[1] Number of cells	nests	P. fuscatus[1] Number of cells	nests	P. fuscatus[2] Number of pupae	nests	P. gallicus[3] Number of cells	nests
1	10	1	24	40	6	48	20	8
2	18	2	42	25	11	24	27	5
3	26	4	49	10	20	17	37	3
4	37	6	65	8	21	6	40	5
5	36	6	61	4	22	2	–	–

All the different methods used in the field show that multiple foundress nests produce more offspring than single foundress nests (table 2). NOONAN (1981) found in contrast to GIBO (1978) only a difference between single- and multiple foundress nests of P. fuscatus, but no correlation between mean reproductive success and a number in excess of two foundresses, probably because of variations among localities of nest sites. Larger associations with more than five foundresses did not generally result in larger nests, probably because of the upper limit of the queen's reproductive capacity. GERVET (1964) observed that queens of P. gallicus laid 5 eggs/day in the mean and 9 eggs/day as a maximum. We found a mean of 3 eggs/day in early nests of the same species in captivity. Oviposition can be increased in later stages to 9 eggs/day, a rate maintained for up to ten days. 12 eggs/day were observed as a maximum.

In captivity, colonies of P. fuscatus started with one, two or three foundresses showed no differences in nest size and reproduction (GIBO, 1974), but multiple foundress colonies were more likely to succeed than single foundress nest. In P. gallicus we obtained clear differences in the number of offspring between different number of foundresses up to three individuales (table 3).

Table 3: Number of offspring emerged during the first 4 months after nest foundation in different size multiple foundress colonies of P. gallicus in captivity.

Number of foundresses	Number of offspring	Number of nests
1	60	9
2	145	29
3	163	4
> 3	125	4

264 · P. F. Röseler

The studies on different *Polistes* species show two clear advantages of multiple foundress nests: a greater probability of success and an increased number of offspring. But, of course, reproduction by foundress decreases the larger an association becomes. So an advantage for the whole population is difficult to see. The total number of reproductives produced within a population might be the same, whether only single foundress colonies are established of which several are destroyed, or whether few, but more successful multiple foundress colonies exist.

3.2 The advantage for foundresses

A dominant female of a multiple foundress association gains most by the presence of subordinates. Since the queen is mostly the only egg-layer, her reproduction is increased. We observed in *P. gallicus* that in early nests a single foundress laid 2,5 eggs/day in the mean and queens of two foundress colonies 3,2 eggs/day, respectively. Two causes are thought to be responsible for the increase in reproductive capacity. Co-foundresses perform most of the dangerous and energetic expensive tasks, so that the dominant seldom leaves the nest. In addition the risk is lowered of the queen being lost during foraging trips. In *P. gallicus*, the dominant females perform only 6–22 % of the foraging flights (PARDI, 1942). STRASSMANN (1981) observed no hunting by *P. annularis* queens. Secondly, the queen has a trophic advantage by trophallaxis and by eating the eggs occasionally laid by subordinates.

What does a foundress gain by joining a dominant foundress as a subordinate? Females can pass their genes to the next generation either by direct reproduction (egg-laying) or by helping a genetically related female with which they share a proportion of genes to rear its offspring. Since reproduction in multiple foundress colonies is increased, a subordinated female can theoretically pass more genes to the next generation in this indirect way than by founding its own colony as a single foundress. The inclusive fitness of a foundress becomes higher than its direct fitness. But this is true only if a subordinate joins a full sister, both of them having the same father. In order to ensure this, foundresses should be able to discriminate between nestmates and non-nestmates.

Observations on several species show that associations are formed in the next spring by former nestmates. WEST EBERHARD (1969) marked future foundresses of *P. fuscatus* on their parental nests in the autumn and recognized in the following spring 18 foundresses; 14 of them started a colony with sisters. NOONAN (1981) found in the same species that 52 % of the foundresses initiated a colony exclusively with sisters. Only 7 % formed associations with non-sisters. In *P. annularis*, foundresses from the same parental nest started a colony together (STRASSMANN, 1981). Some observations on *P. gallicus* show that sisters can occasionally found a colony together (HELDMANN, 1936; RÖSELER, unpubl. observations).

Females of some species have the ability to discriminate nestmates, and they try to exclude non-nestmates from an association (NOONAN, 1981; STRASSMANN, 1981; ROSS and GAMBOA, 1981; POST and JEANNE, 1982). The cues involved in discrimination are nest-specific, probably genetically determined. In *P. gallicus*, in contrast, PRATTE (1982) has shown that foundresses in captivity form associations with nestmates as frequently as with non-nestmates. This is supported by our experiments in which we have never observed that a foundress was not allowed to join an association.

In all the investigations it was not possible to decide whether nestmates are really full sisters. METCALF and WHITT (1977) have shown in their genetic studies using electrophoretic differences of esterase isozymes, that females of *P. metricus* mate twice, and that sperms are not equally used, but in a 9 : 1 ratio. Polyandry means that co-foundresses emerged in the same nest can be more distantly related than full sisters. In that case subordinates should gain more if they found their own nests.

A possible explanation for the high percentage of multiple foundress associations might be the competition for suitable, protected nesting-sites. Most of the species studied tend to start their nests in the vicinity of the natal nest. In this way, nestmates come together at the same places, and the probability is increased that nestmates will form an association. Thus, primary home site recognition seems to increase the density of foundresses which itself then induces the formation of multiple foundress associations (KLAHN, 1979). Nests established away from their natal sites are more likely to be single foundress nests (GAMBOA, 1978).

Subordinated foundresses seldom have the chance to take over a nest and to start direct reproduction, because the probability of survivorship for a dominant foundress is increased in multiple foundress associations. Mortality is normally raised in subordinates which spend a lot of time away fom the nest. STRASSMANN (1981) observed only one of 20 nests of *P. annularis* in which a subordinate became the dominant. In *P. exclamans,* however, the mortality of foundresses was found to be very high, so that co-foundresses have the chance to lay eggs (STRASSMANN, 1981a). Subordinates of other species *(P. gallicus, P. metricus)* are often driven away from the nest by unknown reason at the time, when the first brood emerges (PARDI, 1948; GAMBOA et al., 1978). We have observed the same behaviour on *P. gallicus* nests in captivity. In 12 of 46 multiple foundress nests, subordinates were found dead shortly after the emergence of the first brood; sometimes we have seen that co-foundresses were chased by the queen. In 13 other nests, however, subordinated foundresses survived the queen, but only 4 of them became dominant egg-layers (in < 10 % of all the nests); the other co-foundresses seemed to be too much exhausted by the previous tasks to take over the nests. At present, we do not know what might cause the different development of multiple foundress colonies. In general, there is a tendency for increased longevity of queens in multiple foundress nests. We have found the mean longevity to be as follows: two foundress nests: α-foundress 122 days, β-foundress 106 days; four foundress nests: α-foundress 107 days, β-foundress 105 days, γ- and δ-foundress 77 days.

It has been postulated since GERVET (1964) and WEST EBERHARD (1969) that females with an inferior reproductive capacity will join a strong and more aggressive female with a high reproductive capacity. This conclusion was drawn from the observation that subordinated females have less developed ovaries than dominant females. The consequence should be that different females exist. That hypothesis was at first supported by GIBO (1974). In his studies on *P. fuscatus* in captivity he found that 40 % of single foundresses did not reproduce, and he concluded that in the field these females may have joined a dominant foundress as subordinated helpers. But in later studies on the same species using the technique of colony division, subordinate and dominant females were found to have the same reproductivity (BENDEGEM et al., 1981). DROPKIN and GAMBOA (1981) also concluded that fecundity varies among *P. metricus* foundresses. They observed that ovaries of single foundresses were less developed than in queens of multiple foundress nests, but similar to those of subordinated foundresses. That finding, however, can be interpreted in another way (TURILLAZZI et al., 1982; RÖSELER et al., 1984; see below).

We have investigated the reproductivity of dominant and subordinated foundresses of *P. gallicus* in captivity. After a dominance hierarchy has been established, the females were separated and each female together with a subordinate helper was able to found its own colony (table 4). There was no difference in total reproductivity between previously α-β-foundresses and γ-foundresses. Only the production of females was found to be significantly smaller in colonies headed by a formerly γ-foundress.

Table 4: Number of offspring during the first 4 months after nest foundation of α-, β-, and γ-foundresses of P. gallicus which started separately a colony each female together with a subordinate helper. Data with standard deviation; n.s. = non significant.

	α-foundresses	β-foundresses	γ-foundresses
Number of colonies	6	6	6
Number of total offspring	164 ± 40	175 ± 64	158 ± 74
P		n.s.	n.s.
Number of female offspring	133 ± 40	142 ± 75	102 ± 35
P		n.s.	< 0.1%

Nevertheless, there are some hints that different future foundresses may exist. Deleurance (1952) reported that in P. gallicus some of them performed colony tasks and showed egg-formation prior to hibernation. Strambi et al. (1981) found that two populations of overwintering P. gallicus females exist, the one with a high, the other with a low protein level in haemolymph. Bohm (1972) obtained a different response to daylength according to whether future foundresses of P. metricus had been emerged in June or in July–August. But it is not clear whether the differences observed reflect different fecundities of foundresses in the next spring. Thus, there is to date no evidence for foundresses with an inferior reproductive capacity which determines them to become a subordinated foundress.

4 Endocrine control of dominance and reproduction

Since all hibernated females have a comparable reproductive capacity, the question arises: Have all foundresses which meet at a nesting-site the same chance to become a dominant? Are there certain factors influencing dominant behaviour and favouring a female to achieve the dominant position? What are the mechanisms controlling the sorting of females into dominance hierarchy and, finally, what is responsible for the differentiation in reproductive queens and workerlike co-foundresses?

Hibernated foundresses of Polistes are of different sizes. Observations show that dominant foundresses are mostly, but not always, larger than their co-foundresses (Turillazzi and Pardi, 1977; Noonan, 1981; Dropkin and Gamboa, 1981). Body size, however, is a relative value, differences are valid only within a group. Therefore, the dominant foundress of an association can be smaller than subordinated foundresses of other groups. Studies on P. gallicus in captivitiy show that body size does not contribute to dominance. Since large females, however, were found to have an increased endocrine activity and ovary development, large females have a greater probability to become a dominant than small females (Röseler et al., 1984).

The queen lays all eggs, oogenesis in subordinated foundresses is inhibited. Dominant behaviour is connected to egg-formation. Many observations on different species have shown that the dominant foundress has the most developed ovaries of a colony, and that the social rank of co-foundresses is related to the degree of ovary development (Pardi, 1946, 1948; Gervet, 1964; Röseler, et al., 1980; Dropkin and Gamboa, 1981; Turil-

LAZZI et al., 1982). It seems very likely that the achieving of a dominant position is mediated by factors connected to oogenesis. Egg-formation is generally controlled by hormones, above all by juvenile hormone. Correspondingly, dominant foundresses of *P. gallicus* have larger corpora allata than subordinates, and the activity of ovaries is related to the activity of the endocrine glands. Differences in the volume of corpora allata were found to reflect different synthetic activities, so that the size of the glands can be used as an index of activity (STRAMBI, 1969; RÖSELER et al., 1980; TURILLAZZI et al., 1982). First investigations on endocrine activity and ovary development were performed some days or weeks after the hierarchies had been established. By this, it remained unclear whether differences in the endocrine activity and oogenesis were the consequence of the hierarchy or had caused the ranking of foundresses. We have studied that problem on *P. gallicus* in captivity (RÖSELER et al., 1981; 1984).

Foundresses of *P. gallicus* exhibit clear dominante – subordinate behaviour one day after hibernation, when they meet other foundresses. In the test, immediately after the dominance between two socially naive foundresses was established, the wasps were sacrificed and investigated. 89 % of the females which became dominant one day after hibernation had larger corpora allata than subordinated females, and 85 % of the dominants had better developed oocytes. The activity of both organs is correlated even at that early stage of development (r = 0.49; n = 109).

When we put several females together into a cage, they form a linear dominance hierarchy according to the development of corpora allata and oocytes. Aggressiveness we found to be correlated to the activity of the glands. Females with a corpora allata volume smaller than a certain limit (approx. 220×10^4 μm^3) showed no dominant behaviour, acted immediately as subordinates, and were arranged at the end of the hierarchy. VAWTER and STRASSMANN (1982) reported that high juvenile hormone production by corpora allata in vitro was correlated with aggressive behaviour and high social rank.

During oogenesis, the ovaries of some insect species produce ecdysteroids which are mainly incorporated into eggs. In some species, however, the hormone is also released into the haemolymph. This is true for *P. gallicus*, in which the ecdysteroid titre in ovaries as well as in haemolymph sharply rises during oogenesis (STRAMBI et al., 1977). But, interestingly, even during the early stages of oogenesis there is a clear correlation between size of oocytes and ecdysteroid titre in haemolymph (RÖSELER et al., 1984). The function of ecdysteroids in the haemolymph of adults is still unclear (HOFFMANN et al., 1980), except in mosquitos *(Aedes)*, in which the hormone regulates the synthesis of vitellogenins (HANAOKA and HAGEDORN, 1980), and in crickets, in which a metabolic role of ecdysteroids is postulated (HOFFMANN and BEHRENS, 1982, 1983).

After hibernation the *Polistes* foundress which has more active corpora allata and with it better developed oocytes becomes a dominant, which means that dominant foundresses have a higher titre of juvenile hormone and ecdysteroids in the haemolymph than subordinated foundresses have. We have experimentally tested whether juvenile hormone and 20-hydroxyecdysone can really influence the dominant behaviour. The hormones were injected into foundresses at the end of hibernation and the dominant behaviour was tested one day later. The injection of juvenile hormone as well as of 20-hydroxyecdysone increased the probability that such a foundress became dominant, which had smaller corpora allata and smaller oocytes than the subordinated foundress. The percentage of those foundresses was increased by the hormones to about 50 %, whereas in controls we had obtained only 11 % (foundresses with smaller corpora allata) and 15 % (foundresses with smalles oocytes), respectively (see above). Juvenile hormone and 20-hydroxyecdysone evoked a similar response, but neither hormones acted synergistically. A combined injection of both of them had the same effect as an injection of a single hormone each.

268 · P. F. Röseler

The influence of hormones on ranking foundresses can be clearly seen in foundresses which are of smaller size and have smaller corpora allata and oocytes than the competitor. In untreated controls, only 4 % of foundresses with that threefold disadvantage became dominant. By the injection of hormones the percentage of those dominant foundresses could be increased up to 43 %.

After a dominance hierarchy has been established, an injection of juvenile hormone has no effect on dominance hierarchy in *Polistes*. A subordinated foundress treated with hormone remains subordinated and does not change its behaviour. Similar results were obtained by BARTH and STRASSMANN (1980) in *P. annularis*. Thus, the hierarchy later on is probably not only controlled by hormones, but also by social experience and specific behaviour; pheromones seem not to be involved. This is supported by the observation that workers of *P. biglumis bimaculatus* retained their social position even after they have been ovariectomized (DELEURANCE, 1948). The behaviour of workers, on the other hand, can be influenced by juvenile hormone treatment. BARTH et al. (1975) showed that repeated topical application of juvenile hormone increased the aggressive behaviour of *P. annularis* workers and induced egg-formation, finally resulting in a disruption of the social structures of colonies.

At the end of hibernation, foundresses of *P. gallicus* have a different endocrine activity responsible for ranking foundresses. How can such differences develop among foundresses? In the following experiments we have tried to increase the endocrine activity during overwintering and to increase the chance by that treatment to become a dominant. Overwintering foundresses were divided into several groups: Some wasps remained in the darkness of the cold-room (= controls), others were daily taken out of the room and exposed to sunlight and room temperature for 15 min and 60 min respectively. After 10 days the dominance reaction was tested against controls, and the endocrine activity and oocyte growth were estimated (table 5). After treatment with one hour light and elevated temperature daily corpora allata and oocytes of foundresses were enlarged. The probability of becoming a dominant was increased to 86 %. The 15 min treatment, in contrast, had no effect, corpora allata and oocytes were not enlarged and the probability of winning an encounter was found to be 50 %. In the field, such differences in endocrine activity can be due to differences in the microclimate of hibernation sites, or due to varying amounts of time elapsing after the end of hibernation. Foundresses investigated immediately after being taken out of their natural hibernation sites showed large differences in their corpora allata volume among the foundresses of one site as well as between the two sites studied (Mean corpora allata volume: site 1 = 280 ± 87 × 10^4µm^3; site 2 = 356 ± 72 × 10^4µm^3).

Table 5: Influence of activation by light and temperature on volume of corpora allata, length of oocytes, and dominant behaviour in overwintering foundresses of *P. gallicus* in captivity.

	Activation 15 min/day	control	Activation 60 min/day	control
Number of foundresses	18	17	16	18
C. allata-volume (x 10^4 µm^3)	329	332	343	267
Length of occytes (mm)	0.54	0.55	0.56	0.48
Percentage of dominants	50%	50%	86%	14%

The dominant foundress tries to monopolize reproduction. The mechanisms so far known to be involved in the control were reviewed by West Eberhard (1977). In *Polistes* wasps, queen control is performed by a specific dominant behaviour and by differential egg-eating. So far there is no evidence that pheromones could be involved. When a dominance hierarchy is established, the endocrine activity and oogenesis of subordinates become more and more inhibited, whereas the endocrine and reproductive activity of the dominant is markedly increased. During that divergent development a very interesting phenomenon occurs. The corpora allata of the dominant *P. gallicus* foundress are larger and oogenesis is stimulated more, the more subordinated co-foundresses are arranged beneath them (Turillazzi et al., 1982; Röseler et al., 1984; see also Dropkin and Gamboa, 1981). Thus, a β-female of a multiple foundress association can have more active corpora allata than a single foundress or than a β-female of a two foundress association.

The regulation of endocrine activity in Polistes wasps is probably not only a simple switch on – off mechanism, but the activity can be adjusted to different levels. This result is difficult to explain. It seems that subordination by a dominant can be in part compensated by dominating other subordinates. Turillazzi et al. (1982) discussed the importance of trophic advantage. The queen seldom leaves the nest, so that energetically expensive tasks like hunting are reduced; moreover, the dominant experiences the trophic advantage by trophallaxis and, occasionally, egg-eating. In this way, the β-female of a multiple foundress association with more than two foundresses can also exploit subordinates. Behavioural aspects, however, should also be considered (Röseler et al., 1984). A β-female in a two foundress colony experiences all the domination by the queen, whereas in larger associations the domination is shared among all foundresses. In general, domination not only subordinates co-foundresses, but also has a positive effect on the dominant itself.

5 Discussion

Polistes species which form multiple foundress colonies seem to have developed different strategies to ensure the reproductive success of nests and of foundresses. At the end of hibernation a female is faced with three options: founding a nest as a single foundress, becoming a dominant foundress in an association, or joining a dominant foundress as a subordinate. Since subordinate foundresses in most species have no chance for direct reproduction, the reproductive success of subordinates is maximized only if the foundress joins a full sister and helps to raise its offspring, and if the total reproductive output is increased. This system is highly evolved in species in which foundresses are able to discriminate between nestmates and to exclude non-sisters. In *P. gallicus*, in which nestmate discrimination seems not to exist, the probability of foundress associations formed by nestmates is increased by the behaviour that foundresses tend to return to the natal nest site.

Since some assumptions underlying the hypothesized evolution of foundress associations are not completely fulfilled, the theories cannot explain the origin of multiple foundress colonies, and the validity of the theories still remains to be investigated. A hypothesis for the evolution of foundress associations based on the co-evolution of dominant-subordinate behaviour was presented by Pratte and Gervet (1980a). An association can only be formed if both behaviours are present. The behavioural prerequisite (dominant – subordination) was observed to exist not only in species with multiple foundress colonies, but also in species which very seldom form multiple foundress nests (Perna et al., 1978). With this prerequisite the evolution of multiple foundress colonies requires no sister associations. Multiple foundress colonies probably evolved due to densities of foundresses competing for suitable nesting-sites and using the dominant – subordinate behaviour.

For comparison, bumblebee queens of *Bombus hypnorum* often return to their natal nest sites in the spring and compete for the limited number of suitable holes. All the queens behave aggressively and do not show subordination, so that frequently one of the competitors is killed. In some nests we have observed up to four different queens before the emergence of the first workers. A foundress association cannot be formed, in contrast to *Polistes,* because of the lack of subordinate behaviour in nestfounding queens.

An important prerequisite for the evolution of multiple foundress colonies not considered up to now is the sensitivity of the endocrine system in responding to behavioural signals. Only by that mechanism can the queen control reproduction within the colony.

After hibernation, all foundresses have a comparable reproductive capacity. There is no clear evidence for the existence of inferior females. When foundresses meet at nesting-sites, the dominance hierarchy is established. Small differences among foundresses are used for sorting them into dominance. Foundresses with the highest endocrine activity become the dominants. The correlation between endocrine activity, ovary development and dominant behaviour ensures that only those females which indicate that they have at present the highest reproductive capacity become reproductive foundresses.

The connection between reproductivity and dominance behaviour is widespread in social insects. The results on *Polistes* show that dominant behaviour might be mediated by juvenile hormone and ecdysteroids. It is, however, at present not possible to decide whether both hormones directly influence the behaviour in *Polistes.* More investigations are required before precise conclusions on the effect of both hormones on dominant behaviour can be drawn.

Acknowledgement

The studies on *P. gallicus* cited here were performed in collaboration with the research group of Alain Strambi, CNRS, Marseille, France. I thank all members of both groups in Würzburg and Marseille for their unfailingly generous help, their skilful assistance, and their valuable discussions. The work was supported by Deutsche Forschungsgemeinschaft and by Centre National de la Recherche Scientifique.

References

Akre, R. D., Reed, H. C. (1983): Evidence for a queen pheromone in *Vespula* (Hymenoptera: Vespidae). Can. Ent. *115,* 371–377.

Barth, R. H., Strassmann, J. (1980): Hormones and dominance in paper wasps. Amer. Zool. *20,* 1193 (abstr.).

Barth, R. H., Lester, L. J., Sroka, P., Kessler, T., Hearn, R. (1975): Juvenile hormone promotes dominance behavior and ovarian development in social wasps *(Polistes annularis).* Experientia *31,* 691–692.

Bendegem, J. P. van, Gibo, D. L., Alloway, T. M. (1981): Effects of colony division on foundress associations in *Polistes fuscatus* (Hymenoptera: Vespidae). Can. Ent. *113,* 551–556.

Bohm, M. K. (1972): Effects of environment and juvenile hormone on ovaries of the wasp, *Polistes metricus.* J. Insect Physiol. *18,* 1875–1883.

Bohm, M. K., Stockhammer, K. A. (1977): The nesting cycle of a paper wasp, *Polistes metricus* (Hymenoptera: Vespidae). J. Kans. Ent. Soc. *50,* 275–286.

Deleurance, E. P. (1948): Le comportement reproducteur est indépendant de la présence des ovaires chez *Polistes* (Hyménoptères Véspides). C. R. Acad. Sci., Paris, 227, 866–867.

Deleurance, E. P. (1952): Le polymorphisme social et son déterminisme chez les guêpes. «Structure et Physiologie des sociétés animales», Colloque Int. du CNRS, Paris, 141–155.

Dropkin, J. A., Gamboa, G. J. (1981): Physical comparisons of foundresses of the paper wasp, *Polistes metricus* (Hymenoptera: Vespidae). Can. Ent. 113, 457–461.

Evans, H. E., West Eberhard, M. J. (1973): The wasps. David & Charles, Newton Abbot, pp. 265.

Gamboa, G. J. (1978): Intraspecific defence: Advantage of social cooperation among paper wasp foundresses. Science 199, 1463–1465.

Gamboa, G. J. (1980): Comparative timing of brood development between multiple- and single-foundress colonies of the paper wasp, *Polistes metricus*. Ecol. Ent. 5, 221–225.

Gamboa, G. J. (1981): Nest sharing and maintenance of multiple nests by the paper wasp, *Polistes metricus* (Hymenoptera: Vespidae). J. Kans. Ent. Soc. 54, 153–155.

Gamboa, G. J., Heacock, B. D., Wiltjer, S. L. (1978): Division of labor and subordinate longevity in foundress associations of the paper wasp, *Polistes metricus* (Hymenoptera: Vespidae). J. Kans. Ent. Soc. 51, 343–352.

Gervet, J. (1964): La ponte et sa régulation dans la société polygyne de *Polistes gallicus* L. (Hyménoptère Vespidé). Ann. Sci. Naturelles, Zool., 12ᵉ Sér., T6, 601–778.

Gervet, J. (1964a): Le comportement d'oophagie différentielle chez *Polistes gallicus* L. (Hymen. Vesp.). Ins. sociaux 11, 343–382.

Gibo, D. L. (1974): A laboratory study on the selective advantage of foundress associations in *Polistes fuscatus* (Hymenoptera: Vespidae). Can. Ent. 106, 101–106.

Gibo, D. L. (1978): The selective advantage of foundress associations in *Polistes fuscatus* (Hymenoptera: Vespidae): A field study of the effects of predation on productivity. Can. Ent. 110, 519–540.

Gibo, D. L., Metcalf, R. A. (1978): Early survival of *Polistes apachus* (Hymenoptera: Vespidae) colonies in California: a field study of an introduced species. Can. Ent. 110, 1339–1343.

Hanaoka, K., Hagedorn, H. H. (1980): Brain hormone control of ecdysone secretion by the ovary in a mosquito. In «Progress in ecdysone research» (ed. by Hoffmann, J. A.), 467–480.

Heldmann, G. (1936): Über das Leben auf Waben mit mehreren überwinterten Weibchen von *Polistes gallica* L. Biol. Ztbl. 56, 389–400.

Hoffmann, J. A., Lagueux, M., Hetru, C., Charlet, M., Goltzene, F. (1980): Ecdysone in reproductively competent female adults and in embryos of insects. In «Progress in ecdysone research» (ed. by Hoffmann, J. A.), 431–465.

Hoffmann, K. H., Behrens, W. (1982): Free ecdysteroids in adult male crickets, *Gryllus bimaculatus*. Physiol. Ent. 7, 269–279.

Hoffmann, K. H., Behrens, W. (1983): Ecdysteroids – a class of metabolic hormones in adult crickets? In «Biosynthése, metabolisme, mode d'action des hormones d'invertebres», Colloque Int. du CNRS, Strasbourg, 117.

Ikan, R., Gottlieb, R., Bergmann, E. D., Ishay, J. (1969): The pheromone of the queen of the oriental hornet, *Vespa orientalis* F. J. Insect Physiol. 15, 1709–1712.

Ishay, J., Ikan, R., Bergmann, E. D. (1965): The presence of pheromones in the oriental hornet, *Vespa orientalis* F. J. Insect Physiol. 11, 1307–1309.

Kemper, H., Döhring, E. (1967): Die sozialen Faltenwespen Mitteleuropas. pp. 180, Parey-Verlag.

Klahn, J. E. (1979): Philopatric and nonphilopatric foundress associations in the social wasp, *Polistes fuscatus*. Behav. Ecol. Sociobiol. 5, 417–424.

Metcalf, R. A., Whitt, G. S. (1977): Intra-nest relatedness in the social wasp *Polistes metricus*. Behav. Ecol. Sociobiol. 2, 339–351.

Metcalf, R. A., Whitt, G. S. (1977a): Relative inclusive fitness in the social wasp *Polistes metricus*. Behav. Ecol. Sociobiol. 2, 353–360.

Noonan, K. M. (1981): Individual strategies of inclusive-fitness-maximizing in *Polistes fuscatus* foundresses. In «Natural selection and social behavior» (ed. by Alexander, R. D. and Tinkle, W. D.), 18–44.

Pardi, L. (1942): Ricerche sui Polistini. V. La poliginia iniziale in *Polistes gallicus* L. Boll. Ist. Ent. Univ. Bologna 14, 1–106.

Pardi, L. (1946): Ricerche sui Polistini. VII. La «dominiazione» e il ciclo ovarico annuale in *Polistes gallicus* (L.). Boll. Ist. Ent. Univ. Bologna 15, 25–84.

Pardi, L. (1948): Dominance order in Polistes wasps. Physiol. Zool. *21*, 1–13.

Pardi, L. (1980): Le vespe sociali: biologia ed evoluzione del comportamento. Accad. Naz. Lincei: Contrib. Centro Linc. Interdiscipl. Sc. Mat. e appl. N. *51*, 161–221.

Perna, B., Marino Piccioli, M. T., Turillazzi, S. (1978): Osservazioni sulla poliginia di *Polistes foederatus* (Kohl) (Hym. Vesp.) in dotta in cattivita. Boll. Ist. Ent. Univ. Bologna *34*, 55–63.

Post, D. C., Jeanne, R. L. (1982): Recognition of former nestmates during colony founding by the social wasp *Polistes fuscatus* (Hymenoptera: Vespidae). Behav. Ecol. Sociobiol. *11*, 283–285.

Pratte, M. (1982): Relations antérieures et association de fondation chez *Polistes gallicus* L. Ins. sociaux *29*, 352–357.

Pratte, M., Gervet, J. (1980): Influence des stimulations sociales sur la persistence du comportement de fondation chez la guêpe Poliste, *Polistes gallicus* L. (Hymen. Vesp.). Ins. sociaux *27*, 108–126.

Pratte, M., Gervet, J. (1980a): Le modèle sociobiologique, ses conditions de validité dans le cas des sociétés d'hyménoptères. Ann. Biol. *19*, 163–201.

Röseler, P.-F., Röseler, I., Strambi, A. (1980): The activity of corpora allata in dominant and subordinated females of the wasp *Polistes gallicus*. Ins. sociaux *27*, 97–107.

Röseler, P.-F., Röseler, I., Strambi, A. (1981): Rôle des corpora allata dans l'établissement de la hierarchie sociale chez *Polistes gallicus*. Bull. Int. Section Française UEIS, Toulouse, 112–113.

Röseler, P.-F., Röseler, I., Strambi, A., Augier, R. (1984): Influence of insect hormones on the establishment of dominance hierarchies among foundresses of the paper wasp, *Polistes gallicus*. Behav. Ecol. Sociobiol. *15*, 133–142.

Ross, N. M., Gamboa, G. J. (1981): Nestmate discrimination in social wasps (*Polistes metricus*, Hymenoptera: Vespidae). Behav. Ecol. Sociobiol. *9*, 163–165.

Spradbery, J. P. (1973): Wasps. An account of the biology and natural history of social and solitary wasps. pp. 408, Sidgwick & Jackson, London.

Spradbery, J. P. (1973a): The European social wasp, *Paravespula germanica* (F.) (Hymenoptera: Vespidae) in Tasmania, Australia. Proc. VIIth Int. Congr. IUSSI, London, 375–380.

Strambi, A. (1969): La fonction gonadotrope des organes neuroendocrines des guêpes femelles du genre *Polistes* (Hyménoptères). Influence du parasite *Xenos vesparum* Rossi (Strepsiptères). Thèse Doct. Sci. Nat., Paris, pp. 159.

Strambi, A., Strambi, C., Reggi, M. de (1977): Ecdysones and ovarian physiology in the adult wasp *Polistes gallicus*. Proc. VIIIth Int. Congr. IUSSI, Wageningen, 19–20.

Strambi, C., Strambi, A., Augier, R. (1982): Protein level in the haemolymph of the wasp *Polistes gallicus* L. at the beginning of imaginal life and during overwintering. Action of the strepsipterian parasite *Xenos vesparum* Rossi. Experientia *38*, 1189–1191.

Strassmann, J. E. (1981): Wasp reproduction and kin selection: reproductive competition and dominance hierarchies among *Polistes annularis* foundresses. Florida Ent. *64*, 74–88.

Strassmann, J. E. (1981a): Evolutionary implications of early male and satellite nest production in *Polistes exclamans* colony cycles. Behav. Ecol. Sociobiol. *8*, 55–64.

Strassmann, J. E. (1981b): Kin selection and satellite nests in *Polistes exclamans*. In «Natural selection and social behavior» (ed. by Alexander, R. D. and Tinkle, W. D.), 45–58.

Turillazzi, S., Pardi, L. (1977): Body size and hierarchy in polygynic nests of *Polistes gallicus* (L.) (Hymenoptera Vespidae). Monitore Zool. Ital. (N. S.) *11*, 101–112.

Turillazzi, S., Marino Piccioli, M. T., Hervatin, L., Pardi, L. (1982): Reproductive capacity of single foundress and associated foundress females of *Polistes gallicus* (L.) (Hymenoptera Vespidae). Monitore Zool. Ital. (N. S.) *16*, 75–88.

Vawter, L., Strassmann, J. (1982): Juvenile hormone production in Polistine wasps. Proc. IXth Int. Congr. IUSSI, Boulder, 22 (abstr.).

West, M. J. (1967): Foundress associations in Polistine wasps: dominance hierarchies and the evolution of social behavior. Science *157*, 1584–1585.

West Eberhard, M. J. (1969): The social biology of Polistine wasps. Misc. Publ. Mus. Zool., Univ. Michigan, Nr. *140*, 1–101.

West Eberhard, M. J. (1975): The evolution of social behavior by kin selection. Quart. Rev. Biol. *50*, 1–34.

West Eberhard, M. J. (1977): The establishment of reproductive dominance in social wasp colonies. Proc. VIIIth Int. Congr. IUSSI, Wageningen, 223–227.

Yoshikawa, K. (1955): A Polistine colony usurped by a foreign queen. Ecological studies of Polistes wasps II. Ins. sociaux *2*, 255–260.

Fortschritte der Zoologie, Bd. 31 · Hölldobler/Lindauer (Hrsg.): Experimental Behavioral Ecology
G. Fischer Verlag · Stuttgart · New York · 1985

Contrasts between insects and vertebrates in the evolution of male display, female choice, and lek mating

Jack W. Bradbury

Dept. of Biology, University of California, San Diego, La Jolla, CA 92039, USA

Abstract

Researchers with similar interests but studying different taxa often construct theoretical paradigms which reflect the particular adaptations shown in the taxon they study. It is often illuminating to apply definitions and constructs developed for one taxon to another very different taxonomic group. Current research on mating system evolution of insects and vertebrates respectively is a case in point. A number of criteria have been proposed to distinguish lek mating in vertebrates from alternative systems. When applied to insects, the most common mating patterns appear to fit some of the criteria but not others. In this chapter, it is suggested that the best way to accomodate both taxa in a common paradigm is to treat the proposed criteria as continuous variables instead of discrete alternatives and to accept that they may vary independently of each other. This in fact solves some definitional problems within each taxon as well: recent studies of exploded leks have shown that some of the original discrete criteria were met whereas others were not. Replacing each discrete criterion with an independent variable acknowledges this type of variation. While this type of approach allows for consideration of an infinite number of variable combinations, clearly not all combinations are found. A brief review of vertebrates and insects indicates both similarities and differences in the combinations of variable values found. A number of testable propositions to explain these convergences are suggested. Most focus on the different life history economics and mobilities of the two taxa. In short, it is probably not useful to argue about whether a given taxon has «leks» or not. Instead, one should consider a vertebrate lek as a special case of a suite of strategic adaptations, any one of which might take different values in other taxa facing different ecological constraints. Viewed this way, the differences between the taxa are not a hindrance, but on the contrary a necessary source of variation to characterize each adaptation and identify any correlations between adaptations.

1 Introduction

Most sociobiological research presumes that there are general rules for social evolution which apply across all taxonomic groups. Despite this, most of us tend to work with a limited number of taxa and our own perspectives are often limited by the alternatives which exist in our favored systems. Periodically, bodies of research which have evolved around separate taxa are brought together and the result is usually a major advance in our understanding of those presumed general rules. HAMILTON's classic papers (1964) on kin selection were motivated by patterns observed in social insects, and although their generality was not initially appreciated, the concepts have now permeated much of our thinking about vertebrate as well as invertebrate social evolution. Studies of mating system evolution in insects and vertebrates have similarly undergone long periods of independent development. Much of the theory developed for vertebrates has only recently been applied to insects, and many of the important insect examples are still unfamiliar to vertebrate workers. It is also true that several major contributors to mating system theory (e. g. JEFF PARKER) have begun with insect perspectives and too rarely have their ideas been applied to vertebrate systems. Clearly, we are now in a period when researchers on mating system evolution in the two groups of taxa are comparing notes and the field is undergoing rapid change as a result (e. g. BAKER, 1983; THORNHILL and ALCOCK, 1983; and others cited in later sections below). Since this Symposium is very much in accord with such a period of contrast and exchange, I would like to devote my contribution to considering similarities and differences in the evolution of one type of system present in both groups: Lek Mating. Leks have been the subject of several recent papers in the entomological literature (see below), and I have spent the last 10 years working on several avian and mammalian lek species. Recent insect work has certainly changed my views on the general rules which must govern lek evolution, and new developments in vertebrate examples should perhaps receive a bit more attention among entomologists.

2 Definitions of lek mating

In every field, one is inclined to categorize phenomena as a precondition to making contrasts. Despite the best intentions, we are all limited in identifying criteria by the examples at hand. A case in point is the definition of a «lek mating sytem». Most workers agree that an absence of male parental care is a necessary component in the definition of lek mating (Cf. LACK, 1968; SNOW, 1963). Beyond this, there is considerable disagreement. ALEXANDER (1975) was the first to distinguish between «resource based leks» and «non-resource based leks». In both cases, reproductively active males are clustered, but in the former case females visit the site at least in part to gain access to the resource, whereas only males (and matings) are available in the latter case. The distinction seems important because the cues used in mate choice are bound to differ in the two contexts and this in turn will influence the direction and intensity of sexual selection that results.

Based on work with birds and mammals, I suggested (BRADBURY, 1977) that «lek» be restricted to cases where: a) there is no male parental care, b) males occur on territories which are spatially clustered within a population's accessible range, c) the territories of males contain no resources which influence female visits or mate choice, and d) once a female visits a male assembly, she has the freedom to select a mate. The first criterion was aimed at excluding storks or gulls where the other 3 conditions may be met, but mating is clearly monogamous. The second was intended to focus attention on those systems where the interactions of clustered males facilitated and affected mate choice by females. The third excluded Alexander's first category for the reason given above: one expected the form and dynamics of sexual selection to vary depending on whether resource quality or male phenotype was more important in female choice. Finally, the last category was intended to distinguish between typical vertebrate leks, in most of which females can make free choices, and many insect swarms where they apparently cannot (DOWNES, 1969; EICKWORT and GINSBERG, 1980; CATTS, 1982). Again, one would expect sexual selection to follow different trajectories in the two systems.

This restrictive definition, and even that of ALEXANDER, have occasioned no little controvery. The recent field studies of «promiscuous» vertebrate species which fit criteria a, c, and d, but which show male clustering only when suitable habitat is patchy (e.g. ruffed grouse, some bower birds), suggest that the second criterion may unnecessarily deflect our attention away from forms which are otherwise under selective pressures similar to those of classical lek species (GULLION, 1976; BOAG, 1965; PRUETT-JONES and PRUETT-JONES, 1982). LOISELLE and BARLOW (1978), working on fish mating systems, and LEUTHOLD (1966), working on ungulates, suggest that the role of resources in effecting differential male mating success varies continuously and it is unhelpful to impose an artificial boundary between the two extremes. BAKER (1983) makes a similar point for insect systems. Recent work on the provisioning of females by males in Mecopterans (THORNHILL, 1976, 1981), empid flies (DOWNES, 1970; ALCOCK, 1973), and Orthopterans (via spermatophores; Cf. LEOPOLD, 1976), many of which exhibit male clustering and/or active display, further confounds the issue of resource quality vs. male phenotype in mate selection. On top of these considerations, it is also now clear that even where males do not defend resources, the spatial disposition of resources needed by females may still determine indirectly the patterns of male dispersion (PARKER, 1978; BRADBURY, 1981; BRADBURY and GIBSON, 1983). Finally, several authors have argued either that some female insects DO have a chance to choose when approaching swarms, or else that they do not need to choose since preselection by the males themselves has occurred prior to female visits (Cf. ALCOCK and THORNHILL, 1983 for most recent review).

I am now persuaded that the latter three criteria used in my definition of lek represent particular values for several orthogonal variables which can in principle vary independently with ecological conditions and taxonomic predilection. The lesson to be learned from contrasts between insect and vertebrate systems is that we need a broader framework in which both the classical leks of avian and mammalian species and the immense swarms of mayflies are obtained as special cases. If in retrospect, we find that the variables in such a framework are often correlated, it is at that point that one is justified in distinguishing between common patterns and setting down more formal definitions.

The framework I shall recommend is based on the notion of PARKER (1978) and THORNHILL and ALCOCK (1983) that males will distribute themselves nonrandomly according to the spatial dispersion of at least some of the potential sites where females can be encountered. Some potential encounter locations are clearly dependent on resource distributions: these include oviposition sites, female emergence sites, foraging sites, and microclimatic refuges (PARKER, 1978). Other sites, as discussed below, are not close to resources but may yet be determined by resource distributions: these include transit bottlenecks and so-called «arbitrary» sites. I thus presume that for every species, some type of encounter site can be distinguished as a major determinant of male dispersion. Given the determination of male dispersion by one of these sites, males may vary in their proximity to the site: males aggregating around resources may actually set up territories on the resource (as in many vertebrates), or they may sit on adjacent trees and cliff faces (as in some insects). In short, the first set of parameters one must specify includes the type of encounter site (or sites) favored by a particular species, and the degree of proximity to these sites that males adopt. If one wanted to preserve the distinction of ALEXANDER, one might collapse these two variables into one: consistent proximity to a resource demonstrably required by females. Notice that this shifts attention away fom the role of resources in biasing mate choice to their role in determining male dispersion.

The second required parameter would describe the actual spatial pattern of males which results from the adopting of a given type of encounter site and a given degree of proximity to such sites. These dispersions would vary with the encounter site dispersion, the degree of proximity to such sites adopted, and the rules of male settlement. Clearly, males which settle on dung pats could be clustered, random, or uniformly distributed depending on a variety of factors. The third and final parameter I would invoke would summarize the degree to which the female instead of the male determines the identity of successful males.

Leks as originally defined by myself and others constitute one set of values for these three variables. Whatever one wants to call the other variants, it seems fair to expect the general rules which predict classical leks under one set of conditions to be able to account for these other systems under different conditions. In the remainder of this paper, I shall use contrasts between insects and vertebrates to bracket the factors which appear to constrain these three parameter values and which may lead to significant correlations between them. In the end, I shall reconsider what we might want to mean when we call one system a «lek» and another something else.

3 Types of encounter sites and male proximity to them

Several entomological workers have enumerated the types of sites at which insect males might concentrate to encounter females (ALEXANDER, 1975; PARKER, 1978; ALCOCK, et al. 1978; BAKER, 1983; THORNHILL and ALCOCK, 1983). These include: emergence sites of virgin females, oviposition sites, foraging sites, sites with optimal microclimates, transit bottlenecks for females, major orientation cues for females, and arbitrary sites (vis., none of the above). The emphasis in the insect literature has been that males will go wherever they get the most effective access to females. If there are several types of sites, or if one type is dominated by a few males, then one may find several male strategies within the same species (e. g. ALCOCK, JONES and BUCHMANN, 1977; ALCOCK, 1979; CADE, 1979; review in THORNHILL and ALCOCK, 1983).

Vertebrate researchers have generated equivalent lists (e. g. EMLEN and ORING, 1977; WITTENBERGER, 1981; KREBS and DAVIES, 1981) and although the results are similar, there are some disjoint components. Male birds and mammals do not defend emergence sites since most species exhibit a significant delay between birth or hatching and sexual maturity: one does not find male hornbills waiting outside a tree hole to pounce on emergent fledglings. Males do aggregate at and often defend oviposition sites in a variety of fish, anuran, and avian species, and defense of parturition sites occurs in certain mammals. Defense of foraging resources is common in vertebrates. Defense of refuges with favorable microclimates for females occurs in bats. The degree to which vertebrate species which do not fit one of the above categories can be ascribed to male aggregation around female transit bottlenecks, over orientation cues, or due to arbitrary selection of cues is a topic of considerable discussion and will be reviewed below. One pattern common in mammals and fish, but rare in insects is the continued defense of a mobile group of females. The rarity of this behavior is not due to an inability of males to defend a single female: in fact, this behavior is quite common in a variety of species (e. g. PARKER, 1970). On the other hand, male insects very rarely defend entire groups of females at once. This is presumably because many insect females mate once after emergence and either do not form stable enough associations or do not live long enough to warrant male defense (THORNHILL and ALCOCK, 1983). In short, vertebrates and insects show considerable overlap in the sites at which males may encounter females, and thus in the available male strategies, but the lists are not identical.

Note that which type of site is used by a particular species of male is usually dependent on the dispersion of all potential encounter sites. For example, close proximity to foraging sites may be favored over other alternatives because foraging sites are easier to find, attract more females per «patch», or last longer than either oviposition or emergence sites. More subtly, when all critical resources for females are sufficiently scattered, an intermediate «cross roads» or node of female movements may be the better site. Two conditions of the resource distribution are thus necessary before proximity to transit bottlenecks or transit nodes are favored: a) that no resource itself is sufficiently concentrated that male settlement near the resource is a better strategy than near a node; and b) that the resources which control female movements are appropriately distributed to generate spatial heterogeneities in female movements. Female movements may be further concentrated if females must pass over or through some topographic feature to navigate between separated resource patches (e. g. BAKER, 1972, 1983).

In this regard, we do not know whether the so-called «arbitrary» sites are truly arbitrary, or whether thay also are modulated by resource distributions and female transit routes. There is certainly no theoretical reason why such arbitrary sites might not evolve. PARKER (1978) has suggested one scenario in which initial occupation of sites by males occurs because of some non-arbitrary benefit such as access to a major transit node or settlement in a location where female movements are more easily detected (e. g. hilltops, tall trees, etc.). This male preference could then lead to development of a female search image for such sites. The initial advantage to a female mutant with such an image would be its quicker ability to locate the most males and thus to reduce the costs of mate search and/or comparison. This female preference would then select for refined settlement choices by males. The resulting coevolutionary feedback between male site preference and female search image could easily shift the type of site from one of obvious utility to one of arbitrary specificity. The process is identical to that of sexual selection for other male traits by female choice (LANDE, 1981; KIRKPATRICK, 1982).

The question remains whether such sites are arbitrarily specific, remain tied to some specific location where females are more easily encountered anyway, or arise from some combination of these two processes. In some cases, sites which initially appeared to be arbitrary have later turned out to contain significant resources required by females (e. g. ponds used by bullfrogs, EMLEN, 1976; HOWARD, 1978). Certainly, additional cases in both taxa are likely to be found. Similarly, some sites which themselves are not resource or transit nodes may permit better surveillance of such adjacent sites and thus be of functional benefit to males (Cf. THORNHILL and ALCOCK, 1983). Even where there seems a strong correlation between sexual aggregations and arbitrary cues, it is not clear that this is strong evidence for high specificity in the cues (DOWNES, 1969; HÖLLDOBLER, 1976; DAVIDSON, 1982; ALCOCK, 1981). For example, in the Pogonomyrmex species in which the same Palo Verde trees are used by successive generations of alates for mating (HÖLL-DOBLER, 1976; DAVIDSON, 1982), it would be of interest to contrast the effects on male and female visitation of tree form modification vs. tree relocation relative to perennial ant colonies in the area. The fact that the same trees are used in successive years does not require a highly specific search image. In fact, initially random settlement by males at a number of similar sites would usually result in higher local densities at points intermediate between the supplying colonies. The subsequent release of male secretions which attracted nearby males from less settled points would then exaggerate the initial settlement patterns and produce the perennial usage seen. In other words, the repeated use of the same trees need not imply a highly sophisticated search image, but could instead result from a general favoring of all large trees coupled with aggregative male settlement. Similar problems exist in vertebrate lek species where there are detectable similarities found among utilized lek sites, but not all sites meeting such conditions are occupied in a given year (Cf. BRADBURY, 1981; BRADBURY and GIBSON, 1983). The longer lives of vertebrates further confound the interpretation of perennial use of lek sites because males in many species tend to return to the same locations in which they were successful in prior years (e. g. KRUIJT, et al., 1972). In short, in vertebrates there is no clear-cut evidence for fixed and arbitrary search images as the primary determinants of lek location; for some insect studies, the evidence seems more compelling (e. g. LEDERHOUSE, 1982), but in others the necessary controls are lacking.

However rigorously we define arbitrary and transit sites, it still appears that vertebrates are much less likely to occupy sites distant from resources or female groups than are insects. Among the insects, many *Ephemeroptera* (BRITTAIN, 1982), *Diptera* (DOWNES, 1969), *Hymenoptera* (ALCOCK, et al., 1978; KIMSEY, 1980; EICKWORT and GINSBERG, 1980), *Lepidoptera* (SHIELDS, 1967; LEDERHOUSE, 1972), *Trichoptera* (TOZER, RESH, and SOLEM, 1981), and *Coleoptera* (HANSEN, et al. 1971; HAGEN, 1962) appear to use sites at some distance from any emergence, oviposition, or foraging resource to await mates. As we shall note later, some of these species form «leks» in the restricted vertebrate sense (above), and others form swarms of varying configurations. Among vertebrates, such behavior is more rare. Leks, even counting more dispersed-male species, are uncommon in all of the vertebrate groups (Cf. BRADBURY, 1981; ORING, 1982; LOISELLE and BARLOW, 1978). Swarming, even at resources, occurs rarely in vertebrates, the only clear examples being temperate bats (review in BRADBURY, 1970), and possibly some cetaceans (ROGER PAYNE, personal communication). By far the majority of vertebrates establish residence in close proximity to resources needed by females or defend the females themselves for long periods.

The conditions which ought to favor intermediate or arbitrary siting of males relative to resources instead of over or immediately adjacently to resources have been spelled out by a number of authors on both taxa (EMLEN and ORING, 1977; BRADBURY and VEHRENCAMP, 1977; BRADBURY, 1981; ORING, 1982; THORNHILL and ALCOCK, 1983). The basic argument is that scattered resources which are hard to find, occur in patches of restricted richness, or last for short periods may be insufficient attraction to enough females to make resource proximity a better strategy than occupation of some other site. The fact of the matter is that no one to date has actually quantified the cost of the alternatives and made a rigorous test of this notion. Whereas it might be possible to perform such a test using vertebrate species which show intraspecific variation in adoption of resource vs. «arbitrary» sites (e. g. topi, MONTFORT-BRAHAM, 1975), it would perhaps be no more difficult to use parallel variation in insects, such as carpenter bees (MARSHALL and ALCOCK, 1981). In fact, it might be easier with an insect system to vary artificially food, emergence sites, and other relevant resources than in the vertebrate systems.

To understand the different emphasis given arbitrary and transit encounter sites by insects when compared to vertebrates, one would ideally do the above tests on both taxa. Perhaps one would find that even scaling for allometric differences, the resources are more finely dispersed for insects, or alternatively, that the costs for insects of search and defense go up faster with changes in resource dispersion than they do for vertebrates. There are a variety of factors which could generate the observed taxonomic biases in ways compatible with existing theory. However, until such economic contrasts are available, we shall have neither adequate tests of such theory nor the kinds of within-model refinement which make such theories more robust.

4 Patterns of male dispersion

Regardless of the type of encounter site adopted by males, the full range of male dispersion patterns may be encountered. Clearly, if one male can control an entire site, and sites are rare relative to males, other males may do best to occupy locations near to but not on the preferred site. If no male can control the site, then one may find a dense aggregation of males on the location. A variety of intermediates are of course possible. As suggested earlier, the observed pattern of males will depend on the relative densities of males and sites, the dispersion of the sites, and, perhaps most important, the settlement rules by which males distribute themselves.

Settlement rules have been proposed for both insects (PARKER, 1978) and vertebrates (BRADBURY and GIBSON, 1983). Both approaches assume that males have some idea about how many females are likely to pass through a particular encounter site. In both, the simplest cases presume that males occupy sites such that expected fitnesses are equal. This is an ideal free distribution in the sense of FRETWELL and LUCAS (1970). The difference between the two models is that PARKER treats each female as a fixed resource: that is, there is a fixed number of females likely to visit any given site and the site at which a given female is likely to mate is known. This leads to the prediction that if 10 females mate at site A and 4 females mate at site B, males ought to settle in the two sites in the ratio of 5 : 2. In Parker's model, settlement by a male at one site has no bearing on the fitness of males at an adjacent but separate encounter site.

In our model (called the «hotspot» model in prior papers), a female is allowed to move between encounter sites. We allow her an equal probability of mating at any of the occupied sites within her normal home range. This means that settlement of a male at one site within the home range of a given female devalues her worth (in fitness units) to males at other sites within her range. It does not affect the fitness of males at sites more than one female home range away fom the settled site. Settlement thus tends to equalize the summed fractional paternities of all males. Whereas PARKER's males settle all available sites in proportion to the number of females expected there, our males tend to ignore potential encounter sites intermediate between the best encounter sites. This generates more clustering than occurs in PARKER's example, and it produces a positive correlation between the sizes of female home ranges and the degree of male aggregation.

The simplest case for both models assumes that each male at a site has an equal chance of mating with any female there. Both models then go on to consider the case of despotic settlement in which early settlers can expect a higher fraction of matings than later males. In PARKER's model, the typical example presumes that male territoriality results in a non-equitable partitioning of matings, whereas in ours, either territoriality or differential attraction of females can generate the despotic mating distribution. In both models, the general settlement results are similar in despotic and free settlement, but later settlers tend to adopt less desirable encounter sites sooner in the despotic case. In our system, the correlation between female home range size and male aggregation is preserved in the despotic case, but the overall levels of male aggregation are reduced.

In short, PARKER's model maps males directly onto the dispersion of all acceptable encounter sites; our model maps males onto the same dispersion, but it either settles fewer of the sites or it increases the variance in males per site over that in PARKER's model. Perhaps more important, the dispersion of males in PARKER's analysis is invariant with female home range (within the constraint that these ranges are small relative to encounter site dispersion); in our model, two populations with exactly the same encounter site dispersion might exhibit quite different degrees of male aggregation due to differences in female home range size. The factor which determines which model applies is the ratio of female home range size and the average distance between potential encounter sites. Where encounter sites are discrete patches (which is usually the case for resources such as food, oviposition sites, emergence sites, microclimatic refuges, and TRUE arbitrary sites), such a contrast ought to be fairly straight-forward. Presumably female ranges are set by the most scattered of these sites; if males select this same type of site for mating, they will probably settle by PARKER's rules. If in contrast, males adopt an encounter site which is more closely spaced than that setting the female range size, then our model will apply.

The situation is more complex for transit nodes and continously distributed resources. Here there is not a finite set of potential settlement sites against which the final male distribution can be compared. In fact, there is a surface which describes the probability of female encounter, and it is obvious that settlement at any one peak will devalue the surrounding points within a distance of one female home range. In general, such a model always shows some local devaluation and should thus be sensitive to female range size.

In many insects, foraging and oviposition occur at the same site. If emergence sites are not relevant (as females must mature after emergence), and if the foraging and oviposition sites are easily found and occupied, female ranges should match the distribution of occupied encounter sites and PARKER's models should apply. This is apparently the case for dungflies and several other Dipterans which PARKER has examined: in most cases, his predictions match very well with observed dispersions and behaviors (PARKER, 1970, 1972, 1974). Unfortunately, no one has yet examined dispersions of insect males with regard to availability of encounter sites in species where one might expect a large difference between female range size and the dispersion of the occupied sites. Part of the problem is that identification of encounter site suitability must be made independent of the observed male distribution: in cases, such as arbitrary cues, where the male distribution is used to help define what a suitable site is (e. g. ALCOCK, 1983b; DAVIDSON, 1982), it is impossible to perform the requisite contrasts. One contrast which could be made more easily is to look for correlations (either intra- or interspecifically) between female range size and male dispersion. As noted below, this must be done in such a way as to evaluate the possibilities of other mechanisms which might also generate such a correlation. Where the alternatives are unlikely, and the correlation holds, the hotspot model may be indicated.

In vertebrates, one is faced with similar problems. I have not yet tried to compare the two models for resource-oriented encounter site settlement in vertebrates. Other workers more familiar than I with such species would be better able to make these contrasts. However, within vertebrate lek species, there are a number of groups in which a good correlation between female range and male dispersion is obtained, and where alternative reasons for such a correlation have been disproved or are thought unlikely (BRADBURY, 1981; BRADBURY and GIBSON, 1983). The variation in male dispersion seen in groups such as grouse, in which uniformly distributed males occur in small home range forms, exploded leks occur in moderate home range forms, and classical leks occur in large home range species, thus seems quite compatible with our proposed male settlement rules. There are a number of dispersed species, such as bower birds and the birds-of-paradise, which are currently under study and for which not only the correlations between home range and male dispersion, but also the mapping of males on known «hotspots», ought to be available soon for detailed tests of the model.

In short, male dispersion varies widely among both insects and vertebrates. At the moment, dispersion of available encounter sites seems sufficient to explain the dispersions of males in many forms; for the balance, in both taxa, female home range may be the additional parameter which is required to explain the observed variations.

5 Degrees of female choice

The final parameter of interest is the degree to which females are able to choose a mate, or instead have a mating imposed on them by males. At the phenomenological level, it is this parameter which seems to show some of the most marked differences between insects and vertebrates. There are several grades possible (modified from BORGIA, 1979):

1. Grade 1: a female is free to visit several males and select a mate from them using phenotypic cues of males and without harassment or sacrifice of access to critical resources.
2. Grade 2: a female is free to visit several males, but the latter restrict female access to a critical resource in exchange for mating favors.
3. Grade 3: a female is approached and chased or harassed by aggressive males, but she remains able, perhaps at no small cost, to refuse matings.
4. Grade 4: a female is immediately chased and mounted by one or more males and has no overt choice of a mate. Any non-randomness in male success is strictly due to intrasexual interactions between males.

One might expect *a priori* that the degree of female choice might not be independent of either the type of encounter site adopted by males or their disperion. Where males occupy resource sites, the costs to female fecundity or survival of avoiding a mating with a particular male may be quite high. This need not be true for arbitrary sites unless they are very widely dispersed. Similarly, where males are more widely dispersed on large territories, it should in general be easier for females to avoid particular males in favor of other ones (assuming female ranges are large enough to contain several males). Where males are densely clumped and territorial boundaries do not exist or are poorly respected, continuous interference by adjacent males could greatly limit female choice.

One of the points now clear to me from recent work is that these correlations, while reasonable, may not be binding. For example, male dungflies aggregated over dung pats, (a food and oviposition site), generate at best a Grade 3 and more usually a Grade 4 situation (PARKER, 1970; BORGIA, 1981, 1982). In contrast, many *Drosophila*, which also aggregate over combined food and oviposition sites, exhibit elaborate courtship by males to females, and although there may be some jostling between males, the situation seems closer to Grade 1 than to other grades. Insect species with dispersed or loosely aggregated male territories in arbitrary sites show a tendency to be Grade 3 or Grade 4: examples where females can visit several territories, but are rushed and jumped by males include tarantula hawks (ALCOCK, 1981), and the flies *Physiphora demandata* (ALCOCK and PYLE, 1979) and *Cuterebra spp.* (CATTS, 1982). On the other hand, females of the black swallowtail butterfly are able to pass through the territories of several such males and thus to shop for a mate (LEDERHOUSE, 1982). Euglossine bees also show loosely clustered male territories at which females appear to have reasonable freedom of choice (KIMSEY, 1980). In contrast to vertebrates where Grade 1 is more likely for such male dispersions, swallowtails and euglossines appear to be uncommon exceptions to a general insect pattern of reduced female choice where males are loosely aggregated on arbitrary territories.

The same taxonomic bias seems to recur in the degree of female choice for highly clustered males over arbitrary or transit sites. Whereas most insect swarms of males show Grade 4 behaviors, most vertebrate leks allow the female relatively unconstrained choice of a mate (DOWNES, 1969; ALCOCK, et al., 1978; EICKWORT and GINSBERG, 1980; THORNHILL and ALCOCK, 1983; BRADBURY and GIBSON, 1983). There are some exceptions on both sides. Among the insects, the lekking *Drosophila* are very similar in their behavior to classical leks of vertebrates (SPIETH, 1974; PARSONS, 1977, 1978). The several forms of lekking fireflies appear to have retained a considerable amount of female leverage in refusing unwanted mates (LLOYD, 1979). Among the vertebrates, some birds-of-paradise (LeCROY, et al., 1980), small leks of grouse (HAMERSTROM and HAMERSTROM, 1960) and buff-breasted sandpipers (MYERS, 1979) exhibit high levels of male interference or dominance on leks. Females seem to exercise no mate choice in some temperate bats where the nearest analog to the observed male dispersion is probably an insect swarm (Cf. review in Bradbury, 1970).

It has become fashionable recently to argue that many female insects which visit mating swarms have more choice of a mate than meets the eye. Davidson (1982) recently argued that females approaching *Pogonomyrmex* swarms were likely to be retaining some degree of choice because there was positive assortative mating according to size. In fact, the pattern of size association she reports is more likely explained by male preferences for larger females and subsequent competition between males for such females, than for joint choice by both sexes (Parker, 1983). Thornhill and Alcock (1983) suggest that female honeybees may be able to discourage or allow additional matings after a preceeding copulation by retaining or removing, respectively, the plug formed by the prior male's detached genitalia in their own genital orifice. A similar mechanism may apply in some midges (Downes, 1978). This method, if it occurs, does not of course give the female any control over her first mate. Even if one allows that there is SOME residual female choice in insect swarms, the degree of choice is clearly less than that in classical vertebrate lek systems.

In short, for each type of male dispersion and encounter site, there are obvious exceptions to the simple notions of facilitated avoidance suggested earlier. Overall, insects seem to exhibit reduced female choice even when males are territorial and only loosely clustered; vertebrates, particularly at transit or arbitrary encounter sites, tend to retain considerable female choice even when males are highly aggregated. Two classes of explanations for these patterns have been suggested. The first compares the benefits and costs for each sex of persisiting when a male and female disagree on whether a mating should occur. The most general case occurs in species where males are totally indiscriminate and it is the female which may want to avoid a mating (Cf. Thornhill and Alcock, 1983).

Parker (1979, 1983) has developed several models outlining options and thresholds for female abandonment of choice. I shall not repeat these here, but the sense of them can be seen in the following simple contrast. Consider a female which could either expend some cost, C, to locate a male with some phenotypic cue value B, or she could select males at random at no additional costs and obtain a male of mean cue value M. Let p be the probability that with investment C, she actually locates or is able to distinguish a male of trait B from the average male. Let $W(B)$ be the number of grand-offspring this female achieves, and $W(M)$ be the grand-offspring of a non-discriminating female. For choice to be favored, it must be the case that

$$p[W(B)-C] + (1-p)[W(M)-C] > W(M)$$

or rewriting, that

$$[W(B)-W(M)]/C > 1/p$$

This basically says that the gain in fitness through choice, relative to the costs of that choice, should be larger than the reciprocal of the discrimination probability for that cost. For fixed B, M, C, and function $W(B)$, a female with poor discrimination abilities for a given cost C requires a higher relative benefit of choice to justify the behavior than one with good discrimination abilities at the same cost. The cost to find a male with cue B when the mean is M will of course depend on the variance in male cues in the population, how far the female must travel between males, and how such travel, exposure, and time are scaled into losses of fecundity and survival. Densely aggregated males might lead to lower search costs, but they may concomitantly increase the costs of resisting unwanted mates. Such tradeoffs may be complex. The numerator of the left side of the equation is more complex yet. For cases where males provide some environmental benefit to females, such as access to a resource, the difference between W(B) and W(M) might be quite large. Where the only benefits are genetic, such as the likelihood that a more actively displaying male will produce sons who are themselves more active displayers, the achieved difference between the mated father and the mean will be devalued in the female's sons by a) the degree to which display is heritable, and b) the degree to which sons with a higher cue value are exposed to greater survival risks prior to mating. To justify choice for a given C and p, a low heritability and strong normalizing selection on males will have to be compensated by a very steep W function. In contrast, a shallow W function will require mild selection on males and a higher heritability. As several workers have pointed out, this may lead to a paradox since the execution of strong choice will reduce the amount of heritable variation in male cues until the benefit of choice no longer meets the inequality (BORGIA, 1979; TAYLOR and WILLIAMS, 1982; PARKER, 1983). However, LANDE (1977) has argued that if the trait is polygenic, there will be sufficient back-mutation and recombination to maintain a steady level of heritable male variation; continued female choice would then be favored.

If this model is appropriate, it suggests that the left hand side of the inequality above is more likely to be smaller than the right in insects than it is in vertebrates. This could be true if a) insects were less able to discriminate between males for a given cost than vertebrates; b) the cost of discrimination increased more rapidly for a given (B-M) than in vertebrates; c) insects had lower levels of heritable variation in cues than vertebrates; or d) the dependence of fitness on male cues is steeper in vertebrates. Quite frankly, we have no numbers as yet to test any of these possibilities. One would think that once arriving at a dense aggregation of males insects, the cost to a female of finding suffcient options would be small and thus choice favored. The difficulty may be that whereas a vertebrate female can leave a lek and either return later or go to another lek if harassed, the average female insect does not have sufficient time or energy to exercise this option. The alternative option of remaining at the site and fending off unwanted males can also become expensive. Still, why should *Drosophila* favor female choice both over foraging and oviposition sites and at arbitrary lek sites?

One factor may be that males, as well as females, are somewhat discriminating in some species. PARKER (1978) considers such cases in his general treatment. The gist of the argument, as with females, is that persistence pays for a male only when the chances of finally mating with the female exceed those of searching for and mating with an alternative female. As pointed out by THORNHILL and ALCOCK (1983), the latter probability depends greatly on the operational sex ratio. They suggest that males in many swarms over arbitrary sites are visited by females only at slow rates and most of these females mate only once. Since male longevity in such a swarm is limited, males which aggressively mount any visiting female are favored. The drosophilids and a few other taxa of insects are unusual in that females are cyclically receptive and each female thus makes several visits to mating sites. This effectively increases the ratio of encountered females per male and *a priori* would increase the benefits of males abandoning any one unreceptive female for a more receptive one. As THORNHILL and ALCOCK (1983) suggest, some male discrimination between receptive and non-receptive females would then be favored. Were females to outstrip males in the arms race between male discrimination and the ability of receptive but unwilling females to feign non-receptivity, the emphasis on courtship and a more Grade 1 mating system would result (Cf. PARKER, 1983). Perhaps this is what has occurred in drosophilids and the few other insects with Grade 1 mate choice. It certainly could apply to many of the vertebrate leks where Grade 1 choice appears to be the rule. In summary, if male and female generally disagree over mating preferences, the most likely explanations for the taxon-specific (and exceptional) distributions of different grades of mate choice will be obtained by careful economic contrasts between the sexes in the benefits and costs of persistence. These in turn will be affected by the dispersions, life histories, heritabilities, and other extrinsic factors which are common to each taxon and differ among related species.

The second type of explanation for the absence of female choice in either taxon rests on the notion that where females do not appear to contest male advances, they must be in favor of them. In other words, the behaviors of males among themselves and the choices of females, if they were exercised, would be exactly congruent. In such a case, females do not need to exercise any choice: the males do it for them. The notion that females benefit by mating with the most aggressive or dominant males pervades much of the recent insect literature (e. g. BORGIA, 1979; DAVIDSON, 1982; PARKER, 1983; THORNHILL and ALCOCK, 1983), and until recently, seemed a reasonable interpretation of the vertebrate lek litera- ture (WILLIAMS, 1966; TRIVERS, 1972; ZAHAVI, 1975; WILEY, 1974; BORGIA 1979). The link between aggressive males in insect swarms and successful males in vertebrate leks was generated by a presumed preference of females in the latter case for central territories on leks and a consequent competition by males for such sites. In the insect swarms, males fought for the females directly; in the latter, they fought for sites which females preferred. Even in some insects, males fight for central territories and females appear to select males on the basis of the resulting patterns of ownership (LEDERHOUSE, 1982). Thus both systems really could be using the same mechanism, and the apparent differences in female choice are illusory.

It now appears that this link was fragile at best. The evidence for center-preferences in vertebrate leks was inferred from a) the correlation between male reproductive success and relative location, and b) competition by males to obtain territories closest to the lek centers (WILEY, 1974; BALLARD and ROBEL, 1974; BUECHNER and ROTH, 1974). The problem is that both supportive observations could also be generated by centripetal competition among less successful males to set up territories near males which were successful for reasons other than location. One assumption of the first interpretation is that there is some arbitrary convention which defines the site preferred by both sexes. If so, one expects the location of successful males to be as stable as the location of the arbitrary cues, and males which replace central males should ascend to high mating status. It now appears that available data for the more carefully-studied vertebrate leks either goes against these predictions, or is equivocal (Cf. review by BRADBURY and GIBSON, 1983). In fact, there is increasing support for female discrimination among males on the basis of male display performance and subsequent clustering of unsuccessful males around successful ones (HARTZLER, 1972; DE VOS, 1983; KRUIJT, DE VOS, BOSSEMA, and BRUINSMA, unpublished; BRADBURY and GIBSON, 1983 and unpublished observations).

Why then might female insects accept the outcomes of aggressive male encounters in most species, but most vertebrate females and certain exceptional insects utilize other phenotypic cues of males to exercise choice? One interpretation by some workers is that the cues used by females in either case are those most likely to confer general adaptive benefits on both sons and daughters of discriminating females (BORGIA, 1979; THORN- HILL, 1980; THORNHILL and ALCOCK, 1983; PARKER, 1983). As an example, suppose that foraging ability were a heritable trait that was expressed in daughters as higher fecundity or survival and in males as higher competitive abilities in access to mates. The cues used by females to select males might thus be body size or dominance status, where this was the best indicator of male foraging success, or male performance display, where this was a better indicator of foraging ability. The switch between accepting male aggression and using some other cue would thus depend on which type of male cue was best correlated with the output of both sons and daughters.

The problem with this notion is that the intervening variable of foraging ability adds an additional devaluation term to the numerator (above) in the female choice inequality. Using the same example, the critical heritability is that for foraging ability, and the devaluations are the correlation coefficients between male foraging ability and competitive ability, and female fecundity or survival and foraging ability. It is well known that the correlations between status and some trait such as body size, stamina, and the like need not be very high even when dominance status is very clear-cut and stable (LANDAU, 1951). Thus even if female choice of males was easier (since males did the work of choosing), and even if daughters gained somewhat by that choice, the net gain in fitness would be devalued by the imperfect correlations between traits as well as the levels of heritability. If devalued enough, the gain would not warrant adopting this form of choice. Perhaps more pertinent, such choice might not be resistant to invasion by an alternative form of female choice which did not operate under the constraint of optimizing son and daughter fitness, but instead focused on traits in males which were more closely correlated with current male competitive success and thus benefitted sons only (Cf. KIRKPATRICK, 1982; BRADBURY and GIBSON, 1983).

If one insists that female insects are accepting male decisions because that is the best genetic choice open to them, and if the type of adaptive cue scenario in the preceeding paragraph is deemed not operating, is there any reasonable way to explain the differences between the taxa in the observed grades of female choice? If there is, it is not yet clear to me. I could imagine a sensory argument which assumed that insects were less able than vertebrates to recognize bizarre mutant male displays which had no adaptive value to daughters but which tried to capture the attention of receptive females. It is possible that once such a cue was established by chance or sensory predisposition, it could «runaway» and govern all subsequent mate choice (LANDE, 1981; KIRKPATRICK, 1982). The difficulty with such an argument is the number of exceptional insects which do show elaborate courtship at arbitrary locations with Grade 1 female choice. In lieu of such an argument, my own feeling is that the economic contrasts appropriate to contests between male and female persistence (noted earlier) will provide the most reasonable explanations of the patterns we have been discussing.

6 Conclusions

Do insects have leks? How should we define leks? I am persuaded by my review of both literatures that there may turn out to be specific combinations of type of encounter site, male dispersion, and degree of female choice which recur repeatedly in both vertebrates and insects. There are certainly insects with aggregated males, no nearby resources, and Grade 1 female choice which could be called «leks» by the classical vertebrate criteria. Despite this, I think we either need to formulate a whole host of additional definitions (e. g. no-choice swarms, no-choice dispersed territories, etc.), or else remain with the notion that these three variables can evolve sufficiently independently that any finite set of fixed definitions will always leave some species outside our dictionary. Both approaches are valuable. The first is so because it stresses the clear correlations which must arise in some variable combinations: males cannot as easily adopt a Grade 2 approach when aggregating over arbitrary sites as they can over a resource. Once correlations appear, one must examine their generality across taxa. This forces refinement and/or rejection of the basic categories. With regard to my old definition, it is now obvious that it is not the absence of resources within territories which should distinguish lek from non-lek species, but instead the degree to which males regulate access to those resources to obtain matings.

Bell birds and Epauletted Bats may both court females from within territories which contain resources needed by females; they do not however use controlled access to these resources as leverage in obtaining females (B. SNOW, 1973; BRADBURY, 1981).

The second approach often has as much value in explaining what we see as in what we don't: no one is likely to define a mating system category which doesn't appear in their favored organisms. Using a multivariable format, we can see what parts of the parameter space are never occupied and ask why not. This then allows one to add new taxa as they are described: perhaps they will fill the empty parameter space or perhaps they will only reinforce any existing clusters of points. In this chapter, I have tried to accomodate insects and vertebrates into a more common framework. The result has been both a reinforcement of some existing patterns common to both groups, and the occupation of parameter spaces not shared by the two larger taxa. Next year, maybe someone else can tackle snails and ctenophores.

References

Alcock, J. (1973): The mating behavior of *Empis barbatoides* Melander and *Empis poplitea* Loew (Diptera: Empidae). J. Nat. His. 7, 411–420.

Alcock, J. (1979): The behavioral consequences of size variation among males of the territorial wasp *Hemipepsis ustulata* (Hymenoptera: Pompilidae). Behaviour 71, 322–335.

Alcock, J. (1981): Lek territoriality in the tarantula hawk wasp *Hemipepsis ustulata* (Hymenoptera: Pompilidae). Behav. Ecol. Sociobiol. 8, 309–317.

Alcock, J. (1983a): Territoriality by hilltopping males of the great purple hairstreak, *Atlides halesus* (Lepidoptera, Lycaenidae): convergent evolution with a pompilid wasp. Behav. Ecol. Sociobiol 13, 57–62.

Alcock, J. (1983b): Constancy in the relative attractiveness of a set of landmark territorial sites to two generations of male tarantula hawk wasps (Hymenoptera: Pompilidae). Anim. Behav. 31, 74–80.

Alcock, J., E. M. Barrows, G. Gordh, L. J. Hubbard, L. Kirkendall, D. Pyle, T. L. Ponder, and F. G. Zalom (1978): The ecology and evolution of male reproductive behavior in the bees and wasps. J. Linn. Soc. London, Zool. 64, 293–326.

Alcock, J., C. E. Jones, and S. L. Buchmann (1977): Male mating strategies in the bee *Centris pallida* Fox (Hymenoptera: Anthophoridae). Amer. Nat. 111, 145–155.

Alcock, J. and D. W. Pyle (1979): The complex courtship behavior of *Physiphora demandata* (F.) (Diptera: Otitidae). Zeit. für Tierpsych. 49, 325–335.

Alexander, R. D. (1975): Natural selection and specialized chorusing behavior in acoustical insects. pp. 35–77, in Insects, Science and Society. D. Pimentel, ed. New York, Academic Press.

Baker, R. H. (1972): Territorial behaviour of the nymphalid butterflies, *Aglais urticae* and *Inachis io*. J. Anim. Ecol. 41, 453–469.

Baker, R. H. (1983): Insect territoriality. Ann. Rev. Entomol. 28, 65–89.

Ballard, W. B. and R. J. Robel (1974): Reproductive importance of dominant male greater prairie chickens. Auk 91, 75–86.

Barrows, E. M. (1976): Mating behavior in halictine bees. II. Microterritorial and patrolling behavior in males of *Lasioglossum rohweri*. Zeit. für Tierpsych. 40, 377–389.

Boag, D. A. (1965): Population attributes of blue grouse in southwestern Alberta. Can. J. Zool. 44, 799–814.

Borgia, G. (1979): Sexual selection and the evolution of mating systems. pp. 19–80, in Sexual Selection and Reproductive Competition in Insects. M. S. Blum and N. A. Blum, eds. New York, Academic Press.

Borgia, G. (1981): Mate selection in the fly *Scatophaga stercoraria:* female choice in a male-controlled system. Animal Behaviour 29, 71–80.

Borgia, G. (1982): Experimental changes in resource structure and male density: size-related differences in mating success among male *Scatophaga stercoraria*. Evol. *36*, 307–315.

Bradbury, J. (1970): Social organization and communication. pp. 1–72, in Biology of Bats, Vol. III. W. Wimsatt, ed. New York, Academic Press.

Bradbury, J. (1977): Lek mating behavior in the hammerheaded bat. Zeit. für Tierpsych. *45*, 225–255.

Bradbury, J. (1981): The evolution of leks pp. 138–169, in Natural Selection and Social Behavior: Recent Research and Theory. R. D. Alexander and D. W. Tinkle, eds. New York, Chiron Press.

Bradbury, J. and R. Gibson (1983): Leks and mate choice. pp. 109–138, in Mate Choice. P. P. G. Bateson, ed. Cambridge, Cambridge University Press.

Bradbury, J. and S. L. Vehrencamp (1977): Social organization and foraging in emballonurid bats. III. Mating systems. Behav. Ecol. Sociobiol. *2*, 1–17.

Brittain, J. E. (1982): Biology of mayflies. Ann. Rev. Entomol. *27*, 119–147.

Buechner, H. K. and R. Schloeth (1965): Ceremonial mating behavior in Uganda kob *(Adenota kob thomasii)*. Zeit. für Tierpsych. *22*, 209–225.

Cade, W. (1979): The evolution of alternative male strategies in field crickets. pp. 343–379, in Sexual Selection and Reproductive Competition in Insects. M. S. Blum and N. A. Blum, eds. New York, Academic Press.

Catts, E. P. (1979): Hilltop aggregation and mating behavior in *Gasterophilus* (Diptera: Gasterophilidae). J. Med. Entomol. *16*, 461–464.

Catts, E. P. (1982): Biology of New World botflies: Cuterebridae. Ann. Rev. Entomol. *27*, 313–338.

Davidson, D. W. (1982): Sexual selection in harvester ants (Hymenoptera: Formicidae: Pogonomyrmex). Behav. Ecol. Sociobiol. *10*, 245–250.

Doolan, J. M. (1981): Male spacing and the influence of female courtship behaviour in the bladder cicada, *Cystosoma sundersii* Westwood. Behav. Ecol. Sociobiol. *9*, 269–276.

Downes, J. A. (1969): The swarming and mating flight of Diptera. Ann. Rev. Entomol. *14*, 271–298.

Downes, J. A. (1970): The feeding and mating behaviour of the specialized Empidinae (Diptera): observations on four species of *Rhamphomyia* in the high arctic and a general discussion. Canad. J. Entomol. *102*, 769–791.

Downes, J. A. (1978): Feeding and mating in the insectivorous Ceratopogoninae (Diptera). Memoirs Entomol. Soc. Can. *104*.

Eickwort, G. C. and H. S. Ginsberg (1980): Foraging and mating behavior in Apoidea. Ann. Rev. Entomol. *25*, 421–446.

Emlen, S. T. (1976): Lek organization and mating strategies in the bullfrog. Behav. Ecol. Sociobiol. *1*, 283–313.

Emlen, S. T. and L. W. Oring (1977): Ecology, sexual selection, and the evolution of mating systems. Science *197*, 215–223.

Frankie, G. W., S. B. Vinson, and R. E. Colville (1980): Territorial behavior of *Centris adani* and its reproductive function in the Costa Rican dry forest (Hymenoptera: Anthophoridae). J. Kansas Entomol. Soc. *53*, 837–857.

Fretwell, S. D. and H. L. Lucas (1969): On territorial behavior and other factors influencing habitat distribution in birds. I. Theoretical development. Acta Biotheoret. *19*, 16–36.

Gullion, G. W. (1976): Re-evaluation of «activity clustering» by male grouse. Auk *93*, 192–193.

Hagen, K. S. (1962): Biology and ecology of predacious Coccinellidae. Ann. Rev. Entomol. *7*, 289–326.

Hamerstrom, F. N. and F. Hamerstrom (1951): Mobility of the sharp-tailed grouse in relation to its ecology and distribution. Amer. Midl. Nat. *46*, 174–226.

Hamilton, W. D. (1964): The genetical evolution of social behavior. I, II. J. Theor. Biol. *7*, 1–52.

Hanson, F. E., J. F. Case, E. Buck, and J. B. Buck (1971): Synchrony and flash entrainment in a New Guinea firefly. Science *174*, 161–164.

Hartzler, J. E. (1972): An Analysis of Sage Grouse Behavior. Ph. D. Dissertation Thesis. Missoula, Montana: University of Montana, 234 pp.

Holldobler, B. (1976): The behavioral ecology of mating in harvester ants (Hymenoptera: Formicidae: *Pogonomyrmex*). Behav. Ecol. Sociobiol. *1*, 405–423.

Howard, R. D. (1978): The evolution of mating strategies in bullfrogs, *Rana catesbeiana*. Evol. *32*, 850–871.

Janetos, A. C. (1980): Strategies of female mate choice: a theoretical analysis. Behav. Ecol. Sociobiol. 7, 107–112.

Kimsey, L. S. (1980): The behavior of male orchid bees (Apidae, Hymenoptera, Insecta) and the question of leks. Anim. Behav. 28, 996–1004.

Kirkpatrick, M. (1982): Sexual selection and the evolution of female choice. Evol. 36, 1–12.

Krebs, J. R. and N. B. Davies (1981): An Introduction to Behavioural Ecology. Sunderland, Massachusetts, Sinauer Associates.

Kruijt, J. P., G. J. de Vos, and I. Bossema (1972): The arena system of black grouse. pp. 399–423 in, Proc. XVth Intl. Ornithol. Congr. Leiden, E. J. Brill.

Kruijt, J. P., G. J. de Vos, I. Bossema, and O. Bruinsma (unpubl.): Sexual selection in black grouse. Unpublished manuscript.

Lack, D. (1968): Ecological Adaptations for Breeding in Birds. London, Chapman and Hall.

Lande, R. (1977): The influence of mating system on the maintenance of genetic variability in polygenic characters. Genetics 86, 485–498.

Lande, R. (1981): Models of speciation by sexual selection on polygenic traits. Proc. Nat. Acad. Sci., USA 78, 3721–3725.

Landau, H. G. (1951): On dominance relations and the structure of animal societies, I. Effect of inherent characteristics. Bull. Math. Biophysics 13, 1–19.

LeCroy, M., A. Kulupi, and W. S. Peckover (1980): Goldie's bird-of-paradise: display, natural history, and traditional relationships of people to the bird. Wilson Bull. 92, 289–301.

Lederhouse, R. C. (1982): Territorial defense and lek behavior of the black swallowtail butterfly, *Papilio polyxenes*. Behav. Ecol. Sociobiol. 10, 109–118.

Leopold, R. A. (1976): The role of male accessory glands in insect reproduction. Ann. Rev. Entomol. 21, 199–221.

Leuthold, W. (1966): Territorial behavior of Uganda kob. Behaviour 27, 255–256.

Lloyd, J. E. (1971): Bioluminescent communication in insects. Ann. Rev. Entomol. 16, 97–122.

Lloyd, J. E. (1979): Sexual selection in luminescent beetles. pp. 293–342, in Sexual Selection and Reproductive Competition in Insects. M. S. Blum and N. A. Blum, eds. New York, Academic Press.

Loiselle, P. V. and G. W. Barlow (1978): Do fishes lek like birds? pp. 31–76, in Contrasts in Behavior, E. S. Reese and F. J. Lighter, eds. New York, Wiley and Sons.

Marshall, L. and J. Alcock (1981): The evolution of the mating system of *Xylocopa varipuncta* (Hymenoptera: Anthophoridae). J. Zool. 193, 315–324.

McAlpine, D. K. (1979): Agonistic behavior in *Achias australis* (Diptera, Platystomatidae) and the significance of eyestalks. pp. 221–230, in Sexual Selection and Reproductive Competition in Insects. M. S. Blum and N. A. Blum, eds. New York, Academic Press.

Montfort-Braham, N. (1975): Variations dans la structure sociale du topi *Damaliscus korrigum* Ogilby, au Parc National de l'Akagera, Rwanda. Zeit. für Tierpsych. 39, 332–364.

Myers, J. P. (1979): Leks, sex, and buff-breasted sandpipers. Amer. Birds 33, 823–825.

Oring, L. (1982): Avian mating systems. pp. 1–92, in Avian Biology, Vol. VI. D. Farner, J. King, and K. Parkes, eds. New York, Academic Press.

Parker, G. A. (1970): The reproductive behaviour and nature of sexual selection in *Scatophaga stercoraria* (L.) (Diptera: Scatophagidae). II. The fertilization rate and the spatial and temporal relationships of each sex around the site of mating and oviposition. J. Anim. Ecol. 39, 205–228.

Parker, G. A. (1972): Reproductive behaviour of *Sepsis cynipsea* (L.) (Diptera: Sepsidae). I. A preliminary analysis of reproductive strategy and its associated behaviour patterns. Behaviour 41, 172–206.

Parker, G. A. (1974): The reproductive behaviour and the nature of sexual selection in *Scatophaga stercoraria* (L.) (Diptera: Scatophagidae). VIII. The behaviour of searching males. J. Entomol. (A) 48, 199–211.

Parker, G. A. (1978): Evolution of competitive mate searching. Ann. Rev. Entomol. 23, 173–196.

Parker, G. A. (1979): Sexual selection and sexual conflict. pp. 123–166, in Sexual Selection and Reproductive Competition in Insects. M. S. Blum and N. A. Blum, eds. New York, Academic Press.

Parker, G. A. (1982): Phenotype limited evolutionarily stable strategies. pp. 173–201, in Current Problems in Sociobiology. B. R. Bertram, T. H. Clutton-Brock, R. I. M. Dunbar, D. I. Rubenstein, and R. Wrangham, eds. Cambridge, Cambridge University Press.

Parker, G. A. (1983): Mate quality and mating decisions. pp. 141–166, in Mate Choice. P. P. G. Bateson, ed. Cambridge, Cambridge University Press.

Parsons, P. A. (1977): Lek behavior in *Drosophila* (Hirtodrosophila) polybori Malloch-an Australian rainforest species. Evol. *31*, 223–225.

Parsons, P. A. (1978): Habitat selection and evolutionary strategies in *Drosophila:* an invited address. Behav. Genet. *8*, 511–526.

Pruett-Jones, M. A. and S. G. Pruett-Jones (1982): Spacing and distribution of bowers in Mac-Gregor's bowerbird *(Amblyornis macgregoriae)*. Behav. Ecol. Sociobiol. *11*, 25–32.

Shields, O. (1967): Hilltopping. J. Res. Lepid. *6*, 69–178.

Snow, B. (1973): Notes on the behavior of the white bellbird. Auk *90*, 743–751.

Snow, D. (1963): The evolution of manakin displays. pp. 553–561, in Proc. 13th Intl. Ornith. Cong., Vol. I.

Spieth, H. T. (1974): Courtship behavior in *Drosophila*. Ann. Rev. Entomol. *19*, 385–405.

Taylor, P. D. and G. C. Williams (1982): The lek paradox is not resolved. Theoret. Pop. Biol. *22*, 392–409.

Thornhill, R. (1976): Sexual selection and nuptial feeding behavior in *Bittacus apicalis* (Insecta: Mecoptera). Amer. Nat. *110*, 529–548.

Thornhill, R. (1980): Competitive charming males and choosy females: was Darwin correct? Florida Entomol. *63*, 5–30.

Thornhill, R. (1981): *Panorpa* (Mecoptera: Panorpidae) scorpionflies: systems for understanding resource-defense polygny and alternative male reproductive efforts. Ann. Rev. Ecol. System. *12*, 355–386.

Thornhill, R. and J. Alcock (1983): The Evolution of Insect Mating Systems. Cambridge, Mass.: Harvard University Press. 547 pp.

Trivers, R. L. (1972): Parental investment and sexual selection. pp. 136–179, in Sexual Selection and the Descent of Man, 1871–1971. B. G. Campbell, ed. Chicago, Aldine Press.

Tozer, W. E., U. H. Resh and J. O. Solem (1981): Bionomics and adult behavior of a lentic caddisfly, *Nectopsyche albida* (Walker). Amer. Midl. Nat. *106*, 133–144.

Velthuis, H. H. W. and J. M. F. de Camargo (1975): Observation on male territories in a carpenter bee, *Xylocopa (Neoxylocopa) hirsuitissima* Maidl (Hymenoptera, Anthophoridae). Zeit. für Tierpsych. *38*, 409–418.

de Vos, G. J. (1983): Social behavior of black grouse: an observational and experimental field study. Ardea *71*, 1–103.

de Vries, P. J. (1980): Observations on the apparent lek behavior in Costa Rican rain forest *Perrkhybis pyrrha* (Pieridae). J. Res. Lepid. *17*, 142–144.

Wiley, R. H. (1974): Evolution of social organization and life history patterns among grouse (Aves: Tetraonidae). Quart. Rev. Biol. *49*, 209–227.

Williams, G. C. (1966): Adaptation and Natural Selection. Princeton, N. J.: Princeton University Press. 207 pp.

Wittenberger, J. F. (1981): Animal Social Behavior. Boston, Duxbury Press.

Zahavi, A. (1975): Mate selection – a selection for a handicap. J. Theor. Biol. *53*, 205–214.

IV. Social Organization

Fortschritte der Zoologie, Bd. 31 · Hölldobler/Lindauer (Hrsg.): Experimental Behavioral Ecology
G. Fischer Verlag · Stuttgart · New York · 1985

From solitary to eusocial: need there be a series of intervening species?

CHARLES D. MICHENER

Departments of Entomology and of Systematics and Ecology, and Snow Entomological Museum, University of Kansas, Lawrence. Kansas 66045, USA

Abstract

Bees of the genus *Ceratina* are ordinarily solitary but certain species have social tendencies. In some the mother regularly breaks down partitions between cells, inspects and cleans them, and then reconstructs the partitions. Such behavior is probably not related to social interactions among adults. Perhaps all species form prereproductive assemblages of the young adults reared in a nest, often with their mother since females of some species may live for three years. Interactions in these assemblages include direct transfer of nectar. Foraging individuals may also deposit food on the nest walls from which it is eaten by others. Probably in such assemblages mutual tolerance and other behaviors evolved that permitted formation of colonies of adults.

Most such colonies contain two bees. Within a population colonies are less common than nests occupied by single females. A colony probably usually consists of sisters or of a mother and daughter. Sometimes the members are mated females eith enlarged ovaries (probably quasiosocial) but sometimes only one bee is mated and has enlarged ovaries (queen) while the other has slender ovaries and an empty spermatheca (worker). Queens are ordinarily larger than workers and do not forage while workers are smaller and do the foraging. If the colony consists of sisters it is semisocial; if it consists of a mother and daughter it is eusocial. Eusociality could arise within a population of basically solitary bees by fixation of eusocial behavior already sometimes expressed; there need not be a series of intervening species.

In halictine bees most species are either solitary or eusocial; once eusocial tendencies arise they probably quickly become fixed. This may be because halictids nest in the ground where nests can be found in a two-dimensional search by predators, while *Ceratina* and allodapines nest in stems and twigs where search must be three-dimensional. The advantage of a guard at the nest entrance, impossible for solitary forms but common for colonies of two or more, would be greater for halictids.

1 Introduction

A traditional method of thinking about the evolution of an attribute, particularly if an ancestral and a derived state are easily recognizable, is to look for organisms intermediate for the attribute, i. e., links among existing forms. Such intermediates are then placed with the extremes in a logical sequence from ancestral to derived, and one postulates that the evolution of the attribute followed that sequence. This comparative method of reconstructing evolution, i. e., looking for species whose attributes constitute links in a chain, has been in use since the time of DARWIN and has led to numerous evolutionary scenarios, including those that most of us use, to one degree or another, in explaining the evolution of eusocial insects from their solitary ancestors. WHEELER (1923) postulated seven steps from solitary insects that scatter their eggs to eusocial insects. Evans (1958) envisioned an ethocline of 13 steps from parasitic pompilid wasps to the most highly eusocial vespids. Similar sequences have been postulated for bees. Thus MICHENER (1958) discussed the evolutionary routes followed by bees from solitary to eusocial, and WILSON (1971, p. 99) explained these routes in some detail, reporting on the «evolutionary steps to eusociality in the bees» as envisioned by MICHENER (1969).

Caution in acceptance of the evolutionary interpretations suggested by such sequences has been voiced. Thus MICHENER (1974a, p. 47) noted that while it is tempting to look at the ethoclines as evolutionary sequences, the primitively eusocial mode of life has probably arisen not only from subsocial and from semisocial ancestral species, as suggested by earlier studies, but may also have arisen in some cases directly from solitary antecedents within a species. [Explanations of some terms, adjusted for use with *Hymenoptera*, are as follows: A *solitary* female mass provisions cells in her nest, closes them, and has no contact with her growing offspring. A *subsocial* group consists of immature offspring (eggs, larvae, etc.) and their mother who cares for them progressively. A *quasisocial* colony consists of adult females working on the same cells without caste differentiation or division of labor; all lay eggs. *Semisocial* and *eusocial* colonies have at least behaviorally and reproductively differentiated castes, workers and queens; those of semisocial colonies are of the same generation, those of eusocial colonies are not (e. g., mother and daughters). For further explanation see MICHENER (1974). The term eosocial was introduced by SAKAGAMI and MAETA (1977) for quasisocial colonies involving two generations. A *colony*, for this paper, is a group of nest-making adult females; subsocial groups and prereproductive assemblages (see below) are not considered colonies.]

The present paper is intended to emphasize the viewpoint that while the scenarios usually cited, involving a series of species intermediate between the solitary and the eusocial conditions, may in some cases be correct, they are sometimes wrong. There is increasing evidence that the primitively eusocial way of life can arise, among bee taxa having appropriate potentials, without intervening stages in the sense of *species* that are semisocial, subsocial, etc. The potential exists for direct development of eusociality involving individuals within a hitherto solitary bee population.

2 Ceratina

2.1 Life history; solitary behavior

The genus *Ceratina* is ordinarily considered to consist of solitary bees. Studies of European and North American species (MALYSHEV, 1913; KISLOW, 1976) have shown that each nest is made by a single female. The adults are long lived, and overwintering groups of adults of both sexes are common in the old nest burrows. The bees disperse and mate in the spring. (One of the Japanese species, C. *flavipes*, disperses in the autumn but mating is in the spring.) In spring each female excavates her own new nest (in the two species studied in detail by KISLOW), or in some species such as C. *japonica* old nest burrows are often reused (SAKAGAMI and MAETA, 1977 and in press). Even in such cases, although one female may remain in the old nest, and although she might start provisioning a cell before all of her associates (sisters or daughters) have left, only one working female is usually present in each nest that is being provisioned.

Each nest is a burrow in the pith of a dead stem, subdivided by partitions of pith fragments to form a series of cells, each of which is mass provisioned by the mother and provided with a single egg. When the young bees emerge as adults, they crowd their way toward the nest entrance, past younger siblings, destroying the partitions and often (in some species nearly always) rebuilding them to reform the cells. Ultimately, when all the young have matured, the partitions are cleared away and a group of adults, siblings and sometimes their mother, is found together in the burrow. They remain there through the autumn and winter (or disperse in the case of *C. flavipes*), thus completing the cycle. Such groups in temperate species have been called prehibernation assemblages but a more appropriate term is prereproductive assemblages, considering tropical as well as temperate species. Most species that have been studied in detail have only one generation per year but *C. iwatai* in Japan is bivoltine and some species in the tropics are believed to have several generations annually, as does *C. okinawana* in southern Japan and *C. dallatorreana* in California. With modifications required by the voltanism and climate, the life cycle as outlined above is characteristic of the many species of *Ceratina*, a genus of numerous subgenera and considerable morphological diversity found in all continents.

Kislow (1976) and Sakagami and Laroca (1971) both give good reviews of behavioral and life history observations of *Ceratina* species in all parts of the world. While the major studies have been made in temperate areas, *Ceratina* nests in the tropics also are ordinarily provisioned by individual bees. Likewise the related genera *Pithitis* and *Manuelia* are, so far as known, solitary at the time of nest construction and provisioning. In short, there are no species of *Ceratina* or of closely related genera that consistently work as colonies of adults.

Solitary nest construction and provisioning (and egg laying) as outlined above have been verified by my examination of many nests of *Ceratina (Zadontomerus) calcarata* and *C. (Z.) strenua* in the vicinity of Lawrence, Kansas. In no case did there seem to be two or more bees working together. More impressive are the hundreds of nests of the same species examined weekly and frequently X-rayed to determine their internal conditions by Kislow. She reported no instance of bees working together in making or provisioning cells. The presumably similarly solitary *C. callosa* (probably really *C. chalybea;* Daly, 1983) studied by Malyshev is in the subgenus *Euceratina*. Excellent studies of several Japanese species of the subgenera *Ceratina* and *Ceratinidia* by Sakagami and Maeta (1977, 1982, and in press) also show that the majority of nests were built, provisioned, and the eggs laid by lone females.

Ceratina species show a number of features unusual for solitary bees. Two of these deserve emphasis here. First, long life of the adults has already been mentioned. Kislow as well as Sakagami and Maeta (1977) demonstrate that the mothers may protect immature progeny from natural enemies. Moreover, mothers are often associated for a time with their adult progeny. In the species studied by Kislow and Malyshev such mothers die in the autumn without further reproductive activity at an age of about one and a quarter years. Sakagami and Maeta (1977) found that some females of *C. (Ceratinidia) japonica* and *C. (C.) flavipes* survive and reproduce in a second summer, thus living for more than two years, and a few hibernate the following winter; one in captivity laid a single egg in her third summer when she would have been nearly three years old. Katayama and Maeta (1979) reported that some females of *C. (Ceratina) megastigmata* survive for three years, i. e., function in three brood-rearing seasons; two females reared broods of offspring in the third year (in captivity).

Second, the prereproductive assemblages of young adults of both sexes, sometimes with their mother, are well known. The bees are more or less active, and often interact with one another for several months of late summer and autumn in temperate species. They tolerate their siblings although there is a certain amount of butting and pushing according to Kislow. There is also food transfer among them. Kislow reports seeing a female bring a little pollen into the burrow on her scopae and place it on the wall, from which it was eaten by a male bee. Sakagami and Maeta (1977) found such behavior to be commonplace; in late summer and autumn both mothers and older juvenile females foraged and returned with pollen loads. Such pollen was consumed by the nestmates. Small amounts of nectar have also been seen on burrow walls (Daly, 1966). Kislow reports one incident in which a bee appeared to take food from the mouthparts of another individual. Such behavior (nectar transfer) is of regular occurence in prereproductive assemblages of C. japonica.

2.2 Colonies of mature adults

There has been scattered evidence of small colonies of adults in some nests of various unrelated species of Ceratina. Under seasonally anomalous laboratory conditions Chandler (1975) reported eusocial colonies of Ceratina calcarata. I examined many nests of Ceratina (Calloceratina) laeta near Kourou, French Guiana, at different times of year. Of these 25 contained an egg or young larva or a partially provisioned cell. Most such nests contained only one adult bee; a few contained one or more additional adult females that were unworn juveniles presumably not yet dispersed from the earlier use of the stem by a prereproductive assemblage. One nest, however, contained a cell being provisioned, a large adult female with sperm cells in the spermatheca and enlarged ovaries, and a smaller female with somewhat worn wings, showing that she was not a juvenile adult as yet not dispersed. She had slender ovaries and no sperm cells in the spermatheca. There are no behavioral data but it was tempting to think of the first as queenlike and the second as workerlike.

I made similar casual observations of occasional nests containing a workerlike individual, or even two such individuals, in Ceratina (Ceratina) braunsiana in South Africa and Ceratina of the subgenus Ceratinidia in Java. Dissections, in the few cases where they were made, showed the smaller bee to have slender ovaries and often to be unfertilized. A single nest of C. australiensis, however, was found to contain a cell just provisioned and two adult females, both with enlarged ovaries (Michener, 1962). Again there were no behavioral data.

Recent studies of Japanese species (Sakagami and Maeta, 1977, 1982, and in press) have added greatly to the available information on colonies in Ceratina. Among over 3000 field nests of C. (Ceratinidia) flavipes, nearly all contained solitary mothers. Note that this is the species which disperses in autumn, so that in spring when nests are being established, the females are mostly isolated from one another. In the closely related C. japonica, however, the prereproductive assemblages persist through the winter and dispersal sometimes seems to be incomplete in the spring; at least this may well be the explanation of the frequency of colonies in this species. Of 230 new nests 1.3 percent contained more than one female, but among 203 reused nests (built the preceeding year and presumably used for prereproductive assemblages) the equivalent figure is 31.0 percent. For all nests, an estimated 19.2 percent were inhabited by two or more mature females. Of these, 82.6 percent contained two females, the rest, three except for one nest with four. Of 103 reused nests of C. (Ceratina) okinawana, 12.6 percent contained two females. A few colonies have also been recorded for *Ceratina iwatai* and *C. megastigmata,* both in the subgenus *Ceratina.*

The same authors were able to produce artificially a few colonies of *C. japonica* by crowding – liberating numerous females in a cage with few potential nests. Colonies were formed more readily with females of different sizes than with females of about the same size. Ordinarily the occupant of a nest defends it against would be joiners. This helps to explain the rarity of colonies among new nests in the field.

The females within colonies of *C. japonica* are diverse in their relationships. For simplicity of expression the following comments are in terms of two-bee colonies. In over 81 percent of the field colonies, both bees matured the preceding summer. The rest contained one such bee along with an old bee, in its second reproductive summer. In about half the colonies, the two bees had similar ovarian development, commonly both enlarged and capable of producing eggs. Such a colony is quasisocial and may consist of bees belonging to the same generation (commonly sisters) or to different generations (?mother and daughter). In the remaining colonies, one of the bees had enlarged ovaries while the other had markedly less enlarged or slender ovaries. This suggests division of labor (see below); if the bees are of the same generation (?sisters) the colony is semisocial, if they are of different generations (?mother and daughter) the colony is eusocial.

Twenty-one field collected, semisocial or eusocial nests each contained at least one inseminated bee with enlarged ovaries and one uninseminated individual with slender ovaries; only two contained an inseminated individual with slender ovaries or an uninseminated one with enlarged ovaries. Thus as in most social insects, egg-layers (queens) are usually mated and those that do not lay or that lay less (workers) are usually not mated.

The correlates of caste are similar to those in common social Hymenoptera. Among females from colonies, there is a positive relationship between body size, ovarian enlargement, and insemination. In most semisocial or eusocial colonies, the queen is larger than the worker. When the bees are reproductively more or less equivalent, as in quasisocial associations, size differences are usually less.

Reproductivity, measured by the number of completed cells, is greater for colonies than for lone bees. Reproductivity per female, however, remains constant. Thus two-bee nests are usually deeper than solitary nests and contain about twice as many cells when finished. This is so whether there is reproductive nonequivalence and apparent division of labor as in eusocial and semisocial associations or reproductive equivalence as in quasisocial colonies.

SAKAGAMI and MAETA were able to make detailed behavioral observations of lone as well as colonial *C. japonica* in observation nests. A lone female on sunny days commonly forages in the mornings and early afternoons, then guards (= rests with posterior end toward nest entrance) and manipulates the pollen in the cell being provisioned until late afternoon or early evening when she lays an egg. In two-female nests with division of labor, the smaller female often behaves much like a lone individual. However, when the smaller bee returns, the larger one often faces outward and buccal transfer of nectar occurs before the forager goes to deeper parts of the nest. During most of the day the larger female spends much time guarding but in late afternoon she frequently eats her nestmate's egg on the food mass, remanipulates it, and lays her own egg. In various nests such successive ovipositions, always with oophagy, were observed seven times. Except in one nest containing two bees of about the same size, prolonged daytime guarding in twelve colonies was always by the large individual. In the same colonies no foraging by large individuals was observed, again with the exception of the colony with little size difference. Eggs were laid either by the large individual only or by both, but more often by the large one. (There are few data on behavior in colonies of similar-sized bees which might have been quasisocial).

Sakagami and Maeta (1982) also produced artificial observation colonies of two other species of *Ceratina* by the same methods used with *C. japonica*. For *C. okinawana*, which occasionally forms colonies in the field, the results are not very different from those obtained with *C. japonica*. *C. flavipes*, however, almost never forms colonies in the field. Of 13 multifemale nests produced in a cage by crowding, 10 were unstable and produced no brood; food transfer was not observed and the bees soon dispersed or died. Interestingly, guarding occured in all cases and was mainly by the larger bee of each pair, as in *C. japonica*. In three nests two bees did remain together for 71 to 88 days; colonies were formed, in two of which cells were constructed and provisioned. In the nest that produced no cells the large bee foraged and also transferred food to the small one. In the other two nests, one of which was semisocial, the other eusocial, passing of individuals in the burrow was less easy than in the case of *C. japonica*, food transfer in one nest was seen from large to small but in the other it was the reverse, foraging was by both bees or only by the large one, guarding was by both or only the small one. In one nest foraging by the small individual and guarding by the large one were established, as in *C. japonica*. Thus interactions were considerably more mixed, and not so suggestive of ordinary eusocial Hymenoptera, as in *C. japonica*. The only exception to this statement concerns egg laying, which in both nests was primarily by the larger individual.

2.3 Subsocial *Ceratina*

Although all *Ceratina* females mass provision their cells, some species are subsocial in the sense of contacting and actively caring for their young. This is in contrast to solitary bees which mass provision, oviposit in, and then abandon their cells or at least have no contact with their developing progeny. Some *Ceratina* species, likewise, are fully solitary and do not care for their larvae except to remain in and presumably guard the nest entrance. For example, Sakagami and Maeta (1977) found that in *C. iwatai* cell partitions, larval feces, etc., are not removed until the beginning of the prereproductive phase. In *C. megastigmata* removal of partitions and feces occurs soon after the youngest larva has finished feeding. In both species a minority of the nests contains colonies of adults. From this I judge that colony formation is not causally related to the continuing care of larvae. Such care, now fully established for some *Ceratina* species, is most unusual among bees; it reinforces our understanding of the tendency of these bees to interact with conspecifics.

Females of various species, during and after nest provisioning, regularly open the cells containing their progeny. Kislow, with the help of X-ray photographs, found mothers of two *Zadontomerus* species deep in their nests and associated with every stage from egg to pupa. Sakagami and Maeta (1977), using observation nests, were able to observe directly mothers of two species of the subgenus *Ceratinidia* re-entering their cells and going deep in the nests, and report more such activity associated with older immatures than with eggs and young larvae. Obviously a female can work her way down the nest burrow without damaging delicate stages such as eggs and young larvae. Of course such activity involves destruction of partitions between cells. Although partitions are occasionally omitted, they are normally rebuilt as the mother moves up and down the nest. In both *Zadontomerus* and *Caratinidia* she regularly cleans cells by incorporating the fecal pellets of larvae and other debris into the bottom of the burrow or into the partitions between cells. Sakagami and Maeta found that a mother may return repeatedly to a given cell, removing recently voided feces with each visit. Kislow found that she responds to a dead egg by shortening the cell, filling in around the pollen mass with particles of pith; by completely destroying the affected cell, breaking up the pollen mass and incorporating it into cell partitions to produce one long plug (i. e., thick partition) between cells; or rarely by merely removing a partition to produce a long cell containing an unused food mass and an immature bee.

Inspection, cell cleaning, cell modification, destruction and reconstruction of partitions between cells, and movement of immature stages for short distances within the nest are characteristic of various unrelated species. The subgenera *Zadontomerus* and *Ceratinidia*, in which such behavior is fully documented, are not closely related; fragmentary data suggest similar behavior in species of other subgenera. Thus lack of partitions between older immature stages and empty cells containing larval feces before emergence of young adults have been reported for various species (SAKAGAMI and LAROCA, 1971) and presumably are results of the mother's attention to immature stages.

3 Comparative comments

3.1 Xylocopinae

This subfamily is divisible into two tribes, the Xylocopini (large carpenter bees) and the Ceratinini (small carpenter bees). The latter includes the genera already mentioned, *Ceratina*, *Pithitis*, and *Manuelia*. In addition it includes the allodapine bees, or alternatively these are put in a separate tribe, Allodapini. Allodapine bees are morphologically quite different from other Ceratinini and have many derived characters; they might have arisen from the *Ceratina* group but could not be ancestral to it. Thus there are strong reasons to believe that the solitary or subsocial mode of life of *Ceratina* is ancestral for the genus, derived from the solitary mode of life of most other bees, and not from that of any ancestor that lived in colonies of adults.

Allodapines nest in pithy stems as does *Ceratina* but the burrow is not divided into cells by partitions; in nearly all genera the immature stages live in frequent contact with one another, and are moved about by the adults and fed progressively, not by mass provisioning. Thus a nest containing a mother and her young progeny is obviously subsocial, unlike subsocial *Ceratina* whose partitions and mass provisioning obscure the subsociality. (For reviews see MICHENER, 1971, 1974a, b). It is now apparent that there is more similarity in behavior between allodapines and *Ceratina* such as *C. japonica* than had been realized. The following is a list of some major features of *Ceratina* and allodapine biology.

(1.) Nests of all *Ceratina* and allodapine species are either always or usually made by lone females.

(2.) In some *Ceratina* species and probably all allodapine species a minority of the nests contains colonies of two or more females. In the allodapine *Allodapula dichroa* only 3 percent of the nests contained colonies of mature adults; at the other extreme, in *Braunsapis facialis* and *B. leptozonia* 34 and 38 percent of the nests contained such colonies (MICHENER, 1971).

(3.) In *Ceratina* such colonies are usually in old nests and therefore probably consist of bees that were in the same prereproductive assemblage – probably usually sisters or a mother and her daughter(s). The same is probably true of allodapines but prereproductive assemblages are less obvious in the tropics; also colonies probably arise when young females remain in their mothers' nests as workers, without an obvious prereproductive phase.

(4.) Much less commonly colonies are found in new nests. In these cases the bees may have the same average relationship to one another as the bees in the local population. However, they may well be able to recognize former nestmates or their relatives; at least some halictid bees have such abilities (GREENBERG, 1979; SMITH, 1983). If this is true for Ceratinini, even colonies in new nests may commonly consist of close relatives.

(5.) Adult females in colonies may be similar in reproductive ability. In this case they are probably similar behaviorally and in size, although data supporting this statement are sparse. Such quasisocial colonies are uncommon or temporary in allodapines.

(6.) In other colonies adult females may be quite different in reproductive ability. One may have enlarged ovaries with an oocyte ready to become an egg while the other has slender ovaries without or with few enlarged oocytes. Such bees differ behaviorly and in size. The bee with larger ovaries, the queen, at least in *Ceratina japonica,* is the principal egg-layer, the principal guard, the minimal forager, and is usually inseminated. The bee with smaller ovaries, a worker, lays fewer eggs or none, rarely guards, is the principal forager, and is often uninseminated. The queen is larger than the worker. Bees in such a colony may be of the same generation (semisocial) or of different generations (eusocial). The same statements probably apply to allodapines, whose nests are initially occupied by a mother and her young (subsocial); when young females mature one or a few may remain and become workers while the mother becomes a queen (eusocial); if she dies one of her daughters presumably becomes the new queen with other daughters being workers (semisocial); as workers die off they may be replaced by porgeny of the new queen (again eusocial); etc.

(7.) In ovarian development, behavior and size, there are all intermediates between queens and workers.

(8.) Workers may be reproductively disadvantaged and hence prone to join other bees, but at least some of them in *Ceratina japonica* and probably in allodapines are capable of provisioning and laying by themselves if orphaned. Items 9 to 11 likewise are based on C. *japonica* but probably apply also to allodapines.

(9.) Loss of a worker leads to foraging by the former queen, now alone. She behaves like any other lone individual.

(10.) There is little obvious agonism between colony members. However, queens sometimes eat the eggs laid by workers. The reverse has not been seen.

(11.) If the adults in a colony with division of labor differ noticably in age, the older one is ordinarily the queen.

(12.) Food transfer by regurgitation between colony members occurs frequently.

(13.) In *Ceratina,* although the cells are mass provisioned, adult females of some species open cells containing immature stages, remove feces, and reconstruct partitions between cells. Thus a solitary nest contains a group (the mother and her immature offspring) that can be regarded as subsocial because of the direct and continuing care of the young by their mother. In allodapines there are no cells and the adults feed the larvae progressively, remove feces, etc.

(14.) Such care of growing young is not universal in *Ceratina.* For example in C. *iwatai* the mother does not open, inspect, or clean the cells during the growth of her progeny. Nests of this species inhabited by single females would be solitary, not subsocial, by all standards. Probably no allodapine is solitary by all standards; a lone female caring for her young is subsocial.

(15.) In both *Ceratina* and allodapines in late summer and autumn adult males and females remain together in their nest burrows. In the tropics similar associations are presumably briefer and less obvious. Such prereproductive assemblages probably consist largely of siblings, often with the mother as well. Contact among the individuals and limited food transfer occur.

(16.) Most and perhaps all types of interactions seen among adults in colonies of *Ceratina* can also be seen in prereproductive assemblages. The same is likely to be true for allodapines.

(17.) No storage of significant amounts of food for adult consumption occurs in the nests or in prereproductive assemblages except that in the genus *Allodapula* significant amounts of pollen are sometimes stored.

This brief review shows the similarity in nesting and social behavior between allodapines and *Ceratina* such as *C. japonica*.

The Xylocopini or large carpenter bees share with the *Ceratina* group of Ceratinini many biological features. There are similar prereproductive assemblages. Except for these, some species (e. g., *Xylocopa pubescens*) are solitary. So far as known no species opens cells and inspects or cleans the growing young; thus none is subsocial. But some species have some nests that contain two to several working adult females instead of only one. Food transfer occurs much as in *Ceratina*. Often the relationships are communal, with different females using different branches of the nest, something that is impossible for *Ceratina* because narrow stems do not permit branching nests. In other species, e. g. *X. sulcatipes*, quasisocial and semisocial relationships have been reported and since mothers often survive and are associated with their adult progeny, eusocial associations are possible. Data are sparse and difficult to obtain because the nests are in wood; the best information comes from X-ray examination of nests in boards (GERLING, HURD and HEFETZ, 1983). Few ovarian and spermathecal examinations have been made.

3.2 Apidae

This family, which may have had a common origin with the Xylocopinae (possibly they are sister groups), needs no detailed attention here because early stages in its social evolution are extinct or inadequately studied. The subfamily Euglossinae contains both solitary and slightly social species, but details are largely lacking. The subfamily Bombinae has initially subsocial associations which become primitively eusocial colonies with maturation of the first workers, and the Meliponinae and Apinae consist of the only highly eusocial bees.

3.3 Halictini

The only remaining group of bees in which eusocial behavior has evolved is the Halictidae. This family in not at all related to the xylocopine-apid complex, except that both are bees (superfamily Apoidea). Nearly all of the eusocial halictids are in the tribe Halictini and the following remarks concern that group only. In the Halictini, as in the Xylocopinae, the question arises as to whether eusocial behavior evolved via a series of species exhibiting progressively higher social levels, or alternatively, directly from a solitary or polymorphic species. [There are few subsocial species, for brood cells, once closed, are not opened for addition of food or for cleaning except in a few of the most fully eusocial species of *Lasioglossum* (subgenus *Evylaeus*). Their eusociality is certainly a derived condition in a limited group of *Evylaeus* and has nothing to do with early stages of evolution of halictine eusocial life.]

In the Halictini there are many solitary species as well as many eusocial species. Nests of the latter commonly start with a single female (later to become the queen of a colony) rearing a female-biased or all female brood, most or all of which become workers. There are no regularly quasisocial species and only one that is reportedly semisocial. There may be groups of nest foundresses that are quasisocial or semisocial, as in *Polistes*, but these conditions are temporary and for most species unusual; single foundress colonies are more common. There are also other temporary situations in which the colonies are not eusocial. For example, if the queen dies and is replaced by one of her workers, as happens regularly in *L. (Dialictus) zephyrum*, there is necessarily a stage when the colony is semisocial before the old workers die and are replaced by the porgeny of the new queen, returning the colony to the eusocial condition.

Considering more specifically the American species of the subgenus *Dialictus* of *Lasioglossum*, a large group of morphologically monotonous, closely related species, one finds solitary as well as eusocial species. The solitary ones are similar in mode of life to other solitary burrowing bees. The better known eusocial ones such as *L. (D.) zephyrum* and *imitatum* commonly live in colonies of several females (for a review see MICHENER, 1974). Such forms shed little light on the actual origin of eusociality unless one considers the ontogeny of colonies relevant. However, species of *Dialictus* exist that regularly live in minimal eusocial groups. The best known examples are *L. (D.) breedi* and *seabrai* (MICHENER, BREED, and BELL, 1979). As in most species, nests are started by lone females, but so far as known all that survive obligately develop colonies. The average number of adult females per nest is about 1.5; in nests containing colonies of two or more bees, the average number is 3.0 and 2.3 respectively, for the two species. Even in species with such small mature colony sizes (the maximum number of females found in a nest was 4), the organization is usually eusocial; the queens have developed ovaries and are inseminated, the workers have more slender ovaries and usually are uninseminated. No significant size difference between the castes was found. In a few nests there were two bees with more or less equally developed ovaries – perhaps quasisocial colonies that developed after loss of a queen, allowing ovarial enlargement of two workers. Foraging in *L. breedi* is largely by uninseminated individuals, regardless of ovarian size, suggesting that queens tend to remain in their nests as in other eusocial colonies.

4 Discussion

Important contributors to the potential for colony formation, at least in Xylocopinae, must have been the prevalence of prereproductive assemblages and of long lived adults. Prereproductive assemblages occur even in the fully solitary species of *Ceratina* and *Xylocopa*, suggesting that mutual tolerance and defense, food exchange, foraging for nestmates, etc., evolved in connection with such assemblages, before and probably prerequisite to evolution of nesting colonies of adults. Once evolved, the behavior associated with assemblages could also function in reproductive colonies of adults, where longevity also would be important in permitting co-occurence of adults of different ages and generations. Beyond the stage in which mature females of various ages could live together, there seems to have been no necessary sequence of stages leading to eusociality.

The importance of the *Ceratina* data for an understanding of the origin of eusocial behavior is that when they live in colonies, these bees lack uniformity in social relationships. It is as though whatever two females remain together or join one another, whether they are sisters, mother and daughter, or perhaps unrelated bees, interactions result. Within the same species there exists a whole gamut of social categories. The colonies can be quasisocial, semisocial, or eusocial, all at low frequency in the same species of bee. For the first, in which both bees (in a 2-bee colony) are fully reproductive, one only needs to imagine the evolution of the ability of the bees to tolerate one another during the nest making phase, as well as during the prereproductive phase. For semisocial and eusocial arrangements, however, one female is the principal reproductive and the other is less reproductive or even nonreproductive. Within a predominantly solitary or subsocial species one must imagine the evolution of the potential for the reproductively less competent individual to function as a worker and the reproductively more competent individual, as a queen.

The differences between the worker and queen morphs in *Ceratina japonica* and probably in other species of diverse subgenera, and certainly in various allodapines, are remarkably similar to those found in familiar eusocial insects. Large body size, large ovaries, insemination, reduced foraging, receipt of food in the nest, and probably a tendency to destroy eggs laid by a worker, all go with the *Ceratina* queens; small size, small ovaries (hence reduced egg laying activities), frequently lack of insemination, active foraging, and food transfer to the queen in the nest are all attributes of workers. Most of the same features differentiate the castes in colonies of allodapine bees. Among allodapines caste differences seem least in those species that only rarely produce colonies of mature adults. That all these caste differences go hand in hand suggests that they must have evolved through selection to form the *associations* of characteristics. They go hand in hand not only in these bees but in eusocial insects generally: hence the association of features of the castes hase occurred repeatedly, must therefore be important, and begins at least in bees at an extraordinarily early stage in the evolution of sociality.

It is not difficult to envision evolution of such castes as a result of increased inclusive fitness of the worker, control by the queen, mutual advantage, or a combination of these. The high frequency with which uninseminated females of *Ceratina japonica* become workers suggests that reproductively disadvantaged bees can increase their (inclusive) fitness by joining relatives. However, in each of the three nests in which the order of joining of bees to form a colony is known, a large bee (ultimately a queen) joined a small bee (ultimately a worker) that had already started the nest. It may or may not be legitimate to interpret this as a large bee forcing itself like a parasite on a small one and thereafter controlling it.

In spite of the censuses indicating that reproductivity per *Ceratina* is the same whether alone or in colonies, the result might be quite different if all nests started could be followed throughout a nesting season. Many lone females may be destroyed by predators, so that they do not appear in censuses, i. e., guards in colonies may reduce the number of nests destroyed. If this is true, both bees in a colony must have higher fitnesses than they would if they were alone in spite of the fact that the number of cells per bee in completed nests is the same.

Evolution of castes in Xylocopinae has occurred in situations in which cooperative nesting must not be a major advantage; if it were, there would be Xylocopinae with colony behavior fixed. Instead, eusocial life is a minority condition in all Xylocopinae in which it is known. Selection has somehow been effective enough to assemble the potentials for the attributes of each caste without leading to high frequency or fixation of colonial life. Presumably the association of caste attributes, such that a queen, for example, always has a given list of characteristics, is genetically specified. But the particular caste into which a given individual will develop is under environmental control. This is true of most eusocial insects, and evidently of *Ceratina japonica* also, since the functions (hence caste) of an individual can vary according to its associates or lack of them.

The existence of a minority of nests containing colonies, some of them with castes (i. e., semisocial and eusocial), in various species of *Ceratina,* in most allodapines, and perhaps also in *Xylocopa,* suggests that this polymorphism or at least a potential for it arose in a remote common ancestor of the modern species and has persisted, without ever proceeding to fixation. Presumably from such polymorphic ancestral types, forms arose in the Apidae that consistently showed similar social behavior, so that species rather than individual colonies could be regarded, for example, as eusocial.

For the Halictini the virtual absence of subsocial, communal, quasisocial, semisocial, etc., species, especially in American *Dialictus,* supports the view that, as in the *Ceratina* group, there is no need to postulate the existence of a series of species occupying intermediate social levels from solitary to eusocial. Indeed there is evidence that such series do not exist. The species exhibiting, in maximal colony development, the intermediate social levels such as semisociality, mostly belong to different phyletic lines (EICKWORT and SAKAGAMI, 1979).

It is more difficult to envision the evolution from solitary to eusocial in Halictini than in the xylocopine-apid complex because halictine nests are usually inhabited either by solitary or by eusocial bees. Selection for eusocial attributes in Halictini must be sufficiently strong to associate the various features of each morph and also to carry the process to fixation so that populations and species quickly become characterized by the existance of the morphs, i. e., by eusociality. Again, of course the morphs are not genetically specified; in the absence of a queen a worker can become a queen and intermediates between the casts are common. But the potential to develop into one morph or the other must have evolved and after the young or juvenile adult period, most individuals can be identified by behavior and dissections as members of one caste or the other. (For details on one species see BROTHERS and MICHENER, 1974).

Perhaps nest sites influence the evolution of sociality in *Ceratina* and in Halictini. *Ceratina* nests are normally dispersed because the dead broken stems which they occupy are dispersed. The nest entrances are widely scattered in three-dimensional space and wingless parasites and predators must search in a maze of stems and twigs most of which do not lead to nests. It follows that parasite and predator pressure on *Ceratina* is probably only moderate (although the advantages of guards have been demonstrated) and that the advantages of colonial life may not be enough to lead to fixation of polymorphism and sociality. Presumably such advantages are countered by disadvantages, at least for a worker capable of independent life; perhaps they are sufficient to prevent fixation of the polymorphism, and in some forms like *Ceratina flavipes* may prevent colony formation entirely. Halictini, on the other hand, usually nest in the ground. On the two-dimensional surface, especially if suitable sites are few or if for other reasons the nests are aggregated, parasite and predator pressure is often high. For this reason guards may be more important than in the Ceratinini and probably the tendency is to go all the way toward colony formation as a fixed way of life once the process starts.

Acknowledgments

I am indebted to S. F. SAKAGAMI and Y. MAETA for the use of their paper in press on *Ceratina japonica* and for reading and commenting upon a manuscript version of my section on *Ceratina*. C. J. KISLOW provided a copy of her dissertation with excellent photographic prints of figures. For useful comments on the manuscript I am indebted to WILLIAM T. WCISLO and DAVID W. ROUBIK. This paper is a product of NSF grant BNS82-00651.

Contribution number 1883 from the Department of Entomology, University of Kansas.

References

Brothers, D. J. and C. D. Michener (1974): Interactions in colonies of primitively social bees III. Ethometry of division of labor in *Lasioglossum zephyrum*. Jour. Comp. Physiol., 70, 129–168.

Chandler, L. (1975): Eusociality in *Ceratina calcarata* Robt. Proc. Indiana Acad. Sci., 84, 283–284.

Daly, H. V. (1966): Biological studies of *Ceratina dallatorreana*, an alien bee in California. Ann. Entom. Soc. Amer., 59, 1138–1154.

– (1983): Taxonomy and ecology of Ceratinini of North Africa and the Iberian Peninsula. Syst. Entom., 8, 29–62.

Eickwort, G. C. and S. F. Sakagami (1979): A classification of nest architecture of bees in the tribe Augochlorini, with description of a Brazilian nest of *Rhinocorynura inflaticeps*. Biotropica, *11*, 28–37.

Evans, H. E. (1958): The evolution of social life in wasps. Proc. 10th Internat. Congr. Entom. (Montreal), *2*, 449–457.

Gerling, H. E., P. D. Hurd, Jr., and A. Hefetz (1983): Comparative behavioral biology of two middle east species of carpenter bees (*Xylocopa* Latreille). Smithsonian Contr. Zool., no. 369, i-iii + 1–33 pp.

Greenberg, L. (1979): Genetic component of bee odor in kin recognition. Science, *206*, 1095–1097.

Katayama, E. and Y. Maeta (1979): Brood development and adult activities of a small carpenter bee, *Ceratina megastigmata*. Kontyu, *47*, 139–157.

Kislow, C. J. (1976): The comparative biology of two species of small carpenter bees, *Ceratina strenua* F. Smith and *C. calcarata* Robertson. Ph. D. dissertation, Univ. of Georgia, Athens, Georga, USA, iii + 1–221 pp.

Malyshev, S. (1913): Life and instincts of some *Ceratina*-bees. Horae Soc. Entom. Rossicae, *40(8)*, 1–58, pl. 3 (in Russian, English summary).

Michener, C. D. (1958): The evolution of social behavior in bees. Proc. 10th Internat. Congr. Entom. (Montreal), *2*, 441–447.

– (1962): The genus *Ceratina* in Australia, with notes on its nests. Jour. Kansas Entom. Soc., *35*, 414–421.

– (1969): Comparative social behavior of bees. Ann. Rev. Entom., *14*, 299–342.

– (1971): Biologies of African allodapine bees. Bull. Amer. Mus. Nat. Hist., *145*, 219–302.

– (1974a): The social behavior of the bees. Cambridge, Mass.: Harvard Univ. Press.

– (1974b): Polymorphismus bei allodapinen Bienen, pp. 246–256, *in* G. H. Schmidt, Sozialpolymorphismus bei Insekten, Stuttgart: Wissenschaftliche Verlagsgesellschaft MBH.

Michener, C. D., M. D. Breed, and W. J. Bell (1979): Seasonal cycles, nests, and social behavior of some Colombian halictine bees. Revista Biol. Tropical, *27*, 13–34.

Sakagami, S. F. and S. Laroca (1971): Observations on the bionomics of some neotropical xylocopine bees, with comparative and biofaunistic notes. Jour. Fac. Sci., Hokkaido Univ. (6, Zool.) *18*, 57–127.

Sakagami, S. F. and Y. Maeta (1977): Some presumably presocial habits of Japanese *Ceratina* bees, with notes on various social types in Hymenoptera. Insectes Sociaux, *24*, 319–343.

Sakagami, S. F. and Y. Maeta (1982): Further experiments on the artificial induction of multifemale associations in the principally solitary bee genus *Ceratina*, pp. 171–174, *in* M. D. Breed, C. D. Michener, and H. E. Evans (eds.), The Biology of Social Insects, Proc. 9th Congr., Internat. Union Study Soc. Insects., Boulder, Colo., Westview Press.

Sakagami, S. F. and Y. Maeta (in press): Multifemale nests and rudimentary castes in the basically solitary bee *Ceratina japonica*. Jour. Kansas Entom. Soc., *57*.

Fortschritte der Zoologie, Bd. 31 · Hölldobler/Lindauer (Hrsg.): Experimental Behavioral Ecology
G. Fischer Verlag · Stuttgart · New York · 1985

The principles of caste evolution

EDWARD O. WILSON

Museum of Comparative Zoology, Harvard University, Cambridge, Massachusetts 02138, USA

Abstract

Caste and division of labor are at the core of colony organization in social insects, because they determine the efficiency of energy utilization and resource allocation. In this review I present some of the generalizations that have emerged during the study of these phenomena, especially those encountered in ants during the past ten years.

Castes in ants and other advanced social insects are either physical, marked by anatomical differences, or temporal, based on programmed changes in behavior as a function of aging. The percentages of these castes existing in each colony are largely the outcome of adaptive demography; that is, the schedules of natality and survivorship appear to have been shaped by natural selection at the colony level. Thus the first adult worker brood of the leafcutter ant *Atta cephalotes* consists of workers that just span the minimum range required to collect fresh vegetation and raise fungi on it. This demographic property maximizes the number of individuals that the founding queen produces and presumably reduces to a minimum the chance that any size-group will go extinct before the appearance of the second brood.

Another basic principle of caste evolution in ants is that all physical subcastes (majors, minors, and intermediates) have been generated during evolution by relatively simple modifications in allometric growth. The 44 genera with polymorphic species (the remaining 219 are entirely monomorphic) can be placed within a straightforward array of evolutionary grades ranging from mild allometry and unimodal size-frequency distributions to complete dimorphism. In all species so far studied, allometry is accompanied by alloethism, the size-dependent change in response thresholds and frequency of performance of certain social behaviors.

The division of labor among these various physical and temporal castes is often tightly regulated by feedback loops, the nature of which has only recently begun to receive systematic attention in experimental studies. In *Pheidole dentata*, for example, the major workers are activated for colony defense by the minor workers when the latter report the presence of fire ants or thief ants (genus *Solenopsis*) by means of odor trails combined with other chemical cues. The magnitude of the majors' reaction, and with it the overall pattern of colony response, changes with the intensity of signals received by both minors and majors during the invasion. On the other hand, other colony-level responses are now known in which feedback and regulation are lacking. Thus the percentage of major workers produced by *P. dentata* colonies is independent of the frequency and intensity of attacks on them by *Solenopsis;* there appears to be no way to adjust defense expenditures to the degree of stress.

Optimization studies, employed to identify the selective agents and to evaluate their effectiveness, are in the earliest stages of development. An example is presented of an experimental study on *Atta,* where the foraging (and leaf-cutting) size group was found to be the one that provides the maximum net energetic yield, as opposed to the maximization of other conceivable performances – or no maximization at all.

As such analyses increase in number, and can be synthesized into a more nearly complete picture of colony functioning, it will become useful again to treat the colony as a superorganism and to build exact models based on the interplay of individual- and colony-level selection.

1 Introduction

It is possible to distinguish two very general problems in the study of social insects, to which all other topics and theoretical reflection play a tributary role. The first is the origin of social behavior itself. Entomologists are especially interested in the advanced state called eusociality, which characterizes all of the ants and termites and a small percentage of aculeate wasps and bees. This evolutionary grade is defined as the combination of three features, namely care of the young by adults, overlap in generations, and a division of labor into reproductive and nonreproductive castes.

The last of the traits, the existence of a subordinate or even completely sterile worker caste, is the rarest of the three. It is also by far the most significant with reference to further evolutionary potential, for when individuals can be turned into specialized working machines, an intricate division of labor can be achieved and a relatively complicated social organization becomes attainable even with a relatively simple repertory of individual behavior. It does not matter, to use a rough metaphor, if the separate pieces of a clock are relatively simple in construction, so long as they can be shaped to serve particular roles and then fitted together into a working whole. You cannot construct a proper clock if every little piece is also required to keep some sort of time on its own. By the same token natural selection cannot readily form a complex colony if every member must complete a full life cycle on its own. But reproductive sterility and the origin of a worker caste imply substantial altruism of the kind most difficult to achieve in evolution, since it is directed not to offspring but to nephews, nieces, brothers, and sisters. There is still a great deal of uncertainty concerning the conditions under which the twelve or so phyletic lines of insects (eleven in the aculeate Hymenoptera, one in the Isoptera) have worked against the main evolutionary currents to attain this kind of altruism. What are the relative contributions of kin selection and parental manipulation? What ecological constraints and nest site preferences are most likely to add to the inclusive fitness of the altruistic workers? These questions are the focus of a great deal of continuing theoretical and experimental work, which has reached a quite sophisticated level during the past decade.

The second major problem in the study of social insects, with which I will be concerned in this essay, can be called *colony design,* or, more fully, the strategic design of colonies. Once a sterile worker caste is in place, that is, once the equivalent of the less-than-independent levers and wheels of the clock can be manufactured, the important consideration becomes the best arrangement of castes and division of labor for the functioning and reproduction of the colony as a whole. In an earlier study (WILSON, 1968) I argued that the colony can be most effectively analyzed if treated as a factory within a fortress. Natural selection operates so as to favor colonies that contribute the largest number of mature colonies in the next generation, so that the number of workers per colony is only of incidental importance. In other words, the key measure is not how big, or strong, or aggressive a colony of a particular genotype can become but how many successful new colonies it generates. Hence the functioning of the workers in gathering energy and converting it into virgin queens and males is vital. This part of colony functioning constitutes the factory. But the colony is simultaneously a tempting target for predators. The brood and food stores are veritable treasure houses of protein, fat, and carbohydrates. As a consequence colonies must have an adequate defense system, which often takes the form of stings and poisonous secretions and even specialized soldier castes. This set of adaptations constitutes the fortress.

The ultimate currency in the colony fitness equations is energy. The workers appear programmed to sweep the nest environs in such a way as to gain the maximum net energetic yield. Their size, diel rhythms, foraging geometry, recruitment techniques, and methods of food retrieval are the qualities most likely to be shaped by natural selection. But even as energy is being collected and distributed to the queen and brood, the colony is subject to predation. A certain number of individuals must be sacrificed in periodic defenses of the colony and during the riskier steps of the daily foraging expeditions. The loss of energy required to replace them is entered on the debit side of the fitness ledger.

Colony design then becomes essentially a problem in economics. I have suggested use of the similar expression «ergonomics» to acknowledge that work and energy are the sole elements of calculation, and nothing like human-like transactions with credits and money is involved (WILSON, 1968; OSTER and WILSON, 1978).

The core of ergonomic organization is division of labor, based upon a system of roles and castes. This is the topic on which I have concentrated my own research during the past ten years and will partly summarize here. I propose to cover the main principles of ergonomics and caste evolution, but because the literature documenting them is now so large the examples presented will be taken principally from my own research. This has the additional advantage of bringing with it a greater degree of familiarity, but in making the restriction it is not my intention to imply that the excellent research being conducted by others is any less important; see for example the reviews by SCHMIDT et al. (1974), OSTER and WILSON (1978).

2 Caste, task, role

The aim of any ergonomic (as well as any human-economic) analysis is the prescription of a complete balance sheet, and to this end it is necessary to define as precisely as possible the agents entailed. A *caste* is a set of colony members, smaller than the total colony population, that specialize on particular tasks for prolonged periods of time. Ordinarily, and perhaps in the social insects invariably, the set is distinguished by some kind of additional marker – a larger size, some other kind of anatomical feature, a different age, or even some less apparent physiological trait. To make the classification somewhat more formal, a physical caste is one distinguished not only by its form of labor but also by one or more distinctive anatomical traits, while a temporal caste is set apart by a combination of particular behavior patterns and age. So far as known, all physical castes within a given colony of ants have the same genotype. The differences among them are based on variation in size or some other incidental quality determined during individual development, and not upon differences in genes. A *task* is a set of behaviors that must be performed to achieve some purpose of the colony, such as repelling an invader or feeding a larva. A set of closely linked tasks can be defined as a *role*, even if the acts are otherwise quite different. It is generally true, for example, that in ants the act (task) of grooming the queen is closely linked with the very different acts of regurgitating to the queen and removing freshly deposited eggs. All of these responses can be considered part of the single role of queen care, and it is conceivable that the role might be filled by one, two, or more castes, depending on the species.

The linkage between castes and roles is close, and in the case of the more complex forms of morphological and behavioral variation, it is sometimes necessary to employ roles to distinguish castes. In the leaf-cutter ant *Atta sexdens*, for example, size variation is continuous, and all of the size groups together perform a total of 22 tasks. The physical castes cannot be separated as discontinuous groups from one another on the basis of any known set of discrete anatomical traits. Instead, four castes have been defined on the basis of «role clusters», which are more or less segregated as distinctively shaped sets of activity curves. They are, respectively: gardener-nurses, within-nest generalists, forager-excavators, and defenders (see Figure 1). This discretization is only partial, and finer, arbitrary subdivisions at the lower end of the size scale are possible.

3 Adaptive demography

A key principle of caste evolution is the adaptive nature of colony demography (Wilson, 1968). Ordinary demography, of the kind found in nonsocial organisms, in social vertebrates, and in more primitively social insects such as subsocial wasps and bees, is a function of the individual parameters of growth, reproduction, and death. A large amount of documentation from free-living and laboratory populations supports the general belief that growth and natality schedules are direct adaptations shaped by natural selection at the level of the individual (May et al., 1981; Krebs and Davies, 1981). On the other hand, the size and age structure of the population as a whole are epiphenomena, in the sense that they reflect the individual-level adaptations but do not constitute adaptations in their own right. Thus a sharply tapered age distribution in many species of fishes and birds results

Fig. 1: The four physical castes of the leaf-cutter ant *Atta sexdens,* defined on the basis of size and role clusters. The frequency curves, which have been smoothed by eye, are of workers of different size that perform each of 22 tasks; the frequency curves fall into four groups called role clusters. (From Wilson, 1980a).

from a high birth rate and a high mortality schedule throughout the life span, but in itself does not contribute to the survival of the population or the individual members. The exact reverse is the case of the eusocial insect colony defined as a population. The demography, not its causal parameters, is directly adaptive. The workers are for the most part sterile; their birth and death schedules have meaning only with reference to the survival and reproduction of the queen. Hence the unit of selection is the colony as a whole. The traits of the colony are the larger features of demography, the age and size frequency distributions. What matters are such higher-level traits as the number of very large adults available to serve as soldiers, the number of small young adults functioning as nurses, and so on through the entire caste roster and behavioral repertoire. Each species has a characteristic age-size frequency distribution, and the evidence is strong that this colony-wide trait is not an epiphenomenon, but has been shaped by natural selection, constituting a direct adaptation.

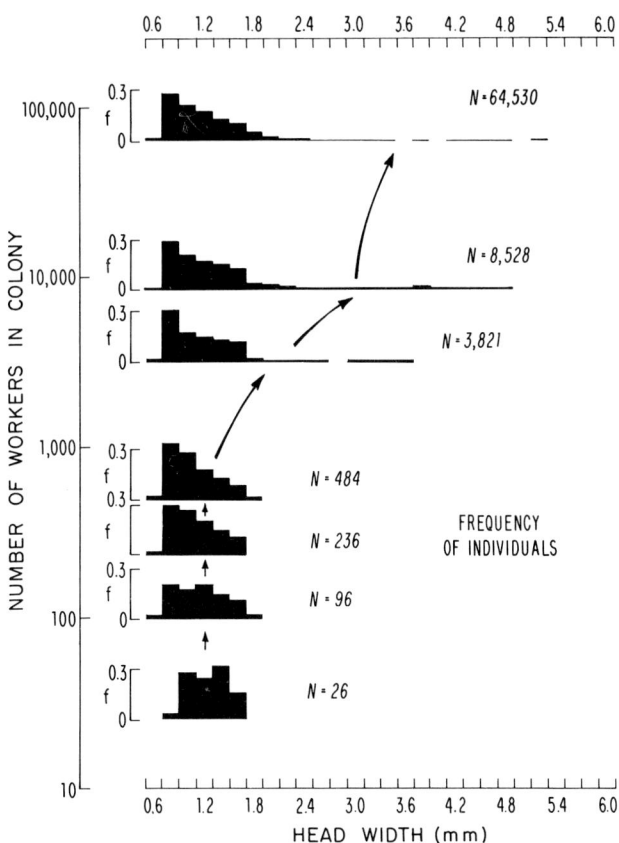

Fig. 2: The ontogeny of the caste system in the leaf-cutter ant *Atta cephalotes* is reflected strikingly in the changes in the size-frequency distribution that occur with colony growth. Shown here are seven representative colonies from the field in Costa Rica and author's laboratory. N, the number of workers in each colony, based on complete censuses; f, the frequency of individuals according to size class. (From WILSON, 1983b).

A striking example of adaptive demography is provided by developmental changes in the caste system of the leaf-cutter ant *Atta cephalotes* (WILSON, 1983b). Beginning colonies, started by a single queen from her own body reserves, have a nearly uniform size-frequency distribution across a relatively narrow head-width range of 0.8–1.6 mm. The key to the arrangement is that workers in the span 0.8–1.0 mm are required as gardeners of the symbiotic fungus on which the colony depends, while workers with head widths of 1.6 mm are the smallest that can cut vegetation of average toughness. This range also embraces the worker size groups most involved in brood care. Thus, remarkably, the queen produces about the maximum number of individuals which together can perform all of the essential colony tasks. As the colony continues growing, the worker size variation broadens in both directions, to head width 0.7 mm or slightly less at the lower end to over 5.0 mm at the upper end, and the frequency distribution becomes more sharply peaked and strongly skewed to the larger size classes (see Figure 2).

A more physiological question immediately arises from the observed colony ontogeny of *Atta:* which is more important in determining the size-frequency distribution, the size of the colony or its age? In order to learn the answer, I selected four colonies 3–4 years old and with about 10,000 workers and reduced the population of each to 236 workers, giving them a size-frequency distribution characteristic of natural young colonies of the same size collected in Costa Rica. The worker pupae produced at the end of the first brood cycle possessed a size-frequency distribution like that of small, young colonies rather than larger, older ones. Thus colony size is more important than age.

The *Atta* example is just an extreme case of what appears at least on the surface to be programmed colony demography among ant species. However, the physiological control mechanisms remain almost entirely unexplored. The «rejuvenation» effect in *Atta cephalotes* indicates that a feedback loop of some kind is involved, as opposed to an irreversible maturation of the size-frequency distribution; but its nature has not been investigated.

4 Allometry and alloethism

Another basic principle of caste evolution in ants is that all worker subcastes appear to have originated ultimately from allometric growth. In simplest terms, the different forms, designated usually as minors, medias, and majors, differ from one another by size, and the size variation is accompanied by differences in body proportions. Thus majors, the largest workers, typically possess heads that are larger relative to the rest of the body than is the case in the minors and medias. In ant species with simpler forms of differentiation the relation can be approximated by the power function $y = bx^a$, where x is one dimension (say width of the pronotum), y is another dimension (say head width), and a and b are fitted constants characteristic of the species. The power function is in fact the defining property of allometry in the original, strict sense. It is of considerable importance that the pattern of allometry that characterizes a given colony is genetically prescribed, but the size attained by individual workers is not.

Of the 263 living genera of ants known worldwide, only 44 possess polymorphic species, in which the worker caste is differentiated into easily recognized subcastes. By standard techniques used in phylogenetic systematics, it has been possible to infer with some confidence which are primitive caste systems and which are derived. The following sequence has occurred repeatedly and independently in many separate evolving lines of ants, as deduced from the comparison of related species showing different stages of advancement (WILSON, 1953). First, the size variation of the workers within colonies broadens and is accompanied by simple allometry, usually including a disproportionate widening of the head, a decrease in the total behavioral repertory, and some degree of specialization – in most cases for defense. Next, the size-frequency distribution is skewed to the larger size classes; then it becomes bimodal, with peaks corresponding to what are now easily recognizable minor and major castes. In some but not all of the species occupying this evolutionary grade, the allometry has become diphasic or triphasic; that is, the allometric curve breaks at one or two points, so that the slope (a in the equation $y = bx^a$) changes value once or twice. This advance either speeds up or slows down the shifts in proportion, and it complicates the overall pattern of subcaste differentiation. Finally, in some of the most advanced species, in genera such as *Acanthomyrmex, Oligomyrmex, Pheidole*, and *Zatapinoma*, the medias drop out, the size-frequency curve is divided into two discrete curves, and the two allometric curves are separated and come to possess different slopes. Paradoxically, this last step simplifies the caste system somewhat by changing its base from continuous size variation and allometry over a broad segment of the size range to a straightforward two-state polymorphism.

The paramount quality of allometric evolution in ants is that all evolving lines (so far as can be reasonably inferred) started with a single allometric curve and stayed with it until the final stage of complete dimorphism, when at last the curve was broken and the two segments evolved in an outwardly independent manner. No phylogenetic group in ants has

5mm

Fig. 3: The caste system of the genus *Atta*, here exemplified by *A. laevigata*, is among the most extreme found in ants, yet it is still based upon single allometry curves combined with size variation. (From OSTER and WILSON, 1978).

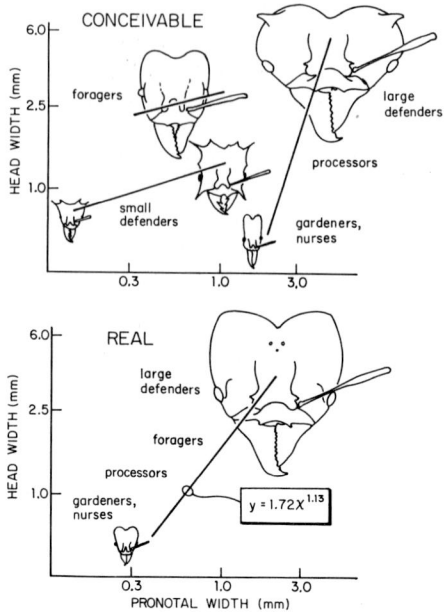

Fig. 4: A conceivable array of *Atta* castes is compared with the actual array in *A. sexdens,* in order to illustrate the principle that the evolution of ant castes is based on a single allometric curve and hence constrained in a fundamental manner. (After WILSON, 1980a).

relied on multiple allometric lines. If it had, this property alone would have permitted the rapid evolution and fine-scale adjustment of a much larger number of specialized worker castes from the outset. In Figures 3 and 4 I have illustrated this principle with a depiction of what actually exists in the highly polymorphic *Atta sexdens,* in contrast to an imaginary example of what *might* have evolved with the addition of only one more allometric curve.

Closely coordinated with the allometry of the physical caste systems is *alloethism,* the regular change in behavior patterns as a function of size. In both species on which measurements have been taken, the fire ant *Solenopsis geminata* and leaf-cutter *Atta sexdens,* the curves were found to possess steeper slopes than the corresponding allometric curves of the anatomical structures employed in the behavior (WILSON, 1978, 1980a). Part of the pattern in the fire ant species is illustrated in Figure 5.

An important feature of both allometry and alloethism in ants is the clearly adaptive function in all cases thus far carefully studied. The extreme, sometimes bizarre anatomical productions are not incidental to some general process of differential growth, nor are the remarkable shifts in behavior with increases in body size neutral by-products of larger or smaller brains. On the contrary, each species has a distinct morphological and behavioral program in its caste differentiation which, in all cases so far analyzed, has proved closely related to its principal life habits.

The correlation between the caste system and colony natural history is strikingly illustrated in the fire ants. The more primitive pattern of *Solenopsis invicta* is typical of almost all of the fire ant species, which comprise the subgenus *Solenopsis* of *Solenopsis* (as opposed to the thief ants, which comprise the subgenus *Diplorhoptrum*). The allometry of

S. invicta is very slight: the majors have heads that are only somewhat shorter, broader, and more quadrate with reference to the remainder of the body (see Figure 6). The behavioral differences are also modest, since the majors perform the same tasks as the minors with the exception of caring for the eggs and young larvae. Workers in these larger size classes simply handle pieces of brood, prey, and soil particles that are correspondingly larger in size. Hence transport and nest excavation appear to be enhanced by the polymorphism, although that subjective impression has not yet been put to a quantitative test. The more important point is that *Solenopsis geminata* has added something entirely new. Allometry is steep, so that the larger medias and majors are grotesque creatures possessing massive heads and blunt, toothless mandibles. These two features together contribute to a substantial increase in the crushing power of the ants. I was able to show that the largest workers are in fact specialized for milling seeds, the majors so much so that they have become restricted to the smallest behavioral repertory thus far recorded in the social insects – milling and self-grooming. *Solenopsis geminata* has undergone this striking revision in its caste system and division of labor as part of its trend toward granivory, which is the most extensive known among the fire ant species.

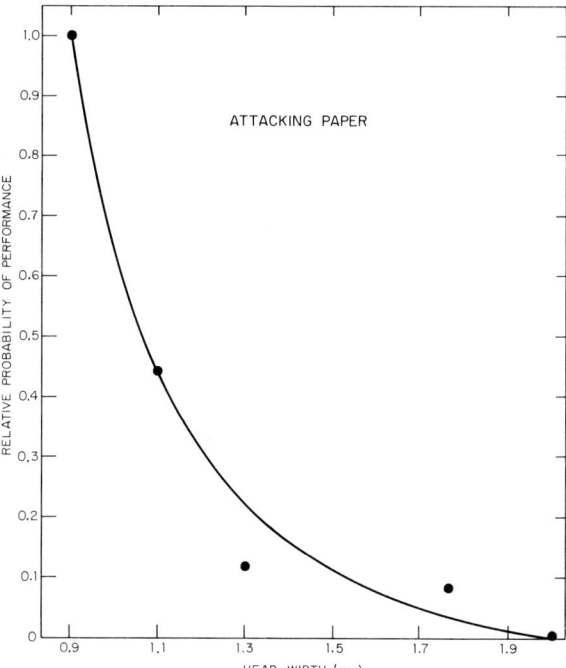

Fig. 5: Part of the alloethic curve for aggressive response by workers of the fire ant *Solenopsis geminata* to a disturbance of the nest. «Relative probability» is defined as the fraction of workers responding in a size group relative to the highest fraction responding in any size group (in this case the group head width 0.9 mm). (From WILSON, 1978).

Fig. 6: The worker caste systems of two fire ant species, the red imported fire ant *Solenopsis invicta* and the native granivorous form *S. geminata*. The outlines shown are the heads of workers at the two extremes of size variation; that is, a small minor worker contrasted with a large major worker. Also presented are the size-frequency distributions of random samples of workers from large laboratory colonies of the two species. (From WILSON, 1978).

5 The superorganism

From about 1900 to 1950, many biologists and philosophers developed a keen interest in holism and emergent evolution. They often turned to colonies of social insects as prime examples of superorganisms, by which is meant aggregates of individuals so well organized that they take on the attributes of true organisms. These early expositions were almost entirely limited to recognizing various sorts of analogies. For example, the queen and spermatheca were compared with the reproductive organs and the workers with the variously differentiated soma, trophallaxis was cited as the equivalent of circulation, soldiers were thought the parallel of the immune system, and so on. While initially stimulating, the entire elaborate exercise eventually exhausted its possibilities. The limitations of a primarily analogical approach became increasingly apparent when investigators turned more to the fine details of communication and caste, and the expression «superorganism» was all but dropped from the technical literature by the 1960s.

The time may be at hand for a revival of the superorganism concept. There are two reasons, both stemming from the increased information and technical competence acquired by entomologists during the analytic phase of the 1960s and 1970s. The first is the beginning of a sound developmental biology of the insect colony, and the second is the rapid improvement of optimization analysis in behavioral ecology and sociobiology.

The new developmental biology entails an understanding of the way in which castes are determined, their ratios regulated, and their actions coordinated through communication. There is a prospect now of drawing analogies at a deeper level, consisting in the precise comparison of these organizational processes with their equivalents in the growth and differentiation of tissues in organisms. I do not believe it too much to suggest that insect sociobiology will in fact contribute to a future general theory of biological organization based upon quantitatively defined principles of feedback, quality control, amplification and cascading effects, and optional spatial arrangements. As WILLIAM M. WHEELER pointed out in 1927, the ant colony offers a notable advantage in studies of a physiological nature over conventional organisms. Its parts – the workers and other colony members – can be temporarily separated from one another and reassembled without severe damage to the remainder of the colony. It is as though a conventional physiologist could remove a hand, dissect its parts, record its physiology and behavior while separated from the arm, and then reconstruct and reattach it with only a modest amount of disturbance. Furthermore, as I will report shortly, this procedure offers the great additional advantage of being repeatable with the very same colony, so that other potentially complicating factors, such as genetic structure, age, and colony size, are kept tightly controlled.

6 Feedback and spatial arrangement

As an example of a complex and precise form of feedback, consider the phenomenon of enemy specification in *Pheidole dentata*. This colony-level defensive reaction has certain behavioral parallels with the immune response of the vertebrate body that make it all the more interesting. *P. dentata*, like most other members of its genus, is completely dimorphic. The minor workers possess body proportions that are ordinary for myrmicine ants, and they participate in all of the 22 tasks recorded for entire *P. dentata* colonies, including defense (WILSON, 1976a, b). The majors have exceptionally large heads, filled mostly with massive adductor muscles that pull the sharp mandibles together like miniature wire clippers. Their overall repertory is much more limited than that of the minors, consisting in the performance of only five tasks.

When scouts of most ant species approach close to a *P. dentata* nest, they are typically met and dispatched by the minor workers. But if the territorial invaders are fire ants or thief ants, in other words, members of the genus *Solenopsis*, they evoke an entirely different response. Minor workers first touch the intruders, often grappling with them briefly, and then run back and forth between the site of contact and the nest, laying an odor trail from the poison gland of the sting. The combination of the trail pheromone and *Solenopsis* odor adhering to the bodies of the minor workers galvanizes the majors into action. They follow the trail out to the intruder and meet them in combat, sometimes succumbing to the bites and the potent *Solenopsis* venom but just as often eliminating their opponents by cutting them to pieces. Often only a single *Solenopsis* worker is sufficient to draw out ten or more majors, which then continue to patrol the area for an hour or longer. This diligence helps to «blind» nearby *Solenopsis* colonies to the presence of the *Pheidole* colonies. The maneuver is a distinct advantage to a *Pheidole* colony, since the workers of a *Solenopsis* colony outnumber its own workers by as much as a hundred to one and move in quickly to destroy and consume the *Pheidole* colony when alerted to its presence by successful scouts.

The entire alarm-defense response is based upon feedback loops and differential response to varying levels of severity in the challenge from the *Solenopsis*. Laboratory studies with fire ants have shown that in the earliest stages the number of majors recruited increases with the number of intruders encountered, and hence depends on the amount of trail pheromone detected and the number of minor workers reporting back that are laden with the distinctive *Solenopsis* scent. When the fire ants invade in larger numbers the strategy changes. Now fewer trails are laid, and the *Pheidole* majors fight closer to the nest along a shorter perimeter. When the invasion becomes still more intense, a truly radical shift in tactics occurs: the minors abscond with their brood and scatter out of the nest in all directions, leaving the fighting majors to their fate. Later, if the fire ants vacate the scene, the survivors may return to the site, rear a new crop of majors, and carry on as before.

Similar feedback occurs in labor allocation in ant colonies, and the nature of the loop can sometimes be detected by experimentally removing castes that are specialized for a particular task. In *Atta* colonies most leaf cutting is performed by media workers with head widths ranging from 1.8 to 2.4 mm (with a mode within 2.0–2.2mm), although workers as small as 1.6 mm or as large as 3.6 mm also participate. In one experiment on four colonies of *A. cephalotes,* I removed more than 90 percent of the workers in the size group from 1.8 through 2.2 mm. Contrary to expectation, the colonies did not respond by adding workers from the adjacent size classes to the leaf-cutter force; in other words, there was no increase in workers smaller than 1.8 mm or larger than 2.2 mm. Yet the rate of leaf harvesting remained unaffected, due to the fact that excess workers in the adjacent size classes were already present on a stand-by basis in the foraging area. Moreover, the few survivors in the prime group increased their individual activity by approximately five times. In unmodified colonies, the prime foragers tend to displace others from the edges of the leaves, where most cutting takes place. When these individuals are removed, the auxiliaries participate more freely (WILSON, 1983a).

I have found it useful to make a distinction between two kinds of flexibility on the part of social insects, and according to level of organization. Both responses contribute to social homeostasis. A colony as a whole shows a certain degree of *resiliency* in each task. Thus, even though most of the prime foragers of *Atta cephalotes* were removed in the experiment just cited, the colony continued to perform as well as ever – although at approximately one-third less energetic efficiency. The colony was therefore almost totally resilient in mechanical performance, although with a substantial loss in net energetic yield.

Colony-level resiliency depends on the degree of individual behavioral *elasticity*, which is defined as the amount by which the repertory of individual workers is modified when the colony is placed under stress. In the case just cited, the surviving *Atta* workers proved elastic enough in behavior, increasing their level of activity by as much as five times, to confer nearly complete resiliency to the depleted foraging force.

A far more striking example of elasticity is found in the Neotropical ant *Pheidole guilelmimuelleri.* The major workers of this species are proportionately very large compared to the minor workers, even by the standards of the highly dimorphic *Pheidole*. Their heads are massive, thickwalled, and extremely modified for cutting and crushing. In an undisturbed colony the majors display very low levels of activity and a restricted repertory, confined mostly to self-grooming, occasional bouts of seed milling, and participation in colony defense. However, when all of the minor workers were experimentally removed, the majors showed a quite surprising degree of behavioral expansion. They increased their repertory by 4.5 times, from 4 to 18 kinds of acts, now performing most of the tasks limited previously to the minor workers, while their overall rate of activity, in tasks per individual per unit time, grew almost 20-fold. Another Neotropical species, *P. pubiventris*, displayed a similar but slightly less marked shift under the same experimental conditions (WILSON, 1984).

Students of social insects still know very little about such feedback mechanisms and the magnitude of homeostasis in most categories of behavior and adaptive demography. They have also just begun to examine the geometry of labor allocation within nests and its relation to caste differentiation. A central aspect of this category of organization is the pattern of change in the behavior of individual workers – in other words the differentiation of temporal castes – and its relation to the location of the workers in and around the nests. In theory, two extreme possibilities in the evolution of temporal castes exist. First, workers can undergo changes in responsiveness to various kinds of stimuli in a strongly discordant manner as they grow older, so that each task is addressed by a distinctly

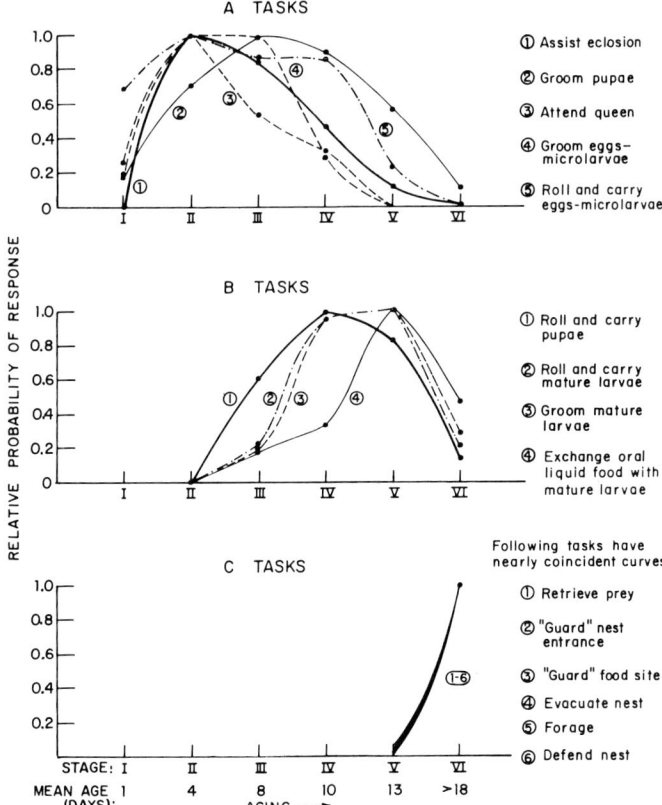

Fig. 7: The discrete partitioning of clusters of tasks by workers of *Pheidole dentata* according to age. The relative probabilities of response (definition: see caption of Figure 5) are given for 15 tasks; stages I–VI are different ages estimated from the degree of exoskeleton darkening and calibrated with individuals marked at the time of eclosion. (From WILSON, 1976b).

different frequency distribution of workers belonging to different age groups. Because these age-frequency distributions change almost gradually from one task to another in covering many such tasks, the resulting temporal caste system is referred to as «continuous.» At the opposite extreme, the aging worker can undergo changes in responsiveness to different stimuli in a highly concordant manner, so that all of the tasks are attended by one or relatively few frequency distributions of workers belonging to different age groups. The resulting temporal caste system has been referred to as «discrete», and the evolutionary process leading to it has been called behavioral discretization (Wilson, 1976b).

In one of the first species studied with this distinction in mind, *Pheidole dentata,* the caste system proved to be closer to the discrete pattern, although not extreme in form (see Figure 7). A close examination of the data displayed in the figure shows that the particular manner in which *P. dentata* colonies are discretized results in an increase in their spatial efficiency. For example, it is energetically more efficient for a particular ant grooming a larva to regurgitate to it as well, or for the worker standing «guard» at the nest entrance to join in excavation when the entrance is buried by a cave-in. The other juxtapositions documented in Figure 6 make equal sense when the spatial arrangement of the colony as a whole is considered. The queen, eggs, first instar larvae (microlarvae), and pupae are typically clustered together and apart from the older larvae, although the positions are constantly being shifted and pupae in particular are often segregated for varying periods of time well away from other immature stages. Thus the *A*-ensemble of workers can efficiently care for all of these groups, moving from egg to pupa to queen with a minimum of travel. The mean free path of a patrolling worker, to put the matter another way, is minimized by such versatility; it utilizes the least amount of energy in travelling from one contingency to another. It makes equal sense for *A* workers to assist the eclosion of adults from the pupae, since the latter developmental stage is already under their care.

7 Caste optimization

The simple fact of the occurrence of evolution is easy to document at the level of both single genes and complex traits controlled by genes at multiple loci. It is also relatively easy to demonstrate the adaptive nature of the evolving traits in most cases, by careful analyses of the function of the phenotypic traits and their effect on survival and reproduction. But it is an entirely different matter to judge such cases of evolution with reference to optimization. In practical terms, we are required to ask how well a species has performed in the course of its evolution, and whether there exists an attainable adaptive peak toward which the species is still moving. Such questions, despite their abstract flavor, are not merely philosophical exercises but truly scientific in nature, that is, soluble by means that can be objectively repeated and verified. The answer to them, if well formulated, can help to predict such important phenomena as the rate and direction of evolution, the impact of a newly imported species on its host environment, and the outcome of competitive interactions between pairs of species.

Under most circumstances, and in the biology of most species, the measure of optimization is obviously going to be technically forbidding. In biology as in engineering, optimization implies an optimum, a goal with reference to which the system may or may not have been ideally designed. Only when the nature of the goal is precisely identified may we presume to use such familiar terms as «suboptimum», «transitional,» and «maladaptive» with any degree of confidence. The complete analysis of optimization, or strategic analysis as it might equally well be called, requires the following four components (Oster and Wilson, 1978): (1) a state space, designating the conceivable parameters such as size and behavioral response and their relevance to the goal; (2) a set of conceivable strategies, such as foraging procedures, caste structure, division of labor, and pattern of colony development; (3) the goal itself, consisting in one or more optimization criteria, or fitness functions, including net energetic yield during foraging; (4) a set of constraints, defined by those states and strategies beyond the reach of the species and hence outside the scope of analysis (we know, for example, not to expect ants that weigh ten kilograms or have metal jaws).

In most studies of behavioral ecology and sociobiology, optimization models are very difficult to design in a way that satisfies the formal and rigorous demands of the four criteria. But this is not an unusual circumstance for biological disciplines in general. It is equally impracticable to test Mendelian genetics with redwoods or to advance the cellular biology of learning with butterflies. The study of animal behavior seeks paradigmatic species that are easily managed in the field and laboratory, as well as phenomena that are relatively unambiguous with reference to the question asked. The biologist should always keep in mind August Krogh's rule of biological research: for every problem there exists an organism ideally suited to its solution. Moreover, an often unappreciated bonus awaits the successful completion of an optimization study. By appropriate experimental design it is possible to learn which fitness criteria actually hold in nature, in other words, which selection pressures have been most active in shaping the trait under consideration. Indeed, the data may indicate that *no* feasible criterion is approached closely, so that the trait can be identified with some confidence as maladaptive or at least substantially suboptimal. So much for the baseless charge sometimes heard that natural selection theory is «panglossian,» circular in logic, and not susceptible to rigorous testing.

Ant castes are exceptionally well suited for optimization studies in sociobiology. The reason is that individual worker ants are full organisms with ordinary, whole patterns of social behavior, yet they are also clearly specialized for particular well-defined tasks. This restriction is extreme in certain highly specialized castes and in particular the major workers of the dimorphic species, which may perform only one or several tasks during their entire lifetime and which possess bodies and behavioral repertories clearly modified to that end. Thus well-defined anatomical structures and behavioral acts can be more readily assayed with reference to the four elements of optimization models; we really are able to specify a restricted and relatively easily defined state space, a set of strategies, testable fitness functions, and measurable constraints.

Consider the case of the prime foraging caste of the leaf-cutter ants of the genus *Atta*, which I recently studied with reference to ergonomics (WILSON, 1980b). As noted, these insects, which possess head widths from 1.8 to 2.4 mm (and a mode of 2.0–2.2 mm), comprise less than ten percent of the work force and do little else except forage and cut vegetation. Here, then, was an opportunity to learn whether the *Atta* colony as a whole, and the leaf-cutting size class in particular, is optimized with reference to foraging. To do so, I began by conceiving three alternative a priori criteria of evolutionary optimization that are consistent with my own understanding of *Atta* biology. These are the reduction of predation by means of evasion and defense during foraging, the minimization of foraging time through skill and running velocity during foraging, and energetic efficiency, which must be evaluated on the basis of both the energetic construction costs of new workers and the energetic cost of maintenance of the existing worker force.

In order to measure the performance of various size groups within the *A. sexdens* worker caste in isolation, I devised a «pseudomutant» technique. At the start of each experiment, groups of foraging workers were thinned out until only individuals of one size class were left outside the nest. Measurements were then made of the rate of attraction, initiative in cutting, and performance of each size group at head-width intervals of 0.4

mm. Other needed measurements were made in body weight, oxygen consumption, and running velocity for each of the size classes.

The pseudomutant technique has the great advantage of permitting the same colony to be used over and over again, with the experimenter modifying it in a precise manner as though it were a mutant in a certain trait, but with little or no alteration of the remainder of its traits. In other words, there is no genetic noise or pleiotropism to confuse the analysis. The procedure used in the *Atta* experiments is roughly comparable to an imaginary study of the efficiency of various conceivable forms of the human hand in the employment of a tool. In the morning we painlessly pull off a finger and measure performance of the four-fingered hand, then restore the missing finger at the end of the day; the next morning we cut off the terminal digits (again painlessly) and measure the performance of a stubby-fingered hand, restoring the entire fingers after the experiment; and so on through a wide range of variations and combinations of hand form. Finally, we are able to decide whether the natural hand form is near the optimum.

The data from the pseudomutant scanning revealed that the size-frequency distribution of the leaf-cutter caste in *Atta sexdens* conforms closely to the optimum predicted by the energetic efficiency criterion for harder varieties of vegetation, such as thick, coriaceous leaves. The distribution is optimum with reference to both construction and maintenance costs (see Figure 8). It does not conform to other criteria conceived prior to the start of the experiments.

I next constructed a model in which the attraction of the ants to vegetation and their initiative in cutting were allowed to «evolve» genetically to uniform maximum levels. The theoretical maximum efficiency levels obtained by this means were found to reside in the head-width 2.6–2.8 mm size class, or 8 percent from the actual maximally efficient class. In the activity of leaf cutting, *A. sexdens* can therefore be said not only to be at an adaptive optimum but also, within at most a relatively narrow margin of error, to have been optimized in the course of evolution. In other words, there appears to be no nearby adaptive peak that is both higher and attainable by gradual macroevolution.

Fig. 8: The principal foraging caste of leaf-cutter ants *(Atta sexdens)*, comprising workers in the size range 1.8–2.4 mm, is also the most efficient in net energetic yield during foraging. The cost criterion used in the measurements depicted here is oxygen consumption, reflecting the energetic cost to maintain workers of various sizes within the colony. (From WILSON, 1980b).

Not all such studies reveal optional responses or even adaptive mechanisms of the sort intuitively expected. For example, what would be the physiological response of an *Atta* colony, as opposed to the purely behavioral reaction described earlier, if a large part of its foraging specialists were suddenly removed by some catastrophe outside the nest? One prudent response on the part of a colony would be to manufacture a higher proportion of workers in the 1.8–2.2 mm size class during the next brood cycle to make up the deficit. However, when I removed over 90 percent of this group in experimental colonies, no differential increase in the production of 1.8–2.2 mm workers could be detected in comparison with sham-treated control colonies. As a consequence, this group remained underrepresented in the foraging arenas by about 50 percent at the end of the first brood cycle, a period of eight weeks.

Another striking example of a feedback loop that did not evolve is stress-induced change in the production of major workers in the ant *Pheidole dentata*. What happens when a colony is attacked repeatedly over a long period by fire ants, the enemy to which its alarm-defense system is specially tuned? An obvious adaptation would be to raise the production of majors (increase defense expenditures, to put it in more familiar human terms) until the stress is relieved. But this response could not be induced by Ardis Johnston and myself in laboratory colonies. We stressed *P. dentata* colonies heavily through four brood cycles by regularly forcing them to fight and destroy *Solenopsis invicta* workers. Contrary to our own expectation, the proportion of majors did not change significantly from colonies stressed with another species of ant *(Tetramorium caespitum)* or from the proportion that prevailed prior to the experiments, when the colonies were free of any pressures through many brood cycles (JOHNSTON and WILSON, 1984).

8 Future directions in caste research

The examples I have cited from my own research, which are paralleled in some instances by the work of other investigators, suggest the richness of caste and division of labor among the 10,000 or more living species of ants. But they also reveal how little we have learned of the underlying control mechanisms. It seems probable that as research proceeds, feedback loops of various kinds, including inhibitory pheromones, facilitation, competitive sequestering of nutrients, competitive displacement of one caste by another at particular tasks, and yet others, will sometimes be discovered in circumstances where they are least expected, and just as often found lacking where they were intuitively most expected. The pattern that appears might first resemble an irrational patchwork of mechanisms, as indeed it seems thus far in *Atta*. Yet there is no reason to suppose that meaningful trends will fail to emerge as studies become more detailed.

LUMSDEN (1982) has recently reexamined the superorganism concept in a more formal and systematic manner that can serve as a useful framework for additional empirical research. He points out that three key features in insect societies need to be linked in models in order to make quantitative predictions about the optimization of caste systems and division of labor. They are the form of the caste system, including the often large differences in energetic costs of different size groups; the quality of interaction among members of the various size groups; and the remarkably short-term, stochastic nature of the colony's memory in terms of past nutritional states, pheromone levels, and the like. Of special immediate interest is the second feature, the modes of interaction. Each species must possess an ergonomic interaction matrix, such that the mutual effects of individuals belonging to different size groups can be cooperative, interfering, or both. The matrix will have measurable effects on the net energetic yield due to foraging and processing of food, as well as defense.

In LUMSDEN's conception, natural selection will tend to shape the ergonomic interaction matrix in a way that maximizes the net energetic yield of the colony as a whole. The ultimate superorganismic traits are the matrix and the yield. The proximate mechanisms are the various modes of communication and feedback which, as I have stressed in this summarization of principles, are just beginning to come under close scrutiny.

It is encouraging to look to the more distant future, when empirical studies might be joined closely to theoretical modeling of the kind advanced by OSTER and WILSON (1978) and LUMSDEN (1982). We might then find it possible to marry the emerging generalizations of caste evolution with those of developmental biology, creating a deeper and more heuristic analogy between organism and superorganism and bringing the study of social insects into still closer alignment with the remainder of biology.

Acknowledgment

The author's personal research reported in this review has been supported by a series of grants from the National Science Foundation, the latest of which is NSF BSR-8119350.

References

Johnston, A., and E. O. Wilson (1984): Correlates of variation in the major/minor ratio of the ant *Pheidole dentata* (Hymenoptera: Formicidae). Ann. Ent. Soc. Amer. in press.

Krebs, J. R., and N. B. Davies (1981): *An introduction to behavioural ecology.* Sinauer Associates, Sunderland, Mass. x + 292 pp.

Lumsden, C. J. (1982): The social regulation of physical caste: The superorganism revived. J. Theoret. Biol. *95*, 749–781.

May, R. M., ed. (1981): *Theoretical ecology: Principles and applications,* second edition. Sinauer Associates, Sunderland, Mass. ix + 489 pp.

Oster, G. F., and E. O. Wilson (1978): *Caste and ecology in the social insects* (Monographs in Population Biology No. 12). Princeton University Press, Princeton, N. J. xvi + 352 pp.

Schmidt, G. H., ed. (1974): Sozialpolymorphismus bei Insekten: Probleme der Kastenbildung im Tierreich. Wissenschaftliche Verlagsgesellschaft MBH, Stuttgart. xxiv + 974 pp.

Wheeler, W. M. (1927): *Emergent evolution and the social.* Keegan Paul, Trench, Trubner, London. 57 pp.

Wilson, E. O.(1953): The origin and evolution of polymorphism in ants. Quart. Rev. Biol. *28*, 136–156.

– (1968): The ergonomics of caste in the social insects. Amer. Nat. *102*, 41–66.

– (1976a): The organization of colony defense in the ant *Pheidole dentata* Mayr (Hymenoptera: Formicidae). Behav. Ecol. Sociobiol. *1*, 63–81.

– (1976b): Behavioral discretization and the number of castes in an ant species. Behav. Ecol. Sociobiol. *1*, 141–154.

– (1978): Division of labor in fire ants based on physical castes (Hymenoptera: Formicidae: *Solenopsis*). J. Kans. Entomol. Soc. *51*, 615–636.

– (1980a): Caste and division of labor in leaf-cutter ants (Hymenoptera: Formicidae: *Atta*). I. The overall pattern in *A. sexdens.* Behav. Ecol. Sociobiol. *7*, 143–156.

– (1980b): Caste and division of labor in leaf-cutter ants (Hymenoptera: Formicidae: *Atta*). II. The ergonomic optimization of leaf cutting. Behav. Ecol. Sociobiol. *7*, 157–165.

– (1983a): Caste and division of labor in leaf-cutter ants (Hymenoptera: Formicidae: *Atta*). III. Ergonomic resiliency in foraging by *A. cephalotes.* Behav. Ecol. Sociobiol. *14*, 47–54.

– (1983b): Caste and division of labor in leaf-cutter ants (Hymenoptera: Formicidae: *Atta*). IV. Colony ontogeny of *A. cephalotes.* Behav. Ecol. Sociobiol. *14*, 55–60.

– (1984): The relation between caste ratios and division of labor in the ant genus *Pheidole* (Hymenoptera: Formicidae). Behav. Ecol. Sociobiol. in press.

Fortschritte der Zoologie, Bd. 31 · Hölldobler/Lindauer (Hrsg.): Experimental Behavioral Ecology
G. Fischer Verlag · Stuttgart · New York · 1985

Termite polygyny: the ecological dynamics of queen mutualism

BARBARA L. THORNE

Museum of Comparative Zoology, Harvard University, Cambridge, Mass. 02138 USA

Abstract

Polygyny, the existence of more than one fertilized and egg-producing queen within a social insect colony, is a mechanism by which an insect society, and its individual queens, can side-step ecological and evolutionary constraints encountered by closely related, obligately monogynous species. Colony growth rate, probability of survival, age of first reproduction, resistence to predation, and ability to exploit resources may all be enhanced by the coexistence of multiple queens. Although polygynous females must share reproductive output and may not survive as the reigning queen as the colony ages, there are significant mutualistic advantages to joining multiple queen associations. This paper surveys the phyletic distribution of polygyny in termites, and focuses on a comparison of the ecological dynamics of polygyny in the New World species *Nasutitermes corniger* (MOTSCHULSKY) and the African termite *Macrotermes michaelseni* (SJÖSTEDT). Finally, ecological and evolutionary convergences between multiple queen associations in the phylogenetically independent orders Isoptera and Hymenoptera are examined.

1 Introduction

Social behavior enables insect colonies to escape some of the morphological, physiological, and neurological limits faced by closely related solitary insects. The increased biological flexibility of an insect society also results in expanded ecological adaptability. Castes are one example of behavioral dynamics mediating such ecological resilience. Division of labor within a colony enables specialization, and also permits concurrent rather than sequential accomplishment of tasks (OSTER and WILSON 1978). Queens, specializing in egg production, are tended and fed by workers, and can therefore allocate their entire time and augmented energy budgets to reproduction. This reproductive specialization, coupled with the ability of many social insect colonies to replace dead or senescent reproductives, enables insect societies (and in many cases individual queens) to function as perennials while most of their solitary relatives are confined to an annual life cycle. As perennials queens achieve a much higher fecundity than as annuals, and their fertile progeny are not all dispersed into the same «basket» of time and space. Labor castes and group living also enable many social insect colonies to build elaborate nests which render their living environment relatively homeostatic, allow food storage or cultivation, and/or give protection from predators. Solitary insects are rarely able to invest in intricate nest construction, and they use simple or existing cavities or shelters for refuge, oviposition, and brood care.

Polygyny is a condition in which multiple fecund queens coexist and are cared for by nonreproductive castes within a single colony. This is another behavioral method by which an insect society, and its individual queens, can evade ecological and evolutionary constraints faced by closely related, obligately monogynous species. The cumulative productivity of multiple queens confers a mutualistic advantage to each contributor (THORNE 1984). In both Hymenoptera and Isoptera, growth rates of polygynous colonies are higher than those possible for monogynous colonies of the same age (e. g. METCALF and WHITT 1977; GIBO 1978; WEST-EBERHARD 1978a; THORNE 1982a, 1984; DARLINGTON 1984). Increased colony population size can result in increased fecundity and probability of survival for both the colony and individual queens (see GIBO 1974, 1978; GAMBOA 1978; THORNE 1984). Larger societies may be able to exploit available resources more effectively. For a colony, multiple queens insure that the death of one fertile female will not kill the colony; in this sense, polygyny is a mode of risk minimization (e. g. WEST-EBERHARD 1978b; BARTZ and HÖLLDOBLER 1982; THORNE 1982a; DARLINGTON 1984). Thus social behaviors and organization, including polygyny, increase the ecological flexibility and resilience of an insect colony as compared with a solitary relative.

This paper focuses on polygyny in termites, first surveying its phyletic distribution and then comparing dynamics in the only two species in which multiple primary queens have been studied, *Nasutitermes corniger* (MOTSCHULSKY) in Central America (THORNE 1982a, b, c; 1984) and *Macrotermes michaelseni* (SJÖSTEDT) in Kenya (DARLINGTON 1984). Analysis shows that even though the two species appear different, both show (1) a mutualistic advantage to multiple queen association, and (2) the advantages of polygyny in allowing escape from ecological constraints. Finally, I examine ecological and evolutionary convergences between polygynous associations in the independent orders Isoptera and Hymenoptera.

2 Phyletic distribution of multiple primary queens in termites

Termite reproductives are of three morphological forms depending upon developmental origin. «Primary» or «first-form» queens are derived from alates, and have conspicuous plates on the dorsal thorax marking abcission points of the nuptial wings. After the mating flight, alates pair, search for a nest site, mate, and initiate new colonies. In Higher termites (family Termitidae) the female ovarioles enlarge and the abdomen becomes physogastric. These primary reproductives have the highest potential fecundity of the three reproductive forms.

«Nymphoid» and «ergatoid» reproductives, derived from nymphs and workers respectively, are termed ‹supplementary› or ‹neotenic› reproductives. They normally differentiate only upon death or senescence of the original primary queen, and they obligatorily remain in the natal nest. Multiple supplementary reproductives are relatively common in colonies of some termite species, particularly in the Lower termite families. However, because female and male primary forms are the only potentially independent, dispersive reproductives, they are regarded as the true queens and kings, and will be the focus of this report.

Although generally considered rare in termites, literature accounts report multiple alate-derived queens in colonies of 38 species (15 genera) of Isoptera, representing all 4 subfamilies of the phylogenetically advanced family Termitidae (Table I). This list is undoubtedly conservative. Extensive field surveys of termite colony reproductive status have been few because royal compartments in many species are not readily accessible (e. g. mound, log, or subterranean nests). Since polygyny appears facultative, numerous colonies must be sampled to estimate its frequency in any particular species and habitat.

Most of the entries in Table I are accounts of a single colony housing multiple primary queens. It is therefore premature to compare polygynous species, but some patterns are suggested. Although the number of associated queens is variable among and within taxa, the Nasutitermitinae have the largest number of polygynous species and the highest queen counts. Multiple primary kings are found commonly in the royal chambers of polygynous colonies in all subfamilies. Queens within an association are generally of approximately the same size and pigmentation. Exceptions to this pattern appear to be cases of mother-daughter affiliations (reported in several species of *Macrotermes* and *Odontotermes*). Multiple reproductives are almost always found in the same queen cell, often sharing single chambers within the cell.

«Adultoid» reproductives are primary replacement reproductives: in some species, mature alates may remain within the natal nest and assume the reproductive position(s) from dead or senescent parents. Experimental removal of established queens with subsequent observation of one or more young primaries documents this replacement route in *Macrotermes natalensis, Odontotermes badius, O. latericius* (COATON 1949), *Astalotermes quietus* (NOIROT 1956), and *Macrotermes michaelseni* (DARLINGTON 1978, 1984; SIEBER and DARLINGTON 1982). The mode of formation of polygynous associations in most species is unknown. Primary foundresses and adultoid replacement reproductives are morphologically indistinguishable. In a number of cases (particularly within the Apicotermitinae, Termitinae, and Macrotermitinae), however, colony age or direct observations suggest multiple adultoid replacements. Such replacements are siblings (or possibly half-siblings if the colony was originally polygynous).

Comparison of polygyny in *Nasutitermes corniger* and *Macrotermes michaelseni*

Polygyny has been investigated in only two termite species. Fortunately, these two focal species are phylogenetically and geographically disparate: *Nasutitermes corniger* (Nasutitermitinae) is Neotropical while *Macrotermes michaelseni* (Macrotermitinae) is an Old World termite. Juxtaposing a comparable phenomenon in such dissimilar species is likely to be more striking than comparisons between closely related species. Many gaps exist in our understanding of the ontogeny of polygynous associations in each species, but available data suggest that some of the patterns and processes of multiple queen colonies are quite different in *Nasutitermes corniger* and *Macrotermes michaelseni*.

Nasutitermes corniger is an ecologically and economically dominant termite throughout rainforest, gallery forest, shrublands and disturbed areas of Central America. It is reported to range south into Columbia, Ecuador and Venezuela (THORNE 1980). Colonies of up to one million individuals are composed of two worker castes, nasute soldiers, and a seasonal reproductive brood. The arboreal carton nests have a network of intercalated galleries surrounding the dense, fist-sized royal cell. Data reported here were collected by the author in areas of young second growth near the Panama Canal, Republic of Panama.

Macrotermes michaelseni is a common termite in semi-arid grasslands in Kenya. Major and minor mandibulate soldiers and major and minor workers staff colonies of up to 5.25 million termites (DARLINGTON 1982). The termites forage on grass litter, and culture fungus within the mound. *M. michaelseni* builds earthen mounds, with a closed ventilation system. Fungus combs surround nursery chambers, which embed a capsule-like royal cell positioned centrally in the hive (DARLINGTON 1977). Observations and data summarized

Table I

	Site	# Primary Queens	# Primary Kings	Queens Approx. Same Size?	Same Queen Cell?	Adultoids?	Reference
Apicotermitinae							
Apicotermes desneuxi Emerson	Africa	2	?	?	?	?	BOUILLON 1964 p. 183
Apicotermes kisantuensis Sjöstedt	Africa	2	2	?	?	?	BOUILLON 1964 p. 183
Astalotermes quietus (Silvestri)	Africa	3–9	?	yes	?	yes	NOIROT 1956 p. 146, and pers. comm.
Ateuchotermes tranquillus (Silvestri)	Africa	11[a]	2	?	?	yes	SILVESTRI 1914–15 p. 54
Termitinae							
Cubitermes aemulus Silvestri	French Guinea	4	2	?	?	yes	SILVESTRI 1914–15 p. 100
Cubitermes curtatus Silvestri	French Guinea	7	?	?	?	yes	SILVESTRI 1914–15 p. 103
Cubitermes sankurensis Wasmann	Africa	2	2–4	?	?	?	BOUILLON and LEKIE 1964 p. 209
Microcerotermes amboinensis Kemner	Indonesia	1	?	?	?	?	WEYER 1930 p. 378
Microcerotermes parvus (Haviland)	South Africa	2	2	?	yes	?	WARREN 1909 p. 125
	Ivory Coast	6+[b]	2[b]	yes	no[d]	yes	NOIROT 1956 p. 150, and pers. comm.
Microcerotermes sikorae (Wasmann)	Madagascar	2	?	?	yes	?	SJÖSTEDT 1914 p. 9
Paracapritermes primus Hill	Australia	5[c]	1	?	?	yes	HILL 1942 p. 418
Pericapritermes heterorotus Silvestri	Guinea	3	1	?	yes	?	SILVESTRI 1914–15 p. 139
Protocapritermes krisiformis (Froggatt)	Australia	12	?	?	?	yes	HILL 1942 p. 416
Termes hospes (Sjöstedt)	Ivory Coast	10+[a,e]	> 1	yes	?	yes	NOIROT 1956 p. 151, and pers. comm.
Termes kraepelinii (Silvestri)	Australia	several	?	?	?	yes	HILL 1942 p. 393
Termes panamaensis (Snyder)	Panama	9	1	yes	?	?	NMNH collection
Nasutitermitinae							
Araujotermes parvellus (Emerson)	Brazil	24	2	yes	no[f]	?	A. E. MILL, pers. comm.
Nasutitermes amboinensis (Kemner)	Indonesia	16	?	yes, no[g]	no?[h]	?	WEYER 1930 p. 376, 378

	Site	# Primary Queens	# Primary Kings	Approx. Same Size?	Same Queen Cell?	Adultoids?	Reference
Nasutitermes corniger (Motschulsky)	Panama	2–33–55?j	2–17	yes	yes	sometimes (w/budding)	DUDLEY & BEAUMONT 1889a p. 61; 1890 p.158, 161, 167–8. 1889b p. 88, 106–7; DIETZ & SNYDER 1923 p. 295; MOLINO & ZETEK (NMNH collection); THORNE 1982a, b; PRESTWICH, RETTENMEYER (pers. comm.)
	Costa Rica						
Nasutitermes costalis (Holmgren)	West Indies	7–8	4–7	?	?	?	NMNH collection
N. morio Banks^l	Cuba	9	1	yes	?	?	BARBOUR & BROOKE, MCZ collection
N. sanchezi Banks^l	Jamaica	2–5	2–6	yes	?	?	HUBBARD, NMNH collection
Nasutitermes ephratae (Holmgren)	Panama	5	?	yes	?	?	ZETEK & MOLINO, NMNH
	Mexico	6	>1	24–32 mm	yes	?	BECKER 1961 p. 81
	Brazil	2	2	?	yes	?	MATHEWS 1977 p. 166
	Costa Rica	12	?	?	yes	?	H. JACOBSON, pers. comm.
Nasutitermes ripperti (Rambur)	Jamaica	4	2	yes	implied	?	ANDREWS 1911 p. 202–4
Nasutitermes sp. (near latus)	Philippines	9	5	?	yes	?	C. K. STARR, pers. comm.
Nasutitermes sp.	Uruguay	6, 7	2	yes	?	?	PARKER, NMNH collection
Macrotermitinae							
Hypotermes obscuriceps (Wasmann)^k	Ceylan	2	2	yes	yes	?	ESCHERICH in Hegh 1922 p. 174
Macrotermes bellicosus (Smeathman)	Erythrée	2	?	no	yes	?	SILVESTRI in Hegh 1922 p. 173
Macrotermes gilvus subsp. malayanus (Haviland)	Malaya	2–8	6	?	yes	?	RIDLEY 1910 p. 157

Species	Site	# Primary Queens	# Primary Kings	Queens Approx. Same Size?	Same Queen Cell?	Adultroids?	Reference
Macrotermes michaelseni (Sjöstedt)	Kenya	2–7	1–3	usually	yes[i]	often	DARLINGTON 1978 p. 22–53; 1984
Macrotermes natalensis (Haviland)	Zaire[m]	3	?	yes	yes	?	BEQUAERT 1921 p. 194–6
		4[n]	2	?	?	?	HEGH 1922 p. 173
Microtermes havilandi Holmgren	South Africa	2	1	no	yes, no	yes	COATON 1949 p. 149
Odontotermes badius Holmgren	South Africa	3–4	?	?	?	?	WARREN 1909 p. 125
Odontotermes bangalorensis Holmgren	South Africa	2–4	?	no	yes	yes	COATON 1949 p. 338
	India	6	1	yes	yes	?	HOLMGREN 1913 p. 107, 109
Odontotermes brunneus Hagen	India	1	2	?	no	probably	HOLMGREN 1912 p. 785
Odontotermes latericius Holmgren	South Africa	3	2	no	no	yes	COATON 1949 p. 376–8
		4–6	?	?	yes	?	WARREN 1909 p. 121
Odontotermes obesus (Rambur)	India	2–3	2	no	yes	implied	ROONWAL & GUPTA 1952 p. 293–4
		2	2	yes	yes	?	ROONWAL & CHHOTANI 1962 p. 975–6
Odontotermes redemanni Wasmann	India	4	2	yes	yes	?	ESCHERICH in Hegh 1922 p. 174
		2+	?	yes	yes	?	MUKERJI & RAYCHAUDURI 1942 p. 175
Odontotermes vulgaris (Haviland)	South Africa	2	2	?	yes	?	WARREN 1909 p. 123
Odontotermes wallonensis (Wasmann)	India	2	2	?	yes	?	HOLMGREN 1913 p. 110
		3	2	yes	yes	?	MATHUR & CHHOTANI 1960 p. 623

a Incomplete coloration.
b Additional primary reproductives present, not counted or collected.
c Implication that females are very young; not necessarily egg-laying.
d No defined queen cell(s); queens found relatively close together.
e Colony only partially sampled; may have been additional reproductives.
f Queens found in proximate cells.
g Different colonies.
h Queens found wandering, possibly from disturbance during nest dissection, therefore status of queen cell occupation is questionable.
i Dudley & Beaumont do not mention whether the "55 queens" are physogastric or dealate imagoes. They are not in the MCZ collection with Beaumont's other specimens.
j Synonymous with N. costalis according to T. E. Snyder (1949).
k Formerly Odontotermes obscuriceps; nomenclature revised according to Roalle 1970

here are based on extensive sampling by J. P. E. C. DARLINGTON around Kajiado, in the Rift Valley Province of Kenya (DARLINGTON 1984 and pers. comm.)

Research methods for the two studies were similar. Colony population size and caste ratio data were derived from complete colony dissections and volumetric subsampling of removed termites. *Nasutitermes* nests were inactivated by refrigeration; *Macrotermes* colonies were fumigated with methyl bromide. All sampled *Nasutitermes* colonies were completely dissected and sampled for population size. Nest population was assessed in only a small proportion of *Macrotermes* colonies. Most nests were opened live for other purposes, and the royal cell was excavated to determine queen status.

At least in the sampled habitats, multiple primary queens are relatively common in both termite species. Of 361 mature queenright *Macrotermes michaelseni* mounds, 84 (23 %) contained 2 or more physogastric queens. In *Nasutitermes corniger*, 25 of 76 (33 %) queenright colonies housed more than one queen.

3.1 Similarities

There are a number of similarities between the two species. First, with the exception of a single colony in each species, all queens are found within a single royal cell in the termitaria. In *Macrotermes,* all females share the same chamber (one exception). *Nasutitermes* queens commonly occupy a single chamber, although in some nests chambers containing queen groups may be stacked like apartment tiers within the royal cell. Second, associated queens appear to be of the same age, as judged by pigmentation, degree of physogastry, and fresh weight. In *Macrotermes michaelseni* there are a few exceptions to this pattern (N=3 of 90 observations, DARLINGTON 1984), but these rare cases appear to be transient eclipses of queen replacement (a senescent mother being succeeded by one or more young daughters). Third, polygyny is not restricted to immature nests. Multiple queens are frequently present in alate-producing colonies (see THORNE 1983). Fourth, boosted by the cumulative egg production of multiple queens, polygynous colonies grow larger than a conspecific monogynous colony headed by a queen of the same age. At least in *N. corniger,* such polygynous colonies also grow faster (THORNE 1982, 1984). Fifth, multiple primary kings are occasionally found in colonies of both *Macrotermes* and *Nasutitermes,* but in each case the usual situation is one male even if there are multiple females. Multiple kings are sometimes found in immature *N. corniger* colonies, or as an apparently transient phase of king replacement in mature colonies of both species (THORNE 1982a, b, 1984; DARLINGTON 1984). Finally, no aggression has been observed among cohabiting queens in either species. However, neither of these studies focused specifically on queen-queen behaviors.

3.2 Differences

Differences between polygyny in *Macrotermes* and *Nasutitermes* are in some cases quite dramatic. First, size, pigmentation, and morphological data (attrition of antennal segments) indicate that polygynous *Nasutitermes* queens are relatively young individuals (THORNE 1984). The weight distribution of individual *Nasutitermes* queens in large groups is markedly skewed toward the smaller size classes (Fig. 1). Monogynous queens (stippled bars) are more evenly distributed through all weight classes, and many reach sizes never attained by multiple queens. Polygynous queens are always a light cream color, while monogynous females frequently have darker pigmentation characteristic of older individuals. In contrast, *Macrotermes* queen associations may have young or old queens (although females *within* any one group are apparently of the same age). Polygynous

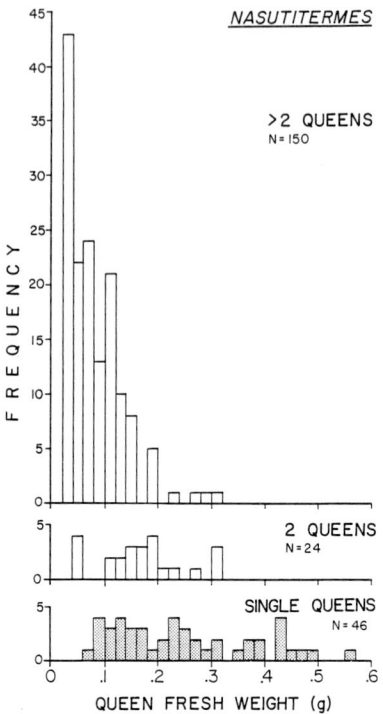

Fig. 1: Histogram of fresh weight distribution of monogynous *N. corniger* queens (stippled bars), queens in two queen groups, and queens in larger polygynous associations.

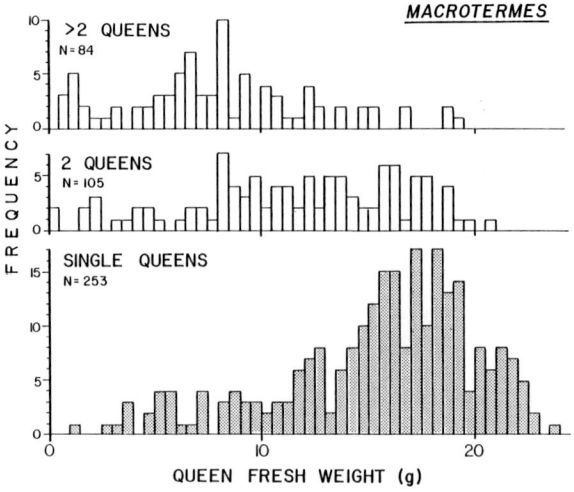

Fig. 2: Histogram of fresh weight distribution of monogynous *M. michaelseni* queens (stippled bars), queens in two queen groups, and queens in larger polygynous associations. Redrawn from DARLINGTON 1984.

queen weights are distributed over most of the range covered by single queens, with no modes to suggest that only large, small, or intermediate weight queens are found in groups (Fig. 2). Further, some polygynous *Macrotermes* queens have darkly pigmented abdomens indicating that they are elderly (DARLINGTON 1984).

Relative queen weight is a second major difference between the species. The largest *Nasutitermes corniger* queen found was just over 1/2 gram. *Macrotermes* queens range up to 24 grams (abcissas, Figs. 1 and 2). An average *Macrotermes* queen is nearly 100 times heavier than an average *Nasutitermes* queen.

A third difference between the two species is that the largest number of *Macrotermes* queens found together was 7 (N=10 of 84 (12%) of the polygynous groups had more than 3 queens), while up to 33 cohabiting females were found in *Nasutitermes corniger* (N=9 of 25 (36%) of the groups housed more than 3 queens). *Nasutitermes* colonies therefore have much larger numbers of queens, in a considerably higher frequency, than in *Macrotermes*.

A fourth difference between *Macrotermes* and *Nasutitermes* is in the mode of formation of polygynous colonies. Figure 3 is a diagramatic representation of possible derivations of polygyny in termites, and transition routes between monogyny and polygyny (a comparative scheme for ants is presented in HÖLLDOBLER and WILSON 1977). In both *N. corniger* and *M. michaelseni*, observations and experiments suggest that multiple queen colonies can be formed by pleometrosis after an alate flight. In *Nasutitermes corniger*, mature colonies can actively bud and seed the satellite daughter nest with alates from the parental colony (THORNE 1982a, b). Budding has not been observed in *Macrotermes michaelseni*. If alate brood are present, a *Macrotermes* colony whose queen dies can replace her (and the king if necessary) with female and male alate progeny (SIEBER and DARLINGTON 1982). Such queen replacement may be observed by experimentally removing a queen and re-sampling the colony a year later, or recent replacement may be inferred when a large termitaria is excavated and found with only small or lightly pigmented young reproduc-

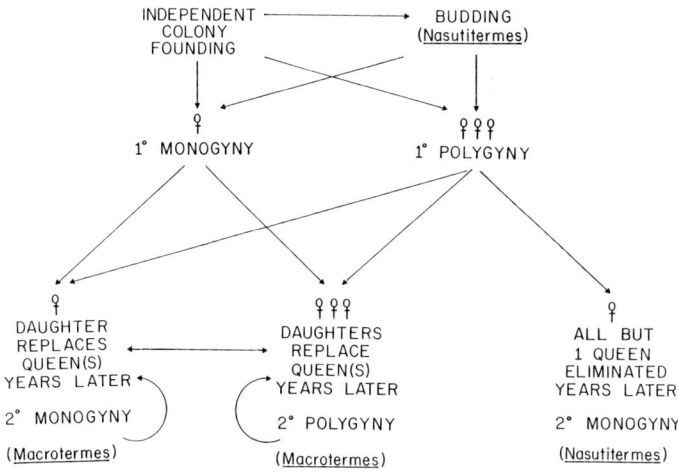

Fig. 3: Possible derivations of polygyny in termites, and transition paths between monogyny and polygyny in *Nasutitermes corniger* and *Macrotermes michaelseni*. When a transition route is thought to be used primarily by one species and not the other, the generic name of the species favoring the option is given in parentheses.

tives in a colony of mature soldiers and workers. Queen replacement appears to be common in *Macrotermes michaelseni*. Such requeening may occur in *Nasutitermes corniger*, but it has not been observed. The present study focused on young nests in recently disturbed habitats. Queen replacement might be more common in older *N. corniger* colonies.

Multiple queens could arise if one or more daughters join their mother and become egg producers. In such a case, colony dissection would reveal a large, darkly pigmented queen accompanied by one or more lightly pigmented, probably smaller, females. This has never been observed in *Nasutitermes corniger,* and has been found only rarely (N = 3 cases) in *Macrotermes michaelseni.* In all cases the older queen appeared senescent and in poor health, so it is likely that overlap of reproductive generations is temporary and that such maturation of daughters is in anticipation of replacing their mother. Note that all methods of polygynous colony formation excepting pleometrosis after an alate flight definitely result in associations of sister or half-sister queens. Cofounders grouping after nuptial flights may or may not be sibs.

Observations suggest that nearly all cases of *Nasutitermes corniger* polygyny are the result of pleometrosis following the alate flight, or as a result of parental colony budding. In contrast, the majority of *Macrotermes michaelseni* multiple queens are apparently replacement reproductives occupying large, established mounds (Darlington 1984 and pers. comm.). If this general pattern is confirmed, it infers that accelerated colony growth rates are advantageous to young *N. corniger* colonies while the cumulative egg production boost of multiple queens is a benefit to large, mature *M. michaelseni* societies.

A fifth interspecific difference is that in *Macrotermes* colonies there is a very high correlation between the number of queens in a and their cumulative weight (Fig. 4A). No such relationship holds among *Nasutitermes corniger* queens (Fig. 4B). Thus egg production of *Macrotermes* colonies appears to jump significantly with queen number, while productivity of *Nasutitermes* depends on both queen number and size.

Furthermore, Darlington (1984) reports that productivity of two small *Macrotermes* queens is functionally equivalent to that of a single large queen. The population size of a

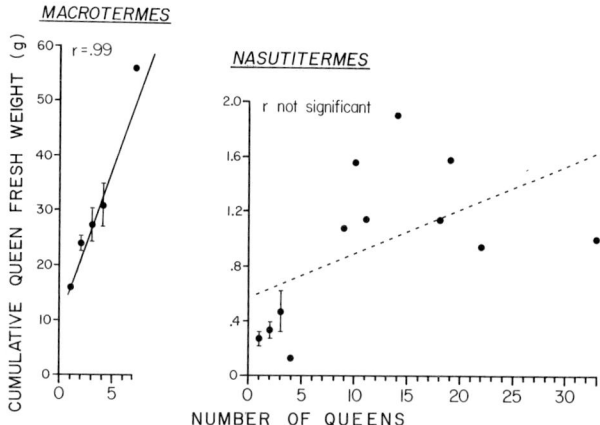

Fig. 4: Correlations between number of queens in a polygynous association and their combined fresh weight in A. *Macrotermes michaelseni* and B. *Nasutitermes corniger.* Standard errors are shown in error bars. (Graph A redrawn from Darlington 1984).

colony headed by two 10 gram queens is comparable to that of a colony housing a single 20 gram queen. No such pattern holds for *Nasutitermes corniger*. Data for egg production appear in THORNE (1982a, 1984); data for neuter population size are presented in Figure 5. 95 % confidence limits of the monogynous and polygynous principal axis correlation lines do not overlap, indicating that, for a given total weight, one large queen is more productive than two smaller ones. (It should be noted, however, that through partnership in a polygynous association, a small queen can be part of a large, rapidly growing colony – an impossibility for a small solitary female).

Cumulative productivity differences between *Macrotermes* and *Nasutitermes* may be due to the striking differences in queen weight. Because all *Nasutitermes* queens are tiny compared with any *Macrotermes* queen, a larger percentage of their body weight is head and thorax. *Macrotermes* queen weight is essentially all abdomen. Therefore, adding *Macrotermes* queen weights may give a more representative index of potential egg productivity than adding *Nasutitermes* queen weights.

Finally, a sixth difference between the two species is in the stability of polygyny. In *Nasutitermes corniger*, evidence suggests that queen number is reduced over time, eventually resulting in monogyny (THORNE 1982a, b, 1984). In *Macrotermes michaelseni*, polygynous associations may be long-lived and stable (DARLINGTON 1984).

3.3 The ecology and evolution of polygyny in *N. corniger* and *M. michaelseni*

Underlying these similarities and differences in details of multiple queen dynamics, however, the ecological constraints changed by polygyny are analogous in *Nasutitermes corniger* and *Macrotermes michaelseni*. Multiple queens enable these termite societies to evade risks and restrictions posed by physiological limits on growth rate and body size of individual queens (including limits to queen growth rate due to a low energy surplus returned by a small foraging force), and by any one queen's eventual mortality. In *N. corniger*, polygyny appears most common early in the colony life cycle when an amplified growth rate rapidly boosts a young society out of the vulnerable «incipient colony» size class. In *M. michaelseni*, polygyny is found among all age classes, with a significant proportion of cases appearing to be replacement reproductives in established mounds.

Using LESLIE matrix projections and the example of *N. corniger*, THORNE (1984) showed that with either a slight increase in the probability of survival during early age classes or with a decrease in the age of first reproduction, females in polygynous groups have an equal or higher expected fitness than queens attempting to initiate colonies, and boost them to the reproductive threshold, alone. Such projections account for the probability of elimination from the association as time progresses. The chance of being the one surviving queen is «worth» the risk of elimination. Colonies with single foundresses grow more slowly and therefore may have a lower probability of survival in the precarious incipient colony size class. A bigger termite colony with an increased buffer provided by larger numbers of soldiers and workers can withstand biotic and abiotic disturbances (an ant raid, an ant-eater attack, drought, famine) with more resilience than a smaller counterpart. Furthermore, single foundress colonies take longer for their neuter population to reach a size at which the colony can successfully rear alate brood. Thus each queen in a polygynous group benefits from the mutualism via a higher probability of survival and/or an increased probability of reproduction in early age classes. An adaptive value of polygyny is not dependent on kin selection; it can be modeled effectively based solely on mutualism.

The same arguments may also apply to pleometrotic *M. michaelseni* colonies, but replacement reproductives in mature colonies require a different explanation. DARLING-

TON (1984) argues that multiple M. *michaelseni* queens enable an absolute increase in a mature colony's population size. For example, the largest colony excavated in her study (5.25 million termites) was headed by 7 fully mature (middle aged) queens, the largest association found in M. *michaelseni* (DARLINGTON 1978, pers. comm.). The combined fresh weight of these queens was 55.9 g, far above the possible weight (and thus egg production capacity) of any single queen (DARLINGTON 1984).

A complete explanation for the evolution of polygyny, however, must address the question of why potentially independent young queens would forego autonomous colony foundation and instead join a multiple association. In a polygynous colony, energy devoted to rearing the fertile brood must be divided, equally or unequally, among progeny of all queens. A monogynous queen does not have to share reproductive output.

Why might a M. *michaelseni* female alate become a replacement queen within her natal nest rather than attempt to found her own colony following a dispersive nuptial flight, and how might an increased mature population size in a M. *michaelseni* mound favor the queens within? Replacement reproductives acquire several advantages over foundresses. By assuming the throne of an established colony, they receive a 'dowry' of a soldier and worker support staff, a pre-constructed termitaria, and deed to a proven microhabitat (the mound is known to be in an adequate resource environment because at least one alate brood was reared successfully). This inheritance translates into a substantial savings in time and energy. Resources which an incipient colony (and its queen) must allocate towards these basics can, in an established colony, be channeled directly into reproduction. Thus replacement queens probably receive the same major advantages as pleometrotic queens, albeit with even greater assurance. They are likely to have a higher probability of survival (once they obtain a reproductive position), and they can expect an earlier age of first reproduction. Furthermore, growth rates of individual replacement queens are ex-

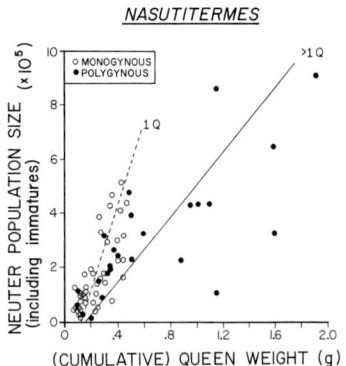

Fig. 5: Principal axis lines of queen fresh weight vs colony neuter population size correlations for monogynous N. *corniger* colonies (open circles; dashed line), and cumulative queen fresh weight vs neuter population size for polygynous N. *corniger* colonies (solid circles; solid line). For single queen colonies, $y = 1,575,532 \times - 202,807$; $r = 0.77$. 95 % confidence limits on the slope of the principal axis are 1,278,339 and 2,079,079. The polygynous correlation line is $y = 602,870 \times - 87,376$; $r = 0.74$. 95% confidence limits on the slope are 446,235 and 928,844. Non-overlap of the 95 % confidence limits indicates that the lines are distinct, and that monogynous queens are more productive than an equivalent biomass of smaller queens.

pected to be higher than for either haplo- or pleometrotic foundresses because the existing foraging force can immediately tend and feed the new reproductives (SIEBER and DARLINGTON 1982).

All of the above arguments hold for single as well as for multiple replacement reproductives. Some *M. michaelseni* colonies house only one replacement; others requeen with 2 or 3 females (DARLINGTON 1978, 1984). Presently, we lack data on the process of queen replacement. How and when are replacements «chosen» amidst the throngs of alate princesses, or do candidates compete for queen status? Nonreproductive colony members would favor multiple replacements if they boost colony reproductive output. Although a single female might «prefer» to reign as the sole replacement, the cost of defending that position may be high enough that she tolerates one or two partners. Multiple replacement reproductives are close kin (sisters if the natal nest was monogynous). Costs of shared reproductive output are thus minimized by the inclusive fitness benefits of producing nieces and nephews.

Cumulative egg production from multiple replacement queens increases the population size of their colony. If the proximate resource environment is sufficiently rich, more foragers can more effectively explore and exploit the habitat. This increased energy input might result in a larger fertile brood (alate) output. Such escalated productivity coupled with inclusive fitness payoffs could, on a per queen basis, compensate for the shared origin of the alate brood.

If polygyny confers such advantages to a colony and to individual queens within the association, why are the minority of dissected *N. corniger* or *M. michaelseni* colonies polygynous? Variability in the number of replacement *M. michaelseni* queens is discussed above. Current evidence from *N. corniger* suggests that polygyny is restricted to relatively young colonies. Sampling from a broader age class distribution, one expects that many societies will have already made the transition to monogyny. Furthermore, polygyny in incipient colonies appears to be facultative. A queen which founds singly must build her colony's population alone, but if successful, she also assumes the uncontested throne of a mature, alate-producing nest. Polygyny is expected to be most common in young *N. corniger* colonies located in habitats with resources rich enough to support rapid growth, and with predator and/or competitor pressure strong enough to give large colonies a survival and reproductive advantage. Even in such habitats, however, not all colonies will be polygynous because – in the hurried quest for nest sites – some tandem alate pairs may not have time to search for additional cofounders, especially if the density of alates landing in the areas is low. In incipient *Macrotermes* colonies, these same influences may explain facultative polygyny.

Thus while the ontogeny of polygynous *N. corniger* and *M. michaelseni* colonies differ, some of the ecological and evolutionary advantages of multiple queens appear similar. At the colony level, polygyny insures against incidental death of any one female. To the participating queens, polygyny confers a mutualistic advantage in that they are part of an ensemble which, cumulatively, can be more productive on a per queen basis.

4 Polygyny in the Isoptera and Hymenoptera: A case of convergent evolution?

Polygyny occurs in many groups of eusocial Hymenoptera, including polybiine wasps (WEST-EBERHARD 1969, 1973, 1978a) and a number of ant genera (reviewed in BUSCHINGER 1974, HÖLLDOBLER and WILSON 1977). Multiple egg-layers (usually foundresses) are prevalent in many species of primitively social bees and wasps (e. g. MICHENER 1974, WEST-EBERHARD 1978a). Polygyny in species of the phylogenetically independent orders Isoptera and Hymenoptera may have envolved in response to similar ecological constraints.

Polygyny in eusocial Hymenoptera originates 1) through pleometrosis; 2) via budding or swarming from a mature colony; or 3) by secondary polygyny (addition of or replacement by daughters) (reviewed in HÖLLDOBLER and WILSON 1977, WEST-EBERHARD 1978a, b, 1982). These are the same pathways known to generate associations of multiple primary queens in termites.

Wasp cofoundresses are frequently close kin (e. g. WEST 1967, GIBO 1974, 1978, GAMBOA 1978, WEST-EBERHARD 1978a, 1982). Associated termite queens are definitely related if they colonize a bud, or if they replace a parent in the natal nest. Queens may or may not be close relatives in termite colonies founded by pleometrosis following alate flights.

Cofounding Hymenoptera queens often develop intra-group dominance and gonad size hierarchies. Behavioral rank normally parallels gonad size hierarchies (e. g. WALOFF 1957, WEST 1967, JEANNE 1972, HÖLLDOBLER and WILSON 1977, WEST-EBERHARD 1978b, BARTZ and HÖLLDOBLER 1982). Such hierarchies result in differential egg production among females, and many hymenoptera colonies become literally or functionally monogynous before producing the first alate brood (e. g. WEST 1967, GAMBOA 1978, GIBO 1978, WEST-EBERHARD 1978b, BARTZ and HÖLLDOBLER 1982). Termite queens within a polygynous *Nasutitermes corniger* or *Macrotermes michaelseni* colony are normally of the same size, and no behavioral dominance hierarchy has been observed. Data suggest, however, that polygynous *N. corniger* colonies do make a transition to monogyny, although not always before production of a fertile brood. Such long term polygyny originating from pleometrosis is unknown in wasps and has not been clearly demonstrated in ants. Polygynous associations in *Macrotermes michaelseni* (in many cases replacements) appear stable over time.

In cases where it has been evaluated, the probability of survival of a polygynous Hymenoptera colony (and therefore of successful queens) is higher than for sympatric monogynous conspecifics (e. g. WALOFF 1957, GIBO 1974, 1978, GAMBOA 1978, BARTZ and HÖLLDOBLER 1982, TSHINKEL and HOWARD 1983). Enhanced survivorship can be due to a decreased predator or parasite pressure because more females are present to guard the incipient colony, a decreased probability of a nest being usurped by a foreign queen, an accelerated growth rate enabling escape from the vulnerability of a small colony, or to a combination of these factors.

Production of non-reproductive progeny is important for colony survival, and also as support staff for rearing alate brood. WEST-EBERHARD (1978b) described «temporary queens» in *Metapolybia aztecoides:* multiple females who lay worker eggs, thus boosting the number of nurses and foragers. The number of queens is then reduced to one prior to laying eggs destined to become fertile progeny. This single queen, supported by the enlarged worker force contributed by her polygynous predecessors, can produce many more reproductive progeny than would have been possible had the nest been continuously monogynous. *Metapolybia aztecoides* colonies cycle between polygyny and monogyny (single queens are replaced by groups of inseminated offspring). Many eusocial Hymenoptera colonies, and the termite *Nasutitermes corniger,* maintain a single queen after the transition to monogyny. Like *Metapolybia aztecoides,* colonies profit from the polygynous pulse, but only in the early age (size) classes. In *N. corniger,* multiple queens may produce alates before the transition to monogyny. Cofounding queens assume the risk of not reigning as the sole survivor, but they may survive long enough to produce some fertile progeny. The payoff is substantial for the single successful queen. Membership in a stable *Macrotermes michaelseni* queen association permits each queen to be part of large, productive colony. The mean weight (and thus egg laying capacity) of polygynous queens is less than that of single queens (Fig. 2), but replacement reproductives likely grow more quickly than foundresses, and are thereby compensated by an earlier age of reproduction.

Thus the ecological factors of early age class probability of survival and expected per queen reproductive output appear to have influenced the evolution of polygyny in the phylogenetically independent Isoptera and Hymenoptera. Parallels in social behavior, colony organization, caste polymorphism, life histories, and foraging behavior between the two orders have been of marked interest: polygyny is a further example of convergent patterns.

Acknowledgements

Special thanks to Dr. J. P. E. C. DARLINGTON of the National Museums of Kenya for allowing me to cite her extensive data on polygyny in *Macrotermes michaelseni,* and for helpful discussion of some of the points presented in this paper.

H. JACOBSON, A. E. MILL, C. NOIROT, G. D. PRESTWICH, C. RETTENMEYER, and C. K. STARR generously provided personal observations of multiple primary queen associations, enabling me to expand the species and geographic lists in Table I.

I appreciate useful comments by J. P. E. C. DARLINGTON, B. HÖLLDOBLER, S. C. LEVINGS, and K. P. SEBENS on earlier versions of this manuscript.

Portions of this research were supported by Harvard University, the Smithsonian Tropical Research Institute, NSF Dissertation Improvement Grant DEB-80-16415, and the American Association of University Women.

References

Andrews, E. A. (1911): Observations on termites in Jamaica. Journal of Animal Behaviour *1*, 193–228.

Bartz, S. H. and B. Hölldobler (1982): Colony founding in *Myrmecocystus mimicus* Wheeler (Hymenoptera: Formicidae) and the evolution of foundress associations. Behavioral Ecology and Sociobiology *10*, 137–147.

Becker, G. (1961): Beobachtungen und Versuche über den Beginn der Kolonie-Entwicklung von *Nasutitermes ephratae* Holmgren (Isoptera). Zeitsch. Angew. Ent. *49*, 78–94.

Bequaert, J. (1921): Insects as food. How they have augmented the food supply of mankind in early and recent times. Natural History *21*, 191–200.

Bouillon, A. (1964): Etude de la composition des sociétés dans trois espècies d'*Apicotermes* Holmgren. Pages 181–196 *in* A. Bouillon, editor. Etudes sur les termites africanis. Masson, Paris.

Bouillon, A. E. & R. Lekie (1964): Populations, rythme d'activite diurne et cycle de croissance du nit de *Cubitermes sankurensis* Wasmann (Isoptera, Termitinae). Pages 197–213 *in* A. Bouillon (ed.) Etudes sur les termites africanis. Masson, Paris.

Buschinger, A. (1974): Monogynie und Polygynie in Insektensozietäten. In: G. H. Schmidt (ed.) Sozialpolymorphismus bei Insekten. Wissenschaftliche Verlagsgesellschaft, Stuttgart. pp. 862–896.

Coaton, W. G. H. (1949): Queen removal in termite control. Farming in South Africa *24*, 335–338.

Darlington, J. P. E. C. (1977): Nest structure and distribution of the population within the nest of the termite *Macrotermes subhyalinus*. Proc. 8th Int. Congr. IUSSI, Wageningen.

Darlington, J. P. E. C. (1978): Populations of nests of *Macrotermes* species in Kajiado and Bissell. Annual Report, International Centre of Insect Physiology and Ecology *6*, 22–23.

Darlington, J. P. E. C. (1982): Population dynamics in an African fungus-growing termite. In: Breed, M. V., C. D. Michener & H. E. Evans (eds). The Biology of Social Insects. Westview Press, Boulder, Colorado. pp. 54–58.

Darlington, J. P. E. C. (1984): Multiple primary reproductives in the termite *Macrotermes michaelseni* (Sjöstedt). Insect Science and its Application, in press.

Dietz, H. F. and T. E. Snyder (1923): Biological notes on the termites on the Canal Zone and adjoining parts of the Republic of Panama. United States Department of Agriculture Journal of Agricultural Research 26, 279–302.

Dudley, P. H. and J. Beaumont (1889a): The termites or so-called «white ants» of the Isthmus of Panama. Journal of the New York Microscopical Society 5, 56–70, 111–112.

Dudley, P. H. and J. Beaumont (1889b): Observations on the termites, or white-ants of the Isthmus of Panama. Transactions of the New York Academy of Science. 1, 85–114.

Dudley, P. H. and J. Beaumont (1890): Termites of the Isthmus of Panama. Part II. Transactions of the New York Academy of Science. 9, 157–180.

Gamboa, G. J. (1978): Intraspecific defense: Advantage of social cooperation among paper wasp foundresses. Science 199, 1463–1465.

Gibo, D. L. (1974): A laboratory study on the selective advantage of foundress associations in *Polistes fuscatus*. Canadian Entomologist 106, 101–106.

Gibo, D. L. (1978): The selective advantage of foundress associations in *Polistes fuscatus* (Hymenoptera: Vespidae): A field study of the effects of predation on productivity. Canadian Entomologist 110, 519–540.

Hegh, E. (1922): Les Termites. Brussels.

Hill, G. F. (1942): Termites (Isoptera) from the Australian region. Council for Scientific and Industrial Research, Commonwealth of Australia. 479pp.

Hölldobler, B. and E. O. Wilson (1977): The number of queens: An important trait in ant evolution. Naturwissenschaften 64, 8–15.

Holmgren, N. (1912): Termites from British India (Bombay) collected by Dr. J. Assmuth, S. J. Journal of the Bombay Natural History Society 21, 774–793.

Holmgren, N. (1913): Termites from British India (near Bombay, in Gujerat and Bangalore), collected by Dr. J. Assmuth, S. J. Part II. Journal of the Bombay Natural History Society 22, 101–117.

Jeanne, R. L. (1972): Social biology of the neotropical wasp *Mischocyttarus drewseni*. Bulletin of the Museum of Comparative Zoology 144, 63–140.

Mathews, A. G. A. (1977): Studies on termites from the Mato Grosso State, Brazil. Academia Brazileira de Ciencias, Rio de Janeiro, Brazil.

Mathur, R. N. and O. B. Chhotani. 1960. Three queens in mounds of *Odontotermes wallonensis* (Wasmann) (Termitidae: Isoptera) Indian Forester 86, 623–624.

Metcalf, R. A. and G. S. Whitt (1977): Relative inclusive fitness in the social wasp *Polistes metricus*. Behavioral Ecology and Sociobiology 2, 353–360.

Michener, C. D. (1974): The Social Behavior of the Bees. Belknap Press of Harvard University Press, Cambridge, Mass.

Mukerji, D. and S. Raychaudhuri (1942): Structure, function, and origin of the exudate organs in the abdomen of the physogastric queen of the termite *Termes redemanni* Wasmann. Indian Journal of Entomology, New Dehli 4, 173–199.

Noirot, C. (1956): Les sexués de remplacement chez les termites supérieurs (Termitidae). Insectes Sociaux 3, 145–158.

Oster, G. F. and E. O. Wilson (1978): Caste and ecology in the social insects. Princeton University Press, Princeton, New Jersey.

Ridley, H. N. (1910): A termite's nest with 8 queens. Journal of the Straits Branch of the Royal Asiatic Society, Singapore. 54, 157.

Roonwal, M. L. and O. B. Chhotani (1962): Termite «*Odontotermes obesus* (Rambur)»: royal chamber with four queens and two kings. Journal of the Bombay Natural History Society 59, 975–976.

Roonwal, M. L. and S. D. Gupta (1952): An unusual royal chamber with two kings and two queens in the Indian mound-building termite *Odontotermes obesus* (Rambur) (Isoptera, Termitidae). Journal of the Bombay Natural History Society 51, 293–294.

Ruelle, J. E. (1970): A revision of the termites of the genus *Nasutitermes* from the Ethiopian region (Isoptera: Termitidae). Bulletin of the British Museum (Natural History) Entomology 24, 363–444.

Sieber, R. and J. P. E. C. Darlington (1982): Replacement of the royal pair in *Macrotermes michaelseni*. Insect Science and its Application *3*, 39–42.

Silvestri, F. (1914–1915): Contribuzione alla conoscenza dei Termitidi e Termitofili dell' Africa occidentale. I. Termitidi. Bollettino del Laboratorio di Zoologia Generale e Agraria della R. Scuola Superiore dAgricoltura in Portici *9*, 3–145.

Sjöstedt, Y. (1914): Termiten aus Madagaskar eingesammelt von Hern. Dr. W. Kaudern 1911–1912. Arkiv for Zoologi *8*, 1–19.

Snyder, T. E. (1949): Catalog of the termites (Isoptera) of the world. Smithsonian Institution Publication 3953, Washington, D. C.

Thorne, B. L. (1980): Differences in nest architecture between the Neotropical arboreal termites *Nasutitermes corniger* and *Nasutitermes ephratae*. Psyche *87*, 235–243.

Thorne, B. L. (1982a): Polygyny in termites: multiple primary queens in colonies of *Nasutitermes corniger* (Motschulsky) (Isoptera: Termitidae). Insectes Sociaux *29*, 102–117.

Thorne, B. L. (1982b). Reproductive plasticity in the Neotropical termite *Nasutitermes corniger*. in P. Jaisson, editor. Social Insects in the Tropics. Vol I. Université Paris-Nord, Paris. pp. 22–29.

Thorne, B. L. (1982c): Multiple primary queens in termites: phyletic distribution, ecological context and a comparison to polygyny in Hymenoptera. in M. D. Breed, C. D. Michener & H. E. Evans (eds) The Biology of Social Insects. Westview Press, Boulder, Colorado. pp. 206–211.

Thorne, B. L. (1983): Alate production and sex ratio in colonies of the Neotropical termite *Nasutitermes corniger* (Isoptera; Termitidae). Oecologia *58*, 103–109.

Thorne, B. L. (1984): Polygyny in the Neotropical termite *Nasutitermes corniger:* Life history consequences of queen mutualism. Behavioral Ecology & Sociobiology *14*, 117–136.

Thorne, B. L. and C. Noirot (1982): Ergatoid reproductives in *Nasutitermes corniger* (Motschulsky): Isoptera, Termitidae. International Journal of Insect Morphology and Embryology *11*, 213–226.

Tshinkel, W. R. and D. F. Howard (1983): Colony founding by pleometrosis in the fire ant, *Solenopsis invicta*. Behavioral Ecology and Sociobiology *12*, 103–113.

Waloff, N. (1957): The effect of the number of queens of the ant *Lasius flavus* (Fab.) (Hym. Formicidae) on their survival and on the rate of development of the first brood. Insectes Sociaux *4*, 391–408.

Warren, E. (1909): Notes on the life histories of Natal termites, based on the observations of the late G. D. Haviland. Annals of the Natal Museum. Vo. II, Part I. pp. 113–128.

West, M. J. (1967): Foundress associations in polistine wasps: dominance hierarchies and the evolution of social behavior. Science *157*, 1584–1585.

West-Eberhard, M. J. (1969): The Social Biology of Polistine Wasps. Miscellaneous publications, Museum of Zoology, University of Michigan *140*, 1–101.

West-Eberhard, M. J. (1973): Monogyny in «polygynous» social wasps. Proceedings VII International Congress IUSSI, London, 396–403.

West-Eberhard, M. J. (1978a): Temporary queens in *Metapolybia* waps: Nonreproductive helpers without altruism? Science *200*, 441–443.

West-Eberhard, M. J. (1978b): Polygyny and the evolution of social behavior in wasps. Journal of the Kansas Entomological Society *51*, 832–856.

West-Eberhard, M. J. (1982): The nature and evolution of swarming in tropical social wasps (Vespidae, Polistinae, Polybiini). In: P. Jaisson (ed), Social Insects in the Tropics, Vol. I. Proc. IUSSI symposium, Mexico 1980. pp. 97–128.

Weyer, F. (1930): Beobachtungen über die Entstehung neuer kolonien bei tropischen Termiten. Zool. Jahrb (Syst) *60*, 327–380.

Fortschritte der Zoologie, Bd. 31 · Hölldobler/Lindauer (Hrsg.): Experimental Behavioral Ecology
G. Fischer Verlag · Stuttgart · New York · 1985

The honeybee queen and the social organization of her colony

H. H. W. Velthuis

Laboratory of Comparative Physiology, University of Utrecht, The Netherlands

Abstract

This paper deals with the mechanisms by which the honeybee queen dominates her workers and how laying worker bees compare to the queen. Queen pheromones are produced by the mandibular glands, the tergal glands and the Arnhard glands. The chemicals in the mandibular gland secretion mainly belong to the fatty acids in the C_6–C_{10} range. The various effects of the queen on the workers constitute one syndrome of reactions; there are no separate stimuli causing specific effects. This complex stimulation of the workers is still unsufficiently known. Learning plays a major role.

The various grades of laying workers can be considered as a series of developmental stages in adult life from workers towards queenlike individuals. Abiotic factors, colony conditions and individual ability determine success or failure in this process towards reproduction. Its competitive nature is reflected in the trophallactic interactions, leading to food exchange. Laying workers are offered food more frequently due to their being distinct. The chemical composition of their mandibular gland secretion has been studied. Some changes in the blend of chemicals occur with the emergence of functional groups of bees, but in general these changes do not explain the differentiation of laying workers. Apart from the mandibular glands other discriminators are present. Among these are probably the tergal glands.

1 Introduction

Thirty years ago the important discovery was made that queen honeybees exercise control over their workers by means of chemical emanations. Simultaneously, Butler (1954), Pain (1954) and de Groot and Voogd (1954) published papers in which they maintained that extracts from queens could affect bees in the same manner as did a living queen. The interpretations of their results differed from the very beginning, and several of the questions that arose at that time are still relevant and in part unsolved. Butler used the term ‹queen substance› to denote a single component and some authors still use it as the popular name for 9-oxo-trans-2-decenoic acid (9-ODA), while others include in the term all the chemicals that are involved in the regulation of the worker by the queen.

The discovery that several sources produced different chemical components of this queen substance stimulated the discussion on their mode of action. Initially, the idea that found most support was that each of these substances had its own particular way of entering into the workers' system and subsequently had its own, specific effect. At present it seems generally accepted that these substances together constitute a complex stimulus, leading to a syndrome of reactions. The complexity of the relation between queen and worker concerns the processing of the information the worker receives from the queen and its subsequent translation into responses, rather than the multifunctional properties of the substances involved. These problems focus on the stimulus-response relationship between queen and individual worker. But both queen and worker are members of the colony which, as a unit, responds to environmental factors. In this ecological setting the queen is no longer the exclusive sovereign but is strongly influenced by the actions of the workers. Very little is known about this adaptation.

The organization of the colony should be understood in the sense that its function is to produce sexuals. The intriguing interweaving of cooperation and competition, so apparent in many features of social insects, becomes increasingly important. On the one hand the honeybee colony functions as a unit in which the queen produces the eggs and the workers tend the brood and care for the nest, and on the other hand each worker possesses a pair of ovaries and would be able to produce eggs, were she not prevented from doing so by the queen. The analysis of this situation has been a matter of interest to physiologists and ethologists, and its ultimate properties have also become an area for theoretical investigations. Therefore, I shall deal at length with laying workers, which are of special interest, since in several social bees reproduction by workers is a normal event, whereas in others, like the honeybee, it is only an aberrant development without any actual consequences for the gene pool.

2 The stimulus complex of the queen

2.1 Chemical identity

Three sources of queen pheromones are known: the mandibular glands (Butler and Simpson, 1958), the tergal glands (Velthuis, 1970b; Vierling and Renner, 1977) and the Arnhard glands on the tarsi (Lensky and Slabezki, 1981). The morphology of these glands has been studied by Altenkirch (1962), Lukoschus (1956, 1962), Nedel (1960), Renner and Baumann (1964), Cruz-Landim (1967), Hemstedt (1969) and da Costa (1982). Of these sources, only the mandibular gland pheromones have been studied chemically. The secretion is characterized by the presence of several classes of substances, the most prominent of which are the fatty acids ranging from 6 to 10 carbon atoms. The known substances are listed in Table 1. An interesting aspect is the great variability of the secretion both in its composition and in the relative amounts of the substances reported. I consider this variation as essential for the understanding of social relationships.

The two most important substances are the 9-ODA, predominant in the secretion of mature queens, and 10-hydroxy-decenoic acid (10-HDA), which is the only or the major component found in worker mandibular glands, especially in nurse bees. Crewe (1982) was able to demonstrate race-specific variation in the ratio 9-ODA/9-HDA (9-hydroxy-decenoic acid) in queens, and a considerable variation in the ratio 10-HDA/10-HDDA (10-hydroxy-decanoic acid) in worker mandibular glands, and royal jelly has been reviewed by Boch and Shearer (1982).

Of the many substances listed in Table 1 a pheromonal function could be attributed only to the 9-ODA. The latter is found in queens of all four species of *Apis* (Shearer et al., 1970) and functions as a sex attractant. It is from this function that the social one, the relation between queen and workers, was probably derived (Velthuis, 1976, 1977;

Table 1: The mandibular gland secretion of queens and worker bees. (sources are 1: BARBIER et al., 1960; 2: PAIN et al., 1960; 3: CALLOW et al., 1964; 4: RUTTNER et al., 1976; 5: BOCH et al., 1979; 6: CREWE and VELTHUIS, 1980; 7: SAIOVICI, 1983).

| substance | reported to be present in | | |
	queen by	queenright worker by	laying worker and false queen by
major components			
9-oxo-trans-2-decenoic acid	1		4
9-hydroxy-trans-2-decenoic acid	3	6	6
10-hydroxy-2-decenoic acid	3	2	6
10-hydroxydecanoic acid	6	5	6
8-hydroxyoctanoic acid	6	6	6
methyl-p-hydroxybenzoate	3		
minor components			
hexanoic acid	5	5	
octanoic acid	5	5	
2-octanoic acid	5	5	
nonanoic acid	3		
decanoic acid	3		
9-oxo-decanoic acid	3		
9-hydroxy-decanoic acid	3		
sebacic acid		5	
p-hydroxybenzoic acid	3		
4-hydroxy-benzyl alcohol		7	
4-hydroxy-benzylaldehyde		7	

MICHENER, 1977) when 9-ODA became involved in the several responses of the workers to the queen (court formation, swarm attraction, inhibition of queen rearing, reduction of ovary development and foraging activity; see VERHEIJEN-VOOGD, 1959; PAIN, 1961; BUTLER and FAIREY, 1964; VELTHUIS and VAN ES, 1964; BOCH et al., 1975 and SIMPSON, 1979). None of the other substances from the mandibular gland, when tested separately, showed any influence on any of the worker responses tested. Some of the substances may perhaps be precursors to real pheromones and others may play a role as keeper substance (see BOCH et al., 1975). On the other hand it should be remembered that the real stimulus probably consists of a blend of components rather than of several substances acting on their own. Research has been concentrated on synergists of 9-ODA, but none of them except the 9-HDA has such a function. BUTLER and SIMPSON (1967) claimed that 9-HDA was involved in the attraction of a swarm by the queen, but this effect has been denied (BOCH et al., 1975). FERGUSON and FREE (1981) report a stimulating effect of 9-HDA on the Nasonof pheromone release by workers at the hive entrance where 9-ODA is not effective. Indeed, 9-HDA is more volatile and could be more useful than 9-ODA for distant communication.

While 9-ODA mimics satisfactorily the attractiveness of a queen for drones, its activity in relation to worker responses is a poor imitation of the mixture secreted by the queen. Indeed, PAIN (1961) claimed already that unstable volatile compounds are involved, which she called »Pheromone II«. Much later, others came to the same conclusion (BOCH et al., 1975; SIMPSON, 1979; FERGUSON et al., 1979; FERGUSON and FREE, 1981; VELTHUIS,

1982). In contrast to what is generally believed I maintain that, in spite of the attention that has been paid to queen substance, we do not know its chemical nature in the broad sense.

2.2 Biophysical properties

The probability that the chemical nature of the stimulus is a rather complex one gives rise to questions concerning the physical aspects of the message and how it reaches the worker bee: some substances may be hardly volatile and only by touching the queen will the worker be able to smell her; other substances are more volatile, permitting detection from a distance. The importance of bodily contact was stressed long ago (Verheijen-Voogd, 1959; Velthuis, 1970 b, 1972), so was the importance of odour perception at short range (van Erp, 1960; Butler and Fairey, 1963). By electrophysiological methods EAG's and single-cell responses were obtained by puffing air, carrying 9-ODA, over worker and drone antennae (Kaissling and Renner, 1968; Beetsma and Schoonhoven, 1966; Adler et al., 1973). Within the hive, however, the active space of a volatile substance may become rather limited if the body surface of queen and worker absorb it; then again, it is only by contacting such a surface that the worker can obtain its information. Indeed, Butler et al. (1973) were unable to detect movements of prospective court bees towards the queen when they were on the combs. One and the same substance, therefore, may have merely an arrestant function inside the hive but will have an attractant function outside.

In fact several biophysical mechanisms are involved. We know this from the observations of Jŭska (1978), who found an exponential decline of the arrestant effect of traces left behind by a queen in a cage. A similar exponential decline characterizes the attention paid to a court bee by other workers after her stay with the queen (Jŭska et al., 1981). The time constants of the exponential functions are of the order of magnitude of 10–15 min. This quick disappearance contrasts with the long-lasting effectivity of pure 9-ODA and extracts from queens and of queens from museum collections, in relation to court behaviour and ovarial inhibition. There are apparently at least two different dispersal mechanisms.

2.3 Production and reception

Little is known about the important quantitative aspect of production and release. Measurements have been restricted to the determination of amounts of 9-ODA present within the mandibular gland; about 100–300 μg is generally present in a queen and quantities of up to 1500 μg have been found occasionally (Pain et al., 1967, 1974; Pain and Roger, 1976; Shearer et al., 1970; Boch et al., 1975). How much of this material is used on a daily basis or during certain behaviours? Probably not much, for after swarming queens still contain much material; furthermore, Butler et al. (1973) and Boch et al. (1975) report a positive rather than a negative correlation between attraction (of workers and drones, resp.) and the amounts 9-ODA present later on. Therefore, the signal emitted will not change considerably in time.

With regard to the nature of the stimulus it is of importance that bees distinguish between virgin and mated queens (Butler and Simpson, 1956) although the amount of 9-ODA in queen's glands is not necessarily different. Furthermore, bees are perfectly able to recognize their own queen in choice tests (Velthuis and van Es, 1964; Boch and Morse, 1974; Ambrose et al., 1979), indicating that both innate and learned components play a role. Individual odour blends emanating from the queen and the general colony odour may be involved. Even the learned odour of a paint mark may elicit behaviour originally directed towards the queen (VELTHUIS, 1972; BOCH and MORSE, 1979). It is this versatile character of the stimulus complex that makes it difficult to give a satisfactory and operational definition of ‹queen substance›.

3 Some responses

3.1 Retinue behaviour

The queen patrols in that area of the colony where brood is reared and where young bees tend the brood. It seems obvious that reactions to the presence or absence of the queen will be found primarily in the young bees. Workers respond either by a quick retreat or by turning their head towards her. Bees give way as soon as she moves and if she passes by, they are unable to follow. The release of retinue is apparently bound up with the body surface of the queen and her immediate surroundings.

The queen is hardly touched by the outstretched worker antennae, which barely move. The mandibles of the workers are generally open, pointing downwards. Often a droplet is held between the mandibles, supported by the basal part of the otherwise withdrawn tongue, irrespective of the position relative to the queen. ALLEN (1955) states that only 1–5 feedings occur per egg produced. The mean duration of a feeding is about 45 sec. A court bee hardly ever refuses to feed the queen.

The extension of the tongue by workers is another aspect of court behaviour. This precludes, of course, food offering. The frequency is rather variable. BUTLER (1954) regarded tongue extrusion as an essential element of retinue behaviour whereby bees would obtain queen substance by licking the queen, but later (1973, 1974) he retracted that argument.

A behaviour that resembles court behaviour is the »balling« of a queen. Balling occurs mainly as a reaction to human interference. It implies an increase in the number of bees surrounding the queen, sometimes to over 60. These bees are therefore very close to each other, forming a tight ball of several layers of bees, preventing the queen from moving. Those that are closest to the queen touch her with the full length of their antennae and with their tongue and mandibles. Some bees may seize her wings, legs, antennae or tongue if food begging has occurred. Such aggressive bees may even climb on to the queen and may attempt to sting, and sometimes actually do so. During most of this balling the queen remains motionless. If undisturbed, balling usually changes into retinue behaviour. Because of this gradual transition and because of the relatedness of several behavioural elements I am inclined to interpret balling and retinue as two intensities of one and the same system.

WALTON and SMITH (1969, 1970) and YADAVA and SMITH (1967 a, 1971 b) made a thorough study of balling, especially in relation to virgin queens introduced into cages with workers from a colony. They demonstrate the involvement of the queens' mandibular glands. But queens whose antennae are removed are not balled; they apparently react to a stimulus provided by the workers examining the queen.

3.2 Queen rearing

Preparatory to swarming, new queens are reared in swarm cells. First of all queen cups are built, in which the queen deposits an egg. Such eggs often disappear, as do the larvae developing from them (ALLEN, 1956, 1965). Swarm cells are thought to be constructed as a response to insufficient production or distribution of queen pheromones.

Emergency queen cells are constructed only as a response to the sudden disappearance of the queen. Some worker cells are transformed into queen cells. First of all, the outer rim of the horizontal, hexagonal cell is changed into a round rim and from that a vertical, hanging queen cell is constructed. The worker larva in the cell is fed like a queen larva as soon as the rim of its cell is transformed; this occurs about 7–10 hrs after the removal of the queen. Nurse bees probably react to the different cell types in order to deliver the appropriate food.

The causal organization of queen rearing from swarm cells and from emergency cells may be identical; its occurrence is more subject to a gradual change in the colony. The process, therefore, is less predictable. An important factor is whether the queen is able to reach the cell and to kill the larva. If this is prevented, as in some commercial breeding methods, many queens can be reared in a queenright colony. The queen apparently controls only the first differentiation of the larva.

In the colony only a limited number of queen cells are constructed. This may be related to the production of pheromones from the queen pupae (Boch, 1979; Koeniger and Veith, 1983).

Once the cells are sealed, the colony has to decide whether to use the cells for supersedure or swarming, or to tear them down again, which happens frequently. Here an interplay of external factors and colony conditions occur. In the latter the queen and her pheromones are again involved.

3.3 The workers' ovaries

Generally, there is only a limited number of bees whose ovaries are activated and then only the initial stages of oogenesis occur. However, once swarming preparations are being made, workers often have well developed oocytes and may occasionally lay an egg. Highly developed ovaries may also occur in wintering bees (Maurizio, 1954).

Removal of the queen enhances this process but the queen is not the only factor that governs the state of the ovary of the individual worker. Race differences and seasonal influences occur related to nutrition in the larval stage; in the adult worker the balance between the availability of protein and the colony's demands determines how much protein is left for oogenesis. Furthermore, workers do affect each other and as a result of this, group size is a variable.

What determines which bee out of a group is to activate its ovaries? Age is the most important factor; most probably it is the younger workers whose ovaries are to be activated. Their physiology is adapted for the maintenance of a high protein level in the haemolymph (Engels, 1974). Although there is a correlation between degree of exposure to queen pheromones and ovary development at the population level (Velthuis, 1970 a, 1976), it is of interest that this is not true at the individual level. This points to the preponderant effect of exchange – probably of a nutritive and of a communicational nature – on the process of oogenesis. There is also social control of the actual egg laying. Perepelova (1929) already distinguished between ‹anatomical› and ‹functional› laying workers. It is still not known, however, what determines this difference.

3.4 The integration at colony level

The foregoing responses cannot be explained solely by regular contact or absence thereof between queen and each individual worker. Apparently workers that encounter their queen and stay in her court for a sufficient period of time subsequently transmit a message to other colony members (Butler, 1954; Verheijen-Voogd, 1959). The message is derived from the mandibular glands of the queen (VELTHUIS, 1972). Worker bees, while contacting the queen, obtain some of her pheromones, either via their antennae or their tongue. In subsequent contacts with nestmates their message is passed on as long as the substance remains on their body. Such workers, called messenger bees by SEELEY (1979), are most often engaged in antennal contacts with nestmates, walk more, thereby dispersing the message, and perform fewer labour acts than their nestmates. The amount of substance on their bodies must be extremely small if the message is 9-ODA; Seeley estimated this to be less than 0.1 ng! FERGUSON and FREE (1980) claim that the first workers that a messenger bee meets also obtain sufficient queen substance to be perceived by nestmates. Like the messenger bee these secondary messengers have an increased number of contacts. In contrast to SEELEY, FERGUSON and FREE found that both messenger bees and secondary messengers became engaged in an increased number of food transfers. These effects of participation in the court ceased, however, within 5 min, rather a short time in comparison to the times reported by VELTHUIS (1972) and SEELEY (1979). This is probably connected with the fact that their colony is much smaller; their bees are therefore much more in contact with the queen.

Although this system of distribution is of importance, the queen herself distributes the information by moving within the brood area. We can deduce this from the fact that a queen without mandibular glands, and thus unable to provide the messenger substance, can head a colony in an apparently perfect way and a considerable period of time (NEDEL, 1960; VELTHUIS, 1970b). Such queens have a court because of their tergal glands (VELTHUIS, 1970b; VIERLING and RENNER, 1977). LENSKY and SLABEZKY (1981) discovered that the Arnhard glands on the tarsi provide another pheromone. These foot-prints are involved in the inhibition of queen cup construction. The model devised by LENSKY and SLABEZKY for the regulation of this behaviour is, however, primitive in that it does not include the other means by which this and other behaviours are regulated.

4 The laying worker

4.1 Its occurrence in the colony

If a colony is dequeened and rearing a new queen is prevented, the colony will produce laying workers. Not only the queen, but also the brood (JAY, 1970, 1972) and the reciprocal effect between workers (VELTHUIS et al., 1965) interfere with oogenesis. The moment the queen is removed the once stable colony sets forth on a developmental pathway along which brood production ceases and ageing of its members takes place. Against this social background individual worker bees compete for a chance to reproduce. Each individual has a restricted period of life during which it is optimally equipped to become a laying worker. Therefore, certain age classes produce many more laying workers than others, since only a few per cent of the individuals will actually lay eggs.

The development of laying workers is accompanied by the occurrence of aggressiveness. Although aggressive bees are characterized by having, to some extent, activated ovaries, there is no direct correlation between laying eggs and being aggressive (VELTHUIS, 1976). We can distinguish 3 groups of workers: those that lay eggs or behave as if they do so, those that are aggressive towards each other and towards the laying workers, and the remaining majority of the colony, which we may call the undifferentiated ones. Laying worker bees were once aggressive bees; they need some days for the transition, during which period they are rather inactive. When they become egg layers, especially at the beginning, they often go through the behavioral sequence of egg laying without producing the egg. The duration of their laying worker phase is very much influenced by the conditions inside and outside the colony. Sometimes they are very severely attacked and may be killed. Then laying workers disappear within a few days of becoming laying workers. In other observation hives, for a number of bees this phase may last much longer; we observed laying workers being reproductive for periods of 25 and 30 days. They always disappear suddenly; only once did we find a former laying worker that became a forager for 2 days. Therefore, the developmental process of a laying worker and of a forager can be considered as alternative pathways, which may diverge already early in adult life, for we found bees becoming aggressive at an age of 5 days and egg laying may start at an age of 7–10 days.

4.2 False queens

This special type of laying worker (Sakagami, 1968) deserves our attention because it attains the social position of the queen: the false queens have a court, overt aggressiveness in the colony ceases and the false queens strongly inhibit other workers from becoming egg layers. The number of false queens is always rather restricted. Their behaviour is distinct from that of laying workers. They walk over the comb like queens and lay their eggs singly in the centre of the cell (laying workers place eggs irregularly and often put many together in the same cell). False queens have a prolonged life. They occur only rarely in nature, but we are able to produce them experimentally by mixing different races of bees. Especially the *A. m. capensis* worker may become a false queen if placed amidst young workers of other races. The most noteworthy peculiarity of *A. m. capensis* workers is the fact that they produce diploid eggs by automictic parthenogenesis (Onions, 1912; Jack, 1916; Ruttner, 1976), their daughters being genetically identical (Verma and Ruttner, 1983).

We followed the development of a freshly emerged *capensis* worker into a false queen by video-recording her contacts with the *mellifera* nestmates. In her first days she was not very distinct but gradually her behaviour became different. She moved more rapidly over the comb, bumping against other workers, walking over and under them. *Mellifera* workers on the other hand tend to stop and wait until their nestmates move aside or make a detour. There was also a change in the nature of the head-to-head contacts. Generally, bees offer and ask for food which, in a certain percentage of contacts, leads to food transmission. *Capensis* workers offer food only when very young; when they are older, the *mellifera* workers chiefly offer food to them. At an age of 5–7 days the *capensis* may have a court and may start ovipositing. Ruttner, Koeniger and Veith (1976) have shown that she produces 9-ODA by that time.

These observations led us to ask two other questions. First, does trophallaxis play a role in the ontogeny of a common laying worker and secondly, what is the nature of the communication between worker bees when they enter upon trophallaxis?

4.3 Trophallaxis

One difficulty in the analysis of trophallaxis in a honeybee colony is that the partners of individuals that are studied generally remain anonymous as far as their own history is concerned. At best, age classes can be distinguished. Such studies, therefore, tend to accentuate the randomness of food exchange and neglect individual differentiation.

In order to avoid these problems we (Korst and Velthuis, 1982) reduced the colony to 2–5 bees of the same age. With 2 animals together a difference often develops between them; one specializes in asking for food, the other in offering. The frequency with which these behaviours lead to food transfer is rather low. Perhaps the performance has a function on its own. But even with a low rate of response one individual gains more from its partner than it gives. In groups of 5 bees essentially the same process has been found, but bees have here the possibility to select or avoid certain partners. It was also possible to demonstrate that bees, when taking the initiative to ask or to offer, take into account the identity of a partner (Fig. 1).

In some, but not in all groups distinct hierarchies were found. It is interesting to note that the animal that receives the most food has a hindgut that contains hardly any pollen grains and its ovaries are best developed. It probably got its protein from the other individuals. At the same time, the animal with the lowest behavioural rank has a hindgut brimfull of pollen and has resting ovaries. It could well be that this animal performed the digestion for the others.

Let us now return to the queenless observation hive and see how trophallactic interactions relate to aggressive bees and laying worker bees. We placed individually marked bees, aged 1–2 days, in a queenless observation hive. As soon as they differentiated into aggressive workers their trophallactic contacts were sampled on a daily basis. This sampling continued for those that became laying workers later on. As has been explained already, this transition takes a few days, and during this period the bees are rather inactive. This made it possible for us to recognize future laying workers and to concentrate on them during this period.

Interesting results were obtained, especially after the laying workers had been separated into two groups: the more active laying workers (the prominent ones, generally characterized by a long period of egg laying) and those that laid for a brief period only (the minor laying workers). As Table 2 shows, the prominent laying workers have high relative values for asking compared to offering, for being offered compared to being asked, and they experience trophic advantage. The minor laying workers have high negative values for

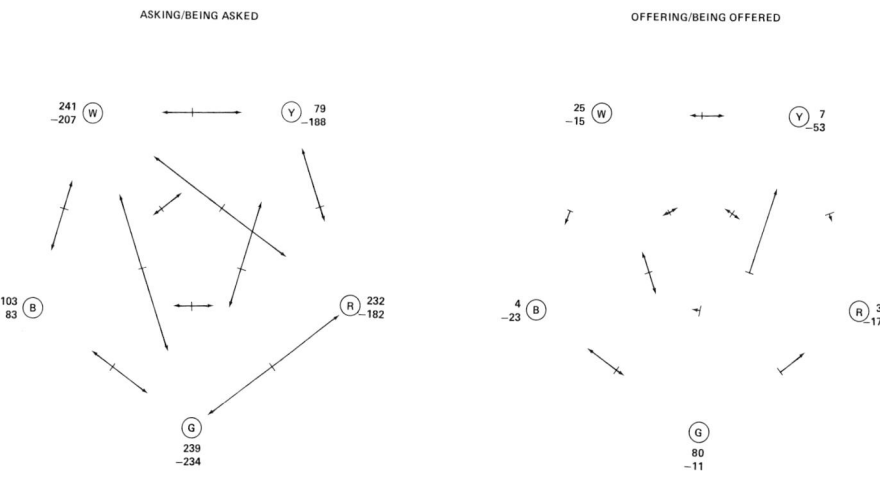

Fig. 1: The frequency and the distribution pattern of the initiatives *asking* and *offering* within a group of five *A. m. capensis* worker bees. The length of each arrow between two bees indicates the number of initiatives taken by and directed at each of them. The total score for each type of initiative taken by and directed at each individual bee is given by positive and negative numbers resp. The figure illustrates the non-randomness of these interactions.

Table 2: Trophallactic interactions of aggressive and laying workers. These interactions are given in the ratio $\frac{\text{asking } - \text{ offering}}{\text{asking } + \text{ offering}}$ for their initiatives and in the ratio $\frac{\text{being offered } - \text{ being asked}}{\text{being offered } + \text{ being asked}}$ for the initiatives taken by their partners.

	major LWB	minor LWB	AWB
$\frac{A-O}{A+O}$ before egg laying period	+0.55	−0.27	−0.05
during egg laying period	+0.58	−0.33	−0.07
$\frac{B_o-B_a}{B_o+b_a}$ before egg laying period	+0.22	−0.30	−0.11
during egg laying period	+0.19	−0.45	+0.02

these ratios, whereas the aggressive bees, as a group, are intermediate. The disadvantages experienced by the minor laying workers probably contributed to their early disappearance.

Not in every case does such a differentiation in the laying workers occur. As already mentioned, in some years only minor laying workers developed. In their trophallactic contacts they gained from the undifferentiated workers, but lost even more to the aggressive ones. We consider environmental factors such as weather and an abundance of flowers to be the most important determinants for the duration of egg-laying.

4.4 Mandibular gland content

MONTAGNER and PAIN (1971) suppose that pheromones are involved in the regulation of trophallactic behaviour and KORST and VELTHUIS (1982) suggest that pheromonal differences could be involved in the labour distribution within the colony. When one observes the decisiveness of an aggressive bee approaching a laying worker and the suddenness of its attacks even if the laying worker seems to be at rest, it is relatively easy to assume that there is pheromonal recognition. As a first possible source the mandibular gland of the worker needs to be investigated.

In young bees, functioning as nurse bees, the gland produces 10-HDA and some other substances, which are also found in worker and royal jelly. Therefore the gland is thought to be involved in larval nutrition and eventually in caste determination. Essential components for queen development do not stem from this gland, however, since PENG and JAY (1977, 1979) were able to rear queens using workers deprived of their mandibular glands. In older bees, functioning as guards or foragers, the gland produces 2-heptanone, an alarm pheromone. Laying workers and false queens are able to produce 9-ODA (RUTTNER et al., 1976; HEMMLING et al., 1979; CREWE and VELTHUIS, 1980) but the laying condition is not always associated with the production of this substance. The presence of 9-ODA does not imply being treated as a queen by nestmates, and in small groups of queenless *capensis* workers they may all produce this substance, but only a few will become laying workers. In fact the mandibular gland secretion of workers ranges from a most workerlike composition (principally 10-HDA) to a most queenlike one (containing 9-ODA as the major component). Perhaps the extent to which the secretion is queenlike is of greater importance than the presence or absence of certain substances.

In an effort to elucidate this matter, we raised bees of different races under different circumstances and sampled their mandibular glands as the groups became older. The composition of the secretion was studied by means of GC and MS. A first group consisted of *capensis* workers that were to become false queens. A second group consisted of the descendants of a *capensis* queen mated to *carnica* drones. Some of them were left with their mother queen in an observation hive, others were placed among young *mellifera* bees so that they could become laying workers. The third group of bees were sister *mellifera* workers; some were placed in the queenright colony, others in a queenless portion of it where differentiation into aggressive and laying workers occurred.

The composition of the mandibular glands of these bees is summarized in Table 3. *Capensis* false queens produce large amounts of 9-ODA as well as several compounds that have not yet been identified. The relative occurrence of known substances does not change considerably with age. In the F_1, *capensis* × *carnica*, queenright bees demonstrate very little effect of age on the mixture of substances but if they are orphaned a change occurs. This is rather a sudden occurrence involving an increase in 9-HDA and 8-HDA and the appearance of 9-ODA at an age of 8–12 days. Before and after this change the secretion is of rather constant composition. Although the acquisition of a reproductive function is accompanied by a change in the mandibular gland secretion, this change probably does not precede oogenesis, and the causal relation seems weak.

Table 3: The composition of mandibular gland secretion in workers of various descend and physiological condition (average percentages).

		1OHDA	1OHDDA	9HDA	9ODA	8HOA	other known	unknown
capensis								
false queens,	8 days	3.6		7.0	69.0	3.5	5.0	12.0
	24 days	2.6		5.0	45.0	4.2	2.2	42.0
hybrid capensis × carnica								
laying workers,	8 days	41.0	4.5	12.0		6.5		35.0
	25–30 days	25.5	2.5	27.0	19.5	10.5		15.0
in colony with queen,	8 days	65.5	9.5	7.0		4.0		14.0
	25 days	64.5	15.5	4.5		4.5		11.0
mellifera								
in colony with queen,								
	7–17 days	73.0	17.0	2.0		3.5		
	20–36 days	76.0	15.0	1.5		2.0		
in queenless hive,								
undiffer.	7–17 days	77.0	17.0	2.0	[1]	2.0		
	20–36 days	73.0	18.5	1.5		3.0		
aggress.	7–17 days	75.5	15.5	1.0		4.0		
	20–36 days	70.0	20.0	1.0		5.0		
egg layer	7–17 days	77.0	17.0	1.5		2.5		
	20–36 days	75.0	17.0	2.0		4.0		

[1] in several bees, irrespective of the category, under queenless conditions traces of 9ODA have been detected.

In the *mellifera* there is hardly any qualitative difference, either in relation to age, or in relation to presence or absence of their queen. Especially for this race an age- or function-dependent type of secretion, serving communication, seems of little importance, at least in the present set of data. Furthermore, as in the queen, the eventual involvement of the mandibular gland in communication between workers is sufficiently supported by other, and probably more important, mechanisms. This can be concluded from a study by SAIOVICI (1983), who removed mandibular glands from young *capensis* workers. This did not interfere with the bees becoming egg layers in groups of *mellifera*, nor did it reduce their inhibitory effect on the *mellifera*'s ovaries. Preliminary observations by BILLEN (unpubl.) show that laying *capensis* workers possess active tergal glands, which so far have been considered as exclusive to queens.

5 Concluding remarks

The foregoing observations on the origin and the continued existence of laying workers have been made with the expectation that mechanisms will become known which may possibly also govern the division of labour under queenright conditions. This goal has not yet been achieved. Instead, we are aware of the many gaps in our understanding of the communication mechanisms and of the consequences of such communication for behaviour – from food exchange to egg laying. Indeed remarkably little is yet known about the more classic problems related to source, chemistry and biological functions of the queen pheromones and to the labour distribution between the workers as a result of these pheromones; in addition, the way in which the colony responds to, the environmental fluctuations is completely unknown. Only by knowing about these mechanisms will it be possible for us to distinguish whether and when a worker bee has the choice between being selfish or altruistic, if such a distinction has any significance at all at a causal level.

It seems to me as if we really have only a rather superficial knowledge of the honeybee, in the sense that only the very general correlations are known but not the causal relations leading to them. It is, however, through these relationships that we may gain further insight into the evolution of the social structure of the honeybee.

Acknowledgements

It is with pleasure that I mention the kind cooperation of Miss F. VAN VLIET, Mrs A. VAN DER KERK, Mrs S. M. MC NAB, M. A., L. THEUNISSEN and M. VAN GEFFEN in the various stages of this study.

References

Adler, V. E., Doolittle, R. E., Shimanuki, H. & Jacobson M. (1973): Electrophysiological screening of queen substance and analogues for attraction to drone, queen, and worker honey bees. J. econ. Entomol. 66, 33–36.
Allen, M. D. (1955): Observations on honeybees attending their queen. Brit. J. anim. Behav. 3, 66–69.
– (1956): The behaviour of honeybees preparing to swarm. Brit. J. anim. Behav. 4, 14–22.
– (1965): The production of queen cups and queen cells in relation to the general development of honeybee colonies, and its connection with swarming and supersedure. J. apicult. Res. 4, 121–141.

Altenkirch, G. (1962): Untersuchungen über die Morphologie der abdominalen Hautdrüsen einheimischer Apiden (Insecta, Hymenoptera). Zool. Beiträge (n. F.) 7, 161–238.

Ambrose, J. T., Morse, R. A. and Boch, R. (1979): Queen discrimination by honey bee swarms. Ann. Entomol. Soc. Amer. 72, 673–675.

Barbier, M. and Lederer, E. (1960): Structure chimique de la ‹substance royale› de la reine d'abeille (Apis mellifera). C. R. Acad. Sci. Paris 250, 4467–4469.

Beetsma, J. and Schoonhoven, L. M. (1966): Some chemosensory aspects of the social relations between the queen and the worker in the honeybee (Apis mellifera L.). Proc. K. Ned. Akad. Wet. C 69, 645–647.

Boch, R. (1979): Queen substance pheromone produced by immature queen honeybees. J. apicult. Res. 18, 12–15.

– and Morse, R. A. (1974): Discrimination of familiar and foreign queens by honey bee swarms. Ann. Entomol. Soc. Amer. 67, 709.

– and – (1979). Individual recognition of queens by honey bee swarms. Ann. Entomol. Soc. Amer. 72, 51–53.

– and Shearer, D. A. (1982): Fatty acids in the heads of worker honeybees of various ages. J. apicult. Res. 21, 122–125.

–, – and Young, J. C. (1975): Honey bee pheromones: field tests of natural and artificial queen substance. J. Chem. Ecol. 1, 133–148.

–, – and Shuel, R. W. (1979): Octanoic and other volatile acids in the mandibular glands of the honeybee and in royal jelly. J. apicult. Res. 18, 250–253.

Butler, C. G. (1954): The method and importance of the recognition by a colony of honeybees (Apis mellifera) of the presence of its queen. Trans. Roy. Entomol. Soc. London 105, 11–19.

– (1973): The queen and the ‹spirit of the hive›. Proc. Roy. Entomol. Soc. London C 37, 59–75.

– (1974): The world of the honeybee. Collins, London, 2nd ed.

–, Callow, R. K., Koster, C. G. and Simpson, J. (1973): Perception of the queen by workers in the honeybee colony. J. apicult. Res. 12, 159–166.

– and Fairey, E. M. (1963): The role of the queen in preventing oogenesis in worker honeybees. J. apicult. Res. 2: 14–18.

– and Simpson, J. (1956): The introduction of virgin and mated queens directly and in a simple cage. Bee World 37 105–114, 124.

– – (1958): The source of the queen substance of the honey-bee (Apis mellifera L.). Proc. Roy. Ent. Soc. London A 22, 120–122.

– (1967): Pheromones of the queen honeybee (Apis mellifera L.) wich enable her workers to follow her when swarming. Proc. Roy. Ent. Soc. London A 42, 149–154.

Callow, R. K., Chapman, J. R. and Paton, P. N. (1964): Pheromones of the honeybee: chemical studies of the mandibular gland secretion of the queen. J. apicult. Res. 3, 77–89.

Costa Leonardo, A. M. (1982): Ciclo de desenvolvimento das glândulas mandibulares de Apis mellifera L. (Hymenoptera: Apidae) e a regulação social na colônia. Diss. Inst. Biociências, São Paulo.

Crewe, R. M. (1982): Compositional variability: the key to the social signals produced by honeybee mandibular glands. In (M. D. Breed, C. D. Michener and H. E. Evans, Eds.) The biology of social insects, 318–322. Westview, Boulder.

– and Velthuis, H. H. W. (1980): False queens: a consequence of mandibular gland signals in worker honeybees. Naturwissenschaften 67, 467–469.

Cruz-Landim, C. da (1967): Estudo comparativo de algumas glândulas das abelhas (Hymenoptera, Apoidea) e respectivas implicações evolutivas. Arq. Zool. (São Paulo) 15, 177–290.

Engels, W. (1974): Occurrence and significance of vitellogenins in female castes of social Hymenoptera. Amer. Zool. 14, 1229-1237.

Erp, A. van (1960): Mode of action of the inhibitory substance of the honeybee queen. Insectes Sociaux 7, 207-211.

Ferguson, A. W. and Free, J. B. (1980). Queen pheromone transfer within honeybee colonies. Physiol. Entomol. 5, 539-366.

– (1981): Factors determining the release of Nasonov pheromone by honeybees at the hive entrance. Physiol. Entomol. 6,11 15–19.

– –, Pickett, J. A. and Winder, M. (1979): Techniques for studying honeybee pheromones involved in clustering, and experiments on the effect of Nasonov and queen pheromones. Physiol. Entomol. 4, 339–344.

Groot, A. P. de and Voogd, S. (1954): On the ovary development in queenless worker bees (Apis mellifera L.) Experientia 10, 384.

Hemmling, C., Koeniger, N. and Ruttner, F. (1979): Quantitative Bestimmung der 9-oxodecensäure im Lebenszyklus der Kapbiene (Apis mellifera capensis Escholtz). Apidologie 10, 227–240.

Hemstedt, H. (1969): Zum Feinbau der Koschewnikowschen Drüse bei der Honigbiene Apis mellifica (Insecta, Hymenoptera). Z. Morph. Tiere 66, 51–72.

Jack, R. W. (1916): Parthenogenesis amongst the workers of the Cape honey-bee: Mr. G. W. Onions' experiments. Trans. Ent. Soc. Lond. 64, 396–404.

Jay, S. C. (1970): The effect of various combinations of immature queen and worker bees on the ovary development of worker honeybees in colonies with and without queens. Can. J. Zool. 48, 169–173.

– (1972): Ovary development of worker honeybees when separated from worker brood by various methods. Can. J. Zool. 50, 661–664.

Jûska, A. (1978): Temporal decline in attractiveness of honeybee queen tracks. Nature, London 276, 261.

–, Seeley, T. D. and Velthuis, H. H. W. (1981): How honeybee queen attendants become ordinary workers. J. Insect Physiol. 27, 515–519.

Kaissling, K. E. and Renner, M. (1968): Antennale Rezeptoren für Queen Substance und Sterzelduft bei der Honigbiene, Z. vergl. Physiol. 59, 357–361.

Koeniger, N. and Veith, J. J. (1983): Identification of a glyceride (glyceryl-1, 2-dioleata-3-palmitate) as a brood pheromone of the honey bee (Apis mellifera L.) Apidologie 14, 59.

Korst, P. J. A. M. and Velthuis, H. H. W. (1982): The nature of trophallaxis in honeybees. Insectes Sociaux 29, 209–221.

Lensky, Y. and Slabezki, Y. (1981): The inhibitory effect of the queen bee (Apis mellifera L.) footprint pheromone on the construction of swarming queen cups. J. Insect Physiol. 27, 313–323.

Lukoschus, F. (1956): Untersuchungen zur Entwicklung der Kasten-Merkmale bei der Honigbiene (Apis mellifera L.). Z. Morph. Ökol. Tiere 45, 157–197.

– (1962): Zur Entwicklung von Leydigschen Hautdrüsen bei der Honigbiene. Z. Morph. Ökol. Tiere 51, 261–270.

Maurizio, A. (1954): Pollenernährung und Lebensvorgänge bei der Honigbiene. Landwirtsch. Jb. Schweiz 69, 115–182.

Michener, C. D. (1977): Aspects of the evolution of castes in primitively social insects. Proc. 8th Int. Congress IUSSI, Wageningen, 2–6.

Montagner, H. and Pain, J. (1971): Etude préliminaire des communications entre ouvrières d'abeilles au cours de la trophallaxie. Insectes Sociaux 18, 177–192.

Nedel, J. O. (1060): Morphologie und Physiologie der Mandibeldrüse einiger Bienen-Arten. Z. Morph. Ökol. Tiere 49, 139–183.

Onions, G. W. (1912): South African ‹fertile› worker bees. Agric. J. Un. S. Afr. 3, 720–728.

Pain, J. (1954): Sur l'ectohormone des reines d'abeilles. C. R. Acad. Sci. Paris 239, 1869–1870.

– (1961): Sur la phéromone des reines d'abeilles et ses effets physiologiques. Ann. Abeille 4, 73–153.

–, Barbier, M. and Roger, B. (1967): Dosages individuels des acides céto-9-décène-2 oique et hydroxy-10 décène-2 oique dans les têtes des reines et des ouvrières d'abeilles. Ann. Abeille 10, 45–52.

– and Roger, B. (1976): Variation de la teneur en acide céto-9 décène-2 oique en function de l'âge chez les reines vierges d'abeille (Apis mellifica ligustica S.) C. R. Acad. Sci. Paris 283, 797–799.

–, – and Theurkauff, J. (1974): Mise en évidence d'un cycle saisonnier de la teneur en acides céto-9 et hydroxy-9 décène-2 oique des têtes de reines vierges d'abeille. Apidologie 5, 319–355.

Peng, Y.-S. and Jay, S. C. (1977): Larval rearing by worker honey bees lacking their mandibular glands. I. rearing by small numbers of worker bees. Can. Entomol. 109, 1175–1180.

– (1979): Larval rearing by worker honey bees lacking their mandibular glands II. rearing by larger number of bees. Can. Entomol. 111, 101–104.

Perepelova, L. I. (1929): Laying workers, the egg-laying activity of the queen, and swarming. Bee World 10, 69–71.

Renner, M. and Baumann, M. (1964): Über Komplexe von subepidermalen Drüsenzellen (Duftdrüsen?) der Bienenkönigin. Naturwissenschaften 51, 68–69.

– and Vierling, G. (1977): The secretion of the tergite glands and the attractiveness of the queen honeybee to drones in the mating flight. Behav. Ecol. Sociobiol. 2, 329–338.

Ruttner, F. (1976): Die Bienenrassen Afrikas. Verh. 25. Int. Bienenz. Kongr. Apimondia, 334–364.

– , Koeniger, N. and Veith, H. J. (1976): Queen substance bei eierlegenden Arbeiterinnen der Honigbiene (Apis mellifera L.). Naturwissenschaften 63, 434.

Saiovici, M. (1983): 9-Oxodecenoic acid and dominance in honeybees. J. apicult. Res. 22, 27–32.

Sakagami, S. F. 1968): The false-queen: fourth adjustive response in dequeened honeybee colonies. Behaviour 13, 280–296.

Seeley, T. D. (1979): Queen substance dispersal by messenger workers in honeybee colonies. Behav. Ecol. Sociobiol. 5, 391–416.

Shearer, D. A., Boch, R., Morse, R. A. and Laigo, F. M. (1970): Occurrence of 9-oxodec-trans-2-enoic acid in queens of Apis dorsata, Apis cerana, and Apis mellifera. J. Insect Physiol. 16, 1437–1441.

Simpson, J. (1979): The existence and physiological properties of pheromones by which worker honeybees recognize queens. J. apicult. Res. 17, 233–249.

Velthuis, H. H. W. (1970a): Ovarian development in Apis mellifera worker bees. Ent. exp. et appl. 13, 377–394.

– (1970b): Queen substances from the abdomen of the honeybee queen. Z. vergl. Physiol. 70, 210–222.

– (1972): Observations on the transmission of queen substance in the honey bee colony by the attendants of the queen. Behaviour 41, 103–129.

– (1976): Egg laying, aggression and dominance in bees. Proc. XV Int. Congr. Entomol., Washington 436–449.

– (1977): The evolution of honeybee queen pheromones. Proc. 8th Int. Congr. IUSSI, Wageningen, 220–222.

– (1982): Communication and the swarming process in honeybees. In: (M. D. Breed, C. D. Michener and H. D. Evans, Eds.) The biology of social insects, 323–328. Westview, Boulder.

– and Es, J. van (1964): Some functional aspects of the mandibular glands of the queen honeybee. J. apicult. Res. 3, 11–16.

–, Verheijen, F. J. and Gottenbos, A. J. (1965): Laying worker honeybee: similarities to the queen. Nature 207, 1314.

Verheijen-Voogd, C. (1959): How worker bees perceive the presence of their queen. Z. vergl. Physiol. 41, 527–582.

Verma, S. and Ruttner, F. (1983): Cytological analysis of the thelytokous parthenogenesis in the Cape honeybee (Apis mellifera capensis Escholtz). Apidologie 14, 41–48.

Vierling, G. and Renner, M. (1977): Die Bedeutung der Tergittaschendrüsen für die Attraktivität der Bienenkönigin gegenüber jungen Arbeiterinnen. Behav. Ecol. Sociobiol. 2, 185–200.

Walton, G. M. and Smith, M. V. (1969): Balling behavior of worker honey bees. Am. Bee J. 109, 300–301, 305.

– (1970): Effect of mandibular gland extirpation on acceptance of the queen honey bee. J. econ. Entomol. 63, 714–715.

Yadava, R. P. S. and Smith, M. V. (1971a): Aggressive behaviour of Apis mellifera L. workers towards introduced queens. I Behavioural mechanisms involved in the release of worker aggression. Behaviour 29, 212–236.

– (1971b): Aggressive behavior of Apis mellifera L. workers towards introduced queens. II Role of mandibular gland contents of the queen in releasing aggressive behavior. Can J. Zool. 49, 1179–1183.

Fortschritte der Zoologie, Bd. 31 · Hölldobler/Lindauer (Hrsg.): Experimental Behavioral Ecology
G. Fischer Verlag · Stuttgart · New York · 1985

Cooperative breeding strategies among birds*

Stephen T. Emlen and Sandra L. Vehrencamp

Animal Behavior in the Division of Biological Sciences, Cornell University, Ithaca, NY 14853, USA,
and Dept. of Biology at the University of California, San Diego, La Jolla, CA 92039, USA

Abstract

In this paper we address several fundamental questions pertaining to the evolution of altruism by examining the phenomenon of cooperative rearing of young among brids.

We argue that an individual bird should cooperate in the rearing of offspring other than its own *only* when its opportunities for reproducing successfully on its own are severely curtailed. Ecological constraints arising from prolonged habitat saturation or from large, unpredictable fluctuations in resources critical for reproduction can restrict breeding opportunities and lead to the evolution of cooperative breeding societies. Under such circumstances, the lifetime inclusive fitness of non-breeding individuals which aid close relatives rear offspring may exceed that of individuals which abandon nesting activities altogether.

Even in cooperative societies, competition between helpers (hopeful reproductives) and breeders (actual reproductives) can be intense. We model the conflicting interests as well as the available options of breeder and helper alike and conclude that the *form* of the cooperative breeding system – whether highly asymmetrical (as in helper-at-the-nest species) or largely equitable (as in some communal nesting species) – is dependent upon the difference in dominance levels of the participants. In the past, cooperatively breeding birds have been portrayed as living in totally harmonious, aid-giving societies. Contrary to this portrayal, we suggest that they represent societies faced with severe ecological hardships which restrict the opportunities for younger, subordinate individuals to breed on their own. They also represent societies in which competitive conflicts of interest between different group members reach extreme limits. Viewing the various forms of cooperative breeding in terms of the balance of interests between conflicting group members, with dominants having greater behavioral leverage than subordinates, provides a useful framework for understanding each system and the evolutionary forces that shaped it.

---

* This article is modified from a chapter by the same title which appeared in Perspectives in Ornithology, pages 93–120, A. H. Brush and G. A. Clark, eds. Cambridge University Press 1983.

1 Introduction

The cooperative rearing of young is a topic of considerable interest to both biological and social scientists. Such behavior reaches its extreme development in many eusocial insect societies, where vast numbers of individuals live their entire lives as sterile workers, rearing young but never themselves becoming reproductives (Wilson, 1971). Such sterile castes have not yet been reported among vertebrates. But there are numerous instances in which individuals of vertebrate species (most of them avian) forego breeding for a signific-ant portion of their adult lives, and spend such time helping to rear young that are not their own offspring. These extra individuals care for their foster offspring by bringing food and by helping to alert and protect the young against predators. Avian helpers also may play roles in nest construction and incubation. Recent reviews (Brown, 1978; Emlen, 1978) have compiled evidence showing that pairs breeding with the assistance of such «helpers» generally achieve a significantly higher reproductive success than pairs breeding alone.

There are three fundamental questions surrounding the topic of cooperative breeding in animals. First, what role have ecological factors played in promoting the development of such aid-giving societies? Second, how can such seemingly altruistic behavior be explained in terms of natural selection theory? And third, what behavioral tactics will members of such societies adopt to maximize their own fitness when interacting with others?

In the following article, we attempt to address each of these three topics. Before doing so, however, it is necessary to define our terms. We define an *auxiliary* as any mature, non-breeding member of a reproducing group. It may or may not provide aid in the rearing of young. *Cooperative breeding* refers to any case where individuals in addition to the two genetic parents provide care in the rearing of young. These cases can be subdivided into two types. In *Helper-at-the-nest* systems, auxiliaries contribute physically, but not geneti-cally, to the young being reared. Auxiliaries serve as helpers, but they do not engage in sexual activity with the breeding pair. *Communal breeding* systems are those in which parentage of the offspring is shared. In the case of shared paternity, more than one male has a significant probability of fathering some of the offspring. With shared maternity, multiple females have a significant probability of contributing eggs to a communal clutch. Although this subdivision is by no means absolute, we feel that it is useful in modelling questions about ecological determinants, as well as behavioral tactics, that are important for the evolution and maintenance of cooperative breeding systems.

2 The ecological determinants of helping-at-the-nest

Approximately 5 percent (300) of the living avian species are known to exhibit aid-giving behavior during breeding, and the vast majority of these are of the helper-at-the-nest type. The list includes species belonging to a wide variety of taxonomic groups, inhabiting a broad range of geographic locations and habitats, and filling the spectrum of ecological niches. This diversity has stifled the search for common ecological de-nominators, and has caused some workers to conclude that no common thread underlies the parallel evolution of cooperative breeding in birds. While agreeing that aid-giving behaviors have undoubtedly evolved independently many times in the class Aves, and that each species can be understood fully only when studied in conjunction with its own, unique, ecology and history, we nevertheless propose that certain broad ecological generalizations can be made about the necessary and sufficient conditions that have led to the evolution of cooperative breeding systems.

In most helper-at-the-nest species, the auxiliaries are younger than the breeders; indeed they are usually grown offspring of the breeders (BROWN, 1978; EMLEN, 1978). Let us consider any post-breeding group of birds comprising parents and maturing offspring. There are two behavioral options available to the maturing individuals: they can disperse and attempt to become established as independent breeders in the upcoming nesting season, or they can remain with their parents in their natal groups through the next season. In the latter case, they face a second subset of options: to help or not to help the group's breeders in rearing the next generation of nestlings. Our first question is: «Under what conditions will grown offspring postpone dispersal and remain in their natal groups»?

There is a large body of literature discussing the gains that accrue to individuals by virtue of living in groups. The two most cited benefits include a) increased alertness and protection against predators, and b) enhanced efficiency in localization and exploitation of patchy, ephemeral food resources (ALEXANDER, 1974; BERTRAM, 1978).

Surprisingly, neither of these factors usually is implicated in studies of cooperative breeders. Instead, field workers consistently stress the difficulties that younger birds have in finding vacant territories, obtaining mates, or breeding successfully alone. We suggest that the selective pressures favoring group living in most helper-at-the-nest species are fundamentally different from those favoring grouping in other types of avian aggregations such as nesting colonies, foraging flocks, or gregarious roosts.

2.1 Constraints on the option of independent breeding

If foraging and/or anti-predation benefits from the primary reason for gregariousness in cooperative breeders, then the average fitness of individual group members should increase as some function of increasing group size up to an optimum size, and decrease thereafter. KOENIG (1981 a) applied this logic to an analysis of the published data available for cooperatively breeding birds. He found that annual, *per-capita* reproductive success showed no consistent pattern with group size. Of 16 cases analyzed, pairs were the most productive units in 7, pairs were roughly equivalent to larger groups in 5, and groups were most successful (on a per-capita basis) in only 4. KOENIG further predicted that if cooperative groups formed because of inherent benefits of grouping, then the most frequently observed group sizes should coincide with the most productive group size as determined by per-capita success. Such was not the case: although in 12 cases pairs were equally or more productive than larger groups, in all cases the observed mean group size exceeded two. From these analyses, KOENIG (1981 a) concluded that most cooperatively breeding birds live in groups because they are «forced» to do so by severe ecological constraints that limit the option of younger birds to become established as independent breeders.

The idea is not new; it was first formulated by SELANDER (1964) during his study of helpers in tropical wrens. It was generalized by BROWN (1974) and recently it has been expanded and developed into more specific models by WOOLFENDEN and FITZPATRICK (1978), GASTON (1978 a), KOENIG and PITELKA (1981), and EMLEN (1981, 1982 a). What is new is the realization that the ecological constraints concept can be generalized to encompass all categories of cooperative breeders. Furthermore, data are becoming available which, for the first time, allow a test of the major predictions of the model.

In its most concise form, the model states that when ecological constraints exist which severely limit the possibility of personal, independent reproduction, selection will favor delayed dispersal and continued retention of grown offspring within their natal units. It is the restriction upon independent breeding more than any inherent gain realized by grouping per se that leads to the formation of cooperative breeding units. Differing proximate factors can be responsible for limiting the option of personal reproduction in different species. To date, three categories of constraining factors have been suggested:

2.1.1 Shortage of territory openings

Many cooperative breeders are permanently territorial species that inhabit stable or regularly predictable environments. Further, many have specific ecological requirements such that suitable habitat is restricted. All available high-quality habitat becomes filled or «saturated». Unoccupied territories are rare, and territory turnovers are few. As the intensity of competition for space increases, fewer and fewer individuals are able to establish themselves on quality territories. Assuming that occupancy of a suitable territory is a prerequisite for reproduction, the option of breeding independently becomes increasingly limited. A new individual can become established as a breeder only (a) when it challenges and defeats a current breeder on an occupied territory, (b) when it competes to fill a vacancy that results from the death of a nearby breeder, or (c) when it buds-off or inherits a portion of the parental territory itself. The non-breeder must wait until it attains sufficient age, experience and status to enable it to obtain and defend an independent territory.

The notion of habitat saturation does not explain why auxiliaries do not disperse into more marginal habitats where competition is less. Koenig and Pitelka (1981) propose that a second factor is necessary for the evolution of cooperative breeding in permanently territorial species. Not only must optimal habitat be saturated, but marginal habitat must be rare. When this is the case, a maturing individual is severely constrained either from establishing itself as an independent breeder in the optimal habitat or successfully surviving and breeding in an outlying area. By this model, cooperative breeding is predicted to occur in those species whose ecological requirements are sufficently specialized that marginal habitat is rare, or which occupy habitats that are physically restricted or relict in distribution.

2.1.2 Shortage of sexual partners

A parallel argument can be made emphasizing the shortage of sexual partners rather than spatial territories. Many species of cooperatively breeding birds have a skewed sex ratio, with an excess of males (Rowley, 1965; Ridpath, 1972; Dow, 1977; Reyer, 1980).The reason for such skewing is poorly understood, but its effect is to increase competition for mates, leading to a demographic constraint on the option of becoming established as an independent breeder.

2.1.3 Prohibitive costs of reproduction

A major stumbling block to the acceptance of the generality of the breeding constraints model lies in the realization that many species of cooperatively breeding birds reside in areas where the concepts of ecological saturation or shortage of marginal habitat simply do not apply. This is especially true of arid and semiarid environments in Africa and Australia. Not only are cooperative breeders common in such environments, but many are either nomadic or inhabit areas subject to large scale, unpredictable, fluctuations in environmental quality (Rowley, 1965, 1976; Harrison, 1969; Grimes, 1976). The carrying capacity in such environments changes markedly and erratically from year to year. Avian populations, with their relatively low intrinsic rates of increase, cannot keep pace with these changes. Consequently, the degree of habitat saturation (if any) changes dramatically across seasons. We cannot speak of any consistent shortage of territory openings as the driving force in the evolution of cooperative breeding. But we can still speak of constraints on the option of independent breeding.

In variable and unpredictable environments, erratic changes in the carrying capacity create the functional equivalents of breeding openings and closures (EMLEN, 1981; 1982 a). As environmental conditions change from year to year so, too, does the degree of difficulty associated with successful breeding. In benign seasons, abundant food and cover decrease the costs to younger, less experienced individuals of dispersing from their natal groups and breeding independently. In harsher seasons, the costs associated with such reproductive ventures increase, eventually reaching prohibitive levels. As conditions deteriorate, breeding options become more constrained, and the constraints hit first at the younger, more subordinate individuals. The predicted outcome is the continued retention of such individuals in the breeding groups of older (usually parental) individuals.

2.2 Tests of the constraints model

The ecological constraints model predicts that the frequency of occurrence of nonbreeding auxiliaries will vary directly with (a) the degree of difficulty in obtaining a territory (for permanently territorial species), (b) the degree of skew in the population sex ratio (for species facing a shortage of mating partners), and (c) the level of environmental harshness (for species in erratic, unpredictable habitats). Relevant data for testing these predictions are available for three species of cooperative breeders. We have analyzed and plotted them in Figures 1 a–c.

The first graph shows the effect of territory constraints on the retention of offspring in the Acorn Woodpecker, *Melanerpes formicivorous*. This species lives in permanently territorial groups of from 2–15 individuals. During breeding, only a single nest is tended at any one time, and most or all group members help to incubate the eggs and feed and defend the young. Yearling individuals either emigrate and attempt to become independent breeders, or remain with their natal groups. Those that remain postpone breeding themselves and play full roles in their group's cooperative breeding attempts. Figure 1a plots the annual incidence of yearling «helpers» as a function of the proportion of all territories that became vacant during the preceeding year (the annual turnover rate). The figure incorporates data reported by MAC ROBERTS and MAC ROBERTS (1976), STACEY and BOCK (1978) and STACEY (1979), as well as unpublished results kindly provided by P. STACEY and W. KOENIG, R. MUMME and F. PITELKA. Acorn Woodpecker populations from Arizona, New Mexico, and coastal California, are pooled in the diagram.

The second example comes from studies of IAN ROWLEY on cooperatively breeding *Malurus* wrens in Australia (1965, 1981). These are classic helper-at-the-nest species, and

Fig. 1: The occurrence of helpers plotted as a function of the severity of ecological constraints for three species of cooperative breeders. A. Acorn Woodpeckers *(Melanerpes formicivorous)*. B. Malurus wrens (● = *M. cyaneus* and ■ = *M. splendens)*. C. White fronted Bee-eaters *(Merops bullockoides)*. See text for details.

breeding units consist either of simple pairs or trios (the helper virtually always being a male). Figure 1b graphs the percentage of breeding groups with a (male) helper as a function of the shortage of sexual partners (using the ratio of females to males in the population as the index of demographic constraint).

The third example is taken from Emlen's (1981, 1982a) work on the White-fronted Bee-eater, *Merops bullockoides*. This is an example of a colonial, cooperative breeder that inhabits the erratic, unpredictable environment of the Rift Valley of Kenya. The survival of nestlings is strongly influenced by the food supply, and reproductive success varies greatly across different seasons[1]. The food supply, in turn, is highly dependent upon the pattern of local rainfall. Consequently, Figure 1c plots the percentage of the population serving as helpers in each of 13 colonies, using a measure of rainfall as the index of ecological constraint (the log of total rainfall occurring in the month preceeding breeding).

Although the proximate factors responsible for the constraint upon independent breeding differ among these three species, in each case the intensity (magnitude) of the constraint is a good predictor of the incidence of helpers.

The retention of non-breeding auxiliary individuals in their natal groups is the usual first step in the evolution of cooperative breeding. By itself, however, it is insufficient to explain the development of actual helping behavior. We must also consider the question: «When should a retained auxiliary help in the rearing of the next generation of nestlings?»

3 The adaptive advantage of helping

Helping behavior is an intriguing phenomenon from the standpoint of evolutionary theory because of its seemingly altruistic nature. The auxiliary that feeds and defends nestlings other than its own not only incurs the costs and risks of alloparental care, but it also improves the reproductive success of other individuals in the population relative to its own. Evolutionary theory predicts that helping should only evolve when it actually benefits the individual helper. The focus of much current research on helper-at-the-nest species is on identifying the ways in which helpers might benefit from helping.

In formulating a testable hypothesis for investigating the selective advantage of helping, it is necessary to establish an alternative behavioral strategy as a reference point for comparison. The obvious alternative to helping is not helping. However, there are few cases of retained auxiliaries that do not also aid the breeding pair in some way. Rather, non-helpers typically disperse and attempt to breed independently. Therefore, the usual alternative strategy is dispersal from the natal territory at the age of sexual maturity and independent breeding thereafter. The evolutionary hypothesis specifically predicts that the fitness of birds that help during their lives will be equal to, or greater than, the fitness of birds that attempt early dispersal and breeding. Such a comparison incorporates the fitness effects of both delayed reproduciton and helping. Thus the question: «Why do helpers provide aid at the nest of others?» is closely tied to the question of why the auxiliaries remain on their natal territory.

How might helping behavior be adaptive to the helper? We discuss five general types of advantages that may accrue to helpers. The first deals with the potential benefits of delayed reproduction, while the second through fifth deal specifically with the question: «Why help?».

---

[1] Unpublished data of S. T. Emlen indicate nestling starvation rates range from 25–45% of hatchlings.

3.1 Survivorship advantage from delayed breeding

As the prospects for breeding independently become increasingly poor, it will become advantageous for certain individuals to forgo reproduction until conditions are better. Younger, subordinate birds will be more influenced by constraining factors of the types discussed in the previous sections than older, experienced individuals. By remaining on the parental territory and delaying reproduction, a young bird can increase its chances of surviving through the difficult waiting period and thereby improve its chances of becoming a breeder in the future when conditions are more favorable.

If the short-term cost of not reproducing is more than compensated for by improved longevity, then the survivorship advantage alone is sufficient to explain the evolution of delayed breeding. However, improved survivorship may be only one component of the total benefits that result in a higher lifetime reproductive success for delayed reproducers compared to non-delayers.

3.2 Breeding experience

Several studies of helpers-at-the-nest species have indicated that experienced breeders are more successful in rearing offspring than inexperienced breeders, and that older helpers provide more effective aid than younger ones (WOOLFENDEN, 1975; LAWTON and GUINDON, 1981). These findings suggest that one advantage of helping during the first year or two of life may be improved breeding expertise. In order for breeding experience to be the sole explanation for the helping phenomenon, however, the amount of improvement in a helper's subsequent reproductive success as a breeder would have to outweigh the cost of its not reproducing during the helping years. This will only be true if helping is a more effective learning process than actual breeding. While helping may be a less risky method of learning, it seems unlikely that it is a more effective one.

Consequently, the attainment of breeding experience is unlikely to be the sole advantage of helping. However, it may well be an important contributory factor. The most likely benefit of breeding experience occurs in conjunction with the survival advantage of remaining on the natal territory when ecological conditions for independent breeding are constraining. The breeding experience of helping provides a bonus to auxiliaries who are otherwise forced to remain with their parents. In this case the improvement in a helper's subsequent reproductive success as a breeder need only outweigh the cost of the aid for the helping to be advantageous.

3.3 Parentally manipulated helping

Helping may function to assure the young bird of continued membership in the group. Youngsters that remain on their natal territory may impose a cost on their parents. The young may not only reduce the level of food on the territory and compete with the new generation for food, but they also may disrupt the breeding pair's reproductive efficiency by interfering with nest construction, interrupting copulation and incubation, and attracting predators to the nest (ZAHAVI, 1974). Helping to rear nestlings may be the «price» the youngsters must pay to be allowed to remain on the parental territory (GASTON, 1978 a). Parents should be selected to expel young that do not help. Parents are in a position to demand such aid, because it is the youngster that stands to benefit most from retention (EMLEN, 1982 b). If the amount of aid an auxiliary provides is determined by parental pressure, then it should be the case that the greater the benefit of retention to the helper, the greater the helping effort the parents can demand (see next section).

In most cooperative species, helpers do improve the reproductive success of the breeders (Brown, 1978; Emlen, 1978). However, helpers usually do not work as hard as the parents themselves, and this is reflected by the fact that per capita reproductive success usually declines with increasing group size (Koenig, 1981 a). In most species, there is variation in the amount of help given as a function of age, sex, and group size. Proof of the parental manipulation hypothesis for the «advantage» of helping will rest upon its ability to predict these variations in helper effort.

3.4 Laisons for the future

Given that auxiliaries are temporarily constrained from breeding and remain on the natal territory as «hopeful reproductives», helping behavior may function in part to speed up the auxiliary's ascendency to breeding status by cementing bonds and creating laisons for future cooperative ventures. There are several mechanisms by which this might work.

(1.) Helping may heighten the dominance position of the helper relative to other group members and improve its position in the queue for breeding slots on the parental territory or on neighboring territories.

(2.) Helping may produce potential laisons that later help the auxiliary to attain breeding status. In some helper-at-the-nest species, coalitions of siblings or half-siblings disperse together. Such groups of dispersers, it has been claimed, have a greater chance of winning territorial disputes than do solitary individuals (Ridpath, 1972; Ligon and Ligon, 1978; Gaston, 1978 b; Koenig, 1981 b). To the degree that the social bonds formed during helping itself are important for the development of these coalitions, we may conclude that helping in one season may increase a helper's prospects for breeding in future years (Ligon and Ligon, 1978).

(3.) By helping cooperate in territorial defense, an auxiliary may bring about an expansion of the natal territory. Cases of such expansion being followed by the auxiliary budding off a portion of the natal area as its own have been reported in jays and babblers (Woolfenden and Fitzpatrick, 1978; Gaston, 1978 a). If an auxiliary remains on its natal territory until the death of one or both of its parents, it may take over the entirety of the territory. This is a widespread practice among both cooperatively breeding birds and mammals. By such an «inheritance» process, ownership of a high quality territory can be passed down through generations, remaining in the same family lineage well beyond the lifespans of individual members.

3.5 Increased inclusive fitness via collateral kin

All of the above mentioned benefits of helping increase the fitness of a helper via the direct or personal component of inclusive fitness, i. e., lifetime production of offspring (West-Eberhard, 1971; Brown, 1980). A second type of genetic gain inherent in helping behavior involves that component of inclusive fitness attributable to gene copies through collateral kin[2] (termed the indirect (Brown, ibid.) or kin (West-Eberhard, ibid.) component). The debate over the importance of kin selection has led to an unfortunate and, in our opinion, unproductive controversy.

It is true that for the vast majority of helper species for which data are available, the helpers are predominantly grown offspring that remain with their parental groups and help to rear full or half sibs. Thus the indirect component of inclusive fitness is large and could prove to be a major factor in the evolution of helping behavior. Some workers,

---

[2] Collateral kin are genetic relatives other than dircect descendants.

however, have mistakenly taken this correlation of group relatedness with helping as the sole evidence to build a case for the essentiality of kin selection in the evolution of seemingly altruistic behaviors. Other workers have erred in the opposite direction. By finding ways in which individual helpers gain personally through helping (i. e., points A, B and D above), they have concluded that kin selection is either unimportant to understanding helping behavior, or that kin selection does not even exist.

Both approaches are too narrow in outlook and miss the point. Evolution is the process of changing gene frequencies in a population throught time. Natural selection does not distinguish between a gene copy produced by a direct descendent and one fostered by a collateral kin. All gene copies are tallied, irrespective of who or what was responsible for their survival in the population. The interesting question, then, is not whether kin selection exists or not, but rather whether collateral kin interactions (as opposed to personal offspring production) have been an important or essential component in the evolution of helping behavior.

To take this debate out of the realm of semantic argument and into the realm of quantitative biology, Vehrencamp (1979) has devised a simple index for determining the relative importances of direct and indirect selection to the current evolutionary maintenance of a behavioral trait. I_k, the kin index, calculates the proportion of the total gain in inclusive fitness that is due to the indirect component of selection for any type of cooperation among kin, compared to the non-cooperative situation:

$$I_k = \frac{W_{RA} - W_R)\, r_{ARy}}{(W_{AR} - W_A)\, r_{Ay} + (W_{RA} - W_R)\, r_{ARy}}$$

where $(W_{RA} - W_R)$ is the change in lifetime reproductive success of the recipient, R, when it is aided by the donor, A,

$(W_{AR} - W_A)$ is the change in lifetime reproductive success of the donor, A, when it provides aid to R,

r_{ARy} is the relatedness of A to R's young, and

r_{Ay} is the relatedness of A to its own young.

The index is applicable only to situations in which the net change in inclusive fitness of A (i. e., the denominator) is positive. When I_k is greater than 1, there is a net cost to A's direct fitness and pure kin selection is acting. When I_k is less than zero, then A is manipulating R at a net cost to R's direct fitness. When I_k is between 0 and 1, both the direct and indirect components are increased by the cooperation, and the value of the index gives the proportion that is due to the indirect component.

Rowley has calculated I_k for the Splendid Wren, (Malurus splendens), an Australian helper-at-the-nest species (1981). He found that the value of I_k ranged from 0.35 to 0.51 for a typical male helper. This suggests that both the direct and indirect component are increased via the helping behavior, and that the direct component is slightly more important than the indirect component. Preliminary calculations on other cooperative breeders also yield values of I_k between 0.4 and 0.5 (Vehrencamp, 1979).

If one considers these five points together, helping behavior ceases to present the evolutionary paradox that it first appeared to do. Severe ecological constraints often eliminate or greatly restrict the option of independent breeding. When viewed against the backdrop of this constraint, a number of possible adaptive functions can be proposed for helping behavior. These range from direct improvements in a helper's lifetime reproductive success to improvements in the indirect component of fitness by aiding close collateral kin. The differing importance of such factors for each type of cooperative system remains one of the principal challenges of future work on cooperative birds.

368 · St. T. Emlen and S. L. Vehrencamp

4 The communal breeding perspective: balancing the within-group conflict

Despite the fact that most cooperatively breeding avian species are characterized by one-sided helping behavior, one cannot dismiss the communal breeding systems. In these species, egg-laying and/or fertilization are shared, so that the fitness benefits as well as the «parental» care costs are more equitably distributed among group members. Many workers have conceived of the communal breeders as belonging to a totally separate and distinct category from the helper species. However, communal and helper systems differ in only one key parameter: the probability that a helper simultaneously will be a reproductive. We refer to this as the degree of bias in current personal reproductive benefits. The degree of bias is a continuously varying characteristic, ranging from no bias (i. e. equal division of reproductive benefits) to a very high bias (i. e. zero personal reproductive benefits to some members). Intermediate levels are found in many of the so-called equitable communal breeders.

This perspective on cooperative breeding now forces the investigator of helper-at-the-nest species to address a third question: «Why don't helpers reproduce communally along with their parents?». Once the communal breeding strategy is established as an alternative hypothesis to helping, the focus of research is shifted away from just the helper. The breeder/helper *relationship* is now viewed as a general dominant/subordinate interaction in which the interests and strategies of the two parties diverge to different degrees. This view forces us to recognize that the cooperatively breeding group is composed of competing individuals with conflicting strategies. Different individuals hold different options and different leverages for imposing their «will» on the group. The social result of these conflicts, in terms of the degree of bias and type of cooperative society, must represent the balance among the various competing interests.

4.1 Types of conflicts

Emlen has employed this approach in evaluating the nature of behavioral interactions in helper species (Emlen, 1982 b). In modelling the conflict between helpers and breeders, he used the inclusive fitness equations of Trivers (1974), West-Eberhard (1975) and Vehrencamp (1979) to establish the zones of conflict. The direction of the conflict, i. e. whether the breeder or the helper had the greatest leverage, changed depending on two critical variables: (a) the severity of the ecological constraints on younger, subordinate individuals, and (b) the magnitude of the advantage (or disadvantage) of group living.

The results of his analysis are summarized graphically in Figure 2 a and b. Each figure is a two-dimensional schematic representation of the fitness consequences of continued retention of an auxiliary. The fitness of a breeder increases from left to right while that of an auxiliary increases from bottom to top. The vertical and horizontal lines passing through the center of each figure represent positions at which retention of the auxiliary results in a zero change in *direct fitness* of breeder and helper respectively. Thus the direct fitness of a breeder is increased in all areas to the right of the vertical line while its *inclusive fitness* is increased in all areas to the right of the line marked B-B. Similarly, the *direct fitness* of an auxiliary is increased by the association with a breeder in all areas above the horizontal line, while the auxiliary's *inclusive fitness* is increased in all areas to the right of the line marked H-H.

When retention and helping benefit both helper and breeder, there is clearly no conflict and helping will evolve (speckled zone). Similarly, when retention and helping are disadvantageous to both parties, helping will not evolve (white zone). But, because of certain asymmetries in the inclusive fitness equations, there are two zones of breeder/helper con-

Fig. 2: Fitness space diagrams for breeders and helpers of two different degrees of relatedness. r_{AR_y} = coefficient of relatedness between an auxiliary and the young of the breeder (whom it usually helps to rear). r_{AR_y} = coefficient of relatedness between a breeder and the young of the auxiliary. The inclusive fitness of a breeder is increased through the retention of a helper in all areas to the right of line B-B; the inclusive fitness of an auxiliary is increased by such an association in all areas to the right of line H-H. Speckled areas indicate zones where continued association is mutually beneficial. Striped and cross-hatched areas represent zones of conflict, in which one party gains, but he other loses, by the association. Two distinct types of breeder-helper conflict, and the behaviors expected with each, are described in the text. Note that as the degree of relatedness between breeder and helper decreases, the zones of conflict increase (modified from EMLEN, 1982 b).

flict over the issue of helping (EMLEN, 1982 b). The size of these conflict zones increases as the degree of relatedness between breeder and helper decreases (compare Figs. 2 a and b).

Type I Conflict (striped zone), typifies helper-at-the-nest societies. Severe ecological constraints effectively prohibit dispersal and independent breeding by yearlings, yet retention of such auxiliaries results in a loss to the personal fitness of the breeder via competition, interference, greater conspicuousness to predators, etc. This means that the auxiliary gains, but the breeder loses, from retention. Assuming that the breeder is dominant over the auxiliary, the breeder will either expel the subordinate from the group or demand that the subordinate aid in the care of its young so as to increase the fitness of the breeder above the breeder retention tolerance line (labelled B-B). Notice that retention of related auxiliaries can evolve even when there is a cost in direct fitness to the breeder, since the improved survival chances of a retained auxiliary can increase the indirect component of the breeders' inclusive fitness.

In Type II Conflict (cross-hatched zone), the breeder gains from the presence of the auxiliary but the auxiliary loses from retention. This will occur when ecological constraints against novice breeders are slight but there is a direct benefit of group living *to breeders*. Even though the breeder would still benefit from the presence of the helper, the breeder has little leverage to prevent helper dispersal. The only option the breeder has is to entice the auxiliary to stay by «forfeiting»[3] some of its fitness benefits via shared fertilization, shared egg-laying, or reciprocation of helping (EMLEN, 1982 b). The dominant breeders must allow the helper a large enough genetic contribution to the clutch to increase the helper's fitness above *its* retention tolerance line (labelled H-H). *This leads to a communal breeding system with a lower degree of bias.*

---

[3] The term «fitness forfeiting» is used in the sense of ALEXANDER (1974).

This model illustrates the nature of conflicts within groups, and shows how the options and leverages of the different group members change as a function of changing environmental conditions. Furthermore, it specifically shows that the strongly biased helper-at-the-nest system can evolve only when the helper stands to gain more from retention in the long run than the breeder does, whereas lower-biased communal systems evolve when the breeder gains more than the helper.

4.2 How much bias?

Following up this conflict approach, we can now pursue the question of how much fitness the dominant must forfeit to keep the helper in the group. A short-term model of inclusive fitness costs and benefits is required and the boundary conditions for such a model are that both the helper and breeder must break even, i. e., all solutions must lie within the speckled area of the fitness space of Figure 2. Furthermore, this model assumes that, within the limits set by the subordinate's options, the dominant individual has the greatest leverage to push the fitness advantage in its favor. Given these assumptions, it is a simple matter to solve for the optimal degree of bias (Vehrencamp, 1983).

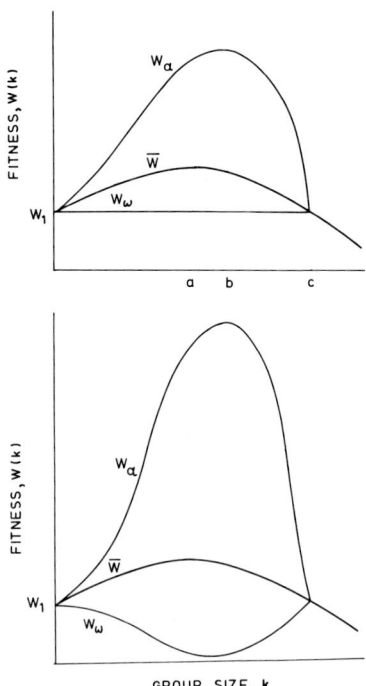

Fig. 3: The maximum degree of bias in fitness that can be generated between dominants and subordinates in groups containing (top) unrelated individuals, and (bottom) individuals related by a coefficient of relatedness r = .25. $\overline{W}$ is the average or per capita fitness of group members, W_α is the fitness of the dominant, and W_ω is the fitness of a subordinate. The distance between the W_α and W_ω curves represents the amount of bias possible at that group size. See text for further explanation.

Take the simplest case of a group of unrelated individuals where grouping benefits all group members on average. The function relating the per capita reproductive success to group size, k, is given by $\overline{W}$ (k) (Figure 3 top). For each unit of fitness that the dominant can usurp from a subordinate, one unit of fitness accrues to the dominant. For simplicity we also assume that there is only one dominant in the group and that all subordinates are affected by the same amount. The dominant cannot lower the fitness of any one subordinate below the fitness of a solitary breeder, $\overline{W}$ (l), otherwise subordinates will be selected to leave and breed solitarily. The lowest possible fitness of a subordinate in a group, $W_\omega(k)$, is therefore depicted as a horizontal line intersecting $\overline{W}$ (l). The fitness increment of the dominant, $W_\alpha(k)$, is the difference between $\overline{W}$ (k) and $\overline{W}$ (l) times the number of subordinates. The bias in fitness is therefore reflected in the degree to which the fitness of dominant and subordinate diverge. Clearly the greater the average benefit to grouping compared to solitary living, the greater the bias can be.

For groups of related individuals, a similar graph can be derived, but in this case the subordinates leave the group when their *inclusive fitness* would be greater if they bred solitarily (Figure 3 bottom). Here, the direct fitness of the subordinate can go well below the direct fitness of a solitary breeder, and the higher the degree of relatedness, the greater the bias can be. As in the unrelated case, grouping and biasing can only occur when there is a net benefit to grouping, when $\overline{W}$ (k) > $\overline{W}$ (l).

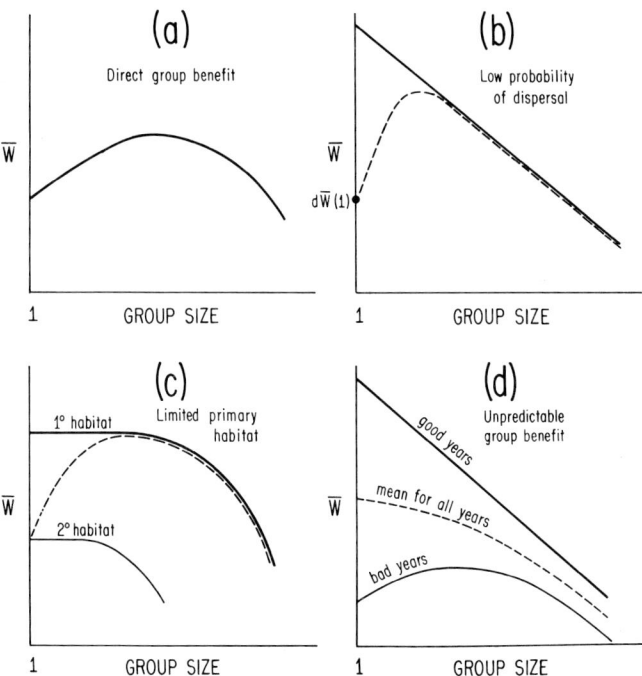

Fig. 4: Four ways to generate a benefit to grouping: (A) direct group benefit, (B) low probablity of dispersing to the optimal solitary situation, (C) limited primary habitat with no disadvantage due to grouping, and (D) direct benefit to grouping occurring unpredictably in poor years only. See text for further explanation.

Given that parents are dominant over their offspring and can control dispersal, group composition, and the degree of bias, certain sets of ecological conditions can be shown to lead to specific types of cooperatively breeding societies, e. g. egalitarian (communal) breeding among relatives, strongly biased breeding with relatives, or moderately biased breeding among non-relatives (Vehrencamp, 1983).

As we saw earlier, there are several situations in which grouping can be advantageous. These conditions are depicted graphically in Figure 4. When group breeding leads to a per capita increase in fitness compared to solitary breeding, there is a direct benefit to group living (Fig 4 a). Communal cooperative breeding will result if there are no strong ecological constraints. The White-winged Chough, *Corcorax melanorhanphus*, provides an example of such a society (Rowley, 1978).

In another case, grouping could lead to net decrease in per capita fitness compared to solitary breeding (Fig 4 b, solid line). However, if the constraints against becoming an independent breeder are high, the intrinsic benefit of independent breeding must be devalued accordingly. This leads to an effective «hump» in the $\overline{W}$ (k) curve and grown offspring may be «forced» to remain on their natal territories (Fig 4 b, dashed line). As discussed previously, this appears to have been the most common cause of grouping among helper-at-the-nest species. The probability of dispersing successfully, here denoted as d, can be calculated for permanently territorial species as the number of breeding slots available relative to the number of auxiliaries competing for them and is an inverse measure of the level of habitat saturation or ecological constraint. This condition can only lead to groups of close relatives since the groups form by retention of natal members. The florida Scrub Jay, *Aphelocoma coerulescens*, is a well-studied example (Woolfenden, 1975).

Another situation in which grouping might be favored is illustrated in Fig. 4 c. Here there is a primary, high quality, habitat which is limited, and a secondary habitat which can support only pairs but which is not limited. The two types of habitats must be close by or arranged in a mosaic so that dispersers have a choice between them. Large groups will occur on good territories, small groups or pairs on the poorer territories. This situation is graphically similar to the Verner-Orians polygamy model (Orians, 1969) and can lead to communal groups of non-relatives. Cooperative breeding in the Grove billed Ani, *Crotophaga sulcirostris,* has been explained in this manner (Vehrencamp, 1978).

Finally, the conditions for grouping may change unpredictably from year to year (Fig 4 d). If grouping is disadvantageous in good years and advantageous in bad years, then birds will hedge their bets by attempting to breed solitarily in most years, but will switch to groups if conditions deteriorate. If there is only a short time for breeding, some birds will initiate breeding but give up their nest to help others during bad times. The model predicts that only close relatives will be willing to accept this cost *and* be in a position to benefit from grouping via heightened inclusive fitness. This situation can lead to a facultative helper-at-the-nest system in which helping is most prevalent in poor years. The society of the White-fronted Bee-eater, *Merops bullockoides,* fits this pattern (Emlen, 1981, 1982 a).

In summary we have shown how a small set of ecological and social factors determine whether or not cooperative breeding is advantageous, and what form of cooperation will result. Typically, cooperatively breeding species have been described as living in harmonious, aid-giving groups. We believe this description to be exaggerated. Rather, such species live in societies faced with severe ecological hardships which restrict the opportunities for maturing young to become independent breeders. They also live in societies in which competitive conflicts of interest between different group members reach extreme limits. Viewing the various forms of cooperative breeding in terms of the balance of interest between conflicting group members, with dominants having greater behavioral leverage than subordinates, provides a more useful framework for understanding each system and the evolutionary forces that shaped it.

Acknowledgments

The research of the authors has been supported by the National Science Foundation through grants number BNS-76-81921 and BNS-79-24436 (STE) and DEB-78-25230 and DEB-80-022167 (SLV). Some of the ideas in this paper were developed while STE was a Visiting Fellow at the Center for Advanced Study in the Behavioral Sciences at Stanford.

References

Alexander, R. D. (1974): The evolution of social behavior. Annu. Rev. Ecol. Syst. 5, 325–383.

Bertram, C. C. R. (1978): Living in groups: predators and prey. In J. R. Krebs and N. B. Davies, (eds.). Behavioral ecology: an evolutionary approach. pp. 64–96. Oxford, Blackwell Scientific Publications.

Brown, J. L. (1974): Alternative routes to sociality in jays – with a theory for the evolution of altruism and communal breeding. Am. Zool. 14, 63–80.

Brown, J. L. (1978): Avian communal breeding systems. Annu. Rev. Ecol. Syst. 9, 123–156.

Brown, J. L. (1980): Fitness in complex avian systems. In H. Markl. (ed.). Evolution of social behavior: hypothesis and empirical tests. Pp. 115–128, Verlag Chemie, Weinheim.

Dow, D. D. (1977): Reproductive behavior of the Noisy Miner, a communally breeding honeyeater. Living Bird 16, 163–185.

Emlen, S. T. (1978): The evolution of cooperative breeding in birds. In J. R. Krebs and N. B. Davies (eds.). Behavioral ecology: an evolutionary approach, pp. 245–281. Oxford, Blackwell Scientific.

Emlen, S. T. (1981): Altruism, kinship and reciprocity in the White-fronted Bee-eater. In R. D. Alexander and D. Tinkle (eds.). Natural selection and social behavior: recent research and new theory. pp. 217–230. New York, Chiron Press.

Emlen, S. T. (1982 a): The evolution of helping. I. An ecological constraints model. Am. Nat. 119, 29–39.

Emlen, S. T. (1982 b): The evolutuon of helping. II. The role of behavioral conflict. Am. Nat. 119, 40–53.

Gaston, A. J. (1978 a): The evolution of group territorial behavior and cooperative breeding. Am. Nat. 112, 1091–1100.

Gaston, A. J. (1978 b): Demography of the Jungle Babbler, Turdoides striatus. J. Anim. Ecol. 47, 845–879.

Grimes, L. G. (1976): The occurence of cooperative breeding behavior in African birds. Ostrich 47, 1–15.

Harrision, C. J. (1969): Helpers at the nest in Australian passerine birds. Emu 69, 30–40.

Koenig, W. D. (1981 a): Reproductive success, group size, and the evolutuon of cooperative breeding in the Acorn Woodpecker. Am. Nat. 117, 421–443.

Koenig, W. D. (1981 b): Space competition in the Acorn Woodpecker: Power struggles in a cooperative breeder. Anim. Behav. 29, 396–409

Koenig, W. D. and F. A. Pitelka (1981): Ecological factors and kin selection in the evolution of cooperative breeding in birds. In R. D. Alexander and D. Tinkle (eds.). Natural selection and social behavior: research and new theory, pp. 261–180. New York, Chiron Press.

Lawton, M. F. and C. F. Guindon (1981): Flock composition, breeding success, and learing in the Brown Jay. 83, 27–33.

Ligon, L. D. and S. H. Ligon (1978): The communal social system of the Green Woodhoopoe in Kenya. Living Bird 17,159–198.

MacRoberts, M. H. and B. R. MacRoberts (1976): Social organization and behavior of the Acorn Woodpecker in central coastal California. Ornithol. Monogr. *21*, 1–115.

Orians, G. A. (1969): On the evolution of mating systems in birds and mammals. Am. Nat. *103*, 589–603.

Reyer, H.-U. (1980): Flexible helper structure as an ecological adaptation in the Pied Kingfisher *(Ceryle rudis)*. Behav. Ecol. Sociobiol. *6*, 219–227.

Ridpath, M. G. (1972): The Tasmanian Native Hen, *Tribonyx mortierrii*. CSIRO Wildl. Res. *17*, 1–118.

Rowley, I. (1965): The life history of the Superb Blue Wren, *Malarus cyaneus*. Emu *64*, 251–297.

Rowley, I. (1976): Co-operative breeding in Australian birds. In H. Frith and J. H. Calaby (eds.). Proceedings of the XVI International Ornithological Congress (Canberra, Australia), p. 657-666.

Rowley, I. (1978): Communal activities among White-winged Choughs, *Corcorax melanorhamphus*. Ibis *120*, 178–197.

Rowley, I. (1981): The communal way of life in the Splendid Wren, *Malurus splendens*. Z. Tier-psychol. *55*, 228–267.

Selander, R. K. (1964): Speciation in wrens of the genus Campylorhynchus. Univ. Calif. Publ. Zool. *74*, 1–224.

Stacey, P. B. (1979): Habitat saturation and communal breeding in the Acorn Woodpecker. Anim. Behav. *27*, 1153–1166.

Stacey, P. B., and C. E. Bock, (1978): Social plasticity in the Acorn Woodpecker. Science *202*, 1297–1300.

Trivers, R. L. (1974): Parent-offspring conflict. Am. Zool. *14*, 249–264.

Vehrencamp, S. L. (1978): The adaptive significance of communal nesting in Groove-billed Anis *(Crotophaga sulcirostris)*. Behav. Ecol. Sociobiol. *4*, 1–33.

Vehrencamp, S. L. (1979): The roles of individual, kin and group selection in the evolution of sociality. In P. Marler and J. G. Vandenbergh (eds.). Handbook of behavioral neurobiology, pp. 351–394. Vol. 3. New York, Plenum.

Vehrencamp, S. L. (1983): A model for the evolution of despotic versus egalitarian societies. Anim. Behav. *31*: 667–682.

West-Eberhard, M. J. (1975): The evolution of social behavior by kin-selection. Q. Rev. Biol. *50*, 1–33.

Wilson, E. O. (1971): The Insect Societies. Cambridge, Mass., Belknap Press.

Woolfenden, G. E. (1975): Florida Scrub Jay helpers at the nest. Auk *92*, 1–15.

Woolfenden, G. E. and J. W. Fitzpatrick (1978): The inheritance of territory in group-breeding birds. BioScience *28*, 104–108.

Zahavi, A. (1974): Communal nesting by the Arabian Babbler: a case of individual selection Ibis *116*, 84–87.

Fortschritte der Zoologie, Bd. 31 · Hölldobler/Lindauer (Hrsg.): Experimental Behavioral Ecology
G. Fischer Verlag · Stuttgart · New York · 1985

Helping, cooperation, and altruism in primate societies

CHRISTIAN VOGEL

Institut für Anthropologie, Georg-August-Universität, Göttingen, F.R. Germany

Abstract

Altruism and cooperation are among those theoretical concepts which have been fundamentally reevaluated by modern evolutionary biology in regard to their adaptive function
and ultimate causation. This paper reviews various types of helping, mutual support,
cooperation and altruistic acts within nonhuman simian primate societies following the
perspective of their assumed evolutionary significance as well as their functional adaptation to the respective species-specific social settings. It is shown that helping, altruistic
behavior, and cooperation are strongly biased toward close kin, particularly among
females which in the majority of simian primates form the continuous and stable element
of reproductive social units by remaining within their natal troop throughout their
lifetime, whereas the males migrate. In those cases where males form the stable center of
the social organization and females are transients, as for instance in chimpanzees, nepotistic behavior is accordingly more common among the males. Reciprocity, however, constitutes an additional motivation for altruistic acts among relatives as well as between
unrelated individuals, especially among individuals occupying adjacent ranks within their
troop's social hierarchy. As has been documented by several longterm longitudinal field-
studies adequate rewarding of altruistic investments may be delayed for several months or
even years under certain social circumstances. For reasons of controversial indications
emerging from field observations and laboratory research the question of whether or not
nonhuman primates possess true «empathetic» or «sympathetic» capabilities must at
present remain unresolved.

1 Introduction

Thirty years ago, HEBB and THOMPSON (1954) noted: «There is a great deal of anecdotal material to suggest the existence of altruism and cooperation in primate societies –, but
the evidence in general has been so poor that ZUCKERMANN (1932) had to conclude that no
altruism exists.»

However, the situation changed dramatically when evolutionary biologists and, in particular, sociobiologists began to analyze intensively the complementary concepts of competition and cooperation in order to uncover the modalities under which cooperation,
helping, and altruistic behavior could have evolved. In part, by adapting these concepts to
the respective requirements of argumentation, terms like altruism, cooperation, helping
etc. have been redefined several times and, of course, sometimes in confusingly divergent
ways.

376 · Ch. Vogel

Therefore, my first task will be to define these terms as I shall use them through this paper.

Helping, primarily, is an asymmetrical interaction within a dyadic context, one individual protecting another individual from being harmed, or one individual aiding, assisting, or supporting another individual to reach its goal or to complete its intended action. Helping may be reciprocated, it may be altruistic or selfish, it may or may not be consciously intended, and its motivation may be classified as nepotistic, opportunistic, hedonistic or something else.

Cooperation is a collaborative behavior of two or more individuals directed toward a common goal or to the production of some common behavioral effect. The partners of a cooperative act are operating simultaneously and are mutually coordinated, they may act in complementary roles («division of labor»), but not in «essentially different roles» (which would serve as a criterion of Kummer's, 1967, «tripartite relationships»). All partners gain benefit, whatever it may be, as a direct result of their joint action (compare Wrangham's, 1982, concept of «mutualistic interaction»). Note that we are neither referring to a particular type or quality of reward nor to the criterion of whether or not the partners actually gain more than they would if acting alone. Although the latter result might be intended, it should not by itself function as a component of the descriptive definition. It should further be noticed that our concept of cooperation is different from what has been called «cooperation» in the game-theoretical approaches like «prisoners dilemma», which includes, in particular, «reciprocal altruism» (e. g. Axelrod and Hamilton, 1981). By definition cooperation is here limited to non-altruistic interactions.

The most controversial concept of those dealt with here is undoubtedly «*altruism*». In humanities and social sciences it has frequently been emphasized that «we have to know more about an incident than the behavioral outcome before we can decide whether or not it *is* altruistic. – The classical issues associated with altruism are *motivational*» (Krebs, 1978). We shall come back to this issue in the final part of this paper. However, here we adopt the restrictive definition coined by evolutionary biologists: *Altruism* is defined as behavior that benefits another individual at some cost to the altruist; costs and benefits being measured in terms of *individual fitness*. Note that by this definition a self-sacrificing parent or grandparent does not act altruistically, whereas a person who acts correspondingly in favor of a sibling or nephew etc. would be labeled as altruist on the basis of the above definition (see also Bertram, 1982).

In defining «*reciprocal altruism*» I follow Packer (1977): «Reciprocal altruism implies the exchange of altruistic acts between unrelated individuals as well as between relatives. If the benefits to the recipient of an altruistic act exceed the costs to the altruist, and if the recipient is likely to reciprocate at a later time, then the cumulative benefits for both individuals will have exceeded the cumulative costs of their altruism».

The counterpart of altruistic is *selfish*: a behavior is considered as being selfish if it serves the *personal fitness* of the actor, irrespective of whether or not it serves the fitness of others as well.

The last terminological differentiation I should make in advance is that between «alliance» and «coalition». For convenience I shall call an *alliance* any cooperative ad hoc formation of individuals acting together toward a common goal, whereas *coalitions* are long-term relationships between two or more particular individuals mutually reciprocating altruistic acts, irrespective of whether or not the benefits are delayed in time (see also Bertram, 1982).

The examples given in this paper are (a) confined to simian primates, (b) primarily focused on free-ranging conditions, and (c) limited to intra-group interactions. Further, I am not concerned here with the whole complex of parental cooperation in raising offspring (a cooperation which is particularly developed in several monogamous primate species). Finally, I do not refer to basic questions of general relationships between cooperation and competition with respect to the evolution of social life and social groupings in primates, units which are per se «cooperative» systems within a competitive setting, as for instance WRANGHAM (1980) argued on the basis of his «feeding competition model». Here I concentrate on actual, directly observable interactions between particular individuals or classes of individuals within social units.

In doing so I will not dwell on more or less singular, occasional, sometimes even anecdotal observations of one individual «helping» another, e. g. of a chimpanzee removing irritants from a conspecific's eye, or cleaning the recipient's teeth, but, I shall confine my examples to regularly observable interactions within the typical, sometimes even species-specific social settings.

2 Cooperation

Let us begin with two classical examples of cooperation. The first one deals with cooperative displays, which among primates are most perfectly developed in form of the famous mutually coordinated «duets» of some of the monogamous hylobatids (Genera: *Hylobates* and *Symphalangus*). These acustically as well as optically impressive pair-ceremonies, characterized by complementary role-taking, appear to serve a combination of distinct functions: (1) territorial advertisement and territorial spacing; (2) demonstration of pair solidarity toward neighbors as well as foreigners; and (3) if the «duet» is complete, to keep other potential sexual partners at a distance, and if the «duet» is incomplete, to attract potential complementary sexual partners (e. g. SERPELL, 1981). The common rewards are the maintenance or acquisition of nutritional as well as reproductive resources.

The second example concerns the obviously intentional cooperation during predatory episodes among chimpanzees *(Pan troglodytes)*. Mutually coordinated actions of adult males were observed with regard to stalking, cornering, and chasing the prey (TELEKI, 1973). Anticipatory capabilities of the actors have been inferred by the observers in all these contexts. The «hunting»-parties comprised up to 5 adult males, and the prey was immediately divided among the cooperating males, who then further distributed pieces of meat to other troop members (e. g. TELEKI, 1973; SUZUKI, 1975). It seems difficult to assess the substantial advantage (if any!) of «hunting» *cooperatively* compared to singly predating from the data published so far. In any case, this is true cooperation in the sense of our above definition.

These two examples are rather out of the ordinary illustrations of cooperation among nonhuman primates confined to highly specialized contexts. In general, cooperative and/or helping interactions among primates are directly or indirectly linked with reproductive strategies in specific ecological and/or social settings.

3 The «helper-at-the-nest» situation

By this metaphor a social and reproductive configuration has been characterized in which non-reproducing sons and/or daughters altruistically help their parents to raise their offspring. Among primates this classical pattern has been developed by the tiny marmosets (Family: Callitrichidae). The primarily insectivorous Callitrichids, owing to special ecological pressures, are adapted to an opportunistically «colonizing» reproductive style (see

Eisenberg, 1978; Ford, 1980). Marmosets produce twins or even triplets twice a year. The newborns weigh about one-fifth to one-quarter as much as their mother. Therefore, it appears plausible that this type of reproduction requires the active support of other family members (e. g. Epple, 1975, 1978; Ingram, 1977). Usually this active support is provided by the breeding male of the strictly monogamous pair, i. e. the biological father. However, additional and demonstrably significant help (by carrying the babies, bringing them back to the mother for suckling, and even sharing food with them) ist frequently provided by elder siblings of the infants. From laboratory research we know that these other family members are inhibited in their own reproduction by the mere presence of the dominant breeding pair. Thus, even fully adult daughters do not ovulate, their sexual activities are completely suppressed as are those of adult sons. This is an almost classical example of the «helper-at-the-nest»-situation, the best we can find in nonhuman primates. In evolutionary terms the «helpers» may gain in *inclusive fitness* on the long run, but this has still to be proven by long-term field data.

Another frequently quoted, but much less unequivocal and less extreme type of helping others to rear their offspring has been described as «aunt behavior» (Hinde et al., 1964; Hinde and Spencer-Booth, 1967; Jay, 1965) or «allomothering», «infant sharing» and «infant transfer», which in its most developed form seems to be a characteristic trait of colobine social behavior (e. g. Hrdy, 1976, 1977; McKenna, 1979, 1981). During their first weeks of life, langur infants (*Presbytis entellus*) spend a considerable amount of day time with «allomothers» who carry them around, sometimes grooming and cradling them, but, sometimes undoubtedly exploiting and even severely mistreating the infants (see below). However, at least as far as elder siblings are involved, which have proven to be the most careful and assiduous allomothers (Vogel, 1984), there is a slight approximation to the «helper-at-the-nest» situation, which may be explained in evolutionary terms of *kin selection* by increasing the inclusive fitness of the helpers.

4 Reciprocal relations

The most famous example of male-male coalitions reciprocating altruistic acts has been reported by Packer (1977) among *Papio anubis*. By gestures one male solicits the support of another who may join him in threatening and attacking a third male who is consorting with an estrous female. «On six occasions the formation of a coalition directed against a consorting male resulted in the loss of the female by the opponent. In all six cases the female ended up with the enlisting male of the coalition; the solicited male generally continued to fight the opponent while the enlisting male took over the female. In each of those cases the solicited male risked injury from fighting the opponent while the enlisting male gained access to an estrous female» (Packer, 1977). The female was taken over by the male who had solicited, and not necessarily by the dominant male of the pair (Packer, 1979). More importantly, «thirteen different pairs of males reciprocated in joining coalitions at each other's request on separate occasions. Individual males which most frequently gave aid were those which most frequently received aid. These results suggest that preferences for particular partners may be partly based on reciprocation» (Packer, 1977). It was at least unlikely that the coalition partners were close relatives, since anubis baboon males are typical transients. However, it seems likely that «the number of offspring that a male sired as a result of participating in reciprocating coalitions would be greater than if he did not» (Packer, 1977). Packer's observations fit well to those of De Vore (1965) and Hausfater (1975) who had already reported that in *Papio anubis* as well as in *Papio cynocephalus* subordinate males sometimes gained access to estrous consort females of higher ranking males by cooperatively harassing the latter.

The counterpart, reciprocal female-female coalitions, has been described by DUNBAR (1979, 1980) in *Theropithecus gelada*. Among geladas dominance rank within the matrilines seems to be determined, at least in part, by the relative aggressiveness of individual females. However, since individual aggressiveness, and hence individual rank as well, have been shown to follow an inverted J-shaped function of age, and since the number of a female's offspring correlates positively with her dominance rank, females should try to reach their optimum position as early as possible, and then, should attempt to prevent rank decline through older ages. The author argued convincingly that these goals could best be reached by forming a stable age-graded female-female longterm coalition. This supposition could be verified by DUNBAR's observations. The age-graded relationship is reciprocal only in the long term, though in the short term it is asymmetrical. It has been shown «that females who form (such) coalitions gain a life-time reproductive advantage over those who do not because coalitions with younger females help to prevent the decline in rank that would otherwise occur in old age. It is argued that females prefer to form coalitions with daughters rather than with unrelated females because the mother-daughter relationship is the only bond of sufficient strength to provide the basis for an investment which is asymmetric in the short term and reciprocal only over the length of a life-time. Any benefits that accrue from kin selection are considered to be secondary» (DUNBAR, 1980). Of course, if these conclusions hold true, then we are dealing with one of the most impressive examples of «delayed benefit» (BERTRAM, 1982) which has been described so far in nonhuman primate societies.

Papio hamadryas provides another example of considerably delayed rewards for altruistic investments, in this case, of a male in favor of a female. An initial form of the hamadryas «one-male unit» consists of a young adult (or subadult) male having «adopted» a juvenile (or even infant) female, taking the role of the mother with every semblance of solicitous maternal care, supporting the juvenile female in any respect of daily life. The growing female herself «seems to transfer the mother's role into the male», and this situation persists into adulthood. «Throughout adult life, a female under extreme stress will cling to the male's back or be embraced by him in the way of the infant» (KUMMER, 1967). This peculiar relationship develops into a stable sexual and social consortship as the female matures. Thus, the male by adopting the mother's role invests altruistically into a longterm interindividual relationship which rewards him only months or even more than two years later (SIGG et al., 1982) in the currency of sexual favors and, ultimately, of reproductive success. This is another most intriguing example of «delayed benefit» (BERTRAM, 1982) in reciprocal relationships.

5 Help, support, and cooperative defense in reproductive contexts

In several species it has been observed that particularly estrous females do solicit and receive support from their respective male consort partners. For instance, SEYFARTH (1978 a) in a detailed study of a *Papio ursinus* troop found «that six of eight females were supported by adult males when they received aggression from other females proportionally more often during sexual consortship than at other times». These supports, however, never did induce any changes in female rank. On the other hand, SEYFARTH (1978 b) was also able to show that the majority of male aids occurred outside sexual consortship, and appeared to be unrelated to changes in female reproductive state. «Each male showed a clear preference in the distribution of these aids, giving the majority to the individual with whom he also shared most frequent proximity, grooming, etc.» Hence, immediate sexual favors are obviously not the main factor provoking male-female support.

Cooperative female support on behalf of preferred males has been observed in several primate species. Since, as SILK and BOYD (1983) noted, «the effectiveness of female mate choice may be influenced by male rank insofar as rank influences both male tenure and access to females, both males and females are expected to have an interest in the outcome of competitive interactions among adult males». Females, of course, act accordingly if preferred males are challenged. They are more likely to do so when a male is established in the troop and is already responsible for a number of their offspring. For instance, HRDY (1977) as well as our team observed langur females *(Presbytis entellus)* jointly defending their established male leader against aggressive males from all-male bands, which tried to oust the leader. HRDY argued that the main interest of these females supporting the father of their infants was to avoid infanticide by a new leader male (see below).

A particular type of (longterm) male-male support are the relationships between «leader» and «follower» within the reproductive units of *Papio hamadryas* first described by KUMMER (1968). A young adult (or subadult) male enters the one-male unit by adopting submissive behavior that makes him acceptable to the harem-leader. The two males gradually develop something like a «working partnership» (CROOK, 1971). The males adopt a sort of complementary role-taking, the leader keeping the part of a «decider» while the follower adopts the function of watching the surroundings and, sometimes, herding the females. As the older male ages, the younger male acquires sexual access to an increasing number of females of the harem; the leader, however, still retaining control of group movement and daily routine. A complex system of mutual «notification» is set up between them to avoid «misunderstandings». It seems difficult to explain why a healthy harem-leader should accept a competitor in the form of the follower. I think the only plausible reason could be that leader and follower are close relatives, as ABEGGLEN (1984) suspected. An aging male could gradually diminish the competition on behalf of his own reproduction, if he is in an effective position to enhance substantially the reproductive chances of close relatives, and by this increase his own inclusive fitness.

Longterm coalitions between particular males conquering and defending bisexual troops, and so gaining or maintaining access to reproductive females, have also been described for *Alouatta seniculus* by SEKULIC (1983).

There are also female-female «attack alliances» against particular males. For example, unrelated female rhesus monkeys *(Macaca mulatta)* band together in fights against adult male troopmates (KAPLAN, 1977); alliances of female geladas *(Theropithecus gelada)* dominate their male harem-leader, who for his part dominates each single female of his unit (BRAMBLETT, 1970); female alliances in vervet monkeys *(Cercopithecus aethiops)* are able to drive away otherwise dominant males (SEYFARTH, 1980); and cooperative attacks of females against particular males preceded the latter's emigration in *Macaca mulatta* (e. g. LINDBURG, 1971) and *Macaca fuscata* (e. g. KURLAND, 1977). In *Presbytis entellus* the females of a troop have been observed jointly attacking intruding males in contexts of male «take-overs». They furiously defended mothers and infants against presumably or actually infanticidal males (HRDY, 1974, 1977; VOGEL and LOCH, 1984; SOMMER, 1984). If the participating females are nonrelatives this behavior might be explained in terms of potential reciprocal altruism, otherwise it could be considered as an altruistic act in defense of kin, and hence, of own inclusive fitness, whereas in the long run it is rather doubtful whether or not the females are really able finally to prevent infanticide (HRDY; SOMMER, 1984).

6 Cooperative hampering or even suppressing reproduction of other consexuals: intrasexual competition

This has been described for both sexes. For instance DE VORE (1965) reported that even high ranking males of *Papio anubis* sometimes were prevented from completing copulation through persistent cooperative harassment and physical interruptions by lower ranking males of the troop. Killing the offspring of another male, of course, is a much more drastic and effective strategy to gain reproductive advantage at the expense of a competitor (e. g. HRDY, 1977, 1979; CHAPMAN and HAUSFATER, 1979; HAUSFATER and VOGEL, 1982; VOGEL and LOCH, 1984; SOMMER, 1984). This, however, is not a cooperative act.

WASSER (1981, 1983) has shown by his field data on *Papio cynocephalus* that females compete with each other on two levels: that of male choice and that of reproductive inhibition of competitors. The «ratio» behind the strategy: «a female is likely to increase her relative personal fitness each time she inhibits another female». Among WASSER's yellow baboons adult females «mediated reproductive inhibition in consexuals» by forming offensive alliances following the tactic: «attack those whose reproduction is easiest to inhibit». However, easiest to inhibit are the reproductive capabilities of females during the most stress-sensitive reproductive phases, i. e. during preovulatory estrus and during early pregnancy. Actually, premature termination of estruses as well as abortions induced by social harassment have now been reproted from several species of free-ranging primates (e.g. WASSER, 1981; PEREIRA, 1983; SOMMER, 1984). The participation of particular females in these attack alliances should, therefore, depend on «common interests» among the allies, mediated by their reproductive state at the respective time of alliance formation, and on the dominance rank relations between allies and victims. Close relatives as victims should be excluded. These predictions were confirmed by WASSER's observations.

It is consequently not surprising that this type of female-female competition continues after parturition as well. One of the most effective ways of reducing the fitness of competitors would be to mistreat or harm infants of non-(or distantly)related females. This, though mostly overlooked, is an aspect of the so-called «aunt behavior» or «allomothering» (see WASSER and BARASH, 1981). HRDY (1976, 1977), KURLAND (1977), WASSER (1981, 1983) and VOGEL (1984) described incidents of apparently deliberately harming, endangering and even injuring infants of other females by allomothers among macaques, baboons, and langurs. Hence, HRDY (1981) is correct in stating that allomothering, with all its complexities, provides a striking illustration of the fine line between cooperation and exploitation between a female helping a troop-mate and one helping herself at a troop-mate's expense. Real helping and «pseudohelping» are the two facets of allomothering (VOGEL, 1984).

However, the complement to male infanticide is female infanticide, which has so far been described only in four cooperative incidents among the chimpanzees *(Pan troglodytes)* of the Gombe Reserve (Tanzania). GOODALL (1977, 1979) reported that two adult females, mother and daughter, belonging to a high-ranking lineage cooperatively killed and cannibalized two infants of a particular low-ranking female and two infants of a particular middle-ranking mother respectively. It is not yet clear whether this behavior should be considered as abnormal and hence maladaptive, or whether it was prompted by mere need or appetite for meat and the two females just took the easiest prey (which seems unlikely, however), or whether mother and daughter pursued a particular reproductive strategy by eliminating the offspring of other non-related female troop members in order to reduce the number of competitors for their own offspring. In this connection it should be emphasized that in contrast to the majority of other nonhuman primate societies (in particular the «female-bonded societies», Wrangham, 1980) adult females in chimpanzee breeding units are most frequently not close genetic relatives, and so the victims were probably not related to the infanticidal females.

7 Helping and cooperation as tools to raise reproductive chances mediated through dominance rank and kinship

Particularly in female cercopithecines, there are strong correlations between kinship, dominance rank, and reproductive success. For instance, female macaques form stable linear rank orders according to three general rules: (1) females outrank all unrelated females outranked by their maternal relatives; (2) adult females rank immediately above their daughters (and their immature sons); (3) adult sisters rank in inverse order of their ages (e. g. Silk and Boyd, 1983).

Kaplan (1977) observed in rhesus monkeys *(Macaca mulatta)* that «females aiding unrelated females against other unrelated females tended to help those animals ranked closer to them in the dominance hierarchy against animals who were more distantly ranked». He argued that supporting unrelated females of adjacent rank may stabilize the existing hierarchy among females, «the stable and central part of the rhesus monkey social group». However, since reciprocity generally seems to be infrequent among unrelated females, Silk (1982) admitted the question to be unresolved of why females form alliances to support unrelated females in the absence of reciprocity. De Waal (1978 a) claimed «redirected aggression» as an explanation of the prevailing «actor alliances» (in which the aggressive party of a dyadic encounter receives support) among unrelated female *Macaca fascicularis*, whereas Silk and Boyd (1983) argued that animals «form alliances in support of non-relatives in order to reduce the fitness of the aggressor».

Kinship, however, appears to be the primary matrix of helping and cooperation in primate societies. Since higher primates are characterized by a considerable longevity, social units can easily comprise three generations with all their possible ramifications in degrees of relatedness among troop members.

Massey (1977) found that within her study troop of *Macaca nemestrina* during agonistic «defender aids» (those aids provided on behalf of the victim of an ongoing aggressive interaction) the animals discriminated clearly between family members and non-family members. Moreover, they distributed their aids significantly according to the gradation of the coefficients of relatedness. «They chose to aid relatives of closer degrees of relatedness more often than relatives more distantly related». Reciprocity was common among family members (excluding mother-infant aids due to the highly unequal cost-benefit ratios involved). So true coalitions were observed only among members of the same genealogy. The author concluded «that kin selection and reciprocal altruistic selection may act conjunctively for family members which do reciprocate aids».

Within the «female-bonded» nepotistic social systems of ceropithecines acts of help and cooperation among females are in general strongly biased toward members of the own matriline. This has been documented e. g. by Kaplan (1977, 1978) and Berman (1980) for *Macaca mulatta*; by Kurland (1977) and Watanabe (1979) for *Macaca fuscata*; by Massey (1977) for *Macaca nemestrina*; by De Waal (1978 a) for *Macaca fascicularis*; by Silk (1982) for *Macaca radiata*; by Paul (in prep.) for *Macaca sylvanus*; by Cheney (1977) for *Papio ursinus;* and by Fairbanks (1980) for *Cercopithecus aethiops*.

In «female-bonded» societies males are transients, leaving their natal troop mostly (but not always) before, during, or shortly after reaching their full reproductive maturity. However, it has been observed that brothers or half-brothers later joined the same bisexual troop, and mutual support might be of essential importance in order to establish favorable positions within these reproductive settings.

For example, MEIKLE and VESSEY (1981) reported that among the free-ranging rhesus monkeys *(Macaca mulatta)* of La Cueva (Puerto Rico), young males frequently transferred into the same social group as their elder brothers. In these cases the authors observed that brothers spent more time close to each other than to other males, formed aggressive alliances with their brothers more frequently than with other males, and disrupted each other's interactions with estrous females less frequently than expected by chance. Males who had brothers within their non-natal troop remained within that troop significantly longer than males without brothers, and, of course, the length of time a male spent in a troop was positively associated with the male's dominance rank and, probably, also with his reproductive success. Therefore, the authors concluded that «HAMILTON's model of inclusive fitness remains a plausible explanation of nepotism among monkey brothers». SADE (1968) as well as BOELKINS and WILSON (1972) reported additional cases of fraternal associations outside the males' natal troops from rhesus monkeys of Cayo Santiago.

Similarly, in chimpanzees *(Pan troglodytes)* RISS and GOODALL (1977) described the successful challenge of the α-male by a team of two brothers, who were mutually supporting each other in raising their rank positions within the male dominance hierarchy. The authors suggested that the frequently observed longterm coalitions between pairs of chimpanzee males are regularly formed among brothers, which would be most effective since male chimpanzees generally remain in their natal troop. By «pushing» an elder brother into a dominant position the younger brother would not only benefit directly from reciprocation, but also through increasing his inclusive fitness, since there are indications that dominant males are able to inhibit successfully copulations of lower ranking males and thus, to enhance their own chances to inseminate estrous females (e. g. TUTIN, 1975; DE WAAL, 1978 b).

8 Helping and rank acquisition in «female-bonded» societies

There are several studies on helping and cooperation in relation to rank acquisition of adolescent females particularly in macaque and savannah baboon societies (e. g. BERMAN, 1980, for *Macaca mulatta*; CHENEY, 1977, for *Papio ursinus*; WALTERS, 1980, vor *Papio cynocephalus*).

For instance, CHENEY (1977) found in *Papio ursinus* that immatures received a considerable proportion of aids from those adult females who ranked adjacent to their mothers and with whom their mothers most frequently interacted. Offspring of high-ranking mothers were more frequently and more successfully aided, and consequently the existing rank hierarchy tended to be perpetuated across generations. CHENEY described a striking difference in alliance formation among immatures and coalitions between adult females. Immature animals formed aggressive alliances primarily with members of high-ranking matrilines, whereas adult females formed coalitions primarily with individuals of adjacent rank. It therefore seems necessary to assume «that over time the formation of alliances will be influenced by an additional factor: namely the animals will learn to cease to form alliances with those individuals who fail to reciprocate them», e. g. individuals of high-ranking matrilines on behalf of individuals of low-ranking matrilines. Hence during their ontogenetic development individuals will learn to ally primarily with animals who reciprocate, that is, with individuals of adjacent rank. «Reciprocal alliances between adjacently ranked animals might therefore be regarded at least in part as the result of compromises that animals adopt during development between the potential benefits to be derived from alliances with high-ranking individuals and the high cost entailed by lack of reciprocity». CHENEY's model, thus, predicts «that the pattern of alliances among adult females will be dependent upon the interaction between an individual's rank and the probability of reciprocity, and that over time reciprocal alliances will generally involve those of adjacent rank», which in savannah baboons, of course, are also most likely to be closely related.

Studying rank acquisition in *Papio cynocephalus*, WALTERS (1980) coined the concept of «targeted» vs. «non-targeted» females, in order to distinguish between females to which a certain adolescent female attempted to become dominant (targeted females), and those females to which the same adolescent female behaved submissively and always remained subordinate (non-targeted females). WALTERS' «examination of non-dyadic agonistic interactions revealed that adolescents frequently intervened against targeted females, but never against non-targeted females, but aided non-targeted females against adolescents. Interveners were unrelated adult females and other adolescents as well as kin. Targeting was determined by birth rank (the rank of the adolescent's mother at the time of the adolescent's birth) and did not depend upon interventions by the mother» (in some cases even the mother may become a targeted female of her own daughter, if the mother had declined in rank since the time of birth of her daughter!). By this mechanism each adolescent female finally reaches her «proper» position within the rank hierarchy, at least in part, by virtue of aid from other females, even if the mother had previously died. «Thus, who intervened for whom in interactions involving adolescent and adult females was governed more by rank relationships than by kin relationship or social bonds (e.g. grooming relationships). Animals were extremely reluctant to intervene against the existing or expected (based on birth rank) hierarchy», and by this they reinforced the transmitted dominance hierarchy among matrilines. «The great difference between the behavior of adolescents toward targeted and non-targeted females implies that young females recognize their position in their society, and the data indicate that this recognition is based on birth rank». Moreover, the other females too must have a perception of their own «proper» relationship with all adolescent female troop-mates. The social organization, in general, might be regarded as a conservative and rather stable compromise between the competetive strategies to maximize personal as well as inclusive fitness.

9 Helping, altrusim, and empathy

Let us return to the initially mentioned notion that the «classical issues associated with altruism are motivational» (KREBS, 1978). Everybody knows that for most «naive» people the concept of altruism is a part of the system of ethical values, and as such «truly altruistic behavior is evidence of Man as his best» (HATFIELD et al. 1978). So it ought to be absolutely unselfish. However, even among humanists it is controversial whether or not this moralistic measure might actually be applicable to man. Most psychologists, of course, would agree with COHEN's (1978) statement that «man operates, in a motivational sense, from point of view of self-interest» even if this self-interest might be as high-grade as to stand for «the desire of being morally superior» (WISPÉ, 1978). Following COHEN's definition: «altruism can be defined as an act of desire to give something gratuitously to another person or group because he, she, they, or it needs it or wants it», three significant elements arise: first, the desire to give something; second, the motivation to give it regardless of whether or not it will be rewarded; and third, the «empathetic» feeling for the needs of others. Thus, «empathy» is a central concept with respect to altruism. ARONFREED (1970) even defined «that any time a person's behavior is controlled by empathetic processes his behavior should be labeled ‹altruistic›». Hence, if we don't know anything about the «desire to give» and about «selfishness vs. unselfishness» of motivations in nonhuman primates, perhaps we might, at least, be able to decide whether or not they are capable of something like «empathy».

However, from field data published so far, there is not the slightest evidence that monkeys or even apes show signs of sympathetic empathy or «compassion» toward suffering, seriously wounded, or even dying conspecifics; not even reactions like warming, cleaning, protecting, or providing privileged access to food, similar to the so-called «invalid care» among dwarf mongoose *(Helogale undulata rufula)* as reported by RASA (1976), have been found. The sad story of the male chimp's «Mc Gregor's» disease described by van LAWICK-GOODALL (1971) in her famous book «In the Shadow of Man» stands as a vivid illustration of the lack of any compassion among his familiar troopmates.

On the other hand, from laboratory experiments there are clear indications of empathetically mediated reactions and «altruistic» acts in apes and monkeys. For instance a chimpanzee (HEBB, 1949) and even rhesus monkeys (STEPHENSON, 1967) actively saved their companions from aversive stimuli, by brachially pulling them away from a place or object of risk. Moreover, experiments by MIRSKY et al. (1958), MILLER et al. (1963), MILLER et al. (1967), and by MASSERMANN et al. (1964) demonstrated that rhesus monkeys (if reared non-isolated!) react empathetically to communicative signals of distress (optical as well as acoustical signals) of their fellow monkeys and that their empathetic reactions mediated altruistic responses (KREBS, 1971).

In conclusion, the question of whether or not nonhuman primates possess «true» empathetic or sympathetic capabilities remains (for the time being) unresolved, at least in the light of definitions such as: «empathy is the self-conscious awareness of the consciousness of the other» (WISPÉ, 1968), or: sympathy designates the «tendency on the part of one social partner to identify himself with the other and so to make the other's goal to some extent his own» (HUMPHREY, 1976). Such conceptualisations presume other mental concepts, like «personal identity», «self-perception» or «self-consciousness» and «self-esteem» which are even more controversial with regard to their applicability to non-human creatures.

However, all the acts of helping and cooperation among non-human primates reported in this paper can be interpreted without any implications as to unselfish and empathetic motivations.

And finally, with regard to human morality I agree with KUMMER (1978) that «obviously, deviation from selfish opportunism is neither a strictly necessary nor a sufficient criterion of morality».

Acknowledgements

I am grateful to ECKART VOLAND for valuable suggestions and to PAUL WINKLER for critical comments and technical help.

References

Abegglen, J.-J. (1984): On socialization in hamadryas baboons. Bucknell University Press, Lewisburg.
Aronfreed, J. (1970): The socialization of altruistic and sympathetic behavior: Some theoretical and experimental analyses. In: Altruism and helping behavior (ed. J. Macaulay & L. Berkowitz) Academic Press, New York, 103–126.

Axelrod, R., Hamilton, W. D. (1981): The evolution of cooperation. Science *211*, 1390–1396.

Berman, C. M. (1980): Early agonistic experience and rank acquisition among free-ranging infant rhesus monkeys. Internat. J. Primatol. *1*, 153–170.

Bertram, C. R. (1982): Problems with altruism. In: Current problems in sociobiology (ed. King's College Sociobiology Group) Cambridge University Press, Cambridge, 251–267.

Boelkins, R. C., Wilson, A. P. (1972): Intergroup social dynamics of the Cayo Santiago rhesus *(Macaca mulatta)* with special reference to changes in group membership by males. Primates *13*, 125–140.

Bramblett, C. A. (1970): Coalitions among gelada baboons. Primates *11*, 327–333.

Chapman, M., Hausfater, G. (1979): The reproductive consequences of infanticide in langurs: A mathematical model. Behav. Ecol. Sociobiol. *5*, 227–240.

Cheney, D. L. (1977): The acquisition of rank and the development of reciprocal alliances among free-ranging immature baboons. Behav. Ecol. Sociobiol. *2*, 303–318.

Cohen, R. (1978): Altruism: Human, cultural, or what? In: Altruism, sympathy, and helping (ed. L. Wispé) Academic Press, New York, 79–100.

Crook, J. H. (1971): Sources of cooperation in animals and man. In: Man and beast: Comparative social behavior (ed. J. F. Eisenberg & W. S. Dillon) Smithsonian Institution Press, Washington, 235–260.

De Vore, I. (1965): Male dominance and mating behavior in baboons. In: Sex and behavior (ed. F. A. Beach) J. Wiley & Sons, Chichester, 266–289.

Dunbar, R. I. M. (1979): Structure of gelada baboon reproductive units. I. Stability of social relationships. Behaviour *69*, 72–87.

Dunbar, R. I. M. (1980): Determinants and evolutionary consequences of dominance among female gelada baboons. Behav. Ecol. Sociobiol. *7*, 253–265.

Eisenberg, J. F. (1978): Comparative ecology and reproduction of New World monkeys. In: The biology and conservation of the Callitrichidae (ed. D. Kleiman) Smithsonian Institution Press, Washington, 13–22.

Epple, G. (1975): The behavior of marmoset monkeys (Callithricidae). In: Primate behavior, vol. 4 (ed. L. A. Rosenblum) Academic Press, New York, 195–239.

Epple, G. (1978): Reproductive and social behavior of marmosets with special reference to captive breeding. In: Primates in medicine, vol. 10 (ed. E. I. Goldsmith & J. Moor-Jankowski) S. Karger, Basel, 50–62.

Fairbanks, L. A. (1980): Relationships among adult females in captive vervet monkeys: Testing a model of rank-related attractiveness. Anim. Behav. *28*, 853–859.

Ford, S. M. (1980): Callitrichids as phyletic dwarfs, and the place of the Callitrichidae in Platyrrhini. Primates *21*, 31–43.

Goodall, J. (1977): Infant killing and cannibalism in free-living chimpanzees. Folia primatol. *28*, 259–282.

Goodall, J. (1979): Life and death at Gombe. National Geographic *155*, 592–621.

Hatfield, E., Walster, G. W., Piliavin, J. A. (1978): Equity theory and helping relationships. In: Altrusim, sympathy, and helping (ed. L. Wispé) Academic Press, New York, 115–140.

Hausfater, G. (1975): Dominance and reproduction in baboons *(Papio cynocephalus)*: A quantitative analysis. Contributions to primatology, vol. 7, S. Karger, Basel.

Hausfater, G., Vogel, C. (1982): Infanticide in langur monkeys (genus *Presbytis*): Recent research and a review of hypotheses. In: Advanced views in primate biology (ed. A. B. Chiarelli & R. S. Corruccini) Springer-Verlag, Berlin–New York, 160–176.

Hebb, D. O. (1949): Temperament in chimpanzees: I. Method of analysis. J. Comp. Physiol. Psychol. *42*, 192–206.

Hebb, D. O., Thompson, W. R. (1954): The social significance of animal studies. In: Handbook of social psychology, vol. 1 (ed. G. Lindzey) Addison-Wesley, Cambridge.

Hinde, R. A., Rowell, T. E., Spencer-Booth, Y. (1964): Behavior of socially living rhesus monkeys in their first 6 months. Proc. Zool. Soc. Lond. *143*, 609–649.

Hinde, R. A., Spencer-Booth, Y. (1967): The effect of social companions on mother-infant relations in rhesus monkeys. In: Primate ethology (ed. D. Morris) Weidenfield & Nicolson, London, 267–286.

Hrdy, S. B. (1974): Male-male competition and infanticide among the langurs *(Presbytis entellus)* of Abu, Rajasthan. Folia primatol. *22*, 19–58.

Hrdy, S. B. (1976): Care and exploitation of nonhuman primate infants by conspecifics other than the mother. In: Advances in the study of behavior, vol. 6 (ed. J. S. Rosenblatt, R. A. Hinde, E. Shaw & C. Beer) Academic Press, London–New York, 101–158.

Hrdy, S. B. (1977): The langurs of Abu. Harvard University Press, Cambridge.

Hrdy, S. B. (1979) Infanticide among animals: A review, classification, and examination of the implications for the reproductive strategies of females. Ethol. Sociobiol. *1*, 13–40.

Hrdy, S. B. (1981): The woman that never evolved. Harvard University Press. Cambridge.

Humphrey, N. K. (1976): The social function of intellect. In: Growing points in ethology (ed. P. P. G. Bateson & R. A. Hinde) University Press, Cambridge, 303–317.

Ingram, J. C. (1977): Interactions between parents and infants and the development of independence in the common marmoset *(Callithrix j. jacchus)*. Anim. Behav. *25*, 811–827.

Jay, P. (1965): The common langur of North India. In: Primate behavior (ed. I. De Vore) Holt, Rinehart & Winston, New York, 197–249.

Kaplan, J. R. (1977): Patterns of fight interference in free-ranging rhesus monkeys. Am. J. Phys. Anthropol. *47*, 279–288.

Kaplan, J. R. (1978): Fight interference and altruism in rhesus monkeys. Am. J. Phys. Anthropol. *49*, 241–249.

Krebs, D. (1971): Infrahuman altruism. Psychol. Bull. *76*, 411–414.

Krebs, D. (1978): A cognitive-developmental approach to altruism. In: Altruism, sympathy, and helping (ed. L. Wispé) Academic Press, New York, 141–164.

Kummer, H. (1967): Tripartite relations in hamadryas baboons. In: Social communication among primates (ed. S. Altmann) Chicago University Press, Chicago, 63–71.

Kummer, H. (1968): Social organization of hamadryas baboons. Chicago University Press, Chicago.

Kummer, H. (1978): Analogs of morality among nonhuman primates. In: Morality as a biological phenomenon (ed. G. S. Stent) Abakon, Berlin, 35–52.

Kurland, J. A. (1977): Kin selection in the Japanese monkey. Contributions to primatology, vol. 12, S. Karger, Basel.

Lawick-Goodall, J. van (1971): In the shadow of man. W. Collins & Sons, London.

Lindburg, D. G. (1971): The rhesus monkey in North India: An ecological and behavioral study. In: Primate behavior, developments in field and laboratory research, vol. 2 (ed. L. A. Rosenblum) Academic Press, New York, 1–106 (1971).

Massermann, J. H., Wechkin, S., Terris, W. (1964): «Altruistic» behavior in rhesus monkeys. Am. J. Psychiatry *121*, 584–585.

Massey, A. (1977): Agonistic aids and kinship in a group of pigtail macaques. Behav. Ecol. Sociobiol. *2*, 31–40.

McKenna, J. J. (1979): The evolution of allomothering behavior among colobine monkeys: Function and opportunism in evolution. Am. Anthropol. *81*, 818–840.

McKenna, J. J. (1981): Primate infant caregiving behavior. In: Parental care in mammals (ed. D. J. Gubernick & P. H. Klopfer) Plenum Press, New York, 389–416.

Meikle, D. B., Vessey, S. H. (1981): Nepotism among rhesus monkey brothers. Nature (Lond.) *294*, 160–161.

Miller, R. E., Banks, J. H., Ogawa, N. (1963): Role of facial expression in «cooperative-avoidance conditioning» in monkeys. J. Abnormal Social Psychol. *67*, 24–30.

Miller, R. E., Caul, W. F., Mirsky, I. A. (1967): Communication of affects between feral and socially isolated monkeys. J. Personality Social Psychol. *7*, 231–239.

Mirsky, I. A., Miller, R. E., Murphy, J. V. (1958): The communication of affect in rhesus monkeys: I. An experimental method. J. Amer. Psychoanal. Ass. *6*, 433–441.

Packer, C. (1977): Reciprocal altruism in *Papio anubis.* Nature (Lond.) *265*, 441–443.

Packer, C. (1979): Male dominance and reproductive activity in *Papio anubis.* Anim. Behav. *27*, 37–45.

Pereira M. E. (1983): Abortion following the immigration of an adult male in yellow baboons. Am. J. Primatol. *4*, 93–98.

Rasa, O. A. E. (1976): Invalid care in the dwarf mongoose *(Helogale undulata rufula).* Z. Tierpsychol. *42*, 337–342.

Riss, D., Goodall, J. (1977): The recent rise to the alpha-rank in a population of free-living chimpanzees. Folia primatol. *27,* 134–151.

Sade, D. S. (1968): Inhibition of son-mother mating among free-ranging rhesus monkeys. Science & Psychoanalysis *12,* 18–38.

Sekulic, R. (1983): Male relationships and infant deaths in red howler monkeys *(Alouatta seniculus).* Z. Tierpsychol. *61,* 185–202.

Serpell, J. A. (1981): Duetting in birds and primates: A question of function. Anim. Behav. *29,* 963–965.

Seyfarth, R. M. (1978 a): Social relationships among adult male and female baboons. I. Behaviour during sexual consortship. Behaviour *64,* 204–226.

Seyfarth, R. M. (1978 b): Social relationships among adult male and female baboons. II. Behaviour throughout the female reproductive cycle. Behaviour *64,* 227–247.

Seyfarth, R. M. (1980): The distribution of grooming and related behaviours among adult female vervet monkeys. Anim. Behav. *28,* 798–813.

Sigg, H., Stolba, A., Abegglen, J.-J., Dasser, V. (1982): Life history of hamadryas baboons: Physical development, infant mortality, reproductive parameters and family relationships. Primates *23,* 473–487.

Silk, J. B. (1982): Altruism among female *Macaca radiata:* explanations and analysis of patterns of grooming and coalition formation. Behaviour *79,* 162–188.

Silk, J. B., Boyd, R. (1983): Cooperation, competition, and mate choice in matrilineal macaque groups. In: Social behavior of female vertebrates (ed. S. K. Wasser) Academic Press, New York, 315–347.

Sommer, V. (1984): Kindestötungen bei indischen Langurenaffen *(Presbytis entellus)* – eine männliche Reproduktionsstrategie? Anthropol. Anz. *42,* 177–183.

Stephenson, G. R. (1967): Cultural acquisition of a specific learned response among rhesus monkeys. In: Neue Ergebnisse der Primatologie/Progress in Primatology (ed. D. Starck, R. Schneider & H.-J. Kuhn) G. Fischer, Stuttgart, 279–288.

Suzuki, A. (1975): The origin of hominid hunting: A primatological perspective. In: Socioecology and psychology of primates (ed. R. H. Tuttle) Mouton, The Hague, 259–278.

Teleki, G. (1973): The predatory behavior of wild chimpanzees. Bucknell University Press, Lewisburg.

Tutin, C. E. G. (1975): Exceptions to promiscuity in a feral chimpanzee community. In: Contemporary primatology (ed. S. Kondo, M. Kawai & A. Ehara) S. Karger, Basel, 445–449.

Vogel, C. (1984): Infant transfer among common Indian langurs *(Presbytis entellus)* near Jodhpur: Testing hypotheses concerning the benefits and risks. In: Current primate researches (ed. M. L. Roonwal, S. M. Mohnot & N. S. Rathore) Scientific Publishers, Jodhpur.

Vogel, C., Loch, H. (1984): Reproductive parameters, adult male replacements and infanticide among free-ranging langurs *(Presbytis entellus)* at Jodhpur (Rajasthan), India. In: Infanticide: Comparative and evolutionary perspectives (ed. G. Hausfater & S. B. Hrdy) Aldine Publishing Co., New York, 237–255.

Waal, F. B. M. de (1978 a): Join-aggression and protective-aggression among captive *Macaca fascicularis.* In: Recent advances in primatology, vol. 1 (ed. D. Chivers & J. Herbert) Academic Press, London–New York, 577–579.

Waal, F. B. M. de (1978 b): Exploitative and familiarity-dependent support strategies in a colony of semi-free living chimpanzees. Behaviour *66,* 268–312.

Walters, J. (1980): Interventions and the development of dominance relationships in female baboons. Folia primatol. *34,* 61–89.

Wasser, S. K. (1981): Reproductive competition and cooperation: General theory and a field study of female yellow baboons *(Papio cynocephalus).* Ph. D.-Dissertation, University of Washington.

Wasser, S. K. (1983): Reproductive competition and cooperation among female yellow baboons. In: Social behavior of female vertebrates (ed. S. K. Wasser) Academic Press, New York, 349–390.

Wasser, S. K., Barash, P. P. (1981): The selfish «allomother»: A comment on Scollay and DeBold (1980). Ethol. Sociobiol. *2,* 91–93.

Watanabe, K. (1979): Alliance formation in a free-ranging troop of Japanese macaques. Primates *20,* 459–474.

Wispé, L. (1978): Introduction. In: Altruism, sympathy, and helping (ed. L. Wispé) Academic Press, New York, 1–9.

Wrangham, R. W. (1980): An ecological model of female-bonded primate groups. Behaviour 75, 262–300.

Wrangham, R. W. (1982): Mutualism, kinship and social evolution. In: Current problems in sociobiology (ed. King's College Sociobiology Group) Cambridge University Press, Cambridge, 269–289.

Zuckerman, S. (1932): The social life of monkeys and apes. K. Paul, Trench, Trubner & Co., London.

V. Physiology and Societies

Fortschritte der Zoologie, Bd. 31 · Hölldobler/Lindauer (Hrsg.): Experimental Behavioral Ecology
G. Fischer Verlag · Stuttgart · New York · 1985

The social physiology of temperature regulation in honeybees

BERND HEINRICH

Zoology Department, Marsh Life Science Building, University of Vermont,
Burlington, VT 05405, USA

Abstract

It has been known for a long time that the internal temperature of honeybee colonies is regulated to within 0.5° of 35°C at both low and high ambient temperatures. The mechanisms of thermoregulation that have been identified include increased heat retention and heat production at low ambient temperatures, and fanning and evaporation of water at high temperatures. Similar thermoregulatory mechanisms are also used by most vertebrate homeotherms and in many insects as individuals. However, thermoregulating individuals have sensors that detect temperature changes, a centrally-located thermostat, and a neural communication system that acts to produce a coordinated response. Do the colonies of social insects have analogous mechanisms? Little work has been done to elucidate details affecting the apparently coordinated thermoregulatory responses of a bee society consisting of tens of thousands of individuals. I here review the data so far available and propose that responses observed in colonies as a whole could potentially be understood in terms of individuals acting behaviorally and physiologically to regulate their own body temperature, in the context of the proximal and evolutionary constraints and possibilities afforded by their social life. This model, although largely consistent with the data so far available, still needs considerable testing, and pertinent experiments are suggested.

1 Introduction

Sociality in bees is roughly correlated with ability to maintain a constant nest temperature. For example, as far as we know none of the solitary or semi-social bees regulate nest temperature, but primitively social bees, like bumblebees, regulate nest temperature within relatively wide limits, while the highly eusocial bees regulate nest temperature fairly precisely. The microclimate control may promote a greater sociality, although it is also possible that the greater sociality promotes better microclimate control. At the present time it may not be possible to separate cause and effect, but perhaps insights can be gained by examining the details of the thermoregulatory mechanisms.

Honeybee colony thermoregulation has been studied for over a century, but so far no one model of thermoregulation has proven adequate for winter and summer hives as well as swarm clusters that have left the hive. SIMPSON (1961) in his review concludes «In effect, the bees keep the center of their cluster at a constant temperature in summer and its periphery above the vital minimum in winter.» Recent work on thermoregulation in swarms (HEINRICH, 1981 a and b) is not fully compatible with previous models of colony thermoregulation. Although the regulation of both heat loss and heat production have repeatedly been identified as colony thermoregulatory mechanisms, very little is known about the role of the individual bees and how or whether they might be coordinated by communication to produce the appropriate colony response.

Honeybees are able to regulate their own body temperature by controlling both heat production by shivering (ESCH, 1960 CAHILL and LUSTICK, 1976) and heat loss by evaporating fluid from their mouthparts (HEINRICH, 1980), and the mechanisms of nest thermoregulation could conceivably be based on individual responses of bees which collectively affect nest temperature. On the other hand, it could involve a coordinated social response with information transfer and division of labor, or a combination of individual and colony responses. My intention in this paper is to explore the mechanisms of thermoregulation in honeybees in order to differentiate the possible alternatives, and to suggest critical experiments where data are so far lacking.

2 «Superorganisms,» and keeping warm in clusters

It is generally maintained that the honeybee colony acts like a «superorganism» in its thermoregulatory response (SOUTHWICK and MUGAAS, 1971, SOUTHWICK, 1982). The implication of such a view is that the thousands of individuals of the colony are not acting on their own, but rather that they subordinate their individual actions for a coordinated response, much like the cells and organs of an organism such as a mouse or a bird act under control of integration centers to produce a unified response.

There are numerous observations that seem to support the superorganism model of thermoregulation. For example, if one lowers the air temperature surrounding a swarm (HEINRICH, 1981 a) or a winter cluster of bees (SOUTHWICK and MUGAAS, 1971) core temperature tends to *increase* while the temperature of the cluster periphery is maintained above some minimum (Fig. 1). The physics of heat flow dictate that the higher the core temperature relative to the outside, the greater the rate of heat flow to the bees on the cluster periphery. The interpretation of these results and premises is therefore in apparent accord with the «superorganisms» model where the core bees are increasing their temperature in order to help defend the vital minimum temperature of their hivemates on the periphery. Conversely, the bees on the swarm periphery are preserving a minimum body temperature rather than the much higher body temperature they prefer when alone, and thus they help to economize the colony's often limited food supplies. A mouse or other homeotherm shows analogous responses, and these responses are also interpreted in terms of mechanisms and adaptive significance of the organism as a whole, rather than in terms of benefit to the various parts involved.

The mechanisms whereby the colony responses are achieved have been compared to those of vertebrate homeotherms. A mouse or other homeotherm, for example, releases or conserves heat from the body core by circulatory shunts and by varying its insulation. The swarm varies the circulation of air with heat through it to affect control of core temperature (HEINRICH, 1981 a). Also, as air temperatures decline bees in the swarm periphery crowd closely together and plug exit holes through which beat might escape from the core (Fig. 2). Like a mouse huddling into a ball in the cold, the swarm, too, contracts presenting a minimum surface area to the air for heat loss (Fig. 1).

Regulation of heat loss is only one potential mechanism of maintaining a stable temperature. Regulation of heat production to offset heat loss is another. Lowering of air temperature around a swarm causes an increase in its total rate of heat production (HEINRICH,

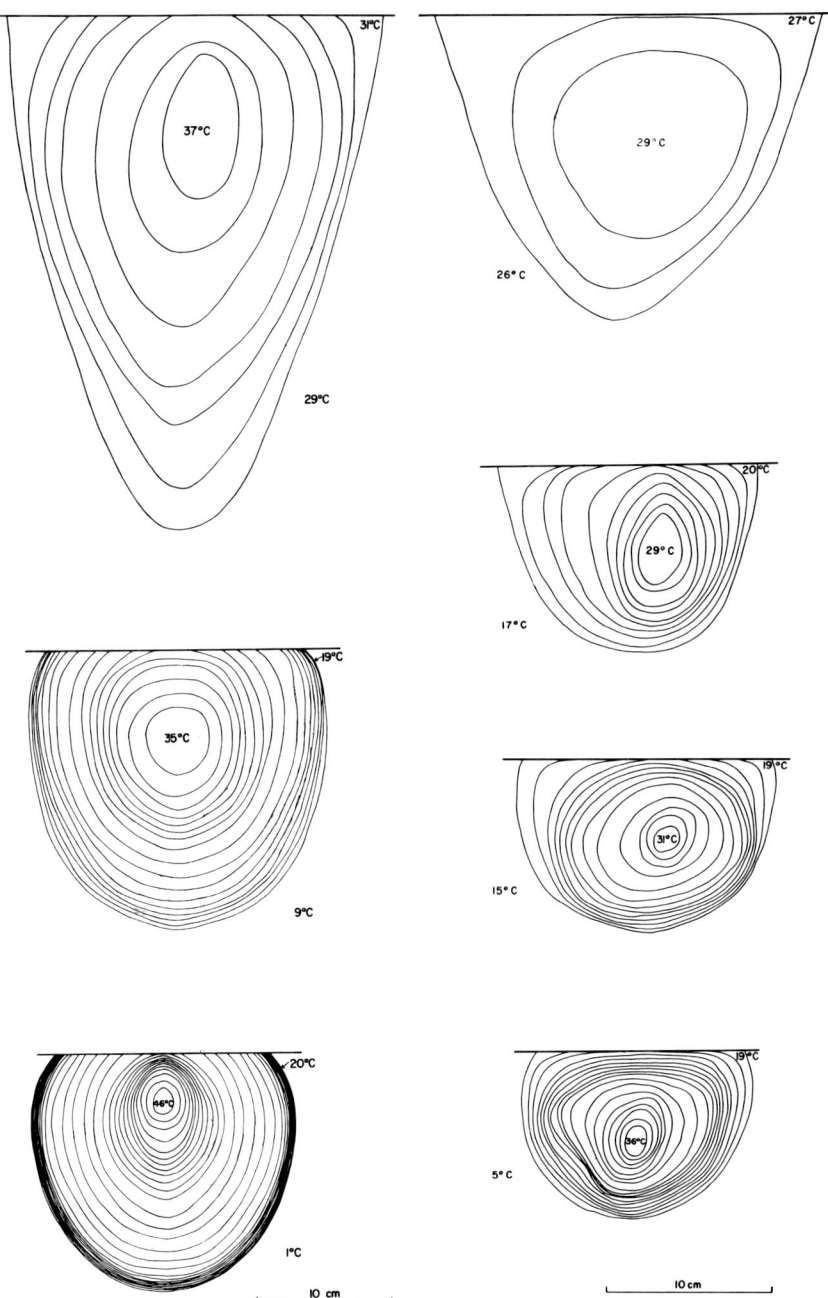

Fig. 1: Swarm shapes, and temperatures (in 1 °C isotherms) of one captive swarm of 16,600 bees (left) at 29 °C, 9 °C and 1 °C (HEINRICH, 1981 b) and of another captive swarm of 5,284 bees at 26 °C, 17 °C, 15 °C, and 5 °C (Heinrich, 1981 a).

1981 a). A vertebrate homeotherm behaves similarly. In a homeothermic vertebrate the thermoregulatory responses are controlled in the hypothalamic region of the brain. Sensory receptors on the organisms' periphery and in the hypothalamus itself monitor body temperature. When body temperatures decline below specific set-points located in the hypothalamus, neural commands are sent to the appropriate organs and these effect a coordinated response to the temperature challenge. Similarly, if a honeybee swarm or colony has bees on the periphery that act as receptors of temperature changes, which convey information about temperature to others that respond appropriately independently of their own needs, then the analogy of the «superorganism» might hold. If on the other hand bees receiving the temperature stimulus on the swarm periphery do not communicate the information to hivemates within the core so that they can respond appropriately to counteract the stimulus, then the «superorganism» model is inappropriate as a tool for promoting a greater understanding of the underlying mechanisms.

In examining the details of a swarm's responses, discrepancies between the vertebrate model and that of the swarm superorganism become apparent. First, a swarm can be divided, and both parts, with or without queen, continue to regulate their temperatures as before (Heinrich, 1981 a) (It is so far not known if the response declines with time.). Secondly, swarm core temperature is often not regulated at one specific set-point. As other workers had observed with winter clusters (Himmer, 1932; Southwick and Mugaas, 1971; Ritter, 1978), I found that temperatures in the core of swarm clusters often tended to increase as air temperature decreased. The swarm periphery was maintained above 13°C, near the bees' chill coma temperature. Although these results do not comform to the model of thermoregulation by vertebrate homeotherms, they nevertheless do not contradict the superorganism model. Indeed, as other workers had interpreted for winter clusters (Himmer, 1932; Simpson, 1961; Southwick and Mugaas, 1971), I also initially attributed the increase in core temperature as the demonstration of a «superorganism» response, where the bees in the center of the swarm attempted to maintain the bees in the swarm periphery above their chill coma temperature by increasing the temperature gradient and therefore the heat flow to the periphery.

I designed experiments to test this model, but the idea that the core bees were responding to the temperatures felt by the mantle bees was not supported (Heinrich, 1981 a). First, at low air temperatures individually marked bees on the mantle remained in place for hours, and days; they did not appear to exchange places with those in the center. Most of the exchange of bees between mantle and core took place at the higher air temperatures. When physical exchange of bees between core and mantle was prevented by a physical barrier (a screen sock), thermoregulation of the swarm remained unaltered. Clearly, there are no «messenger» bees shuttling about between the core and the periphery, telling the bees inside the swarm when to increase their heat production. Secondly, air (with presumptive pheromones) pumped from the center of one swarm located in the warm into one in the cold, and vice versa, failed to alter the thermoregulatory response, indicating that bees were not communicating possible thermal needs by pheromonal messages. Thirdly, perhaps the buzzing of chilled bees conveys information that is heeded by core bees. However, sound recordings from the periphery with a microphone about which the bees were clustered also had no effect on altering swarm core temperature. In summary, the core bees appear to play little active role in swarm thermoregulating and they do not respond to mantle bees.

Individual bees, if given a choice, seek out environmental temperatures near 35°C (Heran, 1952), close to the thoracic temperature they regulate outside the hive while in flight (Heinrich, 1979) while caged in small groups (Cahill and Lustick, 1976), as well as while living in the summer hive (Himmer, 1932; Simpson, 1961). However, in one large

In contrast to the «superorganism» model and in support of the above hypothesis, a series of experiments indicated that the bees on the swarm *periphery* affected core temperature. The mantle bees, by crowding inward when they experience low air temperature contract the swarm cluster. At low air temperatures, the bees were arranged shingle-like over the swarm surface (Fig. 2), as had been described for winter hive clusters (SIMPSON, 1961). The contracted swarms, unlike the expanded ones at air temperatures above 20°C, were apparently solid masses of bees without ventilatory channels (Fig. 4), as the bees from the exterior had crawled into the interior, plugging these channels as air temperature decreased. Heat produced by the core bees was then trapped within the swarm. When I transferred a swarm from 1°C to 16°C I observed an immediate *decline* in core temperature even as mantle temperature increased. It is likely that as the mantle bees became less crowded together as they warmed, air channels were created that caused heat loss from the core. At high air temperatures swarms routinely became elongated and less dense (Figs. 1 and 4). They contained channels for air flow, and air in the channels was cooler than the bees themselves.

If bees on the swarm mantle were responding to low air temperatures appropriately to conserve or release heat from the swarm core, the question remains: what is their stimulus for doing so? The data indicate that they respond, in large part, directly to the temperature they experience, and attempt to maintain their own body temperature at appropriate levels (HEINRICH, 1981 a).

At low air temperatures bees on the swarm mantle can warm themselves by crawling into the air passageways of the swarm, and by crowding their thoraxes close together and shivering when necessary. As the swarm structure becomes very tight, mantle bees are less able to force their way into the interior. When thus «trapped» on the periphery they may be subjected to very low temperatures where they become chilled and less able to shiver and to move, and presumably to replenish their food supplies from colony-mates. When taken to higher air temperatures where they can shiver vigorously (BASTIAN and ESCH,

Fig. 4: Average crowding of bees within swarms calculated from swarm shape (Fig. 1) at different air temperatures. Filled circles = swarm of 5,284 bees. Crosses = swarm of 16,600 bees. Dotted line = a heap of 7,000 dead bees (HEINRICH, unpublished).

1970) they regulate a relatively high thoracic temperature (HEINRICH, 1981 a). Bees from the edge of winter clusters will immediately shiver and produce a large thoracic temperature increase if fed honey (ESCH, 1960). However, by being physically and energetically restricted from maintaining a continuous high body temperature at the edge of the cold bee cluster, the mantle bees are normally reduced to defending the minimum body temperature required to maintain sufficient motor control for crawling, and to remain attached to the swarm.

The core bees, however, may not be total victims of the actions of the mantle bees. If they become too heated by the tightly-packed mantle bees, they may counteract by crawling closer to the swarm periphery. By doing so they loosen the internal swarm cluster, which also cools the other bees that could potenially become overheated. I conclude that a major feature of this model of temperature control of swarms, where individual bees attempt to regulate their own temperature, does not fit the «superorganism» concept. However, presumably some of the bees' thermoregulatory responses may have evolved specifically in the social context, and there may be some features of the thermoregulatory behavior that are unique to the social context that do fit the superorganism concept. These presumed features have not yet been identified.

Thermoregulation of bees in their winter nests is poorly understood. However, like swarms, winter nests lack brood, and similarities in the mechanisms of thermoregulation can be expected.

As air temperature is lowered, the winter bee cluster contracts. As in swarms, during cluster contraction the outermost bees point their heads inward with their thoraxes close together, while their abdomens are exposed to the cold (SIMPSON, 1961). Conversely, as air temperature increases, the bee cluster expands. Obiously both the contraction of the cluster as well as increased heat production could increase the temperature of the core, but the two have never been adequately separated.

HIMMER (1933) observed that the edge of the cluster seldom declined below 10°C, the minimum temperature at which the bees could crawl and still hang onto the cluster. Since bees that cooled below this temperature would be lost from the hive, he speculated that mantle temperature (rather than that in the core of the bee cluster) is the most critical variable that the winter hive cluster tries to maintain.

As I later observed for swarms (HEINRICH, 1981 a), HIMMER (1933) and SOUTHWICK and MUGAAS (1971) also observed the curious behavior that as air temperature fell below 7–8 °C temperature on the cluster mantle remained independent of air temperature, while temperatures in the core often *increased*. (When air temperature increased above 10°C, however, the temperature of the mantle increased in parallel with air temperature). HIMMER and SOUTHWICK and MUGAAS all concluded that the central bees generated heat to keep the bees at the edge at the minimum (defined variously at 8°C to 15°C). HIMMER said «Es handelt sich also um eine typische Wärmeregulierung einer Tiergemeinschaft als biologische Einheit» (It is a matter of a typical thermoregulation of an animal society acting as a unit). In his review SIMPSON (1961) as well as SOUTHWICK and MUGAAS (1971) and SOUTHWICK (1982) in studies of the winter cluster also came to the same conclusion that the bee colony functions as a «superorganism» where «A honeybee cluster thermoregulates so as to maintain a constant surface temperature at low ambient temperature.»

Although the detailed studies performed on swarms have not yet been done on the winter cluster, the data at the present time suggest that the same basic mechanisms apply to both, provided certain important differences are taken into account.

Unlike in swarm clusters, which are temporary aggregations of a few hours or several days, bees in the winter may stay in a cluster for several weeks, moving periodically to feed at new combs with honey and then forming a new cluster. While moving, the swarm

cluster is temporarily loosened or destroyed, potenially cooling all of the bees. Perhaps some of the moving may account for the large variation in temperature (14.5 °C–32 °C) that has been observed in winter hives (HIMMER, 1933. SOUTHWICK and MUGAAS, 1971). Circadian cycles of activity and heat production (KRONENBERG and HELLER, 1982; SOUTHWICK, 1982) also account for variation of hive temperature.

During the periods when bees move at low ambient temperature, there may be great increases in overall hive metabolism (SOUTHWICK, 1982). However, temporary increases of metabolism and food consumption are to be expected as many individuals, without the benefit of the cluster, are each attempting to regulate their own body temperature by increasing their rate of heat production (ALLEN, 1959; ESCH, 1960; CAHILL and LUSTICK, 1976). The metabolism of the tightly contracted winter cluster, in contrast, increases only slightly, even at sub-zero temperatures, and the metabolic rate of these winter clusters (SOUTHWICK, 1982) differs little from that obeserved in resting swarm clusters (HEINRICH, 1981 a). As reviewed by SIMPSON (1961), records of the amounts of food consumed by colonies in winter usually fail to show any definite correlation with outside temperature. As I have described for swarms, apparently much of the thermoregulatory response can therefore be explained by individuals crowding tightly together, trapping heat within the cluster.

One major difference between swarms and winter clusters, however, concerns the physiology of the individual bees. Following prolonged exposure to cold, bees acclimate (HERAN, 1952). Bees from the winter nest in temperature-preference tests in a temperature gradient, choose temperatures averaging 32.8 °C but as low as 28 °C, while summer bees choose temperatures near 35–38 °C (HERAN, 1952). Furthermore, winter bees have lower chill-coma temperatures than summer bees (FREE and SPENCER-BOOTH, 1960). Presumably these differences could alone account for both the lower core and mantle temperatures observed between winter hive clusters and summer swarms (Fig. 5).

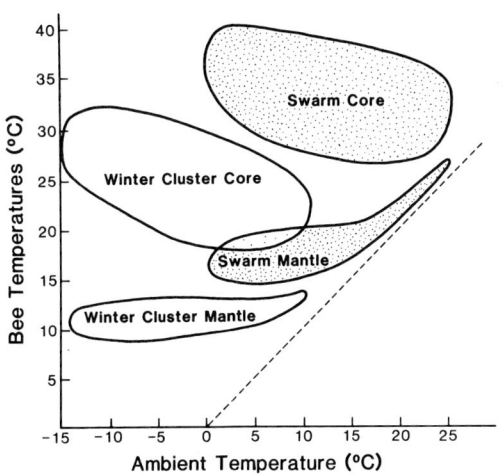

Fig. 5: Swarm and winter cluster temperatures as a function of air temperature. The cloud diagrams exclude the extremes but enclose at least 80 % of the observed temperatures. Data was derived from the following sources: Swarms (HEINRICH, 1981 a), winter cluster cores (SOUTHWICK and MUGAAS, 1971), winter cluster mantle (interpreted from review by SIMPSON, 1961).

3 «Superorganisms» and keeping cool

Honeybees not only elevate nest temperature at low air temperatures, they also prevent overheating of the nest at high ambient temperatures (LINDAUER, 1954; LENSKY, 1964). The classic experiments by LINDAUER (1954) of honeybee colonies subjected to high temperatures suggest that nest cooling involves a highly coordinated social response. In part, the response is a modification of the bee's food storage behavior. Additionally, the thermoregulatory behavior could involve modifications of responses that aid the individuals to regulate their own body temperature, that secondarily affects hive temperature.

As a first response to high hive temperature, bees clustered upon the combs disperse. If they are not sufficiently cooled by dispersing they may leave the hive. Bees that leave the colony presumably lower their own body temperature, but in so doing they also provide space within, so that air circulation can occur and the hive can cool. Expansion of winter clusters or swarms at elevated temperatures has the same effect.

LINDAUER (1954) observed further that bees began to fan and carry in water that evaporated and cooled the hive when it continued to be heat-stressed. As hive temperatures increased and the need for water for evaporative cooling increased, the foragers switched from collecting concentrated nectar to dilute nectar or to pure water. However, the switsch-over did not occur because the water carriers were aware of the need of water for temperature regulation within the hive. Rather, it occurred because other bees eagerly accepted the dilute nectar or water being brought even at the entrance of the colony, while those carrying concentrated nectar could not unload their cargo and consequently did not recruit. It cannot be presumed, however, that the bees were aware of the hive's needs and behaved accordingly. The bees from the nest interior that accepted the water regurgitated it and evaporated it from droplets on their extruded mouthparts (LINDAUER, 1954), which we now know to be the primary mechanism whereby individual bees prevent overheating of their own body temperature (HEINRICH, 1980). Evaporative cooling within the hive would act to reduce hive temperature, regardless of whether it occurs primarily off the comb, or from the individual bees. Thus, bees that accept water to cool themselves would also be acting to regulate hive temperature. So far it is not known if cool bees in a hot hive are willing to accept water for the hive, or if hot bees in a cool hive accept water.

In addition to individual bees holding and evaporating fluid, LINDAUER (1954) observed the bees that received the water from water carriers to regurgitate onto the upper sides of the honeycombs, in the same way that dilute nectar is deposited so that it may be concentrated to become honey. Deposition of pure water cannot be accounted for on the basis of individual cooling, but the bees may not know what else to do with liquids. However, since the deposition of water in combs has taken on the function of cooling the hive, rather than the individual bee, it has assumed social significance. The behavior now aids the hive directly, rather than indirectly through what aids the individual hive members.

Temperature regulation of the hive also involves a third response – fanning. Bees fan after bringing dilute nectar or water into the hive possibly in response to high humidity. The bees also fan in response to other noxious stimuli, such as smoke, excessive CO_2, and invasions of small ants (personal observation).Whether or not they respond by fanning to high temperature (NEUHAUS and WOHLGEMUTH, 1960), as such, is not clear. However, regardless of the various stimuli involved that induce fanning, the behavior affects hive temperature. Are there possibly individualistic behaviors that may have originally formed the basis for the hive's over-all response, and to what extent do these behaviors still form the basis of this overall response?

Bees aligning themselves in chains to create unidirectional air flow (NEUHAUS and WOIILGEMUTH, 1960), appear to show an integrated colony response for optimal cooling of the hive. However, they might also be attempting to cool themselves, without reference to hive needs. Several kinds of small-bodied insects, such as butterflies (HEINRICH, 1972), syrphid flies (HEINRICH and PANTLE, 1975), and cicindelid beetles (KENNETH R. MORGAN, personal communication), fly when heat-stressed, thereby cooling themselves convectively. A bee fanning with its wings also necessarily drives air over itself for cooling. Like an individual insect seeking a drafty place, a second bee could enhance its own cooling by standing in the slip-stream of a second, etc. As a result, the bees would align themselves in chains and unidirectional flow would automatically be created, and cooling of the hive would be optimized. If nest fanning evolved from individuals trying to cool themselves one might expect that the hottest bees would fan first, and that they would initially align themselves outside the nest, pushing cool air over themselves and into it, rather than drawing warm air out of the hive and over themselves.

Many observations indicate that bees that fan do not respond to hive temperature, *per se*. NEUHAUS and WOHLGEMUTH (1960) observed that foragers, particularly those carrying pollen, often fanned before entering the hive. The temperature of the air in the vicinity of the antennae bearing the thermoreceptors (HERAN, 1952) is of no effect in stimulating fanning (NEUHAUS and WOHLGEMUTH, 1960). The body temperature of the bees, however, may be relevant. At least in the Arizona desert, most of the pollen carriers returning to the hive have empty honeycrops and, unlike nectar carriers, they almost never extruded liquid from their mouthparts (PAUL D. COOPER, personal communication). The pollen foragers had much higher thoracic temperatures (average = 43°C). Like NEUHAUS and WOHLGEMUTH (1960), Cooper reports that the pollen carriers «almost always stop and fan upon alighting before entering the hive,» drawing air from the outside of the hive to the inside. Since the fanners presumably had no knowledge of temperature within the hive, it is difficult to rationalize their behavior except in terms of response to their own body temperature. The returning pollen foragers only fanned for short durations. It would be of great interest to know what their body temperatures were when they stopped fanning. Whether or not the bee's fanning behavior is related to individual thermoregulation is so far unexamined. However, if the bees indeed fan to affect their own body temperature, it is significant that through their sociality, they have evolved to do it primarily in the vicinity of the hive, where it immediately benefits colony mates as well.

4 The effect of brood

Of major impact on colony thermoregulation is the presence of brood. The brood is incapable of regulating its own temperature (HIMMER, 1933) and it is sensitive to changes in temperature. In the summer nest the brood nest is maintained at 35°C ± 0.5°C (SIMPSON, 1961). Temperatures higher than 36°C caused developmental abnormalities, principally of the wings (HIMMER, 1933). How does the regulation of brood temperature relate to the model of bees acting primarily to affect their own body temperature? Have responses evolved to modify or channel the worker's «selfish» behavior so that the colony benefits?

Within a colony of tens of thousands of individuals, each is capable of shivering to produce heat (BASTIAN and ESCH, 1970). The heat produced as a by-product of the normal activity and resting metabolism of many individuals, and the colony-wide heating that results, frees the individuals for numerous tasks at the same time that the brood is deriving the benefit of the bees' metabolic heat. In order to heat the brood the workers need only remain in the vicinity of it. Thus, it is possible that the temperature control of brood could be explained in terms of individuals regulating their own body temperature, provided they did it precisely enough with the added behavioral response that the bees are *attracted* to the brood so that they stay in its vicinity sufficiently long to be cooled or heated by it, so that they can respond if temperature between the two differ.

Bees that are not in flight not only attempt to regulate their own thoracic temperature near 35°C by adjusting their rate of heat production (CAHILL and LUSTICK, 1976) but they also choose temperatures near 35°C in a temperature gradient (HERAN, 1952). Therefore, heat produced by the brood and the bees upon it should provide additional incentive for bees to crowd together upon the brood at low air temperatures, amplifying attraction based on pheremonal stimuli. Bees already attracted and producing heat would provide nuclei for the attraction of still more bees seeking warmth.

It has previously been thought that there were major differences between «winter» and «summer» thermoregulation (SIMPSON, 1961). It is likely, however, that the differences observed reflect primarily the presence or absence of brood and that without brood, clusters of summer bees behave similarly to those of winter (RITTER, 1978). Brood, indeed, has a strong attraction to the worker bees (KOENIGER, 1978), and the shifting of the worker force to areas containing brood should predictably have a major effect on heat distribution within the hive. It would be of interest to know if bees are more attracted to warm brood where they could warm themselves, or to cold brood where they must shiver to keep themselves warm.

The inter-relationships between the bees' crowding upon the brood, regulating their own body temperature, and warming of the brood and stabilizing its temperature have so far not been elucidated. It remains unclear if the bees produce heat only to maintain their own body temperature elevated, or to elevate the temperature of the brood. Circumstantial evidence suggests that although the bees may act to regulate their own body temperature, they also respond specifically to brood temperature, *per se*. For example, the bees have numerous thermo-receptors on their antennae (HERAN, 1952), which could serve to monitor brood temperature but which are unlikely to be involved in monitoring their own body temperature. In order to determine if bees respond to brood temperature, as such, KRONENBERG and HELLER (1982) allowed bees to build comb around a water-cooled device in order to control brood temperature, and found that lowering of brood temperature resulted in crowding of the bees upon the comb and in elevation of the colony's metabolic rate. This result suggests but does not prove that the bees regulate brood temperature as such, rather than merely attempting to regulate their own body temperature. As already mentioned, it is difficult to experimentally separate brood from body temperature, since experimental reductions of temperature of the brood upon which the bees are located would affect the bees upon the brood as well.

5 Conclusion

Thermorgulation of honeybee colonies involves many responses. Many if not most of these responses can be understood, in part, in terms of the individual bees regulating their own body temperatures. This perspective offers a single model to account for thermoregulation of not only winter and summer nests, which were previously thought to be qualitatively different, but also of swarms. Responses of individuals acting for their own survival were presumably selected because they also enhanced colony survival and reproduction. Modifications of these responses that aided the colony as a whole could theoretically be superimposed, so that the «superorganism» concept might apply in varying degrees to different functions.

The superorganism concept is obviously highly useful in understanding many aspects of honeybee colony organization. However, with respect to thermoregulation, the superorganism concept is a tool that applies only to a limited extent in framing questions on colony mechanisms. The concept that the individuals interact on the basis of their own thermoregulatory needs is a tool that has so far been applied only to a limited extent, and it promises to provide new insights. Finally, I speculate that regulation of brood temperature evolved as a by-product of individual temperature regulation. In a large social insect colony with thousands of metabolically active individuals, heat is produced that inevitably increases the temperature in the environs of the brood. As reasoned elsewhere for individual thermoregulation (Heinrich, 1977) the brood must evolve to specialize its metabolic functions near the elevated temperature it normally experiences.

Acknowledgements

Writing of this paper was supported by NSF grant BSR-8116662. I thank the Akademie der Wissenschaften und Literatur of Mainz for sponsoring the symposium. I am also grateful to Margaret Heinrich and Dr. Joan Herbers reading drafts of the manuscript and making many helpful comments and criticisms.

References

Allen, M. D. (1955): Respiration rates of worker honeybees of different ages at different temperatures. J. Exp. Biol. *36*, 92–101.

Bastian, J. and Esch, H. (1970): The nervous control of the indirect flight muscle of the honeybee. Z. vergl. Physiol. *67*, 307–342.

Büdel, A. (1958): Ein Beispiel der Temperaturverteilung in der Bienentraube. Z. Bienenforsch. *4*, 63–66.

Cahill, K. and Lustick, S. (1976): Oxygen consumption and thermoregulation in Apis mellifera workers and drones. Comp. Biochem. Physiol. *55A*, 355–357.

Esch, H. (1960): Über die Körpertemperaturen und den Wärmehaushalt von Apis mellifera. Z. vergl. Physiol. *43*, 305–335.

Free, J. B. and Spencer-Both. (1958): Observations on the temperature regulation and food consumption of honeybees *(Apis mellifera)*. J. Exp. Biol. *35*, 930–937.

Free, J.B. and Spencer-Booth, H.Y. (1960): Chill-coma and cold death temperatures of Apis mellifera. Ent. Exp. and Appl. *3*, 222–230.

Heinrich, B. (1972): Thoracic temperature of butterflies in the field near the equator. Comp. Biochem. Physiol. *43 A*, 459–467.

– (1977): Why have some animals evolved to regulate a high body temperature? Amer. Natur. *111*, 623–640.

– (1979):Thermoregulation of African and European honeybees during foraging, attack, and hive exits and returns. J. Exp. Biol. *80*, 217–229.

– (1980): Mechanisms of body temperature regulation in honeybees, Apis mellifera. I. Regulation of head temperature. J. Exp. Biol. *85*, 61–87.

– (1981 a): The mechanisms and energetics of honeybee swarm temperature regulation. J. Exp. Biol. *91*, 25–55.

– (1981 b): Energetics of honeybee swarm thermoregulation. Science *212*, 565–566.

– and Pantle, C. (1975): Thermoregulation in small flies (Syrphus sp.): Basking and shivering. J. Exp. Biol. *62*, 599–610.

Heran, H. (1952): Untersuchungen über den Temperatursinn der Honigbiene *(Apis mellifica)* unter besonderer Berücksichtigung der Wahrnehmung strahlender Wärme. Z. vergl. Physiol. *34*, 179–206.

Himmer, A. (1932): Die Temperaturverhältnisse bei den sozialen Hymenopteren. Biol. Rev. 7, 224–253.

Koeniger, N. (1978): Das Wärmen der Brut bei der Honigbiene (Apis mellifera L.) Apidologie 9, 305–320.

Kronenberg, F. and Heller, H. C. (1982): Colonial thermoregulation in honeybees (Apis mellifera). J. Comp. Physiol. 148, 65–76.

Lensky, Y. (1964): Comportement d'une colonie d'abeilles a des temperatures extremes. J. Ins. Physiol. 10, 1–12.

Lindauer, M. (1954): Temperaturregulierung und Wasserhaushalt im Bienenstaat. Z. vergl. Physiol. 36, 391–432.

Neuhaus, W. and Wohlgemuth, R. (1960): Über das Fächeln der Bienen und dessen Verhältnis zum Fliegen. Z. vergl. Physiol. 43, 615–641.

Ritter, W. (1978): Der Einfluß der Brut auf die Änderung der Wärmebildung in Bienenvölkern (Apis mellifera carnica). Verh. Dtsch. Zool. Ges. 220, Gustav Fischer Verlag, Stuttgart, 1978.

Simpson, J. (1961): Nest climate regulation in honeybee colonies. Science 133, 1327–1333.

Southwick, E. E. (1982): Metabolic energy of intact honeybee colonies. Comp. Biochem. Physiol. 71 A, 277–281.

– and J. N. Mugaas. (1971): A hypothetical homeotherm: The honeybee hive. Comp. Biochem. Physiol. 40 A, 935–944.

Fortschritte der Zoologie, Bd. 31 · Hölldobler/Lindauer (Hrsg.): Experimental Behavioral Ecology
G. Fischer Verlag · Stuttgart · New York · 1985

Feeding behaviour of nurse bees, larval food composition and caste differentiation in the honey bee *(Apis mellifera L.)*

J. Beetsma[1]

Laboratory of Entomology, Agricultural University, Wageningen, Netherlands

Jan de Wilde was scheduled to present a paper on «Problems and Issues in the Study of Caste Development in Social Insects». We were all shocked and deeply saddened when we learned of the sudden death of Professor de Wilde, only two weeks before the commencement of this conference.

The editors are grateful to Dr. Beetsma who, on very short notice, agreed to come to Mainz and present to us the latest findings on caste differentiation in honey bees.

1 Introduction

Caste development in social insects is induced by extrinsic factors. Climatic factors and consequently the availability of food outside the colony affect the conditions within the colony that ultimately regulate the development of castes.

In the social Hymenoptera both trophogenic factors and the activity of the corpora allata play an important role in caste development (de Wilde and Beetsma, 1982).

The most detailed understanding of caste differentiation concerns the honey bee.

According to de Wilde (1975) the female castes of the honeybee can be considered as «ecomorphs». Genetically identical individuals are induced by environmental factors to develop into either queens or workers. «The intricate programmes of development lie in readiness from the very beginning of embryonic development, and need only to be «switched on» by one or a combination of extrinsic factors» (de Wilde, 1976).

The role of juvenile hormone in the process of caste differentiation has been demonstrated by Wirtz and Beetsma (1972), Wirtz (1973), Goewie and Beetsma (1976), Goewie (1978) and Ebert (1978).

Juvenile hormone is considered to act as a «mediator» between the nutritional environment of the larva and the differentiation of caste characteristics.

Concerning the mechanism different hypotheses have been put forward (see review by Beetsma, 1979).

The activity of the corpora allata (CA) in younger larvae seems not to be regulated by the medial neurosecretory cells (MNSC) in the brain. Both Goewie (1978) and Rembold and Ulrich (1982) found undifferentiated MNSC in these larvae and therefore they suggest that the activity of the CA is regulated by another system.

---

[1] Dedicated to the memory of my scientific-«father» Jan de Wilde.

Different results were obtained concerning the moment of the initial activity of the MNSC in older larvae of both castes. Rembold and Ulirch (1982) found that outgrowth of axons and incorporation of ^{3}H-uridine into RNA of the MNSC is delayed by one larval instar in worker larvae when compared to queen larvae. Therefore they suggest an earlier change from unknown system to the MNSC to regulate the activity of the CA in queen larvae.

Whereas Rembold and Ulrich (1982) found stainable neurosecretory granules in the MNSC only in the last instar queen larvae, Goewie (1978) demonstrated these granules already in 3-day-old larvae, irrespective of the transfer or non-transfer of larvae into queen cells.

In addition Goewie (1978) found considerable amounts of neurosecretory material in the CA-innervating axons from the MNSC only at the end of larval development. Therefore he suggested that the CA activity is inhibited by the MNSC.

2 Production of larval food

In the honeybee colony, queens and workers can be reared simultaneously both in the presence and in the absence of the queen. Queen rearing is released by the partial or complete absence of queen pheromones (Butler, 1954). Secondary releasers of this specific behaviour in nurse bees may be the shape, size and orientation of the queen cell and signals emanating from the larva. Until recently the discrimination between the nurse bees feeding queen and/or worker larvae was based on age of the bees and composition of larval food in relation to the content of the mandibular and hypopharyngeal glands of the bees.

Now a new approach of the problem has become possible by measuring the activity of the hypopharyngeal (HP) glands.

Brouwers (1983) developed a method to measure the rate of incorporation of C^{14}-leucine into the proteins of extirpated HP glands *in vitro*. Brouwers (1983) compared the size, protein content and activity of HP glands of bees of different ages with those of known nurse bees, collected from an observation hive.

It appeared that the activity of full-grown HP glands of summerbees showed conspicuous variation. In only one-third of these bees did the activity reach a level as found in the HP glands of bees collected when depositing food in a brood cell (> 800p.mol./h). Recent data indicate that the average activity of HP glands differs between nurse bees feeding queen and worker larvae.

3 Frequency and length of feedings

Both Brouwers (Wageningen) and Ebert (Würzburg) have studied the feeding behaviour of nurse bees in worker cells. In addition Brouwers (in preparation) recorded the offering of food in queen cells. Observations could be carried out by using video apparatus. The video camera was provided with a special recording tube that could be used at low intensities of red light. Using a time-lapse tape recorder the behaviour of the nurse bees could be recorded continuously over several days.

The frequency and length of feedings in queen and worker cells are completely different. Whereas in queen cells a bee offered food for a short time (< 50 seconds) about every five minutes throughout the whole period of larval development, in worker cells the frequency and duration of offering of food changed with the age of the larva.

In worker larvae after the offering of food at the moment of hatching it sometimes took 12 hours before the larva received food again. Older larvae were fed 1–2 times per hour. The length of feedings generally increased with the age of the larva (50 to 250 seconds), but after the age of about 70 hours short feedings (< 50 seconds) occurred in addition.

At this moment we can only guess about differences in the quality of food offered within a short or a long period. On the one hand it is obvious that secondary releasing factors of feeding behaviour present in the cell play a role. On the other hand, however, the physiological condition of the nurse bees should be considered as well.

4 Compositon of larval food

To obtain a complete view of the course of changes in composition of the food of the larvae of both castes during their development, BROUWERS (in preparation) collected food samples at intervals of 12 hours and measured the content of some major components on a dry weight basis.

Among other differences he found a total sugar content of about 20 % in royal jelly and about 15 % in worker jelly collected from cells containing 1–3 day old larvae.

Very conspicuous, however, were the differences in the glucose–fructose ratio between royal jelly and worker jelly (BROUWERS, in press).

The glucose-fructose ratio of royal jelly was at the first day of larval development about 1.7, decreased slowly with increasing age of the larvae, but remained higher than 1.

In worker jelly, however, this ratio started at a level of about 1.3, decreased until the larval age of about 60 hours and remained more or less constant at a level of about 0.7.

The glucose-fructose ratio in the abundant food of the small number of larvae in the initital brood nest of a hived swarm is exceptionally low during the first few days.

It is suggested that glucose stimulates and fructose inhibits the rate of food consumption by the larva, or alternatively that glucose, as opposed to fructose, is readily metabolized.

When the glucose-fructose ratio is high, increased larval growth is only realized when large amounts of food are offered to the larva, as is the case in the queen cell.

References

Beetsma, J. (1979): The process of queen-worker differentiation in the honeybee. Bee Wld. *60* (1), 24–39.

Brouwers, E. V. M. (1982): Measurements of hypopharyngeal gland activity in the honeybee. J. apic. Res. *21* (4), 193–198.

Brouwers, E. V. M. (in press): The glucose-fructose ratio in the food of the honeybee larva. J. apic. Res.

Butler, C. G. (1954): The importance of «queen substance» in the life of a honeybee colony. Bee Wld. *35*, 169–176.

Ebert, R. (1978): Die Bedeutung der Schwerkraft bei der longitudinalen Orientierung der weiblichen Honigbienenlarve (Apis mellifera L.) und deren Beeinflussung durch hormonale Faktoren. Ph. D. Thesis, University of Würzburg.

Goewie, E. A. (1978): Regulation of caste differentiation in the honeybee (Apis mellifera L.). Meded. Landb. Hogesch. Wageningen *78* (15), 76 pp. Thesis.

Goewie, E. A. and Beetsma, J. (1976): Induction of caste differentiation in the honeybee (Apis mellifera L.) after topical application of JH-III. Proc. K. Ned. Akad. Wet. C79 (5), 466–469.

Rembold, H. and Ulrich, G. (1982): Modulation of neurosecretion during caste determination in Apis mellifera larvae. pp. 370–374 from the biology of social insects (Proc. IXth. Congr. I. U. S. S. I., Boulder, August 1982) ed. M. D. Breed, C. D. Michener and H. E. Evans. Westview Press, Boulder, Colorado.

Wilde, J. de (1975): An endorcrine view of metamorphosis, polymorphism and diapause in insects. Am. Zool. *15*, 13–27.

Wilde, J. de (1976): Juvenile hormone and caste differentiation in the honeybee (Apis mellifera L.) p. p. 5–20 from Phase and caste determination in insects ed. M. Lüscher Oxford & New York, Pergamon Press.

Wilde, J. and Beetsma, J. (1982): The physiology of caste development in social insects. Advances in Ins. Physiol. *16*, 167–246.

Wirtz, P. (1973): Differentiation in the honeybee larva. Meded. Landb. Hogesch. Wageningen *73* (5), 155 pp. Thesis.

Wirtz, P. and Beetsma, J. (1972): Induction of caste differentiation in the honeybee (Apis mellifera L.) by juvenile hormone. Ent. exp. appl. *15*, 517–520.

Fortschritte der Zoologie, Bd. 31 · Hölldobler/Lindauer (Hrsg.): Experimental-Behavioral Ecology
G. Fischer Verlag · Stuttgart · New York · 1985

Individual and family recognition in subsocial arthropods, in particular in the desert isopod *Hemilepistus reaumuri*

K. E. LINSENMAIR

Zoologisches Institut der Universität Würzburg, F. R. Germany

Abstract

Individual recognition in the non-eusocial arthropods is, according to our present knowledge, predominantly found in the frame of permanent or temporary monogamy. In some cases, e. g. in stomatopods and possibly other marine crustaceans too, individual recognition may serve to allow identification of (i) individuals within dominance hierarchies or (ii) neighbours in territorial species thus helping to avoid the repetition of unnecessary and costly fights. Kin recognition is experimentally proven only in some isopod species (genera *Hemilepistus* and *Porcellio*) and in the primitive cockroach (termite?) *Cryptocercus*. The «signatures» or «discriminators» used in the arthropods are chemical. It is assumed that the identifying substances are mainly genetically determined and in this paper I shall discuss possible evolutionary origins. The main part of this account is devoted to the presentation of some aspects of the highly developed individual and kin identification and recognition system in the desert isopod *Hemilepistus reaumuri* – a pure monogamous species in which pairs together with their progeny form strictly exclusive family units. Amongst other things problems of (i) mate choice, (ii) learning to recognize a partner, (iii) avoiding the unadaptive familiarization with aliens are treated. Monogamy under present conditions is for both sexes the only suitable way of maximizing reproductive success; an extremely strong selection pressure must act against every attempt to abandon monogamy under the given ecological conditions. The family «badges» which are certainly always blends of different discriminator substances are extremely variable. This variability is mainly due to genetical differences and is not environmentally caused. It is to be expected that intra-family variability exists in respect of the production of discriminator substances. Since the common badge of a family is the result of exchanging and mixing individual substances, and since the chemical nature of these discriminators requires direct body contacts in order to acquire those substances which an individual does not produce itself, problems must arise with molting. These difficulties do indeed exist and they are aggravated by the fact that individuals may produce substances which do not show up in the common family badge. An efficient learning capability on the one hand and the use of inhibiting properties of newly molted isopods help to solve these problems. In the final discussion three questions are posed and – partly at least – answered; (i) why are families so strictly exclusive, (ii) how many discriminator substances have to be produced to provide a variability allowing families to remain exclusive under extreme conditions of very high population densities, (iii) what is the structure of the family badge and what does an individual have to learn apart from the badge in order not to mistake a family member for an alien or vice versa.

1 Introduction

Before animals can reproduce they have to come to numerous decisions requiring special recognition and classification performances. They have to discern self from non-self, their species from others and nearly always different categories within their species: females, males, young etc. Additionally they often have to distinguish between sub-categories, e. g. females in different phases of their reproductive cycle or young of different ages. Under special conditions, still more sophisticated capabilities have been selected, those for individual and for kin recognition. These are the topic of my account, – as far as arthropods are concerned – with the exception of the eusocial species (cf. Michener 1985, this Vol.)
Only a very few species within the huge number of non-eusocial arthropod species are known to possess either or both of these abilities, and in most of these few cases our knowledge is still very limited. Therefore I shall only mention a few studies, partly to exemplify which environmental conditions may favour the selection of such capabilities and which their probable present adaptive value is. I shall mainly concentrate on some selected features of the highly developed mechanisms of identification (sensu Beecher 1982) and recognition of individuals and kin in the desert isopod *Hemilepistus reaumuri* (Linsenmair and Linsenmair 1971, Linsenmair 1972, 1975, 1979, 1984). The first aspect, that of the individual's or kin's identifying cues, will be dealt with predominantly, but not exclusively, since the second aspect, the decoding of the signals provided by individuals or kingroup members about their identity is comprehensively treated and reviewed in this volume by Shermann and Holmes.
Individual recognition requires that, independent of the site of encounter, a single individual can be sorted out of a larger homogeneous group of conspecifics by means of reliable identifying characteristics and that this individual is treated in a way which pre-supposes earlier experience with it. As far as kin specific recognition is concerned, an analogous definition proves to be true, omitting the final restriction: kin can in some species be recognized without previous direct contact (e. g. Blaustein and O'Hara 1981, 1982; Buckle and Greenberg 1981; Greenberg 1979; Holmes and Sherman 1982, 1983; Sherman and Holmes, this Vol.; Waldmann 1981; Wu et al 1980).

2 Individual and kin identification and recognition in non-eusocial arthropods

As far as we know, individual «signature» systems (Beecher 1982) and recognition mechanisms in the group alluded to are found mostly in connection with temporary or permanent monogamy. Following Wickler and Seibt (1981) a distinction is made between a «mate guarding» monogamy and a «shared duty» monogamy.

2.1 Individual identification and recognition of mates in monogamous species

In the *mate guarding monogamy* of the clown shrimp *Hymenocera picta* (Seibt 1974, 1980; Seibt and Wickler 1979; Wickler and Seibt 1981) males seem to have consider-able difficulties in finding unpaired females. Once a male has found a suitable mate it seems to pay him to stay with his iteroparous female, most probably because leaving her and searching for a new one would on average be more costly in terms of time expenditure and/or reduction of his probability to survive. The attachment in this case is asymmetric with males being strongly attached to the partner and females much less so. The adaptive value for a male of recognizing his female individually is presumably to be seen in protection against confusion; mistaking a new female for the former one – if this female is still alive and still offers good reproductive prospects – would too often result in uncompensated time losses. The question of why females recognize their male partners too is more difficult to answer, and until now there seems to have been no satisfactory hypothesis to account for this fact. The individual recognition cues are chemical characteristics and are – contrary to conditions in many other species – effective over long distances. Nothing is known about the chemical nature of the compounds used. The cleaner shrimp *Stenopus hispidus* lives in pairs too, the partners being capable of individual recognition (JOHNSON 1977). Possibly the adaptive value of this capability is the same as in the *Hymenocera* mentioned above, but this assumption is not yet proven.

In the *shared duty monogamy* which may originate from a mate guarding monogamy (as I assume has been the case in *Hemilepistus*, cf. LINSENMAIR 1984) resources vital for reproduction cannot – under present ecological conditions – be secured or handled by one individual alone; the cooperation of at least two conspecifics is necessary. In some cases, as in the carrion beetle *Necrophorus vespilloides* (PUKOWSKI 1933), the essential resource must not be left (and has only to be defended against conspecific competitors for a short period). If under such circumstances each partner wards off only consexual rivals – a feature not only of *Neocrophorus* but also of the snapping shrimp *Alpheus ornatus* (KNOWLTON 1980) – a monogamous social and mating system may result although partners do not recognize each other individually. In cases such as that of *Hemilepistus*, where the vital burrow has to be defended for a very extended period alternately by one pair partner against competitors of both sexes (also during periods of temporary absence of the mate from the den) an anonymous relation of the partners cannot suffice. Mutual individual recognition of mates is then a necessary precondition for securing this resource reliably.

Besides *Hemilepistus, Cryptocercus*, which was formerly considered a primitive cockroach but is more probably a very primitive termite, seems to be the only other non-eusocial arthropod to have reached a level of social evolution which in some respects is comparable to that of the desert isopod *Hemilepistus* (SEELINGER and SEELINGER 1983). *Cryptocercus punctulatus* clearly lives in monogamous pairs or in closed family communities. The animals dwell in the rotten wood of fallen logs and by feeding on the wood they construct in time rather complicated burrows consisting of a number of chambers connected by galleries. In laboratory experiments G. and U. SEELINGER could demonstrate that these burrows are defended – mainly by the adult pair – against alien conspecifics and they assume that they possibly also deter predators (of the young). Foreign adult or juvenile roaches can be discerned from the mate and from the pair's own young – by unknown chemical identifying substances. The question of the adaptive value of the monogamous pair formation in *Cryptocercus* has to be considered still open. One adult alone could probably fulfill all tasks but its chance of surviving the extremely long time of at least 3, possibly 5, years of broodcaring could be too low.

2.2 Individual recognition and rank orders

In many vertebrates rank orders and mutually accepted territory borders are an outcome of aggressive encounters between conspecifics. By individual recognition members of a rank order or «dear neighbours» can avoid repeating already settled disputes. CALDWELL

(1979) has proved that the mantis shrimp *Gonodactylus festai* can potentially learn to recognize conspecifics individually. These highly aggressive stomatopods equipped with potentially lethal weapons fight for scarce holes. Possibly they recognize their neighbours, they certainly recognize and avoid for some time those individuals which have defeated them in a previous battle. Since there is a high risk of severe injuries in fights, the adaptive value of the identification and recognition of individuals in this respect is obvious.

2.3 Kin recognition

Kin recognition, very common in mammals, birds and the eusocial Hymenoptera (cf. e. g. the relevant articles in this Vol.), is experimentally proven in the non-eusocial arthropods besides *Hemilepistus* (see below) and one subsocial Canarian *Porcellio* species (Linsenmair 1984 and unpubl.) only in *Cryptocercus* (Seelinger and Seelinger 1983). In the latter, trophallaxis with symbiont transfer is of paramount importance for larvae during the first two instars, i. e. during the first year of their life. Which valuable advantages the family offers its members in the following 2–4 years, remains at the moment a matter of speculation; possibly it is defense of the adults against predators on the young.

2.4 Nature and origin of the individual – or kin-specific signatures

Individual and kin recognition in the group of arthropods discussed here seems always to be mediated by chemical means. (The assumption of Vannini and Gherardi (1981) that the crab *Potamon fluviatile* might use optical cues to identify conspecific individuals was deduced from results gained under very artificial conditions; confirmation of these results by experiments performed under more natural conditions is required.)

With the exception of *Hemilepistus* we know hardly anything about the chemical properties of the substances used, literally nothing about their degree of variability and their origin. Assuming that these substances are chiefly genetically determined (and not predominantly acquired from the surroundings) which is known to be the case in *Hemilepistus* and which is not improbable in all other species mentioned, the question arises of what the initial variability has been on which selection could have started to work. I can distinguish two main «substrates».

1) Due to variability in their enzymatic equipment, members of a population always differ to some extent in their metabolism. If a repeatedly used vital resource, e. g. a burrow, has to be left temporarily and has to be found again under difficult conditions under which external cues for (i) reorientation to the animal's own (ii) and differentiation between its own and an alien burrow are unreliable or lacking, individual variability in metabolic endproducts (showing up in secretions, faeces and urine, for instance) which had no direct previous value could gain great importance by offering themselves as cheap labels. If those substances were used we could expect a great deal of preadaptation on the decoding side of the system. Many of these compounds could already have gained sign character in connection with e. g. food choice (preference and avoidance) at earlier times. (Furthermore the normally highly developed capacity in arthropods to acquire and process chemical information will always allow the identification of many compounds with no previous biological significance.) Primitive bees and wasps (Steinmann 1973, 1976) and isopods (*Porcellio* spec., Linsenmair 1979) mark their burrow entrances individually, enabling them to find their burrow even under difficult conditions of high dwelling densities. In both groups this could have been a basis for the further development of a signature system.

2) The species-specific signals could represent the other possible starting point (cf. GREENBERG 1979). In order – for example – to find the optimum balance between out-breeding and inbreeding, those individuals will be favoured which are able to use the variability always present within the species-specific features to learn what their near relatives are like, and then, in choosing a mate, to avoid conspecifics which are too similar or too different from the relatives (e. g. BATESON 1980, 1982, 1983). This does not require the ability for individual recognition but to reach it from this level should pose no very difficult evolutionary problems.

3 Individual- and family-specific recognition in the desert isopod *Hemilepistus reaumuri*

3.1 Individual recognition of the mate

3.1.1 *The monogamous pair: formation and behavior*

Hemilepistus family groups stay together for 9 to 10 months after the birth of the young. By the end of the two- to four-month hibernation period the previous bonding of the family members to one another and to their burrow has been dissolved. As soon as they appear above ground, most of the animals leave their birthplace forever, maintaining (by astromenotaxis) constant walking directions for considerable distances (LINSENMAIR in prep. (I)). These directions are chosen at random. This has been demonstrated by marking > 3500 isopods. The distribution of the sites of recovery revealed neither indications of a family-specific nor a population-specific directional bias. Before attempting to set up a new den, the animals travel at least several tens of meters, and sometimes more than a kilometer.

About 8 days after leaving their family burrow, at the earliest, the first emigrants settle down. Sometimes they take over an empty burrow or succeed in evicting a previous occupant, usually they construct a burrow (for details see LINSENMAIR and LINSENMAIR, 1971; LINSENMAIR, 1979, 1984). In most cases (87 %, n=63) the builders of new burrows are females; they dig a tunnel 2–4 cm long and then guard it continuously. In a procedure that usually lasts for hours, a conspecific of the other sex is allowed to enter. By marking the partners in these pairs and observing them for long periods, an observer will notice the following points:

(a) After the first 48 hours of their life together the two partners were in no cases (apart from experimental intervention) found to separate «voluntarily». If a pair does break up it is because one of the partners fails to molt properly, dies, or is driven away by a competitor.

(b) The two partners cooperate in many activities – construction, cleaning and defense of the burrow, providing food (to some extent), and later the care of the young.

(c) In the 9–13 weeks from pair formation to the birth of the young, the burrow is always guarded by one of the partners.

(d) Beginning the second day after pair formation, at the latest, the guard drives away all conspecifics other than its partner, as long as it has had direct contact with its mate within the last 3–12 hours. When the partner demands admittance – e. g. upon its return from foraging – the guard first examines it by touching it with the apical cones of the 2nd antennae, which bear chiefly contact chemoreceptive sensilla (SEELINGER 1977; KREMPIEN 1983), and then as a rule immediately allows it to enter. This special, peaceful treatment of the partner is not site- or situation-specific, and it does not require special behavior on the part of the mate. All that is needed is that the guard is able to touch the returning isopod somewhere on its cuticular surface.

(e) The forager finds its way back to the burrow by means of allo- and idiothetic information, in some cases using an effective search behavior (Hoffmann 1978, 1983a–c, 1984). Having returned, however, it attempts to enter only if it has identified the burrow as its own. The decisive criteria for this identification in the first days after pair formation, are provided by the individual chemical characteristics (see below) of the partner itself – perceived chemotactically.

(f) When a foreign conspecific is – e.g. following experimental manipulation of the guard – allowed direct entry (i.e. entry without the admittance routine) to a burrow, the intruder usually (in 70–90 % of cases, depending on conditions; n > 100; details in Linsenmair in prep. (I)) ejects the guard from the burrow, letting it back in only after a normal admittance procedure. A paired woodlouse admitted by its partner unimpeded to its burrow never behaves in such way, even if it has been experimentally separated from its mate for several days.

(g) Under the climatic conditions prevailing in the normal pair formation season, the female permits copulation only at or in her own burrow and only with her – individually known – male.

(h) After the parturial molt the gravid female accepts only her own male. Conversely, the male behaves peacefully only towards his own female during and after the parturial molt.

3.1.2 Discussion: pair bonding in H. reaumuri

It is evident from the above points (a–h) that *H. reaumuri* forms monogamous pairs. There are two criteria, each of which in itself is regarded as sufficient to categorize a relationship between two heterosexual conspecifics as monogamy (Wickler and Seibt 1981, p. 215), and both are satisfied here:

1. «... the togetherness of two heterosexual adults as a social system».
2. «... a mating system in which an individual reproduces sexually with only one partner of the opposite sex».

The partnership is not simply an association of each member with the burrow, or any other kind of an anonymous monogamy rather the pair is kept together by a mutual attachment of the two individuals – each individually recognized by the other – supplemented by a bonding of the two together to their burrow. The latter bond always proves to be the weaker in conflict experiments. The great significance of the burrow with regard to the cohesion of the pair is that it is the meeting point of the partners, which can notice and identify one another only by direct contact, for they have no mechanisms for long-distance observation of and communication with conspecifics. Without such a meeting point they would quickly lose contact with each other and they never could establish a prolonged pair bond.

The mutual attachment of the partners to one another is evident in

(a) the prolonged cohabitation in very close proximity; after pair formation each member seeks frequent direct antennal and body contact with its partner (and later with its own young), whereas alien ispods are avoided or attacked.

(b) the many behavior patterns related only to the mate (and not to other potential sexual partners), only some of which have been listed above; (see Lamprecht 1973; Wickler 1976).

The partner is individually identified on the basis of extremely varied chemotactically detected characteristics («discriminators»: Hölldobler and Michener 1980) (see below).

3.1.3 Individual recognition: a few selected problems

Of the many questions raised by the existence of monogamy and the ability to identify the partner individually, only a very few can be considered here – and these answered only in broad outline.

3.1.3.1 Do the partners learn to recognize each other in the initial admittance ceremony?

The procedure by which the occupant of a burrow in the field first allows a sexual partner to enter the burrow lasts, depending on different conditions, from ca. 1.5 to more than 48 hours. Here we are concerned only with the question of whether the occupant and the applicant for admission get to know one another during this prolonged interaction. The intensity of the mutual touching during this procedure suggested that they do. The possibility was tested by exchanging conspecifics with the same previous histories, involved in identical parallel experiments, but belonging to different families.

Table I:

A	Is admittance time prolonged by exchange of intruders (females = burrow owners)?	
	Males exchanged[1] every 45 min	Males not exchanged
		Time until admission[2] in min
	122 ± 94 (n = 25)	126 ± 123 (n = 40)

B	Are males individually recognized 60–120 min after 1. admission	
	Males replaced to original female[3]	Males crosswise exchanged[1] [3]
		Time until 2. admission in min
	19,5 ± 18 (n = 20)	17 ± 8 (n = 15)

[1] Exchanged males originated from different families.
[2] Admission is characterized by females allowing males (1) to assume normal guard position within the burrow without pushing them out again for at least a quarter of an hour or (ii) letting them pass into the underneath position.
[3] In experiment B males were replaced 10 min after removal.

In most of the situations tested (see Table I) individual recognition could not be demonstrated. When one of the two interacting animals was exchanged for an alien 1) no delay of the overall process was detectable and 2) at the time of admittance the intruder is not recognizably distinguished from a foreigner by the burrow owner. The only effect observed was that some of the females in the role of intruders, when shifted to another burrow began search behavior after making contact with the alien occupant (see below). The fact that individual recognition was not normally developed in the admittance process, raised the following question.

3.1.3.2 *What is the function of the prolonged admittance procedure in pair formation?*

Under natural conditions, female *H. reaumuri* are strictly semelparous. Even after the earliest possible loss of the offspring – directly after birth (n > 250), or when the eggs were removed experimentally without (n=15) or with damage to the brood pouches (n=20) – in no case was a new clutch produced. With only a single chance for reproduction, and being extremely dependent on her mate for realizing this chance (cf. p. 422), the female can be expected to choose her male with great care. I assume that it is because this choice is so important that the female usually starts to dig a burrow; thereby being in a position to decide whom to admit. How does a female choose? She could evaluate the male directly – for example, by means of the duration and intensity of its striving for admission (for details of the behavior see Linsenmair and Linsenmair 1971). However, all results contradict this presumption. First, in a direct evaluation one would have expected the male not to be admitted solely according to a time program but depending on the result of an examination of the applicant's performances. In that case, however, (i) individual recognition should be established during the admittance procedure and (ii) exchange of applicants should prolong the overall admittance time; as was shown above, neither assumption proved to be true. Second, in laboratory experiments female burrow occupants were presented with males that were (i) greatly handicapped by amputation of the first two pairs of pereiopods, (ii) obviously sick (dying a few days later), or (iii) too small to defend effectively the burrow, dug by a larger female (n ≥ 25 in each case). Choice behavior by direct evaluation should have resulted in the rejection of at least some of these males. The actual result, however, was that all the males that persisted long enough at the entrance were admitted, the times required being not prolonged greatly (Table II).

Table II: Are hampered males refused by female burrow owners?

Admittance time (in hours)	
4 legs amputated	Intact males
16,01 ± 13,2 (n = 28)	12,56 ± 16,25 (n = 30)
No admittance in 48 h	
2	2
Admittance rate	
93%	94%

The experiments were performed only 8 days after termination of hibernation, therefore overall admittance times are rather prolonged. As in all comparable experiments the experimental and the control group consisted of sisters and brothers which all had exactly the same previous history.

Field observations have shown that during the first weeks of the pair-formation phase, everywhere but in the sparsely-inhabited peripheral regions, males – being forced to wait for hours during the admittance procedure – must in this time engage in multiple fights with other males – partly vigorous battles that are very often repeated at intervals of only a few minutes, due to a large number of competitors. Ordinarily the winner is the larger

Table III: Agressive encounters in the field: weights of winners and losers

A Males

	Heavier	Lighter	Significance
Winner	68 (284 ± 28 mg)	23 (266 ± 29)	P ≪ 0,001%
Loser	25 (290 ± 20)	73 (244 ± 39)	χ^2

B Females

Winner	17 (246 ± 19)	9 (237 ± 10)	P = 0,03
Loser	9 (259 ± 15)	19 (204 ± 22)	χ^2

All fights took place without experimental interference at natural burrows. In most cases winners and losers – after reaching a definite decision – were put individually in small containers. They were weighed on a microbalance 1–4 hours later. In a few cases single winners started a new fight immediately after the first one observed. Therefore the number of losers in A exceeds that of winners. The fact that the average weight of those losers which are heavier is slightly higher than the weight of heavier winners is mainly caused by the participation in the aggressive encounters of old parents surviving their first breeding cycle. They are the heaviest but usually are somewhat clumsy and weakened and therefore lose nearly all fights. (They have never been observed surviving until a second pregnancy).

male (see Table III). As a result, during an admittance procedure one male applicant is often replaced by another, sometimes repeatedly. Weakened or small animals usually have no chance of keeping their places long enough to gain entry.

Conclusion. These observations gave rise to the hypothesis that the admittance procedure does indeed serve as a test of the future partner – in an indirect, very effective way that automatically takes into account whether a selection procedure is possible among applicants. In the light of this hypothesis, the results summarized in Table I are not surprising. Even if a conspecific were to become individually identifiable during an admittance procedure, the owner of the burrow should not reject an animal that replaces this already recognized potential sexual partner, because each such change can be expected to bring an improvement. It is also not surprising – indeed, it follows compellingly from the hypothesis – that any applicant (cf. Table II) will eventually be admitted if it persists long enough. After all, if there is no alternative any partner is better than none, and it would be a disadvantage to adhere to absolute criteria. Moreover, after pair formation there is another, indirect test of suitability; an animal that cannot effectively defend its burrow is very likely – if it encounters a superior opponent – to be forcibly expelled. Burrow owners, as just demonstrated, seem not to get acquainted with a potential future sexual partner during the admittance ceremony. But, as already mentioned, females in the role of applicants partly notice an exchange of the burrow owner opposite. (Table IV).

3.1.3.3 Why do about 50% of female applicants give clear indications of recognizing the guard, whereas male applicants do not?

Only to a very limited extent do intruders seem to be able to tell – from the intensity, form and duration of the defense behavior of the guard (and not by chemical cues) –

Table IV: Reactions after transferring intruders to a second burrow with an alien owner

Sex of intruder	Leaving burrow entrance "searching"	Uninterrupted intruding behavior	Significance
Males	1	20	
Females	10 (controls: 1)[1]	12 (controls: 15)	P = 0,002 FEt[2]

After striving for admission for 1–2 hours the intruders were cautiously seized with a forceps and immediately transferred to the entrance of another burrow, identical with the first with the exception that its guard originated from another family (i.e. neither from the intruder's nor the first burrow owner's family).

[1] controls: identically treated but replaced to the first burrow
[2] FEt: Fischer's Exact test

whether the latter is paired or not. For a male intruder the problem of determining that a female burrow guard has no partner is not very difficult; when a burrow is occupied by a pair, the male is almost always present during the activity phase of intruders, and in a series of field observations during 14 activity phases in 86 % (n= 154 pairs) the male was the guard. In these cases brief touching provides the necessary information. When a female with a partner is on guard duty and cannot rapidly drive away an alien male, she will often creep backward into the burrow past her male, «handing over» the task of guard to him. For these reasons, male intruders waste little time in applying to females that already have a partner.

Once a male has found a single female and stays striving for admittance, he loses contact with the burrow only during fights with other males. If, in trying to find his way back after a fight, such a male were often in danger of encountering another single female instead, which would require him to invest more time before being admitted, it would be an advantage to the male to be able to detect his mistake. However, all field observations have indicated that such a situation is so rare and therefore this danger is so uncommon that a special adaptation is not to be expected.

Females seeking admission to a burrow have much more difficulty in finding a single sexual partner. A high percentage of their approaches are likely to be futile (30–60 % depending on how much of the pair-formation phase has elapsed, and if striving for admission for more than 15 minutes is taken as the criterion). Females that have succeeded in locating an unmated male but are distracted by a fight and must then find their way back to his burrow are in great danger of encountering the wrong burrows, occupied by paired males, for these are always much more numerous (the maximal density can reach up to 20 occupied burrows per m^2 during the mating season). Females capable of identifying males individually (and not only by behavioral criteria, which are relatively unreliable) in this situation could often save themselves time-consuming mistakes.

Discussion. In the situation just described, rapid familiarization with an unknown individual would be advantageous to a female. Otherwise, however, it would be more of a disadvantage, and should be suppressed. The social partner is distinguishable from all conspecifics comparable in sex, age, physiological state and so on solely in that it has a familiar badge. By prolonged experimentally enforced tactile contacts an isopod cannot help but get acquainted with an alien conspecific who, in most situations, is then automatically converted to a social partner. Exclusivity of the social units (see p. 431), which is necessary for various reasons, is guaranteed only as long as the learning of another animal's discriminators is limited to the situation of monogamous pair formation (and of contact with one's own young after their birth; cf. LINSENMAIR 1984 and in prep. (II)). But just during the pair-formation phase it is often impossible to avoid prolonged contact with conspecifics that should remain strangers. The simplest way to prevent such familiarization, with a general method that does not require analysis of the specific situation, is to set the frequency of contact required for familiarization so high that only the partners in a pair can achieve it. This assumption could explain why – although the partners in a newly formed pair touch one another often and extensively – 12–24 hours must elapse after admittance before both are demonstrably capable of recognizing one another reliably, whereas in other situations they learn much faster. Of course behavioral variables can play an important role in this process; a paired guard touches an intruder much more rarely than does a single guard, which is in principle prepared to allow entry. (It is not clear whether male and female intruders vary in this regard which then could explain the sex-specific differences of Table IV).

3.1.3.4 Is the pair bond endangered by unavoidable contamination with foreign discriminators?

The discriminators of the desert isopods are strongly polar, practically non-volatile compounds of low molecular weight (LINSENMAIR, SCHILDKNECHT and ESSWEIN, in prep.). They can easily be transferred from one individual to another by direct contact, the individual thereby becoming – depending on the intensity of contact – more or less strongly and long-lasting alienated (LINSENMAIR 1972, 1984, and in prep. (III); see p. 425). Paired guards cannot avoid direct body contact with foreigners during the pair formation period while defending their burrows against alien intruders. When such a guard goes out to forage, in a few cases it is rejected by its partner on its return. In this situation, and this situation alone, 15 of 20 animals responded to the defensive blows of their partners with a very effective behavior: they turned around and presented their hind ends to the guards. This part of the body always remains uncontaminated during defense of the burrow. After it had been touched by the guard's antennae, all individuals were immediately admitted.

In experiments aimed at alienating adult, mated individuals it became apparent that when one member of a pair is forced into body contact with adult foreigners – to an extent that if solely young animals had been involved the contamination would have caused long-lasting rejections by their respective families – its partner guarding the burrow sometimes reacted by no, sometimes by only brief defense. It seemed possible either that the adults are less sensitive than juveniles to foreign discriminators or that they produce less substances which are easily transferable. To test these possibilities, reciprocal contamination experiments were done with adults after hibernation and with almost full-grown (5-month-old) juveniles.

The results of these laboratory experiments are summarized in Table V. They show that the adults (i) transfer less substance than do juveniles under otherwise identical conditions, and (ii) respond less aggressively to foreign substances encountered when examining their partners than do members of families to equally intense contamination of their kin. (Other possible interpretations – that the foreign substances might be less well adsorbed by adults because of differences in the surface properties of the cuticle, and that the adults produce substances less effective in eliciting aggression – have been ruled out by experimental tests outside the scope of the present discussion.)

Conclusions: Our above question can be clearly answered: pair maintenance is not endangered by the unavoidable close contacts with aliens in burrow defense. This poten-

Table V: Alienation of adult pair partners and young family members by direct contact with alien individuals of different age

	Alienated	by	Time of contact	Admittance time ≤ 5 min	> 5 min	Significance
I	Adults	30 Young	1 min	4	13	I : II
II	Adults	30 Adults	1 min	16	8	P < 0,02 χ^2

				Admittance time ≤ 1 hour	> 1 hour	
III	Young	30 Young	1 min	4	18	III : IV
IV	Adults	30 Young	1 min	14	3	P < 0,001 χ^2

The individual to be alienated was placed into a small glass vial and then the thirty unrelated conspecifics of different age (see text) were added.
The isopods could not avoid closest contact which was additionally intensified by shaking the group up very often thus taking care that the test animal was during this procedure permanently amidst the aliens.

tial weak spot is multiply ensured against possible disturbances by suitable adjusted behavior, reduced production of exchangeable badge substances, and altered – lowered – sensitivity to contamination.

3.1.4 What are the adaptive values of monogamy and individual recognition under present-day conditions?

a) To acquire a burrow without undue delay and then to hold it against all competition are absolute prerequisites for the survival and reproduction of a desert isopod. Since these animals have no adaptations for efficient digging, construction of a new burrow is a laborious process which – because of climatic conditions – must begin in spring. The very strong intraspecific (to a lesser extent also interspecific) competition for this vital resource makes it necessary to keep constant guard over it. Adequate food can normally only be found outside the burrow, and a single woodlouse cannot simultaneously guard and forage. In the present situation a burrow can be permanently defended only by the cooperation of at least two adults. These should be able to tell one another apart from foreign invaders. Learning to recognize the partner's individual characteristics is certainly the most reliable solution to this problem (LINSENMAIR and LINSENMAIR 1971; LINSENMAIR 1979, 1984).

b) Even if there were no foraging problem and a desert isopod could stay indefinitely in its burrow, a female during the parturial molt and pregnancy would mostly lose its den to competitors since she cannot defend her burrow effectively enough if at all. Only if she lives together with a male during this critical time does the female have a good chance of reproduction. As a proximate cause, the individual attachment of the male to his female ensures that the pair remains together even after the parturial molt, in which the female loses her sexual attractiveness.

c) For reasons as yet unknown, single gravid females (at least under laboratory conditions) have a very small chance of survival even if all competitors are excluded. We had noticed this phenomenon in our laboratory breeds for some time; in an experiment to study it (LINSENMAIR 1984) 20 females were isolated from their males after the parturial molt, 18 of these females died, either before the birth of the young or before the time when the young would have had a chance to survive alone. In the contol group with pairs kept under otherwise identical conditions, 19 of 20 sisters of the females in the experimental group survived the critical period. It seems very unlikely that these results are pure laboratory artifacts with no relevance to the situation in the field.

d) Moreover, loss of either partner (regardless of sex) within the first two weeks after the birth of the young reduces the mean number of young that survive. In the experimental group there were 23 ± 28 survivors (n = 38 families), 40 % (a significant difference) of the average in the control group, with 40 ± 28 survivors (n=47); there was a particularly large increase in the incidence of total-brood mortality, with 21 % in the control group as compared with 50 % in the experimental group (LINSENMAIR 1979).

3.1.5 Discussion: what makes monogamy the best reproductive method for both sexes?

For females the advantages are so obvious, as the preceding section has shown, that a further discussion seems unneccessary. Males deserve closer consideration in this regard – both in general and among the Peracarida in particular, because their direct parental investment in the young is usually so much less than that of the females. In all such cases one would expect to find a polygamous mating system, relinquished only when conditions select strongly against it (cf. TRIVERS 1972; LINSENMAIR 1979, 1984; WICKLER and SEIBT 1981). Because Hemilepistus males in all our extensive experiments never seem to «play the field», it must be inferred that an attempt to do so would incur risks that would not, on average, be compensated by success with one or more additional females. As analyzed in detail elsewhere (LINSENMAIR 1979, 1984), there are only two situations worth considering in which a male could – theoretically – leave his female without a nearly 100 % risk of losing the investment he had made up to that time, which on average could never be compensated in the future. These situations are as follows:

(a) The male could leave his female immediately after the regular copulation phase, so soon before parturial molt that the female could find another partner but – because she cannot prolong the brief time until parturial molt – has no opportunity for frequent copulation with him. Results so far, though still preliminary, indicate that there is no sperm clumping (LINSENMAIR 1984), so that eggs would always be partly fertilized by sperm from the first male. A method of this sort would require (i) that the males be capable of judging the point of time within the reproductive phase of the population and hence of knowing whether there is enough time left for them to be likely to find an unmated female offering an adequate opportunity for reproduction, and (ii) that the males be very well informed as to the condition of their females, in order to choose the right time to leave them. The requirement in (ii), at least, is certainly not met; the females «withhold» all relevant information from the males (LINSENMAIR 1979, 1984). Still more important, however, is a third point; males forming a pair with a new female should be able to more than compensate the losses they incur by their infidelity towards their first female. Our first results indicate that males choosing the best time to desert their female «had to reckon» that about 50 % of their first females' eggs will be fertilized by the second male. In order to allow for a positive selection of a deserting behavior one basic requirement – besides others left out of consideration here – would be that the new pair's chances for survival (until the male reaches the end of the regular copulation phase for a second time) should exceed 50 %, but this on average is not the case (Shachak 1980; Linsenmair 1984), often their chance does not even reach 10 %.

(b) The second opportunity would arise only some weeks after the birth of the young. But because the climatic and other ecological conditions make it essential to time reproduction accurately with respect to the annual cycle, the females are too well synchronized with one another, thus a male leaving his family at that time would have no chance of finding a female still in a suitable state.

In the present-day situation the desert woodlice have good chances of reproduction only as monogamous pairs. Current conditions of selection certainly stabilize this form of a social and mating system. However, they tell us nothing about the evolution of this highly differentiated and certainly very derivative behavior. The special construction and defense of a permanent burrow in a firm substrate, the formation of pairs in which the partners individually recognize one another, brood care with family-specific recognition of the young – all are crucial adaptations to the ecological conditions of the present biotope and hence prerequisites for inhabiting it. Therefore they cannot have been formed by the selection factors prevailing at present. The early steps must have been taken under other selection pressures, under less severe abiotic ecological conditions (cf. Linsenmair 1984).

3.2 Kin recognition in *H. reaumuri*

The parental pair together with their young – up to 140 of them – constitute a strictly closed community. Foreign conspecifics that appear at the burrow entrance (or within the area around it bounded by the fecal wall) are always attacked by the parents and juveniles (6 weeks of age or older), and outside this boundary they are either attacked or avoided. The members of the cooperative community never behave aggressively to one another «intentionally» (i. e., after tactile examination) until the family group dissolves, unless too close contact has been made with alien conspecifics. This behavior shows that the desert woodlice are not only capable of identifying individuals, but can also distinguish kin from non-kin.

3.2.1 Interfamily variability

In the field, hundreds of experiments and very many more observations have produced no evidence of mistaken identification, despite the fact that at times *H. reaumuri* can live in very dense local populations (up to 14 families with young per m²). The radius within which the family members forage can be as great as 6 m and is usually 1,5–4 m. Given a foraging radius of 2,5 m, with 5 families per m² it is to be expected that members of about a 100 families will come into the vicinity of any particular burrow. Since families in the field remain exclusive even at highest densities, it follows that the variability of the characteristics used for kin identification must be very great.

Well over 50,000 tests involving reciprocal exchange of the juveniles of two families have been carried out, and no two families have ever been found to tolerate one another. Unilateral toleration has been observed. In a systematic cross-exchange test 70 families collected in the field from an area of 50 × 50 m were examined for discriminator coincidence. Of the 4830 repetition-free combinations there were 4 in which the young from one family were not attacked by the members of a single other family. In this case a number of conditions (of animal maintenance and experimental procedure) acted to reduce aggressiveness, so that this misidentification rate of 0.1 % is certain to be an overestimate. But it does indicate that very close resemblances can exist in this frequency.

3.2.2 Nature and origin of the family badge

There is no doubt that the characteristics used for kin identification, the «family badge», are chemical in nature. One of the clearest demonstrations of this is that with suitable solvents extracts can be obtained that when applied to a neutral carrier such as a glass rod can elicit aggression (as foreign conspecifics do); when such extracts are applied to individuals the other members of their family treat them as aliens for a long time.

The density of family-occupied burrows and the great overlap of the foraging areas of neighboring families made it *a priori* highly unlikely that the variety and specificity of kin discriminators would reside in body odors acquired from the surroundings. All the relevant early experiments (LINSENMAIR 1972) and later extensions of them confirm this view. Only one finding need be mentioned, as follows. Hundreds of pairs and families collected in the field were kept unter constant laboratory conditions on the same substrate, and given the same food, for 5–9 months. Many hundreds of woodlouse families bred from those collected in the field have since been maintained for their whole life cycle under these conditions, some of them now in the 4th generation. Unless inbreeding occurred, none of these animals have given any sign of reduced acuity in making the distinction between kin and non-kin (n > 500 cross-tests). Our earlier hypothesis (LINSENMAIR 1972) – that the discriminator substances, with all their diversity and specificity, are genetically controlled secretions, very little influenced by the environment – has now been corroborated by many additional experiments (LINSENMAIR in prep. (III)) and can be regarded as firmly established.

There are several compelling reasons – (i) the degree of variability, (ii) the reproducibly graded aggressive response to members from different alien families (extending in the extreme to unilateral acceptance), and (iii) all the results of mixing experiments (see below) – to conclude that the family badge is always a blend of several components.

3.2.3 Intrafamily variability: individual characteristics

Because emigration of the young (see p. 415) thoroughly mixes the population during the pair-formation period, we have to assume that in more than 99 % of all pairs the partners come from different families, with different badges and corresponding genetic differences. There is no evidence for sex-linkage of the genes responsible for production of the identifying substances. With normal autosomal inheritance, however, variability among the progeny of a pair is to be expected. How, then, can there be a common family badge? Does it really exist? Adoption experiments (LINSENMAIR 1972) in which parents are brought into very close contact with half of the young from another family, thereby compelling them to get acquainted with these juveniles, have shown that as a rule the foster parents will then also accept the other half of the young. This outcome refutes an alternative hypothesis to that of the family badge, namely that mutual acceptance within a family could be a matter of individual recognition alone. The results indicate that the variability of discriminator patterns among family members is somehow reduced or adjusted so that a common badge is achieved.

Given a great primary intrafamily variability in the production of individual discriminator sets, one way to achieve a common family badge could be to make a secondary adjustment, e. g. by confining the spectrum of produced substances within the family to the smallest common denominator. Then the individuals would have to match themselves to some extent to their chemical surroundings. Amputation of the apical cones, the sole structure responsible for badge identification, ought then to cause changes in production, but no such changes have been found (LINSENMAIR 1972; KREMPIEN 1983). Furthermore, week- to month-long integration of single individuals into strange families, during which such individuals soon become fully accepted (and soon «regard themselves as belonging» to the new family; Linsenmair in prep. (III)), ought to be accompanied by changes in production. But when such integrated individuals were isolated immediately prior to a molt and afterward tested to see how their natural and adoptive siblings would respond, the results (Table VI) gave convincing evidence against such a hypothesis. The integrated isopods after removal from their foster family and before molting – were treated in their natural families like foreigners. The alienation could have been either the result of the integrated animals' adjustment to its changed chemical environment or an effect of contamination caused through transferred substances by the foster families' members. The fact that after molting in isolation these individuals were accepted without any aggression in 84 % of all encounters by their genetical kin but only in 15 % by members of their former foster family clearly indicates the lack of an adjustment in discriminator production. It rather points to contamination as the reason for the observed alterations after the integration and before molting in isolation.

b) As the previous experiments indicate, and as we know since a long time (Linsenmair 1972), badge substances are exchanged between animals during body contacts. Members of a family group, living shoulder-to-shoulder within the burrow, cannot avoid this exchange and the consequent intermingling of their secretions. But if the production of the individual discriminators is under extensive genetic control and the family badge is a product of the mixing of the individual discriminators, then – in the absence of special adaptations – in the course of the (very numerous) molts communication problems must arise.

Table VI: Does integration into an alien family change the production of discriminators?

	Test animals	Where tested	Encounter releasing		Significance
			Attacks	No attacks	
A	Not yet moulted[1]	Genetical family	192[2] (N = 22)	3	A : B P ≪ 0,001 (χ^2)
B	Moulted	Genetical family	164 (N = 11)[3]	879	B : C P ≪ 0,001 (χ^2)
C	Moulted	Foster family	522 (N = 17)	92	

Reactions of natural and adaptive siblings towards individuals which had been integrated for 4–8 weeks into foster families and then taken out and tested before and after moulting (in complete isolation). The integrated isopods were removed from their adaptive families about 24 hours prior to the beginning of an ecdysis; they were tested 36–60 hours after terminated ecdysis.

[1] Tests immediately after removal from the foster family.
[2] Number of observed single reactions.
[3] Number of tested isopods.

Table VII: Loss of alien substances by molting

Contaminated individuals	Reactions of uncontaminated family members		Significance
	Attacks	No attacks	
A Before molting	180	3	A : B
		(n = 15 individuals)	
B After molting (24–48 hours after termination)	36	420	B : C P ≪ 0,001
		(n = 15 individuals)	
C Controls: contaminated like A, kept in isolation for the same period as B, but without molts	145	6	A : C not significant
		(n = 10 individuals)	χ^2

The test animals and the controls were contaminated by close direct body contacts with 10 alien conspecifics for 5 min, in A/B 24–48 hours before a molt. For molting individuals were kept in isolation in single uncontaminated containers.

3.2.4 Does molting create problems in communication because of the mixed character of the family badge?

When it molts, each family member discards along with the exuvium all the discriminators it does not itself produce (cf. Table VII; see also Table VI). Observation of undisturbed families reveals that in far fewer than 0.1 % of molts is there any evidence of the newly molted animal being killed (and even in these cases there could be reasons other than communication problems). Here, again, integration experiments and observation of artificially composed groups are useful means of claryfying the situation. We can – as the results summarized in Table VI have proved – safely assume that the substances produced by an integrated animal (which was severely attacked before its integration) depart considerably and permanently from the norm of the adoptive family. If individuals within mixed groups molt 7 days or more after integration, the group or family (if undisturbed) treats them in 96 % of all cases (see Table VIII) not differently from an unmolted mixed group or family member. But if the integrated foreigners are removed shortly before the onset of molting and replaced when molting is completed for more than 36 hours, they are predominantly (in 85 % as the results summarized in Table VI have shown) treated as aliens. Control animals, which had been integrated into families for an equally long time but which did not molt during the four to five-day-period of removal (n=50), were – after being replaced in their foster families – accepted without aggression in 98 % of cases, proving that in the test animals in fact the molting-caused changes were the reason for the altered responses of the adoptive family.

Animals molting within their foster family or mixed group after an integration time of less than 6 days have only a limited chance of surviving (see Table VIII), and all the animals (n=30), which were integrated as singles into pure foster families and which molted there within 36 hours were killed. This dependence of tolerance on integration time could indicate that learning processes are crucially involved in acceptance. But how are we to interpret the difference in response depending on whether the integrated animal molts within the family or in isolation?

Table VIII: Number of individuals surviving complete molts in mixed groups in dependence of time spent in these groups

Days after group formation	Surviving	Killed	Significance
> 2–6	56	24	P ≪ 0,001
7–35	1433	56	χ^2

Killing normally occured during or shortly after shedding the posterior half-exuvium. These animals then were cannibalized.

Preliminary answers to these questions have been given by experiments in which animals – either foreigners integrated into pure families or members of complex or highly complex mixed groups[1] – were removed for molting but returned to the group a shorter time after stripping off the anterior hemiexuvium than was the case in the experiments described above (see Table VI). Animals returned 5–16 hours after the anterior hemiexuvium is shed are attacked only rarely and they hardly ever encounter strong aggression (see Table IX). But if one waits longer, most are attacked. Evidently these early post-molt individuals enjoy temporary protection, which becomes permanent if they are returned to the family or group soon enough.

When a woodlouse is presented an unfamiliar, newly-molted individual, it can easily be seen that the newly-molted half of the body exerts, especially during the first hour after the shedding of the respective hemiexuvium, an inhibitory influence. The results summarized in Table X, however, show clearly that this protection is far from perfect at any time, for in all cases sooner or later (and always within a period of a few minutes only) the foreigner, if placed into an alien family or alien mixed group, is bitten – and the emergence of hemolymph always cancels any inhibition (even that with respect to a normal family

Table IX: Members of mixed groups replaced at different times after molting in isolation into their groups

Time between shedding the anterior hemi-exuvium and test in hours	Reactions of group members		Significance
	Attacks	No attacks	
A 5–16	20	242 (n = 16 individuals)	P ≪ 0,001
B 22–96	180	100 (n = 16 individuals)	χ^2

The isopods were removed about 12–24 hours before molting; they were kept in isolation during the molt and the exact time of shedding the second half exuvium was determined by direct observation. After having been tested in A the animals were isolated again and used for a second time in B.

---

[1] In «complex mixed groups», containing between 60–120 individuals never more than 3 individuals originate from the same family, in «highly complex mixed groups», each of the 60–120 individuals was taken from another family.

Table X: Reaction towards alien conspecifics after touching their newly molted body half

Time between shedding an hemiexuvium and test	Reactions in single encounters		Significance
	Attacks	No attacks	
A 1–14 min	124	397 (n = 20 individuals)	A + B : C P ≪ 0,001
B > 14–30 min	171	419 (n = 23 individuals)	C : D P ≪ 0,001
C > 30–60 min	249	331 (n = 23 individuals)	χ^2
D > 60 min–3 h	149	40 (n = 9 individuals)	

The test animals, seized with a forceps, were presented the controls in such a way that these could touch the newly molted body half only. Often clear signs of inhibition could be observed as follows: controls quickly withdrawing their antennae, retreating some steps, etc. (cf. Linsenmair 1984).

member). Under most conditions the protection only becomes perfect when the members of the family or the mixed group have had a chance to live together with the alien animal for a prolonged period before its molt. It is to be assumed that the isopods could therewith become familiar with the special chemical properties of the deviating group member. Before proceeding to further considerations, we should answer the question of how relevant the results obtained with experimentally altered groups may be for pure families. When members of unaltered families were isolated for molting, and not replaced until 24 hours after its termination the results summarized in Table XI were obtained; they show that the same alienation problems can sometimes arise in natural families, which justifies our experimental procedure.

How can this recognition system – which apparently requires the ability to learn to recognize deviant individuals – function, given that the family badge is a mixture of all the individually produced components? Is it simply a matter of learning all the individual components of the family badge, in order to be able to tolerate then any arbitrary partial combination if it is coupled with the signal «newly molted»? The members of highly complex mixed groups with a great (about 90–95 %) but not complete overlap in the spectrum of families from which the single individuals originated, in many cases tolerate

Table XI: Reactions of pure families towards members isolated during molt and replaced 24–48 hours later

Members of 25 families	Attacks	No attacks
	27 individuals	99 individuals
family No 78/25	17 individuals	4 individuals

These families collected in the field, were kept free of any experimentally caused contaminations. A few families – family No 78/25 is an example – show an extraordinary high incidence of molting-caused alienations.

one another with no aggressiveness, even though they behave very aggressively toward pure families or differently composed mixed groups. The badges of the similar highly complex mixed groups are evidently not distinguished from one another. When members of these mixed groups are isolated for molting and afterwards returned for brief periods, alternately to their own group and to the second group that does not differ detectably in its group badge, they are much more frequently (and with high statistical significance) attacked in the latter group (Table XII). (Observations similar in principle can often be made in pure families that have been divided for long periods, i.e. > 15 days or in complex groups with complete overlap in respect to the families from which members were taken to compose the two or more experimental units.) Accordingly, two groups can have badges indistinguishable from one another and nevertheless comprise differing members (with regard to their production of individual chemical identifiers).

Here, again, experiments in which groups have been assembled experimentally provide critical evidence. A foreign juvenile brought into close contact with young of the control family can alienate between ca. 5 and 20 individuals (depending on the family combination) to such an extent that when they are returned to their uncontaminated family members they are treated as aggressively as foreigners. But when a single alien mingles with a considerably larger number of sibling juveniles from another family, alienation does not occur even after long-term exposure. A single foreigner can produce and transfer only a limited amount of badge substances. If those components which are not contained in the badge of its foster family are distributed among many adoptive siblings, these are diluted below the effectiveness threshold. That is, in the subset of individually produced substances shared by *all* members of the group, the components with respect to which this foreigner (or a single deviant family member) differs from the norm are lacking. We can now understand that two groups may have the same group-specific badge even without complete agreement between the entire sets of discriminator substances produced by each group.

How is such a deviant animal protected when it molts? The decisive point is that in fact the deviant discriminators do not show up in the common badge but – and this certainly is crucial to the deviant's survival – its individual traits are never lost. The family badge can never completely mask an individual's discriminator complex, a complete glossing over individual chemical properties is – according to many experimental results – (LINSENMAIR in prep. (III)) impossible. The physiological basis of this resistance to complete masking presumably (as other findings indicate) lies in a very firm binding of part of the animal's own secretions to the surface of its cuticle. Whereas the family badge can be perceived by touching any member of the group, even if that member itself produces only some components, the detection of individuals producing discriminator substances not present in the

Table XII: Newly molted individuals originating from one of two highly complex mixed groups with identical badges: Are they treated identically in both groups?

Newly molted tested in	Reactions of group members in single encounters		
	Aggressive	Non-aggressive	Significance
Own group	26	191	P ≪ 0,001
Alien group	108	72	χ^2

7 individuals were isolated 20 hours or less before a molt and replaced within 6–20 hours after its termination.

family badge requires that they be touched directly. Within a large group it certainly does not happen that each member touches each other member in every activity period, and it is just as certain that many touches are necessary to identify a deviant conspecific reliably; in this light, the fact (documented above) that the development of tolerance requires relatively long integration times becomes rapidly understandable.

Memory plays a central role in all identification responses, and this is not the least of the reasons why it is difficult to judge the extent of intrafamily variability by using the indirect methods of behavioral experiments. It is therefore impossible to estimate the demands individual and kin recognition make on the learning abilities of the family members. We do not yet know how many components the family badges contain and how many other discriminators may be «concealed», to be learned only through direct contacts with the individual concerned. But there is considerable evidence that very complex combinations of characteristics, including many components that do not appear in the group badge, can be learned.

3.2.5 Inter- and intrafamily communication: discussion

a) Why are the family groups so strictly exclusive?

In the light of our present knowledge, being the result of intensive discussions which have received their strongest impetus from the fundamental contributions of HAMILTON (1964a, b, 1972), the basic answer is trivial: in order for the valuable and costly efforts expended within the social unit on behalf of conspecifics to have an adequate reproductive payoff, these must be confined to relatives. The society must protect itself from both intentional and accidental parasitism, by keeping foreigners out. Because a desert wood-louse family still stays together very long after the time when the juveniles pass the stage of «altricial» nestlings – though they remain thereafter for many additional weeks dependent on parental care and for months on mutual assistance among themselves – the problem of discerning foreigners from family members cannot be solved by, for example, site-specific recognition. For family members to be reliably distinguished from non-members in this case, where many families may dwell nearby, a stable but highly variable identification system allowing accurate and reliable discrimination of kin among a very large number of conspecifics is required. Acquired body odors, from the surroundings or via the food, which seem to be used exclusively (?) or at least as the essential components of the discrimination systems of some eusocial Hymenoptera (reviews: RIBBANDS 1965; MICHENER 1974; WILSON 1971; HÖLLDOBLER and MICHENER 1980), cannot meet these requirements (LINSENMAIR 1972). The signature system evolved by *Hemilepistus*, with its extremely diverse secretions – under genetic control and extremely resistant to most possible external influences – is an excellent solution to the problem of kin recognition under especially difficult conditions resulting from temporary very high dwelling densities and a more or less complete overlap of the foraging grounds of neighbouring families. But this method has one very vulnerable feature: during direct contact substances are exchanged between unrelated animals, rapidly causing alienation from their own families. Therefore such contacts must be avoided at all costs, and as long as the family badge is used for identification the community must remain exclusive. This certainly explains, at least in part, the pronounced aggressiveness exhibited toward alien conspecifics in situations in which it is comprehensible on neither ecological nor sociobiological grounds – it serves to prevent -unintended- contacts (LINSENMAIR in prep. (III)). The danger of those contacts should not be underestimated, for it is only by direct touching with the antennae that identification is possible, and in such close proximity «involuntary» contact may easily occur prior to antennal touching. (Where the density of *Hemilepistus* families was very high we always found indications of relatively large contamination problems.)

b) Interfamily variability. At a conservative estimate, in relatively densely populated regions each isopod burrow lies within the foraging radius of at least 100 families (see p. 424). An estimated upper limit, for very high population densities (10–12 families per m²) and extensive foraging excursions (5–6 m radius) due to food shortage caused by the high numbers of individuals, would be of the order of 1000 families, the members of which could make contact with the inhabitants of a single burrow. Moreover, taking into account that within a complete family, as a rule, there exist at least three distinctly different badges: the male, the female and their progeny differ so greatly from one another that familiarity with the identifying characteristics of one of the three does not result in acceptance of the other two (a result not discussed above; see LINSENMAIR in prep. (III)). It should also be remembered that within the progeny individual variability through «personal» substances not showing up in the family badge is high. Thus the possible number of discriminator sets an individual could encounter at its burrow and mistake for kin may increase by another order, or, as an absolute maximum, another two orders of magnitude.

The estimate of 10^5 different types of identifying characteristics that a family member can encounter, none of which is to be confused with those of its siblings and parents, is probably very high and overestimated. But since we have found not a single case in which two families had the same badge, we can reasonably postulate a discriminator diversity sufficient to ensure that even in the most demanding circumstances misidentifications remain very rare exceptions. The finding of unilateral acceptance in 0.1 % of the cross-combinations in one experiment (i) may well be an overestimate (see p. 424 and LINSENMAIR in prep. (III)) and (ii) offers little threat to exclusivity. That is, a member of a family that cannot distinguish the badge of one other family from its own, so that it «feels at home» when it contacts the marked vicinity of the other family's burrow and may attempt to enter, is recognized as foreign and driven away (presumably because its family badge includes at least one extra component; LINSENMAIR in prep. (III)). Members of the family accepted by the other family never discover this fact, for to them the other family is foreign. Only in exceptional situations – for example, when deprived of their own burrow – might individuals of the more discerning family by a very improbable chance try to enter the burrow that would be «right» for them.

Let us assume, as there are good reasons to do, that badge differences are chiefly or even exclusively qualitative in nature; how many components would then be necessary to produce 10^4–10^6 distinct badges? In our chemical analysis, after a number of purification steps (ESSWEIN in prep.), 8 fractions were obtained which differ considerably from each other in the chemical properties of the compounds included. 7 of these fractions proved effective in our bioassay. If we consider these 7 as 7 independent badge dimensions we would expect each of these classes to comprise not more than between 4 and 10 (on average 8) different substances (provided they lead to phenotypic differences) in order to generate the desired number of repetition free permutations. At the genetic level, a system with 7 loci and 4–10 phenotypes associated with each locus (which, depending on gene interaction, would require 3–5 alleles per locus) would be just adequate to meet the requirement. Such a system, involving the production of only 40–70 different suitable badge substances, should be entirely realizable as far as this point of production is concerned. Nor would such a system make excessive demands on the sensory abilities of these animals, arthropods that orient to their surroundings in general chiefly by way of chemoreception.

c) Intrafamily variability and badge structure. Given normal processes of inheritance, the high interfamily variability must necessarily result in a certain amount of intrafamily variability. These differences among family members are partially masked by the intermingling of individual components that occur automatically on contact. A family badge is thereby produced, a chemical common denominator that is similar enough among at least most if its bearers (apart from the parents) that foreign conspecifics (e. g., adoptive parents) need only become familiar with some larger fraction of the individuals (50–70 % of the progeny) in order subsequently to accept the remainder – animals they have never encountered directly – as members of the group. In this experimental situation the adoptive parents employ a phenotype-matching mechanism (ALEXANDER 1979; HOLMES and SHERMAN 1982, 1983; SHERMAN and HOLMES 1984). This mechanism could also play a role in the intact family; for an animal to remind itself of the family badge and to keep track of any changes of the family badge due e. g. to losses of family members as time goes by, it needs only to touch a few of its siblings.

The family badge has gestalt character (cf. CROZIER and DIX 1979). Each member of a group learns this gestalt independently of its own discriminator production. (The interesting, multi-level problem of how the parents learn to identify their young in the first place and how they avoid eating them, in view of the fact that they always cannibalize young foreign conspecifics, is outside the scope of this discussion; see LINSENMAIR 1984, in prep. (II).) The badge, as would be expected of a gestalt model, is very vulnerable to disturbance, and is more readily made unrecognizable by the addition than by the removal of single components.

The system is greatly complicated by the fact that all members of the *Hemilepistus* families molt at more or less short intervals and in so doing, because of (i) the non-volatility of the discriminators and (ii) their intrafamily variability, alter the badge they bear, sometimes severely. Such alterations must destroy the gestalt character of the badge. A gestalt model alone, then, cannot explain the kin-recognition abilities of *Hemilepistus*.

If molting solely involved the loss of certain components of the common family badge, the family members would – in order to categorize a newly molted individual as belonging to their group or as alien – need to be able to determine whether the discriminators borne by a newly-molted animal amounted to a subset of the family pattern, with no foreign additions. To avoid acceptance of a foreigner that happens to match one of the presumably many possible subsets of the family badge, an additional safety measure would be expected – there must be some sign indicating a recent molt. (Because desert isopods can molt successfully only in burrows, owing to evaporation and other problems, no other assurance would be required.) Although the second part of this scheme does apply to *Hemilepistus* – molting is signalled – the first proposal is too simple. The reason is that the family badge contains only those components that – in a large family – are produced by several individuals. Presumably any component produced by only one or a very few individuals, when distributed among all the family members, is diluted under the threshold of effectiveness and therefore no longer influences behavior. But after such an individual has molted, the deviant substances on its surface become very conspicuous at the same time as more or less large fractions of the common pattern have been lost.

Hemilepistus can and has to learn not only the badge common to the family, but also all those chemical discriminators of deviant individuals which are not represented in the pattern borne by every family member. Such learning is possible only because these substances are bound to the producer's cuticula in a way that reliably prevents their dilution below the detection threshold. It is still not clear what the partial patterns remaining after molting must consist of in order to be acceptable – whether all the single components which are present either as personal or as family discriminators may be freely combined or whether they meet the criterion only in certain combinations, thus restricting the number of possible permutations.

The learning task that a member of a *Hemilepistus* family faces in this context cannot yet be evaluated in detail, but in any case it must be formidable. Although the memory of a

Hemilepistus is very good (LINSENMAIR and LINSENMAIR 1971; LINSENMAIR 1972), it must evidently be continually refreshed, especially in the case of the less common characteristics. Continual learning is probably also necessary because, in the course of time, changes in the badge system develop – owing, for instance, to the death of some family members.

Their permanent capacity for learning makes desert isopods especially suitable subjects for detailed analysis of a differentiated communication system. Because the signals are transmitted by contact chemoreception and not by olfaction (in which case orders of magnitude fewer molecules could be involved), chemical analysis seemed a promising approach, and one that was likely to succeed without the need to extract astronomical numbers of animals. In the event, the chemical properties of the substances have considerably hindered and delayed the analysis (HERING 1981; ESSWEIN 1982), but there are good reasons to believe that we shall soon know the general features of the spectrum of substances employed. This analysis is the most important project currently underway, for there are many questions that can be usefully pursued only after it is completed.

Acknowledgments

This research was supported by the Deutsche Forschungsgemeinschaft (Li 150/6 – 150/10 and SFB 4 «Sinnesleistungen: Anpassungen von Strukturen und Mechanismen»). I would like to express my thanks to EVI KÖPPL, Regensburg and ELISABETH BARCSAY, Würzburg for technical help, I am especially indebted to my wife, Dr. CHRISTA LINSENMAIR, and to DIETER KRAPF for their most valuable help during field work.

References

Alexander, R. D. (1979): *Darwinism and Human Affairs*. Univ. of Washington Press.
Bateson, P. P. G. (1980): Optimal outbreeding and the development of sexual preferences in Japanese quail. Z. Tierpsychol. *53*, 231–244.
– (1982): Preferences for cousins in Japanese quail. Nature *295*, 236–237.
– (1983): Optimal outbreeding. In *Mate Choice*, P. P. G. Bateson (ed), 257–277, Cambridge Univ. Press.
Beecher, M. D. (1982): Signature systems and individual recognition. Am. Zool. *22*, 477–490.
Blaustein, A. R. and R. K. O'Hara (1981): Genetic control for sibling recognition? Nature *290*, 246–248.
– (1982): Kin recognition in *Rana cascadae* tadpoles: maternal and paternal effects. Anim. Behav. *30*, 1151–1157.
Buckle, G. R. and L. Greenberg (1981): Nestmate recognition in sweat bees *(Lasioglossum zephyrum):* Does an individual recognize its own odour or only odours of its nestmates? Anim. Behav. *29*, 802–809.
Caldwell, R. L. (1979): Cavity occupation and defense behavior in the stomatopod *Gonodactylus festai:* evidence for chemically mediated individual recognition. Anim. Behav. *27*, 194–201.
Crozier, R. H. and M. W. Dix (1979): Analysis of two genetic models for the innate components of colony odors in social Hymenoptera. Behav. Ecol. Sociobiol. *4*, 217–224.
Esswein, U. (1982): Über das chemische Familienabzeichen der Wüstenassel *Hemilepistus reaumuri*. Diploma Thesis: Heidelberg University.
Greenberg, L. (1979): Genetic component of bee odor in kin recognition. Science *206*, 1095–1097.
Hamilton, W. D. (1964a): The genetical evolution of social behaviour. I. J. Theoret. Biol. *7*, 1–16.

- (1964b): The genetical evolution of social behaviour. II. J. Theoret. Biol. 7, 17–32.
- (1972): Altruism and related phenomena, mainly in social insects. Ann. Rev. Ecol. Syst. 3, 193–232.

Hering, W. (1981): Zur chemischen Ökologie der Tunesischen Wüstenassel *Hemilepistus reaumuri*. Ph. D. Thesis: Heidelberg University.

Hoffmann, G. (1978): Experimentelle und theoretische Analyse eines adaptiven Orientierungsverhaltens: Die «optimale» Suche der Wüstenassel *Hemilepistus reaumuri* nach ihrer Höhle. Ph. Thesis: Regensburg University.

- (1983a): The random elements in the systematic search behavior of the desert isopod *Hemilepistus reaumuri*. Behav. Ecol. Sociobiol. 13, 81–92.
- (1983b): The search behavior of the desert isopod *Hemilepistus reaumuri* as compared with a systematic search. Behav. Ecol. Sociobiol. 13, 93–106.
- (1983c): Optimization of brownian search strategies. Biol. Cybern. 49, 21–31.
- (1984): Homing by systematic search. In: Varju, D., Schnitzler, H.-U. (Eds): Localization and Orientation in Biology and Engineering, 192–199. Springer Verlag Berlin-Heidelberg.

Hölldobler, B. and Michener, C. D. (1980): Mechanisms of identification and discrimination in social hymenoptera. In *Evolution of Social Behaviour*: Hypothesis and empirical tests. 35–58. Markl, H. (Ed). Dahlem Konferenzen 1980. Weinheim, Verlag Chemie GmbH.

Holmes, W. G. and P. W. Sherman (1982): The ontogeny of kin recognition in two species of ground squirrels. Amer. Zool. 22, 491–517.

- (1983): Kin recognition in animals. Amer. Sci. 71, 46–55.

Johnson, V. R., Jr. (1977): Individual recognition in the banded shrimp *Stenopus hispidus* (Olivier). Anim. Behav. 25, 418–428.

Knowlton, L. (1980): Sexual selection and dimorphism in two demes of a symbiotic, pair-bonding snapping shrimp. Evolution 34, 161–173.

Krempien, W. (1983): Die antennale Chemorezeption von *Hemilepistus reaumuri* (Audouin and Savigny) (Crustacea, Isopoda, Oniscoidea) Ph. D. Thesis: Würzburg University.

Lamprecht, J. (1973): Mechanismen des Paarzusammenhaltes beim Cichliden *Tilapia mariae* Boulanger 1899 (Cichlidae, Teleostei). Z. Tierpsych. 32, 10–61.

Linsenmair, K. E. (1972): Die Bedeutung familienspezifischer «Abzeichen» für den Familienzusammenhalt bei der sozialen Wüstenassel *Hemilepistus reaumuri* AUDOUIN u. SAVIGNY (Crustacea, Isopoda, Oniscoidea). Z. Tierpsychol. 31, 131–162.

- (1975): Some adaptations of the desert woodlouse *Hemilepistus reaumuri* (Isopoda, Oniscoidea) to desert environment. Verh. d. Gesell. ökol. Erlangen, 183–185.
- (1979): Untersuchungen zur Soziobiologie der Wüstenassel *Hemilepistus reaumuri* und verwandter Isopodenarten (Isopoda, Oniscoidea): Paarbindung und Evolution der Monogamie. Verh. Dtsch. Zool. Ges. Stuttgart, 60–72.
- (1984): Comparative studies on the social behaviour of the desert isopod *Hemilepistus reaumuri* and of a Canarian *Porcellio* species. Symp. zool. Soc. London. 53, 423–453.
- I (in prep.): Family dissolving and pair formation in the desert isopod *Hemilepistus reaumuri*.
- II (in prep.): Recognition of the own progeny in the social isopod *Hemilepistus reaumuri*.
- III (in prep.): Experimental analysis of the intrafamily communication in the desert isopod *Hemilepistus reaumuri* and in some subsocial *Porcellio* species.

Linsenmair, K. E. and Linsenmair, Ch. (1971): Paarbildung und Paarzusammenhalt bei der monogamen Wüstenassel *Hemilepistus reaumuri* (Crustacea, Isopoda, Oniscoidea). Z. Tierpsych. 29, 134–155.

Linsenmair, K. E., H. Schildknecht, and U. Esswein (in prep.): The chemistry of the family badge in the social isopod *Hemilepistus reaumuri*.

Michener, C. D. (1974): *The Social Behavior of the Bees*. Cambridge, The Belknapp Press of Harvard University Press.

Michener, C. D. (1985): From solitary to eusocial bees. *Experimental Behavioral Ecology and Sociobiology*. Symposium in memoriam K. VON FRISCH (HÖLLDOBLER, B. and M. LINDAUER eds.) Fortschritte der Zoologie Bd. 31.

Pukowski, E. (1933): Ökologische Untersuchungen an *Necrophorus*. Z. Morph. Ökol. Tiere 27, 518–586.

Ribbands, C. R. (1965): The role of recognition of comrades in the defence of social insect communities. Symp. zool. Soc. Lond. *14*, 159–168.

Seelinger, G. (1977): Der Antennenendzapfen der tunesischen Wüstenassel *Hemilepistus reaumuri*, ein komplexes Sinnesorgan (Crustacea, Isopoda). J. comp. Physiol. *113*, 95–103.

Seelinger, G. and U. Seelinger (1983): On the social organisation, alarm and fighting in the primitive cockroach *Cryptocercus punctulatus* Scudder. Z. Tierpsychol. *61*, 315–333.

Shachak, M. (1980): Energy allocation and life history strategy of desert isopod *Hemilepistus reaumuri*. Oecologia (Berl.) *45*, 404–413.

Sherman, P. W. and W. G. Holmes (1985): Kin recognition: issues and evidence. *Experimental Behavioral Ecology and Sociobiology*, Symposium in memoriam K. von Frisch (Hölldobler, B. and M. Lindauer eds.) Fortschritte der Zoologie Bd. 31.

Seibt, U. (1974): Mechanismen und Sinnesleistungen für den Paarzusammenhalt bei der Garnele *Hymenocera picta* Dana. Z. Tierpsychol. *35*, 337–351.

– (1980): Soziometrische Analyse von Gruppen der Garnele *Hymenocera picta*. *52*, 321–330.

Seibt, U. and W. Wickler (1979): The biological significance of the pair-bond in the shrimp *Hymenocera picta*. Z. Tierpsychol. *5*, 166–179.

Steinmann, E. (1973): Über die Nahorientierung der Einsiedlerbienen *Osmia bicornis* L. und *Osmia cornuta* Latr. (Hymenoptera, Apoidea). Mitt. Schweiz. Ent. Ges. *46*, 119–122.

– (1976): Über die Nahorientierung solitärer Hymenopteren: Individuelle Markierung der Nesteingänge. Mitt. Schweiz. Ent. Ges. *49*, 253–258.

Vannini, M. and F. Gherardi (1981): Dominance and individual recognition in *Potamon fluviatile* (Decapoda, Bradyura): possible role of visual cues. Mar. Behav. Physiol. *8*, 13–20.

Waldman, B. (1981): Sibling recognition in tadpoles: The role of experience. Z. Tierpsychol. *56*, 341–358.

Wickler, W. and Seibt, U. (1981): Monogamy in crustacea and man. Z. Tierpsychol. *57*, 215–234.

Wilson, E. O. (1971): *The Insect Societies*. Cambridge: The Belknapp Press of Harvard University Press.

Wu, H. M. H., W. G. Holmes, S. R. Medina, and G. P. Sackett (1980): Kin preference in infant *Macaca nemestrina*. Nature *285*, 225–227.

Fortschritte der Zoologie, Bd. 31 · Hölldobler/Lindauer (Hrsg.): Experimental Behavioral Ecology
G. Fischer Verlag · Stuttgart · New York · 1985

Kin recognition: issues and evidence

Paul W. Sherman and Warren G. Holmes

Section of Neurobiology and Behavior, Cornell University, Ithaca, New York 14853; and Department of Psychology, University of Michigan, Ann Arbor, Michigan 48109

Abstract

Investigators from a diversity of backgrounds and theoretical orientations have employed a multitude of techniques to investigate why and how animals recognize their genetic relatives. From an ultimate or evolutionary perspective, it appears that kin recognition abilities serve both to facilitate nepotism and prevent its misdirection, and to preclude close inbreeding and optimize outbreeding. From a proximate perspective, we believe that the ontogenies of all known cases of kin recognition involve learning, and that most are based on the spatial distribution of relatives or on rearing association between related individuals. In this paper we also describe an additional mechanism that facilitates recognition between relatives in the absence of spatial or associational cues. This new mechanism, phenotype matching, depends on learning about one's own phenotype or those of known relatives, and then comparing phenotypes of conspecifics whose relatedness is unknown against this template. After discussing studies of phenotype matching in insects, amphibians, birds, and mammals we summarize the results of our own field and laboratory investigations of kin recognition in Belding's ground squirrels *(Spermophilus beldingi)*. Our work along with comparative investigations of three other species of ground squirrels suggests that phenotype matching abilities are highly developed in the more nepotistic sex (females) of the most social species.

1 Introduction

In a variety of situations individuals may increase their fitness by adjusting their behavior as a function of genetic relatedness to conspecifics. Recently it has become apparent that there are several proximate mechanisms which facilitate the assessment of relatedness. These kin recognition mechanisms do not reveal relatedness *per se;* rather they provide means of assessing social or phenotypic variables that correlate with relatedness.

We define kin recognition (synonyms are kin identification and kin discrimination) as the differential treatment of conspecifics as a function of their genetic relatedness. Thus kin recognition is inferred whenever differential treatment is based on kinship, regardless of whether classes of relatives (for example, siblings as opposed to cousins) or individual relatives (sibling A versus cousin B) are identified. This definition involves no assumptions about cognition or intention; neither does it require that one specific developmental path be followed for kin-correlated behavior to emerge.

Our understanding of how kin are identified has expanded rapidly in the last five years (reviewed by Holmes and Sherman 1982, 1983). Interest in this topic is largely due to two theoretical developments in evolutionary biology. The first is W. D. Hamilton's (1964) concept of inclusive fitness. Under this hypothesis individuals can affect their reproductive success and thus their evolutionary fitness not only through the direct production of offspring and associated parental efforts, but also by assisting both descendant and collateral relatives in their reproductive efforts. Voluminous evidence supporting Hamilton's «kin selection» hypothesis has accumulated (e. g., Alexander 1979; Kurland 1980; Sherman 1981b; Hoogland 1983) and there is no longer any doubt that genetic relatedness mediates cooperation and competition in numerous social species.

The second theoretical advancement that has focused attention on kin recognition is the idea of «optimal outbreeding» (Bateson 1978). Whereas the genetic penalties of close inbreeding have long been recognized (reviewed by Hoogland 1982), recent investigators have suggested that extreme outbreeding may also be disadvantageous (Shields 1982). In other words, one component of mate choice may involve striking an optimal balance between inbreeding and outbreeding (Bateson 1980, 1982; Cowan 1979). Some recent empirical information seems to support this hypothesis (reviewed by Bateson 1983).

Neither the kin selection nor the optimal outbreeding hypothesis requires the existence of any particular mechanism to bring about kin-correlated behavior. Indeed, in his land-

Fig. 1: A lactating female Belding's ground squirrel *(Spermophilus beldingi)* gives an alarm call at the approach of a terrestrial predator. This female is a member of an extensively studied population at Tioga Pass, California. Research in which more than 3,000 ground squirrels have been marked individually and observed unobtrusively has shown that alarm calls are usually given by resident females with living mothers, sisters, or offspring nearby rather than by males or by females who are not resident or who have no offspring or other living kin. This pattern of calling tendencies, together with a population structure in which females are sedentary and males are nomadic, suggests that alarm calls function to alert relatives and are thus expressions of nepotism (Photo courtesy of G. D. Lepp/Bio-Tech Images).

mark paper HAMILTON (1964, pp. 21–25) described several possible kin recognition mechanisms, and added (p. 24) that «... the situations in which a species discriminates in its social behaviour tend to evolve and multiply in such a way that the coefficients of relationship involved in each situation become more nearly determinate.» In recent years theoretical discussions of potential mechanisms for identifying kin have been offered by ALEXANDER (1979), HÖLLDOBLER and MICHENER (1980), SHERMAN (1980), BEKOFF (1981), HOLMES and SHERMAN (1982), and BLAUSTEIN (1983). After reviewing these treatments, we summarize empirical information which suggests to us that at least three different kin recognition mechanisms operate in nature. Each of these mechanisms requires learning, but what is learned and how the information is used are different. In this paper, we compare and contrast these mechanisms and describe the selective circumstances, both ecological and social, that may have led to the evolution of each. Finally, we synopsize the results of our five-year laboratory and field investigation of kin recognition in Belding's ground squirrels (*Spermophilus beldingi*: Fig. 1) in light of these mechanisms.

2 Mechanisms of kin recognition

2.1 Spatial distribution

When relatives are distributed predictably in space, nepotism (favoring kin) may occur as a result of location-specific behavior. Under this mechanism, locations rather than conspecifics themselves are recognized and individuals adjust their behavior as a function of proximity to some reference point such as a nest site or burrow. Close inbreeding might also be minimized (GREENWOOD et al. 1978) or outbreeding optimized (PRICE and WASER 1979) if individuals avoided mating with conspecifics that were encountered at particular locations (e. g., too close to home). The spatial distribution mechanism depends on a close and consistent correlation between places where conspecifics are encountered and genetic relatedness. Thus it requires either viscosity of kin groups or nonrandom dispersal of kin. The reliability of this mechanism is obviously reduced to the degree that nonkin can infiltrate into groups of relatives.

Cues based on location frequently mediate parental recognition of offspring among birds, especially during the early development of young. In many cases, avian parents learn to recognize their nest or nest site rather than the chicks themselves; adults continue using location-specific cues up to the time when their chicks become mobile and broods intermix. This is exemplified by comparing species that differ in degrees of coloniality and the age at which fledging occurs (e. g., BIRKHEAD 1978). For example kittiwakes *(Rissa tridactyla)*, which nest in small cracks on sheer cliff faces, often with only one nest per crack, and whose young fledge at five weeks, accept unrelated young experimentally transferred into their nest up until their own chicks are five weeks old (CULLEN 1957); thereafter, foreign chicks are rejected. Loosely colonial, marsh-nesting Franklin's gulls *(Larus pipixcan)* accept foreign chicks in their nest until their own young fledge and begin to stray, at about two weeks of age (BURGER 1974). Various species of highly colonial, ground nesting gulls, whose young are mobile within a few days of hatching, begin to identify their nestlings rather than simply the nest site when their own young are three to five days old (BEER 1970).

Studies of bank swallows *(Riparia riparia)* have provided further insights. These birds, which nest colonially in sand banks, apparently learn the spatial location of the nest hole they have excavated. Parents will feed both their own young and experimentally introduced foreign chicks, up to the time their own offspring fledge at about two weeks of age

(Hoogland and Sherman 1976; Beecher et al. 1981a). Conversely, they ignore their own unfledged chicks when these are experimentally transferred to nearby nest burrows. Just prior to fledging, chicks begin to produce individually distinctive «signature» calls that parents learn. Parents use these calls to discriminate their own from alien young, so that once natural mixing of fledglings among nests has commenced, parents will feed only their own chicks at home and will seek out and feed misplaced offspring in other nest burrows. After fledglings have abandoned nest burrows, parents continue to rely on calls to locate and subsequently feed only their own offspring (Beecher et al. 1981b).

2.2 Association

Association is probably the most common pathway leading to kin recognition in nature. Under this mechanism, relatives must predictably interact in unambiguous social circumstances, in which kinship is rarely confused due to the mixing of unequally related individuals. Thus, kin recognition involves learning the phenotypes of familiar associates and later recalling them; such learning may be based on the timing, rate, frequency, or duration of their social interactions. Here the term «association» refers to opportunities that individuals have to interact rather than to a particular type of learning process (e. g., associative learning). Rearing environments such as the natal nest or burrow often provide ideal settings for the operation of this mechanism because they typically separate or exclude asymmetrically related individuals.

Association is the usual mechanism of recognition between mothers and their offspring in mammals (Michener 1974; Michener and Sheppard 1972; Holmes in press). For instance, mutual recognition between cows and their pups in Galapagos fur seals *(Arctocephalus galapagoensis)* and sea lions *(Zalophus californianus)* is based on familiarity with each other's vocalizations, and appears soon after pup birth (Trillmich 1981). Furthermore, in several colonial gull species *(Larus),* three to five day old chicks learn to recognize as parents individuals whose vocalizations they hear most frequently at the nest (Beer 1970). Obviously, the ability of goslings to «imprint» on parents or parent-like objects (Lorenz 1935; Hess 1973) suggests learned recognition as a result of association during a sensitive period of development.

One well-studied example of the association mechanism is the work of Leon (1975, 1978) on Wistar rat pups *(Rattus norvegicus).* Leon has shown that rat pups learn to discriminate an odor present in their mother's fecal material when they are about two weeks old. The odor is produced by microbial action in the dam's gut and its chemical composition depends on her diet. After learning their mother's odor, pups offered a choice between their own dam and an unfamiliar lactating female prefer to approach their mother; they are also attracted to her odor over that of an unfamiliar lactating female. These preferences disappear when both females are fed identical diets. Finally, pups prefer one unfamiliar lactating female over another if the diet of one of them matches that of their own dam.

Recognition of siblings also depends on learning during direct interactions in some species. Captive spiny mice *(Acomys cahirinus)* that were placed in a test arena more frequently huddled with littermates with whom they were familiar than with unfamiliar nonlittermates (Porter et al. 1978). When *A. cahirinus* littermates were reared apart, they later behaved as if they were not siblings. Finally, when nonsiblings were reared by the same dam, they later huddled together as if they were biological siblings (Porter et al. 1981).

Thus far the term «association» has meant direct social interactions between individuals later treated as kin. However, mediated recognition by association is also possible. If two unfamiliar relatives first interact in the presence of a third conspecific related to each and familiar to both (a «go-between»), recognition between the previously unfamiliar individuals may be facilitated. For instance, either full-siblings or maternal half-siblings born in sequential litters may sometimes learn to recognize each other as a result of mutually associating with their common parent or parents (SHERMAN 1980).

Females may mediate recognition between sire and offspring in some species (BEREN-STAIN et al. 1981). For example, LABOV (1980) allowed wild-strain male and female house mice *(Mus musculus)* to mate and then separated the pairs twelve hours later. At various times before parturition, a male was placed in each female's cage and allowed to remain there. Sometimes a male was reunited with his prior mate, but in other cases the male was housed with a female inseminated by another male. LABOV reported that the probability of a male's killing his partner's pups varied inversely with the length of cohabitation prior to parturition, regardless of whether a male joined a female he had actually inseminated or one inseminated by another male. In this case, the length of male-female cohabitation apparently affected the behavior of mated males toward pups.

As was true for the spatial distribution mechanism, recognition errors – the acceptance of nonrelatives as kin – should occur under the association mechanism if unrelated individuals are inserted into kin groups at an appropriate time and place. Experimentally transferring or «cross-fostering» young so that they are reared by and among nonrelatives induces such errors in cichlid fish (NOAKES and BARLOW 1973), mice (HILL 1974; DEWS-BURY 1982), domestic goats (KLOPFER and KLOPFER 1968; GUBERNICK 1980), and ground squirrels (HOLMES 1984; in press). Cross-fostering has also been used as a tool to investigate the development of parent-offspring and sibling-sibling recognition in bank swallows (HOOGLAND and SHERMAN 1976; BEECHER et al. 1981a; BEECHER and BEECHER 1983) and Belding's ground squirrels (HOLMES and SHERMAN 1982). In both these species, and in many others (e. g., McARTHUR 1982), the appearance of differential treatment of newly cross-fostered young coincides with the time when broods first mix in nature. This suggests that the total frequency or duration of exposure to relatives (BEKOFF 1981) is not as important, under the association mechanism, as are the interactions which occur coincident with or just before the time when unequally related conspecifics first mingle (see also KAREEM 1983).

2.3 Phenotype matching: theoretical issues

Can kin identify each other even if they have not interacted in locations or social circumstances that correlate directly with their relatedness? This is an intriguing question because in many species various relatives do not have obvious locational or associational cues available to indicate kinship. Nonetheless, a growing body of empirical evidence, from insects, amphibians, birds, and mammals indicates the identification of such relatives. We believe that many of these cases involve a process of «comparing phenotypes» (ALEXANDER 1979, p. 116) or «phenotype matching» (HOLMES and SHERMAN 1982, 1983). Under this mechanism, an individual learns about its own phenotypic attributes or those of its relatives by direct association with them or cues associated with them (e.g., their odors), and acquires an image or template of these attributes. When a conspecific whose relatedness is unknown is encountered at some later time, the focal individual matches that phenotype against this learned template. In general, the degree of similarity between the observed and «expected» phenotype is the clue to relatedness. Thus phenotype matching is a perceptual process that may parallel what psychologists call «stimulus generalization» (e. g., MOSTOFSKY 1965), in which an animal's response to an unfamiliar stimulus depends on its similarity to previously learned, familiar stimuli.

Phenotype matching depends on a consistent correlation between phenotypic similarity and genotypic similarity, so that detectable traits are more alike among close relatives than among distantly related or unrelated individuals. These phenotypic traits may have genetic origins, (Kukuk et al. 1977; Greenberg 1979; Breed 1981, 1983), environmental origins (Kalmus and Ribbands 1952), or be derived from a combination of both. Regardless of their source(s), if resemblances in such traits are reliably associated with genotypic similarities they may serve as cues for phenotype matching.

At this point we wish to distinguish explicitly two components that comprise kin recognition processes in general and phenotype matching in particular. First, the *production* component refers to the ways unique phenotypes develop, making individuals or groups distinctive and thus discriminable from others. Second, the *perception* component refers to the ways individuals develop abilities to discriminate among phenotypes. As pointed out by Beecher (1982), the absence of either component precludes kin recognition.

Two different approaches have so far characterized studies of the phenotype-production component. First, mathematical models have been developed to evaluate the amount of information necessary to specify relatedness accurately (e. g., Crozier and Dix 1979; Getz 1981, 1982; Beecher 1982; Lacy and Sherman 1983). These models suggest that accuracy depends on several key factors: the number of independently assorting, detectable traits, their variation and heritability, and the algorithm used to assess kinship based on the traits. A second approach has been an empirical search for the sensory modalities that convey information about the phenotype (e. g., auditory: Beecher et al. 1981b; McArthur 1982; olfactory: Kaplan et al. 1977; Porter and Moore 1981; visual: Miller and Emlen 1975). Terms that have been used to characterize the production component include «discriminator» or «discriminating substance» (Hölldobler and Michener 1980), «signatures» (Beecher 1982), «colony odor» (especially in hymenoptera: Ribbands 1965; Barrows et al. 1975; Kukuk et al. 1977; Crozier and Dix 1979), «recognition cues» (Breed 1981, 1983), and «labeling systems» (Getz 1981, 1982).

2.4 Phenotype matching: empirical evidence

There are three categories of participants in the phenotype matching process we envision. The *observer* is the individual attempting to assess its relationship to an *observed individual*. *Referents* are conspecifics whose phenotypes provide clues about the traits to be expected in various relatives. These referents, from whose phenotypes the template is learned, could be either the observer's familiar relative(s) or the observer itself.

In sweat bees (*Lasioglossum zephyrum*) referents are apparently nestmates. *L. zephyrum* females nest in groups and restrict access to their shared nest burrow by guarding the entrance. Only a single bee acts as a guard at any one time, and guards allow nestmates (usually their sisters) to enter while excluding non-nestmates. In the laboratory, Greenberg (1979) reared guard bees with sisters and later presented guards with unfamiliar conspecifics at nest-hole entrances. Intruders were related to guards with varying degrees of closeness as a result of controlled inbreeding. Greenberg's (1979) results show that the percentage of unfamiliar bees admitted to the nest rose as genetic relatedness between the guard and the unfamiliar intruder increased (Fig. 2a).

In a follow-up experiment, Buckle and Greenberg (1981) reared some *L. zephyrum* solely with non-sisters. In nest-entrance tests these bees admitted unfamiliar intruders if they were the sisters of guards' nestmates, while rejecting their own sisters (Fig. 2b). Buckle and Greenberg (1981) also reared bees in mixed groups of their sisters and non-sisters. They found that these individuals admitted both their unfamiliar sisters and unfamiliar sisters of their (unrelated) nestmates (Fig. 2b). Thus *L. zephyrum* guards discriminate among unfamiliar conspecifics on the basis of their phenotypic similarity to individuals with whom the guards were reared, rather than similarity to their own phenotype.

In the sweat bee case, phenotypic cues used to assess relatedness apparently arise from a genetic source (KUKUK et al. 1977; GREENBERG 1979). In another hymenopteran, nestmate

Fig. 2: Laboratory experiments on kin recognition in sweat bees *(Lasioglossum zephyrum)*. Female *L. zephyrum* guard the entrance to their shared nest, typically admitting only nestmates, which are usually their sisters.

a Guard bees were raised with sisters and later presented with intruders that they had never before encountered. The unfamiliar intruders were related to the guards with varying degrees of closeness as a result of controlled inbreeding. The likelihood that guards would admit intruders to their nest increased with the degree of genetic relatedness between guard and intruder. One possible explanation for the discrimination mechanism is that guards admit unfamilar individuals on the basis of their phenotypic similarity (probably in odor) to nestmates (Redrawn from GREENBERG 1979; copyright 1979 by the AAAS).

b Guard bees were reared in nests of six bees composed either solely of sisters (colony X and colony Y), or of three sisters from one nest and three sisters from another (colony XY). Later, bees from X, Y, and XY colonies were tested as guards as shown (arrows represent unfamiliar intruders seeking entrance to the nest). Guards reared solely with sisters were about three times as likely to admit unfamiliar sisters as unfamiliar, unrelated intruders, allowing 65 % of the unfamiliar sisters to enter as opposed to only 23 % of the unfamiliar, unrelated individuals. However, guards reared in a mixed colony were about as likely to admit their nestmates' unfamiliar sisters as their own unfamiliar sisters, allowing respectively 64 % and 67 % to enter. Guards may have matched the phenotypes of unfamiliar intruders against the phenotypes of bees with whom they were reared and admitted intruders similar to their own nestmates (Redrawn from BUCKLE and GREENBERG 1981).

recognition also appears to be based on phenotype matching but the cues may be of environmental origin. In a recent series of experiments, Pfennig et al. (1983b) brought pupae-laden nests of the paper wasp *Polistes fuscatus* into the laboratory. As each gyne (potential queen) emerged from her natal cell she was assigned to one of four groups: (1) exposure to her natal nest and emerging nestmates for at least five days, (2) exposure to her natal nest but not to nestmates for 4–13 hours, (3) exposure to her natal nest but not to nestmates for only one hour, and (4) exposure to a «foreign nest» and «pseudo-» or «non-pseudonestmates» for 3–5 days. A foreign nest was one to which a female was transferred upon eclosion. Pseudonestmates were created when unrelated gynes were transferred to separate fragments of the same foreign nest; a non-pseudonestmate was a gyne placed on a fragment of a different foreign nest from that to which pseudonestmates had been transferred.

Pfennig et al. (1983b) investigated nestmate recognition by assessing, in a small arena, tolerance values (tendencies of initiators of behavioral interactions to elicit retreat by a recipient) and spatial associations among triplets that were composed of combinations of nestmates, non-nestmates, or pseudonestmates. The researchers reported that gynes exposed to both their natural nest and to nestmates for at least five days (Group 1) were more tolerant of and associated more closely with unfamiliar nestmates than unfamiliar non-nestmates. Similarly, gynes exposed for 4–13 hours (Group 2) or one hour (Group 3) only to their nests showed greater tolerance for and associated more closely with unfamiliar nestmates than unfamiliar non-nestmates. Finally unrelated pseudonestmates, who were exposed to separate fragments of the same but unrelated nest (Group 4), were more tolerant of each other than they were of non-pseudonestmates, who had been exposed to fragments of yet another unrelated nest.

These results suggest that *P. fuscatus* females may absorb chemical cues from the nest soon after eclosion. In less than one hour after emergence, gynes learn these odors, probably from the nest rather than themselves or other nestmates (Shellman and Gamboa 1982; Pfennig et al. 1983a), and use them as a template in the discrimination of nestmates from nonnestmates. This implies that phenotype matching against chemical cues learned from the natal nest underlies nestmate identification in this species. Indeed, in the most stringent test of the matching hypothesis, non-sister gynes exposed to separate fragments of the same foreign nest (Group 4) were more tolerant of each other than of another unrelated gyne that had been exposed to fragments of a different foreign nest. In the wild, *P. fuscatus* females may use their recognition abilities to discriminate between the nests of sisters, with whom they cooperate, and nonrelatives, whose nests they sometimes usurp (Klahn and Gamboa 1983).

The results of several investigations of discrimination in mammals (Gilder and Slater 1978) and birds (Bateson 1978) are also suggestive of phenotype matching with nestmates as referents. In one interesting example, Bateson (1980, 1982) hatched Japanese quail *(Coturnix c. japonica)* in an incubator, reared them with siblings for thirty days, then isolated them for an additional thirty days. At sexual maturity (ca. sixty days of age), the quail were simultaneously presented with five different conspecifics: a familiar sibling, an unfamiliar sibling, an unfamiliar first cousin, an unfamiliar third cousin, and an unfamiliar, unrelated bird. Time spent in front of each stimulus bird, which is an indirect measure of relative mating preference, was recorded. The results, although quite variable, showed that both sexes preferred to stand near their (unfamiliar) first cousins over all the other choice birds. Bateson interpreted these preferences for first cousins in terms of optimal outbreeding, and suggested that the choice mechanism involves comparing phenotypes, with individuals preferring conspecifics whose appearance differs slightly but not greatly from the siblings with whom subjects grew up.

The most recent studies of captive spiny mice suggest that in addition to recognition by association (above), phenotype matching with nestmates as referents can also occur. Previous work indicated that if *A. cahirinus* juveniles were separated for eight days from littermates with whom they were reared, their tendency to huddle with these littermates was abolished (PORTER and WYRICK 1979). It now appears that if the separated littermates are each housed with another of their siblings, they retain their preference for each other (PORTER et al. 1983). In explaining these results, PORTER and his colleagues suggest that littermates' phenotypes (probably odors) «... can influence interactions among *A. cahirinus* weanlings by serving as a learned standard against which odours of conspecifics are compared» (p. 982–983).

The second general class of referents under a phenotype matching mechanism is the observer itself. Although unequivocal evidence for self-matching is not yet available, we believe that various studies point to its existence. For example, self-matching may occur in American toads *(Bufo americanus)*. WALDMAN (1981, 1982) found that in laboratory tests tadpoles reared with their siblings later preferred to associate with those individuals over

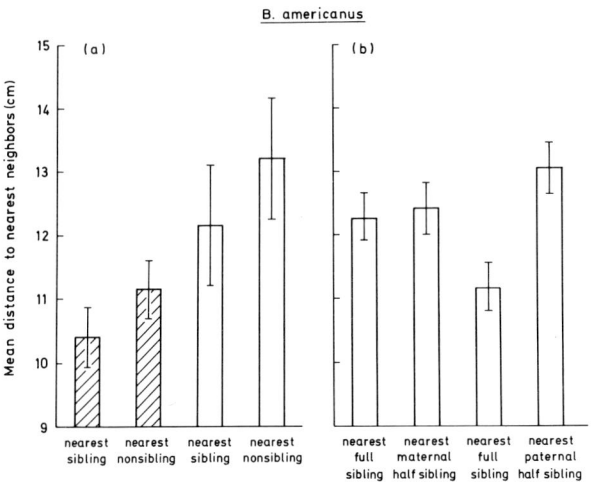

Fig. 3: Laboratory experiments on kin recognition in tadpoles of American toads *(Bufo americanus)*. In each test, two marked groups of tadpoles- either two different sets of full-siblings, full-siblings and their maternal half-siblings, or full-siblings and their paternal half-siblings – that were reared with siblings (hatched) or singly (open) were released into a laboratory pool. Later the distance from each tadpole to its nearest similarly and dissimilarly marked neighbor was recorded.

a Both for tadpoles reared with siblings and for tadpoles reared in isolation, the mean distance to the nearest full-sibling was less than the mean distance to the nearest nonsibling (bars denote 95 % confidence limits).

b Among tadpoles reared alone, there was no difference between the mean distance to the nearest full-sibling and that to the nearest maternal half-sibling; however, the mean distance to the nearest full-sibling was significantly less than that to the nearest paternal half-sibling.

Overall the findings depicted in this figure suggest that some maternal contribution to the egg (such as the jelly) served as a template against which the phenotypes of unfamiliar conspecifics were matched (Redrawn from WALDMAN 1981).

unfamiliar non-siblings. When WALDMAN (1981) divided egg masses early in development and reared each embryo individually in a petri dish, he found that as free-swimming larvae the tadpoles associated more closely with unfamilar siblings than unfamiliar non-siblings. Because in this experiment the rearing procedures eliminated social contact during development, it appears that *B. americanus* tadpoles can identify siblings by means of something learned from their own phenotype (Fig. 3a).

Indeed, WALDMAN (1981) hypothesized that substances contained in the egg or its surrounding jelly might cue recognition. He investigated this by creating paternal half-siblings (one male fertilized the eggs of two females) and maternal half-siblings (some of a female's eggs were fertilized by one male and some by another), then rearing the resulting eggs in isolation. When tested later the tadpoles showed no preference between full-siblings and maternal half-siblings, conspecifics that shared egg jelly derived from the same female. By contrast, the tadpoles preferred to associate more closely with full-siblings than with paternal half-siblings (Fig. 3b). These results are consistent with the hypothesis that sibling recognition in *B. americanus* larvae is cued by some factor associated with the egg or its surrounding matrix.

In related experiments on the Cascade frog *(Rana cascadae)*, BLAUSTEIN and O'HARA (1981) found that tadpoles reared among siblings preferred to swim near those individuals rather than unfamiliar non-siblings in a laboratory tank (also O'HARA and BLAUSTEIN 1981). The preference for siblings is apparently retained after metamorphosis (BLAUSTEIN et al. 1984). Like *B. americanus* larvae, *R. cascadae* tadpoles reared in social isolation later preferred to swim near unfamiliar siblings over unfamiliar non-siblings (BLAUSTEIN and O'HARA 1981). Moreover, in two-choice tests the isolates preferred full-siblings over either maternal or paternal half-siblings, and both sorts of half-siblings over unrelated conspecifics (BLAUSTEIN and O'HARA 1982). These results indicate that the maternal egg jelly might mediate the identification of some but certainly not all discriminable relatives in *R. cascadae*.

Phenotype matching based on self-perception is suggested by a study (WU et al. 1980) of recognition in pigtail macaques *(Macaca nemestrina)*. Laboratory matings of male monkeys with several females each produced multiple pairs of paternal half-siblings. Immediately after they were born, the infants were separated from their mothers and reared by humans. To encourage normal development each youngster was allowed to associate daily with a group of nonkin of the same age. When they were one to twelve months old, 16 of these monkeys were offered choices in a laboratory apparatus among an unfamiliar paternal half-sibling, an unfamiliar conspecific (not closely related to either the subject or its half-sibling), and an empty cage; stimulus animals were matched for sex, age, and weight. WU and her colleagues reported that subjects looked longer at their half-sibling than at either the unrelated monkey or the empty cage, and that they spent significantly more time in proximity to their half-sibling when allowed to approach the three stimuli. To account for these results, DAWKINS (1982, p. 150) has speculated «... my bet is that the monkeys recognize resemblances of relatives to perceived features of themselves.» While this hypothesis is reasonable, we caution that the macaque study has recently been repeated by FREDRICKSON and SACKETT (1984) with quite different results and interpretations (i.e., no recognition of unfamiliar paternal half-siblings was found). Thus whether or not *M. nemestrina* match phenotypes is now in dispute.

Phenotype matching based on self-perception is a plausible mechanism underlying some recently discovered kin recognition abilities of birds and small mammals. For example, male chicks *(Gallus gallus)* that are reared alone apparently «auto-imprint.» As a result they develop a social preference in adulthood for conspecifics or models similar in structure and coloration to themselves (VIDAL 1982; see also SALZEN and CORNELL 1968). In laboratory tests, house mice (*M. musculus*, C. F. L. P. strain) discriminate between unfamiliar paternal half-siblings and unfamiliar, unrelated mice, with the half-sibling pairs showing more «passive body contact» and fewer aggressive interactions in their initial contacts than the unrelated pairs (KAREEM and BARNARD 1982; also KAREEM 1983). Laboratory-reared white-footed deermice *(Peromyscus leucopus)* apparently can distinguish between siblings from parents' subsequent litters and non-siblings, despite not having associated with either prior to testing (GRAU 1982).

Finally, recognition based on phenotype matching may occur in honeybees *(Apis mellifera)*. GETZ et al. (1982) created hives composed of two groups of differently related workers by artificially inseminating one queen with the sperm of two males from phenotypically distinct strains (cordovan and Italian). The investigators discovered that when colony fission occurred the swarm that left the hive contained a slight bias toward full-sisters rather than a random assortment of full- and maternal half-sisters. However, as the authors note, since queens were inseminated with sperm from different strains, the mechanism responsible for the composition of the swarm could have been inter-strain differences in behavior (e. g., the timing of swarming) rather than kin recognition. In a follow-up study, GETZ and SMITH (1983) again used artificially inseminated *A. mellifera* queens to produce three hives containing both full- and maternal half-sisters (i. e., workers were sired by the same male or a male from a different strain). The researchers reported that in arena tests workers were more likely to bite their (different strain) half-sisters than their (same strain) full-sisters, despite having been reared with both.

With the exception of the studies of sweat bees (BUCKLE and GREENBERG 1981) and paper wasps (PFENNIG et al. 1983b), investigations of kin recognition mechanisms have rarely used the kinds of rigorously controlled rearing and testing procedures necessary to elucidate whether phenotype matching is occurring, and if so whether it is based on self-perception or on a template derived from perceptions of other relatives. However, it is clear that phenotype matching is a real possibility and one that merits detailed examination, especially when kin-correlated behavior is observed that cannot be accounted for on the basis of the spatial distribution or association mechanisms.

Table 1: Ecological and social circumstances in which phenotype matching may be favored as a mechanism of kin recognition (after HOLMES and SHERMAN 1982).

I. Multiple Mating
    (a) Maternal half-siblings reared together
    (b) Paternal half-siblings reared apart
    (c) Sire-offspring recognition

II. Inter-brood Aggregation
    (a) Grouped embryos or young
    (b) Cooperative breeding

III. Parasitism
    (a) Intra-specific parasitism
    (b) Inter-specific parasitism

IV. Dispersal or Group Size
    (a) Adult or juvenile relatives disperse
    (b) Large or widely dispersed social group

2.5 Phenotype matching: ecological and social contexts

There are at least four ecological and social circumstances in nature when a phenotype matching mechanism might be favored as a way to recognize kin (Table 1). These are conditions in which spatial or associational cues are typically unavailable or are inaccurate indicators of relatedness. It is important to note that these circumstances will not automatically lead to phenotype matching. However, if optimizing outbreeding or dispensing nepotism are advantageous, these are likely contexts for its evolution.

First, male or female polygamy may select for phenotype matching. If a male mates with several females so that paternal half-siblings are born in the same or different breeding seasons, phenotype matching may be favored when such kin do not grow up together nor live in proximity. Conversely, if a female mates with two or more males during a single receptive period so that her brood is multiply sired (e. g., Hanken and Sherman 1981) or if a female's sequential broods are sired by different males, then spatial or associational cues may not distinguish full- from half-siblings. Furthermore, a male might rely on phenotype matching to identify his offspring among a mate's young (Alexander 1979; Daly and Wilson 1982), especially if the male was unable to guard his mate(s) effectively after copulation or if he was only one of several males to mate with that female.

Second, when differently related young are reared together, as in a communal nest, spatial and associational cues might lead to incorrect kinship assessments. For example, females in many species of frogs, toads, and salamanders deposit eggs in a common microhabitat, and females in several bird species lay eggs in a common nest. As a result, eggs and young that differ in relatedness often develop side by side, a situation which virtually demands some type of phenotype matching if kin recognition is to occur.

Third, brood parasitism within (e. g., Weller 1959) or between species (e. g., Payne 1977; Rothstein 1982) obviously reduces the reliability of spatial proximity or intra-nest associations as indicators of relatedness.

Fourth, dispersal at an early age or large group size may eliminate both spatial and associational cues about kinship. Dispersal from the natal area or group coincident with puberty may preclude older individuals from meeting younger relatives until later in life, when contextual cues about kinship are missing. For example, in many species of birds and mammals, juveniles disperse before full- or half-siblings are born in their parents' subsequent broods (Greenwood 1980; Dobson 1982). Furthermore very large groups, such as those that characterize some social insects and ungulates, may contain so many individuals spread over such an extensive area that some close relatives will not meet until adulthood.

2.6 Recognition alleles

Among mechanisms of kin recognition originally described by Hamilton (1964) was a genetic model that relied on phenotypic assessment but not «phenotype matching». He hypothesized «recognition alleles» that simultaneously caused the expression of a unique phenotypic trait, enabled their bearer to recognize the trait in others, and caused their bearer to preferentially assist conspecifics possessing the trait. Dawkins (1976, 1982) dubbed this the «green beard effect,» metaphorically suggesting that these alleles might code for green beards and also cause their bearers to aid other green-bearded individuals. In contrast to association and phenotype matching, this mechanism postulates that the ability to recognize phenotypic attributes is conferred by the very same alleles that cause the attributes or by alleles tightly linked to them (Alexander 1979).

Both Hamilton and Dawkins deemed the existence of recognition alleles unlikely due to their necessary complexity. Others (e. g., Alexander and Borgia 1978) have argued that such alleles are improbable as a basis for kin recognition because of the costs the behaviors they cause would impose on portions of the genome not shared by the actor and recipient. In other words, the presence of such «selfish» alleles would engender an intragenomic conflict of reproductive interests, with the result that alleles whose effects tended to nullify those of the recognition alleles would spread. Whether hypothetical recognition alleles would indeed be «outlaws» (ALEXANDER and BORGIA 1978), helping themselves at the expense of the rest of the genome, or not (RIDLEY and GRAFEN 1981) is a subject of considerable theoretical interest and debate.

Regardless of the outcome of this discussion, we think that an empirical search for recognition alleles would be difficult at best, because their existence could be inferred only after systematically eliminating all environmental and experiential cues including a subject's experience with its own phenotype. Thus it is not surprising that recognition alleles have never been identified experimentally. Although researchers might wish to heed BLAUSTEIN's (1983) urging and remain open to the existence of recognition alleles, until empirical evidence appears that cannot be understood in terms of our three aforementioned mechanisms, recognition alleles seem hypothetical.

3 Kin recognition in Belding's ground squirrels

For the past five years (1979–83) we have studied kin recognition by Belding's ground squirrels (Fig. 1). Considerable information has been accumulated about the behavioral ecology of this social rodent (SHERMAN 1977, 1980, 1981a, 1981b), allowing us to design laboratory and field experiments that closely approximate conditions under which recognition abilities develop in nature. In brief our results suggest that all three mechanisms, spatial distribution, association, and phenotype matching, are used by *S. beldingi* to identify various relatives; these mechanisms are used under different circumstances and apparently serve different evolutionary functions.

At our study site near Tioga Pass, high (3,040 m) in the central Sierra Nevada of California, Belding's ground squirrels are diurnally active from May through September; the rest of the year they hibernate (MORTON and SHERMAN 1978). Mating occurs within a week of a female's emergence in the spring, and each female typically mates with three or four different males during her single four to six hour receptive period. She rears only one litter of two to eight pups per season. The young are nursed in a solitary burrow until they are about three weeks old, when they emerge above ground. At this point we capture the juveniles, sample their blood for later paternity determinations, and permanently mark them; thus kinship is assessed before littermates mix with neighboring juveniles.

Two to five weeks after they are weaned, juvenile males begin to disperse from their natal area (SHERMAN 1977; HOLEKAMP 1983). They will rarely, if ever, associate again with their mother or sisters. Females by contrast are sedentary from birth, seldom moving very far from their natal burrow. Thus females live near and interact daily with close female relatives. After the spring mating period, some adult males move again. This postbreeding dispersal, coupled with the high mortality characteristic of males (SHERMAN and MORTON in press), virtually precludes matings between fathers and their offspring the following season. In other words males do not inbreed with close kin as a result of permanent dispersal away from places where female relatives are likely to be encountered. Thus outbreeding is enforced via the spatial distribution kin recognition mechanism.

Whereas males do not help rear offspring or assist any other kin, nepotism is important in the social behavior of female *S. beldingi*. Females assist close relatives by giving warning calls when predators appear (Fig. 1), by sharing territories and associated food resources,

450 · P. W. Sherman and W. G. Holmes

and by cooperating to defend nursing pups against attacks by infanticidal members of their own species. Mother-daughter and sister-sister pairs are particularly cooperative, whereas more distant kin such as nieces and cousins are treated the same as unrelated females.

To investigate the effects of sharing a nest on the development of sibling recognition in *S. beldingi*, we manipulated rearing associations in a laboratory study (Holmes and Sherman 1982). Eighteen pregnant females that had mated in the field were captured near Tioga Pass and shipped to the laboratory. Pups born to these females were cross-fostered between dams within three hours of parturition, creating four kinds of rearing groups: siblings reared together by a common dam (either their own mother or a foster dam), siblings reared apart by different dams, non-siblings reared together, and non-siblings reared apart. Subsequent to the experimental transfers most nursing litters contained both biological siblings and non-siblings. Pups were weaned, fattened, and then placed in individual cages in a coldroom for a six-month hibernation period.

Fig. 4: Belding's ground squirrel pups born to females mated in the field were cross-fostered in the laboratory shortly after birth to create four rearing groups: siblings reared together (S. RT.), siblings reared apart (S. RA.), nonsiblings reared together (NS. RT.), and nonsiblings reared apart (NS. RA.). At the age of eight months, pairs from each group were observed in an arena for five minutes and the number of agonistic interactions was recorded.

a The mean number (± S. E.) of agonistic encounters between pairs differing in relatedness and rearing association. The results indicate that both siblings and non-siblings reared together were less aggressive than pairs reared apart. Whereas siblings and nonsiblings reared together were about equally nonaggressive, siblings reared apart were somewhat less aggressive than nonsiblings reared apart. Sample sizes and results of statistical tests are shown.

b The mean number (± S. E.) of agonistic encounters between pairs reared apart (from a), further analyzed to take into account the sex of each pair. This analysis revealed that sisters reared apart were significantly less aggressive than unrelated females reared apart; this was not true for pairs of males or males and females reared apart (From Holmes and Sherman 1982).

Following hibernation, eight month old animals from the four rearing groups were observed during paired-encounter tests in an arena (1 m × 1 m in size), and the frequencies of eleven types of agonistic encounters were recorded. The results showed that young reared together, regardless of relatedness, were less aggressive than young reared apart (Fig. 4a). This was true regardless of sex or whether individuals were reared solely with siblings or with both siblings and nonsiblings. Furthermore, young reared together were about equally nonaggressive, whether or not they were related. Thus our data indicate that association during development mediates differential treatment of littermates.

Interestingly, these same tests revealed that sisters reared apart were significantly less aggressive than unrelated females reared apart (Fig. 4b). By contrast, relatedness did not seem to affect aggression between male-male or male-female pairs that had been reared apart. Thus only the females, the nepotistic sex in the field, behaved as if they could identify sisters despite not having been raised with them.

In describing the association mechanism, we argued that a sensitive period for kin recognition often occurs coincident with the time when young from different broods first mix in nature. Results of a field cross-fostering study, and a follow-up laboratory investigation, indicate such time dependence in S. beldingi (HOLMES and SHERMAN 1982; HOLMES in press). In the field experiment unrelated pups, matched for age with resident young, were inserted into nest burrows of lactating females at Tioga Pass. We found that foster dams accepted as offspring pups transferred into their burrows before the weaning of their own litters (about 25 days post-partum; Fig. 5). Furthermore, foster siblings treated female pups transferred before they were 25 days old as littermates the following season. By contrast, alien juveniles that were introduced into nest burrows after a female's twenty-fifth post-partum day elicited aggression from the potential foster dam, and as yearlings were treated like nonkin by foster sisters.

Fig. 5: To study the development of recognition between mother and offspring in S. beldingi, pups of different ages were cross-fostered into the burrows of lactating females in the field. For pups up to about twenty-five days of age, the percentage of acceptance was high; these pups eventually emerged above ground with the resident pups and behaved as if the foster burrowmates were nestmates. However, the percentage of acceptance dropped dramatically for pups older than twenty-five days, the age when resident pups are normally weaned and first emerge from the nest burrow. The sudden drop in acceptance at this point suggests that the onset of recognition by association coincides with the time when litters first mix in nature. Sample sizes are indicated (From HOLMES and SHERMAN 1982).

In the follow-up laboratory study, pups were also exchanged between females (HOLMES in press). On Days 1 (i. e., 24 h post-partum), 8, 15, and 22, four pups, one from each of four groups, were presented simultaneously outside a female's nest box and the time until she retrieved each was recorded. The stimulus pups were either related-familiar, unrelated-familiar, related-unfamiliar, or unrelated-unfamiliar (related indicates whether or not a pup was the dam's own offspring, and familiar indicates whether or not the pup was reared by the dam). The time between pup introduction and retrieval by the female did not differ among the four categories of young on Days 1, 8, and 15. On Day 22 post-partum, familiar young were for the first time retrieved significantly faster than unfamiliar young. At no time did females seem to distinguish between their own offspring and the young of another female. During paired-encounter tests on Day 29, familiar dam-young pairs were significantly less agonistic than unfamiliar pairs; as in the retrieval study, there was no evidence that relatedness influenced arena encounters. Thus, both the field and laboratory

Fig. 6: Insemination of free-living female *S. beldingi* by more than one male frequently results in litters composed of full-siblings and maternal half-siblings, as shown by electrophoretic paternity exclusion analyses (HANKEN and SHERMAN 1981). Full- and half-sisters were observed in the field and their behavior was compared with that of «littermate sisters» whose exact relatedness was unknown. Numbers in parentheses indicate how many pairs were observed.

Left (a). The mean proportion (± S. E.) of times littermate sisters, full-sisters, and half-sisters fought when they encountered each other (came within 0.5 m. of one another).

Left (b). The mean proportion (± S. E.) of times littermate sisters, full-sisters, and half-sisters chased one another out of a territory following a trespass.

Right (a). The mean proportion (± S. E.) of cooperative chases in which residents were assisted by their littermate sisters, full-sisters, and half-sisters to evict trespassers who had entered their territory.

Right (b). The mean proportion (± S. E.) of chases in which females that were being chased were assisted by their littermate sisters, full-sisters, and half-sisters.

Overall the data suggest that despite being reared together, full-sisters and half-sisters are discriminable; perhaps the mechanism involves phenotype matching (From HOLMES and SHERMAN 1982).

cross-fostering data indicate a time-dependent ontogeny of dam-offspring recognition based on association, with a sensitive period that roughly coincides with the time when free-living young first emerge from their natal burrow.

Multiple mating by female *S. beldingi* typically results in multiple insemination. Electrophoretic paternity exclusion analyses, using eight different polymorphic blood proteins as phenotypic markers, revealed that 64 % to 78 % of litters have multiple sires (HANKEN and SHERMAN 1981; SHERMAN unpubl.). Thus in most litters full-siblings and maternal half-siblings share a common uterine and natal burrow environment. In a field experiment, the behavior of electrophoretically identified full- and maternal half-sisters was observed in 1979–80. The data revealed that as yearlings full-sisters behaved more amicably than half-sisters, in that they fought significantly less often when they met and more frequently permitted each other unmolested access to territories (Fig. 6, left). In addition, yearling full-sisters cooperated more often in chasing distantly related and unrelated intruders from territories, and came to each other's assistance more frequently when one of the pair was chased than did half-sisters (Fig. 6, right).

Among littermates, there are no obvious differences in the kind or extent of postnatal association that would facilitate the observed discrimination between full- and half-sisters. However, it is possible that behavioral differences between littermates might result from intra-uterine associations among fetuses sired by the same male (for examples of *in utero* effects on behavior, see VOM SAAL 1981). Discrimination among full- and half-siblings might also indicate phenotype matching against a pup's own phenotype. The field cross-fostering data (Fig. 5) are consistent with this hypothesis because as yearlings, «accepted» foster sisters were treated like half-sisters rather than full-sisters. Thus, our observations indicate that female Belding's ground squirrels distinguish at least two categories of conspecifics, each composed of at least two groups. First, females either share a natal burrow (nestmates) or they do not (non-nestmates). Second, a female's nestmates are either relatively similar to her phenotypically (in odor, for example), in which case they are treated as full-sisters, or they are not (half-sisters and foster sisters).

4 Kin recognition in the genus Spermophilus

In the last fifteen years field studies of ground squirrels *(Spermophilus)* have provided insights into the evolution of mammalian population dynamics, life history parameters, and social organization (reviewed by ARMITAGE 1981; MICHENER 1983). We highlight four species that have been studied in particular detail: *S. beldingi, S. parryii* (MCLEAN 1982, 1983, in press), *S. richardsonii* (MICHENER, 1973, 1979, 1981; MICHENER and MICHENER 1977; DAVIS in press), and *S. tridecemlineatus* (MCCARLEY 1966; SCHWAGMEYER 1979, 1980, in press; VESTAL and MCCARLEY in press). These studies have documented sexual asymmetries in dispersal similar to those we found in *S. beldingi,* and also the occurrence of nepotism among females but not males. Given the importance of kin-correlated behavior in the females' social structure, interest has recently focused on the proximal mechanisms by which females recognize their kin. A preliminary picture is emerging that relates inter-specific differences in recognition abilities and mechanisms to differences in social organization (Table 2).

For example, neonatal Belding's ground squirrels and thirteen-lined ground squirrels (HOLMES and SHERMAN 1982; HOLMES 1984) were cross-fostered intra-specifically to see how sibling recognition was affected by rearing association and genetic relatedness. Because subjects from both species were cross-fostered, reared, and studied in the same laboratory using similar procedures, inferences drawn from between-species comparisons

Table 2: Results from studies of kin recognition abilities in various ground squirrel species *(Spermophilus)*. The table indicates whether the cited recognition ability was documented in the field (F) or laboratory (L), and whether various categories of kin were (+) or were not (−) recognized when reared together (T) or apart (A).

Species	Category of Kin	Field or Lab Study	Rearing/ Recognition		Reference
S. beldingi	Dam-Offspring	F	T: +;	A: ?	Holmes and Sherman 1982
		L	T: +;	A: −	Holmes in press
	Sibling-Sibling	F	T: +;	A: ?	Holmes and Sherman 1982
		L	T: +;	A: +[1]	Holmes and Sherman 1982
	Maternal Half-Siblings	F	T: +;	A: ?	Holmes and Sherman 1982
		L	T: ?;	A: ?	
	Paternal Half-Siblings	F	T: ?;	A: ?	[2]
		L	T: ?;	A: ?	[2]
S. tridecemlineatus	Sibling-Sibling	L	T: +;	A: −	Holmes 1984
S. parryii	Sibling-Sibling	L	T: +;	A: +[1]	Holmes and Sherman 1982
S. richardsonii	Dam-Offspring	L	T: +;	A: ?	Michener and Sheppard 1972; Michener 1974
	Sibling-Sibling	L	T: +;	A: ?	Sheppard and Yoshida 1971
		L	T: +;	A: +	Davis 1982

?: This rearing regimen was not used for this category of kin.
[1]: Recognition occurred between sister-sister pairs only (see Fig. 4b).
[2]: Field and laboratory studies of paternal half-sibling recognition in *S. beldingi* are currently in progress.

are strengthened. Paired-encounter tests indicate that recognition in female *S. beldingi* can be influenced by both factors (e. g., Fig. 4). In contrast, recognition in *S. tridecemlineatus* may be affected only by rearing association: whereas young that were reared together showed low levels of «exploratory» interactions, young reared apart exhibited high levels of social exploration, regardless of relatedness or sex. In other words, the only individuals thirteen-lined ground squirrel juveniles distinguished in this test were those with whom they had shared a natal nest. Although the significance of this inter-specific difference in kin recognition is currently unclear, it is worth noting that in nature dam-offspring and sister pairs interact frequently and amicably throughout life in *S. beldingi*, whereas amicable interactions in *S. tridecemlineatus* are apparently limited to dams and offspring during the first few weeks post-partum. One possible implication is that some or all of the factors favoring kin recognition by phenotype matching in *S. beldingi* – frequent multiple paternity, extensive kin networks, and widespread nepotism – may be either rare or absent in *S. tridecemlineatus*.

Because *S. parryii* and *S. richardsonii* siblings have also been cross-fostered intra-specifically (Table 2), their abilities to discriminate kin can be added to the comparative picture. Laboratory results for *S. parryii* mirror those for *S. beldingi*: both rearing association and relatedness influence the identification process among females. Like *S. beldingi,* in the field female *S. parryii* that are closely related (i. e., mother-daughter and sister pairs) share home ranges, seldom fight, and frequently interact amicably. In addition, closely related females transport their newly-emerged pups to a common burrow system, and then cooperate to protect these communal nest burrows from intra- and inter-specific predators.

It is more difficult to place the laboratory recognition data on *S. richardsonii* into our comparative perspective because DAVIS (1982) isolated his animals for 75 days immediately prior to testing them; such an isolation during the active season was not experienced by subjects in the other three species and its effects on the recognition process are unknown. This procedural difference notwithstanding, DAVIS's (1982) results suggest that association may not be the sole mechanism of sibling recognition in *S. richardsonii*. First, siblings reared apart remained closer to each other and physically contacted each other more often and for longer periods during dyadic arena tests than did non-siblings reared apart. Second, siblings reared together approached each other more often and made naso-oral contact more frequently than did non-siblings reared together. Unfortunately, small sample sizes precluded analyses by pairs' sexes. However, given the apparent similarities among the social systems and matrilineal kin group structures of *S. richardsonii*, *S. beldingi*, and *S. parryii* populations (reviewed by MICHENER 1983), we predict that phenotype matching occurs in the former species and that such abilities are especially well developed in females.

In conclusion, field and laboratory studies of four ground squirrel species suggest the existence of intriguing similarities and differences in kin recognition abilities and their ontogenies; at least some of these apparently relate to variations in dispersal, polygamy, and nepotism. We anticipate the proliferation of such investigations, and look forward to the development of the comparative picture (Table 2) in scope and detail. Particularly interesting in this regard will be comparisons among the more social *Spermophilus* species (e. g., *S. armatus*, *S. columbianus*) and their more solitary congeners (e. g., *S. franklinii*, *S. lateralis*), as well as parallel studies of prairie dogs *(Cynomys)* and marmots *(Marmota)*. Further research on the ecology and ontogeny of kin recognition abilities among invertebrates and vertebrates, particularly sciurids, seems warranted.

Acknowledgments

Many of the ideas expressed in this paper were presented in our *American Scientist* publication (HOLMES and SHERMAN 1983). For assistance with that work we thank PATRICK BATESON, MARTIN DALY, CYNTHIA KAGARISE SHERMAN, MARTIN L. MORTON, BRUCE WALDMAN, and RICHARD WRANGHAM; for help with the current paper we thank STEPHEN T. EMLEN, CYNTHIA KAGARISE SHERMAN, GEORGE J. GAMBOA, and BERT HÖLLDOBLER. RICHARD D. ALEXANDER's ideas and friendly skepticism were a consistent source of stimulation. WARREN G. HOLMES's research was supported by grants from the University of Michigan; PAUL W. SHERMAN's studies were supported by grants from the National Science Foundation.

References

Alexander, R. D. (1979): Darwinism and Human Affairs. University of Washington Press, Seattle.
Alexander, R. D. and G. Borgia (1978): Group selection, altruism, and the levels of organization of life. Ann. Rev. Ecol. Syst. *9*, 449–474.
Armitage, K. B. (1981): Sociality as a life-history tactic of ground squirrels. Oecologia *48*, 36–49.
Barrows, E. M., W. J. Bell, and C. D. Michener (1975): Individual odor differences and their social functions in insects. Proc. Natl. Acad. Sci. U.S.A. *72*, 2824–2828.

Bateson, P. (1978): Sexual imprinting and optimal outbreeding. Nature 273, 659–660.

Bateson, P. (1980): Optimal outbreeding and the development of sexual preferences in Japanese quail. Z. Tierpsychol. 53, 231–244.

Bateson, P. (1982): Preferences for cousins in Japanese quail. Nature 295, 236–237.

Bateson, P. (1983): Optimal outbreeding. In Mate Choice, ed. P. Bateson, pp. 257–277. Cambridge University Press, Cambridge.

Beecher, M. D. (1982): Signature systems and individual recognition. Amer. Zool. 22, 477–490.

Beecher, I. M. and M. D. Beecher (1983): Sibling recognition in bank swallows (Riparia riparia). Z Tierpsychol. 62, 145–150.

Beecher, M. D., I. M. Beecher, and S. Lumpkin. (1981a): Parent-offspring recognition in bank swallows (Riparia riparia): I. Natural history. Anim. Behav. 29, 86–94.

Beecher, M. D., I. M. Beecher, and S. H. Nichols (1981b): Parent-offspring recognition in bank swallows (Riparia riparia): II. Development and acoustic basis. Anim. Behav. 29, 95–101.

Beer, C. G. (1970): Individual recognition of voice in the social behavior of birds. In Advances in the Study of Behavior, Vol. 3, eds. J. S. Rosenblatt, C. G. Beer, and R. A. Hinde, pp. 27–74. Academic Press, New York.

Bekoff, M. (1981): Mammalian sibling interactions: Genes, facilitative environments, and the coefficient of familiarity. In Parental Care in Mammals, eds. D. J. Gubernick and P. H. Klopfer, pp. 307–346. Plenum Press, New York.

Berenstain, L., P. S. Rodman, and D. G. Smith (1981): Social relations between fathers and offspring in a captive group of rhesus monkeys (Macaca mulatta). Anim. Behav. 29, 1057–1063.

Birkhead, T. R. (1978): Behavioural adaptations to high density nesting in the common guillemot Uria aalge. Anim. Behav. 26, 321–331.

Blaustein, A. R. (1983): Kin recognition mechanisms: phenotypic matching or recognition alleles? Amer. Nat. 121, 749–754.

Blaustein, A. R. and R. K. O'Hara (1981): Genetic control for sibling recognition? Nature 290, 246–248.

Blaustein, A. R. and R. K. O'Hara (1982): Kin recognition in Rana cascadae tadpoles: maternal and paternal effects. Anim. Behav. 30, 1151–1157.

Blaustein, A. R., R. K. O'Hara, and D. H. Olson (1984): Kin preference behaviour is present after metamorphosis in Rana cascadae frogs. Anim. Behav. 32, 445–450.

Breed, M. D. (1981): Individual recognition and learning of queen odors by worker honeybees. Proc. Natl. Acad. Sci. 78, 2635–2637.

Breed, M. D. (1983): Nestmate recognition in honey bees. Anim. Behav. 31, 86–91.

Buckle, G. R. and L. Greenberg (1981): Nestmate recognition in sweat bees (Lasioglossum zephyrum): Does an individual recognize its own odour or only odours of its nestmates? Anim. Behav. 29, 802–809.

Burger, J. (1974): Breeding adaptations of Franklin's Gull (Larus pipixcan) to a marsh habitat. Anim. Behav. 22, 521–567.

Cowan, D. P. (1979): Sibling matings in a hunting wasp: adaptive inbreeding? Science 205, 1403–1405.

Crozier, R. H. and M. W. Dix (1979): Analysis of two genetic models for the innate components of colony odor in social Hymenoptera. Behav. Ecol. Sociobiol. 4, 217–224.

Cullen, E. (1957): Adaptations in the kittiwake to cliff-nesting. Ibis 99, 275–302.

Daly, M. and M. I. Wilson (1982): Whom are newborn babies said to resemble? Ethol. Sociobiol. 3, 67–78.

Davis, L. S. (1982): Sibling recognition in Richardson's ground squirrels (Spermophilus richardsonii). Behav. Ecol. Sociobiol. 11, 65–70.

Davis, L. S. (in press): Behavioral interactions of Richardson's ground squirrels: asymmetries based on kinship. In Biology of Ground-Dwelling Squirrels: Annual Cycles, Behavioral Ecology, and Sociality, eds. J. O. Murie and G. R. Michener. Univ. of Nebraska Press, Lincoln.

Dawkins, R. (1976): The Selfish Gene. Oxford Univ. Press, Oxford.

Dawkins, R. (1982): The Extended Phenotype. Oxford Univ. Press, Oxford.

Dewsbury, D. A. (1982): Avoidance of incestuous breeding between siblings in two species of Peromyscus mice. Biol. Behav. 7, 157–169.

Dobson, F. S. (1982): Competition for mates and predominant juvenile male dispersal in mammals. Anim. Behav. *30*, 1183–1192.

Fredrickson, W. T. and G. P. Sackett (1984): Kin preferences in primates *(Macaca nemestrina)*: Relatedness or familiarity? J. Comp. Psychol. *98*, 29–34.

Getz, W. M. (1981): Genetically based kin recognition systems. J. Theor. Biol. *92*, 209–226.

Getz, W. M. (1982): An analysis of learned kin recognition in Hymenoptera. J. Theor. Biol. *99*, 585–597.

Getz, W. M., D. Brückner, and T. R. Parisian (1982): Kin structure and the swarming behavior of the honey bee *Apis mellifera*. Behav. Ecol. Sociobiol. *10*, 265–270.

Getz, W. M. and K. B. Smith (1983): Genetic kin recognition: honey bees discriminate between full and half sisters. Nature *302*, 147–148.

Gilder, P. M. and P. J. B. Slater (1978): Interest of mice in conspecific male odours is influenced by degree of kinship. Nature *274*, 362–364.

Grau, H. J. (1982): Kin recognition in white-footed deermice *(Peromyscus leucopus)*. Anim. Behav. *30*, 497–505.

Greenberg, L. (1979): Genetic component of bee odor in kin recognition. Science *206*, 1095–1097.

Greenwood, P. J. (1980): Mating systems, philopatry and dispersal in birds and mammals. Anim. Behav. *28*, 1140–1162.

Greenwood, P. J., P. H. Harvey, and C. M. Perrins (1978): Inbreeding and dispersal in the great tit. Nature *271*, 52–54.

Gubernick, D. J. (1980): Maternal «imprinting» or maternal «labelling» in goats? Anim. Behav. *28*, 124–129.

Hamilton, W. D. (1964): The genetical evolution of social behaviour, I. and II. J. Theoret. Biol. *7*, 1–52.

Hanken, J. and P. W. Sherman (1981): Multiple paternity in Belding's ground squirrel litters. Science *212*, 351–353.

Hess, E. H. (1973): Imprinting: Early Experience and the Developmental Psychobiology of Attachment. Van Nostrand Reinhold, New York.

Hill, J. L. (1974): Peromyscus: effect of early pairing on reproduction. Science *186*, 1042–1044.

Hölldobler, B. and C. D. Michener (1980): Mechanisms of identification and discrimination in social hymenoptera. In Evolution of Social Behavior: Hypotheses and Empirical Tests, Dahlem Konferenzen, ed. H. Markl, pp. 35–58. Weinheim, Verlag Chemie.

Holekamp, K. E. (1983): Proximal mechanisms of natal dispersal in Belding's ground squirrel *(Spermophilus beldingi beldingi)*. Ph. D. Thesis, University of California, Berkeley.

Holmes, W. G. (1984): Sibling recognition in thirteen-lined ground squirrels: effects of genetic relatedness, rearing association, and olfaction. Behav. Ecol. Sociobiol. *14*, 225–233.

Holmes, W. G. (in press): The development of dam-young recognition in Belding's ground squirrels. J. Comp. Psych.

Holmes, W. G. and P. W. Sherman (1982): The ontogeny of kin recognition in two species of ground squirrels. Amer. Zool. *22*, 491–517.

Holmes, W. G. and P. W. Sherman (1983): Kin recognition in animals. Amer. Sci. *71*, 46–55.

Hoogland, J. L. (1982): Prairie dogs avoid extreme inbreeding. Science *215*, 1639–1641.

Hoogland, J. L. (1983): Nepotism and alarm calling in the black-tailed prairie dog *(Cynomys ludovicianus)*. Anim. Behav. *31*, 472–479.

Hoogland, J. L. and P. W. Sherman (1976): Advantages and disadvantages of bank swallow *(Riparia riparia)* coloniality. Ecol. Monogr. *46*, 33–58.

Kalmus, H. and C. R. Ribbands (1952): The origin of the odours by which honeybees distinguish their companions. Proc. Roy. Soc. London (B) *140*, 50–59.

Kaplan, J. N., D. Cubicciotti III, and W. K. Redican (1977): Olfactory discrimination of squirrel monkey mothers by their infants. Develop. Psychobiol. *10*, 447–453.

Kareem, A. M. (1983): Effect of increasing periods of familiarity on social interactions between male sibling mice. Anim. Behav. *31*, 919–926.

Kareem, A. M., and C. J. Barnard (1982): The importance of kinship and familiarity in social interactions between mice. Anim. Behav. *30*, 594–601.

Klahn, J. E. and G. J. Gamboa (1983): Social wasps: Discrimination between kin an nonkin brood. Science *221*, 482–484.

Klopfer, P. H. and M. S. Klopfer (1968): Maternal imprinting in goats: Fostering of alien young. Z. Tierpsychol. *25*, 862–866.

Kukuk, P. F., M. D. Breed, A. Sobti, and W. J. Bell (1977): The contributions of kinship and conditioning to nest recognition and colony member recognition in a primitively eusocial bee, *Lasioglossum zephyrum* (Hymenoptera: Halicitidae). Behav. Ecol. Sociobiol. *2*, 319–327.

Kurland, J. (1980): Kin selection theory: A review and selective bibliography. Ethol. Sociobiol. *1*, 255–274.

Labov, J. B. (1980): Factors influencing infanticidal behavior in wild male house mice *(Mus musculus)*. Behav. Ecol. Sociobiol. *6*, 297–303.

Lacy, R. C. and P. W. Sherman (1983): Kin recognition by phenotype matching. Amer. Nat. *121*, 489–512.

Leon, M. (1975): Dietary control of maternal pheromone in the lactating rat. Physiol. Behav. *14*, 311–319.

Leon, M. (1978): Filial responsiveness to olfactory cues in the laboratory rat. In Advances in the Study of Behavior, Vol. 10, eds. J. S. Rosenblatt, C. G. Beer, R. A. Hinde, and M. C. Busnel, pp. 117–153. Academic Press, New York.

Lorenz, K. (1935): Der Kumpan in der Umwelt des Vogels. J. Ornithology *83*, 137–213, 289–413.

McArthur, P. D. (1982): Mechanisms and development of parent-young vocal recognition in the piñon jay *(Gymnorhinus cyanocephalus)*. Anim. Behav. *30*, 62–74.

McCarley, H. (1966): Annual cycle, population dynamics, and adaptive behavior of *Citellus tridecemlineatus*. J. Mammal. *47*, 294–316.

McLean, I. G. (1982): The association of female kin in the Arctic ground squirrel *Spermophilus parryii*. Behav. Ecol. Sociobiol. *10*, 91–99.

McLean, I. G. (1983): Paternal behaviour and killing of young in Arctic ground squirrels. Anim. Behav. *31*, 32–44.

McLean, I. G. (in press): Spacing behavior of female ground squirrels. In Biology of Ground-Dwelling Squirrels: Annual Cycles, Behavioral Ecology, and Sociality, eds. J. O. Murie and G. R. Michener. Univ. of Nebraska Press, Lincoln.

Michener, G. R. (1973): Field observations on the social relationships between adult female and juvenile Richardson's ground squirrels. Can. J. Zool. *51*, 33–38.

Michener, G. R. (1974): Development of adult-young identification in Richardson's ground squirrel. Develop. Psychobiol. *7*, 375–384.

Michener, G. R. (1979): Spatial relationships and social organization of adult Richardson's ground squirrels. Can. J. Zool. *57*, 125–139.

Michener, G. R. (1981): Ontogeny of spatial relationships and social behavior in juvenile Richardson's ground squirrels. Can. J. Zool. *59*, 1666–1676.

Michener, G. R. (1983): Kin identification, matriarchies, and the evolution of sociality in ground-dwelling sciurids. In Advances in the Study of Mammalian Behavior, eds. J. F. Eisenberg and D. G. Kleiman, pp. 528–572. Special Publication No. 7, American Society of Mammalogists.

Michener, G. R. and D. R. Michener (1977): Population structure and dispersal in Richardson's ground squirrels. Ecology *58*, 359–368.

Michener, G. R. and D. H. Sheppard (1972): Social behavior between adult female Richardson's ground squirrels *(Spermophilus richardsonii)* and their own and alien young. Can. J. Zool. *50*, 1343–1349.

Miller, D. E. and J. T. Emlen, Jr. (1975): Individual chick recognition and family integrity in the ring-billed gull. Behaviour *52*, 124–144.

Morton, M. L. and P. W. Sherman (1978): Effects of a spring snowstorm on behavior, reproduction, and survival of Belding's ground squirrels. Can. J. Zool. *56*, 2578–2590.

Mostofsky, D., ed. (1965): Stimulus Generalization. Stanford Univ. Press, Stanford.

Noakes, D. L. G. and G. W. Barlow (1973): Cross-fostering and parent-offspring responses in *Cichlasoma citrinellum* (Pisces, Cichlidae). Z. Tierpsychol. *33*, 147–152.

O'Hara, R. K. and A. R. Blaustein (1981): An investigation of sibling recognition in *Rana cascadae* tadpoles. Anim. Behav. *29*, 1121–1126.

Payne, R. B. (1977): The ecology of brood parasitism in birds. Ann. Rev. Ecol. Syst. *8*, 1–28.

Pfennig, D. W., H. K. Reeve, and J. S. Shellman (1983a): Learned component of nestmate discrimination in workers of a social wasp, *Polistes fuscatus* (Hymenoptera: Vespidae). Anim. Behav. *31*, 412–416.

Pfennig, D. W., G. J. Gamboa, H. K. Reeve, J. Shellman Reeve, and I. D. Ferguson (1983b): The mechanism of nestmate discrimination in social wasps (*Polistes*, Hymenoptera: Vespidae). Behav. Ecol. Sociobiol. *13*, 299–305.

Porter, R. H., J. A. Matochik, and J. W. Makin (1983): Evidence for phenotype matching in spiny mice *(Acomys cahirinus)*. Anim. Behav. *31*, 978–984.

Porter, R. H. and J. D. Moore (1981): Human kin recognition by olfactory cues. Physiol. Behav. *27*, 493–495.

Porter, R. H., V. J. Tepper, and D. M. White (1981): Experiential influences on the development of huddling preferences and «sibling» recognition in spiny mice. Develop. Psychobiol. *14*, 375–382.

Porter, R. H. and M. Wyrick (1979): Sibling recognition in spiny mice *(Acomys cahirinus):* Influence of age and isolation. Anim. Behav. *27*, 761–766.

Porter, R. H., M. Wyrick, and J. Pankey (1978): Sibling recognition in spiny mice *(Acomys cahirinus)*. Behav. Ecol. Sociobiol. *3*, 61–68.

Price, M. V., and N. M. Waser (1979): Pollen dispersal and optimal outcrossing in *Delphinium nelsoni*. Nature *277*, 294–297.

Ribbands, C. R. (1965): The role of recognition of comrades in the defense of social insect communities. Symp. Zool. Soc. London *14*, 159–168.

Ridley, M. and A. Grafen (1981): Are green beard genes outlaws? Anim. Behav. *29*, 954–955.

Rothstein, S. I. (1982): Successes and failures in avian egg and nestling recognition with comments on the utility of optimality reasoning. Amer. Zool. *22*, 547–560.

Salzen, E. A. and J. M. Cornell (1968): Self-perception and species recognition in birds. Behaviour *30*, 44–65.

Schwagmeyer, P. L. (1979): The function of alarm calling behavior in *Spermophilus tridecemlineatus*, the thirteen-lined ground squirrel. Ph. D. Thesis, Univ. of Michigan, Ann Arbor.

Schwagmeyer, P. L. (1980): Alarm calling behavior of the thirteen-lined ground squirrel, *Spermophilus tridecemlineatus*. Behav. Ecol. Sociobiol. *7*, 195–200.

Schwagmeyer, P. L. (in press): Multiple mating and intersexual selection in thirteen-lined ground squirrel. In Biology of Ground-Dwelling Squirrels: Annual Cycles, Behavioral Ecology, and Sociality, eds. J. O. Murie and G. R. Michener. Univ. Nebraska Press, Lincoln.

Shellman, J. S. and G. J. Gamboa (1982): Nestmate discrimination in social wasps: the role of exposure to nest and nestmates (*Polistes fuscatus*, Hymenoptera: Vespidae). Behav. Ecol. Sociobiol. *11*, 51–53.

Sheppard, D. H. and S. M. Yoshida (1971): Social behavior in captive Richardson's ground squirrels. J. Mammal. *52*, 793–799.

Sherman, P. W. (1977): Nepotism and the evolution of alarm calls. Science *197*, 1246–1253.

Sherman, P. W. (1980): The limits of ground squirrel nepotism. In Sociobiology: Beyond Nature/ Nurture?, eds. G. W. Barlow and J. Silverberg, pp. 505–544. Westview Press, Boulder.

Sherman, P. W. (1981a): Reproductive competition and infanticide in Belding's ground squirrels and other organisms. In Natural Selection and Social Behavior: Recent Research and New Theory, eds. R. D. Alexander and D. W. Tinkle, pp. 311–331. Chiron Press, New York.

Sherman, P. W. (1981b): Kinship, demography, and Belding's ground squirrel nepotism. Behav. Ecol. Sociobiol. *8*, 251–259.

Sherman, P. W. and M. L. Morton (in press): Demography of Belding's ground squirrels. Ecology.

Shields, W. M. (1982): Philopatry, Inbreeding, and the Evolution of Sex. State Univ. of New York Press, Albany.

Trillmich, F. (1981): Mutual mother-pup recognition in Galapagos fur seals and sea lions: Cues used and functional significance. Behaviour *78*, 21–42.

Vestal, B. M. and H. McCarley (in press): Spatial and social relationships among relatives in thirteen-lined ground squirrel populations. In Biology of Ground-Dwelling Squirrels: Annual Cycles, Behavioral Ecology, and Sociality, eds. J. O. Murie and G. R. Michener. Univ. of Nebraska Press, Lincoln.

Vidal, J.-M. (1982): «Auto-imprinting»: Effects of prolonged isolation on domestic cocks. J. Comp. Physiol. Psych. *96*, 256–267.

vom Saal, F. S. (1981): Variation in phenotype due to random intrauterine positioning of male and female fetuses in rodents. J. Reprod. Fert. 62, 633–650.

Waldman, B. (1981): Sibling recognition in toad tadpoles: The role of experience. Z. Tierpsych. 56, 341–358.

Waldman, B. (1982): Sibling association among schooling toad tadpoles: Field evidence and implications. Anim. Behav. 30, 700–713.

Weller, M. W. (1959): Parasitic egg laying in the redhead (Aythya americana) and other North American Anatidae. Ecol. Monogr. 29, 333–365.

Wu, H. M. H., W. G. Holmes, S. R. Medina, and G. P. Sackett (1980): Kin preference in infant Macaca nemestrina. Nature 285, 225–227.

Fortschritte der Zoologie, Bd. 31 · Hölldobler/Lindauer (Hrsg.): Experimental Behavioral Ecology
G. Fischer Verlag · Stuttgart · New York · 1985

Coping behaviour and stress physiology in male tree shrews (Tupaia belangeri)

Dietrich v. Holst

Zoologisches Institut, Universität Bayreuth, F. R. Germany

Abstract

In nature, tree shrews (Tupaia belangeri) live singly or in pairs in territories which they defend vigorously against strange conspecifics.

In the laboratory adult males also immediately attack strange intruding males and normally defeat them within a few minutes. After subjugation, victors show no further sign of arousal and pay virtually no attention to the subordinate animals. The latter, however, change their behaviour completely from the moment of subjugation and may be classified in the following two distinct groups:

1. Subdominant animals: These withdraw from situations which could lead to more intense fights by active avoidance behavior. Under such conditions, they are capable of living in dominants' cages, albeit with a very reduced sphere of action, for weeks.

2. Submissive animals: These sit almost continually in a corner of their cages and hardly respond to external stimuli. Even the threats and attacks of the dominants are accepted without the animals attempting to flee or defend themselves and they normally die within less than 20 days.

Serum concentrations of adrenal, thyroidal, gonadal hormones (as well as other physiological parameters) of dominant tree shrews largely correspond to those of controls. Subordinate and submissive animals, however, show distinct stress reactions in all physiological parameters measured. In general, the physiological reactions are qualitatively the same, differing only in degree. There is, however, a clear qualitative distinction between subdominants and submissives with respect to their adrenal functions: Submissives, in relation to dominants, show no change in sympathetic-adrenomedullary activity but an increase in adrenocortical function, the opposite being true for subdominants. The relevance of these physiological reactions for the development of status and coping dependent diseases will be discussed.

1 Introduction

The dispersion of animals within their habitat is largely determined by their social behaviour. The social structure differs between species and may vary also with particular parameters (such as climatic conditions, food shortage, reproductive condition and population density) in a predictable manner. With increasing independence from physical parameters the social ‹environment›, e. g. the interaction between conspecifics, gains in importance, particularly in some insects, in birds and mammals: in these groups each individual is part of the surrounding social sphere of other individuals, which influences their behaviour and physiology constantly.

In this paper I shall present some findings of our research on tree shrews which exemplify the behavioural and physiological responses of male individuals to social conflict in order to clarify their biological significance.

Tree shrews are diurnal mammals, about the size of a squirrel, distributed throughout Southeast Asia. Their systematic position is unclear; while originally considered primates, it now seems more likely that tree-shrews provide a model of the common ancestor of all living placental mammals. They are thus classified as a separate order: Scandentia (Martin, 1969; Starck, 1978). In nature, they usually live in pairs in territories defended vigorously against strange conspecifics of the same sex (Kawamichi and Kawamichi, 1979).

In large laboratory enclosures, as in nature, adult tree shrews of both sexes immediately attack strange conspecifics of their own sex and normally defeat them within a few minutes. Shortly after fighting has ended, the victor shows no further sign of arousal and pays virtually no attention to the subordinate animal. The subordinate tree-shrew, however, crouches in a corner, which it leaves only to feed and drink. It hardly moves at all, spending more than 90 % of the daily activity phase lying motionless in its hiding place and following the movements of the victor with its head.

During the following days, agonistic encounters between the two animals are very rare or do not occur at all. Nevertheless, the subordinate animal dies within less than 20 days.

2 Death as a result of constant «anxiety»

As the following results show, death does not result from the physical exertions of fighting or from wounds received, but rather from the continued presence of the victor. If an adult male is placed into the cage (floor area 120 × 70 cm, height 50 cm) of an unknown male conspecific, it is usually attacked instantly and subdued in less than 2 minutes. Following separation of the two animals by an opaque partition, the loser recovers from the fight nearly as rapidly as the winner. Under such conditions, even when the subordinate animal is subjected to an encounter every day for weeks, it hardly loses any body weight and does not die prematurely. If the two animals are separated after their first fight by a wire mesh partition, so that the loser cannot be attacked but sees the victor constantly, however, it dies within a few days. Thus death is not a (direct) adjunct of social interactions and their physiological consequences, but rather results from central nervous processes in the subordinate animal based on experience (being defeated) and learning (to recognize the victor). To put it anthropomorphously, the subordinate dies of constant «anxiety».

To determine the cause of death of subordinate tree shrews, a male was placed into the cage of an unknown conspecific of the same sex, which subjugated him completely within less than two minutes. Afterwards both animals were separated by a wire mesh partition. Every 1–2 days the figths were repeated. Experimental animals were always healthy adult tree shrews aged between 2 and 5 years (the maximum age reached by tree shrews in our institute's colony is more than 8 years). The animals were maintained under constant conditions (L:D = 12:12 hours; relative humidity 50–60 %) with food and water ad libitum.

Fig. 1: Decrease of body weight of some subordinate tree shrews after initial confrontation.

From the time of first submission, all subordinate animals sat in a corner of the cage or in their sleeping boxes for practically the whole day, hardly responding to external stimuli. They did not even attempt to escape the attacks of the dominant animal, but usually suffered them without any attempt to defend themselves.

Under these conditions, all animals showed a progressive decrease in body weight and died between 2 and 20 days. The daily weight loss was more or less constant for any individual throughout the entire experiment, but differed considerably between individuals (examples: see Fig. 1).

There was a negative correlation between the survival time of subordinate animals in this situation and their daily weight losses (Fig. 2): Daily weight loss is thus a good index of an animal's stress response – at least during this form of acute stress.

On the basis of their daily body weight losses, the animals may be separated into two distinct groups: those which lived 8 days or less in this situation, having daily weight losses above 3 % (type I) and those which survived longer, having daily weight losses below 3 % (type II).

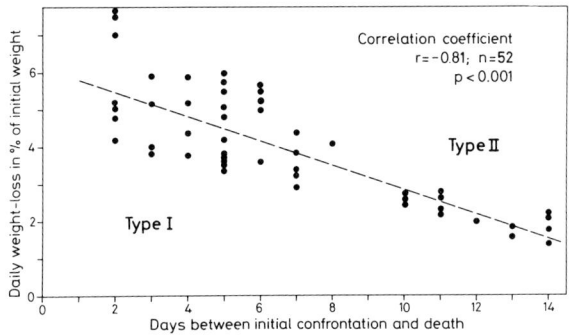

Fig. 2: Relationship between daily loss of body weight and survival time of type I and type II subordinate tree shrews under persistent social stress.

In order to obtain data on the physiological responses of the animals to this stressful situation, blood samples were taken from 48 animals before the experiments were started and every 1–3 days thereafter. Blood samples here as well as in all other experiments were always taken about one hour before onset of light (= activity) period and were used to determine various hormones (by radio-immunoassays) and other clinically important parameters. Due to their daily weight losses, 25 animals were classified as type I animals, the rest as type II.

A clear distinction was evident between type I and type II animals with respect to their kidney function. With only three exceptions the urea nitrogen (and creatinine) values in the serum of type I animals rose within 6 days to more than tenfold of their initial values, leading to death by uraemia (Fig. 3; for further details see v. Holst, 1972), while it remained within the range of controls in the longer surviving type II animals. The cause of death in the latter animals is not yet known.

With respect to all other parameters, the reactions of the individuals of both groups were qualitatively the same, differing only in degree. While all parameters changed very quickly in type I animals (see Fig. 3), the changes in the longer surviving type II animals developed more gradually. They never reached the same degree, evident in type I animals

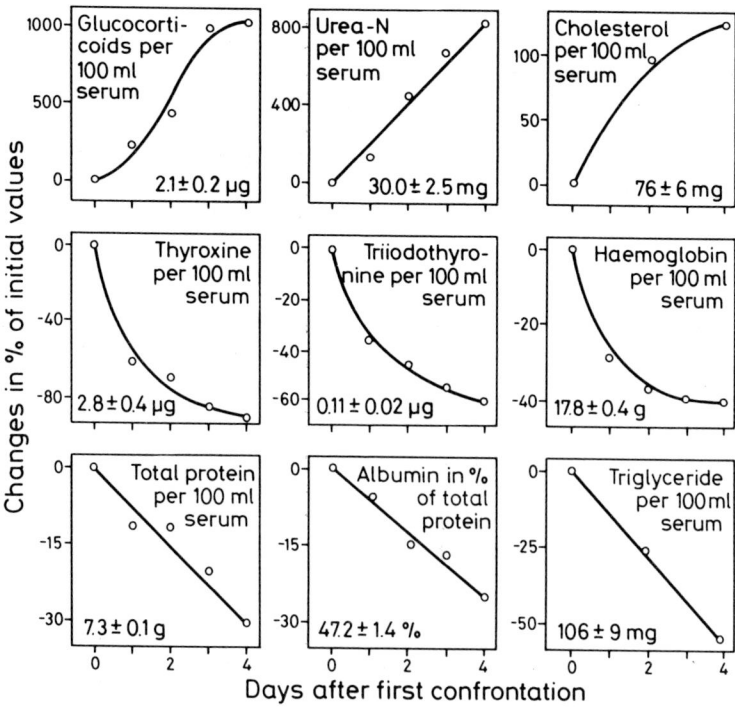

Fig. 3: Some physiological parameters in the serum (resp. blood) of type I subordinate tree shrews, and their changes (as percent of initial values) in the continued presence of dominant animals. The absolute initial values are given, along with their mean errors. All parameters differ significantly ($p < 0.001$) from the initial values within 1–2 days of confrontation (triglycerides after 4 days). For further details see text.

within less than 6 days, even shortly before their death after 10–20 days. However, after 5–8 days all parameters shown in Fig. 3 and many others, were significantly different from intitial values. In addition to the data presented in fig. 3, the weights of testes, epididymides and androgen-dependent glands declined in all animals almost linearly from the moment of subjugation; this result suggests a complete inhibition of the release of gonadotropic hormones by the adenohypophysis. Correspondingly, after less than 10 days all animals had testosterone values in their serum similar to those of castrated males, and they were sterile.

As drastic as these alterations are, we do not, as yet, have an understanding of their consequences regarding the metabolic physiology of the organism as a whole. One main reason is the inadequacy of our information about other hormones (such as epinephrine, insulin, glucagon, growth hormone), which can overlap to a great extent in their effects on metabolic processes with some hormones or may be synergistic, additive or even antagonistic to others. Nevertheless, a few physiological and patho-physiological consequences of this persistent form of stress are evident.

All animals become sterile within a few days and all show a dramatic decrease in body weight. This may be due – at least partly – to the gluconeogenetic activity of the adrenocortical hormones, which increase in all subordinate animals quite dramatically. In addition, the increased glucocorticoid concentrations in the blood result in a drastic decrease in wound healing. While insignificant abraisons or bite wounds, as they may occur in any fight, in dominant animals heal completely within 1–2 days, in subordinates larger subcutaneous wounds may develop. Even more dramatic may be the predicted effect on the immunological system: Based on data from 10 dominant and 14 subordinate individuals, the total count of leucocytes in subordinates did not increase significantly. The number of basophile granulocytes, however, decreased to about 1 %, that of eosinophilic granulocytes to 18 % and that of lymphocytes to 17 % of the values of dominant individuals (and of control animals, respectively; all differences $p < 0.001$). This implies that the healing of wounds and the immune defense against disease, parasites, or cancerous growth would be virtually completely reduced after a few days.

3 Ethological consequences of social conflict and their correlation with physiological changes

The introduction of an individual into the cage or the territory of a strange conspecific is an extremely intense form of stress in a territorial animal such as the tree shrew. To obtain physiological data on a less severe form of stress or even on adaptation to it, two male tree shrews which were unknown to each other were put together in a strange cage (floor area 120 × 70 cm, height 50 cm, with 2 separate sleeping boxes, feeding dishes, and water bottles) (see also v. HOLST et al. 1983). In this situation various responses could be observed. In some cases the confrontation led to high intensity fights and the establishment of a clear dominance relationship between the two within 1–3 days. Firstly, although both animals lived together constantly, the dominant individuals, after establishment of the dominance relationship, usually paid no attention to the subordinates. Attacks against the latter were very rare or even completely lacking. Except for short periods of feeding and drinking, the so-called submissive animals sat in a corner of the cage or in their sleeping boxes for practically the whole day as was the case with the subordinate individuals observed in the first experiment. Even the very rare attacks of the dominants were tolerated, usually without any attempts to flee or to fight back. In this situation, all submissives died within a few days.

In many cases, however, this situation did not result in such immediate and intensive fighting. After less than 4 days, however, and subsequent to low intensity attacks, a dominance structure was established in which the subordinate, by active avoidance behaviour, tried to withdraw from situations which could lead to more intensive fights or – for example if it was cornered – even fought back. Under these conditions, a so-called subdominant – in contrast to a submissive – was capable of living in a dominant's cage, albeit with a reduced sphere of action, for weeks.

Finally, in some pairs low intensity fights occured daily over weeks; these did not, however, result in defined dominance relationships. For most of the time each individual appeared actively to avoid direct confrontations with the conspecific. Since these individuals correspond in their behaviour and their physiological condition to subdominant animals in the presence of the dominant they were classified as such.

So far a total of 58 animals has been investigated; of these 26 were dominant, 18 subordinate and 14 submissive. Some of these individuals were sacrificed between 4–14 days after the stabilisation of the dominance relationship (8 dominants, 10 subordinates, 10 submissives) to gain insight into changes into organ weights and histology. Furthermore, we determined the tyrosine-hydroxylase activities (TyOH) (radioenzymatically) and the norepinephrine concentrations of the left adrenals of the animals. The remaining individuals were kept up to 23 days in the experimental situation. None of the dominant individuals died within this time, but 2 subdominant individuals died on the 20th and 22nd day respectively, and all submissives were dead by the 20th day.

Before the start of the experiments and every 2–5 days thereafter, blood samples were taken from all experimental animals (and 14 control animals kept singly) to determine several physiological parameters. After the dominance relationship had been established (which was the case within the first few days), no significant time dependence with regard to the changes in physiological parameters was found and thus all values for a given parameter of an animal between days 4 and 14 were pooled and the mean considered for further analysis.

Results: The body weight of the dominant animals showed a small but significant increase after establishment of the dominance relationship. Subdominants and submissives showed a drastic decrease in body weight up to about the fourth day of the experiment.

Fig. 4: Body weights (M ± SE) of dominant, subdominant and submissive tree shrews and their changes after the beginning of social confrontation.

Whereas, however, the subdominant animals stabilized at these levels, the body weight of the submissives progressively decreased; the daily weight loss was about 2.5 % of the initial weight, which is within the upper range of the values for submissives type II described in the first experiment (Fig. 4). Correspondingly, there was no apparent difference in the physiological reactions between the latter and submissives in the second experiment.

In the following I shall only consider data that originate from blood samples taken between days 4–14 of social conflict or from organs of animals sacrificed during this period. It has to be mentioned, however, that during the first 3 days even the dominants showed typical stress reactions (among other things a 50 % increase of their serum cortisol values). As can be seen from fig. 5, with the exception of testosterone, the hormone concentrations in the serum of dominant tree shrews as well as all other parameters (including organ weights) largely correspond to those of control animals without direct social contact.

Fig. 5: Some physiological parameters of dominant (D), subdominant (SD), and submissive (SM) tree shrews in percent of those of control animals (C). The absolute values for the control animals are given, along with their mean errors. For further details see text.

There is even evidence of decreased adrenocortical function, since both glucocorticoid hormones as well as adrenal weights show a small (but not significant) decrease. The testosterone concentration in the serum of the dominants, however, is clearly increased (p < 0.05). In the submissives, the serum concentrations of thyroidal and gonadal hormones are lower than in controls or dominant tree shrews (testosterone: p < 0.001; triiodthyronine: p ≈ 0.05). The values of these hormones in the subdominant animals are between those of the dominants and submissives.

A striking difference is evident between submissives and subdominants with respect to their adrenal function (Fig. 5). The cortisol as well as corticosterone concentrations in the serum of dominants and subdominants are within the range of those of controls, while those of submissive animals are increased. As a result, submissive animals – and only these – have very decreased lymphocyte numbers within their blood and show no wound healing (as mentioned for the subordinates in the first experiment).

In contrast, the tyrosine-hydroxylase activity of the adrenal glands in submissives does not differ from that of dominants and controls, but in subdominants it is increased by more than 100 %. The adrenal norepinephrine content in the four groups shows similar changes. This indicates a greatly increased sympathetic activity in the behaviorally active subdominant animals, but not in the passive submissive tree shrews.

The heart rates of 14 tree shrews were measured telemetrically over months; the transmitters were developed in our laboratory; weight including battery: about 1.3 g; duration of continuous registration: about 5 months (for details see Stöhr, 1982). Before social confrontation all animals showed similar marked day/night variations, with daily means about 50 % higher than night values (Fig. 6).

In all cases, social confrontation resulted in a dramatic increase in heart rates during the first day. After one to two days, however, the heart rates of dominant males (n = 5) returned to their original low values; the heart rates of subdominant animals (n = 6), however, showed dramatic increases in the mean frequencies of day values, and even more so in that of night values, thereby reaching, in some cases, night values higher than the daily mean before confrontation (e. g. Fig. 6). This was the case, independent of whether a subdominant was living together with a clear dominant male (as shown in Fig. 6) or

Fig. 6: Mean heart of two male tree shrews before and after begin of social confrontation.

whether both animals were living together without a dominance relationship as subdominants under constant strain.

This increased heart rate points to a constant high activation of the subordinate's sympathetic nervous system in this situation – and this not only during the day when the dominant rival is active and an attack always possible, but also during the night when the animals are completely quiet and sleeping (?) in their separate nest boxes.

It is plausible – and our preliminary histological data support this view – that this situation must lead to damage of the cardiovascular system and probably to heart failure.

Up to now we have been unable to examine submissives (n = 3), since the transmitters were always repelled after 1–2 days, but we have the impression that, in contrast to the active avoiding subdominants, they have a decreased heart rate together with a very reduced blood pressure.

4 Concluding remarks

A social confrontation leading to dominance relationships has apparently no negative effects on dominant tree shrews, even if the position is maintained by fighting. There is even an increase in testicular function and therefore probably also in an increased reproductive capacity. In addition, the data so far point to a small decrease in adrenocortical function (even if this effect is not significant). Subordinate animals, however, show distinct stress reactions in all parameters measured in our laboratory: In general, the physiological reactions are qualitatively the same, differing only in degree. There is, however, a clear distinction between active coping subdominant and passive coping submissive animals with respect to their adrenal functions: that is, the «strategy» of an animal determines (i. e. is correlated with) its physiological response: Active coping with a stressful situation has no apparent effect on adrenocortical function but leads to an increase in sympathetic-adrenomedullary activity and thus may lead to damage of the cardiovascular system, if the situation is maintained over a long period. Passive coping – comparable in human terms with depressive behaviour – has no apparent effects on the sympathetic-adrenomedullary system but leads to adrenocortical activation with its negative effects on wound healing and immune reactions.

Acknowledgements

This work would not have been possible without the cooperation of my colleagues Dr. E. Fuchs and Dr. W. Stöhr whom I would herewith like to thank. Further I would like to thank Mrs. B. Probst and Mrs. I. Zerenner-Fritzsche for their skillful technical assistance.

I am very indepted to Dr. F. Bidlingmaier (University of Munich) for providing antibodies for the determination of cortisol, corticosterone and testosterone. This work was supported by the Deutsche Forschungsgemeinschaft.

References

Holst, D. v. (1972): Renal failure as the cause of death in Tupaia belangeri exposed to persistent social stress. J. comp. Physiol. 78, 236–273.
Holst, D. v.; Fuchs, E.; Stöhr, W. (1983): Physiological changes in male Tupaia belangeri under different types of social stress. In: Biobehavioral bases of coronary heart disease (eds.: T. M. Dembroski, T. H. Schmidt, G. Blümchen), p. 382–390. Karger, Basel.

470 · D. v. Holst

Kawamichi, T.; Kawamichi, M. (1979): Spatial organization and territory of tree shrews (Tupaia glis). Anim. Behav. 27, 381–393.
Martin, R. D. (1968): Reproduction and ontogeny in tree shrews (Tupaia belangeri) with reference to their general behaviour and taxonomic relationships. Z. Tierpsychol. 25, 409–495 and 505–532.
Starck, D. (1978): Vergleichende Anatomie der Wirbeltiere auf evolutionsbiologischer Grundlage. Band 1: Theoretische Grundlagen. Stammesgeschichte und Systematik unter Berücksichtigung der niederen Chordata. Springer: Berlin, Heidelberg, New York.
Stöhr, W. (1982): Telemetrische Langzeituntersuchungen der Herzfrequenz von Tupaia belangeri: Basalwerte sowie phasische und tonische Reaktionen auf nichtsoziale und soziale Belastungen. Dissertation: Universität Bayreuth.

Fortschritte der Zoologie, Bd. 31 · Hölldobler/Lindauer (Hrsg.): Experimental Behavioral Ecology
G. Fischer Verlag · Stuttgart · New York · 1985

Epilogue:

The cognitive dimensions of animal communication

DONALD R. GRIFFIN

The Rockefeller University, 1230 York Avenue, New York, N. Y. 10021–6399 U.S.A.

KARL VON FRISCH was one of those rare scientists endowed with a «green thumb» for eye-opening discoveries about the biological mechanisms that underlie animal behavior. Again and again he showed that scientists had seriously underestimated the perceptual capabilities of so-called lower animals. I suspect that the momentum of unexpected new advances that he helped to inspire will continue far into the future and lead to discoveries that would surprise and delight him.

Around 1912 VON FRISCH upset the firmly established belief that lower vertebrates and all invertebrate animals were color blind. This opinion had been based on what seemed at the time to be sophisticated, quantitative data, chiefly similarity of spectral sensitivity curves to those of color blind human subjects. But elegantly simple experiments showed beyond doubt that fish and honeybees could indeed discriminate hues. Forty years later he effected another major extension of known visual capabilities of animals by demonstrating that honeybees make extensive use of the polarization patterns of light from the blue sky.

In the 1920s and 1930s VON FRISCH and his colleagues proved that many fish have excellent hearing. One of his papers (VON FRISCH 1923) bore the characteristically eloquent title «A catfish that comes when one whistles to him». Yet despite extensive publication of these data, not only in German journals but in English (Science 1930 and Nature 1938) the whole world of underwater sound production and hearing had to be rediscovered by those concerned with practical problems involving underwater sound; and authoritative textbooks continued for years to assert dogmatically that lower vertebrates could not possibly hear because they lack a cochlea of the mammalian form. The acoustic apparatus available to VON FRISCH was crude and uncalibrated by modern standards, but it is a sign of true genius to devise conclusive experiments with simple equipment. This fact is often overlooked by scientists who are so deeply involved in the intracacies of specialized methodology that they forget the danger of sophistication verging into sophistry.

Of course the most revolutionary of VON FRISCH's discoveries was the symbolic communication employed by honeybees. In the scientific climate of opinion prevailing forty years ago it was shocking and incredible to be told that a mere insect could communicate to its companions the direction, distance and desirability of something far away. At least in America, we were still firmly under the spell of behaviorism in psychology and of the reductionistic approach to animal behavior typified by the views of JACQUES LOEB. Therefore many remained skeptical until they could see for themselves the close correlation between the Schwänzeltänze and the location of food or other things about which bees sometimes dance. By decoding the Schwänzeltänze von Frisch provided us with the equivalent of a Rosetta Stone that opened the door to a new and previously unsuspected world.

One of the principal reasons why the symbolic communication of honeybees has revolutionized our ideas about animal behavior is that the Schwänzeltänze have the property known to linguists as displacement. One animal conveys to another information about something that is not present at the time and place where communication takes place. Nothing in the dark beehive or in the behavior of the dancer's sisters contains information about the distance or direction of the food source. This is important because it contradicts the widely held opinion that all animal communication is rigidly linked to immediate physiological conditions within the communicating animal, and that its communicative signals are incidental byproducts of its internal state of fear, hunger, fatigue or the like. At least a few minutes have elapsed since the dancer was exposed directly to stimuli at the food source, and under special conditions this interval may be several hours, as in the marathon dances described by Martin Lindauer (1955).

The Schwänzeltänze resemble human language in symbolism, displacement and versatility more than any other known type of communication employed by animals under natural conditions. But Lindauer and others have now shown how they probably evolved from simpler behavior patterns in other insects. Furthermore a few other animals are known to communicate semantically, and with some degree of displacement. Some species of ants recruit nestmates by communicative gestures conveying more than simple arousal (Hölldobler and Wilson, 1978). And, as reviewed in in this symposium by Marler, vervet monkeys use alarm calls that convey semantic information about the nature of a predator in addition to their state of fear. Thus while the Schwänzeltänze have been called an «evolutionary freak», they are not totally isolated from other known modes of animal communication. And even if only one species communicates in such a symbolic fashion, it is no longer possible to hold to the previous dogma that symbolic communication with the property of displacement is limited to human language. It would seem threatening enough to our visceral feelings of human uniqueness and superiority if one of the great apes were found to communicate symbolically under natural conditions. But when we learned from the classic experiments of Lindauer (1955) that semantically communicative exchanges are used by swarming bees to reach a consensus, the superiority of not only our species but our phylum seemed to be challenged.

One significant reaction to von Frisch's discovery that honeybees employ symbolic gestures to communicate distance and direction was that of Carl Jung (1973). Relatively late in his life he wrote that although he had believed insects were merely reflex automata, «This view has recently been challenged by the researches of Karl von Frisch ... Bees not only tell their comrades, by means of a peculiar sort of dance, that they have found a feeding-place, but ... they also indicate its direction and distance, thus enabling beginners to fly to it directly. This kind of message is no different in principle from information conveyed by a human being. In the latter case we would certainly regard such behavior as a conscious and intentional act and can hardly imagine how anyone could prove in a court of law that it had taken place unconsciously ... We are ... faced with the fact that the ganglionic system apparently achieves exactly the same result as our cerebral cortex. Nor is there any proof that bees are unconscious.»

Many experimental scientists will doubtless be reluctant to place much weight on one of the many and wide ranging comments of even so distinguished a psychiatrist as Carl Jung. Nor are we likely to accept a decisive role for law courts in settling scientific questions. But whether or not we agree with him, Jung has posed a central question. For

VON FRISCH's Rosetta Stone has certainly narrowed the gap between human language and animal communication; and of course human language has always been considered to be closely linked to human thinking. Philosophers concerned with the nature of minds have based some of their fundamental ideas about the uniqueness of human minds on what biologists have told them about animal behavior in general, and communication in particular. JUNG's reaction might be rather general among philosophers if they came to appreciate the versatility of animal communication. Therefore students of animal behavior have an important role to play in this philosophical arena, to encourage philosophers to base their views about human-animal distinctions on scientific facts rather than casual observations of their pet dogs or on elementary and perhaps outdated books on ethology.

Behavioristic psychologists have argued vehemently that mental experiences are of no importance, that they are unworthy of the attention of scientists, and that everything about both animal and human behavior can be better understood and dealt with by totally ignoring them. At least when applied to our own species, this viewpoint is so contrary to common sense that one must blink hard and be sure these colleagues really mean what they seem to be saying. But some of their considered statements are unambiguous. For example a recent rextbook on *Behaviorism, Science and Human Nature* (SCHWARTZ and LACEY 1982) contains the following passage: «If you want to know why someone did something, do not ask. Analyze the person's immediate environment until you find the reward. If you want to change someone's actions, do not reason or persuade. Find the reward and eliminate it. The idea that people are autonomous and possess within them the power and the reasons for making decisions has no place in behavior theory.» If even human beings have no behavioral autonomy and no power to reason or make decisions, it would seem futile to search for such autonomy or decision making in animals. Although this extreme type of behavioristic view is not at all widely shared outside of relatively narrow circles in academic psychology, something quite like it has been taken over implicitly by ethologists and behavioral ecologists.

I have suggested the term «inclusive behaviorists» to include both psychologists who believe that all behavior can best be studied by considering only external contingencies of reinforcement and those biologists who confine their interests to the adaptiveness of animal behavior (GRIFFIN 1984). The leading contemporary behaviorist has recognized for many years that evolutionary selection has influenced the behavior of animals, and presumably to some degree human behavior as well (SKINNER 1966, 1981). He therefore extended his concept of contingencies of reinforcement to include evolutionary selection that has led to the more abundant survival and reproduction of animals that behaved in certain ways. Behavioral ecologists, ethologists, and sociobiologists seldom inquire whether the animals they study think or feel one way or another about what they are doing or about the situations in which they find themselves. Such questions are avoided by concentrating exclusively on the adaptive value of behavior. What inclusive behaviorists have in common is a strong aversion to considering any mental experiences that might occur in the animals they study. It is implicitly assumed that only what the animal *does* can have any effect on its survival and reproduction, so that any mental experiences would have no evolutionary consequences. But this is an assumption, not a demonstrated fact. If what animals do is guided or influenced by any thoughts or feelings they may experience, or if mental experiences themselves affect the animal's well being and reproduction, they could not escape the effects of natural selection.

This neglect of mental experiences is by no means universal among a much wider circle of thoughtful scholars who have been concerned with the nature of minds, whether those of people or animals, and the degree to which thoughts and feelings, beliefs and desires, intentions, expectations and the like do affect behavior. For example, CARLES TAYLOR

(1964, 1970) rejects the customary argument of inclusive behaviorists that mental experiences of animals are beyond the reach of science because they are unobservable and immune from independent and objective verification: «The behaviorist view of science is a closed circle, a self-induced illusion of necessity. For there is no self evidence to the proposition that the mental is unobservable. In a perfectly valid sense I can be said to observe another man's anger, sadness, his eagerness to please, his sense of his own dignity, his uncertainty, love for his girl, or whatever. I can find out these things about another sometimes by just observing him in the common sense of that term, sometimes by listening to what he says ... What people say about themselves is never in principle uncheckable ... Teleological explanation in terms of intentional properties requires no appeal to an interactionism involving the unobservable (TAYLOR 1970, p. 61) ... Future generations may well look upon molar behaviorism with the wonder and awe reserved for some incomprehensible cult of a previous epoch. For the facts of insight, improvisation, goal-direction, and intentionality are so obvious in human behaviour and that of animals which are most similar to us, that it was only by special efforts that they could be overlooked or minimized to the point of appearing tractable to S-R approach.» (p. 67). Similar views have been forcefully expressed by WHITELEY (1973), MACKENZIE (1977) and SOBER (1983). Thus biological students of animal behavior should not feel that the negative dogmatism of inclusive behaviorism is a sacred taboo.

Although inclusive behaviorists have insisted in recent years that any notions such as purpose or intention have no place in explaining animal behavior, the «crypto-phenomenologist» E. C. TOLMAN (1932, 1966) disagreed and developed, within academic psychology, what he called a «purposive behaviorism» that took account of expectancies and purposes. Some behaviorists have argued, mistakenly, that to assume that a goal or purpose affects the behavior of an animal requires that a future event influence what is happening here and now. It is not the future events, but the animal's thinking about them that may well influence its behavior. If we are willing to accept the reality and significance of thinking about what is likely to happen in even the short term future, it becomes reasonable to suppose that animals experiencing such thoughts will prefer one of the outcomes they can think about over others and will attempt to achieve desirable results and avoid unpleasant ones. Anticipating food, they may do those things they believe will help them get food; fearing pain, they may well do what seems likely to help them escape from predators or aggressive companions.

It is important to make clear at this point that whatever speculative extrapolations of VON FRISCH's discoveries I may suggest, he expressed strong doubts that bees or other insects were conscious thinkers. In *Aus dem Leben der Bienen* (English translation 1955) he wrote «There is to my knowledge not one example on record of a really intelligent action having been performed by a honeybee.» (p. 150) But he concludes his very short chapter on «The Bee's Mental Capacity» with a cautiously agnostic disclaimer: «Nobody can state with certainty whether the bees are conscious of any of their own actions.» (p. 151). In a letter written in November 1976, he expanded on this theme:

«The question where in the Animal Kingdom the limits of consciousness are located is one which has gone round and round in my head since my youth. Nevertheless I believe, then as now, that one cannot say anything definite about his question. Personally I have never doubted that animals such as apes, dogs or my parakeet who was a close friend for 15 years have some sort of consciousness and can think to a certain extent. But one can never prove this to those who do not wish to believe it ... The dances of bees are variable and are adapted to changing circumstances. But I do not believe that this is voluntary, considered behavior. They give the overwhelming impression of an instinctive performance. This seems to me to correspond to the development of their central nervous system

... (Yet) it is always better to investigate further, than not to believe in advance in the possibility of progress ... I hope for your sake that your youthful optimism will turn out to be right in the end.»

Three general reasons are commonly advanced for rejecting the possibility that any insect might think consciously about what it does or have any mental states such as beliefs, desires, intentions or the like:

(1) The arthropod nervous system, the bulk of which is located in paired segmental ganglia ventral to the digestive tract, is inherently incapable of flexible or innovative behavior.

(2) Insect behavior is rigidly instinctive, genetically programmed and never adjusted to changing circumstances.

(3) It is inherently impossible to discover what the inner life of another species is like, to them; thus even if insects do have mental experiences we can never hope to learn anything about them.

The first objection, that the arthropod nervous system is incapable of thinking, is really based on the second. Having observed countless instances of rigidity and failure to adapt behavior to changing circumstances in a wide variety of insects, it was only natural to correlate the differences in neuroanatomy of vertebrates and arthropods with these *behavioral* differences. But this correlation was accepted when biologists were limited to the gross anatomy of central nervous systems as a basis for such judgements. Modern neurobiology has disclosed nothing to suggest that the arrangements of neurons and synapses into particular shapes of ganglia, or particular locations within the body are inherently necessary for versatile behavior or thinking. But neurobiologists have not discovered anything to identify whatever properties of brains or their component cells do permit conscious thinking. Ours are not the largest brains, nor the ones with the most extreme lateralization of control over vocal communication. And there is no evidence that Wernicke's or Broca's area of the human cerebral cortex contains special types of neurons or synapses uniquely necessary for conscious thinking.

The essential properties of central nervous systems seem instead to result from interaction of excitation and inhibition at synapses. Complex patterns of excitatory and inhibitory interaction have been demonstrated in arthropod central nervous systems (HUBER 1974; HOYLE 1977; BURROWS 1982). Although there are relatively minor differences in neuron morphology and patterns of arrangement, the basic properties of neurons and synapses do not seem to differ in any fundamental fashion (VOWLES 1961; BULLOCK and HORRIDGE 1965). While only the simpler sorts of neural regulation have been analyzed in detail, no fundamental differences in basic mechanisms have been discovered. Of course insect central nervous systems are very small compared to those of the vertebrate animals with which we are most familiar, and perhaps quantitative differences in mental capabilities can be expected to correlate roughly with size or number of neurons and synapses available in a given central nervous system.

Turning to the second objection on our list, the picture of insect behavior as a set of rigid and unmodifiable instincts has grown up to a large extent because of frequently observed failures of insects to alter their behavior in what *we* can see would be an appropriate fashion. Wasps continue to lay eggs or bring food into nests after an experimenter has opened a hole through which they fall as fast as the wasp replaces them. If live and healthy worker honeybees are annointed with oleic acid, their sisters treat them as corpses. Ants and caterpillars can be induced to follow each other in endless circles. But most if not all of these instances involve conditions well outside of the normal range of circumstances to which the insects in question have become adapted in the course of evolution. Furthermore, as reviewed by THORPE (1963) other insects do repair damaged nests and adapt their behavior to changing circumstances. Having concluded that many insects are thoughtless robots, do we reverse this conclusion when other species behave in a reasonably appropriate fashion? No, we fall back on the assumption that their DNA has been molded by natural selection to provide instructions covering the contingency in question.

Of course insects are quite capable of learning, and indeed even isolated ganglia of mollusks can show to a limited type of associative learning (KANDEL et al. 1983). The whole body of information exchanged via the symbolic dances of honeybees has been learned by the dancer. She has learned not only the location of something urgently needed by the colony but what is in fact needed. This latter type of learning is seldom considered in connection with the symbolic dances, but it is equally important. As reviewed by LINDAUER (1971) worker honeybees spend a great deal of time interacting with their sisters and exchanging materials and pheromones; this provides considerable information as to the needs of the colony. Furthermore the dancer's reception by other bees and the degree to which they do exchange material with her provide information about shortages of sucrose, pollen or perhaps water to cool an overheated hive. This nexus of social communication involves chemical signals which are much more difficult to decode than the symbolic gestures, but it is important to bear in mind that it serves to elicit the searching for what is needed and the dancing about its location and desirability. And of course the dancing does not occur at all unless there is some pressing need; beehives favorably situated where all needs are readily supplied may flourish for long periods without any dancing at all.

These and numerous other examples should serve to dispel the myth that insect behavior is totally fixed and never modified by individual experience or adjusted to changing circumstances. To be sure the flexibility has limits, but undue emphasis has been placed on the experiments in which insects behave stupidly when these limits are exceeded. Within a range of circumstances for which they have been adapted in the course of evolution, insects in general, and honeybees in particular, display abundant evidence of versatile behavior, which, as JUNG pointed out, would be interpreted as resulting from conscious thinking if it occurred in our own species. If learning and adjustment of behavior to changing circumstances are criteria for conscious thinking, honeybees, weaver ants, and other insects satisfy these criteria reasonably well – within the range of circumstances for which they have been adapted in the course of evolution.

Of course the scope of insect versatility seems very limited from our human perspective, but this difference may be quantitative rather than a qualitative difference in kind. Honeybees may think consciously about what is important to them and about those challenges and solutions that lie within their competence. Can we be certain that human thinking is capable of dealing with all contingencies? When viewed from a cosmic perspective, are our most highly trained and well informed leaders behaving in a wholly rational fashion in response to the newly arisen threat of nuclear warfare? Or are we following time worn behavior patterns that have been adaptive in the past under radically altered circumstances? In some future century might paleoethologists from another galaxy liken our behavior to that of wasps that continue to lay eggs in a nest where they fall through holes the animal could easily repair?

One of the clearest examples of insect versatility is provided by the behavior of swarming honeybees analyzed by the painstaking observations and experiments of LINDAUER (1955). Workers live only a few weeks during the season when they are active, but swarming often occurs only at intervals of years. Yet when the swarm has emerged from its former cavity older workers that have previously been searching for food begin to search for something entirely different, namely cavities with appropriate properties to house a new colony. And they use the same symbolic gestures to communicate the direction, distance, and desirability of cavities they have discovered. If insects are genetically programmed robots, we must assume that their DNA transmits instructions to look for cavities when faced with this unprecedented situation. But such genetic instructions must also induce the bees not only to search for and dance about cavities they have visited but also to pay attention to the dances of their sisters that are reporting about other cavities. The individual robot bee sometimes changes roles from giving to receiving information about cavities when she stops dancing about the cavity she has found and follows dances of other bees that are more vigorous than her own. She may then fly out to the second cavity; and after visiting it, and assessing its qualities by the sorts of behavior described by SEELEY (1977), she may dance about its location and desirability. This process of exchanging information, and altering behavior on the basis of such information, leads after many hours or a few days to a consensus in which all or almost all the bees are dancing about the same cavity. After some hours of this, they begin to execute the Schwirrlauf or buzzing run, and after this has become very widespread the whole swarm flies off to the new cavity.

It is worthwhile to point out that honeybees do not have a monopoly on semantic communication with the property of displacement. As HÖLLDOBLER and WILSON (1978) described, weaver ants also use simple symbolic gestures when recruiting nestmates, these differing in at least two cases according to whether the recruitment is to gather food or to fight intruders. Furthermore these ants sometimes employ chain communication, in which one ant that has been stimulated by the recruiting gestures and pheromones repeats these signals to others without herself receiving the direct stimulation of the food or attacking intruders.

The versatility of symbolic communication employed by swarming honeybees to reach a consensus is one of the most significant aspects of the whole honeybee «language». Yet it has received surprisingly little attention in the thirty years since its discovery by LINDAUER, and it is not even mentioned in most reviews of honeybee communication. It certainly calls for further detailed investigation. LINDAUER's original observations required continuous watching of individually marked bees over several days, and his successors may find it difficult to summon the energy for comparable investigations. But a variety of methods could be developed to explore the extent to which bees shift roles in communicative exchanges according to the challenges they face. I often wonder whether our conviction that bees are genetically programmed robots has held back investigations that might lead to highly significant new discoveries.

As VON FRISCH and his colleagues and successors have learned of more and more complex and versatile behavior of honeybees, we are forced to postulate that their DNA encodes appropriate instructions for an exponentially expanding list of adaptive behavior patterns under a widening range of circumstances including some, such as swarming, that occur only at intervals much longer than the lifespan of the insects involved. Perhaps it would be simpler for their DNA to instruct bees how to think consciously about the problems they face and the behavior by which they try to solve them. Cognitive explanations of behavior may be more parsimonious than the customary appeal to more and more elaborate detailed instructions specifying what to do under an enormous range of conditions.

Many scientists concerned with animal behavior, such as WALKER (1983) or several of the contributors to a symposium edited by ROITBLAT, BEVER and TERRACE (1983) now recognize the probability that animal cognition is real and significant. But to speak of animal consciousness still seems too radical a departure from the inclusive behaviorism with which we have become so comfortably familiar. While we know far too little to speak with confident certainty about such questions, I suspect that when cognition becomes as complex, versatile, and multifaceted as in the behavior of honeybees, it becomes simpler and more efficient for the animal to think consciously about the many interacting factors that affect its success in life and reproduction. As scientists we tend to isolate particular behavior patterns for investigation and analysis, but the animals must often react appropriately to the interplay between several influences, and it is a special feature of conscious thinking that it can encompass a whole picture and deal with interactions and trade-offs as well as particular relationships. When we find, with the aid of von Frisch's Rosetta Stone, that socially interdependent animals communicate with each other about solutions to the challenges they face, this suggests that they may be thinking about what they are communicating. These communicated messages can be intercepted and interpreted by human observers, and this provides us with the opportunity to learn something at least about what the animals may be thinking.

The third objection listed above is in many ways the most seriously paralytic. If we remain convinced that there is no possible way to learn anything about the subjective mental experiences of another species, we will never try and therefore make no progress. While such an effort is sure to be challenging and fraught with difficulties and confusion, why must we be so pessimistic, *a priori*, when such exciting progress has been achieved in so many other areas of science? To paraphrase von Frisch, «It is always better to investigate further than to reject in advance the possibility of progress.»

It may help place this problem in appropriate perspective to remind ourselves of an elementary philosophical problem. One of the many logically impregnable philosophical positions is that of the solipsist who insists that he is the only conscious being in the universe. If he is adamant and agile in his manipulation of logical arguments, we cannot convince him that other people also experience conscious thoughts and subjective feelings, for he can explain away every piece of evidence we may offer in favor of consciousness in his companions as one or another sort of illusion. Yet no one takes this viewpoint seriously. We reject it not because of logical arguments but for reasons of plausibility and common sense. So much of what we observe in our companions' behavior, especially their nonverbal signals and what they say, indicates so strongly that they also think and feel that we are willing to make this inference with great confidence despite the logically incontrovertible arguments of the solipsist.

Yet when we consider other species, we have been so strongly swayed by the logical impossibility of proving in any absolute sense that they experience conscious thoughts and subjective feelings that we have fallen into an implicit belief in «species solipsism». Many scientific problems are so difficult that only limited progress can be expected at early stages of their investigation, but in most other areas of science this has fortunately not discouraged attempts to understand objects and processes that are not directly observable. For example behavioral ecologists and sociobiologists seek to understand how animal behavior has been influenced by natural selection. They postulate, at least implicitly, that certain behavior patterns of ancestral animals led to their more abundant reproduction. But these events cannot be observed directly, because they involved animals long dead that inhabited environments widely dispersed in space and time and quite impossible to reconstruct. Therefore we are obliged to reconstruct them in our minds, relying on inference and considerations of plausibility to an even greater degree than is necessary to develop a cognitive ethology, based upon data about events occurring in the brains of animals here and now. Furthermore animals often provide us with many types of information about what is going on in their central nervous systems. These include overt behavior and electrical correlates of brain activity such as the event related potentials that are perhaps on the threshold of providing objective indices of certain simple types of human thinking

(GALAMBOS and HILLYARD 1981; DONCHIN et al. 1983). And, last but not least, animals often seem to be communicating their thoughts and feelings to other animals.

Perhaps it is time to consider tentatively a substantial revision in the way which we think about animals and their behavior. I do not claim that the correctness of this cognitive approach to ethology can yet be established by satisfactory evidence. But I believe that it can lead to fruitful working hypotheses to be tested by scientific methods. Even if such investigations eventually disconfirm these hypotheses, or more likely fail to settle the matter conclusively, the effort promises to improve and enrich our understanding of animals and of the relationship between human and animal thinking. This cognitive perspective on ethology has been inspired by KARL VON FRISCH's discoveries, but I do not wish to imply that he would agree with all or even with any of what I am suggesting. Cognitive ethology, at this embryonic stage of its development, analogous to a gastrula or perhaps only a blastula, entails the following tentative hypotheses:

A. Mental experiences such as desires, beliefs, intentions, expectations, hopes that something nice will happen, or fears that something unpleasant may occur, are real and significant, at least in the human mind. Their occurrence in other species is a matter for empirical investigation.

B. Some mental experiences influence behavior; thus they are not inconsequential by-products or illusions.

C. Mental experiences result from the functioning of central nervous systems; they entail no extra-physical events or processes, and they are governed by the principles of natural science. They are presumably processes regulating information flow within central nervous systems, but they also sometimes produce subjective consciousness, at least in our own species.

D. Central nervous systems function through complex excitatory and inhibitory interactions between nerve impulses, local excitation within neurons and neuroendocrine processes, primarily at synapses.

E. Neurons, synapses, neuroendocrine processes and other basic functions that underly cognition are fundamentally similar in all central nervous systems. Thus nothing now known about neurophysiology precludes cognition or consciousness in any animal with a central nervous system.

F. The existance and nature of mental experiences can be inferred to a significant though limited degree from the behavior of people and animals, and especially from their communication about such experiences. Such inferences are testable by using them to predict future behavior, including communicative behavior.

G. Suggestive evidence of the occurrence of mental experiences is supplied by versatility of adaptive behavior in response to changing circumstances, although this cannot exceed the animal's inherent repertoire of capabilities.

H. Stronger evidence of mental experiences and conscious thoughts can be gathered by intercepting and interpreting the communicative signals which two or more animals exchange; in some cases at least, these may be direct reporting of the mental experiences of the communicator.

Inclusive behaviorists can always claim that an unconscious robot could duplicate whatever behavior we may observe in any animal. But they can also apply this «robot story» to their human companions, as exemplified by the passage from SCHWARTZ and LACEY quoted above. Yet we know that our own mental experiences are real and significant, which means that this «robot story» is not a reliable and conclusive reason to deny consciousness. Therefore we can lay it to one side, just as we do the logically watertight arguments of the solipsist.

Before we can fully appreciate the significance and the potential ramifications of cognitive ethology two additional considerations require discussion. The first of these is the widely accepted view that instinctive behavior, controlled primarily by the animal's DNA, cannot under any circumstances be accompanied or influenced by conscious thinking. The second is that conscious thinking about an animal's problems or opportunities would lead to inefficient hesitation or vacillation, and that rigid and mechanical actions would be more effective. What I will call the «Frischian revolution» seems to call both into question, as I have discussed in detail elsewhere (GRIFFIN 1978, 1981, 1984).

G. J. ROMANES (1884) defined an instinct as «reflex action into which there is imported the element of consciousness.» To be sure, ROMANES is no longer looked upon with favor by students of animal behavior; but, like CARL JUNG, he has at least posed a significant question. If we are willing to concede that any animal might be capable of conscious thinking, why must this be limited to thoughts accompanying learned behavior? It is helpful in this context to distinguish those involuntary and reflexive patterns of human behavior such as sneezing over which we have little or no control, but which we are consciously aware of as they happen, from activities of our bodies which do not ordinarily entail conscious awareness, such as intestinal peristalsis or the constriction of the pupils in bright light. There are also intermediate categories such as breathing or postural reflexes which we do not usually think about but which can be brought to conscious attention when we wish to do so. Perhaps insects and other animals think consciously about some of their instinctive actions even though they may not perform them intentionally. During the construction and provisioning of a nest in which will develop offspring the mother wasp cannot live to see, she can scarcely think about the end result of this activity. But this does not preclude thinking about the activities in which she does engage. Perhaps she thinks about digging a burrow or constructing a nest without any concept of the eventual results. This might be roughly comparable to the early stages of human courtship in which males at least seldom give much thought to the possibility that the eventual result may be a baby.

When we dismiss the possibility of conscious thinking in insects or other animals whose behavior is largely instinctive, what we really mean is that it seems impossible for them to know, or think consciously about, the eventual results of what they are doing. But this in no way precludes conscious awareness of the immediate behavior in which they are engaged, or its short term consequences. The mother wasp might want a burrow, grasp and carry away particles of soil with the intention of forming a dark cavity into which she will crawl to lay eggs, even though she has not the remotest notion that the eggs will later hatch into larvae. We have tended to rule out the possibility of any conscious thinking at all because the animal cannot be aware of the longer term results of its behavior.

The idea that conscious thinking would be inefficient seems to have arisen in discussion of laboratory experiments with rats; for instance E. C. TOLMAN's purposive behaviorism was criticised for «leaving the rat lost in thought» at branch points in a maze. But when one considers the normal behavior of a wide variety of animals under natural conditions, it seems possible that at least simple thinking about alternative actions of which the animal is capable, and their likely results, would be helpful in many circumstances. The ability to think in simple «if, then» terms should permit successful solutions to many of the problems faced by animals that must make a living by finding enough food while avoiding predators. Such thoughts on the part of a hungry lion as «If I sneak slowly with my belly to the ground, those gazelles may not run away and maybe I can catch one» or «If I run into those brambles, that dog won't hurt me» on the part of a frightened rabbit seem plausible if we grant animals any capability of thinking at all. Likewise when honeybees dance about an ideal cavity they might think something like «If we all fly in this direction and about this long a time, we can get into that nice dark, dry place.» The subsequent behavior of the bees is certainly consistent with this interpretation, although such evidence is far from conclusive. But it may be possible, by much additional and enterprising investigation, to build up a body of data that will serve to increase or decrease the plausibility of such interpretations.

As scientists we strongly prefer rigorously testable hypotheses, and I wish I could suggest convincing experiments, comparable to those of KARL VON FRISCH, that would prove that a particular animal was or was not thinking a certain thought. Unfortunately, I feel we are in a state comparable to his frame of mind around 1905. But to deny that future investigators could build on what is already known and devise new and improved methods to test hypotheses about what animals may think and feel is to belittle the capabilities of human brains in general, and those of scientists in particular. Especially with the example of KARL VON FRISCH to inspire us, we should be ready, as DENNETT (1983) has put it to «cast off the straightjacket of (inclusive) behaviorism» and develop appropriate strategies and tactics for learning about animal cognition and consciousness. Perhaps these taboos will someday come to seem comparable to the conviction that bees are color blind, that fish are deaf, and that insects could not possibly communicate symbolically about something far away.

References

Bullock, T. H. and G. A. Horridge (1965): Structure and function in the nervous systems of invertebrates. Freeman, San Francisco.

Burrows, M. (1982): Interneurones co-ordinating the ventilatory movements of the thoracic spiracles in the locust. J. Exptl. Biol. 97, 385–400.

Dennett, D. C. (1983): Intentional systems in cognitive ethology: The «Panglossian paradigm» defended. Behav. Brain Sci. 6, 343–355. See also commentaries ibid 355–390.

Donchin, E., G. McCarthy, M. Kutas, and W. Ritter (1983): Event-related brain potentials in the study of consciousness. In: Consciousness and Self-regulation, Advances in Research and Theory, Vol. 3, ed. by R. J. Davidson, G. E. Schwartz and D. Shapiro, Ch. 3, p. 81–121, Plenum, New York.

Frisch, K. von (1923): Ein Zwergwels, der kommt, wenn man ihm pfeift. Biol. Zbl. 43, 439–446.

– (1930): The sense of hearing in fishes. Science 71, 515.

– (1938): The sense of hearing in fish. Nature (London) 141, 8.

– (1955): The dancing bees, an account of the life and senses of the honey bee. Harcourt Brace, New York.

Galambos, R. and S. A. Hillyard (1981): Electrophysiological approaches to human cognitive processing. Neurosci. Res. Prog. Bull. 20, 141–264 + vi.

Griffin, D. R. (1978/1980): Prospects for a cognitive ethology. Behav. Brain Sci. 1, 527–538. See also commentaries ibid 1, 555–629 and 3, 615–623.

– (1981): The question of animal awareness, 2nd. ed. Rockefeller Univ. Press, New York. Paperback William Kaufman, Los Altos, California.

– (1984): Animal thinking. Harvard Univ. Press, Cambridge, Mass.

Hölldobler, B. and E. O. Wilson (1978): The multiple recruitment system of the African weaver and Oecophylla longinoda (Latreille) (Hymenoptera, Formicidae). Behav. Ecol. Sociobiol. 3, 19–60.

Hoyle, G. ed. (1977): Identified neurons and behavior of arthropods. Plenum, New York.

Huber, F. (1974): Neural integration (central nervous system). In: The Physiology of Insecta, 2nd. ed., Vol. IV, ed. by M. Rockstein, p. 4–100. Academic Press, New York.

Jung, C. (1973): Synchronicity, a causal connecting principle. Princeton Univ. Press, Princeton, N. J.

Kandel, E. R., Abrams, T., Bernier, L., Carew, T. J., Hawkins, R. D., and Schwartz, J. A. (1983): Classical conditioning and sensitization share aspects of the same molecular cascade in Aplesia. Cold Spring Harbor Symposia on Quantitative Biology 48, 821–830.

Lindauer, M. (1955): Schwarmbienen auf Wohnungssuche. Z. vergl. Physiol. *37*, 263–324.
– (1971): Communication among social bees, 2nd. ed. Harvard Univ. Press, Cambridge, Mass.
MacKenzie, B. D. (1977): Behaviourism and the limits of scientific method. Routledge and Kegan Paul, London.
Roitblat, H., T. G. Bever and H. S. Terrace eds. (1983): Animal cognition. Erlbaum, Hillsdale, N. J.
Romanes, G. J. (1969): Mental evolution in animals (1884). Reprint with posthumous essay on instinct by Charles Darwin. ABS Press, New York.
Seeley, T. (1977): Measurement of nest cavity volume by the honey bee *(Apis mellifera)*. Behav. Ecol. Sociobiol. *2*, 201–227.
Schwartz, B. and H. Lacey (1982): Behaviorism, science and human nature. Norton, New York.
Skinner, B. F. (1966): The phylogeny and ontogeny of behavior. Science *153*, 1205–1213.
– (1981): Selection by consequences. Science *213*, 501–504.
Sober, E. (1983): Mentalism and behaviorism in comparative psychology. In: Comparing Behavior: Studying Man Studying Animals. ed. by D. W. Rajecki, Ch. 5 p. 113–142. Erlbaum, Hillsdale, N. J.
Taylor, C. (1964): The explanation of behaviour. Humanities Press, New York.
– (1970): The explanation of purposive behavior. In: Explanation in the Behavioral Sciences, ed. by R. Borger and F. Cioffi, p. 49–79 Cambridge Univ. Press, London.
Thorpe, W. H. (1963): Learning and instinct in animals. 2nd. ed. Harvard Univ. Press, Cambridge, Mass.
Tolman, E. C. (1932): Purposive behavior in animals and men. Appleton-Century, New York.
– (1966): Behavior and psychological man. Univ. of California Press, Berkeley.
Vowles, D. M. (1961): Neural mechanisms in behavior. In: Current Problems in Animal Behaviour, ed. by W. H. Thorpe and O. L. Zangwill, p. 5–29. Cambridge Univ. Press, London.
Walker, S. (1983): Animal thought. Routledge and Kegan Paul, London.
Whiteley, C. H. (1973): Mind in action, an essay in philosophical psychology. Oxford Univ. Press, London.

Subject index